AF361484

Onomasticon Turcicum

Indiana University Uralic and Altaic Series

Denis Sinor, Editor

Volume 172/I

László Rásonyi(†) and Imre Baski

ONOMASTICON
TURCICUM

Turkic Personal Names

as collected by László Rásonyi

Indiana University
Denis Sinor Institute for Inner Asian Studies
Bloomington, Indiana
2007

Copyright © 2007 Indiana University
Denis Sinor Institute for Inner Asian Studies
All rights reserved

Library of Congress Control Number: 2006906304

ISBN 13: 978-0-933070-56-1

ISBN 10: 0-933070-56-X

Preface

Since Ferdinand Justi's *Iranisches Namenbuch* was published in Marburg in 1895[1] and since the publication of CAETANI–GABRIELI's monumental *Onomasticon Arabicum* was started in 1915,[2] interest in the proper, especially the personal, names of the Turks has grown. The Turks, being the third ethnic group of significance in Western and Central Asia, accounts in part for this interest.

Unfortunately, other than in the case of the two great works just mentioned, collecting and organizing data for an Onomasticon Turcicum has been made difficult by the fact that the source material is vast and rather heterogeneous. However, this very circumstance makes Turkic onomatological research especially attractive. Within the fields of linguistics, historical science and ethnography there is something new to say for every branch of Turkology.[3]

Although A. N. SAMOJLOVIČ (1880-1938) had urged the collecting of Turkic onomatological material as early as 1911,[4] no considerable work dealing with names, including both historical and modern data from the whole history and territory of the Turkic world, has been published.

Among Hungarian scholars the idea of collecting all the Hungarian proper names was raised by the historian ISTVÁN HORVÁTH almost a hundred years earlier.[5] Following him – and, considering the importance of onomatology in solving linguistic and historical questions, in the preface of his work *Magyar nyelvkincsek Árpádék korából* [Hungarian language treasures from the age of the Árpáds] of 1854 – JÁNOS JERNEY argued for writing a "Magyar Onomasticon" [Hungarian Onomasticon] and concluded by saying that the knowledge of ancient and modern Asiatic languages as well as an íAsiatic Onomasticoní would also be highly desirable.[6]

At the very beginning of his career, LÁSZLÓ RÁSONYI (1899-1984) turned to Turkic onomatology and began to collect material for an Onomasticon Turcicum, following in the tradition of Hungarian linguistics and Turkic studies inherited from his teachers GYULA (JULIUS) NÉMETH and ZOLTÁN GOMBOCZ. In the course of the subsequent decades he accumulated a large corpus of data, but his long-term university activities in Kolozsvár and Ankara, as well as other tasks and circumstances, were not favourable to the accomplishment of his goal. Nevertheless LÁSZLÓ RÁSONYI collected some 50,000 anthroponyms used by various Turkophone peoples from the beginning of Turkic history until the first half of the twentieth century. He was just at the point of summing up his investigations in 1969, when he lost his failing sight forever and thus could not complete his task.

It was ISTVÁN MÁNDOKY-KONGUR (1944-1992) who at that time helped professor RÁSONYI with the completion and arrangement of the collection. From 1976 on, the author of the present lines assisted with the work on the Onomasticon Turcicum for eight years, with the support of the Research Group for Altaistic Studies and has been a research fellow there since 1993. During the long time spent in these joint efforts, I had the opportunity to become acquainted with the material and with professor RÁSONYI's conception of the treatment and publication of the collection. According to my mentor's will, it became my duty to prepare the collection for publishing and write the introductory study.[7]

Professor RÁSONYI, in one of his articles, said that some of his writings could be used as a kind of introduction to the study of the system of Turkic name-giving. Later, in a letter[8] to the Hungarian Academy of Sciences, he wrote that the planned introduction and bibliography were, by and large, ready in the articles he had published. As a consequence these needed only to be summarized.[9]

On these grounds and under the circumstances that the present book is our common work, I felt authorized to

---

[1] New edition: Hildesheim, 1963. A newer Onomasticon of Iranian names was issued by Abdul Karīm Bihniya almost a hundred years later (*Nām: Pazhūhashī dar nāmha-yi Īrāniān-i mu'āṣir*. Ahwaz, 1981). It is a study of 25,752 men with 1,675 different names, and 12,714 women with 1,283 different names. A newer series edited by M. Mayrhofer: *Iranisches Namenbuch*. Bd. I: *Die altiranischen Namen* (Wien, 1977-79). Bd. II. *Mitteliranischen Personennamen* (Wien, 1986).

[2] The work had been cancelled, but has recently been renewed by scholars in Arabic studies.

[3] Rásonyi, Kayn. p. 71, Rásonyi, P. Cat. p. 207. [Titles in full are given in the paragraph *Bibliographical Abbreviations*, p. LXXXIX.]

[4] Samojlovič, 1911, p. 299.

[5] Tudományos Gyűjtemény [Scientific Collections], Budapest 1821, III, p. 49.

[6] Pest, 1854, p. 83.

[7] It was a great honour for me that Professor Rásonyi, wanting to assure the completion and publication of the Onomasticon Turcicum in the future, concluded an agreement with me on 22 November, 1983 to be his co-author.

[8] Dated October 12, 1978.

[9] Rásonyi, P. Cat., p. 208, where he referred to Rásonyi, Categ.(1953), to his "Türk kadın adları" (1963), "Tarihte Türklük" (1971) and some other articles, the titles of which can be found in the paragraph *Rásonyi's Works on Turkic Onomastics*, p. XV.

take the late Professor RÁSONYI's related studies, authentic drafts and notes from his archive for the basis of the introduction. Thus it reflects fundamentally L. RÁSONYI's onomatological views elaborated in his own writings. As some of these were written almost fifty years ago, here and there I have updated or completed them.

I wish to record my deep appreciation of the helpful comments that I received in preparing this book from a number of colleagues, especially ISTVÁN VÁSÁRY and BENEDEK PÉRI. I am most obliged to the late Professor FERENC TŐKEI, leader of the Research Group for Oriental Studies, and to Professor GYÖRGY KARA, leader of the Research Group for Altaic Studies of the Hungarian Academy of Sciences, for their support which has lasted nearly two decades. My special thanks go to Professor GYÖRGY KARA, who revised the text of the introduction and some of the etymologies. I acknowledge the spontaneous appreciation and kind support I received from the publishers of the Onomasticon Turcicum, particularly from Professor DENIS SINOR, to whom I express my deep sense of gratitude for his overall supervision of the publication and to the thorough revision of the introductory parts of this book.

Finally, I owe my greatest debt of gratitude to my wife, Eszter Moór, and my children, Judit and Sándor, who put up with an often preoccupied husband and father during many long years of the work.

IMRE BASKI

Contents

IV

Introduction

Turkic Onomastics

Onomastics is a relatively young branch of Turkic philology. Aside from exceptional individual efforts of some scholars, not much was done in the early period of Turkic studies and, despite certain achievements of later research, we have to state that it is still a little investigated field.

Modern research of onomastics requires a complex study of linguistic, historical and ethnographical material. The rich variety of name-giving among the Turkic peoples involves a number of social and ethnographical phenomena such as customs, rituals, magical practices and beliefs.

The Beginnings

Even the authors of some early grammatical treatises touched upon the category of proper names. For instance, *Tuhfa*, the Mamluk-Kipchak grammar in Arabic, dating from the 14th century, has a separate section for names. The author notes among others that verbs (e.g., *Alγan* "Took/Taken," *Bükti* "Kneeled down," *Kälgän* "Came," *Kätkän* "Went/Gone"), accidental (random) words and contrived (meaningless) words (e.g., *Qalawun*) may all occur as proper names. He also adds that a major group of personal names rises from common nouns, e.g., *Arslan* "Lion," *Lačïn* "Falcon," *Toγan* "id." The contemporary linguist gave the definition of proper names as follows: proper name is something that is used for distinction only. In the same section it is said about the morphology (structure) of proper names as well. The author states that a proper name can consist of: 1. a single word such as *täñri* "Allah," *payγanbar* "Prophet," *qan* "Khan," etc.; 2. two words, e.g., *Ala-boγa* "Pied Bull," *Qara-käsäk* "Black Cut/Cuttings"; 3. a noun and a verb, e.g., *Kün-doγdï* "The Sun Rose," *Ay-doγdï* "The Moon Rose"; 4. a single verb, e.g., *Bükti* "Kneeled down"; 5. derived words, such as *Alγan* "Took/Taken," *Kälgän* "Came," *Kätkän* "Went/Gone."[10]

Several centuries later, small, specific collections of names appeared, such as KATANOV's name register drawn from the first two volumes of RADLOFF's great collection of folk-poetry.[11] Many personal names are published in RADLOFF's magistral, four-volume dictionary and PEKARSKIJ's similarly rich, three-volume Yakut dictionary.[12] Although MAGNICKIJ's *Čuvašskija jazyčeskija imena*[13] offers a list of 10,567 Chuvash names, this list is regrettably not reliable for the philologist, because it is redundant.

About this time appeared the first attempts at the systematization of Turkic personal names, in only ten pages (from 25 to 35) of M. TH. HOUTSMA's "Ein türkisch-arabisches Glossar."[14] This systematization was very sketchy, not going any deeper than stating the larger semantic and grammatical categories. It is quite obvious that HOUTSMA based his system on the lessons of early Turkic grammatical works, such as *Tuhfa*, noted above. Even so it drew a reaction in Hungary, where interest in Turkic proper and in personal names had been present for some time, due to Hungarians' connections with several Turkic peoples (Khazars, Bulgarians, Pechenegs, Kumanians) throughout the Middle Ages. Thus Z. GOMBOCZ, the author of the first serious study on the subject,[15] relied to a great extent on HOUTSMA.

Because of geographical and historical reasons, Russian scholars started to study Turkic proper names quite early. From the 18th c. G. F. MILLER, P. I. RYČKOV, S. U. REMEZOV, V. N. TATIŠČEV must be mentioned.[16] RADLOFF and his followers collected highly valuable material on Turkic personal names. V. A. GORDLEVSKIJ (1876-1956) also published studies which dealt with the Turkish anthroponyms. One of these articles[17] is especially important, because it inspired A. N. SAMOJLOVIČ to write a polemical article, in which he directed attention to the importance of the collecting and researching all Turkic personal names.[18] In this fundamental study he outlined the tasks to be performed: "Следовало

---

[10] *Tuhfa*, pp. 31, 191-192.

[11] Katanov, *Alfavitnyj ukazatel* (1888).

[12] Pek., (1917-30).

[13] Magn., (1905).

[14] Houtsma, (1894).

[15] Gombocz, ÁTSz. (1915).

[16] See the related paragraphs in A. N. Kononov, *Biobibliografičeskij slovar' otečestvennyh tjurkologov*. Moskva, 1974.

[17] Gordlevskij, V. A., "Roždenie rebenka i ego vospitanie," Ètnogr. Obozr. 1910, vyp. 3-4, p. 168.

[18] Samojlovič, 1911, pp. 298-299.

бы составлять *полные алфавитные списки* с подробными указаниями в каких случаях, в какую историческую эпоху, кому и почему давалось или дается данное имя. Впоследствии явилась бы возможность произвести весьма интересное в культурно-историческом отношении *сравнительное исследование личных имен всех тюркских народов.*"[19] His message is to compile a kind of *Onomasticon Turcicum* and to call for the comparative study of the anthroponyms of all Turkic peoples. He himself gathered more than a thousand Altay Turkic, Turkmen, Kazakh and Nogay personal names, which were partly published in 1917.[20]

Additional scholars of the 19th and early 20th c., such as V. V. BARTOL'D, F. E. KORŠ, N. F. KATANOV, N. ARISTOV, N. I. ZOLOTNICKIJ, Č. Č. VALIHANOV, I. I. BEREZIN, G. N. POTANIN, A. I. LEVŠIN, S. E. MALOV, N. K. DMITRIEV, all contributed to the progress of Turkic onomastics.[21] It was K. G. MALICKIJ (1928) who first wrote about the system of name-giving.

In his dictionary HOUTSMA published quite a number of Turkic anthroponyms originating in animal names. Following him, ZOLTÁN GOMBOCZ defended the totemistic origin of part of the "animal > human being"-names.[22] Many names of this kind gradually left the totemistic nature and formed other psychological categories.[23]

A contemporary of GOMBOCZ, the famous Slavist JÁNOS MELICH formulated a very important methodological principle for Hungarian onomatologists. As early as 1907, he pointed out that the correspondence of one medieval Hungarian name to a Turkic word is not enough; only several examples could demonstrate that the word was used also as a personal name among the Turks.[24]

Hungarian linguists and historians (PAIS, NÉMETH, MELICH, LIGETI, RÁSONYI, GY. GYÖRFFY, CZEGLÉDY, etc.), through the study of Hungarian proper names of Turkic origin, have demonstrated the role of Turkic peoples who later became integrated into the Magyars. The historian L. FEKETE (1927) first pointed out Turkish names of verbal origin. MELICH's short article "Ajtony" (an old Hungarian personal name of Turkic origin, going back to *altïn~altun* "gold") is to be regarded as the first methodological study of a high standard from the point of view of Turkic onomatology in Hungarian scientific literature.

JULIUS NÉMETH's 1930 monograph on how the Hungarians of the Conquest emerged (*A honfoglaló magyarság kialakulása*) definitely demonstrated the presence and the leading role of the successive Turkic peoples in the Carpathian Basin during the 9th and 10th centuries.[25]

Of very high scholarly standard and rich in data is GYULA MORAVCSIK's Byzantinoturcica (1943), a magnificent work which revealed a wealth of Turkic (Pecheneg, Tatar, Turkish) proper names occuring in Byzantine sources.[26]

In 1950 J. SAUVAGET gave an essential account of Mamluk names and surnames.[27] Most of his data have been taken from biographies of al-Manḥal aṣ-Ṣāfi, published by G. WIET in 1932. He reminded us that there was no direct relationship between a name and the ethnic origin of its bearer, and the detection of such a connection cannot be expected from onomastics. However, he added, personal names given by the Mamluks changed from time to time in accordance with the changing circumstances and it was not only the matter of fashion. In the end the author considered it too early to set the whole question forth in its full entirety.[28]

PAUL PELLIOT, the great French orientalist, contributed to the knowledge of Middle Turkic proper names as well. In his fundamental work *"Notes sur l'histoire de la Horde d'Or* (1949), he analyzed the names of the Golden Horde with utmost care and competency. Following him, his compatriot LOUIS BAZIN devoted a few articles to the old Turkic names and titles.

The Turks of Turkey have also shown some interest in the matter of old names, although this interest, as we can see in BESİM ATALAY's work "Türk büyükleri veya Türk adları" (1935), is more for practical reasons: it presents a corpus of commonly known historical names for the choice of new family names. Seemingly, for this latter purpose, more guides (e.g., KARAUĞUZ 1934, ORBAY 1935, KIRIŠ 1938, etc.) were published during the Turkish language reform and later. *Hayat Mecmuası,* the Turkish weekly magazine, for example, was printed during the 1950s and in every issue there was a list of Turkish names with useful explanations.[29]

Turkish philologists and ethnographers - for instance, H. Z. KOŞAY (1927), F. KIRZIOĞLU (1949), M. YUSUFOĞLU (1949) - published some smaller publications on personal names collected from the vernacular speech. A. CAFEROĞLU

---

[19] Ibid.

[20] Samojlovič 1917; see more in Blagova 1998b, p. 45.

[21] T. D. Džanuzakov, Razvitie tjurkskoj onomastiki v SSSR. In: Tjurk. Onom. p. 14.

[22] op. cit., pp. 8-20.

[23] Rásonyi, P. Cat., p. 207.

[24] MNy. III, 1907, p. 167.

[25] Németh, HMK. Recently reedited by Á. Berta.

[26] Byz. Turc.

[27] Noms et surnoms de mamelouks: JA 1950, pp. 31-58.

[28] Sauvaget, p. 33.

[29] Schimmel, p. 96.

(1942) published important name-lists from the East and South-East of the country and attached them to his dialectal collections.

Rásonyi's Part in the Study of Turkic Onomastics

László Rásonyi (1899-1984)

LÁSZLÓ RÁSONYI (originally Nagy, then Rásonyi Nagy), eminent Turkologist, was born in Liptószentmiklós (now Liptovsky Mikuláš in Slovakia) on 22 January 1899. His education began in Kőrösbánya in County Hunyad, Transylvania (now Baia de Criş in Romania), continued in Mezőtúr, where he graduated in 1917. In the same year, he enrolled at the University of Budapest where he learned Turkic philology from GYULA (JULIUS) NÉMETH, Hungarian linguistics from ZOLTÁN GOMBOCZ, and Hungarian history from DÁVID ANGYAL. He received his diploma in education and obtained his doctoral degree in Turkology as well as in Hungarian linguistics and history (1921).

For a while he worked in the Library of the Hungarian Academy of Sciences, where he became senior librarian in 1935. He married Piroska Török, the daughter of high-school teachers from Transylvania. He has one son and two daughters. He published more than 100 studies from 1922 onwards and worked almost to his last day.

He obtained research scholarships on three occasions and received three academic prizes. In 1934 he was invited to Ankara by the Turkish Philological Society to deliver a lecture. The outcome of this public lecture was that President Kemal Atatürk of Turkey decided to create a new chair of Hungarology in the recently established University of Ankara. L. RÁSONYI was invited to fill the chair in 1935.

While working in Ankara, RÁSONYI also organized a Hungarian Institute there and was instrumental in inviting BÉLA BARTÓK to Turkey to carry out ethnomusicological research of folk songs. After the temporary return of Northern Transylvania to Hungary in 1941, Professor RÁSONYI was appointed to the chair of Turkic linguistics and history of the Turkic peoples at the University of Kolozsvár (now Cluj-Napoca, Romania), where he established a Turkic Institute. In the postwar years he lived in Budapest where he was given the task of developing the Oriental Collection, a new section within the Library of the Hungarian Academy of Sciences, where he worked until his retirement in 1962.

Hearing of his retirement, the University of Ankara again invited him to fill the long unoccupied chair of Hungarology; thus for the second time L. RÁSONYI became professor of Hungarology (teaching mainly Turkic and Hungarian linguistics and history), from 1962 until 1971. After returning to Hungary, at the age of 72, he became a member of the board of directors of the Kőrösi Csoma Society.

His many-sided scholarly activity and his main achievements may be summarized as follows:

He advanced Turkic onomatological studies and outlined the concept of the Onomasticon Turcicum. He gave a detailed explanation and phonetic analysis of medieval Kumanian proper names, in which he concluded that the Kumanian language was not uniform: it had several dialects. For more details of his studies on the Turkic onomatology, see the related paragraphs below.

His study of Kumanian history led to the realization of the key importance the presence of the Kumanians constituted in the Carpathian region in the Middle Ages for Bulgaria, Hungary and Romania.

RÁSONYI provided a new explanation for the word *székely*, the ethnonym of the Hungarians of South-East Transylvania.[30]

Investigating many 11th-12th century Transylvanian place names, he showed their Turkic origin, which clearly preceded the first appearance of Romanian settlers in the area.[31]

He proved the Turkic origin of some two dozen Hungarian words, adding to hundreds of others previously identified.[32]

He showed conclusively that in the Transylvania of early medieval times there existed a Turkic ethnic group, called *bulaqs* or *blaqs*, who preceded the Magyars (Hungarians) as well as the Romanians there. The *blacus* (plural *blachi* or *blaci*) of Anonymus could not have referred to the *vlachs* (Romanians), but to this Turkic people in Central Transylvania. They were of Western Turkic-Karluk origin according to RÁSONYI.[33]

In his last years he started to survey the origin of the Hunyadi family and succeeded in showing that John (János) Hunyadi's father's name (*Vayk*) and his grandfather's name (*Šorbe*), as well as the use of the raven in the family coat of

---

[30] A székely név eredete: MNy. 56 (1960), pp. 186-194; L'origine du nom *székely* (sicule): ALingu. 11 (1961), pp. 175-188; Sekeller ve adlarının menşei: Türk Kültürü, S. 113, Y. X,5, 1972, pp. 289-294.

[31] Ortaçağda Erdel'de Türklüğün İzleri: II. Türk Tarih Kongresi Yazıları Yazıları. İstanbul, 1937, 18 pp. (Belleten, 1938, pp. 107-122.

[32] Török jövevényszavainkhoz: MNy. 30 (1934), pp. 157-160; Török adatok a Magyar Etymologiai Szótárhoz: NyK 51 (1941-1943), pp. 98-115, 280-308; Jövevényszavaink és az anatóliai tájszavak. In: Melich Emlékkönyv. Bp. 1943, pp. 314-317; Macarca "gyermek" kelimesi ve "Ermyak" adı. In: Reşid Rahmeti Arat İçin. Ankara, 1966, pp. 382-387; L'origine du hongrois *igen* "oui": AOH 25 (1972), pp. 413-414; Török jövevényszavainkhoz: MNy. 74 (1978), pp. 180-186.

[33] Bulaqs and Oγuzs in Mediaeval Transylvania: AOH XXXIII (1979), pp. 129-151.

arms, point to a Tatar-Kuman origin.[34]

He wrote the first comprehensive synthesis of the history of all the Turkic peoples.[35]

Rásonyi's Part in the Study of Turkic Onomastics

It is not accidental that RÁSONYI's interest turned to Turkic names, since among his professors there were such eminent scholars as ZOLTÁN GOMBOCZ (1877-1935), the famous Hungarian linguist whose article "Árpád-kori török személyneveink" [Our Anthroponyms of Turkic Origin from the Age of the Arpads] had already been published.[36] Also the Turkologist GYULA (JULIUS) NÉMETH (1890-1976), though still young, was having an impact. Presumably on the inspiration of his professors, LÁSZLÓ RÁSONYI began to study Hungarian personal and place names of Turkic (mostly Kumanian) origin.[37]

He wrote his PhD thesis[38] on the anthroponyms of Kumanian origin preserved in medieval Hungarian documents (1921). In this early study he already demonstrated a thorough methodological grounding and knowledge of an extremely wide range of sources. He considered JÁNOS MELICH and ZOLTÁN GOMBOCZ as his masters in onomatology. In his etymologies RÁSONYI carefully explored the Turkic equivalents (parallels or analogies) of the name in question which too had been stressed by GOMBOCZ.[39] He emphasized the condition that the name dealt with should fit into the Turkic name-giving system. The Kuman names of the dissertation were generally taken from GYÁRFÁS,[40] but he used other sources as well. The etymologies of the 34 Kumanian names were refined, and in some places changed, in his later works. Meanwhile, he augmented the lexical and onomatological data to enhance his findings.

The work, with some modification, was published as *Adalékok török tulajdonneveinkhez* [Contributions to Our Turkic Proper Names].[41] The suggested etymologies are more or less acceptable even today. Only in 7 of the 34 examples can we see sizeable lexicological or phonetic difficulties (e.g., *Aydud, Barag, Köndüz, Kördük, Ügütej*).

The articles on Turkic (mainly Kumanian) proper names issued in the following years indicated that the Kipchak "chapter" of Turkic onomatology had become LÁSZLÓ RÁSONYI's chief scholarly interest and activity.[42] Being a Hungarian Turkologist, he was well aware of the importance of the Kumanians, one of the most important branches of the medieval Kipchaks who played a significant role in Hungarian history and whose language left its impact on Hungarian vocabulary. The heritage of the Hungaro-Kumanian relations is still alive in Hungary.[43]

Besides the Kumanian proper names used in Hungary, he dealt with the problems of Kuman names adopted by other peoples, e.g., *Karaiman, Basaraba*.[44] Meanwhile he continued work on his collection of names, which would enable him to analyze Turkic proper names on a larger basis and to summarize the results. In 1953 he published a fundamental article about the classification of Turkic anthroponyms, "Sur quelques catégories de noms de personnes en turc"[45] which was of considerable influence both at home and abroad.

A similar study of great importance is "Les noms de nombre dans l'anthroponymie turque" in which he demonstrated the *magical background of naming children with numbers*.[46] Personal names bearing belief in the *magical power of certain numbers*[47] seemed common in the Indo-European, Semitic, Turkic and other languages. In Kazakh, for example, there have been names formed of numerals 1-10; 20-100; 1,000; 10,000. It is interesting, however, that females were not given such names.[48] Thanks to RÁSONYI's research, the particular role of numbers in Turkic name-giving has become more apparent. His attention focused on the numerals from 2 to 10, 12, 30, 40, 60, 70, 80, 90, 100, 1,000, 10,000 as anthroponyms; he demonstrated this in numerous examples taken from different periods and among various Turkic

---

[34] "The Old-Hungarian Name Vajk - a Note on the Origin of the Hunyadi Family": AOH 36 (1983), pp. 419-428.

[35] *Dünya Tarihinde Türklük* Ankara, 1942, 266 pp. New edition: *Türk Devletinin Batıdaki Vârisleri ve İlk Müslüman Türkler* Ankara, 1983, 240 pp.; also Tarihte Türklük. Ankara, 1971, I-VIII, 420 pp.

[36] See Gombocz, ÁTSz.

[37] "I am grateful to Professor Németh for having stimulated me, when I was his student, a young novice in Turcology, to go in for Turkish onomastics" he wrote in 1976. (Rásonyi, P. Cat., p. 208.)

[38] Kún személyneveinkről. Bp., 1921 (Manuscript).

[39] Gombocz, ÁTSz. 4.

[40] Gyárfás: A Jász-kunok története (1870-1885).

[41] Rásonyi, Adalékok (1923).

[42] See *Rásonyi's Works on Turkic Onomastics*, p. XV.

[43] Ligeti, 1974, p. 149.

[44] MNy. XXVI (1930), MNy. XXIX (1933), also his Bas., and Val.-Turc. The latter reviewed by T. L. in *Ungarische Jahrbücher* VIII (1928), pp. 187-188, by C. Tagliavini in *Studi Rumeni* IV (1929-1930), pp. 187-188.

[45] Rásonyi, Categ.

[46] Rásonyi, Nombre, 1961. Reviewed by T. Žanuzakov: Venger γalïmïnïñ onomastika žönïndegï eñbekterï. In: *Voprosy kazahskogo i ujgurskogo jazykoznanija* Alma-Ata, 1963, pp. 220-222.

[47] See Abulg./Desm. p. 12 on the sacred character of number 9. For additional material, see Blagova 1997, p. 691.

[48] Žanuzakov, op. cit., p. 13.

peoples. Although single numbers are rarely used as personal names, they often form the first member of compound names including ethnonyms. First of all "lucky numbers" were widely used in anthroponyms. In the compound names the number refers to the order of the infant's birth in the family (a similar custom is practised in China) or to the age of the father at the time of birth, and finally, to the (fabulous) number of years wished for a new-born to live.[49]

He was the first to give due attention to the sociological, psychological and onomatological aspects of the Turkic female names. In this study he presented the extended semantic classification which did not change much in his later works.[50]

RÁSONYI's studies on the proper names of Kuman (Kipchak) origin in his later works constituted one of the main areas of research from the very beginning. In the middle 1950s, he devoted two major papers to toponyms of Kumanian origin of Kiskunság (Lesser Kumania), Hungary. In the first one he analysed the origin of the place names ending in *-la~-le* (*Kargala, Csengele, Ügüle*);[51] in the second, he reviewed the historical background and elucidated the origin of 23 toponyms.[52] In his later studies published in Turkish,[53] then in Hungarian, he added more place names, e.g., *Bezther, Kalas, Ketelegaska, Orgowan, Zomokzallasa.*[54]

He summed up results achieved over four decades in the paper "Kuman özel adları" published in Turkey.[55] This large study contains all the Kumanian proper names that he had so identified. He underlined that the Kumans consisted of several ethnic and dialectal groups, a circumstance that should be taken in consideration in the study of their proper names. The list contained 350 names with the necessary apparatus including the possible etymologies. 165 names of Kuman origin once used in Hungary, only 20 remained unexplained or with no certain etymology. At the end of the article we find the Turkish version of his classification in 1962 (see *Categories of TurkicAanthroponyms* below). It is unfortunate that several headwords and cross-references are missing and that many misprints remain.

LÁSZLÓ RÁSONYI extended his research to some morphological features of the names examined. He dealt with the morphemes of names and devoted a considerable study to the imperative forms of protective names and to their adverbial components.[56]

In connection with the word-stock of the names he stated that a great number of the Turkic anthroponyms had been formed from words that were outdated (archaic) or not used in the contemporary language at all.

In the last decade of his life he returned to the question of the common toponyms of Bashkirs and Hungarians. By connecting certain Bashkir and Hungarian toponyms he tried to prove the existence of the Hungarian substratum in Magna Hungaria. Although his results were not received favourably by all researchers, he directed attention once again to the problem.[57]

He slightly modified his classification in 1976. The categories "Names from names," "Hypocoristica" and "Dignities" disappeared but "Fashion names" and "Women's names" were added. This ties in with the supposition that he did not consider his system to be final.

This brief review of LÁSZLÓ RÁSONYI's oeuvre suggests that he succeeded in developing the results of his forerunners. RÁSONYI surpassed HOUTSMA and SAUVAGET in his onomatological research not only with the wealth of his data, but also in the interpretation and classification of the names collected.[58] His system of classification has been applied and enlarged by other researchers.[59]

Onomasticon Turcicum – Rásonyi's Collection of Turkic Names

It was in 1932 that the Hungarian Academy of Sciences announced a competition for a project of the onomasticon of Turkic anthroponyms and ethnonyms. The 1,000 Pengő[60] Feridun-prize was awarded to LÁSZLÓ RÁSONYI for his work entitled "A draft plan of the 'Vocabulary of Turkic Anthroponyms and Ethnonyms' with specimens."[61]

During his research scholarship in Berlin (1924-25) he had attended the lectures of W. BANG and F. W. K. MÜLLER, and also enriched his collection of Turkic proper names. In 1929 he had applied for a scholarship to Helsinki with the aim of studying the vast material of Russian publications available in Finnish libraries. He also wished to collect

---

[49] Ligeti, loc. cit.

[50] Rásonyi, Frauenn. (1962).

[51] MNy. LII (1956), pp. 52-61.

[52] Acta Ling. Hung. VII (1957-58), pp. 73-146).

[53] In: Németh Armağanı. Ankara, 1962, pp. 341-352.

[54] MNy. LXVII (1966), pp. 164-170.

[55] Rásonyi, KÖA (1966-69).

[56] Rásonyi, Imp. (1962).

[57] Ligeti 1974, p. 150.

[58] Ligeti, op. cit.

[59] Such as V. A. Nikonov, A. G. Šajhulov, T. Žanuzakov, etc.

[60] An outdated Hungarian currency.

[61] Akadémiai Értesítő [Bulletin of the Hungarian Academy] XLII, 1932, pp. 142-145.

additional Turkic (mainly Kazakh) anthroponyms. Meanwhile he got acquainted with the actual works of Russian Turkologists. Thus by the time the above mentioned competition was announced (1932), he already had a large collection of names, supported by a fair number of publications on the subject, and experience as an onomatologist.[62] The committee of the Academy, in its evaluation of RÁSONYI's competition work, pointed out that " not only had the candidate laid the foundations for Turkic onomatology, a discipline which incidentally has hardly been studied, but he also managed to put it [i.e., the task, I.B.] all into an almost final form. He went through the Arabic and Persian historical literature with great ambition, looked over all the available Russian official publications in which Turkic names could be found... we propose that the Honourable Academy should award a prize to the work and entrust the author with placing the completed manuscript of his work at the disposal of the Academy as soon as possible."[63]

Although the collection was considered a unique work and its reception at the Academy was positive, it was not published for more than half a century. This can be explained first of all with the unexpected turns in LÁSZLÓ RÁSONYI's life: the long-term university assignment in Kolozsvár and Ankara, failing eyesight, and so on. He wanted to finish and publish his Onomasticon after having retired. According to his plans, declared on several occasions, he would publish several volumes on Turkic names (e.g., ethnical names too), first of which would be on personal names only.

The competition work presented under the password   (on 366 lists of a size 17x21 cm), included an eight-page foreword, followed an arrangement under headwords of 250 Turkic anthroponyms and 100 ethnical names and their variants from different peoples and languages. The collection, which at that time presumably already consisted of several thousand items, increased during the following decades until it reached its present volume. On the basis of our estimation, there are approximately 60,000 10x7 cm cards. The preliminary index of headwords, compiled on the basis of this collection and published in 1986, contains about 25,000 items.[64]

On each card of the collection there is a name (personal or/and family name) of one or more individuals, with the time (year or century) of occurrence, the ethnic or language affiliation, the title (if any) or any other feature (or deed) of the person, plus a short reference to the source. All data concerning the same person are included under two different headwords if the person's names, both personal or second (paternal, family, nick-) names, are of Turkic origin. It should be noted that in this collection we find predominantly original Turkic names.

Having entered all the data on the computer, we can be more exact concerning the extent of the collection. As published here, it consists of 31,500 personal names plus 7,700 toponyms and 2,300 ethnonyms which were originally anthroponyms. In the present Onomasticon there are also some 4,000 references and more than 10,000 entries that provide the possible meaning(s) of the headword, which are followed by short etymological explanations or references to the related entries.

The structure of the *Onomasticon Turcicum* and the manner of publishing were essentially thought out by LÁSZLÓ RÁSONYI. Some details, however, were fixed during our work together. With Professor RÁSONYI, we arranged the names into entries (articles) on the basis of their etymology. The idea of processing the collection on computer and the way of presenting the data in the Onomasticon as well as solving the relevant part-tasks are the result of IMRE BASKI's research and experiments done after the death of LÁSZLÓ RÁSONYI in 1984.[65]

Notes on the Sources Used by Rásonyi

Due to the many decades of collecting and the great variety of sources, the data are not homogeneous. There are many incomplete entries which have insufficient information on the person and the age he lived in. In such cases, even the approximate fixing of the time when the bearer of the name lived would require time-consuming research. In some cases the completion of the incomplete cards and the correction of the defective data are inevitable, but it seems impossible to add all the missing details for the whole collection. Moreover, since we do not have all the sources at our disposal that LÁSZLÓ RÁSONYI used, the publication of the collection would be delayed further.

L. RÁSONYI drew his data from more than half a thousand sources, including Arabic and Persian historical sources, maps, vocabularies, travel books and simple articles from different periodicals.[66] For early historical data it is almost impossible to determine the exact ethnic and language relations (dialect) of a person, because chroniclers were educated men and followed certain normative literary norms when taking names down. From the point of view of quantity of names available, RÁSONYI arranged his sources into five major categories: I. 1-10 items (e.g., Anan'ev; Gayretullah),

---

[62] See the list of *Rásonyi's works on Turkic onomastics*, p. XV.

[63] Akadémiai Értesítő [Bulletin of the Hungarian Academy] XLII, 1932, pp. 153-155.

[64] Baski 1986.

[65] For the details, see Baski 1997. The Hungarian Academy of Sciences has effectively supported I. Baski's efforts from the very beginning, making it possible for him to spend the major part of his time working on the collection. The work was promoted from 1983 to 1988 by the Research Group for Oriental Studies directed by late Acad. Prof. F. Tőkei, then from 1993 to date by the Research Group for Altaic Studies directed by Prof. G. Kara to whom special thanks and gratitude must be expressed for his manifold help and encouragement.

[66] For a short list of his sources see Rásonyi, Kayn. pp. 74-96.

Rásonyi's Works on Turkic Onomastics

II. 10-100 items (e.g., Arīb; Grod., Vojna; Müller, Pfahl.), III. 100-1000 items (e.g., DAI; Grod., Pril.; HRS; Iyās; Potanin, Pred.), IV. 1,000-10,000 items (e.g., MIB; MIK), V. 10,000- items (e.g., AOA; AOK; AOP; SOK; SOV).

In the section *Bibliographical Abbreviations* we have also listed the most significant works which essentially have not been used in the Onomasticon Turcicum because of the timelimit (1984) and because of the simple fact that we were not in possession of most of them. We are firmly convinced, however, that for those who intend to do further research on Turkic onomastics these bibliographical items will provide a certain guidance.

Rásonyi's Works on Turkic Onomastics

1. *Kún személyneveinkről*. Budapest 1921, 38 pp. (Bölcsészdoktori értekezés [Thesis of Doctor of Philosophy], manuscript.).
2. *Török eredetű magyar tulajdonnevek*: KCsA I (1922), pp. 237-239.
3. *Adalékok török tulajdonneveinkhez*: NyK XLVI (1923), pp. 124-135.
4. *Kulán és Szoltán*: MNy. XXII (1926), p. 348.
5. *Bula*: MNy. XXII (1926), pp. 212-213.
6. *Karcag*: MNy. XXII (1926), pp. 348-349.
7. *Borcsol és Csertán*: MNy. XXII (1926), pp. 132-133.
8. *Bokor és Bakony*: MNy. XXIII (1927), pp. 561-571.
9. *Taksony*: MNy. XXIII (1927), p. 274.
10. *Kajtor*: MNy. XXIII (1927), p. 594.
11. *Valacho-Turcica*: Aus den Forschungsarbeiten der Mitglieder d. Collegium Hungaricum dem Andenken R. Graggers gewidmet: FMUI. Berlin (1927), pp. 1-29.
12. *Komócsin*: MNy. XXIII (1927), pp. 52-53.
13. *Török eredetű helynevek*: NyK XLVI (1927), pp. 464-469.
14. *Ormán*: MNy. XXIV (1928), pp. 23-28.
15. *Becs*: MNy. XXIV (1928), p. 210.
16. *A Brassó név eredete*: MNy. XXIV (1928), pp. 311-318.
17. *Kál és társai*: MNy. XXV (1929), p. 121 (Together with Dezső Pais).
18. *Kalacs*: MNy. XXV (1929), pp. 124-127.
19. *Régi családnevek keletkezése*: Új Barázda (1929 /03. 31./)).
20. *Mire tanítanak a helynevek?*: Új Barázda (1929 /06. 23./).
21. *Karaiman, Caraiman herceg*: MNy. XXVI (1930), pp. 392-393.
22. *Mire tanítanak a magyarság régi törzs-és népnevei?*: Magyarság (1930 /08. 10./).
23. *A honfoglaló magyarsággal kapcsolatos török tulajdonnevekhez*: MNy. XXVIII (1932), pp. 100-105.
24. *A Szörény név etymológiájához*: MNy. XXVIII (1932), pp. 308-309.
25. *Baszaraba*: MNy. XXIX (1933), pp. 160-171.
26. *Der Volksname Берендѣй*: Seminarium Kondakovianum VI. Praha (1933), pp. 119-126.
27. *Az oláh államiság kialakulása*: MNy. XX (1933), pp. 160-171.
28. *Türk has isimleri I-II*: Hakimiyet-i Milliye. Ankara (1934 /10-11 Nisan/).
29. *Contributions à l'histoire des premières cristallisations d'état des Roumains*: Archivum Europae Centro-Orientalis I (1935), pp. 221-53.
30. *Kolbászszék*: MNy. XXXII (1936), pp. 266-267.
31. *Contributions à l'histoire des premières cristallisations d'état des Roumains. L'origine des Basarabas.* Budapest (1936), 38 pp. (Études sur l'Europe Centre-Orientale III).
32. *Les noms de tribus dans le Слово о полку Игореве*: Rásonyi - Rasovsky - Toll: Замѣтки к Слово. Praha (1936), pp. 1-9 (Sem. Kond. 8).
33. *Zur Frage der Eigennamen bei Anonymus*: Ungarische Jahrbücher (Gedenkschrift Zoltán von Gombocz) 15 (1936), pp. 548-554.
34. *Ortaçağda Erdel'de Türklüğün İzleri*: II. Türk Tarih Kongresi Yazıları. İstanbul, (1937), 18 pp. (Offprint.).
35. *Ortaçağda Erdel'de Türklüğün İzleri*: Belleten II (1938), pp. 107-122.
36. *Tuna havzasında Kumanlar*: Belleten III (1939), pp. 401-422.
37. *Selçük adının menşeine dair*: Belleten III (1939), pp. 377-384.
38. *A   névhez*: MNy. XXXVI (1940), pp. 291-294.
39. *Makut - Maklár*: MNy. XXXVII (1941), pp. 116-118.
40. *Török adatok a Magyar Etymológiai Szótárhoz*: NyK LI (1941-1943), pp. 98-115, 280-308.
41. *Dünya Tarihinde Türklük*. Ankara 1942, 266 pp.

42. *Bō-kolabur*: Türk Tarih Kurumu Halil Ethem Hâtira Kitabı. Ankara (1947), pp. 242-248.

43. *Sur quelques catégories de noms de personne en turc*: ALingu. III (1953), pp. 323-353.

44. *Mit mondanak Szolnok megye földrajzi nevei?*: Jászkunság 3 (1956), pp. 75-80.

45. *A kiskunsági -lï, -li, > -la, -le képzős földrajzi nevek*: MNy. LII (1956), pp. 52-61.

46. *Köncsög és Kötöny*: Pais Emlékkönyv. Budapest (1956), pp. 435-441.

47. *Les noms toponymiques comans du Kiskunság*: ALingu VII (1957-1958), pp. 73-146.

48. *Miscellanea Arabo-Turcica*: I. Goldziher Memorial Vol. II. Jerusalem (1958), pp. 133-135.

49. *A Tantó családnév eredete*: MNy. LIV (1958), p. 545.

50. *A székely név eredete*: MNy. LVI (1960), pp. 186-194.

51. *Les noms de nombre dans l'anthroponymie turque*: AOH XII (1961), pp. 45-71.

52. *Zu den Namen der ersten türkischen Herren von Jerusalem*: AOH XIII (1961), pp. 89-95.

53. *L'origine du nom székely (sicule)*: ALingu. 11 (1961), pp. 175-188.

54. *Über die geographischen Namen Tortillou und Tatrang*: UAJb. XXXIII (1961), pp. 245-251.

55. *Kiskunság'da Kumanca Yer Adları*: Németh Arm. Ankara (1962), pp. 341-352.

56. *Der Frauenname bei den Türkvölkern*: UAJb. XXXIV (1962), pp. 223-239.

57. *Les noms de personnes impératifs chez les peuples turques*: AOH XV (1962), pp. 233-243.

58. *Başkurt ve Macar yurtlarındaki ortak coğrafî adlar üzerine*: Bilimsel Bildiriler 1963. Ankara (1964), pp. 105-112.

59. *Türk Özel Adlarının Kaynakları*: Türkoloji Dergisi I (1964), pp. 71-101.

60. *Türklükte kadın adları*: TDAYB 1963 (1964), pp. 63-87.

61. *Macarca "gyermek" kelimesi ve "Yermyak" adı*: Reşid Rahmeti Arat İçin (1966), pp. 383-387 (Türk Kültürünü Araştırma Estitüsü Yayınları: 19).

62. *A Kiskunság középkori helyneveihez*: MNy. LXII (1966), pp. 164-170.

63. *Kuman Özel Adları*: Türk Kültürü Araştırmaları III-IV-V-VI (1966-1969), pp. 71-144.

64. *Les anthroponymes Comans de Hongrie*: AOH XX (1967), pp. 135-149.

65. *Türk Özel Adları ve Leksikografyası*: Bilimsel Bildiriler 1966. Ankara (1968), pp. 39-47.

66. *Sekeller ve adlarının menşei*: Türk Kültürü X (1972), pp. 289-294.

67. *The Psychology and Categories of Name Giving Among the Turkish Peoples*: Hungaro-Turcica. Budapest (1976), pp. 207-223.

68. *Azonos földrajzi nevek a baskír és a magyar földön*: MNy. LXXII (1976), pp. 48-53.

69. *Bulaqs And Oguzs In Mediaeval Transylvania*: AOH XXXIII (1979), pp. 129-151.

70. *Remnants of Theophoric Names in Turkic Name Giving*: Belleten XLVI /182/ (1982), pp. 291-296.

71. *The Old-Hungarian Name Vajk. - a Note on the Origin of the Hunyadi Family*: AOH XXXVI (1983), pp. 1-3.

72. *Török eredetű magyar személynevek*: Forrás XV /7/. Kecskemét (1983 /július/), pp. 78-84.

The Recent State of Turkic Onomastics

Russian (later Soviet) scholars have played a significant role in the promotion of onomatological research from the very beginning,[67] but the greatest progress was made in the late 50s of the 20th century. Lately, the major part of the results in Turkic anthroponymy has been achieved due to V. A. NIKONOV's efforts.[68] Much research has been done, many articles, dissertations, over 50 books, and about 50 dictionaries of names have been written and various materials have been published on Turkic onomastics since then.[69] Thus we have already had numerous dictionaries, guides, alphabetical lists, for instance, of Bashkir, Gagauz, Kazakh, Tatar, and Turkmen, anthroponyms, but they cannot be considered complete, because outdated and ill-sounding names have been left out by the editors, even though they would be of special value for the research. Most of these dictionaries do not provide references to components of names which are not in an initial position. Thus the components remain hidden and only indirectly accessible to the users.[70]

Especially valuable are the investigations of N. A. BASKAKOV's, who, writing and editing the Nogay, Karakalpak, Oyrot (Altay) and Hakas dictionaries, always added lists of personal names. Later he analyzed over 300 Russian family names of Turkic origin.[71]

Thanks to the activity of our forerunners, a new generation of onomatologists has been brought up in the Soviet Union. Some of its representatives received academic degrees (3 doctors of sciences, over 50 candidates of sciences) in onomastics between 1940 and 1982.[72] These specialists work in groups/sectors of onomastics of academic institutes or teach at universities. Consequently, a great number of advanced degree work on Turkic onomastics has been written at several universities. These works may be very important for scientific research, because most of them are based on fieldwork and may supply new, yet unknown material.

With so many researchers of Turkic onomastics and with the increasing interest in the results of this new branch, several conferences and seminars have been held in the different regions - e.g., in the Volga-Region (1969, 1971, 1973, 1976), in the Caucasus (1976), in Central Asia (1969, 1978, 1980, 1981, 1983). At the 1st All-Soviet Conference on Personal Names (Moscow, 1968) the anthroponymy of Turkic peoples was presented by dozens of lectures. The papers read usually have been collected and published in separate books such as *Onomastika* (1966, 1969), *Antroponimika* (1970), *Êtnografija imen* (1971), *Istoričeskaja onomastika* (1977), *Êtničeskaja onomastika* (1984), rich sources for further research.[73]

Unfortunately, there are no specific journals for (Turkic) onomastics in the republics of the former Soviet Union. Dozens of significant papers on Turkic onomastics came out in different lingustic journals, such as in *Sovetskoe jazykoznanie* [Soviet Linguistics], *Voprosy jazykoznanija* [Problems of Linguistics], *Sovetskaja tjurkologija* [Soviet Turkology], etc.

One of the current tasks of modern Turkic anthroponymy is the systematization and processing of the available material with the aim of inner reconstruction of the system of Ancient Turkic anthroponyms.[74] A preliminary study on this task has been done by G. F. BLAGOVA (1997). In the chapter "Antroponimika" [Anthroponymy] in the collective work *Sravnitel'no-istoričeskaja grammatika tjurkskih jazykov. Leksika* [Comparative Grammar of Turkic Languages Lexicon] (1997), she attempted the formal and semantic reconstruction of anthroponymycal units. She stated that the units in question did not exist in isolation or as a lifeless mass, but constituted dynamic interrelationships. It has been proved that the semantic model of the world concept of the Ancient Turks was reflected in their personal names.[75]

Intensive research in the field of Turkic onomatology is being made in the Turkic Republics themselves, such as Uzbekistan, Azerbaijan, Kirghizia, Turkmenistan, Chuvashia, Tatarstan, Bashkiria, Altay Republic, Hakasia, Yakutia and Tuva. Many onomatological studies appeared in West Turkestan and a number of bibliographies offer valuable material for name research. It must be noted, however, that research of anthroponyms has lagged significantly from that of the toponyms.[76]

Researchers of academic institutes in Tatarstan, Bashkiria, Kazakstan, etc., have set up card files of proper names

---

[67] See above, p. IX.; cf. also Džanuzakov, 1984, 15, where he enumerates the main representatives from the different republics.

[68] Blagova, 1998b, p. 45.

[69] Cf. Tjurk. Onom. p. 3; Džanuzakov, op. cit. p. 13.

[70] Blagova, 1998b, p. 46.

[71] Bask., Fam. (1979); Reviewed by I. Baski: AOH XLI (1987), 135-138 pp.

[72] Tjurk. Onom. p. 3.

[73] Nikonov, p. 85; Tjurk. Onom. p. 3.

[74] Blagova, 1998b, p. 53.

[75] Blagova, 1997, pp. 619, 723.

[76] Tjurk. Onom. p. 3; T. D. Džanuzakov, Razvitie tjurkskoj onomastiki v SSSR. In: Tjurk. Onom. pp. 13-15, 22-23.

which contain tens of thousands of data from different sources. These files are continuously being enriched and searched, which is quite promising for the progress of Turkic onomatology in the future.

In Hungary, the great generation of scholars of the second half of the 20th century continued searching the early Turco-Hungarian relations. In this field, study of old Hungarian proper names played a significant part. Numerous minor writings, mainly etymologies, were written on ethnonyms (by CZEGLÉDY, GYÖRFFY, MARTINKÓ, MOÓR, NÉMETH, PAIS, RÁSONYI, etc.), on toponyms (by BLAŠKOVIČ, GYÖRFFY, KÁLMÁN, LIGETI, MOÓR, PAIS, RÁSONYI, SINOR, etc.), on personal names (by BÁRCZI, BENKŐ, GYÖRFFY, LIGETI, NÉMETH, PAIS, RÁSONYI, SCHEIBER, etc.).[77]

The younger generation of Hungarian orientalists, have also investigated the inherited traditional onomatological topics. In this respect mention should be made of ZS. KAKUK, I. MÁNDOKY-KONGUR, A. RÓNA-TAS, J. TORMA, I. VÁSÁRY, etc.

One of the traditional fields of Hungarian Turkology is the study of historical, cultural and linguistic influence of the Ottoman conquest. L. FEKETE, ZS. KAKUK, J. NÉMETH, I. SUGÁR, J. TOMPA, etc., published a number of significant works on Turkish names (and Hungarian names of Turkish origin).

Concerning the Ottoman elements of Hungarian, ZS. KAKUK published the richest material, Turkish proper names included, and made the most profound studies.[78] She selected the personal names from the material available in the Hungarian archives of the 16th-17th centuries and discussed them in her separate study titled "Quelques catégories de noms personnes turcs."[79] The title of the article, however, is misleading, because it focuses not on the categories but on the Turkish personal names found in various Hungarian sources of the 16th and 17th centuries. As for the categories listed at the beginning of the article, it is a regrettable simplification of RÁSONYI's system taken over by the author together with some obvious mistakes.[80]

Hungarian research of Kuman names began with GOMBOCZ,[81] NÉMETH and RÁSONYI. In this field the activity of ISTVÁN MÁNDOKY KONGUR (1944-1992) offered promise. In the old birth registers he identified a number of Kuman names. These were partly nicknames, partly surnames, originally anthroponyms. Some were used to differentiate families bearing the same surname. He found, for instance, that one of GYULA NÉMETH's grandmothers had the surname *Köszömös* (< Kumanian *Küsemiš*).[82]

JÓZSEF TORMA (1943-2000), another gifted Hungarian Turkologist did fruitful fieldwork among the Bashkirs and the Turks of Central Asia. Studying questions of the magic elements of Bashkir folk medicine and other customs, he gathered evidence on the traditional name-giving. He contributed two articles (1990, 1992) and some sections in his books (1997, 1999) to the theme. In the last but one, he dealt with the extremely important problem of the teleological function of naming. In a chapter of his last book devoted to the memory of his colleague ISTVÁN MÁNDOKY KONGUR who passed away untimely, he compared the Kuman and Kazakh anthroponyms grouping them into nine categories.

The activity of scholars in Turkey is being continued in the recent period (from 1950) when hundreds of Turkish names (BANARLI 1950, ÖNDER 1955, ONGAN 1956, etc.), dozens of valuable articles on Turkish naming customs (DALBOY 1956, TAHSİN 1960, ARICAN 1960, ÖZERGİN 1970, etc.) were published in the ethnographic journal *Türk Folklor Araştırmaları* (İstanbul, 1945-1972). Here we must stress the activity of AHMET CAFEROĞLU, the outstanding Turkish linguist, because he was among the first to deal with some general questions of Turkic (Azerbaijani, Turkish, Uyghur, etc.) names (see his works of 1931, 1952, 1961).

From 1962 till 1971 RÁSONYI worked in Ankara. At that time he published several works of great importance for Turkic onomatology[83] and was considered to be the only serious and prestigious researcher of Turkic personal names in Turkey. Years after RÁSONYI returned home, T. GÜLENSOY complained: "Türk kültürüne uzun yıllar hizmet ederek ölümsüz eserler bırakan Rasonyi'nin Macaristan'a dönmesiyle bu sahanın [onomatology] sözcülüğünü yapacak ikinci bir ilim adamı kalmamıştır" [Leaving behind immortal works, after serving the Turkish culture for many years, RÁSONYI returned to Hungary without leaving a successor to promote this field (onomatology)].[84] As far as we can learn from the words of AYDİL EROL, the situation did not change much in the subsequent nearly twenty years: "Memleketimizde bu güne değin kişi adları sahasında yapılan çalışmalar, ne yazık ki, bir kaç makalenin sınırını aşmamakta, onlar da üç beş kelimeyle – hattâ bazıları bir tek kelimeyle – sınırlı kalmaktadır." [It is a pity, that until today works done in the field of personal names in our country have not surpassed the margins of several articles which deal with one or two, sometimes

---

[77] For the titles see chapter *Bibliographical Abbreviations (Bibliography)*, p. LXXXIX.

[78] S. Kakuk, *Recherches sur l'histoire de la langue osmanlie des XVIe et XVIIe siècles. Les éléments osmanlis de la langue hongroise.* Budapest, 1973, 660 pp. (BOH 19.)

[79] AOH XXVIII (1974), pp. 1-37.)

[80] For the false classifications of this kind see Nikonov, op. cit., pp. 94-95.

[81] Gombocz, ÁTSz.

[82] Mándoky Kongur, István, *A kun nyelv magyarországi emlékei.* Karcag, 1993, p. 142.

[83] See Nos. 55, 57, 59, 61, 63 in his bibliography (p. XV).

[84] Atsız Armağanı, 1976, p. 257; quoted in Erol I, and Erol II, pp. IV, VIII.

with only one single word (=name)].[85]

Indeed, from the 1950s until the end of the 1980s, only short papers on anthroponyms (KIRZIOĞLU 1961, ÇAĞATAY 1962, YUND 1981, ATSIZ 1984, S. SAKAOĞLU 1984, etc.) and toponyms (GAZİMİHAL 1958, YUND 1960, GÜLENSOY 1979, ERÖZ 1966, etc.) appeared in Turkish. Of great interest are also the short articles on surviving Anatolian popular customs and beliefs concerning name-giving (e.g., ÜLKÜTAŞIR 1963, ÖZERGİN 1970, YETİŞEN 1972, etc.).

Interest in place names has grown during the last two decades nevertheless the study of personal names continue to dominate. Most articles present the toponymy of a settlement or region in general (e.g., ÖNDER, 1982, SEVİNÇ 1983, YEDİYILDIZ 1984, HALİT EREN 1988, GÜNAY 1989, OY 1990, BAYKARA 1991, etc.). Only a few of the studies deal with specific problems of Turkish toponyms (e.g., ERÖZ 1986, KIRZIOĞLU 1988, TEKİN 1990, etc.).

The papers of the first symposium on Turkish toponyms[86] demonstrate the significant progress which was done in Turkish onomatology in general, and in toponymy in particular. Some scholars regularly deal with proper names; for example, FAHRETTİN KIRZIOĞLU wrote his first article on personal names in 1949; MEHMET ERÖZ, TUNCER GÜLENSOY and SAİM SAKAOĞLU also have many years of experience in name research. Professor TUNCER GÜLENSOY has collected more than 20,000 entries for his research project titled "Onomasticum Mongolicum-Turcicum." His collection has not been published yet, the pieces of data sorted and explained are still on index cards.[87]

Among the publications issued in the last decades we can find several guidebooks on Turkish personal (first) and family names (soyadı). These books are meant to help when naming children thus they may also serve language engineering (e.g., KUTLU 1969,[88] PAR 1981, ÇELİK 1991, İLAHİYATÇI 1992, ERK 1997, etc.). Such books were published on the Turkish toponyms as well (e.g., ACAROĞLU 1988, GÜLENSOY 1995, etc.).

Recently more voluminous works and articles have appeared. The first is AYDİL EROL's *Adlarımız* (1989) which contains about 3,000 personal names selected from different ages and scenes of Turkic history. The second edition of the book was published in 1992. The number of names has been enlarged to 5,000 items. Unfortunately the majority of these names is of Arab-Persian origin, which is always referred to, while the exact affiliation of the Turkic (e.g., Kuman, Kazakh, Tatar, etc.) names is not shown. Despite its size, the book cannot be considered a thorough and valid guidebook of names, because in numerous cases explanations are missing, or the interpretation given is not based on reliable research.[89]

YILMAZ KURT's sizeable monographs (1990, 1991, 1994) provide diachronic material from different regions of Anatolia. The author analyses his data meeting the contemporary standards of historical onomatology.

The study of ethnonyms in Turkey has, unfortunately, fallen behind. From the very few studies published so far on this topic, NECDET SEVİNÇ's monograph on the ethnonyms and toponyms of Gaziantep (1983) must be praised for its thoroughness.

FARUK SÜMER's (1924-1995) voluminous work *Türk Devletleri Tarihinde Şahıs Adları* (1999) is to be mentioned amongst the very few monographs of scientific value. SÜMER was well known as an outstanding historian and expert of Oghuz history. After his death, was issued a much awaited reference book by him on Turkic history which hopefully will be a reliable resource in the hands of linguists-Turkologists as well.

SAİM SAKAOĞLU, professor at Selçuk Üniversitesi, Konya, Turkey, has dealt with Turkish onomastics as well. He has written valuable articles in this field for almost twenty years. The first volume of his comprehensive work on Turkish onomastics titled *Türk Ad Bilimi I. (Giriş)* has been published very recently (2001) as a consecutive publication of Türk Dil Kurumu.[90]

Lately, scholars from Western countries have studied mainly modern Turkish names (e.g., BAŞGÖZ, BULLIET, SPENCER, SCHIMMEL, etc.).

Bibliographies

1. *Türk Folklor ve Etnografya Bibliyografyası*. IV (1974-1984). A. Özmen, M. Muhtar Kutlu, G. Erginer (ed.). Ankara, 1999.
2. Malinskaja, B. A. and Šabat, M. C. (eds.), *Onomastika*. Ukazatel' literatury - izdannoj v SSSR za 1971-1975 gg. s pril. za 1918-1962 gg. M. 1978, 301 pp.
3. Caferoğlu, A., *Bibliographia Onomastica:* Turquie (Türkiye): Onoma 3-14 (1952-1969).
4. Rásonyi, L., *Türk Özel Adlarının Kaynakları*: Türkoloji Dergisi I (1964), pp. 71-101.
5. *Inostrannaja literatura po toponimike*. Bibliografičeskij obzor. M. 1965, 40 pp.

---

[85] Erol I, p. IV, Erol II, p. IV.
[86] Türk Yer Adları Sempozyumu (Ankara, 1984).
[87] Gülensoy, 1999, p. 4.
[88] 1,000 female and 6,000 male names are provided for this purpose.
[89] The book was sternly criticized by H. Eren (Türk Dili 495 (1993), pp. 216-238).
[90] At the time of writing, we have not had access to these books.

6. Caferoğlu, A. and Trubačev, O. N., *Bibliographia Onomastica:* Altaic: Onoma 15-16 (1970-1971), pp. 777-787; pp. 722-736.

7. Zinin, S. I., *Onomastika respublik Srednej Azii i Kazahstana.* Kratkij bibliografičeskij ukazatel' literatury za 1917-1972 gg. Taškent, 1974, 36 pp.

8. Gorjačeva, T., *Bibliographia Onomastica:* Altaic: Onoma 18, 23. 3-4 (1974, 1979), pp. 239-247; pp. 691-692.

9. Gorjačeva, T. and Mikesy, S., *Bibliographia Onomastica:* Altaic: Onoma 20. 2-3 (1976), pp. 533-542.

10. Nafaszov, T., Begmatov, E. A. and Karaev, S. (eds.), Onomastika Uzbegistana. (Bibliografičeskij ukazatel' konca XIX. veka - 1988. g.). Taškent, 1989.

11. Nasrattinoğlu, İrfan, [Title unknown] Türkeli Gazetesi 15-16 Ekim, 1994.

12. Bozyiğit, A. E., *Türk Adbilimi Bibliyografyası.* Ankara, 1995, 190 pp.

Name-Dictionaries on Turkic Languages

Personal names

1. *Azerbaycan kişi adları.*

2. Atalay, Besim, *Türk Büyükleri veya Türk Adları.* Istanbul, 1935.

3. Kutlu, Şemsettin, *Türkçe Kadın ve Erkek Adları.* Ankara, 1969. (TDK Yayınları S. 281).

4. Gafurov, Alim, *Lev i Kiparis Vostočnye imena.* M. 1971.

5. Begmatov Ê. A., Uzbek ismlari imlosi *Pravopisanie uzbekskih imjon.* Tashkent, 1972, 383 pp.

6. Bol'šakov, I. V. and Subaeva, R. H., *Spravočnik tatarskih ličnyh imen.* Kazan', 1973, 99 pp.

7. Asanaliev, Ü. and Kosalov, İ. S., *Qïrÿïz Adam Attarïnïñ Sözlügü Praktikalïk qoldonmo.* Frunze, 1979.

8. Žaparov, Š. (ed.), *Slovar' kirgizskih ličnyh imen.* Praktičeskoe posobie. Otv. red. U. Asanaliev, pod obščej red. I. S. Kolosova. Sostavitel' Š. Žaparov. Frunze, 1979, 464 pp.

9. Sattarov, G. F., *Tatar isemnäre süzlege.* Kazan, 1981, 255 pp.

10. Kusimova, T., *Baškirskie imena* Bašqort isemdäre. Ufa, 1982, 136 pp.

11. Žanuzakov, T., *Očerk Kazahskoj onomastiki.* Ličnye imena (pp. 126-163), Kosmonimy (pp. 163-164), Êtnonimy (pp. 164-174). Alma-Ata 1982, 175 pp.

12. Mirzäjev, O. M., *Adlarïmïz* - Naši imena. Bakï,1986, 296 pp.

13. Gafurov, Alim, *Imja i istorija. Ob imenah arabov, persov, tadžikov i tjurkov.* (Slovar' arabskih, persidskih, tadžikskih i tjurkskih imen). M. 1987, 220 pp.

14. Žanuzakov, T. and Esbaeva K. S., *Qazaq esïmderï - Kazahskie imena.* Anïqtama sözdïk - Slovar' - spravočnik. Alma-Ata, 1988, 480 pp.

15. Dron, I. V. and Kuroglo, S. S., *Sovremennaja gagauzskaja toponimija i antroponimija.* Otv. red. T. A. Gajdoraš. (Slovar' gagauzskih familij i prozvišč, pp. 116-180; Slovar' gagauzskih imen, pp. 181-202 (Mužskie imena, pp. 181-194; Ženskie imena, pp. 195-202). Kišinev 1989, 214 pp.

16. Erol, Aydil, *Şarkılarla Şiirlerle Türkülerle ve Tarihî Örneklerle Adlarımız.* Ankara, 1989, 277 pp.

17. *Spravočnik turkmenskih ličnyh imen.* Ašhabad, 1989.

18. Butanaev, V. Ja., *Xöray attarï.* Xakasskie ličnye imena. Abakan, 1990(?), 108 pp.

19. Kupusovič, Amina, *Muslimanska imena u Opširnom popisu 60 sanskog sandžaka iz 1604 godine:* Prilozi za orijentalnu filologiju 40/1990. Sarajevo, (1991), pp 267-308.

20. Ozenbašlï, Ê. M., *Qïrïmtatar adlarï Krymskotatarskie imena.* Aqmesjit ó Simferopol,' 1992, 47 pp.

21. İlahiyatçı, Kaya Hüsameddin, *Çocuk İsimleri Ansiklopedisi.* Gonca Yayınevi, ? 1992.

22. Erol, Aydil, *Şarkılarla Şiirlerle Türkülerle ve Tarihî Örneklerle Adlarımız* (genişletilmiş - geliştirilmiş 2. baskı). Ankara, 1992, 468 pp. (Türk Kültürünü Araştırma Enstitüsü Yayınları: 124, Seri: 1, Sayı A. 24).

23. Kajbullaev, Š. Ê., *Krymskotatarskie imena* Proishoždenie i značenie. Simferopol' 1994, 81 pp.

24. Bayerle, Gustav, *Pashas, Begs and Effendis: A Historical Dictionary of Titles and Terms in the Ottoman Empire.* Istanbul, 1997.

25. Yurtsever, Erk, *Türkçe Adlar Derlemesi.* Istanbul, 1997, 128 pp. [A collection of Turkic anthroponyms, ethnonyms and toponyms.]

26. Gülensoy, Tuncer, *Açıklamalı Kırgız Kişi Adları Sözlüğü.* (Kadın - Erkek).

27. Amanoğlu (Quliyev), Ebülfez, *Eski Türk Onomastik Sözlüğü.* Baku, Elm, 1999, 124 pp.

28. Sümer, Faruk, *Türk Devletleri Tarihinde Şahıs Adları.* I-II. Istanbul, 1999, 878 pp. (Türk Dünyası Araştırmaları Vakfı).

Toponyms

1. *Slovar' toponimii Kryma.* Kartoteka [Cardfile].
2. Iznoskov, I. A., *Opyt istoriko-geografičekogo slovarja Kazanskogo uezda.*
3. Maksimovič, L. M. and Ščekatov, A. M., *Geografičeskij slovar' Rossijskogo gosudarstva.* M. 1801-1809.
4. Semenov-Tjan-Šanskij, P. P., *Geografičesko-statističeskij slovar' Rossijskoj imperii.* I-V. SPb. 1863-1885.
5. Mostras, G., *Dictionnaire géographique de l' Empire Ottoman.* St.Pétersburg, 1873.
6. Candar, Avni, *Anadolu Coğrafya Luğatı Sınaçları* 1 – Ankara. Ankara, 1938, 96 pp.
7. Äbdirahmanov, A. (Abdrahmanov, A.), *Qazaqstannïñ žer-su attarï.* Alma-Ata, 1959, 219 pp.
8. *Tolkovyj slovar' geografičeskih nazvanij Azerbajdžanskoj SSR.* Baku, 1960.
9. Isaev, Tokombaev, Aliev (et al.), *Slovar' geografičeskih nazvanij Kirgizii.* (Project). Frunze, 1962.
10. Konkašpaev, T. K., *Slovar' kazahskih geografičeskih nazvanij.* Alma-Ata, 1963, 185 pp.
11. Karaev, S. K., *Rusko uzbekskij slovar' geografičeskih nazvanij.* Tashkent, 1964.
12. Rototaev, P. S., *Kratkij slovar' gornih nazvanij Kabardino-Balkarii.* Nal'čik, 1969, 100 pp.
13. Kokov, Dž. N. - Šahmurzaev, S. O., *Balkarskij toponimičeskij slovar'.* Nal'čik, 1970, 170 pp.
14. *Slovar' geografičeskih terminov i drugih slov, vstrečajuščihja v toponimii Azerbajdžanskoj SSR.* M. 1971.
15. Volostnova, M. B., *Slovar' geografičeskih terminov i drugih slov, vetrečajučšihsja v toponimii Tuvinskoj ASSR.* M. 1971, 114 pp.
16. Juzbašev, R., Äliyev, K., Sädiyev, *Azerbayjanïn joyrafi adlarï.* Baqï, 1972
17. Kojčubaev, E., *Kratkij tolkovyj slovar' toponimov Kazahstana.* Alma-Ata, 1974, 275 pp.
18. Äbdïrahmanov, A. Ä., *Toponimika žäne êtimologiya.* Almaty, 1975, 206 pp.
19. Hasanov, H. H., *Geografik nâmlar maᶜnâsi.* Tâshkent, 1978
20. Molčanova, O. T., *Toponimičeskij slovar' Gornogo altaja.* Gorno-Altajsk, 1979, 397 pp.
21. Karaev, S. K., *Tolkovyj slovar' geografičeskih terminov.* (Na uzbekskom jazyke). Tashkent, 1979.
22. Kamalov, A. A. (Ed), *Slovar' toponimov baškirskoj ASSR.* Ufa, 1980, 200 pp.
23. Konkobaev, K., *Toponimija Južnoj Kirgizii.* Frunze, 1980, 171 pp.
24. Matveev, A. K., *Geografičeskie nazvanija Urala.* Kratkij toponimičeskij slovar'. Sverdlovsk, 1980, 318 pp.
25. Bagdaryn, S., *Toponimy Jakutii.* Yakutsk, 1982.
26. Garipova, F. T., *Tatarstan gidronimnarï süzlege.* Kazan, 1984, 224 pp.
27. Dron, I. V. and Kuroglo, S. S., *Sovremennaja gagauzskaja toponimija i antroponimija.* Otv. red. T. A. Gajdoraš. (Slovar' gagauzskih familij i prozvišč, pp. 116-180; Slovar' gagauzskih imen, pp. 181-202 (Mužskie imena, pp. 181-194; Ženskie imena, pp. 195-202). Kišinev 1989, 214 pp.
28. Garipova, F., *Tatarstan gidronimnarï süzlege.* Kazan, 1990.
29. Yurtsever, Erk, *TAMGA. Asya'daki Türkçe Coğrâfî Adlar Derlemesi.* Istanbul, 1994.
30. Gülensoy, Tuncer, *Türkçe yer adları kılavuzu.* Ankara, 1995.
31. Yurtsever, Erk, Türkçe Adlar Derlemesi. Istanbul, 1997, 128 pp. [A collection of Turkic anthroponyms, ethnonyms and toponyms.]

Ethnonyms

1. Žanuzakov, T., *Očerk Kazahskoj onomastiki.* Ličnye imena (pp. 126-163), Kosmonimy (pp. 163-164), Êtnonimy (pp. 164-174). Alma-Ata 1982, 175 pp.
2. Atanijazov, Soltanša, *Slovar' turkmenskih êtnonimov.* Ašhabad, 1988, 179 pp.
3. Lezina, I. N. and Superanskaja, A. V., *Slovar'-spravočnik tjurkskih rodoplemennyh nazvanij.* I-II. M. 1994, 466 pp. (Biblioteka Rossijskogo êtnografa)
4. Yurtsever, Erk, *Türkçe Adlar Derlemesi.* Istanbul, 1997, 128 pp. [A collection of Turkic anthroponyms, ethnonyms and toponyms.]
5. Karatayev, Olcobay, *Kırgız Etnonimler (Boy ve Kabile Adları) Sözlüğü.* Bişkek, 1993 (Kırgızstan-Türkiye Manas Üniversitesi Yayınları: 40)

Turkic Anthroponyms

General Notes on Turkic Name-giving

Name-giving has always played a very important part in the life of different peoples. It was especially meaningful with the nomads, where naming was a kind of scintillating poetry, which functioned on the basis of a traditional system accompanied by a series of old customs and ceremonies which reflected their ideology. Notwithstanding the traditional naming conventions, name-giving by the nomadic Turks was full of lightness, idea, imagination, fantasy and invention. Turkic anthroponyms imply melody, rhyme and alliteration, pun and metaphor, polysemy and monosemy, myth and religion. Considering these features, it can be stated that traditional Turkic name-giving must be regarded as a specific genre of the living folk-poetry. As can be supposed, the earliest Old Turkic sources the folklore (mainly epics) paid special importance to the naming ceremony and usually Turkic names were preferred.[91] The existence of a well-developed traditional naming system with the Turks is evident, for example, in Old and New Uyghur sources and the Yakut documents of 17th and early 18th centuries.[92]

Process of Name-giving

Name-giving has always been a very important event in the life of individuals and, of course, their families. A newborn was named for a lifetime and it had to be done in memorable circumstances. It must be noted, however, that in some cases temporary names were given.

The real process of naming and the motives behind the name-giving can be traced to concrete descriptions supplied by different sources. Unfortunately, we have very few reliable descriptions. This is why we are often compelled to rely on analogies; otherwise the motive of name-giving and the meaning of a name can only be determined by speculation, which may be misleading.

Below, in terms of analogies, we present some examples for traditional naming in the past taken mainly from L. RÁSONYI's archive.

Traditional Naming Ceremonies/Customs:

1. Kacha, Koybal and Sagay ethnic groups in Hakasia, 1896: [...] Two or three days later another feast is held where people gathered for the name-giving. The newborn is held either by the midwife or the mother. The midwife offers some wine to the oldest man and says: "Give a name (to the child)!" He finds out a name and gives it to the child at this very moment. Then the father stands up and bows to that man saying: "You gave a name to my child!" Then the midwife offers some wine to the guests and collects gifts "for the tooth." People give either one or twenty Kopecks, buttons, rings, small crosses, etc. The parents take the things gathered. The feast ends like this and the guests leave.

Ceremonies following the childbirth are almost all the same with the Koybal, Kacha and Sagay people. When the newborn is taken to the church, the priest gives the child a Russian name.[93]

2. Karagass or Tofalar, early 20th c.: [...] This time someone from the respected guests, on the request of the father, gives the child a Karagass name. Mostly the name of the naming person himself, or that of his wife, mother, daughter or son is given. Or the name of another respected person is given even if he is not present. Only the name of a dead man cannot be given, because, as the Karagass say, it may be bad for the child. The father gives the man who named his child the hide of a deer and some meat, usually one leg of it. If childbirth took place in a lonely tent and there is no respected guest present at the eating of the meat, the name of the child is given by the parents themselves.[94]

3. Kazakhs:

3.1. Early 19th c.: [...] They give names to children sometimes at the moment of the birth, sometimes around one year of age, or when they begin to walk. It is only the caprice of father and mother that directs the selection of names. Sometimes a child is given a name according to the place of birth or the circumstances preceding the confinement, or according to the appearance of the newborn. Others receive the name of the person who enters the tent first after the childbirth; many parents try to give similar [i.e., related] names to all their sons.[95]

3.2. 2nd half of the 19th c.: [...] After the child was born and the necessary prayer was said by the mullah or some

---

[91] Ögel I, pp. 316, 533.

[92] Sadvakasov-Mahpirov, p. 29; Mahpirov, 1988 p. 51; Rudnyh, p. 221.

[93] Katanov, Otč. II, pp. 12-15, 42.

[94] Vasil'ev, V. N., Kratkij očerk byta karagasov: Êtnogr. Obozr. 1910, pp. 46-76.

[95] Levchine p. 356.

other educated man, the mother gives him/her a name. The Kazakh anthroponyms mesmerise us with their originality. If the child was born on a rainy day, the mother names him *Jañ yurča* "Rainy, Mackintosh." Women neighbours, having heard of the childbirth, gather round the mother and the talks begin: *Bay-bul* "Be Rich!" says one of them turning to the newborn: *Bay-bulsïn* "Let Him Be Rich!" says the other upholding the previous. The mother catches this phrase, converts it to anthroponym and names her child with it. There exist even such "strange" names that cannot be either translated or pronounced in ordinary company. Female names are also thought up by the mother and almost all of them sound nicer than the male names.[96]

3.3. End of the 19th c.: [...] On the fortieth day the newborn is given a name with certain solemnity again. The name is given by respected men of the aul or by the mullah. According to the Kazakhs the name of the child significantly affects his/her fate. They give their children the names of deceased relatives who lived their lives in affluence or that of famous persons. So that the child may not be bewitched and will not be ill, they sometimes give him an ugly name, such as *İt-ayaq* "Dog-Leg," *Qara-küčük* "Black Puppy," etc. Lately, thanks to the mullahs, the names of Muslim prophets have come into fashion among the Kazakhs.[97]

3.4. End of the 19th c.: [...] The newborn is dressed up [...] they celebrate a small feast called *bïsïk-toy* (cradle-feast), a feast for entertaining the women of the aul [...] The mullah is invited in order to give a name to the newborn. Children are usually given the names of deceased parents or relatives, preferring those who lived their lives in affluence and excelled in bravery and riding. Nowadays, more and more names of Muslim saints can be found among the Kirghiz [=Kazakhs] which is due to mullahs who are busy introducing the names of prophets so unusual for the Kirghiz.[98]

3.5. End of the 19th c.: [...] After the childbirth they slaughter a domestic animal. Lads are given a kid (goat) for playing *kükbüre*. Old men are entertained and the name is given.[99]

4. Chuvash, late 19th c.: The family where children died previously and who want to prevent child-death invite a quack besides the midwife on the day of birth. The quack waits outside in the courtyard. Right after the confinement the midwife swathes the child in rags and takes him out in the street. The quack immediately picks him up and brings him into the house saying: "I have found a child. I'll sell him, buy him! Maybe you need this child?"

"Where did you find him?"

"I found him in the garbage." (Sometimes he answers: "I found him in the spring.")

Then the midwife pays five Kopeks for him, takes him and cuts his navel. Thereafter she washes him and gives him the name *S'uppi* which he will bear forever. Then the quack takes the baby again and does some incantation in order to avert the evil eye.[100]

4.1. Chuvash, end of the 19th c.: On the next major feast after the birth of the little child he is given a name. This old heathen ceremony takes place within a narrow circle with prayers. The closest relatives and the midwife are invited. The naming normally takes place on the day following that particular feast for which they make preparations in advance with brewing. Around the morning meal the invited people are already gathering. The housewife puts a big plate in the middle of the table; on the plate there is a loaf topped with cheese. The kinsmen surround the table, a woman from the clan takes the dish with both hands and, turning towards the slightly open door, prays like this:

> *In the name of God, amen, Lord,*
> *we give (him) child-name,*
> *we give (the name) "Crow"* [this varies].
> *Be he sound and healthy,*
> *be he a ploughman,*
> *may he grow old (as we do),*
> *may he live until he puts his sandal on inversely,*
> *until he calls the old "uncle," when seeing them,*
> *until he calls the young "kinfolk," when seeing them.*
> *may he take care of his father and mother,*
> *be he of sound health,*
> *grow he big.*
> *May he have offspring, boys and girls.*
> *Let our clan not die out,*
> *let it go forever and ever.*
> *We grow old and die,*

---

[96] Sozontov, pp. 6-7.

[97] Kustanaev, pp. 37-38.

[98] Ibragimov, p. 124; cf. also Šile, Kirgizy. Êtnografičeskij očerk": Priroda i ljudi, 1879, aprel', p. 44.

[99] Grod., I, p. 98.

[100] Magn., Mat, pp. 196-198.

may he be blessed by us,
be he healthy and happy, amen.

Right after the prayer, the door must be closed quickly so that these words will not go out of the house. Then the praying old woman cuts the loaf into pieces, puts some cheese on each and gives everyone one piece each, then holding this cheese bread in the right hand, they pray again as they did before. The prayer is recited by the same old woman again. Then they sit down to eat and drink. If the newborn is a boy, the joy and the revelry is greater. Before leaving, the guests give a few Kopeks as a gift and the midwife too gets her payment that day.[101]

5. Turks of Turkey: Some days after the birth, the religious leader (hodja, mufti, imam, etc.) or the eldest of the family (grandfather, father) recites an *ezan* in a low voice into the right ear of the newborn, and saying your name is so-and-so, repeats the previously chosen name thrice. This final name is also called *ezan adı* (ezan-name, whispered in the left ear), while the temporary name given by the midwife is the *göbek adı* (umbilical name, whispered in the right ear). Sometimes names from the Koran are chosen as umbilical names.[102] In the region of Tokat two names may be given from which the umbilical name is considered the final (basic) one and only that one is used. As is reported by GORDLEVSKIJ, the Turkish village people bear one name but they have two: one given by the imam, the other chosen from the well-known names which are easy to remember and pronounce.[103]

Naming feasts differ only a little throughout Anatolia. Usually a banquet is given with entertainment. Relatives, close friends, respeted personalities are invited, the *Mevlût* is chanted, an *ezan* is recited while the child is turned toward Mecca.

In Samsun, Turkey, the umbilical name is replaced three days later without any feasts. The seventh day the cradle-feast (*beşik töreni*) is celebrated instead. In some places (e.g., in Tokat) the Koran and a gun are held when naming. In several places of Anatolia no special feasts are celebrated.

5.1. Turks, early 20th c., Istanbul, Turkey: On the day of name-giving all the relatives gather in the house. Usually it is the parents' taste that decides what name is chosen. If someone's children died before, they are named as *Dursun~Tursun* (Be Him/Her Healthy!, May He/She Survive!), *Durmuš* (Survived), girls only as *Yeter* (Enough of Dying!) In the case of an emergency, they depart from the Muslim norms and turn to the ancient traditions.[104]

5.2. Turks, late 20th c., village Hal, Turkey: Five *ezan*s are read after the birth, then they whisper the umbilical name *Muhammed Mustafa* in the ears of boys, and the umbilical name *Fatma* in the ears of girls. (In the past mostly the names of the companions of the Prophet Muhammad (Turk. *sahabe*) or those of their wives were chosen.) Then the child is given the [final] name. In Hal the names of historical personalities, beloved persons or relatives are usually chosen. Furthermore, the name of the baby's father or grandfather may also be given; the name of mother's father is less preferred.[105]

5.3. Turks, late 20th c., Silifke, Turkey: The midwife, cutting the umbilical cord, gives the newborn the name decided before or preferred by herself; this is the umbilical name (göbek adı). In a few days the newborn's [final] name is chosen. Friends, acquaintances, relatives are invited and entertained; an animal is killed for sacrifice. If there is a well-known beloved person in the family, his/her name is given. An *ezan* is recited in a low voice to the right ear of the newborn, then his/her name is pronounced three times loudly.[106]

5.4. Turkmen of Turkey, 20th c., village Kazandağı: To give the child a name they set up a "naming assembly" (Ad Takma Derneği). In this region newborns remain without a name usually for a month, even for six months. Then the father kills a sheep or a goat, and invites the friends and acquaintances. After entertainments the naming takes place. This ceremony must be done in the case of boys.[107]

6. Uzbeks of Khiva, 2nd half of the 19th c.: After *Batïr-bay*'s communication, in the town of Khiva the child is named seven days after the birth. If a boy was born and his father takes one of the four highest positions, the name is given by the *khan* himself; the son of a *mullah* is named by the *kadi, mufti* or the *reis*; the son of an average resident (*puqara*) is named by someone of the relatives, or by the father or mother, or finally, by the elder (*aq-saqal*) of the district. The choice of names is conducted by indications.[108]

7. Bashkirs, early 19th c.: When a Bashkir wife delivers a child, a mullah is called to say some prayers over the newborn and give him a name.[109]

---

[101] Mészáros I, pp. 408-410.

[102] In Silifke, Samsun, Havza, Tokat, Aydın, Tekirdağ, cf. Noyan pp. 6-8.

[103] Noyan, loc. cit., Gordlevskij 1913, p. 133.

[104] Gordlevskij, 1913, p. 129.

[105] Nermin Erdentuğ, Hal köyü'nün etnolojik tetkiki. Ankara, 1975, p. 99.

[106] Noyan, p. 6-7, Schimmel p. 15.

[107] Rıza p, 213.

[108] Samojlovič, pp. 299-300.

[109] P. R.-n: Moskovskij Telegraf, XLVIII, 261 (1832).

Main Points of Turkic Name-giving

Time of Naming

The time of naming varies greatly among non-Turkic peoples as well. The Chukch, for example, gave names on the 5th day while the ancient Greeks named their children on the 10th.[110]

In the old Turkic epics, the hero or the marriageable young man was given his final name only after he had proved his heroic courage by demonstrating some prowess. Then the assembly of the *il/el* or the *boy* (lan) confesses him a grown-up member of the community.[111] Traces of this custom are evident in such terms as *oγlan at* "child/boy-name,"[112] *är at* "büluğa erdikten sonra erkeğe verilen isim" [name given to a man (child) who attained the age of puberty],[113] *ayaγ at* "name (title?) of honour"[114] (cf. *ayağ* "hürmet, saygı").[115] Some instances are as follows: "Oğlan atım Şubuş Inal, er atım Kümül Öğe," "Atım Çor, ayağ atım Kar Yazmaz."[116]

Among the modern Turkic peoples the following main differences have been observed:

1. The names were given right after birth by the Yakuts, Tuvas (seldom), Bashkirs, Tatars of Minusinsk (Hakas). Bashkir children first were named with an "umbilical name" (*kendek ad*) which was changed some days later. This served as a magic purpose against evil spirits.[117] The same custom is known in Silifke, Turkey, where the umbilical name (*göbek adı*) is given first.[118]

2. In some regions of Turkey (Samsun, Tokat, etc.) the naming feast is celebrated on the 3rd or the 7th or even the 40th day after birth. Monday, Thursday or Friday are considered auspicious; in several places Tuesday, Wednesday and Saturday are generally not favored.[119] Among the Gagauz of the 19th and the 20th centuries the names were given on the second or third day after birth by the father. This meant receiving the newborn into the family. Two or three weeks later the second name, the official Christian name was given by the priests and usually was usually quite different from the first name.[120]

2. Uzbeks of Khiva and the Turkmen/Truhmen, Turks gave names on the 7th day.[121]

3. As the Yakut epic poems show, the old Yakuts named their children with temporary names only when they began to sit (7th or 8th month); they gave them the second (final) names when they began to shoot arrows.[122] The names were seldom given right after birth by the Tuvas, who usually gave names several weeks or months and even years after birth. It was not uncommon to give a boy his "male name," in his 10th year of age or later. Till then he simply was called "boy," "little boy" or "son." Even if he was named not much later after birth, he was considered to have completed his 1st year, because they included the embryonic time.[123]

4. In some regions of Turkey, the naming feast is celebrated on the 40th day after birth.[124]

The Naming Person

Naming was always an honourable duty for a person of any rank. It was quite usual that the name was given by a respected (older) man, a religious or secular leader, e.g., a *mullah* or an *aq-saqal* (e.g., in Hakas, Karagass, Kazakh, Bashkir, Turkish, etc.). The importance of the deed may be rendered by the words of Dede Qorqut: "...adïnï ben virdüm, yašïnï Allah virsün..." [I gave him a name, may Allah give him life], he said naming *Buγač (Boγač).*[125] It is quite usual in the folklore that heroes are named either by great wandering minstrels such as Dede Qorqut, or sacred (mystic, legendary) persons such as Xïzïr (Hızır, Kidir, Qïdïr).[126]

Generally, it was one of the parents who named their children (Kazakhs, Kara-Nogays, Turks, etc.). In wealthy or

---

[110] SLINM pp. 337, 369.
[111] cf. also Gökalp, Z., Türk Medeniyeti Tarihi, İstanbul, 1974. p. 293, Ekici p. 13.
[112] Amanoğlu 1996, p. 111.
[113] Gabain (1988), p. 262.
[114] Amanoğlu, 1996, p. 111.
[115] Gabain, (1988), p. 263.
[116] Amanoğlu, 1996, p. 111.
[117] Blagova, 1998b, p. 63 (after Kusimova).
[118] Noyan, p. 6.
[119] Noyan, p. 6.
[120] Kuroglo, p. 182.
[121] see above point 6; cf. Volodin, p. 53, Noyan, pp. 6-8,
[122] İnan, 1976, pp. 138-139.
[123] SLINM, p. 305.
[124] Noyan, p. 6.
[125] DQorqErgin p. 83; Ekici p. 13.
[126] Ögel I, pp. 316, 533.

noble families the naming person was someone of a higher rank as we have seen above with the Uzbeks of Khiva. Among the Tatars of Crimea, for example, the father's mother names the first child, while parents or close relatives give names to the subsequent children.[127] There are, however, slight differences in this respect.

Motives of Name-giving

Motives that influence the name-giving constitute a kind of system on which we have built up the classification of Turkic anthroponyms (see p. XXXVII below). The known motives have been arranged into minor or major categories. Thus the more detailed explanations with examples on the motives mentioned here can be found below (see paragraph *Categories of Turkic Anthroponyms*, p. XXXIX). In connection with the motives behind the name-giving, we must deal with some other factors which influence the naming, such as the custom of giving *related names*, the tendency of giving *foreign* and *fashion names*, *taboo-names* and *bynames*. In the 1930s the authorities of different countries (e.g., the Soviet Union, Turkey) restricted name-giving *by the force of law*, which severely limited the operation of the traditional systems.[128]

Related Names[129]

There are anthroponyms which not only distinguish but put their bearer into a specific system of social relations, associating the person with a certain group in society.[130] Personal names of this kind are called *rhyming/related names*,[131] *name-relations* in English; *Namenfeld, Sinngruppe, Namenbündel, Gruppenbenennung, Korrelationsbildung, Zwillingsbildung, Drillingsbildung*, in German, or *név-korrelációk (=name-correlations)*,[132] *névkapcsolatok (=name-relations)*[133] in Hungarian; *antroponimičeskie serii* or *svjazannye imena* in Russian.[134]

Children in a social unit (e.g., a family) are named in such way that their names form a complex series of names on semantic and/or formal features. Thus *related names* are considered as a group of names characterised by the same prefixes and affixes; as a series of names of which certain segments/morphemes are identical or similar; finally as a set of names given to twins according to tradition.[135]

Even after preliminary studies we can state that the custom of giving related names is widespread across continents and is known by peoples quite distant from each other such as the Arabs, Chinese, English, Koreans, Tibetans, Turks, from different historical periods.[136]

The custom of giving related names in various Turkic communities/societies has been little known or unsatisfactorily researched until recently. Although researchers of Turkic anthroponymy noticed the custom, its real nature and the extent and intensity of its use have not yet been fully explored. It is not known whether this custom is old or if it is a novelty in Turkic anthroponymy.[137]

In Turkic linguistic literature only a few researchers have dealt with the phenomenon in question: RÁSONYI (1961),[138] NIKONOV (1974), GAFUROV (1964), KALILOV (1980), SAADIEV (1970), URAKSIN (1970), ROJZENZON and ISAEVA (1971), ROJZENZON and BOBOHODŽAEV (1978), ŠATINOVA (1980), ŠATINOVA (1980), ŽAPAROV (1989), SCHIMMEL (1989) and SATTAROV (1990). The most detailed among them is NIKONOV's summarising article in which he focuses on twins' names in Bashkir, Tatar, Kazakh, Kirghiz, Turkmen and Uzbek. A fairly good study was published by ROJZENZON and BOBOHODŽAEV. They presented related names of Uzbek brothers and sisters. It is unfortunate that the authors have not added the parents' names; therefore, we cannot state whether they are related to their children based on their names.

Some references to this naming phenomenon had already been made in the middle of the 19th century. From LEVCHINE's comment we can learn that giving related names was popular among Kazakhs: "beaucoup cherchent à donner

---

[127] Kajbullaev, p. 5.

[128] Turkey: "Soy Adı Nizamnamesi" [Regulation of Surnames] (28th June, 1934); this occurred almost at the same time in all Soviet republics (Žanuzakov p. 31.).

[129] For a complete study on this see Baski 2000.

[130] Krjukov, M. V., O sociologičeskom aspekte izučenija kitajskoj antroponimiki. In: Onomastika. Moskva, 1969, p. 36.

[131] Schimmel, p. 16.

[132] As termed by L. Rásonyi in one of his drafts, see footnote 138.

[133] Pais, D., Szempontok Árpád-kori személyneveink vizsgálatához. In: Névtudományi vizsgálatok. Budapest, 1960; Fehértói, K., Az Árpád-kori névvonatkoztatás vitás kérdései. In: Névtudomány és Művelődéstörténet. Zalaegerszeg, 1989, p. 223.

[134] Rojzenzon and Isaeva pp. 37-40; Nikonov 1973a; Nikonov, Imja i obščestvo. Moskva, 1974.

[135] Rojzenzon and Bobohodžaev, p. 144.

[136] Nikonov, pp. 136-137.

[137] Nikonov, p. 138; Rojzenzon and Bobohodžaev, p. 144.

[138] Rásonyi, Jerus., pp. 89-95, in which he devoted a shorter paragraph to the qestion. The draft contents of Onomasticon Turcicum, outlined by L. Rásonyi himself and found in his archive, suggests that he also intended to touch on the question of "névkorrelációk" [=name-correlations].

à tous leurs fils des noms semblables, en se réglant sur celui de l'aîné. J'ai connue, par example, quatre frères nommés *Arghin-Boï, Altchi-Baï, Altyn-Baï, Mindi-Baï*."[139]

In some later works we can find similarly brief statements of the name-relations among different Turkic peoples. For the Kirghiz, for instance, it was desirable to give harmonising names within the family. Thus every girl in a family could be given a name ending in *-ayïm* "lady, mistress," e.g., *Qan-ayïm // Beg-ayïm // Gül-ayïm*.[140] It is also known that in Karakalpak the correlating names are not rare.[141] Moreover, in modern Uyghur families it is fairly common to give such names.[142]

This phenomenon is known in some old and several modern Turkic languages, such as Karakhanid, Khorezmian, Old Oghuz/Turkmen, Mamluk, Seljuk, Chaghatay, Altay,[143] Azerbayjani, Bashkir,[144] Karakalpak, Kazakh, Kirghiz,[145] Nogay, Tatar,[146] Turkish, Turkmen, New Uyghur,[147] and Uzbek.[148] It must be noted that because of the scantiness of studies on the question, there is insufficient data to determine the actual extent and proportion of this phenomenon in name-giving.

NIKONOV, analysing the name-relations of twins, pointed to some phonetic and semantic features of related names in languages of different types. At the end of his study he outlined three *stages of the name-relations* as follows: 1. *close name-relations* of twins; 2. *loose name-relations* of members of the family; 3. *distant name-relations* between children of nonrelated families being acquainted or befriended.[149] Having no data for the last stage, we can only show instances of the first two stages.

NIKONOV's principles used in formal analysis of the related names are rather simple. He examined the phonetically related names only, comparing the harmony at the beginning and at the end of the names. The identity of the initial parts of the names he called *anaphora*,[150] e.g., between the names of twin brother and sister: *Fanil // Farida (Färidä)*, of twin brothers: *Ayrat // Aydar*, etc. The identical parts at the end are called *epiphora*[151] which form *rhymes*, e.g., Tatar twin brothers *Niyaz // İlyas, Aydar // İldar, Nur-sinä // Göl-sinä*, etc. The latter type is more frequent, in NIKONOV's opinion, because the final syllable is stressed in Turkic languages. In some cases the harmony is so complete that it covers almost the whole name, therefore it cannot be described either as *anaphora* or *epiphora*, e.g., in the case of Tatar twin brothers *Rišat // Rifat, Mars // Marsel*, of twin brothers and sisters *Farid (Färid) // Farida (Färidä), Damir // Damira, İrek // İrkä*, etc.[152]

The co-authors ROJZENZON and BOBOHODŽAEV analysed the morphological features of related names, presenting their material in lists arranged according to correlating prepositions and postpositions of names, consistently separating the male, female and mixed relations within the lists.[153]

Here we would like to offer a more complex and detailed system. All available name-relations will be arranged according to the related persons. Then they will be analysed on their linguistic (formal and semantic) features.

Name-relations according to related persons are as follows:

1. Relations with the grandparents' names.[154] The widespread custom of giving names related with the grandfather's or father's name has been explained by SATTAROV with the cult of ancestors.[155]

2. Relations with the parents' names.

3. Relations among brothers' and sisters' names.

3.1. Relations among twins' names.

Considering the *linguistic types of name-relations* we can differentiate three *general types*:

---

[139] Levchine, p. 356.

[140] Kalilov, p. 96.

[141] Nasyrov and Tolstova: SLINM, p. 155.

[142] Sadvakasov and Mahpirov, p. 30.

[143] Šatinova, 1980.

[144] Šakurov, 1980.

[145] Žaparov, 1989, pp. 77-86.

[146] Sattarov, 1990.

[147] Sadvakasov and Mahpirov 1988, pp. 26-35.

[148] Rojzenzon and Isaeva (1971), and Rojzenzon and Bobohodžaev (1978).

[149] Nikonov, p. 141. A specific kind of distant name-relations existed in old Hungarian, too. The names of servants, footmen and the representatives of the same profession who lived together, in several cases had related names (see footnote 133).

[150] (<Greek) consecutive language or prosodic units beginning with the same word or group of words;

[151] (<Greek) the same word or group of words at the end of the consecutive verses or sentences;

[152] Nikonov, pp. 131-132.

[153] Op. cit., pp. 146-149.

[154] Number of occurences in our material is given in parenthesis so that their proportion can be estimated. The total number of related names in our collection is around 500 to date.

[155] Sattarov, 1990, p. 69-70.

I. *Names related by semantic aspects only* (less frequent).

II. *Names related by semantic and formal aspects.*

III. *Names related by formal aspects only.*

Within the major types there are several *subtypes* as outlined below:

1. Types of semantic relations:

   1.1. full identity: Names which are identical from both semantic and phonetic aspects.

For example: Selj. 12th c. *Il-arslan* (father) - *Terken-χatun* (mother) > *Terken-χatun* (daughter); Selj. *Arslan-doɣmiš* (father) > *Arslan-doɣmiš* (son); Tat. 20th c. *Mine-mullah* (father) > *Mine-mullah* (son); Bashk. 1718 *Yannïq ~ Yantïq!* (father) > *Yantïq* (son); Kzk. 19th c. *Xaydar-bek* (father) > *Xaydar-bek* (son);

This phenomenon can also be regarded as *inheritance of names* which exists in different communities in different forms. It exists among the Cheremiss, Chukchi (Siberia), Eskimo, Ewe and Akan (Western Africa), etc.[156] Among the Greeks, beginning with the Hellenic era, the name of a father and his son, and that of a mother and her daughter are often identical.[157]

An Arab child almost never bears a name identical with his father's or mother's.[158] This has been noted by A. SCHIMMEL: "...boys were in many cases called after a deceased grandfather, girls after a grandmother. Among the Arab tribes in early times the maternal grandfather's name was often given to a son... Sometimes a deceased uncle or aunt's name was given: the father's name appears only, and not very often, when he died before the boy was born....and even when a boy bore his grandfather's name he would often be called by a nickname, as was customary, for example, in Tashqurghan."[159]

Very similar customs can be observed among some Turkic peoples. The Tatars of Crimea, for example, tend to choose the name of a close relative or friend if he is a kind man. The Bashkir do not give the newborn his/her living (grand-)father's or (grand-)mother's name.[160] Kazakh newborns often get the names of their deceased parents, close relatives or famous persons.[161] To the contrary, among the Karagass it is forbidden to give the name of a dead man.[162] The Gagauz usually give their son the name of the grandfather so that the clan would not die out. This custom may well be in connection with the cult of ancestors.[163] Naming with names of ancestors (grandparents, aunts, uncles) is fulfilled by the contemporary Greeks according to a rather complicated system that binds the related families vertically. A boy is never given the same name as his father.[164] Similarly, Russians gave the name of an ancestor (mainly that of a grandfather or grandmother) to their children.[165] Among the Tadjiks, likewise, naming children with names (or parts of names) of deceased ancestors - brothers, sisters, uncles, aunts and other relatives - is a fairly widespread phenomenon. As a result the related names connect several generations. Those who bear the names of their ancestors are treated with special care and attention. All this is based on the belief in immortality of the soul and that the name is the soul of man.[166]

Perhaps the motive behind the *commemorative names* (I., p. XXXIX) in Turkic is connected with the beliefs and ideas mentioned above.

   1.2. Identical semantic parts in related names:

Here we list related names of which certain parts are identical from semantic (or etymological) point of view. Very frequently we can see the secondary components of names (e.g., *-bay, -bek, -χan, -χatun, -gül,* etc.) in name-relations. Their relating function, however, may be problematical considering the circumstance when almost every man can bear a name ending, for example, in *-bay, -bek,* etc.

   1.2.1. Identical beginning parts:

Maml. 1480 *Öz-bek* (father) > *Öz-demir* (son); Turk. 1432 *Xaji-ali* (father) > *Xaji-χatun* (daughter); Tat. 20th c. *Mine-mullah* (grandfather) > *Mine-mullah* (father) > *Mine-χarim* (son); Bashk. 1754 *Qutlu-yul* (father) > *Qutlu-bulat* (son); Uzb. 20th c. *Dil-rabâ // Dil-šad // Dilâra* (daughters); Uzb. 1969 *Saidi-asman* (grandfather) > *Saidi-qarim* (father)

---

[156] SLINM, pp. 20, 208, 338, 341, 352.

[157] SLINM, p. 370.

[158] SLINM, p. 57; Schimmel, p. 16.

[159] Schimmel, pp.. 14-15.

[160] Kusimova, 1971, p. 53.

[161] Kustanaev, pp. 37-38; Ibragimov, p. 124.

[162] Vasil'ev, V. N., Kratkij očerk karagasov: Ětnogr. Obozr. 1910, p. 56.

[163] Kuroglo, pp. 182, 185.

[164] Ivanova, Ju. V. in SLINM, p 102-103.

[165] Nikonov, p. 137.

[166] Rahimov, R. R., Dve zametki po antroponimii Zeravšanskoj doliny. In: Onomastika Srednej Azii. Moskva, 1978, pp. 187, 189, 190, 191

> *Saidi-axral* (son) ;

1.2.2. Identical ending parts (dominating):

Uyg.~Karakh. 895 *Taš-temir* (father) > *Toq-temir* (son); Selj. 13th c. *Qïlïč-arslan* (father) > *Toγrïl-arslan* (son); Turk. 1583 *Hïzïr-balï* (father) > *Gülüm-balï* (son); Az. 20th c. *Xoš-awaz* // *Gül-awaz* // *Min-awaz* (daughter); Bashk. 1735 *Qas-pulat* (father) > *Bek-bulat* (son); Uzb. 20th c. *Fayz-ulla* // *Gayb-ulla* // *Xayr-ulla* // *Sad-ulla* // *Murâd-ulla* (sons); Uzb. 20th c. *Sait-qul* // *Sana-qul* // *Mustafa-qul* // *Tura-qul* (sons).

1.3. Names belonging to same semantic categories:

1.3.1. Related beginnings (dominating type):

Oghuz *Ay-xan* "Moon-Khan" // *Yïldïz-xan* "Star-Khan/Prince" (sons); Az. *Baš-xanum* "Head Madam" (mother) > *Kečäl-Ašïr* "Bald Ashïr" (son) // *Daz-γïz* "Bald Girl" (daughter); Bashk. 1968 > // *Tan-sïlu* "Dawn-Beauty"// *Kön-sïlu* "Sun-Beauty" (daughter); Kzk. > *Kenžä Qara Bayïs* "Youngest Black Pasturage / Herding" // *Qunan Qara Bayïs* "Three Year Old Black Pasturage / Herding" // *Dönön Qara Bayïs* "Four Year Old Black Pasturage / Herding" (sons); Kirg. 1969 ? (mother)> // *Ay-nur* "Moon Light" // *Čolpon* "Morning Star" (daughters);

1.3.2. Related ending parts:

Selj. 1073 *Alp-arslan* "Hero Lion" (father) > *Böri-bars* "Wolf Tiger/Panther" // *Melik-šah* (sons); Tat. 1624 *Bek-temir* "Lord-Iron / Strong Iron?" (father) > *Bek-bulat* "Lord Steel" / "Strong Steel" (son); Bashk. 1678 *Qal-tay* "Foal with Birthmark" (father) > *Aq-tanay* "White Calf" (son); Kzk. 19th c. *Altïn-bas* "Golden Head" (son) // *Altïn-šaš* "Golden Hair" (daughter);

This type also exists in Arabic: "Often brothers are all called after the Qur'anic prophets if the father bears the name of a prophet."[167] A fairly early occurrence is the Mogul (Chaghatay) *Šïr-beg* > *Qablān-beg* "Leopard Prince son of Lion Prince."[168]

1.4. Synonyms:

1.4.1. Synonyms in beginning parts:

Turk. 20th c. *Alev* "Flame" (son) // *Ateš* "Fire" (daughter); Az. *Kečal-Ašïr* "Bald Ashir" (son) // *Daz-γïz* "Bald Girl/Daughter" (daughter); Crm. *Palwan-sultan* "Hero Wrestler Sultan" // *Batïr-xan* "Brave Khan / Warrior Khan" (sons); Kzk. 19th c. *Dust* "Friend" (father) > *Yuldaš* "Mate / Companion" (son); Uzb. 20th c. *Xuday-berdi* "God Gave (Him)" // *Egäm-berdi* "God/Lord Gave (Him)" // *Rähim-berdi* "The Gracious/Merciful (God) Gave Him" (sons);

1.4.2. Synonyms in ending parts:

Crm. *Palwan-sultan* "Hero Wrestler Sultan" // *Batïr-xan* "Brave Khan / Warrior Khan" (sons); Kzk. 1968 *Ali-bay* "Ali rich man"// *Ali-bek* "Ali Lord" (son);

1.5. Antonyms:

Examples with antonyms in beginning parts:

Selj. 11th c. *Eksik* "Defective / Imperfect" (father) > *Artïq* "Superfluous, surplus" (son); Khorezm. 12th c. *Atsïz* "Nameless" (father) > *Atlïγ* "Having (A Name)" (son); Turk. *Doγu-xan* "East Khan" // *Batu-xan* "West Khan" (son); Trkm. 1970 *Oγul-senem* "Son Darling/Beauty" // *Bibi-senem* "Lady/Girl Darling/Beauty" (daughter); Tat. 17th. c. *Bay-sit* "Rich (man) Seyit" (father) > *Qul-sit* "Slave Seyit" (son); Tat.(Mish.) 1793 *Yaqšï-γul* "Good Slave" (father) > *Yaman-γul* "Bad/Evil Slave" (son); Alt. 19th c. *Qïsqa-qïlan* "Short Hairy" // *Uzun-qïlan* "Long Hairy" (son);

1.5.1. Antonym in ending part:

Bashk. 1715 *Bek-qul* "Lord Slave" (father) > *Bek-bay* "Lord Rich (man)" (son);

1. 6. Other types of semantic relations:

1.6.1. Cross-linked semanticly related (mostly identical) parts:

Selj. *Arslan-doγmïš* "Lion Born" // *Qara-arslan* "Black Lion" (sons) Selj. 13th c. *Soñqur-tegin* "Falcon Prince" // *Er-toγrul* "Manly Sparrowhawk" (sons); Maml. 1438/39 *Bars-bay* "Chieftain Master" (father) > *Bay-bars* "Rich/Chieftain Panther" (son); Trkm. 19th c. *Geldi-xan* "Came Khan" (father) > *İl-geldi* "Empire Came" (son); Tat.(Sib.)? 1629 *Qulada* "Yellow(ish) Grey; Brown?" // *Qara-qula* "Black Yellow(ish) Grey" (sons); Bashk. 1709 *Aq-gilde* "White Came" (father) > *Kildi-bay* "Came Rich(man)" (son);

1.6.2. Names of folklore or literary heroes in relations:

Alt. *Lamart* // *Čumart* (son), heroes of a tale; Turk. twin brother and sister: *Kerem* // *Aslï*, heroes of a love story;

1.6.3. Logical link:

In some relations we can find a specific logical link that connects the names, e.g: Selj. 12th c. *Qïlïč-arslan* (II) >

---

[167] Schimmel, p. 16.

[168] Ibid.

Sanǰar-šah (son); where *qïlïč* 'sword' -> *sanǰar* "he who will stab/thrust; stabber";

1.6.4. Ideological, political, etc. notions in relations:

Turk. 20th c. *Hürriyet // Uhuvvet // Musavat* (son), "Freedom, Fraternity, Equality";

1.6.5. Relations originating in islamic tradition:

1.6.5.1. Names of twins:

Trkm. 1970 *Xasan-ali // Xusain-ali* (sons); Trkm. 1970 *Patma // Ayša* (daughters); Trkm. 1970 *Xesen-ǰemal* (son) // *Xusun-ǰemal* (daughter); Trkm. *Abdïlla // Seydïlla* (sons) Trkm. *Xïdïr // İlyas* (sons) Kmk. 1968 *Гasan // Гusen* (sons); Kzk. *Batpa // Zuhra* (daughters); Kzk. 1968 *Husen* (son) // *Fatima* (daughter); Kzk. 1968 *Üsen* (son) // *Batna-kül (<Fatima)* (daughter); Kirg. 1969 *Asan~Asan-bek // Üsön~Üsön-bek* (sons); Kirg. 1969 // *Patma // Zuhra* (daughters); Uzb. 1960's // *Fatima // Zuhra* (daughters); Uzb. 1960s *Xuseyn* (son) // *Fatima* (daughter); Uzb. 1965 *Ayše // Zuhra* (daughters); Uzb. 1969 *Xasan* (son) // *Zuhra* (daughter); Uzb. 20th c. *Xasan* (son) // *Fatima* (daughter); Uzb. 20th c. *Xusen* (son) // *Zuhra* (daughter);

A considerable number of twins' names belong to this group. It should be emphasised that related names of Arab-Persian origin normally are to be arranged into the relevant group matching their type of formal relation.

The above subgroups (1.1-1.6) represent the different degrees/stages of semantic relations/links among related names. It seems that among the Turks it was not usual to give the children names fully identical with those of the parents and grandparents. But it was more frequent to give names with identical beginning and/or ending parts. The role of certain components (e.g., *-bay, -bek, -qul, -xanïm, -qïz,*) in the function of a relating part seems problematic, because in some languages they are almost compulsory parts of personal names primarily given not for the sake of relating. Presumably, synonyms and antonyms among the related names can also be considered as a curiosity.

2. Types of formal (phonetic, morphological) relations:

2.1. Full identity:

See point 1.1. for the examples and explanations.

2.2. Identical parts in (compound) names:

2.2.1. Identical parts in the beginning parts:

Tat. 1966 *Min-γata* (father) > *Min-zifa* (daughter); Tat. 1967 *Min-zakir* (father) > *Min-tagir* (son); Bashk. 1754 *Qutlu-yul* (father) > *Qutlu-bulat* (son); Uzb. 20th c. *Gül-bahâr // Gül-nâra // Gül-čehrä // Gül-sara* (daughters); Uzb. 20th c. *Abdu-xayri // Abdu-xamid // Abdu-γani // Abdu-xalil* (sons);

2.2.2. Identical ending parts (dominating):

Uyg.~Karakh. 895 *Taš-temir* (father) > *Toq-temir* (son); Selj. 13th c. *Qïlïč-arslan* (father) > *Toγrïl-arslan* (son); Az. 20th c. *Xoš-awaz // Gül-awaz // Min-awaz* (daughters); Crm. 1633 *Ay-temür~Ay-demir // Qan-temür* (son); Bashk. 1735 *Qas-pulat* (father) > *Bek-bulat* (son); Kzk. 19th c. *Nur-tay* (father) > *Yusuf-tay* (son);

2.3. Linking parts in single names:

Some of the names in relations listed in this group are nearly identical. In most cases only one sound differs; therefore, they could well be considered as identical names.

2.3.1. Linking beginning parts:

Turk. 20th c. *Neǰdet // Neǰmi* (sons) // *Neǰmiye* (daughter); Bashk. 1968 *Salim-yan* (father) > *Salix-yan* (son); Kzk. *Nörmönbet* (father) > // *Tünüköy // Künüköy* (daughters); Kzk. 1968 *Ergiz-bay // Segiz-bay* (son); Kirg. *Qoňuš* (father) > *Qoňur-yan* (daughter); Uzb. 20th c. *Tâǰï-bây // Xâǰï-bây* (sons); Uzb. 20th c. *Xali-qul // Ali-qul* (son);

2.3.2. Linking ending parts (dominating):

Tat. 1967 *Sufiya* (mother) > *Alfïya* (daughter); Bashk. 1968 *Qamilä* (mother) > *Nazilä* (daughter); Kzk. 1968 *Külzira // Nazira* (daughters); Nog. 1967 *Sabirat // Qabirat* (daughters); Kirg. 1969 *Ay-nura // Gül-nara* (daughter); Alt. 19th c. *Aranay // Šaranay~Čaranay* (sons); Uzb. 20th c. *İbâdat // Šaxâdat // Saâdat* (daughter); Uzb. 20th c. *Xašim // Nasim // Nayim* (sons);

Here we have arranged the related names in which the second or final part consisted of two or more harmonising syllables. Similar relations with one harmonising syllable have been considered as rhyming correlations (see 2.5 below).

2.3.3. Related male and female names (mostly of Arabic origin):

Tat. 1967 *Damir* (son) // *Damira* (daughter); Tat. 1966 *Munira* (mother) > *Munir* (son); Bashk. 1968 *Rim* (son) // *Rima* (daughter);

Recently Bashkir and Tatar have used specific suffixes (e.g., *-a, -ä, -iyä, -sa, -sä, -za, -zä, -ra, -rä*) forming female names.[169]

2.4. Alliteration:

---

[169] Sattarov, 1990, p.211.

Because the alliteration is very popular in Turkic prosody, it is no wonder that it plays a significant role in name-relations.

Bulg. *Qobrat* (father) > *Qotïraγ* (son); Turk. *Ayfer* // *Aydil* // *Aynur* // *Aydïn* (son); Az. 1968 *Nasiba* // *Nagiba* (daughter); Tat. 1967 *Ayrat* // *Aydar* (son); Bashk. 1968 *Fakiya* (mother) *Fanira* (daughter); Kzk. 19th c. *Arγïn-bay* // *Alčï-bay* // *Altïn-bay* // *Mindi-bay* (son); Uzb. 20th c. *Maxida* // *Mavluda* // *Mavjuda* // *Maᶜbuda* (daughters);

2.5. Rhyming

Selj. *Ïr-taš* (father) > *Mawdūd* // *Masᶜūd* (sons); Turk. 20th c. *Engin* // *Ersin* (son); Tat. 1967 *Aydar* // *Ildar* (sons); Bashk. 1709 *Qutlumbet* (father) > *Bikmet* (son); Kzk. 1968 *Bolat* // *Manat* (sons); Uzb. 20th c. *Muxabbat* // *Nazâqat* // *Sanâat* // *Salâmat* (daughters); Uzb. 20th c. *Qarim* // *Qazim* // *Xašim* // *Âlim* // *Salim* (sons);

2.5.1. Rhyming suffixes (as relating morphemes):

Oghuz/Trkm. 13th c. *Suwarjïq* ~ *Suwarjik* // *Ögürjik-alp* (sons); Selj. 1160, 1675 *Qaymaz* (father) > *Satmaz* (son); Selj. 1156 *Qaymaz* (father) > *Sïqmas* ~ *Soqmas?* (son); Bashk. 1756 *Qadïrmet* (father) > *Iškinä* // *Bekkinä* (sons); Bashk. 1712 *Azimbet* (father) > *Düskey* // *Nurkey* (sons); Kzk. *Nörmönbet* (father) > *Tünüköy* // *Künüköy* (daughters); Kzk. *Šayïrqay* // *Šarqay* // *Qaqtïrqay* (sons); Bashk. 1783, 1792 *Saγïndïq* ~ *Saγandïq* (father) > *Süyündük* (son);

2.6. Other types of relations

For examples see point 1.6.

In some cases the beginnings are relate to the endings or vice versa. Thus a kind of cross-link connects the semantically related parts, e.g., the second part of the mother's name will be the first part of the daughter's name: Tat. *Minafa* (mother) > *Nafisa* (daughter).

Notes on twins' names:

Among several Turkic peoples, twin brothers and sisters are given *traditional Arabic name-pairs*. Thus some scholars state that the practice of giving the twins related names (e.g., in Uzbek) derives from the Islamic culture. In Tatar and Bashkir, however, there are few relations according to Islamic tradition, but giving the twins phonetically related names is very frequent.[170] The same phenomenon can be observed in Modern Uyghur[171] and Turkmen.[172]

In NIKONOV's opinion all the twins' names in Kazakh of contemporary Chimkent, Kazakhstan are related. Some twenty-eight percent of them are formed under Islamic tradition, seventy-two percent, however, are phonetically related. Among the latter the names related by *epiphora* are predominant by fort-four percent, while twenty-four percent are almost identical, having of course (nearly) identical endings as well. Thus sixty-eight percent of relations are related by *epiphora*. Almost the same proportions have been determined in contemporary Kirghiz.[173]

In our material, too, the proportion of the traditionally related names is, approximately, only twenty-five percent of all twins' names (see 1.6.5.), while nearly half are related phonetically only and these are relations of a newer type, e. g.: Az. 1968 // *Zagida* // *Zagira* (daughters); Tat. 1967 *Glus* // *Flus* (sons); Tat. 1967 *Mars* // *Marsel* (sons); Tat. 1967 *Nafis* // *Fanis* (sons); Tat. 1967 *Xalim* // *Salim* (sons); Bashk. 1968 *Rim* // *Rif* (sons); Kzk. 1968 *Zaure* // *Saule* (daughters); Kzk. 1968 *Berik* // *Serik* (sons); Uzb. 1969 *Qamil* // *Qabul* (sons);

Sometimes the names of the twins are not related, but one of the boys may be called *Egiz-bay* (Kirg.), *Igez-bay* (Bashk.) or *Igezäk* (Bashk.).[174]

A newer method is to repeat the (secondary) components at the end of the twins' names: Trkm. 1970 *Oγul-senem* // *Bibi-senem* (daughters); Bashk. 1968 *Tan-sïlu* // *Kön-sïlu* (daughters); Kzk. 1968 *Alim-žan* // *Ɣalim-žan* (sons); Kzk. 1968 *Ergiz-bay* // *Segiz-bay* (sons); Kirg. 1969 *Arstan-bek* // *Rustan-bek* (sons); Uzb. 1969 *Tulkin-jan* // *Erkin-jan* (sons);

About twenty percent of twins' names in our collection are related by both semantic and formal aspects and are usually not traditionally Islamic names, e.g.,: Kirg. 20th c. *Žanïš* // *Bayïš* (sons); Turk. 20th c. *Serab* // *Mehtap* (daughters) "Mirage" // "Moonlight";[175] Turk. 20th c. *Alev* (son) // *Ateš* (daughter); Turk. 20th c. *Qutlu* // *Mutlu* (sons); Bashk. 1968 *Minne-gül* // *Min-nur* (daughter); Kzk. 1968 *Ali-bay* // *Ali-bek* (son); Kirg. 1969 *Ay-nur* // *Čolpon* (daughter); Kirg. 1969 *Nur-bek* (son) // *Nur-gül* (daughter); Kirg. 1969 *Tālay-bek* (son) // *Tālay-gül* (daughter);

Otherwise we have sorted twins' names into different groups based on their linguistic features.

The above subgroups represent the different degrees/stages of formal identity among the related names. We are well aware that the system suggested is far from being final or perfect. Maybe some of the groups should be united while others divided into newer subgroups.

---

[170] Nikonov, p. 131, Schimmel 17

[171] Nikonov, 1984, pp.196-197.

[172] Muhamedova, 1957, p. 45.

[173] Nikonov, pp. 132-133.

[174] Nikonov, SLINM, p. 73.

[175] Schimmel, p. 17.

During their long history, Turkic peoples borrowed anthroponyms from many other peoples they came in contact with. Thus the foreign layer of Turkic personal names consists of Sanskrit, Tibetan, Mongol, Arab, Greek, Iranian, Kalmyk, Russian, German, and other names. The influence of different religions can be observed in the Turkic anthroponymy as well.

Turkic peoples, before converting to Islam, believed in other religions (e.g., Shamanism, Buddhism, Manicheism, (Nestorian) Christianity), and never neglected their own Turkic personal names.[176] But because of the crushing influence of the Islamic names, the traditional (national) name-system sustained a serious loss.[177] Due to Islam, widespread in the Turkic world, the Muslim (Hebrew, Arabic, Persian) names provided the major group of the foreign names.

In YUSUPOV's opinion, even in the Volga-Bulghar inscriptions of 10th century we can trace the influence of Islam on anthroponyms. It must be noted that not all anthroponyms of Arabic-Iranian origin are connected with the world of Islam. Some are pre-Islamic (Aramaic), such as the names of some prophets; others have been taken from the everyday spoken Arabic-Persian language.[178] The same phenomenon has been observed in Turkmen where only a minor part of the anthroponymy has been influenced by Arabic and Persian names of religious content.[179]

The influence of Islam on name-giving of Bashkirs begins in the 14th c., but, according to genealogies published by KUZEEV, two centuries later the original (Turkic) names still outnumbered the Muslim ones.[180] This influence did not yet reach all the Kirghiz in the 17th century.[181]

The Tatar genealogies also testify that the anthroponyms were homogeneously Turkic and developed for centuries according to their inner laws. In the 13th-14th century, written sources of the Golden Horde, however, show the growing influence of Arabic-Persian names. Yet, the common people bore their traditional Turkic personal names which were preferred even in the 16th century.[182] The influence of Islam and Islamic names became stronger in the 17th and 18th centuries as the aftermath of the resistance to forced Christianization. That was a transitional period when Turkic and Arabic-Persian names were mixed. The original structure types were preserved as well. In the third period (beginning in the early 19th century.) the Turkic-Tatar anthroponyms were actually replaced by Islamic names. The proportion of the latter was ninety percent which reached ninety-seven and a half percent by the end of the 19th century. Composite names predominated while the proportion of mixed personal names (Tatar-Arabic / Tatar-Persian) was relatively insignificant.[183]

Some of the Turkic tribes and peoples became acquainted with Christianity, which happened at different times, mainly following the Russian invasion of the region in question. At the beginning of the 17th century, Yakuts, for example, had an advanced anthroponymical tradition in which Russian names occurred very rarely, but the situation changed in the mid-19th century when Yakuts were finally converted to Christianity. National names were displaced by Russian names.[184] In the Altay region, missionary work began in the first half of the 19th century, and by the mid-19th century Russian farmers were settling there. Altay Turks took over a part of the Russian names but changed their phonetic appearance. They also made names from common nouns borrowed from Russian.[185]

The majority of modern Gagauz names is of Byzantine (Old Hebrew, Old Greek and Latin) origin. These names can be found in the Christian calendar.[186]

In Kazakh sources Russian names appeared in the 18th century, but they were taken over in large numbers only after the October Revolution of 1917. In the Soviet era new names were born in accordance with the new way of life, while outdated ones disappeared.[187]

The presence of Russian anthroponyms is recently significant in the anthroponymy of the peoples of former Russian and Soviet realms. Such Russian names of the new type were borrowed by different Turkic peoples: *Marlen* (Marx + Lenin), *Vladlen* (Vladimir + Lenin), *Kommuna, Bolševik, Kolhoz-bek, Kosmos-bek, Gagarin*, etc.[188]

Part of the foreign names spread among the Turks was due to *fashion* (see below). Through Russian, several

---

[176] Mahpirov, 1988, p. 48.

[177] Noyan, p. 11.

[178] Gordlevskij, 1913 p. 132; Žanuzakov p. 15.

[179] Muhamedova, 1957, p. 45.

[180] Two-thirds of names were of Kipchak-Turkic origin (Garipov, 1973, p. 55).

[181] Nikonov, pp. 89-90.

[182] Ahmetzjanov, pp. 101-107; The same was observed in the Crimea in the late 15th and early 16th centuries: only 14-16 names of 100 were Muslim (Seljametev, p. 115).

[183] Ahmetzjanov, loc. cit. On the influence of Islam on Tatar and Bashkir names, see also Šajhulov, 1975.

[184] Rudnyh, p. 221.

[185] Šatinova, 1971, p. 68.

[186] Kuroglo, pp. 182, 185.

[187] Žanuzakov, p. 15, 95; Nikonov, 1984, p. 195.

[188] Kalilov, p. 97, Žanuzakov, p. 96.

internaticnal names were borrowed, e.g., *Elvira, Ernst, Everest, Indira* (Indira Gandhi), *Luiza, Magellan, Marat, Žanna* (Jeanne d'Arc), etc.[189]

Nowadays Turks (in general, as well as those of Turkey) tend to give their own national names again.[190]

Fashion Names

Names may become fashionable due to different cultural and/or religious influences.

Fashion names occur also among Turkic Peoples, for example, many *Turs*, eighteen *Tümens* and some sixty *Qïlïčs*, etc. figure in RÁSONYI's collection. The most characteristic names that have become fashionable can be found among the militarized feudal Egyptian Mamluks. After the sultan reigning from 1260 to 1277 had vanished, *Bey-bars* was in use so long that in the end it became a fashion name and the chronicles mention more than forty. We also find thirty *Öz-bek*s and ten *Arγun*s.

Turkic peoples in general, and the Kazakhs in particular, name their children gladly with names of famous persons. But then again, because of fashion, it is frequent that the son of a Kazakh with a Muslim name bears a pagan (that is, a Kazakh) name, e.g., *Sarybaj (Sarï-bay) Kasymov (Qasïm)* and *Batyr (Batïr) Jusufov (Yusuf)*.[191]

Some of the fashion names are difficult to separate from those *names decisive of fate*, where parents give *names of great personalities* with the idea of having the child *pursue a similar career*. Presumably such a name, the name of a great man, is given in great masses even after decades have passed, when it has lost its original psychological onoma-magic background and has been degraded into a fashion name. Above, we have seen the name of the two great Seljuk sultans, *Qïlïč-arslan* (I. 1092-1107; II. 1156-1192). Somewhat later, it was still surviving in the name of ten further *Qïlïč-arslan*s. The multitude of the name *Turuntay* among the Mamluks, for example, gives it the impression of being a fashion name.

PNfem:[192] We have no entries because of the insignificant number of women's names compared to men's name, all the more as the name *Bäzäk* "Schmuck, Zierat" [jewel, ornament][193] from the Syrian-Nestorian inscription around 1324 could be included here, supposing all the ten women lived in the same period. *Ay-χatun* "Moon Princess" might also have become a fashion name. Rašïd ad-Dïn was among the first to mention it as her daughter in his last will.[194]

Taboo-Names

The concealing of names is widespread among various peoples of the world. Melanesians conceal their own names; they do not utter the name of their wife and that of anyone missing.[195] It is a universal phenomenon that spouses do not normally call each other by name.[196] Some peoples (e.g., Ewe of W. Africa, Tunguz, Nanay, Nganasan, Vietnamese) call the parents by the name of their first-born child.[197]

The tradition of *taboo-names* is known with the Turkic peoples as well. *Taboo* means, in this case, prohibition on using (uttering) certain names for certain persons in the society (family). Under the circumstances referred to above, using bynames or terms of relationship as substitutes for prohibited names is quite usual. In the Turkic dialects of Altay such bynames are called *sola* or *šola*.[198] The Kazakhs, for example, used the prohibited names in their distorted form, e.g., *Sambet (<Mambet), Sali (<Ali), Mursïn (<Tursïn)*, etc.[199]

As the lesson of the Altay Turks shows, the prohibition of names takes effect on two levels: 1. one must not call by name an older person (male and female); 2. a daughter-in-law and her relatives must not call by name the elder relatives (males and females) on the husband's side; similarly, the husband and his relatives must not call by name the elder relatives on the wife's side. One must not utter even the common noun identical with the name of a relative whose name is taboo. In this case the word in question must be substituted with a synonym.[200]

As for Kazakhs, GRODEKOV reports the following: "... A good wife must not call her husband's relatives and all his branch by name, but she must call them by common kinship terms or honorary titles, e.g., *ata* (father-in-law), *mirza* (gentleman), etc. A less shy wife calls them by name, but only behind their back. Although it is not as blameworthy, it is

---

[189] Nikorov, 1984, p. 195, Kalilov, p. 97.

[190] Šatinova, 1971, p. 69, Noyan, p. 11.

[191] SKSO, VIII, p. 200

[192] In paragraphs beginning with "Pnfem," we make notes on the typical features and/or distinctions regarded in female (feminine) names). Normally, here we only list some of the relevant women's names.

[193] Chwol., Syr.-nest. (NF.) p. 24 etc.

[194] Browne, p. 84.

[195] SLINM, p. 349.

[196] SLINM, p. 217, 324.

[197] SLINM, p. 99, 221, 225, 341, 345, 348.

[198] Hak.(Sag., Koyb.) *sola* "der Zuname, der Titel" (Radl. IV, 550), Shor, Hak.(Kacha) *šola* "der Name, das Wort, mit dem man gewisse Personen benennt, dessen Namen man nicht aussprechen darf" (Radl. IV, 1030).

[199] Žanuzakov, 1971a, p. 103.

[200] Šatinova, 1971, pp. 65-66.

unseemly to utter words which are parts of names of the husband's relatives."[201] In these cases Kazakh wives must use appropriate synonyms.[202]

Bynames and Second Names

While the primary function of a personal name is to identify and distinguish its bearer within the community, it is hindered by the high uniformity (for instance, in Christian and Muslim anthroponymy), and they cannot be distinguished. Thus a byname (Ar. *laqab*) is given to a person to distinguish him from others who bear the same name. Giving bynames is directed by the general motives of name-giving, but this time the outlook, the inner features and habits, father's job or the position of the person are predominant.[203] A person may have several bynames during his/her life. In New Uyghur, for instance, everyone may have even four bynames at the same time: 1. a patronymical byname (common for a family), e.g., *qosaq* "stomach," *taz* "bald," *pañ* "deaf," *toqu* "lame," etc.; 2. an individual byname (on the personal features and habits); 3. a collective byname (common for dwellers of a settlement); 4. an ethnic byname (denoting people of a region). It must be noted that Uyghur women do not normally have any bynames.[204]

As is known, Turks in the distant past, especially the members of the upper class, had several names during their lifetime. Most of them were not legal (confessed) but descriptive names (mostly bynames and titles) changed with the age and position of the person in society. For example, *Bumïn-qaɣan* got the title *Elig-qaɣan* and *Qutluɣ-χan* was named *El-täriš* when they became the rulers of the *el*.[205]

Sometimes the title or the byname may replace the original (basic) name.[206]

In the opinion of some scholars, giving bynames or nicknames began when the Turks converted to Islam and lasted till the Ottoman period. In high society, women frequently used Persian nicknames.

Nowadays giving bynames is common mainly in the provinces. The mother's name seldom turns into a nickname or family name, but her ill-fame or evil features may serve as a base of one's byname. Otherwise, nicknames are frequently used together with female names.[207]

Before the October Revolution in a Kazakh aul everyone got an adequate byname.[208] Sometimes bynames/nicknames are given for protective purposes, as for example with the Chuvash, Kazakhs and Yakuts, many of whom bear double names.[209] Taboo-names (see p. XXXIII) can also be some kind of second (false) names.[210] With similar purpose, Altay Turks were named with "misleading names," Turkmen were given beside "right names" (čïn adï) also were given "false names" (yalan adï) as second names. A Karakalpak child, being seriously ill, usually got a second, misleading homely name.[211] In the region of Muğla, Turkey, the same is seen: a sickly, fragile child is given a new name; the previous name was said to be not useful/suitable.[212]

Traditionally, Bashkirs got two names: the first one, the *yürgäk iseme* (nappy-name) was given by the midwife (*kendek inäy ~ kendek äbey*). Doing so, the midwife ties a hand of the newborn with a silk yarn whispers the baby's name in the infant's ear, then she swaddles him/her. It is believed that the first name and the silk yarn protects the child from evil spirits. The second (official) names were given by the elderly (*aq saqal*) or the parents, later on by the *mullahs*.[213]

Besides the official name, which was a Russian christened name, given at birth, Yakuts, Altay Turks (in the middle of 19th century), Chuvash, etc., later got a *second name* (a national byname or nickname) which was used instead of the official name and could displace it. Yakuts, as observed by GRICENKO, used their bynames parallel with the christened names, sometimes supplemented them (e.g., *Bïrtanï Süödär*, Fedor, by nickname B.; *Toytoχ Kilgäräy*, Grigorij, by nickname Toytoχ, etc.). Similarly in Chuvash, people distinguished one another with bynames since they did not have family-names.[214] In some cases the unofficial names were given first. According to S. S. KUROGLO the existence

---

[201] Grod., I, p. 100.

[202] Potanin, II, p. 98.

[203] Gordlevskij summarized the motives of giving nicknames in Turkish (1913, p. 134). Nicknames of families were formed in Turkish in this way. On the semantics and motives of nicknames in Tatar dialects see Šajhulov 1976. For more details on the nickname or *laqab* in Islamic languages, see Schimmel pp. 50-67.

[204] Sadvakasov and Mahpirov, pp. 28-29.

[205] Amanoğlu, 1996, p. 111, Blagova 1998b, p. 62 (after L. N. Gumilev).

[206] As is seen, for example, in Turkmen (cf. Muhamedova 1957, p. 46).

[207] Gordlevskij, 1913, pp. 132, 135, 136, Noyan, op. cit.

[208] Žanuzakov, p. 26.

[209] Magn. p. 11 (after Zolotnickij), Grod. I, p. 99; Ibragimov, p. 125; Rudnyh, op. cit. p. 223; Gricenko, p. 156.

[210] The same in Kalmyk, cf. Pjurbeev p. 196, in Yakut, cf. Gricenko p. 156.

[211] Muhamedova, 1957, p. 46, Blagova 1998b, p. 63.

[212] Noyan, p. 7. On change of name see Schimmel pp. 72-73.

[213] Kusimova, 1971, pp. 52-53.

[214] SLINM, pp. 359-360; Rudnyh, op. cit. p. 223; Šatinova 1971, p. 68; Žanuzakov p. 27, Kuroglo p. 183 after Vajnštejn, Mahpirov, 1988, p. 48, Gricenko p. 155, Magn. pp. 8, 11, Danilova and Enžaeva p. 62.

of such double names may be explained by the dual belief of the folk and the survival of old traditions.[215]

In RUDNYH's opinion the original Yakut names turned into second names because of christening (in 18th century) and the christened names, which were not comprehensible could not be remembered as used easily in everyday life. Even the kinship was kept in evidence on the second names and not on the Russian official names but sometimes the latter turned intosecond names fitting in with the norms of Yakut language.[216] He also argues that *second names* in Yakut are not identical with the *bynames* as is thought by some researchers.[217]

Some Tatars of Minusinsk (Hakas) also have "Tatar" names beside the christened ones.[218] The Gagauz of the 19th-20th centuries normally had two names. The first one was given by the parents, the second a Christian one by the priests. One is never called by the second (official) name.[219]

As for the grammatical function of the bynames, they constitute the determinant part of a composite name in which the determiner is the basic (primary or original) personal name. This is the most frequent structure of composite names.

General Notes on Women's Names[220]

Since there is no grammatical gender in Turkic, Turkic female names do not normally differ in external features, but they usually do in semantics (see p. XXXIV).

The quantity of women's names in different sources is twenty or thirty times less than that of men's names.[221] In Arabic and Persian sources relating the Mamluk and Seljuk Turks of the Middle Ages one can hardly find any women's names; although several sources mention the beauty of the Turkic women, who could be purchased as slaves for high prices in Kipchak. Also in Maḥmūd al-Kāšyarī's vocabulary, altogether four women's names can be found besides the fifty-two 11th century men's names listed.

Very poor are the Russian, Latin and Byzantine sources on the Kipchak Turks, the Pechenegs, the Kumans, and the Altur Orda Turks, too. Although Magnitskij publishes 10,567 Chuvash names in his collection *Čuvašskija jazyčeskija imena*,[222] he does not say which are women's names.

All this is the outcome of the inferior social position of the women. They have no state function worthy of mention by historiographers. Among primitive nomads, it is general practice that at the arrival of some stranger or guest the women at once become invisible; they draw back into the depths of the tent. There are of course exceptions: the Bāburnāne and Humāyūnnāme, written by the great sovereigns of India, just as Gülbeden-χanïm's memoirs also mention women belonging to their dynasty.

When the Cossacks of Yermak conquered Küčüm-χan's Western Siberian Empire, the Russian sources[223] listed all the names of some thirty women belonging to Küčüm's household.

The text-monuments of the Uyghurs living outside the world of Islam, however, mention far more women's names, especially the *Pfahlinschriften*,[224] which contain out of 768, the names of 60 to 70 noblewomen, mostly in reference to abstract notions. Not only the Manichean and Buddhist Uyghur monuments, but also the epitaphs of Nestorian Turks[225] in Syriac in the Semirečie mention many female names.

We owe much to N. A. BASKAKOV, who, in writing and editing the Karakalpak, Oyrot [=Altay] and Hakas dictionaries, paid particular attention to personal and clan names and was able to offer more than 900 female names.[226]

Notes on the Usage of Turkic Personal Names.

One of the most distinctive features of Turkic anthroponymy is the immense variability of personal names.

---

[215] Kuroḡlo, p. 183, Seljametev p. 114.

[216] Rudnyh, p. 225.

[217] Rudnyh, op. cit. p. 222.

[218] Kostrov, p. 229.

[219] Kuroḡlo, p. 183.

[220] Based on Rásonyi, P. Cat. pp. 218-219. Gordlevskij, 1913, p. 136 wrote a meager ten lines on the theme altogether.

[221] Mahpirov 1988, p. 51.

[222] Magn.

[223] e.g., AI.

[224] Müller, Pfahl.

[225] Chwol., Syr.; Chwol., Syr.-nest.; Chwol., Syr.-nest. (NF).

[226] KkRS, OjrRS, HRS.

Among the present-day Uyghurs living in Kazakhstan, for example, 311 boys shared 197 names, thus sixty-three percent of them bore different names. In the same time 1000 provincial Russian boys got 40-50 kinds of names, so only 0.05 percent of them had different names. The favourable proportion of the Uyghur names is due to abundance of compound names. Out of 30 components, for instance, 870 different names can be created. In the countryside seventy percent of the Uyghur boys got compound names. The situation in towns is quite different since only twenty-five percent were named with compound names. This fact indicates the process of extinction of compound personal names which can be seen more clearly in Azerbaijan, Tatarstan and Uzbekistan, and primarily in towns. It seems likely that rural inhabitants prefer giving compound names. In 1961 fifty-seven percent of Uzbek country boys got compound names, while the proportion was twenty-one percent in Samarkand. The proportion of simple names of Uyghurs was sixteen percent in the country, fifty-two percent in Alma-Ata.[227]

ERGAZIEVA investigated some 150 Kazakh documents of the late 18th and the early 19th centuries that abound in personal names. She found that 60% of names were of Kazakh, 39% of Arab-Persian origin at the end of the 18th century. There were no Mongolian and Russian names at all. This composition changed slightly both in quality and quantity between 1800 and 1828. The anthroponyms of Kazakh origin represented seventy-two percent, the Arab-Persian names came to twenty-six percent and a very few represented Mongolian (0.5 percent) and Russian (0.3 percent) personal names. All that testifies to faint Islamic influence. All these names were used all over the language area, which shows the integrity of the Kazakh language. Most of these names are used even today, a part of which are of obscure origin. Compared with recent Kazakh anthroponymy, it must be stated that the structural models/patterns remained almost unchanged. There are few simple names in both periods. The compounds add up to ninety percent of all names.[228] We note that ERGAZIEVA considers simple names with secondary components as compound names.

In contemporary Bashkir the proportion of Arabic names is seventy-four percent (seventy-eight percent of female, seventy-two percent of male names), that of Iranian names is eight percent (twelve percent female, five percent male names), while only eighteen percent (ten percent female, twenty-three percent male names) are of Turkic origin.[229]

Semantics of Turkic Anthroponyms

In Turkic languages almost every lexical unit (word) can be used as a proper, especially personal, name. This is valid also for Arabic: "As Leone Caetani stated it at the beginning of his Onomasticon Arabicum,[230] one could as well compose a complete dictionary of Arabic [from names] since almost every word has appeared, at some point of history, as a proper name. The same can be said for the Persian and Turkish [Turkic!, I. B.] areas, and for Muslim India."[231]

Traditional anthroponyms are formed of words meaning animals, plants and things used most frequently in everyday life. Thus any list of lexical-semantic groups would always be incomplete and imperfect. The forerunner of lexical-semantic classification was HOUTSMA, who enumerated names meaning animals, heavenly phenomena, inanimate things and honorific titles among simple names.[232]

One of the recent attempts is ŽANUZAKOV's, in which there are groups such as words of 1.livestock-breeding, 2. natural phenomena, 3. domestic and wild animals, 4. jewellery, precious stones and metals, 5. flora, 6. terms of kinship, 7. numbers, 8. toponyms, 9. household utensils, 10. foods, etc. Such lists were and are compiled by other researchers as well.[233] Recently BLAGOVA, in her classification of mixed character, set up the semantic structure of Old Turkic personal names. This structure, originally elaborated for Old German names, consists of 12 main groups (with several subgroups), e.g., time and space, flora, fauna, sacred sphere, human-centered sphere, social-legal sphere, world of things, abstract ideas, attributes (!), predicates (!), etc. As can be seen, these semantic categories are rather broad.[234]

Male and female names differ mainly in semantics. In women's names, for example, pieces of women's clothes and the necessities of the everyday life, beauty, fineness, names of flowers, etc., are presented, see e.g., Altay Turk. *Sïrya* "Ear-rings," *Oymoq* "Thimble," *Dindi* "Pearl (Necklace)" Turkish *Gül, İnji, Altïn*, etc. In men's names, in the same way, we find the names of the tools and objects which normally men deal with, e.g., *Čaqpï* "Snare / Trap," *Malta* "Axe," etc.[235]

---

[227] Nikonov, 1984, p.

[228] Ergazieva, pp. 209, 210.

[229] Garipov, 1973, p. 58.

[230] Caetani and Gabrieli, p. 59.

[231] Schimmel, p. IX.

[232] Houtsma, pp. 28-29.

[233] Žanuzakov, p. 92, also Ahmetzjanov, 1980, pp. 124-129, Ahmetzjanov, (1991) pp. 78-87, Haciyev,, 1996, Taklamakanlı , pp. 194, 207 209, etc.

[234] Blagova 1997, pp. 702-717.

[235] Šatinova 1971, p. 68, Noyan p. 9.

There are also some words applicable as both female and male names, e.g., *Ay-bek ~ Ay-χaniïm, Tolun-bey ~ Tolun-χaniïm ~ Dolun-bike, Atsïz-bek ~ Atsïz-qatun, Bayram-χan ~ Bayram-begüm.*[236]

Our classification offered below is based on semantic-typological (motivational) categories, where the motive behind name-giving is preferred to the meaning (semantics) of the word.

Classification of Turkic Anthroponyms

Theoretically, all kinds of classifications are conventional and mostly far from being perfect. This is also valid for the classifications of Turkic personal names. Within the last half-century several systems were offered by Turkologs. Besides the common categories most invented newer ones as well.[237] However, V. A. NIKONOV claims that a classification should be built up multileveled, not mixing the different levels (e.g., origin and function) within one level.[238]

Yet, we must raise the question: Can Turkic anthroponyms be systematized at all? If yes, on what principles? At this point it is worth taking in consideration L. LIGETI's comments: Turkic name-giving (anthroponymy) has never had fixed and constant rules. Besides, we must reckon with place and time, the features of the social formation in which we examine the anthropyms, with the anthroponymical customs of the neighbouring peoples and with a series of other circumstances. It is noteworthy that certain types of personal names are attached to a particular historical epoch, for instance the anthroponyms formed from ethnonyms largely go back to the Mongol era or subsequent times. The names, however, which refer to the place of birth, are much younger, usually not prior to the 17th-18th centuries.[239]

L. LIGETI stated that RÁSONYI's imposing classification is to be regarded provisional, a framework to be completed from time to time.[240] According to the outstanding Russian onomatologist V. A. NIKONOV the more detailed the classification is, the more it needs correction.[241]

Even so, L. RÁSONYI has succeded in setting up a basic system of categories of personal names which, fundamentally, has been accepted and adopted by other scholars whether they refer to it or not. V. A. NIKONOV and his Tatar colleague G. F. SATTAROV claim that at present RÁSONYI's semantic classification is to be considered the most complete.[242]

Seemingly, RÁSONYI based his system on HOUTSMA's much simpler essay. Thus BLAGOVA is in error saying that HOUTSMA's correct and reasonable classification remained unnoticed in onomatology.[243] Another source of his classification could be the semantic-typological system of Turkic ethnonyms developed by GY. NÉMETH.[244] Nevertheless, motives behind ethnonyms are mostly different from those behind anthroponyms; thus the lesson of the analogies is not always usable.[245]

Rásonyi s Classification of 1953[246]

1. Totemistic names; **2.** Group of omen-names:[247] **a)** Names expressing an immediate wish for the child's future; **b)** Protective names; **c)** Symbolic names; **d)** Names expressing a wish of the parents addressed to the gods/deities; **3.** Fortuitous names: **a)** The name of the object caught sight of after birth; **b)** The name of the animal caught sight of after birth; **c)** The first word pronounced by the mother or father after birth; **d)** The name of the first person entering the tent (or the aul); **e)** The meteorological phenomena; **f)** The name of the month or day of birth; **g)** Historical event at the time of birth; **h)** The name of the characteristic place near the scene of birth; **i)** The name of the enemy, people or tribe defeated at the time of birth; **j)** Numbers (the age of the father or grandfather, or the order of the infant in the family); **4.** Names which

---

[236] Noyan p. 9.

[237] About the recent classifications of Turkic anthroponyms see the notes in Blagova, 1998b, pp. 50-53.

[238] Nikonov, SLINM p. 7.

[239] L. Ligeti, Le professeur L. Rásonyi: AOH XXVIII (1974), p. 149.

[240] Ligeti, ibid.

[241] Nikonov, 1974, p. 102.

[242] Nikonov, 1974, p. 95, Sattarov 1990, p. 11. About the classifications of Turkic anthroponyms in general and about Rásonyi's system in particular, see Blagova 1997, pp. 619-620, and Blagova 1998b, pp. 49-53.

[243] Blagova, 1998b, p. 50.

[244] Németh, HMK pp. 54-101.

[245] Benkő, Név és történelem. Bp., 1998, p. 45.

[246] Rásonyi, Categ., pp. 323-329. This classification was determined as "classification on motives" (R. motivacionnaja klassifikacija) by Blagova, 1998b, p. 50.

[247] Mistakenly called "omen-names" instead of "desiderata" or "intentional" names.

are not in connection with magic concepts and cannot be arranged in the above categories.[248]

Women's Names in Rásonyi's System

In his first classification[249] RÁSONYI did not establish a special category or even a subgroup for women's names. Nearly ten years later in a larger study[250] on that question, he used the same categories he created for men's names. Another decade later in his summarising work *The Psychology and Categories of Name Giving Among the Turkish Peoples*,[251] he set up a new category, *Women's Names*, saying "We must devote a separate class to women's names because, although *their category is equal to that of men's names* [italics mine, I. B.], the psychology of names given to women is quite often different."[252]

The emotions of parents may differ according to the gender of the child, but this difference seems not enough to justify the creation of a special category for women's names.[253] Normally, no such a category is adopted in the onomatological literature.[254] Therefore, we prefer to deal with the peculiarities of female names at the relevant category together with the male names below.

---

[248] This is the least elaborate category: a mixed and obscure group of theophoric names, bynames, related names, etc. L. Rásonyi himself

stated that the presented categories could be multiplied.

[249] Rásonyi, Categ.

[250] Rásonyi, Frauen.

[251] Rásonyi, P. Cat.

[252] Op. cit., p. 218.

[253] Nikonov, 1974, p. 102.

[254] cf. Nikonov, 1974, Žanuzakov, (1982), Šajhulov 1983, Sattarov 1990.

The semantic-typological categories of Turkic names seem to be quite specific in comparison with those of the Indo-European and Uralic languages.[255] This is why a reliable system would be useful for comparative purposes for the linguists-onomatologists of quite different languages.

The semantic-motivational classification used here is based on RÁSONYI's system elaborated in his articles.[256] The real advantage of this system is that it is not merely a semantic classification. It also tries to demonstrate the motives (in RÁSONYI's terms: "the psychology") of name-giving. In the classification shown below the main categories (I/1, I/2, I/3; II/1, II/2, II/3; III/1-14) refer here to the motives, while the subgroups usually reflect the semantic characteristics.

When updating and developing RÁSONYI's classification, we applied the results of other onomatologists, first of all those of NIKONOV, who adopted RÁSONYI's system and developed and spread it among the researchers of names in his country.[257]

I. Commemorative Names (Memorativa)[258]

These are or were originally names of another person, a god, a totem, or an idea exalted, now applied to a new bearer to connect him or her with the primary bearer. They are given on the basis of ancient animistic and totemistic beliefs and may be divided into further groups and subgroups.[259]

I/1 Totemistic Names[260]

The North American Indian word *totem* - misunderstood by Europeans - basically means an animal, but also a plant, with which a certain group of people cultivates a family relationship, for which reason it enjoys respect and regard since certain animals, according to primitive prelogical ideas, are quicker, faster, stronger, more courageous than man.

Totemism was widespread in Australia, Oceania, Indonesia, parts of Africa and also in South America.[261] We are now mainly concerned with the North-American variety of totemism, as it shows greater similarity to the totemism of the old Turkic peoples. Otherwise it has not yet been decided whether the old Turks had not borrowed totemism from some other cultural community.

The most valuable data on the totemism of the Turkic peoples is conveyed by the chronicle of Rašīd ad-Dīn (1247-1318). The part having some importance for us has become known since HOUTSMA's study *Die Ghuzenstämme*[262] appeared. According to Rašīd ad-Dīn, the twenty-four Oghuz tribes belonged to six groups, each group of four having its own *ongun*. HOUTSMA and GOMBOCZ spelled this word, in an easily understandable mistake, as *uygun*. The interpretation of *ongun* according to the modern Türkçe Sözlük[263] is, among others, "İlkel toplumlarda topluluğun ondan türediği sanılarak kutlu tutulan hayvan, totem" [=A kind of animal bringing success and blessing, in primitive societies one or the other community or tribe believes itself to be descendent of]. The *ongun*s of the six groups are birds of prey: *šahin* 'hawk', *qartal* 'eagle', *tavšanjïl* 'golden eagle', *soñγur* 'falcon', *üč-quš* '?', *čaqïr* 'goshawk'. The tribes refrained from hunting their blessing-bringing *ongun*. That means, we face here the kind of totemism that W. WUNDT called "entsagender Totemismus."[264]

The connection of totemism to shamanism has also come up, especially in ZÉLÉNIN's most valuable work "Kul't ongonov."[265] Rašīd ad-Dīn does not say that the tribal groups honoured their *ongun*. Much earlier than Rašīd ad-Dīn, Ibn Faḍlān, who travelled to the Volga-Bulgarians, wrote in 926 that in one of their groups the *crane* while in another the *snake* were rendered cultic homage. The similarly early Gardīzī wrote about the 11th century Kirghiz that one of their groups imparted honours on the *cow*, others to the *wind*, the *tortoise*, the *falcon*, or the *magpie*. The Orkhon Turks believed themselves to be descendants of the *wolf*. That is why they pinned a golden wolf's head at the tip of their banner.

Kézai's chronicle derives the members of the Árpáds, the first dynasty of the Hungarians "de genere *Turu.l*." Again according to Kézai, it was a depiction of the bird *turul* that ornamented Attila's banner. GOMBOCZ has also written

---

[255] Benkő, loc. cit.
[256] Rásonyi's Categ., Frauen., KÖA, Anthr., P. Categ.
[257] V. A. Nikonov, (Imja i obščestvo, 1974, pp. 96-102), A. G. Šajhulov (1974, 1983b), T. Žanuzakov (1982), G. F. Sattarov (1990).
[258] This category was not defined in Rásonyi's system.
[259] Nikonov, 1974, p. 101, Šajhulov, op. cit. pp. 9-20, Sattarov, op. cit. pp. 14-49.
[260] based on Rásonyi, P. Cat. pp. 209-210.
[261] cf. Das Fischer Lexikon, Völkerkunde, Frankfurt a. M. 1959.
[262] WZKM II., pp. 219-233.
[263] Ankara, 1966; cf. also TS
[264] Völkerpsychologie, II. 2, p. 254.
[265] Akademija Nauk SSR. 1936.

about the *Turul*-clan, adding that *Turul* was once a widely used personal name in the 13th century[266]. The *turul* is also a bird of prey, the name of a smaller species of hawks. In Chagatay and Turkish (Osmanli) it is called *toγrul/toğrul*. It used to be a widespread personal name among the Turks, too: the founder or the Seljuk dynasty himself was called *Toγrul-beg*.[267]

Now we have arrived at the statement of the fact that although totemism, from an onomatological point of view, is basically of paramount importance to tribal and clan-names, yet a corpulent group of personal names has to be referred to here as well.[268] We have seen this in the case of *Turul*.

One of the numerous examples is *Boz-qurt* "Grey Wolf." *Boz-qurt* Ibn Sulaimân occurs in Asia Minor in 1480;[269] *Kök-büri* "Blue Wolf" is Irbil's *ata-beg* in 1190.[270] In the description of the Bayaut tribe, Rašid ad-Dīn also mentions a very early *Kök-büri*.[271] The earliest layer of these names must be in connection with totemistic concepts.[272] The personal names *Uqu* "Owl," *Yïlan* "Snake" and *Ayu* "Bear" seem to be primarily totemistic.[273] Names of this kind such as, e.g., Kirg., Chag. *Turumtay* "ein kleiner Raubvogel, der Neuntödter,"[274] were used among the Egyptian Mamluks on such a large scale, and we find so many data in Makrīzī's,[275] Ibn Iyâs',[276] and Ibn Taghrībirdī's[277] chronicles that we may even say it had become a *fashion name*.[278] The same refers to the name *Aq-quš*.[279] The names *Boγday* "Wheat" and *Arpa* "Barley" probably owe their existence to *plant totemism*.

Another part of the numerous *animal names* used as anthroponyms are *incidental* (p. XLVIII), others *symbolic* (p. XLVI), while still others may belong to the group of *protective names* (p. XLIV).

PNfem: We cannot relate female names which are doubtlessly totemistic, unless *Ayu-bikä*[280] "Bear Dame/Lady" and *Arslan-χatun* "Lion Princess/Queen" belong here.

I/2 Theophoric Names[281]

A very important category in Turkic name-giving is that of theophoric names. These names are represented in great abundance among the Turkic peoples, probably more commonly used than those of the Indo European peoples. In the *Onomasticon Turcicum* some 90 items from different ages and different Turkic peoples belong here, like *Täñri-berdi*, *Täñri-bergen* and *Täñri-bermiš* "God-Given" (in their corresponding forms), which are partly names of historical persons. The name of God could be replaced by different words, for instance in *Oγan-berdi*, in the Islamic cultural sphere *Alla(h)-berdi ~ Alla(h)-bergen, Aq-berdi (<Xaq-berdi) ~ Aq-bergen (<Xaq-bergen), Xuday-berdi ~ Xuday-bergen*. The belief that God can be also an indirect cause of conception is reflected in names like *J̌an-berdi* "(the divine) Soul-given."[282]

Theophoric names may consist of the verbal part only, e.g., *Berdi ~ Verdi ~ Virdi*; *Bermiš ~ Vermiš, Aldï ~ Almïš, Bolmuš*. The latter two evidently refer to the lacking ablative form of God's name: 'Taken from God', 'Become from God'. All these Turkic names can rightly be regarded as *remnants of theophoric names* (see also 7.2. on p. LXI). The most common types are *Berdi* "(He who) Gave" and *Bolmuš* "(He Who) Became." The latter can be found in the Orkhon inscriptions in Bilgä-qaγan's attribute: *Tängritäg Tängridä Bolmuš Türk Bilgä qagan* "The Heaven-like and Heaven-born

---

[266] Gombocz, ÁTSz. p. 15

[267] The anthroponyms mentioned in the forthcoming parts of the introduction as examples without indicating the source, can be found in full among the headwords in the Onomasticon.

[268] cf. Gordlevskij 1913, p. 131, also Németh 1971. Nikonov is sceptical about using totem-names as anthroponyms (op. cit. p. 101). Sattarov, however, accepts this possibility (Sattarov 1990, pp. 14-49).

[269] Zambaur, pp. 158, 159.

[270] Ibid. p. 228.

[271] RaD/Ber. I, 177, see also Houtsma p. 33.

[272] Ilimbetov p. 90.

[273] Potanin IV, p. 177, Rásonyi, Categ. p. 325.

[274] Gombocz, ÁTSz. p. 13.

[275] Makrīzī.

[276] Iyâs.

[277] Ibn Taghrīb.

[278] see the paragraph beginning on page XXXIII.

[279] Gombocz, ÁTSz. p. 8.

[280] Proben, III, 187 /226

[281] In his first classification, L. Rásonyi did not set up a separate category for the theophoric names (Rásonyi, Categ. p. 330), he only made, among others, a faint reference to them under No. 4. Later on however, "The Theophoric Names" appeared as an independent category under No. IV. But at the same time he assigned a part of the theophoric names to the protective names (cf. Rásonyi, P. Catcg p. 217). Since recent research has confirmed the latter concept, we do not deal with theophoric names only in this paragraph. For more on Islamic names of this kind, see in Schimmel pp. 18-19.

[282] Rásonyi, Theoph. p. 291.

Turkic Bilgä qagan."[283]

Theophoric names may also have a *protective function* (see II/2.4).

The names of this group preserve not only *theonyms*, but the reminiscence of ancient animism, that is, different cults, such as the cult of animals (wolf, dog, bear), fish, plants, earth, water, planets, etc.

For example: *Arïslan* "Lion," *Yul-bars* "Tiger," *Toyγon* "White Falcon," *Täkä* "He-goat, Ram," *Alma* "Apple," *İmän* "Oak," *Ay-doγdï, Ay-tuγan* "Moon Was Born," *Ay-bars* "Moon Panther," *Ay-demir* "Moon Iron," *Ay-zade* "Moon Son," *Kün-tuγdï* "Sun Was Born," *Kündäy~Küntäy* "Sun-Like," *Kön-timer* "Sun Iron," *Yoldïz* "Star," *Čolpan* "Venus," *Diñgez* "Sea," *Diñgez-bay ~ Diñgez-bäk* "Sea Lord," *Täñre-qul, Xuday-qul* "God('s) Slave," etc. [284]

PNfm: We do not have data for theophoric women's names. SATTAROV and ŠAJHULOV, however, list the female names *Ay-sili* "Moon Beauty," *Ay-bikä, Ay-bikäč* "Moon Princess," *Ay-göl* "Moon Flower," *Kön-bikä* "Sun Princess," *Kön-sïlu* "Sun Beauty," *Yoldïz* "Star," *Čulpan* "Venus," *Su-sïlu* "Water Beauty," *Diñgez-bikä* "Sea Princess," *Aq-quš* "Swan," *Döyä-γoš* "Ostrich" etc., among the cultic names.[285]

I/3 Names of Honoured Persons (Ancestors, Rich Acquaintances, etc.)

These names reflect respect for heroes, well-known people, ancestors, close relatives after their death, and friends.[28·5] The custom of naming Turkmen children in honour of their ancestors (grandfather, grandmother) is described in detail by MUHAMEDOVA.[287]

Actually the *majestic names* in RÁSONYI's classifications should be dealt with here. Anthroponyms formed from other anthroponyms as the names or honorific titles of sovereigns and high-ranking personalities were originally regarded as symbolic names. Later they were transferred to the separate subgroup II/D ("Erhabene Namen," "Meşhur adlar," "Noms majesteux")[288] created for them but abandoned after the independent category of *Fashion names* which emerged in the latest classification.[289]

The names of this kind may also be classified in the group of *Symbolic names* (see p. XLVI).[290]

The great Seljuk sultan's name *Arslan* was given to ten persons in the course of the subsequent decades. We might enumerate many further examples, but as soon as these names became popular, they lost their original content, so that it is difficult to draw a line between the category of *names decisive of fate* and *fashion names* (see p. XXXIII) a part of which may doubtlessly be considered as commemorative or/and desiderata names.

For example: Maml. *Bey-bars*, Maml. *Özbeg*, Uzb. *Uluγ-bek*, Bashk. *Salawat*, etc.

PNfem: *Arslan-xatun* "Lion Lady" from the Seljuk dynasty; *Selčük-xatun* "Seljuk Lady," *Selčük-paša* "Seljuk Lady/Darling," etc.

II. Desiderata or Intentional Names[291]

The majority of Turkic personal names, against a psychological background of a more or less *magical (teleological) character*, springs forth from the notion of good and harmful spirits. The first group of these are the *desiderata names* which express the parents' *wish, protection* and *intention* towards the spiritual world. The mystification of names demands the choice of desiderata names with which parents appeal to fate for the child's good qualities, life, success and happiness. The basis of giving such names is a plea.[292]

We distinguish names clearly expressing other good wishes, further on abstract names symbolizing *power, wisdom, the good and the beautiful*. The delimitation of symbolic names decisive of fate is fairly tentative. For instance, the name of many animals may belong to this group, but we cannot accurately separate them from *totemistic* (see p. XXXIX) or *incidental* names (see p. XLVIII).

II/1. Names Decisive of Fate

Most *imperative names* (see pp. LV, LV, LIX) belong to this group. Some express a *wish* at the newborn's first manifestations of life; some wish richness, power, fortune, success, health, long life, etc., to the infant. Every imperative name is a clearly expressed good wish.

---

[283] Rásonyi, op. cit. p. 293.

[284] Nikonov, op. cit. p.101, Sattarov, op. cit pp. 49-68, Šajhulov, op. cit. pp. 11-20.

[285] Sattarov and Šajhulov, loc. cit.

[286] Gordlevskij, 1913, p. 133, Nikonov, 1974, p. 102, Žanuzakov, op. cit. p. 25, Sattarov, op. cit. p. 68, Kusimova, 1971, p. 53.

[287] Muhamedova, 1957, pp. 43-44.

[288] Rásonyi, Frauen., p. 231, KÖA p. 142, Anthr. p. 148.

[289] Rásonyi, P., Categ. p. 218.

[290] Rásonyi,, Categ. p. 326-327, Nikonov op. cit. p. 103.

[291] Mistakenly called as "Omen" names in Rásonyi, Categ., p. 325 and in his Frauen., p. 231, but corrected in his P. Categ., p. 214.

[292] Nikonov op. cit. pp. 30, 98.

Another verbal form frequently used for such names is the participle of indefinite preterite with the suffix *-mïš* (cf. structures, p. LIII), for instance *Toqtamïš* "Stopped," one of the numerous medieval bearers of this name was a member of the ruling house of the Golden Horde (1376-1396).

PNfem: Imperative names are few, and naturally the names of wild beasts symbolizing power are also rare; there are no names of weapons, but all the more numerous are the *abstract names* meaning especially *beauty, virtue* and the like.

II/1.1 Names wishing to stop the birth or death of children in the family

Toqta "Stand," a khan of the Golden Horde (1291-1312), whose name has been very frequent also among the Kazakhs until recent times; *Toqtamïš* "Stopped," *Ötegen~Ötemis* "Fulfilled, Achieved (wish), Child Being Paid for," *Tölegen, Tölemis, Tölendi* "Paid / Bought / Bought off / Redeemed (child)," *Orïn-basar* "Deputy,"[293]

If a child passes away, Turkmens have a custom of giving subsequent boys names like *Övez* : "Compensation, indemnification," *Durdï,* "Stayed, survived," *Övez-durdï* "Compensation Has Stayed / Survived," *Övez-geldi* "Compensation Has Come," *Övez-mïrat, Öde* "Compensate," etc. If the children do not survive again, they may select from *Mïrat-durdï, Oraz-durdï*, etc.[294]

Besides innumerable Kazakh and other Turkic *Tur* "Stand! Stay!" and even *Bek-tur* "Stand Firm; Hold out," *Tursun* and Turkish/Azeri *Dursun* "Hold on" are attested in several cases.

PNfem: Tursun-gül, Qal-biyke, Tur-tärim, appear in a Nestorian inscription;[295] but these three names might belong to the *desiderata names* (category II/1.4).

II/1.2 Names wishing the child birth (birth of a daughter)

If a girl was born after a lot of boys in a Kirghiz family, they named her *Qïzdar-qan* "Girls' Khan" which means they want more daughters to be born.[296] In these circumstances the Turkish feminine *Dilek* "Wish" expresses the same.[297]

II/1.3 Girls' names wishing the birth of a son

Typical group of female anthroponyms. Such names were given to girls when the parents expected boys, but only girls were born.[298]

PNfem: Kirg. *Burulča~Burulču* "Turn to Other Direction," an imperative with diminutive suffix. It expresses the wish for the birth of no more daughters but a son. The same is expressed by the name *Yeter* "Enough (of girls)" used at many places in Anatolia, *Döndi, Döne, Bïktïk, Son-gül, Tamam*,[299] etc., cf. also Trkm. *Gïz-yeter* "Enough of Girls," Kzk. *Qïs-taman* 'id.', Kzk. *Qïz-tumas* "Girl Won't Be Born," Trkm. *Oɣul-gerek* "We Must Have a Son; It Must Be a Son," *Oɣul-dursun* "May the Son Stay/Survive!," *Oɣul-durdï* "Son Stayed/Survived," *Oɣul-sabïr* "Son Patience," *Oɣul-jemal* 'Son Beauty', *Besdir/Bessir* 'Enough', *Doyduq* '(We) Got Full/Satisfied', *Dōlun* 'Get Full/Satisfied!',[300] Kzk. *Ulan-gerek* "Son is Needed,"[301] *Gül-dursun* "The Rose Hold Stop / Hold Stop Flower" i.e., the birth of girls;[302] *Tursun-gül* "Stop/Hold Flower," *Doğsun-oğli* "A Son should Be Born to Them"[303] , Kirg. *Toqto-bübü* "Wait, Shamaness!,"[304] *Tur-χatun* "Stop Lady," *Ul-bolsïn ~ Ul-bolsun* "It should Be a Son; Let It Be a Son"; Kirg. *Ūl-qan* "Son Khan," *Ūl-bek* "Son Lord,"[305] *Ul-tuɣan* "Son Was Born" (the latest girl was named so, when lots of girls were born before), *Ul-tuwar* "(She) Will Bear a Son,"[306] *Žanïl~Žanïl-χan* "Make a Mistake!" (i.e., "Bear a Son!").[307]

II/1.4 Names wishing health and/or strength

Bek-bol "Be Strong/Healthy!" *Bek-bolsun* "Let Him Be Strong/Healthy," *Esän* "Healthy, Sound," *Isän-tur* "Live Healthy!" *Taš-ba* "Stone Lord," *Bekem-bay* "Strong Lord," etc.

A part of names of metals and minerals may also belong here: *Ay-temir* "Moon Iron," *Bek-timer* "Hard Iron,"

---

[293] Žanuzakov, 1971a, p. 101; Sattarov.

[294] Muhamedova, 1957, pp. 41-42, Zaj.; 1971, p. 334.

[295] Chwolson, Syr.-nest., pp. 78, 90.

[296] Kalilov, p. 93.

[297] Schimmel, p. 20.

[298] Kalilov, p. 93, Žanuzakov, 1971a, p. 100, cf. also Schimmel p. 42.

[299] Erol, II.

[300] Muhamedova 1957, p. 42.

[301] Mihajlov, Tuzemcy Zakasp. Obl. Ashabad, 1900, p. 54, Žanuzakov 1971a p. 100.

[302] Samojlovič: ŽS 1911, p. 298.

[303] DQorq./Rossi, p. 161.

[304] Žanuzakov 1971a p. 101.

[305] Kalilov p. 93.

[306] Žanuzakov, 1971a, p. 100 (after Č. Valihanov, Izbrannye proizvedenija, 1958, p. 163).

[307] Žanuzakov 1971a, p. 100.

II/1.5 Names wishing longevity

Certain protective names (see p. XLIV) may express the idea of longevity. With this aim one gives the child the name of the father or someone who was long-lived in the family or clan.[308]

Ölmez "Immortal," *Tursun* "Stay (Alive),"[309] *Qalsïn* "Remain (=Survive)," *Toχto~Tuχta* "Stay (Alive)!"[310] *Ömür-zaq* "Long life," *Miñ-žasar* "He Will Live to Be a Thousand," etc.

Some numbers used as personal names may also express the wish of longevity.[311]

PNfem: Tümän-qutluγ "Having Ten Thousandfold Happiness," *Yüz-bikä* "May She Live (to be) a Hundred; Lady (of One) Hundred," *Ülmäs-bikä* "Immortal Lady."

II/1.6 Names wishing beauty

PNfem: Ay-čuwaq "Moon Beam," Kzk. *Altïn-šaš* "Golden Hair,"[312] *Ay-kümüš* "Moon Silver," *Altïn-ay* "Gold Moon," *Qara-čač* "Black Hair," *Kümüš-ay* "Silver Moon," *Suluw* "Beautiful, Pretty; Handsome," *Güzel~Gözäl* "Beautiful."

II/1.7 Names wishing positive mental or moral qualities

Aqïl-bay "Wit Lord," *Batïr* "Hero," *Jar-bol* "Be a Companion," *Er-bolsun* "Be a Man."

There are countless names meaning abstract notions of *good* and *beautiful*, e.g., *Tügäl* "Perfect," *Özü-bek* "Strong in Body," his sons, the khans of the Golden Horde *Jani-bek* "Strong in Soul" and *Tïnï-bek* "Strong in Soul," *Bilgä* 'Wise; "Sage," *Sävinč* "Joy," *Türk* "Power," *Ögrünč* "Gaiety; Mirth," *Ärdäm~Erdäm* "Virtue; Merit," *Inanč* "Confidence; Faith."

PNfem: Irïs "Happiness," *Qut-χatun* "Happiness Queen," *Qutluγ-tärim* "Happy Princess," *Ögrünč-tigin* "Joy Prince," *Tüzün-silik-χunčuy* "Clean/Fair Princess," *Urazlï* "Happy," *Sävüg* "Love, Lovely," *Körkli-yaχšï* "Beautiful Good," *Turu-bek* "Right Gentleman," *Aruw-χan* "Pure/Fair Lady."

II.1.8 Names wishing happiness, good luck, wealth

Among the nomads the amount of domestic animals (sheep, cattle, horses, etc.) was considered the measure of wealth, fortune and happiness. That is why certain anthroponyms formed from names of domestic animals may belong to the present category.[313]

Bay-bol "Be Rich," *Bay Büre* "Rich Wolf," *Qol-bas* "Defeat Army-flank"; Uzb. *Yuz-bây* "Rich (Having) One Hundred [his father got 100 sheep]," *Miñ-bây* "Rich (Having) One Thousand [his father got 1000 sheep]," *Qoylï-bay* "Rich In Sheep,"[314] *Tüye-bay* "Rich In Camels," *Baqït* "Happiness," *Baqtï-bek* "Happy Lord," *Qotlï-bay* "Happy Lord,"[315] *Qutlï-yar* "Lucky Companion/Fellow," *Qälli-bek* "Lord With Birthmark," *Irïslï* "Happy," *Saray* "Palast."

PNfem: Sevin-beg "Be Glad Lord," *Süyün-bike* "Be Glad Lady," *Gülsün* "Smile/Laugh"; *Baqtï-gül* "Happy Flower (=girl),"[316] *Qutlï-gül* "Lucky Rose (=girl)."

The Eastern Anatolian *Beş-bine* "For Five Thousand" is a peculiar name used only for females; it shows the parents' wish that the child could be sold; i.e., married for 5,000 Turkish liras.[317]

As *qal* and *meñ* "birthmark" was considered to be the sign of divine care and happiness, the anthroponyms (mainly of females) with these components may also be listed here, e.g., *Meñli* "Having a Birthmark," *Narlï* "Having a Red Birthmark," *Qalli-gül* "Flower (=girl) With Birthmark," etc. The roots of naming with these words go back to the matriarchal clan.[318]

II/1.9 Names wishing success

Hind-al "Take (=conquer) India!"; Bābur-šah writes in his memoirs that in 1518 when the birth of his son was reported to him, news of the taking of Bhīra arrived at the same time. This he understood as a *good omen* and ordered that his son be given the name *Hind-al.*[319] That is why this name may well be listed also in the group of incidental names (see subgroups III/9-10).

---

[308] Gordlevskij, 1913, p. 132; Noyan p. 14.

[309] Grod I, p. 99.

[310] Ibid.

[311] Kalilov, p. 94.

[312] Sultan'jaev, 1970, p. 75

[313] cf. Nikonov, op. cit. p. 98.

[314] Ibid.

[315] Ibid

[316] Ibid

[317] Önder, Göle p.1182.

[318] Kalilov, p. 95.

[319] Bábarnámah ed. by A. S. Beveridge, 1905, GMS I, 220/a.

After the name reform of 1934, such Turkish family names with *double imperative* appeared in Turkey replacing the old Osmanli surnames: such is the new family name of a photographer, e.g., *Gör-al* "See and Take It," of a poet *Bul-ver* "Find and Give" and finally the name of a vali (governor) of Istanbul *Yener Vural* [*Vur-al!*] "Victor-Beat and Grab."

To this category belong the optative names, too, e.g., Turkish *Göre* "Let Him/Her See."

II/1.10 Names wishing dignitaries, power

Names of dignitaries[320] are frequently attested as early as the eighth century among the Uyghurs: *Tegin* "Prince," *İnaq* "Councellor; Minister," *Tarχan* "Priviledged; Nobleman," etc. Uyghur names related to the government of tribal confederation and the empire, respectively, can also be listed here, such as *İl-täber*, *İl-aldï*, *İl-tüzmüš*, *İl-tüzer*, *İl-basar*, *Basar-aba*.[321]

Atalïq, Basqaq, Čawuš, Bäk-min "I (Am) a Lord," *Kilde-bäk* "A Lord Has Come,"[322] *Tarqan, Tutuq, Uruñu.*

PNfem: *Biče-aγa* "(Her) Highness the Lady," *İl-qutadmïš-tängrim* "Her Divine Majesty Who Brought a Blessing for the Realm," *İl-tutmïš-χan* "She Who Held the Empire," *Qunčuy-täñrim* "Princess Highness," *Sultanïm* "My Sultan," *Sultan-bike* "Sultan Lady."

See also category I/3.

II/1.11 Names wishing a good profession, prosperous business or trade

SATTAROV reckons the anthroponyms meaning jobs among the desiderata names,[323] but we think they may be classifiable under group I/3 and III/5 as well.

Ayuwčï "Bear-leader," *Belči* "Guide," *Bïčaqčï* "Cutler," *Yamčï* "Postmaster," *Qašuqčï* "Maker of (wooden) Spoons," *Qoyčï* "Shepherd," *Malčï* "Shepherd; stockbreeder," *Ormančï* "Forester, Woodman," *Ölöñči* "Grass Collector/Seller," *Sabančï* "Farmer, Ploughman, Peasant," *Taγašï* "Shoeing Smith," *Tüšekči* "Maker or Seller of Beds/Couches."

PNfem: *Dadu-χatun* "Child's Nurse," *D'aqačï* "Maker of Collars," *İnekči* "Cowgirl."

II/2. Protective Names (Apotropaeon)

This category is one of the most important groups of Turkic names. Such names are given with the aim of making the harmful and evil spirits believe that the parents do not like or despise the child and his/her death would not cause any grief to the parents, so that it is not worthwhile to do any harm to the child. Other names want to mislead harmful spirits, so that they do not know whose child it is, or believe that the child is ugly, impure, bad, etc. In this respect, RALPH FOX writes: "The Kirghiz Kazakhs are sadly superstitious... Such is their fear of evil spirits that mothers, in terror of their jealousy, commonly christen children with unlovely or unflattering names. They are called after feeble animals, or endowed with sorry qualities, in the hope, that such terrified humility will be beneath the notice of the evil spirits."[324]

IBRAGIMOV claims almost the same: The newborn child is protected from the evil eye with utmost care. Whatever disease happens to him, they ascribe it to that mysterious cause. All Kirghiz [=Kazakh] old women know incantations against affection by the evil eye (*küz tiyü*).[325] To protect the child against evil eye and not to cause him any illness by mentioning his name frequently, they give the child different *bynames* (see p. XXXIV) beside his name. Such bynames are given to boys: *Jaman-bala* "Ugly, Bad Child," *Tentek-bala* "Silly (Naughty) Child," *Jindï-bala* "Mad Boy," *Uru-bala* "Thief Boy," etc. Girls are given bynames like this: *Qara-čaš* "Black Hair," *Qoy-köz* "Sheep Eye," *Uzun-čaš* "Long Hair(ed)," etc. By using these bynames the Kirghiz [Kazakhs] substitute the virtual names of their children.[326]

When children still die one after another in a family, they try to propitiate fate this way: they give the child a shaming name[327] and connect it with the idea of longevity; by giving him the name *Küčük-bay* ["Puppy Lord"] they say: why will he not stay in life like a puppy? Such names are not infrequent: *Küte-bar* ["He Has an Ass"], *Boq-küt* ["Shit Ass"], *May-küt* ["Fat Ass"], *İt-ayaq* ["Dog Leg"], *Qatpa* ["a kind of camel-disease"]. An only child, either male or female, gets a silver ring into his or her nose when children died before in the family.[328]

PNfem: Protective names are less frequently given to females than to males. Why protect the female infant if it is not as valuable as the boy, and as soon as she grows up, she will not stay with her family, but goes to another. At best one

---

[320] For the particular titles see chapter *"Secondary Components,"* p. LXII.

[321] See Rásonyi, Categ. pp. 332-337 and Rásonyi, Bas. pp. 29, 31.

[322] Šajhulov, op. cit. p. 27.

[323] Sattarov, op. cit. p.130.

[324] Fox, p. 149.

[325] It must be noted that mullahs too deal out mascots against affection by the evil eye.

[326] Ibragimov, p. 125.

[327] Šatinova, 1971, p. 67.

[328] Grod. I, p. 99.

wishes to get a great deal of money for her.

Studying of protective names encounters some difficulties since the so called "unlovely or unflattering names" (even the words) have been left out from most dictionaries and name-lists because of certain inconceivable bashfulness.[329]

The protective names may be divided into several subgroups such as:

II/2.1 Names meaning something abhorring or worthless

The Kazakhs, Kirghiz, Turkmen, etc., for instance, often gave nasty (sometimes second) names, hoping that children will be healthy, long-lived and will not be bewitched. RADLOV called these names "misleading names" (R. obmannye imena) which, in fact, were protective names.[330]

Boq "Excrement," *Belden-boq* "Feculent to the Belt," *İt-boq* "Dog's Dirt," *Qomuq* "Horse Dung" *İt-ködön* "Dog's Butt" *Köten* "Butt, Ass," *Täzäk* "Dry Dung (used as fuel)," *Tükrünč* "Spit, Spittle," *D'aman ~ Žaman* "Malvolent," *Baγay* "Bad," *Čoqoy* "Coarse Leather Shoe," *Sasïq-baš* "Stinking Head," *Sirke* "Pus," *Tezek* "Peat, Turf, Excrement," *Tüktü* "Hairy," etc.

PNfem: Yaman "Bad," *Dizenteriya* "Dysentery,"[331] *Poktuγ-kiriš* "Stretched Bowstring," *D'ïtu* "Disgustingly Smelling," *Čolbanaχ* "Sensul, Lewd, Immoral, Bawdy," *Sasï-bikä* "Stink Lady," etc.

II/2.2 Names suggesting that the child is similar to despised animals or people

Čičqan "Mouse," *İt-küčüjük* "Puppy, Whelp," Yak. *İt-oγoto* "Puppy," *Ehe-oγoto* "Bear's Cub,"[332] *Et-almas ~İt-almaz* "(Even) a Dog Won't Take Him/Her," *Et-teymes* "(Even) a Dog Won't Touch It," *Qara-et* "Black Dog," *Kurak* "Crow," *Sart-qalmaq* (name of a people despised by the Kirghiz), *Arap* "Arab" (whose figure is not attractive and is so horrible that even evil spirits would not hurt someone with such a name.).[333]

PNfem: Chuv. *T'šəG'es'* "Swallow" (given as a protective name if two children died in the family earlier).[334]

II/2.3 Personal names confusing the evil spirits

It was thought that one might mislead the evil spirits in two ways:

1. By giving anthroponyms meaning that the child does not exist or it does not belong to the parents anymore (as they have bestowed or sold it to others after the birth or the baby was found). If more newborns had died in the family earlier, they gave the next baby to the midwife who adopted him/her as her son/daughter for a while. This kind of feigned selling was observed with several Turkic peoples, such as Bashkirs, Kirghiz, Chuvash, Turks, etc.[335] In Yakut even the feigned stealing of children was observed. In this case the child was brought back three days later having a new name.[336] In Samsun, Turkey, for example, after several child-deaths in a family they would sell the newborn to a friend whose children always live; they dress the child in the underclothes and frocks of this friend's children. In this case the newborn is given names like *Temel, Yašar, Bākī, Hayātī* "Vital."[337]

2. By giving girls' names to boys.[338] The Kazakhs too used to give their daughters male names (e.g., *Altay, Bolat, Qanapiγa*) and vice versa. Girls with male names played with boys and were dressed and educated like boys. This custom no longer survives.[339]

As has been seen, giving such protective names was accompanied by certain magical ceremonies, especially when children did not stay alive in the family.[340]

Atsïz "Nameless," *Bolmaz* "Non Existent," *Kebek* "Bran, Shorts" (a name given to a child who "was sold"),[341]

---

[329] see, for example, Atanijazov, 1988

[330] Sozontov pp. 6-7; Pantusov, Kirg. p. 39; Grod. I, p. 99; Samojlovič: ŽS 1911, pp. 297-298; Radl., Aus Sib., p. 176; Kustanaev pp. 37-38; Danilova and Enžaeva p. 61.

[331] Nikonov, op. cit. p. 100.

[332] Gricenko, p. 156 notes that sometimes names of dogs also were given to children, and at the same time dogs were named with children's names.

[333] Gordlevskij, 1913, p. 132.

[334] Mészáros p. 409

[335] For the similar custom with the Chuvash see Magn., Mat., pp. 196-198. Cf. also Gordlevskij, 1913, p. 132; Kusimova, 1971, p. 53; Kalilov, p. 93.

[336] Gricenko, p. 157.

[337] Noyan, p. 7.

[338] The latter method was used by the Arabs as well. The pre-Islamic Arabs often gave their sons names which were grammatically analogical to women's names. This is a survival of name-magic, some kind of concealment from evil spirits that may kill male offspring (Gafurov, p. 45). In order to distract the interest of the jinns (evil spirits) they often dress up little boys in girls' clothes (Schimmel p. 21).

[339] Žanuzakov, 1971a, p. 101.

[340] For more details in Kirghiz, see Abramzon, Rožd.; Kalilov, p. 93. On Bashkir magical protection see Torma, 1997, chapters 3, 4, 5.

[341] Kalilov, p. 93.

Satïlɣan~Satïlmïš "Sold, Disposed of," *Tab-aldï* "Found"; *Tört-aba* 'Four Fathers',[342] *Beš-kempir~Bes-kempir* 'Five Old Women', *Altï-qurtqa* 'Six-Old-Women',[343] *Jeti-köt* '(Born From) Seven Vulvas'.[344] (RINTCHEN relates also the Kazakh custom whereas the women present at the birth hold the newborn between their own opened thigs one after other. Whose child is it?), *Qara-qïz* 'Black-girl', the name of one of Chinggis Khan's great-grandsons.

PNfem: *Qurtqa* "Old Woman," *Yädi-qurtqa(-xatun)* "Seven Old Women," *Satïlmïš-xatun* "Lady Already Sold," *Satu-bikä* "Sale Lady; Lady for Sale?," etc.

II/2.4 Anthroponyms that aim to frighten evil spirits

Sometimes the protective name asserts that the child had been given by a fearsome monster (God) or strong animal that can frighten away the harmful spirits.[345] It is not impossible that by giving theophoric names (see p. XXXIV) we may also reckon with *magic ideas: to protect the infant against evil spirits*.[346] Maybe, names like *Täñri-berdi, Xuday-berdi, Alla-berdi* were given with this aim.

If sick, weak children were born into the family, the next child received the name of a strong wild animal.[347] In connection with these and other similar names, the supposition may come up that the protective role is performed by the *totem animal*.[348] In order to form a definite opinion, however, it would be advantageous to collect the psychological data of naming still existent among the Kazakh and the smaller Turkic peoples in the Altay Mountains who preserve the traditions.

Ayu "Bear," *Arstan* "Lion," *Büre* "Wolf," *Böri-berdi* "Given by the Wolf," *Altï-bars* "Six Panthers," *Börümüš* (Son of the Wolf),[349] *Yolbars~Jolbars* "Tiger," *Tülkü* "Fox."

II/3 Symbolic Names

The symbolic names too express a wish to influence the child's future but in a less apparent, metaphoric way, via *word magic*. A. SCHIMMEL writes: "Everywhere one finds that by calling a child by the name of a saint or a hero (including film stars!) parents hope to transfer some of the noble qualities, the heroism or beauty of their patron to the child, and thus to make him participate in the patron's greatness."[350] The names of honoured persons, different dignities, wild or domestic animals and certain objects indicate who or what the infant would resemble.[351]

Thus we listed the *pet-names (hypocoristica)*[352] in the appropriate subgroups of the symbolic and fortuitous names.

PNfem: Although the girl is of less value, the mother's love often manages to outdo the father's evaluation and a pet-name given is retained.

II/3.1 Anthroponyms meaning wild and domestic animals, birds of prey

Animal names have changed to symbolic ones, according to what characteristic features they possessed which the parents considered desirable with regard to the infant, such as *brave, aggressive temper, power, speed*, while in the case of one or the other domestic animal its size is the symbol of the appreciated or useful feature.

The ancient anthroponyms formed from the names of wild animals and birds of prey may belong to *commemorative names* (p. XXXIX). The major part of names of domestic animals, however, should be regarded among the *incidental names* (p. XLVIII).

In the chronicles referring to the Near East, and especially to the Mamluks, the number of names *Arslan* "Lion," *Bars* "Panther," *Buɣa* "Bull" is considerable. Besides these, there occurs very early an *Il-Arslan* "Empire-Lion,"[353] later in Rāwandī's chronicle as the name of a Shah of Khoresm (1156-1172) and also in Qazwīnī.[354]

Further examples: *Il-bars* "Empire Panther," *Ay-bars* "Moon Panther," *Jol-bars* "Tiger," *Il-buɣa* "Empire Bull,"

---

[342] Juwaynī, pp. 52, 81, 84.

[343] P. Pelliot and L. Hambis, *Histoire des campagnes de Gengis khan*. Leiden, 1951, p. 240.

[344] Rintchen, Xaradom, Les superstitions des mongols et des kazakh de la Mongolie septentrionale: ROr. XX (1956), p. 22.

[345] E.g., in Kirghiz (cf. Kalilov). The Arabs suppose that names expressing the idea of "bitter", "war" or "dog" may be frightening (Schimmel, p. 20).

[346] Rásonyi, P. Cat. p. 217.

[347] Kalilov, p. 93.

[348] In Bashkir, cf. Ilimbetov, pp. 89-90.

[349] Proben, V, p. 250.

[350] Schimmel, p. IX.

[351] Kusimova, 1971, p. 53.

[352] In Rásonyi's original classification of 1953 (cf. his Categ.), a group of anthroponyms like this was not established. In some of his later works, however, the pet-names were dealt with under a separate category No. V (cf. Frauen. p. 238; KÖA p. 143) which, in his P. Categ., was listed among the categories of women's names (category VI, p. 221) only.

[353] Juwaynī, II, pp. 12, 14, 15.

[354] See Qazw.

Buyra "Male Camel" (earliest among others, the name of an Uyghur sovereign[355]), *Qars* "Steppe Fox," *Tülkü-bay* "Fox Lord," *Qočqar* "Billy-Goat" (this name occurs on innumerable occasions among the Turkic peoples), *Berqut* "Eagle."

PNfem: *Arslan-xatun* "Lion Princess/Queen," *Ayu-bikä* "Bear Lady."

See also category of totem-names on p. XXXIX.

II/3.2 Names of precious metals and stones

We may not pass over the *Temir~Demir* "Iron" name, which is so extremely popular with every Turkic people and well represented in RÁSONYI's collection. Similar is the name *Bulat* "Steel." These names may also express the wish for a healthy life.

Further examples: Kirg. *Almaz-bek* "Diamond Gentleman," *Taš-bay*, "Stone Lord," *Taš-bolot* "Stone Steel," *Bek-temir* "Prince Iron," *Čoyun-bek* "Cast Iron Prince."[356]

PNfem: *Ay-kümüš* "Moon Silver," *Altïn-ay* "Gold Moon," *Altïn-arïγ* "Golden Virgin," *Altïn-gül* "Golden Rose/Flower," *Jaqut~Yaqut* "Ruby," *Kümüš-ay* "Silver Moon."

II/3.3 Names of weapons

Names of *weapons* may also occur as personal names, e.g., *Balta* "Ax; Hatchet," *Oq* "Arrow," *Süñgü* "Lance."

The frequent *Qïlïč* "Sword" (about 60 persons in the Onomasticon) occurs mainly among the medieval Turkic peoples, sometimes also in compounds, as e.g., *Qïlïč-arslan*, the name of two mighty Seljuk sultans in the 12th century. The most eloquent is the *Otqa-könmiš-qïlïč* "Sword-Tempered-in-Fire" preserved in a runiform inscription from before 750.[357]

II/3.4 Names of various tools

A part of these anthroponyms may also be listed among the incidental names (p. XLVIII).

Ezär "Saddle," *İyne* "Needle," *İres* "Screw," *Qaba (I.)* "Spinning Wheel," *Qayčï* "Scissors," *Qayraq* "Hone, Oil-stone," *Pasqa* "Hammer, Mallet," *Saban (I.)* "Plough," *Ütük* "Iron (tool)," etc.

PNfem: *Xïptïjax* "Little Scissors," *İyneček* "Little Needle," *İynelik* "Needle case, pincushion," *Oymoq* "Thimble," etc.

II/3.5 Names of respected persons

In RÁSONYI's original classification these were mentioned only in the group of *Symbolic names*. Later they were arranged into a separate category ("VI. Namen nach Namen") while the so-called "Majestic names" were treated under the category of *Desiderata names*.[358] Finally, the category "VI. Namen nach Namen" disappeared.[359]

The name of a famous, respected person could be given wishing the same features to the child. Because of this possibility we have set up this subgroup.

For the examples see category I/3.

II/3.6 Anthroponyms suggesting greatness, power

Teñiz~Deñiz with the meaning "Sea" expresses infinite greatness.[360] The Arabic and Persian sources on medieval Turkic peoples (Abulfidā, al-Bondārī, etc.) mention some twenty-five persons of historical importance whose name was *İl-deñiz*. LIGETI makes it very probable that the name of the Mongol *Chinggis-khan* ought to be included here.[361]

The name *Tümän* "Ten Thousand; Great Number" has a similar psychological background some twenty examples can be quoted from different times and ethnic groups of Turkic peoples. The earliest are the Uyghur *Tümän*, is also the name of a Mamluk in Ibn Iyās's chronicle.[362]

II/3.7 Anthroponyms meaning something nice, fine, lovely

A part of *pet-names (Hypocoristica)* doubtlessly belongs to this category.

PNfem: *Ay* "Moon," *Ay-čäčäk* "Moon Flower," *Mah-čičäk* "Moon Flower"[363], *Čečäk-xatun* "Flower Lady," *Jewher* "Jewel," *Alma* "Apple," *Selvi* "Ciprus," *Elif* "Alif (slim, straight like the first letter of the Arabic alphabet)," *Bal-šeker* "Honey Sugar," *Jennet* "Paradise," *Almaz~Almas* "Diamant," *İpek* "Silk," *İnci* "Pearl," *Zümrüd-xatun*

---

[355] Atalay, Ad. p. 39; DTS p. 120.

[356] Kalilov, p. 94–95.

[357] Thomsen, Stein p. 186.

[358] Cf. Rásonyi, Frauen. p. 231, Anthr. p. 149,

[359] Cf. Rásonyi, P. Categ.

[360] Relating to several data, see MNy. XXVIII (1932), p. 102.

[361] Ligeti: NyK. XLVIII (1925), p. 139.

[362] Iyās I. pp. 279-292.

[363] Gülbeden, pp. 281, 283.

"Emerald Lady."[364]

See also groups II/1.8, III/13.

III. Fortuitous Names (Omen-Names ~ Incidental Names)[365]

"Nomen est omen," as the Romans said with more or less intensity , also serves as a psychological background for Turkic personal names; most conspicuous, however, in the case of fortuitous names, are names prompted by an incident ("noms fortuites"). Thus we have come to call this group definitely *omen names*. These names have many categories, just as an incident may happen in many different ways. Some researchers, however, do not accept this concept, saying, in a system with exact structure there is no place for so called "incidental" names, because all names are motivated.[366] Indeed, one of the motives behind naming is based on the magical message of an incident which occurred at or after birth, when parents usually are in the state of increased sensibility and they attach importance to each phenomenon.

PNfem: They play a lesser role athan in men's names, for onomamagic ideas generally are less important in the psychology of giving women's names because of the lesser value of women. Nevertheless, a few examples could be mentioned here, too.

III/1 A Conspicuous Feature (e.g., Colour, Deficiency, etc.) of Infant

In the ancient clan system colours were considered holy.[367]

Ala-köz "Having Multi Coloured Eyes," *Aq-qaš* "Having White Eyebrows," *Aq-mañlay* "Having White Forehead," *Aqsaq~Čatan* "Lame," *Kök-bay* "Blue/Sky Lord," *Qara-baš* "Black Head," *Qara-qaš* "Having Black Eyebrows," *Qïzïl-bäk* "Red Lord," *Maylu* "Fat," *Sarï-malay* "White (Blond, Red) Boy," *Yïlamïš* "Cried," *Sulamïš* "Breathed (deeply)," *Tögäl-bay* "Perfect Lord," *Arïq-bäk* "Meagre Lord," *Kim-bay* "Immature Lord," Kzk. *Šala-bay~Šala-bek*, *Leker* "id. (premature child),"[368] *Tuq-bay* "Full, Satisfied Lord," *Köläč* "Jolly, Smiling."

PNfem: *Bota-göz* "Camel Eye," *Xara-χïs* "Black Girl," *Yöz-sïlu* "Face Beauty," *Qara-qaš-sïlu* "Beauty Having Black Eyebrows," *Qalli-gül* "Flower (=girl) with Birthmark," *Meñlig-tegin* "Princess with a Birthmark;' *Meñli-qatun* "Lady Having a Birthmark," *Aq-begim* "White Lady," *Apaq-begim* "My Snow White Lady,"[369] *Narlï* "Having a Red Birthmark," *Sarï-pas* "Yellow (Blond, Red) Head," *Tas-paš* "Bald Head," *Toq-saba* "Plump Leather Bottle," *Tuq-bikä* "Full, Satisfied Lady," *Uyqučï* "Sleepy, Drowsy.Í

III/2 First Object (Instrument, Tool, Weapon, etc.) Seen at Birth

Described in several sources among different Turkic peoples,[370] such as the Tatars of Minussinsk,[371] Kirghiz,[372] Truhmen,[373] Bashkirs.[374]

Ara-bay "Saw Gentleman," *Balta-bay* "Axe Gentleman," *Qadaq* "Spike," *İšek* "Door," *Tïrmaš* "Rake; Harrow," *Totqoš* "Clamp, Hold," *Qazan* "Cauldron," *Doqmaq* "Wooden Hammer," *Saban* "Plough," *Sandïq* "Chest."

PNfem: *Umčï* "Dummy," *D'üstük* "Ring," *İynelik* "Needle Case, Pincushion," *İyneček* "Small Needle," *Qurut* "Cheese," *Qïmïs* "Koumis, Kumiss," *Susqučaq* "Small Ladle," *Könök* "Bucket," *Ton* "Fur," etc.

III/3 First Animal Seen or Mentioned after Birth

It should be noted, that some anthroponyms formed of animal names may be considered as symbolic names (p. XLVI) and more rarely as totem names (p. XXXIX). Most of the female names of this group are also very suitable for symbolic-hypocoristic names.

Q,y-keldi "Sheep has come."

PNfem: *Ayu-bikä* "Bear Lady," *As* "Ermine," *Buzaw* "Calf," *Dudu-bibi* "Parrot Lady," *Qardïyač* "Swallow," *Qaz* "Goose," *Qoy-bala* "Lamb," *Qoyon* "Rabbit," *Ördäk* "Duck," *Selän* "Snake," *Tülgü* "Fox."

---

[364] Ibn al-Athïr/Tornb. I, p. 125.

[365] Called "Descriptive names" by Nikonov 1974, and after him by Šajhulov, 1978, Žanuzakov, 1982 and Sattarov, 1990.

[366] M. U. Monraev: OnomPov. 2, p.65; Blagova 1997, p. 620.

[367] Sadyhov, p. 213; Taklamakanlı, p. 194.

[368] Žanuzakov, 1971a p. 102.

[369] Gülbeden p. 227.

[370] Radl., Aus Sib. I, p. 315.

[371] Kostrov p. 229.

[372] Almásy p. 717.

[373] Volodin, p. 25, 53.

[374] Torma, 1997, p. 67.

III/4 First Plant (Flower, Tree, Fruit, etc.) Seen or Mentioned after Birth

Most of the female names of such meaning are very suitable for symbolic names given with hypocoristic purposes.

Alma~Alma-bay "Apple," *Qaraɣay,* Tat. *Aq-tiräk,* "White (Silver) Poplar," Tat. *Kük-tiräk* "Poplar."[375]

PNfem: Alma-äčä "Apple Sister," *Alma-qan* "Apple Khan," *Qabaq* "Marrow, Pumpkin" (the daughter of Nogay Khan), *Quzuq* "Nut," *Törčuq* "Cone of Cembra Pine."

III/5 First Person Seen after Birth (or a Guest Appearing)

O'Donovan's evidence is very important in this respect: "I [...] asked, why these babies were brought to my house, and what was the reason for this general presentation? It turned out, that Tekke's newly-born children are, as a rule, called after any distinguished strangers who may be in the oasis at the time of the births, or have resided there a short time previously, or after some event intimately connected with the tribe."[376]

Jandaral "General (who was just passing by the yurt),"[377] *Qoščï* "Bird Catcher," *Urmančï* "Forester," *Kerbende* "Donkey (or Camel) Drover," *Odonovan-beg, Odonovan-ҳan* (after the name of the famous traveller Edmond O'Donovan, incidentally turning up at the yurt),[378] *Dögdör-bay* "Doctor Lord," *Toqtor-bay* 'id.,' *Bay-geldi* "Master/Lord Has Come," *Xoja-keldi* "Hodja Has Come."

Pnfem: Daifa-ҳatun "Woman Guest,"[379] *Ayïljï* "Guest," *Miralay* "Colonel."[380]

III/6 First Word Pronounced at the Confinement

Names often are given based on the words or phrase pronounced by the people present at the birth or coming in afterwards.[381]

Bala-boldu "He became a boy,"[382] *Šükür* "Gratefulness, Thankfulness," *Alla-šügür* "Grace to Allah," *Žarïlqasïn* "Thankfulness, Gratefulness (for the birth of the child)," Az. *Umid-var~Umud-var* "There is (some) Hope," *Döza-ɣïz* "Bear/Stand, Daughter!," *Sevdim* "I Liked Him/Her," *Sevindik* "We Were Glad."[383]

PNfem: Boldï-bikeč "It is a Lady; Became a Lady," *D'ayla* "What a Pity!," *Ayazïn-qō* "Be Light!; Moonlight Beauty."

III/7 Astronomical and Meteorological Phenomenon

Yulduz~Yildïz "Star," *Ayaz, Ayaz-bay* "Clear sky," *Aydïn* "Clear, bright," "Moonlight (Houtsma)," *Buran* "Storm," *Kün-toɣdï~Gün-doɣdï* "Sun-Rise, The Sun Has Risen," *Qarlï* "Snowy," *Qar-yaɣdï* "Snow Has Fallen," *Yaɣmur* "Rain," *Yaɣmur-baba* "Rain Father," *Yañɣalič~Yañɣïlïč* "Rainbow,"[384] *Tuman* "Fog," *Yïldïrïm* "Lightning."

PNfem: Ay-qunčuy "Moon Princess," *Ay-duwa* "Moon Rise; The Moon Rises," *Buran-bikä* "Storm Lady," *Yañɣïr-bikä* "Rain Lady," *Qarlï-bikä* "Snowy Lady," *Dulduz-ҳan* "Star-Prince(ss)," *Tolun-bikä* "Full-Moon-Lady" (from Küčüm khan's family), *Tuman-aɣa* "Fog Lady," *Aq-tolun* "White Full Moon," *Tolɣon-ay* "Full Moon," *Šolpan* "Venus."

See also commemorative names, category I (p. XXXIX).

III/8 Year, Season, Month, Day, Part of Day

The names of animals occurring here are the representatives of the ancient *12-year animal-cycle* and mean the appropriate year of the birth.

Aҳšam "Evening," *Atna-ɣul~Yoma-ɣol* "Friday Slave," *Tïčqan-bay* "Mouse Lord," *Qaqa-bay* "Swine Lord," *Yaz-bay* "Spring Lord," *Qïšlïq* "Wintery / Winterly (born in winter)," *Saban-ay* "Plough Month (May)," *Ramazan* "Ramazan (Ar., the ninth month of the year)," *Qantar-bay* "December," *Bazar-keldi* "Sunday Has Come," *Salï-beg* "Tuesday," *Juma-keldi~Yoma-kilde* "Friday Has Come," *Kündüz* "Daytime," *Tañ-batïr* "Dawn/ Daybreak Hero," *Kön-tudï* "Sun Was Born."

PNfem: Ayna-ҳatun "Friday Queen," *Atna-sïlu* "Friday Beauty," *Erte* "Early Comer," *Qïš-bikä* "Winter Prin-

---

[375] Ahmetzjanov, p. 82.

[376] O'Donovan, II, p. 411.

[377] Grod., I, p. 99.

[378] O'Donovan, op. cit.

[379] Rásonyi, Miscellanea arabo-turcica. In: Goldziher Mem., Vol. II., p. 133.

[380] Cafer., Kars p. 291.

[381] Grod., I, p. 99.

[382] PSRL. IV, p. 338.

[383] Sadyhov, 1984, p. 217.

[384] Sattarov, op. cit., p. 173.

cess," *Yaz-bikä* "Spring Princess," *Yaz-göl* "Spring Flower," *Öyle-bikä* "Noon-bikä," *Tañ-nura* "Dawn Beam," *Kön-sïlu* "Sun Beauty."

III/9 Historical or Family Event, Feast

The original name of the Mamluk sultan, Faraǰ ibn Barqūq, reigning from 1398 to 1405, was *Bulγaq* "Verwirrung" with reference to the disturbances at the time of his birth.[385] Very interesting and characteristic is the passage in Hezârfenn's chronicle relating the historical events during the Danishmendi dynasty of Turkmen origin in the eighth decade of the 11th century, translated into German by MORDTMANN:[386]: "zogen die Ungläubigen dem Melik Gazi und Emir Süleiman entgegen...wurden geschlagen. In derselben Nacht wurde dem Melik Gazi ein Sohn geboren, den er *Yayïbasan* nannte, weil die Rebellen an jenem Tage geschlagen wurden." [The unbelievers marched against Melik Gazi and Emir Süleiman ... and were beaten. In the same night Melik Gazi's son was born and he named him as *Yayï-basan*, for the rebels were beaten that day.] The meaning of *Yayï-basan* is: "Defeater of the Enemy."

Bābur-šah writes in his memoirs in 1518 that when the birth of his son was reported to him, news of the taking of Bhīra arrived at the same time. This he understood as a *good omen* and ordered that his son be given the name *Hind-al* "Take-capture-conquer-India."[387] According to RÁSONYI's system it was ranged in group II/1.11 (p. L), but this name was motivated more by the historical event mentioned above than by the wish of Bābur.

See also O'DONOVAN's report in group III/5 above.

Further examples: *Atna-kilde* "Friday has come (born on Friday which was considered a holy day),"[388] *Bäyräm-bay* "Feast Lord," *Yaw-kilde* "The Enemy Came," *Yaw-qačtï* "The Enemy Escaped,"[389] *Yul-birde* "Journey Has Given Him (born on the road)," *Toy-χoǰa* "Feast Hodja," *Bayram* "Festival, Feast (born on a festive day)," *Front-bek* "Front Lord" (born at the time of the war in 1942), *Saban* "Plough (born at plough)," *Saban-ay* "Plough Month," etc.

PNfem: *Atna-ǰamal* "Friday Beauty (which was considered a holy day),"[390] *Bayram~Bayram-sultan* "Feast(-sultan)," *Bäyräm-sïlu* "Feast Beauty," *Bazar-bige* "Market Lady," *Yul-bikä* "Journey Princess (born on the road)," *Tuy-sïlu* "Feast Beauty"; it was during the Second World War that the name *Soγuš-kül* "War Rose" for Kirghiz female infants came into use, further *Keñeš-qan* "Soviet Lady."[391]

BAŠGÖZ, in his "Name and Society" (p. 1), mentions a Turkish girl called *Aysel* "Moon-like," because she was born on the day the first man landed on the moon. Similar explanations may lie behind many normal names.[392]

III/10 Enemy (People, Country, Sovereign) Defeated at the Time of Birth

For this category Batu Khan's bloody period conveys the most data. Among the peoples he defeated, the Hungarians were the most respected. This is clearly inferred by Plano Carpini, a traveller in the region of Qaraqorum in the depths of Inner Asia when in 1246 he relates the big graveyards "in quo sepulti sunt illi, qui in Hungaria interfecti fuerunt; multi enim ibidem occisi fuerunt."[393] Under the influence of the bloody war and the defeat of the Hungarians, and even somewhat later, many gave the name *Maǰar* "Hungarian" to their babies. Innumerable also are the names *Urus* "Russian," *Köten* "Bottom, Ass" and *Könček* "Leather Trousers," the names of the rulers of the defeated Kumans were similarly given to many infants.[394]

III/11 The scene of the delivery

The reason for calling a child by a geographical name is not always clear.[395] The child may have been born in that place or his father may have been staying there during the birth. Otherwise, the symbolic/metaphoric meaning (e.g., greatness, infinity, immortality) of certain toponyms may have been taken into consideration.[396]

Altay "Altay; High mountains," *Bes-tal* "Five-Willows," *Ätil~Itil~Idil* "Big Stream; Volga," Ever since the very beginning to the present time this word has frequently occurred as the name of the infant who was born by the side of

---

[385] Ibn Taghrīb., VI, 2.

[386] ZDMG XXX.

[387] Bábarnámah, ed. by A. S. Beveridge, 1905, GMS I, p. 220/a.

[388] Sattarov, op. cit., p. 169.

[389] Šajhulov, op. cit., p. 23.

[390] Sattarov, op. cit., p. 169.

[391] Abramzon-Sulejmanov.

[392] Schimmel, p. 89.

[393] Sin. Fr. I, p. 44.

[394] Rásonyi, Categ., pp. 337-345.

[395] It is problematic in other Islamic languages (Schimmel, p. 23).

[396] Schimmel, p. 24, Torma 1997, pp. 73-74.

some river. Even the name of Attila, the King of the Huns was originally *Etil*[397].With the addition of the Old Hungarian suffix *-a-*, it has been preserved in the form *Etila ~ Attila*. At the beginning of the 20th century we may find many Kirghiz and Qazaq *Edil-bay ~ Edil ~ İdil* in the statistical publications.[398] The widespread name *Yayïq* with the same meaning also belongs here. Meanwhile, past centuries have also brought many names of this kind: *Aq-tuba-biy* (after the name of the river), *Orman* "Forest."

    Names of towns may also occur as personal names, e.g., *Dimišq-χvāja* "Damascus Hodja" who died in 1330, and his sister *Baγdad-χatun* ("Baghdad Lady"), both from the Azerbaijani Čobanid dynasty.[399]

    Further examples: *Aral-bay* "(Lake) Aral Lord," *Alačuq* "Hut, Shanty," *Jayïq-bäk~Yayïq-bek* "Ural (river) Lord," *Yäyläw~Jäyläw~Yaylï* "Summer Pasture," *Jambul* (born near the mountain Jambul), *Taw-bay~Taw-bäk* "Mountain Lord." *Üzän-bay* "River Lord," etc.

    PNfem: *Aral-bikä* "(Lake) Aral Princess," *Jayïq-bikä~Yayïq-bikä* "Ural (river) Princess," 1286: *Yaylaq* "Summer Pasture," wife to Noγay-χan[400], *Yäyläw-bikä~Jäyläw-bikä* "Summer Pasture Princess," and further toponyms such as *Erzürüm, Suriye, Yemen, Tortum, Mekke, Medine*.[401]

III/12 How Old Was the Father at the Time the Infant Was Born, Which Child Is it in the Family?

    Sometimes it is the age of the father or grandfather that motivates the name-giving. It should be noted that in the Kirghiz folk calendar, *toqson* ["90"] means the three winter months: December, January and February; thus it may mean the time of birth (category III/8) as well.[402]

    A characteristic example is given by GYÖRGY ALMÁSY when he tells that his servant was called *Elli-bay* "Fifty Lord." He was told that this name had been given because the father had been fifty years of age when the son was born.[403] Among the Kazakhs there are a lot of *Otuze*s "Thirty," *Otuz-bay*s "Thirty Lord," *Altï-bay* "Six(th) Lord" was the legendary khan of the Cheremis.

    For more details on the personal names of similar background, see RÁSONYI's work *Les noms de nombre dans l'anthroponymie turque*[404] and the paragraph "Numeral" (p. LIV) in the paragraph "Grammatical Structures" (p. LIII). Names made of different numbers are given by other (non-Turkic) peoples as well.

    Seemingly, names formed of numerals are given to boys exclusively. The custom itself may be explained by the pride of the parents only.[405]

    The *sequence of birth* of the children in the family traditionally could also be a motive in name-giving. These names were formed not exclusively from numerals, but from other parts of speech (nouns, adjectives, etc.), e.g., *täüge* "first" (Tat.), *baš* "first, principal," *al~alγï* "front, primary," *abalaq* "little child," *azaq* "last," *kenje~kinje* "the youngest," *keče~keček* "little."[406]

    Biš-bay "Fifth Lord," Trkm. *Bäšim* "My Five"[407], *Altï-bay* "Six(th) Lord," Trkm. *Yedi* "Seven," *Jide-bay* "Seven(th) Lord," Trkm. *Sekiz* 'Eight', Trkm. *Doquz* 'Nine', *Tuγïz-bay* 'Ninth Lord', Trkm. *Otuz* 'Thirty', *Altmïš* 'Sixty', *Seksen* 'Eighty,' *Toqsan* 'Ninety,' *Aldaγï* 'First,' *Al-tuγan* 'First Born,' *Baš-bay* 'First Lord,' *Berkäy* 'Only Child,' *İke~İke-bay* 'Two Lord (twin),' *Âlïm-bäk* 'My First (biggest) Lord,' *Orta* 'Middle (child),' *Abalaq~Ablaq* 'Little (youngest) Child,' *Kenje~Kinjä* 'The Youngest (son),' *Keček-qol* 'Little Slave,' *Azaqqï* 'Last, Final.'[408]

    PNfem: *Baš-bikä* 'First Lady,' *Kenje* "The Youngest (daughter)," *Kinjä-bikä~Kinyä-bikä* "The Youngest Lady."

III/13 Pet-names (Hypocoristica)[409]

    Here we classify anthroponyms expressing the parents' emotions (love, joy, blandishment, endearment) about the child. They seem to be manifold regarding their meaning, so we can find pet-names in other categories as well. In SCHIMMEL's opinion, for instance, the joy (gratitude) over the birth of a child, particularly a son, is expressed in all

---

[397] Byz. Turc., p. 80.

[398] AOP, AOK, AOAtb., SOV, etc.

[399] Zambaur, p. 255.

[400] Pelliot, Notes pp. 73, 79.

[401] Cafer., Malatya p. 318.

[402] Kalilov, p. 94.

[403] Almásy.

[404] Rásonyi, Nombre.

[405] Muhamedova 1957, p. 44.

[406] Sattarov, op. cit. pp. 174-178.

[407] The Trkm. examples of this paragraph have been taken from Muhamedova (loc. cit.).

[408] cf. Nikonov, op. cit., p. 98; Sattarov, op. cit., 174-178; Šajhulov, op. cit., p. 24.

[409] This category did not exist in Rásonyi's original system (Categ.), but it appeared as a separate category (No. V) in the two subsequent ones (Frauen., KÖA). In his last classification we can find it only as a subgroup (No. VI) of women's names (cf. P. Cat., p. 221).

Islamic languages with *theophoric (or divine) names* (see p. XL).[410] Another, and most usual, way to express endearment in Turkic is by the use of dimininutive-hypocoristic suffixes.

Eräk~Eräk-bay "Nice/Gentle Lord," *Sorayan* "Asked, Wished," *Süyüm* "Joy," *Teläk* "Wish"

PNfem: *Arzu* "Wish," *Sevinǰ* "Joy, Pleasure," *Širin* "Sweet," *Sïylï-xan, Sïylï-qïz* "Beloved / Darling Girl."

See also categories II/1.8, II/3.8.

III/14 An Incident Induced through the Mediation of the Mullah

Here the influence of Islam accompanies the onomamagic ideas inherited from the past and is still extant. The mullah (or one of the elders) is thumbing through the pages of the Koran; at random he puts his finger on a word (or the first letter of the page opened), and on this basis he defines the name of the infant. SCHIMMEL notes that this custom is also widespread on the Indian Subcontinent and in other, predominantly non-Arab countries; and in many cases it leads to strange combinations, as the parents usually do not know enough Arabic to understand the implications of certain expressions (e.g., Turk. *Üzlifat* "Brought Near" from Sūra 81/13: "When Paradise is brought near").[411] The giving of names has been observed in the region of Tokat, Turkey, where names like *Rahîm, Şefik, Kadîr, Kaadir, Ganî,* etc., were chosen in a similar way.

---

[410] Schimmel pp. 18-19.

[411] Ibid., pp. 25-26. This method led to the formation of meaningless names in a population of non-Arab background.

General Notes

According to the common grammatical approach, proper names are to be regarded as nouns and behave like nouns. Since names are formed from different parts of speech, their grammatical structure-types may be outlined on this basis. It is obvious that different kinds of words are not equally involved in forming personal names. Thus some of them are active while the others may not be used in forming names at all.[412] Most names are formed from nouns and adjectives and from their derived forms.[413]

The structure of the Turkic anthroponyms is inherited. Therefore the archaic features of deriving and compounding are preserved, notwithstanding the influence of foreign personal names. Disyllabic names seem to meet the specifications of the Turkic name-patterns. Thus foreign anthroponyms consisting of three or more syllables often get shortened (contracted) to be disyllabic. A great many occurrences of this phenomenon can be observed in Kazakh, New Uyghur, Tatar, etc.[414]

As has been observed, the grammatical (morphological) basis of the Turkic anthroponyms tends to expand.[415]

Although significant efforts were made in Tatar by G. F. SATTAROV and R. H. SUBAEVA, in Kazakh by T. Ž. ŽANUZAKOV, in Uzbek by Ê. A. BEGMATOV, in Yakut by N. P. SKRJABINA, and by G. F. BLAGOVA on the basis of Old Turkic names, the study of the structures of Turkic anthroponyms is still not satisfactory. Some authors focus only on lexical-semantic features, while the others unfortunately simplify the grammatical structure, as is seen, for instance, A. HACIYEV, who differentiated in Azerbaijani four active structure-types (*işläk struktur tipläri*) only: 1. names formed from simple words of different meanings, 2. suffixed simple words, 3. names derived from different stabilized grammatical forms, e.g., *Tapdïq, Yetär, Dönmäz*, 4. compounds with different lexical meanings, e.g., *Qarakişi, Daşdämir, Adïgözäl, Qaryağdï*. A similar system has been set up by TAKLAMAKANLI for Uyghur personal names.

The system of the structure is, of course, much more complex and it requires a far more detailed description.[416]

Almost all structure-types (simple and compound) could be complemented with different *secondary components* (=*comp.*, p. LXII). Such types can be considered as new sub-types of the structures in question (e.g., *N > N+ comp, Adj > Adj+comp, Vimp > Vimp+comp,... N+ N > N+N+ comp, Adj+ N+ comp*). Since we are of the opinion that *secondary components* are unorganic parts of names, we have set up our system based exclusively on *primary components*. In doing so we claim that *secondary components* are always added to complete personal names (*PN*), serving as their supplementary parts. To signal this possibility we have established group III (p. LXI) for personal names with secondary components at their ends.

I. Simple Personal Names

From lexical and structural points of view, simple names differ highly. They may have emerged at different stages of language history from very different etymons. Sometimes their original forms (root morphemes) cannot be determined; their primary meanings remain obscure.

Normally common people bore simple names meaning jobs, domestic animals, etc., or denoting different clans, tribes, etc.[417]

The proportion of simple personal names in modern Uyghur, for example, is sixteen percent in the country, fifty-two percent in Alma-Ata. Almost the same can be seen in Tatar: out of 15,000 personal names fifty percent are simple. In the 10th-13th-century legal documents, 18 names out of 34, that is fifty-three percent, were compound.[418] These data may be misleading since other authors interpret components differently (see p. LXII).

1. Noun (N)

We do not differentiate the logical categories *Concrete Nouns* and *Abstract Nouns* within this group.

1.1. Simple Noun (N)

Abaq, Ay, Alïm, Arbuz, Bajaq, Bal, Baš, Beke, Bike, Bïčaq, Bota, Budaq, Buzaw, Čaqmaq, Čïčqan, Jaba, Ešek,

---

[412] The lesson of Uzbek anthroponymy testifies the same (Begmatov, p. 199).

[413] Šatinova, 1971, p. 67.

[414] Sattarov, 1990, p. 205 ff.

[415] Blagova, 1998b, pp. 58-59.

[416] Moreover, it was raised by Mahpirov (1988, p. 52) that two structure-systems of names might have existed side by side: one for the personal names of gentlefolks and one for the commoners. All that was based on the sharp social contrasts.

[417] Mahpirov, 1988, pp. 51-52.

[418] Nikonov, 1984, p. 193.

Yaɣmur, Kiši, Qaya, Quš, Nar, Nur, Ögüz, Soɣan, Šolpan, Tañ, Temir, Ulja, Ümit, Ürük, Ziyan.

1.2. Derived Noun (N+ suff / N+ suff+ suff)

It seems likely that certain suffixes are exclusively or predominantly used for forming proper, especially personal, names. These suffixes are *specific suffixes* because they have a particular function in forming names. Specific suffixes do not normally occur in common derived nouns, but form proper names only. As the investigations of BESE show, most of them are diminutive-hypocoristic suffixes, e.g., denominale *-č, -čU, -čUK/-čIK, -y, -Ay, -KA, -KAy, -š*, etc. A part of these suffixes were nonspecific (that is, common) suffixes in the past and are preserved as archaic ones in proper names only. That is why the distinction between personal names formed with nonspecific and personal names formed with specific suffixes, as offered by BESE, cannot be done easily.

Compound suffixes like *-čKA, -yKA, -yKAy, -KAč* are also frequently used.

Different diminutive forms of the same name - that is *name-synonyms* - may be derived with different diminutive suffixes from the same noun (or PN), e.g., *Tekeš (~ Tekes) ~ Tekey,* but then again certain nouns (PNs) can be formed only with one of the diminutives, e.g., Tuv. *Xülbüzek* "Little Male Roe (deer)" < *χülbüs,* Tuv. *Kejikkey* "Little Gift" < *kejik.*[419]

1.2.1.1. Denominal Noun (N+ suff)

Abalïq, Ayuwčï, Aqač, Amanlïq, Begič, Belči, Bïčaqčï, Bïyïqlï, Buɣač, Čïnarlï, Činčeylik, D'amandïq, Eminlik, İgilik, İynelik, İnekči, İšey, Yamči, Yollu, Yumay, Yumaš, Kečili, Qazlïq, Otunčï, Sarañuč, Tüktü.

2. Adjective (Adj)

2.1. Simple Adjective (Adj)
Jomart, Juban, Yaqšï, Yaman, Qadïr, Qara, Kečkene, Kem, Kiči, Tatu, Toq, Torï, Uzun.

2.2. Derived Adjective (Adj+ suff)
Čïnarlï, Jiyrenše, Yamantay, Kičigä, Kökše, Toqčïn

3. Numeral (Num)

Numbers usually occur in names as *numeral adjectives* which are the *determinant* parts of composite names. See also pp. XII, LI.

3.1. Definite Numeral

3.1.1. Cardinal Numeral
Altmïš, Eki, İkeš~İkiš, Yetmiš, Yirmisekiz, Yüz, On, On-ikey, Otuz, Toquz, Tört

3.1.2. Ordinal Numeral (OrdNum ~ Num+ suff(-(I)nCI/-(U)nCU)
İkinji.

3.1.3. Num+ suff
Birke "Little One," *Ekilik~Ekilik-bay* "Double, Duality Lord," *Dürtči, Üšlik.*

3.2. Indefinite Numeral (IndNum)
Kzk. *Kem* "Little, Not Enough," *Mol* "Abundant, Much, Plenty, Rich."

4. Verb (V)

Verbs and different verbal forms play a specific part in forming Turkic proper names. Attention was already directed to this feature by GORDLEVSKIJ and SAMOJLOVIČ. A small detail of the theme was elaborated by FEKETE (1927) and by RÁSONYI (1962).[420] Tatar verbal anthroponyms were studied by SATTAROV (1973).

A great number of toponyms were formed using verbal forms and many studies were written on the theme.[421] In modern Uzbek, for example, 3.9 percent of personal names are *deverbal* anthroponyms, the major part of which is represented by male names (3.1percent).[422] As has been observed in Yakut, a great number of bynames (nicknames) are formed from verbs.[423]

The simple verbal personal names in Turkic can also be considered as *sentence-names* by themselves, because

---

[419] Bese, p. 10.
[420] Rásonyi, Imp.
[421] cf. Karmyševa, 1950, Kiekbaev, 1956; Donidze, 1964; Hudžamberdyev, 1970; Rahmatov, 1973; etc.
[422] Begmatov, 1984, p. 200.
[423] Gricenko, p. 158.

LIV

they have the ability of referring to subject (person) and object (see p. LIX).[424]

It is a Turkic phenomenon of verbal personal names that they may be suffixed also with certain diminutive-hypocoristic suffixes. Thus the homonyms of this kind cannot be differentiated easily. For example, OT *Oquy* may be: 1. Gerund of *oqu-* "to read," 2. Imperative of *oqu-* "to read" suffixed with diminutive suffix *-y*.[425]

4.1. Simple Verb (V)

Simple verbs as personal names may be interpreted as simple or defective sentence-names, see pp. LIX, LXI.

4.1.1. Imperative (Vimp2 = 2nd p. sing. imp.)[426]

Aban, Basïl, Köpäy, Qayt, Tat. Yäšä "Live!"[427] Satïb-al, Toqta.

4.1.2. Negative Imperative (NegVimp2)

Ayärba, Qïdïrma, Satma, Tat. Ülmä Don't Die [428]

4.2. Derived Verb (V+ suff / V+ suff+ suff)

4.2.1. Finite Form of a Verb (V+ suff)

4.2.1.1. Imperative (Vimp3 = 3rd p. sing. imp., suffixed with -sUn ~ -sIn)[429]

Baysïn, Bersin, Jarïlγasïn, Demesin, Tursun, Yayrasïn, Yürsin, Kelsin,
Köpäysin, Oñdasïn, Össin, Süysin, Tursun, Ulansïn.

4.2.1.2. Present Forms (Vpres)

4.2.1.2.1. Present Form (Vpres(-A/-y))

Ačïla, Kilä, Surlay, Ulay

4.2.1.2.2. Negative Present Form (Vpres(-mAy))

Aylamay, Kelmäy, Ösmey.

4.2.1.2.3. Aorist (Present-Future) Form (Vaor(-r~-Ar~-Ir~-Ur))

Abar, Atar, Baqar, Basar, Qačar, Öler, Öser, Süyär, Tabar,
Tuγar, Tüzer, Unar.

4.2.1.2.3.1. Negative Aorist (NegVaor(-mAz~-mAt)

Aytmas, Almat, Bermes, Dolanmaz, Qaymaz, Kelmäz, Qorqmaz,
Ölmez, Satmaz, Süymes.

4.2.1.3. Past (Perfect) Form (Vpast)

4.2.1.3.1. Definite (Categorical) Past Form (Vpast(-DI/-DU))

Aldïm, Berdi, Boldï, Döndi, Güvendik, Qaldï, Keldi,
Saγïndïm, Sevindi, Sevindik, Taptïq, Tabïldï, Turdï.

4.2.1.3.1.1. Negative Definite (Categorical) Past Form (NegVpast(-DI/-DU))

Giremedi, Giremedin.

4.2.1.3.2. Indefinite Past Form I (Vpast(-GAn))

Alγan, Buyurγan, Kelgen, Qašqan, Ösken, Ötegen, Ötkän, Turγan.

4.2.1.3.2.1. Negative Indefinite Past Form I. (NegVpast(-GAn))

Azmaγan.

4.2.1.3.3. Indefinite Past Form II (Vpast(-mIš))

Aytmïš, Ašmïš, Beklemiš, Bermiš, Kelmiš, Qaymïš, Qalmïš,
Ögdülmiš, Ötemiš, Tapmïš, Toγmïš, Tölemiš.

4.2.1.3.3.1. Negative Indefinite Past Form II. (NegVpast(-mIš))

4.2.1.4. Future Form (Vfut)

4.2.2. Deverbal Noun (or Derived Verb) (V+ suff / V+ suff+ suff)

Aylanaš, Berdey, Berdiš, Berdike, Berdimän, Boluč, Jiyü, D'ayqaš, D'ayqaš, Dilenč, Edčü, Ïnanč,

---

[424] Bese p. 21.
[425] Bese p. 14.
[426] cf. Rásonyi, Imp.
[427] Sattarov, 1973, p. 42.
[428] Ibid., p. 43.
[429] Cf. Rásonyi, Imp.

Yumuq, Keldiš, Qayqaš, Ötek, Öteš.

4.2.4. Verbal (Non-finite Verb-Form)

It is almost impossible to distinguish the Finite (forms 3rd p. sing. and 1st p. plur.) and Non-Finite Verb-forms in simple names, e.g., *Abar* can be explained in two ways: 1. 'He Engages/Revolts (Aorist), 2. 'Revolting/Countering (person)' (Future Participle).

4.2.4.1. Infinitive (Inf)

For example: *Aytmaq, Almaq, Jiyü, Qïrmaq, Kečü, Köčmek.*

4.2.4.2. Participle (Part)

4.2.4.2.1. Present Participle (Part(-An))

4.2.4.2.2. Past Participle

4.2.4.2.2.1. Part(-DIk/-DUk)

Qaldïq, Kildik, Kördük, Sayïndïq.

4.2.4.2.2.2. Part(-GAn)

Amrayan, Atayan.

4.2.4.2.2.3. Part(-mIš/-mUš)

Bükmiš.

4.2.4.2.3. Present-Future Participle (Part(-r/-Ar, -Ir, -Ur))

Abar, Yašar.

4.2.4.3. Gerund (Ger)

4.2.4.3.1. Ger(-a)

Čočoyo, İnaya, Noňnoyo, Noruluya, Oppoyo.

4.2.4.3.2. Ger(-y)

It must be noted that PNs derived from Ger(-y) are hard to differentiate from PNs consisting of Verb stems (Vimp2) suffixed with diminutive *-y.*

4.2.4.3.3. Ger(-n)

Čočoyōn, Xantayan, Moχoyon, Oloňχolōn, Torulān.

4.2.4.3.4. Ger(-p)

Yandap, Tiläp, Ötep.

II. Compound (Composite) Personal Names

Compound personal names are made according to definite syntactic models (patterns) using almost every major part of speech.[430] These models are nearly the same as those of the common compound words and word groups. Compound names can be divided into two groups: the major *nominal* and the smaller *verbal* groups. The most widespread is the type consisting of two components (e.g., *N+N, N+V, Adj+N,* etc.).[431]

In studying compound anthroponyms significant efforts were made in Tatar by G. F. SATTAROV and R. H. SUBAEVA, and in Yakut by N. P. SKRJABINA. Relying basically on Old Turkic anthroponyms and making use of the lesson of modern Turkic names, BLAGOVA tried to reconstruct the Ancient Turkic structure types of compound personal names. First of all she separated 91 units of anthroponymy (*R. antroponimičeskaja edinica*) which are - in the author's approach - independent [=simple, I. B.] names (e.g., *ajas~ajaz, ata, ba:ba*) or components (e.g., *qarluyač, qyz*) or both (e.g., *julduz, kün, oyul*). The system of structures reconstructed by BLAGOVA seems quite simple: 1. reconstructed nominal component + noun, 2. noun + reconstructed nominal component (and its third person possessive form), 3. reconstructed verbal component + noun, 4. noun + reconstructed verbal component. It can be simplified as follows: 1. Noun + Noun, 2. Verb form + Noun, 3. Noun + Verb form.[432]

Concerning our conception of components see general notes above and the same in the chapter *Secondary Components* on page LXII.

Grammatical components which usually form compound names have been listed and described in the previous section. Since most of these components are used also as simple personal names, it seems problematic to decide whether an ordinary word (noun / verb, etc.) or a well-known, frequently used simple name has been taken as a component of a

---

[430] Žanuzakov, p. 108.

[431] The same is true for toponyms and ethnonyms (cf. Ishakova, 1984, p. 164).

[432] Blagova, 1997, pp. 623-624; Blagova, 1998b, p. 56.

compound name (*PN*+*PN* or *PN*+*comp?*, *PN*+*PN*+*comp?*, etc).

All these types are subordinate constructions, the first part of which is the *determinant* and the subsequent is the *determinated*. A part of these constructions look like common compounds: their components are totally compatible both lexically and syntactically, e.g., *Edgü-temür* "Good Iron," *Ala-buqa* "Spotted Bull," *Boz-quš* "Grey Bird," *Qara-buqa* "Black Bull," *Qara-köz* "Black Eye," *Qïzïl-buqa* "Red Bull." In a significant part of the compound personal names, however, the components are not compatible,[433] which means that the construction in question does not occur in common compounds. These constructions are impossible either syntactically, e.g., *Altmïš-qara* "Sixty Black," *Qulun-qara* "Foal Black" or lexically e.g., *Qutluγ-buqa* "Lucky Bull," *El-buγa* "People Bull," *İl-arslan* "People Lion," *Saray-buqa* "Palace Bull," *Taγ-buqa* "Colt Bull," *Toγan-buqa* "Falcon Bull," and occur only in personal names.[434] The components in this case must be used respectively as single personal names (sometimes as honorific titles). In GAFUROV's opinion both components are independent and the relation between them is thematic or predicative.[435] The idea was already raised by HOUTSMA who called these anthroponyms *double-names* ("Doppelnamen") instead of compound ("zusammengesetzte") names.[436] Thus at least one of the components is taken as a personal name while the other fulfils some additional function and the common rules (both syntactic and semantic) of compounding are ignored.[437]

Aside from the recently dominant Islamic names, some preference is shown to certain original (i.e. Turkic) *primary* (or *basic*) *components*, such as *Ay* "Moon," *Aq* "White/Clean," *Altïn* "Gold," *Arslan* "Lion," *Bay* "Rich," *Bars* "Panther," *Bek* "Noble Man / Strong," *Buγa~Buqa* "Bull," *Bulat* "Steel," *Jan* "Soul / Darling," *Gül* "Flower," *El~İl* "Country, Empire, People," *Er* "Man, Hero," *Esän* "Strong, Healthy," *Xuday* "God," *Qara* "Black," *Qïzïl* "Red," *Qul* "Slave," *Qutluγ* "Lucky, Blessed," *Oγlan, Oγul* "Boy, Son," *Sïlu* "Beautiful," *Tay* "Colt, Foal," *Taš* "Stone," *Täñri* "God," *Temir* "Iron," *Uluγ* "Big, Great."

Giving and using compound names originally was typical in the privileged classes and spread to the lower social strata.[438] The second part of names usually was a *title,* which, over the course of time, lost its original meaning and became a *secondary component* (see p. LXII). Thus the deluge of foreign compound names arriving with Islam was received favourably, because compounding was widely used for making new words in Turkic. Yet the new compound personal names displaced the Turkic compound names.[439]

Compound names are well-liked among the Turkic peoples even today. In 1971, for example, seventy percent of Uyghur country boys were named with composite names.[440] In 18th and 19th century Kazakh, this proportion was seemingly much higher, about ninety percent.[441] In Turkmen during the Soviet period there was a tendency to avoid personal names with two components.[442] For more details see paragraph of statistical data beginning on p. XXXV.

5. Binary Construction: A Compound with Two Components (determinant+ determinated)

5.1. Compound of Two Simple or Derived Nouns

5.1.1. Adjectival or Possessive Construction (N+ N / N+ N+ suff / N+ suff+ N / N+ suff+ N+ suff)
Aγa-dil, Aγac-awuz, Aγač-bašlï, New Uyg. Taš-tömür, Taš-polat.[443]

5.1.2. Genitival Construction (Ngen+ Nposs)

5.1.3. Shortened Genitival Construction (N+ N+ poss(3rd p. sing))
Afšar-eri.

5.2. Adjectival Construction (Adj+ N)

In typical syntactic construction of Turkic languages, the adjectives *aq, boz, kök, qara, sarï,* etc., are polysemantic, which means that their meanings in composites depend on the other component(s) of the name.[444] We regard names like *Qara-bay, Sarï-bay, Suluw-χan, Suluw-bike,* etc., as simple names complemented with secondary components (see

---

[433] Houtsma (p. 33) took note of the phenomenon.

[434] Cf. Bese, pp. 16, 18.

[435] E.g., *Berdi-pulad* "He who was given is steel (=strong, lively)" (Gafurov, 1987, p. 43).

[436] Houtsma, p. 33. He also supposed that these names consisted of the father's and mother's tribal totem-names.

[437] According to Bese (loc. cit.) one of the components is constant [basic?, I. B.], the other one is variable and its sequence follows a definite pattern.

[438] Nikonov, 1984, p. 194; Mahpirov, 1988, p. 51.

[439] Nikonov, 1984, p. 194.

[440] Ibid., p. 192.

[441] Ergazieva, pp. 209, 210.

[442] Muhamedova, 1957, p. 47.

[443] Taklamakanlï (p. 210) claims that components in this constructions are equal, that is we must reckon here with double names.

[444] Žanuzakov, pp. 109-110.

group 8.).

Aq-arslan, Bay-qošqar, Bek-temir, Tulγun-ay.

5.3. Inverse Adjectival Construction (N+Adj)

This type is characteristic to proper names only.[445] ŽANUZAKOV arranges the names like *Qošqar-bay, Bolat-bek, Qoža-bay* into this group, since he considers components *-bay, -bek,* etc. as Adjectives (primary components) and not as Nouns (secondary components).[446] ESPAEVA also interprets the Kzk. *Aqïl-bay* as "Rich in Mind, Clever," *Tur-bek* as "Live Long! Be Strong!" In the same paragraph, however, she determines *-bay* as an "affix of anthropo-lexem,"[447] that is, in our opinion, a *secondary component* (see p. LXII).

Ay-arïγ, Baš-qara, Jan-qara, Jan-sarï, Jan-uzaq, El-aman, Yol-qutluγ, Jol-aman, Jol-žaqsï, Yan-sarï~Jan-sarï, Kül-arïγ, Qul-sarï, Qulun-qara, Taš-qara.

5.3.1. Nposs+Adj

Bašim-kel "My Head (is) Bald."

5.4. Adj+Adj

Aq-arïγ, Aq-sarï, Aq-suluw, Edgü-qutluγ, Yaman-sarï.

5.5. Part+N

Qïrγan-qïlïš, Öskän-tay, Turmïš-temür.

5.6. N+Part

5.6.1. N+Part(-DIk)

Qoč-sevindigi.

5.6.2. N+Part(-An)

Yel-γovan.

5.6.3. N+Part(-Ar)

Bil-yašar, Taγ-ašar, Taš-ašar.

5.6.4. Nacc+Part(-An)

Yaγï-basan.

5.7. Numerical Attributive Construction

5.7.1. Num+N

Bir-jan "One Soul" (man)?, *Bir-tlek* "One Wish," *Bir-soγïr* "One Armful," *Eki-bay* "Two Rich / Two Lord?," *Üš-bay* "Three Rich / Three Lord?,"[448] *Beš-ay, Altï-qulač, Miñ-bulat.*

5.7.2. Num+Part

Altï-qaqradar, Yüz-yašar.

5.7.3. IndNum+Part

Köp-yašar.

5.8. Adv+N

Öte-bay "Very Rich / Super Lord?" *Öte-tlew* "Frank Wish / Sincere Desire / Superwish?"[449]

5.9. Adv+Part

Seyrek-basan.

5.10. Pronoun+N

6. Compound PN with Three (seldom more) Components

This type is less frequent. As the examples show, it is preferred in the names of rulers and folklore (mythical) heroes.[450] In most cases this construction can also be traced back to one or more binary constructions which consist of

---

[445] The phenomenon has been observed in Mongolian languages as well (Pjurbeev, p. 200).

[446] Žanuzakov, pp. 109.

[447] Espaeva, 1984, p. 231.

[448] Žanuzakov, pp. 107-108.

[449] Ibid., p. 108.

[450] As, e.g., in Yakut, cf. Gricenko, p. 162.

various titles, simple names, primary and secondary components:[451] e.g., Uyg. *Qutluγ-kül-bilge, Ay-teñride-qut-bolmïš, Kün-teñride-qut-bolmïš, Il-yïγmïš-inal, Miñ-temür-tutuq, Qapaγan-tegin-qaγan, Tengride-bolmïš-il-itmiš-bilge-qaγan, Barγut-il-qutadmïš, Yabutqar-il-qutadmïš.*[452]

7. Sentence-name[453] *(S(N)+P(V))*

Names arranged in this group have the structure of an independent simple sentence. In some cases these structures are incomplete remnants of sentences, or parts of sentences. These names may preserve old types of constructions.[454]

7.1. Simple Sentence (S+O+P)

7.1.1. Imperative Sentence (P(Vimp))

Qobrat.

7.1.1.1. Imperative-Vocative Sentence (P(Vimp)+S(N/comp))

Az. *Döza-yïz* 'Bear/Stand, Daughter!'[455]

7.1.2. Subject + Predicate (S+P)

This type is rather unusual among common compound words, but is quite a frequent construction of proper names.[456]

7.1.2.0. S(N)+P(Ecp) [457]

Az. *Umid-var* "There is (some) Hope."[458]

7.1.2.0.1 S(N)+P(NegEcp) [459]

**Umid-yoq* "There is no Hope."

7.1.2.1. N+Vimp2 / Adj+Vimp2

Bay-bol, Bay-tur, Bar-bol, Jaman-bol, Jar-bol, Isän-tur, Qara-bol, Molla-bol.

7.1.2.2. N+Vimp3

Bek-sultan-toχtōsun, Jan-bolsun, Dos-bosun, El-bolsïn, Er-bolsun, Gül-tursïn, Mïr-tursun, Ul-bolsïn.

7.1.2.3. N+Vpast(-DI/-DU)

Ay-toγdï, Er-toγdï, Xaq-berdi, Xoja-keldi, Mal-berdi, Žïl-geldi, Oγïl-keldi.

7.1.2.4. N+Vpast(-GAn)

Ayap-bergen, Alda-bergen, It-emgen, Mal-tuγan, Taš-bergen.

7.1.2.5. N+Vpast(-mIš/-mUš)

Ay-toγmïš, El-almïš, El-tutmïš, Kün-bermïš, Qïz-turmïš, Temür-turmïš.

7.1.2.6. Nposs+Vpast(-DI/-DU)

Bašï-gildi, Xojam-berdi, Iyem-berdi, Qanï-gilde.

7.1.2.7. Nposs+Vpast(-GAn)

Qojam-bergen.

7.1.2.8. N+Vpres(-y/-A)

Tat. *Ir-bula* "He Is (or will be) a Man."

7.1.3. Direct Object+Predicate (O(N)+P(V))

7.1.3.1. Indetermined Direct Object+Predicate (O(N)+P(V))

7.1.3.1.1. N+Vimp2

Iz-bas, Il-düz, Qoy-baq, El-tut, Hind-al.

7.1.3.1.2. N+Vpres(-A/-y

Iš-tota "He Works."[460]

---

[451] As it was shown by Ishakova (1984, p. 167) on the lesson of Crimean toponymy.

[452] Taklamakanlı p. 196.

[453] In Rásonyi's drafts we can find the note "Full sentence - nevek [=names]," but nowhere did he deal with the theme in detail. [I. B.]

[454] Žanuzakov, p. 110, Taklamakanlı, p. 210. For more examples see Baski 2000.

[455] Sadyhov 1984, p. 217.

[456] A. N. Kononov, *Grammatika sovremennogo uzbekskogo literaturnogo jazyka.* M.-L., 1960, p. 134.

[457] Ecp = existential copula particula, e.g., *bar / var* "there is; existent."

[458] Sadyhov, 1984, p. 217.

[459] Negative of Ecp (see above) in this case *yok / yoq / joq*, etc. "there is not; non-existent."

[460] Sattarov, 1973, p. 43.

7.1.3.1.3. IndefNum+Vpast(-DI/-DU)

Köp-berdi.

7.1.3.1.4. N+Vpast(-GAn)

İt-emgen.

7.1.3.1.5. N+Vpast(-DI/-DU)

Yaγï-bastï.

7.1.3.2. Determined Direct Object+Predicate (O(Nacc)+P(V))

7.1.5. Indirect Object + Predicate (O(N)+P (V))

7.1.5.1. Ndat+Vimp2

Beske-qal.

7.1.5.2. Nabl+Vpast(-GAn)

Aydan-bergen.
7.1.5.3. Nabl+Vpast(-DI/-DU)
Yazdan-verdi.

7.1.6. Adverb + Predicate

7.1.6.1. Adv+Vimp2

Bek-tur, Bek-tut, Gel-beri.

7.1.6.1. Adv+Vpast(-DI/-Du)

Aman-geldi, İdän-kilde.

7.1.6.2. Adv+Vpast(-GAn)

7.1.6.3. Num+Vpast(-DI/-Du)

Beš-boldï.

7.1.7. Predicate + Subject (P(V)+S(N) / P(V)+S(PN))

It seems to be the inverse of the structures 7.1.2-3. These structures (e.g., *Vimp2+N, Vimp2+Part, Vimp2+Adv, Vpast+N*) occur also in Tatar.[461] In BEGMATOV's opinion the (de)verbal (predicative) part of the construction is the "head" (or key) constituent which is completed with an "auxiliary" nominal complement, e.g., Uzb. *Berdi-šükür, Berdi-ahim, Yândaš-ali [<Yândaš + Ali], Keldi-muχammad [<Keldi + Muχammad], Toydï-murâd, [<Toydï + Murâd], Tursun-muχammad [< Tursun + Muχammad], Turdï-murâd [< Turdï + Murâd], Tuχta-quzi.*[462] The examples show, however, that the nominal components of this structure themselves are independent personal names.

According to BLAGOVA the inverted constructions seem to be modern (new) models.[463]

7.1.7.1. Vpast(-DI)+N

Berdi-alim, Berdi-šükür, Duγdï-tumač, Turdï-bek "Stayed Strong[464] / Stayed Lord / (He Who) Stood, The Strong Lord?" *Berdi-bek* "Gave Strong[465] / Gave-lord / The Strong/Lord, (Who is) Given (by God)?" *Keldi-murza, Turdï-muχammad.*

The element *Berdi* in these names is to be regarded as defective or abbreviated/simplified theophoric name, as is discussed under 7.2. below.

7.1.7.2. Vpast(-mIš/-mUš)+N? or Part+N?

Turmïš-temür?

7.1.8. Predicate + Adverb (P(V)+Adv)

7.1.8.1. Vimp2+Adv

Gel-beri.

---

[461] Sattarov, 1973, p. 42.

[462] Begmatov, 1984, p. 200.

[463] Blagova, 1998b, p. 59.

[464] Žanuzakov's opinion (Žanuzakov, p. 106).

[465] Ibid.

LX

7.1.9. Predicate + Predicate (P(V)+P(V)

7.1.10. Verbal + Predicate

7.1.10.1. Part+ V?

7.1.10.2. Ger+ V (Adverb+ Predicate)

7.1.10.2.1 Ger(-p)+ Vimp2

Aydap-kel, Alïp-qač, Alïp-kel, Satïb-al.[466]

7.1.10.2.2. Ger(-p)+ Vpast(-DI/-DU)

Alïp-kirdi, Satïp-aldï, Tapïp-aldï, Tawïb-aldï, Tiläp-aldï, Tiläp-berdi, Turup-berdi.

7.1.10.2.3. Ger(-p)+ Vpast(-GAn/-KAn)

Tiläp-bergän, Tölep-bergen.

7.2. Defective Sentence ([X]+ P(VP))

Personal names, originally consisting of two (or more) components, which contain only the verbal part of the compound name, can be regarded as *defective sentences.*[467] Most of these names can be traced back to *theophoric names* (see p. XL). Especially three verbs occur in this case: 1. *ber-* "to give" (e.g., *Berdi ~ Verdi ~ Virdi; Bermiš ~ Vermiš*) and is the most common; 2. *al-* "to get, take" (*Aldï,* Almïš); 3. *bol- ~ bul-*
"to be" (e.g., *Bolmïš ~ Bulmïš* "(he who) Became"). The latter two verbs evidently refer to the lacking Ablative form of God's name: "taken from God," "become from God." All these Turkic names can be correctly regarded as abbreviated/simplified theophoric names.[468]

In ŽANUZAKOV's opinion, names like *Jïlqï-bay* and *Malïs-bay* can also be considered as defective sentences from which the basic (verbal) component (in this case *-bolsïn*) is missing. Thus *Jïlqï-bay* would be shortened of **Jïlqï-bay-bolsïn* which would mean "May He be Rich in Horses."

7.2.1. [N/Adv?]+ V

Bergen, Berdi, Boldï, Bolmuš, Keldi, Toymïš, Tüzmiš.

III. Personal Names Complemented with Secondary Components

In the opinion of several researchers this type of name is considered a virtual compound name. In our system it is not a real composite.

8.1. Simple PN+ comp

Aydar-bek, Bay-bek, Ay-suluw, Jïlqï-bay, Qara-bay, Sarï-bay, Suluw-bike, Suluw-χan.

8.2. Compound PN+ comp

Aq-qočqar-bay, Bayyu-eyder-χan, Bek-fulat-bay, Qar-jaw-bay, Täk-qulï-bay, Töre-bay-χanum, Ayde-ber-bek, Bek-oylï-bek, Činar-qulu-bek, Juma-nazar-bek, Qurban-ali-bek, Tatar-χan-bek, Uzun-asan-bek, Aq-tulum-bike, Oyul-sultan-bikeč, Tuyu-šaχ-bikeč, Gül-jamal-ayïm, Nar-jan-gül.

8.3. Sentence PN+ comp

Az. *Döza-yïz* "Bear/Stand Daughter!"[469] NUyg. *Tursun-qïz, Tursun-ay,*[470] *Ay-doydï-bek, Aq-tuwar-bek, Šah-verdi-bek, Teñri-berdi-bek.*

---

[466] Perhaps all may be classified under 4.1.1. of the simple names above. The name *Alïp // Alp "Hero"* may also be considered here.

[467] Rásonyi, Theoph. (1982); Sattarov 1973, p. 45; Begmatov 1984.

[468] Rásonyi, Theoph., p. 292.

[469] Sadyhov, 1984, p. 217.

[470] Taklamakanlı, p. 211.

Secondary Components

General Notes

Secondary components, also called "anthropo-lexems," are inorganic parts of the names since they only refer to sex (*-bay, -gül, -χatun, -biče*), age (*-aγa, -aqay, -ul*), title (*-mullah, -χan, -qan, -sultan*), job (*baqšï, yarγan, mergen*), or lineage (*-apa, -čičä, -yegän, -yeñgä,-oγlu, -taγay, -ulu*) of the person.

Titles, sociopolitical terms, originally were used as additional or *secondary* parts of the personal names of the upper classes and indicated the grade and position of the person in the society. In some cases titles were used instead of names.

Among secondary parts/components of Kazakh personal names of the 18th-19th centuries for instance, such titles dominated as *χan, bahadur, batïr, sultan, bay, biy, bek, murza, tarχan, tüleñgit, mullah, qazï*, etc.[471] Over the course of time, however, these titles spread to the common people and became traditional names, as well as secondary components of personal names, so they could be given even to newborn or little children.[472] BLAGOVA notes that components *bay, bek* and *χan* began to turn into *affixoids* (or *suffixoids*) with hypocoristic meaning in the social circumstances of the post-October period. This tendency was more explicit in Uzbek than, for example, in Tatar.[473]

Terms of kinship are widely used in Turkic anthroponomy as personal names and as secondary components. In SATTAROV's opinion the oldest names are formed of terms of kinship. In families, such terms normally replace the personal names and then may become PN themselves.[474]

Like other researchers, we also tend to regard this type of component as specific affixes (affixoids) which form or sometimes modify personal names. According to A. N. KONONOV and V. A. NIKONOV for example, as a result of frequent use of certain nouns in compound proper names, the second components lose their original meaning turning into a *derivational suffix* [=secondary component in our terms] with diminutive meaning.[475]

Used at the beginning, these frequently used elements of personal names expressed some kind of wish (wish for happiness in general) to the newborn, but later they lost all their lexical meaning in personal names, turning into *auxiliary suffixes (suffixoids)* [=secondary component in our terms] which merely express the idea of "male name" or "female name."[476] Foreign prefixoids and affixoids such as Ar. *-abd* and *-din* became formal even faster. In the end, they express only the idea of belonging to Islam.[477]

Some scholars interpret the term "component" much more widely. In NIKONOV's and his followers' approach for instance, *ay, bay, beg, qul, gül* are to be regarded identical both at the end and at the beginning of composite names, not differentiated between their basic (primary) and secondary functions.[478] This idea becomes clear when they interpret such names as *Bay-bek* "Rich Lord" // *Bek-bay* "Very Rich(!)," *Suluw-bike* "Beautiful Lady" // *Ay-suluw* "Moon Beautiful," *Qara-bay* "Black-Rich(!)" // *Bay-qara* "Rich(!)-Black," *Sarï-bay* "Yellow/Blond Rich(!)," *Bay-sarï* "Rich Yellow/Blond."

SATTAROV and SUBAEVA, for example, consider the "basic component" (R. *opornyj komponent*) to be each part (composite) of the name, e.g., *aq, bars, qara, qïzïl, qïlïč, uraz*, frequently used in different compound names. According to the authors there are some 500 such "components," more than 160 of which are actively used in Tatar. They tried to classify these components based on their lexical-semantic and grammatical features.[479] In BIKBULATOV's opinion, the names formed from terms of kinship are not used as widely as is presented by SATTAROV. For instance, *ir (är)* and *yeget* should be excluded, and names with the components *qïz* and *ata* should be treated more carefully, since these components refer only to the sex.[480]

The usage of secondary components differs highly among various Turkic peoples. On the evidence of recent

---

[471] Ergazieva, p. 210.

[472] Sadyhov, p. 214.

[473] Blagova, 1998b, p. 59.

[474] Sattarov, 1969, p. 56; Žanuzakov p. 113.

[475] A. N. Kononov, *Grammatika sovremennogo uzbekskogo literaturnogo jazyka*. M.-L. 1960, pp. 9-10; Sadvakasov-Mahpirov, p. 31, Nikonov, 1984, p. 194, Zaj. 1971, pp. 325, 328.

[476] As has been observed in New Uyghur, Bashkir, etc., cf. Sadvakasov-Mahpirov pp. 31, 34-35, Kusimova 133, Torma 1997, p. 71.

[477] Nikonov, 1984, p. 194.

[478] Nikonov, 1984, p. 192-193, Sattarov and Subaeva, p. 71, Sattarov 1990, p. 185-186, Blagova, 1997, 1998b. Žanuzakov, (1982) is of same the opinion.

[479] Sattarov and Subaeva p. 65, cf. also SLINM p. 301.

[480] Bikbulatov, p. 107.

data, it is clear that secondary component of male names *-jan* was much loved by Uzbeks (53%), popular with Uyghurs (32%), hardly used with Kazakhs (8%) and almost ignored by Kirghiz (1%). At the same time *-bek* is popular among the Kirghiz (58%), hardly used in modern Kazakh (7%) and Uzbek (1%), not used in Uyghur and Turkmen at all.[481] We can state that the system and usage of the secondary components are characteristic features of anthroponymy of each people.

List of Secondary Components

aba (comp.) "uncle, father, brother"

abay (comp.) "uncle (as an address of elders), grandfather, elder brother"

abïz (comp.) "writer, educated, enlightened man" (<Ar.)

ačqučï 1. (title) "holder of the key" (*<ač-qu*); 2. (title) "treasurer"

aǰi see **χaǰi**.

addin see **addĭn**.

addĭn (addin, eddin, eddĭn, iddin, iddĭn, uddin, uddĭn) (comp.) "of the religion," a very frequent component of compound Arabic personal names. "After 1200, compounds with *ad-dīn* became part and parcel of the name, the person's qualities or rank notwithstanding. This custom however, developed primarily in the Eastern part of the Muslim world. The use of names with *ad-dīn* very soon became a custom in the Middle East as well, as a look at biographical dictionaries shows"; (Schimmel 60-61). <Ar. *ad-dīn (<al-dīn)*

aγa (aqa) 1. (male, rarely female comp.) "elder male relative such as father, brother, uncle or grandfather" (East.T., Kzk.), "elder sister" (East.T.). It is used to express honour or/and respect towards (elder) people of higher rank when addressing them. 2. (title) "chief, master, landowner" (Turk.). As a title it was given to many persons of varying importance employed in government service, usually of a military or non-secretarial character (EI(NE)Index). Coming before other titles, it forms compound titles such as *aγa-χan; aγa-xatun, aγa-bek* which were used as titles of rulers and their wives, e.g., *Tuman-aγa* (Timur's wife). Its variant *aqa* is used in Western Kazakistan, e.g., *Šam-aqa < Šam-γali*.

aγača (fem. title) "lady of higher rank; a high-born woman (when addressing); daughter of a prince." It is a female title in the Bābur-nāme and a common everyday form of address to a noble woman in Eastern Turkestan (Le Coq, Ind. 4).

aγači (aγïči) (title) "treasurer; financier" cf. Selj. *agačï* "maliyeci" (ToganUTT 210); Karakh. *agïči* "Schatz-meister" (MK/Brock.); *aγïči* "treasurer; the keeper of the silk brocades" (Golden).

aγïči see **aγači**.

aγruqčï (title)

aχond see **aχund**.

aχun see **aχund**.

aχund (aχond, aχun, âχun, aqïn, aqun,) (comp.) 1. "(religious) teacher, scholar, mullah, master, rich man" (Az., NUyg., Uzb. <P.); 2. "(folk) poet" (Kzk., Kirg.); 3. *aqun* in Southern Kirghizia used to mean "man educated in Kashghar" (Jud.); 4. Kirg. *aqun* sometimes means the same as component *bay*; 5. (suffixoid) in NUyg. with meaning "male name" only

ay (ây) 1. (fem. comp.) "Moon," as secondary component, refers to females only with dim. meaning. 2. suffixoid meaning "female name" only; According to Kononov (Gram. Uzb. Jaz., M.-L., 1960, p. 128), used in PNs, it is a dim. suff., also used as a suff. of common nouns in Uzbek. See suff. (suffixoid?) *-ay(1)*. Cf. also **ayïm**.

ayïm (fem. comp.) 1. "lady, rich (noble) woman"; "wife" in Kirg. Uzb., and especially a component of female names in the southern dial. of Kirg. (Jud.); 2. "my Moon (=my darling / my dearest)" in hypocoristic function; 3. suffixoid simply meaning "female name." It may be derived from the secondary component **ay** suffixed with the archaic fem. suff. *-(ï)m*, cf. suff. *-m(3)*.

ake (äke, äkä, eke) (comp.) 1. "father" (Kkalp., Kirg.), "father; brother" (and addressing to elder male relatives), in Kirg. dial. *äkä*; 2. used to respectfully address elder men and women (Kirg., Kzk.). In some cases, maybe as a result of compounding, the name gets shortened/contracted and only the first syllable or the first sounds remain and the component is added: Kzk. *Ažeke (< Ažar +-eke), Äbeke (<Äbu +-eke), Doseke (<Dosmaγambet +-eke), Qarake (< Qarbantay + -ake), Qažeke (<Qažïγali +-eke)* (KzRS 570). See also comp. *aγa~aqa* and suffixes *-qa ~ -ke*.

aqa 1. (comp.) the same as **aγa** (see), e.g., in Kzk. in vocative forms of names; 2. (title) "prime minister;

treasurer of state" (in Khiva); 3. (female title) "khan's daughter, princess; female relative of a khan" (Chag.); 4. (title) "marshal, majordomo" (Crim., Chag., Uzb.)

aqay (comp.) "elder brother" (Crm.): "uncle (address to an elder man whose name one doesn't know" (Crm.)

aqïn see **aχund.**

aqun see **aχund.**

alïp see **alp.**

alp (alïp, ālïp) 1. (comp.) "hero; heroic warrior"; 2. (title) used by Seljuk and subsequent rulers; its synonyms are: **batïr,** *čapar* and *sökmen* (EI(NE)Index).

alpad (alpat) (comp.) "rich man, landlord" < **alpaγut** ?

alpaγut (alpad, alpat?) (comp.) "hero, warrior"

alpat see **alpad.**

ana (fem. comp.) "mother" cf. Uyg., Karakh. *ana* "мат'ь (DTS)

anay (fem. comp.) "mother," see also **änäy**

apa-uruñu (comp.) "father-combatant, great-warrior, first-fighter" cf. **apa I.** and **uruñu**

apa I. (title / comp.) "father; chief" (Karakh.)

apa II. (fem. comp.) 1. "older female relative, older sister" (Uyg., Uzb.), 2. "mother" (Karakh.)

apa-čur (title) "chief of a tribe" (Uyg.), cf. **apa I.** and **čur**

apa-ičräki (comp.) "father-official, first official; chief official" cf. **apa I. + ičräki**

apa-tutuq (comp.) "first leader; chief governor" cf. **apa I. + tutuq**

apa-uruñu (title) "chief/first-ensign," cf. **apa** and **uruñu**

araχ see **arïγ.**

arbab (arbâb) 1. (title) "higher clerk of state" (Chag.); 2. (comp.) "respected elder man" (<Ar.)

arï see **arïγ.**

arïγ (araχ, arï) (fem. comp.) "clean, honest"

arslan-ilig (title) "a sub-ruler" (Karakh.)

arslan-qara-qaγan (title) "the eastern qagan" (Karakh.)

arslan-tegin (title) "a sub-ruler" (Karakh.)

arū see **arïγ.**

ata (comp.) 1. "(grand-) father, ancestor" (address to older men and those of higher rank/dignity/respect); 2. "protector, patron" (Kirg.); 3. "wise, holy, venerated," cf. also **dede**

ata-beg (ata-bek, ata-bey) (title) 1. "commander-in-chief of an army," "chieftain; minister, chief of the guards" (Turk.), the title of a high dignitory under the Seljuks and their successors; 2. "tutor; teacher" (Selj., Chag.), cf. **atalïq**

ata-bek see **ata-beg.**

ata-saγun (title) "title of noblemen with the Karluks" cf. **ata** and **saγun**

ataliγ see **atalïq.**

atalih see **atalïq.**

atalik see **atalïq.**

atalïq (atalik, atelik, ataliγ, atalih) 1. (title) "teacher, educator, stepfather, guardian" (Crm., Kuman), 2. "official of higher degree" (Crm.), close counselor and confidant of the sovereign; 3. "higher dignity, vezir, sheyk" (East. T.), cf. **ata-beg.**

ateke (comp., title?) dim.-hypoc. form of **atalïq** (<*atalïq* + *ake*), cf. also **ake**

atelik see **atalïq.**

ālïp see **alp.**

ây see **ay.**

âχun see **aχund.**

baba (bâbâ) 1. (title) "chief"; 2. (comp.) "grandfather" as respectful address to elders people, e.g., *Asrâr-bâbâ* (UzbRS); 3. "father" as an epithet being attached to names of Muslim saints (*aziz*) (UzbRS, Smirnov, Krym. 28)

bača (comp.) "child, boy; friend" cf. Kirg. *bača* "дитя, ребёнок; мальчик; друг" (Jud.).

baγa an Old Turkic title (<Sogd.)

baγa-tarqan (title) part of Tonyuquq's (650-716) title, compound from titles **baγa** (<Sogd.) and **tarqan**

baγain a Proto-Bulgharian title

baγatur (bahadïr, behadïr, behadur, batïr, bātïr, bōtur, buqatïr) (comp. and honorific title) "courageous hero, brave warrior; champion"; <Mo. *bahadur* [بهادر] (Budagov 218).

bahadïr see **baγatur.**

baχsï see **baqšï.**

baχšï see **baqšï.**

bay (bây, pay) 1. (title) "chief; chieftain" (Togan, BTT 53, after Marquart); chief of an *aul* or a region; 2. (comp.) "rich man; noble man, gentleman; owner, master," used as an address or wish for the future (Kzk., Kirg., Bashk., Tat.); 3. (comp.) simply meaning "man"; or "male name"

bay-biče (bay-biše) 1. (fem. title) "first wife, mistress of the home" (Kirg.), *bay-biše* "id." (Kzk.); 2. (fem. comp.) address for married women, similar to madame in French (Budagov)

bay-biše see **bay-biče.**

bayan I. (comp.) "rich man; gentleman"

bayan II. (fem. title) "lady, mistress, madam"

baqši see **baqšï.**

baqsa see **baqšï.**

baqsï see **baqšï.**

baqšï (baqsa, baqši, baχšï, baqsï, paqšï) (comp.) 1. "a Buddhist priest, monk"; 2. "tutor, literate man, writer; practitioner of shamanistic healing (Uzb.), quack doctor; musician, folk-singer"; 3. "wandering minstrel (Trkm., Turk.) (<Mo.<Chin. *po-shih / pâk-dz'i*)

bala (pala, palañ, palan) (comp.) "child (male and female)"

balγïčï see **belgiči.**

balvan see pehlivan.

balwan see pehlivan.

banïw see banu.

banu (banïw, bânu, panu) (fem. comp.), preposotive component of female names "lady, noble woman; bride; princess" (< P.).

baša 1. (title) put after the proper names, it was applied to soldiers and lower grades of officers (esp. Janissaries) and, also to notables in the provinces; not to be confused with paša (see) (EI(NE)Index); 2. (comp.) "man" cf. Turk. (Yürük) baša "erkek" (tribe Karakečili) (BkCivYür. 69)

batïr (bātïr, madïr, matïr, patïr) (comp., title of respect) "brave and strong man, hero, heroic warrior," "member of the military nobility" (Kzk); cf. also bahadur.

bātïr see batïr.

bāzdār (title) "falconer" (< P. bāz "goshawk")

bâbâ see baba.

bây see bay.

bânu see banu.

bäg see beg.

bäy see bey.

bäk see bek.

bälgiči see belgiči.

bärgän see mergen.

beder (bedri) (fem. comp.) "(full) moon on the 14th day," used in the meaning of "the most beautiful girl" (<Ar.)

bedri see beder.

beg 1. (title, sometimes fem. title) "ruler, prince, tribal leader, high military and civil functionaries, the son of a paša (Osm.), lord, chief, commander, emir"; 2. (comp.) "noble man, wealthy man; gentleman" (expressing respect when addressing or mentioning somebody), cf. bey, bek.

begi (beyi, beki) (comp.) "hero; husband," the Mongolized form of Turkic beg (see) or it is derived from beg/bek + suff. -i

begim (beygüm, biyim?) 1. (title) "(my) prince" (East. T., Le Coq, 96); 2. (fem. title) "(my) princess" (in Western Turkestan and India, Le Coq, 96); "daughter of a bek or an emir " (UzbRS); 3. (fem. comp.) "lady, wife of a beg " (Chag., East. T.), cf. beg. It can be derived from beg/bek + fem. suff. -im, cf. suff. -m(3)

begrek-čur (compound title) "notable, prince" cf. Uyg. bägräk "bey, şehzade" (US) see also beyrek, beg and čur

behadïr see bayatur.

behadur see bayatur.

bey (bäy, biy, bi, bï, pi, pï) 1. (title) "ruler, prince; the son of a paša, high civil functionary" (Osm.); "chieftain" (Uzb.), "judge" (Kirg., Kzk.), "member of the high tribal aristocracy" (Kzk.), "orator" (Kzk.), "clerk" (Alt.); 2. (comp.) "landlord; chief; master, notable country gentleman" (Alt., Kzk.); 3. (comp.) expressing respect when addressing someone; cf. also beg, bek

beygüm see begim.

beyi see begi.

beyrek (title) "notable, prince" cf. Uyg. bägräk "bey, şehzade" (US)

bek (bäk, bik) 1. (title) "(feudal) magnate being under the khan; member of the high tribal aristocracy" (Kzk.), "ruler, head of a district or town" (Uzb.), "prince; clerk" (Tat.) 2. (comp.) "noble man, lord, gentleman, man, husband" used for expressing respect (Kzk., Kirg., Uzb., Bashk. etc.), it is very popular (dominant and fashionable) in contemporary Kirgiz (Žaparov); cf. also beg, bey.

bekey (comp.) "little gentleman, master/owner (noble man)" dim. of bek

beki see begi.

bekläri-bek (title) "(lit.) bek of the beks, elder emir" бекляри бекъ / بكلارى بك (Umarī/Tizeng. I, 227, 249), cf. bek

bekleri-bek (title) "chief (the first) of the emirs"

belgiči (bälgiči, balɣïčï) (title?) < *balïqčï (Golden, Khaz. 165).

bendeh see bende.

bende (bendeh, mende) (comp.) "bearer (carrier) of arms; servant, slave" (<P.), cf. also qul, qulï.

bergen see mergen.

bi see bey.

bibi (bïbä) (fem. comp.) "lady, highborn respected woman; mistress; lady of the house; girl," originally, "little old mother, grandmother, woman of high rank" (<P.)

bicä see biče.

biče (bičä, bicä) 1. (fem. title) "queen" (NUyg., Kar.), 2. (fem. comp.) "woman, wife" (Tat., Karch., Balk.).

bigä see bike.

bige (bigä) see bike.

biy see bey.

biyim see begim.

biyke see bike.

bik see bek.

bikä see bike.

bikäč (bikeš, bikäš) (comp.) 1. "girl, bride, spouse; sister-in-law (husband's elder sister)"; 2. "respectful address to a young girl" (Kzk.).

bikäš see bikäč.

bike (biyke, bige, bigä, bikä, biki?) (fem. comp.) 1. "lady, lady of the house, wife, girl"; 2. "sister-in-law (husband's sister)"; 3. "woman having no husband; widow; debauched woman, adulteress."

bikeš see bikäč.

biki see bike.

bitigči see bitigäči.

bitigäči (bitigči) (title) "writer, secretary" (Uyg.).

bĭ see bey.

bĭbä see bibi.

bïruq see buyruq.

boɣra-χan (title) of the sovereign (Karakh.)

boyla (buyla) (title) (Uyg., Proto-Bulg.), e.g., *Boyla-baɣa-tarqan, Boyla-qutluɣ-yarɣan*

boyla-baɣa-tarqan (title) Tonyuquq's (650-716) title, cf. boyla and baɣa-tarqan

boyla-tarχan (buyla-tarχan) see boyla and tarqan

bōtur see baɣatur.

bögä (bökö, bökä, böke, mökä, mögä, mögö, mökö, mökkö, mükü) (comp.) "strong man; wrestler" (Yak.), cf. Chag., Tar. *bökä* "der Starke, der Ringer" (Radl. IV, 1693), Hak.(Sag., Koyb.) *mökö* "stark" (Radl. IV, 2129), < Mo. *böke* "id." (TMEN II, No. 803)

bögö see bögä.

bökä see bögä.

böke? see bögä.

bökö see bögä.

buɣra-ilig (title) of a Karakhanid sub-ruler

buɣra-qara-qaɣan (title) of the western qaɣan Itaraz (Samarkand); cf. boɣra-χan

buyla see boyla.

buyla-tarχan see boyla-tarχan.

buyruq (bïruq) (title) "clerk, copyist."

buqatĭr see baɣatur.

burχan-qulï (burqan-qulï) (comp.) "Buddha's (prophet's) slave / helper / follower"

burqan-qulï see burχan-qulï.

bü see bübü.

bübü (bǔ, bü) (fem. comp.) "shamaness; woman-baqšĭ"

büwi (fem. comp.) "housewife, mistress," refers to the female sex of the name with dim. meaning; used also as a suffixoid

bǔ see bübü.

čabïš (čapïš) (title) "high military rank (dignitary), aid-de-camp."

čayžañ (comp.) "prince, head of a clan"; "zaysan (feudal clerk, official)"

čan see Jan.

čañgši see čañgšĭ.

čañgšĭ (čangši) (title) "historian of the prince's court" (<Chin.)

čapïš see čabïš.

čauš see čawuš.

čavuš see čawuš.

čawuš (čavuš, čauš) (title) "warrant officer; commander; low-ranking military personnel" (<P.), cf. also čabïš.

čawuš-baš (title) "head of doormen (jamitors)," "chef des huissiers" (Turk.), the same as ešik-aɣasï, cf. čawuš

čawuš-beg (čawuš-bek) (title) "head of doormen (jamitors)," "chef des huissiers" (Turk.), the same as ešik-aɣasï, cf. čawuš/ and beg

čawuš-bek see čawuš-beg.

čelebi 1. (title) of the leader of the Mevlevi order; 2. (comp.) "elder son in the family"; 3. (comp.) used as honorific title for a man of upper classes (in later times, often for non-Muslims) meaning "noble man, educated (learned) man, gentleman, landlord" (Turk.) (Budagov 484, TED)

čeri-baš see čeri-bašï.

čeri-bašï (čeri-baš) (title) "commander, general" cf. Kuman *čeri bašy* "Heerführer, armiragius" (CC), Turk. *çeribaşı* "komutan, başbuğ, serdar, serasker" (TS).

čičä (fem. comp.) "elder sister" (in Khiva), "maternal aunt" (in Samarkand) (Uzb.)

čigši (title) "governor, military commander of high rank" (Uyg.) (< Chin. *tz'ŭ-shih* < *ts'ïäk-ṣi*)

čingsang (title) "Minister of State" (<Chin.)

čïqan (comp.) "son of the aunt on maternal side"

čoban see čupan.

čor (čur) (title) 1. "one of the leaders of the five *oq* of the left wing of the nation"; "Among the Western Kök Türks the title *čur* was associated with the left wing of the nation, composed of the five «arrows» (*oq*) of the *Dulo*. Each of the *oq* was ruled by a *čur*." (Golden); 2. "chief of the bägs who ruled a part of the country led by a *yabɣu* or a *šad* " (he wasn't a member of the dynasty and had no independent army) (Golden, Khaz. 180 after Chavannes).

čora see čura.

čul (čulï) (title) a variant of *čur* see čor.

čulï see čul.

čupan (čoban) 1. (title) "helper of the leader of a village"; 2. (comp.) "herdsman, shepherd" (<P. *čūpān*).

čur see čor.

čura (čora, Jora, Jura, šora, sura) (comp.) 1. "slave (son); farmer, peasant; warrior, soldier"; 2. as a blandishing address to children: *čoram!* (Samojlovič); 3. "friend" (Uzb.); 4. Bashk. *sura* "boy; hero, brave man; mate" (Kusimova 1978, 127, Kusimova 133).

čoro (comp.) "follower, the closest fellow-warrior, intimate friend"

Jabɣu see yabɣu.

Jamal (žamal, Jemal) (fem. comp.) "beauty, fineness" (<Ar.), see also sïlu

Jan (yan, yän, čan, zän, žän, žan, žân) (comp., fem. comp.) "soul; life; person; my dear one!, dearest (heart)Ĭ (P.); a very frequent universal component which expresses respect, gentleness and blandishment. Component *Jan* originally could only be attached to the names of Muslim saints or their well-known epithets (e.g., *Jan-χoja* < *Jan-i Xoja* "soul of the Master," "Master" here stands for prophets Ali or Muhammad) (Gafurov 40).

Janïm (Janum) (comp., fem. comp.) "my soul; my life; my dear one!, my dearest (heart) one!" see **Jan** + poss. suff. *-ïm*

Jar see **yar**.

Jawašïgar* (title) a Khazar dignity being under **Kündür Qaγan*

Jebu see **yabγu**.

Jellād (comp.) "hanger" (<Ar.)

Jemal see **Jamal**.

Jiget see **yigit**.

Jigit see **yigit**.

Jïla (title) of Chuvash type

Jora see **čura**.

Jura see **čura**.

darχan see **tarqan**.

daruγa (title) "governor of town, majordomo, police officer" (<Mo.)

datχa (datqa) (title) high dignity born in the Khanates of Kokand and Bukhara

datqa see **datχa**.

dede (comp.) "grandfather, ancestor" used when addressing elder respected men, the same as **ata** (see)

dihqan (comp.) "landlord, smallholder; ploughman; head of a village"; (<P. *dehgan*

dirim see **terim**.

diwan (title) "scribe; secretary; tax-collector" a dignitary in Khiva

dïyqan see **dihqan**.

äčä (eče, eJe) (fem. comp.) "elder sister" cf. Trkm. *eJe* "мама, мать (прибавляется к именам собств. женским при почтительном обращении пожилым женщинам, а также при обращении к сестре отца или деда по отцовской линии)" (TrkmRS)

äynä-bäk (title) may be an inaccurate version of **inaq-bek** (see)

äkä see **ake**.

äke see **ake**.

äl-täbär see **el-täbär**.

änäy (fem. comp.) "mother" cf. Bashk. dial. *änäy* "id." (BRS/Uraksin), see also **anay**

är see **er**.

ärkin see **erkin**.

eče see **äčä**.

eJe see **äčä**.

eddin see **addïn**.

eddïn see **addïn**.

efendi 1. (comp.) "gentleman, master"; (title) given to literate people, members of the clergy, Ottoman princes, army officers up to major (Turk.).

eke see **ake**.

ekey (comp.) dim. of **eke** (see)

el-täbär (il-teber, äl-täbär) (title) "ruler" cf. Golden 147, 149: "The Qagan left a ruler, i.e. an *il teber* "one who steps on the il" at the head of conquered tribes"; "chieftain" (Ligeti, R. tör. nev. II–III, 39), *ältäbär*, is of Juan-juan origin (Doerfer, TMEN II, 203).

el-täriš (il-täriš) (title of respect, throne name) "polity-gathering/collecting" (Golden 137)

elči (ilči) (title) "envoy, ambassador, messenger"; "ruler of a land or people" (East.T.).

elči-beg (title) "ruler," cf. also **elči** and **beg**

elči-čur (title) see **elči** and **čur**

elig (ilig, ilek) (title) "ruler, monarch," Clauson mistakenly read it as *ellig* (Ligeti, R. tör. nev. II-III, 39), "king" (Doerfer, TMEN II, No. 661).

er (ir, är) (comp.) "man; hero(ic) warrior; husband"; used both as a prepositive and postpositive secondary component of male names.

er-tegin (title) cf. **er** and **tegin**

eren (erän) (comp.) "young man; strong, brave man; hero"

ergek (irgek) (comp.) "male (of an animal), man"

eri (comp.) 3rd p. possessive of **er** meaning "man of; hero(ic) warrior of; husband of"

erkin (ärkin, irkin) (title) a title among the Karluks (DTS)

eš (iš) (comp.) "fellow, mate," very frequent in Tat. and Bashk.

ešik-aγasï (title) "head of doormen (janitors)"; "usher (a minor court officer)"; cf. also **išik-ata, čawuš-baš ~ čawuš-beg ~ čawuš-beḱ**.

fakih (comp.) "an expert (specialist) in the religious law of Islam" (Ar.)

fūšï see **fūšïy**.

fūšïy (fūšï) (title) (Uyg.) (<Chin.).

geray see **keräy**.

gerey see **keräy**.

girey see **keräy**.

göl see **gül**.

gözä see **χoJa**.

gözel see **güzel**.

gül (göl, kül) 1. (fem. comp.) "flower (~ beautiful like a flower), rose; nice"; 2. (suffixoid) partly or totally lost its original meaning "rose" (<P.) and expresses dim.-hypoc. meaning referring to the feminine gender of the name. It is very prominent in women's names all over the Islamic world, particularly in the Persian-Turkic areas, used as an expression of tenderness (Schimmel p. 44).

gür-qan (gür-qā) (title) 1. "khan of the Qara-kitats"; a dignity of the Timurids; 2. (<Mo.?).

gür-qā see **gür-qan**.

güzä see **χoJa**.

güzel (gözel) (fem. comp.) "beautiful, nice, pretty"

γan see qan.

γanïš see qanïš.

γaziy see γāzi.

γazïy see γāzi.

γāzi (γazï, γāziy, γāzïy) (comp.) 1. one who fights on behalf of Islam; frontier raider into a non-Muslim country; 2. "victor, winner"; honorific title given to generals for outstanding exploits; war veteran; (<Ar.).

γïs see qïz.

γïz see qïz.

γol see qul.

γoža see χoǰa.

γuǰa see χoǰa.

γul see qul.

γulï see qulï.

γuža see χoǰa.

haǰi see χaǰi.

han see χan.

hïlïw see sïlu.

hoǰa see χoǰa.

χaǰi (χaǰï, haǰi, aǰi, χaži, χäže) (comp.) "hadji, pilgrim" (<Ar.).

χaǰib (χāǰib, ḥāǰib) (title) "doorkeeper; chamberlain, superintendent of the palace, chief of the guard, chief minister" (<Ar.)

χaǰï see χaǰi.

χaγan (title) "ruler, emperor" cf. χaqan?

χaqan (title) "(supreme) ruler, emperor" a title borrowed by the Turks from the Juan-juan, applied to the heads of the various Turkic confederations, in the form qa'an it was borne by the successors of Chinggis Khan (EI(NE)Index), cf. qaγan

χalife (title) "Caliph (=ruler, governor)," the title of the leader of the Muslim community (<Ar.)

χan (χân, han) 1. (title) "khan, (subordinate) ruler"; first used by the T'u-chüeh apparently as a synonym of qaγan, the later χāqān, with which its relationship is obscure; it was afterwards normally applied to subordinate rulers (EI(NE)Index); 2. (comp.) forming hypoc. form of male names (e.g., Baba-χan "Grossväterchen," Beg-χan "mein lieber Beg" in Trkm., cf. Zaj., 1971, 325); In India today, it is a common affix to the names of Muslims of all classes and is often regarded as a surname (EI(NE)Index). See also qan.

χani (fem. title), e.g., in Chag. Bibi-χani

χanife (fem. title?), e.g., in Chag. Bibi-χanife

χanïm (χenim, χänïm) 1. (fem. title) "wife or daughter of the khan" (title of respect); 2. (fem. comp.) "lady (of the house), mistress, madam"; cf. χan + suff. -m(3)

χanïs see qanïš.

χatša (qatša) (fem. comp.)

χatun (χotun) 1. (fem. title) of Sogd. origin borne by the wives and female relations of the T'u-chüeh and subsequent Trk. rulers. It was employed by the Selj. and Khorezm. shahs and even by the various Chinggisid dynasties. It was displaced in Central Asia in the Timurid period by begüm (EI(NE)Index). 2. (fem. comp.) "lady, noble high-born woman; wife"

χaži see χaǰi.

χākim (haqim, χaqim) (title) 1. "governor, leader of a town or district"; 2. "judge" (Ar.).

χân see χan.

χäže see χaǰi.

χenikey see qanïqay.

χïs see qïz.

χoǰa (qoǰa, χoǰa, qoža, qoǰo, hoǰa, χusa, χuža, χuǰa, quža, γoza, γoža, γuǰa, γuža, küzä, gözä, güzä, közä) (comp.) 1. "master, chief, husband"; 2. "hodja, (Muslim) teacher; educated man," originally the descendants of the first caliphs. (<P.) It is used in many different senses in Islamic lands.

χotun see χatun.

χō see quo.

χuǰa see χoǰa.

χusa see χoǰa.

χuža see χoǰa.

hoǰa see χoǰa.

ičiräki see ičräki.

ičirgü (comp.) "inner; confidental (a part of Bulg. titles)" (cf. Byz. Turc. 133: <g>hÜtzirgouÜ</g>)

ičräki (ičiräki) (title) an official (clerk) inside the palace; lit. "being inside"

iddin see addïn.

iddïn see addïn.

igrül (title)

il-bäg (il-bägi) (title) "head of the state/country," cf. el / il "empire, territory, people, peace" and beg / bek

il-bägi see il-bäg.

il-χan (il-qan) (title) "subordinate khan" (Golden p. 290)

il-qan see il-χan.

il-täriš see el-täriš.

il-teber see el-täbär.

il-ügäsi (title) "fame of the empire"; "Ruhm des Reichs," see also ögä

ilči see elči.

ilek see elig.

ilγar-bašï (title) "commander of the light cavalry" (Chag.) (<Mo.)

ilig see elig.

inaγ see inaq.

inaq (inaγ, inaq-bek, inâq) (title) "confidant of a ruler/prince" (Sauvaget 40); "chief of some Uzbek clans in Khiva" (Samojlovič); "person who governs the empire without having the title of khan" (Samojlovič).

inaq-bek see inaq.

inal see ïnal.

inâq see inaq.

ini (comp.) "younger brother"

ir see er.

irgek see ergek.

irkin see erkin.

ispähsalar see sipehsalar.

iš see eš.

išan (title, a religious dignity) "a religious leader of higher rank at the muslims; teacher of a religious community"

iši (fem. comp.) "woman, wife of a noble man, lady"

išik-ata (title) "head of doormen (janitors)," "door-father," one of the highest dignities in the court of the Timurids; cf. also čawuš-baš ~ čawuš-beg ~ čawuš-bek, ešik-aγasï

išikat (title) "head of the merchants"

ïdiq-qut see ïduqut.

ïdïq-qut see ïduqut.

ïduq-qut see ïduqut.

ïduqut (ïduq-qut, ïdiq-qut, ïdïq-qut) (title) an Uyg. title of the supreme rulers

ïnal (inäl, inal, yinal) 1. (title) a high dignity; "confidant of the khan, prince, deputy, etc."; 2. (comp.) "son of a woman from the khan's clan and a man of common origin"

ïnanč-tutuq (title of respect) "faithful tutuq" cf. tutuq

ïnuq (unuq) (comp.) ?

ïšbara (title) ? (<Sanskr.)

yabγu (yavγu, Jabγu, Jebu) (title) "the highest ruler of the Western Türks," used also as a single personal name.

yaysan (title) "the highest administrative (executive) dignity at the Altay Kalmyks" (<Kalm.)

yaysañ see yaysan.

yalabač see yalawač.

yalavač see yalawač.

yalawač (yalabač, yalavač) (title) "messenger, envoy."

yan see Jan.

yar (Jar, žar, yär) (comp.) "friend; girlfriend; fellow, helper; lover" (P.).

yarγan (title or/and comp.) "hangman," e.g., *Boyla-qutluγ-yarγan*

yasaul (yesaul) (title) "commandant; commander, sergeant" cf. *yasaul* "der Anordner, Ausführer der Befehle" (Chag.), "der Unteroffizier der Chanswache" (Uzb.) (Radl. III, 215) (<Mo.).

yavγu see yabγu.

yazïr-bulaš (title) "deputy of the χaqan (qaγan)"

yän see Jan.

yäñgä see yeñgä.

yär see yar.

yegän (yeyän) (comp.) "son of one's daughter or younger sister; grandson; nephew" (Uyg.);

"grandson" (Bashk.), meaning that the boy was born in the home of his grandmother (Kusimova).

yeget see yigit.

yeyän see yegän.

yeñgä (yäñgä) (fem. comp.) "wife of one's (elder) brother."

yesaul see yasaul.

yigit (yeget, Jigit, Jiget, zigit) (comp.) "(brave) young man"

yiltawär (title) the Oghuric form of el-täbär

yinal see ïnal.

yuγruš (title) "official; vizier, minister"

yüs-baši see yüz-baši.

yüz-baši (yüs-baši) (title) "captain"

käräy see keräy.

kănikäy see qanïqay.

ker-bendeh (comp.) "servant (going) on donkeyback," see bende

keräy (kiräy, girey, giray, giräy, gerey, käräy) 1. (title) of the khans of the Crimea (TMEN IV, No. 1709); 2. (comp.) "respected nobleman; gentleman" (Sattarov-Subaeva).

kethudä (kethüdä) (title) "steward, majordomo"; official, directing the homestead, master of the house, head of the family, husband; "principal, headman of a village, title officer in a town, head, chief of the tribe" (<P.).

kethudä-bey (title) "person directing the home affairs of the Ottoman Empire" see kethudä and bey

köl (title)

köl-bilgä-χan (title of the Uyghur khans)

köl-čur (kül-čur) (title) "chief of a small Türgesh force" cf. köl and čor

köl-ärkin see köl-irkin.

köl-irkin (köl-ärkin, kül-irkin) 1. (title) noble men at the Karluks; 2. (comp.) "noble man"

közä see χoJa.

kübäk (comp.) "hero"

küdägü (comp. and title) "son-in-law" (Mo.)

kül I. see köl.

kül II. see gül.

kül-čur see köl-čur.

kül-irkin see köl-irkin.

küli-čur see köl-čur?

kürekle (fem. comp.) "beautiful"

küzä see χoJa.

qadïn (fem. comp.) "mother-in-law"

qadïr (qayïr) (title)

qaγan (title) an independent prince or (supreme) ruler (Türk < Juan-juan), prince of an independent folk; title of the supreme Khazar ruler, cf. χaqan

qayïr see qadïr.

qalγa (qalγay) (title) "deputy, heir," high dignity coming after that of the khan (Crimea).

qalɣay see **qalɣa**.

qam (comp.) "shaman"

qan (ɣan, qān) 1. (title) "ruler, sovereign; dignity lower than that of the qaɣan's"; 2. (fem. comp.) expressing respect with the original meaning of "empress." See also χan.

qanïkey see **qanïqay**.

qanïqay (qanïkey, kănikäy, χenikey) (title) "princess"

qanïm (title) fem. of **qan** suffixed with fem. suff. -(i)m (3)?, cf. also χanïm

qanïš (ɣanïš, χanïš) (fem. title) "wife of the khan" cf. Kirg. *qanïš* "ханша, жена хана" (Jud.).

qapaɣan (qapɣan) (title) ??

qapɣan (title)

qara (comp.) part of the title of the Karakhanid rulers meaning "strong, powerful"

qara-χan (title) of the Karakhanid rulers, cf. **qara** and **χan**

qaračï (title) of the chieftains in the Crimea

qat (fem. comp.) "woman, wife" cf. Alt. *qat* "женщина, жена" (Verb., Sl.)

qatša (fem. comp.) see χatša.

qatun 1. (fem. title) "wife of a khan or prince," 2. (fem. comp.) "lady, noble high-born woman; married woman, wife" (<Sogd.)

qazï see **qādï**.

qādï (qazï, qāzï) (title) "(Muslim) judge, a representative of authority"

qān see **qan**.

qāzï see **qādï**.

qïs see **qïz**.

qïz (qïs, ɣïz, ɣïs, χïs) (fem. comp.) "girl; daughter"; in medieval usage, one of its denotations was "Christian woman" (<"slave girl, concubine") (EI(NE)Index).

qïzï (fem. comp.) "daughter of" cf. **qïz**

qoči (comp.) "adventurous man; robber; brave man"

qočin? (qučin) (comp.) "member of the soldier-caste of Kashghar."

qoⱨa see χoⱨa.

qoža see χoⱨa.

qol see **qul**.

qontaydži (title) "(reigning) prince" (Mo. < Chin.)

qoš-begi see **quš-begi**.

qožo see χoⱨa.

qō see **quo**.

quč (title)

qučin see **qočin**.

qul (qol, ɣul, ɣol) 1. (comp.) "slave (of God), slave boy, male slave, servant; helper; man"; 2. (suffixoid) meaning "male name" only (cf. Kusimova, 133), cf. also **qulï, bende**

qul-kethudāsï (title) high dignity in the corps of Janissaries

qulï see **qulï**.

qulï (quli) (comp.) "slave of" cf. also **qul, bende**.

qulu see **qulï**.

qunčuy (fem. title) "princess; younger female relative in the khan's family (clan); woman of noble origin" (<Chin. *kung-chu*)

quo (qō (qoo)) (fem. comp.) "beautiful, pretty girl" (< Mid. Mo. *qo'a*).

qurči (comp.) "cavalier-guard of the Safavī rulers"; military term with a variation of different meanings, e.g., "he who bears arms, the sword; chief hubtsman, captain of the watch; leader of a patrol, sentinel, inspector, etc." (<P. <Mo. *qorči* "archer") (EI(NE) Index)

qurtɣa see **qurtqa**.

qurtqa (qurtɣa) (fem. comp.) "old woman"

qus-begi see **quš-begi**.

quš-begi (qoš-begi, qus-begi) (title) "master (chief) of birds; master at training hunting birds"; the title of high officials in the Central Asian khānates in the 16th to 19th centuries, probably with the meaning "commander of the royal camp, quartermaster" (EI(NE)Index).

madïr see **batïr**.

mahram (mehrem) 1. (title) a dignity in the courts of the Khanates of Bukhara and Khiva; 2. (comp.) a trustworthy servant.

malik (mälik, melik) (title) "ruler, emperor, sovereign, king" (<Ar.).

matïr see **batïr**.

mälik see **malik**.

märgän see **mergen**.

mehrem see **mahram**.

melik see **malik**.

mende see **bende**.

mendey (comp.) "little slave / young servant," cf. **bende** + suff. -*y*

mergen (mergän, bärgän, bergen, pärgän, pergen, märgän, mirgän, mirgen) I. (comp.) "sharpshooter, archer; brave hunter" cf. Yak. *bergen* "меткий, ловкий; молодец, удалец" (JRS); II. (fem. comp.) "bride; wife of the elder brother" cf. Yak. *bergen* "невестка (жена старшего деверя)" (JRS) > Mo. *mergen*.

mergän see **mergen**.

mir (mïr) (title) "chief, lord, leader, commander, captain, governor, emir?," a title always coming before the main part of the name; (<P.<Ar.).

mirab (title) "person supervising the water-affairs of a town" (<P. *mīr-āb*)

mirgen see **mergen**.

mïr see **mir**.

mïrza (mirza, morza, murza, mursa) 1. (title) "rich (noble) man', originally "the emir's son; the member of the shah's dynasty"; 2. (comp.) "gentleman; literate man," expressing respect, originally coming before the personal name (P.); 3. (comp.) "gentleman, open-handed, hospitable" (Kzk.) (< P. *āmīr zāde*)

mola see **mulla(h)**.

molda see **mulla**.

morza see **mïrza**.

mögä see **bögä**.

mögö see **bögä**.

mökkö see **bögä**.

mökö see **bögä**.

mula see **mulla**.

mulda see **mulla**.

mulla (mullah, mola, mula, molla, molda, moldo, mulda) 1. (title) "chief judge; doctor of Muslim law," a title of function, of religious dignity or profession and of rank; 2. (comp.) "theological student; mullah; any literate (educated) man."

mursa see **mïrza**.

murza see **mïrza**.

mükü see **bögä**.

nama (comp.) "lama" (<Tib.)

nāib (title) "governor, deputy, substitute, delegate; judge, deputy of the judge" (<Ar. *nāʾib*)

noyan (noyon) 1. (comp.) "nobleman"; 2. (title) "prince" (TMEN I, No. 389), "chief of military units of different sizes." "It is a Mongolian title, rendered in the Muslim chronicles of the Mongolian and Tīmūrid periods in the Arabic script as *nuyān, nūyīn, nuyīn,* etc. Under Chinggis Khan and his successors, the title was granted initially as a military rank, and it came to mean "commander" (EI(NE)Index) (<Mo. *noyan / nuyan*)

noyon see **noyan**.

nöker (nökür) (comp.) "helper, fellow; soldier, servant, footman" (<Mo.)

nökür see **nöker**.

oburɣu (comp.) "brave hero, brave man"

oɣlan (olan, ulan) (comp.) "boy"

oɣlï (oɣlu) (comp.) "son of."

oɣlu see **oɣlï**.

oɣul (ōl, ul, ūl, uwul) (comp.) "son, offspring, child"

oyūn (comp.) "shaman"

ordu-beg see **ordu-begi**.

ordu-begi (ordu-beg) (title) "commander of army; prince/chief of the palace; chief of the headquarters"

ōlaχ see **ōlaq**.

ōlaq (ōlaχ) (comp.) "boy"

ōlan see **oɣlan**.

ögä see **ügä**.

ōl see **oɣul**.

öz-čigši (title) cf. **čigši**

pay see **bay**.

paqšï see **baqšï**.

pala see **bala**.

palan see **bala**.

palañ see **bala**.

palwan see **pehlivan**.

panu see **banu**.

paša (pāša) 1. (title) "pasha (the highest title of civil and military officials)"; 2. (comp., also fem.) used for expressing respect or love when addressing someone, cf. Turk. *paša* "saygı veya sevgi hitabı" (Tar. Sözl.), see also **baša**

patïr see **batïr**.

pāša see **paša**.

pählewan see **pehlivan**.

päk see **bek**.

pärgän see **mergen**.

pehlivan (pählewan, pehlivān, balvan, balwan, palwan) (comp.) "wrestler; champion (in battle), warrior, mighty man; valour; hero" (<P.).

pehlivān see **pehlivan**.

pek see **bek**.

pergen see **mergen**.

pi see **bey**.

pï see **bey**.

saɣun (comp.) "nobleman"

saχib (sāχib) (comp.) "protector, master, owner, patron; lord, chief; companion, disciple" (<Ar.)

said see **seyit**.

salïfān (title) "a Khazar or a local prince" who was a vassal of the Khazars (Golden); *salïfān = Sse-li-fa* of the Sui Shu is under the *tegin* and above the *tudun* in the Turkic hierarchy (Minorsky); "a military officer who was sent to direct the army affairs of subject peoples" (Golden)

saltan see **sultan**.

sančï (title)

sañun see **señün**.

sara (sere) (fem. comp.) "lady, mistress" (Ar.)

sardār see **serdār**.

saučï see **sawčï**.

sawčï (saučï) (title) "envoy, negotiator; prophet"

säydä (säyðä) 1. (fem. title) female form of **seyit**; 2. (fem. comp.) "noblewoman," used in address meaning "madam, lady"

säed see **seyit**.

säyðä see **säydä**.

säyed see **seyit**.

säyet see **seyit**.

säñün see **señün**.

seyit (said, säed, säit, säyed, säyet, seyyid, seyt, sit) 1. (comp.) originally one born into the clan of the Prophet Muhammed; 2. (title) "ruler, chieftain, leader"; 3. (comp.) "master; gentleman, landlord, aristocrat"; as a secondary component originally comes before the main component of the name (Cafer., Ağa 90) (<Ar. *sayyid*).

seyyid see **seyit**.

seyt see **seyit**.

señün (säñün, sañun) (title) "Excellency, general" (<Chin. *chiang-chün < tsi̯ang-ki̯uən*).

serdār (serdär, sardār) (title) "chief; supreme military commander"; (lit.) "holding or possessing the head" (<P.<Ar. *sirdār)*.

serdär see **serdār**.

sere see **sara**.

silavanti (comp.) "honest, righteous; virtuous," epithet of Nestorian or Manichaean Christians (Uyg.) (<Sanskr. *čīlavant*)

singil see **siñil**.

siñil (singil) (fem. comp.) "younger sister"

sipähsalar (ispähsalar, sipehsalar) (title) "commander-in-chief, general officer, army commander" (<P.)

sipehsalar see **sipähsalar**.

sit see **seyit**.

sïlïɣ see **sïlu**.

sïlu (sïlïɣ, sïlū, slu, sula, sulï, sulu, sulū, suluw, hïlïw, sülä, sülü) (fem. comp.) "beautiful; nice, pretty (girl)."

sïluw see **sïlu**.

sïlū see **sïlu**.

slu see **sïlu**.

sofï see **sufi**.

soltan see **sultan**.

su-bašï see **sü-bašï**.

subay (title) "officer, light cavalier"

sufi (sūfï, sofï) (comp.) "mystic, Sufi, devotee"

suɣurči (sügürči) (title) "bearer of parasols (umbrellas)" (<Mo.).

sula see **sulï**.

sulï see **sïlu**.

sultan (soltan, saltan) 1. (title) "ruler, sovereign, monarch; holder of power, authority"; 2. (fem. comp.) "woman from the family of the sovereign; daughter or wife of the sovereign" (Chag.), primarily used as a postpositive component; 3. (comp.) frequent component (also a prepositive one) of male names (<Ar. <Syr.).

sulu see **sïlu**.

suluw see **sïlu**.

sulū see **sïlu**.

sura see **čura**.

sü-bašï (su-bašï) (title) 1. "commander of army," cf. *sü bašï* "военачальник" (DTS); 2. "police superintendent" (Turk.).

sügürči see **suɣurči**.

sülä see **sïlu**.

sülü see **sïlu**.

ša see **šah**.

šad 1. (title) the second in power after the *Qagan*, ruled certain parts of the country; by the 10th c. it appears to

have been replaced by *Bäk* (Golden, Khaz. 206-208); 2. (comp.) member of the khan's dynasty (Golden, Khaz. 206-208); 3. (comp.) the khan's younger brother or son could bear this title (Ligeti, R. tör. nev. II-III, 39) (<Ir.)

šadapït (title) seemingly it is in connection with **šad** but there has not been a faultless explanation yet (Ligeti, R. Tör. nev. II-III, 39, cf. also Bombaci: UAJb. 48 (1976), pp. 32-41)

šah (šâh, ša, šā, šay) 1. (title) "king, ruler, emperor, shah"; 2. (comp.) as the first part of compound names it is an attribute of the basic name meaning "the best, the highest, the first, the biggest (in comparison to the others)" (Budagov, I, 663, Sattarov-Subaeva, 1976, 67). Used also as a second or further part of compound names. In the Indian subcontinent, it is appended to the names of persons claiming descent from the Prophet and has today become a surname (<P.)

šayχ see **šeyχ**.

šali see **šäli**.

šā see **šah**.

šâh see **šah**.

šäli (šali) (title) of a monk (friar)

šeyχ (šayχ, šeyk, šïχ, šiχ) 1. (title) "chief of any human group, chieftain; religious leader, head of an order"; 2. (comp.) "old man, an elder, greybeard," expressing respect (<Ar.).

šeyk see **šeyχ**.

šiχ see **šeyχ**.

šïχ see **šeyχ**.

šora see **čura**.

sūfï see **sufi**.

taɣay (comp.) "uncle on maternal side" (<Mo.)

tay-sañun (title) "great/chief general" (<Chin. *ta-chiang-chün < d'âi-tsi̯ang-ki̯uən*), cf. **señün**

tayči (tayču, tayžï, tayčï, tayJï, taysï) 1. (title) "heir of the throne; prince"; 2. (comp.) "(a Mongol) noble man" (<Mo.<Chin. *t'ai-tzŭ < t'âi-tsi*).

tayčï see **tayči**.

tayču see **tayči**.

tayJï see **tayči**.

tayša see **tayši**.

tayši (tayša) 1. (religious title) "elder teacher" 2. (title) "chancellor, clerk, writer"; 3. (comp.) "nobleman" (<Mo.<Chin *t'ai-shih / t'âi-ṣi*).

taysï see **tayči**.

tayžï see **tayči**.

tamɣačï (title) "keeper of the seal; custom-house officer"

tamɣan (title) cf. **tamɣan-čur, tamɣan-tarqan**

tamɣan-tarqan (title) cf. **tamɣan** and **tarqan**

tarɣa (title) 1. "prince, chief of a tribe"; 2. "tax-collector" (< Mo. *daruɣa*)

tarχan see **tarqan**.

tarïqčï-bäg (title) person who distributes *qalan* on behalf of the khan

tarïm 1. (title) "an official of the subordinate states; prince"; 2. (fem. comp.) "woman or child from the khan's clan," *altun tarïm* "wife of the *χaqan*" (Räsänen, Gabain). Cf. **täñrim, terim**.

tarqan (d**arχan, tarχan**) 1. (title of the sovereign) (Khazar); cf. Qïtan *da-la-gan* "second highest official of the subtribe" (Menges: ROr. XVII, 74); W. Bang and A. von Gabain consider it as borrowing from Chinese *dat-guan* (An Ind. 502); 2. (comp.) "free man (exempt of paying taxes)" (very rare in Kzk., probably taken from Bashk. where it was very widely used even in the 18th c., cf. Ergazieva p. 211) < Mo. *darqan*

tarmač (**t⁺armač, talmač, tïlmač**) (title) "translator?"; the name or title of the Khazar general dispatched by P⁺arsbit⁺ to invade Armenia (Golden).

taw-biy (title) "a chief of the mountaineers"

täbär (title) which tribal leaders usually have

täñrim (**teñrim**) (fem. title/comp.) "highborn (noble) woman" (<*täñri* "lord, emperor" + *-m(3)*), cf. also **tarïm, terim**

tärim see **terim**.

tegin (**tekin, tigin, tikin**) (title) "male relatives of the Türk khan" (Kononov, Golden), "the closest male relatives of the khan" (László F.), "prince" (DTS), "heir to the throne, prince" (Gumilev, Golden, Doerfer), "high and old title" (Ligeti).

tekin see **tegin**.

teñrim see **täñrim**.

terim (**tärim, dirim, tirim**) (fem. title/comp.) "highborn (noble) woman" (Thúry), originates from **teñrim** (Clauson). Cf. **tarïm, täñrim**

tikin see **tegin**.

tiräk (title) "supporter" (a dignity/rank third after the *χan/qan*'s)

tiri (title?) cf. *elči-tiri* (DTS)

tirim see **terim**.

tïlmač (title) "interpreter, translator"; one of the highest title at the Pechenegs, maybe a kind of foreign minister (Németh)

toyïn (comp.) "a Buddha-priest" (<Chin.)

toyon (title) "prince" cf. Yak. *toyon* "господин; глава семьи, начальник" (JRS)

toqal (fem. comp.) "the youngest wife"

toña (comp.) "leopard; big, strong man; hero"

törä (**töre, türä, türe**) 1. (title) "prince; title of the khan's son" (Uyg., Chag., Turk.), "head of a district or town" (Shor); 2. (comp.) "respected noble man" (Crm.).

töre see **törä**.

tudun see **tuðun**.

tudun see **tutuñ**.

tuduñ see **tutuñ**.

tuduq see **tutuq**.

tuðun (**tudun, turun**) (title) "commander; person who distributes water for irrigation."

tuγan 1. (title) "ruler, chief, leader"; 2. (comp.) "relative, brother"

turun see **tuðun**.

tutay (fem. comp.) "(elder) brother and/or sister"

tutuγ see **tutuq**.

tutuχ see **tutuq**.

tutuq (**tuduq, tutuχ, tutuγ**) (title) "military leader of a district; governor of a province" (<Chin. *tu-tu < tuo-tuok*).

tutuñ (**tuduñ, tudun?**) (title) "direct representative (governor) of the Khagan; religious title"; "Chinese sources inform us that *Tudun* was a hereditary title given to officers of the government of the Kök Türks who were not of royal blood (Chavannes, Doc.). Their function was to supervise the administration of conquered lands which were left under the nominal rule of their native kings. One of the *Tudun*'s primary concerns was the control of customs duties and taxes." (Golden) (< Chin. *tu-t'ung < tuo-t'uong*)

tün-qatar (title) "night-watchman"

türä see **törä**.

türe see **törä**.

udaγan (comp.) "shamaness"

uddin see **addïn**.

uddïn see **addïn**.

ul see **oγul**.

ulan see **oγlan**.

ulï (comp.) of paternal names meaning "son of so-and-so," widely used in the 15th century. In Kzk. written sources it is often changed for Ar. *bin* (in the 18th century.) or both are used. As component of father's names, beginning from 1810, *ulï* was replaced with Central Asiatic (Tatar) written forms *oγlï~uγlï* (Ergazieva 212).

unuq see **ïnuq**.

uruñu (comp.) "combatant, warrior, fighter, ensign"

uruñu-tutuq (title) "ensign-tutuq," cf. **uruñu** and **tutuq**

uwul see **oγul**.

ūl see **oγul**.

ūs (comp.) "master" (<Trk. *usta*)

ügä (**ögä**) (title) "supreme councilor," it's recent interpretation as *ögä* is based on a false etymology (Ligeti), < Asian Avar or Mongol (Pelliot)

väli (**veli**) (comp.) "owner; master; protector; saint" (<Ar. *walï*)

vekil (title) "agent, representative" (Trkm.), "deputy, Minister of state" (Turk.)

veli see **väli**.

zada see **zäde**.

zat (fem. comp.) "child (daughter)" <P. *zād* "детеныш"

(Miller).

zāda see **zāde**.

zāde (zada, zāda, zāde) 1. (comp., fem. comp.) "child (son or daughter)"; 2. (title, fem. title) "prince, princess" <P. *zād* "детеныш" (Miller); cf. also suffix -*zada*.

zän see **Jan**.

ziebēl (title) second in dignity to the Khagan; the name or title of the Khazar ruler (most probably the ruler of the Western Kök Türks), ca. 627, after Theophanes (Golden, Khaz. 218); cf. **Jabγu ~ Jebu**

zigit see **yigit**.

žamal see **Jamal**.

žan I. 1. (comp.) "uncle"; 2. (title) "high political rank (dignity)"

žan II. see **Jan**.

žar see **yar**.

žân see **Jan**.

žän see **Jan**.

Suffixes

We preferred the term *suffix* to *affix* since both mean nearly the same. In our list consisting of about 300 items, we tried to determine the function of the suffix in question and provide some examples.

In proper, especially personal names, almost every kind of suffixes may occur. Some suffixes (e.g., diminutive-hypocoristic), however, are used much more frequently. A group of suffixes, however, is preserved in proper (personal) names only.[482] These suffixes were called *specific suffixes* by L. BESE. Non-specific suffixes are used in deriving both common nouns and proper names. Separating suffixes from this point of view would require thorough studies both in diachronic and synchronic aspects on a larger body of material.

Here we have listed the elements called *suffixoids (affixoids)* as well. They are primarily not suffixes; they only function as specific suffixes forming personal names. Some *suffixoids* are esentially shortened-contracted forms of certain personal names or secondary components (see p. LXII), e.g., *-mat~-mät, -bet, -imbet, -umbet (<Muχammet)*.

Certain suffixes are attached to shortened-contracted forms of personal names in Kazakh, Kirghiz, New Uyghur, Tatar, etc. When contracting, the name (both simple or compound) gets shortened, while only the first syllable(s) or the first sounds remain[483] and a suffix (mainly a diminutive one or a component), e.g., *-č, -qa(3), -š(1), -qan(1), -ük(1), ake* is added.[484]

List of Suffixes

-a¹   (-ä, -e, -o) den. Nvoc. / Ndim., also diminutive-hypocoristic, unproductive, e.g., *Bapa, Beke, Čeke, Čoto, Ese, Xizila, Toγana, Tükälä.*

-a²   (-ä) den. N / NPfem., Arabic feminine ending forming often female PN from male PN, e.g., *Ay-nura, Anara, Čolpona, Güla, Gül-nara, Maydana, Samara, Tamaγa.*

-a³   (-e) dev. N, dev. Adj., unproductive in Chuvash.

-a⁴   dev. Vpres. / Ger., gerundium continuitatis forming Vpres., e.g., *Ala, Birä, Tosuya.*

-ač   den. Ndim., e.g., *Baltač, Uruzač,* see -č¹.

(-äčük) den. PN, compound suffix, forms personal names only (Erdal 39), e.g., *Ilačuq, Yartačuq, Qutačuq, Simačuq?*

-aχ   den. N / Ndim, e.g., *Adayaχ, Sortanaχ, Tabaraχ,* see -aq¹.

-ay   den. Ndim., e.g., *Abizay, Aranay, Baqay, Bekey, Janay, Joloy, Jüzöy, Esey, Qadiray, Küzänäy, Sabitay, Taγanay, Umbetay,* (Tat. dial.) *Tuqiy (<Tuqay),* see -y¹.

-aka   (-eke) den. Adj./N, forms also Adjectives from Adjectives.

-aq¹   den. Ndim., also hypocoristic, e.g., *Albanaq, Bayaq, Čermišaq, Qazanaq, Qusqunaq, Sazanaq,* see -q².

-aq²   (-aχ, -eh, -äh) den. N / Ndim.?, < P. -aka?

-an¹   (-än, -en, -on, -ön) den. Ndim., also hypocoristic, e.g., *Abizan, Aqan, Baltan, Beken, Buyan, Čoqan, Jeken, Jolon, Däwläkän, Xurtan, Kükön, Toqon, Tuqan, Tükön, Uman.*

-an²   (-än) dev. Part., e.g., *Qurtaran.*

-ar   dev. Vaor./Part., e.g., *Tapar,* see -r.

-as   den. Ndim., e.g., *Boynaγas, Xapčiγas, Pastiγas,* see -š².

-aš¹   (-eš, -oš, -öš) den. N, e.g., *Bazaš, Jüzöš, Kenješ, Köböš, Qalbaγaš, Miltiγaš, Moynaγaš, Multiγaš,* see -š¹.

-aš²   (-eš) den. dim. PN, forms dim.-hypoc. and/or vocative forms of contracted PNs (Sattarov 1970, p. 213-215, Mahmutov: KzRS p. 570). For the way of contracting see the explanation at component ke., e.g., (Kzk:) *Qulaš (<Qulbadan), Maγaš (< Maγawiya),* (NUyg:) *Büwäš (<Büwi-nur), Mekäš (<Mälikä), Noqaš (<Nur-aχmet).*

-ba   dev. N, e.g., *Ayārba,* see -ma.

-ban   den. Adj., according to Erol it goes back to P. *bân* bakıcı" [attendant, guard] (Erol II, 199: Ilban), e.g., *Alaban, Sariban, Tisawban,* see **-man**.

-bas   dev. Vaor. neg., e.g., *Adabas, Munaytbas, Taldabas,* see **-maz**.

-bet   den. PN, suffixoid, forming also female names in Kirg., e.g., *Gülbet, Nurbet* (Žaparov), e.g., *Almanbet, Dostanbet, Jalmanbet, Yalmanbet,*

Maytubet, Ziyanbet, see -ïmbet.

-bïz den. N, poss. suff. 2nd p. plur., e.g., *Aɣabez?*

-č[1] (-ač, -äč, -eč, -ïč, -ič, -uč, -üč, -š, -ïš, -iš, -eš, -äš, -aš, -s, -as, -es, etc.) den. Ndim., forms also contracted PN with dim.-hypoch. meaning. The name gets shortened/contracted and only the first syllable or the first sounds remain and the suffix is added, e.g., Tat. *Nigüč < Nigmätulla, Pätüč < Fätχulla* (cf. Ahmetzjanov p. 94, Sattarov 1970, p. 213-214), e.g., *Ay-bikäč, Aqač, Baltač, Qarač.*

-č[2] (-ač, -äč, -š, -ïš, -iš, -eš, -äš -aš) dev. N, e.g., *Quwanč, Quwaniš.*

-ča[1] (-čä, -če, -čö, -ša, -še, -sa, -se) den. Ndim., also hypoc., borrowed from P., e.g., *Algitča, Boqča, Botča, Qïlča, Nurča, Onča, Tumanča.*

-ča[2] (-čä, -Ja, -Jä, -ša) den. Adj. / Adv.?, meaning "like; resembling (something)," e.g., *Bašča, Bolča, Toqča.*

-ča[3] (-čä, -Ja, -Jä) den. PNfem., PNfem.; forms female personal names from male personal names.

-ča[4] den. N, e.g., *Bašča, Yuwanča*, see -či[1].

-ča[5] den. Ndim., see -či[2].

-čaq[1] (-čäk, -Jaq, -Jaχ, -Jek, -šaq, -šek) den. N / Ndim., also hypoc., e.g., *Alɣučaq, Tanačaq, Toqtučaq, Torɣunčaq.*

-čaq[2] den. Ndim., e.g., *Qadïrčaq, Murunčaq, Satïlčaq, Susqučaq, Toqčaq*, see -čïq[1].

-čaq[3] (-čäk, -ček, -Jaq, -Jek) dev. N / Adj., Adjective of habit; he who likes doing anything, e.g., Alt. *Azïnčaq* "(s)he who likes cooking" (Šatinova 1971, 67).

-čan (-čän, -šañ, -šeñ) den. N / Adj., forms an Adjective or "a noun of connection, by adding *chan* to any word to denote continuous or frequent connection: Ex: *aghrik-chan* = one who is constantly ill, an invalid, *salla-chan* = one who always wears a turban (*salla*)" (Shaw), e.g., *Baščan, Jäyčän, Qayčan.*

-čän (-čën, -čõn, -čõn) den. Ndim., also hypoc., e.g., *Abaɣačän.*

-čä[1] den. Ndim., see -ča[1].

-čä[2] den. Adj. / Adv., see -ča[2].

-čä[3] den. PNfem., see -ča[3].

-čäk[2] den. Ndim., see -čïq[1].

-čän den. Adj., ?, e.g., *Siäkiläčän*, see -čan.

-če den. Ndim., e.g., *Betče, Xurtče, Kekelče, Kökče, Soyanče*, see -ča?[1].

-čey den. N, < -čï + -y?, e.g., *Yuwančey.*

-ček[1] den. Ndim., e.g., *Čepček, Čïñirček, Iyneček, Tüyünček*, see -čïq[1].

-ček[2] dev. Adj., e.g., *Čekülček?*, see -čïq[3].

-či den. N, e.g., *Bälgiči, Dürtči, Egïnči, Emilči,*

Yeläkči, Kilči, Qazanči, Medeči, Ötenči, Tüšekči, see -čï[1].

-čik[1] den. Ndim., e.g., *Aqïnčik, Meñgüčik, Sämänčik*, see -čïq[1].

-čik[2] den. Adj.?, see -čïq[2].

-čil den. Adj./Ndim., e.g., *Qarɣïsčil*, see -čïl.

-čin[1] den. Ndim., see -čïn[1].

-čï[1] (-či, -ču, -čü, -ča, -če, -Je, -Jï, -Ji, -Ju, -Jü, -ši, -šï) den. N, forms nomen actoris, nomen agentis; he who likes (doing) anything, e.g., *Ayuwčï, Altïnčï, Boqčï, D'aqačï, Yamčï, Qašuqčï, Maralčï, Oyïnčï, Ormančï, Sïčqančï, Tomančï, Tönče, Ulančï.*

-čï[2] (-ča) den. Ndim.?

-čï[3] (-če, -či) dev. N / PN?, e.g., *Kilče, Qalčï.*

-čïɣ den. Ndim., cf. -čïq, e.g., *Qačqïnčïɣ.*

-čïq[1] (-čik, -ček, -čuq, -čük, -Jïq?, -Jïk, -Juq, -čaq, -čäk, -sïq, -šik, -šük, -zïχ?, -žïq, -žik, -žuq) den. Ndim., e.g., *Čïñirčïq, Qadïrčïq.*

-čïq[2] (-čik) den. Adj.

-čïq[3] (-ček) dev. Adj.?

-čïl (-čil, -Jïl, -šïl, -šil) den. Adj./Ndim., meaning "like, resembling (something)," e.g., *Aqčïl, D'ayčïl, Xarbaχčïl, Nurmančïl.*

-čïn[1] (-čin, -šïn) den. Ndim.

-čïn[2] (-čin, -čän, -čen, -Jin, -Jün, -šïn) den. Adj., forms Adjectives from Nouns and Adjectives, cf. also -čan; in Pritsak's oppinion it forms tribal names expressing the belonging to the tribe, according to Rašïd-ud-Dïn it is a female suffix (Pritsak 81), e.g., *Bilikčin, Könäkčin, Siraqčin(?), Tülükčin.*

-ču[1] den. N, describing an instrument or tool.

-ču[2] den. N, e.g., *Boqču, Börüčü, Bozɣunču*, see -čï[1].

-ču[3] (-čü, -čï) dev. N, e.g., *Inanču.*

-čuq den. Ndim., e.g., *Buyančuq, Čapčuq, Ilačuq, Qawčuq, Tawčuq*, see -čïq[1].

-čun dev. Vimp., see -sïn.

-čü den. N, see -čï[1].

-čük den. Ndim., e.g., *Irčük, Yegänčük, Küzänčük, Ögäčük, Ölönčük*, see -čïq[1].

-Ja den. Adj. / Adv., e.g., *Bozja, Čayja, Qïzïlja, Nurja, Orduja*, see -ča[2].

-Jaχ den. N / Ndim., e.g., *Xïptïjaχ, Paltïjaχ, Parčajaχ, Torɣïjaχ*, see -čaq[1].

-Jaq den. N / Ndim., e.g., *Aχunjaq, Izïrɣajaq, Qasqajaq, Qïsqajaq, Turajaq*, see -čaq[1].

-Je den. N, e.g., *Ayneje, Eymïrje*, see -čï[1].

-Jek den. N / Ndim., e.g., *Čibijek, Čïñijek, Sïrjek*, see -čaq[1].

-Ji den. N, see -čï[1].

-ǰik   den. Ndim., e.g., *Denǰik*, see -čiq¹.

-ǰïn²   den. Ndim., see -čïn².

-ǰï   den. N, e.g., *Ayranǰï, Damaǰï, İlimanǰï, Qarǰï*, see -čï¹.

-ǰïq   den. Ndim., e.g., *Qundaǰïq*, see -čiq¹.

-ǰïl   den. Adj./Ndim., see -čïl.

-ǰïn²   den. Ndim., see -čïn².

-ǰu   den. N, e.g., *Yapuǰu*, see -čï¹.

-ǰuq   den. N, e.g., *Sultanǰuq*, see -čïq¹.

-ǰün¹   den. Ndim., see -čïn².

-da²   dev. Vpast., see -tï².

-day¹   den. Adj./Adv., see -tay¹.

-day²   den. Ndim., see -tay².

-day³   den. N, see -tay³.

-daq   (-daγ, -taq) den. N?, e.g., *Buzdaq*.

-dar¹   den. Ndim., only in PN from Chinese and Muslim sources of 13th-14th c. (<Mo.).

-dar³   den. Adj.?, e.g., *Temindar*, see -dār.

-das¹   den. N, e.g., *J̌uldas*, see -daš.

-daš   (-däš, -deš, -das, -des, -taš, -täš, -tas, -tes, -las, -les) den. N, forms Nouns of Association indicating that two persons have a common possession of some kind (Clauson), e.g., *Aydaš, Aldaš, İrdaš, Qaldaš, Qïldas, Nomdaš, Serdäš, Yuldaš / Žoldaš / Žoldas*.

-dān   den. Adj. / N, one who knows something (<P.), e.g., *Xoñqurdān*.

-dār   (-dar) den. Adj.?, (<P.), e.g., *Temindar*.

-däy   den. Adj./Adv., e.g., *Säläñäday, Timirday*, see -tay¹.

-de²   dev. Vpast., see -tï².

-dey   den. Adj./Adv., e.g., *Ayandey, Kögüldey, Sabadey, Tuwandey*, see -tay¹.

-deš   den. N, e.g., *Čendeš, Emeldeš*, see -daš.

-di¹   den. Adj., e.g., *Dendi, J̌eldi, Teldï*, see -lï.

-di²   dev. Vpast., e.g., *Berdi, Aq-berdi*, see -tï².

-dik¹   den. Adj., see -lïq.

-dik²   dev. Part. perf., see -tïq².

-dir   den. Adj., see -tïr.

-dï¹   den. Adj., e.g., *Amandï, J̌uldï, Qoblandï, Muzdï, Nazdï, Sazdï*, see -lï.

-dï²   dev. Vpast., see -tï².

-dïq¹   den. Adj., e.g., *Amaldïq, Ondïq*, see -lïq.

-dïq²   dev. Part. perf., e.g., *Toydïq*, see -tïq².

-dïr   den. Adj., see -tïr.

-doy   den. Adj./Adv., e.g., *Qorγoldoy*, see -tay¹.

-dök   den. Adj., e.g., *Töldök*, see -lïq.

-du¹   den. Adj., e.g., *Boqšadu, D'oldu*, see -lï.

-du²   dev. V, see -tï².

-duq¹   den. Adj., e.g., *Burunduq*, see -lïq.

-duq²   dev. Part. perf., see -tïq².

-dur   den. Adj., e.g., *Čawlïdur, Čawundur*, see -tïr.

-dü¹   den. Adj., see -lï.

-dü²   dev. Vpast., see -tï².

-dük¹   den. Adj., see -lïq.

-dük²   dev. Part. perf., see -tïq².

-dür   den. Adj., see -tïr.

-ä   see -a¹.

-ä¹   den. N / NPfem., e.g., *Melikä*, see -a¹.

-ä²   den. N voc., e.g., *Kičigä*, see -a¹.

-ä³   dev. N / Adj. / Adv., e.g., *Čömčörüyä*, see -u.

-äč¹   den. Ndim., e.g., *Erenäč*, see -č¹.

-äčük   den. PN, see -ačuq.

-äy   den. Ndim., e.g., *Bigišäy, İsäkäy, Kilmäkäy, Küzänäy, Telägäy, Tentekäy, Tiläwäy, Tuñusäy*, see -y¹.

-äk   den. N, as dim.-hypoc. suff. is also added to contracted names, e.g., *Abzäk, Küzenäk, Temiräk, Ümiräk,* (NUyg:) *Pätäk (Pati-gül), Setäk (<Setiw-aldi <Satip-aldï), Nuräk (<Nur-aχun)*, see -aq¹.

-äš¹   den. Ndim., e.g., *İtäš*, see -š¹.

-e   see -a¹.

-ey   den. Ndim., e.g., *Adamey, Amaney, Begeney, Kücükey, Tilekey, Ümitey*, see -y¹.

-ek¹   den. Ndim., e.g., *J̌igitek, İtek, Mametek, Sekizek, Ulmetek*, see -q².

-ek²   dev. N, see -q².

-eke   den. Adj./N, see -aka.

-em   den. Nposs., e.g., *İtem*, see -m¹.

-embet   den. PN, e.g., *Erembet, Bekembet*, see -ïmbet.

-enek   den. N, e.g., *Köčenek*.

-eš   den. Ndim., e.g., *Kempïreš*, see -š¹.

-gän¹   den. Ndim., e.g., *Silïpgän*.

-gän²   dev. Vpast / Part., see -γan.

-gär   (-ger?) den. Adj.?

-gen   dev. Vpast / Part., e.g., *Bergen, Aq-bergen*, see -γan.

-genä   den. Ndim. / Adj., see -qïna.

-ger   den. Adj.?, < P., e.g., *Kemäñger*, see -gär.

-gil   dev. imp. 2nd P. sing., see -qïl.

-ginä   den. Ndim. / Adj., see -qïna.

-gün   dev. N, e.g., *Belgün*, see -qïn.

-γač   den. Ndim., see -qač.

-γay   den. Ndim., e.g., *Qatpaγay, Qotïγay, Uranγay*, see -qay.

-γan   (-gän, -qan, -kän) dev. Vpast / N, a conjugational form; as a noun means repeated or habitual action, e.g., *Surγan, Toyγan*.

-γïr   (-gir, -γur, -gür, -qïr), e.g., Azgïr, Kökšägär, Alšagïr, Kemängar, Talgïr.

-γïs   dev. N, e.g., *Aylañγïs*, see -γïč.

-γus   ?, e.g., *Nurγuγus*.

-χ   den. Ndim., see -q².

-χan¹   den. dimPNfem., e.g., *Ayχan, Almaχan,*

-χan²   *Balaχan, Bibiχan, Öteχan, Sayatχan,* see **-qan¹**.

-χan²   dev. Vpast / Part., e.g., *Xapčaχan,* see **-qan²**.

-i   den. Nposs, e.g., *Afšar-eri,* see **-ï**.

-ijek   den. Ndim., e.g., *Sibijek,* see **-ïjaq?**

-iy   den. Ndim., see **-y¹**.

-im¹   den. Nposs., e.g., *Aγa-mahim, Künim, Pirim,* see **-m¹**.

-im²   den. PNfem., see **-m³**.

-im³   dev. N, see **-m⁴**.

-imbet   den. PN, e.g., *Aytimbet, Dilimbet, Kelimbet, Serimbet, Tilimbet,* see **-ïmbet**.

-iš   den. Ndim. / PN, forms dim.-hypoc. and/or vocative forms of PN as a result of contracting. For the way of contracting names see the explanation at the beginning of the chapter., e.g., *Äbiš (<Äbdiraχman), Maγiš (<Maγrifa),* see **-š¹?**

-ï¹   **(-i, -sï, -si)** den. Nposs., 3rd p. sing., e.g., *Xu-day-qulï.*

-ï²   **(-i, -u, -ü)** den. N / PN, e.g., *Gülü, Qanï, Nuru, Özü(-bek), Tinï(-bek).*

-ïjaχ   den. Ndim., see **-ïjaq**.

-ïjaq   **(-ïjaχ, -ijek?)** den. Ndim., e.g., *Qara-qïzïjaq, Tadïjaq.*

-ïy   den. Ndim., see **-y¹**.

-ïq   den. Ndim., e.g., *Amalïq, Qamrïq, Qurtïq, Marazïq, Nawruzïq, Satïq,* see **-q²**.

-ïm   den. Nposs., e.g., *Janïm, Qalïqïm, Mïratïm, Toyïm,* see **-m¹**.

-ïmbet   **(-imbet, -ïmbet, -embet?, -umbet, -mbet)** den. PN, (suffixoid) den. PN, forms personal names only, meaning "Mukhammad," probably a corruption of Ar. *Muχammad,* e.g., *Dosïmbet, Mambet; Alimbet, Qulumbetka, Yambet, Yanïmbet, Biyimbet, İlimbet, Kelimbet, Toqumbet, Yulumbet, Muχambet, Yaqšïmbet, Ulumbet, Urazïmbet.*

-ïnaq   den. Ndim., e.g., *Qïzïnaq?*

-ïnč   dev. N, e.g., *Yïqïnč.*

-ïs   den. Ndim., e.g., *Jolïs,* see **-š¹**.

-ïš   dev. N, e.g., *Sapïš I.?,* see **-š²**.

-y¹   **(-ay, -äy, -oy, -öy, -ïy, -ey)** den. Nvoc. / Ndim., also hypoc.; used for forming contracted names as well, e.g., Tat. *Apay < Γapt-ulla, Timay < Timer-šah, İsmiy < İš-möχämmät, Mämätäy < Möχämmät.,* e.g., *Aqšay, Balay, Kenjekey, Matay, Sabay, Sarïy, Satïy, Tabay, Urazay, Üzäy.*

-y²   dev. Vpres / Gerund., e.g., *Tatïy.*

-yaq   den. Ndim., e.g., *Čalbïyaq.*

-k   den. Ndim., e.g., *Aynek, Čürük, Kenčik, Tipsek,* see **-q²**.

-ka   den. Ndim., diminutive suffix of Russian origin, used also in NUyg., see **-qa1** as well, e.g., *Adika, Tabanka, Tebeneyka.*

-kä¹   den. Ndim., In Sattarov's and Žaparov's opinion it is the dial. variant of *-käy* (Sattarov 1970, p. 215, Žaparov 91), e.g., *(Tat.) Mišerkä, Özenkä, Sayïnkä, Täwkä, Tilkä;* (Kirg.) *Asake, Qake, Mïke, Sake,* see **-qa¹**.

-kä²   den. N/Nvoc., suffixoid., see **-qa³**.

-käč   den. Ndim., see **-qač**.

-käy   den. Ndim., e.g., *Alkäy, Kädäkkäy, Yawkäy, Süläkäy,* see **-qay**.

-käš   den. Ndim., e.g., *Tiñkäš, Törkäš,* see **-qač**.

-käw   den. Ndim., see **-qay**.

-kän   den. (fem.) Ndim., hypoc., e.g., *Süödärkän,* see **-qan¹**.

-ke¹   den. Ndim., perhaps a crasis of *-kiñe* (Clauson xl), e.g., *Ayanke, Aldïke, Janke, Malke, Tayke, Turduke, Üške,* see **-qa¹**.

-ke²   **(-kö)** den. PNdim, suffixoid, forms personal names only, also hypoc., used when forming contracted PNs; perhaps shortened of the component *ake / eke* (see), e.g., *Maylike, Quske, Oruske, Pekliske, Tonke.,* see **-qa³**.

-key   den. Ndim., e.g., *Abdikey, Dosïkey, Mendekey, Nurkey, Sankey, Ütekey,* see **-qay**.

-ken   den. Ndim., e.g., *Töken,* see **-qan¹**.

-kenä   den. Ndim. / Adj., e.g., *Tüskenä,* see **-qïna**.

-kene   den. Ndim. / Adj., e.g., *Eskene,* see **-qïna**.

-ker   den. Adj.?, <P., e.g., *Kerimker.*

-ki   den. Adj., e.g., *Sigidiki,* see **-qï²**.

-kiy   den. Ndim., e.g., (Tat.) *İškiy, Däwläkiy (<Däwlätkäy),* see **-qay**.

-kil   dev. imp. 2nd P. sing., see **-qïl**.

-kinä   den. Ndim. / Adj., e.g., *İškinä, Bekkinä, Betkinä, Qïzkinä,* see **-qïna**.

-kine   den. Ndim. / Adj., see **-qïna**.

-qï   den. Ndim., e.g., *Xasïtaqï?* (Yak.).

-kka   **(-kke)** den. PN, attached to Chuv. names < R. -ka?, e.g., *Māyakka.*

-ko   den. Ndim., <R. -ka?, e.g., *Toyïško,* see **-ka**.

-kö   den. Ndim/PN, see **-qa³**.

-kül   dev. imp. 2nd P. sing., see **-qïl**.

-q¹   **(-k, -aq, -äk, -ek, -ïq, -χ, -ik, -iχ, -oq, -ök, -uq, -üg, -ük)** den. N/Ndim./Adj., productive, e.g., *Ayuq, Ataq, Bayïq, İšek, Yöräk, Yulïq, Yumaq, Küčäk, Qanïq, Sibäk, Šamaq, Toraq.*

-q²   **(-k, -ak, -aq, -äk, -aχ, -iχ, -ik, -oq, -ök, -uq, -ük; -g?)** dev. N / Adj., e.g., *Salpïq. Oraq, Ötek, Ütäk.*

-qa¹   **(-kä, -ke)** den. Ndim. / PN, forming also PN from PN In Sattarov's opinion it is the dial. variant of *-qay* (Sattarov 1970, p. 215) also used in forming contracted names, e.g., *Ayqa,*

-qa[2] (-kä, -qï, -ki, -qo, -γa, -gä) dev. N?

-qa[3] (-ke, -kä, -kö) den. PNdim, suffixoid, shortened from component *ake/eke*, forming contracted vocative forms of PN from PN (Kirg., Kzk.), for the way of contracting names see the explanation at the component **ake** or at the suffix **-č**, e.g., (Tat.) *Urqa* (< *Uraz-γäli*), *Apušqa* (< *Гabd-ulla*), (Kzk:) *Ayke-žan* (<*Ay-gerim*), *Make* (<*Madina*), *Maqa* (<*Maqat*), *Säke* (<*Säbit*), *Take* (<*Tayïr*), *Täke-žan* (<*Täñir-bergen*), *Žake* (<*Žambïl*), *fem. Žake* (<*Žamal*); (Kirg:) *fem. Ayšake, Küske* (<*Küseyin*), *Tükö* (< *Tügöl-bay*), (NUyg:) *Toqa* (<*Toχt(a)-aχun*), *Zaqa* (<*Zakir-jan*), *Saqa* (<*Sal-aχun*), *Säwka* (<*Säwridin*), *Näwka* (<*Näwridin*), (fem:) *Rizka* (<*Rizwan-gül*), *Nurka* (<*Nur-büwi*).

-qač (-γač, -käč, -qaš, -käš, -qas, -käs) den. Ndim., e.g., *Abuqač, Änkäč, Balaqaš, İlkäč, Yulqas, Tiñkäč.*

-qay (-käy, -key, -γay, -gäy, -quy, -käw, -qïy, -kiy, -qa, -kä) den. Ndim., gives PN dim.-hypoc. meaning, comes from the Mo. *-qai* (<*-qan*), e.g., *Abaqay, Abïqay, Almaqay, Čïnïqay, Yaqšïqay, Qudaqay, Sïrmaqay, Tiñkäy, Uranqay.*

-qan[1] (-kän, -kǎn, -ken, -χan, -χân) den. Ndim. / PN (male and fem.), In East. T. *χa:n, χan* which was earlier considered a "title [!] for a lady, affixed to women's names' (Jarring p. 125). Suffixes *-qan* / *-kän* / *-χan* are used in most Trk. languages, among others in Uzb. and NewUyg. for forming female names, in which it may also be regarded as a suffix, a relic of ancient female grammatical gender of Altaic languages (Sadvakasov-Mahpirov, p. 34-35). The suffix *-χan* expresses respect usually added to the main part of male and female names (TrkmRS 686). Suffixes *-qan* / *-ken* form also dim.-hypoc. forms of full and contracted PNs, e.g., *Töken* < *Tölep-bergen* + *-ken, Šaken* <*Šaymerdan*. For the way of contracting names see the explanation at component **ake** and introductory notes above. Cf. also Mo. dim. suff. *-qan* / *-ken* (Cleaves 415), e.g., *Ayïmqan, Bayanqan, Keñesqan, Qallïqan, Šašlïqan, Süyümqan.*

-qan[2] (-kän, -γan, -gän) dev. Vpast / Part., e.g., *Kilgän, Tuqtaγan*, see **-γan**.

-qana den. Ndim. / Adj., e.g., *Tayqana*, see **-qïna**.

-qaš den. Ndim., see **-qač**.

-qïy den. Ndim., see **-qay**.

-qïl (-gil, -kil, -qul, -kül,) dev. imp. 2nd P. sing., forms informal imperatives, e.g., *Satqïl*.

-qïn (-kin, -qun, -kün, -γïn) dev. N, e.g., *Qačqïn, Jetkin, Köčkün.*

-qïna (-γana, -γïna, -genä, -ginä, -γuna, -χuna, -qana, -kene, -kenä, -kine, -kinä) den. Ndim. / Adj., cf. dim. *-kïña:/kiñä:* (Clauson xl), e.g., *Aygïnä, Bekkine, Bikkenä, İškenä, İškine, Küčükinä.*

-qïr (-γïr, -γar, -gär, -gir, -γur, -gür) den. Adj.?, e.g., *Azgïr, Kökšägär, Alšayïr, Kemänγar, Talγïr.*

-quy den. Ndim., see **-qay**.

-qul dev. imp. 2nd P. sing., see **-qïl**.

-la den. Adj., e.g., *Batala, Qutla*, see **-lï**.

-lač (-leč,-las, -das) den. N?, e.g., *Dimlač.*

-laγ (-laq, -lâq) den. N / Ndim., e.g., *Azlaγ.*

-lay[1] den. Adj./Adv., see **-tay**[1].

-lay[2] (-läy) den. N, allomorph of **-tay2**, forming PN with dim.-hypoch. meaning, e.g., *Qïrmalay, Mamalay, Tirmalay, Topčilay.*

-laq den. N / Ndim., cf. also **-naq(1,2)**., see **-laγ**.

-lar (-ler, -dar, -der) den. N, plur.; Very rare in proper names (Žanuzakov 120), expresses emotional emphasis on the basic meaning, e.g., Trkm. *Aylar, Yüzler* (Muhamedova 1957, 35), e.g., *Qaldar-bek, Qïzlar / Qïzdar-bek, Uldar-bek, Žandar-bek.*

-larï (-leri) den. Nposs., plur.; forms family-names, e.g., *Šauluχlarï, Šoññurlarï.*

-lāχ denN, e.g., *Oγuruolāχ.*

-läy den. N, see **-lay**[2].

-ley allomorph of **-tay2**, forming PN with dim.-hypoch. meaning, e.g., *D'ind'iley*, see **-tay**[2].

-li den. Adj., e.g., *Baγčeli, Jeñkli, Kečili, Meñli, Pirli, Ügüli*, see **-lï**.

-lig den. Adj., e.g., *Čäbäglig*, see **-lïγ**.

-lik den. Adj., e.g., *Činčeylik, Ekilik, Tekelik, Üšlik*, see **-lïq**.

-lïr den. Ndim., e.g., *Kätikälïr*, see **-lïr**.

-lï (-li, -lu, -lü, -dï, -di, -tï, -ti, -tu, -tü; -la?, -le?, -nï) den. Adj., see also lïγ, e.g., *Agalï, Burunlï, Jumalï, Mamalï, Sultanlï, Taylï, Uruslï.*

-lïγ (-lig) den. Adj./N, see also **-lï**, e.g., *Qotlïγ.*

-lïq (-lik, -luq, -lük, -dïq, -dik, -dök, -dük, -tïq, -tik, -nïq) den. Adj./N, means "like, resembling (something)," cf. **-teg**; "The adjective of likeness is formed by affixing -dik (which is subject to phonetic variations of the guttural) to a substantive: Ex: qoi-dïq =sheep-like" (Shaw),

-lïr   e.g., *Abalïq, Qazilïq, Turalïq.*

-lïr   (-lïr, -lür, -nïr, -nür) den. Ndim., e.g., *Kätikälïr.*

-lu   den. Adj., e.g., *Doruqlu, Qazlu, Toq-bawlu,* see -lï.

-lü   den. Adj., e.g., *Čeklü, Yünlü, Üslü,* see -lï.

-m¹   (-m, -ïm, -im, -em, -um, -üm) den. N / Nposs., forms 1st p. sing. possessive Nouns, e.g., *Abam, Qoyšum, Toqtum, Utam.*

-m²   den. Ndim. / PNdim., added to the short-ened-contracted PNs forming perhaps their vocative and/or hypochoristic form (for the way of contracting names see the explanation below and at the beginning of the chapter. Cf. Abulg./Desm., note No. 272: "Hâdjim n'est qu'une contraction de Hădji-Mohammed, comme on dit Ischim pour Isch Mohammed, Dostoum pour Dost-Mohammed, Nouroum pour Nour-Mohammed etc.," e.g., *Dostum (<Dost-Muχammad), Išem/Išim (<Iš-Muχammad), Xajim (<Xaji-Muχammad), Qušïm, Nurum (<Nur-Muχammad).*

-m³   (-äm, -im, -um, -üm) den. PNfem., female suffix used mainly in titles and secondary components, it may be a relic of denoting fe-male gender in Altayic languages (Kononov, Gr. Uzb. p. 71, Sadvakasov-Mahpirov pp. 34-35, Ščerbak, Očerki, p. 9), e.g., *(fem. comp:)* -begim, χanïm, -täñrim, -terim, (NUyg:) *Ayšäm, Ay-nuräm, Saniyäm, Gülüm, Büwüm,* (Kirg:) *Ayïm, Begim, Gülüm, Egem, Qanïm, Nurum, Šayïm.*

-m⁴   (-ïm, -im, -em,-um, -üm) dev. N, meaning a single action or sometimes a concrete object., e.g., *Qalïm, Kötem, Ülem.*

-maq   (-mäk, -mek, -mïq) dev. N/ Vinf., forms Abstract Nouns, e.g., *Aymaq, Aytmaq, Baramïq, Qïrmaq.*

-man   (-män, -men, -mön, -ban, -bän, -pan, -pän, -pen) den. Adj., forms also intensive Adjectives from Adjectives. Its origin is still controversial. Sattarov derives the suff. -man from the Ir. suff. -mänd., e.g., *Aqman, Alman, Alaban, Birmän, Sarïban, Dawletman, Qaldaqpan, Qoyman, Qurman, Oručman, Toyman, Toqman, Türkmön, Uqman.*

-mas   dev. Vaor. neg., e.g., *Küčmäs, Qalmas, Sana-mas, Satmas, Toymas, Toñmas, Ülmäs,* see -maz.

-mat   (-mät, -met) den. PN, suffixoid, forms per-sonal names only, meaning "Muχammad," a corruption of Ar. *Mukhammad* (Sattarov, Žanuzakov, Žaparov). Used also as a prefixoid, e.g., in modern Uyghur as in *Metsalï < Muχemmed Salih, Mettursun < Muhemmed*

Tursun, etc. (Taklamakanlı pp. 206, 208), cf. also -ïmbet, e.g., *Bekmat / Bekmet, Ermat, Yarmet, Qulmat, Niyazmat, Nurmat, Nurmet, Šermat, Tašmat, Toqmet.*

-maz   (-mäz, -mes, -mas, -bas) dev. Vaor. neg., e.g., *Satmaz, Taymaz.*

-mbet   den. PN, e.g., *Berdimbet, Qutlumbet, Tatlïm-bet, Ulumbet,* see -ïmbet.

-mäk   dev. Vinf. / N, see -maq.

-män   den. Adj., e.g., *Keldemän, Kenetmän,* see -man.

-mäs   dev. Vaor. neg., e.g., *Ürkmäs, Ütmäs,* see -maz.

-mät   den. PN, e.g., *Yarmät, Yawmät, Tiläwmät,* see -mat.

-me   dev. N, e.g., *Tileme,* see -ma.

-mek   dev. Vinf. / N, e.g., *Köčmek,* see -maq.

-men   den. Adj., e.g., *Edgümen, Külmen,* see -man.

-mes   dev. Vaor. neg., e.g., *Tölemes,* see -maz.

-met   den. PN, e.g., *Aγammet, Berdimet, Nurmet, Toymet, Ulmet,* see -mat.

-mis   dev. V. / Part., outdated in Kzk., see -mïš.

-miš   dev. V. / Part., e.g., *Tölemiš, Ütmiš,* see -mïš.

-mïq   dev. Vinf. / N, e.g., *Baramïq,* see -maq.

-mïs   dev. V. / Part., outdated in Kzk., nowadays used only in dialects, e.g., *Suramïs,* see -mïš.

-mïš   (-mïs, -miš, -mis) dev. V. / Vpast / Part., It was used in Tatar of 17th-18th c. (Ahmetzjanov p. 91). In the late 19th and early 20th centuries it was still productive in Kazakh publicism, but nowadays it is used in dialects only (Žanuzakov p. 111)., e.g., *Jïlamïs, Kilmeš, Qarmïš, Qïdïrmïš, Ötömüš, Tapmïš, Tilemiš, Toqtomuš, Tölömüš, Tumïš.*

-mon   den. Adj., e.g., *Toqomon,* see -man.

-n   (-ïn, -in, -un, -an, -än) den. N / Ndim.?, e.g., *Atan, Kükän, Tömän, Tuqan.*

-n³   (-ïn, -in, -un) dev. Ger., e.g., *Torulän.*

-naχ   den. Adj., e.g., *Xasχanaχ,* see -naq¹.

-naq¹   (-naχ, -näk) den. Adj., see -lïq.

-naq²   den. Ndim., compound dim. suff. < -γïna + -aq?, e.g., *Buznaq.*

-nči   (-nčï, -ïnčï, -inči,) den. Num., see -nčï.

-nčï   (-nči, -ïnčï, -inči, -nJi) den. Num., froms Ordi-nals.

-nJi   den. Num., e.g., *IkinJi,* see -nčï.

-nïr   den. Ndim., hypoc., e.g., *Uybännïr,* see -lïr.

-nür   den. Ndim., e.g., *Noyonnür,* see -lïr.

-ñ   den. Nposs., poss. suff. 2nd p. Sing., e.g., *Tüköñ.*

-o   see -a¹.

-oy   den. Nvoc. / Ndim., e.g., *Qošoy,* see -y.

-oy   den. Ndim., see -y¹.

-oq   den. Ndim., e.g., *Qoyonoq,* see -q².

-ōn	dev. Ger., e.g., *Čočoyōn*.
-öy	den. Ndim., see **-y**[1].
-ök	den. Ndim., e.g., *Ölbözök*, see **-q**[2].
-öš	den. Ndim., e.g., *Kököš, Kötönöš*, see **-š**[1].
-p	(**-ïp, -ep**) dev. Ger., e.g., *Barïp, Küčep, Ütäp, Žarïlqap*.
-pa	dev. N, see **-ma**.
-pa	dev. Vaor. neg., see **-ma**.
-pan[1]	den. Adj., e.g., *Aytpan, Bekpan, Boqpan, Čarïqpan, Espan, Qošpan, Taspan?, Tospan, Uwaqpan*, see **-man**.
-pan[2]	(**-pän**) dev. N, e.g., *Danïspan*, see **-ban**.
-pas	dev. Vaor. neg., e.g., *Adabas, Munaytbas, Taldabas*, see **-maz**.
-r	(**-ar, -är, -er, -ïr, -ir, -or, -ör, -ur, -ür**) dev. Vaor. / Part. / N / Adj., e.g., *Abar, Betär, Tuwar, Yäšär, Kiler*.
-s[1]	den. Ndim., e.g., *Töles?*, see **š**[1].
-s[2]	dev. N, e.g., *Teläs, Töles?*, see **š**[2].
-sa	den. N, e.g., *Mawsa*.
-saq	(**-saχ**) ?, e.g., *Baysaq*.
-sin	dev. Vimp., see **-sïn**.
-siz	den. N, e.g., *Čensiz, Tergewsiz*, see **-sïz**.
-sï	den. Num., poss. suff. 3rd p. Sing., e.g., *Aγasï*.
-sïl	(**-sul**) den. Ndim.?/ den. Adj., cf. **-čïl**, e.g., *Baysïl*.
-sïmaq	den. Adj., "like, similar, resembling something," e.g., *Baysïmaq, Biysïmaq*.
-sïman	den. Adj., "like, similar, resembling something," e.g., *Qoysïman, Qulziman*.
-sïn	(**-sin, -sen, -sun, -sün, -čun(?)**) dev. Vimp, e.g., *Alsïn, Toysïn, Toqtasïn, Ülsen*.
-sïz	(**-siz, -suz, -hïð**) den. N / Adj., e.g., *Atsïz, Burunsïz, Qadïrsïz, Qayγïsïz, Sansïz*.
-sun	dev. Vimp., e.g., *Aγlasun*, see **-sïn**.
-suz	den. N, e.g., *Гuyruqsuz, Qapusuz, Muñsuz*, see **-sïz**.
-sün	dev. V., see **-sïn**.
-süz	den. N, e.g., *Elsüz*, see **-sïz**.
-š[1]	(**-s, -as, -aš, -äš, -äs, -eš, -es, -iš, -ïš, -ïs, -üš**) den. N
-š[2]	(**-s, -as, -aš, -äš, -äs, -eš, -es, -iš, -ïš, -ïs, -üš**) den. Ndim., forms also contracted PN with dim.-hypoc. meaning. The name gets shortened/contracted and only the first syllable or the first sounds remain and the suffix is added, e.g., Tat. *Ïbräš* < *İbragim, Bibeš* < *Bibi-žamal* (Ahmetzjanov 94), e.g., *Adaš, Apas, Baqaš, Baltaš, Čuraš, Dadaš, Qadaš, Teläš, Timäš, Tumas, Ütäš*.
-š[3]	(**-ïš, -iš, -uš, -üš, -yïš, -yiš**) dev. N
-š[4]	dev. N, e.g., see **-č**[2].
-ša[1]	den. Ndim., see **-ča**[1].
-ša[2]	den. Adj. / Adv., e.g., *Batïrša, Tuñaša, Orïnša,*

	Tazša, see **-ča**[2].
-šaq	den. N / Ndim., see **čaq**[1].
-še	den. Ndim., e.g., *Jiyrenše, Näwše*, see **-ča**[1].
-ši	den. N, e.g., *Čerekši, Yükši, Tümenši*, see **-čï**[1].
-šil	den. Adj./Ndim., see **-čïl**.
-šï	den. N, see **-čï**[1].
-šïχ	den. Ndim., e.g., *Awïlšïχ*, see **-čïq**[1].
-šïq	den. Ndim., see **-čïq**.
-šïl	den. Adj./Ndim., see **-čïl**.
-šïn	den. Adj., e.g., *Aqšïn*.
-šïn[1]	den. Ndim., see **-čïn**[1].
-šuq	den. Ndim., e.g., *Qoyšuq, Topšuq*, see **-čïq**[1].
-šük	den. Ndim., e.g., *Külšük*, see **-čïq**[1].
-ta	den. Adj., e.g., *Toyta.*, see **-lï**.
-tay[1]	(**-day, -däy, -dey, -doy?, -täy, -tey, -dïy, -tïy, -toy? -lay, -nay**) den. Adj./Adv., meaning "like, similar"; In Kononov's opinion (Gr. UzbJa. p. 285) it is an "onomo-affix" [=specific affix deriving names] which is used in diminutive or comparative function in derived names (see ST 1975, No. 2, p. 85.) < Mo. Adjective suffix *-dai* (Pelliot, Notes 178), e.g., *Boqtay, Qastïy, Qoryoldoy, Sollontoy*.
-tay[2]	(**-day**) den. Ndim. / Nvoc., expresses also hypocoristic, polite addressing (Kzk.); A. N Kononov named it as "onomoaffix" [=specific affix deriving names] used in dim. function (see ST 1975, No. 2, p. 85) which may be a „component," more correctly a specific suffix forming personal names without adding any special meaning (Žanuzakov p. 11, 113). As a non-specific suffix it can be added to common nouns meaning human beings [and seemingly to personal names] only (KzRS 570, Kononov, Gr. Uzb. 285). < Mo. *-dai* / *-dei*, e.g., *Quwantay, Quwanday*.
-tay[3]	(**-day**) den. N, forms nouns of masculine gender in Mongol (Sattarov 174) from ethnonyms, e.g., *Majartai* "male Hungarian," *Asudai* "male Ossetian/Ias," *Barqudai* "Barqu man" vs. *Barqujin* "Barqu woman"; <Mo. Adj. suff. *-tai/-dai* (Pelliot, Notes 178); in Pritsak's opinion it is a collective suffix which forms tribal names (Pritsak 81).
-tan	(**-tän**) den. Ndim.
-tanï	(**-täni**) den. Ndim.
-taš	see **-daš**.
-tän	den. Ndim., e.g., *Čïbïstän*.
-täy	den. Adj./Adv., e.g., *Üörüktäy*, see **-tay**[1].
-tän	den. Ndim., see **-tan**.
-täni	den. Ndim., see **-tanï**.
-täš	den. N, see **-daš**.
-tey	den. Adj./Adv., e.g., *Aχtey, Devetey*, see **tay**[1].

-tek	den. Adj., meaning "like, similar" cf. -tay¹, e.g., *Aytek, Čiytek, İštek, Qoytek, Nurtek.*
-tek	**(-teg)** den. Adj./Adv.
-tï¹	den. Adj., e.g., *Beysti, Qara-attï, Sütti,* see -lï.
-ti²	dev. Vpast., see -tï².
-tik	den. Adj., e.g., *Čettik, Jemtik,* see -lïq.
-tir	den. Adj., see -tïr.
-tï¹	den. Adj., e.g., *Tïštï,* see -lï.
-tï²	**(-dï, -di, -du, -dü, -ti, -tu, -tü, -da, -de)** dev. Vpast, conjugational suffix; variants -da < -dï; -de < -di can be seen in several names (mainly in Russian sources), e.g., *Čaqtï, Čïqïštï.*
-tïy	den. Adj./Adv., e.g., *Qastïy,* see -tay¹.
-tïq¹	den. Adj., e.g., *Jïltïq, Tïntïq,* see -lïq.
-tïq²	**(-dik, -dïq, -tik, -duq, -dük, -tuq, -tük)** dev. Part. perf., e.g., *Taptïq.,* see -dïq.
-tïr	**(-dïr, -dir, -dur, -dür, -tir, -tur, -tür)** den. Adj.?, collective suff. in Mo. which forms tribal names (Pritsak 81), e.g., *Bayïndïr, Bayandur, Čawlïdur, Čawundur, Jawuldur, Moldur.*
-toy	den. Adj./Adv., e.g., *Sollontoy,* see -tay¹.
-tu¹	den. Adj., e.g., *Aqïstu, Čoqtu,* see -lï.
-tu²	dev. Vpast., see -tï².
-tur	den. Adj., see -tïr.
-tü¹	den. Adj., e.g., *Tüktü,* see -lï.
-tü²	dev. Vpast., see -tï².
-tür	den. Adj., see -tïr.
-u	**(-ï, -i, -ü; -a, -ä)** dev. N, cf. -a, -ä;, e.g., *Oru, Oqšaw.*
-uy	den. Ndim., see -y¹.
-uq¹	**(-ük)** den. Ndim., e.g., *Qurmašuq,* see -q².
-uq²	dev. N, e.g., *Yumuq, Sontōyuq,* see -q².
-um¹	den. Nposs., e.g., *Nurum, Qošum, Qutum,* see -m¹.
-um²	dev. N, see -m³.
-umbet	den. PN, e.g., *Dosumbet, Qulumbet, Toqumbet,* see -ïmbet.
-uš	**(-ïš, -iš, -uš, -üš, -yïš, -yiš)** dev. N, e.g., *Kün-doγuš,* see -š².
-uš¹	dev. N, e.g., *Kün-doγuš,* see -š¹.
-uw	**(-üw, -u, -ū, -ü, -w)** dev. N, (nomen actionis).
-ū	dev. N, see -uw.
-ü	dev. N, e.g., *Jiyü,* see -u.
-üg¹	den. Ndim., see -q, -g? / -k?².
-üg²	dev. N, e.g., *Sevinüg,* see -q².
-üy	den. Ndim., see -y¹.
-ük	den. Ndim., forms also contracted PN with dim.-hypoch. meaning. e.g., Tat. *İšük < İš-möχämmät, İsmük < İsmäγïyl* (Ahmetzjanov p. 94), e.g., *Tümänük,* see -q².
-üm¹	den. N / Nposs., e.g., *Küčüm,* see -m¹.
-ümbet	den. PN, e.g., *Döšümbet,* see -ïmbet.
-ŭk	dev. Vpart., e.g., *Čölkŭk.*
-w¹	den. N?, e.g., *Ejew.*
-w²	dev. N?, e.g., *Oqšaw,* see -uw.
-zïχ	den. Ndim., e.g., *Uqazïχ,* see -čïq¹?.
-žik	den. Ndim., e.g., *Telžïk,* see -čïq¹.
-žïq	den. Ndim., e.g., *Sïrγāžïq,* see -čïq¹.
-žuq	den. Ndim., e.g., *Qoržuq, Quržuq,* see čïq -šuq? / -čuq¹?.

Abbreviations

Language Abbreviations

Alt.	1. Common name of the Altay Turks (and their literary language) living in the Altay and Kuzneckij Alatau mountain area in the Gorno-Altaj (Mountain Altay) Autonomous Republic in Siberia; formerly called Oyrot (1932-1948); 2. Altay-Kizhi, Altay-Kishi, the Southern dialect of the above-mentioned Altay language
Alt.(Kmd.)	Kumandu (Kumandi, Kumandin), formerly Bijskij Kalmyk, dialect of the Altay language
Alt.(Leb.)	Lebed (Qū-kiži, Čalqandu-/Šalqandu-kiži), dialect of the Altay language
Alt.(Tel.)	Teleut (Telenggut, Telenget, Belyj Kalmyk, Gornyj Kalmyk), dialect of the Altay language
Alt.(Tuba)	Tuba/Tuva/Tuma(-Kizhi), Yïš-kiži, earlier Černevye Tatary, dialect of the Altay language
Ar.	Arabic
Arin	see **Hak.(Kacha)**
Arm.	Armenian
Arm.-Kipch.	Armeno-Kipchak (Armeno-Cuman)
Az.	Azeri (Azarbaijani, Azerbaidjani, Azerbeidzhani)
Az.(Ayn.)	Aynallu (Äynallu), archaic dialect of Azarbayjani (Southern Persia)
Az.(Kashk.)	Kashkay, dialect of Azarbayjani
Balk.	Balkar (Balqar, Malqar)
Bashk.	Bashkir (Baškir, Bašqort, Bašqurt)
Bulg.	Bulghar; data from *Jusupov* and *Epigr. Bulg.* till 1360
Bur.	Buryat
Chag.	Chaghatay or Old Uzbek
Cher.	Cheremis (Mari)
Chul.	Chulim or Chulym Tatar
Chul.(Küer.)	Küerik, dialect of Chulim
Chuv.	Chuvash
Crm.	Crimean, Turkic language of the Crimea either Crimean Tatar or Crimean Turkish; used when there is no exact reference to the language in the source
Crm.(Tat.)	Crimean Tatar
Crm.(Turk.)	Crimean Turkish
East.T.	Eastern Turki (East Turki, Eastern Turkic)
East.T.(Tar.)	Taranchi, an Eastern Turki dialect
Gag.	Gagauz
Georg.	Georgian
Hak.	Hakas (Khakas), earlier Abakan Tatars, Minusa Tatars (Tatars of Minusinsk)
Hak.(Blt.)	Beltir, dialect of Hakas
Hak.(Kacha)	Kacha, dialect of Hakas and the former *Arins* (Tumaševa)
Hak.(Koyb.)	Koybal, dialect of Hakas
Hak.(Kyz.)	Kyzyl, dialect of Hakas
Hak.(Sag.)	Sagay (Saghai), dialect of Hakas
Hak.(Shor)	Shor, dialect of Hakas in the district of Taštyp
Hung.	Hungarian
Ir.	Iranian
Kab.	Kabardin
Kalm.	Kalmyk
Kar.	Karaim
Kar.(Crm.)	Crimean Karaim
Kar.(H.)	Karaim from Halich

Kar.(L.)	Karaim from Lutsk
Kar.(T.)	Karaim from Troki
Karakh.	Karakhanid
Karch.	Karachay
Karg.	Karagass, self-designation Tofa (Tofalar, Tubalar), earlier a dialect of Tuva
Kbalk.	Karachay-balkhar
Khal.	Khaladj
Khorezm.	Khorezmian (Chwarasmian)
Khorezm./Chag.	data from the transitional period of 1400-1450, cf. **Khorezm.** and **Chag.**
Kipch.	Kipchak-type old and modern languages in general
Kirg.	Kirghiz, earlier Kara Kirghiz, Dikokamennyj Kirgiz, Burut
Kkalp.	Karakalpak
Kmk.	Kumuk (Kumyk, Kumük)
Kuman	(Coman / Cuman, Koman), Kipchak-type language of the Desht-i Kipchak before the Mongol invasion and that of the Kumans in Hungary
Kzk.	Kazakh, Kazak, earlier Kirghiz, Kirghiz-kaysak, Kirghiz-kazak
Ma.	Mandshu
Maml.	Mamluk, Mameluk (Mamlük), middle Turkic language of mixed (Kipchak, Oghuz) character
Mo.	Mongol
Mordv.	Mordva
MT	Middle Turkic
Nog.	Nogay (Noγay), Nagay (in some Russian sources)
NP.	New Persian
NUyg.	New Uyghur (Uighur), Uyghur Modern
NUyg.(Lob.)	Lobnor, a New Uyghur dialect
Oghuz	Oghuz-type language in general; data taken from an Oghuz-type source with or without exact time of occurrence
Oghuz/Trkm.	data from *Abulg.* (13th c.), *DQorq.* (14th c. - 15th c.), cf. **Oghuz** and **Trkm.**
Osm.	see **Turk.**
OT	Old Turkic, common termin for Uyghur, Türk(ü), Karluk, Karakhanid etc.
Oyr.	see **Alt.**
P.	Persian
Pecheneg	Pecheneg
R.	Russian
Selj.	Seljuk
Shor	Shor, dialects: Kondom, Mras, Aladag, see also **Hak.(Shor)**
Skr.	Sanskrit
Tadj.	Tadjik
Tat.	Kazan Tatar (from 16th c.)
Tat.(Bar.)	Baraba Tatar, dialect of Siberian Tatar
Tat.(Dobr.)	Dobrudja Tatar, dialect of Crimean Tatar
Tat.(GH)	Kipchak-type language of the Desht-i Kipchak and the Golden Horde (till 16th c.); transitive data from *Jusupov* and *Epigr. Bulg.* after 1400
Tat.(Ishim)	Ishim Tatar, dialect of Siberian Tatar
Tat.(Kasim.)	Tatar of Kasimov
Tat.(Lit.)	Tatar of Litvania
Tat.(Mish.)	Misher (Mishar) Tatar
Tat.(Sib.)	Siberian Tatar, a dialectal branch spoken by the Tatars of Western Siberia
Tat.(Tara)	Tara Tatar (Tarlyk, Tatary Tarskie), dialect of Siberian Tatar
Tat.(Tob.)	Tatar of Tobol, dialect of Siberian Tatar
Tat.(Tüm.)	Tatar of Tümen, dialect of Siberian Tatar
Teptär	a transitional dialect between Tatar and Bashkir languages
Tiptär	a transitional dialect between Tatar and Bashkir languages

Tofa(lar)	see **Karg.**
Trk.	Turkic languages in general
Trkm.	Turkmen (Türkmen, Turkoman)
Tung.	Tunghuz
Turk.	Turkish ancient (14th-19th c.) and modern, Anatolian Turkish, Turkish of Turkey, Osmanli (Osm.), Ottoman at some authors
Türk	Old Turkic (Türkü at Clauson)
Tuv.	Tuva, Tuba, Tuvan, Tuvinian; earlier: Soyon, Soyot, Tannu-Tuva, Uryankhay
Uyg.	Uyghur (Uighur)
Uzb.	Uzbek (Özbeg, Özbek)
Yak.	Yakut (Saχa)
Yürük	Turkish language of the nomadic Yürüks of Anatolia and the Balkans
YUyg.	Yellow Uyghur

Other Abbreviations

A	Attribute
abl.	Ablative case
acc.	Accusative case
Adj	Adjective
Adv	Adverb
aff.	affix
aor.	Aorist
c.	century
ca.	circa (Latin); around
caus.	Causative (form of verb)
cf.	confer (Latin), compare
co-op.	Co-operative (form of verb), cf. **Recip.**
comp.	Component; mainly a secondary component of personal names
compar.	Comparative (form or suffix)
dat.	Dative case
den.	Denominal, derived from a noun
desid.	Desiderative (form of verb)
dev.	deverbal, derived from a verb
dial.	dialect, dialectal form
dim.	Diminutive (noun, name or suffix)
e.g.	exempli gratia (Latin), for instance
ed.	edited; editor
eds.	editors
EN	Ethnical name
et al.	et alii (Latin), and others
etc.	et cetera (Latin), and others
excl.	exclamation
fem.	nomen femininum (Latin); female (feminine) name
ff.	and the following pages
fig.	figurative
folkl.	The bearer of the name is a mythical hero, not a real (existing) person, or someone who is mentioned in the folklore (in a folk-tale, a folk-song, etc.)
fut.	Future tense
gen.	Genitive case
Ger.	Gerund
hypoc.	Hypocoristic / endearing form of a name; suffix forming hypocoristic / endearing names
ibid.	ibidem (Latin), in the same place (of source)
id.	idem (Latin), the same (meaning identical with the previous)
imp.	Imperarive (mood of verb)
ind.	indefinite
inf.	Infinitive (of verb)
instr.	Instrumental case
l. cit.	see loc. cit.
lit.	literal sense.
loc.	Locative case
loc. cit.	locus citati (Latin), place cited
N	Noun
n	nominal
Ndim.	Diminutive form of noun
neg.	negative (form of verb)

Num.	Numeral
Nvoc.	Vocative form of noun
O	Object (Direct)
op. cit.	opus citati (Latin), source cited
opt.	Optative form of verb
ord.	ordinal
OrdNum.	ordinal Numeral.
p.	page
P	Predicate
Part.	Participle
pass.	passive form of verb
perf.	perfectum (Latin), perfect
pers.	person
plur.	plural
PN	Proper, or personal name (in general)
PNfem.	Feminine (female) personal name
PNm.	Masculine personal name
poss.	possessive (form, suffix)
pp.	pagines (Latin), pages
pres.	resent tense
publ.	published
recip.	Reciprocal form of of verb, cf. co-op.
S	Subject
sing.	singular
suff.	Suffix; for more detailed information and references on the suffix in question see the section SUFFIXES.
TN	Toponym, place name
transl.	translation, translator, translated
V	Verb
voc.	Vocative form of noun

Bibliographical Abbreviations
(Bibliography) [*]

AAnt.	*Acta Antiqua Academiae Scientiarum Hungariae.* Budapest.
ABAW	*Abhandlungen der Berliner Akademie der Wissenschaften.* Berlin.
Abdimuratov	Abdimuratov, K., *Počemu tak govorim?* (Iz istorii toponimii Karakalpakistana). Nukus 1965.
Abdimuratov 1970	Abdimuratov, K., *Počemu tak nazvano?* (Na materialah karakalpakskoj toponimii). Nukus 1970, 129 pp.
Abdullaev	Abdullaev, F. A., *Kiši âtlarïnïn qïsqartïš usullarï*: **Özbek tili wä ädäb. mäsäläläri** (1960, No. 2).
Abramzon, Êtn.	Abramzon, S. M., *Êtničeskij sostav kirgizskogo naselenija Severnoj Kirgizii*: **TKAÊÊ** IV (1960), pp. 3-137.
Abramzon, Rožd.	Abramzon, S. M., *Roždenie i detstvo kirgizskogo rebenka*: **SMAÊ** XII (1949), pp. 78-138.
Abramzon-Sulejmanov	Abramzon, S. M. - Sulejmanov, Ê., *Byt kolhoznikov kirgizskih selenij Tarhan i Čičkan.* Moskva 1958.
Abulfar.	Pocochio, Edvardo (ed.), *Historia compendiosa Dynastiarum authore Gregorio Abul-Pharajio.* Arabice edita, et Latine versa ab –. Oxoniae 1663.
Abulfar./Budge	Budge, E. A. W. (ed., transl.), *The Chronography of Gregory Abu'l-Faraj 1225-1286, the Son of Aaron, the Hebrew Physician Commonly Known as Bar Hebraeus,* transl. from the Syriac by - -. Vol. I. English Translation. Oxford 1932.
Abulfar. Or.	Pocochio, Edvardo (ed.), *Tārīχ muχtaṣar al-duval.* Historia orientalis Gregorii Abu'l-Faragii. Ed. ab –. Oxoniae 1663.
Abulfidā	Adler, I. G. Chr. (ed.), *Abulfedae Annales Muslemici Arabice et Latine.* Op. et stud. Io. Jacobi Reiskii. Ed. –. I-V. Hafniae 1789-1794.
Abulfidā: RHCHor I	de Slane, Baron MacGuckin (transl.), *Ismail ibn Ali Abulfidā: Ta'rikh* (Mukhtasar fi akhbar al-bašar): **RHCHor** I (1872), pp. 1-186.
Abulg./Desm.	Desmaison, le Baron (publ., transl.), *Histoire des mongole et des tatares par Aboul-Ghazi Behadour khan.* Publ. trad. et annotée par –. Tome II. Traduction. SPb. 1874. (Reprinted in 1970.).
Abulg./Kon.	Kononov, A. N. (ed.), *Rodoslovnaja turkmen. Sočinenie Abu-l-Gazi hana hivinskogo.* Moskva-Leningrad 1958.
Abulg./Rom.	Romanzoff, Nicolai de (ed.), *Abulghasi Bahadür Chani Historia Mongolorum et Tatarorum,* nunc primum tatarice edita auctoritate et memificentia –. Casani MDCCCXXV.
Abulg./Sabl.	Sablukov, C. S. (transl.), Katanov, N. F. (introd.), *Rodoslovnoe drevo tjurkov. Sočinenie Abul-Gazi.* Perevod i predislovie –. S poslesloviem i primečanijami –. Kazan' 1906.
Abū Šāma	Barbier de Meynard, A. C. (ed., transl.), *Shihab al-Din Abu Shama: Muntakhabāt min Kitāb ar-Rawḍatein fī Akhbar id-Dawlatein wa-ssalāḥiyya*: **RHCHor** IV-V (1896-1906). (New edition by A. Hilmy. Cairo 1957-).
Acar	Acar, Kenan, *Türkiye Türkçesinde Bulunmayan veya Az Bulunan Kırım Tatar Adları*: **Türk Dili** 520 (1995), pp. 421-423.
Acaroğlu 1988	Acaroğlu, M. Türker, *Bulgaristan'da Türkçe Yer Adları Kılavuzu.* Ankara 1988. (Kültür ve Turizm Bakanlığı Millî Folklor Araştırma Dairesi, y.: 89, Halk Edebiyatı Dizisi: 12).
Acaroğlu 1991	Acaroğlu, M. Türker, *Gagauzca'da Takma Adlar, Soyadları, Yer Adları*: **Türk Dünyası Araştırmaları** 72 (1991), pp. 111-128.
ADAW	*Abhandlungen der Deutschen Akademie der Wissenschaften zu Berlin.* Klasse für Sprachen, Literatur und Kunst. Berlin.
Adilov - Sadykov	Adilov, M. A. - Sadykov, Z., *Ob azerbajdžanskoj antroponimii*: **SovT** (1971, No. 3.).
ADTCFD	*Ankara Üniversitesi Dil ve Tarih-Coğrafya Fakültesi Dergisi.* Ankara 1942-.
AGWG	*Abhandlungen der Königlichen Gesellschaft der Wissenschaften zu Göttingen,* Philologisch-historische Klasse, Neue Folge. Göttingen.
AH	Caferoğlu, A., *Abû-Hayyân, Kitâb al-İdrâk li-Lisân al-Atrâk.* İstanbul 1931.

---

[*] The bibliography contains approximately 1,400 items.

Ahbar   Lügal, Necati (transl.), *Sadruddîn ebu'l-Hasan ʿAli ibn Nasir ibn ʿAli el-Hüseynî Ahbâr üd-Devlet is-Selçukiyye*. Muhammed İqbal'in 1933de Lahor'da neşrettiği metinden tercüme eden –. Ankara 1943, 150 pp.

Ahlat   Şerif, Muallim Aptürrahim, *Ahlat kitabeleri*. Yazan: –. İstanbul 1932.

Ahmed   Ahmed, Salahuddin, *A Dictionary of Muslim Names*. London 1999, 351 pp.

Ahmetzjanov   Ahmetzjanov, M., *Tatarskie šedžere*. Issledovanie tatarskih šedžere v istočnikovedčeskom i lingvističeskom aspektah po spiskam XIX-XX vv. Glava IV. Analiz antroponimov v šedžere. Kazan 1991, pp. 77-113.

Ahmetzjanov 1980   Ahmetzjanov, M. I., *Drevnetatarskie ličnye imena v rodoslovnyh zapisjah*: **Issl. jazyka.** (Kazan' 1980), pp. 124-136.

AI   *Akty otnosjaščiesja k istorii Južnoj i zapadnoj Rossii (1361-1665)*, sobrannye i izdannye Arheografičeskoju Kommissieju. I-XV. Stpbg.

Aynī: RHCHor II/1   al-ʿAynī, Badr al-Dīn, *Muntakhabāt min al-ʿIqd al-Ǧumān* (Extracts from al ʿIqd al-Ǧuman): **RHCHor** II/1 (1876), pp. 183-250.

Aynī/Tizeng. I   al-ʿAynī, Badraddīn, *ʿIqd-al-ǧumān*: **Tizeng. I**, pp. 475-535.

Aysan - Tuncay   Aysan, A. - Tuncay, S., *Türk Adları Kılavuzu*: Dilimizde Kadın ve Erkek Adları. Ankara 1981, 175 pp.

Aker   Aker, M. Cavid, *Muğla'da Adlarla İlgili Gelenek ve İnanmalar*: **Türk Folklor Araştırmaları** 132 (6) (1960), pp. 2178-79.

Aqsar./Tur.   Turan, Dr. Osman (ed.), *Aksaraylı Mehmed oğlu Kerīmüddin Mahmud: Müsameret ül-ahbār*. Mogollar zamanında Türkiye selçukluları tarihi. Neşreden –. Ankara 1944, 61+366 pp. (Türk Tarih Kurumu Yayınlarından III/I).

Aqsar./Iş.   Işıltan, Fikret, *Die Seltschukengeschichte des Akserayi*. Leipzig 1943. (Sammlung Orientalischer Arbeiten 12. Heft).

Al-Muχibbī/Tizeng. I   al-Muḥibbī, Taqīaddīn ʿAbdarraḥmān al-Qaḍawī, *Tatqīf at-taʿrīf bi'l-muṣṭalaḥ*: **Tizeng. I**, pp. 331-351.

Alatyr.   *Alatyrskie krepostnyja Knigi 1737-1744 godov*: **Letop. ZAK** III (1864), pp. 134-176.

Aliev   Aliev, Tasan Rafi, *Lingvističeskie i ěkstralingvističeskie faktory v antroponimii* Na materiale tjurkskih jazykov: azerb., uzb., kazah., kirgiz., tatar. i baškirskoj. Avtoref. dis. doktora filol. nauk. Institut jazykoznanija AN Kaz. SSR. Alma-Ata 1989, 48 pp.

ALingu.   *Acta Linguistica Academiae Scientiarum Hungaricae*. I-. Budapest 1951-.

Almásy   Almásy, György, *Vándorutam Ázsia szivébe* [My Wanderings into the Heart of Asia]. Budapest 1903.

Altyns.   Altynsarin, I., *Kirgizskaja hrestomatija*. Orenburg 1906.

Amanoğlu 1996   Amanoğlu, E. K., *Eski Türk Onomastiği Üzerine*: **UTK 1996**, pp. 109-116.

Amanoğlu 1999   Amanoğlu, E. K., *Eski Türk Onomastik Sözlügü*. Baku 1999, 124 pp.

Amanž.   Amanžolov, S., *Voprosy dialektologii i istorii kazahskogo jazyka*. Čast' pervaja. Alma-Ata 1959.

Amari   Amari, M. (transl.), *I diplomi arabi del R. Archivio Fiorentino*. Testo originale con la traduzione letterale e illustrazioni di –. Firenze 1863.

Anan'ev   Anan'ev, G., *Karanogajcy, ih byt i obraz žizni*: **SMOK XX**, otd. I, p. 49.

Andrievič, Ist. Sib.   Andrievic, V. K., *Istoričeskij očerk Sibiri, osnovannyj na dannyh*. I-II. Stpbg. 1886.

Aničkov   Aničkov, I. V., *Pamjatniki kirgizskogo narodnogo tvorčestva*: Kirgizskaja bylina o gerojah Ir-Nazare i Bikete: **UZKU** 63/4. (Kazan' 1896), pp. 1-16.

Anjou Okm.   Nagy Imre, Tasnádi Nagy Gyula (ed.), *Anjoukori okmánytár*. I-VII. Szerk. –. Budapest 1878-1891, 1920. (Monumenta Hungariae Historica).

Annaklyčev 1969   Annaklyčev, Š., *Türkmenlerde at daqïlïšï*. Turkmenskie imena. Ašgabad 1969.

Annaklyčev 1970   Annaklyčev, Š., *Motivy vybora imen u turkmen*: **Ličnye imena v prošlom.** (1970).

Antroponimika   *Antroponimika*. M. 1970.

AOA   *Kirgizskoe hozjajstvo v Akmolinskoj oblasti*. Tom V. Akmolinskij uezd. SPb. 1910.

AOAtb.   *Kirgizskoe hozjajtsvo v Akmolinskoj oblasti*. Tom IV. Atbasarskij uezd. SPb. 1910.

AOH   *Acta Orientalia Academiae Scientiarum Hungaricae*. Budapest.

AOK   *Kirgizskoe hozjajstvo v Akmolinskoj oblasti*. Tom I. Kokčetavskij uezd. SPb. 1910.

AOO   *Kirgizskoe hozjajstvo v Akmolinskoj oblasti*. Tom II. Omskij uezd. SPb. 1910.

AOP	*Kirgizskoe hozjajstvo v Akmolinskoj oblasti.* Tom III. Petropavlovskij uezd. SPb. 1910.
APAW	*Abhandlungen der Preussischen Akademie der Wissenschaften.* Philologisch-historische Klasse. Berlin.
Arabš.	Manger, Samuel Henricus (ed.), *Ahmedes Arabsiadae vitae et rerum gestarum Timuri, qui vulgo Tamerlanes dicitur, historia.* Latine vertit et adnotationes adjecit –. I-II. Loevardiae 1767-72.
Arat	Arat, R. R., *Iduk-kut Ünvânı hakkında:* İÜEFTDED 24/25 (1980/1986), pp. 23-33.
ArchKR	Erman, A. (ed.), *Archiv für wissenschaftliche Kunde von Russland.* Hrsg. von –. Berlin 1841-1867.
Aristov	Aristov, N.A., *Zametki ob êtničeskom sostave tjurkskih plemen i narodnostej i svedenija ob ih čislennosti:* ŽS III,vyp. 4 (1896-1897), 182 pp. (Offprint).
Aristov, Opyt	Aristov, N.A., *Opyt vyjasnenija êtničeskago sostava kirgiz-kazakov bol'šoj ordy i karakirgizov.* SPb. 1895, 96 pp.
Arıcan	Arıcan, Saffet, *Bafra'da Adlarla İlgili Gelenek ve İnanmalar:* **Türk Folklor Araştırmaları** 6 (1960).
ArIsslBaškDial.	*Areal'nye issledovanija po baškirskoj dialektologii i onomastike.* Ufa 1988.
Arīb	De Goeje, M. J. (ed.), *Arīb: Tabarī Continuatus,* quem edidit, indicibus et glossario instruxit –. Leyden 1897.
Asanaliev - Kosalov	Asanaliev, Ü. - Kosalov, İ. S., *Qïrɣïz Adam Attarïniñ Sözlügü.* Praktikalïk qoldonmo. Frunze 1979.
Askarova	Askarova, G. N., *Ličnye imena v fol'klore* (na materialah azerbajdžanskih narodnyh dastanov i poêm). Avtoref. kand. diss. Baku 1986, 24 pp.
Aslan	Aslan, Yasin, *Azerbaycan Onomastikası ve Değiştirilmiş Adlar Meselesi:* **Türk Dünyası** 1 (8) (1987), pp. 19-20.
ASlPh.	*Archiv für Slavische Philologie.* Deutsche Akademie der Wissenschaften zu Berlin. Berlin.
Aspekty lingv.	*Aspekty lingvističeskogo analiza* (na materiale raznyh sistem). Moskva 1974.
Astarab.	Köprülüzade, Mehmed Fuad (introd.), *Bezm u Rezm.* Müellifi Aziz ibn Ardaşir Astarabadi. Müderris Köprülüzade Mehmed Fuad Tarafından eser ve müellifi hakkında yazılan bir mukaddimeyi havidir. İstanbul 1928.
Aširaliev	Aširaliev, K., *Qïrɣïz tilindegi adam attarï:* **IAN KirgSSR** t. VI, vyp. I (1964).
Ašm.	Ašmarin, N. I., *Slovar' čuvašskogo jazyka.* I-XVII 1928-1950. (New edition: Thesaurus Linguae Tschuvaschorum by Nikolaj Ivanovich Ashmarin. With an Introduction by Gerhard Doerfer. Volumes I-IV. Bloomington 1968 (Indiana University Publications Uralic and Altaic Series. Vol. 70/1-4)).
Atalay, Ad.	Atalay, Besim, *Türk Büyükleri veya Türk Adları.* Istanbul 1935.
Atalay, Ek.	Atalay, Besim, *Türk dilinde ekler ve kökler üzerine bir deneme.* İstanbul 1942, 382 pp.
Atanijazov 1980	Atanijazov, S., *Tolkovyj slovar' geografičeskih nazvanij Turkmenistana.* Pod red. Azimova P., Babaeva A. Ašhabad 1980, 364 pp.
Atanijazov 1984	Atanijazov, S. A., *Onomastičeskaja rabota v Turkmenii:* **Tjurksk. onom.** (1984), pp. 237-246.
Atanijazov 1988	Atanijazov, S., *Slovar' turkmenskih êtnonimov.* Ašhabad 1988, 179 pp.
Atanïyazov 1970	Atanïyazov, S., *Turkmenistanniñ toponimik sözlügi.* Toponimičeskij slovar' Turkmenistana. Ašgabat 1970, 306 pp.
Atebet	Arat, Reşid Rahmeti (ed.), *Edib Ahmed b. Mahmud Yükneki: Atebetü 'l-Hakayik.* İstanbul 1951.
Atsız	Atsız, Bedriye, *Lâkaplar:* **Tarih ve Toplum** 11 (1984), pp. 26-28.
Attokurov	Attokurov, Sabır, *Kırgız Sancırası.* Bişkek 1995.
AUK	Alektorov, A. E., *Ukazatel' [–] kirgizov:* **IOAIÊK** (1902-1906).
AUK Dobavl.	Alektorov, A. E., *Ukazatel' [–] kirgizov:* **IOAIÊK (Dobavlenie)** (1902-06).
AÜDTCFD	*Ankara Üniversitesi Dil Tarih Coğrafya Fakültesi Dergisi.* Ankara 1942-.
AÜEFAD	*Ankara Üniversitesi Edebiyat Fakültesi Araştırma Dergisi.* Ankara.
AÜSiyBFD	*Ankara Üniversitesi Siyasal Bilgiler Fak-ltesi Dergisi.* Ankara.
ᶜAwfi	Browne, E. G. and Kazwīnī, Mīrzā Muhammad (ed.), *Hubābu 'l-albāb of Muhammad ᶜAwfi.* Leyden 1906. (Persian Historical Texts IV).

Az. Skaz. Bagrija, A. - Zejnally, H. (transl.), Sokalova, Ju. M. (ed.), *Azerbajdžanskie tjurkskie skazki.* Perevod, stat'i i kommentarii –. Pod obščej redakciej –. Moskva 1935.

AzJoɣrAdl. Juzbašev, R., Äliyev, K., Sädiyev, *Azerbayjanïn joɣrafi adlarï.* Baqï 1972.

AzDilOnom. Israfilova, R. D., Mäšädijev, G. H. Jäfärov, *Azärbajjan Dilinin Onomastikasï* (Očerklär). Baku 1987.

AzKişiAdl. *Azerbaycan kişi adları.*

Ālī Nöldeke, Th. (ed.), *Auszüge aus Neschri's Geschichte des Osmânischen-Hauses*: **ZDMG** XIII (1859), pp. 176-218; 333-380.

Āšikp. Giese, Friedrich (ed.), *Die altosmanische Chronik des Ašikpašazade.* Auf Grund mehrerer neuentdeckter Handschriften von neuem herausgegeben von –. Leipzig 1929.

ÁÚO Wenzel Gusztáv, *Árpádkori új okmánytár.* Közzé teszi –. I-XII. Budapest 1860-1874. (Monumenta Hungariae Historica).

Babur Arat, Prof. Reşit Rahmeti (transl.), *Gazi Zahirüddin Muh. Bābur, Vekayi. Babur'un hatirati.* Doğu Türkçesinden çeviren, izahlı endeksi ve notları hazırlayan –. I-II. Ankara 1943-46.

Bagdaryn Bagdaryn, S., *Toponimy Jakutii* (Na jakutskom jazyke). Jakutsk 1982.

Baybars/Tizeng. I *Tārīḫ Baybars / Zubdat al-fikrat fi tārīḫ al-hiǧra*: **Tizeng. I**, pp.76-123.

Bayerle Bayerle, Gustav, *Pashas, Begs and Effendis:* A Historical Dictionary of Titles and Terms in the Ottoman Empire. Istanbul 1997.

Bayhaki Morley, W. H. (ed.), *Tārīh-ī Bayhakī.* Calcutta 1865. (Bibliotheca Indica).

Bayur Bayur, H., *Harizmşah Alâ'üddîn "Tekiş"in adı hakkında*: **Belleten** XIV (1950), pp. 589-594.

Bakč. Nadp. *Bakčesarajskija arabskija i tureckija nadpisi.* Odessa 1849. (Izdanie Odesskago Obščestva Istorii i Drevnostej).

BalkToponSl. Kokov, Dž. N. - Šahmurzaev, S. O., *Balkarskij toponimičeskij slovar'.* Nal'čik 1970, 170 pp.

Balov Balov, A. B., *Velikorusskija familii i ih proishoždenie.* Istoriko-êtnografičeskij očerk: **ŽS** VI, pp. 157-161.

Banarlı Banarlı, Nihad Sâmi, *Türklerde Soyadı*: **Türk Folklor Araştırmaları** 7 (1950), pp. 97-.

Bang Bang, W., *Monographien zur türkischen Sprachgeschichte*: **SHeidAW** 12 Abh. (1918).

Bang 1918 Bang, W., *Beiträge zur türkischen Wortforschung. I-II.*: **Túrán** (1918), pp. 289-310, 516-540.

Banguoğlu Banguoğlu, Tahsin, *Eski Türkçe Bazı Adlar üzerine.* I. Gültekin: **X. Türk Dil Kurultayında Okunan Bilimsel Bildiriler. 1963.** (Ankara 1964), pp. 1-4.

Barth., Turk. I Bartol'd, V. V., *Turkestan v epohu mongol'skogo našestvija.* Č. I. Teksty. SPb. 1898, 201+1 pp.

Barth., Turk. II Bartol'd, V. V., *Turkestan v epohu mongol'skogo našestvija.* Č. II. Issledovanie. SPb. 1900, VII+575 pp.

Barth., Ulugb. Barthold, V. V., *Ulug Beg und seine Zeit* Ed. Walther Hintz. Leipzig 1935.

Bask., Im. polov. Baskakov, N. A., *Imena polovcev i nazvanija poloveckih plemen v russkih letopisjah*: **Tjurk. Onom.**, pp. 48-77.

Bask., Fam. Baskakov, N. A., *Russkie familii tjurskogo proishoždenija.* Moskva 1979, 279 pp.

Bask., Kkalp. Baskakov, N. A., *Karakalpakskij jazyk I.* Materialy po dialektologii (Teksty i slovar'). Priloženie 1: Mužskie imena, pp. 399-402; Priloženie 2: Ženskie imena, pp. 403-404. Moskva 1951, 410 pp.

Bask., Nog. Baskakov, N. A., *Nogajskij jazyk i ego dialekty.* Grammatika, teksty i slovar'. Moskva 1940, 271 pp.

Baskakov 1968 Baskakov, N. A., *Vestiges de taboo et de totémisme dans les langues altaïques.* Moscou 1968.

Baskakov 1970 Baskakov, N. A., *K êtimologii poloveckih sobstvennyh imen v íSlovo o polku Igoreve"* (Šarohan, Končak, Gzak, Kobjak, Ovlur): **Problemy istorii i dialektologii slavjanskih jazykov.** (M. 1970), pp. 252-258.

Baskakov 1973 Baskakov, N. A., *Mifologičeskie i êpičeskie imena sobstvennye v íSlovo o polku Igoreve"*: **Vost. filologija.** (Tbilisi 1973, No 3).

Baskakov 1975 Baskakov, N. A., *Perežitki tabu i totemizma*: **SovT** (1975, No. 2), pp. 3-8.

Baskakov 1977   Baskakov, N. A., *Strukturnye i smyslovye modeli tjurkskih êtnonimov i ih tipologičeskaja klassifikacija*: **Onoma** XXI (1977), pp. 101-110.

Baskakov 1980a   Baskakov, N. A., *Modeli tjurskih êtnonimov i ih tipologičeskaja klassifikacija*: **Onom. vost.** (Moskva 1980), pp. 199-207.

Baskakov 1980b   Baskakov, N. A., *Oğuz, Oğuz-Kağan etimolojisi üzerine*: **İÜEFTDED** 24/25 (1980/1986), pp. 35-37.

Baskakov 1984   Baskakov, N. A., *Imena polovcev i nazvanija poloveckih plemen v russkih letopisjah*: **Tjurksk. onom.** (1984), pp. 48-77.

Baski 1987   Baski I., *A magyarországi kun eredetű tulajdonnevek kutatása*: **A Jászkunság kutatása 1985.** (Kecskemét - Szolnok 1987), pp. 75-92.

Baski 1989a   Baski Imre, *Kun eredetű nevek a török adóösszeírásokban*: **Névtudomány és művelődéstörténet. A IV. Magyar Névtud. Konf. előadásai.** (Zalaegerszeg 1989), 214-217.

Baski 1989b   Baski Imre, *Kun eredetű neveinkről*: **Honismereti Közlemények** 11-12. (Kecskemét 1989), pp. 77-91.

Baski 1995   Baski, I., *A számítógépes tulajdonnévi adatbázisok tervezéséhez*. Egy épülő török adatbázis kezdeti tanulságai: **MNévtKonf. V.** I-II, pp. 499-512.

Baski 2000   Baski, I., *Zusammengesetzte Personennamen als Satzbau im Türkischen*: **Hasan Eren Armağanı.** (Ankara 2000), pp. 48-59.

Basri   Basri, Hasan, *Çarşamba ve Terme'de Adlarla İlgili Gelenek ve İnanmalar*: **Türk Folklor Araştırmaları** 6 (135) (1960), pp. 2238.

BaškÊtnonimija   *Baškirskaja êtnonimija.* AN SSSR Baškirskij filial. Institut istorii, jazyka i literatury. Ufa 1987.

Başgöz 1976   Başgöz, Ilhan, *İnsan Adları ve Toplum*: **Türk Dili** 294 (1976), pp. 164-170.

Başgöz 1983a   Başgöz, Ilhan, *The Meaning and Dimenson of Change of Personal Names in Turkey*: **Turcica** 15 (1983), pp. 201-218.

Başgöz 1983b   Başgöz, Ilhan, *The Name and Society.* A Case Study of Personal Names in Turkey: **Kungl. Vitterhets Historie och Antikvitets Akademiens Konferensar** 12 (1983), pp. 1-14.

Baştav   Baştav, Şerif, *16. Asırda Yazılmış Grekçe Anonim Osmanlı Tarihi.* Giriş ve Metin (1373-1512). Ankara 1973.

Bazin 1981   Bazin, Louis, *"Ata" dans la tradition turque des titulatures*: **AÜSiyBFD** 36 (1981), pp. 87-94. (Özel Sayı).

Bazin, Ata   Bazin, Louis, *"Ata" dans la tradition turque des titulatures*: **Bazin, Les Turcs** (1994), pp. 218-223.

Bazin, Ataman   Bazin, Louis, *Antiquité méconnue du titre d'"ataman"*: **Bazin, Les Turcs** (1994), pp. 224-232.

Bazin, Čavuš   Bazin, Louis, *Antiquité méconnue du titre turc "čavuš"*: **Bazin, Les Turcs** (1994), pp. 233-243.

Bazin, Kül Tegin   Bazin, Louis, *Kül Tegin ou Köl Tegin*: **Scholia. Beiträge zur Türkologie und Zentralasienkunde.** (Weisbaden 1981), pp. 1-7.

Bazin, Qorqut   Bazin, L., *Le nom propre d'homme "Qorqut"*: Discussion étymologique: **UAJb.** XXXVI (1965), pp. 278-283.

Bazin, Les Turcs   Bazin, Louis, *Les turcs, des mots, des hommes.* Budapest 1994. (BOH XLI).

Bazin, T'o-pa   Bazin, Louis, *Recherches sur les parlers T'o-pa* 5e siècle après J. C.: **T'oung Pao** XXXIX (1950), pp. 228-329.

Bálint   Bálint Gábor, *Kazáni-tatár nyelvtanulmányok.* I. Füzet: Szövegek és forditás (1875). II. Füzet: Kazáni-tatár szótár (1876). III. Füzet: Kazáni-tatár nyelvtan (1877). Budapest 1875-1877.

Begmatov 1965   Begmatov, Ê., *Antroponimika uzbekskogo jazyka.* Avtoref. kand. diss. Taškent 1965, 27 pp.

Begmatov 1966   Begmatov, Ê., *Nomlar va odamlar.* Imena i ljudi. Taškent 1966, 51 pp.

Begmatov 1970   Begmatov, Ê. A., *Kiši nomlari imlosi.* Pravopisanie ličnyh imen. Taškent 1970, 115 pp.

Begmatov 1972   Begmatov, Ê. A., *Ůzbek ismlari imlosi.* Pravopisanie uzbekskih imjon. Taškent 1972, 383 pp.

Begmatov 1984   Begmatov, Ê. A., *Glagol'nye antroponimy*: **Tjursk. onom.** (1984), pp. 199-207.

Belleten   I-. Ankara 1937-. (Türk Tarih Kurumu).

BEO   *Bulletin d'Études Orientales. Institut Français de Damas.* I-. Damascus 1931-.

Berchem   Berchem, Max van, *Matériaux pour un Corpus Inscriptionum Arabicarum.* Première Partie. Égypte. Fasc. Premier. Le Caire-Paris 1894. (Mémoires publ. par les membres de la Mission Archéologique Française au Caire. Tome XIX).

Berchem, Jér.   Berchem, Max Van, *Matériaux pour un Corpus Inscriptionum Arabicarum.* Deuxieme partie. Syrie du Sud. T. I. Jérusalem "Haram". Le Caire 1922-1927. (Mém. Inst. Fr. d'Archéol. Or. du Caire XLIII–XLIV).

Berchem, Perg.   Berchem, Max van, *Die muslimische Inschriften*: **ABAW** (1911).

Bernštam   Bernštam, A. I., *K proishoždeniju imeni Manas*: **Manas - geroičeskij êpos kirgizskogo naroda.** (Frunze 1968), pp. 177-191.

Bese   Bese Lajos, *A mongolok titkos története személynevei.* [Anthroponyms of the *Secret History of the Mongols*] Budapest. (Manuscript).

Bese 1978   Bese, Lajos, *Some Turkic Personal Names in the Secret History of the Mongols*: **AOH** XXXII (1978), pp. 353-369.

BGA   de Goeje, M. J. (ed.), *Bibliotheca Geographorum Arabicorum.* I-VIII. Lugduni Batavorum 1870-1894.

Bičeldej   Bičeldej, K. A., *Tuvinskie antroponimy tibetskogo i mongol'skogo proishoždenija.* Novosibirsk 1983, 4 stu.

Bikbulatov   Bikbulatov, N. V., *Antroponimy i terminy rodstva*: **OnomPov. 3.** (Ufa 1973), pp. 100-107.

Björkm.   Björkman, Walter, *Beiträge zur Geschichte der Staatskanzlei in islamischen Ägypten.* Hamburg 1928. (Hamburgische Univ. Abhandl. aus d. Gebiet der Auslandskunde. Bd. 28).

Byz.   *Byzantion.* Revue internationale des études byzantines. I. Paris 1924.

Byz. Turc.   Moravcsik, Gy., *Byzantinoturcica.* II. Sprachreste der Türkvölker in den byzantinischen Quellen. Budapest 1943.

Blagova 1970   Blagova, G. F., *Tjurkskie srednevekovye ličnye ženskie imena*: **Ličnye imena v prošlom.** (Moskva 1970).

Blagova 1997   Blagova, G. F., *Antroponimija*: **SIGTJa. Leksika** (1997), pp. 619-723.

Blagova 1998a   Blagova, G. F., *Drevnie kypčakskie imena v svete rekonstrukcii pratjurkskoj antroponimičeskoj sistemy*: **Orientalika.** (Ufa 1998), pp. 39-43.

Blagova 1998b   Blagova, G. F., *Sravnitel'no-istoričeskoe izučenie tjurkskoj antroponimii v sovremennoj Rossii: real'nost' i perspektivy*: **ROr.** LI (1998), pp. 45-68.

Blagova 1998c   Blagova, G. F., *K harakteristike tipov rannetjurkskih antroponimov*: **VJa.** (1998, No. 4), pp. 180-191.

Blaškovič 1972   Blaškovič, Jozef, *Toponimy starotjurkskogo proishoždenija na territorii Slovakii*: **VJa.** 6. (Moskva 1972), pp. 62-75.

Blaškovič 1973   Blaškovič, Jozef, *Some Toponyms of Turkish Origin in Slovakia*: **AOH** 27 (1973), pp. 191-199.

Blochet, Intr.   Blochet, E., *Introduction à l'Histoire des Mongols de Fadl Allah Rashid ed-Din par –.* Leyden-London 1910. (GMS XII).

BM   Zajączkowski, A., *Słownik arabsko-kipczacki z okresu Państva Mameluckiego.* Bulġat al-Muštaq fī Luġat at-Turk wa-l-Qifẑaq. I-II. Warszawa 1954, 1958.

Bogdan, Br.   Bogdan, J., *Documente şi regesta privitoare la relaţiile Tarii-Rumineşti cu Braşovul şi Ungaria.* Bucureşti 1902.

Bogdan, Doc.   Bogdan, J., *Documentele lui Ştefan cel Mare.* I-II. Bucureşti 1898.

BOH   *Bibliotheca Orientalis Hungarica.* Budapest.

Boyraz   Boyraz, Ş., *Lâkaplar Konusunda Bazı Dikkatler ve Bir Yöre Örneği*: **Türklük Bilimi Araştırmaları** VII (1988), pp. 117-133.

Boyev   Boyev, E. P., *Bulgaristan'da Minzuhar Köyünde Özel Adlar*: **Türk Folklor Araştırmaları** 9 (191) (1965), pp. 3767-3770.

Boyle, Archers   Boyle, J. A., *Some Additional Notes on the Mongolian Names in the History of the Nation of the Archers*: **Researches in Altaic Languages.** Ed. by L. Ligeti. Budapest 1975, pp. 33-42. (BOH XX).

Bol'šakov   Bol'šakov, I. V., *O tatarskih imenah*: **OnomPov. 3** 3. (Ufa 1973), pp. 49-51.

Bol'šakov - Subaeva	Bol'šakov, I. V. - Subaeva, R. H., *Spravočnik tatarskih ličnyh imen*. Kazan' 1973, 99 pp.
Bol'šakova	Bol'šakova, L. P., *Obrazovanie otčestv ot tatarskih imen*: **Antroponimika**. (M. 1970), pp. 80-82.
Bombaci 1966	Bombaci, A., *Qutluɣ bolsun!* (Part Two): **UAJb**. 38 (1966), 21-22 pp.
Bombaci 1970	Bombaci, A., *On the Ancient Turkic Title Eltäbär*: **Proceedings of the IXth meeting of P. I. A. C.** (Naples 1970).
Bombaci 1976	Bombaci, A., *On the Ancient Turkish Title Šadapï_*: **UAJb**. 48 (1976), pp. 32-41.
Bondarskij	Bondarskij M. S., *Ĵâɣrapiya nâmlarniñ luɣati*. Taškent 1959.
Bondārī	Houtsma, M. Th. (ed.), *Histoire des Seldjoucides de l'Irāq par al-Bondārī d'après Imād ad-Dīn al-Kātib al-Isfahānī*. Texte arabe publ. par – : **Houtsma, Recueil** II (1889).
Bozyiğit	Bozyiğit, A. E., *Türk Adbilimi Bibliyografyası*. Ankara 1995, 190 pp.
Brock., GAL	Brockelmann, C., *Geschichte der arabischen Literatur*. I-II. Suppl. I-III. Leiden 1937-49.
Browne	Browne, Edward Granville, *A Literary History of Persia*. Vol. 3. The Tatar Dominion (1265-1502). Cambridge 1951, XI, 586.
BRS	Ahmerov, K. Z. (ed.), *Baškirsko-russkij slovar'*. Okolo 22 000 slov. Moskva 1958.
BRS/Uraksin	Uraksin, Z. G. (ed.), *Baškirsko-russkij slovar'*. Moskva 1996, 865 pp.
Buchari	*Mīr Muḥammad Amīn-i Buchārī's Maǧmūʿah*. Inhalt des Werk's in Teufel. Quellenstudien zur neueren Geschichte der Chanate: **ZDMG** XXXVIII, pp. 235-376.
Budagov	Budagov, Lazar, *Sravintel'nyj slovar' turecko tatarskih narečij, so vključeniem upotrebitel'nejših slov arabskih i persidskih i s perevodom na russkij jazyk*. Sostavil –. I-II. SPb. 1869-71.
Bukej	Bukejhanov, A., *Iz perepiski hana Srednej kirgizskoj ordy Bukeja i ego potomkov*: **Pam. kn. Semip.** (1901).
Bukin	Bukin, Iš-Muhammed (ed.), *Russko-kirgizskij i kirgizsko-russkij slovar'*. Taškent 1883.
Bulatov	Bulatov, A. B., *Ličnye imena u drevnih bulgar* (VI. - XVI vv.): **OnomPov. 2.** (Kazan' 1971), pp. 79-81.
Bull. Ac.	*Bulletin de l'Académie Impériale des Sciences de St.-Pétersbourg*. Petrograd.
Bulliet	Bulliet, Richard W., *First Names and Political Change in Modern Turkey*: **IJMS** 9, pp. 489-495.
Burguière	Burguière, P., *Les noms turcs des personnes*: **Vie et Louange** (1953).
Butanaev	Butanaev, V. Ja., *Xōray attarï*. Xakasskie ličnye imena. Abakan 1990(?), 108 pp.
Butenko	Butenko, N. P., *Russkie sobstvennye imena v Kirgizii i nekotorye voprosy vzaimodejstvija jazykov*. Avtoref. kand. diss. Minsk 1967.
Butenko - Mambetalieva	Butenko, N. P. - Mambetalieva, K., *Kirgizskie imena segodnja*: **Ličnye imena v prošlom**. (1970).
Caetani - Gabrieli	Caetani, Leone - Gabrieli, Giuseppe, *Onomasticon Arabicum* ossia repertorio alfabetico dei nomi di persone e di luogo contenuti nelle principali opere storiche, biografiche e geografiche, stampate e manoscritte, relative all' Islām. Compilato per cure di – –. Volume I. (Fonti – Introduzione), Volume II. A (Aʿābil – ʿAbdallah). Roma 1915, I-XIX, [1]-[314], 1020 pp.
Cafer., Ağa	Caferoğlu, A., *Azerbaycan Onomastiğinde "Ağa"*: **Németh Arm.** (1962), pp. 89-92.
Cafer., An. Dial.	Caferoğlu, A., *Anadolu Dialektolojisi Üzerine Malzeme* 1-2. İstanbul 1940-1941.
Cafer., Chasse	Caferoğlu, A., *Le culte de la chasse dans l'onomastique turque*: **CISO V** t. 2 (1958).
Cafer., Cheval	Caferoğlu, A., *Le culte du cheval dans l'onomastique turque*: **CISO IV** tome 1 (1952), pp. 205-211.
Cafer., Kars	Caferoğlu, A., *Doğu illerimiz ağızlarından toplamalar*. I. Kars, Erzurum ağızları. İstanbul 1942.
Cafer., Köpek	Caferoğlu, A., *Türk Onomastiğinde "Köpek" Kültü*: **TDAYB** (1961), pp. 1-11.
Cafer., Malatya	Caferoğlu, A., *Güney-doğu illerimizden toplamalar*. Malatya ve saire ağızları. İstanbul 1942.
Cafer., Tukyu	Caferoğlu, A., *Tukyu ve Uygurlarda han unvanları*: **THITM** 1 (1931), pp. 105-19.
Caferoğlu	Caferoğlu, A., *Bibliographia Onomastica:* Turquie (Türkiye): **Onoma** 3-14 (1952-1969).
Caferoğlu 1957	Caferoğlu, A., *Türk Onomastiğinde "başlık" yahut "serpuş"*: **VIII. Türk Dil Kurultayında Okunan Bilimsel Bildiriler** (1957), pp. 113-125.

Caferoğlu 1958 Caferoğlu, A., *Azerbaycan Antroponimisine Dair Notlar*: **İÜEFTDED** 8 (1958), pp. 1-7.

Caferoğlu 1961 Caferoğlu, A., *Der Hund in der türkischen Onomastic*: **Int. Kongr. Nknde** VI (1958). (München 1961).

Caferoğlu - Trubačev Caferoğlu, A. - Trubačev, O. N., *Bibliographia Onomastica:* Altaic: **Onoma** 15-16 (1970-1971), pp. 777-787; pp. 722-736.

Candar 1938 Candar, Avni, *Anadolu Coğrafya Luğatı Sınaçları* 1 – Ankara. Ankara 1938, 96 pp.

Castagné Castagné, Joseph, *Les Basmatchis*. Paris 1925.

CC Grönbech, K., *Komanisches Wörterbuch*. Türkischer Wortindex zu Codex Cumanicus. Kopenhagen 1942, 514 pp.

Cemiloğlu Cemiloğlu, İsmet, *Dilimizdeki "Kara" kelimesi hakkında*: **Millî Folklor** 2 (12) (1991), pp. 303-308.

Chavannes Chavannes, E., *Documents sur les Tou-kiue (Turcs) Occidentaux*. SPb. 1903.

Chwol., Syr. Chwolson, D., *Syrische Grabinschriften aus Semirjetschie*. SPb. 1886, 30 pp. (Mémoires de l'Ac. Imp. des Sc. de Spb. Septieme Sér. Tome XXXIV, No. 4).

Chwol., Syr.-nest. Chwolson, D. (ed.), *Syrisch-nestorianische Grabinschriften aus Semirjetschie,* hrsg. und erklärt von –. Nebst einer Beilage: Über das türkische Sprachmaterial dieser Grabinschriften von W. Radloff. SPb. 1890, 168 pp. (Mémoires de l'Ac. Imp. des Sc. de Spb. Septième Sér. Tome XXXVII, No. 8).

Chwol., Syr.-nest. (NF) Chwolson, D. (ed.), *Syrisch-nestorianische Grabinschriften aus Semirjetschie. Neue Folge.* Hrsg. und erklärt von –. SPb. 1897, 62 pp.

Cinlioğlu Cinlioğlu, Halis Turgut, *Tokad'da Adlarla İlgili Gelenek ve İnanmalar*: **Türk Folklor Araştırmaları** 6 (137) (1960), pp. 2286.

CIA *Corpus Inscriptionum Arabicorum.*

CISO IV *Quatrième Congrès International des Sciences Onomastiques.* Tome 1-2. Uppsala 1952.

CISO V *Actes et Mémoires du Cinquième Congrès International des Sciences Onomastiques.* Tome 1-2. Salamanca 1958.

Clauson Clauson, G., *An Etymological Dictionary of Pre-Thirteenth-Century Turkish.* Oxford 1972, XXXVIII, 989 pp.

Clauson, Qapqan Clauson, G., *A note on qapqan*: **JRAS** (1956), pp. 73-77.

Clavijo Clavijo, Ruy Gonçalez de, *Historia del Gran Tamorlan e itinerario y enarracion del viage y relacion de la Embaxada*. Ed. Gonçalo Argote di Medina. Sevilla 1582.

Cleaves Cleaves, F. W., *The Mongolian Names and Terms in the History of the Nation of the Archers by Grigor Akanc^c*: **HJAS** 12 (1949), pp. 400-43.

Conea-Donat Conea, J. - Donat, J., *Contributions à l'étude de la toponymie pétchénégue-comane de la plaine roumaine du Bas-Danube*: **Contrib. Onom.** (1958), pp. 139-170.

Contrib. Onom. *Contributions onomastiques,* publiées à l'occasion du VIe congrès international des sciences onomastiques à Munich du 24 au 28 Août 1958. Bucarest 1958, 184 pp.

Costăch. Costăchescu, M., *Documentele Moldoveneşti înainte de Ştefan cel Mare*. Iaşi 1931-32.

Csánki Csánki, D., *Magyarország történelmi földrajza a Hunyadiak korában*. I-III, V. Budapest 1890-1913.

Čankov Čankov, D. I., *O zaimstvovanii russkih imen hakasami*: **Issl. po sovr. hakas. jaz.** (Abakan 1980), pp. 91-101.

ČRS Sirotkin, M. Ja. (red.), *Čuvašsko-russkij slovar'*. Pod red. –. Okolo 25 000 slov. Moskva 1961.

ČRS/Skvor. Skvorcov, M. I. (ed.), *Čuvašsko-russkij slovar'*. Pod red. –. Okolo 40 000 slov. Moskva 1982.

Čuv. jaz. *Čuvašskij jazyk:* istorija, êtimologija, fonetika. Čeboksary 1991.

Çağatay Çağatay, S., *Türk Kadın Adları*: **TDAY Belleten.** (Ankara 1962).

Çay Çay, Abdülhalûk, *Türk Kadın Adları Üzerine*: **Ötüken** (1975 (V-VII)).

Çelik Çelik, M. K., *Türk Ad ve Soyadı Sözlüğü.* 1991.

Ǧawzī: RHCHor III Sibṭ ibn al-Džavzī, Yusuf, *Muntakhabāt min Kitāb Mirʾāt iz-Zamān*; **RHCHor** III (1884), pp. 517-570.

Ǧuwaynī/Boyle Boyle, J. A., *The History of the World-conqueror by ʿAla-ad-din ʿAta Malik Juwaini*. Ed. –. I-II. Manchester 1958.

XCVI

J̌uwaynī

Qazwīnī, Mirza Muhammad Ibn Abdul-Wahhāb-i (ed.), *The Ta'rikh-i-Jahān-Gushā of Alā'ud'din Atā Malik-i-Juwaynī* (composed in A. H. 658 A. D. 1260). Part I, containing the history of Chingiz khan and his successors. Part II, containing the history of the Khwarizm-shah dynasty. Edited with an introduction, notes and indices from several old Mss. by –. London - Leiden 1912-16. (GMS XVI).

J̌uzǰānī

Nassau-Lees, W. (ed.) - Raverty, H. G. (transl.), *Djuzdjānī, Minhādj ʿAbū ʿOmar ʿOthmān b. Sirādj Muḥammed, Tabaqāt-i Nāṣirī:* A General History of the Muhammadan Dynasties of Asia by Maulānā, Minhāj-ud-Dīn, Abū-ʿUmar-i-ʿUsman. I-II. Calcutta / New Delhi (reprint) 1874 / 1970. (Bibliotheca Indica).

d'Ohsson

d'Ohsson, Abraham Constantin Mouradgea, *Histoire des Mongols depuis Tchingis-Khan jusqu'à Timour-Beg ou Tamerlan.* I-IV. La Haye - Amsterdam 1834-35.

DAI

Dopolnenija k aktam istoričeskim, sobr. i izd. Arheogr. kommissieju. I-XII + Ukazatel'. SPb. 1846-72.

Dalboy

Dalboy, M. Zeki, *Konya'da Adlarla İlgili Gelenek ve İnanmalar:* **Türk Folklor Araştırmaları** 4 (80) (1956).

DAN

Doklady AN SSSR. Serija V. Leningrad.

Danilova 1976

Danilova, L. V., *Čuvašskaja antroponimija Baškirskoj ASSR XVII-XVIII vv.:* **Dial. top. Pov.** (1976), pp. 26-34.

Danilova 1979

Danilova, L. V., *K izučeniju arabsko-iranskih êlementov v čuvašskoj antroponimike:* **Dial. top. Pov.** (1979), pp. 3-15.

Danilova 1980a

Danilova, L. V., *Tendencija k poljarizacii antroponimov v tjurkskih jazykah:* **Issl. po leksike i gramm. tjurk. jaz.** (Taškent 1980), pp. 85-99.

Danilova 1980b

Danilova, L. V., *K izučeniju arabsko-iranskih êlementov v čuvašskoj antroponimike:* **Dial. top. Pov.** (1980), pp. 131-144.

Danilova-Enžaeva

Danilova, L. V. - Enžaeva, T. T., *Imena čuvašej v Baškirskoj ASSR* (po materialam, sobrannym v derevni Zirikly Bižbuljakskogo rajona): **OnomPov. 4**, pp. 61-64.

Dawād.

Roemer, H. R., *Die Chronik des Ibn ad-Dawādārī. Neunter Teil. Der Bericht über den Sultan al-Malik an-Nāsir Muhammad Ibn Qalā'un.* Hrsg. von –. Kairo, Deutsches Arch. Inst., 1960.

Dávid

Dávid Géza, *A simontornyai defterekből:* Timar defteri No. 353 (1565), No. 505 (1570), No. 659 (1580), No. 1030 (1552).

De Guignes

De Guignes, J., *Histoire des Princes Atabeks en Syrie:* **Notes et Extr.** I. (Paris 1787).

Demirtaş

Demirtaş, Faruk, *Bozulus hakkında:* **ADTCFD** VII (1949), pp. 29-60.

Deny

Deny, J., *Grammaire de la langue turque* (Dialecte osmanli). Paris 1921.

Der Islam

Der Islam. Zeitschrift für Geschichte und Kultur des Islamischen Orients. I-. Strassburg 1910-.

Dial. top. Pov.

Dialekty i toponimija Povolž'ja. Čeboksary.

Dimašqī

Mehren, A. F., *Die Rhetorik der Araber nach den wichtigsten Quellen dargestellt und mit angefügten Textauszügen nebst einem Literatur-geschichte.* Anhange vers. Kopenhagen - Wien 1853, VIII, 303, 140 p.

Divaev, Alp.

Divaev, A. A., *Pamjatniki kirgizskogo narodnogo tvorčestva. Alpamyš batyr.* Kirgizskaja poema. Taškent 1901.

Divaev-Anderson

Divaev, A. A. - Anderson, V. N., *Kirgizskaja legenda o vethozav. Velik. Adže:* **IOAIÊK** XXIV (1908), pp. 434-36.

Divaev, Baksy

Divaev, A. A., *Iz oblasti kirgizskih verovanij.* Baksy kak lekar' i koldun: **IOAIÊK** XV/3 (1899).

Divaev, Biket

Divaev, A. A., *Pamjatniki kirgizskogo narodnogo tvorčestva:* Kirgizskaja bylina o Biket Batyre. Kazan' 1897.

Divaev, Čingiz

Divaev, A. A., *Kirgizskij rasskaz o Čingiz-hane:* **ZVOIRAO** XI (1899), pp. 290-292.

Divaev, Šura

Divaev, A. A., *Šura-batyr:* **Sr. Az.** I (1896), pp. 79-135.

Divaev, Dem.

Divaev, A. A., *Demonologičeskie razskazki kirgizov:* **ZIRGOÊtn.** X, pp. 9-75.

Dyrenkova

Dyrenkova, N. P., *Šorskij fol'klor.* Zapisi, perevod, vstupitel'naja stat'ja i primečanija –. Leningrad - Moskva 1940.

DQorq.

Bartol'd, V.V. (transl.), Žirmunskij, V. M. - Kononov, A. N. (eds.), *Kniga moego deda*

Korkuta. Oguzskij geroičeskij epos. Moskva - Leningrad 1962.

DQorq./Ergin   Ergin, Muharrem, *Dede Korkut Kitabı.* I. Giriş - Metin - Faksimile. II. Indeks - Gramer. Ankara 1958-1963. (T.D.K. Yayınlarından, Sayı 169, 219).

DQorq./Gökyay   Gökyay, Orhan Şaik, *Dede Korkut.* İstanbul 1938.

DQorq./Rossi   Rossi, Ettore, *Il "Kitab-i Dede Qorqut".* Citta del Vaticano 1952. (Studi e Testi 159).

Dmitrieva, Barab.   Dmitrieva, L. V., *Jazyk barabinskih tatar.* (Materialy i issledovanija). Leningrad 1981.

Dobrodomov   Dobrodomov, I. G., *Iz poloveckoj onomastiki. Taz Bonjak:* **IAn SSSR, ser. lit. i jazyka** 3. (M. 1964 I. 23), pp. 256-258.

Dobrosm., Turg.   Dobrosmyslov, A. I., *Turgajskaja oblast'.* Istoričeskij očerk. I. Tver' 1902, 267 pp.

Doğru 1985   Doğru, Mecit, *Türkiye'de Macar Yer Adları:* **Belgelerle Türk Tarihi Dergisi** 8 (1985), pp. 50-52.

Dok. Buhar.   Čehovič, O. D. (transl.), Arendsa, A. K. (ed.), *Dokumenty k istorii agrarnyh otnošenij v Buharskom hanstve.* Taškent 1954.

Donidze 1964   Donidze, G. I., *Glagol'nye toponimy v tjurkskih jazykah:* **Toponimika Vostoka** (1964).

Dorn   Dorn, B. (ed.), *Auszüge aus muhammedanischen Schriftstellern betreffend die Geschichte und Geographie der südlichen Küstenländer des Kaspischen Meeres, nebst einer kurzen Geschichte, der Chane von Scheki.* Arabische, persische und türkische Texte hrsg. von –. SPb. 1858.

Dron - Kuroglo   Dron, I. V. - Kuroglo, S. S., *Sovremennaja gagauzskaja toponimija i antroponimija.* Otv. red. T. A. Gajdoraš. (Slovar' gagauzskih familij i prozvišč, pp. 116-180; Slovar' gagauzskih imen, pp. 181-202 (Mužskie imena, pp. 181-194; Ženskie imena, pp. 195-202). Kišinev 1989, 214 pp.

DS   *Türkiye'de Halk Ağzından Derleme Sözlüğü.* I-X. Ankara 1963-1978.

DTCFD   *Dil Tarih Coğrafya Fakültesi Dergisi.* İstanbul.

DTS   Nadeljaev, V. M. - Nasilov, D. M. - Teniševv, Ê. R. - Ščerbak, A. M. (eds.), *Drevnetjurkskij slovar'.* Leningrad 1969.

Dubins'ki   Dubins'ki, A., *Karaimskie ženskie imena v Krymu i ih semantiko-êtimologičeskij analiz:* **SovT** (1979, No. 4), pp. 29-37.

Duqmaq: RHCHor IV-V   Ibn Duqmaq, *Kitāb al-intişār li-Wāsitat ʿIqd al-Amşār:* **RHCHor** IV-V ().

Duqmaq/Tizeng. I   Ibn Duqmāq, *Nuzhat al-anām fi-tārīḫ al-islām:* **Tizeng. I.** (pp. 315-330).

Duman   Duman, Mustafa, *Maçka'da Sığırlara Verilen Adlar.* Derleyen: –: **Türk Folkloru** 7 (76) (1985), pp. 23.

Džanuzakov 1984   Džanuzakov, T. D., *Razvitie tjurkskoj onomastiki v SSSR:* **Tjurksk. onom.** (1984), pp. 13-33.

Džikija   Džikija, M. S., *Tjurkizmy v kartvel'skom antroponimikone.* Dissertacionnyj vestnik doktora filologičeskih nauk. Tbilisi 1995, 46 pp.

Džikija - Gurgenidze   Džikija, M. S. - Gurgenidze, N., *Anthroponyms of Turkic Origin in Georgian Language* (In Georgian). Tbilisi 1994.

Äbdirahmanov 1959   Äbdirahmanov, A. (Abdrahmanov, A.), *Qazaqstanniñ žer-su attarï.* Alma-Ata 1959, 219 pp.

Äbdirahmanov 1975   Äbdirahmanov, A. Ä., *Toponimika žäne êtimologiya.* Almaty 1975, 206 pp.

Äbdirahmanov 1979   Äbdirahmanov, A. Ä., *Qazaqstan êtnotoponimikasï.* Almatï 1979.

Äliäv   Äliäv, Häsän, *Umumi antroponimika problemläri.* Problemy azerbajdžanskoj antroponimiki. Baqï 1985, 125 pp.

Eberhard   Eberhard, W., *Çin'in Şimal Komşuları. Bir Kaynak Kitabı.* Türkçeye Çeviren Nimet Ulutuğ. Ankara 1942.

Eberhard, Ünvan   Eberhard, W., *Bir Kaç Eski Türk Unvanı Hakkında:* **Belleten** (1945), pp. 319-340.

Ecsedy 1965   Ecsedy, Hilda, *Old Turkic Titles of Chinese Origin:* **AOH** XVIII (1965), pp. 83-91.

EI(NE)Index   Bearman, P. J., Bianquis, Th., Bosworth, C. E., Donzel, E. van, Heinrichs, W. P. (eds), *The Encyclopaedia of Islam* New Edition. Under the Editorship of –. Glossary and Index to Vols. I-IX. Leiden - Boston - Köln 2000.

EI(NE)IndexPN   Donzel, E. van (ed.), *The Encyclopaedia of Islam* New Edition. Index of Proper Names to Vols. I-IX. Comp. and ed. by –. Leiden - Boston - Köln 1998.

EI   Houtsma, M. Th., Arnold, T. W., Basset, R., Hartmann, R., *Enzyklopaedie des Islām.*

Geographisches, ethnographisches und bibliographisches Wörterbuch der muhammedanischen Völker. Hrsg. von –. I-V. Leiden - Leipzig 1913-1938.

Ekici Ekici, Metin, *Halk Hikayelerinde Ad Verme*: **Palandöken** 2, S. 4 (1989), pp. 12-13, 18.

Elbir Elbir, Zekiye Gül, *Elâzığ ve Çevresinde Aile Lâkapları.* Derleyen: –: **Türk Folkloru** 8 (1985), pp. 32-33.

Emel'janov Emel'janov, N. V., *Sjužety olonho o rodonačal'nikah plemeni.* Moskva 1990.

Epigr. Bulg. Róna-Tas A. - Fodor S., *Epigraphica Bulgarica.* A volgai bolgár-török feliratok. Szeged 1975. (Studia Uralo-Altaica I).

Erdem *Erdem.* Atatürk Kültür Merkezi Dergisi. Ankara.

Eren 1942 Eren, Hasan, *Török személynevek*: **MNy.** XXXVIII. (1942), 267 pp.

Eren 1946 Eren, Hasan, *Susol*: **MNy.** XLII (1946), p. 57.

Eren 1953 Eren, Hasan, *Türk onomastique'i hakkında*: **Köprülü Arm.** (İstanbul 1953), pp. 127-129.

Eren, TDES Eren, Hasan, *Türk Dilinin Etimolojik Sözlüğü* 2. Baskı. Ankara 1999, 512 pp.

Ergazieva Ergazieva, N. I., *Sistema kazahskih antroponimov v delovyh dokumentah XVIII - načala XIX v.*: **Tjurksk. onom.** (1984), pp. 207-212.

Erol I Erol, Aydil, *Şarkılarla Şiirlerle Türkülerle ve Tarihî Örneklerle Adlarımız.* Ankara 1989, 277 pp.

Erol II Erol, Aydil, *Şarkılarla Şiirlerle Türkülerle ve Tarihî Örneklerle Adlarımız* (genişletilmiş - geliştirilmiş 2. baskı). Ankara 1992, 468 pp. (Türk Kültürünü Araştırma Enstitüsü Yayınları: 124, Seri: 1, Sayı A. 24).

Eröz 1966 Eröz, Mehmet, *Ege bölgesinde yer (köy ve şehir) adları*: **Reşid Rahmeti Arat İçin.** (Ankara 1966), pp.176-188.

Eröz 1984 Eröz, M., *Sosyolojik Yönden Türk Yer Adları*: **TYASB**, pp. 43-53.

Eröz 1986 Eröz, Mehmet, *Sosyolojik Yönden Türk Yer Adları*: **Belgelerle Türk Tarihi Dergisi** 12 (1986), pp. 39-42.

Eröz, Adapazarı Eröz, Mehmet, *Türk Onomastiği Bakımından Adapazarı Yeradları.* Istanbul-Adapazarı.

Ersoylu Ersoylu, Halil, *Oğuz Han'ın Koyduğu Adlar*: **Türk Dünyası Araştırmaları** 33 (1984), pp. 68-76.

Espaeva 1984 Espaeva, K. S., *Leksiko-semantičeskie tipy antroponimov v êpopee "Put' Abaja" M. Auêzova*: **Tjurksk. onom.** (1984), pp. 229-234.

Ethn. *Ethnographia.* Népélet. I-. Budapest 1890-.

ETY Orkun, H. N., *Eski Türk Yazıtları.* Yazan: –. I-IV. İstanbul 1936-1941.

Êtnogr. Obozr. *Êtnografičeskoe Obozrenie.* Moskva. (Ethnographical Review).

EUTS Caferoğlu, A., *Eski Uygur Türkçesi Sözlüğü.* İstanbul 1968. (Türk Dil Kurumu Yayınları 260).

Êtnogr. imen *Êtnografija imen.* Sbornik. Otv. red. V. A. Nikonov, T. T. Stratanovič. Moskva 1971, 263 pp.

Êtnonimy *Êtnonimy.* Moskva 1970.

ÊtnOnom. Nikonov, V. A. (ed.), *Êtničeskaja onomastika.* Otv. red. R. Š. Džarylkasimova. Moskva 1984, 192 pp.

Fahrutdinov Fahrutdinov, R. G., *Ob imeni i titule pravitelja Volžskoj Bulgarii*: **SovT** No 2. (1979), pp. 63-71.

Fakhrī Derenbourg, H. (ed.), *Al-Fakhrī: Histoire du Khalifat et du vizirat par Ibn aṭ-Tikṭakā.* Nouvelle édition du texte arabe par –. Paris 1895. (Bibliothèque de l'École des Hautes Études 105).

Farforovskij Farforovskij, S. V., *Nogajcy.* Tiflis 1909.

Fatyhova Fatyhova, F. F., *Narečenie imen u baškir*: **Issl. po ist. êtn. Başkirii.** (Ufa 1984), pp. 65-73.

Fedotov Fedotov, M. R., *Slovar' čuvašskih nehristianskih ličnyh imen.* Čeboksary 1998, 148 pp.

Fehértói Fehértói, Katalin, *Egy kis névvonatkoztatás* [Telebuga, Nohaj]: **MNy.** LXVIII (1972), pp. 214-216.

Fejér, CD Fejér, Georgius, *Codex Diplomaticus Hungariae Ecclesiasticus ac Civilis.* I-XI. Budae 1829-1844.

Fekete Fekete, L., *Eine Konskription von den Jassen in Ungarn aus dem Jahre 1550*: **AOH** XI (1960), pp. 115-143.

Fekete 1927   Fekete Lajos, *Igék oszmánli-török tulajdonnevekben*: **MNy.** XXIII (1927), p. 284.

Fekete 1934   Fekete Lajos, *Törtel mint személynév*: **MNy.** XXX (1934), 50.

Fekete 1962   Fekete, L., *Beiname (laqab), Personenname (isim) und Apposition (na^c at) in den Ofner Muqāṭa^c a-Deftern*: **AOH** 15 (1962), pp. 97-109.

Fekete 1965   Fekete, L., *Mit Zahlwörtern gebildete osmanisch-türkische Ortsnamen*: **AOH** 18 (1965), pp. 61-71.

Fest. Hirth   *Festschrift für Friedrich Hirth* zu seinem 75. Geburtstag, 16 April 1920. Berlin 1920.

Fest. Thomsen   *Festschrift Vilhelm Thomsen* zur Vollendung des siebzigsten Lebensjahres am 25. Januar 1912, dargebracht von Freunden und Schülern. Leipzig, Otto Harrassowitz 1912.

Fındıkoğlu   Fındıkoğlu, Z. Fahri, *Türk Folklorunda İsim Meselei*: **Türk Folkloru Ar. Derg.** 39 (1952), pp. 609-610.

FMUI   *Aus den Forschungsarbeiten d. Mitglieder d. Ung. Inst. u. d. Collegium Hungaricum in Berlin. Dem Andenken Robert Graggers gewidmet.* Berlin-Leipzig.

Foy   Foy, Karl, *Zu "der Personenname Aydemir und das Wort demir"*: **MSOS** (1900), pp. 216-217.

FOr.   *Folia Orientalia.* Kraków.

Fox   Fox, Ralph, *People of the Steppes.* London 1925.

Fragm. Hist. Ar.   de Goeje, M. I., *Fragmenta historicorum arabicorum et quidem pars tertia operis Kitabo 'l-Oyun wa 'lhadaık fi akhbari 'l-hakaık, et pars sexta operis Tadjaribo 'l-Omami, auctore Ibn Maskowaih,* quae cum indicibus et glossario, edidit –. Leyden 1871.

Gabain   Gabain, A. von, *Alttürkische Grammatik.* 2. Auflage. Leipzig 1950. (Turkish Edition: 1988).

Gabarovskaja   Gabarovskaja, S. F., *Zaimstvovannye sobstvennye imena i tradicionnye prozvišča v jakutskom jazyke*: **Jazyki i lit. narodov Sibiri.** (Novosibirsk 1970), pp. 165-175.

Gafurov 1971   Gafurov, Alim, *Lev i Kiparis.* Vostočnye imena. Moskva 1971.

Gafurov 1987   Gafurov, Alim, *Imja i istorija. Ob imenah arabov, persov, tadžikov i tjurkov.* (Slovar' arabskih, persidskih, tadžikskih i tjurkskih imen). Moskva 1987, 220 pp.

GagRMS   *Gagauzsko-russko-moldavskij slovar'.* (Familii i prozvišča). Moskva 1973, pp. 604-611.

Gayretullah   Gayretullah, Hızır Bek, *Kazak Türklerinde Kişi Adları*: **Türk Kültürü** (1963 (10)), pp. 13-17.

Galkin, Êtn. mat.   Galkin, M. N., *Êtnografičeskie i istoričeskie materialy po Srednej Azii i Orenburgskomu kraju*: **ZIRGOÊtn.** I (1869).

Garbe Festgabe   *Aus Indiens Kultur.* Festgabe Richard von Garbe dem Forscher und Lehrer zu seinem 70. Geburtstag dargebracht von seinen Freunden, Verehrern und Schülern. Im Verein mit Alfred Hillebrandt und Hermann Jacobi herausgegeben von Julius von Negelein. Erlangen [Palm & Henke] 1927.

Garipov   Garipov, T. M., *Baškirskoe imennoe slovoobrazovanie.* Ufa 1959, 223 pp.

Garipov 1973   Garipov, T. I., *O drevnih kypčakskih imenah v antroponimii baškir*: **OnomPov. 3.** (Ufa 1973), pp. 52-58.

Garipov 1981   Garipov, T. M., *Fonetičeskie processy v baškirskih imenah sobstvennyh*: **Vopr. ba. top.** (Ufa 1981), pp. 64-67.

Garipova 1984   Garipova, F. T., *Tatarstan gidronimnarï süzlege.* Kazan 1984, 224 pp.

Garipova 1990   Garipova, F., *Tatarstan gidronimnarï süzlege.* Kazan 1990.

Gejbullaev   Gejbullaev, G. A., *Toponimija Azerbajdžana* (Istoriko-êtnografičeskoe issledovanie). Baku 1986, 190 pp.

Ghibanescu, Isp.   Ghibanescu, Gh., *Ispisoace şi zapise. Documente slavo-romane.* Iaşi 1906.

Ghibanescu, Sur.   Ghibanescu, Gh., *Surete şi izvoade I. Documente slavo-romane.* Iaşi 1906-1907.

Giese   Giese, Fr., *Die altosmanischen anonymen Chroniken in Text und Übersetzung.* Breslau-Leipzig 1922-1925.

Györffy, Buyruq   Györffy, G., *Die Rolle des buyruq in der alttürkischen Gesellschaft*: **AOH** 11 (1960), pp. 169-179.

Gyárfás   Gyárfás, István, *A jász-kunok története.* I-IV. Kecskemét - Budapest 1870-1885.

Györffy 1953   Györffy, Gy., *Török női méltóságnév a magyar kútfőkben* [=Turkic woman's title in Hungarian sources]: **MNy.** 49 (1953), pp. 109-111.

C

Györffy, Bes.	Györffy György, *Besenyők és magyarok*: **KCsA** I. Ergbd. (1939), pp. 397-500.
GMNS	*E. J. W. Gibb Memorial Series. New Series.*
GMS	*E. J. W. Gibb Memorial Series.*
Golden	Golden, Peter B., *An Introduction to the History of the Turkic Peoples.* Wiesbaden 1992, 483 pp.
Golden, Khaz.	Golden, Peter B., *Khazar Studies: An Historico-Philological Inquiry into the Origins of the Khazars.* Budapest 1980.
Gombocz, ÁTSz.	Gombocz, Z., *Árpádkori török személyneveink.* Budapest 1915, 51 pp. (A Magyar Nyelvtudományi Társaság Kiadványai. 16. sz.).
Gordl. Sb.	*Akademiku V. A. Gordlevskomu k ego semidesjatipjatiletiju.* Sbornik statej. Moskva 1953.
Gordlevskij 1913	Gordlevskij, V. A., *K ličnoj onomastike u osmancev*: **Drevnosti vostočnye** IV, vyp. 1. (M. 1913), pp. 129-136.
Gordlevskij	Gordlevskij, V. A., *Roždenie rebenka i ego vospitanie*: **Ètn. Obozr.** 3-4 (1910), p. 168.
Gorjačeva	Gorjačeva, T., *Bibliographia Onomastica*: Altaic: **Onoma** 18, 23. 3-4 (1974, 1979), pp. 239-247; pp. 691-692.
Gorjačeva - Mikesy	Gorjačeva, T. - Mikesy, S., *Bibliographia Onomastica*: Altaic: **Onoma** 20. 2-3 (1976), pp. 533-542.
Gökb., Ed.	Gökbilgin, Tayyib, *Edirne ve Paşa Livası.* İstanbul 1952. (İstanbul Üniv. Ed. Fak. Yayınları 508).
Gökb., Rum.	Gökbilgin, Tayyib, *Rumeli'de Yürükler, Tatarlar ve Evlad-ı Fatihan.* İstanbul 1957. (İstanbul Üniv. Ed. Fak. Yayınları 748).
Gökçen	Gökçen, İbrahim, *Saruhan'da Yürük ve Türkmenler.* İstanbul 1946. (CHP Manisa Halkevi Yayınlarından, Sayı XVI).
Gönüllü 1983a	Gönüllü, A. R., *Alanya Yörüklerinde Bazı Hayvan İsimleri*: **Türk Folkloru** 4 (47) (1983), pp. 12.
Gönüllü 1983b	Gönüllü, Ali Rıza, *Türk Onomastiğinde "Teke"*: **Türk Folkloru** 6 (71) (1983), pp. 11-12.
Gönüllü 1983c	Gönüllü, Ali Rıza, *Türklerin Bazı Hayvanlara verdiği İsimler*: **Türk Folkloru** 5 (53) (1983), pp. 18-21.
Gricenko	Gricenko, K. F., *Ličnye imena i prozvicšča u jakutov*: **Antroponimika.** (M. 1970), pp. 155-166.
Grigor'ev	Grigor'ev, V. V., *O nekotoryh sobytijah v Buhare, Hokande i Kašgare.* Kazan' 1861.
Grod.	Grodekov, N. I., *Kirgizy i karakirgizy Syr-dar'inskoj oblasti.* I. Taškent 1889, VIII+298+(Priloženie) 205 pp.
Grod., Pril.	Grodekov, N. I., *Kirgizy i karakirgizy Syr-dar'inskoj oblasti.* I. Taškent 1889, VIII+298+(Priloženie) 205 pp.
Grod., Vojna	Grodekov, N. I., *Vojna v Turkmenii.* I-IV. SPb. 1883.
Grousset	Grousset, R., *L'empire des steppes.* Paris 1939.
Grum-Gržim.	Grum-Gržimajlo, G. E., *Zapadnaja Mongolija i Urjanhajskij kraj.* I-III. SPb. - L. 1912-1930.
Gubaeva	Gubaeva, S. S., *Patronimija v toponimii Ferganskoj doliny*: **OSA** (1978), pp. 28-37.
Gusejnzade	Gusejnzade, Č. M., *O dvuh drevnetjurkskih antropoformantah*: **SovT** 1987, pp. 111-115.
Gülbeden	Yılgar, Abdürrab (transl.), *Gülbeden Hanım, Hümâyun-name.* Farsçadan çeviren –. Ankara 1944.
Gülensoy	Gülensoy, Tuncer, *Doğu Anadolu Osmanlıcası* - Etimolojik Sözlük Denemesi -. Ankara 1986.
Gülensoy 1977	Gülensoy, Tuncer, *24 Oğuz Boyunun Anadolu'daki İzleri* [Yer Adları Üzerine]: **Türk Halkbilim Araştırmaları Yıllığı** 1977, pp. 73-98.
Gülensoy 1979	Gülensoy, Tuncer, *Anadolu Yer Adları Üzerine Bir Araştırma*: Bazlambaç: **Türk Kültürü** 17 (197) (1979), pp. 41-44.
Gülensoy 1984a	Gülensoy, T., *Elâzığ, Bingöl ve Tunceli İlleri Yer Adlarına Bir Bakış*: **TYASB** (1984), pp. 149-156.
Gülensoy 1984b	Gülensoy, Tuncer, *Elâzığ, Tunceli, Bingöl ve Diyarbakır Yörelerindeki Boy, Soy, Oymak ve Aşiret Adları Üzerine*: **Türk Dünyası Araştırmaları** 28 (1984), pp. 134-156.
Gülensoy 1994	Gülensoy, Tuncer, *Kazakistan'da ve Türkistan'da (Özbekistan'da) Türk Yer Adları ve*

Anadolu'daki İzleri: **Türk Kültürü Araştırmaları** 32 (1994), pp. 157-169.

Gülensoy 1995   Gülensoy, Tuncer, *Türkçe yer adları kılavuzu*. Ankara 1995.

Gülensoy 1999   Gülensoy, Tuncer, *Türk kişi Adlarının Dil ve Tarih Açısından Önemi*: **Türk Dili** 565 (1999), pp. 3-8.

Gülensoy, Kırg.   Gülensoy, T., *Açıklamalı Kırgız Kişi Adları Sözlüğü* (Kadın-Erkek). (1999).

Gürsoy-Naskalı   Gürsoy-Naskalı, Emine, *Türkçe'de Kedi İsimleri*: **Türk Kültürü Araştırmaları** 32 (1994), pp. 181-193.

Gökalp   Gökalp, Z., *Türklerde Aile adları*: İş I, No. 3-4, Temmuz-Teşrin (1934), pp. 193-194.

Hacıyev   Hacıyev, Alahverdi, *Azärbaycan Antroponimik Sistämindä Türk Mänşäli Şähs Adları*: **UTK 1992** (1996), pp. 667-682.

Hakkı, Ves.   Hakkı, İsmail, *Anadolu Türk Tarihi Vesikalarından İkinci Kitap*. Afyon Karahisar, Sandıklı, Bolvadin, Çay, İsaklı, Manisa, Birgi, Muğla, Milas, Peçin, Denizli, Isparta, Atabey, ve Eğirdir'deki Kitabeler ve Sahip, Saruhan, Aydın, Menteşe, Inanç, Hamit oğulları hakkında malumat. Yazan: –. İstanbul 1929.

Halikov   Halikov, A. H., *500 russkih familij bulgaro-tatarskogo proishoždenija* (Bolγar-tatar čïγïšlï 500 rus familiyasï). Kazan' 1992.

Halikov 1995   Khalikov (Halikov), A. Kh., *Rus Tanınan 500 Bulgar-Tatar Türk Asıllı Sülâle*. Istanbul 1995, 111 pp. (Türk Dünyası Araştırmaları Vakfı Yayınları: 131).

Halikova 1973   Halikova, R. H., *Antroponimy v baškirskih dokumentah XVIII. v.*: **OnomPov. 3.** (Ufa 1973), pp. 113-114.

Halikova 1976   Halikova, R. H., *Struktura baškirskih ličnyh imen XVII-XVIII. vv.* Na materiale sežere, istoričeskih i delovyh dokumentov: **OnomPov. 4.** (Ufa 1976), pp. 121-125.

Halikova 1981   Halikova, R. H., *Ličnye imena i toponimy v sežere i aktovyh pamjatnikah baškir 18-19 vv.*: **Vopr. ba. top.** (Ufa 1981), pp. 19-28.

Hamilton, Ouïg.   Hamilton, James Russell, *Les Ouïgours à l'époque des Cinq dynasties d'après les documents chinois*. Paris 1955. (Bibliothèque des Hautes Études Chinoises Vol. X).

Hamilton, Toquz   Hamilton, James Russell, *Toquz Oγuz et On Uyγur*: **JA** 250 (1962), pp. 23-63.

Hamilton, Tutung   Hamilton, James Russell, *Les titres Šäli et Tutung en ouïgour*: **JA** 272 (1984), pp. 425-437.

Hammer   Hammer-Purgstall, Joseph von, *Geschichte der Goldenen Horde in Kiptschak*. Pest 1840.

Hammer, GOR   Hammer-Purgstall, Joseph von, *Geschichte des Osmanischen Reiches*. I-II. Pest 1827-1828.

Hammer, Ilch.   Hammer-Purgstall, Joseph von, *Geschichte der Ilchane, das ist der Mongolen in Persien*. I-II. Darmstadt 1842-1843.

Hammer, Krim   Hammer-Purgstall, Joseph von, *Geschichte der Chane der Krim unter osmanischer Herrschaft vom XV. Jhr. bis zum Ende des XVIII. Jhr.* Wien 1856.

Haneda   Haneda, Tôru, *A propos d'un fragment d'une prière manichéenne retrouvée à Tourfan*: **Mém. R. Dep. TB** 6 (1963), pp. 1-23.

Hanykov, Buh.   Hanykov, N., *Opisanie Buharskago Hanstva*. SPb. 1843.

Hanykov, Karta ZK   Hanykov, N. (ed.), *Karta zemel' kirgizov vnutrennej i maloj ord*. Sost. –: **Žurn. MVD** (1845).

Hanykov, Poezdka   Chanykov, N., *Poezdka iz Orska v Hivu i obratno, soveršennaja v 1740-41 godah* Gladyševym i Muravinym. Izd. –. SPb. 1851.

Harisova   Harisova, Z. A., *Sostav baškirskih imen i familij*: **OnomPov. 3.** (Ufa 1973), pp. 183-186.

Hasanov 1964   Hasanov, H. H., *Geografiya terminlari lugati* (Rusča-uzbekča, Uzbekča-rusča). Tâškent 1964.

Hasanov 1978   Hasanov, H. H., *Geografik nomlar maᶜnosi*. Tâškent 1978.

Haz. Okm.   *Hazai Okmánytár. Codex Diplomaticus Patrius Hungaricus*. I-VIII. Győr - Budapest 1863-1891.

Hedin   Hedin, Sven, *Im Herzen von Asien*. Zehntausend Kilometer auf unbekannten Pfaden. I-II. Leipzig 1903.

Hedin, En färd   Hedin, Sven, *En färd genom Asien 1893-97*. I-II delen. Stockholm 1898.

Hedin, S. Tib.   Hedin, Sven, *Southern Tibet. Discoveries in former times compared with my own researches in 1906-1908*. I-IX. Stockholm 1917-1922.

Hil. Sābī   Amedroz, H. F., *The historical remains of Hilāl al-Sābi*. First part of his Kitab al-Wuzara (Gotha Ms. 1756) and Fragment of his History 389-393 A. H. (B. M. Ms. add. 19 360). Edited with notes and glossary by –. Leyden 1904.

Hisamitdinova 1981 Hisamitdinova, F. G., *Leksiko-semantičeskaja klassifikacija nazvanij naselennyx punktov*: **Vopr. ba. top.** (Ufa 1981), pp. 29-40.

HJAS *Harvard Journal of Asiatic Studies*. Cambridge, Mass. 1936-.

Horošin Horošhin, A. P., *Isčislenie 92-h kolen uzbekov*: **Maev**, pp. 324-28.

Houtsma, Recueil Houtsma, M. Th., *Recueil de textes relatifs à l'histoire des Seldjoucides*. I-V. Leide 1886-1903.

Howorth Howorth, Henry H., *History of the Mongols, Turks and Tatars from the ninth to the nineteenth century*. I-IV +Index. London 1876-1927.

HRS Baskakov, N. A. (ed.), *Hakassko-russkij slovar'*. Sost. A. I. Inkiževekova-Grekul. Pod red. –. Moskva 1953.

HŞ Heuser, F., *Türkisch-deutsches Wörterbuch*. Verfasst und hrsg. von F. Heuser. 5. verb. Aufl. Wiesbaden 1962.

Hudūd Minorsky, V. (Ed., transl.), *Hudūd al-ᶜĀlam. "The Regions of the World"*. A Persian Geography. Edited, translated and annotated by –. London 1937. (GMNS).

Hudžamberdyev 1970 Hudžamberdyev, Ja., *Glagol'nye toponimy*: **Mat.-y VII Naučno-teoret. konf. prof.-prep. sostava Karšinskogo gos. ped. in-ta.** (Samarkand - Karši 1970).

Hudžamberdyev 1974 Hudžamberdyev, Ja., *Istoriko-etimologičeskoe issledovanie toponimii Surhandar'inskoj oblasti*. Taškent 1974.

Hungaro-Turcica Káldy-Nagy, Gy. (ed.), *Hungaro-Turcica*. Studies in Honour of Julius Németh. Budapest 1976, 364 pp.

Hvol'son, Zam. Hvol'son, D., *Predvaritel'nye zametki o najdennyh v Semirečenskoj oblasti sirijskih nadgrobnyh nadpisjah*: **ZVOIRAO** I (1887), pp. 84-109.

Hvol'son, Nest. (I) Hvol'son, D., *Nestorianskie nadpisi iz Semireč'ja*: **ZVOIRAO** I (1887), pp. 217-221.

Hvol'son, Nest. (II) Khvol'son, D., *Dopolnenija i popravki k stat'jam "Nestorianskie nadpisi iz Semireč'ja"*: **ZVOIRAO** I (1887), pp.303-308.

IAN *Izvestija Akademii Nauk*. Moskva.

IAN KirgSSR *Izvestija Akademii Nauk Kirgizskoj SSR, serija obščestvennyh nauk*. Frunze.

Ibn Abdaẓẓāhir/Tizeng. I Ibn Abdaẓẓāhir, *ar-Rawd aẓ-ẓāhir fī sīrat al-muluk aẓ-ẓāhir*: **Tizeng. I**, pp. 46-64.

Ibn al-Athīr, Atab. Ibn al-Athīr, Ali b. Muχammad, *Taᶜ rīkh al-Dawlah al-Atābakīyyah Mulūk al-Mawṣil*: **RHCHor** II/2 (1876), pp. 1-394.

Ibn al-Athīr (I) Ibn al-Athīr, Ali b. Muχammad, *Al-Kāmil fi 'l-Taᶜrīkh*: **RHCHor** I (1872), pp. 189-744.

Ibn al-Athīr (II/1) Ibn al-Athīr, Ali b. Muχammad, *Al-Kāmil fi 'l-Ta'rīkh*: **RHCHor** II/1 (1876), pp. 1-180.

Ibn al-Athīr/Tornb. Tornberg, C. J. (ed.), *Ibn al-Athīr, Al-Kāmil fi 'l-Ta'rīχ* (Chronicon quod perfectissimum inscribitur). Ed. –. I-XII. Leiden 1851-1876.

Ibn Bībī III Houtsma, M. Th. (ed.), *Recueil de textes relatifs à l'histoire des Seldjoucides*. Vol. III. Histoire des Seldjoucides d'Asie Mineure. Leide 1902, XV, 408 pp.

Ibn Bībī IV Houtsma, M. Th., *Recueil de textes relatifs à l'histoire des Seldjoucides*. Vol. IV. Histoire des Seldjoucides d'Asie Mineure. Leide 1902, XVIII, 358 pp.

Ibn Bat. Defrémery, M. C. - Sanguinetti, B. R. (transl.), *Voyages d'Ibn Batoutah*, texte arabe accompagné d'une traduction par –. Vol. I-IV, Index. Paris 1854-59.

Ibn Fadl. Togan, A. Zeki Validi (ed.), *Ibn Fadlan's Reisebericht*. Hrsg. von –. Leipzig 1939. (Abhandlungen für die Kunde des Morgenlandes XXIV/3).

Ibn Khaldūn/Quatrem. Quatremere, É. M. (ed.), *Prolegomenes d'Ibn Khaldun*. Text arabe. Publ. d'après manuscrits de la Bibliothèque Impériale par –. 1-3. Paris 1858. (Notices et extraites des manuscrits de la Bibl. Imp. et autre bibliothèques. 16-18.).

Ibn Khaldūn/Tizeng. I Ibn Khaldūn, *Kitāb al-mubtada' wa'l-ḫabar fī ayyām al-ᶜarab wa'l-ᶜağam wa'l-barbar*: **Tizeng. I**, pp. 365-394.

Ibn Khallikan Wüstenfeld, F. (ed.), *Ibn Challikani vitae illustrium vivorum*. Arabice edidit, variis lectionibus, indicibus que locupletissimus instruxit –. Fasc. 1-13. Gottingae 1835-50.

Ibn Khallikan/de Slane de Slane, Baron MacGuckin (transl.), *Ibn Khallikan's Biographical dictionary*. Translated from the Arabic by –. I-IV. Paris 1843-1871. (Oriental Translation Fund).

Ibn Saᶜīd Tallquist, Dr. Knut L. (ed.), *Ibn Saᶜīd, Kitāb al-Maġrib fī ḥulā al-Maġrib*. Buch IV. Geschichte der Ihšīden. Herausgegeben von –. Leiden 1899.

Ibn Šaddād, Alep   Sourdel, Dominique, *La Description d'Alep d'Ibn Šaddād*. Édition critique d'al-Aᶜlāq al-Haṭira. Tome I, section 1. Damascus 1953, XXXII pp. + 232 pp.

Ibn Šaddād, Nawād.   Ibn Šaddād, Behā' ud-Dīn, *An-Nawādir as-Sulṭāniyyah wa-l-maḥāsin al-Jūsufiyyah*. Ta'lif al-Qādī-l-Imām al-ᶜĀlim Behā' ud-Dīn –, Abī-l-maḥāsin Jūsuf –, al-maᶜruf bi Ibn Šaddād: **RHCHor** III (1884), pp. 1-370.

Ibn Taghrīb.   Popper, W. (ed.), *Abu 'l-Mahasin ibn Taghrî Birdî's Annals entitled An-Nujûm az-Zahira fi Mulûk Misr wa 'l-Kahira*. Vol. I-VII. Ed. by –. Berkeley, California 1909-1936. (University of California Publications in Semitic Philology).

Ibragimov   Ibragimov, I. I., *Êtnografičeskie očerki kirgizskago naroda*: **Russkij Turkestan** 2, pp. 120-152.

Idrisov   Idrisov, A., *Qïrɣïz tilindegi ïsïmdar*. Lično-sobstvennye imena v kirgizskom jazyke. Frunze 1971, 128 pp.

IIAN   *Izvestija Imperatorskoj Akademii Nauk*. SPb.

IIRGO   *Izvestija Imperatorskago Russkago Geografičeskago Obščestva*. St. Petersburg.

IJMS   *International Journal of Modern Science*.

Iyās   Ibn Iyās, *Bada'iᶜ al-Zuhūr fi Wakā'-iᶜ al-Duhūr*. I-III. Būlāq 1311-12 (1893-94).

Ilimbetov   Ilimbetov, F. F., *Ličnye imena kak istočnik pri izučenii drevnih verovanij baškir*: **Onom-Pov. 3.** (Ufa 1973), pp. 89-95.

IM   Battal, A. (ed.), *Ibnü-Mühennâ Lûgati*. (İstanbul nüshasının Türkçe bölüğünün endeksidir.). İstanbul 1934, 109 pp.

ImÊtnIst.   *Imja – Êtnos – Istorija*. Moskva 1989.

InLitTopon.   *Inostrannaja literatura po toponimike*. Bibliografičeskij obzor. Moskva 1965, 40 pp.

Int. Kongr. Nknde   *Internationaler Kongress für Namenkunde*. München.

IOAIÊK   *Izvestija Obščestva arheologii, istorii i êtnografii pri Kazanskom Universitete*. Kazan'.

IOAIÊK (Dobavlenie)   *Izvestija Obščestva arheologii, istorii i etnografii pri Kazanskom Universitete. Dobavlenie.* Kazan'.

Ionescu   Ionescu, P. C. F., *Noms de personne roumains d'origine turc osmanli*: **V. Milletler Arası Türkoloji Kongr., Tebliğler. Türk Dili 1** (1985). İstanbul 1987, pp. 139-141.

IOO IRGO   *Izvestija Orenburgskogo Otdela IRGO*.

Ipat.   *Letopis' po Ipatskomu spisku*. Izd. Arheogr. Komm. SPb. 1871.

Issl. jazyka   *Issledovanie jazyka drevnepis'mennyh pamjatnikov*. Sbornik statej. Kazan' 1980.

Ismailova - Ovčinnikova   Ismailova, S. A. - Ovčinnikova, E. I., *Ličnye imena i ih varianty v kirgizskom jazyke*: **Voprosy onomastiki** Vyp. 14. (Sverdlovsk 1980), pp. 131-139.

IstorOnom.   *Istoričeskaja Onomastika*. Moskva 1977.

Ivanov   Ivanov, P. P., *Hozjajstvo Džujbarskih šejhov*. K istorii feodal'nogo zemlevladenija v Srednej Azii v XVI-XVII vv. Moskva - Leningrad 1954, 375 pp.

Ivanov, Vosstanie   Ivanov, P. P., *Vosstanie Kitaj-kipčakov v Buharskom hanstve. 1821-1825.* Istočniki i opyt ih issledovanija. Moskva - Leningrad 1937, 130 pp.

Iznoskov   Iznoskov, I. A., *Spisok naselennyh mest Mamadyšskago uezda*. Sostavlen –: **Trudy AS IV**, pp. 116-148.

IzvSrAzKMuz.   *Izvestija Sredne-Aziatskogo komiteta po delam muzeev i ohrany pamjatnikov stariny, iskusstva i prirody*. Taškent.

İdr. Haş.   İzbudak, Veled, *El-İdrak Haşiyesi*. İstanbul 1936.

İlahiyatçı   İlahiyatçı, Kaya Hüsameddin, *Çocuk İsimleri Ansiklopedisi*. Gonca Yayınevi 1992.

İlgaz   İlgaz, Kadriye, *İstanbul'da Doğum ve Çocukla ilgili Adetler ve İnanmalar*: **Türk Folkloru Ar. Derg.** 93 (1957), pp. 1481-1482.

İnan 1940   İnan, Abdülkadir, *Göçebe Türk Destanlarında Kahramanlar-Doğumları, Ad Almaları ve Hüviyetleri*: **Yücel** Nu. 66 (1940), p. 243.

İnan 1958   İnan, Abdülkadir, *İslâmdan Sonra Türkçe Adlar*: **Türk Dili** VII (1958), p. 494.

İnan 1976   İnan, Abdülkadir, *Eski Türk Dini Tarihi*. İstanbul 1976. (Kültür Bakanlığı, Kültür Eserleri 9)

İşçiler 1962a   İşçiler, Salim Sami, *Tekirdağ'da Kadın ve Erkek Adları*: **Türk Folklor Araştırmaları** 7 (158) (1962), pp. 2848-2850.

İşçiler 1962b   İşçiler, Salim Sami, *Tekirdağ'da Gül'lü Adlar*: **Türk Folklor Araştırmaları** 7 (161)

	(1962), p. 2922.
İÜEFTDED	*İstanbul Üniversitesi Edebiyat Fakültesi Türk Dili ve Edebiyatı Dergisi*. İstanbul.
JA	*Journal Asiatique*. Paris.
Jakūbī	de Goeje, M. (ed.), *Kitāb al-aᶜlāk an-nafīsa auctore Abū Alī Ahmed ibn Omar ibn Rosteh. Kitāb al-Boldān auctore Ahmed ibn abī Jakūb ibn Wādhih al-Kātib al-Jakūbī*. Leyden 1892. (BGA VII).
Jankowski 1992	Jankowski, H., *On Crimean Tatar Toponymy*: **Altaic Religious Beliefs and Practices.** (Bp. 1992), pp. 179-182.
Jankowski 1994	Jankowski, H., *Mongolian Loanwords in the Crimean Toponymy*: **Bamberger Zentralasienstudien** (1994), pp. 61-73.
Jankowski 1998	Jankowski, H., *Etymology of the Polish-Lithuanian-Byelorussian Tatar Name Lehimberdi*: **Studia Etymologica Cracoviensia** 3. (Kraków 1998), pp. 13-16.
Jankowski 1999	Jankowski, H., *Polonya Tatarlarının Adları*: **UTK 1996**, pp. 569-578.
Jarilov, Kyz.	Jarilov, A. A., *Kyzylcy i ih hozjajstvo*. Jur'ev 1899, 366 pp. (Byloe i nastojaščee sibirskih inorodcev, vyp. III).
Jarilov, Tel.	Jarilov, A. A. - Kon, F., *Byloe i nastojaščee sibirskih inorodcev*. Teleckie inorodcy. I-III. Minusinsk - Jur'ev 1899.
Jarring	Jarring, G., *An Eastern Turki-English Dialect Dictionary –*. Lund 1964.
Jastrow	Jastrow, Otto, *Die Familiennamen der Türkischen Republik*. Bildungsweise und Bedeutung: **Erlanger Familiennamen-Colloqium.** (Neustadt an der Aisch 1985), pp. 101-110.
Jaz. Prikam.	*Jazyki i onomastika Prikam'ja*. Sb. statej A. S. Gantman (red.). Perm' 1973.
Jegorov 1986	Egorov, N. I., *Ženskie ličnye imena nizovyh čuvašej-jazyčnikov I.*: **Kul'tura i byt** (1986), pp. 88-104.
Jegorov 1987	Egorov, N. I., *Ženskie ličnye imena nizovyh čuvašej-jazyčnikov II*: **Kul'tura i byt** (1987), pp. 54-71.
Jervis	Jervis, Thomas Best, *Military Topographical Map of the Krima Peninsula*. I-X. London 1817.
Jireček	Jireček, K., *Überreste der Petschenegen und Kumanen auf der Balkanhalbinsel*. Prag 1889. (SB. der Böhm. A. d. W.).
Johnson	Johnson, Francis, *A Dictionary Persian, Arabic and English* by –. London 1852.
Joki	Joki, Aulis J., *Wörterverzeichnis der Kyzyl-Sprache*. Helsinki 1953, 47 pp. (Studia Orientalia. Edidit Societas Orientalis Fennica XIX:1).
Jorga, Notes	Jorga, N., *Notes et extraits pour servir à l'histoire des Croisades au Xme siècle*. I-XIII. Bucarest 1915-1916.
JRAS	*The Journal of the Royal Asiatic Society of Great Britain and Ireland*. London.
JRGS	*Journal of the Royal Geographical Society*. London.
JRS	Slepcov, P. A. (ed.), *Jakutsko-russkij slovar'*. Moskva 1972.
JSFOu.	*Journal de la Société Finno-Ougrienne*. Helsingfors.
Jub. sb. Bart.	*Jubilejnyj sbornik V. V. Bartol'du*. Taškent 1927.
Jud.	Judahin, K. K. (ed.), *Kirgizsko-russkij slovar'*. Moskva 1965.
Justi	Justi, F., *Iranisches Namenbuch*. Marburg 1895, XXVI+526 pp. (New Edition: Hildesheim, 1963.).
Jusupov	Jusupov, G. V., *Vvedenie v bulgaro-tatarskuju epigrafiku*. Moskva - Leningrad 1960.
Jusupov 1970	Jusupov, G. V., *Antroponimy v bulgarotatarskoj êpigrafike*: **Ličnye imena v prošlom.** (M. 1970), pp. 248-252.
Yetişen	Yetişen, Rıza, *Naldöken Tahtacıları*: Köyde Doğum ve Ad Verme: **Türk Folklor Araştırmaları** 14 (279) (1972), p. 6450.
Yund 1961	Yund, Kerim, *Adlarla İlgili Gelenek ve İnançlar VIII*. (Silifke): **Türk Folklor Araştırmaları** 6 (138) (1961), p. 2303.
Yund 1981	Yund, Kerim, *Kişi Adlarında Renk*: **Türk Folkloru** 2 (22) (1981), pp. 4-7.
Yurtsever 1994	Yurtsever, Erk, *TAMGA Asya'daki Türkçe Coğrâfî Adlar Derlemesi*. Istanbul 1994. (TürkDünyası Araştırmaları Vakfı).
Yurtsever 1997	Yurtsever, Erk, *Türkçe Adlar Derlemesi*. Istanbul 1997, 128 pp.
Yusufoğlu	Yusufoğlu, Mehmet, *Şer'iye defterlerinde Türkçe kişi adları*: **Anıt Dergisi** 3, 4, 6. (Konya

CV

1949).

Kafesoğlu 1966 Kafesoğlu, İbrahim, *Tarihte 'Türk' Adı*: **Reşid Rahmeti Arat İçin.** (Ankara 1966), pp. 306-319.

Kafesoğlu 1985 Kafesoğlu, İbrahim, *Bilge Kağan'ın Adı ve Lâkabı*: **Türk Dünyası Araştırmaları** 35 (1985), pp. 4-8.

Kajbullaev Kajbullaev, Š. Ê., *Krymskotatarskie imena* Proishoždenie i značenie. Simferopol' 1994, 81 pp.

Kakuk 1955 Kakuk, Zs., *Tabán*: **Nyelvőr** 79 (1955), p. 105.

Kakuk 1974a Kakuk, S., *Anthropnymes turcs mahométans*: **The Muslim East** 1974, pp. 161-173.

Kakuk 1974b Kakuk, S., *Quelques Catégories de noms de Personne Turcs*: **AOH** XXVIII (1974), pp. 1-35.

Kakuk 1988 Kakuk, Zs., *Török személynevek hódoltságkori forrásainkban*: **Keletkutatás** (1988), pp. 13-28.

Kalačev Kalačev, A. K., *Neskol'ko slov o poêzii telengetov*: **ŽS** VI (1896), pp. 489-500.

Kalilov Kalilov, K., *Imjanarečenie u kirgizov v prošlom i nastojaščem*: **OSA 2** (1980), pp. 91-100.

Kamalov Kamalov, A. A., *Nekotorye aspekty izučenija baškirskih narodnyh geografičeskih terminov*: **Vopr. ba. top.** (Ufa 1981), pp. 4-18.

Kamāladdīn al-Dahhan, Sami (ed.), *Umbar b. Ahmad Kamal al-Din: Zubdat al-Talab min Ta'rikh Halab.* (Histoire d'Alep par Kamāl ad-Din Ibn al-ᶜAdīm). I-III. Damascus 1951, 1954, 1968. (Institut Français de Damas).

Kamāladdīn, Bughyah Barbier de Meynard, A. C. (ed., transl.), *Muntakhabāt min Bugyah ṭalab fi taᶜrikh Halab li-Kamāl ad-Dīn Ibn al-Adīm*: **RHCHor** III (1884), pp. 695-732.

Kamāladdīn: RHCHor III Barbier de Meynard, A. C. (ed., transl.), *Muntakhabāt min Ta'rikh Halab li-Kamāl ad-Dīn Ibn al-Adīm*: **RHCHor** III (1884), pp. 577-690.

Karaağaç Karaağaç, Günay, *"Söyén Bike" Adı Hakkında*: **Türk Dili ve Edebiyatı Araştırmaları Dergisi** 8 (1994), pp. 25-29.

Karabacek Karabacek, J., *Das erste Auftreten der Türken*: **M. S. Pap. Rainer** I (1887), pp. 93-107.

Karaboran Karaboran, H. Hilmi, *Türkiye'de Mevkii Adları Üzerine Bir Araştırma*: **TYASB**, pp. 97-148.

Karaev 1964 Karaev, S. K., *Rusko-uzbekskij slovar' geografičeskih nazvanij.* Taskent 1964.

Karaev 1979 Karaev, S. K., *Tolkovyj slovar' geografičeskih terminov.* (Na uzbekskom jazyke). Taskent 1979.

Karakuş Karakuş, İdris, *Türkçe Ad Bilim (Onomastik)'de Hayvan Adları*: **Erdem** 9 (27), 1. 97. (1997), pp. 1143-1151.

Karamanlıoğlu Karamanlıoğlu, Ali Fehmi, *Kıpçak Türkçesi Grameri.* Ankara 1994, 164 pp.

Karatayev Karatayev, Olcobay, *Kırgız Etnonimler (Boy ve Kabile Adları) Sözlüğü.* Bişkek 1993 (Kırgızistan-Türkiye Manas Üniversitesi Yayınları: 40)

Karaulov Karaulov, N. A., *Balkary na Kavkaze*: **IOAIÊK** XXIII, pp. 49-66.

KarRPS *Karaimsko-russko-pol'skij slovar'*. Familii. Moskva 1974, pp. 674-680.

Karta Eniseja *Karta bassejna verhnej časti reki Jeniseja*: **IIRGO** (1912).

Karta JAR *Karta južnoj pograničnoj časti aziatskoj Rossii.* I-XXIV.

Karta Kazan. Rittih, A. (ed.), *Karta narodonaselenij Kazanskoj gubernii po plemenam.* (Priloženie k Materialam dlja Êtnografii Rossii).

Katanov Katanov, N. F., *Alfavitnyj ukazatel' sobstvennyh imen, vstrečajuščihsja v pervom i vtorom tome obrazcov narodnoj literatury tjurkskih plemen,* sobr. V. Radlovym. SPb. 1888.

Katanov, Otč. Katanov, N., *Otčet o poezdke,* soveršennoj s 15 maja po 1 sentjabra 1896 goda v Minusinskij okrug Enisejskoj gubernii: **UZKU** LXIV/3; LXIV/5-6, pp. 1-50; pp. 1-53.

Katanov, Star. Kaz. Katanov, N., *Tatarskie rasskazy o Staroj Kazani*: **IOAIÊK** XXX, vyp. 3 (1920), pp. 287-300.

Katanov: ZIRGOÊtn. *Poezdka k karagasam v 1890 g.*: **ZIRGOÊtn.** XVI (XVII?), vyp. 2 (3?) (1891 (1892?)), pp. 133-230.

Katarinskij Katarinskij, V., *Kirgizsko-russkij slovar'*. Orenburg 1897.

Katona Katona, Lajos, *Omurtag*: **KCsA** II (1929-1932), pp. 384-387.

Kazancev Kazancev, I., *Opisanie kirgiz-kajsak.* SPb. 1867.

Kálmán 1974   Kálmán, B., *Sismánd*: **MNy.** LXX (1974), pp. 205-206.

KB I   Arat, R. R., *Kutadgu Bilig*. I. Metin. İstanbul 1947.

KB III   Arat, R. R. (ed.), *Kutadgu Bilig*. İndeksi neşre hazırlayanlar: Kemal Eraslan, Osman F. Sertkaya, Nuri Yüce. İstanbul 1979.

KCsA   *Kőrösi Csoma Archivum*. Budapest.

Kekulé   Kekulé, S., *Über Titel, Ämter, Rangstufen un Anreden in der offizieller türkischen Sprache*. Halle 1892.

Kenesbaev   Kenesbaev, S. K., *Ob ispol'zovanii sobstvennyh imen v kazahskom jazyke v naricatel'nom značenii*: **SovT** (1973, No. 1), pp. 87-91.

Kenesbaev - Džanuzakov   Kenesbaev, S. K. - Džanuzakov, T. D., *O leksičeskih plastah onomastiki kazahskogo jazyka*: **SovT** (1976, No. 3), pp. 78-88.

Kiekbaev 1956   Kiekbaev, Dž. G., *Voprosy baškirskoj antroponimii*. Uč. zap. Bašk. gos. ped. in-ta im. K. A. Timirjazeva, vyp. 3. Ufa 1956, No. 2.

Kindī   Guest, Rhuvon (ed.), *The Governors and judges of Egypt or Kitāb al'Umarā' (el Qulāh) wa Kitāb el Qudāh of El-Kindī*. Together with an appendix derived mostly from Raf ᶜel Işr by Ibn Hajar. Edited by –. Leyden - London 1912. (GMS XIX).

Kırzıoğlu 1949   Kırzıoğlu, Fahreddin, *Kuzeydoğu Anadolu'da Kullanılan Türkçe Erkek Adları*: **Türk Folklor Araştırmaları** 5 (1949), pp. 76.

Kırzıoğlu 1961   Kırzıoğlu, M. Fahrettin, *Çemizgezek ile Keği ve Sincar'da Eski Türkçe Erkek Adları*: **Türk Dili** CXI (1961), p. 121.

Kırzıoğlu 1966   Kırzıoğlu, M. F., *Köroğlu Boyları'nda Oğuz Düzeni Sayıları* (İkili-Dörtlü-Altılı-Onikili-Yirmidörtlü Düzen): **Reşid Rahmeti Arat İçin.** (Ankara 1966), pp. 323-330.

KkRS   Baskakov, N. A. (ed.), *Karakalpaksko-russkij slovar'*. Moskva 1958.

Klimov - Êdel'man   Klimov - Êdel'man, *K êtimologii Albasty i Almasty*: **SovT** No. 3. (1979), pp. 57-63.

KmkRS   Bammatov, Z. Z. (ed.), *Kumyksko-russkij slovar'*. Moskva 1969.

Kn. Metriki Lit.   Pogodin, M. - Dubenskij, M. D., *Kniga posol'skaja Metriki Velikago Knjažestva Litovskago*. Izd. –. Moskva 1843.

Kojčubaev   Kojčubaev, E., *Kratkij tolkovyj slovar' toponimov Kazahstana*. Alma-Ata 1974.

Kojčubaev   Kojčubaev, E., *Kratkij tolkovyj slovar' toponimov Kazahstana*. Alma-Ata 1974, 275 pp.

Kokovcov   Kokovcov, P. K., *K siro-tureckoj êpigrafike Semireč'ja*: **IIAN** (1909), pp. 773-796.

Konkobaev 1980c   Konkobaev, K., *Toponimija Južnoj Kirgizii*. Frunze 1980, 171 pp.

Konkobaev 1985   Konkobaev, K., *Razvitie i perspektivy kirgizskoj onomastiki*: **Onom. Kirg.** I. (1985), pp. 111-115.

Konšin, Pam.   Konšin, N., *O pamjatnikah stariny v Semipalatinskoj oblasti*: **ZSOIRGOSemip.** I, pp. 1-32.

Konšin, Mat. I-III   Konšin, N., *Materialy dlja istorii Stepnago Kraja (1824) I-III.*: **Pam. kn. Semip.** (1900), pp. 1-117.

Konšin, Mat. V   Konšin, N., *Materialy dlja istorii Stepnago Kraja V.*: **ZSOIRGOSemip.**, pp. 1-107.

Konšin, Oč.   Konšin, N., *Očerki êkonomičeskago byta kirgiz Semipalatinskoj oblasti*: **Pam. kn. Semip.** (1901 / 1902).

Kornilov   Kornilov, T. E., *Slovar' sobstvennyh imen Povolž'ja i sopredel'nyh territorij*.

Koroškin   Koroškin, A. P., *Itinéraires de l'Asie centrale*: recueil d'itinéraires et de voyages dans l'Asie centrale et l'Extrême-Orient. Paris 1878.

Korsakov   Korsakov, D. A. (ed.), *Sbornik materialov po istorii Kazanskogo kraja v XVIII veke*, izdannyj pod redakciej –: **IOAIÊK** XVIII, pp. 1-56, pp. 1-368.

Koržanov   Koržanov, I. I., *Ne musul'manskie imena u tatar Ul'janovskoj oblasti*: **OnomPov. 4.** (Saransk 1976), pp. 81-83.

Kostrov   Kostrov, N., *Očerki byta minusinskih tatar*: **Trudy IV. A. S.** II (1877/1884), pp. 208-248.

Koşay 1921a   Koşay, H. Z., *Krimi és kazáni tatár tulajdonnevek*: **KCsA** I (1921-1925), p. 324.

Koşay 1921b   Koşay, H. Z., *Adalékok a török tulajdonnevekhez*: **KCsA** I (1921-1925), p. 321.

Koşay 1927   Koşay, H. Z., *Türk Adlarına Ait Araştırma*: **Türk Yurdu** V (1927), pp. 120-126.

Kow.   Kowalewski, J. É., *Dictionnaire mongol-russe-français*, par –. I-III. Kasan 1844-1849.

Kowalski   Kowalski, T., *Sir Aurel Stein's Sprachaufzeichnungen in Ainallu-Dialekt aus Südpersien*. Kraków 1937, 71 pp. (Mém. de la Commission Orientaliste No. 29).

Köyl. 1928   *Köylerimizin adları.* İstanbul 1928, 1932.
Köyl. 1968   *Köylerimiz* (1 Mart 1968 durumu). Ankara 1968, 790 pp.
Köprülü Arm.   *60. Doğum Yılı Münasebetiyle Fuad Köprülü Armağanı.* İstanbul 1953.
Köprülü   Köprülü, M. Fuad, *Zur Kenntnis der alttürkischen Titulatur*: **KCsA** I. Ergbd. (1939), pp. 327-344.

Köprülü, Anad. İsl. Köprülü, F., *Anadolu'da İslâmiyyet*: **Dârülfünün Edeb. Fak. Mecmuası** II/4 (1922), p. 392.

Köprülü, Unvan   Köprülü, F., *Eski Türk unvanlarına ait notlar*: **THITM** 2 (1939), pp. 17-31.
Köprülüzade   Köprülüzade, Mehmed Fuad, *Türk onomastique'i hakkında*: **Tarih Dergisi** I (2) (1950), pp. 221-236.

Krasovskij   Krasovskij (ed.), *Materialy dlja Geogr. i Stat. Rossii, sobr. oficerami general'nago štaba.* I-III. Oblast' sibirskih kirgizov, sost. –. SPb. 1868.

KrymTatIm. 1992   Sosnovskij, S. K. (Ed.), *Krymskotatarskie imena.* Spravočnik. Simferopol' 1992, pp. 1-62.
Kronheim   Kronheim, W., *Die Tschuwaschen.* Ein ethnographischer Beitrag: **ArchKR** III (1843).
KSz.   *Keleti Szemle.* Budapest.
Kul'tura i byt   *Kul'tura i byt nizovyh čuvašej.* Čeboksary.
Kungursk. akty   Titov, A. A. (ed.), *Kungurskie akty XVII veka (1668-1699 g.).* Izdanie A. G. Kuznecova. Redaktor –. SPb. 1888.

Kupusovič   Kupusovič, Amina, *Muslimanska imena u Opširnom popisu 60 sanskog sandžaka iz 1604 godine*: **Prilozi za orijentalnu filologiju** 40/1990. (Sarajevo 1991), 267-308 pp.

Kurbanov   Kurbanov (Gurbanov), Afat, *Azerbayjan dilinin onomatologiyasï.* Baqï 1988.
Kurdjumov   Kurdjumov, M. G., *Opisanie aktov hranjaščihsja v arhive Imperatorskoj Arheografičeskoj Kommissii.* I. Akty Kungurskie, II. Akty Solikamskie. SPb. 1909.

Kuroglo   Kuroglo, S. S., *Ličnye imena u gagauzov*: **Istor. onom.** (Moskva 1977), pp. 180-188.
Kurt, Adana   Kurt, Yılmaz, *Adana Sancağında Kişi Adları*: **Tarih Araştırmaları Dergisi** 15 (26) (1990-1991), pp. 169-252.

Kurt, Çorumlu   Kurt, Yılmaz, *Çorumlu Kazası Kişi Adları* (XVI. yüzyıl): **OTAM** 6 (1995), pp. 211-247.
Kurt, Kozan 1990   Kurt, Yılmaz, *Kozan (Sis) Sancağında Kişi Adları*: **Türk Kültürü Araştırmaları** 28 (1990), pp. 365-378.

Kurt, Kozan 1994   Kurt, Yılmaz, *Kozan'da Şahıs Adları*: **Belleten** 58 (223) (1994), pp. 607-633.
Kusimova   Kusimova, T., *Başkirskie imena* Başqort isemdäre. Ufa 1982, 136 pp.
Kusimova 1970   Kusimova, T. H., *Iz istorii ličnyh imen baškir*: **Ličnye imena v prošlom.** (M. 1970), pp. 241-248.

Kusimova 1971   Kusimova, T. H., *Nekotorye obyčai narečenija imen u baškir*: **OnomPov.** 2 (1971), pp. 52-54.

Kusimova 1973   Kusimova, T. H., *Antroponimy v baškirskih šežere*: **OnomPov.** 3. (Ufa 1973), pp. 66-71.
Kusimova 1976   Kusimova, T. H., *Baškirskie ličnye imena v revizskih skazkah 1859 g.*: **OnomPov.** 4. (Ufa 1976), pp. 126-128.

Kusimova 1988   Kusimova, T. H., *Istoriko-tipologičegkaja obščnost' antroponimov, svjazannyh s ritualaem baškir i turkmen*: **Voprosy sov. tjurkol. konf.** (1988), pp. 192-197.

Kustanaev   Kustanaev, Hudabaj, *Êtnografičeskie očerki kirgiz Perovskago i Kazalinskago uezdov.* Taškent 1894.

Kutlu   Kutlu, Şemsettin, *Türkçe Kadın ve Erkek Adları.* Ankara 1969. (TDK Yayınları S. 281).
Kuzeev   Kuzeev, R. G., *Baškirskie Šežere.* Sostavlenie, perevod tekstov, vvedenie i kommentarii –. Ufa 1960.

Kuzeev, Oč.   Kuzeev, R. G., *Očerki istoričeskoj êtnografii baškir.* Ufa 1957.
Kuzeev, Rodo.-plem. Kuzeev, R. G., *Rodo-plemennoj sostav baškir v XVIII veke:* **Vopr. bašk. fil.** (1959), pp. 60-71.

Kuznecov   Kuznecov, Inn., *Istoričeskie Akty XVII stoletija (1633-99).* Materialy dlja istorii Sibiri. Vyp. 2. Sobral i izdal –. Tomsk 1890, 99 pp.

Kúnos   Kúnos, Ignác, *Kisázsiai török nyelvjárások* I. Brusza-Ajdin vidéki nyelvmutatványok (népdalok); II. Brusza vidéki szólások: **NyK** XXII (1890-92), pp. 113-156; 261-298.

Kúnos 1904   Kúnos, Ignác, *A dunai tatárok nyelvéről*: **KSz.** V (1904), pp. 297-304.
Kúnos, Volksm.   Kúnos, Ignác, *Kasantatarische Volksmärchen.* Auf Grund der Sammlung von Ignác Kúnos

herausgegeben von Imre Baski und Zsuzsa Kakuk. Budapest 1989, 220 pp. (Keleti Tanulmányok - Oriental Studies 8).

KzRS — Musabajev, G. (ed.), *Kazahsko-russkij slovar'*. Otv. red. –. Alma-Ata 1954, 575 pp.

KzTS — Oraltay, H. - Yüce, N. - Pınar, S. (transl.), *Kazak Türkçesi Sözlüğü*. Tercüme: –. İstanbul 1984, 328 pp. (Türk Dünyası Araştırmaları Yayını, 8).

Qalānisi — Amedroz, H. F. (ed.), *Ibn al-Qalānisī: Dhail Ta'rikh Dimashq* History of Damascus 363-555 a.H. by Ibn al-Qalānisī, from the Bodleian Ms. Hunt. 125. Being a continuation of the history of Hilāl al-Sābi. Ed. by –. Leyden 1908, 48+397 pp.

Qalāūn/Tizeng. I — Qalāūn, Sayf al-Dīn, *Tašrīf al-ayyām wa'l-ᶜuṣūr basīrat al-muluk al-manṣūr*: **Tizeng. I**, pp. 65-69.

Qawānīn — Telegdi, S., *Eine türkische Grammatik in arabischer Sprache aus dem XV. Jhdt.*: **KCsA** (1937), pp. 282-326.

Qazw. — Browne, E. G. - Nicholson, R. A. (ed.), *The Ta'rikh-i-Guzīda or "Select History" of Hamdullah Mustawfi-i-Qazwīnī*. Compiled in A. H. 750 (A. D. 1330), and now reproduced in facsimile from a manuscript dated A. H. 857 (A. D. 1453) with an introduction by –. I. Leyden - London 1910. (GMS XIV).

Qazw./Gantin — Qazwīnī, Xamdallāh, *Târîkh-e Gozîde par Hamd Ollâh Mostoufi Qazwînî*. Les dynasties persanes pendant la période musulmane, depuis les Saffârides jusques et y compis les Mogols de la Perse en 1330 de notre ere [] par J. Gantin. Paris 1903, IX, 623 pp.

QTDS — Musabaev, G., Kenesbaev, S., Kaliev. G., etc. (ed.), *Qazaq tiliniñ dialektologiyalïq sözdigi*. Almatï 1969, 426 pp.

QTTS — Keñesbaev, I. K., *Qazaq tiliniñ tùsindirme sözdigi*. I-II. Almatï 1959-1961.

Laptev, Materialy — Laptev, *Materialy po Kazak-kirgizskomu jazyku* Sobr. –. Moskva 1900, 148 pp.

Lavr. — *Letopis' po Lavrentievskomu spisku*. SPb. 1872.

Le Coq, Buch-Fragm. — Le Coq, A. von, *Ein manichäisches Buch-Fragment aus Chotscho*: **Fest. Thomsen**, pp. 145-154.

Le Coq, Hellas — Le Coq, A. von, *Auf Hellas Spuren in Osttürkistan*. Berichte und Abenteuer der II. und III. Deutschen Turfan-Expedition. Leipzig 1926, 166 pp.

Le Coq. Ind. — Le Coq, A. von, *Türkische Namen und Titel in Indien*: **Garbe Festgabe,** pp. 1-7.

Le Coq. Man. — Le Coq, A. von, *Türkische Manichaica aus Chotscho*. I-III. Berlin 1910-1922. (ABAW p-h Klasse, 3).

Le Coq, Namenl. — Le Coq, A. von, *Osttürkische Namenliste mit Erklärungsversuch*: **Hedin, S. Tib.** IX, Part 2, pp. 93-114.

Le Coq, Urkunden — Le Coq, A. von, *Handschriftliche uigurische Urkunden aus Turfan*: **Túrán** (1918), pp. 449-460.

Letop. AK — *Lêtopis' Arhivnoj Kommissii*.

Letop. ZAK — *Lêtopis' Zanjatij Arhivnoj Kommissii*.

Levchine — Levchine, Alexis de, *Description des Hordes et des steppes des Kirghiz-Kazaks ou Kirghiz-Kaïsaks*. Traduite du russe par Ferry de Pigny. Revue et publié par E. Charrière. Paris 1840. (Cf. Levšin).

Levšin — Levšin, A., *Opisanie kirgiz-kazač'ih, ili kirgiz-kajsakskih ord i stepej*. I-III. SPb. 1832.

Ličnye imena v prošlom — *Ličnye imena v prošlom, nastojaščem i buduščem*. Moskva 1970.

Ligeti 1933 — Ligeti Lajos, *Dzsingisz Khán neve*: **NyK** 48 (1933), pp. 338-341.

Ligeti 1962a — Ligeti, L., *Sur deux mots comans*: **AAnt.** XXX (1962), pp. 167-174.

Ligeti 1962b — Ligeti, L., *Dengizikh és Bécs állítólagos kun megfelelői*: **MNy.** LVIII (1962), pp. 146-152.

Ligeti, MTT — Ligeti, Lajos, *A mongolok titkos története*. Közreadja –. Budapest 1962.

Ligeti, R. tör. nev. I — Ligeti, Lajos, *Régi török eredetű neveink I*: **MNy.** 74 (1978), pp. 257-274.

Ligeti, R. tör. nev. II-III — Ligeti, Lajos, *Régi török eredetű neveink II-III*: **MNy.** 75 (1979), pp. 26-42; pp. 129-141.

Ligeti, Vocab. — Ligeti, Louis, *Un vocabulaire sino-ouigour des ming*: **AOH** XIX (1966), pp. 117-199, pp. 257-314.

Lit. Tat. — Dobrjanskij, F. (ed.), *Akty o Litovskih Tatarah*. Akty Izdavaemye Vilenskoju Kommissieju Dlja Razbora Drevnih Aktov. Tom XXXI. Vil'na 1906, XL, 586 pp.

Liu — Liu, Mau-Tsai, *Die chinesischen Nachrichten zur Geschichte der Ost-Türken (T'u-Küe)*. I-II. Wiesbaden 1958. (Göttinger Asiatische Forschungen, 10).

Ljutš Ljutš, Ja. (ed.), *Kirgizskaja hrestomatija. Sbornik obrazcov narodnoj literatury kirgiz turkestanskogo kraja*. Sostavil –. Taškent 1883.

Lomakin Lomakin, N., *O poluostrove Mangyšlake i putjah ottuda v raznye punkty Zakaspijskago kraja:* **Zap. Kavk. Otd. IRGO** VIII, 10, pp. 1-42.

Maev Maev, N. A. (ed.), *Ežegodnik. Materialy dlja statistiki Turkestanskago kraja*. Pod red. –. I. SPb. 1872.

Magn. Magnickij, V. K., *Čuvašskija jazyčeskija imena*. Kazan' 1905, 101+4 pp.

Mahpirov 1979 Mahpirov, V. U., *Antroponimy v "Divanu lugat-ittjurk" i "Kutadgu Bilig":* **SovT** (1979, No 4.), pp. 22-28.

Mahpirov 1980 Mahpirov, V. U., *Sobstvennye imena v pamjatnike XI v. "Divanu lugat-it-tjurk" Mahmuda Kašgarskogo*. Avtoref. kand. diss. Alma-Ata 1980, 30 pp.

Mahpirov 1985 Mahpirov, V. U., *Strukturno-funkcional'noe razvitie antroponimičeskih formantov v tjurkskih jazykah*. Na materiale ujgurskoj antroponimii: **SovT** (1985, No. 4), pp. 37-44.

Mahpirov 1988 Mahpirov, V., *Antroponimy ujgurskih juridičeskih dokumentov (k postanovke problemy):* **Issl. po ujg. jazyku.** (Alma-Ata 1988), pp. 47-52.

Mahpirov 1990 Mahpirov, V. U., *Drevnetjurkskaja onomastika* (Imena sobstvennye v Divanu lugat-it turk Mahmuda Kašgarskogo). Alma-Ata 1990, 158 pp.

Mahpirov 1997 Mahpirov, V. U., *Imena dalekih predkov:* istočniki formirovanija i osobennosti funkcionirovanija drevnetjurkskoj onomastiki. Almaty 1997, 299 pp. (Institut Vosotkovedenija. Trudy Centra Ujgurovedenija).

Mahrnāmag Müller, F. W. K., *Ein Doppelblatt aus einem manichäischen Hymnenbuch. (Mahrnâmag):* **APAW** V, 1912, pp. 1-40.

Mayer Mayer, L. A., *Saracinic Heraldry*. Oxford 1932.

Makrīzī Quatremère, M. (transl., ed.), *Histoire des sultans mamlouks de l'Égypte, écrite en arabe par Taki-eddin Ahmed Makrīzī*, Trad. en français et accompagnée de notes phil., hist., géogr. par –. I-IV. Paris 1837-1845.

Makrīzī, Khit. Wiet, G. (ed.), *Al-Makrīzī, al-Mawā'iẓ wa 'l-I'tibār fi Dhikr al-Khiṭaṭ wa 'l-Āthār*. I-IV. Būlāq - Kairo 1853-1854. (MIFAO, I-V, 1911-27?).

Makrīzī/Tizeng. I al-Maqrīzī, [1:] *Kitab as-sulūk li ma'rifat duwal al-muluk* / [2.:] *al-Mawā'iẓ wa 'l-i'tibār fi dikr al-ḫiṭaṭ wa'l-āthār:* **Tizeng. I**, pp. 417-442.

Maqqarī Maqqarī, Ahmed ibn Muhammad al-, *The History of the Mohammedan Dynasties in Spain:* Extracted from the Nafhu-t-tīb min ghosni-l-Andalusi. I-II. London 1840-1841.

Malickij Malickij, K. G., *Sistema naimenovanija u korennogo naselenija goroda Taškenta:* **IzvSrAzKMuz.** (1928, vyp. 3).

Malov, Enisej. Malov, S. E., *Enisejskaja pis'mennost' tjurkov*. Moskva - Leningrad 1952.

Malov, Pam. Malov, S. E., *Pamjatniki drevnetjurkskoj pis'mennosti. Teksty i issledovanija*. Moskva - Leningrad 1951.

Malov, Pam. Mong. Malov, S. E., *Pamjatniki drevnetjurkskoj pis'mennosti Mongolii i Kirgizii*. Moskva - Leningrad 1959.

Marco Polo Polo, Marco, *The Description of the World*. Transl. annot. by. A. C. Moule, and P. Pelliot. I-II. London 1938.

Markov Markov, V., *Šahseveny na Mugani*. Istoriko - Êtnografičeskij očerk. Sostavil –. Tiflis 1890, pp. 1-62. (Priloženie k l. vyp. XIV. toma ZKOIRGO).

Marquart, Chron. Marquart, J., *Chronologie der alttürkischen Inschriften*. Leipzig 1898.

Marquart, In. Marquart, Jos., *Historische Glossen zu den alttürkischen Inschriften:* **WZKM** XII (1989), pp. 157-200.

Marquart, Kom. Marquart, Jos., *Über das Volkstum der Komanen:* **Osttürk. Dialektst.**, pp. 25-238.

Marquart, Streifz. Marquart, Jos., *Osteuropäische und ostasiatische Streifzüge*. Leipzig 1903.

Mas'ūdī de Goeje, M. (ed.), *Kitāb at-Tanbīh wa 'l-Išrāf auctore Al-Mas'ūdī*, ed. –. Leiden 1894. (BGA VIII).

Mas'ūdī, Prairies Maçoudi, *Les Prairies d'or*, textes et traduction par C. Barbier de Meynard et [A.] Pavet de Courteille. I-IX. Paris 1861-1877. (Collection d'ouvrages orientaux publiée par la société asiatique).

Mat. Dagest. Grjumberg, G. E. (ed.) - Bušuev, S. K. (introd.), *Materialy po istorii Dagestana i Čečni*.

Mahačkala 1940.

Matveev Matveev, A. K., *Geografičeskie nazvanija Urala*. Kratkij toponimičeskij slovar'. Sverdlovsk 1980, 318 pp.

MB Qastam. Behcet, Mehmed, *Kastamonu asar-i kadimesi*. İstanbul 1923.

Mehren Mehren, A. F., *Revue des monuments funéraires du Kerafat ou de la ville des morts hors du Caire*. Par –: **Bull. Ac.** XVI. (Spbg. 1871), pp. 513-.

Mejer Mejer, L., *Kirgizskaja step' Orenburgskago vedomstva*. SPb. 1865. (Materialy dlja Geografii i Statistiki Rossii, sobrannye oficerami general'nago štaba).

Meyendorff Meyendorff, *Voyage d'Orenbourg à Boukhara, fait en 1820*. Paris 1826.

Mel'gunov Mel'gunov, G., *(Zamečanija) o južnom berege Kaspijskago morja*. Priloženie k III-mu tomu ZIAN, No. 5. SPb. 1863.

Melich 1924 Melich, J., *Mohamedán-török személynevek Turóc megye XIII. századi nemességénél*: **MNy.** XXII (1924), p. 196.

Melich, HM Melich, János, *A honfoglaláskori Magyarország*. Budapest 1925-29. (A Magyar Nyelvtudomány kézikönyve I/6).

Melikov Melikov, T. D., *Azerbaycan Türkçesinde Soy Adları*: **UTK 1992** (1996), pp. 57-60.

Memmedov 1990 Memmedov, Yunus, *Orhon-Yenisey Abidelerinde Adlar*. 1990.

Memmedov 1996a Memmedov, Yunus, *Onomastik vahidlärlä luγät vahidläri arasinda leksik-semantik älagä*: **UTK 1992** (1996), pp. 683-692.

Memmedov 1996b Memmedli (Memmedov), Y., *Eski Türkçe'de Šahıs Adları ve Unvanları*: **TDAYB 1994** (1996), pp. 95-110.

Menažiev 1964 Menažiev, Ja. M. – Azamatov, H. A., *Ismiñiznin maᶜnosi nimä? Čto oboznačaet Vaše imja?* Toškent 1964.

Menažiev 1968 Menažiev Ja. M., Abdurahmanov D., Azamatov H. A., Begmatov Ê., *Ismiñiznin maᶜnâsi nimä? Čto oboznačaet Vaše imja?* Tâškent 1968, 98 pp.

Mende Mende, Gerhard von, *Der nationale Kampf der Russlandtürken*. Berlin 1936.

Menges Menges, K. H., *The Names of the Päčänäg*: **Byzantion** XVII (1944-45), pp. 256-280.

Mém. R. Dep. TB *Mémoirs of the Research Department of the Toyo Bunko* (The Oriental Library). Tokyo 1963.

Mészáros *Csuvas népköltési gyűjtemény*. I. A csuvas ősvallás emlékei. II. Közmondások, találós-mondások, dalok, mesék. Budapest 1909, 1912, VI+ 471 pp., IX +540 pp.

Mészáros, MH Mészáros, Gy., *Magna Hungaria*. A baskir-magyar kérdés. Budapest 1910, 144 pp.

MG Ank. *Millî Gazete*. Ankara.

Mihaylova Mihaylova, Mariya - Mrıvkarova, *Bulgaristan Tatarlarının özel isimlerinin biçimleri*: **IV. Uluslar Arası Türk Dil Kurultayı** (1982).

Mikkola Mikkola, M., *Avarica*: **ASlPh.** XLI (1927), pp. 158-160.

Miller, Ist. Sib. Miller, G. F., *Istorija Sibiri*. II. Moskva - Leningrad 1941.

Mirch. Bujeh Wilken, Fr., *Mirchond's Geschichte der Sultane aus dem Geschlechte Bujeh*. Berlin 1835.

Mirch. Gasnevid. Wilken, Fr. (ed.), *Mohammedi filii Chondschahi vulgo Mirchondi Historia Gasnevidarum persice*. Berlini 1832.

Mirch. Seldsch. Vullers, J. A. (ed.), *Mirchondi Historia Seldschukidarum*. Persice edidit –. Gissae 1838.

Mirzäjev Mirzäjev, O. M., *Adlarimïz - Naši imena*. Bakï 1986, 296 pp.

Miskawayh *The Tajārib al-umam or history of Ibn Miskawayh (Abu ᶜAli Aḥmad b. Muḥammad) ob. A. H. 421*. Reproduced in facsimile from the Ms. at Constantinople in the Āyā Sūfiyya Library. With a summary and index by Leone Caetani principe di Teano. Vol. V. A. H. 284 to 326. Leyden - London 1913. (GMS VII, 5).

MIT I Volin, S. L., Romaskevič, A. A., Jakubovskij, A. Ju. (ed.), *Materialy po istorii turkmen i Turkmenii*. Tom I. VII-XV vv. Arabskie i persidskie istočniki. Ed. –. I-II. Moskva - Leningrad 1939. (Trudy Instituta Vostokovedenija XXIX).

MIT II Struve, V. V., Borovkov, A. V., Romaskevič, A. A., Ivanov, P. P. (ed.), *Materialy po istorii turkmen i Turkmenii*. Tom II. XVI-XIX vv. Iranskie, Buharskie i Hivinskie istočniki. Ed. –. Moskva - Leningrad 1938. (Trudy Instituta Vostokovedenija XXIX).

MIB I *Materialy po istorii Baškirskoj ASSR*. Tom I. Baškirskie vosstanija v XVII i pervoj polovine XVIII vv. Moskva - Leningrad 1936.

MIB II   *Materialy po istorii Baškirskoj ASSR.* Tom II. Moskva - Leningrad 1940.

MIB III   *Materialy po istorii Baškirskoj ASSR.* Tom III. Êkonomičeskie i social'nye otnošenija v Baškirii v pervoj polovine XVIII v. Moskva - Leningrad 1949.

MIB IV   Demidova, N. F. (ed.), *Materialy po istorii Baškirskoj ASSR.* Tom IV. Êkonomičeskie i social'nye otnošenija v Baškirii. Upravlenie Orenburgskim kraem v 50-70-h godah XVIII v. 2 č. Sost. –. Moskva 1955.

MIB V   Demidova, N. F., Vasil'ev, M. (ed.), *Materialy po istorii Baškirskoj ASSR.* Tom V. Moskva 1960.

MID   *Materialy po istorii Dagestana.* III.

MIK IV   *Materialy po istorii Kazahskoj SSR (1785-1828 gg.).* Tom IV. Moskva - Leningrad 1940.

MIKk.   *Materialy po istorii karakalpakov.* 1935. (Trudy Instituta Vostokovedenija VII).

MK/Atalay   Atalay, B. (transl.), *Divanü lugat-it-Türk tercümesi.* Ankara 1939-1941, 1943.

MK/Brock.   Brockelmann, C., *Mitteltürkischer Wortschatz.* Nach Maḥmūd al-Kāšyarīs Dīvān Luγāt at-Turk. Budapest - Leipzig 1928. (BOH I.).

MKOP   *Materialy po kazahskomu obyčnomu pravu.* Sbornik I. Alma-Ata 1948.

MNévtKonf. V   *Az V. Magyar Névtudományi Konferencia előadásai.* (Miskolc, 1995. augusztus. 28-30). I-II. Budapest-Miskolc 1997. (MNYTK 209. sz.).

MNy.   *Magyar Nyelv.* I-. Budapest 1904-.

Molčanova   Molčanova, O. T., *Toponimičeskij slovar' Gornogo Altaja.* Gorno-Altajsk 1979, 397 pp.

Molčanova 1970   Molčanova, O. T., *Motivirovannye ličnye imena u altajcev*: **Ličnye imena v prošlom.** (1970).

Moravcsik   *see* **Byz. Turc.**

Moravcsik 1930   Moravcsik, Gy., *Az onogurok történetéhez II.*: **MNy.** XXVI (1930), pp. 89-109.

Moravcsik 1933   Moravcsik, Gy., *Die Namenliste der bulgarischen Gesandten am Konzil von 869-870*: **Izvestija na Istoričesk. Družestvo v Sofija** XIII (1933), pp. 8-23.

Moroškin   Moroškin, M., *Slavjanskij imenoslov ili [].* SPb. 1867, 214 pp.

Moskal'cev   Moskal'cev, A., *Izsledovanie vakufov v Taškentskom uezde*: **Sb. Syr-D.** IV (1895), pp. 31-84.

Mouraviev   Mouraviev, N. N., *Voyage en Turkmanie et à Khiva.* (Aperçu des tribus turcomans). Paris 1823.

MSOS   *Mitteilungen des Seminars für orientalische Sprachen an der (Königlichen) Friedrich-Wilhelms-Universität zu Berlin.* Berlin.

Mubárakhsháh   Denison Ross, E. (ed.), *Taʿrīkh-i Fakhru'd-dīn Mubáraksháh,* being the historical introduction to the Book of Genealogies of F. Mub. Marvar-rúdī completed in A.D. 1206. Edited by–. London 1927.

Muh. Ibrahim   Houtsma, M. Th. (ed.), *Histoire des Seldjoucides du Kerman par Muhammed Ibrahim.* Texte persan publ. par –: **Houtsma, Recueil** I. (Leyden 1886).

Muhamedova 1957   Muhamedova, Z. B., *K voprosu o ličnoj onomastike u turkmen*: **Trudy. IJAL AN Turkm. SSR** II. (Ašhabad 1957), pp. 34-48.

Muhamedova 1965   Muhamedova, Z. B., *Ličnaja onomastika u turkmen*: **Pitannja onomastiki.** (Kiiv 1965), pp. 151-157.

Muhamedova 1978   Muhamedova, Z. B., *Neskol'ko slov ob antroponimah v "Oguz-name" iz sočinenija Salar-baba*: **OSA.** (M. 1978), pp. 169-171.

Munkácsi   Munkácsi Bernát, *Baskir helynevek*: **Ethn.** XIII (1902), pp. 15-25.

Murav'ev   Murav'ev, N. N., *Putešestvie v Turkmeniju i Khivu v 1819 i 1820 godah,* gvardejskogo General'nogo Štaba kapitana Nikolaja Murav'eva, poslannaogo v sii strany dlja peregovorov. 1-2. Moskva 1822.

Murzaev 1979   Murzaev, Ê. M., *Geografija v nazvanijah.* Moskva 1979, 166 pp.

Müller, Hofstaat   Müller, F.W.K., *Der Hofstaat eines Uiguren-Königs*: **Fest. Thomsen,** pp. 207-13.

Müller, Pfahl.   Müller, F.W.K., *Zwei Pfahlinschriften aus den Turfanfunden.* Berlin 1915.

Müller, Uig.   Müller, F.W.K., *Uigurica I-III.* Berlin 1908-1910-1922. (ABAW)

Nafiz-Hakkı   Nafiz, R. - Hakkı, I., *Anadolu Türk Tarihi Tetkikatından Sivas Şehri.* İstanbul 1928.

Nalivkin-Dozon   Nalivkin, V. P., *Histoire du Khanat de Khokand.* Trad. par Baron M. Dozon [d'Ohsson]. Paris 1889, 272 pp. (Publications de l'École des Langues Orientaux Vivantes).

Nalyvkin, Kokand.	Nalyvkin, V., *Kratkaja istorija Kokandskogo hanstva.* Kazan' 1885.
Napier	Napier, Robert Cornelius, *Diary (1857-60) of a Tour in Khorassan.* Appendix: Notes on the Yomut Tribe by Kazi Synd Ahmad: **JRGS** XLVI (1876)
Nasawï	Houdas, O. (transl.), *Histoire du sultan Djelal ed-Din Mankobirti, prince du Kharezm.* Par Mohammed an-Nasawi. Texte arabe et trad. franç. par –. Paris 1891-1895. (Publications de l'École des Langues Orientaux Vivantes, Sér. III, Tome 9-10.).
Nasilov	Nasilov, V. M., *Onomastika ohotnič'ego byta tuvincev, ujgurov i kazahov:* **SovT** (1970, No. 3), pp. 71-78.
Nasyrov-Poljakov	Nasyrov-Poljakov, *Skazki kazanskih tatar:* **IOAIÊK** XVI ().
Nazaroff	Nazaroff, P. S., *Hunted through Central Asia* by –. Rendered into English from the Russian of the Author's Manuscript by Malcolm Burr. Edinburgh-London 1932. (New Edition: Oxford 1993).
Nâmî	Nâmî, Hasan, *Havza'da Adlarla İlgili Gelenekler:* **Türk Folklor Araştırmaları** 6 (134) (1960), p. 2221.
Nebol'sin	Nebol'sin, P. I., *Inorodcy Astrahanskoj gubernii:* **VIRGO** II (3-4) ().
Necatigil	Necatigil, B., *Edebiyatımızda isimler sözlüğü.* İstanbul 1966.
Nepljuev	Vitevskij, V. N., *I. I. Nepljuev i Orenburgskij kraj v prežnem ego sostave do 1758 g.* Istoričeskaja monografija –. Kazan' 1897, 962 pp. (Pril. 198 pp.).
Nešri	Nöldeke, Th., *Auszüge aus Neschri's Geschichte des Osmânischen-Hauses:* **ZDMG** XIII, XV (1859), pp. 176-218; 333-380.
Németh 1921	Németh Gyula, *Turán:* **MNy.** XVII (1921), p. 109.
Németh 1925	Németh Gy., *A Debrecen név eredete:* **Klebelsberg-Emlékk.** (Bp. 1925), pp. 139-141.
Németh 1930a	Németh, Gyula, *Der Name Gül-Baba:* **KCsA** II (1930), p. 379.
Németh 1932	Németh Gyula, *A Kobrat és Eszperüch nevek eredete:* **MNy.** XXVIII (1932), pp. 5-11.
Németh 1958	Németh, Gy., *Feriz bég:* **MTA Nyelv- és Irod. Oszt. Közl.** 13. (Bp. 1958), pp. 89-94.
Németh 1961	Németh J., *Reise um zwei kiptschakische Ortsnamen in Ungarn* [Karcag and Debrecen]: **UAJb.** XXXIII (1961), pp. 122-727.
Németh 1964	Németh, J., *Feriz Beg von Kruševac, 1454:* **Der Islam** 39 (1964), pp. 192-196.
Németh 1965	Németh, J., *Kereit, Kérey, Giray:* **UAJb.** XXXVI (1965), pp. 360-365.
Németh 1969	Németh J., *Dva kipčakskih geografičeskih nazvanija v Vengrii:* **Issl. po tjurkologii.** (Alma-Ata 1969), pp. 26-34.
Németh 1971	Németh, J., *Noms ethniques turcs d'origine totémistique:* **Studia Turcica** (1971), pp. 349-359. (BOH XVII.).
Németh 1973	Németh, J., *Das Wolga-Bulgarische wort baqšï 'gelehrter Herr' in Ungarn:* **İslam Tetkikleri Estitüsü Dergisi** V. (İstanbul 1973), pp. 165-170.
Németh Arm.	J. Eckmann - A. S. Levend - M. Mansuroğlu (ed.), *Németh Armağanı.* Ankara 1962, 393 pp. (Türk Dil Kurumu Yayınları, Sayı 191).
Németh, Árpád-kori	Németh Gy., *Árpád-kori törökjeink* (Kié volt a nagyszentmiklósi kincs?): **NéNy.** III (1931), pp. 169-185.
Németh, HMK	Németh, Gyula, *A honfoglaló magyarság kialakulása.* Budapest 1930 (1991).
Németh, Inschr.	Németh, J., *Die Inschriften des Schatzes von Nagy-Szent-Miklós.* Budapest - Leipzig 1932, 84 pp. (BOH II.).
Németh, Kobrat	Németh, J., *Die Herkunft der Namen Kobrat und Esperüch:* **KCsA** II (1932), pp. 440-447.
NéNy.	*Népünk és Nyelvünk.* Budapest.
Nikiforov	Nikiforov, N. A., *Anosskij sbornik.* Sobranie skazok altajcev s primečanijami G. N. Potanina: **ZSOIRGO** XXXVII. (Omsk 1915).
Nikol'skij	Nikol'skij, N., *Hristianstvo sredi čuvaš srednjago Povolž'ja v XVI-XVIII vekah.* Istoričeskij očerk: **IOAIÊK** XXVIII, pp. 1-416.
Nikonov	Nikonov, V. A., *Imja i obščestvo.* Moskva 1974, 277 pp.
Nikonov 1971	Nikonov, V. A., *Sovremennyj imennik uzbekov:* **Vopr. onom.** (1971).
Nikonov 1972	Nikonov, V. A., *Razmeževanie ličnyh imen po polu u tjurkskih narodov:* **SovT** (1972, No. 2).
Nikonov 1973a	Nikonov, V. A., *Obyčaj svjazannyh imen u turkajazyčnyh narodov:* **SÊ** No. 6 (1973), pp. 82-89.

Nikonov 1973b	Nikonov, V. A., *Aktual'nye processy v antroponimii tatar i baškir*: **OnomPov. 3.** (Ufa 1973), pp. 9-21.
Nikonov 1974	Nikonov, V. A., *Ličnye imena turkmen*: **Polevye issl. In-ta êtnogr. AN SSSR.** (Moskva 1974).
Nikonov 1975	Nikonov, V. A., *Sostojanie i žadači onomastičeskih issledovanij Kavkaza*: **Vopr. Jaz.** (1975, No 4.).
Nikonov 1976	Nikonov, V. A., *Ličnye imena kumykov i nogajcev*: **Onomastika Kavkaza.** (Mahačkala 1976).
Nikonov 1978	Nikonov, V. A., *Sredneaziatskie materialy dlja slovarja ličnyh imen*: **OSA** (1978), pp. 153-161.
Nikonov 1980	Nikonov, V. A., *Formy sredneaziatskih familij*: **OSA** 2 (1980), pp. 120-127.
Nikonov 1984	Nikonov, V. A., *Ličnye imena sovremennyh ujgurov*: **Tjurksk. onom.** (1984), pp. 189-199.
Nižegorod. platež.	Veselovskij, S. (ed.), *Nižegorodskija platežnicy 7116 i 7120 gg.* Prigotovil k pečati i redaktiroval –. Moskva 1910.
NyK	*Nyelvtudományi Közlemények.* Budapest.
Noyan	Noyan, Bedri, *Ad Vermede Gelenekler.* Türkçe İnsan Adları ve Aile Adları Hakkında: **Türk Kültürü Dergisi** 246 (1983).
Notes et Extr.	*Notes et Extraits des Manuscrits de la Bibliothèque du Roi.* Paris.
NRS	Baskakov, N. A. (ed.), *Nogajsko-russkij slovbar'.* Moskva 1963, 562 pp.
Nurulu	Nurulu, Mina Hanım, *Türk Menşeli Rus Lakabları*: **Türk Dünyası Araştırmaları** 74 (1991), pp. 21-25.
Nuržanova	Nuržanova, D. K., *Kazahskaja kosmonimija*: **Êtnogr. imen** (1971), pp. 234-236.
Nuwairī	al-Nuwairī, Šihāb ad-Dîn Ahmad Ibn Abdalwahhab, *Nihāyat al-Arab fi Funūn al-Adab.* 1-10 j. 2. tab. Qāhira 1929-33. ((New Edition: Cairo 1985)).
Nuwairī/Tizeng. I	al-Nuwairī, Šihābaddīn Ahmad Ibn Abdalwahhab, *Nihāyat al-ᶜarab fi funūn al-adab*: **Tizeng. I**, pp. 128-171.
O'Donovan	O'Donovan, Edmond, *The Merv Oasis.* Travels and adventures (1879-81): I-II. (London 1882).
OB	*Orientalische Bibliographie / Oriental Bibliography.* I-. Berlin 1887-.
Obz. Zakasp. Obl.	*Obzor Zakaspijskoj oblasti za 1890 goda.* Priloženie I. Vedomost' o razpredelenii plemen i rodov tuzemnago naselenija po uezdam i aulam za 1890 god. SPb. 1892.
Oğuz K. Dest.	Bang, W. Rahmeti, G. R. (ed.), *Oğuz Kağan Destanı.* İstanbul 1936.
OjrRS	Baskakov, N. A. (ed.), *Ojrotsko-russkij slovar'.* Sost. N. A. Baskakov i T. M. Toščakova. Pod obšč. red. –. Moskva 1947.
Ongan	Ongan, Halit, *XV'inci Yüzyıla Ait Bursa Şer'iyye Sicillerinde Geçen Bazı Türkçe Kişi Adları*: **Türk Etn. Derg.** IV (1962), pp. 32-36.
Ongan, Adl.	Ongan, Halit, *Şer'iye sicillerinde geçen Türkçe kişi adları*: **Türk Etn. Derg.** I (1956), pp. 92-94.
Ongan, Ank. I	Ongan, Halit, *Ankara'nın Bir Numaralı Şer'iye Sicili 1583-1584.* Ankara 1958, 194+4 pp.
Ongan, Ank. II	Ongan, Halit, *Ankara'nın İki Numaralı Şer'iye Sicili 1588-1590.* Ankara 1974, 222 pp.
Onomastika 1966	*Onomastika.* Kiev 1966.
Onomastika 1969	*Onomastika.* Sbornik statej. Moskva 1969.
Onomastika (Bibl.)	Malinskaja, B. A. - Šabat, M. C. (eds.), *Onomastika.* Ukazatel' literatury - izdannoj v SSSR za 1971-1975 gg. s pril. za 1918-1962 gg. Moskva 1978, 301 pp.
OnomKavk. 1976	*Onomastika Kavkaza.* Sbornik statej. Mahačkala 1976, 329 pp.
OnomKavk. 1980	*Onomastika Kavkaza.* (Mežvuzovskij sbornik statej). Ordžonikidze 1980, 191 pp.
OnomKirg.	*Onomastika Kirgizii.* Vyp 1. Frunze 1985, 180 pp.
OnomPov. 1	*Onomastika Povolž'ja.* Materialy I-oj Povolžskoj Konferencii po onomastike. 1. Ul'janovsk 1969, 284 pp.
OnomPov. 2	*Onomastika Povolž'ja.* Materialy II-oj Povolžskoj Konferencii po onomastike. 2. Gor'kij 1971, 373 pp.
OnomPov. 3	*Onomastika Povolž'ja.* Materialy III-ej konferencii po onomastike Povolž'ja. 3. Ufa 1973, 431 pp.
OnomPov. 4	Nikonov, V. A. - Mokšin, N. F. (ed.), *Onomastika Povolž'ja.* Otv. red. –. 4. Saransk 1976,

353 pp.

OnomPov. 5 *Onomastika Povolž'ja.* V-aja konferencija po onomastike Povolž'ja. 26-28-ogo sentjabrja 1989 g. Volgograd 1989.

OnomPov. 6 *Onomastika Povolž'ja 6.* Moskva 1991, 200 pp.

OnomPov. 7 Džarylgasinova R. Š. - Suprun, V. I. (eds.), *Onomastika Povolž'ja:* materialy Sed'moj konferencii po onomastike Povolž'ja. Moskva 1997, 200 pp.

OnomTat. Zakiev, M. - Sattarov, G. F., *Onomastika Tatarii.* Kazan' 1989, 119 pp.

OnomUzb. Nafasov, T. N. (ed.-in-chief) - Begmatov, E. A. (ed.), *Onomastika Uzbekistana:* tezisy II-oj respublikanskoj naučno-praktičeskoj konferencii (g. Karši, 11-16 sentjabrja 1989 g.). Taškent 1989, 207 pp.

Onom. vost. Murzaev, Ê. M. (Ed.), *Onomastika vostoka.* Moskva 1980, 285 pp.

Oppenheim von Oppenheim, Max Freiherr (ed.), *Inschriften aus Syrien, Mesopotamien und Kleinasien.* Gesammelt im J. 1899. Mit Beiträgen von Max von Berchem, Julius Euting und Bernhard Moritz hrsg. von –. Leipzig 1913. (Aus d. Beitr. z. Assyriologie und semit. Sprachwiss. Bd. VII, Heft 1 und 2).

Or. Bibl. *Orientalische Bibliographie.* 1. Berlin 1887.

Oruzbaeva Oruzbaeva, B. O., *Kyrgyzsko-altajskie paralleli v pover'jah i tabu.*

Oruzbaeva 1980 Oruzbaeva, B. O., *O sobstvennyh imenah v épose "Manas":* **OSA** 2 (1980), pp. 67-80.

Oruzbaeva 1985 Oruzbaeva, B. O., *Ob odnom kirgizskom étnoantroponime:* **Onom. Kirg.** I. (1985), pp. 116-118.

OSA Nikonov, V. A. - Rešetov, A. M. (ed.), *Onomastika Srednej Azii.* Moskva, Nauka 1978, 226 pp.

OSA 2 Umurzakov, S. U., Oruzbaeva B. O. (et al., ed.), *Onomastika Srednej Azii 2.* Frunze 1980, 309 pp.

Osttürk. Dialektst. Bang, W. - Marquart, J., (ed.), *Osttürkische Dialektstudien.* Berlin 1914. (AGWG, Band XIII/1).

OZ *Otečestvennye zapiski.* SPb.

Ozenbašlï Ozenbašlï, Ê. M., *Qïrïmtatar adlarï.* Krymskotatarskie imena. Aqmesjit - Simferopol' 1992, 47 pp.

Ögel I Ögel, B., *Türk mitolojisi.* (Kaynakları ve açıklamaları ile destanlar). 3. Baskı. I. Ankara 1998, 644 pp.

Ögel II Ögel, B., *Türk mitolojisi.* (Kaynakları ve açıklamaları ile destanlar). 3. Baskı. II. Ankara 1995, 610 pp.

Önder, Göle Önder, Ali Riza, *Göle'de İnsan İsimleri:* **Türk Folklor Araştırmaları** 7 (74) (1955), pp. 1180-1182.

Önder, Hınıs Önder, Ali Riza, *Hınıs'ta İnsan İsimleri:* **Türk Folklor Araştırmaları** 6 (69) (1955), pp. 1099-1100.

Örnek Örnek, S. V., *Türk Folklorunda Ad Seçme ve Ad Koyma:* **Boğaziçi Üniversitesi Halk Bilim Yıllığı** (1975), pp. 101-102.

Özbaş Özbaş, Ömer, *Folklor derlemeleri. İlbeyli Türkmenleri arasında.* Gaziantep 1940.

Özergin Özergin, Kemal, *Türklerde Lâkab Alma Adetine Dair:* **Türk Folklor Araştırmaları** 12 (249) (1970).

Özön Özön, Mustafa Nihat, *Osmanlıca - Türkçe Sözlük.* Istanbul 1977.

Paas. Paasonen, H., *Csuvas szójegyzék.* Budapest 1908.

Pais Pais, Dezső, *Magyar Anonymus. Béla király jegyzőjének könyve a magyarok cselekedeteiről.* Budapest 1926.

Pais Emlk. *Pais Emlékkönyv.* Budapest 1956.

Pais - Rásonyi Pais, Dezső - Rásonyi N., László, *Kál és társai:* **MNy.** XXV (1929), p. 121. (Together with Dezső Pais).

Pam. kn. Semip. *Pamjatnaja knižka Semipalatinskoj oblasti.* Semipalatinsk 1902.

Pam. kn. Semir. *Pamjatnaja knižka i adreskalendar' Semiréčenskoj oblasti na 1900 g.* Vérnyj 1900.

Pam. kn. Turg. *Pamjatnaja knižka Turgajskoj Oblasti 1899 goda.* Orenburg 1899.

Pantusov, Kirg. Pantusov, N. N. (ed., transl.), *Obrazcy kirgizskoj narodnoj literatury,* sobrannye i perevedennye –. Spb. 1890.

Pantusov, Pesni   Pantusov, N. N. (ed., transl.), *Tarančinskija pesni.* Sobr. i perevedeny –. SPb. 1890. (ZIR-GOEtn. XVII. vyp. 1).

Pantusov, Tar.   Pantusov, N. N. (ed., transl.), *Obrazcy tarančinskoj narodnoj literatury,* sobrannye –. Kazan' 1909.

M. S. Pap. Rainer   Karabacek, J. (ed.), *Mitteilungen aus der Sammlung der Papyrus Erzherzog Rainer.* I-III. Wien 1887-1897.

Par   Par, Arif Hikmet, *A'dan Z'ye Ansiklopedik Türk Adları ve Soyadları Sözlüğü.* İstanbul 1981.

Pašaev   Pašaev, A. M., *Prozvišča v azerbajdžanskom jazyke.* Avtoref. kand. diss. Baku 1987.

Patkanov   Patkanov, S., *Statističeskija dannyja pokazyvajuščija plemennoj sostav naselenija Sibiri, jazyk i rody inorodcev.* Tom II. Tobol'skaja, Tomskaja i Enisejskaja gubernii. SPb. 1911-1912.

PdC   Pavet de Courteille, M., *Dictionnaire turk - oriental.* Paris 1870.

Pek.   Pekarskij, E. K., *Slovar' jakutskogo jazyka.* Sost. –. I-III. Petrograd - Leningrad 1917-1930.

Pelissier   Pelissier, Robert, *Mischär-Tatarische Sprachproben.* Berlin 1919, 47 pp.

Pelliot   Pelliot, P., *Notes sur l'histoire de la Horde d'Or,* suivies de quelques noms turcs d'hommes et de peuples finissant en "-ar (-är), -ur (-ür), -ïr (-ir)". Paris 1949, pp. 7-223. (Oeuvres posthumes de P. Pelliot II.).

Petrov 1985   Petrov, L. P., *Iz istorii cuvašskih dohristianskih imen:* **Voprosy tradicionnoj i sovremennoj kul'tury i byta čuvašskogo naroda.** (Čeboksary 1985), pp. 60-77.

Petrov 1986   Petrov, L. P., *Ličnye imena zakamskih čuvašej-jazyčnikov:* **Kul'tura i byt** (1986), 104 pp.

Petrov 1987   Petrov, L. P., *Êtimologija čuvašskih dohristianskih imen I.:* **Voprosy fonetiki, grammatiki i onomastiki čuvašskogo jazyka.** (Čeboksary 1987), pp. 72-79.

Petrov 1988a   Petrov, L. P., *Êtimologija čuvašskih dohristianskih imen II.:* **Iss. po êtim. i gramm. čuv. jazyka.** (Čeboksary 1988), pp. 19-35.

Petrov 1988b   Petrov, L. P., *Iz istorii čuvašskih dohristianskih imjon:* SovT (1988, No. 4.), pp. 21-25.

Petrov 1991   Petrov, L. P., *Êtimologija čuvašskih dohristianskih imen III.:* **Čuvašskij jazyk: istorija, êtimologija, fonetika.** (Čeboksary 1991), pp. 32-46.

Petrov 1991b   Petrov, L. P., *Ličnye imena zakamskih čuvašej-jazyčnikov:* **Čuv. jaz.,** pp. 47-65.

PÉLOV   *Publications de l'École des Langues Orientaux Vivantes.* Paris.

Pjurbeev   Pjurbeev, G. C., *Antroponimy i apeljativy v kalmyckom jazyke:* **Tjurkol. issledovanija.** (M. 1976), pp. 194-201.

PKRS   *Polnyj kirgizsko-russkij slovar'.* Orenburg 1903.

Pojarkov   Pojarkov, F. V., *Kirgizskija legendy, skazki i verovanija* Kara-kirgizskija legendy: **Pam. kn. Semir.** (1900).

Pokrovskij   Pokrovskij, I., *Bortničestvo (pčelovodstvo), kak odin iz vidov natural'nago hozjajstva i promysla bliz Kazani v XVI-XVII vv.:* **IOAIÊK** XVII (1901), pp. 67-73.

Poliv.-Kras.   Polivanov, V.N. - Krasovskij, V.E., *Materialy istoričeskie i juridičeskie rajona byvšago prikaza kazanskago dvorca.* Simbirsk 1898.

Popov, Snoš.   Popov, A. N., *Snošenija Rossii s Hivoju i Buharoju pri Petre Velikom:* **ZIRGO** IX (1853), pp. 237-425.

Poppe   Poppe, N., *Das mongolische Sprachmaterial einer Leidener Handschrift.* Türkische Eigennamen mit mongolischer Übersetzung: **IAN** (1927), pp. 1252-53.

Potanin   Potanin, G.N., *Očerki Severo-Zapadnoj Mongolii.* I-IV. SPb. 1881-83.

Potanin, Pred.   Potanin, G.N., *Kazak-kirgizskija i altajskija predanija, legendy i skazki* [Appendix:] Ukazatel' sobstvennyh imen [Ed. by A. N. Samojlovič, pp. 192-198]: **ŽS** XXV (1916), pp. 47-198.

Prinz 1911   Prinz, Gyula, *Ázsia szívében / Utazásaim Belső-Ázsiában.* Budapest 1911, 80 pp.

Prinz 1945   Prinz, Gyula, *Utazásaim Belső-Ázsiában.* Budapest 1945, XVI, 312 pp.

Pritsak   Pritsak, O., *Stammesnamen und Titulaturen der Altaischen Völker:* **UAJb.** 24 (1952), pp. 49-104.

Pritsak, Yowar   Pritsak, O., *Yowár und Καβαρ / Kāwar:* **UAJb.** XXXVI (1965), pp. 378-393.

Proben   Radloff, W., *Proben der Volksliteratur der türkischen Stämme Süd-Sibiriens.* I-X. SPb. 1866-1904.

Proben IX	Katanov, N.F. (ed.), *Mundarten der Urianchaier (Sojonen), Abakan-Tataren und Karagassen.* (W. Radloff, Proben der Volksliteratur IX). SPb. 1907.
Protok. Turk.	*Protokoly zasedanij i soobščenija členov Turkestanskago Kružka ljubitelej archeologii.* IV, V. Taškent 1899.
Pröhle, Balk.	Pröhle, W., *Balkarische Studien*: **KSz.** XV (1914-15), pp. 165-276.
Pröhle, Kar.	Pröhle, W., *Karatschajisches Wörterverzeichnis*: **KSz.** X (1909), pp. 83-150.
PRS	*Persidsko-russkij slovar' v dvuh tomah.* I-II. Moskva 1970.
PSRL	*Polnoe sobranie russkih letopisej.* I-XXIII. Stpbg. / Petrograd 1868-1916. (New Edition: Vols. I-X, Moskva, 1962-1970).
PSRL (Russk. Hr. I)	*Russkij hronograf.* Čast' I. Chronograf redakcii 1512 goda: **PSRL** XXII (1911), VII, 568 pp.
PSRL (Russk. Hr. II)	*Russkij hronograf.* Čast' II. Hronograf zapadno-russkoj redakcii: **PSRL** XXII (1914), IX, 289.
PSZRI	*Polnoe sobranie zakonov Rossijskoj imperii.* I-XL. SPb.
RaD	Semenov, A. A. - Petruševskij, I. P., *Rašid-ad-din, Sbornik letopisej.* Tom I, kniga pervaja, per. L. A. Hetagurova, red. A. A. Semenova; kniga vtoraja, per. O. I. Smirnovoj, prim. B.I. Pankratova i O.M. Smirnova, red. A. A. Semenova; Tom II, per. Ju. P. Verhovskogo, prim. Ju.P. Verhovskogo i B. I. Pankratova, red. I. P. Petruševskogo. Moskva 1952-1960.
RaD/Ber. I	Berezin, I.N. (transl.), *Sbornik letopisej. Istorija mongolov, sočinenija Rašid-Êddina.* Vvedenie: o tureckih i mongol'skih plemenah. Perevod s persidskago, s vvedeniem i primečanijami –. I. SPb. 1858.
RaD/Ber. II	Berezin, I.N. (transl.), *Sbornik letopisej. Istorija mongolov, sočinenie Rašid-Eddina.* Istorija Čingizhana do vosšestvija ego na prestol. Persidskij tekst, s predisloviem –. II. SPb. 1868.
RaD/Ber. III	Berezin, I.N. (transl.), *Sbornik letopisej. Istorija mongolov, sočinenie Rašid-Eddina.* Istorija Čingizhana ot vosšestvija ego na prestol do končiny. Russk. perevod s primečanijani –. III. SPb. 1888.
RaD/Blochet	Blochet, E. (ed.), *Djami el-tévarikh. Histoire générale du monde par Fadl Allah Rashid ed-Din. Tarikh-i Moubarek-i Ghazani.* Histoire des Mongols, éditée par –. Tome II. Contenant l'histoire des empereurs mongols successeurs de Tchinkkiz Khagan. Leyden-London 1911. (GMS. XVIII/2).
RaD/Erdmann	Erdmann, Franz (ed.), *Vollstaendige Uebersicht der Aeltesten turkischen, tatarischen und mongolischen Voelkerstamme* nach Reschid-Ud-Din's Vorgange bearbeitet v. –.
RaD/Jahn	Jahn, Karl (ed.), *Geschichte Gazan-han's aus dem Ta'rih-i-mubarak-i-Gazani des Rashid al-Din Fadlal-lah b. Imad al-daula Abul-hair.* Hrsg. n. d. Mss. v. Stambul, London, Paris und Wien. Mit einer Einleitung, kritischen Apparat und Indices von–. London 1940. (GMNewS. XIV).
RaD/Quatrem.	Quatremère, E., *Notes and commentary in Rashīd ad-Dīn, Histoire des Mongols de la Perse.*
Radl.	Radloff, W., *Versuch eines Wörterbuches der Türk-Dialekte.* I-IV. SPb. 1893-1911.
Radl., Altuig.	Radloff, W.W., *Altuigurische Sprachproben aus Turfan*: Nachrichten über die [] Expedition nach Turfan. I. SPb. 1899.
Radl., Aus Sib.	Radloff, W., *Aus Sibirien.* Lose Blätter aus meinem Tagebuche. Von –. I-II. Leipzig 1893.
Radl., Inschr.	Radloff, W., *Die alttürkischen Inschriften der Mongolei.* Petersburg 1895, XI+460 pp.
Radl., Phon.	Radloff, W.W., *Phonetik der nördlichen Türksprachen.* Leipzig 1883.
Radl., USp.	Radloff, W., *Uigurische Sprachdenkmäler.* Materialen nach dem Tode des Verfassers mit Ergänzungen von S. Malov herausgegeben. Leningrad 1928.
Ramstedt	Ramstedt, G.J., *Kalmükisches Wörterbuch.* Helsinki 1935.
Ramstedt, Uig.	Ramstedt, G.J., *Zwei uigurische Runenschriften*: **JSFOu.** XXX (1913).
Rásonyi 1921	Rásonyi, L. (as R. Nagy László), *Kún személyneveinkről.* Budapest 1921, 38 pp. (Bölcsészdoktori értekezés [Thesis of Doctor of Phylosophy]. Manuscript.).
Rásonyi 1922	Rásonyi, L. (as R. Nagy László), *Török eredetű magyar tulajdonnevek* [=Hungarian Proper Names of Turkic Origin]: **KCsA** I (1922), pp. 237-239.
Rásonyi 1926a	Rásonyi L., *Kulán és Szoltán* [Hungarian personal names of Turkic origin]: **MNy.** XXII (1926), p. 348.

Rásonyi 1926b   Rásonyi L., *Bala*: **MNy.** XXII (1926), pp. 212-213.

Rásonyi 1926c   Rásonyi Nagy László, *Karcag*: **MNy.** XXII (1926), pp. 348-349.

Rásonyi 1926d   Rásonyi, Nagy L., *Borcsol és Csertán* [Kuman ethnical names]: **MNy.** XXII (1926), pp. 132-133.

Rásonyi 1927a   Rásonyi, N. László, *Bokor és Bakony*: **MNy.** XXIII (1927), pp. 561-571.

Rásonyi 1927b   Rásonyi N. László, *Taksony*: **MNy.** XXIII (1927), p. 274.

Rásonyi 1927c   Rásonyi Nagy László, *Kajtor*: **MNy.** XXIII (1927), p. 594.

Rásonyi 1927e   Rásonyi Nagy László, *Komócsin*: **MNy.** XXIII (1927), pp. 52-53.

Rásonyi 1927f   Rásonyi Nagy, L., *Török eredetű helynevek* [=Placenames of Turkic Origin]: **NyK** XLVI (1927), pp. 464-469.

Rásonyi 1928a   Rásonyi N. László, *Ormán*: **MNy.** XXIV (1928), pp. 23-28.

Rásonyi 1928b   Rásonyi, L., *Becs*: **MNy.** XXIV (1928), p. 210.

Rásonyi 1928c   Rásonyi, L., *A Brassó név eredete*: **MNy.** XXIV (1928), pp. 311-318.

Rásonyi 1929a   Pais Dezső - Rásonyi N. László, *Kál és társai*: **MNy.** XXV (1929), p. 121. (Together with Dezső Pais).

Rásonyi 1929b   Rásonyi, L., *Kalacs*: **MNy.** XXV (1929), pp. 124-127.

Rásonyi 1929c   Rásonyi, L., *Régi családnevek keletkezése*: **Új Barázda** (1929 /03. 31./)).

Rásonyi 1929d   Rásonyi, L., *Mire tanítanak a helynevek?*: **Új Barázda** (1929 /06. 23./).

Rásonyi 1930a   Rásonyi, L., *Karaiman, Caraiman herceg*: **MNy.** XXVI (1930), pp. 392-393.

Rásonyi 1930b   Rásonyi, L. (Kázsmárki), *Mire tanítanak a magyarság régi törzs-és népnevei?*: **Magyarság** (1930 /08. 10./).

Rásonyi 1932a   Rásonyi, L., *A honfoglaló magyarsággal kapcsolatos török tulajdonnevekhez*. [= To the Trukic Proper Names Related with the Old Hungarians]: **MNy.** XXVIII (1932), pp. 100-105.

Rásonyi 1932b   Rásonyi, L., *A Szörény név etymológiájához*: **MNy.** XXVIII (1932), pp. 308-309.

Rásonyi 1933a   Rásonyi László, *Baszaraba*: **MNy.** XXIX (1933), pp. 160-171.

Rásonyi 1933b   Rásonyi, L., *Der Volksname Берендѣй*. **Seminarium Kondakovianum VI.** (Praha 1933), pp. 119-126.

Rásonyi 1933c   Rásonyi L., *Az oláh államiság kialakulása*: **MNy.** XX (1933), pp. 160-171.

Rásonyi 1934   Rásonyi, L., *Türk has isimleri I-II.*: **Hakimiyet-i Milliye.** (Ankara 1934 /10-11 Nisan/).

Rásonyi 1936a   Rásonyi Nagy László, *Kolbászszék*: **MNy.** XXXII (1936), pp. 266-267.

Rásonyi 1936b   Rásonyi, L., *Les noms de tribus dans le Слово о полку Игореве*. **Rásonyi - Rasovsky - Toll: Замѣтки к Слово.** (Praha 1936), pp. 1-9. (Sem. Kond. 8).

Rásonyi 1936c   Rásonyi, L., *Zur Frage der Eigennamen bei Anonymus*: **Ungarische Jahrbücher (Gedenkschrift Zoltán von Gombocz)** 15 (1936), pp. 548-554.

Rásonyi 1937   Rásonyi, L., *Ortaçağda Erdel'de Türklüğün İzleri*: **II. Türk Tarih Kongresi Yazıları.** (İstanbul 1937), 18 pp. (Offprint.).

Rásonyi 1938   Rásonyi, L., *Ortaçağda Erdel'de Türklüğün İzleri*: **Belleten** II (1938), pp. 107-122.

Rásonyi 1939a   Rásonyi L., *Tuna havzasında Kumanlar*: **Belleten** III (1939), pp. 401-422.

Rásonyi 1939b   Rásonyi, L., *Selçük adının menşeine dair*: **Belleten** III (1939), pp. 377-384.

Rásonyi 1940   Rásonyi, L., *A βοοκολαβραζ névhez*: **MNy.** XXXVI (1940), pp. 291-294.

Rásonyi 1941   Rásonyi, L., *Makut - Maklár*: **MNy.** XXXVII (1941), pp. 116-118.

Rásonyi 1941-1943   Rásonyi, L., *Török adatok a Magyar Etymologiai Szótárhoz*: **NyK** LI (1941-1943), pp. 98-115, 280-308.

Rásonyi 1942   Rásonyi, L., *Dünya Tarihinde Türklük.* Ankara 1942, 266 pp.

Rásonyi 1947   Rásonyi, L., *Bō-kolabur*: **Türk Tarih Kurumu Halil Ethem Hâtira Kitabı.** (Ankara 1947), pp. 242-248.

Rásonyi 1956a   Rásonyi, L., *Mit mondanak Szolnok megye földrajzi nevei ?*: **Jászkunság** 3 (1956), pp. 75-80.

Rásonyi 1956b   Rásonyi Nagy László, *A kiskunsági -lï, -li, > -la, -le képzős földrajzi nevek*: **MNy.** LII (1956), pp. 52-61.

Rásonyi 1956c   Rásonyi, Nagy László, *Köncsög és Kötöny*: **Pais Emlékkönyv.** (Budapest 1956), pp. 435-441.

Rásonyi 1958a	Rásonyi, L., *Miscellanea Arabo-Turcica*: **I. Goldziher Memorial Vol.** II. (Jerusalem 1958), pp. 133-135.
Rásonyi 1958b	Rásonyi, L., *A Tantó családnév eredete*: **MNy.** LIV (1958), p. 545.
Rásonyi 1960	Rásonyi, L., *A székely név eredete*: **MNy.** LVI (1960), pp. 186-194.
Rásonyi 1961a	Rásonyi, L., *Zu den Namen der ersten türkischen Herren von Jerusalem*: **AOH** XIII (1961), pp. 89-95.
Rásonyi 1961b	Rásonyi, L., *L'origine du nom székely (sicule)*: **ALingu.** 11 (1961), pp. 175-188.
Rásonyi 1961c	Rásonyi, L., *Über die geographischen Namen Tortillou und Tatrang*: **UAJb.** XXXIII (1961), pp. 245-251.
Rásonyi 1964a	Rásonyi, L., *Başkurt ve Macar yurtlarındaki ortak coğrafî adlar üzerine*: **Bilimsel Bildiriler 1963.** (Ankara 1964), pp. 105-112.
Rásonyi 1964b	Rásonyi, L., *Türklükte kadın adları*: **Türk Dili Araştırmaları Yıllığı - Belleten 1963** (1964), pp. 63-87.
Rásonyi 1966	Rásonyi, L., *Macarca "gyermek" kelimesi ve "Yermyak" adı*: **Reşid Rahmeti Arat İçin** (1966), pp. 383-387. (Türk Kültürünü Araştırma Estitüsü Yayınları: 19).
Rásonyi 1972	Rásonyi, L., *Sekeller ve adlarının menşei*: **Türk Kültürü** X (1972), pp. 289-294.
Rásonyi 1976	Rásonyi, L., *Azonos földrajzi nevek a baskír és a magyar földön*: **MNy.** LXXII (1976), pp. 48-53.
Rásonyi 1979	Rásonyi, L., *Bulaqs And Oguzs In Mediaeval Transylvania*: **AOH** XXXIII (1979), pp. 129-151.
Rásonyi 1983a	Rásonyi, L., *The Old-Hungarian Name Vajk* - a Note on the Origin of the Hunyadi Family: **Acta Orientalia Hungarica** XXXVI (1983), pp. 1-3.
Rásonyi 1983b	Rásonyi, L., *Török eredetű magyar személynevek*: **Forrás** XV /7/. (Kecskemét 1983 /július/), pp. 78-84.
Rásonyi, Adalékok	Rásonyi, L. (as R. Nagy László), *Adalékok török tulajdonneveinkhez* [=Contributions to our Turkic Proper Names]: **NyK** XLVI (1923), pp. 124-135.
Rásonyi, Anthr.	Rásonyi, L., *Les anthroponymes Comans de Hongrie*: **AOH** XX (1967), pp. 135-149.
Rásonyi, Basaraba	Rásonyi, L., *Contributions à l'histoire des premières cristallisations d'état des Roumains. L'origine des Basarabas.* Budapest 1936, 38 pp. (Études sur l'Europe Centre-Orientale III).
Rásonyi, Categ.	Rásonyi, L., *Sur quelques catégories de noms de personne en turc*: **ALingu.** III (1953), pp. 323-353.
Rásonyi, Frauenname	Rásonyi, L., *Der Frauenname bei den Türkvölkern*: **UAJb.** XXXIV (1962), pp. 223-239.
Rásonyi, Imp.	Rásonyi, L., *Les noms de personnes impératifs chez les peuples turques*: **AOH** XV (1962), pp. 233-243.
Rásonyi, Kayn.	Rásonyi, L., *Türk Özel Adlarının Kaynakları*: **Türkoloji Dergisi** I (1964), pp. 71-101.
Rásonyi, Kisk.	Rásonyi, L., *Kiskunság'da Kumanca Yer Adları*: **Németh Arm.** (Ankara 1962), pp. 341-352.
Rásonyi, Kisk. helyn.	Rásonyi, L., *A Kiskunság középkori helyneveihez*: **MNy.** LXII (1966), pp. 164-170.
Rásonyi, KÖA	Rásonyi, L., *Kuman Özel Adları*: **Türk Kültürü Araştırmaları** III-IV-V-VI (1966-1969), pp. 71-144.
Rásonyi, Leksik.	Rásonyi, L., *Türk Özel Adları ve Leksikografyası*: **Bilimsel Bildiriler 1966.** (Ankara 1968), pp. 39-47.
Rásonyi, Nombre	Rásonyi, L., *Les noms de nombre dans l'anthroponymie turque*: **AOH** XII (1961), pp. 45-71.
Rásonyi, NTK	Rásonyi, L., *Les noms toponymiques comans du Kiskunság*: **ALingu** VII (1957-1958), pp. 73-146.
Rásonyi, P. Cat.	Rásonyi, L., *The Psychology and Categories of Name Giving Among the Turkish Peoples*: **Hungaro-Turcica.** (Budapest 1976), pp. 207-223.
Rásonyi, Theoph.	Rásonyi, L., *Remnants of Theophoric Names in Turkic Name Giving*: **Belleten** XLVI /182/ (1982), pp. 291-296.
Rásonyi, Val.-Turc.	Rásonyi-Nagy, L., *Valacho-Turcica:* Aus den Forschungsarbeiten der Mitglieder d. Collegium Hungaricum dem Andenken R. Graggers gewidmet: **FMUI** (1927), pp. 1-29.
Rāwandī	Iqbâl, Muh. (ed.), *The Râḥat-uṣ-ṣudûr wa âyat-us-surûr,* being a history of the Saljûqs by Muhammad ibn ʿAlî ibn Sulaymân ar-Râwandî. London-Leyden 1921. (GMNewS. II.).

Räs. Räsänen, M., *Versuch eines etymologischen Wörterbuches der Türksprachen.* Helsinki 1969.

Räs., Lautg. Räsänen, M., *Materialen zur Lautgeschichte der Türkischen Sprachen.* Helsinki 1949.

Räs., Morph. Räsänen, M., *Materialen zur Morphologie der türkischen Sprachen.* Helsinki 1957.

Rec.T.Trad. *Recueil des textes et des traductions I.* Paris. (Publ. de l'École des Langues Or. Viv. III Sér.).

Rec. V. As. C. *Itinéraire de l'Asie Centrale: Recueil d'itinéraires et de voyages dans l'Asie Centrale et l'Extrême-Orient.* Paris 1878.

Rec.Voy. *Recueil de voyages et de mémoires.* Paris.

Redh. Redhouse, J. W., *A Turkish and English Lexicon.* Londres 1890. (New Impression: Constantinople 1921; Reprint: Beyrut 1974; Istanbul 1968 (Latin); English-Turkish: Istanbul 1969).

Refik, Anad. Refik, Ahmet, *Anadolu'da Türk Aşiretleri (996-1200).* İstanbul 1930.

Reg. Hieros. Röhricht, Reinhold (ed.), *Regesta Regni Hierosolymitani (MXCVII-MCCXCI).* Oeniponti 1893.

Rekogn. *Rekognoscirovka ozera Balhaš.* Proizvedena instrumental'no korp. voen. topogr. kapitanom Kartykovym i štabs kapitanom Ivanovym v 1903 goda: **IIRGO** XL (1904).

Rezun Rezun, D. Ja., *Rodoslovnaja sibirskih familij.* Novosibirsk 1993, 247 pp.

RHCHor *Recueil des historiens des croisades.* Publié par le soins de l'Académie des Inscriptions et Belles-Lettres. Historiens orientaux. Historiens arabes. I-V. Paris 1872-1906.

RHO *Revue Historique publiée par l'Institut d'Histoire Ottomane.* (=Tarih-i Osmanī Enǰümeni Meǰmuasï). İstanbul

Riza Riza, Ali (Yalman Yalgın), *Cenupta Türkmen Oymakları.* I-V. İstanbul-Ankara-Adana 1933-1939.

Rytschkow Rytschkow, P., *Orenburgische Topographie, oder umständliche Beschreibung der Orenburgischen Gouvernements.* Transl. by Jacob Rodde. I-II. Riga 1771. (Transl. from Ryčkov, P. I., Orenburgskaja topografija. SPb. 1762).

RKarBalkS Sujunčeva, H. I., Urusbieva, I. H. (ed.), *Russko-karačaevo-balkarskij slovar'.* Moskva 1965.

RKzS Sauranbaev, N. T., *Russko-kazahskij slovar'.* Moskva 1954.

Rodosl. kn. *Rodoslovnaja Kniga knjazej i dvorjan rossijskih i vyezžih.* I-II. Moskva 1787.

Rojzenzon-Bobohodžaev Rojzenzon, L. I. - Bobohodžaev, A., *Antroponimičeskie serii u uzbekov Nuraty (Samarkandskaja oblast'):* **OSA** (1978), pp. 144-152.

Rojzenzon-Isaeva Rojzenzon, L. I. - Isaeva, A. I., *Ob antroponimičeskih serijah:* **Vopr. onom.** 1 (1971), pp. 37-40.

ROr. *Rocznik Orientalistyczny.* Kraków.

Rosp. Taškent *Rospisanija: nočnym uličnym storožam i dvornikam g. Taškenta:* **TV (Prib.)** 90 (1903).

Rototaev Rototaev, P. S., *Kratkij slovar' gornih nazvanij Kabardino-Balkarii.* Nal'čik 1969, 100 pp.

Röhrborn Röhrborn, Klaus, *Uigurisches Wörterbuch.* Sprachmaterial der vorislamischen türkischen Texte aus Zentralasien. Wiesbaden 1977-.

Rubruck Rubruck, W. de, *Voyage en Orient du frère Guillaume de Rubruck de l'ordre des frères mineurs, l'an de grace 1255.* Ed. by F. Michel an T. Wright: **Rec. Voy.** IV. (Paris 1839), pp. 205-396.

Rudnyh Rudnyh, A. I., *Vtorye imena u jakutov:* **Antroponimika** (1970), pp. 219÷228.

Russk. Arhiv *Russkij Arhiv.* I-. Moskva 1888-.

Sīrat Sadeque, Dr. Syedah Fatima, *Baybars I of Egypt.* Part III. Dacca 1956.

S. Vostokov. *Sbornik Vostokovedenija.*

Saadčev Saadčev, Š. M., *Kategorial'naja diferenciacija azerbajdžanskih antroponimov:* **SovT** (1989, No. 3), pp. 51-60.

Sadyhov 1984 Sadyhov, Z. A., *Sistema azerbajdžanskih ličnyh imen:* **Tjurksk. onom.** (1984), pp. 213-220.

Sadykov Sadykov, Z. A., *Ličnye imena v azerbajdžanskom jazyke.* Avtoref. diss. kand. Baku 1975.

Sakaoğlu 1979 Sakaoğlu, S., *Türkçede soyadları:* **AÜEFAD** 2 (11) (1979), pp. 375-421. (Ahmet Caferoğlu Özel Sayısı).

Sakaoğlu 1981	Sakaoğlu, Necdet, *Divriği'de Aile Adları, Boylar ve Oymaklar*: **Türk Folkloru** 2 (19) (1981), pp. 13-17.
Sakaoğlu 1984a	Sakaoğlu, S., *İnsan Adlarından Kaynaklanan Yer Adlarımız*: **TYASB**, pp. 259-264.
Sakaoğlu 1984b	Sakaoğlu, Saim, *Soyadlarımız Üzerine 1.*: **Türk Dili** 388-389 (1984), pp. 244-249.
Sakaoğlu 1992	Sakaoğlu, S., *Türklerde Ad ve Ad Verme Gelenekleri*: **Türk Aile Ansiklopedisi** 1. (Konya 1992), pp. 2-11.
Sakaoğlu 1995	Sakaoğlu, Saim, *Anadolu'da Bölgelere Has Kişi Adları*: **Türk Dili** 520 (1995), pp. 376-382.
Sakaoğlu 2001	Sakaoğlu, S., *Türk Adbilimi. I. Giriş.* Ankara 2001, 156 pp. (Türk Dil Kurumu Yayınları: 780; Ad Bilimi Çalışma Grubu: 1).
Samojlovič 1911	Samojlovič, A. N., *K voprosu o narečenii imen u tureckih plemen*: **ŽS** XX, II (1911), pp. 297-300.
Samojlovič 1917	Samojlovič, A. N., *Ukazatel' sobstvennyh imen*: **Potanin, Pred.** (1917), pp. 192-198.
Samojlovič 1927	Samojlovič, A. N., *Odin iz spiskov "Rodoslovnogo dreva turkmenskogo" Abul'gazi-hana*: **Doklady** (1927), pp. 39-42.
Saparova	Saparova, G., *Ženskaja antroponimija turkmen hasarli*: **Antroponimika.** (M. 1970), pp. 77-80.
Satybalov	Satybalov, A., *K voprosu o ličnoj onomastike u kumykov*: **Sovetskoe jazykoznanie** II (1936), pp. 95-107.
Sattarov	Sattarov, G. F., *Tatar isemnäre süzlege.* Kazan 1981, 255 pp.
Sattarov 1969	Sattarov, G. F., *Soslovnye tituly i drevnetatarskie ličnye imena*: **OnomPov.** 1 (1969), pp. 52-59.
Sattarov 1970a	Sattarov, G. F., *Ètapy razvitija i očerednye zadači tatarskoj onomastiki.* Posobie k speckursu "Tatarskaja onomastika". Kazan' 1970, pp. 1-87.
Sattarov 1970b	Sattarov, G. F., *Böyek Oktyabr'dan soň tatar onomastikasi üsešeneň qayber tendenciyalare*: **Učen. zan. KGPI** vyp.74 (1970), pp. 219-233.
Sattarov 1971	Sattarov, G. F., *Tatarskaja onomastika za 50 let*: **Uč. Zap. Kaz. Ped. Instituta,** (1971), 95 pp. 52-66.
Sattarov 1972	Sattarov, G. F., *Tatar onomastikasïnda aq häm qara süzläre*: **Tatar tel beleme mäs'äläläre, 4 nče kitap, KGU** (1972), pp. 29-41.
Sattarov 1972b	Sattarov, G. F., *Bulgarizmy v toponimii i antroponimii Tatarskoj ASSR*: **Konf. po tat. jaz. posv. 50-let. SSSR.** (Kazan' 1972), pp. 76-78.
Sattarov 1972c	Sattarov, G. F., *Tatarstan ASSR Zelenodol'sk rajonynyň boryngy tatar häm čuvaš antroponimnarynnan jasalgan avyl atamalary*: **Tatar tel beleme mäsaläläre, 5-nče titap, KGU** (1972), pp. 130-151.
Sattarov 1973	Sattarov, G. F., *Tatarstan ASSR'niň antropotoponimnarï.* Tatarstan avïllarïniň issemnäre. Kazan 1973, 296 pp. (Kazan Universtetï näšrijatï.).
Sattarov 1975	Sattarov, G. F., *Antropotoponimija Tatarskoj ASSR.* Avtoref. doktora fil. nauk. Kazan' 1975, 90 pp.
Sattarov 1975	Sattarov, G. F., *Otčestva i kategorija vežlivosti v tatarskoj antroponimii*: **SovT** (1975, No. 1), pp. 80-86.
Sattarov 1977	Sattarov, G. F., *Leksiko-semantičeskie i tematičeskie gruppy i razrjady tatarskih lično-individual'nyh i semejno-rodovyh prozvišč*: **SovT** 3 (1977), pp. 2-35.
Sattarov 1977b	Sattarov, G. F., *Ètnonimy v toponimi i antroponimii Tatarii*: **Issl. po tat. jaz.** (Kazan' 1977), 20-63 pp.
Sattarov 1978	Sattarov, G. F., *Tatarskaja antropotoponimija i etnolingvističeskie svjazi*: **SovT** 3 (1978), pp. 22-32.
Sattarov 1979	Sattarov, G. F., *Nazvanija naselennyh punktov Tatarii proizvodnye ot ličnyh imen*: **SovT** 2 (1979), pp. 37-47.
Sattarov 1980	Sattarov, G. F., *Tatarskaja onomastika i ètnogenez*: **Tezisy dokl. i soobščenij III VTK.** (Taškent 1980), pp. 188-189.
Sattarov 1981	Sattarov, G. F., *Tatar isemnäre süzlege.* Kazan 1981.
Sattarov 1985	Sattarov, G. F., *Tatarskaja onomastika i ètnogenez.* (k voprosu ispol'zovanija onomastičeskih dannyh v kompleksnom izučenii ètnogeneza): **Tjurkskoe jazykoznanie**

(1985), pp. 309-314.

Sattarov 1990 Sattarov, G. F., *Tatar antroponimikasï*. Kazan 1990, 277 pp.

Sattarov-Subaeva Sattarov, G. F. - Subaeva, R. H., *Osnovnye komponenty složnyh ličnyh imen v tatarskom jazyke*: **OnomPov.** 4 (1976), pp. 65-73.

Sauvaget Sauvaget, J., *Noms et surnoms de Mamelouks*: **JA** CCXXXVIII (1950), pp. 31-58.

Sauvaget: BEO II Sauvaget, J., *Décrets mamelouks de Syrie* (premier article): **BEO** II (anné 1932). (Paris 1932), pp. 1-52.

Sauvaget: BEO III Sauvaget, J., *Décrets mamelouks de Syrie* (deuxième article): **BEO** III (année 1933). (Le Caire 1934), pp. 1-29.

Sauvaget: BEO XII Sauvaget, J., *Décrets mamelouks de Syrie* (troisième article): **BEO** XII (années 1947-1948). (Beyrouth 1948), pp. 1-60.

Sauvaire Sauvaire, H. (transl.), *Description de Damas*. Trad. de l'arabe par –: **JA** III-VII (1894-1897).

Sb. OGV *Sbornik statej pomeščennyh v Orenburgskih gubernskih vedomostjah za 1862 god.* Ufa 1862.

Sb. Syr-D. *Sbornik materialov dlja statistiki Syr-Dar'inskoj oblasti.* Taškent 1891.

SBAW *Sitzungsberichte der Bayerischen Akademie der Wissenschaften.* Philologisch-historische Klasse.

Scheiber Scheiber, S., *Arszlán*: **Nyelvőr** 77 (1953), pp. 468-469.

Schiefner Schiefner, A., *Heldensagen der Minussinschen Tataren*: **Bull. Ac.** XV. (SPb. 1856).

Schimmel Schimmel, A., *Islamic Names*. Edinburgh 1989, 137 pp.

Schmitz Schmitz, Andrea, *Die Erzählung von Edige. Gehalt, Genese un Wirkung einer heroischen Tradition.* Wiesbaden 1996.

SDD *Türkiye'de Halk Ağzından Söz Derleme Dergisi.* I-VI. Istanbul - Ankara 1939-1952.

Sädiyev Sä°diyev, Š., *Adlar nečä aranmišdïrï. Kakie imena nravjatsja.* Baqï 1969.

Seādeddīn Seādeddīn, *Tāӡ et-tevārīχ*. I-II. İstanbul 1862.

Sejdakmatov Sejdakmatov, K., *Slovar' kirgizskih ličnyh imen*: **OSA** 2 (1980), pp. 306-307.

Seyirci Seyirci, Musa, *Afyonkarahisar'da Aile Lâkapları*. Derleyen: –: **Türk Folkloru** 8 (1985), pp. 25-26.

Seldj. Nameh Schefer, Ch. (ed.), *Quelques chapitres de l'abrégé du Seldjouq Nameh composé par l'émir Nassir Eddin Yahia*: **Rec.T.Trad.** V, pp. 1-102.

Seljametev Seljametev, L. M., *Imja i legenda*: **OSA** 2 (1980), pp. 112-119.

Sem. Kond. *Seminarium Kondakovianum.* Recueil d'études archéologie, histoire de l'art, études byzantines. I-. Prague 1927-.

Semenov Semenov, A. A., *Buharskij traktat*: **S. Vostokov.** 5 (1948), pp. 137-53.

Sergeev Sergeev, A., *Nogajcy na Moločnyh vodah (1790-1832 g.).* Istoričeskij očerk. Simferopol 1912.

Seroševskij Seroševskij, V.L., *Jakuty.* Opyt êtnografičeskago izsledovanija. Pod red. N. I. Veselovskago. I. SPb. 1896, XII+719 pp. (IIRGO).

Seroševskij, Razsk. Seroševskij, V.L., *Jakutskie razskazy.* SPb. 1895.

Sertkaya Sertkaya, O. F., *"İnel Kağan" mı? - "İni İl kağan" mı?*: **Atsız Armağanı.** (İstanbul 1976), 376-419 pp.

Sev. Sevortjan, Ê.V., *Êtimologičeskij slovar' tjurkskih jazykov* (Obščetjurkskie osnovy na glasnye). Moskva 1974, 767 pp.

Sevim-Yücel Sevim, Ali - Yücel, Yaşar, *Türkiye Tarihi I-IV.* Ankara 1990.

Sevinç Sevinç, Necdet, *Gaziantep'te Yer Adları ve Türk Boyları, Türk Aşiretleri, Türk Oymakları*: **Türk Dünyası Araştırmaları** 26 (1983), pp. 1-138.

Shaikh Uwais Van Loon's, J.B., *Ta ᶜrikh-i Shaikh Uwais.* (History of Shaikkh Uwais). An important Source for the history of Adharbaijan in fourteenth century. Gravenhage 1954.

Shaw Shaw, R. B., *A Grammar of the Language of Eastern Turkistan*: **IASB** XLVI (1877).

SHeidAW *Sitzungsberichte der Heidelbergen Akademie der Wissenschaften* Philologisch-historische Klasse. Heidelberg.

Sib. Let. *Sibirskija Letopisi.* SPb. 1907. (Izdanija Imperatorskoj Archeografičeskoj Kommissii.).

Sib. Vest. Spasskij, G. (ed.), *Sibirskij Vestnik.* Izd.–. I. SPb. 1819-.

CXXII

Sin. Fr.   Wyngaert, P. Anastasius van den (ed.), *Sinica Franciscana*. Vol. I. Itinera et relationes fratrum minorum saeculi XIII et XIV, collegit ad fidem codicum redegit et adnotavit –. Ad Claras Aquas 1929.

Sinor   Sinor, D., *Pusztaszer* [Toponym]: **MNy.** LXIX (1973), pp. 482-483.

SIGTJa. Leksika   Tenišev, Ê. R. (ed.), *Sravnitel'no-istoričeskaja grammatika tjurkskih jazykov* Leksika. Moskva 1997.

Sysoev   Sysoev, V.M., *Karačaj v geografičeskom, bytovom i istoričeskom otnošenii*. 1913, pp. 1-156. (Sbornik Materialov dlja Opisanija Kavkaza, XLIII).

Syzdykov   Syzdykov, A., *Ob odnoj kirgizskoj rukopisi*: **IOAIÊK** XIII, pp. 354-63.

Skrjabina   Skrjabina, N. P., *Ličnye naimenovanija v dokumentah jasačnogo sbora XVII v. na territorii Jakutii*: **Sobstvennye imena v sisteme jazyka.** (Sverdlovsk 1980), pp. 140-144. (Voprosy onomastiki, vyp. 14).

SKSO   *Spravočnaja knižka Samarkandskoj oblasti.* Samarkand 1893.

SlGeogrKirg.   Isaev, Tokombaev, Aliev etc., *Slovar' geografičeskih nazvanij Kirgizii* (Proekt). Frunze 1962.

SlGeogrTerm.   *Slovar' geografičeskih terminov i drugih slov, vstrečajuščihja v toponimii Azerbajdžanskoj SSR.* Moskva 1971.

SLINM   Krjukov, M. V. (ed.-in-chief), *Sistemy ličnyh imen u narodov mira*. Moskva 1989, 383 pp.

SlKazGeogrNazv.   Konkašpaev, T. K., *Slovar' kazahskih geografičeskih nazvanij*. Alma-Ata 1963, 185 pp.

SlMestGeogrNazv.   Murzaev, Ê., - Murzaev, V., *Slovar' mestnyh geografičeskih terminov*. Moskva 1959.

SlToponBašk.   Kamalov, A. A. (Ed), *Slovar' toponimov baškirskoj ASSR*. Ufa 1980, 200 pp.

SMAÊ   *Sbornik Muzeja Antropologii i Êtnografii.*

Smirnov, Krym.   Smirnov, V.D., *Krymskoe hanstvo pod verhovenstvom Otomanskoj Porty do načala XVIII. veka*. SPb. 1887, XXXV+772 pp.

Smirnov, Sultany   Smirnov, E.T., *Sultany Kenisara i Sadyk*. Biografičeskie očerki. Taškent 1889, IV+83+133 pp.

Smyrnov   Smyrnov, Jean, et Boyer, Paul, *Les populations finnoises des bassins de la Bolga et de la Kama*. In: *l'Année sociologique* 2: 226-9. (1899?)

SMOK   *Sbornik materialov dlja opisanija mestnostej i plemen Kavkaza.* I-. Tiflis 188-.

Sobernh.   Sobernheim, Moritz, *Matériaux pour un Corpus Inscriptionum Arabicorum*. II. Syrie du Nord. I-II. Caire 1959. (Mémoires publ. par les Membres de la Mission Archéologique Française au Caire).

Sobolev   Sobolev, L.K., *Geografičeskija i statističeskija svedenija o Zeravšanskom okruge*. Priloženie 15: Spisok naselennyh mest Zeravšanskago okruga: **ZIRGOStat.** IV (1870/74?), pp. 163-721.

SODž.   Rumjancev, P.P. (ed.), *Materialy po obsledovaniju tuzemnago i russkago starožil'českago hozjajstva i zemlepol'zovanija v Semirečenskoj oblasti*. Kirgizskoe hozjajstvo. Tom III. Džarkentskij uezd. Sobrannye i razrabotannye pod rukovodstvom –. SPb. 1912-13.

SOK   Rumjancev, P.P. (ed.), *Materialy po obsledovaniju tuzemnago i russkago starožil'českago hozjajstva i zemlepol'zovanija v Semirečenskoj oblasti*. Kirgizskoe hozjajstvo. Tom II. Kopal'skij uezd. Sobrannye i razrabotannye pod rukovodstvom –. SPb. 1912-13.

Sokolov   Sokolov, G., *Russkija imena i prozvišča v XVII veke*. Kazan' 1891.

Sopieva   Sopieva, G. K., *Leksičeskie istočniki ličnyh imen u turkmen*: **OSA**, pp. 177-182.

SOV   Rumjancev, P.P. (ed.), *Materialy po obsledovaniju tuzemnago i russkago starožil'českago hozjajstva i zemlepol'zovanija v Semirečenskoj oblasti*. Kirgizskoe hozjajstvo. Tom IV. Vernenskij uezd. Sobrannye i razrabotannye pod rukovodstvom –. SPb. 1912-13.

SovT   *Sovetskaja tjurkologija.* I-. Baku.

Sozontov   Sozontov, Taras, *Kirgiz iz okrestnostej Gur'eva-gorodka*: **Sb. OGV** (1862), Ufa.

SPAW   *Sitzungsberichte der Preussischen Akademie der Wissenschaften.* Philologisch-historische Klasse. Berlin.

Spencer   Spencer, Robert F., *The Social Context of Modern Turkish Names*: **Southwestern Journal of Anthropology** 17, no. 3 (1961), pp. 205-218.

Sprav. Im.   Superanskaja, A. V. (ed.), *Spravočnik ličnyh imen narodov RSFSR*. Izdanie vtoroe, pererabotannoe i dopolnennoe. Pod red. –. Moskva 1979, 571 pp.

Sprav. Im. 1987 Superanskaja, A. V., *Spravočnik ličnyh imen narodov RSFSR.* Izdanie 3-e, ispravlennoe. Pod red. –. Moskva 1987, 630 pp.

Sprav. Im. 1965 Baskakov, N. A. (ed.), *Spravočnik ličnyh imen narodov RSFSR.* Pod red. –. Moskva 1965.

SprTurkmLI *Spravočnik turkmenskih ličnyh imen.* Ašhabad 1989.

Spuler Spuler, B., *Die Goldene Horde.* Die Mongolen in Russland, 1223-1502. Leipzig 1943.

Sr. Az. *Srednjaja Azija.* I-. Taškent 1896-.

SRH Szentpétery, E. (ed.), *Scriptores Rerum Hungaricarum Tempore Ducum Regumque Stirpis Arpadianae Gestarum.* I-II 1937-38.

SÊ *Sovetskaja Êtnografija.*

Stein Stein, Aurel, *Sand-buried ruins of Khotan.* Personal Narrative of a Journey of Archeological and Geographical Exploration in Chinese Turkestan. London 1903, XLIII, 523 pp.

Stein, Inn. Asia Stein, A., *Innermost Asia.* Detailed Report of explorations in Central Asia. 1-4. Oxford 1928.

Steingass Steingass, F.A., *A Comprehensive Persian-English Dictionary.* London 1930.

Su Su, Ekrem Kâmil, *Balıkesir ve Civarında Yürük ve Türkmenler.* İstanbul 1938. (Balıkesir Halkevleri Yayınlarından, sayı 20).

Subaev Subaev, R. S., *Tatarstan ASSR Čüprälä rajonï awïllarïnïñ onomastikasï.* Kazan' 1976.

Sugár Sugár, I., *Az Egerben 1687. után megtelepedett törökök személynevei* [=Personal names of the Turks settled in the town of Eger after 1687]: **MNy.** LXIX (1973), pp. 203-210.

Sulajmanov Sulajmanov, Ê., *Nekotorye imena pirov-pokrovitelej remesel i domašnih promyslov u kirgizov*: **OSA** 2 (1980), pp. 282-289.

Sultan'jaev 1970 Sultan'jaev, O. A., *Ob osnovah položitel'noj êkspressii v kazahskih imenah*: **Antroponimika** (1970).

Superanskaja - Lezina Superanskaja, A. V. - Lezina, I. N., *Slovar' êtnonimov tjurkskih narodov.* I-II. Moskva 1994.

Superanskaja 1984 Superanskaja, A. V., *Onomastičeskij kontinuum*: **Tjurksk. onom.** (1984), pp. 5-12.

Suprunenko Suprunenko, G. P., *Iz drevnekyrgyzskoj onomastiki*: **SovT** (1970, No.3.), pp. 79-81.

Suzd. *Letopis' po Suzdal'skomu spisku*: **PSRL** ().

Sümer Sümer, Faruk, *Avşarlara dair*: **Köprülü Arm.** (İstanbul 1953).

Sümer 1984 Sümer, Faruk, *Eski Türklerde İsim Koyma Geleneklerinden*: Atsız: **Millî Kültür** 47 (1984), pp. 4-5.

Sümer 1999 Sümer, Faruk, *Türk Devletleri Tarihinde Şahıs Adları.* I-II. Istanbul 1999, 878 pp. (Türk Dünyası Araştırmaları Vakfı).

Sümer, Aga Sümer, Faruk, *Eski Türk Devletlerinde Aga Unvanı*: **Türk Dünyası Araştırmaları** (38) (1985), pp. 58-66.

Sümer: DTCFD Sümer, F., *Bayındır, Peçenek ve Yüregirler*: **DTCFD** XI (2-4) (1953), pp. 317-322.

Süssheim Süssheim, Carl, *Das Geschenk aus der Saldschunkengeschichte* von dem Wesir Muhammad B. Muhammad B. Muhammad B. Abdallah B. Al-Nit, am al-Husaini Al-Jazdi zum ersten Male hrsg. von —. Leiden, 1909.

Šajhulov 1974 Šajhulov, A. G., *K voprosu o leksiko-semantičeskoj klassifikacii baškirskih i tatarskih ličnyh imen*: **Aspekty lingv.**, pp. 312-317.

Šajhulov 1975 Šajhulov, A G., *Islam i baškirsko-tatarskaja antroponimičeskaja sistema I.*: **Tezisy konferencii aspirantov i molodyh sotrudnikov Inst. Vost. AN SSSR.** (M. 1975).

Šajhulov 1977 Šajhulov, A. G., *K probleme vyjavlenija antroponimičeskoj tipologii v imenah tjurkskogo i finno-ugorskogo proishoždenija*: **Tezisy naučn. konf. po obšč. voprosam dialektologii i istorii jazyka.** (M.-Nal'čik 1977).

Šajhulov 1978 Šajhulov, A., *Tatarskie i baškirskie ličnye imena tjurkskogo proishoždenija.* Moskva 1978, pp. 1-25. ().

Šajhulov 1978a Šajhulov, A. G., *Tatarskie i baškirskie ličnye imena tjurkskogo proishoždenija* [Thesis of Ph. D. dissertation]. Moskva 1978.

Šajhulov 1981 Šayhulov, A., *Antroponimičeskie sistemy tatarskogo i baškirskogo narodov.* Ufa 1981, pp. 1-20.

Šajhulov 1981a Šajhulov, A. G., *K probleme vyjavlenija tipologii antroponimov tjurkskogo i finno-ugorskogo proishoždenija*: **Lingv. geogr. i problemy ist. i jaz. č. II.** (Nal'čik 1981).

CXXIV

Šajhulov 1983b Šajhulov, A. G., *Tatarskie i baškirskie ličnye imena tjurskogo proishoždenija.* Ufa 1983, pp. 1-71.

Šajhulov 1984a Šajhulov, A. G., *Leksiko-semantičeskaja obščnost' baškirskoj i kazahskoj antroponimii*: **Êtničeskaja onomastika.** (Moskva 1984).

Šajhulov 1984b Šajhulov, A. G., *Zakonomernosti i tendencii zaimstvovanija russkih ličnyh imen (na materiale sovremennoj tatarskoj i baškirskoj antroponimii)*: **Tjurksk. onom.** (1984), pp. 220-229.

Šajhulov 1991 Šajhulov, A. G., *Tematičeskie gruppy tatarskih i baškirskih ličnyh imen doislamskogo perioda*: **Nominacija v onomastike.** (Sverdlovsk 1991), pp. 137-142. (Voprosy onomastiki, vyp. 19).

Šakurov 1980 Šakurov, R. Z., *Rifmovanie imen u baškir*: **Onom. vost.** (Moskva 1980), pp. 43-48.

Šakurov 1981 Šakurov, R. Z., *Sobytija i imena geroev krest'janskoj vojny 1773-1775 gg. v toponimii Južnogo urala*: **Vopr. ba. top.** (Ufa 1981), pp. 44-50.

Šatinova 1971 Šatinova, N. I., *K istorii altajskih imen*: **Êtnografija imen.** (M., Nauka 1971), pp. 65-70.

Šatinova 1980 Šatinova, N. I., *Rifmovanie ličnyh imen u altajcev*: **Onom. vost.** (Moskva 1980), pp. 39-42.

Ščeglov Ščeglov, I. L., *Truhmeny i nogajcy Stavropol'skoj gubernii.* Stavropol' 1910.

Šejb. Berezin, I. (ed.), *Šejbaniada.* Istorija mongolo-tjurkov na džagatajskom dialekte, s perevodom, primečanijami i priloženijami izdal –. Kazan' 1849. (Biblioteka Vostočnyh Istorikov, vyp. 1).

Šipova Šipova, E. N. (ed.), *Slovar' tjurkizmov v russkom jazyke.* Alma-Ata 1976, 444 pp.

Şölen Şölen, Hikmet, *Aydın ili ve Yürükler.* Aydın 1945.

T'oung Pao *T'oung Pao,* ou Archives concernant l'histoire, les langues, la géographie, ethnographie et les arts de l'Asie Orientale. Paris – Leyde.

Tabarī, Annal. De Goeje, M.J. (ed.), *Kitāb Aχbār ar-Rasūl wa'l-Mulūk.* Annales quot scripsit Abu Djafar Mohammed ibn Djarir at-Tabari. I-III. Leiden 1879-1901.

Tahsin Tahsin, Hasan, *Samsun'da Adlarla İlgili İnanmalar*: **Türk Folklor Araştırmaları** 6 (133) (1960).

Taklamakanlı Taklamakanlı, A. P., *Uygur kişi adları Üzerine*: **TDİD** I (1996), pp. 193-211.

Tan. Tar. Sözl. *Tanıklariyle Tarama sözlüğü.* I-IV. Istanbul-Ankara 1943-1957.

Tar. Rashidi Elias, N. (ed.) - Denison Ross, E. (transl.), *The Tarikh-i Rashidi of Mirza Muhammed Haidar Dughlat.* A history of the Moghuls of Central Asia. An English version ed. by–. The translation –. London 1895.

Tar. Sözl. *Tarama sözlüğü.* I-VI. Ankara 1963-1972.

Tar. Zend. Beer, E., *Das Tarikh-i Zendiye.* Leiden, 1888.

Tarǰ/Houtsma Houtsma, M. Th., *Ein türkisch-arabisches Glossar.* Nach der leidener Handschrift herausgegeben und erläutert von –. Leiden 1894.

Tarǰ/Toparlı Toparlı R. - Çögenli M. S. - Yanık, N. H., *Kitâb-i mecmû-i tercümân-i Türkî ve Acemî ve Mugalî.* Ankara 2000, 165 pp. + 63 pp. facsimile.

Tarzimanov Tarzimanov, F. V., *O tatarskih, baškirskih i čuvašskih imenah*: **OnomPov. 1** (1969).

TatRS *Tatarsko-russkij slovar'.* Moskva 1966.

Tazebayoğlu Tazebayoğlu, S., *Kilis'te Ad Verme Adetleri*: **Halk Bilgisi Haberleri** 9 (1940), p. 57.

TDAYB *Türk Dili Araştırmaları Yıllığı. Belleten.* Ankara. (Türk Dil Kurumu Yayınları).

TDİD *Türk Dünyası İncelemeleri Dergisi.* İzmir.

TED *Shorter Redhouse Turkish-English Dictionary.* İstanbul 1972.

Temir Temir, Ahmet Dr., *Manghol-un Niuça Tobça'an (Yüan-Chᶜao Pi-shi).* Moğolların Gizli Tarihi I. Tercüme. Ankara 1948.

Temir, Caca Temir, Ahmet, *Kırşehir Emiri Caca oğlu Nur el-Din'in 1272 tarihli Arapça-Moğolca vakfiyesi.* Ankara 1959.

Tezcan Tezcan, Semih, *Eski Türkçede Buyla ve Baga Sanları Üzerine*: **TDAY.** (Ankara 1977).

THİTM *Türkiye Huhuk İlimleri Tarihi Mecmuası.* İstanbul.

Thomsen, Fragm. Thomsen, Vilhelm, *Fragments of a Runic Turkish Manuscript*: **Stein, Inn. Asia** (1928), pp. 1082-83.

Thomsen, Inscr. Thomsen, V., *Inscriptions de l'Orkhon* déchifrées par–. (I. L'alphabet. II. Transcription et traduction des textes). Première livraison. Helsingfors 1894, 224 pp. (MSFOu. V.).

Thomsen, Stein Thomsen, V. (ed., transl.), *Dr. M.A. Stein's Manuscripts in Turkish "runic" Script from*

Miran and Tun-huang. Publ. and translated by–: **JRAS** (1912), pp. 181-227.

Thomsen, Turcica Thomsen, Vilhelm, *Turcica.* Études concernant l'interprétations turques de la Mongolie et de la Sibérie. Par –. Helsingfors 1916, 107 pp. (MSFOu. XXXVII).

THTD *Türk Hukuk Tarihi Dergisi.* Ankara.

Thúry, Behdset Thúry, József, *A "Behdset-ül-Lugat" czímű csagatáj szótár.* Budapest 1903.

Tihrânî Tihranî, Abu Bakr-i, *Kitâb-i Diyârbakriyya.* (Ak-Koyunlular Tarihi) I-II. Yayınlayanlar: Necati Lugal, Faruk Sümer, giriş ve notlar F. Sümer. Ankara 1962.

Tillo Tillo, A.A., *Pervaja narodnaja perepis' v Kirgizskoj stepi,* proizvedennaja v Nikolaevskom uezde Orenburgskago kraja dejstv. členom Orenburgskago Otdela –: **IIRGO** IX (1873), pp. 77-.

Titov Titov, V., *Bogatyrskija poemy minusinskih tatar:* **VIRGO** XV (1855).

Tizeng. I Tizengauzen, V. G. (ed., transl.), *Sbornik materialov, otnosjaščihsja k istorii Zolotoj Ordy.* Tom I. Izvlečenija iz sočinenij arabskih. SPb. 1884, 564 pp.

Tizeng. II Tizengauzen, V. G. (ed., transl.), *Sbornik materialov, otnosjaščihsja k istorii Zolotoj Ordy.* Tom II. Izvlečenija iz persidskih sočinenij sobrannye – i obrabotannye A. A. Romaskevičem i S. L. Volinym. Moskva - Leningrad 1941, 308 pp.

Tjumencev Tjumencev, L. A., *Antropotoponimy Astrahanskoj oblasti:* **Antroponimika** (1970).

Tjurksk. onom. Kajdarov, A. T. (ed.), *Tjurkskaja onomastika.* Alma-Ata 1984, 247 pp.

TYASB *Türk Yer Adları Sempozyumu Bildirileri.* Ankara 1984, 285 pp.

Tynyšp. Tynyšpaev, M., *Materialy k istorii kirgiz-kazakskogo naroda.* Taškent 1925.

TKA *Türk Kültürü Araştırmaları.* Ankara.

TKAÊÊ *Trudy Kirgizskoj Arheologo-êtničeskoj Êkspedicii.* Moskva.

TM *Türkiyat Mecmuası.* İstanbul.

TMEN I Doerfer, G., *Türkische und Mongolische Elmente im Neupersischen* Bd. I. Mongolische Elemente im Neupersischen. Wiesbaden 1963.

TMEN II Doerfer, G., *Türkische und Mongolische Elmente im Neupersischen* Bd. II. Türkische Elemente im Neupersischen. Wiesbaden 1965.

TMEN III Doerfer, G., *Türkische und Mongolische Elmente im Neupersischen* Bd. III. Türkische Elemente im Neupersischen. Wiesbaden 1967.

TMEN IV Doerfer, G., *Türkische und Mongolische Elmente im Neupersischen* Bd. IV. Türkische Elemente im Neupersischen. Wiesbaden 1975.

TMİB *Türkiye Mülki İdare Bölümleri ve Bunlara bağlı Köyler, Belediyeler* (1 Haziran 1970 durumu). İstanbul 1970.

TMYK *Türkiyede Meskun Yerler Kılavuzu.* I-III.

Togan, BTT Togan, A. Zeki Velidi, *Bugünkü Türkili Türkistan ve yakın Tarihi.* İstanbul 1981.

Togan, UTT Togan, A. Zeki Velidî, *Umumî Türk Tarihi'ne Giriş.* İstanbul 1981, 537 pp.

Toksöz Toksöz, Ü., *Anne ve Çocuk* (pp. 261-273: Çocuğumuza ne İsim Koyalım?). Ankara 1968.

TolkSlGeogr. *Tolkovyj slovar' geografičeskih nazvanij Azerbajdžanskoj SSR.* Baku 1960.

Tolstova Tolstova, L. S., *Drevnevostočnye antroponomičeskie associacii v karakalpakskom istoričeskom fol'klore:* **Onom. vost.** (Moskva 1980), pp. 67-71.

Tolstova 1980 Tolstova, L. S., *Toponimy i êtnonimy v antroponimii karakalpakov:* **OSA** 2 (1980), pp. 101-105.

Tompa Tompa, J., *Feriz bég:* **Nyelvőr** 83 (1959), pp. 350-351.

TOOIK *Trudy Orenburgskogo Obščestva Izučenija Kirgizskogo Kraja.* Orenburg 1921.

ToponAzerb. *Nekotorye toponimy rajonov Azerbajdžana.* Baku 1978.

Torma 1992 Torma, J., *Magic and Name-giving among the Bashkir:* **Altaic Religious Beliefs and Practices.** (Bp. 1992), pp. 361-369.

Torma 1996 Torma, J., *Kun-kazak egyezések a névanyagban:* **Valóság** (1996, V), pp. 93-101.

Torma 1997 Torma, J., „…A tűznek mondom!" (A baskir népi orvoslás mágikus elemeinek mai rendszere). Bp. 1997, 189 pp.

Torma, 1999 Torma, J., *Bérem bélő, Íkem ígő.* - Mándoky Kongur István emlékére -. Karcag 1999, 107 pp.

Torma - Hisametdinova Torma, J. - Hisametdinova, F. G., *Mágia és névadás a baskiroknál* [=Magic and name-giving among the Bashkir]: **Keletkutatás.** (Budapest 1990 (ősz)), pp. 63-80.

TOUAK   *Trudy Orenburgskoj Učenoj Arhivnoj Kommissii.* Orenburg.

Tör   Tör, Nükhet, *Siz Kimlerdensiniz veya Soyadlarımızın Hikâyesi*: **Türk Dili** 616 (2003), pp. 399-407.

Tr. Syr-D. OSK   *Trudy Syr-Dar'inskogo Otdela Statističeskoj Kommissii.*

TrkmRS   Baskakov, N.A. - Karryev, B.A. - Hamzaev, M.Ja. (ed.), *Turkmensko-russkij slovar'.* Moskva 1968.

TRS   Mustafaev, Ê. M.-Ê. - Starostov, L. N. (ed.), *Turecko-russkij slovar'.* Moskva 1977.

Trudy AS IV   *Trudy Četvertago Arheologičeskago sezda v Rossii, byvšago v Kazani.* I-II. Kazan' 1884.

TS   Eren, Hasan (ed.), *Türkçe Sözlük.* Ankara 1988.

TT   Bang, W. - Gabain, A.von, *Türkische Turfan-Texte.* I-VI: **SPAW.** (Berlin 1929-34).

TT VII-X   Arat, G. R. - Gabain, A.von, *Türkische Turfan-Texte*: **APAW / ADAW** VII-X (1936-1958).

TTDS   Mahmutova, L. T., *Tatar teleneň dialektologik süzlege.* Kazan 1969.

Tuhf.   Atalay, B., *Ettuhfet-üz-zekiyya fil-lûgat-it-türkiyye.* İstanbul 1945.

Tuhfa   Fazylov, Ê. I. - Zijaeva, M. T. (transl., ed.), *Izyskannyj dar tjurkskomu jazyku.* (Grammatičeskij traktat XIV v. na arabskom jazyke). Pod red. A. N. Kononova. Taškent 1978, 450 pp.

Tumaševa   Tumaševa, D. G., *Könbatïš seber tatarларï tele.* Grammatik očerk häm süzlek. Kazan 1961.

Tupikov   Tupikov, N.M., *Slovar' drevne-russkih sobstvennyh imen.* SPb. 1903, 858 pp.

Turan   Turan, Osman, *Türkiye Selçukluları Hakkında Resmi Vesikalar.* Metin, Tercüme ve Araştırmalar. Ankara 1958.

Turan, İlig   Turan, O., *İlig unvanı hakkında*: **Türkiyat Mecmuası** 7-8 (1942), pp. 192-199.

Turan 1942   Turan, Osman, *Soyadı Meselesi*: **Bozkurt Mecmuası** 2, Nu. 1, 2 (1942).

Turan: Belleten XII   Turan, O., *Selçuk devri vakfiyeleri III.* Celaleddin Karatay vakıfları ve vakfiyeleri: **Belleten** XII (45) (1948), pp. 17-172, lev. XI-XXXVI (faks.).

Turk. Kraj   *Turkestanskij Kraj.*

TuvRS   Tenišev, Ê.R. (ed.), *Tuvinsko-russkij slovar'.* Moskva 1968.

Túrán   *Túrán.* Zeitschrift für osteuropäische, vorder- und innerasiatische Studien. Budapest 1918.

Türk Etn. Derg.   *Türk Etnografya Dergisi.* Ankara.

TürkFolklBibl.   *Türk Folklor ve Etnografya Bibliyografyası IV* (1974-1984). Ankara 1999.

TürkiyeDTürkBibl.   *Türkiye Dışındaki Türkler Bibliyografyası.* I-II. Ankara 1992.

TürkmTopon.   *Türkmenistannïn toponimiyasï.* Ašgabad 1981.

Türkoloji Dergisi   *Türkoloji Dergisi.* Ankara.

TV   *Turkestanskie Vedomosti.* Taškent.

TV (Prib.)   *Pribavlenie k No. 90 oficial'noj časti "Turkestanskih Vedomostej".* Taškent 1903.

TVORAO   *Trudy Vostočnogo otdelenija Imperatorskogo Russkogo arheologičeskogo obščestva.* SPb.

UAJb.   *Ural-Altaische Jahrbücher.* Wiesbaden.

Uğur   Uğur, Ahmet, *Türkmen ve Avşarlarda Ad Verme Veya Adlandırma Adetleri*: **Türk Dünyası Tarih Dergisi** 5 (55) (1991), pp. 12-14.

UjgRS   Nadžip, Ê. N. (ed.), *Ujgursko-russkij slovar'.* Mužskie sobstvennye imena / Ženskie sobstvennye imena. Moskva 1968, pp. 816-825.

Uyguner 1983a   Uyguner, Muzaffer, *Bilecik'te Aile Adları 1.*: **Türk Folkloru** 4 (47) (1983), pp. 4-5.

Uyguner 1983b   Uyguner, Muzaffer, *Bilecik'te Aile Adları 2.*: **Türk Folkloru** 5 (53) (1983), pp. 12-13.

Uyguner 1985   Uyguner, Muzaffer, *Kandıra'dan Derlenen Aile Lâkapları* Derleyen: –: **Türk Folkloru** 7 (73) (1985), p. 18.

Umarī   Taeschner, F., *Al-Umarī: Bericht über Anatolien in seinem Werke "Masālik al-absār fi mamālik al amsār".* Zum ersten Male hrsg. v. –. Leipzig 1929.

Umarī/Tizeng. I.   al-ʿUmarī, Ibn Faḍlallāh, *[1.:] Masālik al-absār fi mamālik al-amsār; [2.:] At-taʿrif fi-'l-muṣṭalaḥ aš-šarīf*: **Tizeng. I**, pp. 207-251.

Unat   Unat, Faik Reşit, *Şehdi Osman Efendi Sefaretnamesi*: **Tarih Vesikaları** I (1942), pp. 1-57.

Uraksin   Uraksin, Z. G., *Osnovnye kriterii vybora imen u baškir*: **Ličnye imena v prošlom.** (1970).

Uraz   Uraz, Murat, *Türk Adları.* Istanbul 1935, 175 pp.

Urechi-Picot   Urechi, G. - Picot, É. (transl.), *Chronique de Moldavie depuis le milieu du XIVe siècle jusqu'a l'an 1594.* Texte roumain avec trad. française, notes historiques, tableaux généalogiques glossaire et table par Émile Picot. Paris 1878, 662 pp. (Publications de l'École des Langues Orientaux Vivantes).

URS Baskakov, N.A. - Nasilov, V.M., *Ujgursko-russkij slovar'*. Moskva 1939.

URS/Nadžip Nadžip, Ê. N. (ed.), *Ujgursko-russkij slovar'*. Mužskic sobstvennye imena. Ženskie sobstvennye imena. Moskva 1968, pp. 816-825.

US Caferoğlu, A., *Uygur sözlüğü*. I-III. İstanbul 1934-38.

Usāma Dérenbourg, H. (ed.), *Ousama ibn Mounkidh, un émir syrien au premier siècle des croisades (1095-1188)* par –. Deuxième partie, texte arabe. Paris 1886-1889. (Publications de l'École des Langues Orientaux Vivantes, II. Sér., Vol. XII.).

Usmanova Usmanova, M. G., *Toponimy jugo-vostočnoj baškirii*: **Vopr. ba. top.** (Ufa 1981), pp. 83-86.

Useinov Useinov, Sejran, *Krymskotatarskie imena*. Spravočnik. Simferopol' 1992, 62 pp.

UzbRS Borovkov, A.K. (ed.), *Uzbeksko-russkij slovar'*. Moskva 1959, 839 pp.

UZKU *Učenye zapiski Kazanskogo Universiteta*. Kazan'.

Uzunçarş., Anad. Uzunçarşılıoğlu, İ.H., *Anadolu Beylikleri ve Akkoyunlu, Karakoyunlu Devletleri*. Ankara 1937.

Uzunçarş., Küt. Uzunçarşılıoğlu, İsmail Hakkı, *Bizans ve Selçukiylerle Germiyan ve Osman Oğulları zamanında Kütahya şehri*. Yazan: –. I-. İstanbul 1932. (Anadolu Türk Tarihi Notlarından).

Ülkütaşır Ülkütaşır, M. Şakir, *Türklerde adverme ile ilgili âdet ve inanmalar*: **Türk Kültürü** 10 (1963), pp. 7-12.

Ülkütaşır - Koşay Ülkütaşır, M. Ş. - Koşay, H. Z., *Türklerde Ad Verme ve Türk Adları*: **Türk Folklor Araştırmaları** 8 (175) (1963?).

Ün *Ün* Isparta Halkevi Mecmuası. I-. Isparta 1934.

Vajnštejn Vajnštejn, S. I., *Ličnye imena, terminy rodstva i prozvišča u tuvincev*: **Onomastika.** (M. 1969).

Valieva Valieva, T. I., *Tatarstan ASSR Alabuγa rayonï tatar awïllarïnïň onomastikasï*. Kazan' 1976.

Valihanov, Sobr. Valihanov, Č.Č., *Sobranie sočinenij v pjati volumah*. I-V. Alma-Ata 1961.

Valihanov, Soč. Veselovskij, N. I. (ed.), *Sočinenija Čokana Čingisoviča Valihanova*. Izd. pod redakcieju d. č.–. SPb. 1904. (ZGO po otd. E. XXIX.).

Vámbéry, Vázlatok Vámbéry, Á., *Vázlatai Közép-Ázsiából*. Újabb adatok az oxusmelléki országok népismereti társadalmi és politikai viszonyaihoz. Pest 1868, 385 pp.

Vel.-Zern., Bašk. Vel'jaminov-Zernov, V.V., *Istočniki dlja izučenija tarhanstva, jalovannago baškiram russkimi gosudarami*. SPb. 1864, pp. 1-48. (Priloženie k IV-omu tomu ZIAN, No. 6.).

Vel.-Zern., Crim. Véliaminof-Zernof, V., *Matériaux pour servir à l'histoire du Khanat de Crimée*. Extraits. publées par –. SPb. 1864.

Vel.-Zern., Dict. Veliaminof-Zernof, V., *Dictionnaire djagatai-turc*. Saint-Pétersbourg 1869.

Vel.-Zern., Haïder Vélïaminof-Zernof, V., *L'Emir Haïder de Boukhara et ses trois fils*: **Bull. Hist. AI** XVI, pp. 275-83.

Vel.-Zern., Kasim. Vel'jaminov-Zernov, V.V., *Izsledovanie o Kasimovskih carjah i carevičah*. SPb. 1863-87, I-IV.

Velics-Kamm. Velics, Antal (transl.) - Kammerer, Ernő (ed.), *Magyarországi török kincstári defterek*. Kiadja a Magyar Tudományos Akadémia történelmi bizottsága. Ford. –. Bevezetéssel ellátta és sajtó alá rendezte –. I-II. Budapest 1886-90.

Verb., In. Verbickij, V.I., *Altajskie inorodcy*. Sbornik êtnografičeskih statej i izsledovanij altajsk. missionera protoiereja –. Pod redakciej A. A. Ivanovskago. Moskva 1893.

Verb., Sl. Verbickij, V. (ed.), *Slovar' altajskago i aladagskago narečij tjurkskago jazyka*. Kazan' 1884.

Veselovskij, Pam. Veselovskij, N. I. (ed.), *Pamjatniki diplomatičeskih i torgovyh snošenij Moskovskoj Rusi s Persiej*. Izd. pod red. –. 1. tom. Carstvovanija Fedora Ioannoviča. SPb. 1890, 458 pp. (TVORAO, Vol. XX).

Veselovskij, Kirg. Veselovskij, N., *Kirgizskij razskaz o russkih zavoevanijah v Turkestanskom krae*. Tekst, perevod i priloženija. SPb. 1894, X+82; IV+125 pp.

Veselovskij, Nog. Veselovskij, N. I., *Han iz temnikov Zolotoj Ordy. Nogaj i ego vremja*: **ZRAN** (1922).

Veselovskij, Onom.	Veselovskij, S. B., *Onomastikon.* Drevnerusskie imena, prozvišča i familii. Moskva 1974.
Veselovskij, Unk.	Veselovskij, N.I. (ed.), *Posol'stvo k zjungarskomu hun-tajčži Cêvan Rabtanu kapitana ot artillerii Ivana Unkovskago i putevoj žurnal ego za 1722-24 gody.* Izd.–. Stpbg. 1887, XLVI + 277 pp. (ZIRGOÊtn. X. vyp. 2.).
VFGOČJA	*Voprosy fonetiki, grammatiki i onomastiki čuvašskogo jazyka.* Čeboksary 1987.
Vinnikov	Vinnikov, Ja.R., *Rodo-plemennoj sostav i rasselenie kirgizov na territorii južnoj Kirgizii*: **TKAÊÊ** I (1956), pp. 136-81.
VIRGO	*Vestnik Imperatorskago Russkago Geografičeskago Obščestva.* SPb.
Voenn. Sb.	*Voennyj sbornik.*
Volodin	Volodin, A.A., *Truhmenskaja step' i truhmeny*: **SMOK** XXXVIII, otd. 1 (1908), pp. 1-98.
Volostnova	Volostnova, M. B., *Slovar' geografičeskih terminov i drugih slov, vetrečajučšihsja v toponimii Tuvinskoj ASSR.* Moskva 1971, 114 pp.
Vopr. ba. top.	Uraksin, Z. G. (Ed.), *Voprosy Baškirskoj Toponimiki.* Ufa 1981, 86 pp.
Vopr. bašk. fil.	*Voprosy baškirskoj filologii.* Moskva 1959.
Vopr. onom.	*Voprosy onomastiki.* 1-. Samarkand 1971-.
Vroonen	Vroonen, E., *Les noms des personnes en Orient.* Le Caire 1946.
Wassaf	Hammer-Purgstall, J. (ed., transl.), *Geschichte Wassaf's.* Persisch herausgegeben und deutsch übersetzt von –. Wien 1856.
Weil, Abbas	Weil, J., *Geschichte des Abbaside Chalifats in Egypten.* I-II. Stuttgart 1860.
Weil, Chalif.	Weil, J., *Geschichte der Chalifen* nach handschriftlichen, grösstenteils noch unbenutzten Quellen bearbeitet von –. I-V. Mannheim 1846-1862.
Wickenhauser, Moldawa	Wickenhauser, Franz Adolph, *Moldawa oder Beiträge zu einem Urkundenbuche für die Moldau und Bukowina.* Theil 1-2. Wien 1862-1877.
Wiet	Wiet, G., *Les biographies du Manhal Sāfi.* Le Caire 1932. (Mémoires présentés à l'Institut d'Égypt, t. XIX).
Wittek	Wittek, P., *Der Stammbaum der Osmanen*: **Der Islam** XIV (1924), p. 94-100.
Wittek, Gag.	Wittek, P., *Les Gagaouses, les gens de Kaykāūs*: **ROr.** XVII (1951-52), pp. 12-24.
WZKM	*Wiener Zeitschrift für die Kunde des Morgenlandes.* Wien.
Zaj. 1971	Zajączkowski, Wl., *Die turkmenischen Personennamen*: **FOr.** XIII (1971), pp. 323-342.
Zaj., Suf.	Zajączkowski, A., *Sufiksy imienne i czasownikowe w języku zachodniokaraimskim* (Przyczynek do morfologji języków tureckich). W Krakowie 1932.
Zaj., Zwizki	Zajączkowski, A., *Związki językowe Połowiecko-Słowianskie.* Wrocław 1949.
Zakir'janov	Zakir'janov, K. Z., *Ličnye imena u baškir, voznikšie v sovetskoe vremja*: **Ličnye imena v prošlom** (1970).
Zambaur	Zambaur, E. de, *Manuel de Généalogie et de Chronologie pour l'Histoire de l'Islam.* Avec 20 tableaux généalogiques hors texte et 5 cartes. Texte. Hanovre 1927, 388 pp.
ZKOIRGO	*Zapiski Kavkazskogo Otdela IRGO.* Tbilisi.
ZDMG	*Zeitschrift der Deutschen Morgenländischen Gesellschaft.* Leipzig.
Zehireddin/Dorn	Dorn, B. Dr. (ed.), *Sehir-eddin's Geschichte von Tabaristan, Rujan und Masanderan.* Persischer Text, hrsg. von - –. SPb. 1850. (Muhammed. Quellen zur Gesch. d. südlichen Küstenländer des Kaspischen Meeres I.).
Zelenin, Perm.	Zelenin, D. K., *Velikorusskie skazki Permskoj gubernii*: **ZIRGOÊtn.** XLI, pp. 476-.
Zelenin, Vjat.	Zelenin, D. K., *Velikorusskie skazki Vjatskoj gubernii*: **ZIRGOÊtn.** XLII, pp. 422-25, 543.
Zenker	Zenker, J. Th., *Dictionnaire turc-arabe-persan.* I-II. Leipzig 1866-1876.
Zetterst.	Zetterstéen, K.V. (ed.), *Beiträge zur Geschichte der Mamluken-sultane in den Jahren 690-741 der Higra.* Nach arabischen Handschriften hrsg. v. –. Leiden 1919, XVI+118+330 pp.
Zichy Okm.	Nagy, I. (et al., ed.), *A zichy vásonkeői gróf Zichy-család idősb ágának okmánytára.* Szerk. Nagy Imre, Nagy Iván, Véghely Dezső, Kammerer Ernő, Dőry Ferencz, Lukcsics Pál. I-XII. Pest, Budapest 1871-1931.
Zieme, Mat. I	Zieme, Peter, *Materialen zum uigurischen Onomasticon I*: **TDAYB 1977** (1978), pp. 71-84.
Zieme, Mat. II	Zieme, Peter, *Materialen zum uigurischen Onomasticon II*: **TDAYB 1978-1979** (1981), pp. 81-94.
Zieme, Mat. III	Zieme, Peter, *Materialen zum uigurischen Onomasticon III*: **TDAYB** (1984), pp. 267-283.
Zieme, Samb.	Zieme, Peter, *Samboqdu et alii: einige alttürkische Personen-namen im Wandel der Zeiten*:

Zinin
Journal of Turkology 2/1. (Szeged 1994), pp. 119-133.

Zinin, S. I., *Onomastika respublik Srednej Azii i Kazahstana*. Kratkij bibliografičeskij ukazatel' literatury za 1917-1972 gg. Taškent 1974, 36 pp.

ZIAN
Zapiski Imperatorskoj Akademii Nauk. SPb.

ZIRGO
Zapiski Imperatorskago Russkago Geografičeskago Obščestva. St. Petersburg.

ZIRGOGeogr.
Zapiski Imperatorskago Russkago Geografičeskago Obščestva po Otdel. Geografii. St. Petersburg.

ZIRGOStat.
Zapiski Imperatorskago Russkago Geografičeskago Obščestva po Otdel. Statistiki.

ZIRGOÊtn.
Zapiski Imperatorskago Russkago Geografičeskago Obščestva po Otdel. Êtnografii. I-. Sankt-Peterburg 1867-.

Zlatarski
Zlatarski, V.N., *Istorija na bălgarskata dăržava prez srednite vekove*. I/1-2, II, III. Sofija 1918-1940.

Zolotn.
Zolotnickij, N. I., *Kornevoj čuvašsko-russkij slovar'*, sravnennyj s jazykami i narečijami raznyh narodov tjurkskago, finskago i drugih plemen. Sostavlen –. Kazan' 1875.

Zolotn., Alf.
Zolotnickij, N. I., *Alfavitnyj spisok drevnih istoričeskih imen* preimuščestvenno vstrečajuščihsja v istoričeskih aktah i služaščih k objasneniju nazvanij naselennyh mestnostej Kazanskoj gubernii. Sostavil –: **Trudy AS IV** 2, pp. 154-160.

ZOOIRGO
Zapiski Orenburgskago otdela Imperatorskago Russkago Geografičeskago Obščestva. I-. Kazan' 1870-.

ZOOO
Zapiski Orenburgskago Otdela Obščestva.

ZRAN
Zapiski Rossijskoj Akademii Nauk.

ZSOIRGO
Zapiski Zapadno Sibirskago Otdela IRGO.

ZSOIRGOSemip.
Zapiski Semipalatinskago podotdela ZSOIRGO.

Zülfikar
Zülfikar, Hamza, *Kadın, Hanım, ve Benzeri Adlar Üzerine*: **Türk Dili** 55 (434) (1988), pp. 96-101.

ZVOIRAO
Zapiski Vostočnago Otdelenija Imperatorskago Russkago Archeologičeskago Obščestva. I-. Sanktpeterburg (Petrograd) 1886-.

Žanuzakov - Esbaeva
Žanuzakov, T. - Esbaeva K. S., *Qazaq esimderi - Kazahskie imena*. Anïqtama sözdik - Slovar' - spravočnik. Alma-Ata 1988, 480 pp.

Žanuzakov - Belousov
Žanuzakov, T., Belousov, Ja. (et al., ed.), *Qanday esimdi ŭnatasïz - Kakoe vybrat' imja?* Alma - Ata 1968.

Žanuzakov 1960
Žanuzakov, T., *Nekotorye voprosy onomastiki kazahskogo jazyka*: **Voprosy istorii i dialektologii kazahskogo jazyka** 3. (Alma-Ata 1960).

Žanuzakov 1963
Žanuzakov, T. Ž., *Venger yalïmïnïñ onomastika žönindegi eñbekteri*: **Voprosy kazahskogo i ujgurskogo jazykoznanija.** (Alma-Ata 1963), pp. 220-222.

Žanuzakov 1965b
Žanuzakov, T., *Qazaq tilindegi žalqï esimder*. Almatï 1965.

Žanuzakov 1965a
Žanuzakov, T., *Iz istorii razvitija onomastiki kazahskogo jazyka*: **Pitanija onomastiki.** (Kiev 1965).

Žanuzakov 1970
Žanuzakov, T. Ž., *Social'no-bytovye motivy v kazahskoj antroponimike*: **Ličnye imena v prošlom.** (1970), pp. 194-200.

Žanuzakov 1971a
Žanuzakov, T. Ž., *Obyčai i tradicii v kazahskoj antroponimike*: **Êtnogr. imen** (1971), pp. 100-103.

Žanuzakov 1971b
Žanuzakov, T., *Qazaq esimderiniñ tarihi*. Lingvistiqalïq žäne tarihi-êtnografiyalïq taldau. Almatï 1971, 216 pp.

Žanuzakov 1971c
Žanuzakov, T., *Osnovnye tipy i sostav tjurkskoj onomastiki V-VIII vv.*: **IAN KazSSR, ser. obšč.** No 1. (Alma-Ata 1971), pp. 61-65.

Žanuzakov 1974a
Žanuzakov, T., *Esimder sïrï - Tajny imen*. Alma - Ata 1974, 132 pp.

Žanuzakov 1976b
Žanuzakov, T. Ž., *Voprosy russko-kazahskogo antroponimičeskogo vzaimodejstvija*: **Pitannja sučasnoi onomastiki.** (Kiiv 1976), pp. 156-159.

Žanuzakov 1976c
Žanuzakov, T., *Osnovnye problemy onomastiki kazahskogo jazyka*. Avtref. dokt. fil. nauk. Alma-Ata 1976, 129 pp.

Žanuzakov (1982)
Žanuzakov, T., *Očerk Kazahskoj onomastiki*. Ličnye imena (pp. 126-163), Kosmonimy (pp. 163-164), Êtnonimy (pp. 164-174). Alma-Ata 1982, 175 pp.

Žanuzakov 1985
Žanuzakov, T., *Sostojanie i perspektivy razvitija kazahskoj onomastiki*: **Tjurkskoe**

                            jazykoznanie (1985), pp. 351-355.

Žanuzakov 1990   Žanuzakov, T., *Qazaqstan geografiyalïq ataulariniñ sözdigi*. (Žezqazɣan oblïsï). Almatï 1990, 295 pp.

Žaparov 1979   Žaparov, Š. (ed.), *Slovar' kirgizskih ličnyh imen*. Praktičeskoe posobie. Otv. red. U. Asanaliev, pod obščej red. I. S. Kolosova. Sostavitel' Š. Žaparov. Frunze 1979, 464 pp.

Žaparov 1980   Žaparov, Š., *Imena bliznecov*: **OSA** 2 (1980), pp. 105-112.

Žaparov 1984   Žaparov, Š., *Problemi tjurkskoj onomastiki na XV Meždunar. kongr. po onomastike*: **SovT** (1984, No. 5), pp. 94-95.

Žaparov 1985a   Žaparov, Š., *Ob êtnoantroponimah kyrgyz, nogaj, uzbek i arap*: **Onom. Kirg.** I. (1985), pp. 119-131.

Žaparov 1985b   Žaparov, Š., *O dinamike i statistike sovremennyh kirgizskih imen*: **Onom. Kirg.** I. (1985), pp. 131-145.

Žaparov 1989   Žaparov, Š., *Qïrɣïz adam attarï*. Kirgizskie ličnye imena. Frunze 1989, 113 pp.

Žaparov-Konkobaev 1984 Žaparov, Š. Ž. - Konkobaev, K. K., *Onomastika v Kirgizii*: **Tjurksk. onom.** (1984), pp. 235-237.

Ždanko   Ždanko, T.A., *Očerki istoričeskoj êtnografii Karakalpakov*. Moskva - Leningrad 1950.

Žirm., Epos   Žirmunskij, V.M., *Tjurkskij geroičeskij êpos*. Leningrad 1974.

ŽS   *Živaja Starina*. Periodičeskoe izdanie Otdelenija Êtnografii IRGO. I-. Stpbg. (Petrograd) 1891-.

Žumagulov - Isabekova   Žumagulov, Č. - Isabekova, A. B., *Russko-kirgizskij slovar' onomastičeskih terminov*. Frunze 1985, 77 pp.

Žurn. MVD   *Žurnal Ministerstva Vnutrennih Del*. SPb.

Using the Onomasticon

Entries and Headwords

The basic unit of the Onomasticon Turcicum is the *entry*. Each entry is a block of etymologically related names, explanations and different references beginning with a *primary headword*. Primary headwords are made prominent by bold print capitals and set out slightly from the printed column. The same applies for the reference entries. The entries follow in a special alphabetic order (see p. CXXXV).

Types of Headwords

Most headwords in the Onomasticon are *primary headwords* which are followed by the entry. The *reference headwords* are followed by the headwords of a *basic entry* with the etymologically related *name variants* listed. Name variants considered to be secondary ones (like **Birdi~Birde, J̌ilan~Žilan, Demir~Timer, J̌üz~Žüz**, etc.) are presented in the basic entries under the related primary headwords (e.g., **BERDİ, YILAN, YÜZ, TEMİR**, etc.). *Reference headwords* (in this case **BİRDİ, BİRDE, ǰİLAN, DEMİR, ŽİLAN, ŽÜZ**, etc.) facilitate finding the basic entry, the complete information on the name variant in question and, of course, the other variants of the actual primary headword, for instance "**BİRDİ** see **BERDİ**," "**ǰİLAN** see **YILAN**," "**DEMİR** see **TEMİR**," etc. The homonymous headwords are differentiated with roman numbers (e.g., **ADAŠ I., ADAŠ II., ULAŠ I., ULAŠ II.**).

The *primary components* of the *compound (composite) names* are separated by a hyphen either in single names (e.g., **Qulan-ayaq, Man-tabar**) or in headwords (e.g., **QULAN-AYAQ, MAN-TABAR**).

The *secondary components* (see p. LXII), are detached from the primary components by a hyphen (e.g., **Qulan-bay, Man-bay**). Names with secondary components at their endings (e.g., ***Ay-aba, Ay-bek, Ay-χan, Ay-tegin***, etc.) are given inside the entry of their primary (first) component in alphabetical order (in the case of the above examples, under the headword **AY**).

Structure of the Entries

An entry is headed by a *primary headword*. Each entry consists of one or more *units* (basic units of names, unit of etymology and unit of references). The kernel of a *fundamental unit (*or of a *name-unit)* inside the entry is the *name*. The fundamental units are sorted according to the following *principles*: **1.** The names – printed in bold – together with the available set of data, follow one another according to the special alphabet shown below (p. CXXXV) disregarding the chronology and language-ethnic they belong to. **2.** Homonymous names (e.g., Trkm. **Baba-ǰan** ~ Kzk. **Baba-ǰan** ~ Uzb. **Baba-ǰan**) taken from different languages (dialects or ethnic communities) are sorted into the ethno-linguistic groups (Oghuz, Kipchak, Altaic, Turki) they belong to. In the case of homonymy, the Old and Middle Turkic names precede the Modern Turkic ones. **3.** Homonymous names belonging to the same language (or ethnic community) are put in chronological order.

The *layout of a fundamental unit of name* with the attached pieces of information follows the subsequent pattern: **1.** Each unit begins with an *ethnical (or language) abbreviation* (see Language Abbreviations, p. LXXXIII) referring to the nationality of the person or the ethnical-language surroundings the source emerged from. **2.** The *time* (year or century) when the bearer of the name lived or the source was created. **3.** It is followed by the *name* which has been established or reconstructed from the source data. **4.** The *source data* are given in square brackets which, in most cases, show the name found in the actual source(s) in letter-perfect form. **5.** Then, if possible, we also try to provide a more precise determination of the bearer of the name. Abbreviation " *(fem.)*" indicates a female bearer, " *(folkl.)*" shows the name is from a folklore source. **6.** At the end of each name-unit, *Bibliographical abbreviations* (in round brackets) close the name-unit. A semicolon separates the name-units from each other. A full stop (dot/period) follows the last one.

Symbol "◇" indicates the beginning of the *etymological unit* where we, as much as possible, try to give the *etymology of the headword* and/or supply the related data from dictionaries. If several are possible, these are listed under Roman numbers. Unfortunately, in several instances we were not able to ascertain any meanings.

Symbol "⇨", at the end of the entry, refers to the *etymologically related headwords*. In case of compound names we only refer to the entries of the components so as to avoid the duplication of vocabulary data. When presenting a derived name we usually refer to the basic headword and the suffix used. For the more exact determination of the suffix in question, it is recommended to turn to the section "Suffixes" (beginning on p. LXXVI).

Notice **"See also"** at the end of several entries introduces the *onomatological references* where we list the name-synonyms that are the semantically related headwords and the headwords in which the actual headword is present as a second component. Thus the reader can find further compounds in which the headword in question is represent

Tables of Transcriptions

Onomasticon Turcicum	Cyrillic modern	Arabic	Turkish modern	Radlov's system
a	а	ا / آ	a	a
â (=å)	a, o (Uzb.)			
ā	aa		â	ā
b	б	ب	b	б
c	ц		ts	ц
č	ч	چ / ج	ç	ч
ǰ	дж, ж, җ, ч	ج	c	џ
d	д	د	d	д
ð	з̧	ذ		
d'	дь			j
ä	ä, ә, аь	ا	e	ä
å			ê	å
e	е	ايـ / يـ / ۂ	e	е, э
ē	ее, ээ	ايـ / آ / ا	ê	
ĕ / ə	ĕ			
ė	е, э			
f	ф	ف	f	ф
g	г	ݣ / ك	g, ğ	г
γ	г, гъ, ғ, ҕ	غ	g, ğ	ҕ
h	h, х, гь, х	ه	h	h
χ	х	ح / خ	h	x, h
i	и, i	ى	i	i
ī	и(й)	اِ / يـ / بِر	î	ī
ï	ы, и	ايـ / يـ / ی	ı	ы
ï̄	ыы	ايـ / بِر		
ĭ	i, ă			ï̄
y	й	ى	y	j
i̯				
k	к	ك	k	к
q	к, къ, қ, қ	ق	k	k
l	л	ل	l	л, l
m	м	م	m	м
n	н	ن	n	н
ñ	ҥ, нъ, нг, ҥ	ݣ / ـنك		ҥ,
o	о, ў	او / او	u	o
ō	оо			ō
ȯ	о			
ö	ө, оь, ö, ё, ў	او / او	ö	ö
ő	өө, öö			ő

Onomasticon Turcicum	Cyrillic modern	Arabic	Turkish modern	Radlov's system
p	п	پ / ب	p	п
r	р	د	r	р
s	с	ص / س	s	с
s'	ç			
θ	ç	ث		
š	ш	ش	ş	ш
u	у	ا وُ / وُ	u	у
ŭ	ў, ү			ў
ū	уу			у
u̇	ү			
ü	у, ү, уь, ÿ, ю	ا وُ / وُ	ü	ÿ
ü̃	үү, ÿÿ			ÿ
v	в	ۋ / و / ف	v	в
w	в, у, ў	و	v	w
u̯	в, у			
z	з	ض / ز / ظ	z	з
ž	ж	ژ	j	ж

Alphabetical Order of the Headwords and Names

a, ā, â, ă, b, c, č, J, d', d, ð, ä, ä̆, e, ē, f, g, γ, ġ, ğ, h, χ, i, ĭ, ï, ï̆, ĭ, y, k, q, l, m, n, ñ, o, ō, ȯ, ö, ȫ, p, r, s, θ, š, t, u, ŭ, ū, u̇, ü, ü̃, v, w, u̯, z, ž

ONOMASTICON

A

ABA   Türk? 876-880 **Aba** [ابا التركی] (Ṭabarī, Annal.
III, 1900, 1903, Ibn al-Athīr/Tornb. VII, 217, 228);
Türk 893 **Aba** [احمد بن ابا], Aχmed, Aba's son
(Ṭabarī, Annal. III, 2138); Tat.(GH) 14th c. **Aba**
[Αμπα], a christened Tatar (Byz. Turc. 68); Trkm.
1557/58, 16th c. **Aba / Aba-bek / Aba-serdār**
[ابا سردار طاینه اوحلو / Аба (Аба-бек, Айя)], from
the Oχlu tribe (Dorn 204, 413, MIT II, 36, 60, 61, 63,
67, 69, 70, 71); Kuman 1183 **Aba-owlï** [Обовлы
Костуховичъ (Костуковичъ)], a Polovets (Ipat. 427,
440, Rásonyi, KÓA 78). ✧ I. 'Father, uncle, brother'
cf. *aba* 'Onkel von Vaterseite' (Chag.), 'der Vorfahr'
(Chag., Turk.), 'der Vater' (Hak.), 'älterer Bruder'
(Hak.(Kacha)) (Radl. I, 620), Kirg. *aba* 'дядя (по
мужской линии)' (Jud.). Used also as a secondary
component of male personal names. Cf. also Trk. *aba*
(Clauson, Räs., Sev.); II. 'Bear' cf. Hak.(Sag., Koyb.,
Kacha) *aba* 'der Bär' (Radl. I, 620).

ABA-QULAQ   Shor 19th-20th c. **Aba-qulaq**
(Dyrenkova 188, 192). ✧ 'Bear(s)-ear'. ⇨ **ABA** +
QULAQ.

ABAČÏ   Mo. 14th c. **Abačï / Abaǰï** [Абасı / Абаджи], a
commander of Noγay (RaD I/1, 195, Erol II).

ABADAN   Kkalp. 20th c. **Abadan** [Абадан], fem.
(KkRS 777); Trkm. 20th c. **Ovadan** [Ovadan], fem.
(Zaj. 1971, 336); Trkm. 20th c. **Ovadan** [Овадан], fem.
(TrkmRS 480). ✧ 'Flourishing, healthy; beautiful' cf.
Karakh. *abadan* 'mâmûr' (Atebet), Kkalp. *abadan*
'благоустроенный'(KkRS), Trkm. *ovadan*
'красивый, нарядный, изящный' (TrkmRS), <P.
ābādān (Johnson), cf. also P. PN *Abādān* (Justi).

АБАГАČĀN   Yak. **Abaγačān / Amaγačān**
[Аб(м)аҕачан] (Pek.). ✧ 'Dear little uncle' cf. Kuman,
Chaǧ., Alt.(Tel.) *abaγa* 'Vatersbruder, Onkel' (Radl. I,
622), Yak. *abaγa* 'дядя (старший брат отца)' (JRS)
+ suff. -*čān.*

ABAXAY   Hak. 19th c. **Abaχay-arï** [Абахай-ары],
fem (Potanin IV, 618). ✧ 'Fair-lady(-clean/honest)' cf.
Hak. PN *Abaχay* 'дама, красавица'(Butanaev). ⇨
ABAQAY.

ABAY   Kzk. 18th c. - 19th c. **Abay** [Абай], first modern
Kazak poet, died in 1904 (Tynyšp. 70); Kzk. 19th c.
Abay [Абай] (Tynyšp. 6). ✧ I. 'Uncle (as an address of
elders), grand-father, elder brother'. Used also as a
secondary component (as a title of respect) (Žanuzakov,
Sattarov); II. 'Attention, attentive, nice; careful' cf.
Kzk. *abay* 'die Aufmerksamkeit, aufmerksam' (Radl. I,
621); Sattarov: Kirg., Kzk. *Abay* 'saq [watchful,
careful], iγtibarlï [attentive]' (Sattarov); III. Shortened
Kazak-like form of *İbrahim* (Žanuzakov-Esbaeva 458).

⇨ **ABA** + dim. voc. suff. -*y.*

ABAQ   Chuv. 18th-19th c. **Abak, Abek** [Абакъ /
Абекъ] (Magn. 24); Selj. 1095 **Abaq** [ابق], ibn Abdu'l
Rïzzaq (Kamāladdīn: RHCHor II, 121, 121-123); Selj.?
1139,   1154   **Abaq** [ابق بن محمد بن بوری]
(Kamāladdīn: RHCHor II, 273-74, 305); Chag. 1553
Abaq [Абак], emir (Ivanov 140, 144, 145); Chag. 1560
Abaq [Абак], a mirza (Ivanov 104, 114, 325); Chag.
1561 **Abaq** [Абак], fem. (Ivanov 292); Kzk. 19th c.
Abaq [Абакъ], according to tradition he is the
forefather of the tribe of Abak-kireys (Potanin II, 3);
Chag. 1559 **Abaq-bike** [Абак-бике], fem. (Ivanov 99,
140); Chag. 1568 **Abaq-χoǰa** [Абак-ходжа Тараби]
(Ivanov 289); Chag. 1558 **Abaq-sultan** [Абак
Султан] (Ivanov 120); Tat. 1534 **Ābāq** [لباق / (?)],
fem. (Jusupov 5). ✧ 'Idol' cf. Crm. *abaq* 'das
Götzenbild' (Radl. I, 621). See also **QAMÏS-ABAQ.**

ABAQAY   Chuv. 18th-19th c. **Abakay** [Абакай]
(Magn. 24). ✧ 'Aunt; wife; lady, noble woman,
empress' cf. Trk. *afaqay* (Sev.). ⇨ **APA** + dim.
suff. -*qay.*

ABALÏQ   Türk / Uyg.? 865 **Abalïq** [ا بلح / ا بلج], al-
Turkī (Ṭabarī, Annal. III, 1598-99). ✧ 'He who has an
uncle'? ⇨ **ABA?** + suff. -*lïq.*

ABAM   Tat.(Lit.) 1552 Abam [Абамъ] (Kn. Metriki Lit.
64). ✧ 'My father, my uncle, my brother'. ⇨ ABA +
poss. suff. -*m.*

ABAN   Tat.(Sib.) 1640 **Aban** [Абан] (Miller, Ist. Sib. II,
463); Karakh.? 1063/64 **Aban-χan** [ابن حان التركی /
Abân], Khan of the Türks (Kamāladdīn: RHCHor I,
294-96, Zambaur); Uzb. 19th c. **Aban / Xoǰa-aban?**
[Ходжа Абан] (Ivanov, Vosstanie 118). ✧ 'Engage!
Face (the enemy)!' cf. Turk. *aban-* 'sich auf etwas
stützen, um zu wiederstehen, nicht einverstanden sein'
(Radl. I, 623), also Rásonyi, Imp., p. 237.

ABAR   Türk? 9th c. **Abar-tegin** [ابر تکین] (Ṭabarī,
Annal. III, 1879). ✧ 'Rebellious; He engages;
Revolting' (Németh, HMK 104-105), cf. Osm., Chag.
aba- 'absagen, ungehorsam sein' (Radl. I, 620) +
suff. -*r.*

ABARIŠ   Trkm. 1851 **Abariš** [Абариш], chieftain of
the Penderak tribe (MIT II, 248).

ABAŠ   Chuv.? 18th-19th c. **Abaš** [Абашъ] (Magn. 24).
✧ I. 'Elder male relative; father's brother' cf. Tat. PN
Abaš (Sattarov); II. Shortened-contracted form of Tat.
Γabdulla < Ar. Abdullah (Sattarov). ⇨ **ABA** + dim.
suff. -*š.*

ABAŠÏ   Tat. 19th c. **Abašï / Abaši** [Abaši, Hasan-'Ata]
(Mende 133). ✧ I. 'Hunter' cf. Mo. *abači* (<Trk.)
'Jäger' (TMEN I, No. 1); II. 'Ghost, which the children
are frightened with' cf. Karakh. *abačy* 'Gespenst, mit
dem man die Kinder shreckt' (MK/Brock.), *abači*
'бука, пугало' (DTS).

ABAT   Kkalp. 20th c. **Abat** [Абат] (KkRS 772); Kkalp.
20th c. **Abat-žan** [Абатжан] (KkRS 772). ✧

'Flourishing; wealthy' cf. Kkalp. *abat* 'благоустроенный, зажиточный' (KkalpRS), <P. *ābād* (Johnson).

ABĀSÏYA   Yak. **Abāsïya / Abāsïyïn** [Абасыја / Абасыјын] (Pek.). ✧ 'Evil (spirit)' cf. Yak. *abāsï* 'зло, злое начало - общее название многочисленных злых существ (духов)' (Pek.).

ABĀSÏYÏN see **ABĀSÏYA**

ABĀSÏLLAY   Yak. **Abāsïllay** [Абасыллаи], a nickname (Pek.). ⇨ **ABĀSÏYA**.

ABĀSÏTÏYÏÑ   Yak. **Abāsïtïyïñ** [Абасытыјыӈ] (Pek.). ✧ 'Became an evil spirit'? Cf. Yak. *abāsïtïy-* 'превращаться в *abāsï* приобретать дурные качества или свойства' (Pek.). See also **ABĀSÏYA**.

ABĀSÏTÏÑÏ   Yak. **Abāsïtïñï** [Абасытыӈы] (Pek.). ⇨ **ABĀSÏYA**. See also **ABĀSÏYA**.

ABBAZ   Karakh. 11th c. **Abbaz** ['Abbaz] (DTS). ✧ Abbas (Ar.), 'One who frowns a lot' (Ahmed).

ABJÏ-TEMÏR   Tat. 1601 **Abjï-temir / Abji-temir** [Абжитемир Тохташев], (Miller, Ist. Sib. II, 169). ✧ 'Hunter-Iron' cf. Trk. *abčï* 'Jäger' (TMEN II, 582). ⇨ **TEMÏR**.

ABJÜR   Nog. 20th c. **Abjür** [Абджуьр Зуйур увлы], one of Baskakov's informants from the aul of Nökis (Bask., Nog. 143).

ABDAKEY   Hak. 19th-20th c. **Abdakey** [Абдакей], fem. (HRS 353). ✧ Yevdokiya (R.).

ABDAL   NUyg. 19th c. **Abdal** [ابدال], a dervish? (Le Coq, Namenl. 93); Trkm. 1770 **Abdal-χoǰa** [Абдальходжа], a "mutevelli" [administrator, esp. a trustee of a waqf or mortmain property] (MIT II, 347); *EN:* Yürük 1863-73 **Abdal (ašireti)** [Abdal aşireti], a nomadic tribe in the district of Adala (Şölen 94); *TN:* Turk. **Abdal-oγlu** [Abdaloğlu] (Köyl.). ✧ 'Monk, hermit, recluse' cf. East.T. *abda:l / ebda:l* (Ar.) 'Abdal, a tribe of beggars living in different parts of Eastern Turkestan; they are said to be the descendants of the Umayyads, who are said to have caused the death of Imam Husain' (Jarring).

ABDAN   Kzk. 19th c. **Abdan** [Абданъ] (AOK 2). ✧ 'Strong, severe' cf. Chag., East.T., Kzk. *abdan* (P.) 'stark, fest, kräftig' (Räs.; Radl. I, 634); P. *abdān* 'a family, a great tribe; worthy' (Johnson).

ABDEY   Bashk. 1749 **Abdey** [Абдей Кузянов] (MIB III, 468). ✧ 'Little Abdi'. ⇨ **ABDÏ** + dim. suff. -*y*.

ABDEK   Hak. 19th-20th c. **Abdek** [Абдек], fem. (HRS 353). ✧ Yevdokiya (R.). See also **ABDAKEY**.

ABDÏ   Turk. 1485 **Abdi** [Abdi] (Gökb., Ed. 157); Turk. 15th c. **Abdi-hoǰa** [Abdi-Hoca] (Gökb., Ed. 157); Kkalp. 20th c. **Äbdi-bay** [Әбдибай] (KkRS 772); *TN:* Turk. 20th c. **Abdi-paša** [Abdipaşa] (Köyl.). ✧ I. 'Slave (of), servant (of) (first component of Arabic PNs); Slave/servant of God, Creature of God', cf. Turk. (Osm.) *abd* (Özön), Kzk. *Abdi-* (Žanuzakov), < Ar.

ᶜabd 'servant (male), used with the attributes of Allah to form compound names' (Ahmed). In the theology *ᶜabd* means 'the creature', in the Qur'ān, the angels are also called *ᶜabd* (EI(NE)Index); II. Shortened form of Ar. PN Abdullah or Abdurrahman. (Özenbaşly, Erol II).

ABDÏKEY   Bashk. 1735 **Abdikey** [Абдикей Ишеевъ] (Vel.-Zern., Bašk. 21); Tat. 1764 **Aptikey** [Аптикей Киненеев] (MIB II/2, 105); Bashk. 1750 **Aptikey** [Аптикей Сытыев] (MIB III, 475). ✧ 'Little Abdi; little servant'. ⇨ **ABDÏ** + dim. suff. -*key*.

ABDÏŠ   Kirg. **Abdiš** [Абдиш] (Jud. 652). ✧ 'Little Abdi'. ⇨ **ABDÏ** + dim. suff. -*š*.

ABDÏŠÏRÏP   NUyg.(Tar.) **Abdiširip-aqun** [Abdischirip Achun / Абдішіріп Акун] (Proben VI, 9 /10/). ✧ Abdul Sharif (Ar.) 'Servant of the Noble/Highborn', cf. Ar. Sharif (Ahmed), also NUyg. PN *Abdušerip* (UjgRS), Est.T. *šeri:f / šer'ip* 'holy, sacred, noble' (Jarring). ⇨ **ABDÏ**.

ABDÏ   Yak. **Abdï** [Абды], a nickname (Pek.); *EN:* Yak. **Abdï** [Абды], a clan-name (Pek.).

ABDÏ-QALAQ   Kzk. 19th c. **Abdï-qalaq** [Абдыкалакъ] (SOK 270). ✧ 'Abdi-big-spoon' cf. Kzk. *qalaq* 'совок, крыло' (KzkRS); Tat., Tob. etc. *qalaq* 'ein grosser Löffel' (Radl. II, 227). ⇨ **ABDÏ**. See also **QALAQAY, QALAQ-PAS, QALAQSÏZ**.

ABDÏ-SUΓUR   Kzk. **Abdï-suγur** [Абдысугур] (Tynyšp. 66). ✧ 'Servant of Suγur'. ⇨ **ABDÏ** + **SUΓUR**.

ABDÏLDA   Kirg. **Abdïlda** [Абдылда], fem. (Jud. 128); Kzk. 19th c. **Qabdïlda** [Кабдыльда] (SOK 34). ✧ Abdullah (Ar.), cf. Kzk. PNs *Abdolla / Abdulla / Abdilda / Γabdolla / Qabdolla*, etc. (Žanuzakov 127), Tat. PNs *Abdulla / Γabdulla / Γabduq / Γabdïq*, etc. (Sattarov).

ABDUL   Alt. 19th-20th c. **Abdul** [Абдул] (OjrRS 207); Hak. 19th-20th c. **Abdul** [Абдул] (HRS 348). ✧ '(God's) Slave' The first component of Arabic compound names such as *Abd-ul-kerim, Abd-ul-basir* etc. It may also be the shortened form of Ar. *Abdullah, Abdulāziz, Abdullātif* etc. (Özön), Ar. *ᶜabd-ul-* 'slave of'.

ABEK see **ABAQ**

ABÏKA   Chuv. 18th-19th c. **Abika** [Абика] (Magn. 24). ⇨ **ABÏ?** + suff. -*ka*.

ABÏŠ see **ABÏŠ**

ABÏ   Karakh. 11th c. **Abï** [abï] (DTS). ✧ 'Elder male relative' cf. Hak.(Koyb.) *abï* 'die Frau' (Radl. I, 625), Tat. dial. *abïj / apïj* < voc. of *aba / apa* (Sev.), Tat. *abïy* 'дядя; старший брат' (TatRS), Bashk. dial. *abïy=aγay* 'старший брат; дядя; отчим' (BRS/Uraksin). ⇨ **ABA**.

ABÏČ   Uyg. 12th c. - 14th c. **Abïč** [Абıч] (Radl., USp. 671, DTS, EUTS). ✧ 'Elder relative' cf. Trk. *abïč* 'älterer Verwandte' (Sev. 61).

ABÏDAL   Yak. **Abïdal** [Абыдал], byname of a Shaman (Pek.).

ABÏГ see **ABÏQ**

ABÏKE   Kirg. **Abïke** [Абыке], Manas' younger brother (Jud. 21). ✧ 'Little Abï; Dear little uncle'. ⇨ **ABÏ** + suff. -ke or comp. *eke*.

ABÏKEY   Chuv. 18th-19th c. **Abïkey** / **Abigey** [Абекей / Абигей / Абыкей] (Magn. 24). ✧ 'Little Abï; Little dear uncle'. ⇨ **ABÏ** + dim. suff. -key/.

ABÏQ   Uyg. 13th-14th c. **Abïγ** (Zieme, Mat. II, 92); Uyg. 12th c. - 14th c. **Abïq** (Radl., USp. 117, EUTS, DTS). ✧ I. 'Hidden' (Bese 13); II. 'Fence' cf. Uyg. *abïq* 'die Einzäunung, der Zaun' (Radl. I, 626), Karakh. *abï-* 'скрывать, прятать' (DTS) + suff. -q.

ABÏQAY   Tat.(Mish.) 1777 **Abïqay** [Сулейман / Сюлэйман Абыкаев] (MIB V, 59); Bashk. 1759 **Abïqay** [Абыкай Арасланов] (MIB IV/2, 26); Bashk. 1770 **Abïqay** [Абыкай Муталлыпов] (MIB IV/1, 342). ✧ '(Dear) Little Abï'. ⇨ **ABÏ** + dim. suff. -qay/.

ABÏLAY   Kzk. **Abïlay** (Radl. I, 657); Tat. 1779 **Ablay** [Елдаш Аблаев], a tarχan (MIB V, 82); Bashk. 1776 **Ablay** [Барак Аблаев] (MIB V, 33, 34, 79); Bashk. 1782 **Ablay** [Ильяс Аблаев] (MIB V, 133); Kzk. 19th c. **Ablay** [Аблай], son of Qïrqïz in the Kazak popular tradition (Potanin II, 150); Uzb.? 1683-99 **Ablay** [Облай] (DAI X, 387); Kzk. 18th c. **Ablay-qan**, the famous Khan Abul Khayir (Kzk. Äbilqayïr / Äbilχayïr) (Radl., Aus Sib. I, 200, Togan, BTT 173-176); Tat. 1779 **Abläy** [Елбарыс Абляев] (MIB V, 81); Chuv. 18th-19th c. **Abley** [Аблей] (Magn. 24); Bashk. 1757 **Abley** [Абызай Аблеев] (MIB IV/1, 159); Bashk. 1760 **Abley** [Юлборис Аблеев] (MIB IV/1, 197). ✧ 'Little (dear) Abï/Abul'; Shortened popular-dialectal form of Ar. Abul Khayr among the Kirghiz and Kazaks (Erol II, 3, Toğan, BTT 174, 176).

ABÏMAN   Tat.(Tob.) 1638 **Abïman** [Корум Абыманов (тобольский бухарец)], coming from Bukhara to the Tobol region (Miller, Ist. Sib. II, 453). ⇨ **ABÏ** + suff. -man?

ABÏN   Kzk. 19th c. **Abïn** [Абен Бектасовъ] (AUK 471). ✧ 'Be comforted! Cheer up!' cf. Karakh. *abïn-* 'утешиться, насладиться' (DTS), Uyg. *abïn-* 'sich beruhigen, behaglich fühlen' (Radl. I, 626), also Rásonyi, Imp., p. 237.

ABÏS-KELDİ see **ABÏZ-GİLDİ**

ABÏS   Oghuz 12th c. **Abïš-χatun** [Абиш-хатун], or Terken (Tergen, mistakenly Türkân) Xatun from the Bayat (Biyat) tribe is the mother of Horezmšah Muhammed (1098-1128), cf. Togan, UTT 432; there was another [?] Terken (Türkân) Xatun, a Karakhanid princess, the wife of Malik Šah (1072-1092), cf. Togan, ibid. 198 (after Qazw.) (RaD II, 199); Oghuz/trkm. 1265 **Abïš-χatun** [ابش], ruler of the Atabegate of Fars (1263-1264), then wife of Mengü Temür (1266-1280)

(Qazw. 509). ✧ 'A part of the leg above the kneepan' (Erol II), cf. Turk. *abïš* 'der Winkel zwischen den Beinen' (Radl. I, 630). See also **QOŠ-ABÏŠ**.

ABÏTAY   Hak.(Kacha) 1634 **Abïtay** [Абытай] (Miller, Ist. Sib. II, 417). ✧ 'Namesake' cf. Shor *abïday* 'der Namensvetter' (Radl. I, 630).

ABÏZ   Alt. 19th c. **Abïs-qam** [Абысъ-камъ], his other (Khalkha) name was Tarχan-bö (Potanin IV, 289); Chuv. 18th-19th c. **Abïz** [Абызъ] (Magn. 24); Tat. 20th c. **Abïz** [Абыз] (Sattarov); Tat. 20th c. **Abïz-bay** (Sattarov); Tat. 20th c. **Abïz-bike** [Абызбикэ], fem. (Sattarov); Bashk. 1765 **Abïz-yar** [Абизяр Сакбаев] (MIB IV/1, 313); Nog. 20th c. **Awïz-uwlï?** [Байнан Авез увлы], father of one of Baskakov's informants from the settlement Terekli-mektep (Bask., Nog. 144); Kzk. 19th c. **Awuz** [Аузъ] (SOV 156); *EN:* Kzk. **Abs** / **Abz** [Абс / Абз] (Tunyšp. 68, 73, 75); *TN:* Chuv. **Abïz(ova)** [Абызова], district of Yadrinsk (Korsakov 306); *TN:* Tat. 18th c. **Abïzovo** [Абызово], a village in the district of Tetjušinsk (Korsakov 332). ✧ I. 'Respected elderly man; educated man; the chief (leader) of a clan or village' (Sattarov), cf. *abïz* 'ein Gelehrter' (Tat.), 'russischer Priester' (Kzk.) (Radl. I, 629), Bashk. *abïz* 'просвещённый и почитаемый (о человеке)' (BRS (Uraksin)), Trk. *abuz, abyz* 'Gelehrter; russischer Priester' (Räs.); II. 'The Protector, The Keeper' It is one of Allah's several attributes forming the first part of Arabic personal names (cf. Ar. *Hafiz*); III. 'Guard, watchman; a man who knows the whole Quran by heart', cf. Osm. *hafiz, hafïz* (Özön); (<Ar.). See also **QARQ-ABÏZ**.

ABÏZ-GİLDİ   Bashk. 1740 **Abïs-keldi** [Абескельди] (MIB I, 405); Bashk. 1735 **Abïz-gildi** [Абызгилди Рысаевъ], a tarχan (Vel.-Zern., Bask. 15); Bashk. 1740 **Abïz-gildi** [Абыз-гильда (Хафиз кильди)], name of 3 persons at the time of the revolt of 1740 (MIB I, 385, 396, 397); Bashk. 1756 **Abïz-gildi** [Абызгильды Чюраманов] (MIB IV/1, 123); Bashk. 1784 **Abïz-gildi** [Тунгатар Абызгильдин] (MIB V, 154); Bashk. 1784 **Abïz-gildi** [Байтуган Абызгильдин] (MIB V, 155). ✧ An Abïz (see) has come (into the world), has been born'. Maybe a real Abïz has come to the place during or after the birth. ⇨ **ABÏZ** + **KELDİ**.

ABÏZAY   Bashk. 1664 **Abïzay** [Абызайко Тетее] (MIB I, 193); Bashk. 1725 **Abïzay** [Абызай Игибаев] (MIB III, 235); Bashk. 1738 **Abïzay** [Абызай Биметев] (MIB I, 143); Bashk. 1738 **Abïzay** [Абызай] (MIB III, 393); Bashk. 1744 **Abïzay** [Абызай Кадяков] (MIB III, 415); Bashk. 1754, 1755 **Abïzay** [Мастей Абызаев] (MIB IV/1, 79, 95); Bashk. 1754, 1755 **Abïzay** [Мастей Абызаев] (MIB IV/1, 79, 95); Bashk. 1756 **Abïzay** [Абызай Юнусов] (MIB IV/1, 122); Bashk. 1757 **Abïzay** [Абызай Аблеев] (MIB IV/1, 159); Bashk. 1761 **Abïzay**

[Абызай Токаев] (MIB IV/1, 220). ❖ '(Dear) Little Abïz'. ⇨ **ABÏZ** + dim. suff. *-ay*.

ABÏZAN Bashk. 1735 **Abïzan** [Абызанъ] (Vel.-Zern., Bašk. 24); Bashk. 18th c. **Abïzan** [Абзан Уркеев] (MIB V, 71); Bashk. 1760 **Abïzan** [Абызан Мрякеев] (MIB IV/1, 199); Bashk. 1761 **Abïzan** [Абызан Токусев] (MIB IV/1, 221); Bashk. 1770 **Abïzan** [Абызан Алдаров] (MIB IV/1, 343); Bashk. 1772 **Abzan** [Шукур Абызанов] (MIB IV/2, 405); Bashk. 1789 **Abzan** [Кунакбай Абзанов] (MIB V, 260); Bashk. 1790 **Abzan** [Абзан Утеганов] (MIB V, 295); Bashk. 1789 **Abzän** [Аптикей Абзянов] (MIB V, 260); Bashk. 1789 **Abzän** [Байда Абзянов] (MIB V, 254). ❖ '(Dear) Little Abïz'. ⇨ **ABÏZ** + dim. suff. *-an*.

ABLAY see **ABÏLAY**

ABLAYLÏ Kzk. 19th c. **Ablaylï** [Оплайлы] (SODž. 120). ❖ Coming or being from a place called Ablay, maybe from the Kalmyks' town Ablay Kent (cf. Toğan, BTT 292). ⇨ **ABÏLAY** + suff. *-lï*.

ABLAQAY Tat.(Mish.) 1775 **Ablaqay** [Аблакай] (MIB IV/2, 417). ❖ I. 'Little Abla', cf. Ar. fem. PN *Abla* 'well-rounded, perfectly formed, a woman possessing a beautiful figure' (Ahmed), and the dim. suff. *-qay*; II. Shortened of Ar. Abdullah (Kaybullaev).

ABLÄY see **ABÏLAY**

ABLEY see **ABÏLAY**

ABLU Bashk. 1695 **Ablu** [Аблу Тулубаев] (MIB I, 90).

ABRAŠ Bashk. 1718 **Abraš** [Абраш] (MIB III, 169). ❖ 'Itchy, mangy; eczematous'? cf. Turk. *abraš* 'schorfig (grindig) unter dem Schwanze (von Pferden)' (Radl. I, 633) (Ar.).

ABRAM Hak.(Sag.) 19th-20th c. **Abram** [Абрам] (Katanov, Otč. 8). ❖ Avraam (R.).

ABRĀSQA Karg. **Abrāsqa** (Katanov, Otč. 7, 8). ❖ Abraška (R.).

ABRU Bulg. 1320 **Abru** [ابر / Абру], fem. (Jusupov 2). ❖ 'Decorum, honour' cf. Az. *abru / abrï* 'die Ehre, Achtbarkeit' (Radl. I, 633).

ABS see **ABÏZ**

ABU-BAQÏR Kzk. 19th c. **Abu-baqïr** [Абубакыръ] (AOA 130); Kzk. 19th c. **Aw-baqïr** [Ау-бакыръ] (SOV 38); Kzk. 19th c. **Aw-baqïr** [Ау-бакыръ] (AOK 10); Kzk. 19th c. **Aw-baqïr** [Ау-бакыръ] (AOO 54); Kzk. 19th c. **Aw-baqïr** [Ау-бакыръ] (AOAtb. 2); Kkalp. 20th c. **Äbüw-bäkir** [Әбүүбәкир] (KkRS 772). ❖ Abu Bakr (Ar.) 'Father of the young camel', Abu Bakr al-Siddiq (632-634) was one of the first "rightly guided Khalifas" (Ahmed), cf. also Ar. *ab* 'father' used as a *kunya* (nickname), making a compound whose first part is *Abu* 'father of' (Ahmed). ⇨ **BAQÏR.**

ABUJA Turk. 1584 **Abuja** [ابوجه / Iboca] (Ongan, Ank. I, 162). ❖ I. 'Uncle' cf. Turk. dial. *abuca* 'amca' (DS),

Turk. *abca, abuca* 'amca' (Tar. Sözl.) II. 'Elder sister' cf. Turk. dial. *abuca, abıca* 'abla, büyük kızkardeş' (DS I, 1-3; Gülensoy).

ABUҐAY see **BUҐAY**

ABUQAČ Chag. 15th c. **Abuqač-bahadur** [ابوکاج بهادر / Абукаджъ Бахадуръ] (Šejb. LXII). ❖ 'Little father' cf. Chag. *abū* 'Väterchen' (Radl. I,631) + dim. suff. *-qač*.

ABUL-ҐĀZÏ Kzk. 19th c. **Abul-ɣāzï** [Aboul-Ghazy] (Levchine 356). ❖ Abul Ghazi (Ar.) 'Father of the conqueror, father of the hero' (Ahmed), cf. also comp. *ɣāzi*.

ABULAT see **AY-BULAT**

ABUT Tat. 1636 **Abut** [Абут Мешкеров] (Miller, Ist. Sib. II, 435). ❖ Abid (Ar.)?, 'Worshipper, adorer' (Ahmed), cf. also Abit/Âbid (Kaybullaev; Erol II, 4).

ABUTAQ Bashk. 1770 **Abutaq** [Мустаким Абутаков] (MIB IV/1, 345).

ABŪ-MELİK Selj. 11th c. **Abū-melik**, a Turkic leader, the brother of Qutulmïš at Skylitzes (Byz. Turc. 54). ❖ Abū-Malik (Ar.) 'Father of the king'. Cf. Ar. *ab* 'father' used as a *kunya* (nickname), making a compound whose first part is *Abu* 'father of' (Ahmed). ⇨ **MELİK.**

ABZAY see **ABÏZAY**

ABZAN see **ABÏZAN**

ABZÄK Bashk. 1737 **Abzäk** [Сююшъ Абзяковъ] (Nepljuev 426). ❖ '(Dear) Little Abïz'. ⇨ **ABÏZ** + dim. suff. *-äk*.

ABZÄN see **ABÏZAN**

AČAY Alt. 19th-20th c. **Ačay** [Ачай] (OjrRS 207). ❖ 'Elder brother, uncle' cf. Alt. *ača* 'Bruder, Onkel; Väterchen' (Radl. I, 502) + voc.-dim. suff. *-y*.

AČAQ Khorezm./Chag. 1410/11 **Ačaq-behadur** [Аджак-бехадур] (MIT I, 531). ❖ 'Embrace, hug'? cf. Chag. *ačaq* 'id.' (Radl. I, 502). See also **TİNİG-AČAQ, UZUN-AČAQ.**

AČANAY Yak. **Ačanay** [Ачанаи] (Pek.).

AČARAMAN-ČAČARÏAMAN Yak. **Ačaraman-čačarïaman, čačïraman, Ačïraman-čačïraman, Ačïrïman-čačïriman,** [Ачараман-Чачарыаман (Чачыраман) / Ачыраман-Чачыраман / Ачырыман-Чачырыман], an abāsï-bogatyr [= evil warrior/hero] (Pek.).

AČÏ see **AJÏ**

AČÏK-AČ Chuv. 18th-19th c. **Ačik-ač** [Ачикач] (Magn. 31). ⇨ **AČÏQ?**

AČÏR Uzb. 18th c. **Ačir-bi** [Ачерби], envoy from Khiva (Nepljuev 668). ❖ 'A kind of plant' cf. Chag. *ačir* 'Name einer Pflanze' (Radl. I, 510).

AČÏ see **AJÏ**

AČÏBÏ-ČAČÏBÏ Yak. **Ačïbï-čačïbï, Ačïma-čačïma** [Ачыбы Чачыбы / Ачыма Чачыма], a fabulous heroine (Pek.).

AČÏQ Chuv. 18th-19th c. **Ačik** [Ачикъ] (Magn. 31);

Uyg. 12th c. - 14th c. **Ačïq** (Radl., USp. 215, 258, DTS). ✧ 'Open, clear' cf. Uyg., Karakh. *ačuq* 'открытый, ясный' (DTS). See also **AΓZÏ-AČÏQ, AWÏZ-AČÏQ.**

AČÏL Hak. 19th-20th c. **Ačïl** [Ачыл], fem. (HRS 353); Kirg. 20th c. **Ačïl-bek** [Atchil-bek], a basmačï leader (Castagné 76); Uzb. 20th c. **Âčïl** [Очил] (Begmatov 1984, 203); Uzb. 20th c. **Âčïl-bek** [Очилбек] (Begmatov 1984, 203). ✧ 'Open out! Flower!' (Begmatov), cf. Uzb. *âčïl-* 'открываться; расцветать, распускаться'.

AČÏLA Uzb. 20th c. **Âčïla** [Очила], fem. (Begmatov 1984, 203). ✧ 'He/she opens out; He/she flowers/flourishes' cf. Uzb. *âčïl-* 'открываться; расцветать, распускаться'.

AČÏLDÏ Uzb. 20th c. **Âčïldï** [Очилди] (Begmatov 1984, 203). ✧ 'He/she opened out; He/she flowered/flourished' cf. Uzb. *âčïl-* 'открываться; расцветать, распускаться'.

AČÏLÏDDÏN Uzb. 20th c. **Âčïliddin** [Очилиддин] (Begmatov 1984, 203). ⇨ **AČÏL?** + comp. *addin.*

AČÏMA-ČAČÏMA see **AČÏBÏ-ČAČÏBÏ**

AČÏN Bashk. 1757 **Ačïn** [Тавла Ачин] (MIB IV/1, 157).

AČÏNTAT Tat. 1606 **Ačïntat / Ačïntat** [Матамас Ачентатов] (MIB I, 154).

AČKAY Chuv. 18th-19th c. **Ačkay** [Ачкай] (Magn. 31); Chuv. 18th-19th c. **Ačkey** [Ачкей] (Magn. 31). ✧ 'Little money, little coin'. ⇨ **AQČA** + dim. suff. *-y.* See also **AQSAY.**

AČQA see **ALTÏN-AČQA**

AČQÏ Uyg. 12th c. - 14th c. **Ačqï** (Radl., USp. 141, DTS). ✧ 'Key' cf. Uyg. (Lob.) *ačqu* (Radl. I, 514; Sev.). See also **YETMÏŠ-QARA-AČQÏ, ÜKÜŠ-QARA-AČQÏ.**

AJA Hak. 19th-20th c. **Aja** [Ача] (HRS 348). ✧ 'Elder brother; uncle (father's brother)' cf. Hak. *aja* 'старший брат, дядя по отцу' (HRS), cf. also Mo. *aja.*

AJAΓAN Crm.(Tat.) **Ajaγan-bek** [اجاغان بك] (Bakč. Nadp. 42). ✧ 'Feeling pain, sorrow' Participle of the verb *aja-,* cf. *āja-, ajï-* 'горкнуть, болеть' (Sev.; Radl. I, 502).

AJAL Trkm. 18th c. **Ajal** [Аджаль], a seyit (comp.) (MIT I, 489). ✧ 'Death' cf. Trkm. *ajal* (Ar.) 'smert;6 konhina' (TrkmRS) < Ar. *ājal.*

AJAP Trkm. 20th c. **Ajap** [Ağap], fem. (Zaj. 1971, 335); Trkm. 20th c. **Ajap** [Аджап] (TrkmRS 29). ✧ 'Splendid, beautiful' cf. Trkm. *ajap / ajāyip* 'великолепный, прекрасный, изумительный' (TrkmRS) (<Ar.).

AJAR Kirg. **Ajar** [Ажар], fem. (Jud. 108, 547); Kkalp. 20th c. **Ažar** [Ажар], fem. (KkRS 777). ✧ '(Girl) with nice complexion or charming appearance' cf. Kirg. *ajar* 'красивый цвет лица; приятное, симпатичное лицо; обаятельная внешность' (Jud.), Kkalp. *ažar* 'вид, облик; цвет лица' (KkRS). See also **BÏYBÏ-AŽAR.**

AJAR-MÄS Kkalp. 20th c. **Ajar-mäs** [Аджармäс], fem. (Bask., Kkalp. 139). ✧ 'Lively, cheerfurl pretty girl', in Russian translation of Baskakov it is 'Аджербойкая' [=Adžer the nimble, the quick-witted], cf. Kkalp. *mäs* 'веселый, радостный' (KkRS). ⇨ **AJAR.**

AJATUR Nog. 20th c. **Ajatur** [Мусурбий Аджатур увлы / Мусорбий Аджатуров], father of Baskakov's informant from the aul of Nökis (Bask., Nog. 143).

AJĀN Kirg. **Ajān** [Ажаан], this name may originate from the name of an Oirat governor in the valley of Chuy who was ill-famed of his wickedness (Jud. 23). ✧ 'Evil, wicked' cf. Kirg. *ajān* 'злой, злющий' (Jud. 23). This name may originate from the name of an Oirat governor in the valley of Chuy who was ill-famed of his wickedness (Jud.).

AJÏ-KELDÏ see **XAJÏ-KELDÏ**

AJÏMÄS see **ÏT-JEMÄS**

AJÏ Tat.(GH) 1369, 1374 **Ačï-χoJa** [Ачихожа / Ачихажа], envoy of the Golden Horde (PSRL IV, 69,VIII, 17, 22, XXIII, 118); Nog. 20th c. **Ajï** [Аджы Лукъман увлы], one of Baskakov's informants from the aul of Nökis (Bask., Nog. 143); Nog. 20th c. **Ajï** [Аджы Байрам увлы / Аджи Байрамов], one of Baskakov's informants from the aul of Ïrγaqlï (Bask., Nog. 143); Kirg. **Ajï-bay** [Ажыбай] (Jud. 79); Kuman / Tat. 13th c. **Ajï-bay** ['Ατζηπάϊ], a christian Tatar (Byz. Turc. 78); Bashk. (?<Tat.) 1772 **Ajï-bay** [Аджибай Азылов] (MIB IV/2, 409); Kirg. **Ajï-bay, Aju-bay** [Ацыбаі], one of Manas' comrades-in-arms (Proben V, 40 /41/, 185); Kzk. 19th c. **Ajï-sultan** [Аджи-султанъ] (Potanin II, 150); Bashk. 1772 **Azï-bay** [Азибай Асынов] (MIB IV/2, 410); Kzk. 1794 **Ažï-bay** [اجبای / Ажибай] (MIK IV, 158); Kzk. 19th c. **Ažï-bay** (Ljutš 153); Kzk. 19th c. **Ažïmbet** [Ажимбетъ] (AOK 10); *TN:* Tat. 18th c. **Ačï / Ači** [Ачы / Ачи], used in names of villages and peoples (Sattarov). ✧ I. 'Bitter, hot' It may be a protective name (Sattarov); cf. Kuman *ačу* (CC), Tat. *ačï* 'горький, кислый' (TatRS); Kirg. *aši* (Jud.), Kzk. *aši* (RKazS), Kkalp. *ašši*, Bashk. *asï, äse* 'кислый, горький' (BaRS); also Trk. *ājï* (Sev.); II. 'Hadji' (<Ar.), cf. Kirg. *ajï* 'хаджи' (Jud.), also Kzk. PNs *Ăži, Ăži-bay, Ăži-bek, Ăži-γali* (Žanuzakov-Esbaeva). See also **XAJÏ.**

AJÏ-BUJU Yak. **Ajï-buJu** [Ацы Буцу], a Yakut folklore hero (Pek.). ✧ Arji Burji (qan) (<Mo.).

AJÏ-BULAT Nog. 20th c. **Ajï-bulat** [Аджыбулат Ибрахим улы Акъсый / Аджибулат Ибраимович Аксиев], one of Baskakov's informants from the aul of Üykön-χalq (Ikon-halk), Cherkess Autonomous Oblast'

(Bask., Nog. 143). ❖ 'Hadji/pilgrim-steel'. ⇨ AJÏ + BULAT. See also XAJÏ.

AJÏ-GELDİ see XAJÏ-KELDİ

AJÏ-KELDİ see XAJÏ-KELDİ

AJÏ-MAXMET   Nog. 20th c. **Ajï-maχmet** [Ибрахим Аджымахмет Къумратулы], one of Baskakov's informants from the aul of Üykön-χalq (Ikon-halk), Cherkess Autonomous Oblast' (Bask., Nog. 143). ❖ 'Hadji-Makhmed' (Ar.). ⇨ AJÏ / XAJÏ + MAXMED.

AJÏ-MAMBET   Nog. 20th c. **Ajï-mambet** [Аджымамбет Сапыот(!) увлы / Ажимамбет Сануотова], one of Baskakov's informants from Sarï-awul (Bask., Nog. 144). ❖ 'Hadji/pilgrim-Mukhammad'. ⇨ AJÏ / XAJÏ + MAMBET.

AJÏQAY   Nog. 20th c. **Ajïqay** [Ахшалы Аджыкай келинъи / Ахшалы Ажекаева], husband of Aχšalï, one of Baskakov's informants from the aul of Qutlubay (Bask., Nog. 144); Kzk. 19th c. **Äžiqay** [Ажикай] (AOK 98). ❖ 'Little Hadji / (Dear) Little Ajï'. ⇨ AJÏ / XAJÏ + dim. suff. -qay.

AJÏNAY   Yak. **Ajïnay-bōtur** [Ацынаи ботур], a legendary hero (Pek.).

AJU see **AJÏ**

AJUP   Bashk. 1763 **Ajup** [Аджюп Абдуллин], Ajup Abdullin (MIB IV/2, 45).

AD'ÏMAŠ   Alt. 19th-20th c. **Ad'ïmaš** [Адымаш], fem. (OjrRS 211).

ADA   Chuv. 18th-19th c. **Ada-bay** [Адабай] (Magn. 24).

ADA-ГUL see **ADİNA**

ADABAS   Hak. 19th-20th c. **Adabas** [Адабас] (HRS 348). ❖ '(S)He will not name (it)'? cf. Hak. *ada-* 'называть, именовать кого-что-л. давать имя кому-чему-л.' (HRS), Alt. *ada-* 'называть, именовать, давать имя' (OjrRS) + suff. -bas (< -mas).

ADAГÏYĀN   Yak. **Adaγïyān** [Адаҕыйан], nickname for males (Pek.). ❖ 'Being officious' cf. Yak. *adaγïy~adaγay* 'о шамане или знахаре: сознавая важность своего назначения или своей роли быть медлительным в своих движениях' (Pek.). Cf. Mo. *adayi-*.

ADAГÏNA   Yak. **Adaγïna** [Адаҕына], byname of a mythic woman, with very short legs (Pek.) (Pek.). ❖ 'Short legged' cf. Yak. *adaγïy~adaγay* 'о шамане или знахаре: сознавая важность своего назначения или своей роли быть медлительным в своих движениях' (Pek.). Cf. Mo. *adayi-*. See also **ADAГÏYĀN**.

ADAX see **ADAQ II.**

ADAY I.   Hak. 19th-20th c. **Aday** [Адай] (HRS 348); Hak. 19th-20th c. **Aday** [Адайко] (HRS 348). ❖ 'Dog' (Butanaev) cf. Hak. *aday* 'собака' (HRS). See also **SARÏГ-ADAY**.

ADAY II.   Kzk. 19th c. **Aday** [Адай] (AOK 38); *EN:* Kzk. **Aday** [Адай] (Tynyšp. 73).

ADAY III.   Uyg. 13th c. **Aday-tutuŋ** [adaj tutuŋ] (DTS). ❖ 'Nestling; (fig.) child, darling' cf. Uyg. *adaj* 'id.' (DTS), Uyg. *adayu* 'Secimli, aziz, değerli, yavru' (EUTS).

ADAYAX   Hak. 19th-20th c. **Adayaχ** [Адайах] (HRS 348). ❖ 'Little Puppy' (Butanaev). ⇨ **ADAY I.** + dim. suff. -aχ.

ADAQ I. see **AYAQ**

ADAQ II.   Hak. 19th-20th c. **Adaχ** [Адах], fem. (HRS 353); Alt. **Adaq** [Адакъ] (Radl. I, 45, 212, 303). ❖ 'The last; (The) Last born (child); The worst' cf. Tel. *adaq* 'der letzte; geringste, schlechteste; der nach der Wahl zurückgelassene' (Radl. I, 45, 212, 303), Alt.(Tel.) *adaq* 'der letzte, schlechteste, geringste, der nach der Wahl zurückgelassene' (Radl. I, 478) (<Ar.).

ADAL   Khorezm. 13th c. **Adal-χan** [اdالخان / Адалъ-ханъ] (RaD/Ber. I, 185, II, 21, 25, 90). ❖ 'Clean, sacred'? Kirg. *adal* 'id.' (Radl. I, 482) (<Ar. *ḥalal* 'rein, heilig').

ADAM   Uyg. 12th c. - 14th c. **Adam** [Adam] (EUTS); Kirg. 1635 **Adam** [Адам] (Miller, Ist. Sib. II, 427); *EN:* Kzk. 18th c. - 19th c. **Adam-χoja** [Адамходжа] (Tynyšp. 74). ❖ 'Man' cf. Tat.(Bar., Tob.), Kar., Kzk., Turk. *adam* 'der Mensch, der Mann' (Räs.), Tat. *adäm* (TatRS) (<Ar.).

ADAM-SART   Kirg. 1869 **Adam-sart**, sultan of the Suan-tribe (Radl., Aus Sib. II, 387-88). ❖ 'Man-Sart; Man-merchant' cf. Uyg., Chag., Alt., Kzk., Turk. *sart* 'der Sarte (der türkisch sprechende Städtebewohner Mittelasiens); (Uyg., Chag.) 'der Kaufmann', (Alt.) 'ein Geschlechtsname der Altajer', (Kzk.) 'alle Städtebewohner Mittelasiens' (Radl. IV, 335). ⇨ **ADAM.**

ADAM-TOГRÏL   Uyg. 12th c. - 14th c. **Adam-toγrïl** (Radl., USp. 90, DTS). ❖ 'Man-falcon' (Blagova 1997, 707), Falcon-Man; Courageous falcon'. ⇨ ADAM + TOГRÏL.

ADAMAN see **ATAMAN**

ADAMEY   Chuv. 18th-19th c. **Adamey / Adämey** [Адамей / Адемей] (Magn. 25). ❖ 'Little man'. ⇨ ADAM + dim. suff. -ey.

ADAR   Uyg. 12th c. - 14th c. **Adar** [Adar] (EUTS); Uyg. 12th c. - 14th c. **Adar-qïz**, fem. (Radl., USp. 210, 212, DTS). ❖ 'He who will shoot/throw; Shooter'? ⇨ **ATAR I.?**

ADAŠ I. see **ATAŠ**

ADAŠ II.   Uzb. 20th c. **Adaš** [Адаш] (Begmatov 1984, 201); Uzb. 20th c. **Adaš-ây** [Адашой], fem. (Begmatov 1984, 201); Uzb. 20th c. **Adaš-χân** [Адаш], fem. (Begmatov 1984, 201); Uzb. 20th c. **Adaš-χoja** [Адашхўжа] (Begmatov 1984, 201); Uzb. 20th c. **Adaš-qul** [Адашкул] (Begmatov 1984, 201). ❖ 'Be lost!; Wander!' (Begmatov), cf. Uzb. *adaš-* 'бродить, странствовать, заблуждаться' (UzbRS).

ADAŠ-MURAT   Uzb. 20th c. **Adaš-murâd** [Адашмурод] (Begmatov 1984, 201). ✧ 'Be lost - Murat! Wander-Murat!' (Begmatov). ⇨ **ADAŠ II.** + **MURAT.**

ADÄK   Tat.(Sib.) 1622 **Adäk** [Адяков Енигей] (Miller, Ist. Sib. II, 291). ⇨ **ADAQ II.?**

ADÄMEY see **ADAMEY**

ADİ   Chuv. 18th-19th c. **Adi** [Ади] (Magn. 25). ✧ 'Father-in-law' cf. Chuv. *aDi* 'Schwiegervater' (Paas.).

ADİKA   Chuv. 18th-19th c. **Adika** [Адика] (Magn. 25). ✧ 'Little father-in-law'. ⇨ **ADİ** + dim. suff. *-ka*.

ADİL   Tat. 20th c. **Adil** [Адил] (Sattarov); Bashk. 1778 **Adil / Adiley** [Сейфулла Адилев (Адилеев / Адклеев)] (MIB V, 74); Kirg. **Adïl** [Адыл] (Jud. 41, 182, 676); Tat. 1777 **Adïl-ša** [Рахмангулъ Адилшин] (MIB V, 60); Tat. 1764 **Adïl-ša / Adïl-šä?** [Адильше Астаев] (MIB IV/1, 279); Bashk. 1776 **Adul-bay / Abdulay?** [Адулбай Теметов / Абдулай Теметев] (MIB V, 39); Kkalp. 20th c. **Ädil-χan** [Әдилхан] (KkRS 772). ✧ Adil (Ar.), 'Just, honest, upright, righteous' (Ahmed), 'Truthful; Fair' cf. Kirg. *adïl, adil* (Ar.) 'справедливый' (Jud.), Az., Osm., Kzk., Uyg. *adil* (<Ar.) 'gerecht, Gerechtigkeit' (Radl. I, 492). See also **BAY-ADÏL.**

ADİLÄ   Tat. 20th c. **Adilä** [Адилэ], fem. (Sattarov). ✧ Adila, fem. of Adil (Ar.), 'Honest, upright, rightous' (Ahmed).

ADİLQAN   Kirg. **Adïlqan** [Адылкан], fem. (Jud. 72). ⇨ **ADİL** + suff. *-qan(1)*.

ADİM   Chuv. 18th-19th c. **Adim / Adïm** [Адимъ / Адымъ] (Magn. 25). ✧ 'My father-in-law'. ⇨ **ADİ** + poss. suff. *-m*.

ADİMEY   Nog. 20th c. **Adimey** [Адимей Халил улы Миж], one of Baskakov's informants from the aul of Adil-χalq (Bask., Nog. 143).

ADİNA   Trkm. 1809 **Adina** [Адина Нияз аталык] (MIKk. 103); Trkm. 1832 **Adina** [Адина Курт-хан], from the Salïr tribe (MIT II, 229, 430,431, 460); Trkm. 1851/52 **Adina** [Адина Клыч-хан], from the Küčik (Küčik) clan of the Yomut tribe (MIT II, 248); Uzb. 1810 **Adina** [Адина Мурад бехадыр] (MIKk. 110); Bashk. 1738 **Adna-bay?** [Адна-бай Пеляков] (MIB I, 144); Bashk. 1742 **Adna-bay** [Аднабай Тляковъ] (MIB III, 511); Bashk. 1777 **Adna-bay** [Аднабай Ябакаевъ] (MIB V, 52); Tat. 18th c. **Adna-γul** [Аднагулов] (MIB V, 559); Tat. 1763 **Adna-γul** [Ермакъ Аднагуловъ], a Tatar captain ("sotnik") (PSZRI XVI, 322); Bashk. 1712 **Adna-γul** [Аднагулов] (MIB III, 82); Bashk. 1734 **Adna-γul** [Муратъ Аднагуловъ] (Vel.-Zern., Bašk. 10); Bashk. 1735 **Adna-γul** [Кутла Аднагуловъ], a tarγan (Vel.-Zern., Bašk. 14); Bashk. 1735 **Adna-γul** [Аднагулъ Муашевъ], a tarγan (Vel.-Zern., Bašk. 16); Bashk.

1735 **Adna-γul** [Адагулъ Араслановъ], a tarγan (Vel.-Zern., Bašk. 19); Bashk. 1735 **Adna-γul** [Аднагулъ Юсуповъ], a tarγan (Vel.-Zern., Bašk. 22); Bashk. 1735 **Adna-γul** [Аднагулъ Сююндюковъ], a tarγan (Vel.-Zern., Bašk. 24); Bashk. 1735 **Adna-γul** [Аднагулъ Аднашевъ] (Vel.-Zern., Bašk. 25); Bashk. 1795 **Adna-γul** [Кучумъ Аднагуловъ] (IOAIÊK XXVIII, 589); Bashk. 1735 **Adna-γul / Ada-γul?** [Танагулъ Адагуловъ], a tarγan (Vel.-Zern., Bašk. 19); Chuv. 18th-19th c. **Adna-kul** [Аднакулъ / Аднагулъ] (Magn. 25); Bashk. **Aðna / Aðna-bay** (Sprav. Im. 68); Bashk. 18th c. **Aðna-bay** [Азнабай], six persons in the early 18th c. took part in the revolt of the Bashkirs (MIB I, 310, 396); Bashk. 1792 **Aðna-bay** [Итбай Азнабаев] (MIB V, 328); Bashk. 20th c. **Aðna-bay** (Kusimova 28); Bashk. 20th c. **Aðna-bay** [Айна] (Kusimova 28); Bashk. 1712 **Aðna-γul** [Азнагул] (MIB III, 82); Oghuz/Trkm. **Ayïna-χan** [Айына-хан], Usra-χan's father (Muhamedova: OSA 170); Oghuz/Trkm. 13th c. **Ayne** [اينه / Айне], an Awshar Khan (Abulg./Kon. 795, 800); Turk.? 1348 **Ayne-bäg (-bäy)** ['Αϊνάπεης], a commander (Byz. Turc. 81); Kipch. 13th c. **Ayne-bek** [Айнэ-бек], Kipchak's son (RaD I/1, 96); Kzk. 19th c. **Ayne-bek** [Айнебекъ] (SOK 160); Kzk. 19th c. **Ayne-bek** [Айнебекъ] (AOO 2); Kzk. 19th c. **Ayne-bek / Aynï-bek** [Айныбекъ] (SOV 28); Yürük 16th c. **Ayne-χan** [اينه خان] (Gökb., Rum. 104); Trkm. 20th c. **Annagül** [Annagül], fem. (Zaj. 1971, 338); Trkm. 20th c. **Anna** [Anna], fem. (Zaj. 1971, 341); Kkalp. 20th c. **Anna** [Анна], fem. (KkRS 777); Kkalp. 20th c. **Anna-qul** [Аннакул] (KkRS); Trkm. **Anna-soltan** [Аннасолтан], fem. (Sopieva: OSA 180); Bashk. **Atna-γul** [Salach Atnagulov] (Mende 170); Kzk. 19th c. **Azna-bay** [Умурзакъ Азнабаевъ] (Grod., Pril. 119); Kzk. 19th c. **Azna-bay** [Азнабай] (SOV 114); Kzk. 19th c. **Azna-bay** [Азнабай] (SOK 74); Kzk. 19th c. **Azna-bay** [Азнабай] (AOO 22); Kzk. 19th c. **Azna-bay** [Азнабай] (AOA 54); Kkalp. 1740 **Azna-bay-bi** [Азнабай-Би] (Hanykov, Poezdka 19); Kzk. 19th c. **Azna-bek** [Азнабекъ] (SOK 302); Trkm. 20th c. **Anna** [Анна], fem. (TrkmRS 44); Turk. 1402 **Eyne / Îne?** [Εἰενε], a Turkish commander (Byz. Turc. 121); Yürük 1543 **Eyne-χan** [Eynehan] (Gökb., Rum. 177, 179, 181, 189, 193, 194, 201, 226, 233). ✧ 'Friday; born on Friday' cf. Kuman, Crm., Kar. *ayna* 'Freitag', Turk. *Äinä* 'id.' (findet sich in Eigennamen von Oertlichkeiten), Kar. *äynä* 'id.' (Radl. I, 659) Chag. *adina* (< P. اينه) 'Freitag' (Radl. I. 494), Bashk. *aðna* 'неделя' (BRS), Trkm. *ānna* 'пятница' (TrkmRS), NUyg.(Tar.) *azna* 'Freitag' (Radl. I, 577). Sauvaget cites the name in the form of *äynä-bäk* mistakenly interpreting it as the variant of the title *inaq/inaγ* 'the confident of the prince' (p. 40) (<P.). Cf. also Bashk.

"aðna (yoma) kön tïwɣan", its Russian form in Bashkir is *Aznabaj* (Kusimova 28).

ADİS Nog. 20th c. **Adis** [Суьлеймен Ишамакъай (!) улы Адис / Сулейман Имамакеевич Адисов], father of one of Baskakov's informants from the aul of Qañlï (Bask., Nog. 143).

ADÏ-YEKÄ Uyg. 12th c. - 14th c. **Adï-yekä** (Radl., USp. 130, DTS). ⇨ **YEKÄ?**

ADÏ-YOQ Tuv. 19th c. **Adï-yaq** (<Adï-yoq) [Адыјак], fem. (Proben IX, 20); Alt. 19th-20th c. **Adï-yoq** [Адыйок] (OjrRS 207). ✧ 'Unnamed; Nameless' (OjrRS), 'Ring-finger'? ⇨ **AT + YOQ**. See also **ATSÏZ**.

ADÏBAS Alt. 19th-20th c. **Adïbas** [Адыбас] (OjrRS 207). ✧ '(S)He will not name (it)'? ⇨ **ADABAS.**

ADÏJAX Hak. 19th-20th c. **Adïjaχ** [Адыҷах] (HRS 348); Hak. 19th-20th c. **Adïjaχ** [Адыҷах], fem. (HRS 353). ✧ 'Little Stirring-spoon' cf. Hak.(Sag.) *adï* 'Rührlöffel; Stab mit einer Kugel an einem Ende' (Radl. I, 489) + dim. suff. *-jaχ*.

ADÏJAŇ Hak. 19th-20th c. **Adïjañ** [Адыҷанъ] (HRS 348). ✧ 'Darling, nestling, child'? cf. Hak. PN *Adïyan* 'id.' (Butanaev).

ADÏYĀ Tuv. 19th c. **Adïyā** [Адыја] (Proben IX, 141). ✧ 'Darling, nestling, child'? cf. Hak. PN *Adïyan* 'id.' (Butanaev).

ADİL see **ADİL**

ADÏLƔA Yak. **Adïlɣa** (Ān-adïlɣa) [Адылҕа], a mythical name (Pek.). ✧ 'A kind of axe' cf. Yak. *adïlɣa* 'id.' (JRS).

ADİM see **ADİM**

ADÏNAQ Alt. 19th-20th c. **Adïnaq** [Адынак] (OjrRS 207). ✧ 'Shooter, rifleman'? cf. Alt. *at-* 'стрелять'(OjrRS 207), also Hak. PN *Adïnaχ* (Butanaev).

ADÏNAŠ Alt. 19th-20th c. **Adïnaš** [Адынаш] (OjrRS 207). ✧ 'Shooting'? cf. Alt. *at-* 'стрелять' (OjrRS 207).

ADÏS Alt. 19th-20th c. **Adïs** [Адыс] (OjrRS 207). ✧ 'Grid, railings' cf. Alt. *adïs* '1. загон [sheepfold, pinfold] 2. деревянная решётка для сушки творога, сыра [wooden grid for drying curd, cheese] (OjrRS).

ADÏŠ Alt. 19th-20th c. **Adïš** [Адыш] (OjrRS 207). ✧ 'Shooting, firing' cf. Alt. *adïš* 'стрельба, перестрелка', *adïš-* [<at-] 'совместно стрелять, перестреливаться' (OjrRS). ⇨ **ADUŠ?**

ADÏTER Bashk. 1735 **Adïter** [Адитерь Аюгаринъ] (Vel.-Zern., Bašk. 19).

ADLO Hak. 19th-20th c. **Adlo** [Адло] (HRS 348).

ADNA see **ADİNA**

ADNA-ƔUL see **ADİNA**

ADNA-QUL see **ADİNA**

ADNAČÏQ Tat.(Lit.) **Adnačik / Adnačïq** [Адначикъ Мансуревичъ] (Lit. Tat. 105, 106); Tat.(Lit.) 1592

Adnačïq [Фатма Адначиковна], fem. (Lit. Tat. 105). ✧ 'Little Friday'. ⇨ **ADİNA** + dim. suff. *-čïq*.

ADNAŠ Bashk. 1735 **Adnaš** [Аднагулъ Аднашевъ] (Vel.-Zern., Bašk. 25); Bashk. 1742 **Adnaš** [Илиш Аднашев] (MIB III, 511); Bashk. 1764 **Adnaš** [Араслан Аднашев] (MIB IV/1, 295). ✧ 'Little Friday'. ⇨ **ADİNA** + dim. suff. *-š*.

ADRUQ Uyg. 926 **Adruq** [A-tou-you (*â-tor-üoɣ)], title of the Uyghur ruler of Kanchou (Hamilton, Ouïg. 145, 72). ✧ 'Elect; prominent, outstanding; different'; 'Choisi, élu' (Hamilton, Ouïg., ibid.), cf. OT *adruq* 'verschieden, abgesehen von' (<*adru-* 'auswählen') (Gabain 292), *adruq* 'ausgewählt' (TT VII, 80), *adruq, aðruq* ' разный, различный' (DTS).

ADU Chuv. 18th-19th c. **Adu-bay** [Адубай] (Magn. 25).

ADUŠ Alt. 19th-20th c. **Aduš** [Адуш] (OjrRS 207). ✧ 'Shooting, rifle-fire'? cf. Alt. *adïš* 'стрельба' (OjrRS). ⇨ **ADÏŠ?**

AÐÏMAS Bashk. 1780 **Aðïmas** [Бигильда Адзимясов] (MIB V, 104); Bashk. 1735 **Aðïmas / Aðïmäs / Adzimäs** [Адзимяс] (Vel.-Zern., Bašk. 25). ✧ 'He who won't go off the rail (fig.); He won't be impertinent; He won't be naughty' cf. Bashk. *aðï-* 'озорничать; свихнуться; развращаться' (BRS).

AÐNA see **ADİNA**

AÐNAY Bashk. 1737 **Aznay** [Азнай] (MIB I, 311); Bashk. 1740 **Aznay** [Азнай Кучюпкулов] (MIB I, 439); Bashk. 1754 **Aznay** [Абулхаир Азнаев] (MIB IV/1, 83); Bashk. 1760 **Aznay** [Юлай Азнаев] (MIB IV/2, 160); Bashk. 1770 **Aznay** [Азнай Тимашев] (MIB IV/1, 349). ✧ 'Little Friday'. ⇨ **ADİNA** + suff. *-y*.

AÐNAQAY Bashk. 1754 **Aðnaqay** [Азнакай Муллакаев] (MIB IV/1, 83); Bashk. 1755 **Aðnaqay** [Азнакай Кинзин] (MIB IV/1, 99, IV/2, 45); Nog.? 1734 **Aðnaqay / Aznaqay?** [Азнакай Явгилдин], a tarχan (Vel.-Zern., Bašk. 11). ⇨ **ADİNA** + dim. suff. *-qay*.

AÐNALÏ Bashk. 1690 **Aðnalï** [Игимбетка Езналеевъ] (Vel.-Zern., Bašk. 30); Bashk. 1791 **Aðnalï** [Чермыш Азналин] (MIB V, 301). ✧ '(Child) of Friday; Friday's (baby)' cf. Bashk. PN *Aðnalï* (Kusimova). ⇨ **ADİNA** + suff. *-lï*.

AF-TEGİN see **AQ I.**

AFAJAN Turk. 19th c. **Afajan-oɣlu / Aɣajan-oɣlu?**, a Zeybek (Kúnos 1891, 119). ✧ 'Like poison; very sharp; excitement' cf. Turk. dial. *afacan* (DS).

AFAQ see **APAQ**

AFRASÏYAB OT, Karakhanid. 11th c. **Afrasyab / Afrasiyab** [Afrasyab / afrasijab], a mythical (legendary) sovereign of Turan, forefather of the Karakhanids and Seljuks (MK/Atalay 829, MIT I, 398, 431, 439, 508, DTS). ✧ Afrasiyab (P.), 'Troublesome, painful; infuriated, angry, passionate' (Erol II).

AFŠAR Selj. 1133 **Afšar-eri** [Αὐσάραρις], a Turkic commander (Byz. Turc. 91). ✧ 'Afshar; one of the Oghuz tribes'.

AGALÏ Chuv. 18th-19th c. **Agalï** [Агали] (Magn. 24). ✧ 'Having a plough; equipped with a plough' cf. Chuv. *aGa* 'Pflug' (Paas.). + suff. *-lï*.

AGAN Chuv. 18th-19th c. **Agan** [Аганъ] (Magn. 24).

AGANDEY Chuv. 18th-19th c. **Agandey** [Агандей] (Magn. 24). ⇨ **AGAN?** + suff. *-dey*.

AGANEY Chuv. 18th-19th c. **Aganey** [Аганей] (Magn. 24). ⇨ **AGAN?** + suff. *-ey*.

AGANKA Chuv. 18th-19th c. **Aganka** [Аганка] (Magn. 24). ⇨ **AGAN?** + suff. *-qa*.

АГ-BAY see **AQ I.**

АГ-BÄZ Bashk. 1757 **Aγ-bäz** [Салиш Агбезов] (MIB IV/1, 142); Bashk. 1761 **Aγ-bäz** [Агбез Абдуллин] (MIB IV/1, 220); Bashk. 1788 **Aγbes** [Агбес Урусметев (Уразметев)] (MIB V, 238); Bashk. 18th c. **Aγbez** [Агбез] (MIB IV/1, 220). ✧ 'White sort of textile' cf. Bashk. *bäz* 'бязь' [frieze, nettle-cloth] (BRS). It may be the short form of **АГÏ-BÄZ** too. ⇨ **AQ I.**

АГ-BES see **АГ-BÄZ**

АГ-BEZ see **АГ-BÄZ**

АГ-DÖWLET see **AQ-DAWLET**

АГ-IŠ see **АГÏŠ**

АГ-IŠ see **АГÏŠ**

АГА Az. 19th-20th c. **Aγa** [Aγa Hesen (<Ağa Hasan)] (Cafer., Ağa 90); Trkm. 20th c. **Aγa** [Aga] (Zaj. 1971, 325); Kmk. **Aγa** [Ага] (KmkRS 27); Az. 19th c. - 20 th c. **Aγa / Aγa-bey**, an Azerî folk poet (Cafer., Ağa 89); Az. 20th c. **Aγa-begim-aγa**, fem. (Cafer., Ağa 92); Chag. 1554 **Aγa-biče** [Ага-биче], fem. (Ivanov 133); Kkalp. 20th c. **Aγa-biy** [Агабий] (KkRS 772); Chag. 1559 **Aγa-bike** [Ага-бике], fem. (Ivanov 104, 105, 178, 187); Chag. 1566 **Aγa-biki** [Ага-бики], fem. (Ivanov 160, 246); Az. 19th-20th c. **Aγa-jan**, an Azerî poet in Iran (Cafer., Ağa 89); Chag. 1558 **Aγa-χatun** [Ага-Хатун], fem. (Ivanov 236); Az. 19th-20th c. **Aγa-mirze** (Cafer., Ağa 91); Chag. 1558 **Aγa-sultan** [Ага Султан] (Ivanov 146, 128); Az. 20th c. **Aχanïm** (<Aγa-χanïm), from the dialect of the Mugan group (Cafer., Ağa 92); *TN:* **Aγa-jan** [Агаджанъ], a settlement south of Dizah (ZIRGOStat. II, 51). ✧ 'Master; (rich) person of authority; respected elderly man or woman'; Normally the word *aγa* means an elder male relative such as father, brother or grand-father, cf. OT *aqa, aγa* (DTS), Trk. *a:γa* (Sev.), as a title and component of antroponyms, however, it is used to express honour, respect or the higher social status of the person. Cf. Chag., Osm., Az. *aγa, aqa* (Budagov), Kkalp., Kmk. *aγa* (KkRS, KmkRS) etc. Cf. also Cafer., Ağa, 89-92.

АГА-DİL Kzk. 19th c. **Aγa-dil** [Агадилъ] (SOK 164). ✧ 'Father's heart' cf. P. *dil* 'heart'. ⇨ **АГА.**

АГА-KİŠİ Az. 19th-20th c. **Aγa-kiši**, son of Hacı Çelebi from the Şeki Khans (Cafer., Ağa 89). ✧ 'Master-Man', 'Respected elder man' cf. Türk, Kuman, Chag., Crm., Turk., etc. *kiši* 'der Mensch' (Radl. II, 1392). ⇨ **АГА + KİZİ.**

АГА-MAH Chag. 16th c. **Aγa-mah** [Ага-Max], fem. (Ivanov 89, 90, 129). ✧ 'Respected, high-born beautiful lady'. ⇨ **АГА + MAH.**

АГА-MAHİM Chag. 1564 **Aγa-mahim** [Ага-Махим], fem. (Ivanov 118, 120, 177, 178, 179, 229). ✧ 'My fair lady'. ⇨ **АГА-MAHİM.**

АГА-TAY Chag. 15th c. **Aγa-tay** [اغاطای], a Shaybanid (Šejb. LII); *EN:* Kzk. 18th c. - 19th c. **Aγa-tay-batïr** [Агатай-батыр], a personal name of ethnonymic origin (Tynyšp. 73). ✧ 'Elder colt (foal)'. ⇨ **АГА + TAY** or suff. *-tay(2)*?

АГА-TAŠ Chag. 15th c. **Aγa-taš** [اغا طاش], a Shaybanid (Šejb. LII). ✧ 'Brother-stone', 'Fellow-Aγa'? ⇨ **АГА + TAŠ / АГАDAŠ?**

АГABEZ Bashk. 1763 **Aγabez (<*Aγabïz)** [Агабез Утяганов] (MIB IV/1, 269). ✧ 'Our Aγa; our master'? ⇨ **АГА + poss. suff. *-bïz.***

АГABÏZ see **АГABEZ**

АГАС-AWUZ Tat.(Tob.) **Aγac-aus** [Agazaus / Аβацаус] (Proben IV, 260 /324/). ✧ 'Wood-mouth'. ⇨ **АГАČ + AWUZ.**

АГАČ Yürük 16th c. **Aγač** [Ağaç], among the Yürüks of Kocacık (Gökb., Rum. 102); Selj. / Khorezm.? 14th c. **Aγač-eri** [اغاچری], emir at the time of Öljeytü Khan (1304-1316). The name is also known as that of an ancient Turkic tribe (ToganUTT 170, 258, etc.) (Aqsar./Iš. 111; Aqsar./Tur. 302, 303, 305); Hak.(Sag.) 19th-20th c. **Aγïs** [Кам-аβыс], Qam-aγïs (=Aγïs the shaman, see QAM) (Proben IX, 567). ✧ 'Tree; wood; (man of) wood (ethnonym)' cf. Turk. *ağaç* (TS, TRS), Hak.(Sag.) *aγïs* 'Baum, Holz, hölzern' (Radl. I, 167). See also **QOŠ-АГАČ, QUN-АГАČ, TEL-АГÏŠ.**

АГАČ-BAŠLÏ Tat.(GH) 1327 **Aγac-bašlï** ['Αγατζπασλής], a Tatar commander (Byz. Turc. 55). ✧ 'Having wooden head'. ⇨ **АГАČ + BAŠ + suff. *-lï*.**

АГАČ-ERİ Maml. 14th c. **Aγač-eri** [اغاچری / Agaçeri] (Tarj/Houtsma 45, Tarj/Toparlı 42). ✧ 'Man of wood'. ⇨ **АГАČ + ER + poss. suff. *-i*.**

АГАČA Chag. 1560 **Aγača** [Агач], fem. (Ivanov 280); Az. 19th-20th c. **Aγča**, fem. (Cafer., Ağa 91). ✧ 'Woman, wife; (old) lady of higher rank; daughter of a prince' Also used as a female title, later on as a secondary component. Cf. East T. *aγačä ~ aγače* 'woman, wife, old lady' (Jarring), Chag. *aγača* 'se dit des femmes par opposition à *begim* et *χanim* 'dame'' (PdC), *aγača* 'госпожа' (Budagov), Uyg. *aγača ~ aχača* 'старшина, староста' (Budagov), Uyg. *aγača* 'la fille d'un prince impérial' (Ligeti, Vocab.).

АГАČЇ see **АГЇČЇ**

АГАЈЇQ Trkm. 1879-1881 **Aɣajïq** [Agha Jik], from the Göklen tribe (O'Donovan I, 225). ✧ 'Little *Aɣa*'. ⇨ **АГА** + dim. suff. *-jïq*.

АГАDAŠ Az. 19th-20th c. **Aɣadaš**, a poet from Azerbaijan (Cafer., Ağa 89-90). ✧ 'Fellow-*Aɣa*'? ⇨ **АГА** + suff. *-daš*. See also **АГА-ТАŠ?**

АГАY Chuv. 18th-19th c. **Agay** [Агай] (Magn. 24); Kmk. **Aɣay** [Агай] (KmkRS 27); Alt. 19th c. **Aɣay** [Агеев], a warrior (bogatyr) (Verb., In. 147); Hak. 19th-20th c. **Aɣay** [Агай], fem. (HRS 353); Kirg. **Aɣay-qan** (Radl. I, 1090). ✧ 'Respected elderly man; brother; uncle etc.' It is used for accosting elderly men politely. Cf. Kmk. *aɣay* 'вежливое обращение к старшему по возрасту мужчине, дядя' (KmkRS), Kirg. *aɣay* 'почтительное обращение к старшему мужчине' (Jud.), Tuv. *aɣay* 'княгиня, жена нойона' (TuvRS), Tat. *aɣay* 'дядя, дядюшка' (TatRS), Tel. Tat. *aɣay* 'Brüderchen, Onkel' (Radl. I, 145). ⇨ **АГА** + suff. *-y*.

АГАМ-ALİ Az. 19th c. **Aɣam-ali-oɣlu** [Agamaly-Oglu] (Mende 173); Az. 19th c. **Aɣam-eli-oɣlu** (<**Aġam-ali**) (Cafer., Ağa 91). ✧ 'My master (uncle) *Ali*'. ⇨ **АГА** + **ALİ** + poss. suff. *-m*.

АГАМ-ELİ see **АГАМ-ALİ**

АГАМ-OГUS Yak. **Aɣam-oɣus (Ala-moñus?)** [Аҕам Оҕус / Ала Моҥус?] (Pek.). ✧ '(My) Elder bull' cf. Yak. *aɣat* 'пожилой, старший' (Pek.), *oɣus* 'бык' (JRS). ⇨ **АГА** + poss. suff. *-m*. See also **ÖGÜZ, ÖKÜZ**.

АГАММЕТ Az. 19th-20th c. **Aɣammet (<Aġa mehmet)** (Cafer., Ağa 90). ✧ Shortened of Aɣa-Ahmet or Aɣa-Mehmet. ⇨ **АГА** + suff. *-met?*

АГАN-АМЕТ Trkm. 1717 **Aɣan-amet** [Аганаметъ] (ZIRGO IX, 327). ✧ ?-Ahmet. ⇨ **АХМЕТ**.

АГАNDAY Kirg. **Aɣanday** [Agandai / Аҕандаи], Kösqaman's son, Čaɣanday's (!) brother (Proben V, 218 /220/).

АГАSЇ Az. 1765 **Aɣasï-χan**, a khan; later the name was also used fo Prophet ᶜAli (Cafer., Ağa 90); *TN:* Az. 19th-20th c. **Aɣasï-bek**, an „oba" [nomad encampment] (Cafer., Ağa 90). ✧ 'His master'. ⇨ **АГА** + poss. suff. *-sï*. See also **İS-АГАSЇ**.

АГАW Kmk. **Aɣaй / Aɣaw** [Агав] (KmkRS 27). ✧ 'Uncle (as respectful address of male elders)' cf. Kmk. *aɣaй / aɣaw* [аѓав] 'вежливое обращение к старшему по возрасту мужчине; дядя' (KmkRS). ⇨ **АГА**. See also **АГАY**.

АГĀYЇ Yak. **Aɣāyï** [Аҕајы], a nickname for men (Pek.).

АГČA I. see **AQČA**

АГČA II. see **АГАČA**

АГČA-QUГU Trkm. 20th c. **Aɣča-quɣu** [Ağca Kuğu],

fem. (Özbaş 24).

АГDUQ Uyg. 8th c. - 9th c. **Aɣduq-bitgäči**, clerk, scribe (Le Coq, Man. I, 28, III, 43; DTS). ✧ 'Sponger, hanger-on of unknown origin' cf. OT *agduk* 'bozuk, belirsiz, değişik', *agduk kişi* 'kim olduğu belli olmıyan sığıntı adam' (MK/Brock./Atalay IV, 9), *aɣduq* 'Eindringling unbekannter Herkunft' (MK/Brock.), *aɣduq* 'изменчивый', *aɣduq kişi* 'скрытный человек' (DTS).

АГЇ Kzk. **Aɣï-bay** [Agy Bai / Аҕы Баі] (Proben III, 74 /96/). ✧ 'Riches, wealth; treasure; generous' cf. Uyg. *agı* '1. servet, varlık, hazine; 2. göz yaşı' (EUTS). See also **YEGÄN-АГЇSЇZ**.

АГЇ-BÄZ Bashk. 1731 **Aɣï-bäz** [Агыбесь] (MIB III, 286); Bashk. 1750 **Aɣï-bäz** [Агибез Утеганов] (MIB III, 472). ✧ 'White sort of textile'. ⇨ **АГ-BÄZ.**

АГЇČЇ Selj. 12th c. **Aɣačï / Aɣïčï** [Agacı], emir of Alparslan ibn Daud (Ahbar 21); Tat.(GH) 14th c. **Aquči?** [Ακύζης], a christened Tatar (Byz. Turc. II, 60). ✧ 'Treasurer' (a title) cf. Uyg., Karakh. *aɣïčï* 'Schatzmeister' (MK/Brock., DTS), *aɣı:čï* 'treasurer; the keeper of the silk brocades' (Clauson), *agaçı* 'maliyeci' (Togan, UTT 210).

АГЇYA Yak. **Aɣïya / Aɣïya-bātïr** [Аҕыја-батыр омургу], a fabulous bogatyr (warrior) (Pek.).

АГЇLAÑ Hak.(Sag.) 19th-20th c. **Aɣïlañ-qō** [Аҕылаҥ-ко], fem. (Proben IX, 340, 352).

АГЇLDAY Tat.(Bar.) **Aɣïlday / Aɣïlday-mergen** [Агылдай(-Мергенъ)] (Nikiforov 110, 127).

АГЇR-OГLAN Turk. **Aɣïr-oɣlan** [Ağıroğlan], a village in Turkey (Köyl.). ✧ 'Serious boy; difficult boy' cf. Turk. *ağır adam* 'serious-minded man; bore, dull person' (TED). ⇨ **OГLAN**.

АГЇS see **АГАČ**

АГЇŠ Tat.(Lit.) 1592 **Aɣïš / Aɣ-ïš / Aɣ-iš** [Янъ Агишевичъ] (Lit. Tat. 111); Tat.(Mish.) 20th c. **Aɣïš / Aɣ-ïš / Aɣ-iš?** [Агиш], family names (Sattarov); Bashk. 1687 **Aɣïš / Aɣ-ïš / Aɣ-iš** [Агыпышка / Огышко] (MIB I, 78); Bashk. 1706 **Aɣïš / Aɣ-ïš / Aɣ-iš** [Агыш] (MIB III, 27); Bashk. 1732 **Aɣïš / Aɣ-ïš / Aɣ-iš** [Балтас Агышев] (MIB III, 308); Bashk. 1753, 1756, 1757 **Aɣïš / Aɣ-ïš / Aɣ-iš?** [Солтан (Султан) Агишев] (MIB IV/1, 68, 127, 140, 191); Bashk. 1738, 1753, 1761 **Aɣïš / Aɣ-ïš / Aɣ-iš(ev)** [Чюрагул Агишев] (MIB III, 387, 440, MIB IV/1, 68, 230); Bashk. 1751 **Aɣïš / Aɣ-ïš / Aɣ-iš(ev)** [Утеган Агышев] (MIB IV/1, 57); Kirg. **Aɣïš / Er-aɣïš** [Er Agysch / Ер Аҕыш], „der chinese Er Agysch" [=the Chinese Aɣïš the Hero] the name of a women's man, hero of a short epic (Proben V, 23 /24/, Jud. 21, 527); Chag. 1573 **Aɣïš-biy / Aɣ-ïš-biy / Aɣ-iš-biy?** [Агиш-бий] (Ivanov 46, 190); Nog.?, Kzk.? **Aɣïš-murza, Aɣ-ïš-murza, Aɣ-iš-murza?** [Агиш Мурза] (Žirm., Epos 430). ✧ I. 'Honest friend (fellow)' (< AQ + İŠ) for the

Tat., Bashk. names (Sattarov); II. 'Whitish; milk-white' for the Kirg., Nog. names; cf. kirg. *aɣïš* 'беловатый, молочно-белый' (Jud.). ⇨ **AQ I.** + **EŠ**. See also **Bİ-AГЇŠ, ŠİRİN-AГЇŠ, TEL-AГЇŠ**.

AГЇŠ-QALQAN-AM Kzk. **Aɣïš-qalqan-am**, fem. (Radl., Phon. XLII, 1). ⇨ **+ AM?**

AГЇŠ-QOJOŠ Kirg. **Aɣïš-qojoš** [Agysch Kodschosch / Аɓыш Коцош] (Proben V, 162 /163/). ✧ 'White (grey-haired) master' cf. Kirg. *aɣïš* 'беловатый, молочно-белый', *qojo* 'ходжа, благочестивый старец, хозяин, господин' (Jud.) + dim. *-š < -č* (Räs., Morph. 92). ⇨ **AГЇŠ + XOJAŠ**.

AГЇT Tat. 1609 **Aɣït** [Агит] (Miller, Ist. Sib. II, 209).

AГЇZLU Maml. 14th c. **Aɣïzlu** [اَغِـزْلو] (Sauvaget 37). ✧ 'Having (big) mouth' (Sauvaget 37). ⇨ **AWÏZ** + suff. *-lï*.

AГRAQ Khorezm. 13th c. **Aɣraq** [Сейф-эддинъ Меликъ Агракъ], the Khorezmshah's retainer (RaD/Ber. III, 80, 81, RaD I/2 221, 222).

AГRUQČЇ Khorezm. 13th c. **Aɣruqčï** [Агрукчи] (RaD II, 14. 155). ✧ I. An ancient title; II. 'Seriously ill' cf. Karakh. *aɣruq* I. 'груз, имущество, скарб, тяжелобольной' (DTS) + suff. *-čï*.

AГZЇ-AČIQ Turk. 20th c. **Aɣzï-ačïq** [Yukarı Ağzıaçık], toponym, a village in the province of Konya, Turkey (TMİB 582). ✧ 'His/her mouth is open; Open-mouthed' cf. Turk. *ağız* 'mouth' (TED). ⇨ **AČIQ**.

AГZЇ-BÜYÜK Turk. 20th c. **Aɣzï-büyük** [Ağzıbüyük], toponym, a village in the provinces of Adana and Çankırı, Turkey (TMİB 15, 245). ✧ 'His/her mouth is big; Big-mouthed' cf. Turk. *ağız* 'mouth' (TED). ⇨ **BÜYÜK**.

AГZЇ-QARA Turk. 16th c. **Aɣzï-qara** [Muhiddin Mehmed Ağzîkara], (died in 1599), a famous kadi (judge, governor of a kaza) and calligrapher. According to the source, his name is a typical nickname: „Muhiddin'e yaz çok yazdığından, kaleminin ucunu daima ağzına sürdüğünden ve mürekkepten iyi bir tat duyduğundan dolayı Ağzıkara lakab verilmiştir." [= Muhiddin was given the nickname (Aɣzïkara) because he did lots of writing smearing his pen on his mouth while enjoying the flavour of the ink] (Tuhfetül hattatın, Ün 3 (1936), 360). ✧ 'Black-mouthed' cf. also Osm. *ağzı kara* 'who enjoys giving bad news, morbid; who intrigues, backbites' (TED). ⇨ **QARA**.

AHRAM-DAГ Maml. 14th c. **Ahram-daɣ** [اهرام ضاغ / Aχrām-dāġ] (Sauvaget 49). ✧ 'Holy, prohibited mountain' (= Pride like a holy mountain), cf. Osm. *ahram* (Ar.) 'Kutsal, özel yerler, topraklar' (Özön) + Osm. *dağ* 'mountain' (Ibid.), Sauvaget 49: „la montagne des Pyramides". ⇨ **TAГ**.

AX-BULAT see **AQ-BULAT**

AX-ČUBAR see **AQ-ČUWAR**

AX-ČURA see **AQ I.**

AX-KEREY Chuv. 18th-19th c. **Aχ-kerey** [Ахкерей] (Magn. 30); Chuv. 18th-19th c. **Aχ-kirey** [Ахкирей] (Magn. 30). ✧ 'White/honest-nobleman'. ⇨ **AQ I.** + **KERÄY**.

AX-KİBEK Tat.? 1572 **Aχ-kibek** [Муртазалей Ахкибековъ], a prince, christened as Mihail Kajbulin (DAI I, 381). ✧ 'White bran/shorts'? ⇨ **AQ I.** + **KEBEK?**

AX-KİLDA see **AQ-KİLDİ**

AX-KİREY see **AX-KEREY**

AX-KÜBEK see **AQ-KÖBEK**

AX-MOLA see **AQ I.**

AX-PAY see **AQ I.**

AX-PARЇS see **AQ-BARS**

AX-PARS see **AQ-BARS**

AX-POLDЇ Tat.? 1556 **Aχ-poldï** [Ахполдей] (PSRL XIII, 265). ✧ 'He/she became (was born) white/honest'. ⇨ **AQ I.** + **BOLDЇ**.

AX-SAN see **AQ-SAN**

AX-TĀN see **AQ-TĀN**

AX-TİMER see **AQ-TEMİR**

AX-TİMİR see **AQ-TEMİR**

AXALLЇ Trkm. **Aχallï** [Ахаллы] (Sopieva 180). ✧ 'From Aχal; born in Aχal' cf. the placename *Aχal* + suff. *-lï*.

AXAN see **AQAN**

AXANЇM see **AГA**

AXAR Kzk. **Aχar** [Ахаръ], fem. (Sb. Syr-D. IX, 50). ✧ 'Be/become white!' cf. Alt., Hak., Kirg., Kzk., Tat., etc. *aɣar-* 'weiss werden, bleich werden' (Radl. I, 145), also Rásonyi, Imp., p. 237.

AXЇMBET see **AQЇMBET**

AXЇN see **AQЇN**

AXЇNAY Kzk. 18th c. - 19th c. **Aχïnay** [Ахынай] (Tynyšp. 72, 75). ⇨ **AQЇN?** + suff. *-ay*.

AXMAN see **AQMAN**

AXMER Bashk. 20th c. **Aχmär** [Ахмəр / Ахмар] (Sprav. Im. 69); Bashk. 1759 **Aχmer** [Ахмер Кадырметев] (MIB IV/2, 26); Bashk. 1776 **Aχmer** [Ахмер Юлдашев] (MIB V, 51); Bashk. 1779, 1780 **Aχmer** [Ахмер Козяков (Кузяков, Кузиков)], from the village Kozjakovo (MIB V, 88, 106); Bashk. 1783, 1784 **Aχmer** [Ахмер Атянев] (MIB V, 139, 152). ✧ 'Red, redish' cf. Ar. احمـر (Budagov).

AXMET Karakh. 13th c. **Aχmad** [aḥmad], Edib Ahmed ibn Mahmud Yükneki, the author of the poem 'Atäbätu 'l-ḥaqāyïq (DTS); Tat.(Lit.) 1593 **Aχmet** [Хозбей Охметевичъ Адамовичъ] (Lit. Tat. 168); Nog. 20th c. **Aχmet** [Şikar / Шыкъар (!) Амеш (!) къызы / Шыкыр Амитова], father of one of Baskakov's informants from the aul of Nökis (Bask., Nog. 143); Nog. 20th c. **Aχmet-jan** [Муса Батал улы Ахметджан / Муса Беталович Ахметджанов], one of Baskakov's informants from the aul of Qañlï (Bask., Nog. 143); Kirg. **Aqmat** [Акмат] (Jud. 260,

480); Kirg. **Aqmat-bek** [Акматбек] (Jud. 636); Alt. 19th-20th c. **Aqmet** [Акмет] (OjrRS 207); Kkalp. 20th c. **Ämet** [Әмет] (KkRS 772); Bashk. 1675 **Emet** [Сюергул Еметов] (MIB I, 200). ✧ Ahmad (Ar.) 'The Most Praised', one of the names of Muhammad (Ahmed). See also АГАН-АМЕТ, ČAY-AXMET, ER-AMET, QAL-AXMET, QOĴA-AXMET, KUL-AXMAT, SEN-EXMET, SENT-AXMET, TÄŽÏ-AXMET, TEN-AXMET, TÏL-AXMED.

AXŠA see **AQČA**

AXŠALÏ   Nog. 20th c. **Axšalï** [Ахшалы Аджыкай келинъи / Ахшалы Ажекаева], one of Baskakov's informants from the aul of Qutlubay (Bask., Nog. 144). ✧ 'Having money; rich' cf. Crm., Tat. *aqčalï* 'Geld habend', Alt., Kirg. *aqčalü* 'Geld habend, reich' (Radl. I, 122). ⇨ AQČA + suff. -lï.

AXTEY   Bashk. 1659 **Axtey** [Карьмышка (Кармышка) Ахтеевъ], a tarχan (Vel.-Zern., Bašk. 37, 38). ✧ 'White little man'? ⇨ AQ I. + suff. -tey?

AXUNĴAQ   Kzk. 19th c. **Axunĵaq** [Ахунджакъ] (SODž. 156). ✧ 'Little imam, preacher; schoolmaster'. ⇨ AXUND + dim. suff. -ĵaq.

AXUND   Kkalp. 19th c. **Aɣum-bay** (<Aɣun-bay) [Джума Мурадъ Агумбаевъ] (Grod., Pril. 141); Kkalp. 19th c. **Aɣum-bay** (<Aɣun-bay) [Джума Мурад Агумбаев] (Grod., Pril. 141); Kkalp. 1750 **Aɣun** [Агун Мрак шах] (MIKk. 221); Kzk. 1819 **Aɣun-bay** [Агунбай] (MIK IV, 325); Az. 19th c. **Aχund** [Feth-Ali Achundov] (Mende 173). ✧ 'Imam, preacher; schoolmaster' Used also as a component of personal names; cf. Chag., Az. etc. *aχun, aχund* (< P. اخوند) 'der Obermulla, Achun' (Radl. I, 135), Osm. *ahund* 'theologian, preacher, schoolmaster in Iran' (TED).

AÏMBET see **AYÏMBET**

AY see **AY**

AY   Oghuz 13th c. **Ay**, one of the sons of the legendary Oghuz Khagan (Oğuz K. Dest. 15, DTS); Karakh. **Ay** [Ay] (MK/Atalay 831); Karakh. 11th c. **Ay** [Ai], a slave (MK/Brock. 240, MK/Atalay 831); Alt. **Ay**, fem. (Katanov, Otč. 11); Hak.(Sag.) 19th-20th c. **Ay** [Ai], a folklore hero whose brothers were Kün and Ot (Proben IX, 220); Oghuz? 1175 **Ay-aba** [اى ابه], Jamāladdīn ~, the mamluk (gulām?) of Atabek Pehliwān (Rāwandī 331, 340, 344 etc., Ahbar 122, 123); Selj. 1153, 1160 **Ay-aba** [اىابه /اى به / ایبه] / ал-Муайид Ай-аба / Айба Муайид], emir Al-Muayyid ~, ruler of Nishapur (Juwaynī II, 15, 16, 17-19, Abulfidā III, 578-79, ᶜAwfī I, 302, MIT I, 324, 356, 357, 390, 392-404, 405, 407, 408, 437, 445); Hak. 19th-20th c. **Ay-araχ** [Айарахъ], fem. (Titov 202); Alt., Hak. 19th-20th c. **Ay-arïɣ**, fem. (Radl. I, 5); Tuv. 19th c. **Ay-arïɣ** [Айарыгъ], daughter of Ay-qan in a Soyot tale (Potanin IV, 570); Bashk. 1785 **Ay-bay** [Еркей Айбаев] (MIB V, 170); Maml.

14th c. **Ay-bala** [ایبلا / Aybala], fem. (Tarĵ/Houtsma 57, Tarĵ/Toparlı 43); Kzk. 19th c. **Ay-bala** [Айбала] (Grod., Pril. 194); Kirg. **Ay-bala** [Айбала] (Jud. 956); Uyg. **Ay-bäg** [Ay Bäg] (Zieme, Mat. I, 74); Bashk. 20th c. **Ay-bäk / Ay-bik** [Айбәк / Айбик] (Kusimova 29); Maml. 14th c. **Ay-be** [ایبا / Ayba] (Tarĵ/Houtsma 57, Tarĵ/Toparlı 42); Maml. 14th c. **Ay-beg / Ay-bek** [ایبك / Aybeg] (Tarĵ/Houtsma 57, Tarĵ/Toparlı 42); Oghuz 1192/93 **Ay-bek** [العزیزی ایبك], mamlūk/gulām (=slave) of al-Malik al-Aᶜziz (Ibn Šaddād, Nawād.: RHCHor III, 308, 333); Selj. 1094 **Ay-bek** [Ibek?], Yusuf ibn ~ from Haleb (Weil, Chalif. III, 151); Selj. 1193 **Ay-bek** [ایبك الافطس] (Ibn Šaddād, Nawād.: RHCHor III, 365); Selj. 1194 **Ay-bek** [ایبك الصلاحى] (Ibn al-Athīr/Tornb. XII, 77); Selj. 1201 **Ay-bek** [ایبك قطب الدین الغورى] (Ibn al-Athīr/Tornb. XI, 115, XII, 61, 68, 111 ff.); Selj. 1203 **Ay-bek** [ایبك غلام], sultan's governor in Sind (Qazw. 411, 412); Selj. 1223 **Ay-bek** [ایبك الشامى] (Ibn al-Athīr/Tornb. XII, 270, 285); Maml. 1218, 1228/29 **Ay-bek** [ایبك], Izzaddīn Ay-bek, Ašrāf's mamlūk (Ibn al-Athīr/Tornb. XII, 222, 317, Ibn al-Athīr, Atab.: RHCHor II/1, 177-78, Abulfar./Budge I, 374, Juwaynī II, 176, 179); Maml. 1250-57 **Ay-bek** [ایبك التركمانى], Izzaddīn Ay-bek al-Turkmānī, a Mamluk sultan in Turānshāh,,s days (Iyās I, 87, 90, 96, II, 70, 210, Makrīzī I, 2, Weil, Chalif. I, 4-8); Maml. 13th c. - 14th c.? **Ay-bek** [التفلسى ایبك], ~ al-Tiflīsī (Duqmaq:RHCHor IV, 96); Maml. 1252 **Ay-bek** [ایبك الد ویدار الصغیر], Mujāhidaddīn ~ (Fakhrī 74, 111, 453, 454); Maml. 1259 **Ay-bek** [ایبك الافرم الصالحى], Izzaddīn Ay-bek, the commander of the fortress of Cairo (Iyās I, 99, 109, 119, Duqmaq:RHCHor IV, 18, 19, Ibn Taghrīb. VI, 445, Weil, Chalif. I, 109-10, Zetterst. 16, 23); Maml. 1286, 1294 **Ay-bek** [ایبك الموصلى], Izzaddīn ~ the regent of Karak (Makrīzī III, 83); Maml. 1293, 1307 **Ay-bek** [ایبك الخازندار طوید], regent in Tarabulūs, treasurer, died in 1307 (Iyās I, 115, Zetterst. 23, Makrīzī III, 145, IV, 114, 271); Maml. 1294 **Ay-bek** [ایبك حتاىى], Hisāmaddīn (RaD/Jahn 42); Maml. 1298 **Ay-bek** [ایبك الموصلى], Abdullah's son, a regent in Tripolis, where his mausoleum was built (Mayer 83, Sobernh. I, 84); Maml. 1299 **Ay-bek** [ایبك الموصلى], Izzaddīn. an emir (Dawād. 13); Maml. 1302 **Ay-bek** [ایبك والى البرید], Izzaddīn ~ Neĵibi, the chief of the post in Damascus (Makrīzī IV, 194); Maml. 1303 **Ay-bek** [ایبك الحموى], Izzaddīn ~, an emir (Dawād. 113); Maml. 1309 **Ay-bek** [ایبك الخزندار], Izzaddīn ~ an emir, treasurer (Dawād. 205); Maml. 1309/10 **Ay-bek** [ایبك], Izzaddīn ~ al-Baɣdādī, envoy from Baybars II (Iyās I, 151, 174, Zetterst. 97, Weil, Chalif. I, 282);

Maml. 1325 **Ay-bek** [ايبك الجمالى] (Zetterst. 176, 196); Maml. 1330 **Ay-bek** [ايبك الحسامى], Izzaddīn (Zetterst. 201); Maml. 1332 **Ay-bek** [عزلدين أيبك] (Dawād. 366); Maml. 1340/41 **Ay-bek** [ايبك الاشترا] (Iyās I, 174); Maml. 1345 **Ay-bek** [ايبك المصرى نا ظر لـحـرمين], Izzaddīn ~ from Egypt (Berchem, Jér. II, 426, 430); Maml. 14th c. **Ay-bek** [ايبك العزى], Izzaddīn ~, the coqueror (Zetterst. 1); Maml. 1467/68 **Ay-bek** [ايبك الملك المعز] (Ibn Taghrīb. VII, 842); Chag. 15th c. **Ay-bek** [Ibak / Ибекъ Ибрахим], a Shaybanid sultan, rival of Shaybanī khan (Šejb. LXVII, Togan, UTT 361, 493); Trkm. 1707 **Ay-bek** [ايبك] (Refik, Anad. 141); Kzk. 19th c. **Ay-bek** [Айбекъ] (SOV 24); Kzk. 1870 **Ay-bek** [Бака Айбеков] (Grod., Pril. 129); Selj. / Turk. 13th c., 1308/1309, 1312 **Ay-bek** [ايبك لرومى], Oghuz (Türkmen) emir from Anatolia (Iyās I, 148, Zetterst. 20, 24, Dawād. 250); Oghuz/Trkm. 1247 **Ay-bek / Ay-beg?** [Aybeg], envoy [„nuntius Tartar"] to Pope Innocent IV from the Tatar prince of Persia „Bajothnay" (Reg. Hieros. 303); Selj. 12th c. **Ay-bek / Ay-beg?** [ايبه] (Muh. Ibrahim 104); Selj. 12th c. **Ay-bek / Ay-beg?** [ايبه ايازى] (Muh. Ibrahim 108, 116); Selj. 12th c. **Ay-bek / Ay-beg?** [دراز / ا يبك /], Bahāaddīn ~ Ayāzī (Muh. Ibrahim 62, 63); Selj. 12th c. **Ay-bek / Ay-beg?** [دراز ايبك] (Muh. Ibrahim 62, 63); Maml 1261 **Ay-bek / Ay-beg** ['Aîbâg], Izzaddīn. the lord of 'Emâdîâh (Abulfar./Budge I, 442); Selj. / Khorezm.? 12th c. **Ay-bek / Ay-beg?** [ايبه], Ǧamāladdīn ~ (Muh. Ibrahim 52, Juwaynī I, 114 /116/); Chuv. 18th-19th c. **Ay-bekey** [Айбекей] (Magn. 25); Tat. 20th c. **Ay-bikä** [Айбикэ], fem. (Sattarov); Bashk. 1738 **Ay-bikä** [Айбика], fem. (MIB III, 380); Tat. 1539/40 **Ay-bikäč** [اى بكاج / Ай-бикäч], fem. (Jusupov 64); Kzk. 19th c. **Ay-bike** [Айбике], fem. (AOO 38); Kkalp. 20th c. **Ay-böke** [Айбөке], fem. (KkRS 777); Selj. 1136 **Ay-čur** [ايجور كند افرنجى] (Qalānisi 259, 277); Tat. 20th c. **Ay-jamal** [Айжамал], fem. (Sattarov); Kzk. **Ay-jan** [Айджанъ], fem. (ІОАІЁК XXII, 643); Kzk. 19th c. **Ay-jigit** [Ай Джигитъ] (Grod., Pril. 111); Maml. 14th c. **Ay-dägin / Ay-digin** [ايدكين / آيدكين / Aydigin] (Tarǰ/Houtsma 57, Tarǰ/Toparlı 42, Sauvaget 40); Shor 19th-20th c. **Ay-ergek** (Dyrenkova 60); Trkm. 20th c. **Ay-gül** [Aygül], fem. (Zaj. 1971, 339); Kkalp. 20th c. **Ay-gül** [Айгул], fem. (KkRS 777); Kirg. **Ay-γaniš** [Айганыш], fem. (Jud. 28); Kzk. 19th c. **Ay-γul** [Айгул] (AOK 10); Oghuz/Trkm. 13th c. **Ay-χan** [اى خـان / Ай-хан], Oγuz-qan's son (RaD I/1, 76, Abulγ./Kon. 425, 510, 515); Alt. 19th c. **Ay-χan** (Verb., In. 139, 140, 145); Kzk. 19th c. **Ay-χanïm** [Aï-Khanym / Айханым], fem. (Levšin III, 96, Levchine

356); Selj. 12th c.? **Ay-χatun** [اى خـاتون], two of Saladin's concubines bore the name ((after Nuwairī) Makrīzī I, 2); Khorezm. 14th c. **Ay-χatun**, one of Rašidaddīn's daughters (Browne 84); Trkm. 18th c. **Ay-χoǰa** [Ай-ходжа], brother of Kün-χoǰa (MIT II, 208, 209, 210); Oghuz 13th c. **Ay-qaγan**, in the Oghuz-legend (Oğuz K. Dest. 11); Karakh. 11th c. **Ay-qaγan**, fem. (Radl. II, 72, DTS); Alt., Hak. 19th-20th c. **Ay-qan** [Ai-Kān] (Radl. I, 5, 71); Hak. 19th-20th c. **Ay-qan** (Radl. II, 105, HRS 348); Tuv. 19th c. **Ay-qan**, in a Soyot folktale (Potanin IV, 569); Kzk./?Kirg. 19th c. **Ay-qazï** [Айкази] (Grod., Pril. 180); Kzk. 19th c. **Ay-qïz** [Ай-кызъ], fem. (Potanin, Pred. 94); Kirg. **Ay-qoǰo** [Айкожо] (Jud. 48); Hak.(Sag.) 19th c. **Ay-qō** [Ai Ko], fem. (Proben IX, 343-346); Uyg. 8th c. **Ay-qunčuy**, fem. (Müller, Pfahl. 23); Alt., Hak. 19th-20th c. **Ay-mergen** [Ai-Märgän] (Radl. I, 5); Kkalp. 20th c. **Ay-mïrza** [Аймырза] (KkRS 772); Uzb. 1887 **Ay-mïrza** [Ай-мирза] (Moskal'cev 34); Alt. **Ay-mögö** (Radl. II, 313); Alt. 19th c. **Ay-mökö** [Ай-Моко-богатырь], a folklore hero (bogatyr) (Verb., In. 145, 153, 154); Alt., Hak. 19th-20th c. **Ay-mökö** (Radl. I, 5); Kzk. 19th c. **Ay-pay** [Айпай] (SODž. 10); Maml. 14th c. **Ay-sili** [ايسلى / Ayseli] (Tarǰ/Houtsma 78, Tarǰ/Toparlı 44); Uyg. **Ay-sïlïγ** [Ay Sïlïġ] (EUTS); Tat. **Ay-sïlu** [Aysélu], fem. (Kúnos, Volksm. 106); Tat. 20th c. **Ay-sïlu** [Айсылу], fem. (Sattarov 29); Trkm. 20th c. **Ay-soltan** [Aysoltan], fem. (Zaj. 1971, 337); Kkalp. 20th c. **Ay-suluw** [Айсулуў], fem. (KkRS 777); Kirg. **Ay-sulū** [Айсулуу], fem. (Jud. 80); Bashk.(< Tat.?) 18th c. **Ay-sülä** [Айсюля Кулушев] (MIB IV/1, 174); Oghuz/Trkm. 1163 **Ay-tegin** [Ай-тегин], governor of Herat (MIT I, 402, 403); Selj. 1063, 1070/1071 **Ay-tegin** [ايتكين السليما نى], a governor of Baghdad (Ibn al-Athīr/Tornb. X, 23, 62, Bondārī 44, 80, Kamāladdīn: RHCHor II, 22, 23, 31, Rāwandī 106, 109); Selj. 1065, 1102, 1103 **Ay-tegin** [ايتكين الحلبى غلام تتش], Ay-tegin al-Halebī, the servant (slave) of Tutuš, he occupies the fortress of Œmèse (Ibn al-Athīr/Tornb. X, 169, 227, Kamāladdīn: RHCHor III, 591, Kamāladdīn II, 147); Selj. 1084/85, 1104/05 **Ay-tegin** [غلام تتش] (Qalānisi 117, 145, 149); Selj. 1105 **Ay-tegin** [ايدكين ايتكين], born in Haleb, the liege lord of Bosra (Ibn al-Athīr: RHCHor I, 224); Selj. 1131/32 **Ay-tegin** [ايتكين / Aîtikîn], a eunuch executed by sultan Sandjar (1117-1157) (Ibn al-Athīr, Atab.: RHCHor II/2, 81); Selj. 1160 **Ay-tegin** [ايتكين ماهروى], an emir made blind by Muχammad II (1153-1159) ibn Melikshah III (1152-1153) (Qazw. 453); Maml. 1260, 1261, 1264 **Ay-tegin** [البندقدارى / ايدكين], emir, nā°ib of Aleppo or/and Damascus, (d. in 1285) (Sīrat 122 (34), Abulfidā IV, 632-33, Weil,

Abbas I, 23, 31, Makrīzī II, 13, III, 82); ⇨. Maml. 1281 **Ay-tegin**, Alāaddīn ~ Fakhrī, an emir (Makrīzī III, 43); Maml. 1325 **Ay-tegin** [ايدكين], Izzaddīn (Zetterst. 188, 189); Maml. 1334 **Ay-tegin** [ايدكين] (Dawād. 378); Kzk. 19th c. **Ay-tekin** [Нарбай Айтекинъ] (Grod., Pril. 195); Uyg. 1288 **Ay-terim**, „Frau des Juchanan Bešgu" (Chwol., Syr.-nest. 32); Uyg. 1316 **Ay-terim**, fem. (Chwol., Syr.-nest. 21); Kkalp. 20th c. **Ay-žamal** [Айжамал], fem. (KkRS 777); Kzk. **Ay-žan** [Айжан], beautiful daughter of a khan (Žirm., Epos 407); Kkalp. 20th c. **Ay-žan** [Айжан], fem. (KkRS 777); *TN:* Kzk. **Ay-bikä** (Karta JAR XI); *TN:* Kzk. **Ay-jan** [Айджанъ] (Karta JAR XI); *TN:* Chag.? **Ay-χanïm** [Ai-Khánim], ruins of a fort called Ai-Khánim (Tar. Rashidi 220,221). ✧ 'Moon' As the first part of compound (mainly female) personal names it has got methaphorical meanings such as 'nice, good, pleasant pretty girl (woman)'. Used also as a secondary component of female names referring to the female sex of them (see Secondary Components). In the system of symbols of the eastern peoples the 'full moon' symbolizes the nice-looking face of a girl. *Ay* as component of personal names may as well mean: 'pretty, beautiful, dear, noble; saint, sacred; white, clean; bright; precious; rich; happy, lucky' etc. (Sattarov). According to an old tradition the children born in the evening after the Moon rose or by full Moon were given names containing *ay* (Ibid. 26-27). *Ay-bek, Ay-beg, Ay-bäg* 'Moon' *-bek*; 'Moon-prince' (Tarǰ/Houtsma 57, Blochet, Poppe 1252, Németh, HMK 132, Sauvaget 39, Salemann, Noch einmal d. Seldsch. Uhr. 224, cf. also -BEK). *Ay-qan* 'Mondfürst' (Radl. I, 5, 71). The Trk. fem. name *~χatun* equals with Mo. *Saraχatun* (Poppe 1253). *Ay-gül* 'Moon-flower' (Baskakov: OSA 139, Nikonov 156-157). *Ay-tegin (-tekin)* probably means 'a prince with a nice face', 'prince whose face is nice like the Moon', cf. the meanings given by the editors of the sources and other authors: 'belle lune' (Ibn al-Athīr/Tornberg: RHCHOr. I, 224), ما هروى (ماهروى) *~tegin* 'au visage aussi beau que la lune' (Qazw. 453), 'prince lune' (Sauvaget 40), 'Hold-herceg' [=Moon-prince] (Németh, HMK 132-33). Some editors read the name as *Aïdekin* (Quatremère), *ay-dägin* (Sauvaget) etc. See also **AYDÏÑ-AY, AQ-AY, ALTÏN-AY, AWSUN-AY, BEŠ-AY, GÜL-AY, XURSAN-AY, İT-AY, YARQÏN-AY, YÜZ-AY, KÜL-AY, KÜMÜŠ-AY, QURBAN-AY, SABAN-AY, ŠADAM-AY, TOBA-AY, TOΓUZ-AY, TULΓUN-AY, TURDÏ-AY, UMAQ-AY, UMSUN-AY, URMAN-AY.**

AY-AYAZ Uyg. 8th c. **Ay-ayaz-ïnal** (Müller, Pfahl. 23). ✧ 'With nice-looking face', in Müller's interpretation: 'Moonlit night' (Müller, Pfahl. 32). ⇨ **AY + AYAZ.**

AY-ALTÏN Alt. 19th c. **Ay-altïn** [Ай-Алтын богатырь], folkl., the khan of the 3rd heaven (Verb., In. 139); Hak. 19th-20th c. **Ay-altïn** [Аялтын] (HRS 348). ✧ 'Moon-gold'. ⇨ **AY + ALTÏN.**

AY-ARAX see **AY**

AY-BADAQ Kirg. **Ay-badaq** [Айбадак], fem. (Jud. 230, 699). ✧ 'Moon-Badaq'? ⇨ **AY + BADAQ.**

AY-BAQ Kzk. 19th c. **Ay-baq** [Айбакъ Исаходжаевъ] (Grod., Pril. 198). ✧ 'Moon-luck (hapiness)'. ⇨ **AY + BAQ.**

AY-BALAQ Maml. 1314 **Ay-balaq** [علا'الـدين الايـبلتى], a Mamluk envoy to Desht-i Kipchak (Tizeng. I, 256, 265 /after Al-Malik An-Nāsir/). ✧ I. 'Moon-Fish'? II. 'Moon-leg'? ⇨ **AY + BALAQ.**

AY-BARS Maml. 14th c. **Ay-bars** [ايبرس / Aybars] (Tarǰ/Houtsma 57, Tarǰ/Toparlı 41). ✧ 'Moon-panther' (Németh, HMK 132). ⇨ **AY + BARS.**

AY-BAS see **AY-BAŠ**

AY-BAŠ Kzk. 19th c. **Ay-bas** [Айбасъ] (SODž. 28); Kzk. 19th c. **Ay-bas** [Айбасъ] (SOK 102); Kzk. 19th c. **Ay-bas** [Айбасъ] (SOV 12); Kzk. 19th c. **Ay-bas-qul** [Ai-Baskul / Ай-бас-кулъ] (Potanin, Pred. 109, Proben III, 229 /270/); Kzk. 19th c. **Ay-bas-pay** (SOK 184); Kzk. 1792 **Ay-baš** [Айбаш] (MIK IV, 137); Crm.(Tat.) 1636 **Ay-baš** [ايباش محمد] (Vel.-Zern., Crim. 175); Kirg./Uzb.? 19th c. **Ay-baš** [Айбашъ Атакараевъ] (SKSO VIII, 219, 223); Tat. 20th c. **Ay-baš / Ay-buš** [Айбашев / Айбушев], family names (Sattarov); *EN:* Kzk. 18th c. - 19th c. **Ay-bas** [Айбасъ] (Tynyšp. 73). ✧ 'Moon-head; having a head like the Moon; full moon'. ⇨ **AY + BAŠ.**

AY-BER Uyg. 1339 **Ay-ber**, fem. (Chwol., Syr.-nest. (NF) 38). ✧ 'Moon-give'? cf. Kzk. PNs *Ay-berdi, Aybergen* (Žanuzakov-Esbaeva). ⇨ **AY.**

AY-BOL Kzk. 19th c. **Ay-bol** [Айболъ] (SOK 272); Tat. 20th c. **Ay-bul** [Айбул] (Sattarov). ✧ 'Be (like the) Moon! Be as beautiful as the Moon' (Rásonyi, Imp. 238, Sattarov). ⇨ **AY + BOL.**

AY-BUΓA Selj. 11th c. **Ay-buγa** [Ay Buğa], an emir at the time of Alp-Arslan (1063-1072) (Ahbar 21). ✧ 'Moon-bull'. ⇨ **AY + BUQA.**

AY-BUL see **AY-BOL**

AY-BULAY Uzb. 19th c. **Aybulay** [Ядыгеръ Айбулаевъ] (SKSO III, 170). ✧ 'Moon-?'. ⇨ **AY + BULAY.**

AY-BULAT Chuv. 1737 **Abulat** [Абулатъ] (Alatyr. 135); Tat. 20th c. **Ay-bulat** [Айбулатов], family name (Sattarov); Bashk. 1719 **Ay-bulat** [Айбулат Менглибаев] (MIB III, 186); Bashk. 1764 **Ay-bulat** [Айбулатов] (MIB IV/2, 104); Alt. 19th c. **Ay-molot** [Ай-Молот-богатырь], a bogatyr (hero) (Verb., In. 139, 153). ✧ 'Moon-steel'. ⇨ **AY + BULAT.**

AY-BUŠ see **AY-BAŠ**

AY-BUTA Kzk. 19th c. **Ay-buta** [Айбута Рахметов]

(Grod., Pril. 199). ❖ 'Moon-camel-foal'. ⇨ **AY + BUTA.**

AY-BÜRČÜL Hak.(Sag.) **Ay-bürčül** [Акъ-Сабдаръ-Адтыгъ-Айбюрчюлъ], fem. (Kostrov 237). ❖ 'Having a moon-like (=nice) face' (Kostrov); cf. AY + *bürčül*. The whole name *Aq-sabdar-adtïγ Ay-bürčül* means: (A girl) with a moon-like face having yellow (fawn-coloured)? horse. (cf. Hak. *aχ sabdar* 'сиво игреневый' (HRS), Kzk., Shor *šabdar* 'ein hellgelbes Pferd mit weissem Schwanze und weissen Weichen' (Radl. IV, 989), Kzk. *šabdar* 'игрений, игреневый (масть лошади)' (KzRS). ⇨ **AY.**

AY-ČÄČÄK see **AY-ČEČÄK**

AY-ČEČÄK Uyg. **Ay-čäčäk** [Ay çäçäk], fem. (EUTS); Uyg. 8th c. **Ay-čäčäk**, a princess (Müller, Pfahl. 10); Khorezm. 1231 **Ay-čäčäk** [اى جيجاك], mother of the shah Jelāleddīn Meñgü-berdi (Nasawī 40); Tat. 20th c. **Ay-čäčäk** [Айчәчәк], fem. (Sattarov). ❖ 'Flower, beautiful like the Moon' (Sattarov). ⇨ **AY + ČEČÄK.**

AY-ČUR see **AY**

AY-ČÜRÖK Kirg. **Ay-čürök** [Айчүрөк], fem. (Jud. 67, 487). ❖ 'Moon-Duck'. ⇨ **AY + ČÜRÖK.**

AY-DALAY Alt. **Ay-dalay** [Аідалаі], fem. (Radl. I, 655). ❖ 'Moon-Sea/Loss'. ⇨ **AY + TALAY.**

AY-DAŠ see **AY-TAŠ**

AY-DEÑİZ Selj. 1205 **Ay-deñiz** [التـدكز ىاى] (Ibn al-Athīr/Tornb. XII, 155,164-66). ❖ 'Moon-Sea'. ⇨ **AY + TEÑİZ.**

AY-DOΓDÏ see **AY-TOΓDÏ**

AY-DOΓDU see **AY-TOΓDÏ**

AY-DOΓMÏŠ see **AY-TOΓMÏŠ**

AY-DOΓMUŠ see **AY-TOΓMÏŠ**

AY-DOL Hak. 19th-20th c. **Ay-dol** [Айдол] (HRS 348). ❖ 'Moon-be full'? cf. Hak. *tol-* 'наполняться, исполняться' (HRS). ⇨ **AY.** See also **AY-DOLAY, AY-TOLAN, AY-TOLDÏ, AY-TOLÏY, AY-TOLU, AY-TOLUM, AY-TOLUZU.**

AY-DOLAY Hak. 19th-20th c. **Ay-dolay** [Ai-Толузу (Ai-Долаі)] (Radl. I, 5); Hak.(Koyb.) 19th c. **Ay-dolay** [Ай-долай] (Katanov, Otč. II, 12-15); Hak.(Sag.) 19th-20th c. **Ay-dōlay** [Ai-долаі] (Proben IX, 242, 345). ❖ 'Full-Moon' (Radl. I, 5; Butanaev), cf. Hak.(Sag.) *tola* 'die Fülle; voll' (Radl. III, 1191). ⇨ **AY + TOLAY I.?** See also **AY-TOLÏY.**

AY-DOS see **AY-DOST**

AY-DOST Kzk. 19th c. **Ay-dos** [Айдос] (MIK IV, 312, 319); Kzk. 19th c. **Ay-dos** [Айдос] (SOK 114); Kkalp. 20th c. **Ay-dos-baba** [Айдосбаба] (KkRS 772); Kzk. 19th c. **Ay-dos-batïr** (Ljutš 139); Kkalp. 1856 **Ay-dost-biy** [Айдост-бий] (MIT II, 559). ❖ 'Moon-friend'. ⇨ **AY + DOST.**

AY-DUA see **AY-DUWA**

AY-DUΓAN see **AY-TUΓAN**

AY-DUT Kuman 1329 **Ay-dut** [Aydud] (Anjou Okm. II, 404). ❖ 'Moon-Strawberry' (Németh, HMK 132, Rásonyi, Adalékok 129, Rásonyi, Anthr. 136). ⇨ **AY + DUT.**

AY-DUWA Kuman 1270 **Ay-duwa / Ay-dua** [Aydua, Edua, Cydua; puella Cumana], mistress of the Hungarian King László IV. (1272-1290) (SRH I, 473, 474, II, 44, 45). ❖ 'Moon-rise; The moon rises' (Rásonyi, KÖA 84, Ligeti 1986, 103, 116, 411, 412, 541), cf. Kuman *toγ-/tuv-* 'geboren werden' (CC). ⇨ **AY.**

AY-GİLDE see **AY-KELDİ**

AY-YARÏQ Kzk. 1785 **Ay-yarïq** [Айярыкъ] (MIK IV, 60). ❖ 'Moon-bright/light'. ⇨ **AY + YARUQ.**

AY-YÏLDÏS Alt. / Shor **Ay-yïldïs** [Ai-Jылдыс], fem. (Radl. I, 5). ❖ 'Moon-star' (Radl.). ⇨ **AY + YÏLDÏZ.**

AY-KEL Kzk. 19th c. **Ay-kel** [Айкель] (AOK 10). ❖ 'Moon-come'. ⇨ **AY + KEL.**

AY-KELDİ Bashk. 1709 **A-gilde** (<Ay-gilde) [Атламыш Агилдин] (MIB I, 204); Tat.? 1684 **A-gildey** (<Ay-gildey?) [Косенко Агельдѣевъ], servant (of noble origin) of prince Saltanbek Čerkasskij (DAI XI, 133); Bashk. 1664 **Ay-gilde** [Сеиткул Айгильдеев] (MIB I, 185); Chuv. 18th-19th c. **Ay-gildi** [Айгилда] (Magn. 25); Bashk. 1764 **Ay-gildi** [Байряш Айгильдин] (MIB IV/1, 287); Kzk.? 1737 **Ay-gildi** [Айгильдъ(а)], a captain (Nepljuev 427); Selj. 1100, 1147 **Ay-keldi** [آمـد صاحب يـنـال بـن ابـرهيم], İbrahim's son (Qalānisi 138, 167, 285). ❖ 'The moon has come (=risen)'. ⇨ **AY + KELDİ.**

AY-KÖLÜM Kirg. **Ay-kölüm** [Айкөлүм], one of Manas' names (epithets) (Jud. 76). ❖ 'My large-hearted, my noble-minded' cf. Kirg. *ayköl* 'великодушный, благородный' (<*ay* 'луна' + *köl* 'озеро') (Jud.). ⇨ **AY + KÜL (KÖL).**

AY-KŠİ Kzk. 1846 **Ay-kši** [Бикбулат Айкшиев], a mulla (MKOP 153). ❖ 'Moon-man'. ⇨ **AY + KİŠİ.**

AY-KÜMÜŠ Kirg. 20th c. **Ay-kümüš** [Айкүмүш], fem. (Kalilov 95).

AY-KÜN Alt., Shor 19th-20th c. **Ay-kün** (Radl. I, 5); Hak.(Sag.) **Ay-kün** [Ai Күн], one of the devils (Proben IX, 255-258). ❖ 'Moon-Sun'. ⇨ **AY + KÜN.**

AY-QAQ Hak. 19th-20th c. **Ay-qaq** [Айкакъ], fem. (Titov 223). ❖ 'Moon-?'. ⇨ **AY + QAQ?**

AY-QANAT Alt., Hak. 19th-20th c. **Ay-qanat** (Radl. I, 5). ❖ 'Moon-Wing'. ⇨ **AY + QANAT.**

AY-QARAQ Kirg.? 12th c. **Ay-qaraq** [ايقـراق / Айкаракъ], envoy of the Kirghiz to Djingis-khan (RaD/Ber. I, 131). ❖ 'Moon-eye/pupil; Moon-darling'. ⇨ **AY + QARAQ.**

AY-QÏLÏŠ Shor 19th-20th c. **Ay-qïlïš** (Dyrenkova 14). ❖ 'Moon-sable'. ⇨ **AY + QÏLÏČ.**

AY-QUT Turk. 1540 **Ay-γut** [ايغود / Aygud kethudâ], chief of the „Cemâat-i Gevherlü" according to a defter from Diyarbakır (Demirtaş 48); Oghuz 13th c. **Ay-γut-alp** [Aygutalp / Aykut Alp], one of Osman Bey's friends (Sevim-Yücel II, 3, 5, Erol II, 44); Turk. 1583 **Ay-qut / Ay-γut?** [ايـقود] (Ongan, Ank. I, 152). ✧ I. 'Moon-chance/luck (happiness)'; II. 'Reward, compensation, gift' (Erol II). ⇨ **AY + QUT.**

AY-QUTLUΓ Oghuz **Ay-qutluγ** [اى قوتلع] (Ālī 185, also Wittek 94.); Oghuz **Ay-qutluγ** [اى قتلغ] (Nešrī 185); Oghuz **Ay-qutluq** [ايـقو تـلق], forefather of the Ottoman dynasty (Āšikp. 5). ✧ 'Moon-lucky/happy, Moon-blessed'. ⇨ **AY + QUTLUΓ.**

AY-QUTLUQ see **AY-QUTLUΓ**

AY-MAΓAMBET Kzk. **Ay-maγambet** (Žirm., Epos 400). ✧ 'Moon-Mukhammed'. ⇨ **AY + MUXAMMED.**

AY-MANÏS see **AY-MAÑÏS**

AY-MAÑÏS Alt. 19th c. **Ay-mañïs / Ay-manïs** [Айманыс-богатырь] (Verb., In. 142, 145, 146, 148, 149, 162-165); Shor 19th-20th c. **Ay-mañïs / Ay-moñus?** (Radl. I, 891). ✧ 'Moon-Silk' cf. Alt., Koyb., Kacha *mañïs* 'die Seide' (Radl. I, 891). ⇨ **AY.**

AY-MEÑGÜ Uyg. 1270, 1336 **Ay-meñgü** [Aimangku, Ai-Magku, Ai mangu] (Chwol., Syr.-nest. 23, 78, 102). ✧ 'Moon-eternal'. ⇨ **AY + MEÑGÜ.**

AY-MEREKE Kkalp. 20th c. **Ay-mereke** [Аймереке], fem. (KkRS 777). ✧ 'Moon-feasting, Moon-festival'. ⇨ **AY + MEREKE.**

AY-MÏRZA see **AY**

AY-MOLOT see **AY-BULAT**

AY-MÖGÖ see **AY**

AY-MÖKÖ see **AY**

AY-MURAT Kkalp. 20th c. **Ay-mïrat** [Аймырат] (KkRS 772); Kkalp. 20th c. **Ay-murat** [Аймурат] (KkRS 772). ✧ 'Moon-Wish'. ⇨ **AY + MURAT.**

AY-NAZAR Kkalp. 20th c. **Ay-nazar** [Айназар] (KkRS 772). ✧ 'Moon-Glance'. ⇨ **AY + NAZAR.**

AY-NOΓO Alt. 19th c. **Ay-noγo** [Ай-Ного], a hero (Verb., In. 146). ✧ 'Moon-?'. ⇨ **AY.**

AY-NURA Kirg. 20th c. **Ay-nura** [Айнура], fem. (Nikonov: OSA 157). ✧ 'Moon-light, moon-beam'. According to data of 1969 in Frunze 91 girls out of 1000 were named so while in the northern territories of Khirgizia this amount was only 44. The presence of the name with other Turkic peoples (Az., Trkm., Kzk.) is much lower. ⇨ **AY + NUR** + fem. suff. *-a.*

AY-ÖLÜTČI Uyg. 12th c. - 14th c. **Ay-ölütči** [aj ölütči], god Yama's commander of the army (DTS). ✧ 'Moon-killer' cf. Uyg., Karakh. *ölütči* 'убийца' (DTS). ⇨ **AY.**

AY-PARČA Uzb. 19th c. **Ay-parča** [Айпарча], fem. (SKSO III, 150); Kkalp. 20th c. **Ay-parša** [Айпарша], fem. (KkRS 777). ✧ 'Moon-piece' cf. AY + Chag., Osm. *parča* 'das Stück, der Theil, das Fragment' (Radl. IV, 1157), Kkalp. *parša* 'кусок, клочок; обломок, осколок; обрывок' (KkRS). ⇨ **AY + PARČA.** See also **PARŠA-GÜL.**

AY-PARŠA see **AY-PARČA**

AY-PAS see **AY-BAŠ**

AY-SABAQ Shor 19th-20th c. **Ay-sabaq**, daughter of Aq-salγïn and the wife of Aba-qulaq in a legend (Dyrenkova 192). ✧ 'Moon-Thread'. ⇨ **AY + SABAQ.**

AY-SABAR Hak.(Sag.) 19th-20th c. **Ay-sabar** [Ai Sabar / Ai Сабар], a folklore hero, Kün-sabar's elder brother(?) (Proben II, 141 /143/). ✧ 'Moon-finger/toe' cf. Alt. *sabar* 'der Finger, Zeh' (Radl. IV, 416). ⇨ **AY + SABAR.** See also **KÜN-SABAR.**

AY-SABÏR Hak.(Sag.) 19th-20th c. **Ay-sabïr** [Ai Sabyr / Ai Сабыр], a folklore hero, Kün-sabïr's brother (Proben II, 71 /72/). ✧ 'Moon-Patience/strength'. ⇨ **AY + SABÏR.** See also **KÜN-SABÏR.**

AY-SALÏQ Kzk. 19th c. **Ay-salïq** [Айсалыкъ] (SODž. 104). ✧ 'Moon-Kind/honest'. ⇨ **AY + SALÏQ.**

AY-SARÏ Maml. 14th c. **Ay-sarï** [ايـنَساوُوْا / ايساوو Aysaru], fem. (Tarǰ/Houtsma 58, Tarǰ/Toparlı 44); Kzk. 19th c. **Ay-sarï** [Айсары] (SKSO VIII, 223); Kkalp. 20th c. **Ay-sarï** [Айсары], fem. (KkRS 777); *TN:* Kzk. **Ay-sarï** [Айсары], toponym, a settlement in the county of Kökčetau. Its name may originate from the ethnonym Ay-sarï, cf. Bay-sarï (Kojčubaev 19). ✧ I. 'Moon-yellow'; II. 'Blessed, bountiful, good, beautiful' (cf. Tarǰ/Toparlı 44: 'Mübarek gibi'). ⇨ **AY + SARÏ.** See also **BAY-SARÏ.**

AY-SÄNEM Kkalp. 20th c. **Ay-sänem** [Айсәнем], fem. (KkRS 777). ✧ 'My bright (sparkling) moon'. It is the parallel of P.-Ar. *Māh-i Sānā* 'Moon-brightness'. ⇨ **AY + SANAM.**

AY-SEREK Kzk. 19th c. **Ay-serek** [Айсерекъ] (SOK 278). ✧ 'Moon-Lively/careful'. ⇨ **AY + SEREK I.**

AY-TAY Kzk. 19th c. **Ay-tay** [Айтай] (SODž. 158); Uzb. 1854 **Ay-tay-bay** [Ай-Тай-бай] (Moskal'cev 40). ✧ 'Moon-foal'. ⇨ **AY + TAY** or suff. *-tay(2)?*

AY-TANSÏQ see **AY-TAÑSÏQ**

AY-TAÑSÏQ Kzk. 19th c. **Ay-tañsïq** [Айтансыкъ] (AOO 26). ✧ 'Moon-overjoyed, Moon-merry' cf. Kzk. *tañsïq* 'sich wundernd, vor Freude erregt; selten', Chag. *tañsuq* 'das Wunder, wunderbar' (Radl. III, 813-814). ⇨ **AY.**

AY-TAS see **AY-TAŠ**

AY-TAŠ Tat. 1754 **Ay-daš** [Айдаш] (MIB IV/1, 81); Tat.? 1764 **Ay-daš** [Айдаш Зюмаев] (MIB IV/1, 292); Tat. 20th c. **Ay-daš** [Айдашев] (Sattarov); Bashk. 1779, 1785 **Ay-daš** [Айдаш] (MIB V, 81, 166); Alt., Hak. 19th-20th c. **Ay-tas** [Ai-тас] (Radl. I, 5); Kzk. 18th c. - 19th c. **Ay-taš-bahadïr** [ايحا ش بها در],

from the Bay-baqtï tribe (MIK IV, 52, 540). ✧ 'Moon-Stone'; 'Moon-like nice and stone-like hard (child)' (Sattarov), cf. also Radl. I, 5, Barth., Turk. I, 254, Németh, HMK 132, Erol II. Sattarov regards *Aydaš* (<*ay* + suff. *-daš*) as a different name and explains it as 'Beautiful, nice like the Moon' (op. cit.). ⇨ **AY + TAŠ.**

AY-TÄÑRİ Uyg. 795-804 **Ay-täñri** (Ligeti, R. tör. nev. II-III (1979), 42); +.; ✧ 'Moon, Moon-God' cf. Uyg. *aj täŋri* 'божество Луна'; *Ai täñri-dä ülüg bulmiš qutluɣ bilgä*, the title of the Uygur ruler *Huai-sin qaɣan* in Chinese transcription (DTS). ⇨ **AY + TÄÑRİ.**

AY-TEL Bashk. 18th c. **Ay-del / Adel?** [Айдел (Адел) Калгулятов] (MIB III, 310); Kzk. 19th c. **Ay-tel-bay** [Айтельбай] (SOV 138). ✧ 'Moon-lonely (child)'. ⇨ **AY + TEL.**

AY-TELÄŠ Kzk. 1803, 1820 **Ay-teläš-biy** [Айтеляшъ-бий], one of the chiefs of the Jilder (Čümekey) tribe in Kiši Žüz (Sib. Vest. IX, 114, MIK IV, 514). ✧ 'Moon-wished/awaited (child)'? ⇨ **AY + TİLÄŠ.**

AY-TELEÜ Kzk. 19th c. **Ay-teleü** [Айтелеу] (SOK 300). ✧ 'Moon-wish'. ⇨ **AY + TİLÄW.**

AY-TEMİR Selj.? **Ay-demir** [ايدمـر], Falakuddīn Muhammad ibn ~ (Fakhrī 111, MSOS II-III.); Maml. **Ay-demir** [ايـدمـر الزردكاش], Izzaddīn ~, a nā'ib, in an inscription on a bronze stand (Mayer 87); Maml. 13th c. **Ay-demir** [ايـدمـر الاشـرفى], governor of Aleppo (Mayer 86); Maml. 1260, 1263 **Ay-demir** [ايدمـر], Izzaddīn ~ al-Halebī, emir, the nā'ib (viceroy) of Egypt, governor of Karak, commander of the fortress of Cairo (Makrīzī I, 116, 209, II, 13, Makrīzī, Khit. I, 383, Weil, Chalif. I, 19); Maml. 1271/72 **Ay-demir** [ايـدمـر الظا هـرى], nā'ib of Damascus (died in 1300 or 1303 at Shakhāb) (Aynī: RHCHor II/1, 245, Makrīzī IV, 223,224-5, Mayer 84-85); Maml. 1280 **Ay-demir** [Izz-eddin-Aïdemur-alhadj], an emir died in 1280 (Makrīzī III, 38, Weil, Chalif I, 127); Maml. 1282 **Ay-demir** [ايـدمـر الطهـا:] (Iyās I, 115); Maml. 1287, 1290 **Ay-demir** [Izz-eddin Aïdemur-Seïfi], Izzaddīn ~ „Seïfi", an emir, silaχdār, mutawalli of Kus? (Makrīzī III, 90, 106-8, Weil, Chalif. I, 166); Maml. 1294 **Ay-demir** [ايـدمـر الفخـرى] (Iyās I, 127); Maml. 1300 **Ay-demir** [ايـدمـر القشا ش], Aïdemur-Schemsi-Kaschschâsch Shakhāb, the governor of „Scharkiah" and „Garbiah" (Makrīzī IV, 224-5, Zetterst. 118); Maml. 1301 **Ay-demir** [ايـدمـر] (Iyās 143, 145); Maml. 1302, 1320 **Ay-demir** [ايدمـر الرفا] (Dawād. 88, Zetterst. 118); Maml. 1308 **Ay-demir** [ايـدمـر الحسامى] (Dawād. 155); Maml. 1308/09 **Ay-demir** [ايـدمـر الخطيرى], Izzaddīn ~, emir, the mosque in Bulaq bears his name (Iyās I, 148, 166, Makrīzī, Khit. I, 312, also Zetterst.); Maml. 1309 **Ay-demir** [ايـدمـر الـدوادار], Izzaddīn ~ al-Dawādār (Dawād. 185,

Zetterst. 37); Maml. 1310 **Ay-demir** [ايـدمـر الحطيرى] (Dawād. 211); Maml. 1310 **Ay-demir** [ايـدمـر الظاهـرى], Izzaddīn ~ al-ẓāhirī (Zetterst. 95); Maml. 1320 **Ay-demir** [ايدمـر اليونسى] (Zetterst. 145); Maml. 1320 **Ay-demir** [ايدمـر الكبكى] (Zetterst. 168, 184); Maml. 1320, 14th c. **Ay-demir** [ايـدمـر الـزر دكا ش] (Zetterst. 157); Maml. 1321 **Ay-demir** [الشحاعى نـاظر الحـرمين] [ايـدمـر] (Berchem, Jér. I, 250); Maml. 1327 **Ay-demir** [ايـدمـر دقـماق], an emir (Dawād. 343, 357, 377); Maml. 1331 **Ay-demir** [ايـدمـر اميـر خـازنـدار], emir (treasurer) (Iyās 166); Maml. 1332 **Ay-demir** [ايـدمـر السيفى] (Dawād. 369); Maml. 1334 **Ay-demir** [ايـدمـر], Izzaddīn ~ (Dawād. 378); Maml. 1340/41 **Ay-demir** [ايـدمـر النـا صـرى], Izzaddīn ~ (Iyās I, 175); Maml. 14th c. **Ay-demir** [ايـدمـر النـتيب] (Zetterst. 118); Maml. 14th c.? **Ay-demir** [ايـدمـر الشيخى] (Dawād. 299, Zetterst. 155); Maml. 14th c. **Ay-demir** [ايـدمـر العلاىى], Izzaddīn ~ (Zetterst. 149); Maml. 14th c. **Ay-demir** [ايـدمـر الصندى] (Zetterst. 155); Maml. 14th c.? **Ay-demir** [ايـدمـر العمرى], Izzaddīn ~ (Zetterst. 194); Maml. 14th c.? **Ay-demir** [ايـدمـر الكوندكى], Izzaddīn ~ (Zetterst. 164); Maml. 14th c. **Ay-demir** [الجمتدار] [ايـدمـر], name of 17 persons (Dawād. 354); Maml. 14th c. **Ay-demir** [ايـدمـر الصالـحى] (Duqmaq:RHCHor IV, 77); Maml. 14th c. **Ay-demir** [ايـدمـر المحيوى] (Duqmaq:RHCHor IV, 109, 110); Maml. 1361 **Ay-demir** [ايـدمـر الـدوادارالكيـر], from Great Dawādār (Iyās I, 209); Maml. 1366/67 **Ay-demir** [ايـدمـر الشامى], from Sham (Iyās I, 220); Maml. 1368/69 **Ay-demir** [ايـدمـر الخطايـى] (Iyās I, 224); Maml. 1373 **Ay-demir** [العزى ايـدمـر / Aydämür al-Ārūkī], died in 1374 being 70 years old, he had lots of dignities such as the nā'ib of Aleppo, Tripolis and the general commander of the army (Mayer 85-86, Sobernh. 118); Maml. 1373/74 **Ay-demir** [ايـدمـر], nā'ib of Tripolis (Iyās I, 228); Maml. 1376/77 **Ay-demir** [ايـدمـر الشمسى], commander of the fortress in Kairo (Zetterst. 213, Weil, Chalif. I, 527); Kmk. 1722 **Ay-demir** (PSZRI VI, 810); Crm. 17th c.? **Ay-demir** (Smirnov, Krym. 512); Tat.? 1651 **Ay-demir** [Айдемиръ], a murza (AI IV, 159); Maml. 1329-30 **Ay-demür** [ايـدمـون اميـر جنـدار / Âïdemoûr], an emir (of security, police) in Syria (Ibn Bat. II, 154); Maml. 14th c. **Ay-demür / Ay-dämür** [ايـدمـر / اَيْدَمُر / Aydemür] (Tarj/Houtsma 68, Tarj/Toparlı 42); 1698 **Ay-temir** [Айтемировъ], a Russian family-name of Turkic origin (DAI XII, 393); Bashk. 1713 **Ay-temir** [Айтемировъ] (MIB III, 100); Kzk. 19th c. **Ay-temir** [Айтемиръ] (SKSO VIII, 226); Oghuz 1354 **Ay-temür** [ا يتمور], emir, who rose against the Muzaffarids (Qazw. 660);

Crm. 1633 **Ay-temür** / **Ay-demir** [اىتیمور / Ай-Демиръ], Qan-temür's (Kantemir's) brother (Vel.-Zern., Crim. 117, Smirnov, Krym. 512); Turk. 1455 **Ay-temür** / **Ey-timür?** [اىتمور], Gökbilgin reads it as „Eytimür" (Gökb., Ed. 168); Tat. 20th c. **Ay-timer** [Айтимер] (Sattarov 29). ✧ 'Moon-iron' cf. Poppe: IAN 1927, 1253, Németh, HMK 132. ⇨ **AY** + **TEMİR**. See also **QAN-TEMİR**.

AY-TEMUS Hak. 19th-20th c. **Ay-temus** [Айтемусъ] (Titov 190). ✧ 'Moon-hero' (Titov). ⇨ **AY**. See also **KÜN-TEMUS**.

AY-TEMÜR see **AY-TEMİR**

AY-TEN Kzk. 19th c. **Ay-ten** [Айтенъ / Айтенов] (AOAtb. 22); Kzk. 19th c. **Ay-ten** [Айтен / Айтеновъ] (AOK 70); Kzk. 19th c. **Ay-ten** [Айтен / Айтеновъ] (AOO 30). ✧ 'Moon-body, Moon-figur' (Erol II), 'Having Moon-like body, beautiful' (Kaybullaev). ⇨ **AY** + **TEN**.

AY-TERÄK Chuv. 18th-19th c. **Ay-teräk** [Айтерякъ] (Magn. 25). ✧ 'Moon-support(er)'. ⇨ **AY** + **TİRÄK**.

AY-TES Hak.(Blt.) 19th-20th c. **Ai-tås** [Ai-тэс] (Proben IX, 613); Hak. 19th-20th c. **Ay-tes** [Айтес] (HRS 348). ✧ 'Moon-quick'. ⇨ **AY** + **TEZ**.

AY-TİNKE Kzk. 19th c. **Ay-tïnke** [Айтинке] (SODž. 82). ✧ I. 'Moon-(silver)-coin' cf. Uyg., Kzk., Tat. *tïn* 'ein Kopeken, ein Heller' (Radl. III, 1360); II. 'Moon-squirrel'? cf. Kuman, Chag., Hak., Turk. *tïn* 'das Eichhörnchen'. ⇨ **AY** + dim. suff. *-ke*.

AY-TOΓDÏ Selj. 12th c. **Ay-doγdï** [بن لمعروف بشمله / ايـدغـدى بـن كشطغان] (Bondārī 287); Selj. 1300 **Ay-doγdï** [اىطغدى], Osman's cousin (Āšikp. 22, 24); Maml. 1260, 1267/68 **Ay-doγdï** [ايـدغـدى الـركنى], an emir Alā'addīn ~ al-Hass al-Ruknī (Sīrat 154; 57, Berchem, Jér. I, 197); Maml. 1261 **Ay-doγdï** [ايـدغـدى], Alā'addīn ~ (Abulfidā IV, 632-33); Maml. 1261, 1264 **Ay-doγdï** [ايـدغـدى / Djemâl-eddin-Idagdi-Azizi], an emir (Sīrat 172, 174; 71-72, Makrīzī II, 13); Maml. 1279 **Ay-doγdï** [Ala-eddin Idagdi-Harrâni], nā'ib of Karak (Makrīzī II, 170, III, 10); Maml. 1281 **Ay-doγdï** [Aïdagdi], Alā'addīn ~ „Sarkhudi"(?), the nā'ib of the province Gazah (Makrīzī III, 43); Maml. 1289 **Ay-doγdï** [ايـدغـدى ابـنعبد الله بـالكبى], died in 1289 (Berchem, Jér. I, 204); Maml. 1297, 1305 **Ay-doγdï** [ايـدغـدى شتيـر / Ala-eddin-Idagdi-Schoukaïr] (Zetterst. 47-49, Makrīzī IV, 46, Weil, Chalif. I, 213 ff., Dawād. 135, 175); Maml. 1305 **Ay-doγdï** [Idagdi Schekrizouri], a Mamluk envoy then a vizier (minister) in Maghreb (Makrīzī IV, 246, 253); Maml. 1306 **Ay-doγdï** [ايـدغـدى القليلى], Alā'addīn ~ Al-qalīlī, together with Alā'addīn ~ Alχwārazmī he was sent on a mission to Maghreb (Zetterst. 132, 145, 154, Makrīzī IV, 253); Maml. 1306, 1317 **Ay-doγdï** [ايـدغـدى الخوارزمى],

Alā'addīn ~ Alχwārizmī together with Alā'addīn ~ Alqalīlī was sent on a mission to Maghreb (Zetterst. 132, 145, 154, Nuwairī 145, 167); Maml. 1309 **Ay-doγdï** [ايـدغـدى الجمال], Alā'addīn ~, an emir (Dawād. 172); Maml. 1310 **Ay-doγdï** [ايـدغـدى الجمالى], Alā'addīn ~ (Zetterst. 140); Maml. 1310 **Ay-doγdï** [ايـدغـدى اللاىى], an emir (Dawād. 212); Maml. 1320 **Ay-doγdï** [ايـدغـدى التقوى], an emir (Dawād. 299, 300, Zetterst. 155, 168); Maml. 14th c. **Ay-doγdï** [ايـدغـدى / Aydoğdı] (Tarǰ/Houtsma 57, Tarǰ/Toparlı 41); Maml. 14th c. **Ay-doγdï** [ايَـدُغَـدى] (Sauvaget 40); Maml. 14th c. **Ay-doγdï** [Айдогды] (Tuhfa 409); Trkm. 19th c. **Ay-doγdï** [Айдагды / Айдагдыев] (Ščeglov I, 353, 356); Trkm. 20th c. **Ay-doγdï** [Aydogdï] (Zaj. 1971, 333); Oghuz (Trkm.) 1152 **Ay-doγdï** [التـركمـاىى / شمله ايـدغـدى] (Ibn al-Athīr/Tornb. XI, 106-7, 217-19 etc.); Trkm. 1812 **Ay-doγdï-bek** [Ай-догды-бек], from the Sariq tribe (MIT II, 383); Trkm. 1867 **Ay-doγdï-χan** [Ай-догды-хан], from the Göklen tribe (MIT II, 311); Turk. 1517 **Ay-doγdu** [Aydoğdu], from the Kayı tribe in the region of Menteşe (Belleten XII 1948, 609); Yürük 16th c. **Ay-doγdu** [Aydoğdu], from the Yürüks of Kocacık (Gökb., Rum. 104, 210, 219); Turk.? 1133 **Ay-toγdï** ['Αϊτουγδῆς], a Turkic commander of the army (Byz. Turc. 58 (cited by Sauvaget as well)); *TN:* Turk. 20th c. **Ay-doγdu** [Aydoğdu], toponym, villages in the administrative provinces of Ağrı, Amasya, Bursa and Denizli (TMİB 52, 61, 223, 278, 280). ✧ 'The Moon rose; The moon has risen' (Tarǰ/Houtsma 57, Sauvaget 40, Zaj. 1971); cf. *Ay-doγdï* 'la lune est levée' ou 'une lune est née' (Sauvaget 40); *Ay-toγdï* [اىتغنى] 'der Mond ist aufgegangen' (Poppe 1252). ⇨ **AY** + **TOΓDÏ**. See also **KÜN-TOΓDÏ**.

AY-TOΓLÏ Tat.(GH) 1320 **Ay-toγlï** [اىتُغلى / اىتغلى / Аитоглы], Özbek's envoy to Egypt (Duqmaq/Tizeng. I, 320, 327, Ayni/Tizeng. I, 489, 519, Zetterst. 140). ✧ 'Moon-yearling lamb' (Zetterst. 79). ⇨ **AY** + **TOQLÏ**.

AY-TOΓMÏŠ Selj. 1213 **Ay-doγmïš** [اىد غمش / Idogmisch] (Abulfidā IV, 251); Maml. 1259 **Ay-doγmïš** [Idgamisch] (Makrīzī I, 83); Maml. 1320, 1342 **Ay-doγmïš** [ايـدغمش], Alā'addīn ~, an emir(-i aχur), Master of the Horse of the ruler Muhammad al-Nāsir I (1293-1341), governor of Damascus, died in 1342 (Dawād. 298, 357, Zetterst. 226, Iyās I, 166, 177, 181, Weil, Chalif. I, 362, 417, 432 ff.); Maml. 14th c. **Ay-doγmuš** [ايَـدُغُمُش / ايـدغمش] (Tarǰ/Houtsma 57, Tarǰ/Toparlı (facs. 31a)); Maml. 1290 **Ay-doγmuš**, Alā'addīn ~, a clerk in Tarābulus (Tripolis) (Björkm. 164, 168); Turk. **Ay-doγmuš** [اىسلوغمش] (Ongan, Ank. I, 152); Selj. 12th c. **Ay-toγmïš** [اىتغمش], an emir in Iraq (Rāwandī 395, 402 etc.); Maml. 1205 **Ay-toγmïš**

[اﯾﺘﻐﻤﺶ ﺷﻤﯩﻰ اﻟﺪﯾﻦ   ﻣﻤﻠﻮك اﻟﺒﻬﻠﻮان] (Ibn al-Athīr/Tornb. XII, 156-58, 194-97, 200); Khorezm.? 13th c. **Ay-tuɣmïš** [Айтугмыш] (RaD I/2, 159); Uyg. 8th c. **Ay-tuɣmïš-sañun** (Müller, Pfahl. 23); *TN:* Selj.? 12th c. **Ay-doɣmïš** [أﯾﺪ ﻏﻤﺶ اﻟﺠﻮﺑﺎ ن], a masjid (small mosque) (Ibn Šaddād, Alep 84, 85); *TN:* Turk. 1455 **Ay-doɣmuš** [Aydoğmuş], a village (Gökb., Ed. 277); *TN:* Turk. 20th c. **Ay-doɣmuš** [Aydoğmuş], toponym, villages in the provinces of Afyon, Ankara and Isparta (TMİB 38, 86, 431). ✧ I. 'Moon-relative' cf. Uyg. *toɣmïš* 'родственник' (DTS); II. 'The Moon rose' (Sauvaget 40). ⇨ AY + ТОГМÏŠ. See also AY-ТОГDÏ.

AY-TOXTA Uzb. 20th c. **Ây-toxta** [Ойтӱхта], fem. (Begmatov 1984, 205). ✧ 'Moon-Stop'. ⇨ AY + TOQTA. See also BAY-TOXTA, EŠ-TOXTA.

AY-TOLAN Tat.(Tüm.) **Ay-tolan** [Аітолан], a princess from Tümen (Proben IV, 300 /372/). ✧ '(Time of the) full Moon'; II. 'Moon-Horse'. ⇨ AY + TULAN.

AY-TOLDÏ Karakh. 11th c. **Ay-doldu** [Аідолду] (Radl. I, 161, 176, II, 579, DTS). ✧ 'The Moon has become full'. ⇨ AY + TOLDÏ.

AY-TOLÏY Hak. 19th-20th c. **Ay-tolïy-qan** [Ай-толый Канъ] (Titov 210). ✧ 'The Moon is becoming full'. ⇨ AY + TOLAY I.? See also AY-DOLAY, AY-TOLDÏ.

AY-TOLU Kar.(Crm.) **Ay-tolu** [Аітолу], fem. (Radl. I, 5). ✧ 'Full Moon'. ⇨ AY + TOLU.

AY-TOLUM Kzk. 19th c. **Ay-tolum** [Айтолумъ] (SOK 114). ✧ 'My full Moon'. ⇨ AY-TOLU.

AY-TOLUZU Alt., Hak. 19th-20th c. **Ay-toluzu** [Ai-Толузу (Ai-Долаі)] (Radl. I, 5). ✧ 'Full Moon' (Radl. I, 5) cf. *ay-tolu-su* 'the full(ness) of the Moon'. ⇨ AY + TOLU + poss. suff. *-su*. See also AY-DOLAY.

AY-TUГ Uzb. 20th c. **Ây-tuɣ** [Ойтуғ], fem. (Begmatov 1984, 205). ✧ 'Moon-bear!' (Begmatov), 'Be born Moon(-like beautiful)!' cf. Türk, Kuman, Chag. *toɣ-* 'geboren werden; aufgehen (von Sonne); ersteigen' (Radl. III, 1158). ⇨ AY.

AY-TUГAN Kzk. 17th c. **Ay-duɣan** [Алипка Айдуганов] (IOAIÊK XXIX, 342); Crm.(Tat.) 1688 **Ay-tuɣan** [ﺗﻠﻤﺎج ﺗﻮﻏﺎ ن], an interpreter (Vel.-Zern., Crim. 797); Tat.(Tüm.) 1632 **Ay-tuɣan** [Атуганка Акулıев] (Miller, Ist. Sib. II, 399); Bashk. 1758 **Ay-tuɣan** [Айман Айтуганов] (MIB IV/1, 160); Kzk. **Ay-tuɣan** (Protok. Turk. IV, 133); Kzk. 1820 **Ay-tuɣan** [Айтуганъ], a chieftain (Sib. Vest. IX,120); Kzk. 19th c. **Ay-tuɣan** [Айтуганов] (AOO 18, 54); Kzk. 19th c. **Ay-tuɣan** [Айтуган] (Potanin II, 5); Kzk. 19th c. **Ay-tuɣan** [Бай-Адилъ Айтугановъ] (Grod., Pril. 108); Kzk. 1859 **Ay-tuɣan** [Айтуганъ] (ZIRGOÊtn. I, 211); Uzb. 20th c. **Ây-tuqqan?** [Ойтуққан], fem. (Begmatov 1984, 205); Uzb. 20th c. **Ây-tuwɣan** [Ойтувған], fem. (Begmatov 1984, 205); *EN:* Kzk. 18th c. - 19th c. **Ay-tuɣan** [Айтуган] (Tynyšp. 72); *TN:* Turk. 20th c. **Ay-doɣan** [Aydoğan], a village in the province of Çorum, Turkey, the name is originating from the personal name Yıldırım Aydoğan (TMİB 78, 266). ✧ 'The Moon has been born (or has risen)', 'Born under Moon-light' (Torma 1992, 364), cf. Potanin (loc. cit.) who quotes certain Teñgis-bay: 'назван так потому будто бы что родился во время новолуния (ай - месяц, туган - рожденный)' [=(The bearer of the name) was named like this because he might have been born at the time of new Moon (*ay* - moon, *tugan* - born)]. A typical male name in Kazak (Sultan'jaev 1970, p. 75). ⇨ AY + TUГAN I. See also KÜN-TUГAN.

AY-TUГMÏŠ see **AY-TOГMÏŠ**

AY-TUWAQ Kzk. 19th c. **Ay-tuwaq** [Айтуакъ] (AOAtb. 42). ✧ 'Moon-hoof'? ⇨ AY + TUWAQ.

AY-TUWAR Kzk. 1803, 1817, 1819 **Ay-tuwar** [اﯾﻄﻮار / Айтувар] (MIK IV, 311, 318, 323, 513); Kzk. 1820 **Ay-tuwar** [Айтуваръ] (Sib. Vest. IX, 106); Kzk. 19th c. **Ay-tuwar** [Айтуваръ] (Grod., Pril. 171); Kzk. 19th c. **Ay-tuwar** [Айтуаръ] (SOK 200); Kkalp. 20th c. **Ay-tuwar** [Айтуўар] (KkRS 772). ✧ 'The Moon will be born; the moon rises' cf. Kzk. *tuw-* ' родиться' (KzRS). ⇨ AY + TUГAR.

AY-TUŽAR Kzk. 19th c. **Ay-tužar** [Айтужаръ] (SOK 268).

AY-ŽAMAL see **AY**

AY-ŽAMAL see **AY**

AY-ŽAN see **AY**

AYA-GÜZ Kzk. 19th c. **Aya-güz** [Аягузъ] (SODž. 18); Kzk. 19th c. **Aya-güz** [Аягузъ] (SOK 150). ✧ 'Best-eye'? cf. Kzk. *aya* 'der Beste' (Radl. I, 198). ⇨ KÖZ.

AYAB see **AYAP**

AYAB see **AYÏP**

AYAB-BERGEN see **AYAP-BERGEN**

AYAČÏ Mo. 13th c. **Ayačï** [اﺑﺎﺟﻰ / Аячи], 8th son of Šaybān (Šibān) khan (RaD II, 75, Abulg./Desm. 191); Maml. **Ayačï** [اﯾﺎﺟﻰ اﻟﺴﺎﻗﻰ], an emir (Dawād. 367); Maml. 1332 **Ayačï** [اﯾﺎﺟﻰ], an emir (Dawād. 368). ✧ 'Cup-bearer'? cf. Uyg. *ayaqčï*, Chag. *ayaqči* 'Mundschenk' (Radl. I, 199).

AYAГAQ Kzk. 19th c. **Ayaɣaq** [Аягакъ] (AOP 14).

AYAQ Uyg. 12th c. - 14th c. **Ayaq** [kiŋsün ajaq] (Radl., USp. 112-13, DTS); Khorezm./Chag. 1460 **Ayaq** [اﯾﺎق / Аяк / мирза Аяк], byname of Osman Quñrat's brother from the Quñrat tribe whose real name was Muhammed Ali (MIT I, 540); Maml. 1332 **Ayaq** [اﻻﻣﯩﺮ أﯾﺎق اﻟﺠﺎﻣﺪار], an emir, cup-bearer (Dawād. 366); Kzk. 19th c. **Ayaq** (Grod., Pril. 104); *TN:* Uyg. 12th c. - 14th c. **Adaq-tutuq** [Adak tutuk / adaq tutuq], a settlement, originally a patronym (Blagova 709) (Radl., USp. 114-15, EUTS, DTS). ✧ I. 'Foot' cf. in several Trk. languages: *ayaq I.* 'id.' (Radl. I, 202, Sev.); II. 'Cup' cf. all Trk. dial. *ayaq* 'Schale, Napf, Topf' (Radl. I, 201). See also **ALČÏN-ADAQ, ALTÏN-AYAQ, AT-AYAQ, BAZ-AYAQ, ǰULDÏ-AYAQ, XÏZ-AYAX, İT-AYAQ, YALÏN-AYAQ, KİÑSÜN-AYAQ, KÖK-AYAQ, KÜMÜS-AYAQ, QALÄ-AYAQ, QARA-AYAQ, QÏQÏR-ATAX, QOS-AYAQ, QULAN-AYAQ, QUT-AYAQ?, QUŠ-AYAQ, SARČ-AYAQ, SARÏČ-AYAQ, ŠÏY-AYAQ, TOBA-AYAQ, ÜŠ-AYAQ.**

AYAQ-İŠ Kzk. 19th c. **Ayaq-iš?** [Аякишъ Умурзаковъ] (AUK 235).

AYAL Yak. **Ayal** [Аjал], one of the forefathers of Yakuts, Argïn's son (Pek.).

AYAN I. Tat.(Lit.) 1594 **Ayan** [Аянъ Ахметеевичъ] (Lit. Tat. 199). ✧ '(One) with hard step/tread' cf. Crm. *ayan*, Kzk. *ayañ* 'Starker Schritt' (Radl. I, 209, 210).

AYAN II. Kzk. 19th c. **Ayam-bay (<Ayan-bay)** [Аямбай] (AOK 106); Kzk. 19th c. **Ayam-bay (<Ayan-bay)** [Аямбай] (SOK 50); Kzk. 19th c. **Ayam-bek (<Ayan-bek)** [Аямбек] (SOK 264); Kzk. 1819 **Ayan** [Айян] (MIK IV, 325); Kzk. 19th c. **Ayan** [Айен] (SOK 264). ✧ 'Omen/presage / augury /sign; clear' cf. Kzk. *ayan* 'известие /вообще сверхъестественное)' (Ilm.), *ayan* 'ясный; явный; известный' (KzRS). See also **YÜZE-YAN.**

AYANKE Kzk. 19th c. **Ayanke** [Аянке] (AOK 94). ✧ 'Little omen/sign'. ⇨ **AYAN II.** + suff. *-ke.*

AYAP see **AYÏP**

AYAP-BERGEN Kzk. 19th c. **Ayab-bergen** [Аяббергең] (Grod., Pril. 89); Kzk. 19th c. **Ayap-bergen** [Аяпбергең] (AOK 10); Kkalp. 20th c. **Ayap-bergen** [Аяпбергең] (Bask., Kkalp. 78, KkRS 772); Kzk. 19th c. **Ayap-pergen** [Аяппергең] (AOO 38, 58); Kzk. 19th c. **Ayap-pergen** [Аяппергең] (AOO 38). ✧ 'A wicked/deficient (person) has given him' cf. AYÏP; II. 'Given/born regretted, feared' cf. the gerund of Kzk. *aya-* 'щадить; сжалиться' (KzRS), Kkalp. *aya-* 'жалеть;]адить' (KkRS). ⇨ **AYÏP + BERGEN.**

AYAS see **AYAZ**

AYAŠ Yürük 1543 **Ayaš** [Ayaş] (Gökb., Rum. 188). ✧ 'Drunk' cf. Turk. dial. *ayaş=ayyaş* (DS).

AYAZ Karakh. 11th c. **Ayas** [ajas], a slave (MK/Brock., DTS); Turk. 1501 **Ayas** [Hacı Ahmed bin Ayas] (Gökb., Ed. 461); Yürük 1543 **Ayas** (Gökb., Ed. 188); Hak. 19th-20th c. **Ayas** [Аяс / Аёс] (HRS 348); Oghuz 1057 **Ayaz** [اياز], Aymaq's son, the servant of the Ghaznavid ruler Mahmud (998-1030), died in 1057 (Ibn al-Athīr/Tornb. IX, 439); Oghuz? 12th c. **Ayaz** [اياز], ~ Naṣraddīn, the atabek of Sultan Muhammad Arslan (Rāwandī 256, 259); Oghuz/Trkm. 13th c. **Ayaz** [اياز / Айаз], a slave (Abulg./Kon. 1300-13016, 1319); Kuman 1521 **Ayaz** [Johanne Ayaz] (Gyárfás III, 754);

Selj. 11th c. **Ayaz** [اياز غلام ملكشاه], Melikšah's (1072-1092) servant (Qazw. 453-456); Selj. 1100 **Ayaz** [اياز], an emir (Rāwandī 153-154 etc.); Selj. 1101 **Ayaz**, Melikšah's (1072-1092) servant and Berkyāruq's (1094-1104) retainer who became the proprietor of Hamadān (Ibn al-Athīr/Tornb. X, 205, Weil, Chalif. III, 145); Selj. 1104 **Ayaz**, an emir, regent, the „ghāwur" of Türkyārūq [=Berk-yaruq!] Sultan's (1094-1104) son, died in 1104 (Abulfar./Budge I, 238-39); Selj. 1111-1113 **Ayaz** [اياز], Ayaz ibn İlġazi, the son of İlġāzi (the proprietor of Māridīn), one of the commanders in the war against the crusaders (Ibn al-Athīr/Tornb. X, 340, 346, 351-53, Ibn al-Athīr: RHCHor I, 280, 298, ǰawzī: RHCHor III, 553, 555, Abulfar./Budge I, 247, Sevim-Yücel 155, 168); Selj. 12th c.? **Ayaz** [طغرلتكين اياز], Toγrïl-tegin Ayaz (Bondārī 297); Selj. 1190/91 **Ayaz** [اياز الطويـل], one of Saladin's bodyguards, died in 1190/91 (Ibn Šaddād, Nawād.: RHCHor III, 199, 253); Selj. 1191/92 **Ayaz** [اياز المـهـراني] (Ibn Šaddād, Nawād.: RHCHor III, 284-85); Selj. 1200 **Ayaz** [اياز / Ayaz], brother-in-law of Sokman (Sevim-Yücel 166); Selj. 1226 **Ayaz** [اياز / Ayaz], Esedüddin ~, an emir, Alā'addīn Keykubād's commander of the army (Sevim-Yücel 115, 116); Khorezm. 13th c. **Ayaz** [ajaz] (Atebet, DTS); Maml. 1327 **Ayaz** [اياز], ~ ad-Dawādārī, an emir coming from Dawādār (Dawād. 329); Maml. 1332 **Ayaz** [اياز الساقى], an emir (Dawād. 366); Maml. 14th c. **Ayaz** [اياز] (Sauvaget); Turk. **Ayaz** [اياز] (Ongan, Ank. I, 152); Bashk. 1746 **Ayaz** [Аяз] (MIB III, 434); Bashk. 1760 **Ayaz** [Аяз Бакшаев] (MIB IV/1, 189); Bashk. 1761 **Ayaz** [Аяз Тогушаев] (MIB IV/1, 205); Kirg. **Ayaz** [Аяз] (Jud. 47); Selj. 1072 **Ayaz / İyaz?** [اياز], ~ ibn Alp-Arslan (1063-1072) an emir (incorrectly read as *İyaz* in MIT I, 376-77) (Ibn al-Athīr/Tornb. X, 51-53); Turk. 1515 **Ayaz-aγa** [Ayas Ağa] (Gökb., Ed. 74); Kzk. 19th c. **Ayaz-bay** [Аяз-бай] (SOV 152); Kzk. 19th c. **Ayaz-bay** [Аяз-бай] (SOK 40, 122, 152, 254); Selj. 1160 **Ayaz-bek** [بك عياز], Šemsülmülk [Šamsu'lmulk] ibn Hüseyin (Ahbar 104); Uzb. **Ayaz-bek** [Аязъ-бекъ], from Samarkand (ZIRGOStat. IV, 243); Turk. 15th c. **Ayaz-paša** ['Αγιάπασας], head of Yanissaries (Byz. Turc. 56); Turk. 1526 **Ayaz-paša**, a pasha (Byz. Turc. 56); *TN:* Turk. 1516 **Ayaz-bey** [Ayazbey], in the name of a village (Gökb., Ed. 74). ✧ 'Clear; clean; having a nice face' cf. OT *ajas I.* 'heiter, klar' (MK/Brock.), *ajas II.* 'имя собственное (даётся рабам с красивым лицом)' (MK/Brock. DTS), Maml. *ayaz* 'heiterer Himmel' (Tarǰ/Houtsma), Maml. *ayaz, ayas* 'clair, serein, sans nuage' (Sauvaget 39), Kuman *ajaz* 'heiter, unbewölkt' (CC), Kirg. *ayaz* 'чистый, прозрачный, ясный; мороз' (Jud.). See also **AY-AYAZ, ARÏΓ-**

AYAZ.

AYAZ-KÜŠ Selj. 1191/92, 1194 **Ayaz-küš** [اياز کوش],
Sayfaddïn ~, an emir, one of Saladin's commanders of
the army (Ibn al-Athīr/Tornb. XII, 45, Ibn al-Athīr,
Atab. RHCHor II/1, 48). ❖ 'Clear/clean -
strength/power'? ⇨ **AYAZ + KÜČ?**

AYAZÏN Hak. 20th c. **Ayazïn-χō** [Айазын Хоо], fem.
(Butanaev); Hak.(Sag.) 19th-20th c. **Ayazïn-qō**
[Ayasïn-ko], folkl., the bride of the bogatyr (hero)
(Proben IX, 258, Schiefner 383). ❖ 'Let her pity'
(Butanaev). ⇨ **AYAZ?**

AYĀN-QUYĀN Yak. **Ayān-quyān** [Аjан-Куjан],
folk., name of an abāsï-shaman (Pek.).

AYĀR Selj. 1086 **Ayār** [ايار] (Kamāladdīn: RHCHor
II, 100); OT(Qarluq) 1162 **Ayār-bek** [Айяр-бек], a
commander from among the Qarluqs of Mawarannahr
(MIT I, 445). ❖ 'True, real, genuine' cf. OT *ajar*
'проба /металла)' (DTS).

AYĀRBA Yak. **Ayārba** [Аjарба], folkl., a nickname
(Pek.). ❖ 'Don't cry!' cf. Yak. *ayār-* 'горланить,
реветь, кричать, шуметь, тревожить' (Pek.). +
neg. suff. *-ba (<-ma)*.

AYČUQ Uyg. 1310 **Ayčuq-terim** [Aizuk Terim], fem.
(Chwol., Syr.-nest. 18). ❖ '(Dear) little Moon'. ⇨ **AY**
+ dim. suff. *-čïq*.

AYDA Bashk. 1770 **Ayda-γul** [Кучум Айдагулов]
(MIB IV/1, 345); Bashk. 1789 **Ayda-γul** [Реим
Айдагулов] (MIB V, 250, 252). ❖ I. Ayda (Ar.)
'Returning, visitor' (Ahmed); II. 'Moon?' cf. Bashk.
PN *Ayδa-γol* (<*ay* + *qol*) (Kusimova).

AYDAQ Trkm. 1843 **Aydaq-yüzbašï** [Айдак-
юзбаши] (MIT II, 492).

AYDAQAY Bashk. 18th c. **Aydaqay** [Илиш
Айдакаев] (MIB IV/1, 120); Bashk. 1756 **Aydaqay**
[Итамган Айдакаев] (MIB IV/1, 120); Bashk. 1783
Aydaqay [Айдакай] (MIB V, 139); Bashk. 1787
Aydaqay [Иман Айдакаев] (MIB V, 204). ❖ 'Little
Ayda'. ⇨ **AYDA** + dim. suff. *-qay*.

AYDAN-BERGEN Uzb. 19th c. **Aydan-bergen**
[Айданбергенъ] (SKSO III, 20). ❖ 'Given by the
Moon'. ⇨ **AY + BERGEN.**

AYDAP-KEL Kzk. 19th c. **Aydap-kel** [Айдабкель]
(SOK 14). ❖ 'Driving-come (here)' cf. Alt., Crm.,
Hak., Kirg., Kzk., Tat. *ayda-* 'treiben, vertreiben' (Radl.
I, 49). ⇨ **KEL.**

AYDAR Crm.(Tat.) 1480 **Aydar** [Айдаръ / Андаръ /
Идаръ], a prince of the Crimea (PSRL IV, 134, VI,
223, VIII, 205, XXIII, 180, Zolotn., Alf. 155); Tat.(Lit.)
1590 **Aydar** [Асанъ Айдаровичъ] (Lit. Tat. 65, 66,
270); Tat. 1445 **Aydar** [Айдаръ], a prince of Kazan
(PSRL VI, 172); Kzk. **Aydar** [Эркäм Аidar / Еркäм
Аidар], a folklore hero (Proben III, 270 /321/); Alt.
1642, 1652 **Aydar** [Aidar / Айдаръ], a Tölös prince at
the Lake Teletsk (Teleckoe ozero) (Andrievič, Ist. Sib.

I, 97, Radl., Aus Sib. I, 176, 179); Tat.(GH) / Tat. 1429,
1431, 1433 **Aydar** [Айдаръ], a prince of the Horde
(PSRL XII, 9, 147, PSRL (Russk. Hr.), 431); Kirg.
Aydar-qan [Аiдар Кан] (Radl. I, 450, Proben V, 7 /7/,
Jud. 27); Kzk. 19th c. **Aytar** [Карамулда Ходжа
Айтаров] (Grod., Pril. 51). ❖ I. 'Mop or tussock (of
hair)' cf. Kzk. *aydar* 'чуб; коса; пучок волос,
оставленный на макушке (у мальчиков)' (KzRS,
Potanin, Pred. 76), Kirg. *aydar* I. 'id.' (Jud.); II. '(He)
Who will drive (*cattle* and perhaps *enemy*) out' cf. Kzk.
ayda- 'гнать, изгонять' (KzkRS), Kirg. *ayda-* 'id.'
(Jud.). See also **ALTÏN-AYDAR, DUŠ-AYTAR,
ǰAN-AYDAR, ǰÏLQÏ-AYDAR, QAZ-AYDAR,
QOY-AYDAR, QOS-AYDAR, MAL-AYDAR, MÏN-
AYDAR.**

AYDAR-ALÏ Bashk. 1756 **Aydar-alï** [Айдаралы
Юсупов] (MIB IV/1, 111). ❖ It may be derived from
the Ar. *Haydar Ali* 'Lion-Ali', the sobriquet and the
personal name of the 4th Caliph. ⇨ **XAYDAR + ALÏ.**

AYDAR-AT Kzk. 19th c. **Aydar-at** [Айдаратъ] (AOO
46). ❖ I. Haydar-Horse? II. 'Drive-Horse'? ⇨
XAYDAR + AT? / AYDAR + AT?

AYDAS Alt. **Aydas** (Radl. III, 1011). ❖ 'Outstanding;
bigger' cf. Tel., Shor, Kacha, Küä. *aydas* 'überragend,
vor andern hervorragend, grösser' (Radl. I, 51).

AYDĀRÏAX see **AYDĀRÏAQ**

AYDĀRÏAX-BÄRGÄN see **AYDĀRÏAQ**

AYDĀRÏAQ Yak. **Aydārïaq-bärgän** / **Aydārïaχ-
bärgän** [Аидарыак(х) бäргäн], a mythical hero
(bogatyr) (Pek.). ❖ 'Noisy dare-devil' cf. Yak. *aydār-*
'шуметь' (JRS).

AYDE-BER Kzk. 19th c. **Ayde-ber-bek**
[Айдебербекъ] (SODž. 6). ❖ 'Come on, give it!' cf.
Kzk. *äyda* 'айда' (RKzkS). ⇨ **BER.**

AYDÏQ Maml. 1332 **Aydïq** [ايدق], an emir (Dawād.
368).

AYDÏM see **AYDÏN**

AYDÏM-AY see **AYDÏÑ-AY?**

AYDÏN Kzk. 19th c. **Aydïm-bay** (<Aydïn-bay)
[Айдымбай] (SOV 6); Turk.? 14th c. **Aydïn**
['Αϊδίνης], a Turkish prince coming from the dynasty
of Aydınoğulları and its descendants (14th/15th c.)
(Byz. Turc. 57-58); Turk. 14th c. **Aydïn**
[مراد بن ايد ين], in an inscription on a grave from
Tokat (Uzunçarş., Küt. I, 49); Turk. 1405 **Aydïn** [Haсı
Aydın] (Gökb., Ed. 200); Turk. 1464 **Aydïn** [Aydın]
(Gökb., Ed. 327); Turk. 1563 **Aydïn**, a sipahi (spahi,
cavalry soldier) around Pápa, Hungary (Velics-Kamm.
II, 300); Turk. 1565 **Aydïn** [Memi bin Aydın] (Dávid);
Turk. 1570 **Aydïn** [Aydïn Atmaǰa] (Dávid); Turk. 1570
Aydïn [Aydın Atmaca] (Dávid); Turk. 1570 **Aydïn**
[Aydın Atmaca] (Dávid); Turk. 1583 **Aydïn** [Aydın]
(Ongan, Ank. I, 150, 152); Yürük 1543 **Aydïn** [ايد ين /
Aydın] (Gökb., Rum. 103, 175, 182, 186, 187, 196,

212); Az. **Aydïn** (Radl. I, 53); NUyg. 19th c. **Aydïn** [ايد ين / Aidin] (Le Coq, Namenl. 93); Bashk. 1735 **Aydïn / Aydïm?** [Аидым Ешляпов] (Vel.-Zern., Bašk. 24); Selj. 13th c. **Aydïn-alp** [ايد ين الب] (Ibn Bībī III, 61); Turk. 1503 **Aydïn-bey** [Aydın Bey] (Gökb., Ed. 478); Turk. 1412 **Aydïn-šeyh** [Aydın Şeyh] (Gökb., Ed. 24); Tuv. 19th c. **Aydïñ** [Аідыҥ] (Proben IX, 122); *TN:* NUyg. 19th c. **Aydïn**, toponym (Le Coq, Namenl. 92). ❖ 'Clear, light, bright' cf. Az., Turk. *aydïn* 'Glanz, Hell, Schein; Lichtloch' (Radl. I, 52, 53).

AYDÏÑ see **AYDÏN**

AYDÏÑ-AY Tuv. 19th c. **Aydïñ-ay?** [Аідымаі], fem. (Proben IX, 80). ❖ 'Bright Moon'. ⇨ **AYDÏN + AY.**

AYDÏR Hak. 19th-20th c. **Aydïr** [Айдыр] (HRS 348).

AYDOÑ Hak. 19th-20th c. **Aydoñ** [Айдонъ] (HRS 348). ❖ 'Moon-boy' (Butanaev).

AYDOTA Hak. 19th-20th c. **Aydota** [Айдота], fem. (HRS 353). ❖ Avdot'ya (R.) (Butanaev).

AYDU Chuv. 18th-19th c. **Aydu-bay** [Айдубай] (Magn. 25).

AYDUK Chuv. 18th-19th c. **Ayduk** [Айдукъ] (Magn. 25).

AYGÏL Kzk. 1846 **Aygil** [Айгиль], a biy (Konšin, Mat. V, 101).

AYGÏNÄ Maml. 14th c. **Ayginä** [ايكينا / Aygine], fem. (Tarǰ/Houtsma 57, Tarǰ/Toparlı 44). ❖ '(Dear) Little Moon'. ⇨ **AY** + dim. suff. -ginä.

AYΓÏR NUyg. 19th c. **Ayγïr** [ايغير / Aighir] (Le Coq, Namenl. 93); Alt. 19th c. **Asqïr** [Аскыр] (Katanov, Otč. 12). ❖ 'Stallion' (Le Coq, Namenl. 93), cf. Uyg., Alt., Kirg., Kzk., Tat., etc. *ayγïr* 'Hengst' (Radl. I, 15), Hak. *asqïr* 'der Hengst' (Radl. I, 544), Hak.(Sag.) *asχïr* 'жеребец' (HRS). See also **ASQÏR, ČOQ-ADΓÏR, ČUBAR-AYΓÏR, TORÏ-AYΓÏR.**

AYΓU-TÏLÄY Kzk. 19th c. **Ayγu-tiläy** [Калубекъ Айгу-Тилаевъ] (Grod., Pril. 93). ⇨ ? + **TÏLÄ** + dim.-voc. suff. -*y*. See also **BAY-TÏLÄY.**

AYΓUY see **ALΓUY**

AYXAN Kkalp. 20th c. **Ayχan** [Айхан], fem. (KkRS 777). ⇨ **AY** + suff. -*χan(1)*.

AYÏN-ŠAYÏN-ŠÏKŠÏRGE Alt. **Ayin-šayin-šikširge** [Аинъ-Шаинъ-Шикширге] (Nikiforov 31, 37, 41, 43).

AYÏT see **AYT**

AYÏJÏ see **AYUWČÏ**

AYÏΓ-ÖGLÏ Uyg. 10th c. **Ayïγ-ögli** [ajïγ ögli] (DTS). ❖ 'Evil-minded, ill-willed' (DTS), cf. Uyg., Karakh. *ajïγ* 'злой' + *ög* ' разум, мысль' (DTS). + suff. -*li*.

AYÏLČÏ Alt. 19th-20th c. **Ayïlčï** [Айылчы], male also fem. name (OjrRS 207, 211). ❖ 'Guest' (OjrRS) <Mo. *ayilčï(n)*.

AYÏLZAQ Alt. 19th-20th c. **Ayïlzaq** [Айылзак] (OjrRS 207). ❖ 'One who likes to go to stay with somebody' (OjrRS), cf. also Tel. *ailzaq* 'Mensch, der

sich herumzutreiben liebt, gern zu Gast geht' (Radl. I, 43) < Mo. *ayil + saγ.*

AYÏM Kirg. **Ayïm-bača** [Айымбача], fem. (Jud. 725); Kzk. 19th c. **Ayïm-bibi** [Аимъ-биби], fem. (SKSO IV/2, 34); Kkalp. 20th c. **Ayïm-gül** [Айымгюл], fem. (Bask., Kkalp. 403). ❖ 'Wife; lady; good-looking man or woman' cf. Chag. *ajim* 'Frau, Gattin; Zeichen, Wink' (Radl. I, 223), Kzk. *ajim* 'Frau, Gemahlin' (Ibid.), Kkalp. *Ayïm-gül* 'Госпожа роза' (Baskakov: OSA 141). It is used as a permanent component of female names replacing the word 'wife', and expressing kindness at the same time: '*."khanym"* et *"âim"* ma lune, sont des termes de tendresse entre époux croyants. Le mot *"âim"* est employé dans la conversation des musulmans pour remplacer le mot femme' (Korośkin: Rec. d'it. et de voy. dans l'As. Centrale, 214).

AYÏM-BAČA see **AYÏM**

AYÏMBÄT see **AYÏMBET**

AYÏMBET Bashk. **Ayïmbät / A(y)imbät** [Аембет] (Sprav. Im. 68); Bashk. 1776 **Ayïmbet** [Салават Аимбетев] (MIB V, 683); Bashk. 19th c. **Ayïmbet** [Айымбет] (Samojlovič: ŽS XXIV (1915), 167). ❖ I. 'Moon-Mukhammad' cf. AY + comp. -*imbet*; II. 'Beautiful, nice face' cf. AYÏM + Chag.,Osm., Crm. *bät* 'das Gesicht, die rechte Seite' (Radl. IV, 1617), Kzk. *bet* 'id.' (Radl. IV, 1617). ⇨ **AY / AYÏM.**

AYÏMQAN Kkalp. 20th c. **Ayïmqan** [Айымкъан], fem. (Bask., Kkalp. 403). ⇨ **AYÏM** + suff. -*qan(1)*.

AYÏNA see **ADÏNA**

AYÏP Kzk. 19th c. **Ayab** [Аяб] (AOAtb. 130); Kzk. 19th c. **Ayap / Ayab** [Аяп (Аяб) Мирзабаев] (AOK 14); Kzk. 19th c. **Ayap / Ayab** [Аяп (Аяб) Мирзабаев] (SOK 286); Kzk. 19th c. **Ayap / Ayab** [Аяп (Аяб) Мирзабаев] (Grod., Pril. 129); Kirg. **Ayïp-qan** [Аjып Кан] (Proben V, 106). ❖ 'Wicked; deficient, ill' cf. Uyg., Kuman, Chag., Az., Kzk., Tat.(Sib.), Turk., etc. *ayip (aip)* 'die Schuld, Fehler; Unpassenheit; Schlechtigkeit, Strafgeld für Vergehen' (Radl. I, 59), Kar., Kzk. *ayïp* 'id.' (Radl. I, 223), Kzk. *ayïp* 'вина; изъянъ, недостаток' (KzRS), Kirg. *ayïp* (Ar.) 'вина, провинность; изъян, недостаток' (Jud.), Kkalp. *ayïp*, Qara Nog. dial. *ayap* 'вина, проступок, порок' (Bask., Kkalp. 319) or < *Ayub-qan.* Protective name.

AYÏR Kzk. 19th c. **Ayïr-bek** [Аербекъ] (SOK 50).

AYÏRČĀ Tuv. 19th c. **Ayïrčā** [Аjырча] (Proben IX, 169). ❖ 'Small fork'? cf. Tuv. *ayïr* 'вилы' (TuvRS). + dim. suff. -*čā* / -*ča*.

AYÏT see **AYT**

AYÏTMĪŠ Uyg. **Ayïtmïš** (Müller, Uig. II, 80). ❖ 'Spoke'? cf. OT *ayït-* 'позволять говорить; спрашивать; говорить, сказать' (DTS).

AYÏ-TAYBĬR Yak. **Ayï-taybïr** [Аjы-Таібыр], one of Tosoγor-ūs' two sons (Pek.). ❖ 'Good spirit - Taybïr'?

AYQA Kzk. 19th c. **Ayqa-bek** [Айкабекъ] (SODž. 62).

❖ 'Little Moon'. ⇨ **AY** + dim. suff. -*qa*?

AYQÏM see **AYQÏN**

AYQÏN   Kzk. 19th c. **Ayqïm / Ayqïn** [Айкымъ] (SKSO IV/2, 34); Kzk. 19th c. **Ayqïm-bay** (<**Ayqïn-bay)** [Айкымбай] (SOK 44, 208); Kzk. 19th c. **Ayqïm-bay** (<**Ayqïn-bay)** [Айкымбай] (SOV 70); Kzk. 19th c. **Ayqïm-bek** (<**Ayqïn-bek**) [Айкым-бек] (AOO 46); Chag. 1560 **Ayqïm-biy** (<**Ayqïn-biy)** [Айким-бий] (Ivanov 213); Chag. 1559 **Ayqïn / Ayqïm** [Айким], an emir (Ivanov 206); Kzk. 19th c. **Ayqïn-bay** [Айдынбай] (SOV 70); Kzk. **Ayqïn-bay-batïr** [Айкынбай-батыр] (Protok. Turk. V, 151). ❖ 'Clear; large' cf. Kzk. *ayqïn* 'weit, ausgedehnt, einen grossen Raum einnehmend, ein weiblicher Name' (Radl. I, 12), *ayqïn* 'ясный, явный' (KzkRS).

AYQÏNČÏQ   Bashk. / Tat.? 1735 **Ayqïnčik / Ayqïnčïq** [Кинзекей Айкынчиковъ] (Vel.-Zern., Bašk. 23). ⇨ **AYQÏN** + dim. suff. -*čïq*.

AYLAMAS   Kzk. 19th c. **Aylamas** [Айламасъ] (SOV 76). ❖ 'S/He won' t live through a month' cf. Kzk. 'einen Monat dauern, einen Monat verbringen' (Radl. I, 34).

AYLANAŠ   Alt. 19th-20th c. **Aylanaš** [Айланаш], fem. (OjrRS 211). ❖ 'Turning/going around' (Bese 13), cf. Alt. *aylan-* 'вращаться; обходить кругом' (OjrRS) + suff. -*aš*.

AYLAÑÏS   Kirg. **Aylañïs** [Аілангыс], Kökčö's father (Proben V, 7). ❖ 'Turning'? cf. Kirg. *aylan-* 'двигаться вокруг, кружиться, вращаться; вертеться' (Jud.). + suff. -*γïs*.

AYLUČ   Uyg. 8th c. **Ayluč-tarχan / Aylïč-tarqan** [avluč (ailuč?) tarχan / Aylïç Tarkan] (Müller, Pfahl. 12, Radl., USp. 26, DTS, EUTS).

AYMAΓAL   Kzk. 19th c. **Aymaγal** [Савдабай Аймаγаловъ] (Grod., Pril. 29).

AYMAQ   Karakh.? 1057 **Aymaq** [ايماق ابوالنجم اياز بن], his son Ayaz was one of the servants of the Ghaznavid Mahmud (998-1030), Sebük-tegin's son (Ibn al-Athīr/Tornb. IX, 439). ❖ 'Explanation, speech' cf. Uyg. *ajmaq* 'разъяснение, беседа' (DTS).

AYMAQAN   Kkalp. 20th c. **Aymaqan** [Аймақан] (KkRS 772).

AYMAN   Khorezm./Chag. 14th c. **Ayman**, emir, Timür's officer (Tar. Rashidi 31); Trkm.? / Tadj.? 1376/77 **Ayman** [Айман-сербедар] (MIT I, 517); Bashk. 1712 **Ayman** [Айманов] (MIB III, 80); Bashk. 1714 **Ayman** [Айман Уркуняков] (MIB III, 108); Bashk. 1738 **Ayman** [Ильмекей Айманов] (MIB III, 387); Bashk. 1738 **Ayman** [Кошай Айманов] (MIB III, 387); Bashk. 1758 **Ayman** [Айман Айтуганов] (MIB IV/1, 160); Kzk. **Ayman** [Айман] (MSOS VI/2, 214); Kzk. **Ayman** [Айман] (Žirm., Epos 390); Kzk. 1819 **Ayman** [Айман] (MIK IV, 323); Kzk. 19th c. **Ayman** [Айман] (AOK 14); Kkalp. 20th c. **Ayman** [Айман], fem. (KkRS 777); Kkalp. 20th c. **Ayman** [Айман] (KkRS 772, Bask., Kkalp. 403); Kzk. 19th c. **Ayman / Aymen** [Айман] (SODž. 98, 138); Uzb. 1854 **Ayman-bibi** [Аймен-биби], fem. (Moskal'cev 42); Chag. 1505, 1535 **Ayman-χoǰa** [Aiman Khwája Sultán], a sultan (Tar. Rashidi 125-26, 133, 135 etc.); Kzk. **Aymen** [Аймен], folkl., hero of the Kazak legend „Ayman and Šulpan" (Or. Bibl. XVI, 56); Kzk. 19th c. **Aymen** [Аймен] (AOAtb. 66). ❖ 'Clean, naked' cf. Kkalp. *ayman* 'чистый, голый' (Bask., Kkalp.).

AYMAŠ   Bashk. 1737 **Aymaš** [Аймаш] (MIB I, 315).

AYMÄT see **ALÏP-AYMÄT**

AYMEKEN   Kkalp. 20th c. **Aymeken** [Аймекен], fem. (KkRS 777).

AYMEN see **AYMAN**

AYMET   Bashk. 1757 **Aymet** [Аиметев] (MIB IV/1, 142). ⇨ **AY** + suffixoid -*mat*.

AYMÏN   Khorezm. 13th c. **Aymin-χoǰa** [ايمين / Айминъ Хходжа] (Šejb. LIV).

AYMÏŠ   Kzk. 19th c. **Aymïš** [Аймышъ] (SOV 62); Karch. **Aymuš** [Аймушъ] (SMOK III, 162).

AYMUŠ see **AYMÏŠ**

AYNA I.   Trkm. 20th c. **Ayna** [Айна], fem. (Sopieva 181); Trkm. 20th c. **Ayna** [Ayna], fem. (Zaj. 1971, 338); Trkm. 20th c. **Ayna** [Айна], fem. (TrkmRS 34); Kirg. **Ayna** [Айна], fem. (Jud. 35, 843); Kzk. 19th c. **Ayna-bay** [Айнабай] (SOK 8, 188); Kzk. 19th c. **Ayna-bay** [Айнабай] (SOV 82); Kzk. 19th c. **Ayna-bay** [Айнабай] (SOV 82); Oghuz/Trkm. 1296 **Ayna-bek** [اينه بك شر ا شلكتدوغلى], took part in the revolt against Ghazan and was executed (RaD/Jahn 97, 99); Maml. 1332? **Ayna-bek** [اينبك], an emir (Dawād. 266); Kzk. 19th c. **Ayna-bek** [Айнабекъ] (SODž. 126); Kkalp. 20th c. **Ayna-gül** [Айнагюл], fem. (Bask., Kkalp. 403, KkRS 777); Kirg. 20th c. **Ayna-gül** [Айнагүл], a literary fem. character in one of Aytmatov's short stories (Čingiz Ajtmatov, Povesti i rasskazy. Frunze, 1975); Kzk. **Ayna-qan** [Аіна Қан] (Proben III, 257 /302/); Kzk. 19th c. **Ayna-qul** [Айнакулъ] (SOK 308); Oghuz/Trkm. 14th c. - 15th c. **Ayna-melik** [اينه ملك / Айна-Мелик], fem. (DQorq. 13, DQorq./Rossi 100); Turk. 16th c. **Ayni / Aynǐ** [عينى], Memi's daughter. Eight more persons bore the name at that time (Ongan, Ank. II); Turk. 1506 **Ayni-šah-χatun** [Ayni-Şâh Hatun], fem. (Gökb., Ed. 380); Yürük 1543 **Eyne-begi** [اينه بكى / Eynebeği], several persons among the Yürüks of Kocacık, Turkey (Gökb., Rum. 103, 176, 177, 178, 185, 186, 187, 198, 233); *TN:* Turk. 20th c. **Ayna-oγlu**, a village in the province of Balıkesir, Turkey (TMİB 137). ❖ 'Looking-glass' cf. Trkm. *ayna* 'стекло, зеркало' (Sopieva, Loc. cit.), Kkalp. *ayna* 'стекло, зеркало' (KkRS), Kirg. *ayna* 'зеркало' (Jud.), Osm. *ayna* 'cüma' (TarS), Turk. dial.

ayna / ayni 'anne, hey ana anlamında hitap' (DS). Baskakov mistakenly interprets the Trkm. fem. PN *Ayna-gül* as 'Flower-(made of looking-)glass' (see Baskakov: OSA 139) (<P. *āyina*).

AYNA III.　Hak.(Kacha, Sag., Blt.) 19th-20th c. **Ayna** [Аiна], a devil (Proben IX, 245-48, 370, 478-80, 536). ✧ 'Devil, evil spirit' cf. Uyg. *ayna* 'Şeytan' (EUTS), Alt., Hak. *ayna* 'Teufel, böser Geist' (Radl. I, 17).

AYNA-QAN see **AYNA I.**

AYNA-OƦLU see **AYNA I.**

AYNAROZ　Turk. 1530 **Aynaroz** (Gökb., Ed. 397). ✧ 'Athos (mountain)' cf. Turk. *Aynaroz* (dağı) (HŞ).

AYNE see **ADİNA**

AYNEJE　Turk. 1552 **Ayneje** [اينـجه], fem. (Gökçen 35). ✧ 'Small looking-glass'. ⇨ **AYNA I.** + dim. suff. *-je*.

AYNEK　Maml. 1303 **Aynek** [اينك], governor of Damascus, died in 1303 (Zetterst. 27, 40, Weil, Chalif. I, 192, Sauvaire VI, 246); Kzk. 19th c. **Aynek** [Айнекъ] (SOK 218). ✧ I. 'Window'? cf. Kzk. *aynaq*, Kzk. west. dial. *aynäk* 'das Fenster' (Radl. I, 18); II. 'Little looking-glass'? ⇨ **AYNA I.** + dim. suff. *-k.*

AYNEKE　Kzk. 19th c. **Ayneke** [Айнеке] (SODž. 94). ✧ 'Small looking-glass'. ⇨ **AYNA I.** + dim. suff. *-ke* / comp. *ake.*

AYNİ see **AYNA I.**

AYNĬ see **AYNA I.**

AYRA　Hak.(Kacha) 19th c. **Ayra** [Айра] (Katanov, Otč. II, 42). ✧ 'Little old woman' (Katanov).

AYRANJĬ　Maml. 13th c. - 14th c. **Ayranji** [ايـرنـجى] (Sauvaget 40). ✧ 'One who makes or/and sells *ayran*' cf. 'celui qui fait l'ayran, qu'on tire du lait' (Sauvaget 40), Maml. *ayran* 'Yoğurttan yapılan içki' (AH), Uyg., Chag., Alt., Osm. etc. *ayran* 'ein Getränk aus gegohrener Kuhmilch' (Radl. I, 25). + suff. *-jï.*

AYRĬ　Yürük 1543 **Ayrï / Ayrï?** [ايرى / Ayrï], Erdoğdu's son (Gökb., Rum. 181).

AYRUŠ　Alt. 19th-20th c. **Ayruš** [Айруш] (OjrRS 207). ✧ 'Fork' (OjrRS 207) cf. Alt. *ayruuš* 'вилы' (OjrRS).

AYSA　Tat.(Sib.) 1573 **Aysa** [Аиса] (AI I, 350); Bashk. 1756 **Aysa** [Айса Черекеев] (MIB IV/1, 107); Bashk. 1772 **Aysa** [Мурза Айсин] (MIB IV/2, 410); Bashk. 1777 **Aysa** [Мамбет Айсинь] (MIB V, 57); Bashk. 18th c. **Aysa / Aysan** [Айса (Айсан) Кузеев] (MIB V, 152). ✧ '(Prophet) Jesus' cf. *Ƨaysa, Qaysa* (Ar.) 'God protects (him), God saves (him)' (Sattarov, Kusimova). ⇨ **İSA.**

AYŠA　Selj. 11th c. **Ayša** [Аиша], Alp-arslan's (1063-1072) daughter (MIT I, 376); Kkalp. 20th c. **Ayša** [Айша], fem. (KkRS 777); Kirg. **Ayša** [Айша], fem. (Jud. 59); *TN:* Turk. 20th c. **Ayše-χoJa** [Ayşehoca], a village in the province of Adana (TMİB 16). ✧ Aysha (Ar.), 'the name of the Prophet's favourite wife' (EI I, 228). Beloved female name with the Turkic peoples.

See also **BİYBİ-AYŠA.**

AYŠAKE　Kirg. **Ayšake** [Айшаке], fem. (Jud. 38). ✧ 'Little Aysha'. ⇨ **AYŠA** + suff. *-ke.*

AYŠE-XOJA see **AYŠA**

AYT　Tat.(Sib.) 1637 **Ayit-qul** [Аиткул Ангучаков] (Miller, Ist. Sib. II, 442); Tat. 19th c.? **Ayït** [Süleiman Ajytov, Aitov] (Mende 38, 69); Bashk. 20th c. **Ayït-bay** [Айытбай] (Kusimova 30); Bashk. 20th c. **Ayït-qol** [Айыткол] (Kusimova 30); Tat.? 1731 **Ayt** [Аит Сюкенеев] (MIB III, 293); Tat.(Mish.) 1748 **Ayt** [Аит Чалтин] (Nepljuev 437); Bashk. 1727 **Ayt** [Аит Уразаев] (MIB III, 246); Bashk. 1735 **Ayt** [Аит Янымбетевъ] (Vel.-Zern., Bašk. 13); Bashk. 1764 **Ayt** [Сыртлан Аитов] (MIB IV/1, 277); Bashk. 1777 **Ayt** [Салим Аитов] (MIB V, 59); Bashk. 1782 **Ayt** [Субхангул Аитов] (MIB V, 133); Kzk. 19th c. **Ayt** [Аитъ Усеновъ] (Grod., Pril. 157, 166); Kzk. 19th c. **Ayt** [Аит] (AOP 42); Tat.(Mish.)? 1775 **Ayt / Ayit** [Аит Янбетевъ] (MIB IV/2, 421); Tat.(Mish.)? 1775 **Ayt / Ayit** [Аитъ Алмеевъ] (MIB IV/2, 421); Selj. 12th c. **Ayt-aba**, a small mosque (Ibn Šaddād, Nawād.: RHCHor III, 79); Kzk. 19th c. **Ayt-bay** [Айтбай] (AOAtb. 86); Kzk. 19th c. **Ayt-bay** [Айтбай] (AOK 110); Kzk. 19th c. **Ayt-bay** [Айтбай] (AOP 122); Kkalp. 20th c. **Ayt-bay** [Айтбай] (KkRS 772); Kzk. 19th c. **Ayt-eke / Ay-teke?** [Айтеке] (SODž. 84); Kkalp. 20th c. **Ayt-eke / Ay-teke?** [Айтеке] (KkRS 772); Kkalp. 20th c. **Ayt-gül** [Айтгүл], fem. (KkRS 777); Kzk. 19th c. **Ayt-χoJa** [Аятъ-Ходжа] (Grod., Pril. 60); Kzk. 1817 **Ayt-χoJa** (Ayt-χoža / Ayt-qoJa?) [ايتـوجه / Айтхожа] (MIK IV, 308); Kkalp. 20th c. **Ayt-kül** (<Ayt-gül) [Айткюл], fem. (Bask., Kkalp. 403); Tat.? 1822 **Ayt-küze** [Муллагазы Аиткузин], a Cossack captain (yasaul) of Tatar origin? (TOUAK XXIV, 121); Bashk. 1734 **Ayt-küzä** [Аиткуза Исекеевъ], a tarχan (Vel.-Zern., Bašk. 10); Tat.? 16th c.? **Ayt-qul** [Абыз-Кучумъ Аиткуловъ] (PSZRI X, 983); Tat.(Sib.) 1629 **Ayt-qul** [Аиткул Кызылбаев] (Miller, Ist. Sib. II, 343, 344); Bashk. 1706 **Ayt-qul** [Аиткул Шалдыков] (MIB III, 30); Bashk. 1734 **Ayt-qul** [Аиткул Абыз Кансуяров] (Vel.-Zern., Bašk. 11); Bashk. 1735 **Ayt-qul** [Айткулъ Кулчуковъ] (Vel.-Zern., Bašk. 14); Bashk. 1735 **Ayt-qul** [Байслан Аиткуловъ] (Vel.-Zern., Bašk. 15); Bashk. 1735 **Ayt-qul** [Акзигитъ Аиткуловъ] (Vel.-Zern., Bašk. 18); Bashk. 1735 **Ayt-qul** [Айткулъ Рысовъ] (Vel.-Zern., Bašk. 20); Bashk. 1777 **Ayt-qul** [Сыртлан Аиткулов] (MIB V, 60); Kzk. 19th c. **Ayt-qul** [Ир Айткул] (Ljutš 114); Uzb. 1697 **Ayt-qul** [Тенейко Аиткулов (Анткулов!)], a man from Bukhara in Tobolsk (PSZRI III, 355, Andrievič, Ist. Sib. II, 22); Kzk. 1840 **Ayt-pay** [Айтпай Чонгинъ], from the Middle Horde (Orta Žüz) (Konšin, Mat. V, 16); Kzk. 19th c. **Ayt-pay**

[Айтпай] (AOAtb. 66); Kzk. 19th c. **Ayt-pay** [Айтпай] (AOP 14); Kzk. 19th c. **Ayt-pay** [Айтпай] (SODž. 148); Kzk. 19th c. **Ayt-pay** [Айтпай] (SOV 24, 82); Kzk. 1808 **Ayt-žan** [Аитжан], fem. (MIK IV, 240); Kzk. 19th c. **Ayt-žan** [Айтчанъ] (SOV 68); Kkalp. 20th c. **Ayt-žan** [Айтжан] (KkRS 772); Bashk. 1784 Ḡayit-bay [Гаитбай] (MIB V, 157); *EN:* Kzk. 18th c - 19th c. **Ayt** [Айт] (Tynyšp. 67, 74); *TN:* Kzk. **Ayt-pay** [Айтпай], a colony in Kazakstan in lat. 47° N and long 72° E (Karta JAR XI). ✧ 'Festive day; born on a festive day' (Kusimova, Loc. cit.; Sattarov: Ḡayït), cf. Kzk. *ait* (<Ar.) 'Feiertag nach dem Ramasan' (Radl. I, 45), *ayt* 'žïlïnda eki ret bolatïn 'Oraza aytï', 'Qurban aytï' dep atalatïn, dini meyram' (QTTS). Kkalp. *ayt* ' рел. праздник' (KkRS). The Russian 'Аит' forms may reflect an original Tat., Bashk., etc. *Ayăt* (< *Ayïï). See also **TUL-AYT**.

AYT-AMAN Bashk. 1775 **Ayt-aman** [Исенбай Айтаманов] (MIB IV/1, 380). ✧ 'Festive day - healthy/sound'. ⇨ **AYT + AMAN**.

AYT-KEŠ Kzk. 19th c. **Ayt-keš** [Айткешъ] (AOP 26). ✧ 'Feast-sable'? ⇨ **AYT + KÏŠ**.

AYT-MAMBET Kzk. 19th c. **Ayt-mambet** [Айтмамбетъ] (Grod., Pril. 144). ✧ 'Mukhammat born on a festive day'. ⇨ **AYT + MAMBET**.

AYT-MÏRAT see **AYT-MURAT**

AYT-MURAT Kkalp. 20th c. **Ayt-murat / Ayt-mïrat** [Айтмурат / Айтмырат] (KkRS 772). ✧ 'Murat, born on a festive day'. ⇨ **AYT + MURAT**.

AYT-NAZAR Kzk. 19th c. **Ayt-nazar** [Аитъ Назаръ Мурсалов] (Grod., Pril. 95). ⇨ **AYT + NAZAR**.

AYT-PAҐA Tat.(Ishim) **Ayt-paγa** [Aitpaga / Аiтпаßа], Bikärä's son (Proben IV, 215 /265/). ✧ 'Feast-Frog'? ⇨ **AYT + BAQA**.

AYT-SUÑQAR Selj. 1039/40 **Ayt-suñqar** [ايد سنقر / Айд Сункар], took part in the fights against the Khorezmians (after Bayhaki) (MIT I, 286). ✧ 'Feast-Falcon'. ⇨ **AYT + SOÑQUR**.

AYT-TER Tat. 1706 **Ayt-ter** [Айттеръ Иликеев], (MIB III, 29, 30, 183); Bashk. 18th c. **Ayt-ter** [Айттеръ Исембаев] (MIB III, 23, 36, 60). ⇨ **AYT + TER**.

AYTAҐ Uyg. 13th c. - 14th c. **Aytaγ** [ايتاغ] (Chwol., Syr.-nest. 98, 142).

AYTAQ Kzk. 19th c. **Aytaq** [Айтакъ] (SOV 62).

AYTALÏN Yak. **Aytalïn-quo** [Айталын Kyo], fem. (Pek); Yak. **Aytalïn** [Аiталын], Pet name of girls in folktales, the name of a shamaness in a tale (Pek.).

AYTALÏN see **AYTALÏN**

AYTAR see **AYDAR**

AYTEY Kzk. 19th c. **Aytey** [Айтей] (AOAtb. 54); Kzk. 19th c. **Aytey** [Айтей] (AOK 94); Kzk. 19th c. **Aytey-bay** [Айтейбай] (SOK 34). ✧ 'Moon-like'. ⇨ **AY +** suff. *-tey*.

AYTEK Tat.? 1599 **Aytek** [Айтекъ], a murza from Siberia (AI II, 21); Kzk. 19th c.? **Aytek(-biy)** [Айтек бий], from the Kiši žüz (Valihanov, Soč. 163). ✧ 'Moon-like'. ⇨ **AY** + suff. *-tek*.

AYTÏMBET Kzk. 19th c. **Aytimbet** [Айтембетъ] (SODž. 26); Kkalp. 20th c. **Aytimbet** [Айтимбет] (KkRS 772); + suff. *-imbet*.; ⇨ **AYT** + suff. *-imbet*.

AYTÏQ Kzk. **Aytïq** [Кыпчакбай Айтыков] (Konšin, Oč. 131). ⇨ **AYT** + dim. suff. *-ïq*.

AYTQA Tat. 1684 **Aytqa** [Айтка Мокшин] (Zolotn., Alf. 155). ✧ 'Feast; place of the feast' cf. Chag. *aitqa* 'im Russischen ist auch торжество (Feierlichkeit) und торг (Handel) eines Stammes; Marktplatz ' (Radl. I, 47). ⇨ **AYT** + dim. suff. *-qa*.

AYTMAQ Kzk. 19th c. **Aytmaq** [Айтмакъ] (SOV 156). ✧ 'Speech' cf. Maml. *ayt-* 'sagen' (Al-Qawānin), *aytmak* 'söylemek, demek' (İM), Kzk., Kirg. *ait-* 'sagen, reden sprechen' (Radl. I, 43). + suff. *-maq*.

AYTMAS Khorezm. 13th c. **Aytmas** [ايتماس], Ögedey's (1229-1241) commander against Jelāleddīn (Abulg./Desm. 146). ✧ 'He doesn't (won't) speak' cf. Turk., Kzk., Kirg. *ait-* 'sagen, reden sprechen' (Radl. I, 43). See also **MÏN-AYTPAS**.

AYTMAT Kirg. 20th c. **Aytmat** [Чингис Чингисович Айтматов], garnd-father of the famous Kirghiz writer (Tchhinguiz Aitmatov, Adieu Goulsary! Moscou, 1976, etc.). ✧ 'Mukhammad born on festive day'. ⇨ **AYT** + suffixoid *-mat*.

AYTMÏŠ Maml. **Aytmïš**, Sayfaddīn ~, an emir (Björkm. 161); Maml. 13th c. **Aytmïš** [ايتمش] (Zetterst. 89); Maml. 1325 **Aytmïš** [سيف الد ين ايتمش المحمدى / Itmiš] (Zetterst. 166, 192); Maml. 1346/47 **Aytmïš** [ايتمش عبدالغنى] (Iyās I, 187); Maml. 1378/79 **Aytmïš** [ا يتمش البجاسى] (Iyās I, 243, 275, 319); Maml. 1382/83 **Aytmïš** [ايتمش الخاصكى] (Iyās I, 256, 257); Maml. 1398/99 **Aytmïš** [الجرجاوى الظاهرى] (Ibn Taghrīb. VI, 2, 4, 7 etc.); Maml. 1400 **Aytmïš** [السيفى ابو العزايم الرجاسى] (Mayer 91, Ibn Taghrīb. VI, 143); Maml. 1421 **Aytmïš** [ايتمش الخضرى الظاهرى] (Ibn Taghrīb. VI, 505, 537); Maml. 1453 **Aytmïš** [ا يتمش المويدى] (Ibn Taghrīb. VII, 412, 824); Maml. 1493/94 **Aytmïš** [ا يتمش البجاسى] (Iyās II, 282); Khorezm./Chag. 1404/05 **Aytmïš** [ايتمش الشعبانى / Itmiš] (Ibn Taghrīb. VI, 128); Maml. 14th c. **Äytmiš** [ايّتمِش] (Sauvaget 39). ✧ 'He spoke' (Sauvaget 39) cf. Maml. *ayt-* 'sagen' (Al-Qawānin), *aytmak* 'söylemek, demek' (İM), Kzk., Kirg. *ait-* 'sagen, reden sprechen' (Radl. I, 43).

AYTPAN Kzk. 19th c. **Aytpan** [Айтпанъ] (SOK 198). ⇨ **AYT** + suff. *-man*.

AYU Bashk. 1756 **Ayu** [А[Ремгулов] (MIB IV/1, 129); Crm.(Tat.) 17th c. **Ayu / Ayï** [ايوعظمت كراى / Айы],

Khan Azamet Girey's sobriquet (Smirnov, Krym. 631); Kzk. 19th c. **Ayu-bay** [Аюбай] (SOV 114); Kzk. 19th c. **Ayu-bek** [Аюбекъ] (SODž. 56); Kzk. 19th c. **Ayu-bek** [Аюбекъ] (SOK 286); Kzk. **Ayu-bike** [Аju Бiкä], fem. (Proben III, 187 /226/); Kzk. **Ayu-bikeš** [Аюбикеш], fem. (Žirm., Epos 405); Tat. 1780, 1796 **Ayu-χan** [Аюхан Уразаев] (MIB V, 103, 104, 362, 363); *TN:* Trkm. **Ayu-bay** [Аю-бай], toponym, a colony (settlement) north of Čarjou (Karta JAR XIX). ✧ 'Bear' cf. Kuman, Alt., Crm., Kirg., Kzk., Tat., Turk. etc. *ayū* 'der Bär; das Sternbild des Bären' (Radl. I, 223), *ayï (ayu, ayuw, ayïw, ayïq)* 'id.' (Sev.).

AYU-ΓARA Bashk. 1735 **Ayu-γara** [Асян Аюгарин], a tarχan (Vel.-Zern., Bašk. 19). ✧ I. 'Bear-black, black bear'?; II. 'Look at the bear; look for a bear'; cf. Bashk. *qara-* 'смотреть, присматривать'. ⇨ AYU + QARA. See also İT-QARA, QULUM-QARA, TAY-QARA.

AYU-QUTURΓAN Tat. 18th c. **Ayu-quturγan** [Аюкутурган], a village (Korsakov 339). ✧ 'The bear became enraged; where the bear becomes enraged' cf. Tat. *qotïr-* 'беситься; разъяриться' (TRS). ⇨ AYU + QUTUR, QUTURMİŠ.

AYUČAN Kzk. 19th c. **Ayučan** [Аючан] (SOK 288). ✧ 'He who likes (hunting for) bears'. ⇨ AYU + suff. -*čan*.

AYUQ Tat. 18th-19th c. **Ayuq** [Аюкъ] (Magn. 31). ✧ 'Little bear'. ⇨ AYU + dim. suff. -*q*.

AYUQA Chuv. 18th-19th c. **Ayuka** [Аюка] (Magn. 31); Kzk. 19th c. **Ayuke** [Аюке] (Grod., Pril. 169); Bashk. 1761 **Ayuqa** [Аюка Илчикеев] (MIB IV/1, 221). ✧ 'Little bear' cf. Kalm. PN *Ayuki ~ Ayuqa*, 'Bear-father; bear-brother; little bear'. ⇨ AYU + suff. -*qa* / (R.) -*ka* or suff. -*qa/-ke* (<*aqa, ake*).

AYUQAYQA Tat.(Mish.) 1682 **Ayuqayqa** [Аюкайка Кемѣев] (AI V, 139). ✧ 'Little bear'. ⇨ AYU + dim. suff. -*qay* + R. (?) dim. suff. -*qa*.

AYUŠ Kzk. 19th c. **Ayuš** [Аюшъ] (SODž. 150). ✧ 'Little bear'. ⇨ AYU + suff. -*š*?

AYUWČİ Tuv. 19th c. **Ayïjï** [Аjыцы] (Proben IX, 54, 214); Bashk./Tat.? 1675 **Ayuwčï** [Аювчи Толонгозин] (MIB I, 200); Bashk./Tat.? 1675 **Ayuwčï** [Чюраш Аювчин] (MIB I, 200). ✧ 'Bear-hunter; Bear-leader' cf. Tat. *ayučï* 'Bärenführer' (Radl. I, 225). ⇨ AYU + suff. -*čï*.

AYVAZ Turk. 20th c. **Ayvaz** [Ayvaz], a village in the province of Denizli (TMİB, Köyl.). ✧ 'Footman, man servant in a mansion; name of the beautiful youth in the popular story of Köroğlu' (TED), cf. Turk. *ayvaz* 'armenischer Hausdiener; der Aufseher; aufsichtsführender Diener über das Küchenpersonal in früheren türk. Wohnhäusern' (?). The name in Turkish dialects may have several meanings such as 'husband; blind; handsome; bold; dumb person; rude' (DS). Cf.

also the names of villages, where Turkomans of Anatolia live, with the same personal name among their components: *Ayvazhacı, Ayvazpınarı*, etc.

AYWU Bulg. 1320/21 **Aywu / Ayuw?** [ايوو], fem. (Epigr. Bulg. 140-41).

AYZA see **AYSA**

AKİYA Kirg. Akiya [Акия], fem. (Jud. 196).

AKÏSTU Chuv. 18th-19th c. **Akïstu-bay** [Акстубай] (Magn. 26).

AQ I. Hak. 19th-20th c. **Aγ-bay** [Аҕбай] (HRS 348); Shor 19th-20th c. **Aγ-ōl** (<**Aq-oġul**), son of the legendary Šul-bay (Dyrenkova 310); Hak.(Kacha) 19th-20th c. **Aγ-ōl** (<**Aq-ōl**) [Аҕ-ол] (Proben IX, 426); Tuv. 19th c. **Aγ-ōl** (<**Aq-ōl**) [Ак-ол (Аголъ)] (Proben IX, 1320); Bashk. 18th c. **Aγ-zigit** [Акзигит Яншибаев] (MIB IV/1, 315); Chuv. 18th-19th c. **Aχ-čura** [Ахчура] (Magn. 31); Bashk. 1709 **Aχ-čura** [Ахчюра] (MIB I, 271); Chuv. 18th-19th c. **Aχ-mola** [Ахмола] (Magn. 31); Hak. 19th-20th c. **Aχ-pay** [Ахпай] (HRS 348); Chuv. 18th-19th c. **Ak-kam** [Аккамъ] (Magn. 25); Chuv. 18th-19th c. **Ak-mendey** [Акмяндей, Акмендей] (Magn. 26); Uyg. 948 **Aq**, envoy of the Uyghurs (Hamilton, Ouïg. 146); Crm. (Turk./Tat.?) 1680 **Aq** [Ак Мехмед] (Vel.-Zern., Crim. 674); Uzb. 1740 **Aq-arbab** [Акъ-Арбабъ], from Khiva (Hanykov, Poezdka 21); Kirg. **Aq-arïγ** [Ак-арыг], fem. (Radl. I, 89); Turk. 20th c. **Aq-baba** [Akbaba], a village in the province of Ordu (TMİB 711); Maml. 1367 **Aq-bay** [اقباى الاحمدى] (Iyās I, 221); Maml. 1398/99, 1400 **Aq-bay** [اقباى اليحياوى الاينالى] (Ibn Taghrīb. VI, 9, Iyās I, 325, II, 109); Maml. 1398/99, 1401/02 **Aq-bay** [اقباى الكركى طاز] (Ibn Taghrīb. VI, 42, 86, Iyās I, 346); Maml. 1398, 1418 **Aq-bay** [اقباى الطرنطايى], governor of Damascus (Ibn Taghrīb. VI, 9, 23 etc., Weil, Chalif. II, 137 etc., Iyās I, 311, 318, 341); Maml. 1400/01 **Aq-bay** [اقباى الخازندار], a treasurer (Iyās I, 337, 338); Maml. 1414/15 **Aq-bay** [اقباى المويدى] (Ibn Taghrīb. VI, 341 etc.); Maml. 1434/35 **Aq-bay** [اقباى اليشبكى الجاموس] (Ibn Taghrīb. VI, 742); Maml. 1451, 1454, 1456 **Aq-bay** [اقباى السيفى جارقطلو] (Iyās II, 54, Ibn Taghrīb. VII, 221, VIII, 200, 228); Maml. 1456 **Aq-bay** [اقباى الجكمى] (Iyās II, 54); Maml. 1465 **Aq-bay** [اقباى المويدى] (Ibn Taghrīb. VIII, 428, 583); Maml. 1478 **Aq-bay** [اقباى الطويل] (Iyās II, 184, 191, 363, 380, III, 25, 29, 73, Weil, Chalif. II, 375); Maml. 1483 **Aq-bay** [اقباى كاشف الشرقيه] (Iyās II, 220, III, 62); Maml. 1483 **Aq-bay** [اقباى], Al-Sayfī, the ruler of the emirs, in an inscription on a copper- (or brass-)-dish (Mayer 176); Maml. 1487 **Aq-bay** [الظا هرى خشقدم] (Iyās II, 241); Maml. 1490 **Aq-bay** [اقباى بنجا نم], nā'ib of Lattakich, according to the inscription from Lattakich (Sauvaget: BEO XII (1948), 47,

Sauvaget 37); Maml. 1496/97 **Aq-bay** [اقباى نايـب غـزه], nā'ib of Gizeh (Iyās II, 306, 308, 359, Weil, Chalif. II, 364); Maml. 1498 **Aq-bay** [اقباى استـا دار الـنـخيره] (Iyās II, 344); Maml.? 1498/99 **Aq-bay** [اقباى رأس نوبه كبير] (Iyās II, 354); Turk.? 1498/99 **Aq-bay** [اقباى نايـب قلعه الشام], nāᶜib of Syria (Iyās II, 352); Turk.? 1516 **Aq-bay** [اقباى بـن قا نصوه] (Iyās III, 3); Kar. 20th c. **Aq-bay** (Pröhle, Kar. 86); Bashk. 1734 **Aq-bay** [Абдулла Акбаев] (MIB III, 325); Bashk. 1783 **Aq-bay** [Еркей Акбаев] (MIB V, 145); Kzk. **Aq-bay** [Кундынар Акбаев] (MKOP 153); Kzk. 19th c. **Aq-bay** [Акбай] (AOAtb. 10, 54); Kzk. 19th c. **Aq-bay** [Чубаш Акбаев] (Grod., Pril. 126, 151); Kzk. **Aq-bayan** [Ak Bajan / Ак Баjан], fem. (Proben III, 268); Maml. 14th c. **Aq-bala** [اقبلا / Akbala], fem. (Tarǰ/Houtsma 50, Tarǰ/Toparlı 43); Kzk. 1920 **Aq-bala** [Ak Bala] (Fox 149, 170); Kirg. **Aq-bala** [Ак Бала], Bolot's father (Proben V, 214 /215/); Chag. 1570 **Aq-begim** [Ак-бегим], fem. (Ivanov 91); Alt. **Aq-bi** [Акъ-би] (Nikiforov 128); Tat. 1776 **Aq-biy** [Якуб Акбіевъ] (PSZRI XX, 456); Alt. 19th c. **Aq-biy** [Ак-бій] (Potanin IV, 369); Chag. 1554 **Aq-bike** [Ак-бике], fem. (Ivanov 134); Nog. **Aq-bikeš** [Ак-бикеш], fem. (Žirm., Epos 403); Kzk. **Aq-bïbä** [Ak Bïbä / Ак Бібä], fem. (Proben III, 68 /89/); Kkalp. 20th c. **Aq-böke** [Акбэке], fem. (KkRS 777); Alt. **Aq-bökö** [Акъ-Бökö] (Nikiforov 148); Trkm. 19th c. **Aq-čan** [Джиомокай Акчанов] (Ščeglov IV, 179); Kzk./Kirg.? 19th c. **Aq-čan** [Акчань], fem. (Grod., Pril. 124); Tat. 1600 **Aq-čura**, a Tatar prince among the Mordwins (Smyrnov 279); Tat. 1601 **Aq-čura** [Беляк Акчурин] (Miller, Ist. Sib. II, 169); Tat. 18th c. **Aq-čura** [Акчура] (Nepljuev 882); Bashk. 1736 **Aq-čura** [Акчура Азакеев] (MIB III, 344); Bashk. 1740 **Aq-čura** [Ашер Акчурин] (MIB I, 398); Tat. 19th c. **Aq-čura-oγlu** [Акчурин], Yusuf Aq-čura-oγlu (R. form: Akčurin), writer (Or. Bibl. XX, 80, Mende 37, 38, 77, 82, 83, 86, 87, 90, 100, 102, 103, 104, 105, 131); Kzk./Kirg.? 19th c. **Aq-ǰan-bige** [Акджанбиг], fem. (Grod., Pril. 147); Kzk. 19th c. **Aq-ǰigit** [Акджигитъ] (AOO 58); Kzk. / Kirg.? 19th c. **Aq-ǰigit** [Акъ-джигитъ] (Potanin II, 3, 4); Kzk. 1822 **Aq-ǰigit** < **Aq-čigit** [Акчигитъ Амантаевъ] (TOUAK XXIV, 131); Tat. 19th c. **Aq-ǰigit-zäde** [Musa Akǧigit-Yade], from Kazan (Mende 74, 178); Bashk. 18th c. **Aq-änäy** [Акэней Ялмантаев] (MIB V, 203); Trkm. 20th c. **Aq-ɣül** [Aqgül], fem. (Zaj. 1971, 339); Alt. 19th c. **Aq-χan** [Ак-хан] (Verb., In. 140, 145); Tuv. 19th c. **Aq-χan** [Акъ-ханъ], in a folktale (Potanin IV, 423); Tat.(Sib.) 1599 **Aq-χanïm** [Акханымъ], a Siberian princess, Küčüm's grand-daughter (AI II, 21,23);

Maml. 1421 **Aq-χoǰa** [اقحجا الاحمدى الظاهرى] (Ibn Taghrīb. VI, 483, 531); Turk.? 14th c. **Aq-χoǰa** [اقحواجه] (Qazw. 716); Az.? **Aq-χoǰa** [اقحواجه], a place in Iran (RaD/Jahn 57, 83); Bashk. 1735 **Aq-küzä** [Аккуза Кочкаров], a tarχan (Vel.-Zern., Bašk. 16); OT 576 **Aq-qaɣan** [Ακκαγα, 'Ακκάγα], princess of an unknown Scythian (=Turkic) tribe whose region was named after her (Byz. Turc. 59, Németh, HMK 191); Alt. **Aq-qan** [Ак Кан], a bogatyr (hero) (Proben IX, 343-52); Hak. 19th-20th c. **Aq-qan** (Radl. II, 105); Hak.(Belt.) **Aq-qan** [Ак Кан], the title of the Russian imperator (=White Khan) (Proben IX, 362, 382, 456 ff.); Shor 19th-20th c. **Aq-qan / Aq-qān** (Dyrenkova 28 ff., 158 ff.); Kirg. **Aq-qanïš** [Акканыш], fem. (Jud. 953); Kzk. 19th c. **Aq-qazï** [Акказы] (AOA 6); Kirg. 19th c. **Aq-qïz** [Аккызъ (Акгизъ)], fem. (Grod., Pril. 26); Kirg. 20th c. **Aq-qïz** [Аккызъ], fem. (Kalilov 95); Turk. 1583 **Aq-qoǰa** [Akkoca], the source mentions 2 persons with this name (Ongan, Ank. I, 150); Kzk. / Uzb.? **Aq-qoǰa** [Аккоджа], Imbars' son (Nepljuev 805); Bashk. 20th c. **Aq-qol** [Аккол, Аккул] (Kusimova 30); Maml. 1310,1325 **Aq-qul** [اقول الحاجب الحاجب الحمدى], Sayfaddīn Aq-qul, an emir (χājib) whose name was mistakenly written as اقول (Dawād. 213, 249, 264 1367, Zetterst. 147, 188); Bashk. 1686 **Aq-qul** [Аккулка Уразаев] (Vel.-Zern., Bašk. 40); Bashk. 1706 **Aq-qul** [Аккул Слевсинов], a tarχan (MIB III, 13); Khorezm. 1221 **Aq-melik** [اقملك / Хумаюн (Ак-мелик)], byname of Xumayun, the commander-in-chief in Mongol service (J̌uwaynī I, 131, MIT I, 493); Kzk. 19th c. **Aq-mirza** [Акмирза Гаибовъ] (SKSO VIII, 204); Tat. 1555 **Aq-mïrza** [Акъ-мырза], from Astrakhan (PSRL XIII, 245); Kkalp. 20th c. **Aq-mïrza** [Акмырза] (KkRS 772); Kzk. 19th c. **Aq-mulda**, a batïr (bogatyr, hero) (Ljutš III); Tat. 1708 **Aq-murza** [Ак-Мурза Урусов] (MIB I, 219); Tat.? 1717 **Aq-murza** [Акъ Мурза], resident in Mersk (PSZRI V, 487); Tat.? 1784 **Aq-murza** [Акмурза] (IAN (Otd. gum. nauk) 1928, 379); Tat. 18th-19th c. **Aq-murza** [Акмурза] (Magn. 26); Bashk. 1706 **Aq-murza** [Акмурза Акзигитов] (MIB III, 28); Kzk.? **Aq-murza** [Ак-Мурза] (Žirm., Epos 430); Kzk. 1823 **Aq-murza** [اق مرظا] (MIK IV, 459, 462); Kzk.? 19th c. **Aq-murza** [Акъ-Мурза], Bekmurza's brother (Potanin II, 4); Nog.? 1649 **Aq-murza** [Акъ мурза] (AI IV, 87); Uzb. 19th c. **Aq-murza** [Акъ-Мурза] (SKSO III, 22); Kzk. **Aq-pay** [Султан Акпай Джолдин] (Pam. kn. Semip. 1898, 44); Kzk. 19th c. **Aq-pay** [Акпай] (AOO 30); Kzk. 19th c. **Aq-pay** [Джан Акпаев] (Grod., Pril. 126, 151); Kzk. 19th c. **Aq-pay** [Акпай] (SODž. 130); Kzk. 19th c. **Aq-pay** [Акпай] (SOK 116, 242); Tat. / Nog.? 1543 **Aq-seyit** [Аксейитъ] (PSRL XIII, 145); Tat. 20th c. **Aq-soltan**

[Аксолтан], fem. (Sattarov); Oghuz 11th c. - 12th c. **Aq-sultan** [اق سلطان], ibn Qutbaddīn Mahmud the (first) Anushteginid Khorezmshah (1098-1128) (Qazw. 498); Khorezm. 1231 **Aq-sultan** [اق سلطان / Ак-Султан / Ак-шах], known as well as Aq-šah [اق شاه], Terken (or Tergen, mistakenly Türkân) Khatun's and Muhammad's son, Khorezmshah Ǯelāleddīn Meñgüberdi's (1220-1231) brother (Ǯuwaynī II, 131, 133, RaD I/2, 214, RaD/Ber. III, 67, 88, MIT I, 476, 503, 594, Nasawī 40, Barth., Turk. 466, 472); Khorezm./Chag. 1412 **Aq-sultan-χanike** [Акъ-Султанъ-Ханике], the Timurid Sultan Mahmud Khan's daughter (Barth., Ulugb. 73); Kkalp. 20th c. **Aq-suluw** [Ақсулуў], fem. (KkRS 777); Karakh. 1094 **Aq-tegin** [انا صرالدوله افتكـن], mistakenly written as Af-tegin (Ibn al-Athīr/Tornb. X, 162); Tat./Bashk. 1737 **Aq-zigit** [Акзигитъ], a Teptär (Nepljuev 427); Bashk. 1712 **Aq-zigit** [Акзигит Карамшаков] (MIB III, 83); Bashk. 1717 **Aq-zigit** [Акзигит Акбашев] (MIB III, 152); Bashk. 1735 **Aq-zigit** [Акзигитъ Аиткуловъ], a tarχan (Vel.-Zern., Bašk. 18); Bashk. 20th c. **Aq-zigit** [Акзигит] (Kusimova 30); *EN:* Kzk. 18th c. - 19th c. **Aq-qoža** [Аккожа] (Tynyšp. 75); Kzk. 18th c. - 19th c. **Aq-šora** [Акшора] (Tynyšp. 71); *TN:* Aq-bay [Акбай], a well south-west of Čerčen (Karta JAR XX); *TN:* Crm.(Tat.) Aq-čora, a place north-east of "Eski-Qïrïm (Jervis III, VIII). ✧ 'White; innocent; clean; honest' in most Trk. languages *aq* 'weiss; rein, unvermischt' (Budagov, Radl. I, 88, Sev., TMEN II, No. 504, etc.). According to Žanuzakov *aq* may mean 'milk, dairy products' and as such expresses the wish of the parents for abundance of dairy food (Žanuzakov p. 109). See also **SAN-DERYOQ-AQ(?)**.

AQ-AY Alt., Shor 19th-20th c. **Aq-ay**, a hero (Radl. I, 5, 89). ✧ 'White Moon' (Radl. I, 5, 89). ⇨ **AQ I. + AY.**

AQ-AMAN Bashk. 1803 **Aq-aman** [Ряк Акамановъ] (PSZRI XXVII, 803). ✧ 'Clean/honest-Healthy'. ⇨ **AQ I. + AMAN.**

AQ-AÑ Kirg. **Aq-añ** [Акаң] (Jud. 63). ✧ 'Legal, rightful game' cf. Kirg. *añ* 'зверь, дикое животное (как предмет охоты)' (Jud.). ⇨ **AQ I.**

AQ-ARSLAN Selj. 1146 **Aq-arslan** [اقارسلان], emir, commander of Ardebil (Bondārī 217, Ahbar 82). ✧ 'White (=noble) lion'. ⇨ **AQ I. + ARSLAN.**

AQ-AS Tat. 1675 **Aq-as** [Акаско] (Kungursk. akty 26). ✧ 'White ermeline (weasel)'. ⇨ **AQ I. + AS.**

AQ-BAKİ Uzb. 1740 **Aq-baki-arbab** [Акбаки-Арбабъ], from Khiva (Hanykov, Poezdka 21). ✧ 'White/honest-eternal'. ⇨ **AQ I. + BAQÏ.**

AQ-BAL Kzk. 19th c. **Aq-pal** [Ак-палъ] (SOK 108). ✧ 'Clean honey'? ⇨ **AQ I. + BAL? / BALA?**

AQ-BALTA Kirg. **Aq-balta** [Акбалта] (Proben V,

186, Jud. 67, 681). ✧ 'White/clean axe'. ⇨ **AQ I. + BALTA.**

AQ-BARAQ Kzk. 19th c. **Aq-baraq** [Акъ-Баракъ] (Potanin II, 6). ✧ 'White dog with long hair'. ⇨ **AQ I. + BARAQ.**

AQ-BARS Chuv. 18th-19th c. **Aχ-pars / Aχ-parïs** [Ахпарсъ / Ахпарысъ] (Magn. 31); Maml. 14th c. **Aq-bars** [Акбарс] (Tuhfa 409). ✧ 'White-Panther, innocent/clean panther'. ⇨ **AQ + BARS.**

AQ-BAS see **AQ-BAŠ**

AQ-BAŠ 20th c. **Aq-baš** [Акбашевъ], a merchant in Sharikhan (Turk. Kraj 1912: 9); Uyg. **Aq-baš** [aqpaš] (Chwol., Syr.-nest. 31); Chag. 1559 **Aq-baš** [Акбаш], an emir (Ivanov 206); Turk. 14th c. **Aq-baš** [اقبـاش] (Āšikp. 36); Yürük 1543 **Aq-baš** [اقبـاش], from the Yürüks of Kocacık (Gökb., Rum. 103); Bashk. 1687 **Aq-baš** [Абдюк Акбашин] (MIB I, 129); Bashk. 1701 **Aq-baš** [Доскей Акбашев] (MIB III, 9); Bashk. 1726 **Aq-baš** [Акбаш] (MIB III, 238); Uyg. 1326, 1327 **Aq-baš / Aq-paš?** [aqpaš], byname of Selibā's (Zalīwā) son, the head of the church (Chwol., Syr. 18, Chwol., Syr.-nest. 66); *EN:* Yürük 1689 **Aq-baš** [اق بـاش], a nomadic tribe (aşiret) in Anatolia (Refik, Anad. 78); *TN:* Kzk. **Aq-bas** [Акбас], toponym, name of a field and a lake coming from the name of a group of clans (Kojčubaev 21); *TN:* Turk. **Aq-baš** [Akbach], toponym, in the province of Bolu (KA(?) 473); *TN:* Crm.(Tat.) **Aq-baš**, toponym, a village on the Tarkhan peninsula (Jervis I.). ✧ 'White head; having white (bald) head; (fig.) old (experienced, sophisticated) man' (Espaeva 1984, p. 231), cf. Chag. *aq baš* 'entblösster Kopf' (Radl. I, 89); II. 'Bird of prey (bigger than a falcon)' cf. Turk. dial. *akbaş* II 'şahinden büyük bir av kuşu' (DS). ⇨ **AQ I. + BAŠ.**

AQ-BAŠ-ATÏQ Türk 7th c. - 9th c. **Aq-baš-atïq** (DTS). ✧ 'White-Head-Famous?' (Blagova 1997, 705).

AQ-BAZAN Bashk. 1761 **Aq-bazan** [Чубай Акбазанов] (MIB IV/1, 215). ✧ 'Nightmare'? cf. Turk. *basan* 'die Unterdrückung, das Alpdrücken', *qara basan* 'id.' (Radl. IV, 1528). ⇨ **AQ I.**

AQ-BAZAR Uzb. 1740 **Aq-bazar** [Акъ-базаръ], a mirza (Hanykov, Poezdka 27). ✧ 'White (=good) market'. ⇨ **AQ I. + BAZAR.**

AQ-BELEK Kzk. 19th c. **Aq-belek** [Акбелекъ] (SOV 10); Kzk. **Aq-bilek-suluw** [Ак-Билек-Сулу], fem. (Žirm., Epos 410). ✧ 'White (=clean, fair, honest) benefaction/gift' cf. Kirg. *belek* 'дар, подарок' (Jud.). ⇨ **AQ I. + BELEK.**

AQ-BERDEY see **AQ-BERDİ I.**

AQ-BERDİ I. Tat. 17th c. **Aχ-perdä** [Ахпердя мурза Килдибяков], a murza (IOAIÊK XXIX, 313); Tat.(Tob.) 1637 **Aq-berdey** [Акбердей] (Miller, Ist. Sib. II, 444); Maml. 14th c. **Aq-berdi** [اقبردي]

(Sauvaget 37); Maml. 1413/14, 1465 **Aq-berdi** [اقبردى المنتار الدويدى] (Ibn Taghrīb. VI, 333, 347 etc.); Maml. 1436/37 **Aq-berdi** [اقبردى التاجماسى] (Ibn Taghrīb. VI, 754, VII, 5, 6, 265); Maml. 1438/39, 1461, 1467, 1470/71 **Aq-berdi** [اقبردى الاشرفى] (Ibn Taghrīb. VII, 65, 650, VIII, 625, Iyās II, 123,167, 184); Maml. 15th c. **Aq-berdi** [اقبردى اليوسفى], an emir (Iyās II, 73, 222); Maml. 1450, 1455 **Aq-berdi** [اقبردى الظا هرى الساقى] (Ibn Taghrīb. VIII, 61, 65, 220, 248, Iyās II, 45, 53, 54); Maml. 15th c., 1499 **Aq-berdi** [اقبردى], ibn ʿAli-bay al-Dawādār, a chancellor (of state), died in 1499 (Iyās II, 202-395, III, 105, Weil, Chalif. II, 343, 352, Mayer 65, 66); Maml. 1451 **Aq-berdi** [اقبردى المظفرى] (Ibn Taghrīb. VIII, 158); Maml. 1454 **Aq-berdi** [اقبردى قاسم بن التشاشى] (Iyās II, 45); Maml. 1468/69 **Aq-berdi** الهوارى الاينالى [افبردى] (Iyās II, 108); Maml. 1469/70 **Aq-berdi** [اقبردى بن اصباى الاشرفى برسباى] (Iyās II, 113); Maml. 1475/76 **Aq-berdi** [اقبردى تمساح الظا هرى] (Iyās II, 164); Maml. 1478 **Aq-berdi** [اقبردى الاشتر] (Iyās II, 182); Maml. 1482 **Aq-berdi** [اصباى الاشرفى] (Iyās II, 212); Maml. 1483 **Aq-berdi** [اقبردى تمساح بن ططر الظاهرى] (Iyās II, 260); Maml. 1486 **Aq-berdi** [اقبردى بن بخشايش] (Iyās II, 234); Maml. 1494/95 **Aq-berdi** الظاهرى جتمق] (Iyās II, 260); Maml. 1496/97 **Aq-berdi** [اقبردى تدسحى قا نى] (Iyās II, 329); Tat.(Tüm.) 1632 **Aq-berdi** [Чура Акбердеев] (Miller, Ist. Sib. II, 398); Bashk.? 1754 **Aq-berdi** [Акберды Утегулов], (MIB IV/1, 83); Uzb. 20th c. **Âq-berdi** [Оҡберди] (Begmatov 1984, 202); Bashk. 18th c. **Aq-berdi / Aq-berdä** [Акберда Кусянов] (MIB V, 260); Bashk. 1754 **Aq-berdi / Aq-berdä** [Акберда Алюшев] (MIB IV/1, 83); Trkm. **Aq-berdi-χan** [Ак-Берды-ханъ] (Grod., Vojna II, 198); Bashk. 20th c. **Aq-birðe / Akbirde** [Акбирӟе, Акбирде] (Kusimova); Tat. 1695 **Aq-perdey / Aq-perdi** [Кучюк Акпердеев] (MIB I, 92); *TN:* Chuv. 18th c. **Aχ-perdi(na)** [Ахпердина], a village in Civil'skij ujezd (district) (Korsakov 319). ✧ 'White/luck-Given' (Kusimova). ⇨ **AQ I. + BERDİ.** See also **HAQ-BERDİ.**

AQ-BERDİ II. see **HAQ-BERDİ**

AQ-BERGEN Kzk. 19th c. **Aq-bergen** [Уркумбай Акбергеновъ] (Grod., Pril. 62); Uzb. 20th c. **Âq-bergän** [Оҡберган] (Begmatov 1984, 202); *TN:* Kzk. 19th c. **Aq-bergen** [Ак-бергенъ], in lat. 48 N and long 69 E (Karta JAR XI). ✧ I. 'White/Luck-Given'; II. 'God-given'. ⇨ **AQ I.? + BERGEN** + suff. *-gen.* See also **HAQ+BERGÄN.**

AQ-BEZ Bashk. 1751 **Aq-bez** [Акбез Утяганов] (MIB IV/1, 34.). ✧ 'White hemp-cloth' cf. Turk., Uzb.,

Trkm. *bäz* 'Hanfgewebe' (Radl. IV, 1630), Bashk. *bäz* 'бяз' (BaRS). ⇨ **AQ I.**

AQ-BİLEK-SULUW see **AQ-BELEK**

AQ-BİRĐE see **AQ-BERDİ I.**

AQ-BİRÜ Nog. 1649 **Aq-birü** [Кучюкъ Акбирюевъ] (AI IV, 86). ✧ 'White/honest-giving'? ⇨ **AQ I.**

AQ-BÏYÏQ Yürük 1614 **Aq-bïyïq-oγlu** [Mehmet Akbıyıkoğlu] (Su 28). ✧ 'White moustache' cf. Turk. *bıyık* 'moustache' (TED), Maml. (Kipch.) *byjyk* 'Schnurrbart' (Tarj/Houtsma). ⇨ **AQ I.**

AQ-BOL Kzk. 19th c. **Aq-bol** [Акболъ] (SOK 264). ✧ 'Become white (=clean, honest, etc.)'. ⇨ **AQ I. + BOL.** See also **QARA-BOL.**

AQ-BOLAT see **AQ-BULAT**

AQ-BORUQ Chag. 15th c. - 16th c. **Aq-boruq-sultan** [اق بوروق], a Sheybanid (Šejb. LII). ✧ 'White (castrated) sheep'. ⇨ **AQ I. + BORUQ.**

AQ-BOTA Kirg. **Aq-boto**, from the Qojolor family (Imbault-Huart 67); Kzk. 19th c. **Aq-buta** [Акбутаевъ] (SKSO VIII, 229); Uzb.? 19th c. **Aq-buta** [Досткулъ Акбутаевъ] (SKSO II, 4); Uzb. 1723 **Aq-buta / Aq-buta-bi** [Akbouta / Ak-Bouta-by], lord of Khojend (Nalyvkin, Kokand; Nalivkin-Dozon 72); Kzk. 1803 **Aq-buta-biy** [Акбута бий], one of the chiefs of the Alim-ulï tribe of the Little Horde (Kiši Žüz) (MIK IV, 514); *EN:* Kzk. 18th c. - 19th c. **Aq-bota** [Акбота] (Tynyšp. 66, 73); *TN:* Kzk. **Aq-bota** [Акбота], a field and a lake, going back to the name of a group of Kazak clans (Kojčubaev). ✧ 'A one-year-old white foal of camel'. ⇨ **AQ I. + BOTA.**

AQ-BÖKÖ see **AQ I.**

AQ-BUDAY Tat. 19th c. **Aq-buday** [Акбудай, Акбудаево], a village (P. A. Šino: Volžskie tatary III, 121 (Extract from Sovremennik, 1860, No.81, 82)). ⇨ **AQ I. + BUΓDAY.**

AQ-BUΓA Kipch. 1289-1300 **Aq-buγa** [اق بغا], a Kipchak emir, who went over from Noγay to Toqta's side (Baybars/Tizeng. I, 90, 113, Veselovskij, Nog. 48); Selj. **Aq-buγa** [اقبوغا] (Aqsar./Iş. 88, 101, Aqsar./Tur. 184, 246); Khorezm. 1375 **Aq-buγa** [Ak-Bughá], an emir, the governor of Samarkand (Tar. Rashidi 44-45); Maml. 1308/09 **Aq-buγa** [اقبغا الناصرى] (Iyās I, 149); Maml. 1325 **Aq-buγa** [اقبغا لحسنى] (Zetterst. 140); Maml. 1332/33 **Aq-buγa** [اقبغا الجا شنكير] (Iyās I, 166, Zetterst. 214); Maml. 1342 **Aq-buγa** [عبدالواحد اقبغا], Alā'addīn Aq-buγa (died in 1342), primarily Qalāūn's mamlūk, later the governor of Hims, then an emir of Mohamed al-Nāsir I (1293-1341), since he had had his Madrasah built near Ǧāmiʿ al-Azhar, the school المدرسه الاقبغاويه was named after him (Makrīzī, Khit. I, 383, Zetterst. 148, 224, Weil, Chalif. I, 404, Mayer 67-68); Maml. 14th c.? **Aq-buγa** [اقبغا حا نتاه] (Makrīzī, Khit. I, 426); Maml. 14th c.

Aq-buɣa [اقبغا الطولوتمرى لمعروف با للكا ش],
Abdallāh az-Zāhirī's son, Barqūq's (1382-1399)
mamlūk, later colonel (chiliarch) and the governor of
Kerak, executed in 1400 (Iyās I, 288,308, 324,
Duqmaq:RHCHor V, 20, Ibn Taghrīb. VI, 11, 15, 20,
33, 36 ff., Mayer 69-70); Maml. 1351 **Aq-buɣa**
[Akbugā al-Chāsakī], a sultan (ZDMG XIII, 19); Maml.
1366/67 **Aq-buɣa** [اقبغا چركس], a Cherkess (a mamluk
originated from the Caucasus region) (Iyās I, 217, Ibn
Taghrīb. V, 331); Maml. 1376 **Aq-buɣa**
[اقبغا الشيخو نى] (Iyās I, 232); Maml. 1377 **Aq-buɣa**
[اقبغا السيفى] (Iyās I, 239, Zetterst., 200, 216); Maml.
1378/79 **Aq-buɣa** [اقبغا بلشون] (Iyās I, 244); Maml.
1379/80 **Aq-buɣa** [اقبغا الاجنبى], foreigner from
Anatolia (Iyās I, 249); Maml. 1380 **Aq-buɣa** [صيوان
اقبغا] (Iyās I, 246, 248); Maml. 1389 **Aq-buɣa**
[اقبغا الخوهرى] (Iyās I, 276, 279, Weil, Chalif. II, 6);
Maml. 1389 **Aq-buɣa** [اقبغا الماردينى], a chief
treasurer (Iyās I, 271, 275, Weil, Chalif. I, 552 etc.);
Maml. 1389 **Aq-buɣa** [اقبغا النيل] (Iyās I, 312, Weil,
Chalif. I, 567); Maml. 1398/99 **Aq-buɣa** [الظاهرى
اقبغا الخمالى الاطروش], governor of Damascus (Ibn
Taghrīb. VI, 3, 4, 12 ff., Weil, Chalif. II, 76, 102, Iyās I,
303, 312 etc.); Maml. 1398/99 **Aq-buɣa**
[اقبغا الطرنطا يى] (Ibn Taghrīb. VI, 18, 19); Maml.
1398/99, 1404/05 **Aq-buɣa** [اقبغا], chief of Nūbiya
(Ibn Taghrīb. VI, 6, 173); Maml. 1398-1437 **Aq-buɣa**,
Ibn Taghrībirdī, vol. VI, mentions 17 persons with this
name (Ibn Taghrīb. VI); Maml. 1399 **Aq-buɣa**
[اقبغا الجرجاوى] (Ibn Taghrīb. VI, 25); Maml.
1399/1400 **Aq-buɣa** [اقبغا النتيه] (Ibn Taghrīb. VI, 68);
Maml. 1410 **Aq-buɣa** [اقبغا شيطان] (Ibn Taghrīb. VI,
382, 462); Maml. 1411/12 **Aq-buɣa** [علا الدين
اقبغا التديدى] (Ibn Taghrīb. VI, 300); Maml. 1412
Aq-buɣa [اقبغا اليلبغاوى] (Ibn Taghrīb. VI, 432);
Maml. 1429 **Aq-buɣa** [اقبغا الجمالى الكاشف] (Ibn
Taghrīb. VI, 651, 661); Maml. 1438 **Aq-buɣa**
[اقبغا التمرازى], governor of Damascus (Iyās II, 16,
20, 35, Weil, Chalif. II, 226, Ibn Taghrīb. VI, 35, 361,
VII, 2, 22, 26); Maml. 1438/39 **Aq-buɣa** [النا صرى
اقبغا من مامش التركمانى], of Türkmen origin (Ibn
Taghrīb. VII, 10, 47, 55); Maml. 1449, 1468 **Aq-buɣa**
[اقبغا التركمانى], of Türkmen origin (Ibn Taghrīb. VIII,
45, 141, 143, 720); Maml. 15th c. **Aq-buɣa**
[اقبغا الاسندمرى] (Ibn Taghrīb. VI, 409); Tat.(Sib.)
19th c. **Aq-buɣa**, from a heroic legend (Radl., Aus Sib.
I, 159); Khorezm. 1376/77 **Aq-buɣa-behadur** [Ак-
Буга-бехадур], an emir (MIT I, 517), Khorezm. 13th c.
Aq-buqa [Âkbōkâ], father-in-law of Kaijâtû (Gaykhātû
1291-95) ilkhan (Abulfar./Budge I, 499); Khorezm.?

1289 **Aq-buqa** [اقبوقا], an emir (RaD/Jahn 13, 63, 70,
86, 90). ✧ 'White bull (steer)' (Sauvaget 37). ⇨ **AQ I.**
+ BUQA.

AQ-BULAT   Chuv. (Tat.?) 18th-19th c. **Aχ-bulat**
[Ахбулатъ] (Magn. 30).

AQ-BULAT   Tat.(Sib.) **Aχ-molot** [Ах-молотъ] (Titov
126); Tat. 18th-19th c. **Aχ-pulat** [Ахбулатъ] (Magn.
31); Chuv. 18th-19th c. **Ak-bulat** [Акбулатъ] (Magn.
25); Tat. 1621 **Ak-bulat** [Акбулатъ Бегишевъ]
(Zolotn. 155); Tat. 1634 **Ak-bulat** [Акбулат
Бурнашев] (Pokrovskij 69); Tat.(Mish.) 1743 **Ak-
bulat** [Таир Акбулатов] (MIB III, 539); Chuv. 19th c.
Ak-pulat [Акпулатов] (Zolotn. 158); Kzk. 19th c. **Aq-
bolat** [Акболатъ] (SOK 264); Maml. **Aq-bulat**
[اق بلاط] (Ibn Taghrīb. VI, 331, 332); Tat.(Sib.) 1607
Aq-bulat [Акбулатко] (Miller, Ist. Sib. II, 199);
Bashk. 1685 **Aq-bulat** [Бакей Акбулатов] (MIB I,
77); Bashk. 1710 **Aq-bulat** [Арык Акбулатов] (MIB
III, 63); Bashk. 1779 **Aq-bulat** (MIB V, 81); Bashk.
1783 **Aq-bulat** [Акбулат Ракаев] (MIB V, 143); Kzk.
19th c. **Aq-bulat** [Ак-булатъ] (SOK 44); Hak. 19th-
20th c. **Aq-molat**, a hero (Radl. I, 89, II, 312); Kzk.
19th c. **Aq-polat** [Акъ-полатъ] (Potanin II, 6); *EN:*
Kzk. 18th c. - 19th c. **Aq-bolat** [Акболатъ] (Tynyšp.
69). ✧ 'White (high-alloy) steel; Noble steel' cf. Torma
1992, 363, Sauvaget 37: اق بولاط 'acier blanc';
'Weiss-Stahl' (Radl. I, 89). ⇨ **AQ I. + BULAT.**

AQ-BUM   Kzk. 19th c. **Aq-bum** [Акбюмъ] (SOK 290).
✧ 'White/honest-?'. ⇨ **AQ I.**

AQ-BURA   Bashk. 1759 **Aq-bura** [Акбура Баишев]
(MIB IV/2, 382); *EN:* Kzk. 18th c. - 19th c. **Aq-bura**
[Акбура] (Tynyšp. 68, 70, 74). ✧ 'White camel
stallion'. ⇨ **AQ I. + BUƔRA.**

AQ-BUTA see AQ-BOTA

AQ-ČAČ   Alt. 19th-20th c. **Aq-čač / Aq-čaš** [Акчач,
Акчаш], fem. (OjrRS 207). ✧ 'Having fair hair, blond'
cf. Alt. *čač* 'volosy' (OjrRS). ⇨ **AQ I.**

AQ-ČAL   Kzk. 19th c. **Aq-čal** [Акчолъ] (Grod., Pril.
102, 155); Kzk. 19th c. **Aq-čal** [Акчалъ Кандыбаевъ]
(Grod., Pril. 155). ✧ 'White old (man) having grey
beard'. ⇨ **AQ I. + YAL I.**

AQ-ČAN see AQ I.

AQ-ČAPAN   Kzk.? 19th c. **Aq-čepan (<Aq-čapan)**
[Акчепанъ-ходжа], byname of Abdulla-χan-χodža
(Valihanov, Soč. 145). ✧ 'White gown'. ⇨ **AQ I. +
ČAPAN.**

AQ-ČEPAN see AQ-ČAPAN

AQ-ČIHRE   Chag. 1569 **Aq-čihre-bahadur** [Акчихрэ-
бахадур] (Ivanov 197). ✧ 'Having white (pale) face'.
⇨ **AQ I. + ČIHRE.**

AQ-ČOQRAQLÏ   Crm.(Tat.) 20th c. **Aq-čoqraqlï**,
Osman Aq-čoqraqlï, a Turkish turkologist (Mende 58).
✧ 'With white (clean) spring'; The personal name

probably goes back to the place-names *Aq-čoqraqlï or
*Aq-čoqraq indicating the person's place of origin. Cf.
Crm. čoqraq 'die Quelle' (Radl. III, 2008). ⇨ **AQ I.** +
suff. -lï.

AQ-ČONTAY Hak.(Sag.) **Aq-čontay** (Radl. II, 532). ✧
I. 'White/noble people'? cf. Hak. PN Čontay
'народный' (Butanaev); II. 'White leather bottle'? cf.
Chag. čontay 'ein lederner Beutel' (Radl. III, 532). ⇨
AQ I. + **CONTAY.**

AQ-ČORA see **AQ I.**

AQ-ČUAR see **AQ-ČUWAR**

AQ-ČUY Kzk. 19th c. **Aq-čuy-bek** [Акчуйбекъ]
(SODž. 54). ✧ 'White Chuy'. ⇨ **AQ I.**

AQ-ČUYKE Kzk. 19th c. **Aq-čuyke** [Акчуйке] (SOV
100). ✧ 'White little Chuy' cf. the name of the river
Chu / Chuy (Kirg.), Shu (Kzk.). For more details see
Kojčıbaev 256-57. ⇨ **AQ I.** + suff. -ke.

AQ-ČUWAQ Bashk. (?Tat.) 18th c. **Aq-čuwaq**
[Акчувак Балтин] (MIB V, 295). ✧ 'White sunbeam;
bright sunshine etc.' cf. Tat. dial. čuaq 'погожий,
ясный' (TatRS), Kirg. čubaq 'луч (солнца)' (Jud.),
Kzk. šuaq 'солнечный луч' (KzRS), Kzk. šuaq (čōq)
'der Glanz, der Strahl' (Radl. IV, 1095). ⇨ **AQ I.**

AQ-ČUWAR Chuv. 18th-19th c. **Aχ-čubar**
[Ахчубаръ] (Magn. 31); Tat. 20th c. **Aq-čuwar(ov)**
[Акчуаров], a family name (Sattarov). ✧ 'White-pied'.
⇨ **AQ I.** + **ČOBAR.**

AQ-ČUWAŠ Bashk. 1701, 1714 **Aq-čuwaš** [Акчюаш
Юкачев] (MIB III, 9, MIB I, 105); Bashk. 1709 **Aq-
čuwaš** [Кинзибей Акчувашев] (MIB III, 54); Bashk.
1726 **Aq-čuwaš** [Акан Акчувашев / Акчювашев]
(MIB III, 237); Bashk. 1735 **Aq-čuwaš** [Уразгулъ
Акчувашевъ], a tarχan (Vel.-Zern., Bašk. 16); Bashk.
1737 **Aq-čuwaš** [Актюваш] (MIB I, 324); Bashk.
1772 **Aq-čuwaš** [Юлдажбай Акчювашев] (MIB
IV/2, 406). ✧ 'White/honest Chuvash'? ⇨ **AQ I.** +
ČUWAŠ.

AQ-ĴAL see **AQ-ŽAL**

AQ-ĴARQÏN see **AQ-ŽARQÏN**

AQ-ĴEYDE Kzk. 18th c. - 19th c. **Aq-ĵeyde-batïr**
(Tynyšp. 66). ✧ 'White shirt' cf. Kzk. ĵeydä (=ĵeydäm)
'ein Hemd, welches vorn offen ist' (Radl. IV, 66). ⇨
AQ I.

AQ-ĴOL see **AQ-YUL**

AQ-ĴOL-TAY Kzk. 19th c. **Aq-ĵol-tay** [Акджолтай]
(SODž. 12, 100); Kzk. 19th c. **Aq-žol-tay** [Акжолтай]
(SOV 26, 144). ✧ 'White/clean road (life); (fig.)
Right/honest-life-foal (?)'. ⇨ **AQ-ĴOL** + **TAY** or
suff. -tay(2)?

AQ-ĴUNUS Kzk. **Aq-ĵunus** [Ак Цунус], fem. (Proben
III, 122 /155/); Kzk. **Aq-žonas-batïr** [Ак Жонас-
батыр] (Žirm., Epos 395). ✧ 'White/honest Yunus'. ⇨
AQ I. + **ĴUNUŠ.**

AQ-DAM see **AQ-TAM**

AQ-DAŠ see **AQ-TAŠ**

AQ-DAWLET Nog. 1518 **Aγ-döwlet (<Aq-döwlet)**
[Агдовлет], a Noγay prince (PSRL VIII, 268); Trkm.?
Aw-döwlet [Авдовлет], a prince (PSRL XXIII, 202);
EN: Kzk. 18th c. - 19th c. **Aq-dawlet** [Акдаулет]
(Tynyšp. 75). ✧ 'White/clean-Chance'. ⇨ **AQ I.** +
DÄWLÄT.

AQ-DOΓMUŠ Turk. **Aq-doγmuš** [Akdoğmuş], a
village (Köyl.).

AQ-DON Alt.? / Tat.(Sib.) 1622 **Aq-don** [Акдон
Кымцын (Камцын)], a prince by the Kas river
(Miller, Ist. Sib. II, 274). ✧ 'White-clothing'. ⇨ **AQ I.**
+ **TON.**

AQ-ERKÄČ see **AQ-ERKEČ**

AQ-ERKEČ Kirg. **Aq-erkäč / Aq-erkäš** [Ak Erkätsch /
Ак Еркäш], folkl., fem. (Radl. I, 89, Proben V, 22-23
/22-23/); Kirg. **Aq-erkeč** [Ак Эркеч], folkl., fem.
(Jud. 158, 635). ✧ I. 'White goat (kid)' cf. Kirg. erkeč
'кастрированный козёл (он ведёт стадо овец)'
(Jud.), erkeč 'козел, коза' (Sev.); II. 'White (clean,
nice) little darling' cf. Kirg. erkä, ärkä 'der Liebling'
(Radl. I, 777), erke 'баловень, неженка;
балованный' (Jud.) + dim. suff. -č. ⇨ **AQ I.**

AQ-GİLDE see **AQ-KİLDİ**

AQ-GİLDEY see **AQ-KİLDİ**

AQ-YUL Kzk. 19th c. **Aq-ĵol** [Акджолъ] (SOV 24);
Kzk. 19th c. **Aq-yul** [Акъюлъ] (SKSO VIII, 223). ✧
'White, clean road (=fate, life); White (good, lucky)
journey; wishing a successful life'. ⇨ **AQ I.** + **YOL.**

AQ-KİYİK Kzk. 18th c. - 19th c. **Aq-kiyik** [Ак-киик]
(Tynyšp. 68). ✧ 'White wild goat'. ⇨ **AQ I.** + **KİYİK.**

AQ-KİLDİ Chuv. 18th-19th c. **Aχ-kilda** [Ахкилда]
(Magn. 30); Chuv. 18th-19th c. **Ak-gilda / Ak-gilde?**
[Акгилда] (Magn. 25); Bashk. 1709 **Aq-gilde / Aq-
gildey?** [Килдибай Акгилдеев] (MIB I, 264); Bashk.
1664 **Aq-kildi** [Акилди Енеев] (MIB I, 193); Bashk.
1780 **Aw-gilde** [Кумышбай Авгильдин] (MIB V,
104). ✧ 'White/clean was born; One who was born
white (=fortunate)'. ⇨ **AQ I.** + **KELDİ.**

AQ-KİRPİŠ Kzk. **Aq-kirpiš** [Ак Кірпіш], folklore
hero (Proben III, 258 /304/). ✧ 'White little hedge-
hog?' cf. Kuman, Kzk. kirpi 'der Igel' (Radl. II, 1365).
⇨ **AQ I.** + suff. -š.

AQ-KÖBEK Tat.? **Aχ-kübek** [Ахкубекъ Тогоевъ]
(PSRL XIII, 164); Hak.(Sag.) **Aq-köbek** [Ак Кöбäк],
a bogatyr (Proben IX, 393); Hak.(Sag.) 19th-20th c.
Aq-köbek [Акъ-Кёбек] (ZIRGOÊtn. XXXIV, 274);
Hak. 19th-20th c. **Aq-köbek-χan** [Ахъ-кöбекъ-ханъ],
a Kacha bogatyr (Kuznecov: Drevn. mogily Minuss.
okr. I); Tat.(Bar.) **Aq-köbök** [Ak Köbök / Ак Кöбöк],
(Proben IV, 45 /56/); Alt.(Tel., Leb.) **Aq-köbök** [Ak-
Köbök / Ak Köbök / Ак-кöбöк] (Radl. II, 1283, 1315,
Proben I, 204 (224)); Maml. 14th c. **Aq-kübek**
[اقكبك / اقكبل‎ / Аккубулъ?], from the Toqsoba (recte

Toq-saba) tribe (Nuwairī 539, 541); Tat.? 1532 **Aq-kübek** [Аккубекъ], a prince from Astrakhan (PSRL XIII, 62); Tat.(Tara) **Aq-kübek** [Ак Кübäк] (Proben IV, 181 /142/). ✧ I. 'White foam, scum' (consider Radloff's note in Proben IV, p. 58: „Mein Name ist Ak Köbök (Weiss Schaum)"!), but cf. also Alt., Shor, Kzk., etc. *köbük* 'der Schaum' (Radl. II, 317), Chag., Turk. *köpük* 'id.' (Radl. II, 1311); II. 'White dog; Honest mate' (cf. Sattarov: *Aq-kübäk / Kübäk), cf. Crm., Turk. <i>köpäk* 'der Hund, Jagdhund' (Radl. II, 1310), Maml. *köpek it* 'köpek' (Tarǰ/Toparlı). ⇨ **AQ I. + KÖBÖK / KÖBÜK?**

AQ-KÜBEK see **AQ-KÖBEK**

AQ-KÜČÜK Tat. 1663 **Aq-küčük** [Аккучюк Акпердеев] (MIB I, 162); Tat.(Mish.) **Aq-küčük** [Сюянгул Аккучюков] (MIB III, 503); Bashk. 1734 **Aq-küčük** [Аккычик] (Vel.-Zern., Bašk. 10); Bashk. 1734 **Aq-küčük** [Аккычик] (Vel.-Zern., Bask. 10); Bashk. 1742 **Aq-küčük** [Иткине Аккючюков] (MIB I, 486); Bashk. 18th c. **Aq-küčük** [Аккучук Таиров] (MIB V, 38, 39); Bashk. 1798 **Aq-küčük** [Аккучукъ] (PSZRI XXV, 196); Bashk. 19th c. **Aq-küsük** [Акъ-Кусюкъ] (P. R.-n.: Moskovskij Telegraf, XLVIII, 261 (1832).). ✧ 'White, clean puppy'. ⇨ **AQ I. + KÜČÜK.**

AQ-KÜYÜK Khorezm.? 14th c.? **Aq-küyük** (RaD II, 70). ✧ 'White sadness, bitterness'? II. 'White goat/deer/game'? ⇨ **AQ I. + KÜYÜK / KÍYÍK?**

AQ-KÜSÜK see **AQ-KÜČÜK**

AQ-KÜZ Tat. 20th c. **Aq-küz** [Аккузов / Аккузин, Акузин], family-names (Sattarov); Kzk. 1820 **Aq-küz-batïr** [Аккузъ], chief of the Tabïn tribe (Sib. Vest. IX, 111). ✧ 'White eye'. ⇨ **AQ I. + KÖZ.**

AQ-QAГAZ Kkalp. 20th c. **Aq-qaγaz** [Аққағаз], fem. (KkRS 777). ✧ 'White paper'. ⇨ **AQ + QAГAZ.**

AQ-QAYAQ Kzk. 1782 **Aq-qayaq** [Ak-Kaiak / Акъ-Каякъ], Berdi-χoja's brother (Levchine 266, Levšin II, 275). ✧ 'White butter/cream'? cf. Alt. *qayaq* 'die Butter' (Radl. II, 90). ⇨ **AQ I.**

AQ-QALPAQ Kzk. 18th c. - 19th c. **Aq-qalpaq** [Аккалпак] (Tynyšp. 75). ✧ 'White cap'. ⇨ **AQ I. + QALPAQ.**

AQ-QANÏŠ see **AQ I.**

AQ-QATÏŠ Trkm. 1817 **Aq-qatïš** [Рахматулла Ак-Катыш] (MIT II, 400). ✧ 'White/honest mixture/creature'? ⇨ **AQ I. + QATÏŠ.**

AQ-QAWAQ Trkm. **Ak-kavak** [Akkavak], a Türkmen of Anatolia (Riza III, 71). ✧ 'White poplar' cf. + Turk. *kavak* 'die Pappel' (HŞ). ⇨ **AQ I.**

AQ-QAZÏ see **AQ I.**

AQ-QÏYAL Kirg. **Aq-qïyal-arïγ** [Ак Кыјал-арыг], fem. (Radl. I, 89). ✧ 'White-wild/stubborn'. ⇨ **AQ I. + QÏYAL.**

AQ-QÏYAS Kirg. **Aq-qïyas** [Ak Kyjas / Ак Кыјас], Kök-qïyas' brother (folkl.) (Proben V, 27 /28/). ✧ 'White (clean) worth'. ⇨ **AQ I. + QÏYAS.** See also **KÖK-QÏYAS.**

AQ-QÏLÏČ Chuv. 18th-19th c. **Aχ-kilïč** [Ахилычъ] (Magn. 30); Chuv. 18th-19th c. **Ak-klïš (<Ak-kïlïš)** [Аклышь] (Magn. 25); Trkm. **Aq-qïlïč** [Акъ-Килиджъ] (OZ CVII, 188); Karch. **Aq-qïlïč** [Аккелечь] (Sysoev 129); Tat. 18th-19th c. **Aq-qïlïč / Aq-χïlïč** [Акхилычъ] (Magn. 26); Hak. 19th-20th c. **Aq-qïlïš**, a hero (Radl. I, 89); Hak. 19th-20th c. **Aq-qïlïš** [Канъ Акколышь], a Khan in the epic (Titov 218); Tat. 18th-19th c. **Aq-qlïč** [Аклычъ] (Magn. 25). ✧ 'White (fortunate, noble, clean) sword'. ⇨ **AQ I. + QÏLÏČ.**

AQ-QÏLÏŠ see **AQ-QÏLÏČ**

AQ-QÏŠ Bashk. **Aq-qïš** [Чичкан Аккышев] (MIB III, 185). ✧ I. 'White sable'; II. 'White, clean, bright winter' cf. Bashk. *qïš* 'zima' (BRS). ⇨ **AQ I. + KÍŠ.**

AQ-QÏŠA Bashk. 1709 **Aq-qïša** [Аккыша] (MIB III, 48). ⇨ **AQ-QÏŠ?** + voc. suff. -*a*?

AQ-QLÏČ see **AQ-QÏLÏČ**

AQ-QLÏŠ see **AQ-QÏLÏČ**

AQ-QOČQAR Tat.(Sib.) 1632 **Aq-qočqar** [Акочкар] (Miller, Ist. Sib. II, 391); Bashk. 1663 **Aq-qočqar** [Чюлман Аккочкаров] (MIB I, 176); Bashk. 1666 **Aq-qočqar** [Ераткилка Аккочкаров] (Vel.-Zern., Bašk. 28); Tat. 1737 **Aq-qočqar-bay** [Аккачкарбай] (MIB I, 307); Kzk. 19th c. **Aq-qošqar** [Акъ-кошкаръ] (Potanin II, 3). ✧ 'White ram'. ⇨ **AQ I. + QOČQAR.**

AQ-QOYAN Kzk. 19th c. **Aq-qoyan-toqal** [Акъ-Коянъ-токалъ], according to Kazak tradition, she is the foremother of several clans (subdivisions, branches?) (Potanin, Pred. 57); Alt.(Tuba) 19th c. **Aq-qoyan-toqal** [Акъ-Коянъ-токалъ], fem. (Potanin 560). ✧ 'White hare'. ⇨ **AQ I. + QOYAN.**

AQ-QOYATÏ Alt.(Tuba) 19th c. **Aq-qoyatï** [Ак-койаты] (Potanin 560). ✧ 'White/clean-?'. ⇨ **AQ I.**

AQ-QOYATTÏ see **ALTÏN-QARTÏГA**

AQ-QOŠ see **AQ-QUŠ**

AQ-QOŠQAR see **AQ-QOČQAR**

AQ-QOZÏ Kzk. **Aq-qozi** [Аққозы], a character in the Epic „Put' Abaja" by M. O. Auezov (Espaeva 1984, 231); Kirg.? 19th c.? **Aq-qozu** [Ak-kozu] (Atyns. 93); *EN:* Kzk. 18th c. - 19th c. **Aq-qozï** [Аккозы] (Tynyšp. 68); *TN:* Kzk. **Aq-qozï** [Аккозы], a settlement in the west of the country (Kojčubaev 23). ✧ 'White lamb'; 'Sympathetic like a white lamb' (Espaeva 1984, 231). ⇨ **AQ I. + QOZÏ.**

AQ-QOZU see **AQ-QOZÏ**

AQ-QUYUQ see **AQ-KÜYÜK**

AQ-QULAY Bashk. 1738 **Aq-qulay** [Аккулай] (MIB I, 143); Bashk. 1738 **Aq-qulay** [Аккулай Бикташев] (MIB III, 391); Bashk. 1763 **Aq-qulay** [Бактыгирей Аккулаев] (MIB IV/1, 271, 341). ✧ 'White pleasing/suitable'. ⇨ **AQ I. + QULAY.**

AQ-QUŠ Tat. 20th c. **Aq-qoš** (Sattarov); Bashk. 20th c. **Aq-qoš** [Аккуш] (Kusimova 30); Oghuz/Trkm. 1227 **Aq-quš** [اقش / Akach], a former officer of the Ildenizid Özbek-atabek (Nasawī 152); Selj. 1191/92 **Aq-quš** [اقوش] (Ibn Šaddād, Nawād.: RHCHor III, 239); Selj. 1220/21 **Aq-quš** [اق قوش / اقوش], warrior who fought against Georgians (Ibn al-Athīr, Atab.: RHCHor II/1, 155, 156); Selj. 1305, 1309 **Aq-quš** [اقوش الرومى], coming from Anatolia (Zetterst. 109, Weil, Chalif. I, 290, Dawād. 196); Maml. **Aq-quš** [اقوش العزيزى], Ǧamāladdīn ~ (Zetterst. 43, 131); Maml. 1131 **Aq-quš** [اقوش المملوك الدـركى] (Ibn al-Athīr/Tornb. XII, 245); Maml. 13th c. **Aq-quš** [اقوش / Akousch-Schehâbi], one of the emirs of Tabl-khanah (Makrīzī II/1, 17); Maml. 1254 **Aq-quš** [اقوش / Akesch-Rokni] (Makrīzī I, 58); Maml. 1258 **Aq-quš** [أقوش السلحدار], Ǧamāladdīn ~ (Sīrat 88); Maml. 1260 **Aq-quš** [اقوش / Akousch], Šamsaddīn ~, the commander of Gāzah (Makrīzī I, 108, 210, Weil, Chalif. I, 81); Maml. 1261 **Aq-quš** [اقش البـرلى], Šamsaddīn ~ (Sīrat 122, 34); Maml. 1261 **Aq-quš** [أقوش], in Egypt (Abulfidā IV, 632-33; Ibn al-Athīr: RHCHor I, 804); Maml. 1263 **Aq-quš** [أقوش النـجيبى], governor of Damascus (Iyās I, 99, Makrīzī I, 188); Maml. 1263, 1264 **Aq-quš** [أقوش], Fārisaddīn (Mas'ūdī), an emir, the Mamluk envoy, who went to (Dešt-i) Kipchak to Mongol king (khan) Berke (1257-1266) with presents (Ibn Abdaẓẓāhir/Tizeng. I, 52, Makrīzī I, 212; Weil, Chalif. I, 42, Sīrat 219); Maml. 1269 **Aq-quš** [أقوش البـرلى], Ǧamāladdīn ~ al-Burlī (al-Burunlī), died in 1269, his mausoleum is near Kafr Sīb, Palestina (Mayer 73); Maml. 1280 **Aq-quš** [أقوش الشـدسى], Ǧamāladdīn ~, the vice-regent of Haleb, died in 1280 (Iyās I, 145, Weil, Chalif. I, 114, Zetterst. 118, Abulfidā V, 52-53, Makrīzī III, 28); Maml. 1281 **Aq-quš** [اقوش / Akousch], Ǧamāladdīn ~ Hemsi, the regent in Nabolos (Makrīzī III, 44); Maml. 1282 **Aq-quš** [اقوش / Akousch], Sheykh Ali's brother from the nation „Awirat"(=Oirat) (Makrīzī III, 53); Maml. 1282/83 **Aq-quš** [اقوش الموصلى الحـاجـب], Ǧamāladdīn ~ (Iyās I, 115, 148, Zetterst. 28, Weil, Chalif. I, 258); Maml. 1293 **Aq-quš** [اقو ش] (Iyās I, 125); Maml. 1294 **Aq-quš** [اقو ش], Bahāaddīn ~ (Iyās I, 131); Maml. 1298 **Aq-quš** [اقو ش], Ǧamāladdīn ~, an emir (Dawād. V, 39, 109 ff.); Maml. 1298, 1300, 1310, Å1335 **Aq-quš** [اقو ش الاشـرفى], Ǧamāladdīn ~, an emir, the governor of Karak, the regent of Damascus, Syria, he had a mosque made in Cairo (Iyās I, 151, 161, 185, Weil, Chalif. I, 307, Zetterst. 81, 136, Makrīzī IV, 41,54, Dawād. 41, 63, 110, 117, 218, Björkm. 161, Mayer 72); Maml. 1299 **Aq-quš** [Akousch], Ǧamāladdīn ~ (Kattâl-assaba) (Makrīzī IV, 114); Maml. 1299 **Aq-quš** [اقوش الافـرم لمنصورى], Ǧamāladdīn ~, the governor of Damascus (Iyās I, 139, 143, 171, Zetterst. 46, 99, Makrīzī IV, 114, 126); Maml. 1302 **Aq-quš** [اقوش الشـريفى], Ǧamāladdīn ~ (Zetterst. 95); Maml. 1302 **Aq-quš** [اقوش أمير احور], an emir-i ahur (=Master of the Horse) (Dawād. 88); Maml. 1320 **Aq-quš** [اقو ش الطشلاقى] (Zetterst. 152); Maml. 14th c. **Aq-quš** [اقو ش العجمى] (Duqmaq:RHCHor IV, 18); Maml. 14th c. **Aq-quš** [اقوش / Akkuş] (Tarǰ/Houtsma 50, Tarǰ/Toparlı 41); Tat.(Lit.) 1557 **Aq-quš** [Акушъ уланъ], a cavalry-man armed with a lance (=ulanus) (Kn. Metriki Lit. 152); Tat.(Tüm.) **Aq-quš** [Атуганка Акушев] (Miller, Ist. Sib. II, 399); Bashk. 1730 **Aq-quš** [Аккуш] (MIB III, 277); Bashk. 1739 **Aq-quš** [Аккушев] (MIB III, 406); Selj. 12th c. **Aq-quš** [اقوش], in an inscription (Dörner-Neumann: Forschungen in Kommagene. Berlin, 1939, 100); Selj. / Khorezm.? 12th c. **Aq-quš** [اغوش ازامـر اىعـراق], Naṣraddīn ~, an emir in Iraq at the time of the Xwārizmšāh Alā'addīn Tekiš (1172-1200) (Rāwandī 391 ff.); Khorezm. 1227 **Aq-quš / Aχ-quš** [احش / Akhach], Ǧelāl's officer (Nasawī 138); *TN:* Turk. 20th c. Aq-quš [Akkuş], a village in the province of Ordu, Turkey (TMİB 704). ✧ 'White bird, swan, falcon' cf. Sauvaget 38, Tarǰ/Houtsma 50, Poppe: IAN 1927, 1252; Karabacek (p. 107): „*Âkûsch* ist persisch, so viel als ببـر *bebr* 'Panther', ein ungemein häufiger Name türkischer Mamlûken", also Gombocz, ÁTsz. 8-9. ⇨ **AQ I. + QUŠ I.**

AQ-MADİYAR Kzk. 19th c. **Aq-madiyar** [Акмадіяръ] (SOK 276). ✧ 'White Madiyar' cf. Kzk. *Madiyar*, the name of a clan (Aristov 105). ⇨ **AQ I.**

AQ-MAY Tat. 1658 **Aq-may** [Акмой Щадра] (DAI IV, 140); Tat. 1752 **Aq-may** [Кодряк Акмаевъ] (PSZRI XIII, 737). ✧ 'White, clean fat, grease, butter'. ⇨ **AQ I. + MAY.**

AQ-MAL Chag. 1566 **Aq-mal** [Акмаль] (Ivanov 189). ✧ 'Horses (as riches)' cf. Kzk. *aq mal* 'die Pferde'. ⇨ **AQ I. + MAL.**

AQ-MALÏŠ Kzk. 19th c. **Aq-malïš** [Акмалышъ / Акмалишъ] (AOK 10, 114). ✧ 'White sheep'. ⇨ **AQ I. + MALÏŠ.** See also **AQ-MAL.**

AQ-MAMAY Crm.(Tat.)? **Aq-mamay** [Ак Мамаi] (Proben VII, 127). ✧ 'White mythical monster'. ⇨ **AQ I. + MAMAY.**

AQ-MAÑLAY Crm.(Nog.) **Aq-mañlay** [Акъ Манклай], according to the Noγay tradition she is one of the ancestresses of Noγays (Smirnov, Krym. 77). ✧ 'White forhead'. ⇨ **AQ I. + MAÑLAY.**

AQ-MARAL Kzk. 20th c. **Aq-maral** [Акмарал], in 15 cases out of 1000 this name was given in South-Kazakistan in 1969 (Nikonov: OSA 157). ✧ 'White reindeer-hind'. ⇨ **AQ I.** + **MARAL.**

AQ-MÏČÏQ   Bashk. 1776 **Aq-mïčïq** [Серка Акмычыков] (MIB V, 33); Bashk.(<Tat.) 1776 **Aq-mïčïq / Aq-mïčik** [Серка Акмычиков] (MIB V, 33, 34). ✧ 'White cat' cf. East.T. *mišik* 'die Katze' (Radl. IV, 2166), Kzk. *mïsïq* 'id.' (Radl. IV, 2145). ⇨ **AQ I.**

AQ-MOLAT see **AQ-BULAT**

AQ-NABAT   Trkm. 20th c. **Aq-nabat** [Aqnabat], fem. (Zaj. 1971, 339). ✧ 'A kind of white melon' (Zaj. 1971). ⇨ **AQ I.** + **NABAT.**

AQ-NAZAR   Bashk. 1734 **Aq-nazar** [Акназаръ Качкаровъ], a tarɣan (Vel.-Zern., Bašk. 10); Bashk. 1761 **Aq-nazar** [Акназар Акманаев] (MIB IV/1, 219); Kzk. 19th c. **Aq-nazar** [Акназаръ Ходжабергеновъ] (Grod., Pril. 128); Nog. 1649 **Aq-nazar** [Акъ-Назаръ Кудашаевъ] (AI IV, 123). ✧ 'White/clean-glance/look'. ⇨ **AQ I.** + **NAZAR.**

AQ-ÖLEŇ   Shor 19th-20th c. **Aq-öleň**, a bogatyr (Dyrenkova 154 ff., 386). ✧ 'White/clean grass/meadow' cf. Chag., NUyg.(Tar.) *öläñ* 'saftige Pflanzen, die Pflanze, das Grass, die Steppe, die Wiese' (Radl. I, 1246), Alt. *ölöñ* 'die Pflanze, das Grass, Heu', (Kzk.) 'die Sumpfpflanzen' (Radl. I, 1247). ⇨ **AQ I.**

AQ-PERDEY see **AQ-BERDİ I.**

AQ-POLAT see **AQ-BULAT**

AQ-POZ   Kzk. 19th c. **Aq-poz** [Акпозъ] (SOK 304). ✧ 'Light grey, greyish blue (horse)' cf. Kzk. *aqboz* 'белосивый (о масти лошади0' (KzRS). ⇨ **AQ I.** + **BOZ.**

AQ-PÖRİ   Alt. **Aq-pöri** (Nikiforov 225-28). ✧ 'White light grey wolf'. ⇨ **AQ I.** + **BÖRİ.** See also **BOZ-QURT.**

AQ-PUSPAΓ   Tuv. 19th c. **Aq-puspaɣ** [Акпуспагъ], in a tale (Potanin IV, 578-82). ✧ 'White?'. ⇨ **AQ I.**

AQ-SABDAR-ADTÏΓ see **AY-BÜRČÜL**

AQ-SAYİN   Nog. 1649 **Aq-sayin-murza** [Аксаинъ мурза], a „Nagay" murza (AI IV, 99). ✧ 'White/honest-good' cf. Mo. (<Trk) *sayin* 'gut' (TMEN I, No. 248, III, No. 1336). ⇨ **AQ I.**

AQ-SAYQAL   Kirg. **Aq-sayqal** [Ak Saikal / Ак Саiкал], fem. (Proben V, 194). ✧ 'White/clean-Glance/shine'. ⇨ **AQ I.** + **SAYQAL.**

AQ-SAQAL   Tuv. 19th c. **Aq-saqal** [Аксакалъ] (Potanin IV, 416). ✧ 'White (grey) beard (= elderly, wise man, who may be in charge of a clan or village)'. ⇨ **AQ I.** + **SAQAL.**

AQ-SALDEY   Tat. 1662 **Aq-saldey** [Баняшко Аксалдеевъ] (MIB I, 161). ✧ 'White/clean-?'. ⇨ **AQ I.** + **SALDEY?**

AQ-SALΓÏN   Shor 19th-20th c. **Aq-salɣïn** (Dyrenkova 192). ✧ 'White wind' cf. Shor *salɣïn* 'der Wind' (Radl. IV, 364). ⇨ **AQ I.**

AQ-SAMAN   Tat.(GH) 1335 **Aq-saman** ['Ακσαμάς], a christened Tatar, died in 1335 (Byz. Turc. 60). ✧

'White straw'. ⇨ **AQ I.** + **SAMAN.**

AQ-SAN   Kzk. 19th c. **Aχ-san** [Ахсанъ] (Grod., Pril. 148); Kzk. 19th c. **Aq-sam-bay (<Aq-san-bay)** [Аксамбай] (SODž. 146); Kzk. 19th c. **Aq-sam-bï (<Aq-san-bï)** [Аксамбы] (SOV 60); Kzk. 19th c. **Aq-san** [Джурунъ Аксановъ] (Grod., Pril. 141). ✧ 'White Hip/haunch'. ⇨ **AQ I.**+ **SAN.**

AQ-SANATAY   Kirg. **Aq-sanatay** [Аксанатай], AQ-SANATAY and Qara-sanatay, personages in Kirghiz tales corresponding to „Pravda" (=truth) and „Krivda" (=lie) in Russian folklore (Jud. 632). ✧ 'Having white (=good) intentions' < Mo. *sanātai* 'having [good or bad] intentions (G. Kara). ⇨ **AQ I.** See also **QARA-SANATAY.**

AQ-SARXÏN   Kzk. 19th c. **Aq-sarχïm-bek (<Aq-sarχïn-bek)** [Аксархымбекъ] (SODž. 76). ✧ 'White?'. ⇨ **AQ I.** + **SARQÏN?**

AQ-SARİ   Tat.? 1612 **Aq-sarï** [Аксаринъ], a Cheremis of Tatar origin? (Nižegorod. platež. 6, 221); Tat.? 1675 **Aq-sarï** [Аксарко] (Kungursk. akty 29); Tat.? 1681 **Aq-sarï** [Аксарко] (AI V, 94); Bashk. **Aq-sarï** [Аксары Тлевлетьчюрин] (MIB IV, 122); Kzk. 19th c. **Aq-sarï** [Аксары] (AOO 66); Kzk. **Aq-sarï-bï / Sarï-bï** [Ак Сары Бi / Сары Бi], a man often called Sarï-bï only (Proben III, 94 /120/); Nog. 1649 **Aq-sarï-murza** [Аксары мурза Батырчинъ] (AI IV, 122); *EN:* Kzk. 18th c. - 19th c. **Aq-sarï** [Аксары] (Tynyšp. 70, 73). ✧ 'White (light) yellow'. ⇨ **AQ I.** + **SARİ.**

AQ-SART   Kzk. 1803 **Aq-sart(-sultan)** [Аксарт султан], one of the chiefs of the Bayulï-tribe in Kiši Žüz (MIK IV, 514). ✧ 'White/honest Sart'. ⇨ **AQ I.** + **SART.** See also **QARA-SART.**

AQ-SEYİT see **AQ I.**

AQ-SEKEY   Bashk. 1664 **Aq-sekey** [Аксекеев Якшенметко] (MIB I, 192). ⇨ **AQ I.**

AQ-SERKE   Kzk. 19th c. **Aq-serke** [Аксерке] (SOK 142). ✧ 'White goat'. ⇨ **AQ I.** + **SERKE.**

AQ-SÏY   Nog. 20th c. **Aq-sïy** [Аджыбулат Ибрахим улы Акъсый], one of Baskakov's informants from the aul of Üykön-χalq (Ikon-halk), Cherkess Autonomous Oblast' (Bask., Nog. 143). ✧ 'White (friendly) hospitality' cf. Nog. *sïy* 'угощение; подарок' (NRS). ⇨ **AQ I.**

AQ-SÏLDÏ   Kzk. 19th c. **Aq-sïldï** [Аксылды] (SOK 168). ⇨ **AQ I.** + **SÏLDÏ.**

AQ-SÏN   Kkalp. 20th c. **Aq-sïn-gül** [Акъсынгюл], fem. (Bask., Kkalp. 48, KkRS 777). ✧ 'White figure' cf. Kkalp. *sïn* 'figura' (KkRS); cf. also Baskakov:OSA 139. ⇨ **AQ I.**

AQ-SOÑQUR   Maml. 14th c. **Aq-soñqor / Aq-soñqur** [اقسنقر / Aksunkur] (Tarǰ/Houtsma 50, Tarǰ/Toparlı 41); Selj. 11th c. - 12th c., 1119 **Aq-soñqur** [قسيم الدوله صاحب لموصل اقسنقر / Ak Sonkor, Aksonkur], Ala-tuɣan's (Al-tuɣan's) son, Atabek

Zengi's father, Malikšah's mamluk and the regent of Haleb, the proprietor of Mōsul (Rāwandī 129, Kamāladdīn: RHCHor III, 657, 659, Bondārī 179-181, 204-212 etc., Ibn al-Athīr/Tornb. IX, 377, X, 87, 98, 149-52, 290, Ahbar 50, Fakhrī 96-98, 416, Berchem, Jér. II, 394); Selj. 1086 **Aq-soñqur** [Âksenkûr], appointed lord of Aleppo (Abulfar./Budge I, 231); Selj.? 1086, 1092, 1093 **Aq-soñqur** [أقسنقر ولد عما دالـلين] (Kamāladdīn: RHCHor II, 102, 103-113); Selj.? 1087/88 **Aq-soñqur** [اقسنقر], ~ ibn Abdullāh (Ibn Taghrīb. II, 281, 284); Selj. 1108, 1117 **Aq-soñqur** [اقسنقر البـرستى], Sayfaddīn ~, prince of Hamadān, mamluk of Borsuk (Borsok) (Ibn Taghrīb. II, 356, 362 ff., Weil, Chalif. I, 86, Ibn al-Athīr/Tornb. X, 307, 309, 350-52, 377-80, 422-24, Kamāladdīn II, 177, 178, Kamāladdīn: RHCHor III, 610-13, 647-55, Ahbar 74); Selj. 1115 **Aq-soñqur** [Âksenkûr], emir (amīr) of Habûrâ (Abulfar./Budge I, 247); Selj. 1120 **Aq-soñqur** [ااقسنتر البجارى] (Ibn al-Athīr/Tornb. X, 393-94); Selj. 1123, 1133 **Aq-soñqur** [ااقسنقر الاحد يلى] (Ibn al-Athīr/Tornb. X, 421, 471, 480-83, XI, 166, 177, 280, Qalānisi 238, Ahbar 75, 138); Selj. 12th c. **Aq-soñqur** [اقسنقر], Qasimaddīn ~ (Ibn Šaddād, Nawād.: RHCHor III, 17, 24, 49); Selj. 1153-59 **Aq-soñqur** [پیروزکوهى اقسنتر] (Rāwandī 266); Maml. 1271 **Aq-soñqur** [Ak-Sonkor-Fârekâni], an emir (Makrīzī II, 101, Weil, Chalif. I, 93, 105-6); Maml. 1294 **Aq-soñqur** [Ak-sonkor-Hosâmi], among the murderers of sultan Khalil (1290-1293) (Makrīzī III, 153); Maml. 1296, 1308 **Aq-soñqur** [Ak-sonkor-Kertaba], Šamsaddīn ~, the governor of Hama (Makrīzī IV, 60, 172, Weil, Chalif. I, 211, Qazw. 596); Maml. 1325 **Aq-soñqur** [اقسنقر المشد] (Zetterst. 17, 179, 190, 226); Maml. 1325 **Aq-soñqur** [اقسنقر السلحدار], Šamsaddīn ~ (Zetterst. 181, Dawād. 327); Maml. 1339/40 **Aq-soñqur** [اقسنقر شاد العمايى] (Makrīzī, Khit. I, 309); Maml. 1345, 1347 **Aq-soñqur** [اقسنقر], ~ al-Nāṣirī, the regent of Tripolis, died in 1347 (Iyās I, 185, 187, Mayer 70); Selj. / Khorezm.? 1247 **Aq-soñqur**, Ahmed ibn ~ al-Baġdādī (Turan: Belleten XII (1948), 108, 118, 128); Selj. / Turk. 1332 **Aq-soñqur** [اقسنقر الرمسى], an emir coming from Anatolia (Dawād. 327).

AQ-SOÑQUR Turk. 1378 **Aq-soñqur-aγa** [اق صنتور اغا] (Āšikp. 53, 54). ✧ 'White hawk' (Sauvaget 37: *aq-sonqur* 'gerfaut blanc'). ⇨ **AQ I.** + **SOÑQUR.** See also **BAY-SOÑQUR, QARA-SOÑQUR.**

AQ-SU Kzk. 19th c. **Aq-su-bay?** / **Aq-subay?** [Аксубай] (SOK 16). ✧ 'White (proceeding from thawing of the snow) water'. ⇨ **AQ I. / AQ-SUBAY?**

AQ-SUBAY Chuv. 18th-19th c. **Ak-subay** [Аксубай] (Magn. 26); Tat. 20th c. **Aq-subay** [Аксубай], a family name (Sattarov); *TN:* Chuv. 18th c. **Ak-subay(eva)** [Аксубаева], a village of christened Chuvashs in the district of Čistopol' (Korsakov 222); *TN:* Tat. 18th-19th c. **Aq-subay** [Аксубай], a district and its centre (Magn. 26). ✧ I. 'White (noble, honest) cavalry-man' cf. *subay* 'atlï suġïščï' [= warrior mounted on horse-back] (Sattarov) II. 'Handsome, goodlooking' (Sattarov). ⇨ **AQ I. + SUBAY.**

AQ-SUBAN Crm. **Aq-suban-batïr** [Ак Субан батыр], a character in a tale (Proben VII, 129). ✧ 'Clean/honest Subhan', 'White fame/glory'. ⇨ **AQ I. + SUBXAN?**

AQ-SUFİ Khorezm. **Aq-sufi** [Ак-Суфи], Nanguday-emir's son, the ruler of Khorezm (MIT I, 516, 539). ✧ 'White (clean, honest) Sufi' cf. Ar. PN Sufi ' a mystic' (Ahmed). ⇨ **AQ I.**

AQ-SÜYRİK Kkalp. 20th c. **Aq-süyrik** [Аксуйрик], fem. (KkRS 777); Tat.(Sib.) 1599 **Aq-süyrük** [Аксюйрюкъ], a princess in Siberia, Küčüm-qan's wife (AI II, 17, 20, 23); Kzk. 19th c. **Aq-süyrük** [Аксюйрукъ] (AOO 38). ✧ I. 'White (young, nice) reed' cf. Kzk. *süyrük* 'die weissen Wurzeln des Schilfes (die sind essbar)' (Radl. IV, 797), Kkalp. *süyrik* 'молодая поросль камыша (высотою до одного метра)' (KkRS); II. II. 'White sturgeon'? cf. Tat.(Sib.) *söyrek* 'тогы; осетр' (Tumaševa 191). ⇨ **AQ I.**

AQ-SÜYRÜK see **AQ-SÜYRİK**

AQ-ŠORA see **AQ I.**

AQ-TAY Bashk. 1664 **Аχ-tay** [Ахтай] (DAI IV, 410); Bashk. 1734 **Аχ-tay** [Сапаргулъ Ахтаевъ] (Vel.-Zern., Bašk. 10); Maml. 1252, 1254 **Aq-tay** [اقطاى الجمدار الصالحى / Fâres-eddin-Aktaï], Fārisaddīn ~, a cup-bearer (Makrīzī I, 44, 48, Duqmaq:RHCHor IV, 44, Weil, Chalif. I, 5, 19, Sīrat 86, Abulfidā IV, 536-37, Ibn al-Athīr: RHCHor I, 804); Maml. 1253 **Aq-tay** [اقطاى / Aktaï], Sayfaddīn ~, an emir (Makrīzī I, 43); Maml. 1282 **Aq-tay** [اقطاى / Aktaï], Šihābaddīn ~ (Makrīzī III, 53); Maml. 1304 **Aq-tay** [اقطاى بن مهنا], an emir (Dawād. 127); Maml. 14th c. **Aq-tay** [اقطاى / Aktay] (Tarj/Houtsma 50, 83, Tarj/Toparlï 42); Maml. 1366/67 **Aq-tay** [اقطاى اليلبغاوى], ~ al-Yulbuγāwī (Iyās I, 220); Tat. 1675 **Aq-tay** [Актаевъ] (Kungursk. akty 25); Tat.(Sib.) 19th-20th c. **Aq-tay** [Ак-тай], fem. (Katanov, Otč. 10); Bashk. 1663 **Aq-tay** [اقطاى / Актай] (MIB I, 166); Kzk. 1883 **Aq-tay** [Актай Кулбатиевъ] (Grod., Pril. 93); Uzb. 1515 **Aq-tay-sultan** [Актай-султан], Sufiyan Khan's brother (MIT II, 324). ✧ I. 'White foal' (Sauvaget 37: 'poulain blanc'; Sattarov); II. 'White (male child), whitish' (Sattarov). ⇨ **AQ I. + TAY** or suff. *-tay(1,2)*. See also **QARA-TAY.**

AQ-TAYLAQ Kzk. 18th c. - 19th c. **Aq-taylaq-biy** [Актайлак-бий] (Tynyšp. 71). ✧ 'White camel-foal'.

⇨ **AQ I. + TAYLAQ.**

AQ-TAM Bashk. 1756 **Aq-tam** [Актам Усейнов] (MIB IV/1, 130); Kzk. 19th c. **Aq-tam** [Актамъ] (AOK 82); *TN:* Kzk. **Aq-dam-bay** [Акдамбай-карачека], a kurgan (burial-mound) (Konšin, Mat. V, 29). ✧ 'White kurgan' (place of birth) cf. Kzk. *tam* 'das Grabdenkmal' (Radl. III, 991). ⇨ **AQ I.**

AQ-TAN Kzk. **Aq-tan** [Актанъ Беккулинъ] (Konšin, Pam.19); Kzk. 1819 **Aq-tan** [Актан] (MIK IV, 326); Kzk. 19th c. **Aq-tan** [Кулашъ Актановъ] (Grod., Pril. 99); Kzk. 19th c. **Aq-tan** [Актанъ] (AOO 42); Kzk. 19th c. **Aq-tan** [Актанъ] (SODž. 10); Kzk. 19th c. **Aq-tan** [Актанъ] (SOK 266); Tat. 20th c. **Aq-tan** (<Aq-tañ?) [Астрахан Актанов], family-name (Sattarov); *EN:* Kzk. 1785 **Aq-tan-bī** [اقطان بی], an ethnonym (<personal name), a subdivision of the Čümekey (چومكی) tribe (MIK IV, 52, 53). ✧ 'White dawn; Born at dawn' (Sattarov), cf. also Kzk. PN *Aq-tan* (Žanuzakov-Esbaeva). ⇨ **AQ I. + TAÑ.**

AQ-TAN-BERDİ Kzk. 19th c. **Aq-tam-berdi** (<Aq-tan-berdi) [Актамберды] (SODž. 140). ✧ I. 'White khurghan gave him'?; II. 'White dawn has him/her given (born at dawn)' (see AQ-TAN). ⇨ **AQ-TAM / AQ-TAN? + BERDİ.**

AQ-TANA Kzk. 18th c. - 19th c. **Aq-tana** [Актана] (Tynyšp. 71). ⇨ **AQ I. + TANA I.**

AQ-TANAY Tat. 20th c. **Aq-tanay** [Актанаев], family-name (Sattarov). ✧ 'White little (young) calf'. ⇨ **AQ I. + TANAY I.**

AQ-TARAY Bashk. **Aq-taray** [Буляк Актараев] (MIB IV/1, 52). ⇨ **AQ I. + TARA?**

AQ-TAŠ Chuv. 18th-19th c. **Ak-taš** [Акташъ] (Magn. 26); Selj.? **Aq-taš** [اقتاش شرابسلار] (Ibn Bībī IV, 287); Maml. 1210 **Aq-taš** [اقتاش], mamlūk of Naṣraddīn Allah (Ibn al-Athīr/Tornb. XII, 189, 261); Turk. 1503 **Aq-taš** [Hızır Aktaş] (Gökb., Ed. 484); Tat. 20th c. **Aq-taš** [Акташев] (Sattarov); Hak. 19th-20th c. **Aq-taš**, a hero (Radl. I, 89). ✧ 'White stone'. ⇨ **AQ I. + TAŠ.**

AQ-TAW Tat.(GH) 14th c. **Aq-taw** [Актау], follower of Toqtamïš, a „tümen-bek" (Smirnov, Krym. 149); Chag. 1545 **Aq-taw** [Актау] (Ivanov 230). ✧ 'White mountain'. ⇨ **AQ I. + ТАГ.**

AQ-TAZ Hak. 19th-20th c. **Aχ-taz** [Ахтазъ] (Titov 213); *EN:* Kzk. 18th c. - 19th c. **Aq-taz** [Актаз] (Tynyšp. 71). ✧ 'White bold'. ⇨ **AQ I. + TAZ.**

AQ-TĀN Hak. 19th-20th c. **Aχ-tān** [Ах-Таан] (HRS 348); Hak.(Kacha) **Aq-tān** [Ак Тан] (Katanov, Otč. 8, Proben IX, 558). ✧ 'White jackdaw' (Katanov). ⇨ **AQ I. + TĀN.**

AQ-TEBER Khorezm. 1264 **Aq-teber** [Aktebar], Sayfaddin ~, a cup-bearer in the service of Ǯelāleddīn (1220-31) (Makrīzī I, 238). ✧ 'White trampling (of an animal)'? ⇨ **AQ I. + TEPER.**

AQ-TEMİR Chuv., Tat. 18th-19th c. **Aχ-temir** [Ахтеміръ] (Magn. 31); Tat. 17th c. **Aχ-timer?** [Ахтумерко Шереевъ], governor of Kazan (IOAIÊK XXIX, 344); Tat. 18th-19th c. **Aχ-timer** [Ахтимеръ] (Magn. 31); Chuv. 18th-19th c. **Aχ-timir** [Ахтиміръ] (Magn. 31); Maml. 1363, 1365 **Aq-temir** [اقتمرعبدالغنی], a governor who fought against Nubia (Weil, Chalif. I, 525); Maml. 1377/78 **Aq-temir** [اقتمر], regent (lord) of Damascus (Iyās, I, 239, 240, Weil, Chalif. I, 536); Turk. 1400/01 **Aq-temir** [اقتمر العثما نی] (Iyās I, 246); Selj. / Turk.? 13th c. - 14th c. **Aq-temir** [اقتمر] (Nešrī 209); Khorezm. 1372, 1384 **Aq-temür-bahadur** [اقتیمور / Актимур], Temür's follower (Tar. Rashidi 43, 46, 50, Dorn 140, MIT I, 516, 521); Tat. 20th c. **Aq-timer** [Актимер] (Sattarov); Oghuz/Trkm. 11th c. **Aq-timür** [اقتیمور], a chief, who got Mārdīn from Malikšah (Qazw./Gantin 447). ✧ 'White (good, noble) iron' cf. Sauvaget 37: *ak-tämür* 'fer blanc ou blanc + fer'. ⇨ **AQ I. + TEMİR.**

AQ-TEMÜR see AQ-TEMİR

AQ-TİKEN Kzk. 19th c.? **Aq-tiken** (Atyns. 94). ✧ 'White thorn' cf. *aq tikän* East.T.(Tar.) 'Hippophaë rhamnoides', (Tur.) 'Lycium ruthenicum' (Radl. I, 91, III, 1349). ⇨ **AQ I. + TİKEN.**

AQ-TİMER see AQ-TEMİR

AQ-TİMUR see AQ-TEMİR

AQ-TİŠ Trkm. 1827 **Aq-tiš-beχadïr** [Актиш-бехадыр], from the İmreli tribe (MIT II, 445, 634). ✧ 'White tooth'. ⇨ **AQ I.+ TİŠ.**

AQ-TOLQÏN Kzk. **Aq-tolqïn** [Ак-Толкын], fem. (Žirm., Epos 497). ✧ 'White wave' cf. Kzk. *tolqïn* 'волна' (KzRS). ⇨ **AQ I.**

AQ-TOLUN Tat.(Sib.) 1599 **Aq-tolun / Aq-tulum** [Актолунъ / Актулумъ / Актелунъ], a Siberian princess, Küčüm-qan's fourth wife (AI II, 17, 20, 23); Chag. 1571 **Aq-tulum-bike < Aq-tulun-bike** [Актулум-бике], fem. (Ivanov 243, 244). ✧ 'White (clean, fair etc.) full moon'. ⇨ **AQ I. + TOLUN.**

AQ-TORPAQ Kzk. 19th c. **Aq-torpaq** [Акторпакъ] (SOV 68). ✧ 'White calf in the 2nd year of age'. ⇨ **AQ I. + TORPAQ.**

AQ-TUBA Kzk. 1820 **Aq-tuba-biy** [Актуба-бій], one of the chieftains of the Alim-ulï tribe (Sib. Vest. IX, 115). ✧ 'White/honest - sorrow'? ⇨ **AQ I. + TOBA.**

AQ-TUBAY Chuv. 17th c. **Aχ-tubay** [Пехтемейко Ахтубаев] (IOAIÊK XXI, 341). ⇨ **AQ I. + TUBAY.**

AQ-TUΓAN Chuv. 18th-19th c. **Ak-tuγan** [Актуганка] (Magn. 26); Chuv. 18th-19th c. **Ak-tuvan** [Актуванъ] (Magn. 26); Maml. **Aq-tuγan** [اقطغان بن یاروق الخاج] (Ibn Šaddād, Nawād.: RHCHor III, 56); Maml. 1279, 1282 **Aq-tuγan** [Aktewan, Aktouan], Alā'addīn ~ al-sāki (Makrīzī II, 169, III, 53); Bashk. 1675 **Aq-tuγan** [Токан

Актуганов] (MIB I, 200); Bashk. 1709 **Aq-tuɣan** [Актуган Янгурчин] (MIB III, 49); *TN:* Maml. **Aq-tuɣan**, a small mosque (Ibn Šaddād, Nawād.: RHCHor III, 87). ✧ 'White falcon'. ⇨ **AQ I. + TOΓAN.**

AQ-TUQMAN   Kzk. 1819 **Aq-tuqman** [Актукман] (MIK IV, 325). ✧ 'White/clean full/satisfied (child)'? ⇨ **AQ I. + TOQMAN.**

AQ-TURAQ   Maml. **Aq-turaq** [اقطرق الحاجب], al-Sayfī. doorkeeper (al-ḥājib), his blazon has remained in a mosque in Tripolis (Mayer 71, Sobernh. 109); Maml. 14th c. **Aq-turaq** [اَقْطُرَق] (Sauvaget 37). ✧ 'White/good dwelling place'. ⇨ **AQ I. + TURAQ I.**

AQ-TUT   Chuv. 18th-19th c. **Ak-tut** [Актутъ] (Magn. 26). ⇨ **AQ I.**

AQ-TUWA   Maml. 1421, 1448 **Aq-tuwa** [اقطوه الموساوى الظهرى], an emir (Ibn Taghrīb. VI, 481, 483, 725, 742, VII, 24, 64, VIII, 28, Weil, Chalif. II, 196, Berchem 252); Maml. 1462 **Aq-tuwa** [اقطوه الاشرفى] (Ibn Taghrīb. 794); Maml. 1516 **Aq-tuwa** [اقطوه كاشف الشرقيه] (Iyās III, 73). ✧ 'White/honest (child) is being born'? cf. Chag. *tuɣmaq* 'родиться' (Budagov), Kuman, Alt., Hak., Kirg., Kzk., Tat. *tū-* 'gebären; geboren werden' (Radl. III, 1422). ⇨ **AQ I.** See also **AQ-TUBA?, AQ-TUWAR.**

AQ-TUWAN see **AQ-TUΓAN**

AQ-TUWAR   Chag. 1557 **Aq-tuwar-bek** [Актуар-бек] (Ivanov 224). ✧ 'Born white; white born; white little animal' cf. Chag. *tuɣmaq* 'родиться' (Budagov), Nog. *tuwar* 'скот, скотина' (NRS), Kar. *tuar* 'das Vieh' (Rad. III, 1423). ⇨ **AQ I.**

AQ-TÜŠ   Bashk. 1737 **Aq-tüš** [Актюш Таксыров] (MIB I, 325); Bashk. 1751 **Aq-tüš** [Актюш] (MIB IV/1, 43). ✧ 'White chest, breast' cf. Bashk. *tüš* 'грудь' (BRS). ⇨ **AQ I.**

AQ-UL see **AQ I.**

AQ-ZİGİT see **AQ I.**

AQ-ŽAL   Kzk. 19th c. **Aq-žal-bay** [Акжалбай] (SODž. 98). ✧ 'White (grey) mane'. ⇨ **AQ I.+ YAL.**

AQ-ŽARQÏN   Kzk. 19th c. **Aq-žarqïn** [Акжаркынъ] (SOV 32). ✧ 'White-bright (face)' cf. Kzk. *žarqin* 'светлый; лучезарный' (KzRS). ⇨ **AQ I.**

AQ-ŽONAS see **AQ-JUNUS**

AQA   Turk. 1333 **Aqa** [Aka], from Isparta (Ün 1938, 645); Hak. 19th-20th c. **Aqa** [Ака], fem. (HRS 353); Bashk. 1724, 1728 **Aqa / Aqa-mulla** [Ака-мулла Кумакаев, Ака Кумакаев] (MIB III, 222, 252); Maml. 1399 **Aqa-bay** [اقا باى السلطانى] (Ibn Taghrīb. VI, 25); Kzk. 19th c. **Aqa-bek** [Акабекъ] (SODž. 138). ✧ 'Elder brother; prime minister, treasurer of state; princess or the khan's relative (adding to female names)'. It was attached to basic personal names and earlier was used as a real title but later as a title of respect (secondary component) only. Cf. OT *aqa*

'старший брат' (DTS), Chag., Crm. *aqa* 'älterer Bruder' (Radl. I, 96), Chag. (in Khiva) *aqa* [اقا] 'первый министръ, казначей государственный; поставленное после женскаго имени, означаетъ принцессу или родственницу хана' (Budagov 60), Alt. *aqa* 'старший брат; брат деда по отцу; почтительное обращение к старшим мужчинам' (OjrRS), Chuv. *akka* 'ältere Schwester' (Paas.), *aqqa* 'отец, старший брат (старшая сестра), старший родственник, дед, дядя (вежливое обращение к старшему мучине)' (Sev.), Trk. **āka* <Mo. *aqa* 'älterer Bruder' (Räs.).

AQA-TAY   Chag. 1538 **Aqa-tay** [اقاطاى / Akatay Han], one of the Khorezm Khans, then khan of Khiva, died in 1546? (Abulg./Desm. 245, Erol II, 11). ✧ 'Brother-foal'. ⇨ **AQA + TAY?** or suff. *-tay(2)*?

AQAČ   Bulg. 13th c. - 14th c. **Aqač** [اقج / افخ], Jusupov reads Afaχ (Epigr. Bulg. 96, 97, Jusupov 32). ✧ 'Little sister'. ⇨ **AQA** + dim. suff. *-č.*

AQAY   Karch. **Aqay** [Акай] (Sysoev 128); Tat. 18th-19th c. **Aqay** [Акай] (Magn. 25); Bashk. 1664 **Aqay** [Акайко Кармышев] (MIB I, 192); Bashk. 1730 **Aqay** [Акай Кучюмов] (MIB III, 273); Bashk. 1735, 1736, 1737 **Aqay** [Акай], a principal (Rytschkow I, 72, PSZRI IX, 742, X, 243, MIB III, 366); Bashk. 1740 **Aqay** [Акай Кусюмъ (Кусюмов)] (Nepljuev 143, 146, 151, 168 ff., MIB I, 418); Bashk. 1740 **Aqay** [Акай Камакаев] (MIB I, 439-41); Kzk. 19th c. **Aqay** [Ибрагим Акай] (Grod., Pril. 174); Kzk. 19th c. **Aqay**, (AOK 94); Kmk. / Karch.? 1684 **Aqay** [Акайка Ямамбаевъ Уздень], a Cherkess of Kumuk or Karachay(?) origin (DAI XI, 140); Bashk. 1713 **Aqay / Akey** [Акей Бердыметев] (MIB III, 92); Kmk. 20th c. **Aqay-molla** (KSz. XIII, 140); Hak. 19th-20th c. **Aqïy**, fem. (Katanov, Otč. 13); Kzk. 19th c. **Ekey** [Екей] (SOV 86); Kzk. 19th c. **Ekey** [Екей] (SOK 104); Kzk. 19th c. **Ekey** [Екей] (SOV 142); Kzk. 19th c. **Ekey-bay** [Екейбай] (SOK 248). ✧ I. 'Uncle' (also as second component of personal names expressing title of respect). Cf. Crm. *aqay* 'Anrede an einen fremden Mann, dessen Namen man nicht kennt' (Radl. I, 97), Tuv. *aqïy* 'брат (обращение к старшему брату; дядя (обращение к старшим мужчинам)' (TuvRS). *Aqay* goes back to the vocative form of *aqa* (cf. Sev. 122). II. 'Goggle-eyed' (Possible for Tatar and Bashkir names.) cf. Tat. *aqay: aqay küz* 'пучеглазый, лупоглазый' (TatRS). ⇨ **AQA** + voc. suff. *-y.* See also **AΓAY, İŠ-AQAY.**

AQAL   Kzk. 19th c. **Aqal-bay** [Акалбай] (SOV 64).

AQALDEK   Kzk. 19th c. **Aqaldek (Aqal-bek?)** [Акалдекъ] (SOK 78). ⇨ **AQAL?** + suff. *-lïq.*

AQAN   Kzk. 19th c. **Aχan** [Аханъ] (SOK 208); Kzk. 19th c. **Aqam-bay (<Aqan-bay)** [Акамбай] (SODž. 42); Tat.(Mish.) **Aqan** [Кадырмет Аканов] (MIB III,

25); Bashk. 1706 **Aqan** [Акан] (MIB III, 24); Bashk. 1706 **Aqan** [Алик Аканов] (MIB III, 24, 26); Bashk. 1713 **Aqan** [Акан] (MIB III, 96); Bashk. 1726 **Aqan** [Акан Акчювашев] (MIB III, 237); Bashk. 1745 **Aqan** [Тавлу Аканов] (MIB III, 426); Kzk. 19th c. **Aqan** [Аканъ] (AOA 126); Kzk. 19th c. **Aqan** [Аканъ] (AOK 34, 62, 106); Kzk. 19th c. **Aqan** [Аканъ] (SODž. 156); Kzk. 19th c. **Aqan** [Аканъ] (SOK 180); Kzk. 19th c. **Aqan** [Аканъ] (Grod., Pril. 142); Kzk. 1805, 1820 **Aqan-biy** [Акан бий, Аканъ-бiй], one of the chiefs of the Arɣïn tribe of Kiši Žüz (MIK IV, 324, 512, Sib. Vest. IX, 104). ✧ 'White ruler, White empress' (Butanaev). ⇨ **AQ I. + QAN.**

AQAN-ČULAN Crm.(Tat.) 1580 **Aqan-čulan** [Аканъ-Чуланъ] (Kn. Metriki Lit. 320).

AQANAY Tat. 1675 **Aqanay** [Аканайко] (Kungursk. akty 30); Kzk. 19th c. **Aqanay** [Аканай] (SOV 14); Bashk. 1787 **Aqanay / Aqaney** [Аканей Яммантаев (Ялмантаев)] (MIB V, 203); Bashk. 1709 **Aqanay / Aqeney?** [Акеней Бишинбаев] (MIB III, 49); Bashk. 1630 **Aqanay / Aqinay?** [Аракуска Аканаев, Акинаев], from Ufa (MIB I, 75-76); Tat. 1646 **Aqanay(qa)** [Аканайка Сарамышевъ] (Kurdjumov 189). ⇨ **AQAN?** + suff. -ay.

AQAŠ Tat.? 1656 **Aqaš** [Акашевъ] (PSZRI I, 364); Bashk. 1756 **Aqaš** [Ахбай Акашев] (MIB IV/1, 109). ✧ 'Dear little brother'. ⇨ **AQA** + dim. suff. -š.

AQĀBÏL Yak. **Aqābïl** [Акабыл / Акаjар] (Pek.).

AQĀQÏY Yak. **Aqāqïy** [Акакыи] (Pek.). ✧ Akakij (R.< Gr. akakos).

AQBAN see **AQPAN**

AQČA Turk. 1584 **Aɣča** [اغچه / Ağça] (Ongan, Ank. I, 148); Kzk. 19th c. **Aχša-bay** [Акчабай] (SODž. 58); Kzk. 19th c. **Aχša-bay** [Акчабай] (SOK 90); Khorezm. 13th c. **Aqča** [اقچه برادر ميانخق], in the history of Sultan Tekiš (Ĵuwaynī II, 41, 43); Kzk. 1840 **Aqča** [Акча Ханхожин] (Konšin, Mat. V, 42); Kzk. 19th c. **Aqča** [Акча] (SOK 22, 218); Alt. 19th-20th c. **Aqča**, fem. (OjrRS 211); Tuv. 19th c. **Aqča** [Акча], a tale-teller (Potanin IV, 373); Karg. **Aqča** [Акча], fem. (Katanov, Otč. 8); Kzk. 19th c. **Aqča-bay** [Акчабай] (AOA 6); Kzk. 19th c. **Aqča-bay** [Акчабай] (AOK 98); Kzk. 19th c. **Aqča-bay** [Акчабай] (SODž. 6, 94, 148); Kzk. 19th c. **Aqča-bay** [Акчабай] (SOK 166); Kzk. 19th c. **Aqča-bay** [Акчабай] (SOV 74, 80); Alt. 19th-20th c. **Aqča-bay** [Акча Ханхожин] (OjrRS 207); Maml. 1298 **Aqča-be** [اقجبا المنصورى], Sayfaddīn Aqča-be, an emir (Dawād. 7, 110); Maml. 1320 **Aqča-be**, Sayfaddīn ~ (Zetterst. 143); Maml. 14th c. **Aqča-be / Aqča-ba** [اقچيا / لتجُبَا / Akçaba] (Tarĵ/Houtsma 50, Tarĵ/Toparlı 42); Kzk. 19th c. **Aqča-bek** [Акчабекъ] (SOK 150, 138); Kkalp. **Aqča-χan** [Акча-хан] (Divaev: TOOIK III, 17); Turk. 14th c.

Aqča-qoĵa [اقچه قوجه] (Āšikp. 26, 27, 31-36); Kzk. 1817 **Aqša** [اقچه] (MIK IV, 310); Kzk. 19th c. **Aqša-bay** [Акшабай] (SOK 272); Kzk. 19th c. **Aqša-bay** [Акшабай] (SOV 10); Bashk. 1623 **Aqša-ɣul** [Акшагулъ] (Miller, Ist. Sib. II, 300); Kzk. **Aqša-qan** [Akscha Kan / Акша Кан] (Proben III, 120 /153/); _EN:_ Kzk. 18th c. - 19th c. **Aχša-bek** [Ахшабекъ] (Tynyšp. 72); Kzk. 18th c. - 19th c. **Aqča** [Акча] (Tynyšp. 65, 68); _TN:_ Turk. **Aqča-bey / Aqča-beyli** [Akçabey, Akçabeyli], names of villages (Köyl.); _TN:_ Turk. 20th c. **Aqča-qoĵa** [Akçakoca], a village (TMİB 188). ✧ I. 'Whitish' (Erol II), cf. Crm., Turk. _aqča_ 'weiss, weisslich' (Radl. I, 121), Kzk. _aqša_ 'weisslich' (Radl. I, 128); II. 'Money; (silver) coin' cf. _a:qĵa / aqča_ (Sev.). Cf. also Alt. _Aqča-bay_ 'богатый деньгами' (OjrRS 207); Alt. _aqča_ 'деньги' (OjrRS 211), Tuv. _Aqča_ 'деньги' (Katanov, Otč. 8), Kzk. _aqša_ 'Geld' (Radl. I, 128). See also **ALTÏN-AČQA.**

AQČA-QOĴA see **AQČA**

AQČA-QUƔU Trkm. 20th c. **Aɣča-quɣu** [Ağca Kuğu], fem. (Özbaş 24). ✧ 'White swan' cf. Uyg., Karakh., Chag. _quɣu_ 'der Schwan' (Radl. II, 898, DTS). ⇨ **AQČA.**

AQČA-MAY Alt. 19th-20th c. **Aqča-may** (<Aqča-bay) [Акчамай (Акчабай)] (OjrRS 207). ✧ 'White (clean) fat, grease'. ⇨ **AQČA + MAY.**

AQČAQ Kzk. 19th c. **Aqčaq-pay** [Акчакпай] (SOV 62).

AQČÏL Kzk. 19th c. **Aqčïl** [Акчылъ], (SOK 52). ✧ 'Whitish' cf. Kzk. _aqšïl_ 'слегка белый' (KzRS). ⇨ **AQ I.** + suff. -čïl.

AQĪM Yak. **Aqīm** [Акым] (Pek.). ✧ Yoakim, Yakim (R. Иоаким, Яким).

AQÏ Kirg. **Aqï-bay** [Акыбай] (Jud. 435). ✧ 'Lawful, legitimate (property)' cf. Kirg. _aqï_ 'принадлежащее по праву; то, на что кто-либо имеет неотъемлемое право' (Jud.).

AQÏBÄTLEY Tat.(Sib.)? 1638 **Aqïbätley** [Акынятлей (Акыпятлей?) Бердеев], a Tatar in Ufa (Miller, Ist. Sib. II, 452). ✧ '(The) Last/End; Finish' cf. Osm. _âkıbet_ 'son, bitim; sonuç' (Özön) (<Ar.) + suff. -li.

AQÏY see **AQAY**

AQÏL Bashk. 1670 **Aqïl** [Акылничка Тиникеев] (Vel.-Zern., Bašk. 36); Kzk. 19th c. **Aqïl-bay** [Акылбай] (SOV 50); Kzk. 19th c. **Aqïl-bay** [Акылбай] (SOK 126, 258); Kzk. 19th c. **Aqïl-bek** [Акылбекъ] (AOO 18); Kzk. 19th c. **Aqïl-bek** [Акылбекъ] (SODž. 94); Kzk. 19th c. **Aqïl-bek** [Акылбекъ] (SOK 4); Kzk. 19th c. **Aqïl-bek** [Акылбекъ] (SOV 4); Kzk. 19th c. **Aqïl-bek** [Акылбекъ] (Grod., Pril. 92); _EN:_ Kzk. 18th c. - 19th c. **Aqïl-bek** [Акылбекъ] (Tynyšp. 65). ✧ 'Mind, wit, sense' cf. Turk., Kzk., Kirg. etc. _aqïl_ (Ar.) (Radl. I, 102).

AQÏLAY Kirg. **Aqïlay** [Акылаі], daughter of Šoruq (Proben V, 78 /79/).

AQÏLČA Kzk. 19th c. **Aqïlča** [Акылча] (SOK 276). ✧ 'Wisely'? ⇨ **AQÏL** + suff. -*ča*.

AQÏLDÏQ Kzk. 19th c. **Aqïldïq** [Джанбулгай Акилдыкъ] (Grod., Pril. 103). ✧ 'Smartness'. ⇨ **AQÏL** + suff. -*lïq*.

AQÏM Trkm.? 1867 **Aqïm** [Акым Нияз-аталык] (MIT II, 621); Uzb. 1768 **Aqïm-χan** [Акым-хан], from Khiva (MIT II, 343, 351). ✧ 'Flow, deluge' cf. Trkm. *aqïm* 'течение, поток' (TRS).

AQÏM-BEK see **AQÏN**

AQÏMAY Yak. **Aqïmay** / **Bāy-aqïmay-toyon** [Акымаі: баі Акымаі тоjон], hero in a folktale (Pek.). ✧ 'Forearm'. See also **AQÏMAL**.

AQÏMAL Yak. **Aqïmal-bay-toyon** [Акымал баі тоjон], a hero in a tale (Pek.). ✧ 'Upper arm, muscle' cf. Yak. *aqïmal* 'id.' (Pek.).

AQÏMBET Bashk. 1735 **Aχïmbet** [Ахымбеть Тлеғметев] (MIB III, 336); Kkalp. 20th c. **Aqïmbet** [Акымбет] (KkRS 772); Bashk. 1664 **Aqïmbet** / **Aqimbet?** [Акимбетко Карасманов] (MIB I, 193); Kzk. 19th c. **Aqumbat** [Иса Али Акумбатовъ] (Grod., Pril. 187); *EN:* Kzk. 18th c. - 19th c. **Aχ-ïmbet** [Ахьімбет] (Tynyšp. 71); Kzk. 1735 **Aqïmbet** [Акьімбет] (Tynyšp. 70). ⇨ **AQ I.** + suffixoid -*imbet*.

AQÏN Kzk. **Aχïm-bek** (<**Aχïn-bek**) [Иркимбек Ахимбеков] (Sb. Syr-D. IV, otd. II, 92); Khorezm.? 13th c. **Aχïn** [Ахин] (RaD I/1, 97); Kzk. 19th c. **Aqïm-bay** (<**Aqïn-bay**) [Акымбай] (AOK 86); Kzk. 19th c. **Aqïm-bek** [Акимъ-бекъ Байкопаковъ] (Grod., Pril. 120); Kzk. 18th c. - 19th c. **Aqïm-bek** (<**Aqïn-bek**) [Акьімбек] (Tynyšp. 66); Kzk. 19th c. **Aqïm-bek** (<**Aqïn-bek**) [Акимъ-бекъ] (Grod., Pril. 138); Kzk. 19th c. **Aqïm-bek** (<**Aqïn-bek**) [Акимъ-бекъ / Акимбек] (AOO 50); Kzk. 19th c. **Aqïm-bek** (<**Aqïn-bek**) [Акимъ-бекъ / Акимбек] (SOK 258); Kirg. **Aqïn-bek** (<**Aqïn-bek**) [Акимбекъ Ульджебаев] (Konšin, Mat. I-III, 70); Bashk. 1735 **Aqïn** [Якшигилди Акинъ], a tarχan (Vel.-Zern., Bašk. 20); Kzk. 19th c. **Aqïn** [Акын] (AOP 58); Kzk. 19th c. **Aqïn** [Акынъ] (SODž. 4); Kzk. 19th c. **Aqïn-bay** [Акынбай] (SOK 50, 64); Kzk. 1834 **Aqïn-bek** [Акьімбекъ Бопинъ] (Konšin, Mat. V, 42); Kzk. **Aqïn-mulda** [Акын Мулда] (Proben III, 76 /99/). ✧ 'Poet; folksinger' cf. Kzk. *aqïn* 'поэт, акын' (KzRS, Radl. I, 98-99), Bashk. *aqïn* 'id.' (BRS), Tat. *aqïn* 'акын' (TatRS), Kirg. *aqïn* 'акын (певец-импровизатор); поэт' (Jud.) (<P.).

AQÏNČÏ see **AQÏNJÏ**

AQÏNČIY see **AQÏNJÏ**

AQÏNČÏK Bashk. 1780 **Aqïnčïk** [Ниязгул Акинчиков] (MIB V, 111). ✧ 'Little poet'. ⇨ **AQÏN** + suff. -*čik* / -*čïq*.

AQÏNJÏ Bashk. 1751 **Aqïnči** [Такаев Акынчин] (MIB IV/1, 13); Bashk. 1682 **Aqïnči** / **Aqïnčiy?** [Акинчишко, Акинчий Таникеев] (MIB I, 76, 78 80); Yürük 1543 **AqïnJï** [قنجى], from the Yürüks of Kocacık (Gökb., Rum. 104, 222); Tat. **AqïnJï** [Акынсı] (Gökb., Rum. 236, 242). ✧ 'Soldier' cf. Turk. *aqïnJï* 'zum Rauben ausgeschickter Soldat, Steifzügler' (Radl. I, 100).

AQÏP Yak. **Aqïp** / **Äkïp** [Акып / Äкіп] (Pek.). ✧ Arhipp (R.).

AQÏPČA Hak. 19th-20th c. **Aqïpča** [Акыпча] (Katanov, Otč. 13). ✧ Little Arhipp (R.). ⇨ **AQÏP** + suff. -*ča*.

AQÏR Bashk. 18th c. **Aqïr** [Акыр Уразаев] (MIB III, 168). ✧ 'End, Finish; (The) Last' cf. Kzk., Tat. *aqir* 'der Letzte' (Radl. I, 100) (<Ar.).

AQÏS see **AQÏŠ**

AQÏS-KÏLDÏ Bashk. 1672 **Aqïs-kildi** [Килейка Акзкильдин] (MIB I, 74). ✧ 'Reflection (similarity, likeness) has come (has been born)' cf. Kirg. *aqs, akis* (Jud.), Uzb. *aqs* 'отражение, отображение' (UzbRS) (<Ar.). ⇨ **KÏLDÏ**.

AQÏSTAY Kzk. 19th c. **Aqstay** / **Aqïstay** [Акстай] (AOA 146). ✧ 'S(he) is like a reflection'? cf. Kirg. *aqs, akis* (Jud.), Uzb. *aqs* 'отражение, отображение' (UzbRS) (<Ar.). + dim. suff. -*tay(1)*?

AQÏŠ Bashk. 1763 **Aqïč** / **Aqïs** [Чюраш (Чураш) Акичев, Акысев] (MIB IV/1, 271, 341); Uyg. 12th c. - 14th c. **Aqïs** (Radl., Usp. 115-16; Bashk. 1709 **Aqïs** [Акиш Аишев] (MIB I, 263); Bashk. 1729 **Aqïs** [Байсеке Акышев] (MIB III, 270); Uzb. 1538/39 **Aqïš-sultan** [Акиш-султан], Sufiyan Khan's son (MIT II, 59-60). ✧ 'Flow; river' cf. Turk., Kuman *aqïš* 'id.' (Radl. I, 107).

AQÏT Tat.? 1598 **Aχït-murza** [Ахитъ мурза] (AI II, 3); Kzk. 19th c. **Aqït** [اقىت / Акытъ] (AUK Dobavl. 12).

AQÏTČÏK Bashk. 1735 **Aqïtčik** [Акытчикъ], a „tezik" (Vel.-Zern., Bašk. 25). ⇨ **AQÏT** + suff. -*čik*.

AQMAQ Bashk. 1750 **Aqmaq** [Мурза Акмаков] (MIB III, 475). ✧ 'Fool' cf. Kzk., Kirg., Alt., Chag., Tat., Kuman *aqmaq* 'dumm, thöricht' (Radl. I, 131), Bashk. *aχmaq* 'id.' (BRS).

AQMAN Tat. **Aχman** [Ахмановъ] (DAI IV, 286); Tat. 1680 **Aχman** [Ишпулатко Ахмановъ] (AI V, 93); Bashk. 1706 **Aχman** [Ахман Казакаев] (MIB III, 26); Chuv. 18th-19th c. **Akman** [Акманъ] (Magn. 25); Crm.(Tat.) 1623 **Aqman** [اقمن] (Vel.-Zern., Crim. 24); Bashk. 1715 **Aqman** [Акман] (MIB I, 294); Bashk. 1722 **Aqman** [Акман] (MIB III, 135); Kzk. 1878 **Aqman** [Молла Худай-Берган Акманов, Молла Акман] (Grod., Pril. 92, 120). ✧ 'Very white, snow-white; clean' (Erol II); According to Sattarov it may also be the shortened-contracted form of compound PNs like *Aqmöχämmät, Aqmulla, Äχmätjan,* etc. (Sattarov 30). ⇨ **AQ I.** + suff. *-man.*

AQMAN-TAY Kzk. 19th c. **Aqman-tay** [Акмантай Саджирбаевъ] (Grod., Pril. 159); Kzk. / Kirg.? 19th c. **Aqman-tay** [Акмантай Саджирбаевъ] (Grod., Pril. 159); Kzk. / Kirg.? 19th c. **Aqman-tay** [Акмантай Умурзаковъ] (Grod., Pril. 162); Kzk. / Kirg.? 19th c. **Aqman-tay** [Акмантай Сиджиртаевъ] (Grod., Pril. 165). ✧ 'Very white foal'? ⇨ **AQMAN** + **TAY** or suff. *-tay(2)*?

AQMANAY Chuv. 18th-19th c. **Akmaney** [Акманей] (Magn. 26); Bashk. 1715 **Aqmanay** [Акманай Аканаев] (MIB III, 124); Bashk. 1718 **Aqmanay** [Акманай Темиров] (MIB III, 168); Bashk. 1735 **Aqmanay** [Акмянай Уразбактинъ], (Vel.-Zern., Bašk. 25); Bashk. 1737 **Aqmanay** [Акманай Тоняшев] (MIB III, 364); Bashk. 1761 **Aqmanay** [Акназар Акманаев] (MIB IV/1, 219); Kzk. 19th c. **Aqmanay** [Акманай] (Grod., Pril. 72); Tat. / Bashk.? 1695 **Aqmanay** [Кочкар Акманаевъ] (MIB I, 90); Tat. / Bashk.? 18th-19th c. **Aqmanay** [Акманай] (Magn. 26). ✧ 'Little snow-white'. ⇨ **AQMAN** + suff. *-ay.*

AQMAŠ Kzk. 19th c. **Aqmaš** [Худай Бергянъ Молла Акмашевъ] (Grod., Pril. 120).

AQMAT see **AXMET**

AQMET see **AXMET**

AQNA Hak.(Sag.) **Aqna** [Акна], fem. (Katanov, Otč. 7).

AQPAN Kzk. 19th c. **Aqban** [Шукурь-Бек Акбанов] (Grod., Pril. 140); Kzk. 19th c. **Aqpan** [Акпанъ] (AOP 118); Kzk. 19th c. **Aqpan** [Акпанов] (AOO 22); Kzk. 19th c. **Aqpan** [Акпанъ] (SOK 130, 208); Kzk. 19th c. **Aqpan** [Акпанъ] (SOV 56); *EN:* Kzk. 18th c. - 19th c. **Aqban** [Акбан] (Tynyšp. 75). ✧ 'The coldest days of winter' cf. Kzk. *aqpan* 'die kältesten Tage (Dezember-Januar) des Winters' (Radl. I, 130).

AQPÏRA Uyg. 12th c. - 14th c. **Aqpïra** [Ak Pıra] (EUTS, DTS); Uyg. 12th c. - 14th c. **Aqpïra / Aq-bïra / Aq-bara?** (Radl., USp. 86).

AQPÏS Kzk. 19th c. **Aqpïs-pay** [Апыспай] (SOK 48).

AQRU-ARQÏM Kzk. 19th c. **Aqru-arqïm** [Акруаркымъ] (SODž. 82).

AQSA Chuv. 18th-19th c. **Aksa-bay** [Аксабай] (Magn. 26).

AQSA-KEL-MAMET Nog. 1649 **Aqsa-kel-mamet** [Салтанашъ мурза Акса-Келмаметевъ] (AI IV, 78). ⇨ **AQSA / AQSAQ?** + **KEL-MAMET.**

AQSAQ Khorezm. 14th c. **Aqsaq, Aqsaq Temür** (see also *Temir-aqsaq*), born in 1336, sobriquet of the emir of Samarkhand then that of the well-known khan (1370-1405) (Radl. I, 125); Bashk. 1664 **Aqsaq** [Кызилкурт Аксаков] (MIB I, 192); NUyg. 19th c. **Aqsaq** [اقساق] (Le Coq, Namenl. 93). ✧ 'Lame' cf. *aqsaq* 'hinkend, lahm' (Radl. I, 125). See also **TEMÏR-AQSAQ.**

AQSAQ-SALAR see **SALAR**

AQSAMAŠ Tat.(GH) 1335 **Aqsamaš** ['Ακσαμας], a christened Tatar (Byz. Turc. 60).

AQSAR-ATTÏ see **ALTÏN-TANA**

AQSTAY see **AQÏSTAY**

AQSTU see **AQÏSTU**

AQSUQ see **AQŠUQ**

AQŠAY Tat. 1724 **Aqšay** [Баймаш Акшаев] (MIB III, 227); Tat.(Mish.) 1748 **Aqšey** [Азегуль Акшеев] (Nepljuev 437). ✧ 'Little money, little coin'. ⇨ **AQČA** + dim. suff. *-y.* See also **AČKAY.**

AQŠAQ Uyg. 1339 **Aqšaq** (Chwol., Syr.-nest. 93).

AQŠEY see **AQŠAY**

AQŠÏ Kzk. 19th c. **Aqši-bay / Aqšï-bay** [Акшибай] (AOP 126). ✧ '(Man) denying his or other's sin' cf. Kirg. *aqčï* 'человек, отрицающий сво[или чужу[вину' (Jud.).

AQŠÏ-BURDÏ Bashk. 1737 **Aqšï-burdï** [Сюлюк Акшибурдин] (MIB I, 316). ⇨ **AQŠÏ?**

AQŠÏN Bashk. 1730 **Aqšïn** [Азягул Акшинов] (MIB III, 277). ✧ 'Whitish' (Rásonyi: Mny. 1927, 281-282). ⇨ **AQ I.** + suff. *-šïn.*

AQŠUQ Kzk. 19th c. **Aqsuq-pay** [Аксукпай] (SOK 148); Kzk. 19th c. **Aqšuq** [Акшукъ] (SOK 268).

AQTA Kzk. 19th c. **Aqta-bay** [Актабай] (SOK 114). ✧ I. 'Truthful; fair' (var. of AQTÏ?); II. 'Castrated' cf. Kzk. *aqta* 'холощёный' (KzRS) (P.); III. 'Win a price in singing competition' cf. Kzk., Kirg. etc. *aqta-* 'in Gesängen preisen' (Radl. I, 115); ⇨ **AQTÏ?**

AQTAP-BERGÄN Kzk. 1817 **Aqtap-bergän** [آقتاب بيركان] (MIK IV, 313, 319). ⇨ ? + **BERGEN.**

AQTÏ Tat. 1680 **Aqtï-bay** [Токбай Актыбаевъ] (DAI VIII, 272). ✧ 'Truthful; fair' cf. Kzk. *aqtï* (Radl. I, 119), Kirg. *aqtï* (Jud.) (<Ar. ḥaqq?).

AQU Kzk. 19th c. **Aqu-bay** [Акубай] (SOV 148). ✧ 'Generous'? ⇨ **AГÏ?**

AQU-TAY Khorezm. 13th c. **Aqu-tay** (RaD/Ber. I, 166, 287, RaD I/1, 171). ⇨ **AQU** + **TAY** or suff. *-tay(2)*?

AQUČÏ see **AГÏČÏ**

AQUMBAT see **AQÏMBET**

AQUN Kirg. **Aqun / Aqun-χan** [Акун, Акун-хан] (Jud.). ✧ 'Folk-singer, poet' cf. Kirg. *aqun/aqïn* 'акын /до революции) акын, поэт-письменник /певец-импровизатор); поэт' (P.) (Jud.).

AQURTAY Khorezm.? 13th c. **Aγurtay / Aqurtay** [اقرتاى / Агуртай] (RaD/Ber. I, 166, 287).

AQUŠ see **AQ-QUŠ**

AL Oghuz/Trkm. 13th c. **Al** [ال / Ал], İnal-Yawï-χan's son (Abulg./Kon. 730); Kirg. **Al-ake** [Алаке], (Jud. 28, 88, 541); Chuv. 18th-19th c. **Al-bay** [Албай] (Magn. 26), Tat. 20th c. **Al-bay** [Албаев] (Sattarov); Bashk. 1709 **Al-bay** [Албай Алтыбаев] (MIB III, 44); Kzk.? 19th c. **Al-bay** [Албаевъ] (SKSO III, 18); Chuv. 18th-

19th c. **Al-batïr** [Албатыръ] (Magn. 26); Chuv. 18th-19th c. **Al-bäk** [Алмаметъ] (Magn. 27); Bashk. 1709 **Al-bäk** [Албяк Арасланов] (MIB I, 264); Bashk. 1726 **Al-bey** [Албей Ишимбетев] (MIB III, 239); Bashk. 1717 **Al-bek** [Албек Тенеев] (MIB III, 157); Kzk. 19th c. **Al-bek** [Албекъ] (AOO 30); Kzk. 19th c. **Al-bek** [Албекъ] (SODž. 56); Kzk. 19th c. **Al-bek** [Албекъ] (SOK 186, 214, 298); Chuv. 18th-19th c. **Al-bekey** [Албекей] (Magn. 26); Chuv. 18th-19th c. **Al-gazï** [Алгазинъ] (Magn. 26); Kkalp. 20th c. **Al-γazï** [Алгазы] (KkRS 772); Selj. 1054 **Al-χan** [Αλκαν], a commander of the army of the Seljuk Sultan Tugril Beg (Byz. Turc.); Tat.(Tob.) **Al-χan** [Ал Хан], a prince mentioned together with Kül-χan (Proben IV, 274 /340/); Kzk.? 18th c. **Al-χuja** [Алхуджій] (Nepljuev 716); Chuv. 18th-19th c. **Al-murza** [Алмурза] (Magn. 27); Kzk. 1884 **Al-nökür** [Алнокуръ] (Grod., Pril. 94); Kkalp. 20th c. **Äl-žan** [Әлжан] (KkRS 772); Kzk. **Äl-žän** [Әлжän], Sar-žan's mate (or brother?) (Proben III, 78 /100/); *TN:* Tat. 16th c. - 17th c. **Al-bayevo** [Албаево], a village in the district of Mamadyš (Iznoskov 117); *TN:* Turk. **Al-oγlu** [Aloğlu], a village (Köyl.). ✧ I. 'Blood-red, red, rose-coloured' cf. Kuman, Tat., Crm., Kzk., Osm., Uyg., Chag. *al* (Radl. I, 349), Bashk. *al* 'алый' (BRS); II. 'Take (it)!, Get (it)!' (Imperative name, cf. Rásonyi: AOH 15(1962), 233-243). cf. all Trk. languages *al-* 'nehmen, fortnehmen, zu sich nehmen' (Radl. I, 341); III. 'The first (son)'. According to Sattarov the Tatar names *Al-bay, Alqï* were given to the first son born in the family; cf. Tat. *al* 'передний' (TatRS). *Al-ake* may be the shortened form of *Al-mambet* (<*Al-muχammad*) or a compound of *al* and comp. *-ake*. See also **BOP-AL, DÏMÏM-AL, HÏND-AL, ÏS-AL, YEN-AL?, KES-AL, SATÏB-AL, TEMÏR-AL.**

AL-ALMÏŠ see **EL-ALMÏŠ**

AL-AT Hak. 19th-20th c. **Al-at** (<Ala-at) [Алат] (HRS 348). ✧ 'Pied horse' (Butanaev). ⇨ **ALA + AT.**

AL-BAQTÏ Tat. 20th c. **Al-baqtï** [Албактин], Tatar family-name (Sattarov). ✧ I. 'The first child (son) has looked in (=has been born)' (Sattarov), cf. Tat. *baq-* 'смотреть, взглянуть' (TatRS); II. 'First-(born)-Lucky (child)'. ⇨ **AL + BAQTÏ.**

AL-BARÏS see **AL-BARS**

AL-BARS Chuv. 18th-19th c. **Al-barïs** [Албарисъ] (Magn. 26); Chuv. 18th-19th c. **Al-barïs(ka)** [Албарыска] (Magn. 26); Chuv. 18th-19th c. **Al-bars** [Албарсъ] (Magn. 26); Tat. 20th c. **Al-bars / Al-barc** [Албарцев], Tatar family-names (Sattarov); *TN:* Tat. / Chuv.? **Al-parïs** [Алпарысовы], a village (Alatyr. 138). ✧ I. 'Red panther'; II. 'Heroic, brave panther' (Sattarov); The Hung. *Laborc* may also be derived from *Al-bars* (Melich, HM 19). ⇨ **AL / ALP? + BARS.**

AL-BASAR Kzk. 19th c. **Al-basar** [Албасаръ] (AOO 26). ✧ 'First (son) enters'? ⇨ **AL + BASAR.**

AL-BAŠ Chuv. 18th-19th c. **Al-baš** [Албашъ] (Magn. 26); Bashk. 1756 **Al-baš** [Абдрахман Албашев] (MIB IV/1, 107). ✧ I. 'Red head'; II. 'First head (=chief)'? ⇨ **AL + BAŠ.**

AL-BAT Bashk. **Al-bat** [Албат Аипов] (MIB I, 486). ⇨ **AL + BAT?**

AL-BEČ Chuv. 18th-19th c. **Al-beč** [Албечь] (Magn. 26). ✧ 'First/red-?'. ⇨ **AL.**

AL-BERGEN Kzk. 19th c. **Al-bergen** [Альбергенъ] (SOK 286). ✧ I. '(Child) Given first'?; II. 'Red gave him'? III. 'Allah gave him'? ⇨ **AL? + BERGEN.**

AL-BÏTÏQ Tat.(Sib.) **Al-bïtïq** [Ал Бытык] (Proben IV, 142 /181/). ⇨ **AL + BÏTÏQ?**

AL-BURA Kuman 1284 **Al-pra** (<Al-bra <Al-bura) [Alpra], a prince of the Kumans (SRH II, 207, Fejér, CD V, 3, 258-61, Gyárfás II, 449); Kuman 1388 **Al-pura** [Olpura] (Anjou Okm. I, 169). ✧ 'Red-brown (russet) male camel' (Rásonyi: KÖA 80, AOH 20 (1967), 136). ⇨ **AL + BUΓRA.**

AL-BURZA Chuv. 18th-19th c. **Al-burza** [Албурза] (Magn. 26). ⇨ **AL.**

AL-ČAΓÏR Tat.(Ishim) **Al-čaγïr** [Алчаѣыр], (Proben IV, 202 /248/); Kzk. 19th c. **Al-čaγïr** [Альчагыръ] (AOP 102); Kzk. **Al-šaγïr** [Alschagyr / Алшаѣыр / Алшагыр], Bï-jan's father (Žirm., Epos 400, Proben III, 79 /102/, 134 /170/). ✧ 'Red-grey-eyed; having red-grey eyes'? ⇨ **AL + ČAΓÏR.**

AL-ČÜKÜR Bashk. 1714 **Al-čükür** [Алчюкур Бичюрин] (MIB I, 105). ⇨ **AL?**

AL-DEMÏR see **AL-TEMÏR**

AL-DÏMER see **AL-TEMÏR**

AL-DOLAY Hak. 19th-20th c. **Al-dolay** [Алдолай] (HRS 348). ✧ 'Sly/cunning hare' cf. Hak. PN *Al-bay* 'хитрый бай' (Butanaev). ⇨ **AL + TOLAY II.**

AL-DUΓAN see **AL-TUΓAN**

AL-GERIM Chuv. 18th-19th c. **Al-gerim** [Алгеримъ] (Magn. 26). ⇨ **AL + KERÏM?**

AL-GÏLDE Chuv. 18th-19th c. **Al-gilde** [Алгилда] (Magn. 26); Tat. 20th c. **Al-gilde** [Алгилде] (Sattarov). ✧ 'The first-born; born first' (Sattarov). ⇨ **AL + KELDÏ.**

AL-GÏREY Chuv. 18th-19th c. **Al-girey** [Алгирей] (Magn. 26). ⇨ **AL + KERÄY.**

AL-KEŠ Bashk. 1734 **Al-keš** [Алкешъ Сюндеков], a tarχan (Vel.-Zern., Bašk. 11); Bulg. 1316 **Al-kis** [التيس] (Jusupov 14). ✧ 'Red-brown sable (Mustela nivalis)'. ⇨ **AL + KÏŠ.**

AL-KÏS see **AL-KEŠ**

AL-QAYA Turk. **Al-qaya-oγlu** [Alkayaoğlu], a village (Köyl.). ⇨ **AL + QAYA.**

AL-QARA-ULÏ Oghuz **Al-qara-ulï / Alqïr-awlï** [Алкараулы, Алкыр-аули], Kün-χan's son, the same as Alqa-öyli in AbulGKon, and Alqa-bölük in MK (RaD I/l, 76). ✧ 'Red-black?, Black hero?'. ⇨ **AL** + **QARA** + **UL**? See also **ALQA-ÖYLİ**.

AL-QAŠ Bashk. 1709 **Al-qaš** [Алкаш Телявлеев] (MIB I, 264); Bashk. 1751 **Al-qaš** [Алкаш Сююндюков] (MIB IV/1, 43); Bashk. 1788 **Al-qaš** [Кинзябулат Алкашев] (MIB V, 235). ✧ I. 'Red precious stone' cf. Bashk. *al* 'алый, розовый румяный', + *qaš* 'драгоценный камень' (BRS); II. 'Red eyebrow'. ⇨ **AL** + **QAŠ**.

AL-QÏLÏČ Tat.(Lit.) 1554 **Al-qïlïč** [Алкиличъ], a Tatar prince (Kn. Metriki Lit. 99). ✧ 'Blood-red sword'. ⇨ **AL** + **QÏLÏČ**.

AL-MAMET Chuv. 18th-19th c. **Al-mamet** [Алмаметъ] (Magn. 27); Tat. 1753 **Al-mamet** [Кадырметь Алмаметев] (MIB IV/1, 70). ⇨ **AL** + **MAMET**.

AL-MEREK Kzk. 19th c. **Al-merek** [Альмерекъ] (SODž. 82); Kzk. 19th c. **Al-mrek** [Альмрекъ] (SODž. 36). ⇨ **AL**.

AL-MÏRAT see **AL-MURAT**

AL-MONČUQ NUyg. 19th c. **Al-mončuq** [المونجوق / Al-monchuk] (Le Coq, Namenl. 94). ✧ 'Red trinket, pearl' (Le Coq, Namenl. 94). ⇨ **AL** + **MUNČUQ**.

AL-MUQAN Kzk. 19th c. **Al-muqan** [Альмуканъ] (AOK 6); Kkalp. 20th c. **Äl-muqan** [Әлмукан] (KkRS 772). ✧ I. 'Red/first (?) Mukhammad'; II. 'Red/first Servant'. ⇨ **AL** + **MUQAN**.

AL-MULAT Chuv. 18th-19th c. **Al-mulat** [Алмулатъ] (Magn. 27). ✧ 'Red steel'? ⇨ **AL** + **BULAT**.

AL-MURAT Kkalp. 20th c. **Al-mïrat** [Ал-мырат] (KkRS 772); Kkalp. 20th c. **Al-murat** [Ал-мурат] (KkRS 772). ⇨ **AL** + **MURAT**.

AL-SAY Kzk. 19th c. **Al-say** [Алсай] (AOK 10); Kzk. 19th c. **Al-say** [Алсай] (SOK 154). ⇨ **AL**.

AL-SİYİK Kzk. 19th c. **Al-siyik** [Альсіикъ] (SOV 60). ✧ 'Red/first bone/descendant?' cf. Kzk. *süyäk* 'кость' (Radl.), Tat. dial. *siyäk* 'стебель у растений' (KzRS), Tat. *süök/süäk* 'der Knochen, das Geschlecht, die Abstammung' (TatDS). ⇨ **AL**.

AL-ŠAĞÏR see **AL-ČAĞÏR**

AL-TEMİR Chuv. 18th-19th c. **Al-demir** [Алдемиръ] (Magn. 26); Chuv. 18th-19th c. **Al-dimer** [Алдимеръ] (Magn. 26); Tat.(GH) 1407, 1408, 1409 **Al-tämir?** / **Al-tamïr?** [Алтамыръ / (Артимиръ) / Алтамиръ], a prince of the Horde (PSRL VI, 136, VIII, 82, XI, 205, XXIII, 142); Turk. 15th c. **Al-tämür** [Αλταμούριος], chief dignitary of Turkic origin ("vornehmer Würdenträger (türkischer Herkunft?) in Trapezunt") (Byz. Turc. 65, Sauvaget 38); Kzk. 1819 **Al-temär?** / **Al-tamür?** [Алтамьяр] (MIK IV, 325); Chuv. 18th-19th c. **Al-temir** [Алтемиръ] (Magn. 27). ✧ '(Dark) Red-iron' cf. Sauvaget 38: *al-tämür* 'fer vermeil'. ⇨ **AL** + **TEMİR**. See also **EL-TEMİR**.

AL-TUĞAN Chuv. 18th-19th c. **Al-dugan** [Алдугань] (Magn. 26); Tat.? 18th-19th c. **Al-tugan** [Алтуганъ], among the Mordvas (Magn. 27); Kzk. 19th c. **Al-tuɣan** [Алтуганъ] (SOK 186); Selj. 1100 **Al-tuɣan (<Ala-tuɣan?)** [الاتوغان / التـرغان / Al-Targhân], Aq Soñqor's father, Zeñgi's (ca.1126) grandfather (Kamāladdīn, Bugyah: RHCHor III, 704). ✧ I. 'Red (or pied) falcon' cf. the explanation given by Kamāladdīn: '. Telle est la leçon de notre manuscrit. Mais il faut sans doute ن الاتوغـا *Ala-toughân*, ce qui, en turc oriental, signifie 'faucon au plumage bigarré'. On sait que les surnoms empruntés à la vénerie étaient frequents chez les princes d'origine turque.' (Kamāladdīn, Bughyah: RHCHor III, 704); II. 'Born first' (Sattarov). ⇨ **AL** + **TOĞAN**.

ALA Yürük 1543 **Ala** [الا / Ala], from Koсacık (Gökb., Rum. 103); Chuv. 18th-19th c. **Ala-bay** [Алабай] (Magn. 26); Kzk. 19th c. **Ala-bay** [Алабай] (SODž. 112); Turk. **Ala-bey** [Alabey] (Köyl.); Shor 19th-20th c. **Ala-bey**, the youngest son of Šul-bay (Dyrenkova 310); Kzk. 19th c. **Ala-bek** [Алабекъ] (AOAtb. 38); Kirg. **Ala-ǰan** [Ala-dzsan] (Almásy 296); Tat.(Mish.) 1693 **Ala-ɣul** [Алагул], from Ufa (MIB I, 84); *TN:* Turk. **Ala-bey** [Alabey], a village (Köyl.); *TN:* Uzb. **Ala-χatun** [Алахатунъ], a qïšlaq in the district of Urgut (ZSOIRGOSemip.). ✧ 'Pied; streaked; greyish blue' cf. Turk. *ala* 'unrein, gemischte Farbe, insbesondere schmutziges in Grau schimmerndes Blau' (Zenker), Yak. *ala* 'белобокий, белополосатый, в белых полосах поперек туловища (о рогатом скоте и вообще о животном)' (Pek.); Trk. *a:la, ala* (with several meanings in different Trk. languages) (Sev.). See also **UMBET-ALA**.

ALA-BAS see **ALA-BAŠ**

ALA-BAŠ Alt. 19th c. **Ala-bas** [Ала-бас] (Katanov, Otč. 12); Bashk. 1722 **Ala-baš** [Алабаш Токаев] (MIB I, 115); Bashk. 1756 **Ala-baš** [Абдрахман Алабашев] (MIB IV/1, 119); *TN:* Crm. **Ala-baš**, a Qoñrat man on the Salgir river (Jervis III). ✧ 'Pied head' (Katanov, Otč. 12). ⇨ **ALA** + **BAŠ**.

ALA-BERDİ see **ALLA-BERDİ**

ALA-BOTA Crm. 1505 **Ala-bota-ulan** / **Ala-bata-ulan?** [Ала-бута / Ала-бата-Уланъ / Алабота / Алабата, Ала бата], envoy from the Crimea to Moscow (PSRL XII, 259). ✧ 'Spotted/pied camel-foal'. ⇨ **ALA** + **BOTA**.

ALA-BUĞA Maml. 14th c. **Ala-boɣa** [الابغا] (Sauvaget 38); Maml. 14th c. **Ala-boɣa** [Ала бога] (Tuhfa 141, 409); Maml. 1438/39 **Ala-buɣa** [الا بغا] (Ibn Taghrīb. VII, 90); Tat. **Ala-buɣa** [Елабуга], a town and a province in Tatarstan (Radl. I, 367); 1251 **Ala-buɣa** / **Alï-buɣa** [Алыбуга], a prince (PSRL X, 138); *TN:* **Ala-buɣa** [Алабуга], a place in Turkestan (Barth.,

Ulugb. 89); *TN:* Tat. 1645 **Ala-buɣa** [Алабуга], a river (Miller, Ist. Sib. II, 508); *TN:* Tat. 1742-48 **Ala-buɣa** [Алабухинъ], a Tatar in Cheboksari (IOAIÊK XIV, 539). ✧ I. 'Pied/spotted bull'; Let the newly born boy become as strong as a bull (Sattarov). Baskakov mistakenly traces back the R. names *Albuga, Alabuga* to Trk. ALP-BUГA (Bask., Fam. 155). II. 'Perch' cf. Alt., Tat., Kuman *alabuɣa* 'der Barsch' (Radl. I, 367). ⇨ **ALA + BUQA.**

ALA-ČAY   Yak. **Ala-čay** [Алачаі], fem. (Pek.). ✧ 'Pied pebble' cf. Yak. *čay* 'галька' (JRS). ⇨ **ALA.**

ALA-DOÑOR   Kzk. 19th c. **Ala-doñor** [Аладонгоръ] (SOK 166). ⇨ **ALA.**

ALA-GÖZ see **ALA-KÖZ**

ALA-GÜŠÜK see **ALA-KÜČÜK**

ALA-ХARA   Yak. **Ala-χara** [Ала Хара] (Pek.). ✧ 'Pied-black'. ⇨ **ALA + QARA.**

ALA-YAR see **ALLAH-YAR**

ALA-YONTLÏ   Oghuz/Trkm. 13th c. **Ala-yuntlï / Ala-yontlï** [اليونتلى / Алаюнтли / Ала-йонтлы], Taq-han's (Taġ-han's) son (RaD I/1, 76, Abulg./Kon. 520, 560, 610). ✧ 'Having a pied horse' cf. OT *yunt* 'лошадь' (DTS). ⇨ **ALA + suff. -lï.**

ALA-YUNTLÏ see **ALA-YONTLÏ**

ALA-KÖZ   Turk. 1543 **Ala-göz** [Alagöz Çoban] (Gökb., Rum. 221); Turk. 1552 **Ala-göz** [Dursun ibn Ala-göz] (Dávid); Turk. 1565 **Ala-göz** [Bayezid ibn Ala-göz] (Dávid); Turk. 1570 **Ala-göz**, Mustafa ibn Ala-göz (Dávid); Turk. 1609 **Ala-göz** [Alagöz] (Gökb., Ed. 59); Yürük 1543 **Ala-göz** [Alagöz], among the Yürüks of Anatolia several people bore the name (Gökb., Rum. 103, 175, 185, 198, 206, 207, 215, 216, 217, 219, 221, 223, 224, 226, 227, 228); Tat. 1543 **Ala-göz** [Alagöz] (Gökb., Rum. 237); Uyg. 1324 **Ala-köz**, fem. (Chwol., Syr.-nest. 160); Maml. 1332 **Ala-köz** [الاكز], Sayfaddīn ~, an emir (Dawād. 368, 375); Crm.(Tat.) 1499, 1500 **Ala-köz / Ala-küz** [Салыхда Алакозъ (Алыкозъ / Алакузъ) / Салых Алакузъ / Салыхда (Салыгда) Олаэко], envoy from the sultan of Caffa, Crimea (PSRL XII, 250, XX, 369); *EN:* Kzk. 18th c. - 19th c. **Ala-köz** [Алакоз] (Tynyšp. 68). ✧ 'Hazel eyes; greyish blue eyes' cf. Maml. *ala köz* 'graublaues Auge' (Al-Qawānin), الاكوز < 'qui a l'oeil bleu clair' (Sauvaget 38), Turk. dial. *alagöz* 'Elâ göz' (DS). ⇨ **ALA + KÖZ.**

ALA-KÜČÜK   Kzk. 19th c. **Ala-güšük** [Алагушук] (SOV 48); Kzk. 19th c. **Ala-küčük** [Алакучукъ] (SOK 72); Kzk.? 19th c. **Ala-küšük** [Алакшукъ] (SOK 154); *EN:* Kzk. 18th c. - 19th c. **Ala-küšük** [Алакушук] (Tynyšp. 65, 71). ✧ 'Pied puppy'. ⇨ **ALA + KÜČÜK.**

ALA-KÜŠÜK see **ALA-KÜČÜK**

ALA-KÜZ see **ALA-KÖZ**

ALA-QARAQAN   Yak. **Ala-qaraqan** [Ала-Каракан] (Pek.). ✧ 'Pied rascal, villain' cf. Yak. *qaraqan*

'сорванец, пострел, повеса' (Pek.). ⇨ **ALA.**

ALA-QUŠ   Maml. 1294 **Ala-quš** [الاقوش], Bahāaddīn ~, an emir (Makrīzī IV, 12); Maml. 1325 **Ala-quš** [الاقوش المنصورى] (Zetterst. 165, 174); Maml. 14th c. **Ala-quš** [الاقوش / Alakuş] (Tarǰ/Houtsma 52, Tarǰ/Toparlı 41). ✧ 'Pied bird, magpie?' cf. Alt. *ala quš* 'Elster' (Radl. I, 351). ⇨ **ALA + QUŠ I.**

ALA-MAÑNÏQ   Hak.(Kacha) 19th-20th c. **Ala-mañnïq** (Radl. I, 981). ✧ 'Multi-coloured embroidery' cf. Hak.(Koyb.) *mañnïq* 'gestickt, mit Stickerei versehen' (Radl. IV, 2009). ⇨ **ALA.**

ALA-MOÑUS   Yak. **Ala-moñus** [Ала Монус] (Pek.). ✧ 'Pied, streaked bear (monster)' cf. Yak. *moñus* 'едок, обжора; медведь; баснословное чудовище' (Pek.). ⇨ **ALA.**

ALA-MUNDAR   Turk. **Ala-mundar** [Аламундаръ], a Turkish chief (PSRL (Russk. Hr.), 291). ✧ 'Never-do-well, rascal' cf. Turk., Crm.(Tat.), Kzk. *mundar* 'Taugenichts (Schimpfwort)' (Radl. IV, 2188). ⇨ **ALA.**

ALA-ŠÜGÖR see **ALLA-ŠÜGÜR**

ALA-ŠÜGÜR see **ALLA-ŠÜGÜR**

ALA-TAY   Tat.(Sib.) 1630 **Ala-tay** [Алатай Олешко (Алексей)], a newly christened person (Miller, Ist. Sib. II, 364); Kzk. 19th c. **Ala-tay** [Алатай] (SOV 142); Hak. 19th-20th c. **Ala-tay** [Алатай] (HRS 348); *EN:* Kzk. 18th c. - 19th c. **Ala-tay** [Алатай] (Tynyšp. 70). ✧ I. 'Pied foal'; II. 'Pied' (Sattarov). ⇨ **ALA + TAY** or suff. *-tay(1,2)?* See also **AQ-TAY, QARA-TAY.**

ALA-TUГAN see **AL-TUГAN**

ALA-ZİYAN   Bashk. 1740 **Ala-ziyan-ɣul** [Алазиянгул] (MIB I, 382). ✧ 'Pied loss/damage'? ⇨ **ALA + ZİYAN.**

ALABAN   Kzk. 19th c. **Alaban** [Алабанъ] (SOK 240). ⇨ **ALBAN / ALAMAN?, ALA?** + suff. *-ban?* See also **SARÏBAN.**

ALABÏR   Yak. **Alabïr** [Алабыр], a (demonic vamp?) shamaness (Pek.).

ALAČÏ see **ALAČÏ**

ALAČÏ   Crm.Tat. 1278 **Alači** [Алачи], a monk (Smirnov, Krym. 34); Tat.(GH) 1291 **Alačï / Alaču** ['Αλατζ(ού)], a christened Tatar, died in 1291 (Byz. Turc. 61). ✧ 'Small tent' cf. Mo. *alaču* 'Notzelt' (TMEN II. No. 519). See also **ALAČUQ.**

ALAČON   Hak. 19th-20th c. **Alačon** [Алачон] (HRS 348). ✧ 'Pied' (Butanaev). ⇨ **ALA.**

ALAČU see **ALAČÏ**

ALAČUQ   Tat.(GH) 1302 **Alačuq** ['Αλατζουκ], a christened Tatar (Byz. Turc. 61). ✧ 'Yurt, hut' cf. Chag. *alačuq*, Kirg., Kacha, Tat., Crm.(Tat.) *alačiq* 'Rindenjurte; Hütte aus Zweigen, Sommerküche in Dörfern' (Radl. I, 362), *alajïq, alačuq* (Sev.), also *alaču ~ alačuɣ* 'Notzelt' (TMEN II, No. 519). See also **ALAČÏ.**

ALAJA Turk. 20th c. **Alaja-oɣlu** [Alacaoğlu], a village in the district of Lüleburgas of the province of Kırklareli, Turkey (TMİB 539, Köyl.). ✧ 'Motley, speckled; piebald (horse)' cf. Turk. *alaca* 'id.' (TED).

ALAJAY Maml. 1317 **Alajay** [الجاى الدوادارى], Sayfaddīn ~, an emir (Dawād. 292, 296). ✧ 'Little pied (animal)' cf. Maml. *alaja* 'bunt' (AH, Tarǰ/Houtsma). + dim. suff. *-y*.

ALADAN see **ALDAN**

ALAFRENG Oghuz / Khorezm.? 1304 **Alafreng** [الافرنك], a prince from the Ilkhanid Dynasty, Gayhatu's son (RaD/Jahn 94, 102, 103, 104, Howorth III, 377). ✧ 'European' His father was the governor in Rum when he was born that's why he got this name. (RaD/Jahn 94, 102, 103, 104, Howorth III, 377). Cf. Turk. *alafranqa* (Italian *alla franca*) 'nach europäischer Mode, Sitte, Art' (Radl. I, 367).

ALAXČÏN Yak. **Alaχčïn / Ān-alaχčïn** [Алахчын], spirit of Earth (Pek.).

ALAY Crm.(Tat.) 1527 **Alay** [Алай], a prince from the Crimea peninsula (PSRL VI, 283-84). ✧ 'Crowd; procession; front' cf. Turk. *alay* 'Haufen, Regiment, ein feierlicher Zug' (Radl. I, 353), Chag. *alay* 'Fronte einer Truppe, vordere Reihe, Truppe' (Radl. I, 354), *alay* I. (Sev.).

ALAQ-KÖR Trkm. 1817/18 **Alaq-kör** [Алак Köp] (MIT II, 408). ✧ I. 'With eyes popping out; stupid' cf. Kirg. *alaq* '(о глазах) выпученный; выпуклый' (Jud.); Hak., Tuv. *alaq* 'dumm, thöricht, der Fehler' (Radl. I, 355), *alïq, alaq* 'id.' (Sev.); II. 'Robbery, raid; outlaw' cf. Chag. *alaq* 'Raub, Plünderung' (Radl. I, 355), *alaman, alaq* (Sev.). Originally it is a Mo. name, but appears among the Turks in the 14th c.; III. 'Plain, flat country, field, valley' cf. *alan, aläq* (Sev.). ⇨ **KÖR.**

ALAQ-KÖZ Tat.(Lit.) 1552 **Alaq-köz** [Алакгозъ] (Kn. Metriki Lit. 82). ✧ I. 'With eyes popping out; stupid' cf. Kirg. *alaq* '(о глазах) выпученный; выпуклый' (Jud.); Hak., Tuv. *alaq* 'dumm, thöricht, der Fehler' (Radl. I, 355), *alïq, alaq* 'id.' (Sev.); II. 'Robbery, raid; outlaw' cf. Chag. *alaq* 'Raub, Plünderung' (Radl. I, 355), *alaman, alaq* (Sev.). Originally it is a Mo. name, but appears among the Turks in the 14th c.; III. 'Plain, flat country, field, valley' cf. *alan, aläq* (Sev.). ⇨ **KÖZ.**

ALAQ-TAY Alt. 19th c. **Alaq-tay** [Алактай-богатырь], a bogatyr (hero) (Verb., In. 151, 152). ✧ I. 'With eyes popping out; foal (=child) with eyes popping out; stupid' cf. Kirg. *alaq* '(о глазах) выпученный; выпуклый' (Jud.); Hak., Tuv. *alaq* 'dumm, thöricht, der Fehler' (Radl. I, 355), *alïq, alaq* 'id.' (Sev.); II. 'Robbery, raid; outlaw' cf. Chag. *alaq* 'Raub, Plünderung' (Radl. I, 355), *alaman, alaq* (Sev.). Originally it is a Mo. name, but appears among the Turks in the 14th c.; III. 'Plain, flat country, field,

valley' cf. *alan, aläq* (Sev.). ⇨ **TAY** or suff. *-tay(2)*?

ALAQ-TAŠ Maml. 1308/09 **Alaq-taš** [الاقطش] (Iyās II, 149). ✧ I. 'Stone-like (child) with eyes popping out; stupid' cf. Kirg. *alaq* '(о глазах) выпученный; выпуклый' (Jud.); Hak., Tuv. *alaq* 'dumm, thöricht, der Fehler' (Radl. I, 355), *alïq, alaq* 'id.' (Sev.); II. 'Robbery, raid; outlaw' cf. Chag. *alaq* 'Raub, Plünderung' (Radl. I, 355), *alaman, alaq* (Sev.). Originally it is a Mo. name, but appears among the Turks in the 14th c.; III. 'Plain, flat country, field, valley' cf. *alan, aläq* (Sev.). ⇨ **TAŠ?**

ALAQA Trkm. 20th c. **Alaqa** [Alaqa] (Zaj. 1971, 331); Trkm. 20th c. **Alaqa** [Алака] (TrkmRS 39). ✧ 'Gopher, prairie-dog' cf. Trkm. *alaqa* 'суслик' (TrkmRS).

ALAQAY Bashk. 1760 **Alaqay** [Утяган Алакаев] (MIB IV/1, 187); Bashk. 1764 **Alaqay** [Санзяп Алакаев] (MIB IV/1, 290); Bashk. 1767 **Alaqay** [Алакай Солтанбеков] (MIB IV/1, 324); Bashk. 1771 **Alaqay** [Алакай Халилев] (MIB IV/1, 354); Bashk. 1780 **Alaqay** [Умитей (Умукей) Алакаев] (MIB V, 109); Bashk. 1780 **Alaqay** [Алакай] (MIB V, 117); Kzk. 19th c. **Alaqay** [Бусурман Алакаев] (Grod., Pril. 78); *EN:* Nog. 20th c. **Alaqay** [Алакъай], an Aq-noɣay clan (Bask., Nog. 132, 141). ✧ I. 'An exclamation expressing joy and hapiness' cf. Kzk. *alaqay* 'id.' (KzRS), Tat. *alaqay* (Radl. I, 356); II. 'With eyes popping out' cf. Kirg. *alaɣay, alaqay / alaɣar* 'ясные очи (о красивых больших глазах)' (Jud.); III. 'Stupid'.

ALAM Uzb. 1809 **Alam-bek** [Алам бек] (MIKk. 104). ✧ 'Pain, suffering; shame' cf. Uzb. *alam* 'боль, страдание, мука; огорчение, досада' (UzbRS).

ALAMAN Tat. 1552 **Alaman** [Алеманъ] (Kn. Metriki Lit. 82); Kzk. 19th c. **Alaman** [Аламанъ] (SODž. 8, 56, 80, 100); Kzk. 19th c. **Alaman** [Аламанъ] (SOV 20, 78); Trkm. 1879 **Alaman-mirza** [Аламанъ] (Grod., Vojna IV, Grod., Pril. 109); Chag.? 15th c. **Alaman-oɣlan** [Alaman Olglan], („vn grâ señor de la Torquia q ha nombre") (Clavijo 60); *EN:* Kzk. 18th c. - 19th c. **Alaman** [Аламан] (Tynyšp. 67). ✧ 'Robber, brigand' cf. Kzk., Trkm., Az., East.T. *alaman* 'Haufe; ein Kriegsschaar, Räuberbande; der Reuber', Kzk. dial. *Alaman* 'войско; народ, общественность; большая мышь, грызун' (Amanž.).

ALAMANDÏ Kirg. **Alamandï** [Аламанды], a singer in the Manas-epos (Proben V, 40 /41/). ⇨ **ALAMAN** + suff. *-li*?

ALAN Kzk. 19th c. **Alam-bay (<Alan-bay)** [Аламбай] (Grod., Pril. 158); Oghuz/Trkm. 13th c. **Alan** [الان / Алан], Dib-Bakuy-χan's chief bek (Abulg./Kon. 660); Maml.? 1379/80 **Alan** [الان الشعبانى] (Iyās I, 248, 254); Maml.? 1401/02 **Alan** [الان الخاصكى] (Iyās I, 341); Maml. 1405/06 **Alan** [الان اليحياوى] (Iyās I, 348); Kzk.

18th c. - 19th c. **Alan** [Аланъ] (MIK IV, 325); Kzk. 1846 **Alan** [Камбаръ Алановъ] (Konšin, Mat. V, 91); Kzk. 19th c. **Alan** [Аланъ] (SOK 188); Kzk. 19th c. **Alan-bay** [Аланбай] (SODž. 114); *TN:* Kzk. **Alambayevskaya** (< **Alam-bay** < **Alan-bay**) [Аламбаевская], a place (village or town) 130 km north-east of Barnaul (Karta JAR IV). ✧ 'Worried, troubled' cf. Kzk., Alt. *alañ* 'unruhig, erstaunt; eine Krankheit der Schafe' (Radl. I, 357) or EN *Alan*?

ALAN-BUΓA　　Turk.　1379/80　**Alan-buγa** [الان بغا العثمانى] (Iyās I, 248). ✧ 'Worried Bull; Restless Bull'. ⇨ **ALAN + BUQA.**

ALANÏ　Türk 8th c. - 9th c. **Alanï-ičiräki / Alanï-ičräki** [Alanï İçreki / alanï ičiräki] (ETY II, 64, DTS).

ALAÑ-GÜZ　Kzk. 19th c. **Alañ-güz** [Алангузъ] (SOK 198). ✧ 'Having large/worried eyes' cf. Kirg. *alañ köz* 'большеглазый' (Jud.). ⇨ **ALAN + KÖZ.** See also **ALAQ-KÖZ.**

ALAÑ-ZİYAN

Bashk. 18th c. **Alan-ziyan-γul** [Аландзіангулъ] (Nepljuev 164, 170); Bashk. 18th c. **Alañ-ziyan-γul** [Алангзіянгул] (MIB I, 382). ⇨ **ALAN + ZİYAN?**

ALAÑQASAR-ÄLİF　　Kzk. **Alañqasar-älif** [الانكتسار الف / Алангксаръ-алифъ], in a legend, his son is Araslan-alif (ZVOIRAO XI, 292). ✧ 'Light-headed; absent-mided; careless' cf. Kzk. *alañγasar* 'невнимательный; рассеянный; легкомысленный' (KzRS), Kirg. *alañγazar* 'недогадливый; глуповатый; легкомысленный' (Jud.). ⇨ **ELİF.**

ALAÑŽÏBAS　Alt. 19th-20th c. **Alañzïbas** [Аланзыбас] (OjrRS 207). ✧ 'Not doubting; unhesitant; determined' (OjrRS 207), cf. Alt. *alañzï-* 'сомневаться; удивляться' (OjrRS).

ALAP　Uyg. 13th c. **Alap** (DTS). ✧ 'Hero'? ⇨ **ALP?** See also **XAYR-ALAP.**

ALAPSU　　Tat.(GH) 13th c. **Alapsu** ['Αλαψοῦ / Αλουψοῦ?], a christened Tatar (Byz. Turc. 61).

ALAS　Bashk. 1706 **Alas** [Алас Карабашев] (MIB IV/1, 122); Bashk. 1735 **Alas** [Аласъ Татлыбаевъ], a tarγan (Radl. I, 364). (Vel.-Zern., Bašk. 25). ✧ 'A kind of cotton' cf. Bashk. *alas* 'пестрядь' (BRS/Uraksin). ⇨ **ALAŠ?**

ALASA　Kzk. 19th c. **Alasa-χan / Alasa-qan** [Аласа-ханъ] (Potanin II, 149). ✧ 'Short' cf. Kzk. *alasa* 'niedrig' (Radl. I, 364).

ALAŠ　Kzk. 19th c. **Alaš** [Алашъ] (SOK 22, 248); Kzk. 19th c. **Alaš** [Алашъ] (SODž. 72); Kzk. 1889 **Alaš-bay** [Алашбаевъ] (AUK 61); Kzk. 19th c. **Alaš-bay-batïr** [الاشباى باطر / Алашбай-батыръ] (Veselovskij, Kirg. 14); Uzb. 1810 **Alaš-bek** [Алаш-бек] (MIKk. 117, MIT II, 376, 386, 399, 400); Uzb. 19th c. **Alaš-biy** [Алаш-бий] (MIKk. 124, 130, 132, MIT II, 390-92,

398-401, 404, 406 etc.); Alt. **Alaš-qam** [Алашъ-камъ /Алашъ-ханъ] (Nikiforov 145, 178-87); Kzk. 19th c. **Alaš-pay** [Алашпай] (SODž. 112); Kzk. 19th c. **Alaš-pay** [Алашпай] (SOK 234); *EN:* Kzk. **Alaš** [Алаш], a Kazak clan (Radl. I, 365); Nog. 20th c. **Alaš-küp** [Алаш куъп], a Qara-noγay clan (Bask., Nog. 137); Alt. **Alaš-qam** [Алашъ-камъ /Алашъ-ханъ] (Nikiforov 145, 178-87). ✧ I. 'Battle-cry of the Kazaks' (Radl. I, 365) II. Common ethnical name of the Kazak, Kirgiz and Tatar peoples (QTTS). A Kazak clan (Radl. I, 365); III. 'Alien, stranger; member of other clan, folk' cf. Kirg. *alaš* 'von einem andern Orte, Volke, fremd' (Radl. I, 365).

ALAW　Kzk. **Alaw / Er-alaᴜ** [Ер-Алау] (Žirm., Epos 395); Crm.(Tat.) **Alaᴜ-batïr** [Алау батыр] (Proben VII, 211). ✧ 'Flame'? cf. Chag. *alau* 'Flamme, Feuer' (Radl. I, 355).

ALAWAY　Kirg. 19th-20th c. **Alaway** [Алавай], guide of the traveller (Prinz 73). ⇨ **ALAW** + dim. suff. *-ay.*

ALĀPÏYA　Yak. **Alāpïya** [Алапыја], fem. (Pek.). ✧ Agafiya cf. R. Агафия (Pek.).

ALBAQÏN　Yak. **Albaqïn** [Албакын], sobriquet of a shaman (Pek.).

ALBAN　　Kzk. 19th c. **Albam-bay (<Alban-bay)** [Албамбай] (SOV 78); Uyg. **Alban** [Alban] (EUTS); Uyg. 12th c. - 14th c. **Alban** (Radl., USp. /No. 76/ 22); Kzk. 19th c. **Alban** [Албанъ] (SODž. 88); Kzk. 19th c. **Alban** [Албанъ] (SOK 238). ✧ 'A kind of tax; obligation, service, duty' cf. Uyg. *alban* 'повинность' [<Mo. *alba(n)*] (DTS), *alban* 'Hizmetle ödenen bir vergi adı' (EUTS), Alt., East.T. *alban* [البان] 'Tribut, Zins, Abgabe; Kronsabgabe' (Radl. I, 433). See also **ALBANAQ, ALBÏNAX.**

ALBANAX see **ALBANAQ**

ALBANAQ　Hak. 19th-20th c. **Albanaχ** [Албанах] (HRS 348); Hak.(Sag.) **Albanaq** [Албанак] (Proben IX, 557); Hak.(Sag.) 19th-20th c. **Albanaq** [Албанак] (Katanov, Otč. 11); Hak.(Koyb.) 19th c. **Albanaq** [Албанакъ] (Katanov, Otč. II, 12-14). ✧ 'Tax; tax-payer (=man)' (Katanov, Butanaev). ⇨ **ALBAN** + dim. suff. *-aq / -aχ.*

ALBANJÏ　Tuv. 19th c. **Albanjï** [Албанцы] (Proben IX, 156). ✧ 'Rate-collector; tax-collector' cf. Tar., East.T. *albanči* 'der Abgabeneinsammler' (Radl. I, 433). ⇨ **ALBAN** + suff. *-jï.*

ALBÏNAX　Hak. 19th-20th c. **Albïnaχ** [Албынах, Албанах?] (HRS 348). ⇨ **ALBANAQ?**

ALBÏS　Bashk. **Albïs** [Албесъ Юсуповъ], a tarγan (Vel.-Zern., Bašk. 27).

ALČARDÏR　Yak. **Alčardïr** [Алчардыр], a hero (Pek.).

ALČÏ　Kzk., Nog. **Alčï / Alšï** [Алшы Смаил, Алчысмаил], byname of an epic hero called İsmail (Žirm., Epos 403); Kzk. 19th c. **Alčï-bay** [Altchi-Baï], Arγïm-bay's, Altïm-bay's and Mindi-bay's brother

(Levchine 356); Uyg. 12th c. - 14th c. **Alču** (Radl., USp. 108, DTS). ✧ 'Lucky, fortunate; succesful' cf. Az., Tat., Crm. *alčï*, Kzk. *alšï* 'die eingebogene Seite des Knöchels' (Radl. I, 425, 429), Kzk. *alši* 'сторона альчика' (KzRS), *alčï* '(счастливая) сторона игральской бабки' (Sev.) < Mo. *alču* 'Spielknöchel' (TMEN II. No. 531). ⇨ **ALÏČ**. See also **TAYDÏQ-ALČI**.

ALČÏN   Kzk. 19th c. **Alčïn** [Альчин] (Potanin II, 7); *EN:* Kzk. 18th c. - 19th c. **Alčïn** [Алчын] (Tynyšp. 71); Kzk. 18th c. - 19th c. **Alčïn-bay** [Алчынбай] (Tynyšp. 66); *TN:* Crm. **Alčïn** [Altschin], a village south-east of Perekop (Jervis II); *TN:* Crm. **Alčïn**, a village south-east of Karasubazar (Jervis VIII); *TN:* Uzb. **Alčïn** [الچين / Алчинъ], a kyshlak in the district of Katta-Kurgan (ZIRGOStat. IV). ✧ I. 'Lucky' (Sattarov); II. 'Falcon' (Sattarov); III. The name of a Trk. tribe (Sattarov). Cf. Chag. *alčin* 'steiler Bergabhang; der Falke, ein Jagdvogel; eine Elle' (Radl. I, 426), Kirg. *alčïn* 'сажень' (Jud.).

ALČÏN-ADAQ   Hak. 19th-20th c. **Alčïn-adaq** [Алчын-адак] (HRS 348). ✧ 'Lucky foot'? ⇨ **AYAQ**.

ALČU see **ALČÏ**

ALDA-BERDİ see **ALLA-BERDİ**

ALDA-BERGEN see **ALLA-BERGEN**

ALDA-YAR see **ALLAH-YAR**

ALDA-NAZAR see **ALLA-NAZAR**

ALDA-SÖGÜR see **ALLA-ŠÜGÜR**

ALDA-SÜGÜR see **ALLA-ŠÜGÜR**

ALDA-ŽİN   Kzk. 19th c. **Alda-žin** [Алдажинъ] (SOK 222). ⇨ **ALLA**.

ALDAY   Kzk. 19th c. **Alday** [Алдай] (AOP 6, 54, 58, 102); Kzk. 19th c. **Alday** [Алдай] (SOK 92, 132). ⇨ **AL / ALLA?** + dim. suff. *-day/-y*.

ALDAQAY   Bashk. 1790 **Aldaqay** [Зиянчура (Зянчура) Алдакаев] (MIB V, 279). ✧ 'Little dear Allah'? ⇨ **ALLA** + dim. suff. *-qay*.

ALDAN   Kzk. 19th c. **Aldam-bay** (<Aldan-bay) [Алдамбай] (SODž. 150); Kzk. 19th c. **Aldan** [Алданъ] (AOA 102); Alt. 19th c. **Aldan** [Алдан], a hero (Verb., In. 134); Uzb. 20th c. **Aldan** [Алдан] (Begmatov 1984, 201); Uzb. 20th c. **Aldan-χân** [Алданхон] (Begmatov 1984, 201); Uzb. 20th c. **Aldan** [Алдан] (Begmatov 1984, 201); Kzk. 19th c. **Aldan / Aladan?** [Аладанъ] (SODž. 90); Uzb. 20th c. **Aldan-ây** [Алданой] (Begmatov 1984, 201); Uzb. 20th c. **Aldan-bây** [Алданбой] (Begmatov 1984, 201); Uzb. 20th c. **Aldan-ĵan** [Алданджан] (Begmatov 1984, 201). ✧ I. 'Be glad, be delighted' cf. Kzk. *aldan-* 'sich über etwas feruen (von Kindern)' (Radl. I, 415); II. 'Be lost! Be confused! Be conned!' (Begmatov), cf. Uzb. *aldan-* 'обмануться, впасть в заблуждение' (UzbRS). See also **ADAŠ I., SEVİN**.

ALDAN-MURAD   Uzb. 20th c. **Aldan-murâd**

[Алданмурод] (Begmatov 1984, 201). ⇨ **ALDAN?** + **MURAT**.

ALDAR   Chuv. 18th-19th c. **Aldar** [Алдаръ] (Magn. 26); Tat. 20th c. **Aldar** [Алдар], a hero in several Tatar folktales (Sattarov); Bashk. 1729 **Aldar** [Алдар Мамбетев] (MIB III, 267); Bashk. 1746 **Aldar** [Алдар Уразметев] (MIB III, 444); Bashk. 18th c. **Aldar** [Алдаръ] (Nepljuev 124); Bashk. 1754 **Aldar** [Иман Алдаров] (MIB IV/1, 89); Bashk. 1758 **Aldar** [Алдар Ултюков] (MIB IV/2, 20); Bashk. 1777 **Aldar** [Мрадым Алдаров] (MIB IV/2, 20); Bashk. 1788 **Aldar** [Курманай Алдаров] (MIB V, 223); Bashk. 1796 **Aldar** [Явдуш Алдаров] (MIB V, 361); Bashk. 18th c. **Aldar / Aydar / Ardar** [Алдар (Айдар, Ардар) Исекеев], took part in the revolts of 1705-11, 1735-36 and 1740 (MIB I, 224, 262, 405, 413); Bashk. 1734 **Aldar-bay** [Алдарбай Исекеевъ], a tarχan (PSZRI IX, 338, Vel.-Zern., Bašk. 9, 27); *EN:* Kzk. 18th c. - 19th c. **Aldar-biy** [Алдар-бий] (Tynyšp. 73). ✧ I. 'Deceiver, liar; a child (who) will cheat the evil ghoasts', a protective name (Sattarov), in most Trk. languages *alda-* 'betrügen, hinter's Licht führen, beschwindeln etc.' (Radl. I, 412-13), Tat.(Tob.), Crm. *aldar* 'der Betrüger' (Radl. I, 415); II. 'Famous; brave, glorious' (Mo. aldar).

ALDAR-KÖSE   Kzk. **Aldar-köse** [Алдыръ-кöсе] (IOAIÊK XX, 227); Kzk. 19th c. **Aldar-köse** [Алдаръ-косе], a very popular hero in Kzk. folktales (Potanin IV, 364-65, Potanin, Pred. 71, MSOS VI, 2, 214); Kzk. 19th c. **Aldar-köse** [Алдаръ Kосе] (AUK 82, 498); Kzk. 19th c. **Aldar-köse** [الداركوسه / Алдаръ-Köсе] (Pantusov, Kirg. 31); Kkalp. 20th c. **Aldar-köse** [Алдаркөсе] (KkRS 772); Kzk. **Aldar-küsä** [Aldar-Kusa / Алдаръ-куса] (Sb. Syr-D. XII, otd. II, 10, MSOS VI, 2, 214). ✧ 'Rascal, villain' (Radl.), (lit.) 'Deceiver/liar beardless' or 'Brave beardless'. ⇨ **ALDAR + KÖSE**.

ALDAS see **ALDAŠ**

ALDAŠ   Kzk. 19th c. **Aldas** [Алдасъ] (AOP 14); Tat.(Sib.)? **Aldaš** [Алдашко], Aldaško, but in the index Aldan is given, an envoy of Ješken tayša (Miller, Ist. Sib. II, 505, 526); Bashk. 1735 **Aldaš** [Алдашъ Еликеев], a tarχan (Vel.-Zern., Bašk. 16); Bashk. 1770 **Aldaš** [Алдаш Алдаров] (MIB IV/1, 342); Kzk. 19th c. **Aldaš** [Алдашъ] (SOV 92); Kzk. 19th c. **Aldaš-bek** [Аубурбай Алдашбековъ] (Grod., Pril. 151); NUyg. 1877 **Aldaš-datχa** [Алдашъ-датха], a man from Kashghar (Smirnov, Sultany 131); ⇨. Kzk. 19th c. **Aldaš-pay** [Альдешпай] (SODž. 84); Kzk. 19th c. **Aldïs-pay** [Алдыспай] (SOK 284). ✧ 'Cheat each other' cf. Kzk., Tat., Turk. *aldas- / aldaš-* 'einander betrügen' (Radl. I, 417, 418).

ALDAT   NUyg. **Aldat**, Sven Hedin's guide (Hedin I). ✧ 'Cheat/trick (him)!' (Imperative name) cf. Alt., Crm.,

Kar., Kzk., Tat. *aldat-* 'betrügen, betrügen lassen' (Radl. I, 416).

ALDİVER Chuv. 18th-19th c. **Aldiver** [Алдиверъ] (Magn. 26).

ALDÏ Chuv. 18th-19th c. **Aldï** [Алди] (Magn. 26); Kzk. 19th c. **Aldï-bay** [Альдыбай, Альдебай] (SODž. 88, 134, 150); Kzk. 19th c. **Aldï-bay** [Альдыбай, Альдебай] (SOK 204); Kzk. 19th c. **Aldï-bek** [Алдыбек, Альдибек] (SODž. 42, 98); Kirg. 12th c. **Aldï-er** [Aldi-er, Aldi'er], a Kirghiz chieftain (Temir 239, Ligeti, MTT 239); Chuv. 18th-19th c. **Aldu-bay** [Алдубай] (Magn. 26). ✧ I. '(He/she/somebody) Took; bought; got; has taken (the child)' cf. most Trk. languages *al-* 'to take, get, buy etc.' (Radl., Sev.) II. 'The first, best (child)' cf. Kzk. dial. *aldï* 'burïn, ülken; ilgeri, kelešek, bolasaq' (QTTS), Kirg. *ald/aldï* 'передняя часть; лучший' (Jud.), Kkalp. *aldï* 'передний, передовой, лучший' (KkRS). See also **EL-ALDÏ, YEL-ALDÏ, SATÏP-ALDÏ, SURAP-ALDÏ, TABÏP-ALDÏ, TİLEP-ALDÏ.**

ALDÏ-GİREY Crm.(Tat.)? 1693, 1708? **Aldï-girey** [Алди-гирей, Альди Гирей], a Cherkess prince/murza (AI V, 403, DAI XII, 279, MIKk. 157). ⇨ **ALDÏ** + **KERÄY.**

ALDÏY Kzk. 19th c. **Aldïy** [Альдий] (AOAtb. 2). ⇨ **ALDÏ** + (R.?) dim. suff. *-y.*

ALDÏKE Kzk. 19th c. **Aldïke** [Альдеке] (AOP 90); Kzk. 19th c. **Aldïke** [Альдеке] (SODž. 12); *EN:* Kzk. 18th c. - 19th c. **Aldïke** [Альдеке] (Tynyšp. 72). ⇨ **ALDÏ** + suff. *-ke.*

ALDÏKEY Kzk. 19th c. **Aldïkey** [Альдекей] (AOP 2); Kzk. 19th c. **Aldïkey** [Альдекей] (SOV 114). ⇨ **ALDÏKE** + dim. suff. *-y.*

ALDÏQ Chuv. 18th-19th c. **Aldik** [Алдикъ] (Magn. 26); Kzk. 19th c. **Aldïq** [Альдыкъ] (AOAtb. 30); Kzk. 19th c. **Aldïq** [Альдыкъ] (AOK 62); Tat.(Lit.) 1594, 1595 **Alduq** [Яхута Альдуковна Асанова], a princess, Asan Alejevič's wife (Lit. Tat. 210). ✧ 'We (have) bought him/her' cf. Trk. *al-* (Sev.).

ALDÏM Kzk. 19th c. **Aldïm-bay** [Альдембай] (SODž. 52); Kzk. **Aldïm-bek** [Альдимбекъ] (Konšin, Oč. 100). ✧ 'I (have) bought it'. See also **ALDÏQ.**

ALDÏN Chuv. 18th-19th c. **Aldin** [Алдинъ] (Magn. 26); Chuv. 18th-19th c. **Aldinka** [Алдинка] (Magn. 26); Chuv. 18th-19th c. **Aldun-bay** [Алдунбай] (Magn. 26). ✧ 'You (have) bought it'.

ALDÏR-ΓUŠ Bashk. 1770 **Aldïr-γuš** [Алдыргуш Атменев] (MIB IV/1, 349). ✧ 'Big cup - open-mouthed'? Cf. Bashk. *aldïr* 'чаша /большая деревянная для кумыса)' + *γuš* 'обжора' (BRS).

ALDÏŠ see **ALDAŠ**

ALDU see **ALDÏ**

ALÄÜKÖ Kzk. 19th c. **Aläükö** [Алеуко], Aleke's son (Potanin, Pred 95); Kirg. **Aläükö** [Аляүкö], a Khan in the Manas epic (Proben V, 165 /167/). ✧ Shortened turkicized of Ar. Ala-ud-Din 'glory of religion' (Ahmed). ⇨ **ALŌKE?** + suffixoid *-kö.*

ALEKE Kzk. 19th c. **Aleke** [Алеке], Aleükö's father (Potanin, Pred 95); Kzk. 19th c. **Alke** [Алке] (SOV 66). ✧ I. 'Little Ali'; II. Shortened-contracted of Al-muχammet?; III. Identical with Aläükö and Alōke? ⇨ **ALİ** + comp. *ake* or suffixoid *-ke.*

ALEM Bashk. 1735 **Alem** [Алемъ Ишметевъ], (Vel.-Zern., Bašk. 17); Kkalp. 1740 **Alem-bay-bi / Alem-bay-batïr** [Алембай-Би] (Hanykov, Poezdka 19); Turk. 1455 **Alem-χatun** [Alem Hatun], fem. (Gökb., Ed. 193); Turk. 15th c. **Alem-šah** [Alemşah] (Baştav 186); Turk. 1494 **Alem-šah-χatun** [Alemşah Hatun], fem. (Gökb., Ed. 36); *EN:* Trkm. 17th c. **Alem-beglü** [علم بكلو / Alembeğlu], a *cemaat* near Kangrı, Turkey (Refik, Anad. 66). ✧ 'World, people' cf. Tat., Az., Crm. etc. *aläm* (Ar. علم) 'die Welt, das Volk, die Leute, das Jahrhundert, die Zeit' (Radl. I, 371). See also **DÜNYA, JİHAN.**

ALEM-ERDİN Tat.? 1552 **Alem-erdin-aziy** [Алемӗрдінъ-азій] (PSRL XIII, 173). ⇨ **ALEM.**

ALEMAS see **ALMAZ**

ALFAMÏŠ see **ALPAMÏŠ**

ALGA-BAY see **ALQA**

ALGAY Chuv. 18th-19th c. **Algay** [Алгай] (Magn. 26). ⇨ **ALΓA I.** + dim. suff. *-y.*

ALGANEY Chuv. 18th-19th c. **Alganey** [Алганей] (Magn. 26). ⇨ **ALΓAN** + dim. suff. *-ey.*

ALGİT Chuv. 18th-19th c. **Algit** [Алгитъ] (Magn. 26); Chuv. 18th-19th c. **Algit-murza** [Алгитмурза] (Magn. 26). ✧ 'Tax' cf. Chag. *alγit* 'Steuer, Zins, Erpressung' (Radl. I, 396).

ALGİTČA Chuv.? 18th-19th c. **Algitča** [Алгитча] (Magn. 26). ⇨ **ALGİT** + dim. suff. *-ča.*

ALΓA Kzk. 19th c. **Alγa-bay** [Алгабай] (SOK 42); Kzk. 19th c. **Alγa-bay** [Алгабай] (SOV 26, 92, 104). ✧ 'Forward! Ahead!' cf. Kzk. *alγa* (KzRS, QTTS).

ALΓAYAQ Hak.(Kacha) 19th-20th c. **Alγayaq** [Алңајак] (Proben IX, 542). ✧ 'Small boiler, small caldron, kettle' cf. Hak. PN *Alγayaχ* 'id.' (Butanaev), also Alt. *alγay/alγïy* 'небольшой котелок (дорожный)' (Verb., Sl.). + dim. suff. *-aq / -q.*

ALΓAN Chuv. 18th-19th c. **Algan** [Алганъ] (Magn.); Maml. 14th c. **Alγan** [Алган] (Tuhfa 409); Kzk. 19th c. **Alγan** [Алганъ] (SOK 202). ✧ '(The child) has been bought or taken away' (Protective name) cf. Trk. *al-* 'to buy, to get' (Sev.).

ALΓÏM-BERDİ Tat.(Lit.) 1591 **Alγïm-berdi** [Альгимбердъ Селимшичъ] (Lit. Tat. 87). ✧ 'Given by the meeting (born at the time of the meeting)'? cf. Chag. *alγïn* 'die Versammlung' (Radl. I, 394). ⇨ **ALΓÏN(-TİMÜR)** + **BERDİ.** See also **ALQÏM-BİRDİ.**

ALΓÏN-TİMÜR   Khorezm. 13th c. - 14th c. **Aľyïn-timür-tutuq / Aľyïn-temür-tutuq** [Алгин-Тимур-Тутук] (RaD I/2, 152). ✧ 'Meeting-Iron'? cf. Chag. *aľyïn* 'die Versammlung' (Radl. I, 394). ⇨ **TEMİR.**

ALΓÏSAY   Bashk. 1737 **Aľyïšay** [Алгышай батыр], a hero (batyr) (MIB I, 346). ✧ 'Blessing' cf. Alt., Crm., Kuman, Kar., Uyg. *aľyïš* 'der Segen' (Radl. I, 395). + suff. -*ay.*

ALΓUČAQ   Tat.(Sib.) 1632 **Aľyučaq** [Алгучак, Агучак, Айгучак] (Miller, Ist. Sib. II, 398, 450); Tat.(Bar.) 1699 **Aľyučaq** [Алгучакъ Чагировъ (Чагуровъ)] (PSZRI III, 563). ✧ 'Taking, getting'? cf. Chag. *aľyu* 'das Nehmen' (Radl. I, 396). + dim. suff. -*čaq.*

ALΓUY   Khorezm./ Tat.(GH) 1282/83, 1287, 1290 **Aľyuy** [الغى / Алгуй], Mengü Temür Khan's (1267-1280) son, a khan of the Golden Horde (Nuwairī 134, 155, Ipat. 591, 592, 594, Lavr. 499). ✧ 'Taking, getting'? cf. Chag. *aľyu* 'das Nehmen' (Radl. I, 396). + dim. suff. -*y.*

ALΓUTİK   Shor 19th-20th c. **Aľyutik** (Dyrenkova 306).

ALİ   Tat.(GH) 1428 **Ali-baba** [Алибаба], a Tatar prince (PSRL VIII, 95); Bashk. 1778 **Ali-batïr** [Алибатыр Букбашев] (MIB V, 79); Oghuz/Trkm. 13th c. **Ali-čora** [على جوره / Али-чора] (Abulg./Kon. 1345, 1360, 1365); Trkm. 1731 **Ali-quli-bek** [Али-кули-бек] (MIT II, 134); Trkm. 1851 **Ali-quli-bek** [Али-кули-бек], a commander from the clan/tribe Sarulilü in the service of Nadir (MIT II, 302); Nog. 20th c. **Ali-murza** [Али Мурза Шора увлы / Алимурза Шураев], one of Baskakov's informants from the aul of Qarayas (Bask., Nog. 144); Kkalp. 20th c. **Äliy** [Әлий] (KkRS 772); Tat.(Mish.) 18th c. **Qali** [Кали Шемеев] (MIB III, 102); Kzk. 19th c. **Qali** [Кали] (SOK 54); Kzk. 19th c. **Qali** [Кали] (AOK 102); Kzk. 19th c. **Qali** [Кали] (AOA 74); Tat.(Mish.) 1735 **Qali / Qaliy?** [Кали (Калий) Мутеев] (MIB III, 330, 331); Kzk. 19th c. **Qali-bay** [Калибай] (SOK 154, 174); Kzk. 19th c. **Qali-bek** [Калибекъ] (SOK 52); Kzk. 19th c. **Qali-bek** [Калибекъ] (AOP 18, 90); Kzk. 19th c. **Qali-bek** [Калибекъ] (SODž. 68, 76, 100, 104, 124); Kzk. 19th c. **Qali-bek** [Калибекъ] (AOP 38); Kzk. 19th c. **Qali-bek** [Калибекъ] (SOV 10, 98); Kirg. 19th c. **Qali-yul** [Калигулъ Алибековъ], a Kirghiz nobleman (manap) (Konšin, Mat. V, 104); Kzk. 19th c. **Qali-mulda** [Калимулда] (SOK 166); Kzk. 19th c. **Qali-murza** [Калимурза] (SOV 62); Kzk. 19th c. **Qali-pek** [Калипекъ] (SOK 36); Kzk. 1803 **Qalu-bay** [Калубай], chief of the Ĵayalbaylï (Kiši Ĵüz) tribe (MIK IV, 516); Kzk. 19th c. **Qalu-bek** [Калубекъ] (Grod., Pril. 93); *TN:* Kzk. 19th c. **Qali-bek** [Калибекъ] (AOP 126). ✧ Prophet Ali (Ar.); A frequently used component of male names. It was taken from the name of the fourth Caliph *Ali bin Abi Tālib,*

the relative and son-in-law of the Prophet (Özön). *Ali-quli* 'Servant (follower) of (the prophet) Ali'. The variant *Γali* is widely used in Western Kazakistan. ⇨ **ĀLİ.** See also **AYDAR-ALİ, AΓAM-ALİ, AŠÏR-ALİ, BAY-ALİ, BAYRAM-ALİ, BEG-ALİ, BERDİ-ALİ, BERK-ALİ, BEZ-ALİ, BÏYÏQ-ALİ, ČÏN-ALİ, ĴAN-ALİ, ĴUMA-ΓALİY, DAWLET-ALİ, DERBİS-ALİ, ER-ALİ, ERGÄŠ-ALİ, ES-ALİ, ESÄN-ALİ, XASAN-ALİ, İYMAN-ΓALİY, İSÄN-ALİ, İSHAQ-ALİ, İŠ-ALİ, YAR-ALİ, YÂNDÂŠ-ALİ, KENĴE-ALİ, KÖČEK-ALİ, QAČİ-ΓALİ, QAD-ALİ, QAYÏR-ΓALİY, QODÏR-ALİ, QOŠ-ALİ, QUMUQ-ALİ, QURBAN-ALİ, MÄMBET-ALİ, MEN-ALİ, MEÑLİ-ALİ, MÏRZA-ΓALİY, NAZAR-ALİ, NUR-ALİ, ORAZ-ALİ, OTAR-ALİ, ÖSÄR-ALİ, PİR-ALİ, SAYD-ALİ, SAPAR-ALİ, SAV-GALEY, SEYİT-ΓALİY, SOLTAN-ALİ, SÜYÜNČ-ALİ, SÜYÜR-ΓALİ, ŠER-ALİ, Šİ-ΓALE, ŠÜKÜR-ALİ, TAXTAR-ALİ, TİLEK-ALİ, TÏN-ALİ, TOXTA-ALİ, TOY-ALİ, TUR-ALİ, TURDÏ-ALİ, TURΓUN-ALİ, TURSUN-ALİ, TÜRKMEN-ALİ, URAZ-ALİ, ÜTEM-ALİ, ZİYAN-ALİ.**

ALİ-BERDİ   Nog. 20th c. **Ali-berdi** [Мухаммед Али Алиберди / Мухаммед Алиевич Алибердиев], one of Baskakov's informants from the aul of Erkin-yurt (Oray-awul) (Bask., Nog. 143). ✧ 'Ali gave him; Given by Ali'. ⇨ **ALİ + BERDİ.**

ALİ-BUTA?   Kzk. 19th c. **Ali-buta? / Ali-buti?** [Юсуфъ Алибутiевъ] (Grod., Pril. 148). ✧ 'Ali-camel(-foal)'? ⇨ **ALİ + BOTA.**

ALİB see **ELİF**

ALİGER   Chuv. 18th-19th c. **Aliger** [Алигеръ] (Magn. 27).

ALİY   Tat.(Sib.) 1598/99, 1601 **Ali(y) / Aley?** [Алей], a prince, Küčüm-qan's son (AI II, 3-5, 17, 18, 21-23, Miller, Ist. Sib. II, 165, 178, 189); Kzk. 19th c. **Qaliy** [Калий] (AOAtb. 10). ⇨ **ALİ** + suff. -*y.* See also **ÄBÜW-ALİY, ER-ΓALİY.**

ALİYQAN   Kirg. **Qaľïyqan** [Калыйкан], fem. (Jud. 124). ⇨ **ALİ** + suff. -*qan(1).*

ALİYUQ   Balk. 20th c. **Aliyuq** [Alijúq] (Pröhle, Balk. 201).

ALİK   Hak. 19th-20th c. **Alik** [Алик] (HRS 348).

ALİKEY   Tat. 1552 **Alikey** [Аликѣй] (PSRL XIII, 202); Bashk. 1750 **Alikey** [Аликей Карашманов] (MIB III, 472-73); Bashk. 1759 **Γalkey** [Галькей Касимов] (MIB IV/2, 26). ✧ 'Dear little Ali'. ⇨ **ALİ** + dim. suff. -*key.*

ALİM   Uzb. 1722 **Alim** [Ермончук Алимов], from Bukhara (Veselovskij, Unk. 170); Uzb. 20th c. **Alim** [Алим] (UzbRS); Tat. 18th-19th c. **Alim / Älim** [Алимъ] (Magn. 27); Kzk. 19th c. **Alim-bala** [Алимбала] (SOK 224); Kzk. 19th c. **Alim-ĵan** [Алимджанъ] (Grod., Pril. 155); Uzb. 1808-1816

Alim-qan, a khan in Khokand (Nalivkin-Dozon 95); Kirg. **Alim-qul** [Алимкул] (Jud. 18); Uzb. 18th c. **Alim-qul** [Алимкулъ], from Khokand (Nepljuev 721); Kzk. 19th c. **Alïm-bay** [Алымбай] (AOO 42); Kzk. 19th c. **Alïm-bay** [Алымбай] (SKSO II, 14); Kzk. 19th c. **Alïm-bay** [Алымбай] (SODž. 90); Kzk. 19th c. **Alïm-bek** [Алымбекъ] (SOK 12); Kzk. 19th c. **Alïm-qul** [Алымкулъ] (AUK 897); Kzk. 19th-20th c. **Alum-qul-biy (Alïm-quli-biy?)** [Alumkul-bij], chieftain of the Jitem-tübe („Gyitimtübe") tribe (Prinz 328); Kkalp. 20th c. **Älim-bay** [Әлимбай] (KkRS 772); Kzk. 19th c. **Älim-bek** [Алим-бекъ Татыбаевъ], KonšinP 19 (Grod., Pril. 162); Bashk. 1761 **Älim-γul** [Алимгул Козяков] (MIB IV/1, 215); Tat. 19th c. **Γalim-jan** [Galimǧan Galiev (Müderris)], from Kazan (Mende 103); Tat. 19th c. **Γalim-jan** [Galimǧan Ibrahimov], from Kazan (Mende 15, 43, 78, 100, 155, 164, 170, 174, 175, 178); *EN:* Kzk. 18th c. - 19th c. **Alim / Älim** [Алим] (Tynyšp. 74); Kzk. 18th c. - 19th c. **Alim-ulï** [Алим-ули] (Tynyšp. 74). ✧ 'Scholar, learned man, scientist' cf. Kirg. dial. *alim / älim* 'способность' (Jud.), Turk. *alim* 'учёный', *alîm* 'мудрый, знаюший' (TRS), Uzb. *âlim (olim)* 'учёный' (UzbRS), Az., Kzk., Turk. *alim* 'gelehrt' (Radl. I, 385) (<Ar.) <Ar. ʿālim عالم. See also **BERDİ-ALİM, İŠ-ALİM**.

ALİM-BERDİ Uzb. 20th c. **Âlim-berdi** [Алимберди] (Begmatov 1984, 202). ✧ 'Educated/learned (man) has him/her given'. ⇨ **ALİM + BERDİ**.

ALİM-BUL Kzk. 19th c. **Alim-bul** [Алимбулъ] (SKSO VIII, 203). ✧ 'Be/become a scholar' cf. Kzk. *bol-* 'бывать, становитъся' (KzRS). ⇨ **ALİM + BOL**.

ALİM-JANÏS Kzk. 19th c. **Alim-janïs** [Алимджанысъ] (SOV 52); *EN:* Kzk. 18th c. - 19th c. **Alïm-janïs** [Алымджаныс] (Tynyšp. 65). ✧ 'Come back as a scholar'. ⇨ **ALİM.**

ALİMAN Uzb. 19th c. **Aliman** [Баташъ Алимановъ] (SKSO III, 182).

ALİMBET Kzk. 18th c. **Alimbet-batyr** [Алимбетъ батыръ] (Nepljuev 747); Kkalp. 20th c. **Älimbet** [Әлимбет] (KkRS 772); *EN:* Kzk. 18th c. - 19th c. **Alimbet** [Алимбет] (Tynyšp. 68, 69, 70). ⇨ **ALİ / ALİM + suff. -(m)bet?**

ALİME Kzk. 1863 **Alime** [Алимэ и Калим], her sister was called Qalime (ZIRGOGeogr. I, 440); Kkalp. 20th c. **Äliyma** [Әлийма], fem. (KkRS 777). ✧ The Arabic female form of *Alim* (<Ar.). ⇨ **ALİM + suff. -a/-ä.**

ALÏ-BUΓA see ALA-BUΓA

ALİČ Kzk. 19th c. **Alïč** [Алычь] (AOK 34); NUyg. **Alič-bek** [Алычъ-бекъ] (Valihanov, Soč. 150); *TN:* Tat. 18th c. **Alič-tarχan** [Аличъ-Тарханъ], a village (Zolotn., Alf. 163, Korsakov 247). ✧ 'The winner; the gain; chance' cf. Türk *alič* 'счастье, счастливая доля' (DTS), East.T. *ališ* 'a taking, a marrying' (Jarring), Osm. *aliǰ* [=*alič*] 'eine der vortheilhaften (gewinnenden) Seiten des Knöchels (beim Spiele), das Knöchelspiel' (Radl. I, 378). See also **ALČİ.**

ALİJAQ Oghuz/Trkm. 13th c. **Alïjaq-bek** [بيك عليجاق / Алыджак-бек] (Abulg./Kon. 1090). ⇨ **ALİ + dim. suff. -jaq?**

ALÏΓ Hak.(Blt.) 19th-20th c. **Alïγ-ōl** [Алыӊ-ол], (Katanov, Otč. 9). ✧ 'Stupid (lad)' (Katanov), cf. Karakh. *alïγ* 'плохой' (DTS), Alt. *alïγ* 'thöricht, dumm' (Radl. I, 373), Trk. *alïγ* 'albern' (TMEN II, No. 535).

ALÏΓ-ŠARJAN Hak.(Sag.) **Alïγ-šarjan** [Алыг Шарцан], a bogatyr (folklore hero) (Proben IX, 330-335). ✧ 'Stupid Šarjan'. ⇨ **ALÏΓ.**

ALİKE Kzk. 18th c. - 19th c. **Alïke** [Алыке] (Tynyšp. 68). ⇨ **ALİ + suffixxoid -ke < -ake.**

ALÏQ Bashk. 1706 **Alïq** [Алик Аканов], (MIB III, 24, 26); Bashk. 1735 **Alïq-bay** [Алекбай Тевекеевъ], a tarχan (Vel.-Zern., Bašk. 23); Kzk. 19th c. **Alïq-pay** [Алыкпай, Аликпай] (SOK 59, 70). ✧ I. 'Stupid; bad'?; II. 'Caprice, stubbornness' cf. Karakh. *alïq I* 'прихоть, капризы, своеволие' (DTS). ⇨ **ALÏΓ?**

ALÏQ-PAŠ Kzk. 19th c. **Alïq-paš** [Аликпашъ] (AOK 6). ✧ 'Stupid Head', 'Stubborn Head'. ⇨ **ALÏΓ / ALÏQ + BAŠ.**

ALÏQAY Tat.(Tüm.) 1632 **Alïqay** [Иван Алыкаев] (Miller, Ist. Sib. II, 399). ⇨ **ALÏQ + suff. -ay.** See also **ALİKEY?**

ALÏM see ALİM

ALÏM Tat.(Sib.) 1607 **Alïm** [Алымъ], a Vogul of Tatar origin (Miller, Ist. Sib. II, 203); Kirg. **Alïm** [Алым] (Jud. 85, 290, 570). ✧ I. 'Tax; debt' cf. Karakh. *alïm* 'der Schuld' (MK/Brock.), Alt., Crm., Kzk., Turk. *alïm* 'das Nehmen, der Kauf; Abgabe, Steuer; Geschenk zur Bestechung' (Radl. I, 384), Tat. *alïm* 'приём, способ; охват; размах; хватка' (TatRS), Kirg. *alïm* 'дань, налог' (Jud.); II. 'Strength, power' cf. Kzk. *alïm* 'мощь, сила' (KzRS).

ALÏM-SARÏQ Kirg. **Alïm-sarïq** [Алымсарык] (Jud. 526). ⇨ **ALÏM + SARÏQ?**

ALÏMQAN Kirg. **Alïmqan** [Алымкан], fem. (Jud. 820-21). ⇨ **ALÏM + suff. -qan(1).**

ALİN Chuv. 18th-19th c. **Alïn** [Алинъ] (Magn. 27); Chuv. 18th-19th c. **Alïn(ka)** [Алинка] (Magn. 27); *TN:* Kuman 1389 **Alïn.** [Alonnype (= Alon's clan)], a settlement (Gyárfás III, 511); *TN:* Kuman 1395 **Alïn.** [(possessio) Olunipe (=Olun's clan)] (Gyárfás III, 526). ✧ 'Forehead' cf. Kuman *alin* 'Stirn' (CC), Karakh. *alin* 'Stirn, Vorderseite eines Berges' (MK/Brock.). See Rásonyi: Mny. XXXII, 267, KÖA 79, Anthr. 135. See also **PĀQ-ALİN.**

ALÏN-QARA Kzk. 1794 **Alïn-qara** [قرا الين / Алын

Kapa] (MIK IV, 158). ✧ 'Forehead-black'. ⇨ ALÏN + QARA.

ALÏNJA Oghuz/Trkm. 13th c. **Alïnja-χan** [ن / النجهكا / Алынджа-хан], Kök-χan's son (Abulg./Kon. 155, 170).

ALÏNJÏ Oghuz 1098 **Alïnjï (=Ïkinji?)** [النجى / Алынджи ибн Кочкар / Икинджи ибн Кочкар], Qočqar's son, a Khorezmshah (MIT I, 383-84, 442).

ALÏP see ALP

ALÏP-AYMÄT Kirg. **Alp-aymät / Alïp-aymät** [Alyp Aimät / Алп-Аімät] (Proben V, 171 /173/). ⇨ ALP + AY + suff. -mät.

ALÏP-ARASLAN see ALP-ARSLAN

ALÏP-ERDÄM OT 481 **Alïp-erdäm** (Németh, HMK 168?). ✧ 'Hero(ic)-benefactor'. ⇨ ALP + ERDÄM.

ALÏP-KEL Kzk. 19th c. **Alïp-kel** [Алыпкель] (SODž. 32). ✧ 'Take (it) and come'? cf. Ger. of Kzk. *al-* 'to take' (see AL). ⇨ KEL.

ALÏP-KÏRDE Tat.(Sib.) 1635, 1640 **Alïp-kirde / Alïp-kirdey?** [Алыпкирдей Идяков, Алыбкирдей Итяков, Алыпкирдейко] (Miller, Ist. Sib. II, 430, 473). ✧ I. 'Hero/warrior / came in (was born)'; II. '(He) took (it) and went/came in'?, cf. Tat. *al-* 'to take' and *kir-* 'to come in; to go in'. ⇨ ALP?

ALÏP-QAČ Nog. 19th c. **Alïp-qač** [Алыбъ-качъ], a Qara Noγay (Anan'ev 49); Kzk. 19th c. **Alïp-qač / Alïp-qaš** [Алыпкашъ] (AOAtb. 50). ✧ 'Take (it) and run away' (AOAtb. 50), cf. *al-* 'to take, to get, to buy, etc.'. ⇨ QAČ. See also ALÏP-KEL, ALÏP-QAČAR.

ALÏP-QAČAR Uzb. **Alïp-qačar-aqa** [Алиб Качар Ака] (Ivanov 208). ✧ '(He) takes (it) and runs away with (it)'. ⇨ QAČAR. See also ALÏP-QAČ.

ALÏP-QARA see ALP-QARA

ALÏP-QAŠ see ALÏP-QAČ

ALÏŠ Kzk. 19th c. **Alïs-pay** [Алыспай] (AOAtb. 34); Kzk. 19th c. **Alïs-pay** [Алиспай] (SODž. 28); Kzk. 19th c. **Alïs-pay** [Алыспай] (SOK 134, 172); Kzk. 19th c. **Alïs-pay** [Алыспай] (SOV 94); Tat. 1552 **Alïš** [Алышъ] (Kn. Metriki Lit. 82); Bashk. 1710 **Alïš** [Сюрмей Алиышев] (MIB III, 63); Bashk. 1756 **Alïš** [Алиш Уразгулов], (MIB IV/1, 119); Bashk. 1760 **Alïš** [Алиш Усеев], (MIB IV/1, 187); Kzk. 19th c. **Alïš** [Алышъ] (SOK 245); Kzk. 19th c. **Alïš** [Алышъ] (AOO 50); Kzk. 19th c. **Alïš** [Алишъ] (SODž. 66); Uzb. 19th c. **Alïš** [Алышъ Игамбердиев] (SKSO III, 162); Kzk. 19th c. **Alïš-pay** [Алишпай] (AOK 22); Kzk. 19th c. **Alïš-pay** [Алышпай] (AOK 22); Kzk. 19th c. **Alïš-pay** [Алишпай] (SOK 210); Kzk. 19th c. **Alïš-pay** [Алишпай] (SOV 16); Kzk. 19th c. **Alïš-pay** [Алышпай] (SOK 210); Kzk. 19th c. **Alïš-pay** [Алишпай] (SOV 16). ✧ 'Fight' cf. Tat. *alïš* 'схватка' (TatRS), Kzk. *alïs* 'der Kampf' (Radl. I, 379).

ALÏŠAY Tat.(Sib.) 1580 **Alïšay** [Алышай], Küčümqan's yasaul (commander, judge?) (Sib. Let. 323); Bashk. **Alïšay** [Алишай Караспанов] (MIB IV/1, 164). ⇨ ALÏŠ + dim. suff. -ay.

ALKÄY Tat. 1731 **Alkäy** [Алкей Абулатов] (MIB III, 293). ✧ I. 'Little red'; II. 'Little Ali'? ⇨ AL / ALI + dim. suff. -käy.

ALKE see ALEKE

ALQA Chuv. 18th-19th c. **Alga-bay** [Алгабай] (Magn. 26); Chuv. 18th-19th c. **Alka / Alga** [Алка] (Magn. 27); Uyg. **Alqa** [Alka] (EUTS); Bashk. **Alqa** [Алка Булатов] (MIB IV/1, 246); Kzk. 19th c. **Alqa-bay** [Алкабай] (SOK 118); Kzk. 19th c. **Alqa-bek** [Алкабекъ] (SODž. 56). ✧ '(Ear)ring' cf. Kzk., Tat., Crm.(Tat.) *alqa* (< Ar. حلقة) 'der Ring, Ohrring' (Radl. I, 389), Chuv. *alqa* 'серьга' (ČRS). ⇨ ALГA I. See also ČASÏR-ALQA.

ALQA-BÖLÜK Oghuz/Trkm. 11th c.? **Alqa-bölük** [الله ايولى], Kün-χan's third son known in AbulG as Alqa-öyli, in RaD as Alqïr-awlï and Al-qara-ulï (MK/Brock.). ✧ 'Gift of (the tribe) Alqa'? cf. *Alqa*, an Oghuz tribe (DTS). ⇨ ALQA + BÖLEK. See also QARA-ÖYLÏ, AL-QARA-ULÏ.

ALQA-ÖYLÏ Oghuz/Trkm. 13th c. **Alqa-öyli** الله ايولى / Алка-ойли], Kün-χan's third son known in MK as Alqa-bölük (Abulg./Kon. 515, 545, 590). ✧ 'Having a round yurt?' cf. *Alqa*, the name of an Oghuz tribe (DTS), cf. Chag. *öy* 'das Haus, die Jurte' (Radl. I, 1171), Trkm. *öy* 'кибитка' (TrkmRS) + suff. -li = *öyli* 'having a yurt', cf. also Chag. *öylüg~öylük* 'ein Haus habend, verheirathet; der Haupt der Familie; die Frau' (Radl. I, 1176). ⇨ ALQA. See also QARA-ÖYLÏ, AL-QARA-ULÏ.

ALQAY Tat. 18th-19th c. **Alqay** [Алкай] (Magn. 27); Tat.? 1612 **Alqay** [Алкай Карауловъ] (Nižegorod. platež. 48, 201); Tat. 20th c. **Alqay** [Алкаев] (Sattarov). ✧ I. 'Small (ear)ring'; II. 'The first born child'. ⇨ I. ALQA, II. AL + dim. suff. -y / -qay. See also ALKÄY?

ALQAR Kzk. 19th c. **Alqar** [Алкаръ] (SOV 110).

ALQAŠÏ Uyg. 12th c. - 14th c. **Alqašï** [alqašï] (DTS). ✧ 'Boasting, praising (each other)' (Blagova 1997, 717).

ALQÏ Tat. 20th c. **Alqï** [Алкин] (Sattarov); Tat. 19th c. **Alqï / Alqa?** [Seid-Gerei Alkin] (Mende 84, 99, 102, 103); Tat. 19th c. **Alqï(n) / Alqa?** [Iljas Alkin] (Mende 126); Kzk. 19th c. **Alqï-bay** [Алькибай] (AOAtb. 26). ✧ '(Child) born first' (Sattarov), cf. Kzk. *alγï* 'передний, первый' (KzRS). ⇨ AL + suff. -qï. See also AL, ALQAY, ALKÄY, AL-TUГAN.

ALQÏM-BÏRDÏ Chag. 15th c. **Alqïm-birdi-bahadur (<Alqïn-birdi)** [التيم بيردى / Алгкымъ Бирди Баhадуръ], Šeybani-χan's retainer (Šejb. LXV). ✧ 'My first born gave; He gave my first born (child)'. ⇨

ALQÏ + BERDİ. See also **ALГÏM-BERDİ.**

ALQÏR-AULİ *see* **AL-QARA-ULİ**

ALQÏR-AWLİ *see* **AL-QARA-ULİ**

ALLA Tat. 1862 **Ala-yar-bek** (Nalyvkin, Kokand. 251); Kzk. 19th c. **Alda-bay** [Алдабай] (SOK 24); Tat. 15th c. **Alda-yar** [Алдаяръ], a prince of the Kasimov-Tatars (Vel.-Zern., Kasim.); Chuv. 18th-19th c. **Aldï-yar** [Алдеяръ / Алдіяръ] (Magn. 26); Kzk. 19th c. **Aldï-yar** [Алдиаръ] (AUK 873); Kkalp. 20th c. **Alla-bay** [Аллабай] (KkRS 772); Bashk. 18th c. **Alla-güzä** [Туннук Аллагузин] (MIB IV/1, 109); Bashk. 18th c. **Alla-güzä** [Балыхчы Аллагузин] (MIB IV/1, 109); Bashk. 1756 **Alla-güzä** [Аллагузя Биктемиров] (MIB IV/1, 109); Tat. 20th c. **Alla-γuja** [Аллагужа] (Sattarov); Tat. 1502 **Alla-yar** [Аллиаръ], envoy of the Horde (PSRL VI, 49, 244, VIII, 243); Trkm. 1855 **Alla-qulï** [Алла-кули], a yüzbašï (captain) (MIT II, 264); Uzb. 1770 **Alla-qulï** [Алла-кули], from the Qoñgrat tribe (MIT II, 343); Uzb. 1830 **Alla-qulï / Alla-qulï-töre** [Мухаммед-бехадыр-хан Алла-кули], an emir in Khiva (MIT II, 25, 222, 224-26 etc.); Trkm. 1856 **Alla-qulï-vekil** [Алла-кули-векиль], from the İmreli tribe (MIT II, 575); Turk. 19th c. **Allah-yar-bey** [Allah-Jar Bey], a Turk from the Caucasus (Mende 56); Kkalp. 20th c. **Allï-yar** [Аллыяр] (KkRS 772); Chuv. 18th-19th c. **Altï-yar** [Алтіяръ] (Magn. 27). ✧ 'Allah, God' cf. Kkalp. *alla* 'аллах, бог' (KkRS 772), Kzk., Kirg. *alda* 'Gott, Allah' (Radl. I, 412), Kirg. *alda* 'аллах' (Jud.). Normally *Allah*, the name of God, must not be used by itself, but only together with primary or secondary components (cf. Sadyhov 214). On the PNs *Allah-yar / Alla-yar / Alda-yar* consider the explanations: 1. 'God('s)-friend' cf. Kzk., Kirg. *alda* 'Gott, Allah' + *yar*; 2. 'Highness; Your Majesty' Complimentary title of a khan (sovereign ruler), cf. Kirg. *aldayar* (Jud.). (< Ar.).

ALLA-BERDİ Chuv. 18th-19th c. **Ala-berdi** [Алаберди] (Magn. 26); Kzk. 19th c. **Alde-berdi** [Алдеберди] (AOO 58); Kzk. 18th c. - 19th c. **Aldibirdi** [Альдибирдіева] (IOAIÊK XXII, 643); Chag. 1560 **Alla-berdi** [Алла-берды] (Ivanov 117, 128, 171, 220, 224, 310); Trkm. 1816 **Alla-berdi** [Алла-берды], from the Qara-talqanlu tribe (MIT II, 393); Trkm. 1826 **Alla-berdi** [Алла-берды], from the Sarïq tribe (clan) (MIT II, 441); Tat.(Lit.) 1552 **Alla-berdi** [Алъла Берды] (Kn. Metriki Lit.); Uzb. 1793 **Alla-berdi** [Iskender Allaberdiev], a man from Khiva (ArchKR XVIII, 352); Trkm. 1836 **Alla-berdi-atalïq** [Алла-берды-аталык] (MIT II, 467, 557); Khorezm.? 1461 **Alla-berdi-bek** [Алла-берди-бек], an emir (MIT I, 539); Trkm. 1769 **Alla-berdi-bek** [Алла-берди-бек], from the Yomut tribe (MIT II, 342); Uzb.? 1629 **Alla-berdi-bek** [الله بيردى /الجى/ / Аллаберды / Аллабердѣ-бека], courier (envoy) of Shah Abbas (AI IV, 44, Vel.-Zern., Crim. 61); Uzb. 1821 **Alla-berdi-bek** [Алла-берды-бек], from Bukhara, of the Kitay-Kipchak tribe (Ivanov, Vosstanie 69); Trkm. 1809 **Alla-berdi-biy** [Алла-берды-бий] (MIT II, 376); Trkm. 1813 **Alla-berdi-χan / Alla-χan** [Алла-берды-хан / Алла-(берды)-хан] (MIT II, 385); Uzb. 1812 **Alla-berdi-χoja** [Алла-берды-ходжа] (MIT II, 383); Trkm. 1829 **Alla-berdi-yüzbašï** [Алла-берды-юзбаши] (MIT II, 455); Trkm. 1770 **Alla-berdi-uydačï** [Алла-берды-уйдачи] (MIT II, 350); Trkm. 1598 **Alla-verdi-χan** [Алла-верды-хан], an Iranian commander (MIT II, 90); Trkm. 1746 **Alla-verdi-χan** [Алла-верды-хан], sovereign of Fars (MIT II, 177, 178,180); Trkm. **Alla-verdi-šeyh** [Алла-верды-шейхъ] (Grod., Vojna II, 147); 1510 **Allah-birdi** [Alláh Birdi] (Tar. Rashidi 224); **Allâh-bärdi** (Le Coq, Ind. 3); Uzb. 1701 **Allâh-birdi** [Allâhbirdi] (Buchari 263); Uzb. 20th c. **Âllâ-berdi** [Оллоберди] (Begmatov 1984, 202); *EN:* Kzk. 18th c. - 19th c. **Alda-berdi** [Алдаберды] (Tynyšp. 66); Kzk. 18th c. - 19th c. **Alda-berdi** [Альдеберды] (Tynyšp. 74); Kzk. 18th c. - 19th c. **Alda-berdi** [Альдеберлы] (Tynyšp. 75); Nog. 20th c. **Alla-berdi-uruwï** [Аллаберди урувы], an Aq-noγay clan (Bask., Nog. 133, 142). ✧ 'Allah has given (the child)' Such names were given (as protective names) if there were no children, they were sickly or did not survive in the family before (Noyan 6-7). Cf. also Rásonyi, Categ. 330, P. Categ. 217. ⇨ **ALLAH + BERDİ.** See also **XUDAY-BERDİ, OΓAN-BERDİ, SATTAR-BERDİ, TÄÑRİ-BERDİ.**

ALLA-BERGEN Kzk. 20th c. **Alda-bergen** [Алда Бергенъ] (Grod., Pril. 147); Kkalp. 20th c. **Alda-bergen** [Алдаберген] (KkRS 772); Kzk. 19th c. **Alla-bergän-bay** [Аллабергянбаевъ] (Turk. Kraj 1912: 14); Kzk. 19th c. **Alla-bergen** [Миркабай Аллабергеневъ] (Grod., Pril. 80); Kzk. 19th c. **Alla-bergen** [Аллабергенъ] (SKSO II, 14); Kkalp. 20th c. **Alla-bergen** [Аллаберген] (KkRS 772); Kzk. 19th c. **Allah-bergän** [Казбекъ Аллахбергановъ] (Grod., Pril. 185); Kzk. 19th c. **Allah-bergän** [Аллахберганъ] (Grod., Pril. 164). ✧ 'Allah has given (the child)'. See Rásonyi, Categ. 323-352. ⇨ **ALLA + BERGEN.** See also **ALDA-BERGEN, XUDAY-BERGEN, ALLA-BERDİ.**

ALLA-ΓUWAT Bashk. 1735 **Alla-γuwat** [Аллагуватъ Беккуловъ] (Vel.-Zern., Bask. 19.). ✧ 'Allah's power'? ⇨ **ALLA + QUWAT.**

ALLA-YAR *see* **ALLAH-YAR**

ALLA-KEGEN Uzb. 19th c. **Alla-kegen** [Кулчибай Аллакегеневъ] (SKSO III, 178). ⇨ **ALLA + KEGEN.**

ALLA-MURAT Kkalp. 20th c. **Alla-mïrat** [Алламырат] (KkRS 772); Kkalp. 20th c. **Alla-murat**

[Алламурат] (KkRS 772). ❖ 'Allah's wish'. ⇨ **ALLA + MURAT.**

ALLA-NAZAR Kirg. 19th c. **Alda-nazar** [Алда Назаръ Абеловъ] (Grod., Pril. 102); Kkalp. 20th c. **Alla-nazar** [Алланазар] (KkRS 772). ❖ 'Allah's glance'. ⇨ **ALLA + NAZAR.**

ALLA-NİYAZ Kkalp. 20th c. **Alla-niyaz** [Алланияаз] (KkRS 772). ❖ 'Allah's alms / Allah's gift'. ⇨ **ALLA + NİYAZ.**

ALLA-OÑAR Kkalp. 1827 **Alla-oñɣar** [Алла Онгар суфи], a biy (MIKk. 132); Bashk. 1770 **Alla-uñɣar** [Аллаунгар Баксанов] (MIB IV/1, 342); Kzk. 1846 **Alla-uñɣar** [бий Аллаунгаров Баймухамед], a biy (MKOP 157). ❖ 'Let Allah grow him up'. ⇨ **ALLAH + OÑɢAR.**

ALLA-ŠÜGÜR Bashk. 1661-1667 **Ala-šügör(ko)? / Ala-šügür(ko)** [Алашугорко (Алашагурко)], a participant of the revolt of 1661-67 (MIB I, 160); Kzk. 19th c. **Alda-sögür** [Алдасогуръ] (Grod., Pril. 57); Kzk. 19th c. **Alda-sügür** [Алдасугуръ] (SOV 66); Bashk. 1779 **Alla-šügür** [Байбаб Аллашугуров] (MIB V, 102). ❖ 'Thanks to Allah; Grace to God'. ⇨ **ALLA + ŠÜKÜR.**

ALLA-VERDİ see **ALLA-BERDİ**

ALLAH-BERGÄN see **ALLA-BERGEN**

ALLAH-BİRDİ see **ALLA-BERDİ**

ALLAY Yak. **Allay** [Аллаі Араӷас] (Pek.).

ALLAQA Yak. **Allaqa** [Аллака] (Pek.).

ALLAM-BERGEN Kkalp. 20th c. **Allam-bergen** [Алламберген] (KkRS 772). ❖ 'My Allah has given him/her'. ⇨ **ALLA + BERGEN.** See also **ALLA-BERDİ.**

ALLAŠ Kkalp. 20th c. **Allaš** [Аллаш] (KkRS 772); Nog.? 1649 **Allaš-murza** [Аллашъ-мурза Акъ-мурзинъ] (AI IV, 87). ❖ Contracted dim.-hypoc. form of a name with beginning component *Alla(h)*. ⇨ **ALLA + suff. -š.**

ALLEY Chuv. 18th-19th c. **Alley** [Аллей] (Magn. 27). ❖ 'Fifty'. + dim. suff. -*y*.

ALLÏ-YAR see **ALLAH-YAR**

ALMA Kzk. 19th c. **Alma** [Алма] (AOK 30); Kzk. 19th c. **Alma-bay** [Алмабай] (SOK 84, 102, 188); Kzk. 19th c. **Alma-bay** [Алмабай] (SODž. 74); Kzk. 19th c. **Alma-bek** [Альмабекъ] (SODž. 26); Kzk. 19th c. **Alma-bek** [Алмабекъ / Альмабекъ] (SODž. 26, 44,); Uzb. 19th c. **Alma-äčä** [Алма-ача] (TV 1875: 94); Kzk. 19th c. **Alma-gül** [Альмагуль], fem. (Grod. I, 98); Kkalp. 20th c. **Alma-gül** (KkRS 777); Kirg. **Alma-yan** [Alman Jan / Алма Jан], one of the forty retainers of Aq-sayqal (Proben V, 394 /397/). ❖ 'Apple'; *Alma-χan* 'Apple-prince', 'Fürstin Apfel' (Le Coq, Namenl.). Cf. Az., Chag., Kuman, Kzk., Kirg., Tat. etc. *alma* 'der Apfel' (Radl. I, 436), *alma* 'id.' (Sev.).

ALMA-BAŠ Kirg. **Alma-baš** [Алмабаш] (Jud. 709). ❖ 'Apple-head'. ⇨ **ALMA + BAŠ.**

ALMAJÏ Tat.(GH) 1308 **Almajï** ['Αλματζου], a christened Tatar, died in 1308 (Byz. Turc. 63); Turk. 19th c. **Almajï-oɣlu** [Almaȝy-oɣlu] (Kúnos 1891, 119). ❖ 'Someone who raises and/or sells apples'. ⇨ **ALMA + suff. -jï.**

ALMAXAN see **ALMAQAN**

ALMAY Chuv. 18th-19th c. **Almay** [Алмай] (Magn. 27); Tat. 1713 **Almay** [Янгоат Алмаев] (MIB III, 93); Bashk. 1775 **Almay** [Алмай Юнашев] (MIB IV/2, 416); Tat.(Mish.) 1775 **Almey** [Аит Алмеев] (MIB IV/2, 421). ❖ 'Small apple'. ⇨ **ALMA + dim. suff. -y.**

ALMAKA Chuv. 18th-19th c. **Almaka** [Алмака] (Magn. 27). ❖ 'Small apple'. ⇨ **ALMA + dim. suff. -qa.**

ALMAQ Bashk. 1713 **Almaq** [Алмаков] (MIB III, 98). ❖ 'Buying, Taking (Bought child?)' cf. Trk. *al-* 'nehmen, fortnehmen, zu sich nehmen' (Radl. I, 341) + suff. -*maq.*

ALMAQAY Chuv. 18th-19th c. **Almakay** [Алмакай] (Magn. 27); Chuv. 18th-19th c. **Almakey** [Алмакей] (Magn. 27); Tat. 17th c. **Almaqay** [Алмакайко] (IOAIÊK XXIX, 312); Tat. 1675 **Almaqay** [Алмакай], fem. (Kungursk. akty 30); Tat. 1711 **Almaqay** [Алмакай] (MIB III, 73); Tat. 1714 **Almaqay** [Крымкай Алмакаевъ] (MIB III, 117); Bashk. 1706 **Almaqay** [Алмакай] (MIB III, 21); Bashk. 1709 **Almaqay** [Кучкилдей Алмакаев] (MIB I, 264); Bashk. 1770 **Almaqay** [Алмакай Зюбеиров] (MIB IV, 348); Bashk. 1707 **Almekey** [Алмекей Иленчиев] (MIB III, 30); Bashk. 1795 **Almekey** [Альмекей Кильмяков] (IOAIÊK XXVIII, 591). ❖ 'Small apple'. ⇨ **ALMA + dim. suff. -qay.**

ALMAQAN NUyg.? **Almaχan** [Alma χan], from Qara Xōja (Le Coq); Kirg. **Almaqan** [Алмакан], fem. (Jud. 640). ⇨ **ALMA + suff. -qan(1).**

ALMALA Chuv. 18th-19th c. **Almala** [Алмала] (Magn. 27). ❖ 'Having apples'. ⇨ **ALMA + suff. -lï.**

ALMAN Kzk. 19th c. **Alman** [Альманъ] (AOA 82); Kzk. **Alman-bay** [Альманбай] (Sb. Syr-D. IX, 46); Kzk. 19th c. **Alman-bay** [Алманбай, Альманбай] (SODž. 58, 59); Kzk. 19th c. **Almen** [Альменъ] (Grod., Pril. 128); Kzk. 19th c. **Almen-bay** [Алменбай] (SODž. 132). ❖ I. 'Red, reddish' (Rötlich, hochrötlich); II. 'Quick snatching bird of prey' (Schnellgreifend (Raubvogel)), cf. Kirg. *alman* 'хваткий' (Jud.). ⇨ **AL / ALAMAN + suff. -man.**

ALMANBET Kirg. **Almanbet** [Alman Bet / Алман Бет] (Proben V, 6, 225 /226/); Kirg. **Almanbet / Almambet?** [Алмамбет] (Radl. I, 349, Jud. 27). ❖ 'Tiger-like' (Radloff). ⇨ **ALMAN / ALAMAN + suff. -bet.**

ALMANDAY Chuv. 18th c. **Almanday** [Алмандай]

(Magn. 27); Chuv. 18th c. **Almantay** [Алмантай], preserved in the name of the forest called *Almantay hurlïh* < *Almantay hurïnlïhə* near the village Kamennyj Vrag in Saratov government (Ašm. I, 163); Chuv. 18th c. **Almantey** [Алмантей (Алман'дэј)] (Ašm. I, 163); *TN:* Chuv. 18th c. **Almanday** [Алмандаева], a village in the district of Cheboksary (Korsakov 281, Zolotn., Alf. 163). ✧ I. 'Red (male child)'; II. 'Quick snatching as a bird of prey'. ⇨ **ALMAN** + suff. *-day*.

ALMANTA   Bashk. 1728 **Almanta** [Алманта Салдыбаев] (MIB I, 127).

ALMAŇ   Kirg. **Almaň** (Jud. 227). ✧ 'Your Alma' Shortened variant of *Al-mambet'* (Jud. 227). *Almaň* < *Alma (< Al-mambet)* + poss. suff. *-ň*.

ALMAS see **ALMAZ**

ALMAT   Kzk. **Almat** [Альматъ] (Sb. Syr-D. IX, 44); Kzk. 19th c. **Almat** [Алматовъ] (AUK 585); Kzk. 19th c. **Almat** [Альматъ Халбаев] (SKSO VIII, 260); Tat. 1731 **Almet** [Алметь] (MIB III, 293); *TN:* Uzb.? **Almat-sūfi** [Альмат-Суфи], a kyshlak (in Širazskij tumen') (ZIRGOSStat. IV). ✧ I. 'Red Mukhammad'; II. 'He won't take (it); He won't be taken'; III. 'First (born) Mukhammad (=child)'. ⇨ **AL** + suffixoid *-mat* or suff. *-mat* < *-maz*?

ALMATAY   Kzk. 19th c. **Almatay** [Алматай] (SOV 110); Bashk. 1781 **Almatey** [Алматеев] (MIB V, 124). ✧ 'Apple-like' or 'Small apple'. ⇨ **ALMA** + suff. *-tay(1,2)*?

ALMATEY see **ALMATAY**

ALMAZ   Maml. 1317 **Almas** [الماس الحاجب], Sayfaddīn ~ a χājib, an emir (Dawād.); Kzk. 19th c. **Almas** (SOK 118); *TN:* Bashk.? **Almaz**, a village west of Krasnoufimsk (Karta JAR 3). ✧ I. 'Diamond'?; II. '(The dog) Doesn't take', shortened from *İt-almaz*? See also **İT-ALMAZ**.

ALMÄŠ see **ALMÏŠ**
ALMEY see **ALMAY**
ALMEN see **ALMAN**
ALMET see **ALMAT**
ALMÏŠ see **ALMÏŠ**
ALMÏS see **ALMÏŠ**

ALMÏŠ   Chuv. 18th-19th c. **Almiš** [Алмишъ] (Magn. 27); Kzk. 19th c. **Almïs** [Альмисъ] (SODž. 50); Kzk. 19th c. **Almïs** [Альмесъ] (SOK 218); Kzk. 19th c. **Almïs** [Альмесъ] (SOV 114); Kzk. 19th c. **Almïs** [Альмисъ] (SODž. 50); Alt. (Tel.) **Almïs** [Алмысъ], a monster (Kalačev 499); Kzk. 1798 **Almïs-batïr** [Альмес-батыр], 7th descendant of the Dulat tribe, one of the chiefs of the Botbay clan (Tynyšp. 65); Alt. **Almïs-χan** [Алмысъ-ханъ] (Nikiforov 36, 212); Tat. 1724 **Almïš / Almäš** [Умряк Алмяшев] (MIB III, 227); Bulg. 922 **Almïš, Almuš** [المش المس / Алмуш], prince of the Volga Bulgars, the son of Šulki, the emperor of Bulgar (MIT I, 163, Gombocz, ÁTSz. 4, 26

(after Ibn Fadhlan, Ibn Rusta, Gardīzī)); Bulg. **Almuš** [الموش] (Jusupov 9). ✧ 'Bought, Taken'. See also **EL-ALMÏŠ**.

ALMUŠ see **ALMÏŠ**

ALÖKE   Kirg. **Alöke** [Алооке], folkl. (Jud. 87, 158). ✧ 'Small flame'. ⇨ **ALAW** + dim. suff. *-ke*.

ALP   Bulg. 1320/21 **Alïp** [ال ب / aşan awli alïb], Ašan's son (Tekin 88 /186/); Alt. 19th c. **Alïp-χan** [Алып-хан] (Verb., In. 139,152); Hak. 19th-20th c. **Alïp-qan** (Radl. II, 105); Türk 7th-9th c. **Alp** [Alp] (ETY III, 61, 105, 189); Uyg. **Alp** (Haneda 7); Oghuz/Trkm. 14th c. - 15th c. **Alp** [Alp Rüstem], Düren's son (DQorq./Rossi 167, 170, 195, 209, 227); Selj. 1210 **Alp** [الب بن سو لى], on an inscription from Amasya, Turkey (Uzunçarş., Küt. 94); Kuman 1279 **Alp-ar** (<**Alp-är**?) [Alpar], a Kuman notability in Hungary (Gyárfás, II, 338, 438, Endlicher, Monum. r. Hung. Arp. 559-565); Kzk. **Alp-ar** (<**Alp-är**?) [Алпар] (Žanuzakov 130); Tat.(GH) 13th c. **Alp-ata** ['Αλπατάς], a christened Tatar (Byz. Turc. 65); Bulg. 924 **Alp-baγatur** [Αλογοβότοψρ], a Bulghar general (Byz. Turc. 64); Kzk. 19th c. **Alp-bay** [Алпебай] (SODž. 98); Kzk. 19th c. **Alp-bay** [Алпебай] (SODž. 56); Kzk. 19th c. **Alp-bay** [Алпыпай] (SOK 122); Uyg. 762 **Alp-čur** (Mahrnāmag 14); Pecheneg 1255 **Alp-er** [Olper] (ÁÚO VII, 399, also Rásonyi, Slovo 6-7, Rásonyi: AOH XX, 135, Németh, HMK 135); 1227 **Alp-er-χan** (Barth., Turk. 444-45); Oghuz/Trkm. 14th c. - 15th c. **Alp-eren** [Алп-Эрен], İlik-qoja's son (DQorq. 30, DQorq./Rossi 145); Oghuz 1172 **Alp-γazi** [Алп-гази] (MIT I, 406-408); Selj.? **Alp-γāzi** [الب غازى] (Ibn al-Athīr/Tornb. XI, 250, 252); Selj. 1202 **Alp-γāzi** [الب غازى] (Ibn al-Athīr/Tornb. XII, 116, 118, 121); Selj. 13th c. **Alp-γāzi** [الپ غازى], on a gravestone (Uzunçarş., Küt. 57); Khorezm. 1227 **Alp-χan** [الب خان], Jelāl's (1220-1231) officer, who escaped from the Mongols when they captured Samarkand (Nasawī 138, 229, Abulg./Desm. 117); Khorezm? 14th c. **Alp-χan** [Alp-Hān], uncle of Xizr χān at the time of the Xalji dynasty, he was executed (Agha Mehdi Husain, The Rise and Fall of Muhammad bin Tughluq, p. 6); 865 **Alp-inuq** [البينوق الفرغا نى] (Tabarī, Annal. III, 1553, 1554); Crm. 1646 **Alp-mirza** [الپ ميرزا] (Vel.-Zern., Crim. 91, 62); Kzk. 19th c. **Alp-pay** [Алпепай] (SOK 172); Uyg. 762 **Alp-saŋun-ügä** [Alp sangun ügä], alpaγut (Müller, Pfahl. 23); Crm.(Tat.) 1518 **Alp-sultan** [Alp Sultān], a sultan who invaded Moldva with his Tatars from Perekop (Urechi-Picot 259, Istvánfy 87); Khazar 8th c. **Alp-tarχan** [Alpᶜ Tᶜarχan], a general (Golden 150); Türk / Uyg. 8th c. - 9th c. **Alp-tarχan** [alp tarχan] (DTS); Oghuz 10th c. **Alp-tegin** [البتكين], an officer of the Samanid state (Juwaynī II, 1); Oghuz? 961 **Alp-**

tegin [الفتکین] (Ibn al-Athīr/Tornb. VIII, 404, 472, 483-87, IX, 79); Oghuz 962 **Alp-tegin** [البتکین], emir, governor of the Sāmānids in Ghazna, commander (sāχib) of the army in Khorasan, one of the founders of the Ghaznavīd dynasty (Mirch. Gasnevid. 1); Oghuz? 976 **Alp-tegin** [ابو اسحاق بن البتکین] (Ibn al-Athīr/Tornb. VIII, 503); Oghuz? 980 **Alp-tegin** [مغربی البتکین], Abbāsid governor of Syria (Qazw. 511); Oghuz? 1016, 1017 **Alp-tegin** [البتکین لبخاری] / Alp-tegin al–Buxari], a Samanid military commander (Ibn al-Athīr/Tornb. IX, 184, 185, Barth., Turk. 292-93, MIT I, 362, 446); Oghuz? 10th c. **Alp-tegin** [Alptekin], the Ghaznavid Sebük-tegin's father-in-law (Weil, Chalif. 60, Mirch., Qazw.); Oghuz/Trkm. 974, 996 **Alp-tegin** [الافتکین / هنتکین ابو منصور / الب تگین], a Turkic/Oghuz(?) chieftain in the service of the Buwayhids (Mirch. Bujeh 28, Qalānisi 11-21, 46); Oghuz/Trkm. 12th c. **Alp-tegin** [الفتکین الحاجی], a chamberlain killed by Alp-arslan (?) (Kamāladdīn: RHCHor 73); Karakh. 11th c. **Alp-tegin** [alp tegin] (DTS); Karakh. 11th c. **Alp-tigin** [Alp tigin] (MK/Atalay 830); Uyg. 12th c. - 14th c. **Alp-tutuq** [alp tutuq] (DTS); Uyg. 762 **Alp-tutuq-ügä**, tutuq, ügä, the beg of Xočo (Müller, Pfahl. 12); Khorezm.? 14th c. **Alp-unuq** [Алп-Унук] (RaD I/2, 152); Türk 7th c. - 9th c. **Alp-uruñu** [alp uruṇu] (DTS); Türk 7th c. - 9th c. **Alp-uruñu-tutuq** [alp uruṇu tutuq] (DTS). ✧ 'Hero, courageous warrior; champion' cf. Türk, Karakh., Uyg. *alp* 'меткий стрелок; герой, богатырь, отважный, храбрый' (DTS), Alt., Tat., Kzk., Kirg. *alïp* 'ein grosser Held; der Held, der Riese' (Radl. I, 384). It is also used as a secondary (postpositive, rarely prepositive) component of compound personal names, e. g. in *Alp-er* 'Hero(ic) man/warrior' cf. Tat. PN *Alpar* 'id.' (Sattarov), Maml. *alper* 'homme-héros' (AH), cf. also Rásonyi, KÖA 79, Rásonyi, Anthr., 135.

ALP-AYA Karakh. 11th c. **Alp-aya** [alp aja] (DTS). ✧ 'Palm-hero (Sharpshooter?)' (Blagova 1997, 709).

ALP-AR see **ALP**

ALP-ARSLAN Uyg. 767 **Alp-arslan**, the name occurs in the title of an Uyghur khan (Müller, Pfahl. 26); Uyg. 13th-14th c. **Alp-arslan** [Alp Arslan] (Zieme, Mat. II, 90); Selj. 1043 **Alp-arslan** [الب ارسلان] [السلجوقی / الب ارسلان بن طغرل / الب ارسلان بن داود / السلطان عضدالدوله / الب ارسلان بن محمود / الب ارسلان محمد بن داوود / 'Alb 'Arslân / Olub Arslàn / Алп-Арслан], a Seljuk sultan (1063-1072) in Khorasan, the son of Čaγrï-beg; Alp-arslan Sultan (1063-1072), Dawud's son, Mikā'il's (Jaqïrï or Čaγrï beg's) grandson and Seljuq's grand-grandson (cf. ToganUTT 183-184, 201) (Mirch. Gasnevid. 114, Abulg./Kon. 1145, Abulfar./Budge I, 216, Abulfar. 227-229, Bondārī, Muh. Ibrahim 12-14, 17, Ibn al-Athīr/Tornb. IX, 165,212-13, X, 18-20, 22-28, XI, 187,

Ibn Bībī IV, 15); Selj. 11th c. **Alp-arslan** [سیف الدین الب ارسلان] (Muh. Ibrahim 142, 172, 182, etc.); Selj. 1086 **Alp-arslan** [یغی سیان بن الب ارسلان] (Kamāladdīn: RHCHor II, 101, 104, 107, 110, 125, 131 etc.); Selj. 1102 **Alp-arslan**, governor of Rahaba (Weil, Chalif. III, 153); Selj. 1113, 1114 **Alp-arslan** [البارسلان تاج الدوله بن رضوان] (Qalānisi 189-191); Selj. 1134 **Alp-arslan** [الب ارسلان محمد الملك] (Ibn al-Athīr/Tornb. XI, 13); Selj. 1144 **Alp-arslan** [الب ارسلان الخفاجی الملك] (Ibn al-Athīr/Tornb. XI, 66-67); Selj. 12th c. **Alp-arslan** [الب ارسلان بن اتسز], the Khorezmshah Atsïz' (1127-1156) son, a ruler of the Seljuks (1156-1172) who was also known as İl-arslan or İl-aslan (cf. ToganUTT 60) (Qazw. 490-491); Tat.(Sib.) 1599 **Alp-arslan** / **Alïp-araslan** [Алп-Арслан / Алып-Арослан], a prince, the grandson of Küčüm-qan, the ancestor of the princes of Kasymov (AI II, 21, Zolotn., Alf. 155, IOAIÊK XIX, 144); Turk. 1515 **Alp-arslan-bey** [Alp-Arslan Bey] (Gökb., Ed. 82). ✧ 'Hero(ic)-lion'. Also used as part (component) of compound titles (regnal names) of rulers. ⇨ **ALP + ARSLAN.**

ALP-BAŠ-ČİK Uyg. 13th-14th c. **Alp-baš-čik-ügä** [Alp Baš Čik Ügä] (Zieme, Mat. II, 85). ✧ 'Hero-head-?'. ⇨ **ALP + BAŠ.**

ALP-BİLGÄ Uyg. 8th c. **Alp-bilgä-χaγan** (Müller: SBAW (1909), 728). ✧ 'Heroic wise (man)'. ⇨ **ALP + BİLGÄ.**

ALP-BÖRÜ Kirg. **Alp-börü** [Алп-бöрÿ], a man in the Manas-epos (Proben V, 170 (172)). ✧ 'Hero-Wolf'. ⇨ **ALP + BÖRİ.**

ALP-BUΓA Selj.? 1004 **Alp-buγa** [الببغا ابوالفرج] (Ibn al-Athīr/Tornb. IX, 127, 147). ✧ 'Hero-Bull'. ⇨ **ALP + BUQA.**

ALP-BURΓUČAN Türk / Uyg. 8th c. - 9th c. **Alp-burγučan** [alp burγučan] (DTS). ✧ 'Hero(ic)-Burγučan'.

ALP-DEREK Oghuz/Trkm. 1198 **Alp-derek** [Алп-Дерек], Buqu-χan's nephew (MIT I, 448 (after Juwaynī)). ✧ 'Hero-Poplar'. ⇨ **ALP + DEREK.**

ALP-ER-TOÑA Karakh. 11th c. **Alp-er-toña** / **Toña-alp-er** [alp er toṇa / toṇa alp er], legendary ruler of Turan, forefather of the Karakhanids, the same as Afrasiyab (DTS). ✧ 'Hero(ic)-Man/Hero-Leopard'. ⇨ **ALP + ER + TOÑA.**

ALP-EREN see **ALP**

ALP-GERÄY see **ALP-GİREY**

ALP-GİREY Crm.Tat. 1608 **Alp-girey** / **Alp-geräy** [Алпъ-Герай], Selamet-girey (1608-1610) khan's son (Smirnov, Krym. 438-42); Crm.Tat. 17th c. **Alp-girey** / **Alp-geräy** [الپ کرای سلطان / Алпъ-Герай], Murad-girey (1677-1683) khan's son (Smirnov, Krym. 679, Vel.-Zern., Crim. 110). ✧ 'Hero(ic)-gentleman'. ⇨

ALP + KERÄY.

ALP-İLEK Selj. **Alp-ilek** (Belleten I (1937), 308, Németh, HMK 134). ✧ 'Hero-Prince'. ⇨ **ALP + ELİG.**

ALP-YÜREK Selj. **Alp-yürek** [Alpyüräk] (Aqsarāyī 171); Selj. 13th c. **Alp-yürek** [مظفرالدين البيورك], Muẓaffaruddīn Alp-yürek, the supreme commander of the region of Kastamonu, died when Sultan Rükneddin Qïlïč-arslan (1257-1263) revolted against Kaihātū (Aqsar./Iş. 85); Selj. 13th c. **Alp-yürek** [Alp Yürek], emir of Kastamonu, Turkey (Yücel 66-67); Selj. / Turk. 13th c. - 14th c. **Alp-yürek** [البيورك], grandfather of the emir Muẓaffaruddīn Yawlaq-arslan (around 1330) (Ibn Bībī IV, 336-337). ✧ 'Hero(ic) heart; brave man/warrior' Uyg., Kuman, Chag., Alt., Turk. *yüräk* 'das Herz' (Radl. III, 600). ⇨ **ALP.**

ALP-QARA Kzk. 1822 **Alïp-qara** [Алапкара Мусрапов] (TOUAK XXIV, 130); Kzk. **Alïp-qara** [Алипкара], a biy (MKOP 158); 1040 **Alp-qara** [الب قرا] (Ibn al-Athīr/Tornb. IX, 324); Oghuz/Trkm. 1030 **Alp-qara** [Алп-Кара Нирани], an emir (MIT I, 367, 455, 456); Kipch. / Khorezm. 1182 **Alp-qara** [Alp Kara Uran], commander of a Kipchak army in the days of the Khorezmshah Töküš (~Tekeš~Tekiš 1172-1200) (Köprülü: Belleten VII (1940), 20435, Barth., Turk. 365); Kuman/Tat.? 12th c. **Alp-qara** [Αλπιχαρας], a Turkic (Tatar?) chieftain (Byz. Turc. 65). ✧ I. 'Hero(ic) black'; II. 'Black magician' („Noir Enchanteur", BOH XX, 133). ⇨ **ALP + QARA.** See also **ALP-SARÏ.**

ALP-QUŠ Selj.? 1066 **Alp-quš** [البتش السلاحى], an emir (Ibn al-Athīr/Tornb. X, 6, 11, XI, 30, 43); Selj. 1135 **Alp-quš** [البتش الكبير], lord of Isfahān (Ibn al-Athīr/Tornb. XI, 23, 40); Selj. 1139 **Alp-quš** [البتش كونخى] (Ibn al-Athīr/Tornb. XI, 51, 52, 77, 129-30); Selj. 1155 **Alp-quš** [Alp-kuş], an emir, sultan Masʿūd's (1134-1152) retainer (Ahbar 92-94); Maml. 1185 **Alp-quš** [البتش نظام الدين], mamlūk of Qutb ad-Dīn Ilgāzī (Ibn al-Athīr/Tornb. XI, 335). ✧ 'Hero-Bird'. ⇨ **ALP + QUŠ I.**

ALP-QUTLUГ Uyg. 12th c. - 14th c. **Alp-qutluγ** [alp qutluγ] (DTS); Selj. 1195 **Alp-qutluγ** [الب قتلغ الغ همايون], a part of Mengücik Abul-Muẓaffar's sobriquets in an inscription from Divrigi (CIA 3/I, 66-68, Togan, UTT 220). ✧ 'Hero-Happy' (Blagova 1997, 711). ⇨ **ALP + QUTLUГ.**

ALP-SARÏ Selj. 1133 **Alp-sarï?** ['Αλψαρους], commander-in-chief of the town Gangra, mentioned by Theodoros Prodromos (Byz. Turc. 65). ✧ 'Hero-yellow'. ⇨ **ALP + SARÏ.** See also **ALP-QARA.**

ALP-ŠİŇГUR see ALP-ŠİŇQUR

ALP-ŠİŇQUR Uyg. 8th c. **Alp-sïñqur-tigin** [Alp sïnqur tigin], a Manichean prince, Thomsen writes about the source: "seems to have contained a fragment of a legend or tale concerning the conversion to Manichaeism of one Prince Singqur" (Thomsen, Fragm. 1083); Uyg. 762 **Alp-šïňγur-tarχan** [Alp šïngγur t(a)rχan vap čangši] (Müller, Pfahl. 23); Uyg. 762 **Alp-šïñqur-tigin** [Alp šïngqur tigin] (Müller, Pfahl. 23). ✧ 'Hero-Falcon'. ⇨ **ALP + SOŇQUR.**

ALP-TAŠ Uyg. 8th c. - 9th c. **Alp-taš** [Alp Taš] (TT IV, 432); Uyg. 12th c. - 14th c. **Alp-taš** [Türči Alptaš] (Radl., USp. 53). ✧ 'Hero(ic)-stone'. ⇨ **ALP + TAŠ.**

ALP-TOГRİL Uyg. 12th c. - 14th c. **Alp-toγrïl** [Alp Toγrïl] (Radl., USp. 213, 255, DTS); Uyg. 8th c. - 9th c. **Alp-toγrul-tigin** (Müller, Pfahl. 23). ✧ 'Hero-Falcon' (Blagova 1997, 707). ⇨ **ALP + TOГRİL.**

ALP-TOГRUL see ALP-TOГRİL

ALP-TUГAČ Oghuz/Trkm. 13th c. **Alp-tuγač** [الب توغاج / Алп-Тугач], Qara Alp-arslan's son (Abulg./Kon. 860, 865). ⇨ **ALP + TOГAŠ?**

ALP-TURMİŠ Uyg. 12th c. - 14th c. **Alp-turmïš** (Radl., USp. 207, 249, DTS). ✧ 'Hero remained/survived; a hero was born' (Blagova 1997, 711). ⇨ **ALP + TURMİŠ.**

ALP-UNUQ Uyg.? 1209 **Alp-unuq / Alp-utuq** [Алпъ-Утукъ / Алп-Унук], envoy of Činggis Qan to the Uygur idiqut (RaD/Ber. III, 10, 12, RaD I/2, 152). ✧ 'Heroic Little Hunting Bird'? ⇨ **ALP + İNÜK?**

ALP-UTUQ see ALP-UNUQ

ALPAГЏ Turk. 14th c. **Alpaγï** [Alpağı], Saruhan's father (Uzunçarş., Anad. 31). ✧ 'Hero, heroic warrior' cf. Türk *alpaγu* 'герой, богатырь' (DTS).

ALPAMÏS see ALPAMÏŠ

ALPAMÏS-ÄLİF Kzk. **Alpamïs-älif** [Алпамысъ-алифъ], some Arsalañ is better known by people as Alpamïs (Divaev, Čingiz 296). ⇨ **ALPAMÏŠ + ELİF.**

ALPAMÏŠ Kzk. **Alfamïš** [النا ميش], Bay-büre-bay's son? (Divaev, Alp. 5); Kzk. **Alpamïs** [Алпамысъ], some Arsalañ is better known by people as Alpamïs (Divaev, Čingiz 296); Kzk. 18th c. - 19th c. **Alpamïs** [Алпамыс] (Tynyšp.); Kkalp. 20th c. **Alpamïs** [Алпамыс] (Bask., Kkalp. 25, KkRS 772); Kzk. **Alpamïs-batïr** (Divaev, Alp. 1 etc.); Oghuz/Trkm. 14th c. - 15th c. **Alpamïš** [Алпамыш (Алпамыш-Бамси, Алп-Бамси, Алпамыша, Алып-Манаш, Мамыш-бек)], a hero in Central Asiatic folk epics, also known as Alp-bamsi, Alpamïša, Alïp-manaš, Mamïš-bek, originally called Xakim (DQorq. 145, 151, 158, 177, 200, etc., Žirm., Epos 117-348); Kuman? 1185 **Alpamïš** [Ελπουμής, Ελπαμής], a chieftain of Scythian (=Kuman?) origin in the Byzantine army (Byz. Turc. 124). ✧ It is the same as *Alp-bamsi* 'hero (bogatyr) Bamsi' (DQorq. 151).

ALPANTAY Kzk. 19th c. **Alpantay** [Алпантай] (SOK 124). ⇨ **ALBAN / ALPAN + suff. -tay(2).**

ALPAWUT Bashk. 1707 **Alpawut** [Алпаут Тоишев] (MIB III, 37); Bashk. 1738 **Alpawut** [Алпаут

Беккулов] (MIB III, 387); Bashk. 1784 **Alpawut** [Алпаут Аитов] (MIB V, 158, 161); Bashk. 1790 **Alpawut** [Алпаут Балтаев] (MIB V, 276). ✦ '(Outstanding) Heroic young man; hero' cf. Uyg., Karakh. *alpaγut* 'герой, богатырь' (DTS), Uyg., Chag. *albaγut* 'Edelmann; Held' (Radl. I, 433), Kuman, Kar., Tat. *alpaut* 'Edelmann, Gutsbesitzer' (Radl. I, 430-31). ⇨ **ALPAГЇ**.

ALPЇ Uyg. 8th c. **Alpï-tutuγ** [alpï tutuγ], Qumar yegän (Müller, Pfahl. 24). ✦ 'Hero, brave warrior' (Erol II, 21). ⇨ **ALP**.

ALPЇS see **ALTMЇŠ**

ALPS see **ALTMЇŠ**

ALŠEY Tat.? 1739 **Alšey** [Алшей Уразгилъ], a soldier (PSZRI X, 932-33); Tat.? 1739 **Alšey** [Алшей Уразгилъ], a soldier (PSZRI X, 932-33); Tat.? 1739 **Alšey** [Алшей Уразгилъ], a soldier (PSZRI X, 932-33). ⇨ **ALČЇ** + dim. suff. -*y*?

ALŠЇ see **ALČЇ**

ALT-ÖZ Uyg. 1336 **Alt-öz-tegin?** / **Al-tuz-tegin?** [Altöz Tiukin] (Chwol., Syr.-nest. (NF) 30). ⇨ **ÖZ?**

ALTA Az. **Alta** [Алта], Ugur han's daughter (Az. Skaz. 276). ✦ I. 'Deceive! Take in!' II. 'Step!' III. 'Six'. ⇨ **ALTЇ?**

ALTAY Kzk. 1846 **Altay** [бий Анак Алтаев] (MKOP 100, 153); Kzk. 19th c. **Altay** [Джалфусъ Алтаев] (Grod., Pril. 140); Kzk. 19th c. **Altay** [Чалкарбай Алтаев] (Grod., Pril. 188); Kzk. 19th c. **Altay** [Алтай] (AOP 10, 42); Kzk. 19th c. **Altay** [Алтай], a herdsman (Kirg. Stepn. Gaz. 1894, No. 6, AUK 474); Kzk. 19th c. **Altay** [Алтай] (Grod., Pril. 199); Kzk. 19th c. **Altay** [Алтай] (SODž. 140); Kzk. 19th c. **Altay** [Алтай, Альтай] (SOK 244, 308); Kirg. 19th c. **Altay** [Алтай] (Potanin II, 7); Kzk. / Bashk.? 1747 **Altay** [Алтай] (Nepljuev 701); Kzk. 19th c. **Altay-bay** [Алатайбаевъ], a mulla (Pam. kn. Semip. 1898: III, 34); Kzk. 1794 **Altay-batïr** [الطا ى باطر] (MIK IV, 163); Kzk. 19th c. **Altay-bek** [Алтайбекъ] (AOAtb. 114); Kzk. 1794, 1820 **Altay-biy** [الطـاى بـى / Алтай-бий], one of the chiefs of the Alimulï tribe (MIK IV, 164, Sib. Vest. IX, 115); Alt. 19th c. **Altay-χan** [Алтай-хан] (Verb., In. 58); Kzk. 1823 **Altay-mïrza** [الطـاى مـرظا] (MIK IV, 456); *EN:* Kzk. 18th c. - 19th c. **Altay**, an ethnonym? (Tynyšp. 70). ✦ I. 'A kind of fox'?; II. 'The Altay mountains'. See also **QARA-ALTAY, SARЇ-ALTAY**.

ALTAY-BUČAY Alt. (Tel.) **Altay-bučay** [Алтай-Бучай] (Kalačev VI, 492). ⇨ **ALTAY**.

ALTAY-BUČЇ Alt. 19th c. **Altay-buči** [Алтай-Бучи] (Potanin, Pred. 180). ⇨ **ALTAY**.

ALTAY-BUČЇY Alt. **Altay-bučïy** [Алтай Бучый богатырь], a hero in a folktale (Nikiforov 2, 4-11, 13-23). ⇨ **ALTAY**.

ALTAYЇN-SAYЇN-SALAM Alt. 19th c. **Altayïn-sayïn-salam** [Алтаин-Саин-Салам-богатырь] (Verb., In. 143, 159, 160, 161). ⇨ **ALTAY** + **SAYЇN** + **SALAM?**

ALTAQAY Bashk. 1757 **Altaqay** [Алтакай Чюраев (Чюрин)] (MIB IV/1, 145). ⇨ **ALTA** + dim. suff. -*qay* or comp. *aqay?*

ALTAN Kzk. 19th c. **Altan** [Алтанъ], son of Qaraγay who was one of the forefathers of Merkits (Potanin II, 5); Alt. **Altan** [Алтанъ и Шалтан] (Nikiforov 4). ✦ 'Gold' <Mo. PN *Altan*. ⇨ **ALTЇN**.

ALTAN-BUDUQ Alt. **Altan-buduq** [Алтанъ-Будукъ], fem. (Nikiforov 104). ✦ 'Golden decoration of the plaited hair'. ⇨ **ALTAN** + **BUTUQ?**

ALTAN-ČAXČAXAY Yak. **Altan-čaχčaχay** [Алтан Чахчахаi], a folklore hero (Pek.); Yak. **Altan-čaχčāγï-buχatïr** [Алтан-Чахчаҕаi / Алтан-Чахчаҕы-бухаттыр], Ürüñ-ayï-toyon's elder son (Pek.); Yak. **Altan-čaχčāγï-buχatïr** / **Altan-čaχčāγay** [Алтан-Чахчаҕаi / Алтан-Чахчаҕы-бухаттыр], Ürüñ-ayï-toyon's elder son (Pek.). ✦ 'Honey-?' cf. Yak. *altan* 'медь, медный' (JRS). ⇨ **ALTAN?**

ALTAN-ČAXČĀГЇ see **ALTAN-ČAXČAXAY**

ALTAN-ČAXČĀГAY see **ALTAN-ČAXČAXAY**

ALTANAY see **ALTЇN-AY**

ALTЇGEY see **ALTЇKEY**

ALTЇ Kzk. 19th c. **Altï** [Калдыбекъ Бай Алтыевъ] (Grod., Pril. 174); Bashk. 1709 **Altï-bay** [Албай Алтыбаев] (MIB III, 44); Bashk. 1757 **Altï-bay** [Алтыбай Пайтеков] (MIB IV/2, 18); Bashk. 1757 **Altï-bay** [Алтыбай Яныков] (MIB IV/2, 18); Bashk. 1759 **Altï-bay** [Алтыбай (Алтымбай) Апеев] (MIB IV/1, 178-79); Kzk. 18th c. - 19th c. **Altï-bay** [Алтыбай] (Tynyšp. 75); Kzk. 19th c. **Altï-bay** [Алтыбай Кулбаев] (TV 1877, 194); Kzk. 19th c. **Altï-bay** [Алтыбай] (AOP 18, 66); Kzk. 19th c. **Altï-bay** [Алтыбай] (AOAtb. 18, 38); Kzk. 19th c. **Altï-bay** [Алтыбай] (AOK 30); Kzk. 19th c. **Altï-bay** [Алтыбай] (AOA 126); Kzk. 19th c. **Altï-bay** [Алтыбай] (SOK 30, 60, 110, 186); Kzk. 19th c. **Altï-bay** [Алтыбай] (SODž. 124); Kzk. 19th c. **Altï-bay** [Алтыбай] (SOV 88); Kzk. 19th c. **Altï-bay** [Каракбай Алтылаев ю? Алтыбаевщ] (Grod., Pril. 164); Kirg. **Altï-bay** [Алтыбай] (Jud. 42, 423); Uzb. 19th c. **Altï-bay** [Алтыбай Ишназаров] (SKSO III, 162); Khorezm. 1200-1220 **Altï-sultan** / **Altï-soldan?** [Bati. misit contra terram Alti -Soldani / contra terram altisoldani / contra altisoldanum; Altus Soldanus], the Khorezmian sultan Alāeddīn Muhammad II (1200-1220) (Sin. Fr. 113 (after Plano Carpini 672), also Quatremére, Notes et Extr. XIII, 290); Tat.(Sib.) 1603 **Altï-ul** [Урус Алтыулов], a murza (Miller, Ist. Sib. II, 179); Türk 7th c. - 9th c. **Altu** [altu] (DTS); Kzk. 19th

c. **Altu-bay** [Алтубай] (AOAtb. 46); *EN:* Tat.(Sib.) 1603 **Altï-ul** [Алтыулов улус], an ethnic group (Miller, Ist. Sib. II, 179, 181); Nog. 1613 **Altï-ulï** [Алтыулы], an ethnic group of the Great (Ullï) Noγays, which, separated from these, moved to the Aral and Syr-Darya after the death of Sheykh Mamay, the Noγay prince in 1549 (MIKk. 145); *TN:* Uzb. 1851 **Alt-bay** (?<Altï-bay) [Алт бай], a medrese in Urgench (ZIRGO V, 109); *TN:* **Altï-bay** [Алтыбай] (Karta JAR XI); *TN:* Kzk. **Altï-bay** [Алтыбай-соръ], a lake south-west of Krasnodar near the Irtiš river (Karta JAR IV); *TN:* Kzk. 1748 **Altï-bay** [Алтыбаево], a village in the province of Orenburg (Nepljuev 438); *TN:* Kzk. 19th c. **Altï-bay** [Алтыбай], a village near the Čabaqtï river (Tr. Syr-D. OSK 1888, Vyšnegorskij 48). ✧ 'Six' cf. Uyg., Alt., Crm., Hak., Kzk., Tat., Turk., etc. *altï*, Yak. *alta*, Chuv. *oltta* 'id.' (Radl. I, 405), also Blagova 1997, 705. See also **ALTU, MAH-ALTÏ, TEMÜR-ALTÏ.**

ALTÏ-BARMAQ see **ALTÏ-PARMAQ**

ALTÏ-BARS Kuman 1347 **Altï-bars** [Althabarz], a Kuman in Hungary, Beke's father (Gyárfás III, 484); Maml. 1340 **Altï-bars** [علا الـدين الطبرس] (Zetterst. 221); Maml. 14th c. **Altï-bars** [الطيبرس] (Tarǰ/Houtsma 34, 61, Tarǰ/Toparlı /facs. 31a/); Crm.Tat. **Altï-bars** [Алтыбарсъ], an emir in Nogay's days (Smirnov, Krym. 100). ✧ 'Six Panthers' expressing the wish of the parents that the child should live 3 times the 12-year animal cycle, that is (s)he should be long-lived (Rásonyi, Nombre 48, his KÖA 80), cf. also Sauvaget 38, Gombocz, ÁTSz. 37-38, Tarǰ/Houtsma 34, 53, Tarǰ/Toparlı 31a. ⇨ **ALTÏ + BARS.**

ALTÏ-YALÏL Bashk. 1735 **Altï-yalïl** [Алтыялилъ Мурāтаевъ], a tarkhan (Vel.-Zern., Bašk. 27). ⇨ **ALTÏ.**

ALTÏ-QAQRADAR Uzb. 1826 **Altï-qaqradar** [الـتى قـاقـردار], a man from Bukhara (Vel.-Zern., Haïder 280-82). ⇨ **ALTÏ.**

ALTÏ-QAP-YARAŠMAZ(Ï) Uyg. 12th c. - 14th c. **Altï-qap-yarašmaz(ï)** [altï qap jarašmaz(ï)], a constellation and the relevant god (divinity) in astrology (DTS). ✧ '(lit.) Unsuitability of six suits of armour' (DTS). ⇨ **ALTÏ.**

ALTÏ-QOL Kirg. 20th c. **Altï-qol** [Алтыкол] (Kalilov 94). ✧ 'Six fingers' (Kalilov), probably given to a child born with an extra finger. ⇨ **ALTÏ + QOL.** See also **ALTÏ-PARMAQ.**

ALTÏ-QULAČ Turk. 18th c. **Altï-qulač-zāde** [Altıkulaç zâde], in Kastamonu (Uzunçarşılı: Belleten 1974, 243). ✧ 'Six fathoms'? ⇨ **ALTÏ + QULAČ.**

ALTÏ-PARMAQ Turk. 1583 **Altï-barmaq** [الـتى بـرمـاق / Altıbarmak] (Ongan, Ank. I, 152); Crm.T. 1623 **Altï-parmaq-efendi** [Алты-Пармакъ-эфенди], a historiographer, died in 1623 (Smirnov, Krym. 57,

157); Trkm. 1690, 1692 **Altï-parmaq-oγlu** [الـتى بـرمـق اوغـلى / Altıparmakoğlu Hüseyin], in the region of Balıkesir (Refik, Anad. 87, Su 46); *TN:* Turk. 20th c. **Altï-parmaq** [Altıparmak], a village in the province of Tokat (TMİB 822). ✧ 'Six-Fingers', probably given to a child born with an extra finger. ⇨ **ALTÏ + BARMAQ.** See also **ALTÏ-QOL.**

ALTÏ-SAQMAN Oghuz/Trkm. 1039 **Altï-saqman** [Алты-Сакман], a χāǰib (door-keeper) (MIT I, 275 (after Bayhakī)). ✧ 'Six-careful/watchful'? ⇨ **ALTÏ + SAQ?** + suff. *-man.*

ALTÏGEY see **ALTÏKEY**

ALTÏGEN see **ALTÏKEN**

ALTÏKEY 17th c. **Altïgey** (<Altïkey) [Алтигейко Тотишевъ], a Cossack yasaul in Chuvash territory (IOAIÊK XXIX, 341). ⇨ **ALTÏ?** + suff. *-key.*

ALTÏKEN Kzk. 19th c. **Altïgen** [Алтыгенъ] (SOK 218); Kirg.? Kzk. 1824 **Altïken** [Алтыкен] (MIK IV, 463).

ALTÏLAY see **ALTÏ**

ALTÏN Kzk. 19th c. **Altïm** (<Altïn?) [Алтымъ] (SOV 16); Kzk. 19th c. **Altïm-bay** < **Altïn-bay** [Altym-Baï], Arγïm-bay's, Alčï-bay's and Mindi-bay's brother (Levchine 356); Trkm. 20th c. **Altïn** [Altın], fem. (Zaj. 1971, 337); Tat.? 1686 **Altïn** [Алтынъ] (Kungursk. akty 69); Tat. 1717 **Altïn** [Алтынъ], resident in Khiva (ZIRGOÊtn. IX, 324, 329, 333); Tat.(Sib.) 1630 **Altïn** [Алтын], (Miller, Ist. Sib. II, 370, 375); Kzk. 18th c. - 19th c. **Altïn** [Алтын] (Tynyšp. 73); Kzk. 19th c. **Altïn** [Алтынъ] (AOA 62); Kkalp. 20th c. **Altïn** [Алтын], fem. (KkRS 777); Kkalp. 20th c. **Altïn** [Алтын], fem. (Bask., Kkalp. 403, KkRS 777); Kirg. **Altïn** [Алтын], fem. (Jud. 753); Alt. 19th-20th c. **Altïn** [Алтын], fem. (OjrRS 211); Hak. 19th-20th c. **Altïn-araχ** (<Altïn-arïγ) [Алтынарахъ] (Titov 120); Tat. 19th c. **Altïn-arï** [Алтынъ-ары], fem. (Potanin IV, 618); Alt. **Altïn-arïγ** [Алтын Арыг], fem. (Radl. III, 1381); Alt. 19th c. **Altïn-arïγ** [Алтын-Арыгъ], Qara-qan's daughter (Verb., In. 161); Hak.(Kacha) 19th-20th c. **Altïn-arïγ** [Алтын Арыг], hero's sister (Proben IX, 218); Shor 19th-20th c. **Altïn-arïγ**, Aq-qan's wife (Dyrenkova 160 etc.); Tuv. 19th c. **Altïn-arïγ** [Алтынъ-Арыгъ], fem. (Potanin IV, 567); Bashk. 1711 **Altïn-bay** [Алтынбай Актуганов] (MIB III, 72); Bashk. 1714 **Altïn-bay** [Алтын-бай] (MIB I, 105); Bashk. 1791 **Altïn-bay** [Алтын] (MIB V, 309); Bashk. 1827 **Altïn-bay** [Алтынбай Шукуров] (TOUAK XXIV, 182); Kzk. **Altïn-bay** [бий Басан Алтынбаев], a Kazak notability (MKOP 156); Kzk. 19th c. **Altïn-bay** [Алтынбай] (SOK 184); Kzk. 19th c. **Altïn-bek** [Алтынбекъ] (SOK 24, 48); Shor 19th-20th c. **Altïn-čayzañ** [Алтын] (Dyrenkova 128); Shor 19th-20th c. **Altïn-čayzañ** (Dyrenkova 128); Trkm. 20th c. **Altïn-**

Jamal [Altïnğamal], fem. (Zaj. 1971, 337); Alt. **Altïn-ergäg / Altïn-ergäk** [Алтын Ергäг, Алтын Ергäк], a hero (Proben IX, 326, Radl. I, 199); Alt. **Altïn-ergäk** [Алтын-Ергäк] (Radl. II, 1140); Alt. 19th c. **Altïn-ergek** [Алтын-Эргек, Алтын-Ергек], a hero (Verb., In. 139, 141, 142, 144-146, 149, 154, 165); Shor 19th-20th c. **Altïn-ergek** [Алтын] (Dyrenkova 378); Kkalp. 20th c. **Altïn-gül** [Алтынгүл], fem. (KkRS 777); Kkalp. 20th c. **Altïn-gül** [Алтынгюл / Алтынгүл], fem. (Bask., Kkalp. 403, KkRS 777); Alt. 1616 **Altïn-χan** [Алтынъ-ханъ (Кунканчей)] (Andrievič, Ist. Sib. I, 119); Alt. 19th c. **Altïn-χan** [Алтын-хан] (Verb., In. 139, 140, 146, 152, 154); Alt. 19th c. **Altïn-χan** [Алтынъ-ханъ], a hero in a tale (Potanin IV, 556 etc.); Tat.(Kasim.) **Altïn-χanïm** [Алтын Ханым], fem. (Radl. I, 212); Tat.(Sib.) 19th c. **Altïn-irgek** [Алтынъ-Иргекъ] (Potanin 622); Alt. 19th c. **Altïn-irgek / Altïn-ergek** [Алтынъ-Иргекъ / Алтынъ-Эргекъ], a hero (Potanin IV, 572, 573,); Alt. 19th c. **Altïn-qan** [Алтынъ канъ] (Potanin IV, 556); Hak., Alt. 19th-20th c. **Altïn-qan** [Алтын Кан], a hero (Proben IX, 218, 219, 339-46); Shor 19th-20th c. **Altïn-qan** (Dyrenkova 9); Tat.(Minus.) **Altïn-qan** [Алтын-кан] (Radl. II, 195); Alt. **Altïn-qō** [Алтын-коо] (Nikiforov 135, 143); Alt. 19th c. **Altïn-mökö** [Алтын-Моко, Алтын-Мöкö], a hero, khan of the thirteenth sky (Verb., In. 139, 144, 154); Tel. **Altïn-pökö** [Алтын-Пöкö] (Radl. III, 102); Alt. 19th c. **Altïn-tayči** [Алтын-Тайчи] (Verb., In. 140, 145); Shor 19th-20th c. **Altïn-tayči / Külüg-altïn-tayči** [Külüg Altyn Tajčy] (Dyrenkova 164); Alt., Hak. 19th-20th c. **Altïn-tayǰi** [Алтынъ Таицы] (Radl. I, 1282); Nog. 1649 **Altïn-tutay** [Алтын-Тутай] (AI IV, 123); 870 **Altun** [الطون] (Tabarī, Annal. III, 1824); Uyg. 939 **Altun?** [Yi-li-touen (*jäi-lji-tuən > *iäi lji-tuən)], envoy of the Uygurs of Kanchou sent to Chinese court (Hamilton, Ouïg. 146); Uyg. 981 **Altun?** [A-touen], a clan at Etsin Gol(?) (Hamilton, Ouïg. 146); Selj. 1118 **Altun** [الطنام المستظهر] (Ibn Taghrīb. II, 370); Maml 14th c. **Altun** [التون / Alṭun], in Mo. its equivalent is Altan-χatun (Poppe 1253) (Tarǰ/Houtsma 53, Tarǰ/Toparlı 43); Turk.? 1393 **Altun** [الطون], commander of the fort الذجا• in Syria (Arabš. 276 etc.); Kzk. 1786 **Altun** [Алтун] (MIK IV, 75); Uyg. 1264 **Altun-aba** (Chwol., Syr.-nest. (NF) 8); Selj. 1201 **Altun-aba** [التون ابه] (Ibn al-Athīr/Tornb. XII, 107); Selj. 13th c. **Altun-be / Altun-bey** [شمس الدين التون به / بى] (Ibn Bībī III, 308, IV, 125, 212); Maml. 1279 **Altun-be (<Altun-bey)** [Fakhr-eddin-Altounba], regent in the fortress of Kosair (النصير) (Makrīzī II/1, 6); Kzk. 19th c. **Altun-bige** [Алтунъ Бигэ Бахтигельдіева], (fem.) (Grod., Pril. 140); YUyg. 20th c. **Altun-jan**, a young girl (S.

Kakuk, Chants ouigoures: AOH XXV, 416, 422); Chin. 13th c. **Altun-χan** [التون خان], ruler of Xitay [= the Jurchen Empire] in the days of Ögedei (1229-1241) (Juwaynī I, 151, 153); NUyg.(Tar.) 19th c. **Altun-χanïm** [التون خنيم / Алтунъ-ханымъ], fem. (Pantusov, Pesni 25, 113); Oghuz **Altun-qaγan**, in Oghuz epic (Oğuz K. Dest. 17); Oghuz 13th c. **Altun-qaγan** [altun qaγan] (DTS); Chag. 17th c. **Altun-qanïm / χanïm?** [Altun-Khanim], a princess from Khiva (Abulg./Desm. 309); Türk 8th c.- 9th c. **Altun-tay-sañun**, a general in a runic text (Runic Mss. 219?); Türk 8th c. - 9th c. **Altun-tay-sañun** [altun taj saŋun], in a runic text (DTS, Runic Mss. 219); Türk **Altun-tamγan-tarqan** [altun tamγan tarqan] (DTS); Chag.? **Altun-tigin** (Le Coq, Ind. 1); Uyg. 1201 **Altun-toña** [Altun Tunga] (Chwol., Syr.-nest. (NF) 6); Uyg. 1201 **Altun-tuña** (Chwol., Syr.-nest. (NF) 6); *EN:* Nog. 20th c. **Altïn-qoǰa** [Алтын къоджа уьйсин], a branch of the Üysin clan of the Qara-noγays (Bask., Nog. 137). ✧ 'Gold' cf. Uyg., Chag., East.T., etc. *altun* 'das Gold' (Radl. I, 411), Maml. *altun* 'altın' (Tarǰ/Toparlı), also Trk. *altun* (TMEN I, No. 26, II, No. 529, DTS), most Trk. languages *altïn* 'id.' (Radl. I, 405), *altïn* 'id.' (Sev.), etc. Hak. PN *Altïn-tayčï* means 'Golden prince' (Butanaev). Other explanation for *Altïn-arïγ* 'Pure gold' (Titov 120). Blagova interprets *Altun-tay-sañun* as 'Gold-foal-strategist' (Blagova 1997, 706). As for our oppinion cf. comp. of Chin. origin *tay-sañun*. See also **AY-ALTÏN, SAR-ALTÏN.**

ALTÏN-AČQA 1680 **Altïn-ačqa?** [Алтыначка] (DAI VIII, 44). ✧ 'Golden coin'. ⇨ **ALTÏN + AQČA.**

ALTÏN-AY Kzk. 18th c. - 19th c. **Altïn-ay** [Алтынай] (Tynyšp. 66); Kirg. **Altïn-ay** [Алтын Ai], a man in the Manas-epos (Proben V, 107 /108/, Jud. 164); Kirg. 20th c. **Altïn-ay** [Алтынай], fem. (Kalilov 95); Tat.(Sib.) 1607, 1608 **Altïn-ay / Altanay** [Алтынай], a prince, Küčüm-qan's son (Sib. Let. 282, 295, Miller, Ist. Sib. II, 204, 207). ✧ 'Gold-moon'. ⇨ **ALTÏN + AY.**

ALTÏN-AYAQ Tel. **Altïn-ayaq** [Алтын-айак] (Radl. III, 1374). ✧ I. 'Golden foot'; II. 'Golden cup'? ⇨ **ALTÏN + AYAQ.**

ALTÏN-AYDAR Kzk. Kirg.? 19th c.? **Altïn-aydar** [Алтын] (Atyns. 71). ✧ I. 'Golden mop'; II. 'Golden-Aydar (<Xaydar?)'. ⇨ **ALTÏN + AYDAR / XAYDAR?**

ALTÏN-ARAX see **ALTÏN**

ALTÏN-ARBÏY Alt. (Tuv.?) 19th c. **Altïn-arbïy** [Алтынъ-арбый] (Potanin IV, 572). ⇨ **ALTÏN.**

ALTÏN-ARÏ see **ALTÏN**

ALTÏN-ARTČÖL Hak.(Sag.) **Altïn-artčöl** [Алтын Артчол], sister of the hero (bogatyr) (Proben IX, 255, 258, 259). ⇨ **ALTÏN.**

ALTÏN-BAS Kzk. **Altïn-bas** [Алтын Бас], hero of a story in verses (Proben III, 635 /718/); Kzk. 19th c.

Altïn-baš (Ljutš 52). ✧ 'Golden head'. ⇨ **ALTÏN** + **BAŠ.**

ALTÏN-BEL   Kzk. **Altïn-bel** [Алтын Бел], a khan (Proben III, 63 /82/). ✧ 'Golden waist'. ⇨ **ALTÏN** + **BEL.**

ALTÏN-BIŠIK   Uzb. 1512 **Altïn-bišik** [Altyn-Bichik], son of Sultan Bābur (Baber), also called Xuda-yar-χan (or Ilik-sultan), Täñri-yar and Qultuq-χan (or Qutlï-χan); according to a legend, he was born on the road when Bābur was on the run from Samarkand in 1512, so they had to leave him there. He was found and brought up by the tribesmen of Miñ. For newborn was wrapped in precious clothes they named him like this. (Nalivkin-Dozon 63-64). ✧ 'Golden cradle' (Nalivkine 64: 'Berceau d'or'), Uzb. *bešik* 'бешик (деревянная колыбель' (UzbRS). ⇨ **ALTÏN.**

ALTÏN-BUГA see **ALTUN-BUГA**

ALTÏN-BŪ   Bulg. 13th c. - 14th c. **Altïn-bū** [الطن بو] (Jusupov 38). ✧ 'Golden Deer'. ⇨ **ALTÏN** + **BUГU.**

ALTÏN-CABAQ   Tat.(Bar.) **Altïn-cabaq** [Алтын Цабак] (Proben IV, 5 /7/). ✧ 'Golden Bream (fish)'. ⇨ **ALTÏN** + **ČABAQ.**

ALTÏN-ČAČAK see **ALTÏN-ČEČEK**

ALTÏN-ČAГAY   Tuv. 19th c. **Altïn-čaγay** [Алтынъ-Чагай] (Potanin IV, 596). ✧ 'Golden little boy'. ⇨ **ALTÏN** + **ČAГAY.**

ALTÏN-ČEČEK   Alt. **Altïn-čačak** [Алтынъ Чачакъ], fem. (Nikiforov 25-26); Alt. 19th c. **Altïn-čeček** [Алтын-Чечек], in an epic (Verb., In. 150). ✧ 'Golden Flower'. ⇨ **ALTÏN** + **ČEČÄK.**

ALTÏN-ČILTÏS   Alt. 19th c. **Altïn-čiltïs** [Алтынъ-Чилтысъ] (Potanin IV, 561, 587). ✧ 'Golden Star'. ⇨ **ALTÏN** + **YULDUZ.**

ALTÏN-ČÖBE   Tuv. 19th c. **Altïn-čöbe** [Алтынъ-Чобе], fem. (Potanin IV, 566 etc.). ✧ 'Golden arrow'. ⇨ **ALTÏN.**

ALTÏN-JÜSTÜK see **ALTÏN-YÜSTÜK**

ALTÏN-İRGEK see **ALTÏN**

ALTÏN-YÜSTÜK   Alt. **Altïn-Jüstük** [Алтынъ-Джюстюкъ], fem. (Nikiforov 250); Alt. **Altïn-yüstük** [Алтынъ-йустюкъ], fem. (Nikiforov 250); Alt. **Altïn-üstük** [Алтынъ-Ўстўкъ], fem. (Nikiforov 110, 116, 206). ✧ 'Golden Ring' cf. Alt.(Tel.) *yüstük* 'der Fingerring' (Radl. III, 616), Hak.(Sag.), Shor *čüstük* 'der Fingerring' (Radl. III, 2200). ⇨ **ALTÏN.**

ALTÏN-KÖK   Alt. 19th c. **Altïn-kök** [Алтынъ-кокъ] (Potanin IV, 558, 559); Shor 19th-20th c. **Altïn-kŏk,** Altïn-qan's uncle (Dyrenkova 9); Shor 19th-20th c. **Altïn-kŏk,** Altïn-baday's daughter (Dyrenkova 124); Tuv. 19th c. **Altïn-kŏk** [Алтын Кўк], a hero (Proben IX, 255, 259). ✧ 'Gold-blue'? ⇨ **ALTÏN** + **KÖK.**

ALTÏN-QARTAГA see **ALTÏN-QARTÏГA**

ALTÏN-QARTÏГA   Alt. 19th c. **Altïn-qartaγa** [Алтынъ-Картага] (Potanin IV, 569); Tuv. 19th c.

Altïn-qartaγa / **Aq-qoyattï** Altïn-qartaγa [Аккойатты-Алтын-картага] (Potanin IV, 568); Shor 19th-20th c. **Altïn-qartïγa** (Dyrenkova 48, 88). ✧ 'Golden hawk'. ⇨ **ALTÏN** + **QARTÏГA.**

ALTÏN-QÏLÏŠ   Alt., Tuv. 19th c. **Altïn-qïlïš** [Алтынъ-Кылышъ] (Potanin IV, 573). ✧ 'Golden sabre/sword'. ⇨ **ALTÏN** + **QÏLÏČ.**

ALTÏN-QUČQAŠ   Alt. **Altïn-qučqaš** [Алтынъ-Кучкашъ] (Nikiforov 222). ✧ 'Golden nestling' cf. Alt. *qučqaš* 'пташка, пичужка' (OjrRS). ⇨ **ALTÏN.**

ALTÏN-MERIK   Shor 19th-20th c. **Altïn-merik,** Qartïγa-pergen's son (Dyrenkova 24). ✧ 'Golden-shell?' cf. Shor *märik* 'der Strahl (unter dem Hufen)' (Radl. IV, 2092). ⇨ **ALTÏN.**

ALTÏN-OQ   Shor 19th-20th c. **Altïn-oq** (Dyrenkova 144). ✧ 'Golden Arrow'. ⇨ **ALTÏN** + **OQ.**

ALTÏN-PERISTE   Alt. 19th c. **Altïn-periste** [Алтын-Перисте-богатырь], a hero (Verb., In. 144, 154). ✧ 'Golden mile'? cf. Alt. *periste* 'верста' (OjrRS). ⇨ **ALTÏN.**

ALTÏN-PŌS   Alt. **Altïn-pōs** [Алтын Пос], sister of the hero (Proben IX, 251, 254). ✧ 'Golden pregnant' cf. Alt., Hak. *pōs* 'trächtig, schwanger' (Radl. IV, 1288). ⇨ **ALTÏN.**

ALTÏN-SABAQ   Alt. 19th c. **Altïn-sabaq** [Алтынъ-Сабакъ], Altyn-χan's wife (Potanin IV, 556); Hak.(Sag.) 19th-20th c. **Altïn-sabaq** [Алтын Сабак], fem. (Proben II, 173 /176/, 174 /177/); Shor 19th-20th c. **Altïn-sabaq** [āryγ sylyγ Altyn Sabak], fem. (Dyrenkova 56, 170). ✧ 'Golden thread of hair'. ⇨ **ALTÏN** + **SABAQ?**

ALTÏN-SARÏ   Kzk. **Altïn-sarï** [Алтын Сары], a hero (Proben III, 256 /302/); Kzk. 1827 **Altïn-sarï** [Алтынсары Тогумовъ], a Kazak sultan (Konšin, Mat. I-III, 56); Kzk. 19th c. **Altïn-sarï** [Ибрагимъ Алтынсарыновичъ Алтынсаринъ], a noble Kazak of Kipchak origin (Middle Horde, Orta Žüz), his grandfather was Dalgoža Jamgurčin the sergeant-major (AUK 379); Kzk. 20th c. **Altun-sarï** [Ibrahim Altunsari], a Kazak poet (Mende 29). ✧ 'Golden-Blond'. ⇨ **ALTÏN** + **SARÏ.**

ALTÏN-SOLBAN   Alt. **Altïn-solban-märgän** [Алтын Солбан Мäргäн] (Radl. III, 1251). ✧ 'Golden-Venus'. ⇨ **ALTÏN** + **ČOLPAN.**

ALTÏN-SŌM   Shor 19th-20th c. **Altïn-sōm,** a hero (Dyrenkova 152). ✧ I. 'Golden figure'?; II. 'Pure Gold'? ⇨ **ALTÏN** + **SOM.**

ALTÏN-SŪČU   Shor 19th-20th c. **Altïn-sūču-qïs** [Altyn Sūču qys], Aq-qān's daughter (Dyrenkova 24). ✧ 'Golden Swimmer' cf. Alt. *sučï* 'der Schwimmer' (Radl. IV, 779); II. Golden Water-carrier cf. Tat. *sučï* 'der Wasserführer', Chag., East.T. *sučï* 'Wasserträger', (Chag.) 'der Verwalter der Getränke, eine Hofwürde (der Mundschenk)' (Radl. IV, 779). ⇨ **ALTÏN.**

ALTÏN-SŪR   Shor 19th-20th c. **Altïn-sūr** (Dyrenkova 78). ✧ I. 'Golden blaze, golden spark'; II. 'Golden marmot'?; III. 'Golden greyish blue'? ⇨ **ALTÏN + SUR?**

ALTÏN-ŠAQPÏN   Shor 19th-20th c. **Altïn-šaqpïn** (Dyrenkova 64). ✧ 'Golden acacia (Caragana arborescens)' cf. Shor *šaqpïn* 'сибирская акация; der sibirische Erbsenbaum' (Radl. IV, 936). ⇨ **ALTÏN.**

ALTÏN-TAJÏ   Alt. **Altïn-taji** [Алтынъ Таджи], fem. (Nikiforov 17-18). ✧ 'Golden crown/crowned'. ⇨ **ALTÏN + TAJÏ.**

ALTÏN-TADÏ   Alt. **Altïn-tadi** [Алтынъ-Тади] (Nikiforov 116, 208, 209). ✧ 'Golden Tadi'? ⇨ **ALTÏN.**

ALTÏN-TAY   Kzk. 19th c. **Altïn-tay** [Алтынтай] (SOK 28). ✧ 'Golden Foal'. ⇨ **ALTÏN + TAY** or suff. *-tay(2)*?

ALTÏN-TAYJÏ see **ALTÏN**

ALTÏN-TANA   Alt. **Altïn-tana** [Алтынъ-Тана], fem. (Nikiforov 103, 227-30); Alt. **Altïn-tana** [Алтын Тана], hero's daughter (Proben IX, 340, 351-53); Shor 19th-20th c. **Altïn-tana**, Altïn-tayčï's sister (Dyrenkova 164, 387); Tuv. 19th c. **Altïn-tana** [Аксар-атты Алтын-Тана] (Potanin IV, 566); Alt.(Tuba) 19th c. **Altïn-tona?** [Алтынъ-Тона], a character in a tale (Potanin IV, 577). ✧ 'Golden Button' (Dyrenkova 164, 387); 'Golden pearl' (Butanaev). ⇨ **ALTÏN + TANA II.**

ALTÏN-TAS   Alt. **Altïn-tas** [Алтын Тас], a hero (Proben IX, 332, 343-347); Alt. 19th c. **Altïn-tas** [Алтын-Тас-богатырь], a hero (Verb., In. 153); Alt. 19th c. **Altïn-tas** [Алтын-Тас] (Verb., In. 153); Shor 19th-20th c. **Altïn-tas** (Dyrenkova 178). ✧ 'Golden Bald' (Dyrenkova). ⇨ **ALTÏN + TAZ.**

ALTÏN-TOLU   Alt. **Altïn-tolu** [Алтын-толу] (Nikiforov 219, 220). ✧ I. 'Golden present, Golden Ransom' II. 'Full of Gold'; III. 'Golden mirror'. ⇨ **ALTÏN + TOLU.**

ALTÏN-TONA see **ALTÏN-TANA**

ALTÏN-TORÏ   Kzk. 19th c. **Altïn-torï** [Алтынторы Ельторынъ] (AOK 34). ✧ 'Gold-Brown'. ⇨ **ALTÏN + TORÏ.**

ALTÏN-TÜLGÖ   Alt. 19th c. **Altïn-tülgö** [Алтын-Тулгö], fem. (Potanin IV, 578-82). ✧ 'Golden Fox'. ⇨ **ALTÏN + TÜLKÜ.**

ALTÏN-ÜLBEK   Alt. 19th c. **Altïn-ülbek** [Алтын-ульбекъ] (Potanin IV, 560-62). ✧ 'Golden Hook'. ⇨ **ALTÏN.**

ALTÏNCÏ see **ALTÏNČÏ**

ALTÏNČÏ   Tat. 1360 **Altïnčï-bey** [Алтынцыбѣй], envoy of the Tatars (PSRL X, 232); Alt. 19th-20th c. **Altïnčï** [Алтынчы], fem. (OjrRS 211); NUyg. 19th c. **Altunči** [التونچى / Altunchi] (Le Coq, Namenl. 94). ✧ 'Goldsmith'. ⇨ **ALTÏN + suff. -čï.**

ALTÏNÏČ   Tat.? 1686 **Altïnïč** [Алтынычка (Алтаничка) Тойгилдина] (Kungursk. akty 68). ⇨ **ALTÏN + suff. -ïč.**

ALTMÏŠ   Kzk. **Alpïs** [Алпысъ] (Konšin, Oč. 60); Kzk. 19th c. **Alpïs** [Алпысъ] (SOK 14, 34, 104, 150,); Kzk. 19th c. **Alpïs** [Алпысъ] (SOV 124); Kzk. 19th c. **Alpïs** [Алпысъ] (AOP 30); Kzk. 19th c. **Alpïs** [Алпысъ] (AOO 74, 10, 26); Kzk. 19th c. **Alpïs** [Алпысъ] (AOK 6, 50); Kzk. 19th c. **Alpïs-bay** [Алпысбай] (AOAtb. 6); Kzk. 19th c. **Alpïs-bay** [Алпысбай] (AOP 118); Kzk. 19th c. **Alpïs-bay** [Алпысбай] (Grod., Pril. 117); Kzk. 19th c. **Alpïs-bay** [Алпысбай] (AOO 66); Kzk. 19th c. **Alpïs-pay** [Алпыспай] (SODž. 52, 82, 120); Kzk. 19th c. **Alpïs-pay** [Алпыспай] (SOV 72); Kzk. 19th c. **Alpïs-pay** [Алпыспай] (AOP 26, 66); Kzk. 19th c. **Alpïs-pay** [Алпыспай] (SOK 4, 198); Kzk. 19th c. **Alpïs-pay** [Алтыспай] (SOV 72); Kzk. 19th c. **Alps-pay** (<Alpïs-pay) [Алпспай] (SOV 14, 28); Kzk. 19th c. **Alps-pay** (<Alpïs-pay) [Алпспай] (SOK 238); Kzk. 19th c. **Alps-pay** (<Alpïs-pay) [Алпстпай] (SOV 6, 22); Kzk. 19th c. **Altmïš** [Алтмышевъ] (SKSO VIII, 222); NUyg. 19th c. **Altmïš** [التميش / Altmish] (Le Coq, Namenl. 94); Kzk. 1819 **Altmïš-bay** [Алтмышбай] (MIK IV, 324); Kzk. 1863 **Altpïs** [Алтпыс] (ZIRGOGeogr. 411); Kzk. 19th c. **Altpïs-bay** [Алтпысбай] (AOK 130). ✧ 'Sixty (the age of the father or grand-father)' cf. Rásonyi: AOH XII (1961), 45-71); „... *altmïš* = 60, er muss für eine Summe von 60 Goldstücken gekauft worden sein. (Analoga sind die Sklavennamen *Hazārī* p. und *el-Alfī* a., welche beide 'der Tausender' bedeuten, nach dem für den betr. Sklaven bezahlten Preise)." (Le Coq, Ind. 1).

ALTMÏŠ-QARA   Uyg. 12th c. - 14th c. **Alt** (Radl., USp. 130-31); Uyg. 12th c. - 14th c. **Altmïš-qara** [altmïš qara] (DTS, EUTS). ✧ 'Sixty-Black'; 'Sixty-Mighty' (Blagova 1997, 705). ⇨ **ALTMÏŠ + QARA.**

ALTMÏŠ-TÜKÜN   Uyg. 13th c. **Altmïš-tükün** [altmïš tükün] (DTS). ✧ 'Sixty-Spot' (Bese 16, Blagova 1997, 705). ⇨ **ALTMÏŠ.**

ALTOQ see **ARTÏQ**

ALTPÏS see **ALTMÏŠ**

ALTU I. see **ALTÏ**

ALTU II.   Chuv. 18th-19th c. **Altu** [Алту] (Magn. 27); Chuv. 18th-19th c. **Altu-bay** [Алтубай] (Magn. 27). ✧ 'Great, huge'? cf. Cher. *alte* 'id.' (Fedotov).

ALTUҒA   Türk 7th-9th c. **Altuɣa** [Altuɣa] (ETY III, 141). See also **ÄRDÄM-QAÑ-ALTUҒA.**

ALTUN see **ALTÏN**

ALTUN-ABA see **ALTÏN**

ALTUN-AŠUQ   Khorezm.? 14th c. **Altun-ašuq / Altun-asuq** [التون اسوق والتون اشوق] (RnD/Ber. II, 196, 228). ✧ 'Golden helmet'. ⇨ **ALTÏN + AŠUQ.**

ALTUN-BOҒA see **ALTUN-BUҒA**

ALTUN-BU   Maml. **Altun-bu** (Ibn Taghrīb.). ✦ 'Golden-?'. ⇨ **ALTÏN + BU.**

ALTUN-BUΓA   Türk/Uyg.? 8th c. **Altïn-buγa** [الطنبغا العلا] (Mehren XVI, 313); Maml. 1271 **Altun-boγa?** [Jusef Altusbochet], an inhabitant of the Holy Land (Reg. Hieros. 359); Maml. 14th c. **Altun-boγa** [الطنبغا], a Cherkess and a Turk (Sauvaget 38); Oghuz 893 **Altun-buγa** [Altounboga-Fakhr-eddin-?emsi] (Makrīzī II/1, 17); Khorezm. 1282 **Altun-buγa** [Nâser-eddin-Altounbogâ-Khawarizmi], an emir (Makrīzī III, 57); Maml. **Altun-buγa** [الطنبغا], an emir (Berchem 130, 132, 192); Maml. **Altun-buγa** [الطنبغا], 18 persons bear the name in this source. (In the index mistakenly interpreted as [ال طنبغا]) (Iyās); Maml. **Altun-buγa** [الطنبغا] (Duqmaq:RHCHor V, 32); Maml. 1294 **Altun-buγa** [Altoun-boka? le râs-naubah], among the killers of the sultan Khalil (Makrīzī III, 153, Weil, Chalif. I, 192); Maml. 1309 **Altun-buγa** [فخرالدين الطنبغا الاستدار] (Dawād. 180); Maml. 1309/10 **Altun-buγa** [الطنبغا الجمدار], a cup-bearer (Iyās I, 153, Zetterst. 29); Maml. 1313 **Altun-buγa** [الطنبغا الحاجى] (Dawād. 264); Maml. 1314 **Altun-buγa** [علاءالد ين الطنبغا] (Abulfidā V, 284-85); Maml. 1316 **Altun-buγa** [التون بغا / Altoun Bogha], a lieutenant of Sultan Baybars I. (1260-1277) in Aleppo (Abulfidā: RHCHor I, 181); Maml. 1323 **Altun-buγa** [الطنبغا], regent of al-Bireh (Mayer 64-65); Maml. 1340 **Altun-buγa** [Altun buġa al-ʿAlāʾī], regent of Syria (Damascus), died in 1342 (Mayer 63, Abulfidā IV, 132); Maml. 1340/41 **Altun-buγa** [الطنبغا], regent of Syria (Iyās I, 171, Weil, Chalif. I, 421); Maml. 1340/41 **Altun-buγa** [الطنبغا الماردينى], regent of Haleb, died in 1343 (Iyās I, 179, Makrīzī, Khit. I, 308, Zetterst. 202, 203, Weil, Chalif. I, 460); Maml. 14th c. **Altun-buγa** [Šihābaddīn Aḥmad bin Alṭunbuġā] (Björkm. 164); Maml. 14th c. **Altun-buγa** [الطنبغا المعلم], died in 1395/96 (Berchem, Jér. I, 305); Maml. 14th c. **Altun-buγa** [الطنبغا المعلم اللفاف], chief of the silahdārs (custodians of arms), died in1391 (Ibn Taghrīb. VII, 132,137, Weil, Chalif. II, 9); Maml. 14th c. **Altun-buγa** [الطنبغا الجو با نى], regent of Damascus (1390) (Ibn Taghrīb. VII, 368, Iyās I, 247, 249, Weil, Chalif. II, 5); Maml. 1351 **Altun-buγa** [نايب صفد الطنبغا برقاق], governor of Safad (?) (Iyās I, 196); Maml. 1352 **Altun-buγa** [الطنبغا شاد الشرأبخاناه] (Iyās I, 197); Maml. 1366/67 **Altun-buγa** [الطنبغا لمنجكى] (Iyās I, 221); Maml. 1367/68 **Altun-buγa** [الطنبغا اليلبغاوى المعلم] (Iyās I, 221, 248); Maml. 1378/79 **Altun-buγa** [الطنبغا] (Iyās I, 234); Maml. 1387 **Altun-buγa** [الطنبغا الجو نا نى] (Berchem, Jér. II, 312); Maml. 1388 **Altun-buγa** [الطنبغا الحلبى], regent of Haleb (Iyās I, 279, Weil, Chalif. I, 564-65); Maml. 1389 **Altun-buγa** [الطنبغا شادى] (Iyās I, 279); Maml. 1390 **Altun-buγa** [الطنبغا الاشرفى] (Iyās I, 273, 276); Maml. 1398/99 **Altun-buγa** [الطنبغا] (Ibn Taghrīb. VI, 16, 245); Maml. 1398/99 **Altun-buγa** [الطنبغا الحسنى] (Ibn Taghrīb. VI, 17, Weil I, 488-89); Maml. 1398/99 **Altun-buγa** [الطنبغا الخليلى] (Ibn Taghrīb. VI, 9, 17); Maml. 1398/99 **Altun-buγa** [الطنبغا], a regent (Ibn Taghrīb. VI, 28); Maml. 1400/01 **Altun-buγa** [الطنبغا العنبرى] (Iyās I, 335); Maml. 1400/01 **Altun-buγa** [الطنبغا المعروف بسيدى] (Iyās I, 337); Maml. 1400/01 **Altun-buγa** [الطنبغا جاموس] (Ibn Taghrīb. VI, 96, 382); Maml. 1403/04 **Altun-buγa** [الطنبغا] (Ibn Taghrīb. VI, 113); Maml. 1405 **Altun-buγa** [الطنبغا الجكمى] (Ibn Taghrīb. VI, 368); Maml. 1405/06 **Altun-buγa** [الطنبغا الطويك الناصرى] (Ibn Taghrīb. VI, 136); Maml. 1405/06 **Altun-buγa** [الطنبغا الارغونى] (Iyās I, 648); Maml. 1405, 1438 **Altun-buγa** [المرقبى المويدى الطنبغا] (Ibn Taghrīb. VII, 52, 115, 373-74); Maml. 1406/07 **Altun-buγa** [الطنبغا بشلا ق] (Ibn Taghrīb. VI, 195); Maml. 1420 **Altun-buγa** [الظا هرى الطنبغا القرمشى], a regent (Ibn Taghrīb. VI, 330, 334, VII, 579, Weil, Chalif. II, 50 etc.); Maml. 1421 **Altun-buγa** [الطنبغا الصغير الظاهرى] (Ibn Taghrīb. VI, 416, 482); Maml. 1421 **Altun-buγa** [القرشى الالا تا بكى الطنبغا] (Iyās II, 13); Maml. 1422 **Altun-buγa** [الطنبغا الرحبى] (Ibn Taghrīb. VI, 552); Maml. 1425 **Altun-buγa** [الطنبغا فرنج الدمرداشى] (Ibn Taghrīb. VI, 597); Maml. 1430 **Altun-buγa** [الطنبغا مفرق] (Ibn Taghrīb. VI, 664); Maml. 1439/40 **Altun-buγa** [الطنبغا الشريفى الناصرى] (Ibn Taghrīb. VII, 107, 158); Maml. 1447, 1452 **Altun-buγa** [الطنبغا الطر بائى] (Ibn Taghrīb. VIII, 24, 135); Turk. 1448 **Altun-buγa** [الطنبغا العثما نى] (Ibn Taghrīb. VIII, 147); Maml. / Turk.? 1398/99, 1415 **Altun-buγa** [الطنبغا العثمانى الظاهرى], regent of Damascus and Tripolis (Ibn Taghrīb. VI, 3, 4, 12, VII, 326, Iyās I, 279, Weil, Chalif. I, 134); Khorezm.? 14th c. **Altun-buqa** [Алтун-Бука] (RaD II, 154). ✦ 'Golden Bull'. ⇨ **ALTÏN + BUQA.**

ALTUN-BUQA see **ALTUN-BUΓA**

ALTUN-GÖZEKİ   Oghuz/Trkm. 13th c. **Altun-gözeki** [التون كوزكى / Алтун-Гӧзеки], Sundun-bay's daughter, Salor-Qazan-alp's wife (Abulg./Kon. 1440). ✦ 'Golden-?'. ⇨ **ALTÏN.**

ALTUN-QARA   Uyg. 12th c. - 14th c. **Altun-qara** (Radl., USp. 27-28, DTS). ✦ 'Gold-Mighty' (Blagova 1997, 705), 'Gold-Black'. ⇨ **ALTÏN + QARA.**

ALTUN-QUŠ   Maml. 1320 **Altun-quš** [الطنتش] (Zetterst. 148). ✧ 'Golden Bird'. ⇨ **ALTÏN + QUŠ I.**

ALTUN-ŠAŠ   Kzk. **Altun-šaš** [Алтунъ шашъ], fem. (Divaev, Alp. 46). ✧ 'Golden Hair' cf. Alt. *čač* 'volosy' (OjrRS), Shor, Kzk. *šaš* 'die Haare' (Radl. IV, 973). ⇨ **ALTÏN.** See also **AQ-ČAČ, ČÏÑÏR-ČAČ, SULUW-ŠAŠ, UZUN-ČAŠ.**

ALTUN-TAY-SAÑUN see ALTÏN

ALTUN-TAQ   Oghuz 11th c. **Altun-taq** [التونتاق] داد بك حبشى بن / Дад Хабаши ибн Алтунтак (Дадбек Хабаши)], his son Dād Khabashi was an emir in Khorasan (Ǧuwaynī II, 2, 3, etc., Bondārī 259, 260, MIT I, 383-85, 442); Oghuz 11th c. **Altun-taq** [التونتا ق], in the days of the Ghaznavid sultan Masʿūd II (1048) he was the governor of Balkh, then he surrendered himself to the Seljukid Čaqïr-beg (Ahbar 9, 21); Oghuz/Trkm. 1042/43 **Altun-taq / Altun-taš?** [Алтунтак / Алтунташ], doorkeeper (ḥāǧib), the ruler of Balkh (MIT I, 290, 302, 303). ⇨ **ALTÏN + TAQ.**

ALTUN-TAS see ALTUN-TAŠ

ALTUN-TAŠ   Alt. **Altïn-taš** [Алтынъ-Ташъ] (Nikiforov 86);   914   **Altun-taš** [التونتاش هارون الحاجب], doorkeeper (ḥāǧib) (Ibn al-Athīr/Tornb. IX, 155, 184, 282, 294); 10th c. **Altun-taš** [التونتاش] (Bondārī 105, 257); 1041 **Altun-taš** [التونتا ش الحاجب], doorkeeper (ḥāǧib) (Ibn al-Athīr/Tornb. IX, 330-31); 1120 **Altun-taš** (Abulfar./Budge I, 249); Oghuz 1006, 1012, 1014, 1015 **Altun-taš** [التونتاش حاجب], a chieftain in the fights between Mahmud and the Ilkhan, then the regent of Khorezm (died in 1031) (Mirch. Gasnevid. 33, 55, 59, 66, 102-3); Oghuz 1035 **Altun-taš** [هرون بن الطنطاش], the Khorezmshah Harun's father (Abulfidā III, 106-7); Oghuz/Trkm. 1001, 1030 **Altun-taš** [Алтунташ], a door-keeper and (later) Khorezmshah (MIT I, 224, 232, 234-237, 245, 246, 249, 254, 257, 286, 302, 303, 308, 361, 362, 371, 372); Selj. 11th c. **Altun-taš** [امير اخر التونتاش], emir-aҳur of Melikšah (1072-1092) (Rāwandī 455); Selj. 11th c. **Altun-taš** [التون تا ش غلا م], mamluk of Melikšah (1072-1092), he fought against the assasins (Qazw. 518, 519); Selj. 1096 **Altun-taš** [التونتاش احو كربغا] (Ibn al-Athīr/Tornb. X, 176-77); Selj. 1113/14 **Altun-taš** [التونتاش], executed by Alp-arslan (Kamāladdīn: RHCHor 731); Selj. 1122 **Altun-taš** [التونتاش الابرى / Altoun-Tach el Abori], an emir (Ibn al-Athīr, Atab.: RHCHor II/2, 46); Selj. 1147 **Altun-taš** [التونتاش] (Qalānisi 289, 29); Selj.? 1147/48 **Altun-taš** [التونتاش], ruler of Sarkhad (Abū Šāma: RHCHor IV, 52-53); Maml. 1106 **Altun-taš** [صدقه التونتاش مملوك] (Ibn al-Athīr/Tornb. X, 284); Maml. 1280 **Altun-taš** [Schems-eddin-Altountasch], fought at Hims (Makrīzī II/1, 34); Maml. 14th c. **Altun-taš** [الطونتاش / Altuntaş] (Tarǰ/Houtsma 52, 83, Tarǰ/Toparlı 43); 1108, 1113 **Altun-taš, Altun-tegin?** [مودود بن / الطنتكين / الطنطاش] (Abulfidā III, 366-67, 378-79). ✧ 'Golden stone'. ⇨ **ALTÏN + TAŠ.**

ALTUŠ   Bashk. 1756 **Altuš** [Алтуш Васев] (MIB IV/1, 123).

ALURIS   Turk. 14th c. - 15th c.? **Aluris**, Karaman Beyi (Baştav 111).

ALWA   Kzk. 19th c. **Alva** [Алва], fem. (Grod. I, 98). ✧ 'Halva' cf. Kzk. *alwa* 'Žañγaq däninen qant ya bal qosïp istegen tätti tamaq' (QTTS), Turk. *helva* a sweet prepared in many varieties with sesame oil, various cereals, and syrup or honey' (TED) (<Ar.).

AM   Chuv. (<?Tat. / Bashk.) 1737 **Am-bala** [Амбалаевъ] (Alatyr. 135). ✧ 'Vulva' cf. Alt., Crm., Kirg., Kzk., Tat., Turk. *am* weibliche Scham' (Radl. I, 643). See also **AΓÏŠ-QALQAN-AM.**

АМАГ-TÖZÜN   Uyg. 13th-14th c. **Amaγ-tözün** (Zieme, Mat. II, 84). ✧ 'Amaγ-(the)-noble' cf. Uyg. *tözün* 'сдержанный, благородный' (DTS).

АМАГАČĀN see АВАГАČĀN

AMAY I.   Tat. 1720 **Amay** [Амай Кашаевъ] (PSZRI VI, 180). ⇨ **AM / AMA?** + dim. suff. *-ay / -y.*

AMAY II.   Yak. **Amay** [Амаі] (Pek.).

AMAQ   Tat. 1724 **Amaq / Amäk** [Амяк Битяков] (MIB III, 228); Kzk. 19th c. **Amaq-bay** [Амакбаевъ] (SKSO VIII, 230). ⇨ **AM / AMA?** + dim. suff. *-aq / -q.*

AMAL   Kzk. **Amal-bay** [Амалбай Тосаковъ] (Konšin, Mat. 26). ✧ 'Way, tool; craft, slyness' cf. Kirg., Kzk. *amal* 'ein Mittel, mit dessen Hülfe man etwas auszuführen vermag; List, Schlauheit, Gewandtheit' (Radl. I, 645) (<Ar.).

AMALDÏQ   Kzk. **Amaldïq** [Коджабай Амалдыковъ] (Sb. Syr-D. VI Galkin, Êtn. mat., 119); Kzk. 19th c. **Amaldïq** [Амалдык] (AOP 118); Kzk. 19th c. **Amaldïq** [Амолдык] (SOK 142); Kzk. **Amalduq** [Ходжабай Амалдуков] (Sb. Syr-D. III (otd. II), 61); Kzk. 19th c. **Amalduq** [Амалдукъ Джанбулаевъ] (Grod., Pril. 49); Kzk. 19th c. **Amalduq** [Джомартъ Амалдуковъ] (Grod., Pril. 49). ✧ 'Craft, slyness'. ⇨ **AMAL** + suff. *-dïq.*

AMALDUQ see AMALDÏQ

AMALÏQ   Uzb. 1600 **Amalïq / Amallïq?** [Амалыков Мурома], a man from Bukhara (Miller, Ist. Sib. II, 160). ✧ 'Craft, slyness'. ⇨ **AMAL** + dim. suff. *-ïq* or den. suff. *-lïq.* See also **AMALDÏQ.**

AMAN   Trkm. 20th c. **Aman** [Aman], fem. (Zaj. 1971, 341); Trkm. 20th c. **Aman** [Аман], fem. (TrkmRS 43); Chuv. 18th-19th c. **Aman** [Аманъ] (Magn. 27); Kzk. 1817 **Aman** [امان] (MIK IV, 311, 318); Kzk. 1846 **Aman** [Аман Таубаев], a Kazak biy (MKOP 157); Kzk. 19th c. **Aman** [Аман] (AOA 154); Kzk. 19th c. **Aman** [Аманъ], a Kazak biy (Lomakin 37); Kzk. 1870

Aman [Достан Аманов] (Grod., Pril. 128, 157); Kirg. Aman [Аман] (Jud. 352, 962); Uzb. 19th c. Aman [Суандык Аманов] (SKSO III, 156); Kkalp. 20th c. Aman / Aman-bay [Аманбай] (Bask., Kkalp. 37, KkRS 772); Trkm. 1828 Aman-bay [Аман-бай], from the Teke tribe (MIT II, 447); Kzk. Aman-bay [Аманбай] (Altyns. 94); Kzk. 1803 Aman-bay [امان بای] (MIK IV, 211); Kzk. 19th c. Aman-bay [Аманбай] (SOK 118); Kzk. 19th c. Aman-bay [Аманбай] (SKSO IV, otd. II, 34); Kzk. 19th c. Aman-bay [Аманбай] (Ljutš 115); Kzk. 19th c. Aman-bay [Аманбай] (AOK 34); Kzk. 19th c. Aman-bay [Аманбай] (AOA 46); Kzk. 19th c. Aman-bay [Аманбай] (AOP 26); Kirg. Aman-bay [Аманбай] (Jud. 515); Trkm. 1817 Aman-bay-yüzbašï [Аман-бай-юзбаши], a captain (MIT II, 400); Kzk. 19th c. Aman-bek [Аманбекъ] (SOV 158); Kzk. 19th c. Aman-ǰar [Аманджаръ Султанбаевъ] (Grod., Pril. 111); Trkm. 19th c. Aman-γul [Бажигулъ Амангулов] (Ščeglov IV, 189); Kzk. Aman-qul [Аманъ-кулъ] (ZIRGOÊtn. X, vyp. III, 30); Kkalp. 1804 Aman-qulï-biy [Аман-кули-бий] (MIT II, 364); Trkm. 1879 Aman-oγlï [Чоханъ-Аман-оглы] (Grod., Vojna IV, Grod., Pril. 109); *TN:* Kzk.? Aman-bay [Аманбай-соръ], a lake (Karta JAR IV). ✧ 'Healthy; sound, hale; safety' cf. Uyg., Az., Crm., Kzk., Tat., Turk. *aman* 'gesund, wohl, bei Wohlsein; Sicherheit, Schutz' (Radl. I, 643). See also AYT-AMAN, AQ-AMAN, ČEK-AMAN, ǰOL-AMAN, EL-AMAN, ESÄN-AMAN, KÖK-AMAN, QOS-AMAN, QUS-AMAN, MÜLK-AMAN, TÏL-AMAN.

AMAN-ATALÏ Trkm. 1881 Aman-atalï [Аман-Аталы] (Grod., Vojna IV, Grod., Pril. 18, 29). ✧ 'Healthy/sound teacher/guardian'. ⇨ AMAN + ATALÏ(Q)?

AMAN-BERDÏ Uzb. 20th c. Âmân-berdi [Омонберди] (Begmatov 1984, 202). ✧ 'Health gave him/her'. ⇨ AMAN + BERDÏ.

AMAN-ǰOL Kzk. 18th c. - 19th c. Aman-ǰol [Аманджол] (Tynyšp. 69); Kzk. 19th c. Aman-ǰol [Аман-Джолъ Сагаковъ] (Grod., Pril. 71); Kzk. 19th c. Aman-ǰol [Аманджол] (SOV 154); Kzk. 19th c. Aman-ǰol [Аманджол] (SOK 202); Kzk. 19th c. Aman-ǰol [Аманджол] (SODž. 144); Kzk. 20th c. Aman-žol [Аманжолов] (Bibl. izd. AN Kaz. SSR 1951-55. Alma-Ata, 1956, 171-172). ✧ 'Safe and sound road (life)!'. ⇨ AMAN + YOL. See also ǰOL-AMAN.

AMAN-DÄWLET Kzk. 18th c. - 19th c. Aman-däwlet / Aman-daulet? [Амандаулет] (Tynyšp. 75); Trkm. 1812 Aman-dewlet-bay [Аман Девлет-бай], from the Teke tribe (MIT II, 383, 391, 392).

AMAN-DUS Kzk. 19th c. Aman-dus [Амандусъ]

(SOK 160). ✧ 'Healthy friend/mate'. ⇨ AMAN + DOST.

AMAN-GELDÏ Bashk. 1798 Aman-geldi [Амангельди] (PSZRI XXV, 195); Kzk. 18th c. - 19th c. Aman-geldi [Амангельды] (Tynyšp. 72); Kzk. 19th c. Aman-geldi [Амангельды] (SOK 118); Kzk. 19th c. Aman-geldi [Амангельды] (AOO 10, 46); Kzk. 19th c. Aman-geldi [Аменгельды] (SOV 74); Kzk. 19th c. Aman-geldi [Амангельды] (SOV 20); Kzk. 19th c. Aman-geldi [Бейгавулъ Аманъ Гельдіевъ] (Grod., Pril. 79); Trkm. 1858 Aman-geldi-χan [Аман-гельды-хан], from the Kücik clan of the Yomut tribe (MIT II, 590); Trkm. 1859 Aman-geldi-šeyχ [Аманъ-Гельды-шейхъ] (ZIRGOÊtn. I, 195); Bashk. 1772 Aman-gildi [Амангильды Буляков] (MIB IV/2, 407); Uzb. 20th c. Âmân-keldi [Омонкелди] (Begmatov 1984, 202). ✧ 'He/she has come/been born healthy (or in good time); Arrived safe and sound'. ⇨ AMAN + KELDÏ.

AMAN-ΓUL see AMAN

AMAN-QUL see AMAN

AMAN-NÏYAZ Trkm. 19th c. Aman-niyaz [Шалдыбай Аманьязовъ] (Ščeglov I, 352); Kkalp. 20th c. Aman-niyaz [Аманияз] (KkRS 772); Trkm. 1879-1881 Aman-niyaz-qan (O'Donovan II, 216). ✧ 'Healthy alms/sacrifice'. ⇨ AMAN + NÏYAZ.

AMAN-TURDÏ Uzb. 20th c. Âmân-turdï [Омонтурди] (Begmatov 1984, 204). ✧ 'Healthy-lived'. ⇨ AMAN + TURDÏ.

AMANAQ Tat. 1544 Amanaq [Аманакъ (Омонакъ)], a prince in Kazan (PSRL (Russk. Hr.), 525). ✧ '(Dear little) Healthy'. ⇨ AMAN + dim. suff. *-aq / -q*.

AMANDEY see AMANTAY

AMANDÏ Bashk. 1600 Amandï [Беляк Амандынов] (Miller, Ist. Sib. II, 159); Kzk. 19th c. Amandï [Аманды] (SOV 36). ✧ 'Healthy'. ⇨ AMAN + suff. *-dï*.

AMANDÏQ see AMANLÏQ

AMANEY Chuv. 18th-19th c. Amaney [Аманей] (Magn. 27). ✧ '(Little dear) Healthy'. ⇨ AMAN + suff. *-ey*.

AMANKE Khorezm. Amanke (RaD II, 154). ✧ '(Little dear) Healthy'. ⇨ AMAN + suff. *-ke*.

AMANLÏQ Tat. 1600 Amandïq [Беляк (Белян) Амандыков] (MIB I, 152, Miller, Ist. Sib. II, 159); Kzk. 19th c. Amandïq [Амандыкъ], a Kazak biy (Lomakin 33); Kzk. 1785 Amanlïq [Аманлык] (MIK IV, 63); Kzk. 1823 Amanlïq [امانلق] (MIK IV, 457). ✧ 'Health' cf. Crm., Tat. *amanlïq* 'das Wohlsein' (Radl. I, 645). ⇨ AMAN + suff. *-lïq*.

AMANTAY Chuv. 18th-19th c. Amanday [Амандай] (Magn. 27); Chuv. 18th-19th c. Amandey [Амандей] (Magn. 27); Kzk. 19th c. Amantay [Амантай] (SOV

16, 124). ❖ '(Very) Healthy', '(Dear little) Healthy'
(Sattarov). ⇨ **AMAN** + suff. *-tay(1,2)*.

AMAR 1453 **Amar-bey** [Амарбей], a chieftain (PSRL
(Russk. Hr.), 451); Kzk. 19th c. **Amar-qul** [Амаркулъ]
(SOK 88). ❖ 'Quiet, lucky' cf. Mo. *amar* 'спокойный,
благополучный' (Bask., Fam. 19). ⇨ **OMAR?**

AMAR-ZANA see **AMÏR-SANĀ**

AMAŠ Bulg. 1351/52 **Amaš** [اعمش / А˝маш], fem.
(Jusupov 86, 87, (27)). See also **KÖK-AMAŠ**.

AMAT Alt. 19th-20th c. **Amat** [Амат] (OjrRS 207). ❖
'Fancy, dream' (OjrRS).

AMBÏ Uyg. 12th c. - 14th c. **Ambï** [ambi] (Radl., USp.
90, DTS).

AMEKEČ? Bashk. 1770 **Amekač / Ämekäč** [Амекач
Мурзаев] (MIB IV/1, 342).

AMEKEČ Bashk. 1738 **Amekeč / Ämekeč** [Амекеч]
(MIB I, 357). ❖ 'Little Old Woman'. ⇨? + suff. *-keč* /-
eč.

AMELEK Tat. 1624 **Amelek / Ämelek** [Андербышъ
Амелековъ] (Pokrovskij 71).

AMERČİ Kzk. 19th c. **Amerči** [Амерчи] (SOK 198).

AMГA Tuv. 19th c. **Amγa / Añba** [Амңa / Аңба]
(Proben IX, 142).

AMİ Bashk. 1762 **Ami** [Ами Кутлубаев] (MIB IV/1,
238).

AMİN see **EMİN**

AMİNDÏ Kzk. 19th c. **Amindï** [Аминды] (SOV 110).
❖ 'Trustworthy, honest'. ⇨ **AMİN** + suff. *-dï*.

AMÏŠ see **AMİŠ**

AMÏQAN Yak. **Amïqan** [Амыкан, Сынах Амыкан],
forefather of a Yakut clan (Pek.).

AMİN-QÏLAN Alt. 19th c. **Amïn-qïlan** [Амын-
Кылан] (Verb., In. 111). ❖ 'Quiet Klavdiy'? cf. Hak.
PN *Amin* 'spokojnyj' (Butanaev). ⇨ **AMİN** + **QÏLAN**.
See also **QÏSQA-QÏLAN, UZUN-QÏLAN**.

AMİR Alt. 19th-20th c. **Amïr** [Амыр] (OjrRS 207);
Tat.(GH) 1268, 1269, etc. **Amïr-χan** [Амраганъ /
Армаганъ / Аргаманъ / Амрагат / Мираган],
great basqaq (governor) of Vladimir (PSRL III, 61, V,
195, VII, 169, XXIII, 88, Bask., Fam. 19); Balk. 20th c.
Amur-χan / Amïr-χan, forefather of the Amurχalla
[Amur-χanlar] clan (Pröhle, Balk. 201). ❖ 'Quiet,
peace, resting' cf. Alt., Hak. *amïr* 'die Ruhe, der
Frieden, das Ausruhen, die Erholung' (Radl. I, 647), cf.
also Bask., Fam. 19.

AMİR-SANAГA see **AMÏR-SANĀ**

AMİR-SANĀ Alt. 19th c. **Amar-zana** [Амарзана сын
Конгдайча] (Verb., In. 117); Alt. 19th c. **Amïr-sanaγa**
[Амыр-Санага] (Verb., In. 122, 123); Alt. 19th c.
Amur-sana [Амурсана] (Verb., In. 120). ❖
'Quiet/peaceful reason/mind' It was the name of a
Kalmyk Khan from the 17th c. and an epic hero (Erol
II, Bask., Fam. 19). ⇨ **AMÏR** + **SANĀ**.

AMÏŠ Bashk. 1780 **Amiš** [Амиш Кучумов] (MIB V,

111); Kzk. 19th c. **Amïš-Jan** [Амышджанъ] (SOK
44). ❖ + dim. suff. *-š*.

AMRAN see **İMRÄN**

AMRATMÏŠ Uyg. 8th c. **Amratmïš-täñrim**, fem.
(Müller, Pfahl. 23). ❖ 'He/she made himself/herself
love'? cf. Uyg. *amra-* 'любить' (DTS).

AMU Türk / Uyg, 8th c. - 9th c. **Amu** [amu] (DTS). See
also **MAR-AMU**.

AMULJA Oghuz/Trkm. 13th c. **Amulja-χan** [املجهخان
/ Амулджа-хан], Tutek's son (?), Türk's grandson
(Abulg./Kon. 145). ❖ 'Quiet, peaceful' cf. Uyg. *amul*
'sanft, gelassen, ruhig' (Radl. I, 649) + suff. *-ja*.

AMUR see **AMİR**

AMUR-SANA see **AMÏR-SANĀ**

AMUT Kzk. 19th c. **Amut-pay** [Амутпай] (SOK 136).

AN Khorezm. / Tat.? 1380 **An-χoja** [Анхозя], a prince
from the Golden Horde (PSRL VIII, 42); Chuv. 18th-
19th c. **An-murza / Añ-murza?** [Анмурза] (Magn.
28). ❖ 'Mind, reason' cf. Az., Crm., Tat. *añ*
'Auffassungskraft, Geistesschärfe, Scharfsinn' (Radl. I,
183). See also **QARA-AN**.

AN-BAXTA Chuv. 18th-19th c. **An-baχta / An-baχtï?**
[Анбахта] (Magn. 28). ❖ 'Mind/reason has come / has
been born'? ⇨ **AN** + **BAXTÏ**. See also **AN-GİLDİ,
AN-TUГAN**.

AN-BAXTÏ see **AN-BAXTA**

AN-GİLDİ Chuv. 18th-19th c. **An-gildi (<Añ-gildi)**
[Ангилда] (Magn. 28). ❖ I. '(Lit.) Wild/game has
come; (fig.) child has been born' cf. Tat. PN *Añ-kilde*
(Sattarov), also Uyg., Alt., Hak., Kirg., Kzk. *añ* 'Wild,
jedes Thier auf das man Jagd macht; das Maral (cervus
maral)' (Radl. I, 183); II. 'Mind/reason has come'? ⇨
AN + **KELDİ**. See also **AN-BAXTA, AN-TUГAN**.

AN-İNEK Hak. 19th-20th c. **An-inek** [Анинек], fem.
(HRS 353). ⇨ **AN**.

AN-TUGAN Chuv. 18th-19th c. **An-tugan** [Антуганъ]
(Magn. 28). ❖ I. '(Lit.) Wild/game was born; (fig.)
child has been born' cf. Tat. PN *Añ-kilde* (Sattarov),
also Uyg., Alt., Hak., Kirg., Kzk. *añ* 'Wild, jedes Thier
auf das man Jagd macht; das Maral (cervus maral)'
(Radl. I, 183); II. 'Mind/reason has been born'? ⇨ **AN**
+ **TUГAN** I. See also **AN-BAXTA, AN-GİLDİ**.

AN-TURAQ Alt. 19th-20th c. **An-turaq** [Антурак]
(OjrRS 207). ⇨ **AN?** + **TURAQ**.

ANA Alt. 19th-20th c. **Ana** [Ана], fem. (OjrRS 211). ❖
Anna, Anya (<R. fem. PN < Old Hebr.).

ANA-GELDİ see **ANNA-KELDİ**

ANA-QUTLU 14th c. **Ana-qutlu** ['Αναχουτλου],
sobriquet of empress Anna of Trapezunt (1341-1343),
daughter of emperor Alexios II (Byz. Turc.). ❖ 'Anna-
(the)-Happy'. ⇨ **ANA** + **QUTLUГ**.

ANAČAQ Alt. 19th-20th c. **Anačaq** [Аначакj, fem.
(OjrRS 211). ❖ Anna, Anyuta (R.). ⇨ **ANA** +
suff. *-čaq*.

ANADOLU   Yürük 1543 **Anadolu** [اناطولی], several persons of Yürük origin in the same source (Gökb., Rum. 103, 176, 183, 185, 190, 204, 213); Tat. 1543 **Anadolu** [اناطولی] (Gökb., Rum. 236). ✧ 'Anatolia' (placename) (< Turk. < Gr.).

ΑΝΑΓΑΥ   Bulg. 576 **Anaγay** ['Ανάγαιος / 'Αναγαῖος], prince of the Utigurs (Byz. Turc. 97).

ANAQ   Alt. 19th-20th c. **Anaq** [Анак], fem. (OjrRS 211). ✧ Anka, Anna (R.).

ANAQÏ   Alt. 19th-20th c. **Anaqï** [Анакы], fem. (OjrRS 211). ✧ Anka, Anna (R.).

ANAQUŠ   576 **Anaquš** ['Αναγκάστης], a Turkic envoy (Byz. Turc. 69).

ANAL-JÏMA   Yak. **Anal-jïma / Anay-jïma** [Анал-цыма], a legendary girl (Pek.).

ANAR I.   Türk 7th c. - 9th c. **Anar** [anar] (DTS); Selj.? 1139/40 **Anar** [انر], ruler of Baalbek, a minister of Mohammed (Ibn al-Athīr, Atab.: RHCHor II/2, 104, 162, Kamāladdīn: RHCHor II, 261, 269, 272-274). ⇨ AÑĞAR?

ANAR II.   Kirg. 20th c. **Anar-bay** [Анарбай] (Kalilov 95); Kkalp. 20th c. **Anar-gül**, fem. (KkRS 777). ✧ 'Pomegranate (Punica granatum); Red birthmark' (Kalilov), cf. Chag., East.T.(Tar.) *anar* (P.) 'der Granatapfel' (Radl. I, 229).

ANARXAN   Kirg. **Anarχan** [Анархан], fem. (Jud. 139, 230, 754). ⇨ ANAR II. + suff. -χan(1).

ANAS I.   Selj. 12th c. **Anas-uγlï** [محمود انا سوغ لی], amīr-i-bār? (Rāwandī 364, 369). ⇨ ANAS I.

ANAS II.   Alt. 19th-20th c. **Anas** [Анас], fem. (OjrRS 211). ✧ Anastasia (R.).

ANAŠQÏ   Alt. 19th-20th c. **Anašqï** [Анашкы] (OjrRS 207). ✧ Ananiy (R.).

ANATQUS   Tat. 14th c. **Anatqus** ['Ανατκους], a christened Tatar, died in 1339 (Byz. Turc.).

ANBAMEŠ   Maml. 1264 **Anbameš-sadi**, an emir (Makrīzī II, 14).

ANBARJÏ   Khorezm. / Tat.(GH) 13th c. **Anbarjï** [Анбарджи], Meñgü Temür's son (RaD I/1, 120). ✧ 'Storekeeper' cf. Alt., Az., Crm., Kzk. *anbar* 'der Speicher' (Radl. I, 243) (<P.) + suff. -jï.

ANČAS   Hak. 19th-20th c. **Ančas** [Анчас], fem. (HRS 353).

ANČINEK   Hak. 19th-20th c. **Ančinek** [Анчинек] (HRS 348).

ANJAQ   Maml. 1313 **Anjaq** [انجاق] (Dawād. 275).

ANDÏ   Kzk. 18th c. - 19th c. **Andï-χoja** [Андыходжа] (Tynyšp. 73).

ANET   Kzk. 18th c. - 19th c. **Anet** [Анет] (Tynyšp. 68-69).

ANI   Kzk. 19th c. **Ani** [Ani], fem. (Levchine 356).

ANIŠ-XATA   Uyg. 13th c. - 14th c. **Aniš-χata / Āniš-qata?**, fem. (Chwol., Syr.-nest. 98, 142).

ANIŠ   Crm. **Aniš** [Аnышъ], a prince, envoy to/from (?) the Crimea (PSRL?). ⇨ YANÏŠ.

ANKA   Chuv. 18th-19th c. **Anka** [Анка] (Magn. 28).

ANNA see **ADÏNA**

ANNA-BERDÏ   Trkm. **Anna-berdi** [Анна-берди] (Sopieva: OSA 180); Trkm. 1768/69 **Anna-berdi** [Анна-берды], from the Salïr tribe (MIT II, 341); Trkm. 1770 **Anna-berdi-bek** [Анна-бердыбек] (MIT II, 342). ✧ 'Friday-gave (him/her) [=was born on Friday]'. ⇨ ADÏNA + BERDÏ.

ANNA-GELDÏ see **ANNA-KELDÏ**

ANNA-ĞURBAN   Trkm. **Anna-γurban** [Аннагурбан] (Sopieva: OSA 180). ✧ 'Friday-sacrifice'. ⇨ ADÏNA + QURBAN.

ANNA-KELDÏ   Trkm. 1859 **Ana-geldi** [Ана-Гельды] (ZIRGO I, 206); Trkm. **Anna-geldi** [Аннагелди] (Sopieva: OSA 180); Uzb. 20th c. **Anna-keldi** [Аннакелди] (Begmatov 1984, 202). ✧ 'Friday-came; Born on Friday'. ⇨ ADÏNA + KELDÏ.

ANNA-TURDÏ   Uzb. 20th c. **Anna-turdï** [Аннатурди] (Begmatov 1984, 204). ✧ 'Friday-lived/stayed'. ⇨ ADÏNA + TURDÏ.

ANNA-TUWAQ   Trkm. **Anna-tuwaq** [Аннатувак] (Sopieva: OSA 181). ✧ 'Friday - born in „shirt" [caul?]'. ⇨ ADÏNA + TUWAQ.

ANPANÏS   Hak. 19th-20th c. **Anpanis** [Анпанис] (HRS 348). ✧ Afanasiy (R.). See also **OXONŌSOY**.

ANSAQAY   Bashk. 1749 **Ansaqay** [Ансакай Байметев] (MIB III, 465).

ANTAY   Hak. 19th-20th c. **Antay** [Антай], fem. (HRS 353). ✧ 'Having soul; animated' cf. Butanaev: 'имеющий душу'.

ANUR-QAYA   Uyg. 13th-14th c. **Anur-qaya** [Anur Qaya] (Zieme, Mat. II, 91). ⇨ QAYA?

ANUŠ   Oghuz/Trkm. 13th c. **Anuš** [انوش / Ануш], Adam's grandson (Abulg./Kon. 80); Selj. 1096/97 **Anuš-tegin** [Ануштегин Гарча / Мухаммед ибн Ануштегинъ Кутб-ад-дин], father of Qutb ad-Dīn Muhammed (Ay-bek), the Khorezmshah (1097-1128) (MIT I, 384, 442). ✧ 'Faithful' (Abulg./Kon. 80).

ANUŠA   Chag. 17th c. **Anuša-χan** [Ануша-хан], ruler in Khiva (1663-1687) (Ivanov 81, 82). ⇨ ANUŠ + suff. -a.

ANZAQ   Uyg. 1332 **Anzaq** (Chwol., Syr.-nest. (NF) 28).

AÑ see **AN**

AÑ-QUWAT   Crm.Tat. 1506 **Añ-quwat** [Анкуватъ] (PSRL VI, 246). ✧ 'Mind/reason-strength/power' cf. Az., Crm., Tat. *añ* 'Auffassungskraft, Geistesschärfe, Scharfsinn' (Radl. I, 183). ⇨ QUWAT.

AÑĀRÏXSA   Yak. **Añārïχsa** [Анарыхса (тојон)], spirit of Mother-Earth (Pek.).

AÑĀTÏQÏ   Yak. **Xān-añātïqï-uol** [Анатыкы], son of Adaγalāχ Ala Būray-toyon, spirit (deity) of the underground world (Pek.).

AÑBA see **AMГА**

AÑČÏ Alt. 19th-20th c. **Añčï** (OjrRS 207). ✦ 'Hunter' cf. Uyg., Alt., Hak., Kirg., Kzk. *añ* 'Wild, jedes Thier auf das man Jagd macht; das Maral (Cervus Maral)' (Radl. I, 183) + suff. *-čï*.

AÑГAR Bashk. 1758 **Añγar** [Ангар Зиянов] (MIB IV/2, 20). ✦ 'Understand (!); Guess (it)!' cf. Bashk. *añγar-* / *añla-* 'понимать; догадываться' (BRS/Uraksin). ⇨ **ANAR I.?**

AÑГΪ Kirg. **Añγï-čal** [Аңгычал], Yoloy-qan's father, (Aq-)Sayqal's father (Proben V, 193 /194/, 394 /397/ etc.).

AÑÏRDAY Yak. **Añïrday** [Аңырдаі] (Pek.).

AÑÏRSÏYA Yak. **Añïrsïya** [Аңырсыја] (Pek.).

AÑQA Khorezm./Chag. 1412/13 **Añqa** [Анка], emir, ruler of Khorezm (MIT I, 531).

AÑQAS-TÖŠÄK Pecheneg / Kuman? **Añqas-töšäk** / **Añqaš-töšäk?** [Er Aŋkas Töšäk], found in an inscription of a metal mirror (Németh, Inschr. 22); Türk 7th-9th c. **Añqas-töšäk** / **Är-añqas-töšäk** [Er Ankas Töşek / Är Añqas Töşäk] (ETY II, 171). ⇨ **TÖŠÄK.**

APA Uyg. 10th c. **Apa** [A-po, X*â-pwâ], (title of) an envoy of the Uyghurs of Kan-tchou to the Chinese court in 935 (Hamilton, Ouïg. 146); Türk 8th c. **Apa-tarqan** [apa tarqan] (DTS). ✦ I. 'Father; Chief' Used also as a title and secondary component of male names. Cf. Karakh. *apa* III = *aba* II (DTS); II. 'Mother; Elder sister' Used also as a secondary component of female names. Cf. Uyg., Karakh. *apa* I 'старшая родственница, старшая сестра' (DTS), Kzk. *apa* 'старшая сестра, мать' (KzRS), cf. also Sev. See also **SÏRTUŠ-YEGEN-APA.**

APAČ Bashk. 1700 **Apač** [Апач Карсаковъ] (Vel.-Zern., Bašk. 35); Bashk. 1709 **Apač** [Бикей Опачев] (MIB I, 264); Bashk. 1709 **Apač** [Опачь], a mulla (MIB I, 264); Bashk. 1748 **Apač** [Апачевъ] (Nepljuev 437). ✦ 'Little mother; Little sister'. ⇨ **APA** + dim. suff. *-č*.

APAY Bashk. 1735 **Apay** [Каныкай Апаевъ], a tarχan (Vel.-Zern., Bašk. 17); Kzk. 18th c. - 19th c. **Apay** [Апай] (Tynyšp. 69); Tat. 1776 **Apey** / **Apay** [Апей Ибраевъ] (PSZRI XX, 456). ✦ 'Little father; little mother/sister'; 'Elder sister' cf. Bashk. *apay* 'старшая сестра; тёткаъ тётя; мачеха' (BRS/Uraksin), Kzk. *apay* 'сестра (при обращении к старшей)' (KzRS). ⇨ **APA** + suff. *-y*. See also **SART-APAY.**

APAQ Kzk. 19th c. **Afaq-χoJa** [Афакъ-Ходжа Иса-Ходжаевъ] (Grod., Pril. 170); Chuv. 18th-19th c. **Apak** [Апакъ] (Magn. 28); Tat. 1776 **Apaq** [Мамметко Апаковъ] (PSZRI XX, 457); Bashk. 1735 **Apaq** [Апакъ Лавлинъ], a tarχan (Vel.-Zern., Bašk. 21); Bashk. 1738 **Apaq** [Апак Зиянов] (MIB III, 383); Bashk. 1754 **Apaq** [Сабангул Апаков] (MIB IV/1, 83); Bashk. 1756 **Apaq** [Абтюк Апаков] (MIB IV/1, 122); Bashk. 1756 **Apaq** [Юрмакай Апаков] (MIB IV/1, 122); Bashk. 1756 **Apaq** [Артюк Апаков] (MIB IV/1, 107); Chag. 1558 **Apaq-bike** [Апак-бике], fem. (Ivanov 211); Chag. 16th c. - 17th c. **Apaq-χan** / **Afaq-χoJa** [Апак-хан] (Ivanov 77); Crm. 1519 **Apaq-murza** [Апакъ-мурза, Апакъ-князь] (PSRL XIII, 33); Chag. 1566 **Apaq-sultan** [Апак-султан], fem. (Ivanov 218); Hak. 19th-20th c. **Appaχ** [Аппах] (HRS 348); Kzk. 19th c. **Appaq** [Аппак] (Grod., Pril. 57); Kkalp. 20th c. **Appaq**, fem. (KkRS 777); Crm.Tat. 1518 **Appaq** [Аппакъ (Оппакъ)], envoy from the Crimea (PSRL VI, 263, VIII, 268, 269); Hak.(Blt.) 19th-20th c. **Appaq** / **Apaq** [Аппак/ Апак] (Proben IX, 357, 548). ✦ 'Quite White; Snow-white' cf. Kuman, Tat., Turk. *ap-aq* 'ganz weiss', Chag. *ap-aγ* 'id.' (Radl. I, 611), Turk. *apak* 'pure white, all white' (TED).

APAQA Tat. **Apaqa** ['Αποχα], a christened Tatar (Byz. Turc.). ✦ 'Uncle, grandfather, respected elderly man (as an address)' cf. Trk. *abaqa* / *awaqa* 'дядя (по отцу), дедушка, старик; почтенный! (обращение к старшему)' (Sev.), Yak. *abaγa* 'id.' (Pek.) (<Mo.).

APAL Kirg. **Apal** [Апал], fem. (Jud. 943); Kzk. 19th c. **Apal-bay** / **Opal-bay** [Опалбай] (SOK 264); Kzk. 19th c. **Apal-bay** / **Opol-bay** [Ополбай] (SOK 94).

APAN Bashk. 1735 **Apan** [Каникай Апановъ], a tarχan (Vel.-Zern., Bašk. 25); Kkalp. 1724 **Apan** [Апан Кайсаров] (MIKk. 181, 182); Kzk. **Opan** [Опан], fem. (Proben III, 38).

APANAY Tat. 20th c. **Apanay** [Bahruddin Apanaev] (Mende 69); Tat. 20th c. **Apanay** [Abdullah Apanaev (Müderris)] (Mende 99, 102, 103); Bashk. 1757 **Apanay** [Киязь Апанаев] (MIB IV/1, 142); Bashk. 1757 **Apanay** [Нияз Апанаев] (MIB IV/1, 142); Bashk. 1761 **Apanay** [Апанаев], a prince (MIB IV/1, 204). ✦ I. 'Dear little elder sister/brother' (Sattarov); II. 'Afanasiy' (R. < Gr.) (Sattarov). ⇨ **APA** + suff. *-nay*.

APAR Kzk. 19th c. **Apar-bek** [Апарбекъ] (SOK 74); Chag. 1557 **Apar-bike** [Апар-бике], fem. (Ivanov 199). ✦ 'Gracious, kind-hearted' cf. Kzk. *apar* 'gnädig, gütig' (Radl. I, 613) (<Ar.).

APAS Tat. 1686 **Apas** [Апасевъ] (Kungursk. akty 70); Bashk. 1664 **Apas** [Апас] (MIB I, 184); Bashk. 1729 **Apas** [Бекей Апасев] (MIB III, 260); Bashk. 1734 **Apas** [Кудашъ Апасевъ], a tarχan (Vel.-Zern., Bašk. 11); Bashk. 1735 **Apas** [Апасевъ Епановъ], a tarχan (Vel.-Zern., Bašk. 15); Bashk. 1754 **Apas** [Муртаза Апасев] (MIB IV/1, 79); Kzk. 19th c. **Apas** [Апасъ] (SOK 146); Bashk. 1734 **Apas(-mulla)** [Апас мулла Тютеев] (MIKk. 205); *TN:* Bashk. 1792 **Apas** [Халил Апасев], a man from a village called Apaseva (MIB V, 559). ✦ I. 'Elder male relative, brother' (Sattarov); II. Ar. Abbas (according to Sattarov), meaning 'one who frowns a lot' (Ahmed). ⇨ **ABA** + dim.-hypoc. *-ač / -as*.

APČA Hak. 19th c. **Apča** [Апча] (Katanov, Otč. 12). ✧ I. 'Old man' cf. Hak. *Apčay* 'id.' (Butanaev); II. 'Flatterer'? cf. Alt. *apčï* 'der Schmeichler' (Radl. I, 617).

APČAX see **APČAQ**

APČAY Hak. 19th-20th c. **Apčay** [Апчай] (HRS 348); Hak.(Kacha) **Apčay** [Апчаi] (Proben IX, 613). ✧ 'Old man' cf. Hak. *Apčay* 'id.' (Butanaev).

APČAQ Hak. 19th-20th c. **Apčaχ** [Апчах] (HRS 348); Karg. **Apčaq** [Апчак] (Katanov, Otč. 8, 9). ✧ 'Old man, bear' cf. Hak.(Sag.) *apčaq* 'id.' (Radl. I, 617).

APČAN Kzk. 19th c. **Apčan-bay** [Апчанбай] (SODž. 148). ⇨ **APA** + **ǰAN?**

APČANAY Hak. 19th-20th c. **Apčanay** [Апчанай] (HRS 348). ✧ 'Fortune-teller, magician' cf. Hak. PN *Apčïnay* 'id.' (Butanaev).

APČIŠKE Hak. 19th-20th c. **Apčiške** [Апчишке] (HRS 348).

APEY see **APAY**

APENDİ Kirg. **Apendi** [Апенди] (Jud. 746). ✧ 'Odd person'.

APİŠ Bashk. 1756 **Apiš** [Апиш Мангушев] (MIB IV/1, 107); Kzk. 19th c. **Apiš** [Апишъ] (AOK 14).

APİZA Kirg. **Apiza** [Апиза], fem. (Jud. 212). ✧ Fem. form of *Apiz < Abïz* (<Ar. Hafiz). ⇨ **ABİZ.**

APÏYAN Alt. 19th-20th c. **Apïyan** [Апыян] (OjrRS 207).

APÏR Kzk. 19th c. **Apïr-bay** [Апырбай] (SOK 20).

APKİŠEY Bashk. 1757 **Apkišey** [Апкишей Кивя(г)улов] (MIB IV/1, 134). ⇨ **APA** + **KİŠİ?** + suff. *-y*.

APQA Tat. 18th c. **Apqa** [Исмаилъ Апкинъ] (Nepljuev 882). ⇨ **APAQA / APA** + suff. *-qa*.

APQAY Bashk. 1749 **Apqay** [Апкай Мурзанаев] (MIB III, 471). ⇨ **APAQA / APQA** + dim. suff. *-y*.

APPA Turk. **Appa-oγlu**, a Zeybek (Kúnos 1891, 119). ✧ 'Grandfather' cf. Turk. dial. *abba / appa* 'dede, büyükbaba' (DS).

APPAΓAŠ Alt. 19th c. **Appaγaš** (Katanov, Otč. 12). ✧ 'Snow-white' cf. Hak. PN *Appaγas* 'id.' (Butanaev), Alt.(Tel.), Shor *ap-aγaš* 'id.' (Radl. I, 611). See also **APAQ.**

APPAΓÏYĀN Yak. **Appaγïyān** [Аппаҕыjан] (Pek.).

APPAX see **APAQ**

APPAY Tat. 1524, 1529, 1532 **Appay** [Аппай], a soldier (armed with lance) from Kazan (PSRL VI, 264, VIII, 271, 273, 283, XIII, 44). ⇨ **APAY.**

APPAYĀN Yak. **Appayān** [Аппайэн] (Pek.).

APPAYÏS Yak. **Appayïs** [Аппаjыс] (Pek.).

APPĀSAY Yak. **Appāsay** [Аппэсаi] (Pek.).

APPÏS Tat.(Tob.) / Tuv.? 19th c. **Appïs** [Аппыс], byname of a muslim called Abbas (Proben IX, 213).

APRİN Uyg. **Aprin-čor** [Aprin-çor] (EUTS).

APSALAY Hak. 19th-20th c. **Apsalay** [Апсалай] (HRS 348). ✧ Derived from *Apsal* '?' (Butanaev) + suff. *-ay*.

APSALQA Hak. 19th-20th c. **Apsalqa** [Апсалка] (HRS 348). ✧ Derived from *Apsal* '?' (Butanaev) + suff. *-qa*.

APSİLEY Alt. 19th-20th c. **Apsiley** [Апсилей] (OjrRS 207). ✧ Vasiliy (R.).

APSOY Hak. 19th-20th c. **Apsoy** [Апсой] (HRS 348).

APT Kzk. 18th c. - 19th c. **Apt-qul** [Апткул] (Tynyšp. 71). ✧ The shortened(-contracted) form of Ar. Abdurrashid (cf. Radl. I, 616).

APTAQ Bashk. 1776 **Aptaq** [Зиякай / Жиякай Аптаков] (MIB V, 39, 41).

APTAL Bashk. 1744 **Aptal** [Аптал Тохтаров] (MIB III, 415); Bashk. 1761 **Aptal** [Мурат Апталов] (MIB IV/1, 209). ✧ 'Hero, strong man' cf. Uyg. *aptal* 'ein Held, Starker' (Radl. I, 615) (<Ar.).

APTAP-BERGEN Kzk. 1817 **Aptap-bergen** [بيركان افتاب / Аптапберген] (MIK IV, 313, 319). ✧ 'Sunlight gave him/her' cf. Chag., Kirg., NUyg.(Tar.), etc. *aptap* 'der Sonnenschein' (Radl. I, 616) (<P.).

APTAS Kzk. 1862 **Aptas** [Аптасъ] (ZIRGOGeogr. I, 311).

APTEKE Kzk. **Apteke** [Аптäкä] (Radl. I, 616). ⇨ **APT** + comp. *-ake*.

APTİK Hak. 19th-20th c. **Aptik / Aptïk** [Аптик] (Proben IX, 554, HRS 348). ✧ 'Flatterer' cf. Hak.(Sag.), Shor *aptïγ* 'schmeichelnd' (Radl. I, 616).

APTİKEY see **ABDİKEY**

APTİSQA Hak. 19th-20th c. **Aptisqa** [Аптиска] (Proben IX, 557, HRS 348). ✧ 'Charming, enchanter' cf. Hak. *Aptis* 'id.' (Butanaev) + suff. *-qa*.

APTÏL Tat.(Tob.) **Aptïl** [Аптыл], byname of a muslim called Abdul (Proben IX, 121, 124, 174).

APTRAQ Bashk. 1763 **Aptraq** [Аптрак Явгачтын] (MIB IV/2, 45); Bashk. 1763 **Aptraq** [Кисяпай Аптраков] (MIB IV/2, 45). ✧ 'Wonderer, confused, embarrassed' cf. Tat.(Tob.) *aptraq* 'eilig' (Radl. I, 617) + suff. *-q*.

APUQ Bashk. 1777 **Apuq** [Апук Азигулов] (MIB V, 59).

APUŠQA Tat.? 1668 **Apušqa** [Апушкинъ] (Kungursk. akty 2). ⇨ **ABİŠ?** + suff. *-qa*.

AR Hak. 19th-20th c. **Ar-bača** [Арбача] (Katanov, Otč. 13); Kzk. 19th c. **Ar-kül / Ar-qul?** [Аркӱль], in a legend of origin (Potanin, Pred. 56); Kzk. 19th c. **Ar-qul** [Аркулъ] (SOV 12). ✧ I. 'Male, man'?; II. 'Votyak' cf. Tat. *ar* 'der Wotjake' (Radl. I, 244). ⇨ **ER?**

AR-GİLDİ Chuv. 18th-19th c. **Ar-gildi** [Аргилды] (Magn. 29); Bashk. 1740 **Ar-gildi** [Аргилды Бурсукаев] (MIB I, 445). ✧ 'Man/hero has come'. ⇨ **AR / ER** + **KELDİ.**

AR-YARUQ Oghuz/Trkm. 1038 **Ar-yaruk / Ār-yaruq**

[Арьярук] (MIT I, 277). ✧ 'Man/hero - Bright(ness)'.
⇨ ER + YARUQ.

AR-KİL Kzk. 19th c. **Ar-kil** [Аркилъ] (SODž. 106). ✧
'Man/hero - be born!'. ⇨ AR/ER + KEL?

AR-SARÏ see **ER-SARÏ**

AR-TEGİN see **ER**

AR-TUGAN Chuv. 18th-19th c. **Ar-tugan** [Артуганъ]
(Magn. 29). ✧ 'Man/hero - was born!'. ⇨ ER +
TUГAN I.

ARA I. Tat. 1555 **Ara** [Apa], a prince (DAI I, 129);
Tuv. 19th c. **Ara-mergen** [Ара-мергенъ], a hunter
(Potanin IV, 596). ✧ I. 'Adornment, ornament' cf.
Chag. *ara* 'Putz, Zierde' (Radl. I, 248); II. 'Bee'? cf.
Kzk. *ara* 'die Biene' (Radl. I, 248); III. '?' cf. Uyg. *ara*
II. / ara ara, a proper name (<Skr.) (DTS).

ARA II. Kirg. 20th c. **Ara-bay** [Арабай] (Kalilov 92).
✧ 'Saw' (Kalilov) cf. Kirg., Kzk. *ara* 'die Säge' (Radl.
I, 248), Kirg. *arā* 'пила' (Jud.) (< P.).

ARA-BUQA Uyg. **Ara-buγa** [Ara Buġa] (EUTS); Uyg.
12th c. - 14th c. **Ara-buqa** [ara buqa] (Radl., USp. 14,
DTS). ✧ I. 'Ara-bull' (Blagova 1997, 706); II. 'Saw-
bull'? ⇨ ARA I. / ARA II.? + BUQA.

ARA-QAYA Uyg. 13th-14th c. **Ara-qaya-ïnal** (Zieme,
Mat. II, 91). ✧ I. '?-rock'; II. 'Saw-rock'? ⇨ ARA I. /
ARA II.? + QAYA.

ARA-TEMÜR Khorezm. 1291 **Ara-temür** [ارا تيمور]
/ ارا تيمور] (RaD/Jahn 28); Uyg. 12th c. - 14th c. **Ara-
temür / Ara-tämür** [ara temür / Ara Tämür] (Radl.,
USp. 6, EUTS, DTS); Khorezm.? 14th c. **Ara-temür /
Ara-timur** [Ara-Temür Ba'urchi / Ара-тимур], a
steward, a member of the Jüri'et or Jeü'ret, a clan of the
Taichi'ut, was a chiliarch father of Shirin, a concubine
of Abaqa, served under Ghazan (1295-1304) in the
latter's campaigns against Nauruz while viceroy of
Khurāsān (RaD I/1, 192, Boyle, Archers 34). ✧ 'Saw-
iron (=saw)' cf. Kirg., Kzk. *ara temir* 'die Säge' (Radl.
I, 248). ⇨ ARA II. + TEMİR.

ARAJÏN Hak.(Koyb.) 19th c. **AraJïn** [Араджынъ],
fem. (Katanov, Otč. II, 12-15). ✧ 'Drunk, intoxicated'
(Katanov).

АRAГA Karg. **Araγa** [Apaҕa], fem. (Katanov, Otč. 8).
✧ 'Wine' (Katanov).

ARAYİŠ Turk. 15th c. **Arayiš-beygüm** [Arayiş
Beygüm], İskender Mirza's daughter (Uzunçarş., Anad.
62). ✧ 'Good-looking wife of the beg'.

ARAQ Kzk. 19th c. **Araq-pay** [Аракпай] (SOK 12);
Kzk. 19th c. **Araq-pay** [Аракпай] (SODž. 70). ✧
'Brandy'.

ARAQAY Bashk. 1723 **Araqay** [Аракай Бекчюрин]
(MIB III, 219); Bashk. 1731, 1742 **Araqay** [Аракай
Акбашев] (MIB III, 293, 512); Bashk. 1742 **Araqay**
[Аракай Байсланов] (MIB III, 520); Bashk. 1742
Araqay [Аракай Кусюккулов] (MIB I, 486); Bashk.
18th c. **Araqay** [Аракай] (Nepljuev 193). ⇨ ARA I. /

ARA II.? + dim. suff. *-qay*.

ARAL Kzk. 1822 **Aral** [ارال] (MIK IV, 416, 417); Kzk.
19th c. **Aral** [Арал] (Grod., Pril. 176); Kzk. 19th c.
Aral [Тилавберген Аралов] (Grod., Pril. 139); Uzb.
1695 **Aral** [Аралъ], khan in Khiva (DAI X, 384); Kzk.
Aral-bay [Аралбаи] (Proben III, 79); Kzk. 1732 **Aral-
bay** [Аралбай] (Dobrosm., Turg. 10); Kzk. 1734 **Aral-
bay** [Aralbaï] (Levchin (?=Levšin) 155, 172); Kzk.
1734 **Aral-bay** [Аралбай] (PSZRI IX, 303); Kzk. 18th
c. - 19th c. **Aral-bay** [Аралбай] (Tynyšp. 71); Kzk.
19th c. **Aral-bay** [Арасланъ Аралбаевъ] (Grod., Pril.
163); Kzk. 19th c. **Aral-bay** [Аралбай] (SOV 90);
Kzk. 19th c. **Aral-bay** [Аралбай] (AOK 30); Kzk. 19th
c. **Aral-bay** [Аралбай] (AOAtb. 58); Kzk. 19th c.
Aral-bay [Аралбай] (AOP 90); Kzk. 19th c. **Aral-bay**
[Аралбай] (AOO 10); Kzk. 19th c. **Aral-bay**
[Аралбай] (SODž. 158); Kzk. 19th c. **Aral-bay**
[Аралбай] (SOK 72, 228); Kzk. 19th c. **Aral-bay**
[Аралбай] (SKSO III, 8); Kzk. 19th c. **Aral-bay**
[Аралбай] (SKSO III, 8); Kzk. 19th c. **Aral-bay**
[Аралбай] (Pam. kn. Turg. 58); Kkalp. 20th c. **Aral-
bay** [Аралбай] (KkRS 772); Uzb. 19th c. **Aral-bay**
[Аралбай] (SKSO III, 158); Kzk. 19th c. **Aral-bek**
[Аралбекъ] (SODž. 58); Uzb. 1875 **Aral-biy** [Аралъ-
Бій] (Moskal'cev 40); Kkalp.? 1696 **Aral-χan**
[Аралхан] (MIKk. 151); Bashk.? Kzk. 18th c. **Aral-
murza** [Аралъ-Мурза] (Nepljuev 804); *TN:* Bashk.?
Aral-bay [Аралбаева], a village in the Ural (Karta
JAR III); *TN:* Kzk. **Aral-bay** [Аралъ-бай], a place
south of Karkaralinsk (ZIRGOGeogr. I (Karta Oz.
Balhaša)); *TN:* Kzk. 19th c. **Aral-bay** [Аралъ-бай], a
field (AOO 62). ✧ 'Isle (in a river)', Lake Aral or the
name of a tribe, cf. Alt., Kirg., Kzk. *aral*
'Weidengebüsch am Ufer der Flüsse; mit Buschwerk
bedeckte Inseln im Flusse', Chag. *aral* 'Insel; Name
eines Stammes; der Aral-See' (Radl. I, 252). See also
ÜŠ-ARAL.

ARALČİ NUyg. 19th c. **Aralči / Aralči** [ارالچى /
Aralchi] (Le Coq, Namenl. 94). ✧ 'Islander'. ⇨ ARAL
+ suff. *-či.*

ARALГÏ Kzk. 19th c. **Aralγï** [Аралгы] (SOV 108).

ARALÏ Kzk. 19th c. **Aralï-bay** [Аралыбай] (AOP 46).
⇨ ARA II.? + suff. *-lï.*

ARAMSĀR Hak. 19th-20th c. **Aramsār** [Арамсар],
fem. (Katanov, Otč. 11, Proben IX, 557); Hak. 20th c.
Aramsār [Арамсар] (HRS 348). ✧ 'Premature (child)'
cf. Hak. *Aramzar* 'id.' (Butanaev).

ARAN Alt. 19th c. **Aran-tayči** [Аран-Тайчи] (Verb.,
In. 140, 141, 145, 147, 154); Hak. 19th-20th c. **Aran-
tayJï** (Radl. III, 1232). ✧ 'Wealthy' (Butanaev).

ARANAY Alt. 19th c. **Aranay** [Аранай и Шаранай,
Аранай-Чаранай], two brothers (Nikiforov 3, Potanin,
Pred. 180). ✧ 'Little wealthy'. ⇨ ARAN + dim.

suff. -*ay*.

ARAP I. Khorezm. 14th c. **Arap** [Араб] (RaD I/1, 175); Khorezm. 14th c. **Arap**, Samqur's son (RaD I/1, 120); Yürük 1543 **Arap** (Gökb., Rum. 214); Yürük 1543 **Arap** (Gökb., Rum. 202, 214); Kzk. 19th c. **Arap** [Арагъ] (SODž. 116); Kzk. 19th c. **Arap** [Арапъ] (SOK 30); Turk. 1485 **Arap-hoja** [Arab Hoca] (Gökb., Ed. 171); Turk. 1490 **Arap-qadï** [Arab Kadı] (Gökb., Ed. 155); Turk. 1689 **Arap-paša** [Арапъ паша] (Stojanović, St. s. r. i l., 275); Tat.(GH)? 1176, 1177 **Arap-ša** [Арапша], a prince of the (Golden) Horde (PSRL IV, 73, V, 236, VIII, 25-26, XI, 27, XVI, 104, XXIII, 120-121); Oghuz/Trkm. 13th c. **Arap-šaχ**, a Šeybanid (Abulg./Desm. 194). ✧ 'Arab' cf. Uyg., Chag., Kzk., Tat., Turk. *arap* 'id.' (Radl. I, 261).

ARAP II. Hak. 19th-20th c. **Arap** [Арап] (HRS 348). ✧ Arefiy (R.) (Butanaev) < Ar. *harata*.

ARAPÏANA Yak. 20th c. **Arapïana** [Арапына / Арапыана / Күн Өрөпүнä-хотун (Чуонах)], a woman of Russian origin turned into an evil spirit (üör) after her death in the 19th c. (Pek.). ✧ Agrippina (R.).

ARAPÏNA Yak. 20th c. **Arapïna** [Арапына / Арапыана / Күн Өрөпүнä-хотун], a woman of Russian origin turned into an evil spirit (üör) after her death in the 19th c. (Pek.). ✧ Agrippina (R.).

ARAPTAN Bashk. 1745 **Araptan** [Калкан Араптанов] (MIB III, 426); Bashk. 1754 **Araptan** [Араптан Кулчюгулов] (MIB IV/1, 84); Bashk. 1754 **Araptan** [Араптан Кулчюков] (MIB IV/1, 83); Bashk. 1763 **Araptan** [Араптан Улекеев] (MIB IV/1, 267); Bashk. 1764 **Araptan** [Араптан Улекеев] (MIB IV/1, 277); Bashk. 1770 **Araptan** [Калкаман Араптанов] (MIB IV/1, 341); Bashk. 1780 **Araptan** [Бахтияр Араптанов] (MIB V, 117); Bashk. 1789 **Araptan** [Баскун Араптанов] (MIB V, 272); Bashk. 1794 **Araptan** [Токсанбай Араптанов] (MIB V, 338); Bashk. 1798 **Araptan** [Араптанов] (PSZRI XXV, 198).

ARAS see **ORAZ**

ARAS-GELDİ see **ARAZ-GELDİ**

ARASLAN see **ARSLAN**

ARASTULLA Uzb. **Arastulla** [Арастулла Бойалиев] (Rahimov: OSA 184-185). ✧ 'Aristoteles' (Tadjik-Persian form of the ancient Greek name).

ARAŠ-BUΓA Oghuz 1327 **Araš-buγa** [ارش بغا], Abusaid's (1316-1335) envoy to Cairo (Abulfidā V, 374-75). ✧ '?-Bull'. ⇨ ? + **BUQA.**

ARAZ see **ORAZ**

ARAZ-BERDİ Trkm. (Yomud) **Araz-berdi** [Аразберди] (Sopieva: OSA 179). ✧ 'Chance/luck has him/her given'. ⇨ **ORAZ + BERDİ.**

ARAZ-DURDÏ Trkm. (Yomud) **Araz-durdï** [Араздурды] (Sopieva: OSA 179). ✧ 'Chance/luck has stayed/remained'. ⇨ **ORAZ + TURDÏ.**

ARAZ-DURSUN Trkm. (Yomud) **Araz-dursun** [Араздурсун], fem. (Sopieva: OSA 179). ✧ 'May the chance/luck stay/remain'. ⇨ **ORAZ + TURSÏN.**

ARAZ-GELDİ Kzk. 1734 **Aras-geldi-batïr** (Levchin 155, 172); Trkm. (Yomud) **Araz-geldi** [Аразгелди] (Sopieva: OSA 179). ✧ 'Chance/luck has come/been born'. ⇨ **ORAZ + KELDİ.**

ARAZ-TUWAQ Trkm. (Yomud) **Araz-tuwaq** [Аразтувак], fem. (Sopieva: OSA 179). ⇨ **ORAZ + TUWAQ.**

ARAZAN Uyg. **Arazan** [Arazan] (EUTS).

ARBAB-DOST Uzb. 1740 **Arbab-dost** [Арбабъ-Достъ], from Khiva (Hanykov, Poezdka 21). ✧ 'Respected friend' cf. Chag. *arbab* 'hoher Staatsbeamter, Vorsteher; ein (alter) ehrwürdiger Mensch' (Radl. I, 338), Uzb. *arbâb* 'деятель; видное лицо; старостаъ старшина селения или городского квартала (в Бухарском ханстве)' (UzbRS). ⇨ **DOST.**

ARBALYÏN Yak. **Arbalyïn / Ān-arbalyïn / Duon-arbalyïn** [Арбалјын], names of abāsï-shamans (Pek.).

ARBAN Kzk. 19th c. **Arban-batïr** [Арбанъ-батыръ] (Potanin II, 177).

ARBAR Khorezm./Chag. 14th c. **Arbar-aγa**, princess, Timur's wife (Clavijo 52).

ARBÏY see **ALTÏN-ARBÏY**

ARBÏS Hak. 19th-20th c. **Arbïs-qan** [Арбыс-кан] (Radl. II, 105). ✧ 'Having good-luck charm' (Butanaev), cf. Alt.(Tel.) *arbïš* 'die Zauberei, das Besprechen (von Krankheiten)' (Radl. I, 338).

ARBUZ Kuman 13th c., 1289 **Arbuz**, a Kuman notability in Hungary (SRH I, 474, II, 45); Chuv. 1737 **Arbuz** [Арзубъ Янгильдинъ] (Alatyr. 136); Chuv. 18th-19th c. **Arbuz** [Арбузъ] (Magn. 29); Turk. 1485 **Arbuz-ata** (Gökb., Ed. 195). ✧ 'Watermelone' cf. Rásonyi, NTK 79-84, Rásonyi, KÖA 80-81, Rásonyi, Anthr. 136, Erol II.

ARCÏBAŠ see **ARTÏ-BAŠ**

ARČA Kzk. 19th c. **Arča-bay** [Арчабай] (SODž. 126); Kzk. 19th c. **Arča-bek** [Арча-бекъ] (SOV 100); Trkm. 1881 **Arča-sardar** [Арча-сардаръ] (Grod., Pril. 18, Grod., Vojna IV). ✧ 'Pine, juniper' cf. Chag. *arča* 'id.' (Radl. I, 328), Trkm. *arča* 'арча, можжевельник' (TrkmRS).

ARČİ Uzb. 19th c. **Arči-bay** [Арчибай] (SKSO III, 182). ⇨ **ARČA?**

ARČİM Alt. 19th-20th c. **Arčim** [Арчим] (OjrRS 207). ✧ Artem (R. Артём).

ARČÏMAQ Alt. **Arčïmaq** [Арчымак], fem. (Katanov, Otč. 8). ✧ 'Saddlebag' (Katanov), cf. Alt. *arčïmaq* 'grosse Packsäcke' (Radl. I, 324).

ARČUQ Uyg. 13th c. **Arčuq** [arčuq] (DTS). ⇨ **AR +** suff. -*čuq.*

ARČUNİ Uyg. **Arčuni** [Arçuni] (EUTS).

ARJAÑĀTTA Yak. **Arjañatta** [Арцанатта] (Pek.).

ARJAWU Bulg. 1320/21 **Arjawu** [ارجو] (Epigr. Bulg. 140-141).

ARJĬ Tuv. 19th c. **Arjĭ-paqšĭ** [Арц-пакшы], a teacher (Proben IX, 11). ⇨ **AR?** + suff. *-jĭ*.

ARDA Uyg. 12th c. - 14th c. **Arda** [arda] (Radl. I, 319, DTS); Kzk. 19th c. **Arda-bay** [Ардабай] (SOK 250); Kzk. **Arda-bĭ** [Арда бі], a folklore hero, Aq-jūnus' son (Proben III, 166); *TN:* Turk. **Arda**, a village in the province of Giresun, Turkey (Köyl.). ✧ 'Become worse! Decay!' (Bese 11), cf. *arda- / arta-* 'портиться, ухудшаться' (DTS).

ARDAJĬQ Maml. 1321 **Ardajĭq** [ارد اجق / Ардаджукъ] (Duqmaq/Tizeng. I, 321, 328). ✧ 'Little Arda'. ⇨ **ARDA** + dim. suff. *-jĭq*.

ARDAQAY Bashk. 18th. c. **Ardaqay** [Ардакай] (MIB V, 199). ✧ I. 'Little Arda'. ⇨ **ARDA** + suff. *-qay*.

ARDĬ Kzk. 19th c. **Ardĭ-bay** [Ардибай] (Grod., Pril. 123); Tat. 1809 **Ardĭ-bey** [Арди бей] (PSZRI XXX, 888). ✧ '(Grew) tired'.

ARDRAMAR Tat.? 1739 **Ardramar / Ardïramar?** [Ардрамаровъ] (Alatyr. 143). ✧ 'Doesn't (won't) grow tired'.

ARÄMÄN Bashk. 1756 **Arämän** [Арямян Тевлетьчюрин] (MIB IV/1, 122).

AREFE Turk. 1583 **Arefe** [عرفه] (Ongan, Ank. I, 152). ✧ 'Born before the festive day Bayram' (Ar.).

ARGANDEY Chuv. 18th-19th c. **Argandey** [Аргандей] (Magn. 29).

ARGĬ Chuv. 18th-19th c. **Argi-bey** [Аргибей] (Magn. 29). ⇨ **ARGÏ?**

ARΓAČĬ Alt. **Arγačĭ** [Аргачи] (Nikiforov 235). ✧ 'Ingenious, sly'.

ARΓAJAQ Hak.(Koyb.) 19th c. **Arγajaq** [Аргаджакъ], fem. (Katanov, Otč. II, 12-15). ✧ 'Originating from the folk' (Katanov).

ARΓAMAQ Bashk. 1738 **Arγamaq** [Дусмекей Аргамаков] (MIB III, 379); *TN:* Bashk. 1729 **Arγamaq** [Аргамаково], a village (MIB III, 259). ✧ 'Famous and expensive sort of Asiatic saddle-horses' (Bask., Kkalp.; Bask., Fam. 109).

ARΓAN Selj. 1120, 1139 **Arγan** [ارغان], an emir, the χājib of Sultan Maχmud II (1118-1131) (Rāwandī 204, Ahbar 77, 78); Kzk. 19th c. **Arγan-bay** [Аргамбай] (SOV 56); *TN:* Kzk. **Arγan-bay** [Кол. Арган-бай (пр.)], a colony? (Karta JAR X).

ARΓAS Alt. **Arγas** (Katanov, Otč. 8). ✧ 'Laziness (plus) slyness' cf. Alt.(Tel.), Hak. *arγās* 'Faulheit und Schlauheit' (Radl. I, 298).

ARΓAŠ Oghuz/Trkm. 1162 **Arγaš** [Аргаш], an emir (MIT I, 401). ⇨ **ARΓÏŠ?**

ARΓÏ Khorezm. 1300 **Arγï** [بن كيتبوقا / ارغى پسزقونجى], mentioned in Ghazan's (1295-1304)

military expedition to Syria in 1300, by order of the Khan he protected the citizens of Damascus (RaD/Jahn 129). ✧ '?' (<Mo.?).

ARΓÏL Tat.(Tara) **Arγïl** [Argyl / Арвыл] (Proben IV, 129 /166/).

ARΓÏM-BAY see **ARΓÏN**

ARΓÏMAY Alt. 19th-20th c. **Arγïmay** [Аргымай] (OjrRS 207). ✧ 'Saddle-horse of good breed'.

ARΓÏN Bashk. 1784 **Arγïm-bay** < **Arγïn-bay** [Аргымбай Мунгашев], a yasaul (commander) (MIB V, 154, 156); Kzk. 19th c. **Arγïm-bay** < **Arγïn-bay** [Arghim-Baï], Alčï-bay's, Altïm-bay's and Mindi-bay's brother (Levchine 356); Kzk. **Arγïn** (Aristov 286, 308); Yak. **Arγïn** [Аргын], one of the ancestors of Yakuts (Pek.). ✧ I. A Kazak tribe in Kiši-žüz (Lesser/Little Horde); II. 'Tired' cf. Turk. *arγïn* 'müde' (Radl. I, 300). ⇨ **ARΓUN.**

ARΓÏZ Tat. 1691 **Arγïz** [Аргызко] (Kungursk. akty 194).

ARΓO Alt. 19th c. **Arγo** [(Кан) Арго], a heroine (Verb., In. 144, 152); Shor 19th-20th c. **Arγo** [Кан Арго], a bride or a wife of a khan (Dyrenkova 80, 383). ✧ 'Clean, immaculate Khan'. See also **QAN-ARΓO.**

ARΓU-TAY Alt. **Arγu-tay-χan** [Аргутай хан] (Nikiforov 107-108). ⇨ **TAY** or suff. *-tay(2,3)*?

ARΓUDAQ Selj. 11th c. **Arγudaq** [ارغوداق], in the army of Melikšah (1072-1092) (Arabš. II, 698, 700).

ARΓUN Khorezm. 1460 **Arγun(-Xasan)** [Аргун Хасан, сейид-асиль], a notability (MIT I, 540); Maml.? 1332 **Arγun** [ارغون العلايى], an emir (Dawād. 367); Maml. 14th c. **Arγun** [ارغون] (Sauvaget 35); Trkm.? 1824/25 **Arγun-mirza** [Аргун-мирза] (MIT II, 222); Chag. 1564 **Arγun-šah** [Аргун-шах] (Ivanov 210). ✧ I. A Mongol tribe, cf. *Arγun* 'id.' (Radl. I, 302); II. 'Thoroughbred (horse) of Middle Asia' cf. Uyg. *arγun*, Alt.(Tel.), Kirg., Kzk. *arγïmaq* 'mittelasiatisches Vollblutpferd' (Radl. I, 301-302). ⇨ **ARΓÏN.** See also **ARSLAN-ARΓUN.**

ARΓUWAN Kuman 1466 **Orgawan** (Györffy Gy., A kunok feudalizálódása. In: Tanulmányok a parasztság történetéhez Magyarországon a 14. században. Bp. 1953, p. 254); Kuman 1451 **Orgowan** [Johannes dictus Orgowan], a man of Kuman orifgin in Hungary (Szamota-Zolnai, Lexicon Vocabulorum Hungaricarum in Diplomatibus, Budapest, 1902-1906); Kuman 1529 **Orgowan** [Nicolaus Orgowan], in Hungary (Szamota-Zolnai, Lexicon Vocabulorum Hungaricarum in Diplomatibus, Budapest, 1902-1906); *TN:* Kuman 1509 **Orgowan** [descensus Orgowan], a settlement (today *Orgovány*) in Lesser Kumania, Hungary (Gyárfás III, 728). ✧ 'Syringa' cf. Rásonyi, Kisk. 345-52; Rásonyi, KÖA 82, Rásonyi, Anthr. 144, Rásonyi, Kisk. helyn. 166-170.

ARXU Kzk. 19th c. **Arχu-bay** [Архубаевъ] (SKSO

VIII, 206). ⇨ **ARГU?**

ARÏN Hak. 19th-20th c. **Arin** [Арин] (HRS 348). ✧ 'Sacred, clean' (Butanaev), cf. also Chag. *arin* 'ziemlich schön' (Radl. I, 281).

ARİP see **ĀRİF**

ARİS Hak. 19th-20th c. **Aris** [Арис] (HRS 348). ✧ 'Holy, saint' (Butanaev).

ARİSLÄKÄY Bashk. 1796 **Arisläkäy** [Курман Арислякеев] (MIB V, 362).

ARÏNČA Hak.(Kyz.) 19th-20th c. **Arïnča / Orinča** [Арінча], fem. (Katanov, Otč. 13). ✧ 'Holy, clean' cf. Hak. *Arin, Arinče* (Butanaev). ⇨ **ARÏN** + suff. -*če*.

ARÏNKA Hak. 19th-20th c. **Arïnka** [Арунка], fem. (Katanov, Otč. 10). ✧ Orinka (R.).

ARÏ see **ARÏГ**

ARÏГ Kuman 1398 **Arï / Arïy?** [Орѣй], a „Polovets" (PSRL II, 155); Kzk. 19th c. **Arï-bay** [Арыбай] (SODž. 44); Bashk. 1737 **Arï-bike** [Арыбике], fem. (MIB III, 360); Uyg. **Arïy**, Stirftername eines buddh. Sündenbekenntnisses (TT IV, 432); Uyg. 8th c. **Arïy-qatun-täñrim**, an Uyghur princess (Müller, Pfahl. 23); Uyg. 8th c. **Arïy-täñrim**, an Uyghur princess (Müller, Pfahl. 10); Uyg. 12th c. - 14th c. **Arïy-tegin** [arïy tegin] (Radl., USp. 8, DTS); Tat.(Sib.) **Arï-χän** [Api хан] (Proben IV, 190 /235/); Uyg. **Aruγ** [Aruġ] (EUTS). ✧ 'Clean, honest' (Müller, Pfahl. 16: 'Reine'), cf. OT, Uyg., MT *arïy* чистый, незагрязненный; нравственно безупречный, благородный, порядочный' (DTS), Alt., Hak. *arïy* 'rein; heilig' (Radl. I, 272), Uyg. *ariq (3)* 'rein, schön' (Radl. I, 269), Kuman, Kmd. *arï* 'rein, heilig' (Radl. I, 266), Kkalp. *ariw* 'чистый' (Bask.); Kirg. *aruw* 'чистый, миловидный, красивый' (Jud.). Other possible explanations of fem. PNs *Ay-arïy* are: 'Moon-clear', Clear (=immaculate, innocent) Moon'; "die Mondreine" (Radl. I, 5), in Hak. 'чистый месяц' [=clear (immaculate, innocent) Moon] (Titov 202). See also **GÜN-ARÏ, QUL-ARÏQ, TUTA-ARÏ**.

ARÏГ-AYAZ Uyg. 8th c. **Arïy-ayaz-ïnal** (Müller, Pfahl. 23). ✧ 'Clear/clean beautiful face'. ⇨ **ARÏГ** + **AYAZ**.

ARÏГ-TİNİ Uyg. **Arïy-tini** [Arïy Tini], fem. (Zieme, Mat. I, 74). ✧ 'Clean Tini'? (Zieme). ⇨ **ARÏГ**.

ARÏГA Uyg. **Arïya**, wife (aged 30) of Yöläk, aged 55 (Zieme, Mat. I, 80). ✧ 'Oh, Clean/Honest!' (Zieme). ⇨ **ARÏГ** + voc. suff. -*a*.

ARÏX see **ARÏQ I.**

ARÏQ I. Hak. 19th-20th c. **Arïχ / Arïχ-pay** [Арых, Арыхпай] (HRS 348); 13th c. **Arïq** [ارق], an emir (Qazw. 587); Tat. 1624 **Arïq** [Уразла Арыковъ] (Pokrovskij 72); Bashk. 1675 **Arïq** [Аслай Арыков] (MIB I, 201); Bashk. 1708 **Arïq** [Арык] (MIB I, 237); Bashk. 1710 **Arïq** [Арык Акбулатов] (MIB III, 63); Bashk. 1714 **Arïq** [Тоиш Арыков] (MIB I, 105);

Bashk. 1715 **Arïq** [Арык Тепеев] (MIB III, 132); Bashk. 1731 **Arïq** [Иманай Арыков] (MIB III, 292); Bashk. 1737 **Arïq** [Арык Кичинбаев] (MIB I, 325); Bashk. 1737 **Arïq** [Арык] (MIB I, 310); Bashk. 1738 **Arïq** [Елдаш Арыков] (MIB III, 398); Bashk. 1742 **Arïq** [Абан Арыков] (MIB III, 513); Bashk. 1762 **Arïq** [Миндубай Арыков] (MIB IV/1, 244); Kzk. 19th c. **Arïq** [Арыкъ] (SOV 42); Kzk. 19th c. **Arïq** [Арыкъ] (AOK 126); Kzk. 19th c. **Arïq** [Арыкъ] (SOK 34); Kirg. **Arïq** [Арык] (Jud. 920); Alt. 19th-20th c. **Arïq** [Арык] (OjrRS 207); Hak. 19th-20th c. **Arïq** [Арык] (HRS 348); Hak. 19th-20th c. **Arïq** [Арык] (Proben IX, 555, 559); Bashk. 1732 **Arïq-bay** [Арыкбай Сатлыганов] (MIB III, 302); Bashk. 1788 **Arïq-bay** [Яхъя Арыкбаев] (MIB V, 231); Bashk. 1788 **Arïq-bay** [Арыкбай] (MIB V, 231); Kzk. 19th c. **Arïq-pay** [Арыкпай] (SOK 142); Kzk. 19th c. **Arïq-pay** [Арыкпай] (SODž. 28, 64); Kzk. 19th c. **Arïq-pay** [Арыкпай] (SOV 60); Hak. 1685 **Arïq-pay** [Арыкпайка], from the 'Basagar' tribe (Jarilov, Kyz. 6); Uyg. 12th c. - 14th c. **Aruq** [aruq] (Radl., USp. 169, 170, MK/Brock., DTS); Khorezm.? 1284 **Aruq** [اروق / 'Ârok / Oruk], Buqa (Bokâ)'s brother, the governor of Baghdad (Abulfar./Budge I, 478, Wassaf 250). ✧ I. 'Thin, meagre, weak' cf. OT *arïq* 'тощий, худой' (DTS), Alt., Crm., Kar.(L.), Kzk., Tat., Turk. *arïq (1)* 'mager, schwach' (Radl. I, 268). Cf. Hak. PN *Arïχpay* 'тщедушный' [=frail/weak man] (Butanaev); II. 'Dike, trench' cf. Uyg., Kirg., Kzk. *arïq (2)* 'Bewässerungsgräben' (Radl. I, 269). See also **QUL-ARÏQ, TOLON-ARÏQ**.

ARÏQ II. Hak.(Kacha) 19th c. **Arïq** [Арыкъ] (Katanov, Otč. II, 42). ✧ 'Shit' (Katanov). See also **BAYNAQ, BOQ, QOMUQ**.

ARÏQ-TAY 1320, 1349/50 **Arïq-tay** [ارقطاى / سيف الدين], an emir, the governor of Hims, Tripolis, Haleb and Damascus (Dawād. 297, 344, Zetterst. 158, 183, Weil, Abbas I, 350, 430, 435, 484, Sauvaire III, 416, 480); Maml. 1346/47 **Arïq-tay** [ارقطاى] (Iyās I, 184, 189, 190, Sauvaget 35). ✧ 'Skinny, meagre foal' cf. Sauvaget 35: 'poulain maigre'. ⇨ **ARÏQ I.** + **TAY** or suff. -*tay(2)*?

ARÏQ-TÏLÏM Kzk. 19th c. **Arïq-tïlïm** [Арыктылымъ], from the district of Kopal (Maev I, 160). ✧ 'Thin-pigtail/tail'?; 'Thin slice'? ⇨ **ARÏQ I.**

ARÏQLÏ Oghuz/Trkm. 13th c. **Arïqlï** [اريتلى / Арыклы], Irek's son (Abulg./Kon. 1265). ⇨ **ARÏQ I.** + suff. -*li*?

ARÏQLÏ-QAŠ Turk. 20th c. **Arïqlï-qaš** [Арıklıkaş], a village in Turkey (TMİB 10). ⇨ **ARÏQLÏ + QAŠ**.

ARÏM-BAY see **ARİN**

ARİN Kzk. 1840 **Arïm-bay** (<Arïn-bay) [Арымъ-Бай] (ZIRGOÊtn. I, 102); Kzk. 19th c. **Arïm-bay** (<Arïn-

bay) [Арымбай] (SOK 32, 58); Kzk. 19th c. **Arïm-bek (<Arïn-bek)** [Арымбек] (SOK 186); Kzk. 19th c. **Arïn** [Арынъ] (SOK 176); Crm. 18th c. **Arïn-bey** [Арынъбей], chief of the Arïn tribe (Smirnov, Krym. 323); Kzk. 19th c. **Arïn-ɣazï** [Арынгазы] (AOK 2). ✧ Ethnonym *Arïn*? ⇨ **ARUN.**

ARÏS   Kzk. 19th c. **Arïs** [Арыс] (AOK 38); Kzk. 19th c. **Arïs-pay** [Арыспай] (SOV 158).

ARÏSLAN see **ARSLAN**

ARÏSTAM-BAY see **ARÏSTAN**

ARÏSTAN see **ARSLAN**

ARÏSTAN-BUΓA see **ARSLAN-BUQA**

ARÏŠ I.   Uzb. 1722 **Arïš** [Арышъ Китѣевъ], from Bukhara (Veselovskij, Unk. 171); Oghuz/Trkm. 1270 **Arïš-χoǰa** [Ариш-ходжа Маниш] (MIT I, 537); *TN:* Kzk. **Arïš-ata** [Арыш-Ата], a field (territory) in the Aral-region (Kojčubaev 40).

ARÏŠ II.   Alt. 19th-20th c. **Arïš** [Арыш], fem. (OjrRS 211). ✧ Arisha (< R. Irina).

ARÏŠQA   Alt. 19th-20th c. **Arïšqa** [Арышка], fem. (OjrRS 211). ✧ Arishka (< R. Irina).

ARÏZ   Tat. 1663 **Arïz-bay** [Арызбайко] (MIB I, 163); Tat. 1695 **Arïz-bay** [Арызбайко Кутлубаев] (MIB I, 92); Bashk. 1714 **Arïz-bay** [Арызбаев] (MIB I, 105); Oghuz/Trkm. 14th c. - 15th c. **Arïz-qoǰa / Aruz-qoǰa / Uruz-qoǰa?** (DQorq./Rossi 357); Oghuz/Trkm. 14th c. - 15th c. **Aruz / Aruz-qoǰa / Uruz(-qoǰa)** [اروز / Аруз-Коджа (Аруз, Уруз)] (DQorq. 22 etc., DQorq./Ergin 96, DQorq./Rossi 158). ⇨ **ARÏS?**

ARÏSA   Yak. **Arïsa** [Арыса], fem. (Pek.). ✧ Arisha (< R. Arina, Irina).

ARKİLE   Hak. 19th-20th c. **Arkile** [Аркиле] (HRS 348).

ARKİP   Alt. 19th-20th c. **Arkïp** (Katanov, Otč. 10, 12). ✧ Arhip (R.).

ARQA   Chuv. 18th-19th c. **Arka** [Арка] (Magn. 29); Tat.(Ishim) **Arqa** [Арка] (Proben IV, 202); Kzk. 19th c. **Arqa-bay** [Аркабай] (SOK 10, 82, 118, 120, 218, 308); Kzk. 19th c. **Arqa-bay** [Аркабай] (SOV 48, 148); Kzk. 19th c. **Arqa-bay** [Аркабай] (AOP 18); Kzk. 19th c. **Arqa-bay** [Бекмурза Аркабаевъ] (Grod., Pril. 48). ✧ 'Supporter, protector; (lit.) back' cf. Chag., Crm., Kirg., Kzk., Tat., etc. *arqa* 'Rücken, Nacken; Stütze, Schutz' (Radl. I, 285).

ARQA-BAŠ   Kzk. 1867 **Arqa-baš** [Аркабашъ], a kurgan (burial mound) in the region of Vernoje (Alma-Ata?) (ZIRGOGeogr. I, 268). ⇨ **ARQA + BAŠ.**

ARQAY   Bashk. 1751 **Arqay** [Бекбулат Аркаев] (MIB IV/1, 43); Bashk. 1765 **Arqay** [Мендий Аркаев] (MIB IV/1, 311); Bashk. 1776 **Arqay** [Мендияр Аркаев] (MIB V, 35); Kzk. 19th c. **Arqay** [Аркай] (SODž. 128); Kzk. 19th c. **Arqay** [Аркай] (AOP 110). ⇨ **ARQA + dim. suff. -*y*.**

ARQAN   **Arqan** [Арканъ] (PSRL XI, 98). ✧ 'Rope (made of horsehair)' cf. Kzk. *arqan* 'Strick aus Pferdehaar' (Radl. I, 288).

ARQANDAR   Kzk. **Arqandar-batïr** [Аркандаръбатырь] (Valihanov, Soč. 319). ✧ 'Hero who catches (the enemy) with *arqan* (=rope made of horsehair)' cf. Kzk. *arqan* 'Strick aus Pferdehaar' (Radl. I, 288).

ARQAR   Trkm. 1817/18 **Arqar** [Худай-берды Аркар] (MIT II, 407); Kzk. 19th c. **Arqar** [Аркаръ] (SOK 160); Kzk. 19th c. **Arqar** [Аркаръ] (Grod., Pril. 95). ✧ 'Wild sheep (Ovis arkar); wild/mountain goat' cf. Chag., Kzk. *arqar* 'männlicher Argali' (Radl. I, 289), *arqar* 'weibliche Bergziege' (Doerfer, TMEN I, No. 12).

ARQAS   Hak. 19th-20th c. **Arqas** [Аркас] (HRS 348). ✧ The short form of R. Arkadiy / Arkaška (Butanaev).

ARQAŠ   Kzk. **Arqaš-bay** [Аркашбай] (Sb. Syr-D. IX, 48). ✧ 'Little supporter'. ⇨ **ARQA + dim. suff. -*š*.**

ARQĀ   Yak. **Arqā** [Арка] (Pek.).

ARQÏN   Kzk. 1826 **Arqïm-bay (<Arqïn-bay)** [Аркимбай Исбаевъ] (TOUAK XXIV, 167). ✧ 'Slow, calm, serious-minded' cf. Trk. PNs *Arkın, Arkun, Arhun* (Erol II). ⇨ **ARQUN?**

ARQUM-BAY see **ARQUN**

ARQUN   Kzk. 19th c. **Arqum-bay (<Arqun-bay)** [Аркумбай] (SOV 56); Kzk. 19th c. **Arqun** [Аркунъ] (SOK 158). ✧ I. 'Race-horse, racer, runner' cf. Karakh. *arqun* 'скакун, помесь дикого жеребца с домашней кобылой' (DTS); II. 'Slow, calm, serious-minded' cf. Trk. PNs *Arkın, Arkun, Arhun* (Erol II). ⇨ **ARQÏN?**

ARLAY   Bashk. 1762 **Arlay** [Арлай Тюмяков] (MIB IV/2, 302).

ARLAN   Oghuz/Trkm. 13th c. **Arlan** [ارلان / Арлан], Dib-Bakuy-khan's son (Abulg./Kon. 660); Kzk. 19th c. **Arlan** [Арлановъ] (AOK 110). ✧ 'Male wild animal' cf. Kzk. *arlan* 'самец (а хищных животных)' (KzRS).

ARLÏ   Kzk. 19th c. **Arlï-bay** [Арлыбай] (SOK 104); Kzk. 19th c. **Arlï-qul** [Джайдарбекъ Арликуловъ] (SKSO III, 20). ✧ 'Shy, bashful; self-conscious' cf. Crm., Kzk., Turk. *ārlï* 'verschämt, Selbstgefühl habend' (Radl. I, 305).

ARLÏ-QAŠ   Bashk. 1789 **Arlï-qaš** [Арлыкаш Байдяшев] (MIB V, 254). ✧ 'Shy/bashful-Eyebrow'. ⇨ **ARLÏ + QAŠ?**

ARMAΓAN   Turk. 1583 **Armaɣan** [ارمغان] (Ongan, Ank. I, 152); Yürük 1543 **Armaɣan** (Gökb., Rum. 104, 176, 219, 222); Tat. 1543 **Armaɣan** (Gökb., Rum. 235); Tat. 1543 **Armaɣan** (Gökb., Rum. 242). ✧ 'Gift, present' cf. Chag., Turk. *armaɣan* 'Geschenk, Belohnung' (Radl. I, 339), Trk. *armaɣan* 'Geschenk' (Doerfer, TMEN I, No. 465).

ARMAQ   Uyg. **Armaq** (TT IV, 432); Bashk. 1712 **Armaq** [Сулемен Армаков] (MIB III, 84). ✧ 'Gold;

money' cf. Chag. *armaq* 'Gold, Geld' (Radl. I, 339).

ARMAQAY Kzk. 1819 **Armaqay** [Армакай] (MIK IV, 324). ⇨ **ARMAQ** + dim. suff. *-qay*.

ARMAN Chuv. 18th-19th c. **Arman** [Арманъ] (Magn. 29); Kzk. 19th c. **Arman** [Арманъ] (Grod., Pril. 87); Kirg. 20th c. **Armen** (Almásy 113); Kzk. 19th c. **Armen-qul** [Арменкулъ] (SODž. 100). ✧ 'Wish, will' cf. Chag., Kirg., Kzk. *arman* 'Wunsch, Sehnsucht' (Radl. I, 340) (<P.).

ARMANDAY Chuv. 18th-19th c. **Armanday** [Армандай] (Magn. 29). ⇨ **ARMAN** + suff. *-day*.

ARMAŠ Bulg. 13th c. - 14th c. **Armaš** [ارماش] (Jusupov 19). ✧ 'Wish, desire' cf. Kzk. *armaš* 'heftiger Wunsch' (Radl. I, 340).

ARMEN see **ARMAN**

ARMUDAN Az. **Armudan-bek** [Армудан-бек] (Az. Skaz. 501); + suff. *-an* (Miller?) pers. denom.?;

ARNAČ Kzk. 1680 **Arnač(ka)** [Арначка], a Kazak prince (DAI VIII, 42).

ARNAXAY Tat. 1684 **Arnaxay** [Арнахайко, Орнохайко] (DAI XI, 160, 161).

ARNU Kzk. 19th c. **Arnu-bay** [Арнубай] (SOK 4).

AROQ Hak. 19th-20th c. **Aroq** [Арок] (HRS 348).

ARŌS Alt. **Arōs**, fem. (Katanov, Otč. 7).

ARPA-BAL Kzk. 19th c. **Arpa-bal** [Арпабалъ] (SOK 122). ✧ 'Barley-honey'? cf. Crm., Kzk., Turk., etc. *arpa* 'die Gerste' (Radl. I, 333). ⇨ **BAL?**

ARSAY Yak. **Arsay** [Apcai], a nickname (Pek.). ✧ 'Grinner' (Pek.), Yak. *arsay-* 'выставлять зубы' (JRS).

ARSAQ Turk. 1484 **Arsaq** [ارساق] (Āšikp. 188). ✧ 'Cotton reel'? cf. Turk. *arsak* 'iplik makarası' (DS).

ARSALAÑ see **ARSLAN**

ARSALAÑ-ÄLİF Kzk. **Arsalañ-älif / Araslan-älif?** [ارصالانك الیف], in a Kazak legend Alañ-qsar-alif's son (ZVOIRAO 292). ⇨ **ARSLAN?** + **ELİF**.

ARSAN-DUOLAY Yak. **Arsa(ï)n-duolai / Ārsïn-duolay / Ārsan-tuolay (-duolan)** [Арса(ы)н Дуолаі / Арсын Дуолаі / Арсан Туолаі (Дуолаи)], head (father, ataman) of eight generations of evil spirits; a legendary abāsy-bogatyr with eight heads (Pek.).

ARSĀNE Alt. 19th-20th c. **Arsāne** [Арсаане] (OjrRS 207). ✧ Arseniy (R.).

ARSEK Kzk. 19th c. **Arsek** [Арсекъ] (SOK 218).

ARSELAN see **ARSLAN**

ARSÏJAX Hak. 19th-20th c. **Arsïjax** (HRS 348).

ARSLAN Tat. 1555 **Araslan** [Арасланъ] (PSRL XIII, 246); Tat. 17th c. **Araslan** [Михаил Арасланович Кайбулинъ], a prince from Astrakhan (ZVOIRAO XIII, 77); Tat.? 1675 **Araslan** [Семейко Араслановъ] (Kungursk. akty 25); Tat. 1708 **Araslan** [Ярмакъ Араслановъ] (Nikol'skij 271); Tat. 1764 **Araslan** [Араслан] (MIB IV/1, 295); Tat. 18th-19th c. **Araslan** [Ораслан] (Magn.); Tat. 18th-19th c. **Araslan** [Арасланъ] (Magn. 29); Tat.(Mish.) 1708 **Araslan** [Арасланко] (MIB I, 225); Tat.(Mish.) 1748 **Araslan** [Араслан] (Nepljuev 438); Tat.(Sib.) 1605 **Araslan** [Араслан], Aley's son, a prince (Miller, Ist. Sib. II, 190, 193); Bashk. 1709 **Araslan** [Албяк Арасланов] (MIB I, 264); Bashk. 1710 **Araslan** [Кошук Арасланов] (MIB III, 67); Bashk. 1712 **Araslan** [Араслан Самчалин] (MIB III, 83); Bashk. 1715 **Araslan** [Араслан Товлин] (MIB III, 134); Bashk. 1722 **Araslan** [Араслан Бирючаков] (MIB III, 199); Bashk. 1722 **Araslan** [Араслан Аккулов] (MIB I, 109); Bashk. 1731 **Arslan** [Арслан Бекметев] (MIB III, 292); Bashk. 1735 **Araslan** [Арасланъ Епановъ], a tarχan (Vel.-Zern., Bašk. 15); Bashk. 1735 **Araslan** [Адагулъ Араслановъ], a tarχan (Vel.-Zern., Bašk. 19); Bashk. 1750 **Araslan** [Араслан Баслаев] (MIB III, 472); Bashk. 1754 **Araslan** [Кинзя Арасланов] (MIB IV/1, 83); Bashk. 1754 **Araslan** [Кайбулат Арасланов] (MIB IV/1, 83); Bashk. 1759 **Araslan** [Абыкай Арасланов] (MIB IV/2, 26); Bashk. 1763 **Araslan** [Араслан Шемяков] (MIB IV/1, 268); Bashk. 1770 **Araslan** [Араслан Тойкин] (MIB IV/1, 345); Bashk. 1779 **Araslan** [Сафар (Сафер) Арасланов] (MIB V, 96); Bashk. 1789 **Araslan** [Илистан Арсланов] (MIB V, 243); Bashk. 1796 **Araslan** [Гайсар Аразланов] (MIB V, 360); Kzk. 1826 **Araslan** [Арасланъ] (Dobrosm., Turg. 282); Kzk. 1846 **Araslan** [Араслан Джантюрин] (МКОР 152); Bashk. 1722, 1731 **Araslan / Arslan** [Арасланъ / Арслан Бекметевъ], a captain (PSZRI VI, 717, MIB III, 292); Kzk. 19th c. **Araslan (<Arslan)** [Арасланъ] (Grod., Pril. 163); Bashk. 1701 **Araslan-bek** [Араслан-бек] (MIB III, 14); Bashk. 1735 **Araslan-bek** [Арсланбакъ Деветеевъ] (Vel.-Zern., Bašk. 27); Bashk. 1695 **Araslan-bek (<Araslan-bek)** [Рослан-бек] (MIB I, 85); Bashk. 1735 **Araslan-γul** [Арасланъгулъ Атяшевъ], a tarχan (Vel.-Zern., Bašk. 13); Bashk. 1756 **Araslan-γul** [Араслангул Бигишев] (MIB IV/1, 123); Bashk. 1724 **Araslan-tarχan-batïr** [Арслан-тархан-батыр Аккулин] (MIB III, 222); Bashk. 1779 **Arïslan** [Арыслан Арысланбеков] (MIB V, 84); Tat.? 1732 **Arïslan-beg** [Арысланъ Бегъ] (PSZRI VIII, 883); Bashk. 1779 **Arïslan-bek** [Арыслан Арыслан-беков] (MIB V, 84); Kzk. 18th c. - 19th c. **Arïstam-bay (<Arïstan-bay)** [Арыстамбай] (Tynyšp. 68, 75); Kzk. 18th c. - 19th c. **Arïstan** [Арыстан] (Tynyšp. 75); Kzk. 19th c. **Arïstan** [Арыстанъ] (AOK 82); Kzk. 19th c. **Arïstan** [Аристанъ] (Grod., Pril. 109); Kzk. 19th c. **Arïstan** [Джанъ Аристановъ] (Grod., Pril. 110); Kzk. 19th c. **Arïstan-bay** [Арыстамбай] (AOA 150); Kkalp. 20th c. **Arïstan-batïr** [Арыстан-батыр] (Bask., Kkalp. 399); Kzk. 19th c. **Arïstan-bek** [Аристан-бекъ

Атановъ] (SKSO II, 4); Kzk. 19th c. **Arïstan-bek** [Онбаръ Аристан-бековъ] (Grod., Pril. 196); Kzk. **Arïstan-qan** [ارستان قا ن] (Divaev, Biket 5, 27); Hak. 19th-20th c. **Arselan** [Арселан], fem. (HRS 353); 1035? **Arslan** [ارسلان البساسيرى] (Duqmaq:RHCHor IV, 43); 1035 **Arslan** [ارسلان ابولحارت البساسيرى] (Ibn Taghrīb. II, 168); 1190 **Arslan** ['Αρσανῆς], an emir (Byz. Turc. 72); Türk? 576 **Arslan** ['Αρσίλας], a Turkic chieftain (Byz. Turc. 72); Uyg. **Arslan** [Arslan] (EUTS); Uyg. 933 **Arslan** [A-sa-lan], from the Turfan region (Hamilton, Ouïg. 147); Uyg. 12th c. - 14th c. **Arslan** (Radl., USp. 215, 257); Uyg. 1286 **Arslan,** „Scholasticus"? (Chwol., Syr.-nest. (NF) 11); Uyg. 1298 **Arslan,** priest Sergis' son (Chwol., Syr.-nest. 40); Uyg. 1320 **Arslan** (Chwol., Syr.-nest. (NF) 22); Oghuz? **Arslan** [ارسلان حاجب], a χāǰib, the follower of Ghaznavid Mahmūd (998-1030) (Qazw. 435); Oghuz 920 **Arslan** [ارسلان] (Hil. Sābī 429); Oghuz 999 **Arslan** [ارسلان جانب], Mohamed ibn Sebük-tegin's emir (Ibn al-Athīr/Tornb. IX, 103, 133, 155, 323); Oghuz? 11th c. **Arslan** [Arslan el-Besasîri], chieftain of the Turks in the age of the Caliph al-Qaim (1031-1075), executed by Sultan Toγrïl (1038-1063) (Ahbar 15); Oghuz? 11th c. **Arslan** [ارسلان جادب / ارسلان حادب / ارسلان حاذب], a commander of the Ghaznavid Mahmūd (998-1030) (Mirch. Gasnevid. 29); Oghuz 10th c. **Arslan,** doorkeeper (ḥāǰib) (Ahbar 2); Oghuz 1156 **Arslan** [ارسلان بن اتسز], a Khorezmshah Arslan II (1156-1172), Atsïz' son (Ibn al-Athīr/Tornb. XI, 138); Oghuz/Trkm. 1153 **Arslan** [Арслан], an Oghuz (Ghuzz) emir (MIT I, 388); Selj. **Arslan** [درمرو ارسلان امير زاده], a prince in Merv (Juwaynī I, 131); Selj. 1027 **Arslan** [ابو الحرب ارسلان], emir of Tūs (Mirch. Gasnevid. 226); Selj. 1063 **Arslan** [Арслан ибн Тогрул], Alp-arslan sultan (1063-1072), Toγrul's son (MIT I, 402); Selj.? 1153 **Arslan** [الغزى الا مير ارسلان], emir (Ibn al-Athīr/Tornb. XI, 116); Selj. 1160 **Arslan** [ركن الدين ارسلان بن طغرل], Seljuk sultan Rukn ed-Dīn Arslan (1160-1175) the son of Sultan Toγrïl II (1131-1134) (Rāwandī 65, 76, 233 etc.); Khorezm. **Arslan** [Арслан] (RaD II, 75); Khorezm. 13th c. **Arslan** [Арслан], governor of Merv (MIT I, 493); Maml. 1308 **Arslan** [بها'الد ين ارسلان الدوادار], an emir (Dawād. 157, 159 etc.); Maml. 1313 **Arslan** [ارسلان] (Dawād. 276); Maml. 1332 **Arslan** [المنصورة ارسلان نتيب الحلقه] (Dawād. 367); Maml. 14th c. **Arslan** [ارسلان / Arslan] (Tarǰ/Houtsma 46, Tarǰ/Toparlı 42); Maml. 14th c. **Arslan** [ارسلان] (Sauvaget 35); Maml. 14th c. **Arslan** [Арслан] (Tuhfa 409), Maml. 1411/12 **Arslan** [ارسلان], governor of Cairo (Ibn Taghrīb. VI, 317); Turk.? **Arslan** [سليمان ابن ارسلان],

on a gravestone in Ankara? (MG Ank. 35); Turk. 1532 **Arslan** [Ali ibn Arszlān], a Janisary (yeničeri) from Simontornya, Hungary (Velics-Kamm. I, 77); Turk. 16th c. **Arslan,** the source mentions 14 persons having this name (Ongan, Ank. II); Turk. 1583/84 **Arslan,** 7 persons from the period mentioned (Ongan, Ank. I, 152); Turk. 1586 **Arslan** [Arszlān], spāhi of the liva of Szerém, Hungary (Velics-Kamm. I, 355); Turk. 1618 **Arslan** [Arszlān], a reis (commander) in the fortress of Tarcsa, Hungary (Velics-Kamm. I, 409); Yürük 1543 **Arslan** [ارسلان], one of the Yürüks from Kocacık, Turkey (Gökb., Rum. 103, 228, 252); Yürük 1543 **Arslan** (Gökb., Rum. 216, 220, 228); Yürük 1620 **Arslan** (Gökçen 91); Trkm. 1707 **Arslan** [ارسلان بكاول], in the service of Bukhara (Buchari 305); Trkm. 20th c. **Arslan** [Arslan] (Zaj. 1971, 331); Trkm. 20th c. **Arslan** [Арслан] (TrkmRS 52); Crm. 1637 **Arslan** [كوچك / ارسلان] (Vel.-Zern., Crim. 179); Crm. 1689 **Arslan** [ارسلان/چا بقون /] (Vel.-Zern., Crim. 867); Tat. 1543 **Arslan** (Gökb., Rum. 231); Bashk. 1715 **Arslan** [Мамбет Арсланов] (MIB III, 125); Bashk. 1737 **Arslan** [Арслан Мавлутеев] (MIB III, 367); Bashk. 1756 **Arslan** [Арслан Бигишев] (MIB IV/1, 107); Bashk. 1773 **Arslan** [Арслан Тоикинъ] (IOAIÊK XXVIII, 587); Kzk. **Arslan** [Арсланъ] (Levšin III, 96); Kzk. 16th c. **Arslan,** a mighty Kazak prince (Radl., Aus Sib. I, 193); Kzk. 1817 **Arslan** [اروصلا ن] (MIK IV, 303); Kzk. 1820 **Arslan** [Арслан] (MIK IV, 355); Kzk. 19th c. **Arslan** [Арслан Джанибековъ] (Grod., Pril. 91); Kzk. 19th c. **Arslan** [Arslan] (Levchine 356); Nog. 1649 **Arslan** [Арслан], a murza (AI IV, 123); Alt. 19th c. **Arslan** [Арслан] (Verb., In. 149); Selj. **Arslan-aba** [خاصبك انظر ارسلان ابه] / Arslan Chaṣṣbeg b. Begtangri] (Bondārī 192, Ibn al-Nitʿān - Süssheim, S. L. G. d. Seldschukengesch.); Selj. **Arslan-aba** [نصرة الد ين ارسلا ن ا به] (Bondārī 242, 243); Selj. 1150 **Arslan-aba** [ارسلان ابه اتابك], an atabek (Rāwandī 241, 244); Uyg. 1301 **Arslan-aγa** [Арсланъ-Ага] (Hvol'son, Vost. Zam. 119); Crm. 1643 **Arslan-aγa** [ارسلان اغا] (Vel.-Zern., Crim. 261, 333); Uyg. 1301 **Arslan-aqa** (Chwol., Syr.-nest. (NF) 13); Crm. 1637 **Arslan-ali?** [ارسلان على] (Vel.-Zern., Crim. 173); Kkalp. 20th c. **Arslan-bay** [Арсланбай] (KkRS 772); Yürük 1603 **Arslan-bey** (Su 26); Kmk. 1828 **Arslan-bek** [Арсланбек Кандауров] (MID III, 123); Crm. 15th c. **Arslan-bek** [Арсланъ-бекъ] (Smirnov, Krym. 247); Nog. 1654 **Arslan-bek** [Арсланбекъ Каспулатовъ], a murza (AI IV, 208); Alt. 19th c. **Arslan-γan** (<Arslan-qan) [Арсланъ-Г′анъ], ruler of the animals (Potanin IV, 169, 502); Bashk. 1783 **Arslan-γul** [Байгул Арслангулов, Раслангулов]

(MIB V, 147, 295, 300, 409); Oghuz 1018 **Arslan-χan** [ارسلان خان سرف الدوله ابوالمظفر] (Ibn al-Athīr/Tornb. IX, 210, 213); Oghuz 12th c. **Arslan-χan** [محمد ارسلان خان], ruler of Mawarannahr (Rāwandī 174); Oghuz/Trkm. 13th c. **Arslan-χan** [ارسلان خان / Арслан-хан], Toγurmïš's son (Abulg./Kon. 1120, 1125); Oghuz/Trkm. 13th c. **Arslan-χan** [ارسلان خان / Арслан-хан], Quzï-tegin-χan's son (Abulg./Kon. 960, 965, 975, 1005); Oghuz/Trkm. 13th c. **Arslan-χan** [ارسلان خان / Арслан-хан], Asïl-zade's son (Abulg./Kon. 1070, 1115); Karakh. 11th c. **Arslan-χan** [Арслан-хан Сулейман], ruler of Kashgar (1032-1056) (MIT I, 262, 300, 302, 316, 366); Karakh. 12th c. **Arslan-χan** [Мухаммед Арслан-хан], Karakhanid ruler (1102-1130) of Samarkand (MIT I, 386, 387); Karakh. 12th c. **Arslan-χan** [Арслан-хан Махмуд], father of Kemaleddīn, the ruler of Jend (MIT I, 443); Karakh. 13th c. **Arslan-χan** [ارسلان خان / Арсланъ-ханъ], a Qarluq prince, Chingis Khan's contemporary (RaD/Ber. I, 132, III, 43, RaD I/1, 151, Abulg./Desm. 38, 93, Ligeti, MTT 235); Selj. **Arslan-χan** [ارسلان خان قباليغ] (Juwaynī I, 48, 56, 58, 63); Khorezm. 1220/21 **Arslan-χan** [Арслан-хан] (MIT I, 483); NUyg.(Tar.)? 19th c. **Arslan-χan** [Арсланъ-ханъ], a batyr (hero) in Kashgar, fought against the Chinese (Pantusov, Tar. 137); Trkm.? 1847 **Arslan-χan / Aslan-χan** [Арслан-хан, Аслан-хан], emir, Xasan-χan Salar's son (MIT I / II?, 240, 241, 243); Selj. 11th c. **Arslan-χatun** [ارسلان خاتون / 'Arslân Khâtôn], Čaγrï-beg's daughter, Caliph Al-Qāim bi'amrīllah's wife (Qazw. 358, Abulfar./Budge I, 209); Selj. 1058 **Arslan-χatun** [ارسلان خاتون], Dawud's daughter (Ibn al-Athīr/Tornb. IX, 424, 442, 445, X, 13, 77); Uzb. 15th c. **Arslan-χoja** [Арсланъ-Ходжа-тарханъ] (Barth., Ulugb. 80, 83-85); Karakh. 11th c. **Arslan-ilik / Arslan-ilig** [Arslan İlig], honorific title of the Karakhanid rulers (Golden 215); Oghuz 1030 **Arslan-yabγu / Yabγu-arslan / Arslan-bayγu? / Biγu / Piγu-arslan** [پیغو ارسلان / ارسلان بیغو] / Emir Yabgu Arslan / Arslân-Païghou / Арслан Ябгу (Бигу), Арслан ибн Сельджукъ], Seljuk's son, his personal name was Israil (Ahbar 2, Ibn al-Athīr, Atab.: RHCHor II/2, 18, Bondārī 6, MIT I, 321, 362-3, 365-6, 368, 451, 453-4,); Crm. 1635 **Arslan-ketχudā** [ارسلان كتخدا] (Vel.-Zern., Crim. 144, 170); Crm. 1637 **Arslan-mirza** [تمروق اغا / ارسلان مرزه] (Vel.-Zern., Crim. 174); Crm. 1642 **Arslan-mirza** [ارسلان مرزه] (Vel.-Zern., Crim. 275, 460); Khorezm.? 13th c. **Arslan-oγul** [اوقول / ارسلان اغول / ارغول / Arslanaghul], Joči Qasar's grandson, who revolted against Ghazan (1295-1304) and was executed in 1296 (RaD/Jahn 40, 41, 45, 97, 99, 100, 192, Hammer, Ilch. II, 32-34); Oghuz 1116-1117

Arslan-šah [ارسلانشاه بن غزنوى], a Ghaznavid ruler (1116-1117) (Qazw. 361, 363); Oghuz 12th c. **Arslan-šah** [ارسلانشاه بن مسعود بن محمود], a Ghaznevid (Qazw. 405, Mirch. Gasnevid. 128); Oghuz/Trkm. 1211 **Arslan-šah** [ارسلانشاه بن مسعود بن مودود], a Salghurid, died in 1211 (Qazw. 504); Selj. 11th c. **Arslan-šah** [Арслан-шах], Alp-arslan's son (RaD I/2, 103, MIT I, 375, 467); Selj. 11th c. **Arslan-šah** [ارسلانشاه بن طغرلشاه], from Kirmān, better known as Alp-arslan (1063-1072) (Qazw. 479, Juwaynī II, 43); Selj. 1094 **Arslan-šah** [ارسلان شاه صاحب سنجار], proprietor (ruler) of Sinjar (Ibn Taghrīb. II, 304); Selj. 1101 **Arslan-šah** [ارسلان بك بن قاورت بك / ارسلان شاه بن كرما نشاه], a Seljukid in Kirman (Kerman) (Ibn al-Athīr/Tornb. X, 219-20, 363); Selj. 1142 **Arslan-šah** [ارسلانشاه بن كرمانشاه بن قاورد], Kirman-šah's son (Qazw. 536); Selj. 12th c. **Arslan-šah** [سلجوقشاه بن ارسلانشاه], Seljuq-šah's father (Muh. Ibrahim 10, 28, 30-32); Khorezm. 13th c. **Arslan-šah** [ارسلانشاه], grandson of the Khorezmshah Tekiš (1172-1200) (Juwaynī II, 36, 293); Oghuz 919 **Arslan-tegin** [ارسلانتكين / ارسلان تكين الكوركيرى] (Hil. Sābī 407); Karakh. 11th c. **Arslan-tegin** [arslan tegin] (DTS); Uyg. **Arslan-toña** [Arslan Tonga] (TT IV, 432); Uyg. 1300 **Arslan-tuña** [Arslan Tunga], a priest (Chwol., Syr. II, 44); Khorezm./Chag. **Arslan-ügä?** [Арслан-Уга] (RaD I/2, 153); Kzk. 19th c. **Arstam-bay (<Arstan-bay)** [Арстамбай] (Grod., Pril. 49); Kirg. 20th c. **Arstan** [Арстан] (Kalilov 93); Kzk. 1817 **Aruslan-bay (<Arslan-bay)** [اروصلا نباى] (MIK IV, 312, 319); 1625/26 **Aslan** ['Ασλάνος Βόρνικος / Aslan vel Vornic] (Stud. şi doc., Bucureşti, V, 17); Maml. 1455 **Aslan** [اصلا ن بن سليمان بن دلغا در] (Iyās II, 47-48); Maml. 1516 **Aslan** [اصلان], regent of Hims (Iyās III, 47, 51); Az. **Aslan** [Аслан] (Az. Skaz. 306); Karch. 20th c. **Aslan** (Pröhle, Kar. 88); Bashk. 1712 **Aslan** [Аслан Сартов] (MIB III, 85); Turk. 20th c. **Aslan-apa** [Aslanapa], a village in the province of Kütahya, Turkey (TMİB 590); Az.?, Trkm.? 16th c. **Aslan-bek** [ملك على بن اصلان بك] (Dorn 523, 524); Karch. **Aslan-bek** [Асланбекъ Кагиевъ] (Sysoev 135); Turk. 20th c. **Aslan-γāzi** [Aslangazi], a village in the province of Ağrı, Turkey (TMİB 49); Trkm. 1660? **Aslan-χan** [Аслан-хан], ruler of Ferah (MIT II, 115); Trkm. 1750 **Aslan-χan** [اصلان خان], an emir (Das Mujmil et-tārīkh des Ibn Muh. Emīn. Hrsg. v. O. Mann, 32-35, 65); Az.?, Trkm.? 1580 **Aslan-sultan** [اصلان سلطان] (Dorn 289); Nog. **Yaroslan-murza** [Ярослан Мурза (Арслан)] (Žirm., Epos 430); Bashk. 1709 **Raslan-bek** [Расланбек Кашканаев] (MIB III, 53); *TN:* Turk. 20th c. **Aslan-bey**, a village in

the province of Kastamonu, Turkey (TMİB 512); *TN:* Kzk. **Aslan-bek** [Аслан-бекъ], a place near Yarkend (Karta JAR XX). ✧ 'Lion (lit.); (fig.) strong, powerful, mighty man, hero; huge' cf. in most ancient and modern dial. *arslan / araslan / arïslan / arïstan / aslan*, etc. (Radl. II, 327-329; Sev.; TMEN II, No. 453). See also **AQ-ARSLAN, ALP-ARSLAN, BAY-ARSLAN, BEG-ARSLAN, BEGÄČ-ARSLAN, BEKEČ-ARSLAN, BİY-ARSLAN, BULUQ-ARSLAN, ĴAN-ARASLAN, ČİGİL-ARSLAN, ERK-ARSLAN, İL-ARSLAN, YAΓÏ-ARSLAN, YAN-ARASLAN, YAWLAQ-ARSLAN, YİGÄN-ARSLAN, YOLUQ-ARSLAN, KEY-ARSLAN, QARA-ALP-ARSLAN, QARA-ARSLAN, QÏLAN-ARSLAN, QÏLÏČ-ARSLAN, QÏZÏL-ARSLAN, QUL-ARSLAN, QUMAR-ARSLAN, QUTLUΓ-ARSLAN, OΓUL-ARSLAN, PİGU-ARSLAN, SARÏ-ASLAN, SÏRT-ASLAN, TAΓ-ARSLAN, TAÑ-ARSLAN, TOΓAN-ARSLAN, TOΓRÏL-ARSLAN, TOQ-ARSTAN, TOÑA-ARSLAN.**

ARSLAN-ARΓU see **ARSLAN-ARΓUN**

ARSLAN-ARΓUN   Selj. 1054 **Arslan-arγun** [ارسلا ن ارغون], Dawud's son (Ibn al-Athīr/Tornb. IX, 406, X, 34); Selj. 1073 **Arslan-arγun** [ارسلان ارغون بـن الـبـارسلان], Alp-arslan's son (Ibn al-Athīr/Tornb. X, 178-80); Selj. 1065 **Arslan-arγun / Arslan-arγu** [ارسلان ارغون / Арслан Аргу (Арслан Аргун)], Alp-arslan's son, Melik-šah's (1072-1092) brother, Berk-yaruq's (1094-1104) uncle, died in 1097 (Ibn Taghrīb. II, 317, Abulfar. 367, Abulfidā III, Ahbar 59-60, 310-311, Qazw. 451, Rāwandī 143, Zambaur 49, 187, 223, 283, MIT I, 375-76, 381-82). ⇨ **ARSLAN + ARΓUN.**

ARSLAN-BALBAN   Uyg. 12th c. - 14th c. **Arslan-balban** [arslan balban] (Radl., USp. 125, DTS). ✧ 'Lion-Hawk/falcon'? ⇨ **ARSLAN + BALABAN?**

ARSLAN-BALU   Oghuz 992/93 **Arslan-balu / Arslan-yalu?** [Арслан-Балу (Арслан Ялу)], a χāĵib (MIT T, 223-24). ⇨ **ARSLAN.**

ARSLAN-BOΓRA   **Arslan-boγra-sultan** [Arslan-Boghra Sultan], according to an Eastern Turkic legend he fell in a battle against the buddhists (A. Stein, Sand-buried Ruins of Khotan 157). ✧ 'Lion-stallion'. ⇨ **ARSLAN + BUΓRA.**

ARSLAN-BUΓA see **ARSLAN-BUQA**

ARSLAN-BUQA   Selj. 1189/90 **Arslan-buγa** [ارسلان بغا / Arslân-Bogha] (Ibn Šaddād, Nawād.: RHCHor III, 141); Uyg. **Arslan-buqa** [Арслан-Бука, Арсланъ-Буга] (RaD/Ber. III, 12, RaD II, 154); Selj.? 1153 **Arslan-buqa** [ارسلان بوقا التركى] (Ibn al-Athīr/Tornb. XI, 118, 178); Oghuz/Trkm.? 1153 **Arslan-muqa (Arslan-buqa)** [Арслан-Мука (Арслан-Бука)], a Turkic (?) leader (MIT I, 389);

Maml.? **Astan-buγa (<Arstan-buγa <Arïstan-buγa?)** [استنبوغا الـدوا دار] (Arabš. II, 2). ✧ 'Lion-bull'. ⇨ **ARSLAN + BUQA.**

ARSLAN-ĴAZİB   Selj.? 1003, 1030 **Arslan-ĵazib** [ارسلان جـاذب / Арслан ал-Джазиб, Арслан Джазиб; Сулейман-и-Арслан Джазиб;], emir, regent of Tūs (Rāwandī 92, 93, MIT I, 226, 227, 229, 230, 234-5, 250, 265, 277, 288, 321, 352, 360, 363, 366, 439, 456, 463). ⇨ **ARSLAN.**

ARSLAN-GİREY   Crm.Tat. 1689 **Arslan-girey-χan** [ارسلان كـراى حـان], Devlet-girey Khan's son (Vel.-Zern., Crim. 778); Balk. 20th c. **Aslan-gerey** (Pröhle, Balk. 203). ✧ 'Lion-Girey / Hero(ic)-Girey'. ⇨ **ARSLAN + KERÄY.**

ARSLAN-YALU see **ARSLAN-BALU**

ARSLAN-MAZİD   Chag. 1556 **Arslan-mazid** [Арслан Мазид], a mirza (Ivanov 227). ✧ 'Lion-Mazid' cf. Ar. *Mazid* 'increase, excess, maximum' (Ahmed). ⇨ **ARSLAN.**

ARSLAN-MEÑÜ   Türk / Uyg. 8th c. - 9th c. **Arslan-meñü** [arslan meŋü] (DTS). ✧ 'Lion-Eternal/Stable' (Blagova 1997, 705). ⇨ **ARSLAN + MEÑÜ.**

ARSLAN-MİÑ   Uyg. 1297 **Arslan-miñ**, Yusmid's son (Chwol., Syr. II, 40). ✧ 'Lion-thousand'. ⇨ **ARSLAN + MİÑ.**

ARSLAN-MUQA see **ARSLAN-BUQA**

ARSLAN-SÏQ-TOΓRUL   Uyg. 12th c. - 14th c. **Arslan-sïq-toγrul** [arslan sïq toγrul] (Radl., USp. 115-16, DTS). ✧ 'Lion-Little-Falcon' (Blagova 1997, 705). ⇨ **ARSLAN + TOΓRÏL.**

ARSLAN-TAŠ   Selj. 11th c. **Arslan-taš** [ارسلان تـاش], Melikshah's (1072-1092) commander in the battle against the Assassins, proprietor of Sinjar (?) (Qazw. 519); Selj. 1080, 1099 **Arslan-taš** [صاحب سنجـار ارسلان تـاش], lord of Sinjar (Kamāladdīn: RHCHor II, 67, 133, Ibn al-Athīr/Tornb. X, 188); Selj. 1113 **Arslan-taš** [تـمـيـراك بـن ارسلان تـاش], Temirek's father, the lord of Sinjar (Qalānisi 185). ✧ 'Lion-Stone'. ⇨ **ARSLAN + TAŠ.**

ARSLAN-TOΓMÏŠ   Selj. **Arslan-doγmïš** [ارسلا ن دغمش / سنـانالـديـن ارسلان دغمش پـسر], Arslan-doγmïš's son (Aqsarāyī 101, Ibn Bībī IV, 311, 312); Selj.? 1144 **Arslan-doγmïš** [ارسلان دغـمش], Fakhraddīn Qara-arslan's brother (Ibn Bībī IV, 240, 268-271, Abulfar./Budge I, 268); Selj. 13th c.? **Arslan-doγmïš** [ارسلاندغمش اتـابك], an ata-bek, Izzaddīn Sultan's chief (Aqsarāyī 40, Aqsar./İş. 45, 67); Selj. 1249 **Arslan-doγmuš** (Belleten XII, 34, 39); Selj. 1138 **Arslan-toγmïš** [ارسلان دغمش], Dawud ibn Er-taš' son (Qalānisi 267); Selj. 1183 **Arslan-toγmïš** [ارسلا نـدغـمش], Manṣūr Shāhinshah's father?, mentioned in an inscription of Niksār (Uzunçarş., Küt. I, 62). ✧ 'A lion

(=hero, warrior) has been born; Born to be a lion (=hero, warrior, brave man)'. ⇨ ARSLAN + TOFMÏŠ.

ARSLAN-TOFRÏL Selj.? 12th c. **Arslan-toγrïl / Arslan** [ارسلا ن طغرل بن محمد], Seljuk sultan Rukn ed-Dïn Arslan (1160-1175) the son of Sultan Toγrïl II (1131-1134) (Aqsarāyï 9). ✧ 'Lion-hawk / Hero(ic)-falcon'. ⇨ ARSLAN + TOFRÏL.

ARSLAN-TUÑA see ARSLAN

ARSLANAY Tat. 1584 **Arslanay / Arslaney?** [Арсланей Кайбуловичъ (Кайбулы)], a princess from Astrakhan (DAI I, 198). ✧ 'Little lion'. ⇨ ARSLAN + dim. suff. -ay.

ARSLANJÏQ Oghuz? **Arslanjïq** [ارسلانجق], the mythical Afrasiyab's grandfather (Ibn al-Athïr/Tornb. X, 279). ✧ 'Little lion'. ⇨ ARSLAN + dim. suff. -jïq.

ARSLANEY see ARSLANAY

ARSTAM-BAY see ARSLAN

ARSTAN see ARSLAN

ARSU-BAY see ARZÏ

ARŠA Kzk. 19th c. **Arša-bay** [Аршабай], a field (territory) (AOA 50). ✧ 'Juniper tree'.

ARŠÏN Kzk. 19th c. **Aršïn-bek** [Аршинбекъ] (AOP 82).

ARŠUN Oghuz/Trkm. 14th c. - 15th c. **Aršun / Aršuvan** [ارشَوَن / Aršuvan / Eršüven / Аршун], Direk's father (DQorq./Rossi 100, 163, DQorq. 73, 75).

ARŠUN see ARŠÏN

ARŠUVAN see ARŠÏN

ARTA Tat. 1686 **Arta-bay** [Артабай] (Kungursk. akty 70). ✧ 'Survive! / Live in affluence!' cf. Chag., Turk. *arta-* 'gemügen, überleben, in Ueberfluss leben' (Radl. I, 309).

ARTAMÏAN Yak. **Artamïan** [Артамыан] (Pek.). ✧ Artamon (R.).

ARTÏ Uyg. 12th c. - 14th c. **Artï-ïnal / Ārti-ïnal** [artï ïnal] (Radl., USp. 208, 250, DTS). ✧ 'Superfluous(-Noble)' (Blagova 1997, 715), cf. Karakh. *artγu* 'избыточный, лишний' (DTS).

ARTÏ-BAŠ 1603 **Artï-baš** [Артыбашевы], name of several murzas (AI II, 56). ✧ 'Superfluous; outstanding' (Bask., Fam. 215). ⇨ ARTÏ(Q) + BAŠ.

ARTÏQ Kuman 14th c. - 15th c. **Altoq / Oltuq (<*Artuq)** [Nicolaum Oltuk dictum comanum; Althokzallasa, Altokzallasa; Átokháza], name of persons of Kuman origin in Hungary (Zichy Okm. IV, 529-30); Trkm. **Artïq** [Артык], fem. (Sopieva 181); Trkm. 20th c. **Artïq** [Artïq], fem. (Zaj. 1971, 341); Trkm. 20th c. **Artïq** [Артык], fem. (TrkmRS 52); Uzb. 1851 **Artïq** [Мулла-Артык], a mulla (priest) from Khiva (ZIRGO V, 104); Kkalp. 20th c. **Artïq / Artïq-bay** [Артыкбай, Артыкбай] (KkRS 772); Selj. 1084, 1085, 1086, 1087, 1091 **Artïq / Artuq?** [ارتق بن اكسك] ارتق بن اكسك التركمانى / أرتق بن اكسب / Emir

Ortok, filius Acsaki Turcomanus], Eksik's (!) son, the form Eksib is obviously false, an emir, died in 1091 (Kamāladdïn II, 84, 97, 99, Ibn al-Athïr/Tornb. X, 86-87, 96-98, Abulfidā III, 280-281); Selj. 1115 **Artïq / Artuq?** [ايلغازى بن أرتق], Ïl-γāzi's father (Kamāladdïn: RHCHor II, 174, 180 etc.); Kzk. 1825 **Artïq / Artuq** [ارتوق] (MIK IV, 473, 477); Maml. 1313 **Artïq-bahadïr** [ارطق بها در], an emir of a tümen (Dawād. 274); Trkm. 1804 **Artïq-baχšï** [Артык-бахшы], from the Yomut tribe (MIT II, 365); Trkm. 1867 **Artïq-baχšï** [Артык-бахшы], from the Ošaq clan (MIT II, 629); Kzk. 19th c. **Artïq-bay** [Артыкбай] (AOAtb. 66); Kzk. 19th c. **Artïq-bay** [Артыкбай] (AOA 74); Selj. 1077 **Artïq-bek** [ارتق بك] (Ibn Taghrïb. II, 263, 271); Trkm. **Artïq-Jemal**, fem. (Sopieva 181); Trkm. **Artïq-gül**, fem. (Sopieva 181); Khorezm. 1227 **Artïq-χan** [ارتق خان], Sultan Jelal's (1220-1231) officer (Nasawï 138); Kzk. 19th c. **Artïq-pay** [Артыкпай] (SOV 10, 16); Kzk. 19th c. **Artïq-pay** [Артыкпай] (SOK 306); Kzk. 19th c. **Artïq-pay** [Артыкпай] (AOO 18); Kzk. 19th c. **Artïq-pay** [Артыкпай] (AOP 2, 94); Yürük 1543 **Artuk** (Gökb., Rum. 196); OT 1074 **Artuq** ['Αρτουχ], a Turkic chieftain in Byzantine service (Byz. Turc. 72); Oghuz/Trkm. 1084 **Artuq** ['Artûk], a chief, whohe collected the armies of the Türkmen (Abulfar./Budge I, 228, 256); Selj.? **Artuq** [ارتق / اربق] (Qazw. 446); Chag. 16th c. **Artuq** [Артук] (Ivanov 263, 266-268); Yürük 1543 **Artuq** [ارتق], from the Yürüks of Kocacık, Turkey (Gökb., Rum. 102, 196); Oghuz/Trkm. **Artuq / Artïq** [اوتوق ارتوق اورتق], forefather of the Ottoman dynasty (Nešrï 186, Ālï 186, Seādeddïn I, 15); Selj. 1086 **Artuq-beg** [Amîr 'Artûk Bâg], ruler of Jerusalem (Abulfar./Budge I, 230); Trkm. 1859 **Artuq-biy** [Артук-бий] (MIT II, 597, 605, 606); Trkm. 1742 **Artuq-inaq** [Артук-инак] (MIT II, 147-149, 160, 167-171, 177, 181, 334, 335, 345); Chag. 16th c. **Artuq-šeyχ** [Артук шейх] (Ivanov 270); Uyg. 13th-14th c. **Artuq-täñrim** [Artuq Tngrim], fem. (Zieme, Mat. III, 274); Bashk. 1756 **Artuq-ul** [Ялчюгул Артукулов] (MIB IV, 109); *TN:* Kuman 14th c. - 15th c. **Altoq / Oltuq (<*Artuq)** [Althokzallasa, Altokzallasa; Átokháza], a village of Kuman origin in Lesser Kumania, Hungary (Gyárfás III, 532). ✧ 'Superfluous, surplus; the last (child), the end', cf. Türk, Uyg., Karakh. *artïq / artuq* 'больший; избыточный, излишний' (DTS), cf. also Rásonyi, Jerus. 89-93, Rásonyi, KÖA 82, Rásonyi, Anthr. 136, Rásonyi, NTK 76-79, Žanuzakov 131, Sopieva 181, Erol II.

ARTÏQAY Bashk. 1740 **Artïqay / Artïkey?** [Артикей Ишкинеев] (MIB I, 427). ⇨ ARTÏ / ARTÏQ? + suff. -qay / -ay.

ARTÏN Turk. **Artïn / Artin?** (Ongan, Ank. II); Kzk.

19th c. **Artïn-bay** [Артынбай] (Pam. kn. Turg. 60). ✧ 'Proud, having self-respect, dignified' cf. Artun (Erol II.).

ARTŌS Alt. 19th c. **Artōs** (Katanov, Otč. 7).

ARTUQ see **ARTÏQ**

ARTUQAČ Uyg. **Artuqač** [artuqač] (TT IV, 432, 442-45, DTS). ✧ 'Little Superfluous' (Blagova 1997, 715), 'Left, Remainder', 'Last (Child)', 'Little Unwanted (child)', cf. Uyg. *artuk* 'Artık, çok, fazla, arta kalan, son' (EUTS), Türk, Uyg., Karakh. *artuk* 'больший, больше; избыточный, излишний' (DTS). ⇨ **ARTÏQ** + dim. -*ač*.

ARTUQÏŠ Selj. 13th c. **Artuqïš-beg** [ارتوقش بك], Mübarizüddin Behramšah's emir (Ibn Bībī 155, 157-160 etc.). ⇨ **ARTÏQ?** + suff. -*ïš*.

ARU-MAQTÏM Kkalp. **Aru-maqtïm** [Ару-Мактим], from the Nagaylï (Noγaylï) clan (Divaev: OOIKK III, 123). ⇨ **ARÏΓ** + **MAQTÏ** + poss. suff. -*m*.

ARU-MANDAY Alt. **Aru-manday** [Ару-Мандай] (Nikiforov 226-32). ✧ 'Clean (clear) forehead'. ⇨ **ARÏΓ** + **MAÑLAY.**

ARUΓ see **ARÏΓ**

ARUQ Oghuz 1039 **Tegin-aruq** [Тегин-Арук (Артегин)], a χājib in the palace (MIT I, 278, 279, 286, 287, 295). ✧ 'Skinny, meagre' (Blagova 1997, 715), cf. Uyg., Karakh. *aruq* 'усталый, утомленный; худой, исхудалый' (DTS), East.T. *oruq* 'mager, abgemagert' (Radl. IV, 1057). See also **KÜD-ARUQ.**

ARUN Kzk. 19th c. **Arun** [Арун Казангановъ] (AUK 295); Kzk. 1816, 1823, 1827 **Arun-γazï / Harun-γazï?** [هارونغازى / Арунгазы], a sultan (MIK IV, 297, 357, Levchine 298, II, 333, Mejer 36); Uzb. 1851 **Arun-yüzbašï** [Арунъ-Юсъ-Баши], a man from Khiva (ZIRGO IV, 105). ⇨ **ARÏN?**

ARUW-XAN see **ARÏΓ**

ARUWXAN Kkalp. 20th c. **Aruwχan**, fem. (KkRS 777). ⇨ **ARÏΓ** + suff. -*χan(1)*.

ARUWKE Kirg. **Aruwke** [Арууке], fem. (Jud. 88). ✧ 'Clean; Beautiful'. ⇨ **ARÏΓ** + suff. -*ke(2)*.

ARUZ see **ARÏZ**

ARVÏQ Uyg. 8th c. **Arvïq-tañrim**, a princess, the name of a goddess (Müller, Pfahl. 10, EUTS).

ARVUZ see **ERWÜZ**

ARZ see **ARZÏ**

ARZA-MAMET Tat. 1739 **Arza-mamet** [Арзамаметевъ] (Alatyr. 146). ✧ 'Whished Mukhammat'. ⇨ **ARZÏ** + **MAMET.** See also **ARZÏ-MUXAMBET.**

ARZAMAS Tat. 1624-26 **Arzamas** [Арзамас Сенгилдеевъ], tax-payer (Буртас, посопный Татаринъ) (Zolotn. 155).

ARZÏ Chuv. 18th-19th c. **Arsu-bay** [Арсубай] (Magn. 29); Kkalp. 20th c. **Arz-ayïm** (<*Arzï-ayïm*) [Арзайым], fem. (KkRS 777); Kkalp. 20th c. **Arz-eke** (<*Arz(ï)-ake*) [Арзеке] (KkRS 772); Kzk. 19th c. **Arz-γul** (<*Arzï-γul*) [Миканъ Арзгуловъ] (Grod., Pril. 66); Kirg. 1621 **Arza-bay** (<*Arzï-bay*) [Арзабайко] (Miller, Ist. Sib. II, 264); Chuv. 18th-19th c. **Arzï-bay** [Арзыбай] (Magn. 29); Kzk. 19th c. **Arzï-bay** [Арзыбаевъ] (SKSO VIII, 223); Trkm. 20th c. **Arzï-gül** [Arzïgül], fem. (Zaj. 1971, 339); Kkalp. 20th c. **Arzï-gül**, fem. (KkRS 777); Kzk. 19th c. **Arzï-qul** [Арзыкулъ] (SKSO VIII, 223); Kzk. 19th c. **Arzu** [Арзу Имановъ] (SKSO VIII, 204); Kkalp. 20th c. **Arzu** [Арзу] (Bask., Kkalp. 57); Chuv. 18th-19th c. **Arzu-bay** [Арзубай] (Magn. 29); Kkalp. 20th c. **Arzuw** [Арзуў] (KkRS 772). ✧ 'Whish, whished' cf. Uyg., Az., Turk. *arzu* 'Wunsch, Verlangen', (Uyg.) 'der Planet Merkur' (Radl. I, 330), Trkm. *arz* 'жалоба, просьба' (TrkmRS) (<Ar.). *Arzï-gül* is translated bay Baskakov as 'Whished flower, rose' (cf. Baskakov: OSA 140).

ARZÏ-MUXAMBET Nog. 20th c. **Arzï-muχambet** [Арзымухамбет Мустафа увлы], one of Baskakov's informants from the aul of Qara-töbe (Bask., Nog. 143). ⇨ **ARZÏ** + **MUXAMMED.** See also **ARZA-MAMET.**

ARZÏXAN Kkalp. 20th c. **Arzïχan** [Арзыхан], fem. (KkRS 777). ⇨ **ARZÏ** + suff. -*χan(1)*.

ARZÏM Kkalp. 20th c. **Arzïm** [Арзым] (KkRS 772). ⇨ **ARZÏ** + poss. suff. -*m*.

ARZU see **ARZÏ**

ARZUB see **ARBUZ**

ARZUW see **ARZÏ**

AS Karakh. **As** [As], fem. (MK/Atalay 831); Maml. 13th c. - 14th c. **As** [اص السيفى بهادر], one of Qalāūn's (1279-1290) mamluks, then governor of Safad, later chief of the right wing of the Syrian army, died in 1329 (Mayer 93-94); Bashk. 1735 **As** [Аcь / ? Аса Кюлюковъ], a tarχan (Vel.-Zern., Bašk. 18); Maml. 1466, 1467 **As-bay** [اصباى البواب] (Ibn Taghrīb. VIII, 531, 619); Chuv. 18th-19th c. **As-bek** [Асбякъ] (Magn. 30); Kzk. 19th c. **As-janï-bek-χan** [Асъ-Джанибекъ-ханъ] (Potanin, Pred. 171); Hun? 6th c. **As-qan**, a bodyguard of Massaget (= Hun or Alan?) origin in the Byzantine army (Byz. Turc. 75); Uyg. 12th c. - 14th c. **As-qan?**, a clan and a man (Radl., USp. 133-34, 138); Khazar 8th c. **As-tarχan** [As Tarχan] (Golden 151); Karakh. 11th c. **Ās** [ās], by-name used for female slaves (MK/Brock., DTS); *EN:* Nog. 20th c. **As** [Ас урув], Qara Nogay clan (Bask., Nog. 137, 142). ✧ I. 'Ermine' (cf. Ligeti, R. tör. nev. II-III, 136); II. 'As (ethnonym)'? See also **AQ-AS.**

AS-BERGEN Kzk. 19th c. **As-bergen** [Асбергенъ] (SOV 68, 118); *TN:* Kzk. **As-bergen** [Ас-бергенъ] (Karta JAR XI). ✧ 'Ermine?-gave him/her'. ⇨ **AS / AŠ?** + **BERGEN.**

AS-BUΓA Maml. 1386 **As-buγa** [اصبغا] (Berchem, Jér.

I, 300); Maml. 1401/02 **As-buγa** [اصبغا الناصرى] (Iyās I, 342). ⇨ **AS + BUQA.**

AS-ĴANЇ Kzk. 19th c. **As-ĵanï-bek** [Асъ-Джанибекъ-ханъ] (Potanin, Pred. 171). ⇨ **AS + ĴANЇ.**

AS-KİL Bashk. 1735 **As-kil / As-kilä?** [Аскил(а?) Ишимбетевъ] (Vel.-Zern., Bašk. 25). ✧ 'Ermeline, come!'. ⇨ **AS + KEL?** See also **AS-KİLDE.**

AS-KİLDE Tat. 1620 **As-kilde / As-kildey?** [Атай Аскильдѣевъ] (Kurdjumov 121). ✧ 'Ermine came'? ⇨ **AS + KELDİ.** See also **AS-KİL.**

AS-QARA Bashk. 1728 **As-qara** [Аскара Рысмекеев] (MIB III, 259). ✧ 'Ermine-black'? ⇨ **AS + QARA.**

ASA I. Oghuz? 865-870, 874 **Asa-tegin / Sa-tegin** [سا تكين / اسا تكين], governor of Mosul (Tabarī, Annal. III, 1545, 16879, 1788, 1807, 1820 etc., Weil, Chalif. II, 465, 466).

ASA II. Hak. 19th-20th c. **Asa** [Аса] (HRS 353).

ASAY Bashk. 1779 **Asay** [Сулейман Асаев] (MIB V, 83); Kzk. 19th c. **Asay** [Асай] (AOO 58); Tat. 1724 **Asay / Asey?** [Асей] (MIB III, 227); Bashk. 1761 **Asay / Asey?** [Асей Телятев] (MIB IV, 204).

ASAYAH see ASЇYYA

ASAQ Uyg. 12th c. - 14th c. **Asaq** (Radl., USp. 113-114). See also **BAW-ASAQ, TEMİR-ASAQ.**

ASAQAY Bashk. 1754 **Asaqay** [Асакай Тенеев] (MIB IV/1, 83). ⇨ **ASAQ + dim. suff. -ay.**

ASAN 1452 **Asan** [Асанъ / Осанъ] (PSRL VIII, 143); Bulg. 1369, 1375 **Asan** [Асанъ / Осанъ], a prince of the Bulghars (PSRL VIII, 17, 25); Tat.(GH)? 1330 **Asan** [Асанъ], a prince from the Horde (PSRL X, 203); Tat.(GH) 14th c. **Asan** [Асанъ], an outstanding envoy mentioned in a yarlïq of Toqtamïš (Smirnov, Krym. 145); Tat.(GH) 1365 **Asan** [Асанъ / Осанъ], envoy from the Horde (PSRL V, 230, VIII, 13, XXIII, 114); Crm. 1250 **Asan** [Asano Catolico] (Jorga, Notes I, 20); Tat.(Lit.) 1590 **Asan** [Асанъ Айдаробичъ] (Lit. Tat. 65, 66, 270); Tat. 1370 **Asan** [Асанъ], a prince from Kazan (PSRL XI, 12); Tat. 16th c. **Asan** [Асанъ / Осанъ], a Tatar from Kazan who was christened in 1535 and got the name Mikhail (PSRL VI, 297); Tat. 17th c. **Asan** [Асанъ Карачуринъ] (IOAIÊK XXIX, 300); Bashk. 1711 **Asan** [Асан], a murza (MIB III, 75); Bashk. 1714 **Asan** [Тякис Асановъ] (MIB I, 105); Bashk. 1735 **Asan** [Асанъ Байметевъ], a tarχan (Vel.-Zern., Bašk. 22); Bashk. 1735 **Asan** [Чукей Асановъ] (Vel.-Zern., Bašk. 25); Bashk. 1754 **Asan** [Асан Игишев] (MIB IV/1, 83); Bashk. 1764 **Asan** [Асан Тлекеев] (MIB IV, 276); Kzk. 19th c. **Asan** [Асанъ] (SOV 64); Kzk. 19th c. **Asan** [Асанъ] (SOK 74); Kzk. 19th c.? **Asan** (Atyns. 20); Kkalp. 20th c. **Asan** [Асан] (Bask., Kkalp. 399, KkRS 772); Nog. 1587 **Asan** [Асанъ] (PSRL XIII, 119); Nog. 1649 **Asan** [Кожемъ-Бердѣй Асановъ]

(AI IV, 123); Nog. 20th c. **Asan** [Асан Магомет улы Санълыбай / Асан Магометович Санглыбаев], Baskakov's informant from the aul of Erkin-χalq (Bask., Nog. 143); Kirg. **Asan** [Асан] (Jud. 27); Uzb. 1622 **Asan** [Асанъ-Хозяевъ], ruler of Bukhara (AI IV, 43); Salar 19th c. **Asan** [Асан], a Salar (Potanin II, 430); Kkalp. 1740 **Asan-abïz** [Асан абыз] (MIKk. 208); Kzk. **Asan-bay** [Асанбай] (Valihanov, Soč. 382); Kzk. 1622 **Asan-bay** [Асанбай], a prince (Miller, Ist. Sib. II, 289); Kzk. 19th c. **Asan-bay** [Асанбай] (SODž. 34); Kzk. 19th c. **Asan-bay** [Асанбай] (SOK 66); Kzk. 19th c. **Asan-bay** [Асанбай] (Grod., Pril. 112); Trkm. 1840 **Asan-batïr** [Асан-Батыръ] (ZIRGOÊtn. I, 99); 1640 **Asan-bek** [Асан-бекъ], envoy of the Shah (AI IV, 45); Nog. 20th c. **Asan-uwlï** [Барамбай Асан увлы], father of one of Baskakov's informants from the settlement Terekli-mektep (Bask., Nog. 144); Bashk. 1735 **Asän** [Асянъ Аюгаринъ], a tarχan (Vel.-Zern., Bašk. 19). ✧ I. Hasan (Ar.); II. 'Easy, simple'? cf. Chag., Turk. *asan* 'leicht' (Radl. I, 536) (<P.). See also **QOŠ-ASAN, SEYİT-ASAN, UZUN-ASAN.**

ASAN-GİREY Tat.(Sib.)? 1682 **Asan-girey** [Асанъ-Гирей], a prince from Siberia (AI V, 140). ⇨ **ASAN + KERÄY.**

ASAN-ΓAVAS-OΓLU Turk. 19th **Asan-γavas-oγlu**, a Zeybek, probably (H)Asan, son of Γavas (Kúnos 1891, 119?). ⇨ **ASAN + ? + comp. *oγlu*.**

ASAN-QAYDЇ Kzk. 19th c. **Asan-qaydï / Asan-qoydï?** [Асанъ-койды] (Potanin, Pred. 170); Nog. 19th c. **Asan-qaytï** (Ljutš 44). ⇨ **ASAN + QAYDЇ?**

ASAN-QAYTЇ see ASAN-QAYDЇ

ASAN-TÄMÜR Uyg. 13th-14th c. **Asan-tämür** [Asan Tämür] (Zieme, Mat. II, 92). ✧ 'Hasan-Iron'? ⇨ **ASAN? + TEMÜR.**

ASANA Uyg. **Asana** [Asana] (EUTS). ⇨ **ASAN + suff. -a?**

ASAR Turk. 1621 **Asar**, from Isparta (Ün 1938, 645). ✧ I. 'Educator'? cf. Turk. dial. *asar* 'eğitmen' (DS); II. 'Shameless'? cf. Turk. dial. *asar* 'arsız, utanmaz' (DS).

ASAT Hak. 19th-20th c. **Asat** [Асат] (HRS 348).

ASAU see ASAW

ASAW Kzk. 1803, 1820 **Asaw** [Асау], one of the chiefs of the Ĵaγalbaylï tribe (MIK IV, 516, Sib. Vest. IX, 123); Kzk. 1817 **Asaw** [آصاؤ / Асау], chief of the Tabïn tribe (MIK IV, 308); Kzk. 19th c. **Asaw** [Асау] (SOK 154); Kzk. 19th c. **Asaw** [Мамбет Асавовъ] (AUK 877); Kzk. 1825 **Asaw-bay** [اصاو باى] (MIK IV, 469, 476); Kzk. 19th c. **Asaw-bay** [Асаубай] (SOK 32); Kzk. 19th c. **Asaw-bay** [Асаубай] (SOV 30); Kzk. 19th c. **Asaw-bay** [Асаубай] (AOP 118); Kzk. 1822 **Asaw-batïr** [اصاؤ باطور / Асау батыр] (MIK IV, 432, 434); Kzk. 18th c. - 19th c. **Asaw-biy** [Асау-бий]

(Tynyšp. 72). ✧ 'Wild' cf. Kzk. *asau* 'wild' (Radl. I, 536).

ASBEN Kzk. 19th c. **Asben-dirim?** [Асбендирим Нарумов] (AUK 146). ✧ I. 'Sky'? cf. Kirg., Kzk. *aspan* 'der Himmel' (Radl. I, 554) (<P.); II. 'Household utensils'? cf. Kzk. *aspan* 'Geräthschaft, Hausgeräth' (Radl. I, 554) (<Ar. *āsbān*).

ASÄN see **ASAN**

ASEY see **ASAY**

ASEYKTEY Tat.(Lit.) 1592 **Aseyktey** [Асейктей Абрамович] (Lit. Tat. 123). ⇨ ? + suff. *-tey*.

ASГAR see **ASQAR**

ASİL see **ASÏL**

ASİP Hak. 19th-20th c. **Asip** [Асип] (HRS 348). ✧ Osip (R.).

ASÏYYA Bulg. 13th c. - 14th c. **Asïyya / Asayah** [اسيه], fem. (Jusupov 40, Epigr. Bulg. 112, 113).

ASÏ Kzk. **Asï-bay-batïr** [Асыбай-батыр] (Smirnov, Sultany 15). ✧ 'Stubborn, obstinate' cf. Crm., Kzk. *asï* 'ungehorsam, störrisch' (Radl. I, 538).

ASÏГ-BULMÏŠ Uyg. 12th c. - 14th c. **Asïγ-bulmïš / Asïq-bulmïš** [asïγ bulmïš] (Radl., USp. 100-101, DTS). ✧ 'It has got a benefit/gain' (Bese 22), 'Benefit/gain-found' (Blagova 1997, 712), cf. Uyg., Karakh. *asïγ I* 'польза, выгода; прибыль; выгодный, полезный' (DTS). ⇨ **BULMÏŠ.**

ASÏQ Kzk. 19th c. **Asïq-bay** [Асекбай] (SODž. 128); Kzk. 19th c. **Asïq-pay** [Асыкпай] (SOV 74); Kzk. 19th c. **Asïq-pay** [Асыкпай] (SOK 8).

ASÏQ-BULMÏŠ see **ASÏГ-BULMÏŠ**

ASÏL Kzk. 1798 **Asil-biy / Äsil-biy?** [Асиль-бий], a clan of the Dulat tribe (Tynyšp. 65); Bashk. 1754 **Asïl** [Бекчюра Асылов] (MIB IV/1, 83); Kzk. 19th c. **Asïl** [Аселъ] (AOAtb. 6); Kzk. 18th c. - 19th c. **Asïl / Äsil?** [Асиль] (Tynyšp. 66); Maml.? 15th c. **Asïl-bay** [أصل باى الچركسيه], a mamluk of Cherkess (Caucasian) origin (Iyās II, 215, 298, 304, 363, 393); Bashk. 1736 **Asïl-bay** [Асылбай Юсупов] (MIB IV/1, 122); Bashk. 1740 **Asïl-bay** [Асыл-бай Бетекбаев] (MIB I, 384); Bashk. 1778 **Asïl-bay** [Кучкарбай Асылбаев] (MIB V, 67); Kzk. 18th c. - 19th c. **Asïl-bay** [Асылбай] (Tynyšp. 71); Kzk. 19th c. **Asïl-bay** [Асылбай] (SOK 232); Kzk. 19th c. **Asïl-bay** [Асылбай] (SOV 22); Bashk. 1778 **Asïl-bay / Asil-bay** [Кучкарбай Асилбаев] (MIB V, 67); Kzk. 19th c. **Asïl-bek** [Асылбек] (Grod., Pril. 80); Kzk. 19th c. **Asïl-bek** [Асылбекъ] (SODž. 78); Uzb. 18th c. **Asïl-bi** [Sultan-Assyl-by], a sultan, Qučaq-bi's son, known also as Ubeydullah (Nalivkin-Dozon 67); Bashk. 1770 **Asïl-güzä** [Асылгузя Мутачев] (MIB IV/1, 342); Kirg. **Asïl-χan** [Асылхан] (Jud. 97); Oghuz/Trkm. 13th c. **Asïl-zade-χan** [اصل زاده / Асыл-заде-хан], Arslan-χan's father (Abulg./Kon. 1115); Hak.? 1727 **Azïl-bay** [Аечакъ Азылбаевъ] (PSRL VII, 890); Hak. 19th-

20th c. **Azïl-pay** [Азыл-Паи] (Proben IX, 357); Kzk. 19th c. **Esil-bay** [Есильбай] (AOK 90); Kzk. 19th c. **Esil-bay** [Есильбай] (AOK 118); Kzk. 19th c. **Esil-bay** [Есильбай] (SOV 64); Kzk. 19th c. **Esil-bay** [Есильбай], a field (AOAtb. 38); Kzk. 19th c. **Esil-bay** [Есильбай], a field (AOA 154). ✧ 'Real, true, genuine' cf. Kzk., Tat. *asil* 'von guter Race, Herkunft; gut, trefflich, kostbar' (Radl. I, 539), Az. *äsil* 'vortrefflich, theuer, kostbar, echt' (Radl. I, 878), Uzb. *asil* [=*äsil*] 'настоящий, натуральный, неподдельный' (UzbRS) (<Ar.). See also **ČÏN-ASÏL.**

ASÏL-BAS Kzk. 18th c. - 19th c. **Asïl-bas** [Асылбас] (Tynyšp. 73). ✧ 'Genuine/noble head; Valuable/dear head'. ⇨ **ASÏL** + **BAŠ.**

ASÏLAY Bashk. 1664 **Asïlay** [Асылай Тенчурин] (MIB I, 193); Bashk. 1675 **Aslay (<Asïlay)** [Аслай Арыков] (MIB I, 201); Bashk. 1735 **Aslay (<Asïlay)** [Ишки Аслаевъ], a tarχan (Vel.-Zern., Bašk. 17); Bashk. 1735 **Aslay (<Asïlay)** [Шимай Аслаевъ], a tarχan (Vel.-Zern., Bašk. 18). ⇨ **ASÏL** + dim. suff. *-ay?*

ASÏNDAY Alt. **Asïnday** [Асындай], fem. (Katanov, Otč. 8). ✧ 'Kindish' cf. Hak. PN *Asïn<ï>* 'дорогой' and <ï>*Asïnday* (Butanaev) + suff. *-day.*

ASÏR Kzk. 19th c. **Asïr-bay** [Асырбай] (SOV 52); Kzk. 18th c. - 19th c. **Asr-bek (<Asïr-bek)** [Асрбек] (Tynyšp. 68).

ASKEY Bashk. 1748 **Askey** [Аскѣевъ] (Nepljuev 438). ⇨ **AS** + dim. suff. *-key.*

ASKER Turk. 20th c. **Asker** (Önder, Göle); Turk. 20th c. **Asker** (Önder, Hınıs); Balk. 20th c. **Asker-biy** (Pröhle, Balk. 203). ✧ 'Soldier, warrior' cf. Turk. *asker* 'id.' (TED), Balk. *askér* 'Militär, Soldat' (Pröhle, Balk.), Kirg. *asker* 'id.' (Jud.), Kzk. *äsker* 'войско' (KzRS) (<Ar.).

ASQA Chuv.? 18th-19th c. **Aska** [Аска] (Magn. 30); Bashk. 1748 **Asqa** [Аскинъ] (Nepljuev 437). ⇨ **AS** + suff. *-qa.*

ASQABA Khorezm.? **Asqaba** [Аскаба] (RaD II, 17).

ASQAГAR Yak. **Asqaγar** [Аскаӷар] (Pek.).

ASQAR Kkalp. 1839 **Asγar-behadïr** [Асгар бехадыр] (MIKk. 134); Kkalp. 1821, 1822 **Asγar-biy** [Асгар бий] (MIKk. 127); Tat. 1668 **Asqar** [Аскарко] (Kungursk. akty 9); Bashk. 1744 **Asqar** [Аскар Чирюков] (MIB III, 415); Bashk. 1757 **Asqar** [Аскар Юлумбеков] (MIB IV/1, 135); Bashk. 1761 **Asqar** [Калкаман Аскаров] (MIB IV/1, 218); Bashk. 1795 **Asqar** [Мендекей Аскаровъ] (IOAIÊK XXVIII, 590); Kzk. 19th c. **Asqar** [Аскаръ] (AOA 130); Kzk. 19th c. **Asqar** [Аскар] (Grod., Pril. 80); Kzk. 19th c. **Asqar** [Аскаров] (Grod., Pril. 173); Kkalp. 20th c. **Asqar** [Аскъар / Аскар] (KkRS 772, Bask., Kkalp. 82, 399); Kirg. **Asqar** [Аскар] (Jud. 463); Kzk. 19th c. **Asqar-bay** [Аскарбай] (Grod., Pril. 115); Kzk. 19th c. **Asqar-bay** [Аскарбай Игизов] (Grod., Pril. 115);

Kzk. 19th c. **Asqar-bek** [Аскарбекъ] (SOK 30). ✧ I. 'Little (darling), smaller, younger' (Kusimova); II. 'Soldier, warrior' (Kusimova); III. 'Eloquent (man), brave/good at speaking' cf. Kzk. *asqar* 'beredt, kühn in Worten' (Radl. I, 543). ⇨ **ASKER**. See also **ГALİ-ASQAR**.

ASQARD Kzk. 1820 **Asqard** [Аскардъ], a sultan, one of the chiefs of the Tazlar tribe (Sib. Vest. IX, 112).

ASQARİ Nog. 1649 **Asqarï (<Aq-sarï?)** [Аскары Батырчинъ] (AI IV, 87).

ASQĀ Yak. **Asqā** [Аска] (Pek.).

ASQÏR see **AYΓÏR**

ASQUČ Uyg. 12th c. - 14th c. **Asquč-ïnal / Asq-ič-ïnal** [asquč̆inal] (Radl., USp. 208, 250, DTS). ✧ 'Hanger' (Blagova 1997, 717).

ASLAM Maml. 14th c. **Aslam** [ابها 'الد ين أسلام], Qalāūn's (1279-1290) mamluk, then governor of Safad, died in 1346 (Mayer 81-82, also Zetterst. 187). ✧ 'Benefit, prize, bounty' cf. Crm., Kar., Tat. *aslam* 'Vortheil, Nutzen, Gewinnst, Zinsen, Prozente' (Radl. I, 547).

ASLAMČÏ Bashk. 1787 **Aslamčï** [Юзубек Асламчин] (MIB V, 219). ✧ 'Pedlar, hawker' cf. Ta. *aslamčï* 'der Hausirer' (Radl. I, 547).

ASLAN see **ARSLAN**

ASLAN-GEREY see **ARSLAN-GİREY**

ASLARČÏ Bashk. 1751 **Aslarčï** [Девлетбай Асларчин] (MIB IV/1, 43).

ASLÏ Bashk. 1713 **Aslï-bay** [Аслыбай] (MIB III, 105); Yürük 1543 **Aslï-χan** [اصيل خان] / Aslı-han, Asıl-han], from the Yürüks of Kocacık, Turkey (Gökb., Rum. 104, 196, 198, 208, 211, 213, 217); Turk. 1467 **Aslï-paša-χatun** [Aslıpaşa Hatun] (Gökb., Ed. 523); Kkalp. 1740 **Aslu-bay-bi(y)** [Аслубай-Би(й)] (Hanykov, Poezdka 19, MIKk. 108). ✧ 'Noble; reliable, trustworthy' cf. Uyg. *asïl* 'edel, von guter Herkunft' (Radl. I, 547) (<Ar.), Turk. *aslı olmak* 'yeminli olmak; sözünün eri olmak' (DS). ⇨ **ASİL**.

ASLÏQAY Bashk. 1741, 1751 **Aslïqay** [Каипкул Аслыкаев] (MIB III, 413, IV/1, 87). ⇨ **ASLÏ** + dim. suff. *-qay*.

ASLU see **ASLÏ**

ASMAN-TAY see **ASPAN-TAY**

ASMANAQ Tat.(Sib.) 1598/99 **Asmanaq** [Асманакъ / Османакъ], a Siberian prince from Küčüm's family (AI II, 3-5, 17, 20). ✧ 'Sky' cf. Chag., Az., Tat.(Sib.), Turk. etc. *asman* 'der Himmel' (Radl. I, 555) (<P.) + dim. suff. *-aq*.

ASMÏŠ see **AŠMÏŠ**

ASPAN-TAY Kzk. **Asman-tay** [Асмантай], a settlement (Kojčubaev 40); Kzk. 19th c. **Aspan-tay** [Аспантай] (SOK 8). ✧ 'Sky-foal'? cf. Kirg., Kzk. *aspan* 'der Himmel' (Radl. I, 554) (<P.). ⇨ **TAY**? or suff. *-tay(2)*?

ASPANDİYAR Kkalp. 20th c. **Aspandïyar** [Аспандыяр] (Bask., Kkalp. 399, KkRS 772). ✧ 'Isfendiyar' (< P., cf. Justi 142, 308).

ASPARDA Yak. **Asparda** [Аспарда] (Pek.).

ASRAN Uzb. 20th c. **Asran** [Асран] (Begmatov 1984, 201); Uzb. 20th c. **Asran-bek** [Асранбек] (Begmatov 1984, 201); Uzb. 20th c. **Asran-qul** [Асранкул] (Begmatov 1984, 201). ✧ 'Be guarded! Be protected!' (Begmatov), 'Grow up!' cf. Trk. *asra-* 'питать, выращивать, воспитывать, охранять, беречь' (Sev.).

ASTAJAQ Karg. **AstaJaq** [Астацак], fem. (Katanov, Otč. 8). ✧ 'Happy' cf. Hak. PNfem. *Asta (Astačaχ)* 'id.' (Butanaev).

ASTAY Tat. 1764 **Astay** [Адильше Астаев] (MIB IV/1, 279). ✧ 'Ermine-like'. ⇨ **AS** + suff. *-tay(1)*.

ASTAQ Uzb. 19th c. **Astaq** [Астакъ] (SKSO III, 166). ✧ + suff. *-aq*.

ASTANA-QUL-TOQSABA? Uzb. 19th c. **Astana-qul-toqsaba?**, a governor in Khokand (Nalyvkin, Kokand. 168). ✧ 'Yard-Slave-Colonel? / Threshold-Slave-Colonel?' cf. Tob., East T. *astana* 'auf Gräbern aufgeführtes Gebäude' (Radl. I, 550) (<P.), Az. *astana* 'die Schwelle, der Hof, Hofstaat' (Radl. I, 550). ⇨ **QUL** + **TOQ-SABA?**

ASTAW Kzk. 19th c. **Astaw-bek** [Астаубекъ] (SOK 18).

ASTĀPÏY Yak. **Astāpïy** [Астапыі] (Pek.). ✧ Yevstafiy (R.).

ASTÏN Tuv. **Astïn** (Katanov, Otč. 9). ✧ 'Ermeline-squirrel'. ⇨ **AS** + **TÏN**.

ASTRABAL Tat.(GH) 1316, 1317 **Astrabal / Astrabïl / Astrïbal / Yastrabal** [Астрабалъ / Астрабылъ / Астрыбаль / Ястрабалъ], envoy from the Horde (PSRL IV, 48, V, 207, VII, 188, X, 180).

ASTRABÏL see **ASTRABAL**

ASTRÏBAL see **ASTRABAL**

ASTU Kzk. 19th c. **Astu-bay** [Астубай] (SODž. 76).

ASU Kzk. 19th c. **Asu-bay** [Асубай] (SODž. 122); Kzk. 19th c. **Asu-bek** [Асубек] (SOV 10).

ASUΓ Türk **Asuγ** [Asuγ] (ETY II, 135). See also **OΓUL-ASUΓ**.

ASUNA Bashk. 18th c. **Asuna-γul** (Nepljuev 143); Bashk. 18th c. **Asuna-γul** [Асунагулъ Кильмакаевъ] (Nepljuev 143).

AŠ Uyg. 1339 **Aš-tärim / Aš-tarïm?** [Asch Tarim], fem. (Chwol., Syr.-nest. (NF) 33). ✧ 'Feast, treat; food, eatables' cf. Karakh. *aš* 'еда; пища; пир, угощение; званый обед' (DTS). See also **AQ-AŠ, KÖP-AŠ; TOY**.

AŠ-BOLAT Tat. 1557 **Aš-bolat (Eš-bolat?)** (Kn. Metriki Lit. 131). ✧ 'Feast/treat-Steel'; 'Food-steel'? cf. Karakh. *aš* 'еда; пища; пир, угощение; званый обед' (DTS). ⇨ **AŠ** + **BULAT**.

AŠ-BOLDA see **AŠ-BOLDÏ**

AŠ-BOLDÏ   Tat. 1554 **Aš-bolda** (<**Aš-boldï**) [Ашболда] (Kn. Metriki Lit. 103). ✦ 'Feast/treat has been born'. ⇨ **AŠ** + **BOLDÏ**.

AŠ-MURAD see **AŠ-MURAT**

AŠ-MURAT   Kzk. 19th c. **Aš-murad** / **Aš-murat** [Ашмурадъ] (Grod., Pril. 133). ⇨ **AŠ** + **MURAT**.

AŠ-PARS   Chuv. 18th-19th c. **Aš-pars** [Ашпарсъ] (Magn. 31). ✦ 'Feast/treat-Panther'. ⇨ **AŠ I.** / **AŠ II.?** + **BARS** + N/Vimp2+N?

AŠA   Uyg. **Aša** (Zieme, Mat. I, 74, 80). ✦ 'Oh, Food!' (Zieme). ⇨ **AŠ** + voc. suff. -a. See also **XAN-AŠA, QÏZ-AŠA, QUTLUГ-AŠA, MAQ-AŠA, TAP-AŠA, TUZ-AŠA**.

AŠAQ-TEMÜR   Maml. 1399/1400 **Ašaq-temir** [اشتنمر يلبغا الاشتنمرى] (Ibn Taghrīb. VI, 20). ⇨ **АČAQ?** + **TEMİR**.

AŠAN   Uyg. 928 **Ašan** [ašan], envoy of Kan-chou (Hamilton, Ouïg. 147, DTS); Kzk. 19th c. **Ašan** [Курбанъ Айбанъ Ашановъ] (Grod., Pril. 169); Uyg. 12th c. - 14th c. **Ašan-tutuñ** [ašan tutun] (DTS). See also **YAŇÏČUN-AŠAN**.

AŠAN-BUГA   Uyg. 12th c. - 14th c. **Ašan-buγa** [ašan buγa / Äsän Buġa] (DTS, EUTS). ⇨ **AŠAN** + **BUQA**.

AŠAN-QARA   Uyg. 12th c. - 14th c. **Ašan-qara** [ašan qara] (DTS). ✦ 'Food-black' (Bese 18). ⇨ **AŠAN** + **QARA**.

AŠAN-TEMÜR   Uyg. 12th c. - 14th c. **Ašan-temür** [ašan temür] (DTS). ⇨ **AŠAN** + **TEMİR**.

AŠAN-TOГRÏL   Uyg. 12th c. - 14th c. **Ašan-toγrïl** [ašan toγrïl] (DTS). ✦ 'Ašan-Falcon' (Blagova 1997, 707). ⇨ **AŠAN** + **TOГRÏL**.

AŠГABAT   Trkm. **Ašγabat** [Ашгабат] (Sopieva 180). ✦ Ashkabat, capital of Turkmenistan.

AŠİKTAY   Khorezm.? **Ašiktay** [Ашиктай], fem. (RaD II, 203). ⇨ **AŠÏQ?** + **TAY** or suff. -tay(1,2?

AŠÏ   Kzk. 19th c. **Aši-γul** [Ашигулъ] (SOK 6); Uyg. 1341 **Aši-tärim** [Aschi-Tarim], fem. (Chwol., Syr.-nest. (NF) 40). See also **QUTLUГ-AŠÏ**.

AŠÏQ   Kzk. 19th c. **Ašïq** [Ашек] (SODž. 54); Kipch. 1298 **Ašïq** / **Ašik?** [اشق / Ашикъ], a Kipchak chieftain, Noγay's follower (Baybars/Tizeng. I, 88, 111); Tat.(GH) 1260 **Ašïq** / **Ašik?** [Ашикъ] (Ipat. 563, 564); Tat.(GH) 1260, 1261 **Ašïq** / **Ašik?** [Ашикъ] (PSRL II, 199, Ipat. 563, 564); Kzk. 19th c. **Ašïq-pay** / **Ašik-pay?** [Ашикпай] (SOK 60, 220). ✦ I. 'In love, loving; lover' (TED); II. 'A kind of nomad game with knucklebones?' cf. Trk. *ašiq* '(playing) knucklebones; shoulder-blade' (Sev.).

AŠÏQ-QARİB   Crm. **Ašïq-qarib** [Ашык-Карiб] (Radl. II, 1103). ⇨ **AŠÏQ**.

AŠÏM   Kzk. 19th c. **Ašïm** [Ашим] (AOK 14, 122); Kirg. **Ašïm** [Ашым] (Jud. 39, 723); Kzk. 19th c. **Ašïm-bay** [Ашимбай] (SOV 8, 16); Kzk. 19th c. **Ašïm-bay** [Ашимбай] (SODž. 58).

AŠİR   Trkm. **Ašïr** [Ашыр], fem. (Sopieva 179); Trkm. 20th c. **Ašïr** [Ašïr] (Zaj. 1971, 332); Bashk. 1735 **Ašïr** [Аширъ Рысовъ], a tarχan (Vel.-Zern., Bašk. 20); Kzk. 19th c. **Ašïr** [Аширъ] (Grod., Pril. 113); Kirg. **Ašïr-ake** [Ашыраке] (Jud. 189); Trkm. **Ašïr-bibi** [Ашырбиби], fem. (Sopieva 179); Trkm. **Ašïr-γulï** [Ашыргулы] (Sopieva 179). ✦ 'Ashir (the first month of the Muslim lunar year)' (Muhamedova 1957, 40), cf. Kzk. PN *Ašir* (Ir.) '1. десятый; 2. десятый день месяца Мохарама' (Žanuzakov), Trkm. *āšir* 'название первого месяца мусульманского лунного года' (TrkmRS), Crm.(Tat.) *ašir ay* 'месяц муаррем' (KrmRS), < Ar. See also **TAMГUT-AŠİR**.

AŠİR-ALÏ   Kirg. **Ašïr-alï** [Ашыралы] (Jud. 567). ✦ 'Ashir-Ali'. ⇨ **AŠİR** + **ALİ**.

AŠKE   Kzk. 19th c. **Aške** (<**Aš-ake** [Ашке] (SOK 104). ⇨ **AŠ I.** + suff. -ke < -ake.

AŠKEY   Kzk. 19th c. **Aškey** (<**Aš-akey** [Ашкей] (AOK 34). ⇨ **AŠKE** + dim. suff. -y.

AŠQAN   Uyg. 12th c. - 14th c. **Ašqan** [ašqan] (DTS).

AŠQÏN   Kzk. 19th c. **Ašqïn-bay** [Ашгинбай] (AOAtb. 2).

AŠQÏNEY?   Tat. 1611 **Ašqïney?** / **Aškiney?** [Ашгинбай], a prince (Miller, Ist. Sib. II, 220).

AŠMEN   Bashk. 1756 **Ašmen** [Ашмень Куштугулов] (MIB IV/1, 107).

AŠMÏŠ   Uyg. **Asmïš**, Stiftername? (TT IV, 432); Uyg. 12th c. - 14th c. **Ašmïš** [ašmïš] (DTS); Uyg. 9th c. **Ašmïš-täñrim**, a princess (Müller, Pfahl. 10, 16, 23). ✦ 'He who became better, who surpassed somebody' According to Müller: 'die Übertreffende' (Müller, Pfahl. 10, 16, 23), cf. Türk, Karakh., Uyg. *aš-* I 'переходить; переодолевать' (DTS), Chag. *aš-* 'dépasser, franchir' (PdC); II. 'Raised; Multiplied; Enriched, Increased' cf. Uyg. *aš-* II 'увеличивать, прибавлять, умножать' (DTS). ⇨ **AŠ**. See also **İL-AŠMÏŠ**.

AŠPĀDĀ   Uyg. **Ašpādā-buyla** (? **Ašpārā-buyla**) [Ašpādā (ïšbara) buila] (Müller, Hofstaat 210-211). ⇨ **İŠBARA?**

AŠPĀRĀ see **AŠPĀDĀ**

AŠUBUR   Tat.(Sib.) 1640 **Ašubur** / **Aš-ubur?** [Ашубур] (Miller, Ist. Sib. II, 465).

AŠUQ   Uyg. 931 **Tuγ-ašuq** [Tou A-chou], a Türk (T'u-chüeh) envoy at the Chinese court (Hamilton, Ouïg. 147). ✦ 'Helmet' ('casque, cheville'). See also **ALTUN-AŠUQ**.

AŠUR   Trkm. 1828 **Ašur** [Ашур], from the Teke tribe (MIT II, 448); Selj. (Trkm.) 12th c. **Ašur** [عزالدين اشور التركمانى] (Ibn Šaddād, Alep 119); Kzk. 19th c. **Ašur-bay** [Ашурбаевъ] (SKSO II, 8); Trkm. 1720? **Ašur-bek** [Ашур-бек], from the tribe/clan Papalu, ruler of the fortress Quryan (MIT II, 126, 127, 135); Uzb. 1715 **Ašur-bek** [Ашур бек] (MIKk. 165); Uzb. 20th c. **Ašur-bek** [Ашурбековъ], a merchant from Bukhara (Turk. Kraj 1912, 7); Uzb. 20th c. **Ašur-bek**, a basmačï leader, the chief of the Semiz tribe of the Uzbeks (Togan, BTT 427, 452, 467); Trkm. 1628 **Ašur-χan** [Ашур-хан] (MIT II, 104, 109); Uzb. 19th c. **Ašur-qul** [Achour-koul-Divana], the astronomer of the court of Khokand (Nalyvkin, Kokand. 118); Uzb. 20th c. **Ašur-toqsaba** [Achour Toqçaba], a basmačï leader (Castagné 76). ⇨ **AŠÏR.** See also **TAŠ-AŠUR.**

AŠURA Bulg. 1315 **Ašura** [عاشرا / ʿĀšura], fem. (Epigr. Bulg. 132-133).

AŠUT Oghuz **Ašut-beg** [قابى دن اشوت بك], beglerbeg of the right wing (Ibn Bībī III, 89); Oghuz? **Ašut-beg** (Marquart, Kom. 189).

AT Kkalp. 1724 **At-bay** [Атбай Туганов] (MIKk. 182); Kzk. 19th c. **At-eke** [Атеке] (SODž. 52); Kzk. 19th c. **At-eke** [Атеке] (SOK 248); Uyg. 762 **At-χunčuy**, fem. (Mahrnāmag 14, 35); Tat.? 1661 **At-qul** [Аткулов Тюмешка] (Miller, Ist. Sib. II, 546); Chuv. 18th-19th c. **At-murza** [Атмурза] (Magn. 30); Alt. 19th-20th c. **At-pay?** [Атпай] (OjrRS 207); *TN:* Tat. 18th c. **At-bay(eva)** [Атбаева (Алтабаево)] (Korsakov 330). ✧ I. 'Name of a princess; title'; 'Fürstin Name, Ruf' (Mahrnāmag 14, 35); II. 'Horse' cf. all Trk. dial. *at* 'das beschnittene Pferd; Wallach' (Alt., Kzk.), 'das Pferd als Einzelwesen, Reitpferd' (Radl. I, 441). See also **YÏLQÏ; AYDAR-AT, AL-AT, BAYΓUR-AT, ER-AT, QARA-ATTÏ, QARA-DOR-ATTÏ, QULA-ATTÏ, QUŠ-AT, SÏR-AT, TAZ-AT.**

AT-AYAQ Bashk. 1708 **At-ayaq** [Атаяк] (MIB I, 233); Bashk. 1709 **At-ayaq** [Атаяк Назаргулов] (MIKk. 161); Bashk. 1740 **At-ayaq** [Атаяк Мурумбетев] (MIB I, 439); Kzk. 1635, 1654, 1659 **At-ayaq** [Атаяк], a prince (Miller, Ist. Sib. 427, 540, DAI IV, 179). ✧ 'Horse-leg'. ⇨ **AT + AYAQ.** See also **ÏT-AYAQ, QUŠ-AYAQ, QULAN-AYAQ.**

AT-BAΓAR Kzk. 19th c. **At-bayar** [Атбагаръ] (SOV 16). ✧ 'Stud-groom'. ⇨ **AT + BAQAR.** See also **QOY-BAΓAR.**

AT-BASAR Uzb. 20th c. **Ât-bâsar** [Отбосар] (Begmatov 1984, 201). ✧ 'He who will press/overcome horses'. ⇨ **AT + BASAR.**

AT-ČABAR Kzk. 19th c. **At-čabar** [Атчабаръ] (SOK 42); Trkm. 19th c. **At-čapar** [Атъ-Чапаръ Алла Верди] (Murav'ev 94); Kkalp. 20th c. **At-šabar** [Атшабар] (Bask., Kkalp. 399, KkRS 772). ✧ 'Who will gallop/ride at full speed'. ⇨ **AT + ČAPAR.**

AT-ČAPAR see **AT-ČABAR**

AT-ČEMER Kzk. 19th c. **At-čemer** [Атчемеръ] (SODž. 52). ✧ 'Horse-strap (?)' Cf. Trkm. *čemmer* 'верблюѴья подпруга (свитая из шерсти)' (TrkmRS). ⇨ **AT.** See also **BEY-ČEMER.**

AT-ČETER see **AT-YETÄR**

AT-ELŠE Kzk. 19th c. **At-elše** [Ательше] (SODž. 130). ✧ 'Horse-friend'? cf. Kzk. *el* (fig.) 'друг' (KzRS). ⇨ **AT + EL** + dim. hypoc. suff. *-še.*

AT-EMGEN Bashk. 1706 **At-emgen** [Мокшай Атемгенев] (MIB III, 20). ✧ 'Horse-sucked' cf. Kzk. *em-* 'Emmek' (KzTS). ⇨ **AT.** See also **MAY-EMER, ÏT-EMGEN, TAT-EMGEN.**

AT-YETÄR Kzk. 19th c. **At-četer** [Атчетеръ] (SODž. 62); Bashk. 1728 **At-yetär** [Атьетяр Илкаев] (MIB I, 194); Bashk. 1737 **At-zitär** [Анба Атзитаров] (MIB I, 353); Bashk. 1780 **At-ziter** [Кудашман Адзитеров (Адзитерев)] (MIB V, 116, 275). ✧ 'He who will overtake horses'. ⇨ **AT + YETÄR.**

AT-KÏLTÄR Kzk. 19th c. **At-kiltär** [Аткильтаръ Утебаевъ] (AUK 537, 576). ✧ 'Bring a horse' cf. Tat., Tat.(Bar.) *kiltir-* 'kommen lassen, bringen' (Radl. II, 1373). ⇨ **AT.**

AT-KÏRAK see **AT-QÏRAQ**

AT-KÏREY Chuv. 18th-19th c. **At-kirey** [Аткирей] (Magn. 30). ⇨ **AT + KERÄY.**

AT-KÜZÄL Tat. 1620 **At-küzäl** [Аткузял Бякишев] (Miller, Ist. Sib. II, 257). ✧ 'Name/Horse-beauty'? cf. Tat. *güzäl* 'красивый, изящный' (TatRS). ⇨ **AT.**

AT-QAL Yürük 1543 **At-qal** (Gökb., Rum. 103). ⇨ **AT + QAL I.**

AT-QÏRAQ Uyg. **At-kirak / At-qïraq?** [At-kirak; Atkirah, Atkirağ], envoy of the Uyghurs (Temir, Caca 238, Ligeti, MTT 238); Trkm. 1768/69 **At-qïraq** [Ат-Кырак], from the Salïr tribe (MIT II, 341); Kirg. **At-qïraq / At-kiräk?** [Аткирак], an emir from the Kirghiz tribe (RaD I/1, 150). ⇨ **AT.**

AT-QÏRAN Trkm. 1779 **At-qïran-behadïr** [Ат Кыран-бехадыр], from the Salïr tribe (MIT II, 352). ✧ 'Horse-breaking/breaker'? ⇨ **AT + QÏRAN.**

AT-OYNAQ Kzk. 18th c. - 19th c. **At-oynaq** [Атойнак] (Tynyšp. 73). ✧ 'Horse-player/dancer'. ⇨ **AT + OYNAQ.**

AT-OYUNČÏ Alt. 19th-20th c. **At-oyunčï** [Ат-Оюнчы] (OjrRS 207). ✧ 'Rider, jockey' (Ibid.), cf. Alt. *oyïnčï* 'шаловливый, шутник; забавник' (OjrRS). ⇨ **AT.**

AT-ŠABAR see **AT-ČABAR**

AT-TUΓAN Kzk. 19th c. **At-tuyan** [Аттуганъ] (SOK 282); Bashk. 1729 **Atuyan (<At-tuyan)** [Атуган Яргаков] (MIB III, 260). ✧ 'Horse-falcon'?; 'Horse - was born'? ⇨ **AT + TOΓAN?**

AT-ÜYÄK? Bashk. 1776 **At-üyäk?** [Сафар (Сафер) Атюяков] (MIB V, 33, 34). ⇨ **AT.**

AT-ZÏTÄR see **AT-YETÄR**

AT-ZÏTER see **AT-YETÄR**

ATA Oghuz/Trkm. 13th c. **Ata** [اتا / Ата] (Abulg./Kon. 1170); Trkm. **Ata** [Ата] (Sopieva 181); Trkm. 20th c. **Ata** [Ata] (Zaj. 1971, 325); Tat.(Sib.) 1639 **Ata**

[Бугайко Атинов] (Miller, Ist. Sib. II, 453); Trkm. **Ata-bay** (Németh, HMK 67); Chuv. 1613 **Ata-bay** [Атабай] (Zolotn. 155); Chuv. 18th-19th c. **Ata-bay** [Атабай] (Magn. 30); Kzk. 19th c. **Ata-bay** [Атабай Уразбаевъ] (SKSO VIII, 200, 223); Kzk. 19th c. **Ata-bay** [Атабай] (AOA 114); Kkalp. 20th c. **Ata-bay** [Атабай] (KkRS 772); Selj. 12th c. **Ata-bäg / Ata-beg** ['Αταπακας], a Turkic ruler and his descendants (Byz. Turc. 77); Tat.(Sib.) 1623 **Ata-bäk?** [Атабак Корбыцынъ] (Miller, Ist. Sib. II, 292); Selj. **Ata-bek** [Atâbec] (Ibn al-Athīr, Atab.: RHCHor II/2, 45); Kzk. 18th c. - 19th c. **Ata-bek** [Атабек] (Tynyšp. 65); Kirg. **Ata-bek** [Атабек] (Jud. 211, 682); Balk. 20th c. **Ata-biy(larï)** [Atabijları], „Name einer einst leibeigenen (jobbágy, qul) Familie" (Pröhle, Balk. 204); Trkm. **Ata-ĵan** (Sopieva 181-82); Trkm. 20th c. **Ata-ĵan** [Атаджан Таган], a writer (Atadžan Tagan, Za sem'ju rekami. Moskva 1975); Kkalp. 20th c. **Ata-ĵan** [Атаджан] (Bask., Kkalp. 25); Trkm. 1820/21 **Ata-ĵan-bek** [Атаджан-бек] (MIT II, 417-18); Bashk. 1735 **Ata-γul** [Атагулъ Чагыровъ], a tarχan (Vel.-Zern., Bašk. 24); Kzk. 19th c. **Ata-qan** [Атаканъ] (SODž. 132); Kirg. **Ata-qan** [Атакан] (Jud. 842); Kzk. 19th c. **Ata-qazï** [Атаказиевъ] (Grod., Pril. 196); Kzk. 19th c. **Ata-qul** [Атакуловъ] (SKSO VIII, 219); Karakh. 11th c. **Ata-saγun** [ata saγun] (DTS); Uyg. **Ata-tutuñ** (Zieme, Mat. I, 81, Mat. II, 93); Kkalp. 20th c. **Ata-žan** [Атажан] (KkRS 772); *TN:* Tat. 18th c. **Ata-bay** [Атабаева], a village in the district of Tetyushinsk (Korsakov 342); *TN:* Tat. 18th c. **Ata-bay** [Атабаева], a village in the district of Laishevsk (Korsakov 178). ✧ 'Father; grand-father; respected elderly man, uncle (as an addressing)' Desmaison: „Les Turcs donnent. le nom de père (Atâ) aux personnes qu'ils vénérent." Cf. Crm., NUyg.(Tar.), Tat., Tat.(Sib.), Uzb. *ata* 'Vater', Az., Chag., Kzk., Turk. *ata* 'Grossvater, Vorfahr' (Radl. I, 449). Used also as a secondary component of male names expressing honour, respect. *Ata-bek / Ata-beg* is also a wide-spread title with the Seljuks meaning 'Father-Bek' that is „prince, tutor of sovereign's children" used as secondary component of male names, cf. Chag. *ata bäk* 'Erzieher der fürstlichen Kinder' (Radl. I, 451). According to Baskakov *Ata-bek* means 'God's present/gift' (Bask., Fam. 97), in Sopieva's interpretation *Ata-ĵan* is 'родной, любимый отец' that is 'Father-darling' (Sopieva). See also **ČEK-ČEK-ATA, ČÏČAÑ-ATA, ČOLPON-ATA, ČOPAN-ATA, OYSUL-ATA, WAYSÏL-ATA.**

ATA-BAQAN Turk. 20th c. **Ata-bakan**, a village in the province of Ağrı, Turkey (TMİB 51). ✧ 'He who looks after horses'? ⇨ **AT + BAQAN?**

ATA-BERGEN Uzb. 20th c. **Âta-bergän** [Отаберган] (Begmatov 1984, 202). ✧ 'Father has given him/her'.

⇨ **ATA + BERGEN.**

ATA-GELİR Tat. 14th c. **Ata-gelir** ['Αταγελερης], a christened Tatar (Byz. Turc. 76). ✧ '(Grand-)Father comes'? ⇨ **ATA.**

ATA-KELDİ Kzk. 19th c. **Ata-geldi** [Атагельды] (SOV 10, 76); Kzk. 19th c. **Ata-geldi** [Атагельды] (SODž. 56); Uzb. 20th c. **Âta-keldi** [Отакелди] (Begmatov 1984, 202). ✧ '(Grand-)Father has come'. ⇨ **ATA + KELDİ.**

ATA-QARAY Kzk. 19th c. **Ata-qaray** [Айбаш Атакараевъ] (SKSO VIII, 223). ⇨ **ATA + QARAY?** See also **ATÏ-ΓARAY.**

ATA-QOZÏ Kirg. 19th c. **Ata-γozï** [Атагозы] (Potanin II, 6); Kzk. 1785 **Ata-γuzï-bahadïr** [اطا عوزی بهادر / Атагазы], chief of the Aday clan (MIK IV, 52, 54, 75); Kirg. **Ata-qozu** [Атакозу] (Jud. 59). ✧ 'Father-lamb'. ⇨ **ATA + QOZÏ.**

ATA-MURAT Kkalp. 20th c. **Ata-mïrat** [Атамырат] (KkRS 772); Kkalp. 20th c. **Ata-murat** [Ата-мурат] (KkRS 772); Trkm. 1859 **Ata-murat-χan** [Ата-Муратъ-ханъ] (ZIRGOÊtn. 159). ✧ 'Father/Chief-Murat'. ⇨ **ATA + MURAT.**

ATA-NAZAR Kkalp. 20th c. **Ata-nazar** [Атаназар] (KkRS 772). ⇨ **ATA + NAZAR.**

ATA-NİYAZ Trkm. 19th c. **Ata-niyaz** [Атаніязовъ] (AUK 832); Kkalp. 20th c. **Ata-niyaz** [Атанияз] (KkRS 772). ⇨ **ATA + NİYAZ.**

ATA-SARÏ Kzk. 19th c. **Ata-sarï** [Атасары] (SOK 258). ⇨ **ATA + SARÏ.**

ATA-TİLÜ Kzk. 19th c. **Ata-tilü** [Ата Тилу] (Grod., Pril. 33). ⇨ **ATA + TİLÜ.**

ATAB Kzk. 19th c. **Atab / Atap?** [Душибай Атабовъ] (Grod., Pril. 58).

ATAČ Kzk. 1819 **Atač** [Атачь] (MIK IV, 325). ✧ 'Little father'. ⇨ **ATA** + dim. suff. -*č*.

ATAČÏQ Tat./Bashk.? 1728 **Atačik** [тептер Атачик Иликеев] (MIB I, 128). ⇨ **ATA** + dim suff. -*čïq*.

АТАΓAN Alt. 19th-20th c. **Ataγan** [Атаган] (OjrRS 207). ✧ 'Shooting (man), shooter' (OjrRS 207).

ATAY Trkm. 19th c. **Atay** [Атай Мелитньязовъ] (Ščeglov IV, 190); Chuv. 18th-19th c. **Atay** [Атай] (Magn. 30); Tat. 17th c. **Atay** [Атайко Тойдемировъ] (IOAIÊK XXIX, 344); Tat. 1675 **Atay** [Атай] (Kungursk. akty 32); Kzk. 1817 **Atay** [اتای] (MIK IV, 309); Kzk. 19th c. **Atay** [Атай] (AOO 30); Kzk. 19th c. **Atay-bek** [Атайбекъ] (SODž. 4, 120); Uyg. 1362 **Atay-buqa**, father of the prince Hindu (Zieme, Mat. I, 83 (after Cleaves, The Sino-Mongolian Inscription of 1362: HJAs. 12 (1949), p. 87)); Bashk. 1754 **Atay-γul** [Кустень Атайгулов] (MIB IV/1, 85); Kzk. 19th c. **Atey-bek** [Атейбекъ] (SOK 260); *TN:* Crm. **Atay**, a village south of Perekop (Jervis II). ✧ 'Father!, Uncle! (addressing an elderly man)' cf. Bashk. *atay* 'отец;

папа (употреб. и как обращение)' (BRS/Uraksin), Tat. *ăti* 'папа, отец; батюшка' (TatRS). ⇨ **ATA** + dim. suff. *-y*. See also **DÄW-ÄTÄY**.

ATAY-BERGEN Kzk. 19th c. **Atay-bergen** [Атайбергенъ], personal name preserved in the name of a field (AOO 54). ⇨ **ATAY** + **BERGEN**.

ATAY-BOZ Kzk. 19th c. **Atay-boz** [Атайбозъ] (SOK 298). ⇨ **ATAY** + **BOZ.**

ATAYĊİK see **ATAYČIQ**

ATAYRÏ Trkm. 20th c. **Atayrï** [Atayrï], fem. (Zaj. 1971, 338). ✧ 'A sort of spider' (Zaj. 1971), cf. Trkm. *atayrï* 'фаланга' (TrkmRS).

ATAKE Chag. **Atake / Ataka** [اتکی / اٹاکا / اتیکا] (Le Coq, Ind. 3). ✧ Dignity. ⇨ **ATA** + comp. *-ake* or suff. *-ke*.

ATAQ Bashk. 1686 **Ataq** [Атак] (MIB I, 77, 130); Bashk. 1714, 1728 **Ataq** [Навруз Атаков] (MIB I, 107, 124); Kzk. 19th c. **Ataq** [Атакъ] (SODž. 108); Uzb. 19th c. **Ataq** [Атак] (SKSO III, 20); Tat. 1722 **Ataq-qulï** [Атаккулин] (MIB I, 294); Kzk. 19th c. **Ataq-pay** [Атакпай] (SOK 64).

ATAQTÏ-TORU Kzk. 19th c.? **Ataqtï-toru-bay** (Atyrs. 81). ⇨ **ATAQ** + **TORÏ.**

ATAL Kzk. 19th c. **Atal-bay** [Аталбай] (AOP 62).

ATALA Bulg. 6th c. **Atala** [Ἀταλα], a Bulghar warrior (Byz. Turc. 76-77).

ATALÏ see **AMAN-ATALÏ**

ATALÏQ Chuv. 18th-19th c. **Atalïk** [Аталыкъ] (Magn. 30); Trkm. 20th c. **Atalïq** [Atalïq] (Zaj. 1971, 325); Tat. **Atalïq** [Аталык], governor in Kazan (PSRL XIX, 35, 249); Kzk. 18th c. - 19th c. **Atalïq** [Аталык] (Tunyšp. 65, 67, 71-73); Kzk. 19th c. **Atalïq** [Аталык] (AOO 62); Kzk. 19th c. **Atalïq** [Аталык] (SOK 218); Kzk. 19th c. **Atalïq** [Джіянлык Аталыков] (Grod., Pril. 23); Kirg. **Atalïq** [Аталык] (Proben V, 267 /269/). ✧ I. 'Paternity' (Bese 4); II. Title and secondary component meaning: 1. 'teacher, educator, stepfather, guardian' (Crm., Kuman), 2. 'official of higher degree' (Crm.), 3. 'higher dignity, vezir, sheyk' (East. T.). ⇨ **ATA** + suff. *-lïq*.

ATAM Kzk. 19th c. **Atam** [Атамъ] (SKSO VIII, 203); Kzk. 19th c. **Atam-qul** [Атамкулъ Бикетаевъ] (AUK 416). ✧ 'My father'. ⇨ **ATA** + poss. suff. *-m*.

ATAMAN Chuv. 18th-19th c. **Adaman** (<**Ataman**) [Адаманъ] (Magn. 25); Tat.(Lit.) 1592 **Ataman** [Аразъ Атамановичъ] (Lit. Tat. 124); Bashk. 1746 **Ataman** [Атаман Минеевъ] (MIB III, 439); Chuv. 19th c. **Otoman** [Otoman] (Kronheim 96). ✧ 'Chief, leader' (Šipova). ⇨ **ATA** + suff. *-man*. See also **ATMAN**.

ATAMAR Kzk. 19th c. **Atamar** [Атамаръ] (AOP 38).

ATAN Kzk. 1823 **Atan** [اطلان] (MIK IV, 456); Kzk. 1846 **Atan** [бий Атан Исеневъ] (MKOP 154); Kzk.

1846 **Atan** [Чон (Чунг) Атановъ; Атань Исеневъ] (MKOP 100, 156); Kzk. 19th c. **Atan** [Атанъ] (SKSO II, 4); Kzk. 19th c. **Atan** [Атан] (AOA 98); Kzk. 19th c. **Atan** [Атан] (SOV 36); Kzk. 19th c. **Atan** [Атан] (AOk 86); Kzk. 19th c. **Atan-bay** [Атанбай] (SOV 48); Kzk. 19th c. **Atan-bay** [Атанбай] (SODž. 40); Kzk. 19th c. **Atan-bay** [Атанбай] (AOK 34); Kzk. 19th c. **Atan-bay** [Атанбаев] (Grod., Pril. 44); Kzk. 19th c. **Atan-bek** [Мендыбекъ Атонбековъ] (Grod., Pril. 72); Bashk. 1751 **Atan-γul** [Атангул Тойгунов] (MIB IV/1, 43); Bashk. 1756 **Atan-γul** [Сеиткул Атангулов] (MIB IV/1, 128); Bashk. 1756 **Atan-γul** [Чюраман Атангулов] (MIB IV/1, 128); Kzk. 19th c. **Atan-pir** [Атанъ-Пиръ Магомедъ] (Grod., Pril. 92); Bashk. 1783, 1784 **Atän** [Ахмер Атянев] (MIB V, 139, 152); Bashk. 1784 **Atän / Antän?** [Юртума Атянев (Антянев)] (MIB V, 154); Kzk. 19th c. **Aten-bek < Atan-bek?** [Атембек] (SODž. 64); Kzk. 19th c. **Aten-bek < Atan-bek?** [Атенбек] (AOO 58). ✧ '(Castrated/draught) Camel; Camel-foal born first; (fig.) First-born child' cf. Kzk. *atan* 'id.' (KzRS), Bashk. *atan* 'племенной верблюд; верблюжонок, родившийся первым' (BRS/Uraksin). ⇨ **ATAN.**

ATEN-BEK see **ATAN**

ATAN-TAY Kzk. 1822 **Atan-tay** [Акчигитъ Атантаевъ] (TOUAK XXIV, 131); Kzk. 19th c. **Atan-tay** [Атантай] (SOK 4); Kzk. 19th c. **Atan-tay** [Джабага Атантаев] (Grod., Pril. 57); Kzk. 19th c. **Atan-tay** [Атантай] (SOV 50); Kirg. **Atan-tay** [Атантай] (Jud. 79); Kirg. 1827 **Atan-tay** [Атантай] (Konšin, Mat. I-III, 113); Kirg. 19th c. **Atan-tay** [Атантай], from the Sayaq tribe (Valihanov, Soč. 128 etc.); Kirg. 19th c. **Atan-tay** [Атантай] (Potanin II, 3). ✧ 'Castrated camel-foal'. ⇨ **ATAN** + **TAY** or suff. *-tay(1,2)*?

ATANAY Kzk. 19th c. **Atanay** [Атанай] (AOO 18); Kzk. 19th c. **Atanay** [Атанай] (SOV 92). ⇨ **ATAN** + dim. suff. *-ay*.

ATANČE Hak. 19th-20th c. **Atanče** [Атанче] (HRS 348). ✧ 'Little camel'? Derived from Hak. *Atan* 'рабочий верблюд' (Butanaev) + suff. *-ča*.

ATANİK Hak. 19th-20th c. **Atanik** [Атаник], fem. (HRS 353). ✧ Antonina (R.).

ATAR I. Kzk. 19th c. **Atar** [Атар] (SODž. 130); Kzk. 19th c. **Atar-bay** [Атарбай] (AOAtb. 66); Kzk. 19th c. **Atar-bay** [Атарбай] (SODž. 4). ✧ 'He who will shoot/throw; Shooter' (Bese 12), cf. Kzk. *at-* 'стрелять' (KzRS) + aor. suff. *-ar*. See also **BAY-ATAR.**

ATAR II. Yak. **Atar** [Атар] (Pek.).

ATAR-BAS? Yak. **Atar-bas?** [Атарбас] (Pek.). ⇨ **ATAR II. + BAŠ?**

ATAŠ Alt. 19th-20th c. **Adaš** [Адаш], fem. (OjrRS 211); Kzk. 19th c. **Ataš** [Аташ] (AOK 78); Kzk. 19th

c. **Ataš** [Аташ] (SOV 40); Kkalp. 20th c. **Ataš** [Аташ] (KkRS 772); Bashk. 1756 **Ataš-mulla** [Аташ-мулла] (MIB IV/1, 130); *TN:* Kuman 15th c. **Ataš** [Othas ylys zallasa], a village in the district of Kecskemét (Lesser Kumania), Hungary (Gyárfás III, 671). ✧ I. 'Namesake'? (cf. Rásonyi, Anthr. 144, KÖA 123), Kuman, Chag. *ataš*, Kzk. *atas* < *attas* 'Namensvetter' (Radl. I, 457), Alt. *adaš* 'тёзка, одноименный' (OjrRS), Trk. a:тдаш, *ātdaš* (Sev., Clauson).; II. 'Fire, flame'? cf. Uzb. *ataš* 'das Feuer' (Radl. I, 457), Trkm. *ātaš* 'огонь, пламя' (TrkmRS) (<P.); III. 'Bulging (eye)'? cf. Bashk. *ataš* 'выпуклый; выпученный' (BRS/Uraksin); IV. 'Father-like' cf. Bashk. *atas* 'похожий на отца; весь в отца' (BRS/Uraksin); V. 'Train'? cf. Kzk. dial. *ataš* 'поезд' (QTDS). ⇨ **ATA?** + suff. *-š / -s?*

ATAW Kkalp. 20th c. **Ataw-bay** [Атавбай / Атаўбай] (Bask., Kkalp. 399, KkRS 772).

ATBAN Kzk. 19th c. **Atban** [Атбанъ] (SOK 62).

ATÄN see **ATAN**

ATEY see **ATAY**

ATES Bashk. 1764 **Ates / Atas?** [Канмурза Атесев] (MIB IV/1, 291). ⇨ **ATAŠ?**

ATEŠ Trkm. **Ateš** [Атешъ] (Mel'gunov 320); Bashk. 1735 **Ateš** [Канай Атяшевъ], a tarχan (Vel.-Zern., Dict. 13); Kzk. 19th c. **Ateš** [Атешъ] (SOV 64); Trkm. 1816 **Ateš-muχammed-yüzbašī** [Атеш Мухаммед-юзбаши] (MIT II, 390). ✧ 'Fire, flame'? cf. Crm., Turk. *atäš* 'das Feuer' (Radl. I, 458) Uzb. *ataš* 'das Feuer' (Radl. I, 457), Trkm. *ātaš* 'огонь, пламя' (TrkmRS) (<P.). ⇨ **ATAŠ?**

ATГAY see **ATÏQAY?**

ATÏY see **ATÏY**

ATİKE Crm.Tat. 1721 **Atike-sultana** [عا تكه سلطان / Атике-султана], Islam Girey's daughter (Bakč. Nadp. 27).

ATİKEY see **ATÏQAY?**

ATİKES Bashk. 1738 **Atikes** [Касай Атикесев] (MIB III, 391). ⇨ **ATQAS?**

ATİKEŠ Bashk. 1663 **Atigeš? / Atï-geš?** [Атыгеш] (MIB I, 176); Bashk. 1735 **Atikeš** [Атикешъ Дербышевъ], a tarχan (Vel.-Zern., Bašk. 15).

ATÏ Kzk. 19th c. **Atï-bek** [Атыбек] (SODž. 48); *TN:* Kzk. **Atï-bay** [Атыбай] (Karta JAR XI). See also **JAL-ATÏ**.

ATÏ-GEN Kirg. **Atï-gen** [Атыгенъ], one of the legendary forefathers of the Kirghiz (ZIRGO V, 140). ⇨ **ATÏ** + **KEN / KEM?**

ATÏ-ГARAY Kzk. 19th c. **Atï-γaray** [Атыгарай] (SODž. 156). ⇨ **ATÏ** + **QARAY?** See also **ATA-QARAY**.

ATÏ-QUTUMA Bashk. 1735 **Atï-qutuma** [Еникей, Юмакай Атикутуминъ], a tarχan (Vel.-Zern., Bašk. 13). ⇨ **ATÏ**.

ATÏГA Hak. 19th-20th c. **Atïγa** (HRS 348).

ATÏY Kzk. 19th c. **Atiy-bay** [Атийбай] (SOK 92).

ATÏQ Bashk. 1735 **Atïq** [Атыкъ Сююндюковъ], a tarχan (Vel.-Zern., Bašk. 24); Tat.(Sib.) 1581 **Atïq / Atik** [Myrza Atyk], fought against Yermak (Radl., Aus Sib. I, 149, Sib. Let. Remizovsk.? 329); Tat. 1630, 1634 **Atïq / Atïšqa** [Атык, Атышка] (Miller, Ist. Sib. II, 369, 417). See also **AQ-BAŠ-ATÏQ**.

ATÏQA Bashk. 1723, 1726 **Atïqa** [Атика Куеков, Атика Куюков] (MIB III, 239).

ATÏQAY? Kzk. 19th c. **Atγay** [Атгай] (AOO 22, 62, 66); Bashk. 1675 **Atikey** [Байдаш Атикеев] (MIB I, 201); Bashk. 1735 **Atikey** [Атикей Калисевъ], a tarχan (Vel.-Zern., Bašk. 23); Bashk. 18th c. **Atikey** [Батал (Баттал) Атикеев] (MIB V, 415); Bashk. 1760 **Atikey?** [Атикей Девлетев] (MIB IV/1, 199); Kzk. 19th c. **Atïγay** [Атыгай] (Grod., Pril. 23); Kzk. 19th c. **Atïγay** [Атыгай] (AOK 14); Kzk. 19th c. **Atïγay** [Атыгай] (AOA 22); Kzk. 19th c. **Atïγay** [Атыгай] (AOP 30); Kzk. 19th c. **Atïγay** [Атыгай] (AOO 58); Tat. 1763 **Atïqay / Attaqay?** [Аттакаевъ Улла], a captain (PSZRI XVI, 322).

ATÏL Kzk. 19th c. **Atïl** [Атылъ] (SOV 152); Kzk. 19th c. **Atïl-bek** [Атылбек] (SOK 90). ⇨ **ATAL?**

ATÏLAY Kzk. 19th c. **Atïlay** [Атылай] (SODž. 162); Kzk. 19th c. **Atïlay** [Атылай] (SOV 100).

ATÏLAQ Kzk. 1862 **Atïlaq** [Атылакъ Даутовъ] (ZIRGOGeogr. I, 311).

ATÏLLÏQA Yak. **Atïllïqa / Atïllïqaï** [Атыллыка / Атыллыкаы], a bogatyr, the spirit of waters (Pek.). ✧ 'Taking broad steps' cf. Yak. *atïllā-* 'широко шагать, делать широкий шаг' (JRS).

ATÏM Kzk. 19th c. **Atïm-pay** [Атымпай] (SOK 122). ✧ '?' cf. Kzk. PNs *Atïm, Atïmtay* (Žanuzakov-Esbaeva).

ATÏM-TAY Kzk. 19th c.? **Atïm-tay** (Atyns. 118); Kzk. 19th c. **Atïm-tay** [Атымтай] (SOK 56). ⇨ **ATÏM?** + **TAY** or suff. *-tay(1,2)?*

ATÏM-TAY-JOMART Kzk. 19th c.? **Atïm-tay-Jomart**, a very rich man (Atyns. 43). ⇨ **ATÏM-TAY** + **JOMART.**

ATÏP-TAY? Kzk. **Atïp-tay** (Sb. Syr-D. IX, 50). ⇨ **TAY?** or suff. *-tay(1,2)?*

ATÏŠ Karakh. **Atïš** [Atïş / atïš] (MK/Atalay 831, DTS); Kzk. 19th c. **Atïš** [Атышъ / Атишъ] (SOK 76, 234). ✧ 'Shooting' cf. Karakh. *atïš* 'стрельба, перестрелка' (DTS).

ATÏZ Kzk. 19th c. **Atïz-bek** [Атызбекъ] (SODž. 102).

ATKE Chag. 16th c. **Atke** [Атке], a shah (Ivanov 46).

ATQAS Bashk. 1735 **Atqas** [Ялукей Аткасевъ], a tarχan (Vel.-Zern., Bašk. 14); Bashk. 1735 **Atqas** [Мангушъ Аткасевъ], a tarχan (Vel.-Zern., Bašk. 14).

ATQUČİ Chag. 15th c. **Atquči** [انتوجی قولولوق / Атгкучи Гкуллугкъ] (Šejb. LXII). ✧ 'Shooter, warrior' cf. Chag. *atquči* 'der Schütze, Kämpfer' (Radl. I, 456).

ATLAMÏŠ Khorezm./Chag.? 1402 **Atïlmïš? / Atlamïš?** [Atïlmiš], mentioned in the exchange of letters between Timur (Temür) (1370-1405) and the mamluk sultan al-Nāsir Faraj (1405-1412) concerning the extradition of Atïlm'š (Björkm. 129); Kuman 1495 **Atlamïš** [Athlamos], a Kuman in Hungary (Csánki I, 685); Maml.? 14th c. **Atlamïš** [اتلمش] (Tarǰ/Houtsma 30); Maml. 1400 **Atlamïš** [اطلمش] (Ibn Taghrīb. VI, 48, 59); Tat. 1662 **Atlamïš** [Атлемишко] (DAI IV, 285); Bashk. 1709 **Atlamïš** [Атламыш Агилдин] (MIB I, 264). ✧ 'Stepped, jumped'? (Gombocz, ÁTSz. 27), 'Walking on the path of life' (Sattarov) cf. Kuman, Crm., Tat. *atla-* 'schreiten', East. T. *atla-* 'schreiten, überschreiten' (Radl. I, 467).

ATLAN Chuv. 18th-19th c. **Atlan** [Атланъ] (Magn. 30). ✧ 'Mount! Get on horseback!' cf. Kuman, Chag., Crm., Kar., Tat., Turk. *atlan-* 'zu Pferde steigen' (Radl. I, 468).

ATLANAY Bashk. 1693 **Atlanay** [Атланайко Кудеэв], from Ufa (MIB I, 84). ⇨ **ATLAN** + suff. -*ay*.

ATLAR Uzb. 19th c. **Atlar-bek** [Атларъ-бекъ], a kurgan (burial mound) in Khiva (AUK 417).

ATLAS Az. **Atlas** [Hadi Atlasov] (Mende 105, 137, 138); Tat. 1764 **Atlas** [Атлас] (MIB IV/1, 295). ✧ 'A kind of silk' cf. Tat. PN *Atlas* (Sattarov).

ATLÏ Karch. **Atlï** [Атлы] (Sysoev 129); Trkm. 1858 **Atlï-bay** [Атлы-бай], from the Ošaq clan of the Yomut tribe (MIT II, 589, 590); Oghuz 12th c. **Atlï-qan** [اتلى], Tatar-qan's grandson, Atsïz-qan's father (Abulg./Desm. 11); Oghuz 12th c. **Atlïq / Atlïy** [اتليغ بن اتسز / Атлык], Atsïz Khorezmshah's (1127-1156) son, İl-arslan Tāj al-Dunyā (1156-1172) (J̌uwaynī II, 5, 293, MIT I, 442); Kzk. 19th c. **Attï-bay** [Аттыбай] (SOV 54). ✧ I. 'Having a name; famous; named' cf. Uyg., Karakh. *atlïγ* I 'называемый, именуемый; именитый, славный' (DTS), Chag. *atlïγ* 'berühmt' (Radl. I, 470), Kuman, Crm., Tat. *atlï* 'einen Namen habend' (Radl. I, 470); II. 'Having a horse' cf. Türk., Uyg. *atlïγ* II 'имеющий коня; конный' (DTS), Kuman, Alt., Crm., Tat., Turk. *atlï* 'ein Pferd habend; zu Pferde sitzend, beritten' (Radl. I, 469). See also **ATLÏΓ, ATSÏZ.**

ATLÏΓ see **ATLÏ**

ATLÏQ see **ATLÏ**

ATMAǰA Turk. 1488 **Atmaǰa** (Gökb., Ed. 95); Yürük 1543 **Atmaǰa** (Gökb., Rum. 186); Yürük 16th c. **Atmaǰa** [اتمجه], from the Yürüks of Kocacık, Turkey (Gökb., Rum. 103); Trkm. 1692 **Atmaǰa** [اتمجه] (Refik, Anad. 104); Turk. 1570 **Atmaǰa (aydïn)**, from Hungary (Dávid). ✧ 'Hawk' cf. Chag., Turk. *atmaǰa* 'der Habicht' (Radl. I, 473), Turk. *atmaca* 'hawk (Accipiter)' (TED).

ATMAN Bashk. 1761 **Atman** [Атман Тарханов] (MIB IV/1, 216); Kzk. 19th c. **Atman** [Атман] (SOK 36); Bashk. 1770 **Atmen?** [Алдыргуш Атменев] (MIB IV/1, 349). ⇨ **ATAMAN?**

ATMANAY Tat. 1632 **Atmanay** [Акочкар Атманаев] (Miller, Ist. Sib. II, 391); Tat. 1654 **Atmanay** [Атманай Байтерековъ] (AI IV, 236); Nog. 1649 **Atmanay** [Атманай], a murza (AI IV, 87); Crm. 1651 **Atmanay-bek** [اطمناى بك] (Vel.-Zern., Crim. 452, 457).

ATMAS Chuv. 18th-19th c. **Atmas** [Атмасъ] (Magn. 30).

ATMEN see **ATMAN**

ATMÏŠ Chag. 1544 **Atmïš** [Атмыш], an emir (Ivanov 223); Chuv. 18th-19th c. **Atmïš** [Отмешъ] (Magn. 63); Chuv. 18th-19th c. **Atmïš** [Атмешъ] (Magn. 30); Tat. 1631 **Atmïš** [Адията (Одията) Атмышев (Отмышев) Баубеков] (Miller, Ist. Sib. II, 386). ⇨ **ALTMÏŠ?**

ATNA see **ADÏNA**

ATOYAQ Hak. 19th-20th c. **Atoyaq** [Атояк] (HRS 353).

ATRAQ Oghuz 10th c. **Atraq** [Атрак], al-Qatᶜan's son, a chieftain of the Ghuzz (MIT I, 162-63 (after Ibn Faḍlān)).

ATRAW Kzk. 19th c. **Atraw / Atrau** [Атрау] (SOK 148).

ATSAQ Uyg. 12th c. - 14th c. **Atsaq** [atsaq] (Radl., USp. 123, DTS). ✧ 'He who wants to shoot' (Blagova 1997, 713).

ATSÏZ Uyg. 8th c. **Atsïz** [titigči Atsiz], a bricklayer (Müller, Pfahl. 24); Oghuz 12th c. **Atsïz** [انوشتكين / اتسز بن قطب الدين محمد بن / Атсыз ибн Мухаммед ибн Ануштегин], a Khorezmshah (1127-1156) (J̌uwaynī 3-5, 7, 89, 293, Ibn al-Athīr/Tornb. X, 183, 476, XI, 44-45, 58-59, 138 Qazw. 490-91, 814, Bondārī 280-81, Rāwandī 129, 174 etc., Abulg./Desm. 50, MIT I, 316, 318, 319, 339, 341, 348, 356, 384, 392, 435, 442-44, Barth., Turk. 34, 103, 345-56, Togan, UTT 60); Selj. 1076 **Atsïz** [اتسز بن عوف], occupied Damascus, a commander of the army in Syria and Egypt (Abulfidā III, 238-39 etc., Weil, Chalif. III, 110, Ibn Khallikan 121, Ahbar 49); Selj. 1121 **Atsïz** [اتسز بن ترك] (Kamāladdīn: RHCHor II, 201); Oghuz/Trkm. / Selj.? 1071, 1072, 1079, 1095, 1105 **Atsïz** [انسز التركمانى أنسز بن أوق الخوارزمى] (Ibn al-Athīr/Tornb. X, 46, 68, 70, 71, Kamāladdīn: RHCHor 31, 47, 65, Ibn Taghrīb. II, 246, 259, 312, Qalānisi 98, 108-113, 146, Zetterst. 228-231, Björkm. 121); Khorezm. **Atsïz-qan** [اتسیز], Tatar-qan's descendant, Atlï-qan's (Atlïq's) son (Abulg./Desm. 11). ✧ I. 'Nameless; II. 'Without horses', cf. Rásonyi, Jerus. 91, F. Sümer, Eski Türklerde İsim Koyma Geleneklerinden: Atsız: Millî Kültür 47, 1984, pp. 4-5. ⇨ **AT** + suff. -*sïz*.

See also **ATLÏ**.

ATTEY Kirg. 20th c. **Attey** (Almásy 357).

ATTÏ see **ATLÏ**

ATU Chuv. 18th-19th c. **Atu-bay** [Атубай] (Magn. 30); Kzk. 19th c. **Atu-bay** [Атубай] (AUK 570); Chuv. 18th-19th c. **Atu-χan** [Атуханъ] (Magn. 30); Chuv. 18th-19th c. **Atugan / Atu-kan?** [Атуганъ] (Magn. 30).

ATUČÏ Maml. 1320 **Atuči** [اطوجى] (Tizeng. I, 257, 266 /after Al-Malik An-Nāsir/).

ATULU Kmk. 20th c. **Atolu?** (KSz. XIII, 170); Tat.(Sib.) **Atulū-batïr** [Atulu Batyr / Атулу батыр] (Proben IV, 167 /210/, 190 /235/). ⇨ **ATU?** + suff. -lu.

AU see **AW**

AUL see **AWUL**

AULAUČ Uyg. **Aulauč** [aulauč] (DTS).

AULKE Kzk. 19th c. **Aulke (<Aul-ake)** [Аульке] (AOK 74). ⇨ **AWUL** + suffixoid -ke < ake.

AUM Kzk. 19th c. **Aum-bek** [Аумбекъ] (AOO 62).

AUP Kzk. 19th c. **Aup-bay** [Аупбай] (SODž. 104).

AUS see **AWUZ**

AUZ see **AWUZ**

AVAN Chuv. 18th-19th c. **Avan** [Аванъ] (Magn. 24).

AVANDEY Chuv. 18th-19th c. **Avandey** [Авандей] (Magn. 24).

AVANDEY? Chuv. 18th-19th c. **Avendey?** [Авендей] (Magn. 24).

AVANKİN Chuv. 18th-19th c. **Avankin** [Аванкинъ] (Magn. 24).

AVELDEY Chuv. 18th-19th c. **Aveldey** [Авелдей] (Magn. 24).

AVENDİK Chuv. 18th-19th c. **Avendik** [Авендикъ] (Magn. 24).

AVER Chuv. 18th-19th c. **Aver** [Аверъ] (Magn. 24).

AVERİN Chuv. 18th-19th c. **Averin** [Аверинъ] (Magn. 24). ⇨ **AVER**.

AVERKA Chuv. 18th-19th c. **Averka** [Аверка] (Magn. 24).

AVEZ see **AWUZ**

AVLEY Chuv. 18th-19th c. **Avley** [Авлей] (Magn. 24).

AVLUČ Uyg. 8th c. **Avluč / Avluč-tarχan** [Avluç / avluč (ailuč?) tarχan] (EUTS (Müller, Pfahl. 12, 19), DTS).

AVRÏŠ Chuv. 18th-19th c. **Avrïš** [Авришъ] (Magn. 24).

AVRÏŠKA Chuv. 18th-19th c. **Avrïška** [Авришка] (Magn. 24). ⇨ **AVRÏŠ**.

AW Kzk. 19th c. **Aw-bay / Au-bay** [Аубай] (SOK 112); Kzk. 19th c. **Aw-batïr / Au-batïr** [Аубатыръ] (SOK 56); Kzk. **Aw-pay / Au-pay** [Букаш Аупаев], a merchant (Valihanov, Soč. 342); Kzk. 19th c. **Aw-pay / Au-pay** [Аупай] (SOK 256); Kzk. 19th c. **Aw-pay / Au-pay** [Аупай] (AOK 122). ✧ 'Hunting' cf. Kzk. au /

aw 'сети, невод; охота' (KzRS).

AW-BAQÏR see **ABU-BAQÏR**

AW-DÖWLET see **AQ-DAWLET**

AWA Oghuz/Trkm. 13th c. **Awa** [اوا / Ава], Oghuz Khan's legendary grandson, Teñgiz-χan's son (Abulg./Kon. 520, 565, 615). ✧ 'High-quality'? (Kononov).

AWAQ Selj. / Khorezm.? 1071, 1072, 1075, 1079, 1105 **Awaq / Uwaq?** [أنسـز بـن أوق الـخوارزمى / أوق التـركى], Atsïz's or/and Čawlï's father? (Kamāladdīn: RHCHor II, 31, 41, 47, 65, Qalānisi 98, 107-113, 146, Ibn al-Athīr/Tornb. X, 46).

AWAN Kzk. 18th c. - 19th c. **Awan** [Ауан] (Tynyšp. 65).

AWANAŠ Chag. 15th c. - 16th c. **Awanaš** [او اناش / واناش], a Shaybānid (Šejb. LI); Chag. 17th c. **Awanaš-χan / Awanïš-χan?** [اوانش خـان], a Khan in Khiva (Abulg./Desm. 228).

AWAŠBAN Oghuz/Trkm. 13th c. **Awašban-χoĵa** [اواشبان حواجه / Авашбан-ходжа] (Abulg./Kon. 725).

AWAZ Kkalp. 1740 **Awäz-biy** [Авяз-бий] (MIKk. 208); Bashk. 1782 **Äwäz** [Салих Авязев] (MIB V, 133); Kzk. 18th c. - 19th c. **Äwez** [Ауэз] (Tynyšp. 66); Kzk. 18th c. - 19th c. **Äwez-bek** [Ауэз-бек] (Tynyšp. 66); Kkalp. 1715 **Äwez-inaq** [Авез инак], an emir (MIKk. 92); Oghuz/Trkm. 13th c. **Ewez** [عوض / Эвез] (Abulg./Kon. 410); Trkm. 1806 **Ewez-bek-berdï-bek** [Эвез Бек-берды-бек], a Yomut chief (MIT II, 370); Trkm. 1821 **Ewez / Äwäz? / Awaz** [Эвез (Аваз) Мухаммед], an historien and mulla from Khokand (MIT II, 295, 357, 420, 490); Trkm. 1804 **Ewez-bek** [Эвез-бек], from the Salaq tribe (MIT II, 364, 365); Trkm. 1817/18 **Ewez-bek** [Эвез-бек], from the Teke tribe (MIT II, 406); Uzb. 1850 **Ewez-bek** [Эвез-бек] (MIT II, 524); Trkm. 1838 **Ewez-biy** [Эвез-бий], a χoĵa, (MIT II, 473, 475, 477); Trkm. 1838 **Ewez-χoĵa** [Эвез-ходжа], a χoĵa, the Sheykh-ul-Islam (MIT II, 473, 475, 477, 482); Uzb. 1804/05 **Ewez-inaq / Ewez-biy / Ewez-bek / Awaz-bek** [Эвез-инак (Эвез-бек, Эвез-бий, Аваз / Иваз)], from the Qoñrat tribe (MIT II, 24, 202, 258, 296, 341, 353, 355, 356); Uzb. 1804 **Ewez-inâq** [Эвез-инак], an emir from the Mañyït tribe (MIT II, 365); Uzb. 1825 **Ewez-inâq** [Эвез-инак], a commander of the army from Khiva (MIT II, 223). ✧ 'Voice/reputation; fame?' cf. Chag., Az., Tat. *auaz / awaz* 'Stimme, Ton, Klang, Echo, Ruf, Gerücht' (Radl. I, 68), Trkm. *owāz* 'голос, звук; мелодия' (TrkmRS), Uzb. *âwâz* 'голос, звук' (UzbRS), Kzk. *äwez* 'голос, мотив, напев' (KzRS) (<P.).

AWAZ-BERDİ Uzb. 20th c. **Awaz-berdi / Âwâz-berdi** [Авазберди] (Begmatov 1984, 202) ✧ 'Voice/reputation has given him/her'? ⇨ **AWAZ** + **BERDİ**.

AWAZ-TURDÏ   Uzb. 20th c. **Awaz-turdï / Âwâz-turdï** [Авазгурди] (Begmatov 1984, 204); Trkm. **Owāz-durdï-χan** [Овасъ-Дурды-ханъ] (VoennSb. CXXIX, 327). ✧ 'Voice/reputation has stayed/survived'. ⇨ **AWAZ + TURDÏ.**

AWČÏ-PÏRÏM   Az.? **Awčï-pirim** [Овчи-Пирим], a hunter (SMOK VII (2 otd.), 98). ✧ 'Hunter - old man of mine'. ⇨ **AWJÏ + PÏR** + poss. suff. *-im.*

AWČÏ-TARXAN see **AWJÏ**

AWČÏN   Kuman 1096 **Awčïn / Owčïn?** [Овчинъ], a Polovets prince (PSRL I, 104, Ipat. 242 /164/).

AWJÏ   Khazar 683 **Awčï-tarχan** [Awčʿı Tʿarχan] (Golden 154); Uzb. 1839 **Awču / Auču** [Аучу Ишева], from Tashkent (Konšin, Mat. V, 48); Khorezm.? 1312, 1313 **Awjï** [اوجی], one of Toqtay-han's emirs (Dawād. 255, 275); Trkm. 1768 **Awjï** [اوجی], a Türkmen nomadic tribe (aşiret) in the province of Karaman, Turkey (Refik, Anad. 219). ✧ 'Hunter' cf. Uyg., Karakh. *avčï* 'охотник' (DTS).

AWDA   Tat.(Sib.) 1636 **Awda-bek** [Аудабеков Юзеячко] (Miller, Ist. Sib. II, 439).

AWDEY   Kuman? 1259 **Awdey** [Авдѣй], a sculptor (Ipat. 559 /560/).

AWDUL   Tat.(GH) 1338 **Awdul** [Авдулъ], envoy of the Horde (PSRL X, 208). ✧ Abdul (Ar.).

AWΓAR   Tat.? **Awγar / Awγur?** [Авгаръ (Авгуръ)], a prince (PSRL (Russk. Hr.), 316, II, 131).

AWÏLŠÏX   Crm. 1508 **Awïlšïχ** [Абдылъ-Авелшихъ], envoy from the Crimea (PSRL VIII, 279). ⇨ **?** + dim. suff. *-šïχ < -čïq.*

AWÏŠ   Oghuz/Trkm.? **Awïš / Awuš?** [Авеш, Ауш], Yulduz-χan's son, the same as Awšar? (RaD I/1, 76).

AWÏZ-AČÏQ   Kzk. 19th c. **Auz-ačik (<Awuz-ačïq / Awz-ačïq)** [Аузъ-Ачикъ] (Grod., Pril. 89). ✧ 'Mouth-open; Open-mouthed'. ⇨ **AWUZ? + AČÏQ.**

AWÏZ-BĀKÏ   Tat. 1681 **Awïz-bāki** [Авезбакѣй (Овезбакѣй) Кулмаметевъ] (DAI VIII, 319, 320). ⇨ **ABÏZ + BĀKÏ.**

AWÏZÏQ   Kzk. 18th c. - 19th c. **Awïzïq** [Ауэзек] (Tynγšp. 67). ✧ 'Little mouth' cf. Crm., Kzk., Tat. *auz* 'der Mund, die Öffnung' (Radl. I, 82) + dim. *-ïq.*

AWSAR   Kzk. 19th c. **Ausar-bay (<Awsar-bay)** [Аусарбай] (SOK 210); Oghuz/Trkm. 13th c. **Awsar** [اوسار / Авсар], Ögürjik-alp's son (Abulg./Kon. 1235, 1270).

AWSEYN   Tat.(Lit.) 1523 **Awseyn** [Авсеин], a prince (Lit. Tat. 2). ✧ Hüseyn (Ar.).?

AWSÏ   Kzk. 19th c. **Ausï-bay / Awsï-bay** [Аусибай] (SOK 36).

AWSUN-AY   Kzk. 19th c. **Awsun-ay / Owsun-ay** [Овсунъ-Ай], fem. (Grod., Pril. 147). ⇨ **AY.**

AWŠAR   **Aušar** [اوشر] (RaD; Pelliot, 192); Oghuz/Trkm. 13th c. **Awšar** [اوشار / Авшар], Oghuz Khan's grandson, Yulduz-χan's son (Abulg./Kon. 515, 550, 600); Trkm. 1613 **Awšar** [اوشر], a Türkmen ethnic community (cemaat) in Turkey (Refik, Anad. 69); Selj.? 1133 **Awšar-eri** [Αυσαραρις], a Turkic chieftain (Byz. Turc.?). ✧ 'Avshar (ethnonym)' (Pelliot 192, 194, Németh, HMK 32).

AWUL   Kzk. 19th c. **Aul-bay / Awul-bay** [Аульбай] (SOV 16); Kzk. 19th c. **Aul-bek** [Аульбекъ] (AOK 82); Kzk. 19th c. **Aul-bek** [Аульбекъ] (SODž.50, 72, 152); Kzk. 19th c. **Aul-bek** [Аульбекъ] (SOV 76, 148); Kzk. 19th c. **Aul-bek** [Аульбекъ] (SOK 34); Kzk. 19th c. **Aul-bek** [Аульбекъ] (AOP 22). ✧ 'Aul (group of nomad tents); village' cf. Kuman, Crm., Kzk., Tat. *aul* 'Aul, Jurten die an einer Stelle zusammenstehen' (Radl. I, 74), Kzk. *avïl* 'Göçebelik devirdeki bir kaç çadırdan meydana gelen topluluk; Köy' (KZTS). See also **DUS-AWUL.**

AWUZ   Kzk. 19th c. **Awus-pek** [Ауспек] (SOK 32); Kzk. 19th c. **Awuz** [Аузъ] (SODž. 42); Kzk. 19th c. **Awuz-bay** [Аузбай] (AOP 18). ✧ 'Mouth' cf. Tat. (Tob.) *aγac* (=*aγač*) 'tree, wood' (Tumaševa 1961, 97), Tat.(Bar.) *aйus/aйuz* ' рот, уста' (Dmitrieva, Barab., 129), Kzk. *awïz* 'id.' (KzRS). See also **AΓAC-AWUZ, SALQ-AWUZ.**

AWWEL   Bashk. 1780 **Awwel** [Едигар Аввелев] (MIB V, 117).

AZ I.   Kzk. 19th c. **Az** [Джантлеу Азевъ] (AOK 98); Kzk. 19th c. **Az-bay** [Азбай] (AOK 38); Tat.(Sib.) 1634 **Az-bey** [Азбей Чуна] (Miller, Ist. Sib. II, 410); Kzk. 19th c. **Az-bek** [Азбекъ] (SOK 100).

AZ II.   Maml. 14th c. **Ās** [اصٓ] (Sauvaget 37). ✧ 'As (Alan, Osetin)' (Sauvaget 37), cf. Türk *az* IV 'азы, азский народ' (DTS).

AZ-BĀKÏ   Tat. 1662 **Az-bāki** [Азбакѣй Кулмаметевъ] (AI IV, 315). ⇨ **AS? + BĀKÏ.**

AZ-BERDÏ   Tat.(Lit.) 1592 **Az-berdi / Az-berdey** [Нелдеяр Азбердеевичъ] (Lit. Tat. 123); Tat.? 1442, 1445 **Az-berdi / Az-berdey?** [Азбердѣй], a prince of the Horde (PSRL VIII, 111, XII, 62); *TN:* Crm. 19th c. **Az-berdi** [Аз-Берди], a village in the Crimea (Keppen, II, 5. b.); *TN:* Crm. **Az-berdi / Az-berde** [Azberde], a village(?) north-east of Karasubazar (Jervis VIII). ⇨ **AS / AZ + BERDÏ.**

AZ-BERGEN   Kzk. 19th c. **Az-bergen** [Азбергенъ] (SOK 170, 286); Kzk. 1858 **Az-bergen / Aziz-bergen?** [Азберген / Азизберген], a biy (SOK 170, 286). ⇨ **AS / AZ? + BERGEN.**

AZ-BÏ-KÏLDÏY   Tat.(Sib.) 1643 **Az-bi-kildiy** [Азбыкилдей / Абылкилдей] (Miller, Ist. Sib. II, 490). ⇨ **AS / AZ + BÏ + KELDÏ.**

AZ-BUΓA   Turk.? 1432 **Az-buγa**, a Turkic commander (Bogdan, Br. 40). ⇨ **AS / AZ + BUQA.**

AZ-JANÏ-BEK   Kzk. 19th c. **Az-janï-bek** [Азъ-Джанибекъ] (Potanin, Pred. 67). ⇨ **AS / AZ + JANÏ.**

AZA Tuv. 19th c. **Aza / Aza-qan** [Аза], a devil (Proben IX, 8, 19, 44 etc.). ✧ 'Evil spirit, demon' cf. Alt. *aza* 'Teufel, böser Geist' (Radl. I, 557).

AZADE Turk. 1360 **Azade-χatun** [ازاده‌خاتون] (MB Qastam. 80). ✧ 'Free, liberated'. ⇨ **AZAT** + fem. suff. *-e*.

AZAKEY Bashk. 1735 **Azakey** [Акчюра Азакеев] (MIB III, 344).

AZAQ Oghuz **Azaq** [azaq / Азак], an emir of the Ghuzz (MIT I, 310(?), DTS); Maml. 1333/34 **Azaq** [Saifaddīn Azaq an-Nāṣirī], an emir (Björkm. 160). ✧ 'Foot'? (Blagova 1997, 709). ⇨ **AYAQ.**

AZAMAY Bashk. 1754 **Azamay** [Азамай Игишев] (MIB IV/1, 83). ✧ 'He won't be lost'? cf. Bashk. *aδa-* 'теряться' (BRS/Uraksin).

AZAMAT Balk. 20th c. **Azamat** (Pröhle, Balk. 205); Chuv. 18th c. **Azamat** [Азаматова], a village in the district of Cheboksary (Korsakov 282); Bashk.? 18th c. **Azamat** [Биктемир Азаматов] (Nepljuev 347); Bashk. 1783 **Azamat** [Азамат Енабердин] (MIB V, 145); Nog. 1649 **Azamat** [Азаматъ Хорошаевъ], a murza (AI IV, 122); Uzb. 1849 **Azamat** [Азаматъ] (Moskal'cev 76); Kzk. 1919 **Azamat-bek** (Nazaroff 212); Kzk. 1785 **Azamat-biy** [اضامت بى], a chief of a clan (aqsaqal) from the Maša tribe (MIK IV, 52, 53); Nog.? 1682 **Ozamat / Azamat?** [Озаматъ], a murza (DAI X, 161-65). ✧ 'Fine manly youngster; brave man, strong fellow' cf. Kzk. *azamat* 'id.' (KzTS).

AZAMAT-KİREY Nog. 20th c. **Azamat-kirey** [Фатима Азамат Кирей Байыс], father of Fatima, one of Baskakov's informants from the aul of Üykön-χalq (Ikon-halk), Cherkess Autonomous Oblast' (Bask., Nog. 143). ⇨ **AZAMAT** + **KERÄY.**

AZAN Kzk. 19th c. **Azam-bay** (<Azan-bay) [Азамбай] (SODž. 78); Bashk. 1732 **Azan-γul** [Азангул Утешев] (MIB III, 298). ✧ 'Calling for prayer' cf. Kzk., Tat. *azan* 'der Ruf zum Gebet' (Radl. I, 560).

AZANČÏ Bashk. 1795 **Azančï / Azanči** [Азанчей] (IOAIÊK XXVIII, 589). ✧ 'He who calls/invites for prayer' cf. Tat. *azančï* 'der Gebetrufer' (Radl. I, 560). ⇨ **AZAN** + suff. *-čï.*

AZARÏS Uzb. 1717 **Azarïs** [Asaris / Азарысъ], mentioned in the diary of Florio Beneveni (ZIRGO IX, 327, 398).

AZAT Trkm. **Azat** [Азат] (Sopieva 182); Trkm. 20th c. **Azat** [Azat], fem. (Zaj. 1971, 341); Trkm. 20th c. **Azat** [Азат], fem. (TrkmRS 30); Kkalp. 20th c. **Azat** [Азат] (KkRS 772); Bashk. 1771 **Azat-bay** [Кусяпкул Азатбаев] (MIB IV/1, 358); Trkm. 20th c. **Azat-gül**, fem. (Sopieva 182); Bashk. 1735 **Azät** (<Azat?) [Азять Каскиновъ], a tarχan (Vel.-Zern., Bašk. 18); Bashk. 1734 **Azät-qul** (<Azat-qul?) [Азяткулъ Еникеевъ], a tarχan (Vel.-Zern., Bašk. 10). ✧ 'Free,

liberated' (Erol II), cf. Az., Crm., Kar., Kirg., Kzk., Turk. *azat* (<P.) (Radl. I, 561); 'Freedom' (Sopieva 182).

AZAZÏL Tat.(Tara) **Azazïl** [Азазыл] (Proben IV, 132 /170/).

AZDAS Kzk. 19th c. **Azdas-pay** [Аздаспай] (SODž. 136).

AZÄČKA Bashk. 1666 **Azäčka?** [Азячка Аккочкаровъ] (Vel.-Zern., Bašk. 28).

AZÄT see **AZAT**

AZEK see **AZÏQ**

AZER Turk. 20th c. **Azer** (Önder, Göle). ✧ 'Tall, high' cf. Turk. dial. *azer* 'yüksek' (DS).

AZΓAN Uyg. **Azγan** [Azġan], fem. (EUTS).

AZΓANAZ Türk **Azγanaz** [Azγanaz] (ETY II, 121).

AZΓÏR? Maml. 1400/01, 1404/05 **Azγïr / Arγïz / Arγïr / Azγïd / Ozγïr / Uzγïr / Oraγïz / Uraγïz / Ozγara / Uzγara?** [ارغر / ارغذ / وازعره / وارغذ / ارغز / وازعر / ازغد] (Ibn Taghrīb. VI, 96, 176).

AZİ see **XAJİ**

AZİ-BABA see **XAJİ**

AZİ-GİREY see **KERÄY**

AZİK see **AZÏQ**

AZİKEY Chuv. 18th-19th c. **Azekey** [Азекей] (Magn. 25); Bashk. 1718 **Azikey** [Азикей Тиганов] (MIB III, 179, 180); Bashk. 1718 **Azikey** [Азикей Тимганов] (MIB III, 189); Bashk. 1735 **Azikey** [Азикей Кочкаров], a tarχan (Vel.-Zern., Bašk. 16); Bashk. 1735 **Azikey** [Азикей Назаргулов], a tarχan (Vel.-Zern., Bašk. 15); Bashk. 18th c. **Azikey** [Азекей Ератов] (MIB III, 109); Bashk. 1761 **Azikey** [Кудаш Азикеев] (MIB IV/1, 214). ⇨ **XAJİ?** + suff. *-key.*

AZİM Tat. **Azim** [Azimov] (Mende 69); Kirg. **Azim-bay** [Азимбай] (Jud. 93); Kzk. **Azim-Jan** [Azim-Djane / Азимъ-джанъ] (Levšin III, 96, Levchine 356). ✧ Azim (Ar.) 'Mighty, magnificent, glorious' (Ahmed), cf. Kirg. *azïm* 'великий' (Jud.) (<Ar.).

AZİZ Kirg. **Azïz** [Азыз] (Jud. 64); Kzk. 19th c. **Azis-bibi** (<Äziz-bibi) [Азисъ-биби] (SKSO IV, otd. II, 34); Trkm. 20th c. **Āziz** [Åziz] (Zaj. 1971, 327); Trkm. 20th c. **Āziz** [Азиз] (TrkmRS 778). ✧ 'Mighty, strong, illustrious, highly esteemed, dearly loved, beloved' (<Ar. PN *Aziz*), cf. *(Al-)Aziz* in Ar. PNs 'the All-mighty: one of the names of Allah' (Ahmed); cf. also Trkm. *ezïz* 'дорогой, милый, любимый' (TrkmRS), Kirg. *aziz / azïz* 'чтимый, уважаемый, дорогой' (Jud.), Kzk. *äziz / γaziz* 'қымбатты, ардақты, аяулы' (QTTS).

AZİZ-BERDİ Chag.? 1508 **Aziz-birdi-aγa** [Aziz Birdi Aghá] (Tar. Rashidi 185, 187-188); Yürük 1543 **Aziz-virdi** (Gökb., Rum. 231); Uzb. 20th c. **Äziz-berdi** [Азизберди] (Begmatov 1984, 202). ✧ 'The All-mighty (Allah) has given (him/her)'. ⇨ **AZİZ** + **BERDİ.**

AZİZ-BERGÄN   Kzk. 19th c. **Aziz-bergän** [Азизъ-Бергáнъ Дубаевъ] (Grod., Pril. 115); Uzb. 20th c. **Äziz-bergän** [Азизберган] (Begmatov 1984, 202). ✧ 'The All-mighty (Allah) has given (him/her)'. ⇨ AZİZ + BERGEN.

AZİJAQ   Hak.(Blt.) 19th-20th c. **Azïjaq** [Азыцак] (Proben IX, 357). ✧ 'Little'. ⇨ AZ + dim. suff. -jaq.

AZİQ   Chuv. 18th-19th c. **Azek** [Азекъ] (Magn. 25); Tat. 1668 **Azik / Azïq?** [Азикъ Кикѣевъ], first lieutenant (Kungursk. akty 15); Tat. 1715 **Azik (<Azïq)** [Янклыч Азиков] (MIB III, 124-25); Tat. 18th-19th c. **Azik (<Azïq)** [Ази / Азикъ] (Magn. 25); Bashk. 1732 **Azik (<Azïq)** [Азик Бортин] (MIB III, 302, 304); Bashk. 1740 **Azik (<Azïq)** [Азик Камакаев] (MIB III, 411-12). ✧ I. 'Provisions, food'? cf. Alt., Crm., Hak., Kirg., Kzk., Turk., etc. *azïq* 'Proviant, Mundvorrath' (Radl. I, 564); II. 'Advantage, benefit' cf. Uyg. *azïq* 'der Vortheil' (Radl. I, 565); III. 'Little' (as a protective PN), cf. Uyg. *azïq* 'wenig' (Radl. I, 565). See also MAMİR-AZİQ.

AZİL see ASİL

AZİP   Tat.(Sib.) 1599 **Azïp-saltan** [Азепъ-Салтанъ], Küčüm-qan's daughter (AI II, 17, 21, 23). ✧ I. '(The) Sweetest' cf. Turk. *a'zeb* 'daha tatlı, en tatlı' (Özön) (<Ar.); II. 'Bachelor' (Turk. *azeb* 'bekâr, evlenmemiş (erkek)' (Özön) (<Ar.).

AZİR   Kzk. 19th c. **Azir-bay (<Azïr-bay?)** [Азирбай] (Grod., Pril. 142). ✧ 'Ready'? cf. Kirg. *azir* 'готовый' (Jud.) (<Ar.).

AZİRAT   Tuv. 19th c. **Azïrat** [Азырат], fem. (Proben IX, 74).

AZLAГ   Khorezm. 13th c. **Azlaγ-šah** [ابوالمظر ازلاغ شاه السلطان], Terken (or Tergen, mistakenly Türkân) Xatun's son in the family of the Khorezmshahs, died in a battle against the Mongols (Nasawī 25, 62). ⇨ AZ + suff. -laγ / -laq?

AZMAГAN   Kzk. 19th c. **Azmaγan** [Азмаганъ] (AOO 46).

AZMAN   Türk 732 **Azman** [Azman], name of a horse (DTS). ✧ 'Castrated (Ram)' cf. Karakh. *azman* 'кастрированный баран, валух' (DTS).

AZMÄK?   Bashk. 1760 **Azmäk** [Темир Азмяков] (MIB IV/1, 193).

AZMET   Tat. 1764 **Azmet** [Султанак Азметев] (MIB IV/1, 279); Bashk. 1754 **Azmet** [Ишкиня Азметев] (MIB IV/1, 79); Bashk. 1754 **Azmet** [Азмекей Азметев] (MIB IV/1, 79). ⇨ ? + suff. -met.

AZNA see ADİNA

AZNAQAY see ADNAQAY

AZNÄŠ   Tat. 1696 **Aznäš** [Азняшко Казаевъ] (Kungursk. akty 244). ⇨ ADİNA + suff. -š.

AZŌR   Hak.(Blt.) 19th-20th c. **Azōr** [Азор] (Katanov, Otč. 9).

AZPAN   Kzk. 19th c. **Azpan-qul** [Азпанкулъ] (SODž.

14). ✧ 'Castrated (stallion, bull)' cf. Kzk. *azban* 'ein Hengst oder Ochs, der erst im fünften oder sechsten Jahre beschnitten ist' (Radl. I, 581). ⇨ AZMAN.

AŽAR see AJAR

AŽDAR   Trkm. 20th c. **Aždar** [Aždar] (Zaj. 1971, 331); Trkm. 20th c. **Aždar** [Аждар] (TrkmRS 29); NUyg.(Tar.) 19th c. **Aždar-χan** [ميرازدرحان / Миръ-Аждаръ-ханъ] (Pantusov, Tar. 109). ✧ 'Dragon' cf. Az., Turk. *äždäha / äždärha* 'id.' (Radl. I, 916), East.T. *ažderha:* 'id.' (Jarring), Trkm. *aždar / aždarhā* 'дракон; змей' (<P.).

AŽİ see AJİ

AŽİ-KERÄY see KERÄY

ĀXİY   Yak. **Āχïy / Āχïma** [Ахыі / Ахыма], nicknames (Pek.).

ĀXİMA see ĀXİY

ĀLİ   Kirg. **Ālï** [Аалы] (Jud. 27, 42); Kirg. **Ālï-bay** [Аалыбай] (Jud. 27, 42). ✧ 'Heel-piece' cf. Kirg. *ālï* 'подкова /на каблуке)' (Jud.).

ĀLİS   Yak. **Ālïs-luo χän** [Алыс], a hammersmith (Alïs Lukan) in a tale (Pek.). ✧ 'Chaff! Tease!' cf. Yak. *ālïs, ālsar* 'тереться, чесаться; говорить друг другу колкости' (Pek.).

ĀN-ARГİL-OYŪN   Yak. **Ān-arγïl-oyūn** [Ан Аргыл ойун], the first (black) shaman (Pek.).

ĀN-ČAČİN-OYŪN   Yak. **Ān-čačïn-oyūn** [Ан Чачык ойун], shamaness Čïsqïy-udaγan's son (Pek.).

ĀN-JALBĀTĪR   Yak. **Ān-jalbātïr** [Ан-Цалбатыр], a man in a tale (Pek.).

ĀN-JARSİLİ   Yak. **Ān-jarsïlï-buχatïr** [Ан-Царсылы-бухатыр], an abāsï-bogatyr (hero) (Pek.).

ĀN-JÄRSİN   Yak. **Ān-järsïn-buχatïr** [Ан-Царсын-бухатыр], a one-eyed warrior/hero (Pek.).

ĀN-DŪRAY-OBURГU   Yak. **Ān-dūray-oburγu** [Ан Дурай-обургу] (Pek.). ✧ 'Great/glorious - Ān-dūray' cf. Yak. *oburγu* I 'довольно большой; значительный', *oburγu* II 'выражает восторженно-почтительное отношение к высказываемому' (JRS).

ĀN-TAYBĪR   Yak. **Ān-taybïr** [Ан-Таібыр], one of Tosoγor-ūs' two sons (Pek.).

ĀNA   Yak. **Āna** [Ана], fem. (Pek.). ✧ Anna (R.).

ĀNİQA   Yak. **Ānïqa** [Эныка], fem. (Pek.). ✧ Anka (R.) < Anna (R.).

ĀNİSQA   Yak. **Ānïsqa** [Эныска], fem. (Pek.). ✧ Annuška (R.) < Anna (R.).

ĀNNA see ADİNA

ĀÑQA   Yak. **Āñqa** [Аӈка], fem. (Pek.). ⇨ ĀNİQA.

ĀR-YOTAY?   Hak. 19th-20th c. **Ār-yotay?** (Radl. I, 710).

ĀRİF   Kzk. 19th c. **Arip-pay** [Ариппай] (SODž. 42); Turk. 1609 **Ārif** [Ârif Çelebi] (Gökb., Ed. 42); Turk. 1494 **Ārif-aγa** [Ârif Ağa] (Gökb., Ed. 36). ✧ 'Wise; wise man' cf. Turk. *ârif* 'knowing, wise, sagacious;

skilled, expert' (TED), (Ar.).

ÂMÂN-KELDİ see **AMAN-GELDİ**

B

BA-BAXTA see **BAY-BAQTÏ**
BA-BOSUQ see **BAY-BOSUQ**
BA-GELDEY see **BAY-GELDİ**
BA-GİLDEY see **BAY-GELDİ**

BABA   Turk. **Baba** (Önder, Hınıs); Trkm. 20th c. **Baba** [Baba] (Zaj. 1971, 325); Kzk. 18th c. - 19th c. **Baba / Vaba** [Баба, Ваба] (Тynušp. 68); Uzb. 19th c. **Baba-aχond** (Németh, HMK 138 /after Vámbéry/); Trkm. 1855 **Baba-baχšï** [Баба-бахши], from the Yomut tribe (MIT II, 563, 575, 578); Trkm. 1826 **Baba-bay** [Баба-бай], from the Teke tribe (MIT II, 440, 448); Uzb. 1824/25 **Baba-bay** [Баба-бай] (MIT II, 426); Trkm. 1746 **Baba-bek** [Баба-бек], from the Salïr tribe (MIT II, 177); Trkm. 1867 **Baba-bek** [Баба-бек] (MIT II, 310); Kzk. 19th c. **Baba-bek** [Бабабекъ] (SKSO VIII, 232, Grod., Pril. 137); Uzb. 1770, 1779 **Baba-bek** [Баба-бек] (MIT II, 351-53, 359); Uzb. 1854 **Baba-bek** [Баба-бек], from the Qoñgrat tribe (MIT II, 540, 582, 584); Uzb. 1824/25 **Baba-bek-atalïq** [Баба-бек-аталык], from the Nayman tribe (MIT II, 428); Trkm. **Baba-ǰan** (Sopieva 182); Kzk. 19th c. **Baba-ǰan** [Бабаджанов] (AUK 160); Kzk. 19th c. **Baba-ǰan** [Бабаджан Гасанов] (Grod., Pril. 156); Uzb. 19th c. **Baba-ǰan** (Togan, BTT 402); Uzb. 1885 **Baba-ǰan-bay** [Бабаджан-Бай] (Moskal'cev 34); Uzb. 1843 **Baba-ǰan-inaq** [Бабаджан-инак] (MIT II, 490); Kirg. **Baba-dïyqan**, protector of the tillage (Jud. 205); Trkm. **Baba-γulï** [Бабагулы] (Sopieva 182); Trkm. 20th c. **Baba-han** [Babahan] (Zaj. 1971, 325); Chag. 16th c. **Baba-ǰan-sultan / Baba-sultan / Baba-χan** [بابا سلطان / Бабаджан-султан / Баба-султан / Баба-хан], Baraq-sultan's (1540-1553) son, died in 1581 (Šejb. LII, MIT II, 82, 86-88, Togan, BTT 135, 138, 143, 151); Uzb. 1828 **Baba-inaq** [Баба-инак] (MIT II, 451, 467, 506); Kzk. 19th c. **Baba-qan** [Бабаканъ], Merkit's father, a forefather of the Merkits (Potanin II, 5); Yürük 16th c. **Baba-paša** [بابا پاشا], from the Yürüks of Kocacık, Turkey (Gökb., Rum. 103); Trkm. 1804 **Baba-serdar** [Чумче-Баба-сердар], from the Yomut tribe (MIT II, 364). ✧ 'Father, grand-father (mother's father in Trkm.), ancestor; respectful elderly man, chief' (Radl. IV, 1563-64, Sopieva 182). Often used in compound names as a title or component. E. g. *Baba-ǰan* 'Good-natured, nice (elderly) man; Father (as pet name)'.

BABA-ǰAN-BERDİ   Yürük 1543 **Baba-ǰan-berdi**

(Gökb., Rum. 175). ✧ 'Dear father has given him'? ⇨ **BABA(-ǰAN) + BERDİ, BABA + ǰAN-BERDİ.**

BABA-YİGİT   Yürük 1543 **Baba-yigit** [بابا يكيت], from Kocacık (Gökb., Rum. 103, 212). ✧ 'Brave lad; strong fellow' (TED). ⇨ **BABA + YİGİT.**

BABA-KİR   Bashk. 1740 **Baba-kir?** [Бабакир Куласов] (MIB I, 396).

BABA-QALAN?   Uzb. 19th c. **Baba-qalan?** [Бабакалянъ] (SKSO III, 23). ⇨ **BABA + QALAN.**

BABA-NÏYAZ   Trkm. **Baba-nïyaz** [Бабаныяз] (Sopieva 182). ⇨ **BABA + NÏYAZ.**

BABA-NOWRUZ   Trkm.? 1514 **Baba-nowruz** [Баба Ноурузъ], a chief in ǰurǰan (MIT II, 47). ⇨ **BABA + NAWRUZ.**

BABA-SARÏ   Trkm. 1827 **Baba-sarï** [Баба-Сары], from the Teke tribe (MIT II, 445); Trkm. 1881 **Baba-sarï** [Баба-Сары] (Grod., Vojna IV, Grod., Pril. 18). ⇨ **BABA + SARÏ.**

BABA-TUQLAS   Kzk. 19th c. **Baba-tuqlas** [Баба Тукласъ], a character in a tale (AUK 335). ⇨ **BABA.**

BABA-TURMUŠ   Chag. 15th c. **Baba-turmuš** (Barth., Ulugb. 61-63). ⇨ **BABA + TURMÏŠ.**

BABAČAQ   Alt. 19th-20th c. **Babačaq** [Бабачак] (OjrRS 207); Chag. **Babaǰaq-qan** [Bābāǰāk Khān] (Tar. Rashidi 122, 130, 160). ⇨ **BABA + dim. suff. -čaq.**

BABAǰAQ see **BABAČAQ**

BABAǰÏQ   Khazar 703 **Babaǰïq** [Παπατζύς], confidant of the Khazar prince (Byz. Turc. 245). ⇨ **BABA + dim. suff. -ǰïq.**

BABADAY see **BABATAY**

BABAΓAN   Maml. 1399/1400 **Babaγan** [بغان الاينـالى] (Ibn Taghrïb. VI, 25); Tat.(Sib.)? 1621 **Babaγan-tayša** [Бабаган тайша] (Miller, Ist. Sib. II, 268).

BABAY   Chuv. 18th-19th c. **Babay** [Бабай] (Magn. 31); Bashk. 1735 **Babay** [Бабаевъ] (Vel.-Zern., Bašk. 12); Uzb. 18th c. **Babay** [Гумербай Бабаевъ], from Khiva (Nepljuev 883). ✧ 'Grand-father, uncle (as addressing)' (Radl. IV, 1564).

BABAY-BERKUT   Kzk. 19th c. **Babay-berkut** [Бабай-Беркутъ], a writer of articles (AUK 161). ✧ '(Grand-)Father/uncle-Eagle'. ⇨ **BABAY + BÜRKİT.**

BABAQ   Tat. 1686 **Babaq** [Бабак] (MIB I, 77); Bashk. 1757, 1761 **Babaq** [Бабак Нурметев] (MIB IV/1, 142, 204); Bashk. 1740 **Babaq** (<**Baybaq**) [Бабак, Баыбак Токтаров] (MIB I, 427). ✧ 'Grand-father' cf. East.T.(Tar.) *babaq* 'der Grossvater (Kinderwort); das Brustkind' (Radl. IV, 1565).

BABAQAY   Kzk. 1846 **Babaqay** [Бабакай Абилев] (MKOP 154); Kzk. 19th c. **Babekey** [Бабекей] (AOP 62). ⇨ **BABA + suff. -qay.**

BABAL   Kzk. 19th c. **Babal** [Бабалъ] (AOK 30).

BABAN   Alt. 19th-20th c. **Baban** [Бабан], fem. (OjrRS 211). ✧ 'Father' cf. Hak. PN *Paban* 'id.' (Butanaev).

BABAS see **BABAŠ**

BABASAN Tat.(Sib.)? 1580 **Babasan** [Бабасанъ], a murza (Sib. Let. 323).

BABAŠ Kzk. 1820 **Babas** [Бабасъ], chief of the Yappas tribe (Sib. Vest. IX, 120); Kzk. 19th c. **Babas** [Бабас] (Grod., Pril. 128); Kzk. 1868 **Babas** [Бабас] (AOK 10); Kzk. 1794 **Babas-bi** [با ص با بی] (MIK IV, 159); Tat.(Sib.) 1632 **Babaš** [Бабаш Енгилдеев] (Miller, Ist. Sib. II, 398); Tat.(Tob.) 1799 **Babaš** [Смаилъ Бабашевъ] (PSZRI XXV, 658). ⇨ **BABA** + dim. suff. *-š(1) / -s*.

BABATAY Alt. 19th-20th c. **Babaday** [Бабадай], fem. (OjrRS 211); Kzk. **Babatay** [Бабатай], a settlement (Kojčubaev 45); Kzk. **Babatay** [Бабатай] (Nepljuev 807); Kzk. 19th c. **Babatay** [Бабатай] (SOK 104). ⇨ **BABA** + **TAY**? or suff. *-tay(1,2)*?

BABATÏR Chuv. 18th-19th c. **Babatïr (<Bay-batïr?)** [Бабатыръ] (Magn. 31). ✧ 'Rich hero'? cf. Tat. PN *Bay-batïr* (Sattarov). ⇨ **BAY**.

BABEKE Kzk. 19th c. **Babeke (<*Baba-eke)** [Бабеке] (SOK 6). ⇨ **BABA** + comp. *eke*.

BABER see **BÄBER**

BABEŠ Bashk. 1737 **Babeš** [Азик Бабешев] (MIB I, 335). ⇨ **BABÏŠ?**

BABET Kzk. 1734 **Babet** [Бабетъ Теленгутов] (PSZRI IX, 304).

BABÏLDÏ Kzk. 19th c. **Babïldï** [Бабылды] (SOK 72).

BABÏŠ Kzk. 19th c. **Babïš-pay** [Бабышпай] (SOK 106).

BABLAPQA Alt. 19th-20th c. **Bablapqa** [Баблапка], fem. (OjrRS 211).

BABUĠA Tat.(Sib.)? 1623 **Babuγa-tayša** [Бабуга тайша] (Miller, Ist. Sib. II, 304).

BABUL Uzb. 19th c. **Babul-bay** [Султанмурат Бабульбаевъ] (SKSO III, 170).

BAČ Tat.(Sib.) 1680 **Bač** [Бачко] (DAI VIII, 44). See also **ER-BAČ**.

BAČA Uyg. 12th c. - 14th c. **Bača** [bača] (DTS); Tat.(GH) 13th c. **Bača / Рača?** [Πατζά], a christened Tatar, died in 1294 (Byz. Turc.). ✧ 'Male child; boy' Used also as a component of name.

BAČAQ Uyg. 13th-14th c. **Bačaγ / Bačaq?** [Bača[γ] / Bačaq] (Zieme, Mat. III, 272); Uyg. 12th c.-14th c. **Bačaq** [Bačaq] (Radl., USp. 207, 249, Zieme, Mat. I, 75, DTS); Crm.(Tat.) 1537 **Bačaq** [Бачакъ-князь], a prince (PSRL XIII, 115); Uyg. 1340 **Bačaq? / Pašaq?** [Chwol., Syr.-nest. (NF) 38); Uyg. 13th-14th c. **Bačaq-χatun / Bačaγ-χatun** [Bačaγ (Bačaq?) Xatun], fem. (Zieme, Mat. III, 272); Uyg. 12th c.-14th c. **Bačaq-qur[tγa?]-tañrim** [Bačaq Qur??? Tängrim], fem. (Zieme, Mat. I, 75, 82). ✧ 'Christian fast' cf. Karakh. *bačaq* 'id.' (DTS/MK). See also **BAYRAM, URUJ**.

BAČAN Uyg. **Bačan** [Baçan] (EUTS).

BAČARA Uyg. 12th c.-14th c. **Bačara / Bäčäri?** [bačara] (Radl., USp. 89, DTS).

BAČČAİMAN Yak. **Baččaiman** [Баччаіман] (Pek.).

BAČİK Kzk. 19th c. **Bačik-pay / Bačïq-pay?** [Бачекпай] (SOK 80); Kalm.? Mo.? 1646 **Bačik** [Бачик (колмакъ)] (AI IV, 48).

BAČÏM Alt. 19th-20th c. **Bačïm** [Бачым], fem. (OjrRS 211). ✧ 'Quick, nimble'? cf. Kirg. *bačïm* 'schnell, flink' (Radl. IV, 1521).

BAČMAT Alt. 19th-20th c. **Bačmat** [Бачмат] (OjrRS 211).

BAJAQ Kzk. 1819 **Bajaq / Bažaq?** [Бажак] (MIK IV, 325); Turk. 20th c. **Bajaq-oγlu** [Bacakoğlu], a village in the province of Amasya (TMİB 64). ✧ 'Leg, foot' cf. Crm., Turk. *bajaq* 'das ganze Bein, der Schenkel, die Pfote' (Radl. IV, 1522).

BAJAQ-BAŠ Maml. 1298 **Bajaq-baš** [Taïdemur Badjakbasch râs naubah] (Makrīzī IV, 55). ✧ 'Foot-Head'. ⇨ **BAJAQ** + **BAŠ**.

BAJANAQ Turk. 20th c. **Bajanaq** [Bacanak], a village in the province of Ordu (TMİB 705). ✧ 'The husband of one's wife's sister' cf. Turk. *bajanaq* 'id.' (Radl. IV, 1523).

BAJAS? Maml. 1332 **Bajas?** [بجاص], an emir (Dawād. 368).

BAJÏ Turk. 16th c. **Bajï**, fem. (Ongan, Ank. II.). ✧ 'Elder sister; sister; wife; (myst. orders.) title of respect given to the sheikh's wife' cf. Az., Crm., Turk. *bajï* 'die ältere Schwester; eine ältere Frau; die Frau eines Scheich' (Radl. IV, 1523).

BAJÏQ Kzk. 1846 **Bajïq** [Баджик Бишбаев] (MKOP 89); Kzk. 18th c. - 19th c. **Bajïq / Bažik** [باجق / Бажик] (MIK IV, 309).

BAD-SABA Az. **Bad-saba** [Бад-Саба], daughter of a coal dealer (Az. Skaz. 447). ✧ 'Wrong/bad - Saba'? cf. Uzb. *bad* (<P.) 'schlecht' (Radl. IV, 1516). ⇨ **SABA I.?**

BADA Kzk. 19th c. **Bada-pay** [Бадапай] (SOK 82).

BADAY see **BATAY**

BADAQ Chag.? **Badaq-qul** [باداقول / Бадагкул], a Sheybanid (Šejb. XLIX); Kzk. 19th c. **Badaq-pay** [Бадакпай] (SOK 188). See also **AY-BADAQ**.

BADAL Kzk. 19th c. **Badal-bay** [Бадальбай Игамбердіевъ] (SKSO III, 15); Kzk. 19th c. **Badal-bay** [Бадальбай Календаровъ] (SKSO IV, otd. II, 34); Uzb. 19th c. **Badal-bay** [Мулла Мастанъ Бадалбаевъ], a mullah (TV 1876, 83). ✧ 'Replacement, compensation, damages' (child born perhaps after the death of the father), cf. Uzb. *badal / bädäl* 'замена, возмещение' (UzbRS).

BADAM Az. **Badam-ša** [Arif Badamšin] (Mende 105, 3); Tat. 1777 **Badam-ša** [Бадамша Адилшин], a murza (MIB V, 60, 61); *TN:* **Badam-bek** [Бадамбекъ], a place Southwest of Khojend (Karta

JAR XIX). ✦ 'Almond' cf. Kuman, Kzk., Uzb. *badam* 'die Mandeln' (Radl. IV, 1518) (<P.).

BADAN Kirg. 19th c. **Badan** [Баданъ], fem. (Potanin II, 3).

BADANA Kzk. 19th c. **Badana** [Бадана] (AOAtb. 50); Kzk. 19th c. **Badana** [Бадана] (AOK 138). ✦ I. 'Potato-like vegetable' cf. Kzk. *badana* 'Patates gibi bir sebze' (KzTS); II. 'Armor' cf. Kzk. *badana* 'Savaşçıların giydiği zırh' (KzTS).

BADÏŠ Kirg. **Badïš** [Kara Badyš / кара Бадыш] (Proben V, 184 /186/). ✦ 'Seer (of truth)'. See also **QARA-BADÏŠ**.

BADRAQ see **BATRAQ**

BADRUQ Karakh. 11th c. **Badruq** [badruq / Badruk] (DTS, MK/Atalay 831). ✦ 'Flag'? cf. Uyg. *badruq* 'id.' (DTS, TMEN I, No. 727, 824).

BADUR Uyg. **Badur** [Badur] (EUTS). ⇨ **BATÏR**. See also **QUDUΓU-BADUR**.

BAGAČ Chuv. 18th-19th c. **Bagač** [Багачъ] (Magn. 31). ✦ 'Rich man' < R. *bogač* 'id.'.

BAGAČA Chuv. 18th-19th c. **Bagača** [Багача] (Magn. 31).

BAGAČÏ Chuv. 18th-19th c. **Bagači** [Багачи] (Magn. 31).

BAGÏRČA Chuv. 18th-19th c. **Bagïrča** [Багирча] (Magn. 31).

BAΓ Trkm. 19th c. **Baγ-bek** [Нурмухометъ Багбековъ] (Ščeglov IV, 162); Kkalp. 20th c. **Baγ-jan**, fem. (KkRS 777); Tat. **Baw-batïr** [Bau Batyr] (Koşay: KCsA I, 324); Bashk. 1715 **Baw-bek** [Бовбек] (MIB III, 120); Bashk. 1779 **Baw-bek** [Баубек Юсупов] (MIB V, 83); Kzk. 18th c. - 19th c. **Baw-bek** [Баубек] (Tynyšp. 66, 68, 71, 73, 74); Kzk. 19th c. **Baw-bek** [Ситабай Бавбеков] (Grod., Pril. 108); Kzk. 19th c. **Baw-jan** [Бау-жан] (AOAtb. 22); Tat. 1632 **Baw-jan / Baw-čan?** [Кутум Баучанов] (Miller, Ist. Sib. II, 391). ✦ I. 'Tie, string; bunch; connection, link' cf. Türkü/Uyg., Karakh. *baγ* I 'оковы, узы; повязка, узел' (DTS), Kzk. *bau / baw* I 'завязка' (KzRS), cf. also Crm. PN *Bav-bek / Bau-bek* 'l. имя доисламского периода; 2. доверяющий, доверенное лицо' (Kaybullaev); II. 'Garden' cf. Uyg., Karakh. *baγ* II (<Sogd) 'сад; виноградник' (DTS), Kzk. *bau / baw* II 'сад, фруктовый сад' (KzRS). See also **BEK-BAW**, **MÄÑGİ-BAΓ**, **TAS-BAU**.

BAΓ-YASAR Chag. 15th c. **Baγ-yasar**, fought against Muhammad Shaybani, died in 1503 (Tar. Rashidi 165). ⇨ **BAΓ**.

BAΓA I. see **BAQA**

BAΓA II. Uyg. **Baγa** [Baġa] (EUTS); Maml. 1313 **Baγa** [بغا كشكاز من أمرا طلطای] (Dawād. 276); Maml. 1334 **Baγa** [سيف الد ين بغا الدوادار] , an emir (Dawād. 375); Maml. 1313 **Baγa-melik**

[بغا ملك من أمرا طلطای] (Dawād. 276); Uyg. **Qutluγ-baγa-tarqan-ügä**, a title (Ramstedt, Uig. 4-6). ✦ I. An Old Turkic (high) title of Sogdian origin (DTS, Erol II), cf. Türk *baγa* 'eine Würde' (Radl. IV, 1448); II. 'Little, young(er)' (Erol II), cf. Mo. *baγa* 'klein' (TMEN I, No. 91). See also **QUTLUΓ-BAΓA**.

BAΓA-TÄÑRİKÄN Türk 731 **Baγa-täñrikän** [Baγa täñrikän] (ETY I, 128). ⇨ **BAΓA + TÄÑRİKÄN**.

BAΓA-TEMİR Maml. 1332 **Baγa-temir** [بغا تمر] , an emir (Dawād. 367). ✦ 'Little, young(er) Iron'. ⇨ **BAΓA II.? + TEMİR**.

BAΓAY Chuv. 18th-19th c. **Bagay** [Багай] (Magn. 31); Tat.(Sib.)? **Baγay** [Багай Кочурентеев сын] (Miller, Ist. Sib. II, 152); Tat.(Sib.) 1618 **Baγay** [Багай] (Miller, Ist. Sib. II, 244); Alt. 19th-20th c. **Baγay** [Багай], fem. (OjrRS 211). ✦ 'Bad, worthless, good-for-nothing' (OjrRS 211).

BAΓAL Tat.(Sib.) 1609 **Baγal** [Багалъ], a prince (Andrievič, Ist. Sib. I, 45).

BAΓAN I. Alt. 19th-20th c. **Baγan** [Баган] (OjrRS 207). ✦ 'Column, post' (OjrRS 207).

BAΓAN II. Bulg. 772 **Baγan** [Παγάνος], a prince of the Bulghars (Byz. Turc. 239). ⇨ **BAQAN?**

BAΓANALÏ Kzk. 19th c. **Baγanalï** [Баганалы] (AOK 114); *EN:* Kzk. 19th c. **Baγanalï** [Баганалы] (AOK 114). ✦ 'Having columns, posts'? cf. Kzk., Tat. *baγanalï* 'mit Pfählen' (Radl. IV, 1448).

BAΓAR see **BAQAR**

BAΓARÏNYA Yak. **Baγarïnya** [Баҕарынja], Jollōχ Baγarïnya was a famous shaman (Pek.).

BAΓATÏR see **BAΓATUR**

BAΓATUR Crm.(Tat.) 1518, 1519 **Baγatïr / Bahadïr?** [Богатыръ / Багатыръ], Mohammed Girey Khan's son (Qalγa) (PSRL VIII, 268, XIII, 33); Khazar **Baγatur** [Bagatur] (Golden 155); Turk 1329 **Baγatur?** [Μπαχατούρης], a chief of the Turkish army (Byz. Turc. 205); Türk 8th c. - 9th c. **Baγatur-čigši** [baγatur čigši] (DTS); Uyg.? 9th c. **Baγatur-čigši** (Runic Mss. 219); Maml. 1339/40 **Bahadïr** [بهادر البدری], governor of Tripolis, died in 1339/40 (Mayer 94-95); Maml. 14th c.? **Bahadïr** [سيف الد ين بهادر الحموی], chief (reis) of Nubiya (نوبه الجمد اريه) (Mayer 96); Yürük 1543 **Bahadïr** (Gökb., Rum. 207, 215, 218); Tat. 1543 **Bahadïr** (Gökb., Rum. 230); Crm.Tat. **Bahadïr-bek** [بهادر بك] (Vel.-Zern., Crim.); Crm.Tat. **Bahadïr-mirza** [بهادر ميرزا] (Vel.-Zern., Crim.); Crm.Tat. **Bahadïr-šah** [بهادر شاه] (Vel.-Zern., Crim.); Maml. 1332 **Bahadur** [بهادر بن قرمان] (Dawād. 369); Maml. 1332 **Bahadur** [بهادر البدری], an emir (Dawād. 368); Maml. 14th c. **Bahadur** [سيف الدين بهادر], Barqūq's (1382-1389)? nāib (viceroy), died in 1388 (Iyās I, 262, 268, Mayer 96-97); Maml. 14th c. **Bahadur** [Bahādur az̤-z̤āhirī], astādar (viceroy), later the nā'ib of Tripolis, died in 1310 (Mayer 97); Yürük 1543 **Bahadur** (Gökb., Rum. 186); Maml. 1254 **Bahadur / Behadur** (Makrīzī I, 48); Kzk. 19th c. **Batur-bek** [Батуръ-бекъ] (Grod., Pril. 23); Turk. **Bādur-χan-bey** [Бадур-Хан-Бей], in a Turkish destan from Trapezunt (ZVOIRAO XIII, 194); *TN:* Turk. 1519 **Bahādïr**, a village (Gökb., Ed. 258). ✧ 'Brave, warlike, bold, courageous, hero, champion, knight, horseman' (Sauvaget 43), cf. Kuman, Kar. *baɣaïr* 'der Held, kühn' (Radl. IV, 1449), Kuman *bahadur / baɣatur* 'tapfer, brav' (CC), Turk. *bahadïr* 'der Held, der Krieger, tapfer' (Radl. IV, 1466), Turk. *bahadïr* 'alp, kahraman, yiğit' (Eren, TDES) (<P. *bahādur* <Mo. *baɣatur* <Trk.). Used also as a secondary component of male names. Cf. also *baɣatur/bātur* (TMEN II, No. 817). See also **BATÏR**.

BAГČELİ Yürük 1543 **Baɣčeli** (Gökb., Rum. 183). ✧ 'Having a garden'. + suff. *-li*.

BAГDA-GÜL Kkalp. 20th c. **Baɣda-gül** [Багъдагюл / Бағдагул], fem. (Bask., Kkalp. 399, KkRS 777). ✧ 'Flower in the garden' (Baskakov: OSA 139), '(Born) in the garden'? ⇨ **GÜL**.

BAГDAD Turk. 16th c. **Baɣdad** [Hüseyin oğlu Bağdad] (Ongan, Ank. II, 872); Turk. 16th c. **Baɣdad** [İbrahim kızı Bağdad], fem. (Ongan, Ank. II, 1601); Nog. 20th c. **Baɣdad** [Багъдад Исбол Мустафа келинъи / Багдад Мустафаева], one of Baskakov's informants from the aul of Qara-töbe (Bask., Nog. 143). ✧ Baghdad (city) (Erol II).

BAГDALÏYA Yak. **Baɣdalïya** [Багдалыjа] (Pek.).

BAГDAN Uzb.? **Baɣdan-ata** [Багдан-ата], a place north of Samarkand (Karta JAR XIX).

BAГDAŠ Kuman 1451 **Baɣdaš** [Bagdas ilese], a settlement in Kumania Minor, Hungary, named after its chief (Gyárfás III, 626); Kuman? 16th c. **Baɣdaš** [Bağdāša Imre], a man of Ias or Kuman origin in Hungary (Fekete 135); Selj. 11th c. - 12th c. **Baɣdaš** [Alp Yaruq Bağdaš], one of Artuq's sons (Cahen, Le Diyār Bakr au temps des premiers Urtuqides: JA 227(1935), 268); Tat.(Lit.) 1591 **Baɣdaš** [Смегил Мулкоманович Багдашевич] (Lit. Tat.); Tat.(Lit.) 1591 **Baɣdaš** [Ахута Богушовна Багдашевич] (Lit. Tat.); Tat.? 1612 **Baɣdaš** [Богдашка Янбердеев] (Nižegorod. platež.); *TN:* Turk. **Baɣdaš** [باغـد ا ش], a village in the province of Bolu, Turkey (Köyl. 475). ✧ 'Friend, companion' (cf. Rásonyi: NTK 84-85, KÖA 85, AOH 20(1967), 136).

BAГDÏ Selj. 1291 **Baɣdï-yarɣuči** [يـرغـوچـى/ ايلـچـى / بـغـد ى / Boğdī], an envoy (Aqsarāyī 106, 109, Aqsar./Iş. 83); Selj. **Baɣdï-bek / Yaɣdï-bek?** [بـاغـدى بـك / يـاغـدى بـك] (Uzunçarş., Küt. I, 45). ✧ 'Sunbeam, shaft of light' cf. Turk. *baɣdu* 'der Lichtstrahl, Sonnenstrahl' (Radl. IV, 1461).

BAГDÏ-DÖLÖT Kirg. **Baɣdï-dölöt** [Bagdy Dölöt / Бағды Дөлөт Баібичä] (Proben V, 80 /81/). ✧ 'Lucky/Fortunate - Chance/happyness'. ⇨ **BAГDÏ / BAQTÏ? + DÄWLÄT**.

BAГDÏR Alt. 19th-20th c. **Baɣdïr** (OjrRS 207).

BAГЇ Kzk. 19th c. **Baɣï-bay** [Багыбай] (SODž. 52); Trkm. **Baɣï-bek** [Багы-бек], a chief of the begs (beglerbegi) from the Sarïq tribe (MIT 549, 551, 552, 553, 555, 565); Trkm. 1816 **Baɣï-bek** [Багы-бек], a bahadïr from the Yomut tribe (MIT II, 397, 411, 434); Trkm. 19th c. **Baɣï-bek** [Багибекъ] (Ščeglov IV, 189). ✧ I. 'Disobedient, unruly, stubborn' cf. Turk. *baɣï* 'ungehorsam, halsstarrig' (Radl. I, 1449) (<Ar.); II. 'Spell, charm' cf. Turk. *baɣï* 'der Reiz, die Verzückung, die Bezeuberung; das Bündel' (Radl. IV, 1450).

BAГЇL Tat. 1739 **Baɣïl** [Багильдинъ] (Alatyr. 145); Kzk. 19th c. **Baɣïl-bek** [Багильбекъ] (Grod., Pril. 188). ✧ 'Miser, skinflint' cf. Kuman *baɣïl*, Tat.(Tob.) *baqïl* 'geizig' (Radl. IV, 1440, 1452).

BAГЇNDЇQ Bashk. 1768 **Baɣïndïq** [Багындык Муталлапов] (MIB IV/1, 332). ✧ 'We got obedient' cf. Kzk., Tat. *baɣïn-* 'ergeben sein, gehorchen' (Radl. IV, 1450).

BAГЇR Türk 9th c. **Baɣïr** [بـاغـر / بـبـاغـر الـتـركى /] (Mas‘ūdī, Prairies VII, 262); Türk? 862 **Baɣïr** [بـاغـر/ بـاعـر/ الـتـركى] (Tabarī, Annal. III, 1460, 1535-1538 stb.); Türk? 865 **Baɣïr**, one of the respected Türk generals, Mutawakkil's murderer, died in 865 (Weil, Chalif. 384); Türk? 873 **Baɣïr** [بـاغـر الـتـركى] (Fragm. Hist. Ar. 574-77); Az. **Baɣïr** [Bagirov] (Mende 165); Kzk. 19th c. **Baɣïr-bay** [Багорбай] (AOAtb. 58); Trkm.? 1856 **Baɣïr-χan** [Багыр-хан] (MIT II, 272); Trkm.? 1729/30 **Baɣïr-χan / Baqïr-χan?** [Багыр-хан бугаири], officer from the Buɣair (бугаири) clan (MIT II, 131). ✧ 'Liver, heart, relative' cf. Uyg., Karakh. *baɣïr* 'печень, живот, сердце, родственник кровный' (DTS), Az., Crm., Trkm., Turk. *baɣïr* 'die Leber, der vordere Theil eines Dinges; (Trkm.) 'Name eines grossen Auls am Fusse des Kopet-Dag' (Radl. IV, 1451). See also **TAS-BAWUR**.

BAГЇŠ Kzk. 19th c. **Baɣïs** [Багысъ] (SOV 124); Kzk. 19th c. **Baɣïs** [Багысъ] (AOK 42, 82); Kzk. 19th c. **Baɣïs** [Багысъ] (AOP 98); Kzk. 19th c. **Baɣïs** [Багысов] (AOK 50); Kzk. 19th c. **Baɣïs / Baɣïz** [Багызъ] (SODž.); Kzk. 19th c. **Baɣïs-bay** [Багысбай] (AOA 86); Kzk. 19th c. **Baɣïs-pay** [Багыспай] (SODž. 154); Kzk. 19th c. **Baɣïs-pek** [Багыспек] (SODž. 160); Kzk. 19th c. **Baɣïs-pek** [Багыспек] (SOV 106); *EN:* Kzk. 18th c. - 19th c. **Baɣïs** [Багыс] (Tynyšp. 68). ✧ 'Pasturage, herding (together)' cf. Kzk. *baɣïs* 'das Hüten' (Radl. IV, 1453), Kzk. *baɣïs-* 'совместно ухаживать, воспитывать, присматривать' (KzRS). See also **QARA-BAГЇŠ, SARЇ-BAГЇŠ**.

BAГЇŠ Chuv. 18th c. **Bagïš** [Багишева], a village in the district of Yadrinsk (Korsakov 304); Tat. 1624 **Baɣïš**

[Ураз Багишинъ], tax-payer („Буртасъ, посопный Татаринъ ") (Zolotn. 159); Tat. 18th c. **Baγïš** [Багишева], a village in the district of Sviyažsk (Korsakov 360); Bashk. 1635 **Baγïš** [Багиш Тарханов] (MIB I, 90); Kzk. 19th c. **Baγïš** [уста Багиш] (Grod., Pril. 40); Tat.(Sib.)? Bashk.? 1634 **Baγïš** [Багиш], Tarχan-batïr's son (Miller, Ist. Sib. 411, 441); Chag. 1577 **Baγïš-biy** [Багиш-бий] (Ivanov 295, 297); *TN:* Tat.(Sib.) 1750 **Baγïš** [Багышшевскъ], Bagyševsk, a group of yurts in the district of Tümen (VIRGO XXIX, 11, 206); Uzb. **Baγïš-bek** [Багыш-бекъ], a place north of Andijan in the Naryn valley (Karta JAR XIX). ✧ I. 'Gift'? cf. Kuman, Tat. *baγïš* (P.) 'das Geschenk, die Gabe' (Radl. IV, 1453), Chag., Uzb. *baγïš* 'das Geschenk' (Radl. IV, 1455); II. 'Bond, link, joint, joining the family' cf. Chag., East.T. *baγïš* 'das Band, die Binde, das Gelenk; das Strickwerk des Zeltes' (Radl. IV, 1455). See also **BAY-BAΓÏŠ, JÏN-BAΓÏŠ, YURT-BAΓÏŠ, QOY-BAΓÏŠ**.

BAΓÏŠEY Bashk. 1718 **Baγïšey / Baqšay** [Багышай /Бокшай/ Баймаев] (MIB III, 177). ✧ 'Little gift'. ⇨ **BAΓÏŠ** + dim. suff. *-ey*.

BAΓLAN Kzk. 19th c. **Baγlam-bay** (<**Baγlan-bay**) [Богломбай] (SOV 56); *EN:* Kzk. 18th c. - 19th c. **Baγlan** [Баглан] (Tynyšp. 65). ✧ 'Big and thick/fat' cf. Kzk. *baγlan* 'von grossem Wuchse und dick' (Radl. IV, 1458).

BAΓLU-QARA Maml. 1312 **Baγlu-qara** [بغلوقرا الا مير الكرجى] (Dawād. 255). ✧ '?-Black'. ⇨ **QARA.**

BAΓLUN Türk 662 **Baγlun** [بغلون التركى] (Tabarī, Annal. III, 1460, 1461).

BAHADÏR see **BAΓATUR**

BAHADUR see **BAΓATUR**

BAHADUR-AS Maml. 1299, 1303 **Bahadur-as / Behadur-as?** [سيف الدين بهادر اص], an emir (Dawād. 14, 110, 170, Makrīzī IV, 198, Weil, Chalif. I, 282, 295). ⇨ **BAΓATUR + AS.**

BAHAEDDÏN Tat. **Bahaeddin**, an išan? (Mende 30). ✧ Baha-ud-Din (Ar.) 'glory of the religion (Islam)' (Ahmed).

BAHAR Turk. 1583 **Bahar** [بهار], fem. (Ongan, Ank. I, 153); Trkm. **Bahar** [Бахар], fem. (Sopieva 180); Trkm. 20th c. **Bahar** [Bahar] (Zaj. 1971, 335); Trkm. 20th c. **Bahar** [Бахар], fem. (TrkmRS 78); Kzk. 19th c. **Bahar-bay** [Бахарбай Кукаевъ] (SKSO VIII, 207); *TN:* Turk. 20th c. **Baharlar**, (=settlement of Bahars) villages in the province of Manisa and Denizli, Turkey; (TMİB 280, 626). ✧ 'Spring' cf. Trkm., Turk. *bahar* (<P.) 'der Frühling' (Radl. IV, 1465). See also **GÜL-BAHAR**.

BAHARÏMBET Bashk. 1712 **Baharïmbet** [Бахарымбет Чинмурзин] (MIB III, 85). ⇨ **BAHAR** + suffixoid *-ïmbet.*

BAHĀDÏR-GİREY Crm.Tat. 16th c. **Bahādïr-girey-sultan** [بهادر كراى سلطان], Moχammed Girey Khan's son, Mengli Girey Khan's grandson (Vel.-Zern., Crim. 3, 4); Crm.Tat. 17th c. **Bahādïr-girey-χan** [بهادر كراى خان], Crimean Tatar Khan (1637-1641), Selāmet Girey's (1608-1610) son (Vel.-Zern., Crim. 155, 156, 190). ⇨ **BAHADUR + KERÄY.**

BAHŠAYÏŠ Turk. 1583, 1584 **Bahšayiš** (Ongan, Ank. I, 153). ✧ 'Present, gift'? cf. Turk. dial. *bahşış / bakşış* 'evlenecek erkeğin kız tarafına verdiği para ve eşya, başlık' (DS).

BAXČAÑNÏR Yak. **Baχčaññïr** [Бахчанн表ыр] (Pek.).

BAXSÏ see **QÏDAY**

BAXSÏ-TOYONO Yak. **Baχsï-toyono / Doχsun-duyan** [Дохсун-Дуйан / Бахсы тойоно], earlier a man who, because of his sins, was turned into an evil spirit who takes human being's reason away (Pek.). ⇨ **BAQŠÏ + TOYOŇ?**

BAXSÏNAT Yak. **Baχsïnat** [Бахсынат] (Pek.).

BAXSÏTAY see **KÜDÄY**

BAXŠÏ see **BAQŠÏ**

BAXŠÏ-GELDİ Tat.(Lit.) 1548 **Baχšï-geldi** [Бахшикгельдь] (Kn. Metriki Lit. 45). ⇨ **BAQŠÏ + KELDİ.**

BAXT Maml. 14th c. **Baχt-χoja** [بخت حجا] (Mayer 207, Sauvaget 41); Tat.(Sib.) 1629 **Baχt-oul** [Бахтоул], a mirza (Miller, Ist. Sib. II, 359). ✧ 'Chance' cf. Turk. (<P.) *baχt* 'das Glück' (Radl. IV, 1463), Tat. *bäkit* 'Glück' (Radl. IV, 1576).

BAXT-ENEY Kzk. 1634 **Baχt-eney** [Бахтеней (Бехтен, Бехтеней)], a prince (Miller, Ist. Sib. II, 417, 418, 427). ✧ 'Chance-Mother'. ⇨ **BAXT + ENE +** dim. *-y.*

BAXT-URAZ Tat.(Sib.) 1631 **Baχt-uraz** [Якшураз (Якмураз) Бахуразов] (Miller, Ist. Sib. II, 386). ✧ 'Chance-Fast'; 'Chance-Luck'. ⇨ **BAXT + ORAZ.**

BAXTÏ see **BAQTÏ**

BAXTÏ-GELDİ see **BAXTÏ-KELDİ**

BAXTÏ-GİLDEY see **BAXTÏ-KELDİ**

BAXTÏ-GİLDİ see **BAXTÏ-KELDİ**

BAXTÏ-KELDİ Kzk. 19th c. **Baχtï-geldi** [Алтунъ Бигэ Бахтигельдіева], fem. (Grod., Pril. 140); Tat. 1525 **Baχtï-gildey** [Бахтыгильдей], envoy from Kazan to Moscow (Zolotn. 156, 248); Tat. 1524 **Baχtï-kildey** [Бахтыкилдей], a prince from Kazan (PSRL VI, 264, VIII, 271); Tat. 1525 **Baχtï-kildey** [Бахты-Килдѣй] (PSRL XIII, 44); *TN:* Chuv. 18th c. **Baχtï-gildi** [Бахтигилдина], a village in the district of Kozmodemyansk (Korsakov 299). ✧ 'Lucky/Fortunate child has come'. ⇨ **BAQTÏ + KELDİ.**

BAXTÏ-KİLDEY see **BAXTÏ-KELDİ**

BAXTÏYAR Oghuz (Ghuz) 12th c. **Baχtïyar** [Бахтияр], an emir of the Ghuzz (MIT I, 388); Bashk.

1789 **Baχtïyar** [Девлеткильда Бахтияров] (MIB V, 269); Az. **Baχtïyar / Baχtiyar** [Бахтияр] (Az. Skaz. 20-45); Tat. 1510 **Baχtïyar / Baχtiyar** [Бахтіяръ], a prince from Astrakhan (PSRL VI, 48, 244, VIII, 243); Kzk. 19th c. **Baχtïyar / Baχtiyar** [Бахтіяръ] (Grod., Pril. 173). ✧ 'Followed by chance' (Bask., Fam. 32). ⇨ **YAR.**

BAXTLÏ Trkm. 20th c. **Baγtlï** [Bagtlï] (Zaj. 1971, 335); Trkm. 20th c. **Baγtlï** [Багтлы] (TrkmRS 64); Crm. 1782 **Baχtlï-χanïm** [بختلى حا نم / Бахтлы-ханымъ], fem. (Bakč. Nadp. 32); Kzk. 19th c. **Baχtlï-χatun** [Бахтли-Хатун] (Grod., Pril. 120). ✧ 'Fortunate, lucky'; + Adj. suff. *-lï*. ⇨ **BAXT.** See also **QUTLUГ.**

BAY 1548 **Bay** [Бай], envoy (PSRL (Russk. Hr.), 530); Kzk. 19th c. **Bay** [Бай] (AOK 6); Kirg. **Bay** [Бай] (Jud. 88); **Bay-aγa** [بای اغا], from the Zend dynasty (Tar. Zend. IV); Kzk. 19th c. **Bay-ake** [Баяке] (SOK 24); Türk 7th c. - 9th c. **Bay-apa** [bay apa] (DTS); Uzb. 1854 **Bay-baba** [Бай-Баба] (Moskal'cev 42); Uzb. 1919 **Bay-bača** [Ichmat Vaïbatcha], a basmačï from Ferghana (Castagné 81); Kzk. 19th c. **Bay-batïr** (Ljutš 70); Kzk. 19th c. **Bay-batur** [Байбатуръ Сирибаевъ] (Grod., Pril. 162, 164); Yürük 16th c. **Bay-beg** [با بيك], from the Yürüks of Kocacık, Turkey (Gökb., Rum. 103); Tat.(Mish.) **Bay-bek** (IOAIÊK XIX, 142); Kzk. 1740 **Bay-bek** [Байбекъ] (Hanykov, Poezdka 6); Kzk. 19th c. **Bay-bek** [Байбекъ Магомедовъ] (Grod., Pril. 163); Karch. **Bay-čor < Bay-čora?** [Казакъ Байчоровъ] (Sysoev 123); Tat. 1684 **Bay-čur** [Байчур Кулситов] (Zolotn. 156); Bashk. 1663 **Bay-čur** [Байчюрка Илмаметев] (MIB I, 169); Tat. 1557 **Bay-čura** [Байчюра] (PSRL XIII, 281); Tat. 18th-19th c. **Bay-čura** [Байчура] (Magn. 32); Bashk. 1735 **Bay-čura** [Байчура Епанов], a tarχan (Vel.-Zern., Bašk. 15); Trkm. 19th c. **Bay-ǰan** [Бай-джанъ] (Volodin 53); Bashk. 1714 **Bay-ǰigit** [Байджигит Турсунбаев] (MIB I, 105); Uzb. **Bay-ǰigit** [Джумабай Байджигитовъ] (Sr. Az. I, 1896, avg. 16); Uzb. 1875 **Bay-ǰigit** [Бай-Джигитъ Кинджибаевъ] (Moskal'cev 48); Kzk. 19th c. **Bay-eke** [Баеке] (SOK 110); Kkalp. 20th c. **Bay-eke** [Байеке] (Bask., Kkalp. 71, KkRS 772); Tat. 1675 **Bay-gözä** [Турайка Байгозинъ] (Kurdjumov 3); Tat. 1686 **Bay-gözä** [Турайко Байгозинъ] (Kungursk. akty 121); Bashk. 1726 **Bay-gözä** [Наурус Багозин] (MIB III, 239); Bashk. 1735 **Bay-güzä** [Байгуза Кочкаров], a tarχan (Vel.-Zern., Bašk. 16); Bashk. 1735 **Bay-güze / Bay-güzä?** [Байгузе Калпкулов], a tarχan (Vel.-Zern., Bašk. 24); Tat.(Sib.) 1620 **Bay-γul** [Байгул], from Tura (Miller, Ist. Sib. II, 251, 254); Bashk. 1777 **Bay-γul** [Байгул Илышев] (MIB V, 54, 175); Bashk. 1783 **Bay-γul** [Байгул Араслангулов] (MIB V, 147); Maml. 1309 **Bay-χan** [بيخان], a mamlūk (Dawād. 219,

221 etc.); Trkm. 1813 **Bay-χan** [Бай-хан], from the Göklen tribe (MIT II, 211); Kkalp. 20th c. **Bay-χan** [Байхан] (KkRS 772); 12th c. **Bay-χan (?-qan)** (Barth., Turk. 149); Selj. 13th c. - 14th c. **Bay-χoǰa** [بای حواجه / بای حوا جه], Osman's follower (Nešrī 213, Āšikp. 9, 28); Kkalp. 20th c. **Bay-χoža** [Байхожа] (KkRS 772); Kzk. 1820 **Bay-qul-biy** [Байкулъ-бій], one of the chiefs of the Arïïn tribe (Sib. Vest. IX, 103); Trkm. 1859 **Bay-mambet** [Баймамбетъ Маяевъ] (ZIRGOÊtn. I, 158); Chuv. 18th-19th c. **Bay-molla** [Баймолла] (Magn. 32); Chuv. 18th-19th c. **Bay-mulla** [Баймулла] (Magn. 32); Chuv. 18th-19th c. **Bay-murza** [Баймурза] (Magn. 32); Nog. **Bay-murza** [Бай Мурза] (Žirm., Epos 430); Kzk. 19th c. **Bay-ola (<Bay-ulï?)** [Бай Ола Магомедовъ] (Grod., Pril. 95); Tat. 17th. c. **Bay-sit** [Кулситко Байситовъ] (IOAIÊK XXIX, 346); Bashk. 1738 **Bay-sula (<Bay-sulï)** [Байсула Ахматова], fem. (MIB III, 400); Bashk. 1709 **Bay-sulï** [Ерым Байсулеев] (MIB I, 264); Kzk. 19th c. **Bay-sulu** [Байсулу] (SOK 82); Oghuz 11th c. **Bay-tegin** [Байтегин], a commander of the army of the Ghaznawids (MIT I, 286); Selj. 1000 **Bay-tegin** [بایتکین الیاروحی / التركی], fem.? (Hil. Sābī 395); Selj. 1110 **Bay-tegin** [الناجى كشتكين / بایتکین احو] (Qalānisi 166); Bashk. 1750 **Bay-zigit** [Байзигит Сайпяшев] (MIB IV/1, 193); Kkalp. 20th c. **Bay-žan** [Байжан] (KkRS 772); Chuv. 18th-19th c. **Pa-murza (<Pay-murza)** [Памурза] (Magn. 65); Chuv. 18th-19th c. **Pay-mola** [Паймола] (Magn. 65); Hak.(Sag.) 19th-20th c. **Pay-palañ** [Паi Палаӊ], fem. (Proben IX, 391-92); Chuv. 18th-19th c. **Pay-patïr** [Пайпатыръ] (Magn. 65); *EN:* Kzk. 18th c. - 19th c. **Bay-ǰigit** [Байджигит] (Tynyšp. 71); *TN:* **Bay** (Barth., Turk. 480); Kzk. **Bay-bala** [Байбала], a field (Kojčubaev 46); **Bay-χan** (Barth., Turk. 149); Chuv. 18th c. **Bay-murzina (<Bay-murza)** [Баймурзина], a village in the district of Tetyushinsk (Korsakov 346). ✧ 'Rich(man), noble man; master, owner; gentleman' cf. *bay* 'reich', (Kzk., Tat.) 'der Wirth, der Ehemann', (Kzk.) 'der Held, der Anführer' (Radl. IV, 1421). Widely used also as a (secondary) component of Turkic personal names. See also **ǰOLU-BAY, EŠE-BAY, YANÏ-BAY.**

BAY-ADÏL Kzk. 19th c. **Bay-adïl** [Баядылъ] (SOV 76). ✧ 'Rich-Fair'. ⇨ **BAY + ADİL.**

BAY-ALÏ Kzk. 19th c. **Bay-alï** [Баялы] (SODž. 28); *EN:* Nog. 20th c. **Bay-alï** [Байалы урув], Qara-noγay clan (Bask., Nog. 136). ✧ 'Rich-Ali'. ⇨ **BAY + ALİ.**

BAY Uyg. 8th c.? **Bay-apa-čañγšï** (Müller, Uig. II, 81).

BAY-ARSLAN Chuv. 18th-19th c. **Bay-arslan** [Баярсланъ] (Magn. 33); Bashk. 1735 **Bay-slan (<Bay-aslan)** [Байсланъ Аиткуловъ], a tarχan (Vel.-Zern., Bašk. 15); Bashk. 1742 **Bay-slan (<Bay-aslan)**

[Аракай Байсланов] (MIB III, 520); Bashk. 1746 **Bay-slan** (<**Bay-aslan**) [Асан Байсланов] (MIB III, 435); Bashk. 1751 **Bay-slan** (<**Bay-aslan**) [Байслан Ташюреков] (MIB IV/1, 43); Bashk. 1756 **Bay-slan** (<**Bay-aslan**) [Баислан Кизяков] (MIB IV/1, 122); Bashk. 1761 **Bay-slan** (<**Bay-aslan**) [Батыр Байсланов] (MIB IV/1, 204). ✧ 'Rich/Noble lion'. ⇨ **BAY + ARSLAN.**

BAY-ASLAN see **BAY-ARSLAN**

BAY-ATAR Kzk. 19th c. **Bay-atar** [Баятаръ] (AOO 50). ✧ 'Rich Shooter'. ⇨ **BAY + ATAR.**

BAY-BAB Bashk. 1779 **Bay-bab** [Байбаб Аллашугуров] (MIB V, 102). ⇨ **BAY.**

BAY-BAČA see **BAY**

BAY-ВАГАŠ see **BAY-ВАГЇŠ**

BAY-ВАГЇS see **BAY-ВАГЇŠ**

BAY-ВАГЇŠ Kzk. 1629 **Bay-baɣaš** [Байбагаш] (Miller, Ist. Sib. II, 358); Tat.(Sib.) 1623 **Bay-baɣïš** [Байбагиш] (Miller, Ist. Sib. II, 300); Kzk. 20th c. **Bay-paɣïz** (<**Bay-baɣïs**) [Baipagiz] (Almásy 494). ✧ 'Rich Gift/Grant' cf. Kzk. *baɣïš* 'багыш ету' (QTTS). ⇨ **BAY + ВАГЇŠ?**

BAY-ВАГUL Kzk. **Bay-baɣul** (PM Ergh. 43 (Heft.?) 75). ⇨ **BAY + ВАГЇL?**

BAY-ВАXTA see **BAY-BAQTЇ**

BAY-ВАXTЇ see **BAY-BAQTЇ**

BAY-BAYŠA Kkalp. 20th c. **Bay-bayša** [Байбайша], fem. (Bask., Kkalp. 403). ⇨ **BAY + BAYČA?**

BAY-BAQ Kzk. 19th c. **Bay-baq-pay** [Байбакпай] (SOV 30). ✧ 'Rich-Luck'. ⇨ **BAY + BAQ.**

BAY-BAQA Tat. 18th-19th c. **Bay-baqa** [Байбака] (Magn. 32). ✧ 'Rich man looks in (=has been born)' (Sattarov). ⇨ **BAY + BAQA?**

BAY-BAQTЇ Tat. 1624 **Ba-baxta** (<**Bay-baχtï**) [Бабахта Бакшандинъ] (Pokrovskij 72); Tat. 18th-19th c. **Bay-baχta** (<**Bay-baχtï**) [Байбахта] (Magn. 32); Tat.(Sib.), Tat.(Tob.) 1603 **Bay-baχta** (<**Bay-baχtï**) [Байбахта] (Miller, Ist. Sib. II, 179); Bashk. 1735 **Bay-baχtï** [Байбахти Бердыгуловъ], a tarχan (Vel.-Zern., Bašk. 19); Chuv. 18th-19th c. **Pay-baχta** (<**Bay-baχtï**) [Пайбахта] (Magn. 65); *EN:* Kzk. 1785 **Bay-baqtï** [باى يقتى اوروغى / باى بقتى اوروغى / Байбакты], a Kazak clan in the Kiši Žüz (MIK IV, 52, 54); *TN:* Chuv. 18th c. **Baybaχtina** [Байбахтина], a village in the district of Yadrinsk (Korsakov 303); Chuv. 18th c. **Bay-baχti(na)** (<**Bay-baχta** < **Bay-baχtï**) [Байбахтина], a village in the district of Cheboksary (Korsakov 281); Kzk. **Bay-baqtï** [Байбакты], a field (Kojčubaev 46). ✧ 'Rich/Lucky-Fortunate'. ⇨ **BAY + BAQTЇ.**

BAY-BARA Tat. 1620 **Bay-bara** [Чеклубайко Байбаринъ] (Kurdjumov 121, 122). ⇨ **BAY.**

BAY-BARAQ Kirg. **Bay-baraq** [Байбарак] (Jud. 344). ✧ 'Rich-Tousled (dog)' (Jud. 344: 'Lohmač'). ⇨ **BAY + BARAQ.**

BAY-BARЇŠ Chuv. 18th-19th c. **Bay-barïš** [Байбарышъ] (Magn. 32). ✧ 'Rich(man)-Peace', 'Rich-gain/benefit' (Sattarov). ⇨ **BAY + BARЇŠ.**

BAY-BARS Chuv. 18th-19th c. **Ba-barïs** (<**Bay-barïs**) [Бабарысъ] (Magn. 31); Chuv. 18th-19th c. **Ba-bars** (<**Bay-bars**) [Бабарсъ] (Magn. 31); Chuv. 18th-19th c. **Bay-barïs** [Байборысъ] (Magn. 32); Tat. 1698 **Bay-barïs** [Байбарыско, Байбарыска] (Kungursk. akty 267); Tat. 18th-19th c. **Bay-barïs** [Байбарысъ / Байбарисъ] (Magn. 32); Maml. 1260 **Bay-bars** [Baibarz], Sultan Baybars I (1260-1277) „that is Bûndûkdâr" (Abulfar./Budge I, 439); Maml. 1260-1277 **Bay-bars** [الملك الظاهر ركن‌الدين بيبرس البندقداری /بيبرس بن عبدالله الصالحى], sultan Bay-bars I al-ẓāhir (1260-1277) (Makrīzī I, 53, 116 etc., Iyās I, 76 etc., Duqmaq:RHCHor V, 19, 45, 68, Mayer 107-109); Maml. 1320 **Bay-bars** [ركن الدين بيبرس الاحمدى أمير جا ندار], emir of the security guards (Dawād. 296); Maml. 14th c.? **Bay-bars** [Baibars al-Manṣūrī al-χaṭā'ī] (Björkm. 67); Maml. 14th c. **Bay-bars** [بيبرس / Baybars] (Tarǰ/Houtsma 61, Tarǰ/Toparlı 41); Tat. 18th-19th c. **Bay-bars** [Байбарсъ] (Magn. 32); Maml. 1264 **Bay-bars** / **Bey-bars** / **Bi-bars?** [Rokn-eddin-Beïbars-Khass-turk-Kebir-Sâléhi], an emir (Makrīzī II, 13, Duqmaq:RHCHor IV, 90); Maml. 1264 **Bay-bars** / **Bey-bars** / **Bi-bars?** [Rokn-eddin Beïbars-Magrebi], an emir (Makrīzī II, 14); Maml. 1280, 13th c.-14th c. **Bay-bars** / **Bey-bars?** / **Bi-bars?** [ركن‌الدين بيبرس الجالق / Beïbars-Djâlik], Sultan Baybars' emir, died in 1307, buried in Jerusalim (Makrīzī III, 20, 35, Mayer 110); Maml. 1290 **Bay-bars** / **Bey-bars** / **Bi-bars?** [Beïbars-Moëzzi], governor of Qūs (Kous) who fought in Dongola in 1290 (Makrīzī III, 108); Maml. 1301-1313 **Bay-bars** / **Bey-bars** / **Bi-bars?** [الدوادار الكبير / ركن‌الدين بيبرس المنصورى], a chancellor of state and historian (Iyās I, 142, Ibn Taghrīb. VI, 3, 5, Weil, Chalif. I, 191, 337); Maml. 1305 **Bay-bars** / **Bey-bars** / **Bi-bars?** [Bibars-Mouvaffaki-Mansouri] (Makrīzī IV, 250); Maml. 1335/36 **Bay-bars** / **Bey-bars** / **Bi-bars?** [بيبرس حاحب الحجا ب] (Iyās I, 168); Maml. 1341 **Bay-bars** / **Bey-bars** / **Bi-bars?** [بيبرس الاحمدى] (Iyās I, 148, Weil, Chalif. I, 408); Maml.? 14th c. **Bay-bars** / **Bey-bars** / **Bi-bars?** [بيبرس / Beïbars], from around Damascus (Ibn Bat. I, 256); Maml. 1379/80 **Bay-bars** / **Bey-bars** / **Bi-bars?** [بيبرس التمانتمرى] (Iyās I, 249); Maml. 1390 **Bay-bars** / **Bey-bars** / **Bi-bars?** [برقوق بيبرس ابن أحت الظاهر] (Iyās I, 285); Maml. 1401 **Bay-bars** / **Bey-bars** / **Bi-bars?** [بيبرس الركبى] (Iyās I, 328); Maml. 1403/04 **Bay-bars** / **Bey-bars** / **Bi-bars?**

[بيبرس الصغير] (Ibn Taghrīb. VI, 110, 128); Maml. 1407/08 **Bay-bars / Bey-bars / Bi-bars?** [الفارقانى] [بيبرس] (Iyās I, 351); Maml. 1438/39 **Bay-bars / Bey-bars / Bi-bars?** [الاشرفى حال يوسف بن برسباى] [ابيبرس] (Ibn Taghrīb. VII, 88, 466, 483); Maml. 1439/40 **Bay-bars / Bey-bars / Bi-bars?** [بيبرس الساقى] (Ibn Taghrīb. VII, 104); Maml. 1455 **Bay-bars / Bey-bars / Bi-bars?** [بن ططع] [بيبرس الاشرفى الطويك الا شقر] (Iyās II, 53, 156); Maml. 1460/61 **Bay-bars / Bey-bars / Bi-bars?** [بيبرس] (Iyās II, 66, 336); Maml. 1460/61 **Bay-bars / Bey-bars / Bi-bars?** [بيبرسحال العز يز] (Iyās II, 71, 108); Maml. 1461 **Bay-bars / Bey-bars / Bi-bars?** [الجاشنكير] [بيبرس] (Ibn Taghrīb. VII, 689, 839); Maml. 1462 **Bay-bars / Bey-bars / Bi-bars?** [بيبرس احمد بن بكر] (Ibn Taghrīb. VII, 769); Maml. 1479 **Bay-bars / Bey-bars / Bi-bars?** [بيبرس الرحبى] (Iyās II, 188, 230); Maml. 1483 **Bay-bars / Bey-bars / Bi-bars?** [بيبرس اليوسفى] (Iyās II, 220, 248); Maml. 1497/98 **Bay-bars / Bey-bars / Bi-bars?** [بيبرس بن حيور الاشرفى قايتباى] (Iyās II, 340); Maml. 1497/98 **Bay-bars / Bey-bars / Bi-bars?** [بيبرس نايب القلعة] (Iyās II, 332); Maml. 1500/01 **Bay-bars / Bey-bars / Bi-bars?** [بيبرس البهلوان] (Iyās II, 380, 394); Maml. 1516 **Bay-bars / Bey-bars / Bi-bars?** [بيبرس بن عبد الكر يم] (Iyās III, 3); Maml. 1517 **Bay-bars / Bey-bars / Bi-bars?** [بيبرس بن بقر] (Iyās III, 137); Maml. 1520 **Bay-bars / Bey-bars / Bi-bars?** [ابن بنت سير ين] [بيبرس] (Iyās III, 318); Maml. 1297, 1298, 1299, 1309/10 **Bay-bars / Bi-bars / Bey-bars** [الجاشكير] [الجاشكير ثم السلطان الملك المظفر/ بيبرس العثمانى / ركن الدين بيبرس] / Rokn-eddin-Bibars le djaschenkir], Rukneddīn Bay-bars, first an emir then Sultan Bay-bars II al-Muẓaffar (1309-1310) (Abulfidā V, 132, Dawād. 7, 8, 39, Makrīzī IV, 114, Weil, Chalif. I, 279-301 etc., Iyās I, 350); Kuman? 1359 **Bi-bars** [Bybarch vaivoda Olacorum] (Zimmerman, F. - Werner, Urkundenbuch zur Geschichte der Deutschen in Siebenbürgen. Hermannstadt (Nagyszeben), 1892-1902, I, 172); Kuman 1496 **Bi-bars** [Biborcz], a Hungarian „kenez" family of Turkic (Kumanian) origin in Hunyad county (Csánki 164); Tat. 18th-19th c. **Bi-bars** [Бибарсъ] (Magn. 33); Chuv. 18th-19th c. **Pa-baris** [Пабарисъ] (Magn. 64); Chuv. 18th-19th c. **Pa-barïs** [Пабарысъ] (Magn. 64); Chuv. 18th-19th c. **Pi-barïs** [Пибарысъ] (Magn. 66); Chuv. 18th-19th c. **Pi-bars** [Пибарсъ] (Magn. 66); *TN:* Chuv. 18th c. **Bi-bars(ova)** [Бибарсова], a village in the district of Yadrinsk (Korsakov 309). ✧ 'Bay (rich)-leopard' cf. Hist. crois. I, 820: '„le bey-léopard": selon l'auteur du Nodjoum, an 658 [1260], ce nom signifie prince en langue

moghole'; 'Prince-tiger', cf. Sauvaget 43. ⇨ **BAY** + **BARS.** See also **BEY-BARS.**

BAY-BASUQ Kzk. 19th c. **Bay-basuq** [Байбасук] (SODž. 64). ⇨ **BAY** + **BASOQ / BOZUQ?**

BAY-BERDİ Bashk. 1706 **Bay-berdi** [Байберда], a Bashkir serf (MIB III, 30); Maml. 1517 **Bay-berdi / Bi-berdi?** [بيبردى بن كسباى] (Iyās III, 123-147); Chag. 1573 **Bay-berdi-mirza** [Бай-берды-мирза] (Ivanov 189). ✧ 'Rich man has given him'. ⇨ **BAY** + **BERDİ.**

BAY-BERİ Kzk. 19th c. **Bay-beri** [Байберы] (SOV 138); *TN:* Chuv. 18th c. **Bay-beri(na)** (<Bay-beri) [Байберина], a Chuvash village in the district of Tetyushinsk (Korsakov 346). ⇨ **BAY.**

BAY-BİJAN Oghuz/Trkm. 14th c. - 15th c. **Bay-biJan-bek** [باى بيجان] / (Pay Piçen Big) / Бай-Биджан-бек] (DQorq./Rossi 113, 117, 121-24, 130, 134, DQorq. 32, 35, 36, 38, 40, 41, 48, 119, 206, 213, 238). ✧ 'Rich/Noble lifeless/valiant'? cf. Turk. *bican* 'lifeless, spiritless; submisive; valiant' (TED). ⇨ **BAY.**

BAY-BOL Kzk. **Bay-bal?** (<Bay-bol?) [Байбалъ / Тюлюп Байбаловъ] (Patkanov II, 92); Kzk. 19th c. **Bay-bol** [Байболъ] (AOO 42, 50); Kzk. 19th c. **Bay-bol** [Байболъ], a qïstau [winter quarters of nomads] (SOV 8, 28); Kzk. 19th c. **Bay-bol** [Байболъ] (AOP 2); Kzk. 19th c. **Bay-bol** [Байболъ] (Grod., Pril. 69, 169); Kzk. 1820 **Bay-bul** [Байбул] (Sib. Vest. IX/3, 81); Kzk. 19th c. **Bay-bul** [Байбулъ] (AOO 42); Kzk. 19th c. **Bay-bul** [Kabïl-Baybul] (Ljutš 138); Kzk. 19th c. **Bay-bul** [Байбул] (Sozontov); *EN:* Kzk. 18th c. - 19th c. **Bay-bol** [Байбол] (Tynyšp. 71). ✧ 'Be/become rich; become a lord/rich man' (Rásonyi, Imp. 238). ⇨ **BAY** + **BOL.** See also **BEK-BOL, BİY-BOL.**

BAY-BOLAT see **BAY-BULAT**

BAY-BOLDİ Bashk. 1675 **Bay-boldï** [Байболды Елкибаев] (MIB I, 202); Uzb. 20th c. **Bây-boldï** [Бойбўлди] (Begmatov 1984, 201); Chuv. 18th-19th c. **Poy-boldï** (<Pay-boldï) [Пойболда] (Magn. 68). ✧ 'Became rich; became a lord/rich man'. ⇨ **BAY** + **BOLDİ.**

BAY-BOLOT see **BAY-BULAT**

BAY-BOLSÏN Kzk. 19th c. **Bay-bosïn** [Байбасынъ] (SODž. 52); Kzk. 19th c. **Bay-bosïn** [Байбасынъ] (SOK 6); Kzk. 19th c. **Bay-bosun** [Бай-босунъ] (Potanin II, 2); Kzk. 19th c. **Bay-bosun** [Байбасунъ] (SOK 184); Kzk. 19th c. **Bay-bosun** (<Bay-bolsun) [Бай-босунъ] (Potanin II, 2); Kzk. **Bay-bulsïn** [Бай-булсынъ] (Sozontov 6). ✧ 'Let him/her be/become rich' (Sozontov 6). ⇨ **BAY-BUL.**

BAY-BOSÏN see **BAY-BOLSÏN**

BAY-BOSUQ Kzk. 19th c. **Ba-bosuq** (< Bay-bosuq?) [Бабосукъ] (SOV 52). ⇨ **BAY** + **BASOQ / BOZUQ?** See also **BAY-BASUQ, BAY-BUŠUQ.**

BAY-BOSUN see **BAY-BOLSÏN**

BAY-BOTA   Kzk. 19th c. **Bay-bota** [Байбота] (SODž. 126); Uzb. 19th c. **Bay-buta-bi** [Baïbouta-by], early 19th c., Khokand (Nalivkin-Dozon 95). ✧ 'Rich/lord-young camel'. ⇨ **BAY + BOTA.**

BAY-BOZ   Kzk. 19th c. **Bay-boz** [Байбозъ] (SOK 126). ⇨ **BAY + BOZ.**

BAY-BÖRÜ   Tat. 1556 **Bay-börü** [Байберю] (PSRL XIII, 261); Kzk. **Bay-büre** [ایکی تنکلا من بای] [بایبوره بایساری] (Divaev, Alp. 3); Oghuz/Trkm. 14th c. - 15th c. **Bay-büri-beg / Bay-büre-beg / Bay-bura-χan?** [بایبوره بك] / Bay Büre Beg, Pay Püre Big / Бай-Бура-бек, Бай-Бура-хан,] (DQorq./Rossi 112-115, 121, 132, DQorq. 32 etc.). ⇨ **BAY + BÖRİ.**

BAY-BUΓA see **BAY-BUQA**

BAY-BUQA   Uyg. 12th c. - 14th c. **Bay-buγa** [bay buγa / Bay Buġa] (DTS, EUTS); Maml. 1327 **Bay-buγa** [بیبغا الشمسی], an emir (Dawād. 322); Maml. 1346 **Bay-buγa** [بیبغا اروس] (Iyās I, 185); Maml. 1357 **Bay-buγa** [بیبغا الیحیاوی] (Iyās I, 204); Maml. 1357 **Bay-buγa** [بیبغا الشمسی] (Iyās I, 194); Maml. 1400, 1401 **Bay-buγa** [بیبغا السابقی] (Iyās I, 233); Maml. 1421, 1422 **Bay-buγa** [بیبغا المظفری] (Iyās II, 15-23, Ibn Taghrīb. VI 341, 490, VII 183, 258); Maml. 1439 **Bay-buγa** [بیبغا الطیار] (Iyās II, 26); Crm. **Bay-buγa**, a place north-west of Caffa, Crimea (Jervis IX); Uyg. 12th c.-14th c. **Bay-buqa** [بای بوقه] (Radl., USp. 16-17, 55, RaD/Ber. I, 112); Uyg. 13th-14th c. **Bay-buqa** [Bay Buq-a] (Zieme, Mat. II, 92); Khorezm./Chag.? **Bay-buqa** [Бай-бука], Timur-buqa's son (RaD I/1, 175). ✧ 'Rich bull' (Blagova 1997, 711), 'Prince-bull' (Sauvaget 44). ⇨ **BAY + BUQA.**

BAY-BUL see **BAY-BOL**

BAY-BULAT   Kzk. 19th c. **Bay-bolat** [Байболатъ] (SOV 74); Kirg. **Bay-bolot** [Байболот] (Jud. 753); Crm. **Bay-bulat**, a place in the Crimea (Jervis II); Tat. 1662 **Bay-bulat** [Байбулатко] (DAI IV, 285); Tat. 1728 **Bay-bulat** [Байбулатов] (MIB III, 257); Bashk. 1740 **Bay-bulat** [Байбулат Иткусюков] (MIB I, 395); Bashk. 1740 **Bay-bulat** [Байбулат] (MIB I, 377); Kzk. **Bay-bulat** [Байбулатъ Бажентаевъ] (TOUAK XXIV, 161); Kzk. 1824 **Bay-bulat** [Байбулатъ Бажентаевъ] (TOUAK XXIV, 161). ✧ 'Lord-steel'. ⇨ **BAY + BULAT.** See also **Bİ-BULAT.**

BAY-BULDİ see **BAY-BOLDİ**

BAY-BULİQ   Kzk. 19th c. **Bay-bulïq** [Бай-булыкъ] (Potanin II, 177). ⇨ **BAY.**

BAY-BULSİN see **BAY-BOLSİN**

BAY-BURAT   Kzk. 1819, 1829? **Bay-burat** [Байбурат] (MIK IV, 324). ⇨ **BAY + BURAT.**

BAY-BURTLİ   Yürük **Bay-burtlï** (Giese 81); Tat. **Bay-burtlï** (Mende 141). ⇨ **BAY.**

BAY-BUS   Oghuz **Bay-bus** [بایبوس], forefather of the Ottoman dynasty (Āšikp. 50). ⇨ **BAY + BOZ?**

BAY-BUSURMAN   Kzk. 19th c. **Bay-busurman** [Байбусурманъ] (AOA 130). ⇨ **BAY + BUSURMAN.**

BAY-BUŠUQ   Kzk. 19th c. **Bay-bušuq** [Байбушукъ] (SODž. 8). ⇨ **BAY.** See also **BAY-BASUQ, BAY-BOSUQ.**

BAY-BÜRE see **BAY-BÖRÜ**

BAY-BÜRİ see **BAY-BÖRÜ**

BAY-ČAΓAN   Kzk. 1819 **Bay-čaγan** [Байчаган] (MIK IV, 324); Kzk. 19th c. **Bay-čaγan** [Байчаган] (SOK 174); *EN:* Kzk. 18th c. - 19th c. **Bay-čaqan** [Байчакан] (Tynyšp. 67). ⇨ **BAY + ČAΓAN.**

BAY-ČAΓAT   Kzk. 19th c. **Bay-čaγat** [Байчагатъ] (SOV 136). ⇨ **BAY.**

BAY-ČAL   Kzk. 19th c. **Bay-čal** [Байчалъ] (SODž. 108). ✧ 'Rich grey-haired old man'. ⇨ **BAY + ČAL.**

BAY-ČALAQ   Kzk. 19th c. **Bay-čalaq** [Байчалакъ] (SOV 132). ⇨ **BAY + ČALAQ.**

BAY-ČAN   Tat.(Sib.), Tat.(Tob.) 1631 **Bay-čan** [Кутум Байчанов] (Miller, Ist. Sib. II, 385, 386). ⇨ **BAY + ČAN II.**

BAY-ČAŇ   Alt. 19th-20th c. **Bay-čaň**, fem. (OjrRS 211).

BAY-ČAR   Karch. **Bay-čar** [Байчаровъ] (Sysoev 132). ✧ 'Lord-White-head; Lord-Piebald'. ⇨ **BAY + ČAR.**

BAY-ČEL   Kzk. 19th c. **Bay-čel** [Байчелъ] (SOK 88). ⇨ **BAY.**

BAY-ČEN   Kzk. 19th c. **Bay-čen** [Байченъ] (AOK 126). ⇨ **BAY + ČEN / ČİN?**

BAY-ČERKÄS   Kzk. 1820 **Bay-čerkäs** [Байчеркасъ], a chief of a tribe (Sib. Vest. IX, 118). ⇨ **BAY + ČERKES.**

BAY-ČOQ   Kzk. 19th c. **Bay-čoq / Bayčuq? / Bayčïq?** [Баичокъ] (SOK 140). ⇨ **BAY + ČOQ?**

BAY-JAQİP   Kirg. **Bay-jaqïp** [Байжакып] (Jud. 351). ⇨ **BAY + YAQUB.**

BAY-JAMART   Kzk. 19th c. **Bay-jamart** [Байджамарт] (SOK 110). ⇨ **BAY + JOMART.**

BAY-JİN   Kzk. 19th c. **Bay-jin** [Байджинъ] (Grod., Pril. 27). ⇨ **BAY + JİN.**

BAY-JİNBET   Kzk. 19th c. **Bay-jimbet (<Bay-jinbet)** [Байжимбетъ] (SOV 124). ⇨ **BAY-JİN** + suffixoid -*bet*.

BAY-DAM   Kzk. 19th c. **Bay-dam** [Байдамъ] (SOK 102). ⇨ **BAY + DAM?**

BAY-DARAQ   Tat.(Sib.)? 1633 **Bay-daraq** [Баидарак] (Miller, Ist. Sib. II, 405); Kzk. 19th c. **Bay-draq (<Bay-daraq)** [Байдракъ] (SODž. 108). ⇨ **BAY.**

BAY-DAW see **BAY-TAW**

BAY-DAWLET   Kzk. 18th c. - 19th c. **Bay-dawlet** [Байдаулет] (Tynyšp. 75). ⇨ **BAY + DÄWLÄT.**

BAY-DEMİR see **BAY-TEMİR**

BAY-DERMEN Kzk. 19th c. **Bay-dermen** [Байдерменъ] (SOK 56). ⇨ **BAY** + **DÄRMAN.**

BAY-DİLDA Kzk. 19th c. **Bay-dilda** [Байдильда] (SODž. 82); Kzk. 19th c. **Bay-dildi** [Байдильди] (SOK 212). ⇨ **BAY** + **DİLDA.** See also **BEK-DİLLÄ.**

BAY-DİLDİ see **BAY-DİLDA**

BAY-DİMER see **BAY-TEMİR**

BAY-DÏҐAN see **BAY-TUҐAN**

BAY-DUҐAN see **BAY-TUҐAN**

BAY-DUR see **BAY-TUR**

BAY-EDİL? Kzk. 19th c. **Bay-edil?** [Баедиль] (SOK 300). ⇨ **BAY** + **EDİL?**

BAY-GEL Kzk. 19th c. **Bay-gel** [Байгель] (SOV 138); Kzk. 19th c. **Bay-gel** [Байгель] (SOK 246); Kzk. 19th c. **Bay-gel** [Байгель] (AOO 2). ✧ 'Rich(man)-Come!'. ⇨ **BAY** + **KEL.**

BAY-GELDİ Tat.(Sib.)? 1634 **Ba-geldey** (<**Bay-geldiy**) [Багелдей] (Miller, Ist. Sib. II, 418); Tat.(Sib.) 1605 **Ba-gildey** (<**Bay-gildey**) [Багилдей Торкан] (Miller, Ist. Sib. II, 189); Kzk. 19th c. **Bay-geldi** [Байгельды] (SOK 18); Bashk. 1751 **Bay-gilda** (<**Bay-gilde**) [Байгилда Паишаков] (MIB IV/1, 52); Tat. 18th c. **Bay-gildi** [Байгилдина], a village in the district of Civil'sk (Korsakov 318); Chuv. 18th-19th c. **Pa-gilde** (<**Pay-gilde**) [Пагилда] (Magn. 65); Chuv. 18th-19th c. **Pay-kilde** [Пайкилда] (Magn. 65); *EN:* Kzk. **Bay-geldi** [Bay-gäldi] (Németh, HMK 67); *TN:* Crm. **Bay-geldi** [Baigeldii], a place east of Yevpatoriya (Jervis VII). ✧ 'Rich(man) has come (has been born)' cf. Kzk. PN *Baygeldi* (Žanuzakov-Esbaeva). ⇨ **BAY** + **KELDİ.**

BAY-GELDİY see **BAY-GELDİ**

BAY-GİLDEY see **BAY-GELDİ**

BAY-GİREY Chuv. 18th-19th c. **Bay-girey** [Байгирей] (Magn. 32). ⇨ **BAY** + **KERÄY.**

BAY-ҐABÏL Kzk. 19th c. **Bay-ɣabïl** [Байгабылъ], Jan-ɣabïl's brother (Potanin II, 4); Kzk. 19th c. **Bay-ɣabïl** [Байгабылъ] (SOV 58); Kzk. 19th c. **Bay-ɣabïl** [Байгабылъ Таумановъ] (AUK 611); Kzk. 19th c. **Bay-ɣabïl** [Байгабылъ] (SOK 204); Kzk. 19th c. **Bay-ɣabul** [Байгабулъ] (Lomakin 39); Kzk. 19th c. **Bay-ɣabul** [Байгабулъ] (AOO 42). ⇨ **JAN** + **ҐABÏL** / **ҐABUL?** / **QABUL!.** See also **JAN-ҐABÏL, TLÄW-ҐABÏL.**

BAY-ҐABUL see **BAY-ҐABÏL**

BAY-ҐARA see **BAY-QARA**

BAY-ҐASQA Kzk. 19th c. **Bay-ɣasqa** [Байгаска] (AOK 10). ⇨ **BAY** + **QASQA.**

BAY-ҐÏRČAN Nog. 1649 **Bay-ɣïrčan, Bay-ɣïrčañ?** [Байгырчанъ Мамбетькуловъ] (AI IV, 123). ⇨ **BAY.**

BAY-ҐOMÏR Kzk. 19th c. **Bay-ɣomïr** [Байгомыръ] (SOV 14). ✧ 'Rich life'? ⇨ **BAY** + **ÖMÜR?**

BAY-ҐONČAQ Kzk. 19th c. **Bay-ɣončaq** [Байгончакъ] (AOO 46). ⇨ **BAY** + **QONČAQ?**

BAY-ҐULAQ see **BAY-QULAQ**

BAY-ҐULČUQ Kzk. 19th c. **Bay-ɣulčuq** [Байгульчукъ] (SOV 58). ✧ 'Little dear Bay-ɣul'. ⇨ **BAY** + **QULČUQ** + dim. hypoc. suff. *-čuq.*

BAY-ҐURZA Tat. 1702 **Bay-ɣurza** [Ярметко Байгурзинъ] (Letop. ZAK II, 7). ⇨ **BAY.**

BAY-ҐUT see **BAY-QUT**

BAY-ҐUTÏ Kzk. 19th c. **Bay-ɣutï** [Байгуты] (AOO 6). ⇨ **BAY** + **QUT** + poss. suff. *-i?*

BAY-ҐUZA Bashk. 1734 **Bay-ɣuza** [Юсуп Байгузинъ], a tarɣan (Vel.-Zern., Bašk. 11).

BAY-İŠ Tat. 20th c. **Bay-iš** [Баишев] (Sattarov); Tat.(Tüm.) 1633 **Bay-iš** [Баиш] (Miller, Ist. Sib. II, 407); Bashk. 1706 **Bay-iš** [Баиш Айбашев] (MIB III, 26); Kzk. 19th c. **Bay-iš** [Баиш] (AOAtb. 14); Kzk. 19th c. **Bay-iš** [Баешъ] (AOAtb. 58). ✧ 'Rich fellow, mate, friend (child)' (Sattarov). ⇨ **BAY** + **EŠ.** See also **QUL-BAY-İŠ.**

BAY-KEMPİR Kzk. 19th c. **Bay-kempir** [Байкемпиръ] (SOV 32). ⇨ **BAY** + **KEMPİR.**

BAY-KESE Kzk. 19th c. **Bay-kese** [Байкесе] (SOK 214). ✧ 'Rich-Cup'? cf. Kzk. *kese* 'пиалка (чайная чашка)' (KzRS). ⇨ **BAY.**

BAY-KEŠ Tat. 1556 **Bay-keš / Bay-kiš?** [Байкешь] (PSRL XIII, 262). ⇨ **BAY** + **KİŠ?**

BAY-KİŠİ Kzk. 19th c. **Bay-kiši** [Байкишіевъ] (Grod., Pril. 73); Tat.? 1803 **Bay-kši** (<**Bay-kiši**) [Ишгъ Мугамедъ Байкшиевъ] (PSZRI XXVII, 465, 509); Kzk. 19th c. **Bay-kši** (<**Bay-kiši**) [Байкши] (SKSO VIII, 219); Kzk. 19th c. **Bay-kši** (<**Bay-kiši**) [Айджигитъ Байкшіевъ] (SKSO VIII, 220). ✧ 'Rich-Younger' cf. Kzk. *kiši* 'младший; меньше' (KzRS). ⇨ **BAY.**

BAY-KÖPÄK Kzk. 19th c. **Bay-köpäk** [Байкопакъ Мусулмановъ] (Grod., Pril. 126); Kzk. 19th c. **Bay-köpäk** [Байкопакъ] (Grod., Pril. 28, 145); Kzk. 19th c. **Bay-köpäk** [Мингчасаръ Байкопаковъ] (Grod., Pril. 101); Kzk. 19th c. **Bay-köpäk** [Акимъ-бекъ Байкопаковъ] (Grod., Pril. 120); Kzk. 19th c. **Bay-köpäk** [Байкопакъ] (Grod., Pril. 28, 145). ✧ 'Rich Dog'. ⇨ **BAY** + **KÖPÄK.** See also **BAY-KÜČÜK.**

BAY-KÖŠÜK Kzk. 19th c. **Bay-köšük?** [Байкошукъ] (AOA 102). ⇨ **BAY** + **KÖSEK?**

BAY-KŠİ see **BAY-KİŠİ**

BAY-KÜBEK see **BAY-KÖPÄK**

BAY-KÜBEK Kzk. 1822 **Bay-kübek** [Кибекъ Байкубековъ] (TOUAK XXIV, 117); Kzk. 19th c. **Bay-kübek** [Байкубекъ] (Grod., Pril. 81).

BAY-KÜČÜK Bashk. 1675 **Bay-küčük** [Бай-Кучюк Бютюков] (MIB I, 201). ⇨ **BAY** + **KÜČÜK.** See also **BAY-KÖPÄK.**

BAY-QADAN Kzk. 19th c. **Bay-qadan** [Байкаданъ] (SOK 80). ⇨ **BAY.**

BAY-QARA Chag.? 1470 **Bay-qara** [Султан-Хусейн Байкара], Sultan Hüssein Bay-qara (1469-1506), mirza, the Timurid ruler of Khorasan (MIT I, 59-61, 535-541); Turk. 1519 **Bay-qara** (Gökb., Ed. 251); Tat. 1624 **Bay-qara** [Байгора Сатымовъ] (Pokrovskij 70); Tat.(Sib.) 1607 **Bay-qara** [Байгара] (Miller, Ist. Sib. II, 204); Tat.(Sib.) 1609 **Bay-qara** [Байгара Кензин] (Miller, Ist. Sib. II, 209, 210); Kzk. 1814 **Bay-qara** [Байкара Тургаевъ] (TOUAK XXIV, 57); Kkalp. 1822 **Bay-qara** [Байкара], a captain (MIKk. 127); Kirg. 19th c. **Bay-qara** [Байгара], a man in a popular legend (AUK 736); Uzb. 19th c. **Bay-qara** [Байкара Карабаевъ] (SKSO III, 8). ✧ I. 'Lord-Black'?; II. 'Clawn'? cf. Turk. dial. *baykara* 'soytarı, maskara' (DS). ⇨ **BAY + QARA.**

BAY-QATÏČ Tat.(Sib.) 1599 **Bay-qatič** [Байкатычь], a nurse in Küčüm's service (AI II, 20). ⇨ **BAY + QATÏŠ?**

BAY-QATUL Tat.? 1540 **Bay-qatul** [Байкатулъ] (PSRL XIII, 132). ⇨ **BAY.**

BAY-QAZ Bashk. 1756 **Bay-qaz?** [Байкас Кизяков] (MIB IV/1, 122); Kzk. 19th c. **Bay-qaz** [Илкибай Байказовъ] (Grod., Pril. 95). ⇨ **BAY + QAZ.**

BAY-QAZAQ Kzk. 19th c. **Bay-qazaq** [Байказакъ] (SOK 198); Kzk. 19th c. **Bay-qazaq** [Байказакъ] (SOV 100). ⇨ **BAY + QAZAQ.**

BAY-QAZAR Kzk. 19th c. **Bay-qazar** [Байказаръ] (AOO 22). ⇨ **BAY + QAZAR.**

BAY-QOZÏ Kzk. 18th c. - 19th c. **Bay-qozi** [Байкозы] (Tynyšp. 75). ⇨ **BAY + QOZÏ.**

BAY-QUƔUN Kzk. 19th c. **Bay-quγun** [Байкугунъ] (SOK 118). ⇨ **BAY.**

BAY-QULAQ Kzk. 19th c. **Bay-γulaq** [Байгулакъ] (SOV 20); Kzk. 19th c. **Bay-qulaq** [Байкулакъ] (SOK 36); Kzk. 19th c. **Bay-qulaq** [Байкулакъ] (SOV 112); Kzk. 19th c. **Bay-qulaq** [Байкулакъ] (SODž. 138). ⇨ **BAY + QULAQ.**

BAY-QULAN Kzk. 19th c. **Bay-qulan** [Байкуланъ] (SOV 40); Kzk. 19th c. **Bay-qulan** [Байкулановъ] (Grod., Pril. 44). ⇨ **BAY + QULAN.**

BAY-QUT Maml.? 1444/45, 1452/53 **Bay-γut** [لمويدى الاعرج / بيغوت من صفر حجا لمويدى الاعزج / بيغوت من صتر حجا] (Ibn Taghrīb. VII, 137, 153, Iyās II, 43); Maml.? 1469/70 **Bay-γut** [بيغوت] (Iyās II, 114); Kzk. 19th c. **Bay-qut** [Байкутъ] (SOK 238). ✧ 'Rich(man)-Fortune'? cf. Kzk. PN *Bayγut* (Žanuzakov-Esbaeva). ⇨ **BAY + QUT.**

BAY-QUTLÏ Kzk. 18th c. **Bay-qutla** (<Bay-qutlï) [Байкутла] (Nepljuev 762, 763). ⇨ **BAY + QUTLUƔ.**

BAY-MAQAN Kzk. 19th c. **Bay-maqan** [Баймаканъ] (Grod., Pril. 106). ⇨ **BAY + MAQAN.**

BAY-MENDE Kzk. 19th c. **Bay-mende** [Байменде] (AOK 130); Kzk. 19th c. **Bay-mende** [Байменде] (SOV 18). ⇨ **BAY + MENDE.**

BAY-MÖÑKE Kzk. 1825 **Bay-mönke** [باى مونكه / Бай Монке] (MIK IV, 469, 476). ⇨ **BAY + MÖÑKE.**

BAY-NAZAR Kzk. 18th c. - 19th c. **Bay-nazar** [Байназар] (Tynyšp. 70, 71); Kzk. 19th c. **Bay-nazar** [Байнозар] (SODž.); Uzb. 1804 **Bay-nazar-biy** [Бай-Назар-бий], from the Qoñgrat tribe (MIT II, 364). ⇨ **BAY + NAZAR.** See also **BÏY-NAZAR.**

BAY-NÏYAZ Kkalp. 20th c. **Bay-niyaz** [Байнияз] (KkRS 772). ⇨ **BAY + NÏYAZ.**

BAY-PAƔÏS see BAY-BAƔÏS

BAY-SAQAL Kzk. 1820, 1877 **Bay-saqal** [Байсакалъ Тлякинъ / Байсакал / ЛӘя ӘоиӘб], one of the chiefs of the Yappas (Ǧappas) tribe (Sib. Vest. IX, 111, MIK IV, 309); Kzk. 19th c. **Bay-saqal** [Байсакалъ] (TV 1876, 144); *TN:* Kzk. **Bay-saqal** [Бай-сакалъ] (Karta JAR XI). ⇨ **BAY + SAQAL.**

BAY-SALÏQ Kzk. 19th c. **Bay-salïq** [Байсалыкъ] (SOK 222, 302). ⇨ **BAY + SALÏQ.**

BAY-SAN Kzk. 19th c. **Bay-sam-bay** (<Baysan-bay) [Байсамбай] (SOK 8, 180); Kzk. 19th c. **Bay-san-bay** [Байсанбай] (SOK 298, 304). ⇨ **BAY + SAN.**

BAY-SANAQ Kzk. 19th c. **Bay-sanaq** [Байсанакъ] (SOV 152). ⇨ **BAY + SANAQ?**

BAY-SAP Kzk. 19th c. **Bay-sa-pay** (<Bay-sap-pay) [Байсапай] (SOK 188). ⇨ **BAY + SAP / SAPAY?**

BAY-SARA see BAY-SARÏ

BAY-SARÏ Kzk. 19th c. **Bay-sar-bay** (<Bay-sarï-bay) [Байсарбай] (AOK 122); Bashk. 1753, 1760 **Bay-sara** (<Bay-sarï) [Байсара Абызаев] (MIB IV/1, 68, 191); Bashk. 1785 **Bay-sara** (<Bay-sarï) [Байсара Абдрахманов] (MIB V, 168); Maml. 13th c. **Bay-sarï** [بدرالدين بيسرى الظاهرى], one of the mightiest emirs (died in 1297) at the time of Salāmish (Mayer 112, Iyās I, 91, 99, 112, 114); Maml. 1260 **Bay-sarï** [بيسرى] (Sīrat 166); Maml. 1260, 1271/72 **Bay-sarï** [بدرالدين بيسرى الشمسى], an emir; escaping from prison in 1291, as a mark of his respect to Malik-Ashraf-Khalil he changed his nickname Shamsi to Ashrafi (Sīrat 166, Aynī: RHCHor II/1, 245-46, Makrīzī III, 131-33, Weil, Chalif. I, 202, 207, Zetterst. 22); Maml. 1299 **Bay-sarï** [بدرالدين بيسرى], an emir (Dawād. 13); Maml. 1299 **Bay-sarï** [Schems-eddin-Baïsari] (Makrīzī IV, 135); Bashk. 1709 **Bay-sarï** [Урман Байсарыев] (MIB I, 264); Kzk. 18th c. - 19th c. **Bay-sarï** [Байсары] (Tynyšp. 63, 72, 73); Kzk. **Bay-sarï** [باىبوره باىسارى ايكى تنكلا من باى] (Divaev, Alp. 1, 3 etc.); Maml. 1297/98 **Bī-sarï / Bay-sarï?** [بدرالدين بيسرى / Beisari (Bedr Eddin)] (Iyās I, 112, 131, Weil, Chalif. I, 36, 81, 105-108, Makrīzī I, 53,

293); *TN:* Chuv. 18th c. **Bay-sarina** (<Bay-sarï) [Байсарина], a village in the district of Cheboksary (Korsakov 286); Kzk. **Bay-sarï** [Байсары], a lake in Kazak stan (Kojčubaev 48). ❖ 'Lord-yellow/blond'. ⇨ **BAY + SARÏ.**

BAY-SARKE Kzk. 1862 **Bay-sarke** (<Bay-sarïke<Bay-sarï-ake?) [Байсарке Кутеневъ], in the district of Kopal (ZIRGOGeogr. I, 314). ⇨ **BAY + SARKE.**

BAY-SARMÏŠ Kzk. 1877 **Bay-sarmïš** [Кудай Байсармышевъ] (TOUAK XXIV, 80). ⇨ **BAY.**

BAY-SAU Kzk. 1817 **Bay-sau** [باىصاو / Байсау] (MIK IV, 311). ⇨ **BAY + SAW?**

BAY-SEKE Bashk. 1711 **Bay-seke** [Байсеке] (MIB III, 73). ⇨ **BAY + SEKE.**

BAY-SEŇGİR Kzk. **Bay-señgir** [Байсенгыръ] (SOK 222). ⇨ **BAY + SEŇGİR.**

BAY-SERİK Kzk. 19th c. **Bay-serik** [Байсерикъ] (SOK. 278); Kzk. 19th c. **Bay-serik** [Байсерыкъ] (SOK. 278). ⇨ **BAY + ŠERİK II.**

BAY-SERKE Kzk. 19th c. **Bay-serke** [Байсерке] (SOK. 74, 168); Kzk. 19th c. **Bay-serke** [Байсерке] (SOV 100); Kirg. 1876 **Bay-serke** [Бай-Серке], a manap (TV 1876, 183). ⇨ **BAY + SERKE.**

BAY-SİNİR Kzk. 1819 **Bay-sinir** [Байсинир] (MIK IV, 326). ❖ 'Rich-Tendon'? cf. Kzk. *siñir* 'сухожилие' (KzRS). ⇨ **BAY.**

BAY-SİT see **BAY**

BAY-SOŇQUR Khorezm./Chag. 15th c. **Bay-soñqur** [Παϊαγγούρης], Timur's son (Byz. Turc. 240); Khorezm./Chag. 1450, 1452 **Bay-soñqur** [باى سنتر], Šahruχ's (1405-1447) son (Ibn Taghrīb. VIII, 59, 136); Khorezm./Chag. 1450, 1452 **Bay-soñqur** [باى سنتر / Bay Sungur], sultan (1495-1497; died in 1499), Bābūr's father, the ruler of the Timurids in Samarkand (Ibn Taghrīb. VIII, 59, 127 etc., Uzunçarş.? 67); Maml. 1436 **Bay-soñqur** [باىسنتر], commandant of Kirman (Arabš. II, 862); Maml. 1450 **Bay-soñqur** [باى سنتر] محمد بن [(Ibn Taghrīb. VIII, 59); Chag. 15th c. **Bay-soñqur (Bay-suñqar, Bay-suñyar, Bay-soñyur?)** [باىسنغر ميرزا / Báisanghar Mirzá / Байсунгар, Байсункар, Байсанггуръ Мирза], a Timurid mirza, the ruler of Samarkand (1495) (MIT I, 56, 534, II, 53, Tar. Rashidi 119, 154, Šejb. LXX, Radl. III, 442); Turk. 15th c. **Bay-suñyur** [Bay Sungur], from the Akkoyunlular (Uzunçarş., Anad.? 67). ❖ 'A sort of birds of prey' cf. Turk. *baysunyur* 'ein Raubvogel' (Racl. IV, 1430). ⇨ **BAY + SOŇQUR.**

BAY-SUŇÍUR see **BAY-SOŇQUR**

BAY-TABÏN Kzk. 19th c. **Bay-tabïn-qan** (Ljutš 51). ❖ 'Rich-stud'? cf. Chag., Tat. *tabun* 'die Pferdeheerde' (Radl. III, 978). ⇨ **BAY.**

BAY-TAYLAQ Kzk. 19th c. **Bay-taylaq** [Байтайлякъ] (AOO 34); Kzk. 19th c. **Bay-taylaq** [Бай-тайлякъ] (Potanin II, 6); *TN:* Kzk. **Bay-taylaq** [Байтайлак], a field (Kojčubaev 48); Kzk. **Bay-taylaq** [Байтайлак], a field (Kojčubaev 48). ⇨ **BAY + TAYLAQ.**

BAY-TALAQ Kzk. 19th c. **Bay-talaq** [Байталакъ] (SODž. 44). ⇨ **BAY + TALAQ? / TAYLAQ?**

BAY-TALAS Kzk. 19th c. **Bay-talas** [Байталасъ] (SOK 288). ⇨ **BAY + TALAS.**

BAY-TALÏ Kzk. 19th c. **Bay-talï** [Байталы] (SOK 114). ⇨ **BAY + TALÏ.**

BAY-TAN-AT see **BAY-TAÑ-AT**

BAY-TANA Kzk. 18th c. - 19th c. **Bay-tana** [Байтана] (Tynyšp. 66); Kzk. 19th c. **Bay-tana** [Байтана] (SOV 44). ⇨ **BAY + TANA I.**

BAY-TAÑ-AT Kzk. 1823 **Bay-ta-at** [Байтанат] (MIK IV, 457); Kzk. 19th c. **Bay-tan-at** [Байтанатъ] (AOAtb. 58); Kzk. 19th c. **Bay-tan-at** [Аппакъ Байтанатовъ] (Grod., Pril. 57); Kzk. 1819, 1823 **Bay-tañ-at** [باى طانكاط / Байтанат] (MIK IV, 326, 457); Kzk. 1819, 1823 **Bay-tañ-at** [Байтанат] (MIK IV, 326, 457). ⇨ **BAY + TAÑ-AT.**

BAY-TARAQ Kzk. 19th c. **Bay-taraq** [Байтаракъ] (SODž. 120). ⇨ **BAY + TARAQ.**

BAY-TAŠ Kzk. 19th c. **Bay-tas** (Ljutš 74); Kzk. 19th c. **Bay-tas** [Байтасъ Бектасов] (AOO 46); Kzk. 19th c. **Bay-tas** [Байтасъ] (AOO 42); Kzk. 19th c. **Bay-taš** [Байташъ] (SKSO VIII, 226). ⇨ **BAY + TAŠ.**

BAY-TAW Uzb. 1885 **Bay-daw-bay?** [Байдау-бай] (Moskal'cev 50); Kzk. 1846 **Bay-taw** [Джакай Байтаув], a biy (MKOP 156). ⇨ **BAY + ТАГ.**

BAY-TELES see **BAY-TİLÄŠ**

BAY-TELİ Kzk. 19th c. **Bay-teli** [Байтеле] (SOK 262). ⇨ **BAY + TELİ.**

BAY-TEMİR Khorezm.? 14th c. **Bay-demir** [بيدمر / Байдемиръ], regent of Urgench (Ürgenč) at the time of Özbek Khan (1312-1341) (Aynī/Tizeng. I, 486, 526); Maml. 1330 **Bay-demir** [بيدمر] (Dawād. 355); Maml. 1332 **Bay-demir** [بيدمر البدرى], an emir (Dawād. 366); Maml. 1387 **Bay-demir** [بيد مر الخوارزمى], governor of Damascus (Iyās I, 207, 261, Weil, Chalif. I, 545); Maml. 1389 **Bay-demir** [بيد مر المجدى] (Iyās I, 273); Chuv. 18th-19th c. **Bay-demir** [Байдемиръ] (Magn. 32); Chuv. 18th-19th c. **Bay-dimer** [Байдимеръ] (Magn. 32); Tat. 1675 **Bay-temir** [Байтемирко] (Kungursk. akty 24); Bashk. 1706 **Bay-temir** [Байтемир], a tarχan (MIB III, 21); Kzk. 19th c. **Bay-temir** (Ljutš 106); Kzk. 19th c. **Bay-temir** [Байтемиръ] (SOK 254); Kzk. 19th c. **Bay-temir** [Байтемиръ] (SOV 46, 138); Uyg. 12th c.-14th c. **Bay-temür** [Bai-tämür / baj temür] (Radl., USp. 2-3, 8, 34, DTS); Khorezm.? **Bay-temür** [با يتيمور], mentioned among the sons of Tor-qaymïš (?) (تور قايمش)

(RaD/Ber. I, 69); Khorezm. 1295 **Bay-temür** [باى تيمور] (RaD/Jahn 99); Selj. **Bay-temür / Yan-temür?** [باى تمور / يانتمور / Bai Temür], the ancestor of the Ottoman dynasty (Āšikp. 50, Nešrī 186, Seādeddīn I, 10, Wittek 94); Chuv. 18th-19th c. **Bay-timir** [Байтимиръ] (Magn. 32); Maml. 14th c. **Bäy-dämür / Bay-dämür?** [بَيْدَمُرْ] (Sauvaget 44); Turk. 16th c. **Bey-temür** (Ongan, Ank. II, 1140); Chuv. 18th-19th c. **Pay-demir** [Пайдемиръ] (Magn. 65); Chuv. 18th-19th c. **Pay-dimer** [Пайдимеръ] (Magn. 65); Chuv. 18th-19th c. **Vay-dimir** [Вайдимiръ] (Magn. 35); *TN:* Kuman 1419 **Bajdamér-szállása** (<Bay-demir) [Baydamerzallasa], a settlement of Kuman origin in Hungary (Gyárfás III, 566); Turk. 20th c. **Bey-demir**, a village (old name: Rumkuş) in the province of Adana, Turkey (TMİB 13). ✧ 'Rich/noble iron' cf. Rásonyi: Basar. 33, KÖA 89, Adalékok 131-32, Anthr. 137, Blagova 1997, 712. ⇨ **BAY** + **TEMİR**.

BAY-TEMİŠ   Kzk. 19th c. **Bay-temeš** [Байтемешъ] (AOA 114); Kzk. 19th c. **Bay-temiš** [Байтемишъ] (AOO 34). ⇨ **BAY** + **TEMİŠ**.

BAY-TEMÜR see **BAY-TEMİR**

BAY-TERÄK   Tat. 1675 **Bay-täräk** [Байтярякъ] (Kungursk. akty 32); Tat.? **Bay-teräk** [Байтеряк], a murza, Urus-murza's son, forefather of the princely Bay-teräk (R. „Bajterjakovy") clan (Zolotn. 229, Zolotn., Alf. 156); Kzk. 19th c. **Bay-terek** [Байтерекъ] (SOK 150); Kzk. 19th c. **Bay-terek** [Байтерекъ] (SOV 16); Nog. 1542 **Bay-terek** [Байтерекъ] (PSRL XIII, 140); Nog. 1649 **Bay-terek** [Байтерекъ] (AI IV, 87); Nog.? 1693 **Bay-terek** [Азаматъ Байтерековъ], a mirza (AI V, 402); Tat. 1654 **Bay-terek / Bay-teräk?** [Атманай Байтерековъ] (AI IV, 236); Tat.(Sib.) 1598-99 **Bay-terek / Bay-teräk** [Байтерекъ Чеплемишевъ], a murza (AI II, 3, 18, 21); Tat.(Sib.) 1640 **Bay-terek / Bay-teräk** [Кудамышко Байтереков] (Miller, Ist. Sib. II, 473); Kzk. 1817 **Bay-terek / Bay-teräk** [باى تيراك / Байтерек] (MIK IV, 311); Tat.(Sib.) 1621, 1622 **Bay-terek / Bay-teräk / Be(y)-terek?** [Байтерек, Бетерек], a Tatar prince (Miller, Ist. Sib. II, 260, 274, 292); Nog. 1555 **Bay-terik** [Байтерикъ], envoy (PSRL XIII, 249); Kzk. 19th c. **Bay-tiräk** [Джуджасаръ бай Тираковъ] (Grod., Pril. 111); *TN:* Chuv. 18th c. **Bay-teräk(ovo)** [Байтеряково], a village in the district of Tetyushinsk (Korsakov 344). ✧ I. 'Big, old (holy) poplar' (Sattarov: Bay-tiräk!); II. 'Lord/rich-support(er)'; III. 'Lord-healthy' (cf. Sattarov: Terek!). ⇨ **BAY** + **TERÄK / TİRÄK?**

BAY-TEZ   Kzk. 19th c. **Bay-tes** [Байтесъ] (AOO 42); Kzk. 19th c. **Bay-tes** [Байтесъ] (AOO 66). ✧ 'Lord-quick' cf. Kzk. *tez* 'скоро, быстро' (KzRS). ⇨ **BAY** + **TEZ**.

BAY-TİLÄY   Kzk. 19th c. **Bay-tiläy** [Сикимъ-бай Байтилаевъ] (Grod., Pril. 199). ⇨ **BAY** + **TİLÄ** + dim. suff. *-y*.

BAY-TİLÄŠ   Kzk. 19th c. **Bay-teles** [Байтелесъ] (SOK 66); Kzk. 19th c. **Bay-tiläš** [Байтилашъ Кулбаевъ] (Grod., Pril. 125); Kzk. 19th c. **Bay-tles** [Байтлесъ] (SODž. 54); Kzk. 19th c. **Bay-tles** [Байтлесъ] (SOK 300). ⇨ **BAY** + **TİLÄŠ**.

BAY-TİLEK   Kzk. 19th c. **Bay-telek** [Байтелекъ] (SODž. 8); Kzk. 19th c. **Bay-tlek / Bay-tilek** [Байтлекъ] (SOV 62). ⇨ **BAY** + **TİLEK**.

BAY-TİRÄK see **BAY-TERÄK**

BAY-TİMAN   Kzk. 19th c. **Bay-tïman** [Байтыманъ] (SOK 18). ⇨ **BAY**.

BAY-TLEK see **BAY-TİLEK**

BAY-TLEW   Kzk. 1794 **Bay-tlew** [باى تلاو / Байтлеу] (MIK IV, 158); Kzk. 19th c. **Bay-tlew** [Байтлеу] (SOV 10). ⇨ **BAY** + **TİLÄW**.

BAY-TOXTA   Uzb. 20th c. **Bây-toχta** [Бойтӱхта] (Begmatov 1984, 205). ⇨ **BAY** + **TOQTA**.

BAY-TOQ   Kzk. 19th c. **Bay-toq** [Турганъ Байтоковъ] (Grod., Pril. 71); Kzk. 19th c. **Bay-toq** [Байтокъ] (SOV 58). ⇨ **BAY** + **TOQ**.

BAY-TUBAY   Kzk. 19th c. **Bay-tubay** [Байтубай] (AOP 86); Kzk. 19th c. **Bay-tubay** [Байтубай] (SODž. 74). ⇨ **BAY** + **TUBAY**.

BAY-TUΓAN   Bashk. 1784 **Bay-tuγan** [Байтуган Абизгильдин] (MIB V, 155); Kzk. 19th c. **Bay-tuγan** [Байтуганъ] (SOK 286); Kzk. 19th c. **Bay-tuγan** [Байтуганъ] (SOV 28); Kzk. 19th c. **Bay-tuγan** [Байтуганъ] (Grod., Pril. 78); Chuv. 18th-19th c. **Pay-tugan** [Пайтуганъ] (Magn. 65). ✧ I. 'Rich relative' cf. Kzk. *tūyan* 'der Verwandte' (Radl. III, 1431), also Kzk. PN *Baytuyan* (Žanuzakov-Esbaeva); II. 'A rich man, a master (=a boy) has been born; born to be rich'? (Sattarov). ⇨ **BAY**.

BAY-TULAQ   Kzk. 1843 **Bay-tulaq** [Байтулакъ Тенизбаевъ] (Konšin, Mat. V, 59). ⇨ **BAY** + **TULAQ?**

BAY-TUMA   Kzk. 19th c. **Bay-tuma** [Байтума] (SOK 168); Kzk. 19th c. **Bay-tuma** [Байтума] (SOV 38, 64, 104). ⇨ **BAY** + **TUMA**.

BAY-TUR   Chuv. 18th-19th c. **Bay-dur** [Байдуръ] (Magn. 32); Kzk. 19th c. **Bay-tur** [Байтуръ] (SODž. 140); Kzk. 19th c. **Bay-tur / Bay-tur-bay** [Байтуръ / Байтурбай] (SOK 64, 74, 176, 252). ✧ 'Be rich; Become a richman'. ⇨ **BAY** + **TUR**. See also **BEK-TUR**.

BAY-TURSUN   Kzk. 19th c. **Bay-tursun** [Achmed Beitursunov / Ахмед Байтурсунович Байтурсунов], a Kazak writer (TOOIK III, 17 etc., AUK 162); Uzb. 20th c. **Bây-tursun** [Бойтурсун] (Begmatov 1984, 204). ⇨ **BAY** + **TURSİN**.

BAY-TURU Kzk.? **Bay-turu** [Байтуру], on a tombstone south-east of Karkaralinsk (Karta JAR XII). ⇨ **BAY** + **TORЇ**?

BAY-TURUP Kzk. 19th c. **Bay-turup** [Байдтурупъ] (SOK 144).

BAY-TUŠ Tat.(Lit.) 1592 **Bay-tuš** / **Boy-tuš**? [Келдабакъ Бойтушевичъ] (Lit. Tat. 124). ⇨ **BAY** + **TUŠ.**

BAY-TUZ Türk 977 **Bay-tuz** [با يتوز], the Ghaznavid Sebük-tegin's (977-997) enemy (Mirch. Gasnevid. 5-8). ⇨ **BAY** + **TUZ**?

BAY-TÜBET Kzk. 19th c. **Bay-tübet** [Каныбай Байтобетовъ] (Grod., Pril. 56). ⇨ **BAY** + **TÖBET**?

BAY-TÜGEY Kzk. 19th c. **Bay-tügey** [Байтюгеевъ] (AUK 443). ⇨ **BAY** + **TÜGEY.**

BAY-TÜGEL Kzk. 1823 **Bay-tügel(-bi)** [بای توگال بی /] Байтугел бий], a biy (Tynyšp. 72). ⇨ **BAY** + **TÜGÜL**?

BAY-TÜLEK Kzk. 1825 **Bay-tülek** [بايتولك /] Байтулек] (MIK IV, 471, 476). ⇨ **BAY** + **TÜLEK.**

BAY-TÜRKMEN Crm. **Bay-türkmen**, a place in the Crimea (Jervis III). ⇨ **BAY** + **TÜRKMEN.**

BAY-URAM Bashk. 1711 **Bay-uram** [Баюрам Кисякпердин] (MIB III, 80). ✧ 'Rich(man)-street/yard'? cf. Bashk. *uram* 'улица; двор' (BRS). ⇨ **BAY.**

BAY-URAZ Tat.(Sib.) 1596 **Bay-uras** [Баюрас Ларжков] (Miller, Ist. Sib. II, 149, 151); Bashk. 1706 **Bay-uraz** [Баюраз Кусекпердин] (MIB III, 19). ⇨ **BAY** + **ORAZ.**

BAY-UZAQ Kzk. 19th c. **Bay-uzaq** [Шукурбекъ Байузаговъ] (Grod., Pril. 73); Trkm. 19th c. **Bay-zaq** [Байзакъ] (SKSO III, 178); Kzk. **Bay-zaq** [Байзаковъ] (Sb. Syr-D. III. otd. II, 74); Kzk. **Bay-zaq** [Байзакъ-датха] (Smirnov, Sultany 14); Kzk. **Bay-zaq** [Baisak / Баiзак], from the Üysün tribe (Proben III, 72 (94)); Kzk. 18th c. - 19th c. **Bay-zaq** [با يزاق / Байзакъ], chief of the Dulat (Ulu jüz) tribe in the legend about Kenesari (Kenisara?) (ZOOIRGO III, 377); Kzk. 19th c. **Bay-zaq** [Байсакъ] (SOK 182); Kzk. 19th c. **Bay-zaq** [Байзакъ] (SKSO VIII, 207); Kzk. 19th c. **Bay-zaq** [Байзакъ] (SOK 300); Kzk. 19th c. **Bay-zaq** [Баимбетъ Байзаковъ] (Grod., Pril. 59); Kzk. 19th c. **Bay-zaq** [Байзакъ] (AOP 118); Kzk. 19th c. **Bay-zaq** (Ljutš III); Kzk. 19th c. **Bay-zaq** [Байзакъ] (AOAtb. 34); Uzb. (Sart) **Bay-zaq** [Байзакъ Бахшыбаевъ] (Sr. Az. 1896, Avg. I, 14). ✧ 'Rich(ness)-long (=Be rich in your life!?)'. ⇨ **BAY** + **UZAQ.** See also **JAN-UZAQ, ÖMÜR-UZAQ.**

BAY-ZAQ see **BAY-UZAQ**

BAY-ZAQ see **BAY-UZAQ**

BAY-ZİGİT see **BAY**

BAY-ZİLDÄ Kzk. 19th c. **Bay-zildä?** [Байзильда]

(SOK 178). ⇨ **BAY.**

BAYAJЇQ Kzk. 19th c. **Bayajïq** [Баяджик] (SOK 208). ✧ 'Quiet, calm'? cf. Kzk. *bayau* 'ruhig, still, bescheiden' (Radl. IV, 1467) + dim. suff. *-jïq.*

BAYAГUT Uyg. **Bayaγut** (Mahrnāmag 31). ✧ 'Rich, wealthy, richman' cf. Uyg. *bajaγut* 'богатый, состоятельный, богач' (DTS).

BAYAQ Kzk. 19th c. **Bayaq** [Баякъ] (AOA 98); Kzk. 18th c. **Bayaq-batïr** [Баякъ-Батыръ] (Nepljuev 746); Kzk. 19th c. **Bayaq-pay** [Баякпай] (SODž. 16). ✧ 'Little Bay'. ⇨ **BAY** + dim. suff. *-aq.*

BAYAN Kzk. 19th c. **Bayam-bay** (<Bayan-bay?) [Баамбай] (AOO 58); Bulg. 7th c. **Bayan** [Βαίανός], a prince of the Bulghars at the Maiotis, ca. 650 (Byz. Turc. 83-84); Bulg. 8th c. **Bayan** [Βαίανός], a cooper („Binder") of the Bulghar prince Toktos (died in 772) (Byz. Turc. 83-84); Bulg. 9th c.-10th c. **Bayan** [Βαίανός] (Byz. Turc. 83-84); Tat.? 1532 **Bayan** [Боянъ], from the Horde (PSRL VIII, 283); Tat.(Sib.) 1637 **Bayan** [Баянко Буганаков] (Miller, Ist. Sib. II, 445-48); Kzk. 19th c. **Bayan** [Баянъ], fem. (Grod. I, 98); Kzk. **Bayan** / **Bayan-sulū** / **Bayan-suluw** [Bajan / Bajan Sulu / Баjан / Баjан Сулу], heroine of the Kazak poem „Bayan-sulu and Qozï-körpös" (Proben III, 228 /269/, etc.); Uyg. 8th c. **Bayan-čor**, a Kaghan (747-759) (Zieme, Mat. II, 84); Tuv. 19th c. **Payan-ōl** [Пajан-ол] (Proben IX, 40); Tat.(Bar.) **Payan-sïlū** [Пajан Сылу], Qara-qan's daughter (Proben IV, 12); Hak. 19th-20th c. **Payaň** [Паянъ] (HRS 350); Hak.(Blt.) 19th-20th c. **Payaň** [Пajаӊ] (Proben IX, 613); Hak.(Sag.) 19th-20th c. **Payaň** [Пajаӊ] (Proben IX, 455-57); Hak.(Kacha) 19th-20th c. **Payaň** [Пajаӊ] (Proben IX, 558); Hak. 19th-20th c. **Payiň** [Паинъ] (HRS 350); Chuv. 18th-19th c. **Puyan** [Пуянъ] (Magn. 69); *TN:* **Bayan** [Баянъ], a place in the region of Yelisavetopol, in the Caucasus (Karta JAR IX); Kzk.? **Bayan-bay**, a region (Ala-tau) (PM Ergh. 43); Chuv. 18th c. **Buyan(ova)** / **Buyan-kasï** [Буянова, Буян-касы], a village in the district of Civilsk (Tsivilsk) (Korsakov 320). ✧ I. 'Rich (man)' (Németh, HMK 104, Rásonyi, Imp. 234-235), cf. Hak. PNs *Payan, Payin* 'id.' (Butanaev), Mo. (<Trk.) *bayan* 'reich' (TMEN II, No. 714). It is also used as a title and secondary component of male names. II. 'Lady, mistress, madam', title and component of fem. PN, cf. Turk. *bayan* 'id.' (TED); III. 'Staying, life' cf. Kzk. *bayan* 'das Bleiben, das Leben' (Radl. I, 1467). See also **AQ-BAYAN, QUT-BAYAN.**

BAYAN-JÜREK Kzk. **Bayan-žürek** [Баянжурек], a summer pasture in the foot-hills of Jungharia (Kojčubaev 61). ✧ 'Rich(man/lady)-heart'; 'Lady-heart'? cf. Kzk. *žürek* 'сердце' (KzRS). ⇨ **BAYAN.**

BAYAN-SULDUZ Khorezm./Chag. 1372 **Bayan-sulduz** [Шейх-Мухаммед Баян сулдуз], an emir

(MIT I, 516, 517). ⇨ **BAYAN.**

BAYANAY I.   Kzk. 19th c. **Bayanay** [Баянай], a field (AOO 42).

BAYANAY II.   Yak. **Bayanay-bōtur** [Бајанаі ботур] (Pek.); Yak. **Bayanay-toyon** [Бајанаі тојон] (Pek.). ✧ 'Protector (spirit) of hunters and fishermen (in general)' (JRS).

BAYANĀX   Yak. **Bayanāχ** [Бајанах] (Pek.).

BAYANDA   Tat. 1557 **Bayanda** [Боянда], a Tatar envoy (PSRL XIII, 27b). ✧ 'Stay! Live!' cf. Kzk. *bayanda-* 'bleiben, leben' (Radl. IV, 1467).

BAYANDUR   Oghuz/Trkm. 13th c. **Bayandur** [Баяндур], Kök-χan's son (RaD I/1, 76). ✧ 'Very rich' cf. Rásonyi, Imp. 235, Rásonyi, Val.-Turc. 23-24. ⇨ **BAYAN** + suff. *-dur.*

BAYANQAN   Kzk. **Bayanqan** [Baïane-Khan], heroine of the Kazak poem „Bayan-sulu and Qozï-körpöš" (Levchine 109). ⇨ **BAYAN** + suff. *-qan(1).*

BAYAR   Trkm. 20th c. **Bayar** [Bayar] (Zaj. 1971, 325); Trkm. 20th c. **Bayar** [Баяр] (TrkmRS 82); Selj.? **Bayār?** [بیار] (Zehireddin/Dorn 194). ✧ 'Lord, host' (Zaj. 1971), cf. Az., Bashk., Tat., Trkm., Uzb. *bayar* 'der Frohndienst; der Arbeitgeber, Wirth; der Adlige, der russische Gutsbesitzer; der Würdenträger, eine hohe Persönlichkeit' (Radl. IV, 1467), Trkm. *bayar* 'барин; хозяин, господин; чиновник' (TrkmRS).

BAYARDA   Yak. **Bayarda** [Бајарда] (Pek.).

BAYARLÏ   Oghuz? **Bayarlï** [Баярлы], Ay-χan's son (RaD I/1, 176).

BAYAS   Kzk. 1829 **Bayas** [Баяс] (MIK IV, 326).

BAYASÏL   Kzk. 19th c. **Bayasïl** [Баясылъ] (SOK 188); Kzk. 19th c. **Bayasïl** [Баясилъ] (SOK 294).

BAYAŠAL?   Kzk. 19th c. **Bayašal?** [Баяшалъ] (Potanin, Pred. 182).

BAYAT   Oghuz/Trkm. 13th c. **Bayat** [بیات / Баят / Байат], Kün-χan's son (MK/Brock.(Atalay), RaD I/1, 76, Abulg./Kon. 515, 545, 590); Karakh. **Bayat** [Bayat] (MK/Atalay 833); Turk. 1540 **Bayat-kethudā** [بیات], from the defter of Diyarbekir of 1540, he belonged to Bozulus (Demirtaş 50). ✧ I. Ethnonym, the ninth tribe of the Oghuz-Turkmen (DTS); II. 'Eternal (God's epithet)' (Erol II), cf. Karakh., Uyg. *bayat* 'бог' (DTS).

BAYAT-QARA   Uzb. **Bayat-qara**, chief of the Uzbek Bayat tribe (Németh, HMK 84). ⇨ **BAYAT + QARA.**

BAYAZİT   Maml. 1456 **Bayazit** [بایزید التمربغاوی] (Ibn Taghrīb. VIII, 308); Turk. 1455? **Bayazit** [بایزید بن محمد بن عثمان], Mohamed's (1451-1481) son, Osman's grandson? (Ibn Taghrīb. VIII, 263); Bashk. 1757 **Bayazit** [Баязит Киликеев] (MIB IV/2, 19); Bashk. 1779 **Bayazit** [Иксан Баязитов] (MIB V, 82, 165); *TN:* Bashk.? **Bayazitova** [Баязетова], a village (?) south-west of Chelyabinsk (Karta JAR III). ✧ 'White, clean' (Kusimova, Sattarov) (<Ar. / P.?).

BAYBAL   Yak. **Baybal** [Баібал] (Pek.). ✧ Pavel (R.).

BAYBAN   Alt. 19th-20th c. **Bayban** [Байбан] (OjrRS 207). ✧ 'Husband' (OjrRS 207).

BAYBET   Tat. 1829 **Baybet** [Байбетъ Бектургановъ] (PSZRI XXXVI, 29). ⇨ **BAY** + suffixoid *-bet.* See also **BAYMAT.**

BAYBURT   Turk. 16th c. **Bayburt** [با یبرد] (Ongan, Ank. II). ✧ A town near Gümüşhane, Turkey.

BAYČA   Pecheneg 9th c. **Bayča** [Βάϊτζας], chiftain of the first Pecheneg tribe (Byz. Turc. 84); Turk. 15th c. **Bayča** [Πέϊτζάς], a Turkish governor (Byz. Turc. 250); Kuman 1451, 1436 **Bayča** / **Boyča** [Boychazallasa, Baychascalasa], in the name of a village in Hungary (Gyárfás III, 596, 626); Kzk. 19th c. **BayJa** [Микинъ Байджа] (Grod., Pril. 60); Kzk. 19th c. **Bayša** [Байша] (Pam. kn. Turg. 77). ✧ I. 'Little master' (Rásonyi: NyK XLVI, 131, AOH 20: 137, KÖA 89); II. 'Rich' cf. Osm. *bayça* 'zengin' (DS). ⇨ **BAY** + dim. suff. *-ča /-ja.*

BAYČÏQUR   Kzk. 19th c. **Bayčïqur** [Байчикуръ] (SODž. 72).

BAYČÏL   Alt. 19th-20th c. **Bayčïl** [Байчыл], fem. (OjrRS 211).

BAYČÏZAY   Kzk. 19th c. **Bayčïzay** [Байчызай] (SODž. 132).

BAYJA see **BAYČA**

BAYJAQ   Kzk. 19th c. **BayJaq** (<BayJïq?) [Байджаковъ] (SKSO VIII, 224). ✧ 'Little Lord/Master'. ⇨ **BAY** + dim. suff. *-čaq.*

BAYDA   Bashk. 1789 **Bayda** [Байда Абзянов] (MIB V, 254); Kzk. 19th c. **Bayda** [Байда] (SOV 64); Bashk. 1764 **Bayda-γul** [Байдагул Илишев] (MIB IV/1, 285); Bashk. 1695 **Bayda-γul(?ač)** [Байдагулачко] (MIB I, 85). ✧ 'Profit, use, advantage' cf. Kzk. *bayda* 'der Vortheil' (Radl. IV, 1429), also Kzk. PN *Baydabek* (Žanuzakov-Esbaeva) (<Ar.).

BAYDA-BAQ   Kzk. 19th c. **Bayda-baq** [Байдабакъ] (SOV 88). ⇨ **BAYDA + BAQ.**

BAYDA-KEL   Kzk. 1829 **Bayda-kel** [Байдакел] (MIK IV, 324). ⇨ **BAYDA + KEL.**

BAYDAČ   Tat.(Sib.) 1680 **Baydač** [Байдачко] (DAI VIII, 44).

BAYDAY   Kzk. 19th c. **Bayday** [Байдай] (SOK 36).

BAYDAQ see **BAYTAQ**

BAYDAQAY   Kzk. **Baydaqay** [Янгузя Байдакаев] (MIB IV/1, 120). ✧ 'Benefit, advantage'? ⇨ **BAYDA** + dim. suff. *-qay.*

BAYDAL?   Bashk. 1695 **Baydal(ač?)** [Байдалачко] (MIB I, 85).

BAYDALÏ   Kzk. 1820 **Baydalï-biy** [Байдали-бій], one of the chiefs of the Arγïn tribe (Sib. Vest. IX, 102). ✧ 'Helpful, useful, beneficial' cf. Kzk. *baydalï* 'vortheilhaft, nützig' (Radl. IV, 1430).

BAYDAN see **BAYTAN**

BAYDAR   1240 **Baydar** [Байдаръ] (PSRL X, 116); Kzk. 19th c. **Baydar** [Байдаръ] (SODž. 62); *EN:* Nog. 20th c. **Baydar** [Байдар], an Aq-Noɣay clan in the autonomous region of Cherkessk and in the district of Mineralovodsk (Bask., Nog. 135). ⇨ **BAY** + suff. *-dar*.

BAYDARA   Maml. 13th c. **Baydara** [بدرالدين بيدرا المنصورى], governor of Egypt, died in 1293 (Iyās I, 117, Weil, Chalif. I, 176, 192, Makrīzī III, 116, 142); Maml. 1293 **Baydara** / **Bay-dara?** [بيدرا], sultan „Malec el Caher", he was killed (Abulfidā V, 114-15); Maml. 1301 **Baydara** / **Bay-dara?** [بدرالدين بيدرا], an emir, Qalā'ūn's (1279-1290) „ustādār" (Dawād. 64, 65, Björkm. 168).

BAYDAŠ   Chuv. 18th-19th c. **Baydaš** [Байдашъ] (Magn. 32); Bashk. 1675 **Baydaš** [Байдаш Атикеев] (MIB I, 201); Bashk. 1783 **Baydaš** [Ерлыкаш Байдашев] (MIB V, 148); Bashk. 1788, 1789 **Baydaš** / **Baydäš?** [Исергап Байдашев /Байдяшев/] (MIB V, 234, 254). ✧ 'Fellow-Richman' cf. Kzk. PNs *Baytas* *[Bay-tas?]* and *Bektas* *[Bek-tas?]* (Žanuzakov-Esbaeva). ⇨ **BAY** + **TAŠ?** + suff. *-daš?*

BAYDÏ   Kzk. 19th c. **Baydï-bek** [Байдыбекъ] (SOV 30, 152). ✧ 'He grew rich'? cf. Tat. *bay- /bayu/* 'богатеть' (TatRS), Kzk. *bay-(ıt-)* '(birini) zenginleştirme' (KzTS). See also **BAYDÏQ**.

BAYDÏQ   Tat. **Baydïq** [با يدك], in a folktale (Nasyrov-Poljakov 37-40); Kzk. 19th c. **Baydïq** [Байдекъ] (SOK 44). ✧ 'We grew rich' (Sattarov) cf. Tat. *bay- /bayu/* 'богатеть' (TatRS), Kzk. *bay-(ıt-)* '(birini) zenginleştirme' (KzTS).

BAYDÏL   Kzk. 19th c. **Baydïl** [Байдылъ] (SOK 276); Tat. 17th c. **Baydul** [Байдулка Искеевъ], in the region of Kazan (IOAIÊK XXIX, 345).

BAYDÏSQA   Alt. 19th-20th c. **Baydïsqa** [Байдыска] (OjrRS 207).

BAYDOQ   Alt. 19th-20th c. **Baydoq** [Байдок] (OjrRS 207). ⇨ **BAYDÏQ?**

BAYDON   1665 **Baydon** [Байдонъ (Енисейский)] (DAI V, 52).

BAYDU   Alt. 19th-20th c. **Baydu** [Байду] (OjrRS 207); Oghuz/Trkm. 13th c. **Baydu-χan** [Baïdu-Khan], Tatar-Khan's descendant in a legend of origin (Abulg./Desm. 11). ✧ Baidu (Mo.).

BAYDUL see **BAYDÏL**

BAYDUSAN   Kzk. 19th c. **Baydusan** [Байдусанъ] (SOK 180).

BAYDUŠ   Chuv. 18th c. **Bayduš(eva)** [Байдушева], a Chuvash village in the district of Yadrinsk (Korsakov 309).

BAYÄK   Bashk. 1708 **Bayäk** / **Bay-yäk?** [Байяк (Баймек)] (MIB I, 216).

BAYGÍL   Kzk. 1846 **Baygil-bi** [Байгиль би] (Konšin, Mat. V, 101). ✧ 'Become/grow rich! Enrich (yourself)!' cf. Kzk. *bay-* 'богатеть, разбогатеть'

(KzRS) + suff. *-gil*.

BAYƔA   1629 **Bayɣa** [Байга], a Kamass prince (Miller, Ist. Sib. II, 55). ⇨ **BAYQA?**

BAYƔABAT   Kzk. 19th c. **Bayɣabat** [Байгабатъ] (SOV 152); Kzk. 19th c. **Bayɣabat** [Байгабатъ] (SODž. 12).

BAYƔAN   Kzk. 19th c. **Bayɣan** [Байганъ] (SODž. 16, 82); Kzk. 19th c. **Bayqan / Boyqan?** [Бойканъ] (SOV 60).

BAYƔANAQ   Kzk. 19th c. **Bayɣanaq** [Байганакъ] (SOK 46).

BAYƔANLÏ   Kzk. 19th c. **Bayɣanlï** [Байганлы] (SODž. 108).

BAYƔAPAN   Kzk. 19th c. **Bayɣapan** [Байгапанъ] (SOK 22).

BAYƔÏY   Bashk. 1735 **Bayɣïy** [Байгый Гауров], a Bashkir prince? (Vel.-Zern., Bašk. 12).

BAYƔONŠÏ   Kzk. 19th c. **Bayɣonšï? / Bay-ɣonšïn** [Байгоншенъ] (AOO 54).

BAYƔU   Selj. 1029 **Bayɣu / Biɣu?** [بيغو بن ميكا ييل فخر الملك السلجوقى] (Ibn al-Athīr/Tornb. IX, 267, 322-326, X, 22, 191); Kzk. 19th c. **Bayɣu-bay** [Байгубай] (SOK 108).

BAYƔU-EYDER   Kzk. 19th c. **Bayɣu-eyder-χan** [Байгуэйдеръ-хан] (Potanin II, 177). ⇨ **BAYƔU** + **AYDAR?**

BAYƔU-ƔAL   Tat.(Sib.) 1620 **Bayɣu-ɣal** [Байгул Байгугалов], a Tatar from the Tura region (Miller, Ist. Sib. II, 251, 254). ⇨ **BAYƔU** + **QAL I.**

BAYƔUNJĀR   Maml. 1333 **BayɣunJār?** [بيغنجار], an emir (Dawād. 368).

BAYƔUNDÏ   Kzk. **Bayɣundï / Bayɣundïy?** [Байтянъ Байгундыевъ] (TOUAK XXIV, 78).

BAYƔUR   Maml. 1293 **Bayɣur** [بيغور] (Baybars/Tizeng. I, 86, 109, Nuwairī 137, 158). ⇨ ? + suff. *-ɣur*.

BAYƔUS see **BAYQUŠ**

BAYÏQ   Oghuz? 12th-13th c. **Bayïq-beg** [Bayık Beğ], a man in Ibn al-Athīr's chronicle (Ibn al-Athīr/Tornb.) (Erol II, 63); Bashk. 1779 **Bayq / Bayïq?** [Курамша Байков] (MIB V, 83). ✧ 'Precise, accurate' (Sattarov), 'True word' (Erol II), cf. Karakh. *bayïq* 'правдивый, истинный' (DTS), Tat. *bayïq* 'точный, конкретный, определенный' (TatRS).

BAYÏQQA   Yak. **Bayïqqa** [Бајыкка] (Pek.). ⇨ **BĀYKA.**

BAYÏL   Kzk. 19th c. **Bayïl** [Баель] (SODž. 10).

BAYÏM   Crm. 1538 **Bayïm / Bayim?** [Баимъ], envoy from the Crimea (PSRL XIII, 122); Bashk. 1777 **Bayïm / Bayim?** [Баимъ Ялтиковъ] (Vel.-Zern., Bašk. 4); Bashk. 1777 **Bayïm? Bayim?** [Абзанъ Баймовъ] (Vel.-Zern., Bašk. 3); Bashk. 1739 **Bayïm-tarχan / Bayim—tarχan?** [Баимъ-Тарханъ Кидряевъ] (PSZRI X, 982). ✧ 'My master, my owner'

(Kusimova). ⇨ **BAY** + poss. *-ïm*.

BAYÏMBET Kkalp. 20th c. **Bayïmbet** [Байымбет] (Bask., Kkalp. 4); Kzk. **Bayïmbet / Bayimbet?** [Баимбетъ Токбергенсвъ] (Protok. Turk. IV, 76); Kzk. 19th c. **Bayïmbet / Bayimbet?** [Баембетъ Булдурбаевъ] (Grod., Pril. 37). ✧ 'Bay-Muχammad' (Bask., Fam. 83). ⇨ **BAY** + suffixoid *-ïmbet*. See also **BÄYÏMBET**.

BAYÏNDÏR see **BAYUNDUR**

BAYÏR Kzk. 19th c. **Bayïr-bek** [Баирбекъ Джалдибаевъ] (Grod., Pril. 32); Kzk. 19th c. **Bayïr-bek** [Баир бекъ] (Grod., Pril. 146); Uzb. **Bāyir-bek** (É. Dobos, A Tale from Qarabau: AOH XXVII, 170). ✧ 'Hill, desert; rude (man)' Cf. Chag., Trkm. *ba'ir* 'die Wüste, der Bergabhang, der Hügel' (Radl., IV, 1424), Crm., Trkm., Turk. *bayïr* 'der Hügel, die Anhöhe', *bayïr turabï* 'ein grober, ungebildeter Mensch' (Radl. IV, 1469), also Kzk. PN *Bayïr* (Žanuzakov-Esbaeva). See also **QARA-BAYÏR**.

BAYÏRČÏ Alt. 19th-20th c. **Bayïrčï** [Байырчы], fem. (OjrRS 211).

BAYÏRQU Türk **Bayïrqu** [bajïrqu] (DTS). ✧ A tribe living north of the Türks (DTS), cf. also Pelliot, Notes 187.

BAYÏS see **BAYÏŠ**

BAYÏŠ Kzk. 19th c. **Bais / Bayis (<Bayïs)** [Баисъ] (Potanin II, 4); Nog. 20th c. **Bayïs** [Фатима Азамат Кирей къызы Байыс / Фатима Азаматкиреевна Баисова], one of Baskakov's informants from the aul of Üykön-χalq (Ikon-halk), Cherkess Autonomous Region (Oblast') (Bask., Nog. 143); Nog. 20th c. **Bayïs / Bayis?** [Хисаметдин Темирджан улы Баисов], one of Baskakov's informants from the aul of Üykön-χalq (Ikon-halk), Cherkess Autonomous Region (Oblast') (Bask., Nog. 143); Nog. 20th c. **Bayïs-bay** [Байысбай] (Bask., Kkalp. 399, KkRS 772); Kirg. **Bayïš** [Байыш] (Jud. 73, 139, 596); Kzk. 19th c. **Bayïš-bay** [Хаккъ Назаръ Баижбаевъ] (Grod., Pril. 130); Kzk. 19th c. **Bays-pay (<Bayïs-pay)** [Байспай] (SODž. 70, 92); Kzk. 19th c. **Bays-pay (<Bayïs-pay)** [Байспай] (SOV 82); *EN:* Nog. 20th c. **Bayïs-uruwï** [Байыс урувы], an Aq-Noγay clan in the autonomous region of Cherkessk and in the district of Mineralovodsk (Bask., Nog. 135, 142). ⇨ **BAY**.

BAYÏT Kzk. **Bayt-biy (<Bayït-biy)** [Байтбий] (Smirnov, Sultany 18).

BAYÏTĀN Yak. **Bayïtān** [Бајытан] (Pek.).

BAYKE Kzk. 19th c. **Bayke (<Bay-eke)** [Байке] (SOK 282). ✧ 'Little Bay, Rich man'. + suff. *-ke*.

BAYKEY see **BAYQAY**

BAYQA Chuv. 17th c. **Bayka** [Уренейко Байкинъ] (IOΛIÊK XXIX, 348); Khorezm.? **Bayqa** [Байка], fem. (RaD II, 202). ⇨ **BAY?** + suff. *-qa*.

BAYQAY Bashk. 1734 **Baykey** [Емметъ Байкеевъ], a

tarχan (Vel.-Zern., Bašk. 11); Bashk. 1763 **Bayqay** [Байкай Зиянгулов] (MIB IV/1, 271); Bashk. 1777 **Bayqay** [Байкай Кулумбетевъ] (MIB V, 57). ✧ 'Little Richman'? ⇨ **BAY?** + suff. *-qay*.

BAYQAL Bashk. 1757 **Bayqal** [Байкал Урсагулов] (MIB IV/1, 134); Alt. 19th-20th c. **Bayqal** [Байкал] (OjrRS 207); Kzk. 19th c. **Boyqal? / Bayqal** [Бойкалъ] (SOV 58). ✧ from the placename Lake Baykal?

BAYQAN see **BAYΓAN**

BAYQAT Kzk. 19th c. **Bayqat** [Байкатъ] (SOK 22).

BAYQUŠ Tat. 17th c. **Bayγus** [Байгуска Елчюбаевъ], in the region of Kazan (IOAIÊK XXIX, 344); Bashk. 1735 **Bayγus** [Байгузъ], a tarχan (Vel.-Zern., Bašk. 23); Kzk. 19th c. **Bayγus** [Багузъ] (SOK 204); Bashk. 1788 **Bayquš** [Ильяс Байкушев] (MIB V, 235). ✧ 'Owl; (fig.) poor; down-and-out; miserable' cf. Bashk. *bayγoš* 'неясыть (вид совы); бедняга, бедняжка; простак' (BRS/Uraksin), Kzk. *bayγüs* 'бедняга; беспомощный' (KzRS).

BAYLAQ see **BAYLÏQ**

BAYLÄW-KÜYLÄW Kzk. 19th c. **Bayläw-küyläw** [Байляу-куйляу], one of the legendary forefathers of the Kirey tribe of the Middle Horde (Orta Žüz) (Potanin II, 3, Aristov 354).

BAYLÄÜK Kzk. 19th c. **Bayläwük** [Байляукъ] (SODž. 8).

BAYLEW Kzk. 19th c. **Baylew / Bayleü?** [Байлеу] (AOK 122). See also **BAYLEÜ-KÜYLEÜ**.

BAYLÏ Kzk. **Baylï** [Баилы] (Proben III, 68); Uzb. 1813 **Baylï-behadïr / Bayli-behadïr?** [Байли-бехадыр] (MIT II, 385); Maml. 1269, 1277 **Baylï-bek? / Bel-bek?** [بدرالـديـن بيلبك], a treasurer (Iyās I, 99, 112); Kkalp. 1817 **Baylï-yüzbašï** [Байли-юзбаши], from the Čawdar tribe (MIT II, 398, 417, 420, 450, MIKk. 132); Kkalp. 19th c. **Baylï-yüzbašï** [Байлы юзбаши] (MIKk. 132); *TN:* Uzb.? **Baylï-ata** [بـايلى اتـا / Байлы-Ата], a *qišlaq* [winter quarters for nomads] in the region of Katta-Kurgan (ZIRGOStat. IV). ✧ 'Having a richman or master' (Erol II), cf. Kzk. PN *Baylï* (Žanuzakov-Esbaeva). ⇨ **BAY** + suff. *-lï*.

BAYLÏQ Yürük 1543 **Baylïq** (Gökb., Rum. 221); Kzk. 19th c. **Baylïq-bay** [Байлыкбай] (AOA 130); Maml. 1293 **Baylïq-χatun / Baylaq-χatun?** [بيلق حـاتـون / Байлакхатунъ] (Baybars/Tizeng. I, 86, 108, Nuwairī 127, 158). ✧ 'Richness, wealth, well-being' cf. Kkalp. *baylïq* 'id.' (KkRS), Kzk. *baylïq* 'id.' (KzRS), Kuman, Crm., Kzk., Tat., Trkm., Turk. *baylïq* 'Reichtum, die Gebärmutter' (Radl. IV, 1428). ⇨ **BAY** + suff. *-lïq*. See also **LAČÏN-BAYLUQ**.

BAYMAQ Tat. **Baymaq** [Баймакъ] (PSRL XIII, 80); Tat. 1764 **Baymaq** [Улей Баймаков] (MIB IV/1, 279); Kzk. 19th c. **Baymaq** [Дусинъ Баймаковъ] (Grod., Pril. 131); Kzk. 19th c. **Baymaq** [Тангри

Бергянъ Баймаковъ] (Grod., Pril. 81); Bashk. 1708 **Baymek** [Байяк (Баймек)] (MIB I, 216). ✧ I. 'Enrichment; enriching (child)' (Sattarov); II. 'Having skewed (defective) leg' cf. Uzb. *baymaq* 'schiefbeinig' (Radl. IV, 1431); III. 'Lonesome, orphan' (Sattarov).

BAYMAN   Kzk. 19th c. **Bayman** [Байманъ] (Grod., Pril. 25, 27, 57, 91, 158); Kzk. 19th c. **Bayman** [Байманъ] (SKSO III, 15); Kzk. 19th c. **Bayman** [Байманъ] (AOK 130); Kzk. 19th c. **Bayman** [Байманъ] (AOK 54); Kzk. 19th c. **Bayman** [Байманъ] (AOO 6); Uzb. 19th c. **Bayman** [Халбай Баймановъ] (SKSO III, 182); Uzb. 19th c. **Bayman** [Хадыръ Баймановъ] (SKSO III, 168); Kzk. 19th c. **Baymen** [Байменъ] (SODž. 76); Kzk. 19th c. **Baymen** [Байменъ] (SOK 72); Kzk. 19th c. **Baymen** [Байменъ] (SOV 26); Kzk. 1870 **Baymen** [Байменъ Даребаевъ] (Grod., Pril. 128); Kzk. 1870 **Baymen** [Байменъ Даребаевъ] (Grod., Pril. 63). ✧ 'Very rich'? ⇨ BAY + MAN? or suff. *-man / -men*. See also **BAYMEN**.

BAYMANAY   Kzk. 19th c. **Baymanay** [Байманай] (SOV 136). ⇨ **BAYMAN?** + suff. *-ay*.

BAYMANČA   Uzb. 19th c. **Baymanča** [Байманча] (SKSO III, 184); Kzk. 19th c. **Baymenče** [Байменче Акчинъ] (AUK 494). ⇨ **BAYMAN?** + suff. *-ča / -če*.

BAYMAŠ   Tat.(Mish.) 1775 **Baymaš** [Даут Баймашов] (MIB IV/2, 421); Bashk.? 1724 **Baymaš** [Баймаш] (MIB III, 227); Uzb. 20th c. **Baymaš** [Baïmach], a basmačï from Bukhara (Castagné).

BAYMAT   Kzk. **Baymat** [Баиматъ Джонбаевъ] (Sb. Syr-D. IX, 46); Kzk. 19th c. **Baymat** [Байматовъ] (SKSO VIII, 233); Kirg. **Baymat** [Баймат] (Jud. 923); Kirg. **Baymat** [Тас Баймат], one of Manas' comrades-in-arms [čoro] in the Manas epic (Proben V, 70, 71, Jud. 923); Chuv. 18th c. **Baymet** [Байметева], a village in the district of Tetyushinsk (Korsakov 323); Bashk. 1735 **Baymet** [Теменей Байметевъ], a tarχan (Vel.-Zern., Bašk. 21). ⇨ BAY + suffixoid *-mat*. See also **TAS-BAYMAT**.

BAYMEK see **BAYMAQ**

BAYMEN see **BAYMAN**

BAYMENČE see **BAYMANČA**

BAYMET see **BAYMAT**

BAYNA   Türk 7th c. - 9th c. **Bayna-sañun** [bajna saŋun] (DTS).

BAYNAQ   Khorezm. 14th c. **Baynaq** [Байнак Суфи] (MIT I, 519); Kzk. 18th c. - 19th c. **Baynaq** [Байнак] (Tynyšp. 73). ✧ 'Muck, shit, dung' Karakh. *bajnaq / bainaq* 'id.' (DTS, MK/Brock.). See also **ARÏQ II., BOQ, QOMUQ.**

BAYNAQAR   Kzk. 19th c. **Baynaqar** [Байнакаръ] (SODž. 56).

BAYNAN   Nog. 20th c. **Baynan** [Байнан Авез увлы], one of Baskakov's informants from the settlement

Terekli-mekter (Bask., Nog. 144).

BAYNAS   Kzk. 19th c. **Baynas-pay** [Байнаспай] (SODž. 104).

BAYNÄ   Tat.(Sib.) 1638 **Baynä** [Баиня], fem. (Miller, Ist. Sib. II, 449).

BAYPAQ   Kzk. 19th c. **Baypaq** [Байпакъ] (SODž. 134); Kzk. 19th c. **Baypaq** [Байпакъ] (AOAtb. 22). ✧ 'Felt stocking' cf. Kzk. *baypaq* 'войлочные чулки' (KzRS).

BAYPAN   Kzk. 19th c. **Baypan** [Тайлакъ Байпановъ] (Grod., Pril. 110). ✧ 'Good, quiet, polite' cf. Kzk. *baypañ* in the expressions *baypañ žorγa, baypañ minez* (KzRS).

BAYRA   Kzk. 19th c. **Bayra-bay** [Байрабай Байдервишевъ] (SKSO III, 190); *EN:* Nog. 20th c. **Bayra-uruw** [Байра урув], a Qara Noγay clan (Bask., Nog. 137).

BAYRAČ   Trkm. 1651 **Bayrač** [بايراج], a chief of a of the Türkmen tribe (Abulg./Desm. 347). ✧ Ethnonym of a Turkmen clan of the Sarïq tribe (Erol II).

BAYRAQLÏ-TAZ?   **Bayraqlï-taz?** [بيرعلى تاز] (Arabš. II, 642). ✧ 'With a flag - bald' cf. Karakh. *bajraq* 'знамя, флаг' (DTS). ⇨ ? + **TAZ.**

BAYRAM   Selj.? 12th c. **Bayram** [Παιράμης], a Byzantine commander of Turkic origin (Byz. Turc. II, 243); Maml. 1398/99 **Bayram** [بيرم العلا یى] (Ibn Taghrïb. VI, 16); Maml.? 1402 **Bayram** [بيرم بنت برقوق], Barqūq's daughter (Ibn Taghrïb. VI, 106, 111); Maml.? 1412 **Bayram** [بيرم بنت تغرى بردى], fem. (Ibn Taghrïb. VI, 434); Chag. 1558 **Bayram** [Байрам Султан] (Ivanov 202); Turk. **Bayram** [شيخ حاجى بيرم] (Àšikp. 200); Turk. 14th c. **Bayram** [Παιράμης], a Turkish chieftain (Byz. Turc. II, 243); Turk. 1552, 1570 **Bayram** (Dávid); Turk. 1583 **Bayram**, the source mentions 10 persons having this name (Ongan, Ank. I, 153); Turk. 1662 **Bayram**, Yağmur's son from Isparta (Ün 1938, 644,646); Yürük 1543 **Bayram** (Gökb., Rum. 192); Yürük 1543 **Bayram** (Gökb., Rum. 202, 204); Yürük 1543 **Bayram**, from the Yürüks of Kocacık (Gökb., Rum. 101); Trkm. **Bayram** [Байрам], fem. (Sopieva 180); Trkm. 20th c. **Bayram** [Bayram], fem. (Zaj. 1971, 341); Trkm. 20th c. **Bayram** [Байрам], fem. (TrkmRS 67); Tat.(Lit.) 1592 **Bayram** [Ахметъ Байрамъ Сувовичъ] (Lit. Tat. 132); Tat. 1543 **Bayram** (Gökb., Rum. 238); Bashk. 1778 **Bayram** [Токбай Байрямовъ] (MIB V, 69); Bashk. 1779 **Bayram** [Сейфуддин Байрамгуловъ] (MIB V, 86); Nog. 20th c. **Bayram** [Аджы Байрам увлы / Аджи Байрамов], father of one of Baskakov's informants from the aul of Ïrγaqlï (Bask., Nog. 143); Alt. 19th-20th c. **Bayram** [Байрам] (OjrRS 207); Alt. 19th-20th c. **Bayram** [Байрам], fem. (OjrRS 211); Turk. 1482

Bayram / Xaǰï Bayram (Gökb., Ed. 355); Crm. 17th c. **Bayram-aγa** [Байрамъ-ага] (Smirnov, Krym. 557); Turk. 1455 **Bayram-begi** (Gökb., Ed. 25); Trkm. 1841/42 **Bayram-bey** [Байрам Яглы], from the Yomut tribe (MIT II, 484); Trkm. 1513 **Bayram-bek** [Байрам-бек], from the Qaraman clan (MIT II, 57); Bashk. 1740 **Bayram-γul** [Байрамгул Бардыков] (MIB I, 404); Bashk. 1756 **Bayram-γul** [Байрамгул Канчюрин] (MIB IV/1, 122); Selj.? **Bayram-χan**, from the Baharlï tribe, Aqbar's guardian (atalïq) (?); Maml. (Trkm.) 1420 **Bayram-χoǰa** [بيرم حجا التركمانى], of Türkmen origin (Ibn Taghrīb. VI, 473, VII, 24, 104); Maml. 1450 **Bayram-χoǰa** [بيرم حجا الاشرفى] (Ibn Taghrīb. VIII, 82); Tat. 1365 **Bayram-χoǰa** [Байрамъ-хозя], envoy of the Horde (PSRL XVI, 91); Khorezm. 14th c. **Bayram-χoǰa / Bayram-yasaul** [Байрам-ходжа / Байрам-ясаул], a yasaul (MIT I, 515); Maml. 1320 **Bayram-qoǰa** [بيرم قجا] (Tizeng. I, 257, 266 /after Al-Malik An-Nāsir/); Maml. (Trkm.) 1438/39 **Bayram-sūfi** [بيرم صوفى التركما نى] (Ibn Taghrīb. VII, 80, 92); Bashk. 1737 **Baryam-bike** (<Bayram-bike) [Барямбика], fem. (MIB III, 365); Kirg. **Mayram-qan** [Майрам-кан] (Abramzon-Sulejmanov); *TN:* Turk. 20th c. **Bayram-bey**, a village in the province of Giresun, Turkey (TMİB 390); Turk. 1499 **Bayram-dede**, a small mosque (Gökb., Ed. 463). ✧ 'Festival; feast; born on a festive day' cf. Crm., Tat., Turk., Trkm., Uzb. *bayram* 'der Festtag, der Feiertag' (Radl. IV, 1425), Kirg. *mayram* 'праздник (Jud.), also Sauvaget 44. See also **OΓUL-BAYRAM**.

BAYRAM-ALİ Nog. 20th c. **Bayram-ali** [Аджикелди Байрам Али увлы], father of one of Baskakov's informants from the aul of Yaman-γoy, District of Ači-qulaq (Bask., Nog. 143). ⇨ **BAYRAM + ALİ.**

BAYRAM-GELDİ Trkm. **Bayram-geldi** [Байрамгелди] (Sopieva 180). ⇨ **BAYRAM + KELDİ.**

BAYRAM-İLİ Bashk. 1714 **Bayram-ili?** [Байрамили Сарыев] (MIB I, 105). ⇨ **BAYRAM + İLİ?**

BAYRAMLÏ Yürük 1543 **Bayramlï** (Gökb., Rum. 186); Yürük 1543 **Bayramlï** (Gökb., Rum. 206); Yürük 1543 **Bayramlï** (Gökb., Rum. 205); Yürük 1543 **Bayramlï** (Gökb., Rum. 204); Yürük 1543 **Bayramlï** (Gökb., Rum. 200); Tat. 1543 **Bayramlï** (Gökb., Rum. 242); Tat. 1543 **Bayramlï** (Gökb., Rum. 231); Turk. 1583 **Bayramlu** [بيرا ملو] (Ongan, Ank. I). ✧ 'Born on a festive day'. ⇨ **BAYRAM** + suff. *-lï.*

BAYRAMLU see **BAYRAMLÏ**

BAYRAS see **BAYRAŠ**

BAYRAŠ Nog. **Bayras** [Байрасъ], according to the legend of origin of Noγays he is the forefather of Noγays (Smirnov, Krym. 77); Tat.(Lit.) 1591 **Bayraš**

[Дчовберда Байрашевичъ] (Lit. Tat. 82); Bashk. 1738 **Bayräs** [Байряс Табанаев] (MIB I, 145); Bashk. 1701 **Bayräš?** [Байряш Кутушев] (MIB IV/1, 34); Bashk. 1764 **Bayräš** [Байряш Айгильдин] (MIB IV/1, 287). ✧ I. 'Feast', shortened of *Bayram* or *Bayram-γali* (Sattarov), 'Born on a festive day' (Kusimova); II. Shortened of an ancient *Biraš* (Sattarov after K. Nasïyri). ⇨ **BAYRAM (+ EŠ?)** or suff. *-(a)s / -(a)š.*

BAYRÄS see **BAYRAS**

BAYRÏŠ Bashk. 1746 **Bayriš / Bayrïš?** [Байриш] (MIB III, 435). ✧ 'Feast-fellow' / '(Child) born on a festive day'? (contracted-shortened form). ⇨ **BAYRAŠ / BAYRAM + EŠ?**

BAYRÏ Trkm. 20th c. **Bayrï** [Bayrï], fem. (Zaj. 1971, 341); Trkm. 20th c. **Bayrï** [Байры], fem. (TrkmRS 67); Oghuz/Trkm. **Bayrï-χatun** [Байры-хатун], Buqra-χan's wife in the Oghuz-Name by Salar-baba (Muhamedova: OSA 170). ✧ 'The first wife' cf. Trkm. *bayrï* 'первая жена; ветеран' (TrkmRS).

BAYRÏM Alt. 19th-20th c. **Bayrïm** [Байрым], fem. (OjrRS 211).

BAYS see **BAYÏŠ**

BAYSA Tat. 1620 **Baysa** [Байса] (Kurdjumov 121).

BAYSAL Kzk. 19th c. **Bay-sal-bay** [Байсалбай] (Grod., Pril. 97); Kzk. 19th c. **Bay-sal-bay** [Байсалбай] (SODž. 116); *TN:* Kzk. **Bay-sal** [Байсал], a settlement (Kojčubaev 48). ✧ 'Calmness, quietness, patience' (Kojčubaev 48, Espaeva 1984, 231).

BAYSAU Kzk. 18th c. **Baysau-biy** [Байсаубий] (Nepljuev 805, 887).

BAYSE Kzk. 19th c. **Bayse-bay** [Байсебай] (SOV 48). ⇨ **BAYSA?**

BAYSEK Kzk. 19th c. **Baysek** [Байсекъ] (SOK 116).

BAYSEKE Bashk. 1729 **Bayseke** [Байсека Акышев] (MIB III, 271).

BAYSÏL Kzk. 19th c. **Baysïl-bek** [Баисильбекъ] (SOK 218). ⇨ **BAY?** + dim. suff. *-sil?*

BAYSÏMAQ Kzk. 19th c. **Baysïmaq** [Байсымакъ Бадраковъ] (Grod., Pril. 169). ✧ 'Snob; person who longs for richness' cf. Kzk. *baysimaq* 'der den Reichen zu spielen liebt, nach Reichtum strebend' (Radl. IV, 1430). ⇨ **BAY** + suff. *-simaq.*

BAYSÏN Kzk. 19th c. **Baysïn** [Байсын] (SOK 162); *TN:* Kzk. 19th c. **Baysïn-qurγan** [Байсынъ курганъ] (Karta JAR XI); Oghuz **Baysun?** [با يسون], the ancestor of the Ottoman dynasty (Āšikp. 50). ✧ 'Let him/her grow rich' cf. Karakh. *baju-* 'id.' (DTS), Kzk. *bayï-* 'богатеть, разбогатеть' (KzRS) + suff. *-sin.*

BAYSÏŠAQ Kzk. 19th c. **Baysïšaq** [Байсышакъ] (SOK 148).

BAYSLAN see **BAY-ARSLAN**

BAYSUN see **BAYSÏN**

BAYŠA see **BAYČA**

BAYŠAQAY   Bashk. 1756 **Baysaqay** [Байшакай Бикуɹ1аков] (MIB IV/1, 123). ⇨ **BAYČA** + suff. -*qay*.

BAYT see **BAYÏT**

BAYTAQ   Kzk. 19th c. **Baydaq** [Байдакъ] (SOK 44, 206, 256); Kzk. 1823 **Baytaq** [بايطاق / Байтак] (MIK IV, 465); Kzk. 19th c. **Baytaq** [Байтаков], a lieutenant (AUK 842). ✧ 'Large, much, sufficient, enough' cf. Kzk., Tat. *baytaq* 'weit; viel, zahlreich; genug' (Radl. IV, 1429).

BAYTAQAN   Yak. **Baytaqan** [Тімір Баітакан] (Pek.).

BAYTAN   Bashk. 1761 **Baydan** [Ибрай Байданов] (MIB IV/1, 227); Kzk. 19th c. **Baydan** [Байданъ] (AOK 50); Kzk. 19th c. **Baydan** [Байданъ] (AOA 14); Kzk. ⸱820 **Baytan** [Байтанъ], one of the chiefs of the Čaržitim (Orta žüz) tribe (Sib. Vest. IX, 106); Kzk. 19th c. **Baytan** [Абдауфъ Байтановъ] (SKSO IV, otd. II, 13); Kzk. 1827 **Baytän** [Байтянъ Байгундыевъ] (TOUAK XXIV, 78); Kzk. 1846 **Bayten** [Байтен Байгундин] (MKOP 151); Kzk. 19th c. **Bayten** [Байтен] (AOK 90); Bashk. 1738 **Boydan** / **Baydan?** [Бойдан (Байдан) Боиртов] (MIB III, 378).

BAYTÄN see **BAYTAN**

BAYTEN see **BAYTAN**

BAYTÏ   Kzk. 1828 **Baytï-bek** [Даутъ Байтыбековъ] (Dobrosm., Turg. 290); Kzk. 19th c. **Baytï-γul** [Байтыгулъ] (SODž. 64).

BAYTÏQAY   Kzk. 19th c. **Baytïqay** [Байтикай] (AOO 18). ⇨ **BAYTÏ?** + dim. -*qay*.

BAYTÏN   Tat.(Lit.) 1557 **Baytïn** [Бойтинъ Кара] (Kn. Metriki Lit. 131). ⇨ **BAYTAN?**

BAYTLÏ   Kzk. 19th c. **Baytlï** / **Bay-teli?** [Байтлы] (AOAtb. 38).

BAYUNDUR   Oghuz/Trkm. 13th c. **Bayïndïr** [با يندر / Байыɲдыр], Kök-χan's son (Abulg./Kon. 520, 555, 605); Oghuz/Trkm. 14th c. - 15th c. **Bayundur** / **Bayundur-χan** / **Bayïndïr** [Баюндур, Баюндур-хан] (DQorq. 14 etc.); *EN:* Trkm. 1616 **Bayïndïr** [بايندر], Bayındır cemaatı, a nomadic in Yeni İl tribe, Anatolia (Refik, Anad. 76); Turk. 16th c. **Bayïndïr / Bayandïr?** [باينـدر], Bayındır cemaatı, a nomadic in the region of Silifke tribe, Anatolia, Turkey (Faruk Sümer: DTCFD Dergisi XI, 339, 340); *TN:* Turk. 20th c. **Bayïndïr** [Bayındır], a village in the province of Bursa, Turkey (TMːB 222). ✧ 'Fortunate, lucky, happy; rich, prosperous' (Erol II), cf. Turk. *bayındır* 'id.' (TED).An Oghuz tribe, cf. *bajundur* (DTS). Ethnonym, the clan of the Turkmen tribe Gökleñ, cf. Trkm. *bayändär* (Radl. IV, 1468).

BAYUTMÏŠ   Uyg. **Bayutmïš** [Bayutmış] (EUTS). See also **QUTLUΓ-BAYUTMÏŠ**.

BAYZÏŇ   Alt. 19th-20th c. **Bayzïň** (OjrRS 207). ✧ 'Rich' (OjrRS 207).

BAKİR see **BAQÏR**

BAQ   Kzk. 19th c. **Baq-pay** [Бакпай] (SOV 150). ✧ I. 'Look!'? (Sattarov); II. 'Luck; hapiness' cf. Kzk. *baq* 'счастье' (PKzRS), *baqït* 'id.' (KzkRS); III. Variant of BEK (BÄK)? see there. See also **AY-BAQ, BAY-BAQ, BAYDA-BAQ, BUZAW-BAQ, ČİŽEN-BAQ, ǮAYLAW-BAQ, DAWLET-BAQ, EŠKE-BAQ, İL-BAQ, QADÏR-BAQ, QAYDÏ-BAQ, QARAQ-BAQ, QAZÏ-BAQ?, QOY-BAQ, QUTLU-BAQ, QUZ-BAQ, SAR-BAQ, TAŠTAL-BAQ, TUYAN-BAQ, URDA-BAQ.**

BAQ-BAWLÏ   Kkalp. 20th c. **Baq-bawlï** [Бакбавлы] (Bask., Kkalp. 24, 399). ⇨ **BAQ** + **BAW?** + suff. -*lï*.

BAQ-DÖLÖT   Kirg. **Baq-dölöt** (Jud. 112). ✧ 'Luck-happiness'. ⇨ **BAQ** + **DÄWLÄT.**

BAQ-PANBET   Kzk. 19th c. **Baq-panbet** (<**Baq-mambet**) [Бакпанбетъ] (SOK 144). ⇨ **BAQ** + **MAMBET.**

BAQ-TAY   Kzk. 19th c. **Baq-tay** / **Baqtay?** [Бактай] (SOK 182); Kzk. 19th c. **Baq-tay** / **Baqtay?** [Бактай] (SOV 76). ✧ 'Fortune-foal, luck-foal, wealth-foal' or with hypoch. suff. -*tay* 'Fortune-darling, luck-dear', cf. Kzk. PN *Bak-bek* (Žanuzakov-Esbaeva), Kzk. *baq* 'удача, счастье' (KzRS). ⇨ **BAQ+ TAY?** or suff. -*tay(1,2)*?

BAQA   Chuv. 18th-19th c. **Baka** [Бака] (Magn. 32); Oghuz? 967 **Baqa**, a slave, who played part in Diyarbakir (Weil, Chalif. III, 38); Kzk. **Baqa** [Бака], fem. (Sozontov 7); Kzk. 19th c. **Baqa** [Бака] (Grod., Pril. 184); Kzk. 19th c. **Baqa** [Бака] (AOP 122); Nog. 1537 **Baqa** [Бака], a prince (PSRL XIII, 119); Trkm. 1747 **Baqa-sultan** / **Baqa-saltan** [Бака-султан, Бака салтан] (MIT II, 189, PSRL VIII, 17); Hak.(Sag.) 19th-20th c. **Paγa** (Katanov, Otč. 7); Hak.(Koyb.) 19th-20th c. **Paγa** [Паһа], fem. (Katanov, Otč. 13). ✧ 'Frog' (Sozontov 7), cf. Uyg., Karakh. *baqa* 'id.' (DTS), Maml. *baγa* 'лягушка' (Tuhfa), Turk. *baγa* 'der Frosch, das Schildpatt' (Radl. IV, 1448), Alt., East.T. *paqa* 'der Frog' (Radl. IV, 1127), Alt. *paγa* 'лягушка' (Verb., Sl.). See also **AYT-РАГА, BAY-BAQA, İRKE-BAQA, ČÄL-РАГА, QUTLUΓ-ВАГА, URAZ-ВАГА.**

BAQA-BAŠ   Kzk. 1826 **Baqa-baš** [Бакабашъ Утягановъ] (TOUAK XXIV, 167). ⇨ **BAQA** + **BAŠ.**

BAQAY   Chuv. 18th-19th c. **Bakay** [Бакай] (Magn. 32); Tat.(Mish.) 1663 **Baqay** [Бакай] (MIB I, 169); Tat.(Sib.) 1631 **Baqay** [Янгозя Бакаевъ] (Miller, Ist. Sib. II, 386); Bashk. 1709 **Baqay** [Бакай] (MIB I, 264); Kzk. 1846 **Baqay** [Бакай Рахметев], a Kazak biy (MKOP 154); Kzk. 19th c. **Baqay** [Кипчакбай Бакаевъ] (Grod., Pril. 74); Kzk. 19th c. **Baqay** [Суярбай Бакаевъ] (Grod., Pril. 169); Kzk. 1860 **Baqay** [Бакай], a biy, the head of the Bayčigir clan from the Ǧalayïr tribe (ZIRGOGeogr. I, 272); Kirg. **Baqay** [Бакай] (Jud. 31, 697); Kirg. **Baqay-qan** [Бакаи Кан] (Proben V, 3, 5, 6 etc.). ✧ 'Eternal, permanent' (Bask., Fam. 176-177, Sattarov) (<Ar). See also **ÏQ-PAQAY, MONUS-PAQAY, OLONČU-PAҐAY.**

BAQAL see **BAQQAL**

BAQALAQ   Kzk. 19th c. **Baqalaq** [Бакалакъ] (SOK 240).

BAQAMAY   Alt. 19th-20th c. **Baqamay** [Бакамай], fem. (OjrRS 211).

BAQAN   Chag. 1559 **Baqan** [Бакан], a master (of a trade or craft) (Ivanov 110); Bashk. 1732 **Baqan** [Ишперда Баканов] (MIB III, 302); Kzk. 19th c. **Baqan** [Баканъ] (AOP 106); Kzk. 19th c. **Baqan** [Баканъ] (AOP 2). ✧ 'Post (in the centre of the yurt)' cf. Kuman, Chag., Kzk., Uzb. *baqan* 'Stange, mit dem man die Filzdecken der Jurte aufhebt und stüzt' (Radl. IV, 1437). See also **ATA-BAQAN.**

BAQANAY   Tat.(Sib.) 1631 **Baqanay** [Кучук (Кучюк) Баканаев (Боконоев)], from Tümen (Miller, Ist. Sib. II, 385). ⇨ **BAQAN?** + suff. -*ay.*

BAQANAN   Yak. **Baqanan** [Баканан] (Pek.).

BAQAR   Kzk. 19th c. **Baqar** [Бакаръ] (AOO 50); Kzk. 19th c. **Baqar** [Бакаровъ] (AOK 66). ✧ 'He will look after, herd or shepherd (the cattle)' cf. *baq-* 'schauen, hinschauen, sorgen für etwas, hüten (eine Herde)' (Radl. IV, 1435). See also **AT-BAҐAR, BOQ-PAҐAR, QOY-BAQ, QOY-BAQAR, QOS-BAҐAR, QOZÏ-BAҐAR, QULUN-BAҐAR, MAL-BAҐAR, TAY-BAҐAR.**

BAQAŠ   Alt. 19th-20th c. **Baqaš** [Бакаш] (OjrRS 207, Nikonov 94). ✧ 'Little frog' (OjrRS 207, Nikonov 94). ⇨ **BAQA** + dim. suff. -*š.* See also **QOTLU-BAQAŠ.**

BAQŠAL   Uyg. **Baqšal**, Yöläk's daughter (Zieme, Mat. I, 80). ✧ 'Green wood (fig. newly-married woman)' (Zieme).

BAQAUL   Oghuz/Trkm. 13th c. **Baqaul** [باقاول / Бакаул], Zeynal-Gazi's son (Abulg./Kon. 1255). ✧ I. Title, high dignity in the Khan's kitchen.; II. 'Cook' cf. Chag. *baqaul* 'id.' (Radl. IV, 1437).

BAQČÏN   Kzk. 19th c. **Baqčïn** [Бакчынъ] (SOK 44).

BAQÏ   Trkm. 20th c. **Baqï** [Baqï] (Zaj. 1971, 327); Kzk. 19th c. **Baqï-bay** [Бакыбай] (AOK 74); Kzk. 18th c. - 19th c. **Baqï-bek** [Бакыбек] (Tunyšp. 66); Kkalp. 20th c. **Baqïy** (KkRS 772); Trkm. 20th c. **Bāqï** [Бакы] (TrkmRS 69). ✧ 'Eternal' cf. Uzb. *baqi* 'ewig, beständig; das Überbleibsel, der Rest' (Radl. IV, 1442), Chag., Uzb., Trkm. *baqi* 'ewig' (Radl. IV, 1439), Kirg. *baqi* 'вечный' (Jud.); Kzk. *baqi* 'der Knöchel' (Radl. IV, 1439), Kzk. *baqi* 'alle, die Gesammtheit' (Radl. IV, 1439) (<Ar. باقى). See also **AQ-BAKÏ, QURBAN-BAQÏY, MORAÐ-BAQÏ, TURDÏ-BAQÏ, ŠEKER-BAQÏY.**

BAQÏČ   Bashk. 1652 **Baqič** [Бакычко (Бакыко) Качакаевъ] (Vel.-Zern., Bašk. 40).

BAQÏY see **BAQÏ**

BAQÏM-BALA see **BAQÏN**

BAQÏN   Kzk. 19th c. **Baqïm-bala** (<Baqïn-bala) [Бакымбала] (SOK 198); Kzk. 19th c. **Baqïn** [Бакынъ] (AOA 98).

BAQÏR   Tat.(Lit.) 1554 **Bakir-qan / Baqïr-qan?** [Бакиръ-Кганъ / Бакыркганъ] (Kn. Metriki Lit. 86, 103); Kzk. 19th c. **Baqïr** [Бакыръ] (AOAtb. 66). ✧ Bakir / Bakr (Ar.) 'Young camel' (Ahmed). See also **ABU-BAQÏR.**

BAQQAL   Kzk. 19th c. **Baqal** [Бакалъ] (SODž. 8); Kzk. 19th c. **Baqal-bay** [Бакальбай] (SOV 46); Chag. 1560 **Baqqal** [Баккаль], a χoǰa (priest) (Ivanov 144). ✧ 'Grocer' cf. Chag., Turk. *baqal*, Crm., Turk. *baqqal* 'der Kleinhändler, der Krämer' (Radl. IV, 1438) (<Ar.). See also **QARA-BAQAL, SARÏ-BAQAL.**

BAQLÏ   Nog. 1649 **Baqlï** [Баклы], fem. (AI IV, 123). ⇨ **BAQLA?**

BAQRAY   Kzk. 19th c. **Baqray** [Бакрай] (AOK 126).

BAQSA   Kzk. 19th c. **Baqsa** [Бакса Усенъ] (AUK 494). ⇨ **BAQŠÏ?**

BAQSU   Kzk. 18th c. **Baqsu-bay** [Баксубай] (Nepljuev 764). ⇨ **BAQŠÏ?**

BAQŠAY   Bashk. 1760 **Baqšay** [Аяз Бакшаев] (MIB IV/1, 189); **Baqšey** [Тевель бокшей] (PSRL). ✧ Dial. variant of *Baq-šäyeχ* (Sattarov). ⇨ **BAQ.**

BAQŠANDA   Crm. 1539 **Baqšanda** [Бакшанъда] (PSRL XIII, 129); Crm. 1539 **Baqšanda** [Бакшанда] (PSRL XIII, 129); Tat. 1624 **Baqšanda** [Бабахта Бакшандинъ] (Pokrovskij 72); Tat. 17th c. **Baqšanda** [Бакшанда], a landlord from the district of Kazan (Iznoskov 118); Tat. 1549 **Baqšanda / Baqšandu?** [Бакшанду] (PSRL XIII, 157).

BAQŠEY see **BAQŠAY**

BAQŠÏ   Trkm. 20th c. **Baγšï** [Bagšï] (Zaj. 1971, 325); Turk. 16th c. **Baχšï** (Ongan, Ank. II.); Maml. 1497 **Baχšï-bay** [بخشاى], Baχšï-bay Abdulkerim (Iyās II, 306, III, 3, 72); Maml. 1498/99 **Baχšï-bay** [بخشاى], governor of Hama (Iyās II, 354); Maml. 1516 **Baχšï-bay** [بخشاى], governor of Safad (Iyās III, 73); Uyg. 12th c. - 14th c. **Baqšï** [baqšï] (DTS); Trkm. 19th c. **Baqšï** [Бакшиевъ] (Ščeglov IV, 182); Bashk. 1756 **Baqšï** [Бакши Тякин] (MIB IV/1, 123); Kzk. 19th c. **Baqšï-bay / Baqšu-bay** [Бакшубай Тиловаевъ] (Grod., Pril. 190); Bashk. 1737 **Maqšï-γul** [Макшигул Сотингилдин] (MIB I, 349); Bashk. 1772 **Maqšï-γul** [Макшигул] (MIB IV/1, 364); Bashk. 1798 **Maqšï-γul** [Макшигулъ] (PSZRI XXV, 196). ✧ 'Tutor, literate man, teacher; wizard, conjuror, quack doctor', 'Singer' (Zaj. 1871), cf. Uyg., Kuman, Trkm., Uzb. *baqši* 'der Lehrer, der buddhistische Gelehrte; der Schreiber; ein

Volkssänger' (Radl. IV, 1445), Uyg. *paqšï* 'der Lehrer' (Radl. IV, 1132), Uzb. *baqši* 'der Sympathiedoktor' (Radl. IV, 1446), Kzk. *baqsï* 'знахарка' (KzRS), Chag. *baχši* 'der Zauber-Arzt', (East.T.) 'der herumziehende Sänger' (Radl. IV, 1464). Used also as a secondary component of personal names. See also **İN-BAKŠA**.

BAQT-SAN   Kzk. 19th c. **Baqt-san** [Багдсанъ], fem. (Grod., Pril. 192). ⇨ **BAXT + SAN?**

BAQTA see **BAQTÏ**

BAQTÏ   Trkm. 20th c. **Baγtï-gül** [Bagtï Gül], fem. (Zaj. 1971, 339); Chag. 15th c. **Baχtï** [Бахты], Ulug-bek's (1447-1449) concubine, the daughter of an Uzbek called Qasuni (Barth., Ulugb. 116); Tat.(Lit.) 1593 **Baχtï** [Бахтыевичъ], family name (Lit. Tat. 171-72 etc.); Tat.(Sib.) 1632 **Baχtï-bay** [Бахтыбай] (Miller, Ist. Sib. II, 397); Kzk. 18th c. **Baχtï-bay** [Бахтыбай] (Nepljuev 794); Kzk. 19th c. **Baχtï-bay** [Дуранбекъ Бахтибаевъ] (Grod., Pril. 73); Kzk. 19th c. **Baχtï-bay** [Бахтибай] (Grod., Pril. 34); Kzk. 19th c. **Baχtï-bek** [Бахтибекъ] (Grod., Pril. 100); Bashk. 1735 **Baχtï-girey** [Бахты гирей Алдаров], a tarχan (Vel.-Zern., Bašk. 27); Kzk. 19th c. **Baχtï-girey**, a writer of articles (AUK 164); Kzk. 19th c. **Baχtï-gül** [Бахти-гюль], fem. (Grod., Pril. 174); Bashk. 1735 **Baχtï-γul?** / **Baχtï-qul?** [Бахтагул Ногайбаков], a tarχan (Vel.-Zern., Dict. 20); Tat. 1389, 1392 **Baχtï-χoĵa** [Бахтыхозя] (PSRL IV, 97-98, VIII, 64); Bashk. 1756 **Baqta** [Бакта Савелеев] (MIB IV/1, 127); Kzk. 19th c. **Baqta-bay** [Бактабай] (SOK 240); Bashk. 1735 **Baqtï-bay** [Бактыбай Бердиков] (MIB III, 334); Kzk. 1825 **Baqtï-bay** [باقطی بای / Бактыбай] (MIK IV, 470, 476); Kzk. 19th c. **Baqtï-bay** [Бактыбай] (SOK 140); Kzk. 19th c. **Baqtï-bay** [Бактыбай] (AOO 30); Kzk. 19th c. **Baqtï-bay** [Бактыбай] (AOAtb. 62); Kzk. 19th c. **Baqtï-bay** [Бактыбай] (SODž. 50); Bashk. 1763 **Baqtï-girey** [Бактыгирей Аккулаев] (MIB IV/1, 271, 341); Crm.Tat. 1502, 1509 **Baχtï-girey** [Бахты-Гирей (Батикирей, Битикерей)] (PSRL II, 363, 366); Kkalp. 20th c. **Baqtï-gül** [Бакътыгюл / Бакътыгул], fem. (Bask., Kkalp. 403, KkRS 777); Kzk. 19th c. **Baqtu-bay** [Бактубай] (Grod., Pril. 89); Kzk. 19th c. **Baqtu-bay** [Бактубай] (AOK 118). ✦ I. 'Lucky, Fortunate' (Baskakov: OSA 140, Ahmetzjanov 103), cf. Kzk. *baqtï* 'glücklich' (Radl. IV, 1444), Nog. *baqtï* 'счастье' (RNS). According to Baskakov (loc. cit.) *Baqtï-gül* means 'Happy rose'. < Ar. *baχt* 'luck, fortune'; II. Less convincing is: 'Looked (at), saw; (fig.) has come, has been born' (Sattarov, Kusimova). See also **AL-BAQTÏ, AN-BAXTA, BAY-BAQTÏ, EL-BAQTÏ, ESEN-BAXTÏ, İL-BAQTA, QAZA-BAXTÏ, QOM-BAXTÏ, QOŠ-BAXTÏ, QUDAY-BAQTÏ, TON-BAXTA, TİN-BAXTA, URAZ-BAQTÏ.**

BAQTÏRÏ   Yak. **Baqtïrï** [Бактыры], a shaman (Pek.).

BAQTU see **BAQTÏ**

BAQUY-DİB-XAN see **DİB-BAQUY**

BAL   Kzk. **Bal-bay** [Балбаи] (Proben V, 70 /71/); Kzk. 19th c. **Bal-bay** [Балбай] (SOK 104); Tat. 1668 **Bal-bek** [Игитайко Балбеков] (Kungursk. akty 12); Tat. 1543 **Bal-ĵan** (Gökb., Rum. 235, 242); Bashk. 1776 **Bal-gazi** [Балгазя Кайгулов / Балгази Кейгулов] (MIB V, 44, 45); Kzk. 19th c.? **Bal-γoĵa-biy** (Atyns. 28); Kzk. 1846 **Bal-γuĵa** [Балгуджа Янчурин] (MKOP 99); Kzk. 18th c. - 19th c. **Bal-χoĵa** [Балходжа] (Tynyšp. 75); Bashk. 1709 **Bal-közä** [Култей Балкозин] (MIB I, 264); Kkalp. 20th c. **Bal-sïluw / Bal-suluw** [Балсылув / Балсулуў], fem. (Bask., Kkalp. 61, KkRS 777); Kzk. 19th c. **Bal-žan** [Балжанъ], fem. (IOAIÊK XXII, 643); Kkalp. 20th c. **Pal-ĵan** [Палжан], fem. (KkRS 778). ✦ 'Honey' cf. Kuman, Kzk., Tat., Turk., Uzb. *bal* 'id.' (Radl. IV, 1489), Kkalp. *pal II* 'мёд' (KkRS). See also **AQ-BAL, ARPA-BAL, QARA-BAL.**

BAL-DİRÄK   Kzk. 19th c. **Bal-diräk** [Балдиракъ] (Grod., Pril. 76). ⇨ **BAL + TİRÄK.**

BAL-ГАRА   Trkm. 19th c. **Bal-γara** [Балгара Ярыповъ] (ZIRGOÊtn. I, 210). ⇨ **BAL / BALA + QARA?**

BAL-NİYAZ   Kzk. 19th c. **Bal-niyaz** [Балніязъ] (Grod., Pril. 107). ⇨ **BAL + NİYAZ.**

BAL-PAŠ   Kzk. 19th c. **Bal-paš** [Балпашъ] (SOV 100). ⇨ **BAL + BAŠ?**

BAL-ŠEKER   Kzk. **Bal-seker** [Бал-секеръ], fem. (Sozontov 7); Kkalp. 20th c. **Bal-šeker** [Балшекер], fem. (KkRS 777). ✦ 'Honey-sugar' (Sozontov 7). ⇨ **BAL + ŠEKER.**

BALA   Chuv. 18th-19th c. **Bala** [Бала] (Magn. 32); Kzk. 19th c. **Bala-bay** [Джунусъ Болабаевъ] (Grod., Pril. 174); Kkalp. 1822 **Bala-behadïr** [Бала бехадыр] (MIKk. 127); Kzk. 19th c. **Bala-bek** [Балабекъ] (AOA 122); Kzk. 19th c. **Bala-bek** [Балабекъ] (SOK 164, 222); Kzk. 19th c. **Bala-bek** [Балабекъ] (SOV 44); Kzk. 19th c. **Bala-ĵigit** [Баладжигитъ] (AOO 2); 13th c. **Bala-χan** [بالاخان], a commander? from Samarkand (Ĵuwaynī I, 92, Barth., Turk. 444); Yürük 1543 **Bala-χan** (Gökb., Rum. 187); Kzk. 19th c. **Bala-mergen** [Бала-мергенъ] (Potanin IV, 404); Kzk. 19th c. **Bala-pay** [Балапай] (AOK 106); Hak.(Shor) 19th-20th c. **Pala** [Пала], fem. (Katanov, Otč. 11); *TN:* Kzk. **Bala-bek** [Балабек], a hill (Kojčubaev 90). ✦ 'Child' cf. Crm., Kar., Kzk., Kirg., Tat., Trkm., Uzb. *bala* 'das Kind' (Radl. IV, 1491). Cf. Hak. fem. PN *Palan* 'дите' (Butanaev). Used also as a secondary component of personal names.

BALA-BOLAR   Uzb. 20th c. **Bâl-bolar (<Bâla-bolar?)** [Болбӱлар] (Begmatov 1984, 201). ✦ '(The) Child will be living; Enough of children!' (Begmatov). ⇨

BALA + BOL.

BALA-ČUBAY Kzk. 19th c. **Bala-čubay** [Бала-Чубай Кудратъ Бергановъ] (Grod., Pril. 125). ⇨ **BALA + ČUBAY.**

BALA-ГUŠ see **BALA-QUŠ**

BALA-KEK Kzk. 19th c. **Bala-kek** [Балакекъ] (SOK 188). ✧ 'Child-honor (good name, modesty)'? cf. Kzk. *kek* 'intikam; namus, ar' (KzTS). ⇨ **BALA.**

BALA-QUŠ Bashk. 1709 **Bala-γuš** (<Bala-quš) [Балагушев] (MIB I, 264); Bashk. 1770 **Bala-γuš** (<Bala-quš) [Балагуш Бекметев] (MIB IV, 345); Bashk. 1795 **Bala-γuš** (<Bala-quš) [Азанчей Балагушъ Біимбетевъ] (IOAIÊK XVIII, 589). ⇨ **BALA + QUŠ I.**

BALA-TAY Tat. 1702 **Bala-tay** [Балатайка Акпашевъ] (Kurdjumov 331-332). ⇨ **BALA + TAY? OR** suff. *-tay(1,3).*

BALABAN 1207 **Balaban** [بلبان ملوك شاه ارمن] (Ibn al-Athīr/Tornb. XII, 167-69, 180); Selj.? **Balaban** [ملك بلبان] (Ibn Bībī IV, 12); Selj. 1200 **Balaban** [ملك بلبان / Melik Boulban] (Seldj. Nameh 28, 72); Selj.? 1207 **Balaban** [Balaban Chelati Dominus] (Abulfar. 283); Khorezm.? **Balaban** [ملك بلبان] (Ibn Bībī IV, 12); Khorezm. 1206 **Balaban** [Balâbân] (Abulfar./Budge I, 363); Khorezm. 1225 **Balaban** [بلبا ن القداری] (Nasawī 1-7); Khorezm. 1229 **Balaban** [بلبا ن الخلخلی / Belban (Belbân) el-Khelkhaly], Sultan Jelal's (1220-1231) officer (Nasawī 169); Khorezm.? 13th c. **Balaban** [غياث الد ين بلبان / Ghiyâth eddîn Balaban], a sultan (Ibn Bat. III, 152); Khorezm.? 1345 **Balaban** [سيف الد ين بلبا ن السلاح دار] (Chwol., Syr.-nest. (NF) I, 9-10); Maml. **Balaban** [بلبان لمهرانی], an emir (Duqmaq: RHCHor IV, 119, 121); Maml. **Balaban** [بلبان لحبيشی] (Duqmaq:RHCHor IV, 90); Maml. **Balaban** [سيف الدين بلبان] (Zetterst.); Maml. **Balaban** [سيف الدين بلبان الازرق] (Zetterst. 30); Maml. **Balaban** [سيف الدين بلبان الحكيمی] (Zetterst. 134); Maml. **Balaban** [سيف الدين بلبان الفاخری] (Zetterst. 24, 25); Maml. **Balaban** [سيف الدين بلبان الصرختی] (Zetterst. 134); Maml. 1197 **Balaban** [عزالد ين بلبان], a Mamluk chieftain (Abulfidā IV, 168); Maml. 13th c. **Balaban** [Seïf-eddin-Belban-Hemsi], died at Hims in 1280 (Makrīzī III, 39); Maml. 13th c. **Balaban** [سيف الد ين بلبا ن الخا ص ترکی], Qalāūn's (1279-1290) envoy to the Monghols (Zetterst. 160, 168, Makrīzī III, 23); Maml. 13th c. **Balaban** [سيف الد ين بلبان الرکنی], emir, Qalāūn's (1279-1290) envoy to Meñgü Temür (1266-1280) (Makrīzī III, 165); Maml. 1254 **Balaban** [Seïf-eddin Belbân Raschīdi] (Makrīzī I, 57); Maml. 1259 **Balaban** [Belban-Roumi, le dewâdâr] (Makrīzī I, 83); Maml. 1260 **Balaban**

[بلبان الهارو نی], Beybars' I (1260-1277) retainer against Qutuz (Iyās I, 99, Makrīzī I, 83, 112, II, 171); Maml. 1262 **Balaban** [Sayf ed-dîn Balbân ez-Zerdkach] (Sauvaire VI, 228); Maml. 1264 **Balaban** [بلبان / Saif al-dīn Balābān al Zainī Amīr-ᶜAlam], an emir (Sīrat 210); Maml. 1280 **Balaban** [Seïf-eddin Belban Kerimi] (Makrīzī III, 18, Weil, Chalif. I, 117); Maml. 1281, 1298, 1300 **Balaban** [بلبان الطباخی], emir, governor of Haleb (Aleppo) in 1300 (Abulfidā V, 52-53, Dawād. 11, 17, Makrīzī IV, 114, 184, Zetterst. 24, 95, Iyās I, 115, Weil, Chalif. I, 123, 225); Maml. 1294 **Balaban** [سيف الد ين بلبان الحسنی] (Iyās I, 131, Zetterst. 149, 218); Maml. 1300, 1303, 1312 **Balaban** [سيف الد ين بلبا ن طرنه / Bilban Tarna / Balbân Tarna / Sayf-ed-dîn Tarbâ Balbân], emir, until 1312 the governor of Safed, died in 1333, his mausoleum is in Damascus (Dawād. 41, 265, Zetterst. 82, 177, Makrīzī IV, 211, Weil, Chalif. I, 309); Maml. 1306/07 **Balaban** [سيف الد ين بلبا ن الصرخدی], envoy from Egypt to the Kipchak (steppe) (Baybars/Tizeng. I, 95, 119); Maml. 1306/07 **Balaban** [بلبان الحكيمی / سيفالدين بلبان الترکی], envoy from Egypt to the Kipchak (steppe) (Baybars/Tizeng. I, 95, 119, Qalāūn/Tizeng. I, 65); Maml. 1308/09 **Balaban** [بلبان المحمدی] (Iyās I, 148); Maml. 1312 **Balaban** [بلبان البدری], governor of Safed from 1312 (Zetterst. 152, 165, Weil, Chalif. I, 309); Maml. 1320 **Balaban** [بلبان القجتاری] (Zetterst. 148); Maml. 1325 **Balaban** [بلبان الشمسی السلحدار] (Zetterst. 160, 176); Maml. 1325 **Balaban** [بلبان الدمشقی] (Zetterst. 157); Maml. 1332 **Balaban** [بلبان السنانی], an emir (Dawād. 368); Maml. 14th c. **Balaban** [بلبان السنانی الجاشنكير / سيفالدين] (Zetterst. 174, 205, Weil, Chalif. 496); Maml. 1398/99 **Balaban** [بلبا ن الظا هری] (Ibn Taghrīb. VI, 22); Maml.? 1433 **Balaban** [Balbân el Mahmoûdy], the atabek of the army in Damascus, died in 1433 (Sauvaire VI, 222); Maml. 1434 **Balaban** [بلبان نايب درندة], a governor (Ibn Taghrīb. VI, 731); Maml. 1438/39 **Balaban** [بلبان محمد] (Ibn Taghrīb. VII, 73); Maml. 1439 **Balaban** [بلبان] (Iyās II, 26); Maml. 1453 **Balaban** [بلبا ن الزينی] (Ibn Taghrīb. VIII, 182); Maml. 1468 **Balaban** [ا بن بلبان] (Ibn Taghrīb. VIII, 695); Maml. 1482 **Balaban** [بلبان الكا شف] (Iyās II, 213); Turk. **Balaban?** (Baştav 70); Turk. 14th c. - 15th c. **Balaban** [Παλαπάνος], an Ottoman notability (Byz. Turc. 243-44, Sauvaget 43); Turk. 1432 **Balaban** [Балабан бѣг], a commander (Bogdan, Br. 40); Yürük 1543 **Balaban** (Gökb., Rum. 178, 186, 189, 190, 192, 198, 200, 204, 209, 212, 219, 220,223, 225,); Crm. 1289 **Balaban** [Balaban Azardi], resident in Caffa (Actes des notaires génois de Péra et de Caffa. Publ. par G. I. Brătianu, Bucarest 1927, p. 341); Tat. 1543 **Balaban** (Gökb., Rum. 234); Trkm. 1690 **Balaban-beg** [بلبا ن بك / Çiğdem oğlu Balaban beğ], from the Çiğdemlü tribe (Refik, Anad. 84); Turk. 1436-1439 **Balaban-bey** [İzzeddin Balaban Bey] (Gökb., Ed. 173); Turk. 1425 **Balaban-paša** [بلبا ن با شا] (Āšikp. 98); Kzk. 1819 **Balapan** [Балапан] (MIK IV, 324); Kzk. 19th c. **Balapan** [Балапанъ] (SOV 76); Kzk. 19th c. **Balapan** [Балапанъ] (AOA 22); Kzk. 19th c. **Balapan** [Балапанъ] (AOK 86); Kzk. 19th c. **Balapan** [Балапанъ] (SODž. 74); Kzk. 19th c. **Balapan** [Балапанъ] (SOK 274); Kzk. 1794 **Balapan-biy** [بى بالافا ن / Балапан] (MIK IV, 163); *TN:* Turk. 20th c. **Balaban**, a village in the province of İzmir, Turkey (TMİB 470). ✧ I. 'A kind of falcon' (Le Coq, Ind. 2), 'Hunting falcon' (CC), 'Sparrow-hawk' (Sauvaget 43), 'Goshawk, hawk' (Maml.), cf. Kuman *balaban* 'Jagdfalke (falchonus)' (CC), Maml. *balaban* 'Sperber' (Tarj/Houtsma), 'Çakır doğan' [goshawk] (Tarj/Toparlı), Turk., Crm. *balaban* 'eine Sperberart' (Radl. IV, 1494-95); II. 'Nestling', 'Eaglet, Eagle's child' (Sattarov 42, Torma 1992, 366), Kzk. *balapan* 'ein junges Vögelchen' (Radl. IV, 1494); III. 'Having a big head; large, thick' cf. Crm., Turk. *balaban* 'mit grossem Kopfe, gross, dick; eine grosse Trommel' (Radl. IV, 1494-95).

BALAGAY see **BALAQAY**

BALAΓAN Kzk. 19th c. **Balaγan** [Бай-Сакалъ Балагановъ] (Grod., Pril. 53); Kzk. 19th c. **Balaγan** [Уркунбай Балагановъ] (Grod., Pril. 40); Kzk. 19th c. **Balaγan** [Тохтамыш Балаганов] (Grod., Pril. 138); Alt. 19th c. **Balaγan** [Балаганъ], Edzenhan's (Едзсньханъ) sister; this name was also given to Yekaterina II by the Altay-people (Potanin IV, 287, 289). ⇨ **BALA + QAN?**

BALAX see **BÄLÄX**

BALAXAN YUyg. 20th c. **Balaχan**, a young girl (Kakuk, Chants ouigoures: AOH XXV, 416, 422). ⇨ **BALA** + suff. *-χan(1)*.

BALAY Chuv. 18th-19th c. **Balay** [Балай] (Magn. 32); Alt. 19th-20th c. **Balay** [Балай], fem. (OjrRS 211); Kuman/Tat. 1242, 1243 **Balay** [Балай], a Tatar chieftain (hero) (PSRL II, 180, Ipat. 528). ✧ 'Little child' (OjrRS 211). ⇨ **BALA** + dim. suff. *-y*. See also **QUM-BALAY, TAS-PALAY.**

BALAKAŠ Chuv. 18th-19th c. **Balakaš / Balagaš?** [Балагашъ] (Magn. 32).

BALAQ Selj. 1123? **Balaq**, prince of Damascus, Balduin II was his captive (Reg. Hieros. 23); Selj. 1132 **Balaq**, an emir (Ahbar 72, 73); Selj. 1150 **Balaq** [بلاق حسام الد ين] (Qalānisi 306); Selj. 1121 **Balaq** [بلاق بن اسحق] (Kamāladdīn: RHCHor II, 194); Tat. 13th c. **Balaq / Balaγ?** [Βαλάγ], a christened Tatar (Byz. Turc. 85); Uyg. **Balaq-tañrim** [Balaq Tängrim], fem. (Zieme, Mat. I, 74); *TN:* Bashk. 1764 **Balakova** (<**Balaq**) [Балакова], a village (MIB IV/1, 292); Bashk. 1706 **Balaq** [Балак], a small river (MIB III, 17); Bashk. 1734 **Balaq** [Балак], a village (MIB III, 328). ✧ I. 'Fish' cf. Türk, Uyg. *balaq* 'рыба ' (DTS); II. 'Leg (of trousers)' cf. Turk., Kzk., Tat., Türkm., Uzb. *balaq* 'der untere Theil der Hosen; das Hosenbein; (Kzk.) der Venusberg' (Radl. IV, 1492). See also **AY-BALAQ.**

BALAQA Alt. 19th-20th c. **Balaqa** [Балака], fem. (OjrRS 211). ✧ 'Little child'. ⇨ **BALA** + dim. suff. *-qa*.

BALAQAY Chuv. 18th-19th c. **Balagay** [Балагай] (Magn. 32); Kzk. 20th c. **Balaqay** [М. Б. Балакаев], a Kazak linguist (Bibl. izd. AN KazSSR 1951-55. Alma-Ata, 1956, 172). ✧ 'Little child' cf. Tat. *ā balaqayïm* 'o mein Kindchen' (Radl. IV, 1492). ⇨ **BALA** + suff. *-qay*.

BALAMBET Kzk. 19th c. **Balambet** [Баламбетъ] (Grod., Pril. 101). ⇨ **BALA** + suffixoid *-mbet*.

BALAN Khorezm. / Mo.? 1219 **Balan-χan** [Баланъ-ханъ], officer of the Khorezmshah Muχammad Alāaddīn II (1200-1220) (RaD/Ber. III, 57, Byz. Turc. 85). ✧ 'Guelder rose (Viburnum opulus)' cf. Tat. *balan* 'Massholderbeere' (Radl. IV, 1492).

BALANDAY Chuv. 18th c. **Balanday** [Баландай Танчитевъ (Танчишевъ)] (Nikol'skij 97, Alatyr. 136, Letop. ZAK 1864, 136); Tat. 1675 **Balantay** [Балантаевъ] (Kungursk. akty 30); Tat. 1724 **Balantay** [Балантай Булаев] (MIB III, 227). ⇨ **BALAN** + suff. *-day*.

BALANQA Alt. 19th-20th c. **Balanqa** [Баланка] (OjrRS 211). ⇨ **BALAN?** + suff. *-qa*.

BALANTAY see **BALANDAY**

BALAPAQ Kzk. 19th c. **Balapaq** [Балапакъ] (SOV 146).

BALAPAN see **BALABAN**

BALAR Kzk. 19th c. **Balar** [Баларъ] (SOV 114).

BALASŪ Alt. 19th-20th c. **Balasū** [Баласуу], fem. (OjrRS 211).

BALAŠ Kzk. 19th c. **Balaš** [Балашъ] (AOP 46); Kzk. 19th c. **Balaš** [Балашъ] (SOK 278). ✧ 'Dear little child'. ⇨ **BALA** + dim. suff. *-š*.

BALAŠÏQ Kzk. 19th c. **Balašïq** [Балашек] (AOP 62). ✧ I. 'Little child'?; II. 'Tab of a tripod' cf. Kzk. *balašïq* 'петля треножника ' (KzRS). ⇨ **BALA** + dim. *-šïq / -čïq*.

BALAT I. Turk. 1505 **Balat** [Balat], a district in Edirne? (Gökb., Ed. 432).

BALAT II. Kzk. 19th c. **Balat-bek** [Балатбекъ] (SOK 20); Kzk. 19th c. **Balat-bek** [Балатбекъ] (SODž. 58); Kzk. 19th c. **Balat-pay** [Балатпай] (SODž. 92). ⇨

BULAT?

BALAW   Kzk. 19th c. **Balaw** [Балау] (SODž. 162).

BALĀGĬYA   Yak. **Balāgïya** [Балагыja], fem. (Pek.). ✧ Pelageya (R.).

BALBAN   Uyg. 12th c.-14th c. **Balban** (Radl., USp. 215, 257). ⇨ **BALABAN?** See also **ARSLAN-BALBAN.**

BALBAÑ   Kzk. 19th c. **Balbañ** [Балбанговъ] (Grod., Pril. 54). ✧ 'Way of walking; walking proudly' cf. Kzk. *balpañ / balpan* (Radl. IV, 1507).

BALBĀN see **BALABAN**

BALBĀRĬ see **PARBARA**

BALBĬR   Kzk. 19th c. **Balbïr** [Балбыръ] (SOK 4). ✧ 'Soft, mellow' cf. Kzk. *balbïr* 'yumuşak' (KzTS).

BALBRAQ   Kzk. 19th c. **Balbraq** [Балбракъ], a Kazak biy (Lomakin 38). ⇨ **BALBĬR** + suff. *-aq.*

BALČAYBAN   Yak. **Balčayban** [Балчаибан] (Pek.).

BALČİK see **BALČĬQ**

BALČĬBAN   Kzk. 19th c. **Balčïban?** [Балчебанъ] (SOK 44).

BALČĬQ   Oghuz **Balčïq** [بالچیق], forefather of the Ottoman dynasty (Seādeddīn I, 15, Nešrī XIII, 186, Wittek 94); Kzk. 19th c. **Balšaq / Balšïq?** [Балшакъ] (SOK 36). ✧ I. 'Clay, loam'? cf. Crm., Turk., Tat. *balčïq* 'der Lehm, der Thon, der Schlamm, der Schmutz' (Radl. IV, 1505), Kzk. *balšïq* 'der Lehm, der Schmutz' (Radl. I, 1506); II. 'Little child'? ⇨ **BALA?** + dim. suff. *-čïq.*

BALČĬQAY   Kzk. 19th c. **Balčiqay / Balčïqay** [Балчикай] (SOK 28). ⇨ **BALČĬQ** + dim. suff. *-qay.*

BALČUR   Mo.? 13th c. **Balčur** [بالچور / ملك تاتار], ruler of the Tatar, came to Rūm at the time of Er-toγrul (Nešrī XIII, 195).

BALJĬA   Yak. **Baljïa** [Балцыа] (Pek.).

BALDAY   Kzk. 19th c. **Balday** [Балдай] (SOK 186). ✧ 'Honey-like'. ⇨ **BAL** + suff. *-day.*

BALDAN   Kzk. 19th c. **Baldam-bay (<Baldan-bay)** [Балдамбай] (SOV 22); Karch. 20th c. **Baldan**, fem. (Pröhle, Kar. 91). ✧ 'Dear Little Axe' (Sattarov), cf. also Kzk. PN *Baltan* (Žanuzakov-Esbaeva). ⇨ **BALTA** + dim.-hypoc. suff. *-an.*

BALDİMER   Chuv. 18th-19th c. **Baldimer** [Балдимеръ] (Magn. 32). ✧ Vladimir (R.).

BALDĬ   Kzk. 19th c. **Baldï-bay** [Балдыбай] (SOK 168). ✧ 'Honeyed; sweet like honey'. ⇨ **BAL** + suff. *-dï/-lï.*

BALDĬ-BİREK   Kzk. 19th c. **Baldï-birek** [Балдибирекъ] (Grod., Pril. 91). ⇨ **BALDĬ.**

BALDĬŠ   Tat.(Lit.) 1591 **Baldïš** [Балдышевичъ], a Tatar family (Lit. Tat. 82); Tat.(Mish.) **Paldïš-χan** [Paldïšχan] (Pelissier 24); *TN:* Tat.(Mish.) **Paldïš** [Paldïš], a place (Pelissier 24). ⇨ **BALDĬ** + dim. suff. *-š.*

BALDU   Karch. 20th c. **Baldu** (Pröhle, Kar. 91). ⇨

BALTU?

BALDURΓAN   Kzk. 19th c. **Baldurγan-χatun** [Балдурганъ-хатунъ], fem. (Grod., Pril. 193). ✧ '?' cf. Tat. *baldïrγan / baltïrγan*, Kirg. *baltïrγan* 'Bärenkraut (Heracleum sibiricum)' (Radl. IV, 1503).

BALΓA   Kzk. 18th c. - 19th c. **Balγa-bay** [Балгабай] (Tynyšp. 72); Kkalp. 20th c. **Balγa-bay** (KkRS 772); Kzk. 19th c. **Balqa-bek** [Балкабекъ] (AOO 50); Kzk. 19th c. **Balqa-bek** [Балкабекъ] (SOV 72). ✧ 'Hammer' cf. Kzk. *balγa* 'id.' (Radl. IV, 1500), East.T. *balqa* 'id.' (Radl. IV, 1498).

BALΓAYÏR   Bashk. 1769 **Balγayïr?** [Балгаир Кулаков] (MIB IV/1, 336); Bashk. 1715 **Balγayïr-batïr** [Балгаир Батыр] (MIB I, 279).

BALΓAM   Kzk. 19th c. **Balγam-bay (<Balγan-bay?)** [Балгамбай] (SOK 160). ✧ 'Mucus, phlegm' cf. Turk., Uzb. *balγam* (<Ar.) 'der Schleim' (Radl. IV, 1500).

BALΓANČA   1642 **Balγanča** [Балганча], a shaman (DAI II, 262).

BALΓĀNAY   Yak. **Balγānay** [Балганаi] (Pek.).

BALΓÏN   Kzk. 19th c. **Balγïm-bay (<Balγïn-bay)** [Балгымбай] (AOAtb. 38); Kzk. 19th c. **Balγïm-bay (<Balγïn-bay)** [Ахмедъ Балгимбаевъ] (Pam. kn. Turg. 73); Kzk. 19th c. **Balγïm-bay (<Balγïn-bay)** [Балгимбаевъ], a writer of articles (AUK 162). ✧ 'Succulent, juicy'? cf. Kzk. *balγïn* 'saftig' (Radl. IV, 1500), cf. Kzk. PN *Balγïmbay* (Žanuzakov-Esbaeva).

BALX-UDAR   Az. **Balχ-udar** [Балхудар], a fisherman in a tale (Az. Skaz. 54). ✧ 'He who will catch fish'. ⇨ **BALÏQ.**

BALİ   Kzk. 19th c. **Bali-bek** [Балибекъ] (SKSO III, 15).

BALÏ   Turk. 1583/84 **Balï**, twenty-two persons in the source (Ongan, Ank. I, 153 etc.); Turk. 1609 **Balï**, from Isparta, Turkey (Ün 1938, 645); Kzk. 19th c. **Balï-bay** [Мамай Балыбаевъ] (Grod., Pril. 156); Turk. 16th c. **Balï-bey**, the source mentions about 25 persons with this name (Ongan, Ank. II); Kzk. 19th c. **Balï-pay** [Балыпай] (SOK 126); *TN:* Turk. 20th c. **Balï-bey** [Balıbey], a village in the province of Elâzığ, Turkey (TMİB 311); Turk. 20th c. **Balï-šeyh** [Balışeyh, Balışıh], a village in the province of Ankara, Turkey (TMİB 84). ✧ 'Elder brother; grown-up' cf. Turk. dial. *balı* 'büyük kardeş; sevgi gösterilen kimselere denir; veli, ermiş' (DS). See also **JATAN-BALÏ, GÜLÜM-BALÏ, QAYA-BALÏ.**

BALÏ-ČALAN   Yürük 1543 **Balï-čalan** (Gökb., Rum. 236). ✧ 'He who steals the honey'? cf. Turk. *çal-* 'to steal' (TED). ⇨ **BAL?** + Acc. *-i?*

BALÏΓ   Turk.? 15th c. **Balïγ** [Usta Balığ], master of the writer of Bāz-nāme (TMİB VIII/2, 181). ✧ 'Adult, perfect, mature' cf. Turk.(Osm.) *balïγ* 'id.' (TED). See also **TOR-BALÏΓ.**

BALÏXČÏ Bashk. 1756 **Balïχči / Balïχčï** [Балыхчи Аллагузин] (MIB IV/1, 109). ✧ 'Fisherman' cf. Crm., Kar., Tat., Turk. *balïqči* 'id.' (Radl. IV, 1497). ⇨ **BALÏQ** + suff. *-čï.*

BALÏQ Chuv. 18th-19th c. **Balik** [Баликъ] (Magn. 32); Kzk. 19th c. **Balïγ-bek (<Balïq-bek)** [Балгбек] (SOK 122); Uyg. 12th c.-14th c. **Balïq** (Radl., USp. 5); Selj.? **Balïq** [بلق / يلبق / Balik], „Janitor" under al-Kāhir Billa (Abulfar./Budge 293 (193)); Turk.? 14th c. **Balïq** [Μπαλίκας], a ruler in north-west Bulgaria (Byz. Turc. 204); Bashk. 1709 **Balïq** [Балык] (MIB I, 271); Bashk. 1756 **Balïq** [Биктяш Балыков] (MIB IV/1, 117); Kzk. 18th c. - 19th c. **Balïq** [Балык] (Tynyšp. 66); Kzk. 19th c. **Balïq** [Балыкъ] (SOV 92); Kzk. 19th c. **Balïq** [Балик] (SOK 208); Alt.(Tel.) 19th c. **Balïq**, a prince in a legend (Radl., Aus Sib. I, 177, Verb., In. 121); Uzb. 1622 **Balïq** [Чебак Балыков], envoy from Bukhara (Miller, Ist. Sib. II, 287, 289); Kzk. 19th c. **Balïq-bay** [Балыкъ-бай], one of the chiefs of the Kirey tribe (Sib. Vest. IX, 106); Kzk. 19th c. **Balïq-bay** [Балык бай], on of the chiefs of the Kündelen tribe of the Middle Horde (Orta Žüz) (MIK IV, 513); Kzk. 19th c. **Balïq-bay** [Джанкбай Балыкбаев] (Grod., Pril. 131); Kzk. 19th c. **Balïq-bek** [Балыкбекъ] (SODž. 76); Kzk. 19th c. **Balïq-pay** [Балыкпай] (SOV 32, 40); Kzk. 19th c. **Balïq-pay** [Балыкпай] (AOK 74); Kzk. 19th c. **Balïq-pay** [Балыкпай] (SOK 62, 164, 230); Kzk. 19th c. **Balïq-pay** [Балыкпай] (SODž. 54); Kzk. 19th c. **Baluq-bay** [Балукбай] (TOUAK XXIV, 162); *TN:* Uzb. **Balïq-bay** [Балык-бай], a field in Khiva (Karta JAR X). ✧ 'Fish' cf. Kuman, Az., Crm., Kar., Trkm., Turk., etc. *Balïq* 'id.' (Radl. IV, 1496). See also **İT-PALÏQ.**

BALÏQ-QUT Kzk. 19th c. **Balïq-qut** [Балыккут] (MIK IV, 323). ⇨ **BALÏQ + QUT.**

BALÏQAY Kzk. 19th c. **Balïqay** [Ирканъ Баликаевъ] (Grod., Pril. 164). ⇨ **BALÏ(Q)?** + suff. *-(q)ay.*

BALÏQSA Alt. 19th c. **Balïqsa** [Балыкса], Nama's son (Verb., In. 102, 103).

BALÏĎA Yak. **Balï�̃da** [Балыда], a famous shaman (Pek.).

BALKİK Oghuz 10th c. - 12th c. **Balkik?** [Балканак ибн Джабуйя / Балкик ибн Джабуйя], son of the ruler of the Ghuzz (MIT I, 153-54).

BALQA see **BALГA**

BALQAY Kzk. 19th c. **Balqay** [Балкай] (AOP 10). ✧ 'Little Hammer'. ⇨ **BALГA** + suff. *-y.*

BALQAMAN Bashk. 1782 **Balqaman** [Балкаман Боксунов] (MIB V, 131).

BALQAN Trkm. **Balqan** [Балкан] (Sopieva 180); Kzk. 19th c. **Balqan** [Балканъ] (AOO).

BALQANAQ Oghuz 10th c. - 12th c. **Balqanaq** [Балканак ибн Джабуйя / Балкик ибн Джабуйя], son of the ruler of the Ghuzz (MIT I, 153-54).

BALQAŠ Kzk. 19th c. **Balqaš** [Балкашъ] (AOP 66). ✧ 'Marsh with clumps in; boggy place' cf. Kzk. *balqaš* 'id.' (Radl. IV, 1499).

BALQÏ Bashk. 1756 **Balqï / Balqïya?** [Балки (Балкия) Курганов] (MIB IV/1, 107, 119, 122); Kzk. 19th c. **Balqï-bay** [Куликинъ Балкибаевъ] (Grod., Pril. 98); Kkalp. 20th c. **Balqï-bay** [Балкъыйбай] (Bask., Kkalp. 399); Kzk. 19th c. **Balqï-bek** [Балкыбекъ] (SODž. 146); Kzk. 19th c. **Balqï-bek** [Балкыбекъ] (SOV 152, 156); Kzk. 19th c. **Balqï-bek** [Балкыбекъ] (SOK 34); Kzk. 19th c. **Balqï-bek** [Балкыбекъ] (SOK 164). ✧ 'Half-silk' cf. Kzk. *balqï* 'id.' (Radl. IV, 1499).

BALQÏYA see **BALQÏ**

BALQÏM-BAY see **BALQÏN**

BALQÏN Kzk. 19th c. **Balqïm-bay (<Balqïn-bay)** [Балкымбай] (SOV 40). ⇨ **BALГÏN?**

BALQÏŠ Kzk. 19th c. **Balqïš** [Балкышъ] (SOV 14). ⇨ **BALQÏ?** + suff. *-š.*

BALLÏ I. Trkm. 20th c. **Ballï** [Ballï] (Zaj. 1971, 327). ✧ 'With honey; honey-sweet' (Zaj. 1971). ⇨ **BAL** + suff. *-lï.*

BALLÏ II. Karch. 20th c. **Ballï**, fem. (Pröhle, Kar. 91, 237). ✧ 'Cherry' cf. Karch. *bālï* 'Kirsche' (Pröhle, Karch. 91), Balk. *ballı* 'Kirsche' (Pröhle, Balk. 206).

BALMAN Yürük 1543 **Balman** [بالمان], from the region of Yanbolu (Gökb., Rum. 235).

BALMEN Kzk. 19th c. **Balmen** [Бальменъ] (AOP 22). ✧ '?' cf. Kzk. PN *Balman* (Žanuzakov-Esbaeva).

BALPAQ Kzk. 19th c. **Balpaq** [Балпакъ] (SODž. 128). ✧ 'Gopher' cf. Kzk. *balpaq tišqan* 'die Zieselmaus' (Radl. IV, 1506).

BALPAN Kzk. 19th c. **Balpan** [Балпанъ] (SOK 248); Kzk. 19th c. **Balpan-qul** [Балпанкул] (AOK 74). ✧ 'Arrogant, haughty' cf. Kzk. *balpan* 'ein stolzer Gang' (Radl. IV, 1507). ⇨ **BALBAÑ?**

BALPAS Kzk. 1823 **Balpas / Bolpas?** [بالباج / Болпас] (MIK IV, 420, 427).

BALPÏN Kzk. 1860 **Balpïn** [Тленчи Балпыновъ], a biy (ZIRGOGeogr. I, 271). ⇨ **BALPAN?**

BALPÏŠ Kzk. 19th c. **Balpïš** [Балпышъ] (AOP 2).

BALŠAQ see **BALČÏQ**

BALŠÏQ see **BALČÏQ**

BALTA Kuman 1423 **Balta**, a Kuman from Hungary (Gyárfás III, 578); Kuman 1493 **Balta** [Balthazallasa], Baltaszállása (=Balta's settlement), a settlement of Kumanian origin in Hungary (Gyárfás III, 333, 710); Maml. 1398/99 **Balta** [يونس بلطا الظا هرى] (Ibn Taghrīb. VI, 3, 4, 12 etc.); Chag. **Balta** [Balto] (Le Coq, Ind. 4); Tat. 1779 **Balta** [Токташев Балта Аитов] (MIB V, 83); Bashk. 1706 **Balta** [Балта] (MIB III, 18); Bashk. 1727 **Balta** [Балта (Болта) Муняков] (MIB III, 165, 245); Bashk. 1732 **Balta** [Болта] (MIB III,

302, 304); Bashk. 18th c. **Balta** [Болта Илметев] (MIB III, 92); Bashk. 18th c. **Balta** [Болта Исекеев] (MIB III, 523); Bashk. 1760 **Balta** [Балта Имашев] (MIB IV/1, 184); Bashk. 1785 **Balta** [Муса Балтин] (MIB V, 165); Bashk. 1790 **Balta** [Акчувак Балтин] (MIB V, 295); Kzk. 18th c. - 19th c. **Balta** [Балта] (Tynyšr. 68, 70, 72); Kirg. 19th c. **Balta** [Балта] (Potanin II, 5); Uzb. 19th c. **Balta** [Балта Диванъ-беги] (ZIRGOStat. IV, Grod., Pril. 14); Uzb. 19th c. **Balta** [Балта] (SKSO III, 182); Tat. 18th c. **Balta** (>**Boltin**) [Болтинъ] (IOAIÊK XIV, 539); Tat.(Sib.) 1601 **Balta** (>**Boltin**) [Болтин Кошбархан] (Miller, Ist. Sib. II, 169); Trkm. 1740 **Balta-atalïq** [Балта-Аталыкъ], from the Qoñrat tribe (Hanykov, Poezdka 20); Kkalp. 20th c. **Balta-bay** [Балтабай] (KkRS 772); Kkalp. 20th c. **Balta-bay** [Балтабай] (Bask., Kkalp. 30, 399); Kirg. 20th c. **Balta-bay** (Kalilov 92); Uzb. 19th c. **Balta-bay** [Балтабай] (SKSO III, 160); Bashk. 1756 **Balta-γul** [Балтагул Курткашев] (MIB IV/1, 122); Bashk. 1756 **Balta-γul** [Балтагул Куруккашев] (MIB IV/1, 123); Kkalp. 20th c. **Balta-χan** [Балтахъан] (Bask., Kkalp. 19); Tat. 1738 **Balta-mulla** [Балта мулла] (MIB I, 144); Turk. **Balta-oγlu** (Byz. Turc. 244); Trkm. 20th c. **Palta** [Palta] (Zaj. 1971, 331); Trkm. 20th c. **Palta** [Палта] (TrkmRS 512); *EN:* Nog. 20th c. **Balta-mïrza** [Балта-мырза урувы], (=Balta-mïrza's clan) an Aq-noγay clan in the autonomous region of Cherkessk and the district of Mineralovodsk (Bask., Nog. 134, 142). ✧ 'Axe; war-axe' (Sauvaget 43, Rásonyi, KÖA 86, NTK 86, Adalékok, 129, Anthr. 137, Bask., Fam. 154), cf. Kuman, Crm., Kirg., Tat., Trkm., Turk., etc. *balta* 'das Beil, die Axt' (Radl. IV, 1501), Alt., Hak. *palta* 'das Beil' (Radl. IV, 1171). See also **AQ-BALTA, BEK-BALTA, BÏ-BALTA, DAL-BALTA, SAR-BALTA, SARAN-BALTA, TAM-BALTA, URAZ-BALTA; BALTU, KESER, TEBER, TEŠE.**

BALTAČ Bashk. 1754 **Baltač** [Исень Балтачев] (MIB IV/1, 79); Bashk. 1712 **Baltas** [Балтас Исенев] (MIB III, 88); Bashk. 1716, 1718 **Baltas** [Болтась (Балтас) Аблаев] (MIB III, 144, 173, 175); Bashk. 1732, 1770 **Baltas** [Балтас Агышев] (MIB III, 308, IV/1, 341); Bashk. 18th c. **Baltas** [Алпаут Балтасев (Балтачев, Балтаев)] (MIB V, 276, 283, 355); Bashk. 1751 **Baltas** [Тюкан Балтасев] (MIB IV/1, 45); Bashk. 1764 **Baltas** [Кулуй (Колой) Болтасев (Болтачев)] (MIB IV/1, 286); Bashk. 1798 **Baltas** [Балтасевъ] (PSZRI XXV, 195); Tat.(Sib.) 1609 **Baltaš** [Болташ, Балташ], fem. (Miller, Ist. Sib. II, 209, 210); Bashk. 1707 **Baltaš** [Етдашлай Болташев] (MIB III, 31); Bashk. 1761 **Baltaš** [Иткул Балташев] (MIB IV/1, 227); Kzk. 19th c. **Baltaš** [Балташъ] (AOO 2); Kkalp. 1810 **Baltaš** [Балташ, Балаташ] (MIKk. 109, 110). ✧ 'Little axe' According to

Kusimova and Sattarov the Bashk./Tat. PNs *Baltas / Baltač* mean 'master (craftsman) making axes' and go back to forms *baltasï / baltačï* 'id.'. ⇨ **BALTA** + dim. suff. *-č*.

BALTAY Tat. **Baltay** (H. Z. Koşay: KCsA I, 324); Tat. 1624 **Baltay** [Болтай Дербышевъ] (Pokrovskij 72); Bashk. 1740 **Baltay** [Сююндюк Балтаев] (MIB I, 400); Bashk. 1740 **Baltay** [Сююндюк Болтаев] (MIB I, 393); Bashk. 1746 **Baltay** [Балтай Сабаев] (MIB III, 444); Bashk. 1788 **Baltay** [Болтай Ижбулдин] (MIB V, 223); Kzk. 19th c. **Baltay** [Болтай] (SOV 8); Kzk. 19th c. **Baltay** [Болтай] (SOK 270); Trkm. 19th c. **Paltay** [Зармухаметъ Палтаевъ] (Ščeglov IV, 164). ⇨ **BALTA** + voc.-dim. suff. *-y*.

BALTAQA Kzk. 1722 **Baltaqa-abïz** [Болтака-абыз] (MIB I, 299). ⇨ **BALTA?** + suff. *-qa* or comp. *-aqa* < *-ake*?

BALTAQAY Bashk. 1791 **Baltaqay** [Балтакай Кучуков] (MIB V, 313). ⇨ **BALTA?** + suff. *-qay*.

BALTAR Yak. **Baltar** [Мас Балтар], another name of bogatyr Tulayïm (Pek.).

BALTAS Bashk. 1780 **Baltas** [Кулай (Кулаей) Болтасев] (MIB V, 552). ✧ 'Maker or seller of axes, master, woodcutter' (Kusimova).

BALTÏ Kzk. 19th c. **Baltï-bek** [Балтыбекъ] (AOO 50).

BALTU Uzb. 1709 **Baltu**, majordomo (Haushofmeister) of ʿUbaydullāh, sultan of Bukhara (Buchari 316); Chag. 1567 **Baltu-bahadur** [Балту-бахадур] (Ivanov 147); Kzk. 19th c. **Baltu-bek** [Балтубекъ] (AOO 62); Chag.? **Baltu-sultan** [بالتو سلطان], a sheybanid (Šejb. LI, LXXIX). ✧ 'Axe' cf. Uyg. *baltu* 'секира' (DTS), Chag., East.T. *baltu* = *balta* (Radl. IV, 1503). See also **BALTA, KESER, TEBER, TEŠE.**

BALTUR Uyg. **Baltur** [Baltur] (EUTS).

BALTUTA Yak. 1676-79 **Baltuta** [Балтута Тимиряевъ] (DAI VII, 4-45).

BALUQ see **BALÏQ**

BALWAN see **PALWAN**

BAMSÏ-BEYREK Oghuz/Trkm. 14th c. - 15th c. **Bamsi-beyrek** [Бамси-Бейрек] (DQorq. 22 etc.). ⇨ **BAMSÏ + BEYREK.**

BANAY Bashk. 1709 **Banay** [Банай Маймаков] (MIB I, 264). See also **SÏR-BANAY.**

BANČAQ Uyg. 13th-14th c. **Bančaq-tutuñ / Bačaq-tutuñ?** [Bančaq (Bačaq?) Tutuñ] (Zieme, Mat. II, 93).

BANDÏ **Bandï-χan** [оврагъ Банды-ханъ], a precipice (Barth., Turk. 75).

BANÏ Kzk. **Ban-jan** (<**Banï?** / **Banu?** -**jan**) [Банджанъ] (Sb. Syr-D. IX, 44); Kzk. 19th c. **Banï** [Баны] (SODž. 80).

BANÏ-ČIČEK Oghuz/Trkm. 14th c. - 15th c. **Banï-čiček / Banu-čečäk** [با نى چچك / Banı Čičık, Banı Çiçek / Бану-Чечек], Bay Bijan's? (باى بيجان)

daughter (DQorq./Rossi 116, 117, 120, 121, DQorq. 34 etc.). ✧ 'Girl/woman-flower' cf. Turk. *banu* (P.) 'kadın, bayan' (Özön), Tat. fem. *Banu* (Sattarov), Kzk. fem. *Banu* (Džanuzakov), Bashk. fem. *Banïw* (Kusimova). ⇨ ČEČÄK.

BANU-ČEČÄK see **BANÏ-ČİČEK**

BANÜŠ   Alt. 19th-20th c. **Banüš** (OjrRS 207). ✧ Vanyusha, Ivan (R.) (OjrRS 207).

BAÑA   Yak. **Baña** [Баӊа], a shaman (Pek.).

BAPA   Kzk. 19th c.? **Bapa** [Солтабай Бопинъ] (?); Kzk. **Bapa / Bopa**? [Бопа] (Konšin, Mat. V, 43); Kzk. 19th c. **Bapa / Bopa**? [Бопина] (SOK 182); Kzk. 19th c. **Bapa / Bopa** [Бопина] (SOV 134); Kzk. **Bopo** [Sultan Bopo / Бопо төрö] (Proben III, 22 /27/). ✧ 'Truthfulness, honesty; reliability, faithfulness' cf. Tat. PN *Wafa* (Sattarov), Kzk. PN *Bapa / Bafa* (Žanuzakov-Esbaeva), (<Ar.) PN *Wafai / Wafi* (Ahmed).

BAPAY   Kzk. 19th c. **Bapay** [Бапай] (AOA 142); Kzk. 1834 **Bapay / Bopoy**? [Бопой Абулфеизовъ], a Sultan (Konšin, Mat. V, 42). ⇨ **BAPA?** + dim. suff. *-y*.

BAPİŠ   Kzk. 19th c. **Bapiš** [Бапишъ] (Grod., Pril. 165).

BAR   **Bar-bay** [Барбай] (ZIRGOÊtn. XXXIV, 141); Kzk. 19th c. **Bar-bay** [Барбай] (SOK 306); Kzk. 19th c. **Bar-biy** [Барбий] (AOO 50); Hak. 19th-20th c. **Par-öl** [Пароол] (HRS 350). ✧ 'Rich; He has got (sg); there is' cf. Kzk. *bar* 'reich' (Radl. IV, 1472). See also **KÜTİ-BAR, QUTÏ-BAR, MAYZ-BAR, SURÏ-BAR.**

BAR-BOL   Kzk. 19th c. **Bar-bol** [Барболъ] (SOK 274); Uzb. 20th c. **Bâr-bol** [Борбўл] (Begmatov 1984, 201). ✧ 'Be/become rich' (Rásonyi, Imp. 238). ⇨ **BAR + BOL.** See also **BAY-BOL, BEK-BOL, BÏY-BOL.**

BAR-BOLSÏN   Uzb. 20th c. **Bar-bolsïn** [Борбўлсин] (Begmatov 1984, 201); Kzk.? 1551 **Bar-bolsun** [Барболсун Улан] (PSRL XIII, 166). ✧ 'Let him be/become rich'. ⇨ **BAR + BOLSÏN.**

BAR-BOLSUN see **BAR-BOLSÏN**

BARABAŠ   Alt. 19th-20th c. **Barabaš / Bara-baš**? [Барабаш] (OjrRS 207).

BARAČUQ see **BARČUQ**

BARAJUQ see **BARČUQ**

BARAΓAN   Mo.? **Baraγan** [Бараган] (RaD I/1, 96).

BARAY   Kipch.? 1612 **Baray** [Барай Кутумовъ мурза Алѣевичъ / Барай мурза Алѣевичъ Кутумовъ] (DAI I, 303-304). ✧ 'New Moon, Beginning of the Month' (Sattarov) (<Ar.).

BARAKAY   Chuv. 18th-19th c. **Barakay** [Баракай] (Magn. 33).

BARAQ   Kuman 1521 **Baraq** [Demetrius Barag], a Kuman from Asszonyszállás, Hungary (Gyárfás III, 750); Selj. 12th c. **Baraq** [براق] (Usāma 11); Selj. 13th c. **Baraq** [براق], retainer ot the Gürqan, then governor of Kirman till the Mongol invasion (Nasawī 26, 95); Tat.(GH) 1280 **Baraq** [Παράχ], a christened Tatar woman, died in about 1280 (Byz. Turc. 245); Tat.(GH) 1308 **Baraq** [Παράχ], a christened Tatar woman, died in 1308 (Byz. Turc. 245); Turk. 15th c. **Baraq**, a chieftain (Byz. Turc. 86); Turk. 16th c. **Baraq**, a commander of the Ottoman fleet (Byz. Turc. 86); Turk. 1570 **Baraq** [Uruǰ bin Baraq], an Ottoman in Hungary (Dávid); Tat. 1606 **Baraq** [Барак] (MIB I, 154); Tat.(Sib.)? 1605 **Baraq** [Барак] (Miller, Ist. Sib. II, 190); Bashk. 1754, 1761 **Baraq** [Барак Сююндюковъ] (MIB IV/1, 90, IV/1, 215); Bashk. 1776, 1778 **Baraq** [Барак Аблаев], a captain (MIB V, 33, 34, 79); Kzk. 1743 **Baraq** [Баракъ], a Kazak sultan of the Middle Horde (Orta Žüz) (Dobrosm., Turg. 44, MIT II, 335); Kzk. 18th c. - 19th c. **Baraq** [Барак] (Tynyšp. 68, 75); Kzk. 1830 **Baraq** [Шигай Бараковъ] (Konšin, Mat. V, 55); Kzk. 19th c. **Baraq** [Баракъ] (AOP 30, 58); Kzk. 19th c. **Baraq** [Баракъ] (AOK 70, 102, 122); Kzk. 19th c. **Baraq** [Баракъ] (SKSO VIII, 223); Kkalp. 20th c. **Baraq** [Баракъ] (Bask., Kkalp. 399); Oghuz 991 **Baraq / Baraχ** [بارۀ:غلام] (Qalānisi 35); Kzk. 19th c. **Baraq-bay** [Баракбай] (AOA 82); Kzk. 1786 **Baraq-batïr** [Барак батыр] (MIK IV, 73, 109); Turk. 1474 **Baraq-beg** [براق بك], in an inscription of Amasya (Uzunçarş., Küt. I, 120); Turk. 1307/08 **Baraq-čelebi**, a dervish (Wittek, Gag.18, Köprülü: Anad. İsl. II, 1922, 392); Chag. 1538/39 **Baraq-χan** [براق خان / Барак-хан], a Sheybanid, the ruler of Tashkent (Šejb. LI, LXXVIII, MIT II, 59, 68); Khorezm. 13th c. **Baraq-qan**, a Chagatayid ruler (1266-1271) (Tar. Rashidi 3, 299, Togan, UTT 63); Kirg. 1748, 1751 **Baraq-saltan** [Барак салтан], a sultan (MIKk. 220, 223); *EN:* Trkm. 1690 **Baraq** [براق], a community (cemaat) (Refik, Anad. 83); Trkm. 20th c. **Baraq** [Barak türkmenleri], an ethnic group in the vilayet of Gaziantep, Turkey (Özbaş 4, 7 etc.); Nog. 20th c. **Baraq-uruw** [Баракъ урув], a Qara-noγay clan (Bask., Nog. 136); *TN:* Turk. 20th c. **Baraq** [Barak], a village in the province of Ankara, Turkey (TMİB 83); Turk. 20th c. **Baraq** [Barak], the other (old) name of the village Babapınar in the province of Giresun, Turkey (TMİB 385); Crm. **Baraq**, a place north of Kefe (Caffa) (Jervis IX). ✧ 'Having long and thick hair' cf. Kzk., Turk. *baraq* 'mit dichten (langen) Haaren', (Kzk.) 'ein Hund mit krausem Haare' (Radl. IV, 1477), see also Rásonyi, KÖA 86-87, Bas. 11, 15, Anthr. 137. See also **AQ-BARAQ, BAY-BARAQ, İT-BARAQ, QAL-BARAQ, QUL-BARAQ, QOÑUR-BARAQ, QUTLUQ-BARAQ.**

BARAQ-SÏÑΓUR   Uyg. **Baraq-sïñγur** [Barak Sïngγur], Yöläk's youngest son, aged 5 (Zieme, Mat. I, 80). ✧ 'Long-thick-haired dog - ?'. ⇨ **BARAQ.**

BARAQAN   Hak.(Sag.) **Baraqan** [Бараканъ], a bogatyr (hero) (Kostrov 237).

BARAQAT see **BEREKET**

BARAMAY Alt. 19th-20th c. **Baramay** [Барамай] (OjrRS 207).

BARAMAQ see **BARAMÏQ**

BARAMÏQ Kzk. 18th c. - 19th c. **Baramïq** [Барамык] (Tynyšp. 73); Kuman 1354 **Baramuq / Baramaq?** [Baramuk (Baramak) filius Kabak], a man of Kuman origin in Hungary (Gyárfás III, 489, 494, 706). ✧ 'Strengthening, progress'? cf. *barı-* 'korumak, kuvvetlenmek, gelişmek, kökleşmek' (Rásonyi, KÖA 87, Anthr. 137). + suff. *-mïq?*

BARAMUQ see **BARAMÏQ**

BARAN Nog. 20th c. **Baram-bay** < **Baran-bay** [Барамбай Асан увлы], one of Baskakov's informants from the settlement Terekli-mektep (Bask., Nog. 144); Bashk. 1778 **Baran-bay** [Баранбай] (MIB V, 79). ✧ 'Dark (colour of a horse)'? cf. Kzk. *baran* 'dunkelfarben (von Pferden)' (Radl. IV, 1477). See also **QAL-BARAN**.

BARANKÏY Bashk. 1734 **Barankiy?** [Баранкий] (Vel.-Zern., Bašk. 10).

BARAŠ Maml. 1463 **Baraš** [برش الجانبكى] (Ibn Taghrīb. VIII, 479); Tat.(Lit.) 1620 **Baraš** [Афендей Барашевичъ], a prince (Lit. Tat. 293); Tat.(Lit.) 1695 **Baraš** [Baraszu Sudzdziudu (dative form)], an interpreter (Lit. Tat. 497); Tat. 17th c.-18th c. **Baraš** [Išej Barašev], a prince in the country of Mordva (Smyrnov 279); Tat.(Sib.)? 1605 **Baraš** [Барашев Бекбаклуй] (Miller, Ist. Sib. II, 190, 191); Kzk. 1823 **Baraš** [Бараш] (MIK IV, 443). ⇨ **BARÏŠ?**

BARAT Trkm. 1688 **Barat** [Барат], from the Afšar tribe, commander of the fortification Bagvade (MIT II, 120); Kzk. 19th c. **Barat** [Баратъ Юнусовъ] (SKSO VIII, 207); Kzk. 19th c. **Barat-bay** [Маракбай Баратбай] (Grod., Pril. 145); Uzb. 19th c. **Barat-bay** [Хусеинъ Баратбаевъ] (SKSO II, 14); Uzb. 19th c. **Barat-bek** [Баратбекъ Алимбаевъ] (SKSO II, 14); Uzb. 1860 **Barat-bek**, from Kokand (Nalivkin-Dozon 235-37); Uzb. 1826 **Barat-Jan** [براتجان شيرجنك], from Bukhara (Vel.-Zern., Haïder 280-82); Kzk. 19th c. **Barat-pek** [Баратпекъ] (SOK 234).

BARĀ Yak. **Barā-χan-toyon** [Бара], a spirit (Pek.).

BARĀLYÏN Yak. **Barālyïn** [Кытыг(ы)рас Баралйын], a bogatyr (hero) (Pek.).

BARĀNČA Yak. **Barānča / Barānčï / Barāččï** [Кытыг(ы)рас Баранча, Кытыг(ы)рас Баранчы, Кытыг(ы)рас Бараччы] (Pek.). ✧ 'Who goes fast; briskly going' (Pek.).

BARČA Uyg. 12th c. - 14th c. **Barča-toyïn** [barča toyïn / Barça Toyın] (Radl., USp. 48, DTS, EUTS); Kkalp. **Parša-gül**, fem. (Baskakov: OSA 139). ✧ 'All, Whole' (Blagova 1997, 705).

BARČA-TOГMÏŠ Uyg. 12th c.-14th c. **Barča-toγmïš** [Barča (Parča) Toqmïš, Barča toγmïš / Barça Toğmış] (Radl., USp. 48-49, DTS, EUTS). ✧ 'Related-to-all, Relation of all' (Blagova 1997, 705). ⇨ **TOГMÏŠ**.

BARČA-TURMÏŠ Uyg. 12th c.-14th c. **Barča-turmïš** [barča turmïš / Barça Turmış] (Radl., USp. 16-17, DTS, EUTS). ✧ 'All were born' (Blagova 1997, 705). ⇨ **TURMÏŠ**.

BARČÏLA Yak. **Barčïla** [Барчыла] (Pek.).

BARČÏN-SALOR Oghuz/Trkm. 13th c. **Barčïn-salor** [بارجين سالور / Барчын-Салор], Mamïš-bek's (Qarmïš-bay's son's) wife (Abulg./Kon. 1445). ✧ 'Silk-Salor'? cf. Karakh. *barčïn* 'шелковая материя' (DTS). ⇨ **SALÏR**.

BARČUQ Uyg. 13th c. **Barčuq / Baračuq / BaraJuq?** [بارجوق / Barcsuk-art-tigin / Бараджук], ïduq-qut (ruler) of the Uyghurs in Chinggis' times (Juwaynī. I, 32, 34, 63, RaD/Ber. I, 127, RaD I/1, 147, Ligeti, MTT, p. 176). ✧ I. 'Little being/existent'; II. 'Barčuq (town)' (DTS); III. 'Little panther/tiger' <*barsčuq* (Pelliot: T'oung pao 1930, 55; Grousset: L'emp. mo. 485). ⇨ **BAR / BARS?** + dim. suff. *-čuq*.

BARDAM Yak. **Bardam** [Бардам Басылаi (Дерзкий Василий)] (Pek.). ✧ 'Impudent' (Pek.).

BARDAÑ Alt. 19th-20th c. **Bardañ** (OjrRS 207).

BARDAŠ Kzk.? 19th c. **Bardaš** [Бардашев], a writer of articles (AUK 164).

BARDÏ see **BARLÏ**

BARDÏQ see **BARLÏQ**

BARGÏL Kzk. 19th c. **Bargil-bek / Barγïl-bek?** [Баргилбекъ] (SOK 122). ✧ 'Go!' (Rásonyi, Imp. 237).

BARГÏYA see **XARA-BARГÏYA**

BARIS Bashk. 1715 **Baris** [Бекмет Барисов] (MIB III, 123). ✧ 'Baris (=soothsayer, clever)' (Ar.) (Kusimova).

BARÏ Kzk. 19th c. **Barï-bay** [Барыбай] (SOK 104); Kzk. 19th c. **Barï-bay** [Барыбай] (SODž. 78). ✧ Baari (Ar.) 'originator' (Ahmed), one of God's epithets. Cf. also Bashk. PN *Bariy* 'барлыкка килтереүсе, яратыусы' (Kusimova), Tat. PNs *Bariy / Bari* 'id.' (Sattarov).

BARÏQ Kzk. 19th c. **Barïq** [Барыкъ] (SOK 86); Kzk. 19th c. **Barïq / Barik?** [Барикъ] (SOK 146). ✧ 'Substance, fortune, possession; occupation'? cf. Chag. *baruq* 'id.' (Radl. IV, 1482).

BARÏLĀN Yak. **Barïlān** [Барылан] (Pek.). ✧ Varlaam (R.).

BARÏM Khorezm.? 1296 **Barïm** [باريم], mentioned at the time of the revolt led by Arslan-oγul (RaD/Jahn 100); Kzk. 19th c. **Barïm-bek** [Баримбекъ] (SOK 124). ✧ 'Substance, fortune, possession' cf. Türk *barïm* 'die Habe, der Besitz' (Radl. IV, 1481).

BARÏN Bashk. 1740 **Barïn-γul** [Барынгулъ Сабангуловъ] (PSZRI XI, 134).

BARÏS see **BARS**

BARÏSMAZ **Barïsmas-χan** [Барысмас-хан] (RaD

I/2, 208). ✧ 'Won't go together' cf. Kzk. *bariš-* 'zusammen gehen, zusammen besprechen' (Radl. IV, 1479) + neg. aor. suff. -*maz*.

BARÏŠ Crm. 1634 **Barïš-mirza** [بارش ميرزا] (Vel.-Zern., Crim. 144); *TN:* Tat. 18th. **Baryševa (<Barïš)** [Барышева], a village in the district of Tetyushinsk (Korsakov 329). ✧ 'Peace, agreement, reconciliation' cf. Crm., Turk. *bariš* 'id.' (Radl. IV, 1480). See also **BAY-BARÏŠ**.

BARYAM see **BAYRAM**

BARQ-TURMÏŠ Uyg. 12th c. - 14th c. **Barq-turmïš** [barq turmïš] (DTS). ✧ 'The house has remained' (Bese 22), cf. Türk *barq* 'здание, сооружение' (DTS). ⇨ **BARQ + TURMÏŠ.**

BARQA Tat.(Mish.) 1755 **Barqa** [Таты Баркин] (MIB IV/1, 93); Kzk. 19th c. **Barqa** [Барка] (Potanin II, 3); Kzk. 19th c. **Barqa-bay** [Баркабай] (SOK 28); Kzk. 1820 **Barqa-batïr** [Барка батырЪ], chief of the Altïn tribe (Sib. Vest. IX, 112). ⇨ **BAR?** + suff. -*qa*.

BARQUDAY Bashk. / Tat.? 1658 **Barquday** [Ибраимка БаркудаевЪ] (AI IV, 277). ✧ ? (<Mo.?).

BARQUQ Maml. 1386, 1397 **Barqūq** [ابو سعيد برقوق السلطان الملك الظاهر / Μπάρχου], a Mamluk Sultan (1382-1398) (Berchem, Jér. I, 300, Berchem 70, Byz. Turc., 205); Maml. 1438/39 **Barqūq** [برقوق التركى اليمنى] (Ibn Taghrīb. VII, 263); Maml. 1461 **Barqūq** [برقوق الناصرى] (Ibn Taghrīb. VII, 650, 706, Iyās II, 109, 110, 142); Maml. 1468/69 **Barqūq** [برقوق شاد الشرانجانه (الشرأبخاناه؟)] (Iyās II, 102); Maml. 1472/73 **Barqūq** [برقوق نايب الشام], regent of Tripolis (Sham), died in 1473 (Iyās II, 136, 138, Weil, Chalif. II, 335-36, Mayer 103); Maml. 1481 **Barqūq** [برقوق الساقى الاينالى] (Iyās II, 297, 293, 347) ✧ 'Shepherd' Its etymon is not Ar. *barqūq* 'apricot' as it seems, but - after Taghribirdī - it is an arabicized form of the Circassian *mallī khūq*, which means 'shepherd' (Schimmel p. 71).

BARLÏ Kzk. 18th c. - 19th c. **Bardï-bek** [Бардыбек] (Tynyšp. 71); Kzk. 18th c. - 19th c. **Barlï-bay** [Барлыбай] (Tynyšp. 71, 73); Kzk. **Barlï-bay-batïr** [Барлыбай-батырЪ] (Protok. Turk. 151); Kzk. 19th c. **Pardï-bay** [Парды-бай] (SKSO IV, otd. II, 32). ✧ 'Rich, wealthy' cf. Kuman *barli* 'reich' (Radl. IV, 1485), Bashk. *barli* 'богатый, состоятельный, имущий' (BRS/Uraksin).

BARLÏQ Bashk. 1740 **Bardïq** [Байрамгул Бардыков] (MIB I, 404); Kzk.? 19th c. **Barlïq** [Барлык], a writer of articles (AUK); Kkalp. 20th c. **Barlïq-bay** [Барлыкбай] (KkRS 773). ✧ 'Richness, wealth' cf. Kzk., Tat. *barliq* 'das Sein; der Reichtum, die Wohlhabenheit' (Radl. IV, 1485), Bashk. *barliq* 'достаток, богатство' (BRS/Uraksin).

BARMA Khorezm.? **Barma** [Барма] (RaD II, 154).

BARMAQ Kzk. 1768/69 **Barmaq-biy** [Бармак-бий] (MIT II, 340). ✧ 'Finger' cf. Kzk. *barmak* 'палец' (KzRS). See also **ALTÏ-PARMAQ, QOŠ-BARMAQ**.

BARMAQLÏΓ Uyg. **Barmaqlïγ** [Barmaklıg] (EUTS).

BARMAQLÏΓ-JOSUN-BİLLİG Oghuz 13th c. **Barmaqlïγ-josun-billig** [Barmaklığ Çosun Billiğ / barmaqlïγ čosun billig], in the Oghuz legend (Oğuz K. Dest. 27, DTS). ⇨ **BARMAQLÏΓ**.

BARMEN Kzk. 19th c. **Barmen-bay** [Барменбай] (AOA 50); Kzk. 19th c. **Barmen-bay** [Барменбай] (SOK 100).

BARMÏŠ Kzk. 19th c. **Barmïš** [БармешЪ] (SODž. 96).

BARPÏ Kirg. **Barpï** [Барпы] (Jud. 757); NUyg. **Parpï-bay** [Parpi Baj] (Hedin II, 242, 250).

BARS Balk. **Barïs-biy / Baris-biy?** [БаресбiевЪ], family name of a Balkar prince (tau-biy) (Karaulov 52); Türk? 870 **Bars** [على بن بارس] (Tabarī, Annal. III, 1820); Uyg. **Bars**, „the glory of the empire" (il-ügäsi) (Le Coq, Man. III, 43); Crm. 1590 **Bars** [بارس] (Vel.-Zern., Crim. 8); Chuv. 18th-19th c. **Bars** [БарсЪ] (Magn. 33); Türk / Karakh. 906 **Bars** [السامانى بارس الكبير حاجى اسما عيل] (Ibn al-Athīr/Tornb. VII, 365, VIII, 5, 8, 42); Türk / Karakh. 922 **Bars** [بارس], Qara-tegin's servant (Ibn al-Athīr/Tornb. VIII, 91, 92, 95); Maml. **Bars-bay** [ابو النصر برسباى], a sultan (Amari 166); Maml. 1409/10 **Bars-bay** [برسباى الططائى] (Ibn Taghrīb. VI, 238); Maml. 1421, 1438/39 **Bars-bay** [برسباى الحمزاوى النصرى] (Ibn Taghrīb. VI, 513, VII, 62, 65, 79); Maml. 1423, 1435/36 **Bars-bay** [السلطان الملك الاشرف برسباى / Απουνασερ Πουρησπ / Al-Aschraf Saifaddin Barsbai], a sultan of the Mamluks (1422-1438) (Byz. Turc., Uzunçarş., Anad. 43, Sobernh. I, 62, Berchem, Jér. II, 139, Sauvaget: BEO II, 12, 16, Sauvaget 41); Maml. 1438/39 **Bars-bay** [حال يوسف بن برسباى بيبيرس الاشرفى] (Ibn Taghrīb. VII, 88, 466, 483); Maml. 1442 **Bars-bay** [برسباى النا صرى الظاهرى], governor of Tripolis (Sobernh. I, 66); Maml. 15th c. **Bars-bay** [بر سباى الشرفى], İnal Sultan's āmir-i aχūr (Master of the Horse), died in 1473 (Iyās II, 129, 132, Ibn Taghrīb. VII, 547, Mayer 104); Maml. 15th c. **Bars-bay** [برسباى] (Ibn Taghrīb. 14); Maml. 15th c.? **Bars-bay** [الملك الاشرف أبو النصر برسباى الدقماقى الظا هرى], Sultan al-Ashrāf Bars-bay (1422-38) (Iyās I, 72, 309, II, 12-25, 111, 222, 387, III, 8, 35, 55, 302, Ibn Taghrīb. VI, 96, 132, VII, 138, 334, Weil, Chalif. II, 160-213, EI I, 694); Maml. 1450, 1454 **Bars-bay** [برسباى الا ينالى] (Ibn Taghrīb. 80, 205); Maml. 1452/53, 1463 **Bars-bay** [برسباى البجاسى], governor of Damascus in 1463 (Iyās II, 40, 46, 63, Ibn Taghrīb. VII, 149, 239, Weil, Chalif. II, 313 etc.); Maml. 1453 **Bars-bay** [برسباى الموئدى] (Iyās II, 42, 60, Ibn Taghrīb. VII, 224, 375); Maml.

1459 **Bars-bay** [برسباى الخاصكى] (Ibn Taghrīb. VII, 518, 723); Maml. 1460 **Bars-bay** [برسباى الاشرفى] (Ibn Taghrīb. VII, 547, 697); Maml. 1463 **Bars-bay** [برسباى قرا الظا هرى] (Ibn Taghrīb. 455, 605 etc.); Maml. 1467/68, 1474/75 **Bars-bay** [الخازندار يونس برسباى], a treasurer (Iyās II, 156, III, 252, Ibn Taghrīb. VII, 833); Maml. 1468 **Bars-bay** [برسباى قرا المحمدى], a treasurer (Iyās II, 124, 195, 259, Ibn Taghrīb. VII, 706 etc., Weil, Chalif. II, 320, 347); Maml. 1468/69 **Bars-bay** [اميراخور ثانى برسباى], Master of the Horse (title) (Iyās II, 111); Maml. 1471/72 **Bars-bay** [برسباى الشرفى] (Iyās II, 129, 147); Maml. 1477 **Bars-bay** [كاشف الوجه القبلى برسباى] (Iyās II, 180); Maml. 1484 **Bars-bay** [برسباى العلائى] (Iyās II, 2224, 255, III, 22-25); Maml. 1485 **Bars-bay** [برسباى تمربغا الظاهرى حشيش] (Iyās II, 228); Maml. 1492/93 **Bars-bay** [امير جندار برسباى], chief of the guards (Iyās II, 279); Maml. 1493/94 **Bars-bay** [برسباى الصغير] (Iyās II, 282); Maml. 1494/95 **Bars-bay** [برسباى الثور الشريفى] (Iyās II, 290); Maml. 1496/97 **Bars-bay** [برسباى لسلحدار], sword-bearer of the sultan (a title) (Iyās II, 306, 336); Maml. 1497/98 **Bars-bay** [برسباى الاشتر], an emir (Iyās II, 337); Maml. 1516 **Bars-bay** [برسباى الفيل] (Iyās III, 18); Maml. 1520 **Bars-bay** [برسباى اليو سفى] (Iyās II, 229, 326); Maml. 1521 **Bars-bay** [الصحبه] (Iyās III, 248); Maml. 1522 **Bars-bay** [برسباى استادار], an emir (Iyās III, 286, 315); Maml. 1529 **Bars-bay** [برسباى مملوك ودوادار ملك لامرا] (Iyās III, 191, 205, 228); Türk 732 **Bars-beg** [bars beg / Bars bäg] (DTS, ETY I, 38); Khazar 730 **Bars-bek** [Pᶜarsbitᶜ / Barsbek], mother of a qaɣan (Golden 205); Türk 8th c. **Bars-qan-sañun** [bars qan saŋun / Bars qan Sañun] (Runic Mss. 186, 188, DTS, ETY II, 65); Türk **Bars-qan-tudun** [Barsqan /tu/dun [i]šbar[a] kül irkin], a chieftain in the West (Ligeti, R. tör. nev. II-III, 41); Türk 8th c. **Bars-uruñu** [bars uruŋu / Bars Uruñu] (Runic Mss. 187, 189, DTS, ETY II, 66); Chuv. 18th-19th c. **Paris / Parïs** [Парисъ] (Magn. 65); Crm. 17th c.-18th c. **Pars-aɣa** [پارشاغا] (Vel.-Zern., Crim. 826); Crm. 1638 **Pars-mirza** [پارس ميرزا] (Vel.-Zern., Crim. 227). ✧ I. 'Cheetah, hunting panther, ounce; lynx' cf. Ligeti, R. tör. nev. II-III:30, cf. also Németh, HMK 133; *Bars-bay* 'Tiger-Rich' (Sauvaget 41), cf. Kzk., Tat. *barïs* 'der Bars, der Tiger' (Radl. IV, 1479), Türk, Trkm., Turk., Uzb. *bars* 'der Panther, der Tiger, der Leopard', (East.T.) 'der Luchs' (Radl. IV, 1487); II. 'Year of the panther; Born in the year of panther' cf. Rásonyi, Nombre 48. Different interpretations: *Bars-beg* 'Tiger-Prince' (Blagova 1997, 705), *Bars-qan*

'Panther-Khan', 'Tiger-Ruler' (Blagova 1997, 706), *Bars-uruñu* 'Tiger-Flag' (Blagova 1997, 713). See also **AQ-BARS, AY-BARS, AL-BARS, ALTÏ-BARS, AŠ-PARS, BAY-BARS, BEG-BARS, BİL-BARS, BÖRİ-BARS, EL-BARS, EŠ-BARS, ELČİ-ČUR-KÜČ-BARS, İM-BARS, İN-BARS, ÏNAL-BARS, İR-BARS, YAN-BARS, YAŠ-PARS, YOL-BARS, KÄNČÄK-BARS, KİL-BARS, KÜČ-BARS, KÜLÜG-BARS, QAL-BARS, QUL-BARS, QUMAR-BARS, QUTADMÏŠ-BARS, QUTLUƔ-BARS, MEŇGÜ-BARS, OƔUL-BARS, TAY-BARS, TAŠ-SVİT-BARS, TİN-BARS, TOY-BARS, TON-BARÏS, ZEŇİ-PARS.**

BARS-BUQA Maml. 14th c. **Bars-boɣa** [بَرسبُغا] (Sauvaget 41); Uyg. 12th c. - 14th c. **Bars-buɣa** [bars buɣa] (DTS); Maml. 1325 **Bars-buɣa** [سيف الدين برسبغا] (Zetterst. 148, 222); Maml. 1400/01 **Bars-buɣa** [برسبغا] (Iyās I, 330); Maml. 1401/02 **Bars-buɣa** [برسبغا الد وادار] (Ibn Taghrīb. VI, 59, 87, 96); Uyg. **Bars-buqa** [Bars buka] (EUTS); Uyg. 12th - 14th c. **Bars-buqa** (Le Coq, Urkunden 1918, 456, 457); Uyg. 12th c.-14th c. **Bars-buqa** (Radl., USp. 15-16). ✧ 'Tiger-bull' (Blagova 1997, 706). ⇨ **BARS + BUQA.**

BARS-TOƔAN Selj. 1002 **Bars-tuɣan / Bars-toɣan?** [بارسطغان ابو المظفر] (Hil. Sābī 445); Selj. 1030 **Bars-tuɣan / Bars-toɣan?** [بارس طغان حاجب احجاب] (Ibn al-Athīr/Tornb. IX, 286, 309); Selj. 1068 **Bars-tuɣan / Bars-toɣan?** [بارز طغان قطب الدوله والى دمشق], governor of Damascus (Ibn Taghrīb. II, 240); Selj. 1069 **Bars-tuɣan / Bars-toɣan?** [بارزطغان قطب الدين] (Qalānisi 94). ✧ 'Panther-falcon' (Németh, HMK 133). ⇨ **BARS + TOƔAN.**

BARS-TUƔAN see BARS-TOƔAN

BARSA Turk. 1466 **Barsa-ɣatun**, fem. (Gökb., Ed. 343). ✧ I. Derived from *Bars* 'Panther' (Erol II); II. 'Pied goat'? cf. Turk. dial. *barza* 'vücudunun yarısı beyaz, yarısı kara keçi' (DS). ⇨ **BARS + suff. -a.**

BARSA-KİLMEZ Tat.(Tob.) **Barsa-kilmes** [Barsa Kilmäs], a ruler (Radl. IV, 460). ✧ 'If he goes (away)?-won't come (back)'. ⇨ **BARSA.**

BARSAQ Chuv. 18th-19th c. **Barsak** [Барсакъ] (Magn. 33).

BARSƔAN Karakh. 11th c. **Barsɣan** [barsɣan / Barsgan] (DTS, MK/Atalay 832). ✧ A Turkic tribe and town (DTS).

BARSUQ see BORSUQ

BARŠİN Kzk. 19th c. **Baršïn** [Баршинъ Тангбаевъ] (Pam. kn. Turg. 78); *TN:* Kzk. **Baršïn** [Баршын], a village (Kojčubaev 57). ✧ 'Middle-aged person' cf. Kzk. *baršın* 'Yaşı ortayı geçmiş kimse' (KzTS). See also **GÜL-BARŠİN.**

BARŠUƔA Bashk. 1737 **Baršuɣa** [Баршуга] (MIB I,

314).

BARUČÏ Uyg. **Baruči** [Baruçı] (EUTS).

BARUDİ? Tat. 19th c. **Barudi** [Galimğan [Galimjan] Barudi] (Mende 67, 99, 102, 106, 116, 122, 137).

BARUNČU Uyg. 12th c. - 14th c. **Barunču** [barunču] (DTS).

BARUR Chag. 1567 **Barur** [Барур Хафиз] (Ivanov 163).

BARZANAY Bashk. 1751 **Barzanay** [Барзанай (Борсанай) Тюнекаев] (MIB IV/1, 52).

BAS I. see **BAŠ**

BAS II. Yürük 1543 **Bas** (Gökb., Rum. 103, 192, 197). ✧ 'Oppress / crush / conquer (the enemy)!', a frequent part of compound imperative names; cf. Türk, Chag., Kuman, Az., Crm., Kzk., Tat., Trkm., Turk., etc. *bas-* 'drücken, unterdrücken, beherrschen, besiegen' (Radl. IV, 1525), cf. also Rásonyi, Bas.; Rásonyi, Imp. 237. See also **İZ-BAS, QAWM-BAS?, QOL-BAS, MAY-BAS(?), OT-BAS, TAW-BAS.**

BAS-KİREY Chuv. 18th-19th c. **Bas-kirey** [Баскирей] (Magn. 33). ⇨ **BARS?** + **KERÄY.**

BASA Uyg. 13th-14th c. **Basa** (Zieme, Mat. III, 268); Yürük 1543 **Basa** [باصا], from the Yürüks of Kocacık, Turkey (Gökb., Rum. 103); Uyg. 13th-14th c. **Basa-qurtɣa**, Basa Qurtɣa (Zieme, Mat. II,); 1591 **Basa-murza** [Баса мурза] (AI I, 444). ⇨ **BAS II.** See also **JAN-BASA.**

BASA-QAYMÏŠ Uyg. 13th-14th c. **Basa-qaymïš / Basar-qaymïš?** [Basa[r] Qaimïš] (Zieme, Mat. III, 268 (after Cleaves)). ⇨ **BASA + QAYMÏŠ.**

BASA-TEMİR Uyg. 12th c.-14th c. **Basa-temir** [Basa Tämir] (Radl., USp. 215, 258, DTS, EUTS). ✧ 'After-Iron' (Blagova 1997, 704), 'Back/rear Iron' cf. Uyg. *basa* 'Arka' (EUTS), *basa* 'после, следом' (DTS). ⇨ **BASA + TEMİR.**

BASA-TOΓRÏL Uyg. 12th c. - 14th c. **Basa-toɣrïl** [Bäsä Toɣrïl / basa toɣrïl] (Radl., USp. 204-205, 246-247, DTS). ✧ 'After-Falcon' (Blagova 1997, 704, 707). ⇨ **BASA + TOΓRÏL.**

BASAY Kzk. 19th c. **Basay** [Басай] (SOK 94). ⇨ **BAS I.?** + dim. suff. *-ay / -y?*

BASAL Yürük 1543 **Basal** [باصال], from the Yürüks of Kocacık, Turkey (Gökb., Rum. 103, 183, 184); Kzk. 19th c. **Basal-bay** [Басалбай] (SOV 124).

BASALAY Crm. 1538 **Basalay** [Басалай] (PSRL XIII, 119).

BASAMAN Uyg. **Basaman** [basaman], king of the Yakša-demons, protector of the northern countries (DTS). ✧ Vaisravana (<Chin. <Skr.).

BASAMNYÏLĀN Yak. **Basamnyïlān** [Басамнйылан] (Pek.). ⇨ **BASÏMNYÏLĀN.**

BASAN Uyg. 12th c.-14th c. **Basan** [basan / Basan] (Radl., USp. 130-31, DTS, EUTS); Kzk. 1822 **Basan** [Басановъ] (TOUAK XXIV, 121); Kzk. 1846 **Basan** [Басан Алтынбаев], a biy (rich, noble man) (MKOP 156); Kzk. 19th c. **Basan** [Басанъ] (SOK 100); Kzk. 19th c. **Basan** [Басанов], a writer of articles (AUK 164); **Basan? / Yasan?** [الموصل شحنه اسمه باسان], „Praetor Mauselae (Abulfar. 541); Kzk. 19th c. **Basan-bay** [Кулкаръ Басанбаевъ] (Grod., Pril. 38); Uyg. 13th c. **Basan-yalavač** [basan jalavač] (DTS); Kzk. 19th c. **Pasanov (<Basanov)** [Пасановъ] (AOO 30). ✧ I. 'Funeral/burial feast' cf. Karakh. *basan* 'поминки, обрядовое угощение после похорон' (DTS); II. 'Presser; who attacks (the enemy), who defeats (the enemy), taking steps' (Bese 13), cf. *bas-* 'drücken, pressen; unterdrücken, beherrschen, besiegen' (Radl. IV, 1524). See also **AQ-BAZAN, İL-BASAN, YAΓÏ-BASAN, SEYREK-BASAN.**

BASAR **Basar** [Басар], Sasïq's son (RaD II, 76); Maml. 1309 **Basar** [الملوك سيف الدين بثار] (Dawād. 178, 179); Kuman? **Basar-aba** [Basarab] (SRH II, 222); Kuman? 1340 **Basar-aba** [Bazarad], a Vlach chief („voyvoda") (SRH I, 496 etc., II, 284). ✧ 'He who presses; who will overcome (his enemies)' cf. *bas-* 'drücken, pressen; unterdrücken, beherrschen, besiegen' (Radl. IV, 1524), cf. also Rásonyi, Bas. See also **BASAN; AL-BASAR, AT-BASAR, BOQ-BASAR, İL-BASAR, İZ-BASAR, YAW-BASAR, YOL-BASAR, KELDİ-BOQ-BASAR, KİY-BASAR, QUYAN-BASAR, MAY-BASAR, ORÏN-BÂSAR, OT-BASAR, SABÏQ-BASAR, TAY-BASAR, TOQ-PASAR, UL-BASAR.**

BASARAY Chuv. 18th-19th c. **Basaray** [Басарай] (Magn. 33); Bashk. 1709 **Basaray** [Басарей] (MIB I, 263). ✧ 'Seeing; keen/sharp-sighted' cf. Tat. PN *Basarïy* (Sattarov).

BASAT see **BİSAT**

BASBAQ Kzk. 19th c. **Basbaq** [Басбакъ Тузубаевъ] (Grod., Pril. 153). ✧ I. 'One-year-old calf'; II. 'Leather sack' cf. Kzk. *baspaq* 'id.' (Radl. IV, 1539).

BASÏ see **BAŠİ**

BASÏ-ΓARA see **BAŠİ-QARA**

BASÏL Kzk. 19th c. **Basïl** [Базильбекъ] (SODž. 72). ✧ 'Be quiet' cf. Kzk. *basïl-* 'sich beruhigen, still werden' (Radl. IV, 1529-30). See also **SŌRON.**

BASÏMNYÏ Yak. **Basïmnyï-bātïr** [Басымнйы-батыр], a hero (bogatyr) in a tale (Pek.). ✧ 'Hoe / hack' cf. Yak. *bahïmn'ï* 'id.' (JRS).

BASÏMNYÏLĀN Yak. **Basïmnyïlān-buχatïr / Basïmnyïlān-bātïr / Basamnyïlān-bātïr** [Басымнйылан / Басамнйылан], heros (bogatyrs) in tales (Pek.).

BASÏN Kzk. 19th c. **Basïn** [Улмамбет Басиновъ] (Grod., Pril. 99). ⇨ **BAY-BASÏN.**

BASÏQQA Yak. **Basïqqa** [Басыкка] (Pek.); Yak. **Mosōqqo** [Мосокко] (Pek.); Yak. **Mosūqqa** [Мосукка] (Pek.). ✧ Vasyutka (dim. of R. Vasiliy)

(Pek.).

BASÏLAY   Yak. **Basïlay** [Басылаі] (Pek.).   ✦ Vasiliy (R.).

BASÏLAYDÏR   Yak. **Basïlaydïr** [Басылаідыр] (Pek.).   ✦ Vasen'ka (R.), dim. of *Basïlay*.

BASQAQ   Tat. 1742-48 **Basqaq** [Баскаковъ], a Tatar from Čeboksary (IOAIÊK XIV, 539); Kzk. 19th c. **Basqaq** [Джумабай Баскаковъ] (Grod., Pril. 106); Maml. 1335 **Basqaq?** / **Bašqaq?** [سيف الدين بشتاق], an emir (Dawād. 398).   ✦ 'Opressor; the representative of the khan of the Golden Horde (a title)' (Vásáry: AOH 32 (1978), 201-206; Bask., Fam. 23-27, 245).

BASQUN   Bashk. 1737 **Basqun** [Салей Баскунов] (MIB I, 318); Bashk. 1738 **Basqun** [Урсай Баскунов] (MIB III, 387); Bashk. 1756 **Basqun** [Халил Баскунов] (MIB IV/1, 113); Bashk. 1789 **Basqun** [Баскун Араптанов] (MIB V, 272).   ✦ 'Nightmare, pressure' cf. Chag. *basqun* 'das Alpdrücken; das Pressen, der Druck, der Anfall, Überfall' (Radl. IV, 1535).

BASLAY   Bashk. 1750 **Baslay** [Араслан Баслаев] (MIB III, 472).

BASLAN   Bashk. 1735 **Baslan** [Баслан Ерымбетев] (MIB III, 336); Bashk. 1749 **Baslan** [Утеган Басланов] (MIB III, 465).

BASMAN   Kzk. 1809 **Basman** [Басмановъ] (TOUAK XXIX, 37).

BASMÏŠ   Khorezm.? 1301 **Basmïš** [باسميش], a man in the revolt against Saʿdeddīn and Rašīdeddīn (RaD/Jahn 134).   ✦ 'Pressed; overcame' cf. *bas-* 'drücken, pressen; unterdrücken, beherrschen, besiegen' (Radl. IV, 1524) + past(-*miš*). See also **ÏL-BASMÏŠ**.

BASOQ   Kzk. 19th c. **Basoq** [Басокъ] (SOK 248).   ✦ 'Low (in stature), squat, pressed down'? cf. East.T., Turk. *basuk / basïq* 'gedrückt, gepresst, niedrig' (Radl. IV, 1528, 1532) + suff. -*q*. See also **BAY-BASUQ**.

BASPA   Kzk. 19th c. **Baspa-bay** [Баспа бай] (SOK 254); Kzk. 19th c. **Baspa-bek** [Пуласъ бекъ Басбабековъ] (Grod., Pril. 152).

BASSAYA   Yak. **Bassaya** [Бассаja] (Pek.).

BAST   Kzk. 19th c. **Bast** [Лукпанъ Бастовъ] (AOO 46).

BASTAU see **BASTAW**

BASTAW   Kzk. 19th c. **Bastau-bay** [Бастаубай] (SOV 6, 8, 54); Kzk. 19th c. **Bastau-bay** [Бастаубай] (SOK 232); Kzk. 19th c. **Bastau-bay** [Бастаубай] (SODž. 50).   ✦ 'Beginning' (=the first child) cf. Kzk. *basta-* 'anfangen, anführen' (Radl. IV, 1536).

BASTÏ   Maml. 1300 **Bastï** [Seïf-eddin Basti], an emir (Makrīzī IV, 140); Kzk. 19th c. **Bastï-bay** [Бастибай] (SOK 184).   ✦ 'Defeated, opressed'. See also **EL-BASTÏ, ÏZ-BASTÏ, YAI Ï-BASTÏ, QOŽA-BASTÏ**.

BASTÏR   Kzk. 19th c. **Bastïr** [Бастыръ], a Kazak biy (Lomakin 35).

BASTÏRÏQ   Bashk.? 1663 **Bastrïq** [Бастрыков] (MIB I, 174-75, 188).   ✦ 'Pole; pressing pole' cf. Tat. *bastïrïq* 'die Stange, mit der man die Garben und das Heu (auf den Wagen) herabdrückt; der Stock, mit dem man dic Thür verschliesst, der Thorbalken' (Radl. IV, 1537); Bashk. dial. *baϑtïrïq* (=*baϑraw*) 'слега (предназначенная для стягивания воза с сеном или со снопами), гнет (пресс)' (BaRS); Tat. *bastïrïq* 'бастрык, гнет, слега' (TatRS); cf. also the R. nickname *Bastryga* (Бастрыга Еремеев) from 1584 (Veselovskij, Onomastikon).

BASTRÏQ see **BASTÏRÏQ**

BASU   Kzk. 19th c. **Basu-bay** [Басубай] (SODž. 92).

BASUQ see **BAY-BASUQ**

BAŠ   Kzk. 19th c. **Bas-ǰan** [Басджанъ] (SOK 218); Kzk. 19th c. **Bas-eke** [Басеке] (SOK 142); Kzk. 19th c. **Bas-pay** [Баспай] (SOK 74); Kzk. 19th c. **Baš** [Башъ] (AOK 122); Maml. 14th c. **Baš-bay** [بشباي] (Sauvaget 42); Maml. 1408/09 **Baš-bay** [باش باى] (Iyās I, 352); Kzk. 19th c. **Baš-bay** [Ходжабергенъ Башбаевъ] (Grod., Pril. 167); Az. **Baš-χanum** [Баш-ханум], fem. (Az. Skaz. 3); Hak.? 19th-20th c. **Pas** [Пас] (Katanov, Otč. 11); *TN:* Kzk. **Bas-batïr** [Басбатыр], a place in Southern Kazakstan (Kojčubaev 58).   ✦ 'Head; beginning; chief, leader' cf. Türk, Kuman, Chag., Crm., Kirg., Tat., Trkm., Uzb., etc. *baš*, Kar., Kzk. *bas*, Hak. *pas*, Uyg., Alt., Hak. *paš / pǟš* 'der Kopf; der Anfang; der Anführer' (Radl. IV, 1185, 1198, 1200, 1524, 1546-1551). See also **AY-BAŠ, AQ-BAŠ, AL-BAŠ, ALÏQ-PAŠ, ALMA-BAŠ, ALTÏN-BAS, ARQA-BAŠ, ARTÏ-BAŠ, ASÏL-BAS, ATAR-BAS, BAǰAQ-BAŠ, BAQA-BAŠ, BAL-PAŠ, BARA-BAŠ, BATUR-BAŠ, BÏL-BAS, BÏŠ-PAS, BOQ-BAŠ, BOLČOQ-BAŠ, BOZ-PAS, BU-BAŠ, BUYRA-BAS, ČARA-BAS, ČATAL-BAŠ, ČERÏ-BAŠ, ČORA-BAŠ, ČUY-BAŠ, ǰARÏQ-PAS, ǰAW-BAS, DAW-BAS, DELÏ-BAŠ, DEMÏR-BAŠ, EV-BAŠ, ÏKTÜ-SARÏƔ-BAŠ, ÏL-BAŠ, ÏT-BAŠ, YARLÏQ-BAŠ, YEKÄ-BAŠ, YEŠÏL-BAŠ, KÏL-BAŠ, KÖK-BAŠ, KÖPEK-BAŠ, QAƔANAQ-BAS, QAYQA-BAS, QAQ-BAŠ, QAQÏR-BAŠ, QAL-BAS, QALAQ-PAS, QALMAŠ-BAŠ, QANTA-BAŠ, QANZA-BAŠ, QARA-BAŠ, QARAWUL-BAS, QASQA-BAS, QAWM-BAS, QÏYSÏQ-PAS, QÏYSÏN-PAS, QÏL-BAŠ, QÏR-BAS, QOǰA-BAŠ, QOY-BAS, QUQ-BAŠ, QUL-BAŠ, QUÑ-BAŠ, QUÑƔUR-BAŠ, QUR-BAŠ, QURU-BAŠ, QUTADMÏŠ-BAŠ, QUTAN-BAŠ, QUTTU-BAŠ, QUTUR-BAŠ, QUZ-BAŠ, MAY-BAS(?), MAYT-BAS(?), MALÏK-BAŠ, MANA-BAŠ, MATLÏ-BAS, MAW-PAS, MÏYA-BAS, MOQTÏ-BAS, ÖTÄ-BAŠ, ÖTEY-BAS, SALÏQ-PAŠ, SAPAQ-PAS, SARÏ-BAŠ, SARQÏL-BAŠ, SĀR-BAS, SÏRÏ-BAŠ, SODOY-BAŠ, SOR-BAS, SÜYÜR-BAŠ, ŠÏN-BAS, TAQÏR-BAS, TAS-PAŠ, TERÏ-BAŠ,

TİMUR-BAŠ, TİN-BAŠ, TOĠAN-BAS, TOQ-BAS, TOPČİ-BAŠ, TOSTU-BAŠ, TUMAR-BAS, TÜLKÜ-BAS, UQU-BAS.

BAŠ-BUĠA Oghuz **Baš-buɣa** [باش بوغا], forefather of the Ottoman dynasty (Āšikp. 50); Maml. 1404/05 **Baš-buɣa** [ارغون من بشبغا] (Ibn Taghrīb. VI, 90, 129). ✧ 'Head/Chief-bull. ⇨ **BAŠ** + **BUQA**.

BAŠ-QARA I. Uyg. 12th c.-14th c. **Baš-qara** [baš qara] (Radl., USp. 121, DTS). ✧ 'Head-black' (Bese 18, Blagova 1997, 705). ⇨ **BAŠ** + **QARA**.

BAŠ-QARA II. see **BAŠİ-QARA**

BAŠAY Bashk. 1751 **Bašay** [Султангул Башаев] (MIB IV/1, 52); Kzk. 19th c. **Bašay** [Башай] (AOK 38); Kkalp. 18th c. **Bašay-sultan** [Башай султан] (Pam. Sib. Ist. I, 380).

BAŠAQ Maml. **Bašaq?** [يشبك بشق] (Ibn Taghrīb. VII); Kzk. 19th c. **Bašaq** [Башакъ] (SOV 138); Kzk. 19th c. **Bašaq** [Башакъ] (SOK 4); Kzk. 19th c. **Bašaq** [Башакъ] (SODž. 136). ✧ I. 'Little, bad, tenuous, weak' cf. Kzk. dial. *bašaq I* 'id.' (QTDS); II. 'Seed of (water-)melon' cf. Kzk. dial. *bašaq II* 'id.' (QTDS).

BAŠAM Kzk. 19th c. **Bašam-bek** [Башамбекъ] (SODž. 138). ⇨ **BAŠİM?**

BAŠAR Tat. / Bashk. **Bašar** [Магафуръ Башаровъ], a Teptär (ŽS IV, 350); Bashk. 1731, 1735 **Bašar / Bašer** [Башар (Башер) Тоишев] (MIB III, 287, 333). ✧ 'Man / Men'? cf. Tat. PN *Bäšär* 'id.' (Sattarov). ⇨ **BÄŠİR?**

BAŠARA Oghuz 967 **Bašara** [Baschara], servant of „Harndamda Saad Addawlah"? (Weil, Chalif. III, 38).

BAŠČA NUyg. 1864 **Bašča** [Башча] (Valihanov, Soč. 513). ✧ 'Little head'? ⇨ **BAŠ** + dim. suff. -*ča* / suff. -*čï*. See also **BAŠČİ**.

BAŠČİ Uyg. 12th c.-14th c. **Bašči** [Başçı] (DTS, EUTS); Karch. **Bašči** [Бащи] (Sysoev 123); Kzk. 19th c. **Bašči-ɣul** [Бащигулъ] (SODž. 138). ✧ I. 'Chief, leader' cf. (Tat., East.T.) 'der Anführer' (Radl. IV, 1560); II. 'Dealer in sheep-heads' cf. *bašči / bašči* (Turk.) 'der Händler mit Hammelköpfen' (Radl. IV, 1560). ⇨ **BAŠ** + suff. -*čï* / -*či*. See also **BAŠČA, QOL-BAŠČİ**.

BAŠEY Kzk. 19th c. **Bašey** [Башей] (AOP 42); Kzk. 19th c. **Bašey** [Башей], a biy (Lomakin 36).

BAŠEK Kzk. 19th c. **Bašek** [Башекъ] (AOA 82).

BAŠEN Kzk. 19th c. **Bašen** [Башенъ] (AOK 38).

BAŠER see **BAŠAR**

BAŠİ-KEŇ see **BAŠİ-KEŇ**

BAŠİKEY see **BAŠİKEY**

BAŠİR see **BÄŠİR**

BAŠİ Kzk. 19th c. **Basï-bay** [Басыбай] (SOK 138); Kzk. 19th c. **Basï-bay** [Басыбай] (AOK 78); Bashk. 1759 **Bašï** [Баши Кильтянов] (MIB IV/2, 24); Oghuz/Trkm. 13th c. **Bašï-bek** [باشى بيك / Башы-бек],

chief of Dib-Baquy Khan's beks (Abulg./Kon. 660); *TN:* Kzk. 19th c. **Basï-bay** [Басыбай], a field (AOK 46). ✧ 'Chief; head of'. ⇨ **BAŠ** + poss. suff. -*ï*. See also **BAZAR-BAŠİ, YURT-BAŠİ, QÏPČAQ-BAŠİ, QUY-BAŠİ, MİŇ-BAŠİ, NUR-BAŠİ, ORDU-BAŠİ, SÜ-BAŠİ, TÜLKİ-BASİ**.

BAŠİ-BOŠ Turk. **Bašï-boš-oɣlu**, a Zeybek (Kúnos 1891, 119). ✧ 'Free, independent' cf. Turk. *başıboş* 'id.' (TED). ⇨ **BAŠ**.

BAŠİ-BÜYÜK Turk. 20th c. **Bašï-büyük** [Başıbüyük], a village in the province of İstanbul, Turkey (TMİB 457); Yürük 1609 **Bašï-büyük** [Yürükân-i Başıbüyük taifesinden Yaramış bin Kubad], a taife (tribe) of the Yürüks (Gökçen 80). ✧ 'His/her head (is) big'. ⇨ **BAŠ** + **BÜYÜK**.

BAŠİ-GİLDİ Kkalp. 1740 **Bašï-gildi** [Башигильди], from the Qïyat tribe (MIKk. 208); Kkalp. 1740 **Bašï-gildi-abïz** [Башигильди-Абызъ] (Hanykov, Poezdka 20). ✧ 'His head (chief) has come'. ⇨ **BAŠ** + **KELDİ**.

BAŠİ-KEŇ Kzk. 19th c. **Bašï-keň / Baši-keň** [Башикенъ] (Lomakin 40). ✧ 'His head is broad; broad-headed' cf. Kzk., Kirg., Kuman *keň* 'breit, weit, ausgedehnt' (Radl. II, 1067). ⇨ **BAŠ**.

BAŠİ-QARA Kzk. 1794 **Basï-ɣara** [بش قرا / Басыгара] (MIK IV, 162); Kzk. 19th c. **Basï-qara** (Ljutš 138); Kzk. 1794 **Baš-qara (<Bašï-qara)** [بش قرا / Басыгара] (MIK IV, 162); Kzk. 1792 **Bašï-qara** [Башыкара] (MIK IV, 139); Kzk. 1820 **Bašï-qara-biy** [Башикара-бий], one of the chiefs of the Alim-ulï tribe (Sib. Vest. IX, 115). ✧ 'His head is black'. ⇨ **BAŠ** + **QARA**.

BAŠİKEY Bashk. 1709 **Bašïkey / Bašikey** [Башикей] (MIB I, 264). ⇨ **BAŠİ** + suff. -*key*.

BAŠİQ Kzk. 19th c. **Bašïq** [Башикъ] (SODž. 8, 16, 112, 160); Kzk. 19th c. **Bašïq** [Башикъ] (SOK 172); Kzk. 19th c. **Bašïq** [Башикъ] (SOV 114). ⇨ **BAŠ?** + suff. *ïq*.

BAŠİL Kzk. 19th c. **Bašïl** [Башылъ] (SODž. 40).

BAŠİM Kzk. 19th c. **Bašïm** [Башимъ] (AOK 54). ✧ 'My head'. ⇨ **BAŠ**.

BAŠİM-KEL Trkm. 1881 **Bašïm-kel** [Башимъ-Кель] (Grod., Vojna IV, Grod., Pril. 19). ✧ 'My head (is) itchy/bald' cf. Trkm. *kel* 'паршивый, шелудивый; плешивый' (TrkmRS). ⇨ **BAŠ**.

BAŠİN-SİLAVANTİ Uyg. 12th c. - 14th c. **Bašïn-silavanti / Baštïn-silavanti** (Radl., USp. 144). ✧ 'First leader of a religious community' cf. Uyg. *baštïn* 'ilki, önceki' (EUTS), Uyg. *silavanti / šilavanti* (Skr.) 'духовное лицо религиозной общины' (DTS). ⇨ **SİLAVANTİ**.

BAŠQAQ see **BASQAQ**

BAT Kzk. 19th c. **Bat-bay** [Батбаев], a journalist (AUK 164); Kzk. 19th c. **Bat-bala** [Батбала] (SOK

176); Kzk. 19th c. **Bat-pay** [Батпай] (SOK 240); Alt. 19th-20th c. **Bat-pay** [Батпай], fem. (OjrRS 211). ✧ 'Bad, good-for-nothing' cf. Türk, Turk. *bat* 'untauglich' (Radl. IV, 1508); II. 'Quick, nimble' cf. Chag., Sart (Uzb.) schnell, geschwind' (Radl. IV, 1508). See also **AL-BAT, QOL-BAT.**

BATA I. Kzk. 19th c. **Bata-bay** [Батабай] (SOV 134). ✧ 'Prayer, blessing' cf. Kzk. *bata* 'das Gebet, der Segen'' (Radl. IV, 1510) (<Ar.).

BATA II. Yak. **Bata-bātïr** [Бата-батыр], forefather of the Bayaγantay clan from the times of the Russian invasion; the most courageous bātïr (bogatyr) among the people called Khoro (Pek.).

BATAY Tat. 1881 **Baday** [Бадай Сюлеймановъ] (TOUAK XXIV, 4); Kzk. 19th c. **Batay** [Батай] (AOAtb. 50); Shor 1643 **Batay** [Батай], a taxpayer (payer of yasaq) from Kondoma (Miller, Ist. Sib. II, 487). ⇨ **BATA I.?** + dim. suff. -*y*.

BATAL Bashk. 1738 **Batal** [Батал Уркешев] (MIB III, 387); Bashk. 18th c. **Batal / Battal** [Батал (Баттал) Атикеев] (MIB V, 415); Nog. 20th c. **Batal-uwlï** [Муса Батал улы Ахметджан / Муса Беталович Ахметджанов], father of one of Baskakov's informants from the aul of Qañlï (Bask., Nog. 143). ⇨ **BATTAL.**

BATALA Bashk. 1754 **Batala** [Батала Юнусов] (MIB IV/1, 87); Bashk. 1780 **Batala** [Кудаш Баталин] (MIB V, 119). ⇨ **BATA?** + suff. -*la* < -*lï*.

BATAM Kzk. 19th c. **Batam-bay / Batan-bay?** [Батамбай] (SODž. 128).

BATAR Kzk. 19th c. **Batar-bay** [Батарбай], a field (AOA 102). ✧ 'He who will enter' Cf. Türk, Kuman, Az., Crm., Kzk., Tat., Turk., etc. *bat-* 'eindringen, einsinken, untersinken; untergehen; ausfüllen, hineingehen' (Radl. IV, 1508), Alt. *bat-* 'войти, вместиться во что-либо; увязнуть; зайти, закатиться (о солнце, луне, звёздах)' (OjrRS). + suff. -*ar*. See also **ČÏГ-BATAR, TAY-BATAR.**

BATAŠ Karch. **Bataš** [Баташевъ] (Sysoev 119); Tat. 1686 **Bataš** [Баташъ] (Kungursk. akty 68); Tat. 1710 **Bataš** [Баташевъ] (Letop. ZAK II, 25); Uzb. 19th c. **Bataš** [Баташъ] (SKSO III, 182). ✧ 'Little camel' (<R.) byname (<Trk.) (Bask., Fam. 180, 214). ⇨ **BOTAŠ.**

BATČÏ Kzk. 19th c. **Batčï-bay** [Батчибай] (SOK 302).

BATÏ see **BATÏY**

BATÏY Tat. 1726 **Batey / Batiy?** [Батей Тураев] (MIB III, 238); Kzk. 19th c. **Bati / Batï?** [Бати], she was very beautiful (была писанная красавица) (AUK 450); Kzk. 19th c. **Bati-bay** [Батибай] (Grod., Pril. 164); Kzk. 19th c. **Bati-bay** [Батебай] (SODž. 76); Kirg. **Batiy** [Батий], fem. (Jud. 489). ✧ 'Precious stone, jewel' cf. Bashk. PN *Batïy* (Kusimova), Tat. PN *Batu / Batïy* (Sattarov).

BATÏ Kzk. 19th c. **Batï** [Баты] (AOP 65); Nog. 1832 **Batï-murza** [Баты Мурза] (Sergeev 140). ✧ 'West, sunset' cf. *batï* 'der Untergang (der Sonne), der Westen' (Radl. IV, 1511). See also **QUL-BATÏ.**

BATÏP Kzk. 19th c. **Batïp** [Батепъ] (AOK 6).

BATÏR Trkm. 20th c. **Batïr** [Batïr] (Zaj. 1971, 327); Chuv. 18th-19th c. **Batïr** [Батыръ] (Magn. 33); Tat. 1668 **Batïr** [Исекейко Батыревъ] (Kungursk. akty 9); Bashk. 1761 **Batïr** [Батыр Байсланов] (MIB IV/1, 204); Bashk. 1761 **Batïr** [Бигей Батыров] (MIB IV/1, 219); Kzk. 1841 **Batïr** [Ачимтай Батыревъ], a sultan of the Middle Horde (Orta Žüz) (Konšin, Mat. V, 34); Kzk. 19th c. **Batïr-bay** [Батырбай] (SODž. 124); Kkalp. 20th c. **Batïr-bay** [Батырбай] (KkRS 773); Kzk. 19th c. **Batïr-bek** [Чуйбекъ Батырбековъ] (Grod., Pril. 19); Kirg. 19th c. **Batïr-qan**, a high-born person from the Buγu tribe (Almásy 534); Kzk. 18th c. - 19th c. **Batïr-qul** [Батыркул] (Tynyšp. 71); Crm. 1654 **Batïr-mirza** [باطر ميرزا] (Vel.-Zern., Crim. 499); Kzk. 18th c. **Batïr-sultan**, a Kazak khan before 1750 (ArchKR XVIII, 380); Tat.(Mish.) 1755 **Bator** [Мявкей Баторов] (MIB IV/1, 93); Tat.(Mish.) 1755 **Bator** [Бигей Баторов] (MIB IV/1, 93); Alt. 19th c. **Bator** [Батор] (Verb., In. 119); Uyg. 12th c.-14th c. **Batur** [Batur] (DTS, EUTS); Türk 8th c. - 9th c. **Batur-čigši** (DTS); Türk 8th c. - 9th c. **Batur-čigši** [batur čigši] (DTS); Uyg. 762 **Batur-sañun-ügä** (Mahrnāmag 10); Trkm. 20th c. **Bātïr** [Батыр] (TrkmRS 77); Kirg. **Bātïr / Bātïr-bek** [Баатыр, Баатырбек] (Jud. 296, 634, 843); Chuv. 18th-19th c. **Patïr** [Патырь] (Magn. 66); *EN:* Kzk. 18th c. - 19th c. **Batïr-bek-datχa** [Батырбек-датха], a subdivision of the Dulat tribe (Tynyšp. 65). ✧ 'Hero; brave, strong fellow' cf. Türk *batur* 'герой, богатырь' (DTS), Tat., Kzk., Trkm., Uzb., Crm. *batïr* 'tapfer, helden haft, der Held' (Radl. IV, 1511), Trkm. *bātïr* 'богатырь, смельчак, храбрец' (TrkmRS), Hak.(Sag.) *matïr* 'kühn, furchtlos' (Radl. IV, 2045). Used also as a (secondary) component of male personal names. See also **BAГATUR.**

BATÏRAQ see **BATRAQ**

BATÏRČA see **BATÏRŠA**

BATÏRKEY Tat. 1649 **Batïrkey** [Батыркей] (AI IV, 111); Bashk. 1723 **Batïrkey** [Батыркей Иштыков] (MIB III, 217). ⇨ **BATÏR** + suff. -*qay* / -*key*.

BATÏRŠA Kzk. 19th c. **Batïrča** [Батырча] (SODž. 68); Nog. 1649 **Batïrča** [Батырча Янъ-араслановъ] (AI IV, 87); Karch. **Batïrša** [Батырша] (Sysoev 131); Tat. 1776 **Batïrša** [Батырша Адельшинъ] (PSZRI XX, 456); Tat.(Mish.) **Batïrša** [Batyrša] (IOAIÊK XIX, 145); Tat.(Mish.) 1765 **Batïrša** [Сеитбаттал Батыршин] (MIB IV/1, 308); Bashk. 1755 **Batïrša** [Batyrscha Alejev / Abdulla Nasgildin*], a rebellious Bashkir in the 18th c. (Rytschkow II, 22); Bashk. 1794 **Batïrša** [Батырша Алдаров] (MIB V, 338); Kzk.

1753 **Batïrša** [Batyr-Cha], a molla (Levchin 230); Kzk. 19th c. **Batïrša**, a mulla (AUK 228); Kzk. 19th c. **Batïrša** (Ljutš 83); Nog. 1649 **Batïrša** [Батырша Урусов] (AI IV, 85); Crm. 1636 **Batïrša-mirza / Batïr-šah-mirza?** [باطرشاه ميرزا] (Vel.-Zern., Crim. 167). ✧ I. 'Dear little hero'; II. 'Hero(ic) Shah'? cf. Kzk., Bshk. and Tat. PNs *Batïrša* (Žanuzakov-Esbaeva, Kusimova, Sattarov). Sattarov and Kusimova interpret the name *Batïrša* as a compound of *Batïr* and *Šah*. ⇨ **BATÏR** (/ + **ŠAH?**) + / dim.-hypoc. suff. *-ča / -ša*.

BATÏŠ Kzk. 19th c. **Batïš** [Батышъ] (SODž. 70); Kzk. 19th c. **Batïš / Batiš?** [Батишъ] (AOA 26). ✧ I. 'Hero' (Sattarov); II. 'Sunset' cf. Kuman, Tat., Turk. *batïš* 'id.' (Radl. IV, 1514).

BATQAR Uzb. 1836 **Batqar-qan**, the title of Nāsrullah, the great khan of Bukhara and Samarkand (Vel.-Zern., Haïder 277).

BATLEUM Bashk. 1756 **Batleum-bay** [Казак Батлеумбаев] (MIB IV/1, 123).

BATMA see **FATİMA**

BATMAN Kzk. 19th c. **Batman** [Батманъ] (Grod., Pril. 173); Kzk. 19th c. **Batpan-bay** [Батпанбай] (SOV 44). ✧ 'Heavy (old measure of weight varying between 60 and 200 kg)' cf. Kzk. *batpan* 'batman; ağırlık ölçüsü' (KzTS), Chag., Tat., Trkm., Turk., Uzb. *batman* 'ein schweres Gewicht (Dsch. 40 Pfund)' (Radl. IV, 1516).

BATOR see **BATÏR**

BATPA see **FATİMA**

BATPAN see **BATMAN**

BATPANAQ Alt. 19th-20th c. **Batpanaq** [Батпанак], fem. (OjrRS 211). ✧ 'Squat, of small stature, stumpy' (OjrRS).

BATRA Uyg. **Batra** [Batra], fem. (EUTS); Uyg. **Batra-qïz** [batra qïz], fem. (DTS). ✧ 'Queen Badhra' (<Skr.?) (EUTS, Blagova 1997, 708).

BATRAQ Bashk. 1757 **Badraq** [Бадрак Исемметев] (MIB IV/1, 142); Crm. **Batïraq** [Батырак] (Proben VII, 203); Tat. 1624 **Batraq** [Батракъ Теребердѣевъ] (Pokrovskij 72); Tat. 1675 **Batraq** [Батряковъ] (Kungursk. akty 24); Chuv. 18th-19th c. **Patrak** [Патракъ] (Magn. 66). ✧ 'Worker; servant' cf. Tat. (<R.) *batraq* 'der Arbeiter, Schwarzarbeiter' (Radl. IV, 1516); Kzk. *batïraq* 'poor worker, servant in service of the higher classes before the socialist Revolution' (QTTS).

BATÏRÏ-GİLDEY Tat. 1632 **Batrï-gildey** [Бекбаев Батрыгилдейко] (Miller, Ist. Sib. II, 391). ⇨ **BATÏR?** + **KELDİ.**

BATŠAL Bashk. **Batšal** [Батшал Икбердин] (MIB I, 92).

BATTAҐÏYAN-XOSUN Yak. **Battaҕïyan-χosun** [Баттаҕыйан-хосун], a Yakut batïr from the times of Хaptaҕay-bātïr (Pek.).

BATTAL Tat. **Battal** [Abdulbai Battal(ov)] (Mende 132); Kzk. 19th c. **Battal** [Батталъ] (AOP). ✧ Battal (Ar.). See also **SEYİT-BATTAL, TEKE-BATTAL.**

BATTÏQ Kzk. 19th c. **Battïq** [Беткопакъ Баттиковъ] (Grod., Pril. 160). ⇨ **BAT.**

BATTU Kzk. 19th c. **Battu-bay / Buttu-bay** [Джанъ Кутти Баттубаевъ / Буттубаевъ] (Grod., Pril. 104, 105).

BATU Chuv. 18th-19th c. **Batu-bay** [Батубай] (Magn. 33). ✧ 'Batu (=firm, solid, strong)' (Pelliot 28-29) (<Mo.). ⇨ **BATÏ?**

BATUQ Uyg. 12th c.-14th c. **Batuq** [Batuk] (Radl., USp. 55, DTS, EUTS); Bashk. 1776 **Batuq** [Батюк Тангруков] (MIB V, 33). ✧ 'Moor-land, marsh' cf. East.T. *batuq* 'weicher Boden, der Sumpf, der Morast' (Radl. IV, 1514).

BATUR see **BATÏR**

BATUR-BAŠ Kzk. 19th c. **Batur-baš** [Исламбекъ Батурбашевъ] (Grod., Pril. 50). ⇨ **BATÏR + BAŠ.**

BATUR-ČİGŠİ see **BATÏR**

BATURMANČA Bashk. 1722 **Baturmanča-bay** [Батурманчабай] (MIB I, 122). ⇨ **BATÏR + MANČA?**

BAW see **ВАҐ**

BAW-ASAQ Kzk. 1817 **Baw-asaq** [باو اصاق / Бауасак] (MIK IV, 310). ⇨ **BAW + ASAQ.**

BAWEDİN see **BĀBEDİN**

BAWKE Kirg. **Bawke** [Баукä], one of Manas' comrades (Proben V, 40 /41/); Kzk. 19th c. **Bawke-bay** [Баукебай] (SOK 134). ⇨ **ВАҐ** + suff. *-ke* < comp. *-ake*.

BAWKEY Bashk. 1717 **Bawkey** [Илгибай Баукеев] (MIB III, 148). ⇨ **ВАҐ** + suff. *-key* < comp. *-ekey*.

BAWL Kzk. 19th c. **Bawl-bay** [Баулбай] (SOK 60, 108).

BAWLU Turk. **Bawlu-oҕlu** [باولو اوغلى] (Āšikp. 159). ✧ 'Trained' cf. Turk. *bavlï* 'id.' (TRS), also *baulu-*Hunde zur Jagd dressiren' (Radl. IV, 1434). See also **TOQ-BAWLU.**

BAWLUQ Kzk. 19th c. **Bawluq-pay** [Баулукпай] (SOV 14).

BAWM Kzk. 19th c. **Bawm-bay** [Баумбай] (SOK 256).

BAWŠ Tat. 1530 **Bawš** [Баушъ], a man from Kazan (PSRL VIII, 274); Kzk. 19th c. **Bawš** [Баушъ] (SOK 226).

BAWTAN Kzk. 19th c. **Bawtan** [Баутанъ] (AOP 10).

BAZ Selj. 1149 **Baz-aba / Baz-be** [باز به] (Qalānisi 301); Türk 732 **Baz-qaҕan** (DTS); Oghuz 991 **Baz-tegin** [باز تكين] (Kamāladdīn: RHCHor I, 185). ✧ I. 'Peaceful, quiet' cf. Türk *baz: baz qïl-* 'усмирить, замирить' (DTS), Türk, Kar., Crm. *baz* '1. der Friede, die Eintracht, die Ruhe; 2. friedlich' (Radl. IV, 1541);

II. 'Alien, foreigner, stranger, outsider' cf. Karakh. *baz* 'id.' (DTS); III. 'Falcon'? (<P. *bāz*).

BAZ-AYAQ Tat.(Sib.)? 1612 **Baz-ayaq** [Базаякъ], a prince in Siberia (Andrievič, Ist. Sib. I, 44). ✧ 'Falcon-foot'. ⇨ **BAZ** + **AYAQ**.

BAZ-BE see **BAZ**

BAZ-BİRÄ? Tat.(Sib.) 1601 **Baz-birä?** [Базбира Каратаев] (Miller, Ist. Sib. II, 169). ⇨ **BAZ**.

BAZ-QUŠ Selj.? **Baz-quš** [بازکش] (Ibn al-Athīr: RHCHor I, 624). ✧ 'Falcon-bird'. ⇨ **BAZ** + **QUŠ I**.

BAZAY Kzk. 19th c. **Bazay** [Базай] (AOAtb. 54); Kzk. 19th c. **Bazay** [Базай] (AOA 122). ⇨ **BAZ?** + suff. *-ay*.

BAZAQ Uyg. 13th c.-14th c. **Bazaq-tarïm**, fem. (Chwol., Syr.-nest. (NF) 41); Uyg. 13th c.-14th c. **Pazaq** (Chwol., Syr.-nest. (NF) 49); Uyg. 13th c.-14th c. **Pazaq** (Chwol., Syr.-nest. 96, 98); Uyg. 1324 **Pazaq**, fem. (Chwol., Syr.-nest. (NF) 24); Uyg. 1335 **Pazaq** (Chwol., Syr.-nest. 76); Uyg. 1339 **Pazaq** (Chwol., Syr.-nest. (NF) 35); Uyg. 1311 **Pazaq-keyamta**, fem. (Chwol., Syr.-nest. (NF) 18); Uyg. 1341 **Pazaq-tarïm**, fem. (Chwol., Syr.-nest. (NF) 39); Uyg. 1333 **Pazaq-tegin** (Chwol., Syr.-nest. 74). ⇨ **BAZ?** + suff. *-aq*.

BAZAR Trkm. 20th c. **Bazar** [Bazar] (Zaj. 1971, 330); Trkm. 20th c. **Bazar** [Базар] (TrkmRS 66); Kzk. 19th c. **Bazar** [Базаръ] (AOK 46); Kzk. 19th c. **Bazar** [Базаръ Накисовъ] (Grod., Pril. 91); Kkalp. 20th c. **Bazar** [Базар], fem. (KkRS 777); Uzb. 19th c. **Bazar** [Таштымиръ Базаровъ] (SKSO III, 172); Kzk. 19th c. **Bazar-bay** [Базарбай] (AOO 10); Kzk. 19th c. **Bazar-bay** [Базарбай] (SKSO VIII, 201); Kzk. 19th c. **Bazar-bay** [Базарбай] (SOV 150); Kzk. 19th c. **Bazar-bay** [Базаръ-бай] (AUK Dobavl. 5); Kzk. 19th c. **Bazar-bay** [Базарбай] (Grod., Pril. 128); Kzk. 19th c. **Bazar-bay** [Базарбай] (SODž. 56, 92); Kzk. 19th c. **Bazar-bay** [Базарбай] (SOK 104); Uzb. 19th c. **Bazar-bay** [Базарбай] (SKSO III, 176); Uzb. 19th c. **Bazar-bay** [Базарбай] (SKSO III, 168); Uzb. 19th c. **Bazar-bay** [Базаръ-бай] (Grod., Pril. 181); Uzb. 1860 **Bazar-bay** [Bazar-bai-Toksaba] (Nalivkin-Dozon 235); Kzk. **Bazar-batïr** [Базаръ батыръ] (Smirnov, Sultany 15); Kzk. 19th c. **Bazar-bek** [Базарбекъ] (SOV 26, 60); Kzk. 19th c. **Bazar-biče** [Базарбичъ], fem. (Grod., Pril. 120); Kzk. 19th c. **Bazar-bige** [Базаръ бигэ], fem. (Grod., Pril. 142); Kzk. 19th c. **Bazar-biy** [Базорбій], a chieftain (Sib. Vest. IX, 118); Kkalp. 20th c. **Bazar-gül** [Базаргюл / Базаргүл], fem. (Bask., Kkalp. 403, KkRS 777); Bashk. 1760 **Bazar-γul** [Базаргул Юнаев] (MIB IV/2, 160); Bashk. 1768 **Bazar-γul** [Базаргулъ Юнаевъ] (Nikol'skij 275); Bashk. 1783 **Bazar-γul** [Базаргул Кильдикеев] (MIB V, 143); Kzk. 19th c. **Bazar-χan** [Базарханъ] (SOK 92); Kzk. 19th c. **Bazar-qul** [Базаръ-Кулъ] (Grod., Pril. 175); Kzk. 19th c. **Bazar-qul** [Базаркулъ] (SOV 94); Kzk. 19th c. **Bazar-qul** [Базаркуловъ] (SKSO VIII, 226); Kirg. 19th c. **Bazar-qul** [Базаркулъ] (Potanin II, 3); Uzb. 1833 **Bazar-qul-bay** [БазаръКулъ-бай] (Moskal'cev 40). ✧ 'Market; market-place' cf. Turk., Tar., Crm., Trkm., Uzb., Tat., Kar., Kuman *bazar* 'der Markt, der Jahrmarkt; der Korb mit Vorräthen (Turk.); eine Örtlichkeit, an der Buden gebaut sind und wo die Leute der Umgegend sich an gewissen Tagen zum Handel versammeln, an den übrigen Tagen sind diese Örtlichkeiten oft ganz unbewohnt' (Radl. IV, 1542-43) (<P.). In Baskakov's interpretation *Bazar-gül* means "базарная роза; роза базара; хорошая, отборная" [rose from the market, selected rose; nice rose] (Baskakov: OnSrAz. 141). See also **AQ-BAZAR, ES-BAZAR, GÜL-BAZAR**.

BAZAR-BAŠİ Turk. 16th c. **Bazar-baši** (Ongan, Ank. II.). ✧ 'Market-head; Head of the narket'. ⇨ **BAZAR** + **BAŠ** + poss. *-i*.

BAZAR-DOS Kzk. 19th c. **Bazar-dos** [Базардосъ] (SOK 26). ⇨ **BAZAR** + **DOST**.

BAZAR-GELDİ see **BAZAR-KELDİ**

BAZAR-KELDİ Kzk. 19th c. **Bazar-geldi** [Базаргельды] (AOO 42); Kzk. 19th c. **Bazar-geldi** [Базаргельды] (SODž. 80, 150); Kzk. 19th c. **Bazar-keldi** [Базаркельды] (SOV 50). ⇨ **BAZAR** + **KELDİ**.

BAZAR-MÄS Kkalp. 20th c. **Bazar-mäs** [Базармäс / Базармəс], fem. (KkRS 777, Bask., Kkalp. 56). ✧ 'Market - cheerfurl pretty girl' cf. Kkalp. *mäs* 'весёлый, радостный' (KkRS). ⇨ **BAZAR**.

BAZARJA Kzk. 19th c. **Bazarja-χoja** [Базаръ-Джахожинъ] (AUK 792). ⇨ **BAZAR** + suff. *-ja / -ča*.

BAZARXAN Nog. 20th c. **Bazarχan** [Базархан Сарый къызы], one of Baskakov's female informants from Sarï-awul (Bask., Nog. 144). ⇨ **BAZAR** + suff. *-χan(1)*.

BAZARLU Turk. 14th c. **Bazarlu** [Παζαρλους], brother of the Ottoman sultan Urχan (Orχan) (Byz. Turc. 239); Turk. / Yürük? 1551 **Bazarlu** [Hamza ibn Bazarlu] (Gökçen 30); *TN:* Turk. 1475 **Bazarlu-bey** [Bazarlû-Bey], a village in Turkey (Gökb., Ed. 276). ✧ 'Someone having a market' (Erol II). ⇨ **BAZAR** + suff. *-lu / -lï*.

BAZİL Kzk. 19th c. **Bazil-bay** [Базильбай] (SODž. 14); Kzk. 19th c. **Bazil-bek** [Базильбекъ] (SOK 146).

BAZÏQ Bashk. 1737 **Bazïq** [Базык] (MIB I, 327); Bashk. 1693 **Bazuq / Bazïq?** [Чюрюкей Базюковъ] (Vel.-Zern., Bašk. 41); Bashk. 1712 **Bazuq / Bazïq?** [Базюк Акчюрин] (MIB III, 90). ✧ 'Strong, thick' cf. Tat. *bazïq* 'stark, ausdauernd', Kar.(T.) *bazïχ* 'dick' (Radl. IV, 1544), Bashk. *baδïq* 'прочный, крепкии; дюжий; яркий (о свете)' (BaRS). See also **BOYNU-BAZÏQ**.

BAZÏRĠAN Yürük 16th c. **Bazïrɣan** [بازرغان], from the Yürüks of Kocacık, Turkey (Gökb., Rum. 101). ✧ 'Merchant' cf. Turk., Crm. *bazïrg'an* (P.) 'der Kaufmann, der Händler' (Radl. IV, 1545).

BAZMAŠ Alt. 19th-20th c. **Bazmaš** [Базмаш] (OjrRS 211)

BAŽAQAY Kzk. 19th c. **Bažaqay** [Бажакай] (AOK 138) ✧ 'Dear elder sister' cf. Chag., East. T. *baja* 'die ältere Schwester, die Tante' (Radl. IV, 1521) + suff. *-qay*.

BAŽÏ Trkm. 19th c. **Bažï-ɣul** [Бажигулъ Амангуловъ] (Ščeglov IV, 189). ✧ 'Elder sister; elder woman' cf. Az., Crm., Turk. *bajï* 'die ältere Schwester; eine ältereFrau' (Radl. IV, 1523).

BAŽÏQ Kzk. 19th c. **Bažïq-pay** [Бажикпай] (SODž. 88).

BAŽÏN-TAY Kzk. **Bažïn-tay** [Байбулатъ Бажентаевъ] (TOUAK XXIV, 161). ⇨ **TAY?** or suff. *-tay(1,2)*?

BĀBA Alt. 19th-20th c. **Bāba** [Бааба], fem. (OjrRS 211). See also **JAĠA-BĀBA**.

BĀBAY Alt. 19th-20th c. **Bābay** [Баабай] (OjrRS 207).

BĀBEDİN Kzk. **Bawedin** [Кожа Бау-äдiн] (Radl. I, 21); Kirg. **Bābedin** [Баабедин] (Jud. 89). ✧ Baha-ud-Din'' (Ar.).

BĀBER Oghuz/Trkm. 13th c. **Baber** [با بر / Бабер], Boɣra-χan's wife (Abulg./Kon. 890); Chag.? 18th c. **Baber / Babr**, Baber (Babr) ᶜAlī-šāh, a poet in Delhi (Dihli), at the end of the 18th c. (Justi 55); Trkm. 20th c. **Babïr** [Babïr] (Zaj. 1971, 331); Trkm. 20th c. **Babïr** [Бабыр] (TrkmRS 62); Chag. 1497, 1530 **Bābur / Bābur-padša** [Бабур (Захир-уд-дин-Мухаммед) / Бабуръ-падша Ындѣйскiй], the Timurid sultan of Ferghana (1497-1498, 1500-1501), founder (1526-1530) of the Moghul empire (MIT II, 9, 33, 41, 47, 52, 54, 357, PSRL XIII, 65). ✧ 'Lion', 'Tiger' cf. Trkm. *babïr* 'пантера' (TrkmRS) (< P. < Ar.).

BĀČAY Alt. 19th-20th c. **Bāčay** [Баачай], fem. (OjrRS 211).

BĀČČÏYA Yak. **Bāččïya** [Баччыjа] (Pek.).

BĀJAY Yak. **Toyon Bājay** [Тоjон Баџаi], Ulūtuyar Ulū-toyon's younger son (Pek.).

BĀJÏS Yak. **Bājïs** [Баџыс] (Pek.).

BĀDUR see **BAĠATUR**

BĀDUR-XAN-BEY see **BAĠATUR**

BĀY Alt. 19th-20th c. **Bāy** [Баай], fem. (OjrRS 211).

BĀY-BAYANAY Yak. **Bāy-bayanay** [Баi-баjанаi], tutelary deity of hunters and fishers (Pek.). ✧ 'Rich Bayanay' (Pek.). ⇨ **BAY + BAYANAY II**.

BĀYÏR-BEK see **BAYÏR**

BĀYQA Yak. **Bāyqa** [Баiка] (Pek.).

BĀKÏ Kzk. 20th c.? **Baki-bay** [Бакибаевъ], a merchant in Osh, Kirghizstan (Turk. Kraj 1912, 6); Az. 19th c. **Baki-χan** [Bakichanov] (Mende 32); Uzb. 1704 **Bākï**

[Bāqī Toqsabah-i Alčin], from Bukhara (Buchari 280); Oghuz **Bākï / Baki** [باقى], the ancestor of the Ottoman dynasty (Āšikp. 50). ✧ 'Eternal; remaining, surviving' cf. Chag., Trkm., Uzb. (Ar.) *baqï* 'ewig' (Radl. IV, 1439), Turk. *baki* 'tanrı; kalan, artık' (Özön), *baki* 'permanent, everlasting, remaining' (TED). See also **AQ-BĀKİ, AWÏZ-BĀKİ, AZ-BĀKİ, KÜNÄŠ-BAKİ**.

BĀLİ Turk. 15th c. **Bāli**, a judge (kadi) (Gökb., Ed. 149); Turk. 1552 **Bāli**, a man in a conscription made in Hungary (Dávid); Yürük 1543 **Bāli** (Gökb., Rum. 181); Yürük 1543 **Bāli**, name of several persons in the conscription of Yürüks from Kocacık and the nâhiye of Aydos, Turkey (Gökb., Rum. 175-242); Turk. 15th c.-16th c. **Bāli-aɣa**, two persons in the source (Gökb., Ed.); Turk. 15th c.-16th c. **Bāli-bey**, eight persons in the source (Gökb., Ed.); Turk. 1475 **Bāli-čelebi** (Gökb., Ed. 276); Turk. 15th c. **Bāli-paša** (Gökb., Ed. 350, 351). ✧ 'Adolescent, adult; perfect, mature; (myst.) arrived at spiritual perfection' cf. Turk. *baliğ* 'id.' (TED), بالى *bāli* 'alt, abgenutzt' (Zenker). See also **ČOLAQ-BĀLİ, DEDE-BĀLİ, EYMİR-BĀLİ, İSA-BĀLİ, QARA-BĀLİ, TUR-BĀLİ**.

BĀNYA Yak. **Bānya** [Банjа] (Pek.). ✧ Vanya (dim. of R. Ivan) (Pek.).

BĀÑQA see **PĀNQA**

BĀRJÏQ Khazar **Bārjïq** [Bārjïk] (Golden 156).

BĀRDA Yak. **Bārda** [Барда] (Pek.).

BĀSA Yak. **Bāsa** [Баса] (Pek.). ✧ Vasya (dim. of R. Vasiliy) (Pek.).

BĀSQA see **PĀSQA**

BĀŠTŪ Bulg. 10th c. **Bāštū** [Bāštū / Bāštwā], a Muslim envoy (Golden 160).

BĀTÏR see **BATÏR**

BĀZDĀR Selj. 12th c. **Bāzdār** [بازدار] (Muh. Ibrahim 23). ✧ 'Falconer (a dignity)' cf. Turk. *baz* 'Doğan kuşu' (Özön) (<P.), P. *bāzdār* 'сокольничий' (PRS).

BĀZÏM Alt. 19th-20th c. **Bāzïm**, fem. (OjrRS 211). ✧ 'Awl'?

BÂY-BOLDÏ see **BAY-BOLDÏ**

BÄBİKİNÄY Yak. **Bäbikinäy** [Бäбiкiнäi] (Pek.).

BÄBİS Bashk. 1739 **Bäbis** [Бябис Казакаев] (MIB III, 407).

BÄČÄ Uyg. **Bäčä-apa-ičräki** [Bäçä Apa İçräki] (ETY II, 65).

BÄDRÜN Uyg. **Bädrün** [Bädrün] (EUTS).

BÄG see **BEK**

BÄG-ARSLAN see **BEG-ARSLAN**

BÄG-BARS see **BEG-BARS**

BÄG-BUQA see **BEK-BUQA**

BÄG-TAŠ see **BEK-TAŠ**

BÄGİ Yak. **Bägi-suorun-toyon / Bäɣi-suorun-toyon** [Bägi-suorun-toyon / Bäɣi / Бäҕi], Ulū-tuyar Ulū-toyon's son, head of the celestial abāsï-spirits (Pek.).

BÄGİYDÄN Yak. **Bägiydän** [Тiмiр Бäгiiдäн], a

shamaness (Pek.).

BÄGİNÄ Uyg. 12th c.-14th c. **Bäginä** (Radl., USp. 212, 254); Tat. 1671 **Bigine** [Ингольда Бигининъ] (Kurdjumov 327); Bashk. 1707 **Bigine / Bıginey?** [Аднаш Бигинеев] (MIB III, 39). ✧ 'Who does no wickedness' cf. NUyg.(Tar.) *bägünä* 'der nichts Böses thut' (Radl. IV, 1581). ⇨ **BEGNİ.**

BÄGNİ see **BEGNİ**

BÄGÜ Uyg. **Bägü-tutuq** [Bägü Tutuk] (EUTS). ⇨ **BEGİ?**

BÄHBİT Trkm. 20th c. **Bähbit** [Bähbit] (Zaj. 1971, 328); Trkm. 20th c. **Bähbıt** [Бахбит] (TrkmRS 124). ✧ 'Benefit, gain' cf. Trkm. *bäχbıt* 'польза, выгода' (TrkmRS) (<Ar.).

BÄYBÄJİN Yak. **Bäybäjin** [Бäйбäцiн] (Pek.).

BÄYBÄKİN Yak. **Bäybäkin** [Бäйбäкiн], fem. (Pek.).

BÄYBÄLJİN Yak. **Bäybäljin-quo** [Бäйбäлцiн], a girl in a tale (Pek.).

BÄYBÄRİKÄN-ÄMÄXSİN Yak. **Bäybärikän-ämäχsin** [Бäйбäрiкäн], fem. (Pek.).

BÄYGESİ Kzk. 19th c. **Bäygesi** [Байгесы] (SOV 50). ✧ 'Horse-racer'? cf. Kzk. *bäyge* 'скачки; приз на скачках; премия' (KzRS) + suff. *-si / -ši / -či.*

BÄYİMBET Kkalp. 20th c. **Bäyimbet** (KkRS 773). ⇨ **BÄY + İMBET.** See also **BAYMAT.**

BÄK-İŠ Tat.(Sib.) 1620 **Bäk-iš / Baqšï?** [Бякишев (Аткузял) / Бакшиев] (Miller, Ist. Sib. II, 257). ✧ 'Lord-mate/supporter' (Sattarov: *Bigeš / Bigiš*). ⇨ **BEK + EŠ.** See also **BAY-İŠ, BEGİČ.**

BÄKİYÄ Yak. **Bäkiyä** [Tallan-Bäkiyä / Бäкiйä], a worker in a tale (Pek.). ✧ 'Tall and a bit humped' cf. Yak. *bäkiy-* 'быть высоким и сутуловатым' (Pek.).

BÄKİR Bashk. 1687 **Bäkir** [Нагазурка Бакировъ] (Vel.-Zern., Bašk. 45); Bashk. 1735 **Bäkir** [Бякиръ Теникеевъ], a tarχan (Vel.-Zern., Bašk. 16); Bashk. 1759 **Bäkir** [Бякир Мютюгулов] (MIB IV/2, 26); Bashk. 1768 **Bäkir** [Бакир Игимбетев] (MIB IV/1, 332); Bashk. 1770 **Bäkir** [Бакир Азягулов] (MIB IV/1, 345); Kzk. 19th c. **Bäkir-bay** [Базаръ-Кулъ Бакирбаевъ] (Grod., Pril. 175). ✧ I. 'First (child); early ripened/matured (child), quickly grown up (child)' cf. Bashk. PN *Bakir* 'тәүге' (<Ar.) (Kusimova), Tat. PN *Bäkir* 'иртә житлеккән, тиз үскән' (<Ar.) (Sattarov), Kzk. PN *Bäkir* (Žanuzakov-Esbaeva); II. 'Poor, shoddy'? cf. NUyg.(Tar.) *bäkir* 'arm, dürftig' (Radl. IV, 1576) (<Ar.).

BÄKİRDÄN Yak. 19th c. **Bäkirdän** [Бäкiрдäн] (Pek.).

BÄKİRİYİ Yak. **Bäkiriyi-suorun-buχatïr** [Бäкiрiйi], a bogatyr, Käkä-suorun-toyon's son (Pek.).

BÄKİSTÄY Yak. **Bäkistäy** [Öksüküläχ Bäkistäy / Бäкiстäй / Бÿгÿстäй / Бÿкÿстäй], a man in a tale (Pek.). ⇨ **BÜGÜSTÄY / BÜKÜSTÄY.**

BÄKİTTÄ Yak. **Bäkittä** [Küöχ Bäkittä uol / Бäкiттä], a spirit, epithet of a spirit (Pek.).

BÄLÄX Bulg. 1340 **Bäläχ / Balaχ** [بلح / Balaḫ / Бäläх] (Jusupov 47, Epigr. Bulg. 120, 121).

BÄLÄNYİK Yak. **Bälänyik** [Бäläнjiк] (Pek.). ✧ Venedikt (R.).

BÄLGİČİ Khazar 703 **Bälgiči** [Βαλγίτζις], a Khazar governor of the town Bosporos (ca. 703) (Byz. Turc. 86). ⇨ **BELGİ** + suff. *-či.*

BÄLİYPA · Kkalp. 20th c. **Bäliypa**, fem. (KkRS 777).

BÄLTÜLÄK Bulg. 13th c. - 14th c. **Bältüläk** [بلتلك] (Jusupov 39).

BÄPPİRÄY Yak. **Bäppiräy** [Бäппipäi] (Pek.). ✧ Porfiriy (R.).

BÄRÄSKÄYİ Tat.? 1785 **Bäräskäyi** [برسكا یى] (Jusupov 77).

BÄRGÄLYİN Yak. **Bärgälyin** [Bärt Bärgälyin / Бäргäлjiн], a bogatyr in a tale (Pek.). ✧ 'Brave; devil of a fellow; dare-devil' cf. Yak. *bärgän* меткий, искусный; молодец, удалец, витязь' (Pek.).

BÄRGİN-SÄŇÄ see **BERGİN-SEKÄ**

BÄRK-MÄŇGÜ see **BERK-MEŇGÜ**

BÄRKİN-SÄŇÄ see **BERGİN-SEKÄ**

BÄRT-BÄRGÄLYİN see **BÄRGÄLYİN**

BÄŠİR Kzk. 19th c. **Bašir** [Баширъ] (AOO 18); Tat./Bashk. 1823 **Bäšir** [Башировъ], a Teptär (TOUAK XXIV, 141); Bashk. 1749 **Bäšir** [Бяшир Имангулов] (MIB III, 469); Bashk. 1771 **Bäšir** [Башир Мансуров] (MIB IV/1, 354). ✧ Bashir (Ar.) 'bringer of good news, Messenger sent by Allah' (Ahmed).

BÄWEN Kkalp. 20th c. **Bäwen-bala** [Бөÿенбала] (KkRS 773); Kkalp. 20th c. **Bewen-bala / Beven-bala** [Бевен-бала] (Bask., Kkalp. 58 (162)).

BEBİT see **BEYBİT**

BEBEK Trkm. 20th c. **Bäbek** [Bäbek], fem. (Zaj. 1971, 341); Trkm. 20th c. **Bäbek** [Бабек], fem. (TrkmRS 124); Chuv. 18th-19th c. **Bebäk** [Бебякъ] (Magn. 33); Chuv. 18th-19th c. **Bebek** [Бебекъ] (Magn. 33); Oghuz 867 **Bebek-beg** [Babkial / Babkiak / Bamkial / Makial], a Türk chief under Al-Muʿtazz (866-869) (Weil, Abbas II, 401); Oghuz 865 **Bebek-bek** [با بكباك] (Fragm. Hist. Ar. 578); Oghuz 9th c. **Bebek-bek / Beykebek?** [با بكباك / با يكبا ك], a Türk chief (865), governor of Egypt (869) (Tabarī, Annal. III, 1543); Kkalp. 20th c. **Böbik** (KkRS 773). ✧ 'Baby' cf. Trkm. *bäbek* 'крошка, младенец' (TrkmRS), Kzk. *böbek* 'bebek' (KzTS). See also **XİS-PAJAX.**

BEBEKEY Chuv. 18th-19th c. **Bebekey** [Бебекей] (Magn. 33); Kzk. 19th c. **Bebekey** [Бебекай] (SOK 308); Tat.(Mish.) 1748 **Bebkey / Bebekey?** [Бебкей] (Nepljuev 438). ✧ 'Little child' cf. Tat. *bäbäkäy / bäbi* 'ein Kind, das Kindchen' (Radl. IV, 1637, 1638).

BEČAR see **BİČARA**

BEČENE Oghuz/Trkm. 13th c. **Bečene** [بجنه /

Бечене], Kök-χan's son (Abulg./Kon. 520, 555, 605).

BEJİT   Kkalp. 20th c. **Bejit** [Беджит] (Bask., Kkalp. 399).

BEJİTTİ   Alt. 19th c. **Bejitti-χan** [Бежитты-хан] (Verb., In. 166, 167).

BEDİR   Turk. 20th c. **Bedir-χan** [Bedirhan] (Önder, Göle). ✧ Badr (Ar.) 'full moon' (Ahmed).

BEDRÜN   Uyg. 13th c. **Bedrün** [bedrün] (DTS).

BEG see **BEK**

BEG-ALİ   Kkalp. 20th c. **Beg-alï** [Бегалы] (KkRS 772). ⇨ BEK + ALİ.

BEG-ARSLAN   Uyg. **Bäg-arslan** [Bäg Arslan] (EUTS); Uyg. 8th c. **Beg-arslan** [Bäg Arslan] (Müller, Pfahl. 12); Uyg. 12th c.-14th c. **Beg-arslan** (DTS). ✧ 'Prince-Lion' (Blagova 1997, 705), 'High/noble-Lion'. ⇨ BEG + ARSLAN.

BEG-ATAR   Kzk.? 19th c. **Beg-atar** [Бегатаръ] (Maev I, 155). ⇨ BEK.

BEG-BARS   Uyg. 8th c. **Beg-bars** [Bäg bars], a tayši (Müller, Pfahl. 24); Uyg. 12th c.-14th c. **Beg-bars** [Bäg Bars / beg bars] (Radl., USp. 141, EUTS, DTS); Uyg. 8th c. **Beg-bars-sañun** [Bäg bars sangun] (Müller, Pfahl. 23); Chuv. 18th-19th c. **Piχ-pars** [Пихпарсъ] (Magn. 68).

BEK-BARS   Chuv. 18th-19th c. **Pik-barïs** [Пикбарысъ] (Magn. 66); Chuv. 18th-19th c. **Pik-bars** [Пикбарсъ] (Magn. 66).

BEG-BUГA see **BEK-BUQA**

BEG-KÜNKİ   Uyg. **Beg-künki-tay-sañun** [Beg Künki Taisangun Sïrtuš Yägän Apa], ruler of Bešbalïq (Bišbalyq) (Mahrnāmag 10). ⇨ BEK.

BEG-TAŠ see **BEK-TAŠ**

BEG-TEMİR-QUZ   Uyg. 13th c. **Beg-temir-quz** (DTS). ✧ 'Prince-Iron-?'. ⇨ BEK + TEMİR + QUZ.

BEG-TEMÜRLÜ   Turk. 1540 **Beg-temürlü-kethudā**, chief of the ethnic community Güneşlü (Diyarbekir, Turkey) (Demirtaş 56). ⇨ BEK + TEMİR + Adj. suff. -lü / -li.

BEG-TİMUR see **BEK-TEMİR**

BEG-TURMİŠ   Uyg. **Bäg-turmïš** [Bäg Turmış] (EUTS); Uyg. 13th c. **Beg-turmïš** (DTS). ✧ 'Prince-Was-Born' (Blagova 1997, 715). ⇨ BEK + TURMİŠ.

BEG-VERDİ see **BEK-BERDİ**

BEGJİK   Khorezm. 14th c. **Begjik**, a merchant, Toγluq Temür's (1348-1363) life-saver (Tar. Rashidi 9). ✧ 'Little Beg/Lord'. ⇨ BEG + dim. suff. -jik.

BEGÄČ-ARSLAN   Karakh. 11th c. **Begäč-arslan-tegin** [begäč arslan tegin] (DTS); Karakh. 11th c. **Bekeč-arslan-tegin / Bekeč-arslan-tigin** [Bekeç Arslan Tégin / Bekeç Arslan Tigin] (MK/Atalay 833, 834). ✧ 'Prince-Lion(-tegin)' (Blagova 1997, 705). ⇨ BEGİČ + ARSLAN.

BEGÄŠ   Tat. 1841 **Begäš** [Бегашъ Бектауловъ] (Konšin, Mat. V, 34). ✧ 'Prince' cf. Tat. PN Bigäš

(Sattarov).

BEGEY   Tat.? 1598, 1599 **Begey** [Бегѣй] (AI II, 5, 17-18, 20); Bashk. 1730 **Begey** [Бегей Тураев] (MIB III, 272); Kzk. 19th c. **Begey** [Бегей] (AOA 2). ✧ 'Hero; brave man' cf. Tat. PN Bigiy (Sattarov). ⇨ BEGİ. See also TEN-BEGEY.

BEGEM-BAY see **BEKEN**

BEGEN   Kzk. **Begen** [Есемханъ Бегембетевъ] (Konšin, Pam. 4); Kirg. 19th c. **Begen** [Бегень] (Potanin II, 4).

BEGENBET   Kzk. 19th c. **Begenbet** [Бегембетъ] (SOK 48); Kzk. 19th c. **Begenbet** [Бегенбетъ] (SODž. 108). ⇨ BEGEN + suffixoid -bet.

BEGENČ   Trkm. 20th c. **Begenč** [Begenč] (Zaj. 1971, 328); Trkm. 20th c. **Begenč** [Бегенч] (TrkmRS 82); Trkm. 1745 **Begenč / Bekenj?** [Бекендж Али-бек], from the Yomut tribe (MIT II, 172, 173, 178); Trkm. 1826 **Begenč / Bekenj?** [Бекендж], a mulla from the Teke tribe (MIT II, 438); Trkm. 1817/18 **Begenj-bek / Bekenj-serdar** [Бегендж-бек / Бекендж-сердар], from the Teke tribe (MIT II, 403, 447); Trkm. 1817/18 **Bekenj-serdar / Begenj-bek** [Бегендж-бек / Бекендж-сердар], from the Teke tribe (MIT II, 403, 447). ✧ 'Joy, adoration, gaiety' cf. Trkm. begenč 'радость, восторг; веселье' (TrkmRS).

BEGENJ-BEK see **BEGENČ**

BEGENEY   Bashk. 1730 **Begeney** [Касый Бегенеев] (MIB III, 279). ⇨ ? + dim. suff. -ey.

BEGİ   Karakh. 11th c. **Begi** [begi / Begi] (DTS, MK/Atalay 833); Mo. **Beki-bahadur** [Беки-бахадур], Tuqučar's grand-son (RaD I/1, 163); Uzb. 1845 **Beki-Jan-bek / Bekin-Jan-bek?** [Беки Джан-бек / Бекинджан-бек] (MIT II, 498); Uzb. 1826 **Beki-yüzbaši** [Беки-юзбаши] (MIT II, 436, 455, 466, 470, 471, 473, 475, 489, 492); Az., Trkm.? 1306 **Bigi** [بیکی شغاول] (Dorn 10); Tat. 19th c. **Bigi** [Zahir Bigi] (Mende 74, 178); Tat. 19th c. **Bigi / Bigey** [Musa Ğarullah Bigi (Bigeev)] (Mende 54, 55, 74, 79, 80, 103). ✧ 'Hero; husband', the Mongolised form of Turkic Beg. Cf. Karakh. begi I. / beki 'герой' (DTS), Mo. beki, TMEN I, No.114. Used mostly as a secondary component of personal names. ⇨ BEG. See also GÖČ-BEGİ.

BEGİČ   Kipch.? 14th c. **Begič** [Бѣгичка], a prince of Mamay, the (Kipchak?) khan of the Horde (PSRL XI, 43); Tat. 1630 **Begič** [Бегичев Бектул] (Miller, Ist. Sib. II, 369); Tat. 1743 **Begič** [Бѣгичев], a captain (Alatyr. 162); Bashk. 1700 **Begiš** [Бегишка / Бегишъ] (Vel.-Zern., Bašk. 35, 36); Kirg. **Begiš** [Бегиш], fem. (Jud. 633); Tat. 1543 **Begüč** (Gökb., Rum. 235); Tat. 1764 **Bigäš / Bigeš** [Бигаш Мамашев] (MIB IV/1, 279); Tat. 1779 **Bigäš / Bigeš** [Илкей Бигешев (Бигашев)] (MIB V, 82, 93); Tat. 1779 **Bigäš / Bigeš** [Рямгул (Рямкул, Рянгул)

Бигашев] (MIB V, 82); Kzk. 19th c. **Bigäš / Bigeš** [Бигашъ] (AOK 114); Bashk. 1695 **Bigiš** [Бигишев] (MIB I, 91); Bashk. 1750 **Bigiš** [Сюрдяк Бигишев] (MIB III, 472-73). ✧ 'Son of the Khan/Beg; Little/Young Khan/Beg' (title of a khan's son) cf. Karakh. *Bekeç* 'Tekinlerin, Han oğullarının sanı' (MK/Atalay IV, 833), Tat. *Bigäš, Bigäč, Bigiš~Bigeš* (Sattarov), *Beğeç* (Erol II). ⇨ **BEG** + dim. suff. *-ič / -eš / -iš*.

BEGİK   Kzk. 19th c. **Begik** [Бедикъ] (SOK 28).

BEGİM   Chag. 1565 **Begim** [Бегим], fem. (Ivanov 253); Tat.(Lit.) 1594 **Begim** [Бегимовна], a Tatar woman (Lit. Tat. 228); Bashk. 1708 **Begim** [Бегим Кайбула (Кайбулин)] (MIKk. 153); Kkalp. 20th c. **Begim** [Бегим] (KkRS 773); Kkalp. 20th c. **Begim** [Бегим] (Bask., Kkalp. 399); Kzk. 19th c. **Begim-bay** [Бегымбай] (SODž. 156); Chag. 1562 **Begim-bikeč** [Бегим-бикеч], fem. (Ivanov 133); Turk. 15th c. **Beygüm-χatun / Begüm-χatun?** [Beygüm Hatun], wife of Jihan-šah (Cihanşah) (Uzunçarş., Anad. 93); Bashk. 1714 **Bigim** [Бигим Мурзаев] (MIB I, 105); Bashk. 1744 **Bigim** [Бигим Сарманов] (MIB III, 415). ✧ 'My prince', 'My princeess' (title, address (and/or a component of compound names); East.T. بکیم / بیکیم 'an address and title of a prince in Eastern Turkestan; title of a princess in Western Turkestan and India' (Le Coq, Namenl. 96); Title of women; the wife of a *beg/bek*, cf. Chag., East.T. *begim* 'die Frau eines Beg' (Radl. IV, 1581); '. nom [title] que portaient les filles de mirzâs Manghouts, qui passaient dans la couche d'un souverain.' (Abulg./Desm. 229).

BEGİMBET   Kzk. 19th c. **Begimbet** [Бегимбетъ] (SOK 44). ⇨ **BEG, BEGİM?** + suff. *-imbet / -bet?*

BEGİŠ see **BEGİČ**

BEGLÄN   Karakh. 11th c. **Beglän** [beglän / Beglen] (DTS, MK/Atalay 833). ✧ 'Defend/protect yourself!' cf. Karakh. *beglän-* 'оберегать' (DTS).

BEGLER   Yürük 1543 **Begler-χan** [Beğlerhan] (Gökb., Rum. 210); Trkm. 1813 **Begler-χan** [Беглер-хан (Беглербеги-хан)], a member of the Čaušlu/Čapušlu tribe (MIT II, 213, 214, 220, 224, 283-287, 404, 407).

BEGLERČİ   Tat.(GH) 14th c. **Beglerči** [Πεγλερτζου], a christened Tatar (Byz. Turc. II, 249). ⇨ **BEGLER?** + suff. *-či*.

BEGLİ   Turk. 1556 **Begli / Beyli** [Μπεδελη], an Ottoman Pasha (Byz. Turc. II, 205); Yürük 16th c. **Begli-χan / Beyli-χan?** [بکلی حان / Beğli han], from the Yürüks of Kocacık, Turkey (Gökb., Rum. 104). ⇨ **BEG** + suff. *-li*.

BEGLİK   Khorezm.? 1227 **Beglik / Beklek?** [بکلك], an officer of Beklek [or] Özbek atabek (Nasawī 152). ✧ 'Wellfare, wealth' cf. Trkm. *beglik* 'благополучие, привольная жизнь' (TrkmRS), East. T., Crm. *bäglik* 'das zu einem Bege Gehörige; die Würde eines Beg'

(Radl. IV, 1582). ⇨ **BEG** + suff. *-lik*.

BEGMİŠ   Yürük 16th c. **Begmiš** [بیکمش / Begmiş [?]], from the Yürüks of Kocacık, Turkey (Gökb., Rum. 103).

BEGNİ   Türk 732 **Bägni** [Bägni] (ETY I, 178); Türk 8th c. - 9th c. **Begni** (DTS). ✧ 'A kind of beer' cf. Uyg. *bäkini, bäkni* 'bira (içki)' (EUS); MT *bäkni* 'Bier aus Weizen, Hirze oder Gerste' (MK); Maml. *beğni* 'darı sirasi' (IM).

BEGREK   Selj. 12th c. **Begrek / Beyrek** [بکرك], Alp-arslan (1063-1072) Sultan's χājib (Rāwandī 117); Oghuz/Trkm. 14th c.-15th c. **Beyrek**, follower of Salur-qazan (DQorq./Ergin 96, 113); Oghuz/Trkm. 14th c.-15th c. **Beyrek** [بایرك / بامسى باریك / Bamsi Beyrek] (DQorq./Rossi 112-134 etc., 167, 171). ✧ 'Notable, prince' cf. Uyg. *bägräk* 'bey, şehzade' (US); Title used also as a component of male names. See also **BAMSİ-BEYREK**.

BEGÜ-TUTUQ-QÏRQU   Uyg. 12th c.-14th c. **Begü-tutuq-qïrqu-señün** (DTS). ✧ 'Gift/present-tutuq-wrinkled' (Blagova 1997, 712) cf. OT *begü* 'дар, подарок', Karakh. *qïrγu / qïrqu* 'розовый, румяный' (DTS), cf. also comp. *tutuq*. ⇨ **TUTUQ** + **QÏRQU**.

BEGÜČ see **BEGİČ**

BEGÜM see **BEGİM**

BEH-TEMİR see **BEK-TEMİR**

BEHADUR see **BAΓATUR**

BEHİŠT   Trkm. 20th c. **Behišt** [Behišt], fem. (Zaj. 1971, 337); Trkm. 20th c. **Behišt** [Бехишт], fem. (TrkmRS 92). ✧ 'Paradise' cf. Trkm. *behišt* 'рай; райский' (TrkmRS) (<P.).

BEY-BARS see **BAY-BARS**

BEY-BOΓA   Maml. 15th c. **Bey-boγa** [Beyboğa], a mamluk chief (Uzunçarş., Anad. 42, 46). ⇨ **BEK** + **BUQA**.

BEY-BÖYREK   Trkm. **Bey-böyrek** [Beyböyrek / Beyböğrek], hero of a Türkmen tale (Riza III, 68). ⇨ **BEK**.

BEY-BULAT see **BİY-BULAT**

BEY-BUT   Kzk. 19th c. **Bey-but** [Бейбутъ] (SOK 116, 274). ⇨ **BEK** + **BUT**.

BEY-ČEMER   Kzk. 19th c. **Bey-čemer** [Бейчемеръ] (SOK 110). ✧ 'Lord/prince - strap(?)' Cf. Trkm. *čemmer* 'верблюжья подпруга (свитая из шерсти)' (TrkmRS). ⇨ **BEK.** See also **AT-ČEMER**.

BEY-DEMİR see **BAY-TEMİR**

BEY-ΓAWUL   Kzk. 19th c. **Bey-γawul** [Бейгавулъ Аманъ Гельдiевъ] (Grod., Pril. 79). ⇨ **BEK**.

BEY-TEMÜR see **BAY-TEMİR**

BEYAZ   Turk. **Beyaz** (Önder, Hınıs). ✧ 'White' cf. Turk. *beyaz* 'id.' (TED). ⇨ **AQ**.

BEYBİT   Kzk. 19th c. **Bebit-pay** [Бебитпай] (SOV 142); Kzk. 19th c. **Beybit** [Бейбитъ] (SOV 26); Kzk.

19th c. **Bibit** [Кунту Бибитовъ] (SKSO VIII, 201); Kkalp. 1742 **Bibit** [Быбыт], a Sultan (MIB I, 491, 492). ✧ 'Peaceful, quiet, calm' cf. Kzk. (<P.) *beybit* 'ruhig, still, friedlich' (Radl. IV, 1574).

BEYJE Turk. 1448 **BeyJe** [Beyce bin Abdullah] (Gökb., Ed. 266). ⇨ **BEK** + suff. *-je*.

BEYDE Az. **Beyde** [Бейде, Кечаль-Бейде], a man in a tale; as his head was bald he was called Kečal-Beyde (Az. Skaz. 540).

BEYGÜM see **BEGİM**

BEYĞU Khazar **Beyγu** [Бейгу, Ябгу], a Khazar prince (yabγɹ) (MIT 450, 451); Selj. 1037/38 **Beyγu** [Муса ибн Сельджук Ябгу Калян (Бейгу, Муса Ябгу)] (MIT I, 232-33, 246, 248 etc.); OT (Qarluq) 1158 **Beyγu-χan** [Бейгу-хан], chief of the Qarluqs (MIT I, 444). ✧ 'A kind of kite' cf. Turk. 'toγana beŋzer bir newī šikār qušïdur' (Šeyh Suleyman); *piγū* [<Chag. يغو] 'ein Jagdvogel aus der Ordnung der Habichte' (Radl. IV, 1325).

BEYİK I. Bashk. 1664 **Beyik** [Игишко Беиков] (MIB I, 191).

BEYİK II. see **BÜYÜK**

BEYMES Tat. 1689 **Beymes** (<**Bey-imes?**) [Беймеско] (Kungursk. akty 165).

BEYNİ Turk. **Beyni-oγlu**, a Zeybek (Kúnos 1891, 119). ✧ 'Gentleman's (son)' cf. Turk. *beyni* 'Beyin' (TarS I, 528). ⇨ **BEK**. See also **BEGNİ?**

BEYREK see **BEGREK**

BEYS Kzk. 19th c. **Beys** [Бейсъ] (AOO 6); Kzk 19th c. **Beys-pay** [Бейспай] (SOK 20). ✧ 'Paradise' cf. Kzk. *beis* 'das Paradies' (Radl. IV, 1574) (<P. *behišt*).

BEYSE Kzk. 19th c. **Beyse-bay** [Бейсебай] (SOV 18, 56, 126); Kzk. 19th c. **Beyse-bek** [Бейсебекъ] (SOV 18); Kzk. 19th c. **Biyse-bek** [Бийсебекъ] (SOV 90). ⇨ **BEYŠE?**

BEYSEKEY Kzk. 19th c. **Beysekey** [Бейсекей] (AOK 70). ⇨ **BEYSE** + dim. suff. *-key*.

BEYSEM-BAY see **BEYSEN**

BEYSEMBE see **BEYSENBİ**

BEYSEMBİ see **BEYSENBİ**

BEYSEN Kzk. 19th c. **Beyse-bay** [Бейсебай] (AOAtb. 2); Kzk. 19th c. **Beysem-bay** [Бейсембай] (SOV 4); Kzk. 19th c. **Beysen** [Бейсень] (AOA 102); Kzk. 19th c. **Beysen** [Бейсень] (AOP 94); Kzk. 19th c. **Beysen** [Бейсенъ] (AOO 6); Kzk. 19th c. **Beysen** [Бейсенъ] (AOO 10); Kzk. 19th c. **Beysen / Beysem-bay** [Бейсенъ / Бейсембай] (SOV 24). See also **SARSEN**.

BEYSENBE see **BEYSENBİ**

BEYSENBİ Kzk. 19th c. **Beysembe** [Бейсембе] (AOP 74); Kzk. 19th c. **Beysembi** [Бейсембы] (AOO 2); Kzk. 19th c. **Beysembi / Beysembe** [Бейсембе, Бейсембы] (SOV 14, 16); Kzk. 19th c. **Beysenbe** [Бейсенбе] (SOK 60); Kzk. 19th c. **Beysenbe** [Бейсенбе] (AOK 94); Kzk. 19th c. **Biysembe** [Бийсембе] (AOP 118). ✧ 'Thursday' cf. Kzk. *beysämbi* (<P.) 'der Donnerstag' (Radl. IV, 1574), *beysenbi* 'id.' (KzRS).

BEYSENE Tat.(Tob.) **Beysene** [Bäisänä / Бäicänä], fem. (Proben IV, 300 /372/).

BEYSTİ Kzk. 19th c. **Beysti-bay** [Бейстыбай] (SODž. 12). ⇨ **BESTİ? / BEYS?** + suff. *-ti*.

BEYŠE Kirg. **Beyše** [Бейше] (Jud. 887). ⇨ **BEYSE?**

BEK Chuv. 19th c. **Bak-murza / Bik-murza?** [Ilimursa Bakmursin] (Kronheim 96); Türk 7th-9th c. **Bäg-čur** [Bäg Çur] (ETY II, 135); Türk 7th-9th c. **Bäk** [Bäk] (ETY II, 171); Yürük 15th c. **Beg** [بك / Beğ?], From the Yürüks of Kocacık, Turkey (Gökb., Rum. 103); Kirg. **Beg-ayïm**, fem. (Jud. 556); Türk **Beg-čur** (DTS); Trkm. 20th c. **Beg-han** [Beghan] (Zaj. 1971, 325); Kkalp. 20th c. **Beg-zada** [Бегзада], fem. (KkRS 777); Kkalp. 20th c. **Beg-žan** [Бегжан] (KkRS 773); Maml. 14th c. **Bey-χoJa / Bäy-χoJa** [بيخجا] (Sauvaget 44); Maml. 1377, 1378 **Bey-qoJa** [بيقجا الجمالى] (Iyās I, 239); Maml. 1400 **Bey-qoJa** [بيقجا طيفور الشرفى] (Iyās I, 323-24); Uyg. 1304 **Bek?** (Chwol., Syr.-nest. 48); Chag. 16th c. **Bek** [Бек], a mirza (Ivanov 254, 295, 297, 302, 304 etc.); Chag. 16th c. **Bek** [Бек], „emirza" (Ivanov 303); Chag. 1562 **Bek** [Бек], a mir (emir) (Ivanov 98); Bashk. 1616 **Bek** [Бек], a Bashkir murza (Miller, Ist. Sib. II, 235); Kzk. 19th c. **Bek** [Бекъ] (AOO 10); Tat. 20th c. **Bik-Jan**, fem. (Sattarov 48); Kipch. 1180 **Bek-aba** [Бякоба] (Ipat. 421 (435)); Selj. 1135 **Bek-aba** [المحمودى / صاحب البصره / بككابه / بكبه] (Ibn al-Athīr/Tornb. XI, 15-19, 23); Selj. 1135 **Bek-aba** [بك ابه], an emir in the service of Mas'ud of Baghdad (Ibn al-Athīr, Atab.: RHCHor II/2, 90); Kzk. 19th c. **Bek-atay** [Бекатай] (SKSO VIII, 201); Maml. 1521 **Bek-bay** [بكبا ى], an emir (Iyās III, 246); Bashk. 1715 **Bek-bay** [Бекбай Беккулов] (MIB III, 134); Kzk. 19th c. **Bek-bay** [Бекбай] (AOA 130); Kzk. 19th c. **Bek-bay** [Бекбай] (AOA 74); Tat. (Sib.) 1632 **Bek-bay** [Козяш Бекбаев] (Miller, Ist. Sib. II, 398); Tat. (Sib.) 1632 **Bek-bay** [Батыргилдейко Бекбаев] (Miller, Ist. Sib. II, 391); Tat. (Sib.) 1634 **Bek-bay** [Кунюк Бекбаев] (Miller, Ist. Sib. III, 421); Tat. (Sib.) 1646 **Bek-bay** [Бекбайко] (Miller, Ist. Sib. II, 512); Oghuz 969 **Bek-čur**, Mamluk chief of the Hamdanide Seyf ad-Dawlah (Weil, Chalif. III, 38 etc.); Oghuz 969, 989 **Bek-čur** [بكجور] (Kamāladdīn I, 161-172, 177-180); Oghuz 979 **Bek-čur** [بكجور التركى] (Ibn al-Athīr/Tornb. VIII, 502, IX, 59-62); Oghuz 980, 989 **Bek-čur** [بكجور] (Qalānisi 24, 28-31); Selj. 1095 **Bek-čur** [بكجور امير اق سنر] (Ibn Taghrīb. II, 312); Selj. 10th c. **Bek-čur** [بكجور التركى والىحمص], governor of Hims (Ibn Taghrīb. II, 5, 48); Tat. 1676

Bek-čura [Муратка Бекчуринъ] (Kurdjumov 6); Bashk. 1779 Bek-čura [Бекчура Исенгулов (Исянгулов)] (MIB V, 101, 102, 106, 132); Bashk. 1790 Bek-čura [Суяргул (Сюяргул) Бекчурин] (MIB V, 284, 327); Bashk. 1792 Bek-čura [Сюяргул Бекчурин] (MIB V, 327); Bashk. 1792 Bek-čura [Сулейман Бекчурин] (MIB V, 327); Bashk. 1793 Bek-čura [Сулейман (Сюлейман) Бекчурин] (MIB V, 327); Kzk. 19th c. Bek-čura [Бекчурин], a writer of articles (AUK 165); Kzk. 19th c. Bek-ǰan [Карджубай Бекджановъ] (Grod., Pril. 139); Bashk. 1754 Bek-ǰan / Bek-žan [Бекжен Кармяков] (MIB IV/1, 88); Uzb. 1855 Bek-ǰan-bek [Бекджан-бек] (MIT II, 550); 1651 Bek-χan [Бекъ-ханъ] (AI IV, 158); Khorezm. 1372 Bek-χoǰa [Бек-ходжа] (MIT I, 516); Kzk. 19th c. Bek-χoǰa [Бекходжин], a writer of articles (AUK 165); Kzk. 19th c. Bek-yigit [Бекигитъ] (Grod., Pril. 158); Kzk. 19th c. Bek-yigit [Бекигитъ Кутабаевъ] (Grod., Pril. 162); Bashk. 1735 Bek-küzä [Беккуза Кочкаров], a tarχan (Vel.-Zern., Bask. 16); Bashk. 18th c. Bek-küzä [Беккузя Аликеев] (MIB V, 415); Bashk. 1686 Bek-qul [Беккулъ Уразаевъ], a tarχan (Vel.-Zern., Bašk. 41); Bashk. 1706 Bek-qul [Камакай Беккулов] (MIB III, 25); Bashk. 1735 Bek-qul [Ишкуватъ Беккуловъ], a tarχan (Vel.-Zern., Bašk. 19); Bashk. 1735 Bek-qul [Аллагуватъ Беккуловъ] (Vel.-Zern., Bask. 19.); Kzk. 19th c. Bek-qul [Беккулъ] (SOV 44); Kkalp. 20th c. Bek-mïrza [Бекмырза] (KkRS 773); Nog.? Bek-murza [Бек-Мурза] (Žirm., Epos 430); Nog. 1649 Bek-murza [Бекъмурза] (AI IV, 87); Kirg. 19th c. Bek-murza [Бекъ-Мурза], Aq-murza's brother (Potanin II, 4); Uzb. 19th c. Bek-oγlï-bek [Bek-Oghly-bek], early 19th c., Khokand (Nalivkin-Dozon 97); Uzb. 1707 Bek-oγlu-biy [بیك اوغلی بی], from Bukhara (Buchari 298); Kzk. 19th c. Bek-pay [Бекпай] (AOAtb. 2); Kkalp. 20th c. Bek-suluw, fem. (KkRS 777); Kzk. 1790 Bek-šora [بیكچوره / Бекшора] (MIK IV, 136); Oghuz 11th c. Bek-tegin [Бек-тегин], a (Ghaznevid) commander-in-chief (sipehsalār) (MIT I, 239, 240); Khorezm. 1220 Bek-tegin [بکتکین سلاحدار], Alāaddin Muhammad's silaχdār (sword-bearer) (J̌uwaynī I, 116); Uzb. 19th c. Bek-ul? / Bek-qul? [Бекулъ] (SKSO III, 180); Kzk. 19th c. Bek-ulï [Бекулы] (SODž. 154); Bashk. 1735 Bek-zän [Мухамбетъ Бекзяновъ], a tarχan (Vel.-Zern., Bašk. 14); Kzk. 19th c. Bek-žan [Бекжанъ] (AUK 189); Kkalp. 20th c. Bek-žan [Бекжан] (KkRS 773); Kirg. Bek-žan [Бекжан] (Jud. 226); Tat.(Sib.) 1631 Bi-baχša / Bi-baχšï? [Бибахша Кавчуков / Кавчюков] (Miller, Ist. Sib. II, 382); Tat. 1530 Bi-bey [Бибей], a prince from Kazan, court hunter (PSRL VIII, 277); Kzk. 1829 Bi-čan / Bi-ǰan / Bi-žan? [Бичан] (MIK IV, 324); Tat.? Bi-čur [Бичуръ]

(PSRL); Chuv. 18th-19th c. Bi-čura [Бичура] (Magn. 34); Tat.? 1556 Bi-čura [Буччюра], a runner (PSRL XIII, 265); Tat. 1624 Bi-čura [Бичура Янгучеевъ] (Pokrovskij 72); Tat.? 1739 Bi-čura [Бячуринъ] (Alatyr. 143); Bashk. 1714 Bi-čura [Алчюкур Бичюрин] (MIB I, 105); Bashk. 1723 Bi-čura [Бичюринъ] (MIB III, 202); Tat. 1609 Bi-γul [Бигул] (Miller, Ist. Sib. II, 210); Bashk. 1756 Bi-yar / Biy-yar [Усман Бияров] (MIB IV/1, 128); Nog. 1649 Bi-murza [Би мурза Ештерековъ / Иштерековъ / Ищерековъ] (AI IV, 79, 87); Tat.(Sib.) 1598/99 Bi-padša / Bi-badša [Бибадша], a prince from Siberia, Küčüm-qan's son (AI II, 3, 17); Chuv. 18th-19th c. Biχ-čura [Бихчура] (Magn. 34); Chuv. 18th-19th c. Biχ-murza [Бихмурза] (Magn. 34); Chuv. 18th-19th c. Biy-čura [Бийчура] (Magn. 33); Kzk. 19th c. Biy-ǰan [Бийджанъ Тулегеневъ] (SKSO III, 190); Kzk. 19th c. Biy-ǰan [Бийджанъ Юзбаевъ] (Grod., Pril. 23); Kzk. 19th c. Biy-eke [Біеке] (SOV 92); Kzk. 19th c. Biy-eke [Біеке] (SODž. 30); Nog.? Biy-murza [Бий Мурза] (Žirm., Epos 430); Kkalp. 20th c. Biy-žan [Бийжан], fem. (KkRS 777); Tat. 18th-19th c. Bik-čura [Бикчура] (Magn. 34); Bashk. 20th c. Bik-yän [Бикьян] (Kusimova 35); Tat. 1739 Bik-qul [Биккулъ Ардрамаровъ] (Alatyr. 143); Bashk. 1668 Bik-qul [Чурака Биккуловъ] (Vel.-Zern., Bašk. 32); Bashk. 1789 Bik-qul [Биккул Муслюмов] (MIB V, 250); Bashk. 1788 Bik-murza [Бикмурза Куганчин] (MIB V, 234); Oghuz/Trkm. 13th c. Bik-tegin [بیك تکین / Бик-Тегин], Boγra-χan's son (Abulg./Kon. 890); Bashk. 1751 Bik-zän [Бикзянов] (MIB IV/1, 43); Chuv. 18th-19th c. Pi-čura [Пичура] (Magn. 68); Tat. 1739 Pi-čura [Пичура Бячурин] (Alatyr. 143); Chuv. 18th c. Pi-čurina (<Pi-čura) [Пичурина], a village in the district of Cheboksary (Korsakov 285); Chuv. 18th-19th c. Piχ-batïr [Пихбатыръ] (Magn. 67); Chuv. 18th-19th c. Piχ-čura [Пихчурей] (Magn. 68); Chuv. 18th-19th c. Piχ-čura [Пихчура] (Magn. 68); Chuv. 18th-19th c. Piχ-patïr [Пихпатыръ] (Magn. 68); Chuv. 18th-19th c. Pik-batïr [Пикбатыръ] (Magn. 66); Chuv. 18th-19th c. Pik-čura [Пикчура] (Magn. 67); Tat.(Bar.) Pï-qïs [Pi Kys / Пі кыс], fem. (Proben IV, 3 /3/); *TN:* Chuv. 18th c. Pik-čurina (<Pik-čura) [Пикчурина], a village in the district of Cheboksary (Korsakov 281). ✧ I/1. 'Ruler, prince; (feudal) magnate being under the khan'; commander' cf. Türk, Karakh., Uyg. *beg* ' правитель, вождь, бек, князь' (DTS), Kar.(L., T.), Kzk., Tat. *bī, bīy* 'der Fürst, der König, der Herr' (Radl. IV, 1737), Tat. *bik, bi* 'князь, вельможа' (TatRS), Turk. *bäi* 'Fürst, ein Ehrentitel' (Radl. IV, 1568); I/2. 'Emir; head of a district or town', cf. OT, Kuman, Chag., East.T., Crm., Trkm., Uzb. *bäg* 'der Beg, der Beamte (Buchara), der höhere Militärbeamte'

(Radl. IV, 1580), Maml. *bek* [د لِ] 'émir' (Sauvaget 41), Maml. *bey* 'Bey, emir' (Tarj/Toparl), Kzk. *bĭ, bĭy* 'der Richter; weise, Mensch, der schön zu reden versteht' (Radl. IV, 1737); I/3. ' Rich noble man, gentleman; rich man, judge, wise; chief; clerk' cf. Tat. *bik, bi* 'дворянин, господин, чиновник' (TatRS); I/4. *Beg/bäg, bek/bäk, bey, biy, bĭ* are generally used as a secondary component of male (rarely female) names originally expressing title/dignity, later title of respect or simply meaning 'man, noble man, gentleman and husband' cf. Kzk. *bek* 'составная часть собственнх имён (мужских); знатный (бек)' (KZRS), Kirg. *bek* 'бек (феодальный властитель, ниже хана); составная часть личных имён (мужских и женских' (Jud.), Uzb. *bek* 'бек (титул знатного лица; правитель какого-л. района или города в среднеазиатских ханствах в эпоху феодализма); составная часть имён собственных мужских; присоединяется к мужским именам, придавая оттенок уважения' (UzbRS), Bashk. *bäk = bey* 'бей - титул мелких феодалов; вежливое обращение к мужчине' (BRS/Uraksin), Turk. *bey* 'gentleman, Sir; (after name) Mr.; prince, ruler, chieftain; chief, head, master; notable, country gentleman' (TED); II. 'Strong, solid, firm, healthy' cf. Karakh. *bek II* 'крепкий; прочный' (DTS), cf. East.T., Chag., NUyg.(Tar.) *bäk*, Kzk. *bek, bik* 'fest, sehr' (Radl. IV, 1574), Kzk. *bek II.* 'pek, sağlam, çok, bilhassa' (KzTS), Kirg. *bek I* 'крепкий' (Jud.), Tat. *bik* 'sehr stark' (Radl. IV, 1739). – In several occurences the homonyms *bek (bäk)* 'prince, nobleman, etc.' / *bek (bäk)* 'strong, healthy' and *bik* 'prince, nobleman, etc.' / *bik* 'strong, healthy' cannot be separated because both meanings may well be acceptable. That is why the researchers interpret the names in question differently. Thus the interpretation of *Bek-jan* as 'Strong (=young) soul' or 'Prince/noble soul' in Bashkir and Tatar is also possible (cf. Kusimova 35, Sattarov 48). See also **ČAQČAQ-JANÏ-BEK, ÖZ-JANÏ-BEK, ÖZÜ-BEK, TÏNÏ-BEK.**

BEK-BAYBA Bashk. 1675 **Bek-bayba** [Бекбайба Убеховъ] (MIB I, 202). ⇨ **BEK.**

BEK-BAQLUY Tat. (Sib.) 1605 **Bek-baqluy** [Барашев Бекбаклуй] (Miller, Ist. Sib. II, 190, 191). ⇨ **BEK.**

BEK-BALTA Uzb. 1811 **Bek-balta-mirab** [Бек Балга-мираб], a man from the Nüküz clan (MIT II, 381-82). ⇨ **BEK + BALTA.**

BEK-BAS Kzk. 19th c. **Bek-bas** [Бекбасъ] (AOO 58). ✧ 'Opress hard!'. ⇨ **BEK + BAS II. / BAŠ?**

BEK-BAW Tat. 1722 **Bek-baw** [Бекбавка] (MIB I, 116); Bashk. 1760 **Bek-baw** [Миней Бекбовов] (MIB IV/2, 28); Bashk. 1762 **Bek-baw** [Бекбов Улеев] (MIB IV/1, 238); Bashk. 1780 **Bek-baw** [Иткул Бекбовов] (MIB V, 116); Bashk. 1791 **Bek-baw**

[Бекбов Илыкашев] (MIB V, 313); Bashk. 1789 **Bek-baw / Bik-baw** [Бекбов (Бикбов) Кулчумов] (MIB V, 264, 278, 293, 294); Kzk. 19th c. **Bek-paw / Bek-pau** [Бекпау] (SOK 4); Kzk. 19th c. **Bek-paw / Bek-pau** [Бекпау] (AOAtb. 22); Kzk. 19th c. **Bek-paw / Bek-pau** [Бекпау] (SOV 82). ✧ 'Fresh/strong tie/link' cf. Tat. PN *Bik-baw* (Sattarov). ⇨ **BEK + BAГ.**

BEK-BAWÏL Kkalp. 20th c. **Bek-bawïl** [Бекбауыл] (KkRS 773); Kzk. 19th c. **Bek-bawul / Bek-baul** [Бекбаулъ] (SOK 214). ⇨ **BEK.**

BEK-BAWLÏ Kkalp. 20th c. **Bek-bawlï** [Бекбаулы] (KkRS 773). ⇨ **BEK + BAW** + suff. -*lï*.

BEK-BAWUL see BEK-BAWÏL

BEK-BERDI Trkm.? 1580 **Beg-verdi-beg** [بیک بیردی] (Dorn 289); Tat. 1600 **Bek-berdi** [Бекберди] (MIB I, 152); Bashk. 1600 **Bek-berdi** [Бекбердей] (Miller, Ist. Sib. II, 159); Kzk. 19th c. **Bek-berdi** [Бекберды] (AOO 26); Kzk. 19th c. **Bek-berdi** [Бекберды] (Tynyšp. 70, 71); Kzk. 19th c. **Bek-berdi** [Бекъ Берди] (Grod., Pril. 162); Kzk. 19th c. **Bek-berdi** [Бекъ-Берди Бекъ-Матиевъ] (Grod., Pril. 136); Kzk. 19th c. **Bek-berdi** [Бекберды] (SODž. 94); Bashk. 1780 **Bek-berdi / Bek-berde** [Бекберде (Бекберда) Сеитбатталов] (MIB V, 110, 111, 145); Bashk. 1600 **Bek-perdi** [Бекперди Рахмангуловъ], a tarχan (Vel.-Zern., Bašk. 15). ✧ 'Lord/noble man has him/her given' cf. Tat. PN *Bikbirde* 'Бәк бирде, ягъни бәк булыр бала бирде' [A lord was given, that is, a child who will become a lord]. Kusimova mistakenly interprets the Bashk. PN *Bikbirðe* as 'Very (hard/strong) child was given'!. ⇨ **BEK + BERDI.** See also **BAY-BERDI.**

BEK-BERGEN Kzk. 19th c. **Bäk-bergen?** [Бакбергенъ] (SOK 282); Kzk. 19th c. **Bek-bergän** [Бекъ Берганъ] (Grod., Pril. 145); Kzk. 19th c. **Bek-bergen** [Бекбергенъ] (AOO 34); Kzk. 19th c. **Bek-bergen** [Бекбергенъ] (SODž. 64); Kkalp. 20th c. **Bek-bergen** [Бекберген] (KkRS 773); Kzk. 19th c. **Bek-pergen** [Бекпергенъ] (SODž. 154). ⇨ **BEK + BERGEN.**

BEK-BOL Tat. 1691 **Bek-bol(ko)** [Бекболко] (Kungursk. akty 194); Kzk. 19th c. **Bek-bol** [Бекбол] (SOV 12, 30, 32); Kzk. 19th c. **Bek-bol** [Бекбол] (SOK 274, 292); *TN:* Bashk. 1736 **Bekbulovo** [Бекбулово], a village (MIB IV/1, 111). ✧ I. 'Become a rich nobleman, be a lord' (cf. Sattarov: *Bikbul*); II. 'Become/grow strong' (Rásonyi, Imp. 238, 242; Sattarov: *Bikbul*). ⇨ **BEK + BOL.** See also **BAY-BOL, BAY-TUR, BEK-TUR.**

BEK-BOLAT see BEK-BULAT

BEK-BOLSÏN Kzk. 19th c. **Bek-bolsïn** [Бекъ-Болсынъ] (SOK 254); Kkalp. 20th c. **Bek-bosïn**

[Бекбосын] (KkRS 773); Kzk. 19th c. **Bek-bosun** [Бекбасунъ] (SODž. 148); Kzk. 19th c. **Bek-bosun** [Бекбасунъ] (SOV 136); Kzk. 19th c. **Bek-busïn** [Дуястай Бекбусыновъ] (Grod., Pril. 111); Kzk. 19th c. **Bek-busun** [Бекбусунъ Джамбаевъ] (Grod., Pril. 49). ⇨ BEK + BOLSÏN.

BEK-BOSUN see BEK-BOLSÏN

BEK-BOTA   Kzk. 19th c. **Bek-bota** [Бекбота] (SOV 28); Kzk. 19th c. **Bek-buta** [Бекбутиновъ] (SKSO II, 13); Uzb. 19th c. **Be0k0-buta-bek** [Bek-Bouta-bek], early 19th c., Khokand (Nalivkin-Dozon 97); *TN:* **Bikbuta** [بيكبوته / Бикъ-Бута], a settlement in the district of Sugut (Sugutskij tumen') (ZIRGOStat. IV, Pril. 2). ✧ I. 'Rich(man)/prince-young-camel; II. Strong/firm young camel'? ⇨ BEK + BOTA.

BEK-BUQA   Uyg. **Bäg-buqa** [Bäg Buka] (EUTS); Uyg. 13th-14th c. **Bäg-buqa** [Bäg Buq-a] (Zieme, Mat. II, 92); Uyg. 12th c.-14th c. **Beg-buγa** / **Bäg-buqa** [Bäg Buqa, Beg buγa] (Radl., USp.; DTS, Zieme, Mat. II, 92); Uyg. 12th-14th c. **Bek-buqa** (Radl., USp. 16-17, 95-96). ✧ 'High/noble-bull', 'Prince-bull' (Blagova 1997, 710). ⇨ BEK + BUQA.

BEK-BUL see BEK-BOL

BEK-BULAT   Nog. 19th c. **Bek-bolat** [Бекъ-болатъ] (Anan'ev 49); Maml. 1467 **Bek-bulat** [بيك بلاط الاشرفى] (Ibn Taghrīb. VIII, 662); Tat. 1600, 1635 **Bek-bulat** [Бекбулат] (Miller, Ist. Sib. II, 156, 423); Tat. 1624 **Bek-bulat** [Бекбулатъ Бектемировъ] (Pokrovskij 70); Tat. 1675 **Bek-bulat** [Бекбулатко] (Kungursk. akty 24); Tat.(Mish.) 1748 **Bek-bulat** [Бебкей Бекбулатовъ] (Nepljuev 438); Bashk. 1714 **Bek-bulat** [Ермяк Бекбулатов] (MIB I, 105); Bashk. 1734 **Bek-bulat** [Бекбулатъ Якшимбетевъ], a Bashkir tarχan (Vel.-Zern., Bašk. 10); Bashk. 1734 **Bek-bulat** [Бекбулатъ Якшимбетевъ], a tarχan (Vel.-Zern., Bašk. 10); Bashk. 1735 **Bek-bulat** [Бекбулатъ], a Bashkir tarχan (Vel.-Zern., Bašk. 25); Bashk. 1735 **Bek-bulat** [Акмышъ Бекбулатовъ] (Vel.-Zern., Bašk. 21); Bashk. 1735 **Bek-bulat** [Бекбулатъ Каспулатовъ] (Vel.-Zern., Bašk. 25); Kzk. **Bek-bulat** (Hedin I, 367); Kzk. 18th c. **Bek-bulat** [Бекбулатъ], from the Qara-kisek tribe (Valihanov, Soč. 162); Kzk. 19th c. **Bek-bulat** [Бекбулат] (AOO 62); Kzk. 19th c. **Bek-bulat** [Минике Бекбулатов] (Grod., Pril. 85); Alt. 19th c. **Bek-bulat**, Közüm Khan's defeated enemy (Radl., Aus Sib. I, 150); Tat.(Sib.) **Bek-bulat** / **Bey-bulat** [Бекбулатъ / Бейбулатъ], a Khan in Siberia, Yetiger (Yediger)'s son (Sib. Let. (Strog.) 19, Sib. Let. (Esim.) 117, Sib. Let. (Rem.) 319); Uzb. 1740 **Bek-fulat-bay** [Бекфулатъ-Бай], from Khiva (Hanykov, Poezdka 29); Kkalp. 20th c. **Bek-polat** [Бекполат] (KkRS 773); Uzb. 1851/52 **Bek-pulad** [Бек-Пулад], from the Salaq tribe (MIT II, 248); Uzb.

1801 **Bek-pulad-bek** / **Bek-pulad-sufi** [Бек Пулад-бек, Бек Пулад-суфи], from the Nayman tribe (MIT II, 345, 346); Uzb. 1823/24 **Bek-pulad-yüzbašï** [Бек Пулад-юзбаши] (MIT II, 423, 465); Chuv. 18th-19th c. **Biχ-bulat** [Бихбулатъ] (Magn. 34); Tat. 18th-19th c. **Bik-bulat** [Бикбулатъ] (Magn. 33); Chuv. 18th-19th c. **Piχ-bulat** [Пихбулатъ] (Magn. 67); Chuv. 18th-19th c. **Piχ-pulat** [Пихпулатъ] (Magn. 68); Chuv. 18th-19th c. **Pik-bulat** [Пикбулатъ] (Magn. 66); *TN:* Tat. 18th c. **Bikbulatova** [Бикбулатова], a village in the district of Tetyushinsk (Korsakov 340). ✧ I. 'Noble steel, lord-steel'; II. 'Hard/Strong steel' (Kusimova, Sattarov). ⇨ BEK + BULAT. See also BAY-BULAT.

BEK-BUSÏN see BEK-BOLSÏN

BEK-BUSUN see BEK-BOLSÏN

BEK-BUTA see BEK-BOTA

BEK-ČALI   Kzk. 19th c. **Bek-čali** [Бекчали] (SOK 6). ⇨ BEK.

BEK-ČENTEY   Tat. 1772 **Bek-čentey** [Искендер Бекчентеев] (MIB IV/2, 404); Bashk. 1761 **Bek-čentey** [Бекчентей Килдыгулов] (MIB IV/1, 215); Tat. 19th c. **Bik-čäntäy** [Bikčantaev] (Mende 164). ⇨ BEK.

BEK-ČERI   Maml. 14th c. **Bek-čeri** [بكجرى / bägčäri / Bekçeri] (Tarĵ/Houtsma 71, Tarĵ/Toparlı 42). ✧ I. 'Prince-army'. ⇨ BEK + ČERI I.

BEK-ĴEÑAZ?   1352 **Bek-ĵeñaz?** [بيك جكاز], emir, enemy of the Muzaffarïds in Kirmān (Qazw. 651-52).

BEK-DEMİR see BEK-TEMİR

BEK-DİLLÄ   Kkalp. 20th c. **Bek-dillä** [Бекдиллä] (Bask., Kkalp. 399). ⇨ BEG + TİLLA. See also BAY-DİLDA.

BEK-DURDÏ see BEK-TURDÏ

BEK-FULAT see BEK-BULAT

BEK-GEZ   Kzk. 19th c. **Bek-gez** / **Bek-kez?** [Бекгезъ] (Grod., Pril. 36). ⇨ BEK + GEZ?

BEK-KELDİ   Uzb. 20th c. **Bek-keldi** [Беккелди] (Begmatov 1984, 202). ✧ 'Lord has come (has been born)' (cf. Sattarov: *Bigilde / Bikilde* 'id.'). ⇨ BEK + KELDİ. See also BAY-GELDİ.

BEK-QONDÏ   Khorezm./Chag. **Bek-qondï-oγlan** [بيك قوندى اوغلان], a descendant of the Sheybanides (Abulg./Desm. 186 (177)). ⇨ BEK + QONDÏ.

BEK-MEÑGÜ   Uyg. 13th c.-14th c. **Beg-meñgü** / **Bek-meñgü** [Bak-Mangu] (Chwol., Syr.-nest. (NF) 95); Uyg. 1273 **Bek-meñgü** / **Pag-mangu?** [Pag-Mangku / Pag-Mangu] (Chwol., Syr.-nest. 25).

BEK-MÏRAT see BEK-MURAT

BEK-MURAT   Kkalp. 20th c. **Bek-mïrat** [Бекмырат] (KkRS 773); Kkalp. 20th c. **Bek-murat** [Бекмурат] (KkRS 773). ⇨ BEK + MURAT.

BEK-NAZAR   Kzk. 19th c. **Bek-nazar** (Ljutš 108 etc.); Kkalp. 20th c. **Bek-nazar** [Бекназар] (KkRS 773);

Uzb. 18th c. **Bek-nazar-bi** [Bek-Nazar by], from Ferghana (Nalivkin-Dozon 89); Uzb. 1844 **Bek-nazar-biy** [Бек Назар-бий], from Khokand (MIT II, 495). ⇨ **BEK + NAZAR.**

BEK-NİYAZ Kzk. **Bek-niyaz** [بيك نياز], fem. (Divaev, Biket 5, 27). ⇨ **BEK + NİYAZ.**

BEK-POLAT see **BEK-BULAT**

BEK-PULAD see **BEK-BULAT**

BEK-SULTAN-TOXTŌSUN Kirg. 19th c. **Bek-sultan-toχtōsun** [Bek-s'ltan-toχtōsun] (Almásy, Gy., Karakirgiz nyelvészeti jegyzet: KSz. II, 118). ❖ 'Let Bek-sultan stop (and stay here)'; 'Bek-sultan wait a bit' (Almásy: KSz. II, 118). ⇨ **BEK + SULTAN + TOQTASÏN.**

BEK-ŠORA see **BEK**

BEK-TAS see **BEK-TAŠ**

BEK-TAŠ Uyg. **Bäg-taš** [Bäg Taş] (EUTS); Uyg. 12th c.-14th c. **Beg-taš** (Radl., USp. 210, 252, DTS); Kzk. 19th c. **Bek-tas** [Абен Бектасовъ] (AUK 471); Kzk. 19th c. **Bek-tas** [Байтасъ Бектасов] (AOO 46); Kzk. 19th c. **Bek-tas** [Джубанъ Бектасовъ] (Grod., Pril. 82); Kzk. 19th c. **Bek-tas** [Бектасъ Кунаровъ] (Grod., Pril. 126); Kzk. 19th c. **Bek-tas-bay** [Бектасбай] (SOV 148); Selj.? 1104 **Bek-taš** [بكتاش بن تتش بن الب ارسلان] (Ibn al-Athīr/Tornb. X, 258, 281, 327); Selj. 1104, 1106 **Bek-taš** [بكتاش / بقتاش], Tutuq's son, the ruler of Raheba (Rahaba) (Ibn al-Athīr: RHCHor I, 223, 229); Selj.? 1108, 1109 **Bek-taš** [بكتاش], Alp-arslan's (1063-1072) grand-son, Tekiš' (Tekeš') son (Ibn al-Athīr: RHCHor I, 263, 268); Selj.? 1109 **Bek-taš** [بكتاش النهاوندى] (Ibn al-Athīr/Tornb. X, 326); Maml. 13th c. **Bek-taš** [بدر الدين بكتا شالزردكا المنصورى] (Zetterst. 23, 140); Maml. 1294, 1299 **Bek-taš** [بكتاش], an emir (-silaχ) (Iyās I, 131, 139, Makrīzī IV, 116); Maml. 1299, 1325 **Bek-taš** [بدرالدين بكتاش الفجرى / الفاخرى], an emir, a historian (Dawād. 39 (110), Zetterst. 145, 191, Weil., Chalif. I, 255, 266); Maml. 1332 **Bek-taš** [بكتاش النئيب], an emir (Dawād. 365); Maml. 14th c. **Bek-taš** [بكتاش / Bektaš] (Tarĵ/Houtsma 63, 83, Tarĵ/Toparlı 43); Turk.? 1263, 1264 **Bek-taš** [بدرالدين بكتاش], an emir(-silaχ) (Sīrat 151, Makrīzī II, 15, IV, 116); Turk. 1583 **Bek-taš** [بكتاش] (Ongan, Ank. I, 154); Turk. 1583 **Bek-taš** [Bektaş Yaylaoğlu] (Ongan, Ank. I, 120); Yürük 1543 **Bek-taš** (Gökb., Rum. 175); Yürük 1543 **Bek-taš** (Gökb., Rum. 204); Yürük 1543 **Bek-taš** [بكتاش], from the Yürüks of Kocacık, Turkey (Gökb., Rum. 103, 192); Trkm. 1841 **Bek-taš** [Бекташ], an imam (MIT II, 481); Tat. 1543 **Bek-taš** (Gökb., Rum. 232); Bashk. 18th c. **Bek-taš** [Бекташ] (MIB V); Bashk. 1754 **Bek-taš** [Бекташ] (MIB IV/1, 83); Turk. 1487, 1489 **Bek-taš / Beχ-taš?**

[صفىالدين بن روح پاك مولانا بختاش] (MB Qastam. 78); Trkm. 1598 **Bek-taš-sultan / Bek-taš-χan** [Бекташ-султан / Бекташ-хан], a man from the Ustaĵlu clan (tribe?) (MIT II, 99, 100); Tat. 20th c. **Bik-taš** [Бикташев / Биктяшев] (Sattarov 48); Bashk. 20th c. **Bik-taš** [Бикташ] (Kusimova 35); Bashk. 1756 **Bik-taš / Bik-täš?** [Биктяш Балыков] (MIB IV/1, 117); *TN:* Kzk. **Bek-tas-batïr** [Бектасъ-батыръ] (Karta JAR); Turk. 15th c. **Bek-taš**, a village (Gökb., Ed. 20). ❖ I. 'Hard (solid) stone' cf. Le Coq, Ind. 4; Sauvaget 42: < *bäk* 'fort, solide' [in Kipchak], on a ainsi *bäk-taš* 'pierre solide' et *bäk-tämür* 'fer solide'; cf. also Sattarov, Kusimova 35; II. 'Lord/prince-Stone' (Blagova 1997, 704); III. 'Companion of a *bek*' cf. RHCHOr. I, 810: 'Bectach (بكتا ش et بتتا ش Baktach) c'est à dir 'compagnon du bey''. ⇨ **BEK + TAŠ.**

BEK-TAW Kzk. 1803 **Bek-taw** [بقتاو] (MIK IV, 211). ⇨ **BEK + ТАГ.**

BEK-TAWUL Tat. 1841 **Bek-tawul** [Бегашъ Бектауловъ] (Konšin, Mat. V, 34). ⇨ **BEK.**

BEK-TEBERLİ Kzk. 19th c. **Bek-teberli** [Бектеберлы] (SOK 134). ⇨ **BEK + TEBER + suff. -li.**

BEK-TEMİR Uyg. **Bäg-tämir** [Bäg Tämir] (EUTS); Maml. 14th c. **Bäk-tämür** [بَكْتَمُرْ] (Sauvaget 43); Uyg. 13th c. **Beg-temir** (DTS); Türk? 868 **Bek-temir** [بكتمر] (Tabarī, Annal. III, 1987); Selj.? **Bek-temir** [بكتمر] (Masʿūdī 369); Selj. 12th c. **Bek-temir** [Bactamar Chelati Dominus], in the age of Salaheddīn (Abulfar. 414); Maml. **Bek-temir** [بكتمر الحسنى] (Duqmaq:RHCHor IV, 45); Maml. 13th c. **Bek-temir** [بكتمر المنصورى] (Zetterst. 52); Maml. 1297 **Bek-temir** [بكتمر الازرقى] (Iyās I, 135); Maml. 1298, 1300, 1309/10 **Bek-temir** [سيف الدين بكتمر الجوكندار], an emir (Dawād. 7, 41, 109 etc., Iyās I, 154, 174, Weil., Chalif. I, 299, Duqmaq:RHCHor IV, 42, Zetterst. 96, 146, 155, Berchem, Perg. 75); Maml. 1299 **Bek-temir** [بكتمر الابو بكرى] (Iyās I, 137, 157); Maml. 1299 **Bek-temir** [سيفالدين بكتمر السلحدار], governor of Haleb (Iyās I, 127, 144, Makrīzī II, 158, III, 7, Weil, Chalif. I, 234, Zetterst. 2, 47, 129); Maml. 1304 **Bek-temir** [ا لسيفى بكتمر], perhaps the same as Bek-temir ibn 'Abdallah silaχdār, the mamluk of Baybars, then governor of Tripolis, died in 1304 (Mayer 98); Maml. 1308/09 **Bek-temir** [بكتمر الفارسى] (Iyās I, 148); Maml. 1309 **Bek-temir** [سيفالدين بكتمر حاجب الحجان], an emir in Syria (Iyās I, 164, 175, Weil, Chalif. I, 282, Zetterst. 81, 153); Maml. 1310 **Bek-temir** [سيف الدين بكتمر], an emir (Dawād. 207); Maml. 1324 **Bek-temir** [ا لسيفى بكتمر العنمى ا لحسا مى], governor of Alexandria, died in 1324 (Mayer 98-99); Maml. 1325

Bek-temir [بكتمر استا دار] (Zetterst. 192); Maml. 1325 Bek-temir [سيف الدين بكتمر ا لحسا مى الحاجب] (Zetterst. 147, 174, Dawād. 38, 170); Maml. 14th c. Bek-temir [بكتمر بدرجك] (Zetterst.); Maml. 14th c. Bek-temir [بكتمر / Bektemür] (Tarj/Houtsma 63, Tarj/Toparlı 42); Maml. 1352 Bek-temir [بكتمر السعيدى] (Iyās I, 197); Maml. 1363 Bek-temir [سيف الدين بكتمر ا لموٴمنى] (Iyās I, 211, Zetterst. 206); Maml. 1365/66 Bek-temir [بكتمر الشرينى] (Iyās I, 215); Maml. 1370/71 Bek-temir [بكتمر السينى] (Iyās I, 226); Maml. 1398/99, 1405 Bek-temir [الركنى بكتمر], governor of Safed (in 1405) (Iyās I, 321, 348, Weil, Chalif. II, 104, Ibn Taghrīb. VI, 18, 19, 25 etc.); Maml. 1398, 1412 Bek-temir [بكتمر چلق الظاهرى], Bek-temir Ĵelek (Weil: „Buktumur Djelek"), governor of Damascus (Iyās I, 308, 354, Weil, Chalif. II, 126, Ibn Taghrīb. VI, 16, 23, 110 etc.); Maml. 1400/01 Bek-temir [بكتمر] (Iyās I, 328); Tat. 1748 Bek-temir [Бектемиръ Бепкенинъ] (Nepljuev 437); Tat.(Sib.) 1603 Bek-temir [Бектемир] (Miller, Ist. Sib. II, 179, 180); Bashk. 1734 Bek-temir [Бектемир Еникеевъ], a tarχan (Vel.-Zern., Bašk. 10); Bashk. 18th c. Bek-temir [Бектемир Ачаков] (MIB V, 413); Bashk. 1790 Bek-temir [Заит Бектемиров] (MIB V, 282, 319); Bashk. 1798 Bek-temir [Бектемиревъ] (PSZRI XXV, 194); Kzk. 19th c. Bek-temir [Бектымиръ] (SOK 186); Kzk. 19th c. Bek-temir [Бектемиръ Бепкенинъ] (SOV 22); Selj. 1183 Bek-temir / Beg-timur [بكتمر سيف الدين صاحب خلاط / Bûkhtâmar], ruler of Khâlât (Najm) (1185-1193) (Ibn al-Athīr/Tornb. XI, 322, 338, XII, 167-69, Abulfar./Budge I, 362-63, 366, EI I, 718); Tat.(Sib.) 1629 Bek-temir / Beh-temir [Бектемир / Бехтемир] (Miller, Ist. Sib. II, 357); Tat.(Sib.) 1632 Bek-temir / Beh-temir? [Бехтемирев Инка] (Miller, Ist. Sib. II, 398); Maml. 1332/33 Bek-temir / Bek-temür [بكتمر الساقى], [بكتمور السا قى / سيف الدين], chief emir of the Egyptian Sultan al-Malik al-Nāsir; a Mamluk envoy to Kipchak in 1320 (Iyās I, 166, Duqmaq:RHCHor IV, 40, Weil, Chalif. I, 378, Zetterst. 177, 227, Dawād. 302, 323, Nuwairī 148, 170, Aynī/Tizeng. I, 489, 519, Ibn Bat. II, 249); Selj.? Bek-temir / Bek-timur [Бек-Тимур] (RaD I/1, 111); Selj.? Bek-temir / Bek-timur [Бек-Тимур] (RaD II, 74); Turk. 20th c. Bek-temür, a village in the province of Amasya, Turkey (TMİB 62); Yürük 16th c., 1543 Bek-temür [بكتمور / Bektemur], from the Yürüks of Kocacık, Turkey (Gökb., Rum. 103, 227); Kzk. 19th c. Bek-timir [Бектимыръ] (SOK 186); Tat. 18th-19th c. Bik-temir [Биктемиръ] (Magn. 34); Bashk.? 18th c. Bik-temir [Биктемиръ] (Nepljuev 347); Tat. 20th c. Bik-timer [Биктимер] (Sattarov 48); Tat.(GH) 13th c. Bik-timür [بيكتمور /

Биктимуръ], Meñgü Temür's (1266-1280) „beg" from the Tatars (RaD I, 65); Chuv. 18th-19th c. Pi-demer / Pi-demir [Пидемеръ] (Magn. 66); Chuv. 18th-19th c. Pi-demir [Пидемиръ] (Magn. 66); Chuv. 18th-19th c. Piχ-temer [Пихтемеръ] (Magn. 68); Chuv. 18th-19th c. Piχ-temir [Пихтемиръ] (Magn. 68); Chuv. 18th-19th c. Piχ-timer [Пихтимеръ] (Magn. 68); Chuv. 18th-19th c. Piχ-timir [Пихтимиръ] (Magn. 68); Chuv. 18th-19th c. Pik-temir [Пиктемиръ] (Magn. 67); TN: Turk. 20th c. Bek-demir, a village in the province of Bilecik, Turkey (TMİB 157). ✧ I. 'Prince stone'; II. 'Hard (solid) iron' cf. Sauvaget 43: bäk-tämür 'fer solide'. ⇨ BEK + TEMİR.

BEK-TEMİS Kzk. 19th c. Bek-temis [Бектемисъ] (SODž. 154); Kzk. 19th c. Bek-temis [Бектемись] (SODž. 154); Kzk. 19th c. Bek-temis [Бектемисъ] (SOV 44, 112); EN: Kzk. 18th c. - 19th c. Bek-temis [Бектемыс] (Tynyšp. 66). ✧ '?' cf. Kzk. PN Bektemis (Žanuzakov - Esbaeva). ⇨ BEK + TEMİŠ / TEMEŠ?

BEK-TEMÜR see BEK-TEMİR

BEK-TİMUR see BEK-TEMİR

BEK-TOҐDÏ Oghuz / Khorezm.? 11th c. Bek-toγdï [بكطغدى], the Ghaznavid Sultan Masʿud's (1031-1041) chiefttain against the Seljuks (Ahbar 3); Selj. 11th c. Bek-toγdï(-χāĵib) / Bek-tuγdï [بكتغدى حاجب / Бектугды / Буктугды / Ильтугды] (Rāwandī 94, 95, MIT 231-33, 242, 244, 247-253, 255, 261, 265, 267, 276, 277, 280, 287, 295-298, 367, 456, 457). ⇨ BEK + TUҐDÏ.

BEK-TUҐAN Bashk. 1713 Bek-tuγan [Султанай Бектуганов] (MIB III, 94); Bashk. 1778 Bek-tuγan [Илчикей Бектуганов] (MIB V, 66, 70); Bashk. 1714, 1740 Bek-tuγan / Bik-tuγan [Бектуганъ (Биктуган) Акшигулов] (MIB I, 105, 380, 396); Maml. 1326 Bek-tuwan [بكتوان بن عبدلله الشهابى] (Sobernh. I, 55); Chuv. 18th-19th c. Bik-tugan [Биктуганъ] (Magn. 34); Bashk. 1640 Bik-tuγan [Биктугалов Байгул] (Miller, Ist. Sib. II, 175); Chuv. 18th-19th c. Piχ-tugan [Пихтуганъ] (Magn. 68); Chuv. 18th-19th c. Pik-tugan [Пиктуганъ] (Magn. 67). ✧ 'Born strong / Strong brother'? ⇨ BEK + TUҐAN I.

BEK-TUҐDÏ see BEK-TOҐDÏ

BEK-TUҐUŠ Bashk. 1713 Bek-tuγuš [Султанай Бектугушев] (MIB III, 93). ⇨ BEK + TUҐÏŠ.

BEK-TUL Tat. (Sib.) 1630 Bek-tul [Бектул] (Miller, Ist. Sib. II, 369). ⇨ BEK + TOL? See also BEK-TUL.

BEK-TUMAN Maml. Bek-tuman [بكتو مان التربى], [بدرالدين] (Mayer 99). ⇨ BEK + TUMAN?

BEK-TUR Karakh. 11th c. Bek-tur [بَكْتُر] (MK/Atalay I, 455); Kzk. Bek-tur [Бектуръ] (Sb. Syr-D. IX, 44); Kzk. 19th c. Bek-tur [Бектуръ] (SOK 48, 140, 238); Kzk. 19th c. Bek-tur [Бектуръ] (SODž. 22). ✧ I.

'Prince-remain/stay!'; II. 'Be/remain strong (in your place)!' cf. Karakh. *bek tur* 'yerinde sağlam dur' (MK/Atalay I, 455). ⇨ **BEK + TUR**. See also **BAY-TUR, BEK-BOL**.

BEK-TURAN   Kzk. 1838 **Bek-turan** [Бийбатъ Бектурановъ] (Konšin, Mat. V, 57). ⇨ **BEK + TURAN I**.

BEK-TURDÏ   Trkm. 1738 **Bek-durdï-behadïr** [Бек-дурды-бехадыр], from the Teke tribe (MIT II, 157); Trkm. 1804 **Bek-turdï** [Бек-турды] (MIT II, 353); Uzb. 1804 **Bek-turdï** [Бек-турды Теджен] (MIT II, 369); Uzb. 20th c. **Bek-turdï** [Бектурди] (Begmatov 1984, 204). ✧ 'Lord/noble man stayed (alive)/survived'. ⇨ **BEK + TURDÏ**. See also **BAY-TUR, BAY-TURSUN**.

BEK-TURҐAN   Kkalp. 20th c. **Bek-turɣan** (KkRS 773); Kirg. **Bek-turɣan** [Бектурган] (Jud. 952). ⇨ **BEK + TURҐAN**.

BEK-TURҐUN   Uzb. 20th c. **Bek-turɣun** [Бектурғун] (Begmatov 1984, 204). ✧ 'Strong-resident/indigenous (people)'? ⇨ **BEK + TURҐUN**.

BEK-TURSÏN   Kkalp. 20th c. **Bek-tursïn** [Бектурсын] (KkRS 773); Kzk. 19th c. **Bek-tursun** [Бекъ Турсунъ] (Grod., Pril. 199); Uzb. 20th c. **Bek-tursun** [Бектурсун] (Begmatov 1984, 204). ✧ 'May the lord/noble man stay/live!'. ⇨ **BEK + TURSÏN**. See also **BAY-TURSUN**.

BEK-TURSUN see **BEK-TURSÏN**

BEK-TUT   Selj. 12th c. **Bek-tut** [سيف‌الدين بكتوت العز يرى] (Ibn Šaddād, Nawād.: RHCHor III, 133); Maml. 13th c. **Bek-tut** [بكتوت المعزا لجوكندار], in the age of Baybars I (1260-1270) (Iyās I, 99, Weil, Chalif. I, 19); Maml. 13th c.-14th c. **Bek-tut** [Badraddīn Baktūt ar-Rammāḥ al-Hāsindārī], governor of Alexandria died in 1311 (Brock., GAL II, 135); Maml. 13th c., **Bek-tut** [الازرقى] [بدرالدين بكتوت] died in 1297 (Iyās I, 135, Zetterst. 40, Makrīzī IV, 39); Maml. 1261 **Bek-tut** [Schodja-eddin Bektout] (Makrīzī I, 145); Maml.? 1264 **Bek-tut** [Bedr-eddin-Bektout-Medjka-Roumi] (Makrīzī II, 15); Maml. 1279 **Bek-tut** [Bektout Hemsi] (Makrīzī II, 170); Maml. 1280, 1294 **Bek-tut** [بدرالدين بكتوت البلائى] (Iyās I, 131, Makrīzī III, 23, Zetterst. 20, Weil, Chalif. I, 373); Maml. 1282 **Bek-tut** [بكتوت الشمسى] (Iyās I, 115); Maml. 1283 **Bek-tut** [Bedr-eddin-Bektout-Saadi], governor of Hims (Makrīzī III, 62); Maml. 1302/03 **Bek-tut** [الفتاح] [بدالدين بختوت] (Iyās I, 145, Zetterst. 107, 114); Maml. 1306 **Bek-tut** [بدرالدين بكتوت أمير شكار] (Dawād. 145); Maml. 1313, 1348 **Bek-tut** [بدرالدين بكتوت القرمانى], Qalāūn's mamluk, then emir in Damascus died in 1348 (in an inscription on a candlestick) (Dawād. 266, Mayer 100); Maml. 1325

Bek-tut [بدرالدين بكتوت الشيرازى] (Zetterst. 191, 195); Maml. 1332 **Bek-tut** [بكتوت الشيرازى النقيب] (Dawād. 367). ⇨ **BEK + TUT**.

BEK-TUWAN see **BEK-TUҐAN**

BEK-TÜZÜN   Karakh. 964 **Bek-tüzün** [بكتوزون] (Ibn al-Athīr/Tornb. VIII, 409-10, IX, 103); Karakh. 997, 1005 **Bek-tüzün** [بكتوزن وا يح حاجب], governor of Khorāsān (Qazw. 387, 394, Weil, Chalif. III, 61). ⇨ **BEK + TÜZÜN**.

BEK-ZÄN see **BEK**

BEK-ŽENEY   Tat. 1641 **Bek-ženey** [Бекженей Енчаров] (Miller, Ist. Sib. II, 484). ⇨ **BEK + ЈANAY?**

BEKČÄ   Maml. 1332 **Bekčä** [بكجا], an emir (Dawād. 367); Kzk. **Bekšä** [Бекшä] (Proben III, 41 /52/). ⇨ **BEK** + dim. suff. *-čä / -šä*. See also **BEKЈA?**

BEKČI   Chag. 1558 **Bekči / Bikči** [Баба Бекчи / Бикчи] (Ivanov 112, 113, 114, 121, 247). ✧ 'Guard, watchman' cf. Turk. *bäkči* 'der Wächter, die Schildwache' (Radl. IV, 1579).

BEKЈA   Kzk. 19th c. **Bekja** [Кулниязъ Бекджаевъ] (Grod., Pril. 105); Kzk. 19th c. **Bekja (<Bek-qoja?)** [Бекджа] (Grod., Pril. 109). ⇨ **BEK + XOЈA?** See also **BEKČÄ?**

BEKDAŠ   Mo.? **Bekdaš** [Бекдаш], Yesün Tua's son (RaD I/1, 111); Trkm. **Bekdaš** [Бекдаш] (Sopieva 180). ✧ Topopnym, referring to the place of birth (Sopieva).

BEKDELİ   Oghuz/Trkm. 13th c. **Bekdeli** [بيكدلى / Бекдели], Yulduz-χan's son (RaD I/1, 76, Abulg./Kon. 515, 550, 600).

BEKDEZ   Oghuz/Trkm. 13th c. **Bekdez / Bükdüz?** [بوكدوز / بكد ز / Бекдез], Duylï Qayï-χan's inaq-bek (Abulg./Kon. 735). ⇨ **BÜKDÜZ?**

BEKE   Kuman 1347 **Beke** [Beke filium Althabarz], from the Kumans of Hungary (Gyārfās III, 484); Maml. 1332 **Beke** [بكا], an emir (Dawād. 367); Kzk. 1817 **Beke** [بيكا / Беке] (MIK IV, 311,318); Kzk. 19th c. **Beke** [Беке] (SOK 198); Kzk. 1825 **Beke-bay** [بيكا باى / Бекебай] (MIK IV, 469, 476). ✧ I. 'Be strong' II. 'Lady, girl' cf. Rásonyi, KÖA 90, Rásonyi: AOH 20: 137. ⇨ **BİKE**. See also **SAN-BEKE, TEMİR-BEKE**.

BEKEČ-ARSLAN see **BEGÄČ-ARSLAN**

BEKEY   Bashk. 1687 **Bekey** [Акбаш Бекеев] (MIB I, 129); Bashk. 1728 **Bekey** [Ялметь Бекеевъ] (MIB III, 252); Bashk. 1729 **Bekey** [Бекей Апасев] (MIB III, 260); Bashk. 1735 **Bekey** [Колимбетъ Бекеевъ], a tarχan (Vel.-Zern., Bašk. 20); Bashk. 1760 **Bekey** [Бекей Явгильдин] (MIB IV/1, 193); Kzk. **Bekey** [بيكاى / Бекей] (Syzdykov 354); Kzk. 19th c. **Bekey** [Бекей] (SOV 80); Kzk. 19th c. **Bekey** [Бекей] (SOV 124); Kzk. 19th c. **Bekey** [Муратъ Бекеевъ], chief of an aul (Pam. kn. Turg. 39); Kzk. 19th c. **Bekey** [Бекей] (AOO 38); Kzk. 19th c. **Bekey** [Бекей] (AOP 118); Kzk. 19th c. **Bekey** [Бекей] (AOAtb. 54); Kzk. 19th c. **Bekey** [Бекей] (SOK 190); Tat. (Mish.) 1764 **Bekcy** [Бекей Бекмеев] (MIB IV/1, 286); Trkm. 19th c. **Bekey-mulla** [Ханай Бекеймуллаевъ] (Ščeglov I, 349). ✦ 'Little gentleman, master/owner (noble man)' Used also as a secondary component of male personal names. ⇨ **BEK** + dim. suff. *-ey / -y*. See also **ER-BEKEY**.

BEKELEY   Alt. 19th-20th c. **Bekeley** [Бекелей] (OjrRS 207).

BEKEM see **BEKİM**

BEKEMBET   Bashk. 1783 **Bekembet** [Сарбай Бекембетев] (MIB V, 143). ✦ I. 'Lord-Mukhammad'; II. 'Hard/strong Mukhammad'. ⇨ **BEK / BEKEM?** + suffix *-embet / -bet*.

BEKEN   Kzk. 19th c. **Begem-bay** [Бегембай] (AOAtb. 10); Bashk. 1711 **Beken** [Бекен] (MIB III, 98); Kzk. 19th c. **Beken** [Бекен] (AOP 18); Kzk. 19th c. **Beken** [Бекен] (SOK 120); Bashk. 1779 **Beken / Bäkän?** [Бякян Умрясов] (MIB V, 96). ✦ 'Grow strong(er)! Become strong!' cf. Kzk. *bekĭn-* 'укрепиться' (KzRS).

BEKENEY   Tat. (Sib.) 1635 **Bekeney / Benekey?** [Бекеней / Бенекей?] (Miller, Ist. Sib. II, 424).

BEKER   Kzk. 19th c. **Beker-bek** [Бекербекъ] (AOO 14). ✦ 'Fiddling, vain; bachelor' cf. Crm., Trkm., Turk. *bäk'ar* (<P.) 'unverheiratet, der Hagestolz' (Radl. IV, 1575), Kzk. *bekär* 'umsonst, vergleich, ohne Ursache, ungehörig' (Radl. IV, 1575).

BEKET   Kzk. 1803, 1820 **Beket** [Бекетъ], one of the chiefs of the Ĵaγalbaylï tribe, Little Horde (Kiši Žüz) (MIK IV, 516, Sib.Vest. IX, 123); Kzk. 1822 **Beket** [Исельбай Бекетовъ] (TOUAK XXIV, 122); Kzk. 19th c. **Beket** [بيكت / Бекетъ] (Veselovskij, Kirg. 78 (122)); Kzk. 19th c. **Beket** [Бекетъ] (SOK 260); Kzk. 19th c. **Beket** [Бекетъ] (AOAtb. 58); Kzk. 19th c. **Beket** [Бекетъ] (AOK 90); Kkalp. 1722 **Beket** [Бекет] (MIKk. 172); Kkalp. 1722 **Beket** [Бекетъ Пичъ Умергеневъ] (PSZRI VI, 779); Nog. **Beket** [Бекет] (NRS 485); Tat. (Sib.) 1607 **Beket** [Енбай Бекет(ов)] (Miller, Ist. Sib. II, 199); **Beket-batïr** [Бекет-батыр] (Žirm., Epos 392); Kzk. 19th c. **Beket-pay** [Бекетпай] (SOK 84); Kzk. 19th c. **Beket-pay** [Бекетпай] (AOP 26). ✦ 'Post-station'? cf. Kzk. *beket* 'пикет; сторожевой пункт; станция на почтовых трактах' (KzRS); *bekät* (<R.) 'das Piquett' (Radl. IV, 1576), cf. Uzb. *bekat* 'почтовая станция' (UzbRS), cf. also Bask., Fam. 161.

BEKETAY   Kzk. 19th c. **Beketay** [Бекетай Катпиновъ], from Kazalinsk (ZVORIAO X, 89). ⇨ **BEKE + TAY?** or suff. *-tay(1,2)?*

BEKETEY   Bashk. 1735 **Beketey** [Осупъ Бекетеевъ] (Vel.-Zern., Bašk. 17); Bashk. 1735 **Beketey** [Аптимъ Бекетеевъ] (Vel.-Zern., Bašk. 17).

BEKİ see **BEGİ**

BEKİĴEK   Khorezm. 1360, 1361 **Bekiĵek** [Бекиджек], emir of the divān (MIT I, 512, 533). ⇨ **BEGİ / BEGİČ?** + suff. *-(ĵ)ek*.

BEKİL   Kzk. 19th c. **Begil-bek** [Бегильбекъ] (SODž. 142); Oghuz/Trkm. 14th c. - 15th c. **Bekil / Begil** [Бекиль (Бегил)] (DQorq. 83-89, 150, 179, 228-230, 257). ✦ 'Get strong(er), grow stronger' cf. Kzk. *bekil-* 'утверждаться, быть утверждаемым' (KzRS).

BEKİM   Kirg. 20th c. **Bekem-bay** [Бекембай] (Kalilov: OSA 2, 91-95); Bashk. 1734 **Bekim** [Беким Явгильдин], a tarχan (Vel.-Zern., Bašk. 10); Kzk. 19th c. **Bekim-bay / Beküm-bay?** [Бекумбай] (SOV 56). ✦ 'Solid, steady' (Kalilov), 'Healthy, suitable (to do something)' cf. Kzk. *bekäm* 'fest, stark' (Radl. IV, 1576), Kzk. *bekem* 'sağlam', *bekim* 'sağlam, yapabilen, elinden iş gelen' (KzTS), also Kzk. PN *Bekem-bay* (Žanuzakov-Esbaeva).

BEKİN   Uzb. 1845 **Bekin-ĵan-bek / Beki-ĵan-bek?** [Беки Джан-бек / Бекинджан-бек] (MIT II, 498); Uzb. 1858 **Bekin-ĵan-inaq** [Бекинджан-инак] (MIT II, 587). ✦ I. 'Strengthen! Be strong!' cf. Chag. *bäkin-* 'fest, stark werden' (Radl. IV, 1576); II. 'Hide (away)!' cf. Uzb. *bekin-* 'прятаться, укрываться' (UzbRS).

BEKİNÄ   Uyg. 12th c.-14th c. **Bekinä / Bekine** (DTS).

BEKİRÄ   Uyg. 12th c.-14th c. **Bekirä** [Bäkirä / Bekirä] (EUTS, DTS).

BEKİŠ   Maml. 13th c. **Bäkiš**, a Kipchak (AH); Trkm. 1826 **Bekeš-χalife** [Бекеш-халифе] (MIT II, 435, 448, 459, 499, 504, 507, 508, 512, 520, 522-527); Trkm. 1628 **Bekeš-χan** [Бекеш-хан], a man from the Ustajlu clan (tribe?) (MIT II, 103); Kzk. 19th c. **Bekiš** [Бекиш] (AOO 14); Kzk. 19th c. **Bekiš** [Бекиш] (SODž. 102, 128); Kzk. 19th c. **Bekiš** [Бекиш] (AOP 2, 118). ✦ 'Become strong!' cf. Karakh. *bäkiš-* 'fest werden' (MK/Brock.), Chag., Crm. *bäkiš-* 'fest werden' (Radl. IV, 1577), Trkm. *bekeš-* 'крепнуть; усиливаться' (TrkmRS). ⇨ **BEGİČ?** See also **KÜČÄY-BEKİŠ**.

BEKKİNÄ   Tat. 1753 **Bekkinä** [Беккине Тимметев] (MIB IV/1, 70); Bashk. 1744 **Bekkinä** [Беккиня Кусюков] (MIB III, 415); Bashk. 1755 **Bekkinä** [Беккиня Беккулов] (MIB IV/1, 92); Bashk. 1761 **Bekkinä** [Беккиня Назарымбетев] (MIB IV/1, 218); Bashk. 1763 **Bekkinä** [Беккиня Игибаев] (MIB IV/2, 45); Bashk. 1770 **Bekkinä** [Беккиня Минлибаев] (MIB IV/1, 343); Tat. 1764 **Bekkine** [Беккине Усманов] (MIB IV/1, 279); Bashk. 1756 **Bekkine** [Беккине Кадырметев] (MIB IV/1, 113); Bashk. 1776 **Bekkine** [Измаил (Смаил) Беккине] (MIB V, 29). ✦ 'Little prince; Hard /Strong (little child)' cf. Bashk., Tat. PNs *Bikkinä* (Kusimova, Sattarov). ⇨ **BEK** + suff. *-kinä*.

BEKLAR see **BEKLER**

BEKLEMEK   Maml. 1264 **Beklemek** [Seïf-eddin Beklemek], emir, an envoy from Shiraz (Makrīzī I, 238). ✧ 'Awaiting, protecting' cf. Turk. *bäklä-* 'bewachen, behüten' (Radl. IV, 1577).

BEKLEMİŠ   Maml. 14th c. **Bäklämiš** [بَكَلِمِش] (Sauvaget 43); Khorezm.? 13th c. **Beklemiš** [Беклемиш] (RaD I/1, 169); Khorezm.? 1313 **Beklemiš** [بكلمش بن قنجو بغا], envoy of Toqtay (طنطای) (Dawād. 279); Khorezm.? 1319 **Beklemiš** [بكلمش المغلی], a Moghul emir (Dawād. 274); Maml. 1353 **Beklemiš** [بكلمش], governor of Tripolis (Iyās I, 200); Maml. 1393 **Beklemiš** [تكلمش/ بكلمش العلائی] (Iyās I, 291, 297, 327, Ibn Taghrīb. VI, 136, 433); Tat. 1742 **Beklemiš** [Беклемишевъ], from Cheboksary (IOAÏÊK XIV, 539); Tat.(Mish.)? 1198 **Beklemiš** [Беклемишъ], a prince (Keppen, HronUkaz. 360); Tat.(Mish.) 19th c. **Beklemiš** [Беклемиш], son of the Širin prince Baχmet who accepted Christianity, the clan of the Misher princes originates from him (Zolotn. 156); Kzk. 1737 **Beklemiš** [Bēclēmichef] (Levchine 183); Uzb.? 1722 **Beklemiš** [Беклемишевъ Никифоръ], a chieftain („vojvoda") (Veselovskij, Unk. 254); Khorezm. / Mo.? 13th c. **Beklemiš / Biklämiš** [بيكلاميش / Бикламиш], from the people of Hūšin (هوشین) (RaD/Ber. I, 168); Khorezm.? 13th c. **Beklemiš / Biklämiš** [بكلاميش / بيكلاميش / Бикламиш], from the Arlat (ارلات) tribe of the Uryaut (اوریباوت) people in Iran (RaD I, 161). ✧ 'Awaited, protected' cf. Turk. *bäklä-* 'bewachen, behüten' (Radl. IV, 1577), Bask., Fam. 147.

BEKLER   Chag. 1567 **Beklar** [Беклар] (Ivanov 147); Chag. 1562 **Bekler** [Беклер], a χoǰa (Ivanov 250).

BEKLİ   Tat. 1620 **Bekli-bay** [Беклыбай] (Kurdjumov 120, 121); Kzk. 19th c. **Bekti-bay** [Бектыбай], chief of a Kazak aul (settlement) (Pam. kn. Turg. 38); Kzk. 19th c. **Bekti-bay** [Бектыбай] (SOV 26); Kzk. 1863 **Bekti-bay-batïr** [Бектибай-батыръ] (Smirnov, Sultany 32); Oghuz 974 **Bekti-čur** [بكتیجور سباشی الخوارزمی], a superintendent of the Khorezmian army (police?) (Ibn al-Athīr/Tornb. VIII, 467); Kzk. 19th c. **Pehti-bay / Bekti-bay** [Mamon Paluan Peχtibajev] (AUK 131). ✧ 'Having a prince'. ⇨ **BEK** + suff. *-li / -ti*.

BEKMAN   Kkalp. 20th c. **Bekman** [Бекман] (KkRS 773); Uzb. 1838 **Bekman-biy** [Бекман-бий], from the Mañγït tribe (MIT II, 477, 488, 489, 492, 495, 498, 501, 502); 1820 **Bekmen** [Манжукъ Бекменевъ], a soldier (PSZRI XXXI, 429); Kkalp. 20th c. **Bekpan** [Бекпан] (KkRS 773). ⇨ **BEK** + suff. *-man*.

BEKMAT see **BEKMET**

BEKMEN see **BEKMAN**

BEKMET   Kzk. 19th c. **Bekmat** [Бекматовъ] (SKSO VIII, 226); Bashk. 1715 **Bekmet** [Бекмет Барисов]

(MIB III, 123); Bashk. 1735 **Bekmet** [Бекмет Шигаев] (Vel.-Zern., Bašk. 22); Bashk. 1753 **Bekmet** [Бекмет Беккулов] (MIB IV/1, 68); Tat. 1783 **Bikmet** [Бикмет Уразметевъ] (Korsakov 97); Bashk. 1709 **Bikmet** [Бикмет Кутлумбетев] (MIB I, 264). ⇨ **BEK** + suff. *-met*. See also **BAYMAT**.

BEKPAN see **BEKMAN**

BEKPEW   Kzk. **Bekpew / Bekpäü** [Бекпäü / Бекпäÿ] (Proben III, 47 /62/).

BEKSEY   Bashk. 1730 **Beksey** [Бексей Кабин] (MIB III, 277); Bashk. 1747 **Beksey / Beksentey** [Бексей (Бексентей) Тектимекеев] (MIB III, 450); Bashk. 1747 **Beksentey / Beksey** [Бексей (Бексентей) Тектимекеев] (MIB III, 451).

BEKSEN   Kzk. 19th c. **Beksen** [Бексенъ] (AOO 42).

BEKSENTEY   Tat. 1764 **Beksentey** [Бексентей Усманов] (MIB IV/1, 279); Bashk. 1664 **Beksentey** [Боломгозя Бексентеев] (MIB I, 199); Bashk. 1715 **Beksentey** [Бексентей Бикашев] (MIB III, 124); Bashk. 1757 **Beksentey** [Бексентей Токаев] (MIB IV/1, 138); Bashk. 1761 **Beksentey** [Бексентей Токачев] (MIB IV/1, 204); Bashk. 1763 **Beksentey** [Якуп Бексентеев] (MIB IV/1, 267); Bashk. 1747 **Beksentey / Beksey** [Бексей (Бексентей) Тектимекеев] (MIB III, 451).

BEKSİ   Tat. 1713 **Beksi-bay** [Бексыбай Янсыраев] (MIB III, 95).

BEKSİM   Bashk. 1675 **Beksim** [Колчюра Бексимов] (MIB I, 199).

BEKŠÄ see **BEKČÄ**

BEKŠİ   Kzk. 19th c. **Bekši** [Бекши] (SOK 60); Trkm. 1609 **Bekši-χan** [Бекши-хан], governor of Merv (MIT II, 100). ⇨ **BEKČİ?**

BEKTAY   Alt. 19th-20th c. **Bektay** [Бектай], fem. (OjrRS 211). ⇨ **BEK** + **TAY?** or suff. *-tay(1,2)?*

BEKTENE   Kzk. 1629 **Bektene / Bäktänä**, a Kazak prince in Siberia (Radl., Aus Sib. I, 183).

BEKTİ see **BEKLİ**

BEKTÜ   Kzk. 19th c. **Bektü-bay** [Бектубай] (SOK 172).

BEKTÜR   Karakh. 11th c. **Bektür** [bektür / Bektur] (DTS, MK/Atalay 834). ⇨ **BEK** + adj. suff. *-tür*.

BEL   Turk. 1404 **Bel / Beli?** [Πέλης], an Ottoman chieftain (Byz. Turc. II, 251); Kzk. **Bel-χoǰa / Bel-χoža** [Бель-ходжа] (Smirnov, Sultany 18); Kzk. 19th c. **Bel-χoǰa / Bel-χoža** [Бельхожа] (SOV 16); *EN:* Kzk. 18th c. - 19th c. **Bel-χoǰa** [Бельходжа] (Tynyšp. 65); Kzk. 1925 **Bel-χoǰa** [Бельходжа], a clan (Tynyšp. 65). ✧ 'Waist, back, trunk; (fig.) supporter' cf. Kzk. *bel* 'die Taille, das Kreuz' (Radl. IV, 1606), Kzk. *bel* '(перен.) опора' (KzRS). See also **ALTÏN-BEL, ESÄN-BEL, QUM-BEL**.

BEL-ASAR   Kzk. 19th c. **Bel-asar** [Беласаръ] (SODž. 152); Kzk. 19th c. **Bel-asar** [Бельосаръ] (SOV 54);

Kzk. 19th c. **Bel-esar** (**<Bel-asar?**) [Белесаръ] (SODž. 46); Kzk. 19th c. **Bel-esar** (**<Bel-asar?**) [Белесаръ] (SOK 194). ✧ 'He will pass over a (mountain) ridge/pass' cf. Kzk. *bel as-* 'пересечь перевал' (KzRS). ⇨ **BEL.**

BEL-BAQČÏ Uzb. **Bel-baqčï-χan** [Bel-Bakču khan] (Nalivkin-Dozon 250). ⇨ **BEL.**

BEL-BOLSÏN Kzk. 19th c. **Bel-bosïn** [Белбосынъ] (SOV 26). ⇨ **BEL + BOLSÏN.**

BEL-BUL Bashk. 1729 **Belbulova** [Белбулова], a village (MIB III, 265). ⇨ **BEL + BOL.**

BELBAN see BALABAN

BELČER Pecheneg 11th c. **Belčer**, a Pecheneg chieftain, Kegenes' father (or son) (Byz. Turc. II, 86); *TN:* Kuman 1423 **Belčer-χorχan** [Belcherhorhan], a place in Lesser Kumania, Hungary (Gyárfás III, 333, 710). ✧ 'Cross roads' cf. Rásonyi, KÖA 90-91, Rásonyi: AOH 20: 137, Rásonyi, NYK 86-89.

BELČI NUyg. 19th c. **Belči** [بیلچی] (Le Coq, Namenl. 96). ✧ 'Guide'; 'Passführer' (Le Coq).

BELDÄŠ Bashk. 1737 **Beldäš-mulla / Beldaš-mulla** [Белдаш мулла Сююрембетев] (MIB I, 353). ✧ '(Having) Striped stomach (of an animal)' cf. Bashk. *bildäš* 'с поясом другого цвета шерсти вокруг живота (о масти козы или коровы)' (BaRS).

BELDEN-BOQ Kzk. 19th c. **Belden-boq** [Бельденъ-бокъ] (Pantusov, Kirg. 39). ✧ 'From waist - shit/dung'. ⇨ **BEL + BOQ.**

BELÄ-TUΓMA Türk 7th c. - 8th c. **Belä-tuγma** (DTS). ✧ I. 'Belä-Child'; II. 'Belä-button'? (Blagova 1997, 712). ⇨ **TOΓMA.**

BELÄK Tat. 1600 **Beläk** [Беляк Амандынов] (Miller, Ist. Sib. II, 159); Tat. 1601 **Beläk** [Беляк Акчурин] (Miller, Ist. Sib. II, 169); Tat. 1607 **Beläk** [Екшидевлет Беляков] (Miller, Ist. Sib. II, 197); Bashk. 1600 **Beläk** [Беляков Якшаулко] (Miller, Ist. Sib. II, 158, 159); Bashk. 1675 **Beläk** [Беляк] (MIB I, 200); Bashk. 1738 **Peläk** [Адна-бай Пеляков] (MIB I, 144). ✧ I. 'Gift, present' cf. Karakh. *beläk* 'подарок' (DTS); II. 'Arm'? cf. Bashk. *beläk* ' рука (от кисти до плеча)' (BaRS), Tat. *beläk* ' рука от кисти до плеча' (TatRS).

BELÄN Tat. 1600 **Belän** [Белян Амандыков] (MIB I, 152). ✧ 'Be swaddled'? cf. Tat. *bilän-* 'in Windeln gewickelt sein' (Radl. IV, 1763).

BELEY Tat. (Sib.) 1632 **Beley** [Белей Ерденей] (Miller, Ist. Sib. II, 399). ✧ 'Misfortune, bad luck' cf. Tat. *bälä* 'das Unglück' (Radl. IV, 1609) (<Ar.) + suff. *-y.*

BELEK Kirg. **Belek** [Белек] (Jud. 120); Alt. 19th-20th c. **Belek** [Белек] (OjrRS 207). ✧ I. 'Gift, present' cf. Kirg. *belek* 'дар, подарок' (Jud.), Alt. *belek* 'локоть; уст. задаток в виде какой-л. вещи жениху от невесты, выражающий её согласие на

умыкание' (OjrRS); II. 'Polikarp' (<R.) (OjrRS 207). See also **AQ-BELEK.**

BELEK-BULAT Nog.? **Belek-bulat-murza** [Белек-Булат-мурза] (Žirm., Epos 422). ⇨ **BELEK + BULAT.**

BELEKEY Bashk. 1682 **Belekey** [Белекейко Тойголдинъ] (AI V, 139); Bashk. 1779 **Belekey** [Тулпар Белекеев] (MIB V, 101). ✧ 'Little, small, young' cf. Bashk. *bäläkäy* 'маленький; младший' (BRS/Uraksin).

BELEP Kzk. 19th c. **Belep** [Белепъ] (SOV 100).

BELER see BİLİR

BELES Kzk. 19th c. **Beles-pay** [Белеспай] (SOK 32). ✧ 'Hill, hindrance' cf. Kzk. *beles* 'id.' (KzTS).

BELEŠ Tat. 1552 **Beleš** [Белешъ] (Kn. Metriki Lit. 86). ✧ 'Round festal cake with stuffing' cf. Tat. *bäliš* 'eine runde Pastete mit Füllung' (Radl. IV, 1612).

BELGİ Kzk. 19th c. **Belgä-bay?** (**<Belge-bay?**) [Бельгабай] (SOK 242); Kzk. 19th c. **Belge-bay** [Бельгебай] (SODž. 102); Kzk. 19th c. **Belge-bay** [Бельгебай] (AOA 86); Kzk. 19th c. **Belge-bay** [Бельгебай] (SOK 110); Kzk. 19th c. **Belge-bay** [Бельгебай] (SOV 156); Kzk. 19th c. **Belge-bay** [Бельгебай] (SOV 90); Kzk. 19th c. **Belgi-bay** [Бельгибай] (AOAtb. 2, 38); Kzk. 19th c. **Belgi-bay** [Белгыбай] (AOO 50); Kzk. 19th c. **Belgi-bay** [Бельгыбай] (AOK 18); Kzk. 19th c. **Belgi-bay** [Бельгибай] (SOK 148, 270); Kzk. 19th c. **Belgi-bay** [Белгибай] (AOK 46); Kzk. 19th c. **Belgi-bay** [Бельгибай] (SODž. 128); Kzk. 19th c. **Belgi-bay** [Бельгибай] (SOV 94); Kzk. 19th c. **Belke-bay** [Бельгибай] (SODž. 80); Kzk. 19th c. **Belke-bay** [Белькебай] (AOAtb. 2); Kzk. 19th c. **Bilge-bay** [Чубасъ Бильгебаевъ] (Grod., Pril. 101); Kzk. 19th c. **Bïlγï-bay / Bilgi-bay?** [Былгыбай] (AOO 18); Kzk. 19th c. **Bïlγï-bay / Bilgi-bay?** [Былгыбай] (AOA 82). ✧ 'Sign, mark' cf. OT, MT *bälgü* 'Zeichen, Abzeichen' (Gabain; MK), Kar. *bälgi* 'id.', Kzk. *belgä* 'Zeichen, Marke, Merkmal, Beweis' (Radl. IV, 1612), Chag., NUyg.(Tar.) *bälgü* 'Zeichen, Kennzeichen, Wappen' (Radl. IV, 1613). See also **QOS-BELGE.**

BELGİČİ Khazar 703, 704 **Belgiči / Bälgiči** [Belgiči, Bälgiči, Balğıčı (Balıqčı)], governor of the town of Bosporus (Golden 165). ⇨ **BELGİ** + suff. *-či.*

BELGİM see BELGİN

BELGİN Kzk. 19th c. **Belgim-bek** (**<Belgin-bek**) [Бельгимбекъ] (SODž. 162). ✧ 'Clear, evident' (Erol II).

BELGÜN Bulg. 12th c. **Belgün** [Бѣлгун], byname of Asen I (1187-1196) (Zlatarski). ✧ 'Wise' + suff. *-gün.*

BELGÜTEY Kzk. 19th c. **Belgütey** [Бельгутей], according to Kazak traditions he is Chinggis Khan's half-brother (Potanin, Pred. 50).

BELİ Kzk. 19th c. **Beli-bay** [Белибай Меятовъ]

(SKSO II, 14).

BELİN Kzk. 19th c. **Belin-bay** [Белынбай] (SOK 178). ✧ 'Sparrow-hawk'? cf. Chag. *bälin* 'der Sperber' (Radl. IV, 1611).

BELİS Az. **Belis** [Белис], her elder sister is Lačin (Az. Skaz. 540); Kzk. 19th c. **Belis** [Бельиспай] (SOK 94).

BELİŠ Kzk. 19th c. **Belš-pay** (<Beliš-pay) [Белшпай] (SOK 94). ⇨ **BELEŠ?**

BELİT Kzk. 19th c. **Belt-pay** (<Belit-pay) [Бельтбай] (SOK 86).

BELÜK Kzk. 19th c. **Belük-pay / Belük** [Белюкпай, Белюкъ] (SODž. 48, 66).

BENAM-ḠĀZİ Oghuz/Trkm. 13th c. **Benam-γāzi** [بنام غازى / Бенам-Гази] (Abulg./Kon. 1165). ⇨ **ḠĀZİ.**

BENAT Chag. 1555 **Benat-χatun** [Бенат-хатун] (Ivanov 144).

BENÄ Tat.(Sib.) 1623 **Benä** [Беня Теперов], a taxpayer (payer of yasaq) (Miller, Ist. Sib. II, 292).

BENEFŠE Maml. 14th c. **Benefše** [بنفشا / Benefşe], fem. (Tarj/Houtsma 64, Tarj/Toparlı 43). ✧ 'Violet' (Toparlı, loc. cit.).

BENGEYA Bashk. 1740 **Bengeya?** [Бенгея Сатаıшкова], fem. (MIB III, 412).

BENLİ-GERÄY see **MEÑLİ-GİREY**

BENZİYORMUŠ Tat. 1543 **Benziyormuš** (Gökb., Rum. 234); Yürük 1543 **Beñziyormuš / Benziyormuš** [بكزيورمش], from the Yürüks of Kocacık, Turkey (Gökb., Rum. 104, 188, 204, 221, 223, 224, 225, 227, 234). ✧ 'He takes after, he looks like; 'He is/was similar to (his father/mother)' cf. Turk. *bänzä-* 'ähnen, ähnlich sein, gleich sein' (Radl. IV, 1591), *benzemek* 'to resemble, to look like' (TED).

BEÑGİ Trkm. 1867 **Beñgi** [Бенги], from the Qaradašlu tribe (or clan) (MIT II, 632).

BEÑZİYORMUŠ see **BENZİYORMUŠ**

BEPEN Bashk. 18th c. **Bepen** [Бепенъ] (Nepljuev 141); Bashk. 1836 **Bepen** [Бепень] (PSZRI IX, 743); Bashk. 18th c. **Bepen / Bepenä?** [Бепеня] (Nepljuev 160).

BEPEŠ Kzk. 19th c. **Bepeš** [Бепешъ] (AOP 62).

BER Kzk. 19th c. **Ber-bay** [Бербай] (AOK 126). ✧ 'Give' cf. Türk, Kuman, Chag., Kar., Trkm., etc. *bär- / ber-* 'geben' (Radl. IV, 1592-93), *ber-* 'давать' (KzkRS). See also **AY-BER, AYDE-BER, ČEÜL-BER, ES-BER, İG-BER, İL-BER, SALTEN-BER.**

BER-DAWLÄT Crm. 1478, 1479 **Ber-daulät / Ber-dawlät / Ber-dewlet** [Бердоулатъ / Мердоулатъ / Бердоулатъ Ачигирѣевичъ / Бердаоулатъ / Бердійоулатъ / Бердеоулатъ], a prince from the Crimea, son of the Crimean Khan Haji Girey I (1426/1430-1466) (PSRL VI, 223, 278, PSRL VIII, 205 etc., PSRL (Russk. Hr.) I, 500). ⇨ **BER + DÄWLÄT.**

BER-DAWLÏ Kkalp. 20th c. **Ber-dawlï** [Бердавлы]

(Bask., Kkalp. 399). ⇨ **BER + DAWLÏ.**

BERDAQ Kkalp. 20th c. **Berdaq-baqsï** [Бердакъ-бакъсы] (Bask., Kkalp. 76).

BERDALİ see **BERDİ-ALİ**

BERDE see **BERDİ**

BERDEKE see **BERDİKE**

BERDEKEY see **BERDİKEY**

BERDEN Kzk. 1846 **Berden** [Кулдубай Берденев бий] (MKOP 155).

BERDİ Trkm. 19th c. **Berd-bay** (<Berdi-bay) [Екъ-Шенбэ Бердбаевъ] (Ščeglov IV, 164); Nog. 1649 **Berde** [Эбалтары Бердѣевъ] (AI IV, 124); Kmk. 1832 **Berde / Berda?** [Берда Дударов] (MID III, 269); Tat. 1638 **Berdey** (<Berdi(y)) [Бердеев Акыпятлей], a Tatar from Ufa (Miller, Ist. Sib. II, 452); Bashk. 1623 **Berdey** (<Berdi(y)) [Бердеев Кенчегул] (Miller, Ist. Sib. II, 299); Kzk. 19th c. **Berdey** (<Berdi(y)) [Бердеи] (SOK 288); Oghuz/Trkm. 13th c. **Berdi** [بردى / Берди], Ögürjik-alp's son (Abulg./Kon. 1235, 1240); Maml. 15th c. **Berdi** [السيفى برد بك], (az̧-z̧āhirī), the viceroy of Syria, died in 1470 (Mayer 264-65); Maml. 1483 **Berdi** [برد بك المحمدى] (Iyās II, 219, 306); Kzk. 19th c. **Berdi** [Берды] (SODž. 110); Kzk. 19th c. **Berdi** [Тайбекъ Бердіевъ] (Grod., Pril. 182); Kzk. 19th c. **Berdi** [Мирманкулъ Бердіевъ] (Grod., Pril. 45); Kzk. 19th c. **Berdi** [Берды Джаббаркуловъ] (SKSO VIII, 200); Kzk. 19th c. **Berdi** [Берды] (SKSO VII, 224); Uzb. 19th c. **Berdi** [Берды Джіенмуратовъ] (SKSO III, 158); Uzb. 20th c. **Berdi** [Берди] (Begmatov 1984, 202); Kzk. 19th c. **Berdi / Berdi-bay** [Берды / Бердыбай] (AOO 38); Trkm. 1812 **Berdi-atalïq** [Берды-аталык], from the Teke tribe (MIT II, 383); Bashk. 1779 **Berdi-bay** [Алиббай Бердыбаев] (MIB V, 87); Kzk. 19th c. **Berdi-bay** [Бердыбай] (AOK 34); Kzk. 19th c. **Berdi-bay** [Айтуваръ Бердибаевъ] (Grod., Pril. 171); Kkalp. 20th c. **Berdi-bay** [Бердибай] (Bask., Kkalp. 69); Kkalp. 20th c. **Berdi-bay** [Бердибай] (KkRS 773); Uzb. 1875 **Berdi-bay** [Берды-бай] (Moskal'cev 40); Kzk. 19th c. **Berdi-bay / Birdi-bay** [بردى باى / Бирди-бай] (Veselovskij, Kirg. 54); Tat. 16th c. **Berdi-beg**, from the family of the Khans of Astrakhan (Howorth II/2, 352); Khorezm. 14th c. **Berdi-bek** [بيردى بيك], Timur's chieftain (Arabš. II, 454); Tat.(GH) **Berdi-bek**, in a tale from the Crimea together with Toqtamïš and Temir (Proben VII, 110, 212); Maml. **Berdi-bek** [السيفى برد بك] (Mayer 264); Maml. 1405/06 **Berdi-bek** [برد بك و صمغار] (Ibn Taghrīb. VI, 173); Maml. 1405/06 **Berdi-bek** [برد بك الخاز ندار], a treasurer (Ibn Taghrīb. VI, 128, 228); Maml. 1408/09 **Berdi-bek** [برد بك حاجب حلب] (Ibn Taghrīb. VI, 224, 330); Maml. 1409/10 **Berdi-bek**

[برد بك نايب حماه] (Ibn Taghrīb. VI, 204 etc., Weil, Chalif. II, 225, 233); Maml. 1410 **Berdi-bek** [الحمزاوى برد بك] (Ibn Taghrīb. VI, 383); Maml. 1410/11 **Berdi-bek** [برد بك رأس نو به نوروز] (Ibn Taghrīb. VI, 238); Maml. 1433 **Berdi-bek** [برد بك الاسماعيلى] (Ibn Taghrīb. VI, 691); Maml. 1450 **Berdi-bek** [برد بك] (Ibn Taghrīb. VIII, 82, 224, 249 etc.); Maml. 15th c. **Berdi-bek** [برد بك] (Iyās II, 295, 342); Maml. 1450, 1455 **Berdi-bek** [برد بك الجكمى العجمى الاعور] (Ibn Taghrīb. VIII, 158, 357); Maml. 1453 **Berdi-bek** [برد بك الاشرفى / الدوادار الثا نى/] (Ibn Taghrīb. VII, 401, 428, Weil, Chalif. II, 283-85); Maml. 1453, 1516 **Berdi-bek** [برد بك] (Iyās 40, 52, 293, III, 52); Maml. 1456, 1469 **Berdi-bek** [برد بك البجمتدار], an emir (Iyās II, 54); Maml. 1461 **Berdi-bek** [بردبك الطو بك] (Ibn Taghrīb. VIII, 411); Maml. 1467/68 **Berdi-bek** [بردبك التاجى] (Iyās II, 94, 196); Maml. 1467/68 **Berdi-bek** [بردى الابراهيمى الاينالى] (Iyās II, 92); Maml. 1469/70 **Berdi-bek** [برد بك المشطوب اليشبكى] (Iyās II, 113, 122); Maml. 1475/76 **Berdi-bek** [برد بك جر با شكرت] (Iyās II, 160); Maml. 1477 **Berdi-bek** [برد بك سكر] (Iyās II, 177); Maml. 1478 **Berdi-bek** [برد بك المعمار] (Iyās II, 182, 199); Maml. 1483, 1500/01 **Berdi-bek** [برد بك الطو بك المحمدى] (Iyās II, 219, 282, 391); Maml. 1487 **Berdi-bek** [برد بك طرخان الظاهرى جتمق] (Iyās II, 244); Maml. 1495/96 **Berdi-bek** [برد بك المحمدى الاينالى] (Iyās II, 293, 380, Weil, Chalif. II, 379); Maml. 1496/97 **Berdi-bek** [برد بك الا شتر] (Iyās II, 329); Maml. 1517 **Berdi-bek** [برد بك], Khalif Mutevekkil's chancellor (Iyās III, 109, 206); Trkm. 1828 **Berdi-bek** [Берды-бек], from the Bayrač clan (MIT II, 447); Trkm. 19th c. **Berdi-bek** [Бав бекъ Бердыбековъ] (Ščeglov IV, 172); Chuv. 18th-19th c. **Berdi-bek** [Бердибякъ] (Magn. 33); Tat.(Mish.) **Berdi-bek** (IOAIÊK XIX, 142); Bashk. 1735 **Berdi-bek** [Бердыбакъ Кинзинъ] (Vel.-Zern., Bašk. 20); Kzk. 19th c. **Berdi-bek** [Бердыбекъ] (SODž. 84); Kipch. 1356, 1358 **Berdi-bek, Berdi-bek-χan, Berde-bek** [بيردى بيك / بردى بيك / Бердибек-хан Бердебекъ / Бердибекъ (Бердебѣкъ) / Бердибѣкъ], a khan of the Golden Horde (1357-1359), Ǯanï-bek khan's son (Abulg./Desm. 77, PSRL (Russk. Hr.) I, 411, PSRL IV, 63, V, 228, VIII, 10, X, 229, XVI, 87); Trkm. 1809 **Berdi-bek-behadïr** [Берды-бек-бехадыр], from the Yomut tribe (MIT II, 376, 434, 447, 480); Trkm. 1813 **Berdi-biy** [Берды-бий] (MIT II, 385, 407, 408); Uzb.? 20th c. **Berdi-datχa** [Berdi-Datkha], a basmačï from Bukhara (Castagné 77); Bashk. 1675 **Berdi-γul** [Бердыгул Богбеков] (MIB I, 200); Bashk. 1735 **Berdi-γul** [Бердыгулъ Умутбаевъ], a tarχan (Vel.-Zern., Bašk. 16); Bashk.

1735 **Berdi-γul** [Бердыгулъ Тлевкеевъ], a tarχan (Vel.-Zern., Bašk. 15); Bashk. 1735 **Berdi-γul** [Бердыгулъ Араслановъ] (Vel.-Zern., Bašk. 19); Bashk. 1776 **Berdi-γul** [Бердыгул Абдуллин] (MIB V, 42,43); Bashk. 1789 **Berdi-γul** [Калмак Бердыгулов] (MIB V, 259, 272); Trkm. 1854 **Berdi-χan** [Берды-ханъ] (ZIRGOÊtn. I, 173); Tat. 1821/22 **Berdi-χan** [Берды-хан], from the Tatar (!) clan of the Yomut tribe (MIT II, 421, 434, 447, 450, 451); Kzk. 18th c. **Berdi-χoǰa** [Berdi Xodža / Berdy-Khoja], an elder (leader) in a community (Radl., Aus Sib. I, 200, Levchin 265); Kzk. 19th c. **Berdi-χoža** [Бердыхожа] (AUK 792); Uzb. 1814/15 **Berdi-inaq** [Берды-инак] (MIT II, 388, 395, 416); Trkm. 1856 **Berdi-inglis** [Берды-Инглис], from the Yomut tribe (MIT II, 577, 579, 596); Kzk. 19th c. **Berdi-yar** [Бердіяръ] (Grod., Pril. 97); Kzk. 19th c. **Berdi-yar** [Мурза-кулъ Бердыяровъ] (SKSO IV, otd. II, 30); Uzb. 19th c. **Berdi-yar** [Berdy-Yar], from Khokand (Nalyvkin, Kokand. 145); Uzb. 20th c. **Berdi-yâr** [Бердиёр] (Begmatov 1984, 202); Kkalp. 1810 **Berdi-yüzbašï** [Берди юзбаши] (MIKk. 105); Kzk. 19th c. **Berdi-qaγan?** [Берди Кагган] (Grod., Pril. 109); Kzk. 1863 **Berdi-qul** [Бердыкулъ] (ZIRGOGeogr. I, 412); Uzb. 19th c. **Berdi-qul** [Хушвакъ Бердыкуловъ] (SKSO III, 154); Uzb. 19th c. **Berdi-qul** [Бурибай Бердыкуловъ] (SKSO III, 164); Uzb. 19th c. **Berdi-qul** [Ишимъ Бердыкуловъ] (SKSO III, 156); Kzk. 19th c. **Berdi-maγomed** [Берди Магомедъ] (Grod., Pril. 31); Kzk. 19th c. **Berdi-maγommed** [Берди Магоммедъ], Taš-maγommed's son (Grod., Pril. 164); Uzb. 20th c. **Berdi-mälik** [Бердималик] (Begmatov 1984, 202); Kkalp. 20th c. **Berdi-mïrat** [Бердимырат] (KkRS 773); Trkm. 1848 **Berdi-muχammed-bek** [Берды Мухаммед-бек] (MIT II, 517); Kkalp. 20th c. **Berdi-murat** [Бердимурат] (KkRS 773); Trkm. 20th c. **Berdï** [Berdï] (Zaj. 1971, 333); Kirg. 19th-20th c. **Berdu-γul** (Prinz 149); Kzk. 19th c. **Birdi** [Бирды] (SKSO VIII, 207); Kkalp. 20th c. **Perdi-bay** [Пердыбай Садыкъ-улы] (Bask., Kkalp. 60); *EN:* Kzk. 18th c. - 19th c. **Berdi** [Берды] (Tynyšp. 70, 71); *TN:* Chuv. 18th c. **Berde-bek(ova)** (<Berdi-bäk) [Бердебякова], a village in the district of Chistopol' (Korsakov 221). ✦ '(God/He) Has given, gave (him/her)' cf. *bär-, ber-* 'geben' (Radl. IV, 1592-93). A very frequent component of Turkic theophoric names (cf. Rásonyi, Theoph., Bask., Fam. 177). The simple names *Berdi, Bergen, Bermiš* seem to be shortened of compound thephoric names such as *Alla-berdi, Oγan-berdi, Xuday-berdi, Alla-bergen, Teñri-birgen, Xuday-bergen, Teñgri-bermiš* etc. In old Russian sources it is often completed with affix *-y / -yev*, e. g. Tat. *Berde(yev) / Berdi(yev)*, etc. See also **AQ-BERDİ, AQTAN0BERDİ, ALΓÏM-BERDİ, ALİ-BERDİ,**

ALİM-BERDİ, ALQÏM-BİRDİ, ALLA-BERDİ, AMAN-BERDİ, ANNA-BERDİ, ARAZ-BERDİ, AWAZ-BERDİ, AZ-BERDİ, AZİZ-BERDİ, BABA-JAN-BERDİ, BAY-BERDİ, BEK-BERDİ, BÜRİ-BERDİ, ČALAB-BERDİ, ČÏN-BERDİ, JABBAR-BERDİ, JAN-BERDİ, JAW-BERDİ, JOL-BERDİ, DAWLET-BERDİ, EM-BERDİ, ER-VERDİ, ES-BERDİ, ESİ-BERDİ, ET-BERDİ, EWEZ-BERDİ-TAWAR, HAQ-BERDİ, XALÏQ-BERDİ, XAN-BERDİ, XOJA-BERDİ, XOJAM-BERDİ, XOJEND-VERDİ, İČ-EL-BERDİ, İGÄM-BERDİ, İYEM-BERDİ, İK-BERDİ, İMAM-BERDİ, İMAN-BERDİ, İN-BERDİ, İSÄN-BERDİ, İŠ-BERDİ, YAQŠÏ-BERDİ, YANA-BERDİ, YAZ-BERDİ, YAZDAN-VERDİ, YERMÄKLİ-BERDİ?, YİL-BERDİ, YUQ-PERDİ, YUL-BERDİ, KELEM-BERDİ, KERİM-BERDİ, KÖP-BERDİ, KÜN-BERDİ, KÜSÄK-PERDİ, KÜSE-BERDİ, QADÏR-BERDİ, QAY-BERDİ, QAL-BERDİ, QASÏM-BERDİ, QATEŇKLİ-BERDİ, QAZA-BERDİ, QOJAM-BERDİ, QOŠ-BERDİ, QOTA-BERDİ, QUDAY-BERDİ, QUL-BERDİ, QULA-BERDİ, QURBAN-BERDİ, MAL-BERDİ, MÄWLAN-BERDİ, MÄKÄN-XUDAY-BERDİ, MEŇGÜ-BERDİ, MİLLET-VİRDİ, MULLA-BERDİ, NİYAZ-BERDİ, NUR-BERDİ, OΓAN-BERDİ, ORAZ-BERDİ, RAXMAN-BERDİ, RÄHİM-BERDİ, RÄSUL-BERDİ, RÂZÏQ-BERDİ, RÄZZÂQ-BERDİ, SALAM-BERDİ, SATTAR-BERDİ, SÄLİM-BERDİ, SUBHÂN-BERDİ, ŠAH-BERDİ, ŠÜKÜR-BERDİ, TALEP-BERDİ, TAN-BERDİ, TANÏ-BERDİ, TASU-BERDİ, TÄŇİR-BERDİ, TÄŇRİ-BERDİ, TELÄK-BERDE, TERE-BERDİ, TİLÄP-BERDİ, TİLÄW-BERDİ, TOQ-BERDİ, TURUP-BERDİ, ZUBAY-BERDİ.

BERDİ-ALİ Trkm. 19th c. **Berd-ali (<Berdi-ali)** [Ильгильды Бердалиевъ] (Ščeglov IV, 177); Kzk. 19th c. **Berd-ali (<Berdi-ali)** [Кулбаракъ Бердалiевъ] (Grod., Pril. 89); Uzb. 1740 **Berd-ali-bek (<Berdi-ali-bek)** [Бердали-Бекъ], from the Mangut tribe (Hanykov, Poezdka 20); Uzb. 20th c. **Berdi-ali** [Бердиали] (Begmatov 1984, 202); Trkm.? 1817/18 **Berdi-ali-naib** [Берды Али-наиб], from Shakhabad (MIT II, 404); Kzk. 1784 **Berdi-γalï-saltan** [Бердыгалы Салтанъ] (PSZRI XXII, 142, 143); *TN:* Kkalp. **Birdi-ali** [بردیعلی / Бирдиали], a settlement in the tümen of Sheraz (ZIRGOStat. IV). ⇨ **BERDİ + ALİ.**

BERDİ-ALİM Uzb. 20th c. **Berdi-âlim** [Бердиолим] (Begmatov 1984, 202). ⇨ **BERDİ + ALİM** + poss. suff. -*m.*

BERDİ-BEK see **BERDİ**

BERDİ-DUWAN Crm. 1509 **Berdi-duwan** [Лагимъ Бердидуванъ], envoy from the Crimea (PSRL VI, 25, VIII, 251). ⇨ **BERDİ + DUWAN.**

BERDİ-GULĀM Uzb. 20th c. **Berdi-gulâm** [Бердиғулом] (Begmatov 1984, 202). ⇨ **BERDİ + GULĀM.**

BERDİ-YAR see **BERDİ**

BERDİ-KÜWİ Uzb. 20th c. **Berdi-küwi** [Бердикуви] (Begmatov 1984, 202). ✧ 'Given (by)?' cf. Uzb. *küwi* 'леток (в улье)' (UzbRS)? ⇨ **BERDİ.**

BERDİ-QÂBİL Uzb. 20th c. **Berdi-qâbil** [Бердиқобил] (Begmatov 1984, 202). ⇨ **BERDİ + QABUL.**

BERDİ-MÄWLÂN Uzb. 20th c. **Berdi-mäwlân** [Бердимавлон] (Begmatov 1984, 202).

BERDİ-MURAT Uzb. 20th c. **Berdi-murâd** [Бердимурод] (Begmatov 1984, 202). ✧ 'Given (by) Murat'. ⇨ **BERDİ + MURAT.**

BERDİ-NAZAR Kzk. 19th c. **Berdi-nazar** [Берди Назаръ Киргизовъ] (SKSO III, 10); Uzb. 20th c. **Berdi-nazar** [Бердиназар] (Begmatov 1984, 202). ⇨ **BERDİ + NAZAR.**

BERDİ-NÄBİ Uzb. 20th c. **Berdi-näbi** [Бердинаби] (Begmatov 1984, 202). ✧ 'Given (by the) Prophet'. ⇨ **BERDİ + NÄBİ.**

BERDİ-NİYAZ Uzb. 20th c. **Berdi-niyâz** [Бердиниёз] (Begmatov 1984, 202). ✧ 'Given (by) Niyaz'. ⇨ **BERDİ + NİYAZ.** See also **NİYAZ-BERDİ.**

BERDİ-RASUL Uzb. 20th c. **Berdi-räsul** [Бердирасул] (Begmatov 1984, 202). ⇨ **BERDİ + RASUL.** See also **RÄSUL-BERDİ.**

BERDİ-RÄHİM Uzb. 20th c. **Berdi-rähim** [Бердирахим] (Begmatov 1984, 202). ✧ 'Given by the Merciful (God)'. ⇨ **BERDİ + RAHİM.**

BERDİ-ŠÜKÜR Uzb. 20th c. **Berdi-šükür** [Бердишукур] (Begmatov 1984, 202). ✧ 'Given by gratefulness / thankfulness'. ⇨ **BERDİ + ŠÜKÜR.**

BERDİK Bashk. 1735 **Berdik** [Бактыбай Бердиков] (MIB III, 334). ✧ 'We gave (him/her)'? ⇨ **BERDİ** + 1st p. plur. -*k.*

BERDİKE Kzk. 19th c. **Berdeke (<Berdi-eke?)** [Бердеке] (SOK 232); Kzk. 19th c. **Berdike** [Бердыке] (SODž. 12). ⇨ **BERDİ** + suff. -*ke.*

BERDİKEY Bashk. 1701 **Berdikey** [Сатылган Бердыкеев] (MIB III, 11); Bashk.? 1715 **Berdikey** [Колчюра Бердыкеев] (MIB III, 124); Bashk. 1727 **Berdikey / Berdekey** [Бердекей Миллигулов] (MIB III, 244). ⇨ **BERDİ(K)** + suff. -*(k)ey.*

BERDİM Kzk. 19th c. **Berdim-bay** [Бердымбай] (SOK 168); Kzk. 19th c. **Berdim-bek** [Бердымбекъ] (SOK 72); Kzk. 19th c. **Berdim-bek** [Бердимбекъ] (SOV 120). ⇨ **BERDİ?** + 1st p. sing. -*m.*

BERDİMÄN Uzb. 20th c. **Berdimän** [Бердиман] (Begmatov 1984, 202). ✧ 'Given'. ⇨ **BERDİ** + suff. -*män.*

BERDİMET   Bashk. 1713 **Berdimet** [Акей Бердыметев] (MIB III, 92). ⇨ **BERDİ** + suff. *-met.*

BERDİŠ   Tat.(Sib.) 1632 **Berdiš** [Бердишев (Адня Бердишева0] (Miller, Ist. Sib. II, 397); Bashk. 1723 **Berdiš** [Сапай Бердишев] (MIB III, 201); Bashk. 1729 **Berdiš** [Девеней Бердышев] (MIB III, 270); Trkm. 1804 **Berdiš-atalïq** [Бердыш-аталык] (MIT II, 353); Trkm. 1826 **Berdiš-bek** [Бердиш-бек], from the Sarïq tribe (MIT II, 441). ⇨ **BERDİ** + suff. -š.

BERDЇ see **BERDİ**

BERDЇ-ГALЇ see **BERDİ-ALİ**

BERDU see **BERDİ**

BERÄS   Tat.(Mish) **Beräs**, Teleš-murza's son (Pelissier 27); *TN:* Tat.(Mish) **Beräs** [Берясъ ? Верясъ], a placename (Pelissier 24).

BEREBUR   Alt. 19th-20th c. **Berebur** [Беребур] (OjrRS 207). ✧ 'New elections' cf. R. перевыборы 'id.' (OjrRS 207).

BEREKE see **BEREKET**

BEREKEY   Bashk. 1738 **Berekey** [Берекей Игибаев] (MIB III, 393); Bashk. 1750 **Berekey** [Бектемир Берекеев] (MIB III, 475).

BEREKET   Kzk. 19th c. **Baraqat** [Джалгасбай (Джалкасбай) Баракатовъ] (Grod., Pril. 98, 106); Chag. 16th c. **Bereke** [Береке], a „seyid" (Ivanov 9); Maml. 1453 **Bereket** [بركا ت أمير مكه] (Iyās II, 34, Weil, Chalif. II, 390-91); Maml. 1477 **Bereket** [بركا ت بن الجيعان] (Iyās II, 180, 223); Maml. 1492/93 **Bereket** [بركات بن الظريف المقرى] (Iyās II, 278); Maml. 1499/1500 **Bereket** [بركا ت بن قر يميط] (Iyās II, 361); Maml. 1516 **Bereket** [بن موسى المحتسب] (Iyās III, 4, 5, 13); Maml. 1517 **Bereket** [زين الدين بركات] (Iyās III, [بركا ت أحو شرف الدين الصغير] (Iyās III, 108, 181); Maml. 1518 **Bereket** [بركات بن سلمان] (Iyās III, 148); Maml. 1518 **Bereket** [بركا ت بن المبيص] (Iyās III, 149); Maml. 1522 **Bereket** [بركا ت أحو لمستو فى سعد الد ين] (Iyās III, 283); Yürük 1543 **Bereket** (Gökb., Rum. 218, 220); Kkalp. 20th c. **Paraχat** [Парахат] (KkRS 775). ✧ 'Divine gift, blessing' cf. Kzk. *bereke / bereket* 'id.' (KzTS), Kkalp. *paraχat* 'покой, спокойствие' (KkRS), Kuman, Crm., Kzk., Tat., Turk. *bäräkät* 'der Reichtum, der Segen, vortheilhaft, sparsam' (Radl. IV, 1595).

BEREN-QUŠ   Selj.? **Beren-quš** [برنتوش] (Ibn al-Athīr: RHCHor II/2, 188). ✧ '?-Bird'. ⇨ **QUŠ I.**

BERENDEY   Chuv. 18th-19th c. **Berendey** [Берендей] (Magn. 33, 34). ✧ I. Ethnonym (name of a clan or group)? cf. Rasovski: Pečenegi, Torki i Berendei na Rusi i v Ugrii: Seminarium Kondakovianum VI. Praha (1933), pp. 1-66, Rásonyi: Der Volksname Берендѣй: Seminarium Kondakovianum VI. Praha (1933), pp. 119-126, Rásonyi, KÖA p. 92. Rásonyi linked it with participle *beren* (op. cit. p. 123) which is not convincing. A. Erol took over Rásonyi's opinion. II. 'Lamb-like'? cf. Bashk., Tat. *bärän* 'das Lamm' (Radl. IV, 1597). ⇨ **BERENDİ?** + suff. *-dey / -tay(1).*

BERENDİ   Trkm. 1719 **Berendi** [قنق ايباش مع برندى و] (Refik, Anad. 156); *TN:* Turk. 20th c. **Berendi**, a village in the province of Konya, Turkey (TMİB 573); Turk. 20th c. **Berendi**, a village in the province of Antalya, Turkey (TMİB 107). ✧ I. Ethnonym (name of a clan or group)?, cf. Rasovski: Pečenegi, Torki i Berendei na Rusi i v Ugrii: Seminarium Kondakovianum VI. Praha (1933), pp. 1-66, Rásonyi: Der Volksname Берендѣй: Seminarium Kondakovianum VI. Praha (1933), pp. 119-126, Rásonyi, KÖA p. 92. Rásonyi linked it with part. *beren* (op. cit. p. 123) which is not convincing. A. Erol took over Rásonyi's opinion. II. Toponym (name of villages) in Turkey (Erol II: Berendey / Berendi). ⇨ **BERENDEY?**

BERESEYKE   Alt. 19th-20th c. **Bereseyke** [Бересейке] (OjrRS 207). ✧ Firs (R.).

BEREWГUR   Kzk. 19th c. **Berewγur** [Береугуръ] (SODž. 112).

BERGÄN see **BERGEN**

BERGEN   Kzk. 1884 **Bergän** [Баймурадъ Ибинъ Бергановъ] (Grod., Pril. 94); Kzk. 19th c. **Bergem-bay** (<Bergen-bay) [Бергембай] (SOK 14); Kzk. 1794 **Bergen / Bergän?** [بركان] (MIK IV, 160); Kzk. 19th c. **Bergen-bay** [Бергенбай] (SKSO III, 19); Uzb. 1876 **Bergen-bay** [Бергенъбай] (Moskal'cev 52). ✧ '(God/He) Has given, gave (him/her)' cf. *bär- / ber-* 'geben' (Radl. IV, 1592-93) + aff. *-gen / -gän*. A very frequent component of Turkic theophoric names. The simple names *Berdi, Bergen, Bermiš* seem to be shortened of compound thephoric names such as *Alla-berdi, Oγan-berdi, Xuday-berdi, Alla-bergen, Teñri-birgen, Xuday-bergen, Teñgri-bermiš* etc. (cf. Rásonyi, Theoph., Bask., Fam. 177). See also **AYAP-BERGEN, AYDAN-BERGEN, AQ-BERGEN, AL-BERGEN, ALLA-BERGEN, ALLAM-BERGEN, APTAP-BERGEN, AS-BERGEN, ATA-BERGEN, ATAY-BERGEN, AZ-BERGEN, AZİZ-BERGÄN, BEK-BERGEN, ĴABBAR-BERGÄN, DOS-BERGEN, EGÄM-BERGÄN, ES-BERGEN, ESİM-BERGEN, ESİT-BERGEN, HAQ-BERGÄN, XOĴA-BERGEN, XUDAY-BERGEN, İYEM-BERGEN, İMAM-BERGEN, YAQŠÏ-BERGEN, KÄRİM-BERGÄN, KÖJE-BERGEN, KÖZ-BERGEN, QAL-BERGEN, QALÏQ-BERGEN, QAZÏ-BERGEN, QOĴAM-BERGEN, QOŠ-BERGEN, QUDAY-BERGEN, MA-BERGÄN, MALDA-BERGEN, NÄZ-BERGEN, ÖTEP-BERGEN, RÄHMÂN-BERGÄN, RÄHİM-BERGEN, RÄZZÂQ-BERGÄN, SÄLÂM-BERGEN, SÏQÏM-BERGEN, ŠAH-BERGEN, TAŠ-BERGEN,**

TAWUQ-BERGÄN, TÄÑİR-BERGEN, TÄÑRİ-BERGEN, TİLÄW-BERGEN, TİLEP-BERGEN, TÏŠ-PERGEN, TOQ-BERGEN, TOP-PERGEN, TÖLEP-BERGEN, TÜLE-BERGEN, URAZ-BERGEN, ÜTEN-BERGEN, UL-BERGE(?).

BERGİN-SEKÄ Uyg. **Bärgin-sänä** [Bärgin Sängä] (EUTS); Uyg. 12th c. - 14th c. **Bärkin-sänä** [Bärkin-sängä] (Radl., USp. 4-5); Uyg. 12th c. - 14th c. **Bergin-sekä** [bergin sekä] (DTS). ⇨ BERGİN + SEÑÄ.

BERΓUT see **BÜRKİT**

BERXUT see **BÜRKİT**

BERİM Kzk. 19th c. **Berim-qul** (Ljutš 114); Kzk. 19th c. **Berim-žan** [Беримжанъ] (AOP 22). ✧ 'Bribery' cf. Kzk. *bärim* 'Bestechungsgeschenk' (Radl. IV, 1601).

BERİŠ Maml. 1421, 1467 **Beriš** [بريش], Janï-bek's treasurer (Iyās II, 11, 92). ✧ 'Gift, giving, donation' cf. Kuman, Crm., East.T. *bäriš* 'das Geben' (Radl. IV, 1600). See also MEÑGÜ-VİRİŠ.

BERK-ALİ Trkm. 1881 **Berk-ali-χan** [Беркъ-Али-ханъ] (Grod., Vojna II, 145). ✧ 'Strong/firm Ali' cf. Trkm. *berk* 'прочный, крепкий; здоровый' (TrkmRS). ⇨ ALİ. See also TOΓAN-BERK.

BERK-YARUQ Selj. 1094-1105 **Berk-yaruq** [Soltan Barciaruk seu Tarciaruk], a Seljuk sultan (Abulfar. 363); Selj. 12th c. **Berk-yaruq** [بركيارق بن سلطان دغرل], son of the Seljuk Sultan of Iraq Toγrul ibn Arslan (1175-1194) (Rāwandī 347); Selj. **Berk-yaruq / Bärk-yaruq** [بركيارق / ناصرالدين], Nāṣiruddīn Berkyāruq], from the sons of the Seljuk Sultan Qïlïč Arslan ibn Mesᶜūd (Qazw. 482, Aqsar./Iš. 39, Ibn Bībī III, 11-14, IV, 5); Selj. 1091 **Berk-yaruq / Bärk-yaruq** [بركيارق بن ملكشاه] / سلطان ركن الدين ابوالمظفر / Παργιαρούχ / Barkiarok / Tûrkyârûk / Беркиярук], a Seljuk Sultan (1094-1104) (Qalänisi 121, 138-140, Qazw. 361, 433, Ibn al-Athir/Tornb. I, 197, 219, 225, Rāwandī 38, 68 etc., Juwaynī II, 2, Kamāladdīn II, 109, 110, 117, Ibn Taghrīb. II, 291, Bondārī, 86-90, 255-262 etc., Ahbar 52, Abulfar./Budge I, 232, Byz. Turc. II, 245, Reg. Hieros. 1, MIT I, 381-86, 442). ✧ 'Solid-bright (brilliant)' (Németh, HMK 135), cf. Trkm. *berk* 'прочный, крепкий; здоровый' (TrkmRS). ⇨ YARUQ.

BERK-MEÑGÜ Uyg. 13th c.-14th c. **Berk-meñgü** [Barek Mengku] (Chwol., Syr.-nest. (NF) 47). ✧ 'Strong-Eternal' cf. Trkm. *berk* 'прочный, крепкий; здоровый' (TrkmRS). ⇨ BERK + MEÑGÜ.

BERK-TURMÏŠ Uyg. 12th c.-14th c. **Berk-turmïš** (Radl., USp. 6). ✧ 'Stayed firmly' cf. Trkm. *berk* 'прочный, крепкий; здоровый' (TrkmRS). ⇨ TURMÏŠ.

BERKÄM Kzk. 19th c. **Berkäm-bay** [Беркамбай] (Grod., Pril. 82).

BERKE Maml. 14th c. **Bärkä** [بركه] (Sauvaget 41); Mo.? 1370/71 **Berke** [خوند بركة أم الاشرف شعبان] (Iyās I, 226, 290); Maml. 1300 **Berke** [بركة الجوبانى] (Iyās I, 142, 153); Maml. 14th c. **Berke** [بركة رأس نوبة], a chief in Nūbiya (Mayer 101); Khorezm./Chag. 15th c. **Berke**, a Sheybanid Sultan, Yādigār's son (Abulg./Desm. 196 etc.); Maml.? 13th c. **Berke-χan** [حسام الدين ملك الامرا' بركة خان], died at Hims in 1246, his tomb is in Jerusalem (Berchem, Jér. I, 188). ✧ 'Berke' (Mo.), according to Cleaves it means 'a hostage' (p. 416).

BERKEY see **BERKE**

BERKİN I. Uyg. 12th c.-14th c. **Bärkin-sängä / Bärkin-säkä** (Radl., USp. 4-5, Malov 216).

BERKİN II. Kzk. 19th c. **Berkin** [Беркинъ] (SODž. 110).

BERKİŠ Kzk. 19th c. **Berkiš** [Беркиш] (AOAtb. 50); Kzk. 19th c. **Berkiš** [Беркиш] (SOV 84); Kzk. 19th c. **Berkiš-bay** [Беркишбай] (SOK 232). ✧ 'Hold/hang together!; Be strong!' cf. *bärkiš-* (East.T.) 'sich an einander befestigen, vereinigen', (Turk.) 'befestigt sein' (Radl. IV, 1602).

BERKUT see **BÜRKİT**

BERKUTEY Alt. 19th c. **Berkutey** [Еркутей и Беркутей] (Potanin, Pred. 181). ⇨ BÜRKİT + suff. *-ey*.

BERLİ Kzk. 19th c. **Berli / Berle** [Берле] (SOK 164); Kzk. 19th c. **Berli-bay / Berlï-bay** [Берлыбай, Берлибай] (SOK 108, 182).

BERLİKE Kzk. 19th c. **Berlike** [Берлике] (SOK 4). ⇨ BERLİ + suff. *-ke*.

BERLİMBET Kzk. 19th c. **Berlimbet** [Берлимбетъ] (SOK 160). ⇨ BERLİ + suff. *-mbet*.

BERMEN Kzk. 19th c. **Bermem-bay (<Bermen-bay)** [Бермембай] (SODž. 40).

BERMES Kzk. 1808 **Bermes** [Бермес] (MIK IV, 240); Kzk. 19th c. **Birmes** [Шикъ Бирмесъ Шгайбай] (AUK 498). ✧ 'He/she won't give'. ⇨ BER.

BERMET Kirg. **Bermet** [Бермет], fem. (Jud. 35, 921); Kirg. 1969 **Bermet**, fem. (Nikonov: OSA 158). ✧ 'Pearl, beads' cf. Kirg. *bermet* 'перламутр, Кемчуг, бисер' (Jud.).

BERMİŠ Maml. 1366/67 **Bermiš** [برمش العلا یى] (Iyās I, 220); *TN:* Turk. 20th c. **Vermiš** [Vermiş] (TMİB 61). ✧ '(God/He) has given; gave (him/her)' cf. Türk., Kuman, Chag., Kirg., Kzk., Trkm., Uyb., etc. *bär- / ber-* 'geben' (Radl. IV, 1592-93), Az., Turk. *vär- / ver-* 'id.' (Radl. IV, 1967) + aff. *-mïš*. A very frequent component of Turkic theophoric names. The simple names *Berdi, Bergen, Bermiš* seem to be shortened of compound thephoric names such as *Alla-berdi, Oγan-berdi, Xuday-berdi, Alla-bergen, Teñri-birgen, Xuday-bergen, Teñgri-bermiš* etc. (cf. Rásonyi, Theoph.; Bask., Fam. 177). See also ČELEB-VERMİŠ, DOΓRÏ-VERMİŠ, KÜN-BERMİŠ, TAΓ-VERMİŠ,

TÄÑRİ-BERMİŠ.

BERSEҐUR Kzk. 19th c. **Berseɣur** [Берсегуръ] (SOV 42).

BERSİN Kzk. 19th c. **Bersin-bay** [Берсинбай] (SOV 76). ✧ 'Let him/her give'. ⇨ BER + suff. -sin.

BERSTEN Kzk. 19th c. **Bersten** (<Beristen?) [Берстенъ] (AOO 50).

BERTAY Kzk. 19th c. **Bertay** [Бертай] (SODž. 90). ✧ '?' cf. Kzk. PNs Ber-žan, Ber-qayïr, Ber-nar (Žanuzakov-Esbaeva). ⇨ ? + TAY or suff. -tay(1,2)?

BERTİS Kzk. 19th c. **Bertis-pay** / **Bertïs-pay** [Бертыспай] (SOK 28); TN: Kzk. **Bertis** [Бертис], a bay in Lake Balkhash (Kojčubaev 64). ✧ 'A kind of fish'? cf. Tat. bärtäs 'die Quappe' (Radl. IV, 1604).

BERTÜK Bashk. 1779 **Bertük** [Юрмат Бертюков] (MIB V, 96).

BERÜK Bashk. 1754 **Berük** / **Bärük** [Бярюк Чекеев] (MIB IV/1, 83); Kzk. 19th c. **Berük-pay** [Берокпай] (SOV 44).

BERÜM Kzk. 19th c. **Berüm-ǰar** [Нуръ-Мамбетъ Берумджаровъ] (Grod., Pril. 103). ⇨ BERİM?

BERZİ Kzk. 19th c. **Berzi-bek** / **Berzï-bek** [Берзыбекъ] (AOO 18).

BES see **BEŠ**

BES-ČAQPAR Kzk. 19th c. **Bes-čaqpar** [Бесчакпаръ] (SOK 250). ✧ 'Five hammers'? cf. Turk., Alt. čoqmar 'die Keule, der Morgenstern (Waffc)' (Radl. III, 2012). ⇨ BEŠ.

BES-KEMPİR Kzk. 19th c. **Bes-kempir** [Безкемперъ] (SOV 24); Kzk. 19th c. **Bes-kempir** [Бескемпыръ] (SOV 24); EN: Kzk. 19th c. **Bes-kempir** [Безкемперъ] (SOK 156). ✧ 'Five old women'. ⇨ BEŠ + KEMPİR. See also YEDİ-QURTQA.

BES-TAW Kzk. 19th c. **Bes-taw** [Бестау] (AOA 2). ✧ 'Five-Mountain(s)'. ⇨ BEŠ + ТАҐ.

BES-TOQAN Kzk. 19th c. **Bes-toqan** [Бестоканъ] (AOA 134). ✧ 'Five knots/loops'? ⇨ BEŠ + TOQAN.

BES-TORSÏQ see **BES-TORSUQ**

BES-TORSUQ Kzk. 19th c. **Bes-torsuq** [Бесторсукъ] (SOV 26); EN: Kzk. 18th c. - 19th c. **Bes-torsïq** [Бесторсык] (Tynyšp. 65). ✧ 'Five leather bottles'? ⇨ BEŠ + TORSUQ.

BESİK Kzk. 19th c. **Besik-pay** [Бесикпай] (SOV 58). ✧ 'Cradle' cf. Kzk. besik 'лулька, колыбель' (KzRS).

BESİN Kzk. 19th c. **Besim-bay** (<Besin-bay) [Бесимбай] (SOK 130); Kzk. 19th c. **Besim-bek** (<Besin-bek) [Бесымбекъ] (AOK 10); Kzk. 19th c. **Pesin** [Песинъ и Дусинъ] (Grod., Pril. 132). ✧ 'Time of the second prayer' cf. Kzk. besin 'das zweite Gebet' (Radl. IV, 1628) (<P.).

BESKE-QAL Kzk. 19th c. **Beske-qaľ?** [Бескекалъ] (SOK 118). ✧ 'Stay-for-Five'? ⇨ BEŠ? + QAL I. / QAL II.

BESKİ Bashk. 1737 **Beski-bay** [Ирсыбай Бескыбаев] (MIB III, 365).

BESTENEY Nog. 20th c. **Besteney-ulï** [Малик Бестеней улы Оғурлы], father of one of Baskakov's informant from the aul of Erkin-χalq (Bask., Nog. 143).

BESTİ Kzk. 19th c. **Besti-bay** / **Besti-bay** [Бестыбай] (SODž. 110, 136); Kzk. 19th c. **Besti-bay** / **Besti-bay** [Бестыбай] (SOK 24, 54, 82, 126, 218); Kzk. 19th c. **Besti-bay** / **Besti-bay** [Бестыбай] (AOA 110). ✧ 'Five-year-old (horse)' cf. Kzk. besti 'пятилѣтний (лошадь)' (PRS), besti 'id.' (QTTS). ⇨ BEŠ + suff. -ti.

BEŠ Kzk. 19th c. **Bes-bek** [Бесбекъ] (Grod., Pril. 95); Kzk. 19th c. **Bes-pay** [Беспай] (AOK 14); Kzk. 19th c. **Bes-pay** [Беспай] (AOA 102); Kzk. 19th c. **Bes-pay** [Беспай] (AOP 30, 34); Kzk. 19th c. **Bes-pay** [Беспай] (SODž. 126, 148); Kzk. 19th c. **Bes-pay** [Беспай] (SOK 100, 114, 134, 270); Kzk. 19th c. **Bes-pay** [Беспай] (SOV 28, 120); Maml. 1399 **Beš-bay** [بشباى من باكى الظاهرى] (Ibn Taghrīb. VI, 9, 12, 19, 85); Kzk. 1785 **Beš-bay** [بش باى], a principal (MIK IV, 51, 53); Maml. 1431 **Beš-bek** [السيفى بشبك] (Berchem, Perg. 252); Selj. 12th c. **Beš-tegin** [بشتكين غرزة], a groom (Usāma 93); Selj. **Beš-tegin** / **Biš-tegin** [الاميران بيشتكين و بلاق / بشتكين غرزة], an emir (Bondārī 165); Kzk. 1822 **Bis** [بيس] (MIK IV, 416); Kzk. 19th c. **Bis-bay** [Утепъ Бисбаевъ] (Grod., Pril. 78); Kzk. 19th c. **Bis-pek** [Биспекъ] (SOK 284); Kzk. 1846 **Biš-bay** [Баджик Бишбаев] (MKOP 89); Khorezm. 1227 **Biš-tegin** [محمد بن بيشتكين] (Nasawī 156); TN: Kzk. 19th c. **Beš-bay** [Бешбай], a Kazak aul (village) (Grod., Pril. 164). ✧ 'Five' cf. Türk, Chag., Az., Crm., Kar., Trkm., Turk., etc. bäš 'fünf' (Radl. IV, 1635), Kzk. bes 'beš' (KzTS), Tat. biš 'fünf' (Radl. IV, 1787). See also QÏRQ-BEŠ, ON-BES.

BEŠ-AY Mo.? 14th c. **Beš-ay-oɣul?** [بشاى اغل], the Chaghatayid Tarmaširin's (1326-1334) son in Transoxiana (Ibn Bat. III, 43). ✧ 'Five-Moon'. ⇨ BEŠ + AY?

BEŠ-BOLDÏ Uzb. 20th c. **Beš-boldï** [Бешбўлди] (Begmatov 1984, 201). ✧ 'Became five; The fifth child'. ⇨ BEŠ + BOLDÏ.

BEŠ-MULAT Kzk. 19th c. **Beš-mulat** [Бешмулатъ] (SOK 44). ⇨ BEŠ + BULAT?

BEŠ-TEK .14th c. **Beš-tek** [بشتك اتا بك], atabek (tutor, teacher) in Luristan at the end of the 14th c. (Qazw. 723); Maml. 1330 **Beš-tek** [سيف الدين بيشتاك] (Zetterst. 188, 226-228); Maml. 1332 **Beš-tek** [بيشتاك العمرى] (Iyās I, 166, 231); Maml. 1332 **Beš-tek** [سيف الدين بيشتاك الناصرى], an emir (Dawād. 366); Maml. 1338/39 **Beš-tek** [بيشتاك الكريمى] (Iyās I, 170,

177); Maml. 14th c. **Beš-tek** [الناصرى
السيفى بشتاك الملكى], Qalāun nominated him to viceroy
of Syria, died in 1341 (Mayer 104-105, 263-264,
Makrīzī, Khit. II, 34, 70); Maml. 1370/71 **Beš-tek**
[بيشتاك الكريمى] (Iyās I, 226). ✧ 'Five single things;
five mates' cf. Sauvaget 42: 'cinq seulement', Turk. *tek*
'fellow, mate, equal' (TED). ⇨ **BEŠ + TEK.**

BEŠĀRET   Turk. 1540 **Bešāret-beg**, from Diyarbekir,
the chief of the ethnic community (cemaat) Hamza
Hacılu (Demirtaş 49). ✧ 'Good news, joyful tidings;
present given to bearer of good news' cf. Turk. *beşaret*
'id.' (Özön) (<Ar.).

BEŠE   Turk. 16th c. **Beše-bey** (Ongan, Ank. II, 211). ✧
I. 'Pasha, general' different reading of the word *paşa*
(Erol II); II. 'Hard, firm; strong'? cf. Bashk. *beše*
'крепкий; здоровый; упрямый' (BRS/Uraksin). See
also **BÖRİ-BEŠE, QAYA-BEŠE, QATUN-BEŠE.**

BEŠE-TOГRİL   Uyg. 12th c.-14th c. **Beše-toγril** [Bäsä
(Basa?) Toγril] (Radl., USp. 204-5, 246-7). ⇨ **BEŠE +
TOГRİL.**

BEŠEY   Kzk. 19th c. **Bešey** [Бешей] (SOK 296). ✧
'Hard, firm; strong'? cf. Bashk. *beše* 'крепкий;
здоровый; упрямый' (BRS/Uraksin). ⇨ **BEŠE +
suff. -y.**

BEŠGÜ?   Uyg. 1288 **Bešgü? / Bešγu?** [Juchanan
Bešgu] (Chwol., Syr.-nest. 32).

BEŠKÄY   Kzk. 19th c. **Beškäy?** [Бешкай] (AOP 118).

BEŠKE   Kzk. 19th c. **Beške** [Бешке] (AOK 86). ✧
'For/to five'.

BEŠLİ   Turk. 20th c. **Bešli** (Önder, Göle). ✧ 'Fivefold'
(Erol II). ⇨ **BEŠ + suff. -li.**

BET   Kzk. 19th c. **Bet-eke** [Бетеке] (SODž. 134). ✧
'Face'. See also **MAYTU-BET.**

BET-KÖPÄK   Kzk. 19th c. **Bet-köpäk** [Беткопакъ]
(Grod., Pril. 160). ⇨ **BET? + KÖPÄK.**

BETČE   Kzk. 19th c. **Betče** [Бетче] (SOK 118). ✧
'Small face' cf. *bet* 'das Gesicht, die rechte Seite, die
Oberfläche' (Radl. IV, 1617). ⇨ **BET + dim. suff. -če.**

BETENEY   Bashk. 1734 **Beteney** [Сюяргул
Бетенеев] (MIB III, 325).

BETİM   Kzk. 19th c. **Betim / Betїm** [Бетымъ] (AOO
50); Kzk. 19th c. **Betim-bay / Betem-bay** [Бетембай]
(SOV 22). ✧ 'Shame' cf. Kzk. *betim* 'стыд, срам'
(PRS).

BETİŠ   Kzk. 19th c. **Betiš** [Бетышъ] (SODž. 14).

BETKİNÄ   Bashk. 1714 **Betkinä** [Беткиня Баталин]
(MIB III, 108). ⇨ **BET + dim. suff. -kinä.**

BETZEN   Karakh. **Betzen** [Betzen] (MK/Atalay 834).

BEWKEY   Tat./Bashk. 1734 **Bewkey** [Москов
Бевкеев], a Teptär (MIB III, 328).

BEZ-ALİ   Kzk. 19th c. **Bez-ali** [Безали] (AOP 58). ✧
'Swelling-Ali'? cf. Chag., NUyg.(Tar.), Turk. *bäz* 'die
Drüse, die Geschwulst; die Sehne' (Radl. IV, 1631). ⇨
ALİ.

BEZ-BERGEN   Tat. 1600 **Bez-bergen** [Обух
Безбергенев] (MIB I, 152). ✧ 'Swelling?-given' cf.
Chag., NUyg.(Tar.), Turk. *bäz* 'die Drüse, die
Geschwulst; die Sehne' (Radl. IV, 1631). ⇨ **BERGEN.**

BEZ-GÖZ   Tat. 1603 **Bez-göz** [Ычелбердей
Безгозев] (MIB I, 153). ⇨ **KÖZ?**

BEZ-KEMPİR see **BES-KEMPİR**

BEZDİR   Kuman? **Beztür / Beztur** [Beztur „filius
Budli" (genealogiae Arpadi insertus)] (SRH I, 285);
TN: Kuman 1517 **Bezdir** [descensus Beztherzallasa], a
settlement of Kumanian origin in Lesser Kumania
(Gyárfás III, 742). ✧ 'Disgust!' (Rásonyi, Kisk. 343-
44, Imp. 238, KÖA 92, AOH 20:137), 'Oust (the
enemy)!' cf. Kzk. *bezdir-* 'entfernen, forttreiben' (Radl.
IV, 1634).

BEZEY   Bashk. 1664 **Bezey-abїz** [Безей-абыз
Илбуклаев] (MIB I, 192).

BEZELEK   Tat. (Sib.) 1601 **Bezelek-abїz** [Безелек
абыз], from the region of Chat (Miller, Ist. Sib. II,
167). ⇨ **ABİZ.**

BEZERGEN   Tat. 1624 **Bezergen** [Янтимиръ
Безергановъ] (Pokrovskij 70); Tat. 1624 **Bezergen**
[Меней Безергановъ] (Pokrovskij 70); Tat.(Sib.?)
1601, 1610 **Bezergen / Besergen** [Бесерген /
Бесоргген] (Miller, Ist. Sib. II, 169, 218). ✧ 'Merchant'
cf. Turk. *bäzärgän* 'der Kaufmann' (Radl. IV, 1633)
(<P.).

BEZİRJİ   Turk. 16th c. **Bezirji-χatun** [Bezirci Hatun]
(Gökb., Ed. 57). ✧ 'Dealer in linseed oil' cf. Turk.
bezirci 'id.' (TED), *bezir* 'acı, tohumluk patlıcan'
(TarS).

BEZPELDÜK   Tat. 1662 **Bezpeldük** [Безпелдюкъ /
Безпелдючко] (DAI IV, 285, 286, 294, 295). ✧ 'A
kind of hunting bird' cf. Turk. dial. *bezmeldek* 'bir çeşit
av kuşu' (DS); II. 'Five tassels'? cf. BEŠ + Alt. *päldїk*
'Behang des Frauenzopfes' (Radl. IV, 1247).

Bİ see **BEK**

Bİ-AГİŠ   Tat.(Tob.) **Bİ-aγїš** [Бі Аҕыш] (Proben IV,
268 /334/). ✧ 'Lord - honest friend (fellow)'. ⇨ **BEK +
AГİŠ.**

Bİ-BALTA   Chuv. 18th-19th c. **Bi-balta** [Бибалта]
(Magn. 33). ⇨ **BEK + BALTA.**

Bİ-BARS see **BAY-BARS?**

Bİ-BOLDİ   Chuv. 18th-19th c. **Bi-boldї** [Биболда]
(Magn. 33); Chuv. 18th-19th c. **Bi-buldї** [Бибулда]
(Magn. 33); Chuv. 18th-19th c. **Pi-boldї** [Пиболда]
(Magn. 66); Chuv. 18th-19th c. **Pi-buldї** [Пибулда]
(Magn. 66). ⇨ **BEK + BOLDİ.** See also **BAY-BOLDİ.**

Bİ-BUL   Chuv. 18th-19th c. **Bi-bul** [Бибулъ] (Magn.
33). ✧ 'Be/become a Bi(y)!'. ⇨ **BEK + BOL.** See also
BAY-BOL.

Bİ-BULAY   Chuv. 18th-19th c. **Bi-bulay** [Бибулай]
(Magn. 33). ⇨ **Bİ-BUL + suff. -a + dim. -y.**

Bİ-BULAT see **BİY-BULAT**

Bİ-GELDİ Kzk. 19th c. **Bey-geldi** [Бейгельды] (SOK 172); Crm. 1638 **Bi-geldi** [بیكلدی] (Vel.-Zern., Crim. 227); Nog. 1649 **Bi-geldi / Bi-geldey?** [Бигелдѣйко] (AI IV, 123); Chuv. 18th-19th c. **Bi-gilde** [Бигилда] (Magn. 33); Bashk. 1706 **Bi-gilde** [Бигильде] (MIB III, 30); Bashk. 1780 **Bi-gilde** [Бигильда Адзимясов] (MIB V, 104); Tat. 1601 **Bi-gilde / Bi-gildey?** [Менглибай Бигилдеев] (Miller, Ist. Sib. II, 165); Crm. 1689 **Bi-gildi** [Батыръ Бій-гильдыевъ], envoy from the Crimea (Smirnov, Krym. 625); Kzk. **Bi-gildi** [Бигильдый] (Nepljuev 718); Chuv. 18th-19th c. **Pi-gildä? / Pi-geldī** [Пигилда (Пигельде)] (Magn. 66). ✧ '(The) Bi(y) has come'. ⇨ **BEK + KELDİ.** See also **BAY-GELDİ.**

Bİ-YANAS Kzk. 1785 **Biy-yanas** [Биянас] (MIK IV, 63). ✧ 'Lord-stubborn' cf. *janaz* 'eigensinnig, böse, zänkisch, etc.' (Radl. III, 83). ⇨ **BEK.**

Bİ-YARAT Kzk. 19th c. **Bi-yarat-bay / Biy-yarat-bay** [Кишикъ Біяратбаевъ] (Grod., Pril. 193). ⇨ **BEK.**

Bİ-QAŠAR Kzk. 19th c. **Bi-qašar** [Бикошар] (AOAtb. 30). ✧ 'Lord-calf'. ⇨ **BEK + QAŠAR.**

Bİ-MELİK-TEMÜR Maml. 1293 **Bi-melik-temür / Bay-melik-temür?** [بیملك تمر / Баймеликтемиръ], a Kipchak emir (Baybars/Tizeng. I, 86, 109, Nuwairī 137, 158). ⇨ **BEK + MELİK + TEMİR.**

Bİ-TUMAQ? Tat. 1557 **Bi-tumaq?** [Битумагъ Ханикинъ] (Kn. Metriki Lit. 151). ✧ 'Lord-Bastard'? ⇨ **BEK + TUMAQ.**

Bİ-WEDE? Crm. / Turk.? **Bi-wede-sultan?** [بیوده سلطان / Биведе-султана], Ajaγan-bek's daughter (Bakč. Nadp. 42). ⇨ **BEK.**

Bİ-BERJİ Turk. **Biberji-oγlu**, a Zeybek (Kúnos 1891, 119). ✧ 'Seller of pepper' cf. Turk. *biber* 'pepper' (TED) + suff. *-ji.*

Bİ-Bİ Trkm. 20th c. **Bibi** [Bibi], fem. (Zaj. 1971, 334); Trkm. 20th c. **Bibi** [Биби], fem. (TrkmRS 93); Kzk. 19th c. **Bibi** [Биби], fem. (Grod., Pril. 66); Trkm. 20th c. **Bibi-Jemal** [Bibiğemal], fem. (Zaj. 1971, 335); Chag. 16th c. **Bibi-χani** [Биби-хани], fem. (Ivanov 108); Chag. 16th c. **Bibi-χanife** [Биби-ханифе], fem. (Ivanov 139); Chag. 16th c. **Bibi-χatun** [Биби-хатун], fem. (Ivanov 117, 141, 145, 222); Kkalp. 20th c. **Biybi-ayïm** [Биыбиайым], fem. (KkRS 777); Kkalp. **Biybi-gül**, fem. (Baskakov: OSA 141); Kkalp. 20th c. **Biybi-gül** (KkRS 777); Kkalp. 20th c. **Biybi-χatša** [Бийбихатша], fem. (KkRS 777); Kkalp. 20th c. **Biybi-sara** [Бийбисара, Бийбийсара], fem. (KkRS 777, Bask.); Kkalp. 20th c. **Biybi-suluw** [Бийбисулув], fem. (KkRS 777); Kkalp. 20th c. **Biybi-zada** [Бийбизада], fem. (KkRS 777); Kkalp. 20th c. **Biybi-žamal** [Бийбижамал], fem. (KkRS 777); Kkalp. 20th c. **Biybi-žan** [Бийбижан], fem. (KkRS 777). ✧ I. 'Lady; respected woman from the higher society' cf. Chag. 'eine angesehene Frau aus höheren Kreisen' (Radl. IV, 1789); II. 'Lady of the house' cf. Turk. *bibi* 'hanım, hanımefendi' (TS), Az., Uzb., Trkm. *bibi* 'die Frau' (Radl. IV, 1789), Kzk. *bibä* 'ein Fräulein' (Radl. IV, 1789). Title of respect, (secondary) component of female names. III. 'Aunt, elder sister' (Zaj. 1971), cf. Trkm. *bībi* 'почтительное обращение к жёнам духовных лиц; почтительное обращение к старшей систре или к сестре отца' (TrkmRS), Uzb. *bibi* 'бабушка; составная часть имён собственных женских; прибавляется к именам собственным женским при почтительном обращении' (UzbRS). Cf. also Sattarov-Subaeva 1976, 67. See also **XĀNİ.**

Bİ-BİJE Trkm.? 16th c. **Bibije** [بی بیجه], a courtesan in Merv (Abulg./Desm. 258). ✧ 'Dear little lady'. ⇨ **BİBİ** + suff. *-je < -ča(1,3).*

Bİ-BİXAN Chag. 16th c. **Bibiχan** [Биби-хан], fem. (Ivanov 130); Kkalp. 20th c. **Biybiχan** [Бийбихан], fem. (KkRS 777). ⇨ **BİBİ** + suff. *-χan(1).*

Bİ-BİŠ Trkm. 20th c. **Bibiš** [Бибиш], a fem. character in a modern short story (?). ✧ 'Little lady'. ⇨ **BİBİ** + dim. suff. *-š.*

Bİ-BİT see **BEYBİT**

Bİ-ČARA Kuman/Tat.? 1240 **Bičara / Bečara** [Бечаръ / Бичаръ], a Tatar chief („vojvoda") (PSRL X, 116). ✧ 'Poor, helpless' cf. Tat. *bičara* (<P.) 'ein hilfloser, armer Mensch' (Radl. IV, 1781).

Bİ-ČÄ see **BİČE**

Bİ-ČE Chag. 16th c. **Bičä-aγa** [Биче-ага] (Ivanov 144); Chag. 16th c. **Bičä-χatun** [Бича-хатун], fem. (Ivanov 110, 222); Selj. 1141 **Biče** [بجة الترکی] (Kamāladdīn II, 275, 276); Chag. 16th c. **Biče-bike** [Биче-бике], fem. (Ivanov 123); Chag. 16th c. **Biče-jan** [Биче-Джан], fem. (Ivanov 166); Nog. 1557 **Biče(y)** [Бичей], the final -y is a Russian adaptation (PSRL XIII, 284); Kzk. 19th c. **Biže-bay** [Бижебай] (SODž. 98); Kzk. 19th c. **Biži-bay** [Бижибай] (SOK 96). ✧ 'Woman, lady, landlady; empress'. Used also as a secondary component of female name expressing respect. Cf. *bičä* Tat.(Tara) 'die Frau', Kar.(L.) 'die Königin' (Radl. IV, 1781).

Bİ-ČE-DUST Chag. 16th c. **Biče-dust** [Бичэ Дуст], fem. (Ivanov 254). ⇨ **BİČE + DOST.**

Bİ-ČERAX Az. **Bičeraχ?** (<Bičeraq) [Bičerachov] (Mende 143).

Bİ-ČİK Khorezm. / Kuman? **Bičik / Bičig** [Бичигъ], a prince of the Horde (PSRL XVI); Bashk. 1776 **Bičik-qul / Pičik-qul** [Туим (Туюм) Пичиккулов (Бичиккулов)] (MIB V, 33, 34, 79).

Bİ-ČİLEY Tat. 1541 **Bičiley** [Бичилѣй] (PSRL XIII, 100).

Bİ-JAR Turk. 1412 **Bijar-bek** [حمزه بك بن بجار بك], Hamza-bek emir's father (Uzunçarş., Küt. I, 22); Turk.

1417 **Bijar-oγlï** [بجار اوغلى حمزه بك], Hamza-bek, the beglerbeg of Rūm (Rūm ili), Bijar's son (Āšikp. 80). ✦ 'Bījār' (<P. toponym).

BİDAY I. see **BUΓDAY I.**

BİDAY II. Uyg. 12th c.-14th c. **Biday-bïqï / Bidäy-bïqï?** (Radl., USp. 128).

BİDAYČİ Kzk. 19th c. **Bidayčï / Bidayči** [Бидайчи] (SODž. 58, 76); Kzk. 19th c. **Bidayšï / Bidayši** [Бидайши] (AOA 82). ✦ 'Weat-grower'. ⇨ **BİDAY I.** + suff. -čï.

BİDAYŠİ see **BİDAYČİ**

BİDAYŠÏ see **BİDAYČİ**

BİDAL 1554 **Bidal-mirza** [Бидалъ-мирза], a runner (PSRL XIII, 240).

BİDAS Kzk. 19th c. **Bidas-pay** [Бидаспай] (SODž. 64).

BİDE Kzk. 19th c. **Bide-bay** [Бидебай] (Grod., Pril. 179). ✦ 'Muzzle (made of ropes for a camel)' cf. *bidä* 'ein Strick der als Maulkorb dem Kameele angelegt wird' (Radl. IV, 1780). See also **BEY-ČEMER.**

BİDEY Kzk. 19th c. **Bidey-bek** [Бидейбекъ] (SOV 108).

BİDEL Kzk.? **Bidel-bek** [Бидельбекъ], a place south-east cf Lake Aral (Karta JAR XI).

BİDES Kzk. 19th c. **Bides-pay** [Бидеспай] (SODž. 100).

BİÄXÄLÄY Yak. **Biäχäläy** [Біахäläi] (Pek.).

BİÄRÄ Yak. **Biärä** [Біäpä], fem. (Pek.). ✦ Vera (R.).

BİÄSKÄLÄY Yak. **Biäskäläy** [Біäскäläi] (Pek.).

BİGÄŠ see **BEGİČ**

BİGE see **BİKE**

BİGEDER Tuv. 19th c. **Bigeder** [Бигедеръ] (Potanin IV, 422).

BİGEY Bashk. 1740 **Bigey** [Урманчи Бигеев] (MIB I, 427); Bashk. 1761 **Bigey** [Бигей Батыров] (MIB IV/1. 219). ⇨ **BİKE?** + dim. suff. -y.

BİGEŠ see **BEGİČ**

BİGİ see **BEGİ**

BİGİLİČ Bashk. 1737 **Bigilič** [Елисей Бигиличъ] (Nepljuev 17).

BİGİM see **BEGİM**

BİGİNÄK Bashk. 1717 **Biginäk** [Бигиняк] (MIB III, 154).

BİGİNE see **BÄGİNÄ**

BİGİŠ see **BEGİČ**

BİGİŠÄY Bashk. 1738 **Bigišäy** [Бигишай Карабашев] (MIB III, 393); Bashk. 1758 **Bigišäy** [Назик Бигишаев] (MIB IV/1, 164). ⇨ **BİGİŠ** + suff. -äy.

BİGMEN Uzb. 19th c. **Bigmen** [Тохтамратъ Бигменевъ] (SKSO III, 178).

BİXA Oghuz? **Biχa** [Биха], Kök Khan's son (RaD I/1, 76).

BİY see **BEK**

BİY-ARSLAN Tat. 19th c. **Bi-arslan** [Osman Biarslan] (Mende 141); Crm. 1700 **Biy-araslan** [Бий-Араслан] (Smirnov, Krym. 682); Kmk. **Biy-arslan** [Бий-Арсланъ] (Êtnogr. Obozr. 1910, 139); Crm. 1700 **Biy-arslan** [Бий Арсланъ] (Smirnov, Krym. 682). ✦ 'Lord-Lion'. ⇨ **BEK + ARSLAN.** See also **BEG-ARSLAN.**

BİY-BOL Kzk. 19th c. **Biy-bol** [Бийбол] (AOO 60, 66); Kzk. 19th c. **Biy-bol** [Бийбол] (SOK 70, 212). ✦ 'Be/become a prince/rich man'. ⇨ **BEK + BOL.** See also **BAY-BOL, BEK-BOL, BİY-BOL.**

BİY-BOLAT see **BİY-BULAT**

BİY-BULAT Bashk. 1788 **Bey-bulat** [Бейбулат Буракаев] (MIB V, 235); Chuv. 18th-19th c. **Bi-bulat** [Бибулатъ] (Magn. 33); Kzk. 19th c. **Biy-bolat** [Бийболатъ] (AOO 38); Kzk. 19th c. **Biy-bolat** [Бийболатъ] (AOK 26); Nog. 19th c. **Biy-bolat** [Бийболатъ] (Anan'ev 49); Kzk. 19th c. **Biy-bulat** [Бийбулатъ] (Grod., Pril. 132); Chuv. 18th-19th c. **Pi-bulat / Piy-bulat** [Пибулатъ] (Magn. 66). ✦ 'Lord-steel; Prince/chief - steel'. ⇨ **BEK + BULAT.** See also **BAY-BULAT.**

BİY-QANLARÏ Balk. 20th c. **Biy-qallarï (<Biy-qanlarï)**, a family (Pröhle, Balk. 208). ⇨ **BEK + QAN?** + plur. suff. -lar + poss. -ï.

BİY-NAZAR Uzb. 1807 **Biy-nazar** [Бий Назар], an emir (MIT II, 379). ⇨ **BEK + NAZAR.** See also **BAY-NAZAR.**

BİY-SEKEN Kzk. 19th c. **Biy-seken** [Бийсекеновъ] (AOO 30). ⇨ **BEK + SÄKEN.**

BİY-TUΓAN Kzk. 19th c. **Biy-tuγan** [Бійтуганъ] (SOK 88). ✦ I. 'Rich relative'; II. 'A rich man, a master (=a boy) has been born'. ⇨ **BEK.** See also **BAY-TUΓAN.**

BİYBAT Kzk. 1838 **Biybat** [Бійбатъ Бектурановъ] (Konšin, Mat. V, 57). ⇨ **BEYBİT?**

BİYBİ see **BİBİ**

BİYBİ-AYŠA Kkalp. 20th c. **Biybi-ayša** [Бийбиайша], fem. (KkRS 777). ⇨ **BİBİ + AYŠA.**

BİYBİ-AŽAR Kkalp. 20th c. **Biybi-ažar** [Бийбиажар] (KkRS 777). ⇨ **BİBİ + AŽAR.**

BİYBİ-NUR Kkalp. 20th c. **Biybi-nur** [Бибинур], fem. (KkRS 777). ⇨ **BİBİ + NUR.**

BİYBİ-RUWZA Kkalp. 20th c. **Biybi-ruwza** [Бийбируўза], fem. (KkRS 777). ⇨ **BİBİ.**

BİYBİ-SÄNEM Kkalp. 20th c. **Biybi-sänem**, fem. (KkRS 777). ⇨ **BİBİ + SANAM.**

BİYBİT Kzk. 19th c. **Biybit** [Бійбитъ Дуальбаевъ / Бийбит Дуальбаев], a Kazak writer of articles an poet (AUK 312, 431); Kzk. 19th c. **Biybit** [Ташмухамедъ Бійбитовъ] (Grod., Pril. 117). ✦ I. 'Peace-loving, peaceable, quiet' cf. Kzk. *beybit* (<P.) 'ruhig, still, friedlich' (Radl. IV, 1574), Kzk. *beybit: beybit el*

'миролюбивый народ (страна)' (KzRS), cf. also Kzk. PN *Beybit / Beybitžan* (Žanuzakov-Esbaeva); II. 'Become a Biy!' In Rásonyi's opinion it traces back to verb *bit-* 'wachsen' and means 'Deviens un biy!' (Imp. 238).

BİYJA   Kzk. 19th c. **Biyja (<Biy-qoja?)** [Бийджа Бековъ] (Grod., Pril. 64). ⇨ **BEK** + suff. *-ja*.

BİYDAY see **BUΓDAY I.**

BİYÄK   Kzk. 19th c. **Biyäk** [Караманъ Біяковъ] (Grod., Pril. 109).

BİYÄKÄN   Oghuz/Trkm. 13th c. **Biyäkän-alp** [بياكان الب / Биякан-алп] (Abulg./Kon. 1450).

BİYGU   Oghuz/Trkm. 13th c. **Biygu-bek** [بيعو بيك / Бийгу-бек], the eldest of the beks of Dib-baquy Khan (Abulg./Kon. 660).

BİYİK-TURSUN   Kzk. **Biyik-tursun** [Біик-турсунъ], a well named after its owner (?) (KartaJAR XI). ⇨ **BEYİK + TURSÏN.**

BİYİMBET   Bashk. 1735 **Biyimbet** [Биимбетъ Каниевъ], a tarχan (Vel.-Zern., Bašk. 13); Bashk. 1760 **Biyimbet** [Биимбеть Кошаев] (MIB IV/1, 189). ⇨ **BİY** + suff. *-imbet / -bet?*

BİYİNDİK   Bashk. 1719 **Biyindik** [Бииндык Минаев] (MIB III, 181).

BİYİŠ   Bashk. 1701 **Biyiš** [Бииш Тепляков] (MIB III, 14).

BİYLİ   Kzk. 19th c. **Biyli-bay / Biylï-bay** [Бійлыбай] (SOK 204). ⇨ **BEK** + suff. *-li.*

BİYMAN see **BİYMEN**

BİYMEN   Kzk. 19th c. **Biyman / Biymän?** [Гасанъ Біймановъ] (Grod., Pril. 182); Kzk. 19th c. **Biyman / Biymän?** [Бійманъ Юзбаевъ] (Grod., Pril. 23); Kzk. 19th c. **Biymen** [Бійменъ] (SODž. 72, 132); Kzk. 19th c. **Biymen** [Бійменъ] (SOV 32, 138); Kzk. 19th c. **Biman** [Биманъ] (AOK 86). ⇨ **BİYMAN.** See also **BİYMEN-TAY.**

BİYMEN-TAY   Kzk. 1744 **Bimen-tay / Biymen-tay** [بيما نطاى / Биментай] (MIK IV, 159). ⇨ **BİYMEN + TAY?** or suff. *-tay(1,2)?*

BİYMET   Tat. 1690 **Biymet** [Бійметко Салтанаковъ] (Kungursk. akty 178). ⇨ **BEK** + suff. *-met.*

BİYNAŠ   Kzk. 19th c. **Biynaš** [Бійнашъ] (AOP 6).

BİYSEL   Kzk. 1822 **Biysel-bay / Biyseli-bay? / Biyse-ali-bay? / Biys-ali-bay?** [بيسالى باى / Бисельбай] (MIK IV, 416).

BİYSEMBE see **BEYSENBİ**

BİYSÏMAQ   Kzk. 19th c. **Biysïmaq** [Бійсымакъ] (SOV 64). ✧ 'Gentleman-like'. ⇨ **BEK** + suff. *-sïmaq.*

BİYTİ   Kzk. 19th c. **Biyti-γul** [Бійтыгулъ] (AOO 30).

BİYURΓAN see **BUYURΓAN**

BİYÜK see **BÜYÜK**

BİK see **BEK**

BİK-BARS see **BEK-BARS**

BİK-BOTA see **BEK-BOTA**

BİK-ČÄNTÄY see **BEK-ČENTEY**

BİK-ČURA see **BEK**

BİK-YÄN see **BEK**

BİK-KÜČÜK   Bashk. 1773 **Bik-küčük** [Биккучук (Биккучюк) Абышахменев] (MIB IV/2, 413). ✧ 'Strong puppy'? cf. Tat. *bik* 'sehr stark' (Radl. IV, 1739). ⇨ **BEK? + KÜČÜK.**

BİK-QUŠ   Bashk. 1777 **Bik-quš** [Биккуш Мавлютов] (MIB V, 65). ✧ 'Strong bird' cf. Tat. *bik* 'sehr stark' (Radl. IV, 1739). ⇨ **BEK? + QUŠ I.**

BİK-MAY   Tat. 1739 **Bik-may** [Бикмаевъ] (Alatyr. 145). ⇨ **BEK? + MAY.**

BİK-TAGİR see **BİK-TAHİR**

BİK-TAHİR   Tat. 20th c. **Bik-tahir** [Биктачир] (Sattarov 48); Tat. **Bik-tahir / Bik-tagir?** [Biktagirov] (Mende 179). ✧ 'Strong Tahir' cf. Ar. PN *Tahir* 'virtuous, pure' (Ahmed). ⇨ **BEK.**

BİK-TAŠ see **BEK-TAŠ**

BİK-TAW   Kkalp. 1740 **Bik-taw-biy** [Биктав бий] (MIKk. 208, Hanykov, Poezdka 19). ✧ 'High mountain' cf. Kkalp. *biyik* 'высокий' (KkRS). ⇨ **ТАΓ.**

BİK-TÄŠ   Tat. 20th c. **Bik-täš** (Sattarov 48). ✧ I. 'Lord/noble-fire'?; II. 'Strong like the fire' (Sattarov 48). ⇨ **BEK.**

BİK-TEMİR see **BEK-TEMİR**

BİK-TURLİ   Trkm. 19th c. **Bik-turlï** [Биктурли] (ZIRGOÊtn. I, 30). ⇨ **BEK + TURLÏ?**

BİK-UŠAQ   Bashk. 1756 **Bik-ušaq / Bi-qušaq?** [Байшапай Бикушаков] (MIB IV/1, 123). ⇨ **BEK + UŠAQ?**

BİK-ZÄN see **BEK**

BİKČİ see **BEKČİ**

BİKÄY see **BİKEY**

BİKÄŠ   Bashk. 1715 **Bikäš** [Бексентей Бикашев] (MIB III, 124). ✧ I. 'Girl, bride, spouse; sister-in-law (husband's elder sister)', cf. Kzk. *bikäš* 'die ältere Schwester des Mannes' (Radl. IV, 1740), Chag., Kzk., Tat. *bikäč* 'ein Mädchen; eine Braut, ein Mädchen, das Verlobt ist; (Tat.) ein Kuhkalb' (Radl. IV, 1739); II. 'Respectful addressing to a young girl' cf. Kzk. *bikäš* 'eine ehrende Anrede an Mädchen' (Radl. IV, 1740). Also as secondary component of female names. + suff. *-š.*

BİKE   Kzk. 1817 **Bege-žan / Bige-žan** [بيكهجن / Бегежан], a Kazak sultan (MIK IV, 309); Kzk. 1846 **Bige-jan / Bige-žan** [Бигежан Байжанов], a biy (MKOP 155); Selj. 12th c. **Bige-sultan** [Биге-султан], Sultan Sandjar's (1117-1157) daughter (MIT I, 535); Chag. 16th c. **Bike** [Бике], fem. (Ivanov 103, 162,184, 251, 280, 289, 292); Trkm. 20th c. **Bike** [Bike], fem. (Zaj. 1971, 335), Chag. 16th c. **Bike-aγa** [Бике Аγа], fem. (Ivanov 202, 239, 248); Chag. 16th c. **Bike-χan-aγa** [Бике Хан Ага] (Ivanov 298); Chag. 16th c.

Bike-χatun [Бике-хатун], fem. (Ivanov 306); Chag. 16th c. **Bike-sultan** [Бике Султан], fem. (Ivanov 146, 211, 227); Chag. 16th c. **Biki-sultan** [Бики-Султан], fem. (Ivanov 136, 138, 140); Trkm. 20th c. **Bīke** [Бике] (TrkmRS 95). ✧ I. 'Lady, lady of the house, wife, girl', used also as a component of female names expressing respect and blandishment when addressing; (Kirg., Kzk., Tat.), cf. Chag., Kzk., Tat. *bikä* (Radl. IV, 1739), Trkm. *bīke* 'госпожа, хозяйка' (TrkmRS), Tat.(Tob.) *bigä* 'die Frau, die Gemahlin' (Radl. IV, 1741), also Sattarov-Subaeva 65; II. 'Sister-in-law (husband's sister)' cf. Kzk. *bike* 'сестра мужа' (KzRS); III. 'Woman having no husband; widow; debauched woman, adulteress' cf. Chag. *beke* (Vámbéry, Abuška; Thúry, Behdset).

BİKE-DUST Chag. 16th c. **Bike-dust** [Бике-Дуст] (Ivanov 166). ⇨ **BİKE + DOST.**

BİKE-ХABİB Chag. 16th c. **Bike-χabib** [Бике Хабиб], fem. (Ivanov 249). ✧ 'Lady-Friend' cf. Ar. PN *Habib* 'beloved, dear one, friend' (Ahmed). ⇨ **BİKE.**

BİKE-QARŠİ Chag. 16th c. **Bike-qarši** [Бике-Карши] (Ivanov 148). ⇨ **BİKE + QARŠİ?**

BİKE-QASSAB Chag. 16th c. **Bike-qassab** [Бике-кассаб] (Ivanov 124). ✧ 'Lady-Butcher'? cf. Uzb. *qassob / qassâb* 'мясник' (UzbRS). ⇨ **BİKE.**

BİKEY Bashk. 1709 **Bikäy** [Бикай] (MIB I, 264); Tat. 18th c. **Bikey** [Бикей] (Nepljuev 598); Bashk. 1709 **Bikey** [Бикей Опачев] (MIB I, 264). ⇨ **BİKE** + dim. suff. *-y.*

BİKEN Bashk. 1715 **Biken** [Илдыбай Бикенев] (MIB III, 127).

BİKESİ Chag. 16th c. **Bikesi-aγa** [Бикеси Ага] (Ivanov 304).

BİKET Kzk. **Biket** [بیکیت / Бикетъ] (Aničkov).

BİKİ see **BİKE**

BİKİ-TAY Kzk. 19th c. **Biki-tay** [Бикитай] (Grod., Pril. 100). ⇨ **BİKİ + TAY** or suff. *-tay(1,2)?*

BİKİMBET Bashk. 1737 **Bikimbet** [Култай Бикимбетев] (MIB III, 377). ⇨ **BİK** + suff. *-imbet.*

BİKİNÄS Bashk. 1792 **Bikinäs** [Бикиняс Мухамметев] (MIB V, 315).

BİKİŠ Bashk. 1790 **Bikiš** [Тавлы (Тавля) Бикишев] (MIB V, 291, 300).

BİKKİNÄ Bashk. 1739 **Bikkinä** [Биккиня Девлетев] (MIB III, 409). ⇨ **BEK** + suff. *-kinä.*

BİKMEN Tat. 20th c. **Bikmen** [Бикменов] (Sattarov 48); Bashk. 1740 **Bikmen** [Бикмен Тляббердин] (MIB I, 379). ✧ 'Strong, healthy' (Sattarov 48).

BİKMES Bashk. 1715 **Bikmes** [Умир Бикмесев] (MIB III, 124).

BİKMET Tat. 1753 **Bikmet** [Биметь Бикметев] (MIB IV/1, 70); Bashk. 1789 **Bikmet** [Курманай Бикметев] (MIB V, 240). ✧ Shortened-contracted

form of *Bik-möχämmät*, see Bashk. *Bikmät* (Kusimova) and Tat. *Bikmät < Bik-möχämmät* (Sattarov). ⇨ **BEK.**

BİKTİNEY Bashk. 1763 **Biktiney** [Биктиней Игинин] (MIB IV/1, 270).

BİKTÜK Bashk. 1756 **Biktük** [Сейфулла Биктюков] (MIB IV/1, 123).

BİKÜS-BUГA Uyg. 12th c. - 14th c. **Biküs-buγa** [biküs buγa / Bikuş Buġa] (DTS, EUTS); Uyg. 12th c.-14th c. **Biküš-buγa** (Radl., USp. 129). ✧ '?-Bull'. ⇨ **BUQA.**

BİKÜŠ-BUГA see **BİKÜS-BUГA**

BİL Maml. 1254 **Bil-bäg** [بيلبك], Emir Bedreddīn Bilbäg (Berchem 72); Kzk. 19th c. **Bil-ǰan** [Билджанъ Найсенбаевъ] (Grod., Pril. 87); Kzk. 19th c. **Bïl-čan / Bïl-žan / Bil-žan?** [Быльчанъ] (SOK 102, 200). ✧ I. 'Supporter'; II. 'Elephant' cf. Kzk. *bil* 'der Elephant' (Radl. IV, 1759) (<P.). ⇨ **BEL?** See also **DAW-BİL, SARA-BİL.**

BİL-BARS Chag. **Bil-bars** [بيلبارس / Билбарсъ] (Šejb. LI, LII). ✧ I. 'Supporter-Panther'; II. 'Elephant-Panther' cf. Kzk. *bil* 'der Elephant' (Radl. IV, 1759) (<P.). ⇨ **BEL? + BARS.**

BİL-BAS Kzk.? 18th c. **Bil-bas** [Бильбасовъ], a historian (Nepljuev 907, 921). ✧ 'Elephant-Head' cf. Kzk. *bil* 'der Elephant' (Radl. IV, 1759) (<P.). ⇨ **BAŠ?**

BİL-BÜRÜ Alt. 19th-20th c. **Bil-bürü**, fem. (OjrRS 211).

BİL-ČİNAR Tuv. 19th c. **Bil-činar** [Билчинаръ] (Potanin IV, 425). ⇨ **BEL + CİNAR?**

BİL-YAŠAR Kzk. 19th c. **Bil-yašar** [Бильяшар Тукаров] (SKSO VIII, 229). ✧ I. Supporter - long lives'; II. 'Elephant - long lives' cf. Kzk. *bil* 'der Elephant' (Radl. IV, 1759) (<P.). ⇨ **BEL + YAŠAR?**

BİLAL Trkm. 19th c. **Bilal** [Билялъ Кочекбаевъ] (Ščeglov IV, 159). ✧ Bilâl (Ar.).

BİLBİL see **BÜLBÜL**

BİLDE see **BİLDİ**

BİLDİ Kzk. 19th c. **Bilde-bay / Bildi-bay** [Бильдебаевъ] (AOO 26); Kzk. 19th c. **Bilde-bay / Bildi-bay** [Бильдебай] (AOAtb. 50).

BİLÄČKA Bashk. 1675 **Biläčka** [Билячка] (MIB I, 202).

BİLÄN Uyg. 12th c.-14th c. **Bilän (Bilig?)** [Bilän Yaburšu Tutuq] (Radl., USp. 127).

BİLÄN-YEBÜRŠÜ Uyg. 12th c. - 14th c. **Bilän-yebüršü-tutuñ** [bilän jebüršü tutuŋ] (DTS). ✧ 'Together-with-Yebüršü'? (Blagova 1997, 714). ⇨ **BİLÄN.**

BİLÄN-KÜTÄY Uyg. 12th c.-14th c. **Bilän-kütäy / Bilig-kütän?** (Radl., USp. 128, DTS). ✧ 'Together-with-Kütäy'? (Blagova 1997, 714). ⇨ **BİLÄN + KÜTÄY.**

BİLÄÑ Kzk. 19th c. **Biläñ** [Кучинбай Биланговъ] (Grod., Pril. 175).

BİLÄR Bashk. 1756 **Bilär** [Биляр Енебеков] (MIB

IV/1, 128); Bashk. 1787 **Bilär** [Еналь Биляров] (MIB V, 203).

BİLÄRİK   Kirg. **Bilärik** [Bilärik / Біläрік] (Proben V, 170 /172/).

BİLEJİK   Yürük 1577 **Bilejik** [Bilecik] (Gökçen 58).

BİLEY   Bashk. 1761 **Biley** [Билей] (MIB IV/1, 211).

BİLET   Turk. **Bilet** (Önder, Hınıs).

BİLGÄ   Türk 957 **Bilgä** [بلكا بن ونداد] (Ibn al-Athīr/Tornb. VIII, 385); Karakh. 11th c. **Bilgä-beg** (DTS); Uyg. **Bilgä-beg / Bilgä-bäg** [ötükäntäki. bilgä bäg], a prince (Wissensfürst) in Ötükän forest (Le Coq, Man. I, 12); Selj. 1094-1104 **Bilgä-bek** [بيلكا بك غلام], a servant under the Seljuk ruler Berk-yaruq (1094-1104) (Qazw. 45); Selj. 1100 **Bilgä-bek** [بيلكا بك], an emir (Rāwandī 141, 142); Türk? 860 **Bilgä-čur** [بلكا حور / بلكا جور] (Tabarī, Annal. III, 1448, 1449, 1506, 1534, 1580-81, 1615, 1620); Khorezm. 1217/18 **Bilgä-χan** [تاج الدين بلكا خان صاحب اترار / تاج] Тадж-ад-дин Бильге-хан ал Бируни], a historian, a melik of Qara-kitay origin, astronomer and geographer, the ruler of Otrar (Nasawī 22, MIT I, 14, 16, 30, 31, 63, 145, 156, 219, 389, 420, 469, 470); Türk 731 **Bilgä-išbara-tamγan-tarqan** [Bilgä Işbara Tamγan Tarqan] (ETY I, 128); Türk 721 **Bilgä-küli-čur** [Bilgä Küli Çur] (ETY I, 137, 138); Türk 721 **Bilgä-küli-čur** [išbara bilga küli čur / İşbara bilgä Küli Çur], a Türk beg (DTS, ETY I, 137, 139); Türk 721 **Bilgä-küli-čur / İšbara-bilgä-küli-čur** [išbara bilga küli čur] (DTS); Türk 735 **Bilgä-qaγan** [Bilgä qaγan] (ETY I, 22, 58, 70, 72, 118, 120, 130, 54, 164); Uyg. **Bilgä-qaγan** [Tängridä bolmyš il itmiš Bilgä Qaγan] (Ramstedt, Uig. 12-13, 43); Türk 7th-9th c. **Bilgä-šañun** [Bilgä Şañun] (ETY III, 90); Selj. **Bilgä-tegin** [ازاركان دولت سلجوقيان] (Ĵuwaynī II); Selj. 11th c. **Bilgä-tegin** [بلكا تكين], mamluk (gulām?) of Melik-šah I (1072-1092) (Qazw. 486); Karakh. **Bilge-beg** [Bilge beg] (MK/Atalay 834); Selj. 1034 **Bilge-bek / Bilge-tegin** [بلكانك / بلكباك / Бильге-бек (Бильге-тегин)], an emir (a χajib) (MIT I, 229, 237, 241, 384, 442 (after Gardīzī, Ibn al-Athīr and Ĵuwaynī)); Türk 8th c. **Bilge-qaγan / Bilgä-qaγan**, a Turkic ruler (DTS). ✧ 'Wise' cf. Türk, Uyg., Karakh. *bilgä* 'мудрый' (DTS), Uyg. *bilge* 'hakim, bilgili' (EUS). Frequently used also as title of respect when mentioning rulers or high officials, e. g. *Bilgä-bek, Bilgä-čur, Bilgä-χan, Bilgä-išbara-tamγan-tarqan, Bilgä-qaγan, Bilgä-tegin, Bilgä-tonyuquq, Oγuz-bilgä-tamγačï, Tay-bilgä-tutuq*, etc. See also **ALP-BİLGÄ, ČİK-BİLGÄ, EL-BİLGÄ, İNANČ-BİLGE, İNANČU-BİLGÄ, YÄNČÜ-BİLGÄ, KÜL-BİLGÄ, KÜLÜG-BİLGÄ, QADÏR-BİLGÄ, QUTLUΓ-BİLGÄ, OΓUZ-BİLGÄ, TAY-BİLGÄ, TÄÑRİ-BİLGÄ, TÖLÄŠ-BİLGÄ, TUZ-BİLGÄ, TÜZÜN-BİLGÄ.**

BİLGÄ-ČİKŠÄN   Türk 7th c.-8th c. **Bilgä-čikšän** (DTS); Türk 7th-9th c. **Bilgä-čikšin** [Bilgä Çikşin] (ETY III, 116). ✧ 'Wise-Čikšän'. ⇨ **BİLGÄ.**

BİLGÄ-TAČAM   Türk 731 **Bilgä-tačam** [Bilgä Taçam], a Türk qaγan (ETY I, 130). ✧ 'Wise-Tačam'. ⇨ **BİLGÄ + TAČAM.**

BİLGÄ-TALUY   Uyg. 10th c. **Bilgä-taluy** (DTS). ✧ 'Wise sea/ocean' (Blagova 1997, 704), cf. Uyg. *taluj* 'океан, море' (DTS). ⇨ **BİLGÄ.**

BİLGÄ-TONYUQUQ   Türk 735 **Bilgä-tonyuquq** [Bilgä Tonyuquq] (ETY I, 100, 102, 104, 106, 110, 112, 116, 118, 120). ✧ 'Wise Tonyuquq'. ⇨ **BİLGÄ + TONYUQUQ.**

BİLİG   Selj. 1103, 1122, 1124 **Bilig / Bilik?** [بن أرتق بلك بن بهرام بن ارتق بناكسك / بلك بن بهرام بلك غازى] (Kamāladdīn II, 203-221, Ibn al-Athīr, Atab.: RHCHor II/2, 131, Abulfidā III, 339, Ibn al-Athīr/Tornb. X, 252, 432, XI, 72, Qalānisi 170, 208-210, Kamāladdīn: RHCHor III, 633-644); Maml. 13th c. **Bilig / Bilik?** [بدر الدين بلك المسعودى], died at Akka in 1291 (Makrīzī III, 126); Maml. 13th c. **Bilig / Bilik?** [Bedr-eddin Bilik-Scharki], died at Hims in 1280 (Makrīzī III, 39); Maml.? 1261, 1273 **Bilig / Bilik?** [بدرالدين بيليك الخزندار] / l'ēmir Bilik, le khazindâr, a treasurer, an emir (Sīrat 111 (27), Makrīzī II, 115, 123); Maml.? 1271 **Bilig / Bilik?** [l'émir Bedr-eddin Bilik le naïb-assaltanah], a governor (Makrīzī II, 105, Weil, Chalif. I, 77, 105); Maml.? 1279 **Bilig / Bilik?** [Bedr-eddin Bilik-Taïari], governor of Safad (Makrīzī II/1, 8); Maml. 1280 **Bilig / Bilik?** [l'émir Bedr-eddin-Bilik-Halebi], an emir (Makrīzī II/1, 18); Maml. 1298 **Bilig / Bilik?** [Bedr-eddin-Bilik-Fârisi], a χājib (Makrīzī IV, 66); Maml. 1308 **Bilig / Bilik?** [Bedr-eddin-Bilik-Mohsini] (Makrīzī IV, 280); Maml. 1330 **Bilig / Bilik?** [سيف الدين بلك الجمدار] (Zetterst. 186); Maml. 1401/02 **Bilig / Bilik?** [بلك الاحمدى] (Iyās I, 244); Maml.(Kipch.) 1260, 1270 **Bilig / Bilik?** [بيلك عبد الله التجاقى], a mathematician in Cairo (found in manuscripts in Istanbul: 1. Köprülü 949, year H. 658 (1260); 2. Serai: Sultan Ahmed Köşkü 3342, 100, year H. 668 (1270)); Maml.? 14th c. **Bilik** [بلك] (Tarj/Houtsma 30). ✧ 'Wise' cf. Maml. *bilik* (بيليك) 'science, sagesse' et 'sage, savant' (Sauvaget 44). See also **BİLGÄ.**

BİLİG-KÖÑÜL   Türk 9th c. **Bilig-köñül-sañun** [Bilig Köñül Sañun] (Runic Mss. 219, DTS, ETY II, 96); Uyg. 762 **Bilig-köñül-sañun-ügä** (Mahrnāmag 10). ✧ 'Wisdom-mind, wise-mind' (as appellative in Buddhistic terminology 'reason') (Müller, Uig. II, 13), cf. Karakh. *köñül* 'сердце; желание, чувство' (DTS).

BİLİG-TEMİR   Maml. 1299 **Bilig-temir / Bilik-temir?** [بلكتمر المنصورى] (Iyās I, 139). ✧ 'Wise Iron'. ⇨

BİLİG + TEMİR.

BİLİK see **BİLİG**

BİLİKČİN   Tuv. 19th c. **Bilikčin** [Биликчинъ] (Potanin IV, 425). ✧ 'Wise' cf. Alt. *bilik* 'знание, мудрость' (OjrRS). ⇨ **BİLİG** + suff. *-čin*.

BİLİM   Trkm. 1846 **Bilim-atalïq** [Билим-аталык (Билим)], from the Yomut tribe (MIT II, 501, 559, 577, 579, 598, 636); Bashk. 1760 **Bilim-bay** [Билимбаевской завод], a factory (MIB IV/2, 199). ✧ 'Knowledge' cf. Crm., Kzk. *bilim* 'das Wissen' (Radl. IV, 1766), Bashk. *belem* 'id.' (BRS).

BİLİR   Uyg. 7th c. **Bilir**, a prince (Schlegel: MSFOu. IX, 2, 135); Kuman 1292 **Bilir / Beler** [Petrus filius Beler], a christened Kuman nobleman in Hungary (Gombocz, ÁTSz. 33); Uyg. **Bilir-čañsi** (Le Coq, Man. III, 46). ✧ 'He who knows'.

BİLİS   Kzk. 19th c. **Bilis-pek** [Былиспекъ] (SOV 14). ✧ 'Friend, mate' cf. Kzk. *bilīs* 'der Freund, der Bekannte' (Radl. IV, 1766).

BİLİSKE   Kzk. 19th c. **Bilske (<Biliske)** [Бильске] (AOF 30). ✧ 'Dear little friend; Little acquaintance'. ⇨ **BİLİS** + suffixoid *-ke*.

BİLİZ   Uyg. 12th c.-14th c. **Biliz** (Radl., USp. 124, DTS). ⇨ **BİLİS**.

BİLKİŠ   Bashk. 1756 **Bilkiš** [Икчора Билкишев] (MIB IV/1, 109). ✧ 'Wise, educated' cf. Kirg. *bilgič* (Jud.), Tat. *belgeč*, Turk. *bilgiǰ* 'ein grosser Gelehrter, ein Pedant' (Radl. IV, 1769), Kzk. *bilgĭš* 'weise, wissend' (Radl. IV, 1769).

BİLMEY   Tat.(Mish.) 1739 **Bilmey** [Сартан Бильмеев] (MIB I, 373).

BİLMİŠ   Yürük 1543 **Bilmiš** (Gökb., Rum. 216); Yürük 1543 **Bilmiš** [بيلمش] (Gökb., Rum. 216, 240); Tat. 1543 **Bilmiš** (Gökb., Rum. 240). ✧ 'Much knowing, tricky, nimble' cf. Turk. *bilmiš* 'der viel Wissende, bekannt, schlau, geschickt' (Radl. IV, 1773).

BİLNİ   Bashk. 1762 **Bilni-bay** [Умюк Билнибаев] (MIB IV/2, 300-301).

BİLTE   Kzk. 19th c. **Bilte-bay** [Бильтебай] (SOK 174). ✧ 'Wick, fuse'? cf. Kzk. *bilte* 'filtre, fitil' (KzTS).

BİLTEK   Kzk. 19th c. **Biltek-pay** [Бильтекпай] (SOK 150). ✧ 'Stutterer' cf. *biltäk* 'der Stotterer' (Radl. IV, 1770).

BİLTER   Pecheneg 11th c. **Bilter** [Βιλτάρ], a Pecheneg chieftain, Tyrach's father (Byz. Turc. II, 90).

BİMAN see **BİYMEN**

BİMÄK   Tat. 1722 **Bimäk** [Бимяк] (MIB III, 198); Tat. 18th c. **Bimäk** [Амяк Бимяков] (MIB III, 228); Bashk. 1708 **Bimäk** [Урмет Бимяков] (MIB I, 223).

BİMET   Tat. 1753 **Bimet** [Биметь Бикметев] (MIB IV/1, 70). ✧ Contracted-shortened form of *Bi-möxämmät*, in Tat. dial. *Bimät* (Sattarov). ⇨ **BEK** + suffixoid *-met / -mät*.

BİN-BAŠÏ see **MİÑ-BAŠÏ**

BİN-QAL   Yürük 16th c. **Bin-qal** [بنقال], from the Yürüks of Kocacık, Turkey (Gökb., Rum. 103). ✧ 'Thousand - remain/survive!'; 'Thousand-Strength'?; II. 'Thousand Birthmark'. ⇨ **BİN + QAL I. / QAL II.**

BİNDİR   Türk 9th c. **Bindir** [Bindir] (DTS, ETY II, 65).

BİNEKİN   Tat. 1739 **Binekin** [Бинекинъ Алъ-Инидъ] (Alatyr. 141).

BİNTİN   Yak. 1678 **Bintin** [Якунка Бинтинъ] (DAI VIII, 30).

BİNVA   Mo.? **Binva** [Бинва], Deñgiz-χan's son (RaD I/1, 76).

BİR   Uzb. 1862 **Bir-aqa / Mir-bir-aqa** [Миръ-Биръ-Ака] (Moskal'cev 42); Uzb. **Bir-mulla** [Биръ Мулла Кулбаевъ], from Tashkent (Valihanov, Soč. 347); Türk 700-750 **Bir-ügä** (Runic Mss. 187, 189). ✧ 'Only (child), single' cf. Türk., Chag., Crm., Kzk., Turk., etc. *bir* 'ein, eins' (Radl. IV, 1746), Uzb. *bir* 'id.' (UzbRS).

BİR-ĴAN-SAL   Kzk. 19th c. **Bir-ǰan-sal** [برجان صال / Бырджан-салъ] (AUK Dobavl. 3). ⇨ **BİR + ĴAN + SAL.**

BİR-QALÏ   Kzk. 19th c. **Bir-qalï** [Arstangalej Birkaliev] (Mende 76). ⇨ **BİR(K)? + QALÏ.**

BİR-MÏSQAL   Kirg. **Bir-mïsqal** [Бирмыскал], fem. (Jud. 30). ✧ 'A mesure of weight' cf. Kirg. *mïsqal* 'золотник (единица веса)' (Jud.). ⇨ **BİR.**

BİR-NAZAR   Kzk. 19th c. **Bir-nazar** [Бырназар] (SODž. 56). ⇨ **BİR + NAZAR.**

BİRDİ see **BERDİ**

BİRİ-SİYİK   Tat. 1557 **Biri-siyik / Birisiyik** [Бирисиикъ] (Kn. Metriki Lit. 151).

BİRİM   Kzk. 19th c. **Birim** [Бырымъ] (SODž. 86); Kzk. 19th c. **Birim-qul** [Бырымкулъ] (SOV 92).

BİRK-MUXAMMED   Kzk. 19th c. **Birk-muχammed / Birk-muχamed** [Ходжабекъ Биркмухаммедовъ / Биркмухамедовъ] (SKSO VIII, 201, 206). ⇨ **BİR(K)? + MUXAMMED.**

BİRKÄ   Kzk. 19th c. **Birkä / Birqa?** [Бирка Кенджаевъ] (SKSO VIII, 206). ⇨ **BİR** + suff. or suffixoid *-kä / -ke.*

BİRKMAT   Kzk. 19th c. **Birkmat / Birkmad** [Биркмадовъ] (SKSO VIII, 219). ✧ 'The shortened form of Birk-muχammed'. ⇨ **BİRK-MUXAMMED.**

BİRLİ   Kzk. 19th c. **Birli-bay / Bïrlï-bay?** [Бырлыбай] (SOK 172).

BİRMANAY   Kzk. 19th c. **Birmanay** [Бырманай] (SOK 88).

BİRMAT   Kzk. 19th c. **Birmat / Bïrmat?** [Бырмать] (AOP 110). ⇨ **BİR? + suffixoid *-mat.***

BİRÜ   Bashk. 1735 **Birü-bay** [Девлеткулъ Бирюбаевъ], a prince (Vel.-Zern., Bašk. 12); Kzk. **Birü-bay** [Бырубай] (Konšin, Oč. 123); Kzk. 1811 **Birü-bay** [Тубина Бирюбаевъ] (Dobrosm., Turg. 252). See also **AQ-BİRÜ.**

BİRÜČÄK   Bashk. 1722 **Birüčäk?** [Араслан

Бирючаков] (MIB III, 199).

BİRÜY   Kuman/Tat.? 1239 **Birüy** [Бирюй (Бичуръ)], a Tatar chieftain (PSRL II, 177, 339, V, 175, VII, 145).

BİS see **BEŠ**

BİS-UBA   Bashk. 1714 **Bis-uba** [Сырым Бисубин] (MIB I, 105). ✧ 'Five hills' cf. Bashk. *uba* 'курган, холм' (BRS). ⇨ **BEŠ**.

BİSAT   Oghuz/Trkm. 14th c.-15th c. **Bisat / Basat?** [Basat / Бисат], Uruz's son (DQorq./Rossi 169, 193-202, DQorq. 76, 77, 79-83, 104, 111, 133, etc.).

BİSİKEY   Kzk. 19th c. **Bisikey** [Бисикей] (Pam. kn. Turg. 39). ✧ 'Small cradle' cf. Kzk. *besik*? + suff. *-key / -ey*.

BİSTREN   Bashk. 1740 **Bistren** [Жумангузя Бистренев] (MIB I, 397).

BİŠ see **BEŠ**

BİŠ-BUQA   Khorezm.? **Biš-buqa** [Биш-Бука] (RaD II, 74). ⇨ **BEŠ** + **BUQA?**

BİŠ-BULAT   Bashk. 1693 **Biš-bulat** [Бижбулатов] (MIB I, 84). ⇨ **BEŠ** + **BULAT.**

BİŠ-QALLAČ   Uyg.? **Biš-qallač** وپسر عم گورگوز [بیشقلاج ازاتـراك اوپغور] (Ǧuwaynī II, 227). ⇨ **BEŠ?**

BİŠ-QAZAQ   Bashk. 1757 **Biš-qazaq** [Бишказак] (MIB IV/1, 145). ⇨ **BEŠ** + **QAZAQ.**

BİŠ-QURTUQ   Khorezm.? **Biš-qurtuq** [Биш-Куртук] (RaD II, 71). ⇨ **BEŠ?**

BİŠ-PAS   Kzk. 19th c. **Biš-pas** [Бышпасъ] (AOP 118). ⇨ **BEŠ** + **BAŠ?**

BİŠİN   Bashk. 1709 **Bišin-bay** [Акеней Бишинбаев] (MIB III, 49); Kzk. 1791 **Bišin-sultan** [Бишинъ султанъ] (Dobrosm., Turg. 166-67).

BİTER   Kuman 1322 **Biter** [Biter filius Teschench], a Kuman from Hungary (Gyárfás III, 462-63). ✧ 'Growing up; who will grow up' cf. Gombocz, ÁTsz. 32, Rásonyi, KÖA 93, Rásonyi: AOH 20: 137.

BİTİK   Crm. 1542 **Bitäk-mïrza / Bitek-mïrza** [Битякъ-мырза] (PSRL XIII, 143); Kzk. 19th c. **Bitek / Bitäk** [Битакъ] (AOA 102); Kzk. 1794 **Bitik** [بتك / Брик (!)] (MIK IV, 160); Pecheneg 12th c. **Bitik / Bïtïq?** [Πιτικάς / Πιτικάν], a Byzantine chiftain of Scythian (=Pecheneg) origin from the early 12th c. (Byz. Turc. II, 256). ✧ I. 'Script(ure), (holy)book' cf. Chag., Kzk. *bitik* 'die Schrift, das Buch' (Radl. IV, 1775); II. 'Finished' cf. Kzk. *bitik* 'beendigt' (Radl. IV, 160), *bitik* 'id.' (KzRS).

BİTİKEY   Tat. 1551 **Bitikey** [Битикѣй князь], a prince (PSRL XIII, 168).

BİTİM   Kzk. 19th c. **Bitim-bay** [Битимбай] (Grod., Pril. 62); Kzk. 19th c. **Bitim-bek** [Битымбекъ] (SOV 142); Kzk. 19th c. **Bitüm-bay** [Борибай Битумбаевъ] (Grod., Pril. 107). ✧ 'The end, finishing (last child?)' cf. Kzk. *bitim* 'die Entscheidung, die Beendigung' (Radl. IV, 1778).

BİTİN   Kzk. 19th c. **Biten-bay** [Битенбай] (SOK 54);

Tat. 1690 **Bitin** [Булатко Битинъ] (Kungursk. akty 178).

BİTTİ   Yürük **Bitti-bey**, a Yürük chief (Kúnos 1891, 117). ✧ 'Finished, ended (last child)' cf. Chag., Crim., Trkm., Turk., Uzb. *bit-* 'beendigt, fertig sein; geschaffen sein; wachsen' (Radl. IV, 1773) + Vpast(-ti).

BİTÜK   Bashk. 1738 **Bitük** [Сапар Битюков] (MIB III, 391); Bashk. 1740 **Bitük** [Явгилди Битюков] (MIB I, 440).

BİTÜM see **BİTİM**

BİZEN   Karakh. **Bizen** [Bizen] (MK/Atalay 834).

BİŽE see **BİČE**

BİŽİ see **BİČE**

BİKTÄR see **PİKTOR**

BÏAQAR   Yak. **Bïaqar** [Быакар] (Pek.).

BÏALČA   Yak. **Bïalča** [Быалча] (Pek.).

BÏČAQ   Kuman 1490, 1493 **Bïčaq / Bičaq** [Petrus Bichak (Bychak) Capitaneus Cumanorum], one of the chiefs (captains) of the Kumans in Hungary (Gyárfás III, 701, 708); Kzk. 19th c. **Fïčaq** [Фичакъ Ракатовъ] (Grod., Pril. 114); Kzk. 19th c. **Pšaq-pay (<Pïšaq-pay)** [Пшакпай] (SOK 28). ✧ 'Knife, pen-knife' (Rásonyi, KÖA 93, Rásonyi: AOH 20: 137), cf. Crm., Kar., Turk. *bïčaq* 'das Messer' (Radl. IV, 1734), Chag. *bičaq* 'das Messer' (Radl. IV, 1781).

BÏČAQČÏ   Khorezm. 14th c. **Bïčaqčï** [احمد بجتجی / اصحاب الفتی احی Akhy Ahmed Bitchaktchy], a young [noble] man from Azaq (Azov) (Ibn Bat. II, 290, 368). ✧ 'Cutler' cf. Turk. *bïčaqčï* 'das Messerschmied' (Radl. IV, 1435).

BÏČČİĞÏNÄN   Yak. **Bïččïyïnān** [Быччыгынан] (Pek.). ✧ 'Talking meaninglessly' cf. Yak. *bičïyïnai* (Pek.), *bičïyïnai* 'чирликать,]ебетать, лепетать, невнятно говорить' (Pek.).

BÏČİĞAY   Bashk. 1675 **Bïčïyay / Bičïyay?** [Чюнчюра Бычигаев] (MIB I, 199). ⇨ **BİČİK?** + suff. *-ay*.

BÏČİĞÏRAS   Yak. **Bïčïyïras** [Бычыгырас] (Pek.). ✧ 'Dropping; getting wet'? Cf. Yak. *bičïyïrā* 'просачиваться, выступать каплями, течь' (Pek.).

BÏČİRAP   Yak. **Bïčïrap** [Бычырап] (Pek.). ✧ 'Dropping'? Cf. *bičïr-* 'выступать каплями, сочиться (о водянистой жидкости из нарыва)' + R. suff. *-ov* (Pek.).

BÏD'İ   Alt. 19th-20th c. **Bïd'i** [Быдьи] (OjrRS 208).

BÏDAYBÏQÏ   Uyg. 12th c. - 14th c. **Bïdaybïqï / Bïtaybïqï** [bïdajbïqï / Bıtaybıkı] (DTS, EUTS).

BÏDAYÏN   Yak. **Bïdayïn** [Быдайын] (Pek.).

BÏDİN   Uyg. **Bïdïn** [Bıdın] (EUTS). See also **QUDA-BİDİN**.

BÏYAŠ   Nog. 20th c. **Bïyaš** [Седик Быйаш увлы / Седик Бияшев], father of one of Baskakov's informants from the aul of Abram-töbe (Bask., Nog. 144).

BÏYDÏQ Alt. 19th-20th c. **Bïydïq** [Быйдык] (OjrRS 208).

BÏYÏQ-ALİ Turk. 1515 **Bïyïq-ali** [Бıyık-Ali (köy)], a village (Gökb., Ed. 394). ✦ 'Moustache-Ali' cf. Turk. PN *Bıyık* (Erol II). ⇨ **ALİ**.

BÏYÏQLİ Turk. 1446 **Bïyïqlï** [مراد فتیه ابن بیتلی] (MB Qastam. 124). ✦ 'Having a moustache' cf. Turk. *bıyık* 'moustache' (TED), Maml. (Kipch.) *byjyk* 'Schnurrbart' (Tarj/Houtsma). + suff. *-lï*.

BÏQQÏYA see **BÏRQÏYA**

BÏLASÏYA Yak. **Bïlasïya** [Быласыйа] (Pek.).

BÏLATÏAN Yak. **Bïlatïan** [Былатыан] (Pek.). ✦ Platon (R.).

BÏLČAXÏ Yak. **Bïlčaxï** [Былчахы], a shaman (Pek.).

BÏLČİK Kzk. 19th c. **Bïlčik** [Былчикъ] (Pantusov, Kirg. 39). ✦ 'Secretion of eyes, rheum' cf. Kzk. *bılşık* 'göz ağrıdığı zaman gözde meydana gelen kir, çapak' (KzTS).

BÏLÏQ Kirg. **Bïlïq-bay** [Былыкбай] (Jud. 936); Kzk. 19th c. **Bïlïq-pay** [Былыкпай] (AOP 10). ✦ 'Sinful, unsound, tainted' cf. Kirg. *bilïq* 'непутёвый, гнусный; пакость, мразь, нечисть' (Jud.), Kzk. *bilïq* 'verderben (vom Fleische)' (Radl. IV, 1730).

BÏLLAY Yak. **Bïllay** [Былллаи], fem. (Pek.). ✦ '(Lips) hanging down'? Cf. Yak. *billai-* 'губатеть, губастеть' (Pek.).

BÏLLAYA Yak. **Bïllaya** [Быллаjа] (Pek.). ✦ '(Lips) hanging down'? cf. Yak. *billai-* 'губатеть, губастеть'(Pek.).

BÏLTAY Yak. **Bïltay** [Былтаi] (Pek.). ✦ 'Has a finger in every pie' (=R.: Выскочка), cf. Yak. *biltai* (Pek.).

BÏLTARAÑQÏ Yak. **Bïltarañqï** [Былтаранкы], one of the children of the fabulous „Baba Yaga (Ĵaba-bāba)" [Old Witch] of the Yakuts (Pek.). ✦ Derived from Yak. verb *bïltarıı-* (Pek.).

BÏRĴAY Yak. **Bïrĵay, Sïñ-bïrĵay** [Бырцаi] (Pek.). ✦ 'Never-do-well; snivelling brat' (=R.: Сопляк), cf. Yak. *birĵai* 'выдаваться, высовываться' (Pek.).

BÏRĴÏQÏ Yak. **Bïrĵïqï** [Бырцыкы] (Pek.).

BÏRDÏY Yak. **Bïrdïy** [Бырдыи], a shaman living in the first part of the 18th c. in the district (volost') of Megin (Pek.).

BÏRĞÏY Yak. **Bïrγïy** [Быргыи] (Pek.). ✦ 'Boiling, brewing' cf. Yak. *birγïï* 'пышать, бить ключем; кипеть' (Pek.).

BÏRÏS Alt. 19th-20th c. **Bïrïs** [Бырыс], fem. (OjrRS 211).

BÏRQÏYA Yak. **Bïrqïya / Bïqqïya** [Быркыjа, Быккыja], a shaman (Pek.).

BÏRTANÏ Yak. **Bïrtanï** [Быртаны] (Pek.). ✦ 'Loin, groin (of an animal)' cf. Yak. *birta* 'пах у скотины; паховой жир конного или рогатого скота' (Pek.).

BÏTÏGÏRĀN Yak. **Bïtïgïrān** [Бытыгран] (Pek.). ✦ 'Who will breed' cf. Yak *bïtïgïrā* 'там-саям пускать

BÏTÏQ Kzk. 19th c. **Bïtïq** [Бытыкъ] (SOK 10). ⇨ **BÏTÏK?** See also **AL-BÏTÏQ**.

BÏTRU Uyg. 12th c.-14th c. **Bïtru** [Bıtru] (DTS, EUTS).

BÏŽÏR Bashk. **Bïžïr-märgän** [Быжырмарганъ], hero of a Bashkir tale (Zelenin, Perm. 476-79). ✦ 'Smallpox' cf. Bashk. *bižir* '1. зыбь, рябь; 2. рябина (от оспы) 3. рябой, веснушчатый' (BRS); Kzk. *bužur* ' рябина (от оспы)' (PRS).

BÏTÏGÏR Yak. **Bïtïgïr** [Бытыгыр] (Pek.).

BLAQTÏ see **BULAQTÏ**

BLAN see **BULAN**

BOČA Tat. (Sib.) 1608 **Boča, Bača?** [Боча Мостов], a prince (Miller, Ist. Sib. II, 206, 207); Tat. (Sib.) 1598 **Boča-murza / Bača-murza?** [Боча мурза] (Miller, Ist. Sib. II, 18, 151). ✦ I. 'Elder sister; aunt' cf. Chag., East.T., *baja* 'die Ältere Schwester, die Tante' (Radl. IV, 1521); II. 'Sister's or wife's husband' cf. East.T., Tat. *baja* 'der Mann der Schwester (der Frau)' (Radl. IV, 1522).

BOČAN Nog. 1649 **Bočan** [Бочанъ Казыевъ] (Al IV, 123).

BOČČOMUS Yak. **Boččomus** [Боччомус], a shaman (Pek.).

BOČQA Hak.(Kacha) 19th - 20th c. **Bočqa** [Бочка] (Proben IX, 613); Hak.(Kacha) 19th - 20th c. **Pōčqa** [Почка] (Proben IX, 613). ✦ 'Barrel, butt' cf. Hak.(Sag.) *počqa* 'das Fass' (Radl. IV, 1287), (<R.) *bočka*.

BOČTAY Kzk. 1838 **Bočtay** [Бочтай] (Konšin, Mat. V, 15). ⇨ ? + suff. *-tay(1,2)*?

BOČU Kzk. 19th c. **Boču-bay** [Бочубай] (AOP 102).

BOČŪTA Yak. **Bočūta** [Бочута] (Pek.).

BOD'O Alt. 19th-20th c. **Bod'o** [Бодьо], fem. (OjrRS 211). ✦ 'Mash, wash; beer', 'барда после выгонки вина' 'id.' (OjrRS 211), Alt. *bod'o* 'брага' [=home-made beer] (OjrRS).

BODAY I. see **BUĞDAY I.**

BODAY II. see **BOTAY**

BODAP Kzk. 19th c. **Bodap** [Бодапъ] (SOK 16).

BODAŠ Kzk. 19th c. **Bodaš / Badaš?** [Борибекъ Бодашевъ] (Grod., Pril. 25).

BODO? Yak. 1680 **Bodo / Bodoy?** [Чюгинъ Бодоевъ], a prince (DAI VIII, 10, 244, 268).

BODONČAR Kzk. 19th c. **Bodončar** [Бодоньчаръ], Dombaul's son (Potanin, Pred. 49). ✦ 'Little Bodon'?

BODU Kzk. 19th c. **Bodu-bek** [Бодубек] (SODž. 12).

BODUL Yürük 1543 **Bodul** [بودل] (Gökb., Rum. 193).

BODUM Kirg. 19th-20th c. **Bodum-bey** [Bódummbej és [and] Ódummbej] (Prinz 170).

BODUR Turk. 20th c. **Bodur-oγlu**, a village in the province of Çankiri, Turkey (TMİB 250). ✦ 'Short-legged' cf. Turk. *bodur* 'klein an Wuchs' (HŞ), 'kurzbeinig' (Radl. IV, 1677).

ВОГ Bashk. 1675 **Boγ-bek / Baγ-bek?** [Бердыгул Богбеков] (MIB I, 200). ⇨ **BOW?, BAW?**

ВОГА see **BUQA**

ВОГАČ see **BUГАČ**

ВОГАY see **BUГАY**

ВОГAQ Uyg. 1305 **Boγaq / Роγaq?** [Pögak] (Chwol., Syr.-nest.(NF) 16).

ВОГAŠ Kzk. 19th c. **Boγaš** [Богашъ] (SOK 48). ✦ 'Little bull' cf. Kuman, Turk. *boγa* 'der Stier'(Radl. IV, 1648). ⇨ **BUQA** + dim. suff. *-š (<-č)*.

ВОГAZ Türk / Uyg.? 8th c. **Boγaz-tegin** [boγaz tegin] (DTS). ✦ 'Throat, gorge' cf. Uyg., Karakh. *boγaz* 'горло, глотка' (DTS).

ВОГAZJA-FATİMA Oghuz/Trkm. 14th c.-15th c. **BoγazJa-fatima / BoγazJa-fatma / Yaγïz-buγazča-fatima / Yaγïr-buγazča-fatima? / Yawuz-yaγïr-boγazJa-fatma** [بوغازجه فاطمه] / BoğazJa Fātima / Yauz Yağır Boğazca Fatma; Boğazca Fatma / Ягыз-Бугазча-Фатима (Ягыр Бугазча Фатима)], fem. (DQorq./Rossi 130 (Manuscr. Vat. 80v), DQorq. 46). ✦ 'Gluttonous/greedy-Fatima'. ⇨ **ВОГAZ?** + suff. *-ja*.

ВОГAZJA-FATMA see **ВОГAZJA-FATİMA**

ВОГDAMÏŠ Tat.(Sib.)? 1639 **Boγdamïš** [Богдамыш], Ildeney-tayši's envoy (Miller, Ist. Sib. II, 111).

ВОГRA see **BUГRA**

ВОГU Kzk. 19th c. **Boγu-bay** [Богубай] (SOK 80, 132); Kzk. 19th c. **Boγu-bay** [Богубай] (SOV 40, 80); Kzk. 19th c. **Boqu-bay** [Бокубай] (SOK 24); Kzk. 19th c. **Boqu-bay** [Бокубай] (SODž. 128). ✦ 'Deer (stag or hind)' cf. Kzk. *boγu* 'олень (самецъ, самка мараль)' (PRS).

ВОГUГ see **BUГUГ**

ВОГULQA Tat.(Sib.) 1609 **Boγulqa** [Богулка] (Andrievič, Ist. Sib. I, 45).

ВОГUM-BAY see **ВОГUN**

ВОГUN Kzk. 19th c. **Boγum-bay (<Boγun-bay)** [Богумбай] (AOK 98); Kzk. 19th c. **Boγum-bay (<Boγun-bay)** [Богумбай] (SOK 136); Kzk. 19th c. **Boγum-bay (<Boγun-bay / Boqum-bay?)** [Богумбай, Бокумбай] (AOA 82). ⇨ **BOQÏM?**

ВОГUNČU Uyg. 8th c. **Boγunču / Boγurču?** (Müller, Pfahl. 12). ✦ 'Small joint/link' cf. Karakh. *boγun* 'суставъ' (DTS) + dim. suff. *-ču*.

ВОГUS see **ВОГUŠ**

ВОГUŠ Kzk. 19th c. **Boγus-pay** [Богуспай] (SOV 68); Tat.(Lit.) 1582 **Boγuš** [Богушъ Сафьяновичъ] (Lit. Tat. 47); Tat.(Lit.) 1591 **Boγuš** [Яхута Богушовна Багдашевичъ], fem. (Lit. Tat. 82). ⇨ **BUГU?** + suff. *-š*.

ВОГUŠUQ Kzk. 19th c. **Boγušuq** [Богушукъ] (SOV 156). ⇨ **BOUŠ** + suff. *-uq*.

ВОXTUČAQ Tat.(Sib.) 1676 **Boχtučaq / Boχtu-čač?**

[Бохтучакъ / Бохтучачко] (DAI VII, 340). ⇨ **BOQTÏ** + suff. *-čaq*.

BOY Kzk. 19th c. **Boy-bay** [Бойбай] (SOK 110). ✦ 'Body, stature' cf. Kuman, Chag., Crm., Kirg., Kzk., Turk., etc. *boy* 'der Körper; die Gestalt, die Statur, der Wuchs, die hohe Gestalt' (Radl. IV, 1639). See also **QARГA-BOYLÏ; DENE, TEN, TULГA.**

BOY-ŽEKİ Kzk. 19th c. **Boy-žeki** [Бойжеки] (SOV 94). ⇨ **BOY.**

BOYAW Kzk. 19th c. **Boyaw** [Бояу] (AOA 62, 150).

BOYDOY Yak. 1645 **Boydoy?** [Бойдой], a prince (DAI III, 37).

BOYQORJUL Kzk. 19th c. **BoyqorJul** [Бойкорджулъ] (SOK 278).

BOYLA Bulg. 9th c.-10th c. **Boyla** [βοιλᾶς], a Proto-Bulgar rank resp. title (Byz. Turc. II, 93); Bulg. 10th c. **Boyla** [Βουλίας], a commander (Byz. Turc. II, 107); Uyg. **Boyla** [Boyla] (EUTS); Pecheneg / Kuman? **Boyla** [Bojla Čaban] (Németh, Inschr. 25); Türk 8th c. **Boyla-baγa-tarqan** [bojla baγa tarqan / Boyla Baγa Tarqan], Tonyuquq's title (DTS, ETY I, 72); Türk 8th c.? **Boyla-qutluγ-yarγan** [Boyla Qutluγ Yarγan], a title of Tonyuquq (?) (ETY I, 156, DTS, Ramstedt, Uig. 4-6); Uyg. 8th c.? **Buyla** (Müller, Hofstaat 211-212, Marquart, Chron. 42). ✦ A dignity, part of compound titles. Cf. Türk *boila* 'eine Würde' (Radl. IV, 1643).

BOYNAQ NUyg. 19th c. **Boynaq** [بويناق] (Le Coq, Namenl. 96); Kzk. 19th c. **Moynaq** [Мойнакъ] (SODž. 76); Kzk. 19th c. **Moynaq** [Мойнакъ] (AOP 10); Kzk. 19th c. **Moynaq** [Мойнакъ] (AOK 10); Hak.(Sag.) 19th-20th c. **Moynaq** [Моінак] (Proben IX, 468); Kkalp. 20th c. **Moynaq-bay** [Мойнакбай] (KkRS 775); Kzk. 19th c. **Moynaq-pay** [Мойнакпай] (SODž. 54); Kzk. 19th c. **Moynoq? / Moynaq?** [Мойнокъ] (SOV 126); Bashk. 1761 **Muynaq** [Муинак Сюлейманов] (MIB IV/1, 214); Bashk. 1790 **Muynaq** [Муинак Бимурзин] (MIB V, 295); *EN:* Kzk. 18th c. - 19th c. **Moynaq** [Мойнак] (Tynyšp. 73). ✦ I. 'Neck of a camel; II. 'The leather of the neck, a dog with white neck' cf. Kzk. *moynaq* 'id.', Kirg. *moynoq* 'id.' (Radl. IV, 2120), Kkalp. *moynaq* 'бархан; белошеий (кличка собаки)' (KkRS); III. 'Necklace, choker; collar', "Kamelhals; Halsband" (Le Coq 96), cf. Chag. *boynaγ* 'das Halsband' (Radl. IV, 1641); IV. 'Ridge' Karakh. *bojnaq* I 'седловина, горный перевал' (DTS); V. 'Lizard' cf. Karakh. *bojnaq* II 'ящерица' (DTS).

BOYNU-BAZÏQ Maml. 14th c. **Boynï-bazïq** [بويني بازق] (Sauvaget 43). ✦ 'Thick (strong)-necked' (Sauvaget 43: 'qui a le cou épais'), cf. Chag., Az., Turk., Kar.(L.T.), Trkm. *boyun* 'der Hals' (Radl. IV, 1660). ⇨ **BAZÏQ.**

BOYNU-YOГUN Turk. 20th c. **Boynu-yoγun** [Boynuyoğun], a village in the province of Adana,

Turkey (TMİB 9). ✧ 'Thick (stiff) - necked, strong-necked' cf. Chag., Az., Turk., Kar.(L.T.), Trkm. *boyun* 'der Hals' (Radl. IV, 1660) and Turk. *yoğun* 'dicht; kompakt; dickflüssig; steif' (HŞ).

BOYSA   Kzk. 19th c. **Boysa-bay** [Бойсабай] (SOK 106).

BOYŠAN   Tat.(Sib.) 1607 **Boyšan?** [Боишан], prince Altanay's uncle; Altanay was one of Küčüm's sons (Miller, Ist. Sib. II, 204).

BOYU-QÏRA   Uyg. **Boyu-qïra** [Boyu Kıra] (EUTS). ⇨ **BOY + QÏRA.**

BOQ   Kzk. 19th c. **Boq-pay** [Бокпай] (SODž. 134); Kzk. 19th c. **Boq-pay** [Бокпай] (AOO 50); Alt. 19th-20th c. **Boq-ul / Boq-ūl?** [Бокул] (OjrRS 207). ✧ 'Excrement, shit, dung' cf. Chag., Kuman, Crm., NUyg.(Tar.), East.T., Trkm., Uzb. *boq* 'die Excremente, der Mist, der Schmutz' (Radl. IV, 1645). See also **BELDEN-BOQ, İT-BOQ, TOQ-BOQ; ARÏQ II., BAYNAQ, QOMUQ.**

BOQ-BAS see **BOQ-BAŠ**

BOQ-BASAR   Kzk. 19th c. **Boq-basar** (Radl., Aus Sib. II, 387); Kzk. 19th c. **Boq-pasar** [Бокпасаръ] (SOV 34, 40). ✧ 'He who will presse/tread excrement (shit)' cf. *boq* 'die Excremente, der Mist, der Schmutz' (Radl. IV, 1645). ⇨ **BOQ + BASAR.** See also **BOQ-BAS, KELDİ-BOQ-BASAR.**

BOQ-BAŠ   Kzk. 19th c. **Boq-bas** [Бокбасъ] (AOA 22); Bashk. 1778 **Buq-baš** [Алибатыр Букбашев] (MIB V, 79). ✧ 'Shit-head'. ⇨ **BOQ + BAŠ.**

BOQ-QUT   Kzk. 19th c. **Boq-qut** [Боккутъ] (Grod. I, 98). ⇨ **BOQ + QUT?**

BOQ-MURUN   Kirg. **Boq-murun** [Бокмурун] (Jud. 111). ⇨ **BOQ + BURUN.**

BOQ-PAΓAR   Kzk. 19th c. **Boq-paγar** [Бокпагаръ] (SODž. 6). ✧ 'He who looks after the excrement / shit'. ⇨ **BOQ + BAQAR.** See also **QOY-BAQAR, QOZÏ-BAΓAR, QULUN-BAΓAR.**

BOQ-PASAR see **BOQ-BASAR**

BOQ-ŠADU   Uyg. 12th c.-14th c. **Boqšadu / Boqšaltu** [Bokšaltu / boqšadu] (EUTS, DTS). ✧ 'Shit/dung-Shad'? (Blagova 1997, 713). ⇨ **BOQ + ŠAD?**

BOQ-ŠERGÄ   Bashk. 1731 **Boq-šergä?** [Бокшерга] (MIB III, 288).

BOQA see **BUQA**

BOQAY see **BUQAY**

BOQAY-TOQAY   Nog. 1649 **Boqay-toqay** [Бокай-Токай Ажіевъ] (AI IV, 124). ✧ 'Shin-?' cf. Chag. *boγay* 'die Wade' (Radl. IV, 124). ⇨ **BOQAY + TOQAY.**

BOQAN   Kzk. 19th c. **Boqan** [Боканъ] (SOV 76, 100).

BOQČA   Bashk. 1756 **Boqča** [Бокча Ильев] (MIB IV/1, 109); Bashk. 1757 **Boqča** [Бокча Утемышев] (MIB IV/1, 136); Kzk. 19th c. **Boqča-bay** [Бокчабай] (SODž. 12); Bashk. 1756 **Buqča** [Букча Итзимесов]

(MIB IV/1, 107). ✧ 'Haversack, bag, leather bag, sack' cf. Chag., East.T. *boqča* 'die Rolle, der Koffer, der Packsack', Kzk. *boqša* 'Beutel, Sack, den die Frauen sich über den Sattel legen' (Radl. IV, 1647), Tat. *buqča (=boqča)* 'ein Ledersack, Mantelsack' (Radl. IV, 1804).

BOQČÏ   Turk. 1686 **Boqčï / Boqǰi** [Bokdži Ahmed], a prisoner in Buda, Hungary (Hadtörténeti Közlemények 1916, 434); Kzk. 20th c. **Boqču** [Bokcsu] (Almásy 337); Bashk. 1756 **Buqči / Buqčï** [Букчи Идзимясов] (MIB IV/1, 123); Bashk. 1756 **Buqču-bay** [Сатлык Букчюбаев] (MIB IV/1, 128). ✧ 'Dealer in dung; cleaner of cesspools' cf. Turk. *bokçu* 'id.' (TED), Turk. *boqčï* 'der Latrinenreiniger; der Schimpfende, der an das Schimpfen gewöhnte' (Radl. IV, 1647), Tat. *buq* 'der Koth, der Mist; Dreck, eine schlechte Sache' (Radl. IV, 1802). ⇨ **BOQ** + suff. *-čï / -ču.*

BOQDAN   Selj.? **Boqdan-χatun**, fem. (RaD/Quatrem. 111).

BOQÏ   Kzk. 1888 **Boqï-bay** [Бокыбай], a village (Vyšnegorskij: Tr. Syr-D. OSK 1888, 24). ⇨ **BOQ.**

BOQÏM   Kzk. 19th c. **Boqïm-bay** (<**Boqïn-bay?**) [Бокымбай] (SOV 16); Kzk. 19th c. **Boqum-bek** [Бокумбекъ] (SOK 202). ⇨ **BOQ?** + poss. suff. *-im?*

BOQLAN   Kzk. 1817 **Boqlan / Baγlan?** [بوقلن / Баглан(?)] (MIK IV, 309).

BOQLOW   Kuman 1332 **Boqlow** [Kolguna filius Boklow de Philiph], among the Kumans in Hungary (Gyárfás III, 475). ✧ 'Dunghill, muckheap' cf. Rásonyi, NTK 99, Rásonyi, KÖA 93, Rásonyi, Anthr. 138.

BOQOLAP   Tat.(Sib.) 1548 **Boqolap?** [Боколапъ] (Kn. Metriki Lit. 44).

BOQPAN   Kzk. 19th c. **Boqpan** [Бокпанъ] (SOK 170); Kzk. 19th c. **Buqpan** [Букпанъ] (SOK 80, 128). ✧ 'Mucky, dirty'. ⇨ **BOQ?** + suff. *-pan(1).* See also **BOQTÏ.**

BOQPANTAY   Kzk. 19th c. **Boqpantay** [Бокпантай] (SOK 60). ✧ 'Sly, sneaky, underhanded' cf. Kzk. *buqpantay* 'içinden hesaplı, daima samimi olmamak' (KzTS).

BOQSUQ   Kzk. 19th c. **Boqsuq** [Боксукъ] (AOK 46); Tat.(Sib.)? 1634 **Buqsuq** [Буксук Курагай] (Miller, Ist. Sib. II, 410).

BOQSUN   Bashk. **Boqsun** [Боксун] (MIB III, 302).

BOQŠALTU   Uyg. **Boqšaltu / Boq-šadu?** [Bokšaltu / boqšadu] (EUTS, DTS).

BOQŠAN   Bashk. 1675 **Boqšan / Boqman?** [Бокшан (Бокман) Козуметев] (MIB I, 199).

BOQTAY   Khorezm.? 1295 **Boqday?** [بتدای ختاجی] (RaD/Jahn 65); Kzk. 19th c. **Boqtay** [Боктай] (SODž. 76). ✧ 'Shitlike, dunglike, mucklike'. ⇨ **BOQ** + suff. *-tay(1).*

BOQTÏ   Kzk. 19th c. **Boqtï-bay** [Боктыбай] (SOV 118); Kzk. 19th c. **Boqtï-bay** [Боктыбай] (AOO 46);

Alt. 19th-20th c. **Boqtu** [Бокту] (OjrRS 207); Kzk. 19th c. **Boqtu-bay** [Боктубай] (SOV 22); Kzk. 19th c. **Boqtu-bay** [Бокту-бай] (Samojlovič: ŽS XXIV (1915), 167). ✧ 'Very dirty' (OjrRS 207).

BOQU see **BOГU**

BOQUM see **BOQÏM**

BOQUŠ Alt. 19th-20th c. **Boquš** [Бокуш] (OjrRS 207).

BOL Kzk. 19th c. **Bol-žar / Bol-ǰar?** [Больжаръ] (SODž. 18); Tat.(Sib.) **Bul-bek-χan** [Бул Бäк Хан] (Proben IV, 260 /325/). ✧ 'Be!, Live!, Become!' cf. in several Trk. dialects *bol-* 'sein, werden' (Radl. IV, 1669), Uzb. *bol-* 'быть, становиться, существовать, кончать (UzbRS), Tat. *bul-* 'бывать, быть; становиться' (TatRS), Bashk. *bul-* 'быть; становиться' (BRS). Used as second component of compound personal name expresses the wish of the parents (cf. Rásonyi, Imp.). See also **AY-BOL, AQ-BOL, ALİM-BUL, BAY-BOL, BAR-BOL, BEK-BOL, BEL-BUL, BİY-BOL, ČAQQÂN-BOL, ǰAMAN-BOL, ǰAN-BOL, DOST-BOL, EL-BOL, ER-BOL, ES-BOL, ESEN-BOL, ГAYDA-BOL, XAMǰAM-BOL, YAR-BOL, QAR-BOL, QARA-BOL, QARÏQ-BOL, QAZ-BUL, QUT-BOL, MALLA-BOL, MOLLA-BOL, NAR-BOL, SAYÏN-BUL, SERİK-POL, SULTAN-BOL, TAŠ-BOL, TOY-BOL, TOQTA-BUL(?), TOQTÏ-BUL(?).**

BOLAY see **BULAY**

BOLAN Kzk. 19th c. **Bolan-bay** [Садибекъ Боланбаевъ] (Grod., Pril. 34). ✧ 'Mixed' cf. Turk., Crm. *bulan* 'gemischt, umgerührt werden; trübe werden, sich verdüstern' (Radl. IV, 1837). ⇨ **BULAN?** See also **ES-BOLAN.**

BOLAŠ Tat.(Lit.) 1552 **Bolaš** [Болашъ] (Kn. Metriki Lit. 86). ✧ 'Become appeased' cf. East.T. *bolaš-* 'sich versöhnen' (Radl. IV, 1671).

BOLAT see **BULAT**

BOLATKEN Kzk. 19th c. **Bolatken** [Болаткенъ] (SOV 114). ⇨ **BULAT.**

BOLČOY Alt. 19th-20th c. **Bolčoy** [Болчой], fem. (OjrRS 211). ✧ 'Ball, pill' (OjrRS 211).

BOLČOQ-BAŠ Alt. 19th-20th c. **Bolčoq-baš** [Болчокбаш], fem. (OjrRS 211). ✧ 'Round head' (OjrRS 211). ⇨ **BAŠ.**

BOLČOÑÑŪR Yak. **Bolčoññūr / Bolǰoññūr** [Болчоӊнур / Болцоӊнур], a shaman (Pek.). ✧ Derived from Yak. verb *bolčoi-* 'образоваться, вскочить шишке' (Pek.).

BOLČUN Kzk. 19th c. **Bolčum-bek < Bolčun-bek** [Болчумбекъ] (SOV 14). ✧ 'Thick muscles (on legs, and back)' cf. Kzk. *bulšuq* 'id.' (Radl. IV, 1855), Kzk. *bulšïq* 'pazı eti' (KzTS), East.T., Kirg. *bulčuñ* 'der Muskel' (Radl. IV, 1854).

BOLDA see **BOLDÏ**

BOLDAZ Uyg. 12th c.-14th c. **Boldaz** [Boldaz] (DTS, EUTS).

BOLDÏ Kzk. 19th c. **Bolda-bay (< Boldï-bay?)** [Болдабай] (SOV 146); Kzk. 19th c. **Boldï-bay** [Болдыбай] (SOV 110); Kzk. 19th c. **Boldï-bay** [Болдыбай] (SOK 174); Uzb. 20th c. **Boldï-bây** [Бўлдибой] (Begmatov 1984, 201); Chag. 16th c. **Boldï-bikeč** [Болды-бикеч], fem. (Ivanov 88, 90); Uyg. **Boltï-täñrim**, Ata-tutuñ's wife (Zieme, Mat. I, 81, Mat. II, 93); Bashk. 1756 **Buldï** [Ясрябай Булдин] (MIB IV/1, 109); Kzk. 19th c. **Buldu-bay** [Булдубай] (SOK 54, 112, 204). ✧ 'Became (a helper); (the child) has been born'; 'Became/was born; he/she has become/has been born'; 'Enough! I don't want any more!' (Begmatov). Frequently used as a second component of compound names. Cf. Türk, Chag., Kar., Kzk., Trkm., Uzb., etc. *bol-* 'sein, werden' (Radl. IV, 1669), Tat. *bul-* 'sein, werden' (Radl. IV, 1835). See also **BULГAN, BULMÏŠ; AX-POLDÏ, AŠ-BOLDÏ, BAY-BOLDÏ, BEŠ-BOLDÏ, Bİ-BOLDÏ, ǰAN-BOLDÏ, ǰUL-BULDÏ, EL-BOLDÏ, EŠ-BOLDÏ, YAR-BOLDÏ, YAŠ-PULDÏ, QUL-BOLDÏ, QURA-BOLDÏ, NUR-BOLDÏ, PİR-BOLDÏ, PÏŠ-BOLDU, SURA-BOLDÏ, TAY-BOLDÏ, TOY-BOLDÏ.**

BOLDÏQ Khorezm. 1314 **Boldïq-bahadïr?** [بهادر] بلدق المغلى [الامير] (Dawād. 274).

BOLDÏN Kuman 1347 **Boldïn** [Bolden filius Yamulo], from the Kumans in Hungary (Gyárfás III, 484).

BOLDUZ Uyg. 12th c.-14th c. **Bolduz?** (Radl., USp. 1).

BOLГA Kzk. 19th c. **Bolγa-bay** [Туткабай Болгабаевъ] (SKSO III, 20). ✧ 'Mix (it)' cf. *bulγa-* 'mischen, vermischen etc.' (Radl. IV, 1847).

BOLГARA Trkm. 1859 **Bolγara** [Болгара], a runner (ZIRGOÊtn. I, 188).

BOLÏ-QARAY Kzk. 1864 **Bolï-qaray** [Боли-Карай], a manap (Valihanov, Soč. 512). ⇨ **QARAY?**

BOLÏQ Kzk. 18th c. - 19th c. **Bolïq** [بولق / Болыкъ], mentioned in a song (ZOOIRGO III, 301).

BOLÏQ-TOLÏQ Kzk. 19th c. **Bolïq-tolïq**, from the Middle Horde (Orta Žüz) (Ljutš 128). ⇨ **BOLÏQ.**

BOLÏM see **BOLUM**

BOLÏS see **BOLÏŠ**

BOLÏŠ Kzk. 19th c. **Bolïs-pek** [Болыспекъ] (SOV 66); Tat.(Lit.) 1592 **Bolïš** [Кансуба Болишевичъ] (Lit. Tat. 123); Uzb. 20th c. **Bolïš** [Бўлиш] (Begmatov 1984, 201); Uzb. 20th c. **Bolïš-bây** [Бўлишбой] (Begmatov 1984, 201). ✧ I. 'Help(!), support(!)'; 'God (will) help; the child will be living' (Begmatov), cf. Kuman, Chag., Kar. *boluš-*, Kzk., Kar. *bolus-* 'helfen, beistehen' (Radl. IV, 1672), Uzb. *boliš* 'помогать; поддерживать (кого-л.)' (UzbRS); II. 'Helping, supporting; helper, supporter' cf. Kzk. *bolŭs* 'die Hülfe' (Radl. IV, 1671).

BOLQON Kzk. 19th c. **Bolqom-bay (<Bolqon-bay?)** [Болкомбай] (SOK 50). ✧ I. 'A kind of silk'? cf. Kzk.

bulqun 'ein Seidenstoff' (Radl. IV, 1847); II. 'Sable'? cf. Kzk. *bulğın* 'samur' (KzTS).

BOLLOT Yak. **Bollot** [Боллот] (Pek.).

BOLOJUMAR Yak. **Bolojumar** [Болоцумар] (Pek.). ✧ Vladimir (R.).

BOLOM-BAY see **BOLUM**

BOLOT see **BULAT**

BOLOTOY-OXXON Yak. **Bolotoy-oχχon / Molotoy-orχon** [Болотоі Оххон, Молотоі Орхон], one of Ällä's four (six?) sons (Pek.).

BOLPAČ? Kzk. 1822 **Bolpač? / Bolpas?** [بولپاچ / Болпас] (MIK IV, 384, 386). ⇨ **BOLPAŠ, PULPAČ?**

BOLPAŠ Kzk. 19th c. **Bolpaš** [Болпашъ] (SOK 232); Kzk. 1822 **Pulpač** [Бармак Пулпачев] (MIK IV, 414).

BOLPÏQ Kzk. 19th c. **Bolpïq** [Болпыкъ] (SOK 266); Kzk. 19th c. **Bolpïq** [Больпыкъ] (SOV 156).

BOLSÏN Kzk. 19th c. **Bolsun** [Сирибай Болсуновъ] (Grod., Pril. 158); Kzk. 1877 **Bolsun** [Ходжа Гельдибай Болсуновъ] (Grod., Pril. 129). ✧ 'Let him/her be/become'. A frequent part (component) of compound names mainly expressing the parents' wish for the child's future. See also **BAY-BOLSÏN, BEK-BOLSÏN, BEL-BOLSÏN, ČAL-BOSUN, JAN-BOLSUN, DOS-BOSUN, EL-BOLSÏN, ER-BOLSUN, EŠ-BOLSÏN, KÖK-BOLSUN, QUTLUQ-BULSUN, MOL-BOSÏN, UL-BOLSÏN.**

BOLSUN see **BOLSÏN**

BOLTAY see **BALTAY**

BOLTOX Yak. **Boltoχ / Bottoχ** [Болтох, Боттох] (Pek.). ✧ 'Having bulging eyes' cf. Yak. *boltoi* 'выпячиваться, вспучиваться' (Pek.).

BOLTOY Yak. **Boltoy** [Долгуибат Болтоі], byname of a „prince" (Pek.). ✧ 'Having bulging eyes' cf. Yak. *boltoi* 'выпячиваться, вспучиваться' (Pek.). ⇨ **BOLTOX.**

BOLTOÑO Yak. **Boltoño** [Болтоңо], one of the forefathers of the Yakuts from the ulus of Boturus (Pek.). ⇨ **BÖLTÖÑO?, ÜRÜÑ-BAS-BOLTOÑO.**

BOLUČ Karakh. 11th c. **Boluč** [Boluç] (DTS, MK/Atalay 834). ✧ 'Existence, being' (Bese 13). ⇨ **BOL** + suff. *-uč.*

BOLUQČÏ Uyg. 12th c.-14th c. **Boluqčï** (DTS).

BOLUM Kzk. 19th c. **Bolïm** [Болымъ] (SOK 266); Kzk. 19th c. **Bolom-bay** [Боломбай] (SODž. 32); Kzk. 19th c. **Bolum-bek** [Болумбекъ] (SODž. 44, 124). ✧ 'Strength, power' cf. Kzk. *bolŭm* 'das Vermögen, die Gewalt, die Macht' (Radl. IV, 1672), Tat. *bolum* 'мочь, сила' (PRS).

BOLUN see **BULUN**

BOLUŠČÏ Khazar 10th c. **Bolušči** [Boluščı], a commander of the army (Golden 167). ✧ 'Helper'? cf. Tat. *bulišŭči* 'der Gehilfe' (Radl. IV, 1843).

BOLUŠTOP Alt. 19th-20th c. **Boluštop** [Болуштоп]

(OjrRS 208). ✧ 'Brandy-bottle (holding half a litre)' cf. R. *poluštof* (полуштоф) (OjrRS 208).

BONA Kzk. 19th c. **Bona-pay** [Бонапай] (SOK 162).

BONDOQDAR Maml.? 13th c. **Bondoqdar**, byname of Sultan Baybars I (1260-1277) (RaD/Quatrem. 358-59). ✧ Placename.

BONSUZ see **MUÑSUZ**

BOP-AL Kzk. 19th c. **Bop-al** [Бопалъ] (SOK 48). ✧ 'Lead a moral life'? Cf. Kzk. *bop* 'нрав, вкус, церемония, чванство' (PRS); Kzk. *bop* 'der Pope, der Priester' (Radl. IV, 1691), Kzk. *bop=bolŭp* (SOK 48). ⇨ **AL.**

BOPA see **BAPA**

BOPAW Kzk. 19th c. **Bopaw / Bapaw?** [Бопау] (SOK 168).

BOPO see **BAPA**

BORA Kzk. 19th c. **Bora** [Бора Сиксеновъ] (Pam. kn. Turg. 71); Kzk. 19th c. **Bora-bay** [Борабай] (Grod., Pril. 178); Kzk. 19th c. **Boro** [Боро] (AOP 102); Hak. 19th-20th c. **Pora** [Пора] (HRS 351); Hak.(Sag.) **Pora** [Пора богатырь] (Proben IX, 242); Karg. **Pora** [Пора], fem. (Katanov, Otč. 9). ✧ 'Grey, bluish grey' (Katanov, Otč. 9), cf. Hak. *pora* 'сивый, серый (масть лошади)' (HRS). See also **KÖK, SÏPÏY.**

BORA-ГAZÏ-GÏREY Crm.Tat. 1587-1596 **Bora-γazi-girey**, a khan in the Crimea (?). ⇨ **BORA** + **ГAZÏ** + **KERÄY.**

BORAY Chuv. 18th-19th c. **Boray** [Борай] (Magn. 34). ✧ 'A sort of wheat' cf. Tat. *boray* 'полба' (Triticum spelta) (TatRS).

BORAQ Khorezm.? 13th c. **Boraq** [Борак] (RaD I/1, 94, 98); Kzk. 19th c. **Boraq-pay / Buraq-pay?** [Боракпай] (SOV 108). ⇨ **BURAQ.** See also **QOÑUR-BORAQ.**

BORAL Kzk. 19th c. **Boral-bay** [Боралбай] (SOV 78).

BORALÏ Kzk. 19th c. **Boralï** [Боралы] (SOK 256). ✧ 'Mat'? cf. Chag. *bora* 'die Matte' (Radl. IV, 1662). + suff. *-lï.*

BORAN see **BURAN**

BORBAQAY Alt. 19th c. **Borbaqay-qan** [Борбакай-канъ] (Potanin IV, 559). ⇨ **BORBOQ?** + suff. *-ay.*

BORBO see **BORBUY**

BORBOQ Alt. 19th-20th c. **Borboq** [Борбок], fem. (OjrRS 211). ✧ 'Chubby, plump-cheeked' (R. 'пухленькая', OjrRS 211).

BORBON Alt. 19th-20th c. **Borbon** [Борбон] (OjrRS 208).

BORBUY Alt. 19th-20th c. **Borbo / Borbuy** [Борбо, Борбуй] (OjrRS 208); Alt. 19th-20th c. **Borbuy** [Борбуй] (OjrRS 208). ✧ 'Hide, pelt, fur' ('кожаный мех' OjrRS 208); cf. Alt. *borbuy* 'бурдюк; коробочка из высушенного коровьего вымени' (OjrRS).

BORJAQ Trkm. 20th c. **Borjaq** [Borğaq] (Zaj. 1971,

332); Trkm. 20th c. **Bŏrǰaq** [Борджак] (TrkmRS 111). ✧ 'Steppe raspberry (ephedra)' cf. Trkm. *bŏrǰaq* 'эфедра' (TrkmRS).

BORDÏKEY Bashk. 1737 **Bordïkey** [Бордыкей Минлигулов] (MIB III, 364, 365).

BORDÏN Kzk. 19th c. **Bordïn-bay** [Бордынбай] (AOP 94).

BORDU Kzk. 19th c. **Bordu-ɣul** [Бордугулъ] (SOV 12).

BORƔANA Kzk. 1820 **Borɣana-batïr** [Боргана батыръ], one of the chiefs of the Bay-baqtï tribe of the Little Horde (Kiši Žüz) (Sib. Vest. IX, 119).

BORLAQ Karch. **Borlaq** [Борлаковъ], family name (Sysoev 135).

BORLÏ see **BORLU**

BORLU Tat. 1543 **Borlu** (Gökb., Rum. 242); Kzk. 19th c. **Borlu** [Борлу] (SOV 38); Oghuz/Trkm. 14th c.-15th c. **Burla-χatun** / **Borlï-χatun** / **Burlï-χatun** [اوزون بويلو بورلى خاتون / بورلى خاتون] / Borlï Hātūn / boyı uzın Burla Hatun / Бурла-катун, Бурла-хатун], Qazan-beg's wife (fem.) (DQorq./Rossi 123, 131, 139-43, 152, 159, Manuscr. Vat. [Facs.] 87, DQorq./Ergin 96, DQorq. 23 etc.); Kzk. 19th c. **Burlï-bay** [Бурлибай] (SOV 114); Uzb. 19th c. **Burlï-bay** [Бурлибай] (TV 1878, 144); Kzk. 19th c. **Burlu-bay** [Бурлубай Кадырбаевъ] (Grod., Pril. 83). ✧ I. 'Mouse-grey' cf. Tat. *burlï* 'mäuserfarben' (Radl. IV, 1830); II. 'Chalky'? cf. Kzk. *borlŭ* 'von Kreide, mit Kreide' (Radl. IV, 1665). ⇨ **BUR?** + suff. *-lï*.

BORLUQ Uyg. 13th-14th c. **Borluq-čor** (Zieme, Mat. II, 84). ✧ 'Vineyard' cf. Uyg. *borluq* 'виноградник' (DTS).

BORLUQČÏ Uyg. 12th c.-14th c. **Borluqčï** [Borlukçı] (Radl., USp. 24-25, 89, DTS, EUTS). ✧ 'Gardener, vine-grower' cf. Uyg. *borluqčï* 'bağçivan' (US), Uyg. *borluqčï* 'виноградарь' (DTS).

BORNU-BAS Kzk. 19th c. **Bornu-bas** [Барнубасъ] (SOV 40). ⇨ **BURUN + BAS II. / BAŠ?**

BORO Hak. 19th-20th c. **Boro-qan** [Бороканъ] (Titov 214). ✧ 'Bluish grey' (Titov 214).

BOROQUOPAY Yak. **Boroquopay** [Борокуопаі] (Pek.); Yak. **Boropuoqay** [Боропуокаі] (Pek.). ✧ Prokopiy (R.).

BOROLDAY see **BURULDAY**

BOROLƔAY-QU Kirg. 19th c. **Borolɣay-qu** [Боролгай-ку] (Potanin II, 171). ⇨ **QU.**

BORONTAY Maml. 1300 **Borontay** (Makrīzī IV, 142, Weil, Chalif. I, 227). ⇨ **BURUN?** + **TAY?** or suff. *-tay(1,2)*?

BOROŇOT Alt. 19th-20th c. **Boroňot** / **Boroň-ot?**, fem. (OjrRS 211). ✧ 'Blackcurrant' cf. Alt. *boroňot* 'черная смородина' (OjrRS). See also **QARA-QAT**.

BOROPUOQAY see **BOROQUOPAY**

BOROS Alt. 19th-20th c. **Boros** [Борос], fem. (OjrRS 211). ✧ Praskov'ya? (R.).

BOROŠ Alt. 19th-20th c. **Boroš** [Борош], fem. (OjrRS 211). ✧ Praskov'ya (R.).

BOROZOQ Alt. 19th-20th c. **Borozoq** [Борозок] (OjrRS 208). ✧ 'Greyish' (OjrRS 208). ⇨ **BORO.**

BORSOQ see **BORSUQ**

BORSUQ Kzk. 19th c. **Barsuq** [Барсукъ] (AOP 98); Alt. 19th-20th c. **Borsoq** [Борсок], fem. (OjrRS 211); Selj. **Borsuq** [برسق], an emir (Bondārī 70, 156 etc.); Selj.? **Borsuq** [قطب الدين برسق] (Zehireddin /Dorn 250); Selj.? 11th c. **Borsuq** [Προσούχ], a Turkic chieftain (ca. 1080) (Byz. Turc. II, 257); Selj. 11th c. **Borsuq**, one of Melik-šaχ's (1072-1092) followers (slaves) (Ahbar 49); Selj. 1060 **Borsuq** [برسق], an emir (Ibn al-Athīr/Tornb. X, 6, 97, 106 etc.); Selj. 1082 **Borsuq** [Bûrsûk], one of Melik Shah's emirs (Abulfar./Budge I, 227); Selj. 1094/95, 1099 **Borsuq** [برسق], one of Berkyaruq's emirs (Ibn al-Athīr, Atab.: RHCHor II/2, 28, Qazw. 452); Selj.? 1101 **Borsuq** [البكى بن برسق], El-begi's father (Ibn al-Athīr/Tornb. X, 205, 227); Selj.? 1103, 1111 **Borsuq** [اسباسلار برسق بن برسق / برسق بن برسق], ruler of Hammadān? (Iyās X, 243, 356-358, Usāma 54, 56, Qalānisi 174); Selj. 1108/09 **Borsuq** [برسق], chief commander (Ibn al-Athīr/Tornb. I, 258); Selj.? 1134/35 **Borsuq** [برسق بن برسق صاحب خوزستان], ruler of Khuzistān (Ibn al-Athīr, Atab.: RHCHor II/2, 88-89); Selj.? 12th c. **Borsuq** [Προσούχ], a Byzantine chieftain of Turkic [Seljuk?] origin (ca. 1150) (Byz. Turc. II, 257); Kzk. 19th c. **Borsuq** [Жолум Борсуковъ] (Pam. kn. Turg. 69); Selj. 1094-1104 **Borsuq** / **Borsaq?** / **Bursaq?** [اسفهسلار برسق], emir under Berk-yaruq (1094-1104) (RaD/Erdmann 804-805, Rāwandī 145); Kzk. 19th c. **Borsuq-pay** [Борсукпай] (SOK 42); Kzk. 19th c. **Bursïq** [Джаркумбай Бурсиковъ] (Grod., Pril. 106, 112). ✧ 'Badger, brock (Meles vulgaris)' cf. Kipch. *borsuq* (AH), Kzk., Tur. *borsuq* 'der Dachs' (Radl. IV, 1668), Kzk. *borsïq* 'барсук' (KzRS), Kzk. *borsuq* 'id.' (PRS), Tat. *bursïq* 'барсук' (Radl. IV, 1833), R. *barsuk* < Tat. *barsïq* (Šipova).

BORSUL Kzk. 19th c. **Borsul** [Бій Борсулъ] (Valihanov, Soč. 363).

BORSUN Kzk. 19th c. **Borsun** [Борсунъ] (SOK 40).

BORTA Bashk. 1732 **Borta** [Азик Бортин] (MIB III, 302, 304). ✧ 'Deer; draught-horse'? cf. Chag. *borta* 'der Hirsch; das Packpferd' (Radl. IV, 1665).

BORU Kuman 1509 **Boru** / **Boro?** [Valentino Boro], from the Kumans in Hungary (Gyárfás III, 728). ✧ '(Dark) grey' cf. Rásonyi, KÖA 95, Rásonyi: AOH 20(1967), 138.

BORUQ Kzk. 19th c. **Boruq-bay** [Борукбай] (AOP 102). ✧ 'Sheep (ewe)' cf. Kirg. *boruq* 'двухлетний валух' (Jud.). See also **AQ-BORUQ**.

BORULAQ Kzk. 19th c. **Borulaq** [Борулакъ] (AOAtb. 66). ⇨ **BOR + ULAQ?**

BORUOÑQA Yak. **Boruoñqa** [Боруоӈка] (Pek.). ✧ Pron'ka (R.), dim. from R. *Prokopiy*.

BOS see **BOZ**

BOS-PAL Kzk. 19th c. **Bos-pal** [Боспалъ] (SOK 214). ⇨ **BOZ + PAL?**

BOS-TANAY Bashk. 1710, 1711 **Bos-tanay** [Сатыш Бостанаев] (MIB III, 57, 68). ✧ 'Ash-coloured calf'. ⇨ **BOS + TANAY I.**

BOS-UL see **BOZ**

BOSÏN see **BOLSÏN**

BOSÕX Yak. **Bosōχ** [Босox] (Pek.).

BOSŠA see **BOZǦA**

BOSTAN Trkm. 20th c. **Bossan** [Bossan], fem. (Zaj. 1971, 339).

BOSSAN Trkm. 20th c. **Bossan** [Боссан], fem. (TrkmRS 111).

BOSTAN Karch. **Bostan** [Бостановъ], a family name (Sysoev 123, 128); Kzk. 19th c. **Bostan** [Бостанъ] (AOP 18); Kzk. 19th c. **Bostan** [Бостанъ] (SOV 32); Kzk. 19th c. **Bostan** [Бостанъ] (SOK 292); Kzk. 19th c. **Bostan** [Бостанъ] (AOO 2, 6, 10); Kzk. 19th c. **Bostan** [Бостанъ] (AOAtb. 62); Kzk. 19th c. **Bustan** [Бустановъ] (Grod., Pril. 146). ✧ 'Garden' cf. Chag., Turk. *bostan* 'der Garten, der Gemüsegarten' (Radl. IV, 1680-81); Trkm. *bossan* 'бахча; огород' (TrkmRS) (<P.). See also **OГUL-BOSSAN**.

BOSTÏ Kzk. 19th c. **Bostï-bay** [Бостыбай] (AOAtb. 58); Kzk. 1822 **Bostï-bay** / **Bostu-bay** [بوصدو باى / Тархан Бостыбай] (MIK IV, 432, 434); Kzk. 19th c. **Bostu-bay** [Бостубаевъ] (AOO 30); Kzk. 19th c. **Bostu-bay** [Бостубаевъ] (AOP 102).

BOSTU see **BOSTÏ**

BOSUN see **BOLSÏN**

BOSŪCAY Yak. **Bosūčay** [Босучаi] (Pek.).

BOSŪTA Yak. **Bosūta** [Босута] (Pek.). ✧ Vasyuta (R.)?

BOŠAN Kzk. 19th c. **Bošan** [Бошанъ] (AOA 38, 82); Kzk. 19th c. **Bošan** [Бошанъ] (SODž. 18); Kzk. 19th c. **Božan-bay** [Божанбай] (AOP 2). ✧ 'Separate; Be separated! Be free!' (Rásonyi, Imp. 239), cf. Kuman, East.T., Turk. *bošan-* 'sich befreien, frei werden, unabhängig werden, Kzk. *bosan-* 'sich entledigen, sich befreien, sich frei machen' (Radl. IV, 1679).

BOŠTAY Kzk. 19th c. **Boštay** [Боштай] (AOO 42). ✧ 'Free, independent'? cf. Kzk. PN *Boštay* (Žanuzakov-Esbaeva), Kar., Trkm., Turk., Uzb. *boš* 'leer; frei, lose, selbstständig' (Radl. IV, 1688). ⇨ **TAY?** or suff. *-tay(1,2)?*

BOŠTAL Kzk. 19th c. **Boštal** [Боштылъ] (SOK 216).

BOŠUQ Kzk. 19th c. **Bošuq** [Бошукъ] (AOP 22).

BOT Kzk. 19th c. **Bot-bay** [Турабъ Ботбаевъ] (Grod.,

Pril. 168); Kzk. 19th c. **Bot-pay** [Ботпай] (SOV 16); Kzk. 19th c. **Bot-pay** [Ботпай] (AOA 14); *EN:* Kzk. 18th c. - 19th c. **Bot-bay** [Ботбай] (Tynyšp. 65). ⇨ **BUT?**

BOTA Pecheneg 9th c. **Bota** [Βατᾱς / Βατᾱν?] (Byz. Turc. II, 87); Maml. **Bota** [بطا الخاصكى], in the days of Ebu-l-Fath (Iyās I, 73); Maml. 1382 **Bota** [بطا الاشرفى] (Iyās I, 257); Maml. 1389 **Bota** [بطا الطولوتمرى] (Iyās I, 279, 291); Maml. 1390 **Bota** [بطا الدر وا دار] (Iyās I, 293); Trkm.? 1403 **Bota** / **Bütä?** [بوته], an emir (Dorn 185); Kzk. 1817 **Bota-bay** [بوطه باى] (MIK IV, 308); Kzk. **Bota-qan** [Бота Кан] (Proben III, 69 /90/); Kzk. 19th c. **Bota-qan** [Ботаканъ] (SOV 12); Kirg. 19th c. **Botu-bay** [Ботубай] (Potanin II, 5); Kzk. 19th c. **Buta** [Бута Караевъ] (Grod., Pril. 73); Kirg. 19th c. **Buta** [Букбасырбай Бутинъ] (Grod., Pril. 15, 80); Uzb. 1868 **Buta** [Мулла-Бай Бута] (Moskal'cev 54); Kzk. 19th c. **Buta-bay** [Иса Бутабаевъ] (Grod., Pril. 55); Kzk. 19th c. **Buta-bay** [Бутабай] (Grod., Pril. 196); Kzk. 19th c. **Buta-bay** [Бекъ Берди Бутабаевъ] (Grod., Pril. 162); Kzk. 19th c. **Buta-bay** [Бутабай] (SODž. 124); Uzb. 19th c. **Buta-bay** [Бутабай Умарбаевъ] (Sr. Az. I, 1896, Avg. 17); Uzb. 1854 **Buta-bay** [Бутабай] (Moskal'cev 42); Kzk. 19th c. **Buta-bek** [Бутабекъ Сатубалдіевъ] (SKSO VIII, 221); Kzk. 19th c. **Buta-bek** [Бутабекъ Тайляковъ] (SKSO VIII, 201); Kzk. 19th c. **Buta-bek** [Бутабекъ Тайчиновъ] (SKSO III, 18); Kzk. 19th c. **Buta-yar** [Бутаяровъ] (SKSO VIII, 207); Kzk. 19th c. **Buta-yār** [Джуманъ Бутаяровъ] (SKSO III, 20); Kzk. 19th c. **Buta-qul** [Бутакуловъ] (SKSO VIII, 223). ✧ 'Camel, a new-born foal of a camel; (fig.) darling' cf. Chag., East.T., Kzk. *bota* 'ein neugeborenes Kameel, ein Kameeljunges im ersten Jahre' (Radl. IV, 1675), Kirg. *boto* 'id.' (Jud.), Kzk. *Bota-qïs* may be interpreted as 'camel-foal-girl, (fig.) nice girl'; cf. also Sauvaget 42. See also **AY-BUTA, AQ-BOTA, ALA-BOTA, ALİ-BUTA, BAY-BOTA, BEK-BOTA, ǦAN-BOTA, İR-BUTA, İŠ-BUTA, QAN-BUTA, QARA-BUTA, MULLA-BUTA, NAR-BOTA, NUR-BOTA, ON-BOTA, OÑAR-BAY-BUTA.**

BOTAГA Kzk. 19th c. **Botaγa** [Ботага] (Potanin II, 3).

BOTAY Kzk. 19th c. **Boday-bay** [Бодайбай] (SODž. 150); Kzk. 1823 **Botay-biy** [بوطابى / Ботай бий] (MIK IV, 458, 462). ✧ I. 'Little/young camel; (fig.) my darling'; II. 'Short; of short height'? cf. Chag. *boday* 'kurz von Gestalt; ein Gesang der Ösbeken' (Radl. IV, 1677). ⇨ **BOTA** + dim. suff. *-y*. See also **BOTAŠ.**

BOTAM Kzk. **Botam-bay** / **Botan-bay?** [Ботамбай] (Konšin, Oč. 76). ✧ 'My darling'? ⇨ **BOTA** + poss. suff. *-m*.

BOTAN-TAY Kzk. 19th c. **Botan-tay** [Ботантай]

(SODž. 28). ✦ '?' cf. Kzk. PNs *Botan, Botan-bek* (Žanuzakov-Esbaeva). ⇨ **TAY** or suff. *-tay(1,2)?*

BOTASUN Uyg. 12th c.-14th c. **Botasun** (DTS).

BOTAŠ Balk. 20th c. **Botašlarï** (<**Botaš**) [Botašlarï], a family name (Pröhle, Balk. 211); Kzk. 19th c. **Butaš** [Буташъ Халмирзаевъ] (SKSO VIII, 220); Kzk. 19th c. **Butaš** [Буташевъ] (SKSO VIII, 220); Kzk. 19th c. **Butaš** [Буташевъ] (Grod., Pril. 25). ✦ 'Little/young camel-foal; (fig.) my darling'. ⇨ **BOTA** + dim. suff. *-š*. See also **BOTAY**.

BOTČA Karch. **Botča / Botčay?** [Ботчаевъ] (Sysoev 131). ⇨ **BOT** + dim. suff. *-ča?*

BOTÏ Kzk. 19th c. **Botï-bay** [Батыбай] (SOV 60).

BOTÏ-BÖK-TAQDÏ Uyg. 12th c. - 14th c. **Botï-bök-taqdï** [botï bök taqdï] (DTS). ⇨ **BOTÏ** +?

BOTÏ-BÖK-TOQTÏ see **BOTÏ-BÖK-TAQDÏ**
Uyg. 12th c.-14th c. **Er-butï-bük-toγdï / Botï-bök-toqtï?** (Radl., USp. 128).

BOTÏΓAY Kzk. 19th c. **Botïγay** [Ботыгай] (AOO 66). ⇨ **BOTÏ** + suff. *-qay.*

BOTQA Kzk. 19th c. **Botqo-bay** (<**Botqa-bay?**) [Боткобай] (SOK 10). ✦ 'Pulp, squash' cf. Kzk. *botqa* 'gekochte Grütze' (Radl. IV, 1676).

BOTQAY Kzk. 19th c. **Botqay** [Боткай] (SOV 110). ⇨ **BOT / BOTQA?** + suff. *-qay / -y.*

BOTQAT Kzk. 19th c. **Botqat** [Боткатъ] (SOK 22). ⇨ **BAYQAT.**

BOTTÏQ Kzk. 19th c. **Bottïq** [Боттыкъ] (AOO 2).

BOTTOX Yak. **Bottoχ / Boltoχ** [Боттох, Болтох] (Pek.).

BOTU-BAY see **BOTA**

BOZ Kzk. 1794 **Bos-bay** [بوسباى / Босбай] (MIK IV, 162); Kzk. **Bos-Jigit** [Bos Dschigit / Бос џигіт] (Proben III, 336 /408/); Kzk. 19th c. **Bos-Jigit** [Босджигитъ] (AOP 2); Kzk. 1794 **Bos-qul** [Боскулъ] (AOAtb. 34); Kirg. **Bos-ül** [Bos-Ul / бос ул] (Proben V, 151 /153/); Yürük 16th c. **Boz** [بوز], from Kocacık, Turkey (Gökb., Rum. 102); Kzk. 19th c. **Boz** [Бозъ] (SOK 54); 1137/38 **Boz-aba** [بوزابه], ruler (lord) of Huzistan (Ibn al-Athīr, Atab.: RHCHor II/2, 98); 12th c. **Boz-aba** [بوزابه] (Süssheim); Selj. **Boz-aba** [بوزابه] (Aqsar./Iş. 36); Selj. **Boz-aba** [بوزابه] (Bondārī 170, 218-220); Selj. 1137 **Boz-aba** [بوزابه], an emir, rival of Sultan Mesᶜud, died in 1149 (Ahbar 77, 86); Selj. 1142 **Boz-aba** [بوز ا به], an emir (Iyās XI, 39-40, 77-78); Selj.? 1148 **Boz-aba** [بوزبه / بوز ا به] (Qalānisi 294); Selj. 1185 **Boz-aba** [بوزابه], emir Taqi ad-Dīn's mamluk (gulām?) (Iyās XI, 342, 345); Selj. 1186 **Boz-aba** [Bûzabâh], Salaheddin's man (Abulfar./Budge I, 320 (facsim. 369)); **Boz-bey** (Giese 62, 74); Yürük **Boz-bey**, in the legend of origin of the Yürüks from Horzum (Ün II, (1935), 245); Kzk. 19th c. **Boz-Jigit**

[Боздджигитъ] (AOO 6); Kzk. 19th c. **Boz-mïrza** [Бозмрза] (SODž. 108); Kzk.? 19th c. **Boz-oγlan** [بوز اوغلان احمد بيك] (AUK Dobavl. 1); Kirg. **Boz-ül** [Бозуул] (Jud. 350, 896); Chuv. 1737 **Pos-čura** [Посчурину] (Alatyr. 135). ✦ I. 'Grey; ash-coloured' cf. Türk, Chag., Az., Crm., Kzk., Trkm., Uzb. *boz* 'grau, aschgrau, bleich' (Radl. IV, 1681); II. 'Young, new' cf. Kzk. *boz bala* 'молодой паренек' (Žanuzakov 110), Bashk. PN *Buð-yeget* (Kusimova), Kzk. PNs *Boz-žan, Boz-žigit, Boz-tay* (Žanuzakov-Esbaeva). See also **AQ-BOZ, ATAY-BOZ, BAY-BOZ, BAZAR-BOS, ĴAN-BOZ, KÖR-BOZ, QAMBAR-BOZ, QARÏ-BOZ, NUR-BOZ.**

BOZ-AY see **BOZAY**

BOZ-BOΓAN Turk. 1348 **Boz-boγan** [Ποσβογάνης], from the region of Trapezunt, Turkey (A. Hahanov, Hronika Mihaila Panareta 7). ⇨ **BOZ.**

BOZ-ČOLOQ Kirg. **Bos-čoloq** [Бос-чолок], one of Manas' comrades-in-arms [čoro] in the Manas epic (Proben V, 39 /40/). ✦ 'Grey curt, grey short-tailed, (fig.) wolf' cf. *čoloq* 'однорукий или одноногий; безрукий или безногий; с отрезанной часть[руки или ноги; куцый; кургузый' (Jud.). ⇨ **BOZ + ČOLAQ.**

BOZ-DOΓAN 1395 **Boz-doγan** [بوزطوغان] (Astarab 475); Turk.? 1348 **Boz-doγan** [Ποσδογάνης], a Turkish chieftain (Byz. Turc. II, 256). ✦ 'Grey Falcon'. ⇨ **BOZ + TOΓAN.**

BOZ-QARA Kzk. 19th c. **Bos-qara** [Боскара] (AOO 30). ⇨ **BOZ + QARA.**

BOZ-QOYUNLU Trkm. 1690 **Boz-qoyunlu** [بوزقيونلو / Bozkoyunlu Ahmed] (Refik, Anad. 84). ⇨ **BOZ + QOYUNLU.**

BOZ-QURT Turk. 1480 **Boz-qurt** [Bozqurd ibn Sulaïman] (Zambaur 158, 159). ✦ 'Grey wolf'. ⇨ **BOZ + QURT.**

BOZ-QUŠ Maml. 14th c. **Boz-γuš** [بزغش / Bozγuš] (Tarĵ/Houtsma 64, Tarĵ/Toparlı 41); Selj.? 1107/08 **Boz-quš** [بزغش], „prince de Hilla" (Ibn al-Athīr: RHCHor I, 251); Maml. 14th c. **Boz-quš** [بزقوش / Bozkuš] (Tarĵ/Houtsma 64, Tarĵ/Toparlı 41); Turk. 1287 **Boz-quš-bahadur** [Bozkuş Bahadur], commander of Germiyan's army (Uzunçarş., Anad. 36). ✦ 'Grey bird'. ⇨ **BOZ + QUŠ I.**

BOZ-MONAY Kzk. **Boz-monay** [Боз Монаи] (Proben III, 168 /207/). ✦ 'Grey oil?' cf. Kzk. *munay* 'нефть' (KzRS). ⇨ **BOZ?**

BOZ-ÖLEK Kzk. **Boz-ölek** (IOAIÊK XV, 319-20). ✦ 'Grey(ish) dead' cf. Uyg. *öläk* 'der Todte' (Radl. I, 1246). ⇨ **BOZ.**

BOZ-PAS Kzk. 19th c. **Boz-pas** [Бозпасъ] (AOAtb. 50). ✦ 'Grey head'. ⇨ **BOZ + BAŠ.**

BOZ-TAY Kzk. 19th c. **Bos-tay** [Бостай] (SODž. 66,

128). ✧ 'Grey Foal' cf. Kzk. PN *Boztay* (Žanuzakov-Esbaeva). ⇨ **BOZ + TAY** or suff. *-tay(1,2)*?

BOZ-TAYLAQ   Kzk. 19th c. **Boz-taylaq** [Бозтайлакъ / Бозтайлякъ] (SODž. 118). ✧ 'Grey male camel'. ⇨ **BOZ + TAYLAQ.**

BOZ-TEREK   Kzk. 19th c. **Bos-terek** [Бостерекъ] (SOV 62). ⇨ **BOZ + TERÄK.**

BOZAĠAN   Trkm. 20th c. **Bozaɣan** [Bozagan] (Zaj. 1971, 332); Trkm. 20th c. **Bozaɣan** [Бозаган] (TrkmRS 108). ✧ 'Wormwood (Artemisia absinthium), vermouth' (Zaj. 1971), cf. Trkm. *bozaɣan* 'полынь сантолинолистая' (TrkmRS).

BOZAҮ   Kzk. 19th c. **Bozay / Boz-ay?** [Бозай] (AOK 46, 70); Kzk. 19th c. **Bozay / Boz-ay?** [Бозай] (AOA 98); Kzk. 19th c. **Bozay / Boz-ay?** [Бозаемъ Туркэбаевымъ] (AUK 851); Kkalp. 1740 **Buzay-bi** [Бузэй-би], from the Qoñrat tribe (MIKk. 208, Hanykov, Poezdka 19). ✧ I. 'Grey Moon'? II. 'Little Boza'? cf. Kzk. *boza* 'ein aus sauer Milch bereitetes Getränk; gekochte und gesäuerte Weizengrütze' (Radl. IV, 1683), Tat. *buza* 'ein aus Hirse bereitetes Getränk' (Radl. IV, 1867). ⇨ **BOZ + AY? / BOZA?** + dim. *-y.*

BOZAN   1086 **Bozan** [بزان], an emir (Ibn al-Athīr/Tornb. X, 97, 112, 149-52); 1086 **Bozan** [Amîr Bûzân], emir who was appointed chief of Edessa and Melitene (Abulfar./Budge I, 231); 1107 **Bozan** [بزان], an emir (Ibn al-Athīr/Tornb. X, 296, XI, 137); 1167/68 **Bozan** [بوزان], emir, the Turkic chieftain in „Sherizor" (Ibn al-Athīr, Atab.: RHCHor II/2, 242); Selj. 11th c. **Bozan**, ruler of Urfa, Turkey, the Mamluk of Melik-šah I (1072-1092) (Ahbar 50, 52); Selj.? 1085 **Bozan** [Πουζάνος], an emir (Byz. Turc. II, 256); Selj.? 1094/95 **Bozan** [بوزان], Bozan Nūraddīn, the governor of Ḥarrān and Edessa (Ibn al-Athīr, Atab.: RHCHor II/2, 28); Selj.? 1140, 1160 **Bozan** [مجاهدالدين بزان بن مامين ابو الفوارس] (Qalānisi 282, 304, 355); Selj.? 1149/50 **Bozan** [مجاهد الدين بزان] (Abū Šāma: RHCHor IV, 61, 63); Kzk. 1825 **Bozan** [بوزان] (MIK IV, 471, 476). ✧ 'Destroyer' cf. *bozan* 'der Verderber, Vernichter' (Radl. IV, 1683). ⇨ **BUZAN?**

BOZANAQ   Tat.(Lit.) 1554 **Bozanaq** [Бозанакъ] (Kn. Metriki Lit. 99). ⇨ **BOZAN** + suff. *-aq.*

BOZAR   Kzk. 19th c. **Bozar-bay** [Бозарбай] (SOK 82); Khazar 8th c. **Buzar / Buz-er?** [(I)buz(s)er Gliaban(r)], a qaɣan (Golden 182); Kzk. 19th c. **Buzar-bek** [Бузарбекъ] (SOK 14). ✧ 'Destroyer; he who will destroy (his enemy)' cf. Turk. *boz-* 'verderben, besiegen, vernichten' (Radl. IV, 1683), Kzk. *büz-* 'портить; разрушать; нарушать; ломать' (KzRS). See also **BOZAN; ES-POZAR.**

BOZČA see **BOZJA**

BOZJA   Kzk. 19th c. **Bossa** [Босша] (AOA 114); Kzk. 19th c. **Bozča** [Кодукъ Бозчаевъ] (Grod., Pril. 52); Kzk. 19th c. **Bozja** [Нурджай Бозджаевъ] (Grod., Pril. 24). ✧ I. 'Greyish' cf. Kzk. *bozša* 'серенький; белесенький' (KzRS), Turk. *bozja* 'ein wenig grau' (Radl. IV, 1687); II. 'A kind of (ash-coloured) bird' cf. *bozša* 'bir cins kuş' (KzTS). ⇨ **BOZ** + suff. *-ja.* See also **BURULDAY.**

BOZDOM   Kzk. 19th c. **Bozdom-bay** (<Bozdon-bay)? [Боздомбай], a field (AOAtb. 38).

BOZEK I.   Crm.(Tat.) 1507 **Bozek-baχšï**, from the Golden Horde (Vásáry 54).

BOZEK II.   Yak. 1679, 1680 **Bozek** [Мазара Бозековъ], a prince (DAI VIII, 5, 10, 244, 268).

BOZĠUNČU   Kirg. **Bozgunču** [Бозгунчу] (Jud. 481). ✧ 'Fugitive' (Jud. 481). ⇨ **BUSQUN** + suff. *-ču.*

BOZÏM-BEK see **BOZUN**

BOZÏN-BEK see **BOZUN**

BOZOQ see **BOZUQ**

BOZUQ   Oghuz/Trkm. 14th c.-15th c. **Bozoq / Bozuq?** (DQorq./Rossi 170); Bashk. 1728 **Bozuq** [Ешлик Бозюк] (MIB I, 128); Tat. 1506-1519 **Bozuq / Bozïq / Buzuq** [Бозюкъ (Бозекъ / Бузюкъ)], envoy from Kazan (PSRL VI, 246, 252, VIII, 247, 266, XXIII, 202); Tat. 1512 **Buzuq-baqšï** [Бузюкъ-Бакшы] (PSRL XIII, 14). ✧ 'Spoiled, perverse, corrupted' cf. *bozuq* 'verdorben, verderbt, zerstört, vernichtet' (Radl. IV, 1684), 'zerstört, verdorben, vernichtet, zerfallen, in Ruinen' (Radl. IV, 1868), Tat. *bozïq* 'испорченный, неисправный, дефектный' (TatRS).

BOZUM-BEK see **BOZUN**

BOZUN   Kzk. 19th c. **Bozïm-bek** (<Bozïn-bek) [Бозымбекъ] (SOK 262); Kzk. 19th c. **Bozum-bay** (<Bozun-bay) [Бозумбай] (SODž. 48, 94); Kzk. 19th c. **Bozum-bek** (<Bozun-bek) [Бозумбекъ] (SOK 192); Kzk. 19th c. **Bozum-bek** (<Bozun-bek) [Бозумбекъ] (SOV 96); Kzk. 19th c. **Bozun** [Бозунъ] (SOK 236); Kzk. 19th c. **Bozun** [Бозунъ] (SODž. 82); Kzk. 19th c. **Bozun?** [Бозуанъ] (SODž. 54).

BOŽAQAN   Kzk. 19th c. **Božaqan** [Божаканъ] (AOK 22).

BOŽALAW   Kzk. 19th c. **Božalaw** [Божалау] (SOK 34).

BOŽEY   Kzk. 19th c. **Božey** [Божей] (SODž. 108).

BOŽEKE   Kzk. 19th c. **Božeke** [Божеке] (SODž. 36).

BOŽİKEY   Kzk. 19th c. **Božikey** [Божикей] (AOAtb. 14).

BŌ   **Bō-χan** [Βώχανος] (Byz. Turc. II, 108).

BŌQUY   Yak. **Bōquy** [Бокуй] (Pek.). ✧ 'Bow, crouch!' cf. Yak. *bōquy-* 'сгибаться (о ногах), кланяться (приседая)' (Pek.).

BÖBİK see **BEBEK**

BÖDEN   Kzk. 19th c. **Böden / Bödene?** [Боденъ] (AOA 78). ⇨ **BÜDENE?**

BÖDÖ   Alt. 19th-20th c. **Bödö** [Бödö], fem. (OjrRS 211). ✧ Fedora (R.).

BÖDÖGÖY Yak. **Bödögöy** [Бöдöгöi] (Pek.).

BÖDÖN Alt. 19th-20th c. **Bödön / Bödöñ** [Бöдöн] (OjrRS 208). ✦ Fedor / Fyodor (cf. R. Фёдор).

BÖGÄ Karakh. 11th c. **Bögä-yavγusï** [bögä javγusï] (DTS). ✦ 'Hero, brave warrior, strong man; wrestler' cf. Karakh. *bögä / bökä* 'id.' (DTS) (<Mo.) *böke* 'id.' (TMEN II, No. 803). Used also as a component of male names.

BÖGÄ-BUDRAČ Karakh. 11th c. **Bögä-budrač / Bögä-buðrač** [bögä budrač / bögä buðrač] (DTS); Karakh. 11th c. **Bükä-budrač** (DTS). ✦ 'Hero-Budrač'. ⇨ **BÖGÄ + BUDRAČ**.

BÖGEM-BAY see **BÖGEN**

BÖGEN Kzk. 18th c. - 19th c. **Bögem-bay-batïr** (<Bögen-bay) [Богембай-батыр] (Tынуšр. 68). ✦ 'A kind of disease of horse-tail' cf. Kzk. *bögen* 'Atларıн (beygirin) kuyruğunda peydahlanan kaşınma hastalığı' (KzTS), Kzk. *bögen* 'выпадение волос из конского хвоста (болезнь)' (KzTS).

BÖGÜ Uyg. 8th c. **Bögü** [T(ä)ngri Bög[ü] T(ä)ngrikän] (Müller, Pfahl. 6); Uyg.? **Bögü-χaγan** (Müller: SBAW (1909), 729); Uyg. 759-780 **Bögü-χan / Bügü-χan / Bögü-qan** [tngri ilig bögü χan / bögü qan / Bögü ḫan], a ruler (759-780) who was also named as Bilgä-qaγan and under the rule of whom the Uygurs converted to Manichaeanism (762) (TT II, 412-13, Müller, Hofstaat 208-9, Müller, Uig. II, 95, DTS, EUTS); Uyg. 8th c. **Bögü-qaγan**, the Uyghur ruler Bögü-qan (759-780) (DTS). ✦ 'Wise' cf. Türk, Uyg., Karakh. *bögü* 'мудрый; мудрец' (DTS), Kuman *bügü* 'der Weise, der Prophet' (Radl., IV, 1882).

BÖGÜRDLEN Turk. 1544 **Bögürdlen** [Tezvids Bögürdlen], an „ulûfeci" (clerk/secretary of Janissary guards, or palace servants) from Pest, Hungary (Velics-Kamm. II, 32). ✦ 'Bramble, blackberry' cf. Turk. *böğürtlen* 'id.' (TED), *böyürtlen* 'der Himbeerstrauch, der Brombeerstrauch' (Radl. IV, 1697).

BÖYÖN Kirg. **Böyön-χan** [Бöйöн Кан] (Proben V, 1). ✦ 'Tarantula' cf. Kirg. *böyön, böyü, böö* 'тарантул, мизгирь', 'fasciiventris' (Jud.), Turk. *böjä, böyü* 'eine grosse blaue Fliege; die Tarantel' (Radl. IV, 1696).

BÖKČÄ Uyg. 12th c.-14th c. **Bökčä** [Bökçä] (DTS, EUTS).

BÖKEY Kzk. 19th c. **Bökey** [Бокей] (AOO 2); Kzk. 19th c. **Bökey** [Бокей] (SOK 194); Kirg. **Bököy** [Бөкөй] (Jud. 115); Kzk. 19th c. **Bükey** [Букей] (SOK 126); Kzk. 1749, 1801, 1810, 1818 **Bükey-sultan / Bükey-χan** [Букей-Султанъ / Букай-Салтанъ], khan (1749-1818) of the Inner (Little) Horde, Baraq-χan's son, the establisher of the Bukey Horde (PSZRI XXVI, 571-72, XXVII, 654, XXX, 435-38, Radl., Aus Sib. I, 199, MIK IV, 248, Levchine 297, Levšin II, 331). ✦ 'Man with great bodily strength, wrestler (dıminutive form)' cf. Chag., Tar. *bökä* 'der Starke, der Ringer; stark' (Radl. IV, 1693), Kirg. *bökö* 'силач, борец'

(Jud.), Alt. *bökö* 'силач, сильный' (OjrRS). ⇨ **BÖGÄ** + dim. suff. -*y*.

BÖKIŠ Kzk. 19th c. **Bökiš** [Бокишъ] (AOAtb. 30). ✦ 'Humped, hunchbacked, crooked'? cf. Kzk. *bükiš* 'kamburumsu' (KzTS).

BÖKÖN Kzk. **Bökön-bay** [Bökön Bai / Бöкöн Бai] (Proben III, 192 /232/). ✦ 'Antelope' cf. Kzk. *böken* 'id.' (KzRS), Kzk. *böken* 'bögü' (KzTS).

BÖLDIK Kzk. 19th c. **Böldik-pay** [Больдекпай] (SOV 156).

BÖLDIR Kuman 1521 **Böldir** [Stephano Bewlder], from the Kumans in Hungary (Gyárfás III, 754). ✦ 'Annihilate, destroy! (the enemy)' cf. Rásonyi, KÖA 95, Rásonyi: AOH 20(1967), 138; Chag., Turk., Tat., Kzk. *büldür-, böldör-* 'vernichten, zu Grunde richten' (Radl.). See also **JOY**.

BÖLEK Kzk. **Bölek-bay** [بولاکبای / Бöлекбай] (Syzdykov 354); Kkalp. 20th c. **Bölek-bay** [Бöлекбай] (KkRS 773); Kirg. **Bölök** [Bölök / Бöлöк], one of Manas' comrades-in-arms (Proben V, 40 /41/); Kirg. **Bölök-bay** [Бöлөкбай] (Jud. 199); Kzk. 19th c. **Bölük-bay** [Болюкбай] (AOA 2). ✦ 'Part, piece, share; gift; present' cf. Kkalp. *bölek* 'часть; отдел, раздел' (KkRS), Kzk. *bölek* 'часть; другой, особый' (KzRS), cf. Kirg. *bölök* 'часть; другой, не.тот, не тот' (Jud.), Kirg., Kzk. *bölök* 'ander, fremd; ein Mädchen (die sie später in ein anderes aul übersiedelt)' (Radl. IV,1701), Chag., Crm., Kzk., Turk. *bölük* 'der Theil, der Bezirk' (Radl. IV, 1701-02), Chag., East.T., Trkm., Uzb., Kar.(L.) *böläk* 'der Theil, das Geschenk', (Kar.) 'die Heerde' (Radl. IV, 1700). See also **ALQA-BÖLÜK?**

BÖLEK-SUP Tat.(Lit.) 1592 **Bölek-sup** [Тахтамишъ Болексуповичъ] (Lit. Tat. 124). ✦ 'Gift-?'. ⇨ **BÖLEK.**

BÖLEKEY Kzk. 1817 **Bölekey** [بولاکای / Болекей] (MIK IV, 312, 319). ⇨ **BÖLEK** + suff. -*ey*.

BÖLENDI Kzk. 19th c. **Bölendi** [Боленде] (AOAtb. 6). ✦ 'Broke away (from), segregated'? cf. East.T. *bölän-* 'sich trennen' (Radl. IV, 1701).

BÖLÖK see **BÖLEK**

BÖLTEŠ Kzk. 18th c. - 19th c. **Bölteš-biy** [Болтеш-бий] (Tынуšр. 66).

BÖLTÖÑÖ Yak. **Böltöñö** [Бöлтöҥö] (Pek.). ✦ 'With fat face' (Pek.); cf. Yak. *böltöi* 'представляться толстым, широким и выпуклым; выпучиваться' (Pek.).

BÖLTÜÖKÜ Yak. **Böltüökü** [Бöлтÿöкÿ] (Pek.). ✦ Derived from Yak. *böltöi* (Pek.).

BÖLTÜRÜK Kzk. 19th c. **Böltürük** [Больтурукъ] (SOK 282); Kirg. 20th c. **Böltürük** [Бöлтÿрÿк] (Kalilov 93). ✦ 'Wolf-cub' cf. Kzk. *böltürük* 'волченок' (PKRS).

BÖLÜK see **BÖLEK**

BÖÑÄK Uyg. 12th c.-14th c. **Böñäk** (DTS).

BÖRBÖLJÜN Kirg. **Börbölǰün** [Бөрбөлцүн], Kösqaman's son, Dörböljün's (!) brother (Proben V, 218 /220/).

BÖRGELTAY Kzk. 19th c. **Börgeltay** [Бėргельтай], Dombaul's son (Potanin, Pred. 47). ⇨ **TAY** or suff. -tay(1,2)?

BÖRGÖLTÖY Kzk. **Börgöltöy** [Бөргөлтӧi] (Proben III, 66 /86/).

BÖRİ Türk 7th-9th c. **Böri** [Böri] (ETY III, 53); Selj. 1091, 1094, 1101, 1130, 1131 **Böri** [بورى تاج الملوك بن طغـنكين], ruler of Antakya (Turkey) and Damascus died in 1132 (Qalānisi 120-127, Ibn al-Athīr/Tornb. I, 206, 393, 395, IbnTaghrīb. II, 388, 390, Weil, Chalif. I, 86, Kamāladdīn II, 245, 248, Ibn al-Athīr/Tornb. X, 135, 212, 479, XI, 3); Selj. 1139, 1154 **Böri** [أبق بن محمد بن بورى] (Kamāladdīn II, 273-74, 305); Selj. 12th c. **Böri** [شهاب الدين محمود بن تاج الملوك بورى بن طغـكين] (Usāma 74, 141); Selj. 1183 **Böri** [بورى بن ايوب تاج املوك], Saladin's brother, died at Haleb (Abulfidā IV, 58-59); Maml. 1294 **Böri** [بورى السلحدار] (Iyās I, 129); Maml. 1301 **Böri** [بورى] (Iyās I, 132); Maml. 1378/79 **Böri** [بورى الحلبى الاحمدى] (Iyās I, 242); Trkm. 20th c. **Böri** [Böri] (Zaj. 1971, 331); Kzk. 19th c. **Böri** [Бори Кулджановъ] (Grod., Pril. 44); NUyg. 19th c. **Böri** [بورى] (Le Coq, Namenl. 96); Kzk. 19th c. **Böri-bay** [Худай-Бергянъ Борибаевъ] (Grod., Pril. 136); Kzk. 19th c. **Böri-bay** [Борибай Киплатбаевъ] (Grod., Pril. 60); Kzk. 19th c. **Böri-bay** [Толабай Борибаевъ] (Grod., Pril. 119); Kzk. 19th c. **Böri-bay** [Борибай] (Grod., Pril. 107); Kzk. 19th c. **Böri-bay** [Елдибай Борибаевъ] (Grod., Pril. 19); Kzk. 19th c. **Böri-bay** [Борибай] (AOK 102); Kzk. 19th c. **Böri-bek** [Борибекъ] (Grod., Pril. 25); Kzk. 19th c. **Böri-bek** [Чункишъ Борибековъ] (Grod., Pril. 97); Kzk. 19th c. **Böri-bek** [Борибекъ] (Grod., Pril. 25); Kzk. 19th c. **Böri-bek** [Уркунбекъ Борибековъ] (Grod., Pril. 173); Kzk. 19th c. **Böri-qul** [Борикулъ] (Grod., Pril. 25); Bulg. 9th c. **Böri-tarχan** / **Böri-tegin** [Βοριτάκανος / Βοριτακάνος], a Bulgar commander of Belgrad (ca. 853-888) (Byz. Turc. II, 97); Kzk. 19th c. **Börü** [Бору] (SODž. 22); Kirg. 20th c. **Börü** [Бөрү] (Kalilov 93); Kzk. 19th c. **Börü-bay** [Брубай] (AOAtb. 42); Kzk. 1794 **Börü-bay-bi** [بورباى بى] (MIK IV, 159); Trkm. 20th c. **Böri** [Бори] (TrkmRS 115); Bashk. 1723 **Büre** [Бюря Тойгильдин] (MIB III, 209); Bashk. 1771 **Büri** [Елдаш Буриев] (MIB IV/1, 358); Kzk. 19th c. **Büri-bay** [Борибай Камбаровъ] (SKSO VIII, 204); Kzk. 19th c. **Büri-bay** [Бурибаевъ] (SKSO II, 14); Kzk. 19th c. **Büri-bay** [Бурыбай] (Grod., Pril. 78); Uzb.?

1821 **Büri-bay** [Бури-бай], from the Kitay-kipchak tribe (Ivanov, Vosstanie 69); Uzb. 19th c. **Büri-bay** [Бури-бай] (SKSO III, 164, 170); Uzb. 1704 **Büri-bi** [بورى بى قطغان], from the Qataɣan tribe in Bukhara (Buchari 273); Bashk. 1635 **Büri-mirza** [بورى ميرزا] (Vel.-Zern., Bašk. 129, 159); Kirg. 1762 **Büri-saltan** [Бури салтан] (MIKk. 225); Tat.(Sib.) **Büri-χān** [Büri Chan / Бÿpi хан] (Proben IV, 190 /235/). ✧ 'Wolf' cf. Türk., Chag., East.T., NUyg.(Tar.), Trkm. *böri* 'der Wolf' (Radl. IV, 1698), Trkm. *b̄öri* 'волк' (TrkmRS), Uzb. *böri* 'волк' (UzbRS), cf. Bashk. *büre* 'волк' (BRS), Hak.(Sag.), Shor *pürü* 'der Wolf' (Radl. IV, 1397). See also **AQ-PÖRİ**, **ALP-BÖRÜ**, **BAY-BÖRÜ**, **ČOČİ-BÖRİ**, **ČOČUQ-BÖRİ**, **ER-BÖRİ**, **YAW-BÜRİ**, **KÖK-BÖRİ**, **QÏZÏL-BÖRİ**.

BÖRİ-BARS Selj. 1073 **Böri-bars** / **Büri-bars** [بورى بـرس] / Böri Bars / Бурибарс ибн Алп-Арслан], Alp-arslan's (1063-1072) son, Melik-šah's brother (Ibn al-Athīr/Tornb. X, 51, 179-80, Bondārī 85, 257, Ahbar 59-60, MIT I, 376, 382). ✧ 'Wolf-panther' (Németh, HMK 133). ⇨ **BÖRİ** + **BARS**.

BÖRİ-BEŠE 1518 **Böri-beše?** / **Böri-baša?** [بـرى با شا] (Iyās III, 184, 185). ⇨ **BÖRİ** + **BEŠE**.

BÖRİ-OYNAQ Kzk. 19th c. **Böri-oynaq** [Джолдибай Бори-Ойнаковъ] (Grod., Pril. 164). ⇨ **BÖRİ** + **OYNAQ**.

BÖRİ-TEMÜR **Böri-temür** [بورى تيمرر] (RaD/Blochet 15). ⇨ **BÖRİ** + **TEMİR**.

BÖRİM Kzk. 19th c. **Börim-bay** [Боримбай] (SODž. 82); Kzk. 19th c. **Börim-žan** [Бримжанъ] (SOK 212). ✧ 'My wolf'? ⇨ **BÖRİ** + poss. suff. -m.

BÖRKİ Kzk. 19th c. **Börki-bay** [Аджильди Боркибаевъ] (Grod., Pril. 154).

BÖRÖ-JÄSİK Yak. **Börö-ǰäsik** [Бӧрӧ Цäсiк], a deity (Pek.). ⇨ **BÖRİ**.

BÖRÖKÜYÄ Yak. **Böröküyä Bötös** [Бӧрӧкÿjä Бӧтӧс], a legendary bogatyr (Pek.).

BÖRT Uyg. 12th c. - 14th c. **Bört-bay** [bört baj] (DTS); Uyg. **Bürt** [Bürt] (EUTS). See also **QÏTAY-BÖRT**, **QUTADMÏŠ-BÖRT**, **QUTLUF-BÜRT**, **ÖRÄ-BÖRT**.

BÖRTE Kzk. 1823 **Börte-bay-bay** [بورته باى باى / Бортебайбай] (MIK IV, 458, 462). ✧ 'Börte (Chinggis' first wife)' (Mo.), cf. Temir 3; Ligeti, MTT, 66, 94, 99, etc.

BÖRTE-BAY-BAY see **BÖRTE**

BÖRÜ see **BÖRİ**

BÖRÜČÜ Kirg. **Börüčü** [Бөрÿчÿ], one of Manas' comrades-in-arms [čoro] in the Manas epic, Börü's son (Proben V, 184 /186/). ✧ 'Little Wolf'. ⇨ **BÖRİ** + dim. suff. -čü.

BÖRÜŠ Crm.(Tat.), Tat.(Dobr.)? 20th c. **Börüš** (Kúnos 1904, 304); Kirg. **Börüš** [Бөрÿш], one of Manas' comrades-in-arms [čoro] in the Manas epic, Börü's son (Proben V, 248 /250/). ⇨ **BÖRİ**? + suff. -*š*?

BÖTÜK see **PETÜK**

BÖTÜÖK   Yak. **Bötüök** [Бётүöк] (Pek.).

BÖTÜRMİŠ   Türk 5th c. - 7th c. **Bötürmiš-tarqan** [bötürmiš tarqan] (DTS). ✦ 'Completed, fulfilled (wish), healed/cured (child)' cf. Karakh. *bötür-/bütür-* 'заканчивать, исполнять; исцелять' (DTS).

BŎJÖKÖ   Yak. **Bŏjökö** [Бöцöкö] (Pek.).

BŎKÖRÜYÄ   Yak. **Bŏköruyä** [Бöкöрÿйä] (Pek.). ✦ Derived from Yak. *bŏköruï* (Pek.).

BRAN-ГUL see **BARAN**

BRĀČĬS   Yak. **Brāčĭs** [Брачыс] (Pek.). ✦ 'My friend' (<R.) братец 'id.' (Pek.).

BRENDEY see **BERENDEY**

BRİM-JAN see **BÖRİM**

BRUPAL   Yak. **Brupal** [Мус Брупал] (Pek.). ✦ 'The ice disappeared' <R. Led-Propal (Лед-Пропал) 'id.' (Pek.).

BU   Alt. 19th-20th c. **Bu-bay** [Бубай] (OjrRS 208). See also **ALTUN-BU**.

BU-BAŠ   Kzk. 19th c. **Bu-baš** [Джанмирза Бубашевъ] (Grod., Pril. 165). ⇨ **BU**? + **BAŠ**.

BU-QUTLUГ   Khorezm.? 14th c. **Bu-qutluγ**, Amir Timur's private secretary (Tar. Rashidi 46-47). ⇨ **BU** + **QUTLUГ**.

BUBAN   Kzk. **Buban-bay** [Бубанбай] (Sb. Syr-D. IX, 44).

BUBİ see **BUBĬ**

BUBĬ   Tat. **Bubi** [Abdullah Bubi] (Mende 65, 103); Tat. **Bubi** [Gubaidulla(h) Bubi] (Mende 74); Tat. 19th c. **Bubi** [Gebr. Bubi] (Mende 99, 106, 107); Kzk. 19th c. **Bubĭ-qan** [Садыкъ Бубыкановъ] (Grod., Pril. 152).

BUČAQ   Tat.(Lit.) 1552 **Bučaq** [Бучакъ] (Kn. Metriki Lit. 83); Bashk. 1713 **Bučaq** [Каспулат Бучаков] (MIB III, 94). ✦ I. 'Corner'? cf. Chag., Crm., Turk. *bujaq, bučaq* 'der Winkel, die Ecke' (Radl. IV, 1862-63); II. 'Skin, fur'? Chag. *bučaq* 'das Fell' (Radl. IV, 1862).

BUČAÑ   Uyg. **Bučan** [Buçan] (EUTS); Uyg. **Bučañ** [Buçang] (EUTS).

BUČAÑ-ČÏNATUN   Uyg. 13th c. **Bučañ-čïnatun** [bučaŋ čïnatun] (DTS). ⇨ **BUČAÑ**.

BUČAÑ-TEKÄ   Uyg. 13th c. **Bučañ-tekä** [bučaŋ tekä] (DTS). ✦ 'Bučañ-He-Goat' (Blagova 1997, 706). ⇨ **BUČAÑ** + **TEKÄ**.

BUČU   Kzk. 1846 **Buču-bay** [Беркинбай Бучубаев] (MKOP 156); Kzk. 19th c. **Buču-bay** [Бучубай] (SOK 276).

BUČUQUR   Khorezm. 1298 **Bučuqur / Bujuqur** [بوجتور امیر], one of Ghazan's chieftains against Salamïš (RaD/Jahn 121, RaD/Ber. I, 212).

BUČUR   Türk 8th c. **Bučur** (Runic Mss. 187, 189); Türk 8th c. - 9th c. **Bučur** [Buçur] (DTS, ETY II, 67);

Kuman 1354, 1356 **Bučur** [Bwchwr Comanus] (Gyárfás III, 489-91, 494, 706). ✦ 'Thin, nice, short' cf. *bujur* 'dünn, fein, niedrig, kurz' (Radl. IV, 1864).

BUČŪQ   Yak. **Bučuq** [Бучук] (Pek.).

BUJAR   **Bujar** [Буджар] (RaD I/1, 186).

BUJİ   Khorezm. 1220 **Buji-pehlevan** [Буджи-пехлеван] (MIT I, 503).

BUJUГA   Chag. 15th c.-16th c. **Bujuγa / Bučuγa?** [بوجوغه / Буджугга], a Shaybanid (Šejb. LII).

BUDA   Crm.? 1689 **Buda** [Буда, Табунутскiй саитъ] (PSZRI III, 15); Kzk.? 19th c. **Buda-bay-batïr** [باطر بودا بای / Будабай-батыръ] (Veselovskij, Kirg. 16, 24). ✦ 'A bunch (bund) of wood'? cf. Kzk. *būda* 'die Hucke Holz' (Radl. IV, 1858).

BUDAГ see **BUTAQ**

BUDALA   Turk. 1583 **Budala** [بدلا / Budala Salı oğlu] (Ongan, Ank. I, 154); Tat.(Sib.) 1608 **Budala-abïz** [Будала-Абыз], atalïq of Sultan Qanay in Siberia (MIB I, 153). ✦ 'Stupid, silly' cf. Turk. *budala* 'einfältig, albern' (Radl. IV, 1860).

BUDALİ   Yürük 1543 **Budalï** (Gökb., Rum. 209). ⇨ **BUDALA?**

BUDALÏY   Crm. 1534 **Budalïy-murza** [Будалый-мурза] (PSRL XIII, 79). ⇨ **BUDALİ** + R. suff. -*y*?

BUDAN   Kzk. 19th c. **Budan** [Буданъ] (SOK 220); 1670 **Budan-χan** [Буданъ ханъ], ruler of the city of Rešht (Рештъ) (DAI VI, 11). ✦ 'Mestizo; descendant of different folks' cf. Kzk. *būdan* 'ein Abkömmling von zweierlei verschiedenen Thieren; ein Abkömmling von verschiedenen Völkerschaften', (Kirg.) 'ein Racepferd' (Radl. IV, 1860).

BUDASİRİ see **BUDAŠİRİ**

BUDASUN   Uyg. 12th c.-14th c. **Budasun / Bodasun?** (Radl., USp. 98-99).

BUDAŠ   Bashk. 1757 **Budaš** [Исенгул Будашев] (MIB IV/1, 157); Kzk. 19th c. **Budaš** [Будашъ] (SOK 104).

BUDAŠİRİ   Uyg. 12th c.-14th c. **Budasïrï** (Radl., USp. 27-28); Uyg. 12th c.-14th c. **Budaširi** [Budaşiri] (Radl., USp. 6, DTS, EUTS); Uyg. 12th c.-14th c. **Budaširi-baqšï** (Radl., USp. 16-17, DTS). ✦ Derived from Skr. *buddhas'rï*.

BUDİ   Kzk. 19th c. **Budi-bay** [Будибаевъ] (Grod., Pril. 76).

BUDİS   Bulg. 13th c. - 14th c. **Budis / Būdus?** [بودس / Būdus / Будис] (Jusupov 20, Epigr. Bulg. 16).

BUDRAČ   Karakh. 11th c. **Budrač / Buðrač / Buðruč** [Budraç / Budhraç / Budhruç], one of the rulers of Yabaqu (DTS, MK/Atalay 834). See also **BÖGÄ-BUDRAČ**.

BUÐRAČ see **BUDRAČ**

BUГA see **BUQA**

BUГAČ   Oghuz/Trkm. 14th c.-15th c. **Boγač-jan**

[Богач-Джан] (DQorq. 14); Oghuz/Trkm. 14th c.-15th c. **Buγač / Buγač-χan / Boγač?** [بوغاج حان], Dirse-χan's son, because he had killed a bull he was given this name by Dede Qorqut (DQorq./Ergin 83, DQorq./Rossi 104-111). ✧ 'Little bull'? ⇨ **BUQA** + suff. -č. See also **MUΓAČ?**

BUΓAČÏ Kzk. 1630 **Buγačï** [Бугачей], a prince (Miller, Ist. Sib. II, 62).

BUΓAČÏQ Maml. 1389 **Buγačïq** [صرغتمش / بغاجق السيفى] (Iyās I, 276); Khorezm. 13th c. **Buγačuq / Boγačuq?** [Bogacoc nunt. Tartar], Argun Khan's (1284-1291) envoy to the Pope and France (Reg. Hieros. 380); Oghuz/Trkm. 14th c.-15th c. **Buγaǰïq / Boγaǰïq?** [Buγaǰïq (Boγaǰïq) Melik] (DQorq./Rossi 145, 159). ✧ 'Little bull'. ⇨ **BUQA** + suff. -čïq.

BUΓAČUQ see BUΓAČÏQ

BUΓAǰÏQ see BUΓAČÏQ

BUΓAY Chuv. 18th-19th c. **Bogay** [Богай] (Magn. 34); Kzk. 19th c. **Boγay-bay** [Богайбай] (SODž. 106); Tat. 1678-1681 **Buγay** [Бугай], a Tatar Khan (DAI VIII, 38); Tat.(Sib.) 1645 **Buγay** [Бугай / Абугай], a Siberian ruler (sultan), Išim's son, Küčüm's grand-son (Miller, Ist. Sib. II, 508, 516-517, 527, MIB I, 92, 161, 205); Bashk. 1695, 1696 **Buγay** [Бугайко] (MIB I, 97, MIKk. 151); Bashk. 1706 **Buγay** [Умекей Бугаев] (MIB III, 20); Kzk. 19th c. **Buγay** [Бугай] (AOP 110). ✧ 'Little bull' In Baskakov's opinion -y is a Russian adaptation (cf. R. family-name *Bogaevskij*, Bask., Fam. 212). ⇨ **BUQA** + dim. suff. -y. See also **ǰOL-BOΓAY, QARA-BUQAY, TUMAN-BUΓAY.**

BUΓALAQ Tat.(Sib.) 1632 **Buγalaq** (<**Buγalïq?**) [Яков Бугалаков], a new(ly)-christened from Tobol (Miller, Ist. Sib. II, 387-389, 453). ✧ 'Noose' cf. Kzk. *buγalïq* 'die Schlinge zum Einfangen wilder Pferde' (Radl. IV, 1805).

BUΓALÏ Crm. **Buγalï-bay** (Proben VII, 211). ✧ 'Having bulls'. ⇨ **BUQA** + suff. -lï.

BUΓAN Kzk. 19th c. **Buγan** [Буганъ] (AOA 66); Kzk. 19th c. **Buγan-bay** [Буганбай] (Grod., Pril. 80). ✧ 'All'? cf. Tat. *buγan* 'ganz, alle' (Radl. IV, 1805).

BUΓANAQ Crm.Tat. 1637 **Buγanaq** [Баянко Буганаков (Баганаков)], Devletgirey's envoy (Miller, Ist. Sib. II, 445-448). ✧ 'Little Collar-bone, Little clavicle'? cf. Kzk. *buγana* 'die falschen Rippen' (Radl. IV, 1805). ⇨ **BUΓANA** + dim. suff. -q.

BUΓAR Tat.(Mish.) 1775 **Buγar?** [Истикай Бугаров] (MIB IV/2, 417). See also **QUN-BUΓAR.**

BUΓAZČA-FATİMA see BOΓAZǰA-FATİMA

BUΓAZİ Bashk. 1762 **Buγazi / Buγaziy?** [Тевень Бугазиев] (MIB IV/1, 233). ⇨ **BOΓAZ?**

BUΓDAY I. Kzk. 19th c. **Biday / Biyday-bek** [Бицайбекъ] (SOK 60); Chuv. 18th-19th c. **Boday** [Бодай] (Magn. 34); Tat.? Kzk.? 1624 **Buday** [Кунай Будаев], Batïr-tayša's (Batyr Taysha) envoy (Miller,

Ist. Sib. II, 313); Kmk. 1718, 1720 **Buday-χan / Buday-šaw? / Buday-šah?** [Будай ханъ / Будайшавъ] (PSZRI V, 557-558, VI, 167); Selj., Trkm.? Turk.? 1283 **Buday-χatun** [حا تون / ابوداى], fem. (Qazw. 585); Khorezm.? 1306/07 **Buday-χatun** [بوداى حا تون], fem. (Dorn 150); Tat. 1673 **Buday-murza** [Будай мурза (Тарковской)], in a document from Astrakhan (AI IV, 510, DAI VI, 26, X, 472); Khorezm.? 1295 **Buγday** [بتداى احتاجى] [بوغداى احتاجى] (RaD/Jahn 65, 83, 84); Khorezm.? 1295 **Buγday** [بوغداى ابوداجى], a follower of Keyhatu (1291-1295) who sides with Ghazan in 1295 (RaD/Jahn 49, 55, 81); Maml. 1261 **Buγday? / Boγdï?** [الاشرفى] [بها'الدين بغدى] (Sīrat 122 (34)); Khorezm.? 14th c. **Buγday / Buγuday** [بوغداى / Бугдай / Бугудай], the Kereit Al-inaq (El-inaq)'s son, Arpa's brother (RaD/Ber. I, 106, RaD I/1, 101, 135); Kirg. **Būday-bek** [Буудайбек] (Jud. 158). ✧ 'Wheat' cf. *boğday* 'Weizen' (Al-Qawānin), *buğday* 'id.' (IM), Kuman, Chag., NUyg.(Tar.), Tat. *buγday* 'der Weizen' (Radl. IV, 1808), Kar.(T.) *buday* 'der Weizen' (Radl. IV, 1858), Kmk. *budaj* 'Weizen' (Németh, Kumük), Tat. *boday* 'пшеница' (TatRS), Kzk. *biyday* 'пшеница' (KzkRS); *bïday* 'der Weizen' (Radl. IV, 1780). See also **AQ-BUDAY.**

BUΓDAY II. Yak. **Buγday** [Бугдаи] (Pek.).

BUΓRA Karakh. **Boγra-χan** [Bogra Xan] (MK/Atalay 834); Karakh. **Boγra-qara-χan** [Bogra Kara Xan] (MK/Atalay 834); Trkm. 20th c. **Buγra** [Bugra] (Zaj. 1971, 331); Trkm. 20th c. **Buγra** [Бугра] (TrkmRS 117); **Buγra / Boγra** [احمد بن بغرا] (Bondārī 130); 937 **Buγra / Boγra** [بغرا ترك / ابغرا / بنفرا] (Qazw. 345); 10th c.? **Buγra / Boγra** [Baghra], a general of the Samanids (Weil, Chalif. II, 615-616); Karakh. 922 **Buγra / Boγra** [ابغرا] (Ibn al-Athīr/Tornb. VIII, 91, 96); Karakh.? 1018 **Buγra / Boγra** [بغرا حان محمود] (Ibn al-Athīr/Tornb. IX, 213); Karakh. 992, 1000 **Buγra-χaqan / Buγra-χan** [بغرا حاقان هرون بن ايلك] / Hârûn Buğra Xan] (Hil. Sābī 402, 421. 423, Golden 215); Karakh. 11th c.-12th c. **Buγra-χan**, ruler of Kashghar, Balasagun and Khotan (1074-1102/3) (DTS); Chag.? **Buγra-χan** [Bakarra Khan (Elphinstone, Hist. of India, p. 383)] (Le Coq, Ind. 2); Karakh. **Buγra-χan** [بغراحان از قدما'لموك حانيه'ماورا'النهر] / **Boγra-χan** (ǰuwaynī II, 122); Karakh. 10th c.-12th c. **Buγra-χan / Boγra-χan** [Богра-хан Рукн-ад-дин Джемаль-ад-дин], a Karakhanid χan (χaqan) (MIT I, 316-17, 319, 324, 335, 348, 391-95, 397-400, 444, 445); Karakh. 10th c.-12th c. **Buγra-χan / Boγra-χan** [Махмуд Богра-хан ибн Нух Кадыр-хан], Nuχ Qadïr-χan's son (MIT I, 223, 261, 262, 358, 366, 452, 453); Karakh. 993 **Buγra-χan / Boγra-χan** [سليمان ايلك ملك الترك]

بغراخان شهاب الدولة هارون بن] (Ibn al-Athīr/Tornb. IX, 67-70, 323); Karakh. 994 **Buγra-χan / Boγra-χan** [بغرا خان], fought against the Sāmānids (Qazw. 387, 388, 463); Karakh. 1018 **Buγra-χan / Boγra-χan** بغراخان هارون بن قدرخان يوسف] (Ibn al-Athīr/Tornb. XI, 211-13, 358); Selj.? 1247, 1248 **Buγra-χan / Boγra-χan** [بن ابراهيم بن بغرا خان / يوسف / Ibrahim ibn Boğrahan / Boğrahan], mentioned in a vakfiye [deed of trust of a pious foundation] concerning Karatay-mescid (Turan: Belleten XII, 99, 118, 153, 158); Oghuz/Trkm. 13th c. **Buγra-χan / Boγra-χan / Buqra-χan** [بوغرا خان / Богра-хан / Букра хан], Qara-χan's son (Abulg./Kon. 875, 895, 920, 940, 950, 955, 1005, Muhamedova: OSA 170 (after the Oguz-name by Salar Baba)); Karakh. 10th c.- 12th c. **Buγra-qara-χaqan**, one of the rulers of the Karakhanid dynasty (DTS); Karakh. 11th c. **Buγra-qara-χan** [buγra qara χan] (DTS); Selj. 12th c. **Buγra-tegin / Boγra-tegin** [بغرا تگين] (Muh. Ibrahim 48); Selj. 12th c. **Buγra-tegin / Boγra-tegin** [Богра-тегин Бузгуш ал-Джаркани], Sultan Sandjar's (1117-1157) emir (MIT I, 385,399); Kzk. 1846 **Bura** [Бура Кусагулов] (MKOP 151); Uzb. 18th c. **Bura** [Бура], envoy of the Khan of Khiva (Nepljuev 811); Kzk. 19th c. **Bura-bay** [Бурабай] (SODž. 102); Kzk. 19th c. **Bura-bay** [Бурабай] (SOV 76, 132); Bashk. 1706 **Bura-γul** [Бурагул] (MIB III, 20); Bashk. 1757 **Bura-γul** [Бурагул (Бурангул) Умирзаков] (MIB IV/1, 144, 157, 158, 170, 171); Bashk. 1780 **Bura-qan** [Буракан] (MIB V, 103); Bashk. 1789 **Bura-qan** [Сяинзар Бураканов] (MIB V, 262); Kzk. 1817 **Bura-qan** [بوراقان], sultan of the Alim-ulï tribe (MIK IV, 307); Uzb. 1856 **Bura-qul-sufi** [Бура-кулъ-суфи] (Moskal'cev 40); Kzk. 19th c. **Būra** [Буура] (Potanin II, 7); Yak. **Būra / Būra-doχsun** [Бура], a mythological being, Üllär-ätiñ's son (Pek.); Uyg. **Puγra-qan** [Пуңра-кан] (Radl. II, 105). ✧ 'Foal/stallion of a camel' cf. OT, MT *buγra* 'id.' (DTS), Uyg., Alt.(Tel.) *puγra*, Chag., East.T. *buγra* 'der Kameelhengst' (Radl. IV, 1362, 1807), Trkm. *buγra* 'двугорбый вервлюд' (TrkmRS), Kzk. *bura* 'верблюд-производитель' (KzRS), Kzk. *būra* 'der Kameelhengst' (Radl. IV, 1817). E.g.: *Buγra-qara-χaqan* 'Camel-stallion-northern-khan' (Blagova 1997, 704, 706). ⇨ BURA. See also **AQ-BURA, AL-BURA, ARSLAN-BOΓRA, BOZ-QUŠ, ČAW-BURA, QAN-BURA, QARA-BUΓRA, TOQ-BURA.**

BUΓRAČ 871 **Buγrač** [بغراج التركى] (Tabarī, Annal. III, 1842, 1844, 1849, 1891, 1965, 1965, 1988). ✧ 'Little camel'. ⇨ BUΓRA + suff. -č?

BUΓRAJÏQ Oghuz/Trkm. 991 **Buγrajïq** [بغراجق / Boghradjak], the Ghaznavid Mahmud's (998-1030) uncle, died in 991 (Qazw. 395, Weil, Chalif. III, 61);

Oghuz/Trkm. 997 **Buγrajïq** [بغراجق] (Ibn al-Athīr/Tornb. IX, 92, 114). ✧ 'Little camel'. ⇨ BUΓRA + dim. suff. -jïq.

BUΓRAS Kipch. 1320 **Buγras?** [بغراس / Буграсъ], Özbeg Khan's envoy to Egypt (Duqmaq/Tizeng. I, 320, 328). ⇨ BUΓRA?

BUΓU Kzk. 19th c. **Bγu-bay** [Бугубай] (SODž. 50, 116); Kzk. 19th c. **Bγu-bay** [Бугубай] (AOA 30); Kzk. 19th c. **Boγu-bay** [Богубай] (AOAtb. 22); Kzk. 19th c. **Buγu-bay** [Бугубай] (SOK 26, 172, 198); Kzk. 19th c. **Buγu-bay** [Бугубай] (SOK 26, 198); Kirg. 20th c. **Buγu-bay** [Бугубай] (Kalilov 92). ✧ 'Moose elk' cf. Chag., Kzk. *buγu* 'das Elenthier, der Hirsch' (Radl. IV, 1806).

BUΓUDAY see **BUΓDAY I.**

BUΓUΓ Uyg. 759-780 **Buγuγ-χan** [Buγuγ χan / t(ä)ngrikän uiγur buγuγ χan], an Uygur Khan under the rule of whom the Uygurs converted to Manichaeanism (DTS). ⇨ BÖGÜ?

BUΓULJA Khorezm./Chag. 1412/13 **Buγulja** [Бугульджа], ruler of Khorezm (MIT I, 531, 532).

BUΓURČÏ Trkm. **Buγurčï** [Бугурчы] (Sopieva 178). ✧ 'Camel (in the third year of age)' (Sopieva 178, Muhamedova 1957, 39), cf. Turk. *buγur* 'der Kameelhengst' (Radl. IV, 1806). + suff. -čï.

BUΓURTAY Kipch. 1318 **Buγurtay / Buqurtay** [بغرطاى / بترطاى / Бугуртай], Özbeg Khan's envoy to Egypt in 1318 (Duqmaq/Tizeng. I, 318, 325). ✧ I. 'Camel (stallion)' cf. Turk. *buγur* 'der Kameelhengst' (Radl. IV, 1806), 'der Dromedar; Dromedair (mâle)' (Zenk.); II. 'Little bottom/ass' cf. Mo. *buqur* 'bottom, ass'. ⇨ BUΓUR + TAY? or suff. -tay(1,2)?

BUΓUŠ Bashk. 1737 **Buγuš** [Бугуш] (MIB I, 315, 318). ⇨ BUΓU? + suff. -š.

BUXAN Tat. 1764 **Buχan** [Уразметь Буханов] (MIB IV/2, 105).

BUXAR Kzk. 19th c. **Buχar-bay** [Бухарбай] (SODž. 104); Kzk. 19th c. **Buχar-bay** [Бухарбаевъ] (Grod., Pril. 178); Kzk. 19th c. **Buχar-bay** [Бухарбай] (Grod., Pril. 66); Kirg. **Buχar-bay-batïr** [Бухарбай-батыръ] (Smirnov, Sultany 16). ✧ Shortened from the name of Bukhara (Bokhara (<Skr.) or Ir.), the town in Uzbekistan, cf. Tat. PNs *Boχar, Boχaray, Boχar-jan* (Sattarov), Bashk. PN *Boχar* (Kusimova) and Kzk. PNs *Büχar, Büχar-bay* (Žanuzakov-Esbaeva).

BUXAR-DODOR Yak. **Buχar-dodor / Buχar-dodar [dādar] / Buχar-dabar** [Бухар-додор, Бухар-додар, Бухар-дабар], demon of death (Pek.).

BUXARMET Bashk. 1754 **Buχarmet** [Темир Бухарметев] (MIB IV/1, 79); Bashk. 1755 **Buχarmet** [Бухарметь] (MIB IV/1, 105). ⇨ BUXAR + suffixoid -met / -mat.

BUXT-URAZ Tat.(Sib.) 1601 **Buχt-uraz** [Бухтураз Каспирин] (Miller, Ist. Sib. II, 165). ⇨ BAQTÏ +

ORAZ?

BUYAN-KÜKELTAŠ   Chag. 15th c. **Buyan-kükeltaš** [Буянъ-кукельташъ], one of Uluγ-beg's (1393-1449) fathers-in-law (Barth., Ulugb. 116). ✧ 'Good-deed-Foster-brother'. ⇨ **BUYAN + KÜKELTAŠ.**

BUYAN-QAR   Uyg. **Buyan-qar** [Buyan kar] (EUTS). ⇨ **BUYAN? + QAR(A)?** See also **BUYAN-QARA.**

BUYAN-QARA   Uyg. 12th c.-14th c. **Buyan-qara** [Bujan Qara / Buyan kara] (Radl., USp. 34, DTS, EUTS). ✧ 'Good-deed-Black(/much)' (Blagova 1997, 712). ⇨ **BUYAN + QARA.**

BUYAN-ÖZ   Uyg. 1318 **Buyan-öz** (Chwol., Syr.-nest. (NF) 22). ⇨ **BUYAN + ÖZ.**

BUYAN-SIÑΓUR   Uyg. **Buyan-siñγur** [Buyan Sïngγur], Yöläk's son, aged 8 (Zieme, Mat. I, 80). ✧ 'Buyan-Falcon / Good-deed-falcon?'. ⇨ **BUYAN + SOÑQUR?**

BUYAN-TEMÜR   Uyg. **Buyan-tämür** [Buyan Tämür] (EUTS); Uyg. 12th c.-14th c. **Buyan-temür** (DTS). ✧ 'Good-deed-Iron' (Blagova 1997, 712). ⇨ **BUYAN + TEMİR.**

BUYANA   Uyg. **Buyana**, fem. (Zieme, Mat. I, 74). ✧ 'Noble/generous deed; good deed, benefaction' (PN in Vocative form), „O Verdienst!" (Zieme), cf. Uyg. *buyan* 'благодатный поступок, благодеяние; заслуга' (DTS) (< Skr.) + voc. suff. *-a.*

BUYANČOΓ see **BUYANČUQ**

BUYANČUQ   Uyg. 13th-14th c. **Buyančoγ**, fem. (Zieme, Mat. III, 271 (after Gabain)); Uyg. **Buyančuq** [Buyançuk] (EUTS); Uyg. 12th c.-14th c. **Buyančuq** (Radl., USp. 204, 246); Uyg. 12th c.-14th c. **Buyančuq-silavanti** [Buyančuq Silavanti] (Radl., USp. 144, 146, DTS). ✧ '(Little) Luck; (Little) Happiness' cf. Uyg. *buyan* 'hidmet, kut, saadet' (US). ⇨ **BUYAN +** suff. *-čuq.*

BUYANQAY   Yak. 1681 **Buyanqay** [Буянкаевъ] (DAI VIII, 324). ⇨ **BUYAN? +** suff. *-qay.*

BUYAR see **OZAR**

BUYAT   Uyg. **Buyat** [Buyat] (EUTS); Uyg. 8th c. **Buyat-bay** [Buyat bai] (Müller, Pfahl. 10). See also **ÏNAL-BUYAT.**

BUYDAQ   Tat. 1600 **Buydaq** [Буйдак Емачтаев] (Miller, Ist. Sib. II, 159). ✧ 'Bachelor' cf. Tat. *buydaq* 'unverehelicht, ein Hagestolz' (Radl. IV, 1801). See also **KELEN.**

BUYDAN   Tat. 1600 **Buydan** [Буидан Юмачтаев] (Miller, Ist. Sib. II, 152).

BUYLA see **BOYLA**

BUYLA-QUTLUΓ-YARΓAN see **BOYLA**

BUYLAŠ   Chag. **Buylaš-qan**, son of Uyak Sultan, Mirza Haidar's brother-in-law (Tar. Rashidi 161). ⇨ **BOYLA? +** suff. *-š.*

BUYRA-BAS   Nog. 20th c. **Buyra-bas** [Буйра-бас уруғы], an Aq-noγay clan, named after its leader

(Bask., Nog. 135, 142). ✧ 'Curly (haired) head' cf. Kzk. *buyra* 'Saçın kıvırcık olması' (KzTS). ⇨ **BAŠ.**

BUYRA-SAQAL   Kzk. 18th c. - 19th c. **Buyra-saqal** [Буйрасакал], a clan named after its leader (Tynyšp. 75). ✧ 'Curly beard' cf. Kzk. *buyra* 'Saçın kıvırcık olması' (KzTS). ⇨ **SAQAL.**

BUYUNSÏZ   Uzb. 1500 **Buyunsïz** [بويون سيز حسن / Буюнсиз Хасанъ] (Šejb. LXXVI). ✧ 'Not having a neck, without a neck; having a short neck' cf. Chag., Az., Turk., Kar.(L.T.), Trkm. *boyun* 'der Hals' (Radl. IV, 1660) N + suff. *-siz.*

BUYURΓAN   Tat. 1624 **Biyurγan / Bïyurγan** [Каперда Бiюргановъ / Кайперди Бiюргановъ] (Pokrovskij 71); Crm.? 1546 **Bïyurγan / Bïyurγan-seyit** [Абеюрган-сеитъ (Беюрган) / къ сеиту къ Беюргану], (PSRL XIII, 148); Tat. 1612 **Buyurγan** [Буюрганъ Хояшевъ] (Kurdjumov 369); Tat. 1612, 1619 **Buyurγan** [Генгитка (Енгитъ) Буюргановъ / Баюргановъ] (Kurdjumov 117-121, 369, 370). ✧ 'He who (was) ordered (by God)' cf. Kuman, Crm., Kar.(L.T.), Uzb., Trkm., Kzk. *buyur-* 'befehlen; reden' (Radl. IV, 1811).

BUQ-BASÏR   Kzk. 19th c. **Buq-basïr-bay** [Букбасыръ-бай] (Grod., Pril. 15); Kirg. 19th c. **Buq-basïr-bay** [Букбасырбай Бутинъ] (Grod., Pril. 15, 80). ✧ I. 'Shit-trachoma'? cf. Kzk. *basïr* 'Trahoma' (KzTS); II. 'Shit-Basir' cf. Ar. PN *Basir* 'sagacious, endowed with insight' (Ahmed), cf. also Bashk. PNs *Basir / Basïr* (Kusimova). ⇨ **BOQ?** See also **BOQ-BASAR?**

BUQ-BAŠ see **BOQ-BAŠ**

BUQA   Pecheneg 10th c. **Boγa** [Βογᾶς], a Byzantine strategist of Pecheneg origin (?) (Byz. Turc. II, 92); Kzk. 19th c. **Boγa** [Халъ Мурадъ Богиновъ] (Grod., Pril. 178); Kzk. 19th c. **Boqa** [Бока] (AOK 14); Kzk. 19th c. **Boqa-bay** [Бокабай] (Lomakin 32); Türk 7th c. - 9th c. **Buγa** [buγa / Buǵa] (DTS, EUTS); Karakh.? 846, 849-865, 882 **Buγa** [بغا الصغير الشرابى] (Fragm. Hist. Ar. 540-578, Tabarī, Annal III, 1348, 1368, 1380-82, 1386, 1458-61, 1507, Hil. Sābī 145, Jakūbī 262, Weil, Abbas. II, 356, 369, 382, 383, 399, 401, Abulfar. 169, 174-175); Karakh. 869, 880 **Buγa** [محمد بن موسى بن بغا / Mohammed ibn Bogha], a Turkic chieftain who in 869 overthrew Muʿtaz, Musa Ibn Bogha's brother (Weil, Abbas II, 409, 418, Tabarī, Annal. III, 1956, 1988); Selj. **Buγa** [بوغا] (Ibn Bībī IV, 295); Selj. 14th c. **Buγa** [بوغا], takes part in the revolt of Irinjin in Rūm in the age of the Ilkhanid Abū Saʿīd (1316-1335) (Aqsar./İş. 115); Maml. 1325, 1340/41 **Buγa** [بغا الدوادار] (Zetterst. 187, 191, Iyās I, 175); Trkm. 20th c. **Buga** [Buga] (Zaj. 1971, 331); Tat.(Sib.) 1639 **Buγa** [Бугайко Атинов] (Miller, Ist. Sib. II, 453); Karakh.? 862-847, 882 **Buγa / Boγa?** [بغا الكبير / Bogha (der Aeltere)], a general (Fragm. Hist. Ar. 385-563, Tabarī, Annal III, 1174, 1186-93, 1507, 1512 etc.,

Kamāladdīn I, 73, Weil, Abbas. II, 299, 319, 326, 338, 379, 380, Abulfar. 169, 174-175, Mas‘ūdī? 356); Turk. 1365, 1366 **Buγa / Boγa?** [Μπέχνα], a Turkish emir (Byz. Turc. II, 205-206); Uyg. 12th c. - 14th c. **Buγa-qan** [buγa qan] (DTS); Uzb. 1580 **Buγa-uγlï / Boγa-uγlï** [Бога-углы Богадуръ Ханъ] (Moskal'cev 55); Chuv. 18th-19th c. **Buka** [Бука] (Magn. 34); 1355 **Buqa** [امـيـر بـوقـا], a Hazārā emir (Qazw. 667); Uyg. **Buqa** [Buka] (EUTS); Uyg. 1339 **Buqa** (Chwol., Syr.-nest. (NF) 35); Oghuz/Trkm. 1030-1040 **Buqa** [Бука], a chieftain of the Ghuzz (Turkmen) (MIT I, 234, 235, 243, 363, 364); Oghuz/Trkm. 12th c. **Buqa** [بـوقـا قلاووز / Бука], Qutbaddin Muhammad Khorezmshah's (1098-1128) guide (J̌uwaynī I, 120, 121, MIT I, 489); Khorezm. 1289 **Buqa** [بـوقـا], emir who revolted against Arghun and was executed in 1289 (RaD/Jahn 7, 15, 16, 17, 62, Abulfar./Budge I, 470); Chag.? 15th c. **Buqa** [انصرلـديـن بـوقـا], Nasreddin Buqa, from the family of the „Bulı-Timurids" from Qazwīn (Qazw. 849); Bashk. 1745 **Buqa** [Мастюр Букаев] (MIB III, 426); Kzk. **Buqa** [Ишъ-Мухаммедъ Букинъ], author of a Russian-Kazak vocabulary (ZIRGOEtn. X, vyp. 3, 17); Kzk. 19th c. **Buqa** [Букинъ] (AOK 30); NUyg. 19th c. **Buqa** [بـوقـا] (Le Coq, Namenl. 97); Oghuz/Trkm. 13th c. **Buqa / Buγa** [بـوقـا / بـوغـا / Бука], Ögürǰik-alp's son (Abulg./Kon. 1235, 1250); Oghuz/Trkm. 1220 **Buqa / Buqa-pehlivan** [Bouqa le Turcoman / Бука-пехливанъ / Бука-пехлеван], an officer of the Khorezmshah around 1220 (RaD/Ber. III, 69, MIT I, 504, Abulg./Desm. 132); Kzk. 19th c. **Buqa-bay** [Букабай] (AOAtb. 42); Kzk. 19th c. **Buqa-bay** [Букабай] (SOV 14); 1282 **Buqa-čiñsañ** [بـوقـا جنكسانك], Minister of State in Luristan (Qazw. 544, 587); Hak. 19th-20th c. **Puγa** [Пуға] (HRS 351); Hak.(Sag.) 19th-20th c. **Puγa-mökä / Puγa-möke** [Пуӷа Мӧкӓ / Пуга-Мӗке], a folklore hero (Proben IX, 509, 510, ZIRGOEtn. XXXIV, 275); Uyg. 1339 **Puqa** (Chwol., Syr.-nest. 93, 155). ✧ 'Bull; armed bellicose/agressive man' cf. Uyg., Karakh. *buqa* 'быкпроизводитель' (DTS), Türk., East.T., NUyg., Kzk. *buqa*, Chag. *buγa* 'der Bulle', (Radl. IV, 1802, 1804), Maml. *boγa* 'boğa' (Tarǰ/Toparlı), *buqa* 'Stier' (TMEN II, No. 752), cf. also Russian personal and familynames *Buka, Bukiny* (Veselovskij). See also **AY-BUΓA, AQ-BUΓA, ALA-BUΓA, ALAN-BUΓA, ALP-BUΓA, ALTUN-BUΓA, ARA-BUQA, ARAŠ-BUΓA, ARSLAN-BUQA, AS-BUΓA, AŠAN-BUΓA, AZ-BUΓA, BAY-BUQA, BARS-BUQA, BAŠ-BUΓA, BEK-BUQA, BİKÜŠ-BUΓA, BİŠ-BUQA, BULAT-BUΓA, ČAR-BUQA, EL-BUQA, ER-BUQA, ERİM-BUΓA, ESÄN-BUQA, İLČİ-BUΓA, İNČ-BUQA, İŠ-BUQA, IŠ-BUQA, YABLAQ-BUQA, YEKÄ-BUQA, YEL-BUΓA, YÜZ-BUQA, KENT-BUΓA, KER-BUΓA, KET-BUΓA, KÖR-BUΓA, KÜČ-BUΓA, KÜMÜŠ-BUΓA, QARA-BUQA, QÏTAY-BUQA, QÏZÏL-BUΓA, QONČU-BUΓA, QURU-BUQA, QUŠ-BUΓA, QUTLUΓ-BUQA, MELİK-BUQA, MEÑLİ-BUQA, MOÑUL-BUQA, ORDU-BUΓA, ÖRÜÑ-BOΓA, PULAT-BUΓA, SABÏ-BUQA, SAY-BUQA, SAN-BUΓA, SARAY-BUΓA, SARÏ-BUΓA, SASÏ-BUQA, SAWČÏ-BUΓA, SEWİNČ-BUΓA, ŠAΓÏR-BUΓA, TAΓAY-BUQA, TAİR-BUΓA, TAY-BUΓA, TANA-BUQA, TANUŠ-BUΓA, TAŠ-BUΓA, TELE-BUΓA, TEMİR-BUΓA, TEÑİZ-BUΓA, TİMÜR-BUQA, TİN-BUΓA, TOQ-BUΓA, TÖKMİŠ-BUQA, TUΓAY-BUQA, TUY-BUΓA, TUQDUQ-BUQA, TURUN-BUΓA, TÜKRÜNČ-BUQA.**

BUQAΓ Türk 735 **Buqaγ-tutuq** [buqaγ tutuq / Buqaγ Tutuq] (DTS, ETY I, 70). ✧ 'Craw of a bird'? cf. Karakh. *buqaq* 'зоб птицы' (DTS).

BUQAY Kzk. 19th c. **Boqay** [Бокай] (Potanin II, 4); Kzk. 19th c. **Boqay** [Бокай] (AOA 90, 102); Bashk. 1757 **Buqay** [Ибракай Букаев] (MIB IV/1, 157); Bashk. 1763 **Buqay** [Букай Касимов] (MIB IV/1, 253); Kzk. 19th c. **Buqay** [Букай] (SOK 160); Kzk. 19th c. **Buqay** [Чарилкасинъ (Чарулкасынъ) Букаевъ] (Grod., Pril. 65, 111); Kzk. 19th c. **Buqay-χan** [Alichan Bukeichanov] (Mende 102, 145). ✧ 'Little bull'. ⇨ **BUQA** + dim. suff. *-y*.

BUQAQ Bashk. 1754 **Buqaq** [Букак Алимгулов] (MIB IV/1, 83). ✧ 'Goitre, double chin' cf. Kzk. *buqaq* 'der Kropf, das fette Doppelkinn' (Radl. IV, 1805).

BUQAM Uyg. **Buqam-säñün** [Bukam Sängün] (EUTS); Uyg. 12th c.-14th c. **Buqam-säñün** (Radl., USp. 120); Uyg. 12th c. - 14th c. **Buqam-señün** [buqam seŋün] (DTS). ✧ 'My Bull'? ⇨ **BUQA?** + poss. suff. *-m*?

BUQAN Kzk. 19th c. **Buqam-bay** (<Buqan-bay) [Букамбай] (SOK 292); Kzk. 19th c. **Buqam-bek** (<Buqan-bek) [Букамбай] (SODž. 42); **Buqan** [Букан], a runner to „idi-qut" (RaD I/1, 117); Bashk. 1777 **Buqan** [Букан Алимгулов] (MIB V, 65); Türk 576 **Buqan / Buγa-qan?** [Βωχανος], a Turkic chieftain (Byz. Turc. II, 108); Kzk. **Buqan-bay** [Буканбай] (Sb. Syr-D. IX, 52); Kzk. 1710 **Buqan-bay** [Буканъ-Бай], leader of the revolted Kazaks (Nepljuev 135); Kzk. 1792 **Buqan-bay** [Буканбай] (MIK IV, 137); Kzk. 1819 **Buqan-bay** [Буканбай Киикбаев] (MIK IV, 325); Kzk. 19th c. **Buqan-bay** [Буканбай] (Grod., Pril. 25). ✧ 'A kind of antelope, Tatar antelope' cf. Kzk. *buqan* (буконъ) 'Saiga tatarica' (Grum-Gržim. I, 511-14), cf. Mo. *bökön görögesü*, Khalkha *böxön göröös* (Gy. Kara).

BUQANAY Kzk. 19th c. **Buqanay** [Буконай] (SOV 14). ⇨ **BUQAN** + suff. *-ay*.

BUQANČÏ Kzk. 19th c. **Buqančï / Buqančï** [Буканчи]

(SOK 250). ⇨ **BUQAN** + suff. *-čï.*

BUQAR Kzk. 19th c. **Buqar** [Букаръ] (AOP 10); Kzk. **Buqar-bay** [Букарбай], a field north of Lake Balkhash (Krasovskij 379); Kzk. 19th c. **Buqar-bay** [Букарбай] (SOK 138); Kzk. 19th c. **Buqar-bay** [Букорбай] (SOV 142); Kzk. 19th c. **Buqar-bay** [Букарбай] (AOA 78); Kzk. 19th c. **Buqar-bay** [Букарбай] (SOV 120); Kzk. 19th c. **Buqar-bay** [Букарбай], forefather of the İtel clan (Potanin II, 6); *TN:* Kzk. **Bukorbayeva** [Букорбаева], a Kazak aul (village) in the district of Tokalinsk (Patkanov II, 92). ⇨ **BUXAR?**

BUQARA Kzk. 1826 **Buqara** [Буккара Неяновъ] (TOUAK XXIV, 162). ✦ 'Subject, dependant; pauper, beggar, poor' cf. Kirg., Kzk. *buqara* 'untergeben, unterthan, der Unterthan' (Radl. IV, 1803), Turk. *fikara* / *fukara* 'poor, pauper, beggar' (TED) <Ar.

BUQAŠ Bashk. 1740 **Buqaš** [Козяк Букашев] (MIB I, 412); Bashk. 1740 **Buqaš** [Изкозя Букашев] (MIB I, 435); Kzk. **Buqaš** [Букашъ Аупаевъ], a merchant (Valihanov, Soč. 342); Kzk. 19th c. **Buqaš-pay** [Букашпай] (SOK 62). ✦ 'Little bull'. ⇨ **BUQA** + suff. *-š.*

BUQČA see **BOQČA**

BUQČA-BARDAR Uzb. 19th c. **Buqča-bardar** [Séid-Boukcha-bardar], a seyit from Khokand (Nalivkin-Dozon 129). ⇨ **BOQČA.**

BUQČAQ Tat.(Lit.) 1552 **Buqčaq** [Букчакъ] (Kn. Metriki Lit. 86).

BUQČI see **BOQČÏ**

BUQČÏ see **BOQČÏ**

BUQČU see **BOQČÏ**

BUQPA Kzk. 19th c. **Buqpa** [Букпа] (SOV 102); *TN:* Kzk. 19th c. **Buqpa** [Букпа], a field (AOA 2). ✦ 'Thick pulp, squash' cf. Kzk. *buqpa* 'dicke Grütze' (Radl. IV, 1804).

BUQPAN see **BOQPAN**

BUQPAN-TAY Kzk. 19th c. **Buqpan-tay** [Букпантай] (SOK 206). ⇨ **BUQPAN** + **TAY** or suff. *-tay(1,2)?*

BUQRA see **BUĠRA**

BUQSAN Yak. **Buqsan** [Буксан], a child (Pek.). ✦ 'Folding, hooking' cf. Yak. *buqsai-* 'выгибаться, сгибаться' (Pek.).

BUQSUQ see **BOQSUQ**

BUQSUN Bashk. 1770 **Buqsun** [Буксун Муллакаев] (MIB IV/1, 342); Bashk. 1770 **Buqsun** [Буксун Менглигулов] (MIB IV/1, 342).

BUQTUR **Buqtur** / **Buqdur** [Букдур], Deñgiz-χan's son (RaD I/1, 76).

BUQU **Buqu** [Буку] (RaD I/1, 165); Khorezm. 13th c. **Buqu-χan** [از امـرا سلطان جلال‌الـدین مکبرنی], Jelāleddīn Meñgü-berdi Sultan's (1220-1231) emir (Juwaynī II, 185, 186); Uyg.? **Buqu-χan** / **Buqu-tegin** [بوقو تکین / بوقوحـان] (Juwaynī I, 40-44,

192). ⇨ **BUĠU?**

BUQUČ Bashk. 1769 **Buquč** [Муллакым Букучев] (MIB IV/1, 336). ⇨ **BOQUŠ?**

BUQUL Tat.(Sib.)? 1643 **Buqul** [Букул], a tax-payer from Mundus (Miller, Ist. Sib. II, 488, 489).

BUL Kzk. 19th c. **Bul-pek** / **Bulpek?** [Булпекъ] (SODž. 118). ✦ I. 'A kind of (valuable) textile (Haloxylon?)' cf. Kzk. *bŭl* 'красный товар' (KzRS), Kzk. *bul* 'kumaş; değeri, özelliği, para' (KzTS); II. 'Goods, richess, fortune' cf. Kzk. *bul* 'die Waare (der Kaufleute), die Habe, das Vermögen, der Reichtum, der Preis' (Radl. IV, 1834). See also **BEL-BUL, QAZ-BUL, SAYÏN-BUL, TOQTA-BUL(?), TOQTÏ-BUL(?).**

BUL-BEK-XAN see **BOL**

BULA I. Turk. 16th c. **Bula**, fem. (Ongan, Ank. II); Turk. 1583 **Bula-qatun** [بوله قاطون], fem. (Ongan, Ank. I, 154). ✦ 'Aunt (wife of the uncle on mother's side)' cf. Turk. *bula* 'die Tante, die Frau des Onkels von Mutterseite' (Radl. IV, 1836). See also **QATUN-BULA, SÏM-BULA, ŠAH-BULA, TEZ-BULA.**

BULA II. Mo.? **Bula** [بولا / بولا], one of Tura-qaymïš' (توره قايمش) sons (RaD/Ber. I, 69); Tat. 1724 **Bula** / **Bulay?** [Балантай Булаев] (MIB III, 227). ✦ 'Pampered' cf. Kzk. *bŭla* 'холеный; изнеженный' (KzRS), Kzk. *bula* 'hiç zorluk çekmeden, şımarık olarak büyümüş kimse' (KzTS). See also **AY-BULAY.**

BULA-TEMÜR Khorezm. 13th c. **Bula-temür** [بولا تمور], an emir, ancestor of the famous Qazwīnī family (Qazw. 849). ⇨ **BULA II.** + **TEMÍR.**

BULAĠUŠ Bashk. 1773 **Bulaɣuš** [Булагушъ Биимбетевъ (Биимбетев)] (MIB IV/1, 371, IOAIÊK XXVIII, 587). ⇨ **BULA** + **QUŠ I.?**

BULAY Kzk. 19th c. **Bolay** [Болай] (SOV 68); Khorezm. 1299 **Bulay**, Ghazan Khan's chieftain (Makrīzī IV, 132, Weil, Chalif. I, 224, 234); Tat. 1708 **Bulay** [Булайко (Булак) Акбулатов] (MIB I, 225); 14th c. **Bulay(ï)?** [Buláji Dughlát], emir, the author' ancestor who was the first to convert to Islam among the Dughlatids (Tar. Rashidi 6, 7, 38, 55, 53, EI I, 1127); **Bulay-bek** [Булай бекъ], commander of a regiment of the Chinggisids (RaD III, 145); ⇨.; ✦ 'Spoilt, pampered (child)'? ⇨ **BULA II.** + suff. *-y.* See also **AY-BULAY, BÏ-BULAY, ES-BOLAY, İŠ-PULAY.**

BULAQ Selj.? 1198 **Bulaq** [ظهيرالـدين بولق بـن بلنکری], an emir (Ibn al-Athīr/Tornb. XII, 88); Tat.(Sib.) 1643 **Bulaq** [Тетеш Булак] (Miller, Ist. Sib. II, 486); Bashk. 1760 **Bulaq** [Булак Суляков] (MIB IV/2, 160); Tat. 1708 **Bulaq?** / **Bulay** [Булайко (Булак) Акбулатов] (MIB I, 225); Kzk. 19th c. **Bulaq-pay** [Булакпай] (SOK 88); Kzk. 19th c. **Bulaq-pay** [Булакпай] (SOV 56). ✦ I. 'Well, spring' cf.

Chag., Kuman, Kzk., Tat., Turk. *bulaɣ / bulaq* 'die quelle, ein Bach' (Radl. IV, 1837); II. 'Horse with a cut in its leg' cf. Chag. *bulaɣ* 'Pferd mit einem Einschnitt in den Fuss' (Radl. IV, 1837). See also **QARA-BULAQ, SAY-BULAQ, TAY-BULAQ, TES-BULAQ, TETEŠ-BULAQ, TOQ-BOLAQ.**

BULAQAY Kzk. 19th c. **Bulaqay** [Булакай] (SOK 256). ✧ 'Little pampered child'. ⇨ **BULA II.** + suff. *-qay*.

BULAQTÏ Tat.(Mish.) 1775 **Blaqtï** (<**Bulaqtï**) [Блакты Таманов] (MIB IV/2, 417). ⇨ **BULAQ** + den. suff. *-tï*.

BULAM see BULAN

BULAN Kzk. 19th c. **Blan** (<**Bulan**) [Бланъ] (SOV 38); Kzk. 19th c. **Bulam-bay** (<**Bulan-bay**) [Буламбай] (AOAtb. 66); Kzk. 19th c. **Bulam-bay** (<**Bulan-bay**) [Буламбай] (AOO 14); Kzk. 19th c. **Bulam-bay** (<**Bulan-bay**) [Буламбай] (SOV 20); Kzk. 19th c. **Bulam-bay** (<**Bulan-bay**) [Буломбай] (SOK 208); Mo.? 13th c. **Bulan** [بولان / Буланъ], from the Barɣut tribe under the Ilkhanids (RaD/Ber. I, 86); Kzk. 1793 **Bulan** [بولان / Булан] (MIK IV, 149); Kzk. 1817 **Bulan** [بولان / Булан] (MIK IV, 309); Kzk. 19th c. **Bulan** [Буланъ] (AOP 14); Kzk. 19th c. **Bulan** [Буланъ] (AOO 22); Kzk. 19th c. **Bulan** [Булановъ] (AOO 30); Kzk. 19th c. **Bulan** [Буланъ] (SOK 46); Khazar **Bulan / Bülän?** [Bulan (Bülän)], a Khazar qaɣan (Golden 169-171); Kzk. 1829 **Bulan-bay** [Сююндукъ Буланбаевъ] (Konšin, Mat. V, 77); Kzk. 1846 **Bulan-ɣul** [Чулак Булангулов], a biy (notable, country gentleman) (MKOP 158). ⇨ **BOLAN?**

BULANČA Tat. 1600 **Bulanča** [Буланча Кинырев] (Miller, Ist. Sib. II, 159, MIB I, 152); Tat. 1634 **Bulanča** [Буланчин / Булаичин (Баймамет)] (Miller, Ist. Sib. II, 413). ⇨ **BULAN** + suff. *-ča*.

BULANÏQ Yürük 16th c. **Bulanïq** [بولانق], from the Yürüks of Kocacık, Turkey (Gökb., Rum. 103). ✧ 'Turbid; cloudy; dim; enthusiast, eager' cf. Turk. *bulanïq* 'gemischt, umgerührt, trübe, erregt' (Radl. IV, 1838).

BULAR **Bular** [Булар] (RaD II, 73).

BULAŠ Bashk. 1728 **Bulaš** [Уразай Булашев] (MIB I, 128). ⇨ **BULA II.** + suff. *-š?*

BULAT Balk. 20th c. **Bolat** [Bolátları], an Özden family (Pröhle, Balk. 210); Kzk. 19th c. **Bolat** [Болатовъ] (AOO 30); Kzk. 19th c. **Bolat-χan** [Болатханъ] (SOK 32); Kirg. **Bolot** [Болот], Aq-boltoñ's son, one of Manas' comrades-in-arms (Proben V, 40); Kirg. **Bolot** [Öкöм Болот], Yoloy's son, one of Manas' comrades-in-arms (Proben V, 182 /184/); Kirg. **Bolot-bek** [Болотбек] (Jud. 223); **Bulat** [Пулад] (RaD II, 155); 19th c. **Bulat** [Гази Булатовичъ] (AUK 158); Uyg. **Bulat** (Zieme, Mat. I, 74); Uyg. 12th c.-14th c. **Bulat** [Bulat] (DTS, Radl., USp. 98, 208, 249, EUTS); Kipch.? 1407 **Bulat** [Булатъ], a prince of the [Golden] Horde (PSRL VI, 136, VIII, 82-83, XI, 205); Kipch. 1458 **Bulat** [Булатъ], a prince (PSRL XXIII, 142); Maml. 1308 **Bulat** [بولاط الحوكند ار] (Dawād. 155, 393); Maml. 1325 **Bulat** [بلاط] (Zetterst. 190); Maml. 1335/36 **Bulat** [بلاط اليوسى] (Iyās I, 168); Maml. 1376/77 **Bulat** [بلاط السيفى الجاى] (Iyās I, 232, 243); Maml. 1379/80 **Bulat** [بلاط الصرغتمشى] (Iyās I, 249); Maml. 1386 **Bulat** [اصبغا بن بلات] (Berchem, Jér. I, 300); Maml. 1399 **Bulat** [بلاط السعدى] (Iyās I, 318, Ibn Taghrīb. VI, 6, 29, 278); Maml. 1411/12 **Bulat** [بلاط الناصرى الاعرج] (Ibn Taghrīb. VI, 267, 423); Maml. 1412/13 **Bulat** [بلاط الظا هرى] (Ibn Taghrīb. VI, 267, 436); Maml. 1463 **Bulat** [بولاط دوادار اينال] (Ibn Taghrīb. VII, 714, 728); Maml. 1463, 1469/70 **Bulat** [بلاط اليشبكى], governor of Hamah (Ibn Taghrīb. VIII, 439, 476, Iyās II, 114, 148, Weil, Chalif. II, 314); Chag. 16th c. **Bulat** [بولاد / Poulâd], son of Aqatay, the Khan of Khiva (Abulg./Desm. 250); Tat.(Lit.) 1644 **Bulat** [Булатъ] (Lit. Tat. 326 etc.); Chuv. 18th-19th c. **Bulat** [Булатъ] (Magn. 34); Chuv. 18th-19th c. **Bulat** [Пулатъ] (Magn. 69); Tat. 1518, 1529, 1535 **Bulat** [Булатъ], a prince from Kazan (PSRL VIII, 266-67, 273, 291 etc., XIII, 88, PSRL (Russk. Hr.) I, 521); Tat. 1690 **Bulat** [Булатко (Битинъ)] (Kungursk. akty 178); Tat.(Tara) **Bulat** [Булат] (Proben IV, 125 /166/, 202 /248/); Bashk. 1711, 1715 **Bulat** [Булат] (MIB III, 76, 135); Bashk. 1735 **Bulat** [Булатъ Епановъ], a tarχan (Vel.-Zern., Bašk. 15); Bashk. 1761 **Bulat** [Елдубай Булатов] (MIB IV/1, 215); Bashk. 1761 **Bulat** [Култай Булатов] (MIB IV/1, 215); Bashk. 1780 **Bulat** [Булат Кучкеев] (MIB V, 116); Kzk. 1823 **Bulat** [بولات] (MIK IV, 456); Kzk. 1823 **Bulat** [Чубаръ Булатовъ] (TOUAK XXIV, 140); Kzk. 19th c. **Bulat** [Булатъ] (SOK 102); Kzk. 19th c. **Bulat** [Булатъ] (SOK 202); Kzk. 19th c. **Bulat** [Булатъ] (AOP 30); Kzk.? 19th c. **Bulat** [Калмакы Булатов], a writer of articles (AUK 183); Nog. 1649 **Bulat** [Булатъ] (AI IV, 124); Hak. 19th c. **Bulat** [Булатъ] (Titov 129); Maml.? 1299 **Bulat / Bular?** [بولان / بولاد], a mamluk emir from Egypt who fled to Ghazan in 1299 (RaD/Jahn 122, 123); Crm. 1648 **Bulat-aɣa** [بولات اغا] (Vel.-Zern., Crim. 396, 408); Crm. 1708 **Bulat-aɣa** [بولات اغا] (Bakč. Nadp. 27); Crm. 17th c. **Bulat-bahadïr** [بولات بهادر] (Vel.-Zern., Crim. 796); Trkm. 19th c. **Bulat-bay** [Ниазъ-Булатъ-Бай] (Murav'ev I, 48); Bashk. 1740 **Bulat-bay** [Исенгул Булатбаев] (MIB I, 397); Kzk. 19th c. **Bulat-bay** [Булатбай] (AOK 54); Kzk. 1847 **Bulat-batïr** [Булатъ-батыръ] (Konšin, Mat. V, 107); Tat.? 15th c.

Bulat-beg [Булатъ-бѣгъ], a prince, mentioned by the traveller Afanasiy Nikitin (PSRL VI, 332, 346); Uzb./Kzk.? 1717 **Bulat-bey** [Булотбей], resident in Ter (PSZRI V, 487); Kzk. 19th c. **Bulat-bek** [Булатбекъ] (AOK 94); Kzk. 19th c. **Bulat-bek** [Булатбекъ] (AOK 122); Kzk. 19th c. **Bulat-χoǰa** [Булатъ-ходжа], in a legend of origin (Potanin, Pred. 55-57, 61); Bashk. 1737 **Bulat-qan?** [Абдулмаметъ Булаткановъ] (MIB I, 339); Trkm. 1828 **Bulat-mäχrɛm** [Булат-мехрем] (MIT II, 453); Tat. 1558 **Bulat-murza** [Булатъ-мурза] (PSRL XIII, 285); Tat. 1717 **Bulat-murza** [Булатъ-Мурза-Тинбаевъ] (ZIRGO IX, 330); Kzk. 19th c. **Bulat-murza** [Булатъ-мурза], in a legend of origin (Potanin, Pred. 55); Kzk. 19th c. **Bulat-pay** [Бульотпай] (SOV 28); Kzk. 19th c. **Bulat-pay** [Булатъ-пай] (Potanin, Pred. 85-87); Kipch.? 1406, 1407 **Bulat-sultan** [Булатъ султанъ / Булатъ-салтанъ], khan of Golden (or Great) Horde (PSRL (Russk. Hr.) I, 425, PSRL IV, 110, V, 256, VIII, 82, 84, XI, 202, XVI, 157, XXIII, 141); Kzk. 18th c. **Bulat-sultan** [Bulat Sultan] (Howorth II, 685); Khorezm. 14th c. **Fulat / Fulat-sultan** [فولاد سلطان / Foulâd], Shaiban Khan's descendant (Abulg./Desm. 192, Šejb. L, LXXVII); Khorezm./Chag. 1410/11 **Fulat-χan** [Фулад-хан], a Jochid (MIT I, 531); Alt. 19th c. **Molot** [Молот] (Katanov, Otč. 12); Bashk. 1740 **Polat** [Полат Зиликеев] (MIB I, 410); Bashk. 1757 **Polat** [Полат Зиликеев] (MIB IV/1, 144); Kzk. 19th c. **Polat** [Полатъ Джанъ-Тураковъ] (Grod., Pril. 115); Kzk. 19th c. **Polat** [Полатъ] (Grod., Pril. 174); Kkalp. 20th c. **Polat** [Полат] (KkRS 775); Uzb.? 1722 **Polat** [Полатъ], a mulla (Veselovskij, Unk. 178); Trkm. 1823/24 **Pulad-mergen** [Шах Пулад-мерген], a ruler (šah) (MIT II, 423); Khorezm./Chag.? 1376/77 **Pulat** [Пулад] (MIT I, 517); Khorezm./Chag. 1407-1412 **Pulat** [Pulâd], a Jochid on the line of Orda (Zambaur); Chag. 16th c. **Pulat** [پولاد], a Shaybanid (Šejb. XLIX, LI); Turk. 1446 **Pulat** [علی بن پولاد] (MB Qastam. 124); Bashk. 1725 **Pulat** [Мачакбай Пулатовъ] (ZIRGO IX, 393); Bashk. 1757 **Pulat** [Пулат Илтбаев] (MIB IV/1, 150); Bashk. 1757 **Pulat** [Пулатов], a family (MIB IV/1, 150); Bashk. 1757 **Pulat** [Пулат Айметев] (MIB IV/1, 142); Bashk. 1789 **Pulat** [Суюнду (Сеундюк) Пулатов] (MIB V, 267); Kzk. 19th c. **Pulat** [Пулатъ Курчиевъ] (SKSO VIII, 203); Kzk. 19th c. **Pulat** [Пулатъ] (SKSO VIII, 206); Kzk. 19th c. **Pulat** [Пулатъ] (SKSO VIII, 223); Uzb. 19th c. **Pulat** [Ласанъ Пулатовъ] (SKSO III, 174); Uyg. 9th c.-10th c. **Pulat / Bulat** (Radl., Altuig. 59); Uzb. 1845 **Pulat-biy** [Пулатъ-бій Тимуръ-бій оглы] (Moskal'cev 34); Trkm. 1859 **Pulat-χan** [Дуглы-ханъ Пуладъ-хановъ] (ZIRGOÊtn. I, 157); Uzb. **Pulat-χan** [Пулатхановъ], a merchant from Tashkent (Turk. Kraj 1912, 7); Kzk.? 1873 **Pulat-qan** [Poulat-Khan] (Nalivkin-Dozon 258); Trkm. 1817 **Pulat-qul** [Пулат-кул] (MIT II, 401); Uyg.? **Pulat-tegin** [Пулад-тегин] (RaD/Ber. III, 12, RaD I/2, 153). ✧ 'Steel' cf. Uzb., Trkm. *pulat* 'das Stahl' (Radl. IV, 1374), Hak. *molat* 'der Stahl' (Radl. IV, 2126), Kkalp. *polat* 'сталь' (KkRS), Kzk. *bolat* 'сталь' (KzRS), NUyg. *pulat, polat* (Baskakov-Nasilov), Bashk. *bulat* 'булат' (BRS), Tat. *bulat* 'булат' (TatRS), Trkm. *polat* 'сталь' (TrkmRS); R. *Bulatov* (Bask., Fam. 139), (< P.) (Justi 255). See also **AǰÏ-BULAT, AY-BULAT, AQ-BULAT, AL-MULAT, AŠ-BOLAT, BAY-BULAT, BEK-BULAT, BELEK-BULAT, BEŠ-BULAT, ČERİ-BULAT, ČÏN-BULAT, ČOR-BULAT, ČORA-PULAT, ǰAN-BULAT, ǰEM-BULAT, ER-BULAT, EŠ-BULAT, XOR-BULAT, XOŠ-BULAT, İK-BULAT, İL-BULAT, İN-BULAT, İSÄN-BULAT, YAL-BULAT, YAN-BULAT, YAŠ-PULAT, YEÑİ-BULAT, KEMİR-BULAT, KENǰE-BULAT, KOX-BULAT, KORS-PULAT, KÖK-MOLAT, QAY-BULAT, QAYN-BULAT, QARA-BULAT, QARAČA-BULAT, QAS-BULAT, QASA-BULAT, QATÏГ-MOLAT, QOL-BULAT, QUN-BULAT, QUTLU-BULAT, MİÑ-BULAT, MEKLİ-BULAT, MURZA-BULAT, NAR-BULAT, NUR-BULAT, OY-MOLOT, ÖKÖM-BOLOT, PALTA-POLAT, SAY-BULAT, SAYÏN-BULAT, SAN-BULAT, SAP-POLAT, SARÏ-BULAT, Sİ-BULAT, ŠAY-BULAT, ŠİR-BULAT, TAY-BULAT, TAÑ-BOLAT, TAŠ-BULAT, TATTÏ-BOLAT, TAWUQ-BULAT, TAZ-BULAT, TEGİN-BOLAT, TEMİR-BULAT, TİN-BULAT, TOQ-BULAT, TOQTA-BULAT, TOQTÏ-BOLAT, TON-BULAT, TURSUN-PULAT, ULǰA-BULAT, URAS-PULAT.**

BULAT-BUГA Uyg. 12th c.-14th c. **Bulat-buγa** (Radl., USp. 205, 247); Khorezm. 14th c. **Pulat-buγa** [Pulád Bughá], an officer of Timür (Timur Lenk) (Tar. Rashidi 24, 32, 34, 47). ⇨ BULAT + BUQA.

BULAT-KÜKÄǰÄSÜ Kipch.? 1262 **Bulat-kükäǰäsü / Kükäǰür?** [کوکاجور / بلاد کوکاجسو / Пуладъ-Кукаджасу / Кукаджуръ] (Baybars/Tizeng. I, 77, 99). ⇨ BULAT.

BULAT-TEMİR Kuman / Kipch.? 1360, 1366, 1367 **Bulat-temir** [Булатъ-Темиръ (Булакъ-Темеръ / Булакъ Тимеръ / Лубакъ-Темерь)], a prince of the Horde (PSRL IV, 64, V, 229, VIII, 14, XI, 9, XVI, 90, 93); Crm. 17th c. **Pulat-timir** [Пуладъ Тимиръ] (Smirnov, Krym. 140). ⇨ BULAT + TEMİR.

BULATAY Kzk. 19th c. **Bolatay** [Болатай] (SOK 118); Bashk. 1740 **Bulatay** [Булатаев] (MIB I, 384); Kzk. 19th c. **Bulatay** [Булатай] (SOK 78). ⇨ BULA / BULAT? + suff. *-ay* or *-tay(1,2)?*

BULATČÏ Khorezm.? 14th c. **Bulatčï** [پولادچی], an

emir from the Dughlatids (Abulg./Desm. 156, 159, 160); Khorezm.? 14th c. **Pulatčï / Bulatčï?** [Emir Poulâdtchi], Toghluk Temür Khan's (Kashgar) supporter (Abulg./Desm. 165). ⇨ **BULAT** + suff. *-čï*.

BULJĀN Khazar 9th c. **Buljān** [Blučᶜan / Bulčᶜan / Buljän], a general (Golden 171).

BULJĪ Maml.? 1258 **Buljī?** [سيف الد ين بلجى] (Sīrat 88 (10)).

BULDÏ see **BOLDÏ**

BULDU see **BOLDÏ**

BULDUQ Turk.? 1248 **Bulduq-χaǰï** [بلدوق حاجى] (Turan: Belleten XII, 100, 119). ✧ 'Alien, found child' (Erol II), lit. 'We found him/her' cf. Turk. *bul-* 'to find, to reach, to meet' (TED).

BULDUR Kzk. 19th c. **Buldur-bay** [Баембетъ Булдурбаевъ] (Grod., Pril. 37); Kzk. 19th c. **Buldur-bay** [Булдурбай] (Grod., Pril. 37). ✧ 'Foggy, dim; not clear' cf. Kzk. *buldïr* 'sisli, bulanık, aydın değil' (KzTS).

BULĠAİR Bashk. 1746 **Bulγair? / Bulγayïr?** [Булгаир Дюсметев] (MIB III, 435); Bashk. 1746, 1757 **Bulγair? / Bulγayïr?** [Булгаир Десметев (Дюсметев)] (MIB III, 435, IV/1, 140). ✧ Shortened of Ar. Abul-Khair?

BULĠAY Selj. **Bulγay** [بولغاى] (Nešrī 186); Maml. 1299 **Bulγay** [Balgai], one of the emirs of Damascus (Makrīzī IV, 115).

BULĠAQ Karakh. 11 th c. **Bulγaq** [Bulgak] (MK/Atalay 835, DTS); Maml. 13th c., 1299 **Bulγaq** [سيف الد ين بلغاق] (Zetterst. 47, 53, Makrīzī IV, 86, Ibn Taghrīb. VI, 2); Maml. 1307/08 **Bulγaq** [بلغاق بن جفان الحوارزمى] (Berchem, Jér. II, 116, 117); Kzk. 19th c. **Bulγaq** [Булгакъ] (SOV 90, 156); Maml.? 1258 **Bulγaq / Balγaq?** [بلغاق الاشرفى / بـدرالـيـن / Balghāq] (Sīrat 88); Kzk. **Bulγaq / Bulχaq?** [Кулуке Булхаковъ] (Konšin, Pam. 17); Kzk. 19th c. **Bulγaq-pay** [Булгакпай] (SOK 118, 276); Kzk. 19th c. **Bulγaq-pay** [Булгакпай] (SOV 64). ✧ I. 'Seditious; He who foments sedition; rioter' cf. Uyg., Karakh. *bulγa-* 'перемешивать; мутить; досаждать, обижать, печалить; возбуждать недовольство, сеять муту' (DTS); II. 'Proud, high-minded; coquettish' cf. Kzk. *bulγaq* 'stolz einherschreitend (den Kopf nach allen seiten drehend), stolz' (Radl. IV, 1848); III. 'Idler; unstable, untrustworthy man' cf. Kzk. *bulγañ~bulγaq* 'бездельник, празднношатающийся' (Bask., Fam. 49-50) + dev. n suff. *-q*.

BULĠAN Kzk. 19th c. **Bulγan** [Булганъ] (AUK 570); Uzb. 20th c. **Bulγân-bây** [Булгонбой] (Begmatov 1984, 202). ✧ 'Became (a helper); (the child) has been born' cf. Tat. *bul-* 'sein, werden' (Radl. IV, 1835). See also **BOLDÏ**, **BULMÏŠ**; **NUR-BULĠAN**, **UL-BOLĠAN**.

BULĠAR Chuv. 18th-19th c. **Bulgar** [Булгаръ (Торганъ Булгаровъ)] (Magn. 34); Bulg. 6th c. **Bulγar** [Βουλγαρ], a Bulghar prince (Byz. Turc. II, 98); Maml. 1309/10 **Bulγar** [سيف الـدين بلغار] (Iyās I, 151). ✧ I. Bulgar (Ethnonym) (Erol II), cf. also Tat. PN *Bolγar* (Sattarov); II. 'Leather'? cf. Chag. *bulγar* 'das Leder' (Radl. IV, 1850).

BULĠAWUŠ Kzk. 19th c. **Bulγawuš** [Булгаушъ] (SOK 264). ✧ 'Stirrer, a kind of woodden spoon' cf. Kzk. *bɩlǧavɩš* (KzTS).

BULQA Kzk. **Bulqa** [Булька] (Levšin III, 96); Kzk. 19th c. **Bulqa?** [Boulka] (Levchine 356). ✧ 'A kind of Russian bread' cf. Kirg. *bulqa* (<R. *bul'ka*) 'булка; хлеб русского печения' (Jud.).

BULQAY Kzk. 19th c. **Bulqay** [Булкай] (AOP 50). ✧ 'Goods, richess, fortune'. ⇨ **BUL** + dim. suff. *-qay*.

BULMÏŠ Uyg. 12th c.-14th c. **Bulmïš / Bolmïš?** [Bu(o)lmïš, Bulmïš, Bulmış] (Radl., USp. 24-25, 82, 85, 124, DTS, EUTS). ✧ 'Became (a helper); (the child) has been born' cf. Tat. *bul-* 'sein, werden' (Radl. IV, 1835). See also **ASÏQ-BULMÏŠ, MEÑGÜ-BOLMÏŠ; BULĠAN, BOLDÏ**.

BULTAY Kzk. 19th c. **Bultay** [Бултай] (Grod., Pril. 144); Kzk. 19th c. **Bultay / Bultay-batïr**, Qara-batïr's son (Ljutš 50, 52). ⇨ **BUL?** + **TAY** or suff. *-tay(1,2)*?

BULTAN Uyg. 1305 **Bultan / Pultan?** [Pultan] (Chwol., Syr.-nest. (NF) 16).

BULTAŠ Bashk. 1664 **Bultaš** [Булташ] (MIB I, 193).

BULTÏKEY Bashk. 1731 **Bultïkey** [Бултыкей] (MIB III, 292). ✧ 'Dear, valuable, suitable'? cf. Kzk. *buldï* 'kıymetli, fiatlı, işe yarar' (KzTS) + suff. *-key*.

BULTUMAY Alt. 19th-20th c. **Bultumay** [Бултумай], fem. (OjrRS 211).

BULTURUQ Bashk. 1783 **Bultruq (<Bulturuq?)** [Бултрюк Кашкин] (MIB V, 147). ✧ 'A kind of steppe-hen' cf. Kzk. *bulduruq* 'das Steppenhuhn (Ptecocus abnarius)' (Radl. IV, 1854).

BULU Kzk. 19th c. **Bulu-bay** [Булубай] (SOV 134).

BULUČ Selj. 11th c.-13th c. **Buluč / Bulut?** [بلوج / بلوط], a Seljuk from Kirman (Muh. Ibrahim 154, 182). ⇨ **BOLUČ?**

BULUQ Türk 759 **Buluq** [Buluq] (ETY I, 172). See also **QARA-BULUQ**.

BULUQ-ARSLAN Selj. 1200 **Buluq-arslan / Bulaq-arslan** [حسام الـدين بولق ارسلان] (Seldj. Nameh 55, 92). ⇨ **BULUQ** + **ARSLAN.**

BULUN Uyg. 12th c.-14th c. **Bolun** [Bolun] (DTS, EUTS); Uyg. 12th c.-14th c. **Bulun** (Radl., USp. 2-3, Le Coq, Urkunden 1918, 454). ✧ 'Slave; captive' cf. Uyg. *bulun* 'esir; Gefangene' (US, Radl. IV, 1844).

BULUR Karch. **Bulur** [Булуровъ], a Karachay family (Sysoev 128).

BULUT Kzk. 19th c. **Bulut-pay** [Булутпай] (SOV 148). ✧ 'Cloud' cf. Chag., Kuman, Crm., Kar. (L.T.),

Kzk., East.T., NUyg.(Tar.), Trkm., Uzb. *bulut* 'die Wolke, das Gewölk' (Radl. IV, 1845). See also **QARA-BULUT, QASA-BULUT**.

BUMAQ Kzk. 19th c. **Bumaq-pay** [Бумокпай] (SODž. 158). See also **MAM-BUMAQ**.

BUMÏN Türk 6th c. **Bumïn-qaγan** [Bumïn], chieftain of the Türks, founder of the first Türk Khaghanate (DTS, ETY I, 28). ✧ Perhaps of Sogdian origin (Kljaštornyj).

BUN Bashk. 1708 **Bun-güzä** [Темекей Бунгузин] (MIB I, 237).

BUNSUZ see **MUÑSUZ**

BUÑSUZ see **MUÑSUZ**

BUPA Kzk. 1802, 1820 **Bupa** [Бупа], a Kazak Sultan, the chief of the Arγin tribe of Little Horde (Kiši Žüz) (MIK IV, 512, Sib.Vest. IX, 102); Kzk. 1783 **Bupu** (<**Bupa?**) [Boupou] (Levchin 264).

BUPU see **BUPA**

BUR Kzk. 19th c. **Bur-qul** [Уразбай Буркуловъ] (Grod., Pril. 84); *TN:* Kzk. 19th c. **Bur-bay-mola** [Бурбай-мола], a field (AOAtb. 58).

BUR-QUŠ Kzk. 19th c. **Bur-quš** [Буркушевъ] (SKSO VIII, 222). ⇨ **BUR + QUŠ I**.

BUR-TAY Tat.(Lit.) 1552, 1554 **Bur-tay** [Буртай] (Kn. Metriki Lit. 86, 103); Kzk. 19th c. **Bur-tay** [Изтилавъ Буртаевъ] (Grod., Pril. 192). ⇨ **BUR + TAY** or suff. *-tay(1,2)*?

BURA see **BUΓRA**

BURAY Bashk. 1714 **Buray** [Бурай] (MIB I, 106). ⇨ **BUΓRA** + suff. *-y*?

BURAQ Kzk. 19th c. **Braq** (<**Buraq**) [Буратбай Браковъ] (Grod., Pril. 185); Chag.? 15th c. **Buraq** [Буракъ], a prince, Urus-χan's grand-son (Barth., Ulugb. 75-76, 78-79); Turk. 1565 **Buraq**, a spahi (sipahi, cavalry soldier) from Buda, Hungary (Velics-Kamm. II, 349); Yürük 1543 **Buraq** (Gökb., Rum. 189, 190, 192, 224, 225); Tat. 1543 **Buraq** (Gökb., Rum. 240); Kzk. 19th c. **Buraq** [Буракъ] (SOK 208); Turk. (<Ar.?) 1504 **Buraq**, Endüš' son (Gökb., Ed. 428); Turk. (<Ar.?) 1519 **Buraq** [Burak Çelebi] (Gökb., Ed. 332); Yürük 16th c. **Buraq / Baraq?** [براق], from the Yürüks of Kocacık, Turkey (Gökb., Rum. 224); Kkalp. 1820 **Buraq-behadïr** [Бурак бехадыр] (MIKk. 109). ✧ Legendary horse of the Prophet. Cf. Tat.(Tara) *buraq* (<Ar. براق) 'das Pferd' (Radl. IV, 1818), Turk. *Burak* 'Name des Pferdes bei der Himmelfahrt Mohammeds' (HŞ), Kirg. *buraq* 'легендарное вероховое животное' (Jud.).

BURAQAY Bashk. 1709 **Buraqay** [Буракай] (MIB I, 264); Bashk. 1754 **Buraqay** [Буракай Кабясев] (MIB IV/1, 83); Bashk. 1754 **Buraqay** [Унгар Буракаев] (MIB IV/1, 90); Bashk. 1788 **Buraqay** [Буракай Абдуллин] (MIB V, 234); Bashk. 1788 **Buraqay** [Бейбулат Буракаев] (MIB V, 235). ✧ 'Little camel foal' (Torma 1992, 365). ⇨ **BURA** + suff. *-qay / -ay*.

BURALÏ Kzk. 19th c. **Buralï** [Буралы] (SOV 68).

BURALQÏ Kzk. 18th c. - 19th c. **Buralqï-biy** [Буралкы-бий] (Tynyšp. 66). ✧ 'Alien, coming from outside' cf. Kzk. *buralqı* 'id.' (KzTS). See also **ČÏT, YAT, QARÏP, TAT**.

BURALTAY Crm. **Buraltay** [Буралтаи] (Proben VII, 214). ⇨ **TAY?** or suff. *-tay(1,2)*?

BURAN Kzk. 1846 **Boram-bay** (<**Boran-bay**) [Боромбай Баймуратов] (Konšin, Mat. V, 72); Kzk. 19th c. **Boram-bay** (<**Boran-bay**) [Борамбай] (SOV 36); Uyg. **Boran** [Boran] (EUTS); Chuv. 18th-19th c. **Boran** [Боранъ] (Magn. 34); Kkalp. 1810 **Boran** [Боран] (MIKk. 115, 116); Kkalp. 20th c. **Boran-bay** [Боранбай] (KkRS 773); Kzk. 1794 **Boran-bay-mïrza** [کپتان بورانبای مرضه / Капитан Боранбай мурза] (MIK IV, 162); Kkalp. 20th c. **Boran-qul** [Боранкул] (KkRS 773); Bashk. 1744 **Bran-γul** (<**Buran-γul**) [Брангул Иткинин] (MIB III, 415); Kzk. 19th c. **Buram-bay** (<**Buran-bay**) [Бурамбай] (Potanin II, 7); Bashk. 1740 **Buran** [Буран Кулдышев] (MIB I, 422); Kzk. 19th c. **Buran** [Буранъ] (SOV 70); Kzk. 19th c. **Buran** [Курановъ] (SKSO VIII, 222); Uzb. 19th c. **Buran** [Буранъ] (SKSO III, 156); NUyg. 19th c. **Buran** [بوران] (Le Coq, Namenl. 97); Kzk. 18th c. **Buran-bay** [Буранбай] (Nepljuev 762); Kzk. 1811 **Buran-bay** [بورانبای / Боранбай] (MIK IV, 311); Kzk. 19th c. **Buran-bay** [Буранбай] (SODž. 146); Uzb. 19th c. **Buran-bay** [Буранбай Хасановъ] (SKSO III, 172); Kzk. 1792, 1803 **Buran-bay-mïrza** [بورانبای مرزا / Буранбай] (MIK IV, 140, 211); Bashk. 1734 **Buran-γul** [Бурангулъ Едигеровъ], a tarχan (Vel.-Zern., Bašk. 10); Bashk. 1735 **Buran-γul** [Бурангулъ Татыевъ] (Vel.-Zern., Bašk. 15); Bashk. 1754 **Buran-γul** [Бурангул Утяков] (MIB IV/1, 84); Bashk. 1770 **Buran-γul** [Бурангул Култаев] (MIB IV/1, 341); Bashk. 1776 **Buran-γul** [Сеит Бурангулов] (MIB V, 47-49); Bashk. 1790 **Buran-γul** [Рангун Бурангулов] (MIB V, 276, 283); Kzk. 19th c. **Buran-γul** [Бурангулъ] (Lomakin 40). ✧ 'Snowstorm' cf. Turk., Chag. *buraγan*, Turk., Tat. *buran*, Chag. *boraγan*, East.T., Kzk. *boran* 'Sturm, Schneesturm' (Radl. IV, 1662, 1818), cf. Kkalp. *boran* 'буран, снежная вьюга; сильный ветер' (KkRS). See also **DÜLEK-BURAN**.

BURAN-QUŠ Oghuz 12th c. **Buran-quš** [Bāzdār Buranquš], a slave of the Khalife Moqtafi (1138-1160), then that of the ruler of Qazwïn, died in 1140/1141 (Justi 66 (after Ibn al-Athïr/Tornb. X, 477 etc.)). ⇨ **BURAN + QUŠ I**.

BURAN-TAY Kzk. 19th c. **Buran-tay** [Бурантай] (SOK 54). ⇨ **BURAN + TAY** or suff. *-tay(1,2)*?

BURANAQ Alt. 19th-20th c. **Buranaq** [Буранак]

(OjrRS 208).

BURANČÏ Tat. 1777 **Buranča?** (<**Burančï**) [Темиралъ Буранчинъ] (PSZRI XX, 577, 579); Bashk. 1718 **Buranča?** (<**Burančï**) [Буранча] (MIB III, 168); Bashk. 1759 **Buranča?** (<**Burančï**) [Алибай Буранчин] (MIB IV/2, 382); Bashk. 1789 **Buranča?** (<**Burančï**) [Юрали Буранчин] (MIB V, 269); Tat.(Sib.) 1601 **Buranči / Burančï** [Уракчей Буранчеев] (Miller, Ist. Sib. II, 165); Tat.(Sib.) 1605 **Buranči / Burančï** [Янтлеш Буранчеев] (Miller, Ist. Sib. II, 190). ✧ 'Born during snow-storm' (Sattarov, Kusimova). ⇨ BURAN + suff. -*čï*.

BURAS see BURAŠ

BURAŠ Kzk. 19th c. **Buras** [Бурасъ] (AOO 14); Tat. 1783, 1797 **Buraš** [Абдулъ-Гази Токтамышевъ Бурашовъ / Абдулъ-Гази Бурашевъ] (Korsakov 113, PSZRI XXIV, 310); Tat.(Sib.) 1605 **Buraš** [Янгузя Бурашевъ] (Miller, Ist. Sib. II, 190); Bashk. 1734 **Buraš** [Бурашевъ], family-name (Vel.-Zern., Bašk. 10); Bashk. 1734 **Buraš** [Емагулъ Бурашевъ] (Vel.-Zern., Bašk. 10); Bashk. 1756 **Buraš** [Бураш Васев] (MIB IV/1, 122); Bashk. 1773 **Buraš** [Бураш Алимгузин] (MIB IV/2, 411); Tat. 1491 **Buraš-seyit** [Бураш-Сеитъ], commander of Kazan (PSRL VI, 38, VIII, 223, VIII, 223, XII, 228); Bulg. 1291 **Būrāš-bek** [بورا ش بك] (Jusupov 4). ⇨ BUƔRA? + suff. -*š*.

BURAT Kzk. 19th c. **Burat-bay** [Буратбай] (Grod., Pril. 185). ✧ ? See also BAY-BURAT.

BURČ Karakh. 10th c.-12th c. **Burč-tegin / Bur-tegin / Pur-tegin** [Бурч-тегин Ибрахим ибн Наср (Бур-тегин, Пур-тегин)], a Tamɣač Khan (MIT 232, 273-74, 277, 286, 294, 295, 297, 360). ✧ 'Fortress, rook, bastion' cf. Crm. *burč* 'die Befestigung', Turk. *burǰ* 'der Thurm, der Bastion, das Sodiakzeichen' (Radl. IV, 1833), Uzb. *burǰ* 'угловая башня крепостной стены'; *burč* 'долг, обязанность' (UzbRS).

BURČAQ Kzk. 19th c. **Borǰaq / Boržaq / Boršaq?** [Боржакъ] (AOP 90); Bashk. 1716, 1719 **Burčaq** [Казбулат (Каспулат) Бурчаков] (MIB III, 142, 187); Bashk. 1740, 1745 **Burčaq** [Шеганай (Шиганай) Бурчаков (Барсуков, Барчуков, Барчюк)] (MIB I, 378-80 etc., III, 513, 548); Bashk. 18th c. **Burčaq** [Шаганай Бурчаков] (MIB V, 672, 676, 677); Bashk. 1759 **Burčaq** [Шагинай Бурчаков] (MIB IV/2, 167, 168); Kzk. 19th c. **Burčaq** [Бурчакъ] (SODž. 62); Kzk. 19th c. **Burčaq-pay** [Бурчакпай] (SOK 50, 100, 168); Kzk. 19th c. **Burčaq-pek** [Бурчакпекъ] (SOK 66); Kzk. 19th c. **Buršaq** [Буршакъ] (SODž. 66); Kzk. 19th c. **Buršaq-pay** [Буршакпай] (SOK 172). ✧ I. 'Pea' cf. Turk., Trkm, Uzb. *burčaq* 'die Erbse; die Wicke (vicia)' (Radl. IV, 1832), Kzk. *buršaq* 'Erbse, der Hagel' (Radl. IV, 1833), Kzk. *bŭršaq* 'id.' (KzRS); II. 'Hail, hailstone' cf. Kzk. *bŭršaq* ' горох, фасоль' (KzRS); III. 'A rope with

knots for tying lambs' cf. Kzk. *buršaq* 'eine Schnur mit Kügelchen, die man den Lämmern um den Hals legt, wenn man sie anbindet' (Radl. IV, 1833), ' родъ четокъ' (PRS). See also MÏS-BURČAQ, MUZ-BURČAQ.

BURǰAY Kzk. 19th c. **Burǰay** [Алимъ Бурджаевъ] (Grod., Pril. 162).

BURDU Bashk. 1761 **Burdu-ɣul** [Бурей Бурдугулов] (MIB IV/1, 218).

BUREY Bashk. 1761 **Burey? / Bürey?** [Бурей Бурдугулов] (MIB IV/1, 218).

BURƔAN Kzk. 19th c. **Burɣam-bay** (<**Burɣan-bay**) [Бургамбай] (SOK 164); Kzk. **Burɣan-bay** [Сыдыкъ Бургонбаевъ] (Konšin, Pam. 26).

BURƔANAY Yak. **Burɣānay** [Бурҕанаi] (Pek.). ✧ 'Hot-tempered' (=R. 'Вспыльчивый'), cf. Yak. *burɣai-* 'подниматься' (Pek.).

BURƔUČAN Uyg. **Burɣučan** [Burguçan] (EUTS). See also ALP-BURƔUČAN.

BURƔUL-TAY Kzk. 19th c. **Burɣul-tay** [Бургултай] (Potanin II, 149). ⇨ TAY or suff. -*tay(1,2)*?

BURHAN see BURXAN I.

BURXAN I. Turk. 1530 **Burhan** [Burhan] (Gökb., Ed. 501); Yürük 1543 **Burhan** [Burhan], from Silistre (Gökb., Rum. 227, 230); Turk. 15th c. **Burhan-fakih** [Burhan-Fakih] (Gökb., Ed. 84); Turk. 1510 **Burhan-kethudā** [Burhan-Kethudâ] (Gökb., Ed. 428); Uyg. 12th c.-14th c. **Burχan-qulï** [Burχan Quli / Burχan qulï] (Radl., USp. 203, DTS).

BURXAN Uyg. 13th-14th c. **Burχan-qulï-tutuñ** [Bur[χa]n Qulï Tutung] (Zieme, Mat. III, 274).

BURXAN II. Bashk. 1735 **Burχan** [Бурханъ Аиткуловъ] (Vel.-Zern., Bašk. 15); Kzk. 19th c. **Burχan** [Бурханъ] (SOK 26); Kzk. 19th c. **Burχan-baqši** [Бурханъ-Бакши] (Potanin IV, 555). ✧ 'Stentorian, rousing' cf. Kzk. *burqan* 'der Schreihals, der Lautsprechende, der Zänker' (Radl. IV, 1827); or the same as Tat./Bashk. *Borhan* 'Truth(ful)' (Sattarov, Kusimova). ⇨ BURQAN.

BURÏN Kzk. 1826 **Burin? / Burïn** [Сарамбай Буринъ] (TOUAK XXIV, 74); Kzk. 19th c. **Burin-bay? / Burïn-bay** [Буринбаевъ] (SKSO III, 15).

BURÏǰÏ Oghuz/Trkm. 13th c. **Burïǰï-ɣazi** [غازى بوريجى / Бурыджы-Гази] (Abulg./Kon. 1165).

BURÏQ Kzk. 1823 **Burïq** [Куфинбай Бурковъ] (TOUAK XXIV, 139).

BURYUQ-TİRÄK Uyg. **Buryuq-tiräk**, „Stiftername eines buddhistischen Sündenbekenntnisses" (TT IV, 43); Uyg. **Buryuq-tiräk** (TT IV, 432). ✧ 'Clerk/writer - Supporter'. ⇨ BUYRUQ + TİRÄK.

BURQA Kzk. 19th c. **Burqa** [Бурка] (SOK 216).

BURQAY Uyg. **Burqay** [Burkay] (EUTS).

BURQAN Kzk. 19th c. **Burqam-bay** (<**Burqan-bay**) [Буркамбай] (SODž. 144); Kzk. 19th c. **Burqam-bay**

(<**Burqan-bay**) [Буркомбай] (SODž. 108); Kzk. 1820 **Burqan** [Бурканъ], a chief of a tribe (Sib. Vest. IX, 120). ✧ 'Buddha, Prophet, Idol' cf. Kzk. *burqan* 'der Götze, das Buddhabild' (Radl. IV, 1827), Uyg., Hak., Alt. *purqan* 'Buddha; ein von den Shamanen verehrter Geist' (Radl. IV, 1368); II. 'Stentorian, rousing' cf. Kzk. *burqan* 'der Schreihals, der Lautsprechende, der Zänker' (Ibid.). ⇨ **BURXAN I.? / BURXAN II.?** See also **QAN-PURXAN.**

BURQAN-QURMAN Kzk. 1794 **Burqan-qurman-biy?** [بـرقـن قورمـن بـی / Беркын Курман] (MIK IV, 163). ⇨ **BURQAN + QURMAN.**

BURQAS Oghuz/Trkm. 13th c. **Burqas** [بـرقـاس / Буркас], Isik-Ismail's adopted son (Abulg./Kon. 1290).

BURQAT Kzk. 19th c. **Burqat** [Буркатъ] (AOP 74). ✧ 'Buddha, Prophet, Idol' cf. *burqat* 'der Götze, der Götzentempel' (Radl. IV, 1828). ⇨ **BURXAN I.**

BURQÏ Kzk. 1825 **Burqï** [بـورقـه / Буркы] (MIK IV, 471, 476).

BURQU Kzk. 1820 **Burqu-biy** [Бурку-бий], one of the chiefs of the Čümekey tribe (Sib. Vest. IX, 117). ✧ 'Drill, bit' cf. Kzk., Turk. *burɣu* 'der Bohrer, der Drehbohrer' (Radl. IV, 1829).

BURLA see BORLU

BURLAQ Tat.(Sib.) 1629, 1630 **Burlaq** [Бурлак], a murza from Čat (?), a Čat (Čatskij) prince (Miller, Ist. Sib. II, 359, 360, 369, Radl., Aus Sib. I, 181); Bashk. 1734 **Burlaq** [Бурлак Кутлуев] (MIB IV/1, 84). ✧ I. 'Fallow' II. 'Haulier' (<R.) *burlak*; cf. Tat. *burlaq* I. 'залеѢь', *burlaq* II. 'бурлак' (TatRS).

BURLÏ see BORLU

BURLU see BORLU

BURMA Kirg. **Burma** [Бурма] (Jud. 918). ✧ 'Helical; screwed; wily' cf. Kirg. *burma* 'винтовой, винтообразный; колошек в веретене; уловка, неискренность' (Jud.), Kzk. *burma* 'gedreht, schraubenförmig, kraus, gekräuselt' (Radl. IV, 1834).

BURMAN Kzk. 19th c. **Burman** [Бурманъ] (SOV 136); Kzk. 19th c. **Burman** [Бурманъ] (SOK 68).

BURNAS Tat. 19th c. **Burnas** [Abdulazim Burnasev] (Mende 20).

BURNAŠ Tat. 19th c. **Burnaš** [F. Burnaš] (Mende 182).

BURSEY Bashk. 1740 **Bursey** [Бурсей Тулкусев] (MIB I, 435).

BURSÏQ Kzk. 19th c. **Bursïq** [Кучманъ Бурсиковъ] (Grod., Pril. 186); Bashk. 1737 **Bursuq** [Кайка Бурсуков] (MIB I, 318); Kzk. **Bursuq** [Бурсукъ манапъ (небольшаго поколѣнья Кыдыкъ)], head (manap) of the Qïdïq clan (Valihanov, Soč. 59). ✧ I. 'Badger' cf. Tat. *bursiq* = *barsiq* 'der Dachs' (Radl. IV, 1833); II. 'Crinkly, wizened' Chag. *bursuq* = *pursuq* 'gerunzelt, faltig, kraus' (Radl. IV, 1371).

BURSLAN Karakh. 11th c. **Burslan** [Burslan] (DTS, MK/Atalay 835).

BURSUQ see BURSÏQ

BURSUQAY Bashk. 1740 **Bursuqay** [Аргилды Бурсукаев] (MIB I, 445). ⇨ **BURSÏQ** + suff. *-(q)ay?*

BURŠAQ see BURČAQ

BURTAN Kzk. 1817 **Burtan-bay** [بـورطـا نـبـای / Буртанбай] (MIK IV, 313, 319). ✧ I. 'Sanguine, violent, nervous, rude' cf. Kzk. *burtan* 'id.' (KzTS); II. 'Man unnaturally speaking and moving' cf. Kzk. *burtañ / burqañ* 'id.' (Radl. IV, 1827, 1831).

BURTAŠ Tat.(Lit.) 1557 **Burtaš / Bur-taš?** [Бурташъ] (Kn. Metriki Lit. 152); Kzk. 19th c. **Burtaš / Bur-taš?** [Бурташъ] (AOA 110). ✧ 'Hard pisser (a kind of illness)' cf. Kzk. *burtaš* 'Blasenkrankheit, die das Harnlassen erschwert' (Radl. IV, 1831).

BURTU Kzk. 19th c. **Burtu-bay** [Буртубай] (SOK 154).

BURTUČ Kzk. 1819 **Burtuč** [Буртучь] (MIK IV, 326).

BURU Kzk. 19th c. **Buru-bek** [Бурубекъ] (SOK 20).

BURUQ Kzk. 19th c. **Buruq-pay** [Бурукпай] (SODž. 80). ✧ 'Order, command'? cf. NUyg.(Tar.) *būruq ~ burik* 'der Befehl' (Radl. IV, 1821). ⇨ **BUYRUQ?**

BURUL Uyg. 12th c.-14th c. **Burul** (Radl., USp. 127, 236); Kirg. **Burul** [Бурул], fem. (Jud. 658). ✧ 'Apple-grey' cf. Kirg. *būrul* 'чалый' (Jud.), NUyg. *būrul* 'mit gemischten Haare (Pferdefarbe)' (Radl. IV, 1824). See also **KÜČÜM-BUɣRUL, QAŠQA-BŪRUL, TAY-BŪRUL.**

BURULČA Kirg. **Burulča** [Бурулча], fem. (Jud. 30, 918). ⇨ **BURUL** + suff. *-ča.*

BURULDAY Tuv. 19th c. **Borolday** [Бай Боролдай], a Mongol general in Berke's time (Potanin IV, 379); Uyg. 12th c.-14th c. **Burulday** [Buruldaj, Burulday] (DTS, EUTS). ✧ I. 'A kind of ashen grey bird' cf. Chag., Turk. *borulday* 'ein aschgrauer Vogel' (Radl. IV, 1664); II. 'Grey, grey-haired'? cf. Alt. *burul* 'седой; чалый' (OjrRS) + suff. *-day.* See also **BOZJA.**

BURULɣÏ Kipch. 1293 **Burulɣï** [بـرلغـی / Бурулги] (Baybars/Tizeng. I, 137, 158).

BURULQAN Kirg. **Burulqan** [Бурулкан], fem. (Jud. 70). ⇨ **BURUL** + suff. *-qan(1).*

BURUM see BURUN

BURUMAN Kzk. 19th c. **Buruman-qul** [Буруманкулъ] (SOV 104). ⇨ **BURU?** + suff. *-man.*

BURUN Kirg. 1847, 1851 **Burom-bay** (<**Burun-bay**) [Burom Bai / Буромбай], head (manap) of the Buɣu clan (ArchKR XI, 403, ZIRGO V, 141); Kzk. 19th c. **Buron-bay? / Boron-bay? / (<Burun-bay**) [Буронбай / Боронбай] (SODž. 30); Chag. 16th c. **Burum?** [Bouroum], son of Bujuɣa, the Khan of Khiva (Abulg./Desm. 228); Kzk. 1820 **Burum-bay** (<**Burun-bay**) [Бурумбай], one of the chiefs of the Jaɣalbaylï tribe (Sib. Vest. IX, 123); Kzk. 19th c. **Burum-bay** (<**Burun-bay**) [Бурумбай] (SOK 60); Khorezm?

Burun [Бурунъ] (RaD/Ber. II, 29, 30, 32); Kzk. 1797 **Burun-bay** [Бурунбай] (Dobrosm., Turg. 211); Kzk. 19th c. **Burun-bay** [Бурунбай] (Grod., Pril. 180); Uzb. 19th c. **Burun-bay** [Бурунбай] (TV 1876, 78); Kzk. 19th c. **Burun-qul** [Бурункулъ] (SODž. 76); Trkm. 1525/26 **Burun-sultan** [بورون سلطان / Бурун-султан / Бирун-султан] (Dorn 248, MIT II, 51, 58); Kzk. 19th c. **Murum-bay** (<Murun-bay) [Мурумбай] (SOV 152); Kzk. 19th c. **Murum-bay** (<Murun-bay) [Мурумбай] (SODž. 118); Trkm. 19th c. **Murun** [Мурунъ] (AUK 58); Kzk. 19th c. **Murun-bay** [Мурунбай] (SODž. 162); Kzk. 19th c. **Murun-qul** [Мурункулъ] (SOK 30); Kzk. **Murun-žïraw** [Мурун-жырау], a folk singer (Žirm., Epos 396). ✧ 'Nose' cf. Kuman., Crm., Kar.(L.T.), Kzk., Trkm., Turk., Uzb. *burun* 'die Nase, der Schnabel; das Vorgebirge' (Radl. IV, 1821), Alt., Hak., Kzk. *murun* 'id.' (Radl. IV, 2193). See also **BURUNLÏ, BURUNSÏZ; BOQ-MURUN, ČOŇ-MURUN, SAM-BURUN, SAT-BURUN, UZUN-BURUN, ZOR-MURUN.**

BURUNAQ Chag. **Burunaq-sultan** [برناق سلطان / Бернагкъ], a Sheybanid (Šejb. L). ⇨ **BURUN?** + suff. *-aq.*

BURUNČA Bashk. 1776 **Burunča** [Бурунча Даутов] (MIB V, 35, 90, 91). ⇨ **BURUN** + suff. *-ča.*

BURUNDUQ Khorezm.? 1306 **Burunduq** [برندق], an emir (Dorn 145, 179, 390); Chag. 15th c. **Burunduq** [Бурундукъ], head of the vanguard (Barth., Ulugb. 48, 50, 51); Chag.? 1600 **Burunduq** [بورو ند وق], an Arabshahid prince (Abulg./Desm. 291); Tat. 1712 **Burunduq** [Бурундук] (MIB III, 85); Tat. 19th c. **Burunduq** [Burundukov] (Mende 158); Chag. / Uzb.? 1593 **Burunduq-sultan** [بوروندق / برندوق سلطان / Бурундук-султан], a Sheybanid (Šejb. L, MIT II, 82, 91); Kzk. 19th c. **Murundïq** [Мурундыкъ] (AOA 78). ✧ 'Muzzle (a small stick in the nose of a camel which it is directed or driven by)' cf. Chag. *burunduq* 'der Nasenpfloch der Kameele' (Radl. IV, 1824), Kzk. *murundŭq* 'id.' (Radl. IV, 2193). ⇨ **BURUN** + suff. *-duq.*

BURUNLÏ Maml. 14th c. **Burunlï / Burunlu** [برنلو / برنلی] (Sauvaget 41). ✧ 'Having a (big) nose' (Sauvaget 41: 'qui a un grand nez'). ⇨ **BURUN** + suff. *-lï.* See also **BURUNSÏZ.**

BURUNLU see **BURUNLÏ**

BURUNSÏZ Maml. (Trkm.) 1456 **Burunsïz** [برنسز التـركمانى] (Ibn Taghrīb. VIII, 292); Turk. 1583 **Burunsuz** [بور نسوز] (Ongan, Ank. I, 104). ✧ 'Without a nose (=having small nose)'. ⇨ **BURUN** + suff. *-siz.* See also **BURUNLÏ.**

BURUNSUZ see **BURUNSÏZ**

BURUZΓAU Kzk. 19th c. **Buruzγay** [Buruzgay] (Vámbéry, Vázlatok 310). ✧ 'Secluded, wrong, false'?

cf. Kzk. *burıs* 'id.' (KzTS) + dim. suff. *-qay.*

BUSARDU Uyg. 13th-14th c. **Busardu-ïnal** [Busardu Ïnal] (Zieme, Mat. III, 274).

BUSQAN see **BUZQAN**

BUSQUM see **BUSQUN**

BUSQUN Bashk. 1770, 1791 **Busqun** [Калкаман Бускунов] (MIB IV/1, 343, V, 313); Bashk. 1785 **Busqun** [Колкаман Бускунов] (MIB V, 178); Bashk. 1762 **Busqun / Busqum** [Салей Бускунов (Бускум)] (MIB IV/2, 300-301). ✧ 'Refugee; Hidden' cf. Bashk. *boθow* 'таиться, притаиться' (BRS), cf. *Bosqon* (Kusimova).

BUSLUMAN see **MUSULMAN**

BUSTAN see **BOSTAN**

BUSTU Kzk. 1819 **Bustu-bay** [Бустубай] (MIK IV, 326). ✧ 'Escaped'? cf. Chag., Kzk. *bus-* 'Überfälle machen; den Wohnsitz wegen häufiger Überfälle verlassen' (Radl. IV, 1864).

BUSU Yak. **Busu-χan** [Бусухан], a legendary cook (Pek.). ✧ 'Ripe, being cooked' cf. Yak. *bus-* 'вариться, печься, свариться, поспевать, быть готовым для еды (о пище)' (Pek.).

BUSUM Bashk. 1756 **Busum** [Бусум Масаилов] (MIB IV/1, 122).

BUSURMAN Kzk. 1822 **Busurman** [Бусурмановъ] (TOUAK XXIV, 117); Kzk. 1846 **Busurman** [Кумувак Бусурмановъ] (MKOP 151); Kzk. 19th c. **Busurman** [Бусурманъ] (SOK 138); Kzk. 19th c. **Busurman** [Бусурманъ] (AOP 42); Kzk. 19th c. **Busurman** [Бусурманъ] (SOK 12); Kzk. 19th c. **Busurman** [Бусурманъ] (SODž. 152); Kzk. 19th c. **Busurman** [Бусурманъ] (SOV 68); Kzk. 19th c. **Busurman** [Бусурманъ] (Grod., Pril. 78); Kzk. 19th c. **Busurman** [Бусурманъ] (AOP 18). ✧ 'Mohammedan, Moslem'. See also **BAY-BUSURMAN.**

BUŠAČU Uyg. 12th c.-14th c. **Bušaču** (DTS). ✧ 'Cheerless, angry, gruff' (Bese 13), cf. Uyg., Karakh. *buš-* 'печалиться, сердиться' (DTS) + suff. *-(a)ču.*

BUŠAY Kzk. 19th c. **Bušay** [Бушаевъ] (AUK 184); Kzk. 19th c. **Bušay** [Даулетъ Бушаев], Sultan Dawlet Bušayev (AUK 287).

BUŠBAN Kzk. 19th c. **Bušban** [Бужбанъ] (AOO 10). ✧ 'A kind of thick sausage' cf. Kzk. dial. *bužban* 'бүйенге салып істеген шұжық, шұжықтың үлкен түрі' (QTDS).

BUŠÏ Uyg. 13th-14th c. **Bušï-qulï** (Zieme, Mat. III, 280). ✧ 'Alms' cf. Uyg. *bušï* 'пожертвование, покаяние' (DTS) (Chin.). See also **SADAQA.**

BUŠMAN Tat. 1686 **Bušman** [Максимко Бушмановъ] (Kungursk. akty 125).

BUT Kzk. **Bud-bay** [Кюнтушъ Будбаев] (ZIRGOGeogr. I, 272); Kzk. 1803, 1820 **But-bay** [Бутбай], a chief (biy) of a tribe of the Little Horde (Kiši Žüz) (MIK IV, 513, Sib.Vest. IX, 110); Kzk. 1846

But-bay [Бутбай] (MKOP 86); Kzk. 19th c. **But-bay** [Калэндаръ Бутбаевъ] (Grod., Pril. 161); Kzk. 19th c. **But-bay** [Ніязъ Бутбаевъ] (Grod., Pril. 177). ✧ I. 'Leg, thigh' cf. Kuman, Chag., Crm., Kzk., Trkm. etc. *but* 'der Schenkel' (Radl. IV, 1856); II. 'Idol' cf. Chag., Tat., Trkm., Uzb. *but* 'der Götze' (Radl. IV, 1856). See also **BEY-BUT, ČEY-BUT, ČOQ-BUT, QARA-BUT, Šİ-BUT.**

BUT-QAYA Uyg. 12th c.-14th c. **But-qaya** [But Qaya] (Radl., USp. 122). ⇨ **BUT + QAYA.**

BUT-QARA Uyg. 12th c.-14th c. **But-qara** (DTS). ✧ 'Thigh-black' (Bese 18). ⇨ **BUT + QARA.**

BUTA see **BOTA**

BUTAQ Uzb. 1460 **Buday-sultan** [Пир-Будаг-султан], brother of the Uzbek Mustafa-χan (MIT I, 539); Trkm. 1591 **Buday-sultan / Buday-χan** [Будаг-султан / Будаг-хан], a man from the Qajar / Čegeni clan (MIT II, 75, 76, 85, 87, 91, 92, 93, 99); Yürük 1543 **Budak** [بوداق] (Gökb., Rum. 102, 180, 184, 200, 208); **Budaq** [بوداق], from the Zend-dynasty (Tar. Zend. IV.); Turk. 16th c. **Budaq** (Ongan, Ank. II.); Turk. 1570, 1580 **Budaq** [Ahmed bin Budaq, Isa bin Budaq] (Dávid?); Yürük 1575 **Budaq** (Gökçen 49); Yürük 1613 **Budaq** [بداق / Beyazid ibn Budak] (Gökçen 88); Turk. **Budaq-beg**, one of the emirs of the Pürnek (?) [پورناق] clan (Demirtaş 33); Kzk. 19th c. **Budaq-pay** [Будакпай] (SODž. 124); Turk. 1583, 1584 **Budaq** [بداق] (Ongan, Ank. I, 150, 154); Tat.(Lit.) 1548 **Butaq** [Бутакъ] (Kn. Metriki Lit. 45); Kzk. 19th c. **Butaq** [Бутаковъ] (AUK 183); 1589 **Butaq-bek** [Бутакъ бекъ] (Veselovskij, Pam. 124); Trkm. 1881 **Pudaq** [Пудакъ] (Grod., Vojna IV, 18); Trkm. 20th c. **Pudaq** [Pudaq] (Zaj. 1971, 332); Trkm. 20th c. **Pūdaq** [Пудак] (TrkmRS 537). ✧ 'Branch, stick, sucker; seed' cf. Karakh. *butaq / buday* 'ветвь, ветка' (DTS), Kuman, Kzk., Crm. *butaq* 'der Zweig' (Radl. IV, 1857), Turk. *budaq* 'der Schössling, der Zweig, die Weinrebe' (Radl. IV, 1858), Trkm. *pūdaq* 'отросток; ветка' (TrkmRS). See also **ER-BUDAQ, GÜLİ-BUDAQ, QARA-BUDAQ, ŠAH-BUDAQ.**

BUTALÏ Tat.? 1698 **Butalï** [Уразайко Буталинъ], a captain (Kungursk. akty 267). ✧ 'Having camel foal(s)'? ⇨ **BOTA + suff. -lï.**

BUTAŠ see **BOTAŠ**

BUTTU see **BATTU?**

BUTU Kzk. 19th c. **Butu-yul? / Butu-yol** [Усбанъ Бутуголовъ] (Grod., Pril. 75).

BUTUQ **Butuq-χan** [Бутук-хан] (RaD I/1, 165).

BUTUM-BAY see **BUTUN**

BUTUN Kzk. 19th c. **Butum-bay (<Butun-bay?)** [Бутумбай] (AOAtb. 46); *TN:* Kzk. **Butun-bay** [Бутунъ-бай], a kurgan (burial mound) (Konšin, Pam. 29).

BUTUR Trkm. 1690 **Butur** [بوتور] (Refik, Anad. 86). ✧ 'Shameless, impudent; very happy' cf. Kzk. *butur* 'id.' (Radl. IV, 1857).

BUTUŠ Alt. 19th c. **Butuš** [Бутушъ] (Potanin IV, 176, 215).

BUZ Selj. 12th c. **Buz-aba** [بوز ابه], lord (sāχib) of Fars (Rāwandī 231, 239); Kzk. 19th c. **Buz-bay** [Бузбай] (Grod., Pril. 19). ✧ I.'Ice' cf. Kuman, Az., Crm., Kar., Trkm., Turk. *buz* 'das Eis' (Radl. IV, 1866), Chag., Kirg., Kzk., Uzb. *muz* 'id.' (Radl. IV, 2207), Uyg., Alt. *muz* 'id.' (Radl. IV, 2202); II.'Grey' cf. Tat. *buz* 'grau, weisslich' (Radl. IV, 1866). See also **BOZ.**

BUZAČ Türk 9th c. **Buzač-tutuq** [Buzaç Tutuq] (Runic Mss. 219, DTS, ETY II, 96). ✧ I. 'Little (piece of) ice' (Bese 5),; II. 'A kind of drink made of millet' cf. Chag., Tat. *buza* 'ein aus Hirse bereitetes Getränk' (Radl. IV, 1867). ⇨ **BUZ + dim. suff. -č/-ač.**

BUZAĞU Uyg. 8th c. **Buzaγu** [Buzağu] (DTS, EUTS); Kzk. 1819 **Buzaq** [Бузак] (MIK IV, 324); Tat.(Sib.) 1599 **Buzaw** [Бузавъ], a nurse in Küčüm's service (AI II, 20); Kzk. 19th c. **Buzaw?** [Тукубанъ Бузуавовъ] (Grod., Pril. 106); Kzk. 19th c. **Bzaw-bay (<Buzaw-bay)** [Бзаубай] (AOAtb. 6); Kzk. 19th c. **Bzaw-bay (<Buzaw-bay)** [Бзаубай] (SODž. 108). ✧ 'Calf' cf. Türk, Uyg., Karakh. *buzaγu I* 'теленок' (DTS), Kuman, Tat.(Tob.), Kzk. *buzau* 'das Kalb' (Radl. IV, 1867), East.T. *buzaq / buzau* 'id.' (Radl. IV, 1867), Kzk. *buzau* 'id.' (PRS), Alt. *bïza* 'телёнок' (OjrRS).

BUZAQ see **BUZAĞU**

BUZAQAY Tuv. 19th c. **Buzaqay** [Бузакай-Таракай] (Potanin IV, 345).

BUZAN Bulg. 10th c. **Buzan** [Buzan], a 10th century Bulgar chieftain (Golden 183); Bashk. 1770, 1783 **Buzan** [Бузан Исмаков] (MIB IV/1, 349, V, 139). ⇨ **BOZAN?** See also **TULUM-BUZAN.**

BUZAR see **BOZAR**

BUZAW see **BUZAĞU**

BUZAW-BAQ Kzk. 19th c. **Bzaw-baq (<Buzaw-baq)** [Бзаубакъ] (SOV 88). ⇨ **BUZAĞU + BAQ.**

BUZAWMAN Kzk. 19th c. **Bzawman** [Бзауманъ] (SOV 22). ⇨ **BUZAĞU + suff. -man?**

BUZAWTAY Kzk. 19th c. **Bzawtay (<Buzawtay)** [Бзаутай] (AOAtb. 50). ✧ I. Polite and petting form of *Buzaw*; II. '(S)he is like a calf; little calf'. ⇨ **BUZAĞU + suff. -tay(1,2).**

BUZDAQ Bashk. 1738 **Buzdaq** [Буздяк Ишимбетев] (MIB III, 378); Kzk. 1820 **Buzdaq** [Буздакъ], a leader of the Čümekey tribe (Sib. Vest. IX, 122). ✧ 'Young man, fine manly youngster, hero' cf. Kzk. *bozdaq* 'id.' (KzTS). ⇨ **BOZ + suff. -daq.** See also **BUYDAQ, BUZNAK.**

BUZQAN Bashk. 1788 **Busqan** [Бускан Рантанов] (MIB V, 234); Kuman 1333 **Buzqan** [Buzkan filio Arbuz], from the Kumans of Hungary (Gyárfás III,

476). ✧ 'Breaker, destroyer' cf. Türk., Kuman, Kzk., Kar.(L. T.) *buz-* 'zerstören, zerschlagen, verderben, zerbrechen' (Radl. IV, 1866), see also Rásonyi, Adalékok 133, Rásonyi, Anthr. 139, Rásonyi, KÖA 97.

BUZNAQ Tat.? 1543 **Buznaq** [بوزناق] (Jusupov 65). ✧ 'Young man, fine manly youngster, hero'. ⇨ **BOZ** + suff. *-naq*.

BUZUQ see **BOZUQ**

BUZURUQ Uzb.? 19th c. **Buzuruq-χoǰa** [Bouzouroukhodja], governor of Čust („gouverneur de Tchoust") in Ferghana (Nalivkin-Dozon 98). ✧ 'Great, saint' cf. Uzb. *buzruq* 'великий, грандиозный, большой; святой; шутливое название верблюда' (UzbRS) (<P.).

BUŽALTAY Kzk. 19th c. **Bužaltay** [Бужалтай] (SOK 140).

BŪČUGURŪR Yak. **Būčugurūr** [Бучугурур] (Pek.). ✧ Derived from Yak. *būčui* (Pek.).

BŪČUYDĀN Yak. **Būčuydān** [Бучуйдан] (Pek.). ✧ Derived from Yak. *būčui* (Pek.).

BŪDAY see **BUΓDAY I.**

BŪNČUQ Alt. 19th c. **Būnčuq(-qam)** [Буунчукъ камъ], a Teleñit (Teleñut) tale-teller (Potanin IV, 205, 328). ✧ 'Pearl' cf. Crm. *bunčuq* 'die Muscheln, Kügelchen oder Perlen, die man am Halse der Pferde befestigt' (Radl. IV, 1815). See also **MUNČUQ**.

BŪRA see **BUΓRA**

BŪS-ǰALQÏYA Yak. **Būs-ǰalqïya-χotun** [Бусцалкыjа-хотун], Ulūtuyar Ulū-toyon's wife (Pek.). ✧ 'Be boiled splashing/bubling'? cf. Yak. *jalqïya* (Gerund of *jalqïy-*), Yak. *jalqïy-* ' расплескиваться, плескаться, всплескиваться (о молоке), колебаться, колыхаться, волноваться (о море)' (Pek.).

BŪT Yak. **Būt** [Бут] (Pek.). ✧ 'Pound' (<R.) Пуд (Pek.).

BÜBEK Kzk. 19th c. **Bübek-bay** [Бубекбай] (Lomakin 40). ✧ 'Grand-father' cf. East.T. *bübäk* 'der Grossvater' (Radl. IV, 1903).

BÜBÜQAN Kirg. **Bübüqan**, fem. (Jud. 556). ✧ 'Shamaness; woman-baqšï' cf. Kirg. *bübü* 'шаманка, женщина-бахши' (Jud.) + suff. *-qan(1)*.

BÜBÜŠ Kirg. **Bübüš**, fem. (Jud. 288). ✧ 'Little shamaness; Little woman-baqšï' cf. Kirg. *bübü* 'шаманка, женщина-бахши' (Jud.) + suff. *-š*.

BÜDEYLİ Tat. 19th c. **Büdeyli** [Büdeili] (Mende 158).

BÜDENE Kzk. 19th c. **Büdene** [Акманай Буденевъ] (Grod., Pril. 71); Bashk. 1756 **Büdene** [Рахманкул Буденеев] (MIB IV/1, 125); Kzk. 1790 **Büdene-biy** [Бюдене бий (бай)], a bay (rich, noble man) (MIK IV, 129). ✧ 'Quail' cf. Kzk. *bödene* 'перепёлка' (KzRS), 'die Wachtel' (Radl. IV, 1704).

BÜDÜŠ Uyg. 12th c.-14th c. **Büdüš / Büdüš-tutuq** [Büdüş] (DTS, Radl., USp. 115-116, EUTS).

BÜGDÜZ-EMEN Oghuz/Trkm. 14th c.-15th c.

Bügdüz-emen [بيغى قنلو امن] / (Bïyïgï Qanlu) Bügdüz Emen, Bıуıgı Qanlu Emen / Эмен из рода Бэгдюр], Emen from the Begdür (Bügdüz?) clan (DQorq./Rossi 144, 159, 162 etc., DQorq./Ergin 113, DQorq. 30, 58, 73 etc.). ✧ 'Knot (in the tree), humpbacked?'. ⇨ **BÜKDÜZ + EMEN.**

BÜGÖÜ Kzk. **Bügöü** [Бÿгöÿ] (Proben III, 77 /99/).

BÜGÜ see **BÖGÜ**

BÜGÜSTÄY see **TİMİR-BÜKÜSTÄY**

BÜYİK Kzk. 19th c. **Büyik-pay** [Буекпай] (SOV 60). ⇨ **BÜYÜK?**

BÜYÜK Trkm. 1855 **Biyük-χan** [Биюк-хан] (MIT II, 263); Turk. 1583 **Büyük-er** [بيوك ار] (Ongan, Ank. I, 172). ✧ 'Big, tall; great; older, elder, eldest' cf. Chag., Kar. *biyik* 'hoch' (Radl. IV, 1743), Turk. *büyük* 'Big, great; older, elder, eldest' (TED), Bashk. *beyek* 'высокий' (BRS). See also **AΓZÏ-BÜYÜK, BAŠÏ-BÜYÜK, GÖZÜ-BÜYÜK, TABUT-BÜYÜK; ČOÑ, EVREN, YOΓAN, KÄNDÄL, MÄÑKÄ.**

BÜKDÜZ Oghuz/Trkm. 13th c. **Bükdüz** [بكدز / Бÿкдÿз], Teñgiz-χan's son (Abulg./Kon. 520, 560, 615). ✧ 'Knot (in the tree), humpbacked?' cf. Turk. dial. *büğdüz* 'ağacın budak yeri' (DS), *büğdüz~bükrü* 'kambur' (DS). See also **BÜGDÜZ-EMEN.**

BÜKÄČČİYÄ Yak. **Bükäččiyä** [Арбаты Бÿкäччиjä], a shaman (Pek.).

BÜKE Karakh. **Büke** [Büke] (MK/Atalay 834); Kzk. 19th c. **Büke** [Буке] (AOK 2). ✧ 'Wrestler' cf. Turk. *bükä* 'der Athlet, der Ringer' (Radl. IV, 1877), Turk. *bükä* 'der Athlet, der Ringer' (Radl. IV, 1877).

BÜKEY see **BÖKEY**

BÜKEN Bashk. 1740 **Büken-bay** [Букен-бай] (MIB I, 436); Kzk. 19th c. **Büken-bay** [Али-бай Букенбаевъ] (Grod., Pril. 58). ✧ 'Stub, stump; slob' cf. Tat. *bükän* 'der Baumstumpf, der Klotz' (Radl. IV, 1877), Bashk. *bükän* 'чурбан, тумба, обрубок, болван' (BRS).

BÜKİÑ Uyg. 12th c.-14th c. **Bükiñ** [Büking] (DTS, EUTS).

BÜKMİŠ Maml. 1324 **Bükmiš** [بدرالدين بكمش], an emir (Dawād. 315). ✧ 'Bent, curved' cf. Chag., East.T., NUyg.(Tar.), Kzk., Turk. *bük-* 'biegen, beugen' (Radl. IV, 1876).

BÜKTİ Maml. 14th c. **Bükti** [Букти] (Tuhfa 409).

BÜKÜSTÄY see **TİMİR-BÜKÜSTÄY**

BÜLBÜL Trkm. **Bilbil**, fem. (Sopieva: OSA 177); Trkm. 20th c. **Bilbil** [Bilbil], fem. (Zaj. 1971, 342); Trkm. 20th c. **Bilbil** [Билбил], fem. (TrkmRS 96); Turk. 16th c. **Bülbül-χatun** [Bülbül Hatun], fem. (Gökb., Ed. 36); Yürük 1543 **Bülbül-qïzï** [بلبل قيزى], fem. (Gökb., Rum. 193). ✧ 'Nightingale' cf. Trkm. *bilbil* 'соловей' (TrkmRS) (<P.).

BÜLBÜL-KÜYÖ Kzk. **Bülbül-küyö** [Bülbül Küjö / Бÿлбÿл Кÿjö], a bird (Proben III, 488 /563/). ⇨ **BÜLBÜL +?**

BÜLDÄY Kzk. 19th c. **Büldäy** [Бульдяй] (AOP 102). ✧ 'Silky (valuable) cloth'? cf. Kzk. *bülde* 'ipekli kumaş' (KzTS) + suff. *-y*.

BÜLÄK Tat. 20th c. **Büläk** [Бүлэк] (Sattarov); Tat. 20th c. **Büläk** [Бүлэк], fem. (Sattarov); Bashk. 1675 **Büläk** [Бюляк Келдибокбасаров] (MIB I, 199); Bashk. 1714 **Büläk** [Бюляк Илимбетев] (MIB I, 105); Bashk. 1718 **Büläk** [Бюляк Битеев] (MIB I, 289); Bashk. 1722 **Büläk** [Бюляк Кардыгулов] (MIB I, 289); Bashk. 1738 **Büläk** [Елкибай Бюляков] (MIB III, 393); Bashk. 1751 **Büläk** [Бюляк Актараев] (MIB IV/1, 52); Bashk. 1754 **Büläk** [Бюляк Умеров] (MIB IV/1, 83); Bashk. 1754 **Büläk** [Бюляк Тлявбетев] (MIB IV/1, 83); Bashk. 1754 **Büläk** [Узбек Бюляков] (MIB IV/1, 84); Bashk. 1768 **Büläk** [Буляк Тлиумбетев] (MIB IV/1, 407); Bashk. 1772 **Büläk** [Амангильды Бюляков] (MIB IV/1, 407); Bashk. 1789 **Büläk** [Буляк Таиров] (MIB V, 250, 252); Bashk. 1791 **Büläk** [Юртбагуш Буляков] (MIB V, 301); Bashk. 20th c. **Büläk** [Бүлэк] (Kusimova); Bashk. 20th c. **Büläk** [Бүлэк], fem. (Kusimova). ✧ 'Gift, present', given to a newborn whose father or mother died immediately before or after the birth (Sattarov), cf. Bashk. *büläk* 'подарок; дарённый, подаренный' (BRS), Tat. *büläk* 'дар, подарок' (TatRS).

BÜLEK Kzk. **Bülek-batïr** [Булекъ-батыръ] (Protok. Turk. V, 151); Kzk. 19th c. **Bülek-pay** [Булекпай] (SOV 124); Kirg. 19th-20th c. **Bülök-bey** [Bülok-bej] (Prinz 273); Kzk. 19th c. **Bülük** [Булюкъ] (AOK 138). ✧ I. 'Disturbance, riot; robbery with violence; boisterous (lad)' cf. Kzk. *bülīk* 'смута; неурядица, столкновение', *bülīk bala* 'озорник' (KzRS), Kzk. *bülük* 'die Unruhe, die Aufregung; der Raubzug' (Radl. IV, 1894), Kirg. *bülük* 'id.' (Jud.); II. 'Gift'? see BÜLÄK above. See also **MİÑNAN-BÜLEK**.

BÜLEKEY Kzk. 1819 **Büläkäy?** [Булякай] (MIK IV, 324); Kzk. 1815 **Bülekäy?** [Булекай Уралiевъ] (Mejer 28); Kzk. 19th c. **Bülekey** [Булекей] (SOK 70, 118). ⇨ **BÜLÄK / BÜLEK?** + suff. *-äy/-ey*.

BÜLEN Kzk. 1843 **Bülen** [Булень Шанхаевъ] (Konšin, Mat. V, 59); Kzk. 1860 **Bülen** [Булень Тисыбаевъ], a biy, the chief of the Balɣalï clan (of the Jalaɣïr tribe) (ZIRGOGeogr. I, 272).

BÜLKE Kzk. 19th c. **Bülke-bay** [Булкебай] (SOK 280).

BÜLKEN Kzk. 19th c. **Bülken** [Булькенъ] (AOK 42).

BÜLKÜ Kzk. 19th c. **Bülkü-bay** [Булькубай] (SOK 96).

BÜLÖK see **BÜLEK**

BÜLÜK see **BÜLEK**

BÜLÜK Kzk. 19th c. **Bülük / Bülük-pay** [Булюкъ / Булюкпай] (SODž. 100, 128); Kzk. 19th c. **Bülük-pay** [Булюкпай] (SOV 30, 56); Kzk. 19th c. **Bülük-pay** [Булюкпай] (SOK 78). ✧ 'Chaos, huddle, decline; Playful, naughty, boisterous' cf. Kzk. *bülük* 'die Unruhe, die Aufregung, die Uneinigkeit, der Untergang' (Radl. IV, 1894), Kzk. *bülīk bala* 'озорник' (KzRS). See also **SAYÏM-BÜLÜK, UL-BÜLÜK**.

BÜLÜK-GERÄY Crm. 16th c. **Bülük-geräy** [Булюкъ-Герай] (Smirnov, Krym. 422). ⇨ **BÜLEK + KERÄY.**

BÜNEGER Karch. **Büneger** [Бюнегеровъ] (Sysoev 119).

BÜNÜL Uyg. 12th c.-14th c. **Bünül** [Bünül] (DTS, EUTS).

BÜÖGÜL Yak. **Büögül** [Бүöгүл] (Pek.). ✧ Feodul (R.).

BÜÖKÄ Yak. **Büökä / Büö-χān** [Бүöкä] (Pek.).

BÜÖKÄSTÄY Yak. **Büökästäy / Bügüstäy / Miäkästäy** [Бүöкäстäи], a heavenly bogatyr (hero) (Pek.).

BÜÖRSÜN Yak. **Büörsün-bögö** [Бүöрсүн], a legendary hero (Pek.).

BÜÖTTÜR Yak. **Büöttür** [Бүöттүр] (Pek.).

BÜÖTÜL Yak. **Büötül** [Бүöтүл] (Pek.). ✧ Feodul (R.).

BÜRČİ Uyg. **Bürči** [Bürçi] (EUTS).

BÜRČÜY Uyg. 12th c.-14th c. **Bürčüy** (DTS).

BÜRČÜN Uyg. 12th c.-14th c. **Bürčün** (Radl., USp. 83, 231).

BÜRGÄK see **BÜRKÄK**

BÜRGÜN Tuv. 19th c. **Bürgün** [Бюргунъ] (Potanin IV, 167, 208, 212). ✧ 'Gloomy (face)'? cf. Alt. *bürkün* 'пасмурный, мрачный' (OjrRS).

BÜRGÜT see **BÜRKİT**

BÜRİ see **BÖRİ**

BÜRİ-BERDİ Khorezm. 1363 **Büri-berdi** [Бури-берди] (Tizeng. II, 181 /after Yezdī/). ⇨ **BÖRİ + BERDİ.**

BÜRİ-TEMÜR Khorezm. **Büri-temür / Büri-timür** [Бури-Тимур] (RaD II, 14). ⇨ **BÖRİ + TEMİR.**

BÜRKÄK Uyg. 12th c.-14th.? **Bürgäk / Böngäk?** (Radl., USp., Le Coq, Urkunden 1918, 455); Uyg. 12th c. - 14th c. **Bürkäk** [bürkäk] (DTS).

BÜRKİT Maml. 1457 **Berɣut** [الشريف برغوت] (Iyās II, 58); **Berχut** [على برحوط] (Khanikoff, Inscr. musulm. du Caucase: IAs. V/20: 84, 88); Kkalp. 1811 **Berkut-bay** [Беркут бай], a biy (MIKk. 122); Kzk. 19th c. **Berkut-pay** [Беркутпай] (SODž. 24); Kzk. 19th c. **Berkut-pay** [Беркутпай] (SOV 56, 136); Kzk. 19th c. **Berkut-pay** [Беркутпай] (SOK 276, 294); Tuv. 19th c. **Bürgüt** [Бюргутъ] (Potanin IV, 167, 208, 212, 288, 290); Kkalp. 20th c. **Bürkit-bay** (KkRS 773); Kzk. 19th c. **Bürküt-pay** [Бюрку тпай], forefather of the Kazaks (Potanin IV, 17). ✧ 'Eagle, golden eagle' cf. Chag., East.T., Kzk. *bürküt* 'der Berkut (aquila fulva)' (Radl. IV, 1891), Tuv. *bürgüt* 'беркут' (TuvRS), Kkalp. *bürkit* 'berkut' (KkRS), Kzk. *bürkit /*

bürküt 'berkut' (KzRS, PKRS). In Kazak conception, it is the king of birds, who can reach everything, who is able to everything. There are also several occurrences among 16th - 17th c. Russian families such as *Berkut* (Veselovskij, Onom.) (<R.) *berkut* 'id.' (<Kirg.) *bürküt*, Kzk. *bürkit* (Šipova 78). See also **BABAY-BERQUT.**; ✧ 'Golden eagle' cf. Chag., East.T., Kzk. *bürküt* 'der Berkut (aquila fulva)' (Radl. IV, 1891), Kkalp. *bürkit* 'беркут' (KkRS), Tuv. *bürgüt* 'беркут' (TuvRS).

BÜRKÜT see **BÜRKİT**

BÜRLÜK Uyg. **Bürlük** [Bürlük] (EUTS).

BÜRLÜK-QARA Uyg. 12th c.-14th c. **Bürlük-qara** (Radl., USp. 5, DTS). ⇨ **BÜRLÜK + QARA.**

BÜRSEK Bashk. 1712 **Bürsek / Bürsäk?** [Каспулат Бурсяков] (MIB III, 87). ✧ 'Bubbles' cf. Bashk. *börsök* 'маленькие пузырьки, капельки, пупырышки; горошек, крапинки (на ткани)' (BRS).

BÜRT see **BÖRT**

BÜRÜK Kzk. 1756 **Bürük** [Саит Бюрюков] (MIB IV/1, 117); Kzk. 19th c. **Bürük-pay** [Бюрюкпай] (AOP 34). ✧ '(High) Cap' cf. Kzk. *börük* 'шапка' (PKRS), Kzk. *börik* 'börk, başa giyilen nesne' (KzTS). See also **QARA-BÜRÜKLÜ, QÏZÏL-BÜRÜK.**

BÜRÜS Yak. **Bürüs** [Бүрүс] (Pek.). ✧ Bryus (R.), the author of the calendar.

BÜSKÜLÄ Yak. **Büskülä** [Бүскүлä / Бүскүнчä], fem. (Pek.). ✧ ? (<R.)

BÜSKÜNČÄ Yak. **Büskünčä** [Бүскүнчä / Бүскүлä], (fem.) (Pek.).

BÜSÜRÜK YUyg. **Büsürük-χan** (Proben VI, 13). ✧ 'Hermit, ascetic' cf. East.T.(Tar.) *büzürük* 'der Einsiedler, der Eremit' (Radl. IV, 1902).

BÜTČÜ Kzk. 18th. **Bütčü** [Ибрай Бютчюевъ], from Orenburg (Nepljuev 852).

BÜTE Bashk. 1734 **Büte / Büti?** [Чюра Бютеев] (MIB III, 327). ✧ I. 'Talisman; Amulet'? cf. Tat. *böti* 'амулет, талисман' (TatRS); II. 'Young sprout'? cf. Chag., East.T. *bütä* 'ein Schössling, ein Strauch, eine kleine Pflanze' (Radl. IV, 1897).

BÜTEMER Kuman 14th c. **Bütemer** [Buthemer], from the Kumans of Hungary (Gyárfás III, 552, 481, 482). ✧  'Can't be born; won't grow up' cf. Karakh., Uyg. *büt-* 'вырастать, уродиться' (DTS), see Rásonyi, KÖA 97, Rásonyi, Anthr. 138.

BÜTEN Kzk. 19th c. **Bütem-bay (<Bütin-bay)** [Бутембай] (AOP 10). ✧ 'Complete, firm, strong' cf. Kzk. *bütin* 'bütün, parçasız, sağlam' (KzTS).

BÜTÜK Bashk. 1675 **Bütük** [Бай-кучюк Бютюков] (MIB I, 201); Bashk. 1735 **Bütük** [Сапаръ Бютюков] (Vel.-Zern., Bašk. 24). ✧ 'Finished, ended' cf. Chag. *bütük ~ bitik* 'beendigt; die Schrift' (Radl. IV, 1775, 1898).

BÜTÜRMIŠ Uyg. **Bütürmiš** [Bütürmiş], fem. (EUTS); Uyg. 8th c.? **Bütürmiš-ïnal** (Müller, Pfahl. 23); Uyg. 8th c.? **Bütürmiš-täñgrim** [Täkän [tärkän?] qunčui bütürmiš tängrim], a princess (Müller, Pfahl. 10). ✧ 'Finished, ended' cf. Uyg. *bütür-* 'bitirmek' (US).

BÜWÄ YUyg. **Büwä**, fem. (Proben VI, 244). ✧ 'Housewife, mistress' cf. East.T. *bübi* 'eine Dame' (Radl. IV, 1904), see also comp. *büwi.*

BZAU see **BUZAΓU**

BZAW-BAQ see **BUZAW-BAQ**

BZAWMAN SEE BUZAWMAN

C

CONTAY Tat.(Bar.) **Contay-märgän** [Contai Märgän / Цонтаі Мäргäн] (Proben IV, 1(1)). ✧ 'Leather bag' cf. Chag. *čontay* 'ein lederner Beutel' (Radl. III, 2018). See also **AQ-ČONTAY.**

Č

ČABAČOÑ Hak. 19th-20th c. **Čabačoñ** [Чабачонъ], fem. (HRS 356). ✧ 'Owl-people'? cf. Hak. *čaba* 'сова' (HRS) and Hak. *čon* 'народ, публика; население города' (HRS).

ČABAΓA Hak.(Kacha) 19th c. **Čabaγa** [Чабага] (Katanov, Otč. II, 42); Tuv. **Čabaγa** (Katanov, Otč. 9). ✧ '(Big) Foal' (Katanov). See also **QULUN.**

ČABAY I. Kzk. 1747 **Čabay** [Чабай] (Nepljuev 701). ✧ I. 'Present, gift'? cf. Chag. *čaba* 'das Geschenk' (Radl. III, 1928); II. 'Bone (for playing)'? cf. Tat.(Tob.) *čabai* 'Knöchel (zum Spielen)' (Radl. III, 1928). ⇨ **ŠABAY?**

ČABAY II. Hak. 19th-20th c. **Čabay** (HRS 352). ✧ '?' cf. Hak. PNs *Čabay, Čabayaχ* '?' (Butanaev).

ČABAQ Kuman 1419 **Čabaq** [Chabak], among the Kumans of Hungary (Gyárfás III, 566); Kirg. **Čabaq** [Чабак] (Jud. 59); Trkm. / Maml.? 1083, 1085 **Čabaq / Jabaq? / Čïbuq?** [جبق امير التركمان], Türkmen emir (Ibn al-Athīr/Tornb. X, 83, 296, Kamāladdīn II, 91). ✧ 'Carp, small fish' cf. Tat. *čabaq* 'плотва, сорожка' (TatRS), Kirg. *čabaq* 'всякая мелкая рыба, рыбёшка' (Jud.), Bashk. *sabaq* 'плотва, сорога (рыба)' (BRS/Uraksin). See also **ALTÏN-CABAQ.**

ČABAQA Tat.(Lit.) 1592 **Čabaqa** [Чабака Сачкевич] (Lit. Tat. 124). ✧ 'A foal on the second year of age' cf. Hak. *čabaγa* 'ein zweijähriges Füllen' (Radl.III, 1929).

ČABAL Hak.(Koyb.) 19th c. **Čabal** [Чабалъ], fem. (Katanov, Otč. II, 12-15). ✧ I. 'Silly' (Katanov); II. 'Bad' (Butanaev), cf. Hak. *čabal* 'плохой, гадкий, скверный, дурной; зловредный, злой' (HRS).

ČABALQA Hak. 19th-20th c. **Čabalqa** [Чабалка], fem. (HRS 356). ❖ 'Evil, wicked; bad'. ⇨ **ČABAL** + dim. suff. *-qa / -ka*.

ČABAR see **ČAPAR**

ČABAŠ Kzk. 19th c. **Čabaš** [Чабашъ] (SODž. 70). ❖ 'Quiet, peaceful, meek'? cf. Shor *čabaš* 'id.' (Radl. III, 1930).

ČABDAR see **ČAPTAR**

ČABDÏR Kzk. 19th c. **Čabdïr-bay** [Чабдырбай] (SOV 74). ⇨ **ČAPTAR?**

ČABÏJAX Hak. 19th-20th c. **Čabïjax** (HRS 352). ❖ A dignity. Cf. Hak. PNs *Čabï, Čabïčax* 'id.' (Butanaev).

ČABÏKE Kzk. 19th c. **Čabïke?** [Чабыке] (SOV 106). ⇨ ? -- comp. *eke*.

ČABÏKEY Tat. 1540, 1541 **Čabïkey** [Чабыкей, Чабыкěй] (PSRL VIII, 295, XIII, 99). ⇨ ? + dim. suff. *-key*.

ČABÏQ Chuv. 18th-19th c. **Čabïk** [Чабыкъ] (Magn. 91); Kzk. 19th c. **Čabïq** [Чабык] (Lomakin 35). ❖ 'Fast' cf. Crm. *čabïq* 'schnell, schnell laufend' (Radl. III, 1931).

ČABÏR Kzk. 19th c. **Čabïr-bay** [Чабырбай] (SOK 84). ❖ 'Trifle; tiny tot' cf. Kirg. *čabïr* 'мелюзга, мелкота' (Jud.).

ČABÏS Hak. 19th-20th c. **Čabïs** [Чабыс], fem. (Katanov, Otč. 10). ❖ 'Short' (Katanov).

ČABÏS OT? **Čabïs-čor** (Ligeti: MNy. 75: 41); OT? **Čabïs-ïšbara-irkin** (Ligeti: MNy. 75: 41); OT? **Čabïs-tarqan / Čabïs-tarqan?** (Ligeti: MNy. 75: 41).

ČABÏ Karch. 20th c. **Čabï** [Č'abī], fem. (Pröhle, Kar. 96).

ČABLEKEY Kirg. **Čablekey?** (Pojarkov). ❖ 'Swallow' (Pojarkov).

ČABUQ Selj. 11th c.? **Čabuq / Čabuqu?** [جبق], an emir (Bondārī 76). ❖ 'Quick' (<P.) *čabuk, čapuk* 'schnell, gewandt'; cf. also P. *Čāpuk~Čaᶜbuk* (Justi 156).

ČAČA Türk 8th c. **Čača-señün** [čača señün / Çaça Señün / Çaça Säñün], a contemporary of Tonyuquq (DTS, ETY I, 60).

ČAČAQ Alt. 19th-20th c. **Čačaq** [Чачак], fem. (OjrRS 213). ❖ 'Bunch of flowers; tassel, fringe' cf. Alt. *čačaq* 'der Puschel, die Quaste, Franzen', Tat. *čačaq* 'ein Kopfschmuck der Frauen' (Radl. III, 1906).

ČAČAQLÏ Oghuz/Trkm. 13th c. **Čačaqlï** [ججاقلى / Джаджаклы], Salor-qazan-alp's mother (Abulg./Kon. 705, 710); Oghuz/Trkm. 13th c. **Čačaqlï** [ججاقلى / Джаджаклы], Enkeš's wife (Abulg./Kon. 1250-1260); Khorezm.? **Čačaqtu** [Чачакту] (RaD II, 14). ❖ 'Having tassels' cf. Alt. *čačaqtu* 'mit Quasten versehen' (Radl. III, 1906). + suff. *-tu*.

ČAČAQTU see **ČAČAQLÏ**

ČAČÏKEY Kirg. **Čačïkey** [Чачыкей] (Jud. 79, 633). ❖ 'Little fringe, little tassel'? cf. Kirg. *čačï* 'кисть; волосы хвоста; щётка (на ногах лошади)' (Jud.) + suff. *-key*.

ČAČÏQOÑ Hak. 19th-20th c. **Čačïqoñ** [Чачыконъ] (HRS 352); Hak.(Sag.) **Čačïqoñ** [Чачыконǯ] (Proben IX, 557).

ČAJ-ÖL see **YAŠ**

ČADEY Kzk. 19th c. **Čadey** [Чадей] (SODž. 24).

ČADÏN Uyg. 12th c.-14th c. **Čadin / Čädin?** (Radl., USp. 34).

ČADÏŠ Tat.(Sib.)? 1598 **Čadïš** [Чадышъ], a relative from Siberia (AI II, 2).

ČAĞAY Kzk. 19th c. **Čaɣay** [Чагай] (SOV 120); Kzk. 19th c. **Čaɣay** [Чагай] (SOK 234); Kzk. 19th c. **Čaɣay** [Чагай] (SODž. 40); Kzk. 19th c. **Čaɣay-bay** [Алдасогуръ Чагайбаевъ] (Grod., Pril. 57). ❖ I. 'Little boy' cf. Turk., Chag. *čaɣa* 'ein kleiner Knabe; das Kind' (Radl. III, 1842-43). + dim. suff. *-y*. See also **ALTÏN-ČAĞAY, KÖP-ČAĞAY, QAN-ČAĞAY.**

ČAĞALAQ Kzk. 19th c. **Čaɣalaq** [Чагалакъ] (SODž. 6); Kzk. 19th c. **Čaɣalaq** [Чагалакъ] (SOK 62); Kzk. 19th c. **Čaɣalaq** [Чагалакъ] (SOV 90). ❖ 'Gull, mew' cf. *šaɣala* 'id.' (KzRS).

ČAĞALÏ Kzk. 19th c. **Čaɣalï?** [Чагали] (SOK 212). ❖ 'Having children, having a family'? ⇨ **ČAQA** + suff. *-lï*.

ČAĞAMAN Kzk. 19th c. **Čaɣaman** [Чагаманъ] (SOV 4). ⇨ **ČAQA** + suff. *-man*.

ČAĞAN **Čaɣan** [Чаган] (Žirm., Epos 406); Selj. 12th c. **Čaɣan** [چغان], an emir (Rāwandī 402); Maml. 1295 **Čaɣan** [سيف الدين جاغان الحسامى] (Zetterst. 42, 48); Kzk. 19th c. **Čaɣan** [Чаганъ] (SOK 150); Tuv. / Alt.(Sag.)? 19th c. **Čaɣān-qam / Čaɣāñ-qam** [Чаɓан-кам / Чаɓаң-кам], a shaman (Proben IX, 146); Trkm. 20th c. **Čaqan** [Čaqan] (Zaj. 1971, 333); Trkm. 20th c. **Čaqan** [Чакан] (TrkmRS 718). ❖ I.' White' cf. Mo. *čaɣān* 'blanc' (Sauvaget 45); II. 'Festive day at the beginning of January' cf. Alt. *čaɣan* 'праздник в начале января' (OjrRS), Kirg. чаган (в.посе - первый месяц монгольского календаря; начало весны, весенний праздник у калмыков, монголов и китайцев' (Jud.) (<Mo.). See also **BAY-ČAĞAN.**

ČAĞAN-ČUĞURTU-UWAZÏ Tuv. 19th c. **Čaɣan-čuɣurtu-uwazï** [Чаганъ-чугурту-увазы], Uzun-ačaq's sister (Potanin IV, 591). ⇨ **ČAĞAN.**

ČAĞANAQ Kzk. 19th c. **Čaɣanaq** [Чаганакъ] (SODž. 84). ⇨ **ČAĞAN** + suff. *-aq*.

ČAĞANDAY Kirg. **Čaɣanday** [Чаɓандаі], Kösqaman's son, Aɣanday's(!) brother (Proben V, 218/220/); Alt. 19th-20th c. **Čaɣanday** [Чагандай] (OjrRS 210). ❖ I. 'Like a festive day (at the beginning of January), born on a festive day' cf. Alt. *čaɣan* 'праздник в начале января' (OjrRS).

ČAĞAR Karch. **Čaγar** [Чагаровъ] (Sysoev 120); Crm. **Čaγar** (Mende 176); Kzk. 1877 **Čaγar** [Осиръ-бай Чагаровъ] (Grod., Pril. 129); Tuv. 19th c. **Čaγar** [Чаӊар], fem. (Proben IX, 45); Tat.(Sib.) 1599 **Šaγar-bek** [Шагарбекъ], from Küčüm's family (AI II, 20). ⇨ **ČAĞÏR?**

ČAĞARAY Kzk. 19th c. **Čaγaray** [Чагарай] (SODž. 46); Kzk. 19th c. **Čaγaray** [Чагарай] (SOV 64). ⇨ **ČAĞAR** + suff. *-ay.*

ČAĞATAY Yürük 16th c. **Čaγatay** [چاغاتای], from Kocacık, Turkey (Gökb., Rum. 104); Kzk. 19th c. **Čaγatay** [Чагатай] (SOV 68); Uzb. **Čaγatay** [Чагатай Сарымсаков] (TV 1878: 144); Kzk. 19th c. **Šaγatay** [Шагатай] (AOK 86, 130); Kzk. 20th c. **Šaγatay** [Шагатай] (KkRS 776). ✧ I. 'Čaγatay' (Mo.), the name of Chinggis Khan's second son meaning 'The White One', 'He Who is White' (Cleaves 417), cf. also Sauvaget 47; II. 'Brave, honest, sincere' (Bask., Fam.). See also **МОГUL-ČAĞATAY.**

ČAĞBAN-AY Hak.(Blt.) 19th-20th c. **Čaγban-ay** [Чаӊбан-ai] (Proben IX, 362-65). ✧ 'Teal' cf. Hak. PN *Čaγban* 'постный' (Butanaev), Hak. *čaγban* 'id.' (HRS). ⇨ **AY.**

ČAĞÏLÏSA Yak. **Čaγïlïsa** [Чаӊылыса] (Pek.). ✧ 'Having bright eyes'. (<Yak.) *čaγïlïy-* 'сверкать, блистать, сиять' (Pek.).

ČAĞÏN Kzk. 19th c. **Čaγïm-bay (<Čaγïn-bay?)** [Чагимбай] (SODž. 70). ✧ '(A) Little, not much'? cf. Kzk. *şaǧın* 'id.' (KzTS).

ČAĞÏR 1153 **Čaγïr** [جعفر الامير الغزی], an emir (Ibn al-Athīr/Tornb. XI, 116); Bashk. 1708, 1709 **Čaγïr** [Чагыр Яргалов (Ергалов)] (MIB I, 249, 268, MIKk. 160, 161); Bashk. 1735 **Čaγïr** [Атагулъ Чагыровъ], a tarχan (Vel.-Zern., Bašk. 24); Bashk. 1775 **Čaγïr** [Чагыр] (MIB IV/2, 514); Kzk. 19th c. **Čaγïr** [Чагыръ], son of Merkit who was the forefather of the Merkits (Potanin II, 5); Selj. **Čaγïr / Čaqïr** [جعفر / نصيرالدين جقر] (Bondārī 205, Kamāladdīn II, 280, 281); Tat.(Sib.) 1632 **Čaγïr-bay / Čigir-bay?** [Чагирбай (Чигирбай)] (Miller, Ist. Sib. II, 398); Oghuz 999 **Čaγïr-tegin** [جعفر تكين] (Qazw. 391); Kzk. 19th c. **Šaγïr-bay** [Шагырбай] (AOO 70); Kzk. 19th c. **Šaγïr-bay** [Шагырбай] (AOAtb. 30); Kzk. 18th c. - 19th c. **Šaγr-bay (<Šaγïr-bay)** [Шагрбай] (Tynyšp. 68). ✧ 'Grey-eyed; having grey eyes' Cf. Kzk. *šaγïr* 'graue Augen habend (vom Pferde)' (Radl. IV, 938), 'серый (о глазах человека и лошади)' (KzRS). ⇨ **ĴAĞÏR? / ŠAĞÏR.** See also **AL-ČAĞÏR.**

ČAĞÏS Shor 19th-20th c. **Čaγïs-öl** (Dyrenkova 236). ✧ 'Lonely' cf. Hak.(Sag.), Shor *čaγïs* 'allein' (Radl. III, 1847).

ČAĞÏS-ČAYAČÏ Tuv. 19th c. **Čaγïs-čayačï** [Чагысъ-чаячи], a man in a Soyōt tale (Potanin IV, 572). ✧ I. 'Lonely Sister/Aunt'? cf. Hak.(Sag.) *čaya* 'die ältere Schwester, die Tante, die Stiefmutter' (Radl. III, 1852); II. 'Lonely Fire'? cf. Tuv. *čayāčï* 'огонь (как предмет культа)' (TuvRS). ⇨ **ČAĞÏS.** See also **ČAĞÏS-PAYAČÏ.**

ČAĞÏS-PAYAČÏ Alt.(Tub.) 19th c. **Čaγïs-payačï** (Potanin IV, 572). ✧ 'Lonely-brother-in-law (?)' cf. Alt. *paya* 'der Mann der Schwester, der Bruder der Frau' (Radl. IV, 1138). ⇨ **ČAĞÏS** + suff. *-čï.*

ČAĞLAN OT 865, 870 **Čaγlan? / Čuγlan? / Ĵaγlan? / Ĵuγlan?** [جغلان التركی جعلان التركی] (Tabarī, Annal. III, 1615, 1786, 1834-36, 1899, 1920-1924).

ČAĞRAY Kzk. 19th c. **Čaγray** [Чаграй] (AOK 78). ⇨ **ČAĞÏR** + suff. *-ay.*

ČAĞRÏ Uyg. **Čaγrï** [Çaǧrı] (EUTS); Selj. 1116 **Čaγrï** [جغری], Sultan Mahmud's (1092-1094) son (Ibn al-Athīr/Tornb. X, 361-2, 365); Oghuz 1153/54 **Čaγrï / Ĵaγïr?** [Джагыр (Чагры)], a Ghuzz emir (MIT I, 388); Selj. 11th c., 12th c.? **Čaγrï-beg** [Çagrı beğ / čaγrï beg], the same as Čaγrï-tegin (MK/Atalay 835, DTS); Selj. 1028 **Čaγrï-bek** [تتاق بن جغریبك / جغریبك داود / داوود بن ميكاييل بن سلخوق بن David Jagri Beg / Чагры-бек Дауд ибн Микаил ибн Сельджук] (Ibn al-Athīr/Tornb. IX, 267, 321-2, X, 3-4, XI, 227, MIT I, 47, 231, 232, 246, Aqsar. 42, Abulfar./Budge I, 196, Abulfar. Or. /222, 227, 228, 238/ 337, 345, etc.); Selj. 11th c., 12th c.? **Čaγrï-bek / Čaγru-bek** [جغرو بك] (Abulfidā III, 104-5); Selj. 1164 **Čaγrï-χan** [جغری خان بن حسن تكين] (Ibn al-Athīr/Tornb. XI, 205); Karakh. 11th c. **Čaγrï-tegin** [čaγrï tegin], offspring of the Khan-family (DTS); Selj. 11th c., 12th c.? **Čaγrï-tegin**, the same as Čaγrï-beg (-bek) (DTS); Selj. 1165 **Čaγrï-tegin** [جغری تكين حسين] (Ibn al-Athīr/Tornb. XI, 211); Karakh. **Čaγrï-tegin / Čaγrï-tigin** [Çagrı Tégin / Çagrı Tigin] (MK/Atalay 835, 836). ✧ (Title) The name of a child of the khan's family, cf. Togan, UTT 185.

ČAXČAXAY see **ALTAN-ČAXČAXAY**

ČAXČĀĞAY see **ALTAN-ČAXČAXAY**

ČAXČĀĞÏ see **ALTAN-ČAXČAXAY**

ČAXÏR-SAYAN Alt. 19th c. **Čaχïr-sayan** [Чахыръ-Саянъ] (Potanin IV, 370).

ČAY Kzk. 19th c. **Čay-bay** [Чайбай] (SOV 98); Kzk. 19th c. **Čay-bek** [Чайбекъ] (SOV 58, 116); Kzk. 19th c. **Čay-bek** [Чайбекъ] (SODž. 4, 78); Kzk. 19th c. **Čay-bek** [Чайбекъ] (SOK 90). ✧ 'Tea' cf. Kzk. *šay* 'чай' (PRS). See also **ALA-ČAY, ČÏK-ČAY, ÏSÏ-ČAY.**

ČAY-AXMET Kzk. 19th c. **Čay-aχmet** [Чаяхмет] (SOV 126). ⇨ **ČAY?** + **AXMET.**

ČAY-MERDEN see **ŠAH-MERDAN**

ČAYA Uyg. **Čaya** [čaja] (DTS).

ČAYAX Hak. 19th-20th c. **Čayaχ** [Чаях], fem. (HRS 356). ✧ 'Waist, hip' cf. Hak. *čaya* 'поясница' (HRS).

+ dim. suff. -χ / -q.

ČAYASÏNİ Uyg. **Čayasïni** [Çayasıni] (EUTS).

ČAYĀČÏ Karg. **Čayāčï** [Чајачы] (Proben IX, 650). ✧ I. 'Fire' cf. Tuv. *čayāčï* 'огонь (как предмет культа)' (TuvRS); II. 'Creator' cf. Hak.(Sag.), Shor *čayačï* 'der Schöpfer' (Radl. III, 1853).

ČAYČÏ see **ČAYJÏ**

ČAYJA Kzk. 19th c. **Čayja-bay** [Чайжабай] (SODž. 108). ⇨ **ČAYJÏ** + dim. suff. -*ja*.

ČAYJÏ Alt. 19th-20th c. **Čayčï** [Чайчы], fem. (OjrRS 213). ✧ 'Lover of tea' (Ibid.). + suff. -*jï*.

ČAYÏR Kzk. 19th c. **Čayïr-bek** [Чаиръ бекъ] (Grod., Pril.). ✧ 'Nimble, agile, lively' cf. Kzk. *šayïr* 'древесная смола, канифоль; бойкий, расторопный' (KzRS).

ČAYMAN Kzk. 19th c. **Čayman** [Чаиманъ] (SOK 270). ⇨ **ČAY** + suff. -*man*?

ČAYMATAY Kzk. 19th c. **Čaymatay** [Чаиматай] (SOK 32).

ČAYNÏQ Alt. 19th - 20th c. **Čaynïq** [Чайнык], fem. (OjrRS 213). ✧ 'Tea-pot' (<R.) *čajnik* 'id.' (Ibid.).

ČAYSU Uyg. 12th c.-14th c. **Čaysu** [Çaisu] (DTS, EUTS).

ČAYZAΓ Hak. 19th-20th c. **Čayzaγ** [Чайзагъ], a bogatyr in a Kyzyl-Tatar legend (Kostrov 4, 7). ✧ 'Servant, slave (of a prince); clerk of a prince' cf. Hak.(Sag.) *čayzaγ* 'der Dienstmann, der Beamte des Fürsten (in Märchen)' (Radl. III, 1830).

ČAYZAŇ Tuv. 19th c. **Čayzaň-qam** [Чаізаң кам], a shaman (Proben IX, 146). ✧ 'Prince; head of the clan' (Butanaev), 'Feudal official' cf. Tuv. *čayzaň* 'зайсан, феодальный чиновни' (TuvRS) (<Mo.).

ČAKEY Kzk. 19th c. **Čakey** [Чакей] (SOV 80).

ČAKELİ Kzk. 19th c. **Čakeli / Čaq-eli?** [Чакели] (SOV 80). ⇨ **ČAQÏ?**

ČAQ Uyg. 12th c.-14th c. **Čaq-oγlï** [Çakoğlı] (DTS, EUTS); Kzk. 19th c. **Čaq-pay** [Чакпай] (SOK 80); Kzk. 19th c. **Čaq-mergen** [Чакмерген] (SOK 230); Bashk. 1722 **Šaq** [Юсуп Шаков] (MIB I, 289). ✧ I. 'Ugly, worthless, villainous' cf. Tat. *čaq* 'schlecht, untauglich' (Radl. III, 1831); II. 'Time'? cf. *čaq* 'die Zeit, der Zeitpunkt' (Radl. III, 1831).

ČAQA Kzk. 19th c. **Čaqa** [Чака] (SODž. 20); Kzk. 19th c. **Čaqa** [Чака] (SOK 100, 252); Kzk. 19th c. **Čaqa-bay** [Чакабай], according to the legend, this person, the forefather of Abaq-kirey's, was a woman (Potanin II, 3, 6); Kzk. 19th c. **Čaqa-bay** [Чакабай] (AOA 14); Kzk. 19th c. **Čaqa-bay** [Чакабай] (SOV 42); Kzk. 18th c. - 19th c. **Šaqa** [Шака] (Tynyšp. 71); Kzk. 19th c. **Šaqa** [Шака] (AOP 60); Kzk. 19th c. **Šaqa-bay** [Шакабай] (AOA 70). ✧ I. 'Naked' cf. Kzk. *šaqa* 'голый' (KzRS); II. 'Child (male and female), pullet'? cf. Chag. *čaqa* 'das Kind' (Radl. III, 1833), Kuman, Maml., Chag., Turk., Tuv. *čaya* 'ein kleiner

Knabe, das Kind; das Küchlein; das Bärenjunge; das Mädchen, die Sclavin' Kzk. *šaqa* 'genç, sabi ufak çocuk' (KzTS).

ČAQAY Kzk. 1738 **Čaqay** [Чакай] (MIB I, 358); Alt. 19th-20th c. **Čaqay** [Чакай] (OjrRS 210). ⇨ **ČAQA** + suff. -*y*.

ČAQAL Turk. 16th c. **Čaqal** [Çakal Debbağ] (Ongan, Ank. II, 507, 608, 982, 1638); Turk. 16th c. **Čaqal** [Çakal Mehmed] (Ongan, Ank. II, 507, 608, 982, 1638); Trkm. 1690 **Čaqal** [چتال دمورجیلو], from the nomadic Demürcilü tribe (aşiret) (Refik, Anad. 87); Turk. **Čaqal-oγlu**, a Zeybek (Kúnos 1891, 118); Kkalp. 20th c. **Šaγal-bay** [Шагалбай] (KkRS 776). ✧ 'Jackal' cf. Turk. *čaqal* 'id.' (Radl. III, 1833), Kzk. *šaγal, šaqal* 'шакал' (RKzS), Kkalp. *šaγal* 'шакал' (KkRS).

ČAQAN Kipch.? 13th c. **Čaqan?** [Τζαχᾶς], a christened Tatar (Byz. Turc. II, 310); Kuman 1323 **Čaqan** [Chakan], a Kuman from Hungary (Gyárfás III, 463); Selj.? 11th c. **Čaqan?** [Τζαχᾶς], a Turkic [Seljuk?] emir (Byz. Turc. II, 310); Turk. 15th c. **Čaqan** [Ζάγανος], a Turkish commander of the army (Byz. Turc. II, 128); Kzk. 18th c. - 19th c. **Čaqan** [Чакан] (Tynyšp. 66); Kzk. 1830 **Čaqan** [Чаканъ Чунаевъ] (TOUAK XXIV, 192); Kzk. 19th c. **Čaqan** [Аширъ Чакановъ] (Grod., Pril. 113); Kzk. 19th c. **Čaqan** [Курбанъ Чакановъ] (Grod., Pril. 73); Kzk. 19th c. **Čaqan** [Чаканъ] (AOK 14); NUyg. 19th c. **Čaqan** [جاقان] (Le Coq, Nameml. 97); Kirg. **Čaqan-baybiče** [Чакан баібичä], fem. (Proben V, 43 /44/); Kzk. 1819 **Čaqan-mulla** [Чакан мулла] (MIK IV, 323); Kzk. 19th c. **Šaqan** [Шаканъ] (AOA 146); Kzk. 19th c. **Šaqan** [Шаканъ] (AOP 2). ✧ I. 'Battle-axe, war-axe'? cf. Chag. *čaqan* 'die Streitaxt' (Radl. III, 1833); cf. also Rásonyi, KÖA 98, Adalékok 130, Rásonyi, Anthr. 139; II. 'Quick, nimble' cf. Kirg. dial. *čaqan* 'проворный, ловкий' (Jud.), NUyg. *čaqqan* 'проворный, ловкий; бойкий' (UjgRS); III. 'Little' cf. Kirg. *čaqan* 'маленький' (Jud.). See also **QARA-ČAQAN**.

ČAQAPTAY Kzk. 19th c. **Čaqaptay** [Чакаптай] (SOK 72).

ČAQAR **Čaqar** (Byz. Turc. II, 307-8); Kzk. 19th c. **Čaqar** [Чакаръ] (SODž. 58); Kzk. 19th c. **Čaqar** [Чакаръ] (SOV 116); Kzk. 19th c. **Čaqar-bay** [Чакарбай] (SODž. 120). ✧ 'Bold, daring; nimble;' cf. *šaqar* 'бедовый; отчаянный' (KzRS).

ČAQČAY Kzk. **Čaqčay** [Чакчай] (ZIRGOGeogr. I, 443).

ČAQČAQ Kzk. 1797 **Čaqčaq** [Чакчакъ] (Dobrosm., Turg. 211); Kzk. 1802 **Čaqčaq-bey** [Чакчак бей] (MIK IV, 202). ✧ 'Squirrel' cf. Kzk. *šaqšaq* 'Sincap' (KzTS). See also **SAQÏL, SANZÄP, TİYEN**.

ČAQČAQ-JANÏ-BEK Kzk. 19th c. **Čaqčaq-janï-bek** [Чакчакъ-Джани-бекъ] (Potanin, Pred. 67). ⇨

ČAQČAQ + JANÏ.

ČAQÏ Kzk. 19th c. **Čaqï** [Чакы] (SODž. 14, 48, 74); Kzk. 19th c. **Čaqï-bay** [Чакыбай] (SOV 20). ✧ 'Clasp-knife' cf. Turk., Crm. *čaqï* 'das Klappmesser' (Radl. III, 1834).

ČAQÏR Uyg. 12th c.-14th c. **Čaqïr** (Radl., USp. 128); Selj.? 1104, 1105, 1106 **Čaqïr** [جتر بن يعقوب], the same as the later commander of Mosul (Qalānisi 143, 150, 152); Selj.? 1127/28, 1144/45 **Čaqïr** [نصير الدين جتر], commander (ruler) of Mosul, who was killed (Ibn al-Athīr, Atab.: RHCHor II/2, 63, 65, 85, 126, Ibn al-Athīr: RHCHor I, 375, 446, Kamāladdīn 687); Khorezm. 1200 **Čaqïr** [جتر التركى], Khorezmshah (Ibn al-Athīr/Tornb. XII, 104, 152); Turk. 1543 **Čaqïr** [Csakir Szemendre], a Janissary (Velics-Kamm. I, 8); Turk. 16th c. **Čaqïr** [Çakır] (Ongan, Ank. II, 215); Turk. 1552 **Čaqïr** [Ramazán ibn Csákir], an „azâb" (soldier, farm hand) from Szolnok, Hungary (Velics-Kamm. I, 75); Turk. 1552 **Čaqïr** [Júszuf ibn Csákir], an „ulûfeci" (clerk/secretary of Janissary guards, or palace servants) from Szolnok, Hungary (Velics-Kamm. I, 75); Turk. 1560 **Čaqïr** [Sáhin Csákir], a Janissary from Székesfehérvár, Hungary (Velics-Kamm. I, 127); Turk. 1630 **Čaqïr** [Csakir], a Turkish captive in Tokaj, Hungary (Velics-Kamm. II, 745); Yürük 1543 **Čaqïr** [Eyne Çakır] (Gökb., Rum. 189); Yürük 1543 **Čaqïr** [جاقر] (Gökb., Rum. 103, 240); Tat. 1543 **Čaqïr** [Çakır] (Gökb., Rum. 240); Tat.(Mish.) 1755 **Čaqïr** [Илкей Чакиров] (MIB IV/1, 93); Bashk. 1763 **Čaqïr** [Карагул Чакыров] (MIB IV/2, 45); Kzk. 19th c. **Čaqïr** [Сари Чакировъ] (Grod., Pril. 182); NUyg. 19th c. **Čaqïr** [جاقر] (Le Coq, Namenl. 97); Khorezm. / Chag.? 14th. **Čaqïr** [Jákir], (a) good archer (Tar. Rashidi 72); Turk. 1429 **Čaqïr-aγa** [Çakır-Ağa] (Gökb., Ed. 254); Turk. 1543 **Čaqïr-aγa** [Csákir aga], a commander (reis) in Pest, Hungary (Velics-Kamm. I, 19); Turk. 1568 **Čaqïr-aγa** [Csakir aga], commander in chief of Janissaries in Szigetvár, Hungary (Velics-Kamm. I, 201); Turk. 1618 **Čaqïr-aγa** [Csakir aga], a „topçı" (artilleryman) from Tarcsa, Hungary (Velics-Kamm. I, 409); Bashk. 1754 **Čaqïr-bay** [Чакырбай Игиликов] (MIB IV/1, 77); Bashk. 1764 **Čaqïr-bay** [Чакырбай Игилянов] (MIB IV/1, 298); Selj. 1036, 1043 **Čaqïr-bek** [سلجوقى جتربيك], from Khorāsān (Mirch. Gasnevid. 105, 114); Selj. 12th c. **Čaqïr-bek** [الب ارسلان محمد بن جتر بك] (Muh. Ibrahim 12); Turk. 1540 **Čaqïr-kethudā** [Çakır kethudâ], chief of the İlbeglü cemaat (tribe, clan?) according to a defter from Diyarbekir, Turkey (Demirtaş 52); Turk. 20th c. **Čaqïr-oγlu** [Çakıroğlu], a village in the province of Maraş, Turkey (TMİB 642); Karakh. **Čaqïr-toña-χan** [Muhammed Çakır Tonğa Xan] (MK/Atalay 847); Chag. 16th c. **Jaqïr-χoja-biy /**

Čaqïr [Джакир-ходжа-бий], an emir (Ivanov 89). ✧ I. 'Hawk, kite, falcon' cf. Maml. *çağrı* 'doğan' (İM), *çakır* 'doğan envaından' (İdr. Haş.), Turk. *çakır* 'doğan ile atmaca arası bir av kuşu' (TarS); II.'(Having) grey-blue eye' cf. Turk. *çakır* 'graublau [Auge]' (HŞ). See also **EYNE-ČAQÏR, ŠAHİN-ČAQÏR.**

ČAQÏRČA Uyg. **Čaqïrča** [Çakırça] (EUTS). ✧ 'Little hawk (kite, falcon)'. ⇨ **ČAQÏR** + dim. suff. *-ča*. See also **QARA-ČAQÏRČA, QUBA-ČAQÏRČA.**

ČAQÏŠ Kzk. 19th c. **Čaqïš** [Карабала Чакишевъ] (Grod., Pril. 149).

ČAQQÂN-BOL Uzb. 20th c. **Čaqqân-bol** [Чаққонбўл] (Begmatov 1984, 201). ✧ 'Be quick! Be nimble!' cf. Uzb. *čaqqân* 'ловкий, проворный, подвижный', *čaqqân bol!* 'живо! быстро! быстрее!' (UzbRS). ⇨ **BOL.**

ČAQLAQ Kzk. 19th c. **Čaqlaq** [Сабута Чаклаковъ] (Grod., Pril. 171).

ČAQMA Turk. **Čaqma-oγlu**, a Zeybek (Kúnos 1891, 118). ✧ 'Seal; flint;' cf. *čaqma* Turk.: 'das Petschaft, der Tempel', Tat.: 'der FeuerStahl' (Radl. III, 1841).

ČAQMAQ Maml. 14th c. **Čaqmaq** [Чакмак] (Tuhfa 410); Maml. 1399/1400, 1400/01 **Čaqmaq** [جتمق] (Ibn Taghrīb. VI, 31, Iyās I, 330, 338, Weil, Chalif. II, 88); Maml. 1399, 1405 **Čaqmaq** [جتمق الصفوى] (Ibn Taghrīb. VI, 33, 278); Maml. 1420, 1421, 1438/39, **Čaqmaq** [سيف الدين جتمق الارغون شاوى / الارغونى جتمق], governor of Damascus, executed in 1421 (Ibn Taghrīb. VI, 316, 356, 366, 503, 739, 829, VII, 261, 269, Iyās II, 11, 16, Weil, Chalif. II, 113, 160, Mayer 132-133); Maml. 1422 **Čaqmaq** [جتمق العيسوى], an emir (Iyās II, 16); Maml. 1438-1452 **Čaqmaq** [جتمق ابوسعيد], first an emir, later a Mamluk Sultan (1438-1452) (Iyās II, 9, 16 etc., Ibn Taghrīb. VI, 190, 770 etc., VII, 2, 6 etc., Makrīzī, Khit. I, 244, Weil, Chalif. II, 165, 215-48, Berchem (No.) 54, 198, Berchem, Jér. I, 333 etc., Sauvaget: BÉO II, 22-23, 25, 26, XII, 17, Sauvaget 47); Maml. 1452/53 **Čaqmaq** [جتمق الخاصكى], (Iyās II, 41); Maml. 1469/70, 1467/68 **Čaqmaq** [جتمق المؤيدى] (Iyās II, 112, 163, Ibn Taghrīb. VII, 854); Maml. 1476/77 **Čaqmaq** [جتمق النتيه الخاصكى] (Iyās II, 166); Chag. **Čaqmaq** (Le Coq, Ind. 4); Chag. 15th. c. **Čaqmaq** [Чакмак.миръ], one of the emirs of Shahruh (1404-1447) (Barth., Ulugb. 144); Chag. 15th c. **Čaqmaq** [جتماق] / Чагкмагкъ Сотникъ], a captain (Šejb. LXVI); Turk. 1485 **Čaqmaq** (Gökb., Ed. 282); Turk. 1604 **Čaqmaq** [Çakmak], from Isparta, Turkey (Ün 1938, 644); Crm. 1642 **Čaqmaq-atalïq** [جتماق اتالق] (Vel.-Zern., Crim. 321, 827). ✧ 'Lighter' cf. *çakmak* 'Feuerzeug' (HŞ), Turk. *čaqmaq* 'der Feuerstahl' (Radl. III, 1841), 'briquet' (Sauvaget 47), 'Stahl- und Steinfeuerzeug' (Ibid.).

ČAQMAN 1823 **Čaqman** [Чакманъ Дервишъ-Алієнъ], a leader (chief) of a community (TOUAK XXIV, 138); Kzk. 19th c. **Čaqman?** [Чакоманъ] (SODž. 80). ✧ 'Bad, wrong, unfit' cf. Tat. *čaq* 'schlecht, untauglich' (Radl. III, 1831) + suff. *-man*.

ČAQPAQ Tat.? **Čaqpaq-ata** [اطا چنباو] (Divaev, Baksy 310). ⇨ **ČAQMAQ?**

ČAQTA see **ČAQTÏ**

ČAQTÏ Kzk. 19th c. **Čaqta-bay** (<Čaqtï-bay) [Чакабай] (SOV 28). ⇨ **ČAQ** + suff. *-tï*?

ČAQUDU Uyg. 12th c.-14th c. **Čaqudu** [Çakudu] (DTS, EUTS).

ČAL Kzk. 1819 **Čal** [Чалъ] (MIK IV, 323); Kzk. 19th c. **Čal** [Чаловъ] (AOK 86); Kzk. 19th c. **Čal** [Чалъ] (AOK 134); Kzk. 19th c. **Čal** [Чалъ] (SOK 104, 216, 260); Kzk. 19th c. **Čal-bay** [Чалбай] (SOK 6, 114, 132); Kzk. 19th c. **Čal-bay** [Чалбай] (SOV 26, 48); Kirg. **Čal-bay** [Чалбай], one of Manas' comrades-in-arms (Proben V, 39 /40/); Kzk. 19th c. **Čal-mambet** [Чалмымбетъ] (SODž. 90); Crm. 1689 **Čal-mïrza (-murza?)** [مرزا چال] (Vel.-Zern., Crim. 748, 796); Chuv. 18th-19th c. **Čal-murza** [Чалмурза] (Magn. 91); Kzk. 19th c. **Šal** [Шаль] (AOA 98); Kzk. 19th c. **Šal** [Шалъ] (AOK 54). ✧ 'Grey, apple-grey; grey-haired old man, elderly man' cf. Uyg., Turk., Alt. *čal* 'grau; rötlichgrau' (Radl. III, 1874), Kzk., Shor *šal* 'mit grauem Haar, alt, bejahrt; der Graukopf, der Alte' (Rad. IV, 959). See also **AQ-ČAL, BAY-ČAL, QARA-ČAL, QARÏ-ČAL, QÏRĠÏN-ČAL, SARÏ-ČAL, SÏRKÄ-BAY-ŠAL, TAW-ČAL.**

ČAL-BOSUN Kzk. 19th c. **Čal-bosun** [Чалбосунъ] (SODž. 82). ✧ 'Let him be grey-haired (Let him be long-lived)'. ⇨ **BOLSÏN.**

ČAL-QALMAQ Kirg. **Čal-qalmaq** [Чалкалмак] (Jud. 319, 570). ⇨ **ČAL.**

ČALA Kzk. 19th c. **Čala** [Чала] (SOK 140); Kzk. 1846 **Čala-bay** [Бий Маусунбай (Маусамбай) Чалабаев], a biy (MKOP 100, 156); Kzk. 19th c. **Čala-bay** [Чалабай] (SODž. 54, 74); Kzk. 19th c. **Čala-bay** [Чалабай] (SOK 50, 232); Kzk. 19th c. **Čala-bay** [Чалабай] (SOV 8); Bashk. 18th c. **Šala** [Шала Колумбетевъ] (Nepljuev 815); Kzk. 19th c. **Šala-bay** [Шалабай] (AOAtb. 14); Kzk. 19th c. **Šala-bay** [Шалабай] (AOK 2, 30); Kzk. 19th c. **Šala-bay** [Шалабай] (AOO 38); Kkalp. 20th c. **Šala-bay** [Шалабай] (KkRS 776); Kzk. 1817 **Šala-bay / Čala-bay?** [چالاباى / Шалабай] (MIK IV, 311); Kzk. 1825 **Šala-bay / Čala-bay?** [چالا باى / Шалабай] (MIK IV, 468, 475). ✧ 'Incomplete, little, defective' cf. Alt., Kirg., Tat. *čala* 'nicht ganz, nicht volständig, ein wenig, nur teilweise, nicht wie es sich gehört' (Radl. III, 1877), Kkalp. *šala* 'недоделанный, незаконченный; не совсем, не вполне, наполовину; недоносок'

(KkRS), Kzk. *šala* 'nicht fertig gestellt, halbfertig, mangelhaft' (Radl. IV, 961). See also **SARÏ-ĴALA.**

ČALAB-BERDÏ Turk. 1583 **Čalab-verdi** [وىردى چلب / Çalabverdi Şaban oğlu] (Ongan, Ank. I, 155, 173); Yürük 1543 **Čalap-berdi** [بـردى چلـب] (Gökb., Rum. 178); Turk. 16th c. **Čalap-verdi** (Ongan, Ank. II); Yürük 1543 **Čalap-virdi** (Gökb., Rum. 176). ✧ 'God gave (him/her)'. ⇨ **ČALAP** + **BERDÏ.** See also **ALLA-BERDÏ, İGÄM-BERDÏ, OĠAN-BERDÏ, RÄHİM-BERDÏ, TÄÑRİ-BERDÏ.**

ČALAB-VERDÏ see **ČALAB-BERDÏ**

ČALAY Yak **Čalay / Čallāyï** [Чалаі / Чаллаjы], Tïγïn's elder son (Pek.). ⇨ **ČALLĀY, ČALLĀYÏ.**

ČALAQ Kzk. 19th c. **Čalaq** [Чалакъ] (SOK 202); Hak. 19th-20th c. **Čalaq** [Чалак] (HRS 352). ✧ 'Liar' cf. Shor *čalaq = yalaq* 'der Schmeichler' (Radl. III, 156, 1878). See also **BAY-ČALAQ.**

ČALAN Kzk. 19th c. **Čalam-bay (<Čalan-bay?)** [Чаламбай] (SOK 162). See also **BALÏ-ČALAN.**

ČALAP Kzk. 19th c. **Čalap-pay** [Чалаппай] (SODž. 10). ✧ I. 'God' cf. Turk. *Çalap* '(archaic) God' (TED), Turk. *čalab* 'Gott' (Radl. III, 1879); II. 'Watery ayran (yoghurt)' cf. Kzk. *šalap* 'Suluca ayran' (KzTS).

ČALAP-BERDÏ see **ČALAB-BERDÏ**

ČALAP-VERDÏ see **ČALAB-BERDÏ**

ČALBAĠ-ŌL see **ČALBAQ**

ČALBAX see **ČALBAQ**

ČALBAQ Hak. 19th-20th c. **Čalbaχ** [Чалбах], fem. (HRS 356); Alt. **Čalbaq** [Чалбак] (Proben IX, 457); Tuv. 19th c. **Čalbaq-ōl / Čalbaγ-ōl** [Чалбак ол] (Proben IX, 183). ✧ I. 'Broad, big' ('широкий; обширный' /HRS/), 'Broad young man' (широкий юноша /Katanov/); II. 'Tart' ('лепешка' /Butanaev/).

ČALBAT Yak. **Čalbat** [Чалбат] (Pek.).

ČALBÏYAQ Hak.(Belt.) 19th-20th c. **Čalbïyaq** [Чалбыjак] (Proben IX, 362, 366). ✧ 'Little basket' cf. Shor *čalbï* 'grosser Korb, grosse Schachtel' (Radl. III, 1891). + dim. suff. *-yaq*.

ČALČAN Kzk. 19th c. **Čalčan-bay** [Чалчанбай] (SODž. 30).

ČALDAN Kzk. 19th c. **Čaldam-bay (<Čaldan-bay)** [Чалдамбай] (SOK 188); Kzk. 19th c. **Čaldam-bay (<Čaldan-bay)** [Чалдамбай] (SODž. 46, 156); Kzk. 19th c. **Čaldam-bay (<Čaldan-bay)** [Чалдамбай] (SOV 112); Kzk. 19th c. **Čaldam-bek (<Čaldan-bek)** [Чалдамбекъ] (SODž. 10).

ČALDARQA Alt. 19th-20th c. **Čaldarqa** [Чалдарка] (OjrRS 210). ✧ 'Yellow (fawn-coloured?), bay horse' cf. Alt. *čaldar* 'игреневый (масть лошади)' (OjrRS). + suff. *-qa*. See also **ČAPTAR.**

ČALDÏ Kzk. 19th c. **Čaldï-bay** [Чалдыбай] (SOK 94); Kzk. 19th c. **Čaltï-bay** [Чалтыбай] (SOK 200); Kzk. 17th c. **Šaldï** [Шалды], a prince of lesser importance in the region of Ačinsk (Jarilov, Kyz. 4); Kzk. 19th c.

Šaldï [Шалды] (SOK 52); Trkm. 19th c. **Šaldï-bay** [Шалдыбай Атаньязовъ] (Ščeglov I, 352). ⇨ **ČAL?** + suff. *-dï.* See also **ČALLÏ.**

ČALDÏQ   Kzk. 1876 **Čaldïq** [Чальдик], a man resident in the Western Siberian steppe (AUK 357); Bashk. 1706 **Šaldïq** [Аиткул Шалдыков] (MIB III, 30); Kzk. **Šaldïq** [Шалдыкъ Сенгикѣевъ] (DAI VIII, 44-45); Kzk. 1680 **Šaldïq** [Шалдычко (Шалдыкъ) Сенгикѣевъ] (DAI VIII, 44); Kzk. 19th c. **Šaldïq-bay** [Шальдыкбай] (AOA 122). ✧ 'Ride much! Get used to ride much!' cf. Kzk. *šaldïq-* 'viel reiten, sich ans Reiten gewöhnen, durch schnelles Reiten sich müde machen' (Radl. IV, 966).

ČALÏ   Yürük 1543 **Čalï** [چالی] (Gökb., Rum. 180); Trkm. 20th c. **Čalï** [Čalï] (Zaj. 1971, 332); Trkm. 20th c. **Čalï** [Чалы] (TrkmRS 721); Tat.(Lit.) 1518 **Čalï** [Чали] (Kn. Metriki Lit. 44); Kzk. 19th c. **Čalï** [Чалы] (SOV 64); Turk. 15th c. **Čalï-beg** [Τζαλισπεγης], commander of the Ottoman fleet (Byz. Turc. II, 308). ✧ 'Bush' cf. Turk., Crm. *čalï* 'der Strauch, das Gestrüpp' (Radl. III, 1879), Trkm. *čalï* 'солянка кустарниковая' (TrkmRS).

ČALÏKE   Kzk. 19th c. **Čalïke / Čalike?** [Чалике] (SOV 152).

ČALÏQ   Maml. 14th c. **Čalïq** [جالق] (Sauvaget 46); Crm.(Turk.) **Čalïq-oɣlu** [Чалык оӷлу Ібрahім аҕа] (Proben VII, 324). ✧ 'Violent, hidebound' (Sauvaget 46).

ČALÏM   Kzk. 19th c. **Čalïm** [Чалымъ] (SODž. 108); Kkalp. 1740 **Čalïm-bi** [Чалимъ-Би] (Hanykov, Poezdka 19, MIKk. 208); Tat. 1557 **Čalïm-ulan** [Чалымъ-уланъ], from Astrakhan (PSRL XIII, 283). ✧ I. 'Edge of the sword'? Cf. Turk. *čalim* 'die Schneide des Schwertes'; II. 'Dew'? cf. Alt. *čalim* 'der Thau' (Radl. III, 1883).

ČALÏMBET   Kzk. 19th c. **Čalïmbet** [Чалимбетъ] (SOV 52, 54). ⇨ **ČAL** + suffixoid *-ïmbet.*

ČALÏN   Kzk. 19th c. **Čalïm-bay (<Čalïn-bay?)** [Чалимбай] (SOK 50); Kzk. 19th c. **Čalïm-bek (<Čalïn-bek)** [Чалымбекъ] (SOK 60); Kzk. 19th c. **Čalïm-bek (<Čalïn-bek)** [Чалымбекъ] (SOV 60); Kzk. 19th c. **Čalïn-bay** [Чалынбай] (SOV 12). ✧ 'Be hit?' Cf. Turk., Crm., Kar. *čalin-* 'geschlagen werden' (Radl. III, 1881). ⇨ **ČALÏM?**

ČALÏP   Kzk. 19th c. **Čalïp** [Чалипъ] (SOK 82).

ČALÏS   Kzk. 1824 **Čalïs** [Чалысъ Куйгилдинъ] (TOUAK XXIV, 146); Kzk. 1824 **Čalïs** [Чалысъ Куйгильдинъ] (TOUAK XXIV, 146). ✧ 'Wry (awry, slant)' cf. Kzk. *šalïs* 'косой' (KzRS).

ČALÏŠ   Turk. 1583 **Čalïš** [چا لش] (Ongan, Ank. I, 155); Yürük 1516 **Čalïš** [Çalış] (Su 4); Yürük 1543 **Čalïš** [چالیش], from Kocacık, Turkey (Gökb., Rum. 103, 211); Yürük 1553 **Čalïš** [Calış] (Gökçen 35). ✧ 'Work! Strive! Fight!' cf. Crm., Turk. *čalïš-* 'sich abmühen,

sich einer Sache widmen, arbeiten' (Radl. III, 1882).

ČALQA   Kzk. 19th c. **Čalqa-bay** [Чалкабай] (SOK 100). ⇨ **ČAL?** + suff. *-qa.*

ČALQAXTAY   Yak. **Čalqaχtay** [Чалкахтаі уол ättiäбіt] (Pek.). ✧ 'Fat/obese lad cut (it) into pieces' (=Пухлый парень рубил на части), cf. Yak. *čalqaχ + tay* (Pek.). + / suff. *-tay(1,2)?*

ČALQÏ   Kzk. 19th c. **Čalqï-bay** [Чалйыбай] (SOK 8). ✧ 'Scythe'? cf. Kzk. *šalɣï* 'die Sense; die Flügelschlag' (Radl. IV, 965).

ČALLĀY   Yak. **Čallāy** [Чаллаі], one of Är-Soɣotoχ-Ällä's descendants (Pek.). ⇨ **ČALAY.**

ČALLĀYÏ see **ČALAY**

ČALLÏ   Turk. **Čallï-oɣlu,** a Zeybek (Kúnos 1891, 119). ⇨ **ČAL?** + suff. *-lï.* See also **ČALLÏ.**

ČALLÏN   Yak. **Čallïn** [Чаллын] (Pek.).

ČALME   Chag. 16th c.-17th c. **Čalme** [Чальмэ / Чальме] (Ivanov 197, 297, 306, 304-307, 308). ✧ 'A kind of turban' cf. Crm., Tat., Turk. *čalma* 'der Turban' (Radl. III, 1892).

ČALMUR   Kzk. 19th c. **Čalmur** [Чалмуръ] (SODž. 10).

ČALPÏN   Kzk. **Čalpïn** [Чалпынъ] (TOUAK XXIII, 33).

ČALTA   Tat.(Mish.) 1748 **Čalta? / Čaltïn?** [Аитъ Чалтинъ] (Nepljuev 437); Kzk. 19th c. **Čalta-bay** [Чалтабай] (SOV 44). ⇨ **ČALTÏ?**

ČALTÏ see **ČALDÏ**

ČAM-BAY I. see **ĴAN**

ČAM-BAY II. see **ČAN II.**

ČAM-BOL see **ĴAN-BOL**

ČAMA   Hak. 19th-20th c. **Čama** [Чама], fem. (HRS 356). ✧ 'Garlic' (Ibid.), 'Wild garlic' (Butanaev).

ČAMAY   Kzk. 19th c. **Čamay** [Чамай] (SOV 86). ✧ 'Strength, power' cf. Tat.(Tara) *čama* 'die Kraft, das Vermögen' (Radl. III, 1937), Kzk. *šama* 'insan vücudundaki güç - kuvvet' (KzTS) + suff. *-y.*

ČAMAQ   Hak. 19th-20th c. **Čamaq** [Чамак] (HRS 352); Hak.(Sag.) **Čamaq** [Чамак], fem., her R. name was Marija Stepanovna Katanova (Proben IX, 259). ✧ 'Little garlic'. ⇨ **ČAMA?** + suff. *-q?*

ČAMAN   Trkm. 20th c. **Čaman** [Čaman] (Zaj. 1971, 333); Trkm. 20th c. **Čaman** [Чаман] (TrkmRS 721). ✧ 'Lazy, sluggard' (Zaj. 1971), cf. Trkm. *čaman* 'ленивый, вялый' (TrkmRS).

ČAMAŠÏRĴÏ   Turk. **Čamašïrĵï-oɣlu,** a Zeybek (Kúnos 1891, 118). ✧ 'Laundryman'.

ČAMBÏRAY   Tuv. 19th c. **Čambïray** [Чамбырай] (Proben IX, 185).

ČAMČAY see **ČOMČOY**

ČAMDAN   Kzk. 19th-20th c. **Čamdan** [Csamdan], the last independent manap (ruler) of the Sarï-baɣïš Kirghiz (=Kazaks) (Prinz 320). ✧ 'Rage, fume'? cf. Kzk. *šamdan* 'sich innerlich ärgern, wütend sein' (Radl. IV,

994).

ČAMÏN   Kzk. 19th c. **Čamïm-bay** (<**Čamïn-bay?**) [Чамымбай] (SOK 216).

ČAMUQ   Karch. **Čamuq** [Чамукъ] (Sysoev 120).

ČAMZÏ   Tuv. 19th c. **Čamzï** [Чамзы] (Proben IX, 211).

ČAN I. see **JAN**

ČAN II.   Tat.(Bar.) 14th c. **Cān-pay** [Цан Паі], a man who, in the tale, was in the service of Toqtamïš-qan (1382-1397) (Proben IV, 30 /39/); Tat. 20th c. **Can-bay / Cam-bay** (<**Čan-bay**) [Чанбай / Чанбаев / Чамбаев] (Sattarov). ✧ I. 'White'? In some names written in Arabic letters it may be read as *čan* <Mo. *čaγan* 'white' (Sauvaire 46), see ČAΓAN; II. 'Wolf'? <Mo. *čan* (Sattarov).

ČAN-BOL see **JAN-BOL**

ČAN-BULAT see **JAN-BULAT**

ČAN-SABAY   Kzk. 19th c. **Can-sabay** [Чансабай] (SODž. 136). ⇨ **JAN + SABAY?**

ČANA   Kzk. 19th c. **Cana-bay** [Чанабай] (SOV 54). ✧ 'Sleigh'.

ČANAY   Tat.(Lit.) 1555 **Canay** [Чанай] (Kn. Metriki Lit. 113). ⇨ **ČANA + suff. -*y***.

ČANAQ   Crm. 1679 **Canaq-aγa** [چناق اغا] (Vel.-Zern., Crim. 666, 669); Crm. 1689 **Canaq-aγa** [چا ناق اغا] (Vel.-Zern., Crim. 897). ✧ 'Dish, turreen' cf. Chag., Crm., Turk. *čanaq* 'eine irdene Schüssel, Schale, Napf, Terrine' (Radl. III, 1856).

ČANAM   Kzk. 19th c. **Canam-bay** [Пахметъ Чанамбаевъ] (AUK 609).

ČANAR-QUS   Hak.(Sag.) **Canar-qus** [Чанар Кус], a bogatyr (Proben IX, 543, 544). ✧ I. 'Bird of passage' cf. Tuv. *canar quš(tar)* 'перелётные птицы' (TuvRS); II. 'Heat-bird' cf. Hak. PN *Canar Xus* (Butanaev). ⇨ **QUŠ I.**

ČANASÏL   Kzk. 19th c. **Canasïl** [Чанасылъ] (SOK 188).

ČANCA   Alt.? **Canča** [Чанча], fem. (Katanov, Otč. 11).

ČANCÏ   Alt. 19th-20th c. **Canči** [Чанчы] (OjrRS 210).

ČANCÏQ   Alt. 19th-20th c. **Cančïq** [Чанчык] (OjrRS 210). ✧ 'Pouch, little bag' cf. Tuv. *cančïq* 'кисет; фут.лярчик' (TuvRS).

ČANCÏQA   Kzk. 19th c. **Cančïqa-bi / Cančikä-bi?** [Чанчекаби] (SOK 78).

ČANDARLÏ   Turk. 1489 **Candarlï-zäde** [Çandarlı-zade İbrahim Paşa] (Gökb., Ed. 362). ✧ 'Lively' cf. Turk. *candar* 'belebt, lebhaft' (HŞ).

ČANÏ   Kzk. 19th c. **Canï** [Чани] (SODž. 130).

ČANÏMBET   Kzk. 19th c. **Canïmbet** [Чанымбетъ] (SOK 218). ⇨ **JAN + suffäxoäd -*imbet***.

ČANÏŠ   Tat. 1776, 1777 **Canïš** [Ибрагимъ Чанышевъ / Ибрагим Чанышев (Ченышев)], a murza (PSZRI XX, 456, MIB V, 65, 680); Tat.(Mish.) **Canïš** [Чанышевъ], a Misher family (IOAIÊK XIX, 143); Kzk. 19th c. **Canïš-qul** [Чанышкулъ] (SODž. 18);

Kzk. 19th c. **Canïš-qul** [Чанышкулъ] (SOV 108). ⇨ **JAN + suff. -*iš*.**

ČAÑ   Kzk. 1817 **Cañ-bay** [قول جا نكباى] (MIK IV, 311, 318); Kzk. 19th c. **Cañ-bay** [Нурчавъ Чангбаевъ] (Grod., Pril. 197); Kzk. 1817 **Cañ-bay / Šañ-bay / Šan-bay** [جا نكباى / Шанбай] (MIK IV, 311). ⇨ **ČAN I. / II.?**

ČAÑΓÏ-YÜZÜGİ   Bashk. 1763 **Cañγï-yüzügi** [Чанги-Юзюги] (MIB IV/1, 272). ✧ 'Cañγï's ring'? cf. Bashk. *yöðök* 'перстень' (BRS), Alt.(Tel.) *yüstük* 'der Fingerring, der Siegelring' (Radl. III, 616), Kuman, Chag., Tat.(Bar.), Turk. *yüzük* 'id.'(Radl. III, 619) + poss. suf. -*i*.

ČAÑΓÏZ   Bashk. 1776 **Cañγïz / Cañ-güz?** [Чангыз Мустакаев] (MIB V, 38); Kzk. 19th c. **Cañγuz?** [Чангузъ] (SOV 24). ⇨ **ČAÑΓUZ?**

ČAÑΓUZ see **ČAÑΓÏZ**

ČAÑÏY   Alt. 19th-20th c. **Cañïy** (OjrRS 210).

ČAÑÏR   Uyg. 12th c. - 14th c. **Cañïr-tayšï** [čaŋïr tajšï / Çangır Taişi] (DTS, EUTS).

ČAÑŠİ see **ČAÑŠÏ**

ČAÑŠÏ   Türk 7th - 9th c. **Cañsï** [Çañsï] (ETY III, 143); Uyg. **Cañši** [čangši] (Müller, Hofstaat 211, 213); Türk 7th c. - 9th c. **Cañšï** [čaŋšï] (DTS). ✧ 'Historian of the prince's court' (<Chin.), cf. *changshih* 'recorder or remembrancer' (Mayers, Chinese Government No. 34).

ČAPA   Kzk. 19th c. **Capa** [Чапа] (SOK 214). ✧ 'Fast, nimble, skilfully' cf. Kirg. *capa* 'быстро, проворно, ловко' (Jud.).

ČAPAY   Tat.? 1693 **Cepay** [Елтутаръ Чепаевъ], a murza (AI V, 404); Tat. 1752 **Cepay** (<**Čapay**) [Асманъ Чепаевъ] (PSZRI XIII, 737). ✧ 'Famous' (Sattarov), cf. Uyg., Alt. *cap* 'der Ruhm, der Ruf' (Radl. III, 1915) + dim. suff. -*ay*.

ČAPAQ   Kzk. 1820 **Capaq** [Чапакъ], a chieftain of a tribe (Sib. Vest. IX, 121); Kzk. 1846 **Capaq** [Туки Чапаков] (MKOP 155); Kzk. 19th c. **Capaq** [Чапакъ] (SODž. 18). ✧ I. 'Eloquent (man), talkative'? cf. Tat. *capaq* 'beredt, wohlrednerisch' (Radl. III, 1918); II. 'A kind of small fish'? cf. (Tur., Crm.) *capaq* 'ein flacher Fisch' (Radl. III, 1918). ⇨ **ČABAQ?**

ČAPAL   **Capāl / Cap-al**, an emir and poet (Justi 155). ✧ 'Campaign on the enemy's land' („Streifzug in Feindesland" /Justi/).

ČAPAN   Kmk. 1708 **Capan** [Чапан Шавкал / Чапан шевкал кумыцкий], a Kumuk landlord (MIB I, 242, MIKk. 158); Kmk. 1708 **Capan** [Чапан Чапасов] (MIKk. 158); Alt. 19th c. **Capan** [Чапанъ], an informant (Potanin IV, 288); Alt. 19th-20th c. **Capan** [Чапан] (OjrRS 210); Kzk. 19th c. **Capan-bay** [Комакъ Чапанбаевъ] (Grod., Pril. 187); Turk. 1800 **Capan-oγlï / Capan-oγlu?** [چا با ن اوغلى], a derebey (feudal lord) in Anatolia (Uzunçarş., Küt. I, 91); Turk. 1543 **Capan-oγlu** (Gökb., Rum. 175). ✧ 'A kind of special coat, similar to nightgown' cf. Chag., Uzb., Kzk. *čapan* 'ein vorne offener Rock (dem Schlafrock ähnlich, wie ihn die Muhammedaner tragen); ein alter Rock mit Flicken' (Radl. III, 1918), Kirg. *čapan* 'id.' (Jud.), Trkm. *čapan* 'id.' (TrkmRS). See also **AQ-ČAPAN**.

ČAPAR Bashk. 1738 **Čapar** [Мусала Чапаров] (MIB I, 370); *EN:* Crm. 1655 **Toquz-čapar / Toquz-čabar mirzalarï?** [طقوزچبار ميرزالرى] (Vel.-Zern., Crim. 496). ✧ 'Runner, gallopper' cf. Mo. *Čabar* (<Trk.) *čapar*. See also **AT-ČABAR, OT-ČAPAR, TAY-ČABAR**.

ČAPAT **Čapat** [Чапат] (RaD II, 10).

ČAPČAQ Kzk. 19th c. **Čapčaq** [Кадиръ Чапчаковъ] (Grod., Pril. 32). ✧ 'Bucket' cf. *čapčaq* (Alt.) 'der Eimer, das Fass', (Crm., Tat.) 'der Zuber' (Radl. III, 1927).

ČAPČAŇ Alt. 19th-20th c. **Čapčaň** [Чапчаҥ] (Katanov, Otč. 10); Karg. **Čapčaň** [Чапчаҥ], fem. (Katanov, Otč. 8). ✧ 'Quick, lively' (Ibid.).

ČAPČÏN Tat. 1714 **Čapčïn / Čapčin?** [Чапчин Сююндуков] (MIB III, 118).

ČAPČUQ Tat. 1552 **Čapčuq** [Чапчук], a Tatar prince (Zolotn. 160). ✧ I. 'Little fame'? cf. Uyg., Alt. *čap* 'der Ruhm, der Ruf' (Radl. III, 1915); II. 'Arrow with iron head'? cf. Alt. *čap* 'ein Pfeil mit eiserner Spitze' (Radl. III, 1916); III. 'Lie'? cf. Chag. *čap* 'die Lüge, der Betrug, die Prahlerei' (Radl. III, 1916). + dim. suff. *-čuq*.

ČAPÏQ Trkm. 20th c. **Čapïq** [Čapïq] (Zaj. 1971, 333); Trkm. 20th c. **Čapïq** [Чапык] (TrkmRS 723). ✧ 'Scab, mildew' (Zaj. 1971), cf. Trkm. *čapïq* 'обрезанный, срезанный' (TrkmRS).

ČAPÏLDAY Alt. 19th-20th c. **Čapïlday** [Чапылдай] (OjrRS 210).

ČAPQAY Bashk. 1761 **Čapqay** [Чапкай Утегулов] (MIB IV/1, 221). ✧ 'Little fame' cf. Uyg., Alt. *čap* 'der Ruhm, der Ruf' (Radl. III, 1915), cf. also Tat. PN *Čapay* (<*čap*)+ voc. suff. *-ay* (Sattarov) + suff. *-qay*.

ČAPQÏN I. Bashk. 1785 **Čapqïn** [Каюкан Чапкинов] (MIB V, 178, 219); Bashk. 1789 **Čapqïn?** [Чабким Исмаил] (MIB V, 265); Bulg. 1594 **Čapqïn / Čapqun?** [جابتن] (Jusupov 70). ✧ I. 'Messenger, courier' cf. Tat. *čapqïn* 'гонец, курьер, нарочный, конный посыльный' (TatRS); II. 'Tax-collector; Opressor', the term was used in the 16-18th c. among the Tatars of Kazan (Sattarov 212); III. 'Rake, debauchee, naughty, coquettish; rascal, mischievous (child); swift (horse)' cf. Turk. *çapkın* 'id.' (TED).

ČAPQÏN II. NUyg. 19th c. **Čapqïn** [جافتون / جافتين / Chapgin] (Le Coq, Namenl. 98). ✧ 'Snowstorm' (Ibid.); cf. Chag. *čapqun / čabɣun* 'der Angriff; Wind, Regen und Schnee; Schneesturm; ein schnelles Pferd' (Radl. III, 1922), East.T. *čapɣun* 'a very strong wind,

blowing from the mountains' (Jarring).

ČAPPA Kzk. 19th c. **Čappa** [Чаппа] (SOK 32). ✧ 'Trigger, pocket knife' cf. Kzk. *šappa* 'курок; перочинный нож' (KzRS).

ČAPPAŇ Hak.(Sag.) **Čappaň** [Чапчаҥ] (Proben IX, 455, 456).

ČAPPÏJÏQ Tuv. 19th c. **Čappïjïq** [Чаппыжык], fem. (Proben IX, 171).

ČAPRAQ Hak. 19th-20th c. **Čapraq** [Чапрак], fem. (Katanov, Otč. 10); Hak.(Shor) 19th-20th c. **Čapraq** [Чапрак] (Katanov, Otč. 11). ✧ 'Silver ornament' cf. Hak. fem. PN *Čapraχ* 'серебрянные украшения' (Butanaev).

ČAPRAZ Trkm. 20th c. **Čapraz** [Čapraz] (Zaj. 1971, 330); Trkm. 20th c. **Čapraz** [Чапраз] (TrkmRS 723). ✧ 'Silver (or gilded) decoration (on women's clothing)' cf. Trkm. *čapraz* 'id.' (TrkmRS).

ČAPŠÏR Tuv. 19th c. **Čapšïr-öl / Čapšur-ül?** [Чапшурур / Чапшыр-ол] (Proben IX, 65).

ČAPTAR Kzk. 19th c. **Čabdar** [Чабдаръ] (SOK 212); Bashk. 18th c. **Čabdar-bay / Čapdar-bay?** [Чапдарбай, Чапдарбаев] (MIB V, 113, 119, 157, 222, 223, 577, 578, 684); Kzk. 1846 **Čabdar-bek** [Чабдарбек] (MKOP 155); Bashk. 1749 **Čaptar** [Чаптар Сартыков] (MIB III, 460); Bashk. 1760 **Čaptar** [Чаптар Алакаев] (MIB IV/1, 195); Bashk. 1761 **Čaptar** [Чаптар Исенеев] (MIB IV/1, 228). ✧ 'Yellow (fawn-coloured?), bay horse' cf. Alt. *čaptar* 'Pferdefarbe: Fuchs mit weissem Schwanze und weisser Mähne' (Radl. III, 1926), Tat. *čaptar* 'игреневый' (TatRS), Kzk. *šabdar* 'игрений, игреневый' (KzRS), Kzk. *šabdar* 'Kuyruk ve yelesi sarı, vücudunun diğer kısımları kırmızımsı.' (KzTS). See also **ČALDARQA**.

ČAPU Trkm. 1838 **Čapu-yüzbašï** [Чапу-юзбаши] (MIT II, 473). ✧ 'Race, racing (horse); running' cf. Trkm. *čapu* 'id.' (TrkmRS).

ČAR Tat.? **Čar-qul** [Чаркул-Нудуй], a Shaman from the Tatar tribe (RaD I/1, 104). ✧ 'With white head; Spotted, piebald' Cf. *čar* (Kirg.) 'weissköpfig', (Turk., Crm.) 'freiwillig', (Alt.) 'der Schleifstein', 'ein Ochs, ein Arbeitsochs', (Mad. W.[?]) 'ein junger Bär' (Radl. III, 1859), *čār* (Kirg.) 'schekig (Pferdefarbe)' (Radl. III, 1860). See also **BAY-ČAR, KÖK-ČAR, QARA-ČAR, TAW-ČAR**.

ČAR-BUQA Oghuz **Čar-buqa / Čar-buɣa** [چار بوغا / Чар-бука], forefather of the Ottoman dynasty (Āšikp. 50, RaD I/1, 196). ✧ 'Piebold bull; Bull with white head' cf. also Wittek: Der Islam XIV, 94. ⇨ **ČAR + BUQA**.

ČAR-YAR Trkm. 1826 **Čar-yar-qulï-bay / Čār-yār-qulï-bay** [Чарьяр-кули-бай], from the Teke tribe (MIT II, 440, 450, 451). ✧ 'The four friends' (=Abubekir, Omar, Osman, Ali); cf. Trkm. (<P.) *čār* 'четыре', and *yār* 'любимый, возлюбленный,

милый' (TrkmRS). ⇨ **YAR.**

ČARA-BAS Kzk. **Čara-bas** [چرا باس] (Divaev, Baksy 319); Kzk. 1846 **Čara-bas** [бий Кулджабай Чарабасов], a biy (MKOP 100); Kzk. 1803, 1820 **Čara-pas** [Чарапас(ъ)], one of the chiefs of the Čaqčaq tribe of the Middle Horde (Orta Žüz) (MIK IV, 513, SibVestn. IX, 107). ✧ 'Having a head as big as a large (wodden) pot'; „чара - большая котлообразная деревяная чашка, вмещающая иногда въ себѣ около двухъ ведеръ бульона, и бас - голова" (Divaev, Baksy 319). ⇨ **BAŠ.** See also **QUL-ČARA.**

ČARA-PAS see **ČARA-BAS**

ČARĀNĪ Yak. **Čarānï** [Чароны] (Pek.).

ČARΓÏN Kzk. 19th c. **Čarγïn** [Чаргынъ] (SOV 100); Kirg. **Čarγïn** [Чаргын] (Jud. 23, 884); Shor 19th-20th c. **Čarγïn-tayčï**, a bogatyr (Dyrenkova 170).

ČARÏ Kzk. 19th c. **Čarï-bay** [Чарыбай] (SOV 16).

ČARÏQ Kzk. 19th c. **Čarïq** [Чарыкъ] (SOV 100); Turk. 1460 **Čarïq? / Čerkes?** [Τζαρχας], a Turkish emir (cca. 1460) (Byz. Turc. II, 310); Trkm. 1690 **Čarïq-oγlu** [چارق اوغلو] (Refik, Anad. 82); Kzk. 19th c. **Čarïq-pay** [Чарыкпай] (SOK 12, 292); Kzk. 19th c. **Šarïq-pay** [Шарыкпай] (AOO 58); *TN:* Kzk. **Šarïq** [Шарык], a field (Kojčubaev 250). ✧ I. 'Rawhide sandal' cf. Crm., Tat.(Tara), Turk. *čarïq* 'das grobe Schuhzeug der Bauern; der Hemmschuh', (Kirg.) 'Lederstücke, die man um die Füsse bindet' (Radl. III, 1863), Kzk. *šarïq* 'grobe Lederschuhe' (Radl. IV, 953), Kzk. *şarık* 'çarık' (KzTS), Kzk. dial. *čarïq* 'id.' (QTDS); II. 'Stupid, uneducated' cf. Kzk. *şarık* 'okumamış, cahil' (KzTS).

ČARÏQASÏN see **ŽARÏLQASÏN**

ČARÏQPAN Kzk. 19th c. **Čarïqpan** [Чарыкпанъ] (SOK 58). ⇨ **ČARÏQ** + suff. -*pan(1).*

ČARÏM-BAY see **ČARÏN**

ČARÏN Kzk. 19th c. **Čarïm-bay (<Čarïn-bay)** [Чарымбай] (SOV 6, 30); Kzk. 19th c. **Čarïm-bay (<Čarïn-bay)** [Чарымбай] (SOV 80).

ČARÏŇ Alt. 19th-20th c. **Čarïň** [Чарын], fem. (OjrRS 213). ✧ 'Shoulder-blade'? cf. Shor *čarin* 'id.' (Radl. III, 1864).

ČARÏP Kzk. 19th c. **Čarïp-pay** [Чарыппай] (SOV 44, 72).

ČARÏR Uyg. 12th c.-14th c. **Čarïr** [Çarır] (DTS, EUTS).

ČARÏSAY Yak. **Čarïsay** [Чарысаi] (Pek.).

ČARMAQ Tuv. 19th c. **Čarmaq** [Чармак] (Proben IX, 657).

ČARMÏŠ Bashk. 1741 **Čarmïš** [Чармыш (Чермыш) Абдрахманов] (MIB III, 413). ✧ 'Cheremis'.

ČARŠAN Kzk. 19th c. **Čaršan-bay** [Чаршанбай] (Grod., Pril. 40).

ČART Kzk. 19th c. **Čart-pay** [Чартпай] (SOK 120). ✧

'Crack'? cf. Kzk. *šart* 'резкий звук; треск' (KzRS).

ČARTÏM-AY Tuv. **Čartïm-ay** [Чартымай] (Katanov: ZIRGOÊtn. 200). ✧ 'Half-moon' cf. Tuv. *čartïq ay* 'полумесяц' (RTuvS), Hak. *čartï*, Tat.(Bar.) *yartï* 'die Hälfte, halb' (Radl. III, 1868). ⇨ **AY.**

ČARTÏMAY Tuv. 19th c. **Čartïmay / Čartïm-ay** [Чартымай] (Proben IX, 652, 660).

ČARU Kzk. 19th c. **Čaru** [Чару] (SODž. 74).

ČARUQ Uyg. **Čaruq-ügä** [Чарукъ-уга] (RaD/Ber. III, 12). ⇨ **ČARÏQ.**

ČARVA Trkm. 20th c. **Čarva** [Čarba (!)] (Zaj. 1971, 325); Trkm. 20th c. **Čarva** [Чарва] (TrkmRS 724). ✧ 'Stock-breeder, nomad' (Zaj. 1971), cf. Trkm. *čarva* 'id.' (TrkmRS).

ČASAÑTUZ Uyg. **Časañtuz** [Çasangtuz] (EUTS).

ČASÏR-ALQA Uyg. 12th c.-14th c. **Časïr-alqa** (DTS). ✧ '?-earring'? ⇨ **ALQA.**

ČAŠ-KÖK Shor 19th-20th c. **Čaš-kök**, Čaš-salγïn's younger sister from the heroic legend of Aq-qān (Dyrenkova 192). ✧ 'Young cuckoo' cf. Hak.(Shor) *čaš* 'jung' (Radl. III, 1912), Hak.(Sag., Koyb.), Shor *kök* 'der Kuckuck' (Radl. II, 1223). ⇨ **YAŠ.**

ČAŠ-ÖL see **YAŠ**

ČAŠ-PÏLEK Shor 19th-20th c. **Čaš-pilek**, Aba-qulaq's son from the heroic legend of Aq-qān (Dyrenkova 228). ✧ 'Young wrist' cf. Alt., Shor, etc. *piläk* 'das Handgelenk' (Radl. III, 1338). ⇨ **YAŠ.**

ČAŠ-SALΓÏN Shor 19th-20th c. **Čaš-salγïn**, a hero in a heroic legend of Aq-qān (Dyrenkova 192). ✧ 'Young wind' cf. Shor *salγïn* 'der Wind' (Radl. IV, 364). ⇨ **YAŠ.**

ČAŠPAN Tuv. **Čašpan** [Чашпанъ], fem. (Katanov: ZIRGOÊtn. XVII, vyp. III, 165); Tuv. **Čašpan** [Чашпанъ] (Katanov: ZIRGOÊtn. XVII, vyp. III, 165). ✧ 'Wormwood; weed' cf. Tuv. *čašpan* 'полынь; бурьян; сорняк' (TuvRS).

ČAŠTÏ-QÏZ see **SAČLÏ**

ČAT-QASAR Khazar **Čat-qasar** [Čᶜatᶜ Kasar], chamberlain of Awči-tarχan (Golden 173).

ČATAY Bashk. 1776, 1777 **Čatay** [Итяш Чатаев] (MIB V, 51).

ČATAL-BAŠ Turk. **Čatal-baš**, a Zeybek (Kúnos 1891, 118). ✧ 'Forked head' cf. Turk. *çatal* 'fork, pitchfork' (TED). ⇨ **BAŠ.**

ČATÏ Kzk. 19th c. **Čatï-qul** [Чатыкулъ] (SODž. 146). ✧ 'Tripod'? cf. Trkm. *čatï* 'треножник' (TrkmRS).

ČATÏN-XAZÏR Khazar **Čatïn-χazïr** [Čᶜatᶜn Xazr], an Alp-ilut(?) chief (Golden 174).

ČAUŠ see **ČAWUŠ**

ČAVA Karakh. 11th c. **Čava / Čawa** [čava / Çawa] (DTS, MK/Atalay 836).

ČAVUŠ see **ČAWUŠ**

ČAW-BURA Bashk. 1757 **Čaw-bura** [Чавбура Токалов] (MIB IV/1, 157). ✧ 'Fame-camel'? cf. Uyg.

čaw 'der Ruhm' (Radl. III, 1934). ⇨ **BUΓRA**.

ČAW-GİLDE see **YAW-GİLDİ**

ČAWÏN Kzk. 1846 **Čawïn** [бий Чавень Букенев], a biy (MKOP 157).

ČAWKE Kzk. 19th c. **Čawke** [Чавке] (SOV 36); Kzk. 19th c. **Čawke** [Чавке] (SOK 16). ✧ I. 'Jackdaw'? cf. Tat. *čäükä* 'id.' (TatRS), see also SÄWKÄ; II. 'Fame' cf. Uyg. *čaw* 'der Ruhm' (Radl. III, 1934). + suff. *-ke* or suffixoid *-ake*.

ČAWLÏ Selj.? 1076 **Čawlï** [جاو لى بن أوق التركى] (Adīm II, 48); Maml. 14th c. **Čawlï** [جاولى] (Sauvaget 46); Tat.(Lit.) 1557 **Čawlu-bay** [Чавлубай] (Kn. Metriki Lit. 152). ✧ I.'Famous' cf. Uyg. *čaw* 'der Ruhm' (Radl. III, 1934); II. 'Falcon, kite' cf. Chag. *čavli*, Turk. *čavlï* 'ein junger, noch nicht dressirter Falke, ein Sperber' (Radl. III, 1936). + suff. *-li*?

ČAWLÏDUR Selj. 11th c. **Čawlïdur** [جاولدور], on of Alp-arslan's emirs in the battle of Malazgirt (1071) (Ali Selim: Belleten 1962, 125 (taken from Hafiz-i Adru and Selčukname-i Nišaburī)). ✧ I. 'Famous' II. '(He is a) Falcon'. ⇨ **ČAWLÏ** + suff. *-dur*.

ČAWLU see **ČAWLÏ**

ČAWSA Kzk. 19th c. **Čawsa-bay** / **Čausa-bay** [Чаусабай] (SODž. 94).

ČAWTEY Kzk. 19th c. **Čawtey** [Чаутей] (SODž. 44).

ČAWUNDUR Turk. 1540 **Čawundur-kethudā** [چاوندر] / Çavundur kethudâ], chief of the Güzgücek cemaat according to a defter from Diyarbekir (Demirtaş 51). ✧ I. 'Hill'? cf. Turk. dial. *çavundur* 'Düz ovaların ortalarında yükselen yerler' (DS); II. 'River, deluge; heavy rain- or snow-fall'? cf. Chag. *čawun* 'der Fluss, der Strom; sehr starker Regen und Schneefall' (Radl. III, 1935). + Adj. suff. *-dur*.

ČAWUŠ Selj. 11th c. **Čauš** [Σιαύς], envoy of the Seljuk Sultan (Byz. Turc. II, 274); Selj. 12th c. **Čauš-bek** / **Čauš-beg** [جوشبك / Emir Çavuşbeg], an emir, sultan Masʿud's atabek in Mosul (Bondārī 132, 174, Ahbar 68); Turk. **Čauš-oγlu** (Giese 55); Turk. 1444 **Čavuš-bey** [Çavuş Bey] (Gökb., Ed. 37). ✧ 'Warrant officer; commander; 'Chief of the guards (janitors)' Title, secondary component of personal names. Cf. Karakh. *čavuš* (P.) 'младший офицер, командир, непосредственно руководящий воинами в боевых порядках' (DTS), Turk. *çavuş* (hist.) 'halberdier of the sultan; herald, messenger; musician of the palace' (TED).

ČABÏČAXĀN Yak. **Čabïčaχān** / **Čabïča-χān?** [Чабычахан], Čača-χān's wife (Pek.).

ČAČČA Karg. **Čačča** [Чачча (Александра Александровна)], fem. (Proben IX, 658); Yak. **Čačča-χān** (<**Čarča-χān?**) [Чаччахан], a legendary old woman (Pek.). See also **ČARČA**.

ČAJÏN Tuv. **Čajïn** (Katanov, Otč. 8). ✧ 'Paper' (Ibid.).

ČĀL Hak. 19th-20th c. **Čāl** [Чаал] (HRS 352). ✧ 'A young tree' cf. Alt. *čal* 'ein junger Baum, niedriges Gestrüpp, Strauchwerk' (Radl. III, 1875).

ČĀMÏQTÏR Yak. **Čāmïqtïr** [Чамыктыр] (Pek.). ✧ Derived from Yak. *čāmïqlïr* < *čāmïq* 'зверек тарбаган, каменный или алтайский сурок' (Pek.).

ČĀR-YAQLÏ Trkm. 1828 **Čār-yaqlï-bay** [Чаар Яклы-бай], from the Tekke tribe (MIT II, 448). ✧ 'Man with four sides'? cf. P. *čār* 'four' + *yaqlï* 'with sides'. ⇨ **ČAR** + **YAQ** + suff. *-lï*.

ČĀRČAXAN Yak. **Čārčaχan** [Чарчахан, Чаччахан, Чачахан], forefather of the Abaγat clan (Абагатинский род); characters of both sexes in tales (Pek.). ⇨ **ČĀRČA** + suff. *-χan(1)*.

ČĀRDAN Kzk. **Čārdan-bay** [Чарданбай] (Sb. Syr-D. IX, 44).

ČĀS Tuv. 19th-20th c. **Čās** (Katanov, Otč. 10). ✧ 'Hour' (<R.) часъ 'id.' (Ibid.).

ČĀSQA Alt.? 19th-20th c. **Čāsqa** (Katanov, Otč. 10); Hak.(Kyz.) 19th-20th c. **Čāsqa** [Часка], fem. (Katanov, Otč. 13). ✧ 'Cup' (<R.) чашка 'id.' (Ibid.).

ČĀSTAY Hak.(Blt.) 19th-20th c. **Čāstay** / **Čāstïy** [Частаі] (Proben IX, 366). ✧ '(Of) spring' cf. Hak. PN *Častay* 'весенний' (Butanaev).

ČĀSTÏY see **ČĀSTAY**

ČÄBÄGLİG Tuv. 19th c. **Čäbäglig** [Чäбäгліг], fem. (Proben IX, 124). ✧ + suff. *-lig*.

ČÄČČÄN see **ČEČEN**

ČÄČČÄN see **ČEČEN**

ČÄČÄÑ see **ČEČEN**

ČÄDİ-PÜRÜ Hak.(Blt.) 19th-20th c. **Čädi-pürü** [Чäди Пÿрÿ] (Proben IX, 356); Hak.(Blt.) 19th-20th c. **Čädi-pürü** [Чäди Пÿрÿ] (Proben IX, 357). ⇨ **YETİ** + **BÖRİ**.

ČÄDİN Uyg. 12th c.-14th c. **Čädin** / **Čadin?** (Radl., USp. 34).

ČÄKČÄGÄLLÄY Yak. **Čäkčägälläy** [äriän Čäkčägälläy / Чäкчäгäлläі] (Pek.).

ČÄKES Chuv. **Čäkes** / **Čäges** [tʼšʼəges], a pagan female name (Mészáros 215). ✧ 'Swallow'.

ČÄKÜL Türk 7th-9th c. **Čäkül** [Çäkül] (ETY III, 163).

ČÄKÜŠ Uyg. 1339 **Čeküš** [Zakusch] (Chwol., Syr.-nest. (NF) 34). ✧ 'Hammer' cf. Chag., Az. *čäküč* 'id.' (Radl. III, 1954).

ČÄL-PAΓA Karg. **Čäl-paγa** [Чäл-паҕа], a female sorcerer, witch (Proben IX, 634, 635, 637). ✧ 'Wind-frog' (Ibid.). ⇨ **YEL** + **BAQA**.

ČÄLMÄŠ Alt.(Tuba) **Čälmäš** [Tschälmäsch / Чäлмäш], a stupid lad in a tale (Proben I, 279 (302), Radl. I, 1135). ✧ 'Smart, skilful'? Chag. *čälpiš* / *čälbiš* 'geschickt, gewandt' (Radl. III, 1981, 1982).

ČÄMPÄLIS Yak. **Čämpälis** [Чäмпäліс], one of three well-known wrestlers (Pek.).

ČÄN see **JAN**

ČÄNČILÄ Yak. **Čänčilä** [Чäнчилä], old woman, spirit-protector of ermines (Pek.).

ČÄÑÄYÏ Yak. **Čäñäyi-bögö** [Чäңäji-бöҕö], a brave hero, one of Xatan-χañγïlla's famous descendants, forefather of the clans living in the valleys of Amga (Pek.).

ČÄÑÏN Uyg. **Čäñin** [Çängin] (EUTS).

ČÄÑÏNTÄRÏ Uyg. **Čäñintäri-ilči** (Radl., USp. 12).

ČÄÑÜR Uyg. **Čäñür** [Çängür] (EUTS).

ČÄRÏ-DÄMÜR Maml. 14th c. **Čäri-dämür** [جَرِدَمُرْ] (Sauvaget 46). ✧ 'Army-iron'. ⇨ **ČERÏ I.** + **TEMÏR.**

ČÄRÏK-TÄMÜR Maml. 14th c. **Čärik-tämür** [جَرِنْتَمُرْ] (Sauvaget 46). ✧ 'Army-iron' cf. Uyg., Chag., NUyg.(Tar.) *čärik* 'das Heer' (Radl. III, 1967). See also **ČÄRÏ-DÄMÜR.**

ČÄLÄK Yak. **Čäläk** [Чäläк] (Pek.).

ČEBAK Chuv. 18th-19th c. **Čebak** [Чебакъ] (Magn. 91). ⇨ **ČABAQ?**

ČEBŠEK Trkm. 20th c. **Čebšek** [Čebšek], fem. (Zaj. 1971, 338); Trkm. 20th c. **Čebšek** [Чебшек], fem. (TrkmRS 725). ✧ 'Little rabbit/hare; leveret; bunny' cf. Trkm. *čebšek* 'зайчонок' (TrkmRS).

ČEČÄK OT 9th c.-10th c. **Čečäk** [جيجك ام المكتنى], fem. (Tabarī, Annal. III, 2280); **Čečäk / Čičäk** [Tschitschek], Teguder's daughter (Hammer, Ilch. I, 326); Khorezm. 1295, 1300 **Čečäk / Čičäk** [چيچا ك], emir who took part in military expedition to Egypt (RaD/Jahn 59, 86, 91, 95, 99, 127, 130, Hammer, Ilch. II., 33, 98); Tat.? 14th c.? **Čečäk / Čičik** [Τζιτζίχιος] (Byz. Turc. II, 314); Khorezm. / Tat.(GH) 1282 **Čečäk-χatun / Čiček-χatun** [جبجك حا تون / جيجك حا تون / Джиджекхатунъ], Kipchak Khan Meñgü-temür's wife (Qalāūn/Tizeng. I, 66, Makrīzi/Tieseng. I, 418, 428, Makrīzi III, 165); Karakh. 1097 **Čečäk-χatun / Xatun-čečäk?** [حيجك / حا تون جحك / حاتون جنجك], fem. (Karnāladdīn II, 127); Alt. 19th-20th c. **Čeček** [Чечек], fem. (OjrRS 213); Khazar 732 **Čičäk** [Čičäk], a Khazar princess married to Constantine (Copronymus) (Golden 175); Trkm. 1729 **Čičäk-oγlï / Čiček-oγlu** [چيچك اوغلى / Çiçekoğlu Deli Ali], a Türkmen in Anatolia (Refik, Anad. 184); Turk. 1467 **Čiček** [Çiçek bint Abdullah], fem. (Gökb., Ed. 344); Turk. 1584 **Čiček** [چچك / Çiçek], fem. (Ongan, Ank. I, 155). ✧ 'Flower, rose' cf. Chag., Alt., Crm., Tat., etc. *čäčäk* 'die Blume, die Blüthe; die Pocken' (Radl. III, 1988), Turk. *čičäk* 'die Blume' (Radl. III, 2144). See also **AY-ČEČÄK, ALTÏN-ČEČEK, BANÏ-ČIČEK, ČÏNAR-ČEČÄK, GÜL-ČIČEK, QÏR-ČEČÄK.**

ČEČEYGA Tat.(Sib.)? 1645 **Čečeyγa / Čečeygä?** [Чечейга], envoy (Miller, Ist. Sib. II, 505).

ČEČEN Tuv. 19th c. **Čäččän / Čäč-čän?** [Чäччäн], fem. (Proben IX, 180); Tuv. 19th c. **Čäčäñ-qïs** (<**Čäččäñ-qïs**) [Чäчäң кыс], fem. (Proben IX, 163, 164); Chuv. 19th c. **Čečen** [Tschetschen], fem. (Kronheim 96); Bashk. 1756 **Čečen** [Чечен Исенгулов] (MIB IV/1, 120); Bashk. 1776 **Čečen-bay** [Чеченбай Кучуккулов] (MIB V, 35); Tat.(Sib.)? 1635 **Čečen-qatun** [Чечен Катунь], Altïn-qan's mother (Miller, Ist. Sib. II, 427); Alt.(Tuba) 19th c. **Čečin-qïz** [Чечинъ-кызъ], fem. (Potanin IV, 587). ✧ 'Eloquent (man), talkative, tale-teller' cf. Chag., Alt., Crm., Tat.(Bar.) *čäčän* 'schönrederisch, beredt' (Radl. III, 1988-89), Kzk. *šešän* 'beredt, ein kirgisischer Erzähler' (Radl. IV, 1015), Kzk. *šešen* 'красноречивый; оратор' (KzRS), Kirg. *čečän* 'ibid.' (Radl. III, 1989). See also **ERMEN-ČEČEN, YAMČÏR-ČEČEN, YARA-ČEČEN, YEREN-ČEČEN, YÏRENŠE-ŠEŠEN, KÏLDÏŠ-ČEČEN, SARÏ-ČÏČÄN.**

ČEČERON Turk. 19th c. **Čečeron-oγlu**, a Zeybek (Kúnos 1891, 119).

ČEČÏN see **ČEČEN**

ČEGEY Tat.(Sib.)? 1598 **Čegey** [Чегей аталыкъ], father-in-law of the Küčüms (AI II, 4). ✧ 'Thin, meagre; little'? cf. Tuv. *čegey* 'скудный, редкий, малочисленный' (TuvRS). ⇨ **ČÏGÏ?**

ČEGERMÏŠ Selj.? 1103 **Čegermiš / Čigirmiš?** [جـكـر مش] (Adīm II, 148).

ČEGEW Kzk. 19th c. **Čegew-bay** [Чегеубай] (SOK 14).

ČEGÏN Kzk. **Čegin** [Чегынъ] (Konšin, Oč. 64). ✧ 'Knot'? cf. Chag. *čegin* 'der Knoten' (Radl. III, 1958).

ČEGÏRTKE Kirg. **Čegirtke** [Чегиртке] (Jud. 884). ✧ 'Grasshopper, cricket' cf. Kirg. *čegirtke* 'id.' (Jud. 884).

ČEGRÄN see **ČÏGREN**

ČEXRAQ Hak.(Kyz.) 1685 **Čeχraq** [Чехракъ] (Jarilov, Kyz. 6). ⇨ **ČOQRAQ?**

ČEY-BUT Kzk. 19th c. **Čey-but?** [Чейбутъ] (SOK 132). ⇨ **ČÏY + BUT?**

ČEYEK Alt. 19th c. **Čeyek** [Чеек-богатырь] (Verb., In. 146, 148, 149, 164).

ČEYMEN Tat. 13th c. **Čeymen** [Τζειμέν], a christened Tatar (Byz. Turc. II); Tat. 14th c. **Čeymen** [Τζειμέν], a christened Tatar, died in 1344 (Byz. Turc. II). ⇨ **ČÏY?** + suff. -*men?*

ČEYNE Alt. 19th-20th c. **Čeyne** [Чейне] (OjrRS 210). ✧ 'Peony (a kind of flower (Paeonia))' (OjrRS 210).

ČEYNEŠ Alt. 19th-20th c. **Čeyneš** [Чейнеш], fem. (OjrRS 213). ✧ 'A kind of flower (Paeonia)' (OjrRS 213), cf. Mo. *čēne.* + suff. -*š.*

ČEK Kzk. 19th c. **Ček-pay** [Чекпай] (SOK 234). ✧ 'Faultless'? cf. Alt.(Tel.) *čäk* 'fehlerlos, rechtschaffen' Radl. III, 1945).

ČEK-AMAN Kzk. 19th c. **Ček-aman** [Чекаманъ] (AOO 14). ✧ 'Faultless-Hale'? ⇨ **ČEK + AMAN.** See also **ESÄN-AMAN.**

ČEK-ČEK-ATA Kzk. 19th c. **Ček-ček-ata** [Чекъ-

чекъ-ата], protector-spirit of goats (Potanin, Pred. 124). ⇨ **ČEK + ČEK + ATA?**

ČEK-KÜTÜK Bashk. 1756 **Ček-kütük?** [Куртка Чеккутуков] (MIB IV/1, 120). ✧ '?-awaited'? cf. Tat. PN *Kötek* [=awaited male child] (Sattarov), cf. Bashk. *kötö-* 'ждать, ожидать' (BRS/Uraksin). ⇨ **ČEK?**

ČEK-MAMET Tat. 1629 **Ček-mamet** [Чекманет Турубаев] (Miller, Ist. Sib. II, 356). ⇨ **ČEK?** + **MAMET.**

ČEK-SU Kzk. 19th c. **Ček-su** [Чексу] (AOO 46).

ČEK-TEMÜR see **ČIN-TEMÍR**

ČEKÄ Maml.? 1400/01 **Čekä?** [جكا] (Iyās I, 328); Kirg. 1738 **Čekä** [Чека] (MIB I, 356).

ČEKEY Bashk. 1664 **Čekey** [Казанчейко Чекеев] (MIB I, 192); Bashk. 1754 **Čekey** [Бярюк Чекеев] (MIB IV/1, 83); Bashk. 1780 **Čekey** [Чекей Усманов] (MIB V, 115). ⇨ **?** + suff. *-y.*

ČEKENEY Kzk. 19th c. **Čekeney** [Чекеней] (SOK 36).

ČEKER Trkm. 20th c. **Čeker** [Čeker] (Zaj. 1971, 331); Kzk. 19th c. **Čeker** [Чекеръ] (SODž. 76). ✧ 'Drawer' cf. Trkm. *čeker* 'ящик' (TrkmRS).

ČEKES Oghuz/Trkm. 13th c. **Čekes** [چكش / Чекес], chief of the beks of Dib-Bakuy-khan (Abulg./Kon. 660).

ČEKİM Maml. 1399, 1421, 1438/39 **Čekim** [جكم العو ضى] (Iyās I, 313, 346, II, 3, 13, Ibn Taghrīb. VII, 258); Maml. 1421, 1438/39 **Čekim** [جكم], Sultan Yusuf's uncle (Ibn Taghrīb. VI, 529, VII, 7, 16 etc., Weil, Chalif. II, 216-17, 219); Maml. 1438/39 **Čekim** [جكم النوروزى المجنون] (Ibn Taghrīb. VII, 9, 46); Maml. 1468/69 **Čekim** [جكم المحمدى الجشتد مى] (Iyās II, 108); Maml. 1470/71 **Čekim** [جكم الاجرود الاشرفى] (Iyās II, 124); Bashk. 1734 **Čekim** [Чекимъ Явгильдинъ], a tarχan (Vel.-Zern., Bašk. 10). ⇨ **?** + suff. *-im.*

ČEKİM-QARA Maml. 1467/68 **Čekim-qara** [جكم قرا الظا هرى] (Ibn Taghrīb. VII, 833). ⇨ **ČEKİM + QARA.**

ČEKİR Kkalp. 1722 **Čekir-bay** [Чекирбай] (MIKk. 173). ✧ 'Sugar'? ⇨ **ŠEKER?**

ČEKİRMİŠ Selj. **Čekirmiš** [جكرمش] (Qazw. 446); Selj. 1096, 1104, 1107 **Čekirmiš** [Djekirmisch], emir in the region of Diyarbekir and Harran, fought against Tancred at Edessa in 1104 (Weil, Chalif. III, 152); Selj. 1100/101, 1102, 1106/107 **Čekirmiš** [شمس الـدولة جكرمش / جكرمش ولى مـوصـل], governor of Mosul, died in 1106/1107 (Rāwandī 129, Abulfidā III, 360-61, Abulfidā: RHCHor I, 7, 9, Ibn al-Athīr: RHCHor I, 210, 242, Ibn al-Athīr, Atab.: RHCHor II/2, 31-32); + *-miš.*;

ČEKLÜ Tat. 1620 **Čeklü-bay** [Чеклубайко Байбаринъ] (Kurdjumov 121, 122). ⇨ **ČEK?** +

suff. *-lü?*

ČEKTAY? Kzk. 19th c. **Čektay?** [Чектай] (SOV 76). ✧ 'Limit, border'? Kzk. *šek* I 'id.' (KzRS). + suff. *-tay* (1,2)?

ČEKTÄN Kzk. 19th c. **Čektän-bay** [Чектанбай] (AOO 62).

ČEKTİ Kzk. 19th c. **Čekti-bay** [Чектибай] (SODž. 4); Kzk. 19th c. **Čekti-bay** [Чектыбай] (SOV 158). ⇨ **ČEK** + suff. *-ti?* See also **JOГАRΪ-ČEKTİ.**

ČEKÜLČEK Az. **Čekülček-χoja** [Чекулчек-ходжа], fem. (Az. Skaz. 482). ✧ 'Libellula, may-fly' cf. Az. *čekülček* 'чекулчек - стрекоза, иногда прозвище' (Az. Skaz. p. 662).

ČEKÜN Kzk. 19th c. **Čekün-bay?** [Чекунбай] (SOV 56).

ČEKÜR Alt. 1666 **Čekür?** [Чекуръ], tayša of the black Kalmyks (Kuznecov 25-26).

ČEL-SARΪ Alt. 19th c. **Čel-sarï-qan** [Чельсары-канъ] (Potanin IV, 562, 563). ⇨ **YEL + SARΪ.**

ČELBİGÄN see **YÄLBÄГÄN**

ČELEB-VERMİŠ Turk. 152 **Čeleb-vermiš** [جلـبـورمش حلـیمه بنت / Tschalab-virmisch] (Berchem, Perg. 17). ✧ 'God gave him/her, God-given' cf. Turk. *čäläb* 'Gott' (Radl. III, 1977). ⇨ **BERMİŠ.**

ČELEBİ Crm.Tat. **Čelebi** [Čelebiev Čelebiğihan] (Mende 140, 141); Turk. 16th c. **Čelebi-efendi** (Ongan, Ank. II, 416). ✧ 'Gentleman, host, landlord; educated man' cf. Chag., Turk. *čäläbi* 'göttlich, ein Prinz vom Geblüt; Herr (Titel, Anrede eines Europäers); der Hausherr; der Schriftsteller, der Poet, der Gelehrte; gebildet, liebenswürdig, elegant' (Radl. III, 1978).

ČELED Kzk. 19th c. **Čeled** [Челедъ] (SOK 240).

ČELEK Kzk. 19th c. **Čelek-pay** [Челекпай] (SODž. 50). ✧ 'Bucket' cf. Kzk. *čelek* 'id.' (Radl. III, 1977, KzRS).

ČELEKEY Kzk. 19th c. **Čelekey** [Челекѣй] (AOK 70). ✧ 'Little bucket'. ⇨ **ČELEK** + dim. suff. *-ey.*

ČELGÜ Pecheneg? **Čelgü?** (Byz. Turc. II, 311).

ČELİK Turk. 20th c. **Čelik-χan** [Çelikhan İlcesi], preserved in the name of an „ilce" in the province of Adıyaman, Turkey (TMİB 28). ✧ 'Steel'.

ČELİMBET Kzk. 19th c. **Čelimbet** [Челимбетъ] (SOK 252). ⇨ **?** + suffixoid *-(im)bet.*

ČELTÜŠ Bashk. 1738 **Čeltüš** [Екшигул Челтюшев] (MIB I, 143).

ČEMAŠ see **ČEMİŠ**

ČEMEK Chuv. 18th-19th c. **Čemek** [Чемекъ] (Magn. 91).

ČEMEKEY Tat. 1613 **Čemekey** [Урекей Чемекеевъ] (Zolotn. 159); Tat. 18th-19th c. **Čemekey** [Чемекей] (Magn. 91). ⇨ **?** + suff. *-ey.*

ČEMEN Trkm. 20th c. **Čemen** [Чемен], fem. (Nikonov: OSA 161); Trkm. 20th c. **Čemen** [Čemen], fem. (Zaj. 1971, 339); Trkm. 20th c. **Čemen** [Чемен], fem. (TrkmRS 728); Tat.(Sib.) **Čemen / Čimen?** [Чеменко Бирзогилдеев] (Miller, Ist. Sib. II, 521). ✧ 'Bunch (of flowers)' (Nikonov), '(green) field' (Zaj. 1971) cf. Trkm. *čemen* 'букет; луг' (TrkmRS) <P. *čemen* 'лужайка, цветущий луг' (Nikonov: OSA 161).

ČEMENDÜR Selj. **Čemendür** [جمندور], forefather of the Ottoman dynasty (Nešrī 186, Seādeddīn I, 15, Wittek 94). ⇨ **ČEMEN?** + suff. *-dür*.

ČEMİŠ Nog. 1537 **Čemiš-mïrza / Čemäš-mïrza?** [Чемашъ-мырза / Чемиш Мурза] (PSRL XIII, 115, ŽirmEp. 430).

ČEMKEN Bashk. 1738 **Čemken** [Чемкен Ишметев] (MIB I, 145).

ČEMÜRMİR Selj. **Čemürmir?** [جمورمير / جمورهير], forefather of the Ottoman dynasty (Nešrī 186, Ālī, ibid., Wittek 94).

ČEN Kzk. 19th c. **Čen-bay** [Ченбай] (SOK 76); Chuv. 18th-19th c. **Čen-bek** [Ченбекъ] (Magn. 92); Chuv. 18th-19th c. **Čen-bek / Čen-bäk?** [Ченбякъ] (Magn. 92). ✧ 'Place, time'? cf. Kzk. *šen* 'id.' (KzRS). ⇨ **ČİN?** See also **BAY-ČEN.**

ČEN-BULAT see **ČİN-BULAT**

ČENJİM Kzk. 19th c. **Čenjim-bay** (<Čenjin-bay) [Ченжимбай] (SODž. 150).

ČENJİN see **ČENJİM**

ČENJİR Kzk. 19th c. **Čenjir-bek** [Ченжирбекъ] (SOK. 44).

ČENDEY Chuv. 1739 **Čendey** [Чендей Калаевъ] (Alatyr. 142).

ČENEK Chuv. 18th-19th c. **Čenek** [Ченекъ] (Magn. 92).

ČENSİZ Kzk. 19th c. **Čensiz-bay** [Ченсызбай] (SOV 16). ⇨ **ČEN?** + suff. *-siz.*

ČENTİS Kzk. 19th c. **Čentis-bay** [Чентысбай] (SOK 36).

ČEÑGİ Chag. 16th c. **Čeñgi** [Ченги], a chief (mir) (Ivanov 101); Chag. 16th c. **Čeñgi** [Ченги Мухтасиб], a chief (mir) (Ivanov 114). ✧ 'Wandering musician' cf. Turk. *čeñgi* 'herumziehender Musikant' (Radl. III, 1963).

ČEÑİN-TERİ Uyg. 12th c. - 14th c. **Čeñin-teri-elči** [čeŋin teri elči] (DTS). ✧ 'Čeñin-skin/fell' (Blagova 1997, 709).

ČEPAY see **ČAPAY**

ČEPČEK see **ČİPČİK**

ČEPEY Kzk. 1644 **Čepey** [Чепей (Ченеи?)], a prince (Miller, Ist. Sib. II, 493).

ČEPER Trkm. 20th c. **Čeper** [Čeper] (Zaj. 1971, 335); Trkm. 20th c. **Čeper** [Чепер], fem. (TrkmRS 730); Kzk. 19th c. **Čepir-bay** [Чепырбай] (SOK 42). ✧ I. 'Clever, skilful' cf. Trkm. *čeper* 'искусный, умелый' (TrkmRS); II. 'Master'? cf. Kzk. *šeber* 'мастер' (KzRS).

ČEPİR see **ČEPER**

ČEPKEN Bashk. 1787 **Čepken / Čepkän?** [Каскин Чепканов] (MIB V, 219). ✧ 'Stout jacket the sleeves of which are slit, leaving the arms free'? (TED), cf. Alt.(Tel.), Turk. *čäpkän* 'Tuch, Wollenzeug; ein langer Tuchrock; kurzer Tuchrock mit langen, geschlitzten Aermeln' (Radl. III, 1995).

ČEPNİ Oghuz **Čepni** [Чипни / Чепни], Kök-χan's son (RaD I/1, 76, AbulGKon. 520, 555, 605); Turk. 1583 **Čepni** [چبني / Çebni] (Ongan, Ank. I, 155). ✧ I. The name of an Oghuz tribe' cf. MT *čepni* '22 Oğuz bölüğünden biri' (MK); II. 'Mountaineer (villager)'; III. 'Immoral, prostitute'; IV. 'A kind of sheep with long tail' cf. Turk. *çepni* I. 1. 'dağ köylülerine verilen ad', 2. 'Soysuz, ahlâkı bozuk olan kimse'; 3. 'Fahişe' II. 'Kuyruğu uzun bir cins koyun' (DS).

ČEPŠAN Tat.(Sib.) 1599 **Čepšan** [Чепшанъ], a princess in Siberia (AI II, 17, 20, 23).

ČEPTÄRZÄP Bashk. 1798 **Čeptärzäp / Čeptarzäp** [Чептарзяпъ] (PSZRI XXV, 195).

ČER-BAŠ see **ČERİ-BAŠ**

ČER-QARA Bashk. 1735 **Čer-qara?** [Теникей Черкаринъ], a tarχan (Vel.-Zern., Bašk. 24). ⇨ **ČİR?** + **QARA.**

ČERAГ Trkm. 1688 **Čeraγ-bek** [Чераг-бек], from the Afshar tribe (MIT II, 120, 121). ⇨ **ČİRAГ?**

ČERČİ NUyg. 19th c. **Čärči / Čerči** [چرچى] (Le Coq, Namenl. 98); Kuman 1436 **Čerči / Čerče?** [Cherche Bálint / Valentinus Cherchy de Therthelzallasa], from the Kumans in Hungary (Gyárfás III, 596, 676); Turk. 20th c. **Čerči-oγlu** [Çerçioğlu] (TMİB 10). ✧ 'Wandering merchant' (Le Coq 98), cf. Chag., Turk. *čärči* 'der Kleinkramhändler, der Hausirer; Kleinkram' (Radl. III, 1975), Rásonyi, NTK, 118, 142, Rásonyi, KÖA 100, Rásonyi: AOH XX(1967), 139.

ČERDĀQ see **ČERDÄK**

ČERDÄK Karg. 19th-20th c. **Čerdāq** [Чăрдəк] (Katanov, Otč. 10); Bashk. 1675 **Čerdäk** [Чердяк Темирзянов] (MIB I, 199). ✧ 'Loft, garret' cf. R. чердакъ 'id.'.

ČEREKEY Bashk. 1756 **Čerekey** [Айса Черекеев] (MIB IV/1, 107). ⇨ **ČİRİK?** + suff. *-key / -ey.*

ČEREKŠİ Kzk. 19th c. **Čerekši / Čerikši?** [Черекши] (SOV 22). ⇨ **ČİRİK?** + suff. *-ši.*

ČEREMİŠ see **ČERMİŠ**

ČEREN Chuv. 18th-19th c. **Čeren** [Черенъ] (Magn. 92); Tuv. 19th c. **Čeren / Čärän** [Чăрäн] (Proben IX, 52).

ČEREPAN Tat. 1620 **Čerepan** [Черепанъ Ябалаковъ] (Kurdjumov 120,121).

ČERİ I. Uyg. 13th-14th c. **Čärig-ïnal** (Zieme, Mat. III, 274); Kipch. 13th-14th c. **Čärig-tämür** (Zieme, Mat. III, 274 (after B. Ögel)); Chuv. 18th-19th c. **Čer-bay (<Čeri-bay)** [Чербай] (Magn. 92); Crm. 1534 **Čer-**

bey-baqši (<Čeri-bey-baqšï?) [Чербѣй-бакшей], envoy from the Crimea (PSRL VIII, 289); Chuv. 18th-19th c. **Čer-bek** (<Čeri-bek) [Чербякъ] (Magn. 92); Chuv. 1737 **Čeri-bay** [Черебай] (Nepljuev 427); Bashk. 1695 **Čeri-bay** [Ишберда Черебаев], from Ufa (MIB I, 91); Kzk. 19th c. **Čerü-bay** [Черубай] (SODž. 160); Tat.(Mish.) 1755 **Čirü-bay** [Чирюбай Тлянчин] (MIB IV/1, 93); Bashk. 1761 **Čirü-bay** [Чирюбай Клянчин (Тлянчин?)] (MIB IV/1, 218); Bashk. 1794 **Čirü-bay** [Чирюбай Шункаров] (MIB V, 338); Kzk. 19th c. **Čirü-bay** [Искендеръ Чирубаевъ] (Grod., Pril. 61); Bashk. 18th c. **Čirü-bay / Čürü-bay** [Чирюбай (Чурубай) Казмаметев] (MIB V, 51); Bashk. 1771 **Čirü-bay / Čürü-bay** [Чирюбай (Чюрюбай) Ебекеев] (MIB V, 124); Tat. 1777 **Čirü-bay / Čürü-bay? / Čuru-bay?** [Чирюбай (Чурубай) Бабиков] (MIB V, 54, 89, 106); Bashk. 1754 **Čürü** [Чюр[Чюрагулов] (MIB IV/1, 84); Bashk. 1664 **Čürü-bay** [Кугеш Чюрюбаев] (MIB I, 192); Bashk. 1735 **Čürü-bay** [Чюрюбай Кучюков] (MIB III, 336); Bashk. 1779 **Čürü-bay** [Чюрюбай] (MIB V, 89); Bashk. 1781 **Čürü-bay** [Чюрюбай Ебекеев] (MIB V, 89); Bashk. 1736 **Čürü-batïr** [Чюрюбатыр Калмакчурин] (MIB III, 352); Kzk. 19th c. **Šerü-bay** [Шерубай] (AOO 62); *TN:* Kzk. **Šerü-bay-nura** [Шерубай-Нура], a small town (Kojčubaev 251). ✧ 'Army' cf. Kuman *čeri~čejri* 'Heer' (CC), Alt. *čärü* 'das Heer, die Armee' (Radl. III, 1968), Alt. *čerü* 'боец, солдат; войско' (OjrRS), Tat. *čirü* 'das Heer, die Schaar' (Radl. III, 2126), cf. also Gombocz, BTLw. 116. See also **BEK-ČERİ, ГОŠUN, SÜ, ZURUM.**

ČERİ II. Hak.(Sag.) 19th-20th c. **Čēr-bey / Čǎr-bäy?** [Чӑрбӓй] (Katanov, Otč. 7). ✧ 'Worm(s)' (<R.) *červi* 'id.' (Katanov, Otč. 7).

ČERİ-BAŠ Maml. 1331 **Čer-baš / Čeri-baš?** [جـار بـاش], an emir (Dawād. 357, 365); Maml. 1340 **Čeri-baš** (<Čeri-bašï?) [سيف الدين جاريباش] (Zetterst. 205, 210); Maml. 1400 **Čeri-baš** (<Čeri-bašï?) [جربـاش الشيخى] (Ibn Taghrīb. VI, 9, 72, 95, etc.); Maml. 1400 **Čeri-baš** (<Čeri-bašï?) [جـربـاش العمرى] (Ibn Taghrīb. VI, 127, 249); Maml. 1400 **Čeri-baš** (<Čeri-bašï?) [جـربـاش كبـاشة] (Ibn Taghrīb. VI, 235, 246, 329); Maml. 1421, 1424, 1438/39 **Čeri-baš** (<Čeri-bašï?) [جـربـاش قـاشق الكريمى], an emir (Ibn Taghrīb. VI, 416, 493, VII, 36, 38, 39, 51, Iyās II, 17, 57, Weil, Chalif. II, 171, 230); Maml. 1437/38 **Čeri-baš** (<Čeri-bašï?) [جـربـاش الاشرفى مشد سيدى] (Ibn Taghrīb. VII, 9, 20, 104); Maml. 1453 **Čeri-baš** (<Čeri-bašï?) [النـاصرى] (Ibn Taghrīb. VII, 77, 79, 205, Iyās II, 40, 60, 142, 214, Weil, Chalif. II, 256, 302); Maml. 1477 **Čeri-baš** (<Čeri-bašï?) [المحمدى / كرت / كرد المحمدى جـربـاش] (Iyās II, 171); Maml. 1484 **Čeri-baš** (<Čeri-bašï?) [جربـاش المجنون] (Iyās II, 225). ✧ 'Commander, general' cf. Kuman *čeri bašy* 'Heerführer, armiragius' (CC), Turk. *çeribaşı* 'komutan, başbuğ, serdar, serasker' (TS). ⇨ **ČERİ I. + BAŠ(Ï).**

ČERİ-BAŠÏ see **ČERİ-BAŠ**

ČERİ-BULAT Chuv. 18th-19th c. **Čer-bulat** (<Čeri-bulat) [Чербулат] (Magn. 92). ✧ 'Army-steel'. ⇨ **ČERİ I. + BULAT.**

ČERİKTU **Čeriktu?** [Черикту] (RaD II, 14).

ČERİPTAY Kzk. 19th c. **Čeriptay?** [Черыптай] (SOK 92).

ČERKAS see **ČERKES**

ČERKES Khorezm.? 13th c. **Čerkes** [چـركس / Черкес], an emir, attendant of Sulamïš, executed in 1299 (RaD/Jahn 123, MIT I, 531); Khorezm./Chag. 1405/1406 **Čerkes** [Черкес], emir, ruler of Mahan (MIT I, 531); Turk.? **Čerkes** [شـركس / جهـاركس] (Sauvaire 45 (after Aynī)); Turk.? 1405 **Čerkes** [جـركس / جـاركس], in an inscription in Damascus (Sauvaire 45); Turk. 20th c. **Čerkes** [Çerkes] (Önder, Hınıs); Chuv. 18th-19th c. **Čerkes / Čerkäs** [Черкасъ] (Magn. 92); Kzk. 1840 **Čerkes-batïr** [Черкесъ-Батыръ] (ZIRGOÊtn. I, 102). ✧ I. 'Circassian' cf. *čärkäs* 'der Tscherkesse' (Radl. III, 1969), < P. *čahar käs* 'the four tribes of Käs' (Sauvaire: JA (1894), 250-251); II. 'Eagle' Osetin *čärgäs~čärkäs* 'eagle' (Bask., Fam. 136); III. 'Chief of the army' < *čerig ayasï* 'id.' (Bask., Fam. 136 after I. Šinkevič). See also **BAY-ČERKES.**

ČERKEZ Trkm. 20th c. **Čerkez** [Çerkez] (Zaj. 1971, 332); Trkm. 20th c. **Čerkez** [Черкез] (TrkmRS 730). ✧ 'A kind of plant on sodic soil' (Zaj. 1971), cf. Trkm. *čerkez* 'солянка Рихтера; солянка Палецкого' (TrkmRS).

ČERLAQ Bashk. 1738, 1744, 1747 **Čerlaq** [Кузекей Черлаков] (MIB III, 384, 416, 447). ✧ I. 'Polecat, skunk'? Alt. *čarlaq* 'der Iltis' (Radl. III, 1868); II. 'Gull, mew?' cf. Alt. *čarlāq* 'die Möwe' (Radl. III, 1868); 'House cricket'? cf. Turk. *čïrlaq* 'die Grille; der Schwätzer' (Radl. III, 2080).

ČERMİŠ Chuv. 18th-19th c. **Čermiš** [Чермышев] (Magn. 92); Tat. 18th-19th c. **Čermiš** [Чермышъ] (Magn. 92); Bashk. 1664 **Čermiš** [Игилик Чермышев] (MIB I, 191); Bashk. 1717 **Čermiš** [Чермыш Тогулбаев] (MIB III, 154); Bashk. 1740 **Čermiš** [Чермыш Сарбашев] (MIB I, 392); Bashk. 1751, 1750, 1758 **Čermiš** [Чермыш (Чермыж) Юсупов] (MIB III, 472, IV/1, 51, 164); Bashk. 1756 **Čermiš** [Чермыш Сююшев] (MIB IV/1, 125); Bashk. 1791 **Čermiš** [Чермыш Азналин] (MIB V, 301); Bashk. 1760, 1763 **Čïrmïš** [Чирмыш Юсупов] (MIB

IV/1, 188, 270); Bashk. 1754 **Čirmuš** [Чирмуш Кучюкеев] (MIB IV/1, 84). ✧ 'Cheremis' cf. Tat. *čirmeš* 'id.' (TatRS).

ČERMĪŠAQ Bashk. 1761 **Čermīšaq** [Мокша Чермышаков] (MIB IV, 221). ⇨ **ČERMĪŠ** + suff. *-aq*.

ČERÜ see **ČERİ I.**

ČESTAN Nog. 1813 **Čestan-bay** [Мусюрманъ Честанбаевъ] (Sergeev 114).

ČEŠME Oghuz/Trkm. 15th c. **Češme**, „figlia di Ag Melik" (= Aq-melik's daughter) (DQorq./Rossi 145, DQorq./Gökyay 23). ✧ 'Fountain, well' cf. Turk. *čäšmä* 'der Springbrunnen, die Fontaine' (Radl. III, 1994).

ČET-QARA Bashk. 1735 **Čet-qara** (<Četi-qara?) [Елевъ Четкаринъ] (Vel.-Zern., Bašk. 12). ⇨ **ČİT?** + **QARA.**

ČETİK Kzk. 19th c. **Četik-pay** [Четикпай] (SOV 16). ✧ 'Tamarisk'? cf. Chag. *čätik* 'die Tamariske' (Radl. III, 1983).

ČETİR Tat.(Sib.) 1609 **Četir** [Четырь], a prince from Kondinsk (Miller, Ist. Sib. II, 212, 213).

ČETİRMAN Kzk. 19th c. **Četirman** [Четырманъ] (SOK 270). ⇨ **ČETİR?** + suff. *-man.*

ČETPERİK Hak. 19th c. **Četperik** [Чӓтпӓрік], fem. (Katanov, Otč. 12). ✧ 'Four; fourfold' < R. четверикъ 'id.' (Katanov, Otč. 12).

ČETTİK Kzk. 19th c. **Čettïk-pay** / **Čettik-pay** [Четтыкпай] (SOV 104). ⇨ **ČİT** + suff. *-tik.*

ČETTİQ see **ČETTİK**

ČEÜL-BER Tat. 1633 **Čeül-ber** [Чеулберев], a Tatar from Ufa (Miller, Ist. Sib. II, 402, 403).

ČİBİJEK Hak.(Sag.) 19th-20th c. **Čibijek** [Чібіцӓк], fem. (Katanov, Otč. 8, Proben IX, 223, 314). ✧ 'Thread, yarn' (Katanov, Otč. 8, Proben IX, 223, 314). + dim. suff. *-jek.*

ČİBİL Turk. **Čibil-oγlu**, a Zeybek (Kúnos 1891, 119). ✧ 'Naked'? cf. Turk. *čıbıl* 'голый, нагой', *çıpıldak* 'голый, голенький, голыш (а маленьких детях)' (TRS).

ČİBİNTAY see **ČİBİNTAY**

ČİBİQ see **ČİBİQ**

ČİBİL see **ČİBİL**

ČİBİNTAY see **ČİBİNTAY**

ČİBUQ see **ČİBİQ**

ČİBUT Kzk. 1819 **Čibut** [Чибуд] (MIK IV, 326). ✧ 'Jew' cf. Crm. *čıfıt* 'der Jude' (Radl. III, 2102).

ČİČÄK see **ČEČÄK**

ČİČÄN see **SARĪ-ČİČÄN**

ČİČİK see **ČEČÄK**

ČİČKÄ-SİNDU Alt. 19th c. **Čička-sïndu** [Чичкэсынду] (Verbickij 100). ✧ 'Having thin/slim figure' cf. Alt. *čičkä* 'dünn, schmal' (Radl. III, 2146) and Uyg., Kuman, etc. *sïn* 'das Aeussere, die Gestalt'

(Radl. IV, 628), Kzk. *sïn* 'фигура, внешний вид' (KzRS) + suff. *-du (<-lï.)*

ČİČQAN see **ČİČQAN**

ČİJEŇ Hak. 19th-20th c. **Čijeň** [Чиченъ], fem. (HRS 356). ✧ 'Nimble, quick-witted' cf. Hak. *čičeň* 'id.' (HRS 356). ⇨ **ČEČEN?** See also **ČİŽEN-BAQ?**

ČİDER Kirg. **Čidär-qul** [Чідäр кул], a horseherd in the Manas epic (Proben V, 387 /391/); Kzk. 19th c. **Čider-bay** [Чидербай] (SOV 20); Kzk. 19th c. **Čider-bay** [Чидербай] (SODž. 26). ✧ 'Hobble' cf. Chag. *čidär* 'die Fussfesseln der Pferde' (Radl. III, 2144), Kzk. *šider* (шідер) 'тренога, треножник' (RKzS), Kirg. *čider* 'тренога (ремённые путы для стреноживания лошади)' (Jud.).

ČİDİN Uyg. 12th c. - 14th c. **Čidin / Čadin?** [čidin (čadin?) / Çidin] (DTS, EUTS).

ČİGDEM Trkm. 1690 **Čigdem-oγlu** / **Čiydem-ōlu** / **Čidem-ōlu** [Çiğdem oğlu Balaban beğ], from the Çiğdemlü tribe (Refik, Anad. 84). ✧ 'Sunflower, turnsole' cf. Turk. dial. *çiğdem* 'ay çiçeği' (DS).

ČİGEN Kzk. 1846 **Čigen** [Бий Чигень Мусин], a biy (MKOP 100).

ČİGİ Kzk. 19th c. **Čigi-bay** [Чигибай] (SOK 120).

ČİGİL Türk 8th c. (759) **Čigil-tutuq** [čigil tutuq / Çigil Tutuq] (DTS, ETY I, 178). ✧ Ethnical name.

ČİGİL-ARSLAN Uyg. 8th c.-9th c. **Čigil-arslan** [Çigil Arslan Il-tirgüg / Çigil Arslan] (Le Coq, Man. I, 27, DTS, EUTS). ✧ 'Čigil-Lion' (Blagova 1997, 705). ⇨ **ČİGİL + ARSLAN.**

ČİGİM-BAY see **ČİGİN**

ČİGİN Kzk. 19th c. **Čigim-bay** (<Čigin-bay) [Чигимбай] (SOK 76); Kzk. 19th c. **Čigin-bay** [Чигинбай] (SOK 12).

ČİGİR Chuv. 18th-19th c. **Čigir** [Чигирь] (Magn. 92); Bashk. 1682 **Čigir** [Чигирко Андрейковъ] (AI V, 139); Kzk. 1737 **Čigir** [Чигир Енакаев] (MIB I, 346); Kzk. 1846 **Čigir** [Мыкенбай Чигиров], a biy (MKOP 154); Kzk. 19th c. **Čigir** [Бердыкул Чигиров], resident in Tashkent (TV 1878, 124); Tat.(Sib.)? 1616 **Čigir-tayša** [Чигир тайша] (Miller, Ist. Sib. II, 236). ⇨ **ŠEKER.**

ČİGREN Karg. **Čegrän** [Чегрӓн] (Katanov, Otč. 8); Hak. 19th-20th c. **Čigren** [Чигрен] (HRS 352). ✧ 'Red, reddish-brown, bay' (Katanov, Otč. 8, HRS 352), cf. Shor *čigrän* 'fuchsfarben (von Pferden)' (Radl. III, 2115), Alt. *yärän / yägrän* 'fuchsfarben, roth (ein rothes Pferd mit rother Mähne und Schwanz)' (Radl. III, 338). ⇨ **ČEGRÄN.**

ČİGŠİ Türk 8th c. - 9th c. **Čigši** [Çigşi] (ETY III, 90, 121). ✧ A title. <Chin. *čik-ši / tshi-shi.*

ČİGÜY Uyg. 12th c. - 14th c. **Čigüy** [čigüj / Çigüi] (DTS, EUTS).

ČİГAN see **ČİГAN**

ČİHRE Chag. 16th c. **Čihre** [Чихре] (Ivanov 224);

Chag. 16th c. **Čihre-aqa** [Чихре Ака] (Ivanov 223). ✧ 'Face' (<P.) *čährä, čihrä* 'Gesicht, Antlitz, Miene' (Radl. III, 1959), cf. also Budagov I, 502. See also **AQ-ČİHRE, PAYENDE-ČİHRE.**

ČİXAN see **JİHAN**

ČİY Kzk. 19th c. **Čiy-bay** [Чийбай] (SOK 228). ✧ I. '(Bul)rush, covering made of mat' cf. Kzk. *šiy* 'чий (песчаный тростник); цыновка из этого тростника' (KzRS); II. 'Raw, rough' cf. Kzk. *šiyki* 'сырой' (RKzS).

ČİY-QAN Bashk. 1715 **Čiy-qan** [Кулумбет Чийканов] (MIB III, 132); Bashk. 1787 **Čİ-qan (<Čiy-qan?)** [Чура (Чюра) Чиканов] (MIB V, 214). ✧ 'Raw blood, rough blood' cf. Kzk. *šiyki* 'сырой' (RKzS). ⇨ **ČİY + QAN.**

ČİY-MOYİN Alt. 19th c. **Čiy-moyïn** [Чий-моинъ] (Potanin II, 5). ✧ 'Rush-neck (having long neck)'. ⇨ **ČİY + MOYUN.**

ČİY-TEMİR Kzk. 19th c. **Čiy-temir** [Чийтемиръ] (SODž. 106). ⇨ **ČİY + TEMİR.**

ČİYBET Kzk. 19th c. **Čiybet** [Чийбетъ] (SOK 50). ⇨ **ČİY** + suffixoid *-bet*.

ČİYDEM see **ČİGDEM**

ČİYELEY Tat. 1662 **Čiyeley** [Чиелей] (DAI IV, 285).

ČİYİR Kzk. 19th c. **Čiyir-bay** [Чиирбай] (SOK 8).

ČİYTEK Kzk. 19th c. **Čiytek** [Чийтекъ] (AOA 142). ⇨ **ČİY?** + suff. *-tek?*

ČİYTEN Kzk. 19th c. **Čiyten-bay** [Чийтенбай] (AOA 70).

ČİYÜNČİLİ Kzk. 19th c. **Čiyünčili / Čiyünčäli?** [Чіунчалы], because mother could not bear a child for a long time, she regarded the first one as the „bearer of good news" and named it this way (Potanin II, 3). ✧ 'Pleasant (news), Bearer of good news' cf. Kzk. чіюнчи 'good news' (Potanin II, 3). + suff. *-li.*

ČİK see **ČİQ**

ČİK-BİLGÄ Türk 8th c. - 9th c. **Čik-bilgä-čigši** [čik bilgä čigši / Çik Bilgä Çigşi] (DTS, ETY II, 64). ⇨ **ČEK + BİLGÄ.**

ČİKČÄY Tat.(Mish.) 1775 **Čikčäy?** [Муксин Чикчаев] (MIB IV/2, 417); Tat.(Mish.) 1775 **Čikčäy?** [Ысмаил Чикчаев] (MIB IV/2, 417).

ČİKČİ Uyg. **Čikči** [Çikçi] (EUTS).

ČİKEY Bashk. 1712 **Čikey** [Тоняш Чикеев] (MIB III, 83); Tuv. 19th c. **Čikey** [Чикей], a shamaness (Potanin IV, 289); Kzk. 19th c. **Čikey / Čikiy?** [Джулканъ Чикіевъ] (Grod., Pril. 78). ⇨ **ČİY?** + suff. *-key / -y?*

ČİKEL Kzk. 1823 **Čikel-bay / Šikel-bay?** [چیکلبای / Шикелъбай] (MIK IV, 458, 462).

ČİKİR see **ŠEKER**

ČİKİŠ Kzk. 19th c. **Čikiž-bay (<Čikiš-bay)** [Чикижбай] (SOK 290).

ČİKİŽ see **ČİKİŠ**

ČİKŠİN Türk 7th-9th c. **Čikšin** [Çikşin] (ETY III, 116).

ČİKTİ see **ČİQTİ**

ČİQANAR Hak. 19th-20th c. **Čiqanar** [Чиканар] (HRS 352).

ČİQİŠTİ see **ČİQİŠTİ**

ČİL Kzk. 19th c. **Čil-bay** [Чилбай] (AOA 14). ✧ 'Ruffled grouse (Bonasa), francolin (Francolinus)' cf. Chag., Turk. *čil* 'das Haselhuhn' (Radl. III, 2133), Kirg. *čil* 'бородатая куропатка, даурская куропатка' (Jud.), Uzb. *čil* 'куропатка серая' (UzbRS), Kzk. *šil* 'das Haselhuhn' (Radl. IV, 1076). See also **TORLĀ.**

ČİL-MAMBET Kzk. 19th c. **Čil-mambet** [Чильмамбетъ] (SOV 20, 92). ⇨ **ČİL + MAMBET.**

ČİLA see **ČİLA**

ČİLDÄ see **ČİLDİ**

ČİLDİ Kzk. 19th c. **Čildä-bek** [Чильдабекъ] (SODž. 82); Kzk. 19th c. **Čildi-bay** [Чильдыбай] (SOV 60). ✧ 'Hot time of the summer'? cf. Kzk. *šilde* 'жаркое время лета' (KzRS).

ČİLÄK Chuv. 18th-19th c. **Čiläk** [Чилякъ] (Magn. 92). ✧ I. 'Strawberry'? cf. Chag., Turk. *čiläk* 'die Erdbere' (Radl. III, 2135); II. 'Bucket'? cf. Tat. *čiläk* 'der Eimer' (Radl. III, 2135).

ČİLÄW Bashk. **Čiläw** [Чилявъ Чаткаринъ] (PSZRI IX, 338).

ČİLEN Kzk. 19th c. **Čilem-bay (<Čilen-bay)** [Чилембай] (SOV 18); Kzk. 19th c. **Čilem-bay (<Čilen-bay)** [Чилcмбай] (SODž. 210). ✧ 'A kind of berry' cf. Chag., East.T. *čilän* 'eine braune Beere mit einem Steine' (Radl. III, 2136), East.T. *čilan* 'a kind of jujube' (< P. چیلان the jujube-tree)' (Jarring).

ČİLİ Kzk. 19th c. **Čili-bay** [Чилибай] (SODž. 50); Kzk. 19th c. **Čili-bay** [Чилибай] (SOK 150); Tat. 1670 **Čili-bey** [Содыкъ Чилибей] (PSZRI I, 801). ✧ 'Iron ring with chain'? cf. Chag. *čili* 'Halsring von Eisen mit einer Kette (am Halse der Gefangenen)' (Radl. III, 2136).

ČİLİK Kzk. 19th c. **Čilik-pay** [Чиликпай] (SOV 36).

ČİLİM see **ČİLİM**

ČİLPAN see **ČİLPAN**

ČİLTUQ see **ČİLTUQ**

ČİM-BOLAT see **ČİN-BULAT**

ČİM-BULAT see **ČİN-BULAT**

ČİMBET see **ČİNBET**

ČİMÄN-TAY Bashk. 1740 **Čimän-tay?** [Аиткул Чимантаев] (MIB I, 483).

ČİME Alt. 19th-20th c. **Čime** [Чиме], fem. (OjrRS 213). ✧ 'An engravement in the saddle, ornament' cf. *čime* 'насечка у седла, узор' (OjrRS 213).

ČİMEN Crm. 13th c. **Čimen** [Чименъ] (Smirnov, Krym. 34). ✧ 'Meadow, field' cf. Chag., Crm., Turk. *čimen* 'das Kraut, der Rasen, die Wiese' (Radl. III, 2158).

ČİMŠEK Turk. 16th c. **Čimšek** (Ongan, Ank. II, 738); Turk. 1583 **Čimšek** [چمشك] (Ongan, Ank. I, 155). ✧

'Lightening'?

ČÏN-ASÏL see **ČÏN-ASÏL**

ČÏN-BULAT see **ČÏN-BULAT**

ČÏN-DÏMER see **ČÏN-TEMÏR**

ČÏN-GÏLDE see **ČÏN-GÏLDÏ**

ČÏN-GÏLDÏ   Bashk. 1709 **Čin-gilde** [Чингилдей Канчигилдеев] (MIB I, 264); Kzk. 1824 **Čin-gildi** [Кастенъ Чингильдинъ] (TOUAK XXIV, 146). ⇨ **ČÏN** + **KELDÏ**.

ČÏN-PULAD see **ČÏN-BULAT**

ČÏN-TAY   Kzk. 19th c. **Čin-tay** [Чинтай] (SOV 126); Kzk. 19th c. **Čin-tay** [Чинтай] (SOK 80). ⇨ **ČÏN** + **TAY** + / suff. *-tay(1,2)*?

ČÏN-TEMÏR see **ČÏN-TEMÏR**

ČÏN-TEMÜR see **ČÏN-TEMÏR**

ČÏN-TUƔAN   Chuv. 18th-19th c. **Čin-tuɣan** [Чингуганъ] (Magn. 93). ⇨ **ČÏN** + **TUƔAN I.**

ČÏNA see **ČÏNA**

ČÏNAY   Bashk. 1753, 1761 **Činay** [Чинай Бигишев] (MIB IV/1, 230).

ČÏNAQ   Uyg. **Činaq / Činäk** [Çinak / Çinäk] (EUTS).

ČÏNAR see **ČÏNAR**

ČÏNAR-QULU-BEK see **ČÏNAR**

ČÏNATUN   Uyg. **Činatun** [Çinatun] (EUTS).

ČÏNČEY   Alt. 19th-20th c. **Činčey** [Чинчей], fem. (OjrRS 213). ✧ 'Pearl' (OjrRS 213).

ČÏNČEYLÏK   Alt. 19th-20th c. **Činčeylik** [Чинчейлик], fem. (OjrRS 213). ✧ 'Pearly, pearl-'; ⇨ **ČÏNČEY** + suff. *-lik.*

ČÏNČÏK   Bashk. 1675 **Činčik** [Чинчик] (MIB I, 200). ⇨ **ČÏN?** + dim. suff. *-čik.*

ČÏNJÏR   Kzk. 19th c. **Činjir-bay** [Чинджирбай] (SOK 286); Kzk. 19th c. **Činžer-bay / Činžir-bay** [Чинжербай] (SOV 14). ✧ 'Chain'? cf. Kzk. *šinžir* 'die Kette' (Radl. IV, 1070).

ČÏNDALÏ   Kzk. 19th c. **Čindalï** [Чиндалы] (SODž. 70).

ČÏNDÏR   Kzk. 19th c. **Čindir-bay** [Чиндирбай] (SOK 128). ⇨ **ČÏN?** + suff. *-dir.*

ČÏNÄK   Uyg. 12th c. - 14th c. **Činäk** [činäk] (DTS).

ČÏNÄR   Türk 7th-9th c. **Činär** [Çinär] (ETY II, 123).

ČÏNEK   Turk. 20th c. **Činek-oɣlu** [Çinekoğlu] (TMİB 739).

ČÏNET   Kzk.? 18th c. - 19th c. **Činet-batïr** [Чинетъ-батыръ] (Tynyšp. 65).

ČÏNÏKEY see **ČÏNÏQAY**

ČÏNÏ see **ČÏNÏ**

ČÏNÏQAY   Tat. 1624 **Činikey** [Чиникей Караевъ] (Pokrovskij 70); Tat. 1647 **Činïqay** [Чиныкай Мамедкуловъ] (DAI III, 118); Bashk. 1777 **Činïqay** [Чиныкай Емашев] (MIB V, 64); Bashk. 1777 **Činïqay** [Чиныкай (Ченыкай) Емашев] (MIB V, 64). ✧ 'Little cup/glass'? ⇨ **ČÏNÏ** + dim. suff. *-qay.*

ČÏNÏS see **ČÏNÏS**

ČÏNŽER see **ČÏNJÏR**

ČÏÑ-TEMÜR see **ČÏN-TEMÏR**

ČÏÑE   Kzk. 19th c. **Čiñe-bay** [Чингебай] (AOA 30).

ČÏÑEL   Kzk. 19th c. **Čiñel-bay** [Чингельбай] (SOK 190); Kzk. 19th c. **Čiñel-bay** [Чингельбай] (SOV 36); Kzk. 19th c. **Čiñil-bay** [Чингильбай] (SOV 138). ✧ 'Good-looking'? cf. Kirg. *čiñgäl* 'schön' (Radl. III, 2117).

ČÏÑERČEK see **ČÏÑÏRČEK**

ČÏÑÏJEK   Tuv. 19th c. **Čiñijek** [Чингиджекъ], an informant (Potanin IV, 140, 167, 204-205). ⇨ ? + dim. suff. *-jek.*

ČÏÑÏL see **ČÏÑEL**

ČÏÑÏR   Kzk. 1846 **Čiñir / Čiñir-ali / Čiñir-alin?** [Байтюляк Чингир Алин] (MKOP 152).

ČÏÑÏRČEK   Bashk. 1735 **Čiñirček / Čiñerček / Čiñïrčiq?** [Чингирчекъ (Чингерчекъ) Чингырчинъ], a tarɣan (Vel.-Zern., Bašk. 17). ⇨ **ČÏÑÏR** + dim. suff. *-ček.* See also **ČÏÑÏR-ČAČ.**

ČÏÑÏRČÏK see **ČÏÑÏRČÏQ**

ČÏÑÏS see **ČÏÑÏZ**

ČÏÑÏZ   Kzk. 19th c. **Čeñis-pay** [Ченгиспай] (SOV 16); Kzk. 18th c. - 19th c. **Čiñis** [Чингис] (Tynyšp. 74); Kzk. 1839 **Čiñis** [Турсунъ Чингисовъ] (Konšin, Mat. V, 12); Kzk. 1841 **Čiñis** [Джанай Чингисовъ], sultan of the Middle Horde (Orta Žüz) (Konšin, Mat. V, 21); Kzk. 1841 **Čiñis** [Джолда Чингисовъ], sultan of the Middle Horde (Orta Žüz) (Konšin, Mat. V, 21); Kzk. 19th c. **Čiñis-pay** [Чингиспай] (SOV 14, 16); Kzk. 19th c. **Čiñis-pay** [Чингиспай] (SOK 76); Chag. 15th c. **Čiñiz** [Чингизъ], one of Shaybani Khan's followers from the „Bajqïr"s (Šejb. LXV); Kzk. 19th c. **Čiñiz** [Чингизъ], Chokan Valikhanov's father (Protok. Turk. IV, 52); Khorezm./Chag. 1412/1413 **Čiñiz-oɣlan** [Чингиз-оглан] (MIT I, 533); Kzk. 19th c. **Čiñis-pay** [Чингыспай] (SOK 20); Kzk. 19th c. **Čiñiz** [Чингызъ] (SOV 16); Kzk. 19th c. **Čiñiz-bay** [Чингызбай] (SOK 278); Crm. **Čiñiz-qan** [Чыңыз кан], in a Crimean folktale (Proben VII, 160); Kzk. 19th c. **Šiñis-pay** [Шингиспай] (AOAtb. 42). ✧ 'Chinggis Khan' (Mo.). Cf. O. Turan, Çingiz Adı Hakkında: TTK Belleten, CV, 1941, pp. 267-276.

ČÏÑÏRČÏ   Bashk. 1735 **Čiñirči** [Чингирчекъ (Чингерчекъ) Чингырчинъ], a tarɣan (Vel.-Zern., Bašk. 17). ⇨ **ČÏÑÏR** + suff. *-či.*

ČÏÑÏZ see **ČÏÑÏZ**

ČÏÑKÏ   Kzk. 19th c. **Čiñki** [Тасыбекъ Чинкиновъ] (Grod., Pril. 78).

ČÏPČÏK   Kzk. 19th c. **Čepček** [Чепчекъ] (SOV 104); Kzk. 19th c. **Čepček** [Чепчекъ] (SOK 26); Bashk. 1738 **Čipčik** [месегут Чибчиков] (MIB III, 387). ✧ 'Sparrow' cf. Tat. *čïpčïq* 'der Sperling' (Radl. III, 2098).

ČÏPČÏKÄY see **ČÏPČÏQAY**

ČİPNİ see **ČEPNİ**

ČİR Chuv. 18th-19th c. **Čir-bay** [Чирбай] (Magn. 93); Kzk. 19th c. **Čir-bay** [Ахмед Чирбаевъ] (Grod., Pril. 27). ✧ 'Ill, unhealthy, illness' cf. Chag. *čir* 'der Pickel, das Geschwür', (Tat.) 'die Krankheit, das Unwohlsein' (Radl. III, 2122).

ČİRAГ see **ČİRAQ**

ČİRAY see **ČİRAY**

ČİRAN see **JEREN**

ČİRÄ Bashk. 1742 **Čirä** [Чиря Кушаев] (MIB III, 513).

ČİRİ Kzk. 19th c. **Čiri-bek** [Чирибекъ] (SKSO VIII, 224). ✧ I. 'Rotten' cf. Kirg. *čiri* 'faul, verfault', (Radl. III, 2124); II. 'Brave, nimble' cf. Chag. *čiri* 'tapfer, flink' (Radl. III, 2124). See also **ČİRİK**.

ČİRİK Bashk. 1756 **Čirik** [Чирик Тавлетев] (MIB IV/1, 119); Bashk. 1776 **Čirik** [Измаил (Исмаил) Чириков] (MIB V, 47, 48, 49); Bashk. 1744 **Čirük** [Аскар Чирюков] (MIB III, 415); Bashk. 1760 **Čirük** [Ишметь Чирюков] (MIB IV/1, 191); Bashk. 1736 **Čürük** [Ишей Чюрюков] (MIB III, 344). ✧ 'Rotten' cf. *čirik* Alt.(Tel.) 'faul, verfault', (Turk.) 'Eiter, Schmutz' (Radl. III, 2124), Chag., Turk., NUyg.(Tar.) *čürük* 'faul, verfault, verdorben, verrostet, Ohne werth' (Radl. III, 2195). See also **ČİRİ**.

ČİRİN Kzk. 19th c. **Čirin-bek** [Чиринбекъ] (TV 1876: 144). ⇨ **ŠİRİN?**

ČİRKİN Kzk. 19th c. **Čirkin-bek** [Чиркинъ Бекъ] (Grod., Pril. 70); Kirg. **Širkim-beg (<Širkin-beg < Čirkin-bek)** [Шіркім бек], fem. (Proben V, 298 /300/). ✧ 'Ugly' cf. Kzk. *širkin* 'der Ausdruck des Misfallens, ein Schimpwort' (Radl. III, 1074).

ČİRMİŠ see **ČERMİŠ**

ČİRMUŠ see **ČERMİŠ**

ČİRTİN Uyg. 12th c.-14th c. **Čirtin** (DTS).

ČİRÜ see **ČERİ I.**

ČİRÜČİ Tat. 1624 **Čirüči / Čirüčey?** [Чирючей Янгурчеевъ] (Pokrovskij 72); Tat.(Sib.) 1603 **Čirüči / Čirüčey?** [Чирючей] (Miller, Ist. Sib. II, 180, 181). ⇨ **ČERİ I.?** + suff. *-či.*

ČİRÜK see **ČİRİK**

ČİRÜKEY Bashk. 1751 **Čirükey** [Чирюкей] (MIB IV/1, 51). ⇨ **ČİRİK** + suff. *-ey.*

ČİRÜŠ Bashk. 1741 **Čirüš** [Конакбай Чирюшев] (MIB IV/1, 241).

ČİS-QAQON Bashk. 1717 **Čis-qaqon?** [Кулумбет Чискаконов] (MIB III, 148).

ČİSİM Uyg. 12th c.-14th c. **Čisim** [Çisim] (DTS, EUTS); Uyg. **Čizim** [Çizim] (EUTS).

ČİSÜN Uyg. **Čisün** [Çisün] (EUTS); Uyg. 12th c.-14th c. **Čisün** (Radl., USp. 51); Uyg. 12th c.-14th c. **Čisün-señgi** (DTS). ⇨ **ČİSİM?**

ČİŠ Kzk. 19th c. **Čiš-pay** [Чишпай] (SOK 12). ✧ 'Spit, skewer, i.e. thin (child)' cf. Kirg. *čiš* 'der

Bratstock' (Radl. III, 2151).

ČİŠQAN see **ČİČQAN**

ČİT Uyg. **Čit** [čit] (DTS); Kzk. 19th c. **Čit** [Читъ] (AOK 58). ✧ 'Alien, foreign(er)'? cf. Kzk. *šet* 'край, окраина; незнакомый, чужой' (KzRS), Tat. *čit* 'die Grenze, die Seite, der Rand' (Radl. III, 2140). See also **BURALQİ, YAT, QARİP, TAT.**

ČİT-EL Kzk. 19th c. **Čit-el-bay** [Чительбай] (SOK 238). ✧ 'Alien folk, country'. ⇨ **ČİT** + **EL.**

ČİZİM see **ČİSİM**

ČİŽEN-BAQ Tat. 1685 **Čižen-baq** [Чиженбакъ], a taxpayer (payer of yasaq) from Krasnoyarsk (Kuznecov 60). ✧ 'Nimble, quick-witted'. ⇨ **ČEČEN?** + **BAQ.**

ČİŽİR Kzk. 19th c. **Čižir-bay** [Чижирбай] (SOK 120).

ČİŽMAN see **ČİJMAN**

Čİ-QAN see **ČİY-QAN**

ČİDEM see **ČİGDEM**

ČİG Uyg. **Čig-tutuχ** [Çiig Tutuḥ] (EUTS).

ČİRİČİ Kirg. **Čiriči** [Чірычы], Aydar-qan's daughter, Yaqïp-qan's wife in the Manas epic (Proben V, 1).

ČİS Hak. 19th-20th c. **Čis** [Чиис], fem. (HRS 356). ✧ 'Smell'? cf. Hak.(Sag.) *čis* 'der Geruch' (Radl. III, 2147).

ČİBAҲİ see **ČİBAQİ**

ČİBAQİ Yak. **Čïbaqï / Čïbāχï** [Чыбакы, Чыбахы], a shaman (Pek.).

ČİBİAN Yak. **Čïbïan** [Чыбыан] (Pek.).

ČİBİQ Kzk. 19th c. **Čibïq** [Чибыкъ] (SOV 22); Kuman 1266 **Čibuq** [Chybuk], a Kuman notability in Hungary (Gyárfás II, 418). ✧ 'Stick, rod, twig, branch' cf. Maml. *çıbuk* 'Dal' (Tarǰ/Houtsma), Uyg. Alt., Crm., Tat., Turk. *čïbïq* 'die Ruthe, ein dünner Stock; das Pfeifenrohr' (Radl. III, 2099-2100), Crm., East.T., NUyg.(Tar.) *čubuq* 'der Stock, der Prügel', (Crm.) 'das Pfeifenrohr, die Pfeife' (Radl. III, 2185), cf. also Rásonyi, KÖA 100, Adalékok 130, AOH XX(1967), 139. See also **ALTAY-ČUBUQ.**

ČİBİL Kzk. 19th c. **Čibïl** [Чибылъ] (SOV 126); Kzk. 19th c. **Čibïl-bay** [Чибылбай] (SOK 260). ✧ 'Unclean, impure; badness' cf. Alt. *čïbïl* 'die Unreinlichkeit, Unsauberkeit; die Slechtigkeit, die Schande, die Qual' (Radl. III, 2101).

ČİBİNTAY Kzk. 1839 **Čibïntay** [Чибинтай Сагалов] (Konšin, Mat. V, 42, 53); Kzk. 19th c. **Čibïntay** [Чибынтай] (SOK 12). ✧ 'Like a fly' cf. Kzk. *čïbin* 'id.' (KzRS), Tat. *čibïn* 'die Fliege' (Radl. III, 2163). ⇨ **ČİBİN** + suff. *-tay(1).*

ČİČAÑ-ATA Kirg. **Čičañ-ata** [Чычаӊата] (Jud. 77-78). ✧ 'Protector of goats; goats (in general)' cf. Kirg. *čičañata* 'id.' (Jud.), Kirg. *čičañ* 'хвостовые позвонки' (Jud.). ⇨ **ATA.**

ČİČİГRĀN Yak. **Čičïγrān** [Чыгыгран] (Pek.). ✧ 'Chattering; chirrup, twittering' cf. Yak. *čičïγïrā* 'трещать; пищать' (Pek.).

ČĪČĪN   Yak. **Čīčïn** [Чычын] (Pek.).

ČĪČQAN   Khorezm.? **Čičqan** [جيحکان / Чичкан] (RaD/Ber. II, 78,82); Bashk. 1709 **Čičqan** [Девлет Чичканов] (MIB III, 49); Bashk. 1709 **Čičqan** [Чичкан Урыспаев] (MIB III, 54); Bashk. 1719 **Čičqan** [Чичкан Аккышев] (MIB III, 185); Uzb.? 1684 **Čičqan** [Таушко Чичкановъ], a chieftain (DAI X, 384-85, 78); Kzk. 19th c. **Čišqan-bay** [Чишканбай] (SOK 62); Kzk. 19th c. **Čišqan-bay** [Читканбай] (AOAtb. 26); Bashk. 1735 **Čišqan-γul** [Чишкангулъ Мурзагуловъ], a tarγan (Vel.-Zern., Bašk. 14); Alt. 19th-20th c. **Čičqan** [Чычкан], fem. (OjrRS 214). ✧ 'Mouse' (OjrRS 214); cf. Alt. *čičqan* 'die Maus' (Radl. III, 2094). See also **QARA-ČIŠQAN**.

ČĪČQANAY   Bashk. 1756 **Čičqanay** [Мустафа Чичканаев] (MIB IV/1, 123). ⇨ **ČĪČQAN** + suff. *-ay*?

ČĪJMAN   Kzk. 19th c. **Čižman / Čījman** [Чижманъ] (AOA 122).

ČĪDAX   Hak. 19th-20th c. **Čïdax** [Чыдах] (HRS 352); Hak. 19th-20th c. **Čïdaχ** [Чыдах], fem. (HRS 356). ✧ 'Spear, pike' cf. Hak. *čïda* 'штык; копьё' (HRS 352). + suff. *-χ*?

ČĪΓ-BATAR   Uyg. 12th c.-14th c. **Čïγ-batar** [Čïγ Batar / Çıġ Batar] (Radl., USp. 127, 304, DTS, EUTS). ✧ 'Foot - will sink' cf. Uyg. *čïğ* 'ayaq' (US). ⇨ **ČĪQ + BATAR.**

ČĪΓAY   Kzk. 19th c. **Čïγay-bay** [Чыгайбай] (Pantusov). ✧ 'Poor, pauper' cf. Uyg. *čïγay* 'arm, elend' (Radl. III, 2062).

ČĪΓALĪ   Crm. **Čïγalï-qanïm** [Чыγалы Каным], fem. (Proben VII, 129). ✧ 'Feathery; having a tuft'? cf. Turk. *čïγa* 'die Vogelfeder, der Federbusch' (Radl. III, 2062). + suff. *-lï*.

ČĪΓAN   Kzk. 19th c. **Čïγam-bay** (<**Čïγan-bay)** [Чигамбай] (SOV 114); Kzk. 19th c. **Čïγam-bay** (<**Čïγan-bay)** [Чигамбай] (SODž. 82). ✧ 'Poor' cf. Radl. III, 2062-63.

ČĪΓANAQ   Kzk. 1823 **Čïγanaq** [جغاناق / Шиганак] (MIK IV, 459, 462). ✧ I. 'Bay'; II. 'Hinge' cf. Kzk. *šïγanaq* 'залив' (KzRS), Tat. *čïγanaq* 'der Thürbaken, das Scharnier' (Radl. III, 2063).

ČĪΓĪNAY   Kzk. 19th c. **Čïγïnay** [Чыгынай] (SOK 86). ✧ 'Stubborn, persevering' cf. Tat. *čïγïn* 'eigensinnig, halsstarrig' (Radl. III, 2064). + suff. *-ay*.

ČĪXANTAY   Kkalp. 1724 **Čïχantay** [Чихантай Убишев] (MIKk. 182). ⇨ ? + suff. *-tay(1,2)*?

ČĪYĪRDĪ   Kirg. **Čïyïrdï** [Чыйырды], fem. (Jud. 139, 528). ✧ 'Trace, footstep'? cf. Kirg. *čïyïr* 'тропа, след' (Jud.). + suff. *-dï*.

ČĪQ   Kzk. 19th c. **Čik-pay** [Чигпай] (SODž. 56); Kzk. 19th c. **Čik-pay** [Чикпай] (SODž. 72); Uyg. 762 **Čïq-tutuq** (Mahrnāmag 90).

ČĪQ-BILGÄ   Uyg. 750 **Čik-bilgä-čigši** (Runic Mss.

186). ⇨ **ČĪQ + BİLGÄ.**

ČĪQAY   Hak.? 19th-20th c. **Čïqay** [Чыкай], fem. (Katanov, Otč. 13). ✧ Derived from R. чихай (Katanov, Otč. 13).

ČĪQAYĪM   Kzk. 19th c. **Čïqayïm? / Čik-aim?** [Акчолъ Чикаимовъ] (Grod., Pril. 102).

ČĪQAN   Türk 721 **Čïqan / Išbara-čïqan** [İşbara Çïqan] (ETY I, 136); Türk **Čïqan-küli-čur** [ïšbara čïqan küli čur] (DTS); Türk 721 **Čïqan-küli-čur / Išbara-čïqan-küli-čur** [ïšbara čïqan küli čur] (DTS). ✧ 'Nephew on mother-side' (Blagova 1997, 708).

ČĪQAN-TONYUQUQ   Türk 721 **Čïqan-tonyuquq** [čïqan tonjuquq / Çïqan Tonyuquq] (DTS, ETY I, 136). ⇨ **ČĪQAN + TONYUQUQ.**

ČĪQĪ I.   Kzk. 19th c. **Čïqï-bay** [Чикыбай] (SOK 6); Kzk. 19th c. **Čïqï-bay** [Чикыбай] (AOK 50). ✧ 'Share, portion, lot'? cf. Turk. *čïqï* 'der Antheil, das Loos' (Radl. III, 2057).

ČĪQĪ II.   Yak. **Čïqï-ūs** [Чыкы-ус], the youngest of Örün-čä's sons (Pek.). ✧ '?-master' cf. Yak. *ūs* 'мастер' (YakRS).

ČĪQĪRĪNAR   Yak. **Čïqïrïnar** [Чыкырынар] (Pek.).

ČĪQĪŠTĪ   Kzk. 19th c. **Čïqïštï-bay (<Čïqïštï-bay)** [Чикыштыбай] (SOK 266). ⇨ ? + suff. *-tï*.

ČĪQTĪ   Kzk. **Čïqtï-bay / Čïqtï-bay?** [Маканъ Чиктыбаевъ] (Sb. Syr-D. VI, 106). ⇨ **ČĪQ?** + suff. *-tï*.

ČĪLA   Kzk. 19th c. **Čïla-bay / Čïlä-bay?** [Чилабай] (SKSO III, 180); Kzk. 19th c. **Čïla-bay / Čïlä-bay?** [Чилабай] (SOK 86).

ČĪLAN-XAN see YÏLAN

ČĪLAN-MOΓUS   Alt. 19th c. **Čïlan-moγus** [Чылан-Могус-богатырь / Чыланъ Могусъ], a hero (bogatyr) (Verb., In. 140). ⇨ **YÏLAN + MOΓOS.**

ČĪLAŠ   Tat.(Tara) **Čïlaš** [Чылаш], from Tärkäč aul (Proben IV, 149 /188/); Hak.(Blt.) 19th-20th c. **Čïlās** [Чылас] (Katanov, Otč. 9). ✧ 'Naked' cf. Shor *čïlāš* 'id.' (Radl. III, 2086), Alt.(Sag.) *čïlās* 'id.' (Radl. III, 2085).

ČĪLĀS see ČĪLAŠ

ČĪLĀSQA   Hak.(Sag.) 19th c. **Čïlāsqa** [Чыласка], Eple's son (Katanov, Otč. II, 12-15). ⇨ **ČĪLAŠ?** + suff. *-qa*.

ČĪLBAQ   Turk. **Čïlbaq-oγlu**, a Zeybek (Kúnos 1891, 119). ✧ 'Naked' cf. Turk. dial. *cılbak* 'çıplak' (DS).

ČĪLĪM   Kzk. 19th c. **Čïlïm** [Чилымъ] (SOV 72). ✧ I. 'Fishing net' cf. Kzk. dial. *žilim* 'id.' (QTDS), Tat. *jilim* 'невод, рыбачья сеть' (TatRS), Bashk. *yilim* 'невод' (BRS/Uraksin); II. 'Tricky man, sly boots' cf. Kzk. *žilim* 'скрытный, хитрый', *žilim adam* 'хитрый человек' (KzRS).

ČĪLLĀRAY   Yak. **Čïllāray** [Чыллараi] (Pek.).

ČĪLLĪY   Yak. **Čïllïy** [Чыллыi] (Pek.).

ČĪLPAN   Kzk. 1805 **Čïlpan** [Чилпан], chief of the Tana-buγa tribe of the Middle Horde (Orta Žüz) (MIK

IV, 513). ⇨ ČOLPAN?

ČĬLTUQ Kzk. 19th c. **Čiltuq-bay** [Чилтукбаевъ] (Grod., Pril. 97).

ČĬMAQĬ Alt. 19th-20th c. **Čïmaqï** [Чымакы], fem. (OjrRS 214).

ČĬMJAQQAY Tuv. 19th c. **Čïmǰaqqay** [Чымцаккаi] (Proben IX, 98). ✧ 'Soft, mild (character)' cf. Tuv. *čïmčaq* 'мягкий' (TuvRS) + suff. *-qay*.

ČĬMĬL Alt. 19th-20th c. **Čïmïl** [Чымыл], fem. (OjrRS 214). ✧ 'Fly' (OjrRS 214).

ČĬN Tat.(Lit.) 1750 **Čim-bay** (<Čin-bay) [Czymbaiowi Safianowiczowi / Чимбай Сафьяновичъ] (Lit. Tat. 511-13); Kzk. 19th c. **Čin-bay** [Чинбай] (SOV 38, 42); Kzk. 19th c. **Čin-bay** [Чинбай] (SOK 216); Uzb. 18th - 19th c. **Čin-bay** [Чинбай] (Magn. 92); Chuv. 18th-19th c. **Čin-bek / Čin-bäk?** [Чинбякъ] (Magn. 92); Uzb. 1689 **Čin-biy** [Чин-бий] (MIT II, 331); Kzk. 19th c. **Čin-eke** [Чинеке] (SOV 42); Kzk. 19th c. **Čin-χoža** [Чингожа Кибисов], from the region of Semipalatinsk (TV 1876: 129); Kzk. 19th c. **Čin-χoža** [Чингожа] (SODž. 134); Kzk. 19th c. **Čin-ike (<Čin-eke?)** [Чинике] (SOV 58); Bashk. 1712 **Čin-murza** [Бахарымбет Чинмурзин] (MIB III, 85); Bashk. 1748 **Čin-murza** [Чинмурзинъ] (Nepljuev 437); Nog. 1649 **Čin-murza** [Канъ мурза Чинъ-мурзинъ] (AI IV, 92); Nog. 1692, 1693 **Čin-murza** [Чинъ мурза Тинокпатовъ], a murza (AI V, 371); Kirg. **Čïn-qoǰo** [Чынкожо] (Jud. 58); Kzk. 19th c. **Šim-bay (<Šin-bay < Čin-bay)** [Шимбай] (AOP 54); Kkalp. 20th c. **Šin-bek** [Шинбек] (Bask., Kkalp. 54); *TN:* Bashk. **Čin-murza** [Чинмурзина] (MIB III, 192). ✧ I.‘ Chinese' cf. Uyg., Chag., Turk. *čin* 'der Chinese' (Radl. III, 2120); II. 'Hard, well-filled' cf. East.T., NUyg.(Tar.) *čiñ* 'hart, fest gestopft, voll' (Radl. III, 2116); III. 'Real, true, genuine, pure' cf. Uyg., Tat., Turk., Alt. *čin~čïn* 'wahr, gerecht, genau, richtig, wahrhaft' (Radl. III, 2070), Kzk., Hak., Shor, *šïn~čïn* 'wahr, die Wahrheit' (Radl. IV, 1049), Kirg. *čïn* 'истина, правда; истинный, настоящий, действительный' (Jud.), Bashk. *sïn* 'настоящий, натуральный' (BRS/Uraksin). See also **MAMAT-MOÑTUL-ČĬN**.

ČĬN-ALİ Kzk. 1822 **Čin-γali** [Чингалій Урмановъ] (TOUAK XXIV, 132). ⇨ ČĬN + ALİ.

ČĬN-ASĬL Kzk. 19th c. **Čin-asïl** [Чинасылъ] (SODž. 118); Kzk. 1860 **Čin-asïl** [Чинасылъ], a sultan from the Ulaqtï clan of the J̌alayïr tribe (ZIRGOGeogr. I, 271). ✧ I. 'True-genuine' II. 'Of Chinese origin'. ⇨ ČĬN + ASĬL.

ČĬN-ASĬLDĬ Kirg. **Čïn-asïldï** [Чынасылды] (Jud. 598). ✧ 'Real-genuine?; Of chinese origin'? ⇨ ČĬN-ASĬL + suff. *-di.

ČĬN-BERDİ Uzb. 20th c. **Čin-berdi / Čin-berdi?** [Чинберди] (Begmatov 1984, 202). ⇨ ČĬN + BERDİ. See also ČĬN-TURDĬ.

ČĬN-BULAT Kzk. 19th c. **Čim-bolat** [Чимболатъ] (SOV 24); Chuv.? 1624 **Čim-bulat** [Чембулат] (Zolotn. 160); Chuv. 18th-19th c. **Čin-bulat** [Чинбулатъ] (Magn. 92); Chuv. 18th-19th c. **Čin-bulat** [Ченбулатъ] (Magn. 92); Khorezm.? **Čin-pulat** [Чин-Пулад] (RaD II, 17). ✧ 'Genuine (pure) steel'. ⇨ ČĬN + BULAT.

ČĬN-QOŽO see ČĬN

ČĬN-TAY see ČĬN-TAY

ČĬN-TAŠ Chuv. 18th-19th c. **Čen-daš** [Чендашъ] (Magn. 92); Chuv. 18th-19th c. **Čen-deš** [Чендешъ] (Magn. 92). ✧ 'Real/genuine stone'. ⇨ ČĬN + TAŠ.

ČĬN-TEMİR Chuv. 18th-19th c. **Čin-dimer** [Чиндимеръ] (Magn. 92); Bashk. 1714 **Čin-temir (<Čiñ-temir)** [Чинтемир] (MIB I, 105); Kzk. 1794 **Čin-temir (Čiñ-temir)** [چنتيمر / Шитемир юлщъ] (MIK IV, 160); Kzk. 19th c. **Čin-temir (<Čiñ-temir)** [Чинтемир] (SOV 120); Kzk. 19th c. **Čin-temir (<Čiñ-temir)** [Чинтемир] (SOK 36); NUyg.(Tar.) 19th c. **Čin-temür (<Čiñ-temür)** [چنتمور / Чинъ-темюръ] (Pantusov 1-10); Turk. **Čiñ-temür / Ček-temür?** [جكتمور / چكتمور], one of the forefathers of the Ottoman dynasty (Seādeddīn I, 10, Nešrī 186); Chag. 16th c. **Čiñ-temür-sultan** [Chin Timur Sultán], son of Sultan Ahmad Khan (Ahmet Han) (1468-1502) (Tar. Rashidi 161); Kzk. 19th c. **Čin-temir** [Чентымир] (SOV 54); Kirg. **Čïn-temir** [Чынтемир] (Jud. 670); Bashk. / Kzk.? **Sïn-temir** [Sïn-temir] (Divaev, Biket 5); NUyg.(Tar.) **Šim-tömür-batur (<Šin-tömür-batur)** [Schim Tömür / Шiм Тöмÿр Батур] (Proben VI, 168 /221/); Kkalp. 20th c. **Šïn-temir** [Шынтемир] (KkRS 777). ✧ 'Genuine (pure) iron'. ⇨ ČĬN + TEMİR.

ČĬN-TURDĬ Uzb. 20th c. **Čin-turdï** [Чинтурди] (Begmatov 1984, 204). ✧ '(The) Strong stayed / remained / survived'. ⇨ ČĬN + TURDĬ.

ČĬNA Kzk. 19th c. **Čina-bay** [Аябъ-бергенъ Чинабаевъ] (Grod., Pril. 89).

ČĬNAČ-QAYA Uyg. 13th c. **Čïnač-qaya** [čïnač qaja] (DTS). ✧ 'Čïnač-Rock' (Blagova 1997, 704). ⇨ QAYA.

ČĬNAQ Hak. 19th c. **Čïnaq** [Чынак] (Katanov, Otč. 12). ✧ 'Tea-cup'? cf. Alt.(Tel.) *čïnayaq ~ čïna* 'die Theetasse' (Radl. III, 2071). + suff. *-q*?

ČĬNAR Karch. **Činar** [Чинаръ Аджиевъ] (Sysoev 123); Az. **Činar-qulu-bek** [Чинар-Кулу-бек] (Az. Skaz. 291); Trkm. 20th c. **Čïnar** [Čïnar] (Zaj. 1971, 332); Trkm. 20th c. **Čïnar** [Чинар] (TrkmRS 746). ✧ 'Plane-tree, platan' cf. *činar* (Turk.) 'die Platane', (Kirg.) 'die Ulme' (Radl. III, 2071) (<P.). See also **BİL-ČĬNAR, TOL-ǰİNAR(?)**.

ČĬNAR-ČEČÄK Uyg. 10th c. **Čïnar-čečäk-qïz** [čïnar čečäk qïz], fem. (DTS). ✧ 'Čïnar/plane?-Flower'

(Blagova 1997, 705). ⇨ **ČÏNAR + ČEČÄK.**

ČÏNARLÏ   Tat. 1543 **Čïnarlï** [Çınarlı] (Gökb., Rum. 242). ✧ 'Having platans'. ⇨ **ČÏNAR** + suff. -*lï*.

ČÏNAT   Alt. 19th-20th c. **Čïnat** [Чынат] (OjrRS 210).

ČÏNBET   Kzk. 19th c. **Čïmbet-pay** (<**Čïnbet-pay?**) [Чимбетпай] (SOK 202). ⇨ **ČÏN** + suffixoid -*bet*.

ČÏNÏ   Kzk. 19th c. **Činï-bay** [Чиныбай] (SODž. 32); Kzk. 19th c. **Činï-bay** [Чиныбай] (SOV 36); Kzk. 19th c. **Čini-bay** [Чиныбай] (SODž. 158); Kzk. 19th c. **Činï-bek** [Чиныбекъ] (SOK 54); Kzk. 19th c. **Činï-bek** [Чиныбекъ] (SODž. 70, 118); Kzk. 19th c. **Činï-bek** |Чиныбекъ] (AOA 46); Kzk. 19th c. **Činï-bek** [Чиныбекъ] (SOV 74); Kzk. 19th c. **Čïnï-bay** [Ченыбай] (SODž. 42); Kzk. 19th c. **Čïnï-bek** [Ченыбекъ] (SODž. 138); Kzk. 19th c. **Šïnï-bek** [Šini-bek] (Ljutš 118); Kkalp. 20th c. **Šïnï-bek** [Шыныбек] (KkRS 777). ✧ 'Cup, porcelain, glass' cf. Kirg., Tel. *čïna~čïnï* 'die Theetasse' (Radl. III, 2071), Kzk. *šinï* 'das Glas, das Porzelan; rein, gereinigt' (Radl. IV, 1050), Kzk. *šinï* 'стекло' (KzRS).

ČÏNÏS   Kzk. 19th c. **Čïnïs-pay** (<**Čiñis-pay?**) [Чиныспай] (SOK 196). ⇨ **ČÏÑÏZ?**

ČÏNTSU   Uyg. **Čïntsu** [Çıntsu] (EUTS).

ČÏÑAУ   Yak. **Čïñay** / **Ān-čïñay** [Чыңаі, Ан-Чыңаі], the elder of Onoγoy-bāy's two daughters (Pek.).

ČÏÑҐЇS   Tat.(Tara) **Čïñγïs** [Чыңгыс], Surum-qan's son (Proben IV 132 /170/). ✧ 'Great, strong' cf. Chag. *čiñgi::* (<Mo.) 'gross, mächtig' (Radl. III, 2117), also Mo. PN *Čiŋgis* 'Dschingis Chan' (TMEN I, No. 184).

ČÏÑҐЇŠ   Kirg. **Čïñγïš** [Чыңгыш] (Jud. 344).

ČÏÑÏR-ČAČ   Bashk. 1686 **Čïñïr-čač** / **Čiñir-čač?** [Чыңгырчачко Маметевъ] (Vel.-Zern., Bašk. 40). ✧ '?-hair' cf. Alt., Kar., Kzk., etc. *čač* 'das Haar' (Radl. III, 1904). ⇨ **ČÏÑÏR.**

ČÏÑÏZ see **ČÏÑÏZ**

ČÏÑQÏY   Yak. **Čïñqïy** [Чыңкыі] (Pek.).

ČÏPČÏQAY   Bashk. 1675 **Čïpčïqay** / **Čipčikäy** [Юлумбет Чипчикаевъ] (MIB I, 200). ✧ 'Little sparrow' cf. Tat. *čïpčïq* 'der Sperling' (Radl. III, 2098). + suff. -*ay*.

ČÏPLAN   Hak. 19th-20th c. **Čïplan** [Чыпланъ], fem. (HRS 356).

ČÏRAY   Kzk. **Čiray** [Чирай], fem. (Sb. Syr-D. IX, 50); Kkalp. 20th c. **Šïray** [Шырай], fem. (KkRS 779). ✧ 'Face' cf. Tat., Alt., Kar. *čïray* 'das Antlitz, das Gesicht, das Aeussere' (Radl. III, 2075), Kkalp. *šïray* 'черты лица' (KkRS).

ČÏRAQ   Turk. 1431 **Čiraq-bey** / **Čiraγ-bey** (Gökb., Ed. 29); Turk. 16th c. **Čïraq** (Ongan, Ank. II); Turk. 1583 **Čïraq** [چراق] (Ongan, Ank. I, 155); Yürük 1543 **Čïraq** (Gökb., Rum. 177, 183); Yürük 1543 **Čïraq-dede** [دده چراق], from the Yürüks of Kocacık (Gökb., Rum. 101); OT **Ćuraq?** / **Čïraq** [Τζυράκης], a Byzantine clerk of the court of Turkic (?) origin (Byz. Turc. II, 315). ✧ I.

'Apprentice' cf. Turk. *čïraq* 'der Arbeiter, der Knecht' (Radl. III, 2076), *čïraγ* 'ein alter Hausdiener; der Lehrling; der Günstling, der Pflegling'; II. 'Lamp, torch' cf. Turk., Crm. (< P.) 'die Lampe, das Lichtdie Fakel, die Leuchte' (Radl. III, 2077).

ČÏRAN-TAY   Tuv. 19th c. **Čïran-tay** [Чыран-таі] (Proben IX, 98). ⇨ **JEREN?** + **TAY** + / suff. -*tay(1,2)*?

ČÏRAÑATTA   Yak. **Čïrañatta** [Чыраңатта] (Pek.).

ČÏRĀ   Yak. **Čïrā** [Чыра] (Pek.). ✧ 'Ambling horse'? cf. Tuv. *čïrā: čïrā at* 'иноходец' (TuvRS).

ČÏRĀ-QARA   Tuv. 19th c. **Čïrā-qara** [Чыра кара] (Proben IX, 167). ✧ 'Ambling horse - black'. ⇨ **ČÏRĀ** + **QARA.**

ČÏRBAÑ   Tuv. 19th c. **Čïrbañ** [Чырбаң] (Proben IX, 141, 147).

ČÏRBÏL   Tuv. 19th c. **Čïrbïl-qam** [Чырбыл кам], a Shaman (Proben IX, 146).

ČÏRČÏQ   Alt. 19th-20th c. **Čïrčïq** [Чырчык] (OjrRS 210). ✧ 'Wrinkled, wizened' (OjrRS 210).

ČÏRҐALDÏҐ   Tuv. 19th c. **Čïrγaldïγ** [Чырҕалдыҕ] (Proben IX, 143). ✧ 'Jolly, merry, vital' cf. Tuv. *čïrγaldïγ* 'блаженный, счастливый' (TuvRS).

ČÏRQUŠ   Uyg. **Čïrquš** [Çırkuş] (EUTS).

ČÏRMAŠ   Uzb. 20th c. **Čïrmaš** [Чирмаш] (Begmatov 1984, 206); Uzb. 20th c. **Čïrmaš-bâу** [Чирмашбой] (Begmatov 1984, 206). ✧ 'Grasp! Clutch!' (Begmatov) cf. Uzb. *čïrmaš-* 'обвиваться, сцепляться; карабкаться' (UzbRS).

ČÏSTÏҐ   Hak.(Koyb.) 19th c. **Čïstïγ** [Чыстыҕ] (Katanov, Otč. II, 12-15). ✧ 'Stinking' (Katanov).

ČÏTSU   Uyg. **Čïtsu** [Çıtsu] (EUTS).

ČÏTSU-SEİL   Uyg. 12th c. - 14th c. **Čïtsu-seil (senil?)** [čïtsu seil (senil?)] (DTS). ✧ 'May-he-herd-Seil' (Blagova 1997, 716).

ČÏZALÏҐ   Uzb. 1826 **Čïzalïγ** [چزالغ], from Bukhara (Véliaminoff-Zernoff: Bull. Hist. Ac. Spbg., XVI, 280-82).

ČÏZÏÑ   Hak.(Koyb.) 19th c. **Čïzïñ** [Чызың] (Katanov, Otč. II, 12-15). ✧ 'Your stink' (Katanov).

ČÏBÏS   Yak. **Čïbïs** [Чыбыс] (Pek.).

ČÏBÏSTĀN   Yak. **Čïbïstān** [İtüq-Čïbïstān-quo / Чыбыстан], a messenger of the unclean spirits (Pek.). ⇨ **ČÏBÏS** + dim. suff. -*tān*.

ČÏQA   Hak.(Sag.) **Čïqa** [Чыка] (Proben IX, 606).

ČÏPPAÑ   Yak. **Čïppañ** [Чыппан] (Pek.).

ČOBA-YÏQMÏŠ   Uyg. **Čoba-yïqmïš** [Çoba yıkmış] (EUTS); Uyg. 12th c.-14th c. **Čoba-yïqmïš** / **Čuba-yïqmïš** (Radl., USp. 93, DTS). ✧ 'Čoba-Devastated' (Blagova 1997, 716), cf. Uyg., Karakh. *jïq-* 'валить, разрушать' (DTS). See also **YÏQMÏŠ-TAZ.**

ČOBAL   Kzk. 19th c. **Čobal** [Чобалъ] (SODž. 30).

ČOBAN   Khorezm.? 14th c.? **Čoban** [اشیخ حسینا وهو ابن الجوبان / Djoûbân], Shaikh Husain's father (in Shiraz) (Ibn Bat. II, 65); Maml.?

1306 **Čoban** [الامير المغلى جوبان], an emir (Dawād. 149, 231); Maml. 1308 **Čoban** [جوبان], governor of Kerbende (Baybars/Tizeng. I, 96, 120); Maml. 1309 **Čoban** [بدر الد ين جوبان], an emir (Dawād. 170); Maml. 14th c. **Čoban** [جوبان نـائـب ا بن سعيد] (Zetterst. 174, 177, 179); Maml. 14th c. **Čoban** [جوبان الـدودار] (Zetterst. 194); Maml. 1378/79 **Čoban** [جوبان الطبدمرى] (Iyās I, 244); Maml. 1399 **Čoban** [جوبان العثما نى] (Iyās I, 313); Maml. 1442/43 **Čoban** [جوبان] (Ibn Taghrīb. VII, 285); Turk. 1249 **Čoban** [جوبان بن سنقر], noted in the vakfiye of Karatay-mescid (Turan: Belleten XII, 153, 158); Kzk. 19th c. **Čoban** [Чобанъ] (SODž. 104); Chag./ Khorezm.? 14th c.? **Čoban** [Çoban (Emir)], a vezir (emir) of the Ilkhanids (Uzunçarş., Anad. 49); Selj.? 13th c. **Čoban** / **Čopan** [جوبان / چوپان], an emir (Qazw. 588, 591); Khorezm.? 1299, 1327 **Čoban** / **Čuban** [جوبان / امـرا چوبان و سلطان / سربان/ [Sulduz?] / Чобан], an emir, Malik's (Melik's) son from the Sulduz (سولـدوس) folk, Todan's (تـودان) grandson, Rašiduddīn's contemporary, played an imortant role at the time of Ghazan and took part in his war against Egypt, executed by Abu Said in 1327 (RaD/Ber. I, 173, RaD I/1, 175, Abulg./Desm. 175, RaD/Jahn. 88, 111, 122, 123, 127, Hammer, Ilch. II, 33, 299); Khorezm.? / Chag. 14th c. **Čoban** / **Čuban?** [جوبان], Öljeytü's (1304-1316) later Abusaid's (1316-1335) beglerbeg, his daughter is Baɣdād-χatun (see) (Omarī 227, 249); Chag./ Khorezm.? 14th c. **Čoban** / **Čuban?** [جوبان بن تـداون] (Duqmaq/Tizeng. I, 320, 328); Selj. 1211 **Čoban-bey** [Husameddin Çoban Bey], emir of Kastamonu from 1211 (Yücel 64-66); Crm.Tat. 20th c. **Čoban-zāde**, Bekir Sïtqï (1893-1938), the well-known scholar and poet of the Crimean Tatars (Mende 178); Trkm. 20th c. **Čopan** [Čopan] (Zaj. 1971, 325); Trkm. 20th c. **Čopan** [Чопан] (TrkmRS 736); Chuv. 18th-19th c. **Čopan** [Чопанъ] (Magn. 93); Kzk. 19th c. **Šopan** [Шопанъ] (AOAtb. 14). ✧ 'Herdsman' cf. Turk., Crm. *čoban* 'der Hirt' (Radl. III, 2030), Trkm. *čopan* 'чабан, пастух' (TrkmRS), Kzk. *šopan* 'пастух; чабан' (KzRS), cf. also Sauvaget 47.

ČOBAR Kzk. 19th c. **Čobar-bek** [Чобарбекъ] (SOK 202); Kzk. 1794 **Šubar-biy** [چبار بى / Шубар бий] (MIK IV, 165); Kzk. 1790,1794 **Šubar-biy** / **Čuwar-bï?** [چوار بى / Шубар бий] (MIK IV, 132, 134, 165,174). ✧ 'Grey, iron-grey, piebald horse' cf. Chag. *čubar* 'eisengraues Pferd' (Radl. III, 2185), Tat. *čuwar* 'bunt' (Radl. III, 2186), Tat. *čuar (čuwar)* 'пёстрый; вычурный' (TatRS), Tat. dial. *čobar* 'id.' (TatDS), Kzk. *šubar* 'buntfleckig (Pferdefarbe)' (Radl. IV, 1105). See also **AQ-ČUWAR, ČUBAR-AYɣÏR**.

ČOBÏYAQ Hak.(Kacha) 19th-20th c. **Čobïyaq** [Чобыjак] (Proben IX, 511-12). ✧ '?' cf. Hak. PN *Čobïy / Čobïyaχ* '?' (Butanaev) + suff. -*aq*.

ČOBUODAR Yak. **Čobuodar** [Чобуодар] (Pek.).

ČOBUOLAY Yak. **Čobuolay** [Чобуолаі] (Pek.). ✧ 'Be nimble! Be daring' cf. Yak. *čobuolay* 'бойчиться, смелым (бойким) делаться' (Pek.).

ČOBUONNAX Yak. **Čobuonnaχ** [Чобуоннах] (Pek.).

ČOČAQ Tat.(GH) 1279 **Čočaq** / **Čočuq?** [Τζοτζάκ], a christened Tatar, died in 1279 (Byz. Turc. 314); Tat.(GH) 14th c. **Čočaq** / **Čočuq?** [Τζοτζάκ], a christened Tatar in the early 14th c. (Byz. Turc. II, 314).

ČOČĬ-BÖRĬ Türk 7th c. - 9th c. **Čočĭ-böri-sañun** [čočĭ böri sañun] (DTS). ✧ 'Čočĭ-Wolf' (Blagova 1997, 706). ⇒ **BÖRĬ**. See also **ČOČUQ-BÖRĬ**.

ČOČĬT Hak. 19th c. **Čočĭt** (Katanov, Otč. 12). ✧ 'Frighten it'? cf. Alt.(Tel.) *čočĭt* 'Jemanden erschrecken' (Radl. III, 2026).

ČOČQO Alt. **Čočqo** (Nikiforov 81); Hak. 19th-20th c. **Sosqa** [Соска] (HRS 351). ✧ 'Pig, hog, swine' cf. Alt. *čočqo* 'das Schwein' (Radl. III, 2027), Hak. *sosχa* 'id.' (HRS).

ČOČQON Alt. 19th-20th c. **Čočqon** [Чочкон] (OjrRS 210).

ČOČOɣOY Alt. 19th-20th c. **Čočoɣoy** [Чочогой] (OjrRS 210). ✧ 'Pine-cone, fir-cone' (OjrRS 210); cf. Tel. *čočoɣoy* 'die Zapfen der Naderhölzer' (Radl. III, 2026).

ČOČOYO Yak. **Čočoyo** [Чочоjо] (Pek.). ✧ 'Loitering, loafer'? cf. Yak. *čočoy-* 'торчать' (Pek.). ⇒ **ČOČOYŌN** + suff. -*o*.

ČOČOYŌN Yak. **Čočoyōn** [Чочоjон] (Pek.). ✧ 'Loitering, loafer'? cf. Yak. *čočoy-* 'торчать' (Pek.). ⇒ **ČOČOYO** + suff. -*ōn*.

ČOČŌ Yak. **Čočō** [Чочо] (Pek.).

ČOČU see **ČOČUY?**

ČOČU-QÏLÏSÏT Yak. **Čoču-qïlïsït** [Чочу кылысыт] (Pek.).

ČOČUY Karch. **Čoču̇y** / **Čoču?** [Чочуевъ] (Sysoev 120).

ČOČUQ-BÖRĬ Türk 8th c.-9th c. **Čočuq-böri-sañun** [Çoçuq Böri Sañun] (DTS, ETY III, 53). ✧ 'Wolf-cub' cf. Turk., Crm. *čojuq* 'das Kind, das kleine Kind, der Knabe, die Jungen der Thiere' (Radl. III, 2027), Chag. *čočuq* 'das Ferkel' (Radl. III, 2027). ⇒ **BÖRĬ**. See also **ČOČĬ-BÖRĬ**.

ČOČUOBUS Yak. **Čoču̇obus** [Чочуобус] (Pek.).

ČOČUSQUOY Yak. **Čočusquoy** [Чочускуоі] (Pek.).

ČODÏM Kzk. 19th c. **Čodïm-bek** [Чодымбекъ] (SOK 72).

ČOɣAN Turk. 16th c. **Čoɣan-paša** / **Čoqan-paša?** [Tzoganos Paşa], Sancak Bey of Thessalia (Baştav 161). ✧ 'Soapwort (Saponaria officinalis)'? cf. Turk. *čoɣan* 'Seifenkraut' (Radl. III, 2012).

ČOɣDOR Yak. **Čoɣdor-oyūn** [Чогдор оjун], a

shaman, one of shaman Baqanča-Bïtanïa's nine sons (Pek.).

ČOΓÏ   Uyg. 8th c. **Čoγï-tiräk** [Çogı Tiräk] (Müller, Pfahl. 12, 19, EUS, EUTS); Uyg. 12th c.-14th c. **Čoqï** (Radl., USp. 26, DTS); Khorezm./Chag. 1436 **Čoqï** [جوکی], Timür's chieftain, died in 1436 (Arabš. II, 862). ✧ 'Quarrel, brawl, scandal' cf. Uyg., Karakh. *čoγï* 'спор, распря, скандал' (DTS).

ČOΓOLUYA   Yak. **Čoγoluya** [Чоҕолуја] (Pek.).

ČOΓUY   Yak. **Čoγuy** [Чоҕуј] (Pek.). ✧ 'Speaking loudly and nodding lively' cf. Yak. *čoγuy-* 'учащенно кивать головой; говорить бойко (отчетливо), кивая головой; говорить громко (звонко)' (Pek.). See also **TÜRGÄN-ČOΓUY**.

ČOΓUR   Tat.(Sib.)? 1623, 1651 **Čoγur-tayša / Čügür-tayša / Čoqur-tayša?** [Чогур (Чюгур, Чекур, Чокур) тайша] (Miller, Ist. Sib. II, 301, 304, 463, 534). ✧ 'Pipes (musical instrument)'? cf. Alt. *čōqur / čoγor* 'die Rohrpfeife' (Radl. III, 2007, 2014).

ČOXAN   Trkm. 1879 **Čoxan** [Чоханъ-Аман-оглы] (Groc., Vojna IV, Grod., Pril. 109). ⇨ **ČOQAN, ČOΓAN?**

ČOΓAQ   Hak. 19th c. **Čoγaq** (Katanov, Otč. 12). ✧ 'Little liar'? cf. Hak. *čoγ* 'лжец, лгун; ложь' (HRS). + suff. *-aq*.

ČOΓAN   Hak.(Sag.) **Čoγan** [Чоҕан] (Proben IX, 436). ✧ '?' cf. Hak. *čoγ* 'лжец, лгун; ложь' (HRS). ⇨ **ČOΓÏŇ?**

ČOΓČÏQ   Kzk. 19th c. **Čoγčïq** [Чойчекъ] (SODž. 12). ⇨ ? -- suff. *-čïq?*

ČOΓΓORA   Kzk. 19th c. **Čoγγora?** [Чойгора] (SOV 22).

ČOΓÏŇ   Kzk. 19th c. **Čoγim-bay (<Čoγïn-bay)** [Чоимбай, Чоембай] (SOV 40); Kzk. 19th c. **Čoγim-bek (<Čoγïn-bek)** [Чоимбекъ] (SODž. 12). ✧ '(Cast) Iron' cf. Kzk. *šoγïn* 'чугун' (KzRS). ⇨ **ČOYÏŇ, ĴOYÏM.**

ČOYÏŇ   Hak. 19th-20th c. **Čoyïñ** [Чойынъ] (HRS 352); Hak.(Sag.) **Čoyïñ** [Чојыӊ] (Proben IX, 613). ✧ 'Liar'? cf. Hak. *čoγ* 'лжец, лгун; ложь' (HRS). ⇨ **ČOΓÏŇ?**

ČOYKÏ   Kzk. 19th c. **Čoyki-bek?** [Чойкибекъ] (SOV 138). ✧ 'Bent and crooked' cf. Kzk. *şoykı* 'eğri-büğrü, düzgün değil' (KzTS).

ČOYU   Kirg. **Čoyu-bek** [Чоюбек] (Jud. 933).

ČOYUN-ΓULAQ   Kzk. 19th c. **Čoγun-γulaq / Šoyun-γulaq** [Чоюнъ-гулакъ / Шоюнъ-гулакъ] (Potanin, Pred 92-93). ✧ '(Cast) Iron-ear, having iron ears'. ⇨ **ČOYÏN + QULAQ.**

ČOQ   Kzk. 19th c. **Čoq** [Чокъ] (SOK 80); Bulg. 814 **Čoq / Čök / Čük?** [Τζόκος], a Bulghar chieftain, successor of the prince Krum (ca. 814?) (Byz. Turc. II, 314). ✧ I. 'Plenty, much'; II. 'A pagan feast (sprinkling?)' cf. Tat. PN *Čuq* (Sattarov). See also **BAY-ČOQ, SÏKSÄN-ČOQ, TOYÏN-ČOQ.**

ČOQ-ADΓÏR   Uyg. **Čoq-adγïr** [Çok adġır] (EUTS). ⇨ **ČOQ + AYΓÏR.**

ČOQ-BUT   Kzk. 19th c. **Čoq-but** [Чокбутъ] (SODž. 132). ⇨ **ČOQ + BUT.**

ČOQ-MUXAMED   Kzk. 19th c. **Čoq-muχamed** [Чокмухамедъ] (SOV 82). ⇨ **ČOQ + MUXAMMED.**

ČOQ-TUMAQ   Kzk. 19th c. **Čoq-tumaq** [Чоктумакъ] (SODž. 46). ⇨ **ČOQ? + TUMAQ.**

ČOQAY   Tat.(Lit.) 1552 **Čoqay / Čoγay?** [Чокгай] (Kn. Metriki Lit. 86); Kzk. 19th c. **Čoqay-oγlu** [Mustafa Čokaj-Oglu] (Mende 147); Tat.(Lit.) 1557 **Šoqay** [Шокай] (Kn. Metriki Lit. 131); Kzk. 19th c. **Šoqay** [Шокай] (AOP 110); Kzk. 19th c. **Šoqay** [Kungbay Šokay] (Ljutš 128); Kkalp. 20th c. **Šoqay** [Шокъай / Шокай] (Bask., Kkalp. 402, KkRS 776); Nog. 20th c. **Šoqay** [Шокъай Абдухалик увлы], one of Baskakov's informants from the aul of Qoyasulï (Bask., Nog. 144). ✧ I. 'Brave man'?; II. 'Plenty, much'? (Sattarov); III. 'Little pagan feast'? cf. Tat. PN *Čuqay* (Sattarov); IV. 'Nephew' cf. Tat. *Čoqa / Čoqay* (Sattarov). ⇨ **ŠUQAY / ČOQ ?** + suff. *ay.*

ČOQAN   Kzk. 19th c. **Čoqan** [Чоканъ] (AOAtb. 30); Kzk. 19th c. **Čoqan** [Чоканъ Чингизович (Чингисовичъ) Валихановъ], Russian officer, scholar, ethnographer and writer of articles of Kazak origin, died in 1865 (AUK 192, 431); Karg. **Čoqān** (Katanov, Otč. 9). ✧ I. 'Plenty' (Sattarov); II. 'Pagan feast'? (Sattarov); III. 'Cousin on mother side' (Sattarov p. 212: *Čoqa / Čuqan*). ⇨ **ČOQ?** + voc. suff. *-an?*

ČOQAR   Tuv. 19th c. **Čoqar-ōl** [Чокар-ол (Чахролъ)] (Proben IX, 121, 138).

ČOQČA   Kzk. 19th c. **Čoqča-bay** [Чокчабай] (SOV 150). ⇨ **ČOQ?** + suff. *-ča.*

ČOQÏ see **ČOΓÏ**

ČOQO   Kirg. **Čoqo** [Чоко] (Jud. 754). ✧ 'Clay, earth, loam' cf. Kirg. *čoqo~čoro* ' глина, земля' (Jud.).

ČOQTON   Alt. 19th-20th c. **Čoqton** [Чоктон], fem. (OjrRS 213). ✧ 'Be sacrificed'? (<Alt.) *čoqto-* 'кропить на идолов или класть на огонь пищу с восклицанием: чок!' (OjrRS).

ČOQTU   Alt. 19th-20th c. **Čoqtu-bay** [Чоктубай] (OjrRS 210). ✧ 'Flaming, fiery' cf. Alt. *čoqtu* 'огненный' (OjrRS). + suff. *-tu.*

ČOQUR see **ČOΓUR**

ČOL   Chuv. 18th-19th c. **Čol-bay** [Чолбай] (Magn. 93).

ČOLA   Hak. 19th-20th c. **Čola** [Чола], fem. (HRS 356). ✧ 'Soul'? cf. Hak. *čula* '(по суеверным представлениям) душа, духовный двойник человека, который может покинуть тело при жизни' (HRS 356).

ČOLAΓAY   Hak. 19th-20th c. **Čolaγay** [Чолаҕай] (HRS 352). ✧ 'Road'? cf. Hak. *čol* 'путь, дорога' (HRS). ⇨ **ČOLA?** + suff. *-γay.*

ČOLAQ Yürük 1543 **Čolaq** [Çolak], a Yürük from Varna (Gökb., Rum. 215, 239, 243); Yürük 1543 **Čolaq** [Çolak] (Gökb., Rum. 214); Tat. 1543 **Čolaq** [Çolak] (Gökb., Rum. 239); NUyg. 19th c. **Čolaq** [چولاق / Cholak] (Le Coq, Namenl. 99); Kzk. 1817 **Čolaq / Šolaq** [چولاق / Шолак] (MIK IV, 311, 318); Chuv. 18th-19th c. **Čulaχ** [Тулахъ (§Чулахъ)] (Magn. 94); Chuv. 18th-19th c. **Čulak** [Чулакъ] (Magn. 94); Bashk. 1712 **Čulaq** [Коштан Чюлаков] (MIB III, 87); Kzk. 19th c. **Šolaq** [Шолакъ] (AOA 82); Kzk. 19th c. **Šolaq** [Шолакъ] (AOK 46, 122); Kzk. 19th c. **Šolaq** [Шолакъ] (AOP 18). ✧ 'Crippled, disabled' (Le Coq 99), 'One-armed, lame' (Sauvaget 47), cf. also Chag., East.T., NUyg.(Tar.) *čolaq* 'verkrüppelt' (Radl. III, 2023), Turk., Az., Crm. *čolaq* 'einarmig, armlos, mit vertrovknetem Arme', (Az.) 'der Krüppel, der Lahme', (Turk.) 'der Geizhals' (Radl. III, 2023), Kzk. *šolaq* 'verstümmelt, kurz' (Radl. IV, 1030), Tat. *čulaq* 'vertrocknet (von den Armen)' (Radl. III, 2175). See also **BOZ-ČOLOQ, QARA-ČOLAQ.**

ČOLAQ-BĀLİ Yürük 1543 **Čolaq-bāli** [Çolak], a Yürük from Varna (Gökb., Rum. 215, 239, 243). ⇨ **ČOLAQ + BĀLİ.**

ČOLBANAX Hak. 19th-20th c. **Čolbanaχ** [Чолбанах], fem. (HRS 356); Hak. 19th-20th c. **Čolbanaχ** [Чолбанах] (HRS 356). ✧ 'Sensul, lewd, immoral, bawdy' cf. Hak. *čolban* 'приблудный' (HRS). ⇨ **ČOLPAN?** + dim. suff. *-aχ / -aq.*

ČOLLŌNOY Yak. **Čollōnoy** [Чоллоноі] (Pek.).

ČOLMAN-BĬ see **ČOLPAN**

ČOLOX Yak. **Čoloχ** [Чолох] (Pek.). ✧ Derived from *čoloy + -oχ* cf. Yak. *čoloy* 'поднимать голову вверх' (Pek.).

ČOLŌDO Yak. **Čolōdo Ölönö** [Чолодо], fem. (Pek.). ✧ 'Having one eye' cf. Yak *čoloy* 'поднимать голову вверх' (Pek.).

ČOLPAN Bashk. **Čolman-bĭ** [T'šolman bĭ], born on the bank of Čolman (T'šolman), according to a legend of origin, his father was called Qara-tabïn-bĭ (Mészáros, MH 99); Alt. **Čolmon** [Чолмонъ] (Nikiforov 78, 97); Maml. 1467 **Čolpan** [محمد بن جلبان] (Ibn Taghrīb. VIII, 662); Kkalp. 20th c. **Šolpan** [Шолпан], fem. (Bask., Kkalp. 404, KkRS 779); Nog.? **Šolpan** [Шолпан] (Žirm., Epos 390); Kirg. 19th c. **Šolpan** [Шолпанъ] (AUK Dobavl. 3); Kzk. **Šulpan** (MSOS VI, 2, 214); Kzk. **Šulpan** [Aiman i Šulpan], in a Kazak legend (OB XVI, 56). ✧ 'Venus' cf. Uyg. *čolban*, Turk. *čolpan* 'der Planet Venus' (Radl. III, 2025), Tel. *čolmon* 'die Venus' (Radl. III, 2025), Kzk. *šolpan* 'die Morgenröthe' (Radl. IV, 1031), Hak. *solban* 'der Planet Venus' (Radl. IV, 555), cf. also Sauvaget 47: *čolpan* جلبا ن 'étoile du berger'. See also **ALTÏN-SOLBAN.**

ČOLPON-ATA Kirg. **Čolpon-ata** [Чолпоната] (Jud. 77). ✧ 'Protector of sheep; sheep' cf. Kirg. *čolponata* 'id.' (Jud.). ⇨ **ČOLPAN + ATA.**

ČOLTOŠ see **YOLDAŠ**

ČOLUQ Uyg. 12th c.-14th c. **Čoluq** [Çoluk] (Radl., USp. 8, DTS, EUTS). ✧ 'One-armed, disabled; scapegrace, vile' cf. Karakh. *čolaq / čoluq* 'id.' (DTS), Tuv. *čoluq* 'негодяй, подлец; (уст., рел.) жертва, жертвоприношение' (TuvRS).

ČOMA Chuv. 18th-19th c. **Čoma** [Чома] (Magn. 93). ✧ 'Plague'? cf. R. *čuma* 'id.'.

ČOMAQ Kuman 1360 **Čomaq** [Chomak], a Kuman prince (kenez) of the Vlachs from Hateg (Hátszeg) (Kádár III, 232); Karakh. **Čomaq** [Çomak] (MK/Atalay 836); Maml. 14th c. **Čomaq** [جُمَق] (Sauvaget 47); Yürük 1543 **Čomaq** (Gökb., Rum. 228); Chuv. 18th-19th c. **Čomaq** [Чомакъ] (Magn. 93); Bashk. 1709 **Čumaq** [Каштан Чюмаков] (MIB III, 44); Kzk. 19th c. **Šomaq** [Шомакъ] (AOP 30); Tuv. 19th c. **Šumaq-ōl** [Шумак-ол] (Proben IX, 23, 25, 33). ✧ 'Mace, club' cf. Turk. *čomak* 'die Keule' (HŞ), Chag., Turk. *čumaq* 'der Stock mit einer eisernen Kugel an einem Ende, ein Morgenstern' (Radl. III, 2188).

ČOMČOY Yak. **Čomčoy / Čamčay** [Чомчоі] (Pek.). ✧ 'Boast' cf. Yak. *čomčoy* 'особо выдаваться, хвастаться' (Pek.). ⇨ **ČAMČAY.**

ČOMO Yak. **Čomo** [Чомо] (Pek.).

ČOMUR Alt. 19th-20th c. **Čomur** [Чомур], fem. (OjrRS 214). ✧ 'Lily' cf. Alt. *čomur* 'лилия' (OjrRS).

ČOMURČÏ Alt. 19th-20th c. **Čomurčï** [Чомурчы], fem. (OjrRS 214). ✧ I. 'Gathering/picking lilies' (OjrRS 214); II. 'Little lily'. ⇨ **ČOMUR** + dim. suff.? *-čï.*

ČON see **ČOŇ**

ČON-ČURAQ Karg. **Čon-čuraq** [Чончуракъ] (ZIRGOÊtn. XIII, vyp. III, 187). ⇨ **ČOŇ + ČURAQ.**

ČON-ET? Kzk. 1846 **Čon-et?** [Чонет Бердибаев] (MKOP 154). ✧ I. 'Make it big(ger)'? cf. Kzk. *et-* 'делать' (KzRS); II. 'Big meat' cf. Kzk. *et* 'мясо' (KzRS). ⇨ **ČOŇ?**

ČONAY Uyg. 13th c. **Čonay** [Çonai] (DTS, EUTS).

ČONČU Alt.(Tel.) 19th c. **Čonču** [Чончу], an informant (Potanin IV, 321, 328).

ČONJAX Hak. 19th-20th c. **Čonjaχ** [Чончах] (HRS 352). ✧ 'Little Strong; Little Chief'? ⇨ **ČOŇ?** + dim. *-čaq.*

ČONJÏQQA Hak.(Sag.) **Čonjïqqa** [Чонцыкка (Павел)] (Proben IX, 557).

ČONKE Kzk. 19th c. **Čonke / Čoňke** [Чонке] (SODž. 18). ⇨ **ČOŇ** + suff. *-ke.*

ČONMET Chuv. 18th-19th c. **Čonmet** [Чонметъ] (Magn. 93). ⇨ **ČOŇ** + suffixoid *-met.*

ČOŇ Yürük 1543 **Čon** [چون / Çon], from the Yürüks of Kocacık, Turkey (Gökb., Rum. 103, 240); Chuv. 18th-19th c. **Čon-bay** [Чонбай] (Magn. 93); Chuv. 18th-19th c. **Čon-batïr** [Чонбатырь] (Magn. 93); Chuv.

18th-19th c. **Čon-murza** [Чонмурза] (Magn. 93). ✧ 'Big, strong, powerful; elder; chief; magnate' cf. Chag., Kirg., NUyg.(Tar.) *čoñ* 'gross, erhaben, mächtig' (Radl. III, 2016), Kirg. *čoñ* 'большой, огромный, великий; старший; начальник' (Jud.), Hak. *čon?* 'народ, публика; население города' (HRS), Kzk. *šoñ* 'Ülken, däw, zor, žuwan; šonžar, iri feodal' (QTTS), Kzk. *şon (šoñ?)* 'Büyük, kocaman, yüksek; Zengin, mevki sahibi kimse' (KzTS). <Chin. See also **BÜYÜK, EREM, EVREN, YOΓAN, KÄNDÄL, MÄÑKÄ.**

ČOÑ-QARAČ Kirg. 19th c. **Čoñ-qarač / Qarač** [Чонъ-Карачъ] (Valihanov, Soč. 359). ✧ 'Big Qarač; Big Black Man'. ⇨ ČOÑ + QARAČ.

ČOÑ-QOYČU Kirg. **Čoñ-qoyču** [Чоӊ Койчу], Kerim's new name (Jud. 81). ✧ 'Chief shepherd' (Jud. 81). ⇨ ČOÑ + QOYČÏ.

ČOÑ-MURUN Kzk. 18th c. - 19th c. **Čoñ-murun / Čon-murun** [Чон-мурун] (Tynyšp. 71, 75). ✧ 'Big nose'. ⇨ ČOÑ + MURUN.

ČOÑKE see **ČONKE**

ČOPAN see **ČOBAN**

ČOPAN-ATA Kirg. 19th c. **Čopan-ata** [Чопанъ-ата], ancestor of sheep (Potanin II, 153). ⇨ ČOBAN + ATA.

ČOR Uyg. **Čor** [Çor] (EUTS); Chuv. 18th-19th c. **Čor-bay** [Чорбай] (Magn. 93); Türk 7th c. - 9th c. **Čur** [čur / Çur] (DTS, ETY I, 128, 139 II, 134, 135, 136 III, 117, 120, 144); Bashk. 1792 **Čur** [Чур Кинзягулов] (MIB V, 559); Kkalp. 1740 **Čur-aγasï** [Чуръ-Агасы], from the Mañγït tribe (Hanykov, Poezdka 19, MIKk. 208); Chuv. 18th-19th c. **Čur-bay** [Чурбай] (Magn. 94); Kzk. 19th c. **Čur-bala** [Чурбала] (SOK 72); Türk. / Uyg. 8th c. - 9th c. **Čur-tegin** [čur tegin] (DTS). ✧ I. 'A high dignity among the Türks' cf. *čur* 'eine hohe Beamtenwürde' (Radl. III, 2172). Used also as a secondary component of male names (see comp. *čor*); II. 'Period, time' cf. Tat. *čor* 'период, этап, стадия; эпоха' (TatRS). See also **TOQTO-ČUR(?).**

ČOR-BULAT Chuv. 18th-19th c. **Čor-bulat (<Čora-bulat?)** [Чорбулатъ] (Magn. 93). ⇨ ČOR/ČURA + BULAT.

ČORA see **ČURA**

ČORA-BAŠ Chuv. 18th-19th c. **Čora-baš** [Чорабашъ] (Magn. 93). ⇨ ČURA + BAŠ.

ČORA-PULAT Chuv. 18th-19th c. **Čora-pulat** [Чорапулатъ] (Magn. 93). ⇨ ČORA + BULAT.

ČORAXA Hak. 19th-20th c. **Čoraχa** [Чораха] (HRS 352). ✧ 'Gopher; prairie-dog' (HRS 352).

ČORAY Hak. 19th-20th c. **Čoray** [Чорай], fem. (HRS 356).

ČORAQ see **ČURAQ**

ČORAQAY Chuv. 18th-19th c. **Čorakay / Čorakey** [Чоракай, Чоракей] (Magn. 93). ⇨ ČURA + suff. -*qay*.

ČORAL Hak. 19th-20th c. **Čoral** [Чорал] (HRS 352).

ČORAN Hak. 19th-20th c. **Čoran** [Чоранъ] (HRS 352).

ČORΓO Alt. 19th-20th c. **Čorγo** [Чорго], fem. (OjrRS 214). ✧ 'The spout of the teapot' (OjrRS 214).

ČORÏÑ Hak. 19th-20th c. **Čorïñ** [Чорынъ] (HRS 352).

ČORLÏ Trkm. 20th c. **Čorlï** [Čorlï] (Zaj. 1971, 333); Trkm. 20th c. **Čorlï** [Чорлы] (TrkmRS 736). ✧ 'Dirty' cf. Trkm. *čorlï* 'грязный' (TrkmRS).

ČORNAP Hak. 19th-20th c. **Čornap** [Чорнап] (HRS 352).

ČORTAN Kuman 1341 **Čortan** [Dominus dictus Chortan de Peturd], from the Kumans in Hungary (Pesty-Ortvay IV, 70); Kirg. **Čorton** [Чортон] (Jud. 62); Kzk. 19th c. **Šortan** [Шортанъ] (AOP 66); Kzk. 19th c. **Šortan-bay** [Шортанбай] (AOP 78); Kzk. 19th c. **Šortan-bay** [چون / Шортанъ-бай] (AUK Dobavl. 9); Kzk. 19th c. **Šortan-bay** [Шортанъ-бай], originating from the Istek tribe (Potanin, Pred. 112); Kkalp. 20th c. **Šortan-bay** [Шортанбай] (KkRS 776); Kzk. **Šortan-bay / Šortan-bay-qoža** [Шортан Баи] (Proben III, 43 /55/); Kzk. 19th c. **Šortom-bay (<Šortan-bay)** [Шортомбай] (AOO 6). ✧ 'Pike, eel' cf. Turk. *čortan* 'der Aal' (Radl. III, 2021), Alt., Kirg. *čorton* 'der Hecht' (Radl. III, 2021), Kzk., Hak. *šortan* 'der Hecht' (Radl. IV, 1029).

ČORTON see **ČORTAN**

ČOSUN Uyg. **Čosun** [Çosun] (EUTS).

ČOŠÏ Kzk. 19th c. **Čošï-bay** [Чошебай] (SOV 80).

ČOŠUP Kzk. 19th c. **Čošup-pay** [Чошуппай] (SOK 20).

ČOT Alt. 19th-20th c. **Čot** [Чот] (OjrRS 210); Kzk. 19th c. **Čot-bay** [Чотбаевъ] (SKSO VIII, 219); Kzk. 19th c. **Čot-bay** [Чотбай] (SODž. 66). ✧ I. 'Counting board'? <R. *sč'ot, sč'oty* (счёт, счёты) 'counting; counting board'; II. 'Hoe, hack'? cf. NUyg.(Tar.) *čot* 'die Hacke' (Radl. III, 2025).

ČOTÏMAY Karg. **Čotïmay** (Katanov: ZIRGOÊtn. XIII, vyp. III, 194); Karg. **Čōtïmay** [Чотымаi] (Proben IX, 660).

ČOTÏN Kzk. 19th c. **Čotïn** [Чотенъ] (SODž. 102).

ČOTO Tat.(Sib.)? 1638 **Čoto-tayša** [Чото тайша] (Miller, Ist. Sib. II, 110, 111).

ČOTTŌYUQ Yak. **Čottōyuq** [Чоттоjук] (Pek.).

ČŌČO Yak. **Čōčo** [Чочо] (Pek.).

ČŌLUOP Yak. **Čōluop-uola** [Чолуоп], byname of a singer (Pek.).

ČŌTÏMAY see **ČOTÏMAY**

ČÖGDÖNÖ Yak. **Čögdönö / Čögdöñö** [Чöгдöн(н)ö], Omolon's best friend (Pek.).

ČÖKČÖYDÖN see **ÏTÏQ-ČÖKČÖYDÖN-UDAΓAN**

ČÖKÄY Uyg. **Čökäy** [Çökäi] (EUTS).

ČÖKÄYÄÑ Tuv. 19th c. **Čökäyäñ** [Чöкäjäн], fem. (Proben IX, 55).

ČÖKELİK Trkm. 20th c. **Čökelik** [Čökelik] (Zaj. 1971, 331); Trkm. 20th c. **Čökelik** [Чокелик] (TrkmRS 738). ✧ 'Dairy product' cf. Trkm. *čökelik* 'чокелик (молочный продукт)' (TrkmRS).

ČÖKEMEN Kzk. 19th c. **Čökemen** [Абдулла Чокеменов] (AUK 440); Kzk. 19th c. **Šökemen** [Шокеменъ] (AOA 66). ✧ 'Bunch of grass'? < Kzk. *šökö* 'der Grasbüschel' (Radl. IV, 1035). + suff. *-men*?

ČÖKÖT Yak. **Čököt** [Чöкöт] (Pek.).

ČÖQΪ Uyg. **Čöqϊ** [Çökı] (EUTS).

ČÖLBÖ Yak. **Čölbö** [Чöлбö] (Pek.).

ČÖLKŬK Yak. **Čölkŭk** [Чöлкӱк] (Pek.). ✧ 'Swollen, bloated, puffed' < *čölküy+ŭk*, cf. Yak. *čölküy-* 'отекать' (Pek.).

ČÖMČÖRÜYÄ Yak. **Čömčörüyä** [Кӱн-Чöмчöрÿйä], fem. (Pek.). ✧ 'Moving, behaving quickly, lightly' cf. Yak. *čömčörüy-* 'держаться легко, бойко и опрятно' (Pek.) + suff. *-ä*. See also **KŬN-ČÖMČÖRÜYÄ.**;

ČÖMČÜKÄYDÄN Yak. **Čömčükäydän** [Чöмчÿкäйдäн], fem. (Pek.).

ČÖMEN Turk. **Čömen-oɣlu**, a Zeybek (Kúnos 1891, 119). ✧ 'Heap; hut, shed' cf. Turk. *çömen* 'çakıl taşlarından yapılan yığın; ot ve mısır saplarından yapılan küçük yığın; Bostan bekçileri için yapılan kon şeklinde kulübe; çimen' (DS).

ČÖMÖRDŬR Yak. **Čömördŭr** [Чöмöрдÿр] (Pek.). ✧ Derived from Yak. *čömör+lŭr* cf. *čömör* 'медленная и безшумная походка' (Pek.).

ČÖÑÑE Trkm. 20th c. **Čöññe** [Čöŋŋe] (Zaj. 1971, 333); Trkm. 20th c. **Čöññe** [Чонга] (TrkmRS 738). ✧ 'Stupid, silly' (Zaj. 1971), cf. Trkm. *čöññe* 'слабый (о зрении); тупой, глупый' (TrkmRS).

ČÖPPÖLLÖN Yak. **Čöppöllön** [Чöппöллöн] (Pek.).

ČÖRÖK Yak. **Čörök** [Чöрöк] (Pek.).

ČÖRÖKÖ Yak. **Čörökö** [Чöрöкö], a famous Tatar from the ulus (district) of Nyurbinsk (Pek.).

ČÖČÖY Alt. 19th-20th c. **Čöčöy** [Чööчöй], fem. (OjrRS 214). ✧ 'Cup' (OjrRS 214).

ČÖRÖÑÖ Yak. **Čöröñö** [Чöрöнö] (Pek.).

ČÖTİ Alt. 19th-20th c. **Čöti-bek** [Чööтибек] (OjrRS 210).

ČU Uyg. 7th c. - 9th c. **Ču-tutuq** [ču tutuq] (DTS).

ČUBA-YϊQMϊŠ see **ČOBA-YϊQMϊŠ**

ČUBAY Tat. 1633 **Čubay** [Кочербайко Чубаев] (MIB I, 70); Bashk. 1675 **Čubay** [Умир Чюбаев] (MIB I, 200); Bashk. 1761 **Čubay** [Чубай Акбазанов] (MIB IV/1, 215). ⇨ **ČUBA?** + suff. *-y*?

ČUBAQ Kirg. **Čubaq** [Чубак] (Jud. 58, 421, 693). ✧ 'Sunbeam, ray of sunlight' cf. Kirg. *čubaq* 'луч (солнца)' (Jud.). See also **OY-ČUWAQ.**

ČUBALΪ Turk.? 1540 **Čubalï-bey**, attacked Majláth in Transylvania (Urechi-Picot 344). ⇨ **ČUBA** + suff. *-lï.*

ČUBAR-AYɣΪR Kzk. / Kirg.? 19th c. **Čubar-ayɣïr** [Чубарайгыръ], among the legendary ancestors of the Kazaks (Potanin II, 149); *EN:* Kzk. / Kirg.? 19th c. **Čobar-ayɣïr** [Çobar-Aygır], a clan of the Uwaq-girey tribe of the Middle Horde (Orta Žüz) (Togan, BTT 40); *TN:* Kzk. **Šϊbar-ayɣïr** [Schybar Aigyr / Шыбар-аіɓыр], a territory bearing the name of a stallion (Proben III, 231 /272/). ✧ 'Grey / iron-grey stallion'; 'Piebald stallion' (Radloff). ⇨ **ČOBAR + AYɣΪR.**

ČUČU Karakh. 11th c. **Čǔču** [Çuçu], a Turkic poet (DTS, MK/Atalay 837).

ČUJAX Hak. 19th-20th c. **Čujaχ** [Чучах], fem. (HRS 356). ✧ I. 'Small diaper, small nappy'? cf. Alt. *čǔčaq* 'eine kleine Windel' (Radl. III, 2181); II. 'Little coat'? cf. Tuv. *čǔčaq* 'пальтишко, пальтецо (детское)' (TuvRS).

ČUDAYAQ Karg. **Čudayaq** [Чудаякъ] (Katanov: ZIRGOÊtn. XVII, vyp. III, 165); Karg. **Čudayaq** [Чудаjак] (Proben IX, 659).

ČUɣA Turk. 14th c. **Čuɣa** [چوغه / Çuğa], Saruhan Beɣ's brother (Uzunçarş., Anad. 31, Erol II, 107). ✧ 'Brave, courageous, bold' (Erol II).

ČUɣAL Tat.(Sib.) 1632 **Čuɣal** [Евгаштык Чугалов] (Miller, Ist. Sib. II, 398). ✧ 'Keen/sharp thinking (man)' cf. Bashk. *soɣol* 'глубокомыслящий' (BRS).

ČUɣALAY Bashk. 1758 **Čuɣalay** [Канзеи Чюгалаев] (MIB IV/1, 168); Bashk. 1765 **Čuɣalay** [Алмаметь Чюгалаев] (MIB IV/1, 313). ✧ 'Clever' cf. Bashk. *soɣol* 'глубокомыслящий' (BRS). ⇨ **ČUɣAL** + suff. *-ay.*

ČUɣLAN Karakh. **Čuɣlan** [Çuglan] (MK/Atalay 837).

ČUɣUN-ČUɣUTTAY Yak. **Čuɣun-čuɣuttay** [Чугун Чугуттаi], one of Ulü-toyon's four daughters (Pek.).

ČUY-BAŠ Kzk. 1846 **Čuy-baš** [бий Чуйбаш Япанов], a biy (MKOP 155). ✧ 'Hard-head, headstrong'? cf. Bashk. *suy* 'твёрдый (о дереве)' (BRS). ⇨ **ČUY + BAŠ.**

ČUY-TAŠ Kzk. 1846 **Čuy-taš** [бий Кубул Чуйташев], a biy (MKOP 152); Kzk. 1786 **Čuy-taš-batïr** [Чуйташ батыр] (MIK IV, 73). ✧ 'Hard stone'. ⇨ **ČUY + TAŠ.**

ČUYɣAN Tat. 1675 **Čuyɣan** / **Čüygän?** [стрѣлец Андрюша Чюйганов] (Kungursk. akty 35).

ČUYUT Bashk. 1623 **Čuyut-qul** [Чуюткул] (Miller, Ist. Sib. II, 299).

ČUQAJΪ Turk. 1516 **Čuqajï** [Çukacı Karagöz] (Gökb., Ed. 123). ✧ 'Having (or making) flask' cf. Turk. *çuka* چوقه 'Reisekrug mit enger Oefnung, Flasche' (Zenk.).

ČUQAL Bashk. 1708 **Čuqal** [Уряк Чукалев] (MIB I, 234). ✧ 'Armour, blazon for a horse' cf. Chag., Turk. *čuqal* 'Panzer, Panzer für ein Pferd' (Radl. III, 2165).

ČUQTAɣAN Kzk. 19th c. **Čuqtaɣan** [Чуктаганъ Лифасовъ] (Grod., Pril. 100).

ČUQUS Hak.(Blt.) 19th-20th c. **Čuqus** [Чукус] (Katanov, Otč. 9).

ČUL   Khazar 1016 **Čul / Čulï** [Georgius Tzulus] (Golden 177-81).

ČUL-QAZAR   Uzb. 19th c. **Čul-qazar** [Чульказаръ] (SKSO III, 20). ⇨ **ČUL + QAZAR.**

ČULAX see **ČOLAQ**

ČULAQ see **ČOLAQ**

ČULAN see **AQAN**

ČUMAQ see **ČOMAQ**

ČUMAQQAY   Bashk. 1754 **Čumaqay** [Алламрат Чюмъкаев] (MIB IV/1, 83). ✧ 'Little mace, club'. ⇨ **ČUMAQ?** + dim. suff. *-ay / -qay?*

ČUMAN   Bashk. **Čuman** [Чюман] (MIB I, 192); Bashk. 1663 **Čuman** [Чюман Аккочкаров] (MIB I, 176); Bashk. 1695 **Čuman** [Кудабердей Чюманов] (MIB I, 90); Kzk. 19th c. **Čuman** [Шаифъ Чумановъ] (Grod., Pril. 170); Kzk. 19th c. **Čuman** (Levchine 356); Tat. 1662 **Šuman** [Шуманъ] (DAI IV, 284). ✧ 'Lazy, sluggish, sluggard, laggard' cf. Chag. *čuman* 'faul, nachlässig' (Radl. III, 2188).

ČUMAŚ   Tat. 1661 **Čumaš** [Чюмашко Калмеев (Колмеев?)] (MIB I, 159). ⇨ **?** + suff. *-š?*

ČUMČI   Trkm. 1804 **Čumči-baba-serdar** [Чумче-Баба-сердар (Баба-сердар)], from the Yomut tribe (MIT II, 364).

ČUMEY   Chuv. 1739 **Čumey** [Чумѣевъ] (Alatyr. 146).

ČUMIČ   Tat.(Sib.) 1681 **Čumič(ka), Čumič** [Чумичка Ишметевъ] (DAI VIII, 177). ✧ 'Ladle, scoop' cf. Tat. *čumič* 'der Schöpflöffel' (Radl. III, 2189). + suff. *-ka?*

ČUMIQ   Bashk. **Čumïq / Čümik?** [Ракай Чумиков] (MIB V, 170).

ČUNA   Tat.(Sib.) 1634 **Čuna** [Азбей Чуна] (Miller, Ist. Sib. II, 410).

ČUNAY   Bashk. 1760 **Čunay / Čünäy?** [Чюнай Такаев] (MIB IV/2, 28). ⇨ **ČUNA?** + suff. *-y.*

ČUNEY   Hak. 19th-20th c. **Čuney / Čüney?** [Чуней / Чÿней], fem. (HRS 356, Butanaev).

ČUÑUS   Alt. 19th-20th c. **Čuñus** [Чунус], fem. (OjrRS 214).

ČUOČAS   Yak. **Čuočas** [Чуочас] (Pek.).

ČUONA I.   Yak. **Čuona** [Чуона], the youngest of the three daughters of *Ïdäl, Russian emperor Irod [Igor?] in the past (Pek.).

ČUONA II.   Yak. **Čuona / J̌uona** [Чуона / Цуона] (Pek.). ✧ Iona (R. male name).

ČUORDA   Yak. **Čuorda / Čuordaqïs** [Чуорда / Чуордакыс] (Pek.).

ČUORDAQÏS see **ČUORDA**

ČUPTAN   Alt. 19th c. **Čuptan** [Чуптан] (Verb., In. 101).

ČUR see **ČOR**

ČURA   Chuv. 18th-19th c. **Čora** [Чора] (Magn. 93); Tat. **Čora / Čora-batïr** [چورا / چورا باطر], in a Tatar historical legend in verses (IOAIÊK (Dobavlenie) XV, 286); Chuv. 18th-19th c. **Čora-bay** [Чорабай] (Magn. 93); Crm. **Čora-batïr** [Чора Батыр], hero in the Čora-batïr-legend (Proben VII, 21, 124, etc., Radl. I, 654); Chuv. 18th-19th c. **Čora-murza** [Чорамурза] (Magn. 93); Chuv. 18th-19th c. **Čora-pay** [Чорапай] (Magn. 93); Bulg. 1519/20 **Čura** [جورا] (Jusupov, text 4); Chuv., Tat.? 19th c. **Čura** [Чура] (Zolotn. 122, 160); Tat. **Čura** [Чюра Кадышевъ] (PSRL XIII, 125); Tat. 1525 **Čura** [Чюра], a prince in Kazan (PSRL VIII, 271); Bashk. 1706 **Čura** [Чюра Кураев] (MIB III, 26); Bashk. 1735 **Čura** [Чура Кошаевъ], a prince (Vel.-Zern., Bašk. 20); Bashk. 1787 **Čura** [Чура (Чюра) Чиканов] (MIB V, 214); Chuv. 18th-19th c. **Čura-bay** [Чурабай] (Magn. 94); Kzk. **Čura-bay** [Чурабай] (Sb. Syr-D. IX, 56); Kzk. 19th c. **Čura-bay** [Умбетъ Чурабаевъ] (Grod., Pril. 144); Chuv. 18th-19th c. **Čura-batïr** [Чурабатырь] (Magn. 94); Kzk. **Čura-batïr**, Narek's son in a tale (Vámbéry, Vázlatok 324); Bashk. 1735 **Čura-γul** [Чурагулъ Чирикеевъ] (Vel.-Zern., Bašk. 13); Bashk. 18th c. **Čura-γul** [Чурагулъ] (Nepljuev 882); Bashk. 1756 **Čura-γul** [Утей Чурагулов] (MIB IV/1, 123); Bashk. 1756 **Čura-γul** [Утябай Чурагулов] (MIB IV/1, 123); Bashk. 1757 **Čura-γul** [Чурагул Минеев] (MIB IV/1, 142); Bashk. 1787 **Čura-γul** [Култубулат Чурагулов] (MIB V, 214); Chuv. 18th-19th c. **Čura-qan** [Чураканъ] (Magn. 94); Chuv. 18th-19th c. **Čura-murza** [Чурамурза] (Magn. 94); Uzb. 19th c. **J̌ora** [Джура] (SKSO III, 160); Uzb. 19th c. **J̌ora** [Джура Майлибаевъ] (SKSO III, 160); Uzb. 19th c. **J̌ora** [Джура Майлибаевъ] (SKSO III, 160); Uzb. 20th c. **J̌ora** [Жўра] (UzbRS); Uzb. 20th c. **J̌ora** [Жўра], fem. (UzbRS); Uzb. 20th c. **J̌ora** [Джура] (UzbRS 161); Uzb. 20th c. **J̌ora** [Джура], fem. (UzbRS 161); Uzb. 19th c. **J̌ora-bay** [Джурабай] (SKSO III, 8, 152); Uzb. 19th c. **J̌ora-bay** [Джурабай Таировъ] (SKSO III, 152); Kzk. 19th c. **J̌ura-bay** [Ǧurabai] (Mende 70); Kzk. 19th c. **J̌ura-bay** [Джурабай Турдыбаевъ] (SKSO IV, otd. II, 32, 34); NUyg. 19th c. **J̌ura-bek** [Djura Bek], a prince (Hedin, En färd I, 66); Kzk. 19th c. **J̌ura-biy** [Джурабій Касамбаевъ] (TV 1876, 144); Chuv. 18th-19th c. **Šora** [Шора] (Magn. 95); Kkalp. 20th c. **Šora-χan** [Шорахан] (KkRS 776); Nog. 20th c. **Šora-uwlï** [Али Мурза Шора увлы / Алимурза Шураев], father of one of Baskakov's informants from the aul of Qaraγas (Bask., Nog. 144); Kkalp. **Šura** [Шура], in a Karakalpak legend (Divaev 117 etc.); Kzk. 19th c. **Šura-batïr** [Шура-батыръ], a hero in a legend (AUK 295). ✧ I. 'Slave; farmer, peasant; warrior, soldier; hero; friend' (Sattarov), cf. Bashk. *sura* 'слуга; батыр, служащий при ханах и военачальниках' (BRS/Uraksin), Uzb. *jora* 'друг, приятель' (UzbRS); II. '(Land)Lord, chief' cf. Kzk. PN *Šora* (Žanuzakov), Kar.(T.) *čora* 'der Arbeiter' (Radl. III, 2019), Kzk. *şora* 'Eskiden verilen mevki-makam adı' (KzTS), Kkalp.

šora 'совет, председатель аулсовета; лебеда; избалованный' (Bask., Kkalp. 395). Used also as a secondary (hypochoristic) component of male names. See also **BAY-ČURA, Bİ-ČURA, BİK-ČURA, İSEN-ČURA, YAN-ČURA, KİL-ČURA, QOL-ČURA, QUTLU-ČURA, NAΓAY-ČURA.**

ČURA-GİLDİ see **ČURA-KİLDE**

ČURA-KELDİ   Bashk. 1740 **Čura-gildi** [Чюрагилди Кудашев] (MIB I, 454).

ČURA-KİLDE   Chuv. 18th-19th c. **Čura-kilde** [Чуракилда] (Magn. 94). ✤ 'Slave/farmer came (=was born)'. ⇨ **ČURA + KELDİ.**

ČURAY   Trkm. 19th c. **Čuray** [Донай Чураевъ] (Ščeglov I, 357); Chuv. 1739 **Čuray** [Чураевъ] (Alatyr. 146); Tat.(Sib.) 1598 **Čuray** [Чюрай], a prince in Siberia from the family of Küčüm (AI II, 3); Bashk. 1745 **Čuray** [Чюрай Илькеев] (MIB III, 426); Bashk. 1754 **Čuray** [Чюрай Айдаров] (MIB IV/1, 84); Bashk. 1749 **Suray** [Урай Сураев] (MIB III 465). ✤ 'Brave little warrior, champion'. ⇨ **ČURA** + suff. *-y.*

ČURAQ   Chuv. 18th-19th c. **Čorak** [Чоракъ] (Magn. 93); Chuv. 18th-19th c. **Čurak** [Чуракъ] (Magn. 94); Bashk. 1757 **Čuraq** [Чурак Кузянов] (MIB IV/1, 157); Bashk. 1776 **Čuraq** [Кутан Чураков] (MIB V, 42, 43); Bashk. 1788 **Čuraq** [Кузбаш Чураков] (MIB V, 233); Chuv. 18th-19th c. **Šorak** [Шоракъ] (Magn. 95). ⇨ **ČURA** + suff. *-q.* See also **ČON-ČURAQ.**

ČURAQAY   Chuv. 18th-19th c. **Čurakay** [Чуракай] (Magn. 94); Tat.(Mish.) 1755 **Čuraqay** [Чюракай Кадырметев] (MIB IV/1, 93); Bashk. 1740 **Čuraqay** [Илчигул Чуракаев] (MIB I, 400); Bashk. 1745 **Čuraqay** [Чюракай Тюркеев] (MIB III, 426); Bashk. 1759 **Čuraqay** [Чуракай Касимов] (MIB IV/2, 22); Bashk. 1763 **Čuraqay** [Шерып Чюракаев] (MIB IV, 271); Bashk. 1783 **Čuraqay** [Чуракай (Чюракай) Шарымов] (MIB V, 148); Bashk. 1784, 1785 **Čuraqay** [Чуракай (Чюракай) Заитов] (MIB V, 164-166); Bashk. 1785 **Čuraqay** [Валит Чюракаев] (MIB V, 166, 168). ✤ 'Dear little friend' cf. Tat. PN *Čuraqay* (Sattarov). ⇨ **ČURA** + dim.-hypoc. *-qay.*

ČURAMAN   Bashk. 1756 **Čuraman** [Кадраш Чюраманов] (MIB IV/1, 119); Bashk. 1756 **Čuraman** [Абызгильды Чюраманов] (MIB IV/1, 123); Bashk. 1756 **Čuraman** [Чюраман Атангулов] (MIB IV/1, 128); Chuv. 18th-19th c. **Čurman** (<Čuraman) [Чурманъ] (Magn. 94). ⇨ **ČURA** + suff. *-man.*

ČURAŠ   Bashk. 1675 **Čuraš** [Чюраш Аювчин] (MIB I, 200); Bashk. 1706 **Čuraš** [Чюраш Катлыбаев] (MIB III, 30); Bashk. 1706 **Čuraš** [Чюраш] (MIB III, 22); Bashk. 1709 **Čuraš** [Чюрашев] (MIB I, 264); Bashk. 1730 **Čuraš** [Казакай Чюрашев] (MIB III, 276); Bashk. 1734 **Čuraš** [Чюраш Келдышев] (MIB III, 325); Bashk. 1737 **Čuraš** [Чюраш] (MIB I, 314); Bashk. 1753 **Čuraš** [Чураш Карабаев] (MIB IV/1, 68); Bashk. 1763 **Čuraš** [Чураш Акичев] (MIB IV/1, 271); Bashk. 1764 **Čuraš** [Чюраш Карабаев] (MIB IV/1, 299); Bashk. 1770 **Čuraš** [Чураш Акысев] (MIB IV/1, 341); Bashk. 1791 **Čuraš** [Чураш Таиров] (MIB V, 313). ⇨ **ČURA?** + suff. *-š.*

ČUREMEŠ? Chuv. 18th-19th c. **Čuremeš / Čüremeš?** [Чуремешъ] (Magn. 94).

ČURΓUQ Karg. **Čurγuq** [Чургукъ] (ZIRGOÊtn. XVII, vyp. III, 164).

ČURÏ Uyg. 12th c.-14th c. **Čurï / Čüri?** (Radl., USp. 54, DTS).

ČURÏP Kzk. 19th c. **Čurïp-pay?** [Чуриптпай] (SOK 204).

ČURLÏQ Trkm. **Čurlïq-mergen** [Tchourliq Merguène], forefather of the Qoñrat tribe (Abulg./Desm. 53).

ČURU Alt. 19th-20th c. **Čuru** [Чуру], fem. (OjrRS 214).

ČUT Kzk. 19th c. **Čut-bay** [Чутбай] (SKSO VIII, 230); Kzk. 19th c. **Čut-bay** [Чутбай Тагаевъ] (SKSO VIII, 232). ⇨ **ČOT?**

ČUTAY see **ČUTÏY**

ČUTÏY Bashk. 1785 **Čutay / Čutïy** [Чутай (Чутый) Енабардин (Енабердин)] (MIB V, 145, 170, 199, etc.); Kzk. 19th c. **Čutïy / Čutiy / Čutey?** [Чутей] (SODž. 12). ✤ I. 'Shaft of light' cf. Bulg. PN *Čutay/Čutiy* (Sattarov); II. 'Dazzling; very beautiful' (Sattarov after Zäkiev).

ČUWAQAY   Bashk. 1779 **Čuwaqay** [Султангул Чувакаев] (MIB V, 94). ✤ 'Clear (weather)'? cf. Tat. dial. *čuaq* 'погожий, ясный' (TatRS). + dim. *-qay.*

ČUWAŠ Chuv. 18th-19th c. **Čuvaš** [Чувашъ] (Magn. 94); Bashk. 1708 **Čuwaš** [Ишалей Чювашев] (MIB I, 237); Bashk. 1737 **Čuwaš** [Кусмяк Чувашев] (MIB I, 324); Bashk. 1742 **Čuwaš** [Сагыр Чювашев] (MIB I, 486); Bashk. 1751 **Čuwaš** [Абдулгази Чювашев] (MIB IV/1, 51); Bashk. 1760 **Čuwaš** [Кинзекей Чувашев] (MIB IV/1, 187); Bashk. 1762 **Čuwaš** [Яун Чувашев] (MIB IV/1, 244); Bashk. 1777 **Čuwaš** [Мугаш Чувашев] (MIB V, 54); Bashk. 1777 **Čuwaš** [Яун Чувашев] (MIB V, 63); Bashk. 1780 **Čuwaš** [Муаш Чувашев] (MIB V, 106); Kzk. 1842 **Čuwaš** [Матасъ Чувашевъ], from the Middle Horde (Orta Žüz) (Konšin, Mat. V, 22); Kzk. 19th c. **Čuwaš** [Ташъ Магомед Чувашев] (Grod., Pril. 31); Kzk. 19th c. **Čuwaš** [Чувашъ] (AOP 2); Bashk. 1734 **Čuwaš-bay** [Чувашбай Мусинъ], a tarχan (Vel.-Zern., Bašk. 27); Bashk. 1788 **Čuwaš-bay** [Чувашбай (Чювашбай) Девлетбаков], from the village Čuwašbayeva (MIB V, 235); Kzk. 19th c. **Šuaš / Šuwaš** (AOO 34). ✤ 'Chuvash' (Ethnonym) <R. *cuvaš* <Chuv. *čïvaš* <Tat. *jïwaš* 'low-key, modest' cf. Radl. IV, 133. See also **AQ-ČUWAŠ.**

ČUWAŠAY   Bashk. 1707 **Čuwašay** [Ишалей

Чювашаев] (MIB III, 39); Bashk. 1710 **Čuwašay** [Чювашай] (MIB III, 55); Bashk. 1764 **Čuwašay** [Чувашай (Чювашай) Кучкильдин] (MIB IV/1, 303); Bashk. 1765 **Čuwašay** [Яун Чювашаев] (MIB IV/1, 312); Bashk. 1770 **Čuwašay** [Чувашай Юнусов] (MIB IV/1, 350). ⇨ **ČUWAŠ** + suff. -*ay*.

ČUČUĠUS Yak. **Čučuɣus** [Чучугус], a shaman (Pek.).

ČUDA Yak. **Čuda** [Чуда] (Pek.). ✧ Iuda (R.) (Pek.).

ČŪQA Alt. 19th-20th c. **Čūqa** [Чуука], fem. (OjrRS 214).

ČŪSQU Yak. **Čūsqu** [Чуску] (Pek.).

ČUČELEY see **ČUČÜLEY**

ČUČÜK Chag. 16th c. **Čučük-mirza** [Чучук-мирза] (Ivanov 290); Chag.? **Čučük-begim** [چوچوك بيكيم], fem. (Le Coq, Ind. 3 (<Babur name)). ✧ 'Sweet' cf. Chag. *čüčük* 'süss, fade' (Radl. III, 2199).

ČUČÜLEY Bashk. 1750 **Čučeley** [Князь Чючелеев] (MIB III, 473); Tat.(Sib.) 1661 **Čučüley** [Чючюлей (Чучүлей)], Küčüm's grand-son (Miller, Ist. Sib. II, 546). ✧ 'Sweet'? cf. Chag. *čüčü(lük)* 'die Süssigkeit, die Fadheit', *čüčü(män)* 'süss' (Radl. III, 2200) + suff. -*ley* / -*dey*?

ČÜDÄKKÄY Tuv. 19th c. **Čüdäkkäy** [Чүдäккäi], a shaman from the Tülüš tribe (Proben IX, 100). ✧ 'Impure; abominable, disgusting, nasty' cf. Tuv. *čüdek* 'id.' (TuvRS), Shor *čüdäk* / *čüdäɣ* / *čüdüɣ* 'Unreinlichkeit; die Epidemie, das Viehsterben; schlecht, arm, ungesund' (Radl. III, 2198) + suff. -*key* / -*käy*.

ČÜDÜG see **ČÜDÜK**

ČÜDÜK Tuv. 19th c. **Čüdük-ōl** / **Čüdüg-ōl** [Чүдүк-ол] (Proben IX, 106). ✧ 'Bad, poor, weak, unhealthy' Shor *čüdäk* / *čüdäɣ* / *čüdüɣ* 'Unreinlichkeit; die Epidemie, das Viehsterben; schlecht, arm, ungesund' (Radl. III, 2198).

ČÜGIN Yak. 1680 **Čügin** / **Čügün** / **Čuɣun(ko)?** [Чюгинъ (Чюгунъ / Чугунко) Бодоевъ], a prince (PSRL ? VIII, 10, 244, 268).

ČÜY Bashk. 1740 **Čüy-eke** [Сюяргул Чюекин] (MIB I, 381). ✧ I. 'Nail, spike; chock, wedge' cf. Crm., Tat. *čüy* 'der Nagel' (Radl. III, 2189), Tat. *čöy* 'клин; чека' (TatRS).

ČÜYŠE Trkm. 20th c. **Čüyše** [Čüyše], fem. (Zaj. 1971, 338). Trkm. 20th c. **Čüyše** [Чуйше], fem. (TrkmRS 740) ✧ 'Glass, bottle' cf. Trkm. *čüyše* 'id.' (TrkmRS) (<P.).

ČÜLÄY Bashk. 1731 **Čüläy** [Ишкей Чюлаев] (MIB III, 293).

ČÜREY Bashk. 1780 **Čürey** [Москов Чюреев] (MIB V, 113).

ČÜRÖK Kirg. **Čürök** [Чүрθк], fem. (Jud. 46). ✧ 'Duck (layer)' cf. Kirg. *čürök* 'чирок; утка (самка)' (Jud.). See also **AY-ČÜRÖK**.

ČÜRÜ see **ČERİ I.**

ČÜRÜČİY Bashk. 1731 **Čürüčiy?** [Кутлугуш Чюрючей] (MIB III, 284). ⇨ **ČİRÜ?** + suff. -*či*.

ČÜRÜK see **ČİRİK**

ČÜRÜKEY Bashk. 1735 **Čürükey** [Суяр Чурюкеев] (Vel.-Zern., Bašk. 12); Bashk. 1738 **Čürükey** [Чюрюкей Азимбетев] (MIB I, 138); Bashk. 1749 **Čürükey** [Чюрюкай Кадырметев] (MIB III, 471); Bashk. 1761 **Čürükey** [Ялчи Чюрюкеев] (MIB IV/1, 195, 208); Bashk. 1773 **Čürükey** [Чурюкей Касымов] (MIB IV/1, 373). ⇨ **ČÜRÜ** + suff. -*key* / -*ey*?

ČÜS-ALDAY Hak.(Kacha) 19th-20th c. **Čüs-alday** [Чүс Алдаi], an old man (Proben IX, 268). ⇨ **YÜZ** + **ALDAY.**

ČÜSTÜK Karg. **Čüstük** [Чүстүк], fem. (Katanov, Otč. 8). ✧ 'Thimble' (Katanov, Otč. 8). See also **QARA-ČÜSTÜK**.

ČÜWEY Bashk. 1735 **Čüwey** [Чювей Девлетлинъ], a tarχan (Vel.-Zern., Bašk. 18).

ČÜŽE Kzk. 19th c. **Čüže** [Чюжэ], a man of Kirghiz origin in a Kazak tale (Potanin, Pred. 112).

J

JABA Yak. **Jaba** [Цаба] (Pek.).

JABA-BĀBA see **JAĠA-BĀBA**

JABAĠA Kzk. 19th c. **Jabaɣa** [Джабага] (Potanin II, 150). ✧ 'Wool(len), rough wool' cf. Kzk. *jabaɣa* 'die im Frühling geschorene Schafwolle' (Radl. IV, 57).

JABBAR Kzk. 19th c. **Jabbar-qul** [Берды Джаббаркуловъ] (SKSO VIII, 200). ✧ 'Powerful, mighty' one of the epithets of Allah (Ahmed) (<Ar.).

JABBAR-BERDİ Chag. 15th c. **Jabbar-berdi-χan** [Джаббаръ-берди-ханъ] (Barth., Ulugb. 75, 114); Tat.(GH) **Jabbār-birdi** [Djabbâr-Birdi], Toqtamïš-qan's (1382-1397) son (Abulg./Desm., 187); Tat.(GH) **Jabār-birdi** [Jabár Birdi], a Dughlatid emir (amir) (Tar. Rashidi 306, 336, 343, etc.); Uzb. 20th c. **Jabbâr-berdi** [Жабборберди] (Begmatov 1984, 202). ✧ 'The All-compeller (Allah) has him/her given'. ⇨ **JABBAR** + **BERDİ.**

JABBAR-BERGÄN Uzb. 20th c. **Jabbâr-bergän** [Жабборберган] (Begmatov 1984, 202). ✧ 'The All-compeller (Allah) has him/her given'. ⇨ **JABBAR** + **BERGEN.** See also **JABBAR-BERDİ.**

JAJAQLÏ see **ČAČAQLÏ**

JADİGER see **YADÏĠAR**

JADÏQ Nog. 16th c.? **Jadïq-χan** / **Yadïq-χan** [Джадик-хан (Ядик)] (Žirm., Epos 445). ✧ 'Peaceful, gracious'? cf. Kzk. *jatïq* 'id.' (Radl. IV, 45).

JADRA Kzk. 19th c. **Jadra** [Дшадра] (SOV 120). ✧

'Splitting of clouds'? cf. Kzk. *jadra* 'das Auseinandergehen der Wolken mit Regen' (Radl. IV, 47).

JAFAR Selj.? 11th c. **Jafar-tegin** (Ibn al-Athīr/Tornb. IX, 111, 133-134); Kzk. 19th c. **Japar** [Джапаръ] (SOK 44, 160, 182); Kzk. 19th c. **Japar** [Джапаръ] (SOV 148); Kzk. 19th c. **Japar** [Джапаръ] (SODž. 44); Kzk. 19th c. **Japar** [Джапаръ] (AOAtb. 6, 42); Kzk. 19th c. **Japar** [Джапаръ] (AOP 22); Kzk. 19th c. **Japar** [Джапаръ] (AOK 6); Kirg. **Japar** [Жапар] (Jud 329); Kzk. 19th c. **Japar-bay** [Джапарбай] (SOV 64); Kzk. 19th c. **Japar-bek** [Джапарбекъ] (SOV 32); Kzk. 19th c. **Japar-qul** [Джапаркулъ] (SOV 32); Kzk. 19th c. **Japar-qul** [Джапаркулъ] (SODž. 6); Bashk. 1750 **Yapar** [Япар Урусаев] (MIB III, 473); Bashk. 1757 **Yapar** [Япар Митреев] (MIB IV/1, 142); Bashk. 1761 **Yapar** [Япар Кулкаев] (MIB IV/1, 221); Bashk. 1761 **Yapar** [Калай Япаров] (MIB IV/1, 216); Bashk. 1762 **Yapar** [Тунгун Япаров] (MIB IV/1, 251); Bashk. 1763 **Yapar** [Ямансары Япаров] (MIB IV/2, 45); Bashk. 1714 **Yepar** [Епаров Бигузя] (MIB I, 105); Bashk. 1714 **Yepar** [Епаров Тоиш] (MIB I, 105); Bashk. 1734 **Yepar** [Епар Тохтагулов] (MIB III, 322); Bashk. 1780 **Yepar** [Кузяш Епаров], from Yeparovo (MIB V, 103); Bashk. 1785 **Yepar** [Сафар (Сапар) Епаров] (MIB V, 165); Bashk. 1798 **Yepar** [Епаръ] (PSZRI XXV, 195); Tat. 1558 **Yepar-murza** [Епаръ-мурза] (PSRL XIII, 289). ✦ Djafar / Jafar (Ar.), cf. Ar. *ja'far* 'spring, rivulet' (Ahmed). See also **YAΓAFER**.

JAΓA-BĀBA Yak. **Jaγa-bāba** / **Jäbä-bāba** / **Jägä-bāba** / **Jaba-bāba** / **J'aba-bāba** [Џаба-баба / Џага-баба / Џägä-баба / Џäбä-баба], an old woman in the legends who eats human meat and kidnapps children (Pek.). ✦ 'Witch, sorceress' (<R.) *Jaga-Baba / Baba-jaga.*

JAΓALĪMA Yak. **Jaγalïma-bāy-χotun** [Џаҕалыма], a legendary woman (Pek.). ⇨ **JAΓÏLĪMA.**

JAΓÏLÏN Yak. **Jaγïlïn-bāy-toyon** [Џаҕылын], a legendary man (Pek.).

JAΓÏLTAY Chag. 16th c. **Jaγïltay-biy** [Джагилтай-бий], an emir (Ivanov 310). ⇨ **TAY** or suff. *-tay(1,2)?*

JAΓÏR see **ČAΓRÏ**

JAΓRÏ see **ČAΓRÏ**

JAXRAY Kkalp. 20th c. **Jaχray** [Джахърай] (Bask., Kkalp. 72).

JAY-SERIK Kzk. 19th c. **Jay-serik** [Джайсерикъ] (SOK 278). ✦ I. 'Slow/quiet fellow' cf. Kzk. *cay (VIII.)* 'Yavaş, o kadar değil, acelesiz' (KzTS); II. 'Fellow-comuntry-man; steady/quiet mate' Kzk. *cay (III.)* 'Ev, mesken, mekân; Rahat, sakin' (KzTS); cf. also Kzk. PNs *Žaylïbay, Žaytabar* (Žanuzakov-Esbaeva). ⇨ **JAY + ŠERİK II.** See also **KÜN-SERİK.**

JAY-TABAR Kzk. 19th c. **Jay-tabar** [Джайтабаръ]

(SODž. 32). ✦ I. 'He who will find home (quiet place, calmness)' cf. Kzk. *cay (III.)* 'Ev, mesken, mekân; Rahat, sakin' (KzTS); cf. also Kzk. PNs *Žaytabar* (Žanuzakov-Esbaeva).

JAYAN Trkm. 1510 **Jayan-sultan** [Джайан-султан], from the Ustajlu tribe (MIT II, 55).

JAYİK see **JAYÏQ**

JAYÏQ Kzk. 18th c. - 19th c. **Jayïq** [Джаик] (Tynyšp. 66, 73); Kzk. 19th c. **Jayïq** [Джаекъ] (AOK 168); Kzk. 19th c. **Jayïq** [Джаикъ] (Potanin II, 151). ✦ Ural (river), cf. Kzk. *Jayïq* (Radl. IV, 19).

JAYLAW-BAQ Kzk. 19th c. **Jaylaw-baq** [Джайляобак Тастанбаев] (TV 1878: 116). ⇨ **JAYLAW + BAQ.**

JAKE Chag. 16th c. **Jake** [Джаке] (Ivanov 263, 265).

JAKEY Kzk. 19th c. **Jakey** [Джакей] (AOA 10); Kzk. 19th c. **Jakey** [Джакей] (AOP 10). ⇨ **JAKE?** + dim. hypoc. suff. *-y.*

JAQÏP see **YAQUB**

JAQSÏ see **YAQŠÏ**

JAQSÏLÏQ see **YAQŠÏLÏQ**

JAL-ATÏ Hak. 19th-20th c. **Jal-atï** [Джалаты юКугеть тогъщ] (Titov 191). ✦ I. 'Steely' cf. Hak. PNs *Čalat / Čalatï* 'стальной богатырь [=steely warrior]' (Butanaev); II. 'Flame-hero' / 'Grey-horse'? „Пламя-богатырь на сивомъ конѣ" [=flame-hero on grey horse] (Titov). ⇨ **ČAL + AT.**

JAL-MAUS see **YEL-MOΓUS**

JAL-MENDİ Kzk. 19th c. **Jal-mendi** [Джалменды] (SOK 174). ✦ 'Mane-slave' cf. Chag., Turk., NUyg.(Tar.) *bändä* 'Diener, Sklave' (Radl. IV, 1590), Kzk. *bende* 'Pende fert, Bende' (KzTs) (<P.) *bendeh.* ⇨ **YAL + MENDİ.** See also **XUDAY-BENDE, QARA-MENDİ.**

JAL-MÏRZA see **YAL**

JAL-PETEK Kzk. 19th c. **Jal-petek** [Джалпетекъ] (SODž. 80). ✦ 'Mane - foot clout' cf. Chag. *pätäk* 'die Fusslappen' (Radl. IV, 1248). ⇨ **YAL?**

JALĀM Yak. **Jalām** [Џалам] (Pek.).

JALBĀTÏR see **ĀN-JALBĀTÏR**

JALΓASÏN Uzb. 20th c. **Jalγasïn** [Жалғасин] (Begmatov 1984, 202).

JALQÏR Yak. **Jalqïr** [Џалкыр / Дjалкыр] (Pek.). ✦ Derived from Yak. *jalqïy-.* ⇨ **D'ALQÏR.**

JALLAY Yak. **Jallay** [Џаллаи] (Pek.). ✦ 'Having big mouth' (Pek.).

JALMAMBET see **YALMAMBET**

JALTÏS Yak. **Jaltïs** / **D'altïs** [Џалтыс / Дjалтыс] (Pek.); Yak. **D'altïs** [Дjалтыс / Џалтыс] (Pek.). ⇨ **D'ALTÏS.**

JALUR Bulg. 1357 **Jalur** [جالور] (Jusupov 30).

JALWİ Bulg. 1323/24 **Jalwi** [جلو] (Epigr. Bulg. 142-43).

JAMAQ see **YAMAQ**

JAMAL Trkm. 20th c. **Jamal** [Ğamal], fem. (Zaj. 1971, 336); Kzk. 19th c. **Jamal** [Сахабъ Джамалъ], fem. (Grod., Pril. 155); Kirg. **Jamal** [Жамал], fem. (Jud. 93, 528); Trkm. 20th c. **Jamāl** [Җамал], fem. (TrkmRS 319); Kkalp. 20th c. **Žamal** [Жамал], fem. (KkRS 777); Kkalp. 20th c. **Žamal** [Жамал] (KkRS 773). ✧ 'Beauty, grace; beautiful face' cf. Kkalp. *žamal* 'красота' (KkRS), Trkm. *jemal* 'красота, красивое лицо' (Muhamedova 1957, 36) (<Ar.). Used also as a secondary component of female names. See also **NÄZİK-JEMAL**.

JAMAN see **YAMAN**

JAMAN-BALA see **YAMAN**

JAMAN-BOL Kzk. 19th c. **Jaman-bol** [Джаманболъ] (AOO 54). ✧ 'Be/become bad/wicked' (Rásonyi, Imp. 238). ⇨ YAMAN + BOL.

JAMAN-TAΓAU Kzk. **Jaman-taγay** [Џаман Таɓai] (Proben III, 75 /96/). ⇨ YAMAN + TAΓAU.

JAMAN-TURA Uzb. 19th c. **Jaman-tura** [Джамантура] (SKSO III, 158). ⇨ YAMAN + TURA.

JAMART see **JOMART**

JAMBUL Kzk. 20th c. **Jambul** [Джамбул Джабаев], a Kazak poet (SÊ 1946, 4., 230); Kkalp. 20th c. **Žambïl** [Жамбыл] (KkRS 773). ✧ Toponym. ⇨ JAN + BOL.?

JAMČİ Oghuz/Trkm. 13th c. **Jamči** [جامجى / Джамчи] (Abulg./Kon. 525).

JAMÏYLA see **JÄMİYLÄ**

JAMPEİS see **JANPEİS**

JAN Kzk. 19th c. **Čam-bay** (<Čan-bay) [Чамбай] (SODž. 96); Kzk. 19th c. **Čan** [Чанъ] (SOK 58); Kzk. 19th c. **Čan-bay** [Чанбай] (SOK 94); Kzk. 19th c. **Čan-bay** [Чанбай] (SODž. 22, 66); Kzk. 1823 **Čan-čigit** (<Jan-jigit?) [Санбай Чанчигитовъ] (TOUAK XXIV, 139); Oghuz/Trkm. 15th c. **Čan-paša**, fem. (DQorq./Rossi 100, DQorq./Gökyay 3); Tat.(Ishim) **Čǎn-bay** [Чǎнбај] (Proben IV, 196 /242/, 199 /245/); Kzk. **Jan-atay** [Джанатай] (Valihanov, Soč. 319); Yürük 1543 **Jan-beg** [Canbeğ] (Gökb., Rum. 216); Kzk. 19th c. **Jan-jigit** [Джанджигитъ] (SKSO VIII, 223); Bashk. 1740 **Jan-γul** [Джангул Зиянгул Сютяков] (MIB I, 435); Kzk. 19th c. **Jan-γul** [Джангулъ] (Grod., Pril. 131); Kzk. 19th c. **Jan-γul** [Джангулъ] (AOA 114); Trkm.? **Jan-χoja** [Джан-ходжа] (MIT I, 532); Kzk. 18th c. - 19th c. **Jan-χoja-batïr** [Джанходжа-батыр] (Tynyšp. 74); Oghuz/Trkm. 15th c. **Jan-qïz**, fem. (DQorqGökyay 100); Tat. 20th c. **Jan-say** (<Jan-säyet?) [Жансай] (Sattarov); Tat. 20th c. **Jan-säyet** [Жансəет] (Sattarov); Tat.(Lit.) 1585 **Yam-bek** (<Yan-bek) [Селимъ Ямбековичъ] (Lit. Tat. 50-53); Chag. 16th c. **Yam-čura?** [Ямчури], a mir (emir) (Ivanov 306);

Bashk. 1756 **Yam-čura** (<Yan-čura) [Зиянгул Ямчурин] (MIB IV/1, 123); Chuv. 18th-19th c. **Yam-molla** (<Yan-molla) [Яммола] (Magn. 97); Chuv. 18th-19th c. **Yam-murza** (<Yan-murza) [Яммурза] (Magn. 97); Chuv. 18th-19th c. **Yamolla** (<Yan-molla) [Ямолла] (Magn. 97); Chuv. 18th-19th c. **Yamula** (**Yam-mula < Yan-mulla**) [Ямула] (Magn. 97); Chuv. 18th-19th c. **Yamurza** (<Yam-murza < Yan-murza) [Ямурза] (Magn. 97); Crm. **Yan-bay** [Jaнбаi] (Proben VII, 107, 155); Chuv.,Tat. 18th-19th c. **Yan-bay** [Янбай] (Magn. 98); Tat. 1624 **Yan-bay** [Янбай Карачинъ] (Pokrovskij 70); Tat. 1624 **Yan-bay** [Тотай Янбаевъ] (Pokrovskij 71); Tat.(Sib.)? 1609 **Yan-bay** [Янбай мурза], a murza (Miller, Ist. Sib. II, 210); Bashk. 1653 **Yan-bay** [Тоймбетка Янбаевъ (Янбай)] (Vel.-Zern., Bašk. 43); Crm. 1515 **Yan-čura** [Янчура-Дуванъ], envoy (PSRL XIII, 24); Tat. 1711 **Yan-čura** [Янчюре] (MIB III, 76); Tat. 20th c. **Yan-čura** [Янчура] (Sattarov); Bashk. 1728 **Yan-čura** [Янчуринъ (Анчуринъ) Яркей] (PSZRI VIII, 68-69); Bashk. 1761 **Yan-čura** [Янчура Кутлуюлов] (MIB IV/1, 218); Bashk. 1751 **Yan-ekey** [Умют Янекеев] (MIB IV/1, 43); Tat.(Sib.) 1631, 1632 **Yan-gözä** [Янгозя Олякшеев] (Miller, Ist. Sib. II, 386, 397); Bashk. 1756 **Yan-güzä** [Янгузя Байдакаев] (MIB IV/1, 120); Tat.(Sib.) 1631 **Yan-γul** [Янгул Кошкилдеев] (Miller, Ist. Sib. II, 384); Chuv. 18th-19th c. **Yan-igit** (<Yan-yigit) [Янигитъ] (Magn. 99); Tat. 20th c. **Yan-yeget** / **Yän-yeget** [Янъегет] (Sattarov); Tat. 20th c. **Yan-säy** (<Yan-säyet) [Янсəй / Янсəев] (Sattarov); Tat. 20th c. **Yan-säyet** [Янсəет] (Sattarov); Bashk. 1798 **Yan-seyt** / **Yän-seyt** [Янсейтовъ] (PSZRI XXV, 196); Bashk. 1713 **Yan-sïra** [Бексыбай Янсыра] (MIB III, 95); Bashk. 20th c. **Yan-zigit** / **Yän-yeget** [Йəнйегет / Янзигит] (Kusimova); Chuv. 18th-19th c. **Yan-zigit** / **Yän-zigit?** [Янзигитъ] (Magn. 99); Tat.? 1675 **Yan-zigit** / **Yän-zigit?** [Янзигитъ] (Kungursk. akty 31); Tat. 1686 **Yan-zigit** / **Yän-zigit?** [Юкпердка Янзигитов] (Kungursk. akty 119); Bashk. 1761 **Yan-zigit** / **Yän-zigit?** [Янзигит Янатаров] (MIB IV/1, 221); Tat.(Tara) **Yän-bay** [Jan-Bai / Jan Bai / Jaнбаi] (Proben IV, 128 /165/); Bashk. 20th c. **Yän-sura** [Йəнсура / Янсура] (Kusimova); Kzk. 17th / 18th c. **Yen-aqay** (<Yän-aqay?) [Чигир Енакаев] (MIB I, 346); Tat.(Sib.) 1632 **Yen-bay** / **Yän-bay?** [Енбаев Уден] (Miller, Ist. Sib. II, 397, 398); Tat.(Sib.) 1638 **Yen-bay** / **Yän-bay?** [Енбайко] (Miller, Ist. Sib. II, 448, 449); Uzb. 1600 **Yen-bay** / **Yän-bay?** [Енбай Кишташов], from Bukhara (MIB I, 153); Chul. 1697 **Yen-bey** [Енбейко] (Jarilov, Tel. 9); Tat.(Lit.) 1592 **Yen-čura** [Енчура Касимовичъ] (Lit. Tat. 124); Kzk. 19th c. **Žan-aqay** [Исхакъ Жанакаевъ] (Pam. kn.

Turg. 61); Nog. **Žan-bay-biy** [Жанбай-бий] (Žirm., Epos 395); Kkalp. 20th c. **Žan-biyke** [Жанбийке], fem. (KkRS 777); Kkalp. 20th c. **Žan-ɣazï-χan** [Жанғазыхан] (KkRS 773); *EN:* Nog. 20th c. **Ĵan-aqay-uwlu** [Джанакай увлу], a Qara-noɣay clan (Bask., Nog. 136); *TN:* Tat. 18th c. **Yančurino** [Янчурино], a village in the district of Kazan (Korsakov 168). ✧ I. 'Soul' (P.), cf. Chag. *yan* 'die Seite, die Seele' (Radl. III, 79), Uyg., Kuman, Alt. *yañ* 'die Seele' (Radl. III, 57), Tat. dial. *yän* 'id.' (TTDS), Tat.(Bar.) *yan* 'id.' (Tumaševa 1981), Tat.(Sib.) *yän* 'id.' (Tumaševa 1961), Bashk. *yän* 'id.' (BRS), Tat.(Tara) *čän* 'die Seele' (Radl. III, 1960). Used also as a secondary component of male names. II. 'White'? In some names written in Arabic letters may be read as *čän* (<Mo.) *čaɣan* 'white' (Sauvaire 45), see ČAĞAN; III. 'Wolf'? for names with component *čan* (<Mo.) 'id.' (Sattarov). See also ČAĞAN; TAW-ČAN.

ĴAN-AYDAR Tat. 20th c. **Ĵan-aydar** [Җанайдар] (Sattarov); *EN:* Kzk. 18th - 19th c. **Ĵan-aydar** [Джанайдар] (Tynyšp. 72). ⇨ ĴAN + AYDAR.

ĴAN-AQAY-UWLU see ĴAN

ĴAN-ALİ Tat. 20th c. **An-ali (<Yan-ali)** [Анали] (Sattarov); Chag. 1457 **Ĵan-ali** [Джан-Али], a yasaul of the Timurid Sanĵar mirza (MIT I, 535-36); Tat. 20th c. **Ĵan-ɣali** [Җангали] (Sattarov); Bashk. 1713 **Yan-aley (<Yan-ali / Yän-ali)** [Яналей Кунтуков] (MIB III, 100); Tat. 20th c. **Yan-ali** [Янали] (Sattarov); Tat. 1530, 1532, 1535 **Yan-ali / Yän-ali** [Еналей (Аналѣй, Яналѣй)], a ruler (prince Gorodetskij) in Kazan (PSRL VIII, 277, VIII, 282-83, VIII, 291, PSRL (Russk. Hr.) I, 522); Tat. 1779 **Yan-ɣali** [Теней Янгалаев] (MIB V, 83); Tat. 20th c. **Yan-ɣali / Ĵan-ɣali** [Янгали, Җангали] (Sattarov); Tat. 20th c. **Yän-ali** [Енали] (Sattarov); Bashk. 20th c. **Yän-ɣäli** [Йəнғəли / Янгали] (Kusimova); Bashk. 20th c. **Yän-ɣäli** [Йəнғəли / Янгали] (Kusimova); Tat. 20th c. **Yun-ali (<Yan-ali)** [Юнали] (Sattarov). ⇨ ĴAN + ALİ.

ĴAN-ARASLAN see YAN-ARSLAN

ĴAN-ARSTAN see YAN-ARSLAN

ĴAN-BASA Yürük 1543 **Ĵan-basa** [جاناباصا] (Gökb., Ed. 103). ✧ 'Soul (darling) - ?'. ⇨ ĴAN + BASA?

ĴAN-BEK see ĴANİ

ĴAN-BERDİ Maml. 14th c. **Ĵan-berdi** [جانبردي] (Sauvaget 45, 46); Maml.? 1496/97 **Ĵan-berdi** [جانبردى الاشتر الكاشف] (Iyās II, 322, 353, III, 212); Maml.? 1517 **Ĵan-berdi** [جانبردى الغز الى], governor of Syria (Iyās II, 354, 395, III, 3, 308, Weil, Chalif. II, 380, Uzunçarş. 45); Bashk. 1663 **Yam-berdi (<Yan-berdi)** [Ямбердейко] (MIB I, 164); Tat.? 1612 **Yan-berdi** [Богдашка Янбердеев] (Nižegorod. platež.); Bashk. 1717 **Yan-berdi** [Янберде] (MIB III, 154);

Bashk. 1735 **Yan-berdi** [Улметъ Янбердинъ], a tarχan (Vel.-Zern., Bašk. 23); Tat. 20th c. **Yan-birde** [Янбирде] (Sattarov); Tat. 20th c. **Yan-birde** [Янбирде] (Sattarov); Bashk. 20th c. **Yän-birðe** [Йəнбирҙе / Янбирде] (Kusimova); Kzk. 19th c. **Yen-berdi** [Енберды] (SODž. 26). ⇨ ĴAN + BERDİ.

ĴAN-BOL Kzk. 19th c. **Čam-bol (<Čan-bol?)** [Чамболъ] (SOK 126); Kzk. 19th c. **Ĵan-bol** [Джанболъ] (SOK 126); Uzb. 20th c. **Ĵân-bol** [Жонбўл] (Begmatov 1984, 201). ✧ 'Live! Be alive!'. ⇨ ĴAN + BOL. See also ĴAN-BOLDÏ, ĴAN-BOLSUN.

ĴAN-BOLDÏ Kzk. 18th c. - 19th c. **Ĵan-boldï** [Джанболды] (Tynyšp. 68); Tat. 1558 **Yan-buldu(y)** [Янбулдуй] (PSRL XIII, 288). ⇨ ĴAN + BOLDÏ. See also ĴAN-BOL, ĴAN-BOLSUN.

ĴAN-BOLSUN Kzk. 19th c. **Ĵam-bosun (<Ĵan-bolsun)** [Джамбосунъ] (SODž. 82); Kzk. 19th c. **Ĵan-boysun** [Джанбойсун] (Grod., Pril. 165); Kzk. 19th c. **Ĵan-bosun** [Джанбосунъ] (SODž. 82); Kzk. 19th c. **Ĵan-busun (<Ĵan-bulsun)** [Данабекъ Джанъ-бусуновъ] (Grod., Pril. 170); Kkalp. 20th c. **Žan-bosïn** [Жанбосын] (KkRS 773). ⇨ ĴAN + BOLSÏN. See also ĴAN-BOL, ĴAN-BOLDÏ.

ĴAN-BOTA Kzk. 19th c. **Ĵan-bota** [Джанбота] (SOV 6); Kzk. 19th c. **Ĵan-buta** [Джанбута] (SKSO VIII, 200); Kzk. 19th c. **Ĵan-buta** [Джанбута] (Grod., Pril. 183). ✧ 'Soul/darling-young camel'. ⇨ ĴAN + BOTA.

ĴAN-BULAT Chuv. 18th-19th c. **Čan-bulat** [Чанбулатъ] (Magn. 91); Maml. 14th c. **Ĵan-bulat** [جانبلاط] (Sauvaget 46); Maml. 15th c. **Ĵan-bulat** [الملك الاشرف جانبلاط بن يشبك], governor of Syria, commander-in-chief then a Mamluk sultan, died in 1501 (Makrīzī, Khit. I, 244, Iyās II, 256-315, 392, Weil, Chalif. II, 351, 387, Mayer 128); Maml. 1468 **Ĵan-bulat** [جان بلاط الاشرفى] (Ibn Taghrīb. VIII, 726); Maml. 1484 **Ĵan-bulat** [جان بلاطا لخاصكى] (Iyās II, 224, 254); Maml. 1498 **Ĵan-bulat** [جان بلاط الغورى] (Iyās II, 157, 341 etc., Weil, Chalif. II, 366); Maml. 1516 **Ĵan-bulat** [جان بلاط الساقى] (Iyās III, 52); Kzk. 1829 **Ĵan-bulat** [Джанбулатъ] (Konšin, Mat. I-III, 20); Tat. 1675 **Yan-bulat** [Янбулатъ (Янбулатко)] (Kungursk. akty 31); Tat. 20th c. **Yan-bulat** [Янбулат] (Sattarov); Tat.(Sib.) 1603 **Yan-bulat** [Янбулат] (Miller, Ist. Sib. II, 179); *TN:* Chuv. 18th c. **Yan-bulat(ova)** [Янбулатова], a village in the district of Civilsk (Korsakov 321). ⇨ ĴAN + BULAT.

ĴAN-DOS Kzk. 19th c. **Ĵan-dos** [Джандосъ], a biy (Lomakin 33, SOV 108, 158). ⇨ ĴAN + DOST.

ĴAN-DOSAY Kzk. 19th c. **Ĵan-dosay** [Джандосай] (SOV 148). ⇨ ĴAN + DOSAY.

ĴAN-GEL Kzk. 19th c. **Ĵan-gel** [Джангель] (SOK 258, SOV 136). ✧ 'Come to life' (Bese 21). ⇨ ĴAN +

KEL? See also ĴAN-KELDİ.

ĴAN-GELDİ see **ĴAN-KELDİ**

ĴAN-ГABİL see **ĴAN-QABUL**

ĴAN-ГALİ see **ĴAN-ALİ**

ĴAN-KELDİ   Kzk. 19th c. **Ĵan-geldi** [Джангельды] (SOK 72); Nog. 20th c. **Ĵan-geldi** [Къазбек Джангелди увлы Елгитар / Казбек Джанкельдиев], father of one of Baskakov's informants from the aul of Qoyasulï (Bask., Nog. 144); Kirg. 19th c. **Ĵan-geldi** [Мулла Асанъ Джангельдинъ], a manap (AUK 287); Maml.? 1499 **Ĵan-keldi** [خوند جان كلدى] (Iyās II, 362, 372); Tat.(Lit.) 1552 **Ĵan-keldi** [Джанъ Килди] (Kn. Metriki Lit. 65); Uzb. 19th c. **Ĵan-kildi** [Раббія Джанкилдіева], from the region of Tashkent (Sr. Az. 1896 I, avg. 11); Kzk. **Ĵäñ-gäldi** [Dshängäldi / Цäнгäлді] (Proben III, 37 /47/); Chuv. 18th-19th c. **Yan-gilde** [Янгилда] (Magn. 98); Tat. 1624 **Yan-gilde** [Янгилда Еушевъ] (Pokrovskij 71); Tat. 1711 **Yan-gilde** [Янгильде] (MIB III, 76); Chuv. 18th-19th c. **Yan-gilde(y)** [Янгилдей] (Magn. 98); Chuv. 1737 **Yan-gildi** [Арзубъ Янгильдинъ] (Alatyr. 136); Bashk. 1682 **Yan-gildi / Yän-gildi?** [Мамрячко Янгилдинъ] (AI V, 140); Trkm. 1879-1881 **Yan-keldi** [Kari Jan-Kelté], a Khan (O'Donovan I, 222); Kirg. **Yan-keldi** [Jan-keldi / Ян-келді], one of Manas' comrades of arms (Proben V, 40 /41/); Tat. 1645 **Yän-gilde** [Енгилдѣйко Колмаковъ] (AI IV, 23); Bashk. 20th c. **Yän-gilde / Yan-gilde?** [Йӭнгилде / Янгильде] (Kusimova); Kzk. 1817 **Žan-geldi / Yañ-kildi?** [يانككيلدى / Жангельды] (MIK IV, 310); *TN:* Chuv. 18th c. **Yangildina** (<Yan-gildi) [Янгильдина], a village in the district of Čeboksary (Korsakov 285). ✧ 'A soul (=child) has come (has been born)' (Sattarov). ⇨ ĴAN + KELDİ. See also ĴAN-GEL.

ĴAN-QABUL   Kzk. 19th c. **Ĵan-γabïl** [Джангабылъ], Bay-γabïl's brother (Potanin II, 4); Uzb. 18th c. **Ĵan-qabul** [Джанкабулъ], from Khiva (Nepljuev 803). ✧ 'His/her life accepted'? ⇨ ĴAN + QABUL. See also TLÄW-ГABİL.

ĴAN-QARA   Kzk. 18th c. - 19th c. **Ĵan-qara** [Джанкара] (Tynyšp. 73); Nog. 1552 **Yan-γara** [Янгара-багатырь] (PSRL XIII, 179). ⇨ ĴAN + QARA.

ĴAN-QİLİČ   Maml.? 1520 **Ĵan-qïlïč** [جان قلج] (Iyās III, 243, 260). ⇨ ĴAN + QİLİČ. See also YAN-QİLİČ?

ĴAN-QOZÏ   Kzk. 18th c. - 19th c. **Ĵan-qozï** [Джанкозы] (Tynyšp. 75). ⇨ ĴAN + QOZÏ.

ĴAN-QUČÏQ   Kzk. 19th c. **Ĵan-qučïq? / Ĵan-küčik?** [Иръ Мамбетъ Джанкучуковъ] (Grod., Pril. 105). ✧ 'Soul/darling - cancer (sun sign)' cf. Uyg. *qučïq* 'das Sternbild des Krebses' (Radl. II, 1009). ⇨ ĴAN.

ĴAN-QUT   Kzk. 19th c. **Ĵan-qut** [Джанкуть] (SODž. 42); Kzk. 19th c. **Ĵan-qut** [Джанкуть] (SOK 154). ⇨ ĴAN + QUT.

ĴAN-QUTTÏ   Kzk. 19th c. **Ĵan-quttï** [Джанъ Кутти Баттубаевъ / Буттубаевъ] (Grod., Pril. 104, 105). ⇨ ĴAN + QUTLUГ.

ĴAN-MAMET   Nog. 1649 **Ĵan-mamet** [Джанъ-Маметъ мурза Тинмаметев], a murza (AI IV, 84); Tat.(Sib.) 1640 **Yan-mamet** [Янмамет] (Miller, Ist. Sib. II, 471, 472). ⇨ ĴAN + MAMET.

ĴAN-SAY see **ĴAN**

ĴAN-SAQAL   Kzk. 19th c. **Ĵan-saqal** [Джансакалъ] (AOK 2). ⇨ ĴAN + SAQAL.

ĴAN-SARÏ   Tat. 20th c. **Ĵan-sarï** [Җансары] (Sattarov); Kzk. 18th c. - 19th c. **Ĵan-sarï** [Джансары] (Tynyšp. 70, 72); Tat. 20th c. **Yan-sarï** [Янсары / Янсарин / Янсаров] (Sattarov); Bashk. 20th c. **Yän-harï / Yan-harï** [Йӭнһары / Янһары / Янсары] (Kusimova); *TN:* Chuv. 18th c. **Yan-sarina** (<Yan-sarï) [Янсарина], a village in the district of Jadrinsk (Korsakov 306). ✧ 'Soul-yellow (=blond son as dear as our life)' (Sattarov). ⇨ ĴAN + SARÏ.

ĴAN-SÄY see **ĴAN**

ĴAN-SÄYET see **ĴAN**

ĴAN-SÏRT   Kzk. 19th c. **Ĵan-sïrt** [Джансыртъ] (SODž. 98). ⇨ ĴAN + SÏRT.

ĴAN-SUWAN   Kzk. **Ĵan-suwan** [Джансуванъ] (SOK 108). ⇨ ĴAN + SUWAN?

ĴAN-TAY   Kzk. 19th c. **Ĵan-tay** [Джантай] (AOO); Kzk. 19th c. **Ĵan-tay** [Джантай], forefather of the Ĵadïq clan (Potanin II, 6). ⇨ ĴAN + TAY + / suff. *-tay(1,2)*?

ĴAN-TAYLAQ   Kzk. 19th c. **Ĵan-taylaq** [Джантайлакъ] (SOK 16). ⇨ ĴAN + TAYLAQ.

ĴAN-TAS   Kzk. 19th c. **Ĵan-tas** [Джантасъ] (AOP 114). ⇨ ĴAN + TAŠ.

ĴAN-TAW   Kzk. 1829 **Ĵan-taw** [Джантау] (MIK IV, 324). ⇨ ĴAN + TAГ.

ĴAN-TELE   Kzk. 19th c. **Ĵan-tele** [Джантеле] (SODž. 38). ⇨ ĴAN + TELİ? See also ĴAN-TİLİY?

ĴAN-TEMİR   Tat. 20th c. **Ĵan-temir** [Җантимер] (Sattarov); Crm. 1634 **Ĵan-temür** [جا نتمور بك / جانتمور] (Vel.-Zern., Crim. 143, 159, 207, 244); Crm. 1700 **Ĵan-temür / Ĵan-timür?** [Джанъ Тимуръ] (Smirnov, Krym.); Kzk. 19th c.? **Ĵan-temür / Ĵan-timür?** [Джантемировъ] (SKSO VIII, 203); Crm. 1641 **Ĵan-temür-bi** [جانتمور بى] (Vel.-Zern., Crim. 284); Crm. 1628, 1636 **Ĵan-temür-mirza** [جانتمور مرزا], Ali Ghazi Agha's son (Vel.-Zern., Crim. 43, 172); Chuv. 18th-19th c. **Yan-demir** [Яндемиръ] (Magn. 98); Maml. 1398/99 **Yan-temir** [ينتمر المحمّدىّ] (Ibn Taghrīb. VI, 9, 20); Tat. 20th c. **Yan-timer / Yän-timer** [Янтимер] (Sattarov); Tat. 1555 **Yan-timir / Yän-timir**

[Янтимиръ], a prince from Astrakhan (PSRL XIII, 245); Tat. 1624 **Yan-timir** / **Yän-timir** [Янтимиръ Безергановъ] (Pokrovskij 70); Bashk. 1740 **Yän-temir** [Зианчура Янтсмиров] (MIB I, 403); Bashk. 20th c. **Yän-timer** / **Yan-timer** [Йәнтимер / Янтимир] (Kusimova). ✦ 'Let the child be hard (strong) like iron' (Sattarov). ⇨ JAN + TEMİR.

JAN-TEMÜR see **JAN-TEMİR**

JAN-TİLEW   Kzk. 19th c. **Jan-tilew** [Джанъ Тилу Сиритаевъ] (Grod., Pril. 164); Kzk. 19th c. **Jan-tlew** [Джантлеу] (SOK 82); Kzk. 19th c. **Jan-tlew** [Джантлеу] (SOV 10). ✦ 'Soul-wish'? cf. Kzk. PN *Žantilew* (Žanuzakov-Esbaeva). ⇨ JAN + TİLÄW.

JAN-TİLİY   Kzk. 19th c. **Jan-tiliy** [Тангри Кулъ Джан-Тиліевъ] (Grod., Pril. 127). ✦ 'Soul wishes (him/her)' cf. Kzk. *tiläü* 'das Bitten' (Radl. III, 1382), Kzk. *tilev* 'Dilemek' (KzTS), cf. also Kzk. PN *Žantilew* (Žanuzakov-Esbaeva). ⇨ JAN.

JAN-TİMER see **JAN-TEMİR**

JAN-TİRÄK   Kzk. 19th c. **Jan-tiräk** [Джанъ-Тираковъ] (Grod., Pril. 115). ⇨ JAN + TİRÄK.

JAN-TLEW see **JAN-TİLEW**

JAN-TUΓAN   Tat.(Lit.) 1552 **Jan-tuγan** [Джан-Туганъ] (Kn. Metriki Lit. 79); Tat. 20th c. **Jan-tuγan** [Жантуган] (Sattarov); Kzk. 19th c. **Jan-tuγan** [Аманкулъ Джантугановъ] (Grod., Pril. 144); Kzk. 19th c. **Jan-tuγan** [Джанъ-Туганъ] (Grod., Pril. 114); Nog. 20th c. **Jan-tuγan** [Куьн Бийке Йантувгъан келинъи / Кюнбике Янтуганова], husband of one of Baskakov's informants from the aul of İrγaqlï (Bask., Nog. 143); Chuv. 18th-19th c. **Yan-dïgan** [Яндыганъ] (Magn. 98); Chuv. 18th-19th c. **Yan-dugan** [Яндуганъ] (Magn. 98); Chuv. 18th-19th c. **Yan-tugan** [Янтуганъ] (Magn. 99); Tat. 1684 **Yan-tuγan** [Янтуган] (Zolotn. 160); Tat. 1691 **Yan-tuγan** [Янтугановъ] (Kungursk. akty 195); Bashk. 1706 **Yan-tuγan** [Иртуган Янтуганов] (MIB III, 27); Nog. 20th c. **Yan-tuwγan** [Салим Йантувгъан увлы], father of Baskakov's informant from the aul of İrγaqlï (Bask., Nog. 143); Kzk. 19th c. **Žan-tuγan** [Жанъ Туганъ] (SODž. 72); *TN:* Chuv. 18th c. **Yan-dugan(ova)** / **Yän-dugan(ova)** [Яндуганова / Ендуганова] (Korsakov 283). ✦ 'Soul (child, man) has been born'. ⇨ JAN + TUΓAN I.

JAN-TURA   Tat. **Jan-tura** [Selim-Gerei Ğanturin] (Mende 103); Kzk. **Jan-tura** [Джантюра] (Levšin II, 331); Kzk. 19th c. **Jan-tura** [ханъ Джантюри] (AUK 484). ⇨ JAN + TURA.

JAN-TURSUN   Kzk. 19th c. **Jan-tursun** [Джанъ-Турсунъ Джумбатовъ] (Grod., Pril. 175). ⇨ JAN + TURSÏN.

JAN-UZAQ   Kzk. 19th c. **Jan-uzaq** [Джанузакъ] (SODž. 158); Kzk. 19th c. **Jan-uzaq** [Джанузакъ] (AOAtb. 66); Kzk. 19th c. **Jan-uzaq** [Джанузакъ]

(SODž. 158); Kzk. 19th c. **Jan-uzaq** [Джанузакъ] (AOO 10); Kzk. 19th c. **Jan-uzaq** [Санатбай Джанъ Узаковъ] (Grod., Pril. 48); Kirg. 20th c. **Jan-uzaq** [Жанузак] (Jud. 226, Kalilov 95); Bashk. 20th c. **Yan-uðaq** / **Yän-uðaq** [Янузак / Янузак] (Kusimova); Kzk. 1803, 1820 **Yan-uzaq** / **Yan-uzaq-biy** [Янузак / Янузакъ-бій], one of the chiefs of the „Čiklinsk / Čaklinsk" tribe (or clan?) of the Little Horde (Kiši Žüz) (MIK IV, 515, Sib. Vestn. IX, 116); Bashk. 20th c. **Yän-oðaq** [Йәнозак / Янузак] (Kusimova); Kkalp. 20th c. **Žan-ïzaq** [Жаныːзак] (KkRS 773). ✦ 'Soul-long (=Long life)' (Jud. 226). ⇨ JAN + UZAQ. See also **BAY-UZAQ, ÖMÜR-ZAQ**.

JANA see **YAÑI**

JANAY   Kzk. 1841 **Janay** [Джанай Чингисовъ], sultan of the Middle Horde (Orta Žüz) (Konšin, Mat. V, 21); Kzk. 19th c. **Janay** [Джанай] (AOAtb. 22); Kzk. 19th c. **Janay** [Джанай] (AOO 46); Kzk. 19th c. **Janay-bay** [Джанайбай] (SOK 156); Kkalp. 20th c. **Janay-elši** [Джанай-елши] (Bask., Kkalp. 71); Crm. 15th c. **Janay-oγlan** [Джанай-огланъ] (Smirnov, Krym. 213); Tat. 1741 **Yanay** [Janaief] (Levchin 195); Tat.(Mish.) 1748 **Yänäy** [Еней Токбаевъ] (Nepljuev 430, 438); Bashk. 1664 **Yänäy** [Акилди Енеев] (MIB I, 193); Bashk. 1709 **Yänäy** [Янай Улямаев] (MIB I, 264); Bashk. 1776 **Yänäy** [Сатлык Янеев] (MIB V, 39-41); Balk. 20th c. **Zanay** [Zanáj] (Pröhle, Balk. 268); *EN:* Bashk. **Yänäy** [Йәнәй / Еней], a Bashkir tribe (BRS/Uraksin 862). ✦ 'My dear, dearest, darling' cf. Kzk. PN *Žanay* (Žanuzakov-Esbaeva). ⇨ JAN + suff. *-ay*. See also **TOL-ŽANAY; YANAŠ**.

JANBAZ   Yürük 1543 **Janbaz** [جانباز] (Gökb., Rum. 101). ✦ '(Horse) Dealer, swindler' cf. Turk. *jambaz* (<P.) 'der Wiederverkäufer; der Schurke' (Radl. IV, 64).

JANJUN   NUyg.(Tar.) **Janjun** [Dshandsun / Цанцун] (Proben VI, 61, Radl. I, 1010). ✦ 'Governor-general (title)' cf. NUyg. *janjün* / *jañjüñ* 'генерал-губернатор' (UjgRS) (<Chin.).

JANDAL   Trkm. 1768/69 **Jandal** [Джандал], from the Ošaq clan (MIT II, 339).

JANDARAL   Kzk. 19th c. **Jandaral** [Джандаралъ], lived in the district of Chimkent, named after a general who was travelling nearby at the time of birth (Grod. I, 98); Kzk. 19th c. **Jandaral** [Джандаралъ] (SOV 100, 120). ✦ 'General' (Grod. I, 98).

JANDÏ   Kzk. **Jandï-bay** [Ğandybaev] (Mende 118). ✦ 'Lively, alive' cf. Kzk. *jandï* 'belebt, lebendig' (Radl. IV, 24). ⇨ JAN + suff. *-dï* / *-lï*.

JANET   NUyg. / Kzk.? 19th c. **Janet** / **Jenet** [Джанетъ / Дженетъ] (Valihanov, Soč. 363).

JANİ   1409/10 **Jan-bek** (<**Janï-bek**) [جانبك الترمی] (Ibn Taghrīb. VI, 224, 240); 1410 **Jan-bek** (<**Janï-bek**) [جانبك الساقی] (Ibn Taghrīb. VI, 429); 1421 **Jan-bek**

(<Janï-bek) [جانبك الاشرفى] (Ibn Taghrīb. VI, 329, 563, 622); 1437/38 Jan-bek (<Janï-bek) [جانبك دوادار الباسط] (Ibn Taghrīb. VII, 3, 11, 100, 576); 1437/38, 1467/68 Jan-bek (<Janï-bek) [الاشرفى], „Oberstwaffenträger” (Ibn Taghrīb. VII, 9, 23, 104, etc., 829, 846 etc., Weil, Chalif. II, 304, 317 etc.); 1453 Jan-bek (<Janï-bek) [جا نبك الجكمى] (Ibn Taghrīb. VII, 239, 467); 1455 Jan-bek (<Janï-bek) [جانبك الشمسى المويدى] (Ibn Taghrīb. VII, 587); 1461 Jan-bek (<Janï-bek) [جانبك الابلق الظاهرى] (Ibn Taghrīb. VII, 552, 650, Weil, Chalif. II, 273, 304); 1467/68 Jan-bek (<Janï-bek) [جانبك الزينى المويدى] (Ibn Taghrīb. VII, 854); Maml. 1410, 1437 Jan-bek (<Janï-bek) [جانبك الصوفى], a viceroy who escaped to Asia Minor at the time of Bars-bay, died in 1437 (Ibn Taghrīb. VI, 132, 252, VII, 110, 288); Maml.? 1426 Jan-bek (<Janï-bek) [جانبك اليلبغاوى] (Ibn Taghrīb. VI, 607, 670); Maml.? 1433 Jan-bek (<Janï-bek) [الحمرا وى] [جانبك], died in 1433 (Ibn Taghrīb. VI, 340, 495, 691, Weil, Chalif. II, 134, 195); Maml.? 1450 Jan-bek (<Janï-bek) [جانبك النوروزى], governor of Beyrut (Ibn Taghrīb. VII, 346); Maml.? 15th c. Jan-bek (<Janï-bek) [جا نى بك النوروزى / جا نبك النوروزى], governor of Baalbek (Ibn Taghrīb. VII, 65, 149, Iyās II, 45); Maml. 1453-1461 Jan-bek (<Janï-bek) [جانبك التركمانى], Sultan al-Ashraf Inal's (1453-1461) treasurer-in-chief (Ibn Taghrīb. VI, 106, 238, Weil, Chalif. II, 260, 277); Maml.? 1466/67 Jan-bek (<Janï-bek) [جانبك الظاهرى], governor of Damascus (Ibn Taghrīb. VII, 746); Yürük 16th c. Jan-bek (<Janï-bek) [جا نبيك / Canbeğ], from the Yürüks of Kocacık (Gökb., Rum. 103); Janï-beg (Byz. Turc. II, 308); 1340/41 Janï-bek [جا نى بك الناصرى] (Iyās II, 175); 1366/67 Janï-bek [جانى بك اليوسفى] (Iyās I, 220, 224); 1443 Janï-bek [جا نى بك الظاهرى] (Iyās II, 29); 1454 Janï-bek [جانى بك], governor of Zerdekesh (Iyās II, 41); 1457, 1458 Janï-bek [جانى بك الاسماعيلى] (Iyās II, 60, Ibn Taghrīb. VII, 491, 494, etc.); 1467/68 Janï-bek [جانى بك النفيه الظاهرى] (Iyās II, 92, 183); 1468/69 Janï-bek [جا نى بك السيفى تغرى برمش] (Iyās II, 111); 1468/69 Janï-bek [جا نى بك قجا التمشى المويدى] (Iyās II, 100); 1472/73 Janï-bek [جا نى بك قرا العلائى] (Iyās II, 142, Ibn Taghrīb. VII, 382 etc.); 1475/76 Janï-bek [جا نى بك نا يب جده], a governor (Iyās II, 159, 229); 1476/77 Janï-bek [خوند جانى بك الجركسيه] (Iyās II, 168); 1493/94 Janï-bek [المحمودى الظاهرى جتمق] (Iyās II, 284); 1494/95 Janï-bek [جانى بك الحسنى الظاهرى جتمق] (Iyās II, 286); 1495

Janï-bek [جانىبك اقبردى دوادار] (Iyās II, 291); 1496/97 Janï-bek [جانىبك بن تمر باى] (Iyās II, 322); 1496/97 Janï-bek [جانى بك بن ازدمر الصغير] (Iyās II, 306); 1496/97 Janï-bek [جانى بك] (Iyās II, 311, 336); 1497/98 Janï-bek [جانى بك أخو الناصر] (Iyās II, 340); 1519 Janï-bek [جا نى بك كاشف الشرقية] (Iyās III, 201, 203); Khorezm.? 1480 Janï-bek [أخو تانىبك قرا] [جانىبك] (Iyās II, 199); Maml. 14th c. Janï-bek [جانبك] (Sauvaget); Maml. 1415 Janï-bek [البجاس] [جانىبك] (Iyās II, 5, 16); Maml. 1450, 1452/53 Janï-bek [جا نى بك البواب / جا نبك] (Ibn Taghrīb. VII, 212, 214, Iyās II, 40, 220, Weil, Chalif. II, 260); Maml. 1452 Janï-bek [جانى بك] (Iyās II, 36, 145, 318); Maml. 1463 Janï-bek [جانى بك], killed in 1463 as a great „dawādār”, a mausoleum in Cairo was named after him (Mayer 129-131); Maml. 1468/69 Janï-bek [جانى بك الاشقر] (Iyās II, 104, 162); Maml. 1479 Janï-bek [جانى بك أحد مماليك السلطان] (Iyās II, 187); Maml. 1485, 1488 Janï-bek [جانىبك الطويل] [جانى بك الابراهيمى الطويل الا شرفى] (Iyās II, 227, 250); Maml.? 1516 Janï-bek [جا نى بك دوادار طراباى] (Iyās III, 52, 218); Maml.? 1516 Janï-bek [جانى بك العادلى] (Iyās III, 52); Maml.? 1516 Janï-bek [جانى بك القصير] (Iyās III, 44); Chag.? 1480 Janï-bek [جا نى بك أخو سيباى] (Iyās II, 199); Chag.? 1521 Janï-bek [جا نى بك أخو قا يتباى الدوادار] (Iyās III, 247, 291); Kzk. Janï-bek [Џаны Бек], Šaqša's son (Proben III, 47 /62/); Kzk. 16th c. Janï-bek, a Kazak prince at the end of the 16th c. (Radl., Aus Sib. I, 193); Kzk. 18th c. - 19th c. Janï-bek [Джаныбек] (Tynyšp. 68, 71, 75); Kzk. 19th c. Janï-bek [Джанибекъ Нурбаевъ] (Grod., Pril. 182); Kkalp. 20th c. Janï-bek [Джанибек / Джаныбек] (Bask., Kkalp. 74, 100); Nog. 20th c. Janï-bek [Абдулхамит Джанибек], one of Baskakov's informants from the aul of Ašïqulaq (Bask., Nog. 144); Uzb. 20th c. Janï-bek [Djanibek], a basmačï from Bukhara (Castagné 77); 1452/53 Janï-be / Jan-bek (<Janï-bek) [جا نى بك التجماسى الاشرفى / جا نبك] (Iyās II, 40, Ibn Taghrīb. VII, 385); Tat.(GH) 1356, 1378 Janï-bek / Janï-bek-χan [جانى بيك / جانىبيك حان / جانبك / Жанибекъ / Чянибѣкъ / Жанебѣкъ / Чанибекъ / Занибекъ / Занибечекъ / Джани-бек / Джаныбек-хан / Шанибекъ / Шадибекъ / Шадибѣкъ / Алибѣгъ], a ruler of the [Golden] Horde (1342-1357), Özbek-χan's son, Tini-bek's younger brother (Qazw. 677, Ibn Bat. II, 397, PSRL (Russk. Hr.) I, 409, 411, 424-25, PSRL IV, 110, VI, 131, VIII, 78, XI, 32, XVI, 155-157 etc., Abulg./Kon. 1295, 1305, 1315, 1395-1405, Šejb. L, LVII, LXXIII, MIT II, 56); Crm. Janï-bek-qan [Џаныбек кан] (Proben VII, 122, etc.); Kzk. 19th c.

Janï-qul [Джаникулъ] (Grod., Pril. 193); Kkalp. 20th c. Jäni-bek [Джäнибек] (Bask., Kkalp. 62, 76); Nog. 1654 Yanï-bek [Янибекъ], a murza (AI IV, 204); Bashk.? 1535 Zanï-bek? / Janï-bek [Занебѣкъ Кулабердѣевъ] (PSRL XIII, 247); Kkalp. 20th c. Žanï-bek [Жаныбек] (KkRS 773); Kzk.? 19th c.? Žanï-bek-batïr (Atyns. 18); Kkalp. 20th c. Žäni-bek [Жəнибек] (KkRS 773); *EN:* Trkm. Janï-beg [Džanibäg], a clan (Németh, HMK 67). ✧ 'Soul of; His/her soul'? Put together with the comp. *bek* it may mean 'Soul-(of)-prince' (Sauvaget 46: 'prince-âme'); 'His soul (is) strong'. Consider Defrémery's oppinion on the names *Tini-bek* and *Janï-bek*: „L'aîné s'appelle *Tîna bec*; *bec* a le sens d'émir, et *tîn (ten)* celui de corps; c'est donc comme s'il se nommait 'émir du corps'. Le nom de son frère est *Djâni bec. Djân* signifie l'âme; c'est comme s'il s'appelait 'émir de l'âme'." (Ibn Bat. II, 397), cf. also Pelliot, Notes 98-99, Eren 1953, 127-129, Türk Dili 495 (1993), 232-233. ⇨ JAN + suff. -*ï*. See also AS-JANÏ-BEK, AZ-JANÏ-BEK.

JANÏLÏ Kzk. 19th c. Janïlï [Джанылы] (SOK 10). ⇨ JANÏ? + suff. -*lï*.

JANÏM 1438/39 Janïm [جانم من حسنشاه] (Ibn Taghrīb. VII, 260); 1449, 1452, 1453 Janïm [جانم الظاهرى] (Ibn Taghrīb. VII, 224, 375, VIII, 56, 61, 170 etc.); 1453 Janïm [جانم الساقى] (Iyās II, 40, Weil, Chalif. II, 260); 1453, 1460 Janïm [الاشرفى جانم / السيفى /], a governor-in-chief of the province of Damascus (Ibn Taghrīb. VIII, 183, 209-213, 552, 659, 778 etc., BÉO II, 42-43); 1469 Janïm [جانم المجنون الخشقد مى] (Iyās II, 112); 1470/71 Janïm [جانم السيفى تمر باى الزردكا ش] (Iyās II, 123, 159, 191); 1475/76 Janïm [جانم الشرينى] (Iyās II, 158, 195); 1477 Janïm [جانم الاصفر] (Iyās II, 171); 1479 Janïm [جا نم الاعور بن بلباى] (Iyās II, 187); 1480 Janïm [جانم الا عرج] (Iyās II, 196); 1491/92 Janïm [جانم بن مصطفى] (Iyās II, 274); 1495/96 Janïm [جانم بن برسباى أخو قانصوه االنفى] (Iyās II, 297, 309); 1496/97 Janïm [جانم قايتباى] (Iyās II, 326); 1498/99 Janïm [جانم اقجى الابراهيمى] (Iyās II, 360); 1500/01 Janïm [جانم بن قجماس] (Iyās II, 391); 1516 Janïm [جانم الا فرنجى] (Iyās III, 25); 1520 Janïm [جانم الكا شف] (Iyās III, 244); 1520 Janïm [جانم كاشف منغلوطو ليهنسا] (Iyās III, 231); 1521 Janïm [جا نم أمير الحاج] (Iyās III, 246, 281); 1522 Janïm [جا نم السيفى دولا ت باى الاتابكى] (Iyās III, 289); Maml.? 1458 Janïm [جانم بن البهلوان الاشرفى], governor of Damascus (Iyās II, 25, 220, III, 260, Ibn Tahgrīb. VII, 383, 496, Weil, Chalif. II, 277); Maml.? 1491/92 Janïm [جانم المصبغة] (Iyās II, 274, 360, III, 299, Weil, Chalif. II, 366); Maml.? 1494/95 Janïm [جانم] (Iyās II, 287, 296, 379, III, 62); Maml.? 1500/01 Janïm [جانم المحمدى الخشقدمى] (Iyās II, 377 III, 52); Maml? 1516 Janïm [جا نم الطو يـل] (Iyās III, 52, 166); Maml. 1516 Janïm [جانم الابراهيمى] (Iyās III, 74); Bashk. 1779 Žanïm [Сарыгул Жанымов] (MIB V, 96). ✧ 'My soul, My darling' (Sauvaget 46). ⇨ JAN + poss. suff. -*ïm*.

JANKE Kzk. 19th c. Janke [Джанке] (SOK 96); Chuv. 18th-19th c. Yanka [Янка] (Magn. 99). ✧ 'Little soul (darling)'. ⇨ JAN + dim. suff. -*ke*.

JANPEÏS Kzk. 19th c. Jampeis (<Janpeis) [Джампеисъ] (SOV 108). ⇨ JAN?

JANSAD Kzk. 19th c. Jansad [Джансадъ] (SODž. 10). ⇨ JAN?

JANTÏ Kirg. Jantï [Жанты] (Jud. 508). ⇨ JANDÏ?

JAÑA-BERDÏ Kzk. 19th c. Jaña-berdi [Джанга-бердинъ] (AOO 54). ⇨ YAÑÏ + BERDÏ.

JAÑГURČA see YAMГURČÏ

JANÏ-BERGEN Kzk. 1841 Jana-bergen [Джана-бергенъ] (SOK 78); Uzb. 19th c. Janï-bergen [Джанги-бергенъ], from the Kipchak Uzbeks (SKSO III, 191). ⇨ YAÑÏ + BERGEN.

JAÑÏL Kzk. Jañïl [Dshangyl / Цаңыл], fem. (Proben III, 37 /47/); Kzk. Jañïl [Цаңыл], Sarï-qan's widow, Qozï-körpöš's mother (Proben III, 232 /273/); Kkalp. Jañïl [Жаңыл], fem. (KkRS 777); Kirg. Jañïl [Жаңыл] (Jud. 97, 232, 546); Kkalp. 20th c. Jañïl / Žañïl [Джанъыл], fem. (Bask., Kkalp. 403, KkRS 777); Kirg. Jañïl-mïrza [Жаңыл-Мырза] (Jud. 547). ✧ 'Be mistaken' cf. Kkalp. *jañïl-* 'путать, ошибаться' (KkRS), Kirg. *žañïl-* 'ошибаться' (Jud.).

JAÑÏM Kzk. 19th c. Jañïm-χanïm [Джангымъ-ханымъ], Kenisara's second wife (Smirnov 25). ⇨ JANÏM?

JAÑÏZAQ Kzk. 19th c. Jañïzaq-qsï (<Jañïzaq-qïzï?) [Джангызакъ-ксы] (Potanin II, 6). ✧ 'Alone, lonesome' cf. Kzk., Tat. *jañïz / jañγïz* 'allein' (Radl. IV, 17, 18) + suff. -*aq*.

JAÑQ Kzk. 19th c. Jañq [Джанкъ] (SOV 58); Kzk. 19th c. Jañq [Джанкъ], a hunter (Potanin, Pred. 112); Kzk. 19th c. Jañq-bay [Джанкбай] (Grod., Pril. 131). ✧ 'Fight' cf. Uzb. *jank, jänk* 'бой, сражение, битва' (UzbRS).

JAÑQ-SARÏ Kzk. 1785 Jañq-sarï [جنك سارى / Жан-сары], an „aqsaqal" (leader of a smaller community, village) (MIK IV, 51, 53). ⇨ JAÑQ + SARÏ.

JAPAR see JAFAR

JAPEK Kirg. Japek [Жапек] (Jud. 467).

JAPPAS Kzk. 19th c. Jappas [Джаппасъ] (SOK 230).

JAR see YAR

JAR-BOL see YAR-BOL

JAR-QUTLU Maml. 1433 Jar-qutlu [جارقطلو الظاهرى], governor of Damascus (Ibn

Taghrīb. VII, 256, 370, Weil, Chalif. II, 192-93); Maml. 1467/68 **Jar-qutlu** [جـارقطـلو الـدولات بـايـى] (Ibn Taghrīb. VII, 748). ✧ 'Friend-Happy'; Sauvaget interpretes the name as P. *čār* 'quatre' + Trk. *qutlu* 'béni' = 'quatre heureux', 'quatre bonheurs' (p. 45). ⇨ **YAR + QUTLUΓ.**

JAR-MAMBET Kzk. 18th c. - 19th c. **Jar-mambet** [Джармамбет] (Tynyšp. 74). ✧ 'Friend / follower (of) Muḥammad'. ⇨ **YAR + MUXAMMED.** See also **YARMÄT.**

JARΓÏY Yak. **Jarγïy** [Џаргыі / Нјаргыı] (Pek.). ✧ 'Knock(ing)'? cf. Yak. *jarγïy-* 'издавать звук (напр. от ударе топором по доске и вообще по тонкому и звонкому предмету)' (Pek.).

JARΓÏMIAN Yak. **Jarγïmïan / Jarmïγïan** [Џарγымыан / Џармыгыан] (Pek.). ✧ Yermogen, Germogen (R.).

JARÏQ-PAS Kzk. 19th c. **Jarïq-pas** (SOV 76); Kzk. 19th c. **Jarïq-pas** (SOK 130). ✧ 'Bright head'. ⇨ **YARUQ + BAŠ.**

JARÏLΓASÏN Kzk. 19th c. **Jarïlγasïn** [Исенгалий Джарылгасынов] (AUK 433). ✧ 'Let God be your protector' (Žanuzakov), 'Let God bless you; Let God make you happy; Let God forgive you' cf. Kzk. *žarïlqa-* 'одарить кого-н., облагодетельствовать; простить, отпустить грехи' (KzRS), Kzk. *jarïlγa- / jarïlqa-* 'gnädig sein, glücklich machen, Jemanden beschenken' (Radl. IV, 30), cf. also Rásonyi, Imp. 239.

JARLÏQ-TÖRE see **ZARLÏQ**

JARŠANQÏ Oghuz/Trkm. 13th c. **Jaršanqï** [جـارشـانـتى / Джаршанкы] (Abulg./Kon. 1245).

JAS-TÜLÜK Kzk. **Jas-tülük** [Џас Тӱлӱк] (Proben III, 102 (130)). ✧ 'Young child'. ⇨ **YAŠ + TÜLEK.**

JASÏQ Kzk. 18th c. - 19th c. **Jasïq** [Джасык] (Tynyšp. 71); Kzk. 18th c. - 19th c. **Jasïq-bay** [Джасыкбай] (Tynyšp. 73). ✧ 'Not fat, thin, shy, irresolute' cf. Kzk. *jasïq* 'нежирный (о мясе); непитательный; робкий, не энергичный; нерешительный' (KzRS).

JAŠAR see **YAŠAR**

JAŠAW see **YAŠAW**

JATAN-BALÏ Kzk. 19th c. **Jatan-balï** [Джатанбалы] (SOV 144). ⇨ **BALÏ.**

JATÏ-QOÑÏZ Kzk. 19th c. **Jatï-qoñïz / Jeti-qoñïz?** [Джатыконизъ] (SOK 18). ⇨ **YEDI + QOÑUZ?**

JATKE Kzk. 19th c. **Jatke** [Джатке] (AOP 86). ⇨ ? + suff. *-ke.*

JAW-BAS Tat.(Lit.) 1591 **Jaw-bas** [Зелюха Дчовбасовна Балдышевичъ] (Lit. Tat. 82). ✧ 'Attack/oppress the enemy' cf. Chag., Alt., Tat. *yau* 'der Feind' (Radl. III, 16), Turk. *yaw* 'fremd, ein Fremder; feindlich, der Feind' (Radl. III, 289), Bashk. *yaw* 'битва, бой ' (BRS), Kzk. *žau* 'враг, неприятель' (KzRS). ⇨ **YAW(-BASAR) + BAS II.**

See also **JAW-BERDİ.**

JAW-BASAR see **YAW-BASAR**

JAW-BERDİ Tat.(Lit.) 1591 **Jaw-berdi** [Дчовберда Байрашевичъ] (Lit. Tat. 82). ✧ **BERDİ.** See also **JAW-BAS.**

JAW-GİLDE see **YAW-GİLDİ**

JAW-QASTÏ see **YAW-QAČTÏ**

JAWALÏ Selj. / Khorezm.? 1106 **Jawalï** [Jâwâlî], a „Turkish 'Amîr" (Abulfar./Budge I, 239).

JAWGER see **YAWGER**

JAWQAY see **YAWQAY**

JAWQAR see **JEWHER**

JAWULDUR Oghuz **Jawuldur** [Джаулдур], Kök-χan's son (RaD I/1, 76). ✧ Ethnonym, a tribe of the Oghuz branch Üč-oq, cf. *Çavuldur* (Erol II). ⇨ **ČAWUNDUR?**

JAWUR Kzk. 18th c. - 19th c. **Jawur** [Джаур] (Tynyšp. 65).

JĀJAY Yak. **Jājay** [Џаџаі], byname of a woman usually called Agrafena (R.) (Pek.).

JĀQÏP Yak. **Jāqïp** [Џакып / Џакып] (Pek.). ✧ Yakov (R.).

JÂN-BOL see **JAN-BOL**

JÄBÄ-BĀBA see **JAΓA-BĀBA**

JÄDİGÄR see **YADÏΓAR**

JÄGÄ-BĀBA see **JAΓA-BĀBA**

JÄKİM Yak. **Jäkim** [Џäкім] (Pek.). ✧ Yefim (R.).

JÄLDİ-BAY see **YELLİ**

JÄLİSÄY Yak. **Jälisäy** [Џälіcіäі / Дälіcіäі] (Pek.). ✧ Yelisey (R.).

JÄLLÄNÄY Yak. **Jällänäy** [Џäллäнäі / Дjäллäнäі] (Pek.).

JÄMİYLÄ Kirg. **Jamïyla** [Жамыйла], fem. (Jud. 111); Kzk. 19th c. **Jämiylä** [Джамила], fem. (SKSO IV, otd. II, 34); Kkalp. 20th c. **Žämiyle** [Жәмийле], fem. (KkRS 777). ✧ Djamila / Jamila (Ar.) 'beautiful, pretty' (Ahmed).

JÄN-GÄLDİ see **JAN-KELDİ**

JÄNİ-BEK see **JANÏ**

JÄÑİR NUyg.(Tar.) **Jäñir-χoJa / Jäñgir-χoJa** [Dschängir Chodscha / Џäнгір Хоџа] (Proben VI, 6 /7/). ⇨ **JİHANGİR?**

JÄRÄBÄY Yak. **Järäbäy / Järimiäy** [Џäräбäі / Џäріміäі] (Pek.). ✧ Yeremey (R.).

JÄRİÄS Yak. **Järiäs-bärgän** [Џäріäс-бäргäн] (Pek.).

JÄSÄGÄY Yak. **Jäsägäy / D'äsägäy / Jüsügäy / Jösögöy / D'ösögöy / Jüsägäy / Jäsägäy-toyon** [Џäcäräі / Дjäcäräі / Џӱcӱräі / Џöcöröі (Djöcöröі) / Џӱcäräі] (Pek.); Yak. **Jösögöy / Jösögöy-toyon** [Џöcöröі / Џöcöкöі / Дjöcöröі / Џäcäräі (Дjäcäräі) / Џӱcäräі / Џӱcӱräі], a god giving people wealth (that is, plenty of livestock) (Pek.); Yak. **Jüsägäy / Jüsügäy / Jösögöy / Dyösögöy / Jäsägäy / Dyäsägäy** [Џӱcäräі, Џӱcӱräі / Џöcöröі (Djöcöröі),

Цäсäгäi (Djäcäräi) / Сäттä-кÿрÿö-цÿсäгäi-айы], Ayï-toyon's follower, god (protector) of horses (Pek.). ✧ 'God, Christ'; „божество, которое "творчески ниспосылает скот" (под этим именем якуты ныне разумеют Христа" (Pek.). See also **KÖRÖ-JÄSÄGÄY**.

JÄSİN-TURANTAY Yak. **Jäsin-turantay** [Цäсiн Турантаi-частъ], a component of female names (Pek.).

JÄSİN-TURĀXAY Yak. **Jäsin-turāχay** [Цäсiн Турахаi], a spirit of the roads (придорожный дух) (Pek.).

JÄSİÑKÄY Yak. **Jäsiñkäy** [Цäсiҥкäi], a demonic old woman (Pek.).

JÄSTÄYBÄ Yak. **Jästäybä** [Цäстäiбä], petname of one of the children of the legendary witch (Baba-yaga) (Pek.). ✧ 'Having red eyes, with red eyes' cf. Yak. *jäs*.

JÄWHÄR see **JEWHER**

JEBEŠ Khorezm./Mo.? 14th c. **Jebeš** [Джебеш], Ghazan Khan's (1295-1304) wife, Künčük's (Qunčuq's?; see Könček) sister (RaD I/1, 120).

JEBГU see **YABГU**

JEBİL see **EDİL-JEBİL**

JEGE Kzk. 19th c. **Jege-bey** [Джегебеи] (SOK 60); Kzk. 19th c. **Jiki-bay** [Минтибай Джикибаевъ] (Grod., Pril. 91). ✧ 'Lonesome, alone'? cf. Kzk. *žeke* 'отдельный, единоличный' (KzRS), Kzk. *jekä* 'allein, besonders' (Radl. IV, 67) (<P.).

JEYHŪN Trkm. 20th c. **Jeyhun** [Ğeyhun] (Zaj. 1971, 333); Trkm. 20th c. **Jeyhun** [Джейхун] (TrkmRS 323). ✧ 'Raging, stormy, boisterous, wild' cf. Trkm. *jeyhūn* 'бушующий, неукротимый' (TrkmRS) (<Ar.).

JEYİS Kzk. 19th c. **Jeys-pay** (<Jeyis-pay) [Джейспай] (SODž. 64).

JEKEY Kzk. 19th c. **Jekey** [Джекей] (AOK 118). ⇨ **JEKE?** + suff. -*y*.

JEKEL Oghuz/Trkm. 13th c. **Jekel** [جكل / Джекель], Türk's son, Yafes' grand-son (Abulg./Kon. 135).

JEKİP see **YAQUB**

JEKSEM Kzk. 19th c. **Jeksem-bay** [Джексембай] (SOV 24); Kzk. 19th c. **Jeksem-bay** [Джексембай] (SODž. 52); Kzk. 19th c. **Jeksem-bay** [Джексембай] (SOK 182). ⇨ **JEKSEMBİ?**

JEKSEMBİ see **YEKŠENBE**

JEKSENBE see **YEKŠENBE**

JEKÜ Kzk. 19th c. **Jekü-pek?** [Джекупекъ] (SODž. 124).

JEL Kzk. 19th c. **Jel-qïz** [Джель-кызъ], fem. (Potanin, Pred. 94). ✧ 'Wind(-girl).'. ⇨ **YEL**.

JEL-QAYÏP Kirg. **Jelqayïp** [Желкайып] (Jud. 250, 251).

JEL-MAUS see **YEL-MOГUS**

JELAY Kzk. 19th c. **Jelay** [Джелай] (SOK 68).

JELLETQAN Nog. 20th c. **Jelletqan** [Джеллет къан Шапшакъ келинъи], one of Baskakov's female informants from Sarï-awul (Bask., Nog. 144). ⇨ **JELLET** + suff. -*qan(1)*.

JEM Kzk. 19th c. **Jem-bek** [Джембекъ] (SODž. 12). ✧ 'Corn, food' cf. Kzk. *jem* 'das Futter, die Nahrung' (Radl. IV, 91).

JEM-BULAT Trkm. 19th c. **Jem-bulat** [Джембулатовъ] (Ščeglov I, 350, 358). ⇨ **JEM** + **BULAT**.

JEMDİ Kzk. 19th c. **Jemdi-bay** [Джемдыбай] (SODž. 160). ✧ 'Having corn, food.'. ⇨ **JEM** + suff. -*di*.

JEMTİK Kzk. 19th c. **Jemtik** [Джемтыкъ] (AOO 70). ⇨ **JEM** + suff. -*tik*.

JEMÜ Kzk. 19th c. **Jemü** / **Jemu** [Джему] (SODž. 8).

JEN Kkalp. 18th c. - 19th c. **Jen-bek-bi** [Дженбек-би] (MIKk. 208); Kzk. 19th c. **Jen-bikey** [Дженбикей], fem. (Grod., Pril. 116). ✧ 'Sleeve'? cf. Kzk. *jeñ* 'der Aermel' (Radl. IV, 69).

JENAQ Kzk. **Jenaq** [Дженакъ] (Konšin, Oč. 73). ✧ I. 'Stirrup'? cf. Chag. *janaq* 'id.' (Radl. IV, 21); II. 'Little soul'? ⇨ **JAN?** + suff. -*aq*.

JENAVER Turk. **Jenaver-oγlu**, a Zeybek (Kúnos 1891, 118). ✧ 'Beast, wild animal.'.

JEND Turk. **Jend-oγlu**, a Zeybek (Kúnos 1891, 118).

JENDİ Kzk. 19th c. **Jendi-bay** [Джендыбай] (SODž. 40). ✧ 'Overcame' cf. Kzk. *jeñ-* 'besiegen, die Oberhand haben' (Radl. IV, 69).

JENEWİT Kkalp. 20th c. **Jenewi** / **Ženewit** [Дженевит, Женеўит] (Bask., Kkalp. 75, KkRS 773).

JENİL Kzk. 19th c. **Jenil-bay** (<Jeñil-bay) [Дженельбай] (SODž. 134). ✧ 'Sanguine, hot, hasty' cf. Kzk. *jeñil* 'leicht, flink, heftig (von Menschen)' (Radl. IV, 69).

JENNET Trkm. 20th c. **Jennet** [Ğennet], fem. (Zaj. 1971, 337); Trkm. 20th c. **Jennet** [Дженнет], fem. (TrkmRS 324). ✧ 'Paradise' cf. Trkm. *jennet* 'рай, райский' (TrkmRS) (<Ar.).

JEÑİŠ see **YEÑİŠ**

JEÑKİ Kzk. 19th c. **Jeñki-bay** [Дженкыбай] (SOV 92). ✧ 'Victorious hero, warrior' cf. Crm. *jeñk* (<P.) 'der Kampf, der Krieg' (Radl. IV, 70). See also **ГĀZİ**.

JEPS Kzk. 19th c. **Jeps-bay** [Джепсбай] (SODž. 58).

JER-JENİZ Alt. 19th c. **Jer-Jeniz** [Джердженизъ] (Potanin, Pred. 182).

JERDAN Kzk. 19th c. **Jerdan** [Джерданъ Нуракбаевъ] (Grod., Pril. 190).

JEREN Kzk. 1819 **Čiran** [Чиран] (MIK IV, 324); Trkm. **Jeren** [Җерен], fem. (TrkmRS 324); Trkm. 20th c. **Jeren** [Ğeren], fem. (Zaj. 1971, 338); Trkm. 20th c. **Jeren** [Джерен], fem. (TrkmRS 324); Trkm. 1816 **Jeren-yüzbaši** [Джерен-юзбаши] (MIT II, 395). ✧ 'Gazelle' cf. Trkm. *jeren* 'джейран; газель' (TrkmRS), Chag. *čiran* 'die Gazelle' (Radl. III, 2123). See also **YAZ-JEREN, KİYİK**.

JERİYE Kzk. 19th c. **Jeriye-pay** [Джерiепай] (SOV

134). ✧ 'Female slave, concubine' cf. Turk. *cariye* 'id.' (TED) (<Ar.).

JERİT Turk. **Jerid-oɣlu**, a Zeybek (Kúnos 1891, 119). ✧ 'Stick used as a dart in the mounted game; game of jereed; the game of jereed' (TED), cf. Turk. *jirid* 'das Dschiridspiel' (Radl. IV, 142).

JERMEK Maml. 1320 **Jermek** [جرمك النا صرى] (Dawād. 303). ➪ YERMÄK?

JERŠİBAT Kzk. 19th c. **Jeršibat** [Джершибатъ] (Groč., Pril. 76).

JEŠ Selj.? 11th c. **Ješ / Češ?** [جش] (Ahbar 21). ✧ 'Turquoise' cf. Karakh. *češ, čeč* 'бирюза' (DTS).

JETBİS see YETMİŠ

JETEY Kzk. 19th c. **Jetey** [Джетей] (AOAtb. 66). ✧ 'Enough (of children)' cf. Kzk. *jet- (cetüv)* 'Ulaşmak, yarmak; dolmak, yaşını doldurmak; kafi gelmek' (KzTS).

JETİ see YETİ

JETİ-KÖT Kzk. **Jeti-köt** (Rintchen: ROr. XX(1956), 22). ✧ 'Seven arses (vulvas)' (Rintchen: ROr. XX(1956), 22: 'sept vulves'), cf. Kuman, Chag., Alt., Crm., Kzk. *köt* 'die Schamtheile und der Hintern' (Radl. II, 1275). ➪ YETİ.

JETİ-SABAR see YETİ-SABAR

JETİ-TAS Tuv. 19th c. **Jeti-tas** [Джеты Тасъ] (Potanin IV, 345, 348, 721). ✧ 'Seven stones.'. ➪ YETİ + TAŠ.

JETİM see YETİM

JETPİS see YETMİŠ

JETPİS see YETMİŠ

JETTİ Kzk. 19th c. **Jetti-bay** [Ханъ Магомедъ Джетибаевъ], a Kazak Khan (χan) (Grod., Pril. 91). ✧ 'He reached, arrived (= was born)' cf. Kzk. *jet-* 'to reach'.

JEWHER Kkalp. 20th c. **Jawqar** [Джавкъар], fem. (Bask., Kkalp. 403); 1063 **Jewher** [جوهر المتلبى] (Qalānisi 90); 1438/39, 1447 **Jewher** [جوهر المنجكى] (Ibn Taghrīb. VII, 25, 118, 315); 1465/66 **Jewher** [جوهر الارغونى شاوى] (Ibn Taghrīb. VII, 811); Bulg. 13th c.-14th c. **Jewher** [جوهر] / Джäвхäр] (Jusupov 35); Selj. 12th c. **Jewher**, Sultan Sandjar's (1117-1157) retainer (Ahbar 79); Maml.? 1332 **Jewher** [جوهر بن الملك], an emir (Dawād. 368); Maml.? 1460/61 **Jewher** [جوهر النوروزى] (Iyās II, 67, 172); Maml.? 1518 **Jewher** [جوهر نائب مقدم المماليك], a governor (Iyās III, 160); Trkm.? 1441 **Jewher** [جوهر القنتبائى] (Ibn Taghrīb. VIII, 2); Trkm.? 1450, 1468/69 **Jewher** [جوهر التركما نى] (Ibn Taghrīb. VII, 203, 696, Iyās II, 104); Trkm. 1461, 1468 **Jewher** [جوهر التركما نى الهندى] (Ibn Taghrīb. VIII, 412, 434, 695); Khorezm. 14th c. **Jewher-aɣa?** [Yauguyaga], one of Timur's wives (Clavijo 52); Maml.? 1383 **Jewher-**

küčük-χoǰa [جوهر كوچك خواجه], the Muzaffarid Šāh-šuǰā's follower (Qazw. 724); Chag. **Jewher-šah-begüm** [Gauhar Shah Begum], sister of the author Mirza Haydar (Tar. Rashidi 193); Kkalp. 20th c. **Žawhar** [Жаухар], fem. (KkRS 777). ✧ 'Precious stone, diamond' cf. Kzk. *jawqar* (Ar.) 'der Edelstein' (Radl. IV, 7), Turk. *cevher* 'jewel, gem; precious thing or person; ability, capacity, good quality' (TED) (<P<Ar.). See also GÄWHÄR.

JEZ-TİRNAQ Kzk. **Jez-tïrnaq**, a fabulous woman in Kazak mythology (Or. Bibl. XVIII, 65). ✧ 'Copper nail' 'Kupferklauen' (Or. Bibl. XVIII, 65). ➪ TİRNAQ.

JEZİ Kzk. 19th c. **Jezi-bay** [Джезыбай] (AOP 50).

Jİ see JİY

JİBÄK see JİBEK

JİBEK Kkalp. 20th c. **Jibäk** [Джибек], fem. (Bask., Kkalp. 403); Tat. 14th c. **Jibäk / Jibek / Čibäk?** [Τζηπάκις], a christened Tatar from the early 14th c. (Byz. Turc. II, 312); Kzk. 19th c. **Jibek** [Джибекъ], fem. (Grod., Pril. 124, Grod., Vojna I, 98); Kirg. **Jibek** [Жибек], fem. (Jud. 416); Kzk. 19th c. **Jibek / Jibek-qïz / Qïz-Jibek** [قز جيبك / Джибек, Джибеккыз], a man in a folk epic titled „Qïz Jibek" [قصه'قز جيبا ك], Kazan, 1896) (Grod. I, 56, 98, Or. Bibl. XX, 81, AUK Dobavl. 5); Kkalp. 20th c. **Žibek** [Жибек], fem. (KkRS 777). ✧ 'Silk' cf. Kzk. *cibek* 'ipek' (KzTS), Kkalp. *jipek* 'шёлк' (KkRS), Bashk. *yebäk* 'шелк' (BRS). See also İBÄK, QÏZÏL-JİBEK.

JİBUQ see ČİBİQ

JİDÄ Kzk. **Jidä-baj** [Джедабай] (Konšin, Oč. 73); Kzk. 19th c. **Jiyda-bay / Jiydä-bay?** [Джийдабай] (SOV 28); Kzk. 19th c. **Jiyde-bay** [Джийдебай] (SOK 182); Kzk. **Žide-bay** [Жидебай], a forefather of the original inhabitants (Kojčubajev 102). ✧ 'Oleaster, wild olive' cf. Kzk. *jidä* 'der Silberbaum (Elaeagnus angustifolia)' (Radl. IV, 153), Kzk. *žide* 'джида' (KzRS).

JİÄDÄ-BAXSİLA Yak. **Jiädä-baχsïla-toyon** [Џіäдä-ахьыла-тojoн], host (spirit) of the home (Pek.).

JİÄRGİLÄ-BAXSİLA Yak. **Jiärgïlä-baχsïla-toyon** [Џіäргïлä-Бахсыла-тojoн], host (spirit) of the home (Pek.).

JİÄS-XOTŌBO Yak. **Jiäs-χotōbo** [Џіäс-Хотобо], a component of the name of a legendary old woman (abāsï) (Pek.). ✧ 'It is ready' (<R. *Jest' Gotova* / Есть-Готова 'id.') (Pek.).

JİGER Turk. 1583 **Jiger** [جكر] / Ciger] (Ongan, Ank. I, 179); Kzk. 19th c. **Jiger** [Джигеръ] (SOK 38). ✧ 'Liver, strength; darling' cf. *jiger* (Crm.) 'die Leber', (Tat.) 'die Kraft, die Gewalt' (Radl. IV, 136), Turk. *ciger* 'liver; heart, affections; one's child; darling' (TED).

JİGİ Bashk. 19th c. **Jigi-jan** (Mende 183).

JİGİT see **YİGİT**

JİGİTEK   Kzk. 19th c. **Jigitek** [Джигитекъ] (SODž. 118); Kzk. 19th c. **Jigitek** [Джигитекъ] (SOV 74); Kzk. 19th c. **Jigitek** [Джигитекъ] (SOK 66). ⇨ **YİGİT** + dim. suff. -ek.

JİHAN   Hak. 19th-20th c. **Čiχan** [Чихан] (HRS 352); Trkm. 20th c. **Jahan** [Ğahan], fem. (Zaj. 1971, 337); Trkm. 20th c. **Jahan** [Джахан], fem. (TrkmRS 321); Yürük 16th c. **Jihan-beg**, from the Yürüks of Kocacık (Gökb., Rum. 103); Selj. 13th c.-15th c. **Jihan-melik-χatun** [جهانملك خاتون], in an inscription of a tomb in Tokat (Uzunçarş., Küt. I, 55); Bashk. 1740 **Jiyan-γul** [Джиянгулъ Исѣкѣевъ] (Nepljuev 172); Bashk. 1779 **Jiyan-γul** [Джиянгул Табулдин] (MIB V, 83, 84); Tat.(GH) 1541 **Jiyan-χoJa** [جيان خوجه] (Jusupov (text) 7); Kzk. 19th c. **Jiyan-χoJa** [Джіянъ Ходжа кулэ Ходжиновъ] (Grod., Pril. 118); Kzk. 19th c. **Jiyan-qul** [Джіанкуловъ] (SKSO VIII, 222); Trkm. 1735 **Jiyan-vekil** [Джиян-векиль], from the Yomut tribe (MIT II, 333). ✧ 'World, resident of the world' cf. Turk. *jihan* 'die Welt.' (Radl. IV, 137), Tat. *jihan* 'id.' (TatRS), Trkm. *jahan* 'мир, свет' (TrkmRS), also Hak. PN *Čiχan* (Butanaev) (< P.). See also **DUR-JİHAN, MAH-JİHAN, NUR-JAHAN.**

JİHANGİR   Turk. 15th c. **Jihangir** [Cihangir], ruler of the Karakoyunlu state(let) (Uzunçarş., Anad. 64, 93). ✧ 'He who will conquer the world' <P. جهان كير (Jahān-gīr) 'qui conquiest le monde' (Sauvaget 47).

JİY   Kzk. 19th c. **Jiy-bay** [Асилъ Джибаевъ] (Grod., Pril. 30).

JİYDİ   Kzk. 19th c. **Jiydi-bay** / **Jiydï-bay** (<**Jïydï-bay?**) [Джийды-бай] (Potanin, Pred. 66).

JİYEMBET   Kzk. 18th c. - 19th c. **Jiyembet** (<**Jiyenbet**) [Джиембет] (Tynyšp. 66, 68, 69, 70, 71, 73, 75,). ⇨ **JİYEN** + suffixoid -bet.

JİYEN   Kzk. 18th c. - 19th c. **Jiyem-bay** (<**Jiyen-bay**) [Джиембай] (Tynyšp. 65, 69); Kzk. 18th c. - 19th c. **Jiyen** [Джиен] (Tynyšp. 73); Kzk. 18th c. - 19th c. **Jiyen-bay** [Джиенбай] (Tynyšp. 66, 69); Kzk. 18th c. - 19th c. **Jiyen-qul** [Джиенкул] (Tynyšp. 68); Bashk. 1740 **Žiyän-bay** [Жиан-бай Иткустин] (MIB I, 440); Kkalp. 18th c. - 19th c. **Žiyen-alï** [Джиеналы] (Tynyšp. 75); Kkalp. 20th c. **Žiyen-bay** [Жийенбай] (KkRS 773); Kkalp. 20th c. **Žiyen-gül** [Жийенгул], fem. (KkRS 777). ✧ 'Cousin (on mother-side)' cf. Kzk. *jiän, jiyän* 'der Mensch im Verhältnisse zu den Verwandten von Mutterseite' (Radl. IV, 135, 140), Kzk. *jiyen* 'племянник, племянница (по женской линии' (KzRS).

JİYETİL   Kzk. 19th c. **Jiyetil-bay** / **Jetil-bay** [Джіетылбай] (AOK 130).

JİYRENŠE   Kkalp. 20th c. **Jiyrenše** / **Žiyrenše** [Джийренше / Жийренше] (Bask., Kkalp. 400,

KkRS 773); Kzk. 18th c. - 19th c. **Yerenče-batïr** / **Erenče-batïr?** [Еренче-батыр] (Tynyšp. 70). ✧ 'Red, red-blond' cf. Kzk., Tat. *jïrän* 'fuchsfarben, hochroth, hochblond' (Radl. IV, 142), Kkalp. *žiyren* ' рыжий' (KkRS), Kirg. *žēren, žeyren, žērde* ' рыжий' (Jud.), Alt. *yärän, yägrän* 'fuchsfarben, roth (ein rothes Pferd mit rother Mähne und Schwanz)' (Radl. III, 338); Kzk. *žiren* 'рыжий' (KzRS). + suff. -še.

JİYÜ   Kzk. 19th c. **Jiyü-bay** [Джіюбай] (SOK 180). ✧ 'Collection, collecting, gathering'? cf. Kzk. *cïyuv [žïyuw]* 'toplamak, bir yere yïğmak' (KzTS) + suff. -ü.

JİK   Kzk. 1819 **Jik** [Джик] (MIK IV, 324). ✧ 'Slit; seam'? cf. Kzk. *jik* 'die Spalte, Fuge, Nath' (Radl. IV, 136).

JİK-JİK   Az. **Jik-Jik-χanum** [Джик-джик-ханум] (Az. Skaz. 466).

JİKER   Uzb. **Jiker** [Джикеръ] (ZIRGOStat. IV, Pril. 14).

JİKİ see **JEGE**

JİKİ-BURA   **Jiki-bura** [Джики-Бура] (RaD/Ber. II, 116). ⇨ **JEGE** + **BUГRA?**

JİL see **YEL**

JİL-GELDİ see **JİL-KELDİ**

JİL-KELDİ   Kzk. 18th c. - 19th c. **Jil-geldi** [Джильгельды] (Tynyšp. 66, 68); Kzk. 19th c. **Jil-geldi** [Джилгельдіевъ] (Grod., Pril. 101); Kzk. 18th c. - 19th c. **Jil-keldi** [Джилкельды] (Tynyšp. 73); Kzk. 19th c. **Jil-keldi** [Токусбай Джилкелдинъ] (Grod., Pril. 57); Kzk. 19th c. **Jil-keldi** [Джилькельды] (SOK 198); Kzk. 19th c. **Jil-geldi** [Джилгельды] (SOV 8). ✧ I. 'Wind has come' II. 'The (new) year has come'? ⇨ **JİL** + **KELDİ.**

JİL-MAMBET   Kzk. 18th c. - 19th c. **Jil-mambet** [Джильмамбет] (Tynyšp. 75). ⇨ **YEL** + **MAMBET.**

JİLAN see **YÏLAN**

JİLANJİ   **Jilanji** [Джиланджи], Tuγan-buqa's son (RaD I/1, 94). ✧ 'Grower or breeder of gazelles / snakes?' cf. Chag., Crm. *jilan* 'die Gazelle' (Radl. IV, 145). ⇨ **JÏLAN** / **JEREN?** + suff. -ji.

JİLAUN   Khorezm.? 14th c. **Jilaun** [Джилаун], Toqtay-beki's son (RaD I/1, 115).

JİLAW   **Jilaw** [Джилау], an emir (RaD I/1, 112); Kzk.? 19th c. **Jiläw-quš-begi** / **Yilaw-quš-begi** يلاو قوش بكى / [Джиляу] (Veselovskij, Kirg. 2). ✧ 'Rein (of bridle), reins' cf. Chag. *jilau* 'der Zügel' (Radl. IV, 145).

JİLAWQAN   Khorezm. 14th c. **Jilawqan-bahadur** [Джилаукан-бахадур], from the Suldus (Sulduz) tribe of Mongol origin (RaD I/1, 131). ⇨ **JİLAW?** + suff. -qan.

JİLDÏ see **YELLİ**

JİLİS see **JİLİS**

JİLQÏ see **YÏLQÏ**

JİMELDİ   Kzk. 19th c. **Jimeldi?** [Джимельды]

(SODž. 66).

JÏN Kzk. 19th c. **Jin-atay** [Джинатай] (AOAtb. 22); Kzk. 19th c. **Jin-bek** [Джинбекъ Абдиловъ] (Grod., Pril. 72). ✧ 'Devil, evil spirit' cf. Kzk. *jïn* 'ein böser Geist' (Radl. IV, 119), Chag., Turk., NUyg., Kzk. *jin* 'ein böser Geist, ein Plagegeist, ein Dämon' (Radl. IV, 141). See also **BAY-JÏN.**

JÏN-BAΓÏŠ Kzk. 19th c. **Jin-baγïš-bay** [Джинбагишбай] (Grod., Pril. 158). ⇨ **JÏN + BAΓÏŠ.**

JÏN-GILDI Kzk. 19th c. **Jin-gildi** [Джингильды] (SOK 186). ✧ 'Devil (evil) has come (=has been born).'. ⇨ **JÏN + KELDI.**

JÏN-TAY Kzk. 19th c. **Jin-tay** [Исмирза Джинтаевъ] (Grod., Pril. 179). ⇨ **JÏN + TAY + / suff. -tay(1,2).**

JÏNDAN Kzk. 19th c. **Jindan** [Джинданъ] (AOO 54).

JÏNDÏ Kzk. 19th c. **Jindï-bala** [Джинды-бала] (Ibragimov 125); Kzk. 19th c. **Jindu-bay / Jindü-bay?** [Джиндубай] (SOV 20); *TN:* Kzk. **Jindu-bay / Jindü-bay?** [Джинду-бай], a well? (Karta JAR XI). ✧ 'Mad' cf. Kzk. *žindï* 'сумасшедший' (KzRS).

JÏNEL Kzk. 19th c. **Jinel** [Джинель] (SOV 206).

JÏNI Kzk. 19th c. **Jini-bay** [Турганбай Джинибаевъ] (Grod., Pril. 156).

JÏNKIN Kzk. 19th c. **Jinkin-bay** [Давылка Джинкинбаевъ] (Grod., Pril. 91).

JÏNQA Kzk. 19th c. **Jinqa-bay?** [Джинкабай] (SOK 148)

JÏNTAQ Kzk. 19th c. **Jintaq?** [Джинтакъ Исабаевъ] (Grod., Pril. 32).

JÏNÜ Kzk. 19th c. **Jinü (<Jiñü?)** [Джинубай] (Grod., Pril. 186). ✧ 'Victory'? cf. Kzk. *jeñü* 'победить, одолеть' (KzRS).

JÏÑIL Kzk. 19th c. **Jiñil-bay** [Джингильбай] (SOV 148)

JÏÑIS Yak. **Jiñis** [Џиңіс], a Yakut sovereign who ruled over the Yakuts when they were living in their former southern country, according to tradition he was followed by Tïγïn who led the Yakuts to the recent country in the north (Pek.). ✧ Derived from Yak. *čiñïs.*

JÏPA Kzk. 19th c. **Jïpa** [Джипа] (AOP 62).

JÏPAR see **YÏPAR**

JÏPÏS Kzk. 19th c. **Jipïs-bay** [Джипысбай] (SOK 266).

JÏRAL Kzk. 19th c. **Jiral-bay? / Jir-al-bay?** [Джиралбай] (Grod., Pril. 54).

JÏRENČE-ČEŠÄN see **YÏRENŠE-ŠEŠEN**

JÏRINŠE-ŠEŠEN see **YÏRENŠE-ŠEŠEN**

JÏT Kzk. 19th c. **Jit-qul** [Джиткуловъ] (Grod., Pril. 53).

JÏVAN-MERD Chag. **Jivan-merd-sultan** [سلطان جوانمرد / Джеванмердъ Султанъ], a Shaybanid (Šejb. LV, LXXVIII). ✧ '?- (Brave) man' cf. Turk. *märd* 'ein tüchtiger, tapferer Mann; muthig' (Radl. IV, 2096), Turk. *merd* 'Adam, insan; erkek; yiğit' (Özön) (<P.).

JÏZÏQ Kzk. 19th c. **Jiziq-pek / Jïzïq-pek?** [Джизыкпекъ] (SOV 44).

JÏY Yak. **Jïy** [Џы] (Pek.). ✧ Diy (R. male name).

JÏLAN see **YÏLAN**

JÏLÏS Kzk. 19th c. **Jilïs** [Джилысъ] (SODž. 6). ✧ 'Meeting, collecting' cf. Kzk. *jïlïs* 'die Versammlung' (Radl. IV, 146).

JÏLQÏ-AYDAR Kkalp. 20th c. **Jïlqï-aydar** [Джылкъыайдар] (Bask., Kkalp. 400); Kkalp. 20th c. **Žïlqï-aydar** [Жылкъыайдар] (KkRS 774). ✧ 'He who will herd/drive the horses; who will drive (*cattle* and perhaps *enemy*) out'. ⇨ **YÏLQÏ + AYDAR.**

JÏLTÏQ Kzk. 19th c. **Jïltïq** [Джылтыкъ] (SOK 172). ✧ 'One year old'? cf. Kzk. *cïl* 'ыл, sene' (KzTS) + Adj. suff. *-tïq.*

JÏÑΓÏL Kkalp. 20th c. **Jïñγïl-bay** [Джынъгъылбай] (Bask., Kkalp. 400); Kkalp. 20th c. **Žïñγïl-bay** [Жынғылбай] (KkRS 774). ✧ 'Tamarisk' cf. Kkalp. *jïñγïl* 'тамариск (кустарника, который используется для топлива)' (KkRS).

JÏPPÏALA see **SÏTÏ-JÏPPÏALA**

JÏRRÏQ Turk. **Jïrrïq-oγlu**, a Zeybek (Kúnos 1891, 119). ✧ 'A kind of bird' cf. Turk. *cırrık* 'serçeden biraz büyük, eti yenen boz renkli bir kuş' (DS).

JOΓARÏ-ČEKTI Kzk. 18th c. - 19th c. **Joγarï-čekti** [Джогары-чекти] (Tynyšp. 69).

JOXSOΓON-OYŪN-KINÄS Yak. **Joχsoγon-oyūn-kinäs** [Џохсоҕон-ојун-кінäс] (Pek.).

JOXSOΓON-UOLA-KINÄS Yak. **Joχsoγon-uola-kinäs** [Џохсоҕон уола Кинäс], harmful spirit (üör) that makes people bad, sick, etc. (Pek.).

JOY Kzk. 19th c. **Joy** [Джой] (SODž. 74). ✧ 'Annihilate (the enemy)'!; cf. Kzk. *joy-* 'verlieren, vernichten' (Radl. IV, 92). See also **BÖLDIR.**

JOYÏM Kzk. 19th c. **Joyïm** [Джоимъ] (SOV 40).

JOQEY Kzk. 19th c. **Joqey** [Джокей] (AOP 58). ✧ 'Non-existent, poor (in diminutive form)' cf. Kzk. *joq* 'das Nichtsein, eine verlorene Sache, der Arme' (Radl. IV, 92-93). + dim. suff. *-ey.*

JOL-AMAN Kzk. 18th c. - 19th c. **Jol-aman** [Джоламан] (Tynyšp. 68, 69); Kkalp. 20th c. **Žol-aman** [Жоламан] (KkRS 773). ✧ 'Road (=life) healthy, lucky; Have a good (healthy, lucky) road (=life)!'. ⇨ **YOL + AMAN.** See also **AMAN-JOL.**

JOL-BERDI Kzk. 18th c. - 19th c. **Jol-berdi** [Джолберды] (Tynyšp. 73). ⇨ **YOL + BERDI.**

JOL-BOΓAY Kzk. 19th c. **Jol-boγay** [Джолбогай] (SOK 28). ⇨ **YOL + BOΓAY?**

JOL-MAMBET Kzk. 18th c. - 19th c. **Jol-mambet** [Джолмамбет] (Tynyšp. 67); Kzk. 19th c. **Žul-mambet** [Калій Жулмамбетовъ] (AUK 870). ⇨ **YOL + MAMBET.**

JOL-ŽAQSÏ Kzk. 18th c. - 19th c. **Jol-žaqsï** [Джолжаксы] (Tynyšp. 70). ✧ 'Road (=life) good;

Let him have a good (fortunate) life.'. ⇨ **YOL** + **YAQŠÏ**. See also **JOL-AMAN**.

JOLAY Kkalp. 20th c. **Jolay** / **Žolay** [Джолай / Жолай] (Bask., Kkalp. 23, KkRS 773). ✦ 'Migrant, wanderer' (Žanuzakov-Esbaeva 462). See also **YOLDAŠ**.

JOLBARS see **YOLBARS**

JOLČU see **YOLČI**

JOLDAY see **JOLTAY**

JOLDAS see **YOLDAŠ**

JOLÏM-BAY see **YOLUM**

JOLÏMBET see **YOLUMBET**

JOLÏS Kzk. 19th c. **Jolïs** [Джолысъ] (SOV 140). ⇨ ? + dim. suff. *-ïs*? See also **YULÏŠ**?

JOLMA see **JULMA**

JOLOY see **YULAY**

JOLTAY Kzk. 19th c. **Jolday** [Бай Джолдаевъ] (Grod., Pril. 48); Kzk. 19th c. **Joltay** [Джолтай] (AOK 2, 102). ✦ 'Road (male child); (Male child born on) Road','Road(=life)-foal'? Component *-tay* can also be interpreted as dim.-hypoc. suffix as in *Esentay* in Espaeva's oppinion (Espaeva 1984, 231). ⇨ **YOL** + **TAY**? or suff. *-tay(1,2)*. See also **QARA-YOLTOY**.

JOLU-BAY Kzk. 19th c. **Jolu-bay** [Джолубай] (SOK 308). ✦ 'His road(=life) (is) rich, let his road be rich'. ⇨ **YOL** + **BAY** + poss. suff. *-u*.

JOLUMBET see **YOLUMBET**

JOMART Kzk. 19th c. **Jamart** [Газбекъ Джамардовъ] (Grod., Pril. 19); Kzk. 1879 **Jamart** [Джуже Джамартовъ] (Grod., Pril. 130); Trkm. 20th c. **Jomart** [Ğomart] (Zaj. 1971, 327); Trkm. 20th c. **Jomart** [Джомарт] (TrkmRS 326); Kzk. 18th c. - 19th c. **Jomart** [Джомарт] (Tynyšp. 72); Kzk. 19th c. **Jomart** [Джомартъ] (SOV 32); Kzk. 19th c. **Jomart** [Джомартъ] (Grod., Pril. 49); Kzk. 19th c. **Jomart** [Джамартъ] (SOV 20); Kzk. 19th c. **Jumart** [Джумартъ] (SOV 96); Kzk. 19th c. **Jumart** [Джумартъ] (AOK 18); Kzk. 19th c. **Jumart** [Джумартъ] (AOK 46); Kzk. 1817 **Yumart** [Юмартъ Токмановъ] (Mejer 35); Kzk. 19th c. **Žomart** [Жомартъ] (AOP 94); Kzk. 1825 **Žumart** [يومارت / Жумарт] (MIK IV, 471, 476). ✦ 'Generous, free-handed, open-handed' cf. Kar.(T.), Kzk. *jomart* 'freigiebig, reich' (Radl. IV, 101), Trkm. *jōmārt* 'щедрый' (TrkmRS), Tat. *jumart* 'freigiebig' (Radl. IV, 175), Tat. *yumart* 'freigiebig' (Radl. III, 575) (<P.). See also **ATÏM-TAY-JOMART, BAY-JAMART**.

JON-JAGÏLÏ Yak. **Jon-jaɣïlï** [Цон-цаҕылы], one of Är-älläy's six sons (Är-älläy is the forefather of the ulus of Boturus (Pek.).

JON-TAY Kzk. 19th c. **Jon-tay** [Джонтай], forefather of one of the of the Kirey tribes (Potanin II, 4). ⇨ **ČOŇ** + **TAY** or suff. *-tay(1,2)*?

JORA see **ČURA**

JORA Kzk. 1879 **Jora** [Джора] (Grod., Pril. 130); Kzk. 19th c. **Jora-bay** [Товукбай Джорабаевъ] (Grod., Pril. 107). ✦ 'Reason, mind, wit' cf. Kzk. *jora* 'die Bedeutung, der Sinn; die Sitte' (Radl. IV, 96).

JORO Yak. **Joro** [Мария Цоро], fem. (Pek.).

JOSUN-BİLLİG see **BARMAQLÏG-JOSUN-BİLLİG**

JÖŠ see **YUWAŠ**

JÖGÜÖR Yak. **Jögüör** [Цёгүöр] (Pek.). ✦ Yegor (R.).

JÖLYÜT Yak. **Jölyüt** [Цöлјүт], a legendary person (Pek.).

JÖSÖGÖY see **JÄSÄGÄY**

JÖSÖGÖY-AYÏSÏT see **JÖSÖGÖY-AYÏ**

JÖSÖGÖY-AYÏ Yak. **Jösögöy-ayï** [Цöсöгöi-аjы], a god who sends horses from heaven to people he loves; he is believed to be the creator of horses (Pek.). ⇨ **JÄSÄGÄY**.

JÖSÖGÖY-YÄYÄXSÏT see **JÖSÖGÖY-AYÏ**

JÖSÖGÖY-TOYON see **JÄSÄGÄY**

JÖSÖKÖY see **JÄSÄGÄY**

JU see **JUW**

JU-JASAR see **YÜZ-YAŠAR**

JU-JÏLAN Maml. 1262 **Ju-julan** / **Ju-jïlan**? [جوجلان / Джуджуланъ], a Kipchak (Baybars/Tizeng. I, 78, 100). ✦ '?-snake'. ⇨ **JUW** + **YÏLAN** / **YULAN**?

JUBAY Chag. 16th c. **Ju-bay**? / **Jubay**? [Джубай], an emir (Ivanov 153); Kzk. 19th c. **Ju-bay**? / **Jubay**? [Джубай] (SODž. 42); Kzk. 19th c. **Ju-bay**? / **Jubay**? [Джубай] (Grod., Pril. 172). ✦ '(Married) couple' cf. Kzk. *jubay* 'Eheleute, Mann und Frau' (Radl. IV, 174). ⇨ **JUW**?

JUBAN Kzk. 19th c. **Juban** [Джубанъ Бектасовъ] (Grod., Pril. 82); Kzk. 1785 **Juban-bahadïr**? [بهادر جبان], from the Qïzïl-qurt tribe (MIK IV, 52, 54); Khorezm. 14th c. **Juban-bek** / **Čuban-bek**? [Djouban-beg], an emir, Timür-taš's father; „Lorsque l'émir Djouban-beg eut acquis dans le pays d'Iran une telle influence, qu'il était le véritable sultan, son fils Timour-tasch se rendit puissant dans les coutrées de Rousse". (Notes et Extr. XIII, 345); Kzk. 18th c. - 19th c. **Juwan-bek** [Джуанбек] (Tynyšp. 66); Bashk. 1750 **Zuwan** [Касым Зюванов] (MIB III, 472). ✦ 'Thick' cf. Kzk. *juan, juban* 'dick' (Radl. IV, 163).

JUBANČÏ Kzk. 19th c. **Jubančï**? [Ирикъ Джубанчевъ] (Grod., Pril. 38). ⇨ **JUBAN**? + suff. *-čï*.

JUBAŠ Kzk. 19th c. **Jubaš** [Джубашъ] (AOO 54). ✦ 'Friendly, quiet'?; cf. Kzk. *juas, yuwaš* 'friedlich, freundlich, fromm' (Radl. IV, 164). ⇨ **JAW-BAS**?

JUČÏ Uzb. 1689? **Juči-sultan** [Джучи-султан], a khan (MIT II, 332). ✦ 'Djochi (Mo.)'.

JUJAY Kzk. 1884 **Jujay** [Джуджай Сиралиевъ] (Grod., Pril. 93).

JUJE Kzk. 1879 **Juje** [Джудже] (Grod., Pril. 130). ✦ 'Dwarf' cf. Turk. *jujä* / *jüjä* 'der Zwerg' (Radl. IV, 173,

187).

JUDAS Kzk. 19th c. **Judas** [Ташъ-Магоммедъ Джудазовъ] (Grod., Pril. 192). ⇨ **JU?** + suff. *-das?*

JUΓUN Yak. **Juγun** [Цугун], a strong richman who lived far in the south, his son was Onoγoy (Pek.).

JUXXARÏ-MAÑAN Yak. **Juχχarï-mañan-χotun** [Цуххары], a legendary woman (Pek.).

JUQURUDUMUON Yak. **Juqurudumuon** [Цукурудумуон] (Pek.).

JUQUSTAY Kzk. 19th c. **Juqustay** [Джукустай] (SODž. 160). ⇨ **TAY** or suff. *-tay(1,2)?*

JUL see **YOL**

JUL-BULDÏ Kzk. **Jul-buldï** [Джульбульдин] (TOOIK I, 68). ⇨ **YOL** + **BOLDÏ**.

JUL-JÏΓÏN see **ÖRÖS-KÜÖL-JUL-JÏΓÏN**

JUL-SART Kzk. 19th c. **Jul-sart-pay** [Джулсартпай] (SOK 22). ⇨ **JUL / YOL** + **SART**.

JUL-TAY Kzk. 19th c. **Jul-tay** [Джултай] (Grod., Pril. 78); Kzk. 19th c. **Jul-tay** [Ходжабай Джултаевъ] (Grod., Pril. 116); Kzk. 18th c. **Žul-tay** [Жултай Сапулатовъ] (Nepljuev 704, 707). ⇨ **JUL / YOL** + **TAY** or suff. *-tay(1,2)?*

JULA see **YULA**

JULAY see **YULAY**

JULAL Kzk. 19th c. **Julal-bay** [Джулалбай] (Grod., Pril. 101).

JULAN see **YULAN**

JULDÏ see **YOLLU**

JULDÏ-AYAQ Kzk. 19th c. **Juldï-ayaq** [Джулди-Аякъ] (Grod., Pril. 71d). ⇨ **YOLLU** + **AYAQ**.

JULDU see **YOLLU**

JULDUS see **YULDUZ**

JULDUZAY Kkalp. 20th c. **Julduzay** [Джулдузай], fem. (Bask., Kkalp. 403); Kkalp. 20th c. **Žuldïzay** [Жулдызай], fem. (KkRS 777). ✧ 'Little (nice) star'. ⇨ **YULDUZ** + dim. suff. *-ay.*

JULLÏ Trkm. 20th c. **Jullï** [Ğullï] (Zaj. 1971, 330). ✧ 'With horse-blanket/rug' cf. Trkm. *jul* 'попона; одежда' (TrkmRS) + suff. *-lï.*

JULMA Kuman 1292 **Julma / Jolma?** [Keldech filii Gyolma], a Kuman in Hungary (Gyárfás II, 459, ÁÚO XII, 534). ✧ 'Taken away; escaped'? *<yol-, yul-* 'ausreissen, fortnehmen, befreien, erretten' (Gombocz, ÁTSz. 31), also Rásonyi, NTK 135, Rásonyi, KÖA 138, Rásonyi, Anthr. 140.

JULUW-TAŠ Kkalp. 20th c. **Juluw-taš** [Джулувташ], fem. (Bask., Kkalp. 403). ⇨ **TAŠ.**

JUM Kzk. 19th c. **Jum-bay** [Малинбай Джумбаевъ] (Grod., Pril. 60); Kzk. 19th c. **Jum-bay** [Джумбай] (Grod., Pril. 119); Kzk. 19th c. **Jum-bay** [Джумбай] (AOP 30, 74). ✧ 'Friendly, agreeing' cf. Kzk. *jum* 'einstimmig, einig' (Radl. IV, 175).

JUMA Trkm. **Juma** [Жума] (Sopieva: OSA 180); Trkm. 19th c. **Juma** [Джума] (Volodin 53); Trkm. 20th c. **Juma** [Ğuma], fem. (Zaj. 1971, 341); Trkm. 20th c. **Juma** [Джума], fem. (TrkmRS 328); Kzk. 19th c. **Juma** [Джума] (AOO 2); Kzk. 1817 **Juma** [Джума Худаймендіевъ], sultan of the Arγïn tribe (clan) (Mejer 35); Kirg. 19th-20th c. **Juma** [Dšuma], Kirghiz guide of the Almásy-Prinz expedition (Prinz 22); Uzb. 20th c. **Juma** [Djouma], a basmačï from Bukhara (Castagné 77); Kzk. 19th c. **Juma-bay** [Дусамбай Джумабаевъ] (Grod., Pril. 54); Kzk. 19th c. **Juma-bay** [Джумабай] (SKSO IV, otd. II, 36); Kzk. 19th c. **Juma-bay** [Джумабай] (Grod., Pril. 101); Kzk. 19th c. **Juma-bay** [Джумабай] (SODž. 134); Kzk. 19th c. **Juma-bay** [Джумабай] (SOV 48); Kzk. 19th c. **Juma-bay** [Джумабай] (SOV 50); Kzk. 19th c. **Juma-bay** [Молла Джумабай] (Grod., Pril. 145); Uzb. **Juma-bay** [Джума(н)бай Байджигитовъ] (Sr.Az. I, 1896, avg. 17); Uzb. **Juma-bay** [Джумабай Байджигитовъ] (Sr. Az. I, 1896, avg. 16); Uzb. 19th c. **Juma-bay** [Джумабай] (SKSO III, 172); Turk. 20th c. **Juma-biy** [Cuma] (Önder, Göle); Uzb. 1804 **Juma-biy** [Джума-бий] (MIT II, 371); Trkm. **Juma-gözel** [Жумагөзел], fem. (Sopieva: OSA 180); Kzk. 19th c. **Juma-gül-bibi** [Джума Гюль-биби] (Grod., Pril. 154); Kzk. 18th c. - 19th c. **Juma-χan** [Джумахан] (Tynyšp. 71); Kzk. 19th c. **Juma-qul** [Джумакулъ] (SKSO VIII, 207); Kzk. 19th c. **Juma-qul** [Джумакулъ Кулъ Мамбетовъ] (Grod., Pril.142); Trkm.? 1747 **Juma-qulï-bek** [Джума-кули-бек], a Mañγït (MIT II, 189); Kzk. 19th c. **Juma-mirgen** [Джумамиргеневъ] (SKSO VIII, 224); Trkm. **Juma-soltan** [Жумасолтан] (Sopieva 180); Bashk. 1682 **Yoma-güzä** [Ямагуза Ишкаринъ] (AI V, 139); Bashk. 1715 **Yoma-güzä?** [Емагуз Юлушев] (MIB III, 125); Bashk. 1735 **Yoma-güzä** [Емагуза Емагуловъ] (Vel.-Zern., Bašk. 11); Bashk. 1734 **Yoma-γul** [Емагулъ Бурашевъ] (Vel.-Zern., Bašk. 10); Bashk. 1735 **Yoma-γul** [Емагуза Емагуловъ] (Vel.-Zern., Bašk. 11); Bashk. 18th c. **Yuma-güzä?** [Юмагузъ] (Nepljuev 895); Bashk. 1798 **Yuma-güzä** [Юмагузинъ] (PSZRI XXV, 196); Bashk. 1784 **Yuma-γul** [Сультый Юмагулов] (MIB V, 151); Bashk. 1735 **Yuma-γul / Yoma-γul?** [Юмагулъ Иркинъ], a prince (Vel.-Zern., Bašk. 12); Bashk. 1789 **Zuma-güzä** [Зюмагузя Каипов] (MIB V, 115); Bashk. 1789 **Zuma-güzä / Zuma-murza?** [Зюмагузя / Зюмарурзя Бикбов] (MIB V, 271); Kkalp. 20th c. **Žuma** [Жумабек] (KkRS 773); Kkalp. 20th c. **Žuma-bek** [Жумабек] (KkRS 773); Kkalp. 20th c. **Žuma-gül** [Жумагул], fem. (KkRS 777); Tat. 1750 **Žuma-γul? / Žama-γul?** [Жамагуль] (PSZRI XIII, 212); Kzk. 18th c. **Žuma-γul? / Žama-γul?** [Жамагуль], a mulla (Nepljuev 590, 600). ✧ 'Friday', '(Born on) Friday' (Kusimova), cf. Kzk. *juma*, Turk. *jumᶜa* 'der Freitag' (Radl. IV, 175), Bashk. *yoma*, Tat. *yuma* (TatRS)

(<Ar.). Cf. Kkalp. fem. *Juma-gül* 'Friday(=Sunday)-flower' (Baskakov: OSA 140), Bashk. *Yoma-γuža* 'yomala tïuγan' (Kusimova). See also **MÄMBET-JUMA**.

JUMA-DİL Kzk. 19th c. **Juma-dil** [Джумадилъ] (AOO 6); Tat.(Mish.) 1770 **Zuma-dil** [Зюмадиль Бухаров] (MIB IV/1, 343). ⇨ **JUMA + DİL.**

JUMA-ГALİY Kkalp. 20th c. **Juma-γaliy** [Жумағалий] (KkRS 773). ⇨ **JUMA + ALİ +** suff. *-y*.

JUMA-KELDİ Uzb. 20th c. **Juma-keldi** [Жумакелди] (Begmatov 1984, 202); Nog. 20th c. **Juma-keldi-uwlï** [Ходжа Джумакелди увлы], father of Baskakov's informant from the aul of İrγaqlï (Bask., Nog. 143). ✧ 'Friday has come; he was born on Friday'. ⇨ **JUMA + KELDİ.**

JUMA-KÜN Uzb. 19th c. **Juma-kün** (SKSO III, 182). ✧ 'Friday'. ⇨ **JUMA + KÜN.**

JUMA-NAZAR Trkm. 20th c. **Juma-nazar** [Ğumanazar] (Zaj. 1971, 332); Kzk. 19th c. **Juma-nazar-bek** [Джума-Назаръ-бекъ Хайдаровъ] (Grod., Pril. 120). ✧ 'Friday-look'. ⇨ **JUMA + NAZAR.**

JUMA-NİYAZ Trkm. 19th c. **Juma-niyaz** [Диньмухаметъ Джуманьязовъ] (Ščeglov I, 350). ⇨ **JUMA + NİYAZ.**

JUMA-TURDİ Trkm. 20th c. **Juma-durdï** [Ğumadurdï] (Zaj. 1971, 334); Uzb. 20th c. **Juma-turdï** [Жуматурди] (Begmatov 1984, 204). ✧ '(On) Friday stayed / remained / survived'. ⇨ **JUMA + TURDİ.**

JUMAXAN Kkalp. 20th c. **Žumaχan** [Жумахан], fem. (KkRS 777). ⇨ **JUMA +** suff. *-χan(1).*

JUMAY Tat.? 1764 **Jumay** [Айдаш Зюмаев] (MIB IV/1, 292). ⇨ **JUMA +** dim. suff. *-y.*

JUMAQAY Trkm. 19th c. **Jumaqay** [Джіомокай Акчановъ] (Ščeglov IV, 179). ⇨ **JUMA +** dim. suff. *-qay.*

JUMALİ Kzk. 19th c. **Jumalï / Jumali?** [Джумаліевъ] (AUK 770); Kzk. 19th c. **Jumalï / Jumali?** [Джумаліевъ], a pupil (AUK 844). ⇨ **JUMA +** suff. *-lï.*

JUMAN see YUMAN

JUMAN-TAY Kzk. 19th c. **Juman-tay** [Джумантай] (AOO 58). ⇨ **JUMAN + TAY** or suff. *-tay(1,2)?*

JUMART see JOMART

JUMAŠ Kzk. 19th c. **Jumaš** [Джумашъ] (SODž. 64); Kkalp. 20th c. **Jumaš** [Джумаш Къыдырбай-улы], a teacher, Baskakov's informant (Bask., Kkalp. 85); Kkalp. 20th c. **Žumaš** [Жумаш] (KkRS 773). ✧ 'Little Friday'. ⇨ **JUMA +** dim. suff. *-š.*

JUMAŠKE Kzk. 19th c. **Jumaške** [Джумашке] (AOP 130). ✧ 'Little Friday'. ⇨ **JUMAŠ +** dim. suff. *-ke.*

JUMAT Kzk. 19th c. **Jumat** [Джумат] (SOV 114). ✧ 'The fifth day of the Moon-calendar; child born on the fifth day' (Ar.) (Žanuzakov).

JUMBAT Kzk. 19th c. **Jumbat** [Джанъ Турсун Джумбатовъ] (Grod., Pril. 175). ⇨ **JUM +** suffixoid *-bat.*

JUMJUMA Kzk. **Jumjuma** [Цумцума] (Proben III, 684 /771/).

JUNAY see YUNAY

JUNÏ Oghuz/Trkm. 13th c. **Junï** [جونى / Джуны] (Abulg./Kon. 1245).

JUNUŠ Kirg. **Junuš** [Жунуш] (Jud. 32); Kkalp. 20th c. **Žünis** [Жүнис] (KkRS 774). ✧ Yunus (Ar. < Old Hebr.), a Prophet, the biblical Jonah (Ahmed), Turk. *Yonos* 'der Prophet Jonas' (Radl. III, 417, Zenker 977), *Yunus* (يونس) 'Jonah' (J. Penrice, Dictionary of the Korʻan. L., 1873, 166). See also **AQ-JUNUS.**

JUONA Yak. **Juona** [Цуона] (Pek.). ✧ Yona (R.).

JUPAR see YÏPAR

JUR-PAY see JURT

JURA I. Yak. **Jura-bögö** [Цура-бөҕө], a character in a tale (Pek.).

JURA II. see ČURA

JURANTĀYÏ Yak. **Jurantāyï** [Усун-Цурантайы-суруксут], one of Ürüñ-ayï-toyon's sons (Pek.).

JURČİ see YURTČİ

JURT Kzk. 19th c. **Jur-pay (<Jurt-pay)** [Джурпай] (SOV 44); Kzk. 19th c. **Jurt-pay** [Джуртпай] (SOK 170); Kzk. 19th c. **Jurt-pay** [Джуртпай] (SOV 50); Kzk. 19th c. **Jurt-pay** [Джуртпай] (Potanin, Oč. I, 29, 30, 37); Kzk. 19th c. **Žurt-pay** [Журтпай] (SODž. 58). ✧ 'Home, dwelling place, campsite, country, empire' cf. Türk, Kuman, Chag., Alt., Turk. *yurt* 'der Wohnort, Wohnstätte' (Radl. III, 548), Kzk. *jurt* 'das Lager, die Lagerstelle, das Land, das Reich, das Volk' (Radl. IV, 168).

JURUN-TAY Kzk. 19th c. **Jurun-tay** [Джурунтай] (SOV 16). ✧ 'Hem/list - foal'? cf. Kzk. dial. *žürïn* (QTDS). ⇨ **TAY** or suff. *-tay(1,2)?*

JURUO Yak. **Juruo-bögö** [Цуруо-бөҕө] (Pek.).

JURUP-TAY Kzk. 19th c. **Jurup-tay** [Джуруптай] (SOK 188).

JUSAN Kzk. 19th c. **Jusan-bay** [Джусанбай] (SODž. 48); Kzk. 19th c. **Jusan-bay** [Джусанбай] (SOV 16, 42). ✧ 'Vermuth' cf. Kzk. *jusan* 'id.' (Radl. IV, 173).

JUSUN Kzk. **Jusun** [Джусунъ Танабаевъ], a mulla (Pam. kn. Semip. III, 43); Tuv. 19th c. **Jusun-χan** [Джюсунъ-ханъ] (Potanin IV, 375). ✧ 'Rule, order; reminiscence' cf. Kirg. *josun* 'порядок, правило; следы, остатки старого' (Jud.), Chag., East.T., NUyg.(Tar.) *yosun* 'die Regel, Gewohnheit, Sitte, Ordnung' (Radl. III, 441).

JUSUP see YUSUF

JUW Kkalp. 20th c. **Ju-bïke (<Juw-bïke?)** [Джубике], fem. (Bask., Kkalp. 3).

JUWAN see JUBAN

JŬWAN-TAYAQ   Kzk. 19th c. **Jŭwan-tayaq** [Джуантаякъ] (AOK 2). ⇨ **JUBAN + TAYAQ.**

JŪRA   Yak. **Jūra-bögö / Jūra-buχatïr** [Цура-бöҕö], a hero in a tale (Pek.).

JŪRAT   Kirg. **Jŭrat-bek** [Жууратбек], fem. (Jud. 271) ✧ 'A kind of sour milk' cf. Kirg. *žŭrat* 'цельное кислое молоко (без примеси воды и не снятое), варенец' (Jud.).

JŬC see **YÜZ**

JÜNDİ-BAY see **YÜNLÜ**

JÜNDÜ-BAY see **YÜNLÜ**

JŬNEYD   Turk. 1366 **Jŭneyd** [Abdal Cüneyd] (Gökb., Ed. 174); Turk. 1434 **Jŭneyd** [Cüneyd Fakih] (Gökb., Ed. 266). ✧ Junaid (Ar.).

JŬRDİK   Selj. 1169, 1193 **Jŭrdik** [جُرْديك / جورديك / عزالدين], mutevekkil of Jerusalim (Kamāladdīn II, 326, 327, Ibn al-Athīr/Tornb. XI, 223-24, 369, XII, 57, 88, Berchem, Jér. I, 96).

JŬRÜM   Kzk. 19th c. **Jŭrüm-bek** [Джюрюмбекъ] (SOK 20).

JÜRÜPTAY   Kzk. 19th c. **Jürüptay** [Джурюптай] (SOK 28); Kzk. 19th c. **Jürüptay** [Джуруптай] (SOK 188).

JÜSÄGÄY see **JÄSÄGÄY**

JÜSİP see **YUSUF**

JÜSÜ   Kzk. 19th c. **Jüsü-bay** [Джюсубай] (SOV 154); Kzk. 19th c. **Jüsü-pay** [Джусупай] (SOK 210); Kzk. 19th c. **Jüsü-pek** [Джусупекъ] (AOAtb. 2, 38). ✧ Perhaps a short form of *Jüsüp / Jüsip*, cf. Kzk. PNs *Jüsip, Jüsib-äli, Jüsip-bek, Jüsip-qali* (Žanuzakov-Esbaeva). ⇨ **YUSUF.**

JÜSÜGÄY see **JÄSÄGÄY**

JÜSÜP see **YUSUF**

JÜZ-BAY see **YÜZ**

JÜZ-JASAR see **YÜZ-YAŠAR**

JÜZAN   Kzk. 19th c. **Jüzan** [Джюзановъ] (AOK 106).

JÜZİP see **YUSUF**

JÜZÜM   Kzk. 19th c. **Jüzüm** [Дзюзюм] (AOK 34). ✧ 'Grape' cf. Kzk. *žüzim* 'виноград' (RKzS).

D'

D'ADAΓAY   Alt. 19th-20th c. **D'adaγay** [Дьадагай] (OjrRS 208). ✧ 'Open'? cf. Alt. *d'adaγay* 'открытый' (OjrRS).

D'AYAN   Alt. 19th-20th c. **D'ayan** [Дьайан], fem. (OjrRS 211). ✧ 'Grown-up, tall' (OjrRS 211).

D'AYČİL   Alt. 19th-20th c. **D'ayčil** [Дьайчыл], fem. (OjrRS 211). ✧ '(S)he who loves summer' (OjrRS 211). cf. Alt. *d'ay* 'лето' (OjrRS). + suff. *-čil.*

D'AYÏM   Alt. 19th-20th c. **D'ayïm** [Дьайым], fem.
(OjrRS 211). ✧ 'Freedom' (OjrRS 211).

D'AYQAN   Alt. 19th-20th c. **D'ayqan** [Дьайкан], fem. (OjrRS 211). ✧ 'Rise, deluge' (OjrRS 211).

D'AYQAŠ   Alt. 19th-20th c. **D'ayqaš** [Дьайкаш] (OjrRS 208); Alt. 19th-20th c. **D'ayqaš** [Дьайкаш], fem. (OjrRS 211). ✧ 'Swing' cf. Alt. *d'ayqa-* 'качать' (OjrRS). + suff. *-š.*

D'AYLA   Alt. 19th-20th c. **D'ayla** [Дьайла], fem. (OjrRS 211). ✧ 'Oh, oh dear! Ugh! Woe!' (OjrRS 211).

D'AYLAY   Alt. 19th-20th c. **D'aylay** [Дьайлай], fem. (OjrRS 211). ⇨ **D'AYLA** + suff. *-y.*

D'AYLAŠ   Alt. 19th-20th c. **D'aylaš** [Дьайлаш], fem. (OjrRS 211). ⇨ **?** + suff. *-š.*

D'AYTQA   Alt. 19th-20th c. **D'aytqa** [Дьайтка], fem. (OjrRS 211).

D'AQAČÏ   Alt. 19th-20th c. **D'aqačï** [Дьакачы], fem. (OjrRS 211). ✧ 'Maker of collars'? cf. Alt. *d'aqa* 'воротник' (OjrRS 211). + suff. *-čï.*

D'AQALAY   Alt. 19th-20th c. **D'aqalay** [Дьакалай], fem. (OjrRS 211). ✧ 'Catching/Seizing (somebody by the collar)' cf. Alt. *d'aqala-* 'взять за ворот' (OjrRS).

D'AQÏYLA   Alt. 19th-20th c. **D'aqïyla** [Дьакыйла] (OjrRS 208).

D'ALA   Alt. 19th-20th c. **D'ala** [Дьала] (OjrRS 208); Alt. 19th-20th c. **D'ala** [Дьала], fem. (OjrRS 211). ✧ 'Penalty, fine' cf. Alt. *d'ala* 'штраф' (OjrRS).

D'ALAČÏ   Alt. 19th-20th c. **D'alačï** [Дьалачы], fem. (OjrRS 211). ✧ 'Kind, nice; flatterer' (OjrRS 211). + suff. *-čï.*

D'ALADAY   Alt. 19th-20th c. **D'aladay** [Дьаладай], fem. (OjrRS 211). ✧ '(S)he is like (penalty) fine'. See also **D'ALADÏY.**

D'ALADÏY   Alt. 19th-20th c. **D'aladïy** [Дьаладый], fem. (OjrRS 211). ✧ '(S)he is like (penalty) fine' (OjrRS 211). See also **D'ALADAY.**

D'ALAQ see **YALAQ**

D'ALAQAY   Alt. 19th-20th c. **D'alaqay** [Дьалакай] (OjrRS 208); Alt. 19th-20th c. **D'alaqay** [Дьалакай], fem. (OjrRS 211). ✧ 'Kind, nice; flatterer' (OjrRS 208, 211).

D'ALAMAŠ   Alt. 19th-20th c. **D'alamaš** [Дьаламаш], fem. (OjrRS 211). ✧ 'Little ribbon' (OjrRS 211).

D'ALQA   Alt. 19th-20th c. **D'alqa** [Дьалка], fem. (OjrRS 211). ✧ 'Lazy' (OjrRS 211). ⇨ **D„ALQU.**

D'ALQÏR   Yak. **D'alqïr** [Дјалкыр / Цалкыр] (Pek.). ⇨ **JALQÏR.**

D'ALQU   Alt. 19th-20th c. **D'alqu** [Дьалкау] (OjrRS 211). ✧ 'Lazy' (OjrRS 211). ⇨ **D'ALQA.**

D'ALTÏS see **JALTÏS**

D'AMAN see **YAMAN**

D'AMAN-SARA   Alt. 19th-20th c. **D'aman-sara** [Дьамансара] (OjrRS 208). ⇨ **YAMAN + SARÏ / SARA I.?**

D'AMAND'İT Alt. 19th-20th c. **D'amand'it** [Дьамандьит] (OjrRS 208). ❖ 'Stinking'.

D'AMANDÏQ Alt. 19th-20th c. **D'amandïq** [Дьамандык], fem. (OjrRS 211). ❖ 'Evil, wicked' (OjrRS 211). ⇨ **YAMAN** + suff. -*lïq*.

D'AMANQA see **YAMANQA**

D'AMANQA Alt. 19th-20th c. **D'amanqa** [Дьаманка] (OjrRS 208).

D'AMÏRSÏN Alt. 19th-20th c. **D'amïrsïn** [Дьамырсын] (OjrRS 208).

D'ANARU Alt. 19th-20th c. **D'anaru** [Дьанару] (OjrRS 208).

D'AÑ-AY Alt. 19th-20th c. **D'añ-ay (<D'aña-ay?)** [Дьанай], fem. (OjrRS 211); Alt. 19th-20th c. **D'añ-ay (<D'aña-ay?)** [Дьанай] (OjrRS 208). ❖ 'New moon (OjrRS 211); (born at) new moon; (nice) like the new moon'. ⇨ **D'AÑA + AY.**

D'AÑA see **YAÑÏ**

D'AÑAR Alt. 19th-20th c. **D'añar** [Дьанар] (OjrRS 208); Alt. 19th-20th c. **D'añar** [Дьанар], fem. (OjrRS 211).

D'APRAY Alt. 19th-20th c. **D'apray** [Дьапрай] (OjrRS 208).

D'ARAS Alt. 19th-20th c. **D'aras** [Дьарас] (OjrRS 208). ❖ Gerasim (R.).

D'ARDAQ Alt. 19th-20th c. **D'ardaq** [Дьардак] (OjrRS 208). ❖ 'Nacked' (OjrRS 208).

D'ARΓANAT Alt. 19th-20th c. **D'arγanat** [Дьарганат], fem. (OjrRS 211). ❖ 'Bat' (OjrRS 211).

D'ARÏQČÏ Alt. 19th-20th c. **D'arïqčï** [Дьарыкчы] (OjrRS 208). ❖ 'Shining, glittering' (OjrRS 208), 'Bright, cheerful' cf. Alt. *d'arïq* 'светлый; весёлый' (OjrRS). + suff. -*čï*.

D'ARQÏN D'AŽNAY Alt. 19th-20th c. **D'ažnay** [Дьажнай] (OjrRS 208). ❖ 'Young' (OjrRS 208).

D'ĀBÏŠ Alt. 19th-20th c. **D'ābïš** [Дьаабыш] (OjrRS 208). ❖ 'Raining; snowing'? cf. Alt. *d'ā-* 'идти (о дожде, граде, снеге' (OjrRS).

D'ĀRU Alt. 19th-20th c. **D'āru** [Дьаару] (OjrRS 208).

D'EBÄT Hak. 19th-20th c. **D'ebät-qan** (Radl. II, 105).

D'ELENE Alt. 19th-20th c. **D'elene** [Дьелене], fem. (OjrRS 211). ❖ Elena (R. fem.).

D'ELEŠ Alt. 19th-20th c. **D'eleš** [Дьелеш], fem. (OjrRS 211). ❖ Elena (R. fem.) + suff. -*š*?

D'ELKE Alt. 19th-20th c. **D'elke** [Дьелке], fem. (OjrRS 211). ❖ Elena (R.) + suff. -*ke*.

D'EREMEY Alt. 19th-20th c. **D'eremey** [Дьеремей] (OjrRS 208). ❖ Eremey (R.).

D'İBAN Alt. 19th-20th c. **D'iban** [Дьибан] (OjrRS 208). ❖ Ivan (R.).

D'İÄSİNTÄY see **TİMİR-JİÄSİNTÄY**

D'İMİRČİ Alt. 19th-20th c. **D'imirči** [Дьымирчи] (OjrRS 208).

D'İND'İ Alt. 19th-20th c. **D'ind'i** [Дьиндьи], fem. (OjrRS 211). ❖ 'Necklace (made of glass beads), string' (OjrRS 211), cf. Alt. *d'ind'i* 'бисер; жемчуг' (OjrRS).

D'İND'İGEY Alt. 19th-20th c. **D'ind'igey** [Дьиндьигей], fem. (OjrRS 211). ❖ 'Small glass bead, pearl'. ⇨ **D'İND'İ** + suff. -*gey*.

D'İND'İLEY Alt. 19th-20th c. **D'ind'iley** [Дьиндьилей] (OjrRS 208); Alt. 19th-20th c. **D'ind'iley** [Дьиндьилей], fem. (OjrRS 211). ❖ 'Glass beads; pearl' (OjrRS 211), cf. Alt. *d'ind'i* 'бисер; жемчуг' (OjrRS). ⇨ **D'İND'İ** + suff. -*ley*.

D'ÏDU see **D'ÏTU**

D'ÏLAMAŠ Alt. 19th-20th c. **D'ïlamaš** [Дьыламаш], fem. (OjrRS 212). ❖ 'Strawberry' (OjrRS 212).

D'ÏLAN see **YÏLAN**

D'ÏLÏM Alt. 19th-20th c. **D'ïlïm** [Дьылым], fem. (OjrRS 212). ❖ 'Flat, plain; well-fed' (OjrRS 212).

D'ÏMŽAY Alt. 19th-20th c. **D'ïmžay** [Дьымжай] (OjrRS 208). ❖ 'Soft' (OjrRS 208).

D'ÏRAČÏ Alt. 19th-20th c. **D'ïračï** [Дьырачы] (OjrRS 208). ❖ 'Ditch / Bush'? cf. Alt. *d'ïra* 'ров', *d'ïra~d'ïraa* 'кустарник' (OjrRS). + suff. -*čï*.

D'ÏRΓAL Alt. 19th-20th c. **D'ïrγal** [Дьыргал], fem. (OjrRS 212). ❖ 'Gladness, pleasure' (OjrRS 212).

D'ÏRMAY Alt. 19th-20th c. **D'ïrmay** [Дьырмай] (OjrRS 208).

D'ÏTU Alt. 19th-20th c. **D'ïdu** [Дьыду] (OjrRS 208); Alt. 19th-20th c. **D'ïtu** [Дьыту], fem. (OjrRS 212); Alt. 19th-20th c. **Titu** [Титу], fem. (OjrRS 213). ❖ 'Stinking' (OjrRS 212), cf. Alt. *d'ïtu* 'имеющий какой-л. запах, душистый, вонючий' (OjrRS), Alt.(Tel.) *d'ïttū / yïttū* 'einen Geruch, einen Geist habend' (Radl. III, 494-95), Alt.(Tel.) *d'ïdū / yïdū* 'einen schlechten Geruch habend, faulend' (Radl. III, 496).

D'ODAİ Hak. 19th-20th c. **D'odai-qan** (Radl. II, 105). ❖ 'Little Thigh'? cf. Alt. *d'odo*, Uyg., Tat.(Bar.), Chul.(Küer.) *yoda* 'der Oberschenkel' (Radl. III, 440) + suff. -*y*.

D'OΓOSPO Alt. 19th-20th c. **D'oγospo** [Дьогоспо] (OjrRS 208). ❖ 'Don't exhaust him/her!' cf. Alt.(Tel.) *d'oγos-* 'zu Ende bringen, ganz verbrauchen' (Radl. III, 411).

D'OQOQ Alt. 19th-20th c. **D'oqoq** [Дьокок] (OjrRS 208). ❖ 'Not existing?' cf. Alt. *d'oq* 'нет, не существуется, не имеется' (OjrRS).

D'OLDU Alt. 19th-20th c. **D'oldu** [Дьолду] (OjrRS 208). ❖ 'Lawful, legitimate (child?)' (OjrRS 208). + suff. -*du*.

D'ORÏQČÏ Alt. 19th-20th c. **D'orïqčï** [Дьорыкчы] (OjrRS 208). ❖ 'Rider, horseman' (OjrRS 208). + suff. -*čï*.

D'ŌN Alt. 19th-20th c. **D'ōn** [Дьоон] (OjrRS 208). ❖ 'Thick' (OjrRS 208).

D'ÖSÖGÖY Yak. **D'ösögöy** [uottāχ D'ösögöy /

Djöcöröi / Цöcöröi], a god giving people animals with white hair (that is, horses) (Pek.). ⇨ **JÖSÖGÖY.**

D'UDRUQ Alt. 19th-20th c. **D'udruq** [Дьудрук], fem. (OjrRS 211). ✧ 'Fist' (OjrRS 211).

D'URUYT Alt. 19th-20th c. **D'uruyt** [Дьуруйт] (OjrRS 208).

D'ÜSTÜK Alt. 19th-20th c. **D'üstük** [Дьӱстӱк] (OjrRS 208); Alt. 19th-20th c. **D'üstük** [Дьӱстӱк], fem. (OjrRS 212); Alt. 19th-20th c. **Tüstük** [Тӱстӱк] (OjrRS 210); Alt. 19th-20th c. **Tüstük** [Тӱстӱк], fem. (OjrRS 213). ✧ 'Ring' (OjrRS 212) cf. Alt.(Tel.) *yüstük, yüzük* 'der Fingerring, der Siegelring' (Radl. III, 616, 619), Hak.(Sag.), Shor *čüstük* 'der Fingerring' (Radl. III, 2200). ⇨ **YÜZÜKEY, ALTÏN-YÜSTÜK, QARA-ČÜSTÜK.**

D

DABAY Kzk. 19th c. **Dabay** [Дабай Дуйсабаевъ] (Groč., Pril. 80).

DABÏT Yak. **Dabït** [Дабыт / Лабыт] (Pek.). ✧ David (R.).

DABULTAY Kzk. 19th c. **Dabultay** [Дабултай] (SOK 218). ✧ 'He is like a drum' cf. Kzk. *dabïl* 'die Trommel; die Locktrommel für den Jagdvogel' (Radl. III, 1643) + suff. *-tay(1,2)*.

DAD Karakh. 13th c. **Dad-ispähsalar-beg** [dad ispähsalar beg] (DTS); Chuv. 1737 **Dad-ulï** [Дадулинъ] (Alatyr. 135). ✧ 'Gift' cf. P. *dād* 'дар, подарок' (PRS). See also **XUDAY-DAD.**

DADABAL Uzb. 20th c. **Dadabal** [Dadabal], a basmači from Ferghana (Castagné 77).

DADAŠ Az. **Dadaš** [Дадаш], a fisherman (Az. Skaz. 3 etc.). ✧ 'Brother, brave young man; an addressing in East Turkey' (Erol II); 'Brother, uncle, father' cf. Az. PN *Dadaš* 'elder brother' (Mirzäjev 65), Chag., NUyg.(Tar.) *dada* 'der Onkel von Mutterseite, der Vater, Väterchen' (Radl. III, 1640) + dim. suff. *-š(2)*.

DADÏ Kzk. 1737 **Dadï** [Дады] (MIB I, 345); Turk. 1422 **Dadu-χatun** [سلطان محمد دادوسی دادو خاتون], the child's nurse of Sultan Mehmed (Mohamed) I (1413-1421) (Āšikp. 94). ✧ 'Child's nurse' cf. Turk. *tatu* (طا طو) 'Dadı' (TarS).

DADU see **DADÏ**

DAΓÏRDAY Yak. **Daγïrday** [Даӷырдаі], fem. (Pek.).

DAHÏR Kar.(Crm.) **Dahïr** [Даһыр ілän Зöһpä] (Proben VII, 327). ✧ Tāhir (Ar.).

DAXXAK Karakh. 11th c. **Daχχak** [daḫḫak] (DTS). ✧ 'Jeering, mocking' (Ar.) (DTS).

DAIFA Selj.? 1243/44 **Daife-χatun / Daifa-χatun** [ضينه خاتون / Daifa Hatun], died in 1243 (fem.)

(Abulfidā; Erol II, 109). ✧ (<Ar.).

DAİR Kzk. 1846 **Dair / Dayïr** [Бий Даир Джанджигитов], a biy (MKOP 156); Kzk. 1817 **Dair-bay / Dayïr-bay** [داور بای / Даирбай] (MIK IV, 310); Kzk. 1817 **Dair-bay / Dayïr-bay** [داير بای / Даирбай] (MIK IV, 311); Kzk. 19th c. **Dair-bek / Dayïr-bek** [Даирбекъ] (SOK 112); Kirg. 1847 **Dair-bek / Dayïr-bek** [Ичкай Даирбековъ] (Konšin, Mat. V, 107); Mo.? **Dayr** (RaD I/1, 168). ✧ I. 'Round(ed), rotary' cf. Tat. PNs *Dair, Dairä* (Sattarov), Kzk. PNs *Dayïr, Dayïr-bek, Dayïr-žan* (Žanuzakov-Esbaeva); II. 'Monastery' cf. Kzk. PN *Dair* 'id.' (Žanuzakov 135).

DAİRČİ Kzk. 1749 **Dairči** [Сюлейман Даирчиев] (MIB III, 465). ⇨ **DAİR** + suff. *-či.*

DAY-IŠ Kzk. 19th c. **Day-iš** [Дай-ишъ] (Nalivkin: Tr. Syr-D. OSK 1888, 8). ⇨ **TAY + EŠ?**

DAY-MURAP Kzk. 19th c. **Day-murap / Day-murat?** [Даймурап] (SODž. 10). ✧ 'Uncle-Murap/Murat'? cf. Kzk. dial. *dayï* 'naγaši' [relative on mother side] (QTDS), Turk. *dai* 'der Onkel (von Mutterseite)' (Radl. III, 1605), Turk. *dayï* 'der Onkel (mütterlicherseits)' (Radl. III, 1620).

DAYAR Kzk. 19th c. **Dayar-bek** [Даярбекъ] (SOK 4). ✧ 'Ready' cf. Kzk. *dayar* 'fertig, bereit' (Radl. III, 1620).

DAYDĀLA Yak. **Daydāla** [Даідала] (Pek.).

DAYÏR see **DAİR**

DAYÏLA Yak. **Dayïla** [Дајыла] (Pek.). ✧ Daniil, Danila (R.). ⇨ **TAYÏLALÏR.**

DAYRA see **DÄRYA**

DAYRE see **DÄRYA**

DAKEY Kzk. 19th c. **Dakey** [Дакей] (AOK 110). ✧ 'Giant'? cf. Kzk. *däü* 'id.' (KzRS) + suff. *-ke* + *-y.*

DAQAN-ERDİ Uzb. 1740 **Daqan-erdi** [Даканъ-Ерди], from Khiva (Hanykov, Poezdka 28). ✧ 'Peasant, ploughman -?' cf. Uzb. *deχqān* (P.) 'дехканин, крестьянин; земледелец' (UzbRS).

DAQUPLAN Uzb. 1600 **Daquplan** [Дакуплан] (Miller, Ist. Sib. II, 160).

DAL Kzk. 19th c. **Dal-bay** [Далбай] (SOK 186); Kzk. 19th c. **Dal-bay** [Далбай] (SOV 186); Kirg. **Dal-bay** [Далбай] (Jud. 141). ✧ 'Confused, embarrassed' cf. Kirg. *dal* 'растерявшийся, опешивший' (Jud.), Kzk. *dal* 'grade in der Mitte' (Radl. III, 1632).

DAL-PALTA Trkm. 20th c. **Dal-palta** [Dalpalta], from the Kürdili (Barak) tribe (Özbaş 15). ⇨ **DAL + BALTA.**

DALA Oghuz/Trkm. 1029 **Dala** [Дала], the chieftain of the Ghuzz (MIT I, 364); Kzk. 19th c. **Dala-bay** [Далабай] (SOK 96); Kzk. 19th c. **Dala-bay** [Далабай] (AOAtb. 66); Kzk. 19th c. **Dala-bay** [Далабай] (AOP 126); Kzk. 19th c. **Dala-bay** [Далабай] (SOV 114); Kzk. 19th c. **Dala-bay** [Далабай] (SODž. 24). ✧ 'Flatland, steppe' cf. Kzk.,

Tat. *dala* 'die Steppe, die Ebene'; 'die Wüste';
(Chag.,Turk.) 'beissen, stechen'; 'rauben, plündern'
(Radl. III, 1633). See also **YABAN, SÄXRA,
ŠÖLKEY, TÏS.**

DALANTAY   Yak. **Dalantay** [Далантаі], a bogatyr
(Pek.). ✧ 'Waving' cf. Yak. *dalai-* (Pek.).

DALBÏR   Kzk. 19th c. **Dalbïr** [Далбыръ] (AOO 50).

DALDAL   Turk.? **Daldal-oγlu** (Giese 62). ✧ 'Elect,
hero' cf. Kirg. *daldal* 'auserwählt, vortrefflich; der
Held' (Radl. III, 1637).

DALDÏ   Kzk. 19th c. **Daldï-bay** [Дальдебай] (SODž.
6).

DALГÏČ   Yürük **Dalγïč** [دالغچ / Dalgıç], from the
Yürüks of Kocacık, Turkey (Gökb., Rum. 103). ✧
'Diver' cf. Turk. *dalγïč* 'der Taucher' (Radl. III, 1636).

DALİ see **DALÏ**

DALÏ   Kzk. 19th c. **Dalï-bay / Dali-bay?** [Далибай]
(SOV 4); Kzk. 19th c. **Dalï-bay / Dali-bay?** [Далибай]
(SOK 74); Bashk. 1737 **Dalï-batïr** [Далы батыр]
(MIB I, 345). ✧ 'Shoulder-blade' cf. Chag., NUyg.
dalu 'die Schulter, das Schulterblatt' (Radl. III, 1635),
Kirg. *dalï* 'das Schulterblatt' (Radl. III, 1635).

DALÏČÏ   Kirg. **Dalïčï** [Далычы], one of Manas'
comrades-in-arms (čoro) (Proben V, 116 /117/). ✧
'Fortune-teller using the shoulder-blade of sheep' cf.
Kirg. *dalïčï* 'id.' (Jud.).

DALÏM   Kzk. 19th c. **Dalïm-bek / Dalim-bek?**
[Далимбек] (SOK 42).

DALĀXTÏR   Yak.   **Dallāχtïr-daγda-būray**
[Даллахтыр], fem. (Pek.). ✧ Derived from Yak. *dallāχ*
(Pek.).

DAM   Kzk. 19th c. **Dam-bay** [Дамбай] (SODž. 36). ✧
'Roof'? cf. Az., Turk., Crm. *dam* 'das Dach; das Haus'
(Radl. III, 1648). See also **BAY-DAM.**

DAMAЈÏ   Tat.(GH)? 1313 **Damaǰï** [الامیر المغلی دماجی],
a Moghul emir (Dawād. 274). ✧ + suff. *-ǰï.*

DAMAR   Khorezm. 13th c. **Damar-melik** [Дамар-
мелик], a follower of Sultan J̌elāleddïn (1220-1231)
(MIT I, 476). ✧ 'Vein' (Erol II), cf. Az., Turk. *damar*
'id.' (Radl. III, 1650).

DAMBEMČE   Kzk. 19th c. **Dambemče / Dam-bemče?**
[Дамбемче] (SOK 202).

DAMELİ   Kzk. 19th c. **Dameli-bike / Dam-eli-bike?**
[Дамели-бике], fem. (Grod., Pril. 116). ⇨ **DAM + EL**
+ suff. *-li?*

DAN   Kzk. 19th c. **Dan-eke** [Данеке] (AOK 54). ✧
'Steppe, desert' cf. Kzk. *dan* 'id.' (Radl. III, 1621).

DAN-TOY   Kzk. 19th c. **Dan-toy** [Дантой
Алибековъ] (Grod., Pril. 112). ⇨ **DAN + TOY.**

DANA   Crm.(Tat.) 1518 **Dana**, a ḥāfiz/baḫšï from the
Golden Horde (Vásáry 54); Tat. 1529 **Dana** [Дана-
князь] (PSRL XIII, 46); Trkm.? 1821 **Dana-ata**
[Дана-ата] (Samojlovič 1927, 39). ✧ 'Clever, learned,
wise' cf. Kzk., Turk. *dana* 'kenntnissreich, klug,

gelehrt, der Gelhrte' (Radl. III, 1621) (<Ir.).

DANAY   Tat.(Sib.) 1599 **Danay** [Данай / Донай], a
princess from Siberia, a member of Küčüm's family (AI
II, 18, 20-21, 23); Kzk. 19th c. **Danay** [Данай] (SOV
40, 116). ⇨ **DANA** + suff. *-y.*

DANAP   Kzk. 19th c. **Danap** [Койланъ Данаповъ]
(Grod., Pril. 24).

DANDÏ   Kzk. 19th c. **Dandï-bay** [Дандыбай] (SOK
142). ⇨ **DAN?** + suff. *-lï.*

DANİYAR   Tat.(Kasim.) 15th c. **Daniyar** [Даньяр
Касимович] (Vel.-Zern., Kasim.); Kzk. **Daniyar**
[Даніяръ Мендыбаичъ] (ZIRGOGeogr. I, 452); Kzk.
19th c. **Daniyar** [Даніяръ Шадіевъ] (Grod., Pril.
197); Kzk. 19th c. **Daniyar** [Даніяръ] (SODž. 14);
Kkalp. 20th c. **Däniyar** [Дәнияр] (KkRS 773). ✧
'Clever' (Kusimova, Sattarov) (<P.).

DANİŠMEND   Trkm. 11th c. **Danišmend**, „Beiname
des Tāilu, eines Turkomanen aus χwārizm, der mit Alp
Arslan nach Kleinasien kam" (Justi 77 (after Ibn al-
Athïr/Tornb. X, 203)); Trkm. 11th c. **Danišmend**
[Ahmed Gümüštegin Ibn al-Dānišmend / al-
Dānišmend], Ahmed Gümüštegin, the son of Tāilu, also
named al-Dānišmend, the founder of the Dānišmend-
dynasty in 1086 (Justi 77); Khorezm. 1220
Danišmend-χan [Данишменд-хан], commander of
the army (MIT I, 483). ✧ 'Learned man; disciple,
follower'; 'der Gelehrte, in Persien auch Titel eines
Schülers der ʿUlemā oder Doctoren des moslimischen
Rechts' (Justi 77).

DANÏM   Kzk. 19th c. **Danïm-bay** [Данембай] (AOO
38). ⇨ **DAN?** + poss. suff. *-ïm.*

DANÏSPAN   Kzk. 19th c. **Danïspan** [Даныспанъ]
(SOK 78). ✧ 'Learned; wise' cf. Kzk. *danïspan*
'gelehrt, kenntnissreich, weise' (Radl. III, 1623).

DAPAQ   Kzk. 19th c. **Dapaq** [Тукачъ Дапаковъ]
(Grod., Pril. 114).

DAR   Kzk. 19th c. **Dar-bek** [Дарбекъ] (SOV 34); Kzk.
19th c. **Dar-jan** [Шахъ-Ніазъ Дарджановъ] (Grod.,
Pril. 173). ✧ 'Gallows' cf. *dar* (Az., Turk.) 'eng,
schmal, beengt', (East.T., Kzk., Turk.) 'der Galgen'
(Radl. III, 1625, 1626).

DARA   Trkm. 1510 **Dara-bek** [Дара-бек] (MIT II, 56,
57); Kzk. 19th c. **Dara-bek** [Дара-бекъ] (AOA 138).
✧ I. 'Gallows' cf. Kzk. *dara* 'der Galgen' (Radl. III,
1626); II. 'One by one' cf. Kzk. *dara* 'einzeln,
vereinzelt, jeder einzelne' (Radl. III, 1626).

DARAB   Turk. 1473 **Darab-bey** [Dârâb Bey] (Gökb.,
Ed. 13).

DARABÏAN   Yak. **Darabïan / Darïbïan** [Дарабыан /
Дарыбыан] (Pek.). ✧ Larivon, Ilarion (R).

DARABUNG   Mo.? **Darabung** [Дарабунг] (RaD II,
11).

DARBAZ   Kirg. **Darbaz** [Дарбаз] (Jud. 243). ✧
'Hangman' cf. Kirg. *darbaz* 'палач-вешатель;
канатоходец' (Jud.).

DARDAY   Yak. **Darday** [Дардаи] (Pek.). ✧ 'Lanky, wiry; lean man with broad back' (Pek.), cf. Yak. *dardai* (Pek.).

DARXAN see **DARQAN**

DARĬ see **DÄRİ**

DARĬBĬAN see **DARABĬAN**

DARĬYA see **DÄRYA**

DARĬYAXAN   Kirg. **Darïyaχan** [Дарыяхан], fem. (Jud. 754). ⇨ **DÄRYA** + suff. *-χan(1)*.

DARĬM   Yak. **Darïm** [Дарым], legendary name (Pek.).

DARĬN   Yak. **Darïn** [Ulū Darïn / Дарын], a bogatyr (Pek.).

DARĬNČA   Yak. **Darïnča** [Дарынча], Ǯāñï-Darïnča, a Tungus bogatyr of the remote past (Pek.). ⇨ **DARĬN** + suff. *-ča*.

DARYA see **DÄRYA**

DARQAN   Kkalp. 20th c. **Darχan-bay** [Дарханбай] (KkRS 773); Kzk. 19th c. **Darqam-bay (<Darqan-bay)** [Даркамбай] (SOV 88); Kzk. 19th c. **Darqan-bay / Darqïm-bay?** [Даркембай] (AOP 38); Kzk. 19th c. **Darqan-bay / Darqïm-bay?** [Даркембай] (SODž. 36). ✧ I. 'Free; freedom' cf. Kkalp. *darqan* 'вольный, свободный, привольный' (KkRS), Kzk. *darqan* 'die Freiheit' (Radl. III, 1629); II. 'Smith' cf. Kirg. *darqan* 'der Schmied, der Künstler'; III. 'The favourite' cf. Kzk. *darqan* 'der Liebling des Chans, einer den der Chan belohnt hat' (Radl. III, 1629). ⇨ **TARXAN.**

DARMA   Mo.? **Darma-bala** [Дармабала] (RaD II, 154).

DARMĬŠ   Selj.? 1161-1163 **Darmïš** [Дармиш ибн Шиш], a Ghurid hero (MIT I, 441).

DARU   Kzk. 19th c. **Daru-bay** [Дарубай] (SODž. 118). ✧ I. 'Medicine' cf. Kuman, Tat., East.T. *darū* 'das Heilmittel, die Medizin' (Radl. III, 1629); II. 'Gunpowder' cf. Chag., East.T. *daru* 'das Schiesspulver' (Radl. III, 1629). See also **DÄRİ.**

DAŠ see **TAŠ**

DAŠMAN   Bashk. 1664 **Dašman** [Икишко Дашманов] (MIB I, 193). ✧ 'Hard as stone'? ⇨ **TAŠ** + suff. *-man*.

DATĬP   Kzk. 19th c. **Datïp-bek** [Датыпбекъ] (SODž. 154).

DATQA   Kirg. **Datqayïm (< Datqa-ayïm)** [Датқайым], fem. (Jud. 123, 318). ✧ A title, cf. Kirg. *datqa* 'одно из высоких званий, дававшихся в Кокандском и Бухарском ханствах' (Jud.).

DAUΓAR see **DAWKER**

DAVLET see **DÄWLÄT**

DAW   Kzk. 19th c. **Daw-bay** [Давбай Джавдировъ] (Grod., Pril. 114); Kzk. 19th c. **Daw-bay** [Даубай] (SODž. 38); Kzk. 1883 **Daw-bay** [Давбай] (Grod., Pril. 93); Kzk. 1883 **Daw-bay** [Давбай] (Grod., Pril. 131); Trkm. 1722 **Daw-bek** [Даубекъ] (ZIRGO IX, 375); Kzk. 19th c. **Daw-bek** [Даубекъ] (SODž. 74); Kzk. 19th c. **Daw-qul-bay** [Давкулбай Джанъ Тюраевъ] (Grod., Pril. 36). ✧ 'Quarrel' cf. Kuman, Tat., Kzk. *dau* (<Ar.) 'der Streit, der Process' (Radl. III, 1607). See also **ER-DAW.**

DAW-BAS   Kzk. 19th c. **Daw-bas** [Даубасъ] (SOK 114). ⇨ **DAW + BAŠ.**

DAW-BİL   Kzk. 19th c. **Daw-bil** [Давбилъ бекъ] (Grod., Pril. 116). ⇨ **DAW + BİL.**

DAW-QARA   Kzk. 1822 **Daw-qara** [Кутлумбетъ Даукаринъ] (TOUAK XXIV, 122); Kzk. 1846 **Daw-qara** [бий Даукара] (MKOP 157). ⇨ **DAW + QARA.**

DAWACİ   Alt. 19th c. **Dawaci** [Даваци-князь], a prince (Verb., In.). ⇨ **TABĀČİ.**

DAWALĬNTAQ   Kzk. 19th c. **Dawalïntaq** [Дауалентакъ] (SOK 214).

DAWĬL   Kzk. 19th c. **Dawïl-bay** [Кундибай (Кондабай) Давилбаевъ] (Grod., Pril. 159, 160); Kkalp. 20th c. **Dawïl-bay** [Давылбай, Даұылбай] (Bask., Kkalp. 400, KkRS 773); Kzk. 1823 **Dawul-bay** [طولباى / Даулбай] (MIK IV, 459, 462); Kzk. 19th c. **Dawul-bay** [Даулбай] (SODž. 46); Kzk. 19th c. **Dawul-bay** [Даулбай] (AOAtb. 42); Kzk. 19th c. **Dawul-bay** [Даулбаевъ] (Grod., Pril. 116); Kzk. 19th c. **Dawul-bay** [Даулбаевъ] (AUK 879). ✧ 'Storm, tornado' cf. Kkalp. *dawïl* 'буря, ураган' (KkRS), Kzk. *dawl* 'der Wind, der Sturm' (Radl. III, 1607), Kzk. *dawïl* 'буря' (KzRS).

DAWKER   Kzk. **Dauγar-alïp** [Daugar Alyp / Дауғар алып], a character in a tale (Proben III, 282 /336/); Kzk. 19th c. **Dawker** [Таиръ Даукеровъ] (SKSO III, 190). ✧ 'Claimant, litigant, complainant; quarrelsome' cf. Kzk. *davger [dawger]* 'davacı, şikayetçi' (KzTS). ⇨ **DAW** + suff. *-ker*.

DAWLET see **DÄWLÄT**

DAWLET-ALİ   Kzk. 19th c. **Dawlet-ali** [Курпатай Даулеталиевъ] (Grod., Pril. 172). ⇨ **DÄWLÄT + ALİ.**

DAWLET-BAQ   Kzk. 18th c. - 19th c. **Dawlet-baq** [Даулетбак] (Tynyšp. 68, 71). ⇨ **DÄWLÄT + BAQ.**

DAWLET-BERDİ   Kzk. 18th c. - 19th c. **Dawlet-berdi** [Даулетберды] (Tynyšp. 67); Crm. 1427 **Dawlet-birdi** [دولة بردى / Даулетбирди] (Aynī/Tizeng. I, 501,533). ⇨ **DÄWLÄT + BERDİ.**

DAWLET-KELDİ see **DÄWLÄT-KELDİ**

DAWLETČİ   Tat. 1840 **Dawletči** [Давлетчи] (Konšin, Mat. V, 36). ⇨ **DÄWLÄT** + suff. *-či*.

DAWLETEY   Kzk. 19th c. **Dawletey** [Даулетей] (AOA 6). ⇨ **DÄWLÄT** + suff. *-ey*.

DAWLETMAN   Uzb.? 20th c. **Dawletman-bey** [Daouletman-bey-Dotkha], a basmači, Enver's second in command, died in 1922 (Castagné 77). ⇨ **DÄWLÄT** + suff. *-man*.

DAWLĬ Kzk. 19th c. **Dawlĭ-bay** [Кутибай Давлибаевъ] (Grod., Pril. 168). ✧ 'Grumpy' cf. Kzk. *daulï* 'streitsüchtig' (Radl. III, 1608). ⇨ **DAW** + suff. *-lï*. See also **BER-DAWLĬ**.

DAWRAN see **DÄWREN** ·

DAWRUN Kzk. 19th c. **Dawrum-bek** (<**Dawrun-bek**) [Даурумбекъ] (SODž. 158); Kzk. 19th c. **Dawrun-bek** [Даурунбекъ] (SODž. 74). ⇨ **DÄWREN?**

DAWUM Nog. **Dawum** [Даумъ], fem. (AI IV, 123).

DAWUT Kzk. 19th c. **Dawut-pay** [Даутпай] (SODž. 96). ✧ 'Davut, David'.

DAZ-ГĬZ see **TAZ**

DAŽDAN Kzk. 1788 **Daždan-batïr** [Dajdane-Batyr / Даждан Батыръ] (Levšin II, 301, Levchine 280).

DĀDAY Yak. **Dāday** [Дадаи] (Pek.). ✧ 'Be passive/effortless!' cf. Yak. *daday-* 'быть пассивным' (Pek.).

DĀDAR Yak. **Dādar** [Дадар] (Pek.). ✧ Diodor (R.).

DĀYE Turk. 1494 **Dāye-hatun** [Dâye Hatun] (Gökb., Ed. 36). ✧ 'Nanny, child's nurse' cf. Turk. *dâye* 'daya, dadı' (Özön) (<P.).

DÄBDÄKİÄY Yak. **Däbdäkiäy** / **Däbdäkiäyä** [Дäбдäкiäi / Дäбдäкiäjä], fem. (Pek.). ✧ Yevdokiya (R.).

DÄBDÄKİÄYÄ see **DÄBDÄKİÄY**

DÄGDÄ Yak. **Dägdä** [Дäгдä] (Pek.).

DÄGÄČČİN Yak. **Dägäččin** [Дäгäччiн] (Pek.).

DÄKÄYÄ Yak. **Däkäyä** [Дäкäjä] (Pek.).

DÄLGĀX Yak. **Dälgāχ** [Дäлгäх] (Pek.).

DÄLİ see **TELİ**

DÄLİXAN see **DÄLİQAN**

DÄLİQAN Kkalp. 20th c. **Däliχan** [Дäлихан], fem. (KkRS 777); Kkalp. 20th c. **Däliqan** [Дäликъан], fem. (Bask., Kkalp. 403). ⇨ **TELİ** + suff. *-qan(1)*.

DÄLLÄGÄY Yak. **Dällägäy** [Дäллäгäi], former leader of the Meginskiy ulus (Pek.).

DÄM-ETKEN Kkalp. 20th c. **Däm-etken** [Дäметкен], fem. (KkRS 777). ✧ 'Made (some) food'? cf. Kkalp. *däm* 'вкус; пища' (KkRS), *et-* 'делать'(KkRS).

DÄME Kkalp. 20th c. **Däme** [Дäме], fem. (KkRS 777); Kkalp. 20th c. **Däme-gül** [Дäмегүл], fem. (KkRS 777). ✧ 'Hope' cf. Kkalp. *däme* 'надежда, упование; стремление' (KkRS), for Kkalp. *Däme-gül* 'Hope-flower, flower of hoping' see Baskakov: OSA 140.

DÄMEGÖY Kkalp. 20th c. **Dämegöy** [Дäмегөй], fem. (KkRS 777). ✧ 'Charity, (Awaiting for) alms' cf. Kkalp. *dämegöylik* 'ожидание подачки' (KkRS). ⇨ **DÄME.**

DÄMEXAN Kkalp. 20th c. **Dämeχan** [Дäмехан], fem. (KkRS 777). ⇨ **DÄME** + suff. *-χan(1)*.

DÄMEŠ Kkalp. 20th c. **Dämeš** [Дäмеш], fem. (KkRS 777). ⇨ **DÄME** + suff. *-š?*

DÄNEK Tat.(Sib.) 1601 **Dänek** / **Denek?** [Дянек Яншиков] (Miller, Ist. Sib. II, 164).

DÄNİYAR see **DANİYAR**

DÄRİ Kkalp. 20th c. **Däri** [Дäри] (KkRS 773); Kzk. 19th c. **Däri-bay** [Даребаевъ] (Grod., Pril. 128); Kzk. 19th c. **Däri-bay** / **Dari-bay?** [Дарибай Мамбетовъ] (Grod., Pril. 98); Kkalp. 20th c. **Däri-biyke** [Дäрибийке], fem. (KkRS 777); Kkalp. 20th c. **Däri-gül** [Дäригүл], fem. (KkRS 777); Kkalp. 20th c. **Däri-žan** [Дäрижан], fem. (KkRS 777). ✧ 'Medicine' cf. Kzk. *däri* 'лекарство' (RKzS), Kkalp. *däri* 'лекарство; порох' (KkRS), for Kkalp. fem. PN *Däri-gül* 'Medicinal flower' see Baskakov: OSA 139. ⇨ **DARU.**

DÄRİXAN Kkalp. 20th c. **Däriχan** [Дäрихан], fem. (KkRS 777). ⇨ **DÄRİ** + suff. *-χan(1)*.

DÄRİҮA Kkalp. 20th c. **Däriγa** [Дäрийга], fem. (KkRS 777). ✧ 'Gloom, sadness, regret'? cf. Kzk. *darığa* 'pişman olmak, üzülmek, özlemek belirtisi' (KzTS).

DÄRİKÄ Kkalp. 20th c. **Därikä** [Дäрикä], fem. (Bask., Kkalp. 403). ⇨ **DÄRİ?** + suff. *-kä*.

DÄRYA Kzk. 19th c. **Dayra** [Дайра] (SOK 24); Kzk. 1825 **Dayra-bay** [Дайрабай Ульджебай] (TOUAK XXIV, 156); Kzk. 19th c. **Dayra-bay** [Тенгриберди Дайрабаевъ] (Grod., Pril. 109); Kzk. 19th c. **Dayra-bay** [Дайрабай] (Grod., Pril. 187); Kzk. 19th c. **Dayra-bay** [Дайрабай] (AOA 102); Kzk. 19th c. **Dayre-bay** [Дайребай] (SODž. 32); Kkalp. 20th c. **Darya-bay** [Дарйабай] (Bask., Kkalp. 58); Kkalp. 20th c. **Därya-bay** [Дäрьябай] (KkRS 773); Turk. 1565 **Derya-beg** (Dávid). ✧ 'Sea, (big) river' cf. Chag., Turk., Crm., Kar. *dárya* 'das Meer, der Strom, der Fluss, der Wasserschwall', Kzk. *däryä* 'das Meer; ein freigiebiger und reicher Mensch' (Radl. III, 1673), Kkalp. *där'ya* 'большая река' (KkRS), Kzk. *dariya* 'большая река' (KzRS), Kzk. (dial.) *daira* (<دريا) 'ein grosser Fluss' (Radl. III, 1606) <P. *daryā*.

DÄRMAN Kkalp. 20th c. **Därman** [Дäрман] (KkRS 773). ✧ 'Strength, energy; support' cf. Kkalp. *därman* 'сила, энергия; средства, возможности' (KkRS).

DÄW Kkalp. 20th c. **Däw-eke** [Дäүеке] (KkRS 773). ✧ 'Big; Great; Elder; Giant; Hero' cf. Tat. *däw* 'большой, крупный; старший' (TatRS), Bashk. *däw* 'большой, крупный' (BRS/Uraksin), Kkalp. *däw* 'великан, исполин, богатырь; див' (KkRS), Kirg. *dȫ (döö)* 'див, сказочный исполин, великан' (Jud.). See also **QARA-DȪ; BOYŠAN, DUOLANTAY, ÄLLÄY, KETTÄ, QOŽAQ, ULUГ, ZOR.**

DÄW-ÄNÄY Bashk.? 1678 **Däw-änäy** [Девеней Девлетъ Баевъ], a tarγan (DAI IX, 92-93); Bashk. 1713 **Däw-änäy** [Девеней Каныбеков] (MIB III, 107); Bashk. 1729 **Däw-änäy** [Девеней Бердышев] (MIB III, 270); Bashk. 1750 **Däw-änäy** [Маракай Девенеев] (MIB III, 476). ✧ 'Grand-mother' cf. Tat.

däw äni 'бабушка' (TatRS). ⇨ **DÄW**. See also **ENEŠ**.

DÄW-ÄTÄY   Bashk. 1712 **Däw-ätäy** [Деветей] (MIB III, 34); Bashk. 1735 **Däw-ätäy** [Арасланбакъ Деветеевъ], a tarχan (Vel.-Zern., Bašk. 27); Bashk. 1763 **Däw-ätäy** [Деветей Маметев] (MIB IV/1, 268); Bashk. 1779 **Däw-ätäy** [Илимбеть Деветеев] (MIB V, 101). ❖ 'Grand-father; uncle' cf. Tat. *däw äti* 'дедушка; дядя, старший брат отца' (TatRS). ⇨ **DÄW + ATAY**.

DÄW-QARA   Kkalp. 20th c. **Däw-qara** [Дәўқара] (KkRS 773). ⇨ **DÄW + QARA**.

DÄWLÄKÄY see **DÄWLÄTKÄY**

DÄWLÄT   Kzk. 19th c. **Dawlet** [Даулетъ Бушаев], Sultan Dawlet Bušayev (AUK 287); Kzk. 19th c. **Dawlet-bike** [Даулетъ-бик], her sister was called Naz-bike (Potanin II, 4); Uyg. 13th c.-14th c. **Däwlät** [Daulet], fem. (Chwol., Syr.-nest. (NF) 42); Uyg. 1338 **Däwlät** [Dulit], fem. (Chwol., Syr.-nest. (NF) 84); Maml. 1516 **Däwlät** [دولات] (Iyās III, 4); Tat.(Sib.) 1600 **Däwlät** [Девлетев Катаргул] (Miller, Ist. Sib. II, 159); Tat.(Sib.) 1601 **Däwlät** [Девлет Куткилдеев] (Miller, Ist. Sib. II, 164); Bashk. 1707 **Däwlät** [Девлет Савит] (MIB III, 40); Bashk. 1709 **Däwlät** [Девлеть Чичканов] (MIB III, 49); Bashk. 1735 **Däwlät** [Девлетъ Аднагуловъ], a tarχan (Vel.-Zern., Bašk. 14); Bashk. 1739 **Däwlät** [Биккиня Девлетев] (MIB III, 409); Bashk. 1754 **Däwlät** [Девлеть Урускулов] (MIB IV/1, 84); Bashk. 1756 **Däwlät** [Токаш Девлетов] (MIB IV/1, 132); Bashk. 1756 **Däwlät** [Девлеть Биктемиров] (MIB IV/1, 128); Bashk. 1792 **Däwlät** [Девлет Увакаев] (MIB V, 327); Bashk. 1793 **Däwlät** [Габайдулла Девлетев] (MIB V, 331); Kzk. 19th c. **Däwlät / Döwlet?** [Мамакулъ Бай Довлатовъ] (Grod., Pril. 143); Trkm.? 1817/18 **Däwlät-baχši** [Девлет-бахши] (MIT II, 404); Tat.(Sib.) 1599 **Däwlät-baχt(ï)?** [Девлетъ-Бахтъ], (young) wife in the family of Küčüm (AI II, 20); Maml. 1421 **Däwlät-bay** [دولات باى المحمودى] (Iyās II, 43); Maml. 1438, 1461 **Däwlät-bay** [دولات باى سكسن لخاصكى] (Ibn Taghrīb. VII, 10, 554, 697); Maml. 1453 **Däwlät-bay** [دولات باى] (Iyās II, 41); Maml. 1459 **Däwlät-bay** [دولات باى الظاهرى] (Ibn Taghrīb. VII, 518); Maml. 1460 **Däwlät-bay** [دولات باى بن قجماس] (Ibn Taghrīb. VIII, 788); Maml. 1460, 1467 **Däwlät-bay** [دولات باى حمام الاشرفى] (Ibn Taghrīb. VII, 545, 853, Iyās II, 113); Maml. 1461, 1467 **Däwlät-bay** [دولات باى النجمى الاشرفى] (Ibn Taghrīb. VII, 691, 846, 839, Iyās II, 88, 171); Maml. 1467/68 **Däwlät-bay** [دولات باى الابو بكرى المويّدى] (Ibn Taghrīb. VII, 749, 854); Maml. 1470 **Däwlät-bay** [دولات باى اليبا لى] (Iyās II, 118); Maml. 1470/71 **Däwlät-bay** [دولات باى الخازندار], a treasurer (Iyās II, 123); Maml. 1496 **Däwlät-bay** [دولات باى بن اركماس], governor of Haleb (Iyās II, 306); Tat.(Sib.) 1601 **Däwlät-bay** [Девлетбай] (Miller, Ist. Sib. II, 169); Bashk. 1666 **Däwlät-bay** [Канкаска Девлетбаевъ], a tarχan (Vel.-Zern., Bašk. 42); Bashk. 1735 **Däwlät-bay** [Ширий Девлетбаевъ], a tarχan (Vel.-Zern., Bašk. 16); Bashk. 1751 **Däwlät-bay** [Девлетбай Асларчин] (MIB IV/1, 43); Bashk. 1764 **Däwlät-bay** [Девлетбай Иштяков] (MIB IV/1, 291); Maml. 1496 **Däwlät-bay** [دولات باى], a Cherkess (Iyās II, 314); Tat.(Sib.) 1599 **Däwlät-bike** [Девлебака], Küčüm-qan's grand-daughter (AI II, 20); Chag. **Däwlät-γazi** [دولت عازى], a Sheybanid (Šejb. LII); Maml. 1456 **Däwlät-χan** [دولات خان سلطان لى] (Ibn Taghrīb. VIII, 286); Tat.(Lit.) 1582 **Däwlät-yar** [Муртоза Давлят-яровичъ] (Lit. Tat. 48); Uzb. 1767/68 **Däwlät-yar** [Девлет-яр], from the Qongrat tribe (MIT II, 336, 339); Bashk. 1735 **Däwlät-qul** [Девлеткулъ Назаргуловъ], a tarχan (Vel.-Zern., Bašk. 15); Bashk. 1780 **Däwlät-qul** [Девлеткул Адзимясов] (MIB V, 115); NUyg.(Tar.) 19th c. **Däwlät-nazar-šeyχ** [Девлетъ-назаръ-шейхъ] (Pantusov, Tar. 15); Maml.? 1437/38 **Däwlät-šah** [دولات شاه الكردى] (Ibn Taghrīb. VII, 4, Weil, Chalif. II, 194); Maml. 1465 **Däwlät-šah** [دولات شاه الكردى] (Ibn Taghrīb. VIII, 514); Bashk. 1735 **Däwlät-še** [Девлетше Аиткуловъ], a tarχan (Vel.-Zern., Bašk. 15); Tat. 1551 **Däwlät-žar** [Девлетжаръ] (PSRL XIII, 161); Kkalp. 20th c. **Däwlet** [Дәўлет] (KkRS 773); Kkalp. 20th c. **Däwlet-bay** [Дәўлетбай] (KkRS 773); Kkalp. 1740 **Däwlet-bay-bi(y)** [Девлетбай-Би] (Hanykov, Poezdka 19); Kkalp. 20th c. **Däwlet-iyar** (<Däwlet-yar) [Дәўлетияр] (KkRS 773); Turk. 1486 **Devlet** [Devlet binti Abdullah], fem. (Gökb., Ed. 460); Turk. 1583 **Devlet** (Ongan, Ank. I, 155); Chuv. 18th-19th c. **Devlet** [Девлетъ] (Magn. 36); Tat. 1675 **Devlet** [Девлетъ] (Kungursk. akty 31); Turk. 1504 **Devlet-bey** (Gökb., Ed. 472); Turk. 1495 **Devlet-han** [Devlethan bin Tanrıvermiş] (Gökb., Ed. 134); Yürük 1543 **Devlet-han** (Gökb., Rum. 185, 203); Turk. 1540 **Devlet-χan** [Devlet Han kethudâ], chief (kethudâ) of the Uran tribe, according to the defter of Diyarbekir (Demirtaş 51); Yürük 16th c. **Devlet-χan** [Devlet-han], from the Yürüks of Kocacık, Turkey (Gökb., Rum. 104); **Devlet-χatun** [دولت خاتون], in the genealogy of the Mongols (Qazw. 557); Yürük 1543 **Devlet-qïzi** (Gökb., Rum. 234); Selj., Turk.? **Devlet-šah** [دولتشاه], an emir in Afghanistan at the time of the Muzaffarid Mubārizuddīn (Qazw. 643); Khorezm. 1214 **Devlet-šah** [دولتشاه بوكاول], from Khorezm (Qazw. 694-695 etc.); Crm.(Tat.?) 1784 **Devlet-šah, Däwlät-šah?** [Девлетша мурза], a murza (CAN otd. gum. nauk 1928, 379);

Turk. 1494 **Devlet-šah-hatun** (χatun?) [Devletşah Hatun] (Gökb., Ed. 36); Chag.? **Devlet-šeyχ** [شيخ دولت], a Sheybanid (Šejb. XLIX, L); Trkm. 1816 **Dewlet-serdar** [Мир Девлет-сердар] (MIT II, 395); Kirg. **Dölöt** [Bagdy Dölöt / Баҕды Дölöт Баiбiчä], fem. (Proben V, 80 /81/); Trkm. 20th c. **Dövlet** [Dövlet] (Zaj. 1971, 328); Trkm. 20th c. **Dövlet** [Довлет] (TrkmRS 280); Trkm. 20th c. **Döwlet-aγa**, a character in a modern short story (?); Trkm. 1814 **Döwlet-išan** [Мир Доулет-ишан], from the Ĵafar-bay clan (MIT II, 215); Bashk. 1756 **Täwlät** [Тевлеть Елдашев] (MIB IV/1, 123); Bashk. 1756 **Täwlät-čura** [Арямян Тевлеть чюрин (Тлевлеть чюрин)] (MIB IV/1, 122); Bashk. 1756 **Täwlät-čura** [Аксары Тевлеть чюрин (Тлевлеть чюрин)] (MIB IV/1, 122); Bashk. 1756 **Täwlät-qul** [Сюлейман Тевлет кулов] (MIB IV/1, 128). ✧ 'Chance, happiness, wealth, richness; country, homeland' (P. < Ar.), cf. OT *däwlät* (DTS), Kuman, Tat. *däülät* 'das Glück, das Heil, der Reichtum, das Vermögen' (Radl. III, 1657), Turk., Crm. *däwlät* 'das Glück, das Vermögen, der Reichtum; das Reich, die Regierung' (Radl. III, 1695), Trkm. *dövlet* 'богатство, добро' (TrkmRS), Bashk. *däwlät* 'государство; богатство, состояние' (BRS), Kkalp. *däület* 'богатство, состояние; счастье' (KkRS), Kzk. *dâvlet* 'Zenginlik, mal-mülk sahibi olmak' (KzTS). See also **AQ-DAWLET, AMAN-DAWLET, BAΓDÏ-DÖLÖT, BAY-DAWLET, BAQ-DÖLÖT, BER-DAWLÄT, XAN-DÄWLÄT, İGÜ-DÄWLÄT, İŠ-DÄWLÄT, YAN-DÄWLÄT, YAQŠÏ-DÄWLÄT, KÖP-DÄWLÄT, QOŠ-DÄWLÄT, MEÑLİ-DÄWLÄT, MER-DŪLÄT, ŠÄW-DAWLET, ŠÜGÜR-DÄWLÄT, URAZ-DÄWLÄT, ŽAN-DÄWLET.**

DÄWLÄT-BİKÄ see **DÄWLÄT**

DÄWLÄT-ĴAR see **DÄWLÄT**

DÄWLÄT-DURDÏ   Trkm. 1828 **Däwlät-durdï** [Девлет-Дурды], from the Soqtï clan (MIT II, 447). ⇨ **DÄWLÄT + TURDÏ.**

DÄWLÄT-GELDİ see **DÄWLÄT-KELDİ**

DÄWLÄT-GİREY   Crm.(Tat.) 1532 **Däwlät-girey** [Девъleть-Гирѣй], prince, the later Crimean khan (Devlet Giray I, 1551-1577) (PSRL XIII, 61, XIX, 110, 397); Crm.(Tat.) 1572, 1592? **Däwlät-girey-χan** [دو لت کرای حان], Mengli Girey Khan's son? (Vel.-Zern., Crim. 5, 13, 14); Crm.(Tat.) 1592? **Däwlät-girey-sultan** [دولت کرای سلان بن بهادر کرای حان], Bahadir Girey Khan's son? (Vel.-Zern., Crim. 164, 213); Crm.(Tat.) 1692 **Däwlät-girey-sultan** [دولتکرای سلان بن سليم کرای حان], Khan Devlet Girey II (1699-1702), Selim Girey Khan's son (Vel.-Zern., Crim. 718, 723 etc.); Crm.(Tat.) 1531, 1551 **Däwlät-girey(-sultan)** [دو لت کرای / Девлетъ-Гирей],

Crimean Khan Devlet Giray I (1551-1577), Mubarek Girey Khan's son (PSRL VIII, 279, VI, 304, VelZernC 27, 31); Crm.(Tat.) 1624? **Däwlät-girey(-sultan)** [دو لت کرای نورالد ين محمد کرای حان] (Vel.-Zern., Crim. 22, 23); Nog. 1649 **Däwlät-kirey(-murza)** [Девлеть-Кирей мурза], a murza (AI IV, 79); Tat.(Sib.) 1609, 1654 **Devlet-girey** [Девлеть-Кирей / Девлеткирей], Küčüm's grand-son (AI IV, 229, Miller, Ist. Sib. II, 212, 363, 383, 390, 407 etc., 436 etc., 480 etc., 527); Crm.(>Kabard?) 1689 **Divlet-kirey** [Дивлеть-Кирей], a Kabard mirza (AI V, 316).

DÄWLÄT-İYAR see **DÄWLÄT**

DÄWLÄT-KELDİ   Kzk. 18th c. - 19th c. **Dawlet-keldi** [Даулеткельди] (Tynyšp. 75); Crm.(Tat.) **Däwlät-geldi** [Девлеть-гэльди], an atalïq (Smirnov, Krym. 223); Uzb. 20th c. **Däwlät-keldi** [Давлаткелди] (Begmatov 1984, 202); Crm. 1534 **Däwlät-kildey / Däwlät-kilde** [Девлеть-килдѣй] (PSRL XIII, 79); Tat. 19th c. **Däwlät-kilde / Däwlät-kildey** [Devlet Kildêjev], a prince, the chief of the police in Uržum („Tatar converti, sinon musulman") (Smyrnov 195); Tat.(Sib.)? 1599 **Däwlät-kildey / Däwlät-kilde** [Девлеть-килдѣй], mother Qulu-bi's (Külü-bi's?) son (AI II, 20); Tat. 1675 **Däwlät-kildi** [Иванайко Девлеткилдиевъ] (Kungursk. akty 30); Tat. 18th c. **Däwlät-kilde / Däwlät-kildey** [князь Девлеткильдеевъ], a prince from a Russian Family in the province of Kazan (Korsakov 206); Chuv. 18th-19th c. **Devlet-kildä** [Девлеткилда] (Magn. 36); Chuv. 18th-19th c. **Devle-kildä** [Девлекилда] (Magn. 36). ✧ 'Chance / happyness / wealth has come (has been born)'. ⇨ **DÄWLÄT + KELDİ.**

DÄWLÄT-KİLDEY see **DÄWLÄT-KELDİ**

DÄWLÄT-KİLDİ see **DÄWLÄT-KELDİ**

DÄWLÄT-QARA-KÖZ   Trkm.? 1816 **Däwlät-qara-köz** [Девлет Каракоз] (MIT II, 391, 402). ⇨ **DÄWLÄT + QARA + KÖZ.**

DÄWLÄT-MİRAT see **DÄWLÄT-MURAT**

DÄWLÄT-MURAD see **DÄWLET-MURAT**

DÄWLÄT-SAR   Tat.(Mish.) 18th c. **Däwlät-sar** [Абдюкъ Девлетьсаровъ] (Nepljuev 879, 890). ⇨ **DÄWLÄT.**

DÄWLÄTÄK   Crm.(Tat.) 1474 **Däwlätäk / Döwlätäk?** [Довлетекъ], murza, envoy of the Crimea (under Mengli Giray) (PSRL VIII, 180-181, SmirnovKrym. 255); Crm.(Tat.) 1520 **Däwlätäk-bi** [دولتك بى / Devletek bi] (Vel.-Zern., Crim. 3). ⇨ **DÄWLÄT + suff. -äk.**

DÄWLÄTİM   Tat.(Sib.) 1581 **Däwlätim-bay / Devletim-murza** [Дѣвлетимъ Бай, Девлетимъ мурза] (Sib. Let. (Rem.) 319, 320). ✧ 'My chance'. ⇨ **DÄWLÄT + 1st p. sing. poss. suff. -im.**

DÄWLÄTKÄY   Bashk. 1659 **Däwläkäy** [Якши-Иванъ Девлекеевъ] (Vel.-Zern., Bašk. 37); Bashk. 1754

Däwläkäy [Девлекей Мратов] (MIB IV/1, 79); Tat. 18th-19th c. **Däwlätkäy / Däwläkäy** [Девлекей, Девлеткей] (Magn. 36). ✧ 'My little chance'. ⇨ **DÄWLÄT** + suff. *-käy*.

DÄWLÄTLİ Bashk. 1735 **Däwlätli** [Чювей Девлетлинъ], a tarχan (Vel.-Zern., Bašk. 18); Bashk. 1756 **Täwlätli** [Кутук Тевлетелиев] (MIB IV/1, 123). ✧ 'Very happy; distinguished' cf. Turk. *dävlätli* 'sehr glücklich, hoch geehrt' (Radl. III, 1695). ⇨ **DÄWLÄT** + suff. *-li*.

DÄWLET-MURAT Trkm. 1849 **Däwlät-murad-inaq / Däwlät-inaq** [Девлет Мурад-инак, Девлет-инак], one of the chiefs of Teke-Turkmen (MIT II, 520, 536); Kkalp. 20th c. **Däwlet-mïrat** [Дәүлетмырат] (KkRS 773); Kkalp. 20th c. **Däwlet-murat** [Дәүлетмурат] (KkRS 773). ⇨ **DÄWLÄT + MURAT.**

DÄWLET-NAZAR Kkalp. 20th c. **Däwlet-nazar** [Дәүлетназар] (KkRS 773); Kkalp. 19th c. **Döwlät-nazar** [Довлатъ Назаръ] (Grod., Pril. 142). ⇨ **DÄWLÄT + NAZAR.**

DÄWRÄN see **DÄWREN**

DÄWREN Kzk. 19th c. **Dawram-bek (<Däwrän-bek)** [Даурамбекъ] (SOV 42); Kzk. 19th c. **Dawren-bay / Däwren-bay** [Дауренбай] (SODž. 124); Kzk. 19th c. **Dawren-bay / Däwren-bay** [Дауренбай] (SOK 242); Kzk. 19th c. **Dawran-bek / Däwrän-bek** [Дауранбекъ] (SODž. 40). ✧ 'Time, epoch, era' cf. Kzk. PNs *Dauren* (Žanuzakov 136), *Däwren, Däwren-bek* (Žanuzakov-Esbaeva) (<Ar.).

DEBOŠ Karch. 20th c. **Deboš** (Pröhle, Kar. 100).

DEBRE Turk. 1489 **Debre** [Debre] (Gökb., Ed. 156).

DEDE Turk. 1565 **Dede** [Dede bin Derya beg] (Dávid); Turk. 20th c. **Dede** [Dede] (Önder, Hınıs); Yürük 1543 **Dede** two Yürüks (Gökb., Rum. 196). ✧ 'Grandfather; elderly respected man (addressing)' cf. Chag., Turk. *dädä* 'der Grossvater, Väterchen; der Chef der Derwische' (Radl. III, 1682), western Turkic *dede* 'yaşlı büyüklerin ünvanı' (DQorq./Ergin).

DEDE-BĀLİ Yürük 1543 **Dede-bāli** (Gökb., Rum. 181). ⇨ **DEDE + BĀLİ.**

DEGÄŠ Bashk. 1738 **Degäš** [Кугаш Дегашов] (MIB III, 393).

DEHŠET Turk. 20th c. **Dehšet** [Dehşet] (Önder, Göle). ✧ 'Terror, horror' cf. Turk. *dehşet* 'terror, horror, dread, awe; marvelous' (TED). (Ar.).

DEYDER-TÄKEY Bashk. 1675 **Deyder-täkey** [Солгангин Дейдертякеев] (MIB I, 200). ⇨ **?** + **TEKE** + suff. *-y.*

DEYE-PERGEN Kzk. 19th c. **Deye-pergen** [Деепергенъ] (SOK 8). ✧ 'Camel-given'? ⇨ **DEVE?** + **BERGEN.**

DELBE Kzk. 19th c. **Delbe-pay** [Дельбепай] (SOV 122). ✧ 'Rein(s)' cf. Kzk. *delbä~dilbä* 'die Zügel' (Radl. III, 1681).

DELİ see **TELİ**

DELİ-BAŠ Turk. 20th c. **Deli-baš** (Önder, Hınıs). ✧ 'Headstrong, stubborn' cf. Turk. *deli baş* 'своевольный' (TRS). ⇨ **TELİ + BAŠ.**

DELİ-DUMRUL see **DOMRUL**

DELİL Turk. 20th c. **Delil** (Önder, Göle). ✧ 'Guide, leader; evidence; sign' (Erol II) (<Ar.).

DELİMBET Kkalp. 20th c. **Delimbet** [Делимбет] (Bask., Kkalp. 68). ⇨ **TELİ** + suff. *-imbet / -mbet.*

DELÜ see **TELİ**

DELÜ-DUMRUL see **DOMRUL**

DELÜ-DUNDAR Oghuz/Trkm. 15th c. **Delü-dundar / Delü-tundar** [دلو دوندار], Qïyan Seljük's son, his byname was Delü (DQorq./Rossi 121, 122, 144, 157, 161-163, DQorq./Ergin 96).

DELÜ-HALİFE Turk. 1454 **Delü-halife** [Delü Halife] (Gökb., Ed. 162). ✧ 'Caliph; assistant' cf. Turk. *halife* 'Eskiden bir tarikat şeyhinden el alan kimse' (TS). ⇨ **TELİ + XALİFA.**

DELÜ-ŠAHİN Turk. 1455 **Delü-šahin** [Delü-Şahin] (Gökb., Ed. 236). ⇨ **TELİ + ŠAHİN.**

DELÜ-TUNDAR see **DELÜ-DUNDAR**

DEM Kzk. 1819 **Dem-eke** [Демяка] (MIK IV, 323). ✧ 'Breath; rest, quiet' cf. Chag., East.T., Crm., Kzk. *däm~dem* (P.) 'der Hauch, der Athem; das Ausruhen, die Zeit; die Ruhe' (Radl. III, 1697), Turk. *dem* 'breath; drone; instant, time' (TED). ⇨ **DÄME?**

DEM-GELDİ Yürük 1543 **Dem-geldi** [دم كلدى] (Gökb., Rum. 207). ✧ 'Soul has come / Born in time'? cf. Chag., East.T., Crm., Kzk. *däm~dem* (P.) 'der Hauch, der Athem; das Ausruhen, die Zeit; die Ruhe' (Radl. III, 1697), Turk. *dem* 'breath; drone; instant, time' (TED). ⇨ **KELDİ.**

DEM-SU Kzk. 19th c. **Dem-su?** [Демсу] (AOAtb. 2). ⇨ **DEM + SUW?**

DEMEY see **DÜMEY**

DEMENTEY Bashk. 1709 **Dementey** [Дементей] (MIB I, 271). ✧ Dementiy (R.).

DEMENTLİKÄY Bashk. 1682 **Dementlikäy?** [Дементликайко Ижбулаевъ] (AI V, 139).

DEMESİN Kzk. 19th c. **Demesin** [Демесин] (SOK 134, 278, 304); Kzk. 19th c. **Demesin** [Демесын] (SOV 46). ✧ 'Let him/her help/support (us)!' cf. Kzk. *deme-* 'поддержать, помочь ' (KzRS).

DEMEŠ Chuv.? 1737 **Demeš?** [Демешъ], a clerk (scribe) from an office in Yadrinsk (Alatyr. 136). ⇨ **DEM?** + suff. *-eš / -iš.*

DEMİČİ-EREN (<DEMİRČİ-EREN?) see **TEMİČİ**

DEMİR see **TEMİR**

DEMİR-BAŠ Turk. 1528 **Demir-baš** [Fahreddin Demirbaş] (Gökb., Ed. 162). ⇨ **TEMİR + BAŠ.**

DEMİR-BULAT see **TEMİR-BULAT**

DEMİR-ĴAN see **TEMİR**

DEMİR-DAŠ see **TEMİR-TAŠ**

DEMİRJİ see **TEMİRČİ**

DEMÜR-EKİJİ see **DEMÜR-KÜČİ**

DEMÜR-GÜČİ see **DEMÜR-KÜČİ**

DEMÜR-KÜČİ   Oghuz/Trkm. 15th c. **Demür-küči / Demür-güči / Demür-ekiji** [دمور اكجى دموركوجى / Demür Ekigi, Demür Guci, Demür Cuci / Демюр-Кючи] (DQorq./Rossi 136, DQorq./Ergin 97, DQorq. 23). ✧ 'Iron-Strength'. ➪ **TEMİR** + **KÜČ** + poss. suff. -*i*.

DEMÜR-OΓLU see **TEMİR**

DEN-GELDİ   Kzk. 19th c. **Den-geldi** [Денгельды] (SOK 190). ✧ 'Body (man) has come (has been born)'. ➪ **TEN** + **KELDİ.**

DENJİK   Kzk. 19th c. **Denjik-pay** [Денджикпай] (SOK 126). ✧ 'Small body' cf. Kzk. *den* 'der Körper' (Radl. III, 1666). + suff. -*jik*.

DENDİ   Kzk. 19th c. **Dendi-bay** [Дендыбай] (SOK 174). ✧ 'Having small body' cf. Kzk. *den* 'der Körper' (Radl. III, 1666). + suff. -*di*.

DENE   Kzk. 19th c. **Dene-bay** [Денебай] (SOK 92). ✧ 'Body' cf. Kzk. *denä* 'der Körper' (Radl. III, 1666). See also **BOY, DENE, TEN, TULΓA.**

DENESTAN   Kzk. 19th c. **Denestan** [Денестанъ] (SODž. 4).

DENGEM   Kzk. 19th c. **Dengem-bay / Dengim-bay?** [Денгембай] (SODž. 78). ✧ '(Born) in time' cf. Kzk. *däñ* 'die passende Zeit', *däñimä keldi* 'er ist zu mir zu passender Zeit gekommen' (Radl. III, 1660).

DENİ   Kzk. 19th c. **Deni-bay** [Деныбай] (SOK 116). ➪ **DEN.**

DEÑEL   Kzk. 19th c. **Deñel-bay** [Денгельбай] (SOK 44, 90, 166, 230, 302); Kzk. 19th c. **Deñel-bay** [Денгельбай] (SOV 30, 98); Kzk. 19th c. **Deñil-bay** [Денгильбай] (SOK 172). ✧ 'Similar; suitable' cf. Kzk. *däñäl* 'gleich, passend' (Radl. III, 1661).

DEÑGER   Kzk. 19th c. **Deñger-bay / Deñer-bay** [Денгербай] (SOK 194).

DEÑİZ see **TEÑİZ**

DEPE-GÖZ   Oghuz/Trkm. 15th c. **Depe-göz / Tepe-göz** [Тепегöз / Депе-Гэз] (DQorq. 76-78, 80-83, 133, 134 etc., DQorq./Rossi 193-202). ✧ 'One-eyed; Cyclops' cf. Turk. *tepegöz* 'whose forehead is so narrow that his eyes seem near his hair; cyclops (legendary monster)' (TED) <*depe* 'golovaголова [head]' + *gez* 'глаз [eye]' (Bartol'd: DQorq. 275, footnote 6). ➪ **KÖZ.**

DER   Uyg. 1209 **Der-bay** [Дербай], envoy of the Uyghur ïduq-qut to Chinggis Khan (RaD/Ber. III, 10, 12); Kzk. 19th c. **Der-bek** [Дербекъ] (SODž. 86); Kkalp. 20th c. **Der-biyke** [Дербийке], fem. (Bask., Kkalp. 71, KkRS 777); Tat.(Sib.) 1599 **Der-patša** [Дерпадша], Küčüm's daughter (AI II, 20). ✧ 'Genuine, real, true' cf. Kzk. *der* 'echt' (Radl. III, 1670).

DER-GÜČİ   Nog. 1649 **Der-güči (Der-güčey?)**

[Дергучѣй], a murza (AI IV, 17). ➪ **DER** + **KÜČ** + poss. suff. -*i*.

DERBAL   Bulg. **Derbal** [Дербалъ], a Bulghar prince (PSRL (Russk. Hr.) II, 208). ➪ **TERVEL?**

DERBİS see **DERVİŠ**

DERBİS-ALİ   Kzk. 19th c. **Derbis-ali / Derbis-äli** [Дербисалиевъ] (Grod., Pril. 196); Kzk. 19th c. **Dereps-alï** (<**Derbs-alï** < **Derbis-alï?**) [Дерепсалы] (SOK 114). ✧ 'Derviš Ali'; 'Special Ali'? cf. Kzk. *derbes*? 'отдельный, самостоятельный; специальный, особый' (KzRS), cf. also Kzk. PN *Derbis-äli* (Žanuzakov-Esbaeva). ➪ **DERVİŠ?** + **ALİ.**

DERBİŠ see **DERVİŠ**

DERE   Kzk. 19th c. **Dere-bay** [Деребай] (SOK 236). ✧ 'A part of the trough' cf. Kzk. *därä* 'der Untersatz unter der Mulde, aus der man das Vieh tränkt' (Radl. III, 1670).

DEREBEY   Turk. 20th c. **Derebey** [Derebey] (Önder, Hınıs). ✧ 'Feudal lord' cf. Turk. *derebey* 'feudal lord, local potentate, despot; bully' (TED).

DEREK   Kzk. 19th c. **Derek-pay** [Дерекпай] (SOV 4). ✧ 'News, message' cf. Chag. *däräk* 'die Nachricht' (Radl. III, 1670), Kzk. *derek* 'весть' (KzRS). See also **ALP-DEREK, İL-DEREK.**

DEREPS-ALÏ see **DERBİS-ALİ**

DERİM   Kzk. 19th c. **Derim-bay** [ديريمباى / Деримъ-бай] (Veselovskij, Kirg. 78 (122)). ✧ '(Türkmen) tent' cf. Turk. *därim* 'turkmenskaq palatkaė ein türkisches Zelt' (Radl. III, 1672).

DERYA see **DÄRYA**

DERSE   Oghuz/Trkm. 15th c. **Derse-χan / Dirse-χan** [درسه خان / Dirse Han / Дерсе-хан], Boγač-χan's (Buγač-χan's) father (DQorq./Rossi 101-111 (61), DQorq. 14 etc.).

DERVÄ   NUyg.(Tar.) 19th c. **Dervä-quli / Derva-quli?** [Дервакули] (Pantusov, Tar. 15).

DERVİŠ   Kzk. 19th c. **Derbis** [Дербисъ] (SOV 88); Tat. 1624 **Derbiš** [Камай Дербышев] (Pokrovskij 70); Bashk. 1735 **Derbiš** [Кинзяшъ Дербышевъ], a tarχan (Vel.-Zern., Bašk. 15); Bashk. 1762 **Derbiš** [Тышкан Дербышев] (MIB IV/2, 300-301); Bashk. 1770 **Derbiš** [Тлеумбеть Дербышев] (MIB IV/1, 349); Tat.(Lit.) 1592 **Derbiš-čeleb[i** / Дербишчелебка] (Lit. Tat. 118); Turk.? 1454 **Derviš** [درو يش الرومى] (Ibn Taghrīb. VIII, 358); Turk. 1583-1584 **Derviš** [Derviş] (Ongan, Ank. I, 155); Trkm. 1538/39 **Derviš-biy-vekil** [Дервиш-бий-векиль] (MIT II, 60); Bashk. 1769 **Terbiš** [Тербиш Кутлумбетев] (MIB IV/1, 334). ✧ 'Dervish' cf. Tat. *därbiš*, Turk., Crm. *därviš/därbüš* (P.) 'der Derwisch, der Arme' (Radl. III, 1676), Kzk. *derwiš* 'id.' (RKzS). It may be used as a secondary component. See also **DERBİS-ALİ, DERBİS-ALİ, QUL-DERVİŠ.**

DERZİ see **QARA-DERZİ**

DESMEKEY see **DÜSMEKEY**

DESPİNE   Turk. 15th c. **Despine-χatun** [Despine Hatun] (Gökb., Ed. 140). ❖ 'Bracelet' cf. Turk. *destine* (P.) 'id.' (TRS).

DESTAN   Turk. 1583 **Destan-bey** [دستان / Destan Bey] (Ongan, Ank. I, 155). ❖ 'Epos, epic poem; story, novel, tale' cf. Turk. *destan* (TS), Kar.(Crm.) *dästan* (P.) 'eine Geschichte, der Roman, die Fabel' (Radl. III, 1684).

DEŠAN   Kzk. 18th c. **Dešam-bay (<Dešan-bay?)** [Исянъ-Али Дешамбаевъ] (Nepljuev 718).

DEVE   Turk. 20th c. **Deve-oγlu**, a Zeybek (Kúnos 1891, 119); Khorezm. 1295 **Dewe-šahzade** [دوا شهزاده], prince who together with Sārbān overruns Khorasan (RaD/Jahn 97, 146); Kzk. 19th c. **Töyä-biy** [Тоябий] (AOP 110); Kzk. 19th c. **Tüyä-bay** [Оразъ Туябаевъ] (Grod., Pril. 196); Kzk. 19th c. **Tüyä-bay** [Туябай] (Pam. kn. Turg. 76); Kzk. 1794 **Tüye** [Tye] (MIK IV, 162); Kzk. 19th c. **Tüye-bay** [Туебай] (SODž. 144); Kkalp. 20th c. **Tüye-bay** [Туйебай] (KkRS 776); Kkalp. 20th c. **Tüyö-bay** [Тюйёбай] (Bask., Kkalp. 402); Tat. 1500 **Tüwe** [Тюве], a prince (PSRL IV, 135). ❖ 'Camel' cf. Karakh. *tevä / tevi* 'верблюд' (DTS), cf. Uyg., Chag. *tävä* 'das Kameel' (Radl. III, 1127), Chag. *tüyä* 'das Kameel' (Radl. III, 1546), Kzk. *tüye* 'верблюд' (KzRS), Kkalp. dial. *tüyö* 'верблюд' (Bask., Kkalp.), Az., Turk., Crm. *dävä* 'das Kameel' (Radl. III, 1692).

DEVEY   Tat. 1600 **Devey** [Девей Иртишов] (MIB I, 152); Bashk. 1747, 1754 **Devey** [Дюмей Девеев] (MIB III, 450, MIB IV/1, 77); Bashk. 1754, 1764 **Devey / Deväy** [Чурагул (Чюрагул) Девеев (Деваев)] (MIB IV/1, 77, 276, 298); Bashk. 1754 **Tewey** [Тевей Кузьмин] (MIB IV/1, 83); Bashk. 1796 **Tewey** [Сюмекей Тевеев] (MIB V, 363). ❖ 'Little camel'. ⇨ **DEVE** + dim. suff. *-y*.

DEVEKEL   Bashk. 1735 **Devekel** [Девекель Умутбаевъ], a tarχan (Vel.-Zern., Bašk. 16). ⇨ **TÄWÄKKÜL, TÄWKÄL.**

DEVEŠER   Chuv. 18th-19th c. **Devešer** [Девешеръ] (Magn. 36).

DEVLET see **DÄWLÄT**

DEWK   Bashk. 1758 **Dewk** [Деук Бекбовов] (MIB IV/1, 164). ⇨ **DÄW?** + suff. *-k.*

DEWM   Bashk. 1749 **Dewm** [Сапар Деумов] (MIB III, 465); Bashk. 1758 **Dewm** [Салым Деумов] (MIB IV/1, 163); Bashk. 1758 **Dewm** [Деум Тютюков] (MIB IV/1, 163).

DİAL   Kzk. 1634 **Dial / Dïal** [Диал, Дыал], a Kazak prince (Miller, Ist. Sib. II, 61, 418).

DİAMET   Tat.(Sib.) 1638 **Diamet** [Диаметко] (Miller, Ist. Sib. II, 452).

DİB-BAQUY   Oghuz/Trkm. 13th c. **Dib-baquy-χan** [باقوى ديب خان ديب باقوى.حان / Диб-бакуй-хан, Бакуй-Диб-хан], Qayï-χan's son, Oγuz-χan's (grand-)grand-son (Abulg./Kon. 645-655, DQorq. 176). ❖ 'Original, genuine' cf. Turk. *dip* 'Kök, asıl' (TS I, 209).

DİB-YAQUY   Oghuz **Dib-yaquy** [Диб-Якуй], Noah's grand-son (RaD I/1, 76).

DİB-YAW-QUY   Oghuz **Dib-yaw-quy**, according to Rašīd-ud-Dīn he is Oghuz's grand-father (Muhamedova: OSA 169).

DİDAR   Trkm. 20th c. **Didar** [Didar] (Zaj. 1971, 330); Trkm. 20th c. **Dīdār** [Дидар] (TrkmRS 266). ❖ 'Face' cf. Trkm. *dīdār* 'лицо; образ' (TrkmRS) (<P.).

DİÄBÄ   Yak. **Diäbä** [Дiäбä], fem. (Pek.). ❖ Eva (Adam's wife) (R.).

DİÄBÄ-BAXSÏYA   Yak. **Diäbä-baχsïya-χotun** [Дiäбä], a spirit (Pek.).

DİKÄN-ÄRKE?   Kzk. 19th c. **Dikän-ärke?** [Диканарке] (SOK 268). ⇨ **DİKÄN + ERKE.**

DİKÄŠ   Kzk. 19th c. **Dikäš** [Дикашъ] (SOK 14).

DİQAN   Kzk. 19th c. **Diqan-bay** [Дикамбай] (SOV 24). ❖ 'Landlord, smallholder' cf. Kzk. PNs *Diqan / Diqan-bay* (Žanuzakov-Esbaeva), Used also as a secondary component. (<P.) *dehgān*.

DİL   Tat. 1446 **Dil-χoja** [Дыл-хозя], a prince (PSRL XII, 66). ❖ 'Heart' cf. Crm. *dil* (P.) 'das Herz' (Radl. III, 1766), *dīl* (د يـل) 'a dot, the heart, a fold, cote' (Johnson). See also **AΓA-DİL, JUMA-DİL, GÖK-DİL.**

DİLĀWAR   Uzb. 1701 **Dilāwar(-χwāja)** [Chwagah Dilâwar], eunuch of ʿUbaydullâh Sultan of Bukhara (Buchari 257).

DİLBER   Turk. 1509 **Dilber** [Dilber binti Abdullah], fem. (Gökb., Ed. 461); Trkm. 20th c. **Dilber** [Dilber], fem. (Zaj. 1971, 335); Trkm. 20th c. **Dilber** [Дилбер], fem. (TrkmRS 268); Turk. 1487 **Dilber-χatun** [Dilber Hatun], fem. (Gökb., Ed. 205). ❖ 'Beloved, lover' cf. Trkm. *dilber* 'возлюбленная, любимая' (TrkmRS) (<P.). See also **SÄWÜK, SÜYÜM, SÜYÜŠ.**

DİLENČ   Turk. 1693 **Dilenč-oγlu** [ديلنج اوغلى / Dilenç oğlu] (Refik, Anad. 107). ❖ 'Wish, request' cf. Turk. *dile-* 'to wish, to desire; to beg, to ask (for)' (TED). + suff. *-nč.*

DİLENJİ see **TİLENČİ**

DİLİMBET   Kkalp. 20th c. **Dilimbet** [Дилимбет] (KkRS 773). ⇨ **DİL** + suff. *-imbet.*

DİLŠAT   Trkm. 20th c. **Dilšat** [Dilšat], fem. (Zaj. 1971, 335); Trkm. 20th c. **Dilšāt** [Дилшат], fem. (TrkmRS 270). ❖ 'Joyful, happy' cf. Trkm. *dilšāt* 'радостный, весёлый' (TrkmRS).

DİLVAR   Kirg. **Dilvar** [Дилвар], fem. (Jud. 47).

DİLŽA   Kzk. 19th c. **Dilža** [Дилжа] (SOV 62).

DİMAŠQ   Maml./Trkm.? 1315 **Dimašq** [بنجو بان د مشق.حجا], a Moghul emir (Dawād. 289, 345 etc.). ❖ 'Damascus' (Sauvaget 47).

DİMİM-AL   Nog. 1802 **Dimim-al-murza** [Дмималъ мурза Суюншовъ] (Sergeev 77). ⇨ **AL.**

DİMİTRÄY   Yak. **Dimïträy** [Дiмiтpäi] (Pek.). ✧ Dimitriy (R.).

DİMLAČ   Selj. **Dimlač** [دملاج] (Kamāladdīn 618-621). ⇨ ? + suff. -*lač*?

DİN   Tat.(Sib.) 1603 **Din-güzä** [Дингузя Колодат] (Miller, Ist. Sib. II, 181). ✧ 'Religion; religious' cf. Tat. *din* 'религия, вера' (TatRS) (<Ar.).

DİN-MUXAMET   Trkm. 19th c. **Din-muχamet** [Диньмухаметъ Джуманьязовъ] (Ščeglov I, 350). ⇨ **DİN + MUXAMMED.**

DİN-MURZA   Tat.(Lit.) 1592 **Din-murza** [Дервишчелебкахъ   Димурзневич (Димурзиневич)] (Lit. Tat. 118). ⇨ **DİN + MURZA.**

DİNAR   Kirg. **Dinar** [Динар], fem. (Jud. 190). ✧ 'Golden coin' (Kusimova, Sattarov) cf. Kirg. *dinar* (<Ir.) 'динар (монета в Иране и Ираке)' (Jud.) (<Ar.).

DİNİZ-XAN see **TENİZ**

DİÑLİ   Oghuz/Trkm. 13th c. **Diñli** [دينكلى / Дингли], Ögürjik-alp's   son   (Abulg./Kon.   1240,   1270); Oghuz/Trkm. 13th c. **Diñli-bek** [دينكلى بيك / Дингли-бек], chief of the country (il) of Salors (Abulg./Kon. 1100, 1160).

DİREK   Oghuz/Trkm. 15th c. **Direk / Direk-tekür** [Direk Tekür / Дирек], Aršun's (Aršuwan's) son (DQorq. 73, 75). ✧ 'Column, support' cf. Turk. *diräk* 'der Pfahl' (Radl. IV, 1761).

DİRSE see **DERSE**

DİSAN   Kzk. 19th c. **Disan-eke** [Дисанеке] (SODž. 12).

DİSATQAM   Kzk. 19th c. **Disatqam** [Дисаткамъ] (SODž. 74).

DİVĀNE-KÖPEK   Yürük 1543 **Divāne-köpek** [ديوانه كوپك / Dîvâne Köpek] (Gökb., Rum. 176).

DİVĀNE-QAYA   Yürük 1543 **Divāne-qaya** [Dîvâne Kaya] (Gökb., Rum. 183).

DİVEY   Tat.? 1673 **Divey-murza** [Дивей мурза] (DAI VI, 286); Nog. 1571 **Diviy(-murza)** [Дивій мурза Ногайский], a Noγay murza (PSRL III, 173); Crm. 1539 **Diviy-mïrza** [Дивій-мырза] (PSRL XIII, 125). ✧ 'Evil spirit' cf. NUyg.(Tar.) *divä* 'der böse Geist' (Radl. III, 1780). + suff. -*y*?

DİVİY see **DİVEY**

DİZ   Hak. 19th-20th c. **Diz-miki** [Дизъ Мики (Дизъ Сороттогъ)] (Titov 206). ✧ 'Bronze (hero)' (Titov 206); cf. Alt. *yäs* 'das Kupfer, Messing', Hak.(Koyb.) *yes* 'id.' (Radl. III, 376-77).

DİBARDĀN   Yak. **Dïbardān** [Дыбардан], an abāsï-bogatyr (Pek.).

DİBİLİÑSA   Yak. **Dïbïlïñsa** [Дыбылыңса] (Pek.). ✧ 'Thin-long' (Pek.), 'Man with three shadows and seven slynesses; mythical hero (bogatyr) with seven heads' cf. Yak. *Dïbïlïñsa* 1. '(человек) с тремя тенями и семь[хитростями', 2. 'семиголовый богатырь "в

железной лодочке с железным весломˮ' (Pek.). See also **TİMİR-DİBİLİÑSA.**

DİBİRDĀN see **TİMİR-DİBİRDĀN, XORO-DİBİRDĀN,**

DİϒAR   Kzk. 19th c. **Dïϒar-bek** [Дыгарбекъ] (SODž. 4).

DİϒİN   Yak **Dïϒïn** [Дыгын / Тыгын], a famous ancestor of the Yakuts who fought against the Russians, captured by them he was executed (Pek.). ⇨ **TİϒİN.**

DİϒİSA   Yak. **Dïϒïsa** [Дыгыса], Mojuqān's grand-son (Pek.).

DİYİN   Kzk. 19th c. **Dïyin-sulu** [Дыинъ-Сулу], fem. (Potanin, Pred. 98).

DİYÏQ   Yak. **Dïyïq** [Дыjык] (Pek.).

DİYQAN   Kirg. **Dïyqan-bay** [Дыйканбай] (Jud. 822). ✧ 'Peasant, ploughman' cf. Kirg. *dïyqan* 'id.' (Jud.).

DİLBİÑSA   Yak. **Dïlbïñsa** [Дылбыңса], part of the compound name of a Shaman-dress in a tale (Pek.). ✧ 'Clench'? cf. Yak. *tïlbïy* (Pek.).

DİLDA see **TİLLA**

DİLDİ   Kzk. 19th c. **Dïldï-bay** [Дылдыбай] (SOK 178). ⇨ **DİL?** + suff. -*dï*. See also **DİLDA, TİLDİ.**

DİMϒA   Kzk. 19th c. **Dïmϒa-bay** [Дымгабай] (SODž. 150).

DİNDİ   Kzk. 19th c. **Dïndï-bay** [Дындыбай] (SODž. 90). ⇨ **DİLDİ?**

DİÑİZ see **TENİZ**

DİRXAN see **ĀN-DİRXAN**

DİRİŠ   Kzk. 19th c. **Dïrïš** [Дырышъ] (SOV 38). ✧ 'Strive; do your best' cf. Kzk. *tïrïs-* 'стараться' (KzRS).

DİRAY   Yak. **Dïray** [Дыраi] (Pek.).

DYÄSÄGÄY see **JÄSÄGÄY**

DYÖSÖGÖY see **JÄSÄGÄY**

DODOYUS   Yak. **Dodoyus / Doduyus / Doyudus** [Додоjус / Додуjус / Доjудус], nicknames of a rich Yakut (Naharskij nasleg, Vost.-Kangalasskij ulus) (Pek.).

DODOÑO   Yak. **Dodoño** [Додоno] (Pek.).

DODŌÑ   Yak. **Dodōñ-χoruol-ïrāχtāϒï** [Додоn], a king in a Russian tale (Pek.). ✧ 'Dodon-king'.

DODUYUS see **DODOYUS**

DOϒALAQ see **TOϒALAQ**

DOϒAN see **TOϒAN**

DOϒAN-ARSLAN see **TOϒAN-ARSLAN**

DOϒAN-BABA see **TOϒAN**

DOϒAR-ASLAN   Turk. 20th c. **Doϒar-aslan** [Doğaraslan], a village in the province of Kütahya, Turkey (TMİB 589). ⇨ **TUϒAR + ARSLAN.**

DOϒDORUQĀN see **TİMİR-DOϒDORUQĀN**

DOϒDU see **TUϒDİ**

DOϒLU   Turk. 20th c. **Doϒlu-šah** [Doğluşah], a village in the province of Kütahya, Turkey (TMİB 590).

DOϒOYO   Yak. **Doϒoyo-bōtur** [Доɣojo], legendary

person (Pek.).

DOΓORŪSA Yak. **Doγorūsa** [Доҕоруса] (Pek.). ✧ The pet-form of *doγor* (Pek.).

DOΓRÏ-VERMIŠ Maml.? 13th c. **Doγrï-vermiš** [دغرى ورمش], a small mosque in Aleppo (Haleb) (Ibn Šaddād, Alep 78).

DOΓSUN Oghuz/Trkm. 15th c. **Doγsun-oγlï / Toγsun-oγlï** [طوغسون اغلى] (DQorq./ Rossi 162). ✧ 'Let him be born'.

DOΓUM Uzb. 1816 **Doγum-biy** [Догум-бий], from the Mañγït tribe (MIT II, 391, 398, 400, 403, 407, 408, 412, 423, 428, 444, 451).

DOXSUN-DUYAN Yak. **Doχsun-duyan** [Дохсун-Дуйан / Бахсы тойоно], earlier a man who, because of his sins, was turned into an evil spirit who takes human being's reason away (Pek.).

DOYDEY Kzk. 19th c. **Doydey** [Дойдей] (SOV 118). ⇨ TOY?

DOYDUSA Yak. **Doydusa-darχan** [Доідуса], one of the six main ancestors, descendants of Älläy (Pek.).

DOYÏR Kzk. 19th c. **Doyïr-bay** [Доырбай] (SOK 180). ✧ 'Thick whip' cf. Kzk. *doyïr* '16 veya 18 olarak örülen kalın kamçı' (KzTS).

DOYMUŠ. see **TOYMÏŠ**

DOYOMPO Yak. **Doyompo-oγūn** [Дойомпо], a shaman (Pek.).

DOYUDUS see **DODOYUS**

DOQAQ see **TOQAQ**

DOQANJÏ see **TUΓANJÏ**

DOQMAQ see **TOQMAQ**

DOQUR? Mo.? **Doqur-χatun / Doquz-χatun?** [دوقور خاتون] (RaD/Jahn 13, 124).

DOQUZ see **TOQUZ**

DOL Kzk. 19th c. **Dol-bay** [Долбай] (AOO 10); Kzk. 19th c. **Dol-bay** [Долбай] (SODž. 136); Kzk. 19th c. **Dol-bï / Dol-bi?** [Долбы] (AOK 98). ✧ 'Turban-cloth' cf. Chag. *dol* 'das Turbantuch' (Radl. III, 1713-14).

DOLAN Kzk. 19th c. **Dolan** [Доланъ] (SOK 48). ✧ 'Working not smoothly; not accustomed; unskilful; heavy-handed' cf. Kzk. *dolan* 'bir şeye alışık olmayan, eli yatkın olmayan kimse' (KzTS).

DOLANMAZ Yürük 1543 **Dolanmaz** [دولنمز] (Gökb., Rum. 183). ✧ 'He doesn't turn, he will not go round; he will not wander around' cf. Az., Crm., Turk. *dolan-* 'umgeben sein, eingewickelt, umwunden sein' (Radl. III, 1715).

DOLBUN Yak. **Dolbun-(Dabï)-soχχor** [Долбун (Дабы) coxxop] (Pek.).

DOLDA Kzk. 19th c. **Dolda-bay** [Долдабай] (SOV 102). ✧ 'Nervous, irritable, on edge' cf. Kzk. *dolda(n)* 'sinirlenmek, kızmak' (KzTS).

DOLDARÏM? Selj. 1218/19 **Doldarïm / Yïldïrïm?** [بن بدر الدين دلدرم الياروقى / Ibn Bedr-eddyn Dolderim Alyarouky], prince of Tell-Bacher (Ibn al-

Athïr, Atab.: RHCHor II/1, 145).

DOLΓUYBAM Yak. **Dolγuybam** [Долгуйбан] (Pek.). ✧ 'Choppyng, vacillating'? cf. Yak. *dolγuy-* 'колыхаться, качаться, колебаться, двигаться, возмущаться (о воде)' (Pek.).

DOLΓURA Yak. **Dolγura-bāi-toyon** [Долгура-баи-тойон], a character in a tale (Pek.). ⇨ DOLΓURATA.

DOLΓURATA Yak. **Dolγurata** [Долгурата], fem. (Pek.). ✧ Derived from Yak. *dolγura-, dalγïra-* 'затище' (Pek.).

DOLÏM Kzk. 19th c. **Dolïm-bay (<Dolïn-bay?)** [Дольымбай] (AOP 62). ✧ 'Nervous, irritable, stubborn' cf. Kzk. *dolı* 'sinirli, asabi' (KzTS), *dolï* 'упрямый, вспыльчивый, раздражительный' (KzRS) + suff. -*m*.

DOLLŪQ Yak. **Dollūq** [Доллук] (Pek.).

DOLMUŠ Yürük 16th c. **Dolmuš** [طولمش / Dolmuş], from the Yürüks of Kocacık, Turkey (Gökb., Rum. 104). ✧ 'Full, filled, stuffed' cf. Crm., Turk. *dol-* 'gefüllt werden, voll sein' (Radl. III, 1714), Turk. *dolmuš* 'gefüllt' (Radl. III, 1723).

DOLONUQSA see **TİMİR-DOLONUQSA**

DOMİK Kzk. 19th c. **Domik?** [Домикъ] (AOO 54).

DOMRUL Oghuz/Trkm. 15th c. **Domrul / Dumrul / Deli-dumrul / Delü-dumrul** [Duxa Koca oğlı Deli Dumrul / Deli Dumrul figlio di Duha Qoğa / Duḫa Koca oğlı Delü Dumrul / Домрул], Duqa-qoja's son; his nickname was Deli/Delü (DQorq./Rossi 175-186, DQorq. 59-63, 110, 112, 121, etc.). ✧ 'Foolish/brave Domrul'. ⇨ TELİ.

DON see **TON**

DONA Yürük 1543 **Dona** [طوكا], from the Yürüks of Kocacık, Turkey (Gökb., Rum. 103). ✧ 'Let him freeze'? cf. Turk. *don-* 'gefrieren, erstarren, frieren, Kälte fühlen' (Radl. III, 1710-11).

DONAY Trkm. 19th c. **Donay** [Донай Аджибраевъ] (Ščeglov I, 350); Trkm. 19th c. **Donay** [Донай Чураевъ] (Ščeglov I, 357); Kzk. 19th c. **Donay** [Донай] (SOV 50); Kzk. 19th c. **Donay** [Донай] (SOK 206). ✧ '?' cf. Kzk. PN *Donay* (Žanuzakov-Esbaeva).

DONAQAY Karch. **Donaqay / Don-aqay?** [Донакай] (Sysoev 128). ⇨ TON? + comp. *aqay*.

DONDÏ Kzk. 19th c. **Dondï-bay** [Дондыбай] (SOK 204). ⇨ TON + suff. -*dï*.

DONMUŠ Yürük **Donmuš** [Donmuş] (Gökb., Rum. 226). ✧ 'Frozen' cf. Turk. *don-* 'gefrieren, erstarren, frieren, Kälte fühlen' (Radl. III, 1710-11).

DONRUL Yürük 1543 **Donrul** (Gökb., Rum. 214); Yürük 1543 **Donrul** [طوكرول / Donrul], from the Yürüks of Kocacık, Turkey (Gökb., Rum. 103, 189, 197); Yürük 1543 **Donrul** (Gökb., Rum. 224); Yürük 1454 **Donrul-bey** (Gökb., Ed. 162). ⇨ DOMRUL?

DONSUZ Turk. 20th c. **Donsuz-oγlu**, a Zeybek (Kúnos 1891, 119). ✧ 'Not having a cloth'. ⇨ TON +

suff. *-suz*.

DOÑ-QULDAQ Kkalp. 20th c. **Doñ-quldaq** [Донкулдак] (KkRS 773).

DOÑĞUS see **TOÑUZ**

DOR Kzk. 19th c. **Dor-bay** [Дорбай] (SOV 134).

DORBA Kzk. 19th c. **Dorba** [Дорба] (SODž. 96). ✦ 'Sack, bag' cf. Kzk. *dorba* 'torba' (KzTS).

DORBEN Kzk. 19th c. **Dorben (Dörben? / Dürben?)** [Дорбенъ] (SOV 26).

DORGUTİS Turk. 14th c. **Dorgutis?** [Dorgutis], prime minister of Sultan Bayezid I (1390-1403) (Baştav 176).

DORKEM Kzk. 19th c. **Dorkem-bay? (Dörkem-bay / Dürkem-bay <Dörken-bay / Dürken-bay?)** [Доркембай] (SODž. 60); Kzk. 19th c. **Dorkem-bek? (Dörkem-bek / Dürkem-bek <Dörken-bek / Dürken-bek?)** [Доркембекъ] (SODž. 154).

DORMAN Kuman 1273 **Dorman / Durman?** [Дърман], a (Kuman?) boyar in Bulgaria (Zlatarski III, 540). ⇨ **TURMAN I. / TURMAN II.?** See also **URUS-DURMAN.**

DOROPPŪN Yak. **Doroppūn / Dropūn** [Дороппун / Дропун] (Pek.). ✦ Trofim (R.).

DORŌLJUN see **TOÑ-DORŌLJUN**

DORŌLYUN see **TOÑ-DORŌLJUN**

DORUQLU Yürük 1543 **Doruqlu** [دورقلى] (Gökb., Rum. 237). ✦ 'Piled up'? cf. Turk. *doruqlu* 'aufgehäuft' (Radl. III, 237). + suff. *-lu*.

DOS see **DOST**

DOS-BERGEN Kkalp. 20th c. **Dos-bergen** [Досберген] (KkRS 733); Kzk. 19th c. **Dos-pergen** [Доспергенъ] (SODž. 114). ✦ 'Friend has (been) given (=born)'. ⇨ **DOST + BERGEN.**

DOS-BOSUN Kzk. 19th c. **Dos-bosun** [Досбосунъ] (SOK 168). ✦ 'Let him be (our) friend (mate)'. ⇨ **DOST + BOLSÏN.**

DOS-BUL see **DOST-BOL**

DOS-QALİY Kkalp. 20th c. **Dos-qaliy** [Доскалий] (KkRS 773). ⇨ **DOST + ALİ.**

DOS-MAMBET Kzk. 19th c. **Dos-mambet** [Досмамбетъ], a Kazak biy (Lomakin 36). ⇨ **DOST + MAMBET.**

DOS-NAZAR Kkalp. 20th c. **Dos-nazar** [Досназар] (KkRS 773). ⇨ **DOST + NAZAR.**

DOS-NİYAZ Kkalp. 20th c. **Dos-niyaz** [Доснияз] (KkRS 773). ⇨ **DOST + NİYAZ.**

DOS-PERGEN see **DOS-BERGEN**

DOS-POL see **DOST-BOL**

DOSAY Chuv. 1728 **Dosay** [Досайке Тюгеев] (MIB I, 128); Tat. 1624 **Dosay** [Досай Какинъ] (Pokrovskij 70); Tat. 1668 **Dosay** [Досайко Иткиняевъ] (Kungursk. akty 9); Bashk. 1735 **Dosay** [Козекай Досаевъ], a „tezik" (Vel.-Zern., Bašk. 25); Kzk. 19th c. **Dosay** [Досай] (AOO 42); Kzk. 19th c. **Dosay** [Досай] (SOV 4); Kzk. 19th c. **Dosay** [Досай] (SOK 44); Kzk. 1862 **Dosay** [Досай Маркабаевъ], from the district of Kopal (ZIRGOGeogr. I, 309); Nog. 1649 **Dosay** [Досай Сеитовъ] (AI IV, 123). ✦ 'Little friend'. ⇨ **DOST** + suff. *-ay*. See also **ĴAN-DOSAY.**

DOSAN Kzk. 1826 **Dosan** [Досанъ], a Kazak sultan (Konšin, Mat. I-III, 8); Kzk. 19th c. **Dosan** [Досанъ] (SODž. 124); Kzk. 19th c. **Dosan** [Досанъ] (SOK 288); Kzk. 19th c. **Dusam-bay (<Dusan-bay)** [Дусамбай] (Grod., Pril. 54); Kzk. 19th c. **Dusan** [Джолдашъ Дусановъ] (Grod., Pril. 81); Kzk. 19th c. **Dusan** [Дусановъ] (SKSO VIII, 206). ⇨ **DOSTAN?**

DOSİKEY Kzk. 19th c. **Dosïkey** [Досыкей] (AOK 46). ⇨ ? + suff. *-key*?

DOSİM see **DOSTUM**

DOSİMBET Kzk. 18th c.- 19th c. **Dosïmbet** [Досымбет] (Tynyšp. 71). ⇨ **DOS** + suff. *-ïmbet / -bet*?

DOSİN Kzk. 18th c. - 19th c. **Dosïn** [دوسن باطر / Досн] (MIK IV, 164); Kzk. 19th c. **Dosïn-bek** [Досынбекъ] (SOK 182). ⇨ **DOSTUM?**

DOSKE Kzk. 19th c. **Doske** [Доске] (SOV 150); Bashk. 1735 **Düske (<Düseke / Düs-eke?)** [Сырымбет Дюскин] (Vel.-Zern., Bašk. 25). ⇨ **DOST** + suff. *-ke* or comp. *ake*.

DOSMAN Kzk. 19th c. **Dosman** [Досманъ / Досмаинъ] (SOK 288). ⇨ **DOST** + suff. *-man*.

DOST Uzb. 19th c. **Dos** [Башманъ Досовъ] (SKSO III, 174); Kzk. 19th c. **Dos-čan** [Досчанъ] (SODž. 26); Kirg. **Dos-qulu** [Доскулу] (Jud. 346); Kzk. 19th c. **Dos-pay** [Доспай] (SOK 20); Kzk. 19th c. **Dos-pay** [Доспай] (SOV 62, 156); Kzk. 19th c. **Dos-pay** [Доспай] (SOK 44); Kkalp. 20th c. **Dos-žan** [Досжан] (KkRS 773); Chag. 16th c.? **Dost-χan** [دوست خان / Дость Ханъ], a Sheybanid (resident in Khorezm.?) (Šejb. LII); Uzb.? 19th c. **Dost-qul** [Досткулъ Акбутаевъ] (SKSO II, 4); Kzk. 19th c. **Dus-Jan** [Дусджанъ] (Grod., Pril. 50); Kzk. 19th c. **Dust** [Юлдашъ Дустовъ] (SKSO VIII, 220); Kzk. 19th c. **Dust** [Дустъ] (Grod., Pril. 176); Kzk. 19th c. **Dust-bala** [Дустбала] (SKSO VIII, 227). ✦ 'Friend' cf. Kuman, Turk., Kar.(T.) *dost* (P.) 'der Freund' (Radl. III, 1724), Kirg. *dos* 'друг' (Jud.). See also **AY-DOST, AMAN-DUS, ARBAB-DOST, BAZAR-DOS, BİČE-DUST, BİKE-DUST, ĴAN-DOS, EN-DOS.**

DOST-BOL Kzk. 19th c. **Dos-bul** [Досбулъ] (SODž. 20); Kzk. 19th c. **Dos-pol** [Досполъ] (SOV 56); Kzk. 19th c. **Dos-pol** [Досполъ] (SOK 6, 220); Kzk. 19th c. **Dust-bul** [Дустбулъ] (SKSO VIII, 203). ✦ 'Be/become a friend'. ⇨ **DOST + BOL.** See also **DOS-BOSUN, YAR-BOL.**

DOST-EMEL Kzk. 19th c. **Dost-emel** [Достемель] (SOK 122). ⇨ **DOST + EMEL.**

DOST-EMES Kzk. 19th c. **Dost-emes / Dost-emis** [Достемесъ / Достемисъ] (SOK 122). ✧ '(He) is not a friend'. ⇨ **DOST.**

DOST-EMİS see **DOST-EMES**

DOST-KELDİ Uzb. 20th c. **Dost-keldi** [Дӯсткелди] (Begmatov 1984, 202). ✧ 'Friend has come (has been born)'. ⇨ **DOST + KELDİ.**

DOST-QARA Uzb. 1705 **Dost-qara** [Dost Qara], nobleman from Bukhara (Buchari 286). ⇨ **DOST + QARA.**

DOST-MURAT Uzb. 1793 **Dost-murat** [Rachimbai Dostmuratow] (ArchKR XVIII, 352). ⇨ **DOST + MURAT.**

DOSTAN Kzk. 19th c. **Dostan** [Достанъ] (Grod., Pril. 56, 78); Kzk. 1868 **Dostan** [Бабасъ Достановъ] (Grod., Pril. 128); Kzk. 1794 **Dostan-murza** [Достан] (MIK IV, 163); Kzk. 1817 **Dustan** [دوستان] (MIK IV, 303); Kzk. 19th c. **Dustan** [Дустанъ] (Grod., Pril. 152).

DOSTANBET Crm. **Dostanbet-aγa** [Достанбăт ага] (Proben VII, 196). ⇨ **DOSTAN?** + suff. -*bet*.

DOSTMAT Kkalp. 19th c. **Dostmat** [Достъ-Матъ] (Smirnov 72); Tat. **Dusmät** [Дусмят] (Katanov, Star. Kaz. 297); Kzk. 19th c. **Dustmat** [Дустматовъ] (SKSO VIII, 221). ⇨ **DOST** + suffixoid -*mat*.

DOSTU Kzk. 19th c. **Dostu-bay** [Достубай] (SODž. 136). ✧ 'Having a friend'. ⇨ **DOST** + suff. -*tu*.

DOSTUM Kzk. 19th c. **Dosïm-bek (<Dosïn-bek?)** [Досембекъ] (AOP 126); Uzb. 1851 **Dosïm-biy** [Досым-Бйй], Mañγït chief (ZIRGO V, 108); Uzb. 1721 **Dostum-bay** [Dostum Bai], from Florio Beneveni's diary (ZIRGO IX. 397); Kzk. 19th c. **Dostum-bek** [Достумбекъ] (SOK 64); Kzk. **Dosum-qan** [Досум Кан] (Proben III, 68 /89/); Kzk. 19th c., 1820 **Dusum-bek (<Dusun-bek?)** [Дусумбекъ], chief of the İsaq-Kirey tribe (Sib. Vest. IX, 103). ✧ 'My friend' cf. Kzk. PN *Dosïm, Dosïm-bek, Dosïm-žan* (Žanuzakov-Esbaeva). ⇨ **DOST** + poss. suff. 1st p. sing. -*um*.

DOSUM see **DOSTUM**

DOSUMBET Bashk. 1664 **Dosumbet** [Досумбетевъ (Докумбетевъ) Ахтай] (DAI IV, 410). ⇨ **DOST / DOSTUM?** + suff. -*(um)bet?*

DOŠAQ Kzk. 19th c. **Došaq** [Дошакъ] (SOK 306). ✧ '?' cf. Kzk. PN *Dosaq* (Žanuzakov-Esbaeva).

DOWLAY Kzk. 19th c. **Dowlay? / Döwley?** [Довгаевъ] (Grod., Pril. 110).

DOWRUM Kzk. 19th c. **Dowrum-bek** [Доурумбекъ] (SOV 76).

DŌDOY Yak. **Dōdoy** [Додои], a character in a tale (Pek.). ✧ Derived from Yak. *dōdoγor* (Pek.).

DÖBÜK Yak. **Döbük** [Дöбӱк] (Pek.).

DÖGENJİ Yürük **Dögenji** [Döğençi (Döğenci?)] (Gökb., Rum. 223, 232). ✧ 'Weaver' cf. Turk. *döven* 'bez dokuma tezgâhı; tokmak' (DS). + suff. -*ji*.

DÖGER Turk. 1693 **Döger-oγlan** [دوكر اوغلان / Döğer Oğlan], a cemaat [religious and ethnic community] in the regions of Hama and Humus (Refik, Anad. 107); Oghuz/Trkm. 15th c. **Dögür** [دوكور] (DQorq. 158); Oghuz/Trkm.? 13th c. **Düker** [دوكر / Дукер], Ay-χan's son (RaD I/1, 76, AbulGKon. 515, 550, 595). ✧ '?' cf. Pelliot, Notes 191.

DÖGÜR see **DÖGER**

DÖKEN see **DÜKEN**

DÖLEK-ÖVEN see **DÜLEK-BURAN**

DÖLÖT see **DÄWLÄT**

DÖN Kzk. 19th c. **Dön-bay** [Дöнбай] (AOA 126). ✧ 'Hill, mountain, apex' cf. Kzk. *dön* 'tepe' (KzTS).

DÖNDİ Turk. 16th c. **Döndü** (Ongan, Ank. II, 5); Turk. 1584 **Döndü**, fem. (Ongan, Ank. I, 155); Khorezm.? 13th c. **Döndü-χatun / Döndi-χatun?** [خاتون دندى خا تون / دوندى], sixth wife of Mahmud Ghazan Khan (1295-1304) (RaD/Jahn 14, 104). ✧ 'Returned; has returned' Such names are given when only girls are born.

DÖNE Trkm. **Döne**, from the Türkmen in Anatolia (Riza III, 58). ✧ 'Return! Come back!'.

DÖNE-BİLMEZ Oghuz/Trkm. 15th c. **Döne-bilmez** [دونه بلمز دولك اورن / Dönebilmez Dölek Evren], byname of Dölek Evren, the son of Eylik Qoja (DQorq./Rossi 161, 163, 167, 209, 226). ✧ 'Cannot return; will not return' cf. Turk. *dön-* 'to go round; to spin; to turn (back), to return' (TED). ⇨ **DÖNE.**

DÖNÖN see **DÜNEN**

DÖÑGÖLEK-TAS Kzk. 19th c. **Döñgölek-tas** [Донголектасъ] (SOV 108). ✧ 'Ring/hoop - stone' cf. Kzk. *döngelek* 'yuvarlak bilezik gibi demir' (KzTS). ⇨ **TAŠ.**

DÖRMEN Nog. 20th c. **Dörmen** [Осман Халил улы Доьрмен / Осман Халилович Дурменов], one of Baskakov's informants from the aul of Adil-χalq (Bask., Nog. 143).

DÖRT-QULAQ Maml.? 14th c. **Dört-qulaq** [درت قلق] (Sauvaget 47). ✧ 'Four ears; having four ears' (Sauvaget 47). ⇨ **TÖRT + QULAQ.**

DÖŠÜMBET Kkalp. 20th c. **Döšümbet** [Дёшюмбет] (Bask., Kkalp. 56). ⇨ **?** + suff. -*ümbet?*

DÖVRAN Trkm. 20th c. **Dövran** [Dövran] (Zaj. 1971, 328); Trkm. 20th c. **Dövrān** [Довран] (TrkmRS 280). ✧ 'Cheerful/merry times' cf. Trkm. *dövrān* 'веселое, счастливое время' (TrkmRS).

DÖWLÄT-NAZAR see **DÄWLET-NAZAR**

DÖWLET see **DÄWLÄT**

DÖWLET-ГЇLЇČ Trkm. **Döwlet-γïlïč** [Дöвлетгылыч] (Sopieva: OSA 181). ⇨ **DÄWLÄT + QÏLÏČ.**

DÖWLET-NAZAR see **DÄWLÄT-NAZAR**

DÖWLET-TER Tat.(Lit.) 1591 **Döwlet-ter** [Белуха Довлеттеровна Балдышевичъ], fem. (Lit. Tat. 82).

⇨ **DÄWLÄT + TER?**

DRAΓÏŠ Bashk. 1749 **Draγïš** [Сюней Драгишев] (MIB III, 464).

DRAΓUN Bashk. 1770 **Draγun** [Драгун Мрясев] (MIB IV/1, 342); Bashk. 1770 **Draγun** [Буксун Драгунов] (MIB IV/1, 342).

DROPŪN see **DOROPPŪN**

DRUM Kzk. 19th c. **Drum-bay** (<Durum-bay) [Друмбай] (SOK 138).

DRUS-QALDÏ Kzk. 19th c. **Drus-qaldï** (<Durïs-qaldï) [Друскальды] (SOK 268). ✧ 'He (has) remained true, straight, honest' cf. Kzk. *durïs* 'правильный' (RKzS). ⇨ **QALDÏ.**

DRÜK Tat. 1722 **Drük** [Дрюк] (MIB I, 297).

DU Kzk. 19th c. **Du-bay?** [Азизъ-Берганъ Дубаевъ] (Grod., Pril. 115). ✧ 'Big noise' cf. Kzk. *dū* 'grosser Lärm' (Radl. III, 1782).

DUDAL Oghuz/Trkm. 13th c. **Dudal-bay** [دودال باى / Дудал-бай] (Abulg./Kon. 1450).

DUDAR Chuv. 18th-19th c. **Dudar** [Дударъ] (Magn. 37); Trkm. 1804 **Dudar-qul** [Дудар-кул], from the Yomut tribe (MIT II, 365). ✧ I. 'Brother, relative' (Žanuzakov 136, Žanuzakov-Esbaeva) (<Tadj.); II. 'A two-stringed instrument, guitar' cf. Kzk., NUyg.(Tar.) *dudar/dutar* 'id.' (Radl. III, 1793, 1794) (<P.).

DUDÏQ Oghuz/Trkm. 13th c. **Dudïq** [دودق / Дудык], Ögürjik-alp's brother (Abulg./Kon. 1235, 1275).

DUDU see **TOTÏ**

DUDUMAN Trkm. 1692 **Duduman-oγlu** [Dudumanoğlu Ahmed], chief of the Dudumanlu cemaat (Refik, Anad. 104). ⇨ **TOTÏ?** + suff. *-man.*

DUDURΓA Oghuz/Trkm. 13th c. **Dudurγa** [دودرغه / Дудурга], Aw-χan's son (Abulg./Kon. 515, 550, 595).

DUΓDÏ-TUMAČ Trkm. 1859 **Duγdï-tumač** [Дугды-Тумачъ] (ZIRGOÊtn. I, 206).

DUΓLÏ Trkm. 1859 **Duγlï-χan** [Дуглы-ханъ Пуладьхановъ] (ZIRGOÊtn. I, 157).

DUΓUZ see **TOQUZ**

DUYASTAY? Kzk. 19th c. **Duyastay?** [Дуястай] (Grod., Pril. 111). ⇨ **?** + **TAY?** + / suff. *-tay(1,2)?*

DUYDUQ Turk. 1583 **Duyduq** [طو يدق / Duyduk] (Ongan, Ank. I, 155). ✧ 'We felt it, we heard it' cf. Az., Turk., Crm. *duy-* 'hören, fühlen, verstehen, bemerken, ahnen' (Radl. III, 1783).

DUYLÏ-QAYÏ Oghuz/Trkm. 13th c. **Duylï-qayï-χan** [دويلىقايى / Дуйлы-Кайы-хан], İnal-yawï-χan's son (Abulg./Kon. 730-740, 765, 770, 815). ⇨ **TOYLÏ?** + **QAYÏ.**

DUYMUŠ Turk. 1540 **Duymuš-kethudā**, from Diyarbekir (Demirtaş 55). ✧ 'Heard, has been heard'.

DUQA Oghuz/Trkm. 15th c. **Duqa-qoja** [Duha Qoğa / Дука-Коджа], Domrul's father (DQorq. 59, 121, 190, 199).

DUQAQ see **TOQAQ**

DUQAN see **DÜKEN**

DUQSÏTAY Kzk. 19th c. **Duqsïtay** [Дуксытай] (SOK 59). ⇨ **TAY** or suff. *-tay(1,2)?*

DUQUZ see **TOQUZ**

DULA Trkm. 1828 **Dula-baχšï** [Дула-бахши], from the Yomut tribe (MIT II, 449); Trkm. 1818 **Dula-serdar** [Дула-сердар] (MIT II, 408).

DULAN Kzk. 19th c. **Dulan-bay** [Дуланбай] (SOK 252).

DULDUZXAN Balk. 20th c. **Dulduzχan**, fem. (Pröhle, Balk. 217). ⇨ **YULDUZ** + suff. *-χan(1).*

DULLÏ Trkm. 1817 **Dullï-teke** [Дулли-теке], from the Teke tribe (MIT II, 398).

DUM-BERGEN Kzk. 19th c. **Dum-bergen** [Думбергенъ] (SODž. 142). ⇨ **?** + **BERGEN.**

DUMAN see **TUMAN**

DUMRUL see **DOMRUL**

DUNALÏY Kzk. 18th c. **Dunalïy** [Дуналій] (Nepljuev 718).

DUNDAR Oghuz/Trkm. 15th c. **Dundar** [دو ندار / Dundar] (DQorq./Rossi 133, 135, 145, 158, 159). ✧ 'Defender-soldier, rear-guard' cf. Turk. *tundar* 'dümdar, arkayı gözeten, koruyan asker' (TarS), *dümdar* 'арьергард' (TRS) (<P.). See also **DELÜ-DUNDAR.**

DUNDAZ Oghuz/Trkm. 15th c. **Dundaz / Dondar / Dundar / Tundaz / Tundar?** [Dundar, deli Dundar, Tundar / Дондар, Дундар, Тундаз] (DQorq. 22, 29, 31, etc.).

DUNMAS Trkm. 1770 **Dunmas-serdar** [Дунмас-сердар], from the Yomut tribe (MIT II, 345, 346).

DUODARBA Yak. **Duodarba** [Дуодарба] (Pek.). ✧ Derived from Yak. *duoday-* (Pek.).

DUOLAY Yak. **Duolay** [Дуолаі] (Pek.). ✧ Derived from Yak. *duolan.* ⇨ **TUOLAY.** See also **ARSAN-DUOLAY.**

DUOLANTAY Yak. **Duolantay** [Дуолантаі], a legendary bogatyr (hero) (Pek.). ✧ 'Big, grown-up' cf. Yak. *duolan* 'большой ростом, громадный, достугший полной зрелости' (Pek.). See also **BOYŠAN, DÄW, ÄLLÄY, KETTÄ, QOŽAQ, ULUΓ, ZOR.**

DUOLΓAN Yak. **Duolγan** [Дуолҕан] (Pek.).

DUR see **TUR**

DUR-ALİ see **TUR-ALİ**

DUR-BĀLİ see **TUR-BĀLİ**

DUR-JİHAN Turk. 1513 **Dur-jihan-dede** [Dur Cihan-Dede] (Gökb., Ed. 194). ⇨ **TUR** + **JİHAN.**

DUR-DAΓÏ Turk. 1543 **Dur-daγï** [Durdağı] (Gökb., Rum. 177). ⇨ **TUR?**

DUR-QAL Yürük 1543 **Dur-qal** [Durkal] (Gökb., Rum. 225). ⇨ **TUR** + **QAL I.?**

DUR-SİRΓAN Kzk. 19th c. **Dur-sirγan?** [Отачанъ Дурсиргановъ] (Grod., Pril. 186). ⇨ **TUR.**

DURA Yürük 16th c. **Dura** [طورا], from the Yürüks of Kocacık, Turkey (Gökb., Rum. 102). ✧ 'Let him/her live' cf. component *dura-* of *Dura-kadın* 'Yaşaya(!) kadın' (Erol II).

DURAY Yürük 16th c. **Duray** [طورای], from the Yürüks of Kocacık, Turkey (Gökb., Rum. 102). ⇨ **DURA** + suff. *-y*?

DURAN see **TURAN I.**

DURASÏ Yürük 1543 **Durasï** [طوره سی / Durası] (Gökb., Rum. 231). ✧ 'Let him stay/survive!'. ⇨ **TUR.**

DURBAN 14th c.? **Durban** [دوربان قوم] (RaD/Jahn 2); Bashk. 1749 **Durban** [Аит Дурбанов] (MIB III, 469).

DURBĀÏ Yürük 1543 **Durbāi** [Durbâ'i] (Gökb., Rum. 186).

DURDÏ see **TURDÏ**

DURDÏ-KEM Trkm. 1833 **Durdï-kem** [Дурды Кем], a Yomut serdar (chief) (MIT II, 462, 501). ⇨ **TURDÏ** + **KEM.**

DURDÏ-QÏLÏČ Trkm. 1859 **Durdï-qlič** / **Durdï-qïlïč** [Дурды-клычъ] (ZIRGOEtn. I, 210); Trkm. 1828 **Durdï-qlič(-serdar)** / **Durdï-qïlïč(-serdar)** / **Qïlïč-serdar** [Дурды Клыч / Дурды-сердар], a Yomut serdar (chief) (MIT II, 447, 450, 451, 455). ⇨ **TURDÏ** + **QÏLÏČ.**

DURDÏ-SERDAR see **DURDÏ-QÏLÏČ**

DURDU see **TURDÏ**

DURDUΓA Oghuz? **Durduγa** [Дурдуга], Ay-χan's son (RaD I/1, 76).

DURΓUT see **TURΓUT**

DURMAN see **DORMAN**

DURMÏŠ see **TURMÏŠ**

DURMUŠ see **TURMÏŠ**

DURMUŠ-TOPAL Yürük 16th c. **Durmuš-topal** [طورمش طپال / Durmuş topal] (Gökb., Rum. 104). ⇨ **TURMÏŠ** + **TOPAL.**

DURSUN see **TURSÏN**

DURU Yürük 1543 **Duru** [طورى] (Gökb., Rum. 188, 202). ⇨ **DORU?**

DUS see **DOST**

DUS-AWUL Kzk. 19th c. **Dus-awul-bay** [Дусаулбай] (SOK 278). ⇨ **DOST** + **AWUL.**

DUSAN see **DOSAN**

DUSÏQ Kzk. 19th c. **Dusïq** [Уразъ Дусыковъ] (Grod., Pril. 132).

DUSMÄT see **DOSTMAT**

DUSMEKEY see **DÜSMEKEY**

DUSMEN Kkalp. 1722 **Dusmen?** [Дусменъ] (PSZRI VI, 778). ✧ 'Enemy' cf. Kzk. *tuspan* 'der Feind, feindlich, fremd' (Radl. III, 1502).

DUST see **DOST**

DUST-BUL see **DOST-BOL**

DUSTAN see **DOSTAN**

DUSTMAT see **DOSTMAT**

DUSUM see **DOSTUM**

DUŠ-AYTAR Kzk. 19th c. **Duš-aytar** [Душ Айтар] (Grod., Pril. 43). ⇨ **?+AYDAR?**

DUŠTA Uyg. **Dušta** [Dušta] (EUTS).

DUT Karch. **Dut** [Дудовъ], a Karachay family (Sysoev 126). ✧ 'Mulberry' cf. Crm., Turk. *dut* 'die Maulbeere' (Radl. III, 1792). See also **AY-DUT.**

DUTAN Yürük **Dutan** (Gökb., Rum. 193).

DUWA-TEMÜR Chag. 17th c.? **Duwa-temür** [دوا تیمور / Dua Timür], 15th Chaghatay Khan (Abulg./Desm. 158). ⇨ **DUWĀ** + **TEMİR.**

DUWADAQ Kzk. 19th c. **Duwadaq** [Дуадакъ] (AOO 66). ✧ 'Bustard' cf. Kzk. *duadaq* 'die Trappe' (Radl. III, 1783).

DUWAY Kzk. 19th c. **Duway** [Дувай Саватовъ] (Grod., Pril. 170).

DUWAN Kzk. 19th c. **Duwan-bek** [Дуанбекъ] (SODž. 6). ✧ 'District court; district' cf. Kzk. *duwan* (P.) 'das Kreisgericht; der Bezirk' (Radl. III, 1782), *duan* 'қала, губерния' (QTTS). See also **BERDİ-DUWAN, TETLÄYİN-BERDEY-DUWAN.**

DUWĀ Chag. **Duwā-qan** (Zambaur 248).

DUWLU Kzk. 19th c. **Duwlu-bay** [Дувлубай] (SOV 52). ✧ 'Noisy' cf. Kzk. *du* 'шум; галдёж' (KzRS). + suff. *-lu*?

DUZ-MAΓOMET Trkm. 1879 **Duz-maγomet** [Дузъ-Магометъ] (Grod., Vojna IV, Grod., Pril. 109). ✧ 'Salt(y) Muhammad'. ⇨ **TUZ** + **MAXMED.**

DÜBEN Kzk. 19th c. **Düben?** [Дубенъ] (SOV 112).

DÜDİK Bashk. 1709 **Düdik** [Дюдик(ов)] (MIB I, 264). ✧ 'Pipes' cf. Chag., Crm., Turk. *düdük* 'die Schalmei, die Flöte, die Pfeife' (Radl. III, 1811).

DÜDÜ Tat.(Sib.) 1678 **Düdü-bäk?** [Дюдюбак], a Sultan (prince) from Siberia (MIB I, 205). ⇨ **DUDU?**

DÜDÜK Yak. **Düdük-χān** [Дүдүк], Thundergod (Pek.).

DÜGÄČİ Uzb. 1740 **Dügäči-χoja** [Дюгачи-Хаджа], from Khiva (Hanykov, Poezdka 28). ✧ 'Beneficiary, greedy, self-seeker' cf. Chag. *dügä* 'der Nutzen, der Vortheil' (Radl. III, 1801) + suff. *-či.*

DÜGER see **DÖGER**

DÜYSE Kzk. 19th c. **Düysä-bay** [Дабай Дуйсабаевъ] (Grod., Pril. 80); Kzk. 19th c. **Düyse-bay** [Дюйсебай] (SODž. 74); Kzk. 19th c. **Düyse-bek** [Дюйсебекъ] (SOK 206); Kzk. 19th c. **Düyse-bek** [Дюйсебекъ] (SOV 108); Kzk. 19th c. **Düsi-bay** / **Düyse-bay?** [Дусибай] (Grod., Pril. 183). ✧ '?' cf. Kzk. PNs *Düyse-bay, Düysek, Düysekey* (Žanuzakov-Esbaeva).

DÜYSEK Kzk. 19th c. **Düysek** [Дюйсекъ] (AOK 114); Kzk. 19th c. **Düysek** [Дюйсекъ] (SOK 208). ✧ 'Feeling; need'? cf. Kzk. *tüysik* 'ощущение; нужда' (KzRS).

DÜYSEN Kzk. 19th c. **Düysem-bay** (<Düysen-bay) [Дыйсембай] (SOK 162); Kzk. 19th c. **Düysem-bay** (<Düysen-bay) [Дюйсембаевъ] (AUK 322); Kzk.

19th c. **Düysen** [Дюйсенъ] (AOK 98); Kzk. 19th c. **Düysen** [Дюйсенъ] (AOO 34); Kkalp. 20th c. **Düysen** [Дюйсен, Дуйсен] (Bask., Kkalp. 41, 44, KkRS 773); Kkalp. 20th c. **Düysen-bay** [Дуйсенбай] (KkRS 773); Kzk. 19th c. **Düsem (Düsen-bay<Düysen-bay)** [Дюсембай] (SODž. 78); Kzk. 19th c. **Düsem-bek (<Düsen-bek < Düysen-bek)** [Дюсембекъ] (AOO 66); Bashk. 1770 **Düsen** [Сююш Дюсенов] (MIB IV/1, 350); Kzk. 19th c. **Düsin (<Düysin)** [Елдашъ Дусиновъ] (Grod., Pril. 133). ✧ '?' cf. Kzk. PNs *Düysen, Düysen-bay, Düysen-bi* (Žanuzakov-Esbaeva).

DÜKEN Kzk. 19th c. **Döken** [Докенъ] (SOK 154); Kzk. 19th c. **Duqam-bay (<Duqan-bay)** [Дукамбай] (Grod., Pril. 153); Kzk. 19th c. **Duqan, Düken?** [Дукенъ] (SODž. 20); Kzk. 19th c. **Duqan-bay / Düken-bay** [Дукенбай, Дуканбай] (SOK 54, 136). ✧ 'Store, shop, workshop' cf. Kzk. *dökön* 'der Laden, die Fabrik, die Scmiede' (Radl. III, 1729), *düken* 'лавка' (KzRS), Crm., NUyg. *duqan* 'die Werkstatt, die Fabrik', (Crm.) 'der Laden, die Bude' (Radl. III, 1784) (<P.).

DÜKER see **DÖGER**

DÜKÜS Kzk. 1819 **Düküs** [Дюкусь] (MIK IV, 324).

DÜLEK-BURAN Oghuz/Trkm. 15th c. **Dülek-buran / Dülek-vuran / Dülek-uran / Dölek-öven / Dölek-evren / Dülek-evren** [Eliğ Koca oğlı Dölek Öven, Dönebilmez Dölek Evren, Eylik Koca oğlı Dülek Evren / Дюлек-Буран, Дюлек-Вуран, Дюлек-Уран], İylik (Eylik)-Qoja's son (DQorq. 74, 75, 88, 100, 102, 237, 238). ✧ '(Water-)Melon / settled, sober-minded - storm?' cf. Turk. dial. *dölek* 'зелёная (неспелая) дыня; зелёный (неспелый) арбуз; уравновешенный, рассудительный, рассмотрительный (о человеке)' (TRS), *dölek* 'id.' (DS). ⇨ **BURAN?**

DÜLEK-URAN see **DÜLEK-BURAN**

DÜLEK-VURAN see **DÜLEK-BURAN**

DÜMEY Bashk. 1747 **Dümey** [Дюмей Тимекеев] (MIB III, 447); Bashk. 1747 **Dümey** [Иштеряк Дюмекеев] (MIB III, 447); Bashk. 1747, 1754 **Dümey** [Дюмей Девеев] (MIB III, 450, MIB IV/1, 77); Bashk. 1783 **Dümey** [Мавлют Дюмеев] (MIB V, 137); Bashk. 1731 **Dümey / Demey** [Дюмей, Демей] (MIB III, 290-91). ⇨ **TÜMEY?**

DÜNDAR Yürük 16th c. **Dündar** [دونـدار], from the Yürüks of Kocacık, Türkey (Gökb., Rum. 103). ✧ I. 'Jolly, merry'? (Erol II); II. 'Rear-guard'? ⇨ **DUNDAR?**

DÜNDÄKEY Tat. 1675 **Dündäkey** [Дюндякейка] (Kungursk. akty 26).

DÜNEN Kzk. **Dönön** [Дöнöн Кара Баӊыс], three brothers called Kenžä, Qunan and Dönön Qara Baɣïs (Proben III, 253 /297/); Kzk. **Dünen-bay** [Маллябекъ Дуненбаевъ] (Protok. Turk. IV, 76). ✧ 'Three-year-

old male domestic animal' in western Kzk. dial. (Žanuzakov-Esbaeva 462), cf. also Kzk. *dönen* 'самец-трёхлетка (о скоте)' (KzRS).

DÜNYA Trkm. 20th c. **Dünya** [Dünya], fem. (Zaj. 1971, 342); Trkm. 20th c. **Dünyä** [Дунъя], fem. (TrkmRS 292). ✧ 'World' cf. Trkm. *dünyä* 'вселенная, мир (TrkmRS) (<Ar.).

DÜNKE Oghuz/Trkm. 13th c. **Dünke** [دونـکه / Дунке] (Abulg./Kon. 735).

DÜRBET Bashk. 1787 **Dürbet** [Дюрбеть Юлдашев] (MIB V, 219).

DÜRDÄNE Kirg. **Dürdana** [Дурдана], fem. (Jud. 204); Turk. 1509 **Dürdâne** [Dürdâne binti Abdullah], fem. (Gökb., Ed. 461). ✧ 'Pearl' cf. Ar./P. *dur-dāna* 'A single pearl' (Johnson), Kirg. *dürdana* 'id.' (Jud.).

DÜRMEN Bashk. 1729 **Dürmen** [Юнусай Дурменев] (MIB III, 265).

DÜRSÜN Kirg. **Dürsün / Türsün** [Дүрсүн / Түрсүн], one of Manas' comrades-in-arms, always mentioned together with Taylaq (Proben V, 70 (71), 151 (152)).

DÜRTČİ Kzk. 19th c. **Dürtči? / Durtči?** [Дуртчи] (SOK 288). ⇨ ? + suff. *-či*.

DÜSEY Bashk. 1745 **Düsäy / Dusay?** [Яви Дусаев] (MIB III, 426); Bashk. 1745 **Düsey** [Юмаш Дюсеев] (MIB III, 426). ⇨ **DOSAY.**

DÜSEKE see **DOSKE**

DÜSEKEY see **DÜSKEY**

DÜSEKSEN Kzk. 19th c. **Düseksen-bi?** [Дусексембы] (SOV 80).

DÜSEM see **DÜYSEN**

DÜSEMBE Kzk. 1846 **Düsembe** [Дюсембе Курутбаев] (MKOP 101); Kzk. 19th c. **Düsembe** [Дюсембе] (AOO 6); Kzk. 19th c. **Düsembe** [Дюсембе] (AOK 86); Kzk. 19th c. **Düsembi** [Дюсембы] (SOV 8). ✧ 'Monday' cf. Kzk. *düysenbi* 'понедельник' (KzRS), Kkalp. *düyšenbi* 'пятница' (KkRS), Kirg. *düyšembü* 'понедельник' (Jud.), Tat., Turk. *düšämbä* 'der Montag' (Radl. III, 1819).

DÜSEMBİ see **DÜSEMBE**

DÜSEN see **DÜYSEN**

DÜSİN see **DÜYSEN**

DÜSKE see **DOSKE**

DÜSKEY Bashk. 1770 **Düsekey** [Усман Дюсекеев] (MIB IV/1, 342); Kzk. 19th c. **Düsekey** [Дюсекей] (AOA 2); Bashk. 1709 **Düskey** [Дюскей Урсаев] (MIB I, 263); Bashk. 1712 **Düskey** [Дюскей Азимбетев] (MIB III, 85); Bashk. 1757 **Düskey** [Токметь Дюскеев] (MIB IV/1, 157); Bashk. 1760 **Düskey** [Усень Дюскеев] (MIB IV/1, 195, 202); Bashk. 1761 **Düskey** [Усян Дюскеев] (MIB IV/1, 202); Bashk. 1779 **Düskey** [Дюскеев] (MIB V, 81); Tat. 1779 **Düskey / Deskey?** [Кутлугуш Дюскеев (Дескеев)] (MIB V, 81, 93); Bashk. 1761 **Düsükäy** [Дявля Дюсюкаев] (MIB IV/1, 202). ✧ 'Little friend'. ⇨ **DOST + EKEY?**

DÜSMEKEY   Bashk. 1738 **Düsmekey** [Дусмекей Аргамаков] (MIB III, 379); Bashk. 1725 **Düsmekey / Desmekey** [Дюсмекей (Десмекей) Урметев] (MIB III, 234-235).

DÜSÜKÄY see **DÜSKEY**

DÜŠEK   Nog. 1649 **Düšek** [Дюшекъ Мамбетевъ] (AI IV, 123).

DÜŠÜM-QARA   Kkalp. 1827 **Düšüm-qara** [Дюшум-кара] (MIKk. 133). ✧ 'My chest is black' cf. Bashk. *tüš* 'грудь; наковальня' (BRS), Turk. *düš* 'die Schulter' (Radl. III, 1817). ⇨ **QARA.**

DÜZEN   Oghuz/Trkm. 15th c. **Düzen**, Alp Rüstem's father (DQorq./Rossi 195, 209, 227, DQorq./Gökyay 84).

DÜZİ   Kkalp. 20th c. **Düzibay** [Дузибай] (KkRS 773). ✧ 'A kind of wide/broad rope for fixing the central post of the yurt' cf. Trkm. *düzi, düzüyür* 'широкая верёвка (для крепления среднего остова кибитки)' (TrkmRS).

Ä

ÄBDĀNİK   Tuv. 19th c. **Äbdãnik** [Äбдãнiк] (Proben IX, 213). ✧ Yevgeniy (R.).

ÄBDİ see **ABDİ**

ÄBDİ-ΓAPPAR   Kkalp. 20th c. **Äbdi-γappar** [Әбдиғаппар] (KkRS 772). ✧ Abdel Ghaffar / Abdul Ghaffar (Ar.) 'Servant of the All-forgiving' (Ahmed). ⇨ **ABDİ.**

ÄBDİ-ΓÄNİY   Kkalp. 20th c. **Äbdi-γäniy** [Әбдиғәний] (KkRS 772). ✧ Abdul Ghani (Ar.) 'Servant of the All-sufficient' (Ahmed). ⇨ **ABDİ.**

ÄBDİ-KÄMAL   Kkalp. 20th c. **Äbdi-kämal** [Әбдикәмал] (KkRS 772). ✧ Abdel Kamal (Ar.) 'Slave of perfection/completion'. ⇨ **ABDİ + KEMAL.**

ÄBDİ-KÄRİM   Kkalp. 20th c. **Äbdi-kärim** [Әбдикәрим] (KkRS 772). ✧ Abdul Karim / ⁽Abd al-Karim (Ar.) 'Servant of the most Generous' (Ahmed 95). ⇨ **ABDİ + KERİM.**

ÄBDİ-QALÏQ   Kkalp. 20th c. **Äbdi-qalïq** [Әбдиқалық] (KkRS 772). ✧ Abdel Khaaliq (Ar.) 'Servant of the Creator'. ⇨ **ABDİ + QALÏQ.**

ÄBDİ-QÄDİR   Kkalp. 20th c. **Äbdi-qädir** [Әбдиқәдир] (KkRS 772). ✧ Abdul Qadir / ⁽Abd al-Qadir (Ar.) 'servant of the Powerful' (Ahmed 159). ⇨ **ABDİ + QADÏR.**

ÄBDİ-MURAT   Kkalp. 20th c. **Äbdi-mïrat** [Әбдимырат] (KkRS 772); Kkalp. 20th c. **Äbdi-murat** [Әбдимурат] (KkRS 772). ✧ Abdel/Abdul Murad (Ar.) 'Servant of Murad'. ⇨ **ABDİ + MURAT.**

ÄBDİ-RAZAQ   Kkalp. 20th c. **Äbdi-razaq** [Әбдиразақ] (KkRS 772). ✧ Abdur Razzaq / ⁽Abd al-Razzāq (Ar.) 'Servant of the All-provider' (Ahmed). ⇨ **ABDİ.**

ÄBDİ-RÄYİM   Kkalp. 20th c. **Äbdi-räyim** [Әбдирәйим] (KkRS 772). ✧ Abdur Rahim (<⁽Abd al-Rahīm) 'Servant of the most Gracious' (Ahmed). ⇨ **ABDİ + RÄHİM.**

ÄBDİ-RÄSUL   Kkalp. 20th c. **Äbdi-räsul** [Әбдирәсул] (KkRS 772). ✧ Abdur Rasul / ⁽Abd al-Rasul (Ar.) 'Slave of the messenger of Allah'. ⇨ **ABDİ + RASUL.**

ÄBDİ-ŽÄMİL   Kkalp. 20th c. **Äbdi-žämil** [Әбдижәмил] (KkRS 772). ✧ Abdul Jamil (Ar.) 'Servant of the Beautiful', cf. Ar. *jamīl* 'handsome, attractive, impressive' (Ahmed); 'Creature (slave) of the all-gracious (God)' cf. Turk. *cemil* 'admirable; charming; all-gracious (God)' (<Ar.). ⇨ **ABDİ.**

ÄBDİR   Kkalp. 20th c. **Äbdir-χan** [Әбдирхан] (KkRS 772).

ÄBÄK   Tat. 13th c.-14th c. **Äbäk** [ابک / Äбäк] (Jusupov 55). ✧ 'Quick, nimble'? cf. Uyg. *äbäk* 'hurtig, eilig, flüchtig' (Radl. I, 927).

ÄBÄRÄ   Yak. **Äbärä** [Äбäpä], son of Tïγïn, the Yakut ruler whose clan (descending from him) still exists (Pek.).

ÄBEKÄY   Bashk. 1781 **Äbekäy** [Чюрюбай Ебекеев] (MIB V, 124); Chuv. 18th-19th c. **Ebekey** [Ебекей] (Magn. 37). ✧ 'Grand-mother, granny' cf. Bashk. *äbekäy* 'бабушка, бабуся' (BRS), Tat. *äbekäy* 'id.' (TatRS). + suff. *-käy.*

ÄBİL-QASÏM   Tat.(Ishim) **Äbil-qasïm** [Âбiл Касым], a prince (Proben IV, 192 /237/). ✧ 'Qasym's son'. ⇨ **QASÏM.**

ÄBİLXAYÏR   Kkalp. 20th c. **Äbilχayïr** [Әбилхайыр] (Kkalp. 772). ✧ Abul Khayr, a famous Shaybanid Khan in the 15th c. <Ar. Abū'l-Khayr 'father of good work' (Ahmed).

ÄBİRÄČČİ   Yak. **Äbiräčči** [Äбiрäччi], fem. (Pek.). ✧ 'Pock-marked, spotty'? cf. Yak. *äbir.*

ÄBİRÄN   Yak. **Äbirän** [Äбiрäн], fem. (Pek.). ✧ 'Pock-marked, spotty' cf. Yak. *äbir, äbiriän* (Pek.).

ÄBİŠ   Bashk. 1770 **Äbiš** [Абиш Уразманов] (MIB IV/1, 350). ✧ Contracted-diminutive form of *Äbdiraχman*, its variants are *Äbiš-žan Äbišim* 'Dear Äbiš / My Äbiš' (Espaeva 1984, 231).

ÄBÜW-ALİY   Kkalp. 20th c. **Äbüw-aliy** [Әбүүалий] (KkRS 772). ⇨ **ALİ.**

ÄBÜW-BÄKİR see **ABU-BAQÏR**

ÄČÄ   Kuman? 1521 **Äčä** [Echehalma, Ecsezug, Ecserét], main component of several toponyms in Greater Kumania, Hungary (Rásonyi: MNy. XXXVIII, 116, AOH 20(1967), 140, KÖA 103). ✧ 'Elder sister' cf. Karakh. *eče* 'ältere Schwester' (MK), Chag., Trkm. *äčä* 'die ältere Schwester; das Weib, die Gemahlin, Mutter' (Radl. I, 862). See also **MAQ-AČA.**

ÄJÄN Tuv. 19th c. **Äjän / Äjäň-qan** [Äцäн / Äцäň(-кан)], Tuva name of the Manchu emperor (Proben IX, 43-57, 100). ✧ Cf. Mo. *ejen qaγan*. ⇨ **ÄDÄN**.

ÄJİ Kkalp. 20th c. **Äji-qan** [Äджикъан] (Bask., Kkalp. 17). ✧ I. 'Hadji'? cf. Kzk. PNs *Äzi, Äzi-bay, Äzi-bek, Äzi-γali, Äzi-murat* (Žanuzakov-Esbaeva); II. 'Grandmother'? cf. Kzk. *äže* 'id.' (KzRS). ⇨ **XAJİ**?

ÄDÄN Alt.(Tel.) **Ädän-qan**, Chinese emperor (Radl. III, 850). ✧ The title of the Chinese emperor. Cf. Alt.(Tel.) *Ädän* 'der chinesische Kaiser' (< Manju *ecen*) (Radl. I, 850) (<Mo. *ejen qaγan*).

ÄDEN Kkalp. 20th c. **Äden-bay** [Эденбай] (KkRS 772). ⇨ **ÄDÄN**?

ÄDGÜ-QUTLUГ see **EDGÜ-QUTLUГ**

ÄDGÜ-TOГRİL see **EDGÜ-TOГRİL**

ÄDGÜ-TÖZÜN Uyg. 13th-14th c. **Ädgü-tözün** [Ädgü Tözün], fem. (Zieme, Mat. II, 86). ✧ 'Good-noble' cf. Uyg. *tözün* 'сдержанный, благородный' (DTS). ⇨ **EDGÜ**.

ÄDİGÄ see **EDİGE**

ÄDİKEY Kzk. 19th c. **Ädikey** [Адикей] (AOA 18). ✧ '(Dear) Little Ruler' cf. Kzk. PNs *Adi / Ädi* (<Ar.) 'правитель, руководитель' (Žanuzakov, Žanuzakov-Esbaeva).

ÄDİL see **ADİL**

ÄYÄNTÄY Yak. **Äyäntäy-bōtur** [Äйäнтäй-ботур], the legendary Är-soγotoχ's son (Pek.).

ÄYİ Alt.(Tel.) **Äyi**, the first woman, Eve (Radl. I, 726). ✧ Eva (the first woman).

ÄYİMBET Kkalp. 20th c. **Äyimbet** [Эйимбет] (KkRS 772). ⇨ **?** + suff. *-imbet / -bet*?

ÄYTÄ-BULUM Tat.(Ishim) **Äytä-bulum** [Äйтä Булум], a batyr (Proben IV, 215 /264/). ✧ '?' cf. Tat.(Tara) *äitä-* 'treiben, jagen' (Radl. I, 667).

ÄKČİLGÄ see **ÄKČİRGÄ**

ÄKČİRGÄ Yak. **Äkčirgä / Äkčilgä** [Äкчиргä / Äкчилгä] (Pek.). ✧ 'Stick for throwing away' cf. Yak. *äkčirgä* 'дубинка, палка, приспособленная для бросания' (Pek.).

ÄKÄČÄN Yak. **Äkäčän** [Äкäчäн], nickname of a shaman given him in his childhood (Pek.). ⇨ **ÄKKÄČÄN**.

ÄKİLİNÄ Yak. **Äkilinä** [Äкiлiнä / Öкÿлÿнä], fem. (Pek.); Yak. **Ökülünä** [Öкÿлÿнä], fem. (Pek.); Yak. **Ökülünä** [Öкÿлÿнä] (Pek.). ✧ Akilina, Akulina (R.).

ÄKKÄČÄN Yak. **Äkkäčän / Äkäčän** [Äккäчäн], a shaman, one of the children of the legendary witch Äriägiyä (see) (Pek.). ⇨ **ÄKÄČÄN**.

ÄL see **AL**

ÄL-MUQAN see **AL-MUQAN**

ÄL-ŽÄN see **AL**

ÄLBÄS-TÄLBÄS Yak. **Älbäs-tälbäs** [Äлбäс Тäлбäс], a servant (Pek.).

ÄLÄYBÄ Yak. **Äläybä** [Äлäйба] (Pek.). ✧ 'Don't diminish, don't be lost'? cf. Yak. *äläy-* 'уменьшаться в объем, измаляться, протираться' (Pek.).

ÄLÄYÄN Yak. **Äläyän** [Äлäйäн] (Pek.). ⇨ **ÄLÄYBÄ**.

ÄLÄKÜL Türk 8th c., before 750 **Äläkül** (Runic Mss. 187, 189); Uyg. **Äläkül** [Äläkül] (ETY II, 67).

ÄLÄŇGÄ Karg. **Äläňgä** [Äлäнгä], fem. (Proben IX, 659). ✧ 'Door frame, jamb' cf. Alt.(Tel.) *äläňä* 'der Thürpfosten, Thürrahmen' (Radl. I, 812).

ÄLGÜR Uyg. **Älgür** [Älgür] (EUTS).

ÄLİY see **ALİ**

ÄLİYMA see **ALİME**

ÄLİK see **ELİK**

ÄLİK-XANDA Yak. **Älik-χanda** [Äлiк Ханда], one of the forest-ghosts called bayanay (Pek.). ✧ 'Quick evil spirit of home' cf. Yak. *älik* 'скорый; быстрый, проворный', *χanda* 'домовой; название злого духа' (Pek.). ⇨ **ÄLİK**?

ÄLİK-TÜRGÄN Yak. **Älik-türgän** [Äлiк Тÿргäн kici], a legendary hero (Pek.). ⇨ **ÄLİK**?

ÄLİM see **ALİM**

ÄLİM-BÄŇGİ Kzk. 1888 **Älim-bäňgi** [Алимъ-банги] (Nalivkin 16). ⇨ **ALİM**.

ÄLİP-XANDAГAY Yak. **Älip-χandaγay** [Äлiп хандаɓai] (Pek.).

ÄLKÄNÄY see **ÜRÜŇ-ÄLKÄNÄY**

ÄLLÄY Yak. **Älläy** [Äллäi], one of the Yakuts' ancestors of Tatar or Buryat origin (Pek.). ✧ 'Big, huge' cf. Yak. *älläy* 'id.' (Pek.). See also **BOYŠAN, DÄW, DUOLANTAY, KETTÄ, QOŽAQ, SEŇGİR, ULUГ, ZOR**.

ÄLLİK NUyg. 19th c. **Ällik** [اليك] (Le Coq, Namenl. 94). ✧ 'Fifty' (Le Coq 94).

ÄMET see **AXMET**

ÄMİYNA see **EMİNE**

ÄMİN see **EMİN**

ÄMİR-GÄW Maml. 14th c. **Ämir-gäw** [اميركو] (Sauvaget 38). ✧ 'Prince-hero' (<Ar./P.) (Sauvaget 38).

ÄMRÄN see **İMRÄN**

ÄNÄ-SOLİM Tat.(Bar.) **Änä-solïm** [Äнä Солым], a hero, brother-in-law of Altain Sain Sümä (Proben IV, 74 /94/). ✧ 'Mother - Unknown, stranger'? ⇨ **ENE** + **SOLİM**.

ÄNEPİYA Kkalp. 20th c. **Änepiya** [Энепия], fem. (KkRS 777). ✧ Prophets (Ar.) (Žanuzakov 131).

ÄNİYPA Kkalp. 20th c. **Äniypa / Änïpa** [Энийпа], fem. (KkRS 777). ✧ Hanifa (Ar.), fem. of Hanif 'true, one of true faith, upright' (Ahmed).

ÄNÜK Maml. 14th c. **Änük** [انوك] (Sauvaget 38-39). ✧ 'Lion cub' (Sauvaget 38), cf. Maml. *änük* 'chiot, lionceau' (AH), Chag. *änük* 'junger Löwe, junges Raubthier' (Radl. I, 735), Turk. *änik* 'ein junges fleischfressendes Thier (Hund, Wolf)' (Radl. I, 733).

ÄŇÜRÜN see **EŇÜRÜN**

ÄPİYPA Kkalp. 20th c. **Äpiypa / Äpïpa** [Эпийпа],

fem. (KkRS 777). ❖ Habiba (Ar.) 'beloved, darling, sweetheart' fem. of Habib (Ahmed).

ÄPLÄ see **ÄPPİLÄ**

ÄPPİLÄ Hak.(Kacha) 19th-20th c. **Äppilä / Äplä** [Äппілä / Äплä] (Proben IX, 555, 558).

ÄPPİJÄK Hak.(Sag.) 19th-20th c. **Äppİjäk** [Äппіцäк] (Proben IX, 442, 443).

ÄR-JÜZ Türk / Uyg.? 876, 877 **Är-Jüz / Ar-Juz** [ارخوز بن يولغ بن طرخان التركى] (Ibn al-Athīr/Tornb. VII, 214, 227). ⇨ **AR + YÜZ?**

ÄR-KÄRBÄLYİN-OYŪN see **KÄRBÄLYİN**

ÄR-TAŠ OT? Är-taš (Németh, HMK 135 /after Gombocz/). ❖ 'Hero-Stone'. ⇨ **ER + TAŠ.**

ÄRBÄ‍XTÄY Yak. **Ärbäχtäy-bärgän** [Äрбäхтäі / Äрбäхтäі-бäргäн], a legendary hero (Pek.). ❖ 'Thumb-like' cf. Yak. *ärbäχ* 'большой палец; особое орудие для вытягивания из прорубей ремней невода ...' (Pek.).

ÄRČÄNTÄY Karg. **Ärčäntäy** (Katanov, Otč. 9). ❖ Arseniy (R.).

ÄRDÄM-QAÑ-ALTUГA Türk 7th-9th c. **Ärdäm-qañ-altuγa** [Ärdäm Qañ Altuγa] (ETY III, 141). ❖ 'Benefactor-father-Altuγa'? cf. Türk, Uyg. *qañ* 'отец' (DTS). ⇨ **ERDÄM + ALTUГA.**

ÄRDÄNİ Uyg. 8th c. **Ärdäni-χatun-tänrim**, a princess (Müller, Pfahl. 10); Uyg. **Ärdäni Qatun** [Ärdäni Katun], fem. (EUTS). ❖ 'Precious stone' (Müller., Pfahl. 16), cf. Uyg. *ärdäni* (Mo.) 'der Edelstein' (Radl. I, 794).

ÄRADÄL Yak. **Ärädäl** [Äpäдäл], a Yakut hero (Pek.). ⇨ **ÄRİÄDÄL.**

ÄRÄKÄ-JÄRÄKÄ Yak. **Äräkä-Järäkä** [Äpäкä-цäpäкä], gods of the nature, sons of Mother Earth (Pek.).

ÄRÄKKÄY Tuv. 19th c. **Äräkkäy** [Äpäккäi] (Proben IX, 137).

ÄRÄM see **EREM**

ÄRÄM-QARA Uyg. **Äräm-qara** [Äräm Kara] (EUTS); Uyg. 12th c.-14th c. **Äräm-qara** [Äräm Qara] (Radl., USp. 142). ❖ 'Big, strong (child)'. ⇨ **EREM + QARA.** See also **BÜYÜK, ČOÑ, BÜYÜK, EVREN, YOГAN, KÄNDÄL, MÄÑKÄ.**

ÄRÄN-BUГA Maml. 1407 **Ärän-buγa** [اردبغا], Ibn Taghrīb. VI, 198, 428. ⇨ **EREN + BUQA.**

ÄRİDİMÄ-DOXSUN Yak. **Äridimä-doχsun** [Äpiдiмä Дохсун], younger brother of Ärbäχ-jaγïl, a celestial hero (Pek.). ❖ 'Brave, impudent - cotton reel / harpoon?' cf. Yak. *äriy-* 'крутить, вертеть; сучить, обвивать' (Pek.).

ÄRİÄDÄL Yak. **Äriädäl-bärgän** [Äpiäдäл-бäргäн], a legendary hero (Pek.).

ÄRİÄGİYÄ Yak. **Äriägiyä** [Äpiärijä], one of the children of the witch (Ĵaba-bäba) (Pek.).

ÄRİGİR-XARA-ÄRBÄS-OYŪN Yak. **Ärigir-χara-**ärbäs-oyūn [Äpiriр хара Äрбäс ojyн], spirit (ghoast) of large dark forests (Pek.).

ÄRİKMÄS Maml. 14th c. **Ärikmäs** [ارکماس] (Sauvaget 35). ❖ 'He who won't withdraw' (Sauvaget 35).

ÄRİLİKİYÄ-QUOMAY Yak. **Ärilikiyä-quomay** [Äpiлiкijä Kyoмai], a legendary person (Pek.).

ÄRKİN-ÄRÄLÄSÄ Yak. **Ärkin-äräläsä** [Äркін-Äпäläцä], a legendary person (Pek.).

ÄRKLİG Uyg. 761 **Ärklig** (Mahrnāmag 10); Uyg. **Ärklig-qan** [Ärklig Kan] (EUTS). ⇨ **ERK.**

ÄRNİ Bulg. 1320 **Ärni** [ارنى] (Jusupov 2).

ÄSÄN-TÄMÜR see **ESÄN-TEMİR**

ÄSÄNÄ Uyg. **Äsänä** (Zieme, Mat. I, 74). ❖ 'Oh, healthy!' (Zieme). ⇨ **ESÄN** + voc. suff. *-ä*.

ÄSEM see **HÄSEN**

ÄSEN see **HÄSEN**

ÄSİL-BİY see **ASİL**

ÄSKÄL Türk 565 **Äskäl, Eskil** [Ασκήλ], „Fürst des Volkes der Hermichionen (=Türken)" (Byz. Turc. II); Türk? **Äskäl-kül-irkin** [Äskäl kül irkin], from the western tribe (Ligeti: MNy. 75, p. 41); Türk? **Äskäl-nēšaγ-irkin** [Äskäl nēšag irkin], a chieftain from the western tribe (Ligeti: MNy. 75, p. 41).

ÄSREK Kzk. 19th c. **Äsrek** [Асрекъ] (SODž. 80). ❖ 'Drunken'? cf. Kzk. *esrek* <*esirik(tik)* 'опьянение' <*esir-* 'опьянеть' (KzRS).

ÄTRÄČ Bulg. 1316 **Äträč** [اتراج / Äтрäч] (Jusupov 14).

ÄWÄZ see **AWAZ**

ÄWEZ see **AWAZ**

ÄZİYZ Kkalp. 20th c. **Äziyz / Äzİz** [Әзийз] (KkRS 772). ⇨ **AZİZ?**

ÄZİYZA Kkalp. 20th c. **Äziyza** [Әзийза], fem. (KkRS 777). ❖ Aziza (Ar.) 'noble, honourable, dearly loved, beloved' fem. of Aziz (Ahmed).

ÄŽİ see **XAJİ**

ÄŽİ-NİYAZ Kkalp. 20th c. **Äži-niyaz** [Әжинияз] (KkRS 772). ⇨ **XAJİ + NİYAZ.**

ÄŽİXAN Kkalp. 20th c. **Äžiχan** [Әжихан], fem. (KkRS 777). ⇨ **XAJİ** + suff. *-χan(1).*

ÄŽİQAY see **AJİQAY**

ÄŽİR Kkalp. 20th c. **Äžir** [Әжир] (KkRS 772).

ÄLKÄMÄ Kzk. **Älkämä** [Äлкäмäніñ баласы], Munap-batïr's son (In the German translation mistakenly interpreted as Älkämän!) (Proben III, 757 /848/).

E

EBDEK Hak. 19th-20th c. **Ebdek** [Эбдек], fem. (HRS 356). ❖ Yevdokiya (R.).

EBDEKEY   Hak. 19th-20th c. **Ebdekey** [Эбдекей], fem. (HRS 356). ✧ Yevdokiya (R.).

EJEŠ   Trkm. **EJeš** [Эжеш], fem. (Sopieva: OSA 182). ✧ 'Little mother' cf. Trkm. *eje* 'мама, мать' (TrkmRS) + dim. suff. *-š*.

EJEW   Trkm. **EJew** [Эжев], fem. (Sopieva: OSA 182). ✧ 'Little mother' cf. Trkm. *eje* 'мама, мать;' (TrkmRS) + voc. suff. *-w*?

ED'İ   Alt. 19th-20th c. **Ed'i** [Эдьи] (OjrRS 210).

EDAL   Kzk. 19th c. **Edal** [Эдалъ] (AOO 58).

EDČÜ   Uyg. **Ädču-sañun-tirä** [Ädçü Sañun Tirä] (ETY II, 64); Türk 8th c. - 9th c. **Edču-sañun-tirä** [edču sañun tirä] (DTS). ✧ 'Active; organizer, creator'? (Bese 13), cf. Uyg., Karakh. *et-* 'совершать, создавать, строить; устраивать, приводить в порядок' (DTS) + suff. *-či*.

EDE   Yürük 1543 **Ede** [اده], from the Yürüks of Kocacık, Turkey (Gökb., Rum. 102, 208); Kzk. 19th c. **Ede-bay** [Едебай], field (AOO 66). ✧ 'Father, elder brother, grand-father; promising great man' cf. Turk. *ede* 'baba, büyük kardeş, elinden iş gelir büyük adam, dede' etc. (DS).

EDEY   Kzk. 19th c. **Edey** [Едей] (SODž. 24); Hak. 19th-20th c. **Edey** [Эдей], fem. (HRS 356). ⇨ **EDE?** + suff. *-y*?

EDEM   Kzk. 19th c. **Edem-bay (<Eden-bay?)** [Едембай] (SOK 96). ✧ Edhem (Ar.) (Özön).

EDGÄRMİŠ   Uyg. 8th c. **Edgärmiš-täñrim**, fem. (Müller, Pfahl. 23). ✧ 'Corrected, better' cf. Uyg. *edgär-* 'исправлять, улучшать' (DTS).

EDGE see EDİGE

EDGÜ   Türk / Uyg.? 8th c. (before 750) **Edgü-sañun-tirä / Edgü-sañun-tiri** [Äd.ü Sangun Tirä] (Runic Mss. 188); Uyg.? 874, 886 **Edgü-tegin** [Atkutekin / Adlutekin /Atkutkin], governor of Mosul (around 260 a.H.) and Qazwīn at the time of al-Mutamid (Weil, Chalif. II, 450, 465, 469); Uyg.? 880, 882, 890 **Edgü-tegin** [اذكوتكين / يدكوتكين بن ا ساتكين] (Tabarī, Annal. III, 1936, 2024, 2115,); Uyg.? 882 **Edgü-tegin** [انظر يدكوتكين] (Tabarī, Annal. III, 2024); Uyg.? 885 **Edgü-tegin** [اذكوتكين] (Dorn 447); Karakh. 1002 **Edgü-tegin** [اذكوتكين ابوالفتح المو يد] (Hil. Sābī 457); Uyg. 8th c. **Edgü-tutuq-ügä, Ädgü-tutuq-ügä** (Le Coq, Man. III, 46). ✧ 'Good' cf. Uyg. *ädgü* 'iyi, iyilik; üstünlük' (US, EUS). ⇨ **EDİGE.**

EDGÜ-YEGÄN   Uyg. 8th c. **Edgü-yegän-sañün** (Müller, Pfahl. 12). ⇨ **EDGÜ + YEGÄN.**

EDGÜ-QUTLUГ   Uyg. 8th c. **Edgü-qutluγ-ïnal** (Müller, Pfahl. 23). ✧ 'Good-lucky'. ⇨ **EDGÜ + QUTLUГ.**

EDGÜ-TEMÜR   Khorezm. / Uyg.? 12th c.-13th c. **Edgü-temür** [ادكو تيمور پسر جنتمور], the elder son of Jan-temür (Čin-temür?), the governor of Khorasan (Juwaynī II, 230-36, 243, 270); Uyg.? 1384 **Eygü-temür** [ايكو تيمور] (Dorn 165); Khorezm.? 1295 **Eygü-temür-χatun** [ايكو تيمور خاتون], fem. (RaD/Jahn 48). ✧ 'Good (noble)-iron'. ⇨ **EDGÜ + TEMİR.**

EDGÜ-TOГRÏL   Uyg. **Ädgü-toγrïl** [Ädgü Toğrıl] (EUTS); Uyg. 12th c.-14th c. **Edgü-toγrïl** [Ädgü Toγrïl] (Radl., USp. 209, 212, 251, 253, EUS, DTS). ✧ 'Good-bird of prey'. ⇨ **EDGÜ + TOГRÏL.**

EDİGE   Crm. **Ädigä** [Äдігä], hero of the legend, son of Qutlu Qaya (Qutlu-γaya-bï), among his ancestors there are also Qoj(a) Amät, Är Amät, Kär Amät, Temir Qaya (Proben VII, 158, 161-62, Radl. IV, 2112); Kzk. 19th c. **Edge** [Едге] (SOK 250); Kzk. 19th c. **Edige** [Едыге] (AOO 2); Kzk. 19th c. **Edige** [Едыге] (AOK 22); Kzk. 19th c. **Edige** [Едыге] (SOK 120); Kzk. 19th c. **Edige** [Едиге] (SOV 158); Kkalp. 20th c. **Edige** [Едиге] (KkRS 773); Nog. **Edige / Edigü / İdige / İdigü / İdiki / İdikü / İdügü** [Эдига, Эдиге, Эдигу, Идиге, Идигей, Идигу, Идики, Идугу, Идику], famous folklore hero (Žirm., Epos 9, 10, 354-386 etc.); Kzk. 19th c. **İdigä** [Idiga] (Levchine 356); Kzk. **İdige** [Идига] (Levšin III, 96); Kzk. 1846 **İdige** [Рабай Идигин], a biy (MKOP 157); Kzk. 19th c. **İdige-bi** [Идыге-би], according to the Kazak tale in the muslim world there were 4 İdiges, 4 Tursuns and 4 Aχmets (Potanin IV, 404); Maml. 1449 **İdigi** [ايـدكى الظا هـرى] (Ibn Taghrīb. VIII, 45); Maml. 1449, 1467 **İdigi** [ايـدكى الاشـرفى] (Ibn Taghrīb. VIII, 57, 463, 625); Kzk. 1826 **İdigi** [Идиги] (Dobrosm., Turg. 283); Khorezm. 1393 **İdigü-bahadïr / Edigü-bahadïr?**, an emir, Temür's governor in Kirman (Qazw. 754). ✧ 'Good' (<Mo.). ⇨ **EDGÜ.**

EDİGEY   Tat. / Nog.? 1399, 1407 **Edigey** [Ediguy / Edeguy / Едигѣй / Гедигѣй / Едигей / Едигеи / Едегей / Зедегей / Едигерей], a prince („knjaz' velikij") of the Noγay Horde (PSRL XI, 173, XIX, 14, 15, PSRL (Russk. Hr.) I, 425, Clavijo 60); Tat.(Sib.)? 1584 **Edigey / Yedigey?** [Jeligäi (!)], a prince, Yermak's enemy (Radl., Aus Sib. I, 149); Kzk. 19th c. **Edikey** [Эдикѣевъ] (Grod., Pril. 188); Nog. **İdigey** [Идигей], the famous folklore hero (Žirm., Epos 9, 10, 354-386 etc.). ✧ A Russian adaptation of Edige. ⇨ **EDİGE + R. suff. *-y*.**

EDİGÜ see EDİGE

EDİKEY see EDİGEY

EDİL   Crm. **Ädil-sultan** [Äділ Султан] (Proben VII, 215); Kzk. 19th c. **Edel-bay** [Едельбай] (SODž. 34); Kzk. 19th c. **Edel-bay** [Едельбай] (SOV 4); Kzk. 19th c. **Edil** [Едилъ] (AOK 82); Kzk. 19th c. **Edil** [Эдиль] (SOK 12, 224); Kzk. 19th c. **Edil** [Едиль] (SODž. 18); Kzk. 19th c. **Edil** [Едилъ] (AOP 26); Kzk. 19th c. **Edil / Edïl?** [Едыль] (AOP 22, 42); Kzk. 19th c. **Edil / Edïl?** [Едыль] (SOK 42); Kzk. 19th c. **Edil / Edïl?**

[Едыль] (SOV 88); Kzk. 19th c. **Edil / Edîl?** [Едыль] (SODž. 70); Kzk. 1825 **Edil-bay** [ایدولبای / Едильбай] (MIK IV, 470, 476); Kzk. 19th c. **Edil-bay** [Едильбай] (SODž. 146); Kzk. 19th c. **Edil-bay** [Едильбай] (SOK 10); Kzk. 19th c. **Edil-bay** [Едильбай], a field (AOA 46); Kzk. 19th c. **Edil-bay** [Едильбай] (AOAtb. 22); Trkm. 19th c. **Edil-bek** [Эдильбекъ] (Ščeglov IV, 161); Kzk. 1819 **İdil** [ایدولبای / Идил] (MIK IV, 324); *TN:* Trkm. 19th c. **Edil-bay** [Эдильбай], a Turkmen aul [village] (Volodin 27). ✧ 'Volga (river)' cf. Kzk. *Edil* 'die Wolga' (Radl. I, 857), Chag. *Ädil* 'der Fluss Wolga; der Strom, Fluss' (Radl. I, 857), Alt.(Tel.) *Ädäl* 'id.' (Radl. I, 850). See also **BAY-EDİL.**

EDİL-ĴEBİL   Alt. 19th c. **Edil-ĵebil** [Эдиль-Джебиль], fem. (Potanin, Pred. 180). ⇨ **EDİL?**

EDİL-QOĴİL   Alt. 19th c. **Edil-qoĵil** [Эдиль-Коджилъ], fem. (Potanin, Pred. 180). ⇨ **EDİL?**

EDİM   Kzk. 19th c. **Edim** [Едимъ] (SOV 110).

EDİTKE   Kzk. 19th c. **Editke** [Едитке] (AOO 26).

EFENDİ   Turk. 20th c. **Efendi** (Önder, Hınıs); Turk. 16th c. **Efendi-beg**, from the region of Silifke, Turkey (Sümer: DTCF XI, 339). ✧ 'Gentleman; master; title given to literate people, members of the clergy, Ottoman princes, army officers up to major' (TED), cf. also Crm., Turk. *äfändi* 'id.' (Radl. III, 937) (<Greek).

EFENDİ-BULA   Turk. 1583 **Efendi-bula** [افندی بوله] (Ongan, Ank. I, 156). ⇨ **EFENDİ + BULA.**

EFLĀTŪN   Uzb. 1711 **Eflâtûn** [افلاطون قلماق / Iflâtûn (-i Qalmaq)], from the Qalmaq tribe in Bukhara, the last follower of Sultan ʿUbaidullāh who died together with his master in 1711 (Buchari 338, 341). ✧ Plato (the Greek philosopher); 'learned man' (TED), cf. Turk. *Eflâtun* (Özön).

EGDÄČİN   Uyg. **Ägdäčin** [Ägdäçin] (EUTS); Uyg. 12th c.-14th c. **Egdäčin** (DTS).

EGÄM-BERDİ see **İYEM-BERDİ**

EGÄM-BERGÄN see **İYEM-BERGEN**

EGÄN see **EGİN**

EGELTEY   1612 **Egeltey / Egentey** [Егельтей (Егентей) Янчуринъ] (Nižegorod. platež. 43, 195). ⇨ ? + suff. *-tey*.

EGEM-BERDİ see **İYEM-BERDİ**

EGEN see **EGİN**

EGENTEY   1612 **Egeltey / Egentey?** [Егельтей (Егентей) Янчуринъ] (Nižegorod. platež. 43, 195). ⇨ **EGİN?** + suff. *-tey*.

EGİ   Kzk. 19th c. **Egi-bay** [Гаибъ Егибаевъ] (Grod., Pril. 121). ✧ I. 'Good'? cf. Kzk. PN *Egi-bay* (Žanuzakov-Esbaeva), cf. Kar. *ägi* 'gut, schön' (Radl. III, 598); II. 'Master, gentleman'? cf. Chag., NUyg., Uzb. *ägä* 'der Wirth, Herr, Gemahl; Gott' (Radl. III, 694).

EGİM see **EGİN**

EGİN   Kzk. 19th c. **Egim-bay (<Egin-bay)** [Егимбай] (SOK 132, 162); Kzk. 19th c. **Egim-bay / (<Egin-bay)** [Егимбай] (SODž. 134); Kzk. 19th c. **Egim-bay (<Egin-bay)** [Егембай] (SODž. 52); Kzk. 19th c. **Egim-bek (<Egin-bek)** [Егембекъ] (SODž. 58); Kzk. 19th c. **Egin-bay** [Егинбай] (AOO 10); Kzk. 19th c. **Egin-bay** [Егынбай] (AOA 114); Kzk. 19th c. **Egin-bay** [Егинбай] (SOK 214); Kzk. 19th c. **Egin-bay** [Еген-бай] (SOV 40); Kzk. 19th c. **Egin-bay** [Егенбай] (SOV 40); Kzk. 19th c. **Egin-bay** [Егенбай] (SODž. 28, 58, 74); Trkm. **Egin-batïr** [Егянъ-батыръ-кала], a fortress (qala) named after Egïn-batïr (Grod., Vojna II, 143). ✧ 'Plough, field; corn, grain, green crops' cf. Kzk. *egin* 'das Ackern, das Ackerfeld' (Radl. III, 699), Kzk. *egin* 'посевы; хлеб' (KzRS).

EGİNČİ   Kzk. 19th c. **Eginči** [Егенчи] (SOK 238); Turk. 20th c. **Ekinĵi-oγlu** [Ekincioğlu], a village in the province of Sivas, Turkey (TMİB 784). ✧ 'Corn-farmer' cf. Kzk. *eginşi* 'ekinci' (KzTS). ⇨ **EGİN.**

EGİZ see **EKİZ**

EGLEN   Yürük 1543 **Eglen / Eylen?** [اكلن / Eğlen] (Gökb., Rum. 183). ✧ 'Have a good time; amuse yourself' cf. Turk. *eğlen-* 'to have a good time to amuse oneself, to enjoy oneself' (TED).

EGOLAK   Tat.(Sib.)? 1629 **Egolak?** [Еголак], a Tatar murza (Miller, Ist. Sib. II, 360).

EGRĀY   Alt.? 19th-20th c. **Egrāy** [Еграй], fem. (Katanov, Otč. 10). ✧ 'Play!' (<R.) *igraj* (Katanov, Otč. 10).

EGREK see **EKREK**

EGRENĴE   Oghuz/Trkm. 13th c. **Egrenĵe** [اكرنجه / Эгрендже], a man from the İl (folk, country) of Afšars (Abulg./Kon. 900).

EX   Tat. 1747 **Eχ-čura?** [Утяганъ Ехчуринъ] (PSZRI XII, 668). ✧ 'Spindle, bobbin, spool'? cf. Karakh. *ig / ik* 'веретено' (DTS).

EYBEK   **Eybek / Ey-bek?** [Эйбек] (RaD II, 150).

EYDEK   Trkm. 1856 **Eydek-yüzbašï** [Эйдек-юзбаши] (MIT II, 572).

EYGÜ-TEMÜR see **EDGÜ-TEMÜR**

EYLE   Hak. 19th-20th c. **Eyle** [Эйле] (HRS 352).

EYLEN see **EGLEN**

EYLENĴİ   Yürük 1543 **Eylenĵi** [Eğlenci] (Gökb., Rum. 198). ✧ 'Restrained, lingering, slow' cf. Turk. *äiläniĵi* 'zurückgehalten, verspätet, langsam' (Radl. III, 664).

EYLEW   Bashk. 1735 **Eylew** [Ейлевъ Аптуловъ], a tarχan (Vel.-Zern., Bašk. 18).

EYLİK-QOĴA see **ELİG**

EYMİR see **EMİR**

EYMİR   Turk. 1494 **Eymir** [Eymir bin Hasan] (Gökb., Ed. 104); Yürük 1543 **Eymir** [Eymır] (Gökb., Rum. 189, 192, 196, 206); Turk. 1583 **Eymir / İmir ?** [ایمیر]

(Ongan, Ank. I, 163); Yürük 1543 **Eymir-χan** [Eymirhan] (Gökb., Rum. 191); Yürük 1543 **Eymir-šah** [Eymirşah], from the Yürüks of Kocacık, Turkey (Gökb., Rum. 190). ✧ A Turkic tribe (Erol II).

EYMİR-BĀLĬ Yürük 1543 **Eymir-bālĭ** [Eymirâlı] (Gökb., Rum. 190). ⇨ EYMİR + BĀLİ.

EYMİRJE Yürük 1543 **Eymirje** [Eymirce] (Gökb., Rum. 194). ⇨ EYMİR + suff. *-je*.

EYNE see ADİNA

EYNE-ČAQÏR Yürük 1543 **Eyne-čaqïr** [Eyne-Çakır] (Gökb., Rum. 189). ⇨ AYNA I. + ČAQÏR.

EYNEL Yürük 1543 **Eynel** [Eynel], several persons among the Yürüks of Kocacık (Gökb., Rum. 180-190). ✧ 'A part of the cultivated land separated for certain people' cf. Turk. *eynel* 'sürülecek bir tarlanın belirli kimselere ayrılan kısım ya da parçaları' (DS).

EYWAS-QARA Trkm. **Eywas-qara / Owāz-qara?** [Эйвасъ-кара] (Mel'gunov 320). ⇨ AWAZ + QARA.

EKEY see AQAY

EKİ Kzk. 19th c. **Eki-bay** [Екибай] (SOV 130). ✧ 'Two' cf.

EKİ-MŌS Alt. 19th c. **Eki-mōs** [Еки-Моосъ], a hero (bogatyr) (Verb., In. 149, 150); Alt. 19th c. **Eki-mōs-χan** [Еки-Моос-хан] (Verb., In. 139). ⇨ EKİ + МОГОS?

EKİLDÄK Bashk. 1675 **Ekildäk** [Маряк Екилдяков] (MIB I, 200).

EKİLİK Kzk. 1794 **Ekilik / Eklik?** [ايكه ليك ايبكوليك / Еклик] (MIK IV, 158); Kkalp. 1820 **Ekilik-biy** [Экилик бий] (MIKk. 107); Kkalp. 1822 **Ekilik-biy** [Экилик бий], from the Quñyrat tribe (MIKk. 127); Chag. 16th c. **İkilik** [Икилик] (Ivanov 217, 295); Chag. 16th c. **İkilik-bay** [Икилик-бай] (Ivanov 213, 298); Chag. 16th c. **İkilik-biy** [Икилик-бий] (Ivanov 215, 294). ✧ 'Double, twin'? cf. Kzk. *ekilik* 'die Zweiheit' (Radl. I, 681). ⇨ EKİ + suff. *-lik*.

EKİNJİ-OĬLU see EGİNČİ

EKİZ Kirg. **Egiz-bay** [Эгизбай], two rich („bay") brothers called Egiz-bay (Jud. 190); Turk. 1540 **Ekiz-kethudā**, chief of the cemaat-i Çübeklü in a defter of Diyarbekir (Demirtaş 56); Kzk. 19th c. **İgiz** [Аскарбай Игизов] (Grod., Pril. 115); *TN:* Turk. 20th c. **İkiz**, a village in the adiministrative province of Gümüşhane, Turkey (TMİB 398); Maml. **İkiz / İgiz** [ايكـز], a mesjid (Ibn Šaddād, Nawād.: RHCHor III, 78). ✧ 'Twin' cf. Kirg. *egiz* I. 'id.' (Jud.).

EKİZÄK Kzk. 19th c. **Ekizäk** [Махмудъ Экизаковъ] (Grod., Pril. 158). ✧ 'Little twins'? ⇨ EKİZ + suff. *-äk*.

EKKEY Alt. 19th-20th c. **Ekkey** [Эккей], fem. (OjrRS 214). ✧ 'Oh, dear!' < Alt. *eχ!* 'эх (междометие, выражающее сожаление)' (OjrRS), cf. also Hak. male and fem. PN *İke* 'ласковое название ребёнка [blandishing name of a child]' (Butanaev). + suff. *-key /*

-qay.

EKREK Oghuz/Trkm. 15th c. **Ekrek / Egrek** [Egrek / Экрек], Ušun-qoja's elder son (DQorq./Rossi 211-219, DQorq./Gökyay 48, DQorq. 89, 90, 93, 94, 149, 228, 229, 238).

EKSEK-QOJA see EKSİK

EKSİK Selj.? 11th c. **Eksik** [اكسك], اردق بن اكسب / أردق بن], Artuq's father, the form „Eksib" is obviously false (Adīm II, 84, 97, 99, Athīr X, 86-87, 96-98, Abulfidā III, 280-281); Oghuz/Trkm. 15th c. **Eksik-qoja / Eksek-qoja** [Eñse Koca / Эксек-Коджа], Oqči's father (DQorq./Rossi 170, DQorq. 105, 238, 240); Kzk. 19th c. **Öksük-pay** [Оксюкпай] (SOK 100). ✧ 'Defective, deformed; imferfect' cf. *äksik* 'mangelhaft, fehlerhaft; Mangel, Fehler' (Radl. I, 687), Chag., Uyg. *öksük* 'mangelhaft' (Radl. I, 1189).

EL Maml. 1325 **El-baba** [بـدرالـدين جنكلى بـن بـابـا] (Zetterst. 128, 195, 219); Kzk. 19th c. **El-bay** [Ельбай] (AOA 62); Selj.? 1101 **El-begi** [البكى بـن بـر سق] (Ibn al-Athīr/Tornb. X, 205, 227); Maml.? 13th c. **El-begi** [Fârıs-eddin-Albeki assâki], governor of Hems, died in 1303 (Makrīzī II, 170, IV, 223); Maml. 1299 **El-begi** [البكى], a Mamluk emir who escaped to Ghazan in 1299 (RaD/Jahn. 122); Selj.? 1133 **El-begi / El-begü?** [Ελπεγκους], a Turkic chieftain (Byz. Turc. II, 123); Türk 8th c.-9th c. **El-čur** (DTS); Selj.? 1095 **El-χan** [Ελχάνης], a Turkic emir (Byz. Turc. 124); Trkm. 1859 **El-χan** (ZIRGOÊtn. I, 225); Trkm. 1859 **El-χanī / El-χani?** [Джафаръ-Кули-Хан-Эль-Хани] (ZIRGOÊtn. I, 225); Bulg. 1018 **El-inaq / İl-inaq?** [Ελεμάγος, Ελινάγος], a commander (Mutafčiev 205, Zlatarski I/2, 785, Byz. Turc. 123); Khorezm. 13th c. **El-inaq / İl-inaq?** [الينـا ق], an emir (Wassaf 139, 146); Uyg. 12th c.-14th c. **El-qoja** (DTS); Bashk. 1647 **El-mīrza** [ال مـيرزا بـن بى مـيرزا] (Vel.-Zern., Bašk. 412); Tat. 1693 **El-murza** [Азаматъ мурза Ельмурзинъ сынъ Байтерековъ] (AI V, 402); Tat. 1708 **El-murza** [Ель-Мурза], from Astrakhan (MIB I, 219); Nog. 1649 **El-murza** [Ель мурза] (AI IV, 78); Tat.? 1609 **El-murza / İl-murza** [Эль (Илъ) Юсуповъ мурза / Илъмурза Исуповичь] (AI II, 176); Kzk. 19th c. **El-sulï** [Елсулы] (SODž. 76); Selj.? 1073 **El-tegin** [حا قـا ن يلتـكين], ruler (owner) of Samarkand (Ibn al-Athīr/Tornb. X, 52-53, 60); Uyg. **İl** [İl] (EUTS); Uyg. 13th-14th c. **İl** (Zieme, Mat. II, 85 (after TT IV)); Chag. 16th c. **İl** [Иль] (Ivanov 312); Bashk. 1756 **İl** [Бокча Ильев] (MIB IV/1, 109); Maml. **İl-aba** [سيف الـدين ابو بكـر بـن ايلبا] (Ibn Šaddād, Nawād.: RHCHor III, 40); Maml. **İl-aba**, Tuγ-tegin's mamlūk/gulām (?) (Ramazan Şeşen: İslam Tetkikleri Enstitüsü Dergisi, VI, 3-4 (1976), p. 18); Yürük 1543 **İl-bay** (Gökb., Rum. 196); Tat. 1676 **İl-bay** (Kurdjumov 6, 8); Tat. 1702 **İl-bay** [Тюлейко Ильбаевъ], from

Kungursk (Letop. ZAK II, 8); Tat. 18th-19th c. **İl-bay** [Илбай] (Magn. 42); Chuv. 18th-19th c. **İl-batïr** [Илбатыръ] (Magn. 42); Selj.? 1112 **İl-begi** [ايلبكى], an emir, who fought against the crusaders (Ibn al-Athīr: RHCHor I, 280); Yürük 1543 **İl-begi** [İlbeği], from the Yürük (Gökb., Rum. 103, 205, 220, 227); Kzk. 19th c. **İl-begi** [Ильбегиевъ] (Grod., Pril. 72); Kzk. 19th c. **İl-begi** [Чуканбай Ильбегиевъ] (Grod., Pril. 192); Kzk. 19th c. **İl-begi** [Ильбеги] (Grod., Pril. 192); Maml. 14th c. **İl-begi / Äl-bägi** [البكى / İlbegi] (Tarj/Houtsma 58, Tarj/Toparlı 41); Turk. 14th c. **İl-bey** [Hacı İl Bey] (Gökb., Ed. 6); Chuv. 18th-19th c. **İl-bey** [Илбей] (Magn. 42); Turk. 20th c. **İl-beyi** (Önder, Göle); Bashk. 1777 **İl-bek** [Терегулов Илбек Батыршин] (MIB V, 60). Chuv. 18th-19th c. **İl-bek / İl-bäk** [Илбякъ] (Magn. 42); Pecheneg / Kuman? **İl-bek / İl-beg?** (Németh, Inschr. 27); Chuv. 18th-19th c. **İl-čura** [Илчура] (Magn. 44); Selj. 1118 **İl-γāzi** [İlgâzî], emir, the son of Artuq (Abulfar./Budge I, 249); Khorezm. 1219 **İl-χoĵa** [Иль-ходжа / Ильходжа], son of the emir of Nur (MIT I, 503); Uyg. **İl-qoča** [İl Koça] (EUTS); Kzk.? 1817 **İl-murza** [Мустай Ильмурзинъ], a „Cossack" from Orenburg (TOUAK XXIV, 76); Chuv. 19th c. **İl-murza / El-murza** [Ilimursa Bakmursin] (Kronheim 96); Oghuz/Trkm. 13th c. **İl-tegin** [ايـل تـكيـن / Иль-Тегин], Boγra-χan's son (Abulg./Kon. 890, 1005, 1010); Tat. 1446 **Li-bey** (<İl-bey?) [Либей], a prince from Kazan (PSRL VIII, 114); *TN:* Turk. 20th c. **İl-γāzi** [İlgazi], a village in the province of Amasya, Turkey (TMİB 61); Uzb. **İl-mirza-tepe**, a hill in the region of the Zerafshan mountains (Trudy Otd. Ist. Kul't. i Iskusstva Vostoka II, 133, 163). ✧ 'Folk; people, foreign man; country; state; army; power' cf. Trk. *i:l/el* 'народ; люди; страна' (Sev.), Turk. *il* 'administrative province' (TEİ), Tat., Turk. *il* 'das Volk, der Volkstamm, die Gemeinde, das Dorf' (Radl. I, 1472). See also **ČİT-EL, SAS-EL.**

EL-ALDÏ Maml. 14th c. **Äl-aldï / İl-aldï** [الدى / alaldy / İlaldı] (Tarj/Houtsma 52, Tarj/Toparlı 41); Turk. 1540 **İl-aldï**, head of the Dodur (دودور) cemaat according to a defter of Diyarbekir (Demirtaş 54); Turk. 1494 **İl-aldï-hatun** [İl Aldı Hatun], fem. (Gökb., Ed. 425); Turk. 1530 **İl-aldï-sultan** [İl Aldı Sultan (şehzade)] (Gökb., Ed. 380); Khorezm.? **İl-altï / İl-aldï?** [Илъ-алти] (RaD/Ber. II, 82, 83 (text 136)). ✧ 'People/empire - one who has seized' (Bese 19); 'People/folk-taken' (Blagova 1997, 709). ⇨ **EL.** See also **EL-ALMÏŠ.**

EL-ALMÏŠ Uyg. 12th c.-14th c. **El-almïš-sañun** (Radl., USp. 12, DTS); Uyg. **İl-almïš** [İl Almış] (EUTS); Oghuz/Trkm. 15th c. **İl-almïš / Él-almïš**, from Bayïndïr-qan's army (DQorq./Rossi 161, DQorq./Gökyay 78); Uyg. **İl-almïš-tigin** [İl Almış Tigin] (EUTS); Oghuz/Trkm. 14th c. - 15th c. **Ul-almïš?** [Bağrıncı oğlı El-almış / Yağrıncı oğlı İl almış / İl Almış / Улальмиш], Yaγrïnči's (Baγrïnči's) son (DQorq. 74, 237). ✧ 'People/empire - one who has seized' (Bese 19), 'People/folk-taken' (Blagova 1997, 709). ⇨ **EL + ALMÏŠ.** See also **EL-ALDÏ.**

EL-AMAN Trkm. 1505 **El-aman** [Эль Аман] (MIT II, 39, 41, 54); Uzb. 1804, 1810 **El-aman-behadïr** [Эль-аман / Эль-аман-бехадыр], from the Qoñrat tribe (MIT II, 366, 379, 380); Kirg. **El-äman** [Еляман] (Proben V, 143, 161, 168, 171); Kzk. 19th c. **El-eman** [Елеманъ] (AOA 78); Kirg. **El-eman** [Элеман] (Jud. 480); Kzk. 19th c. **İl-aman** [Ильаманъ] (Potanin II, 5); Chag. 16th c. **İl-aman-biy** [Иль Аман-бий], an emir (Ivanov 89). ⇨ **EL + AMAN.**

EL-BAQTÏ Kzk. 19th c. **El-baqtï** [Эльбахты] (SOV 12); Chuv. 18th-19th c. **İl-baχta** [Илбахта] (Magn. 42); Bashk. 1734 **İl-baqtï / İl-baχtï** [Урманчи Илбахтын], a tarχan (Vel.-Zern., Bašk. 10); Bashk. 1735 **İl-baqtï / İl-baχtï** [Илбахти Бердыгуловъ], a tarχan (Vel.-Zern., Bašk. 19); Bashk. 1735 **İl-baqtï / İl-baχtï** [Илбахти Илмаметевъ], a tarχan (Vel.-Zern., Bašk. 17); Chuv. 18th-19th c. **İl-bakta** [Илбакта] (Magn. 42). ✧ 'People/country-lucky'. ⇨ **EL + BAQTÏ.** See also **EL-QUTLU.**

EL-BARX see **EL-BARQ**

EL-BARQ Chuv. 18th-19th c. **El-barχ** [Елбархъ] (Magn. 37); Chuv. 18th-19th c. **İl-barik** (<İl-bark) [Илбарикъ] (Magn. 42); Chuv. 18th-19th c. **İl-bark** [Илбаркъ] (Magn. 42). ✧ '?'. ⇨ **EL.**

EL-BARS Tat. 1779 **El-barïs** [Елбарыс Абляев] (MIB V, 81); Uzb. 18th c. **El-barïs** [Абязъ Елборисовъ], a khan of Bukhara (Nepljuev 840); Chuv. 18th-19th c. **İl-barïs** [Илборысъ] (Magn. 42); Chuv. 18th-19th c. **İl-barïs** [Илбарысъ] (Magn. 42); Uyg. 13th-14th c. **İl-bars** [İl Bars] (Zieme, Mat. II, 85); Chuv. 18th-19th c. **İl-bars** [Илборсъ] (Magn. 42); Chuv. 18th-19th c. **İl-bars** [Илбарсъ] (Magn. 42); Uzb. 15th c. **İl-bars** [البارص / ايلبارس / ايلبارص / البارس,], Yādigār's grand-son, Berke-sultan's son, khan from 1505 (Abulg./Desm. 207); Uzb.? 1621 **İl-bars** [Ильбарс], İsfendiyar-χan's brother (MIT II, 101); Uzb. 1752 **İl-bars** [Илбарсъ Магомедъ Богадыръ ханъ], İl-bars I, a khan from Khiva, executed by Nadir-šah (Nepljuev 77, 781, A. f. w. v. R. XVIII, 382, Zambaur 275, MIT II, 323-325, 333); Uzb. 1734 **İl-bars-χan** [Ильбарс-хан], İl-bars II, a Khan from Khiva (Khorezm) of Kazak origin (MIT II, 137-139, 142-47, 149, 156, 159-62, 166, 169, 195, 196, 258, 292, 293, 334). ✧ 'Folk-panther'. ⇨ **EL + BARS.**

EL-BAS Kzk. 19th c. **El-bas** [Ельбас] (SOK 22). ✧ I. 'Leader of the country/folk'; II. 'Opress the country'? ⇨ **EL + BAŠ; EL + BAS II.?** See also **İL-BAS; EL-**

BASAR, İL-BASAR, İL-BASMÏŠ.

EL-BASTÏ   Maml. 14th c. **İl-bastï / Äl-bastï** [البصتى / İlbaştı] (Tarǰ/Houtsma 58, Tarǰ/Toparlı 43). ✧ '(He) Opressed the country'? ⇨ EL + BASTÏ.

EL-BEKİR   Khorezm.? 1351 **El-bekir / İl-bekir?** [ايـل بكـر], an emir in the history of the Muzaffarïds (Qazw. 651). ⇨ EL + BEKİR.

EL-BEZÄR   Uzb. 20th c. **El-bezär** [Элбезар] (Begmatov 1984, 201). ✧ 'He who will ornament/adorn the country' cf. Uzb. *bezä-* 'украшать, наряжать, оформлять' (UzbRS). ⇨ EL.

EL-BİČİ   Tuv. 19th c. **El-biči-χam** [Ельбичи-хамъ], according to a Tuva tale the first Shaman (woman) (Potanin IV, 288).

EL-BİLGÄ   Türk 732 **El-bilgä** [Elbilgä], El-teriš Khan's wife (ETY I, 34); Türk 8th c. **El-bilgä-qatun**, Kül-tegin's and Bilge-qaγan's mother (DTS). ✧ 'People/empire-wise' (Bese 19, Blagova 1997, 708). ⇨ EL + BİLGÄ.

EL-BOL   Kzk. 19th c. **El-bol** [Ельболъ] (SOV 10); Bashk. 1789 **İl-bul** [Илбул Хусеинов] (MIB V, 271). ✧ 'Be/become (the ruler/owner of the) country (folk)' (Rásonyi, Imp. 238, Sattarov). ⇨ EL + BOL. See also EL-BOLDÏ, EL-BOLSÏN.

EL-BOLDÏ   Bashk. 1719 **El-boldï** [Елболди] (MIB I, 280); Tat.(Lit.) 1548 **El-boldï? / Yäl-boldï?** [Ялбалды] (Kn. Metriki Lit. 44); Tat. 1695 **El-buldï** [Елбудейко (Елдубейко) Девлеткилдеев] (MIB I, 90); Chuv. 18th-19th c. **İl-boldï** [Илболда] (Magn. 42); Tat. 1738 **İl-boldï** [Илболда Ишкин] (MIB I, 144); Bashk. 1755 **İl-buldï** [Илбулда Ишбулдин] (MIB IV/1, 101). ⇨ EL + BOLDÏ. See also EL-BOL, EL-BOLSÏN.

EL-BOLSÏN   Uzb. 20th c. **El-bolsïn** [Элбӱлсин] (Begmatov 1984, 201). ⇨ EL + BOLSÏN. See also EL-BOL, EL-BOLDÏ.

EL-BUΓA see EL-BUQA

EL-BUQA   Uyg. 12th c.-14th c. **El-buγa** (DTS); Khorezm. 1297 **El-buqa / İl-buqa?** [ايـل بوقـا] (RaD/Jahn III); Uyg. 12th c.-14th c. **İl-buγa** (Radl., USp. 137); Uyg. 12th c.-14th c. **İl-buqa** (Radl., USp. 16-17); Uyg. 12th c.-14th c. **İl-buqa** (Radl., USp. 4); Uyg. 13th-14th c. **İl-buqa** [İl Buq-a] (Zieme, Mat. II, 92). ✧ 'People-bull, Bull of the people/folk' (Bese 17, Blagova 1997, 709). ⇨ EL + BUQA.

EL-DEMİR see EL-TEMİR

EL-DİYAR   Kirg. **El-diyar?** [Элдияр] (Jud. 212). ✧ 'Folk-country'? cf. Tat., Bashk. PN *Diyar* 'il, yort' (Sattarov, Kusimova), Turk. *diyar* (Ar.) 'Memleket, ülke' (Özön). ⇨ EL. See also KUY-DİYAR.

EL-DİMİR see EL-TEMİR

EL-ÄMAN see EL-AMAN

EL-EMAN see EL-AMAN

EL-GELDİ see EL-KELDİ

EL-İNANČİ   Türk 7th-9th c. **El-inančï** [El İnançï] (ETY III, 164). ⇨ EL + İNANČU.

EL-YAQŠÏ   Tat. 1534, 1555 **El-yaqšï** [Ѣлъякши, Елъякшы], a princess from Astrakhan (PSRL XIII, 243). ⇨ EL + YAQŠÏ.

EL-KELDİ   Trkm. 1875 **El-geldi** [Ель-Гельды-ханъ] (Voenn. Sb. CXXIX 331); Kzk. 19th c. **El-keldi** [Ельгельди] (AOO 54); Kkalp. 1822 **El-keldi** [Эль-кельди] (MIKk. 127); Uzb. 20th c. **El-keldi** [Элкелди] (Begmatov 1984, 203); Trkm. 1879-1881 **İl-geldi** [Il Geldi], Geldi-χan's son (O'Donovan I, 208); Kzk. 19th c. **İl-geldi** [Ильгельди] (Grod., Pril. 164); Trkm. 19th c. **İl-gildi** [Ильгильды Бердалиевъ] (Ščeglov IV, 177); Bashk. 1695 **İl-gildi** [Илгилди] (MIB I, 85); Bashk. 1727 **İl-gildi** [Калмаметь Илгилдин] (MIB III, 247); Chuv. 18th-19th c. **İl-kilda** [Илкилда] (Magn. 43); Chuv. 18th-19th c. **İn-gildi** [Ингилда] (Magn. 45). ⇨ EL + KELDİ.

EL-KEZÄR   Uzb. 20th c. **El-kezär** [Элкезар] (Begmatov 1984, 203). ✧ 'Country-wanderer; He will wander in the country' cf. Uzb. *kez-* 'бродить; объездить; странствовать' (UzbRS). ⇨ EL. See also YER-KEZER.

EL-KİRMİŠ   Uyg. 12th c.-14th c. **El-kirmiš-sañun** [el kirmiš saŋun] (DTS); Uyg. **İl-kirmiš [İl-körmiš? / İl Kirmiş]** (EUTS). ✧ 'People/empire - one who has entered' (Bese 19), 'Joining the tribal organization' (Blagova 1997, 709), cf. Uyg., Karakh. *kir-* 'входить; появляться' (DTS). ⇨ EL.

EL-QATMÏŠ   Uyg. 12th c.-14th c. **El-qatmïš** (DTS). ✧ 'People/empire - one who became hard' (Bese 19, Blagova 1997, 709). ⇨ EL.

EL-QAV   Uyg. 1341 **El-qav / Eli-qaw?**, fem. (Chwol., Syr.-nest. (NF) 39). ⇨ EL.

EL-QUTLÏ see İL-QUTLUΓ

EL-MARS   Chuv. 18th-19th c. **El-mars** [Елмарсъ] (Magn. 38). ⇨ EL.

EL-MİRAT see EL-MURAT

EL-MURAT   Kkalp. 20th c. **El-mïrat** [Елмырат], colloquial variant of El-murat (KkRS 773); Kkalp. 20th c. **El-murat** [Елмурат] (Bask., Kkalp. 34, KkRS 773); Uzb. 19th c. **İl-murat** [Ильмуратъ Имрмановъ] (SKSO III, 16); Uzb. 19th c. **İl-murat** [Самандаръ Ильмуратовъ] (SKSO III, 15). ⇨ EL + MURAT.

EL-TAY Kkalp. 20th c. **El-tay / Eltay?** [Елтай] (KkRS 773). ⇨ EL + TAY? + / suff. *-tay(1,2)?*

EL-TÄBÄR   Türk 8th c. **El-täbär** [eltäbär], commander of the army of the Az folk (DTS); Uyg. **İl-täbär**, an Uyghur title, from the Iškül tribe (RaD/Ber. I, 126); Uyg. **İl-täbär** [İltäbär] (EUTS); Uyg. 8th c.-9th c. **İl-täbär** (Le Coq, Buch-Fragm. 147); Uyg. 8th c.-9th c. **İl-täbir** (Le Coq, Man. II, 94, Thomsen 182). ✧ 'One who steps on the el/il' (Golden 147, 149), a title of the

Az commanders (DTS), cf. Karakh. *tep-* 'пинать, лягать' (DTS), cf. also Pelliot: T'oung-Pao XXVI (1929), pp. 226-228; Pelliot, Notes 182; Czeglédy Károly, Egy bolgár- török méltóságnév: MNy. XL (1944), p. 179. ⇨ **EL.**

EL-TÄRİŠ Türk 7th c. **El-täriš-qaγan**, Kül-tegin's and Bilge-qaγan's (681-691) father (DTS); Türk 7th c. **El-täriš-qaγan** [Eltäriş / eltäriš qaγan], throne name of Qutluγ-qaγan, Kül-tegin (Köl-tegin) and Bilge-qaγan's father, ruled 681-691 (ETY I, 34, 102, 116, 118, 120, 128, 130, 136, DTS); Türk 7th c. **İl-tiriš** [Il-tiris] (Thomsen 145, 196, Müller, Uig. II, 94-95, Turc. (?) 49, 90, 95). ✧ 'Organizing/gathering the polity, country/state' (Golden 137, Erol II), cf. Türk, Uyg., Chag. *tär-* 'sammeln' (Radl. III, 1060), also *ilt(i)r(i)š* 'König der Türken' (Gabain 311). ⇨ **EL.**

EL-TEMİR Maml.? 1325 **El-demir** [الدمر] خليل بن سيف الدين] (Zetterst. 182, 83); Maml. 1320 **El-demir / İl-demir?** [سيف الدين الدمر الركنى] (Zetterst. 149, 182, WeilChalif. I, 315-16); Maml.? 1320 **El-demir? / İl-demir?** [الدمر امير جاندار سيف الدين], an emir (Duqmaq:RHCHor IV, 41, Dawād. 296, 308); Chuv. 18th-19th c. **El-dimir** [Елдимиръ] (Magn. 37); Uyg. 1305 **El-temir** [Elitimur Pultan] (Chwol., Syr.-nest. (NF) 16); Khorezm.? 1291 **El-temür** [ايلتمور] (RaD/Jahn 32); Uyg. 12th c.-14th c. **El-temür (İl-tämir / İl-tämür)** (Radl., USp. 7, 8, Le Coq, Urkunden 455, DTS); Bulg. 13th c. **El-timir** [Ελτιμιρης], brother of the Bulghar ruler Terter I (1280-1292) (Byz. Turc. 124); Chuv. 18th-19th c. **İ-dimer (<İl-dimer)** [Идимеръ] (Magn. 41); Chuv. 18th-19th c. **İl-demir** [Илдемиръ] (Magn. 42); Chuv. 18th-19th c. **İl-dimer** [Илдимеръ] (Magn. 43); Chuv. 18th-19th c. **İl-dimir** [Илдимиръ / Ильдимиръ] (Magn. 43, 44); Uyg. **İl-tämir** [İl Tämir] (EUTS); Uyg. **İl Tämür** [İl Tämür] (EUTS); Uyg. 13th-14th c. **İl-temür** [El T(ä)mür] (Zieme, Mat. II, 85). ✧ I. 'Country/folk-iron' (Tarǰ/Houtsma 33), 'People-iron' (Bese 19, Blagova 1997, 709); II. 'Hand-iron' (Zetterst. 83); III. 'Red iron' cf. Sauvaget 38: al-tämür 'id.'. ⇨ **EL + TEMİR. See also AL-TEMİR.**

EL-TERGÜG Uyg. 8th c.-9th c. **El-tergüg / İl-tirgüg?** (Le Coq, Man. I, 27, DTS); Uyg. **İl-tirgäk** [İl tirgäk] (EUTS); Uyg. **İl-türgüg** [İl Türgüg] (EUTS). ✧ 'Support of the country (nation)' cf. *tirgük* 'опора' (DTS), cf. also Uyg. *tirgäk jultuz* 'название звезды' (DTS). ⇨ **EL + TERGÜG.**

EL-ТОГАН Türk 7th c.-9th c. **El-toγan-tutuq** [El Toγan Tutuq] (DTS, ETY III, 31); Chuv. 18th-19th c. **İ-dugan (<İl-dugan)** [Идуганъ] (Magn. 41); Chuv. 18th-19th c. **İl-dugan** [Илдуганъ / Ильдуганъ] (Magn. 43, 44); Chuv. 18th-19th c. **İl-tugan** [Илтуганъ] (Magn. 44); Bashk. 1770 **İl-tugan** [Илтуган Унгаров] (MIB

IV/1, 342); Chuv. 18th-19th c. **İn-dugan** [Индуганъ] (Magn. 45). ✧ I. 'Born by the folk', 'Folk-falcon' (Blagova 1997, 709); II. II. 'Chief of the nation was born' cf. Tat. *İl-tuγan / İl-duγan* (Sattarov). ⇨ **EL + ТОГАН / ТУГАН I.**

EL-ТОГДİ Selj. 1041 **El-toγdï** [مسعود الغزنوى] [ايلتغدى حاجب] (Ibn al-Athīr/Tornb. IX, 325). ⇨ **EL + ТУГДİ.**

EL-TUR Tat. (Sib.) 1596 **El-tur** [Елтур] (Miller, Ist. Sib. II, 149). ✧ 'People/folk - be alive / survive!'. ⇨ **EL + TUR?**

EL-TURMİŠ Selj. 1226 **El-turmïš** [الترمش شمس الدين] (Ibn al-Athīr/Tornb. XII, 303). ⇨ **EL + TURMİŠ.**

EL-TUTAR Tat.? 1693 **El-tutar** [Ел-тутаръ Чепаевъ], a murza (AI V, 404). ⇨ **EL + TUTAR.**

EL-TUTMİŠ Uyg. **İl-tutmïš** [İl Tutmış] (EUTS); Oghuz 902 **El-tutmïš (Aldatmïš?)** [الد تمش التركى] (Ibn al-Athīr/Tornb. VII, 357); Maml. 1210/11 **El-tutmïš, İl-tutmïš** [التتمش / ايلتتمش], Mamluk sultan in Delhi (Lahore and Kashmir), India (1210-1211), his names have been preserved on coins (Nasawī 89, Poole, Catalogue of Indian Coins; Sultans of Dehli, p. XXIX); Maml. 1426 **İl-tutmïš** [ايلتتمش / Iltutmyš] (Muḥ. b. Hasan Niẓāmī, Tāǧ al-ma'ātir (Barthold: ZDMG LXI, 192-193)); Uyg. 767 **İl-tutmïš / El-tutmïš**, part of the title of an Uyghur khan (Müller, Pfahl. 26); 1210/11 **İl-tutmïš / İl-etmiš?** [شمس الد ين التتمش سلطان] Šems eddîn Altmyš(!) / Шемс-ад-дин Ильтутмыш], a Slave King in Delhi, India (1211-1236), came of the İberi / Alprī branch of Kara Khitai Turks (Ibn Bat. III, p. XVIII, Ǧuwaynī II, 61, 144, 145, MIT I, 50). ✧ 'He who got/saved the empire'; 'Preserver, defender of the state' (Barthold: ZDMG LXI, 1907, 192-193: „Erhalter des Reiches"); 'Handgrasper, supporter' (Poole p. 295); cf. Türk *il (äl) tut-* 'die Stammgemeinschaft (das Reich) erhalten' (Thomsen 135), Uyg. *il tutmïš* 'das Reich gehalten habende' (Müller., Uig. II, 15); cf. also EI II, 501, Horovitz, The Inscript. of *İltutm.*: Epigr. Indo-Moslemica, 1913. The name of Sultan Šemseddīn *İltutmïš (~El-tutmïš)* was preserved in different incorrect forms such as *Altamš, Altamiš* (cf. Elphinstone, History of India, p. 371, Le Coq, Ind. 1), *Altïtmïš* (cf. A. Müller: Der Islam II, 188), etc. ⇨ **EL. See also EL-TUTAR, İL-TUT.**

EL-TUTMİŠXAN Maml. 13th c., 1309/10 **El-tutmïšχan / İl-tutmïšχan?** [الخا تون التطمشحان], wife of Sultan Bay-bars II (1309-1310) (Makhrīzī, Khit. I, 83). ⇨ **EL-TUTMİŠ + fem. suff. -χan(1).**

EL-TÜBER Kzk. 19th c. **El-tüber** [Ельтуберъ] (SOV 106).

EL-TÜZER Kzk. 18th c. - 19th c. **El-tüzer** [Ельтузер] (Tynyšp. 65); Uzb. 1770 **El-tüzer** [Эльтузер], from the Qoñrat tribe (MIT II, 345); Uzb. 1804/05 **El-tüzer**

[Эльтузер], a khan from Khiva (MIT II, 24, 202-204, 258, 259, 296, 349, 354-356, 358, 359, 362, 368, 370-372); Trkm. 1851 **El-tüzer-χan** [Эльтузер-хан], a serdar, from the Yomut tribe (MIT II, 302, 304); Trkm. 1856 **El-tüzer-inaq** [Эльтузер-инак] (MIT II, 559); Uzb. 1804 **İl-tezer** / **İl-täzär** [Ilteser, Iltazar], Awǰas-inaq's son who became the khan in Khiva at the beginning of the 19th century (ArchKR XVIII, 382, Zambaur); Kzk. 19th c. **İl-tüzär** [Джамбулатъ Ильтузаровъ] (Grod., Pril. 130). ✧ 'He who will arrange/organize the country/people'. ⇨ **EL + TÜZER.** See also **EL-BEZÄR, İL-TÜZMİŠ.**

ELAT Chuv. 18th-19th c. **Elat / Yelat / Yelät?** [Елатъ] (Magn. 37).

ELBESİN Kzk. 19th c. **Elbesin** [Ельбесынъ] (AOA 2).

ELČİ Uyg. 12th c.-14th c. **Elči** (DTS); Tat.? 1716 **Elči** [Яковъ Ельчинъ], a major (Andrievič II, 375); Bashk. 1751 **Elči** [Елчи Якшиев] (MIB IV/1, 84); Kzk. 19th c. **Elči-bay** [Елчибай] (AOA 82); Kzk. 19th c. **Elči-bay** [Ельчибай] (SOK 184); Kzk. 19th c. **Elči-bay** [Ельчибай] (SOV 50); Kzk. **Elči-bek** [Ельчибекъ] (TV 1876, p. 78); Kzk. 19th c. **Elči-bek** [Ельчибек] (SODž. 74); Kzk. 19th c. **Elči-bek** [Ельчибек] (SOK 200); Kzk. 19th c. **Elči-bek** [Элчибекъ] (Lomakin); Türk 8th c.-9th c. **Elči-čur** (DTS); Uzb.? 1770 **Elči-inaq** [Элчи-инак] (MIT II, 345); Kzk. 19th c. **Elčim-bay?** / **Elči-bay** [Ельчимбай] (SODž. 76, 114); Tat. 17th c. **Elčü-bay** [Байгуска Елчюбаевъ] (IOAIÊK XXIX, 344); Uyg. 12th c.-14th c. **İlči** (Radl., USp. 25-26, 41, 50-51); Bashk. 1731 **İlči** [Илчи Солтонаев] (MIB III, 292); Chuv. 18th-19th c. **İlči-bay** [Илчибай] (Magn. 44); Bashk. 1663 **İlči-bay** [Илчибай Бекпердеев] (MIB I, 175); Bashk. 1664 **İlči-bay** [Илчибай Токпердеев] (MIB I, 193); Bashk. 1708 **İlči-bay** [Илчибай Бакеев] (MIB III, 42); Bashk. 1715 **İlči-bay** [Ылчибай] (MIB III, 132); Bashk. 1734 **İlči-bay** [Коземшугур Илчибаев] (Vel.-Zern., Bašk. 10); Bashk. 1734 **İlči-bay** [Илчибай] (MIB III, 317); Bashk. 1745 **İlči-bay** [Мусалип Илчибаев] (MIB III, 430); Bashk. 1794 **İlči-bay** [Илчибай Канакаев] (MIB V, 338); Khorezm. 1360 **İlči-behadur** [Ильчи-бехадур], an emir (MIT I, 512, 516); Chuv. 18th-19th c. **İlči-bey** [Илчибей] (Magn. 44); Kzk. 19th c. **İlči-bek(-batïr)** [Илчибекъ батыръ] (Valihanov, Soč. 316); Bashk. 1726 **İlči-γul** [Абекей Ильчигулов] (MIB III, 240); Bashk. 1738, 1776 **İlči-γul** [Илчигул Тоймасов] (MIB III, 387, V, 43, 45); Bashk. 1740 **İlči-γul** [Илчигул Чуракаев] (MIB I, 400); Bashk. 1770 **İlči-γul** [Аллаберда Илчигулов] (MIB IV/1, 341); Bashk. 1789 **İlči-γul** / **Elči-γul** [Илчигул (Елчигул) Илкенеев] (MIB V, 260); Khorezm. 1221 **İlči-pehlewān** [پهلوان ایلچی / Ильчи-пехлеван], one of the emirs of Sultan Jelāleddīn Meñgü-berdi, the lord of

Sabzewār (J̌uwaynī II, 153, 169); Bashk. 20th c. **İlse-γol** [Илсеҕол / Ильсигул] (Kusimova); Bashk. 1740 **İlsü-γol** [Илсюгол Бетюкбаев] (MIB I, 396); Bashk. 1709 **İlši** [Илши] (MIB I, 264). ✧ 'Envoy', cf. Tat. *ilči* 'der Gesandte, Bote' (Radl. I, 1496), Bashk. *ilse* 'посол, посланник; посланец' (BRS).

ELČİ-ČUR-KÜČ-BARS Türk 7th c.-9th c. **Elči-čur-küč-bars** [Elç Çur Küç Bars] (ETY III, 117, 144). ⇨ **ELČİ + ČUR + KÜČ-BARS.**

ELČİ-TİRİ Uyg. 12th c. - 14th c. **Elči-tiri / İlči-tiri** (Radl., USp. 4-5, DTS). ✧ 'Envoy-Tiri (alive)' (Blagova 1997, 711). ⇨ **ELČİ.**

ELČİKEY Bashk. 1770 **Elčikey** [Елчикай Хошай] (MIB IV/1, 342); Bashk. 1714 **İlčikey** [Урус Ильчикеев] (MIB III, 117); Bashk. 1757 **İlčikey** [Илчикей Биктуганов] (MIB IV/1, 150); Bashk. 1761 **İlčikey** [Аюка Илчикеев] (MIB IV/1, 221); Bashk. 1778 **İlčikey** [Илчикей Бектуганов] (MIB V, 66, 70); Bashk. 1778 **İlčikey** [Илчикей Кадырметев] (MIB V, 94, 265). ✧ 'Dear little envoy' cf. Kzk. PN *İlčekäy* (Sattarov). ⇨ **ELČİ** + suff. -*key*.

ELČİM Kzk. 19th c. **Elčim** [Эльчимъ] (SOK 22); Bashk. 1756 **İlčim** [Илчим Катаев] (MIB IV/1, 109). ⇨ **ELČİ** + poss. suff. -*m*.

ELDAŠ see **İLDAŠ**

ELDEY I. Kzk. 19th c. **Eldey** [Ельдей] (SOK 18, 250).

ELDEY II. Chuv. 18th-19th c. **Eldey** [Елдей] (Magn. 37).

ELDEKEY Chuv. 18th-19th c. **Eldekey** [Елдекей] (Magn. 37).

ELDİ Kzk. 19th c. **Eldi-bay** [Ельдибай] (SOK 10); Kzk. 19th c. **Eldi-bay** [Елдибай] (Grod., Pril. 19, 33); Bashk. 1754 **Eldi-bay / Eldï-bay?** [Елдыбай Кинзегулов] (MIB IV/1, 83); Kzk. 1790 **Eldi-bay / Eldï-bay?** [Елдыбай] (MIK IV, 129); Bashk. 1761 **Eldü-bay** [Елдубай Булатов] (MIB IV/1, 215); Chuv. 1748 **İldi-kan** [Илдиканъ Ишпулдинъ] (PSZRI XII, 942); *TN:* Bashk. 1756 **İldi-bay(evo)** [Ильдыбаево], a village (MIB IV/1, 127). ⇨ **EL?** + suff. -*di* /-*li*.

ELEBES Kirg. **Elebes** [Элебес] (Jud. 196). ✧ 'He won't notice/react'? cf. Kirg. *ele-* 'просеивать (через решето, сито); замечать, обращать внимание; реагировать' (Jud.).

ELEGEY see **İLİKEY**

ELEKEY see **İLİKEY**

ELESKEY Alt. 19th-20th c. **Eleskey** [Элескей] (OjrRS 210). ✧ Aleksey (R.) (OjrRS 210).

ELEW Bashk. 1735 **Elew** [Елев Четкарин] (Vel.-Zern., Bašk. 12); Bashk. 1761 **Elew** [Зайсан Елевов] (MIB IV/1, 221); Kzk. 19th c. **Elew** [Элеу] (AOAtb. 54); Kzk. 19th c. **Elew** [Елеу] (AOAtb. 14); Kzk. 19th c. **Elew** [Елеу] (SOK 240); Kzk. 19th c. **Elew-bay** [Елеубай] (AOP 58). ✧ 'Attention, care' (Espaeva 1984, 231).

ELEWKE Kzk. 19th c. **Elewke** [Елеуке] (AOP 86). ⇨ **ELEW** + suff. -ke.

ELEWLİ Kzk. 19th c. **Elewli** [Елеули] (SOK 164). ✧ 'Noteworthy, remarkable' cf. Kzk. elewli 'id.' (KzRS).

ELEZİM Kzk. 19th c. **Elezim-qul** [Джибнатай Элезимкуловъ] (Grod., Pril. 178).

ELGİTAR Nog. 20th c. **Elgitar** [Къазбек Джангелди увлы Елгитар / Казбек Джанкельдиев], one of Baskakov's informants from the aul of Qoyasulï (Bask., Nog. 144).

ELGÜ Kzk. 19th c. **Elgü-bek** [Ельгубекъ] (SOK 26). ✧ 'Present, now'? cf. Kzk. ălgĭ 'jetzig, jetzt' (Radl. I, 822).

ELGÜR Uyg. 13th c. **Elgür-tutuñ** [elgür tutuŋ] (DTS).

ELİF Bashk. 1779 **Älib-bay** (<Älip-bay) [Алиббай Бердыбаев] (MIB V, 87); Kzk. 19th c. **Älep** [Елепъ] (SOK 220); Kzk. 19th c. **Älep-pay** [Елеппай] (SODž. 102); Kzk. 19th c. **Älïp** [Алибъ] (AOO 10); Kzk. 19th c. **Älip** [Алипъ] (SOK 60); Kzk. 19th c. **Älip** [Елипъ] (SOV 46, 74); Kzk. 19th c. **Älip** [Елипъ] (SOK 42); Tat.? 18th c. **Älip(ka)** [Алипка Айдугановъ], an ataman of the Cossacks (IOAIÊK XXIX, 342); Kzk. 19th c. **Älip-pay** [Алиппай] (SOV 24); Kzk. 19th c. **Älip-pay** [Елиппай] (SODž. 24, 38); Kzk. 19th c. **Älip-pek** [Алиппекъ] (SOK 36); Kzk. 19th c. **Älip-pek** [Елибпекъ] (SODž. 60); Yürük 1543 **Elif**, fem. (Gökb., Rum. 221). ✧ Alif (Ar.) 'friendly, siciable, amicable' (Ahmed), cf. Turk. elif '(Arabic alphabet) name of the first letter' (TED), Kzk. ălip 'der erste Buchstabe des arabischen Alphabets' (Radl. I, 819), Bashk. älep 'id.' (BaRS). See also **ALAÑQASAR-ÄLİF, ALPAMÏS-ÄLİF, ARSALAÑ-ÄLİF**.

ELİFE Turk. 1583 **Elife** [الينا / elife], two girls in the source (Ongan, Ank I, 156). ✧ Alifa (Ar.) 'friendly, siciable, amicable', fem. of Alif (Ahmed). ⇨ **ELİF**.

ELİG Oghuz/Trkm. 14th c. - 15th c. **Elig-qoǰa / İlik-qoǰa / Eylik-qoǰa** [Elig Koca, Eylik Koca / Илик-Коджа], father of Sarï-qulmaš, Dönebilmez Dölek Evren and Alp-eren (DQorq./Rossi 136, 145, 161, 226, DQorq./Ergin 96, DQorq. 23, 30, 74, 100, 236, 237, 250); Khorezm. 1229 **İleɣ-χan** [الغ حان / Ilegh Khān], Jelāl's officer (Nasawī); Karakh. 993, 1017/18 **İlek-χan** [ايلك حان], the title of the Karakhanid ruler Abu Nasr Ahmed ibn Ali, died in 1017/18 (Ibn al-Athīr/Tornb. IX, 70, 76, 91, 111-113); Karakh. 996, 1012/13 **İlek-χan** [ايلك حان / Наср ибн Али, Арслан-Илек (Наср I, Илек-хан)], the title of the Karakhanid ruler Abul-Hasan Nasr ibn Ali (Nasr I, known as Arslan-ilek too), died in 1012/13 (Mirch. Gasnevid. 24, 29, MIT I, 3., 223-227, 229-270, 350-351, 358-361, 366, 451-452); Karakh. 11th c. **İlik** [Ilik], „dans la ville Balâsâgoun un khan nommé Ilik" (Abulg./Desm. 49). ✧ 'Ruler, imperor, king, prince' A title of Karakhanid rulers, used as part of their full name. Cf. Türk, Uyg.

elig 'правитель, государь' (DTS), also Clauson 141-142, Räs., TMEN II, No. 661, Sev. Ilig-er 'Prince-man' (Golden 259); Németh, HMK 134, 192; O. Turan, İlig Unvanı Hakkında: Türkiyat Mecmuası, VII-VIII, İstanbul, 1942. See also **ALP-İLEK**.

ELİK Karakh. 11th c. **Älik** (Radl. I, 651); Uyg. 12th c. - 14th c. **Elik** [elik] (DTS); Kirg. 20th c. **Elik-bay** [Эликбай] (Kalilov 92); Bashk. 1709 **İlik** [Илик Текянов] (MIB III, 49); Bashk. 1734 **İlik** [Араслан Иликов] (MIB III, 325); Chuv. 18th-19th c. **İlik-murza** [Иликмурза] (Magn. 43). ✧ I. 'Wild she-goat' cf. Türk, Uyg., Karakh. elik I 'самка серны, дикой козы (DTS), Bashk. ilek 'косуля, дикая коза' (BRS/Uraksin); II. 'First (born) child'? cf. Uyg., Tat.(Sib.) ilik 'der erste, zuerst' (Radl. I, 1485).

ELİK-TEMÜR Kirg. **Elik-temür / Elik-timür?** [Элик-Тимур], from the Kirghiz tribe (RaD I/1, 150). ⇨ **ELİK + TEMİR.**

ELİM Kirg. **Elim** [Елім] (Proben V, 70 /71/); Kzk. 19th c. **Elim-bek** [Елимбекъ] (SODž. 114); Bashk. 1756 **İlim-ɣul** [Илимгул Теникеев] (MIB IV/1, 122). ✧ 'My country/folk'? ⇨ **EL?** + poss. suff. -im.

ELİP see **ELİF**

ELKE Hak. 19th-20th c. **Elke** [Елке] (HRS 348). ✧ Ilya (R.).

ELLÄY Bashk. 1795 **Elläy? / Yelläy?** [Еллай] (IOAIÊK (Dobavlenie) XXVIII, 59).

ELLİ Kirg. 19th c. **Elli-bay** [Elli-baj], Almásy's guide in Kirghizia (Almásy). ✧ I. 'Fifty'? cf. Kirg. elǖ 'id.' (Jud.); II. 'Breadth of a finger (measure)'? cf. Kzk. eli 'eine Fingerbreite' (Radl. I, 814), cf. also Kzk. PNs Eli-bay, Eli-bek (Žanuzakov-Esbaeva).

ELMAQAY? Bashk. 1709 **Elmaqay?** [Елмакай] (MIB I, 264). ⇨ **ALMA?** + suff. -qay.

ELSÜZ Turk. 1489 **Elsüz** [Muhiddin bin Muslihiddin Elsüz] (Gökb., Ed. 305); Turk. 1574-1595 **Elsüz-piri**, a man from Teke sancağı, cemâat-i Bayındır (Sümer: DTCF XI, 339). ✧ 'Having no country (folk)', cf. Turk. pîr 'Yaşlı, ihtiyar, koca; tarikat kuranlardan her biri' (Özön). ⇨ **EL** + suff. -süz.

ELTAŠ see **İLDAŠ**

ELUMBET Bashk. 1738 **Elumbet? / Elümbet?** [Мряс Елумбетев] (MIB I, 143); Bashk.? 1744 **Elumbet? / Elümbet?** [Елумбеть] (Nepljuev 682, 690); Kzk. 1744 **Elumbet? / Elümbet?** [Елумбетъ] (Dobrosm. 64). ⇨ **EL** + suff. -umbet / -bet?

ELUW see **ELÜ**

ELÜ Kzk. 19th c. **Eluw-bay / Elüw-bay?** [Елуубай] (SODž. 10); Kzk. 19th c. **Elü-bay** [Елюбай] (SOK 114, 176); Kzk. 19th c. **Elü-bay** [Елюбай] (AOP 6, 110); Kzk. 19th c. **Elü-bay** [Елюбай] (SOV 46, 142); Kzk. 19th c. **Elü-bay** [Елюбай] (AOO 46); Kzk. 19th c. **Elü-bay** [Елюбай] (AOK 82, 110); Kzk. 19th c. **Elü-bay** [Елюбай] (AOA 66). ✧ 'Fifty'.

ELÜS Hak. 19th-20th c. **Elüs** [Элӱс], fem. (HRS 356).

ELÜSKÄ Hak.(Sag.) 19th-20th c. **Elüskä** [Елӱскä] (Katanov, Otč. 8). ❖ Ilyushka (R.) (Katanov).

ELVAN Turk. 15th c. **Elvan-oγlu** [Elvan oğlu Hamza] (Gökb., Ed. 198). ❖ 'Of different colours, multi-coloured'? (TED; Erol II) (<Ar).

ELVEND Turk. 1503 Elvend (Gökb., Ed. 484).

EM-BERDİ Kzk. 19th c. **Em-berdi** (<En-berdi?) [Эмберды] (Lomakin 40). ⇨ **EM + BERDİ.**

EMEGELJİN Tuv. 19th c. **Emegeljin / Yemegeljin?** [Емегельджинъ / Емегенъ] (Potanin IV, 99). ❖ Totem-name; One makes such totem if he has no child or cannot have any at all (Potanin IV, 99).

EMEGEN Tuv. 19th c. **Emegen / Yemegen?** (Potanin IV, 99). ❖ Totem-name; One makes such totem if he has no child or cannot have any at all (Potanin IV, 99). ⇨ **EMEGELJİN.**

EMEKEY Bashk. 1710 **Emekey** [Емекей Сабанаев] (MIB III, 67).

EMEL I. Kzk. 19th c. **Emel-bay** [Эмельбай] (SODž. 96). ❖ 'Wish, hope, ideal' (TED), cf. also Alt., Az., Crm., Tat. *ämäl* 'die Angelegenheit, That; das Mittel, das Verfahren die Art und Weise etc.' (Radl. I, 950).

EMEL II. Alt. 19th-20th c. **Emel** [Эмел], fem. (OjrRS 214); Alt. 19th-20th c. **Emil** [Эмил], fem. (OjrRS 214). ❖ 'Kernel, pith, flesh' (OjrRS 214), cf. Alt. *ämäl* 'der innere Theil der Birkenrinde; weicher Kern der Steinfrüchte' (Radl. I, 950).

EMELČİ Alt. 19th-20th c. **Emelči** [Эмелчи], fem. (OjrRS 214); Alt. 19th-20th c. **Emilči** [Эмилчи], fem. (OjrRS 214). ❖ 'One who loves wick (kernel)' (OjrRS 214). ⇨ **EMEL** + suff. *-či*.

EMELDEŠ Tat. 1608, 1618 **Emeldeš / Emeltäš?** [Емелдеш (Емельтяш) Еменеев], a murza (Miller, Ist. Sib. II, 206, 244); Tat. 1535 **Emildeš** [Емилъдешъ] (Kn. Metriki Lit. 113). ❖ 'Mate' cf. Tat.(Bar.) *ämäldäš* 'der Gefährte' (Radl. I, 951). ⇨ **EMEL I.** + suff. *-deš*.

EMEN Oghuz/Trkm. 14th c.-15th c. **Emen** [بيغى قتلو امن / (Bïyïgï Qanlu) Bügdüz Emen, Бıyıgı Qanlu Emen / Эмен из рода Бэгдюр], Emen from the Begdür (Bügdüz?) clan (DQorq./Rossi 144, 159, 162, 167, 170, 195, DQorq./Ergin 113). ❖ Emin? (Ar.). See also **BÜGDÜZ-EMEN.**

EMET see AXMET

EMETČİ Bulg. 1357 **Emetči** [امتجى بكاى / Emetji Bügēy] (Epigr. Bulg. 146-147).

EMİL see EMEL II.

EMİLČİ see EMELČİ

EMİLDEŠ see EMELDEŠ

EMİN Kzk. 19th c. **Amin / Ämin?** [Аминъ] (Grod., Pril. 123); Trkm. 20th c. **Āmin** [Āmin] (Zaj. 1971, 327); Kzk. 19th c. **Emin-bek** (Hedin I, 210); Trkm. 1826 **Emin-serdar** [Эмин-сердар], from the Sarïq tribe (MIT II, 441); Trkm. 20th c. **Emin** [Эмин] (TrkmRS 787). ❖ Amin (Ar.) 'trustworthy, honest, faithful' (Ahmed), cf. also Uyg., Kuman, Chag., Turk., Kar. *ämin* 'sicher, zuverlässig, sich verlassend' (Radl. I, 954), Trkm. *emin* 'доверенное лицо' (TrkmRS) (<Ar.). See also **MAΓLİYAR-AMİN, MUXAMMET-EMİN.**

EMİNE Kkalp. 20th c. **Ämiyna / Ämïna** [Әмийна], fem. (KkRS 777); Turk. 1519 **Emine-χatun** [Emine Hatun], fem. (Gökb., Ed. 233). ❖ Amina (Ar.) 'trustworthy, honest', fem. of Amin (Ahmed).

EMİNEK Turk. 15th c. **Eminek-beg?** [Εμηνάχυς], an Ottoman chieftain (Byz. Turc. II, 124); Crm.?/ Turk. 15th c. **Eminek-bey** [Эминекъ бей], a man under Mengli Girey (Smirnov, Krym. 267 etc.); Trkm. 1515 **Eminek-χan** [Эминек-хан] (MIT II, 324). ⇨ **EMİN** + suff. *-ek*.

EMİNLİK Turk. 1540 **Eminlik-kethudā**, chief of the Begdili cemâat (Demirtaş 52). ⇨ **?** + suff. *-lik*.

EMİR Tat. 20th c. **Amir-χan** [Hüssein Amirchan, F. Amirchan] (Mende 38, 178); Turk. 16th c. **Emir** [Εμήρ], nephew of Sultan Selim I (1512-1520) (Byz. Turc. II, 124); Khorezm. 14th c. **Emir-aγa-χatun** [امير اغا / Emir-Aghâ-Khâtoun], wife of Toγluq-temür (1348-1363) khan of Kashgar (Abulg./Desm. 169); Turk. 1343 **Emir-beg** [Αμηρπεκις], a man identical with Omur-bäg (Ibid.) (Byz. Turc. II, 66); Trkm. 1510 **Emir-bek** [Эмир-бек Мосульский] (MIT II, 50, 51, 56); Turk. 20th c. **Emir-χan** [Emirhan] (Önder, Göle); Trkm.? 1814 **Emir-χan** [Эмир-хан], from the Qajar clan (MIT II, 214, 216); Turk. 1453 **Emir-šah** [Emirşah Çelebi] (Gökb., Ed. 325). ❖ Emïr, Amïr / Āmir (Ar.); cf. Kzk., Turk., etc. *ămir* 'das Befehlen; die Macht, der Wille' (Radl. I, 956).

EMİREK Oghuz 1039 **Emirek** [Эмирек Кутли] (MIT I, 280); Selj.? 1146/47, 1160 **Emirek** [اميرك الجاندار / Amîrec], chief of the army in the service of Zengi (Ibn al-Athīr, Atab.: RHCHor II/2, 152, Ibn al-Athīr/Tornb. XI, 167); Bashk. 1709 **Mräk** [Мряк], a mulla (MIB I, 264); Bashk. 1715 **Mräk** [Мряк Султуков] (MIB III, 79, 124, 222); Bashk. 1715 **Mräk** [Мряк Урметев] (MIB III, 415); Bashk. 1724 **Mräk** [Мряк-мулла (Мряс-мулла) Султуков] (MIB III, 222); Bashk. 1748 **Mräk** [Тогучай Мряков] (MIB III, 452); Bashk. 1749 **Mräk** [Тогусяй Мряков] (MIB III, 468). ❖ 'Little Emir'. ⇨ **EMİR** + suff. *-ek* (<P. dim.)? See also **QARA-MİREK.**

EMİRZA Turk. 15th c. **Emirza?** [Εμηρζές], son of Ogurlu Mohammed from the family of Akkoyunlu (Byz. Turc. II, 124). ❖ 'Prince' cf. P.-Trk. *mirza* 'Prinz' (Byz. Turc. II, 124). ⇨ **MİRZA.**

EMLAK Oghuz/Trkm. 13th c. **Emlak** [املاق / Эмлак], Türk's son, Yafes' grand-son (Abulg./Kon. 135).

EMMET Bashk. 1653 **Emmet** [Эмметь] (Vel.-Zern.,

Bašk. 44); Bashk. 1734 **Emmet** [Эммѣтъ Байкеевъ], a tarχan (Vel.-Zern., Bašk. 11). ✧ Himmat / Himmet (Ar.) 'ambition, endeaviour, resolution' (Ahmed)?

EMO Kzk. 19th c. **Emo-bay?** [Емобай] (AOO 46); Kzk. 19th c. **Emo-bay?** [Эмобай] (SOK 28).

EMREN see **AMRAN**

EMREN see **İMRÄN**

EMÜKE Kzk. 19th c. **Emüke?** [Емуке] (SODž. 6).

EN Uyg. 12th c.-14th c. **En-ïnanč-tutuq** [en ïnanč tutuq] (DTS). ✧ 'Low, short?, humble' cf. Karakh. *en* 'низ, спуск; низкий' (DTS).

EN-DOS? Tat. 1606 **En-dos?** / **Yen-dos?** [Ендос] (Miller, Ist. Sib. II, 193, 218). ⇨ **EN?** + **DOST.**

ENČ-SÄKÄ see **İNČ-SEKÄ**

ENDER Oghuz/Trkm. 13th c. **Ender** [اندر / Эндер] (Abulg./Kon. 1170). ✧ 'Very little, rare' (Erol II) (<Ar.).

ENDİ Kzk. 19th c. **Endi-bay** [Ендыбай] (SODž. 8). ✧ 'Broad, wide' cf. Kzk. *endi* 'широкий' (KzRS).

ENE Trkm. 20th c. **Äne** [Äne], fem. (Zaj. 1971, 334); Trkm. **Ene** [Эне], fem. (Sopieva: OSA 182); Trkm. 20th c. **Ene** [Эне] (TrkmRS 789); Trkm. 20th c. **Ene-Jan** [Энежан], fem. (Sopieva: OSA 182). ✧ 'Grand-mother on father's line; Mother' (Sopieva: OSA 182, Zaj. 1971), cf. Trkm. *ene* 'бабушка, мать; матка; матушка; мамаша' (TrkmRS), Alt.(Tel., Leb.), Shor *änä* 'die Mutter' (Radl. I, 729), also Uyg., Karakh. *ana* 'мать' (DTS). Used as a secondary component of female names when addressing politely.

ENEKEY Hak. 19th-20th c. **Enekey** [Энекей], fem. (HRS 356, Butanaev). ✧ 'Dear little mother'. ⇨ **ENE** + dim. suff. -*key.*

ENEL-BUJA Turk. **Enel-buJa-oγlu**, a Zeybek (Kúnos 1891, 118).

ENESTEY Hak. 19th-20th c. **Enestey** [Энестей] (HRS 352). ✧ 'Grand-mother-like'? cf. Alt.(Tel.) *änäš* 'die Grossmutter' (Radl. I, 733) + suff. -*tey.*

ENEŠ Trkm. **Eneš** [Энеш], fem. (Sopieva: OSA 182). ✧ 'Grand-mother on mother's line' (Sopieva: OSA 182).

ENETÄČ Trkm. **Enetäč** [Энетäч], fem. (Sopieva: OSA 182). ✧ 'Grand-mother on mother's line' (Sopieva: OSA 182).

ENİČÜK Uyg. 12th c.-14th c. **Eničük** (Radl., USp. 244, DTS). ✧ 'Little younger brother' cf. Türk *ini* 'младший брат' (DTS) + dim. suff. -*čük.*

ENKEŠ Oghuz/Trkm. 13th c. **Enkeš** [انكش / Энкеш], a man from the İl of Salor (Abulg./Kon. 1250, 1255); Oghuz/Trkm. 13th c. **Enkeš** [انكش / Энкеш], kethudā of Salor-Qazan-alp (Abulg./Kon. 710); Oghuz/Trkm. 13th c. **Enkeš** [انكش / Энкеш], Otqan's father (Abulg./Kon. 665); Oghuz/Trkm. 13th c. **Enkeš** [انكش / Энкеш] (Abulg./Kon. 1170); Oghuz/Trkm. 13th c. **Enkeš-χoJa** [انكش / Энкеш-ходжа] (Abulg./Kon.

725). ⇨ **?** + suff. -*š.*

ENSE see **EÑSE**

ENÜS Kzk. 19th c. **Enüs-bay?** [Енусбай] (SOK 212).

ENŻEY Chuv. **Enžey**, fem. (Németh, HMK 134). ✧ 'Pearl'. ⇨ **İNJİ.** See also **MERWERT.**

ENŻİ see **İNJİ**

EÑGÜREK Mo.? 13th c. **Eñgürek-boyïn** / **Eñgürek-noyïn?** [انكورك بوين / Engürek], emir, officer of Bayju (Aqsarāyī 38, 39, Aqsar./İş. 44).

EÑSÄGÄY Kzk. **Eñsägäy** [Еңсäгäи] (Proben III, 68 /89/). ⇨ **EÑSE** + suff. -*gäy?*

EÑSE Kzk. 19th c. **Eñse-bay** [Еңгсебай] (SOV 154). ✧ 'Nape' cf. Turk. *änsä*, Kzk. *eñsä* 'der Nacken' (Radl. I, 718, 748).

EÑÜRÜN Uyg. 12th c. - 14th c. **Äñürün-ilči** [Ängürün İlči / eñürün elči] (Radl., USp. 56, EUTS, DTS).

EP-KELDİ Uzb. 20th c. **Ep-keldi** [Эпкелди] (Begmatov 1984, 203). ✧ 'Born in time' cf. Uzb. *epli* 'умелый, ловкий; уместный, подходящий' (UzbRS). ⇨ **KELDİ.**

EPČEY Hak. 19th-20th c. **Epčey** [Эпчей] (HRS 352). ✧ 'Little woman, housewife' cf. Uyg., Alt. *äpči* 'eine Verheirathete Frau, Frau, eine Wirthin, Hausfrau' (Radl. I, 923) + dim. suff. -*y.*

EPTELMAN Chuv. 18th-19th c. **Eptelman** [Эптельманъ] (Magn. 95).

ER Oghuz 1039 **Ar-tegin** [Тегин-Арук (Артегин)], a χājib (janitor?) of the court (MIT I, 278, 279, 286, 287, 295); Turk. 16th c. **Er** [ار] (Ongan, Ank. II, 872); Bulg. 9th c. **Er-atay?** [Ηρατανς], a Bulghar nobleman (Byz. Turc. 132); **Er-čor** [ارجور التركى] (Iyās I, 36); Kzk. 19th c. **Er-Jan** [Ерджан] (SOK 4); Kzk. 19th c. **Er-Jan** [Ерджан] (AOO 14); Kkalp. 20th c. **Er-Jan** [Эрджан] (Bask., Kkalp. 402); Kzk. 19th c. **Er-Jigit** [Ерджигитъ] (SOK 64); Turk. 1583 **Er-qulu** [ارقولى / Erkulu] (Ongan, Ank. I, 156); Crm. 1720 **Er-murza** [Эръ-мурза] (Smirnov, Krym. 325); Kzk. 1822 **Er-murza** [Еръмузаевъ] (TOUAK XXIV, 118); Nog. 1651 **Er-murza** [Эрь мурза Ишъ-мурзинъ] (AI IV, 161); Kkalp. 20th c. **Er-žan** [Ержан] (KkRS 773); Chuv. 18th-19th c. **İr-bay** [Ирбай] (Magn. 45); Chuv. 18th-19th c. **İr-bey** [Ирбей] (Magn. 45); 18th c. - 19th c. **İr-jan** [ايرجان / Ирджанъ], a person in a song about Kenesary (ZOOIRGO III, 373); Kzk. 19th c. **İr-jan** [Ирджанъ Моллабаевъ] (Grod., Pril. 92); Kzk. 19th c. **İr-jan** [Сатубалды Ирджановъ] (Grod., Pril. 185); Kzk. 19th c. **İr-jan** [Ирджанъ], a Kazak biy (Lomakin 35); **İr-qan** [Ir-khan] (Németh, HMK 135 /after Gombocz/); Kzk. 1845 **İr-žan** [Иржанъ Саржановъ] (Konšin, Mat. V, 62). ✧ 'Man; brave heroic man' cf. Uyg., Kuman, Chag., Alt., Crm., Shor, Kar., Turk., etc. *är* 'der Mann, ein starker Mann, ein Held, der Ehemann' (Radl. I, 751), Hak., Kirg., Kzk. *er* 'id.'

(Radl. I, 753), Tat. *ir* 'der Mann, Ehemann, der Held, ein tapferer Mann' (Radl. I, 1456), Chuv. *ar* 'мужчина; муж, супруг' (ČRS/Skvor.). See also **AГAČ-ERİ, QUM-ER, ÖZ-ER.**

ER-ALİ Kzk. 1734, 1761 **Er-ali** [Erali], a Kazak Sultan (Levchin 155, 242, 280); Kzk. 1768/69 **Er-ali-χan** [Эр Али-хан] (MIT II, 339, 340, 342); Kzk. 1791-1794 **Er-ali-χan** [Er-Ali Chan], khan of the Little Horde (Kiši Žüz) (Radl., Aus Sib. I, 98); Kzk. 19th c. **Er-alï** [Ералы] (SOV 136); Kkalp. 20th c. **Er-alï** [Ералы] (KkRS 773); Kzk. 1820 **İr-ali** [Ирали Букеевъ], a Kazak sultan (from the Sergamskij clan of the Great Horde) (Sib.Vest. IX, 101). ✧ 'Heroic Ali; Ali the hero'. ⇨ **ER + ALİ.**

ER-ALİ-DURDÏ Trkm. 1803 **Är-ali-durdï** [Аралидорди Мурадовъ] (PSZRI XXVII, 542); Trkm. 19th c. **İr-ali-durdï** [Ирали Дорди Мурадовъ] (PSZRI XXVII, pril. 20). ⇨ **ER-ALİ + TURDÏ.**

ER-ALÏ see **ER-ALİ**

ER-AMET Crm. **Er-amet** [Äр Амäт] (Proben VII, 161). ⇨ **ER + AXMET.**

ER-AÑQAS-TÖŠÄK see **AÑQAS-TÖŠÄK**

ER-AT Bashk. 1714 **Er-at** [Азекей Ератов] (MIB III, 109); Bashk. 1664 **Er-at-qul** [Ераткул] (MIB I, 192); Bashk. 1745 **Er-at-qul** [Ераткул Тойчин] (MIB III, 432); Bashk.? 18th c. **Er-at-qul** [Ераткуловъ], a chief (staršina) (Nepljuev 141). ✧ 'Man / Men' cf. Bashk. *ir-at* 'мужчины' (BRS), *ir-at* 'мужчина' (BRS/Uraksin).

ER-BAČ Yürük 1543 **Er-bač** [Erbaç] (Gökb., Rum. 180). ⇨ **ER + BAČ.**

ER-BEGUS Nog.? **Er-begus?** [Ер-бегус] (Žirm., Epos 395). ⇨ **ER.**

ER-BEKEY Kzk. 19th c. **Er-bekey** [Ербакей] (SODž. 10). ⇨ **ER + BEK + suff. -ey.**

ER-BOL Kzk. **Er-bol** [Ербол], a character from the epic „Put' Abaja" by M. O. Auezov (Espaeva 1984, 231); Uzb. 20th c. **Er-bol** [Эрбӱл] (Begmatov 1984, 201). ✧ 'Be/become a hero! Be/become a brave man/soldier!'. ⇨ **ER + BOL.**

ER-BOLSUN Kzk. 19th c. **Er-bosun** [Эрьбосунъ] (SOK 44). ✧ 'Let him become a brave heroic man'. ⇨ **ER + BOLSÏN. See also ER-BOL.**

ER-BÖRİ Uyg. 8th c.-9th c. **Er-böri** (DTS). ✧ 'Man-wolf' (Blagova 1997, 706), 'Hero-Wolf'. ⇨ **ER + BÖRİ.**

ER-BUDAQ Turk. 1583 **Er-budaq** [اربداق] (Ongan, Ank. I, 156). ⇨ **ER + BUTAQ.**

ER-BUQA Uyg. 12th c.-14th c. **Er-buqa** (Radl., USp. 24-5); Uyg. 12th c.-14th c. **Er-buqa** [Ar(a/y) Buqa] (Radl., USp. 16-18, DTS); Khorezm.? 13th c. **Er-buqa** [اربو قا], emir of Alāaddin Muhammad II (1200-1220), the Khorezmshah (Juwaynī I, 97); Khorezm. 1220 **Er-**

buqa-pehlevan [Эрбука-пехлеван], an emir (MIT I, 486). ✧ 'Man-bull' (Blagova 1997, 706). ⇨ **ER + BUQA.**

ER-BULAT Chuv. 18th-19th c. **Ar-bulat** [Арбулатъ] (Magn. 29); Chuv. 18th-19th c. **Er-bulat** [Ербулатъ] (Magn. 39); Chuv. 18th-19th c. **İr-bulat** [Ирбулатъ] (Magn. 45); Kzk. 19th c. **İr-bulat** [Ирбулатъ] (Grod., Pril. 150). ✧ 'Man/hero-steel'. ⇨ **ER + BULAT.**

ER-BUTÏ-BÜK-TOГDÏ see **BOTÏ-BÖK-TAQDÏ**

ER-ĴAN see **ER**

ER-DAW Kzk. 19th c. **Er-daw** [Ердау] (SOK 288). ⇨ **ER + DAW.**

ER-DOГAN see **ER-TOГAN**

ER-DOГDÏ see **ER-TOГDÏ**

ER-DOГDU see **ER-TOГDÏ**

ER-ГALİY Kkalp. 20th c. **Er-γaliy** [Ерғалий] (KkRS 773). ✧ 'Hero-Ali'. ⇨ **ER + ALİ.**

ER-YAÑГÏ-KENT see **İRQÏL**

ER-KÖGİS Nog.?, Kzk.? **Er-kögis / Er-qoγïs?** [Ер-Когис] (Žirm., Epos 395). ✧ 'Hero-Kögis'. ⇨ **ER.**

ER-KÖKŠÖ Nog.? **Erke-kökšö** [Эр-кёкшё] (Žirm., Epos 390). ✧ 'Hero-Beautiful, Hero-Good-looking' (Erol II). ⇨ **ER + KÖKČE.**

ER-KÖŠÜK see **KÖŠEK**

ER-QAL Bashk. 1708 **Er-qal** [Чагыр Ергалов] (MIB I, 249). ⇨ **ER + QAL I. / QAL II. ?** See also **EREN-QAL.**

ER-QOSAY Nog.?, Kzk.? **Er-qosay** [Эр-Косай] (Žirm., Epos 390); Kzk. 19th c. **İr-qosay** [Иръ-Косай] (Potanin, Pred. 79). ⇨ **ER + QOŠAY.**

ER-QULA-TAY Alt. 19th c. **Er-qula-tay** [Эр-Кулатай] (Verb., In. 142, 145, 146, 152, 153). ⇨ **ER + QULA-TAY.**

ER-QUŠ Selj. 12th c. **Er-quš** [ارقش بوزهجی] (Muh. Ibrahim 30, 31). ⇨ **ER + QUŠ I.**

ER-MAMBET Kzk. 19th c. **Er-mambet** [Эрмамбетъ] (Lomakin 41). ⇨ **ER + MAMBET. See also YÄR-MÖXÄMMÄT.**

ER-MOLLA Tat.(Sib.) 1620 **Er-mola** [Ермолин Алияр] (Miller, Ist. Sib. II, 251, 254); Tat.(Sib.) 1630 **Er-mola** [Ермолин], Russian family name in the early 17th c. (Miller, Ist. Sib. II, 268, 362). ⇨ **ER + MOLLA.**

ER-MONČUQ Uzb. 1722 **Er-mončuq** [Ермончукъ Алимовъ] (Veselovskij, Unk. 170). ⇨ **ER + MUNČUQ.**

ER-NAZAR Trkm.? 1838 **Er-nazar** [Эр Назар-инак] (MIT II, 472, 488, 489); Kzk. 18th c. - 19th c. **Er-nazar** [Ерназар] (Tynysp. 73); Kkalp. 20th c. **Er-nazar** [Ерназар] (KkRS 773); Uzb. 1852/53 **Er-nazar** [Эр Назар], from the Qoñrat tribe (MIT II, 533, 555, 572). ⇨ **ER + NAZAR.**

ER-SANČMÏŠ Uyg. 12th c. - 14th c. **Er-sančmïš**

(Radl., USp. 128, DTS). ✧ 'Man-defeated' (Blagova 1997, 708), 'Hero-defeated/stabbed' cf. Karakh. *sanč*-'колоть, вонзать; побеждать' (DTS). ⇨ **ER + SANČMĪŠ.**

ER-SARÏ   Kzk. 19th c. **Ar-sarï** [Арсары] (SOK 30); Oɣhuz/Trkm. 13th c. **Ar-sarï-bay** [ارسارى / Арсари-бай], a person from the Salor tribe (Abulg./Kon. 1320, 1330-1340, 1370, 1420); Oghuz/Trkm. 13th c. **Ar-sarï-bay** [ارسارى بى / Арсари-бай], Qul-χaji's son (Abulg./Kon. 1245); Kzk. 19th c. **Er-sari** [Ерсары] (SOK 108); Trkm. 1816 **Er-sarï-χoja** [Эрсари-ходжа] (MIT II, 389); Tuv. 19th c. **Er-saru** [Ep-Capy], in a tale (Potanin IV, 341-48). ✧ 'Er-sarï (a Trkm. clan)' cf. *Ersarı, Erseri* (ToganBTT 73, 75, 234, 616). ⇨ **ER + SARĪ.**

ER-TOɣAN   Turk. 20th c. **Er-doɣan** [Erdoğan], a village in the adninistrative province of Konya, Turkey (TMİB 570); Yürük 1543 **Er-doɣan** [Erdoğan] (Gökb., Rum. 214); Selj. 1241 **Er-toɣan** [ار تغا ن الاتا بك], in an inscription from Denizli, Turkey (Lavdikya 54?); Tat. 1554 **Er-tuɣan** [Ертуганъ], Tsar Jemgurčejev's daughter (PSRL XIII, 243); Tat. 18th-19th c. **İr-tuɣan** [Иртуганъ] (Magn. 46); Bashk. 1706 **İr-tuɣan** [Иртуган Янтуганов] (MIB III, 27); Bashk. 1728 **İr-tu**ɣ**an** [Иртуган Куняков] (MIB I, 127); Bashk. 1780 **İr-tuɣan** [Рахмангул Иртуганов] (MIB V, 109); Bashk. 1798 **İr-tuɣan** [Иртугановъ] (PSZRI XXV, 195). ⇨ **ER + TOɣAN.**

ER-TOɣDÏ   Chag. / Trkm.? 16th c. **Er-doɣdï-χalife** [اوردوغدى حلبنه / اردوغدى / Urdughedi Chalîfah Tekelü], from the Tekelü tribe, the successor of Tahmasp I (1513-1576), conspired against Ismaïl Šāh (Iskender Munšī - Erdmann: ZDMG XIV, 721); Turk. 16:h c. **Er-doɣdu** (Ongan, Ank. II, 397, 1739); Turk. 1609 **Er-doɣdu** [Erdoğdu] (Gökb., Ed. 61); Yürük 1543 **Er-doɣdu** (Gökb., Rum. 181); Turk. 1565 **Er-toɣdï** [Ertogdi], a "spahi" from Szendrő, Hungary (Velics-Kamm. II, 571); Turk. 1583 **Er-toɣdu** [Ertogdi], a "spahi" from the "nahiye" of Heves, Hungary (Velics-Kamm. II, 737). ✧ 'A hero (brave man) was born'. ⇨ **ER + TUɣDÏ.**

ER-TOɣMÏŠ   Uyg. 8th c. **Er-toɣmïš** (DTS). ✧ I. 'A hero has been born; he was born to be a hero'; II. 'Man/husband-relative' (Blagova 1997, 716). ⇨ **ER + TOɣMÏŠ.**

ER-TOɣRUL   Selj. **Er-toɣrïl** [ارطوغـرل] (Ibn Bībī III, 213); Turk. **Er-toɣrïl** [ارطغـرل غـارى / ارطوكـرل], Orχan's father (Āšikp. 5-8, 16, 20, 132); Selj. 13th c. **Er-toɣrul** [Ερτογρούλης], forefather and founder of the Ottoman dynasty (Byz. Turc. 125-126); Turk. 14th c. **Er-toɣrul / Er-toɣrïl** [ارطغـرل / Ερτογρούλης], Sultan Bayezid's son (Āšikp. 59, 66, 67, Byz. Turc. 125-126); Turk. 1454 **Er-tuɣrul-bey** [Ertuğrul] (Gökb.,

Ed. 162); *TN:* Turk. 20th c. **Er-tuɣrul-köy** [Ertuğrulköy], villages in the provinces of Bursa, Eskişehir, Turkey (TMİB 213).

ER-TOQSÏN   Hak.(Sag.) 19th-20th c. **Er-toqsïn** [Ер Токсын / Эръ-Токсынъ] (Proben IX, 295-97, ZIRGOÊtn.XXXIV, 274); Hak.(Sag.) 19th-20th c. **İr-taqsïn** [Иртаксынъ], a folklore hero (Kostrov 238). ✧ 'Hero-prince'. ⇨ **ER + TOQSÏN.**

ER-TOQUŠ   Selj. **Er-toquš / Er-toqus** [ار تـقش / روتـقس] (Aqsarayī 32, Aqsar. 41). ⇨ **ER + TOQÏŠ.**

ER-TOÑA   Uyg. 12th c. - 14th c. **Er-toña** (DTS). ✧ 'Man/Hero(ic)-Leopard; Man-Hero'. ⇨ **ER + TOÑA.**

ER-TUɣRUL see ER-TOɣRUL

ER-TÜSTÜK   Kzk. 19th c. **Er-tüstük** [Еръ Тюстюкъ] (Potanin, Pred. 85). ✧ I. 'Hero-breast'?; II. 'Hero-noon'? cf. Kzk. *tüstük* 'eine halbe Tagereise; was sich auf den Mittag (Süden) bezieht' (Radl. III, 1580). ⇨ **ER + TÖŠTÜK.**

ER-VERDİ   Turk. 1583 **Er-verdi** [ار ويـردى] (Ongan, Ank. I, 156). ✧ 'Hero-given; a hero gave him'. ⇨ **ER + BERDİ.**

ERDÄM   Maml.? **Erdäm / Ärdäm** [Ärdäm] (Tarǰ/Houtsma 29); Pecheneg **Erdem?** [Ηρτήμ] (Németh: MNy. 38 (1942), p. 5). ✧ 'Nobility, glory; benefactor' cf. Uyg., Karakh. *erdäm* 'достоинство, доблесть, добродетель; доблестный' (DTS), Maml. *ärdäm, ärdämli* 'vernünftig' (Tarǰ/Houtsma). See also **ALÏP-ERDÄM, İL-ÄRDÄM, ŠİÑɣUR-ÄRDÄM.**

ERDEY   Bashk. 1735 **Erdey / Yerdey?** [Урганакъ Ердеевъ], a tarχan (Vel.-Zern., Bašk. 18). ⇨ **ER? +** suff. -*dey.*

ERDEMEN   Chuv. 18th-19th c. **Erdemen** [Эрдеменъ] (Magn. 95). ⇨ **? +** suff. -*men.*

ERDES see ERDEŠ

ERDEŠ   Kzk. 19th c. **Erdes-pay** [Ердеспай] (SOV 44); Kzk. **Erdeš** [Ердешъ], in a Kazak animal fable (Pojarkov 13); Kzk. 19th c. **İrdaš / İrdäš** [Ирдашъ Ирназаровъ] (SKSO VIII, 232). ✧ 'Fellow man (hero)'? ⇨ **ER +** suff. -*daš (-des / -däš / -deš).*

ERDÜK   Turk. **Erdük-sultan** [Erdük Sultan], İskender Mirza's daughter (Uzunçarş., Anad. 62). ✧ 'We got it'? cf. Turk. *är-* 'erreichen, erlangen' (Radl. I, 755), cf. also PNs *Erdim, Erdin* (Erol II).

ERÄM-QARA   Uyg. 12th c. - 14th c. **Eräm-qara** [eräm qara] (DTS); Uyg. 12th c.-14th c. **Erem-qara / Äräm-qara** [Aräm Qara] (Radl., USp. 142). ✧ 'Big/strong-Black'. ⇨ **EREM + QARA.**

ERÄN-ULUɣ   Türk 7th-9th c. **Ärän-uluɣ** [Ärän Uluɣ] (ETY III, 104); Türk 7th c.-9th c. **Erän-uluɣ** (DTS). ✧ 'Man/warrior-Great' (Blagova 1997, 714) cf. also Németh, HMK 135. ⇨ **EREN + ULUɣ.**

ERĀS   Hak.(Sag.) 19th-20th c. **Erās** [Epääc] (Proben IX, 469). ✧ 'Torture, suffering'? cf. Hak.(Tel.) *erā* 'die

Mühe, Qual' (Radl. I, 755) + suff. *-s*? See also **ERES**.

EREJEB   Trkm. 19th c. **Erejep** [Эреджепъ Мурзаевъ] (Ščeglov I, 350); Kzk. 19th c. **Erežeb** [Ерсжебъ] (AOP 62). ✧ Redjeb (Ar.).

EREKE   Kkalp. 20th c. **Ereke** [Ереке] (KkRS 773). ⇨ **ER**? + comp. *eke*?

ERELDEY   Alt. 19th c. **Ereldey** [Ерельдей] (Potanin IV, 218); Alt. 19th-20th c. **Ereldey** [Ерелдей] (OjrRS 210).

ERELEÑGDÜ-ÖLÖGÖÑ   Alt. **Ereleñgdü-ölögöñ-baγay** [Ереленгдÿ-Öлöгöнъ-багай] (Nikiforov 106).

EREM   Uyg. **Äräm** [Äräm] (EUTS); Chuv. 18th-19th c. **Erem** [Эремъ] (Magn. 95). ✧ 'Big, strong (child)' cf. Tat.(Mish.) *äräm* (< Ar. χaram?) 'zu gut, zu schade, die Vergeudung' (Radl. I, 759), Alt.(Tel.) *äräm* (<Mo.) 'gelt; ein schnellwachsendes Kalb oder Füllen' *äräm bala* 'ein starkes, grosses Kind' (Radl. I, 760). See also **ÄRÄM-QARA, KÖKÜZ-ERÄM; BÜYÜK, ČOÑ, EVREN, YOΓAN, KÄNDÄL, MÄÑKÄ**.

EREMBET   Bashk. 1798 **Erembet** [Ерембетъ] (PSZRI XXV, 195). ⇨ **ER / EREM**? + suff. *-embet / -bet*? See also **ERİMBET**.

EREN   Uyg. **Ärän** [Ärän] (EUTS). ✧ 'Brave man; hero; gentleman' cf. Uyg., Chag., Turk., Kar. *ärän* 'ein tüchtiger Mann, ein Mann von guter Bildung, ein tapferer Mann, ein Gentleman' (Radl. I, 757); Kzk., Kirg. *erän* 'ein Jüngling, kräftiger, tapferer Mann, Held' (Radl. I, 758). See also **ALP-EREN**.

EREN-QAL   Yürük **Eren-qal** [ارن قال], from the Yürüks of Kocacık, Turkey (Gökb., Rum. 103). ✧ 'Remain a brave man / hero / gentleman'? ⇨ **EREN + QAL I**. See also **ER-QAL**.

ERENÄČ   Kzk. 1684 **Erenäč** [Еренячко], a prince (DAI XI, 160, 162); Hak.(Kyz.) 1680 **Erenäč** [Еренячко] (Jarilov, Kyz. 5). ⇨ **EREN**? + suff. *-äč*?

EREÑ   Uzb. 1649 **Ereñ-χan** [Эренг-хан], from Khiva (MIT II, 330, 331, 357). ⇨ **EREN**?

ERES   Shor 19th-20th c. **Eres-tayčї** (Dyrenkova 192). ✧ 'Brave, bold' cf. Tuv. *eres* 'id.' (TuvRS).

EREŽİK   Kzk. 19th c. **Erežik** [Ережикъ] (SOK 254).

ERGÄŠ   Uzb. 20th c. **Ergäš** [Эргаш] (Begmatov 1984, 206); Uzb. 20th c. **Ergäš-bay** [Эргашбой] (Begmatov 1984, 206); Uzb. 20th c. **Ergäš-ĵân** [Эргашжон] (Begmatov 1984, 206); Uzb. 19th c. **İrgäš** [Иргашъ] (SKSO III, 178); Uzb. 19th c. **İrgäš** [Иргашъ Тутымъ Джауліевъ] (SKSO III, 160); Uzb. 19th c. **İrgäš** [Иргашъ Абдіевъ] (SKSO III, 154); Uzb. 19th c. **İrgäš** [Иргашъ Назаровъ] (SKSO III, 15); Uzb. 20th c. **İrgäš** [Irgach], a leader of the basmačïs (Castagné 81); Uzb. 19th c. **İrgäš-bay** [Иргашбай Каттабековъ] (SKSO III, 16); Uzb. 1945-47 **İrgäš-bây** [Иргашбой] (Erohina-Ramazanova: OSA 201). ✧ 'Follow (us)! Join (us)!' cf. Uzb. *ergäš-* 'следовать (чьему-л. примеру)' (UzbRS).

ERGÄŠ-ALİ   Uzb. 20th c. **Ergäš-ali** [Эргашали] (Begmatov 1984, 206). ⇨ **ERGÄŠ + ALİ**.

ERGE-BÜRGE   Kzk. / Kirg.? 19th c. **Erge-bürge** [Ерге-бурге] (Potanin IV, 390). ✧ 'Old - ?' cf. Tuv. *ärgä* 'alt (von Sachen)' (Radl. I, 784).

ERGENE   Khorezm. 14th c. **Ergene-χatun** [Эргене-хатунъ], Arïq-buqa's daughter, Qara Hülegü Khan's wife, the 4th ruler of the Čaγatay Ulus (Barth., Ulugb. 114). ✧ 'Mine, pit; hill, ridge, pass' (Erol II).

ERİ   Kzk. 19th c. **Eri-bay** [Ерибай] (SODž. 14, 146); Kzk. 19th c. **Eri-bay** [Ерыбай] (SOV 138); Kzk. 19th c. **Eri-bek** [Эрибекъ] (SODž. 86). ✧ 'Huge, very big'? cf. Tat.(Bar.) *äri* 'grosskörnig, grobkörnig' (Radl. I, 761), Tat. *ere* 'крупный, большой, высокомерный' (TatRS).

ERİK   Tat. 1706 **Erik** [Кансюер Ерыков] (MIB III, 24); Tat. 1706 **Erik** [Ерык] (MIB III, 24). ✧ 'Strong, powerful' cf. Kuman, Chag., Alt., Hak. *ärik* 'die Kraft; stark, eifrig, heftig', Kzk. *erik* 'die Gewalt, Kraft; der Wille, der freie Wille' (Radl. I, 762, 763).

ERİM   Bashk. 1709 **Erim** [Ерым Байсулеев] (MIB I, 264); Bashk. 1742 **Erim** [Ерым Бухамбет] (MIB I, 487). ✧ I. 'Vermuth' cf. Tat. *ärim* 'id.' (Radl. I, 773); II. 'Hope, wait' cf. Chag., NUyg.(Tar.), Turk. *ärim* 'die Hoffnung, die Erwartung' (Radl. I, 773); III. 'My man/hero'? ⇨ **ER**? + poss. suff. *-m*.

ERİM-BUΓA   Maml. 1325 **Erim-buγa** [سيف الدين ارم بغا] (Zetterst. 149, 184). ⇨ **ERİM + BUQA**.

ERİMBET   Bashk. 1740 **Erimbet** [Еримбет Боскунов] (MIB I, 425); Kkalp. 20th c. **Erimbet** [Еримбет] (KkRS 773). ⇨ **ER** + suff. *-imbet*. See also **EREMBET**.

ERİŠ   Bashk. 1770 **Eriš** [Садык Ерышев] (MIB IV/1, 346); Bashk. 1779 **Eriš** [Салих (Салиш) Ерышев] (MIB V, 102, 106, 131).

ERK-ARSLAN   Uyg. **Ärk Arslan** [Ärk Arslan] (EUTS); Uyg. 12th c. - 14th c. **Erk-arslan-sañun** [erk arslan saŋun] (DTS). ✧ 'Power/might-Lion' (Blagova 1997, 710). ⇨ **ERİK**? + **ARSLAN**.

ERKÄ-SARÏ   Kzk. **Erkä-sarï** [Erkä Sary / Еркä Сары] (Proben III, 258 /304/). ✧ 'Darling-black'. ⇨ **ERKE + SARÏ**.

ERKE   Kirg. **Erke** [Эрке], fem. (Jud.); Bashk. 1735, 1753 **İrkä** [Ирка Якшиев] (MIB III, 337, IV/1, 70); Kzk. 19th c. **İrkä** [Ирка] (Grod., Pril. 101); Kzk. 19th c. **İrkä-bay** [Иркабай] (SKSO VIII, 219); Kzk. 19th c. **İrkä-bay** [Иркабай Иматовъ] (SKSO VIII, 233); Kzk. 19th. **İrkä-bay** [Ирка-бай] (Nalivkin 10); Bashk. 1776 **İrkä-bek** [Иркабек Минглюгужин] (MIB V, 33, 34). ✧ 'Favourite, darling, pampered child' cf. Chag., Alt., NUyg.(Tar.) *ärkä* Kirg. *erke* 'id.' (Jud.), Kzk. *erke* 'id.' (KzRS), Tat. *irkä* 'изнеженный, балованный' (TatRS), Bashk. *irkä* 'изнеженный, избалованный ' (BaRS), Tat. *İrkä* (Sattarov). See also **DİKÄN-ÄRKE?, TAYÏN-İRKÄ.**

ERKE-MÖNDÜR Alt. **Erke-möndür** [Эрке Мöндÿръ] (Nikiforov 9). ⇨ **ERKE + MÖNDÜR.**

ERKE-ŠÜDÜN Alt.(Tel.) 19th c. **Erke-šüdün / Ärkä-šüdün** [Эрьке-Шудюнь / Äркä-Шÿдÿн] (Verb., In. 101, Radl. I, 777). ⇨ **ERKE.**

ERKEK Tat.(Sib.)? 1671 **Ergek** [Эргека], a clan was named after him („rod Ergeki") (AI IV, 473); Kzk. 19th c. **Erkek / Erkäk?** [Шамитъ Эркаковъ] (Grod., Pril. 190); Kzk. 19th c. **Erkek-bala** [Эркекбала] (SODž. 90). ✧ 'Man; Male (of an animal)' cf. Trk. *erkek* (Sev.), Kuman, Chag., Alt., Crm., Turk. *ärkäk* 'männliches Wesen, das Männchen (von Thieren)' (Radl. I, 777), cf. Uyg., Chul.(Küer.), Shor, Alt.(Leb.) *ärgäk* 'der Kater', Shor *ärgäk* 'männliches Wesen' (Radl. I, 784). Used also as a secondary component of male names.

ERKELEY Alt. 19th-20th c. **Erkeley** [Эркелей], fem. (OjrRS 214); Hak.(Sag.) 19th-20th c. **Erkeley** [Еркäläй], fem. (Katanov, Otč. 7). ✧ 'Gentle, tender(-hearted)' (OjrRS 211, 214).

ERKEMEY Alt. 19th-20th c. **Erkemey** [Эркемей] (OjrRS 211). ✧ 'Gentle, tender(-hearted)' (OjrRS 211, 214).

ERKEŠ Alt. 19th-20th c. **Erkeš** [Эркеш] (OjrRS 211). ✧ 'Gentle, tender(-hearted)'. ⇨ **ERKE + suff. -š.**

ERKETEN Alt. 19th-20th c. **Erketen** [Эркетен] (OjrRS 211).

ERKİ see **KÖL-ERKİ**

ERKİL Oghuz/Trkm. 13th c. **Erkil-χoJa** [ارقیل خواجه / Эркиль-ходжа] (Abulg./Kon. 470, 475, 485, 490, 540, 1230).

ERKİN Türk 721 **Ärkin** [Ärkin] (ETY I, 139); Trkm. 20th c. **Ärkin** [Årkin] (Zaj. 1971, 327); Trkm. 20th c. **Erkin** [Эркин] (TrkmRS 792); Kirg. **Erkin** [Эркин] (Jud. 623); Türk 8th c. **Erkin / Uluγ-erkin / İrkin** (Thomsen: ZDMG 78 (1924), 129, DTS (KT 6)); Uyg. **İrkän** [İrkän] (EUTS); Kzk. **İrkem-bek (<İrken-bek)** [Иркемъ-Бекъ] (Sb. Syr-D. VI, Galkin, Êtn. mat. 104); Tat. 20th c. **İrken-bay** [Иркенбай] (Sattarov); Tat. 20th c. **İrken-bek** [Иркенбəк] (Sattarov); Kzk. 19th c. **İrkim-bek (<İrkin-bek)** [Иркимбекъ Ахимбековъ] (Z'VOIRAO XI, 297, Sb. Syr-D. IV, otd. II, 92); Tat.(Sib.) **İrkin** [Иркин] (Andrievič, Ist. Sib. II, 260); Bashk. 1708 **İrkin** [Итемган Иркин] (MIB I, 216); Bashk. 1735 **İrkin** [Юмагулъ Иркинъ], a prince (Vel.-Zern., Bašk. 12); Bashk. 1758 **İrkin** [Байсал Иркин] (MIB IV/1, 164); Kzk. 1700 **İrkin** [Иркинъ], a prince (Andrievič, Ist. Sib. II, 182); Kzk. 19th c. **İrkin** [Омарбай Иркиновъ] (Grod., Pril. 120). ✧ 'Free(man), unbound, independent' cf. Kzk. *erkin* 'свободный' (KzRS), Trkm. *erkin* 'id.' (TrkmRS), Kirg. *erkin* 'id.' (Jud.), Tat. *irken* 'свободный, вольный; привольный' (TatRS), Tat. *irkin* 'breit,

geräumig; frei, ungebunden' (Radl. I, 1466), Tat.(Tüm.) *irgin* 'die Lust, der Gefallen, freier Wille' (Radl. I, 1468); II. A title in the Old Turkic, cf. Thomsen: ZDMG 78 (1924), 129, DTS. See also **KÖL-İRKİN.**

ERKUTEY Alt. 19th c. **Erkutey** [Еркутей и Беркутей] (Potanin, Pred. 181).

ERLEPES Kzk. 1817 **Erlepes** [Ерлепес] (MIK IV, 313, 319); Kkalp. 20th c. **Erlepes-qïzï** [Къалджан Ерлепес-къызы], patronym (Bask., Kkalp. 59).

ERLİ-ГАР see **ERLİ-QAP**

ERLİ-ГАŠ Tat. 1654 **Erli-γaš / Yerlï-qaš?** [Кудашъ Ерлыгашевъ] (AI IV, 236); Bashk. 1783 **Erli-γaš / Yerlï-qaš?** [Ерлыкаш (Ерлычат) Байдашев] (MIB V, 148, 291, 300).

ERLİ-QAP Bashk. 1760 **Erli-gäp? / Erlï-γap?** [Ерлыгап Юртбагышев] (MIB IV. 199); Bashk. 1777, 1788 **Erli-qap / Yerlï-qap?** [Ерлыкап (Ерлыкан) Калкашев] (MIB V, 52, 233); Bashk. 1778 **Erli-qap? / Yerlï-qap?** [Ерлыкап (Ерлычап) Кунакбаев] (MIB V, 69). ✧ 'Shy, bashful'.

ERMEK Kzk. **Ermek** [Ермек] (KzRS); Kzk. 1817 **Ermek** [ايرمك / Ермек] (MIK IV, 311); Kkalp. 20th c. **Ermek** [Ермек] (KkRS 773); Kirg. **Ermek** [Эрмек] (Jud. 680). ✧ 'Joy, pleasure, delight' cf. Kirg. *ermek* 'забава, развлечение, утеха' (Jud.), Kkalp. *ermek* 'id.' (KkRS).

ERMEN Kzk. 18th c. - 19th c. **Ermen** [Ермен] (Tynyšp. 69). ✧ 'Vermuth' cf. Kzk. *ermän* 'Wermuth' (Radl. I, 802).

ERMEN-ČEČEN Alt. **Ermen-čečen** [Ермен-Чеченъ], fem. (Nikiforov 2 etc.).

ERMET Uzb. 19th c. **Ermet** [Каршибай Ерметовъ] (SKSO III, 166). ⇨ **ER + suffixoid -met.**

ERTE Alt. 19th-20th c. **Erte** [Эрте], fem. (OjrRS 214). ✧ 'Early (girl)' (OjrRS 214).

ERTEY Alt. 19th-20th c. **Ertey** [Эртей], fem. (OjrRS 214). ✧ 'Early (girl)' (ORS 214). ⇨ **ERTE + suff. -y.**

ERTEN Tuv. 19th c. **Erten-er? / Erten-erge?** [Ертенъ-ерге], in a tale (Potanin IV, 387-91). ✧ '(Early) Morning' cf. Tuv., Tel., Alt. *ärtän* 'früh an Morgen, morgen, morgen früh' (Radl. I, 1792), Tuv. *erten* 'утро; утром; завтра' (TuvRS).

ERTENA Selj.? **Ertena / Ertana / Eretna?** (Uzunçarş., Anad. 1, 2, 5, 42, 49, 50, 51, 84, 85).

ERTENE Tuv. 19th c. **Ertene-mergen** [Ертене-мергенъ], in a tale (Potanin IV, 416). ✧ 'Pearl, treasure'? cf. Tuv. *ertine* 'id.' (TuvRS).

ERTİS see **İRTİŠ**

ERTİS Kzk. 19th c. **Ertis** [Ертисъ] (AOO 26).

ERÜ Kzk. 19th c. **Erü-bay** [Ерубай] (SOV 34, 106); Kzk. 19th c. **Erü-bay** [Ерубай] (AOAtb. 102); Kzk. 19th c. **Erü-bay** [Ерюбай] (SODž. 130). ✧ I. 'Quiet, restful' cf. Kzk. *erü* 'der Aufenthalt, die Ruhe, das Ausruhen' (Radl. I, 774); II. 'Strength' cf. Kuman (CC) *ärü* 'die Kraft' (Radl. I, 774), *erüv* 'rasch, energisch' (CC).

ERÜK Khorezm.? 13th c. **Erük-χatun** [اروك حا تون], at the time of Argun (1284-1291) and Mahmud Ghazan Khan (1295-1304) (Qazw. 545). ⇨ **ERİK?**

ERVÜZ see ERWÜZ

ERWÜZ Karakh. 11th c. **Erwüz / Ervüz / Erwüz / Arvuz** [Erwüz] (MK/Atalay 838, DTS).

ERZMEN Yürük 16th c. **Erzmen** [ارز من], from Kocacık, Turkey (Gökb., Rum. 102). ✦ 'Respected' cf. Turk. *erz* 'saygı' (DS) + suff. *-men*.

ES Kzk. 19th c. **Es** [Эсъ] (AOP 114); Kzk. 19th c. **Es** [Есь] (AOO 6); Kzk. 19th c. **Es** [Есь] (AOAtb. 118); Chuv. 18th-19th c. **Es-bay** [Есбай] (Magn. 40); Tat.(Lit.) 1552 **Es-eke** [Есеке] (Kn. Metriki Lit. 86); Kzk. 19th c. **Es-eke** [Есеке] (AOK 122); Kzk. 19th c. **Es-eke** [Есеке] (SOV 150); Kzk. 19th c. **Es-ekey** [Есекей] (AOAtb. 10); Kzk. 19th c. **Es-ekey** [Есекей] (SOK 24); Kzk. 18th c. - 19th c. **Es-χoǰa** [Есходжа] (Tynyšp. 66); Kzk. 19th c. **Es-qoža** [Ескожа] (SOV 52); Kirg. 1845 **Es-qoža / Es-qoǰa** [Джангарачъ Эскожинъ] (Konšin, Mat. V, 72); Kzk. 19th c. **Es-pay** [Эспай] (AOP 78); Kzk. 19th c. **Es-pay** [Еспай] (AOK 66); Kzk. 19th c. **Es-pay** [Еспай] (SODž. 52, 102); Kzk. 19th c. **Es-pay** [Еспай] (SOV 70, 150); Kzk. 19th c. **Es-pay** [Еспай] (SOK 72); Kzk. 19th c. **Es-žan** [Есчанъ] (SOK 140); Kzk. 19th c. **Es-žan** [Есчанъ] (SOV 60); Kzk. 19th c. **Es-žan** [Есчанъ-Джабагинъ] (AUK 699); Bashk. 1735 **İs** [Исев Рахмангулов], a tarχan (Vel.-Zern., Bašk. 15); Kzk. 19th c. **İs-bay** [Исбай] (SOK 222); Kzk. 19th c. **İs-ǰan** [Исджанъ] (Grod., Pril. 50); Tat. 1809 **İs-qan** [Исканъ Иманаевъ] (PSZRI XXX, 980, 981); Bashk. 1764 **İs-qan** [Искан Елдашев] (MIB IV/1, 277); Kzk. 19th c. **İs-qul** [Искулъ] (SKSO VIII, 222, 223); Kzk. 19th c. **İs-mirza** [Исмирза] (Grod., Pril. 179); Kzk. 19th c. **İs-pay** [Испай] (SODž. 138); Kzk. 19th c. **İs-žan** [Изжанъ] (SOV 64); Uzb. 1869 **İz-bey** [Избей] (Moskal'cev 40). ✦ I. 'Mind, sense, wit' cf. Kzk. *es* 'das Gedächtniss, der Sinn' (Radl. I, 870), Kzk. *es* 'aqïl, sana' (QTTS), Kkalp. *es* 'сознание, ум, память' (KkRS); II. 'Healthy, sound'; Shortened form of ESEN / ESÄN in compound names.

ES-ALİ Kzk. 19th c. **Es-alï** [Есалы] (SOK 202). ⇨ **ES / EŠ + ALİ.**

ES-BAZAR Kzk. 1819 **Es-bazar** [Ясбазар] (MIK IV, 323). ⇨ **ES / EŠ + BAZAR.**

ES-BER Kzk. 18th c. - 19th c. **Es-ber** [Есбер] (Tynyšp. 65, 67); Kzk. 19th c. **Es-per** [Есперъ] (SOK 72); Kzk. 19th c. **Es-per** [Есперъ] (SOV 86); Kzk. 19th c. **Es-per** [Есперъ] (SODž. 84, 154). ✦ 'Give wit/sense'? ⇨ **ES / EŠ + BER.**

ES-BERDİ Kzk. 18th c. - 19th c. **Es-berdi** [Есберды]

(Tynyšp. 67); Kzk. 19th c. **Esi-berdi** [Эсиберды] (Lomakin 40). ⇨ **ES / EŠ + BERDİ.**

ES-BERGEN Kzk. 19th c. **Es-bergen** [Есбергенъ] (SOV 18, 152); Kkalp. 20th c. **Es-bergen** [Есберген] (KkRS 773); Kzk. 1840 **Es-pergen** [Еспергенъ Садырбаевъ] (Konšin, Mat. V, 25); Kzk. 1845 **İs-pergen** [Испергенъ Садырбаевъ] (Konšin, Mat. V, 63). ⇨ **ES / EŠ + BERGEN.**

ES-BOLAY Kzk. 18th c. - 19th c. **Es-bolay** [Есболай] (Tynyšp. 71); Kzk. 19th c. **İs-bulay** [Арстамбай Исбулаевъ] (Grod., Pril. 49). ✦ 'He / she is becoming a mate/helper'. ⇨ **ES / EŠ + BOLAY.**

ES-BOLAN Kzk. 19th c. **Es-bolan** [Есболанъ] (SOK 140); Kzk. 19th c. **Es-polan** [Есполанъ] (SOK 140). ⇨ **ES / EŠ + BOLAN.**

ES-BOLAT see EŠ-BULAT

ES-BOSİN see EŠ-BOLSİN

ES-BULAT see EŠ-BULAT

ES-XAǰİ Bulg. 880 **Es-χaǰi** ['Εσχάτζης] (Byz. Turc. 126). ⇨ **ES / EŠ? + XAǰİ.**

ES-KELDİ Kzk. 18th c. - 19th c. **Es-keldi** [Ескельды] (Tynyšp. 65); Kzk. 19th c. **Es-keldi** [Ескельды] (SOK 84); Kzk. 19th c. **Es-keldi** [Эскельды] (SOV 80); Kzk. 19th c. **Es-keldi** [Ескельды] (SODž. 32, 132); Kzk. 19th c. **Es-keldi** [Ескельды] (SOV 80); Kzk. 19th c. **Es-keldi** [Ескельда] (SOV 62); Kzk. 18th c. - 19th c. **Es-keldi-bïy** [Ескельды-бий] (Tynyšp. 68). ⇨ **ES / EŠ? + KELDİ. See also EŠ-KELDİ?**

ES-QALİY Kkalp. 20th c. **Es-qaliy** [Есқалий] (KkRS 773). ⇨ **ES / EŠ + ALİ.**

ES-QARA see EŠ-QARA

ES-QUWAT Kzk. 20th c. **Es-quwat** [Ескуўат] (KkRS 773); Kkalp. 20th c. **Es-quwat** [Ескъуват] (Bask., Kkalp. 82). ⇨ **ES / EŠ + QUWAT.**

ES-PERGEN see ES-BERGEN

ES-POL see EŠ-BOL

ES-POLAN see ES-BOLAN

ES-POZAR Kzk. 19th c. **Es-pozar** [Еспозаръ] (SOV 134). ✦ 'He'll make somebody crazy'. ⇨ **ES + BOZAR.**

ES-TAY Kzk. 19th c. **Es-tay** [Естай] (AOAtb. 38); Kzk. 19th c. **Es-tay** [Естай] (AOO 46); Kkalp. 20th c. **İz-tay** [Изтай] (KkRS 774). ⇨ **ES / EŠ + TAY or suff. *-tay(1,2)*?**

ES-TEMİR Tat.(Lit.) 1552 **Es-temir** [Естемиръ] (Kn. Metriki Lit. 86). ⇨ **ES / EŠ + TEMİR.**

ES-TEMİZ Kzk. 19th c. **Es-temis** [Естемисъ] (SODž. 72). ⇨ **ES / EŠ + TEMİZ.**

ESČİ Kzk. 19th c. **Esči-bek** [Есчибекъ] (SODž. 10). ⇨ **ES + suff. *-či*.**

ESÄN Uyg. 13th-14th c. **Äsän**, fem. (Zieme, Mat. III, 273); Maml. 14th c. **Äsän** [اَسَن / Esen], fem. (Tarǰ/Houtsma 48, Tarǰ/Toparlı 43,); Maml. 14th c.

Äsän-bay / Esen-bay [اَسَنْبای / اسنبای / Esenbay]
(Tarj/Houtsma 48, Tarj/Toparlı 43, Sauvaget 35); Uyg.
13th-14th c. Äsän-čor (Zieme, Mat. II, 84); Maml. 14th
c. Äsän-qoĵa [اسنتجا] (Sauvaget 36); Uyg. 12th c. -
14th c. Esän [esän] (DTS); Uyg. 13th c. Esän-tegin
[esän tegin] (DTS); Kzk. 19th c. Esem-bay (<Esen-
bay) [Есембай] (AOO 66); Kzk. 19th c. Esem-bay
(<Esen-bay) [Есембай] (SODž. 12); Kzk. 19th c.
Esem-bay (<Esen-bay) [Есембай] (SOK 106); Kzk.
19th c. Esem-ĵan [Есемджанъ] (SOV 70); Kzk.
Esem-χan (<Esen-χan) [Есемханъ Бегембетевъ]
(Konšin, Pam. 4); Kuman 1106 Esen [Асень], a
"Polovets" prince (PSRL XXVIII, 29); Maml.? 1299
Esen [ایسن], an emir, executed as one of Sulamïš'
followers in 1299 (RaD/Jahn 123); Turk. 16th c. Esen
[Esen] (Ongan, Ank. II); Trkm. 20th c. Esen [Esen]
(Zaj. 1971, 327); Trkm. 20th c. Esen [Эсен] (TrkmRS
77); Kzk. 18th c. - 19th c. Esen [Есен] (Tynyšr. 67, 68,
70, 71, 73); Kkalp. 20th c. Esen [Есен] (KkRS 773);
Uyg. 12th c. - 14th c. Esen / Äsän (Radl., USp. 12-13,
56, 123); Uyg. 12th c. - 14th c. Esen / Äsän [Qusang
Äsän] (Radl., USp. 133-34); Chuv. 18th-19th c. Esen /
Äsen [Асенъ] (Magn. 30); Maml. 1398/99 Esen-bay
[اسنبای امير عشرة] (Ibn Taghrīb. VI, 26); Maml.
1403/04 Esen-bay [اسنبای التركما نی ا لجمالی] (Ibn
Taghrīb. VI, 125, 176); Maml. 1406/07 Esen-bay
[اسنبای], amīr-i aχur (Master of the Horse) (Ibn
Taghrīb. VI, 191, 287); Maml. 15th c. Esen-bay
[اسنبای] (Arabš. II, 38); Maml. 1452/53 Esen-bay
[اسنبای] (Iyās II, 40); Maml. 1456 Esen-bay [الظاهری]
[اسنبای ا لجما ل] (Iyās II, 55); Maml. 1480 Esen-bay
[اسنبای المبشر] (Iyās II, 192, 238-317); Maml. 1493/94
Esen-bay [اسنبای ابرهيم ا لاصم] (Iyās II, 280, 388);
Kzk. 18th c. - 19th c. Esen-bay [Есенбай] (Tynyšr.
65, 73); Kzk. 19th c. Esen-bay [Есенбай] (SOK 74);
Kzk. 19th c. Esen-bay [Есенбай] (SOV 18); Kzk. 19th
c. Esen-bay [Есенбай Даулетовъ], a writer of articles
(AUK 291); Kkalp. 20th c. Esen-bay [Есенбай]
(KkRS 773); Uzb.? 1816 Esen-bay-biy [Эсенбай-бий]
(MIT II, 391); Kzk. 19th c. Esen-ĵan [Эсензянъ], a
Kazak biy (Lomakin 42); Kzk. 19th c. Esen-ĵar
[Есенджаръ] (AOO 38); Uyg. 12th c. - 14th c. Esen-
tutuq / Äsän-tutuq (Radl., USp. 138, 205, 247); Tat.
1779 İsän[Салих Исянов] (MIB V, 83); Bashk. 1785
İsän-bay [Габит Исянбаев] (MIB V, 559); Kzk. 1880
İsän-bay [Исанбай] (Grod., Pril. 174); Bashk. 1831
İsän-γul [Исянгуловъ] (TOUAK XXIV, 199); Kzk.
19th c. İsän-qul [Исанкулъ Казаковъ] (SKSO VIII,
204); Kzk. 19th c. İsem-bay (<İsen-bay) [Исембай]
(Potanin II, 3); İsen [Исенъ] (Karta JAR XI); Chuv.
18th-19th c. İsen [Исень] (Magn. 46); Bashk. 1734
İsen [Исенъ Канаевъ], a tarχan (Vel.-Zern., Bašk.

11); Bashk. 1735 İsen [Исенъ Чоткаровъ], a tarχan
(Vel.-Zern., Bašk. 14); Bashk. 1795 İsen [Азангулъ
Исеневъ] (IOAIÊK (Dobavlenie) XXVIII, 590); Kzk.
1846 İsen [бий Атан Исенев] (MKOP 154); Kzk.
1860 İsen [Исень Даулетовъ] (ZIRGOGeogr. I, 273);
Kzk. 20th c. İsen [Исен Утеулиевъ] (TOOIK III,
182); Tat. 1686 İsen-bay [Исенбаевъ] (Kungursk. akty
120); Tat. 18th-19th c. İsen-bay [Исенбай] (Magn.
46); Bashk. 1772 İsen-bay [Исенбай] (MIB IV/1,
364); Kzk. 20th c. İsen-bay [Исеньбай] (SOK 174);
Kzk. 1847 İsen-bek [Калча Исенбековъ] (Konšin,
Mat. V, 104); Bashk. 1709 İsen-čora [Исенчора]
(MIB I, 271); Bashk. 1735 İsen-čura [Елимчи
Исенчуринъ], a tarχan (Vel.-Zern., Bašk. 23); Bashk.
1779 İsen-čura [Талбытак Исенчурин] (MIB V,
101); Bashk. 1780 İsen-čura [Исенчюра Карисев]
(MIB V, 113); Bashk. 1735 İsen-γul [Исенгулъ
Муайтмасовъ], a prince (Vel.-Zern., Bašk. 12); Bashk.
1779 İsen-γul [Бекчура Исенгулов (Исянгулов)]
(MIB V, 101, 102, 106, 132); Alt. 19th c. İsen-χan
[Исень-ханъ] (Potanin, Pred. 182); Bashk. 1776 İzäm-
bay (<İzän-bay) [Ракай (Аракай) Изямбаев] (MIB
V, 683); Chuv. 18th-19th c. İzän-bay [Изанбай]
(Magn. 41); Chuv. 18th-19th c. İzän-čura [Изанчура]
(Magn. 41); Kzk. 19th c. İzem-bay (<İzen-bay)
[Изембай] (SOV 90); Kzk. 19th c. İzem-bay (<İzen-
bay) [Изембай] (SOV 124); Chuv. 18th-19th c. İzen
[Изенъ] (Magn. 42); Chuv. 18th-19th c. İzen [Изень]
(Magn. 42); Chuv. 18th-19th c. İzen-bay [Изенбай]
(Magn. 42); Chuv. 18th-19th c. İzen-čura [Изенчура]
(Magn. 42); Chuv. 18th-19th c. İzen-murza
[Изенмурза] (Magn. 42); Kzk. 19th c. İzīm-bay
(<İsen-bay?) [Изымбай] (SOK 176); Chuv. 18th-19th
c. İzīn-bay [Изынбай] (Magn. 42); Kzk. 19th c. Sem-
bay (<Esen-bay) [Сембай] (AOP 42); Kzk. 19th c.
Sem-bay (<Esen-bay) [Сембай] (SOV 40, 86); Kzk.
19th c. Sem-bey (<Esen-bey) [Сембей] (SODž. 72);
Kzk. 19th c. Sem-bek (<Esen-bek) [Сембекь] (SOK
174). ❖ 'Healthy, sound, fit' cf. Chag., East.T., Turk.,
Kzk., Kirg., etc. esän, äsän 'gesund, wohl, in gutem
Zustande'; (Chag.) 'unverletzt, wahr, autentisch' (Radl.
I, 873). See also QUDUΓČÏ-ESÄN, QUSAÑ-ÄSÄN.

ESÄN-ALİ Bashk. 1735 Sen-ali (<Esän-ali) [Сеналий
Идзимясовъ], a tarχan (Vel.-Zern., Bašk. 20). ⇨
ESÄN + ALİ.

ESÄN-AMAN Kkalp. 20th c. Esen-aman [Есенаман]
(KkRS 773); Bashk. İsen-aman [Исенаман
Сейтяков] (MIB IV/2, 45). ❖ 'Hale and hearty'
(Kusimova). ⇨ ESÄN + AMAN. See also ČEK-
AMAN?

ESÄN-BAXTÏ Chuv. 18th-19th c. İsän-baχta
[Изанбахта] (Magn. 41); Chuv. 18th-19th c. İsän-
baχta [Изянбахта] (Magn. 42); 1582 Sen-baχta

ESÄN-BUQA

(<Esen-baχtï) [Сенбахта], a Siberian ruler, Maχmet's son (Sib. Let. 319). ⇨ ESÄN + BAQTÏ.

ESÄN-ВОГА see ESÄN-BUQA

ESÄN-BUQA   Äsän-buqa (Le Coq: Túrán 1918, 456, 457); Uyg. 12th c. - 14th c. Esän-buγa [Äsän Buγa] (Radl., USp. 117); Maml. 1309, 1328 Esän-buγa [اسنبغا / Asanboga, Acenbogha], mamlūk of Abulfidā (Abulfidā V, 226-27, Ibn al-athīr: RHCHor I, 186, 802); Maml. 1344/45 Esän-buγa [استبغا استادار الصحبه] (Iyās I, 182); Maml. 1347 Esän-buγa [استبغا المحمودى السلحدار] (Iyās I, 190, 239); Maml. 1361 Esän-buγa [استبغا بن بكتمر / Äsänbuga ibn Bektämür], nāʿib of Aleppo, died in 1375/76 (Iyās I, 210, Mayer 79); Maml. 1377/78 Esän-buγa [استبغا التلبكى] (Iyās I, 242-44); Maml. 1377/78 Esän-buγa [اسنبغا الرومى] (Iyās I, 239); Maml. 1377/78 Esän-buγa [استبغا النظامى] (Iyās I, 239); Maml. 1398/99 Esän-buγa [اسنبغا الظاهرى الز دكاش] (Ibn Taghrīb. VI, 45, 81); Maml. 1398/99 Esän-buγa [اسنبغا المسافرى] (Ibn Taghrīb. VI, 25); Maml. 1398/99 Esän-buγa [اسنبغا لمحمودى] (Ibn Taghrīb. VI, 16); Maml. 1400 Esän-buγa [اسنبغا المصارع] (Ibn Taghrīb. VI, 99, 108); Maml. 1447, 1450, 1452/53 Esän-buγa [ا لطيارى / اسنبغا] (Ibn Taghrīb. VI, 285, 684, VIII, 22, 53, 54, 58, Iyās II, 40, 77); Maml. 1448 Esän-buγa [اسنبغا] (Ibn Taghrīb. VIII, 30); Maml. 1461, 1463 Esän-buγa [اسنبغا الناصرى] (Ibn Taghrīb. VIII, 430, 463); Maml. 1467/68 Esän-buγa [اسنبغا صفرحجا المويدى] (Iyās II, 96); Trkm. 1352 Esän-buγa [استبغا التركما نى] (Iyās I, 197); Tat.? 1471/72 Esän-buγa [اسنبغا التترى اليشبكى] (Iyās II, 219); 1295 Esän-buqa [ا يسان بوقا] (RaD/Jahn 59); Uyg. 12th c. - 14th c. Esän-buqa (Radl., USp. 15-16, DTS); Chag. Esän-buqa [اسنبوقا], 12th Chagatay khan (Abulg./Desm. 158); Uzb. Esän-buqa [Эсень-Бука] (Barth., Ulugb. 89, 90); Turk. 20th c. Esen-boγa [Esenboğa], a village in the province of Ankara, Turkey (TMİB 78); Chag. 15th c. İsen-boγa / İsen-buγa?, a Sultan (1434-1462) in Mawarannahr (Jorga, Notes XIII, 284 /Mesalekalabsar/); Maml.? Sen-boγa [سنبغا / Senboga], emir of the town Kerdema (Jorga, Notes XIII, 339 /Mesalekalabsar/). ✧ 'Healthy (strong) bull; strong/bellicose like a bull' cf. RHCHor. I, 186, 802: 'fort comme un boeuf', Sauvaget 36: *äsän-boga* 'taureau, étalon sain, robuste'. ⇨ ESÄN + BUQA.

ESÄN-GİREY   Chuv. 18th-19th c. Sen-gerey [Сенгерей] (Magn. 75); Chuv. 18th-19th c. Sen-girey [Сенгирей] (Magn. 75). ⇨ ESÄN + KERÄY.

ESÄN-KELDİ   Kzk. Esen-geldi [ايسان كيلدى / Эсенгельди] (Syzdykov: IOAIÊK XIII, 354); Kzk. 19th c. Esen-geldi [Есенгельды] (AOO 38); Trkm. 1768/69 Esen-geldi-meχrem [Эсен Гельды-Мехрем], from the Qoñrat tribe (MIT II, 340); Kkalp. 1805 Esen-keldi [Есенкельди], a mulla (MIKk. 97); Kkalp. 1810 Esen-keldi-biy [Эсен-Кельди бий] (MIKk. 111); Kzk. 19th c. İsän-geldi [Исанъ Гельди] (Grod., Pril. 66, 102); Kzk. 19th c. İsän-gildi [Иссянъ-гильди] (Levšin III, 96); Kzk. 19th c. İsän-gildi [Issian-Ghildi] (Levchine 356); Kzk. 1820 İsän-gildi-biy [Исянъ-гильды бий], a chieftain (Sib. Vest. IX, 118); Kzk. 1820 İsän-gildi-biy [Исанъ-гильды-бій], a chieftain (Sib. Vest. IX, 118); Chuv. 18th-19th c. İsen-gilde [Исенгилда] (Magn. 46); Tat.(Sib.)? 1599 İsen-gilde(y) [Исенгильдѣй Тойлаковъ], a Siberian murza (AI II, 18, 21, 23); Bashk. 1695 İsen-gilde(y) [Исенгилдей Язгутов] (MIB I, 90); Bashk. 1695 İsen-kilde(y) [Исенкилдей] (MIB I, 10); Chuv. 18th-19th c. İzän-gilde [Изангилда] (Magn. 41); Chuv. 18th-19th c. İzen-gilde [Изенгилда] (Magn. 42); Tat. 1624 Sen-gilde(y) [Арзамас Сенгильдеевъ] (Zolotn. 155); Chuv. 18th-19th c. Sen-gildi [Сенгилда] (Magn. 75); Kzk. Señ-keldi [Сенгкельдіевъ] (Grod., Pril. 107-108); Kzk. 19th c. Señ-keldi [Чарикасинъ Сенгкельдіевъ] (Grod., Pril. 107-108); *EN:* Kzk. 18th c. - 19th c. Esen-geldi [Есенгельды] (Tynyšp. 70, 71, 75); Chuv. 18th c. İzen-gildina [Изенгилдина], a village in the district of Tsivil'sk (Korsakov 318). ✧ '(He/She) arrived safe and sound'. ⇨ ESÄN + KELDİ.

ESÄN-QAYA   Uyg. 12th c. - 14th c. Esän-qaya [esän qaja] (DTS). ✧ 'Healthy/unharmed rock' (Blagova 1997, 704). ⇨ ESÄN + QAYA.

ESÄN-TEMİR   Maml.? 14th c. Äsän-dämür [اَسَنْدَمُر], a Turkic man („de race turque") (Sauvaget 36); Maml. 14th c. Äsän-dämür / Esen-demür [اسنبدمر / Esendemür] (Tarǰ/Houtsma 48, Tarǰ/Toparlı 42); Uyg. 12th c. - 14th c. Äsän-tämür (Radl., USp. 16-17); Khorezm.? 1296 Esän-tämür [پسر قونقورتاى شهز اده / ايسنتمور], Qoñγur-tay's son (RaD/Jahn 96, 99); Uyg. 12th c. - 14th c. Esän-temür (DTS); 1346/47 Esen-demir [استدمر الكاملى] (Iyās I, 184); Maml.? 1291 Esen-demir [السيفى أسندمر السلحدار المنصورى], in the inscription on the gravestone of his wife (Mayer 80); Maml.? 1302 Esen-demir [سيف الدين استدمركرجى / Asendémur / Acendemor / Ecendemur], lieutenant of the Egyptian sultan Al-Malik an-Nāsir, governor of Haleb, died in 1310/11 (Iyās I, 152, 154, Weil, Chalif. I, 202, 305, 307, Makrīzī IV, 24, 38, Abulfidā V, 176, 228, Abulfidā: RHCHor I, 165, 802); Maml. 1325 Esen-demir [اسندمر رسول ابىسعيد] (Zetterst. 178); Maml. 1331 Esen-demir [اسندمر العمرى], governor of Tripolis (Zetterst. 176, 214, Ibn Tagrīb. VI, 25, Weil, Chalif. I, 420, 471); Maml. 14th c. Esen-demir

[اسندمر القلنجنى] (Zetterst. 206, 217); Maml.? 1366/67 **Esen-demir** [استدمر الصرغتمشى الناصرى] (Iyās I, 219-239, Weil, Chalif. I, 529); Maml.? 1366/67 **Esen-demir** [استدمر] (Iyās I, 220, 269); Maml.? 1377/78, 1389 **Esen-demir** [استدمر الاشرفى] (Iyās I, 239, 279); Maml. 1392 **Esen-demir** [على بن استدمر] (Iyās I, 296); Maml. 1398/99 **Esen-demir** [اسندمر الاسعردى] (Ibn Taghrīb. VI, 16); Maml. 1412 **Esen-demir** [اسندمر], an amīr-ī-aχur (Master of the Horse) (Ibn Taghrīb. VI, 310); Maml. 1421 **Esen-demir** [اسندمر النورى ا لظا هرى] (Ibn Taghrīb. VI, 561); Maml.? 15th c. **Esen-demir** [ا سند مر الناصرى] (Ibn Taghrīb. VI, 130, Weil, Chalif. I, 518-21); Osm. 1376/77 **Esen-demir** [ا ستد مر العثما نى] (Iyās I, 232); Kzk. 18th c. - 19th c. **Esen-temir** [Есентемыр] (Tynyšp. 73); Kzk. 1785 **Esen-temir** [اوروغى / ا سا ن دمر / Род Есентемир] (MIK IV, 52, 54); Kzk. 19th c. **Esen-temir** [Есентемиръ] (SOK 96); Kkalp. 20th c. **Esen-temir** [Есентемир] (KkRS 773); 13th c. **İsän-timür** [ايسان تيمور / Исанъ-Тимуръ], under the Ilkhans (RaD I, 86); Mo.? 13th c. **İsän-timür** [تيمور ايمن], from the folk سوقيوت (RaD/Ber. I, 199); **İsen-timür** [Исен-Тимур] (RaD II, 17); Chuv. 18th-19th c. **İzän-dimer** [Изандимеръ] (Magn. 41); Chuv. 18th-19th c. **İzen-dimer** [Изендимеръ] (Magn. 42); Chuv. 18th-19th c. **Sen-dimer** [Сендимеръ] (Magn. 75). ✧ 'Healthy-(strong)-iron' cf. also the other interpretations: RaDBer. I, 199: „горячее железо" [hot iron]; de Slane: 'fort comme du fer'; Sauvaget 36: 'fer solide'; Blagova 1997, 715: „Невредимое железо" [healthy/unharmed iron]. ⇨ **ESÄN + TEMİR.**

ESE Kzk. 19th c. **Ese-bay** [Есебай] (SODž. 154); Kzk. 19th c. **Ese-bek** [Есебекъ] (SOV 50); Kkalp. 20th c. **Ese-mïrat** [Есемурат] (KkRS 773); Kkalp. 20th c. **Ese-murat** [Есемурат] (KkRS 773). ✧ I. 'Multiple'? cf. Kkalp. *ese* 'кратность, кратный' (KkRS); II. see ESİ?

ESEY Kzk. 19th c. **Esey** [Есей] (AOK 10); Kzk. 19th c. **Esey** [Есей] (AOO 2); Kzk. 19th c. **Esey** [Есей] (SOV 26); Kzk. 19th c. **Esey** [Есей] (AOP 102); Kzk. 19th c. **Esey** [Есей] (SOK 102); Kzk. 19th c. **Esey** [Есей] (SOV 148); Kzk. 19th c. **Esey** [Есей] (SOV 136); Kzk. 19th c. **Esey-bek** [Есейбекъ] (SOK 40); Tat. 1624 **İsey** [Исей Шесмаилевъ] (Pokrovskij 72). ✧ 'Grow up! Strengthen!' (Žanuzakov 138), cf. Kzk. *esey-* 'подрастать' (KzRS), Tat. *isäy-* 'id.' (TatRS).

ESEK see **EŠEK**

ESEKEN Kirg. 19th c. **Eseken** [Эсекень] (Potanin II, 149).

ESEN see **ESÄN**

ESEN-BOL Kzk. 19th c. **Esem-bol** (<Esen-bol) [Есемболъ] (SOK 120, 298). ✧ 'Be healthy'. ⇨ **ESÄN + BOL.**

ESEN-DEMİR see **ESÄN-TEMİR**

ESEN-GELDİ see **ESÄN-KELDİ**

ESEN-KELDİ see **ESÄN-KELDİ**

ESEN-KÜBEK Kzk. 19th c. **Esen-kübek** [Есенкубекъ] (Lomakin 37). ⇨ **ESÄN + KÖPÄK?**

ESENDİK Kzk. 19th c. **Esendek** (<Esendik) [Есендекъ] (SOK 56). ✧ 'Health, weal, well-being'. ⇨ **ESÄN** + suff. *-dik / -lik.*

ESEP Kzk. 19th c. **Esep-pay** [Есеппай] (SODž. 32). ✧ 'Reckoning, tally' cf. Kzk. *esep* 'счёт, отчёт, расчёт' (KzRS) (<Ar.).

ESER Kzk. 19th c. **Eser-bay** [Есербай] (SOK 20). ✧ 'Fool'? cf. Kzk. *esär* 'dumm, leichtsinnig, albern' (Radl. I, 874).

ESERGEK Kzk. 19th c. **Esergek** [Есергекъ] (SOV 30). ✧ 'Sympathetic'? cf. Kzk. *esirke-* 'сочуствовать' (KzRS).

ESERKEY Kzk. 19th c. **Eserkey** [Есеркей] (AOP 38). ✧ 'Little silly, little idiot' cf. Kzk. *esär* 'dumm, leichtsinnig, albern' (Radl. I, 874) + suff. *-key.*

ESİ Kzk. 19th c. **Esi-bay** [Есыбай] (SOV 60). ✧ I. 'Master, owner, gentleman'? cf. Selj., Osm. *äsi* 'der Besitzer, wirth, Herr' (Radl. I, 875); II. 'Elder brother'? (Erol II). ⇨ **ESE?**

ESİ-BAY see **ES**

ESİ-BERDİ see **ES-BERDİ**

ESİK Kzk. 19th c. **Esik** [Есыкъ] (SODž. 78); Kzk. 19th c. **Esik-pay** [Есикпай] (SODž. 84). ✧ 'Door' cf. Kzk. *esik* 'die Thür' (Radl. I, 875).

ESİK-AΓASÏ 1720 **Esik-aγasï?** [Ески-Кагасы], mentioned among similar names (titles) such as Tüfenkči-agasï (Туфенкчи-Агасы), Qular-aγasï (Куларъ-Агасы) (ibid., p. 362) (ZIRGO IX, 348). ✧ 'Head of doormen (title)' cf. also comp. *ešik-aγasï.* ⇨ **ESİK + AΓA.**

ESİL see **ASÏL**

ESİLİ Yürük 1543 **Esili** (Gökb., Rum. 188, 189).

ESİM Kzk. 19th c. **Esim** [Есимъ] (SOV 158); Kzk. 18th c. - 19th c. **Esim-bek** [Есымбекъ] (Tynyšp. 68, 71); Kzk. 19th c. **Esim-bek** [Есимбекъ] (SOV 14); Kzk. 19th c. **Esim-bek** [Есымбекъ] (SODž. 130); Kzk. 19th c. **Esim-bek** [Есымбекъ] (SOK 258); Kzk. 1862 **Esim-bek** [Есимбекъ Таникинъ], from the district of Kopal (ZIRGOGeogr. I, 311); Kzk. **Esim-χan** [Эсимъ-ханъ] (Grod. 26); Kzk. **Esim-qan** [Esim Kan / Ecім Kaн] (Proben III, 68 /89/); Kzk. 19th c. **Esin-bay** (<Esim-bay) [Есинбай] (SODž. 6). ✧ 'Name' cf. Kzk. *esim* 'id.' (KTTS).

ESİM-BERGEN Kkalp. 20th c. **Esim-bergen** [Есимберген] (KkRS 773). ⇨ **ESİM + BERGEN.**

ESİN-BAY see **ESİM**

ESİRGÄB see **ESİRGEP**

ESİRGÄDİ Uzb. 20th c. **Esirgädi** [Эсиргади]

(Begmatov 1984, 206).

ESİRGEP Kzk. 19th c. **Esergep / Esepgep?** [Есепгепъ (Есергеп?)] (SOV 96); Uzb. 20th c. **Esirgäb** [Эсиргаб] (Begmatov 1984, 206). ✧ 'Sympathizing, regretting'? cf. Kzk. PN *Esirkep* (Žanuzakov-Esbaeva), Kuman, Chag., Az., Turk. *äsirgä-* 'mitleidig sein, traurig sein, gnädig sein; nicht gern geben' (Radl. I, 877).

ESİT-BERGEN Kkalp. 20th c. **Esit-bergen** [Еситберген] (Bask., Kkalp. 400). ⇨ **?+BERGEN.**

ESKE Kzk. 19th c. **Eske-bay** [Ескебай] (SOK 100). ⇨ **ES / EŠ?** + suff. *-ke.*

ESKEY Kzk. 19th c. **Eskey** [Ескей] (AOK 10). ⇨ **ES** + suff. *-key.* See also **SAR-ESKEY.**

ESKENE see **İŠKİNÄ**

ESLAM see **İSLAM**

ESLİ Oghuz/Trkm. 13th c. **Esli** [ايسلى / Эсли-хан], İl-tegin's son (Abulg./Kon. 1010); Kzk. 19th c. **Este-bay / Esti-bay** [Эстебай] (SOK 62); Kzk. 19th c. **Este-bay / Esti-bay** [Эстебай] (SOV 50); Kzk. 18th c. - 19th c. **Esti** [Есты] (Tynyšp. 65); Kzk. 19th c. **Esti-bay** [Эстыбай] (AOP 18); Kzk. 19th c. **Esti-bay** [Эстыбай] (SOK 64, 140); Kzk. 19th c. **Esti-bay** [Эстыбай] (SODž. 54). ✧ I. 'Strong, big, grown-up'? cf. Chag., Crm., Kar. *äsli* 'gross, stark; erwachsen' (Radl. I, 884); II. 'Brainy, clever'? cf. Crm. *äslï* 'klug' (Radl. I, 884), Kzk. *estï* 'klug, verständig' (Radl. I, 885), Tat. dial. *isle* 'сознательный, понятливый' (TatRS), Tat.(Tob.) *islï* 'verständig, vernünftig' (Radl. I, 1531).

ESMEN Kzk. 19th c. **Esmem-bay (<Esmen-bay?)** [Есмембай] (SODž. 90); Kzk. 19th c. **Espan** [Еспанъ] (AOP 42); Kzk. 19th c. **Espen-bek** [Еспенбекъ] (SOK 116). ✧ 'Brainy, smart'? cf. Kzk. PN *Esman, Espembet* (Žanuzakov-Esbaeva). ⇨ **ES** + suff. *-men.*

ESMEZ Turk. 1540 **Esmez-kethudā**, chief of the Tek(?) clan (cemaat) according to a defter from Diyarbekir (Demirtaş 51). ✧ 'Won't blow, does not bluster' cf. Turk. *es-* 'wehen, blasen' (Radl. I, 871). + suff. *-mez.*

ESPAN see **ESMEN**

ESPEN see **ESMEN**

ESPENBET Kkalp. 20th c. **Espenbet** [Еспенбет] (KkRS 773). ✧ 'Brainy Mukhammed' cf. Kzk. PN *Espembet* (Žanuzakov-Esbaeva). ⇨ **ESMEN** + suffixoid *-bet.*

ESPERÜX Bulg. 7th c. **Esperüχ / Ešberüχ** ['Ασπαρούχ], a Bulghar prince (644-702) (Byz. Turc. 75-76). ✧ '?' cf. Németh, HMK 135.

ESPİR Kzk. 19th c. **Espir** [Эспиръ] (SODž. 86).

ESTE see **ESLİ**

ESTEK Chuv. 18th-19th c. **Estek** [Эстекъ] (Magn. 95); Kzk. 19th c. **Estek** [Есьтекъ] (AOA 98); Kzk. 19th c. **Estek-bay** [Естекбай] (AOK 102); Kzk. 19th c. **Estek-pay** [Естекпай] (SODž. 50); Kzk. 19th c. **Estek-pay** [Естекпай] (SODž. 58). See also **SAR-ESTEK.**

ESTEN Kzk. 18th c. - 19th c. **Estem-bek (<Esten-bek)** [Естембай] (Tynyšp. 65); Kzk. 19th c. **Estem-bek (<Esten-bek)** [Естембекъ] (SOV 50). ✧ '?' cf. Kzk. PN *Esten* (Žanuzakov-Esbaeva).

ESTİ see **ESLİ**

EŠ Kkalp. 20th c. **Eš-bay** [Ешбай] (KkRS 773); Kzk. 19th c. **Eš-batïr-χaʃi** [Ешъ-Батыръ-хаджи] (AUK 829); Kkalp. 20th c. **Eš-eke** [Ешеке] (KkRS 773); Nog. 1649 **Eš-qoʃa** [Бекъ Эшкожинъ], a murza (AI IV, 123); Chuv. 18th-19th c. **Eš-patïr** [Ешпатыръ] (Magn. 40); Kkalp. 20th c. **Eš-žan** [Ещан] (KkRS 773); Tat. 1648 **Eško?** [Ешко Улешев] (Miller, Ist. Sib. II, 528); Kzk. 19th c. **İš** [Ишъ] (SKSO VIII, 201, 206); Tat. 20th c. **İš-bay** [Ишбай] (Sattarov); Bashk. 18th c. **İš-bay** [Ишбай Кучаков] (MIB V, 70, 83, 84); Bashk. 20th c. **İš-bay** [Ишбай] (Kusimova); Kzk. 19th c. **İš-bay** [Ишбай Кёзбергеновъ], author of the book Boz oγlan Ahmed-bek (Kazan 1889) (OB. XV, 78, AUK Dobavl. 1); Bashk. 1778 **İš-bay / İš-pay** [Ишбай (Ишпай) Кинзягулов] (MIB V, 267); Kkalp. 20th c. **İš-čan** [Ишчан] (Bask., Kkalp. 64); Chuv. 18th-19th c. **İš-čora** [Ишчора] (Magn. 48); Chuv. 18th-19th c. **İš-čura** [Ишчура] (Magn. 48); Kzk. 19th c. **İš-ʃan** [Ишджанъ Иръ Ніязовъ] (Grod., Pril. 187); Uzb. 1875 **İš-ʃan** [Иш-Джанъ] (Moskal'cev 48); Nog. 1555 **İš-ekey** [Ишекей], a Noγay envoy (PSRL XIII, 249); Kzk. **İš-γazi** [Ишъ-газы] (Levšin III, 96); Kzk. 19th c. **İš-χoʃa** [Аятъ-Ходжа Ишъ-Ходжаевъ] (Grod., Pril. 60); Bashk. 1675 **İš-közä** [Итимген Ишкозин] (MIB I, 199); Bashk. 1777 **İš-küzä** [Ишкузя Тускаев] (MIB V, 124); Bashk. 1779 **İš-küzä** [Ишкузя Бадряшев] (MIB V, 62, 86); Bashk. 1779 **İš-küzä** [Ишкузя Бавачев] (MIB V, 83, 84); Bashk. 20th c. **İš-qol** [Ишкол / Ишкул] (Kusimova); Bashk. 1787 **İš-qul** [Ишкул Меняев] (MIB V, 207); Bashk. 1789 **İš-qul** [Ишкул Абдулменов] (MIB V, 269); Bashk. 1790 **İš-qul** [Ишкул Макшеев] (MIB V, 294, 295); Bashk. 1791 **İš-qul** [Ишкул Ишменев] (MIB V, 301); 1614 **İš-mirza** [Ишъ-мирза] (AI III, 444); Kzk. 19th c. **İš-mirza** [Ишъмирза] (SKSO VIII, 222); Bashk. 20th c. **İš-murza** [Ich mourzine], a basmačï (Castagné 80); Chuv. 18th-19th c. **İš-patïr** [Ишпатыръ] (Magn. 48); Kzk. 19th c. **Š-pek (<Eš-pek)** [Шпекъ] (SOV 110). ✧ 'Friend, mate, fellow, companion; help, helper' (Sattarov, Kusimova, Žanuzakov), cf. Türk, Karakh. *eš* 'друг, приятель, сподвижник' (DTS), Kirg. *eš* 'опора, поддержка; надежда; друг' (Jud.), Tat. *iš* 'der Gefährte' (Radl. I, 1545-46), Bashk. *iš* 'пара, чета; ровня' (BaRS). Used mainly as first component of personal names. See also **BAY-İŠ, BEK-İŠ, DAY-İŠ, QARA-İŠ, QUL-BAY-İŠ, TOY-İŠ.**

EŠ-BAΓANBET see **EŠ-MAQAMBET**

EŠ-BARS   Chuv. 18th-19th c. **Eš-pars** [Ешпарсъ] (Magn. 40); Chuv. 18th-19th c. **Eš-pars** [Шпарсъ] (Magn. 95); Tat. 20th c. **İš-bars** [Ишбарс] (Sattarov); Chuv. 18th-19th c. **İš-paris** [Ишпарисъ] (Magn. 48); Chuv. 18th-19th c. **İš-parïs** [Ишпарысъ] (Magn. 48); Chuv. 18th-19th c. **İš-pars** [Ишпорсъ] (Magn. 48); Chuv. 18th-19th c. **İš-pars** [Ишпарсъ] (Magn. 48). ✧ 'Friend-panther, fellow-panther' cf. Tat. *İš-bars* (Sattarov). ⇨ **EŠ + BARS.**

EŠ-BOL   Kzk. 18th c. - 19th c. **Es-bol** [Есбол] (Tynyšp. 65, 70, 74); Kzk. 1823 **Es-bol** [ايسبول / Есбол] (MIK IV, 459, 462); Kzk. 19th c. **Es-pol** [Есполъ] (AOAtb. 62); Kzk. 19th c. **Es-pol** [Еспол] (SOV 40, 54, 64, 84); Kzk. 19th c. **Es-pol** [Еспол, Эсполъ] (SOK 10, 170, 218, 220); Kzk. 19th c. **Es-pol** [Еспол] (SODž. 16); Bulg. 9th c. **Eš-bul** ['Ισβουλος], a Bulghar chieftain (Byz. Turc. 141); Nog. 20th c. **İs-bol** [Исбол Мустафа], father of one of Baskakov's informants from the aul of Qara-töbe (Bask., Nog. 143); Kzk. 19th c. **İs-bul** [Мидабай Исбуловъ] (Grod., Pril. 114); Tat. 20th c. **İš-bul** [Ишбул] (Sattarov); Kzk. 19th c. **İš-bul** [Ишбуловъ] (SKSO VIII, 204). ✧ 'Be a helper, a companion (for younger brothers)!' (Sattarov; Žanuzakov 138). ⇨ **EŠ + BOL.**

EŠ-BOLDÏ   Uzb. 20th c. **Eš-boldï** [Эшбӱлди] (Begmatov 1984, 201); Nog. 1649 **Eš-buldu** [Ешбулдуй Итешевъ] (AI IV, 80); Bashk. 1735 **İš-boldï** [Ишбольда Темиров] (MIB III, 337); Bashk. 1761 **İš-boldï** [Ижболда Муйкашев] (MIB IV/1, 211); Bashk. 1784 **İš-boldï** [Халил Ижболдин] (MIB V, 154); Tat. 20th c. **İš-buldï** [Ишбулды] (Sattarov); Bashk. 1755 **İš-buldï** [Илбулда Ишбулдин] (MIB IV/1, 101); Bashk. 1758 **İš-buldï** [Ижбулде Солтанов] (MIB IV/1, 160); Bashk. 1773 **İš-buldï** [Ишбулды Наурузов] (MIB IV/2, 130); Bashk. 1780 **İš-buldï** [Ижбулда Мустаев] (MIB V, 109); Bashk. 1798 **İš-buldï** [Ижбулдинъ] (PSZRI XXV, 196); Bashk. 20th c. **İš-buldï** [Ишбулды] (Kusimova); Chuv. 18th-19th c. **İš-poldï** [Ишполда] (Magn. 48); Chuv. 1748 **İš-puldï** [Илдиканъ Ишпулдинъ] (PSZRI XII, 942); Chuv. 18th-19th c. **İš-puldï** [Ишпулта] (Magn. 48); *TN:* Bashk.? **İšbuldina** [Ишбулдина], a village south of Verhneuralsk (?). ✧ 'Helper, companion, son was (born)' (Sattarov). ⇨ **EŠ + BOLDÏ.**

EŠ-BOLSÏN   Kkalp. 20th c. **Es-bosïn** [Есбосын] (KkRS 773); Uzb. 20th c. **Eš-bolsïn** [Эшбӱлсин] (Begmatov 1984, 201); Kzk. 19th c. **Eš-bosïn (<Eš-bolsïn)** [Ежбосынъ] (SOV 110). ✧ 'Let him/her be/become (our) mate/friend'. ⇨ **EŠ + BOLSÏN.**

EŠ-BUL see **EŠ-BOL**

EŠ-BULAT   Kzk. 19th c. **Es-bolat** [Есболатъ] (SODž. 62); Kzk. 19th c. **Es-bolat** [Есболатъ] (SOV 112); Tat. 1624 **Es-bulat** [Есбулат Урусовъ] (Zolotn. 157); NUyg. 1770 **Eš-pulad-atalïq** [Эш Пулад-аталык] (MIT II, 343); Chuv. 18th-19th c. **Eš-pulat** [Ешпулатъ] (Magn. 40); Tat. 1675 **İš-bulat** [Ижбулатка] (Kungursk. akty 24); Tat. 1698 **İš-bulat** [Ижбулатовъ], a captain (Kungursk. akty 267); Tat. 1706 **İš-bulat** [Ижбулатъ] (Kurdjumov 342); Tat. 1784/85 **İš-bulat** [اشبولاط / Ишбулат] (Jusupov 76); Tat. 18th-19th c. **İš-bulat** [Ижбулатъ] (Magn. 41); Bashk. 1707 **İš-bulat** [Ижбулат Камышев] (MIB III, 40); Bashk. 1768 **İš-bulat** [Токтамышъ Ижбулатовъ] (Nikol'skij 276); Bashk. 1787 **İš-bulat** [Ижбулат Тляуф] (MIB V, 214); Tat. 1675 **İš-pulat** [Ишпулатко Ишинбаевь] (Kungursk. akty 21); Tat. 1680 **İš-pulat** [Ишпулатко] (Kungursk. akty 45); Tat. 1680 **İš-pulat** [Ишпулатко] (AI V, 93); Tat. 18th-19th c. **İš-pulat** [Ишпулатъ] (Magn. 48); Tat. 18th-19th c. **İz-bulat / İš-bulat?** [Избулатъ] (Magn. 41). ✧ 'Mate/friend-steel'. ⇨ **EŠ + BULAT.**

EŠ-BULDU see **EŠ-BOLDÏ**

EŠ-KELDİ   Chag. 16th c. **Eš-keldi** [Эш Келди] (Ivanov 190); Kzk. 19th c. **İs-keldi** [Исъ-кельды] (Lomakin 34); Chuv. 18th-19th c. **İš-kilde** [Ишкилда] (Magn. 48); Tat. 20th c. **İš-kilde** [Ишкилде] (Sattarov); Bashk. 1744 **İš-kilde** [Ишкильда Бекбаев] (MIB III, 415); Bashk. 1750 **İš-kilde** [Ишкильда Урманов] (MIB III, 472); Bashk. 1753 **İš-kilde** [Мулла (Муса, Мустай) Ишкильдин] (MIB IV/1, 68); Bashk. 1756 **İš-kilde** [Мурзябяк Ишкильдин] (MIB IV/1, 122); Bashk. 1756, 1761 **İš-kilde** [Ишкильда Ишеев] (MIB IV/1, 123, 211); Bashk. 1779 **İš-kilde** [Кучербай Ишкильдеев] (MIB V, 94); Bashk. 20th c. **İš-kilde** [Ишкилде] (Kusimova); Bashk. 1735 **İš-kildi** [Ишкилди Каскаевъ], a prince (Vel.-Zern., Bašk. 17). ✧ 'Friend (mate, fellow) came (was born)' (Sattarov, Kusimova). ⇨ **EŠ + KELDİ.** See also **ES-KELDİ.**

EŠ-QARA   Uyg. **Äš-qara** [Äş kara] (EUTS); Kzk. **Es-qara** [Ескара], a field (Kojčubajev 87); Kzk. 19th c. **Es-qara** [Ескара] (SOV 116); Uyg. 12th c. - 14th c. **Eš-qara** (DTS); Kirg. **Eš-qara** [Эшкара] (Jud. 17); Uyg. **İš-qara** [İşkara] (EUTS); Uyg. 12th c. - 14th c. **İš-qara** [İš qara] (Radl., USp. 169-170, 215, 257); Tat. 20th c. **İš-qara** [Ишкара] (Sattarov); Bashk. 1682 **İš-qara** [Ямагуза Ишкаринъ] (AI V, 139); Bashk. 1714 **İš-qara** [Ишкара Кулушев] (MIB III, 116); Bashk. 1745 **İš-qara** [Ишкара] (MIB III, 428); Bashk. 1769 **İš-qara** [Ишкара Султанов] (MIB IV, 336). ✧ I. 'Fellow-Black/Mighty/Strong' (Blagova 1997, 708); II. 'Fellow (friend), look! (be born!)' (Sattarov). ⇨ **EŠ + QARA.** See also **İŠ-BAQ.**

EŠ-MAQAMBET   Kkalp. 20th c. **Eš-baγanbet** [Ешбағанбет] (KkRS 773); Kzk. 19th c. **Eš-**

maqambet [Ешмакамбетъ] (SOV 70). ⇨ **EŠ +
MAQAMBET.**

EŠ-MĬRAT see **EŠ-MURAT**

EŠ-MURAT   Kkalp. 20th c. **Eš-mïrat** [Ешмырат]
(KkRS 773); Kkalp. 20th c. **Eš-murat** [Ешмурат]
(KkRS 773); Uzb. 1767/68 **Eš-murat** [Эш Мурад],
from the Qoñrat tribe (MIT II, 336, 339). ⇨
EŠ+MURAT.

EŠ-NAZAR   Trkm. 1801 **Eš-nazar** [Эш Назар
(Эшэк-сойган)], a mulla (MIT II, 345); Kkalp. 20th c.
Eš-nazar [Ешназар] (KkRS 773). ⇨ **EŠ+NAZAR.**

EŠ-NİYAZ   Kkalp. 20th c. **Eš-niyaz** [Ешнияз] (KkRS
773); Uzb. 1770 **Eš-niyaz-bay** [Эш Нияз-бай] (MIT
II, 347). ⇨ **EŠ + NİYAZ.**

EŠ-PARS see **EŠ-BARS**

EŠ-TAN   Hak.(Kyz.) 1685 **Eš-tan** [Ештанъ] (Jarilov,
Kyz. 6). ⇨ **EŠ+TAN.**

EŠ-TOXTA   Uzb. 20th c. **Eš-toχta** [Эштўхта]
(Begmatov 1984, 200). ✧ 'Stand/stay as mate/helper!'.
⇨ **EŠ + TOQTA.**

EŠE see **EŠI**

EŠEK   Tuv. 19th c. **Äšäk** [Атучи Аксага Ашякъ
(Аксакалъ ашякъ)] (Potanin IV, 416); Kzk. 19th c.
Esek [Есекъ] (SOV 98); Khorezm. 1295 **Ešek**
[اشك توغلى] (RaD/Jahn 98); Nog. 1649 **Eštek** [Бекъ
мурза Ештековъ] (AI IV, 87). ✧ 'Donkey' cf.
Alt.(Tel.), Shor *äštäk* 'der Esel' (Radl. I, 912), Balk.
išäk (=R. *išak*) 'Maulesel' (Karaulov: IOAKaz. XXIII),
Nog. *ešek* 'осёл' (RNogS), Kzk. *esek* 'осёл' (RKzS).

EŠEK-SOYҐAN   Trkm. 1801 **Ešek-soyɣan** [Эш
Назар (Эшэк-сойган)], byname of Eš-nazar mulla
(MIT II, 345). ✧ 'He who flayed a donkey; Donkey-
Skinner' cf. Trkm. *soy-* 'сдирать (кожу, кожицу с
чего-л.); забивать, резать (скот)' (TrkmRS). ⇨
EŠEK.

EŠEK-TEMİR   Maml.? 1364, 1373, 1380 **Ešek-temir**
[Seifeddīn Ešektimür al-Māridāni], governor of Haleb,
later that of Damascus (Weil, Chalif. I, 511, 545). ✧
'Donkey-iron'. ⇨ **EŠEK + TEMİR.**

EŠER   Alt. 19th-20th c. **Ešer** [Эшер] (OjrRS 211).

EŠI   Kkalp. 20th c. **Eše-bay** [Ешебай] (KkRS 773);
Kirg. **Eši** [Эши] (Jud. 181); Bashk. 1734 **İši-bay**
[Байзигит Ишибаев] (MIB III, 325). ✧ 'His
helper/supporter'? ⇨ **EŠ?** + poss. suff. -*i*.

EŠİM   Kkalp. 20th c. **Ešim** [Ешим] (KkRS 773); Kirg.
Ešim [Эшим] (Jud. 640); Kkalp. 1714 **Ešim(-sultan)**
[Эшим султан], from the Karakalpak princes (töre)
(MIKk. 91); Chag. 1645 **Ešim-χan** [Эшим-хан], ruler
of Tashkent (Ivanov 77). ✧ 'My helper/supporter'? ⇨
EŠ? + poss. suff. -*m*.

EŠİMBET   Kkalp. 20th c. **Ešimbet** [Ешимбет] (KkRS
773); Tat. 20th c. **İšembät** [Ишембэт] (Kusimova);
Bashk. 20th c. **İšembät** [Ишембэт / Ишимбет]
(Kusimova); Bashk. 1735 **İšimbet** [Ишимбет

Усейнов], a tarχan (Vel.-Zern., Bašk. 22); Bashk.?
1735 **İšimbet** [тезикъ Иишмбеть Иштыковъ], a
Tadjik? (Vel.-Zern., Bašk. 25); Bashk.? 1735 **İšimbet**
[Аскиле Ишимбетеву], a Tadjik? (Vel.-Zern., Bašk.
25). ⇨ **EŠ** + suffixoid -*imbet*. See also **İŠ-MAMET.**

EŠİMUT   Kipch.? 1276 **Ešimut?** [Ешимутъ], envoy
from the Horde (PSRL II, 207).

EŠKE-BAQ   Kzk. 19th c. **Eške-baq** [Ешкебаковъ]
(AOO 26). ⇨ **EŠ+BAQ.**

EŠKEY   Kzk. 19th c. **Eškey** [Ешкей] (AOP 26); Tat.
20th c. **İškäy** [Ишкэй] (Sattarov); Tat. 20th c. **İškäy**
[Ишкэй] (Kusimova); Bashk. 1773 **İškäy** [Ишкай
Кашкаев] (MIB IV/2, 415); Bashk. 1701, 1731 **İškey**
[Ишкей] (MIB III, 11, 293); Bashk. 1723 **İškey**
[Ишкей], fem. (MIB III, 11, 202); Bashk. 1735 **İškey**
[Ишкей Кошаевъ], a tarχan (Vel.-Zern., Bašk. 13);
Bashk. 1735 **İškey** [Ишкей] (Vel.-Zern., Bašk. 13). ✧
'Little friend, little fellow'. ⇨ **EŠ** + suff. -*key.*

EŠKEN see **EŠKEN**

EŠKEN   Kzk. 19th c. **Eskem-bay** (<**Esken-bay**)
[Ескембай] (SODž. 62); Kzk. 19th c. **Esken** [Эскенъ]
(AOP 122); Tat.(Sib.) 1651 **Ešken** [Эшкенъ], a tayša
(Andrievič I, 108). ✧ 'Little friend, little fellow'. ⇨ **EŠ**
+ suff. -*ken.*

EŠLÄP   Bashk. 1735 **Ešläp** [Тюрюмъ Ешляповъ], a
tarχan (Vel.-Zern., Bašk. 24).

EŠLİK   Bashk. 1728 **Ešlik / Ešläk** [Ешлик (Ешляк)
Бозюк] (MIB I, 128).

EŠTÄMİ see **İSTÄMİ**

EŠTEK see **EŠEK**

ET-BERDİ   Bashk. 1734 **Et-berdi** [Етберди Каниев],
a tarχan (Vel.-Zern., Bašk. 10). ✧ '(He was) given by a
dog'. ⇨ **İT + BERDİ.**

ET-JİMÄS see **İT-JEMÄS**

ET-YEMEZ   Turk. **Et-yemez-oɣlu**, a Zeybek (Kúnos
1891, 119). ✧ 'He doesn't (won't) eat any meat' (NyK
XXII, 119), cf. Turk. *et* 'flesh; meat' (TED), Uyg.,
Chag., Alt., Crm., Kirg., Turk. etc. *yä-* 'essen' (Radl.
III, 312), Kzk. *že-* 'есть, кушать' (KzRS).

ET-TAŠLAY   Bashk. 1707 **Et-dašlay** [Етдашлай
Болташев] (MIB III, 31). ✧ 'The dog leaves him/her'
cf. Bashk. *tašla-* 'покидать, оставлять' (BaRS). ⇨
İT.

ETEGEN   Bashk. 1715 **Etegen** [Этегень Егумбетев]
(MIB III, 120).

ETEK   Tat.(Mish) **Ätäk-χan** (Pelissier 24); Kzk. 19th c.
Etek-bay [Етекбай] (AOA 22); Kzk. **Etek-pay**
[Етекпай] (SODz. 116); Kzk. 19th c. **Etek-pay**
[Етекпай] (SOV 100, 118); Kzk. 19th c. **Etek-pay**
[Етекпай] (AOP 10). ✧ 'Bottom' cf. Kzk. *etek*
'подол; пола, подошва (горы, возвышенности)'
(KzRS).

ETİL   Tat.? 1321 **Etil** ['Ιτίλης], an Alan (Tatar?) in the
army of the Bulghar ruler Georg II (Byz. Turc. 142);

Tat./Bashk. 1737 **İdel** [Курметъ Иделевъ], a Teptär (Nepljuev 427); Bashk. 1792, 1793 **İdel-bey / İdil-bey** [Шамагана Идильбеев] (MIB V, 328); Kzk. 19th c. **İdil** [Идыль], a hunter (Potanin, Pred. 112); Kzk. 19th c. **İdil** [бай Идиль] (Potanin, Pred. 110); Chuv. 18th-19th c. **İdil-bay** [Идылбай] (Magn. 41); Bashk. 1795 **İdil-bay** [Идильбай Муратовъ] (IOAIÊK (Dobavlenie) XXVIII, 590); Bashk. 1760 **İdil-bäk** [Култень Идилбяков] (MIB IV/1, 199); *TN:* 19th c. **İdel-bay** [Иделбай], a tomb north of the Caspian sea (IIRGO XVI); **İdil-bay(eva)** [Идильбаева], a village (Karta JAR 3). ✧ 'River Volga' The Turkic name of the river. Cf. Karakh. *Etil* (DTS).

ETKER   Alt. 19th c. **Etker** [Эткерь], Erlik's servant (Verb., In. 100).

ETMEKČİ   Maml. 14th c. **Etmekči** [اَتْمَكُجِي] (Sauvaget 35). ✧ 'Baker' cf. Maml. *etmekçi* 'id.' (Tarj/Toparlı 105).

ETRÜK   Türk 7th c. - 9th c. **Etrük** [etrük] (DTS).

ETTİK   Kzk. 19th c. **Ettik-bay** [Еттыкбай] (SOK 122).

ETÜL   Hak. 19th-20th c. **Etül** [Этӱл], fem. (HRS 356).

ETÜMİŠ   1223 **Etümiš?** [Ετούμης], a Turkic governor (Byz. Turc. 127).

EV-BAŠ   Yürük 1543 **Ev-baš** [Evbaş] (Gökb., Rum. 227). ✧ 'Head of the house'. ⇨ **EW + BAŠ.**

EVAY   Bashk. 1770 **Evay** [Хасян Еваев] (MIB IV/1, 350).

EVDEY   Hak. 19th-20th c. **Evdey** [Эвдей] (HRS 352). ✧ Avdey (R.).

EVɣİNÄK-İSMİN   Uyg. 10th c. **Evɣinäk-ismin** [evɣinäk ismin] (DTS).

EVREN   Oghuz/Trkm. 15th c. **Evren** [اورن] (DQorq./Rossi 162); Yürük 1543 **Evren** [اورن], from the Yürüks of Kocacık (Gökb., Rum. 103). ✧ 'Big, tall man; handsome; hero' cf. Turk. dial. *evren* 'büyük, yüksek; boylu boslu, iri yarı, yakışıklı; kahraman, yiğit' (DS), *evran, evren* 'dragon, monster; great, saint' (TED). See also **BÜYÜK, ČOŇ, YOƔAN, KÄNDÄL, MÄŇKÄ.**

EVRENOS see **EVRENOZ**

EVRENOZ   Yürük 1543 **Evrenos** (Gökb., Rum. 208); Turk. 1397 **Evrenos-bey** (Gökb., Ed. 23); Turk. **Evrenoz-bey** (Baştav 60, 61, 62, 66, 68, 73, 100, 102, 103, 109, 112, 116).

EW   Tat. 1623 **Ew-aɣa / İw-aɣa?** [Евага, Ивага], a prince (Miller, Ist. Sib. II, 292).

EWĀZ-DURDİ-SERČE   Trkm. 1881 **Ewāz-durdï-serče-sardar** [Эвазъ-Дурды-Серче-сардаръ] (Grod., Vojna II, 143). ⇨ **OWĀZ-DURDİ + SERČE.**

EWEZ see **AWAZ**

EWEZ-BERDİ-TAWAR   Uzb.? 1818 **Ewez-berdi-tawar** [Эвез-берды Тавар] (MIT II, 412). ⇨ **EWEZ + BERDİ.**

EWEZ-QARAUL   Trkm. 1826 **Ewez-qaraul** [Эвез-караул], from the Soqtï (Suqtï) tribe (MIT II, 441).

EWEZLİ   Trkm. 1826 **Ewezli** [Эвезли], a mulla from the Sarïq tribe (MIT II, 440).

EWLÜ   Tat.(Sib.) 1607 **Ewlü-bay** [Евлубай] (Miller, Ist. Sib. II, 204). ✧ 'Having a house (=married)' cf. *äwli, ävli* 'verheiratet (von Männern)' (Radl. I, 943).

EWLÜŠ   Tat. 1541 **Ewlüš** [Евлушъ] (PSRL XIII, 100).

EWTEK   Tat. 1532 **Ewtek-baqšï** [Евтекъ бакшей (Бакшей) / Евтекъ-бакшей], envoy from Kazan (PSRL VIII, 282, XIII, 69, XX, 416).

EWÜŠ   Tat. 1623 **Ewüš** [Евушев Емамлик] (Miller, Ist. Sib. II, 304); Tat. 1624 **Ewüš** [Янгилди (Янгилда) Еушевъ] (Pokrovskij 71).

EZDİN   Turk. 1489 **Ezdin** [ازدین / Ezdin] (Gökb., Ed. 157).

EZÄR   Hak.(Sag.) 19th-20th c. **Ezär** [Эзäр] (Proben IX, 259). ✧ 'Saddle' Cf. Hak.(Sag.) *ezär* 'der Sattel' (Radl. I, 892).

EZEYÄK   Tat.(Sib.) 1635 **Ezeyäk** [Езеяк] (Miller, Ist. Sib. II, 585).

EZERMEN   Yürük 1543 **Ezermen** [ازرمن / Ezermen] (Gökb., Rum. 196).

EZGÄNÄ   Türk 7th c. - 9th c. **Ezgänä** [Äzgänä / ezgänä] (ETY III, 170, DTS).

EŽEKE   Kzk. 19th c. **Ežeke** [Ежеке] (SOV 64). ✧ 'Little grand-mother'? cf. Kzk. *äže* 'бабушка' (KzRS) + suff. *-ke.*

EŽİ-GÄLDİ   Kzk. **Eži-gäldi** [Eshigäldi / Ежігäлди] (Proben III, 279 /332/). ✧ 'His/her pair/mate came'. ⇨ **EŠ + KELDİ.**

F

FAYÏQ   Turk. 1583 **Fayïq** [فایق / Fayık], a slave (servant) of Hungarian origin (Ongan, Ank. I, 157).

FAKİR   Chag. 15th c.- 16th c. **Fakir-sultan** [فقیر سلطان], a Shaybanid (Šejb.). ✧ 'Poor' cf. *faqir* 'arm, elend, der Fakir' (Radl. IV, 1909).

FARMAN see **FERMAN**

FARMANLİ see **FERMANLİ**

FATİMA   Kirg. **Batma** [Батма], fem. (Jud. 943); Kirg. **Batma-ǰan** [Батмажан], fem. (Jud. 351); Kzk. 19th c. **Batpa** [Батпа, Заура], Fatima and Zuhra - the names of girls-twins (Grod. I, 98); Nog. 20th c. **Fatima** [Фатима Азамат Кирей къызы Байыс], one of Baskakov's informants from the aul of Üykön-χalq (Ikon-halk), Cherkess Autonomous Oblast' (Bask., Nog. 143); Turk. 15th c. **Fatma-hatun** [Fatma Hatun], several persons in the source (Gökb., Ed.); Kkalp. 20th c. **Patïyma** [Патыйма], fem. (KkRS 778); Kkalp. 20th

c. **Patpa** [Патпа], fem. (KkRS 778). ✧ Fatima (Ar. fem.). See also **ВОГАZЈА-FATİMA**.

FATMA see **FATİMA**

FELEMEZ   Turk. **Felemez** (Önder, Hınıs).

FEODORČUQ   Tat. 1327 **Feodorčuq** [Феодорчюкъ], a Tatar chieftain (voevoda) (PSRL X, 194). ✧ 'Little Feodor' cf. R. male name Feodor (SlRLI) + dim. suff. -*čuq*.

FERAH   Turk. 1528 **Ferah-šad-hatun** [Ferahşad Hatun] (Gökb., Ed. 379). ✧ Farah (Ar.) 'Joy, happiness, delight' (Ahmet).

FERHAD   Turk. 15th c. **Ferhad**, several persons (Gökb., Ed.). ✧ Ferhad (Ar.).

FERMAN   Kzk. 19th c. **Farman-bek** [Фарманъ-бекъ] (Grod., Pril. 154); Turk. **Ferman** (Önder, Hınıs); Kzk. 19th c. **Parman** [Парманъ] (Grod., Pril. 57); Kzk. **Parman-bek** [Parman Bek / Парман Бек] (Proben III, 251 /296/); Trkm. 20th c. **Perman** [Perman] (Zaj. 1971, 329); Trkm. 20th c. **Perman** [Перман] (TrkmRS 524). ✧ 'Order (of God?), command' cf. Turk. *färman* 'der Ferman, der Befehl' (Radl. IV, 1924), Uzb. *farmon (färmān)* 'указ' (UzbRS), Tat. *parman* (P.) 'der Befehl' (Radl. IV, 1161), Trkm. *permān* 'указ, приказ' (TrkmRS) (<P.). ⇨ **BARMEN?**

FERMANLÏ   Kzk. 19th c. **Farmanlï** [Фарманлы] (Grod., Pril. 186); Turk. **Fermanlï** (Önder, Hınıs). ✧ 'Having orders'. ⇨ **FERMAN** + suff. -*lï*.

FERRUH   Turk. 1528 **Ferruh** [Hacı Ferruh] (Gökb., Ed. 37). ✧ Ferrukh (Ar.).

FİČAQ see **BİČAQ**

FİSTAW   Kzk. 19th c. **Fistaw-bay** [Отаганъ Фиставбаевъ] (Grod., Pril. 150).

FİŠ   Kzk. 19th c. **Fiš-Jan** [Фишджанъ] (Grod., Pril. 43).

FİNDÏQ   Turk. 1528 **Fïndïq** [Fındık Fakih] (Gökb., Ed. 47). ✧ 'Hazel-nut'.

FİRTÏNA   Turk. 20th c. **Fïrtïna**, a Zeybek (Kúnos 1891, 118); Turk. 20th c. **Fïrtïna-oγlu**, a Zeybek (Kúnos 1891, 118). ✧ 'Storm' cf. Turk. *fïrtïna* 'der Sturm' (Radl. IV, 1953).

FORUZAT   Tat. 1530 **Foruzat** [Форузатъ], envoy from Kazan (PSRL VIII, 277).

FRONT   Kirg. 20th c. **Front-bek** [Фронт-бек] (Abramzon 109). ✧ 'Front' the name of a child born at the time of the war (<R.).

FULAD see **BULAT**

G

GAWHÄR see **GÄWHÄR**
GÄNČ see **KENČ**
GÄWHÄR   Kzk. 1969 **Gauχar** [Гаухар], 25 Kazak

girls out of 1000 got this name in Chimkent (Nikonov: OSA 158); Chag. 1550 **Gawhär-bike** [كوهر بيكه / Гавхäр-бикä] (Jusupov 66); Uyg. 1338 **Gäuher-naz** [Gauher Naz] (Chwol., Syr.-nest. (NF) 40); Uyg. 1342 **Gäüher-tärim** [Gauher Tarim], fem. (Chwol., Syr.-nest. (NF) 40); Tat. 1536 **Gäwhär-šad?** [Ковгоршадъ / Ковъгоршадъ / Горшадна], a princess from Kazan (PSRL VIII, 291, XIX, 326, 328, 390 XIII, 88); Kkalp. 20th c. **Gäwχär** [Гäўхəр], fem. (KkRS 777); Selj. 1073 **Gevher** [Gevher, Mehd ül-Irak], Melik-šah's daughter (Ahbar 40); Turk. 1519 **Gevher** [كوهر / Gevher Melik Sultan / Cem Sultan kızı], Djem Sultan's daughter (Gökb., Ed. 380); Turk. 1583 **Gevher** [كوهر / Gevher], fem. (Ongan, Ank. I, 157); Az. **Gevher-aγa**, fem. (Cafer., Ağa 92); Turk. 16th c. **Gevher-han** [Gevher Han binti Sultan Selim], Sultan Selim's daughter (Gökb., Ed. 501); Selj. 1146 **Gevher-χatun** [خاتون كوهر], Sultan Mas⁽ūd's (1134-1152) daughter (Rāwandī 227, 467); Selj. 12th c. **Gevher-χatun** [كوهر خاتون], Sultan Muχammad's wife (Rāwandī 132); Trkm. 20th c. **Gövher** [Gövher], fem. (Zaj. 1971, 338); Trkm. 20th c. **Gövher** [Гёвхер], fem. (TrkmRS 195); Maml. 14th c. **Güher** [كهار / gühär / Güher], fem. (Tarǰ/Houtsma 99, Tarǰ/Toparlı 44). ✧ 'Pearl, precious stone, brilliant, diamond' cf. Karakh. *gävhär* (P.<Ar.) 'жемчуг' (DTS), Kkalp. *gäwhar* 'жемчужина, жемчуг, перл; драгоценный камень; бриллиант, алмаз' (KkRS), Trkm. *gövher* 'женчуг' (TrkmRS), NUyg. *gōhär* 'der Edelstein, Karfunkel' (Radl. II, 1584) (<P.) جوهر ناز 'die köstliche Perle' (ChwolSyrNF 40), cf. also the P. personal names *Gauhar, Gōhar, Gūhar* which go back to Ar. *ǰauhar* 'jewel' (Justi 112). See also **JEWHER**.

GÄWHÄR-TAŠ   Selj. **Gähär-taš** (<Gäwhär-taš?) [بدرالدين كهرتاش / Kahr taš] (Ibn Bībī IV, 299); Maml.? 1302 **Göhär-daš** (<Göwhär-daš?) [كهرداش], Sayfaddīn ~, an emir (Dawād. 80). ✧ 'Precious stone'. ⇨ **GÄWHÄR** + **TAŠ**.

GEJE-GİDEN   Turk. **Geje-giden-oγlu** (Kúnos 1891, 119). ✧ 'Going by night; he who goes (away) at night' cf. Turk. *gece* 'night, at night' and *git-* 'to go (away), to lead (road)' (TED).

GEDAY   Chag. **Geday-sultan** [كداى سلطان / Гедай] (Šejb. LI, LXXIX).

GEDÜK   Turk. **Gedük** [كدوك احمد پاشا], Gedük Ahmed-paša (Āšikp. 166-70, 175-178, 180, 198).

GEGİL   Bashk. 1740 **Gegil** [Геглев Кинзеев] (MIB I, 404).

GEY-MUNČUQ   Az. **Gey-munčuq** [Гей-Мунчук] (Az. Skaz. 559). ⇨ **KEY+MUNČUQ**.

GEYİK see **KİYİK**

GEKPİŠ   Uzb. 1740 **Gekpiš-atalïq** [Гекпишъ-Аталыкъ], from Khiva (Hanykov, Poezdka 29).

GEL-BERİ   Turk. 20th c. **Gel-beri** [Gelberi] (TM IV,

164); Turk. **Gel-beri-sultan** [Gelberi Sultan] (Németh 1930a, 379). ✧ 'Come here/back!' (Rásonyi, Imp. 239). ⇨ **KEL.**

GELDİ see **KELDİ**

GELGEN Kirg. 19th c. **Gelgen-bi** [Гельгенъ-би] (Potanin II, 162).

GENJE see **KENJE**

GENJE-MİRAT see **GENJE-MURAT**

GENJE-MURAT Kkalp. 20th c. **Genje-mïrat** [Генжемырат] (KkRS 773); Kkalp. 20th c. **Genje-murat** [Генжемурат] (KkRS 773).

GENJEN Kzk. 19th c. **Genjen** [Геньдженъ] (Grod., Pril 174).

GENJİŠ Kzk. 19th c. **Genjiš** [Генджишъ], fem. (Grod., Pril. 29). ⇨ **KENJE?** + suff. -š.

GENDİ Kzk. 19th c. **Gendi-bay** [Буканбай Гяндибаевъ] (Grod., Pril. 25). ✧ 'With abundant treasure, rich, wealthy'? cf. Kzk. PN *Kendi* (Žanuzakov-Esbaeva), Kzk. *ken* 'bol hazine, zenginlik' (KzTS) + suff. -li.

GENENDİK Trkm. 19th c. **Genendik** [Генендыкъ Тагандурдыиевъ] (Ščeglov I, 354).

GERƏY see **KERÄY**

GERELİ Turk. **Gereli**, hero of Zeybek folksongs (Kúnos 1891, 116).

GEZ NUyg. 19th c. **Gez** [كز] (Le Coq, Namenl. 101). ✧ I. 'Arrow' (Le Coq) cf. Chag. *gäz* 'id' (Radl. II. 1574); II. 'Seat; linear measure'? cf. Chag. *gäz* 'der Sessel, Lehnstuhl'; (Chag., Turk.) (P.) 'ein Längemass, die Elle, Arschin' (Radl. II. 1574). See also **BEK-GEZ.**

GEZDAN Kzk. 19th c. **Gezdan-bay** [Гезданбай] (Grod., Pril. 144).

GİČ-GELDİ Trkm. 20th c. **Gičgeldi** [Gičgeldi] (Zaj. 1971, 334). ✧ '(S)he came late' cf. Trkm. *gič* 'поздно, поздний' (TrkmRS). ⇨ **KELDİ.**

GİYİK see **KİYİK**

GİLDEY see **KİLDEY**

GİNJE see **KENJE**

GİNEKEY Trkm. 19th c. **Ginekey** [Гинекеевъ] (Ščeglov I, 354).

GİRAY see **KERÄY**

GİREY see **KERÄY**

GİREYLİ see **KERÄYLİ**

GİREMEDİ Yürük 16th c. **Giremedi**, from the Yürüks of Kocacık, Turkey (Gökb., Rum. 104). ✧ 'He/she could not go/get in'.

GİREMEDİN Yürük 1543 **Giremedin** (Gökb., Rum. 117). ✧ 'You couldn't get in'.

GÖČ-BEGİ Yürük 1543 **Göč-begi** [كوچبكى / Göçbeği], from the Yürüks of Kocacık, Turkey (Gökb., Rum. 103, 178); *TN:* Turk. 1577 **Göč-begi** [Göç-beği], a village (Gökb., Ed. 218). ✧ 'Bek (leader) of wandering' or born at the time of wandering' cf. Turk. *göç* 'der Umzug; die Wanderung (der Nomaden)' (HŞ). ⇨ **BEK.**

See also **GÖČ-ERİ.**

GÖČ-ERİ Turk. 16th c. **Göč-eri** [كوجرى] (Ongan, Ank. II, 1386); Turk. 16th c. **Göč-eri** [Göçeri ibn İbrahim], from the region of Tarsus (Sümer: DTCFD XI, 339); Yürük 1543 **Göč-eri** [Göçeri] (Gökb., Rum. 103, 177, 196, 227, 228); Tat. 1543 **Göč-eri** [Göçeri] (Gökb., Rum. 236); *TN:* Turk. 20th c. **Göč-eri** [Göçeri], a village in the province of Adıyaman, Turkey (TMİB 30). ✧ 'Man (hero, soldier) of wandering (born at the time of wandering)'. ⇨ **ER.** See also **GÖČ-BEGİ.**

GÖČEBE see **KÖČEBE**

GÖČER-SÜLÜK Trkm. 1690 **Göčer-sülük** [كوجر سولك] (Refik, Anad. 82). ⇨ **KÖČER** + **SÜLÜK.**

GÖDE Turk. 1584 **Göde-bey** / **Göde-beg** [كو ده بك / Gödebey] (Ongan, Ank. I, 153). ✧ A male name (Erol II).

GÖGSEN Yürük **Gögsen-k'âhya** / **Göysen-k'âhya** [Gögsen kâhya], from the aširet of Tecirli (Riza V, 14).

GÖHÄR-DAŠ see **GÄWHÄR-TAŠ**

GÖK-DİL Yürük 1543 **Gök-dil** [كوكدل] (Gökb., Rum. 195). ✧ 'Free soul (heart)' cf. Turk. *dil* (P.) 'Gönül; Cesaret, yürek; İstek, niyet; yarı' (Özön). ⇨ **KÖK.**

GÖK-GÖZ see **KÖK-KÖZ**

GÖKČÄ see **KÖKČE**

GÖKČE see **KÖKČE**

GÖKMEN Yürük 1543 **Gökmen** (Gökb., Rum. 176). ✧ 'Blue-eyed ve blond' (Erol II). ⇨ **KÖK** + suff. -men.

GÖL-NÄZİK Tat. **Göl-näzik** [كل نازك] (Nasyrov-Poljakov 29-34). ✧ 'Nice flower' cf. Tat. *Nazik* 'Nice, kind, gentle' (Sattarov). ⇨ **GÜL.**

GÖLČÜ Yürük 1543 **Gölčü** (Gökb., Rum. 226). ⇨ **KÜL?** + suff. -čü / -jü.

GÖNDÜL Yürük 1543 **Göndül?** [كوندل], from Silistre (Gökb., Rum. 228).

GÖNÜLSÜZ Turk. 1495 **Gönülsüz** (Gökb., Ed. 134); Turk. 1494 **Gönülsüz-bey** (Gökb., Ed. 395). ✧ 'Humble, modest; unwilling' (TED).

GÖRE Yürük 1543 **Göre** (Gökb., Rum. 103).

GÖRÜNJİ Turk. 1491 **Görünjï** [Görüncî Kâtip] (Gökb., Ed. 103).

GÖZEL see **GÜZEL**

GÖZÜ-BÜYÜK Trkm. 1690 **Gözü-büyük-oγlu** [كوزى بيوك اوغلى] (Refik, Anad. 85); *EN:* Turk. 1576 **Gözü-büyükler** [Gözübüyükler] (?); *TN:* Turk. 20th c. **Gözü-büyük** [Gözübüyük], a village in the province of Çorum, Turkey (TMİB 259). ✧ 'Having big eyes; His eyes are big'. ⇨ **KÖZ** + **BÜYÜK.**

GULĀM Trkm. 1649 **Gulām-behadïr** [Гулям-бехадыр] (MIT II, 329). ✧ 'Boy, young man; slave' cf. Turk. (Ar.) *gulâm* 'der Knabe, der Jüngling' (HŞ). See also **BERDİ-GULĀM.**

GULĀMXAN NUyg.(Tar.) 19th c. **Gulāmχan**

[كولام حان / Гулямъ-ханъ], fem. (Pantusov III-II, 107).
⇨ **GULĀM** + suff. *-χan(1)*.

GÜJÜM Trkm. 20th c. **Güjim** [Гуджим] (TrkmRS 217); Trkm. 20th c. **Güjüm** [Гуджюм] (Zaj. 1971, 332). ✧ 'Elm(-tree)' cf. Trkm. *güjüm* 'ильм (дерево)' (TrkmRS).

GÜDE Yürük 1543 **Güde** (Gökb., Rum. 103).

GÜL Uzb. **Gùl-bibi** [Gul-bibi] (Nazaroff 44); Trkm. 20th c. **Gül** [Gül], fem. (Zaj. 1971, 339); Trkm. 20th c. **Gül** [Гюль], fem. (TrkmRS 219); Kkalp. 20th c. **Gül-ayïm** [Гулайым], fem. (KkRS 777); Turk. 16th c. **Gül-baba**, a dervish, resident in Buda, Hungary (Németh 1930a, 379); 1262/63 **Gül-beg**, Jemâl ad-dîn Gûlbâg, lord of Gâzarttâ (Abulfar./Budge I, 443, 444); Kkalp. 20th c. **Gül-bïybi** [Гулбийби], fem. (KkRS 777); Trkm. 20th c. **Gül-Jamal** [Gülğamal], fem. (Zaj. 1971, 339); Kkalp. **Gül-Jamal** [Гюльджамал], fem. (Baskakov: OSA 142); Trkm. 1873 **Gül-Jamal-ayïm** [Гульджамаль-аимъ] (Smirnov 73); Kkalp. **Gül-Jan** [Гульджан], fem. (Baskakov: OSA 142); Trkm. 1879-1881 **Gül-Jemal** [Gul Djemal] (O'Donovan II, 261); Turk. 1583 **Gül-dede** [كل دده] (Ongan, Ank. I, 173); Kzk. 19th c. **Gül-χanïs** [Гуль-ханысъ / Гульханысъ], a heroine of an epic (Divaev, Šura 89, Grod. I, 98); Kkalp. 20th c. **Gül-qatša** [Гулқатша], fem. (KkRS 777); Turk. 1471, 1485 **Gül-šah / Gül-šah-χatun** [Gülşah binti Abdullah, Gülşah Hatun], fem. (Gökb., Ed. 345, 319); Kkalp. 20th c. **Gül-žamal** [Гулжамал], fem. (KkRS 777); Kkalp. 20th c. **Gül-žan** [Гулжан], fem. (KkRS 777). ✧ 'Flower, rose' cf. Kirg. *kül, gül* 'цветок' (Jud.). Also a very frequent secondary component of female names. E. g. Kkalp. *Gül-ayïm, Biybi-gül* 'Lady-rose' (Baskakov: OSA 141), Kkalp. *Gül-jan* 'Rose-dear (darling)' (Baskakov: OSA 142), Kkalp., Trkm. *Gül-jamal* 'Beautiful flower' (O'Donovan) or 'Rose-beauty' (Baskakov: OSA 142). See also **BAΓDA-GÜL**.

GÜL-AY Karch. **Gül-ay** [Гулаевъ], a Karachay family (Sysoev 119); Kirg. **Gül-ay** [Гулай], fem. (Jud. 603). ✧ 'Rose/flower-Moon' cf. Turk. *Gülay*, Kkalp. *Gülayım* (Erol II). ⇨ **GÜL** + **AY**.

GÜL-AYÏM see **GÜL**

GÜL-ĀBÏ Turk. 1583 **Gül-ābi** [كلا بى / Gülâbi], several persons in the source (Ongan, Ank. I, 157). ✧ I. 'Rose/flower-brother' (Erol II), cf. Turk. *abi / ağabey* 'elder brother, used also as title of respect in addressing nonrelated persons' (TED); II. 'A kind of melone'? cf. Trkm. *gülabï* 'id.' (TrkmRS).

GÜL-BAΓDÏYA Bashk. 1765 **Gül-baγdïya / Göl-baγdïya** [Гулбагдыя Чурюкеева], fem. (MIB IV/1, 315). ⇨ **GÜL**.

GÜL-BAHAR Maml. 14th c. **Gül-bahar** [كلهار / Gülbahār], fem. (Tarj/Houtsma 98, Tarj/Toparlı 44); Turk. 1480 **Gül-bahar** [Gülbahar binti Abdullah (Ayşe

Hatun azadlısı)] (Gökb., Ed. 461); Trkm. 20th c. **Gül-bahar** [Гулбахар], fem. (Sopieva: OSA 180); Turk. 1468 **Gül-bahar-χatun**, Abdullah's daughter, mother of Sultan Bāyezid II (1481-1512) (Gökb., Ed. 320); Turk. 1529 **Gül-bahar-χatun**, Abdüssamed's daughter, mother of Yavuz Sultan Selim (Gökb., Ed. 46). ✧ 'Flower of spring'. In Sopieva's interpretation 'Blooming spring' („цветущая весна") (Sopieva: OSA 180). ⇨ **GÜL** + **BAHAR**.

GÜL-BARŠÏN Kzk. 19th c. **Gül-baršïn** [Гульбарчинъ], fem. (Grod. I, 98); Kkalp. 20th c. **Gül-paršïn** [Гулпаршын], fem. (KkRS 777). ✧ 'Rose-absent-minded; pondering-rose' (Baskakov: OSA 142). ⇨ **GÜL** + **BARŠÏN**.

GÜL-BAZAR Kkalp. 20th c. **Gül-bazar** [Гулбазар], fem. (KkRS 777). ✧ 'Rose of bazar; rose from the bazar (=nice, selected rose)' (Baskakov: OSA 141). ⇨ **GÜL** + **BAZAR**.

GÜL-ČIČEK Maml. 14th c. **Gül-čiček** [كلچيچك / Gülçiçek], fem. (Tarj/Houtsma 98, Tarj/Toparlı 43). ⇨ **GÜL** + **ČEČÄK**.

GÜL-JAN see **GÜL**

GÜL-JEMAL see **GÜL**

GÜL-JEMİLE NUyg.(Tar.) 19th c. **Gül-jemile** [كل جميله / Гюль-джемиле], fem. (Pantusov, Tar. 47). ✧ 'Flower/rose - Jamila' cf. Ar. fem. *Jamila* 'beautiful, pretty' (Ahmet). ⇨ **GÜL**.

GÜL-ÄNDÄM NUyg.(Tar.) 19th c. **Gül-ändäm** [كل اندام / Гюль-андамъ], fem. (Pantusov, Tar. 47). ✧ 'Flower-like figure/stature' (P.) cf. Tat., Bashk. fem. PN *Göländäm* (Kusimova, Sattarov), Tat. PN *Ändam* 'body, stature, trunk' (Sattarov) (<P.). ⇨ **GÜL**.

GÜL-HÄSÄM see **GÜL-HÄSEM**

GÜL-HÄSEM Kkalp. **Gül-häsäm** [Гюльхасам], fem. (Baskakov: OSA 141); Kkalp. 20th c. **Gül-häsen** [Гулхэсен], fem. (KkRS 777). ✧ 'Flower-beautiful', 'Beautiful rose' (Baskakov), cf. Kkalp. *häsem* 'красивый, симпатичный' (KkRS). ⇨ **GÜL**.

GÜL-HÄSEN see **GÜL-HÄSEM**

GÜL-QĀQÏ Kirg. **Gül-qāqï** [Гулкаакы], fem. (Jud. 308). ⇨ **GÜL**.

GÜL-LEYLUN NUyg.(Tar.) 19th c. **Gül-leylun** [كل ليلون / Гюлъ-Лейлунъ], fem. (Pantusov, Pesni 4, 80). ✧ 'Flower/Rose Leylun'. ⇨ **GÜL**.

GÜL-MUΧAMMED Trkm. 19th c. **Gül-muχamed** [Гуль-Мухамедъ] (Volodin 53); 1614 **Gül-muχammed-mirza** [Гюль-Мухаммедъ] (AI III, 444). ✧ 'Flower-Muχamed' (Volodin). ⇨ **GÜL** + **MUΧAMMED**.

GÜL-NAR Trkm. 20th c. **Gül-nar** [Gülnar], fem. (Zaj. 1971, 339); Kkalp. 20th c. **Gül-nar** [Гулнар], fem. (KkRS 777); Kirg. **Gül-nar** [Гулнар], fem. (Jud. 190); Maml. 14th c. **Gül-nār** [كلهار / Gülnār], fem.

(Tarǰ/Houtsma 98, Tarǰ/Toparlı 44). ✦ I. 'Noble-flower (rose)' cf. Kkalp. *nar* 'благородный; храбрый' (KkRS); II. 'Flower of pomegranate' (Baskakov: OSA 141). ⇨ **GÜL + NAR.** See also **GÜL-NARA.**

GÜL-NARA Bashk. 20th c. **Gül-nara (<Gül-nar),** very popular female name (1968) (Nikonov: OSA 158-60); Kzk. 20th c. **Gül-nara (<Gül-nar),** 30-40/1000 of the girls in the districts of Jambul (J̌ambul) and Southern Kazakstan (1969) (Nikonov: OSA 158-60); Kirg. 20th c. **Gül-nara (<Gül-nar),** 23-17/1000 of the girls in Kirghizistan (Nikonov: OSA 158-60); Uzb. 20th c. **Gül-nara (<Gül-nar)** [Гулнора], 34/1000 of the girls in Samarkand (1965) (Nikonov: OSA 158-60). ✦ 'Flower of pomegranate'. One of the most frequented Turkic female names. Under Tadjik influence *nara* arose from Tadj. *anor* 'гранат' (Nikonov: OSA 158-60). ⇨ **GÜL + NAR.** See also **GÜL-NAR.**

GÜL-PARŠÏN see **GÜL-BARŠÏN**

GÜL-SA see **GÜL-SÄ**

GÜL-SARA Kkalp. 20th c. **Gül-sara** [Гулсара], fem. (KkRS 777). ✦ 'Best / selected / high quality rose' (P.) (Baskakov: OSA 141). ⇨ **GÜL + SARA I.**

GÜL-SARAXAN Kirg. **Gül-saraχan** [Гулсарахан], fem. (Jud. 818). ⇨ **GÜL + SARA I.** + suff. *-χan(1).*

GÜL-SARÏ Kkalp. 20th c. **Gül-sarï** [Гюлсары, Гулсары], fem. (Bask., Kkalp. 403, KkRS 777). ✦ 'Yellow rose' (Baskakov: OSA 141). ⇨ **GÜL + SARÏ.**

GÜL-SÄ Kkalp. 20th c. **Gül-sä** [Гулса], fem. (KkRS 777). ✦ 'Beautiful rose' (Baskakov: OSA 142). ⇨ **GÜL-SÄNEM.**

GÜL-SÄNEM Kkalp. 20th c. **Gül-sänem** [Гюлсänem, Гулсänem], fem. (Bask., Kkalp. 403, KkRS 777). ✦ 'Flower/rose-darling'; 'Beautiful rose' (Baskakov: OSA 142), cf. Bashk. fem. PN *Sänä* 'Bright beam' (Kusimova), Tat. fem. PN *Sänam* 'Beloved darling of mine' (Sattarov) (<Ar.). ⇨ **GÜL.**

GÜL-SEVER Tat. (Mish.) 1759 **Gül-sever** [Гульзевер Салихова], fem. (MIB IV/1, 183). ✦ 'Lover of flowers (roses)' cf. PN *Sever* 'Sevgi besler, gönül verir, hoşlanır, etc.' (Erol II), Aor./Part. of *sev-* 'to love, to like; to pet, fondle' (TED). ⇨ **GÜL.**

GÜL-SÏFAT Tat.(Sib.) 1599 **Gül-sïfat / Gül-sïfat?** [Гулсыфатъ], a Siberian princess, Küčüm's daughter (AI II, 17, 20, 23). ✦ 'Rose-like; having an appearance of a rose/flower' cf. Turk. *sıfat* (Ar.) 'quality; appearance' (TED). ⇨ **GÜL.**

GÜL-ŠAT Kkalp. 20th c. **Gül-šat** [Гулшат], fem. (KkRS 777). ✦ 'Rose-glad; glad rose/flower' (Baskakov: OSA 142). ⇨ **GÜL + ŠAT.**

GÜL-ŠÄR Kkalp. 20th c. **Gül-šär** [Гулшар], fem. (KkRS 777). ✦ 'Sad rose' cf. Kkalp. *šär, šäri* (P.) 'грустный, печальный' (Baskakov: OSA. 141). ⇨ **GÜL.**

GÜL-ŠEHRİ Turk. 1485 **Gül-šehri** [Kızıl Delü oğlu] (Gökb., Ed. 183). ✦ 'New Moon of rose' cf. Turk. *şehr*

'yeni ay, hilâl' (Özön) (<P.), cf. also Turk. PNs *Şehrigülserin, Şehriyâr, Şehriye* (Erol II). ⇨ **GÜL.**

GÜL-ŠENE Turk. 1473 **Gül-šene** [Gülşene binti Abdullah], fem. (Gökb., Ed. 346). ✦ I. 'Rose garden; Flower garden' cf. Turk. PN *Gülşen* 'id.' (Erol II), Turk. *gülşen* 'id.' (TED); II. 'Rose/Flower - Cheerful'? cf. Turk. *şen* 'joyous, cheerful' (TED) (<P.). ⇨ **GÜL +** fem. suff. *-ä(1).* See also **GÜL-ZAR.**

GÜL-TURSÏN Kkalp. **Gül-tursïn** [Гюльтурсын], fem. (Baskakov: OSA 141). ✦ 'Let the rose/flower live' (Baskakov). ⇨ **GÜL + TURSÏN.**

GÜL-ZAR Kkalp. 20th c. **Gül-zar** [Гулзар], fem. (KkRS 777). ✦ 'Rose garden; Flower garden' (Erol II), cf. Turk. *gülzar* 'id.' (TED) (<P.). ⇨ **GÜL.** See also **GÜL-ŠENE.**

GÜL-ZÄBİYRÄ Kkalp. 20th c. **Gül-zäbiyrä** [Гулзәбийра], fem. (KkRS 777). ✦ 'Energetic-rose' (Baskakov: OSA 142). ⇨ **GÜL.**

GÜL-ZİYRÄ Kkalp. 20th c. **Gül-ziyrä** [Гулзийра], fem. (KkRS 777). ✦ 'Smart, nice rose' (Baskakov: OSA 142). ⇨ **GÜL.**

GÜL-ŽÏRÄ Kkalp. 20th c. **Gül-žïrä** [Гюлжирä], fem. (Bask., Kkalp. 38). ⇨ **GÜL + ČİHRE?**

GÜLJÜ Yürük 1543 **Güljü / Göljü?** (Gökb., Rum. 226). ⇨ **GÜL +** suff. *-jü.*

GÜLDAR Kzk. 19th c. **Güldar** [красавица Гульдаръ], fem. (AUK 570). ⇨ **GÜL +** suff. *-dār.*

GÜLDİRSİN Kkalp. 20th c. **Güldirsin** [Гулдирсин] (KkRS 773).

GÜLDÜK Yürük 1543 **Güldük** [كولدك] (Gökb., Rum. 221). ✦ 'We laughed (smiled)' cf. Turk. *gül-* 'laugh, smile' (TED).

GÜLÄLEK Trkm. **Gülälek** [Гуләлек] (Sopieva: OSA 177); Trkm. 20th c. **Gülälek** [Gülälek], fem. (Zaj. 1971, 339). ✦ 'Field poppy, red poppy' (Zaj. 1971, Sopieva), cf. Trkm. *gülälek* 'мак красный' (TrkmRS).

GÜLEK Yürük 1543 **Gülek** [كولك] (Gökb., Rum. 180). ✦ 'Ridiculous; smiling' cf. Trkm. *gülek* 'id.' (TrkmRS).

GÜLXAN Kkalp. 20th c. **Gülχan** [Гулхан], fem. (KkRS 777). ⇨ **GÜL +** suff. *-χan(1).*

GÜLİ-BUDAQ Trkm. 1620 **Güli-budaq** [كو لى بـدا ق], from Anatolia (Refik, Anad. 61). ⇨ **GÜL + BUTAQ.**

GÜLİKEY Trkm. 19th c. **Gülikey** [Кенже Гуликеевъ] (Ščeglov IV, 165).

GÜLİM Kkalp. 20th c. **Gülim-xan** [Гулимхан], fem. (KkRS 777). ✦ 'My lady-rose' (Baskakov: OSA 142). ⇨ **GÜL +** poss. suff. *-im.*

GÜLİMBET Kkalp. 20th c. **Gülimbet** [Гулимбет] (KkRS 773). ⇨ **GÜL +** suff. *-imbet.*

GÜLİSTAN Turk. 16th c. **Gülistan** (Ongan, Ank. II); Kkalp. 20th c. **Gülistan** [Гулистан], fem. (KkRS 777). ✦ 'Rose garden; rosy-cheeked' (Erol II) (<P.). ⇨ **GÜL +** suff. *-(i)stan.*

GÜLLER Az. **Güller** [жена Ахмеда Гуллер], fem. (Az. Skaz. 245). ✧ 'Roses' (Erol II). ⇨ **GÜL** + plur. suff. *-ler*.

GÜLLİ Turk. 1583 **Gülli**, fem. (Ongan, Ank. I, 157); Az. **Gülli-χanum** [Гюлли-ханум], fem. (Az. Skaz. 482); Turk. 1485 **Güllü-χatun**, Yahşi Fakih's granddaughter (Gökb., Ed. 175). ✧ 'Flowered, in blossom' (Erol II). ⇨ **GÜL** + suff. *-li*. See also **İKİ-GÜLLİ**.

GÜLLİ-ГАХ-ГАХ Az. **Gülli-γaχ-γaχ-χanum** [Гюлли-Гах-Гах-ханум], fem. (Az. Skaz. 42). ✧ 'Having roses/flowers -?' cf. Turk. *kâh kâh* 'at times, now and then' (TED). ⇨ **GÜL** + suff. *-li*.

GÜLLÜ see **GÜLLİ**

GÜLME Yürük 1543 **Gülme** [كولمه], from Filibe (Gökb., Rum. 233). ✧ 'Laughing, laughter; jest, joke' cf. Turk. *gülme* 'id.' (TED).

GÜLSİM Kkalp. 20th c. **Gülsim** [Гулсим], fem. (KkRS 777). ✧ 'Beautiful rose' (Baskakov: OSA142). ⇨ **GÜL-SÄNEM.**

GÜLSÜN Yürük 1935 **Gülsün**, fem. (Naci Kum Atabeyli, Gülsünün Düğünü: Ün II, (1935), 277); Turk. 20th c. **Gülsün-oγlu**, a Zeybek (Kúnos 1891, 119). ✧ 'Let him/her smile' (Rásonyi, Imp. 239), cf. Turk. *gül-* 'to laugh' (TED) + imp. suff. *-sün*.

GÜLÜM Kzk. 19th c. **Gülüm** [Гюлумъ] (Grod., Pril. 110). ✧ I. 'My flower! (addressing)' (Erol II); II. 'Laugh' (Erol II) cf. Turk. *gülme* 'id.' (TED).

GÜLÜM-BALÏ Turk. 1583 **Gülüm-balï** [كولم بالى], Hızır-balı's son (Ongan, Ank. I, 157). ⇨ **GÜL** + **BALÏ / BĀLİ?**

GÜLÜMQAN Kkalp. 20th c. **Gülümqan** [Гюлюмкъан], fem. (Bask., Kkalp. 403). ⇨ **GÜLÜM** + suff. *-qan(1)*.

GÜLÜNJE Tat. 1543 **Gülünje** [كولنجه / Gülünce] (Gökb., Rum. 236). ✧ 'Ridiculous' cf. Turk. *gülünj* 'das Gespött, lächerlich' (Radl. II, 1642) + suff. *-e*.

GÜMİS-AY see **KÜMÜŠ-AY**

GÜMLÜ Turk. 1526, 1568 **Gümlü** [Murad Bey bin Gümlü] (Gökb., Ed. 230); Turk. 1481, 1568 **Gümlü / Gümlü-oγlu** (Gökb., Ed. 229, 230); Turk. 1481 **Gümlü-bey** (Gökb., Ed. 229).

GÜMRİ Yürük 1453 **Gümri** [كومرى] (Gökb., Rum. 192, 226). ✧ 'Small earthen pot; small earthenware cooking pot' cf. Turk. dial. *gümrü = güdü I* 'küçük çömlek, güveç' (DS).

GÜMÜŠ see **KÜMÜŠ**

GÜMÜŠ-AY see **KÜMÜŠ-AY**

GÜN-ARÏ Turk. **Gün-arï-bey**, Karaman's son (Uzunçarş., Anad. 4). ⇨ **GÜN** + **ARÏГ.**

GÜN-DOГDÏ see **KÜN-TOГDÏ**

GÜN-DOГMUŠ see **KÜN-TOГMÏŠ**

GÜN-DÖYEN Trkm. **Gün-döyen-bey / Gün-dögen-bey?** [Gündöğen Bey], a former chief of the nomadic Sarï-kečili tribe (Riza III, 35). ✧ 'Sun-

Beating/Thrashing'? cf. Turk. *döv-/döğ-* 'to beat, to thrash' (TED). ⇨ **KÜN.**

GÜNDÜZ Turk. 14th c. **Gündüz** [Κουντούζης], son of Sultan Murad I (1362-1389) (Byz. Turc. 168); Yürük 1543 **Gündüz** (Gökb., Rum. 182, 232); Trkm. 1484 **Gündüz** [كندز / كوندوز], among the Türkmen taking possession of Çukurova, Turkey (Āšikp. 188, 225, Sümer: DTCFD XI, 331); Tat. 1543 **Gündüz** (Gökb., Rum. 232, 235, 239); Selj./Trkm. 13th c. - 14th c. **Gündüz / Gündüz-alp / Gündüz-bey** [كوندز / Ιουδουζάλπης / Sarubatı (Gündüz Alp)], Oghuz prince, Er-toγrul's son, brother Osman-bey I (1280-1324) (Nešrī 196, Byz. Turc. 139, Sevim-Yücel II, 3); Selj./Trkm. 13th c. **Gündüz-alp**, Er-tuγrul's relative (either his father or son), see the other GÜNDÜZ-items (Ibn Bībī III, 61, 218); Selj./Trkm. 13th c. **Gündüz-alp**, probable father of Ertuγrul-bey, the forefather of the Ottoman dynasty (Toğan, UTT 324, Sevim-Yücel II, 2); Turk. **Gündüz-bey**, from the region of Denizli (Kúnos 1891, 115); *EN:* Turk. 1863-73 **Gündüz-ašireti**, a nomadic tribe in the region of Manisa (Akhisar, Gölmarmara), Turkey (Gökçen 95); *TN:* Turk. 20th c. **Gündüz-bey**, a „bucak" in the province of Malatya, Turkey (TMİB 611). ✧ 'Daytime' (Erol II), cf. Turk. 'id.' (TED).

GÜNEŠ Oghuz/Trkm. 13th c. **Güneš** [كونش / Гүнеш] (Abulg./Kon. 1250); Turk. 1467 **Güneš-χatun** [Güneş Hatun], fem. (Gökb., Ed. 523). ✧ 'Sun' (TED).

GÜRJİN Turk. **Gürjin-oγlu** [Gürӡyn oγlu], a Zeybek (Kúnos 1891, 118).

GÜREY see **KÜREY**

GÜVENDİK Turk. 16th c. **Güvendik**, eight persons in the same source (Ongan, Ank. II); Turk. 1583 **Güvendik** [كوندك], name of three persons in the source (Ongan, Ank. I, 157); Yürük 1543 **Güvendik** [كوندك], from the yürüks of Kocacık, Turkey (Gökb., Rum. 103, 204, 228); Turk. 1540 **Güvendik-kethudā**, chief of the Hüseyin Hajīlu in a defter from Diyarbekir (Demirtaş 49); Turk. 16th c. **Güvendik-oγlu** [Ahmed Güvendik-oğlu] (Ongan, Ank. II). ✧ 'We trusted in him; we relied on him' cf. Turk. *güvän-* 'sich anvertrauen, trauen, sich stützen auf' (Radl. I, 1652).

GÜZÄL see **GÜZEL**

GÜZEL Trkm. **Gözel** [Гөзел], fem. (Sopieva: OSA 177); Trkm. 20th c. **Gözel** [Gözel], fem. (Zaj. 1971, 336); Trkm. 20th c. **Gözel** [Гөзел], fem. (TrkmRS 197); Uzb. 1972 **Güzäl** [Гузал], fem. (Erohina-Ramazanova: OSA 202); Turk. 16th c. **Güzel**, fem. (Ongan, Ank. II, 1110). ✧ 'Beautiful, pretty, good, nice; beauty, belle' cf. Turk. *güzel* 'id.' (TED), Trkm. *gözel* 'красавица; красивый, прекрасный' (TrkmRS). See also **HÄSEN, KÜRKLİ, KÖRKLÄ, KÖRTLÄ, NİGĀR, SİLÏГ, ZİFA.**

Г

ГАBAYDULLA   Kzk. 19th c. **Гabaydulla** [султанъ Габайдулла или Обайдулла] (AUK 157). ✧ Aḃidullah? (Ar.) 'worshipper of Allah' (Ahmed).

ГАBİ   Bashk. 1763 **Гabi** [Габи Исенбаев] (MIB IV/1, 267).

ГАBİRİLLA see **XABRİLLA**

ГАJAR   Trkm. 20th c. **Гajar** [Gaǧar] (Zaj. 1971, 331). ✧ 'Gryphon' cf. Trkm. *γaǰar* 'черный гриф' (TrkmRS).

ГАDAY   Uzb. 20th c. **Гaday** [Gadai], a basmačï from Bukhara (Castagné 79).

ГАDAM   Trkm. 20th c. **Gadam** [Gadam] (Zaj. 1971, 330); Trkm. 20th c. **Гadam** [Гадам] (TrkmRS 137). ✧ 'Step' cf. Trkm. *γadam* 'id.' (TrkmRS).

ГАFLET   Oghuz/Trkm. 15th c. **Гaflet-qoja** [غلت قوجه], Šer Šemsäddin's father (DQorq./Rossi 144). ✧ 'Carelessness' cf. Crm., Turk. *γaflät* (Ar.) 'die Nachlässigkeit, Sorglosigkeit' (Radl. II, 1549-1550).

ГАGUY   Mo.? 13th c.? **Гaγuy** [Гагуй] (RaD I/1, 192).

ГАİB   Kzk. 19th c. **Гaib** [Гаибовъ] (SKSO VIII, 204). ✧ 'Lost, missing' cf. Turk. *gaip* (Ar.) 'id.' (TED).

ГАУ   Tat.(Tüm.) 1631 **Гaу** [Исенмамет Гаев] (Miller, Ist. Sib. II, 386); Kzk. **Гaу-bek** [Гайбекъ] (Sb. Syr-D. IX, 46). ✧ 'Panther' cf. Chag. *gaj* [غى] 'párduc [=panther]' (Thúry 51).

ГАУJİM   Turk. **Гayǰïm-oγlu**, a Zeybek (Kúnos 1891, 119).

ГАУDA-BOL   Kzk. 19th c. **Гayda-bol** [Гайдаболовъ] (Grod., Pril. 40). ✧ 'Be returning'? ⇨ **AYDA + BOL.**

ГАУDAN   Selj. **Гaydan** [غيدان], an Emir (Aqsarāyï 83).

ГАУİT see **AYT**

ГАУLİ   Trkm. 20th c. **Гaylï** [Gaylï] (Zaj. 1971, 330). ✧ 'Snow-stormy' cf. Trkm. *γaylï* 'сопровождаемый метелью, бурей; вьюжный' (TrkmRS).

ГАУMİŠ see **QAYMİŠ**

ГАУR see **XAYR**

ГАУSAR   Bashk. 1750 **Гaysar** [Гайсар Уразлин] (MIB III, 473); Bashk. 1775 **Гaysar** [Гайсар Яркеев] (MIB IV/1, 376); Bashk. 1789 **Гaysar** [Гайсар Еркеев] (MIB V, 250); Bashk. 1796 **Гaysar** [Гайсар Арасланов] (MIB V, 360). ✧ Gaysar (Ar.) (Kusimova).

ГАУSГАN   12th c.? **Гaysγan** [Gâisgân], the Turkish governor of Antioch when it was besieged by the crussaders (Abulfar./Budge I, 235).

ГАLAY-EMET   Bulg. 1319/20 **Гalay-emet** [غلای اماه / Galāy Emēt] (Epigr. Bulg. 126-127). ✧ Ali-Aχmet? (Ar.), cf. Tat. PN *Гali-äχmät* (Sattarov).

ГАLANDAR see **QALÄNDÄR**

ГАLBİR   Kzk. 19th c. **Гalbir** [Галбиръ] (Grod., Pril. 171). ✧ 'Canister, tin' cf. Kzk. *qalbir* 'жестяная банка' (KzRS).

ГАLDAN   Kzk.? 19th c. **Гaldan** [Галдан] (Verb., In. 119, 120). ✧ '?' (<Mo.?). ⇨ **QALDAN.**

ГАLDİ   1541 **Гaldï** [Галдѣй] (PSRL XIII, 113). ⇨ **QALDİ?**

ГАLİ-ASQAR   Kzk. 19th c. **Гali-asqar** [Галиоскаръ] (SOK 162). ✧ 'Ali('s) soldier'. ⇨ **ALİ + ASKER.**

ГАLİM see **ALİM**

ГАLKEY see **ALİKEY**

ГАN-TİMUR see **QAN-TEMİR**

ГАNDİM   Trkm. 20th c. **Гandïm** [Gandïm] (Zaj. 1971, 332); Trkm. 20th c. **Гandïm** [Кандым] (TrkmRS 151). ✧ 'A kind of bush' cf. Trkm. *γandïm* 'джузгун' (TrkmRS).

ГАPALAW   Karch. 20th c. **Гapalaw** [Гар ʿaláu] (Pröhle, Kar. 103).

ГАRA see **QARA**

ГАRГА see **QARГА**

ГАWXÄR see **GÄWHÄR**

ГАZ see **QAZ**

ГАZ-BOYLU   Turk. 19th c. **Гaz-boylu-oγlu** (Kúnos 1891, 119). ✧ 'Goos-statured'. ⇨ **QAZ + BOY + suff. -lu.**

ГАZAN   Kipch.? **Гazan** [Газан], Kipchak's descendant from the Ĵalayïr tribe (RaD I/1, 96); Khorezm.? 13th c. **Гazan** [Καζάνης / Газан-хан], Ilkhanid (1295-1304) (Byz. Turc. 146, MIT I, 52-53, 56, 506-507, 513); Khorezm./Chag. 1410/11 **Гazan** [Газан], an emir (MIT I, 531-32); 13th c. **Гazan-bahadur** [Газан-бахадур], Qutluγ-buqa's son (RaD I/1, 142). See also **QUTLU-ГAZAN.**

ГАZİR   Alt. 19th c. **Гazïr-γam** [Газыръ-гамъ], a shaman in a tale from the Altai (Potanin IV, 290). ✧ 'Despot, tyrant; angry, annoyed' cf. Alt. *qazïr* 'гневный, грозный, жестокий' (OjrRS).

ГАZİ   Tat.(Mish.) 1757 **Гāzi** [Мещеряк Курманай Газиев (Газев)] (MIB IV/1, 135, 290, 291). ✧ Ghazi (Ar.) 'conqueror, hero, gallant soldier' (Ahmed), used also as a secondary component of male names (see). See also **BENAM-ГĀZİ, İČ-ГĀZİ; ĴENKİ.**

ГÄNİY   Kkalp. 20th c. **Гäniy** [Фәний] (KkRS 773). ✧ Ghani / Ghaniyy (Ar.) 'rich, wealthy, prosperous' (Ahmed). See also **ÄBDİ-ГÄNİY.**

ГİLİČ-DURDİ   Trkm. **Гïlïč-durdï** [Гылычдурды] (Sopieva: OSA 181). ⇨ **QÏLÏČ + TURDİ.**

ГİMMAT see **QÏYMAT**

ГİZ-DURDİ   Trkm. 20th c. **Гïz-durdï** [Gïzdurdï], fem. (Zaj. 1971, 335). ✧ 'The daughter stayed/survived'; 'The daughter will long live' (Zaj. 1971). ⇨ **QÏZ + TURDİ.**

ГОГUČİK   Chul. 1674 **Гoγučik** [Гогучековъ сынъ Кулунгайко] (Jarilov, Tel. 8).

ГOQUM Turk. 20th c. Гoqum-oɣlu, a Zeybek (Kúnos 1891, 119).

ГORLAQ Bashk. 1667 Гorlaq [Севергунко Горлаков] (AI IV, 373). ⇨ **QURLAQ?**

ГORLAN Tat. 1682 Гorlan [Горлан] (MIB I, 206).

ГOSMAN see **OSMAN**

ГOŠA Trkm. 20th c. Гоšа [Гоша] (Sopieva: OSA 181); Trkm. 20th c. Гoša [Goša] (Zaj. 1971, 330); Trkm. 20th c. Гoša [Гоша] (TrkmRS 191). ✧ 'Pair; mate, companion' cf. Trkm. γоša 'два; пара' (TrkmRS).

ГOŠUN Trkm. 20th c. Gošun [Gošun] (Zaj. 1971, 327); Trkm. 20th c. Gošun [Гошун] (TrkmRS 192). ✧ 'Army' cf. Trkm. γošun 'армия, войска' (TrkmRS), Trk. qošun 'Truppe' (TMEN I, No. 282) (<Mo.). See also **BEK-ČERI, SÜ, ZURUM.**

ГUBER Kzk. 1803 Гuber-batïr? [Губер батырь], one of the chiefs of the Aday tribe, Kiši Ĵuz (MIK IV, 575); Kzk. 1820 Гuber-batïr? [Губеръ-батыръ], on of the chiefs of the Bayulï tribe (Sib. Vest. IX, 118).

ГUYRUQSUZ Turk. 20th c. Гuyruqsuz-oɣlu, a Zeybek (Kúnos 1891, 119). ✧ 'Without tail; Having no tail'. ⇨ **QUYRUQ** + suff. -suz.

ГUMER see **ÖMÜR**

ГUMRÏ Trkm. Гumrï [Гумры], fem. (Sopieva: OSA 178). ✧ 'Turtle-dove; wild pigeon' (Sopieva: OnSrAz. 178).

ГUNČA Trkm. 20th c. Гunča [Gunča], fem. (Zaj. 1971, 339); Trkm. 20th c. Гunča [Гунча], fem. (TrkmRS 210). ✧ 'Bud' cf. Crm., Turk. qonǰa 'die Knospe' (Radl. II, 547), Trkm. γunča 'бутон' (TrkmRS) (<P.).

ГUNTURUNTAY Yak. 19th c. Гunturuntay [Гунтурунтай] (Potanin IV, 637).

ГUR see **QUR**

ГURBAN see **QURBAN**

ГURBAN-BERDI see **QURBAN-BERDI**

ГURBAN-DURDI see **QURBAN-TURDI**

ГURSANJÏ Khorezm. 13th c. Гursanĵï / Гursanši / Гuršayĵï, byname of Sultan Rukneddïn (the /grand-/son of Alāaddin Muhammad II, 1200-1220), lived 1205-1222 (Ĵuwaynī II, 208-210).

ГURSANŠÏ see **ГURSANJÏ**

ГURŠAYĴÏ see **ГURSANJÏ**

ГUSMAN see **OSMAN**

ГUZ Oghuz 1119/20 Гuz-oɣlï [غزغلى / Ghozz-Oghli], Sultan Maχmud's atabek, executed by Sultan Sandjar (Ibn äl-Athïr: RHCHor I, 321,785); Selj. Гuz-oɣlï [غزغلى], Sultan Sanjar's χāĵib (Rāwandī 168); Selj. Гuz-oɣlï [غزغلى السلاحى] (Bondārï 185, 188, 189). ✧ 'Ghuz' (ethnonym).

ГUZDAW Kzk. 19th c. Гuzdaw [Нурджау Гуздавовъ] (Grod., Pril. 83).

ГUVANČ SEE QUWANČ

H

HAQ-BERDI Kzk. 1820 **Aq-berdi** [Акберди] (Sib. Vest. IX, 118); Kirg. **Aq-berdi** [Акберди] (Jud. 181); Kzk.? 19th c.? **Haq-berdi** [Хакберды] (SKSO III, 19); Uzb. 20th c. **Haq-berdi** [Хакберди] (Begmatov 1984, 200, 202); *EN:* Kzk. 18th c. - 19th c. **Aq-berdi** [Акберды] (Tynyšp. 66). ✧ 'God-Given', meaning „May God save/protect him/her" (Sattarov 199, Erol II, 178), cf. Chag., Az., Crm., EastT., Turk. *haq* (<Ar.) 'die Wahrheit, das Recht, die Richtigkeit, Gott' (Radl. II, 1742), Trkm. *χaq* 'истина, правда; (разг.) худай' (TrkmRS). Cf. also Ar. PN Haqq 'true, real, right, just', Al-Haqq 'the Truth', one of the names of Allah (Ahmed). ⇨ **BERDI**. See also **ALLA-BERDI, HAQ-BERГÄN, XUDAY-BERDI, XUDAY-BERGEN, OГAN-BERDI, SATTAR-BERDI.**

HAQ-BERGÄN Uzb. 20th c. **Haq-bergän** [Хакберган] (Begmatov 1984, 202). ✧ 'God-Given', meaning „May God save/protect him/her" (Sattarov 199, Erol II, 178), cf. Chag., Az., Crm., EastT., Turk. *haq* (<Ar.) 'die Wahrheit, das Recht, die Richtigkeit, Gott' (Radl. II, 1742), Trkm. *χaq* 'истина, правда; (разг.) худай' (TrkmRS). ⇨ **BERGEN.** See also **HAQ-BERDI.**

HAZĀR Khazar 737 **Hazār-tarχān** [Hazār Tarχän], a military commander (Golden 181). ✧ 'Thousand' cf. Karakh. *hāzar* 'тысяча' (DTS) (<P.).

HÄSÄM-GÜL see **HÄSEN**

HÄSEN Kzk. 19th c. **Äsem-bay** [Асембай] (SOV 74); Kzk. 20th c. **Äsem-kül** [Асемкуль], fem. (Sultan'jaev 1970, p. 75); Kkalp. **Häsäm-gül**, fem. (Baskakov: OSA 141); Kkalp. 20th c. **Häsen-gül** [Хәсенгүл], fem. (KkRS 779). ✧ 'Beautiful, nice (rose, flower)' Kkalp. *häsem* 'красивый, симпатичный' (KkRS), Kzk. *äsem* 'id.' (KzRS). (<P.) حسن *häsän* 'id.' (PRS), cf. Turk. *hasen* 'güzel, iyi, hoş' (Özön) (<Ar.) See also **GÜL-HÄSEM; GÜZEL, KÜRKLI, KÖRKLÄ, KÖRTLÄ, NIGÄR, SILÏГ, ZIFA.**

HÄSIYET Trkm. 20th c. **Häsiyet** [Häsiyet] (Zaj. 1971, 336); Trkm. 20th c. **Häsiyet** [Хасиет], fem. (TrkmRS 713). ✧ 'Character' cf. Trkm. *χäsiyet* 'характер, поведение' (TrkmRS) (<Ar.).

HEMRĀ Trkm. 20th c. **Hemrā** [Hemra] (Zaj. 1971, 326); Trkm. 20th c. **Hemrā** [Хемра] (TrkmRS 696). ✧ 'Companion, fellow traveller' cf. Trkm. *hemrā* 'id.' (TrkmRS) (<P.).

HESEL Trkm. 20th c. **Hesel** [Hesel] (Zaj. 1971, 336); Trkm. 20th c. **Hesel** [Хесел], fem. (TrkmRS 697). ✧

'Honey' cf. Trkm. dial. *hesel* 'id.' (TrkmRS) (<Ar.).

HİYLİ   Kzk. 19th c. **Hiyli-bay** [Хийлибай] (SOK 88).

HİND-AL   Khorezm. / Chag. 14th c. **Hind-al**, Šāh Mīrzā's son, successor of his brother Šīrāšāmuk, and ruled as Qutbeddīn (1386-1396) (Justi 129); Khorezm. / Chag. 16th c. **Hind-al**, Bāber's / Bābur's (1497-98, 1500-1501) son, a poet, died in a battle on 19 November, 1551. He was just born when his father was taking Hind(ustan) (Justi 129). ✧ 'Take Hindustan!' (Rásonyi, Imp., p. 237, Erol II), 'Conqueror of Hindustan' (Erol II). ⇨ **AL**.

HİNDİ   Trkm. 1610 **Hindi** [هندى], from Syria (Refik, Anad. 62); Trkm. 1690 **Hindi-kethudā** [هندى كتحدا] (Refik, Anad. 87); NUyg. 16th c. **İndi-bay** [اىندى باى / Indi Bai], resident in Khiva (Abulg./Desm. 269). ✧ 'Indian (being from India), Hindu' cf. Uyg. *indi* 'hindisch' (Radl. I, 1450), Trkm. *χindi* 'id.' (TrkmRS).

HİNDU   Oghuz 1199/1200, 1219 **Hindu-χan** [Хинду-хан], nephew of the Khorezmshah Muχammed ibn Tekeš (1200-1220), proprietor of Yazyr (MIT I, 448, 47:). ✧ 'Hindu' (ethnonym).

HİNŽİ-GÜL see **İNŽİ**

HİTAY see **QİTAY**

HÖKKÄ   Karg. **Hökkä** [Хöккä] (Proben IX, 658).

HÖÑGÄYÄK   Karg. **Höñgäyäk** [Хöҥгäjäк (Михаилъ Матвеевичъ Конгояковъ)] (Proben IX, 660).

HÜMMET   Trkm. 20th c. **Hümmet** [Hümmet] (Zaj. 1971, 328); Trkm. 20th c. **Hümmet** [Хуммет] (TrkmRS 708). ✧ 'Strength, power; endeavour' cf. Trkm. *hümmet* 'сила; мощь' (TrkmRS) (<Ar.).

X

XABAX-MÄYİ   Yak. **Xabaχ-mäyi** [Хабах-Мäji] (Pek.). ✧ 'Bladder/bubble-head' (Pek.).

XABAYA   Yak. **Xabaya** [Хабаjа] (Pek.).

XABAYAS   Yak. **Xabayas** [Хабаjас] (Pek.).

XABARČA   Yak. **Xabarča** [Хабарча], one of Moγujān's 9 sons (Pek.).

XABJİΓRİAY   Yak. **XabJïγrïay** / **XabJïγïrïay** [Хабцыгрыаi / Хабцыгырыаi] (Pek.). ✧ 'He screams like a patridge; he drivels nonsense' cf. Yak. *χabJïγ(ï)rä-* 'испускать звук, подобный тому, какой испускают куропатки, кричать как куропатка, говорить чепуху, болтать с видом знатока' (Pek.).

XABİDAL-XARA   Yak. **Xabïdal-χara-buχatïr** [Хабыдал-хара-бухатыр], an *abāsï*-bogatyr (hero, warrior) (Pek.). ⇨ **QARA**.

XABİQİYA   Yak. **Xabïqïya** [Хабыкыjа], a hero from the descendants of Xarañaččï-Sürük (Pek.).

XABİRİLLA see **XABRİLLA**

XABRİLLA   Yak. Габïrïlla [Габырылла] (Pek.).

XABİP   Trkm. 20th c. **Xabïp** [Набïп / Хабып] (Zaj. 1971, 325). ✧ 'Friend' (Zaj. 1971), cf. Trkm. *χabïp* 'id.' (<Ar.).

XABİTA   Yak. **Xabïta** [Хабыта] (Pek.).

XABRİLLA   Yak. **Xabrïlla** / **Xabïrïlla** [Хабрылла / Хабырылла / Габырылла] (Pek.). ✧ Gavriil, Gavrila (R.).

XABRİS   Yak. **Xabrïs** / **Xabrïrïs** (<Xab(ï)rïlla) [Хабрыс / Хабрырыс], a shaman living in the *ulus* of Boturus, Xosχoyor's contemporary (Pek.). ✧ Gavriil (R.). See also **XABRİLLA**.

XABU   Hak. 19th-20th c. **Xabu** [Хабу] (HRS 352). ✧ 'Tinder, matchwood' cf. Hak. *χabo* 'трут' (HRS).

XAČİYA   Yak. **Xačïya** [Хачыjа] (Pek.). See also **XALLĀN-XAČİYA**.

XAČMAZ see **QAČMAZ**

XAJ-ANAY see **XAJİ**

XAJ-ERİ   Maml. 1293 **Xaj-eri** [حاجرى] (Baybars/Tizeng. I, 86, 109). ✧ 'Man (hero, soldier) of pilgrims' cf. Turk. *haj* (Ar.) 'die Pilgerfahrt nach Mekka' (Radl. II, 1763). ⇨ **ER**.

XAJ-SÖGER   Tat. / Kipch.? 150 **Xaj-söger** / **Xaz-söger?** [Хазсогерь], a Tatar prince (PSRL VI, 47, 243, VIII, 241).

XAJ-UMAR see **XAJİ-UMAR**

XAJAR   Uzb. 1896 **Xajar** [Хаджаръ], fem. (Sr. Az. I (15 Aug., 1896)). ✧ 'Stone, rock, gravel' (Erol II) (<Ar.).

XAJJAS see **XALJAS**

XAJİ   Crm. 1474, 1500 **Azi-baba** [Азибаба], envoy from the Crimea (PSRL VI, 32, 44, VIII, 178, VIII, 238); Kzk. 18th c. **Azi-bäk-batïr** [Азибякъ-Батыръ] (Nepljuev 746); Bashk. 18th c. **Azi-γul** [Азегулъ] (Nepljuev 433); Bashk. 1770 **Azi-γul** [Бакир Азягулов] (MIB IV/1, 345); Bashk. 1777 **Azi-γul** [Салих Азигулов] (MIB V, 58); Kkalp. 20th c. **Äži** [Әжи] (KkRS 772); Kkalp. 20th c. **Äži-bay** [Әжи] (KkRS 772); Kzk. 18th c. **Xaj-anay** [Хаджанай], fem. (Nepljuev 791); Trkm. 19th c. **Xaji** [Мамай Хаджиевъ] (Ščeglov IV, 190); Trkm. 20th c. **Xajï** [Hağï] (Zaj. 1971, 326); Trkm. 20th c. **Xaji** [Хаджи] (TrkmRS 680); Crm.(Tat.) 1598 **Xaji** [Хази Адамовичъ татарка], fem. (Lit. Tat. 272); Uzb. 19th c. **Xaji** / **Гaji?** [Гурапъ Гаджіевъ] (SKSO III, 158); Khorezm./Chag. 1400, 1404 **Xaji-baba** [Хазибаба бесерменинъ] (PSRL IV, 108, 145, V, 253, VI, 131, VIII, 75); Kzk. 1726 **Xaji-bay** [Khadjibaï] (Levchin 154); Khorezm.?, Kipch. 1377, 1378 **Xaji-bey** [Хазибей / Хазибѣй], a „voevoda" of the Tatars / a prince of the Horde (PSRL IV, 74, V, 237, VIII, 33, XVI, 106 (Letop. Avraamki)); Turk. 1396 **Xaji-bek-**

čelebi [حاجى بك چلبى], retainer of Ahmed the Sultan of Sivas, Turkey (Astarab. 508); Turk. 1432 **XaJï-χatun** [Hacı Hatun binti Hacı Ali], fem. (Gökb., Ed. 272). ✧ 'Hadji; pilgrim; title of respect in village communities' cf. Az., Tat. *hajï*, Crm., Turk. *haji* (Ar.) 'der nach Mekka reisende, der Pilgrim; ein unruhiges Kind; Ehrentitel der Leute, die die Pilgerfahrt nach Mekka unternommen haben; Ehrentitel der Honorationen in den Dorfgemeinden' (Radl. II, 1764-1765), Trkm. *χajï* 'id.' (TrkmRS) (<Ar.). *XaJi-χatun* is a 'Muslim woman who has performed the pilgrimage; an elderly lady' cf. Turk. *hacı hanım, hacı kadın* 'id.' (TED). See also **ES-XAJİ, TUL-AZİ.**

XAJİ-GELDİ see **XAJİ-KELDİ**

XAJİ-GİREY see **KERÄY**

XAJİ-KELDİ   Nog. 20th c. **AJï-keldi / AJi-keldi** [Аджикелди Байрам Али увлы], one of Baskakov's informants from the aul of Yaman-γoy, District of Ači-qulaq (Bask., Nog. 143); Trkm. **XaJi-geldi** [Хаджи-Гельды] (Mel'gunov 320). ✧ 'Hadji/pilgrim-Came; A Hadji/pilgrim was born'. ⇨ **AJÏ + KELDİ.**

XAJİ-QARA   Trkm. 19th c. **XaJi-qara** [Темиръ Хаджикараевъ] (Ščeglov IV, 173). ⇨ **XAJİ + QARA.**

XAJİ-RAMAZAN see **RAMAZAN**

XAJİ-UMAR   Karch. **XaJ-umar (<XaJi-umar)** [Хаджумаръ Чагаровъ] (Sysoev 120). ⇨ **XAJİ + OMAR.**

XAJİMÄ   Bulg. 14th c. **XaJimä** [حجم / Hajima / Хаджимä], fem. (Jusupov 41, Epigr. Bulg. 114, 115). ⇨ **XAJİ.**

XAJÏ-ŠAD-GELDİ see **ŠAD-GELDİ**

XAJAT   Trkm. 20th c. **XaJat** [Hağat] (Zaj. 1971, 336); Trkm. 20th c. **XāJat** [Хаджат], fem. (TrkmRS 680). ✧ 'Need(ed), necessity, want' cf. Trkm. *χāJat* 'нужда, надобность' (TrkmRS) (<Ar.). See also **OΓUL-XAJAT.**

XADAT   Hak. 19th-20th c. **Xadat** [Хадат] (HRS 352).

XADİJA   Kzk. 19th c. **XadiJa** [Хадиджа], fem. (Grod., Pril. 155); Turk. 1450 **XatiJe** [Hatice binti Tanrıvermiş], fem. (Gökb., Ed. 273); Turk. 1495 **XatiJe** [Hatice binti Câfer] (Gökb., Ed. 464); Kkalp. 20th c. **Xädiyša** [Хәдийша], fem. (KkRS 779); Kkalp. 20th c. **Qatïyša** [Къатыйша / Қатыйша], fem. (Bask., Kkalp. 403, KkRS 778); Kkalp. 20th c. **Qätiyša** [Қәтийша], fem. (KkRS 778). ✧ Khadija (Ar. fem.) the first wife of Muhammad (Ahmed), 'Premature' cf. Kzk. fem. PNs *Xadiša* (Žanuzakov 160), *Qadiša* (Žanuzakov-Esbaeva).

XADİČ see **QADÏŠ**

XAΓAN see **QAΓAN**

XAXAY   Yak. **Xaχay** [Xaxai], fem. (Pek.). ✧ 'Lion' cf. Yak. *χaχay* 'лев, царь зверей' (Pek.).

XAXAYALÏR   Yak. **Xaχayalïr** [Хахаялыр] (Pek.).

XAXAYAR   Yak. **Xaχayar** [Хахаjар] (Pek.).

XAXAYDĀN   Yak. **Xaχaydān** [Хахаiдан], a shamaness (Pek.).

XAXANÏ   Yak. **Xaχanï** [Хаханы], one of the ancestors of the people in Vilyuysk (Pek.).

XAYAX   Hak. 19th-20th c. **Xayaχ** [Хаях], fem. (HRS 355). ✧ 'Butter' (Butanaev).

XAYARAÑ   Yak. **Xayarañ / Käyäräñ** [Хаjараҥ / Кäjäрäҥ], one of the ancestors of the Yakuts, Tüört-ügül's son, Älläy's and Omoγoy's father (Pek.).

XAYAT   Uzb. **Xayat-žan** [Хоятжанъ Ачильдибаевъ], a merchant from Bukhara (Turk. Kraj 1912:5). ✧ 'Life' (TED). See also **ÖMÜR.**

XAYĀLİ   Turk. 16th c. **Xayālï-bey** [Hayâlî Bey Vizeli Hamza Çelebi oğlu], died in 1557 (Gökb., Ed. 63, 64, Necatigil 139). ✧ 'Imaginary, fantastic; shadow theatre player' (TED).

XAYBU   Kzk. 1862 **Xaybu-bek** [Хаибубекъ Саиновъ] (ZIRGOGeogr. I, 311).

XAYDAR   Tat.? 19th c. **Xaydar** [Chaidarov] (Mende 115); Kzk. 19th c. **Xaydar-bek** [Хайдарбекъ Хайдарбековъ] (SKSO III, 190); Kzk. 19th c. **Xaydar-bek** [Хайдарбекъ], Xaydar-bek's father (SKSO III, 190). ✧ 'Lion' (Ar.), epithet of Prophet Ali (DTS). See also **QARA-XAYDER.**

XAYLO   Hak. 19th-20th c. **Xaylo** [Хайло] (HRS 352). ✧ 'Mattock; pick-axc'.

XAYR   Maml. 1448 **Xayr-bek** [الاجرود] (Ibn Taghrīb. VII, 164, 207, 212, etc.); Maml. 1449 **Xayr-bek** [خير بك المويدى] (Ibn Taghrīb. VIII, 51, 208); Maml. 1450 **Xayr-bek** [خير بك الا شتر المو يدى] (Ibn Taghrīb. VII, 212, 420 etc.); Maml. 1450, 1455 **Xayr-bek** [خير بك النوروزى] (Ibn Taghrīb. VIII, 59, 100, 248); Maml. 1456 **Xayr-bek** [خير بك الاشرفى] (Ibn Taghrīb. VIII, 371); Maml. 1457, 1467 **Xayr-bek** [خير بك البهلوان] (Ibn Taghrīb. VII, 483, 700, VIII, 626, 710); Maml. 1463 **Xayr-bek** [خير بك الظاهرى] (Ibn Taghrīb. VIII, 474, 495); Maml. 1516 **Xayr-bek** [السيفى خير بك], Inal's mamlūk, colonel (chiliarch), leader of the campaign to Hidjāz, died in 1516 (Mayer 138-39, Iyās II, 324, 362); Maml. 1522 **Xayr-bek** [خير بك], governor of Aleppo, then of Egypt in the Ottoman era, died in 1522 (Mayer 136-37, Iyās III, 3, 62); Khorezm. 13th c. **Xayr-χan / Γayr-χan?** [غاير خان], governor İnalčïq (İnalčuq)'s byname (Ĵuwaynī I, 60, 61, 64-66); Uzb. 20th c. **Xāyir-bek** [السيفى خير بك / Hāyirbek], a character in a tale (É. Dobos, A Tale from Qarabau: AOH XXVII, 170); Kkalp. 20th c. **Qayïr-bay** [Қайырбай] (KkRS 774); Kzk. 19th c. **Qayïr-bay** [Кайербай] (SOK 72); Kzk. **Qayr-bek** [Kair-bek] (Almásy 494); Kzk. 19th c. **Qayr-bek** [Каирбекъ] (SODž. 148); Oghuz 1114

Qayr-χan / Qayïr-χan? [قیر خـان بن قراجه], lord of Hims (Abulfidā III, 382-83, 420-21). ✧ I. 'Good, welfare benefit' (DTS), Uzb. χayr 'добро, благо; милостыня, подаяние, пожертвование' (UzbRS), Crm. χayïr 'das Almosen' (Radl. II, 1661), Turk. *hayïr* 'der Vortheil, Profit' (Radl. II, 1747); II. 'Alms, pittance' cf. Uyg., Kzk. *qayr* 'gut, vortrefflich; die Wohltat, Gunst' (Radl. II, 20), Tat. *qayïr* 'das Almosen' (Radl. II, 99), Kkalp. *qayïr* 'милостыня, подаяние' (KkRS), cf. Ar. χayr 'good' (Redh.). See also **QUTLU-XAYÏR**.

XAYR-ALAP Kzk. 19th c. **Xayr-alap** [Хайралапъ] (Grod., Pril. 129); Kzk. 19th c. **Xayr-lap** (<Xayr-alap) [Хаирлаповъ] (Grod., Pril. 135); Kzk. 19th c. **Qayralap** [Кайралапъ] (AOK 102); Kzk. 19th c. **Qayr-alap** [Кайралапъ] (SOV 84). ⇨ **XAYR + ALP?**

XAYR-TEMÜR Selj.? **Xayr-temür** [خیر تمور], an emir at the time of the muzaffarīd Mubārizuddīn (Qazw. 642). ⇨ **XAYR + TEMİR.**

XAYT see **QAYT**

XAYT Kzk. 19th c. **Xayt-bay** [Хаитбай] (Grod., Pril. 34). ⇨ **QAYT?**

XAYTA Turk. **Xayta-oγlu**, a Zeybek (Kúnos 1891, 119). ✧ 'Thief' (NyK XXII, 119).

XAYTÏQ Yak. **Xaytïq** [Хаітык] (Pek.).

XAYTÏM Kzk. 19th c. **Xaytïm-bay** [Хайтымбай] (SKSO III, 178).

XAQAN see **QAΓAN**

XAL see **QAL II.**

XAL-QÏDÏR Kzk. 19th c. **Xal-qïdïr** [Халькыдыровъ] (SKSO VIII, 204). ⇨ **QAL I./ QAL II.? + XÏZÏR.**

XAL-MAΓOMET Kzk. 19th c. **Xal-maγomet** [Халъ-Магомедъ] (Grod., Pril. 34). ⇨ **QAL II. + MAXMED.** See also **XAL-MUXAMMED.**

XAL-MAXAMMED see **QAL-MUXAMED**

XAL-MUXAMED see **QAL-MUXAMED**

XAL-MURAD see **QAL-MURAT**

XAL-TAŠ Kzk. 19th c. **Xal-taš** [Хашимъ Халташевъ] (Grod., Pril. 58). ⇨ **QAL II. + TAŠ.**

XALAB Maml. 14th c. **Xalab** [Халаб] (Tuhfa 410). ✧ Halab (Aleppo) (Ar.), a town in Syria.

XALAT Kzk. 19th c. **Xalat** [Халатъ] (SKSO VIII, 200). ✧ 'Gown' cf. Kzk. χalat 'халат' (RKzS).

XALĀNTAY Yak. **Xalāntay** [Халантаі], fem. (Pek.). ✧ 'Flood, deluge' cf. Yak. χalān 'разлив воды, половодье, наводнение рек, речек; вода, происходящая от таяния снега весной' (Pek.) + suff. -tay.

XALČA Kzk. **Xalča** [Хальча] (Sb. Syr-D. IX, 50). ⇨ **QALČA?**

XALJAS Yak. **XaJJas** [Хаццас] (Pek.); Yak. **XalJas** [Халцас] (Pek.); Yak. **XalJas-bärgän** [Халцас-бäргäн], fem. (Pek.).

XALDAY Hak. 19th-20th c. **Xalday** [Халдай] (HRS 352). ✧ 'Man of humble/lowly origin/birth' (Butanaev) cf. Hak. χal 'могущественный; отважный, неустрашимый; неотзывчивый; неопытный, бестолковый, непонятливый' (HRS) + suff. -day.

XALDÏ see **QALDÏ**

XALÄ Kmk. 1689 **Xalä-bek** [Халебекъ мурза Кумыцкий], a Kumuk murza, in a document from Astrakhan (AI V, 316). ✧ 'Aunt on mother side; auntie, dame (addressing)' cf. Kmk. dial. χala 'тётя, тётушка' (KmkRS).

XALFA see **XALİFA**

XALXALİMA see **TİMİR-XALXALİMA**

XALİ Kzk. 19th c. **Xali-bay** (AUK 206); Kzk. 1879 **Xali-qul** [Халикулъ] (Grod., Pril. 130). ✧ 'Empty; free' cf. NUyg.(Tar.), Tat.(Tob.) χali 'leer, frei; die Oede, Einsamkeit' (Radl. II, 1676).

XALİČA Kzk. **Xaliča / Xaličä** [Биби Халича], fem. (CKSO IV, otd. II, 38).

XALİFA Tat. 19th c. **Xalfa** [Ibrahim Chalfin] (Mende 20, 38); Tat. 19th c. **Xalfa** [M. S. Chalfina], fem. (Mende 178); Kzk. 19th c. **Xalifa** [Биби Халифа Хасанбаева], fem. (SKSO IV, otd. II, 34); Kirg. **Qalïypa** [Калыйпа] (Jud. 905). ✧ 'Caliph' cf. Tat., Turk. χalfa (Ar.) 'der Subalternbeamte; die älteren Schüler der Medressen' (Radl. II, 1678), Kzk. χalifa 'id.' (KTTS).

XALİL Nog. 20th c. **Xalil** [Осман Халил улы Доьрмен / Осман Халилович Дурменов], father of one of Baskakov's informants from the aul of Adil-χalq (Bask., Nog. 143). ✧ Khalil (Ar.) 'friend' (Ahmed).

XALİM Trkm. 1863 **Xalim-bek** [Халим-бек] (MIT II, 608). ✧ Halim (Ar.) 'patient, tolerant' (Ahmed).

XALİZAT NUyg.(Tar.) **Xalizat** [Chalimsat[!] / Хализат], a doctor (physician) (Proben VI, 25).

XALÏASKAY Yak. **Xalïaskay** [Халыаскаі] (Pek.). ✧ 'Wild' cf. Yak. χalïan 'дикий, бешеный, нескромный (о лошади)' (Pek.).

XALÏΓÏAY Yak. **Xalïγïay** [Халыгыаі] (Pek.).

XALÏQ-BERDİ Kzk. 19th c. **Xalïq-berdi** [Халыкъ-Берды Разыкбердыевъ] (SKSO IV, otd., III, 13); Kzk., Tat.? 19th c. **Xalïq-berdi** [Халыкъ-Берды и Кадыръ-Берды], from Qara-tüb(e), Qadïr-berdi's brother (TV 1876, 132). ✧ 'Khaliq gave him'. ⇨ **QALÏQ +BERDİ.** See also **XALÏQ-BERGÄN.**

XALÏQ-BERGÄN Uzb. 20th c. **Xâlïq-bergän** [Холикберган] (Begmatov 1984, 202); Kzk. 19th c. **Qalïq-bergen** [Калыкбергенъ] (SOK 96). ✧ 'Khaliq gave him'. ⇨ **QALÏQ + BERGEN.** See also **XALÏQ-BERDİ.**

XALÏQTAY see **XĀN-XALÏQTAY**

XALLĀN-XAČÏYA Yak. **Xallān-χačïya** [Халлан Хачыіа], a shaman (Pek.).

XALLİ see **QALLÏ**

XALLİ see **QALLÏ**

XALMAN see **QALMAN**

XALMAT Kzk. 19th c. **Xalmat** [Халь-матъ] (Nalivkin 8). ⇨ **QAL I./II.?** + suffixoid -*mat*.

XALMEN see **XALMAN**

XALTARAX Hak. 19th-20th c. **Xaltara\chi** [Халтарах] (HRS 352). ✧ 'Worker of a mine, proletarian' (Butanaev).

XAM-ČÜGÜL Uzb. **Xam-čügül**, in a tale from Qarabau (É. Dobos, A Tale from Qarabau: AOH XXVII, 173). ✧ 'Humped'? cf. Uzb. *\chiam* 'согнутый, сгорбленный (UzbRS) + *čügül*?

XAMAN see **XALMAN**

XAMJAM-BOL Uzb. 20th c. **Xamjam-bol** [Хамжамбўл] (Begmatov 1984, 201). ⇨ **BOL.**

XAMDAN NUyg. 19th c. **Xamdan-bay**, a servant (Hedin II, 250). ✧ 'Intimate friend, constant companion' (<P.). ⇨ **XEMDEM.**

XAMİR Karakh. **Xamir** [Xamir] (MK/Atalay 839).

XAMUŠ Khorezm.? 1227 **Xamuš** [خاموش / Khamouch], Özbek-atabek's son (Nasawī 129).

XAMZA Turk. 15th c. **Xamza** [Elvan oğlu Hamza] (Gökb., Ed. 198); Turk. 1525 **Xamza-bey** (Gökb., Ed. 426, 396); Chag.? 15th c. - 16th c. **Xamza-sultan** [حمزه سلطان], a Shaybanid (Šejb.); *TN:* Turk. 1485 **Xamza-beglü**, a village (Gökb., Ed. 426, 396); Turk. **Xamza-bey** [Hamsabey], a place (village?) in Asia Minor (PM Ergh. 116 (Taf. 2)). ✧ Hamza (Ar.) 'lion' (Ahmed).

XAN Turk. 1583 **Xan-a\gamma a** [خان اغا / Hanağa], fem. (Ongan, Ank. I, 158); Kzk. 19th c. **Xan-bay** [Ханбай] (Grod., Pril. 149); Tat.(Mish.) **Xan-bek** [خان بيك / Chan-bek] (IOAIÊK (Dobavlenie) XIX, 142); Crm. 1644 **Xan-qul** [Ханкулъ], a messenger from the Crimea (AI III, 399); Kzk. 19th c. **Xan-qul** [Ханкулъ] (SKSO VIII, 233); Trkm. 20th c. **Xān-qulï** [Hanqulï] (Zaj. 1971, 326); Chag. **Xan-qulï(-sultan)** [سلطان خان قلى], a Shaybanid (Šejb. LII); Tat.(Sib.)? 1599 **Xan-zāda** [Ханзада], a princess of Siberia in Küčüm's family (AI II, 18, 20, 23); Turk. 1489 **Xan-zāde** [Hanzâde], Aydın Bey's daughter (Gökb., Ed. 212); Trkm. 20th c. **Xān** [Han] (Zaj. 1971, 326); Trkm. 20th c. **Xān** [Хан] (TrkmRS 686); *EN:* Kzk. 18th c. - 19th c. **Xan-\chioja** [Ханходжа] (Tynyšp. 68). ✧ I. 'Ruler, imperor (title)' cf. Karakh. *\chian* 'хан, правитель' (DTS), Trkm. *\chiān* 'id.' (Trkm.); II. Secondary component of personal names, title, title of respect usually coming after the main part of male names (TrkmRS). Cf. East. T. *\chia:n, \chian* 'title for a lady, affixed to women's names' (Jarring). See also **QAN, QUNAQ-ŠOL-XAN, TAY-XAN.**

XAN-AŠA Uyg. 1338 **Xan-aša**, fem. (Chwol., Syr.-nest. (NF) 85). ⇨ **XAN + AŠA** + suff. -*a*.

XAN-BERDİ Khorezm 1227 **Xan-berdi** [خان بردى /

Khan Berdi], Jelal's commander (Nasawī 138); Maml. 1258 **Xan-berdi** [عزالدين بن خان بردى / ʿIzzal-dīn b. Khān Bardī] (Sīrat 88). ⇨ **XAN + BERDİ.**

XAN-DÄWLÄT Chag. **Xan-däwlät** [خان دولت], a Shaybanid (Šejb. LI). ⇨ **XAN + DÄWLÄT.**

XAN-GELDİ see **XAN-KELDİ**

XAN-GELDİ see **XAN-KELDİ**

XAN-KELDİ Trkm. 19th c. **Xan-geldi** [Ханъ-Гельди] (Murav'ev I, 38); Kzk.? 18th c. - 19th c. **Xan-geldi** [Шушала Хан гельдинъ] (ZOOIRGO IV, 99); Trkm. 1767/68 **Xan-geldi-biy** [Хан Гельды-бий], a \chiakim from the region of Aral (MIT II, 336-340); Trkm. 1767/68 **Xan-geldi-inaq** [Хан Гельды-инак], a \chiakim from the region of Aral (MIT II, 336-340); Tat.(Lit.) 1620 **Xan-kelde(y)?** [Ханкелдей Барашъ] (Lit. Tat. 293); Tat.? 1552 **Xan-kilde(y)** [Ханъкилдѣй], a prince (PSRL XIII, 176); Uzb. 20th c. **Xân-keldi** [Хонкелди] (Begmatov 1984, 203); *EN:* Kzk. 18th c. - 19th c. **Xan-geldï** [Хангельды] (Tynyšp. 66, 67, 68, 73). ✧ 'The Khan has come'. ⇨ **XAN + KELDİ.** See also **QAN-KELDİ.**

XAN-KİLDE see **XAN-KELDİ**

XAN-LEYLUN NUyg.(Tar.) 19th c. **Xan-leylun** [خان ليلون / Ханъ-Лейлунъ], fem. (Pantusov, Pesni 3, 79). ⇨ **XAN.**

XAN-SÜWER-BİYİM see **QAN-SÜYÄR**

XANAX Hak. 19th-20th c. **Xana\chi** [Ханах] (HRS 352).

XANAY Trkm. 19th c. **Xanay** [Ханай Бекеймуллаевъ] (Ščeglov I, 349).

XANAT-MİLTÏQ Hak. 19th-20th c. **Xanat-mïltïq** [Ханат-Мылтык] (HRS 352). ⇨ **QANAT + MİLTÏQ.**

XANČERLİ Turk. 1542 **Xančerli-sultan** [Hançerli Sultan], daughter of Şehzade Mahmud (Bâyezid II) (Gökb., Ed. 69). ✧ 'Having a dagger (khanjar); armed with a dagger' cf. Turk. *\chianjärli* 'mit einem Dolche bewaffnet' (Radl. II, 1666). ⇨ **XANJAR** + suff. -*li*.

XANJAR Trkm.? 1817/18 **Xanjar-\chian** [Ханджар-хан] (MIT II, 199). ✧ 'Khanjar (short curved dagger)' cf. Az. *\chianjar*, Crm., Turk. *\chianjär* (Ar.) 'ein krummer Dolch' (Radl. II, 1666).

XANDAΓAN Yak. **Xanda\gamma an** [Хандаҕан] (Pek.).

XANİ-KÖR-SERDAR see **KÖR**

XANİJE Crm. 1741 **Xanije** [Ханидже], Abdullah's daughter (Bakč. Nadp. 24). ⇨ **QANÏ** + suff. -*je*. See also **XANİŠA.**

XANİM Kzk. 19th c. **Xanïm** [Ханымъ], fem. (Grod., Pril. 115); Kkalp. 20th c. **Xanïm** [Ханым], fem. (KkRS 779); Kzk. **Xanïm-jan** [Khanym-Djane / Ханымъ-джанъ], fem. (Levšin III, 96, Levchine 356); Turk. 1528 **Xanïm-\chiatun** [Hanım Hatun], Yavuz Sultan Selim's daughter (Gökb., Ed. 515); Kzk. 1878 **Xanum** [Ханумъ], fem. (Grod., Pril. 137). ✧ 'Wife or daughter of the khan; lady of the house; title of respect' Used also as a secondary component of female names. Cf. Crim., Turk. *χanïm* 'die Chanin, Chanstochter, eine vornehme Dame, die Hausfrau' (Radl. II, 1664); cf. Chag. *χanïm* (خانم) 'A title in the Bābur-nāme', recently used in Eastern Turkestan when addressing a woman (Le Coq, Ind. 4), Uzb. *χanïm* 'госпожа; дама; красотка; присоединяется к женским именам, придавая оттенок уважения' (UzbRS).

XANÏMAY Uzb. 20th c. **Xanïmay**, from a tale (É. Dobos, A Tale from Qarabau: AOH XVII, 173). ⇨ **XANÏM** + dim. suff. *-ay* or fem. comp. *ay.*

XANÏŠ see **QANÏŠ**

XANÏŠA Kzk. 19th c. **Xanïša** [Ханиша], fem. (Grod., Pril. 134). ⇨ **QANÏ** + suff. *-ša.* See also **XANÏJE**.

XANYAS-ÄMÄXSÏN Yak. **Xanyas-ämäχsin** / **Xanyas-χotun** [Ханјас Хотун / Ханјас әмәхсін], a woman-spirit (Pek.).

XANYAS-XOTUN see **XANYAS-ÄMÄXSÏN**

XANTAYAN Yak. **Xantayan** [Хантајан], a person from the ulus of Bayaγa (Pek.). ✧ 'Throwing his head back'? cf. Yak. *χantay-* (Pek.).

XANTAQA Yak. **Xantaqa** [Хантака] (Pek.).

XANTĀXAN Yak. **Xantāχan** [Хантахан] (Pek.).

XANUM see **XANÏM**

XAPAY Karch. **Xapay** [Хапаевъ], a Karachay family (Sysoev 120). ⇨ **QAPAY?**

XAPČAXAN Yak. **Xapčaχan** [Хапчахан] (Pek.). ✧ 'Contraction, clenching'? cf. Yak. *χapčay-* 'теснить, стеснять; суживаться' (Pek.) + suff. *-χan.*

XAPČÏΓAS Hak. 19th-20th c. **Xapčïγas** [Хапчыгас] (HRS 352). ✧ 'Little sack, bag' cf. Hak. *χarčïχ* 'мешочек; кисет; кошелёк (HRS) + suff. *-as?*

XAPÏTÏAN Yak. **Xapïtïan** [Хапытыан] (Pek.); Yak. **Xappïtïan** [Хаппытыан] (Pek.). ✧ Kapiton (R.).

XAPPAΓ-ČÏLĀN Yak. **Xappaγ-čïlān** [Харрач-чылан], a girl in tales (Pek.).

XAPPÏYÏQ Yak. **Xappïyïq** [Хаппыјык] (Pek.).

XAPPÏTÏAN see **XAPÏTÏAN**

XAPSÏM Yak. **Xapsïm** / **Xapsïn** [Хапсым / Хапсын] (Pek.). ✧ Akepsim (R.).

XAPSÏN see **XAPSÏM**

XAPTASÏN-XALÏQÏS-KÜLÜK-SÜÖDÄR-BUXATÏR Yak. **Xaptasïn-χalïqïs-külük-süödär-buχatïr** [Хаптасын-Халыкыс-Күлүк-Сүөдәр бухатыр] (Pek.).

XARA see **QARA**

XARA-AXSÏR Hak. 19th-20th c. **Xara-aχsïr** [Хара-Ахсыр] (HRS 352). ✧ 'Black stallion'. ⇨ **QARA** + **AYΓÏR**. See also **QARA-BUΓRA**.

XARA-BARΓÏYA Yak. **Xara-barγïya-toyon** [Хара Баргыја тојон], a demon-shaman born from a frog (Pek.). ⇨ **QARA**.

XARA-BÄKÏRDÄN Yak. **Xara-bäkirdän** [Хара-Бәкірдән] (Pek.). ⇨ **QARA** + **BÄKÏRDÄN**.

XARA-XÏZÏJAX see **QARA-QÏZÏJAQ**

XARA-XOY see **QARA-QOY**

XARA-XUČA see **QARA-QUČA**

XARA-MOYÏN see **QARA-MOYÏN**

XARA-MUYUZTU Tuv. 19th c. **Xara-muyuztu** [Хара Муюзту] (Potanin IV, 420). ✧ 'Having black horn, with black horns'. ⇨ **QARA** + **MÏYÜZ** + suff. *-tu.*

XARA-PARLAS Hak. 19th-20th c. **Xara-parlas** [Харапарлас] (HRS 352). ⇨ **QARA** + **PARLAS**.

XARA-PUΓA see **QARA-BUQA**

XARA-TAY see **QARA-TAY**

XARAJÏAL-MOXSOΓOL Yak. **Xarajïal-moχsoγol** [Харацыал-Мохсоғол] (Pek.). ✧ 'Black falcon' (Pek.). See also **XĀRJÏT-MOXSOΓOL**.

XARAΓDAN Yak. **Xaraγdan** [Харагдан], a new-born boy (Pek.).

XARAQDAN Yak. **Xaraqdan** [Харакдан], a new-born boy (Pek.).

XARAMAN see **QARAMAN**

XARAÑ Hak. 19th-20th c. **Xarañ** [Харанъ] (HRS 352). ✧ I. 'Black'? cf. Hak. *χara* 'id.'; II. 'Unobserved, unnoticed'? cf. Hak. *χaran* 'незаметно, исподтишка' (HRS), Alt.(Tel.), Shor *qaran* 'unbemerkbar, unmerklich, undeutlich' (Radl. II, 154).

XARAS Hak. 19th-20th c. **Xaras** [Харас], fem. (HRS 355).

XARBAXČÏL Hak. 19th-20th c. **Xarbaχčïl** [Харбахчыл] (HRS 352). ✧ I. 'Hasty; flustered' cf. Hak. *χarbaχ: χarbaχ-χurbaχ* 'торопливо, поспешно'; II. 'Handful' cf. *χarbaχ* 'горсть' (HRS) + suff. *-čil.*

XARČÏX Hak. 19th-20th c. **Xarčïχ** [Харчых], fem. (HRS 355). ✧ 'Tick' (HRS 355).

XARΓA see **QARΓA**

XARÏAJA Yak. **Xarïaja-bärgän** [Харыаца-бäргän / Хоруоца], a character in a tale (Pek.). ✧ I. '?- brave man' cf. Yak. *bergen* 'меткий, ловкий; молодец, удалец' (JRS); II. '? - Bride' cf. Yak. *bergen* 'невестка (жена старшего деверя)' (JRS). ⇨ **XORUOJA** + **MERGEN**.

XARMĀS Bulg. 13th c. - 14th c. **Xarmās** [حرماس] (Jusupov 18).

XAROX Hak. 19th-20th c. **Xaroχ** [Харох] (HRS 352).

XARŌL see **QARA**

XASAN Kkalp. 20th c. **Äsen** [Әсен] (KkRS 772); Bashk. 1748 **Xasan** [Хасан Иштереков] (MIB III, 454); Trkm.? 1813 **Xasan-bay-biy** [Хасанбай-бий] (MIT II, 385); Trkm.? 1835 **Xasan-χan** [Хасан-хан Сары Аслан] (MIT II, 231, 233). ✧ Hasan (Ar.) 'handsome, beautiful, goodlooking' (Ahmed). See also **ÏL-XASAN**.

XASAN-ALÏ Chag. 16th c. **Xasan-ali** [Хасан Али Калынбаф ходжа] (Ivanov 115, 150). ⇨ **XASAN** + **ALÏ**.

XASAR Uyg. 762 **Xasar-tegin** (Mahrnāmag 9).

XASXA Yak. **Xasχa** [Хасха] (Pek.).

XASXANAX Hak. 19th-20th c. **Xasχanaχ** [Хасханах] (HRS 352). ✧ 'Having white forehead'. ⇨ **QAŠQA** + suff. *-naχ*?

XASÏYĀN Yak. **Xasïyān** [Хасыjан] (Pek.). ✧ Kas'yan (R.).

XASÏTAQÏ Yak. **Xasïtaqï** [Хасытакы] (Pek.). ✧ Derived from Yak. *χasïtā* (Pek.) + suff. *-qï*.

XASQÏYDĀN Yak. **Xasqïydān-quo** [Хаскыiдан-куо], fem. (Pek.).

XAT-QALDAY Kzk. **Xat-qalday** [Хаткальдай] (Sb. Syr-D. IX, 52). ⇨ ? + **QALDAY**?

XATAY Khorezm.? 1298 **Xatay-oγul** [حتای اغول], a prince, died in 1298 (RaD/Jahn 118). ✧ 'Chinese'.

XATALAMAY Yak. **Xatalamay-bärgän** [Хаталамаi Бäргäн], one of the four sons of Älläy (Pek.).

XATAM Trkm. 20th c. **Xatam** [Hatam] (Zaj. 1971, 327); Trkm. 20th c. **Xātam** [Хатам] (TrkmRS 691). ✧ 'Generous, open-handed' cf. Trkm. *χātam* 'щедрый' (TrkmRS) (<Ar.). See also **SAXÏ**.

XATAMALAY Yak. **Xatan-χatamalay / Xatamallay** [Хатамалаi / Хатан-Хатамалаi (Хатамаллаi)], one of Är-älläy's six (!) sons (Pek.).

XATAMTAY Kzk. 19th c. **Xatamtay** [Хатамтаевъ] (SKSO VIII, 225). ✧ Hatem Tayy (Ar.).

XATAÑAYĀQ-ÄSÄKÄN Yak. **Xatañayāq-äsäkän** [Хатаңаjак äсäкäн], protective spirit of common sables and hazel-grouses (Pek.).

XATÏJE see **XADÏJA**

XATÏM Oghuz? 10th c. - 12th c. **Xatim-bek** [Хатим-бек (Итимад-уд-довле)], Abbas' vezīr (MIT I, 11). ✧ 'Keeper of the seal (title)'? (Ar.) cf. Turk. *hâtim (hatm)* 'mühür basan, mühürleyen' (Özön).

XATÏ Tat.? 1689 **Xatï-murza** [Хаты мурза], in a document from Astrakhan (AI V, 316).

XATÏRAÑ Crm. **Xatïrañ** [Хатыраң / Хараман], Xaraman's brother (Proben VII, 34). ✧ 'Resin, pitch, tar' cf. Crm. *χatïrañ* 'id.' (Radl. II, 1682).

XATU Kzk. 19th c. **Xatu-bay** [Хату бай] (SODž. 76).

XATUN see **QATUN**

XATUN-BULA see **QATUN-BULA**

XAZANQA see **QAZANQA**

XAZAR see **QAZAR**

XĀČÏLĀN Yak. **Xāčïlān-quo** (<Xappaγ-čïlān) [Хачылан-куо], a girl in tales (Pek.).

XĀKÏM Kzk. 19th c. **Äkim-bay** [Екимбай] (SOV 60); Trkm. 1851 **Xakim-ata** [Хаким-ата], a sheykh (MIT II, 285); Trkm. 1740 **Xakim-atalïq / Xakim-biy** [Хаким-аталык], a Mañγït atalïq (MIT II, 140, 141, 162, 206); Trkm. 1826 **Xakim-biy** [Хаким-бий], a qušbegi (MIT II, 443); Kzk. 19th c. **Xakim-žan** [Хкимжанъ Минайдаровъ] (AUK 444); Kzk. 19th c. **Käkim-bek** [Какимбекъ] (SODž. 44). ✧ I. 'Judge; ruler, magistrate' cf. Turk. *hâkim* 'ruler, governor,

judge, magistrate' (TED), Turk. *haqim* 'der Richter; der Verwalter, Fürst' (Radl. II, 1744), Kkalp. *χäkim* ' хаким, правитель области (наследственная должность в бывшем Хивинском ханстве, утверждавшаяся ханом)' (KkRS), Kzk. *äkim* 'der Befehlshaber, Chef' (Radl. I, 681); II. 'Wise, clever; chief, leader' cf. Kzk. *äkim* '(билеуші,) басқарушы, басшы' (QTTS), cf. also Kzk. PNs *Kakim-žan / Käkim-žan* (Žanuzakov 144, Žanuzakov-Esbaeva). (<Ar.).

XĀLÏQ Trkm. 20th c. **Xālïq** [Halïq] (Zaj. 1971, 326); Trkm. 20th c. **Xālïq** [Халык] (TrkmRS 685). ✧ 'God' (Zaj. 1971), cf. Trkm. *χālïq* 'id.' (TrkmRS) (<Ar.).

XĀN-XABAR Yak. **Xān-χabar** [Хан-хабар] (Pek.). ✧ 'Blood?-be angry' cf. Yak. *χān* 'кровь; кровяной; кровавый' (JRS) and *χabar-* 'сердиться, яриться' (Pek.).

XĀN-XALÏQTAY Yak. **Xān-χalïqtay** [Хан Халыктаi] (Pek.).

XĀN-XARAXĀN Yak. **Xān-χaraχān** [Хан-Харахан] (Pek.).

XĀND Turk. 1529 **Xānd-χatun** [Hând Hatun], Ahmed Bey's daughter (Gökb., Ed. 54).

XĀNÏ Turk. 1507 **Xānï-χatun** [Hânî Hatun], fem. (Gökb., Ed. 379).

XĀNYĀR-ÄMÄXSÏN Yak. **Xānyār-ämäχsin** [Хаnjар äмäхсiн], fem. (Pek.).

XĀNNĀX-SÄGÄLÄN Yak. **Xānnāχ-sägälän** [Ханнах Сäгäлäн] (Pek.).

XĀRJÏT-MOXSOΓOL Yak. **Xārjït-moχsoγol** [Харџыт Мохсоҕол] (Pek.).

XÂL-TURDÏ Uzb. 20th c. **Xâl-turdï** [Холтурди] (Begmatov 1984, 204). ✧ 'Birthmark has stayed/survived'. ⇨ **QAL II.** + **TURDÏ**. See also **TURDÏ-XÂL**.

XÄDÏYŠA see **XADÏJA**

XÄKÏM Kkalp. 20th c. **Häkim** [Хәким] (KkRS 776); Kkalp. 20th c. **Häkim-bay** [Хәкимбай] (KkRS 776); Kkalp. 20th c. **Häkim-zada** [Хәкимзада] (KkRS 776); Trkm. 20th c. **Xekïm** [Hekim / Хеким] (Zaj. 1971, 326). ✧ 'Sage, philosopher, doctor' cf. Kuman *haqim* 'der Arzt' (Radl. II, 1744), Turk. *hakîm* 'sage, of great wisdom, philosopher; God; physician, doctor of medicine' (TED), Trkm. *χekïm* 'доктор, мыслитель; мудрец' (TrkmRS), Kzk. *äkim* 'билеуші (басқарушы, басшы)' (QTTS) (<Ar.).

XÄKÏM-NÏYAZ Kkalp. 20th c. **Xäkim-niyaz** [Хәкимнияз] (KkRS 776). ⇨ **XÄKÏM** + **NÏYAZ.**

XÄMÏYDA Kkalp. 20th c. **Xämiyda** [Хәмийда], fem. (KkRS 779). ✧ Female form of Hamid (Ar.). ⇨ **XÄMÏYT.**

XÄMÏYT Kkalp. 20th c. **Xämiyt** [Хәмийт] (KkRS 776). ✧ Hamid (Ar.).

XÄMRA Kzk. **Xämra** [Hämrä] (Proben III, 452 /527/).

XEKÏM see **XÄKÏM**

XEMDEM Trkm. 1610 **Xemdem** [حمدم], from Anatolia

(Refik, Anad. 61). ❖ 'Intimate friend, constant companion' (<P.), cf. Turk. *hemdem* 'id.' (TED).

XÏJAX Hak. 19th-20th c. **Xïjaχ** [Хычах] (HRS 356). ❖ 'Passionate; eager, greedy' cf. Hak. *χïja* 'страсть, желание; жадность' (HRS) + dim. suff. -*χ*.

XÏDAÑAS Hak. 19th-20th c. **Xïdañas** [Хыданъас], fem. (HRS 355).

XÏDÏMAY Hak. 19th-20th c. **Xïdïmay** [Хыдымай], fem. (HRS 355).

XÏDÏÑ Hak. 19th-20th c. **Xïdïñ** [Хыдынъ], fem. (HRS 355). ❖ '(Your) Virgin / Girl'? cf. Hak. fem. PN *Xïdï* 'дева' (Butanaev).

XÏDÏR see **XÏZÏR**

XÏDÏR-UҐRÏ Crm. **Xïdïr-uγrï / Xïdïr-uγlï?** [Хыдыръ-угъы] (Smirnov 70). ⇨ **XÏZÏR?**

XÏDRAY Hak. 19th-20th c. **Xïdray** [Хыдрай], fem. (HRS 355). ❖ 'Pock-marked, having small-poxes' cf. Hak. *χïdïr* 'рябой' (HRS) + suff. -*ay*.

XÏLĀÑ Hak. 19th-20th c. **Xïlāñ** [Хылаанъ] (HRS 352). ⇨ **QÏLAN?**

XÏNAN Hak. 19th-20th c. **Xïnan** [Хынан] (HRS 352). ❖ 'Earthworm; long-legged'? cf. Hak. *χïna* 'глист, глиста' (HRS).

XÏPČAQ see **QÏPČAQ**

XÏPTÏJAX Hak. 19th-20th c. **Xïptïjaχ** [Хыптычах], fem. (HRS 355). ❖ 'Little scissors' cf. Hak. *χïptï* 'ножницы' (HRS) + dim. suff. -*jaχ*.

XÏRĀÑ Hak. 19th-20th c. **Xïrāñ** [Хыраанъ] (HRS 352).

XÏS see **QÏZ**

XÏS-PAJAX Hak. 19th-20th c. **Xïs-pajaχ** [Хыспачах], fem. (HRS 356). ❖ 'Baby-girl' cf. Hak PN *Pačaχ* 'младенец' (Butanaev), consider also Hak. fem. PN *Xïspa / (dim.) Xïspačaq* '?' (Butanaev). ⇨ **QÏZ.** See also **BEBEK.**

XÏS-TORAY Hak. 19th-20th c. **Xïs-toray** [Хысторай], fem. (HRS 356). ⇨ **QÏZ + TORAY?**

XÏSXÏLÏX Hak. 19th-20th c. **Xïsχïlïχ** [Хысхылых], fem. (HRS 356). ❖ 'Flamingo' (Butanaev).

XÏSPÏN Hak. 19th-20th c. **Xïspin** [Хыспін], fem. (HRS 356). ❖ 'Girl'? cf. Hak. fem. PN *Xïspin* 'производное от Хыс - дева' (Butanaev). ⇨ **QÏZ + suff.** -*pin?*

XÏSTA Hak. 19th-20th c. **Xïsta** [Хыста], fem. (HRS 356). ❖ 'Spend the winter' cf. Hak. *χïsta-* 'проводить зиму, зимовать' (HRS).

XÏSTAN Hak. 19th-20th c. **Xïstan** [Хыстан], fem. (HRS 356).

XÏSTAR Hak. 19th-20th c. **Xïstar** [Хыстар], fem. (HRS 356).

XÏSTONČE Hak. 19th-20th c. **Xïstonče** [Хыстонче], fem. (HRS 356). ❖ '?' cf. Hak. fem. PN *Xïstonča* derived from *Xïston* '?' (Butanaev) + suff. -*ča / -če*.

XÏTXAX Hak. 19th-20th c. **Xïtχaχ** [Хытхах], fem. (HRS 356).

XÏZ-AYAX Hak. 19th-20th c. **Xïz-ayaχ** [Хызаях] (HRS 352). ⇨ **QÏZ + AZAQ.**

XÏZA see **QÏZA**

XÏZAY see **QÏZAY**

XÏZAN Hak. 19th-20th c. **Xïzan** [Хызан] (HRS 352); ❖ '?' cf. Hak. PN *Xïzan* (Butanaev).

XÏZANAX Hak. 19th-20th c. **Xïzanaχ** [Хызанах] (HRS 352). ❖ '?' cf. Hak. PN *Xïzanaχ* (Butanaev). ⇨ **QÏZAN + dim. suff.** -*aχ*.

XÏZANČE see **QÏZĀNČA**

XÏZARAY Hak. 19th-20th c. **Xïzaray** [Хызарай], fem. (HRS 355). ❖ 'Saint virgin' (Butanaev).

XÏZÏJAX see **QÏZÏJAQ;**

XÏZÏJEÑ Hak. 19th-20th c. **Xïzïjeñ** [Хызычень], fem. (HRS 355).

XÏZÏL see **QÏZÏL**

XÏZÏLA Hak. 19th-20th c. **Xïzïla** [Хызыла], fem. (HRS 355). ❖ 'Red(dish girl)'. ⇨ **QÏZÏL + suff.** -*a*.

XÏZÏNOY see **XÏZÏNAY**

XÏZÏNAY Hak. 19th-20th c. **Xïzïnay** [Хызынай], fem. (HRS 355); Hak. 20th c. **Xïzïnoy** [Хызыной] (Butanaev). ❖ 'Little virgin' cf. Hak. fem. PN *Xïzïnay* (Butanaev). ⇨ **XÏZÏÑ + suff.** -*ay*.

XÏZÏÑ Hak. 19th-20th c. **Xïzïñ** [Хызынъ], fem. (HRS 355). ❖ 'Virgin' cf. Hak. fem. PN *Xïzïn / Xïzïnas* 'дева' (Butanaev).

XÏZÏR Trkm. 20th c. **Xïdïr** [Hïdïr] (Zaj. 1971, 326); Trkm. 20th c. **Xïdïr** [Хыдыр] (TrkmRS 709); Turk. 15th c. - 16th c. **Xïzïr** [Hızır], 36 persons in the same source (Gökb., Ed.); Oghuz/Trkm. 13th c. **Xïzïr / Xïdïr / Xïzïr-bay / Xïdïr-bay / Xïzïr-čora / Xïdïr-čora** [خضره جوره / خضر / خضر / Хызыр-бай / Хыдыр-бай / Хызыр-чора / Хыдыр-чора], a slave's son (Abulg./Kon. 1345, 1350, 1360); Turk. 15th c. **Xïzïr-baba** [Hızır Baba] (Gökb., Ed. 36); Yürük 1543 **Xïzïr-dede** [Hızır-dede] (Gökb., Rum. 101); Tat.(GH) 1360 **Xodïr / Xïdïr?** [Ходырь], a Tatar prince (R. tsar = sovereign) (Suzd. 504); Kzk. **Qïdïr** [Кыдыр] (Proben III, 259 /305/); Kkalp. 20th c. **Qïdïr** [Кыдыр] (KkRS 774); Kkalp. 20th c. **Qïdïr** [Къыдыр] (Bask., Kkalp. 5); Hak. 19th-20th c. **Qïdïr** [Кыдыр] (Katanov, Otč. 10); Kzk. 19th c.? **Qïdïr-ata** [Kïdïr-ata] (Atyns. 85); Kzk. 19th c. **Qïdïr-bay** [Кыдырбай] (SOK 74); Kkalp. 20th c. **Qïdïr-bay** [Къыдырбай] (Bask., Kkalp. 85, KkRS 774); Kkalp. 20th c. **Qïdïr-bay** [Джумаш Къыдырбай-улы], a teacher, Baskakov's informant (Bask., Kkalp. 85); Bashk. 1791 **Qïzïr** [Кызыр Кусяшев] (MIB V, 313); Kzk. 19th c. **Qïzïr** [Кызыръ] (AOA 122). ❖ Khizr / Khidr (Ar.) 'green' (Ahmed); 'Hizir (legendary person who attained immortality by drinking from the water of Life)' (TED), cf. Turk. *Xïzïr* 'der Name des Propheten. Elias' (Radl. II, 1724), Crm. *Xidir* 'id.' (Radl. II, 1729), Kzk. *Qïdïr* 'der Prophet Chizr' (Radl. II, 790), Trkm. *χïdïr* 'Хызр' (TrkmRS)

(<Ar.). See also **TEKNEJİ-XÏZÏR.**

XÏZÏR-YENİ-ČERİ Yürük 1543 **Xïzïr-yeni-čeri** [Hızır Yeniçeri] (Gökb., Rum. 214). ✧ 'Hizir - Janissary / Hizir-bully?' cf. Turk. *Yeniçeri* 'Janissary; swashbuckler, bully' (TED). ⇨ **XÏZÏR.**

XÏZNOŃ Hak. 19th-20th c. **Xïznoń** [Хызнонъ] (HRS 352).

XÏZR-İLİYAS Kkalp. 20th c. **Xïzr-iliyas / Qïdïr** [Хъызр-Илияс, Къыдыр] (Bask., Kkalp. 5). ✧ 'Prophet Ilyas (Elias)' cf. Ar. PN *Khidr / Khizr* and *Ilyas* (Ahmed). ⇨ **XÏZÏR + İLYAS.**

XOBAN Az. **Xoban** [Хобан], a maidservant (Az. Skaz. 610).

XOBOČOQ Yak. **Xobočoq** [Хобочок], a shaman (Pek.).

XOBOX Yak. **Xoboχ** [Хобох] (Pek.).

XOBOXTŌX Yak. **Xoboχtōχ** [Хобохтох] (Pek.).

XOBULDEY Kzk.? 19th c. **Xobuldey-mergen** [Хобульдэй-мэргэнъ] (Potanin II, 181).

XOČČORDŪR Yak. **Xoččordūr** [Хоччордур] (Pek.).

XOJA Chag. 16th c. **Xoja** [Ходжа], several persons (Ivanov 233, 236, 258, 263); Turk. 1583 **Xoja** [خواجه / Hoca], the source mentions 2 persons with this name (Ongan, Ank. I, 159); Trkm. 20th c. **Xoja** [Hoğa] (Zaj. 1971, 326); Trkm. 20th c. **Xoja** [Ходжа] (TrkmRS 700); Tat. 1502 **Xoja** [Хозя], a Tatar envoy (PSRL VI, 49, 244, VIII, 243); Nog. 20th c. **Xoja** [Ходжа Джумакелди увлы], Baskakov's informant from the aul of İrγaqlï (Bask., Nog. 143); Uzb. 19th c. **Xoja** [Choğa (Chodžaev) Feizulla] (Mende 90, 170); Chag. 16th c. **Xoja-bek** [Ходжа-бек] (Ivanov 159); Uzb. 1770 **Xoja-qulï-inaq** [Ходжа-кули-инак], from the Qoñrat tribe (MIT II, 343); Tat. 1502 **Xoja-soltan?** (<-sultan) [Хозя-салтанъ], a Tatar prince (PSRL VI, 49, 244); Chag. 16th c. **Xojaγa** (<Xoja-aγa) [Ходжага] (Ivanov 234); Chag. 16th c. **Xojaγa** (<Xoja-aγa) [Ходжага маулана] (Ivanov 234, 239); Chag. 16th c. **Xojaγa** (<Xoja-aγa) [Ходжага], a mirza (Ivanov 163); Chag. 16th c. **Xojaγa** (<Xoja-aγa) [Ходжага мулла] (Ivanov 184); Kkalp. 20th c. **Xoža-bay** [Хожабай] (KkRS 776); Kkalp. 20th c. **Qoj-eke** (<Qoja-eke) [Къоджеке] (Bask., Kkalp. 76); Selj.? 1352 **Qoja** [قجا], a bearer of arms (Iyās I, 194); Kkalp. 20th c. **Qož-eke** (<Qoža-eke) [Кожеке] (KkRS 774); Kkalp. 20th c. **Qoža-bay** [Кожабай] (KkRS 774); *EN:* Kzk. 18th c. - 19th c. **Xoja-γul** [Ходжагул] (Tynyšp. 71, 75); Kzk. 18th c. - 19th c. **Qoža-bek** [Кожабек], a clan (Tynyšp. 66); *TN:* Turk. 20th c. **Qoja-bey** [Kocabey], a village in the province of Artvin?, Turkey (TMİB 117). ✧ I. 'Hodja, (Muslim) teacher; educated man (originally the descendants of the first caliphs)' cf. Turk. *hoca* 'id.' (TED), Trkm. *χoja* 'ходжа' (TrkmRS), Maml. *qoja* 'Şeyh, ulu, efendi' (Tarj/Toparlı); Kzk. *qoža* 'der Lehrer, Mulla, Geistliche' (Radl. II, 646),

Kirg. *qožo* 'ходжа; благочестивый старец; хозяин, господин' (Jud.), Kzk. *qoža* 'хозяин дома' (KzRS). Used also as secondary component of male names. (<P.<Ar.); II. 'Master (of the house); old man; husband' cf. Karakh. *qoča / χoja* 'старый, старик' (DTS), Maml. *qoja* 'Herr' (Tarj/Houtsma); Kzk. *qoža* 'хозяин дома' (KzRS), Chag., Crm., Turk. *qoča, qoja* 'alt, der Greis; der Ehemann; gross, moralisch stark' (Radl. II, 616, 618), Turk. *koca* I. 'husband; elderly man, elder', *koca* II. 'Old, aged; ancient; large, great' (TED). Its Bashkir variants *χuža, γuža, küzä* are listed by Kusimova. Used also as a secondary component. (<P. خواجه, *khwaja* (Johnson 540) <Ar.). See also **QOJA.**

XOJA-BERDİ Chag. 16th c. **Xoja-berdi** [Ходжа-берды] (Ivanov 108, 117); Uzb. 20th c. **Xoja-berdi** [Хўжаберди] (Begmatov 1984, 202); Kzk. 1741 **Qoža-berdi / Bašlïq-qoža-berdi** [Башлыкъ-Коже-Берды] (Nepljuev 182). ✧ 'Hodja gave him'. ⇨ **XOJA + BERDİ.** See also **XOJA-BERGEN, XOJAM-BERDİ.**

XOJA-BERGEN Kzk. 1820 **Xoja-bergän** [Ходжа Берганъ], a chieftain (Sib. Vestn. IX, 116); Kzk. 19th c. **Xoja-bergän** [Ходжа Берганъ] (Grod., Pril. 95); Uzb. 20th c. **Xoja-bergän** [Хужаберган] (Begmatov 1984, 202); Kzk. 19th c. **Xoja-bergen** [Ходжа Бергенъ Караджигитовъ] (Grod., Pril. 171); Kzk. 19th c. **Qoža-bergen** [Кожаберген] (Altyns. 2); Kzk. 1868 **Xoja-bergen** [Акназаръ Ходжабергеновъ] (Grod., Pril. 128); Kzk. 19th c. **Qoja-bergen?** [Коджебергенъ] (Potanin II, 6). ✧ 'Hodja gave him' cf. Kzk. PN Qoža-bergen (Žanuz.-Esbaeva). ⇨ **XOJA + BERGEN.** See also **XOJA-BERDİ, XOJAM-BERDİ.**

XOJA-GELDİ see **XOJA-KELDİ**

XOJA-KELDİ Kzk. 19th c. **Xoja-keldi** [Ходжа Келды] (SKSO II, 13); Uzb. 20th c. **Xoja-keldi** [Хўжакелди] (Begmatov 1984, 203); Kzk. 19th c. **Qoža-geldi** [Кожегельды] (SODž. 34); Kzk. 19th c. **Qoža-geldi / Qoš-geldi?** [Кожгельды] (SOK 252); *EN:* Kzk. 18th c. - 19th c. **Xoja-geldi** [Ходжагельды] (Tynyšp. 71, 75); Kzk. 18th c. - 19th c. **Qoža-geldi** [Кожагельды], a clan (Tynyšp. 70). ✧ 'Hodja has come'. ⇨ **XOJA + KELDİ.**

XOJA-MURAT Kkalp. 20th c. **Xoža-murat** [Хожамурат] (KkRS 776); Kkalp. 20th c. **Qoža-mïrat** [Қожамырат] (KkRS 774); Kkalp. 20th c. **Qoža-murat** [Қожамурат] (KkRS 774). ⇨ **XOJA + MURAT.**

XOJAGA see **XOJA**

XOJAYÏQ Chag. 16th c. **Xojayïq?** [Ходжайек] (Ivanov 161, 180).

XOJAL-DİWANAY Kzk. 19th c. **Xojal-diwanay** [Али Ходжальдиванаевъ] (SKSO VIII, 201).

XOJALAQ Uyg. 14th c. **Xojalaq-bahadïr** [خواجهلاق بهادر / Ходжалагкъ Б.], Uyghur chief (Šejb. LIV).

XOJAM Chag. 16th c. **Xoǰam-yar** [Ходжам Яр] (Ivanov 170). ✧ 'My Hodja'. ⇨ **XOJA** + poss. suff. *-m*.

XOJAM-BERDİ Chag. 16th c. **Xoǰam-berdi** [Ходжам-берды] (Ivanov 281); Uzb. 1705 **Xoǰam-berdi** [خواجم بيردى] (Buchari 286, 295, 318); Uzb. 1705, 1707, 1709 **Xoǰam-berdi** [خواجم بيردى / Chwâgumbirdi-i Kinnagas], nobleman from Bukhara (Buchari 286, 295, 318); Uzb. 20th c. **Xoǰam-berdi** [Хўжамберди] (Begmatov 1984, 202); Trkm. 1829 **Xoǰam-berdi-yüzbašï** [Ходжам Берды-юзбаши] (MIT II, 455); Bashk. 1664 **Küzem-berdi** [Кузембердейко Тетиков] (MIB I, 193); Bashk. 1776 **Quǰam-berdi** [Бухарметь Кужамбердин] (MIB V, 47-49). ✧ 'My hodja gave him'. ⇨ **XOJA** + **BERDİ**. See also **XOJA-BERDİ**, **XOJA-BERGEN**.

XOJAM-ŠÜKÜR? Kzk. 1817 **Xoǰam-šükür** [حوجا مشكر / Хожамешкер] (MIK IV, 310). ⇨ **XOJAM** + **ŠÜKÜR**.

XOJAŠ Tat.(Bar.) **Xoǰaš** [Хоцаш], a hero from Täpkäč aul (Proben IV, 166 /209/); Kirg. 19th c. **Qoǰos** [Коджосъ] (Potanin II, 4); Kzk. 19th c. **Qoǰas** [Кожасъ] (AOK 102); Chag. 15th c. **Quǰaš-mïrza** [قوجاش ميرزا / Qoudjâsch Mirza], defeated by the Sheybanid Berke-sultan (Abulg./Desm. 202); Tat. 1629 **Quǰaš** [Кужаш] (Miller, Ist. Sib. II, 360); Bashk. 1786 **Quǰaš** [Кужаш Арасланов] (MIB V, 198). ⇨ **XOJA** + suff. *-š*. See also **AГÏŠ-QOJOŠ**.

XOJEND-VERDİ Trkm. 1851 **Xoǰend-verdi** [Ходженд-верды], from the Yomut tribe (MIT II, 302). ✧ 'Khodjend (Tn.) gave him/her'. ⇨ **BERDİ**.

XOJİM Kzk. **Xoǰïm** / **Qoǰïm?** [قوجم / Хожимъ] (Syzdykov 354).

XOJUГUR Yak. **Xoǰuɣur** [Кусаҕан Хоцугур], Qusaɣan ~, a character in a tale (Pek.). ✧ 'Tall, slim' cf. Yak. *χoǰoɣor* 'стройный, высокий' (Pek.).

XODAY-KELDİ Kirg. **Xoday-keldi** [Khodai-Keldi], a mergen, Almásy's guide (Almásy 296). ⇨ **XUDAY** + **KELDİ**.

XODĀ-BERDİ see **XUDAY-BERDİ**

XODĀ-BİRGEN see **XUDAY-BERGEN**

XODÏR I. Hak. 19th-20th c. **Xodïr** [Ходыр] (HRS 352). ✧ I. 'Itch, scab' cf. Hak. *χodïr* 'чесотка, парша, короста' (HRS). ⇨ **XİZİR**.

XODÏR II. see **XİZİR**

XOҮČU see **QOYČİ**

XOYÏÑ Hak. 19th-20th c. **Xoyïñ** [Хойынъ], fem. (HRS 355). ✧ 'Bosom' cf. Hak. *χoyïn* 'пазуха' (HRS).

XOQQAY Karg. **Xoqqay** [Хоккай] (Katanov: ZIRGOÊtn. XVII, vyp. III, 187).

XOLLÏ see **QALLÏ**

XOLUONYAY Yak. **Xoluonyay** [Холуоҥjai], Uot ~, one of the four female spirits of four roads connecting all three worlds (Pek.).

XOLURDĀN Yak. **Xolurdān** [Холурдан], Timir Xolurdān Udaɣan, an abasï-shamaness (*abāsï udaɣan*) (Pek.). ✧ 'Iron-?-shamaness' (Pek.).

XOMAY Hak. 19th-20th c. **Xomay** [Хомай], fem. (HRS 355). ✧ 'Bad, disgusting' (HRS).

XON-GEYEK Karg. **Xon-geyek** [Хонгеекъ], a family (Katanov: ZIRGOÊtn. XVII, vyp. III, 214).

XONA Kzk. 19th c. **Xona-bek** [Хонабекъ] (SOK 8).

XONČOLŪN Yak. **Xončolūn**, **Xončolūn-toyon** [Хончолун / Хончолун-тojон] (Pek.). ✧ 'Strech yourself; straighten'? cf. Yak. *χončoy-* 'выставляться горизонтально, выпрямляться' (Pek.).

XONDÏR see **QONDÏR**

XONYOÑNŪR Yak. **Xonyoññūr** [Хонjоҥнур], fem. (Pek.).

XONNORUN Yak. **Xonnorun** [Хоннорун] (Pek.).

XONOX Yak. **Xonoχ** [Хонох] (Pek.).

XONOXO Yak. **Xonoχo** [Хонохо] (Pek.).

XONTORUN Yak. **Xontorun** [Хонторун], a 7-year-old boy who died of headache and became a famous *üör* (Pek.).

XOÑXOYBOX Yak. **Xoñχoyboχ** [Хонҥхоiбох] (Pek.). ✧ 'A man with sunken cheeks' cf. Yak. *χoñχoy-* 'впадать' (Pek.).

XOÑQURDĀN Yak. **Xoñqurdān-buχatïr** [Хонҥкурдан бухатыр] (Pek.). ✧ 'Throated voice hero' cf. Yak. *χoñqur* (Pek.) + suff. *-dān*.

XOÑQURU Yak. **Xoñquru (-χotun)** [Хонҥкуру (хотун)], goddess of fire (Pek.).

XOÑOLOY-XORSUNA Yak. **Xoñoloy-χorsuna** [Хонҥолоi-хорсуна], *abāsï ataman* (chief) of the evil spirits (Pek.).

XOPOT Yak. **Xopot** [Хопот] (Pek.).

XOR-BULAT Chuv. 18th-19th c. **Xor-bulat** [Хорбулатъ] (Magn. 91). ✧ 'Free (independent) steel' cf. Tat. male name *Xör-bulat* 'id.' (Sattarov). ⇨ **XUR / QUR?** + **BULAT**.

XORASANLÏ Oghuz/Trkm. 13th c. **Xorasanlï** [خراسانلى / Хорасанлы], Oɣuz-χan's descandant (Abulg./Kon. 525). ✧ 'Coming from (or living in) Khorasan'.

XORAZ Trkm. 20th c. **Xoraz** [Horaz] (Zaj. 1971, 331); Chuv. 18th-19th c. **Xoraz** [Хоразъ] (Magn. 91); Kzk. 19th c. **Xuraz** [Хуразъ] (Grod. I, 98); Trkm.? 1823/24 **Xuraz-atalïq** [Хураз-аталык] (MIT II, 423); Trkm.? 1746 **Xuraz-bek-atalïq** [Хураз-бек-аталык (Хураз-инак)], Artuq-inaq's brother (MIT II, 177, 181, 334, 335, 348); Tat. 1681 **Qoraz** [Коразко Кочуковъ] (Kurdjumov 16); Tat. 1668, 1696 **Quraz** [Куразка (Куразко) Кучюковъ] (Kungursk. akty 12, 132); Tat. 1675 **Quraz** [Куразъ] (Kungursk. akty 35); Kzk. 18th c. **Quraz-bek** [Куразбекъ] (Nepljuev 809, 811, 813). ✧ 'Cock, buck, dandy; having a good descent' cf. Kzk.

qoraz 'der Hahn; der Stutzer; anständig, von gutem Herkommen' (Radl. II, 552), Trkm. *χoraz* 'петух' (TrkmRS) (<P.).

XORUOJA   Yak. **Xoruoja / Xarïaja** [Хоруоџа / Харыаца] (Pek.).

XORUOJAY   Yak. **Xoruojay-bärgän** [Хоруоцаи-бäргäн], silver bogatyr (hero), son of the eagles' god (Pek.). ⇨ **XORUOJA** + **BÄRGÄN** + suff. -*y*.

XOŠ   Selj. 1192/93 **Xoš-tegin** [خشتكين الجراجى / Khochtékîn el-Djerādjī] (Ibn Šaddād, Nawād.: RHCHor III, 308). ✦ 'Pleasant, nice, good' cf. Karakh. *χoš* ' радостный, веселый' (DTS), Maml. *hoš* '*yahšï* = gut' (Al-Qawānīn), Kuman, Kirg. *qoš* 'gesund, wohl, glücklich' (Radl. II, 637), Kzk. *qoš* ' будь здоров' (KzRS), (<P.) *χoš~χuš* 'nice, good, pleasant' as second component of P. compound names (Justi).

XOŠ-BULAT   Chuv. 18th-19th c. **Xoš-pulat** [Хошпулатъ] (Magn. 91); Chuv. 18th-19th c. **Xož-bulat** [Хожбулатъ] (Magn. 90). ✦ 'Good/excellent steel' cf. Tat. *Xuš-bulat* 'id.' (Sattarov). ⇨ **XOŠ** + **BULAT.**

XOŠ-XAL   Uzb. 1701 **Xoš-χal-bi** [خوشحال / Chwušḥâl Bi-i Qatafân], a treasurer-in-chief (Oberkämmerer) from Bukhara, from the Qatafân tribe (Buchari 265). ✦ 'Pleasant, good state; good power/strength' cf. Tat. *χal* 'I. положение; обстоятельство, случай, II. сила, моıц; бодрость ' (TatRS). ⇨ **XOŠ.**

XOŠ-KELDİ   Trkm. 20th c. **Xoš-geldi** [Hošgeldi] (Zaj. 1971, 334); Maml. **Xoš-keldi** [السيفى حشكلدى], a treasurer mentioned in an inscription without date on a copper tray (Mayer 141-42); Maml. 1438/39 **Xoš-keldi** [حشكلدى اليشبكى] (Ibn Taghrīb. VII, 80); Maml. 1438/39 **Xoš-keldi** [حشكلدى الناصرى بهلوان] (Ibn Taghrīb. VII, 65); Maml. 1441-69 **Xoš-keldi** [حشكلدى], name five persons in the source (Ibn Taghrīb. VIII); Maml. 1452 **Xoš-keldi** [حشكلدى] (Ibn Taghrīb. VII, 225, 444); Maml. 1453, 1467/68 **Xoš-keldi** [حشكلدى القوامى الناصرى] (Ibn Taghrīb., VII, 435, 522, Iyās II, 83, 115); Maml. 1454 **Xoš-keldi** [حشكلدى السيفى قجتار جغتاى] (Ibn Taghrīb. VIII, 245, 246); Maml. 1455 **Xoš-keldi** [حشكلدى الزردكاش] (Iyās II, 53); Maml. 1461 **Xoš-keldi** [حشكلدى الكوجكى] (Ibn Taghrīb. VII, 76); Maml. 1461/62 **Xoš-keldi** [حشكلدى اليوسفى] (Iyās II, 73, 81, 89, 312, 395); Maml. 1467/68 **Xoš-keldi** [حشكلدى قرا الحسينى] (Ibn Taghrīb. VII, 854); Maml. 1468 **Xoš-keldi** [حشكلدى الخازندار الصغير] (Ibn Taghrīb. VIII, 690); Uzb. 20th c. **Xoš-keldi** [Хушкелди] (Begmatov 1984, 203); Chag. 16th c. **Xuš-keldi-bay** [Хушкельди-бай] (Ivanov 154, 155, 157); Bashk. 1734 **Uš-kildi** [Ушкилди Мусинъ], a tarχan (Vel.-Zern., Bašk. 27). ✦ '(S)he is welcome' cf. Maml. *hoš* '*yahšï* = gut' (Al-

Qawānīn) (<P.), Bashk. *χuš kildeň* 'добро пожаловать' (BRS/Uraksin), see also the names beginning with *Xoš-*. Such names were given when the long awated child was born to the parents not having any children before (Zaj. 1971, p. 334). ⇨ **XOŠ** + **KELDİ.**

XOŠ-QADEM   Maml. 1441-1469 **Xoš-qadem** [خشتدم], name of several persons in the source (Ibn Taghrīb. VIII); Maml. 1447 **Xoš-qadem** [خشتدم الناصرى] (Iyās II, 30, 55); Maml. 1450 **Xoš-qadem** [خشتدم الظاهرى الرومى] (Ibn Taghrīb. VIII, 91); Maml. 1455 **Xoš-qadem** [خشتدم دوادار] (Ibn Taghrīb. VIII, 276); Maml. 1455 **Xoš-qadem** [الملك الظاهـر] [خشتدم الناصرى] (Ibn Taghrīb. VIII, 276); Maml. 1464 **Xoš-qadem** [ابوسعيد خشتدم], a sultan in Egypt (Sauvaget: BÉO XII, 23); Maml. 1474/75 **Xoš-qadem** [خشتدم الوريـر] (Iyās II, 154); Maml. 1475/76 **Xoš-qadem** [خشتدم الزينى] (Iyās II, 157); Yürük 1543 **Xoš-qadem** [Hoşkadem] (Gökb., Rum. 204). ✦ 'Auspicious, lucky (lit. having lucky foot)' (Erol II), cf. Ar. *qadem* 'foot (measure)'. ⇨ **XOŠ.**

XOŠ-PULAT see **XOŠ-BULAT**

XOŠ-WAQÏT   Kzk. 19th c. **Xoš-waqt** [Хошвактъ] (SKSO III, 10); Kzk. 19th c. **Xoš-waqt** [Хошвактъ] (SKSO VIII, 230); Kzk. 19th c. **Xuš-waqt** [Хушвактъ] (SKSO VIII, 206); Kzk. 19th c. **Xuš-waqt** [Алимкулъ Хушвактовъ] (SKSO VIII, 200); Kzk. 19th c. **Xuš-waqt** [Хушвактъ] (SKSO VIII, 225); Uzb. 1821 **Xuš-waqt-quš-begi** [Хушвакт-кушбеги], from Bukhara (Ivanov, Vosstanie 67, 69, 70). ✦ 'Pleasant, nice time; (born) in (good) time' cf. Kzk. *waqït* ' время' (KzRS). ⇨ **XOŠ.**

XOŠ-WAQT see **XOŠ-WAQÏT**

XOŠKE   Uzb. 1704 **Xoške** [خوشكه], an *ataliq* from the Yüz tribe (Buchari 272). ✦ 'Pleasant, beautiful, nice, good; sweet' (P.) (TED, Özön). ⇨ **XOŠ** + dim. suff. -*ke* or < comp. -*ake*.

XOTAMÏŠ   Trkm. 1768 **Xotamïš** [حوطامش / Hotamış], chief of a clan in Anatolia (Refik, Anad. 219). ✦ 'He lived' cf. Turk. dial. *hota-* 'yaşamak' (SDD).

XOŽ-BULAT see **XOŠ-BULAT**

XOŽA see **XOJA**

XŌČÏYAX   Hak. 19th-20th c. **Xŏčïyaχ**, fem. (HRS 355). ✦ 'Nice, pretty' cf. Yak. *χŏčayaχ* 'красивенький, красивый (напр. о ткани)'.

XŌJOŇ   Yak. **Xōjoň** [Хоцоң] (Pek.). ✦ 'Certain kind of rhytmic moving' cf. Yak. *χojoň* 'особый вид движения под такт ритму в песне или особый ритм под такт движению' (Pek.).

XUBAX   Hak. 19th-20th c. **Xubaχ** [Хубах] (HRS 352). ✦ 'Pale' cf. Hak. *χuba* 'бледный; бледножёлтый; светлокрасный; светлокоричневый' (HRS).

XUČQAR see **QOČQAR**

XUDA I. see **QUDA I.**

XUDA II. see **XUDAY**

XUDA-BENDE see **XUDAY-BENDE**

XUDAY Maml. 1301 **Xuda-bende** [بن ابغا
حدا بنده بن أرغون] (Dawād. VI, 212); Khorezm.? 14th
c. **Xuda-bende-χan** [Mohammed Khodhâbendeh /
Мухаммед Худабандэ-хан], king of the „Tatars",
who converted to Islam (RaD I/1, 42, Ibn Bat. II, 114-
115); Uzb. 1512 **Xuda-yar** [Khoudaiar-Khan], son of
Sultan Bābur (Baber), also called Altïn-bišik [=Golden
Cradle] (Nalivkin-Dozon 64); Uzb. 1833 **Xuda-yar-biy**
[Худаяр-бий], from the Qïyat tribe (MIT II, 464, 466,
568); Chag. 16th c. **Xuda-yar-χaǰi** [Худай Яр-
хаджи] (Ivanov 143); Chag. 16th c. **Xuda-yar-χoǰa?**
[Худаяр-хаджа] (Ivanov 151); Kzk. 1794 **Xuday-
bende, Quday-bende** [حداى بنده] (MIK IV, 163);
Bashk. 1798 **Xuday-γul** (PSZRI XXV, 196); Chag.
16th c. **Xuday-qulï** [Худай-кули], several persons
(Ivanov 151, 166, 211, 225); Uzb. 1689 **Xuday-qulï-
inaq** [Худай-кули-инак] (MIT II, 331); Kzk. 1817
Xuday-mende [Джума Худаймендіевъ], sultan of
the Arγïn tribe (clan) (Mejer 35); Kzk. 1786 **Xuday-
mendi** [Khoudaï Mendy / Худай-Менды], a sultan of
the Middle Horde (Orta Žüz) (Levchine 283, Levšin II,
306); Kzk. 1840 **Xuday-mendi** [Худаймендыi], sultan
of the Middle Horde (Orta Žüz) (Konšin, Mat. V, 14);
Kzk. 19th c. **Xuday-mindi** [Иръ Магомедъ Худай-
Миндіевъ] (Grod., Pril. 43); Crm. 1531 **Quda-yar**
[Кудодаръ], a murza (PSRL VIII, 278); Tat. 1532
Quda-yar [Кудояръ / Кудалыяръ], envoy from
Astrakhan (PSRL VIII, 284); Kkalp. 20th c. **Quda-yar**
[Кудайар] (Bask., Kkalp. 11); Kkalp. 20th c. **Quda-
yar** [Кудаяр] (KkRS 774); Kirg. **Quda-yar** [Кудаяр]
(Jud. 798); Bashk. 1734 **Quda-mendi** [Кудаменди
Мусинъ], a tarχan (Vel.-Zern., Bašk. 27); Bashk. 1719
Quday-bende-baγatïr [Кудай-Бенде-Багатыр
султан] (MIB I, 280); Bashk. 1734 **Quday-γul**
[Кудайгулъ Бурашевъ], a tarχan (Vel.-Zern., Bašk.
10); Tat. 1506 **Quday-qul** [Кудайкулъ], a prince from
Kazan (PSRL XIII, 1); Tat. 1534 **Quday-qul**
[Кудайкулъ-уланъ] (PSRL XIII, 81); Tat. 1551
Quday-qul [Кудайгулъ-уланъ / Кудугулъ-уланъ]
(PSRL XIII, 168); Tat. 1505 **Quday-qul / Xuday-qul**
[Петръ Кудайкулъ (Худай-кулъ)], a christened
prince from Kazan (PSRL VI, 51, 244, VIII, 245, IX,
22, 227); Kzk. 19th c. **Quday-mende** [Кудаймендe]
(SODž. 58); Kzk. / Kirg.? 19th c. **Qutay-mendi**
[Кутай-Менды] (Potanin IV, 405); *EN:* Kzk. 18th c. -
19th c. **Xuday-bek** [Худайбек] (Tynyšp. 66); Kzk.
18th c. - 19th c. **Xuday-qul** [Худайкул], a clan
(Tynyšp. 65, 66, 71, 74, 75). ✧ 'God' cf. Tuv. *χuda*,
Tat.(Tob.) *χuday*, *χudā* 'Gott' (Radl. II, 1735-36),
Alt.(Tel., Leb.), Hak.(Koyb.), Shor, Chul.(Küer.), Kzk.,

Kirg. *quday* 'Gott' (Radl. II, 998), Turk. *χüda* 'id.'
(Radl. II, 1738) (<P.) *χuday*, خداى '(Self-existent) God'
(Johnson). *Xuda(y)-yar / Quda-yar* means 'God's
friend'. See also **ALLA, ОҐАН, TÄÑRİ.**

XUDAY-BERDİ Turk. 16th c. **Xuda-verdi**, 9 persons
in the source (Ongan, Ank. II); Turk. 1583 **Xuda-verdi**
[Hudaverdi], 3 persons in the source (Ongan, Ank. I,
161); Chag. 15th c. - 16th c. **Xuday-berdi**
[حداى بردى], a Shaybanid (Šejb. LI); Chag. 16th c.
Xuday-berdi-mirza [Худай-берды-мирза] (Ivanov
221); Chag. 16th c. **Xuday-berdi-sultan** [Худай-
берды-султан] (Ivanov 28); Chag. 16th c. **Xuday-
berdi** [Худай-берды] (Ivanov 132, 159, 170, 171);
Trkm. 1768/69 **Xuday-berdi-bay** [Худай-берды-бай],
from the people of Čaγatay (MIT II, 342); Trkm.
1817/18 **Xuday-berdi** [Худай-берды Аркар] (MIT II,
407).

XUDAY-BERDİ-TAWUQ Trkm. 1823 **Xuday-berdi-
tawuq** [Худай-берды Таук], a military leader (MIT
II, 423).

XUDAY-BERDİ Trkm. 1880 **Xuday-berdi**
[Нургельды Худай-Бердіевъ] (Grod., Vojna IV, 39);
Bashk. 1783 **Xuday-berdi** [Худайберда] (MIB V,
148); Bashk. 1789 **Xuday-berdi** [Мунаатмас
Худайбердин] (MIB V, 259); Kkalp. 1740 **Xuday-
berdi-bi** [Худайберды-Би] (Hanykov, Poezdka 19,
MIKk. 208); Uzb. 16th c. - 17th c. **Xuday-berdi**
[Худай-берды], several persons (Ivanov 358); Uzb.
1804 **Xuday-berdi-inâq** [Худай-берды-инак], from
Khiva (MIT II, 364); Uzb. 1804 **Xuday-berdi** [Худай-
берды], a governor from the Nüküz tribe (MIT II, 353);
Uzb.? 1813 **Xuday-berdi-bek** [Худай-берды-бек]
(MIT II, 387); Uzb. 19th c. **Xuday-berdi** [Каршибай
Худайбердіевъ] (SKSO III, 172); Trkm. 20th c.
Xuday-berdï [Hudayberdï] (Zaj. 1971, 333); Trkm.
1881 **Xuday-verdi-χan** [Худай-Верды-ханъ] (Grod.,
Vojna IV, Grod., Pril. 18); Maml. 1516 **Xudā-berdi**
[حدابردى الاشرفى], emir, governor of Alexandria, died
in 1516 (Iyās III, 3, 26, 75, 80, 87, Mayer 140); Maml.
1547 **Xudā-berdi** [حضا بردى الظا هرى], builder of the
Pilgrim's Road, died around 1547 (Mayer 141); Turk.
1552 **Xudā-verdi** (Dávid); Turk. 1570 **Xudā-verdi**
(Dávid); Turk. 1580 **Xudā-verdi**, Kurd bin ~ (Dávid);
Turk. 1580 **Xudā-verdi**, Hasan bin ~ (Dávid); Turk.
1629 **Xudā-verdi** [Khudaverdi], a spāhi in Buda,
Hungary (Velics-Kamm. I, 450); Turk. 1630 **Xudā-
verdi** [Khudáverdi], a Turk from Cserépvár, Hungary
(Velics-Kamm. I, 745); Yürük 1543 **Xudā-verdi**
[Hudā-verdi] (Gökb., Rum. 101); Yürük 1543 **Xudā-
virdi** [Hudâ-virdi] (Gökb., Rum. 177, 189, 219); Yürük
16th c. **Xudā-virdi** [حدا ويردى], from the Yürüks of
Kocacık, Türkey (Gökb., Rum. 101); Uzb. 20th c.
Xudây-berdi [Худойберди] (Begmatov 1984, 202);

Turk. **Xüdä-värdi** (Radl. II, 1738); Turk. 1540 **Xüdä-virdi-kethudā** [Hüdâvirdi kethudâ], in a defter of Diyarbekir (Demirtaš 51); Bashk. 1623 **Quda-berdey** (<Quda-berdi) [Ангишай Кудабердеев] (Miller, Ist. Sib. II, 299); Bashk. 1695 **Quda-berdey** (<Quda-berdi) [Кудабердей Чюманов] (MIB I, 90); Tat. 1601 **Quday-berdey** (<Quday-berdi) [Кудайбердей] (Miller, Ist. Sib. II, 169); Bashk. 1600 **Quday-berdey** (<Quday-berdi) [Канай Кудайбердеев] (Miller, Ist. Sib. II, 158, 159, MIB I, 151); Bashk. 18th c. **Quday-berdi** [Сеит (Сагит) Кудайбердин], (MIB V, 673); Bashk. 1789 **Quday-berdi** [Сулейман Кудайбердин] (MIB V, 254, 291, 300); Tat. 1752 **Quday-berdi(y)** [Курдай Бердей Уразметевъ] (PSZRI XIII, 737); Tat.(Tara) **Quday-birdī** [Kudai Birdi / Кудаи Бірді], Ïsän's son (Proben IV, 166 (202)); Bashk. 1756 **Quðay-berdi?** [Кузайберды] (MIB IV/1, 109); *EN:* Kzk. 18th c. - 19th c. **Xuday-berdi** [Худайберды], a clan (Tynyšp. 66, 68, 70, 71, 73, 75). ✧ 'God-given; God has given (him)' (Sauvaget 47, Rásonyi, Theoph. 291-296, Zaj. 1971) Such names were given if there were no children, they were sickly or did not survive in the family before (Noyan 6-7). ⇨ XUDAY + BERDĪ + suff. -di. See also **ALLA-BERDĪ, ČALAB-BERDĪ, XUDAY-BERGEN, ÏGÄM-BERDĪ, ОГAN-BERDĪ, RÄHĪM-BERDĪ, SATTAR-BERDĪ, TÄÑRĪ-BERDĪ.**

XUDAY-BERDÏ see **HUDAY-BERDÏ**

XUDAY-BERGEN Tat. **Xoday-birgen** (H. Z. Košay: KCsA I, 324); Kkalp. 19th c. **Xuda-bergän-bi** [Худай Бергянъ] (Xanykov, Poezdka 19); Kzk. 19th c. **Xuday-bergän** [Джуманъ Худай Бергяновъ] (Grod., Pril. 175); Kzk. 19th c. **Xuday-bergän** [Худай Бергянъ Молла Акмашевъ] (Grod., Pril. 120); Kzk. 1878 **Xuday-bergän** [Худай Берганъ Молла Акмановъ] (Grod., Pril. 92); Trkm. 1821/22 **Xuday-bergen** [Худай-берген-бай], from the Er-sarï tribe (MIT II, 421); Trkm. 1841/42 **Xuday-bergen-yüz-bašï** [Худай-берген-юзбаши / Худай-берген Орус], from the Yomut tribe (MIT II, 482, 498, 566); Kzk. **Xuday-bergen** [Худайбергенъ Баетовъ] (Smirnov 14); Uzb. 19th c. **Xuday-bergen** [Иръ-Мухаммедъ Худайбергеневъ] (Sr. Az. I (1896), avg. 17); Uzb.? 1855 **Xuday-bergen-biy** [Худай Берген-бий] (MIT II, 553, 555); Trkm. 1804 **Xuday-bergen(-bek)** [Худай-берген (бек)] (MIT II, 365, 366, 369); Uzb. 20th c. **Xudây-bergän** [Худойберган] (Begmatov 1984, 202); Kzk. 1771 **Quday-bergen** [Kudai Bergen], tarχan (Rytschkow, P., Tagebuch. Riga 1774, p. 341); Kzk. 19th c. **Quday-bergen** [Кудайбергенъ] (SOV 68); Kzk. 19th c. **Quday-bergen** [Кудайбергенъ] (SODž. 84); Kzk. 19th c. **Quday-bergen** [Кудайбергенъ] (SOK 46); Kkalp. 20th c. **Quday-bergen** [Кудайберген] (KkRS 774); Kzk. 1817

Quday-bergen / Quday-bergän? [قداى بيركان] (MIK IV, 312, 319); *EN:* Kzk. 18th c. - 19th c. **Xuday-bergen** [Худайберген], a clan (Tynyšp. 71). ✧ 'God-given; God gave him' cf. Rásonyi, Theoph. 291-296. ⇨ **XUDAY + BERGEN + suff. -gen.** See also **ALDA-BERGEN, ALLA-BERGEN, XUDAY-BERDĪ, ČALAB-BERDĪ, ОГAN-BERDĪ, SATTAR-BERDĪ, TÄÑRĪ-BERDĪ.**

XUDAY-DAD Khorezm.? **Xuday-dad** [پولادچی / خدایداد بن امیر / Khoudâï-Dâd], follower of Toγluq-temür Khan of Kashghar (Abulg./Desm. 169); Nog. 1649 **Xuday-dat (Xuday-naš?)** [Худайнашъ мурза Шейдякъ-мурзинъ] (AI IV, 87); Nog. 1649 **Xuday-dat (Xuday-nat?)** [Худайнатъ мурза Саръ-Исуповъ] (AI IV, 78, 87); Bashk. 1777 **Xuday-tat** [Худайтат Апуков] (MIB V, 59); Khorezm./Chag. 1423 **Quday-dat** [Кудаидатъ (Куйдадать)], ruler of the Horde (PSRL V, 262, VI, 142, VIII, 92). ✧ 'God-given present; God's present (aid)' cf. Turk. *dâd* 'bahşiş, vergi' (Özön) (<P.), Tat. *Xodaydad* (Sattarov). ⇨ **XUDAY.**

XUDAY-MENDĪ see **XUDAY-BENDE**
XUDAY-MĪNDĪ see **XUDAY-BENDE**
XUDAY-NAŠ see **XUDAY-DAD**
XUDAY-NAT see **XUDAY-DAD**

XUDAY-NAZAR Chag. 16th c. **Xuday-nazar** [Худай Назар Тархан], a tarχan (Ivanov 202); Uzb. **Xuday-nazar** [Худай-Назаръ-Чулакъ] (Smirnov 70); Uzb. 1826 **Xuday-nazar** [خدای نظر شغاول], from Bukhara (Vel.-Zern., Haïder 280-282); Bashk. 1787 **Quday-nazar** [Близяк (Бинзяп) Кудайназаров] (MIB V, 214); Kkalp. 20th c. **Quday-nazar** [Кудайназар] (KkRS 774); Kirg. **Quday-nazar** [Кудайназар] (Jud. 17). ⇨ **XUDAY + NAZAR.**

XUDAY-ŠÜKÜR Uzb. 1887 **Xuday-šükür** [Худай-Шукуръ-бай] (Moskal'cev 44); Kzk. 18th c. - 19th c. **Quday-sügür** [Кудайсугуръ] (ZOOIRGO IV, 99); Tat. 1629 **Quday-šügür** [Кудайшугур] (Miller, Ist. Sib. II, 358). ⇨ **XUDAY + ŠÜKÜR.**

XUDAY-VERDĪ see **XUDAY-BERDĪ**
XUDĀ-BERDĪ see **XUDAY-BERDĪ**
XUDĀ-VERDĪ see **XUDAY-BERDĪ**

XUYÏX Hak. 19th-20th c. **Xuyïχ** [Хуйых] (HRS 352). ✧ 'Smell of the burnt food on the funeral feast' cf. Hak. PN *Хуиχ* 'запах гари от пищи сжигаемой на поминках' (Butanaev).

XULA-TAY see **QULA-TAY**

XUMA NUyg.(Tar.) **Xuma-χan** [Chuma Chan / Хума Хан] (Proben VI, 200 /262/). ✧ Khuma (P.) a woman's name (Jarring).

XUMAR Khorezm. **Xumar** [سلطانی عوارزم / خمار ازاتراك] (Juwaynī I, 97-99); Khorezm. 1220 **Xumar** [Хумар], Türkān-χatun's relative (MIT I, 486,

4٤7, 504); Uyg. 762 **Xumar-čur** [Liŭlāng χūmār čūr] (Mahrnamag 11); 878 **Xumar-tegin** [خمارتکین], خمارتکین] (Tabarī, Annal. III, 1922); 1174/75 **Xumar-tegin** [خمارتکین / Khamartekîn], Salăh ad-Dīn's emir and saver (Ibn al-Athīr: RHCHor I, 619); Oghuz? 1037 **Xumar-tegin** [Хумар-тегин куранхан, гулям], a slave-soldier (gulām) in Ghaznevid service (MIT I, 259); Karakh.? 993 **Xumar-tegin** [خمارتکین البهای] (Hil. Sābī 383); Selj. **Xumar-tegin** [الطغرائی] خمارتکین] (Bondārī 18, 21); Khorezm. 13th. **Xumar-tegin** [Khoumâr Tékine], defended Urgendj against the Mongols at Chinggis' time (Abulg./Desm. 37, 118, Hudūd 349, 364); Uyg. **Qumar** [Kumar] (EUTS); Uyg. 8th c. **Qumar** [Qumar ygän alpï tutuγ] (Müller, Pfahl. 24); Kzk. 19th c. **Qumar-bay** [Кумарбаевъ] (SKSO VIII, 221); Kzk. 19th c. **Qumar-bay** [Кумарбай] (SOK 56); Kzk. 19th c. **Qumar-bay** [Кумарбай] (SKSO VIII, 226); Uzb. 19th c. **Qumar-bay** [Кумарбай] (SKSO III, 174); Kzk. 19th c. **Qumar-bek** [Кумарбекъ] (SODž. 66, 122); Kirg. **Qumar-yan** [Кумар-Jан], one of the forty followers of Aq-sayqal (Proben V, 394 /397/); 1183 **Qumar-tegin** [Kûmârtakîn] (Abulfar./Budge I, 315, 329); Selj. 1232 **Qumar-tegin** [خماردکین / Chamardekin] (Abulfidā IV, 396-97). ✧ I. 'Gambling' cf. Chag., Turk. *qumar* 'das Hasardspiel' (Radl. II, 1045), Kzk. *qŭmar* I. 'азарт' (KzRS); II. 'Intense emotion, wish' cf. Kzk. *qŭmar* II. 'сильное желание, страсть (KzRS) (<Ar.).

XUMAR-TAŠ 1104/05 **Xumar-taš** [السلیمانی] خمارتانن] (Ibn Taghrīb. II, 346); 1137 **Xumar-taš** [خمارتا شالوالی] (Qalānisi 252); 1145 **Xumar-taš** [خمارتا ش الحافظی ابو المظفر] (Qalānisi 272); Oghuz/Trkm. 1031 **Xumar-taš** [Хумарташ], a door-keeper and commander-in-chief of Turkmen (MIT I, 234, 235); Selj. **Xumar-taš** [خمارتاش] (Bondārī 76); Selj.? 12th c. **Xumar-taš** [محمد خمارتاش] (Muh. Ibrahim 104). ⇨ **XUMAR / QUMAR? + TAŠ.**

XUNUM Bashk. 1737 **Xunum-bike** [Хунумбике], fem. (MIB III, 368).

XUÑƦURAQ Tat.(Sib.)? 1629 **Xuñγuraq** [Пыркей Хунгураков] (Miller, Ist. Sib. II, 344, 345).

XUR Chag. 16th c. **Xur-χatun** [Хур-хатун], fem. (Ivanov 138). ✧ 'Free, independent'? ⇨ **QUR?**

XURAM Tat.(Tob.) **Xuram-can** [Churam Zan / Хурам Цан] (Proben IV, 273 /339/). ✧ Khurram (P.) 'cheerful, glad, fresh' (Ahmed).

XURAZ see **XORAZ**

XURČU Hak. 19th-20th c. **Xurču** [Хурчу], fem. (HRS 355). ✧ 'Thimble' cf. Hak. *χurču* 'наперсток (HRS).

XURDAQ Chag. 16th c. **Xurdaq** [Хурдак, маулана] (Ivanov 92); Chag. 16th c. **Xurdaq** [Хурдак, мулла] (Ivanov 218, 253); Chag. 16th c. **Xurdaq** [Хурдак,

ходжаъ мир] (Ivanov 173, 230).

XURİ Yürük 1543 **Xuri-qïzï** [حوری قیزی / Hûri-Kızı], fem. (Gökb., Rum. 224). ✧ 'Houri; angel, darling; beautiful girl' cf. Turk. *huri* 'die Huri' (HŞ), *huri* 'cennet kızı; sevgili' (Özön) < P.

XURMA Trkm. 20th c. **Xurma-χatun** [Hurma (hatun)], fem. (Özbaş 69). ✧ 'Date, date palm (Phoenix dactylifera); sweet, nice (lady)' cf. Az., Turk., Crm. *χurma* 'die Palme, Dattelpalme, Dattel' (Radl. II, 1734).

XURMAN see **QURMAN**

XURMET see **QURMET**

XURSANAY Kzk. 19th c. **Xursanay** [Хурсанъ-ай], fem. (SKSO IV, otd. II, 38); Uzb. 19th c. **Xursanay** [Хурсанъ-ай], from Bukhara (SKSO VIII). ⇨ ? + suff. -*ay*.

XURSUL 1541 **Xursul** [Хурсулъ] (PSRL XIII, 100).

XURTAN Hak. 19th-20th c. **Xurtan** [Хуртан] (HRS 352). ✧ 'Worm' cf. Hak. *χurt* 'червь, червяк' (HRS) + suff. -*an*.

XURTČE Hak. 19th-20th c. **Xurtče** [Хуртче], fem. (HRS 355). ✧ 'Worm' cf. Hak. *χurt* 'червь, червяк' (HRS) + suff. -*če*.

XUSEYN see **QUSAYIN**

XUSN-NİGĀR Chag. 15th c. **Xusn-nigār-χanike?** [Хуснъ-Нигаръ-Ханике], Ulug-bek's third wife (Barth., Ulugb. 116). ✧ 'Beauty-sweetheart, very beautiful woman' (Ar., P.), cf. Tat. *Xösne* (Sattarov), Bashk. *Xösnä* (Kusimova) 'id.'. ⇨ **NİGĀR.**

XUŠ-KELDİ see **XOŠ-KELDİ**

XUŠ-WAQT see **XOŠ-WAQÏT**

XUŠAY Chag. 16th c. **Xušay-χafiz** [Хушай Хафиз] (Ivanov 299). ⇨ **XOŠ** + suff. -*ay* or comp. *ay*?

XUŠANDRA Alt. **Xušandra-χan** [Хушандра(-ханъ)] (Nikiforov 247).

XUT see **QUT**

XUTADMÏŠ see **QUTADMÏŠ**

XUTLUƦ-ÜZÜK Uyg. **Xutluγ-üzük** (Müller, Uig. II, 81). ⇨ **QUTLUƦ + ÜZÜK.**

XUZÏBAN Kzk. 19th c. **Xuzïban** [Иманкулъ Хузибановъ] (Grod., Pril. 193).

XÜDĀ-VERDİ see **XUDAY-BERDİ**

XÜKÜMET Trkm. 1854/55 **Xükümet-χan** [Хукумет-хан], a ruler of Meymene (MIT II, 260, 264, 265, 544). ✧ 'Government' cf. Trkm. *χökümet* 'id.' (TrkmRS) (<Ar.).

İ

İ-DEMER see EL-TEMİR
İ-DİMER see EL-TEMİR
İ-DZİMÄS see İT-ĴEMÄS

İBA see **İYBA**

İBAĴ Chag. 16th c. **İbaĵ-oɣlan** [Ибаджь-Огланъ] (Barth., Ulugb. 25-26).

İBAYXAN Kkalp. 20th c. **İbayχan** [Ибайхан], fem. (KkRS 777). ✧ Derived from some PN İbay + suff. -χan(1).

İBAT Kzk. 19th c. **İbat-χoĵa** [Ибатъ Ходжа] (Grod., Pril. 70). ✧ 'Slaves (of God)' (Erol II.) (Ar.).

İBDEY Hak. 19th-20th c. **İbdey** [Ибдей] (HRS 348). ✧ 'Like a tent (yurta), House-like' cf. Hak. ib ' юрта; дом (HRS) + suff. -dey.

İBÄK Chuv. 1737 **İbäk** [Ибяковъ] (Alatyr. 135); Bashk. 1757 **İbik** [Каиткул Ибиков] (MIB IV/1, 134). ✧ 'Silk' cf. Chag., Turk. ipäk 'die Seide' (Radl. I, 1566). See also **ĴİBEK**.

İBİK see **İBÄK**

İBİKEY Bashk. 1717 **İbikey** [Табай Ибыкеев] (MIB III, 148).

İBİN Kzk. 1884 **İbin** [Ибинъ Ергановъ] (Grod., Pril. 94). ✧ 'Shining, brilliant'? cf. Chag. ibin 'glänzend' (Radl. I, 1569).

İBİŠİK Kzk. 1820 **İbišik-murza** [Ибишикъ мурза], chief of a tribe (Sib. Vest. IX, 121).

İBRAHİM Karakh. **İbrahim** [İbrahim] (MK/Atalay 840); Uyg. / Karakh.? **İbrahim / İbrayim** [ibrahim / ibrajim] (DTS); Kkalp. 20th c. **İbrayїm** [Ыбрайым] (KkRS 777). ✧ Ibrahim (Ar.) 'kind father', a Prophet, the biblical Abraham (Ahmed).

İBRAY Tat.(Mish.) 18th c. **İbray** [Ибрай Темиргозинъ] (Nepljuev 882); Bashk. 1728 **İbray** [Ибрай Емяков] (MIB III, 253); Bashk. 1739 **İbray** [Ибрай] (MIB I, 375); Bashk. 18th c. **İbray** [Ибрай], from Orenburg (Nepljuev 852); Bashk. 1781 **İbray** [Япей Ибраевъ] (Korsakov 29); Kzk. 19th c. **İbray** [Ибрай] (AOP 82); Kzk. 19th c. **İbray** [Ибрай] (AOK 86); Kzk. 19th c. **İbray** [Ибрай] (AOO 54); Bashk. 18th c. **İbray-mulla** [Ибрай мулла] (Nepljuev 599, 600); Kkalp. 20th c. **İbray** [Ыбрай] (KkRS 777). ✧ Diminutive of Ar. Ibrahim (Kusimova, Sattarov, Žanuzakov 142). ⇨ **İBRAHİM**. See also **İBRAQ, İBRAŠ**.

İBRAYİM see **İBRAHİM**

İBRAQ Bashk. 1735 **İbraq** [Ибрак Тымыковъ], a tarχan (Vel.-Zern., Bašk. 13); Bashk. 1757 **İbraq** [Ибрак Ичтякин] (MIB IV/1, 157); Bashk. 1760 **İbraq** [Ибрак Иманов] (MIB IV/2, 385). ✧ Diminutive of Ar. Ibrahim (Sattarov). See also **İBRAY, İBRAŠ**.

İBRAQAY Bashk. 1757 **İbraqay** [Ибракай Букаев] (MIB IV/1, 157). ✧ 'Little İbrahim'. ⇨ **İBRA(Q)** + dim. suff. -(q)ay. See also **İBRAY, İBRAQ, İBRAŠ**.

İBRAŠ Bashk. 1735 **İbraš** [Ибрашъ Килинъ], a tarχan (Vel.-Zern., Bašk. 25); Bashk. 1745 **İbraš** [Ибраш Кутуев] (MIB III, 548); Bashk. 1787 **İbraš** [Ибраш Илаков] (MIB V, 207). ✧ Diminutive of Ar. Ibrahim (Sattarov). See also **İBRAY, İBRAQ**.

İBUČİR Khazar 700 **İbučir? / Bučur?** [Ιβούζηρος Γλιαβάνος], a noble Khazar, the brother-in-law of the emperor Iustinianus II (cca. 700) (Byz. Turc. 136).

İČ-EL-BERDİ Tat. 1603 **İč-el-berdi(y) / İč-el-berde(y)** [Ычелбердей Безгозев] (MIB I, 153). ⇨ **? + EL + BERDİ**.

İČ-ГĀZΪ Kzk. 19th c. **İč-ɣāzї** [Ich-Ghasy] (Levchine 356). ⇨ **EŠ? + ГĀZİ**.

İČ-TÄKÄ Bashk. 1757 **İč-täkä?** [Ибрак Ичтякин] (MIB IV/1, 157). ⇨ **EŠ + TEKE?**

İČEY see **İŠEY**

İČİMEK Tat.(Sib.) 1578 **İčimek** [Ичимокъ есаулъ] (Sib. Let. (Rem.) 325).

İČKÄY Kirg. 1847 **İčkäy** [Ичкай Даирбековъ] (Konšin, Mat. V, 107).

İČKÄRMİŠ Uyg. **İčkärmiš-їnal** [İçkärmiş ınal] (EUTS). See also **İL-İČKÄRMİŠ**.

İĴAN Kzk. 19th c. **İĵan / İ-ĵan?** [Иджанъ] (SODž. 98).

İĴİMÄS see **İT-ĴEMÄS**

İDÄ Kzk. **İdä-ɣul** [Идягуловъ] (TOUAK XXIV, 87). ✧ 'Gentleman, master; Lord, God' cf. Türk, Karakh. idi 'хозяин, владелец; обладатель; господин (о боге)' (DTS).

İDÄGÄ Uyg. **İdägä** [İdägä] (EUTS); Crm. **İdägä-bї** [Iдягä бi], a character in a tale (Proben VII, 99); Uyg. 10th c. **İdägä-toyїn** [idägä tojїn] (DTS); TN: 19th c. **İdege** [Идеге], a tomb north of Caspian sea (IIRGO XVI). ⇨ **EDGÜ?**

İDEGER see **İDİGER**

İDEHER see **İDİGER**

İDEL see **ETİL**

İDELÄK see **İDELEK**

İDELEY Chuv. 18th-19th c. **İdeley** [Иделей] (Magn. 41). ⇨ **ETİL?** + suff. -ey.

İDELEK Chuv. 18th-19th c. **İdelek / İdeläk** [Иделекъ] (Magn. 41). ⇨ **ETİL?** + suff. -ek.

İDİ-QURT Uyg. 12th c. - 14th c. **İdi-qurt** [idi qurt / İdi Kurt] (Radl., USp. 4-5, DTS, EUTS); Uyg. 12-14th c. **İti-qurt** [iti qurt] (DTS). ✧ 'Master/owner-Wolf' (Blagova 1997, 706), cf. Türk, Karakh. idi 'хозяин, владелец; обладатель; господин (о боге)' (DTS). ⇨ **QURT**.

İDİČÄ Kzk. 19th c. **İdičä? / İdigä?** [Идича (Идига?)] (Kazancev 79). ✧ '?' cf. Türk, Karakh. idi 'хозяин, владелец; обладатель; господин (о боге)' (DTS) + suff. -čä.

İDİGE see **EDİGE**

İDİGEY see **EDİGEY**

İDİGER Tat. 1542 **İdiger / İdeger / İdeher** [Идигеръ / Идегеръ / Идехеръ], a prince from Astrakhan (PSRL XIII, 143).

İDİGÜ see **EDİGE**

İDİKİ see **EDİGE**

İDİKÜ see **EDİGE**

İDİL see **ETİL**

İDRİS   Uyg. / Karakh. **İdris** [idris] (DTS); Selj. 1089 **İdris** [ادريس بن طغان شاه], Toγan-šaχ's son (Kamāladdīn II, 105); Bashk. 1763 **İdris** [Идрись Муашев] (MIB IV/1, 271); Kzk. 19th c. **İdris** [Идрысъ] (SOK 48); Kzk. 19th c. **İdris** [Идрысъ] (SOV 44); Turk. **İdriš-oγlu**, a Zeybek (Kúnos 1891, 119). ✧ Idrīs (Ar.) Quranic name sometimes equated with Enoch (TED).

İDUKİ   Oghuz/Trkm. 13th c. **İduki-biy** [ايدكى بى / Идуки-бий], Qutlï-Qïyalï's son, the chief of the Mañγïts (Abulg./Kon. 325).

İDÜGÜ see **EDİGE**

İG   Oghuz/Trkm. 13th c. **İg-bek-čora** [ايك بيك / Игбек-чора], son of a slave (Abulg./Kon. 1345, 1370, 1385); Bashk. 1756 **İk-bay** [Икбай Ижбаев] (MIB IV/1, 128); Bashk. 18th c. **İk-čura** [Икчюре] (MIB III, 76); Bashk. 1756 **İk-čura** [Икчюра Билкишев] (MIB IV/1, 109). ✧ I. 'Noble'? (Németh, HMK), 'Good' cf. Bashk. PN *İg-däwlät* 'Good-Chance' (Kusimova); II. 'Illness'? cf. Uyg., Chag. *ik* 'die Krankheit, das Uebel' (Radl. I, 1415), Karakh. *ik* 'id.' (MK/Brock.); III. 'Spool, spindle'? cf. Tat. PN *İk-baqtï* which, according to Sattarov, would be derived from Karakh. *ig / ik / jig* 'веретено' (DTS).

İG-BER   Kzk. 19th c. **İg-ber** [Игберъ] (AOK 6). ✧ 'Give goodness'? ⇨ **İG.**

İG-MAMET   Bashk. 1695 **ig-mamet** [Иг-Мамет Каздеулов] (MIB I, 90). ✧ 'Good Mamet'. ⇨ **İG + MAMET.** See also **İGMET, İGİ-MUXAMMET.**

İG-TEMÜR   Crm. 1689 **İg-temür-bek** [مير شيرين / اكتيمور بك] (Vel.-Zern., Crim. 767). ⇨ **İG + TEMİR.**

İGDİR   Oghuz/Trkm. 13th c. **İgdir** [ايكدر / Игдир], Teñgiz-χan's son (Abulg./Kon. 520, 560, 615).

İGÄM-BERDİ see **İYEM-BERDİ**

İGÄN-BERDİ see **İYEM-BERDİ**

İGEN I.   Chuv. 18th-19th c. **İgen** [Игенъ] (Magn. 40); Chuv. 18th-19th c. **İgen-bay** [Игенбай] (Magn. 40); Bashk. 1763 **İgin** [Биктиней Игинин] (MIB IV/1, 270); Chuv. 18th-19th c. **İgin-bay** [Игинбай] (Magn. 40). ✧ 'Corn' cf. Tat. *igen* 'хлеб, хлеба (TRS), Tat., Tat.(Tob.), Bashk. *igĭn* 'der Acker; das Getreide' (Radl. I, 1426), Tat. *İgen-bay* (Sattarov).

İGEN II. see **İKEN**

İGİ   Tat.(Mish.) 1755 **İgi-bay** [Сайдак Игибаев] (MIB IV/1, 93); Bashk. 1664 **İgi-bay** [Игибайко Тилдигулов] (MIB I, 192); Bashk. 1723 **İgi-bay** [Игибай] (MIB III, 202); Bashk. 1725 **İgi-bay** [Абызай Игибай] (MIB III, 235); Bashk. 1727 **İgi-bay** [Игибай Калмаков] (MIB III, 243); Bashk. 1735 **İgi-bay** [Муса Игибаевъ], a tarχan (Vel.-Zern., Bašk. 22); Bashk. 1737 **İgi-bay** [Игибай Кулгараев] (MIB I, 326); Bashk. 1738 **İgi-bay** [Берекей Игибаев] (MIB III, 393); Bashk. 1754 **İgi-bay** [Игибай] (MIB IV/1, 83); Bashk. 1761 **İgi-bay** [Игибай] (MIB IV/1, 216); Bashk. 1763 **İgi-bay** [Беккиня Игибаев] (MIB IV/2, 45). ✧ 'Good' (Kusimova). ⇨ **EKİ?**

İGİ-MUXAMMET   Bashk. 1798 **İgi-muχammet** [Иги мухамметъ] (PSZRI XXV, 195). ✧ 'Good Mukhammed'. ⇨ **İGİ + MUXAMMED.** See also **İG-MAMET, İGMET.**

İGİČEK   Bashk. 1717 **İgiček** [Шабай Игичеков] (MIB III, 154); Bashk. 1717 **İgiček** [Якип Игичеков] (MIB III, 150). ⇨ **İGÄ / İGİ?** + suff. *-ček / -čik.*

İGİLİK   Bashk. 1764 **İgilek** [Амир Игиляков] (MIB IV/1, 298); Bashk. 1664 **İgilik** [Игилик Чермышев] (MIB I, 191); Bashk. 1675 **İgilik** [Каскин Игиликов] (MIB I, 199); Bashk. 1744 **İgilik** [Сакырбай Игиликов] (MIB III, 417); Bashk. 1754 **İgilik** [Чакырбай Игиликов] (MIB IV/1, 77). ✧ 'Goodness, kindness, charity'. ⇨ **İGİ** + suff. *-lik.*

İGİM   Bashk. 1704 **İgim-bay** (<**İgin-bay**?) [Игимбай] (Kurdjumov 341); Bashk. 1715 **İgim-bay** (<**İgin-bay**?) [Игимбай] (MIB III, 133); Bashk. 1717 **İgim-bay** (<**İgin-bay**?) [Игимбай Игитев] (MIB III, 158). ✧ I. 'Goodness' II. 'Corn, grain (crop)' cf. Bashk. *igen* 'id.', also Tat. PN *İgen-bay* (Sattarov). ⇨ **İGİ / İGEN I.?**

İGİMBET   Bashk. 1690 **İgimbet** [Игимбетка Езналеевъ] (Vel.-Zern., Bašk. 30); Bashk. 1714 **İginbet** [Ишекей Игинбетев] (MIB III, 113); Bashk. 1717 **İginbet** [Ишикай Игинбетев] (MIB III, 154); Bashk. 1724 **İgimbet** [Игимбет] (MIB III, 219, 222); Bashk. 1735 **İgimbet** [Игимбетъ] (Vel.-Zern., Bašk. 18); Bashk. 1761 **İgimbet** [Утяш Игимбет] (MIB IV/1, 219); Bashk. 1768 **İgimbet** [Бакир Игимбетев] (MIB IV/1, 332). ✧ Cf. Tat. PNs *İgi-bulat, İgi-däwlet* (Sattarov). ⇨ **İGİ / İYE?** + suff. *-(i)mbet.* See also **İG-MAMET, İGİ-MUXAMMET, İGMET.**

İGİN see **İGEN I.**

İGİNBET see **İGİMBET**

İGİNKA   Chuv. 18th-19th c. **İginka / İginkä?** [Игинка] (Magn. 40). ⇨ **İGEN I.** + suff. *-ka / -kä.*

İGİŠ   Bashk. 1664 **İgiš** [Игишко Беиков] (MIB I, 191); Bashk. 1754 **İgiš** [Асан Игишев] (MIB IV/1, 83); Bashk. 1754 **İgiš** [Азамай Игишев] (MIB IV/1, 83). ⇨ **İGİ** + suff. *-š.*

İGİT see **YİGİT**

İGİZ see **EKİZ**

İGMET   Bashk. 1764 **İgmet** [Игмет Уразметев] (MIB IV/1, 291). ✧ 'Good chance' cf. Bashk. PN *İγ-däwlet* (Kusimova). ⇨ **İGİ** + suff. *-met.* See also **İG-MAMET.**

İGMİŠ   Khorezm.? **İgmïš** [Игмыш] (RaD II, 193).

İGNAS Hak. 19th-20th c. **İgnas** [Игнас] (HRS 348). ❖ Ignatiy (R.). See also **İQİNĀČAY**.

İGÜ-DÄWLÄT Bashk. 1760 **İgü-däwlät** [Ягафер Игудявлет] (MIB IV, 188). ❖ 'Good chance' cf. Bashk. *İɣdäwlät* (Kusimova). ⇨ **İG / İGİ + DÄWLÄT**.

İFNĀÑ Hak. 19th-20th c. **İɣnāñ** [Игнаанъ] (HRS 348); Hak.(Sag.) 19th-20th c. **İɣnāñ** [Иҕнаҥ] (Katanov, Otč. 8, Proben IX, 556).

İHTİYAR Yyrük 1543 **İhtiyar**, from the Yürüks of Kocacık, Turkey (Gökb., Rum. 102, 189). ❖ I. 'Old man' cf. Turk. *ihtiyar* (Ar.) (Özön); II. 'Free will; freedom' NUyg. *iχtiyār* 'der freie Wille, die Gewalt, das Ansehen' (Radl. I, 1424).

İXUǨ Bulg. 13th c. **İχuǩ** [ﺝﺍﺣ / Aḥaǰ / Ихудж] (Jusupov 50, Epigr. Bulg. 124, 125).

İYBA Hak. 19th-20th c. **İba** [Иба] (HRS 348); Kkalp. 20th c. **İyba-gül** [Ийбагүл], fem. (KkRS 777). ❖ 'Well-bred, shy' (Baskakov: OSA 140), cf. Kzk. *ība* (Ar.) 'die Wohlerzogenheit, Höfflichkeit, Sitte' (Radl. I, 1569).

İYÄ see **İYE**

İYÄDĀ Karg. 19th-20th c. **İyädā** (Katanov, Otč. 10). ❖ 'Food' <R. *jeda* „ѣда (еда)" (Katanov).

İYE Kzk. 19th c. **İyä-bek** [Иябекъ] (SODž. 150). ❖ 'Master, owner, host; Lord (God)' cf. Uyg. *ijä* 'хозяин, господин (о боге)' (DTS), Uyg. *igä* 'хозяин; дух, божество' (DTS), Kkalp. *iye* 'хозяин, владелец' (KkRS), Kzk. *iye* 'id.' (KzRS), Tat. *iyä* 'der Herr, Wirth' (Radl. I, 1434), Chag., Turk. *ikä* 'der Herr, Wirth' (Radl. I, 1416), Uzb. *egä* 'хозяин; бог, господь' (UzbRS), for more data cf. also *eye* (Sev.).

İYEM-BERDİ Uzb. 20th c. **Egäm-berdi** [Эгамберди] (Begmatov 1984, 202); NUyg. 20th c. **Egäm-berdi** [Egämbärdi], Le Coq's servant at his 3rd expedition (Le Coq, Hellas 137); Kzk. 19th c. **Egem-berdi** [Эгемберди Усековъ] (Grod. 7); Kzk. 19th c. **İgäm-berdi** [Игамберди] (SKSO II, 14); Kzk. 19th c. **İgäm-berdi** [Маулянберды Игамбердіевъ] (SKSO II, 13); Kzk. 19th c. **İgäm-berdi** [Игамберди] (SKSO III, 115); Kkalp. 19th c. **İgäm-berdi** [Игамберди], a settlement (qïšlaq) (ZIRGOStat. IV); **İgän-berdi** [Нурметъ Иганъ-Бердыевъ], from the village Ača-maylï (TV 1876, 132); Kkalp. 20th c. **İyem-berdi** [Ийемберди] (KkRS 774); Kzk. 19th c. **İkäm-berdi** [Икамъ берди] (Grod., Pril. 193); Kzk. 19th c. **Yem-berdi (<İyem-berdi)** [Ембердыј] (SOV 96). ❖ 'My Lord (God, Master) gave him' ⇨ **İYE + BERDİ + poss. suff. -m**.

İYEM-BERGEN Uzb. 20th c. **Egäm-bergän** [Эгамберган] (Begmatov 1984, 202); Kkalp. 20th c. **İyem-bergen** [Ийемберген] (KkRS 774); Kkalp. 20th c. **Yem-bergen (<İyem-bergen)** [Емберген] (KkRS 773). ❖ 'My Lord (Master) gave him'. ⇨ **İYE + BERGEN + poss. suff. -m**.

İYGİLİK Kirg. **İygilik** [Ийгилик] (Jud. 962). ❖ 'Good deed' cf. Kirg. *iygilik* 'доброе дело' (Jud.). ⇨ **İGİ**.

İYMA-MÏRAT see **İYMA-MURAT**

İYMA-MURAT Kkalp. 20th c. **İyma-mïrat** [Иймамырат] (KkRS 774); Kkalp. 20th c. **İyma-murat** [Иймамурат] (KkRS 774). ⇨ **İMA? + MURAT**.

İYMAN Kkalp. 20th c. **İyman-bay** [Ийманбай] (KkRS 774). ❖ Iman (Ar.) 'belief, faith in Allah' (Ahmed), cf. Kkalp. *iyman* 'вера; символ (мусульманской) веры' (KkRS), Uyg., Chag., Tat., Turk. *īman* (Ar.) 'der wahre Glaube' (Radl. I, 1571).

İYMAN-ГALİY Kkalp. 20th c. **İyman-ɣaliy** [Ийманғалий] (KkRS 774). ⇨ **İYMAN + ALİ**.

İYMAŠ Kkalp. 20th c. **İymaš** [Иймаш] (KkRS 774). ❖ Shortened form of İmametdin (Ar.) (Kusimova).

İYNE Yürük 1522 **İyne-χoǰa** [ﻪﺟﻮﺧ ﻪﻨﻳﺍ / İne hoca] (Su 4). ❖ 'Needle' cf. Alt., Az., Kzk., Tat. *inä* 'id.' (Radl. I, 1442). See also **TAQAR, TEBEN, TEBENEYKA, TEMENE, TEMENEY**.

İYNEČEK Alt. 19th-20th c. **İyneček** [Ийнечек], fem. (OjrRS 212). ❖ 'Small needle'. ⇨ **İYNE + dim. suff. -ček**.

İYNELİK Alt. 19th-20th c. **İynelik** [Ийнелик], fem. (OjrRS 212). ❖ 'Needle case, pincushion'. ⇨ **İYNE + suff. -lik**.

İYSA see **İSA**

İYSATAY Kkalp. 20th c. **İysatay** [Ийсатай] (KkRS 774). ⇨ **İSA + suff. -tay(1,2)?**

İYSEN-ГALİY see **İSÄN-ALİ**

İYT-BAŠ see **İT-BAŠ**

İYT-ǰEMES see **İT-ǰEMÄS**

İYT-EMER see **İT-EMER**

İYT-KÖTÖN Alt. 19th-20th c. **İyt-kötön** [Ийт-Кётён] (OjrRS 208). ❖ 'Arse of the dog'. ⇨ **İT + KÖTÄN**.

İYT-QULAQ Alt. 19th-20th c. **İyt-qulaq** [Ийт-Кулак] (OjrRS 208). ❖ 'Dog's ear'. ⇨ **İT + QULAQ**.

İYT-ŽEMES see **İT-ǰEMÄS**

İK see **İG**

İK-BERDİ Bashk. 1695 **İk-berdi** [Икберди] (MIB I, 92); Bashk. 1737 **İk-berdi** [Икберди Ахманаев] (MIB III, 372); Bashk. 1756 **İk-berdi** [Икберда Сайтяшев] (MIB IV, 106). ⇨ **İG + BERDİ**. See also **İG-BER**.

İK-BULAT Tat.(Lit.) 1592 **İk-bulat** [Икбулат Ясюкевичъ] (Lit. Tat. 117). ⇨ **İG + BULAT**. See also **İG-TEMÜR**.

İK-GİLİM Tat.(Lit.) 1554 **İk-gilim** [Икгилимъ] (Kn. Metriki Lit. 111). ❖ 'Noble (good) / bad (sick, wicked) science, knowledge'? cf. Tat. *ɣiylem* 'наука; знание' (TatRS), Bashk. *ɣilem* 'id.' (BRS) (<Ar.). ⇨ **İG?**

İK-TURГAN Kzk. 19th c. **İk-turɣan** [Майлибай Иктургановъ] (Grod., Pril. 123). ⇨ **İG + TURГAN**.

İKBAL   Selj. 13th c. **İkbal** [اقبال / Iqbāl], Aq-boγa's brother, took part in Sülemiš's revolt (Aqsarāyī 246, Aqsar./Iş. 101). ✧ 'Fate, chance, success' cf. Turk. *ikbal* (Ar.) 'die Gunst des Schicksals, das Glück' (HŞ).

İKÄY   Bashk. 1709 **İkäy?** [Килки Икаев] (MIB I, 264). ⇨ **İGÄ?** + suff. -*y*.

İKÄM-BERDİ see **İYEM-BERDİ**

İKE   Kzk. 19th c. **İke** [Ике] (Grod., Pril. 57); Chuv. 18th-19th c. **İke-bay** [Икебай] (Magn. 42); Kzk. **İke-bay** [Икебай] (Patkanov II, 94); Kzk. 19th c. **İki-bay** [Джанбойсунъ Икибаевъ] (Grod., Pril. 165). ✧ 'Host, landlord, master' cf. Chag., Turk. *ikä* 'der Herr, Wirth' (Radl. I, 1416)? ⇨ **EKİ?** See also **ON-İKEY**.

İKEN   Hak. 19th-20th c. **İgen** [Игенъ] (HRS 348); Hak. 19th-20th c. **İken** [Икен] (HRS 348). ✧ Innokentiy (R.). See also **İLLÄKÄNTÄY**.

İKEŠ   Chuv. 18th-19th c. **İkeš** [Икешъ] (Magn. 42); Bashk. 1664 **İkiš** [Икишко Дашманов] (MIB I, 193). ⇨ **İKE?** + suff. -*š*.

İKİ-GÜLLİ   Az. **İki-gülli** [Ики-Гюлли], fem. (Az. Skaz. 487). ✧ 'Having two flowers (roses)'. ⇨ **EKİ** + **GÜL** + suff. -*lli*.

İKİČ see **İKİČİ**

İKİČİ   Uyg. **İkič-toyïn** [İkiç toyın] (EUTS); Uyg. 12th c. - 14th c. **İkiči** [ikiči / İkiçi] (DTS, EUTS); Uyg. 12th c. - 14th c. **İkiči-toyïn** (Radl., USp. 130-131). ✧ 'Second' (Blagova 1997, 705).

İKİLİK see **EKİLİK**

İKİM   Chag. 16th c. **İkim-biy** [Иким-бий] (Ivanov 213, 294). ✧ 'Good (child) of mine'. ⇨ **İG**. See also **İGİ**.

İKİNJİ   Oghuz 1096/97 **İkinji (Alïnjï?)** [النجى / Икинджи ибн Кочкар (Алынджи ибн Кочкар)], a Khorezmshah, Qočqar's son (MIT I, 383-84, 442). ✧ 'Second (child)'. ⇨ **EKİ** + suff. -*nji*.

İKİŠ see **İKEŠ**

İKİZ see **EKİZ**

İKLÜN   Hak. 19th-20th c. **İklün** [Иклүн], fem. (HRS 353).

İKMAT see **İGMET**

İKON   Hak. 19th-20th c. **İkon** [Иконъ] (HRS 348). ✧ Ikon (R.).

İKOS   Hak. 19th-20th c. **İkos** [Икос] (HRS 348).

İKSAN   Bashk. 1762 **İksan** [Иксан Елдашев] (MIB IV/1, 238); Bashk. 1775 **İksan** [Иксан Ибрагимов] (MIB IV/1, 380); Kzk. 19th c. **İksen** [Иксенъ] (SOK 44). ✧ 'Favour, benevolence, kindness, goodness; gift' cf. Turk. *ixsān* (Ar.) 'id.' (TED), Bashk. PN *İxsan* (Kusimova).

İKSEN see **İKSAN**

İKTÜ   Uyg. **İktü** [İktü] (EUTS); Uyg. **İktü / Öktü?** [Külüg ïnanč tutuq iktü] (Radl., USp.).

İKTÜ-SARÏG-BAŠ   Uyg. 12th c. - 14th c. **İktü-sarïγ-baš** [iktü sarïγ baš] (DTS). ✧ 'Domestic animal-yellow/blond-head' cf. Karakh. *iktü* 'домашнее

животное' (DTS). ⇨ **İKTÜ** + **SARÏ** + **BAŠ**.

İQUÑGUR-BAŠ   Kzk. 1820 **İquñγur-baš** / (<**Quñγur-baš?**) [Икунгурбаш бий], one of the chiefs of the Kazak Qara-kitan tribe (Sib. Vest. IX, 114). ⇨ **?** + **QOÑUR** + **BAŠ**.

İL see **EL**

İL-ALDÏ see **EL-ALDÏ**

İL-ALMÏŠ see **EL-ALMÏŠ**

İL-ALTÏ see **EL-ALDÏ**

İL-AMAN see **EL-AMAN**

İL-ARSLAN   Oghuz 1163 **İl-arslan / İl-aslan** [ايل ارسلان / Абу-л-Фатх Иль-Арслан ибн Атсыз], the Khorezmshah İl-arslan (1156-1172), son of the Khorezmshah Atsïz (Ibn al-Athīr/Tornb. XI, 193, 208, 247, MIT I, 46, 319, 402, 443-445, Ahbar 103, Qazwīnī 368, Juwaynī II, 12, 14, 15, Rāwandī 472); Uyg. 13th-14th c. **İl-aslan** [İl Aslan] (Zieme, Mat. II, 85); Uyg. 13th-14th c. **İl-arslan-tigin** [İl Arslan Tigin] (Zieme, Mat. II, 85); *EN:* Yürük 16th c. **İl-arslan** [ايل ارسلان], a cemâat among the Yürüks of the sandjak of Hamid (Sümer: DTCFD XI, 339). ✧ 'The lion of the country' cf. P. *Šēr-i kišwar* 'Löwe des Landes' which is obviously the translation of the Turkic *İl-arslan* (Justi 296); 'People-Lion' (Bese 16). ⇨ **EL** + **ARSLAN**.

İL-ASLAN see **İL-ARSLAN**

İL-AŠMÏŠ   Uyg. 8th c. **İl-ašmïš-tigin** (Müller, Pfahl. 23). ⇨ **EL** + **AŠMÏŠ**.

İL-BAXTA see **EL-BAQTÏ**

İL-BAXTÏ see **EL-BAQTÏ**

İL-BAQTÏ see **EL-BAQTÏ**

İL-BAQ   Kzk. 19th c. **İl-baq** [Илбакъ] (Grod., Pril. 24). ✧ 'Take care of the country (folk)'. ⇨ **EL** + **BAQ**.

İL-BAQTA see **EL-BAQTÏ**

İL-BARÏS see **EL-BARS**

İL-BARQ see **EL-BARQ**

İL-BARS see **EL-BARS**

İL-BASAN   Yürük 1543 **İl-basan** (Gökb., Rum. 184, 233); *TN:* Turk. 1540 **İl-basan**, a village (Gökb., Ed. 450, 451). ⇨ **EL** + **BASAN**. See also **İL-BASAR, İL-BASMÏŠ**.

İL-BASAR   Selj. 1292/93 **İl-basar** [ايلبصار / Ilbasār], got the yarlïq of an eyālet in Rūm (Aqsarāyī 180, Aqsar./Iş. 87); Khorezm.? **İl-basar / İl-yasar?** [ايل يسار] (RaD/Blochet 112, Aynī/Tizeng. I, 93, 94, 117-19, 484, 513). ⇨ **EL** + **BASAR**. See also **İL-BASAN, İL-BASMÏŠ**.

İL-BASMÏŠ   Kipch. 1296, 1299 **İl-basmïš** [ايل باسميش / İlbasmış Kıpçak / Ильбасмыш], a Kipchak emir in Diyarbekir, Ghazan's emir in 1296 (RaD/Jahn 99, 127, RaD 76, Togan, UTT 244, 253, Hammer, Ilch. II, 86 (Wassaf)); Tat. 1302 **İl-basmïš** [Велъбласмышъ Татаринъ / Велъбласмыш Михаилович] (Lavr. 501 (Suzd.)); Uyg. 8th c. **İl-basmïš-tigin** (Müller,

Pfahl. 23). ⇨ **EL + BASMÏŠ**. See also **İL-BASAN, İL-BASAR**.

İL-BAŠ Chuv. 18th-19th c. **İl-baš** [Ильбашъ] (Magn. 44); Selj. 13th c. - 15th c. **İl-baš-oγlï / İl-bašï-zāde** [ايلباش اوغلى / ايلباشى زاده احمد], in an inscription of the djami called İl-baš-oγlï (Uzunçarş., Küt. 91). ⇨ **EL + BAŠ**.

İL-BATÏR see **EL**

İL-BER Chuv. 18th-19th c. **İl-ber** [Илберъ] (Magn. 42). ⇨ **EL + BER**.

İL-BOLDÏ see **EL-BOLDÏ**

İL-BUΓA see **EL-BUQA**

İL-BUQA see **EL-BUQA**

İL-BUQLAY Bashk. 1664 **İl-buqlay** [Безей-абыз Илбуклаев] (MIB I, 192). ⇨ **EL**.

İL-BUL see **EL-BOL**

İL-BULAT Chuv. 18th-19th c. **İl-bulat** [Илбулатъ] (Magn. 42). ⇨ **EL + BULAT**.

İL-BULDÏ see **EL-BOLDÏ**

İL-DEGİZ see **İL-DENİZ**

İL-DENİZ Selj. 1146 **İl-deñiz** [شمس الدين], lord (ruler) of Kenje (Genje) (Ibn al-Athīr/Tornb. XI, 63, 87, 176-79); Selj. 1149 **İl-deñiz** [الدكز] (Ibn al-Athīr/Tornb. XI, 87); Türk? 1073 **İl-deñiz / İl-degiz?** [الدكز متدم الاتراك بمصر] (Ibn al-Athīr/Tornb. X, 58, 60, 61); Kipch. 1161 **İl-deñiz / İl-degiz** [Ildeñiz], atabek, ruler in Azerbayjan (Abulfidā III, 582-83, Aqsarāyī 24, Aqsar./İş. 36, 37); Karakh.? 1075, 1076 **İl-deñiz / İl-degiz?** [الدكز التركى] / Il dügüz, dux Turcarum aliquis] (Abulfidā III, 228-29, Qalānisi 109); Selj. 1139, 12th c. **İl-deñiz / İl-degiz** [شمس الدين ايلدكز / Шемс-ад-дин Ильдегиз], atabek, the real ruler of the Seljuk empire in Iraq around 1164, forefather of the Ildegizids (Qalānisi 261-65, Rāwandī 22, 37, 233, Qazw. 466, 467, 472, Bondārī 222, 231-33, 242-44, 297, 299, 301, MIT I, 402); Selj. 1148/49 **İl-deñiz / İl-degiz?** [Ildeguiz as-Sultânî], an emir (Ibn Khallikan/de Slane IV, 116, 127); Selj. 12th c. **İl-deñiz / İl-degiz?** [Ильдегиз] (RaD I/2, 102); Selj. 12th c. **İl-deñiz / İl-degiz** [پهلوان بن ايلدكز] (Muh. Ibrahim 51, 89, 90, 133); Selj. 12th c. **İl-deñiz / İl-degiz** [ايلدكز] (Muh. Ibrahim 51, 55, 90); Selj. 1170/71 **İl-deñiz / İl-degiz?** [ايلد كز] / Ildeguiz (Yeldokouz) Chems ed-Dîn], ruler of Hamadān and Isfahān (Aynī: RHCHor II/1, 188, 277); Selj. 1264 **İl-deñiz / İl-degiz** [Scherf-eddin Aldekiz-Karaki], an emir (Makrīzī II, 13); Maml. 1312 **İl-deñiz / İl-degiz?** [شمس الدين الدكز السلحدار], an emir, silaχdār (Dawād. 243); Maml. 1320 **İl-deñiz / İl-degiz?** [الدكز المنصورى] (Zetterst. 151, 157); Türk? 1035/36 **İl-deñiz / İl-degüz? / İl-digüz?** [الدكوز اسد الدوله التركى] (Ibn Taghrīb. II, 179, 180 etc.). ⇨ **EL + TEÑİZ**.

İL-DEREK Khorezm. 1219/1220 **İl-derek** [Илдерек], a ruler (melik) (MIT I, 504). ⇨ **EL + DEREK**.

İL-DUΓAN see **EL-TOΓAN**

İL-ÄRDÄM Uyg. 8th c. **İl-ärdäm** (Müller, Pfahl. 23). ✧ 'Glory of the folk (country); benefactor of the folk (country)'. ⇨ **EL + ERDÄM**.

İL-ÄVİRMİŠ Uyg. 13th-14th c. **İl-ävirmiš** [İl Ävirmiš] (Zieme, Mat. II, 85); Uyg. 13th-14th c. **İl-ävirmiš-alp-qutluγ-arslan-ata-ügä-bäg-qadïr-baš** [İl Ävirmiš Alp Qutluγ Arslan Ata Ügä Bäg Qadïr Baš] (Zieme, Mat. II, 93-94). ⇨ **EL**.

İL-GEREY Chuv. 18th-19th c. **İl-gerey** [Илгерей] (Magn. 42). ⇨ **EL + KERÄY**.

İL-GİLDİ see **EL-KELDİ**

İL-ΓAŠAY Bashk. 1737 **İl-γašay** [Илгашай] (MIB I, 327). ⇨ **EL**.

İL-XASAN Yürük 1543 **İl-χasan** [İlhasan] (Gökb., Rum. 215). ⇨ **EL + XASAN**.

İL-İČKÄRMİŠ Uyg. 8th c. - 9th c. **İl-ičkärmiš-ïnal** [Il ičkärmiš ïhal] (Müller, Pfahl. 23); Uyg. 8th c. - 9th c. **İl-ičkärmiš-inal / İl-ičkärmiš-ïnal** (Müller, Pfahl. 23); Uyg. 8th c. - 9th c. **İl-ičkärmiš-tigin** (Müller, Pfahl. 23). ✧ 'He who directed the nation' cf. Uyg. *ičgär-* ~ *ičkär-* 'einführen, in Gehorsam führen, unterwerfen, heimkehren' (Gabain). ⇨ **EL**.

İL-İGMÏŠ see **İL-YÏΓMÏŠ**

İL-İTMİŠ Uyg. 13th-14th c. **İl-itmiš** (Zieme, Mat. II, 84); Türk **İl-itmiš-qutluγ bilgä**, (qara türgäš) from Chinese transcription (Ligeti, R. tör. nev. II–III, 41); Uyg. **İl-itmiš-tigin** [İl İtmiş Tigin] (EUTS); Uyg. 8th c. **İl-itmiš-tigin** (Müller, Pfahl. 23). ✧ 'He organized the El/İl (country)' (Zieme: 'Reich eingerichtet'), cf. Türk., Karakh. *et-* 'создавать, строить; устраивать, приводить в порядок' (DTS). ⇨ **EL**.

İL-İNANČ Uyg. **İl-inanč-tiräk** [İl İnanç Tiräk] (EUTS); Uyg. 8th c. **İl-ïnanč-tiräk** (Müller, Pfahl. 23). ✧ 'Trusted Country(wide)' (A high dignity.). ⇨ **EL + İNANČ + TİRÄK**.

İL-YÏΓMÏŠ Khorezm. 1388 **İl-igmïš-oγlan** [Иль-Игмыш-оглан] (MIT I, 524); Selj.? 12th c. **İl-yïγmïš** [Ελεγμός], a Turkic (Seljuk?) commander (Byz. Turc. 122); Uyg. **İl-yïγmïš-tängrim** [İl Yïgmïš Tängrim] (EUTS); Uyg. 8th c. **İl-yïγmïš-tängrim** (Müller, Pfahl. 24); Uyg. 8th c. - 9th c. **İl-yïγmïš-tutuq** (Le Coq, Man. III, 46). ⇨ **EL + YÏΓMÏŠ**.

İL-KÄLMİŠ Uyg. 13th-14th c. **İl-kälmiš-täñrim** [İl Kälmiš Tngrim], fem. (Zieme, Mat. II, 93). ⇨ **EL + KELMİŠ**.

İL-KİKÄDMİŠ Uyg. 8th c. **İl-kikädmiš-sañγun** (Müller, Pfahl. 10). ✧ 'Praised by the folk/country'? cf. Uyg. *kögädmäk / kökädmäk* 'methetmek, övmek' (EUTS). ⇨ **EL**.

İL-KÖRMİŠ Uyg. 13th-14th c. **İl-körmiš** [İl Körmiš] (Zieme, Mat. II, 85). ⇨ **EL-KİRMİŠ?**

İL-KÜL   Türk **İl-kül-šad-baɣa Ïšbara-qaɣan**, from Chinese transcription (Ligeti, R. tör. nev. II-III, 41). ⇨ **EL + KÜL.**

İL-QAYA   Uyg. **İl-qaya** [İl Kaya] (EUTS); Uyg. 8th c. **İl-qaya** [Il ügäsi ata ügä il qaya sïɣïr tarχan ügä qanmïš] (Müller, Pfahl. 23); Uyg. 8th c. **İl-qaya** [Il ügäsi isik ädgü tutuq ügä il qaya] (Müller, Pfahl. 10). ✦ 'Rock, cliff of the country (folk)' (Müller). ⇨ **EL + QAYA.**

İL-QARÏŠUR   Uyg. 13th-14th c. **İl-qarïšur** [İl Qarïšur / Savïšur / Sävišür?] (Zieme, Mat. II, 85). ✦ 'Folk/country will quarrel' cf. Uyg., Karakh. *qarïš- II* 'встречаться; сражаться; враждовать, ссориться' (DTS). ⇨ **EL.**

İL-QAŠ see **İLİ-QAŠ**

İL-QATMÏŠ   Uyg. **İl-qatmïš** [İl Katmïš] (EUTS); Uyg. 8th c. **İl-qatmïš** (Müller, Pfahl. 10). ✦ 'The empire got strong' cf. *qat-* 'fest werden, hart werden' (Radl. II, 277-79). ⇨ **EL.**

İL-QAVŠURMÏŠ   Uyg. 13th-14th c. **İl-qavšurmïš** [İl Çavšu[rmïš]], fem. (Zieme, Mat. II, 87, 89). ✦ 'Folk/country - united' cf. Karakh. *qawušur- / qavšur-* 'соединять, складывать' (DTS). ⇨ **EL.**

İL-QONDÏ   Tat. 1675, 1668 **İl-ɣondï** [Истекайка Ильгондинъ (Илгондинъ)] (Kungursk. akty 1, Kurdjumov 3, 4); Kzk. 1881 **İl-ɣundï** [Ильгунда] (ZOOIRGO 99); Kzk. 18th c. **İl-qundï** [Илкундый] (Nepljuev 718). ⇨ **EL + QONDÏ.**

İL-QORA   Uzb. 19th c. **İl-qora / İl-qara** [Илкора Ишбутиновъ] (SKSO III, 10). ⇨ **EL + QARA.**

İL-QUTADMÏŠ   Uyg. **İl-qudatmïš** [İl Kudatmïš] (EUTS); Uyg. 8th c. **İl-qutadmïš (-täñgrim)** (Müller, Pfahl. 23); Uyg. 8th c. **İl-qutadmïš-tiräk** (Müller, Pfahl. 23). ⇨ **EL + QUTADMÏŠ.**

İL-QUTLÏ see **İL-QUTLUɣ**

İL-QUTLUɣ   Bashk. 1765 **El-qutlï / İl-qutlï?** [Елкутла Хабибовъ] (MIB IV/1, 318); Khorezm. 13th c.? **İl-qutluɣ** [Иль-Кутлуг] (RaD II, 202). ✦ 'People/country-lucky'. ⇨ **EL + QUTLUɣ.** See also **EL-BAQTÏ.**

İL-MEKEY   Bashk. 1738 **İl-mekey** [Ильмекей Айманов] (MIB III, 387); Bashk. 1756 **İl-mekey** [Кузябердя Илмекеев] (MIB IV/1, 109). ⇨ **EL + MEKEY?**

İL-MEÑGÜ   Tat.(GH) 1312 **İl-meñgü? / İt-meñgü?** [Ϊτμενκού], a christened Tatar, died in 1312 (Byz. Turc. 143). ⇨ **EL + MEÑGÜ.**

İL-MUXAMMED   Nog. 20th c. **İl-muχambet** [Абдулджалил Илмухамбет увлы / Абдулжалил Ильмухаммедов], father of one of Baskakov's informants from the aul of İrɣaqlï (Bask., Nog. 143). ⇨ **EL + MUXAMMED.**

İL-MURAT see **EL-MURAT**

İL-NAZAR   Trkm. 19th c. **İl-nazar** [Ильназаръ] (Ščeglov I, 356). ⇨ **EL + NAZAR.**

İL-OÑɣURT-QARČUQİ   Uyg. 8th c. - 12th c. **İl-oñɣurt-qarčuqi** (Müller, Uig. II, 81). ⇨ **EL +?**

İL-ÖGÄSİ   Uyg. 8th c. - 12th c. **İl-ögäsi Yegän-sewüg-tutuχ** [Il ügäsi jägän-säwäg tutuχ] (Fest. Thomsen 211); Uyg. **İl-ügäsi-ata** [İl Ügäsi Ata] (EUTS). ✦ A dignity. ⇨ **EL + ÖGÄ** + poss. suff. *-si*.

İL-ÖTÜKÄN   Uyg. **İl-ötükän** [İl Ötükän] (EUTS). ⇨ **EL + ÖTÜKÄN.**

İL-SABAN   Tat.? 1259/60 **İl-saban** [ايل سبان / Yl-Sabban], chief of the Tatars (Aynī: RHCHor II/1, 215). ✦ 'Folk/country - ploughing/plowing'. ⇨ **EL + SABAN I.**

İL-SARAY   Chuv. 18th-19th c. **İl-saray** [Илсарай] (Magn. 44). ⇨ **EL + SARAY.**

İL-TATɣU   Uyg. **İl-tatɣu** [İl Tatġu] (EUTS). ⇨ **EL.**

İL-TEBEN   Bashk. **İl-teben** [ايلتبان], a character in a legend (Mészáros, MH 77 (after a historian of the 16th c. called Hisamuddin)); Bashk. 1737 **İl-teben / İl-tebän?** [Илтебан Степанов], a captain (opposing the revolt) (MIB I, 318). ⇨ **EL + TEBEN.**

İL-TEMİR see **EL-TEMİR**

İL-TEZER see **EL-TÜZER**

İL-TİRGÄK see **EL-TERGÜG**

İL-TİRGER   Chag. 16th c. **İl-tirger** [Иль Тиргер] (Ivanov 218). ✦ 'Have the folk gathered/united!' cf. Karakh. *ter-/tir-* 'собирать, копить' (DTS). ⇨ **EL +** caus. suff. *-gir*. See also **İL-TİRMİŠ.**

İL-TİRGÜG see **EL-TERGÜG**

İL-TİRMİŠ   Uyg. 13th-14th c. **İl-tirmiš-täñrim** [İl Tirmiš Tngrim], fem. (Zieme, Mat. II, 85). ✦ 'He who gathered/united the folk' cf. Karakh. *ter-/tir-* 'собирать, копить' (DTS). ⇨ **EL.** See also **İL-TİRGER.**

İL-TİTLİ   Bashk. 1675 **İl-titli** [Ильтитли] (MIB I, 200). ⇨ **EL + TİT?** + suff. *-li*.

İL-TOQ   Kzk. 19th c. **İl-toq** [Ильтокъ] (Potanin II, 4); Kzk. 19th c. **İl-toq** [Ильтокъ] (SOK 248); Kzk. 19th c. **İl-toq** [Ильтокъ] (SOK 248). ⇨ **EL + TOK.**

İL-TUɣAN see **EL-TOɣAN**

İL-TUɣDÏ see **EL-TOɣDÏ**

İL-TUQU   Khorezm. 1220-1221 **İl-tuqu** [Илтуку], İlči-pehlevan's son (MIT I, 481). ⇨ **EL + TOQ?** + poss. suff. *-u*.

İL-TURMÏŠ see **EL-TURMÏŠ**

İL-TUT   Tat. 1744 **İl-tut** [Илтутов] (MIB III, 421). ⇨ **EL + TUT.** See also **EL-TUTAR, EL-TUTMÏŠ.**

İL-TUTMÏŠ see **EL-TUTMÏŠ**

İL-TÜRGÜG see **EL-TERGÜG**

İL-TÜZER see **EL-TÜZER**

İL-TÜZMİŠ   Selj. 12th c. **İl-düzmiš** [ابن الدزمش], preserved in the name of a public bath and small mosque in Aleppo (Ibn Šaddād, Alep 134, 23); Türk 8th c.-9th c. **İl-tüzmiš** (TT IV, 432, 434, 438); Uyg. 13th-14th c. **İl-tüzmiš** [İl T[üz]miš] (Zieme, Mat. II, 85); Uyg. 8th c.-9th c. **İl-tüzmiš-sañun**, fem. (Müller, Pfahl. 23). ✧ 'Hc who arraned/organized the country/people'. ⇨ **EL + TÜZMİŠ.** See also **EL-TÜZER.**

İL-ÜGÄSİ-ATA see **İL-ÖGÄSİ**

İL-ÜSÜNMİŠ Uyg. 12th c. - 14th c. **İl-üsünmiš** [İl üsünmiš] (Radl., USp. 216, 258). ⇨ **EL.**

İLAKE Hak. 19th-20th c. **İlake** [Илаке] (HRS 348).

İLBEY Hak. 19th-20th c. **İlbey** [Илбей] (HRS 348). ✧ 'Great, big, large' (Butanaev).

İLČEN Kzk. 1860 **İlčen** [Илченъ Кульмамбетевъ] (ZIRGOGeogr. I, 272).

İLČİ see **ELČİ**

İLČİ-BUГA Khorezm. 1376/1377 **İlči-buγa** [Ильчи-Буга], an emir (MIT I, 517-18). ⇨ **ELČİ + BUQA.**

İLČİ-FİRAQ Khorezm. 1458 **İlči-firaq** [Ильчи-Фирак (Махмуд Туркестани)], envoy of Sultan Husein, better known as Mahmud Turkestanī (MIT I, 537). ⇨ **ELČİ.**

İLČİKEY see **ELČİKEY**

İLČİMBET Bashk. 1761 **İlčimbet** [Илчимбеть Туканов] (MIB IV/1, 215); Bashk. 1777 **İlčimbet** [Ильчимбеть Токтаров] (MIB V, 51); Bashk. 1779 **İlčimbet** [Ракай (Ракаш) Илчимбетев] (MIB V, 100, 101, 104). ✧ Cf. Tat. PN *İlče-möχämmät* (Sattarov). ⇨ **ELČİ** + suff. *-mbet*.

İLČİNEY Bashk. 1731 **İlčiney / İlčikey?** [Ишметь Илчинеев] (MIB III, 292). ⇨ **ELČİ** + suff. *-key?*

İLČÜK Uyg. 12th c. - 14th c. **İlčük** (Radl., USp. 203). ⇨ **EL** + suff. *-čük.*

İLJİRBE Hak.(Kacha) 19th c. **İlJirbe** [Ильджирбе], fem. (Katanov, Otč. II, 42). ✧ 'Small chain' (Katanov).

İLDAŠ Uyg. 1335 **Eltaš** [Eltasch] (Chwol., Syr.-nest. (NF) 30); Chuv. 18th-19th c. **İldaš** [Илдашъ] (Magn. 42); Bashk. 1791 **İldaš** [Темирбай Илдашев] (MIB V, 309); Chuv. 18th-19th c. **İldäš** [Илдяшъ] (Magn. 43); Uyg. 13th c. - 14th c. **İldaš? / İltaš** (Chwol., Syr.-nest. (NF) 45, 46); Uyg. 1317 **İldaš? / İltaš** (Chwol., Syr.-nest. 140). ✧ 'Fellow-countryman' cf. Bashk. *ildäš* 'id.' (BaRS). ⇨ **EL** + suff. *-daš.*

İLDAŠ-QANA Uyg. 1317 **İldaš-qana? / İltaš-qana** [Iltaš-Kana] (Chwol., Syr.-nest. 59). ⇨ **İLDAŠ + QANA?**

İLDÄŠ see **İLDAŠ**

İLDEŠ Alt. 19th-20th c. **İldeš** [Илдеш] (OjrRS 208). ✧ Ilya (R.). See also **İLKA, İLJĀ, İJJĀ.**

İLÄBÄNTİ Tuv. 19th c. **İläbäntï** [Ілябäнтї] (Proben IX, 63, 64, 73, 76, 81). ✧ Leontiy (R.).

İLÄY see **İLEY**

İLÄK see **ELİG**

İLÄKÜ Uyg. 13th c. **İläkü** [iläkü], in documents from Turfan (DTS).

İLÄPPİN Hak.(Sag.) **İläppïn** [Іляппїн], fem. (Proben IX, 606).

İLÄŠ Uzb. 20th c. **İläš** [Илаш] (Begmatov 1984, 202); Uzb. 20th c. **İläš-bek** [Илашбек] (Begmatov 1984, 202); Uzb. 20th c. **İläš-Jân** [Илашжон] (Begmatov 1984, 202); Uzb. 20th c. **İläš-qul** [Илашкул] (Begmatov 1984, 202). ✧ 'Be alive!' (Begmatov), cf. Uzb. *iläš-* 'зацепляться; приставаться' (UzbRS).

İLEG see **ELİG**

İLEY Bashk. 1778 **İläy** [Иляй Азнагильдин] (MIB V, 79); Tat. 1779 **İley** [Ахмер Илеев] (MIB V, 83); Bashk. 1737 **İley-bay** [Илей-бай] (MIB I, 330).

İLEK see **ELİG**

İLEK-TÜRK'ĀN Karakh. 11th c.? **İlek-türk'ān / İlek-türkmen** [Илек-туркмен (Илек-туркан)], a khan in Balasagun (MIT I, 444). ⇨ **ELİG? + TERKEN.**

İLEK-TÜRKMEN Karakh. 1158 **İlek-türkmen / İlek-türk'ān** [Илек-туркмен (Илек-туркан)], a khan in Balasagun (MIT I, 444). ⇨ **ELİG? + TERKEN.**

İLEKEY see **İLİKEY**

İLEKSEÑ Hak. 19th-20th c. **İlekseñ** [Илексенъ] (HRS 348). ✧ Aleksey (R.).

İLENČİ Bashk. 1707 **İlenči** [Алмекей Иленчиев] (MIB III, 30). ✧ I. 'Reddish' cf. Bashk. *elän I.* 'рысистый' (BaRS); II. 'Maker of a kind of light upper clothes' cf. Bashk. *elän II.* 'верхняя лёгкая одежда' (BaRS).

İLENDEY Chuv. 19th c. **İlendey** [Ilcndeï] (Kronheim 96).

İLGE see **İLGİ**

İLGİ Chuv. 19th c. **İlge-bi** [Ilgebi], fem. (Kronheim 96); Bashk. 1717 **İlgi-bay** [Илгибай Баукеев] (MIB III, 148). ✧ 'The first born' cf. Kuman, Tat.(Sib.) *ilki* 'der erstere, der frühere' (Radl. I, 1490).

İLHAM Uzb. **İlham** [Ильхам] (URS 177); 19th c. **İlham-Jan** [Eminğan Ilhamğanov] (Mende 102); Uzb. 20th c. **İlham-Jan** [Илхамджан] (Erohina-Ramazanova: OSA 202). ✧ 'Inspiration, divine revelation' cf. Uzb. *ilχom / ilχâm* 'вдохновение; воодушевление' (UzbRS) (<Ar.)

İLİ Kzk. 19th c. **İli-bay** [Или-бай Рахимбаевъ] (Grod., Pril. 58); Kzk. 19th c. **İli-bay** [Илибай] (SODž. 158); Kzk. 19th c. **İli-bay** [Илибай] (SOK 280); Kzk. 19th c. **İli-bek** [Илибековъ] (SKSO VIII, 225); *TN:* Kzk. 19th c. **İli-bay** [Илибай], a field (AOK 58). ✧ 'River İli'? See also **BAYRAM-İLİ?**

İLİ-QAŠ Bashk. 1756 **İl-qaš** [Исябяк Иликашев] (MIB IV/1, 122); Bashk. 1756 **İli-qaš** [Сарап Иликашев] (MIB IV/1, 122); Bashk. 1791 **İli-qaš?** [Бекбоз Илыкашев] (MIB V, 313). ⇨ **İLİ? + QAŠ.**

İLİČÜK Uyg. 13th-14th c. **İličük**, fem. (Zieme, Mat. III, 272); Uyg. 12th c. - 14th c. **İličük / İlinčük** (Radl., USp. 212, 253). ✧ 'Little king'? (Zieme). ⇨ **ELİG** + dim. suff. *-čük.*

İLİG see **ELİG**

İLİGEY see **İLİKEY**

İLİGİ Uyg. 13th-14th c. **İligi**, fem. (Zieme, Mat. III, 271). ✧ 'First-born'? cf. Uyg., Tat.(Sib.) *ilik* 'der erste, zuerst' (Radl. I, 1485).

İLİK I. see **ELİK**

İLİK II. see **ELİG**

İLİKEY Kzk. 19th c. **Elegey** [Елегей] (SOK 156); Tat. 1618 **Elekey** / **Elekäy** [Елекай Кудашев], a murza (Miller, Ist. Sib. II, 244); Chuv. 18th-19th c. **İlekey** [Илекей] (Magn. 43); Kzk. 19th c. **İlekey-qan, Elekey-qan** [ايلكاى قان / Elekey-kan / Илекей-ханъ] (Veselovskij, Kirg. 80, Ljutš 134); Tat.(Tüm.) 17th c. **İligey** [Илигей] (Nepljuev 453); Tat. 1706 **İlikey** [Аиттерь Иликеев] (MIB III, 29, 30, 183); Tat. / Bashk.? 1728 **İlikey** [Атачик Иликеев], a Teptär (Tiptär) (MIB I, 128); Bashk. 1675 **İlikey** [Иликей Колюбаев] (MIB I, 200); Bashk. 1707 **İlikey** [Иликей Бекбаев] (MIB III, 35); Bashk. 1710 **İlikey** [Иликей] (MIB III, 65); Bashk. 1713 **İlikey** [Иликей] (MIB III, 105); Bashk. 1714 **İlikey** [Иликей Тирисев] (MIB I, 107); Bashk. 1715 **İlikey** [Ыликей, Иликей] (MIB III, 133, 134); Bashk. 1737 **İlikey** [Иликей] (MIB I, 339); Bashk. 1740 **İlikey** [Иликей Миндуров] (MIB I, 405); Bashk. 1740 **İlikey** [Иликей Умряков] (MIB I, 392); Bashk. 1753 **İlikey** [Юмай Иликеев] (MIB IV/1, 68, 79); Bashk. 1761 **İlikey** [Иликей Сакиров] (MIB IV/1, 218); Bashk. 1770 **İlikey** [Иликей Екупов] (MIB IV/1, 345); Bashk. 1714 **İlikey** / **İlekey** [Иликей (Илекей) Тересев] (MIB III, 119). ✧ I. 'The little first (born) child'?; II. 'Little wild she-goat'? ⇨ **ELİK / ELİG?** + dim. suff. *-ey* / *-key*.

İLİMANJÏ Turk. **İlimanjï-oγlu** (Kúnos 1891, 119). ✧ 'Worker of docks' cf. Turk. *iliman, liman*, Kuman, Crm. *liman* (Greek) 'der Hafen' (Radl. II, 1489, III, 758) + suff. *-ji*.

İLİMBET Bashk. 1675 **İlimbet** [Юлкутлу И.лимбетев] (MIB I, 202); Bashk. 1714 **İlimbet** [Бюляк Илимбетев] (MIB I, 105); Bashk. 1735 **İlimbet** [Илимбеть Исенеевъ], a tarχan (Vel.-Zern., Bašk. 15); Bashk. 1735 **İlimbet** [Илимбеть Исенгуловъ], a tarχan (Vel.-Zern., Bašk. 23); Bashk. 1735 **İlimbet** [Илимбет Гауров], a tarχan (Vel.-Zern., Bašk. 12); Bashk. 1779 **İlimbet** [Илимбеть Деветеев] (MIB V, 101). ⇨ **EL / ELİM?** + suff. *-(im)bet*.

İLİMDAR Turk. 20th c. **İlimdar** (Önder, Göle). ✧ 'Possessor of knowledge; learned man' (Erol II), cf. Turk. *ilim* 'science, knowledge' (TED) + suff. *-dar*.

İLİN I. see **İLİN**

İLİN II. Kzk. 19th c. **İlin-bay** [Илынбай] (SOK 86); *T.N:* Kzk. **İlin-bay-say** [Илинбай-сай], a field in the district of Kopal (ZIRGOGeogr. I, 314).

İLİS Alt. 19th-20th c. **İlis** [Илис] (OjrRS 208).

İLİSTAN Bashk. 1789 **İlistan** [Илистан Арасланов] (MIB V, 243).

İLİSTİK Yak. **İlistik** [Ілістік] (Pek.). ✧ 'Tiredness' cf. Yak. *ilistī*, nomen actionis of *ilisin* (Pek.).

İLİŠ Tat. 1718 **İliš** [Илыш Кулушев] (MIB III, 168); Bashk. 1712 **İliš** [Шембет Илишев] (MIB III, 86); Bashk. 1734 **İliš** [Илиш Токеев] (MIB III, 322); Bashk. 1738 **İliš** [Сафар Илишев] (MIB I, 145); Bashk. 1742 **İliš** [Илиш Аднашев] (MIB III, 511); Bashk. 1756 **İliš** [Илиш Тлевбердин] (MIB IV/1, 122); Bashk. 1756 **İliš** [Илиш Айдакаев] (MIB IV/1, 120); Bashk. 1760 **İliš** [Ширым (Ширим) Илишев] (MIB IV/1, 191, IV/2, 45); Bashk. 1761 **İliš** [Илиш Кудашев] (MIB IV/1, 221); Bashk. 1762 **İliš** [Илиш Имасаев] (MIB IV/1, 241); Bashk. 1764 **İliš** [Байдагул Илишев] (MIB IV/1, 285); Bashk. 1777 **İliš** [Байгул Илышев] (MIB V, 54). ✧ 'Friend of the nation' (Sattarov). ⇨ **EL + EŠ.**

İLİT Kzk. 19th c. **İlit** [Илитъ] (SODž. 112).

İLİN Hak. 19th-20th c. **İlin** [Илин] (HRS 348); Karg. **İlin** [Ilîn] (Katanov, Otč. 9). ✧ 'Ilya's (day)' (R.) shortened of R. *Il'in (den')* [=(day) of Ilya], cf. Hak. PN *İlin* 'Ильин день' (Butanaev) (<R.).

İLYAS Nog. 20th c. **İliyas** [Таджыбай Илийас увлы / Таджибай Илиясов], father of one of Baskakov's informants from the settlement Terekli-mekter (Bask., Nog. 144). ✧ 'Elias'. See also **XÏZR-İLİYAS.**

İLYUK Chuv. 19th c. **İlyuk** [Iljuk] (Kronheim 96). ✧ Ilyuk (R.), hypoc. of R. Il'ja.

İLKA Hak. 19th-20th c. **İlka** [Илка] (HRS 348); Hak.(Sag.) 19th-20th c. **İlkä** [Ілкä] (Katanov, Otč. 8). ✧ Il'ya (R.). See also **İLJÄ, İJJÄ, İLDEŠ.**

İLKÄČ Tat. 20th c. **İlkäč** [Илкәчев] (Sattarov); Bashk. 1780 **İlkäč** [Илкач] (MIB V, 115); Bashk. 1780 **İlkäč** [Казанбай Илкачев] (MIB V, 103); Bashk. 1780 **İlkäč** [Рыскул Илкачев] (MIB V, 115); Bashk. 1756 **İlkäš** [Сарап Илкашев] (MIB IV/1, 106); Bashk. 1757 **İlkäš** [Илкаш Рысов] (MIB IV/1, 157); Bashk. 1770 **İlkäš** [Бекбай Илкашев] (MIB IV/1, 342); Bashk. 1789 **İlkäš** [Илкаш] (MIB V, 263). ✧ Diminutive-hypochoristic form of İl. (Sattarov). ⇨ **İL** + dim. suff. *-käč*.

İLKÄY see **İLKEY**

İLKÄŠ see **İLKÄČ**

İLKEY Chuv. 18th-19th c. **İlgey** [Илгей] (Magn. 42); Tat. 20th c. **İlkäy** [Илкиев, Илкәев, Илкин] (Sattarov); Bashk. 1728 **İlkäy** [Атьетяр Илкаев] (MIB I, 124); Bashk. 1758 **İlkäy** [Илкай Янабердин] (MIB IV/1, 169); Bashk. 1784 **İlkäy** [Мукай Илькаев] (MIB V, 158); Bashk. 20th c. **İlkäy** [Илкай] (Kusimova); Chuv. 18th-19th c. **İlkey** [Илкей] (Magn. 43); Tat.(Mish.) 1755 **İlkey** [мещер Илкей Чакиров] (MIB IV/1, 93); Bashk. 1664 **İlkey** [Илькей] (MIB I, 188); Bashk. 1712 **İlkey** [Илкей], fem. (MIB III, 84); Bashk. 1737 **İlkey** [Кускей

Илкеев] (MIB I, 321); Bashk. 1745 **İlkey** [Чюрай Илькеев] (MIB III, 426); Bashk. 1750 **İlkey** [Мурзай Илкеев] (MIB III, 479); Bashk. 1760 **İlkey** [Илкей Уразаков] (MIB IV/2, 35); Bashk. 1779 **İlkey** [Илкей Бигешев (Бигашев)] (MIB V, 82, 93); Bashk. 1784 **İlkey** [Микей Илькеев] (MIB V, 158). ❖ Diminutive-hypochoristic form of *İl* (Sattarov, Kusimova). ⇨ **EL** + dim. suff. *-käy / -key.*

İLKEN Tat. 20th c. **İlken** [Илкен] (Sattarov). ❖ 'First child' (Sattarov).

İLKENEY Bashk. 1789 **İlkeney** [Илчигул (Елчигул) Илкенеев] (MIB V, 260). ❖ 'First child' (Sattarov). ⇨ **İLKEN** + dim. suff. *-ey.*

İLKİ Tat. 18th c. **İlki** [Аиса Илкинъ] (Nepljuev 824, 825); Bashk. 1735 **İlki** [Илке Исенгулов(у)], a tarχan (Vel.-Zern., Bašk. 23); Kzk. 19th c. **İlki** [Ишъ Магоммедъ Илки Хайдаровъ] (Grod., Pril. 164); Kzk. 19th c. **İlki-bay** [Молла Илки-бай Алиджановъ] (Grod., Pril. 173); Kzk. 19th c. **İlki-bay** [Илкибай] (Grod., Pril. 95); Kzk. 19th c. **İlki-bay** [Илькебай] (SOV 140). ❖ 'First child' cf. Kuman, Tat.(Tüm., Tob.) *ilki* 'der erste, der frühere, zuerst' (Radl. I, 1490). ⇨ **İLKEN.**

İLLÄKÄNTÄY Yak. **İlläkäntäy** [Ілläкäнтäі / Ляkiäнтäі / Лягіäнтäі] (Pek.). ❖ Innokentiy (R.). See also **İKEN.**

İLLİ Trkm. 20th c. **İlli** [Illi] (Zaj. 1971, 327); Trkm. 20th c. **İlli** [Илли] (TrkmRS 351). ❖ 'He who has an *il* (country)' cf. Trkm. *īlli* 'имеющий родину' (TrkmRS). ⇨ **EL** + suff. *-li.*

İLMAN Chag. 16th c. **İlman-bahadur** [Ильман-бахадур], an emir (Ivanov 320). ⇨ **EL** + suff. *-man.*

İLMES Bashk. 1756 **İlmes-qul** [Усман Ильмескул] (MIB IV/1, 108). ❖ '?' cf. Turk. PN *İlmez* (Erol II).

İLMET Bashk. 18th c. **İlmet** [Болта Илметев] (MIB III, 92). ⇨ **EL** + suff. *-met.*

İLON Hak. 19th-20th c. **İlon** [Илон], fem. (HRS 353). ❖ Alyona (R.) cf. Hak. fem. *İlona* (Butanaev).

İLONA Hak. 19th-20th c. **İlona** [Илона], fem. (HRS 353). ❖ Alyona (R.) cf. Hak. fem. *İlona* (Butanaev).

İLSE see **ELČİ**

İLŠA Kzk. 18th c. **İlša / İlšä?** [Ильша мулла] (Nepljuev 850). ⇨ **EL** + suff. *-ša / -ča.*

İLT Bashk. 1757 **İlt-bay** [Пулат Илтбаев] (MIB IV/1, 150). ❖ 'Take him/her (away)' cf. Tat., Tat.(Bar., Tob.) *ilt-* 'fortbringen' (Radl. I, 1493).

İLTAŠ see **İLDAŠ**

İLTÄK Bashk. 1776 **İltäk-bay** [Сырмакай Илтякбаев] (MIB V, 47-49). ⇨ **EL** + suff. *-tek?*

İLTEY Kzk. 1809 **İltey** [Илтей] (Dobrosm., Turg. 250). ⇨ **EL** + suff. *-tey?*

İM Kzk. **İm-bek** [Имбек Урумбаев] (TV 1878, 144); Kzk. 19th c. **İm-Jan** [Имчанъ] (Lomakin 40). ❖ 'Sign (of property) in the ear of an animal' cf. Alt. *im* 'ein Eigenthumszeichen am Ohre des Haustieres; ein Zeichen mit der Hand, Wink' (Radl. I, 1571), Kzk. *ïm* 'знак, мимика' (KzRS).

İM-BARS Uzb. 18th c. **İm-bars** [Имбарсъ] (Nepljuev 805). ⇨ **İM + BARS.**

İMA Bashk. 18th c. **İma** [Имагулъ] (Nepljuev 202). ❖ Ima (shortened from *Imametdin* (Ar.), e. g. Bashk. PNs *İmay, İmaš* (Kusimova). See also **İMAY.**

İMAY Tat. 1713 **İmay** [Имай Кулаев] (MIB III, 96); Bashk. 1709 **İmay** [Имай] (MIB I, 253); Bashk. 1761 **İmay** [Имай Кулдыбаев] (MIB IV/1, 221). ❖ Shortened-contarcted from Ar. *İmametdin* (Kusimova) + suff. *-y.*

İMAYČA Kzk. 19th c. **İmayča** [Имайча Хумкіевъ] (Grod., Pril. 175). ⇨ **İMAY** + suff. *-ča.*

İMAQ Bashk. 1756 **İmaq / İmäk?** [Имак Абдрахманов] (MIB IV/1, 123). ❖ '?' cf. Kzk. PN *İmaq* (Žanuzakov-Esbaeva).

İMAQAY Bashk. 1764 **İmaqay / İmanay?** [Имакай Асанов] (MIB IV/1, 299). ⇨ **İMA(Q)** + suff. *-(q)ay.*

İMAM Nog. 20th c. **İmam** [Имам Мурза увлы], one of Baskakov's informants from the Sarï-awul (Bask., Nog. 144); Uzb. 19th c. **İmam** [Кулай Имамовъ] (SKSO III, 180); Nog. 20th c. **İmam-akey** [Суьлеймен Ишамакъай (!) улы Адис / Сулейман Имамакеевич Адисов], father of one of Baskakov's informants from the aul of Qañlï (Bask., Nog. 143); Kzk. 19th c. **İmam-bay** [Имамбай] (SOV 118); Kzk. 19th c. **İmam-bay** [Имамбай] (SOK 44); Kzk. 19th c. **İmam-bek** [Имамбекъ] (SOK 32); Trkm. 20th c. **İmām** [İmam] (Zaj. 1971, 326); Trkm. 20th c. **İmām** [Имам] (TrkmRS 770). ❖ Imam (Ar.) 'prayer leader; religious leader, chief, model, etc.' (Ahmed), cf. Chag., Tat., Tat.(Tob.), Turk. *imam* 'ein muhammedanischer Geistlicher' (Radl. I, 1573), Trkm. *imām* 'id.' (TrkmRS).

İMAM-BERDİ Kzk. 19th c. **İmam-berdi** [Имамберлы (?)] (SOK 200); Kzk. 19th c. **İmam-berdi** [Имамъ Берды Танатаевъ] (TV 1876, 76); Uzb. 20th c. **İmâm-berdi** [Имомберди] (Begmatov 1984, 202). ⇨ **İMAM + BERDİ.;** ⇨ **İMAM + BERDİ.**

İMAM-BERGEN Uzb. 20th c. **İmâm-bergän** [Имомберган] (Begmatov 1984, 202); Kzk. 19th c. **İmam-bergen** [Имамбергенъ] (SOK 50). ⇨ **İMAM + BERGEN.**

İMAN Tat.(GH) 1347 **İman** [Iman Yūsuf], a kātib (scribe) of the Golden Horde (Vásáry 54); Tat. 1753 **İman** [Иман Рысов] (MIB IV/1, 72); Tat. 20th c. **İman** [Иман / Иманов / Иманский] (Sattarov); Tat.(Mish.) 1708 **İman** [Иманко] (MIB I, 225); Tat.(Mish.) 1755 **İman** [мещер Иман Зянгиров] (MIB IV/1, 93); Bashk. 1710 **İman** [Иман Табысев] (MIB III, 64); Bashk. 1734 **İman** [Иманъ Агышевъ], a tarχan (Vel.-Zern., Bašk. 9, 15); Bashk. 1734 **İman** [Даутъ Имановъ], a tarχan (Vel.-Zern., Bašk. 11); Bashk. 1735 **İman** [Иманъ Теникеевъ], a tarχan (Vel.-Zern., Bašk. 16); Bashk. 1735 **İman** [Иманъ Рысаевъ], a tarχan (Vel.-Zern., Bašk. 15); Bashk. 1754 **İman** [Темирбай Иманов] (MIB IV/1, 183); Bashk. 1754 **İman** [Умер Иманов] (MIB IV/1, 183); Bashk. 1754 **İman** [Иман Алдаров] (MIB IV/1, 89); Bashk. 1756 **İman** [Иман Янышев] (MIB IV/1, 128); Bashk. 1756 **İman** [Ялчи Иманов] (MIB IV/1, 125); Bashk. 1757 **İman** [Иман Айдаров] (MIB IV/1, 139); Bashk. 1760 **İman** [Ибрак Иманов] (MIB IV/2, 385); Bashk. 1762 **İman** [Иман Кучюков] (MIB IV/1, 241); Bashk. 1763 **İman** [Мазан Иманов] (MIB IV/2, 45); Bashk. 1770 **İman** [Иман Купландин] (MIB IV/1, 343); Bashk. 1778 **İman** [Мунас Иманов] (MIB V, 67); Bashk. 1787 **İman** [Иман Айдакаев] (MIB V, 204); Bashk. 1787 **İman** [Иман Нурушев] (MIB V, 165); Bashk. 1793 **İman** [Кидряс Иманов] (MIB V, 335); Bashk. 20th c. **İman** [Иман] (Kusimova); Kzk. 19th c. **İman** [Иманъ Абдулаевъ] (Grod., Pril. 188); Kzk. 19th c. **İman** [Арзу Имановъ] (SKSO VIII, 204); Kzk. 19th c. **İman** [Иманъ] (AOK 38); Kzk. 19th c. **İman** [Иманъ] (SOV 92); Kzk. **İman-bay** [Иманбай] (Pam. kn. Semip. 61); Kzk. 19th c. **İman-bay** [Иманбай] (SOK 290); Kzk. 19th c. **İman-bay** [Иманбай] (SOK 6); Kzk. 19th c. **İman-bay** [Иманбай] (SOV 102); Bashk. 1722 **İman-batïr** [Иман батырь] (MIB I, 113); Tat. 20th c. **İman-bäk** [Иманбәк] (Sattarov); Bashk. 1734 **İman-γul** [Имангул] (Vel.-Zern., Bašk. 15); Bashk. 1734 **İman-γul** [Имангулъ Мурзагуловъ], a tarχan (Vel.-Zern., Bašk. 14); Bashk. 1777 **İman-γul** [Муса Имангулов] (MIB V, 51, 235); Bashk. 1785 **İman-γul** [Имангул (Емангул) Яхшигулов] (MIB V, 166, 168, 223, 224); Bashk. 1798 **İman-γul** [Имангулъ] (PSZRI XXV, 196); Bashk. 1740 **İman-γul-bay** [Имангул-бай] (MIB I, 439); Uzb. 1856 **İman-qul-bay** [Иманъ-кул бай] (Moskal'cev 40); *TN:* Kzk. **İman** [Иман], a field (Kojčubaev 109); Kzk.? **İman-bay** [Иманбай аулъ], a settlement in Kainskij okrug (district) (Patkanov II, 260); **İman-γul** [Имангуль] (Karta JAR XI). ✧ '(True) faith, belief, believing in the faith of Islam; religion' cf. Uyg., Chag., Tat., Turk. *iman* 'der wahre Glaube' (Radl. I, 1571), Bashk. *iman* 'вера, религиозное убеждение; совесть' (BaRS), (<Ar.). See also **KERİ-İMAN.**

İMAN-BERDİ Kzk. 19th c. **İman-berdi** [Иманберды] (SODž. 20). ⇨ **İMAN + BERDİ.**

İMAN-NİYAZ Kzk. 19th c. **İman-niyaz** [Иманыязъ] (SODž. 84). ⇨ **İMAN + NİYAZ.**

İMANAY Tat. 19th c. **İmanay** [Иманай] (Potanin, IV, 770); Bashk. 1717 **İmanay** [Артыков Иманаев] (MIB III, 161); Bashk. 1731 **İmanay** [Иманай Арыков] (MIB III, 292); Bashk. 1738 **İmanay** [Иманай] (MIB III, 387); Bashk. 18th c. **İmanay** [Иманаев], a mulla (MIB V, 416); Bashk. 1753 **İmanay** [Аблай Иманаев] (MIB IV/1, 68); Bashk. 1754 **İmanay** [Иманай Асанов] (MIB IV/1, 79); Bashk. 1757 **İmanay** [Иманай Карасев] (MIB IV/1, 136); Bashk. 1780 **İmanay** [Ибрай (Ибрак) Иманаев] (MIB V, 113, 119); Bashk. 1780 **İmanay** [Иманай Кадырбаков] (MIB V, 116); Bashk. 1780 **İmanay** [Иманай Кинзин] (MIB V, 145); Bashk. 1783 **Manay** [Кадыргул Манаев] (MIB V, 139); Kzk. 19th c. **Manay** [Манай] (AOK 38). ⇨ **İMAN** + suff. *-ay / -y.*

İMANČA Kzk. 19th c. **İmanča** [Иманча] (SODž. 156). ⇨ **İYMAN** + suff. *-ča.*

İMAŠ Bashk. 1789 **İmaš** [Имаш Кансюяров] (MIB V, 249); Bashk. 1798 **İmaš** [Имашъ] (PSZRI XXV, 195); Kzk.? **İmaš** [Давлетьяр Имашевъ] (TOOIK I, 52). ✧ Shortened from Ar. *İmametdin.* ⇨ **İMA** + suff. *-š.*

İMBETEY Bashk. 1735 **İmbetey** [Имбетей Каскаевъ], a tarχan (Vel.-Zern., Bašk. 17). ✧ Corruption of Ar. Mukhammad. See also suffixoid -*imbet* + suff. *-ey.*

İMDAT Turk. 20th c. **İmdat** [İmdat] (Önder, Göle). ✧ Imdad (Ar.) 'help, aid, support' (Ahmed).

İMÄČ Bashk. 1757 **İmäč** [Алимбеть Имячев] (MIB IV/1, 145); Bashk. 1757 **İmäč** [Муса Имачев] (MIB IV/1, 157); Bashk. 1737 **İmäs** [Кибиняс Имясев] (MIB III, 365); NUyg.(Tar.) 19th c. **İmeš** [Имешь], fem. (TV 1876, 135); Bashk. 1757 **İmič** [Алимбеть Имичев] (MIB IV/1, 157); Kzk. 19th c. **İmiš** [Имишъ] (SOK 16). ✧ Shortened of *İmametdin* cf. Bashk. PN *İmaš* (Kusimova) and Tat. PN *İmametdin* 'leader of communal prayer' (Sattarov). + suff. *-č / -š(1).*

İMÄS see **İMÄČ**

İMEĬE Yürük 1543 **İmeĭe** [İmece] (Gökb., Rum. 213, 215, 217, 219, 241 etc.). ✧ 'Work done for the community by the whole village' cf. Turk. *imece* 'die gemeinsame Arbeit' (HŞ).

İMEKEY Bashk. 1732 **İmekey** [Имекей Тюмяков] (MIB III, 310); Kzk. 19th c. **İmekey** [Имекей] (AOK 86); Tat.? 17th c. **İmikey** [Имикейка Ишпулатовъ], a Cossack ensign (officer) in Chuvashia (IOAIÊK XXIX, 341).

İMEN see **İMİN**

İMEN-GİLDE Chuv. 18th-19th c. **İmen-gilde** [Именгилда] (Magn. 44); Chuv. 18th-19th c. **İmen-gilde(y)** [Именгилдей] (Magn. 44). ⇨ **İMAN + KELDİ.**

İMENČÄ Chuv. 18th-19th c. **İmenčä** [Именча] (Magn. 44). ✧ 'Little poplar; little oak' cf. Tat., Tat.(Bar) *imän* 'die Eiche, die Pappel' (Radl. I, 1573) + suff. *-čä / -ča.*

İMENEY   Chuv. 18th-19th c. **İmeney** [Именей] (Magn. 44). ✧ 'Little poplar; little oak' cf. Tat., Tat.(Bar) *imän* 'die Eiche, die Pappel' (Radl. I, 1573). ⇨ **İMANAY?** + suff. *-ey*.

İMENEK   Chuv. 18th-19th c. **İmenäk** [Именякъ] (Magn. 44); Chuv. 18th-19th c. **İmenek** [Именекъ] (Magn. 44). ✧ I. Healthy, sound, uninjured' II. 'Little poplar; little oak' cf. Tat., Tat.(Bar) *imän* 'die Eiche, die Pappel' (Radl. I, 1573). ⇨ **İMİN?** + suff. *-ek*.

İMENKA   Chuv. 18th-19th c. **İmenka** [Именка] (Magn. 44). ✧ 'Little poplar; little oak' cf. Tat., Tat.(Bar) *imän* 'die Eiche, die Pappel' (Radl. I, 1573) + suff. *-ka*.

İMENTEY   Tat. 1704 **İmentey** [Сементей Иментеевъ] (Kurdjumov 338). ✧ 'Poplar-like; oak-like' cf. Tat., Tat.(Bar) *imän* 'die Eiche, die Pappel' (Radl. I, 1573) + suff. *-tey*.

İMEŠ see **İMÄČ**

İMİČ see **İMÄČ**

İMİKEY see **İMEKEY**

İMİL   Crm. 1541-1542 **İmil** [Имил-царевичь] (PSRL XIII, 137, 142); Bashk. 1745 **İmil** [Маткуш Имилев] (MIB III, 427).

İMİN   Chuv. 18th-19th c. **İmen** [Имень] (Magn. 44); Kzk. 19th c. **İmin / İmïn?** [Имынъ] (SOV 124); Crm. 1541-1542 **İmin-girey / İmil-girey** [Имин-Гирѣй-салтан / Имил-царевичь / Имин-царевичь / Имин-Кирѣй] (PSRL 137, 142). ✧ 'Healthy' cf. Tat. *imĭn* 'ungefährlich, unverletzt, sicher, bei gutem Wohlsein' (Radl. I, 1574), *imin* 'здоровый; безопасный; благополучный' (TatRS).

İMİR   Oghuz/Trkm. 13th c. **İmir / İmur?** [ايمر / Имур / Имир], Taγ-χan's son (RaD I/1, 76, Abulg./Kon. 520, 560, 610). See also **YAŠ-İMİR**.

İMİŠ see **İMÄČ**

İMİT   Bashk. 1675 **İmit-bay** [Имитбай] (MIB I, 200). ⇨ **ÜMİT?**

İMLİK   Kzk. 19th c. **İmlik** [Имликъ] (SOK 248, 268).

İMRAN   Uyg. **İmran** ['imran] (DTS). ✧ Imran (Ar.), the father of Maryam (Ahmed).

İMRÄN   Oghuz/Trkm. 14th c. - 15th c. **Amran (Ämrän) / İmran (İmrän)** [Begil oğlı Emren / Амран (Имран)], Bekil's (Begil's) son (DQorq. 83, 85, 89, 179, 188, 227, 228, 229, 230, 233, 237, 257); Oghuz/Trkm. 15th c. **Emren**, Begil's son (DQorq./Rossi 202, 205-211) ✧ 'Be Loved!; Wish! Desire!' cf. Turk. PN İmren (Erol II), Turk. *ämrän-* 'wünschen' (Radl. I, 963), *imren-* 'to long for, to desire; to covet' (TED). See also **SEWİL**.

İMRE   Kzk. 19th c. **İmre** [Имре] (SOK 20). ✧ 'Lover; brother' (see Erol II: Emre).

İMÜR see **İMİR**

İN   Maml. 1366/67 **İn-bek** [اينبك البدرى] (Iyās I, 217, 232, 242); Bashk. 18th c. **İn-zän-γul** [Куватъ Инзянгуловъ] (Nepljuev 865). ✧ 'Mark/cut on ears' cf. Bashk. *in* 'метка (на ушах животных)' (BRS/Uraksin); II. 'Dung of sheep'? cf. Karakh. *in* II. 'помет овец' (DTS).

İN-BAKŠA   Chuv. 18th-19th c. **İn-bakša** [Инбакша] (Magn. 45). ⇨ **İN** + **BAQŠĬ**.

İN-BARS   Chuv. 18th-19th c. **İn-bars** [Инбарсъ] (Magn. 45). ⇨ **İN** + **BARS**.

İN-BERDİ   Maml.? 1455 **İn-berdi** [اينبردى] (Iyās III, 52); Tat. 1633 **İn-berdi / İn-berdey** [Инбердей Тоганаев] (Miller, Ist. Sib. II, 402). ⇨ **İN** + **BERDİ**.

İN-BERGEN   Kzk. 19th c. **İm-bergen** [Имбергень] (Grod., Pril. 117); *TN:* Kzk. 19th c. **İn-bergen** [Инбергень], a qïstaw (winter pasture, settlement). ⇨ **İN** + **BERGEN**.

İN-BULAT   Tat. 1776 **İn-bulat** [Инбулатовъ] (PSZRI XX, 457). ⇨ **İN** + **BULAT**.

İN-DEMER see **İN-TEMİR**

İN-DİMER see **İN-TEMİR**

İN-DUGAN see **EL-TOΓAN**

İN-GİLDİ see **EL-KELDİ**

İN-QSA   Kzk. 19th c. **İn-qsa-bay** [Инксабай] (Grod., Pril. 192). ⇨ **İN**.

İN-ÖZ   Türk 8th c. **İn-öz-inänčü** [In Öz Inänçü] (ETY II, 108, 112). ⇨ **İN** + **ÖZ?**

İN-TEMİR   Chuv. 18th-19th c. **İn-demer** [Индемеръ] (Magn. 45); Chuv. 18th-19th c. **İn-dimer** [Индимеръ] (Magn. 45); Chuv. 18th-19th c. **İn-temir** [Интемиръ] (Magn. 45). ⇨ **İN** + **TEMİR**.

İN-ZÄN-ΓUL see **İN**

İNA   Bashk. 1789 **İna-bay** [Инабай] (MIB V, 269).

İNAQ   Oghuz 1160 **İnaq** [Ихтияр-ад-дин Инак (Исак, Айтак?)], an emir (MIT I, 397-99, 404, 554); Uyg. 12th c. - 14th c. **İnaq-quli / İnaq-quli?** (Radl., USp. 210, 152); Uyg. **İnaq-quli** [Inak kulı] (EUTS). ✧ 'Confident of a prince'; 'chief of some Uzbek clans in Khiva' (Samojlovič); 'person who governs the empire without having the title of khan' (Samojlovič). Title used as a secondary component of male names.

İNAL see **ÏNAL**

İNAL-YAWÏ   Oghuz/Trkm. 13th c. **İnal-yawï-χan** [اينال ياوى خان / Инал-Йавы-хан] (Abulg./Kon. 675, 725, 730). ⇨ **ÏNAL** + **YAWÏ**.

İNAL-YAWQUY   Oghuz/Trkm. **İnal-yawquy** [Инал Йав Куй], descendant of Oghuz by Salar-baba (Muhamedova: OSA 170). ⇨ **ÏNAL**.

İNAL-ÖZ see **ÏNAL-ÖZ**

İNAL-SAYRU-YAWQUY   Oghuz/Trkm. **İnal-sayru-yawquy** [Инал Сайру Йав Куй], Oghuz's descendant by Salar-baba (Muhamedova: OSA 170). ⇨ **ÏNAL**.

İNAN   Turk. 16th c. **İnan** (Ongan, Ank. II, 191, 571, 149). ✧ 'Believe, trust!' (Erol II).

İNANČ see **ÏNANČ**

İNANČ-BİLGE   Selj. 11th c. **İnanč-bilge** [Инанч Бильге Улуг Джандар-бек], an emir (MIT I, 314-15). ⇨ **ÏNANČ + BİLGÄ.**

İNANDÏ   Turk. 16th c. **İnandï-bey** [İnandı Bey] (Ongan, Ank. II). ✧ 'Believed' cf. Turk. *inan-* 'to believe' (TED).

İNČ-BUQA   Uyg. **İnč-buqa** [İnç Buka] (EUTS); Uyg. 12th c. - 14th c. **İnč-buqa / İnč-buɣa** (Radl., USp. 12, DTS). ✧ 'Quiet-Bull' (Blagova 1997, 715), 'Peace(ful), calm bull' cf. OT *inč* 'Frieden, Ruhe, still, ruhig' (Gabain), Karakh. *inč* 'покой, спокойный ' (DTS). ⇨ **BUQA.**

İNČ-QAYA   Uyg. 13th-14th c. **İnč-qaya** [İnč Qaya] (Zieme, Mat. II, 91). ✧ 'Peace(ful), calm rock' cf. OT *inč* 'Frieden, Ruhe, still, ruhig' (Gabain), Karakh. *inč* 'пэкой, спокойный ' (DTS). ⇨ **QAYA.**

İNČ-SÄGÄ see **İNČ-SEKÄ**

İNČ-SÄNGÄ see **İNČ-SEKÄ**

İNČ-SEKÄ   Uyg. 12th c. - 14th c. **İnč-sekä** [inč sekä] (DTS). ✧ 'Peace(ful)-Sekä', 'Quiet-Sekä' (Blagova 1997, 714), cf. OT *inč* 'Frieden, Ruhe, still, ruhig' (Gabain), Karakh. *inč* 'покой, спокойный ' (DTS). ⇨ **SEÑÄ.**

İNČKİ   Uyg. **İnčki** [İnçki] (EUTS); Uyg. **İnčki / İnčkü?** / İnčgü (Radl., USp. 12, DTS). ✧ 'Calm, quiet' cf. Uyg. *inčgü, inčkü* 'спокойный' (DTS).

İNČÜ-URUÑU   Uyg. **İnčü-uruñu** [inčü urungu sängün apačur], a chief of a tribe (Haneda 4, 7). ✧ 'Slave-warrior' cf. Uyg. *inčü* 'köle' (EUTS). ⇨ **URUÑU.**

İNJİ   Chuv. **Enži-bey** (Németh, HMK 134); Kkalp. **Hınji-gül** [Hindži-gül], fem. (Baskakov: OSA 139); Kkalp. 20th c. **Hinži-gül** [Хинжигүл], fem. (KkRS 779); Turk. 1583 **İnji** [انجى / İnci] (Ongan, Ank. I, 163); Turk. 1546 **İnji-dede** [Şeyh İnci Dede] (Gökb., Ed. 445, 456); Turk. 1482 **İnjü-bajï** [İncü Bacı] (Gökb., Ed. 355); Turk. 1450 **İnjü-χatun** [İncü Hatun], İlyas' daughter (Gökb., Ed. 274); Turk. 1497 **İnjü-χatun** [İncü Hatun], Abdullah's daughter (Gökb., Ed. 465). ✧ 'Pearl' cf. Turk. *inci* 'die Perle' (HŞ), Kkalp. *hinži* 'жемчуг (KkRS), Chuv. *əndžə* 'id.' (Németh, HMK 134). See also **YÄNČÜ.**

İNJÜ see **İNJİ**

İNDİ see **HİNDİ**

İNDİR   Tat.?, Kzk.? 1677 **İndir-Jan / İndir-čan?** [Индырчанъ / Индырчанко Кебековъ] (DAI VII, 252-60).

İNÄČİ see **İNÄČÜ**

İNÄČÜ   Uyg. **İnäči** [İnäçi] (EUTS); Uyg. 12th c. - 14th c. **İnäči** (Radl., USp. 210, 251, 252); Uyg. **İnäčü** [İnäçü] (EUTS).

İNÄČÜK   Uyg. 12th c. - 14th c. **İnäčük** [inäčük / İnäçük] (DTS, EUTS). ✧ 'Little excrement'? cf. Karakh. *in* 'помет овец' (DTS) + dim. suff. *-čük.*

İNÄKÄY   Bashk. 1757 **İnäkäy** [Инякай Яманаев] (MIB IV/1, 157). ✧ 'Little needle' cf. Tat. *inä / enä* 'игла, иголка' (TatRS) + suff. *-käy.*

İNÄL see **İNAL**

İNÄL-QUČ   Uyg. 12th c. - 14th c. **İnäl-quč** [inäl quč] (DTS); Uyg. **İnal-quč** [Inal Kuç] (EUTS). ✧ 'Noble-quč' (Blagova 1997, 710), 'İnäl-embrace!'? cf. Uyg. *quč-* 'обнимать; обхватить руками' (DTS). ⇨ **İNAL.**

İNÄL-ÖZ   Karakh. 11th c. **İnäl-öz** [inäl öz] (DTS). ✧ 'Noble-Life' (Blagova 1997, 710). ⇨ **İNAL + ÖZ.**

İNE   Turk. 1583 **İne-bey / Ayne-bey?** [اينه بك / Ine bey] (Ongan, Ank. I, 163); Turk. 16th c. **İne-beyi** (Ongan, Ank. II); Khorezm.? **İne-bek** [Инэ-бек] (RaD I/1, 99); Turk. 16th c. **İne-han** (Ongan, Ank. II); Turk. 1552 **İne-χan**, Süleyman's son (Dávid); Turk. 1552 **İne-χan**, Karagöz's son (Dávid); Turk. 1565 **İne-χan**, Murad's son (Dávid); Turk. 1570 **İne-χan-aɣa** (Dávid). ⇨ **ENE?**

İNEKČİ   Alt. 19th-20th c. **İnekči** [Инекчи] (OjrRS 212). ✧ 'Cowgirl' (OjrRS 212).

İNESTEY   Hak. 19th-20th c. **İnestey** [Инестей] (HRS 348). ✧ 'Share; Money'? cf. Hak. PN *İmestey* derived from *İmes / İbes* 'часть; деньги; рубль' (Butanaev).

İNİK   Uyg. **İnik** [İnik] (EUTS).

İNKÄ   Bashk. 1706 **İnkä** [Явгоста Инькин] (MIB III, 28); Kzk. 19th c. **İnkä-bay** [Инкабай] (Grod., Pril. 71); Bashk. 1778 **İnkä-güzä** [Кубахта (Кубакты) Инкагузин] (MIB V, 71, 110, 269). ⇨ **İN?** + suff. *-kä.*

İNKÄM   Kzk. 19th c. **İnkäm-bek** [Инкамбекъ] (SODž. 156).

İNKİ   Kzk. 19th c. **İnki-bay** [Инкибай] (Grod., Pril. 179).

İNQAR   Kzk. 19th c. **İnqar-bay** [Инкарбай] (SOK 148). ✧ 'Negation, denial' cf. Turk. *inkâr* (Ar.) 'das Leugnen, das Ableugnen' (HŞ), Uzb. *inkâr (inkor)* 'отрицание ' (UzbRS).

İNS   Maml. 1497 **İns-bay** [أنس باى] (Iyās II, 332, III, 26, 257); Maml. 1498 **İns-bay** [أنس باى], governor of Alexandria (Iyās II, 344); Maml. 1499 **İns-bay** [أنسباى شاد الشرابخانات] (Iyās II, 367). ✧ 'Friend, fellow, companionable, amicable' cf. Ar. انس (*ins*) 'Genosse, Freund; geselliger Mensch'.

İNSAN   Bashk. 1770 **İnsan** [Инсан Яхьин] (MIB IV/1, 345). ✧ 'Man' cf. Tat. *insan* (Ar.) 'keše' (TatRS).

İNSİ   Kzk. 19th c. **İnsi-bay** [Инсыбай] (SOV 156).

İNTİ   Kzk. 19th c. **İnti-bay** [Интыбай] (SOK 156).

İNÜK   Bulg. 1338 **İnük** [اينوك / Инук] (Jusupov 25); Bulg. 1382 **İnük** [اينوك / Инук] (Jusupov 44). ✧ 'Little hunting bird' cf. *in* 'Jagdvogel' (Räs.) + dim. suff. *-k.*

İÑÄ   Uyg. 12th c. - 14th c. **İñä** [iñä / İngä] (DTS, EUTS).

İÑÄL   Uyg. **İñäl** [İngäl] (EUTS).

İÑGÄ   Uyg. 12th c. - 14th c. **İñgä** (Radl., USp. 133-34).

İÑGÄL   Uyg. 12th c. - 14th c. **İñgäl** (Radl., USp. 130-131).

İÑGEJEK   Hak. 19th-20th c. **İñgejek** [Ингечек], fem. (HRS 353). ✧ 'Littl needle' cf. Hak. fem. *İngeček* 'иголочка' (Butanaev).

İÑGLİS   Kzk. 1819 **İñglis** [Инглис] (MIK IV, 324). ✧ 'English'.

İÑNES   Hak. 19th-20th c. **İñnes** [Инънес] (HRS 348). ✧ 'Rod for carrying buckets' cf. Hak. *iñnes* 'коромысло ' (HRS).

İP   Kzk. 19th c. **İp-pek** [Иппекъ] (SOK 304). ✧ 'Smartness, skilfulness' cf. Kzk. *ep* ' ловкость; удобный момент ' (KzRS).

İP-ALAQ   Kzk. 19th c. **İp-alaq** [Ипалакъ] (SOK 164). ⇨ **İP** + **ALAQ**.

İPİ   Kzk. 19th c. **İpi-bay** [Ипыбай] (SOV 88).

İPPİLE   Hak. 19th-20th c. **İppile** [Иппиле] (HRS 348).

İPTİS   Hak. 19th-20th c. **İptis** [Иптис] (HRS 348). ✧ 'Accurate' cf. Hak. PN *İptis* (Butanaev).

İR see **ER**

İR-ALİ see **ER-ALİ**

İR-BARS   Chuv. 18th-19th c. **İr-bars** [Ирбарсъ] (Magn. 45). ⇨ **ER** + **BARS**.

İR-BULAT see **ER-BULAT**

İR-BUTA   Kzk. 19th c. **İr-buta** [Ирбутаевъ] (SKSO VIII, 226). ✧ 'Man/hero-young-camel'. ⇨ **ER** + **BOTA**.

İR-GÖKŠE   Kzk. 19th c. **İr-gökše** [Иръ-Гокше] (Potanin, Pred. 79). ⇨ **ER** + **KÖKČE**.

İR-XUSAYN   Tat. 1784/85 **İr-χusayn** [اير حسين / Ирхусайн] (Jusupov 76). ✧ 'Hero-Husain' (Ar.). ⇨ **ER** + **QUSAYİN**.

İR-KÖPÄK   Kzk. 19th c. **İr-köpäk** [Иръ-Копакъ Илянговъ] (Grod., Pril. 58). ⇨ **ER** + **KÖPÄK**.

İR-QAN   Kzk. 19th c. **İr-qan** [Ирканъ] (Grod., Pril. 164). ⇨ **ER** + **QAN**.

İR-QOSAY see **İR-QOSAY**

İR-MUXAMMED   Uzb. 19th c. **İr-muχammed** [Иръ-Мухаммедъ Худайбергеневъ] (Sr. Az. I (1896), avg. 17). ⇨ **ER** + **MUXAMMED**.

İR-NİYAZ   Kzk. 19th c. **İr-niyaz** [Моллабай Иръ Нiязъ] (Grod., Pril. 133); Kzk. 19th c. **İr-niyaz** [Ирнiязъ] (Grod., Pril. 91). ⇨ **ER** + **NİYAZ**.

İR-SARÏ   Tuv. 19th c. **İr-sarï-müge** [Иръ-сары-муге], a character in a tale (Potanin IV, 584). ⇨ **ER** + **SARÏ**.

İR-TAY   Kzk. 19th c. **İr-tay** [Иртай] (SOK 206). ⇨ **ER** + **TAY** or suff. *-tay(1,2)*?

İR-TAQSÏN see **ER-TOQSÏN**

İR-TAL   Kzk. 19th c. **İr-tal-bay** [Ирталбай] (Grod., Pril. 136). ⇨ **ER** + **TAL**.

İR-TAŠ   Selj. 1042 **İr-taš** [Иrташ], his sons were called Mawdūd and Masʿūd (MIT I, 372, 373, 375). ⇨ **ER** + **TAŠ**.

İR-TUΓAN see **ER-TOΓAN**

İRANJİ   Khorezm. 1457 **İranji** [Иранджи] (MIT I, 536).

İRAPSİN   Hak. 19th-20th c. **İrapsin** [Ирапсин], fem. (HRS 353). ✧ Yerofey (R.) cf. Hak. PN *İrepsin* derived from *İrep* 'Ерофей' (Butanaev).

İRBİS   Alt. 19th-20th c. **İrbis** [Ирбис] (OjrRS 208). ✧ 'Panther' cf. Alt. *irbis* 'барс ' (OjrRS). See also **BARS**.

İRBİZEK   Alt. 19th-20th c. **İrbizek** [Ирбизек] (OjrRS 208). ✧ 'Little panther'. ⇨ **İRBİS** + dim. suff. *-ek*.

İRČET   Hak. 19th-20th c. **İrčet** [Ирчет] (HRS 348).

İRČÜK   Uyg. **İrčük** (Radl., USp. 93); Uyg. **İrčük** [İrçük] (EUTS). ✧ 'Little man' cf. Uyg. *ir* 'er, erkek' (EUTS), Németh, HMK 135. ⇨ **ER**? + dim. suff. *-čük*.

İRJALİ   Uzb. 19th c. **İrjali** [Баймуратъ Ирджалiевъ] (SKSO III, 191).

İRJİN   Hak. 19th-20th c. **İrjin** [Ирчин] (HRS 349). ✧ 'Manly, virile, unwearying' cf. Hak. PN *İrčin* 'мужественный, неутомимый' (Butanaev).

İRDAŠ see **ERDEŠ**

İRDÄN see **İRDEN**

İRDEMEY   Chuv. **İrdemey** [Самандей Ирдемеев] (MIB IV/1, 275).

İRDEN   Kzk. 19th c. **İrdän** [Ирданъ] (SKSO III, 14); Uzb. 19th c. **İrdän** [Ирданъ Ишназаровъ] (SKSO III, 156); Kzk. 19th c. **İrden** [Ирденъ] (AOK 26). ✧ 'Brave, heroic'? cf. Hak. PN *İrden* (Butanaev).

İRDİ   Khorezm./Chag. 1458 **İrdi-yasaul** [Ирди-ясаул], a χoja (MIT I, 537).

İRÄN see **İREN**

İRÄNDÄY see **İRENDEY**

İRÄSKÄ   Hak. 19th-20th c. **İräskä / İräska?** [Иряска] (HRS 349). ✧ 'Little man' cf. Hak. PN *İres* 'мужчина' (Butanaev).

İREK   Oghuz/Trkm. 13th c. **İrek** [ايرك / Ирек, сын Джаджаклы], Jajaqlï's son (Abulg./Kon. 1265). ✧ The motive of giving this name has been explained in the source as follows: since this boy came from the folk (country) *İl-bečene* he was given the name *İrek*. Among the Turks there is a tradition to give the dogs names like *İrek* or *Serek*.

İREM   Bashk. 1761 **İrem-qul** [Янмулла Иремкулов] (MIB IV/1, 221). ✧ I. 'Omen'? cf. Chag. *irim* 'id.' (Radl. I, 1463); II. 'My man/hero'? ⇨ **ERİM**?

İREN   Chuv. 18th-19th c. **İrän** [Иранъ] (Magn. 45); Chuv. 18th-19th c. **İren** [Иренъ] (Magn. 46).

İRENČİ   Chuv. 18th-19th c. **İrenči** [Иренчи] (Magn. 46). ⇨ **İREN** + suff. *-či*.

İRENDEY   Chuv. 18th-19th c. **İrändäy** [Ирандай] (Magn. 45); Chuv. 18th-19th c. **İrendey** [Ирспдсй] (Magn. 46); Chuv. 18th-19th c. **İrentey** [Ирентей] (Magn. 46). ⇨ **İREN** + suff. *-dey*.

İRENÄK   Chuv. 18th-19th c. **İrenäk** [Иренякъ] (Magn. 46); Kzk. 1666 **Erenäk / İrenäk** [Еренякъ (Иренякъ / Яренякъ / Ярначка) Ишеевъ], a prince (DAI V, 40-44). ⇨ **İREN** + suff. *-äk*.

İRENEY   Chuv. 18th-19th c. **İreney** [Иреней] (Magn. 46). ⇨ **İREN** + suff. *-ey*.

İRENTEY see **İRENDEY**

İREPİY   Hak. 19th-20th c. **İrepiy** [Ирепий] (HRS 348). ✧ Yerofey (R.) cf. Hak. PN *İrepey* derived from *İrep* 'Ерофей' (Butanaev).

İREŠ   Hak. 19th-20th c. **İreš** [Ирес] (HRS 348). ✧ 'Screw' cf. Hak. *ireš* 'винт ' (HRS).

İRGÄŠ see **ERGÄŠ**

İRGE   Kzk. 19th c. **İrge-bay** [Иргебай] (AOA 14); Kzk. 19th c. **İrge-bay** [Иргебай] (SODž. 6); Uzb. 1873 **İrge-bay** [Джумабай Иргебаев] (Moskal'cev 40). ✧ 'Base'? cf. Kzk. *irge* 'основание; нижняя часть решётки юрты' (KzRS).

İRGENEY   Chuv. 1670 **İrgeney(ka)** [жена ... Иргенейка], fem. (Poliv.-Kras. 64). ✧ 'Free(man), unbound' cf. Tat.(Tüm.) *irgin* 'die Lust, der Gefallen, freier Wille' (Radl. I, 1468), Tat. *irkin* 'frei, ungebunden, ungehindert' (Radl. I, 1466). ⇨ **ERKİN** + suff. *-ey*.

İRGİMEK   Bashk. 1764 **İrgimek** [Мемедели (Мухамедвали) Иргимеков] (MIB IV/1, 286).

İRGİZ   Kzk. 19th c. **İrgiz-bay** [Мамбетъ Иргизбаевъ] (Grod., Pril. 150); Kzk. 19th c. **İrgiz-bay** [Майдубай Иргизбаевъ] (Grod., Pril. 66); Kzk. 1822 **İrgïz-bay** [Иргызбаевъ] (Konšin, Mat. I-III, 50). ✧ İrγïz (river).

İRİ   Kzk. 19th c. **İri-bay** [Ирибай] (SOK 256). ✧ 'Large, huge' cf. Kzk. *iri* 'крупный, большой' (KzRS). See also **QOJA-İRİ**.

İRİ-QAP   Kzk. 19th c. **İri-qap** [Ирикабъ] (Grod., Pril. 27). ✧ 'Large pot' cf. Kzk. *qap* 'geniş çuval' (KzTS). ⇨ **İRİ**.

İRİBSİN   Alt. 19th c. **İribsin-χan** [Ирибсынъ-ханъ] (Potanin II, 179).

İRİK-МАГОМЕТ   Trkm. 1879 **İrik-maγomet** [Ирикъ-Магометъ] (Grod., Vojna IV (Grod., Pril. 109)). ⇨ **İREK?** + **MAXMED**.

İRİM   Kzk. 19th c. **İrim-bay / İrïm-bay** [Ирымбай] (SOK 216); Kzk. **İrim-qul** [Иримкуль] (Sb. Syr-D. IX, 46). ✧ 'Omen (good or bad); prophecy' cf. Alt., Chag., NUyg.(Tar.), Tat. *irim, ïrïm* 'ein gutes und ein böses Omen; die Weissagung, Wahrsagung, das Omen, der Aberglaube' (Radl. I, 1370).

İRİS   Kzk. 19th c. **İris** [Ирисовъ] (SKSO VIII, 200); Kzk. **İris** [Бекатай Ирисовъ] (SKSO VIII, 201); Kzk. 19th c. **İris-bay** [Ирисъ-бай Яхшибаевъ] (Grod., Pril. 23); Kzk. 19th c. **İris-bay** [Ирисбай] (Grod., Pril. 25); Kzk. 19th c. **İris-bay** [Ирисбай] (Grod., Pril. 83); Kzk. 19th c. **İris-bay** [Ирисбай] (Grod., Pril. 144); Kzk. 19th c. **İris-bay** [Ирисбай] (Grod., Pril. 100); Kzk. 19th c. **İris-bay** [Ирисбай Болабаевъ] (Grod., Pril. 173); Uzb. **İris-bay** [Ирисбаевъ] (Moskal'cev 48); Kzk. 19th c. **İris-bek** [Аскаръ Ирисбековъ] (Grod., Pril. 173); Kzk. 19th c. **İris-gül** [Ирисъ-Гюль], fem. (Grod., Pril. 137); Kzk. 19th c. **İris-χan** [Ирис-ханъ] (Grod., Pril. 118); Kzk. 19th c. **İris-qul** [Ирискуловъ] (SKSO VIII, 222); Kzk. 1820 **İrïs-bay** [Ырысбай], chief of the Teläw tribe (Sib. Vest. IX, 112). ✧ 'Happiness, luck, success' cf. Kuman, Alt., Kzk. *irïs, rïs* 'das Glück, die Wohlfahrt, der Erfolg' (Radl. I, 1368).

İRİS-MUXAMMED   Kkalp. 1709 **İris-muχammed / Rïs-mambet** [Ирис-Мухаммед (Рысмамбет)], a Karakalpak khan (MIKk. 58, Pam. Sib. Ist. 380). ⇨ **İRİS** + **MUXAMMED**.

İRİSAQ   Bashk. 1756 **İrisaq** [Казяр Ирисаков] (MIB IV/1, 123).

İRİZ   Uyg. **İriz** [İriz] (EUTS). ⇨ **İRİS?**

İRÏS see **İRİS**

İRÏŠ   Kzk. 19th c. **İrïš** [Ирышъ] (SOK 164).

İRKÄ see **ERKE**

İRKÄY   Uyg. 12th c. - 14th c. **İrkäy** [irkäj / İrkäy] (Radl., USp. 30, DTS, EUTS). ✧ 'Little man'? (Németh, HMK 135). ⇨ **ER** + dim. suff. *-käy*.

İRKÄN see **ERKİN**

İRKÄNT   Uyg. 12th c. - 14th c. **İrkänt** [irkänt] (DTS).

İRKE-BAQA   Bashk. 1751 **İrke-baqa** [Иркебака] (MIB IV/1, 55). ⇨ **İRKE** + **BAQA**.

İRKENEY   Bashk. 1729 **İrkeney** [Секе Иркенеев] (MIB III, 264). ⇨ **ERKİN** + suff. *-ey*.

İRKİM-BEK see **ERKİN**

İRKİN see **ERKİN**

İRKİNÄ   Crm.? 1689 **İrkinä** [Иркиня, табунутский саитъ] (PSZRI III, 15). ⇨ **ER(KİN)?** + suff. *-(kin)ä*?

İRQÏL   Oghuz **İrqïl-χoja** [Эрйанги-Кент Иркыл-ходжа], Kün-χan's councillor (RaD I/1, 86).

İRQOS   Hak. 19th-20th c. **İrqos** [Иркос], fem. (HRS 353).

İRQUS   Hak. 19th-20th c. **İrqus** [Иркус], fem. (HRS 353).

İRLEPES   Kzk. 19th c. **İrlepes** [Ирлепес Тютебетовъ] (TV 1877, 69).

İRMAN   Kzk. 19th c. **İrman** [Ирманъ] (SKSO III, 20); Uzb. 19th c. **İrman** [Ильмуратъ Ирмановъ] (SKSO III, 16); Uzb. 19th c. **İrman** [Ирманъ] (SKSO III, 172); Uzb. 19th c. **İrman** [Ирманъ] (SKSO III, 18). ⇨ **ER** + suff. *-man*?

İRMAT   Kzk. 19th c. **İrmat / İrmät?** [Норматъ Ирматовъ] (SKSO VIII, 232); Kzk. 19th c. **İrmet** [Ирметъ Абдибаевъ] (SKSO IV, otd. III, 14). ⇨ **ER** + suff. *-mat*?

İRMÄK   Tat.(Sib.) 20th c. **İrmäk** [Ирмәк] (Sattarov); Bashk. 1707 **İrmäk** [Ирмӓк Богданов] (MIB III, 31);

Bashk. 1718 **İrmäk** [Кульмет Ирмяков] (MIB III, 169); Bashk. 1738 **İrmäk** [Темир Ирмяков] (MIB I, 357, 367); Bashk. 1761 **İrmäk** [Уразмет Ирмяков] (MIB IV/1, 227); Bashk. 20th c. **İrmäk** [Ирмәк, Ирмяк] (Kusimova); Kzk. 1820 **İrmäk** [Ирмякъ Мурза], one of the chiefs of the Tazlar tribe (Sib. Vest. IX, 112); Kzk. 19th c. **İrmäk** [Турди Ирмаков] (Grod., Pril. 153); Kzk. 19th c. **İrmäk** [Орасбай Ирмаковъ] (Grod., Pril. 50); Kzk. 19th c. **İrmäk-bay** [Уренкъ-бай Ирмакбаевъ] (Grod., Pril. 52); Kzk. 19th c. **İrmek** [Доскулъ Ирмековъ] (Pam. kn. Turg. 59); Kzk. 19th c. **İrmek** [Мурзагулъ Ирмековъ] (Grod., Pril. 144). ✧ 'Comforting, solacing; fun' Bashk. *irmäk* 'забава, потеха' (BaRS), *İrmäk* 'künel yïwatqïs' (Kusimova), Tat.(Tara, Tob.) *irmäk* 'die Unterhaltung, die Belustigung' (Radl. I, 1471). ⇨ **ERMEK?**

İRMÄŠ Bashk. 1707 **İrmäš** [Ирмяш Урмячев] (MIB III, 35); Bashk. 1731 **İrmäš** [Мрясь Ирмяшев] (MIB III, 294); Bashk. 1738 **İrmäš** [Ирмяш Курмасев] (MIB I, 143); Bashk. 1746 **İrmäš** [Полат Ирьмяшев] (MIB III, 444); Bashk. 1754 **İrmäš** [Пулат Ирмяшев] (MIB IV/1, 79); Bashk. 1764 **İrmäš** [Медияр Ирмяшев] (MIB IV/1, 277); Bashk. 1728 **İrmiš** [Ирмиш] (MIB I, 123).

İRMÄT see **İRMAT**

İRMEK see **İRMÄK**

İRMET see **İRMAT**

İRMİŠ see **İRMÄŠ**

İRSAY Bashk. 1763 **İrsay** [Ирсай Яхшигулов] (MIB IV/2, 45); Bashk. 1709 **İrsay / İrsay?** [Ирсай] (MIB I, 264). ✧ 'Clever, saint' (Kusimova).

İRSALİ Kzk. 19th c. **İrsali** [Ирсали Магомедовъ] (Grod., Pril. 110); Kzk. 1820 **İrsali-batïr** [Ирсали батыръ], chief of the Bay-baqtï tribe (Sib. Vest. IX, 119).

İRSAN Bashk. 1795 **İrsan / İrsän?** [Бектемиръ Ирсановъ] (IOAIÊK XXVIII, 589).

İRSÏ Tat. 1737 **İrsï-bay** [Ирсыбай Бескыбаев] (MIB III, 365). ✧ 'Singer' cf. Bashk. *yïrsï* 'id.' (BRS).

İRTİŠ Kzk. 19th c. **Ertis** [Ертисъ] (AOO 26); Kzk. **Ertis-pay** [Ертыспай] (Konšin, Oč. 94); Kzk. 19th c. **Ertis-pay** [Ертыспай] (SOK 280); Tat. 1600 **İrtiš** [Девей Иртишов] (MIB I, 152). ✧ Irtish (river) cf. Kzk. TN *Ertis* (Kojčubaev).

İRTÏŠAQ Tat.(Ishim) 1580 **İrtïšaq** [Иртышакъ царь] (Sib. Let. (Rem.) 318).

İRUSLAN Chuv. 18th-19th c. **İrïslan** [Ирысланъ] (Magn. 46); Chuv. 18th-19th c. **İruslan** [Ирусланъ] (Magn. 46); Nog. 1551 **Uruslan** [Урусланъ], a murza (PSRL (Russk. Hr.) I, 532). ✧ Ruslan (R.<Trk. *arslan* /Šipova/). ⇨ **ARSLAN.**

İRUŠ Bashk. 1735 **İruš** [Ирушъ Кюлюковъ], a prince (Vel.-Zern., Bašk. 18).

İRÜ Kzk. 1805 **İrü-bay** [Ирюбаевъ] (PSZRI XXVIII, 1325). ✧ 'Strong'.

İS see **ES**

İS-AĞASÏ Kzk. 19th c. **İs-aɣasï** [Исагасы] (Potanin II, 4). ✧ 'Master of work/service'? cf. Kzk. *is* 'iş, hizmet' (KzTS). ⇨ **ES / EŠ? + AĞA + poss suff. *-sï*.**

İS-AL Kzk. 19th c. **İs-al** [Исалъ] (SOK 202). ✧ 'Get a mate/helper';'Get work/service!'? cf. Kzk. *is* 'iş, hizmet' (KzTS). ⇨ **ES / EŠ + AL.**

İS-ALİ see **İŠ-ALİ**

İS-BOL see **EŠ-BOL**

İS-BUL see **EŠ-BOL**

İS-BULAY see **ES-BOLAY**

İS-MADİYAR Kzk. 19th c. **İs-madiyar** [Исмадіаръ Ташевъ] (SKSO VIII, 204). ✧ 'Mate-Madiyar / Service-Madiyar'? cf. Kzk. *is* 'iş, hizmet' (KzTS), Kzk. *Madiyar*, the name of a clan (Aristov 105). ⇨ **ES / EŠ?**

İS-MAĞOMED Kzk. 19th c. **İs-maɣomed** [Исъ Магомедъ Исъ Аліевъ] (Grod., Pril. 180); Kzk. 19th c. **İs-maqombet** [Исмакомбетъ] (SOK 308). ✧ I. 'Mate-(of)-Maɣomed'; II. 'Healthy Maqombet' cf. Kzk. *Es-maɣambet* (Žanuzakov-Esbaeva), Tat. PN *İš-möxämmät* (Sattarov). ⇨ **ES / EŠ? + MAXMED.**

İS-MAQOMBET see **İS-MAĞOMED**

İS-PEMBET Kzk. 19th c. **İs-pembet** [Испембетъ] (Lomakin 40). ⇨ **İZ I. + MAMBET.** See also **İZ-BAĞAMBET.**

İS-PERGEN see **ES-BERGEN**

İS-TÄWLET see **İŠ-DÄWLÄT**

İS-TEMİR see **İŠ-TİMER**

İS-TİLÄW Kzk. 19th c. **İs-teleü** [Истелеу] (SOK 212); Kzk. 19th c. **İs-tiläw** [Изтилавъ Буртаевъ] (Grod., Pril. 92). ✧ 'Mind-wish/desire'; 'Mate/helper-desire'? ⇨ **ES / EŠ + TİLÄW.**

İSA Kkalp. 20th c. **İysa** [Ийса] (KkRS 774); Uyg. **İsa** ['isa] (DTS); Turk. 1458 **İsa** [İsâ Halife] (Gökb., Ed. 176); Turk. 1485 **İsa** [İsâ Fakih], a defterdar (Gökb., Ed. 429); Turk. 1503 **İsa** [İsâ], „dizdar" of Turhal kalesi (Gökb., Ed. 483); Khorezm.? **İsa(-qalämči0** [Иса-Калямчи] (RaD II, 213); Kzk. 19th c. **İsa-bay** [Мусабекъ Исабаевъ] (Grod., Pril. 198); Kirg. **İsa-bek** [Ысабек] (Jud. 636). ✧ Isa, a Prophet, the biblical Jesus (Ahmed) (<Ar.). See also **QARA-İSA.**

İSA-BĀLİ Yürük 1543 **İsa-bāli** [İsâ Bâli] (Gökb., Rum. 181). ⇨ **İSA + BĀLİ.**

İSAKEY Nog. 20th c. **İsakey / İsaqay** [Исакей Мана Оғурлы / Исакай Манаевич Огурлиев], one of Baskakov's informants from the aul of Erkin-yurt (Oraɣ-awul) (Bask., Nog. 143). ✧ '(Dear) Little İsa' cf. Kzk. *İsaqay* (Žanuzakov-Esbaeva). ⇨ **İSA + suff. *-key.***

İSAR Uzb. 19th c. **İsar** [Ташъ Тамиръ Исаровъ] (SKSO III, 164).

İSATOY Hak. 19th-20th c. **İsatoy** [Исатой] (HRS 349).

İSÄK   Tat. 20th c. **İsäk** [Исәк] (Sattarov); Bashk. 1756 **İsäk** [Шакай Исяков] (MIB IV/1, 122); Bashk. 1756 **İsäk** [Темергут Исяков] (MIB IV/1, 122). ✧ 'Bump, swelling' cf. Kzk. *isäk* 'die Geschwulst' (Radl. I, 1525).

İSÄKÄY   Tat. 16th c. - 17th c. **İsäkäy** [Исәкәй] (Sattarov); Tat. 1668 **İsäkäy** [Исекейко Батыревъ] (Kungursk. akty 9); Tat.(Mish.) 1758 **İsäkäy** [Исекей Алмеев] (MIB IV/1, 169); Bashk. **İsäkäy** [Алдарбай Исекеевъ], a tarχan (PSZRI IX, 338); Bashk. 1734 **İsäkäy** [Аиткузъ Исекеевъ] (Vel.-Zern., Bašk. 10); Bashk. 1734, 1735 **İsäkäy** [Алдарбай Исекеевъ], a tarχan (Vel.-Zern., Bašk. 9, 27); Bashk. 1735 **İsäkäy** [Исекей Зиямбетевъ], a prince (Vel.-Zern., Bašk. 17); Bashk. 18th c. **İsekey / İsäkäy?** [Болта Исекеев] (MIB III, 523). ✧ 'Comforting, solacing; fun' (Sattarov). ⇨ **İSÄK?** + dim. suff. *-äy*. See also **İSÄKİ, İRMÄK**.

İSÄKİ   Tat. 20th c. **İsäki** [Исәки] (Sattarov). ✧ Shortened dialectal variant of *İsäkäy* (Sattarov). ⇨ **İSÄKÄY**.

İSÄN see **ESÄN**

İSÄN-ALİ   Kkalp. 20th c. **İysen-γaliy** [Ийсенғалий] (KkRS 774); Tat. 1538 **İsän-ali** [Исеньелѣй] (PSRL XIII, 125); Tat. 20th c. **İsän-ali** [Исәнали] (Sattarov). ⇨ **ESÄN** + **ALİ**.

İSÄN-BAXTA see **ESÄN-BAXTÏ**

İSÄN-BERDİ   Bashk. 1713 **İsän-berde** [Исенберде] (MIB III, 100); Tat.(Mish.) 1693 **İsän-berdi** [Исенберди], from Ufa (MIB I, 84); *TN:* Kzk. **İsen-berdi** [Исен-берды] (Karta JAR X). ✧ 'Healthy-given/born / Healthy-given (by God); (A) healthy (man/woman) gave it'? ⇨ **ESÄN** + **BERDİ**.

İSÄN-BUQA see **ESÄN-BUQA**

İSÄN-BULAT   Chuv. 18th-19th c. **İsän-bulat** [Изанбулатъ] (Magn. 41). ✧ 'Sound Steel' cf. Tat. PN *İsän-bulat* (Sattarov). ⇨ **ESÄN** + **BULAT**.

İSÄN-GELDİ see **ESÄN-KELDİ**

İSÄN-GİL see **İSÄN-KİL**

İSÄN-GİLDİ see **ESÄN-KELDİ**

İSÄN-GİLDİ-BİY see **ESÄN-KELDİ**

İSÄN-YUL   Bashk. 1763 **İsän-yul** [Абдулла Исеньюлов] (MIB IV/2, 45). ⇨ **ESÄN** + **YOL**.

İSÄN-KİL   Chuv. 18th-19th c. **İsän-gil** [Изенгилъ] (Magn. 42); Tat. 20th c. **İsän-kil** [Исәнкил] (Sattarov). ✧ 'Come (be born) healthy' (Sattarov). ⇨ **ESÄN** + **KEL**.

İSÄN-TUR   Tat.(Sib.) 1621 **İsän-tur** [Исентуръ] (Miller, Ist. Sib. II, 263). ✧ 'Live healthy'. ⇨ **ESÄN** + **TUR**.

İSÄNDÄY   Chuv. 18th-19th c. **İsändäy** [Исендей] (Magn. 46); Chuv. 18th-19th c. **İsändäy** [Изяндей] (Magn. 42). ⇨ **ESÄN** + suff. *-däy*.

İSÄNÄK   Chuv. 18th-19th c. **İsänäk** [Изянякъ] (Magn.

42). ⇨ **ESÄN** + dim. suff. *-äk*.

İSÄNKÄ   Bashk. 1666 **İsänkä** [Исенка] (Vel.-Zern., Bašk. 28). ⇨ **ESÄN** + dim. suff. *-kä*.

İSEY see **ESEY**

İSEYDİK   Bashk. 1740 **İseydik** [Исейдык Алимбетев] (MIB I, 404).

İSEK   Chul. 1609 **İsek** [Исекъ], a prince (Andrievič, Ist. Sib. I, 45). ✧ According to Sattarov, Tat. *İsäk* is the dial. variant of *İsäkäy* (Sattarov). ⇨ **İSAKEY?**

İSEKE   Kzk. **İseke** [Исеке] (Divaev, Kirgizskaja pesnja: ZVOIRAO X, 90). ✧ Diminutive-contracted form of PN İset (Divaev). ⇨ **İSET** + comp. *eke*.

İSEKEY see **İSÄKÄY**

İSEL see **İSİL**

İSEL   Kzk. 1822 **İsel-bay** [Исельбай Бекетовъ] (TOUAK XXIV, 122).

İSEM   Bashk. 1758 **İsem / İsīm?** [Исемь Ямметев] (MIB IV/1, 163); Kzk. 19th c. **İsim** [Исимъ] (Potanin, Pred. 110); Kzk. 1862 **İsim** [Исимъ Джадаевъ], a sultan in the district of Kopal (ZIRGOGeogr. I, 306); Kzk. 1862 **İsim** [Исимъ Мамырхановъ] (ZIRGOGeogr. I, 311); Kzk. **İsim-biy / İsïm-biy** [Исымъ-бий] (Divaev, Šura 79); Kzk. 19th c. **İsïm** [Исымъ] (Grod., Pril. 144). ✧ '?' cf. Kzk. PN *İsem-bek* (Žanuzakov-Esbaeva), cf. Kzk. *is* 'iş, hizmet' (KzTS)? ⇨ **ES?** + suff. *-im*.

İSEMBET see **İSENBET**

İSEMÄL   Bashk. 1735 **İsemäl** [Исемьялъ Лачиновъ], a tarχan (Vel.-Zern., Bašk. 15).

İSEMMET see **İSENBET**

İSEN see **ESÄN**

İSEN-GİLDE see **ESÄN-KELDİ**

İSENBET   Bashk. 1695 **İsembet** [Исембетка Тлевлинъ] (Vel.-Zern., Bašk. 32); Bashk. 1755 **İsemmet** [Исемметь] (MIB IV/1, 105); Bashk. 1695 **İsenbet** [Исенбет] (MIB I, 85); Bashk. 1735 **İsenbet** [Кусякъ Исенбетевъ], a tarχan (Vel.-Zern., Bašk. 19). ⇨ **ESÄN** + suff. *-bet / -met*.

İSER-ГАР   Bashk. 1740 **İser-γap** [Исергап (Сулумов) Сюлюмов] (MIB I, 400, 434); Bashk. 1749 **İser-γap** [Исергап] (MIB III, 458); Bashk. 1754 **İser-γap** [Исергап Алабердин] (MIB IV/1, 83); Bashk. 1757 **İser-γap** [Исергап Муштумов] (MIB IV/1, 157); Bashk. 1788 **İser-γap** [Исергап Байдашев] (MIB V, 234, 254); Bashk. 1788 **İser-γap** [Исергап Бекбов] (MIB V, 178); Bashk. 1789 **İser-γap** [Исергап Байдяшев] (MIB V, 254); Kzk. 1846 **İser-γap** [бий Исергаб] (MKOP 153); Kzk. 19th c. **İsir-qap** [Исиркабъ] (Grod., Pril. 104); Kzk. 19th c. **İsir-qap** [Исиркабъ] (Grod., Pril. 23); Kzk. 19th c. **İsir-qap / İsir-käp** [Ораз Исиркябовъ] (Grod., Pril. 177). ✧ I. 'Hunting-bird-sack; skullcap put on the head of a hunting bird'? cf. Chag. *isir* 'ein Jagdvogel' (Radl. I, 1527), Türk, Alt., Az., Crm., Hak., Kirg., Kzk., Turk., etc. *qap* 'der Sack, Beutel, die Tasche; das Futteral, Ueberzug; die Scheide' (Radl. II, 400); II. 'Stupid sack / Scapegrace-sack'? Kzk. *eser* 'yaramaz, akılsız' (KzTS), Kzk. *esär* 'dumm, leichtsinnig, albern' (Radl. I, 874).

İSERGÄN Bashk. 1788 **İsergän** [Исерган Байдашев] (MIB V, 234). ✧ 'Dazed, drunken' cf. Bashk. *iθer-* 'пьянеть; хмелеть' (BRS/Uraksin).

İSERKE Uzb. 1882 **İserke-bay** [Исерке-бай] (Moskal'cev 48). ✧ 'Little hunting-bird' cf. Chag. *isir* 'ein Jagdvogel' (Radl. I, 1527) + suff. *-ke*.

İSET Kzk. 18th c. **İset** [Исетъ] (Nepljuev 766, 783); Kzk. 1827 **İset** [Турсунбай Исетевъ] (TOUAK XXIV, 173). ✧ 'Izzat [=glory]' (<Ar.) cf. Kzk. *İzat-bek* (Žanuzakov).

İSETAY Kzk. 1837 **İsetay** [Исетай], from the Inner Horde (Mejer 53). ⇨ **TAY** or suff. *-tay(1,2)*?

İSFAHAN Maml. 1437 **İsfahan-šah-χatun** [اسنهان شاه خاتون], the dead emir Mahmud's daughter (Berchem, Jér. I, 323). ✧ 'Isfahan (a town)'.

İSFENDİYER Turk. 1528 **İsfendiyer-bey** [İsfendiyer Bey] (Gökb., Ed. 328-330). ✧ İsfendiyar (P.) 'Pehlivan [=wrestler, hero]' (Erol II), cf. also Tat. PN *Äsfändiyär* (Sattarov).

İSHAQ Karakh. **İshaq** [İshak] (MK/Atalay 841); Tat. 16th c. **İsqaq** [Искакъ (Исаак)], when taking Kazan he was the commander of the Kazak cavalry from Arsk (Iznoskov 122); Tat. 1748 **İsqaq** [Искаковъ] (Nepljuev 437); Kzk. 19th c. **İsqaq** [Искакъ] (SOK 146, 160, 182); Kzk. 19th c. **İsqaq** [Искакъ] (SOV 116); Kzk. 19th c. **Saqaq** (<İsqaq) [Сакакъ] (SOK 12, 230); Kzk. 19th c. **Saqaq** (<İsqaq) [Сакакъ] (SOV 64, 144); *TN:* Tat.? **Iskakova** [Искакова], a village in the Ural mountains south-west of Verhneuralsk (?). ✧ Ishaq (Ar.) 'a Prophet, the biblical Isaac' (Ahmed) (<Hebr.).

İSHAQ-ALİ Turk. 15th c. **İshaq-ali** [Ισακαλης], a governor (Byz. Turc. 140). ✧ 'Ishāq (=Isaac)-Ali' (<Ar.). ⇨ **İSHAQ + ALİ.**

İSHAQİ **İshaqi** [Ajaz Ishaki] (Mende 38, 75, 85, 88, etc.).

İSİG Türk 8th c. - 9th c. **İsig-sañun** [isig saŋun / Isig Sañun] (DTS, ETY II, 91); Uyg. **İsig-tarχan** [İsig Tarḫan] (EUTS). ✧ 'Friendly' cf. Karakh. *isig* 'горячий, теплый; приветливый' (DTS).

İSİGÄ see **İSİKÄ**

İSİK Oghuz/Trkm. 13th c. **İsik-İsmail** [اسق اسماعيل / Исик-Исмаил] (Abulg./Kon. 1285).

İSİKÄ Uyg. 13th-14th c. **İsigä** (Zieme, Mat. II, 92); Uyg. 12th c. - 14th c. **İsikä** [isikä / İsikä] (Radl., USp. 4, DTS, EUTS).

İSİL Kzk. 19th c. **İsil-bay** [Исильбай] (SOK 184); Bashk. 1695 **İsïl-bay** / **İsïl-buy?** [Исыл-бай Меллыбай] (MIB I, 92).

İSİM see **İSEM**

İSİR-QAP see **İSER-ГАР**

İSİR-KÄP see **İSER-ГАР**

İSİL see **İSİL**

İSKÄNDÄR see **İSKENDER**

İSKEY Tat.? 17th c. **İskey** [Байдулка Искеевъ] (IOAIÊK XXIX, 345); Tat.? 17th c. **İskey** [Искей Тойдимерко], a Cossack ataman in the region of Tsivil'sk (IOAIÊK XXIX, 341). ⇨ **ES?** + suff. *-key*.

İSKENDER Tat. 20th c. **İskändär** [Искəндəр] (Sattarov); Bashk. 20th c. **İskändär** [Искəндəр] (Kusimova); Kkalp. 20th c. **İskender** [Искендер] (KkRS 774); Turk. 16th c. - 17th c. **İskender-bey** [İskender Bey], several persons in the source (Gökb., Ed.); Kzk. **İskendir** [Искендир] (Žanuzakov); Tat. 1519 **İskindar** [اسكيندر] (Jusupov 60). ✧ Alexander (<Ar. form of the Greek male name).

İSKENDİR see **İSKENDER**

İSKENE Kzk. 19th c. **İskene** [Искене] (AOO 14). ⇨ **ES?** + suff. *-kene*.

İSKİNDAR see **İSKENDER**

İSQAQ see **İSHAQ**

İSQAR see **İSQAR**

İSQAT see **İSQAT**

İSLAM Crm. 1522 - 1534 **İslam** [Исламъ (Асламъ)], prince, Muχammad Girey's son (PSRL III, 199, VIII, 278, 289 etc.); Tat. 1608 **İslam** [Исламка Барсуковъ] (Kurdjumov 55); Tat. 20th c. **İslam** [Ислам] (Sattarov); Bashk. 20th c. **İslam** [Ислам] (Kusimova); Kkalp. 20th c. **İslam** [Ислам] (KkRS 774); Kzk. **İslam** / **Eslam** / **Slam** [Ислам, Еслам, Слам] (Žanuzakov); Uzb.? 19th c. **İslam-bay** [Исламбай], from a Kipchak tribe (clan) (SKSO III, 191); NUyg.? 19th c. **İslam-bay** [Islam Baj, tjänare], a servant (Hedin); Kzk. 19th c. **İslam-bek** [Исламбекъ] (Grod., Pril. 50); Crm. 1532 **İslam-bi** [Исламъ-би], a prince (PSRL XIII, 61); Bashk. 1737 **İslam-γul** [Юлдашев (Исламгул)] (MIB I, 318); Bashk. 1783 **İslam-γul** [Исламгул Султангулов] (MIB V, 147); Yürük 1543 **İslām** [Durmuş ve İslâm] (Gökb., Rum. 186); Turk. 1528 **İslām-bey** [Hacı İslâm Bey] (Gökb., Ed. 54); Trkm. 20th c. **İslām** [İslam] (Zaj. 1971, 328); Trkm. 20th c. **İslām** [Ыслам] (TrkmRS 772). ✧ 'Islam (religion); Muslim' (<Ar.) *islām* 'submission, surrender (to the will of Allah)' (Ahmed).

İSLĀM see **İSLAM**

İSLÄKÄY Bashk. 1777 **İsläkäy** [Имангул Ислакаев] (MIB V, 62, 66).

İSLEMES Trkm. 1591 **İslemes-χan** [Ислемес-хан] (MIT II, 77). ✧ '(S)He won't strive; (S)He won't work hard' cf. Trkm. *islä-* 'wollen, streben' (Radl. I, 1531).

İSMAİL Oghuz 11th c. **İsmail** [Исмаил ибн Алтунташ, Исмаил Хандан ибн Алтунташ], son of the Khorezmshah Altun-taš (MIT I, 249, 257, 286,

306-308, 372); Oghuz 11th c. **İsmail** [بـن سبكتكين] / Исмаил ибн Себуктегин], Sebük-tegin's son (Ibn al-Athīr/Tornb. X, 91-92, MIT I, 29); Bashk. 1796 **İsmail** [Измаил / Исмаил Юлдашев] (MIB V, 362); Kzk. 19th c. **Smayl** [Ибрагимъ Смайловъ] (AUK 232). ✧ Ismail (Ar.) 'a Prophet, the biblical Ishmael' (Ahmet).

İSMAQ Tat. 20th c. **İsmaq** [Исмак] (Sattarov); Bashk. 1756 **İsmaq** [Исмак Кусекеев] (MIB IV/1, 123); Bashk. 1763 **İsmaq** [Исмак Касаев] (MIB IV/2, 45); Bashk. 1772 **İsmaq** [Исмак Муксин] (MIB IV/1, 364); Bashk. 20th c. **İsmaq** [Исмак] (Kusimova). ✧ 'Bountiful, open-handed' (Kusimova) (<P.).

İSMAQAY Bashk. 1757 **İsmaqay** [Исмакай Изжимасов] (MIB IV/1, 151). ✧ 'Little Generous' cf. Tat. PN *İsmaq* (Satarov) (<P.).

İSMET Kkalp. 20th c. **İsmet** [Исмет] (KkRS 774). ✧ 'Chastity, purity; honour, innocence' cf. Turk. *ismet* (Ar.) 'id.' (TED).

İSMİR Türk / Uyg. 8th c. - 9th c. **İsmir** [ismir] (DTS).

İSRAİL Selj. 11th c. **İsrail** [Исраил ибн Сельджук], Selčük (Seljuk)'s son (MIT I, 229, 350-4, 462-3).

İSRİK Bashk. 1729 **İsrik** [Исрык] (MIB III, 270). ✧ 'Drunk' cf. Tat. *isïrïk* 'betrunken, betäubt' (Radl. I, 1527).

İSTABAN Kirg. 19th c. **Staban / İstaban** [Стабанъ / Истабанъ] (Potanin II, 6).

İSTÄK Kzk. 1820 **İstäχ-bay** [Истяхбай], a chief from the Uwaq tribe (Sib. Vest. IX, 107); Kzk.? 1734 **İstek** [Муса Истековъ] (PSZRI IX, 341); *TN:* **İstek-bay** (Karta JAR XI). ✧ I. 'Bashkir' cf. Kzk. *İstäk* 'der Baschkire' (Radl. I. 1533); II. 'Wish, desire' cf. Karakh. *istäk* 'Suche, Verfolgung' (MK/Brock.), Crm., Turk. *istäk* 'id.' (Radl. I. 1533).

İSTÄK-TOLU Maml. 1317 **İstäk-tolu** [استتطلو / Istactolu] (Abulfidā V, 314-15). ⇨ **İSTÄK + TOLU.**

İSTÄMİ Türk 6th c. **İstämi-qaγan / İštämi-qaγan / İštemi** [I(e)štämi kaγan / istämi qaγan / İstemi kagan / İštemi], one of the kaghans (552-575/576) of the western Türks (Németh, HMK 168, DTS, ETY I, 28, Golden 127). See also **KENČ-ESTEMİ.**

İSTÄK Hak. 19th c. **İstäk** [Істäк] (Katanov, Otč. 12). ✧ 'Crowbar' cf. (R.) стягъ 'id.' (Katanov).

İSTÄNČÄ Karg. **İstänčä** [Істäнчä] (Katanov, Otč. 9). ✧ Sten'ka (R.) (Katanov).

İSTÄNKÄ Hak. 19th c. **İstänkä** [Істäнка] (Katanov, Otč. 12). ✧ Sten'ka (R.) (Katanov).

İSTEK see **İSTÄK**

İSTEKÄY Tat. 1668, 1675 **İstekäy** [Истекайка Илгондинъ / Истечко Илгондинъ / Истекайка Ильгондинъ] (Kungursk. akty, 1, 20, Kurdjumov 3, 4); Tat.(Mish.) 1775 **İstikäy** [Истикай Бугаров] (MIB IV/2, 417). ⇨ **ESLİ** + suff. *-käy.*

İSTİÄBÄ Yak. **İstiäbä / Sibiätä** [Істіäбä / Сібіäтä],

fem. (Pek.). ✧ Yelisaveta (R.).

İSTİKAY see **İSTEKÄY**

İSTİKÄY see **İSTEKÄY**

İSTİLÄN Tat. / Bashk.? 1773 **İstlän-bay** [Истлянбай Азаматов] (MIB IV/2, 132).

İSTLÄN see **İSTİLÄN**

İŞ see **EŞ**

İŞ-AQAY Tat. 1739 **İš-aqay** [Ишакаевъ], a murza (Alatyr. 146); Uzb. 19th c. **İš-aqay** [Суяръ Ишакаевъ] (SKSO III, 174). ⇨ **EŞ + AQAY.**

İŞ-ALEY see **İŞ-ALİ**

İŞ-ALİ Kzk. 19th c. **İs-ali** [Исъ Алиевъ] (Grod., Pril. 180); Bashk. 1707 **İš-aley (<İš-ali)** [Ишалей Чювашев] (MIB III, 39); Bashk. 1722 **İš-aley (<İš-ali)** [Ишалей] (MIB I, 114); Bashk. 1751 **İš-aley / İš-ali** [Аббез Ишалев] (MIB IV/1, 51); Bashk. 1783 **İš-ali** [Ишали Кускильдин] (MIB V, 139, 199); Kzk. 19th c. **İš-ali** [Канай Ишалиевъ] (Grod., Pril. 172); Bashk. / Tat.? 1736 **İš-ali** [Ишали] (PSZRI IX, 743); Bashk. 1731 **İš-äli** [Ишелы Кайдалын] (MIB III, 292); *TN:* Bashk. 1701 **İšäleyeva** [Ишелеева], a village (MIB III, 14). ✧ 'Mate/helper-Ali' cf. Tat. PNs *İš-γali / İš-ali / İš-alï* (Sattarov), Kzk. PN *Es-äli* (Žanuzakov-Esbaeva). ⇨ **EŞ + ALİ.**

İŞ-ALİM Bashk. 1763 **İš-alim** [Ишалим Мусин] (MIB IV/2, 45). ⇨ **EŞ + ALİ** + suff. *-m.*

İŞ-BAQ Tat. 20th c. **İš-baq** [Ишбак] (Sattarov). ✧ 'Fellow (friend), look! (be born!)' (Sattarov). ⇨ **EŞ + BAQ.** See also **İŞ-QARA.**

İŞ-BARS see **EŞ-BARS**

İŞ-BERDİ Bashk. 1695 **İš-berde** [Ишберда Черебаев], from Ufa (MIB I, 91); Bashk. 1777 **İš-berde** [Ишберда (Ишбурда) Кутлугильдин] (MIB V, 65); Tat.(Sib.)? 1580 **İš-berde / İš-berdey** [Ишбёрдёй], a prince (Sib. Let. (Rem.) 337); Crm. 1653 **İš-berdi-behadïr** [اشبـردى بهادر] (Vel.-Zern., Crim. 322); Crm.(Tat.) 1493 **İš-berdi**, a baχšï / χafïz of the Golden Horde (Vásáry 54); Bashk. 1790 **İš-berdi** [Исергап Ишбердин] (MIB V, 275); Bashk. 1793 **İš-berdi** [Утей Ишбердин] (MIB V, 329); Tat. 20th c. **İš-birde** [Ишбирде] (Sattarov); Bashk. 20th c. **İš-birδe** [Ишбирзе / Ишбирди] (Kusimova); Chuv. 18th-19th c. **İš-perde** [Ишперда] (Magn. 48); Tat. 1716 **İš-perde** [Ишперда Ишелин] (MIB III, 139); Bashk. 1732 **İš-perde** [Ишперда Баканов] (MIB III, 302); Bashk. 1753 **İš-perde** [Ишперда Ишмурзин] (MIB IV/1, 68); Chuv. 18th-19th c. **İš-pirdä / İš-pirdäy** [Ишпирдай] (Magn. 48); Chuv. 18th-19th c. **İš-pirde** [Ишпирда] (Magn. 48); Chuv. 18th-19th c. **İš-pirte** [Ишпирта] (Magn. 48). ✧ 'Son, helper was born' (Sattarov), 'Mate, fellow, helper was given'. ⇨ **EŞ + BERDİ.**

İŞ-BİRDE see **İŞ-BERDİ**

İŠ-BİRÐE see **İŠ-BERDİ**

İŠ-BOLDÏ see **EŠ-BOLDÏ**

İŠ-BUQA   Uyg. **İš-buγa** [İş buġa] (EUTS); Uyg. 12th c. - 14th c. **İš-buqa** (Radl., USp. 16-17). ⇨ **EŠ + BUQA.**

İŠ-BUL see **EŠ-BOL**

İŠ-BULA   Bashk. 1682 **İš-bula** [Дементликайко Ижбулаевъ] (AI V, 139); Kzk. 19th c. **İš-bula** [Ишбула] (Grod., Pril. 65). ✧ 'He is a mate/helper' cf. Türk, Chag., Kar., Kzk., Trkm., Uzb., etc. *bol-* 'sein, werden' (Radl. IV, 1669), Tat. *bul-* 'sein, werden' (Radl. IV, 1835). ⇨ **EŠ.** See also **EŠ-BOL.**

İŠ-BULDÏ see **EŠ-BOLDÏ**

İŠ-BUTA   Uzb. 19th c. **İš-buta** [Ишбутиновъ] (SKSO III, 10); Kzk. / Kirg.? 19th c. **İš-buta** [Ишбутиновъ] (SKSO III, 10). ✧ 'Mate-young-camel; (fig.) mate-darling'. ⇨ **EŠ + BOTA.**

İŠ-DÄWLÄT   Kzk. 19th c. **İs-täwlet** [Иставлетъ] (Grod., Pril. 66); Tat. 20th c. **İš-däwlät** [Ишдәүләт] (Sattarov); Bashk. 1664 **İš-däwlät** [Иждевлетко Кабанов] (MIB I, 192); Bashk. 1790 **İš-däwlät** [Иждевлеть Мухаметев] (MIB V, 295); Bashk. 20th c. **İš-däwlät** [Ишдәүләт / Ищдавлет] (Kusimova); Tat. 1681 **İš-däwlät(ka)** [Иждевлетка], fem. (Kurdjumov 16); Bashk. 1790 **İš-täwlät** [Иштевлет Мухаммедев] (MIB V, 254). ✧ 'Mate-Chance/Luck'? cf. Kzk. PN *Es-däwlet* (Žanuzakov-Esbaeva). ⇨ **EŠ + DÄWLÄT.**

İŠ-KEREY   Chuv. 18th-19th c. **İš-kerey** [Ишкерей] (Magn. 48). ⇨ **EŠ + KERÄY.**

İŠ-KİL   Chuv. 18th-19th c. **İš-kil** [Ишкилъ] (Magn. 48); Tat. 20th c. **İš-kil** [Ишкил] (Sattarov). ✧ 'Friend (mate), be born!' (Sattarov). ⇨ **EŠ + KEL.**

İŠ-KİLDİ see **EŠ-KELDİ**

İŠ-KÜZÄ see **EŠ**

İŠ-QARA see **EŠ-QARA**

İŠ-QUWAT   Bashk. 20th c. **İš-qïwat** [Ишкыуат / Ишкуват] (Kusimova); Bashk. 1735 **İš-quwat** [Ишкуватъ Беккуловъ], a tarχan (Vel.-Zern., Bašk. 19); Bashk. 1751 **İš-quwat** [Ишкуат Тоймасов] (MIB IV/1, 34); Tat. 20th c. **İš-quwät** [Ишкуатов] (Sattarov). ⇨ **EŠ + QUWAT.**

İŠ-МАГМЕТ see **İŠ-MAMET**

İŠ-MAMET   1542 **İš-maγmet** [Ишмагметъ-мырза] (PSRL XIII, 143); Bashk. 1677, 1678 **İš-mamet** [Ишмаметь], a tarχan (AI V, 29, DAI IX, 92-93); Bashk. 1735 **İš-mamet** [Ишмаметъ Юсуповъ], a tarχan (Vel.-Zern., Bašk. 20); Tat. 20th c. **İš-mämät** [Ишмәмәт] (Sattarov); Chuv. 18th-19th c. **İš-memet** [Ишмеметъ / Ишмеметь] (Magn. 48). ⇨ **EŠ + MAMET.**

İŠ-MÄMÄT see **İŠ-MAMET**

İŠ-MEMET see **İŠ-MAMET**

İŠ-PARİS see **EŠ-BARS**

İŠ-PARÏS see **EŠ-BARS**

İŠ-PARS see **EŠ-BARS**

İŠ-PATÏR see **EŠ**

İŠ-PERDE see **İŠ-BERDİ**

İŠ-PERDİ see **İŠ-BERDİ**

İŠ-PİRDE see **İŠ-BERDİ**

İŠ-POLDÏ see **EŠ-BOLDÏ**

İŠ-PULAY   Chuv. 1764 **İš-pulay** [Ишпулай Рысаев] (MIB IV/2, 103). ⇨ **İŠ-BULA** + dim. suff. *-y.*

İŠ-PULAT see **EŠ-BULAT**

İŠ-PULDÏ see **EŠ-BOLDÏ**

İŠ-SAY   Kkalp. 1740 **İš-say-batïr** [Ишсай-Батыръ] (Hanykov, Poezdka 19). ✧ 'Mate-Worthy/Steady?' cf. Kzk. *say* I. 'готовый, достойный' (KzRS). ⇨ **EŠ.**

İŠ-SAT   Trkm. 19th c. **İš-sat** [Ишсатъ] (Lomakin 39). ✧ 'Mate-Fortune'? ⇨ **EŠ + SAT.**

İŠ-TÄWLÄT see **İŠ-DÄWLÄT**

İŠ-TEKEY   Bashk. 1738 **İš-tekäy** [Иштекай Кукчеев] (MIB III, 387); Chuv. 18th-19th c. **İš-tekey** [Иштекей] (Magn. 48). ⇨ **EŠ + TEKEY.**

İŠ-TERÄK   Tat. 1693 **İš-teräk** [Давыдко Иштеряков], resident in Kazan (MIB I, 84); Tat. 1764 **İš-teräk** [Иштеряк Утеганов] (MIB IV/2, 106); Tat. 1768 **İš-teräk** [Колманъ Иштеряковъ] (Nikol'skij 271); Bashk. 1757 **İš-teräk** [Канзяш Иштеряков] (MIB IV/1, 157); Nog. 1614 **İš-terek** [Иштерекъ], a Noγay (AI III, 12, 22-25, 411-414 etc.); Nog. 1649 **İš-terek** [Чебанъ мурза Иштерековъ], a murza (AI IV, 97, 100); Nog. 1651 **İš-terek** [Иштерекъ] (PSZRI I, 248); Tat. 1681 **İš-tiräk** [ايشتيراك / Иштиräк] (Jusupov (text) 10); Tat. 20th c. **İš-tiräk** [Иштирәков] (Sattarov). ✧ 'Friend-supporter'; Traditionally twin brothers were called *İš-tiräk* and *Quš-tiräk* (Sattarov). ⇨ **EŠ + TİRÄK.**

İŠ-TEREK see **İŠ-TERÄK**

İŠ-TİMER   Tat. 1695 **İs-temir** [Истемир] (MIB I, 90); Chuv. 18th-19th c. **İš-timer** [Иштимеръ] (Magn. 48); Tat. 20th c. **İš-timer** [Иштимер] (Sattarov); Chuv. 18th-19th c. **İš-timir** [Иштимыръ] (Magn. 48). ✧ 'Let the son be as hard (strong) as iron' (Sattarov). ⇨ **EŠ + TEMİR.**

İŠ-TİRÄK see **İŠ-TERÄK**

İŠ-TUΓAN   Tat. 18th-19th c. **İš-tuγan** [Иштуганъ] (Magn. 48); Tat. 20th c. **İš-tuγan** [Иштуган] (Sattarov); Bashk. 1740 **İš-tuγan** [Иштуган] (MIB I, 381); Bashk. 1756 **İš-tuγan** [Иштуган Мешаров] (MIB IV/1, 111); Bashk. 1759 **İš-tuγan** [Иштуган Мещерев] (MIB IV/2, 382); Bashk. 1762 **İš-tuγan** [Иштуган Мишаров] (MIB IV/1, 246); Bashk. 1787 **İš-tuγan** [Исергап Иштуганов] (MIB V, 203); Bashk. 20th c. **İš-tuγan** [Иштуган] (Kusimova). ✧ 'A friend, mate (of the other sons) is born' (Sattarov). ⇨ **EŠ + TUΓAN I.**

İŞ-TUQAY Tat. 20th c. **İš-tuqay** [Иштукай] (Sattarov); Bashk. 1772 **İš-tuqay** [Иштукай Ялмятев] (MIB IV/2, 408). ⇨ **EŠ** + **TOQAY.**

İŞAN Trkm. 19th c. **İšan** [Ишанъ] (Lomakin 39); Kzk. 19th c. **İšan-bay** [Ашмурадъ Ишанбаевъ] (Grod., Pril. 133); Kzk. 19th c. **İšan-bek** [Ишанбекъ] (Grod., Pril. 130); Kzk. 19th c. **İšan-qul** [Ишанкулъ] (SKSO VIII, 207); Kzk. 19th c. **İšan-qul** [Ишанкулъ] (SKSO IV, otd. II, 32); Trkm. 20th c. **İšān** [Išan] (Zaj. 1971, 326); Trkm. 20th c. **İšān** [Ишан] (TrkmRS 365). ✧ I. 'Believe!; Be a believer' cf. Chag., East. T. *išan-* 'glauben, Zutrauen haben, goffen auf' (Radl. I, 1550); II. 'A religious leader of higher rank at the muslims; teacher of a religious community' (A religious dignity). Used also as a component of personal names.

İŞAN-TAY Kzk. 19th c. **İšan-tay** [Ишантай] (SOK 232). ⇨ **İŠAN** + **TAY** or suff. *-tay(1,2)*?

İŞBİT Kzk. 19th c. **İšbit** [Ишбитъ] (AOP 34).

İŞČÄN Uyg. 13th c. **İščän** [iščän] (DTS). ✧ 'Diligent; hard worker' cf. Uyg., Karakh. *iš* 'дело, работа' (DTS) + suff. *-čän.*

İŞÄNÄY Kzk. 1629 **İšänäy** [Išänäi], a Kazak prince in Siberia (Radl., Aus Sib. I, 183). ⇨ **İŠAN** + suff. *-äy.*

İŞEY Tat.(Sib.) 1645 **İčey / İšey?** [Ичей] (Miller, Ist. Sib. II, 512); Tat. 16th c. - 17th c. **İšäy** [Ишәев / Ишеев] (Sattarov); Kzk. 19th c. **İšäy** [Ишай] (AOP 66); Trkm. 19th c. **İšey** [Муса Ишеевъ] (Ščeglov I, 351); Tat. 16th c - 17th c. **İšey** [Išej Barašev], a Tatar prince in Mordovia (Smyrnov 279); Tat. 1708 **İšey** [Ишей Кашкарин], a Tatar from Astrakhan (MIB I, 219); Bashk. 1735 **İšey** [Ишей] (MIB III, 343); Bashk. 1735 **İšey** [Абдикей Ишеевъ], a tarχan (Vel.-Zern., Bašk. 21); Bashk. 1736 **İšey** [Ишей Чюрюков] (MIB III, 344); Bashk. 1754 **İšey** [Ишей Шакарымбетев] (MIB IV/1, 85); Bashk. 1756 **İšey** [Ишкильда Ишеев] (MIB IV/1, 123); Bashk. 1756 **İšey** [Алимгул Ишеев] (MIB IV/1, 123); Bashk. 1756 **İšey** [Азигул Ишеев] (MIB IV/1, 123); Bashk. 1788 **İšey** [Валиш Ишеев] (MIB V, 238); Bashk. 1790 **İšey** [Салих Ишеев] (MIB V, 288); Kzk. 1666 **İšey** [Еренякъ Ишеевъ] (DAI V, 40-44); Kzk. 1666 **İšey** [Ябялякъ Ишеевъ], a prince (DAI V, 43, VII, 341); Tat. 1645 **İšey / İčey?** [Ичей] (Miller, Ist. Sib. II, 512). ✧ I. 'Little fellow, mate, son'; II. 'Multiply! Breed!' (Sattarov), cf. Tat. *išäy-* 'viel werden, sich vermehren' (Radl. I, 1552). ⇨ **EŠ?** + dim. suff. *-ey.*

İŞEM see **İŞİM**

İŞİ-BAY see **EŠİ**

İŞİBAN Tat.(Sib.) 1564 **İšiban** [Ишибанъ], a Siberian sultan (DAI I, 170).

İŞİG Uyg. **İšig** [İşig], fem. (EUTS).

İŞİK-TUĞLİ Kipch. **İšik-tuγlï** [Ишик-Туглы], Kipchak's descendant (successor?) (RaD I, 1, 96).

İŞİKÄY see **EŠKÄY**

İŞİM Tat. 1537 **İšim** [Ишимъ князь], a prince from Astrakhan (PSRL XIII, 120); Tat. 1623 **İšim** [Карабаш Ишимов] (Miller, Ist. Sib. II, 300, 435); Tat. 1764 **İšim** [Ишим Сеитов] (MIB IV/1, 287); Tat. 1776 **İšim** [Амиръ Ишимовъ] (PSZRI XX, 456); Tat./Bashk. 1723 **İšim** [тептер Ишим Кинзеев], a Teptär (MIB III, 212); Bashk. 1735 **İšim** [Ишимъ Кызыкуртовъ], a tarχan (Vel.-Zern., Bašk. 20); Bashk. 1738 **İšim** [Спир Ишимов] (MIB III, 378); Bashk. 1744 **İšim** [Ишим Кансуяров] (MIB III, 415); Bashk. 1761 **İšim** [Бакир Ишимов] (MIB IV/1, 204); Kzk. 1635 **İšim**, a Kazak-kirgiz khan (Radl., Aus Sib. I, 194); Kzk. 18th c. **İšim** [Ишимъ], Nurali's son (Nepljuev 798); Kzk. 1832 **İšim** [Ишимъ Ючинъ] (Konšin, Mat. I-III, 34); Kzk. 1846 **İšim** [Ишимовъ] (Konšin, Mat. V, 91); Kzk. 19th c. **İšim** [Ишимъ] (Grod., Pril. 25); Kzk. 19th c. **İšim-bay** [Ишимбай Саксанбаевъ] (SKSO VIII, 221); Uzb. 19th c. **İšim** [Ишимъ] (SKSO III, 156); Kkalp. 18th c. **İšim / Ešim** [Ишим (Эшим)], a Karakalpak khan, Küčük (Qučuq?)'s relative (MIKk. 57); Tat.(Sib.) 1582, 1601-1631 **İšim / İšim?** [Ышимъ / Ишим], one of Küčüm-qan's sons (Sib. Let. (Esip.) 282, Miller, Ist. Sib. II, 166, 234-38, 300, 435, Radl., Aus Sib. I, 151); Bashk. 1714 **İšim-bay** [Ишим-бай Утемышев] (MIB I, 105); Kzk.? 1744 **İšim-bay** [Елдашъ Ишимбаевъ], a rebel (Nepljuev 217); Bashk. 1633 **İšim-bay? / İšin-bay?** [Ишинбайко (Ишимбайко, Шинбайко, Ышинбайко) Кулушев], a captain (MIB I, 70); Bashk. 1758 **İšim-bay? / İšin-bay?** [Кузметь Ишинбаев] (MIB IV/1, 169); Uzb. 16th c. **İšim-bi** [بی ایشم / Ischim-Bi], from Khiva (Abulg./Desm. 281); Bashk. 1756 **İšim-čura** [Ишимчура Баимбетев] (MIB IV/1, 122); Kzk. 1809 **İšim-χan** [Ишимъ ханъ] (Dobrosm., Turg. 250); Kzk. 1809 **İšim-χan** [خان ایشم] (MIK IV, 242); Uzb. 1717 **İšim-χoja** [Ишимъ-Ходжа (Хаджа)], from Khiva (ZIRGO IX, 324); Uzb. 1865 **İšim-χoja** [Ишимъ ходжа] (Moskal'cev 60); Kzk. 1795-1797 **İšim-qan / İšim-χan** [Išim kan / Ишим-Ханъ], a khan of the Kiši-žüz (PSZRI XXVII, 140, Radl., Aus Sib. I, 198); Kkalp. 1740 **İšim-murza** [Ишимъ-Мурза] (Hanykov, Poezdka 19); Kzk. 1782 **İšim-saltan?** [Ишимъ-Салтанъ] (PSZRI XXI, 406, XXII, 143, Nepljuev 791); *TN:* Bashk. **İšimbayeva** [Ишимбаева], a village (Karta JAR 3); Bashk. **İšimčurina** [Ишимчурина], a village in the Ural mountains (Karta JAR 3). ✧ I. 'My mate, my friend, my companion'; II. Shortened-contracted form of PN *İš-muχammed.* ⇨ **EŠ** + suff. *-m/-im.*

İŞİM-ČUWAQ Kkalp. **İšim-čuwaq** [Ишим-Чювак Девлетгиреев], a Karakalpak sultan (MIB I, 492). ⇨ **İŠİM.**

İŞİM-MUXAMET Kkalp. 1722 **İšim-muχamet-χan** [Ишимъ Мугаметъ Ханъ / Ишим Мухаммед], a

Karakalpak khan (PSZRI VI, 777, 779, MIKk. 58). ⇨
IŠIM + MUXAMMED.

IŠIRÄ   Uyg. 12th c. - 14th c. **Iširä** [iširä / İşirä] (DTS, EUTS).

IŠKÄY see **EŠKEY**

IŠKENEY   Bashk. 1791 **İškeney** [Ишкеней Ишметов] (MIB V, 307). ✦ 'Little friend/mate' cf. also Tat. PN *İškenä* (Sattarov). ⇨ **EŠKEN** + suff. -*ey*.

IŠKİ   Bashk. 1735 **İški** [Ишки Аслаевъ], a tarχan (Vel.-Zern., Bašk. 17).

IŠKİN   Kzk. 19th c. **İškim-bay** (<**İškin-bay**) [Кулъ Магомедъ Молла Ишкимбаевъ] (Grod., Pril. 91); Tat. 1724 **İškin** [Юмакай Ишкин] (MIB III, 227). ⇨ **EŠ** + suff. -*ken*. See also **IŠKİNÄ**.

IŠKİNÄ   Kzk. 19th c. **Eskene** [Ескене] (AOK 134); Kzk. 19th c. **Eskene** [Ескене] (AOA 26); Tat. 20th c. **İškenä** [Ишкенин] (Sattarov); Bashk. 20th c. **İškenä** [Ишкенə / Ишкина] (Kusimova); ⇨ **İŠ**. Tat. 1731 **İškinä** [Юней Ишкикин(!)], cf. Tat. İškenä < İškenin by Sattarov (MIB III, 293); Bashk. 1702 **İškinä** [Ишкиня (Ишкине)] (MIB III, 16, 18); Bashk. 1713 **İškinä** [Минлиш Ишкинин] (MIB III, 103); Bashk. 1730 **İškinä** [Якшигул Ишкинин] (MIB III, 280); Bashk. 1751 **İškinä** [Ишкиня Урузбаев] (MIB IV/1, 51); Bashk. 1753 **İškinä** [Усман Ишкинин] (MIB IV/1, 68); Bashk. 1754 **İškinä** [Ишкиня Азметев] (MIB IV/1, 79); Bashk. 1756 **İškinä** [Ишкине Кадырметев] (MIB IV/1, 113); Bashk. 1764 **İškinä** [Ишкиня Мустаев] (MIB IV/1, 276); Bashk. 1764 **İškinä** [Ишкиня Ишмамбетев] (MIB IV/1, 285); Bashk. 1770, 1787 **İškinä** [Ишкиня Минлибаев] (MIB IV/1, 343, V, 219). ✦ 'Little friend/mate'. ⇨ **EŠ** + hypoc. suff. -*kinä* / -*kenä*.

IŠKİNÄY   Bashk. 1740 **İškinäy** [Артикей Ишкинеев] (MIB I, 427). ⇨ **IŠKİNÄ** + suff. -*y*.

IŠMAY   Tat. 1724 **İšmay** [Канбой Ишмаев] (MIB III, 228). ✦ Dialectal [shortened] variant of *İš-möχämmät* (Sattarov). ⇨ **EŠ** + **MUXAMMED.** See also **EŠ-MAQAMBET.**

IŠMAN   Tat. 20th c. **İšman** [Ишманов] (Sattarov); Uzb. 19th c. **İšman** [Ишманъ] (SKSO III, 22); Uzb. 19th c. **İšman** [Сафарбай Ишмановъ] (SKSO III, 162); Bashk. 1709 **İšmen** [Ишмен] (MIB III, 49); Bashk. 1754 **İšmen** [Максют Ишменев] (MIB IV/1, 79); Bashk. 1754, 1761 **İšmen** [Минлибай Ишменев] (MIB IV/1, 79, 204); Bashk. 1756 **İšmen** [Ишмен Кущигулов] (MIB IV/1, 123); Bashk. 1770 **İšmen** [Темир Ишменов] (MIB IV/1, 342); Bashk. 1780 **İšmen** [Ишмен] (MIB V, 116); Bashk. 1792 **İšmen** [Халил Ишменов] (MIB V, 559). ✦ 'Mate, pair; equal' (Sattarov). ⇨ **EŠ** + suff. -*man* / -*men*.

IŠMAT   Kzk. 19th c. **İšmat** [Ишматовъ] (SKSO VIII, 207); Kzk. 19th c. **İšmat** [Ишматъ] (SKSO VIII, 223); Uzb. 20th c. **İšmat** [Ichmat Baïbatcha], a basmačï from Ferghana (Castagné 81); Tat.(Sib.) 1681 **İšmet** [Чумичка Ишметевъ] (DAI VIII, 177); Bashk. 1735 **İšmet** [Алемъ Ишметевъ], a tarχan (Vel.-Zern., Bašk. 17); Bashk. 1735 **İšmet** [Ишметъ Юсуповъ], a tarχan (Vel.-Zern., Bašk. 22); Bashk. 1738 **İšmet** [Чепкен Ишметев] (MIB I, 145). ✦ I. 'Fellow Mukhammed' shortened of *İš-muχammed* (Sattarov); II. 'Respect'? cf. Uyg. *išmät* 'Hochachtung' (Radl. I, 1563) (<Ar.) ⇨ **EŠ** + suff. -*mat*. See also **IŠMET, IŠMAMET.**

IŠMÄY   Bashk. 1785 **İšmäy** / **İšmey?** [Рахмангул Ишмеев] (MIB V, 558). ✦ Shortened-contracted form of Tat. *İš-möχämmät* (Sattarov) or Bashk. *İš-möχämät* (Kusimova), see headwords İš-mamet, İš-mämät, Eš-maqambet + suff. -*(ä)y*.

IŠMÄK   Tat. 1768 **İšmäk** [Ураз Ишмаковъ], from the protectorate of Tambov (Nikol'skij 274); Bashk. 1701 **İšmäk** [Деветка Ишмяковъ], a tarχan (Vel.-Zern., Bašk. 29); Bashk. 1734 **İšmäk** [Асан Ишмяков] (MIB III, 325); Bashk. 1740 **İšmäk** [Ишмок Кусяков] (MIB I, 396); Trkm. 1881 **İšmek-bay** [Ишмекъ-Бай] (Grod., Pril. 18). ✦ Shortened-contracted form of Tat. *İš-möχämmät* (Sattarov) or Bashk. *İš-möχämät* (Kusimova), see headwords İš-mamet, İš-mämät, Eš-maqambet + suff. -*(ä)y*.

IŠMEK see **IŠMÄK**

IŠMEKEY   Bashk. 1735 **İšmekey** [Ишмекей Куреев], a tarχan (Vel.-Zern., Bašk. 23); Bashk. 1707 **İšmikey** [Ишмикей Богданов] (MIB III, 31). ✦ Shortened-contracted form of Tat. *İš-möχämmät* (Sattarov), see headwords İš-mamet, İš-mämät, Eš-maqambet + suff. -*key*.

IŠMEN see **IŠMAN**

IŠMENEY   Bashk. 1791 **İšmeney** [Ишкул Ишменеев] (MIB V, 301). ⇨ **IŠMAN** + suff. -*ey*.

IŠMET see **IŠMAT**

IŠMETDİN   Nog. 20th c. **İšmetdin-äfendi** / **İsmetdin-efendi** [Мухаммет Иймин Ишметдин Аьфенди улы Къарас / Мухаммед-Имин Исметдин Эфенди Карасов], father of one of Baskakov's informants from the aul of Erkin-χalq, Cherkess Autonomous Oblast' (Bask., Nog. 143, 158). ⇨ **İŠİM** + comp. *eddin*.

IŠMİKEY see **IŠMEKEY**

IŠTAN   Bashk. 1755 **İštan** [Иштан Унгаров] (MIB I, 101). ✦ I. 'Mate of dawn (friend/child born at dawn)' cf. Tat. PN *İš-tañ* (Sattarov); II. 'Under-pants'? cf. Chag. *ištan* 'die Unterhosen' (Radl. I, 1561).

IŠTÄMİ   Türk 6th c. **İštämi-qaγan** [Στεμβισχάγαν] (Byz. Turc. 291).

IŠTEY   Bashk. 1772 **İštey** [Иштей] (MIB IV/1, 364); Bashk. 1794 **İštey** [Абдулгафер Иштеев] (MIB V, 339). ✦ 'Friendly; mate-like' cf. Tat. PN *İštay*

(Sattarov). ⇨ **EŠ** + suff. *-tey*. See also **İŠTEK**.

İŠTEK   Bashk. 1664 **İštäk** [Иштяк Карагызов] (MIB I, 186); Bashk. 1764 **İštäk** [Девлетбай Иштяков] (MIB IV/1, 291); Bashk. 1777 **İštäk** [Сарыгул Иштаков] (MIB V, 57); Tat. 1706 **İštek** [Иштек Байбулатов] (MIB III, 24); Kzk. 19th c. **İštek-pay** [Иштекпай] (SOV 68); Bashk. 1723 **İštik** [Батыркей Иштыков] (MIB III, 217). ✦ 'Friendly'. ⇨ **EŠ** + suff. *-tek*. See also **İŠTEY**.

İŠTEMİ see **İSTÄMİ**

İŠTİM   Uzb. 19th c. **İštim** [Худай Назаръ Иштымовъ] (SKSO III, 168).

İT   Bashk. 1754 **İt-bay** [Итбай Канчюрин] (MIB IV/1, 83); Bashk. 1757 **İt-bay** [Ярман Итбаев] (MIB IV/1, 150, 153); Bashk. 1761 **İt-bay** [Рякай Итбаев] (MIB IV/1, 218); Bashk. 1763 **İt-bay** [Балтясь Итбаев] (MIB IV/1, 259); Bashk. 1792 **İt-bay** [Итбай Азнабаев] (MIB V, 328); Bashk. 1793 **İt-bay** [Итбай Азнабаев] (MIB V, 328); Kzk. 19th c. **İt-bay** [Итбай] (AOK 70); Kzk. 19th c. **İt-bay** [Итбай] (AOK 138); Kzk. 19th c. **İt-bay** [Итбай] (AOO 46); Kzk. 19th c. **İt-bay** [Итбай] (SOV 124); Kzk. 19th c. **İt-čan** (<İt-žan) [Итчанъ] (SODž. 160); Kzk. 19th c. **İt-ǰan** [Итджанъ] (SOK 4); Kzk. 19th c. **İt-ǰigit** [Итджигитъ] (SOK 272); Kzk. 19th c. **İt-eke** [Итеке] (SOK 208); Crm. 16th c. **İt-χoǰa** [Итъ-ходжа] (Smirnov, Krym. 422); Tat. 1690 **İt-qul** [Иткулка] (Kungursk. akty 179); Bashk. 1695 **İt-qul** [Иткулов] (MIB I, 85-86); Bashk. 1732 **İt-qul** [Иткул] (MIB III, 299); Bashk. 1734 **İt-qul** [Иткулъ] (Vel.-Zern., Bašk. 10); Bashk. 1735 **İt-qul** [Иткулъ Янымбетевъ], a tarχan (Vel.-Zern., Bašk. 13); Bashk. 1761 **İt-qul** [Иткул Балташев] (MIB IV/1, 227); Bashk. 1780 **İt-qul** [Иткул Бекбовов] (MIB V, 116, 263); Kzk. 1846 **İt-qul** [Иткул Баубеков], a biy (MKOP 157); Maml. 1313 **İt-oγlï** / **İt-oγlu** [ايت أغلى] (Dawād. 274); Kuman 1190, 1193 **İt-oγlï** / **İt-ulï?** [Итоглый (Итогды) / Итылый], a Lukomorskiy Polovets (Ipat. 452, 454, PSRL II, 675); Kzk. 19th c. **İt-pay** [Итпай] (SOK 230); Kzk. 19th c. **İt-pay** [Итпай] (SOV 88); Kzk. 19th c. **İt-pay** [Итпай] (AOP 34); Uyg. **İt-tarχan** [İt Tarḫan] (EUTS); Uyg. 8th c. - 12th c. **İt-tarχan** (Müller, Pfahl. 10); Kzk. 19th c. **İt-žan** [Итжанъ] (AOO 18). ✦ 'Dog' cf. Uyg., Chag., Kuman, Alt., Az., Hak., Turk. etc. *it* 'der Hund' (Radl. I, 1498), Kzk. *iyt* 'it' (KzTS).

İT-AY   Kzk. 19th c. **İt-ay** / **İtäy?** [Итай] (AOK 130). ⇨ **İT + AY.**

İT-AYAQ   Bashk.? **İt-ayaq** [Куты-баръ Ить-аяковъ] (ZVOIRAO X, 194); Bashk. 1778 **İt-ayaq** [Итаяк] (MIB V, 79); Bashk. 1798 **İt-ayaq** [Сафар (Сафер) Итаяков] (MIB V, 79); Kzk. 19th c. **İt-ayaq** [Итаякъ] (SODž. 6); Kzk. 19th c. **İt-ayaq** [Итаякъ] (Grod. I,

98); Kzk. 19th c. **İt-ayaq** [Ить-аякъ] (Pantusov, Kirg. 39). ✦ 'Dog('s)-leg'. ⇨ **İT + AYAQ.**

İT-ALMAZ   Trkm. 20th c. **İt-almaz** [Italmaz] (Zaj. 1971, 334); Uzb. 20th c. **İt-âlmas** [Итолмас] (Begmatov 1984, 203). ✦ 'The dog won't take him' (Samojlovič 1911; Gordlevskij 1913, p. 132). The newborn is put in the place of the dog. If the dog does not hurt him/her, the evil spirits will not hurt him/her either (Kusimova 1971, p. 53). ⇨ **İT + ALMAZ.** See also **İT-ĴEMÄS.**

İT-BARAQ   Oghuz/Trkm. 13th c. **İt-baraq-χan** [خان براق / Ит-Барак-хан] (Abulg./Kon. 275, 330). ⇨ **İT + BARAQ.**

İT-BAS see **İT-BAŠ**

İT-BAŠ   Alt. 19th-20th c. **İyt-baš** [Ийт-Баш] (OjrRS 208); Alt. 19th-20th c. **İyt-baš** [Ийт-Баш] (OjrRS 208); Kzk. **İt-bas** [Итъ-бас] (Kustanaev 37); Bashk. 1777 **İt-baš** [Итбаш Сюярымбетев] (MIB V, 52); Kzk. 19th c. **İt-pas** [Итпасъ] (AOK 2); Kzk. 19th c. **İt-pas** [Итпасъ] (SOV 120); Kzk. 19th c. **İte-bas** (<İt-bas?) [Итебасъ] (SOV 62); Kzk. 19th c. **İtï-bas** (<İt-bas?) [Итыбасъ] (SOK 50). ✦ 'Dog's head'. ⇨ **İT + BAŠ.**

İT-BÄRT   Türk 7th-9th c. **İt-bärt** / **İrt-bärt?** [İt Bärt] (ETY II, 137). ✦ 'A kind of tax'? (DTS).

İT-BOQ   Bashk. 1761 **İt-boq** [Итбок Чакыров] (MIB IV/1, 214). ✦ 'Dog's excrement (shit)'. ⇨ **İT + BOQ.** See also **QOMUQ.**

İT-ĴEMÄS   Kzk. 18th c. **Et-ǰimäs** / **Aǰimäs?** [Аджимясъ] (Nepljuev 717); Bashk. 1777 **İ-ǰimäs** (<İt-ǰimäs) [Расул (Рясулъ) Иджимасов] (Vel.-Zern., Bašk. 3, MIB V, 545); Bashk. 1783 **İ-ǰimäs** (<İt-ǰimäs) [Девлеткул Иджимясов] (MIB V, 149); Bashk. 1798 **İǰimäs** (<İt-ǰimäs) [Иджимясовъ] (PSZRI XXV, 196); Bashk. 1756 **İd-zimäs** (<İt-dzimäs) [Букчи Идзимясов] (MIB IV/1, 123); Bashk. 1735 **İdzimäs** (<İt-dzimäs) [Сюнчали Идзимясов], a tarχan (Vel.-Zern., Bašk. 20); Bashk. 1737 **İdzimäs** (<İt-dzimäs) [Идзимас] (MIB I, 331); Bashk. 1756 **İdzimäs** (<İt-dzimäs) [Сатубалды Идзимясов] (MIB IV/1, 123); Bashk. 1756 **İdzimäs** (<İt-dzimäs) [Албяк Идзимясов] (MIB IV/1, 123); Kkalp. 20th c. **İyt-ǰemes** [Ийтджемес] (Bask., Kkalp. 400); Kkalp. 20th c. **İyt-žemes** [Ийтжемес] (KkRS 774); Kzk. 19th c. **İt-šemes** [ايتشما س / Итчемисъ] (Veselovskij, Kirg. 72 /117/); Bashk. 1756 **İt-zimes** [Сатып Итзимесов] (MIB IV/1, 107); Bashk. 1756 **İt-zimes** [Букча Итзимесов] (MIB IV/1, 107); Bashk. 1757 **İt-žimäs** [Исмакай Изжимасов] (MIB IV/1, 151); Bashk. 1776 **İ-ǰimäs** (<İt-žimäs) [Итжимас (Иджимяс) Унданов (Ундадов)] (MIB V, 39, 40, 41). ✦ 'Dog won't eat (him)'. ⇨ **İT.**

İT-ĴİMÄS see **İT-ĴEMÄS**

İT-EMER Kkalp. 20th c. **İyt-emer** [Ийтемер] (KkRS 774); Kzk. 19th c. **İt-emär** [Итемаръ] (SODž. 122); Chuv. 18th-19th c. **İt-emer** [Идемеръ] (Magn. 41). ✧ 'Dog sucker' cf. Kzk. *em-* 'сосать' (KzRS). ⇨ **İT**. See also **MAY-EMER**.

İT-EMGÄN see **İT-EMGEN**

İT-EMGEN Bashk. 1675 **İt-emgän** [Итамген] (MIB I, 199); Bashk. 1708 **İt-emgän** [Итрмган Иркин] (MIB I, 216); Tat.(Sib.)? 1650 **İt-emgen** [чатский мурза Итегменъ] (Andrievič, Ist. Sib. I, 110); Kzk. **İt-emgen** [Сары Итемгеновъ] (Valihanov, Soč. 347); Kzk. 1824 **İt-emgen** [Итемгенъ] (Konšin, Mat. I-III, 6); Kzk. 1846 **İt-emgen** [бий Итемген Кутякаев] (MKOP 155); Kzk. 19th c. **İt-emgen** [Итемгенъ] (SOV 24); Kzk. 19th c. **İt-emgen** [Итемгенъ] (AOO 70); Kzk. 19th c. **İt-emgen** [Ить-эмгенъ] (Pantusov, Kirg. 39); Kzk. 19th c. **İt-eñmän (<İt-emgän)** [Итэнгмянъ] (Potanin II, 5); Kzk. 19th c. **İt-eñmen (<İt-emgen)** [Итэнгмэнъ] (Potanin II, 4); Bashk. 1756 **İt-imgän** [Итимган Айдакаев] (MIB IV/1, 120); Bashk. 1675 **İt-imgen** [Итимген Ишкозин] (MIB I, 199); *EN:* Kzk. 18th c. - 19th c. **İt-emgen** [Итемген] (Tynyšp. 67, 70, 72). ✧ '(He) sucked a/the dog' cf. Kzk. *em-* 'Emmek' (KzTS). ⇨ **İT**. See also **AT-EMGEN, MAY-EMER, MAY-İMGEN, TAT-EMGEN**.

İT-EÑMÄN see **İT-EMGEN**

İT-EÑMEN see **İT-EMGEN**

İT-ESKİN Kzk. 19th c. **İt-eskin** [Итескынъ] (AOO 14). ⇨ **İT**.

İT-İMGÄN see **İT-EMGEN**

İT-KEREY Chuv. 18th-19th c. **İt-kerey** [Иткерей] (Magn. 47). ⇨ **İT + KERÄY**.

İT-KÜČÜK Bashk. 18th c. **İt-küčük** [Иткучуков] (MIB V, 279); Bashk. 1770 **İt-küčük** [Айдагул Иткучуков] (MIB IV/1, 345); Bashk. 1787 **İt-küčük** [Иткучюк Сангушев] (MIB V, 214, 215); Bashk. 1740 **İt-küsük** [Бай-Булат Иткусюков] (MIB I, 395). ✧ 'Dog('s)-puppy'. ⇨ **İT + KÜČÜK**.

İT-KÜSÜK see **İT-KÜČÜK**

İT-QARA Tat.? 1357 **İt-qara** [Иткара], envoy from the Horde (PSRL X, 229); Kzk. 19th c. **İt-qara** [Иткара] (Potanin II, 3); Kzk. 19th c. **İt-qara** [Иткара] (SOV 30). ⇨ **İT + QARA**.

İT-QARİY Bashk. **İt-qariy** [Иткарий Ярамбетев] (MIB IV/1, 334). ⇨ **İT + QARAY?**

İT-QURUQ Tat.(Sib.) 1598 **İt-quruq** [Иткурюкъ] (AI II, 2). ⇨ **İT-QURUQ / QUYRUQ?**

İT-QUSTİ Bashk. 1706 **İt-qustï** [Каныкай Иткустин] (MIB III, 26); Bashk. 1734 **İt-qustï** [Иткусте], a tarχan (Vel. Zern., Bašk. 10); Bashk. 1740 **İt-qustï** [Жуанбай Иткустин] (MIB I, 440); Bashk. 1675 **İt-qustu** [Иткусту Ишпердин] (MIB I, 200). ✧ 'Dog-younger brother' cf. Bashk. *qustï* 'младший брат, братишка' (BRS/Uraksin). ⇨ **İT**.

İT-QUSTU see **İT-QUSTİ**

İT-PALÏQ Kzk. 19th c. **İt-palïq** [Итпалык] (AOK 2). ⇨ **İT + BALÏQ**.

İT-PAS see **İT-BAŠ**

İT-SEMİS see **İT-SEMİŠ**

İT-SEMİŠ Uyg. 8th c. - 12th c.? **İt-semiš / İt-semis? (<İt-semiz?)** [It-semis] (Müller, Pfahl. II). ⇨ **İT + SEMİŠ**.

İT-ŠEMES see **İT-JEMÄS**

İT-TİMES see **İT-TİMEZ**

İT-TİMEZ Bashk. 1675 **İt-times (<İt-timez)** [Иттимес Козубаев] (MIB I, 200). ✧ 'Dog won't touch (him)' cf. Kuman, Alt., Kar., Kirg., Kzk., Tat. *tī-* 'berühren, anrühren; treffen, erreichen' (Radl. III, 1343). ⇨ **İT**.

İT-ZİMES see **İT-JEMÄS**

İT-ŽİMÄS see **İT-JEMÄS**

İTÄČUQ Türk 8th c. - 9th c. **İtäčuq** [itäčuq / İtä-çuq] (DTS, ETY II, 91).

İTÄŠ Bashk. 1754 **İtäš** [Итяш Янкеев] (MIB IV, 83); Bashk. 1777 **İtäš** [Итяш Чатаев] (MIB V, 51); Nog. 1649 **İteš** [Ешбулдуй Итешевъ] (AI IV, 80). ✧ 'Puppy'. ⇨ **İT + dim. suff. -äš**.

İTE-BAS see **İT-BAŠ**

İTEY Chuv. 18th-19th c. **İtey** [Итей] (Magn. 47); Kzk. 19th c. **İtey** [Итей] (SODž. 140). ✧ 'Little dog, puppy'. ⇨ **İT + suff. -ey**.

İTEK Kzk. 19th c. **İtäk** [Итакъ] (SODž. 116); Chuv. 18th-19th c. **İtäk / İdek** [Итякъ (Идекъ)] (Magn. 47); Oghuz 815 **İtäk / İtek** [Itach, Inach, Itjach?], a Turkic chief in the service of the Abbasid caliphs al-Mamūn and al-Mutawakkil (Weil, Abbas II, 317, 239-40, 348-350); Kzk. 19th c. **İtek** [Итекъ] (SOV 150); Kuman 1283, 1284, **İtek / İtik** [Ityk / Itok / Itek], among the Kumans of Hungary (Gyárfás II, 447, 450, 459); Bashk. 1717 **İtik** [Итик Итеев] (MIB III, 147); Bashk. 1737 **İtik** [Мамаш Итыков] (MIB I, 319); Kzk. 19th c. **İtik-bay / İtïk-bay?** [Итыкбай] (SODž. 58); *TN:* Tat. 1522 **İtäk** [Итяково поле] (PSRL (Russk. Hr.) I, 538); Kzk. 19th c. **İtek** [Итекъ], a winter pasture (SOV 18). ✧ 'Puppy' cf. Maml. (Trkm.) *itük* 'Jung eines Hundes' (Tarǰ/Houtsma), cf. also Rásonyi, Adalékok 126, Rásonyi, KÖA 106, Rásonyi, Anthr. 140-41. ⇨ **İT + dim. suff. -ek**. See also **İT-KÜČÜK**.

İTEKEY Chuv. 18th-19th c. **İtekey** [Итекей] (Magn. 47); Chuv. 18th-19th c. **İtigey (<İtikey)** [Итигей] (Magn. 47); Bashk. 1770 **İtikey** [Итыкей Рахмангулов] (MIB IV/1, 343). ✧ I. 'Little puppy'?; II. 'Boots'? cf. Tat. *itek* 'сапог, сапоги' (TatRS). ⇨ **İTEK + dim. suff. -ey**. See also **İTKÄY**.

İTEM Kzk. 19th c. **İtem-bek** [Итембекъ] (SOV 56); Nog. 1649 **İtem-bek** [Итембекъ], a murza (AI IV, 123); Bashk. 1713 **İtim / İtïm?** [Итым Кангильдин]

(MIB III, 100); Kzk. 19th c. **İtim-qul / İttïm-qul?** [Иттымкулъ] (AOO 54). ✧ 'My dog'. ⇨ **İT?** + poss. suff. -*em*.

İTEN Kzk. 19th c. **İten** [Итенъ] (SOV 100); Kzk. 19th c. **İten** [Итенъ] (AOP 42).

İTEŠ see **İTÄŠ**

İTİ Bashk. 1754 **İti / İtiy?** [Жюнтай Итиев] (MIB IV/1, 84); Kzk. 19th c. **İti-bay / İtï-bay?** [Итыбай] (AOA 78); *TN:* Kzk. / Uzb. **İti-bay / İtï-bay** [Итыбай], a place south-west of Lake Aral (Karta JAR X).

İTİ-KÄN Uyg. **İti-kän** [İti-kän], Bögü-qaγan, an Uyghur ruler (US, EUTS). ⇨ **İTİ.**

İTİGEY see **İTEKEY**

İTİGİ Kzk. 19th c. **İtigi** [Итыги] (AOP 66).

İTİGİL Kzk. **İtigil** [Итыгиль] (ZIRGOGeogr. I, 526).

İTİX-BATA Bashk. 1675 **İtix-bata?** [Тентикей Итихбатин] (MIB I, 202).

İTİK see **İTEK**

İTİKEY see **İTEKEY**

İTİKŠA Bashk. 1723 **İtikša (<İtikši?)** [Итыкша Кутыев] (MIB III, 201). ✧ 'Boot-maker' cf. Tat. *itïkčï* 'id.' (Radl. I, 1503).

İTİM see **İTEM**

İTİNEY Bashk. 1745 **İtiney** [Итиней Килмаев] (MIB III, 548). ⇨ **İTEN?** + suff. -*ey*.

İTİ-BAS see **İT-BAŠ**

İTKÄY Tat.(Mish.) 18th c. **İtkäy** [Иткай] (Nepljuev 194); Kzk. 19th c. **İtkäy / İtgäy** [Итгай] (SOK 78); Chuv. 18th-19th c. **İtkey** [Иткей] (Magn. 47). ✧ 'Puppy'. ⇨ **İT** + dim. suff. -*käy*.

İTKE Bashk. 1706 **İtke** [Иткин] (MIB III, 27); Kzk. 19th c. **İtke** [Итке] (AOK 10). ⇨ **İT** + suff. -*ke*.

İTKİNÄ Bashk. 1675 **İtkinä** [Иткиня Кудашманов] (MIB I, 201); Bashk. 1711 **İtkinä** [Менеть Иткинин] (MIB III, 75); Bashk. 1713 **İtkinä** [Смаил Иткинин] (MIB III, 100); Bashk. 1735 **İtkinä** [Нурушъ Иткининъ], a tarγan (Vel.-Zern., Bašk. 25); Bashk. 1738 **İtkinä** [Иткиня Ксюков] (MIB III, 393); Bashk. 1740 **İtkinä** [Янгилда Иткинин] (MIB I, 396); Bashk. 1742 **İtkinä** [Иткине Аккучюков] (MIB I, 486); Bashk. 1742 **İtkinä** [Тиим-бай Иткинин] (MIB I, 486); Bashk. 1742 **İtkinä** [Иткине Сеитов] (MIB I, 486); Bashk. 1742, 1760 **İtkinä** [Таиш Иткинин] (MIB III, 513, IV/1, 200); Bashk. 1744 **İtkinä** [Брангул Иткинин] (MIB III, 415). ✧ 'Puppy'. ⇨ **İT** + dim. suff. -*kinä*.

İTKİNÄY Tat. 1668 **İtkinä / İtkinäy?** [Досайко Иткиняевъ] (Kungursk. akty 9). ✧ 'Little puppy'. ⇨ **İT / İTKİNÄ?** + suff. -*kinä* +-*y*.

İTMÄN 1612 **İtmän** [Итманка Байковъ] (Nižegorod. platež. 58, 213). ⇨ **İT** + suff. -*män*.

İTMİŠ Uyg. 762 **İtmiš** (Mahrnāmag 11); Uyg. 762

İtmiš-χatun, fem. (Mahrnāmag 15). See also **İL-İTMİŠ.**

İTPASLİN Hak. 19th-20th c. **İtpaslin** [Итпаслин] (HRS 349).

İTTİM see **İTEM**

İTÜKEY Bashk. 1782 **İtükey** [Итюкей Султанов] (MIB V, 132). ✧ 'Little puppy'. ⇨ **İTEK** + dim. suff. -*ey*.

İWAZ Turk. 1489-1490 **İwaz** [عواض / İvaz, veledi İsâ mahalle] (Gökb., Ed. 218). ✧ 'Backlog, reserve' cf. Turk. *ivaz* 'der Ersatz, die Ersatzgabe, das Entgelt' (HŞ).

İZ I. Kzk. 19th c. **İs-pek** [Испекъ] (SODž. 134); Kzk. 19th c. **İz-bay?** [Избой] (SOK 142). ✧ 'Footstep' cf. Kuman, Chag., Crm., Kar., Kirg., Kzk., Turk. *iz* 'die Spur' (Radl. I, 1536), Uyg., Alt. *is* 'id.' (Radl. I, 1524).

İZ II. see **ES**

İZ-BAΓAMBET Kkalp. 20th c. **İz-baγambet** [Избағамбет] (KkRS 774). ⇨ **İZ I.?** + **MUXAMMED.**

İZ-BAS Kzk. 1819 **İs-bas** [Исбасъ] (MIK IV 323); Kzk. 19th c. **İz-bas** [Избасъ] (SOK 196); Uzb. 20th c. **İz-bâs** [Избос] (Begmatov 1984, 201). ✧ 'Follow (your ancestors)'. ⇨ **İZ I.** + **BAS II.** See also **İZ-BASAR, İZ-BASAR, İZ-BASTÏ.**

İZ-BASAR Kzk. 19th c. **İs-basar** [Ишмурадъ Исбасаровъ] (SKSO VIII, 230); Kzk. 19th c. **İs-basar** [Сбасоръ] (SOK 250); Kzk. 19th c. **İz-basar** [Избасаръ] (SKSO III, 190); Kzk. 19th c. **İz-basar** [Збосаръ] (SODž. 14); Kzk. 19th c. **İz-basar** [Избсаръ] (SODž. 52); Kkalp. 20th c. **İz-basar** [Избасар] (KkRS 774). ✧ 'He will follow (his parents, ancestors); heir, successor' cf. Kzk. *iz(in) bas-* 'следовать за кем-либо' (KzRS). ⇨ **İZ I.** + **BASAR.** See also **İZ-BAS, İZ-BASQAN, İZ-BASTÏ.**

İZ-BASQAN Kkalp. 20th c. **İz-basqan** [Избасқан] (KkRS 774). ✧ 'He followed (us); he is our follower' cf. Türk, Kuman, Chag., Az., Crm., Kirg., Kzk., Tat., Trkm. etc. *bas-* 'drücken, pressen; unterdrücken, beherrschen, besiegen' (Radl. IV, 1525). ⇨ **İZ I.** + **BAS II.** See also **İZ-BAS, İZ-BASAR, İZ-BASTÏ.**

İZ-BASTÏ Uzb. 20th c. **İz-bâstï** [Избости] (Begmatov 1984, 201). ✧ 'He followed (us); he is our follower' cf. Türk, Kuman, Chag., Az., Crm., Kirg., Kzk., Tat., Trkm. etc. *bas-* 'drücken, pressen; unterdrücken, beherrschen, besiegen' (Radl. IV, 1525). ⇨ **İZ I.** + **BAS II.** See also **İZ-BAS, İZ-BASAR, İZ-BASQAN.**

İZ-BÂS see **İZ-BAS**

İZ-YAŠ Bashk. 1764 **İz-yaš / İðäš?** [Изъяш Каныбеков] (MIB IV/, 298). ⇨ **İZ I.** + **YAŠ?**

İZ-MUXAN Kkalp. 20th c. **İz-muχan** [Измухан] (KkRS 774). ⇨ **İZ I.?** + **MUQAN.**

İZ-TAY see **ES-TAY**

İZ-TELEK Crm. / Nog.? 1550 **İz-telek** [Изтелекъ], a

murza (PSRL (Russk. Hr.) I, 532). ⇨ İZ I.? + TİLEK.

İZAN see **ESÄN**

İZBAN Kkalp. 20th c. İzban [Избан] (KkRS 774).

İZJİ Yürük 1543 İzji [ایزجی / İzci] (Gökb., Ed. 208). ✧ 'Tracker; guide' cf. Turk. *izci* 'id.' (TED).

İZDEN Kkalp. 20th c. İzden [Изден] (KkRS 774).

İZÄN see **ESÄN**

İZÄN-GİLDE see **ESÄN-KELDİ**

İZEL Kzk. 19th c. İzel-bay [Изелбай] (SOK 236).

İZEN see **ESÄN**

İZEN-GİLDE see **ESÄN-KELDİ**

İZEREK Tat. 1651 İzerek [Кунестейко Изерековъ], a prince from the Mras region (AI IV, 148).

İZİMBET Kkalp. 20th c. İzimbet [Изимбет] (KkRS 774). ⇨ İSENBET?

İZMEN Tat. 1776 İzmen [Адилъ Изменевъ] (PSZRI XX, 456).

İZZET Uzb. 1873 İzed-bibi [Изедъ-Биби], fem. (Moskal'cev 38); Kzk. 19th c. İzzät-bibi [Иззатъ-биби] (Grod., Pril. 128); Trkm. 20th c. İzzat [İzzat] (Zaj. 1971, 328); Trkm. 20th c. İzzat [Ыззат] (TrkmRS 767). ✧ Izzat (Ar.) 'honour, fame, power' (Ahmed), cf. NUyg.(Tar.) *izät* 'die Ehrenbezeugung' (Radl. I, 1538), Uzb. *izzat* 'уважение' (UzbRS) (<Ar.).

İŽENEY Tat.(Sib.) 1642 İženey [Иженей], a prince (Andrievič I, 113); Kzk. 1652 İženey [Мергенъ Иженей] (DAI III, 379, 382); Kzk. 1659 İženey [Иженей], a princess (DAI IV, 179,). See also **MERGEN-İŽENEY**.

İ

İLKÄ see **İLKA**

İSTİ Kzk. 18th c. - 19th c. İsti-bay [Истыбай] (ZOOIRGO 1882, IV, 99); Kzk. 19th c. İsti-bay [Истыбай] (SODž. 136); Kzk. 19th c. İsti-bay [Истыбай] (SOK 264); Kzk. 19th c. Sti-bay [Стыбай] (SOV 88, 94). ✧ 'Smelly, stinking' cf. Kzk. *isti* 'einen Geruch habend' (Radl. I, 1534).

İSŪS Yak. İsūs (Kristiäs) [I-сус / I-сус Křістіäс] (Pek.) ✧ Jesus (Christ).

İŠ-ÄLİ see **İŠ-ALİ**

Ï

ÏAMALJÏN Yak. Ïamaljïn [Ыамалцын] (Pek.).

ÏBRAY see **İBRAY**

İBRAYÏM see **İBRAHİM**

ÏČÏM Yak. Ïčïm [Ычым], a shaman (Pek.).

ÏČÏNĀN Yak. Ïčïnān [Ычынан] (Pek.).

ÏJJĀ see **ÏLJĀ**

ÏJİLER Hak. 19th-20th c. Ïjiler [Ычилер], fem. (HRS 356).

ÏDÏQ Kzk. 19th c. Ïdïq-bay [Ыдыкбай] (AOK 90). ✧ 'Fate, fortune' cf. Uyg. *idïq* 'das von Gott geschickte Verhängniss'; (von Gott) gesendet, glücklich, gesegnet' (Radl., I, 1381-82).

ÏĞDU see **ÏQTU**

ÏYĀQÏN Hak.(Sag.) 19th-20th c. Ïyāqïn [Ыйакын] (Katanov, Otč. 8); Karg. Ïyāqïn (Katanov, Otč. 9). ✧ 'Deacon' (<R.) дьяконъ (Katanov).

ÏYĀQÏP Hak.(Blt.) 19th-20th c. Ïyāqïp [Ыйакып] (Katanov, Otč. 10). ✧ Yakov (<R. <Ar.). ⇨ YAQUP.

ÏYBĀN Hak.(Blt.) 19th-20th c. Ïybān [Ыйбан] (Katanov, Otč. 10). ✧ Ivan (R.).

ÏYÏQTAY Yak. Ïyïqtay-bōtur [Ыјыктаі-ботур], a bogatyr (warrior) (Pek.).

ÏQ-PAQAY Bashk. 1775 Ïq-paqay [Ыкпакай Бухаров] (MIB IV/2, 416). ⇨ BAQAY?

ÏQĀYÏS Yak. Ïqāyïs [Ыкајыс] (Pek.). ✧ Byname given to a man for his erratic (defective) trunk. (Pek.)

ÏQĀNAY Yak. Ïqānay [Ыканаі] (Pek.).

ÏQÏNĀČAY Yak. Ïqïnāčay [Ыкыначаі] (Pek.). ✧ Ignatiy (R.). Scc also **ÏGNAS**.

ÏQPA Uyg. 12th c. -14th c. Ïqpa (Radl., USp. 93).

ÏQTÏM Kzk. 19th c. Ïqtïm-bay [Иктымбай] (SOK 10). ✧ 'Escaped'? cf. Kzk. *ïq-* 'идти по ветру; спасаться от непогоды' (KzRS).

ÏQTU Uyg. 12th c. -14th c. Ïqtu / Ïγdu, a title? (Radl., USp. 130-131).

ÏLA Hak.? 19th-20th c. Ïla [Ыла] (Katanov, Otč. 10).

ÏLABÏRANTÏY Hak.(Sag.) 19th-20th c. Ïlabïrantïy [Ылабырантый] (Katanov, Otč. 7). ✧ Lavrentiy (R.).

ÏLAČÏN see **LAČÏN**

ÏLAČUQ Uyg. Ïlačuq (Zieme, Mat., I, 74). ✧ I. 'Little Ïla (river)' (Zieme, Mat. I, 77-78); II. 'Little Ïl(?)' (Hamilton) + dim. suff. -*čuq* / -*ačuq*?

ÏLAQ Bashk. 1787 Ïlaq [Ибраш Илаков] (MIB V, 207); *TN:* Bashk. 1738 Ïlaq [Илак], a village in the district of Girey (MIB III, 397). ✧ 'Kid' cf. Kzk. *ilaq* 'das Zicklein, ein einjähriges Rehkalb' (Radl., I, 1374), Bashk. *ïlaq* 'козлёнок' (BRS).

ÏLARÏN Yak. Ïlarïn-χotun [Ыларынхотун], goddess-host of the horse-court (Pek.).

ÏLAS Yak. Ïlas [Ылас] (Pek.).

ÏLJĀ Yak. Ïjjā [Ыцца] (Pek.); Yak. Ïljā [Ылца] (Pek.). ✧ Il'ya (R.). See also **ÏLKA, ÏLDEŠ**.

ÏLJĀNA Yak. Ïljāna [Ылцана], fem. (Pek.). ✧ Ul'yana (R.).

ÏLĞUM Bashk. 1735 Ïlγum [Ілгумъ Кюлюковъ] (Vel.-Zern., Bašk. 18).

ÏLÏBÏR Yak. **Ïlïbïr** [Ылыбыр] (Pek.).

ÏLÏQ Oghuz **Ïlïq** [Ылыкъ], Buqra-χan's cook in the Oγuz-nāme by Salar-baba (Muhamedova: OSA 171). ✧ 'Warm'? cf. Karakh. *iliγ* 'id.' (DTS), Turk. *iliq* 'warm, lauwarm' (Radl. I, 1375).

ÏMÄM see **ÏMAM**

ÏMÏYALAN Yak. **Ïmïyalan-quo** [Ымыjалан, Ытык-Ымыjалан-куо], fem. (Pek.).

ÏMÏYÏXĀN Yak. **Ïmïyïχān** [Ымыjыхан] (Pek.).

ÏNAXSÏT Yak. **Ïnaχsït-χotun** [Инахсыт-хотун Маңан Маңхалын], an old woman, the protector of calves (Pek.).

ÏNAYA Yak. **Ïnaya** [Ынаjа] (Pek.). ✧ 'Burly, portly' cf Yak. *ïnay-* 'вздуваться, выпячиваться (о брюхе), пузатеть ' (Pek.).

ÏNAQ see **ÏNAQ**

ÏNAL Karakh. **Ïnal** [İnal], fem. (MK/Atalay 841); Maml. 1481 **İnal** [ملك الامرا ٵ ينال الاشرفى], in an inscription of Lattakich (Sauvaget: BEO XII (1948), 46, Sauvaget 40); Maml. 1489 **İnal** [السيفى اينال الاشرفى], mentioned in inscriptions in Hama and Damascus, the governor of Hama; „Possibly identical with Aynāl al-Ashqar al-Ashrafī, who died of the plague in 1491/92" (Mayer 89-90, Sauvaget: BEO III, 5, Sauvaget 40); Oghuz/Trkm. 13th c. **İnal-γāzi** [اينا ل غازى / Инал-Гази], Er-sarï-bay's son (Abulg./Kon. 1165, 1245); Oghuz/Trkm. 13th c. **İnal-χan** [اينا ل حان / Инал-хан] (Abulg./Kon. 670, 680); Türk 712-716 **İnäl-qaγan** [inäl qaγan / inel kagan], Qapaγan-qaγan's son (DTS, ETY I, 110, 114); Türk 8th c. - 9th c. **İnäl-uruñu** (DTS); Uyg. **İnal** [Inal] (EUTS); Uyg. **İnal** [Inal] (EUTS); Uyg. 8th c. - 9th c. **İnal** [yna ïnal alï] (Haneda 4); Oghuz 876 **İnal** [ينال ده هزار غلام ابن طلحه] (Ibn al-Athīr/Tornb. VII, 210); Oghuz 936 **İnal** [ينال الكبير] (Miskawayh V, 511); Oghuz 946 **İnal** [ينال كوشه] (Ibn al-Athīr/Tornb. VIII, 337, 340, 341); Oghuz 1099 **İnal** [ينال بن انوشتكين الحسامى] (Ibn al-Athīr/Tornb. X, 195, 227-29, 266); Karakh. **İnal** [Inal], fem. (MK/Atalay 840); Selj. **İnal** [ابرهيم بن ينال بن سلجق] (Bondārī 8, 9, 13, etc.); Selj.? 1007 **İnal** [بامرالله] (Ibn al-Athīr/Tornb. IX, 140, 141); Selj. 1042, 1048, 1049 **İnal** [ينال الطويل قايد الحاكم] , a chieftain, Toγrul-beg's brother who passes to Irak (Mirch. Bujeh 52, 53, Weil, Chalif. III, 88, 98, Abulfidā III, 130-31); Selj. 1096, 1100 **İnal** [ينال صاحب امد] (Qalānisi 131, 138); Selj.? 1133 **İnal** [Ἰνάλης], a Turkic chieftain (Byz. Turc. 139); Selj. 1141 **İnal** [ينال يوسف الحاجب] (Qalānisi 274); Selj. 1167 **İnal** [ينال بن حسان قطب الدين المنبجى] (Ibn al-Athīr/Tornb. XI, 217, 318, etc.); Selj. 1175 **İnal** [قطب الدين ينال بن حسان], Saladin's enemy (Abulfidā IV, 24); Maml. 1389 **İnal** [اينال اليوسفى],

governor of Haleb in 1389 (Iyās I, 243, 291, Ibn Taghrīb. VI, 5, 12, 143, Weil, Chalif. I, 536, 566); Maml. 1398/99, 1438/39 **İnal** [اينال حطب العلائى] (Ibn Taghrīb. VI, 9, 25, 28, VII, 259, Iyās II, 321); Maml. 1400 **İnal** [اينال الرجبى] (Ibn Taghrīb. VI, 339); Maml. 1401/02 **İnal** [اينال المظفرى] (Ibn Taghrīb. VI, 108); Maml. 1404/05 **İnal** [اينال المنقار الجلالى] (Ibn Taghrīb. VI, 173, 190); Maml. 1404/05, 1410/11 **İnal** [اينال], a treasurer (Ibn Taghrīb. VI, 127, 250); Maml. 1415 **İnal** [اينال الصطلا نى], an emir, governor of Haleb in 1415 (Iyās II, 5, Ibn Taghrīb. VI, 202, 228, etc., Weil, Chailf. II, 134); Maml. 1421 **İnal** [اينال الشيخى] (Ibn Taghrīb. VI, 346, 393, 402, 500); Maml. 1421 **İnal** [اينال الظاهرى ططر] (Ibn Taghrīb. VI, 560); Maml. 1421 **İnal** [اينال العلائى الناصرى] (Ibn Taghrīb. VI, 237, 520); Maml. 1421, 1438/39 **İnal** [اينال النوروزى] (Ibn Taghrīb. VI, 469, 497 etc., VII, 258, 593); Maml. 1423, 1425, 1439/40 **İnal** [اينال الششمانى الناصرى] (Ibn Taghrīb. VI, 569, 593, VII, 87, 102); Maml. 1425 **İnal** [اينال طاز البهلوان] (Ibn Taghrīb. VI, 606); Maml. 1427, 1439/40 **İnal** [اينال المويدى اخوقشتم] (Ibn Taghrīb. VI, 796, VII, 105, 153); Maml. 1430 **İnal** [اينال السلحدار], a bearer of arms (Ibn Taghrīb. VI, 669); Maml. 1432 **İnal** [اينال الظاهرى ابزا] (Ibn Taghrīb. VI, 692); Maml. 1432, 1453-1460 **İnal** [اينال العلائى الناصرى جرود الملك الاشرف / Ìnâl Saifad-dîn Alā'i], emir, governor of Ghaza (1432), later a Mamluk sultan of Egypt (1453-1460), died in 1461 (Mayer 88, Ibn Taghrīb. VII, 5, 10, 63, 66, Makrīzī, Khit. I, 244, Iyās I, 356, II, 26-101, 128-364, III, 174, Berchem 271, 272, 420, etc.); Maml. 1436/37 **İnal** [اينال الظاهرى النتيه] (Ibn Taghrīb. VI, 771, VII, 6, 10); Maml. 1437 **İnal** [اينال الابوبكرى الاشرفى] (Ibn Taghrīb. VI, 727, 751, VII, 1, 7, 8, 12, Weil, Chalif. 211, 230); Maml. 1438/39 **İnal** [اينال اليوسفى], an emir (Ibn Taghrīb. VII, 33, 257, Weil, Chalif. II, 221); Maml. 1438/39 **İnal** [اينال الحمار] (Ibn Taghrīb. VII, 261); Maml. 1438/39 **İnal** [اينال الظاهرى] (Ibn Taghrīb. VII, 10, 159); Maml. 1438, 1439/40 **İnal** [اينال الجكمى], governor of Damascus in 1438 (Zambaur 31, Iyās II, 27, Ibn Taghrīb. VII, 5, 10, 12); Maml. 1449, 1453 **İnal** [احمد بن اينال] (Ibn Taghrīb. VIII, 54, 175, 182); Maml. 1452 **İnal** [الناصرى] (Ibn Taghrīb. VII, 375); Maml. 1455 **İnal** [اينال الكملى] (Ibn Taghrīb. VII, 463); Maml. 1457 **İnal** [اينال الجلبا نى التجنى] (Ibn Taghrīb. VII, 597); Maml. 1460 **İnal** [اينال الاشرفى الطويل], governor of Haleb in 1260 (Iyās II, 53, Weil, Chalif. II, 281); Maml. 1461 **İnal** [اينال الصصلا نى] (Ibn Taghrīb. VIII, 428); Maml. 1467 **İnal** [ا ينال الششما نى] (Ibn Taghrīb. VIII,

560); Maml. 1467/68 **Ïnal** [ضع ينال ا] (Ibn Taghrīb. VI, 199, 226, VII, 824); Maml. 1468 **Ïnal** [اينال الاشتر], governor of Haleb (Iyās II, 71, 74, 141-159, 275, Ibn Taghrīb. VI, 176, VII, 555, 705 etc., Wcil, Chalif. II, 333); Maml. 1471/72 **Ïnal** [اينال الحكيم] (Iyās II, 128-163); Maml. 1474/75 **Ïnal** [اينال الخنيف], a chief treasurer (Iyās II, 151, Weil, Chalif. II, 361); Maml. 1475/76 **Ïnal** [قى الاسحا ينال ا] (Iyās II, 163, 204); Maml. 1481 **Ïnal** [اينال السلحدار], custodian of arms (Iyās II, 205, 225, 313, 341); Maml. 1482 **Ïnal** [الملك الاشرف اينال], a sultan (Berchem, Jér. II, 160); Maml. 1484 **Ïnal** [اينال الخسيف] (Iyās II, 225-320, Weil, Chalif. II, 361); Maml. 1490 **Ïnal** [الحاجب] [اينال الفتيه] (Iyās II, 263, 284); Maml. 1493/94 **Ïnal** [اينال السلحدار نايب طرابلسى], custodian of arms of the governor of Tripolis (Iyās II, 281, Weil, Chalif. II, 364); Maml. 1496/97 **Ïnal** [اينال السلحدار الصغير], custodian of arms (Iyās II, 328); Maml. 1516 **Ïnal** [ا ينال خاز ندار طر ا باى], a treasurer (Iyās III, 91); Maml. 1516 **Ïnal** [ا ينال خازندار قانى باى], a treasurer (Iyās III, 52); Maml. 1516 **Ïnal** [اينال الاعور] (Iyās III, 71); Maml. 1516 **Ïnal** [اينال بن جا نى بك] (Iyās III, 44); Maml. 1519 **Ïnal** [ا ينال السيفى طر ا باى] (Iyās III, 191, 318); Yürük 1543 **Ïnal** [Inal] (Gökb., Rum. 205); Kirg. 13th c.? **Ïnal** [اينال / inâl], title of the chiefs (princes) of the Kirghiz (RaD/Ber. I, 130, Abulg./Desm. 43); Oghuz 938 **Ïnal / Yanal?** [بن ينال الترجمان محمد], a translator (Miskawayh V, 568-69, 571, 578); Maml. 1399 **Ïnal-bay** [ا ينال باى] (Iyās I, 318, II, 259, III, 30); Maml. 1399 **Ïnal-bay** [اينال باى بن قجما س] (Iyās I, 313-350, Ibn Taghrīb. VI, 9, 18, 28 etc.); Maml. 1450 **Ïnal-bay** [اينال باى الخاصكى] (Ibn Taghrīb. VIII, 73, 83); Maml. 1456 **Ïnal-bay** [الابراحيمى اينال باى] (Iyās II, 234); Maml. 1468/69 **Ïnal-bay** [اينال باى ميق] (Iyās II, 108, 111); Maml. 1481 **Ïnal-bay** [ا ينال باى الاسحاقى] (Iyās II, 206); Maml. 1496/97 **Ïnal-bay** [ا ينال باى], governor of Tripolis (Iyās II, 314-319); Uyg. **Ïnal-čur** [Inal Çur] (EUTS); Uyg. 8th c. **Ïnal-čur** (Müller, Pfahl. 24); Khorezm. 13th c. **Ïnal-χan** [ينال خان], Khorezmshahid, governor of Otrar, executed by Chinggis (Nasawī 34 etc.); Maml.? 1476 **Ïnal-χākim** [السيفى اينال حكيم], atabek of the soldiers in Haleb, died in 1476 (Mayer 89); Türk 7th c. - 9th c. **Ïnal-ögä** (DTS); Selj.? 1018 **Ïnal-tegin** [ينا لتكين] (Ibn al-Athīr/Tornb. IX, 211); Selj.? 1018 **Ïnal-tegin** [احمد بن ينالتكين] (Ibn al-Athīr/Tornb. IX, 211, 267, 300, 333); Khorezm. **Ïnal-tegin** [خوارزمشاه] [ينالتكين] (Bondārī 232, 233); Selj.?/ Khorezm.? 1016 **Ïnal-tegin** [ينالتكين صاحب جيش خوارزم], fought

against Mahmud, died in 1016 (Mirch. Gasnevid. 64); Türk / Uyg.? **Ïnal-tudun-kül** (Ligeti, R. tör. nev. II-III, 41); Türk 8th c. **Ïnal-uruñu** (Runic Mss. 186, 188); Uyg. **Ïnal-uruñu** [Ïnal Uruñu] (ETY II, 65, 66); Oghuz (Ghuz) 1095 **Yinal** [Йинал], the younger chieftain of the Ghuz (MIT I, 161, 163); Selj. 11th c. **Yinal** [Αβραμιος Αλείμ / Ибрахим Йинал (Ибрахим-и-Йинал)], (step-)brother of the Seljuk prince Toγrul-bek (Jorga, Notes 38, MIT I, 246, 269-71, 322, 355, 372). ✧ 'Son of a woman from the khan's clan and a man of lowly/common origin; man of noble descent; high-born' cf. *inäl / ïnal* II. 'id.' (DTS), Pelliot, Notes 182-183, Doerfer, TMEN IV, No. 1900. Used also as a title meaning 'a high dignity, confident of the khan, prince', etc. Other interpretation of *Ïnäl-ögä*: 'Noble-Wise' (Blagova 1997, 710), of *Ïnäl-qaγan*: 'Noble-Qaγan' (Blagova 1997, 710), of *Ïnäl-uruñu*: 'Noble-Flag' (Blagova 1997, 710).

ÏNAL-BARS Uyg. **Ïnal-bars** [Inal Bars] (EUTS); Uyg. 12th c. - 14th c. **Ïnal-bars** (Radl., USp. 140); Uyg. 8th c. - 9th c. **Ïnal-bars / Ïnal-baš?** (Müller, Pfahl. 23). ⇨ **ÏNAL + BARS.**

ÏNAL-BUYAT Uyg. **Ïnal-buyat** [Inal Buyat] (EUTS). ⇨ **ÏNAL + BUYAT.**

ÏNAL-ÖZ Karakh. **Ïnal-öz** [Ïnal öz] (MK/Atalay 841); Karakh. **Ïnal-öz** [Inal öz] (MK/Atalay 840). ⇨ **ÏNAL + ÖZ.**

ÏNALČÏQ Khorezm. 13th c. **Ïnalčïq** [اينالچق / اينالجوق / Inaltchiq], governor of Otrar, whose ill-considered action caused Chinggis' western campaign, his byname was *Γayr-* or *Xayr-χan* (J̌uwaynī I, 60, 61, 64-66, Abulg./Desm. 105); Uyg. **Ïnalčuq** [Inal Çuk] (EUTS); Uyg. 12th c. - 14th c. **Ïnalčuq** (Radl., USp. 206); Uyg. 12th c. - 14th c. **Ïnalčuq?** [Inalquč] (Radl., USp. 33); Khorezm. 13th c. **Ïnalčuq** [ملقب بغايرحان] [اينالجق], ruler (governor) of Otrar (J̌uwaynī 60); Khorezm. 13th c. **Ïnalčuq** [Ïnâshlṭk (Ïnâl shuk)] (Abulfar./Budge I, 357). ⇨ **ÏNAL + suff. -čïq.**

ÏNALČUQ see ÏNALČÏQ

ÏNANAΓ Oghuz? 1058 **Ïnanaγ** [Ïnânâgh], the captain of the host of the Ghûzzâyê (Abulfar./Budge I, 213).

ÏNANČ Turk. 1329 - 1339 **Ïnanč-bey / Ïnanč-bey** [Ïnanç Bey], Ibn Batuta met him in Denizli, Turkey (Uzunçarş., Anad. 38, 92); Selj. 11th c. **Ïnanč-bek / Ïnanč-bek?** [Инанч-бек ибн Сельджук] (MIT I, 457); Khorezm. 1220 **Ïnanč-χan / Ïnanč-χan?** [Бедр-ад-дин Инандж-хан], an emir, χājib (MIT I, 39, 477-80, 482); Uyg. 12th c. - 14th c. **Ïnanč** [Inanç] (DTS, EUTS); Oghuz 845 **Ïnanč** [اينانج الصحيع ايتا] (Qazw. 323); Pecheneg 1086 **Ïnanč** [Νεάντζης], a Pecheneg refugee (fugitive) (Byz. Turc.); Selj. 1099 **Ïnanč** [اينانج], emir of Berkyaruq (Qazw. 452); Selj. 12th c. **Ïnanč** [هسام الدين اينانج والى رى], a governor of Rey

(Rāwandī 259, 266 etc., Ahbar 90); Selj. 12th c. **İnanč** [اینادج] (Muh. Ibrahim 51); Selj. 1160 **İnanč** [اینا نج حا كم رى] (Qazw. 469, 471); Selj. 1191/92 **İnanč** [اینانج / Inanedj] (Ibn Šaddād, Nawād.: RHCHor III, 274); Karakh. **İnanč-beg** [Inanç Beg] (MK/Atalay 840); Selj. **İnanč-beg / İnač-beg?** [ایناج / اینانج بك سنقر صاحب الرى] (Bondārī 233, 283, 296-300 etc.); Khorezm. 1216 **İnanč-χan** [اینانج خان], emir Oγul-χaǰib (اغل حاجب) got this laqab from sultan Muhammad Alāaddīn ibn Tekeš (1200-120) as an honour (Nasawī 11); Selj. 12th c. **İnanč-χatun** [اینا نج خاتون], Atabeg Muhammad-pehlewān's wife (Rāwandī 336, 337 etc,); Selj. 1100 **İnanč-yabγu Aχor-beg** [اینانج يبغو احـربك] (Rāwandī 145, 146). ✧ 'Belief, trust' cf. Uyg., Crm., Turk. *inanč* 'der Glaube, das Vertrauen' (Radl. I, 1362). See also **EL-İNANČÏ, İL-İNANČ, KÜLÜG-İNANČ, QUTLUΓ-İNANČ, QUTLUΓ-İNANČ-MAXMUD, OΓUL-İNANČ.**

İNANČ-MAXMUD Selj. 1190 **İnanč-maχmud / Qutluγ-ïnanč / Qutluγ-ïnanč-maχmud** [قتلغ اینانج بن بهلوان / Kutluğ Inanç Mahmud], Pehlivan atabeg's and İnanč-χatun's son, the grand-son of emir İnanč (Rāwandī 347, 348 etc., Ahbar, Bondārī 302). ⇨ **İNANČ + MAXMUD.**

İNANČ-SAČU Uyg. 12th c. - 14th c. **İnanč-sаču** [ïnanč sаču] (DTS). ✧ 'Trust-fringe/frill' (Blagova 1997, 712). ⇨ **İNANČ + SAČU.**

İNANČ-TİRÄK Uyg. 8th c. - 9th c. **İnanč-tiräk** (Haneda 4). ⇨ **İNANČ + TİRÄK.**

İNANČČÏ Uyg. 12th c. - 14th c. **İnanččï** [Inanççı] (DTS, EUTS). ✧ 'Trustworthy' (Blagova 1997, 714).

İNANČČÏ-MEÑÜ Uyg. 12th c. - 14th c. **İnanččï-meñü / İnančï-meñü** (DTS). ✧ 'Trustworthy-Eternal' (Blagova 1997, 714). ⇨ **İNANČČÏ + MEÑGÜ.**

İNANČU Türk 8th c. **İnanču** [Inançu / İnançu] (Runic Mss. 187, 189, DTS, EUTS, ETY II, 67); Türk 7th-9th c. **İnanču-alp** [İnançu Alp] (ETY III, 105); Türk 732 **İnanču-apa-yarγan-tarqan** [İnançu Apa yarγan tarqan], a Türk beg mentioned in the Orkhon inscriptions (ETY I, 54); Türk 732 **İnanču-čur** [ïnanču čur / İnançu Çur] (DTS, ETY I, 52). ✧ 'Belief; faith, trust' cf. Uyg., Karakh. *inan-* 'верить, доверять' (DTS) + dev. suff. *-ču*.

İNANČU-BİLGÄ Türk 7th c. - 9th c. **İnanču-bilgä** [ïnanču bilgä / İnançu Bilgä] (DTS, ETY III, 133); Türk 8th c. - 9th c. **İnanču-bilgä-tiräk** (Fest. Thomsen 211). ✧ 'Belief-Wise'; 'Trustworthy-Wise' (Blagova 1997, 714). ⇨ **İNANČU + BİLGÄ.**

İNANČU-KÜLÜG Türk 7th c. - 9th c. **İnanču-külüg-čigši** [İnançu Külüg Çigşi] (DTS, ETY III, 90). ✧ 'Trustee-Famous' (Blagova 1997, 714). ⇨ **İNANČU + KÜLÜG.**

İNAÑ-UΓRAČ Türk **İnañ-uγrač** [ïnaŋ uγrač] (DTS); Türk 7th c. - 9th c. **İnañ-uγrač** [ïnaŋ uγrač] (DTS). ⇨ **UΓRAČ.**

İNDÏ Kirg. **İndï-bay** (Jud. 745).

İNDU Uyg. 12th c. -14th c. **İndu** [ïndu / Indu] (Radl., USp. 4-5, DTS, EUTS).

İNÏLÏR Yak. **İnïlïr** [Ынылыр] (Pek.).

İÑALÏ-UDAΓAN Yak. **İñalï-udaγan** [Ыңалы-удаҕан], İñalï-shamaness, Mr Moon's daughter (Pek.). ⇨ **UDAΓAN.**

İÑQABÏL-XOSUN Yak. **İñqabïl-χosun** [Ыңкабыл-Хосун] (Pek.).

İRAY Yak. **İray** [Ыраi] (Pek.).

İRĀY Yak. **İrāy** [Ыраi / Ыраi] (Pek.).

İRBÏ-QUONDAY Yak. **İrbï-quonday** [Ырбы-Куондаi], a fabulous *abāsï* (Pek.). ✧ 'İrbï the horseman, rider' cf. Yak. *quonday* (<R. конный [=horse-]) (Pek.).

İRΓÏM Kzk. 19th c. **İrγïm-bay / İrγïn-bay?** [Ыргымбай] (AOP 10).

İRÏS Alt. 19th-20th c. **İrïs** [Ырыс], fem. (OjrRS 214); Kkalp. 20th c. **İrïs-biyke** [Ырысбийке], fem. (KkRS 779); Kkalp. 20th c. **İrïs-gül** [Ырысгюл / Ырысгул], fem. (Bask., Kkalp. 404, KkRS 779); Kzk. 19th c. **Rïs / Rïs-qul** [Рысъ / Рыскулъ] (SKSO VIII, 224); Kzk. 18th c. - 19th c. **Rïs-bay** [Рысбай] (Tynуšр. 65, 75); Kzk. 1723 **Rïs-bek-batïr** [Рысбек-батыр] (Tynуšр. 65); Kkalp. 20th c. **Rïs-biyke** [Рысбийке], fem. (KkRS 778); Bashk. 1790 **Rïs-qul** [Рыскул Юлдашев] (MIB V, 275); Kzk. 18th c. - 19th c. **Rïs-qul** [Рыскул] (Tynуšр. 71); Kzk. 19th c. **Rïs-qul** [Turar Ryskulov] (Mende 161). ✧ 'Chance, happiness; fortune; wealth' cf. Kuman, Alt., Hak. *rïs* 'das Glück, der Wohlstand' (Radl. III, 719), Kzk. *ırıs* 'devlet, zenginlik, nasip' (KzTS), consider also Kkalp. *İrïs-gül* 'Rose bringing chance' (Baskakov: OSA 140).

İRÏSÏMBET Kzk. 18th c. - 19th c. **Rsïmbet (<İrïsïmbet)** [Рсымбет] (Tynуšр. 71). ⇨ **İRÏS + suff. -imbet.**

İRŌMQA Alt. **İrōmqa** (Katanov, Otč. 13). ✧ 'Stemmed glass, goblet, brandy glass' <R. *rjumka / рюмка* (Katanov).

İRZA Kkalp. 20th c. **İrza** [Ырза] (KkRS 777). ✧ 'Harmonious; satisfied' cf. Kkalp. *irazï, irza bol-* (KkRS) (<Ar.)

İSA see **İSA**

İSAQ Kirg. **İsaq** [Ысак] (Jud. 845). ⇨ **İSHAQ?**

İSÏ Bashk. 1763 **İsï-bay** [Чюраш Ысыбаев] (MIB IV/1, 274). ✧ 'Heat, hot'? cf. Turk. *isï* 'heiss; die Hitze' (Radl. I, 274).

İSÏ-ČAY Kzk. 19th c. **İsï-čay / İsï-čay** [Исычай] (SOK 208). ✧ 'Hot tea'. ⇨ **İSÏ + ČAY.**

İSÏQ Kzk. 19th c. **İsïq** [Исикъ] (AOO 22); *EN:* Kzk. 18th c. - 19th c. **İsïq** [Ысык] (Tynуšр. 73). ✧

'Miserable, piteous' cf. Kzk. *isïq* 'Mitleid erregend, erbärmlich' (Radl. I, 1388).

ÏSÏL see **ÏSÏL**

ÏSQAR Bashk. 1723 **Ïsqar** [Искар Кулашев / Иска Кулушев] (MIB III, 203). ✧ 'Piercing cold, keen frost' cf. Kirg. *isqar* 'die schneidende Kälte' (Radl. I, 1391).

ÏSQAT Kzk. 19th c. **Ïsqat** [Искатъ] (SODž. 12). ✧ 'Propitiatory gift (sacrifice)' cf. Kzk. *isqat* 'die Sühngeschenke, die man macht, um dem Seelenheil eines Verstorbenen zu nützen' (Radl. I, 1391).

ÏSLAM see **ÏSLAM**

ÏSLAM-GÏREY Crm. 1534 **Ïslam-girey** [Ысламъ-Гирѣй], Crimean Khan Islam Girey I (1532) (PSRL XIII, 84). ⇨ **ÏSLAM + KERÄY.**

ÏSNÖP Hak.(Sag.) 19th-20th c. **Ïsnöp** [Ыснoп] (Katanov, Otč. 7). ✧ 'Sheaf' <R. *snop* / снопъ (Katanov).

ÏSTAQ Alt. 19th-20th c. **Ïstaq** [Ыстак] (OjrRS 210). ✧ Stah (R.).

ÏSTAPĀN Yak. **Ïstapān** / **Ïstappān** [Ыстапан / Ыстаппан] (Pek.); Karg. **Ïstappan** [Ыстаппан] (Katanov, Otč. 8). ✧ Stepan (R.).

ÏSTAPPAN see **ÏSTAPĀN**

ÏSTAPPĀN see **ÏSTAPĀN**

ÏSTŌQ Hak. 19th-20th c. **Ïstōq** [Ысток] (Katanov, Otč. 10). ✧ 'Haystack' <R. *stog* (pronounced as *stok*) / стог (Katanov).

ÏSTŌN Hak.(Sag.) 19th-20th c. **Ïstōn** [Ыстон] (Katanov, Otč. 11). ✧ 'Moan, groan' (<R.) стонъ (Katanov).

ÏŠ Uyg. 12th c. - 14th c. **Ïš** (DTS). ✧ 'Soot, grime; fog, mist'. See also **YAN-ÏŠ, USTA-YAN-ÏŠ, TUMAN.**

ÏŠ-BUQA Uyg. 12th c. - 14th c. **Ïš-buqa** [iš buqa] (DTS). ✧ 'Fog/mist-bull' (Blagova 1997, 704). ⇨ **ÏŠ + BUQA.**

ÏŠBARA Uyg. **Ïšbara** [Işbara] (EUTS); Türk 6th c. **Ïšbara-yabɣu** [Σπαρζευγοῦν], a Türk qaɣan (Byz. Turc. 290). ✧ A high dignity.

ÏŠBARA-TARQAN Türk 731 **Ïšbara-tarqan** [Işbara Tarqan] (ETY I, 130). ⇨ **ÏŠBARA + TARQAN.**

ÏŠÏQ Yürük 1543 **Ïšïq** [Işık] (Gökb., Rum. 202). ✧ 'Light, glaze' (<Ar.). See also **QARA-ÏŠÏQ.**

ÏŠÏQ-TEMÜR Maml. 14th c. **Ïšïq-temür** [اشتمر] (Sauvaget 36). ✧ 'Light/glaze-iron' (Sauvaget 36). ⇨ **ÏŠÏQ + TEMÏR.**

ÏT-QAYA Uyg. 13th-14th c. **Ït-qaya-ïnal** [Ït Qaya Ïnal] (Zieme, Mat. II, 91). ✧ 'Dog-rock'. ⇨ **ÏT + QAYA.**

ÏT-SAMAN Uyg. 12th c. - 14th c. **Ït-saman** [Ït Saman / ït saman] (EUTS, DTS). ✧ 'Dog-straw' (Blagova 1997, 707). ⇨ **ÏT + SAMAN.**

ÏTÏQ-ČÖKČÖYDÖN Yak. **Ïtïq-čökčöydön-udaɣan** [Ытык Чөкчөйдөн удаган], fem. (Pek.). ✧ 'Respected squating (shamaness)' (Pek.).

ÏTÏQ-SUBAYDĀN Yak. **Ïtïq-subaydān** [Ытык субайдан], fem. (Pek.).

ÏTÏLLA Yak. **Ïtïlla** [Ытылла] (Pek.).

ÏTÏQQA Yak. **Ïtïqqa** [Ытыкка] (Pek.).

ÏVAZ Turk. 1442 **Ïvaz** [Hacı Ivaz] (Gökb., Ed. 280); Yürük 1543 **Ïvaz**, frequent name (Gökb., Rum. 194, 213 etc.). ⇨ **AYVAZ?**

ÏZARГAЈAX see **ÏZÏRГAЈAQ**

ÏZÏQÏY Kzk. 19th c. **Ïzïqïy** [Ызыкый] (SODž. 68). ✧ 'Pitiable, miserable'? cf. Kzk. *isïq* 'Mitleid erregend, erbärmlich' (Radl. I, 1388) + suff. -(ï)y.

ÏZÏRГA see **SÏRГA**

ÏZÏRГAЈAQ Hak. 19th-20th c. **Ïzarɣaȷax** [Ызарғачах], fem. (HRS 356); Hak.(Blt.) 19th-20th c. **Ïzïrɣaȷaq** [Ызырғацак], fem. (Katanov, Otč. 9). ✧ 'Little earring' cf. Hak. fem. PN *Ïzïrɣačax* dim. of *Ïzïrɣa* (Butanaev). ⇨ **SÏRГA** + dim. suff. -ȷaq / -čax.

ÏZMÏYAN Kkalp. 20th c. **Ïzmïyan-töre** [Ызмыйан-төре] (Bask., Kkalp. 75).

ÏZOT Hak. 19th-20th c. **Ïzot** [Ызот] (HRS 352).

ÏSTÏY Yak. **Ïstïy** [Ыстыı], one of At-küsäñäy's four sons, forefather of the contemporary Ïstïy-clan (Pek.). ✧ 'Catch in the pan, burn on; black' cf. Yak. *istïy* (Pek.).

Y

YABAГU see **YABГU**

YABAQ Bashk. 1756 **Yabaq** [Аднакай Ябаков] (MIB IV/1, 129); Kzk. 1819 **Yabaq** [Ябак] (MIKk. IV, 325). ✧ 'Foal (till the first year of age)' cf. Bashk. *yabaq* 'жеребёнок до годовалого возраста, которому обрезают гриву и хвост' (BRS).

YABAQAY Bashk. 1777 **Yabaqay** [Аднабай Ябакаев] (MIB V, 52). ⇨ **YABAQ** + suff. -ay.

YABAL Nog. 1502 **Yabal** [Ябалъ (Ягалъ)], envoy (PSRL XII, 254).

YABALAQ Tat. 1675 **Yabalaq** [Ябалакъ] (Kungursk. akty 32); Tat. 1675 **Yabalaq** [Ебалакъ (Ебалачко) Чюваковъ] (Kungursk. akty 38); Tat.? 1675 **Yabalaq** [Ябалакъ Сюаковъ] (Kungursk. akty 32); Bashk. 1798 **Yabalaq** [Ебалакъ] (PSZRI XXV, 195); Kzk. 1666 **Yabalaq** [Ябалакъ (Ябоомъ)], a Kazak prince (DAI V, 43, VII, 341); Tat.(Sib.) 1580 **Yabalaq** / **Abalaq** [Ябoлакъ (Ябoлокъ) / Ябалакъ (Абалакъ) / Абалакъ Агышевъ], a ruler of Siberia, son of the prince Mar (Sib. Let. (Strog.) 18, Sib. Let. (Esip.) 115, 183, Sib. Let. (Rem.) 318); Maml. 1300 **Yabalaq** / **Yablaq** [يبلق / Яблакъ], a Kipchak, Toqta's follower (Baybars/Tizeng. I, 90, 113); Tat. 1620 **Yabalaq** / **Yebalaq?** [Черепанъ Ебалаковъ (Ябалаковъ)] (Kurdjumov 120, 121); Tat. 1620

Yabalaq / Yebalaq? [Беклыбай Ебалаковъ (Ябалаковъ)] (Kurdjumov 120, 121); Kirg. 1824 **Yapalaq** [Алимбекъ Япалаковъ] (Konšin, Mat. I-III, 70); *TN:* Tat. 18th c. **Yebalakova** [Ебалакова], a village in the district of Svijažsk (Korsakov 360); Tat. 18th c. **Yebalakovo** [Ебалаково], a village in the district of Tetyushinsk (Korsakov 338). ✧ 'Owl' cf. Chag., Tat., Crm., Alt.(Tob.), NUyg.(Tar.) *yapalaq* 'die Eule' (Radl. III, 262), Crm., Tat. *yabalaq* 'die Eule' (Radl. III, 277).

YABAN Bashk. 1757 **Yaban** [Ябан Карагулов] (MIB IV/157); Chuv. 18th-19th c. **Yaban(ka)** [Ябанка] (Magn. 96); Bashk./ 1756 **Yapan** [Япан Юлаев] (MIB IV/1, 122); Bashk. 1756 **Yapan** [Япан Тупиев] (MIB IV/1, 106); Kzk. 1846 **Yapan** [Чуйбаш Япанов] (MKOP 155). ✧ 'Desert, flatland, steppe, field; wilderness' cf. Türk/Uyg., Chag., Crm., Tat.(Tob.), Turk. *yaban* 'die Ebene, Steppe, Wildniss, Eiröde, Wüste' (Radl. III, 275), Turk. *yaban* 'wild' (HȘ), Tat. *yapan* 'die Steppe, das Feld' (Radl. III, 261). See also **DALA, SÄXRA, ŠÖLKEY, TÏS**.

YABASUN Uyg. **Yabasun** [Yabasun] (EUTS).

YABASUNTU Uyg. 12th c. - 14th c. **Yabasuntu** (DTS).

YABAŠ see **YAWAŠ**

YABATU Uyg. 12th c.- 14th c. **Yabatu** [Yabatu] (DTS, EUTS).

YABAW Trkm. 1851/52 **Yabaw-χan** [Ябав-хан], a wog (or breeder of camels) (MIT II, 248).

YABDU Uyg. 12th c. - 14th c. **Yabdu** (DTS).

YABDU-TERÄK Uyg. 12th c. - 14th c. **Yabdu-teräk** [jabdu teräk] (DTS); Uyg. **Yabdu-tiräk** [Yabdu Tiräk] (EUTS); Uyg. 12th c. - 14th c. **Yabdu-tiräk** (Müller, Pfahl. 13, 19); Uyg. 12th c. - 14thc. **Yapdu-teräk** (DTS). ✧ I. 'Yabdu-poplar?'; II. 'Yabdu-supporter?'. ⇨ **TERÄK / TİRÄK**.

YABDU-TİRÄK see **YABDU-TERÄK**

YABГU Türk, Khazar 7th c. **Ĵabğu** [Yabğu Qağan], ruler of the western Kök Türks and the Khazars (= Baγa-šad, the younger brother of Ton Yabğu) (Golden 187); Khazar 625 **Ĵebγu** [Ζιέβηλ], a chieftain of the Khazars (Byz. Turc. 130); Selj. 1037/38 **Yabγu** [Муса ибн Сельджук Ябгу Калян (Бейгу, Муса Ябгу)], (title? of) the chieftain of all Turkmen-Seljuks, Toγrul-bek's uncle; according to Romaskevič, here Yabγu is not a title any more, but a personal name (MIT I, 232-33, 246, 248, etc.); Selj. 11th c. **Yabγu / Bayγu?** [مسی یبغو بن سلجوق / مسی ببغوكلان / Músá Payghú Kalán], got Ghazna and India in the middle of the 11th c., known as Arslan-yabγu in other sources (Qazw. 437, Rāwandī 87, 102 etc.); Selj. 1040 **Yabγu / Bayγu / Biγu?** [بیغو / یبغو / Iabgu], „qui tunc Turcis imperabat" (Abulfidā III, 102-103); Selj. 1051 **Yabγu / Bayγu / Biγu?** [بیغو], from Khorasan (Mirch.

Gasnevid. 118-119); Oghuz 10th c.? **Yabγu / Beyγu (Biγu?)** [Ябгу (Бейгу)], a prince mentioned together with Seljuk and Dukak (MIT I, 450, 451); Selj. **Yabγu / Yabaγu / Biγu** [Yabâgû (Bîghû)], Amīr Saljûk's son (Abulfar./Budge I, 196); Uyg. 9th c. **Yabγu / Žabγu** (Mahrnāmag 39); Uyg. 12th c. - 14th c. **Yabγu-bäg** (Radl., USp. 30); Uyg. **Yavγu** [Yavġu] (EUTS). ✧ The highest ruler of the western Türks (a title) (DTS), used also as a single personal name.

YABÏR Oghuz **Yabïr** [یا بیر \ یا بر / Yâbir], Oghuz's grand-son (Abulg./Desm. 27-28); Alt. 19th c. **Yabïr-χan** [Ябыр-хан] (Verb., In. 54). ✧ 'He who defeats anyone'; Desmaison: 'qui renverse tout ce qui se rencontre devant lui'; Sablukov: 'низлагающий все встрѣчайущееся'.

YABÏRA Uyg. 12th c. - 14th c. **Yabïra / Yapïra / Yäbirä?** [Yabïra] (Radl., USp. 95, DTS, EUTS).

YABLAQ-BUQA Uyg.? 13th c. **Yablaq-buqa? / Yaylaq-buqa? / Baylaq-buqa?** [یابلاغ بوقا / Яйлакъ-буга], son of the Uyghur Körguz in Iran (RaD/Ber. I, 117). ⇨ **YABALAQ + BUQA.**

YABUQ Chuv. 18th-19th c. **Yabuk** [Ябукъ] (Magn. 96); Bashk. 1756 **Yabuq-γul** [Туляк Ябукгулов] (MIB IV/1, 120). ✧ 'Skinny, lean, thin' cf. Tat. *yabïq* 'abgezehrt, abgemagert, mager' (Radl. III, 279); Kar.(L.) *yabuq* 'bedeckt, verdeckt, versteckt' (Radl. III, 284).

YABUNSU Uyg. 12th c. - 14th c. **Yabunsu / Yapunsu** [Yabunsu] (Radl., USp. 205, 247, DTS, EUTS); Uyg. 12th c. - 14th c. **Yapunsu-silavanti** (Radl., USp. 144).

YABURŠU Uyg. 12th c. - 14th c. **Yaburšu** [Yaburşu] (EUTS); Uyg. 12th c. - 14th c. **Yaburšu-tutuq** [Bilän Yaburšu Tutuq] (Radl., USp. 127); Uyg. 12th c. - 14th c. **Yaburšu-tutuñ / Yapuršu-tutuñ** (DTS).

YABUT 1643 **Yabut** [Ябут] (Miller, Ist. Sib. II, 488).

YAČANQÏR Uyg. **Yačanqïr** [Yaçankır] (EUTS); Uyg. 12th c. - 14th c. **Yačanqïr** (DTS). ✧ 'Shy, bashful' cf. Karakh. *jačan-* 'стыдиться, смущаться' (DTS) + dev. suff. *-qïr/-γïr?*

YADГAR see **YADÏGAR**

YADÏGAR Kkalp. 20th c. **Ĵadiger** [Джадигер] (Bask., Kkalp. 98); Kkalp. 20th c. **Ĵädigär** [Джädигäр] (Bask., Kkalp. 22); Trkm. 1554/55 **Yadγar** [Ядгар Мухаммед-султан], a tarχan (MIT II, 62, 63, 70, 72); Chag. 16th c. **Yadγar-bike** [Ядгар-бике], fem. (Ivanov 133); Uzb. 19th c. **Yadïger** [Ядыгеръ] (SKSO III, 170); Chuv. 18th-19th c. **Yatker** [Яткеръ] (Magn. 100); Turk. 1504 **Yādigār-bey** [Yâdigâr Bey] (Gökb., Ed. 472); Chag. 15th c. - 16th c. **Yādigār-χan** [یادكار خان] (Šejb. LI); Tat. 20th c. **Yädgär / Yädkär / Yädegär** [Ядгарь / Ядкарь / Ядегəр] (Sattarov); Tat. 1639 **Yädigär** [Едигер Брыков] (Miller, Ist. Sib. II, 453); Tat.(Sib.)? **Yädigär** [Ебигеръ (Гедегеръ /

Егитеръ / Едигаръ / Етигоръ / Итогиръ)], identical with Yädigär-Maγmet, ruler of Kazan (Sib. Let. 19, 89, 90, 117, 118, 133, 186, 202, 247, 274); Bashk. 1613 **Yädigär** [Едигерко Уркел] (MIB I, 84); Bashk. 1734 **Yädigär** [Едигеровъ], a Bashkir family (Vel.-Zern., Bašk. 10); Bashk. 1750 **Yädigär** [Едигар Тогузаков] (MIB III, 474); Bashk. 1780 **Yädigär** [Ибильаминь Едигаров] (MIB V, 117); Bashk. 1780 **Yädigär** [Шерып Едигаров] (MIB V, 117); Bashk. 1780 **Yädigär** [Едигар Аввелев] (MIB V, 117); Tat./Nog.? 1446 **Yädigär** [Едигеръ], a prince of the Horde; identical with the ruler of Kazan Yädigär-Maγmet? (PSRL (Russk. Hr.) I, 436); Bashk. 1623 **Yädigär** / **Yädägär** [Едегер (Едигер)] (Miller, Ist. Sib. II, 300); Bashk. 20th c. **Yäðegär** [Йəзегəр / Ядкар] (Kusimova); Kirg. **Yedigär** [Jeдiгäp] (Proben V, 144); 1548 **Yediger** / **Yädigär?** [Едигеръ / Ядигеръ?], a prince (PSRL (Russk. Hr.) I, 530); Tat. 1552, 1563 **Yediger** / **Yädigär** / **Yädigir** [Едигирь Магметъ / Едигеръ-Магметъ (Симеонъ) / Едигер (Ядигар)], a prince from Astrakhan, lived among the Nogays and ruled in Kazan from 1552 (PSRL XIII, 179, AI I, 330, Žirm., Epos 455, 460, 461); Kkalp. 20th c. **Žädiger** [Жəдигер] (KkRS 773); *TN:* Kzk.? **Yadγar-bay** [Ядгарбай], a village (qïšlaq) and trench in the region of Sugut (Sugutskij tumen') (ZIRGOStat. IV, Pril. 2). ✧ 'Present, reminder' cf. Turk. *yadïgar* 'das Andenken, Geschenk' (Radl. III, 211) (<P.) *yadgar*, *Yadgar* (personal name).

YADUK Chuv. 18th-19th c. **Yaduk** [Ядукъ] (Magn. 97). ⇨ **YATÄK / YAT** + suff. -*äk*.

YAFÄθ Karakh. **Yafäθ** [jafäθ] (DTS); Karakh. **Yafes** [Yafes] (MK/Atalay 858). ✧ The biblical Yafet (Ar.), Noah's son (Ahmed).

YAGİPER see **YAΓAFER**

YAΓAFER Chuv. 19th c. **Yagiper** [Jagiper] (Kronheim 96); Bashk. 1756 **Yaγafer** [Ягафер Алдаров] (MIB IV/1, 130); Tat. 1539-1540 **Yaγfar** [يغنر / Йагфар] (Jusupov 64); Tat. 20th c. **Yägäfär** [Ягəфəр] (Sattarov); Bashk. 20th c. **Yägäfär** [Йəгəфəр] (Kusimova); Tat. 20th c. **Yäγfär** [Ягъфəр] (Sattarov); Tat. 1781 **Yegäfer** [Егафер Юмашев] (MIB V, 126); Bashk. 1740 **Yeγafer** [Егафер Елдашев] (MIB I, 398). ✧ Djafar / Jafar (Ar.) <*ja'far* 'spring, rivulet' (Ahmet). See also **JAFAR**.

YAΓALAČ Tat.(Sib.) 1675 **Yaγalač(ka)** / **Yeγalač(ka)?** (DAI VII, 341).

YAΓAN Uyg. 12th c. - 14th c. **Yaγan-burqan-qulï** (DTS); Khorezm.? 1225 **Yaγan-taysï?** [يغان طايسى / Yghân Thaïsi], against the Mongols (Nasawī 108); Karakh. **Yaγan-tegin** [Yagan Tégin] (MK/Atalay 858); Karakh. **Yaγan-tcgin** (DTS). ✧ 'Elephant' (DTS). See also **QŪL-YAΓAN**.

YAΓANAQ see **YEKEŇK**

YAΓČUX Uyg. 762 **Yaγčuχ** / **Yaγčuq?** [Yagčuχ Iši], fem. (Mahrnāmag 15). ✧ 'Little plump/fat' cf. Karakh., Uyg. *yaγ* 'жир, масло; мазь' (DTS) + dim. suff. *čuq*.

YAΓJï Turk. 1470 **Yaγjï** [Bĭli ibn Yaḡcï] (Gökb., Ed. 127). ✧ 'Oil-vendor' cf. Turk. *yaγjï* 'Ölpresser, Ölverkäufer' (Zenker).

YAΓDï see **QAR-YAΓDï**

YAΓFAR see **YAΓAFER**

YAΓï-ARSLAN Selj. 1164/65 **Yaγï-arslan** [ياغى ارسلان / Ιαγονπασάν], prince of Malatya, younger son of Gümüš-tekin. RHCOR I, 761: „Abou'l-Fedâ et Ibn el-Athîr écrivent ce nom Yaghi-Arslân, mais les historiens arméniens l'écrivent Yakoub Arslân. Nicetas Choriates nous fournit la leçon Ιαγονπασάν. Ed-Dimechkî. écrit ياغى بصان Yaghi-Basân „qui écrase l'ennemi", et se trouve ainsi d'accord avec l'historien byzantin." (Ibn al-Athīr: RHCHor I, 543, 544). ✧ 'Enemy-lion' cf. Türk, Uyg., Karakh. *yaγï* 'враг' (DTS), Maml. *jagy* 'Feind' (Tarǰ/Houtsma), *yaγı* 'düşman' (Tarǰ/Toparlı). Houtsma writes somewhere that *Yaghi* is „qui foule aux pieds ses ennemies". ⇨ **ARSLAN.**

YAΓï-BASAN Selj. 11th c.? **Yaγï-basan** [محمد اليغيسا نى] (Bondārī 209); Selj. 1080, 1157 **Yaγï-basan** [ياغى بسان بن ملك غازى], son of Melik Ghazi / Melik Shah I. (1072-1092); mentioned in an inscription of Nikshar; Very interesting and characteristic is the passage in Hezârfenn's chronicle, relating the historical events during the Danishmendi dynasty of Türkmen origin in the 1180s, German translation by Mordtmann (ZDMG XXX.): „.. zogen die Ungläubigen dem Melik Gazi und Emir Süleiman entgegen. wurden geschlagen. In derselben Nacht wurde dem Melik Gazi ein Sohn geboren, den er Yaγïbasan nannte, weil die Rebellen an jenem Tage geschlagen wurden." [The unbelievers marched against Melik Gazi and Emir Süleiman. and were beaten. In the same night Melik Gazi's son was born and he named him as Yaγï-basan, for the rebels were beaten that day.] (Uzunçarş., Küt. I, 59, EI I, 953); Selj. 12th c. **Yaγï-basan** [Ιατουπασάνης], an emir from the dynasty of Danishmend (Byz. Turc. 135); Selj. 12th c. **Yaγï-basan** [ياغى بسان], Dānišmend's son (Aqsarāyī 29, Aqsar./Iš. 39, 41); Selj. 1248 **Yaγï-basan** [نظام الدين ياغبصان الملك], a ruler in an inscription of Tokat, Turkey (Uzunçarş., Küt. I, 40); Maml. 14th c. **Yaγï-basan** [ياغى بسان] (Zetterst. 237, 239); Selj. 12th c. **Yaγï-basan-beg** [ياغبصان بك] (Ibn Bībī III, 62, IV, 24); *EN:* Turk. 1563 **Yaγï-basan** [Yağıbasan], an ethnic community (Gökb., Ed. 499); *TN:* Selj. 12th c. **Yaγï-basan** [يغبسا ن], a mosque (Ibn Šaddād, Alep. 86). ✧ 'Defeater of the enemy, he who treads the enemy down' cf. Türk, Uyg., Karakh. *yaγï* 'враг' (DTS), Maml. *jagy* 'Feind' (Tarǰ/Houtsma), *yaγı* 'düşman' (Tarǰ/Toparlı).

Houtsma writes somewhere that *Yaghi* is „qui foule aux pieds ses ennemies". RHCOR I, 761: „Ed-Dimechkî. écrit ياغى بصان Yaghi-Basân „qui écrase l'ennemi", et se trouve ainsi d'accord avec l'historien byzantin." Cf. *Yāghī Basān* türk. Rebellenzwinger (Justi 77). ⇨ **BASAN. See also YAΓÏ-BASTÏ.**

YAΓÏ-BASTÏ Maml.? 1345 **Yaγï-bastï** [Yagy-Basty], died in 1345 (Zambaur 255). ✧ 'Defeated the enemy'. ⇨ BASTÏ. See also YAΓÏ-BASAN.

YAΓÏ-SÏYAN Selj. **Yaγï-sïyan** [ياغى سيان / Yaghi-Siân], ruler of Antiochia (Abulfidā: RHCHor I, 3); Selj. 1084/85, 1098 **Yaγï-sïyan** [الامير ياغى سيان / Yaghi Sian / Yaghi Sianus), a prince (governor) of Antiochia („princeps Antiochiae") (Ibn al-Athīr, Atab.: RHCHor II/2, 17, Ibn al-Athīr/Tornb. X, 18, 158, 169, Reg. Hieros. 1); Selj. 1093 **Yaγï-sïyan** [مويد الدوله ياغى سيان] (Qalānisi 122, 132-135); Selj. 1097 **Yaγï-sïyan** [باغى سيان بن محمد التركمانى صاحب انطاكيه] / Bagi(!) Sejan], lord (ruler) of Antiochia (Abulfidā III, 312-313 etc.); Selj. 1124 **Yaγï-sïyan** [يغى سيان / Yaghi Siân], an Ortokid (Kamāladdīn: RHCHor 646). ✧ '?-Enemy' cf. Türk, Uyg., Karakh. *yaγï* 'враг' (DTS), Maml. *jagy* 'Feind' (Tarj/Houtsma), *yaġı* 'düşman' (Tarj/Toparlı). Houtsma writes somewhere that *Yaghi* is „qui foule aux pieds ses ennemies". ⇨ JAΓÏ. See also YAΓÏ-BASAN.

YAΓÏR-BUΓAZČA-FATİMA see BOΓAZJA-FATİMA

YAΓÏZ-BUΓAZČA-FATİMA see BOΓAZJA-FATİMA

YAΓLAXAR see YAΓLAQAR

YAΓLAQAR Uyg. 9th c. **Yaγlaχar-ïnal** [Yaglaχar Inal] (Mahrnāmag 8, 10, Németh, HMK 84); Türk **Yaγlaqar-qan-ata** [Yaγlaqar qan ata] (ETY I, 156); Uyg. **Yaγlaqar-qan** (DTS); Uyg. / Kirg.? **Yaγlaqar-qan-ata** [Jaγlaqar qan ata] (Ramstedt, Uig. 4-6, Németh, HMK 84).

YAΓMA Oghuz 1000, 1002 **Yaγma** [يغما ابوطاهر] (Hil. Sābī 394, 395, 444); Oghuz/Trkm. 13th c. **Yaγma** [يغما / Йагма], king of Kashmir, Oghuz Khan's enemy (Abulg./Desm. 20-21, Abulg./Kon. 355); Yürük 1543 **Yaγma** [ياغما / Yağma] (Gökb., Rum. 175). ✧ I. A Turkic tribe (DTS); II. 'Robbery; plunder' cf. Turk. *yaγma* 'der Raub, die Plünderung' (Radl. III, 54).

YAΓMAL Yürük 16th c. **Yaγmal** [يغمال] (Gökb., Rum. 103).

YAΓMALÏ Yürük 1543 **Yaγmalï** [Yağmalı] (Gökb., Rum. 233).

YAΓMÏŠ Khorezm. 1295, 1305 **Yaγmïš / Yïγmïš** [ينغميش / يغميش], Ghazan's emir in 1295, the governor of Isfahan, envoy in 1305 (RaD/Jahn 57-60, Hammer, Ilch. II, 23, 147); Türk 8th c. **Yaγmïš-tutuq** [Y(a)γmïš Tutuq / Yagmïş Tutuq] (Runic Mss. 187, 188, DTS,

ETY II, 65). ✧ 'Intimate, confident; follower' cf. Türk *jaγ- II; jaγmïšï ben ertim* 'приближаться; я был его приближенным' (DTS).

YAΓMUR Trkm. 20th c. **Yaγmïr** [Yagmïr] (Zaj. 1971, 330); Trkm. 20th c. **Yaγmïr / Yaγmur?** [Ягмур] (TrkmRS 804); Uyg. 13th-14th c. **Yaγmur** [[Ya]γmur], fem. (Zieme, Mat. III, 273); Oghuz/Trkm. 1031 **Yaγmur** [Ягмур], a chieftain (commander) (MIT I, 235, 237, 243, 260, 363, 364); Selj.? **Yaγmur** [يغمور] (Zehireddin/Dorn 200); Maml. **Yaγmur** [بن شداد يغمر] (Duqmaq:RHCHor V, 126); Maml. 1203, 1264 **Yaγmur** [Djamâl ed-dîn ebn Yaghmoûr el Yâroûky], born in 1203, governor of Damascus, majordomo („majordome supérieur") (Sauvaire IV, 291, Makrīzī I, 100, II, 15); Maml. 1213/14 **Yaγmur** [يغمور المعظمى , عزالدين عمر بن], an architect (Berchem, Jér. I, 132); Maml. 1233 **Yaγmur** [جمالالدين بن يغمور / Ibn Saʿīd 124, 133, 141, Makrīzī II, 25, 28, Maqqarī I, 706); Maml. 1256-1258 **Yaγmur** [جمالالدين يغمور], mentioned in connection with Hülegü's campaign to Irak (Aqsarāyī 5, 55, 60); Maml. 1264 **Yaγmur** [يغمور / amir Jamāl al-dīn Mūsa b. Yaghmūr], the supreme ostāddār (Sīrat 210); Maml. 1310 **Yaγmur** [الامير يغمور الشقيرى], an emir (Dawād. 212); Maml. 1320 **Yaγmur** [يغمور] (Zetterst. 148); Maml. 1400 **Yaγmur** [يغمور بنبها در الدكرى] (Ibn Taghrīb. VI, 342); Maml. 1450 **Yaγmur** [يغمور] (Ibn Taghrīb. VIII, 65); Maml. 1452 **Yaγmur** [يوسف بن يغمور] (Ibn Taghrīb. VII, 232, 375); Turk. 1583 **Yaγmur** [Şeyh Yağmur] (Ongan, Ank. I, 153); Turk. 1662 **Yaγmur** [Yağmur], a person from Isparta, Turkey (Ün 1938, 644); Turk. 1519-1528 **Yaγmur-baba** [Yağmur Baba oğlu Karlı Bey] (Gökb., Ed. 456); Selj. 1160 **Yaγmur-χan** [Ягмур-хан], a Yazyr (Yazγïr) leader (MIT I, 397, 398); Trkm. 1879-1881 **Yaγmur-χan** [Yaghmour Khan] (O'Donovan II, 208); Trkm. 1826 **Yamγur-bek** [Ямгур-бек], from the Salïr tribe (MIT II, 440); *TN:* Turk. 20th c. **Yaγmur-baba**, a village in the province of Ankara, Turkey (TMİB 88); Turk. 1519 **Yaγmurlar** [Yağmurlar], a village in the subdistrict of Samakov, Turkey (Gökb., Ed. 443); Turk. 20th c. **Yaγmurlar** [Yağmurlar (Sülümü)], a village in the province of Ordu, district Mesudiye, subdistrict Yeşilce, Turkey (TMİB 709). ✧ 'Rain' cf. Uyg., Karakh. *yaγmur* 'дождь' (DTS), Maml.(Trkm.) *yagmur* 'yağmur' (Tarj/Toparlı), Trkm. *yaγmïr* 'дождь; дождевой' (TrkmRS), Kirg. *žamγïr* 'дождь' (Jud.). See also **QARA-YAΓMUR.**

YAΓRÏNČÏ Oghuz/Trkm. 14th c. - 15th c. **Yaγrïnčï / Yaγrïnči** [Ягрынчи], Ul-almïš's father (DQorq. 74, 237). ✧ 'Oracle; fortune-teller using burnt shoulderblade of sheep' cf. Chag. *yaγrinči* 'Jemand, der aus angebrannten Schulterblättern wahrsagt' (Radl. III, 51).

YAΓURČİN Tat.(GH) 1274 **Yaγurčin? / Yaγurčin?** [Ягурчинъ / Ягурчина / Ягураина], a Tatar chief (Ipat. 575 /577/). ⇨ **YAMΓURČİ?**

YAX see **YAQ**

YAXAM Bulg. 1323 **Yaχam** [يخم / Йахам] (Jusupov 21).

YAXŠİ see **YAQŠİ**

YAXŠİ-MUXAMMED Trkm. 1858 **Yaχšï-muχammed-daruγa** [Яхши Мухаммед-даруга] (MIT II, 584, 599, 606); Uzb. 1770 **Yaχšï-muχammed** [Яхши Мухаммед], from the Qataγan clan (MIT II, 349); Uzb. / Trkm.? 1867 **Yaχšï-muχammed-pehlevan** [Яхши Мухаммед-Пехлеван] (MIT II, 635). ⇨ **YAQŠİ + MUXAMMED.**

YAXŠİ-MURAD see **YAQŠİ-MURAD**

YAXŠİLİQ see **YAQŠİLİQ**

YAİK Alt. 19th c. **Yaik-χan** [Яик-хан] (Verb., In. 53,76). ✧ I. 'Good spirit'? cf. Alt. *D'ayïq* 'добрый дух, часть существа Ульгена; небожитель, посредник между Ульгеном и людьми' (OjrRS); II. 'Deluge; the Flood' cf. Alt. *d'ayïq* 'наводнение, поток; великий потоп (OjrRS).

YAY Bashk. 1784 **Yay-bay** [Салих Яйбаев] (MIB V, 154); Oghuz/Trkm. 14th c. - 15th c. **Yay-χan** [Yayḫān kešïš] (DQorq./Rossi 143). ✧ 'Bow' cf. Chag, Crm., Turk. *yay* 'der Bogen' (Radl. III, 3). See also **OQČA, SADAQ.**

YAY-ATΓAR Uyg. 8th c. - 12th c. **Yay-atγar-čañγšï** [tarduš tapmïš Yayatγar čangši] (Müller, Pfahl. 22).

YAYA Turk. 1584 **Yaya** [يايا] (Ongan, Ank. I, 168). ✧ 'Pedestrian, foot soldier' (Erol II), cf. Turk. *yaya* 'id.' (TED).

YAYAQ Uyg. 8th c. **Yayaq** [Yayak] (DTS, EUTS); Maml. 1332 **Yayaq** [يا يق], emir, custodian of arms (Dawād. 366). ✧ 'On foot; footman' (Blagova 1997, 711), cf. Chag. *yayaq ~ yayau* 'zu Fuss' (Radl. III, 73).

YAYALU Turk. 16th c. **Yayalu** [يا لو] (Ongan, Ank. II, 1540). ✧ 'Having foot soldiers'? (Erol II). ⇨ **YAYA + suff. -*lu*.

YAYJÏ Oghuz/Trkm. 13th c. **YayJï** [يايجى / Йайджы] (Abulg./Kon. 1240, 1270). ✧ I. 'Archer'; II. 'Fortune-teller (using a bow), witch'; III. 'A town near Bukhara on the river Amu-Darya' cf. Chag., Tat.(Tob.) *yaiči / yaicï* 'der Bogenschütze; der Zauberer, Wahrsager (gewiss ursprünglich mit Hülfe eines Bogens); eine stadt in der Nähe von Buchara' (Radl. III, 14).

YAYÏLMÏŠ Kirg. **Yayïlmïš** [Jaiлмыш] (Proben V, 151 /153/). ✧ 'Spread out; stretched him/herself'? cf. Uyg., Alt., Crm., Kar., Turk. 'ausgebreitet, überschwemmt sein; entfaltet sein' (Radl. III, 77) + suff. *-mïš*

YAYÏN-ΓAL Kzk. 1819 **Yayïn-γal** [Яингал] (MIK IV, 324). ⇨ **QAL I. / II.?**

YAYLAQ Kzk. 19th c. **Jaylaw** [Джайлау] (AOP 14); Kirg. **Jaylō-bay** [Жайлообай] (Jud. 876); Turk. 16th c. **Yayla** [يايلا] (Ongan, Ank. II, 1784); Turk. 1583 **Yayla** [يايلا] (Ongan, Ank. I, 179); Yürük 1543 **Yayla** [يايلا] (Gökb., Rum. 104, 211); Tat. 1543 **Yayla** (Gökb., Rum. 242); Turk. 19th c. **Yaylaq-oγlu**, a Zeybek (Kúnos 1891, 119); Bashk. 1770 **Yäyläw / Yayläü?** [Яилев Илчиев] (MIB IV/1, 342); Bashk. 1757 **Zäylä-γul** [Зяйлягул Кулбулдин] (MIB IV/1, 148); Bashk. 1755 **Zäyläw** [Зайляу Кулбулдин] (MIB IV/1, 99); Bashk. 1776 **Žaylaw** [Куибак Жаилявов] (MIB V, 47). ✧ 'Summer pasture and settlement of the nomads' cf. Chag. *yaylaq* 'der Sommeraufenthalt' (Radl. III, 12), Turk. *yayla* 'ein Sommersitz im Gebirge' (Radl. III, 11), Kzk. *jaylau* 'der Sommeraufenthalt' (Radl. IV, 4), Kirg. *žaylō* 'джайлау, летовка, летнее пастбище' (Jud.), Bashk. *yäyläw* (йәйләү) 'летняя стоянка кочевников' (BRS). ⇨ **YAYLA.**

YAYLÏM Trkm. 20th c. **Yaylïm** [Yaylïš (!)], fem. (Zaj. 1971, 341); Trkm. 20th c. **Yaylïm** [Яйлым], fem. (TrkmRS 808). ✧ 'Meadow; green field; spring field; summer pasture' cf. Trkm. *yaylïm* 'пастбище; луг; весенний луг; летнее пастбище' (TrkmRS).

YAYMA-KÖKÜL Kirg. **Yayma-kökül** [Jaima Kökül / Jaiма Көкүл], one of Manas' comrades-in-arms (Proben V, 40 /41/). ✧ 'Exuberant mop' cf. Kirg. *žayma kökül* 'распущенная чёлка, пышный чуб' (Jud.). ⇨ **KÖKÜL.**

YAYRA Uzb. 20th c. **Yayra** [Яйра], fem. (Begmatov 1984, 206); Uzb. 20th c. **Yayra-χân** [Яйрахон], fem. (Begmatov 1984, 206). ✧ 'Be/live free (happy)! Grow up free (happy)' (Begmatov), cf. *yayra-* 'жить привольно, чувствовать себя свободно, привольно; наслаждаться' (UzbRS).

YAYRASÏN Uzb. 20th c. **Yayrasïn** [Яйрасин], fem. (Begmatov 1984, 206). ✧ 'May he be/live free (happy)! May he grow up free (happy)'. ⇨ **YAYRA.**

YAYSAN Kalm. **Jaysañ** [Jaisang Dumbaul / Думбаул цаисан] (Proben III, 150 /189/); Tat. 1764 **Yaysan** [Яйсан Заитов] (MIB IV/1, 283); Kzk. 1819 **Yaysan** [Яйсан] (MIK IV, 323). ✧ '(title) the highest administrative (executive) dignity at the Altay Kalmyks' cf. Alt. (Tel., Leb., Tuba) *yayzañ* 'ein Saisan, höchter Verwaltungsbeamter der altaischen Bergkalmücken' (Radl. III, 14). See also **QOS-JAYSAN.**

YAYSAÑ see **YAYSAN**

YAQ Bashk. 1735 **Yaχ** [Яхъ Кюлюков], a tarχan (Vel.-Zern., Bašk. 18); Chuv. 18th-19th c. **Yaχ-čura** [Яхчура] (Magn. 101); Bashk. 1735 **Yaq-čura** [Мутюкай Якчурин] (MIB III, 336). See also **YÜZE-YAQ.**

YAQ-TUΓAN Bashk. 1761 **Yaq-tuγan** [Токтар

Яктуганов] (MIB IV/1, 221). ⇨ **YAQ + TUГAN I.**

YAQA Bashk. 1739 **Yaqa / Yaqay?** [Абдрахман Якаев] (MIB III, 409). ✧ 'Collar, choker' cf. Chag., NUyg.(Tar.), Tat., Turk. *yaqa* 'der Kragen' (Radl. III, 25).

YAQAQ Selj. **Yaqaq**, emir Seljuk's father (Ahbar 1). ✧ 'Iron bow' (Ahbar).

YAQAN Uyg. **Yaqan** [Yakan] (EUTS).

YAQAŠ Kzk. **Yaqaš** [Iakach / Якашъ] (Levšin III, 96, Levchine 356); Kzk. 1820 **Yaqaš** [Yakach] (Meyendorff 50). ⇨ **YAQA** + dim. suff. -š.

YAQÏČAY Bashk. 1738 **Yaqïčay?** [Якычай Сырымов] (MIB I, 143).

YAQÏP see **YAQUB**

YAQÏT see **YAQUT**

YAQYA Uyg. **Yaqya** [jaqya] (DTS). ✧ Yahya (Ar.), the biblical John, son of Prophet Zakariya (Ahmed).

YAQŠÏ Kzk. **Jaqsï-bay** [Джаксыбай Кустанов] (?); Kzk. 18th c. - 19th c. **Jaqsï-bay** [Джаксыбай] (Tynyšp. 73); Kzk. 18th c. - 19th c. **Jaqsï-bay** [جاقصى باى], a person mentioned in a song (ZCOIRGO III, 297); Kzk. 19th c. **Jaqsï-bay** [Джаксыбай], an informant (Potanin II, 165); Kzk. 19th c. **Jaqsï-bay** [Джоксы бай] (SOK 164); Kzk. 19th c. **Jaqsï-bay** [Джаксыбай] (SOV 48, 54); Kzk. 19th c. **Jaqsï-bay** [Джаксыбай] (SOK 110, 148); Kzk. 19th c. **Jaqsï-bay** [Джаксыбай] (SODž. 114, 146); Trkm. 20th c. **Yaγšï** [Ягшы] (TrkmRS 805); Trkm. 20th c. **Yaγšï** [Yagšï] (Zaj. 1971, 328); Turk. 1396 **Yaχši** [Γιαξης], an Ottoman commander (Byz. Turc. 113); Turk. 1436-1439 **Yaχši** [Yahşi bin Gazi] (Gökb., Ed. 173); Turk. 1470 **Yaχši** [Yahşi bin İlyas] (Gökb., Ed. 354); Turk. 1485 **Yaχši** [Yahşi], a standard bearer (Gökb., Ed. 80); Turk. 1528 **Yaχši** [Yahşi Fakih bin Dīanişmend] (Gökb., Ed. 43); Yürük 1543 **Yaχši** [Yahşi] (Gökb., Rum. 195, 197, 201, 204, 205, 209, 218, 226, 228); Yürük 1543 **Yaχši** [Yahşi] (Gökb., Rum. 207, 213); Tat. 1543 **Yaχši** [Yahşi] (Gökb., Rum. 231, 233, 235, 242); Turk. **Yaχši-bey** [Yahşi Bey], an Ottoman Bey (Uzunçarş., Anad. 54); Turk. 1519-1528 **Yaχši-bey** [Yahşi Bey] (Gökb., Ed. 431); Turk. 1341 **Yaχši-χan / Yaχši-bey** [يحيى بن قراشى / يخشى خان], Yakhchy khân / Karasi oğlu Yahşihan / Yahşi Bey], sultan/prince of Marmara (Berghama), commander of fleet, Karasi (Karašı's / Karesi's?) son, Demir-χan's brother, died after 1341 (Ibn Bat. II, 316, Jorga, Notes XIII, 366 /Mesalek alabsar/, Uzunçarş., Anad. 34,); Turk. 16th c. **Yaχši-oγlu** (Ongan, Ank. II, 669); Turk. 1621 **Yaχšï** [Yahşı], from Isparta, Turkey (Ün 1938, 645); Maml. 14th c. **Yaχši-bay** [يخشى باى] (Sauvaget 56); Maml. 1437/38 **Yaχši-bay** [المويدى الاشرفى يخشباى] (Ibn Taghrīb. VII, 2, 8, 15); Kzk. 19th c. **Yaχšï-bay** [Нурманъ Яхшыбаевъ] (Grod., Pril. 23);

Turk.? Maml.? 1534 **Yaχšï-beg** [يخشى بك] [الاميرى الخاج] (Sauvaget: BEO III, 13); Trkm. 1833 **Yaχšï-mergen** [Яхши Мерген], from the Gökleñ tribe (MIT II, 464, 465, 469); Bashk. 1714 **Yaqšï** [Явкей Якшиев] (MIB I, 105); Bashk. 1754 **Yaqšï** [Ямчи Якшиев] (MIB IV/1, 84); Bashk. 1754 **Yaqšï** [Елчи Якшиев] (MIB IV/1, 84); Bashk. 1766 **Yaqšï** [Яныбек Якшиев] (MIB IV/1, 320); Bashk. 1770 **Yaqšï** [Якши Рахмангулов] (MIB IV/1, 342); Kzk. 1829 **Yaqšï** [Яккиши] (MIK IV, 323); Tat.(Sib.) 1639 **Yaqšï(y)** [Саруоль Якшеев] (Miller, Ist. Sib. II, 453); Bashk. 1735, 1753 **Yaqšï / Yaqši** [Ирка Якшиев (Якшеев)] (MIB III, 337, IV/1, 70); Bashk. 1756 **Yaqšï-bay** [Якшибай Кинзебаев] (MIB IV/1, 109); Bashk. 1760 **Yaqšï-bay** [Якшибай] (MIB IV/1, 200); Kzk. **Yaqšï-bay** [Кашкаръ Якшибаевъ] (Êtnogr. Obozr. 1915, No 3-4, 62); Kzk. 1919 **Yaqšï-bay** [Yakshi Bai] (Nazaroff 40); Turk. 14th c. **Yaqšï-beg** [Yakší Beg], a person from Konya, Turkey (EI 802); Tat.? 1407 **Yaqšï-bey** [Якшибѣй (Акшибѣй)], a prince of the Horde (PSRL VI, 136, VIII, 83); Tat. 1409 **Yaqšï-bi** [Якшиби], a prince (PSRL XI, 205); Tat. 1409 **Yaqšï-bi** [Якшиби], a prince (PSRL XXIII, 142); Tat.(Mish.) 1775 **Yaqšï-γul** [Ягшигул Курманов] (MIB IV/2, 416); Tat.(Mish.) 1793 **Yaqšï-γul** [Ямангул Ягшигулов] (MIB V, 332); Bashk. 1600 **Yaqšï-γul** [Беляков Якшагул (Якшаулко)] (Miller, Ist. Sib. II, 158, 159); Bashk. 1600 **Yaqšï-γul** [Якшагул] (Miller, Ist. Sib. II, 159); Bashk. 1714 **Yaqšï-γul** [Акшигулов Бектуган] (MIB I, 105); Bashk. 1714 **Yaqšï-γul** [Мятик Якшигулов] (MIB I, 105); Bashk. 1730 **Yaqšï-γul** [Якшигул Ишкинин] (MIB III, 280); Bashk. 1735 **Yaqšï-γul** [Якшигулъ Ногайбаковъ], a tarχan (Vel.-Zern., Bašk. 20); Bashk. 1742 **Yaqšï-γul** [Якшигул Селтешев] (MIB III, 513); Bashk. 1756 **Yaqšï-γul** [Урускузя Якшигулов] (MIB IV/1, 123); Bashk. 1756 **Yaqšï-γul** [Алямгузя Якшигулов] (MIB IV/1, 123); Bashk. 1756 **Yaqšï-γul** [Уразбай Якшигулов] (MIB IV/1, 123); Bashk. 1757 **Yaqšï-γul** [Салтан Якшагулов] (MIB IV/1, 151); Bashk. 1761 **Yaqšï-γul** [Якшигул Сюлюков] (MIB IV/1, 211); Bashk. 1763 **Yaqšï-γul** [Ирсай Яхшигул] (MIB IV/2, 45); Bashk. 1785 **Yaqšï-γul** [Имангул (Емангул) Яхшигулов] (MIB V, 166, 168, 223, 224); Bashk. 1789 **Yaqšï-γul** [Кушали Якшигулов] (MIB V, 267); Bashk. 1738 **Yaqšï-γul / Yäqši-γul?** [Екшигул Челтюшев] (MIB I, 143); Chag. 16th c. **Yaqšï-sufi** [Якши Суфи] (Ivanov 133); Bashk. 1732 **Yaqšiy / Yaqšiy** [Якший Кадыров] (MIB III, 297); Kkalp. 20th c. **Žaqsï-bay** [Жаксыбай] (KkRS 773); *EN:* Kzk. 18th c. - 19th c. **Jaqsï-bay** [Джаксыбай] (Tynyšp. 73); *TN:* Kkalp.? 1724 **Yaqšï-bay** [Якши Бай], a river in the region of Yaik river (MIKk. 180).

❖ 'Good, nice' cf. Karakh., Oghuz *yaqšï* 'хорошый, добрый; хорошо' (DTS), Maml. *yakšï* 'güzel' (Tarǰ/Toparlı), Trkm. *yaɣšï* 'хорошый, добрый' (TrkmRS). See also **ǰOL-ŽAQSÏ, EL-YAQŠÏ, KÖRKELİ-YAXŠÏ, TERMİ-YAQŠÏ.**

YAQŠÏ-BERDİ Bashk. 1663 **Yaqšï-berdi** [Якшиберди] (MIB I, 169). ⇨ **YAQŠÏ** + **BERDİ.** See also **YAQŠÏ-BERGEN.**

YAQŠÏ-BERGEN Kzk. 1819 **Yaqšï-bergän** [Якшиберган] (MIK IV, 323); Kzk. 1819 **Yaqšï-bergen** [Якшиберген] (MIK IV, 323). ⇨ **YAQŠÏ** + **BERGEN.** See also **YAQŠÏ-BERDİ.**

YAQŠÏ-DÄWLÄT Bashk. 1751 **Yaqšï-däwlät** [Якшидевлеть] (MIB IV/1, 43); Tat.(Sib.) 1607 **Yaqšï-däwlät / Yäqši-däwlät?** [Екшидевлет Беляков] (Miller, Ist. Sib. II, 197); Bashk. 1734 **Yaqšï-däwlet / Yaqši-dawlet** [Якшидавлетъ Арасланбековъ], tarɣan (Vel.-Zern., Bašk. 27); Bashk. 1717 **Yaqšï-dewlät** [Султангул Якшидевлятев] (MIB III, 154). ⇨ **YAQŠÏ** + **DÄWLÄT.**

YAQŠÏ-GİLDİ Bashk. 1735 **Yaqšï-gildi** [Якшигилди Акинъ], a tarɣan (Vel.-Zern., Bašk. 21); Bashk. 1735 **Yaqši-gildi** [Якшигилди Касеневъ], a tarɣan (Vel.-Zern., Bašk. 21); Tat.(Sib.) 1623 **Yaqšï-gildi / Yäqši-gilde?** [Якшигилдиев (Екшигилдеев)] (Miller, Ist. Sib. II, 291, 300, 397, 164). ⇨ **YAQŠÏ** + **KELDİ.**

YAQŠÏ-İVAN Bashk. 1659 **Yaqšï-ivan** [Якши-Иванъ Девлекеевъ], a tarɣan from the village Yaqši-ivanov (Vel.-Zern., Bašk. 38); *TN:* Bashk. 1659 **Yaqši-ivanov** [Якшииваново / Якшиван (Якшиваново)], a village in the region of Ufa, Bashkiria (Vel.-Zern., Bašk. 38). ❖ 'Good-Ivan'. ⇨ **YAQŠÏ.**

YAQŠÏ-QADÏM Nog. 1541 **Yaqšï-qadïm** [Якшикадымъ] (PSRL XIII, 134). ⇨ **YAQŠÏ.**

YAQŠÏ-MAГMED Trkm. 1821 **Yaqšï** [Якши-Магмедъ] (Russk. Arhiv 1888, I, 72). ⇨ **YAQŠÏ** + **MAXMED.**

YAQŠÏ-MURAD Trkm. 1838 **Yaɣšï-murad-yüzbašï** [Яхши Мурад-юзбаши] (MIT II, 473, 475, 477); Uzb.? 1855 **Yaqšï-murad-daruɣa** [Якши Мурад-даруга] (MIT II, 555). ⇨ **YAQŠÏ** + **MURAT.**

YAQŠÏ-URAZ Tat. 1631 **Yaqš-uraz** (<Yaqšï-uraz) [Якшураз / Якмураз?] (Miller, Ist. Sib. II, 386). ⇨ **YAQŠÏ** + **ORAZ.**

YAQŠÏBET Kkalp. 1846 **Yaqšïbet** [Куйчтай Якшебетев] (MKOP 152). ❖ 'Good Muxammet'. ⇨ **YAQŠÏ** + suff. (suffixoid) *-bet* <*-imbet.*

YAQŠÏQAY Bashk. 1779, 1780 **Yaqšïqay** [Усман Якшикаев] (MIB V, 89, 106). ⇨ **YAQŠÏ** + dim. suff. *-qay.*

YAQŠÏLĬQ Kkalp. 20th c. **ǰaqsïlïq** [Жақсылық] (KkRS 773); Kzk. 19th c. **Yaɣšïlïq** [Яхшылыкъ] (Grod., Pril. 34); Kzk. 19th c. **Yaɣšïlïq** [Яхшилыкъ] (Grod., Pril. 60); Kipch. 1779 **Yaɣšïlïq-biy** [Яхшилик-

бий], a ruler of the Kipchaks (MIT II, 352, 376); Kkalp. 1820 **Yaɣšïlïq-biy** [Яхшылык бий] (MIKk. 107); Trkm. 19th c. **Yaqšïlïq** [Якшелыкъ] (SKSO III, 178); Tat.(Mish.) 1755 **Yaqšïlïq** [Якшилак Юнусов] (MIB IV/1, 93); Kzk. 19th c. **Yaqšïlïq** [Якшылыкъ Джанкабаевъ] (Grod., Pril. 37); Kzk. 19th c. **Yaqšïlïq** [Турсунбай Якшылыковъ] (Grod., Pril. 37); Kzk. 19th c. **Yaqšïlïq** [Тастубай Якшылыковъ] (Grod., Pril. 37); *EN:* Kzk. **ǰaqsïlïq** (Radl. I, 1098); Kzk. 18th c. - 19th c. **ǰaqsïlïq** [Джаксылык] (Tynyšp. 65, 66,71). ❖ 'Goodness; goodwill'. ⇨ **YAQŠÏ** + suff. *-lïq.*

YAQŠÏMBET Bashk. 1734 **Yaqšïmbet / Yaqšimbet** [Бекбулатъ Якшимбетевъ], a tarɣan (Vel.-Zern., Bašk. 10); Bashk. 1735 **Yaqšïmbet / Yaqšimbet** [Муаймасъ Якшимбетевъ], a tarɣan (Vel.-Zern., Bašk. 19); Bashk. 18th c. . **Yaqšïmbet / Yaqšimbet** [Якшимбетов] (MIB V, 269); Bashk. 1763 **Yaqšïmbet / Yaqšimbet** [Якшимбеть Биктяшев] (MIB IV/1, 271); Bashk. 1791 **Yaqšïmbet / Yaqšimbet** [Сюяргул Якшимбетев] (MIB V, 301); Kzk. 1737 **Yaqšïmbet / Yaqšimbet** [Якшимбет] (MIB I, 339); Kzk. 1740 **Yaqšïmbet / Yäqšimbet?** [Екшимбеть] (MIB I, 404); Bashk. 1664 **Yaqšïnmet** [Якшенметко Аксекеев] (MIB I, 192). ❖ I. 'Good Mukhammad' (Sattarov); II. 'Good folk/people' (Kusimova). ⇨ **YAQŠÏ** + **MUXAMMED** + / suffixoid *-mbet / -imbet.*

YAQŠÏMET Bashk. 1710 **Yaqšïmet / Yaqšimet?** [Якшимет Янгильдин] (MIB III, 68); Bashk. 1729 **Yaqšïmet / Yaqšimet?** [Точибай Якшиметев] (MIB III, 260). ❖ A contraction of the compound PN *Yaqšï-muχammet* meaning 'Good Muhfammed', or PN *Yaqšï* suffixed with suffixoid *-met.* ⇨ **YAQŠÏ** + suff. *-met.*

YAQŠÏNMET see **YAQŠÏMBET**

YAQUB Kirg. **ǰaqïp** [Жакып] (Jud. 95, 697); Kzk. 19th c. **ǰekip** [Джекипъ] (AOK 90); Kirg. **Yaqïp-qan** [Jakyp Kan / Жакып Кан] (Proben V, 1); Uyg. **Yaqub** [ja'qub] (DTS); Nog. 20th c. **Yaqup** [Нуракъай Йакъуп увлы], father of one of Baskakov's informants from the aul of Qara-töbe (Bask., Nog. 143); Nog. 20th c. **Yaqup** [Рахмет Йакъуп улы Сыйкъаллы / Рахмет Якубович Сыйкалиев], father of one of Baskakov's informants from the aul of Üykön-χalq (Ikon-halk), Cherkess Autonomous Oblast' (Bask., Nog. 143); Kkalp. 20th c. **Žaqïp** [Жакъып] (KkRS 773); Kirg. **Žaqïp** [Жакып] (Jud. 95). ❖ Yaqub (Ar.), a Prophet, the biblical Jacob (Ahmet), cf. Kzk. PNs *Žaqïp, Žaqïp-bay, Žaqïp-bek* (Žanuzakov-Esbaeva). See also **BAY-ǰAQÏP.**

YAQUP see **YAQUB**

YAQUŠ Kuman 1462 **Yaquš** [Якушъ (Акушъ)], a messenger (PSRL IV, 222); Tat. 1731 **Yaquš** [Якушка Мамлин] (MIB III, 284); Bashk. 1714 **Yaquš** [Якушко] (MIB I, 106); Kuman 1189 **Yaquš / Aquš?** [Якушъ (Акушъ)], a (Lukomorskiy) Polovets prince

(PSRL II, 142, 323). ✧ Shortened form of *Yaqup /
Yaqub* (Sattarov). ⇨ **YAQ(UB)** + suff. *-(u)š.*

YAQUT Kzk. **J̌aqut** [Джакутъ], fem. (ZIRGOGeogr. I,
529); Kzk. **J̌aqut** [Джакутъ], fem. (ZIRGOGeogr. I,
529); Kzk. 19th c. **J̌aqut** [Джакутъ], fem.
(ZIRGOGeogr. I, 529); Kkalp. 20th c. **Yaqi̇t** [Якыт],
fem. (KkRS 779); Tat. **Yaqut** [يعقوت / Йакут], fem.
(Jusupov 19); Turk. 1407 **Yaqut-paša** [Yakut Paşa]
(Gökb., Ed. 24). ✧ 'Ruby' cf. Kzk. *jaqut* 'der Rubin,
der Edelstein' (Radl. IV, 12), Kuman, Tat., Turk. *jaqut*
'der Rubin' (Radl. III, 30).

YAL Kzk. 18th c. - 19th c. **J̌al-mïrza** [Джалмырза]
(Tynyšp. 66); Chuv. 18th-19th c. **Yal-čora** [Ялчора]
(Magn. 97). ✧ 'Mane' cf. Alt., Uyg., Chag., Turk. *yal*
'die Mähne' (Radl. III, 152), Bashk. *yal* 'грива'
(BRS/Uraksin), Kzk. *žal* 'id.' (KzRS) cf. Kkalp. *jal*
(джал) 'грива, загривок' (Bask.). See also **AQ-ŽAL,
TERİ-ŽAL, UГLİ-YAL.**

YAL-BULAT Chuv. 18th-19th c. **Yal-bulat**
[Ялбулатъ] (Magn. 97). ⇨ **YAL?** + **BULAT.**

YAL-MAMET Bashk. 1787 **Yal-mamet** [Кутурбай
Ялмаметев] (MIB V, 203). ⇨ **YAL + MAMET.**

YALAQ Alt. 19th-20th c. **D'alaq** [Дьалак] (OjrRS
211); Alt. 19th-20th c. **Yalaq / D'alaq** [Яалак /
Дьалак] (OjrRS 211). ✧ 'Flatterer' cf. Alt. *yalaq*,
Alt.(Tel.) *d'alaq* 'der Schmeichler' (Radl. III, 156).

YALAQAY Nog. 20th c. **Yalaqay** [Муслим
Йалакъай увлы / Муслим Ялкаев], father of one
of Baskakov's informants from the aul of Qoyasulï
(Bask., Nog. 144). ✧ I. 'Sweet-toothed; licking' cf.
Kuman., Alt., Tat. *yala-* 'lecken, ablecken' (Radl. III,
154), Kzk. *žalaq* 'лизун' (KzRS); II. 'Creep, crawler,
flatterer; liar' cf. Bashk. *yalaγay* 'id.' (BRS/Uraksin);
III. 'Lazy, layabout' cf. Bashk. dial. *yalaγay* 'id.'
(BRS/Uraksin); IV. 'Cup or bowl (for dogs and cats)'
cf. Crm. *yalaq* 'миска (для кормления собаки,
кошки)' (KrmRS) + suff. *-qay.*

YALANČI Oghuz/Trkm. 14th c. - 15th c. **Yalančï /
Yalanči** [يلنجى / Яланчи], Yartačuq's father
(DQorq./Rossi 121-133, DQorq. 39, 40, 41, 42, 44, 48).
✧ 'Liar' cf. Crm., Turk. *yalanjï* 'der Lügner' (Radl. III,
161).

YALANČÏQ Oghuz/Trkm. 14th c. - 15th c. **Yalančïq**
[يلنجى اوڭلى يلنجيق], Yalančï's son (DQorq./Rossi
121-133). ✧ 'Little lie'? cf. Kuman, Turk. *yalan* 'die
Lüge, lügnerisch' (Radl. III, 161) + suff. *-čïq.*

YALAÑ-TAŠ Uzb. 16th c. **Yalañ-taš** [Jalang-tach], an
architect in Samarkand coming from the Alčin tribe.
„Jalang-tach (pierre polie) était Uzbek de naissance et
de la tribu d'Altchin. Vámbéry, je ne sais pour quelle
raison, en fait un Qalmouq convert à l'islam"
(Koroškin: Rec. V. As. C. p. 215). ✧ 'Polished stone'
„pierre polie" (Koroškin). ⇨ **TAŠ.**

YALAÑ-TUŠ Uzb. 1628 **Yalañ-tuš-behadur**
[Ялангтуш-бехадур], a biy and atalïq, the architect of
famous mosques in Samarkand (MIT II, 109); Trkm.?
1816 **Yalañ-tuš-χan** [Ялангтуш-хан], from the J̌alayïr
tribe (MIT II, 221, 226); Trkm. 1815 **Yalañ-tuš-χan**
[Yalangtush Khan / Ялангтуш-хан], a Djemshidi chief
(O'Donovan II, 226, MIT II, 388, 459, 461). ⇨ **TUŠ.**

YALAWAČ Selj. **Yalawač** [يلواج], forefather of the
Ottoman dynasty (Nešrī 186); Selj.? **Yalawač** [يلواج]
(SE I, 10). ✧ 'Messenger, envoy' (title), cf. DTS, Le
Coq, Ind. 3.

YALČİ see **YALČİ**

YALČİ Tat. 20th c. **Yalčï** [Ялчин], a family (Sattarov);
Bashk. 1757 **Yalčï** [Ялчи Чирков] (MIB IV/1, 151);
Bashk. 1760 **Yalčï** [Ялчи Чюрюкеев] (MIB IV/1,
195); Bashk. 1761 **Yalčï** [Ялчи Чюрюкеев] (MIB
IV/1, 208); Bashk. 1790 **Yalčï** [Исергап Ялчин]
(MIB); Bashk. 1756 **Yalčï / Yalči?** [Ялчи Иманов]
(MIB IV/1, 125); Bashk. 1740 **Yalčï-γul** [Ялчигул
Чюракаев] (MIB I, 434); Bashk. 1756 **Yalčï-γul**
[Ялчигул Артукулов] (MIB IV/1, 109). ✧ 'Hack,
navvy; mercenary' cf. Alt., Tat., Kar.(T.) *yalčï* 'der
Tagelöhner, Knecht, die Magd' (Radl. III, 185).

YALГAŠ Uzb. 20th c. **Yâlγâš** [Ёлғош] (Begmatov
1984, 202); Uzb. 20th c. **Yâlγâš-bây** [Ёлғошбой]
(Begmatov 1984, 202); Uzb. 20th c. **Yâlγâš-bek**
[Ёлғошбек] (Begmatov 1984, 202). ✧ 'Be living; Be
alive' cf. Uzb. *yâlγa- (žalγa-)* 'присоединяться (в
смысле будь живым)' (Begmatov).

YALÏN-AYAQ Turk. 19th c. **Yalïn-ayaq-oγlu** [Jalyn
ajak oγlu], a Zeybek (Kúnos 1891, 119). ✧ 'Barefoot'
cf. Turk. *yalın ayak* 'id.' (TED). ⇨ **AYAQ.**

YALLAQ Uzb. 19th c. **Yallaq** [Яллакъ] (SKSO III,
176).

YALLÏ Nog. 20th c. **Yallï / İyallï** [Сейфулла Ийалли
увлы], father of one of Baskakov's informants from
Sarï-awul (Bask., Nog. 144).

YALMAMBET Kzk. **J̌almambet / J̌almambet-mïrza**
[Цалмам Бет / Цалмам Бет мырза] (Proben III,
122 /156/); Kirg. **Yalmanbet / Yalmambet (<Yal-
mambet?)** [Ялман Бет], one of Manas' comrades-in-
arms (Proben V, 40 /41/). ✧ I. 'Hard/strong
Mukhammad' cf. Chag. *yalman* 'hart, heftig' (Radl. III,
190); II. Perhaps derived from *Yal + Mambet
(<Muχammed).* ⇨ **YALMAN** + suff. *-bet.*

YALMAN Maml. 14th c. **Yalman / Yälbän?**
[يلمان / يالبان / Yalman] (Tarǰ/Houtsma 108,
TarǰToparlı 42); Chuv. 18th-19th c. **Yalman-čura**
[Ялманчура] (Magn. 97). ✧ I. 'A kind of hare/rabbit'
cf. Maml. *jälmän* 'Springhase (jerboa)' (Tarǰ/Houtsma
108); II. 'Hard, strong' cf. Chag. *yalman* 'hart, heftig;
unwegsam (von Gebirgen)' (Radl. III, 190).

YALMAN-TAY Bashk. 18th c. **Yalman-tay** [Аканей
Ялмантаев] (MIB V, 203). ✧ 'Strong Foal'. ⇨
YALMAN + TAY or suff. *-tay(1,2)?*

YALMANBET see **YALMAMBET**

YALMAS Chuv. 18th-19th c. **Yalmas** [Ялмасъ] (Magn. 97).

YALMAT Bashk. 1772 **Yalmat** [Иштукай Ялматев] (MIB IV/1, 408); Bashk. 1728 **Yalmet** [Ялметь Бекеевъ] (MIB III, 252). ⇨ **YAL** + suff. -*mat*. See also **YAL-MAMET, YALMAMBET**.

YALSAQA Türk 8th c. **Yalsaqa-bäg** [Yalsaqa bäg] (ETY II, 112).

YALTEY Bashk. 1779 **Yaltey** [Ялтей (Ялти) Таиров] (MIB V, 91). ⇨ **YAL** + suff. -*tey*.

YALTÏQ Bashk. 1777 **Yaltïq** [Ялтикове и отце ево Баиме] (Vel.-Zern., Bašk. 4). ⇨ **YAL** + suff. -*tïq*?

YALTÏR Kzk. 1819 **Yaltïr** [Ялтыр] (MIK IV, 324); Bashk. 1777 **Yaltïr** / **Yaltïr-tarχan** [Ялътыръ Таймасовъ / Ялтыр-тархан Таймасов / Ялтыр Таймасов], a tarχan (Vel.-Zern., Bašk. 3-4, MIB V, 41, 64, 85). ✧ 'Bright, shining' cf. Bashk. *yaltïr* 'блестящий, лысый' (BRS/Uraksin).

YALUK Chuv. 18th-19th c. **Yaluk** [Ялукъ] (Magn. 97). ✧ 'Lazy, fed up with something' cf. Tat.(Bar., Tob.) *yalïq* 'faul sein, überdrüssig sein' (Radl. III, 165).

YALUKEY Bashk. 1735 **Yalukey** [Ялукей Аткасевъ] (Vel.-Zern., Bašk. 14). ✧ 'Fault, defect' cf. Chag. *yalu* 'das Fehlende' (Radl. III, 171). + suff. -*key*.

YAM Uyg. 12th c. - 14th c. **Yam** (DTS); Uyg. 12th c. - 14th c. **Yam-čur-tu** (Radl., USp. 82, DTS). ✧ I. 'Post-station' cf. Uyg. *yam* 'die Poststation' (Radl. III, 298), Bashk. *yam* 'почтовая станция' (BRS/Uraksin), Tat. *yam* 'почтовая станция' (TatRS); II. 'Rubbish, waste' (DTS)?

YAM-BARÏS see **YAN-BARS**

YAM-BEK see **ǰAN**

YAM-ČURA see **ǰAN**

YAM-MOLLA see **ǰAN**

YAM-MURZA see **ǰAN**

YAMAQ Uzb. 18th c. **ǰamaq-bi** [Djamach-by], a sultan, Asïl-bi's son, better known as Šah-mart-bi (Nalivkin-Dozon 67); Bashk. 1714 **Yamaq** [Ямак Чюкбашев] (MIB I, 105); Kzk. 1819 **Yamaq** [Ямак] (MIK IV, 323). ✧ 'Patch' cf. Uyg., Chag., Turk. *yamaq* 'der Flick' (Radl. III, 299-300).

YAMAN Tat. 1240 **ǰaman** [Τζαμάνης], a chieftain of the Tatars (Byz. Turc. 308); Kirg. 20th c. **ǰaman-bay** (Aytmatov); Kzk. 18th c. - 19th c. **ǰaman-bala** [Джаманбала] (Tunyšp. 71); Kzk. 19th c. **ǰaman-bala** [Джаманъ-бала] (Ibragimov 125); Kzk. 19th c. **ǰaman-γul** [Джамангулъ] (Grod., Pril. 38); Alt. 19th-20th c. **D'aman-uwul** [Дьамануул] (OjrRS 208); Alt. 19th-20th c. **D'aman** [Дьаман], fem. (OjrRS 211); Chuv. 18th-19th c. **Yaman** [Яманъ] (Magn. 97); Bashk. 18th c. **Yaman** [Яманов] (MIB V, 249); Bashk. 1754 **Yaman** [Яман Амангулов] (MIB IV/1, 84); Kzk. 1819 **Yaman** [Яман] (MIK IV, 325); Hak. 19th-20th c. **Yaman** [Яман] (HRS 356); Bashk. 1754 **Yaman** / **Yäman?** [Еман Унгаров] (MIB IV/1, 83?); Kzk. 19th c. **Yaman-bay** [Яманбай] (Grod. I, 98); Kzk. 19th c. **Yaman-bay** [Чутанъ Яманбаевъ] (Grod., Pril. 165); Chuv. 18th-19th c. **Yaman-čura** [Яманчура] (Magn. 97); Bashk. 1758 **Yaman-čura** [Максют Яманчурин] (MIB IV/1, 174); Bashk. 1740 **Yaman-γul** [Алша Ямангулов] (MIB I, 401); Bashk. 1777 **Yaman-γul** [Султан-Мрат (Салтанмрат) Емангулов] (MIB V, 54, 88, 172, 241); Bashk. 1787 **Yaman-γul** [Сеит (Саит) Ямангулов] (MIB V, 203); Bashk. 1790 **Yaman-γul** [Ямангул Мокшин] (MIB V, 295); Kzk. 19th c. **Yaman-qul** [Довлатъ Яманкуловъ] (Grod., Pril. 164); Kzk. 19th c. **Yaman-qul** [Яманкулъ] (Grod., Pril. 65); Kzk. 19th c. **Yaman-qul** [Яманъ Кулъ Магомедовъ] (Grod., Pril. 182); Tat. 1662 **Yeman-γul** [Емангулка Кошкилдиевъ] (DAI IV, 286); Bashk. 1740 **Yeman-γul** [Емангул Емантаев] (MIB I, 404); Bashk. 1798 **Yeman-γul** [Емангулъ] (PSZRI XXV, 195); Bashk. 1798 **Yeman-sura** [Емансуринъ] (PSZRI XXV, 296); *EN:* Kzk. 18th c. - 19th c. **ǰaman-bay** [Джаманбай] (Tunyšp. 69); *TN:* **Yaman** [Яманъ], a place? south of Kashgar (Karta JAR XX). ✧ I. 'Bad, wicked' cf. Alt. *d'aman* 'плочой' (OjrRS), Uyg., Kuman, Alt., Crm., Tat., Turk. *yaman* 'schlecht, böse, untauglich, schuldig' (Radl. III, 301); II. 'Strong, hard' (Kusimova). See also **QAR-YAMAN**.

YAMAN-ǰANDAR Turk. **Yaman-ǰandar** [Şemsüddin Yaman Candar / Şemsüddin Candar / Yaman Candar], an Ottoman Bey from the ǰandar-family of Türkmen origin (Uzunçarş., Anad. 1, 23). ✧ 'Wicked chief of guards' cf. Turk. *candâr* (P.) 'Diri, canlı; Koruyucu kimse, emniyet memuru' (Özön). ⇨ **YAMAN**.

YAMAN-QARA Kzk. 19th c. **Yaman-qara** [Яманъ-Кара] (Grod., Pril. 173). ⇨ **YAMAN** + **QARA**.

YAMAN-SARÏ Kzk. 19th c. **ǰaman-sarï** [Джамансары] (SOV 30); Bashk. 1763 **Yaman-sarï** [Ямансары Япаров] (MIB IV/2, 45); Bashk. 1742 **Yeman-sarï** [Емансары Зыбаев] (MIB III, 513); Bashk. 18th c. **Yeman-sarï** [Еман-сары Епаров] (MIB IV/1, 183); Bashk. 1768 **Yeman-sarï** [Ямансары Яфаров] (MIB IV/1, 332); Bashk. 18th c. **Yeman-sarï** / **Aman-sara** [Емансары (Амансара) Абдусалямов] (MIB V, 406); Bashk. 1764, 1785 **Yeman-sarï** / **Yeman-sar** [Емансары (Емансар) Биганов] (MIB IV/1, 285, V, 170). ⇨ **YAMAN** +**SARÏ**.

YAMANAY Bashk. 1757 **Yamanay** [Инякай Яманаев] (MIB IV/1, 157); Chuv. 18th-19th c. **Yamaney** [Яманей] (Magn. 97). ⇨ **YAMAN** + suff. -*ay*.

YAMANAQ Kzk. 1840 **Yamanaq** / **Yemanaq?** [Еманаковъ] (Konšin, Mat. V, 16); Chuv. 18th-19th c. **Yamanek** [Яманекъ] (Magn. 97). ⇨ **YAMAN** +

suff. *-aq, -ek.*

YAMANČA   Kzk. 19th c. **Yamanča** [Iamantcha / Яманча] (Levšin III, 96, Levchine 356). ⇨ **YAMAN** + suff. *-ča.*

YAMANDAY see **YAMANTAY**

YAMANDEY see **YAMANTAY**

YAMANEY see **YAMANAY**

YAMANEK see **YAMANAQ**

YAMANQA   Alt. 19th-20th c. **D'amanqa** [Дьаманка], fem. (OjrRS 211); Alt. 19th-20th c. **Yamanqa / D'amanqa** [Яманка / Дьаманка] (OjrRS 214). ✧ 'Bad; evil, wicked' (OjrRS 211). ⇨ **YAMAN** + suff. *-qa.*

YAMANSUR   Bashk. 1790 **Yamansur** [Ямансур Мокшин] (MIB V, 295).

YAMANTAY   Chuv. 18th-19th c. **Yamanday** [Ямандай] (Magn. 97); Chuv. 18th-19th c. **Yamandey** [Ямандей] (Magn. 97); Chuv. 18th-19th c. **Yamantay** [Ямантай] (Magn. 97); Kzk. 1846 **Yamantay** [Тлеубай Ямантаев] (MKOP 99); Kzk. 19th c. **Yamantay** [Молла Ямантай] (Grod., Pril. 173); Kkalp. 1846 **Yamantay** [Ямантай], a biy (MKOP 155); Bashk. 1735 **Yemantay** [Емантай Тымыковъ] (Vel.-Zern., Bašk. 13); Bashk. 1758 **Yemantay** [Акиней (Акеней) Емантаев] (MIB IV/1, 169). ✧ 'Bad, wicked'. ⇨ **YAMAN** + **TAY** or suff. *-tay(1,2)?*

YAMAR   Karakh. **Yamar** [Yamar] (MK/Atalay 858).

YAMAŠ   Tat.(Mish.) 19th c. **Yamaš** [Ямашевъ] (IOAIÊK XIX, 143); Bashk. 1756 **Yamaš** [Ямаш Чюрагулов] (MIB IV/1, 106); Bashk. 1756 **Yamaš** [Кутук Ямяшев] (MIB IV/1, 111); Bashk. 1761 **Yamaš** [Утмас Ямашев] (MIB IV/1, 216); Bashk. 1731 **Yemaš** [Бекбулат Емашев] (MIB III, 292); Bashk. 1735 **Yemaš** [Емашъ Мурзинъ] (Vel.-Zern., Bašk. 15); Bashk. 1740 **Yemaš** [Емаш] (MIB I, 404). ✧ I. A kind of bird, cf. Bashk. *yamaš* 'певчий воробей с красной грудкой' (BRS/Uraksin); II. A Bashkir clan (BRS/Uraksin); III. Shortened (dialectal) variant of (Tat.) *Jamaletdin* (Sattarov).

YAMBET see **YANBET**

YAMČÏ   Bashk. 1754 **Yamčï** [Ямчи Якшиев] (MIB IV/1, 84). ✧ 'Postmaster' cf. *yamčï* 'der Postillon, Postknecht' (Radl. III, 311). ⇨ **YAM** + suff. *-či.*

YAMČÏR-ČEČEN   Alt. (Tel.) **Yamčïr-čečen** [Ямчыръ-чеченъ], Altay-bučay's sister (Kalačev 492). ⇨ ? + **ČEČEN.**

YAMĞUR see **YAĞMUR**

YAMĞURČÏ   Kirg. **Jamyïrčï** [Жамгырчы] (Jud. 234); Kzk. **Jañyurča** [Джангурча] (Sozontov 6); Kzk. 19th c. **Jañyurčï / Jañyurča?** [Джангурча] (Sozontov 6); Kirg. **Yamyïrči** [Жамгырчы], a folklore hero (Proben V, 189 /190/); Tat.(GH) 13th c. **Yamyurči** [Ямгурчи] (Smirnov, Krym. 34); Crm.(Tat.) 18th c. **Yamyurči** [يمعورجى / Yamghourtchi], Meñli-Girey-χan's (1724-1730) son (Abulg./Desm. 187); Kzk. 19th c. **Yamyurči** [Далгожа Ямгурчинъ], sergeant-major, Ibragim Altynsarynovič's grand-father (AUK 379); Kzk. 19th c. **Yamyurči** [Экизъ Ямгучиевъ] (Grod., Pril. 169); Tat. 1555, 1557 **Yamyurči / Yamyurčey?** [Ямгурчѣй / Ямгурчей], the penultimate ruler (khan) in Astrakhan (PSRL XIII, 245, Zolotn. 160); Nog. 1480, 1481, 1499, 1507 **Yamyurči / Yamyurčiy?** [Ямгурчій / Ямгурчей], a murza (PSRL IV, 154, VI, 21, 35, 46, 248, VIII, 240, 249, XIX, 8, 203, XX 346, Zolotn. 160); Nog. 1500 **Yamyurči-murza, Yamyurčey-murza?** [Ямгурчей-мурза] (PSRL XII, 253); Chag. 15th c. **Yamyurčï** [Аббасъ МусаЯмггурджи], from the Mañkit tribe (Šejb. LVI); Tat. 14th c. **Yamyurčï** [Γιαμγουρτζέ], a christened Tatar (Byz. Turc. 113); Tat. 1649 **Yamyurčï** [Ямгурчѣй], a murza in Astrakhan (AI IV, 77, 79); Tat.? 1649 **Yamyurčï / Yamyurčiy?** [Ямгурчѣй], a murza (AI IV, 421); Tat. 1552 **Yañyurči** [Янъ-Курчи], a prince (Kn. Metriki Lit. 86); Tat. 1624 **Yañyurči** [Янгурчей Колчуринъ] (Pokrovskij 71); Tat. 1624 **Yañyurči** [Чирючей Янгурчеевъ] (Pokrovskij 72); Bashk. 1664 **Yañyurči** [Янгурчей] (MIB I, 193); Bashk. 1709 **Yañyurči** [Актуган Янгурчин] (MIB III, 49); Bashk. 1735 **Yañyurči** [Янгурчий Каныевъ] (Vel.-Zern., Bašk. 19); Kzk. 1846 **Yañyurči** [Балгуджа Янгурчин] (MKOP 99); Tat. 20th c. **Yañyurčï** [Янгурчиев] (Sattarov); Tat.(Sib.) 1609 **Yañyurčï** [Янгурча] (Miller, Ist. Sib. 209, 210). ✧ I. 'Rainy' (Sozontov 6; Rásonyi, Categ. 328.); II. A kind of bird. The name is applied to several species of waders (Shaw-Scully). ⇨ **YAĞMUR?** + suff. *-čï / -ča.*

YAMÏ   Türk 8th c. **Yamï-qayan** [yamï kagan] (DTS, ETY I, 128); Kzk. 1634 **Yamu-qan?** [Ямокан], a Kazak prince (Miller, Ist. Sib. II, 418). ✧ 'High-ranking, eminence' cf. Alt. *yamï* 'das Ansehen, die einflussreiche, wichtige Stellung, das Amt, die Rangklasse' (Radl. III, 307).

YAMMET see **YANMAT**

YAMTAR   Türk 732 **Yamatar** [Yamatar] (ETY I, 66); Türk 732 **Yamatar / Išbara-yamatar** [Išbara Yamatar] (ETY I, 44). See also **TUDUN-YAMTAR.**

YAMUK   Chuv. 19th c. **Yamuk** [Jamuk] (Kronheim 96).

YAN see **JAN**

YAN-ALİ see **JAN-ALİ**

YAN-ARASLAN see **YAN-ARSLAN**

YAN-ARSLAN   Trkm. 19th c. **Jan-araslan** [Джанъ-Араслановъ] (Ščeglov I, 355); Trkm. 19th c. **Jan-araslan** [Керимъ-Берды Джанъ-Араслановъ] (Ščeglov I, 355); Kzk. 19th c. **Jan-arstan** [Джанарстанъ] (SOV 42); Nog. 1649 **Yan-araslan** [Батырча Янъ-араслановъ] (AI IV, 87); Tat. / Nog.? 1614 **Yan-araslan** [Кутукъ Янараслановъ] (AI III,

23, 411); Nog. 1601 **Yan-raslan** (<Yan-araslan) [Ян Раслан] (Miller, Ist. Sib. II, 169). ⇨ ĴAN + ARSLAN.

YAN-BARS   Chuv. 18th-19th c. **Yam-baris** [Ямбарисъ] (Magn. 97); Bashk. 20th c. **Yan-baris** [Янбарис] (Kusimova); Tat. 20th c. **Yan-bars** [Янбарс / Янбарисов / Янбарцев] (Sattarov); Tat. 1548 **Yan-bars / Yän-bars?**, prince and envoy from Kazan (PSRL (Russk. Hr.) I, 529); Tat. 1531 **Yan-bars-murza / Yän-bars-murza?** [Енъбарсъ-мурза] (PSRL XIII, 167); *TN:* Chuv. 18th c. **Yan-barus(ova)** [Янбарусова], a village in the district of Čeboksary (Korsakov 283). ⇨ ĴAN + BARS.

YAN-BERDİ see ĴAN-BERDİ

YAN-BİRDE see ĴAN-BERDİ

YAN-BULAT see ĴAN-BULAT

YAN-BULDU(Y) see ĴAN-BOLDÏ

YAN-DÄWLÄT   Tat.(Lit.) 1594 **Yan-däwlet** [Яндавлетовичъ], a family (Lit. Tat. 221, 232); Tat.(Sib.) 1598-99 **Yan-däwlet** [Яндевлетъ], a Siberian princess, Küčüm-qan's third wife (AI II, 17, 20, 23). ⇨ ĴAN + DÄWLÄT.

YAN-DEMİR see ĴAN-TEMİR

YAN-DİMER see ĴAN-TEMİR

YAN-DÏĞAN see ĴAN-TUĞAN

YAN-DUĞAN see ĴAN-TUĞAN

YAN-GİLDE see ĴAN-KELDİ

YAN-GİLDİ see ĴAN-KELDİ

YAN-GİREY Chuv. 18th-19th c. **Yan-girey** [Янгирей] (Magn. 98). ⇨ ĴAN + KERÄY.

YAN-GÜZÄ see ĴAN

YAN-ĞALİ see ĴAN-ALİ

YAN-ĞALÏČ see YAN-QÏLÏČ

YAN-ĞARA see ĴAN-QARA

YAN-ĞÏLÏČ see YAN-QÏLÏČ

YAN-ĞULTAN   Bashk. 1726 **Yan-ğultan** [Янгултан Менлибаев] (MIB III, 242). ⇨ ĴAN + QULTAN.

YAN-HARÏ see YAN-SARÏ

YAN-ÏŠ   Tat. 20th c. **Yan-ïš** [Яныш / Янышев / Янишев] (Sattarov); Bashk. 1742 **Yan-ïš** [Яныш Улмяскулов] (MIB I, 486); Bashk. 1751 **Yan-ïš** [Яныш Тукунбетев] (MIB IV/1, 55); Bashk. 1773 **Yan-ïš** [Солтан-мрат Янышев] (MIB IV/1, 374); Bashk. 1740 **Yan-ïš-bay** [Янышбай] (MIB I, 412, 446); Kzk. 1803 **Yan-ïš-biy** [Яныш бий], one of the chiefs of the Alim-ulï tribe of the Little Horde (Kiši Žüz) (MIK IV, 514). ✧ 'Soul-friend' (Sattarov). ⇨ ĴAN + EŠ.

YAN-KELDİ see ĴAN-KELDİ

YAN-QÏLÏČ   Chuv. 18th-19th c. **Yan-ğlïč** [Янглычъ] (Magn. 98); Tat.(Mish.) **Yan-ğalïč** [Янгалычевъ], a Misher family (IOAIÊK XIX, 143); Crm.(Tat.) 1528 **Yan-ğlïč-mïrza** [Янглычъ-мыръза] (PSRL XIII, 46); Tat. 1715 **Yan-qlïč** [Янклыч Азиков] (MIB III, 124,

125); Tat. 1624 **Yen-ğlïč** (<Yan-ğïlïč) [Енглычъ Караевъ] (Pokrovskij 70). ✧ 'Rainbow' cf. *yañ* 'bow' + *qïlïč* 'sword' (Sattarov). ⇨ YAÑ? + QÏLÏČ. See also ĴAN-QÏLÏČ?

YAN-QLÏČ see YAN-QÏLÏČ

YAN-MAMET see ĴAN-MAMET

YAN-NAZAR Kzk. 1820 **Yan-nazar** [Янназаръ] (Sib. Vest. IX, 116). ⇨ ĴAN + NAZAR.

YAN-RASLAN see YAN-ARSLAN

YAN-SARQA   Tat.(Sib.) 1625 **Yan-sarqa** [Янсарка] (Miller, Ist. Sib. II, 320). ⇨ ĴAN-SARÏ + dim. suff. -qa.

YAN-SÄY see ĴAN

YAN-SÏRA see ĴAN

YAN-SUBA   Tat.(Lit.) 1592 **Yan-suba** [Янсуба Шемердеевичъ] (Lit. Tat. 124). ⇨ ĴAN.

YAN-SÜYÄR   Tat. 20th c. **Yan-söyär** [Янсөяр] (Sattarov); Tat.(Sib.) 1598-1599 **Yan-süyer** [Янсюеръ], Küčüm-qan's grandson (AI II, 17, 20-22). ⇨ ĴAN + SEWÄR.

YAN-TELÄŠ   Tat.(Sib.) 1605 **Yan-tleš** (<Yan-teläš) [Янтлеш (Буранчеев)] (Miller, Ist. Sib. II, 190). ⇨ ĴAN + TİLÄŠ.

YAN-TUBA   Tat. 1624 **Yan-tuba** [Янтуба Янбулатовъ] (Pokrovskij 70). ⇨ ĴAN.

YAN-TUĞAY Tat.(Sib.) 1640 **Yan-tuğay** [Янтугай Катюков] (Miller, Ist. Sib. II, 474). ⇨ ĴAN + TOĞAY.

YAN-TUĞAN see ĴAN-TUĞAN

YAN-TUWĞAN see ĴAN-TUĞAN

YAN-URS see YAN-URUS

YAN-URUS Chuv. 18th-19th c. **Yan-urs** (<Yan-urïs) [Янурсъ] (Magn. 99); Bashk. 1723 **Yan-urus** [Янурус Байгузин] (MIB III, 208); Bashk. 1751 **Yan-urus / Yän-urus** [Янурусов (Енурусовъ)] (MIB IV/1, 34, 69, 75). ⇨ ĴAN + URUS.

YAN-UZAQ see ĴAN-UZAQ

YANA Yürük 1543 **Yana** [يانا] (Gökb., Rum. 103); Tat.(Tüm.) 1632, 1651 **Yana-bek** [Гилдей Янабеков (Янебеков)], a murza (Miller, Ist. Sib. II, 391, DAI III, 329); Tat. 1697 **Yana-pay** [Янапайковъ] (Kungursk. akty 246). ✧ '(Once) again'? cf. Chag., Tat., Turk. *yänä* 'von Neuem, abermals, noch' (Radl., III, 329).

YANA-BERDİ   Bashk. 1734 **Yäna-berdi** [Енаберда Сартаевъ], a tarχan (Vel.-Zern., Bašk. 11); Bashk. 1783 **Yäna-berdi** [Азамат Енабердин] (MIB V, 145); Bashk. 1780 **Yäna-berdi / Yäna-bardï?** [Усейн Енабардин] (MIB V, 109); Bashk. 1735 **Yäna-berdi / Yäna-berda** [Енаберда Мустаев] (MIB III, 334); Bashk. 1780 **Yäna-berdi / Yäna-berda** [Енаберда Еныбеков] (MIB V, 115). ⇨ YANA? + BERDİ.

YANAĞLÏ Oghuz/Trkm. 14th c. - 15th c. **Yanağlï-qoĵa / Yanağlu-qoĵa** [Yapağılu Koca; Yapağulu Koca /

Янаглы-Коджа (Янаглу-Коджа)] (DQorq. 78, 79, 83).

YANAΓLU see **YANAΓLÏ**

YANAY see **ǰANAY**

YANAR Uzb. 20th c. **Yânar** [Ёнар] (Begmatov 1984, 202); Uzb. 20th c. **Yânar-bay** [Енарбай] (Begmatov 1984, 202). ✧ 'Shining, sparkling' (Begmatov), cf. Uzb. *yân-* 'гореть; сиять, блестеть' (UzbRS).

YANARČA Kzk. **Yanarča** [Янарча] (Sb. Syr-D. IX, 54).

YANAŠ Tat. 1764 **Yanaš** [Мурзаш Янашев] (MIB IV/1, 304). ✧ 'My dear, dearest, darling' cf. Tat. *žanaš* 'душечка, любимая' (TatRS).

YANBET Bashk. 1690 **Yambet** (<Yanbet / Yänbet?) [Кутлумбетка Ямбетевъ] (Vel.-Zern., Bašk. 37); Tat.(Mish.) 1775 **Yanbet / Yänbet?** [Аит Янбетев] (MIB IV/2, 421). ⇨ **ǰAN** + suff. *-bet*.

YANČAT Tat. 1601 **Yančat** [Янчат] (Miller, Ist. Sib. II, 169).

YANČER Tat.(Sib.) 1601 **Yančer / Yänčer?** [Янчеров Козыбай] (Miller, Ist. Sib. II, 169); Tat.(Sib.) 1641 **Yenčar / Yenčär?** [Енчаров Бекженей] (Miller, Ist. Sib. II, 484). ✧ 'Little soul (darling)'. ⇨ **ǰAN** + Mo. dim. suff. *-čar/-čer*.

YANDAP Uzb. 20th c. **Yândâp** [Ендоп] (Begmatov 1984, 202). ✧ 'Be by (us) / Be/stay alive!' (Begmatov).

YANDÏL Turk. 19th c. **Yandïl-oγlu** [Jandyl oγlu] (Kúnos 1891, 119).

YANDÏR Khorezm.? **Yandïr** [Яндир], Deñiz-χan's son (RaD I/1, 76).

YANGÍT Tat.(Sib.) 1631 **Yangit?** [Янгит] (Miller, Ist. Sib. II, 386).

YANÏ-BAY Bashk. 20th c. **Yanï-bay** [Яныбай] (Kusimova). ✧ 'His soul is rich' (Kusimova). ⇨ **ǰAN / ǰANÏ? + BAY**.

YANÏ-BEK see **ǰANÏ**

YANÏ-ΓUL Bashk. **Yanï-γul** [Тоианъ Яныгуловъ] (Vel.-Zern., Bašk. 25). ✧ 'His soul is slave' cf. Tat. PN *Yan-γol / Yän-γol* (Sattarov). ⇨ **ǰAN / ǰANÏ? + QUL**.

YANÏQ Bashk. 1757 **Yanïq** [Яныков] (MIB IV/2, 18). ✧ 'Soot, burn' cf. Bashk. *yanïq* 'нагар' (BRS).

YANÏM Chuv. 18th-19th c. **Yanïm** [Янымъ] (Magn. 99). ⇨ **YAN**.

YANÏMBET Bashk. 1735 **Yanïmbet** [Янымбеть Уразов], a tarχan (Vel.-Zern., Bašk. 13); Bashk. 1735 **Yanïmbet** [Тоскубай Янымбетев] (MIB III, 336); Bashk. 1735 **Yanïmbet** [Иткулъ Янымбетевъ], a tarχan (Vel.-Zern., Bašk. 13). ⇨ **ǰAN** + suff. *-ïmbet*.

YANKA see **ǰANKE**

YANQUR Kzk. 1819 **Yanqur-bay** [Янкурбай] (MIK IV, 325).

YANMAT Bashk. 1758 **Yammet / Yämmet?** [Исемь Ямметев] (MIB IV/1, 163); Tat.(Sib.) 1640 **Yanmat** [Янмат] (Miller, Ist. Sib. II, 455); Bashk. 1758

Yänmät [Исень Янметев] (MIB IV/1, 163). ⇨ **YANMAMET, ǰAN** + suff. *-mat*.

YANNÏQ Tat. 1718 **Yannïq** [Янтык Янныков] (MIB III, 167).

YANOŠ Yürük 1543 **Yanoš** [Hasan Yanoş] (Gökb., Rum. 213).

YANSAN see **ZAYSAN**

YANTAQČÏ Kirg. **Yantaqčï** [Jantaktschy / Джантакчы] (Proben V, 561 /566/). ✧ 'Someone who deals with thistle'.

YANTÏQ Bashk. 1678 **Yantïq** [Кадышъ Янтиковъ] (Vel.-Zern., Bašk. 33); Bashk. 1718 **Yantïq** [Янтык Янныков] (MIB III, 167); Bashk. 1735 **Yantïq** [Кинзегулъ Янтыковъ], a tarχan (Vel.-Zern., Bašk. 24). ✧ I. 'Slanting, leaning (to one side)' cf. Alt., Tat. *yantïq* 'schief, abschüssig; auf die Seite geneigt' (Radl. III, 92), Bashk. *yantïq* 'покосившийся' (BRS/Uraksin); II. 'Hip; a part of hip-bone' cf. Bashk. dial. *yantïq* = *yanbaš* 'бедренная кость; мосол' (BRS/Uraksin).

YANTÏŠ Bashk. 1763 **Yantïš** [Назар Янтышев] (MIB IV/2, 45).

YANUR-BAS Kzk. 1819 **Yanur-bas** [Янурбас] (MIK IV, 323). ⇨ **BAŠ.**

YAÑA see **YAÑÏ**

YAÑΓURČÏ see **YAMΓURČÏ**

YAÑΓURČÏ see **YAMΓURČÏ**

YAÑΓURSA Tat.? 1680 **Yañγursa / Yañγursä** [Янгурсинъ] (Kungursk. akty 45); Tat. 1680 **Yañγursa / Yañγursä** [Адайко Янгурсинъ] (AI V, 94).

YAÑÏ Kzk. 18th c. - 19th c. **ǰana-bay** [Джанабай] (SOK 78); Alt. 19th-20th c. **D'aña** [Дьана], fem. (OjrRS 211); Tat.(Sib.) 20th c. **Yanï-bay** [Яныбай / Яныбаев / Янабаев] (Sattarov); Uzb. 19th c. **Yaña-bay** [Янгабай Карабаевъ] (SKSO III, 186); Bashk. 20th c. **Yañï-bay** [Яңыбай / Яныбай] (Kusimova); Kzk. 1819 **Yañï-bay** [Янгыбаевъ] (MIK IV, 325); Kzk. 19th c. **Yañï-bay** [Янгибаевъ] (SKSO VIII, 220); Bashk. 1779 **Yañu-bay** [Янгубай Калмаккулов] (MIB V, 80, 90, 91). ✧ 'New(ly born)' (Sattarov, Kusimova) cf. Tat. *yaña* 'neu' (Radl. III, 58), Bashk. *yañï* 'новый, свежий' (BRS), Kzk., Tat. *jaña* 'neu' (Radl. IV, 16). See also **TEYÄR-YAÑÏ**.

YAÑÏ-BERGÄN Kzk. 1817 **Yañï-bergän** [یانكی بیرگان] (MIK IV, 311). ⇨ **YAÑÏ + BERGEN**.

YAÑÏČUN Uyg. **Yañïčun** [Yangıçun] (EUTS).

YAÑÏČUN-AŠAN Uyg. 12th c. - 14th c. **Yañïčun-ašan** (DTS). ✧ 'Willing/ready-to-new-Ašan' (Blagova 1997, 714). ⇨ **YAÑÏČUN + AŠAN**.

YAÑLÏ Kzk. 19th c. **Yañlï** [Джанъ Янглыевъ] (Grod., Pril. 151).

YAÑLÏŠ Uzb. **Yañlïš**, fem. (É. Dobos, A Tale from Qarabau: AOH XXVII, 172); Uzb. 20th c. **Yañlïš**

[Янглиш] (Begmatov 1984, 206). ❖ I. 'Be mistaken!' Begmatov treats it as an imperative name (op. cit. 206), cf. Uzb. *yañliš-* 'ошибаться, заблуждаться' (UzbRS), II. Defective, Faulty, Mistake, Fault' *yañliš* 'ошибка, заблуждение, запутаться' (UzbRS).

YAÑU see **YAÑİ**

YAÑUČİ Tat. 1624 **Yañuči** [Бичура Янгучеевъ] (Pokrovskij 72).

YAP-TOĠRİL Uyg. 12th c. - 14th c. **Yap-toɣrïl** [jap toɣrïl / Yap Toġrïl] (Radl., USp. 205, 247, DTS, EUTS). ❖ '?-Falcon/hawk'. ⇨ **TOĠRİL.**

YAPAĠÏLU Oghuz/Trkm. 14th c. - 15th c. **Yapaɣïlu-qoja** (DQorq./Rossi 195, 196, 201). ❖ 'Having raw wool' cf. Chag., Turk. *yapaɣï* 'unbearbeitete Wolle, der Fliess' (Radl. III, 261) + suff. *-lu.*

YAPAĠU Chag. 16th c. **Yapaɣu-bay** [Япагубай] (Ivanov 106). ❖ 'Raw wool' cf. Chag., Turk. *yapaɣï* 'unbearbeitete Wolle, der Fliess' (Radl. III, 261).

YAPAQ Kzk. 1819 **Yapaq** [Япак] (MIK IV, 325); Kkalp. 20th c. **Žapaq** [Жапак] (KkRS 773). ❖ 'Raw wool' cf. Chag., Turk. *yapaɣï* 'unbearbeitete Wolle, der Fliess' (Radl. III, 261).

YAPALAQ see **YABALAQ**

YAPANČA Tat. 1552 **Yapanča** [Япанча], a prince (PSRL XIII, 202); Tat. 20th c. **Yapanča** [Япанча] (Sattarov); Tat.(Crm.) 1495 **Yapanča** [Япанча], Mengli Girey's servant (PSRL VI, 41, 241, VIII, 232); Tat.(Crm.) 1551 **Yapanča** / **Yepanča** [Япанча (Епанча)], an Ar(skij)? prince (PSRL VI, 307, XIX, 418); Crm. 1497 **Yapanča-saltan** [Япанча-Салтанъ], son of the Crimean ruler (PSRL XII, 244); Tat. **Yapanči** [Япанчи] (Katanov, Star. Kaz. 297); Tat. 20th c. **Yapančï** [Япанчы] (Sattarov); Tat. 1580 **Yapanša** [Japansa], a Tatar prince, fought against Yermak (Radl., Aus Sib. I, 148); Crm. 1528 **Yepanča** [Епанча] (PSRL 46). ❖ 'Child born in the steppe' (Sattarov). ⇨ **YABAN.**

YAPANČİ see **YAPANČA**

YAPANČÏ see **YAPANČA**

YAPAR see **JAFAR**

YAPAŠ Bashk. 1740 **Yapaš** [Татлы Япашев] (MIB I, 404); Bashk. 1740 **Yapaš** [Япаш] (MIB I, 395).

YAPATU Uyg. 12th c. - 14th c. **Yapatu** (DTS). ⇨ **YABDU?**

YAPDU-TERÄK see **YABDU-TERÄK**

YAPEY Tat. 1781 **Yapey** [Япей Ибраевъ] (Korsakov 29).

YAPĠUN Türk/Uyg. 8th c. - 9th c. **Yapɣun** [japɣun / Yapġun] (DTS, EUTS).

YAPÏĠ Uyg. 13th c. **Yapïɣ** (DTS).

YAPÏRA see **YABÏRA**

YAPÏŠ Bashk. 1740 **Yapïš** [Япиш Кайбаков] (MIB I, 404).

YAPLÏŠ Uyg. 12th c. - 14th c. **Yaplïš** [Yaplïş] (DTS,

EUTS).

YAPSA Kuman 1347 **Yapsa** [Japza] (Gyárfás III, 484). ❖ I. 'Cover him/her over; tuck him/her in' (Rásonyi, KÖA 137, Rásonyi, Anthr. 147), cf. Karakh. *yapsa-* 'bedecken, scliessen wollen' (MK/Brock.); II. 'Be glad; be delighted' cf. Alt. *yapsï-* 'entzückt sein, sehr erfreut sein, sich wundern' (Radl. III, 271).

YAPTÏQ Yürük 16th c. **Yaptïq** [ﯾﺎﭘﺪق] (Gökb., Rum. 103). ❖ 'We have done (it)'? cf. Turk. *yap-* 'to do, to make' (TED).

YAPUJU Turk. 19th c. **Yapuju-oɣlu** [Japužu oɣlu], a Zeybek (Kúnos 1891, 119). ❖ 'Builder; architect' cf. Turk. *yapïjï* 'der Erbauer, Maurer, Zimmermann, Architect' (Radl. III, 264).

YAPUNSU see **YABUNSU**

YAPURŠU see **YABURŠU**

YAR Khorezm.? 13th c.? **Jar-bek** [ﺟﺎﺭ ﺑﻚ] (RaD/Jahn 54); Kzk. 19th c. **Jar-murza** [Джармурза] (SODž. 52); Chag. 16th c. **Yar-baba-bahadur** [Яр Баба бахадур] (Ivanov 142); Chag. 16th c. **Yar-bek** [Ярбек (Яр Мухаммед)], the same as Yar-muχammed-mirza (Ivanov 321); Trkm. 1820/21 **Yar-qulï** [Яр-кули Палван], from the Yomut tribe (MIT II, 417, 425); Chuv. 18th-19th c. **Yar-molla** [Ярмолла] (Magn. 100); Chuv. 18th-19th c. **Yar-mula** [Ярмула] (Magn. 100); Chuv. 18th-19th c. **Yar-mulla** [Ярмулла] (Magn. 100); Uyg. 12th c. - 14th c. **Yar-oɣïl** (DTS); Chag. 16th c. **Yar-oɣlï** [Яр-оглы] (Ivanov 208); Uyg. **Yar-oɣlu** [Yaroğlu] (EUTS). ❖ 'Friend, bride-groom; girl-friend, bride; lover; fellow, mate, helper' Frequently used also as a secondary component of male and female names. Cf. Uyg. *yar* (<P.) 'друг' (DTS), Az., Crm., Tat., Turk. *yar* 'die Geliebte, der Genosse, Gefährte, Freund' (Radl. III, 101), Tat. *yar / yär(?)* 'возлюбленный, милый, любимый' (TatRS), Bashk. *yär* 'возлюбленный, возлюбленная' (BRS/Uraksin), Kkalp. *yar* 'любимый, возлюбленный' (KkRS), Kzk. *žar III* 'супруг, супруга; жених, невеста' (KzRS), Kkalp. dial. *jar / žar* 'любимый, милый' (Bask., Kkalp. 338), Tat. *jär* 'другъ' (Ostroumov). See also **ALLAH-YAR, ČAR-YAR, QUL-QUDA-YAR, MÄDİ-YAR.**

YAR-ALİ Maml. 1438/39 **Yar-ali** [ﯾﺎﺭﻋﻠﻰ ﺑﻦ ﻧﺼﺮﺍﻟﻠﻪ ﺍﻟﺨﺮﺍﺳﺎﻧﻰ ﺍﻟﻌﺠﻤﻰ ﺍﻟﻄﻮﯾﻞ] (Ibn Taghrīb. VII, 91, 95 etc.); Trkm. 1850 **Yar-ali-mulla** [Ярали-мулла] (ZIRGOÊtn. I, 32). ❖ 'Friend-Ali; Prophet Ali's friend'. ⇨ **YAR + ALİ.**

YAR-BOL Kzk. 19th c. **Jar-bol** [Джарболъ] (SOV 16, 38, 42, 72); Kzk. 19th c. **Jar-bol** [Джарболъ] (SOK 294); Kzk. 19th c. **Jar-bol** [Джарболъ] (AOP 2); Tat. 20th c. **Yar-bul** [Ярбул / Ярбулов] (Sattarov); Kzk. 1822 **Žar-bul** / **Yar-bol** [ﯾﺎﺭﺑﻮﻝ / Жарбул] (MIK IV, 433, 435). ❖ 'Be/become a friend / a helper' (Rásonyi, Imp. 238, Sattarov). ⇨ **YAR + BOL.** See also **DOST-**

BOL, YAR-BOLDЇ.

YAR-BOLDЇ Kzk. 19th c. **J̌ar-boldï** [Джарболды] (Potanin II, 6); Nog. 20th c. **Yar-boldï** [Мекли Булат Йарболды увлы], father of Baskakov's informant from the aul of Yaman-ɣoy (Bask., Nog. 143). ✧ 'A friend is born; born as friend'. ⇨ YAR + BOLDЇ.

YAR-ÏŠ see **YARÏŠ**

YAR-QAYA Uyg. **Yar-qaya** [Yarkaya] (EUTS); Uyg. 8th c. **Yar-qaya** / **Yär-qaya** (TT IV, 432). ✧ 'Precipice-rock' cf. Karakh. *yar* 'яр, овраг' (DTS), Uyg. TN *Jar* 'название места; название реки' (DTS). ⇨ YAR? + QAYA.

YARA-ČEČEN Alt.(Tel.) 19th c. **Yara-čečen** [Яра-чеченъ] (Potanin IV, 362-63); Alt. 19th c. **Yara-čečen** / **Yara-čäčän** [Яра-Чечен], Ülgen's servant (Verb., In. 98, 100, Radl. III, 104). ✧ 'Be a good *Čečen*' cf. Türk, Uyg., Chag., Kuman, Kar., Tat., Turk., etc. *yara-* 'passend sein, tauglich sein, gefallen' (Radl. III, 104). ⇨ ČEČEN.

YARAB Bashk. **Yarab-qul** [Утей Ярабкулов] (MIB IV/2, 405). ✧ Ya-Rabb! (Ar.) 'Oh God!'.

YARAƔ-SÏLƔA Uyg. 13th c. **Yaraɣ-sïlɣa** (DTS). ⇨ YARAQ.

YARAX see **YARAQ**

YARAQ Chuv. 18th-19th c. **Yaraχ-mula** [Ярахмула] (Magn. 99); Chuv. 18th-19th c. **Yaraχ-pey** [Ярахпей] (Magn. 99); Chuv. 18th-19th c. **Yaraχ-pi** [Ярахпи] (Magn. 99); Chuv. 18th-19th c. **Yarak** [Яракъ] (Magn. 99); Chuv. 18th-19th c. **Yarak-pay** [Яракпай] (Magn. 99); Uyg. **Yaraq** [Yarak] (EUTS); Uyg. 12th c. - 14th c. **Yaraq** (Radl., USp. 114-15). ✧ I. 'Suitable, required, necessary' cf. Türk, Uyg., Chag. *yaraq* 'die Passendheit, das Passendsein, die Möglichkeit, die nöthige Vorbereitung; passend, nöthig' (Radl. III, 105-107), Uyg. *yaraɣ* I 'id.' (DTS); II. 'Armour' cf. Türk. *jaraq* I 'панцирь, кольчуга' (DTS).

YARAMAY Chuv. 1739 **Yaramay** [Ярамаевъ] (Alatyr. 142); Chuv. 18th-19th c. **Yaramay** [Ярамай] (Magn. 99). ✧ 'Not suitable; useless, good-for-nothing' cf. Tat. *yara-* 'годиться, быть годным' (TatRS).

YARAMBET Bashk. 1769 **Yarambet** [Иткарий Ярамбетев] (MIB IV/1, 334). ⇨ YAR / YARAN? + suff. *-ïmbet / -bet*.

YARAMÏŠ Uyg. 762 **Yaramïš** [Orungu Yaramïš] (Mahrnāmag 10); Yürük 1609 **Yaramïš** [يارامش / Yaramïş] (Gökçen 80). ✧ '(H)She Became useful; (H)She Was suitable' (Erol II), cf. Türk, Uyg., Kuman, Chag., Az., Tat., Turk., etc. *yara-* 'passend sein, tauglich sein, gefallen' (Radl. III, 104), Turk. *yara-* 'to be serviceable; to be of useful; to be suitable' (TED). See also **ORUÑU-YARAMÏŠ**.

YARAN Chuv. 18th-19th c. **Yaran** [Яранъ] (Magn. 99); Chuv. 18th-19th c. **Yaran** [Ярань] (Magn. 99); Chuv. 18th-19th c. **Yaran-bay** [Яранбай] (Magn. 99);

Trkm. 20th c. **Yārān** [Yaran] (Zaj. 1971, 326); Trkm. 20th c. **Yārān** [Яран] (TrkmRS 819). ✧ 'Friend, mate, fellow; helper' (Zaj. 1971), cf. Chag. *yaran* 'der Freund, Gefährte' (Radl. III, 109), Trkm. *yārān* 'сторонник, соучастник, союзник; друг' (TrkmRS), Crm. *yarän* 'bekannt, befreundet, der Freund' (Radl. III, 119), plur. of P. *yār*.

YARAN-QAŠ Selj. 1154 **Yaran-qaš** [Яранкаш] (MIT I, 356). ⇨ YARAN + QAŠ? See also **YARÏN-QUŠ**?

YARAŠ Kzk. **Yaraš** [Ярашъ] (Sb. Syr-D. IX, 50); Uzb. 20th c. **Yaraš** [Яраш] (Begmatov 1984, 206); Uzb. 20th c. **Yaraš-ǰân** [Ярашжон] (Begmatov 1984, 206); Uzb. 20th c. **Yaraš-χoǰa** [Ярашхўжа] (Begmatov 1984, 206). ✧ I. 'Suitable' cf. Uyg., Chag., Alt. *yaraš* 'das Passende; die Schönheit, Ansehnlichkeit, Wohlgefälligkeit' (Radl. III, 115); II. 'Become appeased! Resign/reconcile yourself!' (Begmatov), cf. Türk, Uyg., Kuman, Chag., Alt., Crm., Turk. *yaraš-* 'sich versöhnen, in Frieden leben, sich etwas anpassen' (Radl. III, 116), Uzb. *yaraš-* I. '(при)мириться' (UzbRS).

YARAŠPÏDЇ Uyg. 12th c. - 14th c. **Yarašpïdï** [Qayaq Yarašpïdï] (Radl., USp. 127-28); Uyg. 12th c. - 14th c. **Yarašpïdï** (DTS).

YARAZ Oghuz/Trkm. 13th c. **Yaraz** [Яраз], Ay-χan's son (RaD I/1, 76).

YARDAR Kuman 1266 **Yardar** [Jardar], a Kuman nobleman (Dominus de Kumanis) in Hungary (Gyárfás II, 418). ✧ 'Creator?'; *Yardar <*Yaradar <*Yaratar <yarat-*; participle of Kuman *jarat-* 'schaffen, erschaffen' (CC), see Rásonyi, KÖA 137-138, Rásonyi, Anthr. 147.

YARDÏM Yürük 1558 **Yardïm** [ياردم / Yardım ibn Ali] (Gökçen 38). ✧ 'Help(er)' cf. Turk. *yardïm* 'die Hülfe, der Beistand' (Radl. III, 146).

YARGUN Chuv. 18th-19th c. **Yargun** [Яргунь] (Magn. 100). ✧ 'Judge, mayor' (Rásonyi, KÖA 138, Rásonyi, Anthr. 147), cf. Kuman *jarguču* 'Richter, Bürgermeister' (CC). + suff. *-čï*.

YARGUNKA Chuv. 18th-19th c. **Yargunka** [Яргунка] (Magn. 100).

YARGÜČ see **YÜRGÜČ**

YARƔAQ Bashk. 1729 **Yarɣaq** [Атуган Яргаков] (MIB III, 260). ✧ I. 'Thin' cf. Bashk. *yarɣaq* 'тощий, худой' (BRS/Uraksin); II. 'Chatterer, boasting' cf. Türk, Chag., Alt., Kirg., Tat. *yarɣaq* 'ein Pelz ohne Haare, Regenmantel etc.; (Tat.) der Schwätzer' (Radl. III, 136-37).

YARƔAL Bashk. 1709 **Yarɣal** [Яргал] (MIKk. 160-161).

YARƔUČЇ Kuman 1330 **Yarɣučï** [Jurguche cumanus / Jurguche Comano de Kozar] (Gyárfás III, 472). ✧ 'Judge' cf. Chag. *yarɣučï* 'der Richter' (Radl. III, 140).

YARƔUŠ Bashk. 1735 **Yarɣuš** [Яргушъ Мурзинъ], a tarχan (Vel.-Zern., Bašk. 15). ✧ 'Lawsuit, captivity' cf.

Chag. *yarɣuč* 'der Prozess, das Tribunal, Gefängniss' (Radl. III, 140).

YARÏ Chag. 16th c. **Yarï / Yari?** [Яри] (Ivanov 261-68, 271-73); Chag. 16th c. **Yarï / Yari?** [Яри], a mir (Ivanov 129); Chag. 16th c. **Yarï-biy / Yari-biy?** [Яри-бий] (Ivanov 216, 290); Turk. 1505 **Yarï-hoJa** [Yапı Hoca] (Gökb., Ed. 428); Trkm. 1828 **Yarï-šeyχ** [Ярышейх], from the MeJeur (?) clan (MIT II, 448, 462). ❖ I. 'Half'? cf. Turk. *yarı* 'id.' (TED), Trkm. *yārï* 'половина' (TrkmRS), Crm., Turk. *yarï* 'die Hälfte; halb' (Radl. III, 120); II. 'Help, support' cf. Uyg., Kuman, Crm., Turk. *yarï* (<P.) 'die Hülfe, der Beistand' (Radl. III, 120).

YARÏČÏ Uyg. 12th c. - 14th c. **Yarïčï** (Radl., USp. 127); Uyg. 12th c. - 14th c. **Yarïčï** [Yarıçı] (DTS, EUTS). ❖ 'Helper, follower' cf. Uyg. *yarïǰï* 'der Helfer, Unterstützer' (Radl. III, 127).

YARÏQ see **YARUQ**

YARÏQ-TAŠ see **YARUQ-TAŠ**

YARÏQASÏM see **ŽARÏLQASÏN**

YARÏQLÏ Trkm. 1821/22 **Yarïqlï-palwan** [Ярыклы Палван] (MIT II, 421).

YARÏLQASÏN see **ŽARÏLQASÏN**

YARÏM Bashk. 1709 **Yarïm** [Ярым (Ерым) Байсулеев] (MIB I, 264); Bashk. 1740 **Yarïm** [Ярым Шанаев] (MIB I, 438); Trkm.? 1743 **Yarïm-diwan** [Ярым-диван] (MIT II, 334, 337). ❖ 'Half; imperfect' cf. Kuman, Alt., Tat. *yarïm* 'die Hälfte, halb', (Turk.) 'nicht vollständig, unvollständig, unbeendet' (Radl. III, 128).

YARÏN-QUŠ Selj. **Yarïn-quš** [يَرِنتَش] (Bondārī 71, 209); Selj. **Yarïn-quš** [يرنتش قرآن خوان] (Bondārī 177); Selj. **Yarïn-quš** [المؤيّد يرنتش هِرِيوَه] (Bondārī 224, 276); Selj. 1035 **Yarïn-quš** [يرنتش], a falconer, ruler (owner) of Qazwīn (Ibn al-Athīr/Tornb. X, 477-78, XI, 14-15); Selj 1072-1092 **Yarïn-quš** [يرنتش], Melik Shah (1072-1092) sends him to Yemen (Ahbar 50); Selj. 1118-1157 **Yarïn-quš** [يرنتش], one of Sultan Sandjar's (1118-1157) emirs (Rāwandī 179); Selj. 1121 **Yarïn-quš** [سعدالدولة يرنتش الزكوى] (Bondārī 160, 170, 193, 248, Ibn al-Athīr/Tornb. X, 398, 422, 480, XI, 22, 70); Seld. 1142 **Yarïn-quš** [Yarınkuş el-Kâri], an emir, died in 1142 (Ahbar 66); Selj.? 1147 **Yarïn-quš** [يرنتش الخادم] (Kamāladdīn II, 281-282); Selj. 1153-1159 **Yarïn-quš** [يرنتش], a falconer (Bondārī 170, 183, 232, Rāwandī 262); Selj. 1198 **Yarïn-quš** [يرنتش النظام] (Ibn al-Athīr/Tornb. XII, 91, 97); Selj.? 1210 **Yarïn-quš** [احمد بن يرنتش] (Ibn al-Athīr/Tornb. XII, 188). ⇨ **YARAN-QAŠ?**

YARÏP Trkm. 1859 **Yarïp** [Балгара Ярыповъ] (ZIRGOEш. I, 210).

YARÏSÏ-ÖLÜ Turk. 19th c. **Yarïsï-ölü-oɣlu** [Jarysy ölü oɣlu] (Kúnos 1891, 119). ❖ 'Half-dead' cf. Crm., Turk.

yarï 'die Hälfte' (Radl. III, 120). ⇨ **YARÏ.**

YARÏŠ Bashk. 20th c. **Yarïš** [Ярыш] (Kusimova); Tat.(Mish.) 20th c. **Yarïš** (<Yar-iš) [Ярышев] (Sattarov); Bashk. 1761 **Yarïš** (<Yar-iš?) [Ярыш Сумаков] (MIB IV/1, 221); Bashk. 1761, 1762 **Yarïš** (<Yar-iš?) [Ярыш Унгаров] (MIB IV/1, 205, 251); Bashk. 1763 **Yarïš** (<Yar-iš?) [Ярыш Кульшарыпов] (MIB IV/2, 45); Bashk. 1779 **Yarïš** (<Yar-iš?) [Салих (Салиш) Ярышев (Ерышев)] (MIB V, 88, 91, 101, 102, 151, 676); Bashk. 1790 **Yarïš** (<Yar-iš?) [Ярыш Кулчукаев] (MIB V, 279); Maml. 1449, 1453 **Yarïš-bay** (<Yar-iš-bay?) [يرشباى الايناى لمؤيدى / يرشباى الاناى لمؤيدى] (Ibn Taghrīb. VII, 174, 238, VIII, 197, 356). ❖ I. 'Friend, mate' (Sattarov), see YAR+ÏŠ; II. 'Together, side by side' (Kusimova). ⇨ **YARUŠ?**

YARÏŠTÏ Tat. 1554 **Yarïštï** [Ярышты-царевичь], a prince (PSRL XIII, 243). ⇨ **YARÏŠ?** + suff. -*tï.*

YARQAY Tat. 20th c. **Yarqay** [Яркаев] (Sattarov); Tat. 20th c. **Yarqay** [Яркай / Яркаев] (Sattarov); Chuv. 18th-19th c. **Yarok-ay / Yarqay?** [Ярок-ай] (Magn. 100); Bashk. 1728 **Yärkäy** [Яркей Янчуринъ] (PSZRI VIII, 68-69); Bashk. 1749, 1751, 1758 **Yärkäy** [Еркей Ермаков (Ермяков)] (MIB III, 469, IV/1, 34, 166); Bashk. 18th c. **Yärkäy** [Яркей] (Nepljuev 388); Bashk. 1775 **Yärkäy** [Гайсар Яркеев] (MIB IV/1, 376); Bashk. 1786 **Yärkäy** [Яркей Ярмяков] (MIB V, 207); Bashk. 1786 **Yärkäy** [Яркей Касаев] (MIB V, 196); Bashk. 20th c. **Yärkäy** [Йәркәй / Яркей] (Kusimova); Bashk. 20th c. **Yärkäy** [Йәркәй / Яркей] (Kusimova); Bashk. 1783 **Yärkäy / Yerkey?** [Еркей Акбаев (Айбаев)] (MIB V, 145, 170). ❖ 'Little darling; dear friend' cf. Tat. PN *Yarqay* (Sattarov). ⇨ **YAR** + dim. hypoc. suff. -*qay.*

YARQÏM-BAY see **YARQÏN**

YARQÏN Alt. 19th-20th c. **D'arqïn** [Дьаркын] (OjrRS 208); Kzk.? **Yarqïn-ayïm** [Yarkyn-Aïm], a woman in Khokand (Nalivkin-Dozon 178, 244); Kzk. 1786 **Yarqïn-bay** [Яркынбай] (MIK IV, 87); Kzk. **Žarqïn-bay** [Жарқынбай], a character from the epic „Put' Abaja" by M. O. Auezov (Espaeva 1984, 231); *TN:* **Yarqïm-bay** (<Yarqïn-bay) [Яркым-бай], a well (Karta JAR X). ❖ 'Light, bright; nice, good-natured' (Espaeva 1984, 231), 'Shine, glitter' (OjrRS 208), cf. Kuman, Alt. *yarqïn* 'der Glanz, die Helligkeit, der Strahl' (Radl. III, 136), Kzk. *carkın* 'Güler yüzlü, iyi huylu' (KzTS). See also **AQ-ŽARQÏN.**

YARQÏN-AY Kzk. 1846 **Yarqïm-ay** (<Yarqïn-ay?) [Казы Яркымаев] (MKOP 151). ❖ 'Bright Moon' cf. Kzk. PNs *Žurqïn, Žarqïn-bek* (Žanuzakov-Esbaeva). ⇨ **YARQÏN + AY.**

YARLAQAČ see **YARLÏQAŠ**

YARLÏɣAY Tat. 1724 **Yarlïɣay** [Ярлыгаев] (MIB III,

228); Bashk. 1728 **Yarluɣay** [Ярлогай Кулуков] (MIB I, 124). ❖ 'Gracious, forgiving' cf. Uyg., Kuman, Chag., Turk. *yarlïqa-* 'einen Befehl erteilen, ein Dekret erlassen, gnädig sein' (Radl. III, 142-44), Bashk. *yarlïqa-* 'миловать, прощать' (BRS/Uraksin).

YARLÏQ-BAŠ   Kzk. 1819 **Yarlïq-baš** [Ярлыкбаш] (MIK IV, 324). ❖ 'Head of the commands/orders' cf. Uyg., Alt. *yarlïq* 'die Verkündigung, der Befehl' (Radl. IV, 141), Chag. *yarlik* 'der Befehl eines Fürsten, das Dekret' (Radl. I, 143). ➪ **BAŠ**.

YARLÏQAN   Kzk. 19th c. **Yarlïqan** [Ярлыканъ] (SKSO III, 7). ❖ 'Be forgiven, get forgiveness' cf. Tat. *yarlïqan-* 'amnestirt werden' (Radl. III, 142).

YARLÏQAP   Trkm. 1810 **Yarlïqab-bek** [Ярлыкаб-бек], from the Xasan-eli tribe (MIT II, 378); Tat. 20th c **Yarlïqap** [Ярлыкапов] (Sattarov); Bashk. 20th c. **Yarlïqap** [Ярлыкап / Ярлыкап] (Kusimova). ❖ 'Forgiving' cf. Uyg., Kuman, Chag., Turk. *yarlïqa-* 'einen Befehl erteilen, ein Dekret erlassen, gnädig sein' (Radl. III, 142-44), Bashk. *yarlïqa-* 'миловать, прощать' (BRS/Uraksin).

YARLÏQAŠ   Uzb. 19th c. **Yarlaqač** [Ярлакачъ] (SKSO III, 180); Tat. 1554 **Yarlïqaš** [Ярлыкашъ] (Kn. Metriki Lit. 102). ❖ 'Award, prize; gift' cf. Tat. *yarlïqaš* 'die Vergeltung, Belohnung' (Radl. III, 142), Bashk. *yarlïqaš* 'вознаграждение' (BRS/Uraksin), Chag. *yarlïɣaš* 'das Geschenk' (Radl. III, 144).

YARLUƔAY see **YARLÏƔAY**

YARMA   Kkalp.? / NUyg. 1810 **Yarma** [Ораз Али Ярма] (MIKk. 110). ❖ 'Bran; thin soup made of barley or wheat' cf. Chag., Tat. *yarma* 'die Grütze, Gerstengrütze' (Radl. III, 150), Kaklp. *žarma* 'крупа; жидкая похлёбка из толчёного ячменя, пшеницы или джугары' (KkRS).

YARMAČ   Bashk.? 1693 **Yarmač** [Ярмачко Бижбулатов] (MIB I, 84). ➪ **YARMA** + suff. *-č*.

YARMAN   Chuv. 18th-19th c. **Yarman** [Ярманъ] (Magn. 100). ➪ **YAR?** + suff. *-man*.

YARMANČE   Chuv. 18th-19th c. **Yarmanče(y) / Yarmanči?** [Ярманчей] (Magn. 100). ➪ **YARMAN** + dim. suff. *-če*.

YARMANDAY   Chuv. 18th-19th c. **Yarmanday** [Ярмандай] (Magn. 100). ➪ **YARMAN** + suff. *-day / -tay*.

YARMAT see **YARMÄT**

YARMATÏ   Chag. 16th c. **Yarmati** [Ярмати] (Ivanov 124). ➪ **YARMÄT?**

YARMÄT   Uzb. 19th c. **Yarmat-bay** [Абдушукуръ Ярматбаевъ] (SKSO III, 154); Tat. 1702 **Yarmät** [Ярметко Байгурзинъ], a Tatar from Kungur (Letop. ZAK II, 7); Tat. 20th c. **Yarmät** [Ярмэт] (Sattarov). ❖ Shortened-contracted form of *Yar-Möxämmät* in Tatar dialects (Sattarov). ➪ **YAR** + suffixoid *-mät*.

YARMÏS-XARA   Uzb.? 1826 **Yarmïs-χara / Yaramïs-χara / Yaramas-χara?** [يارمسخره / Jarmiskhara], from Bukhara (Vel.-Zern., Haïder 281-82). ❖ I. 'Suitable-Black'? II. 'Good-for-nothing-Black / Bad/Naughty-Black' cf. Uzb. *yaramas* 'негодный; плохой' (UzbRS). ➪ **YARAMÏŠ?** + **QARA**.

YARMÏŠ   Bashk. 1759 **Yarmïš** [Ярмыш Бекчурин] (MIB IV/1, 180). ❖ Shortened-contracted form of *Yar-möxämmät* in Tatar dialects (Sattarov). ➪ **YÄR-MÖXÄMMÄT** + suff. *-(ï)š*.

YAROSLAN see **ARSLAN**

YARTAČUQ   Oghuz/Trkm. 14th c. - 15th c. **Yartačuq** [Yalancı oğlı Yarıncuk / Yalanǧuq, figlio di Yalangi, Yalançı oğlı, Yartaçuk / Яртачук сын Яланчи] (DQorq. 39-42, 44, 48, 140, 206).

YARTÏ   Kzk. 19th c. **Yartï-bay** [Яртибай] (Grod., Pril. 122). ❖ 'Half'. ➪ **YARÏM**.

YARUQ   Chuv. 18th-19th c. **Yarïk** [Ярыкъ] (Magn. 100); Karakh. 948 **Yaruχ** [يارو: صاحب ناصر الدولة] (Ibn al-Athīr/Tornb. VIII, 358); Chuv. 18th-19th c. **Yaruχ** [Ярухъ] (Magn. 100); Chuv. 19th c. **Yaruχ** [Jaruk] (Kronheim 96); Oghuz/Trkm. 996 **Yaruχ-tegin** [يارختكين] (Ibn al-Athīr/Tornb. IX, 86); Chuv. 18th-19th c. **Yaruk** [Ярукъ] (Magn. 100); Uyg. 12th c. - 14th c. **Yaruq** [Yaruk] (Radl., USp. 12, DTS, EUTS); Oghuz/Trkm. 935 **Yaruq** [ياروق] (Ibn al-Athīr/Tornb. VIII, 225); Oghuz/Trkm. 1146/47 **Yaruq** [يارق], Türkmen chief (Ibn al-Athīr, Atab.: RHCHor II/2, 142); Selj. 1093 **Yaruq** [يارُق الحاجب] (Bondārī 75); Selj.? 1164 **Yaruq** [ياروق], „a Frank servant" (Usāma 62); Maml. 14th c. **Yaruq** [ياروق], of Turkmen origin (Sauvaget 56); Türk 7th-9th c. **Yaruq-tegin** [Yaruq tegin] (DTS, ETY III, 118); *TN:* Selj.? 12th c. **Yaruq** [ياروق], a mosque (Ibn Šaddād, Alep 81, 84). ❖ 'Bright(ness), light(ing)' cf. Uyg. *yaruq* ' свет, сияние, блеск, луч ' (DTS), Karakh. *yaruq* светлый, сияющий ' (DTS), Türk, Uyg., Chag., East.T. *yaruq* 'hell, leuchtend, strahlend, glänzend' (Radl. III, 132), Alt., Kuman *yarïq* 'hell, leuchtend'; das Licht, der Glanz' (Radl. III, 121), Kzk. *žarïq* I 'свет, освещение' (KzRS). See also **AY-YARÏQ, AR-YARUQ, BERK-YARUQ, TAÑ-YARÏQ, TEKEŠ-YARUQ**.

YARUQ-TAŠ   Türk? 972 **Yarïq-taš** [مولى سيف الدولة يارقتاش] (Ibn al-Athīr/Tornb. VIII, 502); Selj.? 1096/97 **Yarïq-taš** [يارقطاش اميراالحرا / Ярыкташ], emir, chief of the emirs (Ibn al-Athīr/Tornb. X, 181-82, MIT I, 383); Selj. 1115/16, 1117 **Yarïq-taš** [شمس الخواص يارقطاش], an atabek and the regent (governor) in Aleppo (Ibn al-Athīr: RHCHor I, 296, 309, 385, 863, Abulfidā III, 390-91); Selj. 1103, 1130, 1116 **Yaruq-taš** [يارقطاش شمس الخواص / يارقتاش] (Kamāladdīn II, 149, 174, 179, 245, Ibn al-Athīr/Tornb. X, 357, 463); Selj. 13th c. **Yaruq-taš** [يَارُوقْطَاش], an emir (Ǧuwaynī II, 3). ✧ 'Bright (brilliant) stone'. ⇨ **YARUQ + TAŠ.**

YARUQ-TUΓMÏŠ Oghuz/Trkm. 1030 **Yaruq-tuγmïš** [Яруктугмыш], a commander of the army (MIT I, 234, 235). ⇨ **YARUQ + TOΓMÏŠ.**

YARUŠ Bashk. 1754 **Yaruš** [Яруш] (MIB IV/1, 83). ⇨ **YARÏŠ?**

YAS Nog. **Yas-murza / Yasa-murza?** [Ясъ мурза (Ногайского Ясы мурзы)] (DAI XII, 336). ✧ 'Damage, loss; mourning' cf. Uyg. *yas* 'der Schaden', Uyg., Chag., Turk. *yas* 'die Trauer' (Radl. III, 212).

YAS-ASMAN Bashk. 1773 **Yas-asman?** [Заис Ясасманов] (MIB IV/2, 413).

YASA Chuv. 18th-19th c. **Yasa-bay** [Ясабай] (Magn. 100). ✧ 'Decree, order; law'cf. Chag. *yasa* 'die Verordnung, der fürstliche Befehl, das Gesetz' (Radl. III, 214).

YASADU Uyg. **Yasadu** [Yasadu] (EUTS); Uyg. 13th c. **Yasadu-tutuň** [jasadu tutuŋ] (DTS). ✧ 'Built, constructed'? cf. Türk *yasa-* 'строить, делать, устраивать' (DTS).

YASAK Chuv. 18th-19th c. **Yasak** [Ясакъ] (Magn. 100). ✧ 'Princely order/law, codex' cf. Chag., Tat. *yasaq* 'der fürstliche Befehl, die Verordnung, das Gesetz, der Codex; die Strafe; der Tribut, die Abgaben' (Radl. III, 216. ⇨ **YASA.**

YASAUL Tat.(Sib.) 1634 **Yasaul** [Кутлумерген Ясаулов] (Miller, Ist. Sib. II, 411); Tat.(Sib.) 1634 **Yasaul** [Кутлумемет Ясаулов] (Miller, Ist. Sib. II, 411); Tat. 1600 **Yesaul** [Есаул Сарагулбегов] (MIB I, 152). ✧ 'Commanding, ordering' cf. Chag. *yasaul* 'der Anordner, Ausführer der Befehle', 'der Unteroffizier der Chanswache' (Uzb.) (Radl. III, 215).

YASEMİN Turk. 1583 **Yasemin** [ياسمين] (Ongan, Ank. I, 179). ✧ 'Jasmine' (<Greek) (Erol II).

YASÏR see YAZÏR

YASMEK Kzk. 19th c. **Yasmek** [Ясмекъ] (SOK 164).

YAŠ Tuv. 19th c. **Čaǰ-öl (<Čaš-öl)** [Чацол / Чаш-ол] (Proben IX, 68, 76); Uyg. **Yaš** [Yaš] (EUTS); Maml. 1400 **Yaš-bek** [يشبك الايتمشّى] (Ibn Taghrīb. VI, 349); Maml. 1400 **Yaš-bek** [يشبك الخاصّكى] (Ibn Taghrīb. VI, 344); Maml. 1400 **Yaš-bek** [Yachbek], an emir (Jorga, Notes XIX, LXXXV); Maml. 1400/01 **Yaš-bek** [يشبك بن باكى] (Iyās I, 337); Maml. 1401/01 **Yaš-bek** [يشبك السودو نى] (Iyās I, 345, Ibn Taghrīb. VI, 512, 601 etc., VII, 2, 21, 26, Weil, Chalif., II, 228-31); Maml. 1401/02 **Yaš-bek** [يشبك الاعرج الساقى الظاهرّى] (Ibn Taghrīb. VI, 96, 238); Maml. 1401/02 **Yaš-bek** [يشبك العثمانىّ الظاهرّى] (Ibn Taghrīb. VI, 59, 87, 96, Weil, Chalif. II, 75, 88); Maml. 1405 **Yaš-bek** [يشبك الشعبانى الظاهرى], minister (chancellor) of state (Ibn Taghrīb. VI, 3, 5, 13, 15, VII, 418, Iyās I, 308, 350

etc., Weil, Chalif. II, 99 etc.); Maml. 1407 **Yaš-bek** [يشبك], Yašbek aš-Šaʿbānī, commander-in-chief died in 1407 (in an inscription in the mausoleum of Baalbek) (Mayer 253-54); Maml. 1408 **Yaš-bek** [الموساوىّ الافتم] (Ibn Taghrīb. VI, 198, 200); Maml. 1411 **Yaš-bek** [يشبك اليوسفىّ المؤيّدىّ], governor of Haleb (Ibn Taghrīb. VI, 333 etc., Weil, Chalif. II, 143); Maml. 1415 **Yaš-bek** [يشبك بن از مر], died in 1415 (Ibn Taghrīb. VI, 50, 115, 128 etc., Weil, Chalif. II, 111, 134, Iyās I, 346); Maml. 1421 **Yaš-bek** [يشبك الجكمى], a minister (chancellor) of state (Iyās II, 41, Ibn Taghrīb. VI, 495, 500, VII, 563, Weil, Chalif. I, 162, 166-67); Maml. 1422 **Yaš-bek** [يشبك], Bars-bay's father? (Ibn Taghrīb. VI, 571, 604); Maml. 1431 **Yaš-bek** [يشبك الصوفىّ] (Ibn Taghrīb. VI, 669); Maml. 1431 **Yaš-bek** [يشبك], a treasurer (Berchem 252); Maml. 1435 **Yaš-bek** [يشبك ططر] (Ibn Taghrīb. VI, 842); Maml. 1439/40 **Yaš-bek** [يشبك بشق] (Ibn Taghrīb. VII, 105); Maml. 1447 **Yaš-bek** [يشبك], governor of Tripolis (Sobernh. I, 69); Maml. 1448, 1454 **Yaš-bek** [يشبك طاز المؤيدى] (Ibn Taghrīb. VII, 155, 233, VIII, 200, 248); Maml. 1450 **Yaš-bek** [سلمان شاه المويدى يشبك] (Ibn Taghrīb. VIII, 82, 128); Maml. 1451 **Yaš-bek** [السيفى يشبك الحمزاوى], dawādār, then governor of Ghaza and Safad (Mayer 251); Maml. 1453 **Yaš-bek** [يشبك الناصرى] (Iyās II, 40); Maml. 1453 **Yaš-bek** [يشبك الظاهرى /جتمق/] (Ibn Taghrīb. VII, 389); Maml. 1453 **Yaš-bek** [يشبك القرمى الظاهرى], police superintendent in Cairo (Ibn Taghrīb. VII, 393, 400, Weil, Chalif. II, 254); Maml. 1454, 1455 **Yaš-bek** [يشبك النوروزى] (Ibn Taghrīb. VIII, 59, 158, 200, Iyās II, 52); Maml. 1455 **Yaš-bek** [يشبك بن مهدى] (Iyās II, 51, 90-94 etc., Weil, Chalif. II, 288, 325, 358); Maml. 1463 **Yaš-bek** [يشبك / اش او اوش/ قلق] (Ibn Taghrīb. VII, 714, 728); Maml. 1467 **Yaš-bek** [يشبك البجاسى الاشرفى], governor of Haleb (Iyās II, 67, 104, 228, Ibn Taghrīb. VII, 444, 649, Weil, Chalif. II, 318); Maml. 1467 **Yaš-bek** [الفتيه المؤيّدىّ الدوادار يشبك], a minister (chancellor) of state (Ibn Taghrīb. Vi, 802, Iyās II, 8, 11, 77, 88 etc., Weil, Chalif. II, 319-22); Maml. 1468/69 **Yaš-bek** [يشبك بن حيدار الدوادار], chief of the police in Cairo (Iyās III 102-261, Weil, Chalif. II, 336); Maml. 1468/69 **Yaš-bek** [يشبك المحتسب السيفى] (Iyās II, 103-104, 132, 184 etc., Weil, Chalif. II, 346-53); Maml. 1475/76 **Yaš-bek** [يشبك حلس بن اقبردى الاشرفى] (Iyās II, 151); Maml. 1480 **Yaš-bek** [السيفى يشبك من مهدى], emir of inspector general ("Dawādār Kebir"), regent, major-domo (Mayer 251-53); Maml. 1497 **Yaš-bek** [يشبك قمر العجمى] (Iyās II, 295, Weil, Chalif. II, 361-

64); Chuv. 18th-19th c. **Yaš-mola (Yaš-molla)** [Яшмола] (Magn. 101); Chuv. 18th-19th c. **Yaš-mulda** [Яшмулда] (Magn. 101); Chuv. 18th-19th c. **Yaš-mulla** [Яшмулла] (Magn. 101); Chuv. 18th-19th c. **Yaš-pay** [Яшпай] (Magn. 101); Chuv. 18th-19th c. **Yaš-patïr** [Яшпатыръ] (Magn. 101); Tat.(Tara) **Yäš-yigit** [Jäш Jiriт] (Proben IV, 88 (113)). ✧ 'Young, new' cf. Türk, Uyg., Kuman, Chag., Alt., Az., Turk. etc. *yaš* 'frisch, grün, saftig, feucht; jung (an Jahren)' (Radl. III, 240), Tat., Tat.(Bar.), Turk.(Osm.) *yäš* 'id.' (Radl. III, 379), Kirg. *jaš* 'молодой, свежий ' (Jud.), Shor *čaš (=čas, yaš)* (Radl. III, 1912). See also İZ-YAŠ, QARA-YAŠ, QOJO-JAŠ, MOLDO-JAŠ.

YAŠ-İMİR Bashk. 1706 **Yaš-imir** [Сабанай Яшмиров] (MIB III, 27). ⇨ YAŠ + İMİR.

YAŠ-KİLDA see YAŠ-KİLDİ

YAŠ-KİLDÄ see YAŠ-KİLDİ

YAŠ-KİLDİ Chuv. 18th-19th c. **Yaš-kildi / Yaš-kilda?** [Яжкилда] (Magn. 97); Chuv. 18th-19th c. **Yaš-kildi / Yaš-kildä?** [Яшкилда] (Magn. 101); Bashk. 1735 **Yaš-kildi / Yaš-kildä / İš-gilde?** [Яшкильда (Ишгильде) Ишимбетев] (MIB III, 333). ⇨ YAŠ + KELDİ.

YAŠ-QAMÏŠ Kirg. **Yaš-qamïš** [Jaш Камыш] (Proben V, 151 (153)). ⇨ YAŠ + QAMÏŠ.

YAŠ-MEMET Chuv. 18th-19th c. **Yaš-memet** [Яшмеметъ] (Magn. 101). ⇨ YAŠ + MAMET.

YAŠ-PARS Chuv. 18th-19th c. **Yaš-parïs** [Яшпарысъ] (Magn. 101); Chuv. 18th-19th c. **Yaš-pars** [Яшпарсъ] (Magn. 101); Chuv. 18th-19th c. **Yaš-pars** [Яшпорсъ] (Magn. 101); Chuv. 18th-19th c. **Yaš-parus** [Яшпарусъ] (Magn. 101). ⇨ YAŠ + BARS.

YAŠ-PULAT Chuv. 18th-19th c. **Yaš-pulat** [Яшпулатъ] (Magn. 101); Bashk. 1714 **Yaš-pulat** [Масайко Яшпулатов] (MIB I, 107). ⇨ YAŠ + BULAT.

YAŠ-PULDÏ Chuv. 18th-19th c. **Yaš-puldï** [Яшпулда] (Magn. 101). ⇨ YAŠ + BOLDÏ.

YAŠ-TEMİR Chuv. 18th-19th c. **Yaš-dimer** [Яждимеръ] (Magn. 97); Chuv. 18th-19th c. **Yaš-temir** [Яштемиръ] (Magn. 101); Chuv. 18th-19th c. **Yaš-timer** [Яштимеръ] (Magn. 101). ⇨ YAŠ + TEMİR.

YAŠ-TERÄK Nog. 1649 **Yaš-teräk** [Яштерекъ], a murza (AI IV, 79). ✧ 'Young poplar' cf. Tat. PN *Yäš-tiräk* (Sattarov). ⇨ YAŠ + TERÄK.

YAŠ-TİMER see YAŠ-TEMİR

YAŠ-TÏNKA Chuv. 18th-19th c. **Yaš-tïnka** [Яштынка] (Magn. 101). ⇨ YAŠ.

YAŠ-TUGAN Chuv. 18th-19th c. **Yaš-tugan** [Яштуганъ] (Magn. 101). ✧ 'Born young' cf. Tat. PN *Yäš-tuγan* (Sattarov). ⇨ YAŠ + TUΓAN I.

YAŠ-TUT Chuv. 18th-19th c. **Yaš-tut** [Яштутъ]

(Magn. 101). ⇨ YAŠ + TUT.

YAŠAQ Türk 7th-9th c. **Yašaq** [Yaşaq] (ETY III, 35). ⇨ YAŠÏQ?

YAŠALÏQ Uzb. 19th c. **Yašalïq** [Яшалыкъ] (SKSO III, 154).

YAŠAR Karch. **Jašar-qul** [Джашаркулъ] (Sysoev 120); Chuv. 18th-19th c. **Yašar** [Яшаръ] (Magn. 101); *TN:* Turk. 20th c. **Yašarlar** [Yaşarlar (Kürtköyü)], a village in the province of Konya, Turkey (TMİB 567). ✧ 'Long live(s)' cf. Chag. *yašar-* 'eine Grössere Zahl Jahre leben' (Radl. III, 244), Kzk. *jasa-* 'сделать; сотворить, создать' (KzRS), Kzk. *casav [jasa- / žasa-]* 'Yapmak; yaşamak, hayat sürmek' (KzTS). See also BİL-YAŠAR, BAΓ-YASAR, YÜZ-YAŠAR, KÖP-YAŠAR, QAY-ŽASAR, MİÑ-JASAR(?), MUN-JASAR(?).

YAŠAW Karch. **Jašaw** [Джашау] (Sysoev 120); Chuv. 18th-19th c. **Yašav** [Яшавъ] (Magn. 101). ✧ Life.

YAŠÏK Chuv. 18th-19th c. **Yašïk** [Яшикъ] (Magn. 101). ✧ I. 'Thin, lean'? cf. Kuman *yašïq* 'mager' (Radl. III, 245); II. 'Tortured, weak, not suitable' cf. Kirg. *yašïq* 'gequält, abgemattet, schlecht, untaguglich' (Radl. III, 246).

YAŠQAN Uyg. **Yašqan** [Yaşkan] (EUTS); Uyg. 8th c. **Yašqan-ïnal** (DTS); Uyg. 13th-14th c. **Yašqan-ïnal** [Yaš[qa]n İnal] (Zieme, Mat. III, 273).

YAŠMAK Chuv. 18th-19th c. **Yašmak** [Яшмакъ] (Magn. 101). ✧ 'Veil (worn by Oriental women)' cf. Chag., Turk. *yašmaq* 'der Schleier, mit dem die Frauen Kopf und Brust bedecken' (Radl. III, 252).

YAŠMAS Chuv. 18th-19th c. **Yašmas** [Яшмасъ] (Magn. 101).

YAŠMET Chuv. 18th-19th c. **Yašmet** [Яшметь] (Magn. 101). ✧ Cf. also Tat. PN *Yäš-möχämmät* (Sattarov). ⇨ YAŠ + suffixoid -*met*.

YAŠNAR Uzb. 20th c. **Yašnar** [Яшнар], fem. (Begmatov 1984, 206); Uzb. 20th c. **Yašnar-ây** [Яшнарой], fem. (Begmatov 1984, 206). ✧ '(S)He who will flower/flourish; (S)He will be happy' (Begmatov), cf. Uzb. *yašna-* 'цвести; процветать' (UzbRS).

YAT Chuv. 18th-19th c. **Yat-murza** [Ятмурза] (Magn. 101). ✧ 'Alien, foreigner' cf. Uyg., Chag., Alt., Kar., Tat. *yat* 'fremd, der Fremdling' (Radl. III, 190), Az. *yad* 'fremd' (Radl. III, 207) (<Ir.). See also BURALQÏ, ČİT, QARÏP, QAR-YAT, QUL-YAT.

YAT-KİREY Chuv. 18th-19th c. **Yat-kirey** [Яткирей] (Magn. 100). ⇨ YAT + KERÄY.

YAT-MURZA see YAT

YATAΓAN Turk. 1455 **Yataγan** [Hacı Yatağan] (Gökb., Ed. 194). ✧ 'Heavy curved knife, yataghan; a kind of hunting-knife' cf. Turk. *yataγan* 'eine Art Messer' (Radl. III, 199).

YATAY Tat. 1689/90 **Yatay** [ياتاى] (Jusupov 73).

YATÄK   Tat.(Sib.) 1632 **Yatäk / Yätäk?** [Ятяк] (Miller, Ist. Sib. II, 398).

YATÏ-KÜZ   Chag. 16th c. **Yati-küz** [Яти-Куз Узбек] (Ivanov 303). ✦ '?-eye'. ⇨ **KÖZ.**

YATÏΓMA   Türk 712-716 **Yatïγma** [Yatïγma] (ETY I, 114, 116).

YATÏR   Hak. 19th-20th c. **Yatïr** [Ятыр] (HRS 356).

YATKER see YADÏΓAR

YATMAY   Chuv. 18th-19th c. **Yatmay** [Ятмай] (Magn. 100).

YATMAK   Chuv. 18th-19th c. **Yatmak** [Ятмакъ] (Magn. 100).

YATMAS   Chuv. 18th-19th c. **Yatmas** [Ятмасъ] (Magn. 101); *TN:* Tat. 16th c. - 17th c. **Yatmas** [Ятмасъ (Дусаева)], a village in the disrtict of Mamadyš (Iznoskov 1480).

YAUSÏP see YUSUF

YAVGAN   Chuv. 18th-19th c. **Yavgan** [Явганъ] (Magn. 96).

YAVGANDEY   Chuv. 18th-19th c. **Yavgandey** [Явгандей] (Magn. 96). ⇨ **YAVGAN** + suff. *-dey.*

YAVGANEY   Chuv. 18th-19th c. **Yavganey** [Явганей] (Magn. 96). ⇨ **YAVGAN** + suff. *-ey.*

YAVΓU see YABΓU

YAVLAQ-SARÏΓ   Karakh. 11th c. **Yavlaq-sarïγ** [Yawlaǧ sarıǧ / javlaq sarïγ] (MK/Atalay 859, DTS). ✦ 'Strong-Sage' (Blagova 1997, 705), 'Strong-Blond' cf. Karakh. *javlaq* 'крепкий' (DTS). ⇨ **SARÏ.**

YAW-BASAR   Kzk. 18th c. - 19th c. **J̌aw-basar** [Джаубасар] (Tynyšp. 73); Oghuz/Trkm. **Yaw-basar** [يَوْباسار] (Samojlovič 1927, 40); Kzk. 19th c. **Yaw-basar** [Явбасаръ] (Grod., Pril. 82); Kkalp. 1820 **Yaw-basar** [Яу-басар] (MIKk. 104); Uzb.? 1817 **Yaw-basar-bek** [Яубасар-бек], Qara-behadïr-mirab's son (MIT II, 401); Uzb. 20th c. **Yâw-bâsar** [Ёвбосар] (Begmatov 1984, 201); Kzk. 1734 **Žaw-basar** [Жаубазаръ Каскулатовъ] (PSZRI IX, 341). ✦ 'Oppressor of the enemy; he who will oppress the enemy; going in to battle' cf. Chag., Alt., Tat. *yau* 'der Feind' (Radl. III, 16), Turk. *yaw* 'fremd, ein Fremder; feindlich, der Feind' (Radl. III, 289), Bashk. *yaw* 'битва, бой ' (BRS), Kzk. *žau* 'враг, неприятель' (KzRS). ⇨ **BASAR.** See also **YAW-BASAR, YAW-GİLDE.**

YAW-BÜRİ   Trkm. 1770 **Yaw-büri** [ياو بورى / Яу-бури-наиб], governor of (nä⁽ib) Bek-abad from the Mañγït tribe (MIT II, 348); Chag. 15th c. - 16th c. **Yaw-büri-behadur** [ياو بورى بهار / Явъ Буру Беhадуръ] (Šejb. LIX). ✦ 'Enemy-Wolf' cf. Chag., Alt., Tat. *yau* 'der Feind' (Radl. III, 16), Turk. *yaw* 'fremd, ein Fremder; feindlich, der Feind' (Radl. III, 289), Bashk. *yaw* 'битва, бой ' (BRS), Kzk. *žau* 'враг, неприятель' (KzRS). ⇨ **YAW(-BASAR) + BÖRİ.**

YAW-GİLDE see YAW-GİLDİ

YAW-GİLDEY see YAW-GİLDİ

YAW-GİLDEKÄ   Bashk. 1701 **Yaw-gildkä** (<**Yaw-gildekä**) [Явгилдка Тленчеевъ], a tarχan (Vel.-Zern., Bašk. 29). ⇨ **YAW-GİLDİ** + suffixoid *-kä / -ke.*

YAW-GİLDİ   Tat. (Sib.) 1609 **Čaw-gilde / J̌aw-gilde(y)** [Чавгильдей Теребердеев] (Miller, Ist. Sib. II, 209, 210); Tat.(Sib.) 1629 **Yaw-gilde** [Таганай Яугилдеев] (Miller, Ist. Sib. II, 357); Bashk. 1726 **Yaw-gilde** [Явгильде Айтышев] (MIB III, 242); Bashk. 1734 **Yaw-gilde** [Явгилдинъ] (Vel.-Zern., Bašk. 10); Bashk. 1734 **Yaw-gilde** [Явгилдинъ] (Vel.-Zern., Bašk. 10); Bashk. 1735 **Yaw-gilde** [Явгилда Тевкеев], a tarχan (Vel.-Zern., Bašk. 11); Bashk. 1740 **Yaw-gilde** [Явгилда Кулаев] (MIB I, 404); Bashk. 1740 **Yaw-gilde** [Явгилда Кулаев] (MIB I, 404); Bashk. 1760 **Yaw-gilde** [Бекей Явгильдин] (MIB IV/1, 193); Bashk. 1776 **Yaw-gilde** [Явгильда Исаков] (MIB V, 39, 41); Bashk. 1777 **Yaw-gilde** [Карайган Явгильдин] (MIB V, 52, 53, 204); Bashk. 1784 **Yaw-gilde** [Уязаш Явгильдин] (MIB V, 204); Bashk. 1787 **Yaw-gilde** [Карайган Явгильдин] (MIB V, 204); Bashk. 1714 **Yaw-gildi** [Алтеть Явгилдиев] (MIB I, 105); Bashk. 1734 **Yaw-gildi / Yaw-gilde?** [Азнакай Явгилдин], a Naγaydu (?) tarχan (Vel.-Zern., Bašk. 11); Bashk. 1740 **Yaw-gildi** [Явгилди Битюков] (MIB I, 440); Bashk. 1718, 1726 **Yaw-gildi / Yaw-gilde** [Явгильды (Явгильда) Таулин] (MIB III, 172, 237). ✦ 'The enemy (the war) has come' cf. Chag., Alt., Tat. *yau* 'der Feind' (Radl. III, 16), Turk. *yaw* 'fremd, ein Fremder; feindlich, der Feind' (Radl. III, 289), Bashk. *yaw* 'битва, бой ' (BRS), Kzk. *žau* 'враг, неприятель' (KzRS). ⇨ **YAW(-BASAR) + KELDİ.**

YAW-ΓASTÏ see YAW-QAČTÏ

YAW-ΓAŠTÏQ   Tat.(Sib.) 1632 **Yaw-γaštïq** [Евгаштык Чугалов] (Miller, Ist. Sib. II, 398). ⇨ **YAW-QAČTÏ?** + suff. *-q?*

YAW-QAČ   Uzb. 20th c. **Yaw-qâč** [Явқоч] (Begmatov 1984, 207). ✦ 'Enemy-run!'. ⇨ **YAW(-BASAR) + QAČ?**

YAW-QAČAR   Uzb. 20th c. **Yâw-qâčar** [Ёвкочар] (Begmatov 1984, 201, 207). ✦ 'The enemy will escape' cf. Chag., Alt., Tat. *yau* 'der Feind' (Radl. III, 16), Turk. *yaw* 'fremd, ein Fremder; feindlich, der Feind' (Radl. III, 289), Bashk. *yaw* 'битва, бой ' (BRS), Kzk. *žau* 'враг, неприятель' (KzRS). ⇨ **YAW(-BASAR) + QAČAR.** See also **YAW-QAČTÏ.**

YAW-QAČTÏ   Bashk. 1706 **Yaw-γastï** [Явгосты] (MIB III, 28); Bashk. 1706 **Yaw-γastï** [Явгоста (Явгуста) Инькин] (MIB III, 28); Nog. **Yaw-γaštï / J̌aw-qasti** [Явгашты (Джавкосты)] (Žirm., Epos 502); Tat. 20th c. **Yaw-qačtï** [Яукачтыев (Яукачтиев)] (Sattarov); Tat.(Sib.) 1629 **Yaw-qačtï** [Евгаштин (Неврус)] (Miller, Ist. Sib. II, 358, 447);

Bashk. 1763 **Yaw-qačtï** [Аптрак Явгачтын] (MIB IV/2, 45); Uzb. 20th c. **Yâw-qâčdï** [Евкочди] (Begmatov 1984, 207). ❖ 'The enemy escaped; the war ended' cf. Chag., Alt., Tat. *yau* 'der Feind' (Radl. III, 16), Turk. *yaw* 'fremd, ein Fremder; feindlich, der Feind' (Radl. III, 289), Bashk. *yaw* 'битва, бой' (BRS), Kzk. *žau* 'враг, неприятель' (KzRS) + Past (Imperfect) of Türk., Uyg., Kuman, Chag., Alt., Crm., Turk. etc. *qač-* 'fliehen' (Radl. II, 332), Bashk. *qas-* 'убегать, бежать' (BRS/Uraksin). ⇨ **QAŠTÏÑ?** See also **YAW-QAČAR, YAW-BASAR.**

YAW-TAŠ Selj.? 1256 **Yaw-taš** [Yâwtâsh Baglâr Bâg], the captain of the host of Bêth Rōmîyê, died in 1256 (Abulfar./Budge I, 424). ❖ 'Enemy-stone' cf. Chag., Alt., Tat. *yau* 'der Feind' (Radl. III, 16), Turk. *yaw* 'fremd, ein Fremder; feindlich, der Feind' (Radl. III, 289), Bashk. *yaw* 'битва, бой' (BRS), Kzk. *žau* 'враг, неприятель' (KzRS). ⇨ **TAŠ.**

YAWAČ Selj.? **Yawač** (<Yalawač?) [ياوج] (Ālī).

YAWAQDİN Chag.? 1509 **Yawaqdin-bek** [Явак-Дин-бек] (MIT II, 46).

YAWAN Chuv. 18th-19th c. **Yavan** [Яванъ] (Magn. 96); Yürük 1543 **Yawan** [يوان / Yavan] (Gökb., Rum. 197). ❖ 'Tastless, flavourless' cf. Turk. 'geschmacklos, pfade' (Radl. III, 290).

YAWAŠ Türk **Yabaš** (DTS); Alt.(Tuba) 19th c. **Yabaš** [Ябашъ], one of Erlik's seven sons (Potanin IV, 218); Türk 9th c. **Yabaš-tutuq** [Yabaš Tutuq] (DTS, ETY II, 95); Chuv. 18th-19th c. **Yavaš** [Явашъ] (Magn. 96); Maml. 14th c. **Yawaš** [يَواش / Yavaš], fem. (Tarj/Houtsma 109, Tarj/Toparlı 43); NUyg. 19th c. **Yawaš** [ياواش / Yavash] (Le Coq, Namenl. 122); Selj. / Khorezm.? 11th c. - 12th c. **Yawaš** [يواش], under Tekiš the Khorezmshah (1172-1200) (Rāwandī 402); *TN:* Turk. 20th c. **Yawaš-bey** [Yavaşbey], a village in the province of Samsun, Turkey (TMİB 749). ❖ 'Quiet, gentle; obedient' (Le Coq), cf. Uyg., Turk. *yavaš* 'friedlich, ruhig' (Radl. III, 290).; ❖ 'Peaceful, quiet, calm, silent; mild, weak' cf. Uyg. *yabaš* 'friedlich, friedfertig, ruhig' (Radl. IV, 278), Uyg., Crm., Turk. *yavaš / yawaš* 'id.' (Radl. III, 290).

YAWAŠKA Chuv. 18th-19th c. **Yawaška** [Явашка] (Magn. 96). ⇨ **YAWAŠ** + dim. suff. *-qa?*

YAWDA Bashk. 1753 **Yawda / Yawdï?** [Явда Тюлдин] (MIB IV/2, 426).

YAWDAN Nog. 20th c. **Yawdan** [Йавдан Уьтемалы улы / Явдан Утемалиев], one of Baskakov's informants from the aul of Nökis (Bask., Nog. 143).

YAWGER Bashk. 1785 **Jawger** [Джавгер Давыдов] (MIB V, 178); Bashk. 1756 **Yawgär** [Явгяр Юлушев] (MIB IV/1, 123). ❖ 'Fighter, soldier' cf. Bashk. *yawgir* 'боец, воин' (BRS/Uraksin).

YAWÏ Bashk. 1745 **Yawï?** [Яви Дусаев] (MIB III, 426). See also **İNAL-YAWÏ, QUZİ-YAWÏ, MUR-**

YAWÏ.

YAWÏN Bashk. 1762 **Yawn / Yawun** [Яун Чювашев (Чувашев)] (MIB IV/1, 244, V, 63); Bashk. 1765 **Yawn / Yawun** [Яун Чювашаев] (MIB IV/1, 312). ❖ 'Moisture, rain; born when it rained' (Kusimova), cf. Bashk. *yawïm / yawïn* 'осадки; дождь' (BRS/Uraksin).

YAWKÄY see **YAWQAY**

YAWQAY Kzk. 19th c. **Jawqay** [Джаукай] (AOK 106); Bashk. 1714 **Yawkäy** [Явкей Якшиев] (MIB I, 105). ❖ 'Little enemy' cf. Chag., Alt., Tat. *yau* 'der Feind' (Radl. III, 16), Turk. *yaw* 'fremd, ein Fremder; feindlich, der Feind' (Radl. III, 289), Bashk. *yaw* 'битва, бой' (BRS), Kzk. *žau* 'враг, неприятель' (KzRS) + dim. suff. *-käy.*

YAWLAQ-ARSLAN Selj. 1184 **Yawlaq-arslan** [Hûsâm ad-Dîn Yâwlak 'Arslân], an Ortokid who inherited Mardîn (Abulfar./Budge I, 317); Selj.? 1281 **Yawlaq-arslan** [Muzaffereddîn Yavlak-Arslan] (ADTCFD XXII (1965), 67, 68, 70). ❖ 'Strong, daring lion' cf. Karakh. *javlaq* II. 'крепкий; отважно' (DTS). ⇨ **ARSLAN.**

YAWLÏ Oghuz/Trkm. 13th c. **Yawlï-χan / Qanlï-yawlï-χan** [قاتلى ياولى / Канлы-Йавлы-хан], Tuman-χan's son who had the byname Qanlï (=Bloody) (Abulg./Kon. 805, 810, 815, 835-845). ❖ 'Hostile; militant'? cf. Chag., Alt., Tat. *yau* 'der Feind' (Radl. III, 16), Turk. *yaw* 'fremd, ein Fremder; feindlich, der Feind' (Radl. III, 289), Bashk. *yaw* 'битва, бой' (BRS), Kzk. *žau* 'враг, неприятель' (KzRS) + suff. *-lï.*

YAWMÄT Bashk. 1779 **Yawmät** [Гали Явметев] (MIB V, 87). ❖ 'Enemy-Mukhammad' cf. Chag., Alt., Tat. *yau* 'der Feind' (Radl. III, 16), Turk. *yaw* 'fremd, ein Fremder; feindlich, der Feind' (Radl. III, 289), Bashk. *yaw* 'битва, бой' (BRS) + suff. *-mät.*

YAWUQ Bashk. 1798 **Yawuq** [Яукъ] (PSZRI XXV, 195). ❖ 'Close, near'? cf. Uyg., Chag. *yawuq* 'nah' (Radl. III, 293).

YAWUNBET Bashk. 1756 **Yawumbet (<Yawunbet)** [Яумбет Текеев] (MIB IV/1, 122). ❖ 'Rainfall, moisture; child born in rainy (bad) weather' cf. Bashk. *yawïn* 'осадки' (BRS), Tat. *yawïn* 'der Regen, das schlechte Wetter' (Radl. III, 292) + suff. *-bet.*

YAWUŠ Crm.? **Yawuš** [Явушъ], a prince of the Ars (Arskij knjaz') (PSRL XIX, 418); Bashk. 1735 **Yawuš** [Зьянгул Яушев] (MIB III, 331); Bashk. 1736 **Yawuš** [Явуш] (MIB III, 344); Bashk. 1747 **Yawuš** [Ишаля Яушев] (MIB III, 447); Bashk. 1757 **Yawuš** [Сыртлан Яушев] (MIB IV/1, 142); Bashk. 1761 **Yawuš** [Искендер Яушев] (MIB IV/1, 200); Bashk. 1772 **Yawuš** [Яуш] (MIB IV/1, 367); Bashk. 1798 **Yawuš** [Кукей Яушев] (MIB IV/1, 290); Tat. / Bashk.? 19th c.? **Yawuš** [Veli Bai Javušev] (Mende 99). ❖ 'Enemy-leader / Fight-chieftain' Dial. (shortened) variant of

Yaw-šäyeχ (Sattarov), cf. Chag., Alt., Tat. *yau* 'der Feind' (Radl. III, 16), Turk. *yaw* 'fremd, ein Fremder; feindlich, der Feind' (Radl. III, 289), Bashk. *yaw* 'битва, бой' (BRS), Kzk. *žau* 'враг, неприятель' (KzRS), see also comp. *šeyχ*.

YAWUŠA Bashk. 1776 **Yawuša** [Яуша Мумашев] (MIB V, 51). ✧ 'Man or woman sent out to inquire about a prospective bride and to lead the marriage negotiations' cf. Tat. *yaučï* 'id.' (TatRS).

YAWUZ see **ВОГАZJA-FATİMA**

YAWUZ-YAГЇR-ВОГАZJA-FATMA see **ВОГАZJA-FATİMA**

YAZ Trkm. **Yaz-bibi** [Язбиби], fem. (Sopieva 180). ✧ 'Spring, summer' cf. Türk., Kuman, Chag., Az., Crm., Tat., Turk., etc. *yaz* 'der Frühling; der Sommer' (Radl. III, 225). See also **SARA-YAZ**.

YAZ-BERDİ Trkm. **Yaz-berdi** [Язберди] (Sopieva 180). ✧ 'Spring has him/her given; Born in spring'. ⇨ **YAZ + BERDİ.**

YAZ-JEREN Trkm. **Yaz-jeren** [Язжерен] (Sopieva 180). ✧ 'Spring-gazelle'. ⇨ **YAZ + JEREN.**

YAZ-GELDİ Trkm. **Yaz-geldi** [Язгелди] (Sopieva 180). ✧ 'Spring has come; born in spring'. ⇨ **YAZ + KELDİ.**

YAZ-ГЇLЇČ Trkm. **Yaz-γïlïč** [Язгылыч] (Sopieva 180). ✧ 'Spring-sword'. ⇨ **YAZ + QÏLÏČ.**

YAZ-NUR Trkm. **Yaz-nur** [Язнур], fem. (Sopieva 180). ✧ 'Spring-light'. ⇨ **YAZ + NUR.**

YAZ-SOLTAN Trkm. **Yaz-soltan** [Язсолтан], fem. (Sopieva 180). ✧ 'Empress of the spring'. ⇨ **YAZ + SULTAN.**

YAZARMÏŠ Yürük 1543 **Yazarmiš** [Yazarmış] (Gökb., Rum. 291). ✧ 'He who wrote; (God) wrote (ordered) it'? cf. Kuman, Crm., Tat., Turk. *yaz-* 'schreiben, zeichnen' (Radl. III, 226).

YAZDAN-VERDİ Trkm.? 1847 **Yazdan-verdi-χan** [Яздан-верды-хан], „Zaferanlü" (from the clan Zaferan) (MIT II, 241, 256, 257). ⇨ **YAZ? + BERDİ.**

YAZГUT Bashk.? 1695 **Yazγut** [Исенгилдей Язгутов] (MIB I, 90). ✧ 'Destiny, fate, preordinance' cf. Trkm. *yazγït* 'судьба, рок; предопределение' (TrkmRS).

YAZЇ Pecheneg 860-880 **Yazï** [Γιαζής / Jazy], chief of the Pecheneg Yazï-qabān tribe or Keban (Németh, HMK 84, Byz. Turc. 112, Erol II); *TN:* Turk. 20th c. **Yazï-beyli** [Yazıbeyli], a village in the province of Ankara (TMİB 91). ✧ 'Flat(land); Steppe'? cf. Türk., Uyg., Kuman, Alt. *yazï* 'flach, eben, die Fläche, Ebene, Steppe' (Radl. III, 229).

YAZIJЇ Crm. / Turk.? **Yazïjï-oγlu** [Jazyǧy Oglu] (Mende 73, 3). ✧ 'Writer, writing; scribe' cf. Crm., Kar., Turk. *yazïjï* 'ein Mensch, der Schreibt, ein Schreiber, Schriftsteller, Schriftgelehrter' (Radl. III, 235).

YAZÏK Chuv. 18th-19th c. **Yazïk** [Языкъ] (Magn. 97). ✧ 'Sin; harm, damage' Alt., Tat., Turk. *yazïq* 'die Sünde, das Vergehen, Verbrechen; das Unglück, der Schaden, die Schande' Radl. III, 231).

YAZÏR Oghuz/Trkm. **Yazïr** [يازير / Yâzir], Oghuz' grand-son, Ay-χan's son (Abulg./Desm. 27, Abulg./Kon. 515, 545, 595); Kzk. 1846 **Yazïr-bay** [Талпак Язырбаев], a biy (MKOP 100); Uyg. 12th c. - 14th c. **Yazïr-toña** / **Yäzir-tonγa** / **Yezir-toña** [Yäzir Tonga / jazïr toŋa / jezir toŋa] (Radl., USp. 108, 204, 246, 275, EUTS, DTS); *EN:* Oghuz **Yazïr** (<**Yazγïr?**) [Jazγïr / Yazgïr], one of the 24 (22?) Oghuz tribes (MK/Brock. 244, MK/Atalay IV, 859); Oghuz/Trkm. 13th c. **Yazïr** / **Yasïr** [يازير / Yâzir / Йазыр / Йасыр], Ay-χan's son, Oghuz' grand-son, a chieftain (Abulg./Desm. 27, Abulg./Kon. 515, 545, 595). ✧ 'He who will write', 'He writes' (Pelliot, Notes 191: présent duratif du verbe *yaz-*, avec la forme -*ïr* du suffix); Pelliot reads the name as *Yazïr < Yazγïr <yaz-* 'to write' (Radl. III, 226) + Aor. suff. -*ïr* <-*γïr* (Pelliot, Notes 229). See *Yazïr-toña* 'Yazïr-Panther' (Blagova 1997, 706).

YAZLAMAZ Trkm.? **Yazlamaz-oγlu** [Yazlamazoğlu Ali bey], forefather of the noblest family of „Tecirli oymağı" (tribe of Tejirli) (Riza V, 14). ✧ 'He won't spend the summer' cf. Turk. *yazla-* 'eintreten werden (von Sommer); den Sommer zubringen wo' (Radl. III, 239).

YĀDİGÄR see **YADЇGAR**

YĀÏR Khorezm. 1213 **Yāïr-qan?** [Jâir khân], defender of Bukhara against the Mongols in 1213 (Abulfar./Budge I, 368 /428/).

YÂNDÂŠ Uzb. 20th c. **Yândâš** [Ёндош] (Begmatov 1984, 200); Uzb. 20th c. **Yândâš-bây** [Ендошбой] (Begmatov 1984, 202); Uzb. 20th c. **Yândâš-mirza** [Ендошмирза] (Begmatov 1984, 202). ✧ 'He who stands by (us); He who stays by (us); Supporter' cf. Uzb. *yândâš* 'стоящий бок о бок; находящийся рядом', *yândaš-* 'быть, находиться бок о бок; соприкасаться' (UzbRS).

YÂNDÂŠ-ALİ Uzb. 20th c. **Yândâš-ali** [Ендошали] (Begmatov 1984, 200); Uzb. 20th c. **Yândâš-ali** [Ендошали] (Begmatov 1984, 202). ⇨ **YÂNDÂŠ + ALİ.**

YÄBİRÄ see **YABЇRA**

YÄDİGÄR see **YADЇGAR**

YÄDİGER see **YADЇGAR**

YÄDİM see **YETİM**

YÄЂEGÄR see **YADЇGAR**

YÄGÄ see **YEKÄ**

YÄGÄFÄR see **YAГAFER**

YÄGÄLYİN Yak. **Yägälyin** [Тіmір Järälįіn], a hero in a tale (Pek.).

YÄGRÄK Maml.? 14th c. **Yägräk** [يكرك] (Sauvaget

:56). ✧ 'Better' (Sauvaget 56).

YAΓFÄR see **YAΓAFER**

YÄYLÄW see **YAYLAQ**

YÄKÄ see **YEKÄ**

YÄKÄN Uyg. **Yäkän** [Yäkän] (EUTS).

YÄKÄNČÜK Uyg. **Yäkänčük** [Yäkänçük] (EUTS). ⇨ **YÄKÄN** + suff. *-čük*.

YÄKŠEMBE see **YEKŠENBE**

YÄL-BOΓA see **YUL-BUΓA**

YÄL-BOΓA Selj. 1209/10 **Yäl-boγa** (Németh, HMK 136).

YÄLBÄ Bulg.? **Yälbä / Yelbeh** [يَلبَ / Йäлбä] (Jusupov 40, Epigr. Bulg. 112, 113).

YÄLBÄΓÄN Hak.(Sag.) **Čelbigän** [Челбігäн Кащей Безсмертный] (Proben IX, 248, 302, 463-465); Alt. **Yälbäyän** [Jäлбäӊäн] (Radl. II, 110); Tat.(Bar.) **Yilbägän** [Jiлбäгäн / тäмір Jiлбäгäн], mythical being (Proben IV, 59 /73/, 79 /100/); Tat.(Bar.), Tat.(Tüm.) **Yilbägän** [Jiлбäгäннäр / ÿц Jiлбiгäн], mythical beings (die drei Gebrüder Jilbägän / die siebenhundert Jilbägänen) (Proben IV, 66 /82/, 74 /94/); Tat.(Tara) **Yilbägän / Yilbigän** [Jiлбäгäн / Jiлбiгäн], mythical being (Proben IV, 106 /138/); Tat.(Tüm.) **Yilbigän** [Jiлбiгäн], mythical being(s) in the tale (Proben IV, 319 /398/). ✧ Fabulous man-eater (monster), cf. Alt. *Yälbäyän* 'ein menschenfressendes Ungeheuer von menschlicher Gestalt mit einem, drei, sieben oder zwölf Köpfen, der farbe nach wird von schwarzen und gelben Jelbegenen besprochen' (Radl. III, 357), cf. Shor *čälbägän / čelbägän = t'älbägän* (Radl. III, 1981). See also **SARЇ-ČÄLBÄGÄN**.

YÄLBÄN see **YALMAN**

YÄLÄKČI Uyg. **Yäläkči** [Yäläkçi] (EUTS).

YÄLGÄK Türk **Yälgäk** [Yälgäk] (ETY II, 122).

YÄM-BERDİ see **ĴAN-BERDİ**

YÄMEY Tat. 1730 **Yämey** [Ямей Ямекесбеев] (MIB III, 274). ✧ 'Beauty, finery' cf. Tat. *yäm* 'die Schöhnheit' (Radl. III, 387), also Tat. PNs beginning with *Yäm* (Sattarov) + suff. *-ey*.

YÄMEKES Tat. 1730 **Yämekes** [Ямей Ямекесбеев] (MIB III, 274).

YÄN see **ĴAN**

YÄN-ALİ see **ĴAN-ALİ**

YÄN-BİRĐE see **ĴAN-BERDİ**

YÄN-GİLDE see **ĴAN-KELDİ**

YÄN-GİLDİ see **ĴAN-KELDİ**

YÄN-ΓÄLİ see **ĴAN-ALİ**

YÄN-HARЇ see **ĴAN-SARЇ**

YÄN-OĐAQ see **ĴAN-UZAQ**

YÄN-TİMER see **ĴAN-TEMİR**

YÄN-UĐAQ see **ĴAN-UZAQ**

YÄN-URUS see **YAN-URUS**

YÄNA-BERDİ see **YANA-BERDİ?**

YÄNČÜ Alt. 19th c. **Yänčü** [Енчу], a shaman (Potanin IV, 204, 207); Tat.? 17th c. **Yänčü-bay** [Янчюбайко Кулбаишевъ], from the government of Kazan (IOAIÊK XXIX, 344); Maml. 14th c. **Yünčü** [ينجو / Yünçü], fem. (Tarĵ/Houtsma 108, Tarĵ/Toparlı 43). ✧ 'Pearl' cf. Türk *yänčü* 'die Perle', Chag. *yänjü* 'id.' (Radl. III, 334).

YÄNČÜ-BİLGÄ Türk **Yänčü-bilgä-qaγan** [?] (Németh, HMK 134). ⇨ **YÄNČÜ** + **BİLGÄ**.

YÄNÄY see **ĴANAY**

YÄNÄW Bashk. 19th c. **Yänäw-bay** [Янäубай Енлевовъ] (IOAIÊK XXVIII, 590).

YÄNEKÄY see **YENİKÄY**

YÄNKÄY Bashk. 1735 **Yänkäy** [Янкай Кюлюковъ], a tarχan (Vel.-Zern., Bašk. 18); Bashk. 1754 **Yänkäy** [Итяш Янкеев] (MIB IV/1, 83). ✧ 'My little soul, my darling'. ⇨ **ĴAN** + hypoc. suff. *-qay*. See also **YÄNEKÄY**.

YÄNMÄT see **YANMAT**

YÄR-QARA Tat.(Bar.) **Yär-qara** [Jär Kara / Jäp Kapa] (Proben IV, 79 (101)). ✧ 'Earth-Black' cf. Türk, Uyg., Kuman, Chag., Alt., Turk. *yär* 'dasd Land, die Erde; der Ort' (Radl. III, 334). ⇨ **QARA**.

YÄR-MÖXÄMBÄT see **YÄR-MÖXÄMMÄT**

YÄR-MÖXÄMMÄT Bashk. 1742 **Yär-moχämbät** [Ермухамбеть Ибраев] (MIB III, 517); Bashk. 1742 **Yär-moχämbät** [Ермухамбеть Ибраев] (MIB III, 518); Bashk. 1760 **Yär-moχämmät** [Ермухаммет] (MIB IV/2, 28). ✧ Cf. also Tat. PN *Yar-möχämmät* (Sattarov) and Bashk. PN *Yär-möχämät* (Kusimova). ⇨ **YAR** + **MUXAMMED**.

YÄRÄN-ČÄČÄN see **YEREN-ČEČEN**

YÄRKÄY see **YARQAY**

YÄSRÄ Bashk. 1756 **Yäsrä-bay** (<Yäsirä) [Ясрябай Булдин] (MIB IV/1, 109). ✧ 'Little, small' cf. Tat. *Yäsirä* (<Ar.) (Sattarov).

YÄSTÄY-MÖÑKÖ Tat.(Bar.) **Yästäy-möñkö** [Jästäi Möngkö / Jäctäi Möнкö] (Proben IV, 78 /99/). ✧ 'Brother-in-law-Eternal' cf. Alt.(Tel.) *yästä, yästäs* 'der Mann der älteren Schwester' (Radl. III, 378), Alt.(Tel., Leb.) *möñkü* 'ewig' (Radl. III, 2131). ⇨ **MÖÑKE?**

YÄSÜK Tat.(Lit.) 1592 **Yäsük** [Икбулатъ Ясюкевичъ] (Lit. Tat. 117).

YÄŠ see **YAŠ**

YEDİ see **YETİ**

YEDİ-QURTQA Khorezm.? 13th c. **Yedi-qurtqa-χatun** [بیدی قورتنه خاتون / Еди-Хуртага], Mengü Temür (1266-1280) χan's daughter, Ghazan Ilkhan's (1295-1304) wife (RaD/Ber. I, 101, RaD/Jahn 13). ⇨ **YETİ** + **QURTQA**.

YEDİGEY see **EDİGEY**

YEDİK Kzk. 1726 **Yedik-bay** [Jedikbaï], a head (senior) (Levchin 157). ✧ 'Suitable, fitting, appropriate; diligent, sensible' cf. Uyg., Tat.(Bar.) *yädik* 'erreichend, gehörig, passend; flink, fleissig, verständig' (Radl. III, 371).

YEGÄ see **YEKÄ**

YEGÄN Uyg. **Yägän** [Yägän] (EUTS); Uyg. 830 **Yegän-apa** [Beg Künki Taisangun Sïrtuš Yägän Apa] (Mahrnāmag 10); Trkm. 20th c. **Yegän-bey** [Yeğen-bey], a Türkmen in Turkey (Özbaş 24); Türk 721 **Yegän-čur** (DTS); Uyg. **Yigän** [Yigän] (EUTS); Uyg. 911 **Yigän** [Tchou Yi-yen], an envoy, whose Chinese family name was Tchou (Hamilton, Ouïg. 66); Uyg. 13th-14th c. **Yigän** (Zieme, Mat. II, 86); Türk 7th-9th c. **Yigän-čur** [Yigän] (ETY III, 61); Türk 721 **Yigän-čur** [Yigän Çur] (ETY I, 139); Uyg. 13th-14th c. **Yigän-toña / Yägän-toña** [Ygän Tonga] (Zieme, Mat. II, 86); *TN:* Turk. 20th c. **Yegän-aγa** [Yeğenağa (Tataryeğenağa)], a village in the province of Kırşehir, Turkey (TMİB 550); Turk. 15th c. **Yegän-beg (jāmi)** [يكان بك جامعى], a mosque (in Ankara?) (MG Ank. 51). ✧ 'Nephew, grand-son' cf. Uyg. *ykän, y(ä)kän, y(ä)gän* 'neveu, nièce' (Haneda 3-4, 6), Uyg. *yegän* 'племянник' (DTS), Bashk. *yeyän* 'внук' (BaRS), also a secondary component of names. In the Bashk. it means that the boy was born in the home of his grand-mother (Kusimova 132). See also **EDGÜ-YEGÄN**.

YEGÄN-AΓÏSÏZ Uyg. 8th c. - 12th c. **Yägän-aγïsïz-sañun** [Yägän-aγïsïz sangun] (Müller, Pfahl. 12); Uyg. 12th c. - 14th c. **Yegän-aγïsïz-säñün** (Radl., USp. 12). ⇨ **YEGÄN + AΓÏ** + suff. *-sïz*.

YEGÄN-KÜLÜG Uyg. 12th c. - 14th c. **Yegän-külüg-sañün** (DTS); Uyg. 8th c. - 12th c. **Yegän-külüg-säñün (-sañun?)** [Yägän külüg sangun] (Müller, Pfahl. 10). ✧ 'Nephew-famous' or 'Nephew-famous-strategist'? (Blagova 1997, 708). ⇨ **YEGÄN + KÜLÜK.**

YEGÄN-QARA Uyg. 12th c. - 14th c. **Yegän-qara** (DTS). ✧ 'Nephew-black/mighty' (Blagova 1997, 708). ⇨ **YEGÄN + QARA.**

YEGÄN-QIÑRUL Uyg. 12th c. - 14th c. **Yegän-qiñrul-säñün** (DTS). ✧ 'Nephew-wicked/evil' (Blagova 1997, 708). ⇨ **YEGÄN + QIÑRUL.**

YEGÄNČÜK Uyg. 12th c. - 14th c. **Yegänčük** (Radl., USp. 90, 93, DTS). ✧ 'Little nephew' (Blagova 1997, 708). ⇨ **YEGÄN** + dim. suff. *-čük*.

YEGİN-SİLİG Türk 732 **Yägin-silig** [Yäginsilig] (ETY I, 44); Türk 732 **Yegin-silig-beg** (DTS). ✧ I. 'Nephew-clean/honest'; II. 'Nephew-noble(-prince)' (Blagova 1997, 708), cf. Uyg. *silig / silik* 'arı, temiz, pâk, bakire' (EUTS). ⇨ **YEGÄN + SİLÜ.**

YEGİT see **YİGİT**

YEGİTEY Bashk. 1790 **Yegitey** [Шерып Егитеев] (MIB V, 278). ⇨ **YİGİT** + dim. suff. *-ey*.

YEΓAFER see **YAΓAFER**

YEKÄ Uyg. **Yäkä** [Yäkä] (EUTS); Uyg. 12th c. - 14th c. **Yekä** (DTS); Uyg. 12th c. - 14th c. **Yekä / Yegä** (Radl., USp. 115-116). ✧ 'Alone, lonely' cf. Chag. *yäkä* 'einzeln, einsam, verlassen'; (Kirg.) *yekä* 'einzig,

allein' (Radl. III, 317). See also **TEGRÄNČ-YEKÄ**.

YEKÄ-BAŠ Uyg. 12th c. - 14th c. **Yekä-baš** (Radl., USp. 83, DTS 48). ✧ 'Yekä-Head' (Blagova 1997, 709). ⇨ **YEKÄ + BAŠ.**

YEKÄ-BUQA Uyg. 12th c. - 14th c. **Yekä-buqa / Yäkä-buγa** [Yäkä Buγa] (Radl., USp. 75, 129, DTS). ✧ 'Yekä-Bull'. ⇨ **YEKÄ + BUQA.**

YEKEÑK Oghuz/Trkm. 14th c. - 15th c. **Yekeñk / Yügnek / Yigenek / Yaγanaq** [يَكَنَك / Yügnek, Yigenek (Big Yigenek), Yaganak / Иекенк], Qazï-qoja's son (DQorq./Gökyay 23, DQorq./Rossi 112, 127, 133, 135, 144, 158, 160-65, DQorq./Ergin 113, DQorq. 22, 30, 32, 44 etc. [Manuscr. Vatic. 67]).

YEKŠENBE Kzk. **J̌eksembe** [Джексенбе] (Valihanov, Soč. 347); Kzk. 19th c. **J̌eksembe** [Джексембе] (SOK 42, 258); Kzk. 19th c. **J̌eksembe** [Джексембе] (SOV 16, 22); Kzk. 19th c. **J̌eksembi** [Джексембы] (AOO 46, 66); Trkm. 19th c. **Yäkšembe** [Якшембе] (Volodin 53); Trkm. 19th c. **Yekšenbe** [Екъ-Шенбэ Бердбаевъ] (Ščeglov IV, 164); Kzk. 19th c. **Žeksembe** [Жексембе] (SODž. 20). ✧ 'Sunday' cf. Kzk. *jeksämbï* 'der Sonntag' (Radl. IV, 68), Trkm. *yekšenbe* 'id.' (TrkmRS) (<P.).

YEL Kzk. 19th c. **J̌il-bay** [Джилбай] (AOA 142); Kzk. 19th c. **J̌il-bay** [Джильбай] (SOK 52); Kzk. 19th c. **J̌il-bay** [Джильбай] (SOV 154); Kzk. 19th c. **J̌il-biy** [Джилбий] (Grod., Pril. 29); Maml. 1450, 1467 **Yal-bay / Yel-bay?** [يلباى الاينالى] (Ibn Taghrīb. VIII, 82, 185, 602-617); Maml. 1461 **Yel-bay** [يلباى طاز المجنون] (Ibn Taghrīb. VII, 698, 840); Maml. 1467 **Yel-bay / Bil-bay?** [يلباى الاينالى لمؤيدى/ الملك الظاهر ابونصر/], a Mamluk sultan, died in 1468 (Ibn Taghrīb. VII, 88, 388, Weil, Chalif. II, 230, 251, 316-20); Maml. 1440 **Yel-bay / Yal-bay** [يلباي الظاهري], a governor in Tripolis, mentioned in an inscription in Lattakich (Sauvaget: BEO XII (1948), 47); Maml. 1465, 1468 **Yel-bay / Yal-bay** [يلباى الظاهرى] (Ibn Taghrīb. VIII, 82, 185, 602-617); Maml. 1421, 1444/45 **Yel-χoǰa** [الناصرىَ] [يلخجا من مامش], chief marshal of the court („Oberhofmarschall") (Ibn Taghrīb. VI, 480, 569, 741, VII, 8, 132, 139, Weil, Chalif. II, 238); Maml. 1446 **Yel-χoǰa** [يلخجا من مامش] (Ibn Taghrīb. VIII, 2, 20); Oghuz 981, 982, 983 **Yel-tegin / Yel-tekin** [بلتكين / يلتكين/ التركي / يلتكين التركى / Yeltekin], from the Ikhshids (Ibn al-Athīr/Tornb. IX, 5, 6, 13, Qalānisi 20, 26, 29, Tugan, UTT 179); *TN:* Kzk. 1867 **J̌el-seyit** [Джелъ-Сеитъ], a kurgan (burial mound) in the region of Vernoje (Alma-Ata?) (ZIRGOGcogr. 1, 268). ✧ I. 'Wind' cf. Karakh. *yel* I 'id.' (DTS), Kzk. *žel* 'ветер' (KzRS), Tat. *jil* 'ветер' (TatRS); II. 'Evil spirit, wicked being' cf. Karakh. *yel* II 'злой дух, демоническое существо' (DTS). See also **QUTLU-YÄL**.

YEL-ALDÏ Turk. 19th c. **Yel-aldï-oγlu** [Jel aldy oγlu], a Zeybek (Kúnos 1891, 119). ✧ 'The wind took him'. ⇨ **YEL + ALDÏ**.

YEL-BUΓA Maml. 1388 **Yel-buγa / Yul-buγa?** [يلبغا / يولبوغا], nāꜥib (governor) of Haleb who assaulted Sivas (Astarab. 349, 364 etc.); Maml. 1306 **Yel-buγa** [يلبغا التركمانى] (Iyās I, 147, Weil, Chalif. I, 276); Maml. 1339 **Yel-buγa** [Jelbuġa al-Kāmilī], governor of Haleb and Hama (Björkm. 158); Maml. 1339/40 **Yel-buγa** [سيف الدين يلبغا اليحياوى] / Jelbuġa al-Jaḫjāwī] (Iyās I, 171, 187, Weil, Chalif. I, 463, Björkm. 163); Maml. 1359, 1366 **Yel-buγa** [الخاصكى السيفى يلبغا], amīr-ī majlīs in 1359 then commander-in-chief, died in 1366 (Mayer 249, Iyās I, 184, 187-88, Weil, Chalif IV, 453, 460, 463); Maml. 1367 **Yel-buγa** [يلبغا الناصرى العمرى الخاصكى], chief marshal of the court („Oberhofmarschall"), died in 1367 (Weil, Chalif. I, 518 etc., Iyās I, 207, 211-220, Björkm. 124); Maml. 1367/68 **Yel-buγa** [يلبغا القوصونى] (Iyās I, 222-225); Maml. 1368/69 **Yel-buγa** [يلبغا آص] (Iyās I, 224, Weil, Chalif. I, 521); Maml. 1374/75 **Yel-buγa** [السيفى يلبغا الناصرى], an emir-i χājib, died in 1374/75 (Mayer 248); Maml. 1376/77 **Yel-buγa** [يلبغا السابقى] (Iyās I, 231); Maml. 1377/78 **Yel-buγa** [يلبغا النظامى] (Iyās I, 239); Maml. 1379/80 **Yel-buγa** [يلبغا المنجكى] (Iyās I, 248, 292, Ibn Taghrīb. VI, 127); Maml. 1383 **Yel-buγa** [Yelbuga], governor of Haleb (Uzunçarş., Anad. 46); Maml. 1386 **Yel-buγa** [يلبغا صغير], a treasurer (Weil, Chalif. I, 545, Iyās III, 149); Maml. 1389, 1397 **Yel-buγa** [يلبغا السالمى الظاهرى] (Iyās I, 281, Ibn Taghrīb. VI, 20, Weil, Chalif. I, 565-66); Maml. 1391 **Yel-buγa** [يلبغا الناصرى] (Weil, Chalif. I, 528-29, II, 6, 9, Ibn Taghrīb. VI, 144, 145); Maml. 1397 **Yel-buγa** [ابدالله يلبغا السالمى] (Berchem 70); Maml. 1398/99 **Yel-buγa** [يلبغا الاحمدى لظاهرقّ المجنون], chief marshal of the court („Obersthofmarschall") (Ibn Taghrīb. VI, 3, 5, 6, 9 etc., Iyās I, 307-313 etc., Weil, Chalif. II, 13, 78); Maml. 1399 **Yel-buγa** [يلبغا الحافظى] (Iyās I, 317); Maml. 1399/1400 **Yel-buγa** [يلبغا الاشتمرى] (Ibn Taghrīb. VI, 20); Maml. 1399/1400 **Yel-buγa** [يلبغا المحمودىّ] (Ibn Taghrīb. VI, 16); Maml. 1400 **Yel-buγa** [يلبغا المظفّرى] (Ibn Taghrīb. VI, 341); Maml. 1400 **Yel-buγa** [يلبغا كماج] (Ibn Taghrīb. VI, 349); Maml. 1402/03 **Yel-buγa** [يلبغا السودونىّ] (Ibn Taghrīb. V, 157, Duqmaq:RHCHor V, 10, 19, 24, 71); Maml. 1438/39 **Yel-buγa** [يلبغا البهائى الظاهرى] (Ibn Taghrīb. VII, 53, 57); Maml. 1453 **Yel-buγa** [يلبغا المجنون] (Ibn Taghrīb. VIII, 173); Maml. 1347 **Yel-buγa / Yal-buγa** [السيفى يلبغا الساقى] / Yalbuga al-Yahyāvī], as viceroy (governor) of Syria he was imprisoned and died in 1347, mentioned in an inscription of a well (Mayer 249-251, Iyās I, 184, 187-88, Weil, Chalif IV, 453, 460, 463); Maml. 1448, 1451 **Yel-buγa / Yul-buγa?** [يلبغا الجاركسى], a mamluk of Cherkess origin (Ibn Taghrīb. VIII, 32, 120). ✧ I. 'Wind-Bull' cf. Németh, HMK 136: *Yäl-boγa* 'Szél-bika' [=Wind-Bull]; II. 'Wicked Bull'? ⇨ **YEL + BUQA**.

YEL-ΓOVAN Turk. 19th c. **Yel-γovan-oγlu** [Jel govan oγlu], a Zeybek (Kúnos 1891, 119). ✧ 'He who drives away (pursues) the wind, wind-pursuer' cf. Turk. *kovan* 'that drives away or pursues' (TED). ⇨ **YEL**.

YEL-MOΓUS Kzk. 19th c. **J̌al-maus** [Джалмаусъ] (Potanin II, 146); Karch. **J̌el-maus** [Джелмаусъ], fem. (SMOK III, 158-160); Kirg. **Yel-moγus** [Јелмоɓус] (Proben V, 549 (553)). ✧ 'Wind-warrior/fighter? ' (Németh, HMK 137), cf. Hak. *moγus* 'der Kämpfer' (Radl. III, 2122). ⇨ **YEL + MOΓOS**.

YEL-ORTAY Tat.(GH) 1288 **Yel-ortay / Yel-örtey** [Елортай / Елортей], Temir's son (from the Horde) (PSRL X, 167). ⇨ **YEL**.

YELAYÏR Bashk. 1675 **Yelayïr / Yelair?** [Елаир] (MIB I, 199).

YELBÄGÄY Kirg. **Yelbägäy** [Јелбäräi], one of Manas' comrades-in-arms (Proben V, 39 /41/). ✧ 'Unbuttoned; open' cf. Kirg. *yelbägäy* 'den Gürtel nicht festgebunden habend, so dass die Kleider im Winde flattern' (Radl. III, 357), Kzk. *želbegey* 'нараспашку; внакидку' (KzRS).

YELÄKČİ Uyg. 12th c. - 14th c. **Yeläkči** (DTS). ✧ 'Rider/Riding'? (Blagova 1997, 716) + suff. -*či*.

YELGÄN Kzk. 1741 **Yelgän-biy** [Елган бий] (MIKk. 210).

YELGÄNDÄY Chuv. 18th-19th c. **Yelgändäy?** [Елгандай] (Magn. 37).

YELGİNEY Bashk. 1791 **Yelginey** [Елгиней Елинов] (MIB V, 307).

YELİKEY Bashk. 1735 **Yelikey** [Кулубай Еликеев], a tarχan (Vel.-Zern., Bašk. 16).

YELİMČİ Bashk. 1735 **Yelimči** [Елимчи Исенчуринъ], a tarχan (Vel.-Zern., Bašk. 23). ✧ 'Fisherman, user of fishing net' cf. Tat. *jīlīmčï* 'id.' (TatRS), Bashk. *yilïm* 'невод' (BRS/Uraksin). See also **TORČİ**.

YELİN Bashk. 1791 **Yelin** [Елгиней Елинов] (MIB V, 307). ✧ 'Udder; mane'? cf. Kuman, Chag., East.T., NUyg.(Tar.) *yälin* 'das Euter, das Euter der Stute' (Radl. III, 350); Alt. *yelin (yälä, yal)* 'die Mähne' (Radl. III, 350).

YELİNJE Oghuz/Trkm. 13th c. **Yelinje-χan** [Yèlindjè-Khan], Tatar Khan's son in a legend of origin (Abulg./Desm. 11).

YELLİ Kzk. 19th c. **J̌äldi-bay** [Джялдыбай] (AOA 62); Kzk. 19th c. **J̌ildï-bek** [Джилдыбекъ] (SOV 24);

Trkm. 20th c. **Yelli** [Yelli] (Zaj. 1971, 330); Trkm. 20th c. **Yelli** [Елли] (TrkmRS 304). ✦ 'Windy' cf. Trkm. *yelli* 'ветреный; опухший' (TrkmRS). ⇨ **YEL** + suff. *-li / -di*.

YELMET   Bashk. 1728 **Yelmet** [Елметев] (MIB III, 254). ⇨ **YEL?** + suff. *-met*.

YEMAČTAY   Tat.(Sib.) 1600 **Yemačtay / Yamačtay?** [Буйдак Емачтаев] (Miller, Ist. Sib. II, 159). ⇨ **?** + suff. *-tay(1,2)?*

YEMAMBET see **YEMANBET**

YEMAN see **YAMAN**

YEMAN-SAR see **YAMAN-SARÏ**

YEMAN-SARÏ see **YAMAN-SARÏ**

YEMANBET   Bashk. 1735 **Yemanbet** [Усенъ Емамбетевъ], a tarχan (Vel.-Zern., Bašk. 18). ⇨ **YAMAN** + suff. *-bet*.

YEMANTAY see **YAMANTAY**

YEMAŠ see **YAMAŠ**

YEMÄK   Bashk. 1728 **Yemäk?** [Ибрай Емяков] (MIB III, 253).

YEMEKEY   Bashk. 1715 **Yemekey** [Емекей] (MIB III, 132). ⇨ **YEMÄK?** + suff. *-äy*.

YEN see **ǰAN**

YEN-AL?   Bashk. 1787 **Yen-al? / Yän-al? / Yan-ali?** [Еналь Биляров] (MIB V, 203). ⇨ **ǰAN** + **AL / ALİ?**

YEN-BERDİ see **ǰAN-BERDİ**

YEN-ГЇLЇČ see **YAN-QÏLİČ**

YENA   Tat.(Sib.) 1628 **Yena-bek / Yenä-bek?** [Енабеков Мирзагилдей], a yasaul (commander) (Miller, Ist. Sib. II, 338). ⇨ **YANA?**

YENČAR see **YANČER**

YENDİBAČ   Tat. 1662 **Yendibač / Endibač?** [Ендыбачъ Тарабердѣевъ] (DAI IV, 306).

YENİ   Kzk. 19th c. **Yeni-bay?** [Енибай] (Grod., Pril. 146). ✦ 'Darling' cf. Tat.(Mish.) *yäni* [=ǰani 'жандай кадерле'] (Sattarov). ⇨ **ǰAN / ǰANİ.**

YENİKÄY   Bashk. 20th c. **Yänekäy** [Йәнекәй / Яникей] (Kusimova); Bashk. 20th c. **Yänekäy** [Йәнекәй / Яникей] (Kusimova); Bashk. 1706 **Yänikey / Yanïkey?** [Яныкей Борисов] (MIB III, 26); Tat. 1622 **Yenigey** [Енигей] (Miller, Ist. Sib. II, 291); Tat. 14th c. **Yenikey** [Jenikejev], a Tatar murza on Mordva territory (Smyrnov 276); Tat. 1552 **Yenikey** [Еникей], a chief/commander of ten thousand (soldiers) at the assault of Kazan (Zolotn. 157); Tat. 1777 **Yenikey** [Ханбек Еникеев] (MIB V, 60); Tat. 1777 **Yenikey** [Хансуяр Еникеев] (MIB V, 60); Tat.(Mish.) **Yenikey** [Еникеевъ] (IOAİÊK XIX, 143); Bashk. 1734 **Yenikey** [Еникеевъ] (Vel.-Zern., Bašk. 10); Bashk. 1735 **Yenikey** [Еникей Атикутуминъ], a tarχan (Vel.-Zern., Bašk. 13); Bashk. 1792 **Yenikcy** [Рахмет Еникеев] (MIB V, 319); Tat.(Mish.) 16th c. - 18th c. **Yenikey / Yeniki** [Еникәй / Еники] (Sattarov). ✦ 'Little soul (darling)' cf. Tat.(Mish.) *yäni*

=ǰani 'жандай кадерле [=dear like soul]' (Sattarov)]. ⇨ **ǰAN / ǰANÏ?** + dim. hypoc. suff. *-käy*. See also **YENİ.**

YEÑÄDİ   Uzb. 20th c. **Yeñädi** [Енгади] (Begmatov 1984, 202). ✦ 'Defeated / overcame' (Begmatov), cf. Uzb. *yeñ-* 'побеждать, осиливать, побороть' (UzbRS). See also **YEÑİLDİ.**

YEÑGE   Kzk. 19th c. **Yeñge-bay** [Енгебай] (SOK 188). ✦ 'A woman's sister-in-law or aunt-in-law' cf. Karakh., Uyg. *jeŋgä* 'жена старшего брата или дяди' (DTS), Kzk. *žeñge* 'невестка' (RKzkS).

YEÑİ-BULAT   Uyg. 12th c. - 14th c. **Yeñi-bulat** [Yängi Bulat] (Radl., USp. 52). ⇨ **YAÑÏ** + **BULAT.**

YEÑİLDİ   Uzb. 20th c. **Yeñildi** [Енгилди] (Begmatov 1984, 202). ✦ '(He was) defeated; Lost' (Begmatov), cf. Uzb. *yeñil-* ' быть побеждённым проиграть' (UzbRS). See also **YEÑÄDİ.**

YEÑİŠ   Kirg. **ǰeñiš** [Жениш] (Jud. 693); Trkm. **Yeñiš** [Ениш] (Sopieva 177, 182). ✦ 'Victory, triumph' cf. Trkm. *yeñiš* 'победа, успех, завоевание; торжество' (TrkmRS), Kirg. *ǰeñiš* 'победа, завоевание' (Jud.).

YEPAR see **ǰAFAR**

YEPEY   Bashk. 1735 **Yepäy / Yapay?** [Епай Кусеев], a tarχan (Vel.-Zern., Bašk. 18); Tat.(Sib.)? 1621, 1623 **Yepey** [Епей], a prince (Miller, Ist. Sib. II, 259, 273, 292).

YEPİŠ   Bashk. 1664 **Yepiš** [Тогонай Епишев] (MIB I, 185).

YEPPİM   Karg. **Yeppİm** [Еппім] (Katanov, Otč. 8). ✦ Yefim (R.).

YEPTİG   Alt.? 19th-20th c. **Yeptig** [Ептіг], fem. (Katanov, Otč. 10). ✦ 'Facile, acquiescent'.

YEPTİS   Hak.(Blt.) 19th-20th c. **Yeptis** [Ептіс] (Proben IX, 365).

YER-KEZER   Alt. **Yer-kezer** [Jеръ-кезеръ] (Nikiforov 83-84). ✦ 'Earth-wanderer' (Nikiforov), lit. 'Earth-hero' cf. Alt., Hak. *yär /d'är/ d'er* 'das Land, die Erde, der Ort, Platz' (Radl. III, 338) and Alt. *käzär* 'der Held' (Radl. II, 1174), *kezer* 'витязь, удалой' (OjrRS). See also **EL-KEZÄR.**

YEREMEŠ   Chuv. 18th-19th c. **Yeremeš** [Еремешъ] (Magn. 39).

YEREN-ČEČEN   Alt.(Tel.) **Yärän-čäčän** [Jäpän-Чäчäн] (Radl. III, 196); Alt.(Tel.) 19th c. **Yeren-čečen** [Ереньчеченъ] (Potanin IV, 362); Tat.(Tara) **Yirän-čičän** [Jірäн Чічäн] (Proben IV, 159 (201)). ✦ 'Red-eloquent, talkative (man), orator' cf. Alt.(Tel.) *yärän* 'fuchsfarben, roth (ein rothes Pferd mit rother Mähne und Schwanz)' (Radl. III, 338). ⇨ **ČEČEN.** See also **YİRENŠE-ŠEŠEN.**

YERENČE see **ǰİYRENŠE**

YERİKLİ-BERDİ see **YERMÄKLİ-BERDİ?**

YERKÜČ?   Türk 869 **Yerküč? / Yarγuč(i)?**

Onomasticon Turcicum

Indiana University Uralic and Altaic Series

Denis Sinor, Editor

Volume 172/II

László Rásonyi(†) and Imre Baski

ONOMASTICON
TURCICUM

Turkic Personal Names

as collected by László Rásonyi

Indiana University
Denis Sinor Institute for Inner Asian Studies
Bloomington, Indiana
2007

Copyright © 2007 Indiana University
Denis Sinor Institute for Inner Asian Studies
All rights reserved

Library of Congress Control Number: 2006906304

ISBN 13: 978-0-933070-56-1

ISBN 10: 0-933070-56-X

[يـاركوج الـتـركى] (Ibn al-Athīr/Tornb. VII, 126, 157-58, 177). ❖ '(Long) wide wooden plank used as a peel'? cf. Karakh. *järküč* 'breites, langes Holz zum Umwenden der Brote im Ofen' (MK/Brock.), *jerküč* 'id.' (DTS).

YERMÄK Tat. 18th c. **Yärmäk** [Алей Ярмяковъ], from Orenburg (Nepljuev 809, 824, 825); Tat. 1768 **Yärmäk** [Ярмакъ Давыдовъ] (Nikol'skij 272); Tat. 1768 **Yärmäk** [Ярмакъ Араслановъ] (Nikol'skij 271); Bashk. 1757 **Yärmäk** [Ярмяк Итбаев] (MIB IV/1, 150, 153); Bashk. 1787 **Yärmäk** [Яркей Ярмяков] (MIB V, 207); Tat. 1764 **Yärmek / Yärmäk** [Ярмек (Ярмяк) Ямкин] (MIB IV/1, 290); Chuv. 18th-19th c. **Yermäk** [Ермякъ] (Magn. 39); Tat. 1718 **Yermäk** [Абдил Ермяков] (MIB III, 173); Tat. 1763 **Yermäk** [Ермакъ Аднагуловъ], a Tatar captain („sotnik") (PSZRI XVI, 322); Bashk. 1714 **Yermäk** [Ермяк Бекбулатов] (MIB I, 105); Bashk. 1735 **Yermäk** [Ермякъ Исенчуринъ], a tarχan (Vel.-Zern., Bašk. 23); Bashk. 1735 **Yermäk** [Ермякъ Абитевъ] (Vel.-Zern., Bašk. 25); Bashk. 1738 **Yermäk** [Ермак Полатов] (MIB III, 387); Bashk. 1740 **Yermäk** [Ермак Козяшев] (MIB I, 409); Bashk. 1749, 1758 **Yermäk** [Еркей Ермаков (Ермяков)] (MIB III, 469, IV/1, 166); Bashk. 1754 **Yermäk** [Ермак Тойметев] (MIB IV/1, 83); Bashk. 1757, 1761 **Yermäk** [Ермак Килеев] (MIB IV/1, 140, 204); Bashk. 1771 **Yermäk** [Ермак Каракучюков] (MIB IV/1, 358); Kzk. 19th c. **Yermek** [Ермекъ] (AOO 54); Kzk. 19th c. **Yermek** [Ермекъ] (AOK 66, 102, 130); Kzk. 19th c. **Yermek** [Ермекъ] (AOA 62); Kzk. 19th c. **Yermek** [Ермекъ] (SOK 102, 182, 188); Kzk. 19th c. **Yermek** [Ермекъ] (SODž. 24, 54, 148); Kzk. 19th c. **Yermek** [Ермекъ] (SOV 78); Kzk. 19th c. **Yermek-pay** [Ермекпай] (SOV 26, 28); Kzk. 19th c. **Yermek-pay** [Ермекпай] (AOO 42); *TN:* Kzk. 19th c. **Yermäk** [Ермакъ], a winter pasture (settlement) (SODž. 136). ❖ 'Child, young' <Bulg. *cermik (jermik)* < Chuv. *sarmək* 'jung' (Rásonyi: Macarca 'gyermek' kelimesi ve 'Ermyak' adı: TKAE 19, 382-383).

YERMÄKÄY Chuv. 18th-19th c. **Yermäkäy / Yermekey?** [Ермекей] (Magn. 39). ⇨ **YERMÄK** + suff. *-äy*.

YERMÄKLİ-BERDİ? Tat.? 1407 **Yermäkli-berdi? / Yerikli-berdi** [Ермоклиберди (Ериклиберди)], a prince of the Horde (PSRL VI, 136, VIII, 82-83). ⇨ **YERMÄK? + BERDİ.**

YERMEŠ Kzk. 19th c. **Yermeš / Yermiš?** [Ермешъ] (SODž. 118).

YESTAY Kzk. 19th c. **Yestay?** [Естай] (AOO 46). ⇨ **?** + suff. *-tay(1,2)*?

YEŠİL-BAŠ Trkm. 1690 **Yešil-baš** [يشيـل بـاش / Yeşilbaş] (Refik, Anad. 89). ❖ 'Green head', 'A kind of wild duck' cf. Turk. *yeşil* 'green; verdant; fresh', *yeşilbaş* 'mallard drake (Anas platyrhynchos)' (TED),

Trkm. *yašïlbaš* 'id.' (TrkmRS). ⇨ **BAŠ.**

YETÄR Turk. 20th c.? **Yetär,** fem. (Cafer., An. Dial. I, 213). ❖ I. 'Sufficient'; II. 'Enough (of daughters), no more daughters!' (cf. Erol II: Yeter). See also **AT-YETÄR.**

YETER see YETÄR

YETİ Kzk. 19th c. **Jeti-bay** [Джетыбай] (SOK 78, 142, 180); Kzk. 19th c. **Jeti-bay** [Джетыбай] (SODž. 94, 142, 156); Kzk. 19th c. **Jeti-bay** [Джетыбай] (SOV 94, 140, 148); Kzk. 19th c. **Jeti-bay** [Джетыбай] (Grod., Pril. 34); Kzk. 19th c. **Jeti-bay** [Джетыбай] (AOK 102); Kzk. 19th c. **Jeti-bay** [Жетыбай] (AOK 82); Kzk. 19th c. **Jeti-bay** [Джетебай] (SODž. 32); Kzk. 19th c. **Jeti-bek** [Джетыбекъ] (Potanin, Pred. 94); Turk. 1399/1400 **Yedi(-šah)** [يـدى شـاه], an Ottoman ruler (Ibn Taghrīb. VI, 17); Kzk. 19th c. **Yedi-bay** [Балдиракъ Едибаевъ] (Grod., Pril. 76); Kzk. 19th c. **Yedi-bay / Yeddi-bay?** [Белдирегъ Еддибаевъ] (Grod., Pril. 173); Kirg.? 14th c.? **Yedi-inal** [Jedi-inal], a Kirghiz chief (Ligeti, MTT 239); Kzk. 19th c. **Žet-qatïn (<Žeti-qatïn)** [Жеткатынъ] (SODž. 60); Kzk. 19th c. **Žeti-bay** [Жетыбай] (AOAtb. 10); *EN:* Kzk. 18th c. - 19th c. **Jeti-bay** [Джетыбай] (Tynyšp. 66); Kirg.? 14th c.? **Yedi** [سـدى / بيـدى], a Kirghiz (?) tribe (RaD/Ber. I, 130, III, 163); *TN:* Kzk. **Žeti-bay** [Жетибай], a town-type settlement in the west of the country (Kojčubaev 101). ❖ 'Seven; the seventh child?' cf. Türk, Uyg. *yeti* 'id.' (DTS), Türk, Chag., Kuman *yäti* 'sieben' (Radl. III, 361), Kzk. *žeti* 'id.' (KzRS). See also **TETÄK-YEDİ(?).**

YETİ-SABAR Alt. **Jeti-sabar** [Джеты-Сабаръ], a monster (Nikiforov 97, 99, 102, 105); Alt. **Yeti-sabar-χan** [Јеты-Сабаръ ханъ] (Nikiforov 78). ❖ 'Seven fingers/toes' cf. Alt. *sabar* 'der Finger, Zeh' (Radl. IV, 416). ⇨ **YETİ.** See also **AY-SABAR, KÜN-SABAR.**

YETİLMİŠ Turk. 16th c. **Yetilmiš** [Yetilmiş] (Ongan, Ank. II, 32, 54 etc.); Turk. 16th c. **Yetilmiš** [Yetilmiş] (Ongan, Ank. I, 179). ❖ 'Attained, matured' cf. Chag. *yätil-* 'erreicht sein, erlangt sein, reif sein' (Radl. III, 362).

YETİM Kzk. 19th c. **Jetem-bay / Jetim-bay** [Джетембай] (SODž. 26); Bashk. 1737 **Yädim** [Ядим] (MIB I, 315); Bashk. 1724 **Yetim-čura** [Етимчюра] (MIB III, 228); Trkm.? 1598 **Yetim-sultan** [Етим-султан] (MIT II, 91). ❖ 'Orphan, captive' cf. Uyg. *yädim* 'die Waise' (Radl. III, 374), Karakh. *jetim* 'сирота' (DTS), Chag., NUyg.(Tar.), Crm. *yätim* 'die Waise' (Radl. III, 363), Bashk. *yätim* 'сирота' (BRS/Uraksin), Kzk. *jetim* 'die Waise, der Hörige' (Radl. IV, 82). (<Ar.). See also **ŠAR-ŽETİM.**

YETİMBET Kzk. 19th c. **Yetimbet** [Јэтимбетъ] (SODž. 8). ⇨ **YETİM** + suff. *-bet*.

YETİMÄK Bashk. 1757 **Yetimäk** [Сапер Етимяков] (MIB IV/1, 150). ⇨ **YETİM** + suff. *-äk*.

YETMİŠ Kzk. 19th c. **J̌etpïs** [Джетпысъ] (SOV 22); Kzk. 19th c. **J̌etpis** [Джетписъ] (AOK 90); Kzk. 19th c. **J̌etpïs** / **J̌etbïs** [Джетбысъ] (AOAtb. 10); Tat.(Mish.), Kzk.? **J̌etpïs-bay** / **J̌etbïs-bay** [Джетбысбаевъ] (IOAIÊK XIX, 133); Kzk. 19th c. **J̌etpis-bay** [Джетписъ-Бай] (AOK 94); Kzk.?, Tat.(Mish.)? 19th c. **J̌etpïs-bay** / **J̌etbïs-bay** [Джетбысбаевъ], a writer of articles, the author of „Načal'noe rukovodstvo arabskogo, persidskogo i kirgizskogo jazykov" (AUK 295, IOAIÊK XIX, 133); Kzk. 19th c. **J̌etpis-pay** [Кжетписпай] (SODž. 124); Kzk. 19th c. **J̌etpïs-pay** [Джетпыспай] (SOK 70, 76, 100); Kzk. 19th c. **J̌etpïs-pay** [Джетпыспай] (AOK 58); Kzk. 19th c. **J̌etpis-pay** [Джетписпай] (AOA 142); Kzk. 19th c. **J̌etpïs-pay** [Джетпыспай] (AOA 142); Kzk. 19th c. **J̌etps-pay** (<**J̌etpïs-pay**) [Джетпспай] (SOV 22, 32, 52); Kzk. 19th c. **J̌itpis** [Джитписъ] (SOK 154); Khorezm.? 1304 **Yetmiš** [يتميش / Jatmīš / Jetmisch], executed by Ghazan (1295-1304) (RaD/Jahn 154, Hammer, Ilch. II, 135); Kzk. 19th c. **Yetmiš** [Мамайбекъ Етмишевъ] (Grod., Pril. 25); Uyg. **Yitmiš** [Yitmiş] (EUTS); Uyg. 8th c. - 12th c. **Yitmiš-qatun-täñrim**, fem. (Müller, Pfahl. 23); Kzk. 19th c. **Žetpis-bay?** [Жжетисбай] (SODž. 106). ✧ 'Seventy' cf. Türk, Uyg., Chag., Kar.(T.), Turk. *yätmiš* 'siebzig' (Radl. III, 368), Kirg. *jetpiš* 'id.' (Radl. III, 367), Kzk. *jetpïs* 'id' (Radl. IV, 83).

YETMİŠ-QARA-AČQÏ Uyg. 12th c. - 14th c. **Yetmiš-qara-ačqï** (Radl., USp. 44, DTS). ✧ 'Seventy-mighty-Ačqï', where *ačqï* is a den. N. (nomen actionis) of *ač-* 'открывать; завоевывать; пролагать (путь)' (Blagova 1997, 705). ⇨ **YETMİŠ** + **QARA** + **AČQÏ**.

YEVMİHAYÏR Yürük 1543 **Yevmihayïr** [يوم خير / Yevmihayır] (Gökb., Rum. 241). ✧ 'Day of blessing/fortune' (<Ar.).

YEZİR see **YAZÏR**

YİDİKİ Uyg. 13th-14th c. **Yidiki?** (Zieme, Mat. III, 272).

YİGÄN see **YEGÄN**

YİGÄN-ARSLAN Uyg. 13th-14th c. **Yigän-arslan** / **Yägän-arslan** [Ygän Arslan] (Zieme, Mat. II, 86). ✧ 'Nephew-lion'. ⇨ **YEGÄN** + **ARSLAN.**

YİGÄN-QAYA Uyg. 13th-14th c. **Yigän-qaya** (Zieme, Mat. II, 86); Uyg. 13th-14th c. **Yigän-qaya** [Yigän Qaya] (Zieme, Mat. II, 93). ✧ 'Nephew-rock'. ⇨ **YEGÄN** + **QAYA.**

YİGÄN-TÖZÜN Uyg. 13th-14th c. **Yigän-tözün** / **Yägän-tözün** [Ygän Tözün], fem. (Zieme, Mat. II, 86). ✧ 'Nephew-noble' cf. Uyg. *tözün* 'сдержанный, благородный' (DTS). ⇨ **YEGÄN.**

YİGÄTMİŠ Uyg. 8th c. - 12th c. **Yigätmiš-qatun-täñrim**, fem. (Müller, Pfahl. 22). ✧ 'Got better' cf. *yegät-* 'улучшать ' (DTS).

YİGENEK see **YEKEÑK**

YİGİN-ALP-TURAN Türk 7th c. - 9th c. **Yigin-alp-turan** [jigin alp turan / jigin alpturan] (DTS). ⇨ **YEGÄN** + **ALP** + **TURAN.**

YİGİT Kzk. 19th c. **J̌igit** [Джигитъ] (AOP 98); Crm.(Tat.) 1637 **J̌igit-bek** [جكت بك] (Vel.-Zern., Crim. 174); Bashk. 1717 **İgit** [Игимбай Игитев] (MIB III, 158); Tat. 1543 **Yigit** [Yiğit] (Gökb., Rum. 232); Turk. 1389 **Yigit-beg** / **Yiyit-bey** [يكيت بك / Jijit Bei], pasha of Bāyezīd I (1389-1402) (Nešrī 333, Āšikp. 58, 67); Khorezm. 1227 **Yigit-melik** [سكت ملك / Yiguit Malik], Jelāladdīn Meñgü-berdi's (1220-1231) officer (Nasawī 139). ✧ '(Brave) young man, stripling; brave youngster; youth' cf. Karakh. *yigit* ' юноша, молодой человек ' (DTS), Uyg., Kuman, Chag., Kar. *yigit* 'der Jüngling, junge Mann' (Radl. III, 510), Kzk., Tat. *jigit* 'ein Jüngling, ein junger Mensch, ein tüchtiger Junge' (Radl. IV, 137), Bashk. *yeget* (BRS). Used also as a secondary component of male names. See also **BABA-YİGİT.**

YİGLÄMİŠ Khorezm. 1289 **Yiglämiš** [ييكلاميش], Ghazan's (1295-1304) attendant (RaD/Jahn 16). ✧ I. '(Being) preferred' cf. Karakh. *yeglä-* 'предпочитать ' (DTS); II. '(He/she) got sick' cf. Uyg. *yiklä-* 'krank werden' (Radl. III, 509).

YİL-BERDİ Oghuz/Trkm. 1017 **Yil-berd(i)?** [Йильберд], an emir (MIT I, 379). ⇨ **YEL** + **BERDİ.**

YİLBÄGÄN see **YÄLBÄГÄN**

YİLBİGÄN see **YÄLBÄГÄN**

YİLİG Uyg. **Yilig-čur** [Јılıг Чур], a name engraved in the ceiling of a cave in Yar-hoto (Radl., Altuig. 82). ✧ 'Marrow, medulla' cf. Karakh. *yilig* 'костный мозг ' (DTS).

YİLİM Uzb. 18th c. - 19th c. **Yilim** [Нияз бек Йилим] (MIKk.?). ✧ 'Intrusive'? cf. Uzb. *yelim* 'прилипчивый, назойливый' (UzbRS).

YİMİŠ Uyg. 12th c. - 14th c. **Yimiš** (Radl., USp. 23-24). ✧ 'Fruit' cf. Uyg., Karakh. *yemiš* 'фрукт, плод ' (DTS).

YİNAL see **İNAL**

YİR-TÜŠLÜK Tat.(Tüm.) **Yir-tüšlük** [Јıртÿшлÿк], seventh son of a khan in a folktale (Proben IV, 352 (443)). ⇨ **ER** + **TÖŠTÜK?** See also **ER-TÜSTÜK.**

YİRÄN-ČİČÄN see **YEREN-ČEČEN**

YİRENŠE-ŠEŠEN Kzk. 19th c. **J̌irenše-šešen-χan** [Джиренше-Шешенъ / Джиренше-Шешенъ-ханъ], a person in a tale (Potanin, Pred. 67, Potanin IV, 364); Kzk. 19th c.? **J̌irenše-šešen** (Atyns. 62); Kzk. 19th c. **J̌irenše-šešen** [Джиренше Шешень] (AUK 498); Kzk. 19th c. **J̌irinše-šešen** [Джиринше-Шешень] (AUK 82,); Crm. **Yirenše-šešen** [Јіраншä Шäшäн] (Proben VII, 214); Kzk. 19th c. **Žiyrenče-češän** / **J̌iyrenče-češän** [جيرانچه ديكان چيشان /

Жйренче-чешенъ] (Pantusov 31); Kzk. 19th c. **Žirenče-češän / Jirenče-češän** [ديكان چيشان دجيرانچه] (Pantusov 31). ❖ 'Red eloquent, red talkative (man)' (PotaninP 167), 'Red tale-teller'. ⇨ **JÏYRENŠE + ČEČEN.** See also **YEREN-ČEČEN.**

YÏRMÏSEKÏZ Turk. 19th c. **Yirmisekiz** [يكرمى سكيز / Йирми секизъ], a Turkish scholar (Smirnov, Krym. 111). ❖ 'Twenty-eight'.

YÏRSUV Uyg. **Yirsuv** [Yirsuv] (EUTS).

YÏTMÏŠ see **YETMÏŠ**

YÏDDUГ Uyg. 761 **Yïdduγ-čur** (Mahrnāmag 11).

YÏLГAY Trkm. 20th c. **Yïlγay** [Yïlgay] (Zaj. 1971, 328); Trkm. 20th c. **Yïlγay** [Йылгай] (TrkmRS 377). ❖ 'Eternal, immortal' cf. Trkm. *yïlγay* 'вечный' (TrkmRS).

YÏГDÏ Uyg. 12th c. - 14th c. **Yïγdï** (Radl., USp. 212, 254). ❖ 'Gathered' cf. Uyg. *yïγ-* 'собирать; сдерживать, удерживать ' (DTS).

YÏГMÏŠ Uyg. 8th c. - 12th c. **Yïγmïš-qunčuy** [Yigmiš qun[čui]], fem. (Müller, Pfahl. 23). ❖ 'Gathered' cf. Uyg. *yïγ-* 'собирать; сдерживать, удерживать ' (DTS). See also **ČOBA-YÏQMÏŠ, ÏL-YÏГMÏŠ, OГUL-YÏГMÏŠ.**

YÏQÏNČ Uyg. 12th c. - 14th c. **Yïqïnč-tutuñ** (Radl., USp. 89, DTS). ❖ 'Ravaging, devastation' (Blagova 1997, 714), cf. Karakh. *yïq-* 'валить, разрушать' (DTS) + suff. *-ïnč*.

YÏQMÏŠ-TAZ Uyg. 12th c. -14th c. **Yïqmïš-taz** (DTS). ❖ 'Devastated-Bald' (Blagova 1997, 716). ⇨ **YÏГMÏŠ + TAZ.**

YÏL-BASSAL Kirg. **Yïl-bassal** [Jyl-Bassal / Йыл-басал], khan of the giaours (infidels, non-Muslims) (Proben V, 145).

YÏLAN Alt.(Tub.) 19th c. **Čilan-qan** [Чиланъ-канъ] (Potanin IV, 577, 578); Alt. 19th c. **Čïlan-χan** [Чылан-ханъ], a hero (bogatyr) (Verb., In. 141, 144, 147, 154); Kzk. 19th c. **Jilan** [Джиланъ] (Grod., Pril. 19); Kzk. 19th c. **Jilan** [Джиланъ] (Grod., Pril. 19); Kzk. 19th c. **Jilan** [Джиланъ] (Grod., Pril. 19); Kzk. 19th c. **Jilan** [Джиланъ] (Grod., Pril. 19); Kzk. **Jïlan-baba** [Цылан Баба] (Proben III, 330 /400/); Alt. **D'ïlan-pï** [Дылан Пі] (Radl. III, 1171); Kuman 1266 **Ïlan** [Illan], a chief (dominus) of the Kumans in Hungary (Gyárfás II, 418); Kzk. **Ïlañ** [Илангъ] (Grod., Pril. 79); Kzk. 19th c. **Ïlañ** [Иръ-Копакъ Илланговъ] (Grod., Pril. 58); Alt. **Yïlan-pï** [Дылан-Пі] (Radl. I, 1286, III, 1171). ❖ 'Snake' cf. Türk, Uyg., Kuman, Alt., Az., Kirg., Turk. *yïlan* 'die Schlange' (Radl. III, 482), Kuman *ilan* 'id.' (CC), Chag., NUyg. *ilan* 'die Schlange' (Radl. I, 1475), Hak., Shor *čilan* 'die Schlange' (Radl. III, 2085), Kzk., Tat, *jïlan* 'id.' (Radl. IV, 125), Rásonyi, Adalékok 125, Rásonyi, KÖA 106, Rásonyi, Anthr. 149. See also **JU-JÏLAN, QARA-YÏLAN, NOR-ČÏLAN, TOÑA-YÏLAN.**

YÏLANDAY Chuv. 18th-19th c. **Yïlanday** [Еландай] (Magn. 37). ❖ 'Snake-like'. ⇨ **YÏLAN** + suff. *-day.*

YÏLDÏRÏM Turk. 14th c. **Yïldïrïm** [Ιλδιρίμ], byname of Sultan Bayezid I (1389-1402) (Byz. Turc. 137-138); Turk. 20th c. **Yïldïrïm** (Önder, Göle); *TN:* Turk. 20th c. **Yïldïrïm-aydoγan** [Yıldırım Aydoğan], a village in the province of Ankara, Turkey (TMİB 78). ❖ 'Lightning, lightning-fast' cf. Kar., Turk. *yïldïrïm* 'das Blitz' (Radl. III, 490).

YÏLDÏZ see **YULDUZ**

YÏLÏQ Turk. 19th c. **Yïlïq-oγlu** [Jylyk oγlu] (Kúnos 1891, 119). ❖ 'Frightened, terrified' cf. Turk. *yïlïq* 'erschreckt, eingeschüchtert' (Radl. III, 484).

YÏLÏŠ Bashk. 1785 **Yïlïš** [Байдагул Елышев] (MIB V, 170).

YÏLQÏ Kzk. 19th c. **Jilqï-bay** [Джилкыбай] (AOO 46); Kzk. 19th c. **Jilqï-bay** [Джилкыбай] (AOK 98); Kzk. 19th c. **Jilqï-bay** [Джилкыбай] (SODž. 42); Kzk. 19th c. **Jilqï-bay** [Джилкыбай] (SOK 32, 96); Kzk. 19th c. **Jilqï-bay** [Джилкыбай] (SOV 20, 30, 52); Kzk. 19th c. **Jilqï-bay** [Джилкибай] (AOK 10, 54); Kzk. 19th c. **Jilqï-bay** [Джилкибай] (AOP 118); Kzk. 19th c. **Jilqï-bay** [Сабирбекъ Джилкибаевъ] (Grod., Pril. 195); Kzk. 19th c. **Jilqï-bay** [Джылкосбай (!)] (SODž. 150); Kzk. 19th c. **Jilqï-bay** [Джилкибай] (Grod., Pril. 140); Tat. 20th c. **Yïlqï-bay** [Елкыбай] (Sattarov); Bashk. 1675 **Yïlqï-bay** [Елкибай] (MIB I, 202); Bashk. 1738 **Yïlqï-bay** [Елкибай Бюляков] (MIB III, 393); Bashk. 1751 **Yïlqï-bay** [Ялкибай Кунтыбатов] (MIB IV/1, 52); Bashk. 1751 **Yïlqï-bay** [Елкибаев] (MIB IV/1, 54); Bashk. 20th c. **Yïlqï-bay / Zïlqï-bay** [Йылкыбай / Зилкибай] (Kusimova); Bashk. 1710 **Yïlqï-čura** [Елкычюра Тевеков] (MIB III, 66); Kzk. 19th c. **Žilqï-bay** [Жилкыбай] (AOK 10). ❖ 'Horse; (child) born in the year of the horse' (Sattarov), cf. Türk, Alt., Kuman *yïlqï* 'das Heerdenvieh; Pferde die in Heerden leben' (Radl. III, 485).

YÏMÏŠ Uyg. 12th c. 14th c. **Yïmïš** [Yımış] (DTS, EUTS). ⇨ **YÏMÏŠ?**

YÏMSAMÏT Kkalp. 20th c. **Yïmsamït** [Йымсамыт Усакъ-улы] (Bask., Kkalp. 21 (52)).

YÏPAR Uzb. 19th c. **Jipar** [Джипаръ Дустмухаммедова], from Tashkent (Sr. Az. I, 1896, avg. 10); Kirg. **Jïpar-kül** [Жыпаркүл], fem. (Jud. 971); Kkalp. 20th c. **Jupar** [Джупар], fem. (Bask., Kkalp. 403); Kzk. **Yupar-bay-biše** [Юпар байбише], fem. (Grod. 8); Kkalp. 20th c. **Župar** [Жупар], fem. (KkRS 777). ❖ 'Musk; Perfume, odour' cf. Karakh. *yipar* ' мускус; запах, аромат ' (DTS), *yipar* 'der Moschus' (Radl. III, 499), Kkalp. *župar* 'благовоние; благоухание' (KkRS), Kzk. *žŭpar* 'мускус' (KzRS), Kzk. *jïpar* 'der Moschus' (Radl. IV, 133). See also **KÜZÜ-YÏPAR.**

YÏPAR-ГAZAN-SĀT Uyg. 762 **Yïpar-γazan-sät**, fem. (Mahrnāmag 15, 35). ✧ 'Scent-hoard-shine' (Müller: 'Duft-Schatz-Glanz'). ⇨ **ГAZAN.**

YÏRAQLÏ Nog. 20th c. **Yïraqlï?** [Сайит Еракли увлы / Саит Еракиев], father of one of Baskakov's informants from the aul of Abram-töbe (Bask., Nog. 144).

YÏRÏM Uyg. 12th c. - 14th c. **Yïrïm** [Yırım] (DTS, EUTS).

YÏRYA Uyg. **Yïrya** [Yırya] (EUTS).

YÏRYA-AČQÏ Uyg. 12th c. - 14th c. **Yïrya-ačqï** (DTS). ⇨ **YÏRYA + AČQÏ.**

YÏRTÏJÏ Turk. 19th c. **Yïrtïjï-oγlu** [Jyrtyžy oγlu], a Zeybek (Kúnos 1891, 119); Turk. 19th c. **Yïrtïnjï-oγlu** [Jyrtynžy oγlu], a Zeybek (Kúnos 1891, 119). ✧ 'Murderous; wild; tearing'.

YÏRTÏNJÏ see **YÏRTÏJÏ**

YOГAN NUyg. 19th c. **Yoγan** [يوغان / Yoghan] (Le Coq, Namenl. 123). ✧ 'Big, thick' (Le Coq). See also **BÜYÜK, ČOŃ, EVREN, KÄNDÄL, MÄŃKÄ.**

YOYPUR Kirg. **Yoypur** [Jaipur / Joiнyp / Joiнўp] (Proben V, 70 /71/, 151 /152/).

YOQ Uyg. 1339 **Yoq** (Chwol., Syr.-nest. 92). ✧ 'Not-being, non-existent; abscence' cf. Uyg., Chag., Kom., Az., Crm., etc. *yoq* 'das Nichtsein, Nichtvorhandensein' (Radl. III, 397).

YOQA Uyg. **Yoqa / Yoγa? / Yuqa?** (Radl., USp. 249). ✧ 'Thin' cf. Uyg. *yuqa, yuγa* 'тонкий ' (DTS).

YOQPAR Kzk. 19th c. **Yoqpar** [Iокпаръ] (SODž. 156). ✧ 'Nonsense, idiocy; nothing, trifle'? cf. Tat. *yuq-bar* 'вздор, пустяк' (TatRS).

YOL Kkalp. 20th c. **Jol-mïrza** [Джолмырза] (Bask., Kkalp. 400); Kzk. 18th c. - 19th c. **Jol-seyit** [Джолсеит] (Tynyšp. 66); Kzk. 19th c. **Jol-seyit** [Джолсеитъ] (SODž. 22); Kzk. 18th c. **Jul-bay** [Джулбай] (Nepljuev 807); Kzk. 19th c. **Jul-eke** [Джулеке] (SOK 200); Yürük 1543 **Yol-eri** [Yoleri] (Gökb., Rum. 103); Bashk. 1756 **Yul-aqay** [Умер Юлакаев] (MIB IV/1, 128); Bashk. 1761 **Yul-aqay** [Тавлукай Юлакаев] (MIB IV/1, 221); Kkalp. 20th c. **Žol-mïrza** [Жолмырза] (KkRS 773). ✧ 'Road (=life, future, fate); right way' cf. Türk, Uyg., Chag., Alt., Crm., Kirg., Turk. etc. *yol* 'der Weg, die Linie, das Schicksal' (Radl. III, 430-431), Kzk. *jol* 'der Weg, der richtige Weg, das Schicksal' (Radl. IV, 97), Tat. *yul* 'дорога; путь' (TatRS). – *Yol-eri* means 'Wanderer, goer, traveller'. See also **AQ-JOL-TAY, AQ-YUL, AMAN-JOL, İSÄN-YUL, QARA-YOLU, QUTLU-YUL.**

YOL-BASAR Uzb. 20th c. **Yol-bâsar** [Йулбосар] (Begmatov 1984, 201). ✧ 'He who will step on the right way'. ⇨ **YOL + BASAR.**

YOL-QUTLUГ Khorezm.? 13th c.? **Yol-qutluγ** [Йол-Кутлуг], Arγun-aqa's son (RaD I/1, 121); Uyg. 13th c.

- 14th c. **Yul-qutluq** [Jul Kutluk] (Chwol., Syr.-nest.(NF) 53). ✧ 'Road (=life) fortunate; Let him live fortunate life'. ⇨ **YOL + QUTLUГ.** See also **QUTLU-YUL.**

YOLA Türk 7th c. - 9th c. **Yola** (DTS). ✧ 'Torch, firebrand' cf. Uyg., Karakh. *yola / yula* 'факел, светильник' (DTS).

YOLBARS Kzk. 1739 **Jolbars** [Džolbars Chan], prince of the Great Horde, died in 1739 (Radl., Aus Sib. I, 194); Kzk. 19th c. **Jolbars** [Джолбарсъ] (SOK 68); Kzk. 19th c. **Jolbars** [Джолбарсъ] (SOV 34); Kzk. 19th c. **Jolbars** [Джолборсъ] (AOAtb. 58); Kirg. 20th c. **Jolbors** [Жолборс] (Kalilov 93); Trkm. **Yolbars** [Ёлбарс] (Sopieva 177); Kzk. 1817 **Yolbars** [يولبارس] (MIK IV, 307); NUyg.? 1933 **Yolbars**, a rebel chieftain (leader) in Eastern Turkestan (Hedin, Die Seidenstrasse 9); Bashk. 20th c. **Yulbaris** [Юлбарис] (Kusimova); Bashk. 1758 **Yulbarïs** [Юлбарис Сейтяков] (MIB IV/1, 174); Bashk. 1760 **Yulbarïs** [Юлборис Аблеев] (MIB IV, 197); Bashk. 1762 **Yulbarïs** [Юлбарыс Аблаев] (MIB IV/1, 249); Bashk. 1770 **Yulbarïs** [Юлбарыс Кучумов] (MIB IV/1, 342); Bashk. 1777 **Yulbarïs** [Юлбарис Асанов] (MIB V, 60); Bashk. 1777 **Yulbarïs** [Юлбарис Асанов] (MIB V, 60); Bashk. 1791 **Yulbarïs** [Муллаш Юлбарисов] (MIB V, 313); Kzk. 1822 **Yulbarïs** [Абдулфеизъ Юлбарисовъ], a Kazak sultan (TOUAK XXIV 117); Kzk. 1738 **Yulbarïs / Yulbars** [Joulbars / Юлборусъ], khan of the Greater Horde (Ulu Žüz) (PSZRI X, 614, 616-17, Levchin 156); Kzk. 1794 **Yulbarïs-γazï** [Юлбарыс Газы], a sultan (MIK IV, 177); Tat. 20th c. **Yulbars** [Юлбарс] (Sattarov); Kzk. 1832 **Yulbars** [Али Юлбарсовъ] (Mejer 48). ✧ 'Tiger, panther, leopard' cf. Uyg. *jolbars* 'тигрица' (DTS), Chag., East. T. *yolbars* 'der Panther, Leopard' (Radl. III, 439), Bashk. *yulbarïθ* 'тигр' (BRS/Uraksin), cf. also Bang: KSz. Vol.17, p. 116.

YOLČÏ Kuman 1419, 1455 **Jolčï / Yolčï** [Dioltapalzallasa / Gyolchapalzallasa], preserved in the name of a settlement of the Kumans in Hungary (Gyárfás III, 566, 631); Turk. 20th c. **Yolju** [Yolcu] (Önder, Göle); Yürük 1543 **Yolju** [يولجى / Yolcu] (Gökb., Rum. 188); Uzb. 19th c. **Yulčï-bay** [Хайдаръ Юлчибаевъ] (Sr. Az. I, 1896 (avg. 14)); Kzk. **Yulčï-bek** [Юлчибекъ Сапаковъ] (Protok. Turk. IV 77); Kzk. 19th c. **Yulčï-bek** [Юлчибековъ] (SKSO VIII, 201); Uzb. **Yulčï-bek** [Youltchi-bek] (Nalivkin-Dozon 183). ✧ 'Migrant, wanderer' cf. Türk, Uyg., Chag., Alt., Crm., Kirg., Turk. etc. *yol* 'der Weg, die Linie, das Schicksal' (Radl. III, 430-431), Uyg. *yolčï* 'der Wanderer; der Führer' (Radl. III, 438), for the Kuman names see Rásonyi, KÖA 138, Rásonyi, Anthr. 140.

YOLJU see **YOLČÏ**

YOLDAŠ Alt. 19th c. **Čoltoš** [Чолтошъ

Куранаковъ], Nikiforov's informant (tale-teller) (Nikiforov 2); Kzk. 19th c. **J̌oldas** [Джолдасъ] (AOK 70); Kzk. 19th c. **J̌oldas-bek** [Джолдаспекъ] (Grod., Pril. 19); Kzk. 19th c. **J̌oldas-pay** [Джолдаспай] (SODž. 114); Kzk. 19th c. **J̌oldas-pek** [Джолдаспекъ] (SOV 94); Kzk. 19th c. **J̌oldaš** [Джолдашъ Дусановъ] (Grod., Pril. 81); Kzk. 19th c. **J̌oldos-pay** (<**J̌oldas-pay?**) [Джолдоспай] (SOK 16); Bashk. 1751 **Yeldaš-bay** [Кармангул Елдашбаев] (MIB IV/1, 52); Tat. 1543 **Yoldaš** [Yoldaş] (Gökb., Rum. 243); Tat. 1779 **Yoldaš** [Елдаш Аблаев], a tarχan (MIB V, 82); Tat. 18th-19th c. **Yoldaš** [Елдашъ] (Magn. 37); Tat. 18th-19th c. **Yoldaš** [Елдашъ] (Magn. 37); Tat.(Mish.) 1708 **Yoldaš** [Елдаш Утесмышев / Утямышев] (MIB I, 233); Bashk. 1730 **Yoldaš** [Елдаш Колговов] (MIB III, 277); Bashk. 1735 **Yoldaš** [Елдашъ Кутлуметев] (MIB II, 338); Bashk. 1738 **Yoldaš** [Елдаш Арыков] (MIB III, 398); Bashk. 1739 **Yoldaš** [Карагул Елдашев] (MIB III, 404); Bashk. 1740 **Yoldaš** [Стамгул Елдашев] (MIB I, 398); Bashk. 1740 **Yoldaš** [Елдаш] (MIB I, 447); Bashk. 1740 **Yoldaš** [Егафер Елдашев] (MIB I, 398); Bashk. 1740 **Yoldaš** [Елдаш] (MIB I, 447); Bashk. 1744 **Yoldaš** [Курмаш Елдашев] (MIB III, 415); Bashk.? 1744 **Yoldaš** [Елдашъ Ишимбаевъ] (Nepljuev 217); Bashk. 1756 **Yoldaš** [Мавлюш Елдашев] (MIB IV/1, 120); Bashk. 1756 **Yoldaš** [Селим Елдашев] (MIB IV/1, 207); Bashk. 1756 **Yoldaš** [Абсалом Елдашев] (MIB IV/1, 120); Bashk. 1756 **Yoldaš** [Мавлюш Елдашев] (MIB IV/1, 120); Bashk. 1756 **Yoldaš** [Тевлеть Елдашев] (MIB IV/1, 123); Bashk. 1758, 1764 **Yoldaš** [Елдаш (Юлдаш) Копаев] (MIB IV/1, 165, 294); Bashk. 1761 **Yoldaš** [Елдаш Тураев] (MIB IV/1, 227); Bashk. 1761 **Yoldaš** [Исмагил Елдашев] (MIB IV/1, 227); Bashk. 1761 **Yoldaš** [Елдаш Тураев] (MIB IV/1, 227); Bashk. 1761 **Yoldaš** [Исмагил Елдашев] (MIB IV/1, 227); Bashk. 1762 **Yoldaš** [Иксан Елдашев] (MIB IV/1, 238); Bashk. 1764 **Yoldaš** [Искан Елдашев] (MIB IV/1, 277); Bashk. 1771 **Yoldaš** [Елдаш Буриев] (MIB IV/1, 358); Bashk. 1785 **Yoldaš** [Елдаш Ищдевлетев] (MIB V, 166); Bashk. 1785 **Yoldaš** [Елдаш Ищдевлетев] (MIB V, 166); Bashk. 1785 **Yoldaš** [Елдаш (Юлдаш) Ищдевлетев] (MIB V, 166, 168); Kzk.? 1744 **Yoldaš** [Елдашъ Ишимбаевъ], a rebel (Nepljuev 217); Kzk. 19th c. **Yoldaš** [Елдашъ] (Grod., Pril. 133); Kzk. 19th c. **Yoldaš** [Молла Юнусъ Елдашевъ] (Grod., Pril. 170); Kzk. 19th c. **Yoldaš** [Елдашъ Азиматовъ] (Grod., Pril. 35); Kzk. 19th c. **Yoldaš** [Елдашъ] (Grod., Pril. 133); Kzk. 19th c. **Yoldaš** [Молла Юнусъ Елдашевъ] (Grod., Pril. 170); Kzk. 19th c. **Yoldaš** [Елдашъ Азиматовъ] (Grod., Pril. 35); Uzb.

1873 **Yoldaš** [Mollah-Yoldach-Pançat] (Nalivkin-Dozon 259); Bashk. 1779, 1780, 1782, 1787 **Yoldaš / Yuldaš** [Елдаш Мяскеев (Миксеев) / Юлдаш Маскеев (Мяскеев)], chief of the „Kirgizskaja Volost'" (MIB V, 87, 111, 133, 207); Tat. 20th c. **Yuldaš** [Юлдаш] (Sattarov); Tat. / Bashk.? 1791 **Yuldaš** [Каты Юлдашев], a Teptär (MIB V, 679); Bashk. **Yuldaš** [Юлдаш Юсупов] (MIB V, 109); Bashk. 1737 **Yuldaš** [Юлдашев (Исламгул)] (MIB I, 318); Bashk. 18th c. **Yuldaš** [Юлдашев] (MIB V, 301); Bashk. 1761 **Yuldaš** [Юлдаш Мурзин] (MIB IV/1, 209); Bashk. 1772 **Yuldaš** [Юлдаш Кусяков] (MIB IV/2, 407); Bashk. 1776 **Yuldaš** [Ахмер Юлдашев] (MIB V, 51); Bashk. 1777 **Yuldaš** [Кулсар Юлдашбаев] (MIB V, 64); Bashk. 1777 **Yuldaš** [Юлдаш Кинжин], a captain (MIB V, 544, 545); Bashk. 1777 **Yuldaš** [Усман Юлдашев] (MIB V, 52); Bashk. 1777, 1780 **Yuldaš** [Юлдаш Кутлин] (MIB V, 52, 115); Bashk. 1779, 1780, 1787 **Yuldaš** [Юлдаш Маскеев (Мяскеев, Мяскиев)] (MIB V, 87, 111, 207); Bashk. 1787 **Yuldaš** [Дюрбеть Юлдашев] (MIB V, 219); Bashk. 1787 **Yuldaš** [Юлдаш Сююндюков] (MIB V, 204, 205); Bashk. 1790 **Yuldaš** [Рыскул Юлдашев] (MIB V, 275); Bashk. 1790 **Yuldaš** [Юлдаш Сатлыков] (MIB V, 282); Bashk. 1796 **Yuldaš** [Измаил / Исмаил Юлдашев] (MIB V, 362); Bashk. 1798 **Yuldaš** [Юлдашевъ] (PSZRI XXV, 196); Bashk. 20th c. **Yuldaš** [Юлдаш] (Kusimova); Kzk. 19th c. **Yuldaš** [Хальмухамедъ Юлдашевъ] (SKSO VIII, 201); Kzk. 19th c. **Yuldaš** [Юлдашъ Дустовъ] (SKSO VIII, 220); Kzk. 19th c. **Yuldaš** [Юлдашъ] (SKSO IV, otd. II, 39); Kkalp. 20th c. **Yuldaš** [Юлдаш] (KkRS 776); Uzb. 19th c. **Yuldaš** [Юлдашъ Катагайбаевъ] (SKSO III, 18); Uzb. 19th c. **Yuldaš** [Юлдашъ Халмухаммедовъ] (Sr. Az. I, (1896) avg. 16); Uzb. 19th c. **Yuldaš** [Юлдашъ Кошибаевъ] (SKSO III, 18); NUyg.(Tar.) 19th c. **Yuldaš** [Юлдашъ] (Pantusov, Tar. 15); Bashk. 1789 **Yuldaš / Yoldaš / İldaš?** [Юлдаш (Илдаш, Елдаш) Тляпов] (MIB V, 267); Uzb. 1846 **Yuldaš-bay** [Юлдашъ-бай] (Moskal'cev 40); Uzb. 19th c. **Yuldaš-bay** [Юлдашбай] (SKSO III, 160); Uzb. 18th c. **Yuldaš-bi** [Youlzach-by] (Nalivkin-Dozon 89); Bashk. 1739 **Yuldaš-mulla** [Юлдаш Мулла] (PSZRI X, 869); Bashk. 1772 **Yuldaž-bay** (<**Yuldaš-bay**) [Юлдажбай Акчювашев] (MIB IV/2, 406); Kkalp. 20th c. **Žoldas** [Жолдас] (KkRS 773); Kkalp. 20th c. **Žoldas-bay** [Жолдасбай] (KkRS 773); *EN:* Kzk. 18th c. - 19th c. **J̌oldas** [Джолдас] (Tunуšp. 71). ✧ 'Fellow(-traveler), mate, companion, friend' cf. Kar., Tat.(Bar.), Turk. *yoldaš*, Kar.(L.) *yoldas* 'id.' (Radl. III, 437), Shor *čoldaš* 'Weggefährte' (Radl. III, 2024).

YOLÏГ Türk 8th c. **Yolïγ-te(gin)** [yolïγ te(gin) / Yolïγ tegin], relative of Bilge-qaγan and Kül-tegin composing the funerary inscriptions for them (DTS, ETY I, 28, 54, 72); Türk 732 **Yolluγ-tegin** [Джоллуӈ тäггін], relative of Bilge-qaγan and Kül-tegin (Radl. III, 437). ✧ 'Fortunate, happy, blessed' (Gabain). See also **YOLLU**.

YOLLU Kzk. 18th c. - 19th c. **J̌oldï-bay** [Джолдыбай] (Tynyšp. 71); Trkm. 19th c. **J̌uldï-bay** [Уразбай Джулдыбаевъ] (SKSO III, 178); Kzk. **J̌uldu-γul** [Джульдугулъ] (Harkov, Bibl. dlja čtenija CXXIV, 231); Yürük 1543 **Yollu** (Gökb., Rum. 229); Kzk. 19th c. **Yuldï-bay** [Юлдыбаев] (SKSO VIII, 233); Bashk. 1798 **Yuldu-bay** [Юлдубаевъ] (PSZRI XXV, 196); Kzk. 1819 **Yuldu-bay** [Юлдубай] (MIK IV, 323); Bashk. 1763 **Yullï** [Юллыбай Пулатов] (MIB IV/2, 45). ✧ I. 'Course of life; Long-lived (child)' (Sattarov); II. 'Striped; legal, rightful, proper' cf. Turk. *yollu* 'Wege, Streifen, Striche habend; gestreift; in gehöriger Weise ausgeführt, regelrecht, richtig' (Radl. III, 436). ⇨ **YOL** + suff. *-lï/-lu /-dï /-du*. See also **YOLÏΓ**.

YOLOY see **YULAY**

YOLU-ODÏČI Uzb. 1704 **Yolu-odïči** [يولى اوديچى / Jolu Odyči] (Buchari 278). ⇨ **YOL**?

YOLUQ Türk 876/77 **Yoluγ / Yolïγ?** [ارخوز بن يولغ بن طرخان التركى] (Ibn al-Athīr/Tornb. VII, 214, 227); Khorezm. 1227 **Yoluq-χan?** [اولق خان], Jelāladdīn Meñgü-berdi's (1220-1231) officer (Nasawī 128); Chag. 16th c. **Yuluγ** [Йулуг Хафиз] (Ivanov 155); Bashk. 1735 **Yuluq** [Юлукъ Аблаевъ], a tarχan (Vel.-Zern., Bašk. 17); Tat. (Mish.) 1755 **Yuluq** [Тойна Юлуков] (MIB IV/1, 93). ✧ 'Ransom, offering, sacrifice' cf. Karakh. *joluk* 'Lösegeld, Opfer' (DTS), cf. Uyg., Chag. *yoluq* 'das Opfer; ausgerupft, mit ausgerissenen Haaren' (Radl. III, 433).

YOLUQ-ARSLAN Selj. **Yoluq-arslan** [حسام الدين التبلو يولق ارسلان], a Seljuk from Konya (Ibn Bībī III, 84, IV, 34); Selj. 12th c. **Yoluq-arslan** [يولق ارسلان بن ارسلا نشاه] (Muh. Ibrahim 92, 95, 96); Selj.? 1184, 1186, 1198/99 **Yoluq-arslan** [حسام الدين يولق ارسلان / Youlok-Arslân], sovereign of Maridīn (Abulfidā IV, 65, Ibn al-Athīr/Tornb. XI, 335, XII, 91, 98, Abulfidā: RHCHor I, 54, 75, 863, Zambaur 228, 230); Selj. 1305, 1329 **Yoluq-arslan / Yuluq-arslan?** [الييُورك / مظفرلدين يولق ارسلان بن البورك] [مظفرلدين يولق ارسلان بن] (Ibn Bībī IV, 336, 337, Zambaur 148, MB Qastam 58). ✧ I. 'Ransom-lion'; II. 'Straight-haired lion'? ⇨ **YOLUQ + ARSLAN.**

YOLUQAY Bashk. 1786 **Yoluqay / Yuluqay** [Елукай (Юлукай) Аблязев] (MIB V, 196); Bashk. 1779 **Yuluqay** [Юлукай Умитбаев] (MIB V, 96); Bashk. 1781 **Yuluqay** [Бекбов Юлукаев (Юлкеев?)] (MIB V, 128). ⇨ **YOLUQ** + suff. *-qay.*

YOLUQLÏ Az.? 16th c. **Yoluqlï-beg** [يولقلى بيك ذوالقدر] (Dorn 265, 410). ✧ 'Having a sacrifice'? ⇨ **YOLUQ** + suff. *-lï.*

YOLUM Kzk. 19th c. **J̌olïm-bay** [Джолымбай] (SOV 88); Trkm.? 16th c. **Yolum-bi / Yulum-bi** [يولوم بى نايمان / Yoloum-Bi], governor of Merv, from the Nayman tribe (Abulg./Desm. 255); Bashk. 1757 **Yulum-bek** [Аскар Юлумбеков] (MIB IV/1, 135); Kzk. 19th c. **z1olum** [Жолумъ] (Pam. kn. Turg. 69). ✧ 'My road (=life) (is/will be) rich'. ⇨ **YOL** + poss. suff. *-ïm.*

YOLUMBET Kzk. 18th c. - 19th c. **J̌olïmbet** [Джолымбет] (Tynyšp. 71, 73); Kzk. 19th c. **J̌olïmbet** [Джолымбет] (SOK 300); Kzk. 19th c. **J̌olumbet** [Джолумбет] (Grod., Pril. 156); Kzk. 19th c. **J̌olumbet** [Джолумбетовъ] (AOK 94); Bashk. 1787 **Yolumbet** [Сунарча Елумбетев] (MIB V, 214); Bashk. 1723 **Yolumbet / Yulumbet** [Унгар (Юлумбетев) Елумбетев] (MIB III, 219-20); Bashk. 1675 **Yulumbet** [Юлюмбет Чипчикаев] (MIB I, 200); Bashk. 1731 **Yulumbet** [Юлумбет] (MIB III, 292); Bashk. 1735 **Yulumbet** [Юлумбет Юлмашевъ], a tarχan (Vel.-Zern., Bašk. 18); Bashk. 1735 **Yulumbet** [Юлумбет Ногайчуринъ], a prince (Vel.-Zern., Bašk. 12); Bashk. 1738 **Yulumbet** [Мряц Юлумбетев] (MIB I, 145). ⇨ **YOL** + suff. *-ïmbet / -umbet.* See also **J̌OL-MAMBET.**

YOMA see **J̌UMA**

YOMAYQA Bashk. 1735 **Yomayqa** [Сапаръ Емайкинъ], a tarχan (Vel.-Zern., Bašk. 23). ✧ 'Little Friday'. ⇨ **J̌UMA / J̌UMAY** + suff. *-qa.*

YOMUT Oghuz/Trkm. 13th c. **Yomut** [يموت / Йомут] (Abulg./Kon. 1240). ✧ Ethnonym, a Trkm. tribe.

YOÑΓA Turk. 1583 **Yoñγa** [يونغه] (Ongan, Ank. I, 150). ✧ 'Shavings'? cf. Turk. *yonγa* 'die Spahn, die Hobelspähne' (Radl. III, 418).

YORČUQ Türk / Uyg. 8th c. - 9th c. **Yorčuq-ïnal** (Le Coq, Man., DTS).

YORΓA Uyg. 8th c. - 12th c. **Yorγa** [yaχšïčï (?vaχšïčï) yorγa)] (Müller, Pfahl. 24); Crm.(Tat.) **Yourγa** [Альйко Юрга] (Smirnov, Krym. 121). ✧ 'Amble' cf. Chag., Turk. *yorγa* 'der Passgänger' (Radl. III, 425).

YOSÏPAS Uyg. **Yosïpas** [yosïpas / Yosipas] (DTS, EUTS). ✧ Aesopus (Gr.).

YOSMUT Uyg. **Yosmut** [Yosmut] (EUTS).

YÖKÄSIRI Uyg. 13th c. **Yökäsiri** [Yökäsiri] (DTS, EUTS).

YÖLÄK Uyg. **Yöläk**, aged 55, Arïγa's, 30, husband (Zieme, Mat. I, 80). ✧ 'Support(er)', „Stütze" (Zieme), cf. Uyg. *yöläk* 'опора' (DTS).

YÖRGÜČ see **YÜRGÜČ**

YUBANÏČ see **YUVANÏČ**

YUBUQ Tat. 1706 **Yubuq** [Юбук Бурисов] (MIB III, 24).

YUΓURUŠ Bulg. 9th c. **Yuγuruš?** [᾿Ωκόρσης], a leader of the Bulghars at the time of prince Omurtag (814-831) (Byz. Turc. 350).

YUQ-PERDİ Tat. 1686 **Yuq-perdka (<Yuq-perdike)** [Юкпердка] (Kungusk. akty 119). ✧ 'Poor gave him' cf. Tat. *yuq* '(3) неимущий, бедный' (TatRS). ⇨ **BERDİ.**

YUQA Uyg. 12th c. - 14th c. **Yuqa** (DTS); Alt. 19th-20th c. **Yuqa** [Юка] (OjrRS 211). ✧ 'Thin, slim' cf. Uyg. *yuqa* 'тонкий' (DTS).

YUQAČ Bashk. 1701, 1714 **Yuqač** [Акчюаш Юкачев] (MIB III, 9, MIB I, 105); Kzk. 19th c. **Yuqas-pay** [Юкаспай] (SOK 184). ✧ 'Thin, meagre, lean' cf. Tat. *yuqa* 'dünn, von geringer Dicke' (Radl. III, 538), Kzk. *žuqa* 'тонкий, лёгкий' (KzRS) + suff. -*č*.

YUQAS see **YUQAČ**

YUQAT Bashk. 1729 **Yuqat** [Юкат Беккулов] (MIB III, 265).

YUQUSUŠ Uyg. 12th c. - 14th c. **Yuqusuš** (Radl., USp. 128, DTS).

YUL-BERDİ Bashk. 1783 **Yul-berdi** [Юлберда Кинзебаев] (MIB V, 149). ✧ 'Road/travelling - gave (him/her)', born during travelling (Sattarov), cf. Bashk. PN *Yul-birðe* (Kusimova), Tat. PN *Yul-birde* (Sattarov). ⇨ **YOL + BERDİ.**

YUL-QUTLUQ see **YOL-QUTLUΓ**

YULA Khazar 1016 **Jula?** [Τζούλοος], a prince (Byz. Turc. 314-15); Türk 7th-9th c. **Yula** [Yula] (ETY III, 79); Khorezm.? 14th c.? **Yula-iläk / Yula-ilik** [Юла-илакъ / Юла-иликъ] (RaD/Ber. II, 40). ✧ 'Torch-bearer; Courier' cf. Uyg., Tuv. *yula* 'die Fackel, das Zicht' (Radl. III, 553).

YULAY Kirg. **Joloy** [Жолой], an epic hero, Manas' adversary (Jud. 80, 481); Kzk. **Julay** [Джулай] (Valihanov, Soč. 347); Kirg. **Julay** [Джулай], according to Manas-epos, he is a Mongol Khan (Valihanov, Soč. 73); Kirg. **Yoloy** [Joloi] (Proben V, 160 /162/); Bashk. 18th c. **Yulay** [Салават Юлаев] (MIB V, 678); Bashk. 1777 **Yulay** [Юлай Азналин] (MIB V, 678); Bashk. 1777 **Yulay** [Юлай Тяжиков] (MIB V, 57, 96); Kirg. **Žoloy** [Жолой], a folklore hero, enemy of Manas (Jud. 80, 481). ✧ I. 'Rein, bridle' (Mo.) (Sattarov); II. 'Little torch; courier' (Sattarov); III. 'Little road' (Kusimova), name given to children born on the road. ⇨ **YOL, YULA** + dim./voc. suff. -*y* /-*ay*?

YULAM Bashk. 1709 **Yulam** [Юлам Юртакаев] (MIB I, 264).

YULAN Kkalp. 1827 **Julan-behadïr** [Джулан бехадыр] (MIKk. 131); Bashk. 1763 **Yulan** [Юлан Туканов] (MIB IV/1, 274). ✧ Derived from *Yul* (Kusimova). ⇨ **YOL** + suff. -*an*?

YULBARS see **YOLBARS**

YULČİ see **YOLČİ**

YULDAŠ see **YOLDAŠ**

YULDİ see **YOLLU**

YULDU see **YOLLU**

YULDUZ Kzk. 19th c. **Juldus-bay** [Джулдусбай] (SOK 22); Selj.? 1309 **Yuldus-χatun / İl-dus-χatun?** [ايلدوس خاتون], Oldjaytu-bek's wife, in an inscription of Amasya (Uzunçarş., Küt. I, 101); Oghuz/Trkm. 13th c. **Yulduz** [يولدوز خان / يولدوز بن مينكلى خواجه خان] / Youldouz-khan / Ilduz], Meñli-χoja-χan's son (in a genealogy of Chinggis), the mythical forefather of Chinggis-khan (Abulg./Desm. 64, Šejb. XXVII); Kzk.? 19th c. **Yulduz** [Юлдузовъ], a pupil (AUK 844); Selj.? Trkm.? 1290 **Yulduz** [ايلدوز شاه / شاه يلدوز], a ruler (shah) (Dorn 132); Selj.? Trkm.? 1291, 1294, 1295 **Yulduz** [تاجالدين ايلدوز / تاجالدين يلدز / يلدوز] (RaD/Jahn 56, Dorn 137); Khorezm.? 1200, 1205 **Yulduz / Yïldïz** [تاجالدين يلدز / Tādž ad-dïn Yolduz], took part in the events at Ghazna in 1205 (EI I, 307, Abulfidā IV, 216-17); Oghuz/Trkm. 13th c. **Yulduz / Yulduz-χan** [يولدوز خان / يولدوز بن اوغوزخان], Oghuz-khan's son in the Turkic legend of origin (Abulg./Desm. 22 etc., Abulg./Kon. 425, 510, 515, 550, RaD I/1, 76, MIT II, 426, Šejb. XXIII, DTS); Oghuz 14th c. **Yultuz**, one of the sons of the legendary Oghuz Kaghan (Oğuz K. Dest. 15); Uyg. 1337 **Yuntuz-päk** [Juntuz Päk] (Chwol., Syr.-nest. 141). ✧ 'Star' cf. Crm., Turk. *yïldïz* 'der Stern, das Sternbild' (Radl. III, 491), Uyg. *yuldus*, Kuman, Chag., Kar. *yulduz* 'der Stern, der Sternbild' (Radl. III, 559), Kkalp. *žuldïz* 'звезда' (KkRS). See also **AY-YÏLDÏS, ALTÏN-ČÏLTÏS.**

YULDUZČİ Khorezm. **Yulduzčï** [Юлдузчи] (RaD II, 30). ✧ 'Astronomer' cf. Kuman *yulduzcï* 'der Sterndeuter' (Radl. III, 560). ⇨ **YULDUZ** + suff. -*čï.*

YULÏŠ see **YULUŠ**

YULKEY Bashk. 1794 **Yulkey** [Батал Юлкеев] (MIB V, 338). ⇨ **YOL** + suff. -*key.*

YULLÏ see **YOLLU**

YULMAŠ Bashk. 1735 **Yulmaš** [Юлумбет Юлмашевъ], a tarχan (Vel.-Zern., Bašk. 19). ✧ Shortened-contracted of *Yul-möχämät?*

YULMET Bashk. 1763 **Yulmet** [Иман Юлметев] (MIB IV/1, 268); Bashk. 1763 **Yulmet / Yulmät** [Кабай Юлметев] (MIB IV/1, 268). ✧ Shortened from *Yul-möχamet* (Sattarov). ⇨ **YOL** + suff. -*met.*

YULTAY Bashk. 1754 **Yultay** [Юлуш Юлтаев] (MIB IV/1, 83); Bashk. 1770 **Yultiy / Yultïy** [Юлти Таиров] (MIB IV/1, 347). ✧ 'Long-lived (child)' (Sattarov), cf. Tat. *yul* 'дорога; путь' (TatRS) + suff. -*tay* / -*tïy* (Mo.).

YULTÏY see **YULTAY**

YULTUZ see **YULDUZ**

YULTUZLAY Uyg. 762 **Yultuzlay-tegin** (Mahrnāmag 9). ⇨ **YULDUZ** + suff. *-lay(2)*?

YULU Uyg. 1339 **Yulu** (Chwol., Syr.-nest. (NF) 34). ❖ 'Help' cf. Karakh. *yulu-* 'помогать' (DTS).

YULUГ see **YOLUQ**

YULUQ see **YOLUQ**

YULUQAY see **YOLUQAY**

YULUM see **YOLUM**

YULUMBET see **YOLUMBET**

YULUŠ Bashk. 1756 **Yulïš** [Мансур Юлышев] (MIB IV/1, 109); Bashk. 1709 **Yuluš** [Юлуш] (MIB I, 262); Bashk. 1715 **Yuluš** [Емагуз Юлушев] (MIB III, 125); Bashk. 1735 **Yuluš** [Юлушъ Янтыковъ] (Vel.-Zern., Bašk. 24); Bashk. 1735 **Yuluš** [Утекей Юлушевъ] (Vel.-Zern., Bašk. 23); Bashk. 1745 **Yuluš** [Утекей Юлушев] (MIB III, 427); Bashk. 18th c. **Yuluš** [Девлеткул Юлушев] (MIB V, 415); Bashk. 1754 **Yuluš** [Юлуш Юлтаев] (MIB IV/1, 83); Bashk. 1756 **Yuluš** [Явгар Юлушев] (MIB IV, 123); Bashk. 1756 **Yuluš** [Балтагул Юлушев] (MIB IV, 123); Bashk. 1756 **Yuluš** [Кущигул Юлушев] (MIB IV, 123); Bashk. 1756 **Yuluš** [Тущигул Юлушев] (MIB IV/1, 106); Bashk. 1789 **Yuluš** [Байдагул Юлушев] (MIB V, 241); Bashk. 1790 **Yuluš** [Юлуш Асанов (Исенев)] (MIB V, 282, 319). ❖ I. 'Road-fellow; friend, helper (on the road)' cf. Tat. PN *Yulïš < Yul+Iš* (Sattarov); II. 'Redemption, ransom' cf. Chag. *yuluš* 'das Lösegeld' (Radl. III, 556); III. 'Rescue, salvation' cf. Uyg. *yuluš* 'die Errettung' (Radl. III, 556). ⇨ **YOL** + **EŠ**?

YUMA see **JUMA**

YUMAČTAY Tat. 1600 **Yumačtay** [Бумдан Юмачтаев] (MIB I, 152). ⇨ **TAY** or suff. *-tay(1,2)*?

YUMAГAY see **YUMAQAY**

YUMAY Tat. 1779 **Yumay** [Юмай Мсеев] (MIB V, 83); Bashk. 1653 **Yumay** [Юмай] (Vel.-Zern., Bašk. 44); Bashk. 1716 **Yumay** [Юмай Исенеев] (MIB III, 137); Bashk. 1717 **Yumay** [Юмай] (MIB III, 146); Bashk. 1722 **Yumay** [Юмай] (MIB I, 289); Bashk. 1738 **Yumay** [Юмай Токтагулов] (MIB III, 387); Bashk. 1753 **Yumay** [Юмай Иликеев] (MIB IV/1, 68); Bashk. 1754 **Yumay** [Юмай Исеньюлов] (MIB IV/1, 83); Bashk. 1754 **Yumay** [Юмай Иликеев] (MIB IV/1, 79); Bashk. 1760 **Yumay** [Юмай Рянгулов] (MIB IV/1, 187); Bashk. 1761 **Yumay** [Юмай Аликеев] (MIB IV/1, 230). ❖ Vocative/imperative of *Yuma* 'Servile, fawing, complaisant' (Satttarov). ⇨ **YUMA** + voc./dim. suff. *-y*.

YUMAQ Turk. 16th c. **Yumaq** [Yumak] (Ongan, Ank. II); Yürük 1543 **Yumaq** [Yumak] (Gökb., Rum. 205); Bashk. 1763 **Yumaq** [Юмак Муаитмас] (MIB IV/2, 45); Oghuz/Trkm. 13th c. **Yumaq-bay** [یوماق بای / Йумак-бай] (Abulg./Kon. 1450). ❖ 'Ball/clew (of wool, string)' cf. Turk. *yumaq* 'der Knäuel, Klumpen' (Radl. III, 574). ⇨ **YUMA** + dim. suff. *-q*.

YUMAQAY Tat. 1731 **Yumaqay** [Юмакай Тлекев] (MIB III, 293); Bashk. 1724 **Yumaqay** [Юмакай] (MIB III, 227); Bashk. 1734 **Yumaqay** [Юмакай Кунаевъ], a tarχan (Vel.-Zern., Bašk. 10); Bashk. 1735 **Yumaqay** [Юмакай] (MIB III, 343); Bashk. 1735 **Yumaqay** [Юмакай Атикутуминъ], a tarχan (Vel.-Zern., Bašk. 13); Bashk. 1756 **Yumaqay** [Юмакай Карагушев] (MIB IV/1, 106); Bashk. 1758 **Yumaqay** [Кусядык Юмакаев] (MIB IV/1, 160); Bashk. 1760 **Yumaqay** [Кусюм Юмагаев] (MIB IV/1, 199); Bashk. 1760 **Yumaqay** [Кусюм Юмакаев] (MIB IV/1, 199); Bashk. 1764 **Yumaqay** [Кутуй Юмакаев] (MIB IV/1, 287); Bashk. 1776 **Yumaqay** [Юмакай Бинлибетев] (MIB V, 240); Bashk. 1776 **Yumaqay** [Юмакай Сензяпов] (MIB V, 313); Bashk. 1776 **Yumaqay** [Юмакай (Зюмакай) Солтанмратов] (MIB V, 44); Bashk. 1783 **Yumaqay** [Кусюкбай Юмакаев] (MIB V, 139); Bashk. 1783 **Yumaqay** [Кусюкбай Юмакаев] (MIB V, 139); Bashk. 1798 **Yumaqay** [Юмакаевъ] (PSZRI XXV, 196-197). ❖ 'Liar, bootlicker' cf. Tat. *yumaqay* 'льстивый; льстец, подлиза' (TatRS). ⇨ **YUMA?** + suff. *-qay*.

YUMALAQ NUyg. 19th c. **Yumalaq / Yumulaq?** [یومالاق] (Le Coq, Namenl. 123). ❖ 'Round; sheep-excrement'; 'rund (aber auch=Schafmist)' (Le Coq), cf. Tat.(Bar.), Crm. *yumalaq* 'kugelförmig; die Kugel' (Radl. III, 576). See also **TOMALAQ**.

YUMALDUQ Kzk. 1819 **Yumalduq** [Юмалдук] (MIK IV, 325).

YUMAN Kzk. 19th c. **Juman** [Джуманъ Худай Бергяновъ] (Grod., Pril. 175); Chag. 16th c. **Juman-biy** [Джуман-бий] (Ivanov 78); Kzk. 1829 **Yuman** [Юман] (MIK IV, 323); Bashk. 1731 **Yuman-yul** [Сеит Юмангулов] (MIB III, 292); Kkalp. 20th c. **Žuman** [Жуман] (KkRS 773). ❖ '?' cf. Kzk. PN *Žïman* (Žanuzakov-Esbaeva).

YUMANAY Bashk. 1780 **Yumanay** [Юманай] (MIB V, 115). ⇨ **YUMAN?** + suff. *-ay*.

YUMART see **JOMART**

YUMAŠ Bashk. 1687 **Yumaš** [Юмашка Батраев] (Vel.-Zern., Bašk. 31); Bashk. 1781 **Yumaš** [Егафер Юмашев] (MIB V, 126). ❖ 'Little Friday'. ⇨ **YUMA** + suff. *-š*.

YUMŠAQ Uyg. 12th c. - 14th c. **Yumšaq** [Yumşak] (Radl., USp. 48, DTS, EUTS). ❖ 'Soft; peaceful' cf. *yutšaq* ' мягкий, нетвердый ' (Radl. III, 585).

YUMUQ Kzk. 1819 **Yumuq** [Юмук] (MIK IV, 326). ❖ 'Closed' cf. Chag., Turk. *yumuq* 'zugedrückt, geschlossen (von Mund und Augen etc.) + suff. *-uq*.

YUMURTALÏ Turk. **Yumurtalï-oγlu** [Jumurtaly oγlu] (Kúnos 1891, 119). ❖ 'Having or selling eggs' +

suff. *-li*.

YUMUT Trkm. 1717 **Yumut** [Юмутъ], from Khiva (ZIRGO IX, 327). ✧ 'Gather!' cf. Uyg. *yumit-, yumut-* 'versammeln' (Radl. III, 576).

YUMUTLÏ Bashk. 1740 **Yumutlï** [Юмутлы Кумышев] (MIB I, 468). ⇨ YUMUT + suff. *-li*.

YUNAY Chag. 16th c. **Junay-sufi** [Джунай Суфи] (Ivanov 224); Chag. 16th c. **Junay-šeyχ** [Джунай-шейх] (Ivanov 240); Bashk. 1712, 1714 **Yunay** [Юнай Шелтыков] (MIB III, 90, 116); Bashk. 1719 **Yunay** [Юнай Салтыков] (MIB III, 188); Bashk. 1757 **Yunay** [Юнай Юнусаев] (MIB IV/1, 151); Bashk. 1768 **Yunay** [Базаргуль Юнаевъ] (Nikol'skij 275); Bashk. 1770 **Yunay** [Базаргул Юнаев] (MIB IV/2, 160); Bashk. 1770 **Yunay** [Кучук Юнаев] (MIB IV/1, 342); Bashk. 1770 **Yunay** [Мякалан Юнаев] (MIB IV/1, 342); Bashk. 1785 **Yunay** [Макалап (Макалан, Мякалам) Юнаев] (MIB V, 178); Bashk. 1737 **Yunay-bay** [Юнай-бай Шелтынов (Шелтыков ?)] (MIB III, 367); *TN:* Bashk. 1738 **Yunayevo** [Юнаево] (MIB III, 379). ✧ '?' cf. Bashk. PN *Yunay* (Kusimova) + suff. *-y*?

YUNΓU Karakh. 11th c. **Yunγu** [Yunğu] (MK/Atalay 860). ✧ '(Ritual) washing'? cf. Uyg. *yunγu* 'мытье' (DTS).

YUNNA Bashk. 1737 **Yunna(-tarχan)** [Юнна тархан] (MIB I, 307).

YUNTUZ see **YULDUZ**

YUNUSAY Bashk. 1751 **Yunusay** [Юнусай] (MIB IV/1, 34). ✧ 'Yunus' cf. Turk. *Yonos* 'der Prophet Jonas' (Radl. III, 417). ⇨ JUNUŠ + suff. *-ay*.

YUPAR see **YÏPAR**

YUR-BAŠA see **YURT-BAŠÏ**

YUR-GIL Bashk. 1735 **Yur-gil?** [Юргилъ Юлушевъ], a tarχan (Vel.-Zern., Bašk. 24). ✧ 'Yurt-come!'? ⇨ KEL?

YUR-ΓAL Bashk. 1709 **Yur-γal?** [Юргал] (MIB I, 268). ⇨ QAL I. / QAL II.?

YURALÏ Bashk. 1789 **Yuralï, Yur-ali?** [Юрали Буранчин] (MIB V, 269).

YURΓUN Bashk. 1740 **Yurγun** [Сюяргул Юргунов] (MIB I, 404). ✧ 'Weak, tired' cf. Chag., Turk. *yorγun* 'schlaff, müde, ermüdet' (Radl. III, 426).

YURMAQAY Bashk. 1756 **Yurmaqay** [Юрмакай Апаков] (MIB IV/1, 122).

YURMAT Bashk. 1779 **Yurmat** [Юрмат Бертюков] (MIB V, 96); Khorezm.? 13th c. **Yurmat-bey** [Јурмат-бей], one of the „beys" of Chinggis-Khan in a certain „Dastan" (IOAIÊK XIX, 133). ✧ Ethnonym *Yurmati*?

YURT-BAΓÏŠ Tat. 1716 **Yur-baγïš** (<Yurt-baγïš) [Юрбагыш Токметев] (MIB III, 137); Bashk. 1732 **Yurt-baγïš** [Юртбагыш Юнусов] (MIB III, 302); Bashk. 1760 **Yurt-baγïš** [Ерлыгап Юртбагышев] (MIB IV/1, 199); Bashk. 1764 **Yurt-baγïš** [Ахмер Юртбагышев] (MIB IV/1, 292); Bashk. 1791 **Yurt-baγïš** [Юртбагыш Буляков] (MIB V, 301); Bashk. 1791 **Yurt-baγïš** / **Yurt-baγuš** [Юртбагуш / Юртбагиш Буляков] (MIB V, 301). ✧ 'Looking after the yurt' cf. Bashk., Tat. PN *Yort-baγïš* (Kusimova, Sattarov). ⇨ JURT + BAΓÏŠ.

YURT-BAŠA see **YURT-BAŠÏ**

YURT-BAŠÏ Bashk. 1738 **Yurt-bašï** [Юрбаша (Юртбаша) Исмакаев] (MIB III, 386). ✧ 'Head/leader of the yurt'. ⇨ JURT + BAŠ + poss. *-ï*.

YURTAY Bashk. 1757 **Yurtay** [Асан Юртаев] (MIB IV/1, 145). ⇨ TAY or suff. *-tay(1,2)*?

YURTAQAY Bashk. 1709 **Yurtaqay** [Юлам Юртакаев] (MIB I, 264). ✧ 'Horse with good gait' cf. Chag., Tat.(Bar.) *yortaq* 'ein Pferd, das einen guten Schritt, Trab hat' (Radl. III, 427) + suff. *-ay*.

YURTČÏ Kzk. 19th c. **Jurči** [Джурчи] (SODž. 62); Oghuz/Trkm. 13th c. **Yurtčï** [يورتجى / Йуртчы] (Abulg./Kon. 525); Turk. 16th c. **Yurtčï** [Yurtcı] (Ongan, Ank. II (Num. 1554, 1716)). ✧ 'Chief of a settlement/camp' cf. Chag. *yurtči* 'der Verwalter einer Ansiedlung, eines Lagers' (Radl. IV, 550). ⇨ JURT + suff. *-či*.

YURTÏ Bashk. 1744 **Yurtï** [Юрты Табанаев] (MIB III, 415).

YURTUMA Bashk. 1784 **Yurtuma** [Юртума Атянев (Антянев)] (MIB V, 154).

YURUL-TAŠ Khorezm.? 13th c. **Yurul-taš?** [يُرُل تَاش / Jurultasch] (Wassaf 29). ⇨ TAŠ? or suff. *-taš*?

YURUN-TAY Kzk. 1819 **Yurun-tay** [Юрунтай] (MIK IV, 324). ✧ 'Patch, piece' cf. Chag., Alt., Alt.(Tel.) *yurun* 'der Flick; Lappen, ein Stückchen Zeug' (Radl. III, 546-547). ⇨ TAY? or suff. *-tay(1,2)*?

YUSUF Kzk. 19th c. **Jusup-pay** [Джусуппай] (SOK 286); Kkalp. **Jüsüp** [Джюсюп] (Bask.); Kzk. 19th c. **Jüzip** [Джюзепъ] (AOK 98); Uyg. **Yausip** [jausip] (DTS); Karakh. 11th c. **Yusuf** [yusuf] (DTS); Kzk. 19th c. **Yusuf** [Юсуфъ Алибутиевъ] (Grod., Pril. 148); Oghuz 11th c. **Yusuf-inal** [يوسف ينال / Yūsuf Yīnal (inal)] (Köprülü, Arīs al-Qulūb: Belleten VII, 475, 502); Bashk. 1735 **Yusup** [Юсуповъ], a tarχan (Vel.-Zern., Bašk. 20); Kkalp. 20th c. **Žüsip** [Жүсип] (KkRS 774). ✧ Yusuf (Ar.<Old Hebr.), the biblical Joseph (Ahmed). See also **QARA-YUSUF**.

YUSUF-TAY Kzk. 19th c. **Yusuf-tay** [Юсуфъ Тай Нуръ Таевъ] (Grod., Pril. 196). ⇨ YUSUF + TAY? or suff. *-tay(1,2)*?

YUSUN Kzk. 1846 **Yusun-bay** [Беккожа Юсунбаевъ] (Konšin, Mat. V, 67); Kzk. 19th c. **Yusun-batïr** [Юсунъ-батыръ], in Kazak traditition (Potanin, Pred. 55). See also **SARÏ-YUSUN**.

YUSUP see **YUSUF**

YUSURQAP Trkm. 19th c. **Yusurqap** [Джаназаръ Юсуркаповъ] (SKSO III, 178).

YUŠO-KANİG Uyg. **Yušo-kanig** [yušo kanig] (DTS). ✧ '?' <Sogd. *ysw* (DTS).

YUŠUMUT Khorezm.? **Yušumut** [Юшумут] (RaD II, 10).

YUT Kzk. 19th c. **Yut-bay** [Дусибай Ютбаевъ] (Grod., Pril. 183). ✧ I. 'Swallow!'? cf. Uyg., Chag., Alt., Kirg. *yut-* 'verschlucken, herumschlucken' (Radl. III, 561); II. 'Misfortune, disaster; destitution, poverty' cf. Türk, Uyg., Chag. *yut* 'hoher Schnee und im Frühling nach Thauwetter eintretende Frost, wodurch ein Viehsterben veranlasst wird' (Radl. III, 560); (Alt.) 'das schlechte Wetter, Unglück'; (NUyg.(Tar.)) 'der Misswachs, ein ungünstiges Jahr' (Radl. III, 560), Kzk. *cut* [žut / jut] 'mal mülkten ayrılmak, yokluk' (KzTS).

YUVAN Chuv. 18th-19th c. **Yuvan** [Юванъ] (Magn. 96); Chuv. 18th-19th c. **Yuvan-batïr** [Юванбатыръ] (Magn. 96); Chuv. 18th-19th c. **Yuvan-bey** [Юванбей] (Magn. 96); Chuv. 18th-19th c. **Yuvan-murza** [Юванмурза] (Magn. 96). ✧ 'Thick; rude' cf. Tat. *yu(w)an* 'толстый; полный; низкий; грубый ' (TatRS).

YUVANAČ see **YUVANİČ**

YUVANAY Chuv. 18th-19th c. **Yuvanay** [Юванай] (Magn. 96). ⇨ YUWAN + suff. *-ay*.

YUVANČA Chuv. 18th-19th c. **Yuvanča** [Юванча] (Magn. 96). ⇨ YUWAN + suff. *-ča (<-čï.)*

YUVANČEY Chuv. 18th-19th c. **Yuvančey** [Юванчей] (Magn. 96). ⇨ YUWAN + suff. *-čey (<-čï+-y.)*

YUVANİČ Kzk. 1829 **Yubanïč** [Юбанычъ] (MIK IV, 325); Chuv. 18th-19th c. **Yuvanač** [Юваначъ] (Magn. 96). ✧ 'Consolation (of the parents); amusement' cf. Tat. *yuwanïč* 'die Langsamkeit; der Trost' (Radl. III, 570), 'утешение; развлечение; забава; отрада; услада; утеха ' (TatRS).

YUVAŠKA Chuv. 18th-19th c. **Yuvaška** [Ювашка] (Magn. 96). ⇨ YUWAŠ + suff. *-qa / (R.) -ka*?

YUWAQ Bashk. 1738 **Yuwaq** [Ювак] (MIB III, 345).

YUWAQAY Bashk. 1737 **Yuwaqay** [Ювакай Кошаев] (MIB I, 317). ⇨ YUWAQ + suff. *-ay*.

YUWAŠ Chuv. 18th-19th c. **Yuvaš** [Ювашъ] (Magn. 96); Kirg. **Žōš-bay** [Жоошбай] (Jud. 49). ✧ 'Peaceful, quiet, slow' cf. Kar. (L.), Kar.(T.), Tat. *yuwaš* 'friedfertig, leise, langsam, gemüthlich, zahm' (Radl. III, 572), Kirg. *žōš* [„oow] ' смирный, кроткий ' (Jud.).

YÜGÄY Tat. 1779 **Yügäy** [Сюлюк Югяев] (MIB V, 82). ✧ 'Lime(-tree)' cf. Tat.(Tob.) *yügä* 'die Linde, der Lindenbast' (Radl. III, 593) + suff. *-y*.

YÜGNÄKİ Khorezm. 13th c. **Yügnäki / Yüknäki**, Ahmed Yügnäki is the author of the vocabulary „'Atäbätu 'l-haqājïq" (DTS). ✧ 'Coming/originating from *Yügnäk*' cf. Uyg. TN *Yügnäk* (DTS).

YÜGNEK see **YEKEÑK**

YÜGÜR Uzb. 20th c. **Yügür-bây** [Югурбой] (Begmatov 1984, 206); Uzb. 20th c. **Yügür-bek** [Югурбек] (Begmatov 1984, 206). ✧ 'Run! Be lively/nimble!' (Begmatov), cf. Uzb. *yügür-* 'бегать, скакать' (UzbRS).

YÜKLÜ see **YÜNLÜ**

YÜKŠİ Bashk. 1701 **Yükši** [Мякис Юкшиев] (MIB III, 9). ✧ 'Carman, waggoner' cf. Tat. *yökče* 'возчик, извозчик ' (TatRS) + suff. *-ši*.

YÜN Chuv. 18th-19th c. **Yün** [Юнъ] (Magn. 96); Tat. 20th c. **Yün-čur** [Юньчур] (Sattarov); Chuv. 18th-19th c. **Yün-čura** [Юнчура] (Magn. 96); Tat. 20th c. **Yün-čura** [Юньчура] (Sattarov). ✧ 'Cheap, not dear' cf. Tat. *yün* 'дешевый, недорогой ' (TatRS).

YÜNEY Tat. 1731 **Yüney** [Юней Ишкикин] (MIB III, 293).

YÜNLÜ Kzk. 19th c. **Jündi-bay** [Джюндыбай] (SODž. 162); Kzk. 19th c. **Jündü-bay** [Джундубай] (SOK 78); Oghuz/Trkm. 14th c. - 15th c. **Yünlü-qoĵa / Yüklü-qoĵa? / Yüñlü-qoĵa** [Yüñlü Koca, Yuñlu Koca / Юклю-Коджа] (DQorq. 78, 79, 83); Kzk. 19th c. **Žündü-bay** [Жундубай] (SOK 244). ✧ 'Hairy, shaggy' cf. Az., Kar., Turk. *yün* 'das Thierhaar, die Wolle' (Radl. III, 597), Kzk. *žün* 'шерсть' (KzRS) + suff. *-lü*.

YÜÑLÜ see **YÜNLÜ**

YÜRGÜČ Yürük 1543 **Yörgüč** [يوركج / Yörgüç] (Gökb., Rum. 188); Turk. 1428, 1429 **Yürgüč-paša / Yargüč-paša** [يوركوج پاشا / Lala Yargüç Paşa], in an isnscription of a djami in Amasya (Sevim-Yücel I, 277, Uzunçarş., Küt. 117, 118, 119). ✧ 'Younger brother'? cf. *yürküč* 'der jüngere Bruder' (Radl. III, 607).

YÜRKEY Bashk. 1722 **Yürkey** [Юркей] (MIB I, 294); Bashk. 1749 **Yürkey** [Юркей Исейнов] (MIB III, 460).

YÜRSİN Uzb. 20th c. **Yürsin** [Юрсин] (Begmatov 1984, 206); Uzb. 20th c. **Yürsin** [Юрсин], fem. (Begmatov 1984, 206); Uzb. 20th c. **Yürsin-ây** [Юрсиной], fem. (Begmatov 1984, 206); Uzb. 20th c. **Yürsin-bây** [Юрсинбой] (Begmatov 1984, 206); Uzb. 20th c. **Yürsin-bek** [Юрсинбек] (Begmatov 1984, 206); Uzb. 20th c. **Yürsin-χân** [Юрсинхон], fem. (Begmatov 1984, 206); Uzb. 20th c. **Yürsin-χoĵa** [Юрсинхўжа] (Begmatov 1984, 206); Uzb. 20th c. **Yürsin-mirza** [Юрсинмирза] (Begmatov 1984, 206). ✧ 'Let him/her move/be; Let him/her not die; Let him/her be healthy' (Begmatov), cf. Uzb. *yür-* 'ходить, ездить' (UzbRS).

YÜRTÜKEY Bashk. 1732 **Yürtükey** [Юртукей] (MIB III, 302); Bashk. 1753, 1757, 1761 **Yürtükey** [Минлыбай Юртюкеев] (MIB IV/1, 68, 140, 230); Bashk. 1760 **Yürtükcy** [Юртюкей Сеитов] (MIB IV/1, 187).

YÜRÜ Kzk. 19th c. **Yürü-bay** [Юрюбай] (Grod., Pril. 89). ✧ 'Go, move, live' cf. Uyg. *yüri-* 'in Bewegung sein, gehen, fahren, reiten, leben' (Radl. III, 602), Uyg., Kuman, Chag., Kar., Turk. *yürü-* 'gehen, fahren, leben' (Radl. III, 603).

YÜRÜK Uyg. 12th c. -14th c. **Yürük** [Yürük] (DTS, EUTS); Yürük 1543 **Yürük** (Gökb., Rum. 104, 209). ✧ 'Nomad' cf. Crm., Turk., Chag. *yürük* 'gehend, schnell gehend, laufend, schnell, flüchtig; ein Nomad' (Radl. III, 604).

YÜRÜK-QÏPČAQ Uyg. 12th c. - 14th c. **Yürük-qïpčaq** [yürük qïpčaq] (DTS); Uyg. 13th-14th c. **Yürük-qïpčaq** (Zieme, Mat. II, 92). ✧ 'Nomad-Kipchak' (Blagova 1997, 708).

YÜRÜK-TÜMÄN Uyg. 12th c. - 14th c. **Yürük-tümän** [yürük tümän] (Radl., USp. 16-17, DTS); Uyg. 13th-14th c. **Yürük-tümän** (Zieme, Mat. II, 92). ✧ 'Nomad-ten-thousand' (Blagova 1997, 705), 'Migrating-ten-thousand' (Blagova 1997, 716).

YÜZ Kzk. 19th c. **J̌uc-pay** (<J̌uz-pay) [Джуспай] (SOK 156); Kzk. 19th c. **J̌üz-bay** [Джузбай] (AOAtb. 2); Kzk. 19th c. **J̌üz-bay** [Джузбай] (AOA 98); Kzk. 19th c. **J̌üz-bay** [Джузбай] (AOO 70); Kzk. 19th c. **J̌üz-bay** [Джузбай] (Grod., Pril. 188); Kzk. 19th c. **J̌üz-žan** [Джюзжанъ] (AOK 110); Kzk. 19th c. **Yüz-bay** [Юзбаевъ] (Grod., Pril. 196); Kzk. 1822 **Züs-batïr / Žüs-batïr?** [Зюсъ-батыр] (TOUAK XXIV, 130); Kzk. 19th c. **Žüz-bay** [Жюзбай] (SOK 240); Kzk. 1817 **Žüz-batïr** [جوز باطر / Жуз-батыр], chief of the Bay-ulï tribe (MIK IV, 309). ✧ I. 'Hundred' cf. Türk, Kuman, Chag., Az., Crm., Turk., etc. *yüz* 'hundert' (Radl. III, 616), Uyg., Alt., Tat.(Sib.) *yüs* 'id.' (Radl. III, 614), Kzk. *cüz* 'yüz' 'KzTS), Hak.(Shor, Sag.) *čüs* 'hundert' (Radl. III, 2200); II. 'Face' cf. Türk, Kuman, Chag., Az., Crm., Turk., etc. *yüz* 'das Gesicht, das Antlitz' (Radl. III, 616), Uyg., Alt. *yüs* 'id.' (Radl. III, 614), Hak.(Sag.), Shor *čüs* 'das Antlitz, das Gesicht' (Radl. III, 2200), Kzk. *žüz* 'id.' (KzRS). See also **ÄR-ǰÜZ**.

YÜZ-AY Kzk. 1817 **J̌uz-ay** [بوراى / Жузай] (MIK IV, 312, 319); Kzk. 19th c. **J̌üz-ay-bay** [Джузайбай] (Grod., Pril. 161); Kzk. 19th c. **Yüz-ay** [Юзъ-ай], fem. (Grod., Pril. 30). ✧ 'Face-Moon'? ⇨ **YÜZ + AY?** + dim. suff. -*ay*?

YÜZ-BUҐА see **YÜZ-BUQA**

YÜZ-BUQA Chag. 15th c. **Yüz-buɣa**, a chieftain who lived in the time of Shahruh (1404-1447) (ᶜAbd alRazzāk al-Samarkandī, Matla as-saᶜdain: Notices et Extr. XVI/1, 29); Khorezm. **Yüz-buqa** [Юз-Бука] (RaD II, 72). ⇨ **YÜZ + BUQA.**

YÜZ-YAŠAR Kzk. 19th c. **J̌üz-ǰasar / J̌u-ǰasar?** [Джуджасаръ бай Тираковъ] (Grod., Pril. 111); Bashk. 1719 **Yüz-yašar** [Юзяшар Уразлин] (MIB III, 189). ✧ 'He will live to be a hundred, he will be long-lived' cf. Tat. PN *Yöz-yäšär* (Sattarov). ⇨ **YÜZ + YAŠAR.** See also **MÏÑ-ǰASAR.**

YÜZ-SİR Kzk. 19th c. **Yüz-sir** [Туякбай Юзъ Сировъ] (Grod., Pril. 123). ⇨ **YÜZ.**

YÜZ-TEMİR Karakh.? 975 **Yüz-temir** [يوزتمر] (Ibn al-Athīr/Tornb. VIII, 482-483). ✧ 'Hundred-iron'. ⇨ **YÜZ + TEMİR.**

YÜZE-YAQ Tat.(Tüm.) 1636 **Yüze-yaq** [Юзеяк ?/ Аудабеков Юзеячко] (Miller, Ist. Sib. II, 439). ⇨ **YÜZ + YAQ?**

YÜZE-YAN Tat.(Sib.) 163 **Yüze-yan (Yüze-ayan?)** [Юзеян] (Miller, Ist. Sib. II, 413). ✧ 'His face is clear'. ⇨ **YÜZ + AYAN II.**

YÜZEY Bashk. 1743 **Yüzey / Yöðey** [Юзей Уразаев] (MIB III, 540); Bashk. 1749 **Yüzey / Yöðey** [Кузей Юзеев] (MIB III, 469); Bashk. 1754 **Yüzey / Yöðey** [Юзей Шигимов] (MIB IV/1, 79); Bashk. 1759 **Yüzey / Yöðey** [Юзей Картаев] (MIB IV/2, 24); Bashk. 1760 **Yüzey / Yöðey** [Мукмень Юзеев] (MIB IV/2, 28); Bashk. 1760 **Yüzey / Yöðey** [Юзей Карманов] (MIB IV/2, 384); Bashk. 1777 **Yüzey / Yöðey** [Мурсалим Юзеев] (MIB V, 60); Bashk. 1780 **Yüzey / Yöðey** [Юзей Ракаев] (MIB V, 113); Bashk. 1785 **Yüzey / Yöðey** [Юзей Хузяшев] (MIB V, 168). ✧ I.'Live to be a hundered' cf. Tat. PN *Yözäy / Yüzäy / Yüzī* 'Йөзәй, йөзгә жит' (Sattarov); II. 'Multiply, propagate!' cf. Tat. PN *Yözäy / Yüzäy / Yüzī* 'Күбәй, ишәй' (Sattarov); III. 'Little face'? ⇨ **YÜZ?** + suff. -*ey*?

YÜZEYİM Tat. 1609 **Yüzeyim** [Юзеим Окшеев] (Miller, Ist. Sib. II, 210). ⇨ **YÜZ-AY?**

YÜZEKEY see **YÜZÜKEY**

YÜZÜKEY Bashk. 1770 **Yüzekey** [Бектемир Юзекеев] (MIB IV/1, 350); Bashk. 1790 **Yüzekey** [Юзекей Татлыбаев] (MIB V, 288); Bashk. 1732 **Yüzükey** [Юзюкей Кусекеев] (MIB III, 302); Bashk. 1748, 1752 **Yüzükey** [Юзюкей Сеитов] (MIB III, 454, IV/1, 66); Bashk. 1753 **Yüzükey** [Кадыр Юзюкеев] (MIB IV/1, 68); Bashk. 1756 **Yüzükey** [Сюлейман Юзюкеев] (MIB IV/1, 113); Bashk. 1760 **Yüzükey** [Надыр Юзюкеев] (MIB IV/1, 191); Bashk. 1761 **Yüzükey** [Кадыр Юзюкеев] (MIB IV/1, 230). ✧ 'Little ring' cf. Bashk. *yöðök* 'перстень' (BRS), Alt.(Tel.) *yüstük* 'der Fingerring, der Siegelring' (Radl. III, 616), Kuman, Chag., Tat.(Bar.), Turk. *yüzük* 'id.'(Radl. III, 619) + suff. -*key*?

K

KALAMAN Chuv. 18th-19th c. **Kalaman** [Каламанъ] (Magn. 49).

KALMA Chuv. 18th-19th c. **Kalma** [Калма] (Magn. 49).

KAMİSAR Chuv. 18th-19th c. **Kamisar** [Камисаръ] (Magn. 50). ✧ 'Commander' <R. комисар.

KARİM see **KERİM**

KATİKEY Chuv. 1737 **Katikey** [Черебай Катикѣевъ] (Nepljuev 487).

KAZ-DİMER Chuv. 18th-19th c. **Kaz-dimer** [Коздимеръ] (Magn. 52). ⇨ **QAZ?** + **TEMİR.**

KAZANEY Chuv. 18th-19th c. **Kazaney** [Казаней] (Magn. 49). ⇨ **QAZAN** + suff. *-ey*.

KÄD-TUΓMÏŠ Uyg. 13th-14th c. **Käd-tuɣmïš-tarχan** (Zieme, Mat. II, 88). ✧ '(A) Good/Strong (man) was born; strong-born'. ⇨ **KEY** + **TOΓMÏŠ.**

KÄDÄKKÄY Tuv. 19th c. **Kädäkkäy** [Кӓдӓккӓi], fem. (Proben IX, 90).

KÄDİM see **KEDİM**

KÄDİR see **QADÏR**

KÄKÄGÜ Yak. **Käkägü** [Кӓкӓҥӱ], fem. (Pek.). ✧ 'Having stately posture' cf. Yak. *käkäi* 'откидывать назад (шею, затылок); статно себя держать' (Pek.).

KÄKİM see **XĀKİM**

KÄKİLİK Trkm. 20th c. **Käkilik** [Käkilik], fem. (Zaj. 1971, 338); Trkm. 20th c. **Käkilik** [Кякилик], fem. (TrkmRS 425). ✧ 'Partridge' cf. Trkm. *käkilik* 'кеклик, каменная куропатка' (TrkmRS).

KÄL-KİČ Uzb. 1826 **Käl-kič** [كل كيج / Kalkitch] (Vel.-Zern., Haïder 280-282).

KÄLBÄR Yak. **Kälbär** [Кӓлбӓр] (Pek.).

KÄLBİSTÄY Yak. **Kälbistäy** [Кӓлбicтӓi], part of the name of a heroine in a tale (Pek.).

KÄLİMBET Kkalp. 20th c. **Kälimbet / Qälimbet** [Қәлимбет] (KkRS 774). ✧ 'Birthmark - Mukhammad'. ⇨ **QAL II** + suffixoid *-imbet*.

KÄLYİ Yak. **Kälyi** [Тiллӓх-Калли? (Кӓлji)-Тӓлбicтӓi-куо], part of the name of a heroine in a tale (Pek.).

KÄMAL see **KEMAL**

KÄMİYLÄ Kkalp. 20th c. **Kämiylä** [Кәмийлә], fem. (KkRS 778). ✧ Kamila (Ar.) 'perfect, complete, genuine' fem. of Kamil (Ahmed).

KÄNČ-TURMÏŠ Uyg. **Känč-turmïš-tarḫan** [Känç Turmış Tarḫan] (EUTS). ⇨ **KENČ** + **TURMÏŠ.**

KÄNJİ see **KENJE**

KÄNDÄL Yak. **Kändäl, Kändäl-buχatïr** [Кӓндӓл / Кӓндӓл-бухатыр] (Pek.). ✧ 'Big, tall'? cf. Yak. *kändä* 'большой, высокий'; *kändägär* 'высокий и поддавшийся вперед' (Pek.). See also **BÜYÜK, ČOÑ, EVREN, YOΓAN, MÄÑKÄ.**

KÄNİ Kkalp. 20th c. **Käni-gül** [Кәнигүл], fem. (KkRS 778). ✧ 'Special, curious'; Baskakov: 'особая роза' [special, curious rose] (OSA 141).

KÄNİG Uyg. **Känig** [Känig] (EUTS).

KÄÑİLDEY Kzk. **Käñildey** [Кянгильдей] (Hanykov, Poezdka 19).

KÄRBÄLYİN Yak. **Kärbälyin / Är-kärbälyin-oyūn** [Кӓрбӓлjiн / Ӓр-Кӓрбӓлjiн-оjун], a bloodthirsty black shaman (Pek.). ✧ 'Cut through; annoy' cf. *kärbä* 'точить (о черве), грызть, персрезать; донимать (о человеке)' (Pek.).

KÄRÄY see **KERÄY**

KÄRĂČÄÑ Hak.(Sag.) 19th-20th c. **Kärăčäñ** [Кӓрӑчӓҥ] (Proben IX, 467).

KÄRGÄSİN Yak. **Kärgäsin** [Кӓргӓciн] (Pek.).

KÄRGÜ Uyg. **Kärgü** [Kärgü] (EUTS).

KÄRİ-AČARÏ Uyg. **Käri-ačarï** [Käri Açarı] (EUTS).

KÄRİYMÄ Kkalp. 20th c. **Käriymä** [Кәриймә], fem. (KkRS 778). ✧ Karima (Ar. fem.) 'kind, generous, benevolent, open-handed, noble' (Ahmed). ⇨ **KÄRİM.**

KÄRİM see **KERİM**

KÄRİM-BERGÄN Uzb. 20th c. **Kärim-bergän** [Каримберган] (Begmatov 1984, 202). ✧ 'Given by the most Generous (Allah)'. ⇨ **KERİM** + **BERGEN.**

KÄRLİK Uyg. **Kärlik** [Kärlik] (EUTS).

KÄRPÄSTÏR Yak. **Kärpästïr** [Кӓрпӓcтiр] (Pek.). ✧ 'Travelling, wandering'? cf. Yak. *kärpästä-* 'путешествовать, ехать понемножку' (Pek.).

KÄRŠİN Uyg. **Käršin** [Käršin] (EUTS). ⇨ **KERSİN?**

KÄSİYÄN Yak. **Käsiyän / Kässiyän / Qačïyän** [Кӓcijӓн / Кӓccijӓн / Качыjан] (Pek.); Yak. **Qačïyän** [Качыjан / Кӓcijӓн] (Pek.). ✧ Kas'jan (R.).

KÄSSİYÄN see **KÄSİYÄN**

KÄT-QARA see **KET-QARA**

KÄT-TAŠ see **KED-TAŠ**

KÄTÄLİM Pecheneg 1050 **Kätälim?** [Καταλείμ], a commander (Byz. Turc. 156).

KÄTİRİNÄ Yak. **Kätirinä** [Кӓтipiнӓ], fem. (Pek.). ✧ Yekaterina (R.).

KÄTİRİS Yak. **Kätiris** [Кӓтipic], fem. (Pek.). ✧ Katrisha (Katerinushka) (R.).

KÄTİT-KÄÑİRİ Yak. **Kätit-käñiri** [Кӓтiт Кӓҥipi] (Pek.). ✧ 'Bridge of the nose'? cf. Yak. *käñiri* 'переносье, хребетъ носа' (Pek.).

KÄTİTTÄN-KÄSKİLLÄX Yak. **Kätittän-käskilläχ** [Кӓтiттӓн кӓcкiллӓх], Ürüñ-ayï-toyon's epithet (Pek.).

KÄTKÄ Tat.(Tob.) **Kätkä-balvan** [Кӓткӓ балван] (Proben IV, 270 /336/).

KÄTKÄN Maml. 14th c. **Kätkän** [Кӓткӓн] (Tuhfa 410). ✧ 'He/She's gone'? cf. Maml. *kät-* 'уходить, отправляться' (Tuhfa).

KÄTPĂJİK Tuv. 19th c. **Kätpăjik** [Кӓтпӑцiк] (Proben IX, 98, 109).

KĂJÄY Yak. **Kăjäy / Kădyäy-qïs** [Кӓцӓi, Кӓдjӓi], a demon born from a shamaness, he makes people mad an sick (Pek.).

KĀL-JUMLA Kzk. **Kăl-jumla** [Kăl-Dschumla / Кӑлцумла], Hâmra's sister (Proben III, 452 /527/).

KĀLÜ Crm. **Kălü** [Кӓлÿ], Oraq-mamay-mïrza's

younger brother (Proben VII, 195).

KĀNİKÄY see **QANÏQAY**

KĀRİ-İMAN   Kzk. **Kări-iman** [Käri Iman / Кӑри Iман] (Proben III, 656 /741/). ✦ 'Great true faith'. ⇨ **KERİ + İMAN.**

KĀTİKÄLİR   Yak. **Kătikälir** [Кӑтiкӓлiр], fem. (Pek.). ✦ Katka (R. Катька); dim.-hypoc. of R. fem. *Yekaterina* (Pek.) + dim. suff. *-lĭr.*

KĀTİ   Yak. **Kăti** [Кӑтi], fem. (Pek.). ✦ Katya (Yekaterina) (R.).

KEBE   Kzk. 19th c. **Kebe** [Кебе] (SOK 252); Kzk. 19th c. **Kebe-bay** [Кебебай] (SODž. 144). ✦ 'Tent, small house' cf. Kirg. *kepe* 'шалаш, избушка' (Jud.).

KEBE-TAY   Kzk. 19th c. **Kebe-tay** [Кебетай] (SOV 78). ⇨ **KEBE?** + **TAY** or suff. *-tay(1,2)?*

KEBEY   Hak.(Sag.) **Käbäy** [Кӓбӓй] (Proben IX, 557); Hak. 19th-20th c. **Kebey** [Кебей] (HRS 349). ✦ '?' cf. Hak. PN *Qabay / Kebey* '?' (Butanaev), cf. Alt. *qabay?* 'die Wiege' (Radl. II, 435).

KEBEK   Khorezm. 14th c. **Käbäk**, a prince in Öljeytü's (1304-1316) time (Qazw. 598, 599); Chag. **Käbäk-χan** [Kabak Khán], a Chaghataid (Tar. Rashidi 3); Chag. 1476 **Käbäk-sultan-oγlan** [Kabak Sultán oghlán], from Eastern Turkestan (Tar. Rashidi 90, 91, 95); Chag.? **Käpäk-bäg** (Le Coq, Ind. 4); Tat. 1600 **Kebäk** [Кебяк] (MIB I, 150); Tat. 1600 **Kebäk** [Кебяк Шакеев] (Miller, Ist. Sib. II, 156); Tat.(Tüm.) 1552 **Kebäk / Kebek** [Кѣбякъ-князь / Кебекъ-князь], a prince from Tümen (PSRL XIII, 176, 292); Khorezm.? 1367/68 **Kebek** [كبك الصرغتمشى / Gebeg], a prince in Transoxania (Iyās I, 222, Weil, Chalif. I, 320); Kmk. 1677 **Kebek** [Индырчанъ / Индырчанко Кебековъ] (DAI VII, 252-260); Kzk. 19th c. **Kebek** [Кебекъ] (SODž. 8, 30); Kzk. 19th c. **Kebek** [Кебекъ] (SOK 248); Kirg. **Kebek** [Кебек] (Jud. 65); Maml.? Khorezm.? 1282 **Kebek** [Seïf-eddin-Kebek] (Makrīzī III, 52); Kirg. 19th c. **Kebek-bay** [Кебекбай] (Kalilov 93); Khorezm. 14th c. **Kebek-χan** [Кебекъ-ханъ], Tuva's son (Barth., Ulugb. 8, 9, 14); Kipch.? 14th c. **Kebek-χatun** [الخـاتـون كبك / Kebec khâtoûn], Özbeg Khan's (1312-1341) second wife (Ibn Bat. II, 383, 392); Kzk. 19th c. **Kebek-pay** [Кебекпай] (SOK 14, 72, 90, 106); Kzk. 19th c. **Kebek-pay** [Кебекпай] (SOV 44, 80, 154); Kzk. 19th c. **Kebek-pay** [Кебекпай] (SODž. 30, 64); Kzk. 19th c. **Kepek** [Кепекъ] (AOA 138); Kzk. 19th c. **Kepek** [Кепекъ] (AOO 34); Chag. 16th c. **Kepek-biy** [Кепек-бий] (Ivanov 23); Khorezm. 1322/23 **Kibäk** [Кибякъ] (Aynī/Tizeng. I, 494, 524); Chuv. 18th-19th c. **Kibäk** [Кибякъ] (Magn. 51); Chuv. 18th-19th c. **Kibek** [Кибекъ] (Magn. 50); Kzk. 1822 **Kibek** [Кибекъ Байкубековъ] (TOUAK XXIV, 117); Kzk. 19th c. **Kïbek** [Кыбекъ] (AOO 58). ✦ 'Bran, shorts; dandruff' cf. Karakh. *kebek* 'Kleie, Kopfschuppen' (MK/Brock.); „le mot kebec, en turc

veut dire 'le son (de la farine)' " (Defrémery), Kuman, Crm. *käbäk*, Kzk. *kebäk* 'die Kleie' (Radl. II, 1191), Kirg. *kebek* 'шелуха (проса, ячменя и т. п.); отруби' (Jud.), Tat. *kibäk* 'мякина, отруби' (TatRS), Chag., NUyg.(Tar.), Turk. *käpäk* 'die Kleie, die Schinnen im Haar' (Radl. II, 1186). See also **AX-KİBEK.**

KEBEKČİ   Kzk. 19th c. **Kebekči** [Кебекчи] (SOV 100); Kzk. 19th c. **Kebekči** [Кебекчи] (SOV 98). ⇨ **KEBEK** + suff. *-či.*

KEBEL   Kzk. 19th c. **Kebel-pay** [Кебелпай] (SOK 254).

KEBEN   Kzk. 19th c. **Keben** [Кебенъ] (SOK 282). ✦ 'Haycock' cf. Kzk. *kebän* 'der Heuschober' (Radl. II, 1191-1192).

KEBENÄK   1554 **Kebenäk** [Кебенякъ-князь] (PSRL XIII, 245); Kzk. 19th c. **Kebenek** [Кебенекъ] (SODž. 146); Kzk. 19th c. **Kebenek** [Кебенекъ] (SOK 74). ✦ 'Felt-gown' cf. Kzk. *kebänäk* 'ein Filzrock' (Radl. II, 1192).

KEBES   Bashk. 1734 **Kebes** [Масегутъ Кебесевъ], a tarχan (Vel.-Zern., Bašk. 11); Kzk. **Kibis** [Чингожа Кибисовъ], a Kazak from the county of Semipalatinsk (TV 1876, 129). ✦ I. 'Crooked, inclined, awry' cf. Bashk. *kibes, käweš* 'косой' (BRS/Uraksin); II. 'Proud'? cf. Uyg. *käbäs* 'stolz' (Radl. II, 1193).

KEBİS   Kzk. 19th c. **Kebis-pay** [Кебыспай] (SOV 40). ✦ 'Galoshes' cf. Kzk. *kebis* 'die Galosche' (Radl. II, 1197), 'кожаные галоши (на каблуках)' (KzRS).

KEBLÜ   Turk. 1466 **Keblü-oγlï** [كَبَلو اوغلى] (Āšikp. 164).

KEČÄL   Az. **Kečäl** [Кечаль-Бейде], a man in a tale; as his head was bald he was called *Kečal-Beyde* (Az. Skaz. 540). ✦ 'Bald' (ATSkaz. 540), cf. Chag., Turk. *käčäl* 'kahlköpfig' (Radl. II, 1145). See also **QALDAN, KELEŠ, TAZ.**

KEČERÜK   Karch. **Kečerük** [Кечерюковъ] (Sysoev 132).

KEČİDEK   Khorezm. 1220, 1221 **Kečidek / Keĵidek** [كجيدك / Кеджидек-амирахур], Ĵelāl's (1220-1231) officer, commander of the army, his title was amīr-ī-aχur (Master of the Horse) (Nasawī 68).

KEČİLİ   Maml.? 1335/36 **Kečili** [كجلى] (Iyās I, 168, 187). ✦ 'Having goats' cf. Maml. *käči* 'Ziege' (Tarĵ/Houtsma). + suff. *-li.*

KEČKENE see **KİČKİNE**

KEČKİR   Maml.? 1320 **Kečkir** [كجكـر العلى] (Iyās I, 141).

KEČNEK   Hak. 19th-20th c. **Kečnek** [Кечнек], fem. (HRS 353). ✦ '?' cf. Hak. fem. PN *Kečin / Kečinek* '?' (Butanaev) + suff. *-ek.*

KEČÜ   Kzk. 19th c. **Kečü-bay** [Кечубай] (AOK 30). ✦ 'Wandering, roving'. ⇨ **KEŠÜ.**

KEĴEK see **KEĴİK**

KEJİDEK see **KEČİDEK**

KEJİK Maml. 1299 **Kejek** [Kedjek], among the killers of Lâdjin [Lāčïn?] sultan (Makrīzī IV, 96); Maml. 1264 **Kejik** [Seïf-eddin-Kedjik-Bagdadi] (Makrīzī II, 14). ✧ 'Passage' cf. Uyg. *käjik* 'der Übergang' (Radl. II, 1150).

KED-BORAN Uyg. 13th c. **Ked-boran** [ked boran] (DTS). ✧ 'High-(lit. strong)-whirl-wind' (Bese 15, Blagova 1997, 704), cf. Uyg., Karakh. *ked / ket II* 'сильный, крепкий' (DTS), Mo. *käd* 'gut, tüchtig' (Cleaves 422). ⇨ **KEY + BURAN.**

KED-QAYA Uyg. **Ked-qaya** [ked qaja] (DTS). ✧ 'Strong rock' cf. Uyg., Karakh. *ked / ket II* 'сильный, крепкий' (DTS), Mo. *käd* 'gut, tüchtig' (Cleaves 422). ⇨ **KEY + QAYA.** See also **KED-TAŠ.**

KED-TAŠ Uyg. **Käd-tas** [Käd tas] (EUTS); Uyg. 12th c. - 14th c. **Kät-taš** [Käd (Kät) Taš] (Radl., USp. 258, 215); Uyg. 12th c. - 14th c. **Ked-taš** [ked taš] (DTS). ✧ 'Hard/strong-stone' (Bese 15, Blagova 1997, 714), cf. Uyg., Karakh. *ked / ket II* 'сильный, крепкий' (DTS), Mo. *käd* 'gut, tüchtig' (Cleaves 422). ⇨ **KEY + TAŠ.** See also **KED-QAYA.**

KEDÄY Tat. 1603 **Kedäy** [Кедяй] (Miller, Ist. Sib. II, 180, 181); Kzk. 1823 **Kedey / Kedäy** [كیدای / Кедей] (MIK IV, 458, 462); Kirg. **Kedey-qan** [Кедейкан] (Jud. 686). ✧ 'Poor, miserable' cf. Kzk. *kedäi* (P.) 'arm, dürftig' (Radl. II, 1133), Kirg. *kedey* 'бедный; бедняк' (Jud.).

KEDEY see **KEDÄY**

KEDEL Kzk. **Kedel** [Кеделъ] (ZOOO 1870, 234).

KEDİM Uyg. **Kädim-uruñu** [Kädim Uruñu] (ETY II, 64); Türk 8th c. - 9th c. **Kedim-uruñu** [Kädim Urungu] (Runic Mss. 188, DTS); Kzk. 19th c. **Kiyim-bay** [Киимбай] (SOK 198). ✧ 'Clothes, clothing, suit' cf. Karakh. *kedim / keδim* 'одежда, одеяние' (DTS), Alt., Kzk. *kiyïm* 'die Kleidung' (Radl. II, 1344).

KEDİRÄ Uyg. 12th c. - 14th c. **Kädirä / Kedirä** [Kädirä] (Radl., USp. 83, 86, DTS, EUTS).

KEDİŠ Bashk. 1734 **Kediš** [Укай Кедышев] (MIB III, 322).

KEDRÄS Bashk. 1735 **Kedräs** [Кедрясъ Муллакаевъ], a tarχan (Vel.-Zern., Bašk. 22).

KEGE Kzk. 19th c. **Kege-bay** [Кегебай] (AOP 22).

KEGEY Alt. 19th-20th c. **Kegey** [Кегей], fem. (OjrRS 212).

KEGEM-BAY see **KEGEN**

KEGEN Kzk. 19th c. **Kegem-bay** [Кегембай] (SOV 6, 34); Kzk. 19th c. **Kegem-bay** [Кегембай] (SODž. 134); Pecheneg 1050 **Kegen** [Κεγένης], a commander of the army (Byz. Turc. 158); Kzk. 19th c. **Kegen** [Кегенъ] (SOV 50); Kzk. 19th c. **Kegen-bay** [Кегенбай] (SOK 248); Kzk. 19th c. **Kegen-bek** [Кегенбекъ] (SODž. 6); Kzk. 19th c. **Keken-bay** [Кекенбай] (SOK 100); *TN:* Kzk. 19th c. **Kegen-bay** [Кегенбай], a field between the mountains and the Kegen river (SODž. 280). ✧ Kegen (the name a mountain and a river), according to Kojčubaev (see) it is a variant of OT TN *Kögmen* lit. 'небесные преграды' [=heavenly (sky-high) barriers/ridges]. See also **ALLA-KEGEN.**

KEGLİNČ Karakh.? **Keglinč-tarqan** (DTS).

KEY Türk? 870 **Key-čur** [كیجور التـركی / Keidjur] (Ibn al-Athīr/Tornb. VII, 165, 166, 183, Weil, Chalif. II, 451). ✧ 'Strong; good' cf. Uyg., Karakh. *kej* 'крепко, основательно' (DTS), Uyg. *kät* 'tüchtig, trefflich, fest, gewichtig, zuverlässig' (Radl. II, 1123), Uyg. *ked / ket II.* 'сильный, крепкий' (DTS), Maml. *käi, gäi* 'gut' (Tarǰ/Houtsma), Maml. *key* 'iyi' (Tarǰ/Toparlı), cf. also Mo. PN *Käd Buqa* < *käd* 'gut, tüchtig' (Cleaves 422). See also **KET-BUГA, KET-QARA.**

KEY-ARSLAN Selj. 12th c. **Key-arslan** [محمّـد بن كیارسلان], an emir (Muh. Ibrahim 26). ✧ 'Strong/good lion'. ⇨ **KEY + ARSLAN.**

KEY-DOГDÏ Maml. 1260 **Key-doγdï** [Kidgadi] (Makrīzī I, 90); Maml. 1264 **Key-doγdï** [Ala-eddin-Kaïdagdi-Djeischi], a commander (Makrīzī II, 14); Maml. 1264 **Key-doγdï** [Alem-eddin Kaïdagdi-Dâheri], an emir (Makrīzī II, 14); Maml. 1279 **Key-doγdï** [Kidagdi], emir of the assembly (émir-i-medjlis) (Makrīzī II, 171). ✧ 'Strong/good (man) has been born'. ⇨ **KEY + TOГDÏ.**

KEY-KELDİ Maml. 1320 **Key-keldi** [بـدرالیـن كیكلدی] (Zetterst. 148); Maml. 14th c. **Key-keldi / Käy-keldi** [كَیكَلدي] (Sauvaget 55); Maml. 14th c. **Key-keldi / Käy-keldi** [كَیكلدی / käi-käldi / Keykeldi] (Tarǰ/Houtsma 101, Poppe 1252, Tarǰ/Toparlı 41). ✧ 'Welcome' (Sauvaget 55), 'Strong/good (man) has come'. ⇨ **KEY + KELDİ.**

KEY-KİŠ Kzk. 19th c. **Key-kiš** [Кейкышъ] (SOV 32). ✧ 'Good sable'. ⇨ **KEY + KİŠ.**

KEY-QUWAT Nog. 1649 **Key-quwat** [Кейкуватъ Янмаметъ] (AI IV, 77). ✧ 'Strong/good strength/power'. ⇨ **KEY + QUWAT.**

KEY-TEMİR Maml. 1325 **Key-temir** [كیتمر احو دروط] (Zetterst. 176); Maml. 14th c. **Key-temür / Käy-tämür** [كَیتَمُر / Käy-tämür] (Sauvaget 55). ✧ 'Good/strong iron' (Sauvaget 55); 'Sovereign-iron' (Bese 16). ⇨ **KEY + TEMİR.**

KEYČE see **KEYŽE**

KEYGLÜ Kzk. 19th c. **Keyglü-bay** [Кейглубай] (SOK 162).

KEYİÐ see **KİYİZ**

KEYİK see **KİYİK**

KEYKE Kzk. 19th c. **Keyke** [Койке] (SOV 138). ✧ 'Little good (man)'? ⇨ **KEY + dim. suff. -ke.**

KEYKİMAN Kzk. 19th c. **Keykiman** [Кейкиманъ] (SOV 118); Kzk. 19th c. **Keykiman** [Кейкиманъ]

(SOK 182).

KEYLİ Kzk. 19th c. **Keyli** [Кейлибай] (SOK 64). ✧ 'Strong; good'? ⇨ **KEY?** + suff. *-li*.

KEYME Kzk. 19th c. **Keyme-bay** [Кеймебай] (SOK 124).

KEYNE Kzk. 19th c. **Keyne-bay** [Кейнебай] (SOK 192).

KEYSİK Kzk. 19th c. **Keysik** [Кейсыкъ] (SOK 182).

KEYÜN Kzk. 19th c. **Keyün-bay** [Кеюнбай Дусмагамедовъ] (Grod., Pril. 152).

KEYŽE Kzk. 19th c. **Keyče** [Кейче] (SOK 284); Kzk. 19th c. **Keyže** [Кейже] (AOP 66). ✧ I. 'Different'? cf. Kzk. *key* 'иной' (KzRS); II. 'Little Good'? ⇨ **KEY** + dim. suff. *-še / -če*?

KEKEY Nog. 1649 **Kekey** [Кекѣй] (AI IV, 123).

KEKEL see **KEKİL**

KEKELČE Kzk. 19th c. **Kekelče** [Кекельче] (SOV 118). ⇨ **KEKİL** + suff. *-če*.

KEKEN see **KEGEN**

KEKİ Kzk. 19th c. **Keki-bay** [Май Имканъ Кекибаевъ] (Grod., Pril. 160).

KEKİČ Nog.? 1558 **Kekič-murza** [Кѣкичь-мурза] (PSRL XIII, 289). ✧ 'Stutterer, stammerer'? cf. NUyg.(Tar.), Turk. *käkäč* 'der Stotterer; stumm' (Radl. II, 1060).

KEKİL Trkm. 20th c. **Käkil** [Käkil] (Zaj. 1971, 330); Trkm. 20th c. **Käkil** [Кәкил] (TrkmRS 425); Kzk. 19th c. **Kekel** [Кекель] (SOK 62); Kzk. 19th c. **Kekil** [Кекилъ] (SODž. 1); Kzk. 19th c. **Kekil** [Кекилъ] (SOK 184); Kzk. 19th c. **Kekil-bay** [Кекилъбай] (SOK 100, 280). ✧ 'Mop or tussock (of hair) on the forehead' cf. Kzk. *kekil* 'die Haarbüschel, die man auf den Vorderköpfen der Knaben nicht abrasirt' (Radl. II, 1061), Trkm. *käkil* 'взбитая прядь волос надо лбом; кок' (TrkmRS) (<P.).

KEKİN Kzk. 19th c. **Kekin** [Кекинъ Айчуваковъ] (AUK 759).

KEKİŠ Kzk. 19th c. **Kekiš** [Кекишъ] (SOV 14); Kzk. 19th c. **Kekiš** [Кекишъ] (SODž. 46). ✧ 'Stammering, stutterer' cf. Kzk. *kekeš* 'id.' (KzRS).

KEKİZ Kzk. 19th c. **Kekiz-bay** [Кекизъ-бай Ишъ-Ходжаевъ] (Grod., Pril. 50). ✧ 'Friendly; talkative' cf. Turk. *käkiz* 'gefällig, willfährig; der Sodomite' (Radl. II, 1061).

KEKLİK Maml.? **Keklik / Keygülüg?** [اسحـاق بـن كيفـلغ] (Kamāladdīn I, 97, 105, 127).

KEL Tat.(Lit.) 1591 **Kel-bek** [Сулиманъ Келбекевичъ] (Lit. Tat. 82); Bashk. 1710 **Kel-čura** [Келчюра Кемяков] (MIB III, 66); Bashk. 1722 **Kel-čura** [Мокша Келчюра] (MIB I, 119); Bashk. 1730 **Kel-čura** [Келчюра] (MIB III, 277); Bashk. 1722, 1724 **Kel-čura-bay / Kel-čura** [Келчюра-бай Кисмяков / Келчюра Кесмяков] (MIB I, 109, III, 222); Chuv. 18th-19th c. **Kil-bay** [Килбай] (Magn.

51); Tat. 20th c. **Kil-bay** [Килбай] (Sattarov); Chuv. 18th-19th c. **Kil-bey** [Килбей] (Magn. 51); Tat.(Mish.) 1755 **Kil-čura** [Килчюра Юлаев] (MIB IV/1, 93); Bashk. 1735 **Kil-čura** [Килчура Кутлуметевъ], a tarχan (Vel.-Zern., Bašk. 16); Bashk. 1787 **Kil-čura** [Килчура Смаков] (MIB V, 211); Chuv. 18th-19th c. **Kil-murza** [Килмурза] (Magn. 51). ✧ 'Come (=be born)' (Sattarov), cf. Türk, Uyg., Kuman, Chag., Alt., Crm., Kar., etc. *käl-* 'kommen, ankommen' (Radl. II, 1109). See also **AY-KEL, AYDAP-KEL, ALİP-KEL, AR-KİL, AS-KİL, BAY-GEL, BAYDA-KEL, ǰAN-GEL, GEL-BERİ, İSÄN-KİL, İŠ-KİL, KÖRİN-KEL, QOY-KEL, QUDA-GEL, NAR-KEL, SAN-GEL, ŠAWÏP-KEL, TUR-GEL, URUS-KİL.**

KEL-MAMET Tat.(Sib.) 1623 **Kel-mamet** [Келмамет] (Miller, Ist. Sib. II, 291, 300); Tat. 18th-19th c. **Kil-mamet** [Килмаметъ] (Magn. 51); Uzb. 1696 **Kil-mamet** [Кильмаметъ], a khan in Khiva (DAI X, 384); Tat. 20th c. **Kil-mämät** [Килмəмəт] (Sattarov); Chuv. 18th-19th c. **Kil-memet** [Килмеметъ] (Magn. 51); Tat.(Mish.) 18th c. **Kil-muχammed** [Килмухаммедъ] (Nepljuev 879-90). ✧ 'Come!-Muχammed'? cf. Bashk. PN *Kil-möχämät*, (Kusimova), cf. also Tat. PN *Kil-möχämmät, Kil-mämät* 'Möχämmätneñ ayaq astïndaγï tufraγï' (!) (Sattarov). ⇨ **KEL?** + **MUXAMMED**. See also **KELİMBET**.

KELBÄS see **KELMÄZ**

KELBE Karakh.? 9th c.? **Kelbe-tegin** [كلبا تـكين التـركى] (Ibn al-Athīr/Tornb. VII, 95); Karakh.? 865 **Kelbe-tegin** [كلبا تـكين] (Tabarī, Annal. III, 1523, 1543, 1544, 1555).

KELBİR Kzk. 19th c. **Kelbir-bek** [Кельбырбекъ] (SOV 104).

KELDEBÄN see **KELDEMÄN**

KELDEK Kzk. 19th c. **Keldek / Keltek** [Кельдекъ / Кельтекъ] (SOK 216). ✧ 'Short stick'? cf. Chag. *kältäk* 'ein kurzer Stock, Prügel' (Radl. II, 1122).

KELDEMÄN Tat. 1635 **Keldebän / Keldeban?** [Мурзогилдей Келдебанов] (Miller, Ist. Sib. II, 430, 473); Tat. 1600 **Keldemän, Keldiman?** [Токмаметъ Келдеманов] (MIB I, 152); Tat. 1596, 1603 **Keldemän / Kildemän** [Келдеман / Килдеман] (Miller, Ist. Sib. II, 148, 179, 181). ⇨ **KELDİ?** + suff. *-män?*

KELDİ Kzk. 1877 **Geldi-bay** [Ходжа Гельдибай Болсуновъ] (Grod., Pril. 129); Trkm. 1804 **Geldi-χan** [Гельди-хан], from the İmreli tribe (MIT II, 356, 358, 364, 368, 376, 387, 403, 434, 438); Trkm. 1879-1881 **Geldi-χan** [Geldi Khan] (O'Donovan I, 207); Trkm. 1829 **Geldi-χan-serdar** [Гельди-хан-сердар] (MIT II, 456); Yürük 1543 **Geldi-χatun** [Geldi Hatun], a man(!) (Gökb., Rum. 189); Kzk. 19th c. **Kelde-bay** [Кельдебай] (AOK 62); Tat.(Lit.) 1592 **Kelde-bek** [Келдабакъ Бойтушевич] (Lit. Tat. 124); Kzk. 19th

c. **Kelde-bek** [Кельдебекъ] (AOK 114); Nog. 20th c. **Keldi** [Акъманълай Келди къызы Сали келинъи], father of Aq-mañlay, one of Baskakov's informants from the aul of Ïrγaqlï (Bask., Nog. 143); Uzb. 20th c. **Keldi** [Келди] (Begmatov 1984, 202); Kzk. 19th c. **Keldi / Keldï** [Хусейнъ Ходжа Кельдыевъ] (Grod., Pril. 115); Kzk. 19th c. **Keldi-bay** [Кельдыбай] (AOA 70); Kzk. 19th c. **Keldi-bay** [Кельдыбай] (AOO 34); Kzk. 1817 **Keldi-bay / Kildi-bay** [كيلدى باى / Кельдибай] (MIK IV, 308); Tat.(Mish.) **Keldi-bek** (IOAIÊK XIX, 142); Kzk. 19th c. **Keldi-bek** [Кельдибекъ] (SOV 22); Kzk. 19th c. **Keldi-bek** [Кельдибекъ] (AOK 2, 106); Tat.(Lit.) 1566 **Keldi-yar** [Келдияръ], a Tatar nobleman (boyarin) (Lit. Tat. 4, 7); Chag. 16th c. **Keldi-yar-bahadur** [Кельди-Яр-бахадур], an emir(-zade) (Ivanov 211); Uzb. 20th c. **Keldi-yâr** [Келдиёр] (Begmatov 1984, 202); Uzb. 20th c. **Keldi-qul** [Келдикул] (Begmatov 1984, 202); Kzk. 19th c. **Keldi-pï-γul?** [Кельдпеегулъ] (SODž. 76); Chuv. 18th-19th c. **Kilde** [Килда] (Magn. 51); Bashk. 1798 **Kilde-γul** [Кильдегулъ] (PSZRI XXV, 195); Tat. 20th c. **Kilde-yar** [Килдеяр / Килдеяров] (Sattarov); Bashk. 20th c. **Kilde-yar** [Килдеяр] (Kusimova); Chuv. 18th-19th c. **Kildi** [Килды] (Magn. 51); Bashk. 1709 **Kildi-bay** [Килдибай Акгилдеев] (MIB I, 264); Chuv. 18th-19th c. **Kildi-bäk** [Килдыбякъ] (Magn. 51); Kzk. 17th c. **Kildi-bäk** [Ахпердя мурза Килдибяковъ], near Kazan (IOAIÊK XXIX, 313); Chuv. 18th-19th c. **Kildi-bey** [Килдибей] (Magn. 51); Kuman? / Tat.? 1360, 1361 **Kildi-bek / Kildi-bik** [Килдибекъ / Килдибѣкъ / Кылдибикъ / Килдибекъ], a prince (ruler) of the Horde (PSRL IV, 64, V, 229, VIII 11, X, 233, XVI, 90); Bashk. 1756 **Kildi-yar** [Килдияр Метеев] (MIB IV/1, 123); Bashk. 1787 **Kildi-yar** [Килдияр] (MIB V, 211); *EN:* Kzk. 18th c. - 19th c. **Keldi-bay** [Кельдыбай] (Tynyšp. 74); Kzk. 18th c. - 19th c. **Keldi-bek** [Кельдыбек] (Tynyšp. 68); Kzk. 18th c. - 19th c. **Keldi-γul** [Кельдыгул] (Tynyšp. 71); *TN:* Crm. **Kelde-bay**, a place in the north-west of Crimea (Jervis III); Kzk. **Kelde-bay** [Кельдебай], a field (Krasovskij 381). ✧ 'He/she has come (=has been born)' cf. Türk, Uyg., Kuman, Chag., Alt., Crm., Kar., etc. *käl-* 'kommen, ankommen' (Radl. II, 1109), Tat. *kil-* 'to come, to arrive'. Cf. also Bashk. PN *Kildi-yar* 'A friend came (was born)' (Kusimova); *Keldi-bek* 'появившийся на свет крепким [=born to be strong]' (Gafurov 43). See also **ABÏZ-GİLDİ, AY-KELDİ, AQ-KİLDİ, AQÏS-KİLDİ, AL-GİLDE, AMAN-GELDİ, AN-GİLDİ, ANNA-KELDİ, AR-GİLDİ, ARAZ-GELDİ, AS-KİLDE, ATA-KELDİ, BAXŠÏ-GELDİ, BAXTÏ-KELDİ, BAY-GELDİ, BAYRAM-GELDİ, BAŠÏ-GİLDİ, BAZAR-KELDİ, BEK-KELDİ, Bİ-GELDİ, ČİN-GİLDİ, ČURA-KİLDE, ĴAN-KELDİ, ĴİL-KELDİ, ĴİN-GİLDİ, ĴUMA-KELDİ, DEM-GELDİ, DÄWLÄT-KELDİ, DOST-KELDİ, EL-KELDİ, EP-KELDİ, ES-KELDİ, EŠ-KELDİ, ESÄN-KELDİ, EŽİ-GÄLDİ, GİČ-GELDİ, XAĴİ-GELDİ, XAN-GELDİ, XOŠ-KELDİ, XODAY-KELDİ, XOĴA-KELDİ, İMEN-GİLDE, İS-KELDİ, YAŠ-KİLDİ, YAQŠÏ-GİLDİ, YAW-GİLDİ, YAZ-GELDİ, KEY-KELDİ, KÖČ-KELDİ, KÖP-KELDİ, KÜN-GİLDİ, KÜS-KİLDE, KÜZÜ-GİLDE, QAQA-GELDİ, QAL-KELDİ, QAN-KELDİ, QANAL-GELDİ, QANÏ-GİLDE, QAS-KELDİ, QAT-KELDİ, QOY-GELDİ, QOŠ-KİLDİ, QOZAQ-KİLDE, QOŽA-GELDİ, QUČ-KELDİ, QUDA-GELDİ, QUL-GİLDE, QUNAQ-KİLDİ, QURAT-GELDİ, QURBAN-GELDİ, QURT-GELDİ, QUT-KELDİ, QUTLU-GİLDİ, QUZLA-GİLDİ, MAL-GELDİ, MAN-GİLDİ, MEÑLİ-GELDİ, MES-GİLDİ, MULLA-GİLDİ, MÏRZA-GELDİ, NAR-KELDİ, NŌBAT-GELDİ, NUR-KELDİ, OΓÏL-KELDİ, OLĴA-GELDİ, ORAQ-GELDİ, ORAZ-KELDİ, OS-KİLDİ, POYAN-GİLDE, POS-KİLDE, RÏS-KELDİ, SAFAR-GELDİ, SAV-KELDİ, SULTAN-GELDİ, SOTİN-GİLDİ, ŠAD-GELDİ, ŠAH-KELDİ, TAY-GELDİ, TAMU-GELDİ, TERE-GİLDİ, TİN-GİLDE, TOY-GİLDE, TOL-KİLDE, TON-GİLDE, TOS-KİLDE, TÖRE-KELDİ, TUR-GELDİ, TURA-KELDİ, TUVAN-GİLDE, TÜMÄN-GİLDE, TÜBE-GELDİ, UΓUR-GELDİ, US-KİLDE, UŠ-KİLDİ, ÜSEN-GİLDE, ÜZÜ-GELDİ, ZİW-GİLDE.**

KELDİ-BOQ-BASAR Bashk. **Keldi-boq-basar** [Бюляк Келдибокбасаров] (MIB I, 199). ⇨ **KELDİ + BOQ-BASAR.**

KELDİ-MAXMUD Chag. 15th c. - 16th c. **Kildi-maχmud-sultan** [كيلدى محمد سلطان], a Sheybanid (Šejb. LI, LXXVIII). ⇨ **KELDİ + MAXMUD.**

KELDİ-MUXAMMAD Uzb. 20th c. **Keldi-muχammad** [Келдимухаммад] (Begmatov 1984, 202); Tat. 20th c. **Kilde-möχämmät** [Килдемөхәммәт] (Sattarov). ⇨ **KELDİ + MUXAMMED.**

KELDİ-MURAT Uzb. 20th c. **Keldi-murât** [Келдимурод] (Begmatov 1984, 202). ⇨ **KELDİ + MURAT.**

KELDİ-MURZA Uzb. 20th c. **Keldi-mirza** [Келдимирза] (Begmatov 1984, 202). ⇨ **KELDİ + MURZA.**

KELDİ-URAZ Bashk. 1695 **Kelt-uras (<Keldi-uraz)** [Келтурас] (MIB I, 90). ⇨ **KELDİ + ORAZ.**

KELDİŠ Bashk. 1734 **Keldiš** [Чюраш Келдышев] (MIB III, 325); Chuv. 18th-19th c. **Kildeš** [Килдешъ] (Magn. 51); Tat. 20th c. **Kildeš / Keldiš** [Килдеш /

Келдыш] (Sattarov); Chuv. 18th-19th c. **Kildeš / Kildäš?** [Килдашъ] (Magn. 51); Bashk. 1740 **Kildeš / Kildäš?** [Кудряс Килдашев] (MIB I, 395); *TN:* Chuv. 18th c. **Kildiš(eva)** [Килдишева], a village in the district of Yadrinsk (Korsakov 308). ⇨ **KELDİ + EŠ** + suff. *-(i)š?*

KELDİŠTÜK Nog. 1540 **Keldištük?** [Келдищдукъ] (PSRL XIII, 131-132). ⇨ **KELDİŠ?** + suff. *-tük / -tik.*

KELE Kuman **Kele-bi?** [Keleby], originally an anthroponym preserved in the name of a village in the south of Lesser Kumania, Hungary (cf. Iványi, Bács-Bodrog vármegye helynévtára I., 80) (Rásonyi, KÖA 111-112, Rásonyi, Anthr. 142). ✦ 'Let him come (=be born)'?; According to L. Rásonyi it is the optative of *kel-.* ⇨ **KELİ / KEL.**

KELEY see **KİLEY**

KELEK Oghuz/Trkm. 1372 **Kelek** [Келек] (MIT I, 515); Yürük 1543 **Kelek** [كلك] (Gökb., Rum. 185); Alt.(Tel.) 19th c. **Kelek** [Келекъ] (Potanin IV, 293). ✦ I. 'Melon'?; II. 'A kind of float of the nomad made of leather hose (bottle)' cf. Turk. *käläk* 'ein Floss, welches auf aufgeblasenen Ledersäcken befestigt ist, wie man solche zu Fahrten auf dem Euphrat und Tigris benutzt; eine schlechte, unreife Melone' (Radl. II, 1112).

KELEKE Kzk. 19th c. **Keleke** [Келеке] (SODž. 12). ✦ 'Mocking, mock' cf. Kzk. *keläkä* 'die Verspottung, der Spott' (Radl. II, 1112).

KELEM-BERDİ Tat.(Lit.) 1646 **Kelem-berdi(y)** [Келембердей] (Lit. Tat. 336). ✦ '(Nice) Word-gave; Talker-given'? cf. Crm., Turk. *kälam* 'das Word' (Radl. II, 1112), Tat. PN *Kälim* (Sattarov). ⇨ **BERDİ.**

KELEMČİ Alt. 19th-20th c. **Kelemči** [Келемчи], fem. (OjrRS 212).

KELEMET Balk. **Kelemet** [Келеметовъ], a chief („prince") of the mountaineers (таубiй) (Karaulov 67).

KELEN Kzk. 19th c. **Kelem-bay (Kelen-bay)** [Келембай] (SODž. 34); Kzk. 19th c. **Kelen** [Келенъ] (SODž. 98). ✦ 'Bachelor' cf. Kzk. East. dial. *keleñ* 'бойдақ, көп уақытқа дейін үйленбеген жігіт' (QTDS). See also **BUYDAQ, QAS-KELİN.**

KELEÑ Alt. 19th-20th c. **Keleñ** [Келен], fem. (OjrRS 212).

KELES Kzk. 19th c. **Keles-pay** [Келеспай] (SOV 112). ✦ 'Suitable, lovable' cf. Kzk. *kelis-siz(!)* 'yakışıksız, sevimsiz' (KzTS), also Kzk. PN *Kelis* (Žanuzakov-Esbaeva).

KELEŠ Turk. 20th c. **Keleš** [Keleş] (Önder, Göle). ✦ 'Bald' cf. Turk. *keleş* 'grindköpfig, Glatzkopf, kahl' (HŞ). See also **QALDAN, KEČÄL, TAZ.**

KELGÄNDEK Uzb. 20th c. **Kelgändek** [Келгандек] (Begmatov 1984, 202). ⇨ **KELGEN** + suff. *-dek/-dik.*

KELGEN Uzb. 20th c. **Kelgän** [Келган] (Begmatov 1984, 203); Uzb. 20th c. **Kelgän-ây** [Келганой], fem. (Begmatov 1984, 203); Uzb. 20th c. **Kelgän-bây** [Келганбой] (Begmatov 1984, 203); Kzk. 19th c. **Kelgem-bay (Kelgen-bay)** [Кельгембай] (SOV 40, 54); Kzk. 19th c. **Kelgem-bay (Kelgen-bay)** [Кельгембай] (SOK 64); Maml. 14th c. **Kälgän** [Кäлгäн] (Tuhfa 410); Kzk. 19th c. **Kelgen** [Кельгенъ] (SOK 228); Kzk. 19th c. **Kelgen / Kelken?** [Келкенъ] (AOO 38); Kzk. 19th c. **Kelgen-bay** [Кельгенбай] (SOK 110, 152, 228); Kzk. 19th c. **Kelgen-bay** [Кельгенбай] (SOV 110). ✦ 'He/she has come (has been born)'. ⇨ **KEL** + dev. suff. *-gen.* See also **KÄTKÄN.**

KELİ Kzk. 19th c. **Keli-bay** [Келибай] (SODž. 42); Kzk. 19th c. **Kilï-bay** [Килыбаевъ] (Grod., Pril. 86); Kzk. 19th c. **Kili-bay** [Укманъ Килибаевъ] (Grod., Pril. 75); Kzk. 19th c. **Kïlï-bay** [Кылыбай] (SOK 182). ✦ I. 'Mortar' cf. Tat. *kilï* 'der Mörser' (Radl. II, 1369), Kzk. *keli* 'der Mörser' (Radl. II, 1116), Kzk. *kelï* 'ступа' (RKzS); II. 'Mug, dumbhead, slob' Kirg. *kelebay* 'олух', *kele* 'рогатый скот, корова' (Jud.).

KELİMBET Bashk. 1735 **Kelimbet** [Келимбеть Уразовъ], a tarɣan (Vel.-Zern., Bašk. 13); Kzk. 19th c. **Kelimbet** [Келимбетъ] (SOV 82); Kzk. 19th c. **Kelimbet** [Келимбетъ] (AOK 102); Nog. 1649 **Kelimbet** [Келимбетъ], a murza (AI IV, 87); Tat. 20th c. **Kilembät** [Килембəт] (Sattarov); Bashk. 1754 **Kilimbet** [Казакай Килимбетев] (MIB IV/1, 84). ⇨ **KEL** + suff. *-imbet.* See also **KEL-MAMET.**

KELİÑ Turk. **Keliñ-oɣlu** (Giese 58). ✦ 'Son of the daughter-in-law' cf. in several Trk. languages: *kälin, kelin* 'die Schwiegertochter' (Radl. II, 1117).

KELİRÄK Bashk. 1675 **Keliräk** [Келирак Минлигозин] (MIB I, 200).

KELKEN see **KELGEN**

KELLEJİ Turk. **Kelleji-oɣlu**, a Zeybek (Kúnos 1891, 119). ✦ 'Maker or seller of a certain kind of food (cake)' cf. Turk. *kelle* 'içerisine ceviz, fındık, pirinç ve saire konulan, tencerede pışırılan bir çeşit hamur yemeği' (SDD II, 872).

KELMÄY Tat. 1724 **Kelmäy** [Кулметь Келмаев] (MIB III, 227); Tat. 1661 **Kelmey** [Чюмашко Келмеев] (MIB I, 159); Tat.(Mish.) 18th c. **Kilmäy** [Иткай Килмаевъ] (Nepljuev 194); Bashk. 1745 **Kilmäy** [Итиней Килмаев] (MIB III, 548). ✦ 'He isn't coming; he won't be born'. ⇨ **KEL.** See also **KELMÄZ.**

KELMÄZ Karg. **Kelbäs** [Келбäс] (Katanov, Otč. 8); Bashk. 1715 **Kelmäs** [Кельмесь Тыбаев] (MIB III, 124); Bashk. 1707 **Kilmäs** [Килмясь Уразаев] (MIB III, 39); Bashk. 1749 **Kilmäs** [Бектемир Кильмясев] (MIB III, 460); Bashk. 1795 **Kilmäs** [Беиула Кильмясова] (IOAIÊK XXVIII, 540). ✦ 'He/she won't come, won't be born'. ⇨ **KEL.** See also **KELMÄY.**

KELMEKEY Bashk. 1706 **Kelmekey** [Келмекей

Шаликеев] (MIB III, 27); Bashk. 1706 **Kelmekey** [Келмекей] (MIB III, 27); Bashk. 1735 **Kelmekey** [Келмекей Шигаевъ] (Vel.-Zern., Bašk. 22). ⇨ **KİLMÄK?** + suff. -*ey*.

KELMEN   Tat.(Mish.) 1708 **Kelmän** [Келманко Кулаев] (MIB I, 225); Kzk. 19th c. **Kelmen** [Кельменъ] (SODž. 22); Kzk. 19th c. **Kelmen** [Кельменъ] (SOK 64, 102). ⇨ **KEL?** + suff. -*men?*

KELMENTEY   Tat.(Sib.) 1600 **Kelmentäy** [Сальнян Келментаев] (Miller, Ist. Sib. II, 159); Tat.(Sib.) 1600 **Kelmentey** [Тугака Келментеев] (Miller, Ist. Sib. II, 159); Tat. 1600 **Kelmentey** / **Kelmentäy** [Тугона Келментеев (Келментаев)] (MIB I, 152); Tat. 1600 **Kelmentey** / **Kelmentäy** [Саиняк Келментеев (Келментаев)] (MIB I, 152). ⇨ **KELMEN?** + suff. -*tey*.

KELMİŠ   Khorezm.? 13th c. **Kelmiš-aqa** [اقا کالمیش / Кальмишъ-ака], an Ilkhanid princess (RaD/Ber. I, 150, 167, RaD II, 202); Khorezm.? 13th c. **Kilmiš-aɣa** [Гильмиш-Агга], from the Qoñyrats (Šejb. XLIX). ✧ 'He/she came (was born)'. ⇨ **KEL.** See also **İL-KÄLMİŠ.**

KELPİNEK   Kzk. 19th c. **Kelpinek** [Кельпинекъ] (SODž. 140).

KELSİN   Uzb. 20th c. **Kelsin-bây** [Келсинбой] (Begmatov 1984, 203); Uzb. 20th c. **Kelsin-χân** [Келсинхон] (Begmatov 1984, 203); Uzb. 20th c. **Kelsin-χoĵa** [Келсинхўжа] (Begmatov 1984, 203); Uzb. 20th c. **Kelsin-qul** [Келсинқул] (Begmatov 1984, 203). ✧ 'Let him come! May he be born!'. ⇨ **KEL** + imp. suff. -*sin*.

KELT-URAS see **KELDİ-URAZ**

KELTÄ   Bashk. 1760 **Keltä** [Келта Ниязов] (MIB IV/1, 187). ✧ 'Short' cf. Kirg., Kzk., *keltä*, Chag., Tat. *kältä* 'kurz' (Radl. II, 1121).

KELTEŠ   Kzk. 19th c. **Kelteš** [Кельтешъ] (AOK 94).

KELZÄ   Uyg. 1341 **Kelzä-tegin**, „Scholasticus" (Chwol., Syr.-nest. (NF) 36).

KELŽE   Kzk. 19th c. **Kelže-bay** [Кельжебай] (SODž. 108). ✧ 'Iranian nomad' cf. Chag. *kälčä* 'die als Nomaden lebenden Ureinwohner von Kokand iranischer Abstammung' (Radl. II, 1122-23).

KEM   Kzk. 19th c. **Kem-baba** [Кембаба] (SOV 84); Kzk. 19th c. **Kem-bay (<Ken-bay?)** [Кембай] (SOV 78, 148); Kzk. 19th c. **Kem-bay (<Ken-bay?)** [Кембай] (SODž. 130). ✧ 'Little/few; insufficient, week, poor' cf. Kzk. *kem* (<P.) 'wenig, unzureichend' (Radl. II, 1204). ⇨ **KEN?** See also **DURDİ-KEM, QÏLİČ-KEM.**

KEM-URUS   Tat.(GH)? 1503 **Kem-urus** [Кемъ-Урусъ], envoy of the Horde (PSRL VI, 49, 244, VIII, 243, XII, 257). ⇨ **KEM?** + **URUS.**

KEMAL   Kkalp. 20th c. **Kämal** [Кәмал] (KkRS 774); Trkm. 20th c. **Kemal** [Kemal] (Zaj. 1971, 327); Trkm. 20th c. **Kemāl** [Кемал] (TrkmRS 390); Kzk. 19th c. **Kemel** [Кемелевъ] (AOK 102); Kzk. 19th c. **Kemel-bay** [Кемельбай] (SOK 112); Kzk. 19th c. **Kemel-bay** [Кемельбай] (AOO 18); Kzk. 19th c. **Kemel-bay** [Кемельбай] (SODž. 140); Kzk. 19th c. **Kemel-bek** [Кемельбекъ] (SOK 6); Hak. 19th-20th c. **Qamal** [Камал] (HRS 349); Uyg. 12th-14th c. **Qamal-ügä-ïnal-buyat** [Qamal ügä ïnal buyat] (Müller, Pfahl.). ✧ 'Perfect, faultless; perfection, completeness' cf. Karakh. *kämal / kemal* 'совершенный' (DTS), Trkm. *kemāl* 'совершеннолетие, зрелость; совершенство' (TrkmRS), Kzk. *kemel* 'arzusuna erişmek, herşeyin mükemmel olması' (KzTS), cf. Ar. PN *Kamal* 'perfection, completion, integrity' (Ahmed), see also Kzk. PNs *Kamal, Kemel, Kemel-bay, Kemel-bek* (Žanuzakov-Esbaeva). See also **ÄBDİ-KÄMAL, SEYİT-KÄMAL.**

KEMÄK   Bashk. **Kemäk** [Келчюра Кемяков] (MIB III, 66). ✧ Ethn. *Kimäk?* ⇨ **KEMEK?**

KEMÄÑGÄR   Kzk. **Kemäñgär** [Кемäнгäр] (Proben III, 50 /65/). ✧ 'Wise' cf. Kirg. *kemenger* 'мудрый' (Jud.).

KEME   Kzk. 19th c. **Keme-bay** [Кемебай] (SOK 132). ✧ 'Boat' cf. Kuman, Chag., Alt., East.T. *kämä* 'das Boot', Hak.(Kacha, Koyb., Sag.), Kirg., Kzk. *kemä* 'id.' (Radl. II, 1205), Bashk. *kämä* 'лодка, ялик, чёлн, шлюпка' (BRS). See also **QAYÏQ.**

KEMEY   Tat.(Mish.) 1682 **Kemey** [Аюкайка Кемѣев] (AI V, 139); Bashk. 1711 **Kemey** [Сеит Кемеев] (MIB III, 77); Bashk. 1711 **Kemey** [Баймурат Кемеев] (MIB III, 77); Bashk. 1757 **Kimey** [Кимей Бикметев] (MIB IV/1, 146); Bashk. 1761 **Kimey** [Султи Кимеев] (MIB IV/1, 204); *TN:* Bashk. 1706, 1710, 1714, 1717, **Kemeyeva** [Кемеева], a village (MIB III, 19, 64, 70, 113, 155 etc.). ✧ I. 'Little boat'? II. 'Intimate (heart-to-heart) lady-friend' cf. Bashk. *kemäy (äχirät)* 'наперсница, задушевная подруга' (BRS/Uraksin). ⇨ **KEME** + suff. -*y.*

KEMEK   Kzk. 19th c. **Kemek** [Кемекъ] (SOK 162, 246). ⇨ **KEMÄK?**

KEMEM-BAY see **KEMEN**

KEMEN   Kzk. 19th c. **Kemem-bay (<Kemen-bay)** [Кемембай] (SODž. 104); Kzk. **Kemen** [Кемень] (Vasil'ev 11). ✧ 'A kaftan made of felt' cf. Kirg. *kemän* 'ein Filzrock' (Radl. II, 1206).

KEMENČE   Kuman 1290 **Kemenče** [Kemenche], a Kuman nobleman (SRH I, 474). ✧ 'Violin, fiddle; archery bow' (Rásonyi, KÖA 112, Rásonyi, Anthr. 142), cf. Turk. *kämänče* (P.) 'a little archery bow; a smallsize violin' (Redh.).

KEMENK   Turk. **Kemenk-oɣlu** (Kúnos 1891, 119). ✧ 'Fish spear; harpoon' cf. Turk. dial. *kemenk* 'okun veya zıpkının sivri ucu; balıkçı zıpkını' (SDD).

KEMER see **KEMİR**

KEMGİL Kzk. 19th c. **Kemgil** [Кемгилъ] (AOP 10).

KEMİL Kzk. 19th c. **Kemil-bay** [Кемильбай] (SOK 172). ✧ Kamil (Ar.) 'perfect, complete, genuine' (Ahmed), cf. also Kzk. PN *Kämil-bek* (Žanuzakov-Esbaeva).

KEMİR Kzk. 19th c. **Kemer-bay** [Кемербай] (SODž. 140); Kzk. 19th c. **Kemer-bay** [Кемербай] (SOV 22, 100); Kzk. 19th c. **Kemer-bay** [Кемербай] (SOK 194); Kzk. 19th c. **Kemir** [Кемиръ] (SOV 30); Kzk. 19th c. **Kemir-bay** [Кемирбай] (SODž. 64); Kzk. 19th c. **Kemir-bek** [Кемирбекъ] (SOV 58). ✧ I. 'Chew!'? cf. Kzk. *kemïr-* 'nagen, benagen' (Radl. II, 1209); II. 'Belt, girdle' cf. Kzk. *kemer* 'kemer, deriden süslenerek yapılan kemer' (KzTS). See also **TAŠ-KEMİR**.

KEMİR-BULAT Kzk. 19th c. **Kemir-bulat** [Кемирбулатъ] (SOK 78). ⇨ **KEMİR + BULAT**.

KEMİREK Kzk. 19th c. **Kemirek** [Кемирекъ] (SOK 112). ⇨ **KEMİR?** + suff. *-ek*.

KEMİŠ Kzk. 19th c. **Kemiš** [Кемишъ] (SODž. 26). ✧ I. 'Overthrow (the enemy)' cf. Kuman *kemiš-* 'nieder-, fort-, wegwerfen' (CC); II. 'Deficiency, scantiness' cf. Kzk. *kemis, kemistik* 'недостаток, недочёт' (KzRS).

KEMKE Kzk. 19th c. **Kemke** [Кемке] (AOAtb. 30). ⇨ **KEM?** + dim. suff. *-ke*.

KEMPİR Kzk. 19th c. **Kempïr** [Кемпыръ] (SOK 30); Kzk. 19th c. **Kempïr** [Кемпыръ] (AOA 114); Kzk. 19th c. **Kempïr** [Кемпыръ] (Potanin II, 4); Kzk. 19th c. **Kempïr / Kemper?** [Кемперъ] (AOK 54); Kzk. 19th c. **Kempïr-bay / Kemper-bay?** [Кемпербай] (SOK 84). ✧ 'Old woman' cf. Kzk. *kempïr* 'ein altes Weib' (Radl. II, 1216). See also **BAY-KEMPİR, BES-KEMPİR, ÜČ-KEMPİR**.

KEMPİREK Kzk. 19th c. **Kempïrek / Kemperek** [Кемперекъ] (SOK 280); Kzk. 19th c. **Kemprek** (<**Kempïrek**) [Кемпрекъ] (SOV 8). ✧ 'Little old woman'. ⇨ **KEMPİR** + dim. suff. *-ek*.

KEMPİREŠ Kzk. 19th c. **Kempreš** (<**Kempïreš**) [Нисанъ Кемпрешевъ], a Kazak from Kopal (Pantusov, Kirg. 23). ✧ 'Little old woman'. ⇨ **KEMPİR** + dim. suff. *-eš*.

KEMPİŠ Kzk. 19th c. **Kempiš** [Кемпишъ] (SOK 172); Kzk. 19th c. **Kempiš** [Кемпышъ] (SOV 130).

KEMPREK see **KEMPİREK**

KEMPREŠ see **KEMPİREŠ**

KEN Kzk. **Ken?** [Бырубай Кеневъ] (Konšin, Oč. 123); Kzk. 19th c. **Ken-bay** [Кенбай] (AOP 62); Kzk. 19th c. **Ken-bay** [Кенбай] (SOK 88, 154, 204, 210); Kzk. 19th c. **Ken-bay** [Кенбай] (SODž. 16, 78). ✧ 'Mineral'? cf. Kzk. *ken* 'id.' (KzRS), also Kzk. PN *Ken-bay* (Žanuzakov-Esbaeva). ⇨ **KEM?**

KENČ Trkm. 1598 **Gänč / Gänj-ali-χan** [Гяндж-Али-ханъ] (MIT II, 90); Uyg. **Känč-oγlan** [Känç oğlan] (EUTS); Uyg. **Känč-tängrim** [Känç Tängrim] (EUTS); Uyg. 8th c. - 12th c. **Kenč-täñrim** [Känč tängrim], a princess (Müller, Pfahl. 10); *TN:* Uzb.? / Kzk. **Kenč-pï** [كنج پى / Кунжупай?], a kyshlak (settlement, winter pasture) in the district of Katta-Kurgan, Uzbekistan (ZIRGOStat. IV). ✧ I. 'Child (=young)' cf. Uyg. *kenč* 'ребенок' (DTS), Turk. *gänj* 'jung, frisch, neu' (Radl. II, 1554); II. 'Treasure; riches, wealth' cf. Uyg. *gänj* (<P.) 'сокровисжеъ богатство' (DTS).

KENČ-BERSÜ Uyg. 12th c. - 14th c. **Kenč-bersü** (DTS). ✧ 'Child be given' (Blagova 1997, 716). ⇨ **KENČ**.

KENČ-ESTEMİ Uyg. **Känč-ästämi** [Känç Ästämi] (EUTS); Uyg. 12th c. - 14th c. **Kenč-estemi** [Känčäsdämi] (Radl., USp. 127-128, DTS). ✧ '(The) Youngest Estemi' (Blagova 1997, 708). ⇨ **KENČ + İSTÄMİ**.

KENČ-ТОГMÏŠ Uyg. **Känč-toγmïš-tarχan** [Känç Toğmış Tarḫan] (EUTS); Uyg. **Känč-tuγmïš** [Känç Tuğmış] (EUTS); Uyg. 12th c. - 14th c. **Kenč-toγmïš-tarqan** (DTS). ✧ 'Young(est)-born' (Blagova 1997, 708), 'Young(est)-relative' (Blagova 1997, 716). ⇨ **KENČ + ТОГMÏŠ**.

KENČİ see **KENJE**

KENČİK Kzk. 19th c. **Kenčik** [Кеньчикъ] (SODž. 124). ⇨ **KENČİ** + dim. suff. *-k*.

KENČİM Kzk. 19th c. **Kenčim** [Кемчимъ] (SOV 94); Kzk. 19th c. **Kenčim-bay** [Кемчимбай] (SODž. 62); Kzk. 19th c. **Kenčim-bay** [Кемчимбай] (SOK 118); Kzk. 19th c. **Kenčim-bay** [Кемчимбай] (SOK 156); Kzk. 19th c. **Kenčim-bay** [Кемчимбай] (SOV 18). ✧ 'My younger child (son)'. ⇨ **KENČİ**.

KENČİN Kzk. 19th c. **Kenčin?** [Кенчинъ] (SODž. 124). ✧ 'Your youngest child (son)'? ⇨ **KENČİ** + poss. suff. *-ñ / -n*?

KENJÄ see **KENJE**

KENJE Kzk. 19th c. **Genje** [Генджа], fem. (Grod., Pril. 192); Kzk. 19th c. **Genje-bay** [Генджебай] (Grod., Pril. 130); Kzk. 19th c. **Genje-bay** [Киставбай Генджубаевъ] (Grod., Pril. 186); Kkalp. 20th c. **Genže-bay** [Генжебай] (KkRS 773); Kkalp. 20th c. **Genže-gül** [Генжегүл], fem. (KkRS 777); Kzk. 19th c. **Ginje-qul** [Гинджекулъ Бекташевъ] (Grod., Pril. 28); Kkalp. 20th c. **Känji-bay** [Кänджибай] (Bask., Kkalp. 89); Kzk. **Kenči-bay** [Кенчибай] (Konšin, Pam. 9); Kzk. 19th c. **Kenči-bay** [Кенчибай] (SOV 94); Kzk. 19th c. **Kenjä** [Кенджа Игамбердіевъ] (SKSO II, 14); Kzk. 19th c. **Kenjä-bay** [Кенджабаевъ] (SKSO VIII, 206); Kzk. 19th c. **Kenjä-bay** [Наурузбай Кенджабаевъ] (SKSO VIII, 232); Trkm. 19th c. **Kenje** [Кендже Гуликеев] (Ščeglov IV, 165); Kzk. 19th c. **Kenje** [Кендже] (SOK 80); Kzk. 19th c. **Kenje-bay** [Кенджебай Сулеймановъ] (SKSO VIII, 200); Kzk. 19th c. **Kenje-bay** [Кенджебай] (AOAtb. 14, 42); Kzk. 19th c.

Kenje-bay [Кенджебай] (AOK 66); Kkalp. 20th c.
Kenje-bay [Кенджебай] (Bask., Kkalp. 400); Kzk.
19th c. **Kenje-bek** [Кеньджебекъ] (SODž. 124); Kzk.
19th c. **Kenje-bek** [Кеньджебекъ] (SOK 116); Kzk.
19th c. **Kenje-bek** [Кеньджебекъ] (SOV 26); Kzk.
19th c. **Kenje-bek** [Кенджебекъ], a biy (Lomakin 37);
Kzk. **Kenji-bay** [Кенджибай Матеновъ] (Miropiev /
Divaev, Dem. 11); Kzk. **Kenžä** [Кенжä Кара
Баӊыс], three brothers called Kenžä, Qunan and Dönön
Qara Baÿïs (Proben III, 253 /297/); Tat.(Sib.) 1609
Kenže [Байгара Кензин] (Miller, Ist. Sib. II, 209,
210); Tat.(Sib.) 1609 **Kenže** [Бигул Кензин] (Miller,
Ist. Sib. II, 209); Kzk. **Kenže** [كينجه / Кенже]
(Syzdykov 354); Kkalp. 20th c. **Kenže-bay**
[Кенжебай] (KkRS 774); Kzk. 19th c. **Kinjä-bay**
[Кинджабай] (SKSO II, 16); Kzk. 19th c. **Kinjä-χoja**
[Кинджа ходжа] (SKSO IV otd., III, 14); Kzk. 19th
c. **Kinje-qïz** [Кинджe-Кызъ] (Grod., Pril. 116); Uzb.
1875 **Kinji** [Кинджибай рпут.] (Moskal'cev 48);
Uzb. 1875 **Kinji-bay** [Бай-Джигитъ Кинджибаевъ]
(Moskal'cev 48); Bashk. 1757 **Kinyä-ul** [Апкишей
Киняулов] (MIB IV/1, 134); Bashk. 1735 **Kinzä**
[Бердыбакъ Кинзинъ], a tarχan (Vel.-Zern., Bašk.
20); Bashk. 1745 **Kinzä** [Кинзя Азаматов] (MIB III,
433); Bashk. 1755, 1763 **Kinzä** [Азнакай Кинзин]
(MIB IV/1, 99, IV/2, 45); Bashk. 1784 **Kinzä** [Сеит
(Сагит) Кинзин] (MIB V, 161, 201); Bashk. 1682
Kinzä-γul [Кинзягулка Шугуралѣевъ] (AI V, 139);
Bashk. 1740 **Kinzä-γul** [Кинзягул Тумасов] (MIB I,
397); Tat./Bashk. 1723 **Kinze** [Ишим Кинзеев], a
Teptär (MIB III, 212); Bashk. 1756 **Kinze** [Килдубай
Кинзебаев (Кинзибаев)] (MIB IV/1, 109); Bashk.
1756 **Kinze** [Якшибай Кинзебаев (Кинзибаев)]
(MIB IV/1, 109); Bashk. 1762 **Kinze** [Кусекей
Кинзебаев] (MIB IV/1, 241); Bashk. 1783 **Kinze**
[Юлберда Кинзебаев] (MIB V, 149); Bashk. 1790
Kinze [Москов Кинзебаев] (MIB V, 292, 299, 319);
Bashk. 1749 **Kinze / Kinzä** [Кинзе (Кинзя) Ураев]
(MIB III, 467-468); Bashk. 1758 **Kinze / Kinzä**
[Кинзя (Кинзе) Адналин] (MIB V, IV/1, 163);
Bashk. 1714 **Kinze-γul** [Кинзегул Кулдашев] (MIB
I, 105); Bashk. 1735 **Kinze-γul** [Кинзегулъ
Янтыковъ], a tarχan (Vel.-Zern., Bašk. 24); Bashk.
1735 **Kinze-γul** [Кинзегулъ Гауровъ], a tarχan (Vel.-
Zern., Bašk. 12); Bashk. 1735 **Kinze-γul** [Кинзегулъ
Кулгановъ], a tarχan (Vel.-Zern., Bašk. 18); Tat. 1675
Kinzi-bay [Кинзибаевъ] (Kungursk. akty 25); Bashk.
1709 **Kinzi-bay** [Кугей Кинзибаев] (MIB I, 263);
Bashk. 1715 **Kinzi-bay** [Нурмет Кинзибаев] (MIB
III, 123); Bashk. 1722 **Kinzi-bay** [Кинзибай
Кинзегулов] (MIB III, 198); Bashk. 1725 **Kinzi-bay**
[Кинзибай Литов] (MIB III, 232); Bashk. 1730
Kinzi-bay [Кинзибай] (MIB III, 281); Bashk. 1753

Kinzi-bay [Кинзибай Толунбаев] (MIB IV/1, 68);
Bashk. 1709 **Kinzi-bey** [Кинзибей Акчувашев]
(MIB III, 54); Bashk. **Kinžä-bay** [Киньжабай] (ŽS
IV, 357); *EN:* Kzk. 18th c. - 19th c. **Kenje** [Кендже],
Kazak clan (Tynyšp. 67, 68, 71); Kzk. 18th c. - 19th c.
Kenje-bay [Кенджебай], Kazak clan (Tynyšp. 72,
75); Kzk. 18th c. - 19th c. **Kenje-γul** [Кенджегул],
Kazak clan (Tynyšp. 72, 75); *TN:* Az. **Gänjä** [Гäнцä],
the Azerbaidjan town „Elisabethgrad" (Radl. II, 1554).
✧ 'The youngest child (son or daughter) in the family'
cf. Chag. *kenjä* 'die jüngere Tochter' (Radl. II, 1082),
Kzk. *kenžä* 'das jüngste Kind, der zuletzt geborene
Sohn, das Nesthäkchen' (Radl. II, 1083), *kenže*
'младший из детей; поздний молодняк' (KzRS),
Kirg. *kenže* 'младший ребёнок последыш' (Jud.),
(Kkalp. *kenže* 'последыш' (KkRS), Bashk. *kinyä*
'последыш' (BRS) < Mo. *kenje*.

KENJE-ALÏ Kzk. 19th c. **Keň-jalï** [Кэнгджалы]
(Potanin II, 4). ⇨ **KENJE + ALÏ.**

KENJE-BULAT Kzk. 19th c. **Kenje-bulat**
[Кенджебулатъ] (AOK 10); Kzk. 19th c. **Kenje-bulat**
[Кенжеболатъ] (AOO 42); Bashk. 1788 **Kinzä-bulat**
[Кинзябулат Алкашев] (MIB V, 235). ⇨ **KENJE +
BULAT.**

KENJE-ГAR Kzk. 19th c. **Kenje-γar?** [Кенджегаръ],
fem. (Grod., Pril. 140). ⇨ **KENJE.**

KENJE-QARA Kzk. 1794 **Kenje-qara, Kenže-qara?**
[كينجه قرا مرزا / Кенжекара], a mirza (MIK IV,
159); Kzk. 1846 **Kinže-γara** [Сары-Буня
Кинжегарин], a biy (MKOP 152); *EN:* Kzk. 18th c. -
19th c. **Kenje-qara** [Кенджекара], Kazak clan
(Tynyšp. 68, 73). ⇨ **KENJE + QARA.**

KENJE-TAY Kzk. 19th c. **Kenje-tay** [Кенджетай]
(AOK 42). ⇨ **KENJE + TAY** or suff. *-tay(1,2).*

KENJEKE Kirg. **Kenjeke / Kenjäkä** [Кенцäкä]
(Proben V, 170 /172/). ⇨ **KENJE + suff. -ke / -kä.**

KENJEKEY Kzk. 19th c. **Kenjekey** [Кенджекей],
fem. (Potanin, Pred. 87); Kzk. 19th c. **Kenjekey**
[Кенджекей] (SOV 100); Bashk. 1756 **Kinzäkäy**
[Ужбай Кинзякаев] (MIB IV/1, 123); Bashk. 1756
Kinzäkäy [Тяуш Кинзякаев] (MIB IV/1, 123);
Bashk. 1787 **Kinzekäy** [Кинзекäй] (MIB V, 211);
Bashk. 1712 **Kinzekey** [Сырым Кинзекеев] (MIB
III, 88); Bashk. 1735 **Kinzekey** [Кинзекей
Айкынчиковъ], a tarχan (Vel.-Zern., Bašk. 23);
Bashk. 1760 **Kinzekey** [Кинзекей Чювашев] (MIB
IV/1, 187); Bashk. 1780 **Kinzekey** [Кинзекей
Сююшев] (MIB V, 119); Bashk. 1723 **Kinzikey**
[Кинзикей Зияшев] (MIB III, 209-210); Bashk. 1738
Kinzikey [Сырым Кинзикеев] (MIB III, 393);
Bashk. 1739 **Kinzikey / Kinzekiy?** [Нурушъ
Кинзекіевъ] (PSZRI X, 983). ⇨ **KENJEKE + dim.
suff. -y.**

KENJÏ see KENJE

KENJÜM Kzk. 19th c. **Kenjüm-bay** [Кенджумбай] (Grod., Pril. 115). ⇨ **KENČİM?**

KENDEKEY see **KİNDİKEY**

KENDİLJİ Turk. **Kendilji-oγlu**, a Zeybek (Kúnos 1891, 119). ✧ 'Maker or seller of oil lamps' cf. Turk. *kandilci* 'id.' (TED).

KENDİN Tuv. 19th c. **Kendin / Kändin?** [Кäндін] (Proben IX, 88).

KENDİR Kzk. 19th c. **Kendir-bay** [Кендырбай] (SOK 104); Kzk. 19th c. **Kendir-bay** [Кендырбай] (SOV 84); Kzk. 19th c. **Kendir-bay / Kender-bay?** [Кендербай] (SOK 46); Kzk. 19th c. **Kindir-bek** [Кындырбекъ] (SOK 176). ✧ 'Hemp' cf. Kzk. *kendir* 'der Hanf' (Radl. II, 1081), *kendïr* 'id.' (KzRS).

KENDİS Kzk. 19th c. **Kendis-bek** [Кендысбекъ] (SOK 116).

KENDÜK Kzk. 1817 **Kendük?** [كندوك / Кендук] (MIK IV, 313, 319).

KENÄN see **KENEN**

KENE Oghuz/Trkm. 13th c. **Kene** [كنه / Кене] (Abulg./Kon. 525); Kzk. 19th c. **Kene** [Кене] (SOK 152); Kzk. 19th c. **Kene** [Кене] (AOK 122); Kzk. 19th c. **Kene** [Кене] (AOO 14); Kzk. 19th c. **Kene-bay** [Кенебай] (SOV 88); Kzk. 19th c. **Kene-bay** [Кенебай] (SOK 218); Kzk. 19th c. **Kene-bay** [Кенебай] (AOP 6); Kzk. 19th c. **Kene-bay** [Кенебай] (AOA 54, 74); Kzk. 19th c. **Kene-bay** [Кенебай] (AOK 98); Kzk. 19th c. **Kene-bay** [Кенебай] (SOV 26); Kzk. 19th c. **Kene-bay** [Кенебай] (SODž. 38, 74). ✧ 'Mite' cf. Kzk. *kenä* 'die Zecke' (Radl. II, 1075).

KENE-SARÏ Kzk. **Kenä-sarï / Kene-sarï** [Кенä Сарыı] (Proben III, 71 /92/); Kzk. 19th c. **Kene-sarï** (Ljuš 136); Kzk. 19th c. **Keni-sar-batïr (<Keni-sarï)** (AUK 82). ⇨ **KENE + SARÏ.**

KENE-SAT Kzk. 19th c. **Kene-sat** [Кенесатъ] (SOV 126). ⇨ **KENE + SAT?**

KENEK Kzk. 19th c. **Kenek-pay** [Кенекпай] (SOV 110); Kzk. 19th c. **Kenek-pay** [Кенекпай] (SODž. 96). ✧ 'Bad' cf. Hak.(Kyz.) *känäk* 'schlecht, gering' (Radl. II, 1076).

KENELDİK Kzk. 19th c. **Keneldik** [Кенельдыкъ] (AOP 118).

KENEN Kirg. **Kenän** [Кенäн], Jam-bay's father (Proben V, 40 /41/); Kzk. 19th c. **Kenem-bay (Kenen-bay)** [Кенембай] (SODž. 8, 96); Kzk. 19th c. **Kenen-bay** [Кененбай] (AOAtb. 42); Kzk. 19th c. **Kenen-bay** [Кененбай] (SOK 4); *TN:* Kzk. **Kenen-bay** [Кененбай] (Karta JAR XI). ✧ 'Enough (of children or girls)' Kzk. *kenen* 'достеточный, вполне достаточный; обильный; просторный' (KzRS).; ✧ 'Generous, open-handed' (Žanuzakov 145), cf. Kzk. dial. *kenen* 'бостаншылық, кеншілік, молдық' (QTDS).

KENES see **KEÑES**

KENEŠ Kzk. 19th c. **Keneš** [Кенешъ] (AOP 98); Kzk. 19th c. **Keneš-pay** [Кенешпай] (SOK 300). ⇨ **KEÑES / KENİŠ?**

KENET Kzk. 19th c. **Kenet-pay** [Кенетпай] (SOK 116). ✧ 'Sudden; fortuitous' cf. Kzk. *kenet* 'вдруг, мгновенно, неожиданно' (KzRS). ⇨ **KENT / KENİT?**

KENETMÄN Tat. 1600 **Kenetmän** [Токмаш Кенетманов] (Miller, Ist. Sib. II, 159). ⇨ **KENET +** suff. -*män*.

KENİ-SAR see **KENE-SARÏ**

KENİS see **KEÑES**

KENİŠ Kzk. 19th c. **Keniš-pay** [Кеныьшпай] (SOK 256). ✧ 'Freedom, quiet'? cf. Kzk. *kenis* 'serbestlik, rahatlık' (KzTS).

KENİŠTİ Kzk. 19th c. **Keništi-bay** [Кеныьштыбай] (SOK 180). ✧ 'Free, quiet'. ⇨ **KENİŠ** + suff. -*ti*.

KENİT Kzk. 19th c. **Kenït-pay** [Кеныьтпай] (SOK 82). ⇨ **KENT / KENET?**

KENLÜ Kzk. 19th c. **Kenlü-bay** [Кенлубай] (SOK 76). ⇨ **KEN?** + suff. -*lü* / -*li*.

KENS see **KEÑES**

KENSİG Uyg. **Känsig** [Känsig] (ETY II, 65); Türk 8th c. - 9th c. **Kensig** (Runic Mss. 186, 188, DTS).

KENT Kzk. 19th c. **Kent-bay** [Кентбай] (SOK 20). ✧ 'Town' cf. Kzk. *kent* 'die Stadt' (Radl. II, 1079). ⇨ **KENET / KENİT?**

KENT-BUΓA Kzk. **Kent-buγa** [Kent Buga / Кент Буҕа], a jinn's (demon's) father (Proben III, 48 /63/). ⇨ **KENT + BUQA.**

KENT-QARA Uyg. 12th c. - 14th c. **Kent-qara / Ket-qara?** (Radl., USp. 208, 250). ⇨ **KENT + QARA.**

KENTE Kzk. 19th c. **Kente-bay / Kent-bay** [Кентебай] (SOV 90). ⇨ **KENT?**

KENŽE see **KENJE**

KENŽE-BOLAT see **KENJE-BULAT**

KEÑEL Kzk. 19th c. **Keñel-bay** [Кенгельбай] (SOV 102).

KEÑELDİ Kzk. 19th c. **Keñeldi** [Кенгельды] (SOV 108).

KEÑES Kzk. 19th c. **Kenes** [Кенесъ] (AOO 62); Kzk. 19th c. **Kenes-bay** [Кенесбай] (AOO 2); Kzk. 19th c. **Kenes-pay** [Кенеспай] (SODž. 38, 64, 114); Kzk. 19th c. **Kenes-pay** [Кенеспай] (SOK 184); Kzk. 19th c. **Kenes-pay** [Кенеспай] (AOO 62); Kzk. 19th c. **Kenis-bay** [Кенисбай] (AOK 114); Kzk. 19th c. **Kens-bay** [Кенсбай] (AOA 110); Kzk. 19th c. **Keñes** [Кенгесовъ] (AOK 46); Kzk. 19th c. **Kïnïz-bay?** [Кынызбай] (SOK 232); *EN:* Kzk. 18th c. - 19th c. **Kenes-bay-biy** [Кенесбай-бий], a Kazak clan (Tynyšp.). ✧ 'Advice; adviser' cf. Kzk. *keñäs* 'der Rath, die Berathung' (Radl. II, 1068).

KEŇESQAN Kirg. 20th c. **Keňešqan** [Кенгешкан], fem. (Abramzon-Sulejmanov). ⇨ **KEŇEŠ** + suff. *-qan(1)*.

KEŇEŠ see **KEŇES**

KEŇİR Kzk. 19th c. **Keňir** [Кенгыръ] (SODž. 110); Kzk. 19th c. **Keňir** [Кенгыръ] (AOA 114); Kzk. **Keňir-bay** [Кеңір Баі] (Proben III, 20 /24/).

KEP Kzk. 19th c. **Kep-pay** [Кеппай] (AOO 59). ✧ 'Web, net' cf. Kzk. *kep* 'das Fangnetz für Raubvögel' (Radl. II, 1184).

KEPE Kzk. 19th c. **Kepe** [Кепе] (SODž. 62). ✧ I. 'Grown-up lamb' cf. Kzk. *kepe* 'büyümüş kuzu' (KzTS); II. 'A kind of peat/turf'? cf. Kzk. *kepe* 'tezeğin bir çeşidi' (KzTS).

KEPEK see **KEBEK**

KEPİL Kzk. 19th c. **Kepil-baj** [Кепильбай] (SOV 154). ✧ 'Guarantor' cf. Kzk. *kepil* (Ar.) 'der Bürge' (Radl. II, 1187).

KEPLİN Hak. 19th-20th c. **Keplin** [Кеплин] (HRS 349).

KER Khorezm. 1313 **Ker-bay** [كربای بهادر], a Moghul emir (Dawād. 274); Khorezm. 1312 **Ker-bek** [الامير الكرجی كربك], an emir (Dawād. 255); Kzk. 19th c. **Ker-pay** [Керпай] (SOK 96). ✧ I. 'Monstrosity; giant' cf. Alt. *kär* 'ein Ungeheuer, ein sehr grosses Thier' (Radl. II, 1083), cf. also Németh, HMK 264-66; II. 'Dark brown (horse) with white jowl' cf. Kzk. *ker* 'ein dunkelbraues Pferd mit weissem Maule' (Radl. II, 1084); III. 'Arrogant, disdainful' cf. Kzk. *ker* 'чванливый' (KzRS).

KER-BENDE Khorezm. 14th c. **Ker-bende** [Kherbendeh], the original name of Muχammad Xudabende, „King of the Tatars" (Ibn Bat. II, 114-115). ✧ 'Muleteer' cf. P. *kher* + *bendeh* 'le vale de lâne; muletier' (Defrémery: Ibn Bat. II, 115.). ⇨ **MENDE.**

KER-BUΓA Kkalp. 20th c. **Ker-boγa** [Кербогъа] (Bask., Kkalp. 15); Selj. 1094, 1101 **Ker-buγa** [كربوقا غلام / كربوقا / كربوغا / كر بغا / كر بوغّا / كور بوغا / كر بوغا / Carboga / Corbuga / Corbogha Kauam ed-Daula / Kerbogha / Corbogha / Kior-Bogha], Altun-taš's brother, emir, lord of Harram, Mosul (princeps Mossuliae), etc., fought against Antiochia, died in 1100/1 or 1101/2 (Abulfidā III, 290-291 etc., 308-309 etc., Ibn al-Athīr, Atab. 28-31, Rāwandī 140, Kamāladdīn II, 111, 112, 117, 121, 130, etc., Qazw. 449, 450, Weil, Chalif. III, 152, Reg. Hieros. 1, Kamāladdīn: RHCHor III, 578-584, 707-710, Bondārī 259, Ibn al-Athīr: RHCHor I, 194, 195, 208); Kzk. **Ker-buγa** [Кер-буга] (TOOIK III, 169); Selj. 10th c. **Ker-buγa** / **Kör-buγa?** [مغانون / التركی / كور بغانون / كور] (Tabarī, Annal. II, 1195, III, 1602). ✧ 'Dark brown - bull; Giant-bull'. ⇨ **KER + BUQA.**

KEŇ-BUQA see **KER-BUΓA**

KER-TAY Uyg.? 1338 **Ker-tay** [كرتای السيفی / اسيف الدين] (Sobernh. I, 84). ⇨ **KER + TAY** or suff. *-tay(1,2)*?

KER-TAYLAQ Kzk. **Ker-taylaq** [Кер Таілак] (Proben III, 72 /94/). ⇨ **KER + TAYLAQ.**

KER-TORUN Crm. **Ker-torun** [Кäр-Торун] (Proben VII, 127). ⇨ **KER + TORUN.**

KERČE-BULADÏ Oghuz/Trkm. 13th c. **Kerče-buladï** [كرجه بولادی / Керче-Булады], Alp-Arslan's (1063-1072) daughter (Abulg./Kon. 1450).

KERČEK Kkalp. 1809 **Kerček** [Мухаммед-Нияз-Керчек] (MIKk. 102); Kkalp. 1870 **Kerček-inaq** [Керчек Инак] (MIKk. 107).

KERÄY Crm. 1465, 1475, 1480 **Aji-girey** / **Ači-girey** (<**Xaji-girey**) [حاج كرای / حاجی كرای خان / Атζικερίης / Ази-Гирей / Акигирей / Асирệй / Ачигирей], Crimean Khan Haji Girey I (1426/1430-1466) (PSRL III, 243, VI, 34 etc., VIII, 151, 181, Vel.-Zern., Crim. 3, 261, 739, 896, Byz. Turc.); Kzk. **Ažï-keräy-mïrza** [Ажы Кераi Мырза] (Proben III, 166); Crm.(Tat.) 17th c. **Girey**, Shahin Girey Khan (Mende 58); Bashk. 18th c. **Girey** [Гирей] (Nepljuev 164-165); Alt.(Tel.) **Käräy** [Käpäi], ruler of the hell of this world (Radl. II, 1086); Uyg. 12th c. - 14th c. **Käräy** / **Keräy** [Käräy] (Radl., USp. 19-20, 27-28, DTS, EUTS); Maml.? 1280 **Keray** / **Keräy?** [Keraï], fought at Hims (Makrīzī III, 34); Maml.? 13th c. **Kerey** [كرای], an emir al-Nāsir in Egypt, fought against Esän-demir (Abulfidā and Ibn al-Athīr: RHCHor I, 175, 826); Maml.? 1300, 1310 **Kerey** [سيف الدين كرای المنصوری], an emir (Dawād. 51, 117, 214 etc.); Kzk. 1793 **Kerey** [ئارای / Керей] (MIK IV, 161); Kzk. 19th c. **Kerey** [Керей] (SOV 108, 124); Kzk. 19th c. **Kerey** [Керей] (SOK 96, 162, 206); Alt. 19th c. **Kerey** [Керей], one of Erlik's seven sons (Potanin IV, 218); Kzk. 19th c. **Kerey-bay** [Керейбай] (SOV 36, 56, 86); Kzk. 19th c. **Kerey-bay** [Керейбай] (SOK124); Kzk. 19th c. **Kerey-bay** [Керейбай] (AOO 22); Kzk. 19th c. **Kerey-bay** [Керейбай] (AOP 122); Alt. 19th c. **Kerey-χan** [Керей-хан] (Verb., In. 91, 99); Alt. 19th c. **Kerey-χan** [Керей-хан] (Verb., In. 91, 99); Kzk. 19th c. **Kerey-qul** [Керейкулъ] (SOK 12); Kzk. 19th c. **Kerey-qul** [Керейкулъ] (SODž. 60); Tat. 20th c. **Kiräy** [Кирəй] (Sattarov); Tat.(Ishim), Tat.(Tob.), Tat.(Bar.) 19th c. **Kiräy** / **Käräy-qan** [Ahmed Käräi Kan / Akmet Käräi Kan / Акмет Кäпäi Кан], Aχmet Kiräy Sultan, Küčüm-qan's brother and predecessor (Proben IV, 8 /10/, 212 /261/, 218 /268/, Radl., Aus Sib. I, 153); Kzk. 19th c. **Kiräy-bay** [Кыряйбай] (SODž. 140); Crm.(Tat.) 1522 **Kirey** [Маетме Кирей], ruler of Perekop (Lit. Tat. 1); Crm.(Tat.) 1765 **Kirey** [Кирей Капаев] (PSZRI XVII, 111); Tat.? 1470 **Kirey** [Кирей Амуратовъ] (PSRL VIII, 158, 168); Tat. 18th-19th c. **Kirey** [Кирей] (Magn. 51); Nog. 20th c. **Kirey**

[Куьлджемине Кирей келинъи], husband of one of Baskakov's informants from the aul of Yaman-γoy, District of Ači-qulaq (Bask., Nog. 143); Kzk. 19th c. **Kirey-bay** [Кирейбай] (AOK 130); Kzk. 19th c. **Kirey-bay** [Кирейбай] (AOAtb. 42). ✧ 'Respected nobleman; gentleman' (Sattarov-Subaeva), cf. also Turk. *gäray* 'würdig, ein Titel der Krymchane' (Radl. I, 1555). Used also as a secondary component of personal names. Originally, it is a Mongol ethnonym. Cf. J. Németh, Kereit, Kêrey, Giray: UAJb. XXXVI (1965), pp. 360-365. Other interpretation: 'Razor' (Blagova 1997, 713), cf. Karakh. *keräj* 'id.' (DTS). See also **AX-KEREY, AL-GİREY, ALDÏ-GİREY, ALP-GİREY, AŠÏ-KERÄY, ARSLAN-GİREY, ASAN-GİREY, AŠÏ-KERÄY, AT-KİREY, AZAMAT-KİREY, BAHĀDÏR-GİREY, BAY-GİREY, BAS-KİREY, BORA-ГАZİ-GİREY, BÜLÜK-GERÄY, İL-GEREY, İŠ-KEREY, İT-KEREY, ÏSLAM-GİREY, YAN-GİREY, YAT-KİREY, DÄWLÄT-GİREY, ESÄN-GİREY, MAYETME-KİREY, MEŇ-GİREY, MEŇLİ-GİREY, SAFA-KİREY, SAL-KEREY, SAP-KİREY, SAT-KEREY, SAV-KİREY, SĀDET-GİREY, SĀHİB-GİREY, ŠAHBAZ-GEREY, ŠAHİN-GİREY, TOY-GİREY, TOQTAMÏŠ-KİREY, TUT-KERÄY, ÜTÄMİŠ-KERÄY**.

KERÄYLİ Oghuz/Trkm. 13th c. **Gireyli** [كرايلى / Гирейли] (Abulg./Kon. 525); Oghuz/Trkm. 13th c. **Keräyli** [كرايلى] (Abulg./Desm. 18). ⇨ **KERÄY** + suff. *-li*.

KERÄNĴE Oghuz/Trkm. 13th c. **Keränĵe-χoĵa** [كرانجه حواجه / Керандже-ходжа] (Abulg./Kon. 1065).

KERÄŠ Kzk. 19th c. **Keräš** [Кувандукбай Керашевъ] (Grod., Pril. 131).

KERE Kzk. 19th c. **Kere-bay** [Керебай] (SOV 126). ✧ 'Evidence' cf. Kzk. *kerä* 'das Zeugniss' (Radl. II, 1086). See also **TOLÏ-KERE**.

KEREČ Kirg. **Kereč** [Кереч] (Jud. 920). ✧ 'A kind of medicinal plant (herb)' cf. Kirg. *kereč* 'название горного лекарственного растения' (Jud.).

KEREDE Alt. **Kerede** [Канъ Кереде] (Nikiforov 46). See also **PADÏ-KEREDE**.

KEREY see **KERÄY**

KEREYT Kzk. 19th c. **Kereyt** [Керейтъ] (AOP 26); Kzk. 19th c. **Kereyt-bay** [Керейтбай] (AOK 54). ✧ 'Kereit' Originally a Mo. ethnonym.

KEREK Trkm. 20th c. **Gerek** [Gerek], fem. (Zaj. 1971, 335); Trkm. 20th c. **Gerek** [Герек], fem. (TrkmRS 173); Alt. 19th-20th c. **Kerek** [Керек], fem. (OjrRS 212). ✧ 'Necessary, needed (child)' cf. Alt. *kerek* 'потребность, необходимость' (OjrRS), Trkm. *gerek* 'нужный необходимый' (TrkmRS), Tat. *kiräk* 'нужный необходимый' (TatRS). See also **OГUL-GEREK**.

KEREKE Kzk. **Käräkä** [Käpäkä] (Proben III, 79 /102/).

KEREKÜZ Tat.(Sib.) 1609 **Kereküz** [Керекузъ] (Andrievič, Ist. Sib. I, 45).

KEREN see **KEREŇ**

KEREŇ Kzk. 19th c. **Keren-bay** [Керенбай] (SODž. 110); Kzk. 19th c. **Keren-qul** [Керенкуль] (SOK 214); Kkalp. 1809 **Kereñ** [Нимет Керенг] (MIKk. 103). ✧ 'Great, powerful' cf. Kirg. *keräñ* 'gross, mächtig' (Radl. II, 1090).

KERİK Uyg. 12th c. - 14th c. **Kerik** (DTS). ✧ 'Large, gross; obese, fat' cf. Karakh. *kerik* 'растянутый, обширный' (DTS).

KERİL Kzk. 19th c. **Keril-bay** [Конди Керилбаевъ] (Grod., Pril. 109). ✧ 'Stretch oneself; grow up' cf. Hak., Kzk. *keril-* 'sich ausrecken, sich ausstrecken' (Radl. II, 1096).

KERİM Kkalp. 20th c. **Kärim** [Кəрим] (KkRS 774); Kzk. 19th c. **Kärim-bay** [Каримбай] (SKSO III, 8); KKalp. 20th c. **Kärim-bay** [Кəримбай] (KkRS 774); Kzk. 19th c. **Kärim-qul** [Каримкулъ] (Grod., Pril. 137); Uzb.(Kipch.) 19th c. **Kärim-qul**, a Kipchak from Khokand (Nalivkin-Dozon 194); Trkm. 20th c. **Kerim** [Kerim] (Zaj. 1971, 327); Kirg. **Kerim** [Керим] (Jud. 81); Kirg. **Kerim-aχun** [Керимахун] (Jud. 139, 747); Uzb. 1817/18 **Kerim-atalīq** [Керим-аталык], from the Salaq tribe (clan) (MIT II, 406); Trkm. 1820/21 **Kerim-bek** [Керим-бек] (MIT II, 417); Trkm. 1819 **Kerim-χan** [Керим-хан] (MIT II, 415); Trkm. 1830 **Kerim-χan** [Керим-хан], from the Zafaranlu clan (MIT II, 224); Trkm. 1860 **Kerim-χan** [Керим-хан Зенд] (MIT II, 280); Trkm. 1867 **Kerim-χan** [Керим-хан] (MIT II, 315); Trkm. 20th c. **Kerīm** [Керим] (TrkmRS 393); Uzb. 1840 **Kirim** [Магометъ Киримъ], from Khiva (ZIRGOÊtn. I, 100); Hak. 19th-20th c. **Qarim** [Карим] (HRS 349); Hak. 19th-20th c. **Qarim / Qarïm?** [Карым] (Katanov, Otč. 10); Kzk. **Qarïm-bay** [Карымбаевъ] (TOUAK XXIV, 85); *TN:* Kzk. **Qarïm-bay** [Карым-бай] (Karta JAR XI). ✧ Karim (Ar.), 'kind, generous, benevolent, noble', one of the names (epithets) of Allah (Ahmed), 'Gracious, merciful; goodness' cf. Kirg. *kerim* 'милостивый (эпитет аллаха); милость, доброта' (Jud.), Uyg., Crm., Turk. *kärim* 'gnädig, edelmüthig, wohlthätig, freigiebig' (Radl. II, 1097), also Hak. PN *Karim* (Butanaev), Kzk. PN *Kärim* (Žanuzakov-Esbaeva). See also **AL-GERİM?, ÄBDİ-KÄRİM**.

KERİM-BERDİ Uzb. 20th c. **Kärim-berdi** [Каримберди] (Begmatov 1984, 202); Uzb.? 19th c. **Kärim-birdi** [Игамберды Каримбирдіевъ], a Tajik(?) person with an Uzbek name (SKSO VIII, 209); Tat.(Lit.) 1552 **Kerem-birdey / Kerem-birde?** [Керемъ-Бирдей] (Kn. Metriki Lit. 79); Tat.(GH) 14th c. **Kerim-berdi** [Керимберди], Toqtamïš-qan's son

(Abulg./Desm. 187); Kkalp. 1820 **Kerim-berdi** [Керимберди] (MIKk. 104); Uzb. 16th c. **Kerim-berdi-inaq / Kerim-berdi-atalïq** [Керим-берди-инак / Керим-берди-аталык], an emir (Ivanov 87, 90, 242, MIT II, 348, 375, 384, etc.); Tat.? 1413 **Kerim-berdi(y)** [Керимъ-Бердѣй], a ruler of the Horde (PSRL XI, 219); Trkm. 19th c. **Kerim-berdï** [Керимъ-Берды Джанъ-Араслановъ] (Ščeglov I, 355). ✦ 'The Gracious (Allah) gave (him/her)'. ⇨ **KERİM + BERDİ.**

KERİMKER   Kzk. 19th c. **Kerimker** [Керимкеръ] (SOK 250). ⇨ **KERİM** + suff. *-ker.*

KERİP   Kzk. 19th c. **Kerip** [Керыпъ] (SOK 250). ✦ 'Beggar, cadger' cf. Kzk. *kărip* (Ar.) 'der Bettler, Krüppel, arm, elend' (Radl. II, 1097). See also **QOLČU, TİLENČEK, TİLENČİ.**

KERİT   Kzk. 19th c. **Kerit-bay** [Керитбай] (SOV 56). ✦ 'Strong' cf. Kzk. *kert* 'kuvvetli, güçlü' (KzTS).

KERİLÄ see **KİRİLLÄ**

KERKİ   Trkm. **Kerki** [Керки] (Sopieva 180). ✦ 'Pickaxe' cf. Trkm. *kerki* 'кирка' (TrkmRS).

KERLEK   Kzk. 19th c. **Kerlek-pay** [Керлекпай] (SOK 236). ⇨ **KER?** + suff. *-lik.*

KERLİP   Kzk. 19th c. **Kerlip-pay** [Керлиппай] (SODž. 144).

KERMESEN-SAS   Kzk. **Kermesen-sas** [Кермесенъ-сасъ], fem. (Divaev, Šura 131). ⇨ **SAČ.**

KERMEŠ   Tat.(Lit.) 1592 **Kermeš** [Тубурчикъ Кермешевичъ] (Lit. Tat. 124).

KERNEY   Kzk. 19th c. **Kerney** [Керней] (SOV 110). ✦ 'Reed flute' cf. Kzk. *kernay* 'ney' (KzTS).

KERSİN   Uyg. **Kersin / Kärsin** (Radl., USp. 16-18, DTS). ✦ 'May he stall / May he block [the enemy's way?]' (Blagova 1997, 716), cf. Uyg., Chag., Kuman, Alt., Crm. *kär-,* Kirg., Kzk. *ker-* 'ausspannen, ausstrecken' (Radl. II, 1084), Karakh. *ker-* 'растягивать; преграждать, замыкать' (DTS).

KERSKİČ   Uyg. **Kärskič** [Kärskiç] (EUTS); Uyg. 12th c. -14th c. **Kerskič** [Kärskič] (Radl., USp. 48-49, DTS).

KERTİK   Trkm. 20th c. **Kertik** [Kertik] (Zaj. 1971, 333); Trkm. 20th c. **Kertik** [Кертик] (TrkmRS 393). ✦ 'Score, hack, slash' cf. Trkm. *kertik* 'надрез, метка' (TrkmRS).

KERÜKİ   Uyg. 12th c. - 14th c. **Kerüki** (Radl., USp. 128, DTS).

KERÜNJEK   Oghuz/Trkm. 13th c. **Kerünjek** [كرونجك / Керунджек], bek of Quzï-yawï Khan's council (Abulg./Kon. 665).

KES   Maml. 1444/45 **Kes-bay** [المجنون المويىدى / كسباى الششمانى] (Ibn Taghrīb. VII, 131, 156). ✦ I. 'Quick; fast' cf. Uyg. *käs* 'schnell, flüchtig' (Radl. II, 1154); II. 'Cut' cf. Alt.(Tel.) *käs-* 'schneiden, zerschneiden' (Radl. II, 1154).

KES-AL   Yürük 1543 **Kes-al** [كسال / Kes-al] (Gökb., Rum. 103, 190). ⇨ **KES? + AL?**

KES-YAR   Yürük 1543 **Kes-yar** [كسيار / Kesyar] (Gökb., Rum. 103, 199, 200). ⇨ **KES + YAR?**

KESEK   Kzk. 19th c. **Kcsek-bay** [Кесек-бай] (SODž. 72); Kzk. 19th c. **Kesek-bay** [Кесек-бай] (SOK 30). ✦ 'Lump, ball, hank; piece' cf. Chag., East.T., NUyg.(Tar.), Kar.(L.), Tur. *käsäk* 'das Stück, die Erdscholle' (Radl. II, 1160), Kzk. *kesek* 'ком, комок, кусок' (KzRS). See also **QARA-KESEK.**

KESEKE   Kzk. 19th c. **Keseke** [Кесеке] (SOK 112). ⇨ **KES?** + comp. *eke.*

KESEKLİ   Maml. 1303 **Kesekli** [سيفالـدـين كسكلى], an emir (Dawād. 110). ✦ 'Having cuts, scars' cf. + suff. *-li.*

KESER   Turk. **Keser** (Önder, Hınıs). ✦ 'Axe, hatchet' cf. Turk. *keser* 'Querbeil, Axt' (HŞ). See also **BALTA, BALTU, TEBER, TEŠE.**

KESİK   Kzk. 19th c. **Kesik-pay** [Кесыкпай] (SOV 26); Kzk. 19th c. **Kesik-pay** [Кесикпай] (SOV 16, 120). ✦ 'Being cut; having cuts, scars' cf. Kzk. *kesik* 'разрезанный' (KzkRS).

KESİR   Kzk. 1794 **Kesir** [كسر / Кеср] (MIK IV, 158); Turk. **Kesir-oγlu**, a Zeybek (Kúnos 1891, 119). ✦ 'Break, fracture; harm, damage, misery' cf. Kzk. *kesir* 'вред, зло' (KzRS), Turk. *kesir* 'ломание; разрушение; перелом' (TRS).

KESKEN   Maml. 1312 **Kesken** [سيفالـدـين كسكـن], an emir (Dawād. 258). ✦ 'A kind of mace' cf. Chag. *käskän* 'eine Art Keule' (Radl. II, 1166).

KESMÄK see **KİSMÄK**

KESTAN   Oghuz/Trkm. 13th c. **Kestan** [كستـان قـرا الـب / Кестан-Кара-алп], Qara-alp's byname (Abulg./Kon. 1450).

KESTENJİ   Turk. **Kestenji-oγlu** (Kúnos 1891, 119). ✦ 'Chestnut man, chestnut seller' cf. Turk. *kestaneci* 'id,' (TED).

KESTERE   Hak. 19th-20th c. **Kestere** [Кестере] (HRS 349).

KEŠE   Kzk. 19th c. **Keše-bay** [Кешебай] (SODž. 162). ✦ 'Stupid, dumb' cf. Kzk. *kešä* 'dumm, schwerfällig von Verstande' (Radl. II. 1181).

KEŠEKLİ   Khorezm. 1219 **Kešekli-χan** [Кешекли-Ханъ], an officer in Bukhara at the time of Chinggis' invasion (RaD/Ber. III, 53).

KEŠER   Kzk. 19th c. **Kešer-bay** [Кешербай] (SOV 28). ⇨ **KÖŠER?**

KEŠEW   Kzk. 19th c. **Kešew-bay** [Кешеубай] (SOK 266).

KEŠKEL   Maml. 1279 **Keškel**, appointed to an emir by Qalawun (Makrīzī II/1, 12).

KEŠKENE see **KİČKİNE**

KEŠKİL   Kzk. 19th c. **Keškil** [Кешкилъ] (SODž. 98). ✦ 'Short (nosed)'? cf. Kzk. *keşkil: keşkil tumsıq* 'kısa burun' (KzTS).

KEŠKİN   Kzk. 1817 **Keškin** [كچكن / Кешкин] (MIK IV, 310). ✧ 'Handsome, of striking appearance; courageous'? cf. Kzk. *keskin* 'keskin, yüzü gösterişli, cesaretli' (KzTS).

KEŠLİ   Khorezm. 1220 **Kešli-χan** [كشلى خان / Keshlî khân], chieftain of the Khorezmshah Muhammad, he escaped from Bukhara when the Mongols attacked it (Abulfar. Or. 442, Abulfar./Budge I, 376). ✧ 'Having (making/selling?) quivers' + suff. *-li*.

KEŠNÄ   Kzk. 1790 **Kešnä-bay** [Кешнябай] (MIK IV, 129).

KEŠŠAF   Turk. (Yürük?) **Keššaf-oγlu** (Şölen 13). ✧ 'Explorer, discoverer, investigator' cf. Turk. *keşşaf* 'id.' (TED).

KEŠÜ   Kzk. 19th c. **Kešü-bay** [Кешубай] (AOA 82); Kzk. 19th c. **Kešü-bay** [Кешубай] (AOA 82); Kzk. 19th c. **Kešü-bay** [Кешубай] (SODž. 90); Kzk. 19th c. **Kešü-bay / Kešüw-bay** [Кешубай] (AOO 42); *EN:* Kzk. 18th c. - 19th c. **Kešü-bay** [Кешубай] (Tynyšp. 75). ⇨ **KEČÜ?**

KET-BUΓA   Maml. 13th c. **Ket-buγa** [Kät buγa], from Egypt (Le Coq, Ind. 2); Maml. 1259 **Ket-buγa** [كتبغا / Ketboga], envoy from Syria to Hulagu (Hülägü) (Abulfidā IV, 591); Maml. 1280, 1298, 1303 **Ket-buγa** [زين الدين كتبغا الملقب العادل / Zeïn-eddin-Ketboga naïb-assaltaneh], an emir (of Mongol origin), later a sultan (1295-1297) then the governor of Hamah, died in 1303, his tomb (mausoleum) is in Damascus (Makrīzī III, 12, 27, IV, 2, 21-39, 226, Dawād. 7, 14, 41 etc., Sauvaire VI, 247); Maml. 13th c. **Ket-buqa** [كيد بوقا / Caid Buka Bawargiensis], „turcarum prefectus" (Abulfar. Or. 503). ✧ 'Reliable bull / trustworthy bull' (Le Coq, Ind. 2), 'Strong bull'. ⇨ **KEY + BUQA.**

KET-BUQA see **KET-BUΓA**

KET-QARA   Uyg. **Kät-qara** [Kät Kara] (EUTS); Uyg. 12th c. - 14th c. **Ket-qara** [Kät (Käd) Qara] (Radl., USp. 133-134). ✧ 'Good/Strong-Black'. ⇨ **KEY + QARA.**

KETE   Kzk. 19th c. **Kete-bay** [Кетебай] (SOK 164); Kkalp. 1811 **Kete-bay** [Кете бай], a biy (MIKk. 122); *EN:* Kzk. 18th c. - 19th c. **Kete** [Кете] (Tynyšp. 74, MIK IV, 52).

KETE-KÜŠER   Kzk. 19th c. **Kete-küšer** [Kete-Kušer] (Ljutš 138). ✧ '(He) goes - moves away'? cf. Kzk. *ket-* 'уходить', Kzk. *köš-* 'кочевать' (KzRS).

KETEGEY   Kzk. 19th c. **Ketegey** [Кетегей] (AOA 134). ⇨ **KETİK** + suff. *-ey*.

KETENEK   Alt. 19th-20th c. **Ketenek** [Кетенек], fem. (OjrRS 212).

KETEZET   Alt. 19th-20th c. **Ketezet** [Кетезет], fem. (OjrRS 212).

KETİK   Maml. 14th c. **Ketik** [كَتِك] (Sauvaget 54); Bashk. 1653 **Kitik** [Китикъ тарханъ], a tarχan (Vel.-Zern., Bašk. 43). ✧ I. 'Nick, defective, loss, damage'

cf. Tat. *kitĭk* 'abgebrochen, schartig; der Schaden' (Radl. II, 1375); II. 'Toothless' (Sauvaget 54).

KETİN   Kzk. **Ketin** [Кетинъ] (Konšin, Oč. 64).

KETMEN   NUyg. 19th c. **Ketmen** [كتمان] (Le Coq, Namenl. 105); Kzk. 19th c. **Ketmen-bay** [Кетменбай] (SOV 100); Kzk. **Ketpän** [Кетпän], Qarasay's son (Proben III, 137 /173/); Kzk. 19th c. **Ketpen** [Кетпенъ] (SODž. 84). ✧ 'Hack, pickaxe; a kind arms' cf. Chag., NUyg.(Tar.) *kätmän* 'die Hacke, das Grabscheit, die Haue; eine Waffe' (Radl. II, 1132), Kzk. *ketpen* 'кетмень (мотыга)' (KzRS).

KETPÄN see **KETMEN**

KETPEN see **KETMEN**

KETSÜN   Turk. 1583 **Ketsün** [كتسون / كد سون] (Ongan, Ank. I, 164).

KETTÄ   Kzk. 19th c. **Kettä-bay?** [Кеттабай] (Grod., Pril. 179). ✧ 'Big, great; noble, influential, powerful' cf. Chag., East.T., Uzb., Bashk. *kättä* 'gross, vornehm, mächtig' (Radl. II, 1057). See also **BOYŠAN, DÄW, DUOLANTAY, ÄLLÄY, KETTÄ, QOŽAQ, ULUΓ, ZOR.**

KETTİÑES   Hak. 19th-20th c. **Kettiñes** [Кеттінъес] (HRS 349).

KETÜR-YARU   Uyg. 12th c. - 14th c. **Ketür-yaru** (DTS).

KEWKİN   Kzk. 19th c. **Kewkin** [Кеукынъ] (SODž. 96).

KEZÄK   Alt. 19th c. **Kezäk** [Кезäк] (Katanov, Otč. 12). ✧ 'Piece, part' cf. Alt. *käzäk* 'der Theil, ein Stück' (Radl. II, 1172).

KEŽEM   Kzk. 19th c. **Kežem-bay (Kežen-bay)** [Кежембай] (AOK 82). ✧ 'Get angry; threaten' cf. Kzk. *kežen-, kezen-* 'осердиться; грозить; замахиваться (палкой, нагайкой)' (PKRS).

KİBAR   Turk. 20th c. **Kibar** (Önder, Göle). ✧ 'Distinguished (man); noble, rich' cf. Turk. *kibar* (Ar.) 'id.' (TED).

KİBÄK see **KEBEK**

KİBEK see **KEBEK**

KİBEKEY   Chuv. 18th-19th c. **Kibekey** [Кибекей] (Magn. 50). ⇨ **KEBEK** + dim. suff. *-ey*.

KİBİNÄS   Bashk. 1737 **Kibinäs** [Кибиняс Имясев] (MIB III, 365).

KİBİS see **KEBES**

KİČE   Hak. 19th-20th c. **Kiče** [Киче] (HRS 349).

KİČEMEY   Hak. 19th-20th c. **Kičemey** [Кичемей] (HRS 349). ✧ 'Diligent, hard worker' cf. Hak. PN *Kičemey* (Butanaev).

KİČEŠ   Alt. 19th-20th c. **Kičeš** [Кичееш] (OjrRS 208). ✧ 'Diligence; hard-working; stayer' cf. Alt. *kiče-*

'стараться, быть прилежным, настойчивым'
(OjrRS). + suff. -š.

KİČİ   Trkm. 20th c. **Kiči** [Kiči], fem. (Zaj. 1971, 341);
Trkm. 20th c. **Kiči** [Кичи], fem. (TrkmRS 401);
Kuman 1090 **Kiči / Kici?** [Κιτζῆς], a Kumanian
chieftain (Byz. Turc. 160); Turk. 1418 **Kiji-bey** [Kici
Bey] (Gökb., Ed. 189). ✧ 'Little, small' cf. Kuman *kiči*
'klein' (CC), Kar.(T.), Turk. *kiči* 'klein' (Radl. II,
1381), Turk. *kici, kiçi* 'küçük' (Tar. Sözl.), Alt. *kiči*
'немного, чуточку' (OjrRS), Kzk. *kiši (= kičik)* 'klein'
(Radl. II, 1392). ⇨ **KİČİG.**

KİČİG   Nog. 1531 **Kičig** [Кичигъ Алѣй
(Кичигилѣй)] (PSRL XX, 410); Alt. 19th c. **Kičig**
[Кичиг-Нилигчи богатырь] (Verb., In. 152);
Hak.(Sag.) 19th-20th c. **Kičig-irgek** [Кіvіг Іргäк], a
folklore hero (Proben II, 415, 416, 421, 424); Alt. 19th-
20th c. **Kičig-ōl** (Katanov, Otč. 10); Chag. 16th c.
Kičik [Кичик], an „ustad" (Ivanov 308); Khorezm. /
Maml.? 1280 **Kičik** [Bedr-eddin-Kidjik-Khawarizmi],
an emir (Makrīzī II/1, 18); Chag. **Kičik-beg** [كيچيك بـك
/ Kičik bäg] (Le Coq, Ind. 3); Uzb. 1855 **Kičik-χan-
türä** [Кичикъ-ханъ-тюря] (Valihanov, Soč. 140);
Trkm. 19th c. **Kišik** [Кышикъ Сююндюковъ]
(Ščeglov IV, 163); Kzk. 19th c. **Kišik** [Кишикъ]
(Grod., Pril. 193); Kzk. 19th c. **Kižik / Kišik**
[Кижикъ] (SOV 100). ✧ I. 'Little, small' cf. Uyg. *kijik*
'klein' (Radl. II, 1383), Chag., Alt.(Tel.), NUyg.(Tar.)
kičik 'klein, gering' (Radl. II, 1381), Uyg. *kičig*
'маленький, малый, небольшой' (DTS); II.
'Curved, bent, bowed' cf. Chag. *kišik* 'krumm' (Radl.
II, 1393). ⇨ **KİČİ.**

KİČİGÄ   Uyg. **Kičigä** (Zieme, Mat. I, 74). ✧ 'Oh,
little!' (Zieme). ⇨ **KİČİG** + voc. suff. -*ä*.

KİČİK see **KİČİG**

KİČİM   1431 **Kičim** [Кичимъ-Ахметъ / Кичихъ-
Ахметъ] (PSRL VIII, 96).

KİČİN   Bashk. 1737 **Kičin-bay** [Арык Кичинбаев]
(MIB I, 325).

KİČİNEY   Alt. 19th-20th c. **Kičiney** [Кичиней] (OjrRS
208). ✧ 'Little, small' (OjrRS 208).

KİČİNEK   Alt. 19th-20th c. **Kicinek-bala**
[Кичинекбала], fem. (OjrRS 212). ✧ 'Little, small'
cf. Alt. *kičinek* 'малость; маленький' (OjrRS).

KİČKENE see **KİČKİNE**

KİČKENTAY see **KİŠKENTAY**

KİČKİ-TAY   Bashk. 1754 **Kički-tay** [Рамазан
Кичкитаевм] (MIB IV/1, 86). ⇨ **TAY** or
suff. -*tay(1,2)*?

KİČKİNE   Kirg. 19th c. **Kečkene-bala** [Kecskene-bala],
Almásy's guide (Almásy 558); Kzk. 19th c. **Keškene-
bay** [Кешкенебай] (SOV 152); Kzk. 19th c. **Kičkene-
bay** [Кичкенебай] (SODž. 66); Tat.(Lit.) 1548
Kločkinä [Кичкиня] (Kn. Metriki Lit. 45); Selj. 1077
Kičkine [كجكينـا / Kadjkīna], chamberlain of Sultan
Melik Shah I (1072-1092), fought in Bahrein (De
Goeje: JA 1895, V, 12); Chag. 16th c. **Kičkine-
bahadur** [Кичкинэ-бахадур] (Ivanov 130, 142);
Chag. 16th c. **Kičkine-bike** [Кичкине-бике], fem.
(Ivanov 299); Kzk. **Kičkine-χoJa** [Кичкина-Ходжа]
(Sb. Syr-D. VII, 132); Bashk. 1738, 1753, 1757, 1761,
Kiskinä [Мурза Кискинин] (MIB III, 387, MIB IV/1,
68, 140, 230); Kzk. 19th c. **Kišken-bay (<Kiškene-
bay?)** [Кишкенбай] (AOP 110). ✧ 'Little, small;
young' cf. Kzk. *kiškene* 'маленький' (KzkRS), Kzk.
kiškīne 'sehr klein' (Radl. II, 1393), Kirg. *kičkinekey*
'малюсенький' (Jud.), Bashk. *keskenä*
'малюсенький, крохотный' (BRS/Uraksin).

KİČKÜNČİ see **KÜČKÜNČİ**

KİČMEK   Bashk. 1709 **Kičmek** [Кичмек] (MIB I,
264).

KİČREK   Maml. 14th c. **Kičrek-be / Kičürik-be?**
[كينُحُزْكِبَ / كجوكنـا / küčükinä? / Kiçrekba], fem.
(Tarj/Houtsma 96, Tarj/Toparlı 43). ✧
'Smaller/younger child'. ⇨ **KİČİ?** + suff. -*rek*.

KİDAY   Kzk. 18th c. **Kiday** [Кидай], a biy (Nepljuev
716).

KİDÄN   Tat.(Bar.) **Kïdän-χān** [Kidän Chan / Кідäн
хан] (Proben IV, 143 /182/). ✧ 'Flax' cf. Tat.(Bar)
kidän 'der Flachs, die Leinewand' (Radl. II, 1377).

KİDİS   Hak. 19th-20th c. **Kidis** [Кидис], fem. (HRS
353).

KİGİK   Bashk. 1754 **Kigik-bay** [Кигикбай Кулуков]
(MIB IV/1, 83).

KİGİMAN   Bashk. 1756 **Kigiman** [Кигиман
Каскинов] (MIB IV/1, 130).

KİGİZ see **KİYİZ**

KİY   Kzk. 19th c. **Kiy-bay** [Кийбай] (SOK 218). ✧
'Muck, dung (of sheep)' cf. Kzk. *qïy* 'der Schafmist'
(Radl. II, 687), Kzk. *qïy* 'кизяк из овечьего помёта'
(KzRS). See also **QOY-KİY.**

KİY-BASAR   Kzk. 19th c. **Kiy-basar** [Кийбасаръ]
(SOV 18). ⇨ **BASAR.**

KİYÄ   Kzk. 19th c. **Kiyä-bay** [Киябай] (SOK 14); Kzk.
19th c. **Kiyä-bay** [Киябай] (SOK 216); Kzk. 19th c.
Kiyä-pay [Кияпай] (SOK 298). ✧ 'Causing
misfortune; ill omen' cf. Kzk. *kiyä* 'unglückbringend,
eine schlechte Vorbedeutung' (Radl. II, 1343).

KİYÄZ see **KİYİZ**

KİYİK   Turk. 1350 **Geyik-baba /Giyik-baba?**
[كييك بـابـا] (Āšikp. 44); Trkm. **Keyik** [Кейик], fem.
(Baskakov); Trkm. 20th c. **Keyik** [Keyik], fem. (Zaj.
1971, 338); Trkm. 20th c. **Keyik** [Кейик], fem.
(TrkmRS 387); Kzk. 19th c. **Kiyek** [Киякъ] (SOK 46);
Kzk. 19th c. **Kiyek-pay** [Киякпай] (SODž. 158); Kzk.
19th c. **Kiyek-pay** [Киякпай] (SOK 130, 280, 284);
Bashk. 1775 **Kiyik** [Шерып Кииков] (MIB IV/1,
380); Kzk. 19th c. **Kiyik / Kïyik** [Кыикъ] (AOK 126);
Tat.(Mish.) 18th c. **Kiyik-bay** [Киикбаев] (MIB V, 60,

61); Bashk. 1794 **Kiyik-bay** [Киикбай Култаев] (MIB V, 338); Kzk. 18th c. - 19th c. **Kiyik-bay** [Буканбай Киикбаев] (MIK IV, 325); Kzk. 1820 **Kiyik-bay** [Киикбай], one of the chiefs of the Turï-ayɣïr tribe (Sib. Vest. IX, 108); Kzk. 19th c. **Kiyik-bay** [كيك باى / Киикбай] (Veselovskij, Kirg. 72, 117); Kzk. 19th c. **Kiyik-pay** [Киикпай] (SOK 54); Kzk. 19th c. **Kiyk** [Кійкъ] (AOK 6); Kzk. 19th c. **Kiyk-atay** [Кийкатай] (SOV 98); Kzk. 19th c. **Kiyk-pay** [Кійкпай] (SODž. 126); Kzk. 19th c. **Kiyk-pay** [Кійкпай] (AOP 14); Kzk. 19th c. **Kiyk-pay** [Кійкпай] (SOV 52); Tat. 1668 **Kĭk-bay** [Акбашко Кикбаев] (Kungursk. akty 9); Bashk. 1709 **Kĭk-bay** [Кикбаев] (MIB I, 264); *EN:* Kzk. 18th c. - 19th c. **Kiyik-bay** [Киикбай] (Tynyšp. 72); *TN:* Kzk. **Kiyik-bay** [Киикбай], a brook, stream in Kazakstan (Kojčubaev 134). ✧ 'Wild animal; wild goat; deer; game' cf. Türk, Uyg., Karakh. *keyik* 'олень, лань; зверь вообще' (DTS), Bashk. *keyek* 'зверь; дичь' (BRS), Kzk. *kiyĭk* 'дикая коза' (KzRS), Chag., Alt., Hak., Kzk., Tat. *kĭk* 'ein wild lebendes Thier, wild (wild lebend)' (Radl. II, 1340), Turk. *geyik* 'Hirsch' (HŞ), *geyik* 'Yırtıcı olmayan dört ayaklı yabani hayvan' (Tan. Tar. Sözl. I). See also **AQ-KİYİK, TOQ-KİYİK.**

KİYİM see **KEDİM**

KİYİR Kzk. 19th c. **Kiyir-bay** [Кіирбай] (SOK 8). ✧ 'He/she will dress' cf. Kuman, Alt., Kirg., Kzk., Tat. *kĭ-* 'anziehen, aufsetzen' (Radl. II, 1339).

KİYİZ Bashk. 1722 **Keyiz-bi-bay** [Кеизбибай] (MIB I, 297); Kzk. 19th c. **Kigiz-bay** [Кигизбай] (SODž. 108); Bashk. 1738 **Kiyez** / **Kiyäð?** [Кияз] (MIB III, 381); Bashk. 1750 **Kiyez** / **Kiyäð?** [Киязь Чючелеев] (MIB III, 472); Bashk. 1754 **Kiyez** / **Kiyäð?** [Сююндук Киязев] (MIB IV/1, 79); Bashk. 1758 **Kiyez** / **Kiyäð?** [Уразлы Киязев] (MIB IV/1, 164); Kirg. **Kiyiz-bay** [Кийизбай] (Jud. 902); Kzk. 19th c. **Kiyz-bay** [Кийзбай] (SODž. 92); Kzk. 19th c. **Kĭyz-bay** [Киизбай] (SOV 26); Kzk. 19th c. **Kĭyz-bay** [Кийзбай] (AOA 54); Kzk. 19th c. **Kĭyz-bay** [Киизбай] (SOK 190); Kzk. 19th c. **Kĭyz-bay** [Киизбай] (SODž. 6). ✧ 'Felt' cf. Kar. (L., T.) *kiyiz* 'die Filzdecke' (Radl II, 1344), Chag., East.T., NUyg.(Tar.) *kigiz* 'die Filzdecke' (Radl. II, 1341), Kzk. *kĭyiz* 'кошма, войлокъ' (PKRS), Kuman, Kzk., Tat. *kĭz* 'die Filzdecke, der Woilok' (Radl. II, 1389), Alt., Hak. *kĭs* 'der Filz, Woilok' (Radl. II, 1384), Bashk. *keyeð* 'войлок' (BRS). See also **QARA-QĬS?**

KİYİZ-ҔAP Kzk. 19th c. **Kiyz-ɣap** [Кійзгапъ] (SODž. 22). ✧ 'Felt bag/sack' cf. Kzk. *qap* 'мешок' (KzRS). ⇨ **KİYİZ.**

KİYK see **KİYİK**

KİYZ see **KİYİZ**

KİKÄN Tat. 1728 **Kikän** [Мух. Киканов] (MIB III, 258).

KİKEY Tat. 1668 **Kikey** [Азикъ Кикѣевъ], first lieutenant (Kungursk. akty 15).

KİKEL Tat.(Lit.) 1591 **Kikel** [Войтехъ Кикель (Кикелевичъ)] (Lit. Tat. 108, 110).

KİKEM Kirg. **Kikem** [Кикем] (Jud. 386).

KİKİÄNÄN Yak. **Kikiänän** [Кікіänän], a smith (Pek.).

KİL see **KEL**

KİL-BARS Chuv. 18th-19th c. **Kil-bars** [Килбарсъ] (Magn. 51); Tat. 20th c. **Kil-bars** [Килбарс] (Sattarov). ⇨ **KEL + BARS.**

KİL-BAŠ Chuv. 18th-19th c. **Kil-baš** [Килбашъ] (Magn. 51). ✧ 'Come (be born) - head (child)' (Sattarov). ⇨ **KEL + BAŠ.**

KİL-DEMİR Chuv. 18th-19th c. **Kil-demir** [Килдемиръ] (Magn. 51); Chuv. 18th-19th c. **Kil-dimer** [Килдимеръ] (Magn. 51). ⇨ **KEL + TEMİR.**

KİL-DİMER see **KİL-DEMİR**

KİL-DUҔAN Chuv. 18th-19th c. **Kil-dugan** [Килдуганъ] (Magn. 51). ⇨ **KEL + TUҔAN I.**

KİL-DUTAK Chuv. 18th-19th c. **Kil-dutak** [Килдутакъ] (Magn. 51). ⇨ **KEL + TUTAQ.**

KİL-MAQAY Bashk. 18th c. **Kil-maqay** [Асунагулъ Кильмакаевъ] (Nepljuev 143). ⇨ **KEL + MAQAY.**

KİL-MAMET see **KEL-MAMET**

KİL-MEMET see **KEL-MAMET**

KİL-SARAY Chuv. 18th-19th c. **Kil-saray** [Килсарай] (Magn. 51). ✧ 'Palast made of white clay'? cf. Turk. *kil* (<P.) 'ein weisser Thon, der als Heilmittel gilt' (Radl. II, 1366). ⇨ **SARAY.**

KİLČİ Bashk. 1761 **Kilči-bay** [Килчибай] (MIB IV/1, 214); Chuv. 18th-19th c. **Kilzi-bey** / **Kilǰi-bey?** [Килзибей] (Magn. 51). ✧ 'Man dealing or working with clay' cf. Turk. *kil* (<P.) 'ein weisser Thon, der als Heilmittel gilt' (Radl. II, 1366) + suff. -*či.*

KİLǰİ see **KİLČİ**

KİLDÄŠ see **KELDİŠ**

KİLDEY Tat.(Tüm.) 1632, 1651 **Gildey** [Гилдей Янабеков (Янебеков)], a murza (Miller, Ist. Sib. II, 391, DAI III, 329); Kkalp. 1691, 1694 **Kildey(-murza)** [Кильдей мурза] (DAI X, 375-380, MIKk. 148); *TN:* Tat. 18th c. **Kildey(evo)** [Килдѣево], a village in the district of Svijažsk (Korsakov 352). ⇨ **KELDİ** + suff. -*y.* See also **DÄWLÄT-KİLDEY, ROZMA-GİLDEY.**

KİLDEŠ see **KELDİŠ**

KİLDEŠEY Chuv. 18th-19th c. **Kildešey** / **Kildäšey?** [Килдашей] (Magn. 51). ⇨ **KELDİŠ** + suff. -*ey.*

KİLDİ see **KELDİ**

KİLDİK Chuv. 18th-19th c. **Kildĭk** [Килдыкъ] (Magn. 51). ✧ 'We came'? (< Tat.?). ⇨ **KEL?** See also **KELDİ.**

KİLDİKEY Bashk. 1783 **Kildikey** [Субхангул Кильдикеев] (MIB V, 143); Bashk. 1783 **Kildikey**

[Базаргул Кильдикеев] (MIB V, 143); Bashk. 1765 **Kildĭkey** [Айсан Килдикеев] (MIB IV/1, 313). ⇨ **KELDİ** + dim. suff. *-key.*

KİLDİŠ see **KELDİŠ**

KİLDİŠ-ČEČEN Tat. 1737 **Kildiš-čečen** [Килдыш-чечен] (MIB I, 307). ⇨ **KELDİŠ** + **ČEČEN.**

KİLÄ Tat. 20th c. **Kilä-bay** [Киләбай] (Sattarov). ✧ 'He/she is coming (=is being born)' (Sattarov). ⇨ **KEL.**

KİLÄN Bashk. 1760 **Kilän** [Умиткул Килянов] (MIB IV, 195). ✧ 'Be glad' cf. Tat. *kilän-* 'sich freuen' (Radl. II, 1368). See also **QUWAN, SEVİN.**

KİLÄŠ Bashk. 1756 **Kiläš** [Кайдыбак Кляшев] (MIB IV/1, 120).

KİLĂPİR Yak. **Kilăpir** [Кіläпір] (Pek.).

KİLE-KİTTÄ Chuv. 18th-19th c. **Kile-kittä / Kilä-kitte?** [Килекитдя] (Magn. 51).

KİLEY Bashk. 1722 **Keley** [Келей Юрабай] (MIB I, 289); Tat. 1764 **Kiley** [Килей Тиркин] (MIB IV/2, 105); Bashk. 1663 **Kiley** [Килей Таникеев] (MIB I, 176); Bashk. 1672 **Kiley** [Килейка Акзкильдин] (MIB I, 74); Bashk. 1712 **Kiley** [Тергов Килеев] (MIB III, 84); Bashk. 1738 **Kiley** [Килей Султанов] (MIB III, 384); Bashk. 1747 **Kiley** [Килей Солтанов] (MIB III, 450); Bashk. 1751 **Kiley** [Килей Алеев] (MIB IV/1, 51); Bashk. 1757, 1761 **Kiley** [Ермак Килеев] (MIB IV/1, 140, 204). ✧ Diminutive of KİLÄ 'He/she is coming (=is being born)' (Sattarov). + suff. *-y.*

KİLEKEY Bashk. 1757 **Kilekey** [Ускильда Килекеев] (MIB IV/1, 136). ⇨ **KİLÄ?** + suff. *-key / -käy.*

KİLEMET Kuman/Tat. 1240 **Kilemet** [Килемет] (PSRL X, 116).

KİLGÄRÄY Yak. **Kilgäräy** [Кілгäпäi] (Pek.). ✧ Grigoriy (R.). ⇨ **KİRGÄLÄY, KİRGİÄLÄY.**

KİLGİÄ Yak. **Kilgiä** [Кілгiä] (Pek.). ✧ Grigoriy (R.). ⇨ **KİLGİÄRÄY.**

KİLGİÄ-OҐONYOR Yak. **Kilgiä-oҐonyor** [Кілгiä-оҕонjор] (Pek.). ✧ 'Uncle Grigoriy' (R.). ⇨ **KİLGİÄ.**

KİLGİÄRÄY Yak. **Kilgiäräy** [Кілгiäпäi] (Pek.). ✧ Grigoriy (R.).

KİLGÜN Bashk. 1756 **Kilgün** [Килгун Кузянгулов] (MIB IV/1, 123); Bashk. 1756 **Kilgün** [Хабибулла Килгунов] (MIB IV/1, 123).

KİLİ see **KELİ**

KİLİK Chag. 16th c. **Kilik-bek** [Килик-бек] (Ivanov 159).

KİLİKEY Bashk. 1706 **Kilikey** [Муракай Киликеев] (MIB III, 26); Bashk. 1757 **Kilikey** [Баязит Киликеев] (MIB IV/1, 19). ⇨ **KELİ, KİLİ / KİLİK** + suff. *-key / -ey.*

KİLİMBET see **KELİMBET**

KİLİN Bashk. 1735 **Kilin? / Kilä?** [Ибрашъ Килинъ], a tarχan (Vel.-Zern., Bašk. 25). ⇨ **KELİÑ?, KİLÄ?**

KİLİNEY Bashk. 1714 **Kiliney** [Килинейко] (MIB I, 107). ⇨ **KELİÑ / KİLİN?** + dim. suff. *-ey.*

KİLİÑES Hak.(Kacha) 19th c. **Kiliñes** [Килингесъ], fem. (Katanov, Otč. II, 42);; ✧ 'Velvet' (Katanov: „barhatec"), cf. Alt. *kiliñ* 'бархат, плис' (OjrRS) + dim. suff. *-es.*

KİLKİ Bashk. 1709 **Kilki** [Килки Икаев] (MIB I, 264).

KİLMÄY see **KELMÄY**

KİLMÄK Tat. 20th c. **Kilmäk** [Килмәк / Килмяков] (Sattarov); Bashk. 1726 **Kilmäk** [Ишимбет Кильмяков] (MIB III, 241); Bashk. 1736 **Kilmäk** [Килмякъ], the same as Kilmäk-abïz, leader of rioters (PSZRI IX, 742, X, 243, XI, 135); Bashk. 1737 **Kilmäk** [Кильмяк] (MIB I, 343); Bashk. 1760 **Kilmäk** [Кильмяк Исекеев] (MIB IV/1, 199); Bashk. 20th c. **Kilmäk** [Килмәк / Кильмак] (Kusimova); Bashk. 1736 **Kilmäk-abïz** [Kilmak Abys / Килмякъ Абызъ], leader of the rioters (PSZRI IX, 836, Nepljuev 141, 146, 147 etc., Rytschkow II, 164); Bashk. 1737 **Kilmäk-mulla** [Килмяк-мулла] (MIB I, 314). ✧ 'To come, to be born'; Sattarov: *'Kilgän (tuɣan) bala* (Come/born child)', also Bashk. PN *Kilmäk* (Kusimova). ⇨ **KEL.**

KİLMÄKÄY Bashk. 1758 **Kilmäkäy** [Тюмекей Килмекеев] (MIB IV/1, 160). ⇨ **KİLMÄK** + suff. *-äy.*

KİLTÄN Bashk. 1759 **Kiltän** [Баши Кильтянов] (MIB IV/2, 24).

KİLTİKÄY Kipch. 1293 **Kiltikäy** [كلتكاى / Кильтикай] (Baybars/Tizeng. I, 86, 109, Nuwairī 137, 158). ⇨ **KELDİ?** + suff. *-käy.*

KİLZİ see **KİLČİ**

KİMÄK Chuv. 18th-19th c. **Kimäk** [Кимякъ] (Magn. 51).

KİMÄNSÜ Uyg. **Kimänsü** [Kimänsü] (EUTS).

KİMÄTTÜ Uyg. 12th c. - 14th c. **Kimättü** [Kimätdü / kimättü] (Radl., USp. 130-131, EUTS, DTS).

KİMEY see **KEMEY**

KİMEKEY Chuv. 18th-19th c. **Kimekey** [Кимекей] (Magn. 51).

KİMSÜN Uyg. 12th c. - 14th c. **Kimsün** [Kimzün], a woman slave (Radl., USp. 109, 251, DTS, Zieme, Mat. I, 81); Uyg. **Kimzin** (Zieme, Mat. I, 74); Uyg. **Kimzün** [Kimzün] (EUTS). ✧ '?' Probably of Chinese origin.

KİMTSÜ Uyg. 12th c. - 14th c. **Kimtsü** (DTS).

KİMÜNSÜ Uyg. **Kimünsü** [Kimünsü] (EUTS); Uyg. 12th c. - 14th c. **Kimünsü** (Radl., USp. 133-134).

KİMZİN see **KİMSÜN**

KİN-QAŠ Bashk. 1738 **Kin-qaš?** [Сюндюк Кинкашев] (MIB III, 380). ✧ I. 'Wide Eyebrow' cf. Bashk. *kiñ* 'широкий' (BRS/Uraksin); II. 'Muskeyebrow'? cf. Karakh. *kin* 'мускус' (DTS). ⇨ **QAŠ?**

KİN-QUŠ Bashk. 1713 **Kin-quš? / Kin-qaš?** [Кинкуш(ев)] (MIB III, 105). ✧ 'Musk-bird'? cf. Karakh. *kin* 'мускус' (DTS). ⇨ **KİN-QAŠ?**

KİN-TİMÜR Khorezm. **Kin-timür** [Кин-Тимур] (RaD II, 78). ✧ 'Musk-(uterus?)-iron'? ⇨ **TEMİR.** See also **KİN-TOΓMÏŠ.**

KİN-TOΓMÏŠ Uyg. 12th c. - 14th c. **Kin-toγmïš** [Kin-Toğmış] (DTS, EUTS). ✧ 'Musk-(uterus?)-relative' (Blagova 1997, 716) cf. Karakh. *kin* 'мускус', Uyg. *kin* 'чрево' (DTS). ⇨ **TOΓMÏŠ.** See also **KİN-TİMÜR.**

KİNJÄ-BULAT see **KENJE-BULAT**

KİNJÄ-QAR Kzk. 19th c. **KinJä-qar** [Кинджакаръ] (Grod., Pril. 37). ⇨ **KENJE + QAR?**

KİNJE see **KENJE**

KİNJEKEY see **KENJEKEY**

KİNJİ see **KENJE**

KİNDÄK see **KİNDİK**

KİNDİ Bashk. 1707 **Kindi-bäk** [Сапар Киндибяков] (MIB III, 35).

KİNDİK Tat.(GH) 1341, 1342 **Kindäk** [Киндякъ], envoy of the Horde (PSRL VII, 209, X, 215); Tat.(GH) 1399 **Kindäk** [Киндякъ], a prince (PSRL XI, 176); Chuv. 18th-19th c. **Kindik** [Киндикъ] (Magn. 51); Alt. 19th-20th c. **Kindik** [Киндик] (OjrRS 208); Kzk. 19th c. **Kindik-pay / Kïndïk-pay?** [Кындыкпай] (SOK 226). ✧ 'Navel' cf. Chag., Alt., Hak., Kzk., Kirg. *kindik* 'der Nabel' (Radl. II, 1348).

KİNDİKEY Chuv. 1738 **Kendekey** [Кѣндѣкѣев] (Letop. ZAK (1864), 142); Bashk. 1710 **Kindikey** [Тимяш Киндикеев] (MIB III, 67). ⇨ **KİNDİK +** suff. -*ey.*

KİNDİRÄS Bashk. 1763 **Kindiräs** [Киндряс Мулакаев] (MIB IV/2, 45); Bashk. 1785 **Kindiräs** [Киндрясь] (MIB V, 170).

KİNÄS Yak. **Kinäs-oyūn** [Кинäс-оjун], a very powerful evil spirit (üör), a shaman in the past (Pek.).

KİNE Hak. 19th-20th c. **Kine** [Кине] (HRS 349). ✧ Gena (R.) dim.-hypoc. of R. Gennadiy (Butanaev).

KİNEN Bashk. 1675 **Kinen-bay** [Киненбай] (MIB I, 200); Kzk. 19th c. **Kinen-bay** [Киненбай] (SOK 128). ✧ 'Enjoy, relish' cf. Tat. *kinän-* 'geniessen, sich delectiren an etwas' (Radl. II, 1346).

KİNENEY Tat. 1764 **Kineney** [Аптыкей Киненеев] (MIB IV/2, 105). ⇨ **KENEN +** suff. -*ey.*

KİNİK Bashk. 1735 **Kinik** [Киникъ Качкаровъ], a tarχan (Vel.-Zern., Bašk. 15).

KİNİR Tat. 1600 **Kinir / Kiñir?** [Буланча Кинырев] (Miller, Ist. Sib. II, 159, MIB I, 152).

KİNYÄ see **KENJE**

KİNKÄ Tat. 1696 **Kinkä** [Кинка] (Kungursk. akty 240).

KİNZÄ see **KENJE**

KİNZÄ-BULAT see **KENJE-BULAT**

KİNZÄFER Bashk. 1769 **Kinzäfer?** [Кинзяфер (Канзяфер, Канзяфар, Канзафар) Усеев] (MIB IV/2, 389).

KİNZÄKÄY see **KENJEKEY**

KİNZE see **KENJE**

KİNZEKÄY see **KENJEKEY**

KİNZİ see **KENJE**

KİNZİKEY see **KENJEKEY**

KİNŽÄŠ Bashk. 1735 **Kinžäš** [Кинзяшъ Дербышевъ] (Vel.-Zern., Bašk. 15). ⇨ **KENJE +** suff. -*š.*

KİNŽE-ΓARA see **KENJE-QARA**

KİÑSÜN Uyg. **Kiñsün** [Kingsün] (EUTS).

KİÑSÜN-AYAQ Uyg. 12th c. - 14th c. **Kiñsün-ayaq** [kiŋsün ajaq] (Radl., USp. 112-113, DTS). ✧ 'Kiñsün-Foot' (Blagova 1997, 709). ⇨ **KİÑSÜN + AYAQ.**

KİPČAQ see **QÏPČAQ**

KİPKEY Karch. **Kipkey** [Чёпе Кипкеевъ] (Sysoev 128).

KİR NUyg. 19th c. **Kir** [كير] (Le Coq, Namenl. 106). ✧ 'Dirt(y), smudge' (Le Coq), cf. East.T. *kir* 'dirty, soiled, dirt, (dirty) laundry' (Jarring). See also **BABA-KİR.**

KİRBÄZ Bashk. 1773 **Kirbäz-γul** [Султан Кирбязгулов] (MIB IV/2, 412); Bashk. 1776 **Kirbäz-γul** [Кирбязгул] (MIB V, 41, 42, 43, 96). ✧ 'Brick' cf. Bashk. *kirbes* 'кирпич' (BRS).

KİRÄSTİYÄN Hak.(Sag.) 19th-20th c. **Kirästiyän** [Кірäстійäн] (Katanov, Otč. 8). ✧ 'Peasant' cf. R. крестьянинъ (Katanov).

KİRÄS Karg. **Kiräs** [Kipäc], fem. (Katanov, Otč. 9). ✧ 'Cross' cf. R. крестъ (Katanov).

KİREY see **KERÄY**

KİREYT Kzk. 19th c. **Kireyt** [Кирейтъ] (AOK 98). ✧ 'Coming from the tribe (clan) Kireyit'.

KİREK Chuv. 18th-19th c. **Kirek** [Кирекъ] (Magn. 51). ⇨ **KEREK?**

KİRGÄLÄY Yak. **Kirgäläy** [Кіргäläi] (Pek.). ✧ Grigoriy (R.).

KİRGİÄLÄY Yak. **Kirgiäläy** [Кіргіäläi] (Pek.). ✧ Grigoriy (R.).

KİRİK see **QÏRQ**

KİRİLÄ see **KİRİLLÄ**

KİRİLLÄ Karg. **Kerîlä** (Katanov, Otč. 9); Yak. **Kirilä** [Кіріlä] (Pek.); Yak. **Kirillä** [Кіріллä] (Pek.); Hak.(Sag.) 19th-20th c. **Kirîlä** [Кіріlä] (Katanov, Otč. 8); Yak. **Kirîllä** [Кіріллä] (Pek.); Hak. 19th-20th c. **Krile** [Криле] (HRS 349). ✧ Kirill (R.), cf. R. Кирила (Pek.), Кириллъ (Katanov).

KİRİM see **KERİM**

KİRİSTÄPİÄR Yak. **Kiristäpiär** [Кірістäпіäр] (Pek.). ✧ Hristofor (R.).

KİRİSTİÄS see **QRİSTUOS**

KİRİŠ I. Shor 19th-20th c. **Kiriš** [Поктуг Кириш] (Dyrenkova 176); Turk. **Kiriš-oγlu**, a Zeybek (NYK

XXII, 119). ✧ 'Catgut/bowstring' (Butanaev: Kïrïs).

KİRİŠ II.   Alt. 19th-20th c. **Kiriš** [Кириш] (OjrRS 208). ✧ Grisha (R.), diminutive of R. Grigoriy.

KİRİŠQA   Alt. 19th-20th c. **Kirišqa** [Киришка] (OjrRS 208). ✧ Grishka (R.) diminutive of R. Grigorij.

KİRİLÄ see **KİRİLLÄ**

KİRİLKÄ   Yak. **Kirïlkä** [Кірілкä] (Pek.). ✧ Kirilka (R.), diminutive of R. Kirill (Кирилл).

KİRİLLÄ see **KİRİLLÄ**

KİRİSÄ   Yak. **Kirïsä** [Кіріcä] (Pek.). ✧ Grisha (R.), diminutive of R. Grigoriy.

KİRİSÄLİR   Yak. **Kirïsälïr** [Кіріcäлір] (Pek.). ✧ Grishenka (R.), diminutive of R. Grisha. ⇨ **KİRİSÄ.**

KİRİSKÄ   Hak.(Sag.) 19th-20th c. **Kirïska** [Кіріcкä] (Katanov, Otč. 7, 8). ✧ Grishka (R.).

KİRKİN   Hak. 19th-20th c. **Kirkin** [Киркин] (HRS 349).

KİRLİ   Trkm. 1879 **Kirli** [Кирли Мамедъ-оглы] (Grod., Pril. 109). ✧ 'Dirty' cf. Trkm. *kirli* 'грязный' (TrkmRS). ⇨ **KİR** + suff. *-li*.

KİRPİS   Karg. **Kirpïs** [Кірпіc], fem. (Katanov, Otč. 9). ✧ 'Brick' cf. R. кирпичъ (Katanov).

KİRT   Kzk. 19th c. **Kirt** [Киртъ] (SOK 50). ✧ 'Rustle, crash'.

KİRWAN   Kzk. 19th c. **Kirwan-bay** [Кирванбай] (Grod., Pril. 78). ✧ 'Caravan' cf. Kzk. *kerwen* 'караван' (RKzS).

KİSÄ   Kzk. 19th c. **Kisä-bey / Kisa-bek?** [Кисабекъ] (SOK 230); Bashk. 1776 **Kisä-γul** [Кисягул Янеев] (MIB V, 39). ✧ 'Leather bag; purse' cf. Tat. *kisa* 'der lederne Beutel (der Schneider)', Kzk., Turk. *kisä* 'eine Ledertasche, die an der Seite am Gürtel getragen wird, in welcher man Pulver und Patronen aufbewahrt' (Radl. II, 1385).

KİSMÄK   Bashk. 1724 **Kesmäk** [Келчюра Кесмяков] (MIB III, 222); Bashk. 1722 **Kismäk** [Келчюра-бай Кисмяк(ов)] (MIB I, 109).

KİSTÄN   Hak.(Koyb.) 19th-20th c. **Kistän** [Кістäн], fem. (Katanov, Otč. 13). ✧ 'Mace-Black' cf. R. кистень (Katanov), Chag., Tat. *kistän* 'der Stock zum Butterschlagen, der Prügel' (Radl. II, 1388).

KİSTÄN-QARA   Chag. 16th c. **Kistän-qara** [كيستن قرا سللان / Кистенъ Гкара Султанъ], a Sheybanid sultan (Šejb. LXXIX). ✧ 'Mace-Black' cf. R. кистень (Katanov), Chag., Tat. *kistän* 'der Stock zum Butterschlagen, der Prügel' (Radl. II, 1388).

KİSTÄŠ   Chag. / Uzb. 1600 **Kistäš** [Енбай Кишташев], from Bukhara (MIB I, 153, 160).

KİSTEY   Karg. **Kistey** [Кыштей] (Katanov: ZIRGOÊtn. XVII (III), 153).

KİSTEŠ   Hak.(Shor)? 19th c. **Kisteš** [Кыштеш] (Verb., In. 126).

KİŠ   Chuv. 18th-19th c. **Kiš** [Кишъ] (Magn. 52). ✧ 'Sable' (Ligeti, R. tör. nev. II-III, 137), cf. Karakh.,

Oghuz *kiš* 'соболь' (DTS), Kuman *kiš* 'Zobel' (CC), Nog. *kis* 'соболь' (NRS), Tat. *kiš* 'der Zobel' (Radl. II, 1414), Bashk. *keš* 'соболь' (BRS), Tat. *keš* 'соболь' (TatRS), cf. also Trk. **kīš* (Räs.). See also **AQ-QİŠ?, AL-KEŠ, BAY-KEŠ, KEY-KİŠ, QARA-KEŠ.**

KİŠ-TOΓAN   Selj. **Kiš-toγan** [كشطغان المعروف], an emir, Ay-doγdï's father (Bondārī 230, 287, Ibn al-Athīr/Tornb. XI, 106). ⇨ **KİŠ** + **TOΓAN / TUΓAN I.**

KİŠ-TOΓDİ   Maml. 1264, 1279 **Kiš-toγan** [علا'الـديـن كشتغدى البـهـادرى], died at Akka in 1291 (Zetterst. 152, 156, Makrīzī II, 2, 171); Maml. 1264, 1279 **Kiš-toγan** [علا'الـديـن كشتغدى الشـمـسى], died at Akka in 1291 (Zetterst. 152, 156, Makrīzī II, 2, 171). ⇨ **KİŠ** + **TUΓDİ.**

KİŠÄČÜK   Uyg. 12th c. - 14th c. **Kišäčük** (Radl., USp. 82, DTS). ✧ 'Little sable' (Bese 6). ⇨ **KİŠ** + dim. suff. *-čük.*

KİŠİK see **KİČİG**

KİŠİM   Kirg. **Kišim** [Кишим], fem. (Jud. 168); Kirg. **Kišim-Jan** [Кишимжан], fem. (Jud. 139, 623). ✧ 'My (little) sable'. ⇨ **KİŠ** + poss. suff. *-im.*

KİŠKEY see **TİŠKEY**

KİŠKEN see **KİČKİNE**

KİŠKENTAY   Kzk. 19th c. **Keškentay** [Кешкентай] (SOV 96); Kzk. **Kičkentay** [Акашкаръ Кичкентаевъ] (Voenn. Sb. XLVII, 170); Kzk. 19th c. **Kiškentay** [Кишкентай] (SODž. 88); *TN:* Kzk. **Kičkentay** [Кичкентай] (Karta JAR XI). ✧ 'Little (young child)' cf. Kzk. *kiškentay (=kiškene)* 'маленький; немного' (KzRS). ⇨ **KİČKİNE** + suff. *-tay(1,2)*?

KİŠMİŠ   Kirg. **Kišmiš** [Кишмиш] (Proben V, 192 /194/). ✧ 'Raisin' cf. Kirg. *kišmiš* 'кишмиш', *kišmiš Jem* '(в эпосе) отборный корм для боебого коня' (Jud.).

KİŠTİ   Bashk. 1740 **Kišti** [Кышты (Кишты)], Mindi-γul's wife (MIB I, 399).

KİTÄ   Kzk. 1803, 1820 **Kitä-bay(-biy)** [Китябай-бий], a biy, one of the chiefs of the Čümekey (Jildus) tribe belonging to the Little Horde (Kiši Žüz) (MIK IV, 514, Sib. Vest. IX, 114).

KİTÄP   Bashk. 1714 **Kitäp** [Рыс Китяпов] (MIB I, 105); Bashk. 1714 **Kitäp** [Урмен Китяпов] (MIB I, 105); Bashk. 1723 **Kitäp** [Китяп Тленчеев] (MIB III, 212); Bashk. 1737 **Kitäp** [Китяп Тлечеин (Тленчин?)] (MIB III, 375); Bashk. 1759 **Kitäp** [Чюракай Китяпов] (MIB IV/1, 176); Bashk. 1759 **Kitäp** [Сагандык Китяпов] (MIB IV/1, 176); Bashk. 1760 **Kitäp** [Макуш Китяпов] (MIB IV/1, 184). ✧ 'Book' cf. Bashk. *kitap* 'книга' (BRS/Uraksin), Tat. *kitap* (Ar.) 'das Buch' (Radl. II, 1374).

KİTEY see **QİTAY**

KİTİČ   Bashk. 1761 **Kitič / Kitiš?** [Куват Китичев] (MIB IV/1, 209).

KİTİY   Bashk. **Kitiy?** [Зюбеир Китиев] (MIB IV/1, 285).

KİTİK see **KETİK**

KİTİR   Uyg. 12th c. - 14th c. **Kitir** (Radl., USp. 123).

KİZÄK   Bashk. 1756 **Kizäk** [Мугаш Кизяков] (MIB IV/1, 122); Bashk. 1756 **Kizäk** [Байкас Кизяков] (MIB IV/1, 122); Bashk. 1756 **Kizäk** [Байслан Кизяков] (MIB IV/1, 122); *TN:* Bashk. 1737 **Kizäk** [Кизяк], a village (MIB I, 339). ✧ 'Turf, peat' cf. Tat. dial. *kizäk* 'id.' (TatRS).

KİZÄNÄK   Chuv. 18th-19th c. **Kizänäk** [Кизенякъ] (Magn. 51). ✧ 'Hand' cf. Tat. dial. *kizänäk* 'рука' (TatRS).

KİZİ   Hak.(Sag.) 19th-20th c. **Kizi** [Кізі] (Katanov, Otč. 8). ✧ 'Man' (Katanov).

KİZLİ   Khorezm. 1208 **Kizli** [Кизли], a Turk from the suite of Türkân-χatun, the ruler of Nishapur (MIT I, 449).

KİK see **KİYİK**

KİLİP   Yak. **Kilip** [Кіліп] (Pek.). ✧ Kirik (R.?).

KİŠTÄY   Karg. **Kištäy** [Кіштäі (Спиридонъ Иваровичъ)] (Proben IX, 658, 659).

KLA   Hak. 19th-20th c. **Kla** [Кла], fem. (HRS 353). ✧ Klava (R.)? cf. Hak. fem. PN *Qila(nča)* (Butanaev).

KLAN see **QÏLAN**

KLİS   Hak. 19th-20th c. **Klis** [Клис], fem. (HRS 353). ✧ 'Velvet' cf. Shor *kilis* 'der Sammet' (Radl. II, 1371).

KOX-BULAT   Chuv. 18th-19th c. **Koχ-bulat** [Кохбулатъ] (Magn. 53). ⇨ **KÖK + BULAT.**

KON-MURZA   Chuv. 18th-19th c. **Kon-murza** [Конмурза] (Magn. 52). ⇨ **MURZA.**

KORS-PULAT   Chuv. 18th-19th c. **Kors-pulat** [Корспулатъ] (Magn. 52). ✧ '?-steel'. ⇨ **BULAT.**

KOZAR   Chuv. 18th-19th c. **Kozar** [Козаръ] (Magn. 52).

KÖBDÜK   Kzk. 19th c. **Köbdük** [Кобдукъ] (SOK 106); Kzk. 19th c. **Köbdük** [Кобдукъ] (SOV 14, 116); Kzk. 1823 **Köbdük-biy** [كوبدوك بى / Кобдук бий] (MIK IV, 46, 462).

KÖBÄK see **KÖPÄK**

KÖBÄLÄK   Kzk. 19th c. **Köbäläk** [Кобелекъ] (AOK 98). ✧ 'Butterfly' cf. Kuman *köbäläk* 'der Schmetterling' (Radl. II, 1315).

KÖBEY see **KÖPÄY**

KÖBEK see **KÖPÄK**

KÖBEN   Kzk. 19th c. **Köben** [Кобенъ] (AOK 42); Kzk. **Köbön** [Кобöн], Qarasay's son (Proben III. 134 /170/); Kzk. **Köbön / Köböñ** [كوبانكه] (Divaev, Biket 7, 48); Kzk. 19th c. **Kömen** [Коменъ] (SOK 202). ✧ 'Meagre, weak horse' cf. Hak., Kzk. *köböñ* 'ein Pferd, das sich schnell satt isst, aber nicht viel aushält' (Radl. II, 1316), also Kzk. PN *Köben* (Žanuzakov-Esbaeva).

KÖBEŠ   Kzk. 19th c. **Köbeš** [бій Кобешъ] (Potanin II, 2, 3); Kzk. 19th c. **Köbeš-pay** [Кобешпай] (AOK 14);

Kirg. **Köböš** [Кöбöш] (Jud. 46, 405).

KÖBİRJİN-POYBAS   Hak.(Kacha) 19th-20th c. **Köbirjin-poybas** [Кöбірцін-Поібас], fem. (Proben IX, 545, 546).

KÖBİRGÄN   Hak. 19th c. **Köbirgän**, fem. (Katanov, Otč. 12). ✧ 'Green onion' (Butanaev). See also **SOГAN, SOГONOQ.**

KÖBÖK   Kirg. 19th c. **Köbök** [Кöбöк] (Potanin II, 3); Alt. 19th-20th c. **Köbök** [Кöбöк] (OjrRS 208); *EN:* Nog. 20th c. **Köbök-uruw** [Коьбоьк урув], an Aqnoγay clan in the district of Mineralovodsk (Bask., Nog. 135). ✧ I. A Tatar tribe, cf. Alt.(Tel.) *Köbök* 'ein Tatarenstamm, der am Flusse Ulagan (einem Nebenflusse des Baschkaus) wohnt' (Radl. II, 1315); II. The name of an epic hero, cf. *Ak-Köbök* 'ein in Liedern besungener Held' (Radl. II, 1315). See also **AQ-KÖBEK.**

KÖBÖN see **KÖBEN**

KÖBÖÑ see **KÖBEN**

KÖBÖŠ see **KÖBEŠ**

KÖBRÄK   Tat. 1752 **Köbräk** [Кобрякъ Акмаевъ] (PSZRI XIII, 737).

KÖBÜK   Kzk. **Köbük** [Кöбӱк] (Proben III, 191 /230/). ✧ 'Foam' cf. Alt., Shor, Kzk., etc. *köbük* 'der Schaum' (Radl. II, 317), Chag., Turk. *köpük* 'id.' (Radl. II, 1311). ⇨ **KÖBÖK?**

KÖCÜM see **KÜČÜM**

KÖČ-KELDİ   Uzb. 20th c. **Köč-keldi** [Кӱчкелди] (Begmatov 1984, 202); Bashk. 1780 **Küč-kilde?** [Кучкильда Смаилов] (MIB V, 114, 115); Bashk. 1764 **Küč-kildi / Küč-kilde?** [Чувашай Кучкильдин] (MIB IV/1, 303). ✧ I. 'Time of migration came; Goods and chattels has come' cf. Uzb. *köč* 'имущество, домашние вещи (при перевозке, переселении); рой' (UzbRS); II. 'Strength (=supporter) came'? ⇨ **KÜČ? + KELDİ.**

KÖČ-QONDÏ   Khorezm. 1225 **Köč-qondï** [كوج قندي / Koudj Qandi], Jelāl's (1220-1231) officer (Nasawī 1-7); Khorezm. 1220/21 **Küč-qandï / Köč-qondï?** [Куч-Канди] (MIT I, 483). ✧ 'The nomadic camp settled down' cf. Uyg., Chag. *köč* 'die Reise, Wanderung, Uebersiedlung, der Jurtenzug' (Radl. II, 1287). ⇨ **QONDÏ.**

KÖČÄGÄS   Hak.(Sag.) 19th-20th c. **Köčägäs** [Кöчäгäc] (Proben IX, 432). ✧ 'Puppy' cf. *köčägäš* 'ein junger Hund' (Radl. II, 1289).

KÖČE   Chuv. 18th-19th c. **Köče-bay** [Кочебай] (Magn. 53); Kzk. 1630 **Köče-bay / Köše-bay?** [Кочебай] (Miller, Ist. Sib. II, 373). ⇨ **KÖČÖ?**

KÖČEBE   Maml. 13th c. **Köčebe** [سعد الدين كوجبا الناصرى] (Zetterst. 27, 46); Khorezm. 1225 **Köčebe / Köčebe-kök-χan** [كوجابه كك حان], byname of Jelāl's (1220-1231) emir, Kök-χan (Nasawī 176); Kzk. 19th c. **Köšebe** [Кошебе]

(AOP 106); Maml. 14th c. **Küč-be** [كوجِبا / كوجَبا /
Kücba] (Tarǰ/Houtsma 96, TarǰToparlı 42); *TN:* Selj.
12th c. **Köčebe** [كوجبا النورىَ / مسجد/], a mosque
named after him (Ibn Šaddād, Alep 81); Selj. 12th c.
Köčebe [ابن كوجبا / مسجد/], a mosque named after
him (Ibn Šaddād, Alep 85); Maml. 12th c. **Köčebe**
[كوجبا / مسجد/], a mosque after him (Ibn
Šaddād, Alep 74). ✧ 'Nomad' (Sauvaget 55).

KÖČEBE-KÖK-XAN see **KÖČEBE, KÖK**

KÖČEY Chuv. 18th-19th c. **Köčey** [Кочей] (Magn.
53); Tat. 1774 **Küčäy** [Кучай] (Dobrosm., Turg. 151);
Tat. 20th c. **Küčäy** [Кучай / Кучаев] (Sattarov);
Bashk. 1783 **Küčey** [Кучей Зияшев] (MIB V, 137);
Kzk. 19th c. **Küčey** [Чумекей Кучѣевъ] (Grod., Pril.
85). ✧ 'Nomad', dialectal variant of *Küčerbay*
(Sattarov). See also **KÖČER**.

KÖČEK see **KÖŠEK**

KÖČEK-ALÏ Kzk. 19th c. **Köčeg-alï?** [Кочегалы]
(AOK 34). ⇨ **KÖČEK + ALİ.**

KÖČEM Tat. 1631 **Köčem / Köčel?** [Кочем (Кочел)]
(Miller, Ist. Sib. II, 386).

KÖČENEK Kkalp. 1820 **Köčenek-biy** [Кёченек бий]
(MIKk. 115, 116). ✧ 'Nomad' cf. Uyg., Chag., Alt.,
Kirg. etc. *köč*- 'nomadisieren' (Radl. II, 1282). +
suff. *-enek*.

KÖČER Uzb. 20th c. **Köčär** [Кӱчар] (Begmatov 1984,
203); Uzb. 20th c. **Köčär-ây** [Кӱчарой], fem.
(Begmatov 1984, 203); Uzb. 20th c. **Köčär-qul**
[Кӱчаркул] (Begmatov 1984, 203); Uzb. 20th c.
Köčär-mirza [Кӱчармирза] (Begmatov 1984, 203);
Tat. 1633 **Köčer-bay** [Кочербайко Чубаев] (MIB I,
70); Kzk. 19th c. **Köčer-bay** [Кочербай] (AOK 86);
Tat./Bashk.? 1773 **Küčer-bay** [Кучербай
Арасланов], a Teptär (MIB IV/2, 132); Bashk. 1772
Küčer-bay [Кучербай] (MIB IV/1, 364); Bashk. 1779
Küčer-bay [Кучербаи Ишкильдеев] (MIB V, 94);
Bashk. 1780 **Küčer-bay** [Кучербай Иметбаев] (MIB
V, 115); Kzk. 1811 **Küčer-bay** [Кучербай] (TOUAK
XXIV, 41); Bashk. 1737 **Küčer-mulla** [Кучер-мулла]
(MIB I, 354); *TN:* Kzk. **Küčer-bay-qum** [Кучербай-
кумъ] (Tr. Syr-D. OSK 1888, 74). ✧ 'Nomad' cf.
Maml. *köčäri* [كوجَرِي] „nomade" (Sauvaget 55), Chag.
köčär 'der Nomade' (Radl. II, 1289).

KÖČKÄN Uzb. 20th c. **Köčkän** [Кӱчкан] (Begmatov
1984, 203). ✧ 'Migrated/moved away' cf. Uzb. *köč*-
'переезжать, переселяться' (UzbRS).

KÖČKÄN-MURAD Uzb. 20th c. **Köčkän-murâd**
[Кӱчканмурод] (Begmatov 1984, 203).

KÖČKEN Maml.? 1298 **Köčken** [سيف الـدين كجكن /
Kedjken], fought in Lesser Armenia (Makrīzī IV, 60,
Weil, Chalif. I, 206, 211, Zetterst. 47-49, 110); Maml.
1338/39 **Küč-kün / Köčkän? / Köčikän?** [عبدالله
بن كجكن السيفى/], an emir, died in 1338/39, his name

preserved in an inscription of a mausoleum in
Damascus (Mayer 145, Sauvaget 54, Zetterst. 42, 47-
49, 110). ✧ 'Kite; eagle' cf. Maml. *köckän* 'Kerkes
kuşu' [kite] (AH), *küčkän* 'Adler, Geier'
(Tarǰ/Houtsma).

KÖČKİN Uzb. 20th c. **Köčkin** [Кӱчкин] (Begmatov
1984, 203); Uzb. 20th c. **Köčkin-ây** [Кӱчкиной], fem.
(Begmatov 1984, 203); Uzb. 20th c. **Köčkin-bek**
[Кӱчкинбек] (Begmatov 1984, 203); Uzb. 20th c.
Köčkin-ǰân [Кӱчкинжон] (Begmatov 1984, 203);
Uzb. 20th c. **Köčkin-χoǰa** [Кӱчкинхӱжа] (Begmatov
1984, 203); Uzb. 20th c. **Köčkin-qul** [Кӱчкинкул]
(Begmatov 1984, 203). ✧ 'He who moves/migrates;
Nomad'. ⇨ **KÖČKÄN.**

KÖČMEK Kuman 1283, 1284 **Köčmek / Küčmek?**
[Kuchmek, Kucmeg], a christened Kuman in Hungary
(Gyárfás II, 447, 450); Bashk. 1737 **Küsmäk** [Кусмяк
Чувашев] (MIB I, 324). ✧ 'Wandering' (Rásonyi,
KÖA 118, Rásonyi, Anthr. 143, Gombocz, ÁTSz. 32),
cf. Uyg., Chag., Alt., Kar., Kirg. *köč*-, Tat. *küč*-
'nomadisieren, übersiedeln' (Radl. II, 1287, 1491),
Bashk. *küs*- 'переходить, переселяться'
(BRS/Uraksin) + suff. *-mek*.

KÖČÖ Alt. 19th-20th c. **Köčö** [Кӧчӧ], fem. (OjrRS
212). ✧ 'Soup or squash made of barley' (OjrRS), cf.
Hak. *köčä* 'eine Suppe oder ein Brei aus ganzen
Gerstenkörnern' (Radl. II, 1288).

KÖČPES see **KÖŠPES**

KÖDÄLÄ Tuv. 19th c. **Ködälä** [Кӧдäлä] (Proben IX,
147).

KÖDER Hak.(Kacha) 19th-20th c. **Ködär** [Кӧдäр]
(Proben IX, 558); Hak. 19th-20th c. **Köder** [Кӧдер]
(HRS 349).

KÖDES Hak. 19th-20th c. **Ködēs** [Кӧдеес], fem. (HRS
353); Hak. 19th-20th c. **Ködēs** [Кӧдеес] (HRS 349). ✧
'Pot made of iron' cf. Hak. *ködes* 'горшок, чугун,
чугунок' (HRS).

KÖDĒS see **KÖDES**

KÖDÖN see **KÖTÄN**

KÖDÜLÄ Tuv. 19th c. **Ködülä / Kötïlä / Ködül-aqqï**
[Кӧдӱлä / Кӧтiлä / Кӧдӱл' аккы], Tat. name of the
Kacha person Evgraf Prokop'evič Mohov (Proben IX,
100).

KÖGÄN Tuv. 19th c. **Kögän** [Натсын-Кӧгäн-
Конҕар], a hero (bogatyr) (Proben IX, 131).

KÖGEDEY Kzk. 19th c. **Kögedey** [Когедай], in
Kazak folklore (Potanin II, 150). ⇨ **KÖKÖTÖY?**

KÖGEY-KÖK Shor 19th-20th c. **Kögey-kök**, Öleñ-
tayčї's wife (Dyrenkova 74). ⇨ **KÖGÖY + KÖK?**

KÖGER Kzk. 19th c. **Köger-bay** [Когербай] (AOAtb.
38).

KÖGEREY Hak. 19th-20th c. **Kögerey** [Кӧгерей],
fem. (HRS 353).

KÖGÖY Hak.(Kyz.) 19th-20th c. **Kögöy / Kögöy-qan**
(Radl. II, 105). ✧ 'Dear little! My dearest!' cf. Hak. PN

Kökey 'ласковое название ребенка' (Butanaev).

KÖGÖY-PÜRČÜK Hak.(Kyz.) 19th-20th c. **Kögöy-purčuq** / **Kögöy-pürčük** [Köröi Пурчук / Пÿрчÿк], Kögöy-qan's daughter (Proben II, 667, 677680, 685). ✧ 'Dearest tuft/bud (?)' cf. Turk. *pürčük* 'die Locke' (Radl. IV, 1400), Alt. *pürčük* 'die Blattknospen der Bäume' (Radl. IV, 1400). ⇨ **KÖGÖY.**

KÖGÖN Alt. 19th-20th c. **Kögön** [Köгöн] (OjrRS 208). ✧ 'Fly, horse-fly, gadfly'.

KÖGÖRČİN see KÖGÖRŠİN

KÖGÖRŠİN Kzk. **Kögöršin-qan** [كوكورچن حان / Kögöršin kan] (Divaev-Anderson 434-36); Tat. 20th c. **Kügärčen** [Кÿгəрченев, Кугарчинов] (Sattarov); *TN:* Bashk. 1788 **Kügürčin** [Кугурчинская дорога] (MIB V, 229). ✧ 'Dove' cf. Alt. *kögörčün*, Kzk. *kögöršün* 'die Taube' (Radl. II, 1232), Kzk. *kögirşin* / *kögarşın* [*kögäršin?*] 'güvercin' (KzTS), Tat. *kügärčin* 'die Taube' (Radl. II, 1427).

KÖGÜLDEY Alt. **Kögüldey** [Когульдей] (Nikiforov 117). Alt.(Tel.) **Kögüldey-batïr**, a constellation (Radl. II, 1233); Karg. **Kügüldäy** [Кÿгÿлдäй], fem. (Katanov, Otč. 9); Tat. 1662 **Kükildey** [Кукилдěико] (DAI IV, 286) ⇨ **KÖKÜL** + suff. *-dey* / *-däy*.

KÖXÖ-BŪRAY Yak. **Köχö-būray-toyon** [Köxö-бураi-тоjон], Ulūtuyar-ulū-toyon's son, the chief of nine tribes of evil spirits (Pek.).

KÖXÖRGÖS Yak. **Köχörgös** [Köxöргöc] (Pek.).

KÖY-TEYİK Kirg. **Köy-teyik** [Köi Tejиk] (Proben V, 105 /106/).

KÖYGÖLDÜ Kzk. **Köygöldü** [Köiгöлдÿ] (Proben III, 80 /103/). ✧ 'Trembled' cf. Kirg. *köyköl-* 'zittern, vibriren' (Radl. II, 1217).

KÖK Trkm. 20th c. **Gök** [Gök] (Zaj. 1971, 333); Trkm. 20th c. **Gök** [Гёк] (TrkmRS 199); Turk. 20th c. **Gök-jan-oγlu**, a Zeybek (Kúnos 1891, 119); Oghuz 13th c. **Kök** [Kök], Oghuz Khan's (Oghuz Kaghan's) son in the legend of origin (Oğuz K. Dest. 15, Šejb. XXIII, DTS, EUTS); Crm. **Kök** [Kök Jанбаi] (Proben VII, 160); Selj. **Kök** / **Kök-alp** [كوك الب / كك الب], fhe forefather of Ottoman dynasty; the same as Kök-χan (Āšikp. 50, Nešrī); Oghuz/Trkm. 13th c. **Kök** / **Kök-χan** [كوك / كوكخان / Kouk / Kök-хан], Oghuz Khan's (Oghuz Kaghan's) son in the legend of origin (RaD I/1, 76, Abulg./Desm. 23, Abulg./Kon. 430, 510, 520, 555); Selj. **Kök-alp** [كوك الب] (Ibn Bībī III, 218); Maml. **Kök-bay** [Sayf Koûk bây el Mansoûry], emir-in-chief (Sauvaire VI, 255); Maml. 1455 **Kök-bay** [تربة كوكباى] (Ibn Taghrīb. VII, 466, 584); Oghuz/Trkm. 13th c. **Kök-χan** [كوك حان / Kök-хан], Dib-baquy-χan's son (Abulg./Kon. 150); Kzk. 19th c. **Kök-χan** [Кок-хан] (Verb., In. 139); Khorezm. 1225 **Kök-χan** / **Kük-χan** / **Köčebe-kök-χan** [كوج ابه ككخان / Кукъ-Ханъ], Jelāleddīn's (1220-1231) emir, the commander of the garnison in Bukhara at the time of Chinggis Khan's attack (Nasawī 176, RaD/Ber. III, 53); Shor 19th-20th c. **Kök-qān** (Dyrenkova 74); Kzk. 1850 **Kök-pay** [Кокпай] (Konšin, Mat. V, 103); Kzk. 19th c. **Kök-sulu** [Коксулу] (SOK 122); Tat.(Dobr.) 19th c. **Kök-šora**, a Tatar by the Danube (Kúnos 1904, 304); Oghuz 12th c. **Kük-χan** [Chug chan dux], Mohammed Qutb al-Dīn's I (1098-1128) emir and chieftain (Ǯuwaynī I, 80, 82, Abulfar.); Chuv. 18th-19th c. **Kük-murza** [Кукмурза] (Magn. 53). ✧ 'Blue; sky' (Nöldeke; Tarj/Houtsma). See also **ALTÏN-KÖK.**

KÖK-AYAQ Kzk. 19th c. **Kök-ayaq** [Кокаякъ] (SOK 24). ⇨ **KÖK + AYAQ.**

KÖK-AMAN Kzk. **Kök-aman** [كوكامان / Кокаман] (Divaev, Baksy 318-320). ⇨ **KÖK + AMAN.**

KÖK-AMAŠ Türk 7th c. -9th c. **Kök-amaš-tutuq** (DTS). ✧ 'Blue-Amaš' (Blagova 1997, 705). ⇨ **KÖK.**

KÖK-BAS see KÖK-BAŠ

KÖK-BAŠ Kzk. 19th c. **Kök-bas** [Кобасъ] (SOV 26); Bashk. 1714 **Kök-baš** [Татлы-бай Кокбашев] (MIB I, 105, 106); Tuv. 19th c. **Kök-paš** [Кök-Паш], fem. (Proben IX, 36). ⇨ **KÖK + BAŠ.**

KÖK-BOLSUN Kzk. 19th c. **Kök-bosun** [Кокбосунъ] (SOV 56). ⇨ **KÖK + BOLSÏN.**

KÖK-BOSUN see KÖK-BOLSUN

KÖK-BÖRİ Selj. 1168/69, 1182, 1187/88, 1217 **Kök-böri** / **Kük-büri?** [مظفرالدين كوكبورى / كوكبرى / كيكبورى / Coucbouri / Gueuk-Bouri / Kûkbûrî / Музафферъ-Эддинъ Кукбуру / Музаффар-ад-дин Кукбури ибн Зайн-ад-дин Али], lord of Arbele [Arbil], Harran, Edessa (Ibn al-Athīr, Atab.: RHCHor 244, 360, Abulfidā IV, 50, Abulfidā/Ed. 51, 99, 100, Ibn al-Athīr: RHCHor 653, 656, 678, Abulfar./Budge 1, 372, RaD/Ber. III, 91, RaD I/2, 159); Chag. 16th c. **Kök-böri-sultan** [Кукбури Сультанъ], grandson of Sheybāni, the Uzbek Khan (Šejb. LXXVII); Tat.(Dobr.) **Kök-börö** [Kokböro] (Kúnos 1904, 304); Tat.(Sib.) 1681 **Kök-büri** [Мантабарко Кокбиринъ] (DAI VIII, 177). ✧ 'Grey wolf'. ⇨ **KÖK + BÖRİ.**

KÖK-BUYA Uyg. **Kök-buya** [Kök-Buja] (EUTS). ⇨ **KÖK.**

KÖK-ČAR Uzb. 19th c. **Kök-čar** [Кокчаръ] (SKSO III, 166). ✧ 'Grey-piebald, grey with white head'. ⇨ **KÖK + ČAR.**

KÖK-ČEBİČ Kirg. **Kök-čebič** [Kök Чебiч], one of Manas' comrades-in-arms (Proben V, 39 /41/, 151 /153/). ⇨ **KÖK.**

KÖK-KÖZ Yürük 16th c. **Gök-göz** [كوك كوز], from the Yürüks of Kocacık, Turkey (Gökb., Rum. 103); Kzk. 1785 **Kök-köz-bi** [كوك كوز بى / Коккоз (Кукуз, Куккуз) бий], a chief (aq-saqal) of the Kete tribe (MIK IV, 52, 53, 63, 73 etc.); Tat. 20th c. **Kük-küz**

[Күккүз] (Sattarov); Bashk. 1777 **Kük-küz / Kük-küzä?** [Куккузя Заиров] (MIB V, 57); *EN:* Kzk. 18th c. - 19th c. **Kök-köz** [Коккоз], a clan (Tynyšp. 70). ✧ 'Blue eye; child with blue eyes' (Sattarov). ⇨ **KÖK + KÖZ.**

KÖK-QARČÏГA   Kzk. 19th c. **Kök-qarčïγa** [Кöкъкарчига-бай] (Potanin, Pred. 140). ✧ 'Blue Falcon'? ⇨ **KÖK + QARČÏГA.**

KÖK-QÏYAS   Kirg. **Kök-qïyas** [Кöк Kyjas / Кöк Кыјас], Aq-qïyas' younger brother (Proben V, 28 /28/). ⇨ **KÖK + QÏYAS.** See also **AQ-QÏYAS.**

KÖK-QUNA   Tuv. 19th c. **Kök-quna** [Кöк-куна] (Proben IX, 30, 31). ⇨ **KÖK.**

KÖK-LŪ   Uyg. 12th c. - 14th c. **Kök-lū** [kök lū], a deity (DTS). ✧ 'Blue-Dragon/Snake' cf. Uyg. (<Chin.) *lū* 'дракон; змея' (DTS). ⇨ **KÖK.**

KÖK-MOLAT   Hak.(Sag.) 19th-20th c. **Kök-molat** [Кöк Молат], a folklore hero (bogatyr) (Proben IX, 242). ✧ 'Blue steel/hero' (Titov 118: „синеукладный богатырь ". ⇨ **KÖK + BULAT.**

KÖK-PAŠ see **KÖK-BAŠ**

KÖK-PURBA   Shor 19th-20th c. **Kök-purba**, a folklore heroine (bogatyrša) (Dyrenkova 74). ✧ 'Blue ring' (Dyrenkova). ⇨ **KÖK.**

KÖK-SAL   Kzk. 19th c. **Kök-sal** [Коксалъ] (AOAtb. 6). ⇨ **KÖK + SAL / ČAL?**

KÖK-SÏRГAQ   Kirg. **Kök-sïrγaq** [Кöк Сырҕак], one of Manas' comrades-in-arms (Proben V, 151 /153/). ⇨ **KÖK + SÏRГAQ.**

KÖK-TAY   Hak. 19th-20th c. **Kök-tay** [Кöктай] (HRS 349); Kzk. 19th c. **Kük-tay** [Куктай] (SOK 52); Kzk. 19th c. **Kük-tay** [Куктай] (SODž. 114). ✧ 'Bluish-grey-foal' (Butanaev). ⇨ **KÖK + TAY** or suff. *-tay(1,2)*?

KÖK-TARBA   Karg. **Kök-tarba** [Кокъ Тарба] (Katanov: ZIRGOÊtn. XVII, 164). ✧ 'Blue-magic' cf. Alt., Hak. *tarba* 'die Verhexung, die Besprechung' (Radl. III, 871). ⇨ **KÖK.** See also **SARÏГ-TARBA.**

KÖK-TAŠ   Oghuz? 1029 **Kök-taš** [كوكتاش الغزى] (Ibn al-Athīr/Tornb. IX, 267, 269-71, 275, 348); Oghuz/Trkm. 1030/1031 **Kök-taš** [Кокташ], a chieftain of Turkmen and/or Ghuzz (MIT I, 234-35, 243, 363-64); Bashk. 1693 **Kök-taš** [Васка Кокташевъ], from Kungursk (Kungursk. akty 217). ⇨ **KÖK + TAŠ.**

KÖK-TÄMÜR see **KÖK-TEMÍR**

KÖK-TEMÍR   Uyg. 13th-14th c. **Kök-tämür** [Kök Tämür] (Zieme, Mat. II, 92); Maml. 1313 **Kök-temir** [ككتمر] (Dawād. 276). ⇨ **KÖK + TEMÍR.**

KÖK-TONLÏ   Oghuz/Trkm. 13th c. **Kök-tonlï** [تونلى كوك / Кöк-Тонлы] (Abulg./Kon. 1215, 1220). ⇨ **KÖK + TON + suff. *-lï*.

KÖK-TÖS   Hak.(Blt.) 19th-20th c. **Kök-tös** [Кöк Töc],

a hunter (Proben IX, 364, 365). ✧ I. 'Greyish-blue breast'? cf. Hak.(Sag., Koyb.) *tös* 'die Brust, das Bruststück' (Radl. III, 1265). ⇨ **KÖK.**

KÖKČÄ see **KÖKČE**

KÖKČE   Khorezm.? **Gökče** [Гöкче] (RaD I/2, 159); Yürük 1543 **Gökče** [Gökçe] (Gökb., Rum. 188); Yürük 16th c. **Gökče** [كوك/چه / Gökçe], from the Yürüks of Kocacık, Turkey (Gökb., Rum. 102); Yürük 1576 **Gökče-oγlu** [Gökçeoğlu] (Gökçen 56); Kuman./Tat.? 1318, 1319 **Kökčä** [Кокча / Конча], envoy of the Horde (PSRL X, 181, XVI, 62, XXIII, 99); Selj. 12th c. **Kökče** [نورالدين ككجه], governor of Hamadan (Rāwandī 388, 391 etc.); Kzk. 19th c. **Kökče** [Кокче] (SOK 26); Tat. 1424 **Kökče / Kökčä** [Кохча / Когча / Кокча багатыръ], a hero (bogatyr) (PSRL V, 262, VI, 142, VIII, 92, XX, 232, XI, 239, PSRL (Russk. Hr.) I, 426); Trkm. 1851 **Kökče-bay** [Кокче-бай джафарбайский] (MIT II, 283); Kzk. 19th c. **Kökče-bay / Kökčä-bay?** (SOV 76); Trkm. 1500 **Kökče-sultan** [كوكچه سلطان / Кокча-султан], from the Qaǰar tribe (Dorn 255, 256, 413, MIT II, 61, 70); Kirg. **Kökčö** [Кöкчö] (Proben V, 7, Jud. 27); Kzk. 19th c. **Kökše** [Кокше] (SOK 128); *EN:* Trkm. **Gökčä-bäg**, a Türkmen clan (Németh, HMK 67); Trkm. 1701 **Gökčelü** [كوكچهلو / Gökçelü cemaatı] (Refik, Anad. 130). ✧ I. 'Bluish'; II. 'Pretty, Good-looking', cf. Turk. *gökçe* 'bluish, blue-green; mistletoe (Loranthus europaeus); rock-dove, rock-pigeon; pretty, beautiful person' (TED) <Mo.?, Kalm. PN *Kokča*? ⇨ **KÖK + suff. *-če*. See also **ER-KÖKŠÖ, ÍR-GÖKŠE.**

KÖKČÖ see **KÖKČE**

KÖKČÖ-KÖZ   Kirg. **Kökčö-gös? / Kök-čögös?** [Кöкчöгöс] (Proben V, 226 /228/); Kirg. **Kökčö-kös** [Кöкчöкöс] (Proben V, 111 /112/). ⇨ **KÖKČE + KÖZ.**

KÖKÄY-KÖŠÜK   Kzk. **Kökäy-köšük** [Kököi, Köschük / Kökäi Köшük] (Proben III, 48 /63/). ⇨ **KÖKEY + KÖŠÜK?**

KÖKÄR   Uzb. 20th c. **Kökär** [Кÿкар] (Begmatov 1984, 203); Uzb. 20th c. **Kökär-bek** [Кÿкарбек] (Begmatov 1984, 203); Uzb. 20th c. **Kökär-jân** [Кÿкаржон] (Begmatov 1984, 203). ✧ 'Live!; Grow (up)!' (Begmatov), cf. Uzb. *kükär-* 'зеленеть; расти' (UzbRS).

KÖKÄRSÍN   Uzb. 20th c. **Kökärsin** [Кÿкарсин] (Begmatov 1984, 203). ✧ 'Let him live!' (Begmatov). ⇨ **KÖKÄR + imp. suff. *-sin*.

KÖKE-MAJAR see **MAJAR**

KÖKEY   Kzk. 19th c. **Kökey** [Кокей] (SOK 194). ✧ 'Reason, sense, brain' cf. Kzk. *kökey* 'fikir, akıl, insana özgü asalet' (KzTS). ⇨ **KÖK + suff. *-y*. See also **QARAS-KÖKEY.**

KÖKEM-BAY see **KÖKEN**

KÖKEN Kzk. 19th c. **Kökem-bay (<Köken-bay)** [Кокембай] (SODž. 92). ✧ 'Plant; peach; cherry'? Maml. *kökän* 'Pflanze, Pfirsich, Kirsche' (AH, Tarj/Houtsma).

KÖKEZ Karch. 20th c. **Kökez** [K'ök'éz] (Pröhle, Kar. 111).

KÖKİL Alt. 19th-20th c. **Kökil** [Кӧкил] (OjrRS 208).

KÖKLİ Oghuz/Trkm. 13th c. **Kökli** [كوكلى / Koukli / Кӧкли] (Abulg./Desm. 28 Abulg./Kon. 525). ⇨ **KÖK** + suff. -*li*.

KÖKLİN Hak. 19th-20th c. **Köklin** [Кӧклин], fem. (HRS 353).

KÖKLİS Hak.? 19th-20th c. **Köklis** [Кӧкліс], fem. (Katanov, Otč. 10). ✧ 'Grey-haired, grey-headed' (Butanaev).

KÖKLŎ Hak.(Sag.) 19th-20th c. **Köklŏ** [Кӧклӧ], fem. (Katanov, Otč. 7). ✧ 'Poppet, doll' cf. R. кукла 'id.' (Katanov).

KÖKLÜ Kzk. 19th c. **Köklü-be** [Коглубе] (AOP 34). ⇨ **KÖKLİ?**

KÖKÖ Kirg. **Kökö** [Кӧкӧ] (Jud. 962). ✧ 'Diligent, gluttonous'? cf. Kirg. *kökö: kökö teñir* 'бог', *kökö: kökö qoloqoy* 'человек, который старательно работает, но и поесть любит' (Jud.), < Mo.?, cf. *Kökö* (Ligeti, MTT 202).

KÖKÖNÖY Yak. **Kökönöy** [Кӧкӧнӧi], Küötčüt Kökönöy one of the ten Bayïnays (Pek.).

KÖKÖŠ Alt. 19th-20th c. **Kököš** [Кӧкӧш] (OjrRS 205). ✧ 'Greenish' (OjrRS). ⇨ **KÖK** + suff. -*öš*.

KÖKÖTÖY Kirg. **Kökötöy** [Kam Kökötöi / Кӧкӧтӧй], a shaman (Proben V, 142, Jud. 83, 418). ⇨ **KÖGEDEY?**

KÖKSÜZ Kuman 1096 **Köksüz / Köküs?** [Коксусь / Кокусь], a prince (PSRL I, 104, Baskakov, Im. polov. 67). ✧ 'Not having a clan; without roots' (Baskakov, Im. polov. 67), cf. Kuman *kök* 'Ursprung, Abstammung' (CC). ⇨ **KÖKÜZ** + suff. -*süz*.

KÖKŠÄ see **KÖKČE**

KÖKŚE see **KÖKČE**

KÖKŚÜ Kzk. **Kökšü / Er-kökšü** [Ер Кӧкшӱ], forefather of the Waq (Uaq) tribe, Middle Horde (Orta Žüz) (Proben III, 47 /62/, 88 /112/).

KÖKÜL Alt. **Kökül** [Канъ Кокӱлъ], a khan in a folktale, also mentioned as Kögüldey (Nikiforov 117). ✧ 'Tuft, lock on the crown'? cf. Kirg. *kökül* 'das Stirnhaar; die Haarbüschel, die die Kalmücken auf dem Kopfe nicht scheeren; der Zopf, das Zöpfchen' (Radl. II, 1224). See also **YAYMA-KÖKÜL, QARA-KÖKÖL**.

KÖKÜM Kirg. **Köküm** [Кӧкӱм], Ürbü's father (Proben V, 143 /145/).

KÖKÜÖNÄN Yak. **Kököönän** [Кӧкӱӧнӓн], a smith in a tale (Pek.).

KÖKÜZ Kzk. 19th c. **Köküs** [Кокюсъ] (SOK 248). ✧

'Chest'? Uzb. *küks* [кӱкс] (UzbRS).

KÖKÜZ-ERÄM Uyg. 13th c. **Köküz-eräm** [köküz eräm] (DTS). ✧ 'Chest?-Eräm' cf. Uyg., Karakh. *köküz* 'грудь' (DTS). See also **ERÄM-QARA**.

KÖL Karakh. 11th c. **Köl-irkin** [Köl irkin] (DTS, MK/Atalay 845). ✧ 'Lake'? cf. Türk, Uyg., Karakh. *köl* 'озеро, водоем' (DTS), Chag., Alt., Hak., Kirg., Kzk. *köl* 'der See', (Alt.) 'der Arm eines Flusses', (Hak.(Sag.)) 'der Sumpf' (Radl. II, 1267). ⇨ **KÜL?**

KÖL-BİLGÄ Karakh. 11th c. **Köl-bilgä-χan** [Köl Bilge Xan / köl bilgä xan] (MK/Atalay 845, DTS). ⇨ **KÖL** + **BİLGÄ.**

KÖL-DENEK Alt. **Köl-denek-bökö** [Кӧльденекъ-бӧкӧ] (Nikiforov 79). ✧ 'Lake-idiot'? cf. Alt. *tenek* 'идиот, глупый; шалун' (OjrRS). ⇨ **KÖL.**

KÖL-ERKİ Oghuz/Trkm. 13th c. **Köl-erki-χan** [كول ايركى / خان /] / Кӧль-Эрки-хан], Duylï-qayï-χan's younger brother (Abulg./Kon. 735-745, 760-775, 785-830). ✧ 'Strength/power of lake'? cf. Karakh. *erk* 'цила, воля, могущество, власть' (DTS). ⇨ **KÖL.**

KÖL-İRKİN Türk **Kül-ärkin** (Radl. II, 1466); Türk 735 **Kül-irkin / Beg-kül-irkin** [Sebeg Kül İrkiz / Säbäg Kül İrkiz (!)] (ETY I, 72). ✧ 'Noble man', a Karluk title, and a secondary component of names. ⇨ **KÜL** + **ERKİN.**

KÖLJÜ Tuv. 19th c. **Köljü** [Кӧлцӱ], fem. (Proben IX, 132). ⇨ **KÖL** + suff. -*jü*.

KÖLJÜN Tuv. 19th c. **Köljün / Köljüñ** [Кӧлцӱн / Кӧлцӱң], fem. (Proben IX, 172, 180). ⇨ **KÖL** + suff. -*čin(2)*.

KÖLJÜN-QARA Tuv. 19th c. **Köljüñ-qara** [Кӧлцӱң кара], fem. (Proben IX, 172, 180). ⇨ **KÖLJÜN** + **QARA.**

KÖLÄDĂ Hak.(Sag.) 19th-20th c. **Köládă** [Кӧлядä] (Katanov, Otč. 7). ✧ Born at Christmas R. коляда (Katanov).

KÖLÄY see **KÖLEY**

KÖLEY Hak.(Sag.) 19th-20th c. **Köläy** [Кӧляi] (Proben IX, 553); Hak. 19th-20th c. **Köley** [Кӧлей] (HRS 349); Hak. 19th-20th c. **Köley** [Кӧлей], fem. (HRS 353). ✧ 'Old, desert field' (HRS), cf. Hak.(Sag., Koyb.) *köläy* 'das Brachfeld' (Radl. II, 1268).

KÖLEK see **KÜYLEK**

KÖLEMEN Turk. 1497 **Kölemen** (Gökb., Ed. 133); Yürük 16th c. **Kölemen** [كولهمـن], from the Yürüks of Kocacık, Turkey (Gökb., Rum. 102, 183, 189, 190, 199, 200, 204, 213). ✧ 'Slave' cf. Turk. *kölemen* 'Circassian slave brought up as a warrior; Mameluk (in Egypt)' (TED).

KÖLLÜMÄS Yak. **Köllümäs** [Кӧллӱмäс] (Pek.).

KÖLÖČÖK Alt. 19th-20th c. **Kölöčök** [Кӧлӧчӧк] (OjrRS 208). ✧ Kolechka (R.), hypocoristic form of R. Nikolay.

KÖLÜYÄN Yak. **Kölüyän** [Кӧлӱjӓн] (Pek.).

KÖLÜK Kzk. 19th c. **Kölük-bay** [Колюкбай] (SODž. 144); Kzk. 19th c. **Kölük-pay** [Колюкпай] (SOK 88). ✧ 'Draught animal' cf. Kzk. *kölük* 'das Zugvieh; die Transport mittel (Pferde, Wagen etc.)' (Radl. II, 1272).

KÖMEK Trkm. 20th c. **Kömek** [Kömek] (Zaj. 1971, 329); Kzk. 19th c. **Kömek-bay** [Комекбай] (SODž. 98, 110). ✧ 'Helper, supporter' cf. Chag., Turk. *kömäk* 'die Hülfe, Stütze, Verstärkung' (Radl. II, 1319), Trkm. *kömek* 'помощ, пособие, подкрепление' (TrkmRS).

KÖMEKEY Kzk. 19th c. **Kömekey** [Комекей] (AOK 98, 110). ⇨ **KÖMEK** + dim. suff. *-ey.*

KÖMEN see **KÖBEN**

KÖMÜRDEŠ Maml.? **Kömürdeš** [كمرداش] (Duqmaq:RHCHor IV, 124).

KÖMÜS-ČOMČUKÄYDĀN Yak. **Kömüs-čomčukäydän-quo** [Köмÿc Чöмчÿкäiдäн-куо], Toyon-nyuryun's younger sister (Pek.). ✧ 'Silver-čomčukäydän'. ⇨ **KÜMÜŠ.**

KÖN-DUWDÏ see **KÜN-TOГДÏ**

KÖN-TUГAN see **KÜN-TUГAN**

KÖNČEK Khorezm. 1291 **Könček** [كونجك], emir of Mahmud Ghazan Khan (1295-1304) in Mazenderan (RaD/Jahn 26, 27, Hammer, Ilch. II, 15); Maml. 1363 **Könček** [كنجك الخوارزمى], mamlūk of Khorezmian origin, mentioned in a funeral inscription in Damascus (Mayer 147); Maml. 1293, 1298 **Könček / Künček / Künčük?** [كنجك / كونجك / Кунджукъ / Кунджск], a Kipchak chieftain (Baybars/Tizeng. I, 86, 88, 109, 111, Nuwairī 137, 158, RaD/Ber. I, 132, RaD I/1, 151, 158); Kuman 1333 **Künčeg** [Kunchegh], a Kuman from Hungary (Gyárfás III, 476); Kuman 1347 **Künčeg** [Kumcheg], a chief (captain) of the Kumans from the Čertan clan in Hungary (Gyárfás III, 484); NUyg. **Künček-qan-bek** [Kuntjekkan Bek] (Hedin, En färd II, 188); Khorezm.? 13th c. - 14th c. **Künčük / KünJük?** [Кунджук], Ghazan Khan's (1295-1304) wife (RaD I/1, 120); *EN:* Kuman 1371 **Künčeg** [Kuncheg], a Kumanian clan in Hungary (Gyárfás III, 506); *TN:* Kuman 1509 **Könček / Kenček?** [Kenchekzallasa], a settlement in Lesser Kumania, Hungary (Gyárfás III, 727). ✧ 'Drawers; leather trousers' (Sauvaget 55, Pelliot, Notes 95), cf. Kuman *könček* 'unterhosen, Hosen' (CC), Maml. *könčäk* 'Hosen' (Tarj/Houtsma), *könçek* 'urba' (Tuhf.), *künčäk* 'don' (AH), Turk. *könçek* 'uzun paçalı don, şalvar, don' (DS). The word originally may have meant a kind of leather-trouser of the nomads mentioned by Eberhard as well (Kultur der Randvölker p. 42, 47). Since Karakh., Kzk., East.T. *kön* means curried leather (DTS, İM, Radl. II, 1241). Cf. also Rásonyi, Köncsög., Rásonyi, KÖA 117, Rásonyi, Anthr. 143.

KÖNČEK-QARA Maml.? 1495/96 **Könček-qara** [قرا كنجك] (Iyās II, 293). ⇨ **KÖNČEK + QARA.**

KÖNÄKČIN Hak.(Sag.) **Könäkčin** [Köнäкчiн], fem.

(Proben IX, 429). ✧ 'Little bucket' cf. Uyg., Hak. *könäk* 'ein Eimer, Ledereimer' (Radl. II, 1242) + suff. *-čin.* See also **KÖNÖK.**

KÖNEY Kzk. 1822 **Köney** [كوناى / Конай] (MIK IV, 433, 435). ✧ 'Experienced, sophisticated; pugnacious' cf. Kzk. *köne* 'бывалый, опытный; боевой' (KzRS). + dim. suff. *-y.*

KÖNEKE Kzk. 19th c. **Köneke** [Конеке] (SODž. 16). ✧ I. 'Little experienced, sophisticated; pugnacious' cf. Kzk. *köne* 'бывалый, опытный; боевой' (KzRS); II. 'Deer leather' cf. Kzk. *kön* 'buntes (gelbes) Leder' (Radl. II, 1241). + suff. *-(e)ke.*

KÖNER Kzk. 19th c. **Köner-bay** [Конербай] (SOK 60). ✧ 'Outworn, fading' cf. Kzk. *köner-* 'быть поношенным и потерять цвет' (KzRS).

KÖNÖK Kzk. 19th c. **Könök** [Köнöкъ] (SOK 104); Alt. 19th-20th c. **Könök** [Köнöк], fem. (OjrRS 212); Alt. 20th c. **Könök** [Кöнöк], fem. (Nikonov 94). ✧ 'Leather-bucket' cf. Alt., Kzk. *könök* 'der Eimer; der lederne Melkeimer zum Melken der Stuten' (Radl. II, 1243).

KÖNÖKKÖ Yak. **Könökkö** [Köнöккö] (Pek.).

KÖNÖK Yak. **Könŏk** [Köнŏк] (Pek.).

KÖÑ-KÜNÄN Yak. **Köñ-künän** [Köÿкÿнäн] (Pek.).

KÖP Kzk. 19th c. **Köp-aqay** [Копакай] (AOA 118); Kzk. 19th c. **Köp-pay** [Коппай] (SOK 290); Kzk. 19th c. **Köp-pay** [Коппай] (SOV 30, 84, 58); Kzk. 19th c. **Köp-pay** [Коппай] (AOO 6); Kzk. 19th c. **Köp-pay** [Коппай] (AOAtb. 14); Kzk. 19th c. **Köp-pay** [Коппай] (SODž. 102). ✧ 'Much, many; plenty (of children), a long life (as a wish)' cf. Tat. *küp* 'много; обильно' (TatRS), Bashk. *küp* 'id.'(BRS), Kzk. *köp* 'много; долго' (KzRS), also Kzk. PNs *Köb-žan / Köp-žan* 'huge, mighty' (Žanuzakov 145, 146), *Köp-bay, Köp-žan* (Žanuzakov-Esbaeva).

KÖP-ASAR Kzk. 19th c. **Köp-asar** [Копасаръ] (SOK 292). ✧ 'He eats a lot; He will eat a lot'. ⇨ **KÖP + ASAR.**

KÖP-AŠ Kzk. 19th c. **Köp-aš** [Копашъ] (SOV 84). ⇨ **KÖP + AŠ?**

KÖP-BERDÏ Bashk. 1664 **Köp-berdi** [Копбердейко Метеев] (MIB I, 193); Tat.(Sib.) **Kü-perde (<Küp-berde)** [Кутунай Купердин] (Miller, Ist. Sib. II, 546). ✧ 'He gave a lot; Much was given'? ⇨ **KÖP + BERDÏ.**

KÖP-ČAГAY Kzk. 19th c. **Köp-čaγay** [Копчагай] (SOV 44). ⇨ **KÖP + ČAГAY?**

KÖP-ĴASAR see **KÖP-YAŠAR**

KÖP-DÄWLÄT Tat. 1600 **Köp-däwlät** [Кобдевлет] (MIB I, 151, Ist. Sib. II, 157); Tat. 1600 **Köp-däwlät** [Кобдевлет Конкозов] (Miller, Ist. Sib. II, 157). ✧ 'Very rich, happy'. ⇨ **KÖP + DÄWLÄT.**

KÖP-YAŠAR Kzk. 19th c. **Köp-ĵasar** [Кобджасаръ] (SOV 74, 134); Kzk. 19th c. **Köp-ĵasar** [Кобджасаръ]

(AOO 2); Kzk. 19th c. **Köp-ǰasar** [Кобджасаръ] (SOK 52, 114); Uzb. 20th c. **Köp-yašar** [Купяшар], fem. (Begmatov 1984, 206). ❖ 'He will live long'. ⇨ **KÖP + YAŠAR.**

KÖP-KELDİ Kzk. 19th c. **Köp-keldĭ** [Коп-кельды] (SOK 90); Tat.(Sib.) 1601 **Küp-kilde** [Девлет Купкилдеев] (Miller, Ist. Sib. II, 164). ❖ 'A lot (of them) has come; he came (was born) for long'. ⇨ **KÖP + KELDİ.** See also **KÖP-BERDİ.**

KÖP-SALAN Kzk. 19th c. **Köp-salan** [Копсаланъ] (SOV 106). ❖ 'Much-?'. ⇨ **KÖP + SALAN.**

KÖP-ŠİR Kzk. 19th c. **Köp-šir** [Копъ-Шировъ] (Grod., Pril. 165). ⇨ **KÖP + ŠİR?**

KÖPČİL Kzk. 19th c. **Köpčil-bay** [Копчильбай] (SOV 18). ❖ 'Outgoing, sociable' cf. Kzk. *köpšil* 'человек, любящий общество' (KzRS).

KÖPÄY Kzk. 1829 **Köbey** [Кобей] (Konšin, Oč. 100, Konšin, Mat. V, 20); Kzk. 19th c. **Köbey** [Кобей] (AOP 30); Kzk. 19th c. **Köbey** [Кобей] (SOV 114); Uzb. 20th c. **Köpäy** [Кўпай], fem. (Begmatov 1984, 203); Uzb. 20th c. **Köpäy-ǰân** [Кўпайжон] (Begmatov 1984, 203); Uzb. 20th c. **Köpäy-χân** [Кўпайхон] (Begmatov 1984, 203); Uzb. 20th c. **Köpäy-χoǰa** [Кўпайхўжа] (Begmatov 1984, 203); Uzb. 20th c. **Köpäy-qul** [Кўпайкул] (Begmatov 1984, 203); Uzb. 20th c. **Köpäy-mirza** [Кўпаймирза] (Begmatov 1984, 203); Kzk. 19th c. **Köpey / Köbey?** [Копей] (AOP 82); Tat.(Sib.) 1601 **Kübey** [Кубей Мурат], Küčüm's son (Miller, Ist. Sib. II, 165, 167); Kzk. **Kübey** [Мулла Кубей Токфулатовъ] (ZVORIAO XI, 292); Kzk. **Kübey** [Мулла Кубей] (Sb. Syr-D. XII, otd. II, 17); Kzk. 19th c. **Kübey** [Кубей] (Grod., Pril. 169); Uzb. 19th c. **Kübey** [Кубей] (SKSO III, 180); Bashk. 1756 **Küpey** [Карман Купеев] (MIB IV/1, 109). ❖ 'Multiply! Grow up!'; 'Be lively' (Begmatov), cf. Kzk. *köbčy-* 'viel werden, sich vermehren' (Radl. II, 1315), Kzk. *köbey-* 'çoğalmak, bollaşmak' (KzTS), Tat. *kübäy-* 'sich vermehren' (Radl. II, 1518), Tat. *kübäy-* 'размножаться, увеличиваться' (TatRS), Uzb. *köpäy-* 'множиться, увеличиваться, расти' (UzbRS).

KÖPÄYSİN Uzb. 20th c. **Köpäysin** [Кўпай] (Begmatov 1984, 203); Uzb. 20th c. **Köpäysin** [Кўпайсин] (Begmatov 1984, 203); Uzb. 20th c. **Köpäysin** [Кўпайсин], fem. (Begmatov 1984, 203). ❖ 'Let him/her multiply! Let him/her grow up!'. ⇨ **KÖPÄY.**

KÖPÄK Kuman 1166, 1174, 1185 **Köbäk** [Кобякъ (Бонякъ) Карлыевичъ], a khan (prince) of the Kumans (Polovets) in the region of the Dnepper (PSRL VII, 79, Ipat. 387, Lavr. 375, also Bask., Im. polov. 67); Tat. 1624 **Köbäk** [Утешъ Кобяковъ] (Pokrovskij 72); Tat. 1624 **Köbäk** [Уракай Кобяковъ] (Pokrovskij 72); Tat.(GH) 14th c. **Köbek** [كبك / Koubouk],

Toqtamïš-qan's (1382-1397) son (Abulg./Desm. 187); Kzk. 19th c. **Köbek** [Кобекъ] (SOV 54); Kzk. **Köbek-bay** [Кобекбай], a mulla (Pam. kn. Semip. 1898, III, 40); Kzk. 1794 **Köbek-biy** [Кобек бий] (MIK IV, 161); Kzk. 19th c. **Köbek-pay** [Кобекпай] (SOK 220); Maml.(Trkm) 14th c. **Köpäk** [كبَّك] (Sauvaget 54); Kzk. 19th c. **Köpäk** [Копакъ] (SOK 304); Kzk. 19th c. **Köpäk** [Копакъ Азимбаевъ] (Grod., Pril. 161); Nog.? **Köpäk** [Копак], Musa's son (Žirm., Epos 400); Selj. **Köpek** [سعدالدين كوپك] (Ibn Bībī III, 381, 284); Yürük 1543 **Köpek** [Divâne Köpek] (Gökb., Rum. 176); Yürük 1543 **Köpek** (Gökb., Rum. 186); Tat. 1543 **Köpek** (Gökb., Rum. 232, 233); Chag. 1500 **Köpek-biy** [كپك / كيپك / Копекъ Бий], Sheybanī Khan's follower (Šejb. LXXV); Chag. 1500 **Köpek-mirza** [كپك / كيپك / Кипекъ Мирза / Кёпек-мирза], a Timurid (Šejb. LXXV, MIT II, 52, 53); Uzb. / Trkm.? 1525, 1538/39 **Köpek-sultan** [كپك سلطان / Кёпек-султан] (Dorn 247, 390, 403, MIT II, 60); Kzk. 19th c. **Köppek-bay** [Коппекбай] (SOV 44); Chuv. 18th-19th c. **Kübäk** [Кубякъ] (Magn. 53); Bashk. 1735 **Kübäk** [Кубякъ Кинзягуловъ], a tarχan (Vel.-Zern., Bašk. 24); Bashk. 1753 **Kübäk** [Кубяк Аднагулов] (MIB IV/1, 68); Bashk. 1757 **Kübäk** [Кубяк Аднагулов] (MIB IV/1, 140); Tat. 18th c. **Kübek** [Кубекъ] (Nepljuev 701, 705); Bashk. 1748 **Kübek** [Кубекъ] (Nepljuev 718); Bashk. 1762 **Kübek** [Мосягут Кубеков] (MIB IV/1, 232); Bashk. 1769 **Kübek** [Кубек Кулаев] (MIB IV/1, 336); Kzk. 1738 **Kübek** [Кубек] (MIB I, 358); Kzk. 18th c. **Kübek** [Кубекъ] (Nepljuev 806); Kzk. 18th c. - 19th c. **Kübek** [Кубекъ] (ZOOIRGO 1881, IV, 99); Kzk. 1817, 1820 **Kübek** [Кубекъ Шукуралиевъ], one of the chiefs of the Yappas tribe (Mejer 35, Sib. Vest. IX, 111); Kzk. 1846 **Kübek** [Баркенбай Кубеков] (MKOP 151); Kzk. 19th c. **Kübek** [Кубековъ] (AUK 844); Nog. 1675 **Kübek** [Кунекъ Ураковъ] (PSZRI I, 978); Kzk. 1846 **Kübek-batïr** [Кубекъ-батыръ] (Konšin, Mat. V, 100); Tat.? 1711 **Kübek-murza** [Кубекъ-мурза] (PSZRI IV, 630); Bashk. 1750 **Küpäk** [Купак Девлетьбаев] (MIB III, 475); *TN:* Tat. 18th c. **Köbäk(ova)** [Кобякова], a village in the district of Arsk (Korsakov 259). ❖ 'Dog (with long hair)' cf. Karakh. *köpäk* 'собака' (DTS), Maml.(Trkm.) *köpäk* 'çok tüylü köpek' (AH), *köpäk it* 'Hirtenhund, grosser Hund' (Tarǰ/Houtsma), Bashk. *kübäk* 'собака' (BRS/Uraksin), Uzb. *köppäk* 'дворняга; верный слуга; злой человек' (UzbRS). See also **BAY-KÖPÄK, BAY-KÜBEK, BET-KÖPÄK, DİVÂNE-KÖPEK, İR-KÖPÄK, QARA-KÖBÄK, TURSUN-KÖPÄK(?).**

KÖPEGEN Kzk. 19th c. **Köpegen / Köbegen?** [Копегенъ] (SOK 164). ❖ 'Healthy, sound, strong, stayer' cf. Kzk. *köbegen* 'sağlam, dayanıklı'.

KÖPEY see **KÖPÄY**

KÖPEK see **KÖPÄK**

KÖPEK-BAŠ　Yürük 1543 **Köpek-baš** (Gökb., Rum. 239). ⇨ **KÖPÄK + BAŠ.**

KÖPĒYKE　Karg. 19th-20th c. **Köpēyke** (Katanov, Otč. 10). ✧ 'Kopeyka (Russian small coin)' cf. R. копейка.

KÖPTİRGES　Hak. 19th-20th c. **Köptirges** [Köптіргес] (HRS 349). ✧ 'Tart' (HRS).

KÖR　Kkalp. 20th c. **Kör-oɣlï** [Кёрогълы], a well-known folklore hero (Bask., Kkalp. 76); Turk. **Kör-oɣlu** [Köroğlu] (Önder, Hınıs); Trkm. 1817 **Kör-serdar** [Хани Köp-сердар], from the Teke tribe (MIT II, 401); Oghuz 942 **Kör-tegin** [كورتكين / الد يلمي/] (Hil. Sābī 317); Karakh.? 928 **Kör-tegin** [كورتكبن] (Miskawayh 273); Kkalp. 20th c. **Kör-uɣlï** [Кθруғлы], a well-known folklore hero (KkRS 774). ✧ I. 'Brave, courageous' cf. Karakh. *kür* 'смелый, отважный' (DTS), MK, Radl. II, 1447; II. 'Blind'? cf. Uyg., Crm., Turk. *kör* (<P.) 'blind' (Radl. II, 1248). See also **ALAQ-KÖR, MÜBÄRÄK-KÖR, SABİR-KÖR.**

KÖR-BUГA see **KER-BUГA?**

KÖR-JİÄLYİT　Yak. **Kör-ĵiälyit** [Köp-Џіäлĵіт] (Pek.).

KÖRDĀY　Hak. 19th c. **Kördǟy** [Köрдäй] (Katanov, Otč. 12). ✧ Gordey (R.).

KÖRDÜK　Kzk. 19th c. **Kördük** [Кордюковъ] (AOK 6). ✧ 'We saw him'.

KÖRENKEY　Kzk. 19th c. **Körenkey** [Коренкей] (SOV 72).

KÖRGÜLÄK　Tuv. 19th c. **Körgüläk** [Кöргÿläк], fem. (Proben IX, 114).

KÖRİN-KEL　Kzk. **Körin-kel** [Корин-кель] (TOOIK III, 171-72); Kzk. **Körin-kel** [Коринъ-кель] (TOOIK III, 171-72). ⇨ **KEL?**

KÖRİNE　Kzk. 19th c. **Körine-bay** [Коринебай] (AUK 852).

KÖRKELİ-YAXŠÏ　Oghuz/Trkm. 13th c. **Körkeli-yaχšï** [كوركالى يخشى / Кöркели-Йахшы], Boghra Khan's wife (Abulg./Kon. 900). ✧ 'Beautiful-good' cf. Kzk. *körkölü* 'schön' (Radl. II, 1260), Kuman, Kar. (L.) *körklü* 'schön' (Radl. II, 1261). ⇨ **YAQŠÏ.**

KÖRKLÄ　Uyg. 13th-14th c. **Körklä**, fem. (Zieme, Mat. III, 273). ✧ 'Beautiful' (Zieme). See also **GÜZEL, HÄSEN, KÜRKLİ, KÖRTLÄ, NİGĀR, SÏLİГ, ZİFA.**

KÖRKSÜZ　Uyg. 13th-14th c. **Körksüz**, fem. (Zieme, Mat. II, 83); Uyg. 13th-14th c. **Körksüz-ana-täñrim** [körksüz ana tngrim], fem. (Zieme, Mat. II, 87). ✧ 'Ugly, hideous' cf. Uyg., Karakh. *körksüz* 'некрасивый, неприятный' (DTS). See also **KÖRKELİ-YAXŠÏ, KÖRKLÜ.**

KÖRKÜL　Alt. 19th-20th c. **Körkül** [Кöркÿл] (OjrRS 209).

KÖRKÜZ　Uyg. 1235 **Körküz** [كوركوز / Куркуз],

Ögedey's (1229-1241) Uyghur governor in Khorasan and Mazenderan, between 1235 and 1242, tutor of Chinggis' sons (Togan, UTT 264) (Abulg./Desm. 42, RaD/Ber. I, 117, RaD I/1, 142, II, 14); Khorezm. 1323 **Körküz / Kürküz** [كركز / كوكز / Иса Куркузъ], Özbek Khan's governor (Ibn Khaldūn/Tizeng. I, 372, 388). ✧ I. 'Sign, mark'? cf. Turk. *körküz* 'das Zeichen, Abzeichen, die Probe' (Radl. II, 1261); II. Georges? (Togan, UTT 264).

KÖRÖ-JÄSÄGÄY　Yak. **Körö-Jäsägäy-toyon** [Köpö-цäсäгäi-(Џöсöгöi)-тоjон] (Pek.).

KÖRPE I.　Turk. 16th c. **Körpe** (Ongan, Ank. II); Turk. 1583 **Körpe** [كوربه] (Ongan, Ank. I, 165); Yürük 1543 **Körpe** [كوربه] (Gökb., Rum. 184); Trkm. 1840 **Kürpe** [Хидыръ Курпинъ] (ZIRGOÊtn. I, 97); Trkm. 20th c. **Körpe** [Körpe], fem. (Zaj. 1971, 341); Trkm. 20th c. **Körpe** [Корпе], fem. (TrkmRS 416). ✧ 'Newly born (child, animal), quite young, the youngest, fresh' cf. Karakh. *körpä* 'молодой, свежий' (DTS), Kuman, Turk. *körpä* 'ein neugeborenes Lamm, ganz jung, frisch, delikat' (Radl. II, 1266), Trkm. *körpe I.* 'младший, свежий' (TrkmRS).

KÖRPE II.　Kzk. 19th c. **Körpe** [Корпе] (AOP 126); Kzk. 19th c. **Körpe** [Корпе] (SOV 46); Kzk. 1817 **Körpe-bay** [كورپا باى / Корпебай] (MIK IV, 313, 319); Kzk. 19th c. **Körpe-bay** [Корпебай] (AOA 102); Kzk. 19th c. **Körpe-bay** [Корпебай] (AOP 10); Kzk. 19th c. **Körpe-bay** [Корпебай] (SOK 36); Kzk. **Körpö-bay** [Körpö Bai / Köрпö Баі] (Proben III, 47 /62/); Kirg. **Körpö-yan** [Körpö Jan / Köрпö-Јан] (Proben V, 35 /36/); Kzk. 1819 **Kürpe-bay** [Курьпабаи] (MIK IV, 323); Kzk. 19th c. **Kürpe-bay** [Курпебай] (SODž. 122); Kzk. 19th c. **Kürpe-bay** [Курпебай] (AOA 130); Kzk. 19th c. **Kürpe-bay** [Курпебай] (SOV 6). ✧ 'A kind of blanket' cf. Kzk. *körpe* 'одеяло' (KzRS), Kirg. *körpö* 'мерлушка, курпейка, узенькое одеяльце; молодая(!) люцерна' (Jud.), Chag., Uzb. *kürpä* 'eine Decke aus Kameelhaar oder Kattun' (Radl. II, 1464), Trkm. *körpe II.* 'одеяльце, перинка, мягкая подстилка' (TrkmRS).

KÖRPE-TAY　Kzk. 19th c. **Körpe-tay** [Корпетай] (AOK 22); Kzk. 19th c. **Körpe-tay** [Корпетай] (SOK 26); Trkm. 19th c. **Kürpe-tay** [Курпетай Тлекъ-Аліевъ], (Ščeglov I, 357); Kzk. 19th c. **Kürpe-tay** [Курпатай] (Grod., Pril. 172); Kzk. 19th c. **Kürpe-tay** [Курпетай] (SOK 80, 232); Kirg. **Kürpe-tay** [Курпетай] (Grod. IV). ✧ 'Newly born foal; newly born (the youngest) child'. ⇨ **KÖRPE I. + TAY** or suff. *-tay(1,2)*?

KÖRPEKPES　Kzk. 19th c. **Körpekpes** [Корпекпесъ] (SOK 122).

KÖRPEŠ　Kzk. 19th c. **Körpeš** [Корпешъ] (SODž. 34). ✧ 'The youngest (child)'. ⇨ **KÖRPE I. + dim. suff. -š.**

See also **QOZÏ-KÖRPÖŠ**.

KÖRPÖ see **KÖRPE II.**

KÖRPÖ-QARA   Kzk. 19th c. **Körpö-γara** [Корпогора] (SOV 66). ⇨ **KÖRPE II. + QARA.**

KÖRSEN Kzk. 19th c. **Körsen** [Корсень] (AOP 42). ✧ 'Let him see'?

KÖRTLÄ Uyg. 762 **Körtlä-čur** (Mahrnāmag 10); Uyg. 8th c. **Körtlä-täñrim / Körtlä-qatun-täñrim** [Tängrikän körtlä tängrim / Tängrikän körtlä qatun tängrim], a princess (Müller, Pfahl. 10, 22). ✧ 'Beautiful' cf. Uyg. *körtlä* 'красивый, прекрасный' (DTS). See also **HÄSEN, KÖRKLÄ, KÜRKLİ, PERÏYZA, NİGĀR, SÏLÏΓ, ZİFA.**

KÖRTÜK Alt. 19th-20th c. **Körtük** [Köртÿк] (OjrRS 209). ✧ 'Drift, flurry' cf. Alt.(Tel.) *körtük* 'ein Schneehaufen, eine Schneehäufung' (Radl. II, 1265).

KÖRÜ Uyg. **Körü** [Körü] (EUTS); Uyg. 12th c. - 14th c. **Körü / Kürü?** (Radl., USp. 51).

KÖRÜ-SÏŠÏ Uyg. 12th c. - 14th c. **Körü-sïšï** (DTS).

KÖRÜK Tat.(Mish.) 18th c. **Körük** [Ахметъ Корюковъ] (Nepljuev 882); Bashk. 1737 **Körük** [Корюк] (MIB I, 315); *EN:* Nog. 20th c. **Körük-uruw** [Коьрьук урув], a Qara-noγay clan (Bask., Nog. 137). ✧ I. 'Beauty' cf. Chag. *körük* 'die Schönheit' (Radl. II, 1253); II. 'Bellows, windbag, leather bottle' cf. Uyg., Chag., Alt., Hak., Kzk., Turk. *körük* 'der Blasebalg' (Radl. II, 1252). See also **KÜSÄ-KÜRİK.**

KÖSÄK Bashk. 1701 **Kösäk** [Косяк Камакаев] (MIB III, 31). ✧ 'Club, bludgeon, butt; blockhead' cf. Bashk. *küθik* 'дубина' (BRS/Uraksin), Tat. *küsäk* 'дубина; болван' (TatRS).

KÖSÄT see **KÜZÄT**

KÖSE Tat. 1534 **Kösä(-Aχmat)?** [Козя-Ахматъ (Охматъ)], envoy from Kazan (PSRL VIII, 286-87); Turk. 1288 **Köse** [كوسه مخال / كوسه ميخال], Köse Miχāl, the forefather of the Mikhaloghlis (Āšikp. 14, 16, Nešrī: ZDMG XIII, 199-216); Kkalp. 20th c. **Köse** [Кӧсе] (KkRS 774); Kkalp. 20th c. **Köse** [Кӧсё] (Bask., Kkalp. 43); Crm. **Kösö-bay** [Köcö Баi] (Proben VII, 106); Kzk. 19th c. **Küse-bay** [Кусебай] (SOK 32); Kzk. 19th c. **Küse-bay** [Кусебай] (SODž. 102). ✧ 'A man whose beard will not grow or is very scanty' (Redh.), cf. Kkalp. *kösö* 'безбородый' (KkRS), Crm., Turk. *kösä* 'der Bartlose, Dünnbart' (Radl. II, 1293), Bashk. *küθä* 'безбородый, с редкой бородой' (BRS/Uraksin), Tat. *küsä* 'человек с редкой бородой, безбородый' (TatRS). See also **ALDAR-KÖSE.**

KÖSEK Turk. **Kösek-oγlu**, a Zeybek (Kúnos 1891, 119). ✧ 'Poker, rake (long thin person, spindle-shanks)' cf. Turk. dial. *köseği / kösek* 'ateş karıştırmaya yarayan bir ucu yanmış odun, tahta' (DS VIII).

KÖSEKE Kzk. **Köseke** [كوسكا / Köceke] (Syzdykov 358). ⇨ **KÖSE** + suff. *-ke* or comp. *-eke?*

KÖSEM Kzk. 19th c. **Kösem-bay** [Косембай] (AOP 126). ✧ 'Sheep (ram) who leads the flock; ringleader' cf. Kzk. *kösöm* 'der Leithammel, der Führer, das Haupt einer Gesellschaft (Bande)' (Radl. II, 1295).

KÖSÖ see **KÖSE**

KÖSÖY Yak. **Kösöy** [Köcöi] (Pek.).

KÖSÖYÖN Yak. **Kösöyön** [Köcöjöн], a family (Pek.).

KÖSTÄNKİN Hak.(Sag.) 19th-20th c. **Köstänkin** [Кӧстäнкін] (Katanov, Otč. 8). ✧ Konstantin (R.).

KÖSTEY Maml. 1315, 1316 **Köstey** [السيفى كُستاى النـاصرى], governor of Tripolis, died in 1316 (Sobernh. I, 53, Nuwairī).

KÖSTİNKÄ Hak. 19th-20th c. **Köstinkä** [Кӧстінкä] (Katanov, Otč. 10). ✧ Kostin'ka (R.).

KÖSTÖKÜN Yak. **Köstökün** [Кӧстöкÿн] (Pek.). ✧ Konstantin (R.).

KÖSTÜK Kuman 1183 **Köstük / Qostuq** [Обовл Костукович (Костухович)] (PSRL II, 663, Ipat. 427). ✧ 'Fetter, hobble' (Bask., Im. polov. 69).

KÖSÜNČİ see **KÜZÜNČİ**

KÖŠÄN see **KÖŠEN**

KÖŠEK Trkm. 19th c. **Köček** [Кочекъ Перикеев] (Ščeglov IV, 180); Tat. 20th c. **Köček** [Кӧчеков / Кучуков] (Sattarov); Kzk. 19th c. **Köšäk** [Кошяк] (Potanin II, 4); Trkm. **Köšek** [Кӧшек] (Sopieva 178); Trkm. 20th c. **Köšek** [Köšek] (Zaj. 1971, 331); Kzk. 19th c. **Köšek** [Кошекъ] (AOK 6, 46); Kzk. 19th c. **Köšek** [Кошекъ] (SODž. 32); Kkalp. 20th c. **Köšek-bay** [Кёшекбай / Кӧшекбай] (Bask., Kkalp. 400, KkRS 774); Kzk. 19th c. **Köšek-pay** [Кошекпай] (AOA 18); Kzk. 19th c. **Köšek-pay / Köžek-pay?** [Кожекпай] (SOV 156); Bashk. 1664 **Köšük** [Кошуков] (MIB I, 193); Bashk. 1710 **Köšük** [Кошук Арасланов] (MIB III, 67); Bashk. 1715 **Köšük** [Умир Кошуков] (MIB III, 123); Kzk. **Köšük** [Кöшÿк] (Proben III, 48 /63/); Kzk. 19th c. **Köšük** [Кошукъ] (AOA 102); Kzk. 19th c. **Köšük** [Кошукъ] (SOK 138); Kzk. **Köšük / Er-köšük** [Ер Кöшÿк] (Proben III, 37 /46/); Kzk. 1823 **Köšük-bay / Köček-bay?** [كوچكباى / Кошукбай] (MIK IV, 459, 462); Kzk. 19th c. **Köšük-pay** [Кошукпай] (SOK 182); Kzk. 19th c. **Köšük-pay** [Кошукпай] (AOK 18); Trkm. 20th c. **Köšek** [Кошек] (TrkmRS 417); Kzk. 19th c. **Küšek-pay** [Кушекпай] (SOK 6). ✧ I. 'Young animal; little child' cf. Turk. *köčäk* 'junges Thier, das Junge (hauptsächlich von Kameelen gesagt); ein Tänzer; ein Bursche, Geseller' (Radl. II, 1288), Kzk. *küšik* 'it yavrusu; ufak çocuk' (KzTS); II. 'Young camel' (Zaj. 1971, Sopieva), cf. Turk. *köšäk* 'ein Kameeljunges, ein junges Thier überhaupt' (Radl. II, 1305), Kkalp. *köšek* 'верблюженок' (KkRS), Trkm. *köšek* 'верблюженок-сосунок; детка, деточка, малютка' (TrkmRS), Turk. *küčäk* 'das Kameelfüllen; jedes kleine Ding oder Wesen; ein öffentlicher Tänzer'

(Radl. II, 1491), cf. also *köşek* (Eren, TDES). See also **BOTA, KÜČELÄK, OΓŠUQ; BAY-KÖŠÜK, KÖKÄY-KÖŠÜK.**

KÖŠEKEY Bashk. 1798 **Köšekey** [Кушекай] (PSZRI XXV, 195); Kzk. 19th c. **Köšekey** [Кошекей] (SODž. 128). ⇨ **KÖŠEK** + dim. suff. *-ey.*

KÖŠEKLİ Turk.? 1389 **Köšekli** [كشكلی] (Iyās I, 279). ✧ 'Having a young camel' cf. Turk. *köšäkli* 'mit einem Füllen (Kamelstute)' (Radl. II, 1305). ⇨ **KÖŠEK** + suff. *-li.*

KÖŠEN Kzk. 19th c. **Köšäm-bay** (<Köšän-bay) [Кошамбай] (SODž. 38); Kzk. 19th c. **Köšän** [Кошанъ] (SODž. 36); Kzk. 19th c. **Köšän** [Кошанъ] (AOP 102); Kzk. 19th c. **Köšän** [Кошанъ] (AOK 130); Kzk. 19th c. **Köšän** [Кошанъ Чутаевъ] (SKSO VIII, 202); Kzk. 1817 **Köšen** [كوچن / Кошен] (MIK IV, 311); Kzk. 19th c. **Köšen-bay** [Кошенбай] (SODž. 82). ⇨ **KÜČEN?**

KÖŠENÄY Tat.(Sib.)? 1631 **Köšenäy** [Кошенаев (Антяк)] (Miller, Ist. Sib. II, 386); Tat.(Sib.)? 1640 **Köšenäy** [Кошенаев (Ахмамет)] (Miller, Ist. Sib. II, 476). ⇨ **KÖŠEN?** + suff. *-äy.*

KÖŠER Kzk. 1794 **Köšer-bay** [كوچرباى / Кошербай] (MIK IV, 158); Kzk. 19th c. **Köšer-bay** [Кошербай] (AOK 18, 34, 70, 94); Kzk. 19th c. **Köšer-bay** [Кошербай] (AOO 18, 50); Kzk. 19th c. **Köšer-bay** [Кошербай] (AOP 50); Kkalp. 20th c. **Köšer-bay** [Көшербай] (KkRS 774); Kzk. 19th c. **Köšir** [Коширъ] (SODž. 60); Kzk. 1828 **Küšer-bay** [Кушербай] (Dobrosm., Turg. 288); Kzk. 19th c. **Küšer-bay** [Кушербай] (SOK 48); Khorezm. 1260 **Küšer-bek** [سيف الدين كشربك / Saif al-dīn Kusharbak], envoy of Berke Khan (1257-1266) to Bay-bars I (1260-1277) (Sīrat 157). ✧ I. 'Axle'? Kkalp. *köšer* 'ось' (KkRS); II. 'He will be wandering; he will be a nomad' cf. Kkalp. *köš-* 'переселяться, перекочевывать' (Bask., Kkalp.). See also **KETE-KÜŠER.**

KÖŠPES Kzk. 19th c. **Köčpes** [Кочпесъ] (AOK 38); Kzk. 19th c. **Köšpes** [Көшпесъ] (Potanin, Pred. 134). ✧ 'He won't be wandering'. See also **KÖŠER.**

KÖŠÜ Kzk. 19th c. **Köšü-be** [Кошубе] (AOP 38).

KÖŠÜGEN Kzk. 19th c. **Köšügen** [Кошугенъ] (SODž. 132). ✧ 'Trembled, quivered' cf. Kirg. *köšü-* 'zittern, beben' (Radl. II, 1306).

KÖŠÜK see **KÖŠEK**

KÖŠÜNČİ see **KÜZÜNČİ**

KÖTÄK Kuman 1252 **Kötäk** [Котъякъ], a prince, according to Baskakov (Im.Polov. 69) the same as Kötän (PSRL XV, 396). ✧ 'Much awated (child)' cf. Tat. PN *Kötek* 'id.' (Sattarov), cf. Tat. *kötek: kötä-kötä kötek bul-* II 'ожидая истомиться' (TatRS).

KÖTÄLİ-QAŠQA Kuman 1451 **Kötäli-qašqa** [Ketelegaska], personal name preserved in a placename

in Lesser Kumania, Hungary (Gyárfás III, 626). ✧ 'His spare horse has a blaze on the forehead' (Rásonyi, Kisk. 344, Rásonyi, Kisk. helyn. 165, Rásonyi, Anthr. 142), cf. Chag. *kötäl* 'ein beim Zaume geführtes Pferd' (Radl. II, 1277). ⇨ **QAŠQA.**

KÖTÄN Tat.(Bar.) **Ködön-qan** [Кöдöн Кан] (Proben IV, 46 /58/); Alt.(Tel.) **Ködön-pi** [Кöдöн-Пi] (Radl. II, 1283); Kuman 1202, 1223, 1225 **Kötän** [Котянъ (Котанъ) Сутоевичъ], a Polovets prince (PSRL I, 216, II, 156, III, 39-40, VII, 129-30 etc., Ipat. 481 /488/, 498 /504/, Lavr. 478 etc.); Hak.(Sag.) 19th-20th c. **Kötän-peg** [Котäн-пег], folklore hero (Proben IX, 392, 393); Kzk. 19th c. **Köten** [Котенъ] (AOK 106); Kzk. 19th c. **Köten** [Котень] (SODž. 156); Kzk. 19th c. **Köten** [Котенъ] (AOA 142); Kzk. 19th c. **Köten-bay** [Котенбай] (SOK 50); Uyg. 12th c. - 14th c. **Kütän** [kütän] (DTS, EUTS); Kzk. 1819 **Kütän** [Кутян] (MIK IV, 325); Kuman 1240 **Küten / Köten** [Kuthen, Cumanorum rex], prince of the Kumans moving to Hungary (SRH II, 553-554 etc.). ✧ 'Bottom, ass' cf. Chag. *kötän* 'der Hintern; der Stuhl, Schemel' (Radl. II, 1276), Alt. *ködön* 'der Hintere' (Radl. II, 1283); Concerning the Kuman etymologies cf. Rásonyi, NTK 111-114, Rásonyi, KÖA 118, Rásonyi, Anthr. 143-144, Bask., Im. polov. 69. See also **İYT-KÖTÖN; KÖŠÜK.**

KÖTEN see **KÖTÄN**

KÖTEN-TAY Kzk. 19th c. **Köten-tay / Kötentey?** [Котентей] (SOK 240). ⇨ **KÖTÄN** + **TAY** or suff. *-tay(1,2)*?

KÖTER Kzk. 19th c. **Köter-bay** [Котербай] (AOA 6); *TN:* Kzk. 19th c. **Köter-bay** [Котербай], a field (AOP). ✧ 'Worry, attack (the enemy)!' cf. Chag., East.T. *kötär-* 'aufheben; beunruhigen, angreifen' (Radl. II, 1276).

KÖTİ-BAS Kzk. 1822 **Köti-bas / Köt-bas?** [كوتباس / Котыбас] (MIK IV, 432, 434). ⇨ **KÖT / QUTU?** + **BAS II. / BAŠ?**

KÖTLÖMBET see **QUTLUMBET**

KÖTÖNÖŠ Alt. 19th-20th c. **Kötönöš** [Кöтöнöш] (OjrRS 209). ⇨ **KÖTÄN** + suff. *-öš.*

KÖTPEY Hak. 19th-20th c. **Kötpey** [Кöтпей] (HRS 349).

KÖTÜT Uyg. 8th c. **Kötüt** [Kötüt] (DTS, EUTS).

KÖZ Oghuz/Trkm. 13th c. **Köz-χan** [Коз-хан], Dibbaquy's son (RaD I/1, 76). ✧ 'Eye' cf. Türk, Chag., Kuman, Kzk., Kirg. etc. *köz* 'das Auge' (Radl. II, 1299), Uyg., Alt., Hak. etc. *kös* 'das Auge, der Blick' (Radl. II, 1291). See also **AYA-GÜZ?, AQ-KÜZ, ALA-KÖZ, ALAŇ-GÜZ, BAY-GÜZ, ČAŇ-GÜZ, DÄWLÄT-QARA-KÖZ, DEPE-GÖZ, YATİ-KÜZ, YOMA-GÜZ, KÜK-KÖZ, KÖKČÖ-KÖZ, QAQ-KÜZ, QAMAŇ-KÖS, QARA-KÖZ, QAZ-GÖZ, QAZAQ-KÜZ, QOY-KÖZ, QOYAN-KÖZ, TANA-**

KÜZ, TEMİR-GÜZ, TÏSQAN-GÖZ, ÜČ-GÖZ.

KÖZ-BERGEN   Kzk. 19th c. **Köz-bergen** [Ишбай Кёзбергеновъ], İš-bay's father (OB. XV, 78, AUK Dobavl. 1). ⇨ KÖZ + BERGEN.

KÖZ-QAMAN   Kirg. **Kös-qaman** [Köc Каман] (Proben V, 218 /220/); Kirg. **Köz-qaman** [Көзкаман] (Jud. 619).

KÖZÄK   Bashk. 1740 **Közäk** [Козяк Букашев] (MIB I, 412); Bashk. 1761 **Közäk** [Алимгул Козяков] (MIB IV/1, 215); Bashk. 1709 **Közäk / Kösäk?** [Козяк (Казяк) Тленчеев] (MIB III, 48); Bashk. 1779, 1780 **Közäk / Küzäk** [Ахмер Козяков (Кузяков, Кузиков)], from the village Kozjakovo (MIB V, 88, 106).

KÖZÄM see QOJAM

KÖZÄM-ŠÜGÜR   Tat.(Tüm.) 1633 **Közäm-šügür** [Козямшугурко] (Miller, Ist. Sib. II, 407); Bashk. 1734 **Közäm-šügür** [Коземшугур Илчибаев], a tarχan (Vel.-Zern., Bašk. 10). ⇨ QOJAM + ŠUГUR / ŠÜGÜR.

KÖZÄMİŠ see KÜSÄMİŠ

KÖZÄN see KÜZÄN

KÖZÄŠ   Tat. 1632 **Közäš** [Бекбаев Козяш] (Miller, Ist. Sib. II, 398); Bashk. 1740 **Közäš** [Козяш (Кузяш)] (MIB I, 384); Bashk. 1735 **Küzäš** [Алдакай Кузяшевъ], a prince (Vel.-Zern., Bašk. 12); Bashk. 1756 **Küzäš** [Кузяш Сеинов] (MIB IV/1, 109); Bashk. 1780 **Küzäš** [Кадыр Кузяшев] (MIB V, 116, 275); Bashk. 1780 **Küzäš** [Сейфулла Кузяшев] (MIB V, 106); Bashk. 1780 **Küzäš** [Кузяш Епаров] (MIB V, 103). ⇨ XOJAŠ?

KÖZEY   Kuman? 1280 **Közey** [Козѣй], a Tatar chieftain (Ipat. 581 /582/); Uzb. 1644 **Közey-bek** [Козей-бекъ], envoy from Bukhara (AI IV, 43). ⇨ KÖZ? + suff. -ey.

KÖZEY-NOГAU   Nog. 1645 **Közey-noγay (-naγay?)** [Козѣй-Нагай], envoy from Bukhara (AI IV, 15). ⇨ KÖZEY + NOГAU.

KÖZEN see KÜZÄN

KÖZİYKE   Alt. 19th c. **Köziyke** [Козийке] (Verb., In. 142).

KÖZLİK   Türk? 871 **Közlik-χan** [كزلك حان], lord of Nishapur (Ibn al-Athīr/Tornb. VII, 172-75).

KÖZÜM   Tat.(Sib.) 17th c. **Közüm-qan**, Yermak's (Yermäk's) enemy (Radl., Aus Sib. I, 146); Bashk. 1706 **Küzüm** [Кускей абыз Кузюмов] (MIB III, 25); Bashk. 1736 **Küzüm** [Кузюм Тохтаров] (MIB III, 344); Bashk. 1751 **Küzüm** [Чурагул Кузюмов] (MIB IV/1, 50). ⇨ KÖZ.

KÖZÜNČİ see KÜZÜNČİ

KÖŽENEK   Hak.(Sag.) 19th-20th c. **Köženek** [Кöженек] (Katanov, Otč. 8). ✧ '?' cf. Hak. PN *Köčen / Köčenek* (Butanaev).

KŌSTÄ   Hak.(Sag.) 19th-20th c. **Kōstä** [Кöстä]

(Katanov, Otč. 10, 11). ✧ Kostya (R.).

KRİLE see KİRİLLÄ

KRİSTİÄS see QRÏSTUOS

KUY-DİYAR   Chuv. 1764 **Kuy-diyar / Kuydi-yar?** [Куйдияр Мелеидеев] (MIB IV/2, 103).

KUL-AXMAT   Chuv. 18th-19th c. **Kul-aχmat** [Кулахматъ] (Magn. 53). ⇨ QUL + AXMET.

KURAK   Chuv. 19th-20th c. **Kurak** [Kurak] (Mészáros I, 409). ✧ 'Crow' (Mészáros).

KURBAN-ГALİU see QURBAN-ALİ

KURMUŠKA   Chuv. 18th-19th c. **Kurmuška** [Курмушка] (Magn. 54).

KÜBÄK see KÖPÄK

KÜBÄN   Selj.? 11th c. - 13th c. **Kübän** [Cuban (Cayuci) frater] (Abulfar. 489).

KÜBÄS   Kzk. 18th c. **Kübäs** [Кубясь] (Nepljuev 764).

KÜBE   Tat. (Arin) 1629 **Kübe-yan?** [Кубеян] (Miller, Ist. Sib. II, 342). ✧ I. 'Shell, armour'? cf. Kuman, Chag., Kar., Tat.(Tob., Tara) *kübä* 'der Panzer' (Radl. II, 1517); II. 'Protuberant, bloated, puffy'? cf. Tat.(Tob.) *kübä* 'convex, erhaben' (Radl. II, 1517).

KÜBEY see KÖPÄY

KÜBEK I.   Alt. 19th-20th c. **Kübek** [Кÿбек] (OjrRS 209). ✧ 'Misery, devastation' (OjrRS), Shor *kübäk* 'das Unglück, Verderben' (Radl. II, 1518).

KÜBEK II. see KÖPÄK

KÜBEKEY   Chuv. 18th-19th c. **Kübekey** [Кубекей] (Magn. 53). ✧ 'Puppy'. ⇨ KÖPÄK + suff. -ey.

KÜBEN-TAY   Kzk. 19th c. **Küben-tay** [Кубентай] (SOK 58). ⇨ KÖBEN + TAY or suff. -tay(1,2)?

KÜCÖMÖC   Tat.(Bar.) **Kücömöc** [Кÿцöмöц], a folklore hero (Proben IV, 47 /59/).

KÜČ   Türk 7th-9th c. **Küč** [Küç] (ETY III, 133); Kzk. 19th c. **Küč-bay** [Кучбай] (SKSO II, 16); Selj. **Küč-beg** [كوج بيك / كوج بك] (Nešrī 186, Seādeddīn I, 15); Oghuz? 14th c. **Küč-χan** [كوچ حان منسيك], in the genealogy of the Mongols (Qazw. 558); Türk 7th-9th c. **Küč-kül-tutuq** [(Ö)Kü Çäkül Tutuq / küč kül tutuq] (ETY III, 163, DTS); Karakh. 11th c. **Küč-tegin** [Küç Tégin / küč tegin] (MK/Atalay 846, DTS); Khorezm. 1220-1225 **Küč-tegin** [كوج دكين / Koudj Tékîn], Jelāl's (1220-1231) officer (Nasawī 68); Khorezm. 1220 **Küč-tegin-pehlevan / Küš-tegin-pehlevan** [Куч-тегин-пехлеван (Куш-мегин-пехлевап)] (MIT I, 479, 488, 492); Karakh. **Küč-tigin** [Küç Tigin] (MK/Atalay 846). ✧ I. 'Strength, power; strong' cf. Türk, Uyg., Chag., Alt. *küč* 'die Kraft; kräftig, kraftvoll' (Radl. II, 1489); II. 'Time of migration; Goods and chattels' cf. Uyg., Chag. *köč* 'die Reise, Wanderung, Uebersiedlung, der Jurtenzug' (Radl. II, 1287); Uzb. *köč* 'имущество, домашние вещи (при перевозке, переселении); рой' (UzbRS). See also QABAN-KÜČİ, MÜBÄRÄK-KÜČ.

KÜČ-BARS   Türk 7th-9th c. **Küč-bars** [El(i?)ç Çur Küç

Bars / Elç Çur Küç Bars] (ETY III, 117). ⇨ **KÜČ + BARS.**

KÜČ-BARS-KÜLÜG   Türk 7th-9th c. **Küč-bars-külüg** [Tüz Bay Küç Bars Külüg] (ETY III, 119). ⇨ **KÜČ + BARS + KÜLÜG.**

KÜČ-BARSLÏГ   Uyg. 12th c. - 14th c. **Küč-barslïγ** (Radl., USp. 204, 246, DTS). ✧ 'Having a strong panther'. ⇨ **KÜČ-BARS** + suff. *-lïγ.*

KÜČ-BUГA   Khorezm. 1220-1225 **Küč-buqa-χan / Küč-buγa-χan?** [خان بغا کوچ / خـان بوقه کجـ / Kéchboga khân / Кучъ-бука Ханъ], an emir of Muhammad, the Khorezmshah in Northern Persia, at the time of Ĵebe's and Sübötey's invasion; Ĵelāl's (1220-1231) officer (RaD/Ber. III, 89, Ĵuwaynī I, 116, Nasawī 70). ✧ 'Strength-Bull'. ⇨ **KÜČ + BUQA.**

KÜČ-DOГDÏ   Maml. 14th c. **Küč-doγdï / Küš-doγdï** [کش دغدی / اکشـدغـدی] (Sauvaget 54). ✧ 'Strength has been born; born to be strong/hard' (Sauvaget 54). ⇨ **KÜČ + TUГDÏ.**

KÜČ-KİLDE see **KÖČ-KELDİ**

KÜČ-KİLDİ see **KÖČ-KELDİ**

KÜČ-QÏYAГAN   Türk 7th-9th c. **Küč-qïyaγan-ičreki** [Küç Qïyaγan / Küç Kïyagan içreki] (ETY III, 49). ⇨ **KÜČ + QÏYAГAN.**

KÜČ-TAY   Kzk. 1846 **Küč-tay** [Куйчтай Якшебетев], a biy (MKOP 152). ⇨ **KÜČ + TAY** or suff. *-tay(1,2)?*

KÜČ-TEMÜR   Uyg. **Küč-tämür** [Küç Tämür] (EUTS); Uyg. 12th c. - 14th c. **Küč-temür** (Radl., USp. 27-28, DTS); Khorezm./Chag. 14th c. **Küč-timür** [Kuj Timur], commander of thousands under Timur (1370-1405) (Tar. Rashidi 24); Khorezm./Chag. 14th c.? **Küč-timür** [Куч-Тимур] (RaD II, 17). ✧ 'Power/strength-Iron'. ⇨ **KÜČ + TEMİR.**

KÜČ-TİMÜR see **KÜČ-TEMÜR**

KÜČÄY see **KÖČEY**

KÜČÄY-BEKİŠ   Bashk. 1663 **Küčäy-bekiš** [کوچـای بکیش / Кучай Бекиш] (MIB I, 166). ⇨ **KÖČEY + BEKİŠ.**

KÜČE   Uzb. 1876 **Küče-mergen-bay?** [Кучемергенъ-бай] (Moskal'cev 52).

KÜČEGEN   Chuv. 18th-19th c. **Küčegen** [Кучегень] (Magn. 54).

KÜČEY see **KÖČEY**

KÜČEKEY   Bashk. 1737 **Küčekey-bay** [Кучекей-бай] (MIB I, 334). ⇨ **KÖČE / KÖČEK?** + suff. *-(k)ey.*

KÜČELÄK   Bashk. 1757 **Küčeläk** [Нияз Кучеляков] (MIB IV/1, 157); Bashk. 1776 **Küčeläk** [Савкабай (Сявкабай) Кучеляков] (MIB V, 42, 42, 544, 545); Tat. 1556 **Küčelek** [Кучелекъ] (PSRL XIII, 261); Bashk. 1714 **Küsäläk** [Кусяляк Туганаев] (MIB III, 118); Bashk. 1718 **Küseläk** [Куселяк Лелеев] (MIB III, 175); Bashk. 1776 **Küseläk** [Савкабай

Куселяков] (MIB V, 42); Bashk. 1740 **Küselek** [Кусюм Куселеков] (MIB I, 395); Bashk. 1724 **Küsüläk / Küseläk?** [Кусюляк Туганаев] (MIB III, 232); Kzk. 19th c. **Küselek** [Кушелекъ] (SOV 66). ✧ 'Little/young camel; little thing'? cf. Turk. *kösäläk* 'ein kleines Kameelfüllen; überhaupt ein kleines Dind' (Radl. II, 1305). See also **KÖSEK.**

KÜČEN   Kzk. **Küčen** [Иралы-Кученъ], a Kazak sultan who loved wandering (Protok. Turk. IV, 51). ✧ 'He who loves wandering' cf. Tat. *küčïn-* 'mit seiner ganzen Familie umziehen' (Radl. II, 1492).

KÜČER see **KÖČER**

KÜČİK-ŠEREF   Uzb. 1740 **Küčik-šeref** [Кючикъ-Шерефъ] (Hanykov, Poezdka 21). ✧ 'Young (animal) - honour' cf. Uzb. *šäräf* 'честь, почёт; благородство; достоинство' (UzbRS). ⇨ **KÖČEK.**

KÜČİM see **KÜČÜM**

KÜČKEY   Bashk. 1764 **Küčkey** [Амир Кучкеев] (MIB IV/1, 298); Bashk. 1780 **Küčkey** [Булат Кучкеев] (MIB V, 116). ⇨ **KÜČ** + suff. *-käy.*

KÜČKÜN see **KÖČKEN**

KÜČKÜNČİ   Kzk. 19th c. **Kičkünči-bay** [Кичкюнчибай] (Grod., Pril. 80); Chag. 1510-1531 **Küčkünči-χan** [خان کوجکنجی / Кучкунджи Ханъ], Shaybanī khan's uncle, follower and successor in Turkestan (Šejb. LXXV); Chag. 1529 **Küčkünči-χan** [Кучкунчи-ханъ], from Samarkand (Barth., Ulugb. 102, 116). ✧ 'Nomad; person who likes wandering' cf. Alt. *köčkün* 'das Sichfortbewegen', Tat.(Bar.) *köčkün* 'der Nomade' (Radl. II, 1291).

KÜČÜ   Uyg. 12th c. - 14th c. **Küčü / Küči** (Radl., USp. 112-13, DTS).

KÜČÜGÄY see **KÜČÜKEY**

KÜČÜK   Trkm. 20th c. **Güĵik** [Гуджик] (TrkmRS 217); Trkm. 20th c. **Güĵük** [Güğük] (Zaj. 1971, 331); Khorezm. **Küčük** [Кучук] (RaD II, 69); Tat.(GH) 14th c. **Küčük** [کوجـك / Koutchouk / Кучукъ], Toqtamïš-qan's (1382-1397) son (Abulg./Desm. 187, Šejb. L); Turk. 1583 **Küčük** (Ongan, Ank. I, 165); Yürük 1543 **Küčük** [Küçük] (Gökb., Rum. 190, 204, 241); Yürük 1553 **Küčük** [کوجـك / Küçük ibn Hamza] (Gökçen 35); Balk. **Küčük** [Кучуковъ], a prince (tau-biy) (Karaulov 52); Balk. 20th c. **Küčük** (Pröhle, Balk. 231); Kmk. 1807 **Küčük** [Кучук Таймазов] (MID III, 143); Kmk. 1828 **Küčük** [Кучук Турлув] (MID III, 123); Tat. 1668 **Küčük** [Куразка Кучюковъ] (Kungursk. akty 12); Tat. 1690 **Küčük** [Кураска Кучуковъ] (Kurdjumov 25); Tat. 1695 **Küčük** [Кучюк Акпердеев] (MIB I, 92); Tat.(Sib.) 1645 **Küčük** [Кучюк (Кучук)] (Miller, Ist. Sib. II, 526, 527); Bashk. 1706 **Küčük** [Кучюк Токшеиков] (MIB III, 26); Bashk. 1712 **Küčük** [Кучюк Савельев] (MIB III, 84); Bashk. 1712 **Küčük** [Кучюк] (MIB III, 88);

Bashk. 1735 **Küčük** [Тоганъ Кучуковъ], a tarχan (Vel.-Zern., Bašk. 16); Bashk. 1737 **Küčük** [Кучюк Серняков] (MIB I, 320n); Bashk. 1749 **Küčük** [Кучюк Ицкин] (MIB III, 469); Bashk. 1762 **Küčük** [Иман Кучюков] (MIB IV/1, 241); Kzk. 1832 **Küčük** [Кучукъ Ханхожинъ], a sultan (Konšin, Mat. I-III, 36); Kzk. 1841 **Küčük** [Маджикъ Кучуковъ], a sultan from the Orta Žüz (Konšin, Mat. V, 22); Alt. 19th-20th c. **Küčük** [Кÿчÿк] (OjrRS 209); Bashk. **Küčük-bay** [Kutschukbai], at the time of the Batyrsha-revolt (Rytschkow II, 28); Bashk. 18th c. **Küčük-bay** [Кучукбай Имангулов,] (Nepljuev 882); Bashk. 1761 **Küčük-bay** [Кучюк Баимбетев] (MIB IV/1, 221); Bashk. 1769 **Küčük-bay** [Кучкбай Киккузин] (MIB IV/1, 336); Kzk. 1820 **Küčük-bay** [Кучук бай], a chieftain (Sib. Vest. IX, 121); Kzk. 19th c. **Küčük-bay** [Джанак Кучукбаевъ] (Grod., Pril. 52); Kzk. 19th c. **Küčük-bay** [Кучукбай] (Grod. I, 98); Kkalp. 1709 **Küčük-batïr** [Кучук батыр] (MIKk. 159); Uzb. 1770 **Küčük-bek** [Кучук-бек] (MIT II, 343); Kkalp. 1803 **Küčük-inaq** [Кучук инак] (MIKk. 96); Uyg. **Küčük-ïdïqqut** [Küçük Idıkkut] (EUTS); Turk. 1540 **Küčük-kethudā**, from Diyarbekir (Demirtaş 56); Bashk. 1754 **Küčük-qul** [Кучюккул Уразманов] (MIB IV/1, 83); Nog. 1649 **Küčük-murza** [Кучюкъ мурза Алатуевъ] (AI IV, 86, 87); Kzk. 19th c. **Küčük-pay** [Кучукпай] (SOK 92); Kzk. 19th c. **Küčük-pay** [Кучукпай] (SOK 168); Bashk. 1737 **Küsük** [Кусюк Серенеков] (MIB I, 354); Bashk. 1744 **Küsük** [Беккул Кусюков] (MIB III, 415); Bashk. 1756 **Küsük** [Кусюк Ширшакаев] (MIB IV/1, 122); Bashk. 1761 **Küsük** [Кусюк Якупов] (MIB IV/1, 200); Bashk. 1740 **Küsük-bay** [Жаузбай Кусюкбай] (MIB I, 397); Bashk. 1783 **Küsük-bay** [Кусюкбай Юмакаев] (MIB V, 139); Bashk. 1742 **Küsük-qul** [Аракай Кусюккулов] (MIB I, 486); Kzk. 1794 **Küsük / Küčük-bay** [کوشوك / کوچك بـای / Куçук] (MIK IV, 158). ✧ 'Puppy' cf. Sauvaget 54: „chiot", „chien qui a le queue coupé"; Alt. *küčük* 'щенок' (OjrRS), Alt., Kar. (T.), Turk. *küčük* 'der junge Hund' (Radl. II, 1494), Alt.(Tel.) *qučuq* 'der junge Hund' (Radl. II, 1010), Kzk. *küsük* 'die jungen der Thiere' (Radl. II, 1512), Kzk. *küsik* 'щенок' (KzRS), Bashk. *kösök* 'щенок' (BRS). See also **AQ-KÜČÜK, ALA-KÜČÜK, BAY-KÜČÜK, BİK-KÜČÜK, İT-KÜČÜK, QAN-KÜČÜK, QARA-KÜČÜK, SARÏ-KÜČÜK, TOXTA-KÜČÜK.**

KÜČÜK-TEMÜR Uyg. 12th c. - 14th c. **Küčük-temür** [Küçük Tämür] (Radl., USp. 16-17, DTS, EUTS). ✧ 'Little(?)-Iron' (Blagova 1997, 712), 'Young-Iron'. ⇨ **KÜČÜK + TEMİR.**

KÜČÜKEY Tat.(Tob.) 1678 **Küčügäy** [Метей Кучюгаев] (MIB I, 205); Bashk. 1770 **Küčükey** [Кучукей Игнатьев] (MIB IV/1, 342); Alt. 19th-20th c. **Küčükey** [Кÿчÿкей] (OjrRS 209); Bashk. 1664 **Küsük** [Карашай Кусюков] (MIB I, 193); Bashk. 1734, 1740 **Küsükey** [Кусюкей Кулчюрин] (Vel.-Zern., Bašk. 6, MIB I, 422); Bashk. 1744 **Küsükey** [Беккиня Кусюков] (MIB III, 415). ✧ 'Little puppy'. ⇨ **KÜČÜK** + dim. suff. *-ey*.

KÜČÜM Tat.(Bar.) **Köcüm-qan** [Кöцÿм Кан] (Proben IV, 8 /10/); Tat.(GH) 14th c. **Küčim-baqšï** [Κουτζίμπαξις], a christened Tatar at the court of Andronikos II Palaiologos (Byz. Turc. 170); Tat. 1742-1748 **Küčüm** [Кучумовъ], from Cheboksary (IOAIÊK XIV, 539); Tat.(Sib.) 1645 **Küčüm-χan** [کوجم خان / Кучюм (Кучум)], Tatar khan (sultan) of Siberia (1563-1598) (Abulg./Desm. 177, 179, Miller, Ist. Sib. II, 150, 156, 163-168, 178, 443-449, 508); Bashk. 1730 **Küčüm** [Акай Кучюмов] (MIB III, 273, V, 573); Bashk. 1730 **Küčüm** [Кучюм Улекеев] (MIB III, 273); Bashk. 1757 **Küčüm** [Тимирбай Кучумов] (MIB IV/1, 157); Bashk. 1762 **Küčüm** [Кучюм Сафаров] (MIB IV/1, 238); Bashk. 1770 **Küčüm** [Юлбарис Кучумов] (MIB IV/1, 342); Bashk. 1780 **Küčüm** [Амиш Кучюмов] (MIB V, 111); Bashk. 1784 **Küčüm** [Ряш Кучюмов] (MIB V, 165); Tat.(Mish.) 1775 **Küčüm-bay** [мещеряк Кучюмбай] (MIB IV/2, 417); Hak.(Kacha) 19th-20th c. **Küčüm-qan** [Кÿчÿм-кан] (Proben IX, 541); Khorezm.? Chag.? 14th c.? **Küčüm-sultan** [Kuchum Sultán] (Tar. Rashidi 159); Bashk. 1714 **Küsüm** [Кусюм Кождевлетев] (MIB I, 105); Bashk. 18th c. **Küsüm** [Кусюмъ] (Nepljuev 131, 440); Bashk. 1760 **Küsüm** [Кусюм Юмакаев (Юмагаев)] (MIB IV/1, 199); Bashk. 1764 **Küsüm** [Кусюм Сапаров] (MIB IV/1, 276); Bashk. 1782 **Küsüm** [Кусюм (Кучум) Сюлеев] (MIB V, 132, 133); Bashk. 1789 **Küsüm** [Кусюм Сююндюков] (MIB V, 257); Bashk. 1789 **Küsüm** [Кусюм (Кучум) Айдагулов] (MIB V, 243); Bashk. 1794 **Küsüm** [Кусюм (Кучум) Тюлекеев] (MIB V, 574); Bashk. 1705-1711 **Küsüm-batïr** [Кусюм батырь (Кусюмка, Касюмка)] (MIB I, 215, 224, 253-58); Tat.(Tob.) **Kücim-χan** [Кÿцім хан] (Proben IV, 218 /269/, 253 /316/); *TN:* Bashk. 1780 **Küčüm(ovo)** [Кучюмово] (MIB V, 116). ✧ 'My strength; my power'? cf. *küčüm* 'stark' (Räs., Morph. 106). ⇨ **KÜČ** + suff. *-üm*.

KÜČÜM-BUΓRUL Khorezm.? **Kučüm-buγrul** [قوجم بوغرول / Кучумъ-Бугрулъ] (RaD/Ber. II, 5). ⇨ **KÜČÜM + BURUL?**

KÜČÜP Bashk. 1740 **Küčüp-qul** [Азнай Кучюпкулов] (MIB I, 439).

KÜD-ARUQ Türk 7th-9th c. **Küd-aruq-bäk** [Küd Aruq Bäk / Küd aruk beg] (ETY II, 171); Pecheneg / Kuman? **Küd-aruq-bäk** (Németh, Inschr. 22). ⇨ **ARUQ.**

KÜDÄY Yak. **Küdäy-baχsïtay-üstar** [Кÿдäi Бахсытаi устар], legendary smiths who built iron houses (Pek.); Yak. **Küdäy-baχsïtay** [Кӱдӓи Бахсытаі] (Pek.).

KÜDÄN Uyg. 12th c. - 14th c. **Küdän** (Radl., USp. 248). ✧ 'Guest' cf. Uyg. *küdän* 'der Gast' (Radl. II, 1486).

KÜDÄNÄ Yak. **Küdänä-bärgän** [Кӱдӓнӓ-бӓргӓн] (Pek.).

KÜDER Kzk. 19th c. **Küder-bay** [Кудербай] (SODž. 138); Kzk. 19th c. **Küder-bay** [Кудербай] (SOK 126); Kzk. 19th c. **Küder-bay** [Кудербай] (AOP 66); Kzk. 19th c. **Küder-bek** [Кудербай] (SOK 32). ✧ 'Hope' cf. Kzk. *küder* 'надежда' (KzRS).

KÜDERİ Kzk. 19th c. **Küderï** [Кудеры] (SOV 122); Kzk. **Küdörü-qoža** [Küdörü Kosha / Кӱдӧрӱ Кожа] (Proben III, 33 /41/). ✧ 'A kind of wild animal' cf. Kirg. *küdörö* 'ein wildes Thier, etwas grösser als der Karsak' (Radl. II, 1487), cf. Mo. *küderi* 'musk-deer' (Gy. Kara).

KÜDÖRÜ see **KÜDERİ**

KÜGÄL Pecheneg 9th c. **Kügäl / Küwäl** [Κουελ], chief of the 2nd tribe of the Pecheneg (Byz. Turc. 166).

KÜGÄL-TAŠ see **KÜKEL-TAŠ**

KÜGÄRČEN see **KÖGÖRŠİN**

KÜGEY Bashk. 1709 **Kügey** [Кугей Кинзибаев] (MIB I, 263). ✧ I. 'Be as high/great as sky!', II. 'Blue-eyed child' cf. Tat. PN *Kügäy* (Sattarov); III. 'Young tree'? cf. Bashk. *kügä* 'молодой (о деревьях)' (BRS/Uraksin).

KÜGEŠ Bashk. 1664 **Kügeš** [Кугеш Чюрюбаев] (MIB I, 192). ✧ 'Little swan'? (Sattarov).

KÜGÜLDÄY see **KÖGÜLDEY**

KÜGÜRČİN see **KÖGÖRŠİN**

KÜGÜRT Alt. **Kügürt** [Кӱгӱрт богатырь] (Proben IX, 220). ✧ 'Thunder' cf. Hak., Chul.(Küer.) *kügürt* 'der Donner' (Radl. II, 1427).

KÜYKE Kzk. 19th c. **Küyke-bay** [Куйкебай] (SOV 48). ✧ 'Wellfare; lucky/fortunate happening' cf. Kzk. *küy* 'der Komfort, die Wohlhabendheit; eine günstige Gelegendheit' (Radl. II, 1418) + suff. *-ke*.

KÜYLEK Kzk. 19th c. **Kölek-bay** [Колекбай] (SOK 264); Kzk. 1829 **Küylek** [Куйляк] (MIK IV, 324). ✧ 'Shirt' cf. Kzk. *köylek* 'рубаха' (RKzS). ⇨ **KÖLEK.**

KÜYLEW Kzk. 19th c. **Küylew** [Куйлеу] (Potanin II, 6). ✧ 'Consolation; soothing, calming'? cf. Tat. *köyläw* 'напевать; утешать, успокаивать' (TatRS).

KÜYÜK Bashk. 1723, 1726 **Küyük** [Атика Куюков (Куеков)] (MIB III, 201, 239); Kzk. 19th c. **Küyük** [Куюкъ] (AOO 58); Kzk. 19th c. **Küyük** [Куюковъ] (AOO 14); Kzk. 19th c. **Küyük** [Кююкъ] (AOP 30); Kzk. 19th c. **Küyük** [Куюкъ] (SOV 84); Kzk. **Küyük-bay** [Küjük Bai / Кӱjӱк Баі] (Proben III, 192 /232/); *TN:* Tat. 18th c. **Küyük** [Куюкъ] (Korsakov 249). ✧ 'Burn; sadness, bitterness' cf. Kzk. *küyik* 'ожог; горе, печаль' (KzRS), Kirg. *küyük* 'id.' (Jud.). See also **AQ-**

KÜYÜK, QARA-GÜYÜK.

KÜYÜN Trkm. 1859 **Küyün-mulla** [Куюнъ-мулла] (ZIRGOEtn. I, 199). ✧ 'Be angry'? cf. Kirg., Kzk. *küyün-* 'entbrennen, zornig sein, erregt sein, betrübt sein' (Radl. II, 1434).

KÜK see **KÖK**

KÜK-BÜRİ see **KÖK-BÖRİ**

KÜK-KÜZ see **KÖK-KÖZ**

KÜK-KÜZÄ see **KÖK**

KÜK-SAΓİR Karakh. 1158 **Kük-saγïr** [Кук-Сагыр], Ǧelāleddīn Ali ibn al-Huseyn (MIT I, 444). ⇨ **KÖK + SAΓİR.**

KÜK-SAR Bashk. 1737 **Kük-sar-batïr** [Куксар батыр] (MIB I, 342). ⇨ **KÖK + SARİ.**

KÜK-TAY see **KÖK-TAY**

KÜKČÄ see **KÖKČE**

KÜKČEY Chuv. 18th-19th c. **Kükčey** [Кукчей] (Magn. 53); Bashk. 1738 **Kükčey** [Иштекай Кукчеев] (MIB III, 387). ⇨ **KÖKČE** + dim. suff. *-y.*

KÜKÄ Uyg. **Kükä** [Kükä] (EUTS); Bashk. 1755 **Kükä** [Урман Кукин] (MIB IV/1, 101). See also **QAČAN-KÜKÄ.**

KÜKÄMÄN-QASQA Kzk. **Kükämän-qasqa** [Кукаманъ-каска] (Divaev, Alp. 50). ⇨ **QAŠQA.**

KÜKÄNÄK Chuv. 18th-19th c. **Kükänäk** [Куканякъ] (Magn.53). ✧ 'Dove' cf. NUyg.(Tar.) *kökänäk* 'ein Turteltaube' (Radl. II, 1223).

KÜKEY Bashk. 1734 **Kükey** [Тавлу Кукеев] (MIB III, 322); Bashk. 1764 **Kükey** [Кукей Яушев] (MIB IV/1, 298). ✧ 'Cuckoo' cf. Tat. PN *Küke / Kükiy / Küküy* (Sattarov), Tat. *kükï* 'der Kukuk' (Radl. II, 1423).

KÜKELTAŠ Uzb. 16th c. **Kügältäš** [Kougaltach], from Ferghana (Nalivkin-Dozon 56); Chag. 16th c. **Kükeltaš** [Хасан Кукельташ], a mirza (Ivanov 325); Chag. **Kökeltaš / Göñültaš / Köñültäš?** [كوكلتاش / Gokultas / Gokaltas / Kokultaš / Kokaltaš] (Le Coq, Ind. 3); Khorezm./Chag. 1409/10 **Kükeltaš** [Ала-ад-дин Алика Кукельташ], an emir (MIT I, 530); Chag. 1556 **Kükeltaš** [Ага Махим Кукель таш], fem. (Ivanov 232). ✧ 'Foster-brother' (title) (I. Vásáry, The Institution of Foster-brothers (emildäš and kökeldäš) in the Chingisid States. In: AOH XXXVI (1982), pp. 549-562), cf. Chag. *köñültäš / köñüldäš* 'der Milchbruder, die Milchschwester' (Radl. II, 1238, 1239). Le Coq (loc. cit.) reads it as *Köngültaš*.

KÜKEM-BAQUY Oghuz/Trkm. 13th c. **Kükem-baquy** [كوكم باقوى / Кукем-Бакуй], Arslan-χan's son (Abulg./Kon. 1120-1135, 1155).

KÜKEN Bashk. 1756 **Kükän** [Исимбеть Куканов] (MIB IV/1, 117); Kzk. 1785 **Kükän?** [Кукан] (MIK IV, 60); Bashk. 1718 **Küken** [Кукень Кадраев] (MIB III, 166). ✧ I. 'A kind of fish'? cf. Bashk. dial. *küken / kükyän* 'синец (рыба)' (BRS/Uraksin); II. 'Sloe

(Prunus spinosa)'? cf. Bashk. *kügän* 'тёрн, терновик' (BRS/Uraksin).

KÜKİLDEY see **KÖGÜLDEY**

KÜKSÜN   Hak. 19th-20th c. **Küksün** [Кӱксӱн], fem. (HRS 353). ✧ 'Jug, pitcher' cf. Hak. PN *Küksin* 'кувшин' (Butanaev) <R.?

KÜKSÜÖ-XĀDÏAT   Yak. **Küksüö-χādïat** [Кӱксӱö-Хадыат] (Pek.).

KÜKŠİN   Bashk. 1761 **Kükšin? / Kükše?** [Байдугул Кукшинов] (MIB IV/1, 218); *TN:* Tat. 17th c. **Kükšin** [Кукшинъ], a village in the county of Kazan (IOAIÊK XXIX, 346). ✧ 'Grey-headed, grey-haired; old man' cf. Uyg. *kökčin, kökšin* 'grau, der Greis' (Radl. II, 1229).

KÜKÜLČÜL   Bashk. 1788 **Kükülčül?** [Кутлу гильда Кукулчюлов] (MIB V, 235).

KÜKÜÖ-XAXAT   Yak. **Küküö-χaχat** [Кӱкӱö-Хахат], fem. (Pek.).

KÜL   Türk 7th-9th c. **Kül** [Kül] (ETY III, 158); Kirg. **Kül** [Кул] (Jud. 142); Uyg. 8th c. - 12th c. **Kül-arïγ-čañγši** (Müller, Pfahl. 23); Türk 8th c. - 9th c. **Kül-čigši** [Kül Çigşi] (DTS, ETY II, 65); Uyg. 750 **Kül-čigši** [Kül Čigši] (Runic Mss. 186, 188); Kirg. **Kül-čoro** [Кулчоро] (Jud. 17, 550); Uyg. 762 **Kül-čur** (Mahrnāmag 14, Thomsen, Inscr. 130, 155, Chavannes 340); Türk 721 **Kül-čur / Küli-čur** [Kül Çur / Kül-çur] (ETY I, 70, EUTS); Türk **Kül-čur-tutuq** (Radl. II, 1466); Kzk. **Kül-ǰamal** [Kül Dschamal / Кӱл Џамал], fem. (Proben III, 514 /590/); Tat.(Tob.) **Kül-χan** [Кӱл Хан] (Proben IV, 274 /340/); Uyg. **Kül-qaγan** [Kül-kaġan] (EUTS); Uyg. **Kül-sañun-tiräk** (Müller: Fest. Thomsen 211); Uyg. 8th c. - 9th c. **Kül-sawčï-tarqan** [Kül savčï trqan] (Haneda 4); Uyg. 8th c. - 9th c. **Kül-tarqan** [tonga Kül t(a)rqan] (Le Coq, Man. III, 45); Türk 732 **Kül-tegin / Kül-tägin** [Kül tegin], Bilgä-qaγan's younger brother; Bazin and Hamilton reads *Köl-tegin* (Radl. II, 1466, DTS, ETY I, 42, 44, 46, 48, 50, 52, 54); Türk **Kül-tudun** [Kül tudun] (ETY II, 121, 122); Türk 8th c. **Kül-tudun** (Radl. II, 1466). ✧ I. 'Ash'? (Blagova 1997, 712), e. g. *Kül-tegin* 'Ash-Prince' (ibid. 713); II. A title, a part of compound titles, e. g. *Kül-bilgä-qaγan, Kül-čur, Kül-tarqan, Kül-sangun, Kül-tegin, Kül-tudun, Kül-tutuq?* (Németh, HMK 45). See also **İL-KÜL**.

KÜL-AY   Kirg. **Kül-ay?** [Кулай], fem. (Jud. 70). ✧ 'Flower-Moon'? 'Lake-Moon'? ⇨ **GÜL / KÜL + AY?**

KÜL-BİLGÄ   Uyg. 12th c. - 14th c. **Kül-bilgä** [kül bilgä / Kül Bilgä] (DTS, ETY I, 164); Türk 8th c. **Kül-bilgä-χan** [kül bilgä χan] (DTS); Uyg. 759 **Kül-bilgä-qaγan** [kül bilgä qaγan / Kül-Bilgä kaġan], title of some Uyghur rulers (Ramstedt, Uig. 12-13, 43, DTS, EUTS); Uyg. 8th c. - 12th c. **Kül-bilgä-tāngri-ilig**, an Uyghur Khan (Müller, Pfahl. 6). ✧ 'Ash-Wise' (Blagova 1997, 709); 'Lake-Wise'. Title of some Uyghur rulers. (Németh, HMK 45). ⇨ **KÜL + BİLGÄ.**

KÜL-BÜZÄK   Tuv. 19th c. **Kül-büzäk** [Кӱлбӱзäк], fem. (Proben IX, 45). ⇨ **KÜL.**

KÜL-ĴEMİNE   Nog. 20th c. **Kül-ĵemine** [Куьлджемине Кирей келинъи], one of Baskakov's informants from the aul of Yaman-γoy, District of Ači-qulaq (Bask., Nog. 143). ⇨ **KÜL.**

KÜL-HANĴÏ   Turk. **Kül-hanĵï-oγlu** (Kúnos 1891, 119). ✧ 'Stoker of a bath' (TED), cf. Turk. *külhancı* 'id.', *külhan* 'stokehole of a bath' (TED). ⇨ **KÜL.**

KÜL-SAΓAT   Alt. 19th-20th c. **Kül-saγat** [Кӱлсагат], fem. (OjrRS 212).

KÜL-SARÏΓ   Selj. 11th c. **Kül-sarïγ** [كلسارغ / Kutbeddin Atabek Külsarıǧ], a chieftain of the Seljuk sultan Melik Qutulmïš ibn Arslan Israil (Ahbar 20-21). ⇨ **KÜL + SARÏ.**

KÜLČE   Kzk. 19th c. **Külče** [Кульче] (SOK 180); Kzk. 19th c. **Külče-bay** [Кульчебай] (SOV 16); Uzb. 19th c. **Külči-bay** [Кулчибай Аллакегеневъ] (SKSO III, 178); Bashk. 1798 **Külčü** [Кулчуевъ] (PSZRI XXV, 195); Kzk. 19th c. **Külčü-bek** [Кульчубекъ] (SODž. 44); Bashk. 1623 **Külse-γul?** [Кулзегул] (Miller, Ist. Sib. II, 299). ✧ 'Flat bread baked on an iron sheet (originally in hot ash)' cf. Bashk. *kölsä* 'лепёшка; пресный хлеб, лепёшка (выпекаемое в горячей золе)' (BRS/Uraksin), Bashk. *küljä* 'ein kleines Backwerk' (Radl. II, 1479), Kzk. dial. *külše* 'табаға пісірген нан; етке салатын нан' (QTDS), Uzb. *kulča (külčä)* 'небольшая круглая лепёшка' (UzbRS).

KÜLČİ see **KÜLČE**

KÜLČÜ I.   Bashk. 1754 **Külčü-γul** [Араптан Кулчюгулов] (MIB IV/1, 84). ⇨ **KÜL?** + suff. *-čü.* See also **GÖLČÜ?**

KÜLČÜ II. see **KÜLČE**

KÜLČÜK   Kzk. 19th c. **Külčük** [Кульчукъ] (AOK 38); Kzk. 19th c. **Külĵik** [Инкибай Кульджиковъ] (Grod., Pril. 179); Kzk. 19th c. **Külšük** [Кульшукъ] (AOA 74); Bashk. 1754 **Külčük** [Араптан Кулчюков] (MIB IV/1, 83); Bashk. 1757 **Külčük** [Аиткул Кулчюков] (MIB IV/1, 139); Kzk. 19th c. **Külčük** [Кульчукъ] (AOAtb. 6); Kzk. 19th c. **Külčük** [Кульчукъ] (Pam. kn. Turg. 40); Kzk. 19th c. **Külčük** [Кульчукъ] (SOK 308). ⇨ **KÜL?** + dim. suff. *-čük/-šük, -ĵik/-čik.*

KÜLČÜM   Bashk. 1764 **Gülčüm** [Сюрметь Гулчумов] (MIB IV/1, 277); Bashk. 1708 **Külčüm** [Кулчюмко] (MIB I, 215); Bashk. 1754 **Külčüm** [Кулчюм Мусин] (MIB IV/1, 86); Bashk. 1790 **Külčüm** [Сырметь Кульчумов] (MIB V, 276, 331); Bashk. 1793 **Külčüm** [Сюяргул (Сююргул) Кульчумов] (MIB V, 331); Bashk. 1793 **Külčüm** [Кульчум] (MIB V, 332); Bashk. 1798 **Külčüm** [Кулчумовъ] (PSZRI XXV, 195); Bashk. 1709 **Külčüm-tarχan** [Кулчюм тархан] (MIB I, 264);

Kzk. 19th c. **Külčün-bay** / **Külčüm-bay?** [Кульчунбай] (AOP 106); Bashk. 1790 **Külüčüm** / **Külčüm** [Суярымбеть (Сюярметь) Кулучумов] (MIB V, 276, 277, 283).

KÜLJEŇ Hak. 19th-20th c. **Küljeň** [Кӱлченъ] (HRS 349). ✧ 'Smiling'.

KÜLJİK see **KÜLČÜK**

KÜLDÄY see **KÜLDEY**

KÜLDEY Chuv. 18th-19th c. **Küldäy** / **Qulday?** [Кулдай] (Magn.53); Chuv. 18th-19th c. **Küldey** [Кулдей] (Magn.53); Kzk. 19th c. **Küldey** [Кульдей Джансеитовъ] (Grod., Pril. 23); Kzk. 19th c. **Küldey** [Кульдей] (SOK 62); Bashk. 1709 **Kültey** [Култей Балкозин] (MIB I, 264). ⇨ **KÜL** + suff. -dey?

KÜLDÜR I. Pecheneg 1183 **Küldür** [Кулдюръ (Кундуръ)], a chieftain of the Berendeys (or Chernye Klobuki) (PSRL II, 127, 319, Ipat. 425 /438/).

KÜLDÜR II. Kzk. **Küldür** [Küldür Mamai / Кӱлдӱр Мамаi] (Proben III, 75 /96/); Kirg. **Küldür** [Кӱлдӱр] (Proben V, 117 /118/). ✧ 'Make him laugh!' cf. Uyg., East.T. küldür- 'lachen machen, Gelächter verursachen' (Radl. II, 1477).

KÜLDÜRTÄY see **KÜLTÜRTÄY**

KÜLÄK Chuv. 18th-19th c. **Küläk?** [Кулякъ] (Magn. 54).

KÜLÄNTİMÄ Yak. **Küläntimä** [Кӱлянтiмä], a ruler in a tale (Pek.).

KÜLÄSAL Kkalp. 20th c. **Küläsal** [Кюлäсал / Күләсал], fem. (Bask., Kkalp. 403, KkRS 778).

KÜLÄŠ Kkalp. 20th c. **Küläš** [Кюляш / Күләш], fem. (Bask., Kkalp. 403, KkRS 778).

KÜLEN Kzk. 19th c. **Külem-bay** (<**Külen-bay**) [Кулембай] (AOA 130); Kzk. 19th c. **Külem-bek** (<**Külen-bek**) [Кулембекъ] (SOV 32).

KÜLERA Kzk. 1628 **Külera?** [Кулера], a Kazak princess (Miller, Ist. Sib. II, 340).

KÜLET Kzk. 19th c. **Kület** [Кулетъ] (SOV 48); Kzk. 19th c. **Kület** [Кулетъ] (SODž. 160).

KÜLETEK Kzk. 19th c. **Kületek** [Кулетекъ] (AOK 110).

KÜLGEN Kzk. 19th c. **Külgen** [Кульгенъ] (SOV 14). ✧ 'He/she laughed' cf. Uyg., Kuman, Kzk. etc. kyl- 'lachen' (Radl. II, 1466).

KÜLİ Türk 721 **Küli-čur** [Küli Çur] (DTS, ETY I, 136, 137, 138).

KÜLİPAŠ Kzk. 19th c. **Külipaš** [Кулепашевъ] (AOO 46). ✧ Shortened-hypocoristic form of Gül-baxram / Gül-banu (Žanuzakov 146).

KÜLKÄ Crm. **Külkä** [Кӱлкä] (Proben VII, 197).

KÜLKÜL Yak. **Külkül-bögö-oňonyor** [Кӱлкӱл-бöҕö оҥонjор], a person in a tale (Pek.).

KÜLMÄK Chuv. 18th-19th c. **Külmäk** [Кулмякъ] (Magn. 54). ✧ 'Shirt' cf. Tat. külmäk 'das Hemd' (Radl. II, 1479).

KÜLMÄS see **KÜLMEZ**

KÜLMEN Kzk. 19th c. **Külmen-bay** [Кульменбай Нор Алiевъ] (SKSO III, 18). ⇨ **KÜL** + suff. -men.

KÜLMES see **KÜLMEZ**

KÜLMESİN Kzk. 19th c. **Külmesin**, in a folk-tale (AUK 59). ✧ 'Let him not laugh'.

KÜLMEŠ Kzk. 19th c. **Külmeš** [Кульмешъ] (AOA 78). ⇨ **KÜL**.

KÜLMEZ Kkalp. 20th c. **Külmäs-qan** / **Külmes-χan** [Кюлмäскъан / Күлмесхан] (Bask., Kkalp. 92, KkRS 774); Bashk. 1737 **Külmäs-qul** [Кулмяскул] (MIB I, 335). ✧ 'He won't (does not) smile (laugh)'.

KÜLÖK Kzk. **Külök** [Er Külök / Ер Кӱлök] (Proben III, 127 /162/). ✧ 'Hero'? cf. Uyg., Chag., Hak., Kirg. külük 'der Held; das Rennpferd, der Renner' (Radl. II, 1470).

KÜLPENE Kzk. 19th c. **Külpene** [Кульпене] (SOK 250).

KÜLSE see **KÜLČE**

KÜLŠÜK see **KÜLČÜK**

KÜLTEY see **KÜLDEY**

KÜLTEN Bashk. 1760 **Külten** [Култень Идилбаков / Идилбяков] (MIB IV/1, 199).

KÜLTÜRTÄY Uyg. **Küldirtäy** [Küldirtäy] (EUTS); Uyg. 12th c. - 14th c. **Küldürtäy** / **Kültürtäy** (Radl., USp. 46, DTS).

KÜLÜG Uyg. 8th c. - 12th c. **Yägän-külüg-sañun** (Müller, Pfahl. 10); Türk 7th-9th c. **Külüg** [Külüg] (ETY III, 39, 90, 180); Uyg. **Külüg** [Tängridä qut bulmiš il tutmiš alp külüg] (Müller, Uig. II, 95); Türk 7th c. - 9th c. **Külüg-apa** [Külüg Apa] (ETY III, 122); Türk 7th c. - 9th c. **Külüg-čigši** (DTS); Türk 7th c. - 9th c. **Külüg-čur** [Külüg Çur] (DTS, ETY III, 63); Crm. 1631 **Külüg-oɣlï** [كولوك اوغلی] (Vel.-Zern., Crim. 85, 114, 115 etc.); Türk 749 **Külüg-sañun** [Külüg Sañun] (Runic Mss. 187-188, DTS, ETY II, 66); Uyg. **Külüg-sañün** [Külüg Sängün] (EUTS); Türk 7th c. - 9th c. **Külüg-tutuq** [Külüg Tutuq] (DTS, ETY III, 62); Türk 750 **Külüg-uruñu** [Külüg-Urungu] (Runic Mss. 188, DTS, ETY II, 64); Bashk. 1735 **Külük** [Чувашъ Кюлюковъ], a tarχan (Vel.-Zern., Bašk. 18); Kzk. 19th c. **Külük** [Кулюкъ] (AOO 62); NUyg. 19th c. **Külük** [كولوك] (Le Coq, Namenl. 108). ✧ I. 'Glorious, famous; hero(ic)'; Used also as a part of compound majestic titles. Cf. Türk, Karakh. külüg 'славный, знаменитый' (DTS), Türk. külüg '1. berühmt; 2. der Held, als zweiter Theil von zusammengesetzten Eigennamen' (Radl. II, 1472), Uyg., Hak., Kirg. külüg '1. der Held; 2. (Kirg., Uyg.) das Rennpferd, der Renner' (Radl. II, 1470); II. 'Racehorse, racer; big dog' cf. (Kirg., Uyg.) 'das Rennpferd, der Renner', (Chag.) 'ein grosser Hund' (Radl. II, 1470); III. 'Laugh'? (Le Coq, Namenl. 108). See also **İNANČU-KÜLÜG, YEGÄN-KÜLÜG, KÜČ-BARS-KÜLÜG, TÜZ-**

BAY-KÜČ-BARS-KÜLÜG.

KÜLÜG-BARS   Uyg. 8th c. -12th c. **Külüg-bars** [Külüg bars öktü tiräk] (Müller, Pfahl. 12); Türk/Uyg. 8th c. - 9th c. **Külüg-bars** (Le Coq, Man. III, 46). ⇨ **KÜLÜG + BARS.**

KÜLÜG-BİLGÄ   Uyg. **Külüg-bilgä?** [. al[p] qutluɣ külüg bilgä uiɣur χangan.] (Müller: Fest. Thomsen 209). ⇨ **KÜLÜG + BİLGÄ.**

KÜLÜG-İNANČ   Uyg. **Külüg-inanč** [Külüg İnanç] (EUTS); Uyg. 8th c. - 12th c. **Külüg-ïnanč(-sacu-sañun / -sacu-säñün)** (Müller, Pfahl. 6, DTS); Uyg. 8th c. - 12th c. **Külüg-ïnanč(-tutuq-iktü)** (Müller, Pfahl. 10). ✧ 'Glorious belief'? ⇨ **KÜLÜG + İNANČ.**

KÜLÜG-TİRİG   Türk 7th c. - 9th c. **Külüg-tirig** (DTS). ✧ 'Glorious/famous-Alive'? ⇨ **KÜLÜG + TİRİG.**

KÜLÜGES   Hak. 19th-20th c. **Külüges** [Kÿлÿгес], fem. (HRS 353). ✧ 'Wise; clever' cf. Hak. *külük* 'мудрость; умный, мудрый' (HRS 353).

KÜLÜY   Kirg. **Külüy-qan** [Кулуйкан] (Jud. 528).

KÜLÜK I. see **KÜLÜG**

KÜLÜK II. see **SİRĀNA-KÜLÜK**

KÜLÜKTÄY   Yak. **Külüktäy-bärgän / Külüktän-bärgän** [Кÿлÿктäi-бäргäн / Кÿлÿктäн-бäргäн], a folklore hero (Pek.).

KÜLÜM   Kirg. **Külüm-qan** [Кÿлÿмкан] (Jud. 52). ✧ 'Laugh, smiling'? cf. Chag., Kzk. *külüm* 'das Lachen, Gelächter' (Radl. II, 1473).

KÜLÜSTEY   Tuv. 19th c. **Külüstey-mergen** [Кулюстей-мергенъ] (Potanin IV, 419-21). ✧ 'Laugh, cheerfulness' cf. Hak.(Sag.), Kzk. *külüs* 'das Lachen, die Fröhlichkeit' (Radl. II, 1472) + suff. *-tey*?

KÜMEK   Kzk. 19th c. **Kümek** [Кумекъ] (SOK 282); Kzk. 19th c. **Kümek** [Кумекъ] (SOV 110); Kzk. 19th c. **Kümek-bay** [Кумекбай] (Pam. kn. Turg. 65). ✧ 'Help; helper' cf. Kzk. *kömek* 'помощ' (KzRS).

KÜMEN   Tat.(Lit.) 1593 **Kümen** [Селимша Муступинъ Куминовичъ] (Lit. Tat. 168); Kzk. **Kümen** [Тойбулды Куменевъ (Кушеневъ)] (Konšin, Pam. 21).

KÜMERT   Bashk. 1756 **Kümert?** [Кул Кумертев] (MIB IV/1, 120).

KÜMİN see **KÜMEN**

KÜMİS see **KÜMÜS**

KÜMİŠ see **KÜMÜS**

KÜMİŠ-TAŠ   Alt. **Kümiš-taš** [Кумышъ-ташъ], Kün-χan's son (Nikiforov 185). ⇨ **KÜMÜS + TAŠ.**

KÜMİŠKÄ   Bashk. 1761 **Kümiškä** [Кумышка Мрадымов] (MIB IV/1, 211). ✧ 'Home made brandy' cf. Bashk. *kömöškä* 'самогон' (BRS/Uraksin), Tat. *kömeškä* 'самогон' (TatRS).

KÜMLİ   Turk. 14th c. **Kümli** [Κουμουλίης], a commander (Byz. Turc. 168).

KÜMPES   Kzk. 18th c. - 19th c. **Kömbäs / Kömbes** [كوم باس / Комбас] (MIK IV, 164); Kuman 1475, 1493

Kümpes / Kömpes? (<**Kümpez**) [Kempeczzallasa, Kempeth, Kömpöcz], a Kuman in Hungary whose name preserved in toponyms of Lesser Kumania (Gyárfás III, 677, 709). ✧ 'Cupola, mausoleum' cf. Kzk. *kümböz* 'die Kuppel' (Radl. II, 1529), Kzk. *kümbez* 'кümbet, minare' (KzTS), Tat. *gümbäz* (<P.) 'der Bogen, die Kuppel' (Radl. II, 1656), Kirg. *kümböz* 'купол; надмогильное сооружение; надгробье; мавзолей' (Jud.). For more detailed explanation se Rásonyi, NTK 102-14, and also Rásonyi, KÖA 120, Rásonyi, Anthr. 142.

KÜMSÄ   Uyg. **Kümsä** (Müller, Uig. II, 80); Uyg. 12th c. - 14th c. **Kümsä** (DTS).

KÜMÜL   Türk 7th c. - 9th c. **Kümül-ögä** (DTS).

KÜMÜS see **KÜMÜŠ**

KÜMÜS-AYAQ   Kzk. **Kümüs-ayaq** [Кÿмÿс Айак] (Proben III, 635 /718/). ⇨ **KÜMÜŠ + AYAQ.**

KÜMÜŠ   Kkalp. 20th c. **Kümis** [Кюмис], fem. (Bask., Kkalp. 403, KkRS 778); Maml. 14th c. **Kümiš** [Kümiş], fem. (Tarǰ/Houtsma 98, Tarǰ/Toparlı 43); Tat.(Sib.) 1598-99 **Kümiš** [Кумышъ], Küčüm's son, a Siberian prince (AI II, 3-4, 9, 20, 22); Bashk. 1740 **Kümiš** [Юмутлы Кумышев] (MIB I, 468); Bashk. 1780 **Kümiš-bay** [Кумышбай Авгильдин] (MIB V, 104); Kzk. 1785 **Kümiš-bay** [Кумышбай] (MIK IV, 60); Alt. **Kümiš-qō** [Кумышъ-коо], fem. (Nikiforov 142); Hak. 19th-20th c. **Kümüs** [Кÿмÿс], fem. (HRS 353); Hak.(Sag.) 19th-20th c. **Kümüs-arïɣ** [Кÿмÿс Арыҥ], sister of the hero (bogatyr) (Proben IX, 249-52, 254); Hak.(Kacha) 19th-20th c. **Kümüs-arïɣ** [Кÿмÿс Арыҥ], mother of a hero (bogatyr) (Proben IX, 218); Kzk. 19th c. **Kümüs-bay** [Кумусбаевъ] (Grod., Pril. 70); Hak. 19th c. **Kümüs-irgek** [Кумюсъ-Иргэкъ] (Potanin IV, 618); Uyg. 13th c. - 14th c. **Kümüš**, fem. (Chwol., Syr.-nest. 101); Karakh. 11th c. **Kümüš** [kümüš / Kümüş] (DTS, MK/Atalay 846); Trkm. 20th c. **Kümüš** [Kümüš], fem. (Zaj. 1971, 338); Trkm. 20th c. **Kümüš** [Кумуш], fem. (TrkmRS 421); Kirg. **Kümüš** [Кÿмÿш], fem. (Jud. 32); Kirg. **Kümüš** [Кÿмÿш], fem. (Jud. 905); Karakh.? 882, 897, 905 **Kümüš-čur** [بُـدقة محمد بن كُمْشْجُور] (Tabarī, Annal. III, 2025, 2151, 2198, 2248, Kindī 242); Uyg.? **Kümüš-χatun** [كمش حاتُنْ] (Poppe 1253); Shor 19th-20th c. **Kümüs-qan** (Dyrenkova 88); Karakh.? 11th c. **Kümüš-tegin** [Kümüş tégin] (DTS, MK/Atalay 847); Selj. 1114 **Kümüš-tegin** [كمشتكين البلبكى] (Kamāladdīn II, 170); Selj. 1126, 1147 **Kümüš-tegin** [كمشتكين], an emir of state (Qalānisi 215, 153, 289); Selj. 12th c. **Kümüš-tegin** [كمشتكين جانـدار], Berk-yaruq's atabek (Rāwandī 140); Selj. 1177/78 **Kümüš-tegin** [كمشتكين], lord of Aleppo (Haleb), died in 11177/78 (Ibn al-Athīr: RHCHor 577, 608, 632); Selj. /Trkm.? 1097, 1100 **Kümüš-tegin** [كمشتكين بن طيلو / Kumischtekin /

Cameschtekin, filius Tilu], lord of Malatya, Sivas and other places, commonly called as ibn al-Danišmend (Weil, Chalif. III, 152, Abulfidā III, 324-325); Selj. 11th c. **Kümüš-tegin / Gümüš-tegin?** [كمشتكين / Gumichtikîn], occupied Rakka, died in 1106 (Ibn al-Athīr: RHCHor 237); Karakh. **Kümüš-tigin** [Kümüš tigin] (MK/Atalay 847). ✦ 'Silver' cf. Türk, Karakh. *kümüš* 'серебро' (DTS), Trkm. *kümüš* 'id.' (TrkmRS), Alt. *kümüš* 'id.' (OjrRS), Kzk. *kümis* 'id.' (KzRS). See also **AY-KÜMÜŠ, ŠĬN-GÜMĬS**.

KÜMÜŠ-AY Kkalp. 20th c. **Gümis-ay** [Гумисай], fem. (KkRS 777); Kzk. 19th c. **Gümüš-ay** [Гюмушъ-Ай] (Grod., Pril. 123); Kirg. 20th c. **Kümüš-ay** [Кумушай], fem. (Kalilov 95). ✦ 'Silver Moon'. ⇨ **KÜMÜŠ + AY**. See also **AY-KÜMÜŠ**.

KÜMÜŠ-BUƔA Maml. 14th c. **Kümüš-boya** [كُشبُغا] (Sauvaget 55); *TN:* Selj. 12th c. **Kümüš-buɣa** [كموشبغا الظاهريّ الحاجّ], a mesjid (Ibn Šaddād, Alep 74). ✦ 'Silver-bull' (Sauvaget 55). ⇨ **KÜMÜŠ + BUQA**.

KÜMÜŠ-QARTĬƔA Shor 19th-20th c. **Kümüš-qartïɣa** (Dyrenkova 62). ⇨ **KÜMÜŠ + QARTĬƔA**.

KÜMÜŠ-TAJĬ Alt. **Kümüš-taJi** [Кӱмӱшъ Таджи], fem. (Nikiforov 18); Alt. **Kümüš-taJi** [Кӱмӱшъ-Таджи], fem. (Nikiforov 16, 18). ⇨ **KÜMÜŠ + TAJĬ?**

KÜN Oghuz 13th c. **Kün** [kün] (DTS, EUTS); NUyg. 19th c. **Kün, Gün?** [كون / Kün (Gyn)] (Le Coq, Namenl. 108); Alt.(Tuba) 19th c. **Kün-arïɣ** [Кунарыгъ], Kün-qan's daughter (Potanin IV, 579, 580); Uyg. 8th c. - 12th c. **Kün-arïɣ-ïnal** (Müller, Pfahl. 23); Maml. 1313 **Kün-bay** [كنباى], one of Toqtay's soldiers (Dawād. 275); Maml. 1467/68 **Kün-bay** [كنباى], an emir (Iyās II, 81); Nog. 20th c. **Kün-biyke** [Куьн Бийке Йантувгъан келинъи / Кюнбике Янтуганова], one of Baskakov's informants from the aul of Ïrɣaqlï (Bask., Nog. 143); Oghuz 867, 870, 878 **Kün-čur** [كنجور / البخارى/] (Tabarī, Annal. III, 1636, 1668, 1685, 1840 etc.); Kzk. **Kün-Jan** [Кӱн Џан] (Proben III, 55 /71/); Oghuz/Trkm. 13th c. **Kün-χan** [كون خان بن اوغوز خان / Koun / Кӱн-хан], one of the sons of the legendary Oghuz Khaghan (Khan) (Abulg./Desm. 22, 24-26, Oğuz K. Dest. 15, Šejb. XXIII, Abulg./Kon. 425, 465, 470-480 etc., RaD I/1, 76); Tuv. 19th c. **Kün-χan** [Кунь ханъ] (Potanin IV, 426); Uyg.? **Kün-χatun** [كون خاتون] (Poppe 1253); Trkm. 18th c.? **Kün-χoJa** [Кун-ходжа], Ay-χoJa's brother (MIT II, 208); Alt. **Kün-qan** (Radl. I, 983); Hak.(Sag.) 19th-20th c. **Kün-qan / Qun-qan?** [Кӱн Кан], folklore hero (Proben IX, 220, 453-455); Kzk. 19th c. **Kün-qïz** [Кунъ-кызъ], mentioned together with *Ay-qïz* and *Jel-qïz* (Potanin, Pred. 94); Tat.(Bar.) **Kün-sïlū** [Кӱн Сылу], fem. (Proben IV, 52 /65/). ✦ 'Day; sun' (Jarring). See also **AY-KÜN, JUMA-KÜN, KÜČ-**

KÜN, QAZAN-KÜN, ÖTÖ-GÜN.

KÜN-BERDĬ Tat.(Sib.) 1632 **Kün-berdi** [Кунбердей] (Miller, Ist. Sib. II, 397). ✦ 'Sun-given'. ⇨ **KÜN + BERDĬ**. See also **KÜN-BERMĬŠ**.

KÜN-BERMĬŠ Uyg. **Kün-bärmiš** [Kün Bärmiş] (EUTS); Uyg. 12th c. - 14th c. **Kün-bermiš-säñün** (Radl., USp. 52, DTS); Uyg. 8th c. - 12th c. **Kün-bermiš-tarχan** (Müller, Pfahl. 23). ✦ 'Given by the Sun' (Blagova 1997, 704). ⇨ **KÜN + BERMĬŠ**. See also **KÜN-BERDĬ**.

KÜN-ČOMČÖRÜYÄ Yak. **Kün-čomčörüyä** [Кӱн-Чömчöрÿjä], fem. (Pek.). ⇨ **KÜN + ČOMČÖRÜYÄ**.

KÜN-JÄP Bashk. 1752 **Kün-Jäp / Kün-zäp?** [Кунзяп Утекеев] (MIB IV/1, 63).

KÜN-JÖLŌRÜMÄ Yak. **Kün-Jölŏrümä** [Кӱн Џöлöрӱмä Саркыл-хотун], foremother of the evil spirit Altan Sabaray-toyon and all his family (Pek.). ✦ 'Sun-Jölŏrümä (=holed, full of holes)' (Pek.). ⇨ **KÜN**.

KÜN-JÜÖLLÜT Yak. **Kün-Jüöllüt** [Кӱн Чÿöллÿт] (Pek.). ✦ 'Sun-Jüöllüt' (Pek.). ⇨ **KÜN**.

KÜN-DEÑIZ Selj. **Kün-deñiz** [كيدكر / كندكز], an emir, Sultan Sandjar's (1118-1157) chieftain (Ahbar 61, Bondārī 259, 260, 262). ⇨ **KÜN + TEÑIZ**.

KÜN-DOƔDĬ see **KÜN-TOƔDĬ**

KÜN-DOƔUŠ Oghuz? 816 **Kün-doɣuš** (Fragm. Hist. Ar. 347, 423, Tabarī, Annal. III, 936). ✦ 'Sun-rise' cf. Turk. *doğuş* 'birth' (TED). ⇨ **KÜN + TUƔĬŠ + suff. -*uš***.

KÜN-DUƔAR see **KÜN-TUƔAR**

KÜN-GĬLDĬ Bashk. 1710 **Kün-gildi** [Урмекей Кунгилдин (Кунгильдин)] (MIB III, 60, 62, 63). ⇨ **KÜN + KELDĬ**.

KÜN-KÜBÄYĬΧSÄ Yak. **Kün-kübäyiχsä-χatun** [Кӱн-Кӱбäjiхсä-хатын], wife of the spirit of the Earth Añārïχsa-toyon (Pek.). ✦ 'Highly-respected Sun' (Pek.). ⇨ **KÜN**.

KÜN-MOLTOY Yak. **Kün-moltoy** [Кӱн-молтoi] (Pek.).

KÜN-NĬYAZ Kzk. 19th c. **Kü-nyaz (<Kün-niyaz?)** [Куньязъ] (SOK 222). ⇨ **KÜN + NĬYAZ**.

KÜN-ÖRÖPÜNÄ Yak. 20th c. **Kün-öröpünä-χotun** [Арапына / Арапыана / Кӱн Öрöпÿнä-хотун (Чуонах)], a woman of Russian origin turned into an evil spirit (üör) after her death in the 19th c. (Pek.). ✦ 'Sun-Agrippina' (R.). ⇨ **KÜN**.

KÜN-SABAR Hak.(Sag.) 19th-20th c. **Kün-sabar** [Kün Sabar / Кӱн Сабар], a folklore hero, Ay-sabar's brother(?) (Proben II, 141 /143/). ⇨ **KÜN + SABAR?**

KÜN-SABĬR Hak.(Sag.) 19th-20th c. **Kün-sabïr** [Kün Sabyr / Кӱн Сабыр], a folklore hero, Ay-sabïr's brother (Proben II, 71 /72/). ✦ 'Sun-Patience/strength'. ⇨ **KÜN + SABĬR**.

KÜN-ŠĬƔAR Kkalp. 20th c. **Kün-sïɣar** [Куншыгар] (KkRS 774). ✦ 'The Sun rises' cf. Kkalp. *šiq-*

'выходить; всходить' (KkRS). ⇨ **KÜN.**

KÜN-TEMUS   Hak. 19th-20th c. **Kün-temus** [Куйтемусъ] (Titov 190). ✧ 'Sun-hero' (Titov). ⇨ **KÜN.** See also **AY-TEMUS.**

KÜN-TOГDÏ   Trkm.? 1814/15 **Gün-doγdï-qāzï** [Гюндогды-кази] (MIT II, 388); Yürük 16th c. **Gün-doγdu** [كوندعدى], from the Yürüks of Kocacık, Turkey (Gökb., Rum. 104); Oghuz 1190 **Kön-duwdï** [Кондувдый], a prince of the Torks (''knjaz' Torskij'') (Ipat. 450); Selj.? 1124/25 **Kün-doγdï** [كندغدى / كيدغدى / كُنُدغدى] / Condoghdi), an emir(-in-chief) of sultan Mohamed (Ibn al-Athīr, Atab.: RHCHor II/2, 51, Bondārī 123, 211); Maml. 1299, 1332 **Kün-doγdï** [كندغدى التجترى], a governor (Dawād. 15); Maml. 14th c. **Kün-doγdï** [كندغدى / Kündoğdı] (Tarǰ/Houtsma 99, Tarǰ/Toparlı 41); Maml. 14th c. **Kün-doγdï** [Кундогды] (Tuhfa 410); Karakh. 11th c. **Kün-toγdï** [kün toγdï] (DTS); Selj./Trkm. 13th c. **Kün-toγdï** / **Kün-doγdï** [كون طوغدى], Er-toγrul's brother (Nešrī 140, Āšikp. 6); Kuman 1183, 1185, 1191, 1192 **Kün-tuwdï** / **Kün-tuγdï** [Кунтувдѣй / Кунътугдыя /], a prince (Ipat. 425 /438/, 430 /442/, 450-453); Bashk. 1709 **Kün-tüdï** [Кунтуди] (MIB I, 264); *TN:* Turk. 20th c. **Gün-doγdu** [Gündoğdu], a village in the province of Antalya, Turkey (TMİB 107); Turk. 20th c. **Gün-doγdu** [Gündoğdu], a village in the province of Balıkesir, Turkey (TMİB 145); Turk. 20th c. **Gün-doγdu** [Gündoğdu], a village in the province of Adıyaman, Turkey (TMİB 28); Turk. 20th c. **Gün-doγdu** [Gündoğdu], a village in the province of Bursa, Turkey (TMİB 221); Turk. 20th c. **Gün-doγdu** [Gündoğdu], villages in the province of Bursa, Turkey (TMİB 213, 221); Turk. 20th c. **Gün-doγdu** [Gündoğdu], a village in the province of Burdur, Turkey (TMİB 204). ✧ 'The Sun was born (rose); The Day was born' (Blagova 1997, 704), cf. also Sauvaget 55: „le jour a paru", „le soleil s'est levé"; Poppe 1253: „die Sonne ist aufgegangen". ⇨ **KÜN? + TUГDÏ.** See also **AY-TOГDÏ.**

KÜN-TOГMÏŠ   Turk. 16th c. **Gün-doγmuš** (Ongan, Ank. II, 1512); Turk. 1540 **Gün-doγmuš-kethudā**, chief of the Karkın cemaat (Diyarbekir, Turkey) (Demirtaş 57); Maml. 14th c. **Kün-doγmïš** [كندغمش / Kündoğmıš] (Tarǰ/Houtsma 99, Tarǰ/Toparlı 41); Selj. 12th c. **Kün-toγmïš** / **Gün-doγmïš?** [Κουντογμής], a commander of the army (Byz. Turc. 163); *TN:* Turk. 20th c. **Gün-doγmuš** [Gündoğmuş İlcesi], a district in the province of Antalya, Turkey (TMİB 102). ✧ 'The Sun was born (rose); The Day was born'. ⇨ **KÜN + TOГMÏŠ.** See also **KÜN-TOГDÏ.**

KÜN-TUГAN   Tat.(Mish.) 1713 **Kön-tuγan** [Бикей Контуганов] (MIB III, 102); Crm.(Tat.)? 1542 **Kün-tuγan** [Кунтуган (Кунъ-Туганъ) Дуан], envoy of the ruler of Perekop (Kn. Metriki Lit. 21); Kzk. 19th c. **Kün-tuγan** [Кунтуганъ] (AOP 2); Kzk. 19th c. **Kün-tuγan** [Тлеубай Кунтугановъ] (Pam. kn. Turg. 78). ✧ 'The sun rose', 'A sun-like bright child has been born' (Sattarov). A typical female name in Kazak (Sultan'jaev 1970, p. 75). ⇨ **KÜN + TUГAN I.** See also **AY-TUГAN.**

KÜN-TUГAR   Tat. 1777 **Kün-duγar** [Кундугаръ] (PSZRI XX, 577, 579); Uzb. / Trkm.? 1538 **Kün-tuγar** [كون تغار بهادر] / Koun-Toughâr Behâdour], from the Quñgrat tribe (Abulg./Desm. 243); Kkalp. 20th c. **Kün-tuwar** [Кюнтувар / Күнтуұар] (Bask., Kkalp. 400, KkRS 774); *TN:* Kzk. **Kün-tuwar** [Кунтуар], the name of a field (Kojčubaev 157). ✧ 'The sun rises; the day will begin'. ⇨ **KÜN + TUГAR?** See also **AY-TUWAR.**

KÜN-TUW   Kzk. 1823 **Kün-tuw** [كون طو / Кунту] (MIK IV. 457); Kzk. 19th c. **Kün-tuw** [Кунту] (SOV 60); Kzk. 19th c. **Kün-tuw** [Кунту Бибитовъ] (SKSO VIII, 201); Kzk. 19th c. **Kün-tuw-bay** [Кунтубай] (SOV 140). ⇨ **KÜN + TUW.**

KÜN-TUWAR see **KÜN-TUГAR**

KÜN-TUWDÏ see **KÜN-TOГDÏ**

KÜN-TŪDÏ see **KÜN-TOГDÏ**

KÜN-TÜYMES   Nog. 20th c. **Kün-tüymes** [Куьн-Туьймес] (Bask., Nog. 249).

KÜN-ŽARÏQ   Kzk. 19th c. **Kün-žarïq** [Юнусъ Кунжарыков] (AUK 623). ⇨ **KÜN + YARUQ.**

KÜNČ   Türk 7th c. - 9th c. **Künč-tutuq** [Künç Tutuq] (DTS, ETY III, 169).

KÜNČE   Khorezm.? Kipchak.? 1388 **Künče-oγlan** [Кунче-оглан] (MIT I, 823). ✧ 'Little sun'? cf. Hak. PN *Künče* 'солнышко' (Butanaev). ⇨ **KÜN +** suff. -*če*.

KÜNČIÑ   Uyg. 10th c. **Künčiñ** (DTS).

KÜNČUK see **KÖNČEK**

KÜNJUK see **KÖNČEK**

KÜNDÄY I.   Selj. 1132, 1143 **Kündäy** [كندايجور] (Qalānisi 233, 277).

KÜNDÄY II.   Yak. **Kündäy** [Күҥдäi] (Pek.).

KÜNDÄLİKĀN   Yak. **Kündälikān-toyon** [Күҥдäлiкäн-тojoн] (Pek.).

KÜNDEČ   Karakh.? 900? **Kündeč** / **Kündečik?** [كنداج / اسحاق بن كنداجيق / اسحاق بن] [Kamāladdīn I, 80. 81, Arīb 63).

KÜNDEČIK   Karakh.? / Khazar 917 **Kündečik** [كنداج / بن محمد بن اسحاق بن كنداجيق / اسحاق بن / طرخان], Isχaq's father (Kündečik / Qundajïq al-Xazarī) (Arīb 63, Kamāladdīn I, 80, 81, Golden 202: a well-known general of the ᶜAbbāsid Caliphate).

KÜNDER   Kzk. 19th c. **Künder-bek** [Кундербекъ] (AOAtb. 38). ✧ 'He will grudge, will be possessive' cf. Kzk. *künde-* 'завидовать, ревновать' (KzRS).

KÜNDİ see **KÜNDÜ**

KÜNDÜ Alt. 19th-20th c. **Kündi** [Кӱнди] (OjrRS 209); Alt. **Kündü-χan** [Куьндю-ханъ (Куньду-ханъ)] (Nikiforov 78, 99-109). ✧ I. 'Khan with sun(shine?)' (Nikiforov), 'Inhabitant of the Sun-world', cf. Alt.(Tel.) *kündü* 'eine Sonne habend (=unter der Sonne wohnend)' (Radl. II, 1444); II. 'Respect, honour' (OjrRS), cf. Alt. *kündü*? 'die Ehrfurcht, Höflichkeit' (Radl. II, 1444) (<Mo.).

KÜNDÜY Alt. 19th-20th c. **Kündüy** [Кӱндӱй] (OjrRS 209). ✧ 'Sun-like' (OjrRS). ⇨ **KÜNDÜ**.

KÜNDÜLEY Alt. 19th-20th c. **Kündüley** [Кӱндӱлей] (OjrRS 209). ✧ 'Sun-like'.

KÜNDÜMEY Karg. **Kündümey** [Кӱндӱмäй], fem. (Proben IX, 632).

KÜNDÜR Khazar **Kündür**, high dignity (lofty title) in the Khazar hierarchy, the substitute of the Qaγan-bek (Golden 200-202); Kirg. **Kündür** [Кӱндӱр] (Proben V, 71).

KÜNDÜZ see **GÜNDÜZ**

KÜNÄR Tat.(Tüm.) **Künär-sulū** [Кӱнäр Сулу], Barsa-kilmäs-padïša's daughter (Proben IV, 364 /460/).

KÜNÄS Yak. **Künäs-oyūn** [Кӱнäс-оjун], a shaman (Pek.).

KÜNÄŠ-BAKİ Chag. 16th c. **Künäš-baki** (Ivanov 211). ✧ 'Sun-eternal' cf. Turk. *künäš* 'die Sonne' (Radl. II, 1440). ⇨ **BAQÏ**.

KÜNÄYİ Yak. **Künäyi-bātïr** [Кӱнäji-батыр], a folklore hero (Pek.).

KÜNE Oghuz/Trkm. 13th c. **Küne** [كونه / Кӱне] (Abulg./Kon. 525).

KÜNEY Bashk. 1737 **Küney(e)?** [Кунея Бутякова], a widow (MIB III, 356).

KÜNESTEY Tat. 1651 **Künestey** [Кунестейко Изерековъ], a prince from the Mras region (AI IV, 148).

KÜNET Alt. 19th-20th c. **Künet** [Кӱнет] (OjrRS 209); Alt. 19th-20th c. **Künet** [Кӱнет], fem. (OjrRS 212). ✧ 'The sunny side of a mountain' (OjrRS).

KÜNGENE Kzk. 19th c. **Küngene** [Кунгене] (AOP 78).

KÜNİ-TİRİG Türk 7th c. - 9th c. **Köni-tirig** [Köni Tirig] (ETY III, 62); Türk 7th c. - 9th c. **Küni-tirig** (DTS). ✧ 'Küni-Alive' (Blagova 1997, 714). ⇨ **TİRİG**.

KÜNİM Kzk. **Künim-ǰan** [Кунимджанъ], Keni-sarï-χan's wife (Smirnov, Sultany 25). ⇨ **KÜN** + poss. suff. *-im*.

KÜNİN-KÖRKLİ Oghuz/Trkm. 13th c. **Künin-körkli** [كونين كورلى / Кӱнин-Кöркли], Yumak-bay's daughter, Qarqïn Qonaq-alp's wife (Abulg./Kon. 1450); Oghuz/Trkm. 13th c. **Künin-körkli** [كوركاى / كوركلى / كونين / Кӱнин-Кöркли], Qondï-bay's daughter, Biyäkän-alp's wife (Abulg./Kon. 1450). ✧ '?-beautiful'

cf. Kuman, Kar. *körklü* 'schön' (Radl. II, 1261).

KÜNKER Alt. 19th c. **Künker** / **Künker-χan** [Кункеръ / Кункеръ-ханъ] (Potanin, Pred. 182, Potanin IV, 321).

KÜNKİ Uyg. 762 **Künki-tay-sañun** [Beg Künki Taisangun Sïrtuš Yägän Apa], lord of Biš-balïq (Beš-balïq) (Mahrnāmag 10). See also **BEG-KÜNKİ**.

KÜNTEK Kzk. 19th c. **Küntek** [Кунтекъ] (SODž. 140).

KÜNTÜŠ Kzk. 1860 **Küntüš** [Кюнтушъ Будбаевъ], chief of the J̌alayïr clan (ZIRGOGeogr. I, 272).

KÜÖGÄLǰİN Yak. **Küögälǰin-udaγan** / **Küögälyin-udaγan** [Кӱöгäлцин / Кӱöгäлjiн], a shamaness (Pek.). ✧ 'Circling quietly' cf. Yak. *küögälǰii* 'тихо и плавно двигаться (кружиться)' (Pek.).

KÜÖKÄ-ǰĀSÏN Yak. **Küökä-ǰāsïn** [Кӱöкä Цасын], a being living in the sky (Pek.).

KÜÖRÄÑKİN Yak. **Küöräñkin** [Кӱöpäнкiн] (Pek.).

KÜÖTÄSKİ Yak. **Küötäski** [Кӱöтäскi] (Pek.).

KÜP-QAS Bashk. 1750 **Küp-qas** [Мустафа Купкасов] (MIB III, 479). ⇨ **KÖP +?**

KÜPÄ Uyg. **Küpä** [Küpä] (ETY II, 64).

KÜPÄ-YARÏQ Türk 750 **Küpä-yarïq** [küpä jarïq] (Runic Mss. 188, DTS). ⇨ **KÜPÄ + YARUQ**.

KÜPÄS Alt. 19th-20th c. **Küpäs** (Katanov, Otč. 10). ✧ 'Merchant' cf. R. купецъ (Katanov).

KÜPEY see **KÖPÄY**

KÜR Trkm. 1859 **Kür** [Уразъ-Мурадъ-Кюръ] (ZIRGOÊtn. I, 195). See also **MAY-KÜR, URAZ-MURAD-KÜR**.

KÜRǰESKE Hak. 19th-20th c. **Kürǰeske** [Кӱрцäскä / Кӱрческе], fem. (Proben IX, 553, HRS 353).

KÜRÄ Pecheneg 967, 971, 972 **Kürä** [Куря], a prince (PSRL VII, 288, VII, 291, 314, Lavr. 72, Ipat. 48 /56/); Kuman 1096 **Kürä** [Куря] (PSRL II, 221, Lavr. 223, Ipat. 161). ✧ 'Flee, fly' cf. Karakh. *kürä-* 'бежать' (DTS).

KÜRÄBİR Türk 750 **Küräbir-uruñu-sañun** [Küräbir Ur(u)ŋu S(a)ŋun / Küräbir Uruñu Sañun] (Runic Mss. 187-88, DTS, ETY II, 66).

KÜRÄK Tuv. 19th c. **Küräk** [Кӱräк], fem. (Proben IX, 120). ✧ 'Scoop, shovel' cf. Uyg., Kuman, Chag., Alt., Turk., etc. *küräk* 'die Schaufel, der Spaten' (Radl. II, 1449), Tuv. *χüürek* 'лопата' (TuvRS).

KÜRÄL Bashk. 1751 **Küräl** [Нуркей Курялев] (MIB IV/1, 34).

KÜRÄLDÄY Tuv. 19th c. **Küräldäy-mergän** [Кӱräлдäи Мергäн] (Proben IX, 249-54). ✧ 'Bronze' cf. Mo. *kurel* 'Bronze' (Schiefner XXXII).

KÜRÄÑ see **KÜREN**

KÜREY Bashk. 1601 **Gürey** [Гуреев (Досай)] (Miller, Ist. Sib. II, 166); Tat. 1729 **Kürey** [Юсуп Куреев] (MIB III, 259); Bashk. 1735 **Kürey** [Уразгильди Куреевъ], a tarχan (Vel.-Zern., Bašk. 23).

KÜREMSÄ   Tat.(GH) 1250, 1260 **Küremsä /
Qurïmsa?** [Куремься / Куремса], a Tatar prince and
commander (Ipat. 535 (539), PSRL II, 184, 197 etc.).

KÜREN   Kirg. **Küräñ** [كورانك / Курангъ], a χan in a
legend (ZVOIRAO XI, 292-95); Kzk. 19th c. **Kürem-
bay** (<Kuren-bay) [Курембай] (SODž. 56); Kzk. 19th
c. **Küren-bay** [Куренбай] (SOK 288). ✧ 'Brown' cf.
Alt., Hak. *küräñ* 'id.' (Radl. II, 1450), Kzk. *küren*
'kahverengi' (KzTS), Turk. *küräñ* 'braun (eine
Pferdefarbe)' (Radl. II, 1451).

KÜRENKEY   Kzk. 19th c. **Kürenkey** [Куренкей]
(SOK 288); Kzk. 19th c. **Kürenkey** [Куренкей] (SOK
116); Kzk. 19th c. **Kürenkey** [Куренкей] (SOV 94);
Kirg. 20th c. **Kürenkey** [Мураталы Куренкеев], a
people's artist (Hudožniki Sovetskoj Kirgizii. Moskva,
1951). ⇨ **KÜRÄÑ?** + suff. *-key / -käy*.

KÜREŠČİ   Turk. 15th c. **Küreŝči** [Κυρίτζης], byname
of Sultan Muhammed I (1402-1421) (Byz. Turc. 175).
✧ 'Wrestler'.

KÜRGÜŠ   Alt. 19th-20th c. **Kürgüš** [Кÿргÿш] (OjrRS
209). ✧ 'Big tub/vat'? cf. Alt.(Tel.) *kürgü* 'ein grosses
Birkenrindengefäss zum Aufbewahren der Gerste'
(Radl. II, 1460) + suff. *-š*.

KÜRİT   Hak. 19th c. **Kürit** [Кÿріт] (Katanov, Otč. 12).
✧ 'He/she smokes' cf. R. куритъ (Katanov).

KÜRKÄ   Kipch.? 1229 **Kürkä** [كوركا / Kourka], prince
of the Kipchak (Qifǰāq) tribe (Nasawī 172). ✧ 'Side
rod/rail of a tent'? cf. Chag. *kürgä* 'die Stäbe in den
Wänden des Zeltes' (Radl. II, 1459).

KÜRKEY   Bashk. 1738 **Kürkey** [Куркей] (MIB I,
145). ✧ 'Little Turkey (bird)'? cf. Bashk. *kürkä*
'индейка' (BRS/Uraksin) + dim. suff. *-y*.

KÜRKEK   Tat. 1665 **Kürkek** [Куркекъ Канбиревъ]
(DAI V, 39).

KÜRKLİ   Tat. 14th c. **Kürkli-bikä** [كوركلى بيكا], fem.
(Jusupov 67). ✧ 'Beautiful' cf. Tat. fem. PN *Kürekle-
bikä* (Sattarov), Kuman, Kar. *körklü* 'schön' (Radl. II,
1261), Tat. *kürekle* 'красивый, изящный,
благовидный' (TatRS). See also **HÄSEN, KÖRKLÄ,
KÖRTLÄ, PERİYZA, NİGĀR, SİLİГ, ZİFA.**

KÜRKÜ   Hak. 19th-20th c. **Kürkü** [Кÿркÿ], fem. (HRS
353). ✧ 'Grouse' (HRS), cf. Hak. *kürkü* 'das Birkhuhn'
(Radl. II, 1458).

KÜRLEÜT   Kzk. 19th c. **Kürleüt** [Курлеутъ] (AOO
66); Kzk. 19th c. **Kürleüt** [Курлеутъ] (AOA 102).

KÜRMEKEY   Bashk. 1798 **Kürmekey** [Курмекеевъ]
(PSZRI XXV, 196).

KÜRPE see **KÖRPE II.**

KÜRPE-TAY see **KÖRPE-TAY**

KÜRRE   Trkm. **Kürre** [Кÿрре] (Sopieva 178). ✧
'Little donkey'.

KÜRSE   Bashk. 1789 **Kürse-bay** [Курсебай
Аиткулов] (MIB V, 240).

KÜRSİKEY   Kzk. 19th c. **Kürsikey** [Курсикей] (SOK

200). ✧ 'Small tripod' cf. Kzk. dial. *kürsi* 'мосы'
[=tripod] (QTDS) + suff. *-key*.

KÜRSÜ   Yak. **Kürsü** [Кÿрсÿ], one of Moǰuqān's 9 sons
(Pek.).

KÜRSÜK   Bashk. 1790 **Kürsük** [Курсюк Куштеев]
(MIB V, 295).

KÜRT   Turk.? 1496/97 **Kürt-bay** [كرتباى], governor of
Beyrut (Iyās II, 308).

KÜRTE   Kzk. 19th c. **Kürte-bay** [Куртебай] (SOK
140). ✧ 'Winter-clothing made of leather (or cloth)' cf.
Kzk. *kürte* 'işlenmiş deriden veya kumaştan yapılan kış
elbisesi' (KzTS).

KÜRTEÑ   Hak. 19th-20th c. **Kürteñ** [Кÿртенъ], fem.
(HRS 353).

KÜRÜ   Uyg. 12th c. - 14th c. **Kürü** (DTS).

KÜRÜNDÜK   Bashk. 1754 **Küründük** [Гутер
Курюндюков] (MIB IV/1, 83). ✧ 'We were seen, we
appeared' cf. Uyg., Kuman., Alt., Hak., Kzk. *körün-*
'gesehen werden, zu sehen sein, sichtbar sein, sich
zeigen' (Radl. II, 1254).

KÜRÜN   Tuv. 19th c. **Kürün-öl** [Кÿрÿн ол] (Proben
IX, 166).

KÜS-KİLDE   Bashk. 1664 **Küs-kilde** [Кускилдей]
(MIB I, 185); Bashk. 1756 **Küs-kilde** [Кускильда
Туганаев] (MIB IV/1, 130); Bashk. 1756 **Küs-kilde**
[Абызан Кускильдин] (MIB IV/1, 130); Bashk. 1783
Küs-kilde [Ишали Кускильдин] (MIB V, 139, 199).
✧ 'The caravan has come; the hive arrived'? cf. Bashk.
Küskilde (Kusimova), Bashk. *küs* 'рой; толпа людей;
летовка' (BRS/Uraksin). ⇨ **XOŠ-KELDİ?**

KÜSÄ-KÜRİK   Tat.(Bar.) **Küsä-kürik-sulü** [Küsä
Kŭrik sulū / Кÿcä Кÿрік сулу], fem. (Proben IV, 166
/210/). ⇨ **KÖSE?** + **KÜRİK.**

KÜSÄ-PERDİ see **KÜSE-BERDİ**

KÜSÄDİK   Bashk. 1758 **Küsädik / Küθädik?**
[Кусядык Юмакаев] (MIB IV/1, 160). ✧ 'We
wished/wanted him/her' cf. Bashk. *köθä-* 'желать,
хотеть' (BRS/Uraksin).

KÜSÄYÜK   Uyg. **Küsäyük-täñrim** [Küsäyük
Tängrim], fem. (Zieme, Mat. I, 75). ✧ 'Wanted,
wished'? cf. Uyg. *küsä-* 'wünschen' (Zieme).

KÜSÄK   Tat. 1737 **Küsäk** [Кузмяш Кусяков] (MIB
III, 375); Bashk. 1772 **Küsäk** [Юлдаш Кусяков]
(MIB IV/2, 407); Bashk. 1776 **Küsäk** [Уразбай
(Урусбай) Кусяков] (MIB V, 47, 48, 49); Bashk. 20th
c. **Küsäk** [Кÿсәк / Кусяк] (Kusimova); Bashk. 1740
Küsäk-bay [Кусяк-бай] (MIB I, 446). ✧ 'Desired,
wanted, awaited child' (Kusimova, Sattarov).; ✧ I.
'Wanderer; wandering' (Kusimova), cf. Bashk. *küse-*
'переходить, переселяться' (BRS/Uraksin); II.
'Club' cf. Bashk. *küθäk* 'дубина' (BRS).

KÜSÄK-PERDİ   Bashk. 1711 **Küsäk-perdi** [Баюрап
Кусякпердин] (MIB III, 80). ⇨ **KÜSÄK + BERDİ.**

KÜSÄKÄY   Bashk. 1778 **Küsäkäy** [Кусякай

(Кусепей) Аптраков] (MIB V, 68, 271); Bashk. 1791 **Küsäkäy** [Кусякай (Кусекей) Суюндуков] (MIB V, 311, 395); Bashk. 1664 **Küsäkey** [Кусäкейко Тюменчюрин] (MIB I, 192); Tat. 1675 **Küsekäy** [Кусекайка] (Kungursk. akty 25); Tat. 1686 **Küsekäy** [Кусекайко Салкаевъ] (Kungursk. akty 118); Tat. 1764 **Küsekey** [Кусекей Сюлеев] (MIB IV/1, 283); Bashk. 1734 **Küsekey** [Кусекей Тоймасовъ] (Vel.-Zern., Bašk. 11); Bashk. 1756 **Küsekey** [Кадыргул Кусекеев] (MIB IV/1, 123); Bashk. 1756 **Küsekey** [Исмак Кусекеев] (MIB IV/1, 123); Bashk. 1762 **Küsekey** [Кусекей Кинзебаев] (MIB IV/1, 241); Bashk. 1764 **Küsekey** [Кусекей Таянкин] (MIB IV/1, 300); Bashk. 1788 **Küsekey** [Кусекей Сююндюков] (MIB V, 234). ✧ 'Little bald (child)'. ⇨ **KÖSE** + suff. *-key / -käy*.

KÜSÄLÄK see **KÜČELÄK**

KÜSÄMBET   Bashk. 1786 **Küsämbet < Küsänbet?** [Кусямбеть Девлетбаев] (MIB V, 196). ✧ 'Chief' cf. Bashk. *küsäm* 'предводитель' (BRS/Uraksin) + suff. *-bet*.

KÜSÄMIŠ   Uyg. **Közämiš** [Közämiş / Közäмiш] (Radl. II, 1301, EUTS); Uyg. 13th-14th c. **Küsämiš**, fem. (Zieme, Mat. III, 280); Karakh. 11th c. **Küsämiš** [küsämiš] (DTS); Uyg. 8th c. - 12th c. **Küsämiš-täñrim** (Müller, Pfahl. 10). ✧ 'Wished, wanted (child)' (Müller, Pfahl. 15), cf. Uyg., Karakh *kösä- / küsä-* 'желать; тосковать' (DTS), Bashk. *köθämeš* 'любимое блюдо (о пище)' (BRS/Uraksin).

KÜSÄN   Uyg. 13th-14th c. **Küsän-ba?-ïnal** [Küsän Ba[? / Ïna]l] (Zieme, Mat. III, 274); Uyg. 13th-14th c. **Küsän-čor** [Küsän Čor], a scribe (clerk) (Zieme, Mat. III, 274). ✧ I. The Old Turkic name of the town Kucha (Quča), cf. Zieme, ibid.; DTS; II. 'Polecat, skunk'? ⇨ **KÜZÄN.**

KÜSÄNBET see **KÜSÄMBET**

KÜSÄP   Bashk. 1735 **Küsäp** [Кусяпъ Кутуевъ] (Vel.-Zern., Bašk. 14); Tat. 1737 **Küsäp-batïr** [Кусяп-батыр] (MIB I, 307); Bashk. 1771 **Küsäp-qul** [Кусяпкул Азатбаев] (MIB IV/1, 358). ✧ 'Wished, awaited child' cf. Bashk. PN *Köθäp-qol* (Kusimova), Tat. PN *Kösäp-qol* (Sattarov), Bashk. *köθä-* 'желать, хотеть' (BRS/Uraksin). See also **KÜSÄMIŠ.**

KÜSÄŠ   Bashk. 1770 **Küsäš** [Кусяш Якупов] (MIB IV/1, 342). ⇨ **KÖSE** + dim. suff. *-š*.

KÜSÄTMIŠ   Uyg. 8th c. - 12th c. **Küsätmiš-täñrim**, fem. (Müller, Pfahl. 23).

KÜSE see **KÖSE**

KÜSE-BERDİ   Bashk. 1675 **Küsä-perdi** [Кусяперди Кутлубаев] (MIB I, 200); Tat.(Sib.) 1632 **Küse-berdi / Küse-berdey?** [Кусебердей] (Miller, Ist. Sib. II, 398). ⇨ **KÖSE** + **BERDİ.**

KÜSEK   Kzk. 19th c. **Küsk-bay** [Кюскбай] (SODž. 40).

KÜSEKEY see **KÜSÄKÄY**

KÜSELÄK see **KÜČELÄK**

KÜSELEK see **KÜČELÄK**

KÜSEPEY   Bashk. 1756 **Küsepey** [Кусепей Кинзябаев] (MIB IV/1, 109). ⇨ **KÖČE?**

KÜSKE   Hak. 19th-20th c. **Küske** [Кÿске], fem. (HRS 353). ✧ 'Mouse' (HRS).

KÜSKEJEK   Hak. 19th-20th c. **KüskeJek** [Кÿскäцäк], fem. (Katanov, Otč. 11). ✧ 'Little mouse' (HRS) (Katanov), cf. Alt.(Kmd.) *küskäjäk* 'die Maus' (Radl. II, 1501). ⇨ **KÜSKE** + dim. suff. *-jek*.

KÜSKEY   Bashk. 1706 **Küskey** [Кускей] (MIB III, 25); Bashk. 1709 **Küskey** [Кускей Утешев] (MIB III, 51); Bashk. 1737 **Küskey** [Кускей Илкеев] (MIB I, 321); Bashk. 1706 **Küskey-abïz** [Кускей абыз Кузюмов] (MIB III, 25). ⇨ **KÜČKEY?**

KÜSKELEY   Hak.(Sag.) 19th-20th c. **Küskäläy** [Кÿскäläи], fem. (Proben IX, 553); Hak. 19th-20th c. **Küskeley** [Кÿскелей] (HRS 349). ✧ 'Mouse-like'? ⇨ **KÜSKE** + suff. *-ley*.

KÜSKEŠ   Hak.(Shor) 1630 **Küskeš** [Кускеш] (Miller, Ist. Sib. II, 368). ✧ 'Little mouse'? ⇨ **KÜSKE** + suff. *-š*.

KÜSKÜ   Hak. 19th-20th c. **Küskü** [Кÿскÿ], fem. (HRS 353). ✧ 'Autumnal; Born in autumn' cf. Alt., Hak. *küskü* 'herbstlich' (Radl. II, 1502).

KÜSMÄK see **KÖČMEK**

KÜSMIS   Kzk. 19th c. **Küsmis** [Куссмисъ] (AOA 2).

KÜSTEN   Bashk. 1754 **Küsten** [Кустень Атайгулов] (MIB IV/1, 85).

KÜSTİ   Bashk. 1779 **Küsti** [Кусти Тянишев] (MIB V, 94).

KÜSÜ   Kzk. 1846 **Küsü-bay** [Байбулат Кусубаев] (MKOP 156).

KÜSÜK see **KÜČUK**

KÜSÜKEY see **KÜČUKEY**

KÜSÜLÄK see **KÜČELÄK**

KÜSÜM see **KÜČUM**

KÜSÜNČİ   Uyg. 12th c. - 14th c. **Küsünči** [küsünči] (DTS).

KÜSÜŠ   Uyg. **Küsüš**, fem. (Zieme, Mat. I, 74, 78). ✧ 'Wish' (Zieme).

KÜŠEK see **KÖŠEK**

KÜŠEKEY. see **KÖŠEKEY**

KÜŠELEK see **KÜČELÄK**

KÜŠEN   Kzk. 19th c. **Küšen** [Кушеновъ] (AOO 30); Kzk. 19th c. **Küšen** [Кущенъ] (AOO 55). ✧ 'Struggle, swot' cf. Kzk. *küšen-* 'тужиться' (KzRS), East.T. *küčän-* 'sich anstrengen' (Radl. II, 1492).

KÜŠER see **KÖŠER**

KÜŠİD   Trkm. 1881 **Küšid-χan** [Kouchid Khan / Кушидъ-ханъ], commonly known as *Baba Khan* (Voenn. Sb. 1881, No. 11, 186, O'Donovan II, 126).

KÜŠİNÄY   Bashk. 1740 **Küšinäy** [Кушинай

Кӑраккусюк] (MIB I, 396).

KÜŠLÜK Bashk. 1798 **Küšlük** [Кушлюкъ] (PSZRI XXV, 195); Khorezm. 13th c.? **Küčlük-χan / Küšlük-χan** [كوجلوك خان / Кушлук-хан], a commander of Bukhara (RaD I/1, 106, 131, Abulg./Desm. 109). ⇨ **KÜČ** + suff. *-lük*.

KÜTÄY Bashk. 1664 **Kütäy** [Кутейко], a tarχan (MIB I, 193); Bashk. 1735 **Kütäy** [Кутей Умитеевъ], a tarχan (Vel.-Zern., Bašk. 22). ✧ 'Little ass' cf. Kuman, Chag., Alt., Crm., Kzk. *köt* 'die Schamtheile und der Hintern' (Radl. II, 1275), Tat. *küt* 'der Hintern' (Radl. II, 1480). + suff. *-äy*. See also **BİLÄN-KÜTÄY**, **KÜTKEY**.

KÜTÄN see **KÖTÄN**

KÜTEK Kzk. **Kütek** [Кутекъ] (Dobrosm., Turg. 471). ✧ 'Little ass'? cf. Kuman, Chag., Alt., Crm., Kzk. *köt* 'die Schamtheile und der Hintern' (Radl. II, 1275), Tat. *küt* 'der Hintern' (Radl. II, 1480). + suff. *-ek*.

KÜTEMEY Bashk. 1739 **Kütemey** [Кутемей Якшигулов] (MIB III, 405).

KÜTİ Trkm. 20th c. **Küti** [Küti] (Zaj. 1971, 336); Trkm. 20th c. **Küti** [Кути], fem. (TrkmRS 423). ✧ 'Fat, plump' cf. Trkm. *küti* 'толстый, объёмистый' (TrkmRS).

KÜTİ-BAR Kzk. 19th c. **Küti-bar** [Кутебаровъ] (AUK 153); Kzk. 19th c. **Küti-bar** [Кутебаръ] (Grod. I, 98); Kzk. 1816 **Kütü-bar** [Кутюбар] (MIK IV, 301). ✧ 'He/she has an ass (lit.); he/she is brave' cf. Kzk. *kötü bar* 'er ist kühn' (Radl. II, 1275).

KÜTKEY Hak. 19th-20th c. **Kütkey** [Куткей] (HRS 349). ✧ 'Little ass' cf. Hak. PN *Kutkey [Kütkey!]* 'задница' (Butanaev), Kuman, Chag., Alt., Crm., Kzk. *köt* 'die Schamtheile und der Hintern' (Radl. II, 1275), Tat. *küt* 'der Hintern' (Radl. II, 1480). + dim. *-key*.

KÜTÜ-BAR see **KÜTİ-BAR**

KÜTÜJEK Hak. 19th-20th c. **Kütüjek** [Кӱтчек] (HRS 353).

KÜVČÜ Uyg. **Küvčü** [Küvçü] (EUTS).

KÜZÄK Chuv. 18th-19th c. **Küzäk** [Кузякъ] (Magn. 53); Bashk. 1762 **Küzäk** [Кузяк Товенеев] (MIB IV/1, 233); Bashk. 1735 **Küzäk-batïr** [Кузякъ Батырь Кутумбетевъ], a tarχan (Vel.-Zern., Bašk. 21). ⇨ **KÜSÄK?**

KÜZÄKÄY see **KÜZEKEY**

KÜZÄM Bashk. 1770 **Küzäm-γul** [Кузямгул Сатлыков] (MIB IV/1, 342).

KÜZÄN Bashk. 1760 **Közän** [Козян Кемяков] (MIB IV/1, 184); Bashk. 1675 **Közen** [Кашак Козенбаев] (MIB I, 200); Bashk. 1749 **Küzän** [Абдей Кузянов] (MIB III, 468); Bashk. 1765 **Küzän** [Кузян Курчин] (MIB IV/1, 320); Bashk. 1765 **Küzän** [Мукай Кузянов] (MIB IV/1, 310); Bashk. 1756 **Küzän-γul** [Килгун Кузянгулов] (MIB IV/1, 123); Bashk. 1756 **Küzän-γul** [Суумбай Кузянгулов] (MIB IV/1, 123);

Kzk. 19th c. **Küzem-bay (<Küzen-bay)** [Кузембай] (SODž. 40); Kzk. 19th c. **Küzem-bay (<Küzen-bay)** [Кузембай] (SOV 42); Chuv. 18th-19th c. **Küzen** [Кузень] (Magn. 53); Bashk. 1757 **Küzen** [Айдак Кузенев] (MIB IV/1, 157); Tat. 1711 **Küzen-bay** [Мусей Кузенбаев] (MIB III, 68); Kzk. 19th c. **Küzen-bay** [Кузенбай] (AOAtb. 14). ✧ 'Polecat, skunk' cf. Karakh. *küzün* 'хорек' (DTS), Kuman, Alt. *küzän* 'der Iltis' (Radl. II, 1506), Bashk. *köðän* 'хорек' (BRS), Tat. *közän* 'хорь, хорёк' (TatRS), Kzk. *(sasïq) küzen* 'хорек' (RKzS, KzRS). See also **TOQ-GÜZÄN**.

KÜZÄNČÜK Uyg. **Küzänčük** [Küzänçük] (EUTS); Uyg. 12th c. - 14th c. **Küzänčük** (Radl., USp. 214). ✧ 'Litle polecat (skunk)'. ⇨ **KÜZÄN** + dim. suff. *-čük*.

KÜZÄNÄY Chuv. 18th-19th c. **Küzänäy** [Кузеней] (Magn. 53). ⇨ **KÜZÄN** + dim. suff. *-äy*.

KÜZÄŠ see **KÖZÄŠ**

KÜZÄT Uyg. 750 **Küzät**, fem. (Müller, Uig. II, 81, DTS); Kzk. 19th c. **Küzet-bay** [Кузетбай] (AOP 122). ✧ 'Guard, watch' cf. Uyg. *küzät* 'караул, стража' (DTS), Kzk. *küzet* 'караул; охрана' (KzRS).

KÜZEY Bashk. 1710 **Küzey** [Кузей Сююнгулов] (MIB III, 64); Bashk. 1713 **Küzey** [Сатлык Кузеев] (MIB III, 90); Bashk. 1729 **Küzey** [Кутан Кузеев] (MIB III, 260); Bashk. 18th c. **Küzey** [Айса (Айсан) Кузеев] (MIB V, 152); Tat.(Arin) 1636 **Küzey** [Кузейко] (Miller, Ist. Sib. II, 439); Bashk. 1793 **Küzey / Küzäy?** [Кузей Шакиров] (MIB V, 332); Bashk. 1623 **Küzey / Küzey-qul** [Кузей Кулметев / Кузейкул / Кузеикул (Кузенкул) Маметев] (Miller, Ist. Sib. II, 299-300); Bashk. 1623 **Küzey-qul** [Кузейкул] (Miller, Ist. Sib. II, 299). ✧ I. 'Little eye' cf. Bashk. *küðäy* 'id.' (BRS/Uraksin); II. One of the clans of the tribe Ayli.

KÜZEKÄY see **KÜZEKEY**

KÜZEKE Kzk. 19th c. **Küzeke** [Кузеке] (SOK 230).

KÜZEKEY Bashk. 1786 **Küzäkäy** [Кузякай Юнусов] (MIB V, 196); Bashk. 1798 **Küzäkäy** [Кузякай] (PSZRI XXV, 195); Bashk. 1728 **Küzekäy** [Кузекай Бакшаев] (MIB III, 253); Bashk. 1738 **Küzekey** [Кузекей Черлкаков] (MIB III, 384); Bashk. 1763 **Küzekey** [Амир Кузекеев] (MIB IV/1, 276); Bashk. 1793 **Küzekey** [Кузекей (Кузекай) Купландин] (MIB V, 331); Bashk.? 1735 **Qozï-qay** [Козекай Досаевъ] (Vel.-Zern., Bašk. 25). ⇨ **KÜSÄKÄY?**

KÜZEM-BERDİ see **XOJAM-BERDİ**

KÜZEM-ENKEY Tat.(Sib.) 1598 **Küzem-enkey** [Куземенкѣй], a prince from Siberia (AI II, 7).

KÜZEMET Tat. 1695 **Küzemet** [Куземетко Кутлугуданов] (MIB I, 92).

KÜZEN see **KÜZÄN**

KÜZENÄK Chuv. 18th-19th c. **Küzenäk** [Кузенякъ] (Magn. 53); Tat.(Sib.)? 1623 **Küzenek / Küzenäk /**

Küsenäk / Küzen [Кузенек (Кузен, Кузенак, Кусеняк)], a tayša (Miller, Ist. Sib. II, 236, 301). ⇨ **KÜZÄN** + dim. suff. *-äk.*

KÜZER   Kzk. 19th c. **Küzer-bay** [Кузербай] (SOV 78).

KÜZET see **KÜZÄT**

KÜZMÄŠ   Bashk. 1737 **Küzmäš** [Кузмяш Кусяков] (MIB III, 375).

KÜZMET   Bashk. 1745 **Küzmet** [Кузметъ] (MIB III, 424).

KÜZÜ   Tat.(Sib.) 1633 **Küzü-bay** [Кузюбайко (Кузюбалко)] (Miller, Ist. Sib. II, 402); *TN:* Bashk. 1730 **Küzü-bay(eva)** [Кузюбаева], a village (MIB III, 277).

KÜZÜ-GİLDE   Tat.(Sib.) 1632 **Küzü-gilde** [Кузюгилдеев] (Miller, Ist. Sib. II, 397). ⇨ **KÜZÜ** + **KELDİ.**

KÜZÜ-YÏPAR   Bashk. 1735 **Küzü-yïpar?** [Кузюепаръ Чириковъ] (Vel.-Zern., Bašk. 12). ⇨ **KÜZÜ** + **YÏPAR.**

KÜZÜM see **KÖZÜM**

KÜZÜNČİ   Uyg. 12th c. - 14th c. **Küzünči / Közünči / Kösünči / Kösünči** [Közünçi / kösünči / küzünči] (Radl., USp. 82, EUTS, DTS). ✦ 'Breeder or seller of polecats (skunks)'. ⇨ **KÜZÄN** + suff. *-či.*

KÜZÜŠ   Alt. 19th-20th c. **Küzüš** [Кÿзÿш] (OjrRS 209).

KÜBÄ   Yak. **Kübä** [Кÿбä] (Pek.).

KÜCÄ   Tat.(Tob.) **Kücä-bay** [Кÿцä Баи] (Proben IV, 216 /266/). ✦ 'Fast-meal' cf. Tat.(Tara) *kücä* 'die Fastenspeise' (Radl. II, 1499).

KÜCİM see **KÜČÜM**

KÜR   Tat.(Tob.) **Kür-batïr** [Кÿр батыр], a person in a tale (Proben IV, 258 /323/).

Q

QABA I.   Bashk. 1730 **Qaba** [Бексей Кабин] (MIB III, 277); Kzk. **Qapa?** [Сабир Капин] (TOOIK I, 61). ✦ 'Spinning wheel' cf. Bashk., Tat. *qaba* 'прялка' (BRS/Uraksin, TatRS), Kzk., Tat. *qaba* 'id.' (Radl. II, 434). See also **QUTLUΓ-QABA.**

QABA II.   Turk. 1544 **Qaba** [Kaba bin Urudzs], a merchant in Pest, Hungary (Velics-Kamm. II, 9, 41). ✦ 'Rough, rude, puffy, mighty' cf. Turk. *kaba* 'id.' (TED), Crm., Kzk., Turk. *qaba* 'dicht (von Haaren), (Nog., Turk.) dick, geschwollen, (Turk.) grob, plump' (Radl. II, 433).

QABA-SAQAL   Turk. **Qaba-saqal**, a Zeybek (Kúnos 1891, 119); *TN:* Turk. 20th c. **Qaba-saqal**, a village in the adninistrative province of Adana (TMİB 9). ✦ 'Rough beard'. ⇨ **QABA II. + SAQAL.**

QABA-SAR   Kzk. 19th c. **Qaba-sar** [Кабасаръ] (SOK 86). ⇨ **QABA?** + **SARÏ.**

QABAY   Türk 7th-9th c. **Qabay** [Qabay] (ETY III, 80); Bashk. 1763 **Qabay** [Кабай Юлметев] (MIB IV/1, 268); Kzk. 19th c. **Qabay-bay** [Кабайбай] (SOK 6); Hak.(Kacha) 19th-20th c. **Qabāy** [Кабаи (Парфён)] (Proben IX, 558); Bashk. 1675 **Qapey? / Qabey?** [Капей Утешев] (MIB I, 201). ✦ 'Cradle' (Sattarov), cf. Alt. *qabay* 'die Wiege' (Radl. II, 435).

QABAQ I.   Kuman 1354, 1493 **Qabaq** [Baramuk (Baramak) filio Kabak] (Gyárfás III, 489, 706); Turk. 1583 **Qabaq** [قاباق] (Ongan, Ank. I, 167, 171). ✦ 'Pumpkin' cf. Chag., Crm., Tat., Turk. *qabaq* 'der Kürbis' (Radl. II, 437), Kuman *qabaq* 'Kürbis, cucurbita' (CC), cf. also Rásonyi, Adalékok 129, Rásonyi, KÖA 107, Rásonyi, Anthr. 141.

QABAQ II.   Alt.?, Hak.? 19th-20th c. **Qabaq** [Кабак] (Katanov, Otč. 11). ✦ 'Tavern, boozer' cf. Alt., Tat. *qabaq* (R.) 'die Branntwein kneipe' (Radl. II, 436).

QABAQJÏQ   Oghuz/Trkm. 13th c. **QabaqJïq** [قاباجيق / Кабакджык] (Abulg./Kon. 1235, 1275). ⇨ **QABAQ** + dim. suff. *-Jïq.*

QABAQLÏ   Kkalp. 1696 **Qabaqlï-χan** [Кабаклы хан] (MIKk. 151); Uzb. 1684 **Qabaqlï-χan** [Кабаклы ханъ], from Khiva (DAI X, 384); Turk. **Qabaqlï-oγlu**, a Zeybek (Kúnos 1891, 119). ⇨ **QABAQ I.** + suff. *-lï.*

QABALA   Tat. 1713 **Qabala** [Кабала Кельмаев] (MIB III, 98). ✦ 'Mascot, good-luck charm' cf. Tat. *qabala* 'id.' (TatRS).

QABAM-BAY see **QABAN**

QABAN   Kzk. 19th c. **Qabam-bay** (<Qaban-bay) [Кабамбай] (SOV 48, 106); Kzk. 19th c. **Qabam-bay** (<Qaban-bay) [Кабамбай] (AOK 70); Uyg. **Qaban** [Kaban] (EUTS); Kuman 1190 **Qaban** [Кобанъ], a Polovets prince, Urus-aba's son (Ipat. 451, 452); Khorezm.? **Qaban** [Кабан] (RaD II, 194); Bashk. 1744 **Qaban** [Кабан Сирюев] (MIB III, 416); Bashk. 18th c. **Qaban** [Иждевлетко Кабанов] (MIB I, 192); Kzk. 1829 **Qaban** [Кабан] (MIK IV, 324); Kzk. **Qaban-bay** [Kaban Bai / Кабан Баи], forefather of the Qara-kesäk tribe (Proben III, 47 /62/); Kzk. 19th c. **Qaban-bay** [Кабанбай] (Potanin II, 7); Kzk. 19th c. **Qaban-bay / Qoban-bay?** [Кобанбай] (SOK 210); Kzk. 19th c. **Qaban-bay? / Qoban-bay? / Qobon-bay?** [Кобонбай] (SODž. 108); Kzk. 19th c. **Qaman** [Каманъ] (SOK 188); Kirg. **Qaman** [Каман] (Proben V, 70 /71/, 136, 152); *EN:* Kzk. 18th c. - 19th c. **Qabam-bay-batïr** (<Qaban-bay-batïr) [Кабамбай-батыр], a Kazak clan (Tynyšp. 71); *TN:* Bashk. 1705, 1725, 1727, 1744, 1752, 1755, 1762 **Qabanovo / Qaban** [Кабаново, Кабан], a village (MIB III, 16, 234, 243, 416, IV/1, 64, 96, 238). ✦ 'Boar; (=hero, warrior)' cf. Kuman, Chag., Az., Kzk. *qaban* 'der Eber, das wilde Schwein; der Held, Kämpfer' (Radl. II, 439),

Kirg. *qaman* 'кабан (дикий), вепрь' (Jud.), cf. also Gombocz, ÁTSz. 18; Sattarov; Bask., Im. Polov. 67. See also **KÖS-QAMAN**.

QABAN-KÜČİ Oghuz/Trkm. 14th c. - 15th c. **Qaban-küči** [Qıyan Guği, Kaban Güci, Kıyan Güci / Кабан-Кючи] (DQorq. 23). ⇨ **QABAN + KÜČ**.

QABAŠ Kzk. 1819 **Qabaš** [Кабаш] (MIK IV, 324); Kzk. 19th c. **Qabaš** [Кабашевъ] (Grod., Pril. 65). ⇨ **ABAŠ**.

QABDA Uyg. 12th c. - 14th c. **Qabda** [Kabda] (Radl., USp. 127, 236, DTS, EUTS).

QABDÏQ Kzk. 19th c. **Qabdïq-pay** [Кабдыкпай] (SOV 118). ⇨ **ABDÏLDA**.

QABDÏLDA see **ABDÏLDA**

QABDÏR Kzk. 19th c. **Qabdïr** [Кабдыръ] (SOK 34).

QABÄS Bashk. 1754 **Qabäs** [Буракай Кабясев] (MIB IV/1, 33). ✧ 'The Archer'? (P.) cf. Tat. *Qawäs, Qawis* (Sattarov).

QABİKE Kzk. 19th c. **Qabike** [Кабике] (SOK 302). ✧ 'Strong, powerful' cf. Kzk. PN *Qabi* 'id.' (Žanuzakov 143) (<Ar.) + suff. -*ke*.

QABİL see **QABUL**

QABİLDÄŠ Tat.(Sib.) 1600 **Qabildäš** [Кабельдяш / Кобельдяш] (Miller, Ist. Sib. II, 159). ✧ Qabil (Ar.) (Ahmed) + suff. -*däš*.

QABÏČAQ Tat.(Sib.) 1675 **Qabïčaq** [Кабычакъ (Кабачачко) Курундаевъ] (DAI VII, 333). ✧ 'Sack; shirt; purse' cf. Alt., Hak. *qabičaq* 'der Beutel, das Glückshemd' (Radl. II, 452).

QABÏQAY Tat.(Sib.) 1675 **Qabïqay** [Кабыкай] (DAI VII, 333).

QABÏL see **QABUL**

QABÏLAN see **QAPLAN**

QABÏR Hak. 19th-20th c. **Qabïr** [Кабыр] (HRS 349). ✧ Gavriil (R.) personal name (HRS).

QABRİS Hak 19th-20th c. **Qabris** [Кабрис] (HRS 349). ✧ Gavryusha (R.) (Butanaev).

QABU Alt. 19th-20th c. **Qabu** [Кабу] (OjrRS 208). ✧ 'Net used for hunting wild animals' (OjrRS).

QABUL Kzk. 19th c. **Qabil-bek** [Кабилъ-бекъ] (Grod., Pril. 138, 154); Kkalp. 18th c. - 19th c. **Qabil-biy** [Кабил-бий] (Ivanov: MIK 84); Kzk. 19th c. **Qabïl** [Kabil-Baybul] (Ljutš 138); Kzk. 19th c. **Qabïl** [Кабылъ] (SODž. 72); Kzk. 19th c. **Qabïl** [Кабылъ] (AOK 10); Kzk. 19th c. **Qabïl** [Кабылъ] (Potanin II, 5); Kkalp. 20th c. **Qabïl** [Къабыл / Қабыл] (Bask., Kkalp. 76, KkRS 774); Kkalp. 1822 **Qabïl(-biy)** [Кабыль бий] (MIKk. 127); Bashk. 1776 **Qabïl / Qabul** [Кабыл (Кабул) Алагузин] (MIB V, 35, 67, 69, 85); Kzk. 19th c. **Qabïl-bay** [Кабылбай] (SKSO II, 16); Kkalp. 20th c. **Qabïl-bay** [Кабылбай] (KkRS 774); Uzb. 1875 **Qabïl-bay** [Кабылбай] (Moskal'cev 48); Kzk. 19th c. **Qabïl-Jan** [Кабыльджанъ] (SKSO IV, otd. III, 13); Oghuz/Trkm. 13th c. **Qabïl-χoJa /**

Qabil-χoJa? [خواجه قبل / Кабиль-ходжа], chief-bek of Dib-baquy-χan (Abulg./Kon., 660); Kzk. 19th c. **Qabïl-pay** [Кабелпай] (SODž. 128); Kzk. 19th c. **Qabul** [Кабулъ] (AOO 10); Kzk. 19th c. **Qabul** [Кабулъ] (SKSO VIII, 205); Kzk. 19th c. **Qabul** [قابول] (SKSO VIII, 205); Kzk. 19th c. **Qabul-bay** [Кабулбай] (SOV 50); Uzb. 1851 **Qabul-bay** [Кабулъ-бай], chief of the town Urgench (ZIRGO V, 109); *EN:* Kzk. 18th c. - 19th c. **Qabïl-bek** [Кабылбек], a clan (Tynyšp. 66). ✧ 'Acceptance, agreement; all right' cf. Kzk. *qabïl* 'id.' (KzRS), Kkalp. *qabïl* 'id.' (KkRS), Turk. *qabul* 'id.' (TED), Bashk. *qabul* 'id.' (BRS). (<Ar.). See also **BAY-ГАBÏL?**, **BERDİ-QABUL**, **JAN-QABUL**, **TÄW-QABÏL**, **TLÄW-QABÏL**, **TOBA-QABÏL**.

QAČ Kzk. 19th c. **Qač-bay** [Тилавли Качбаевъ] (Grod., Pril. 150); Kzk. 19th c. **Qač-bay** [Мусакиръ Качбаевъ] (Grod., Pril. 150). ✧ 'Flee; run away!' cf. Türk, Uyg., Chag., Alt., Crm., Kirg., Kzk., Tat., Turk., etc. *qač-* 'fliehen; abhanden kommen' (Radl. II, 332). See also **ALÏP-QAČ, YAW-ГAŠTÏQ, YAW-QAČ**.

QAČA Hak. 19th-20th c. **Qača** [Кача] (HRS 349).

QAČAČ Karakh. **Qačač** [Kaçaç] (MK/Atalay 841).

QAČAГAN see **QAŠAГAN**

QAČAY Hak. 19th c. **Qačay** [Качай], fem. (Katanov, Otč. 12). ⇨ **QAČA** + suff. -*y*.

QAČAQ Chuv. 18th-19th c. **Kačak** [Качакъ] (Magn. 50); Turk. 20th c. **Qačaq** [Kaçak] (Önder, Göle); Kzk. 19th c. **Qačaq-pay** [Качакпай] (SOK 128); Kzk. 19th c. **Qašaq-bay / QaJaq-bay?** [Кажакпай] (Pam. kn. Turg. 64). ✧ 'Runaway; fugitive' cf. Tat. *qačaq* 'беженец; беглец; вольница (TatRS), Chag., Az., Turk. *qačaq* 'die Flucht; flüchtig; (Az.) der Feigling'.

QAČAL Trkm. 1550 **Qačal** [Качаль Шах-верди / Шах-верды-бек Качаль], Šah-verdi-sultan's byname (MIT II, 60, 61, 69, 70).

QAČALAY Tat.(Lit.) 1592 **Qačalay** [Качалай] (Lit. Tat. 123); Tat.(Lit.) 1592 **Qačalay** [Качалаевичъ] (Lit. Tat. 119, 122).

QAČAN-KÜKÄ Uyg. 12th c. - 14th c. **Qačan-kükä** [Kaçan Küka] (Radl., USp. 91, DTS, EUTS). ✧ 'Escaped-Kükä' cf. Az., Crm., Turk. *qačan* 'geflohen, der Flüchtling' (Radl. II, 334), Türk, Uyg., Chag., Alt., Crm., Kirg., Kzk., Tat., Turk., etc. *qač-* 'fliehen; abhanden kommen' (Radl. II, 332). ⇨ **KÜKÄ** + past. part. suff. -*an*.

QAČANAQ Bashk. 1632 **Qačanaq** [Качанако Кырпычаков] (Vel.-Zern., Bašk. 39). ⇨ **QAČAN?** + suff. -*aq*.

QAČAR Chag. 16th c. **Qačar** [Качар], a mulla (Ivanov 208); Yürük **Qačar-oγlu** (Giese 90, 125); *EN:* Trkm. 1732 **Qačar** [قجر / Kaçar cemaatı], a cemaat (religious ethnic community) in the region of Bozdağı, Turkey (Refik, Anad. 187). ✧ 'He will flee / run away' cf. Trk.

qač- 'fliehen' (Radl. II, 332). See also **ALÏP-QAČ, ALÏP-QAČAR, YAW-QAČ, YAW-QAČAR, YAW-QAČTÏ**.

QAČATAY   Tat.(Lit.) 1557 **Qačatay** [Качатай], a prince (Kn. Metriki Lit. 152). ⇨ **?** + **TAY** or suff. *-tay(1,2)*?

QAČÏ see **QAČÏ I.**

QAČÏ-ГАLÏ   Tat. 1532 **Qači-ɣali-murza / Qači-ɣaley-murza?** [Качигалей / Качигалѣй-мурза], a murza in Kazan (PSRL VIII, 276-277, XIII, 56). ⇨ **QAČÏ I.** + **ALÏ.**

QAČÏГÏ   NUyg.(Tar.) **Qačïɣï-bay** [Katschigi Bai / Качіɟi Баі], Orduɣa-bay's slave (Proben VI, 154 /203/).

QAČÏ I.   Kzk. 1630 **Qači-bay** [Качебай], a prince (Miller, Ist. Sib. II, 374); Tat. 1362 **Qači-bey / Qač-bey** [Качибей (Качбей, Качзей)], a prince (PSRL II, 350). ⇨ **ХAЈÏ?**

QAČÏ II.   Alt. 19th-20th c. **Qačï** [Качы] (OjrRS 208).

QAČÏYĀN see **KÄSÏYĀN**

QAČÏLÏŠ   Maml. 1320 **Qačïlïš** [قجليش] (Iyās I, 159, 161,).

QAČÏN   Alt. 19th-20th c. **Qačïn** [Качын] (OjrRS 208).

QAČÏR   Hak.(Kyz.) 19th-20th c. **Qačïr** [Качыр] (Katanov, Otč. 13). ✧ 'Drive, chase!' (Katanov).

QAČÏRSU   Uyg. 12th c. -14th c. **Qačïrsu** [Kaçırsu] (DTS, EUTS). ✧ 'May he make (the enemy) escape' (Blagova 1997, 716).

QAČQAR see **QAŠQAR**

QAČQÏN   Kzk. 19th c. **Qačqïm-bay (<Qačqïn-bay)** [Качкымбай] (AOK 34); Bashk. 1735 **Qačqïn** [Качкынъ Тымыковъ] (Vel.-Zern., Bašk. 13); Bashk. 1769 **Qačqïn** [Качкен Айсов] (MIB IV/1, 334); Bashk. 1793 **Qačqïn** [Качкин Ильясов] (MIB V, 335); Bashk. 1826 **Qačqïn** [Качкиновъ] (TOUAK XXIV, 71); Kzk. 19th c. **Qačqïn** [Катбаръ Качкиновъ] (Grod., Pril. 48); Kzk. 19th c. **Qačqïn** [Избасаръ Качкиновъ] (Grod., Pril. 139); Bashk. 1754 **Qačqun** [Качкун Усейнов] (MIB IV/1, 83); Bashk. 1761, 1763, 1777 **Qačqun / Qačqïn** [Качкун (Качкин) Самаров] (MIB IV/1, 45, 215, V, 65); Tat. 1748 **Qasqïn** [Умяшъ Каскиновъ] (Nepljuev 437); Tat.(Mish.) 1755 **Qasqïn** [Каскин Тоймасов] (MIB IV/1, 93); Bashk. 1675 **Qasqïn** [Каскин Игиликов] (MIB I, 199); Bashk. 1706 **Qasqïn** [Каскын] (MIB III, 22); Bashk. 1709 **Qasqïn** [Каскын Татлыев] (MIB III, 51); Bashk. 1710 **Qasqïn** [Каскын Татлымбетев] (MIB III, 64); Bashk. 1735 **Qasqïn** [Азять Каскиновъ], a tarɣan (Vel.-Zern., Bašk. 18); Bashk. 1741, 1743 **Qasqïn** [Кункас (Конкас) Каскинов] (MIB III, 508, 514); Bashk. 1754, 1764 **Qasqïn** [Каскин Самаров] (MIB IV/1, 83, 300); Bashk. 1756 **Qasqïn** [Кигиман Каскинов] (MIB IV/1, 130);

Bashk. 1756 **Qasqïn** [Каскын Марсалимов] (MIB IV/1, 109); Bashk. 1757 **Qasqïn** [Каскин Кутлыхозин] (MIB IV/1, 139); Bashk. 1759 **Qasqïn** [Абдулла Каскионов] (MIB IV/2, 22); Bashk. 1783 **Qasqïn** [Сююндюк Каскинов] (MIB V, 130); Bashk. 1787 **Qasqïn** [Каскин Чепканов] (MIB V, 219); Kzk. 19th c. **Qašqïm-bay (<Qasqïn-bay)** [Кашкимбай] (AOK 78); Kzk. 19th c. **Qašqïm-bay (<Qasqïn-bay)** [Кашкимбай] (AOO 38); Kzk. 19th c. **Qašqïm-bay (<Qasqïn-bay)** [Кашкымбай] (SOK 116); Kzk. 19th c. **Qašqïm-bay (<Qasqïn-bay)** [Кашкымбай] (AOP 14); Kzk. 19th c. **Qašqïm-bay (<Qasqïn-bay)** [Кашкымбай] (SOV 60); Kzk. 19th c. **Qašqïn** [Кашкенъ] (SODž. 20); Kzk. 19th c. **Qašqïn** [Аузъ-Ачикъ Кашкиновъ] (Grod., Pril. 89); Kzk. 19th c. **Qašqïn** [Кашкынъ] (AOP 42); Kzk. 19th c. **Qašqïn** [Кашкынъ] (SOK 48); Kzk. 19th c. **Qašqïn** [Кашкынъ] (SODž. 64); Kzk. 19th c. **Qašqïn** [Кашкынъ] (AOK 46); Kzk. 19th c. **Qašqïn** [Кашкымъ] (AOO 26); Kzk. 19th c. **Qašqïn** [Кашкенъ] (AOP 94); Kzk. 19th c. **Qašqïn** [Кашкинъ] (Grod., Pril. 89); Kzk. **Qašqïn-bay** [Кашкинбаевъ] (Konšin, Pam. 13); Kzk. 19th c. **Qašqïn-bay** [Кашкынбай] (AOP 22); Kzk. 19th c. **Qašqïn-bay** [Кашкынбай] (SODž. 108, 130); Bashk. 1756 **Sqasqïn < Qasqïn** [Скаскин Чюин] (MIB IV/1, 130); *TN:* Bashk. 1783 **Qasqïnovo** [Каскиново], a village (MIB V, 130). ✧ 'Runaway, fugitive' cf. Alt., Az., Crm. Kar.(T.), NUyg., Tat., Turk. *qašqun* 'die Flucht' (Radl. II, 342) *qačqïn* 'der Flüchtling' (Radl. II, 341), Hak. *qasqïn* 'id.' (Radl. II, 354), Bashk. *qasqïn* 'беглец' (BRS/Uraksin). See also **QARA-QAČQÏN, QAŠAГAN.**

QAČQÏNČÏГ   Kuman 1469 **Qačqïnčïɣ** [Kachkanchiw], earlier a desert (steppe), nowadays a settlement in Lesser Kumania, Hungary (Gyárfás III, 663). ✧ 'He who flees/runs away'; for more detailed explanation see Rásonyi, NTK 97-99, Rásonyi, KÖA 107, Rásonyi, Anthr. 151. ⇨ **QAČQÏN** + suff. *-čïɣ.*

QAČQUN see **QAČQÏN**

QAČMAZ   Maml. 14th c. **Qačmas** [قِنْجماس] (Sauvaget 52); Maml. 1436/37 **Qačmas** [اقبردى التاجماسى] (Ibn Taghrīb. VI, 754, VII, 5, 6, 265); Maml. 13th c. **Qačmaz** (Tarǰ/Houtsma 30). ✧ 'Won't flee/run away' (Sauvaget 52, Rásonyi, KÖA 108, Rásonyi, Anthr. 141). ⇨ **QAČMAR.**

QAČU   Tat.(Sib.) 1661 **Qaču-yar** [Качуяр], Küčüm's grand-son (Miller, Ist. Sib. II, 546).

QAЈAR   NUyg.(Tar.) 19th c. **ХaЈar-χoЈa** [حجر حوجه / Хаджаръ-Ходжа], fem. (Pantusov, Tar. 163 /118/); Trkm. 1879-1881 **QaЈar-χan** [Kadjaı Khan] (O'Donovan II, 126); *EN:* Turk. **QaЈar**, a Zeybek clan (aşiret) in the region of Tire, Turkey (Kúnos 1891, 117);

Yürük 1863-1873 **Qaǰar-ašireti**, in the region of Manisa, Turkey (Gökçen 95). ⇨ **QAČAR?**

QAǰULAY Khorezm./Chag.? 1410 **Qaǰulay-behadur** [Каджулай-бехадур] (MIT I, 532).

QAD-ALİ Bashk.? 1737 **Qad-ali / Qad-aliy?** [Ишали-батырь Кадалеев] (MIB III, 367). ✦ Shortened-contracted of *Qadïr-ali*? Cf. PNs: Tat. *Qadïyr-γalī* (Sattarov), Kzk. *Qadïr-yali* (Žanuzakov-Esbaeva). ⇨ **QADÏR + ALİ.**

QADA-ESÜRÜK Uyg. 12th c. - 14th c. **Qada-esürük** [Kada Äsrük] (DTS, EUTS). ✦ 'Qada-(the-)enthusiastic' cf. Türk, Karakh. *esrük, esürük* 'возбужденный; пьяный' (DTS).

QADAY Karch. **Qaday** [Кадай] (Sysoev 131); Hak. 19th-20th c. **Qaday** [Кадай] (HRS 349); Tuv. 19th c. **Qaday** [Кадай], a 62-year-old woman (Proben IX, 95, 110). ✦ 'Old woman' cf. Tuv., Hak.(Kacha) *qaday* 'eine alte Frau' (Radl. II, 307).

QADAÑ Hak. 19th-20th c. **Qadañ** [Каданъ], fem. (HRS 353). ✦ 'Quick; fast' cf. Kzk. *qadañ* 'schnell' (Radl. II, 310).

QADAR Türk/Uyg. 8th c. **Qadar**, fem. (Le Coq, Buch-Fragm. 147, DTS).

QADAŠ Karg. **Qadaš** [Кадаш], fem. (Katanov, Otč. 9); Chag. 16th c. **Qadaš / Qadaš-bahadur** [Кадаш, Кадаш-бахадур] (Ivanov 216, 217). ✦ 'Relative, brother' cf. Türk, Karakh. *qadaš* 'родич, родственник, родной; брат' (DTS).

QADEMLİ Yürük 1543 **Qademli** [قدملى], from the Yürüks of Kocacık, Turkey (Gökb., Rum. 105, 227). ✦ 'Lucky, auspicious; bringing chance' cf. Turk. *kademli* 'id.' (TED), 'dessen Fuss Glück bringt; glückbringend' (HŞ).

QADİY Hak. 19th-20th c. **Qadiy** [Кадий] (HRS 349); Hak. 19th-20th c. **Qadiy** [Кадий], fem. (HRS 353). ✦ Shortened of R. Arkadiy (Butanaev).

QADİK Hak. 19th-20th c. **Qadik** [Кадик] (HRS 349).

QADÏ see **QAZÏ**

QADÏR Kkalp. 20th c. **Kädir-bay / Qädir-bay** [Кәдирбай] (KkRS 774); Uyg. 12th c. -14th c. **Qadïr** (DTS); Kzk. 19th c. **Qadïr** [Кадыръ] (Potanin II, 4); Kkalp. 20th c. **Qadïr** [Къадыр] (Bask., Kkalp. 53); Uyg. 12th c. -14th c. **Qadïr-čigši** (DTS); Bashk. 1735 **Qadïr-γul** [Кадыргулъ] (Vel.-Zern., Bašk. 12); Karakh. 11th c. **Qadïr-χan** [Кадыр Хан / Кадыр-хан], Xarun Boγra-χan's son (DTS, MIT I, 232, 321, 361, 438, 439, 454-455, MK/Atalay 841); Khazar 758-764 **Qadïr-il-täbär** [Xatʿirlitʿbēr], commander of one of the constituent hordes of the Khazar army (Golden 198); Kirg. **Qadïr-qul** [Кадыркул] (Jud. 638); Hak. 19th-20th c. **Qadr < Qadïr** [Кадр] (HRS 349); Kkalp. 20th c. **Qädir** [Кәдир] (KkRS 774); *EN:* Kzk. 18th c. - 19th c. **Qadïr-bek** [Кадырбек], a clan (Tynyšp. 75); Bashk. 1798 **Qadïr-γul** [Кадыргулъ] (PSZRI XXV, 195);

Kzk. 18th c. - 19th c. **Qadïr-γul** [Кадыргул], a clan (Tynyšp. 73); Kzk. 18th c. - 19th c. **Qadïr-qul** [Кадыркул], a clan (Tynyšp. 73); Kzk. 19th c. **Qadïr-qul** [Кадыркулъ] (SOV 8); *TN:* Kzk.? **Qadïr-bay** [Кадырбай], a well (Karta JAR X). ✦ I. 'Strickt, severe, unmerciful' cf. Karakh., Uyg. *qadïr* 'суровый, жестокий, лютый' (DTS); II. Qadir (Ar.) 'able, powerful, mighty' (Ahmed), one of Allah's epithets, cf. Kkalp. *qadïr* 'авторитет' (KkRS), Kzk., Turk. *qadïr* 'mächtig, einflussreich' (Radl. II, 325), Turk. *kadir* 'mighty, powerful, strong' (TED). See also Golden, Khaz. 198. III. 'Respect; honour, value' cf. Kkalp. *qädir* (<Ar.) 'уважение; честь; почет; достоинство, ценность' (KkRS), Kzk., Tat. *kädir* 'die Macht, Trefflichkeit; die Ehre, Freundlichkeit' (Radl. II, 1138-1139). See also **ÄBDİ-QÄDİR.**

QADÏR-BAQ Bashk. 1784 **Qadïr-baq** [Сеит (Сагит) Кадырбаков] (MIB V, 154). ⇨ **QADÏR + BAQ.**

QADÏR-BERDİ Chag. 16th c. **Qadïr-berdi** [Кадыр-берды] (Ivanov 325); Bashk. 1784 **Qadïr-berdi** [Баимбеть Кадырбердин] (MIB V, 165); Kkalp. 1822 **Qadïr-berdi** [Кадыр берди] (MIKk. 127); Uzb. 18th c. **Qadïr-berdi** [Кадырбердыбай Худайбердинъ] (Nepljuev 803); Chag.? 16th c. **Qadïr-berdi-oγlan** [Кадир-берды-оглан] (Ivanov 199); Tat.(GH) 1419 **Qadïr-birdi / Qadïr-berdi** [قادربردى / Qâdir-Birdi / Кадирбирди / Кадыр-бäрдi султанъ], Toqtamïš-qan's son (1382-1397) (Aynī/Tizeng. I, 500, 532, Abulg./Desm. 187, Proben VII, 117); *EN:* Kzk. 18th c. - 19th c. **Qadïr-berdī** [Кадырберды], a clan (Tynyšp. 70). ⇨ **QADÏR + BERDİ.**

QADÏR-BERGEN Kkalp. 1810 **Qadïr-bergen** [Кадырберген], a biy (MIKk. 107). ⇨ **QADÏR + BERGEN.**

QADÏR-BİLGÄ Uyg. 12th c. - 14th c. **Qadïr-bilgä** [Kadır Bilgä] (Radl., USp. 277, EUTS). ⇨ **QADÏR + BİLGÄ.**

QADÏRAY Bashk. 1735 **Qadray** [Кадрай Девлетлинъ], a tarχan (Vel.-Zern., Bašk. 18). ⇨ **QADÏR + dim. suff. -ay.**

QADÏRČAQ Bashk. 1735 **Qadïrčaq** [Рашъ Кадырчаковъ], a tarχan (Vel.-Zern., Bašk. 18). ⇨ **QADÏR + suff. -čaq. See also QADÏRČİK.**

QADÏRČİK Bashk. 1734 **Qadïrčiq** [Кадырчик] (MIB III, 327); Bashk. 1734 **Qadïrčiq** [Кадырчиковъ], a tarχan (Vel.-Zern., Bašk. 9); Bashk. 1734 **Qadïrčiq** [Кадырчиковъ], a tarχan (Vel.-Zern., Bašk. 10); Bashk. 1761 **Qadïrčiq** [Бактияр Кадырчиков] (MIB IV/1, 221). ⇨ **QADÏR + suff. -čiq. See also QADÏRČAQ?**

QADÏRMET Tat. 1753 **Qadïrmet** [Кадырметь Алмаметев] (MIB IV/1, 70); Bashk. 1756 **Qadïrmet** [Беккине Кадырметев] (MIB IV/1, 113); Bashk. 1756 **Qadïrmet** [Ишкине Кадырметев] (MIB IV/1,

113); Bashk. 1759 **Qadïrmet** [Ахмер Кадырметев] (MIB IV/2, 26); Bashk. 1798 **Qatïrmet** [Катерметъ] (PSZRI XXV, 195). ⇨ **QADÏR** + suff. *-met*.

QADÏRSÏS see **QADÏRSÏZ**

QADÏRSÏZ   Kzk. 19th c. **Qadïrsïs** [Кадырсысъ] (Grod., Pril. 37); Kzk. 19th c. **Qadïrsiz** [Кадырсызъ] (SOV 130); Kzk. 19th c. **Qadïrsïz** [Кадырсызъ] (SODž. 108). ✧ 'Worthless, good-for-nothing'. ⇨ **QADÏR** + suff. *-sïz*.

QADÏŠ   Tat.(Lit.) 1582 **Xadïč** [Хадычъ Шабановичъ] (Lit. Tat. 44); Tat.(Lit.) 1592 **Qadïš** [Кадышевичъ] (Lit. Tat. 116, 118); Tat. 1533, 1543 **Qadïš** [Кодышъ (Кадышъ) / Кадышъ-князь], a prince from Kazan (PSRL VIII, 282, XIII, 69, 147, Zolotn. 157); Tat.(Mish.) 19th c. **Qadïš** [Кадышевъ] (IOAIÊK XIX, 143); Tat.(Sib.) 1640 **Qadïš** [Татуй Кадышев], taxpayer („jasačnyj") (Miller, Ist. Sib. II, 463); Bashk. 1678 **Qadïš** [Кадышъ Янтиковъ] (Vel.-Zern., Bašk. 33); Bashk. 1735 **Qadïš** [Батыръ Кадышевъ], a tarχan (Vel.-Zern., Bašk. 18); Bashk. 1755 **Qadïš** [Кулман Кадышев] (MIB IV/1, 101); Bashk. 1758 **Qadïš** [Ибрай Кадышев] (MIB IV/1, 163); Tat.(Bar.) **Qadïš-mergen** [Кадыш Мäргäн] (Proben IV, 58 /72/). ✧ 'Relative; brother' (Sattarov). ⇨ **QADAŠ.**

QADR see **QADÏR**

QADRAY see **QADÏRAY**

QADRÄS   Bashk. 1670 **Qadräs / Qaðräs?** [Кадрясъ Аллакаевъ] (Vel.-Zern., Bašk. 37); Bashk. 18th c. **Qadräs / Qaðräs?** [Кадрясъ] (Nepljuev 687).

QAFAR   Kzk. 19th c. **Qafar** [Кафаръ], a biy (Lomakin 35). ✧ Ghafar (Ar.) 'pardoner, merciful' (Ahmed), cf. Kzk. PN Γafar (Žanuzakov-Esbaeva).

QAΓAN   Khazar 965 **Xaγan** [Каганъ / Хаганъ / Хоганъ], a prince of the Khazars (PSRL (Russk. Hr.) I, 312-313, PSRL (Russk. Hr.) II, 163, PSRL V, 106, VII, 287 Lavr. 63, Ipat. 42 /48/); Türk? 870 **Xaqan** [Ahmed Ibn Chakan], Al-Muhtadi was held in his house until he was executed (Weil, Chalif. II, 420); Türk? 912 **Xaqan** [Alfath Ibn Chakan] (Weil, Chalif. II, 368).

QAQAN   Karakh. **Xaqan** [χaqan] (DTS).

QAΓAN   Karakh.? 8th c. - 9th c. **Xaqan** [الراوى / حاقان بن صبّاح] (Tabarī, Annal. III, 602); Karakh.? 833-847 **Xaqan** [حاقان الخادم] (Fragm. Hist. Ar. 468, 532); Karakh.? 863, 866 **Xaqan** [حاقان ارطوج / مزاحم بن / Muzahim Ibn Chakan] (Weil, Chalif. II, 394, Tabarī, Annal. III, 1481, 1588, 1591, 1617-1619, 1693); Karakh.? 870 **Xaqan** [سلمة بن حاقان] (Tabarī, Annal. III, 1811); Karakh.? 896 **Xaqan** [حاقان البلخىّ / المفلحى] (Kindī 241); Karakh.? 903, 917, 918 **Xaqan** [حاقان المفلحى / Chakan Almuflihi], commander of the army of the Caliph Almuklafi (Weil, Chalif. II, 529, Miskawayh V, 115, Arīb 19, 67); Karakh.? 912, 920 **Xaqan** [يحيى بن حاقان / Mohammed Ibn Ubeid Allah Ibn Jahja Ibn Chakan], a vezir under Muktadir (Weil, Chalif. II, 367, 547, Arīb 79, Masʿūdī 46, 47, 361, 379); Karakh.? 919 **Xaqan** [احمد بن عبيدالله بن حاقان] (Arīb 72-73); Karakh.? 925 **Xaqan** [حاقان بن احمد] (Miskawayh V, 225, 244); Karakh.? 932 **Xaqan** [احمد بن حاقان] (Arīb 159, 174, 182); Türk **Qaγan-čor** [Ïšbara qaγan čor], in Chinese transcription (Ligeti, R. tör. nev. II-III, 41); Tat.(Mish.) **Qaγan-bek** [Каган-бекъ] (Ahmarov: IOAIÊK XIX, 142); Khorezm.? **Qän-bay** [قاان باى] (Šejb. XLIX). ✧ '(Supreme) Ruler, emperor' Used generally as a secondary component (title) in majestic names (see comp. qaγan / χaqan).

QAΓANAQ-BAS   Kkalp. 20th c. **Qaγanaq-bas** [Қаҕанақбас] (KkRS 774). ✧ 'Caul/chorion-head' cf. Kkalp. qaγanaq 'околоплодная оболочка' (KkRS). ⇨ **BAŠ.**

QAΓARLÏQ   Oghuz/Trkm. 13th c. **Qaγarlïq** (DTS). ✧ 'Snowy' (Blagova 1997, 704).

QAΓAZ   Kzk. 19th c. **Qaγaz-bek** [Кагазбек] (SOK 22); *TN:* Kzk. **Qaγaz-bay** [Кагазъ-бай], a place south-west of Aral Sea (Karta JAR XI). ✧ 'Paper' cf. Kkalp. qaγaz 'бумага' (KkRS). See also **AQ-QAΓAZ.**

QAΓDÏΓAS   Hak.(Blt.) 19th-20th c. **Qaγdïγas** [Каҕдыҕас] (Proben IX, 361); Hak.(Kacha) 19th-20th c. **Qaγdïγas** [Каҕдыҕас], a folklore hero (Proben IX, 386).

QAΓΓAN   Kzk. 19th c. **Qaγγan** [Берди Кагганъ] (Grod., Pril. 109).

QAΓÏ   Kzk. 19th c. **Qaγï** [Кагы] (AOP 34). ✧ 'Nag, reprove' cf. Crm. qaγï- 'tadeln, schimpfen' (Radl. II, 73).

QAΓÏDLU   Kzk. 19th c. **Qaγïdlu** [Кагыдлу] (AOO 58).

QAΓÏNČAR   Kzk. 19th c. **Qaγïnčar** [Кагинчаръ], Dombaul's son (Potanin, Pred. 49). ✧ 'Little Qaγïn'?

QAΓÏR   Alt.(Tel.) 19th c. **Qaγïr** [Каҕыр], a mythical being, Erlik's servant, the most powerful of the evil spirits (Radl., II, 74); Alt.(Tel.) 19th c. **Qaγïr-γān** [Каҕырҕан / Кагыръ-ханъ], a mythical being, mediator between Ülgen and Erlik (Radl., II, 74, Verb., In. 44).

QAHARMAN see **QAHRAMAN**

QAHRAMAN   Tat. 20th c. **Qaharman** [Каharман] (Sattarov); Bashk. 1788 **Qaγarman** [Каҕарман Исмаилов / Измаилов] (MIB IV/1, 313, V, 231); Bashk. 20th c. **Qaharman** [Каharман / Каҕарман] (Kusimova); Turk. 18th c. **Qahraman-bey**, in the region of Çorum, Turkey (Uzunçarşılı: Belleten 1974, 218). ✧ 'Hero, heroic; wrestler' (Kusimova, Sattarov), Turk. kahraman (P.) 'hero, brave, heroic' (TED), Budagov II, 100, Bashk., Tat. qaharman 'герой, мужественный, отважный' (BRS/Uraksin, TatRS).

QAY   Karakh. **Qay** [Kay] (MK/Atalay 843); Selj. 1159 **Qay-aba** [قيه], an emir (Ibn al-Athïr/Tornb. XI, 167);

Crm. 1784 **Qay-aɣa** [Кай ага], a murza in the Crimea (IAN (Otd. gum. nauk) 1928, 379); Maml.? 1480 **Qay-bey** [Кайбей], a sultan in Egypt (AI I, 137); Kzk. 19th c. **Qay-molda** [Каймолда] (SOK 12); Bashk. 1783 **Qay-murza** [Габит Каймурзин] (MIB V, 143); Crm.? 1682 **Qay-temir** [Кайтемиръ мурза], a murza (DAI X, 165); *TN:* Maml. 12th c. **Qay-aba**, a mesjid (small mosque) (Ibn Šaddād, Alep 75). ✧ I. A Trk. (Kipchak) ethnical (tribal) name, cf. Karakh. *qaj* 'одно из тюркских племен' (DTS, Sattarov, Erol II); II. 'Hard, strong' (Sattarov, Erol II). ⇨ **QAYĬ.**

QAY-BERDĬ Bashk. 1713 **Qay-berdi** [Кайберде (Кайберда)] (MIB III, 100); Tat. 1624 **Qay-perdi** [Кайперди Біюргановъ] (Pokrovskij 71); Tat. 1624 **Qay-perdi, Qay-perdä?** [Кайперда Дербышевъ] (Pokrovskij 70). ⇨ **QAY + BERDĬ.**

QAY-BULAT Bashk. 1754 **Qay-bulat** [Кайбулат Арасланов] (MIB IV/1, 83); Nog. 1678 **Qay-bulat** [Кайбулатъ Тинокпатовъ] (DAI VIII, 25). ⇨ **QAY + BULAT.**

QAY-DAWL Tat.(Sib.)? 1583 **Qay-dawl** [Кайдаулъ (Чайдаулъ / Закайдамъ)], a murza (Sib. Let. 345-47); Kzk. 19th c. **Qay-dawl** [Кайдаулъ] (AOP 62, 114). ✧ 'Strong wind/storm' cf. Kzk. *daul* 'der Wind, der Sturm' (Radl. III, 1607). ⇨ **QAY.**

QAY-NAZAR Kirg. **Qay-nazar** [Кайназар] (Jud. 93). ⇨ **QAY + NAZAR.**

QAY-SAQĬQ Uyg. 12th c. - 14th c. **Qay-saqïq** [Kay Sakık] (Radl., USp. 153-154, DTS, EUTS). ⇨ **QAY + SAQ**? + dim. suff. *-ïq.*

QAY-SALAN Kzk. 19th c. **Qay-salan** [Кайсаланъ] (SODž. 40). ⇨ **QAY + SALAN.**

QAY-SĬMAN Kzk. 19th c. **Qay-sïman? / Qay-suman** [Кайсоманъ] (SOV 102). ⇨ **QAY + SĬMAN.**

QAY-SUMAN see **QAY-SĬMAN**

QAY-ŽASAR Kzk. 19th c. **Qay-žasar** [Кайжасаръ] (SOV 12). ✧ 'Strong-lives'. ⇨ **QAY + YAŠAR.**

QAYA Uyg. **Qaya** [Kaya] (EUTS); Turk. 16th c. **Qaya** (Ongan, Ank. II.); Turk. 1565 **Qaya** [Nasuχ bin Qaya] (Dávid); Turk. 1570, 1580 **Qaya** [Qaya bin İlyas] (Dávid); Turk. 1583 **Qaya** [قيا] (Ongan, Ank. I, 164); Turk. 20th c. **Qaya** (Önder, Göle); Yürük 1543 **Qaya** [قيا] (Gökb., Rum. 187, 208); Yürük 1543 **Qaya** (Gökb., Rum. 187, 195, 207, 208); Turk. 15th c. **Qaya-beg / Qaya-bey?** [Καγιάπεγ], a commander of the army (Byz. Turc. 145); Turk. 1467 **Qaya-bey**, Kasım-bey's son (Gökb., Ed. 328); Crm. 1718 **Qaya-χanïm** [قايا خانم / Каja-ханымъ] (Bakč. Nadp. 36); Uyg. 13th-14th c. **Qaya-oñ-totoq-bäg** [Qaya Ong Totoq Bäg] (Zieme, Mat. II, 87, 89); *TN:* Turk. 20th c. **Qaya-bey**, a village in the province of Ağrı, Turkey (TMİB 52). ✧ 'Rock' cf. *qaya* 'скала' (DTS). See also **AL-QAYA, ANUR-QAYA, ARA-QAYA, BUT-QAYA,**

ČĬNAČ-QAYA, DĬVĀNE-QAYA, ESÄN-QAYA, İL-QAYA, İNČ-QAYA, ĬT-QAYA, YAR-QAYA, YĬGÄN-QAYA, KED-QAYA, QAŠ-QAYA, QUL-QAYA, QULDU-QAYA, QUTLUГ-QAYA, MEÑLĬG-QAYA, SELĬ-QUTLUГ-QAYA, TÄMĬR-QAYA.

QAYA-BALĬ Turk. 1583 **Qaya-balï** (Ongan, Ank. I, 164); Tat.(Lit.) 1557 **Qaya-balï** [Каябалы] (Kn. Metriki Lit. 151). ⇨ **QAYA + BALĬ / BALĬ.**

QAYA-BEŠE Turk. 1583 **Qaya-beše** [قيا باشه / قيا بشه], fem. (Ongan, Ank. I, 164). ⇨ **QAYA + BEŠE.**

QAYA-TEMĬR Maml. 1332 **Qaya-temir** [قياتمر], an emir (Dawād. 368). ⇨ **QAYA + TEMĬR.**

QAYAJA Yürük 1543 **Qayaja** (Gökb., Rum. 194). ⇨ **QAYA** + suff. *-ja.*

QAYAQ Uyg. **Qayaq** [Kayak] (EUTS). ✧ 'Cream' cf. Karakh. *qayaq* 'сливки' (DTS). See also **AQ-QAYAQ.**

QAYAQ-YARAŠPĬDĬ Uyg. 12th c. - 14th c. **Qayaq-yarašpïdï** (Radl., USp. 127-28, DTS). ⇨ **QAYAQ + YARAŠPĬDĬ.**

QAYALĬ Yürük 1543 **Qayalï** (Gökb., Rum. 195, 231). ✧ 'Rocky'. ⇨ **QAYA** + suff. *-lï.*

QAYAN Kipch. 1262 **Qayan** [قيان / Каянъ] (Baybars/Tizeng. I, 78, 100); Maml. 1263 **Qayan** [Kaïan] (Makrīzī I, 222); Tat.(Sib.) 1630 **Qayan** [Каян (Коян)], a prince from Tubinsk (DAI IV, 179-80, Miller, Ist. Sib. II, 362, 366-68); Oghuz/Trkm.? / Chag.? **Qayan** [Каян] (Radl. III, 251); Maml. 1450 **Qayan-bay** [قايت باى] (Ibn Taghrīb. VII, 214, 383); *TN:* Tat. 1689 **Qayanova** [Каянова], a village (Kungursk. akty 167). ✧ 'Lively, quick'? cf. Turk. *qayan* 'lebhaft, schnell, hastig; ein reissender Bergfluss, ein Wasserfall; ein Mongolenstamm' (Radl. II, 91), Kuman, Alt., Az., Hak., Turk. *qay-* 'ausgleiten, gleiten' (Radl. II, 3) + part. suff. *-an.*

QAYARĬM Turk. 16th c. **Qayarïm-bey** [Καϊάρμπες], a commander of the army (Byz. Turc. 146).

QAYBĬS Tat.(Mish.) 1682 **Qaybis** [Кайбиско Узѣевъ] (AI V, 139). ⇨ **QAYMĬŠ?**

QAYBULA Tat. 1554 **Qaybula** [Кайбула] (Kn. Metriki Lit. 99); Tat. 1552, 1555 **Qaybula (Qay-bulat?)** [Кайбула (Кайбалъ / Кайбалу) Ахкубековичъ], a prince from Astrakhan (PSRL XIII, 144, 177, XIX, 112-113, 153, DAI I, 129). ✧ 'Gift of the invisible Allah' cf. Crm.(Tat.) PNs *Qaybulla / Qaybula* (Kaybullaev) (<Ar.).

QAYČĬ see **QAYČĬ**

QAYČĬ Kzk. 19th c. **Qayči-bek** [Кайчибекъ] (SOV 74); Kzk. 19th c. **Qayči-bek** [Кайчибекъ] (SODž. 102); Kzk. 19th c. **Qayču-bay** [Кайчубай] (SOK 218); Kzk. 19th c. **Qayču-bek** [Кайчубекъ] (SODž. 74). ✧

'Scissors' cf. Alt., Tat. *qaycї* 'die Schere' (Radl. II, 41), Kzk. *qayšї* 'ножницы' (KzRS).

QAYČU see QAYČĬ

QAYČUMAN Kzk. 19th c. **Qayčuman** [Кайчуманъ] (SOV 76). ⇨ **QAYČĬ?** + suff. *-man*.

QAYČUMAS Kzk. 19th c. **Qayčumas** [Кайчумасъ] (SODž. 12).

QAYDALĬ Bashk. 1731 **Qaydalї** [Ишелы Кайдалын] (MIB III, 292).

QAYDAMĬŠ Yürük 1543 **Qaydamїš** [قيدەمش] (Gökb., Rum. 235). ✧ 'He came back, returned' cf. Turk. dial. *kayta(mak)* 'geri gelmek' (DS VIII).

QAYDAN Maml. 1335 **Qaydan** [مظفرالدين قيدان], an emir (Dawād. 389); Maml. 14th c. **Qaydan** [قيدان الرومى] (Zetterst. 226); Yürük 1543 **Qaydan** [قيدان], from Silistre (Gökb., Rum. 229); Kzk. 19th c. **Qaydan** [Кайданъ] (AOA 2).

QAYDAWQ Kzk. 19th c. **Qaydawq** [Кайдаукъ] (AOO 54).

QAYDĬ Kzk. 19th c. **Qaydї-bay** [Кайдыбай] (SOK 302). See also **ASAN-QAYDĬ**.

QAYDĬ-BAQ Bashk. 1756 **Qaydї-baq?** [Кайдыбак Кляшев] (MIB IV/1, 120). ⇨ **QAYDĬ + BAQ**.

QAYDUM Pecheneg 9th c. **Qaydum** [Καϊδούμ], chief of the 5th of the Pecheneg tribe (Byz. Turc. 146).

QAYƔALAƔ Karakh.? 881, 904, 906 **Qayɣalaɣ** [كَيْغَلَغْ / كيغلغ التركى / ابراهيم بن كيغلغ] (Tabarī, Annal. III, 1967, 2241, 2255); Karakh.? 905-916, 933 **Qayɣalaɣ** [احمد بن كيغلغ], commander of the army under Al-Muqtafī; governor of Egypt in 933 (Ibn al-Athīr/Tornb. VII, 373, VIII, 69, 168, 247, Miskawajh V, 42, 43, 45, 102, Ibn Saʿīd IV, 10-12, 164, Weil., Chalif. II, 525, 528, 534, Kindī 269, 273, 279, 282-86, 532); Karakh.? 909 **Qayɣalaɣ** [ابراهيم بن كيغلغ] (Miskawayh V, 73); Alt. **Qayɣalaq / Qan-qayɣalaq** [Кан-Кайралак] (Katanov 25). ✧ 'Wonderful, marvellous, famous' (Katanov), cf. Alt.(Kmd.), Hak. *qayɣalaq?* 'die Schwimmhölzer am Netz' (Radl. II, 8). See also **QAN-QAYƔALAQ**.

QAYƔALAQ see QAYƔALAƔ

QAYƔĬLĬ Maml. 1332 **Qayɣїlї** [قيغلى] (Dawād. 369). ✧ 'Grief, sad, mournful' cf. *qayɣu* 'печаль, горе, скорбь' (DTS).

QAYƔĬLĬQ Kzk. 1823 **Qayɣїlїq** [Кайгилик] (MIK IV, 444). ✧ 'Gloom, sadness' cf. Kuman, Kzk., Tat., Turk., etc. *qayɣї* 'die Trauer, Betrübniss, der Kummer' (Radl. II, 8) + suff. *-lїq*.

QAYƔĬSĬZ Yürük 1543 **Qayɣusuz** (Gökb., Rum. 236); Tat. 1543 **Qayɣusuz** (Gökb., Rum. 236); Turk. **Qayɣusuz-oɣlu**, a Zeybek (Kúnos 1891, 119). ✧ 'Careless, light-hearted'.

QAYƔUL Tat.(Sib.) 1642 **Qayɣul** [Карагуш Кайгулов] (Miller, Ist. Sib. II, 485). ✧ 'Guard,

watch'? cf. Alt.(Tel.) *qayɣul* = *qaraɣul* 'die Wache, das Bewachen' (Radl. II, 10). See also **QARAWUL**.

QAYƔUSUZ see QAYƔĬSĬZ

QAYĬ Oghuz/Trkm. 13th c. **Qayї / Qayї-bay** [قا یى باى / Qayï / Кайи / Кайы / Кайы-бай], Kün-χan's son (RaD I/1, 76, DQorq./Rossi 96, Abulg./Kon. 513, 540, 590, 645, 1445); Selj. 1156 **Qayї-aba** [قى ابه / Kayï-aba el-Kumaç], an emir, died in 1156 (Ahbar 87); Oghuz? **Qayї-alp** [قى / قنه / قيه الپ], forefather of the Ottoman dynasty (Āšikp. 5, Wittek 94); *EN:* Yürük 1560 **Qayї** [قاىى / Kayı nam cemaatı], a community (cemaat) of the Türkmen (Yürük?) in the district (kaza) Sanduklu, Turkey (Refik, Anad. 3). ✧ I. A Turkic (Oghuz) ethnical (tribal) name (EN), cf. Karakh. *qaj* 'одно из тюркских племен' (DTS), Oghuz EN *Kayı* (Erol II); II. 'Hard, strong' cf. Tat. PNcomp. *Qay* (Sattarov), *Kayı* (Erol II). ⇨ **QAY**. See also **DUYLĬ-QAYĬ**.

QAYĬČAQ Chag.? 1533 **Qayїčaq** [Kájichak], malik of Kashmir (Tar. Rashidi 441). ⇨ **QAYĬ?** + suff. *-čaq / -čїq*.

QAYĬQ Kzk. 19th c. **Qayq-bay** [Яртибай Каикбаевъ] (Grod., Pril. 122). ✧ 'Boat' cf. Alt., Crm., Kzk., Tat., Turk. *qayїq* 'das Boot' (Radl. II, 93). See also **KEME**.

QAYĬMTU Uyg. 12th c. - 14th c. **Qayїmtu / Qayїmtu-baqšї** [Kayımtu] (DTS, EUTS).

QAYĬN Kzk. 19th c. **Qayn-bay** [Каинбай] (SODž. 92); Bashk. 1770 **Qayn-qul** [Чапкун Каинкулов] (MIB IV/1, 343). ✧ I. 'Birch' cf. Bashk. *qayїn* 'берёза' (BRS), Alt. *qayїñ* 'берёза' (OjrRS); II. 'Member of the family of one's wife or husband'? cf. Kzk. *qayїn* 'родня жены' (KzRS), Bashk. *qäyen(bikä), qäyen(yeñgä)* 'id.' (BRS).

QAYĬÑČĬ Alt. 19th-20th c. **Qayїñčї** [Кайыпчы] (OjrRS 208). ✧ 'Seller of birch'? cf. Alt. *qayїñ* 'берёза' (OjrRS). + suff. *-čї*.

QAYĬP Trkm. 20th c. **Гаyїп** [Gayїp] (Zaj. 1971, 327); Trkm. 20th c. **Гāyїp** [Гайып] (TrkmRS 144); Kkalp. 20th c. **Qayїp** [Къайып / Қайып] (Bask., Kkalp. 41, KkRS 774); Kirg. **Qayїp** [Кајып], Qara-börük's father (Proben V, 77 /79/); Kzk. 1750 **Qayp** [Каïp] (Levchin 224); Uzb. 1750 **Qayp** [Kaip], Batïr-sultan's son (ArchKR XVIII, 380); Kzk. 1717 **Qayp / Qayp-qan** [Каïp / Kaip khan], a khan (Levchin 150, AUK 227); Kkalp. 1734 **Qayp-χan** [Каип-хан] (PSZRI IX, 304). ✧ 'Absence; loss; not being' cf. Tat., Turk. *qaip* 'unsichtbar' (Radl. II, 46), Trkm. *ɣāyїp* 'исчезнувший, скрывшийся' (TrkmRS), Kkalp. *qayїp* 'отсутствие', *ɣayїp* 'скрытое, неведомое' (KkRS); Kirg. *qayїp* 'скрытый, незримый' (Jud.) (<Ar.). See also **JEL-QAYĬP**.

QAYĬP-NAZAR Kkalp. 20th c. **Qayїp-nazar** [Қайыпназар] (KkRS 774). ⇨ **QAYĬP + NAZAR**.

QAYĬR see XAYR

QAYÏR-ГALİY   Kkalp. 20th c. **Qayïr-γaliy** [Қайырғалий] (KkRS 774). ✧ 'Good/blessing Ali' cf. Kzk. PN *Qayïr-γali* (Žanuzakov-Esbaeva). ⇨ **XAYR** + **ALİ.**

QAYÏRГAS   Hak.(Sag.) 19th-20th c. **Qayïrγas** [Кайырђас] (Proben IX, 429-432). ✧ I. 'Roll, parcel, bundle'; II. 'Hone, oilstone' cf. Alt.(Tel.), Shor *qayïrγaš* 'ein Bündel, Knäuel; ein Stein zum Schleifen der Sicheln' (Radl. II, 96).

QAYÏS   Kzk. 19th c. **Qayz-bay** (<Qayïs-bay) [Каизбай] (SODž. 54). ✧ 'Strap, thong; belt' cf. Kzk. *qayïs* 'кайыс' (KzTS).

QAYÏTMİŠ   Turk. 16th c. **Qayïtmïš-beg**, from the Musullu of Akkoyunlus tribe, fell in the battle against Shah Ismail (Demirtaş 32). ✧ 'Returned' cf. Turk. (archaic) *kayıtmak* 'to return' (TED).

QAYÏW   Kkalp. 20th c. **Qayïw / Qayuw** [Къайув / Қайьıў] (Bask., Kkalp. 14, KkRS 774). ✧ 'Fine seam, fine sewing'? cf. Kkalp. *qayïü* 'сшивание чего-л. мелкой строчкой' (KkRS).

QAYKE   Kzk. 19th c. **Qayke** [Кайке] (AOA 34); Kzk. 19th c. **Qayke** [Кайке] (Grod., Pril. 62). ⇨ **QAYQA?**, **QAY** + suff. *-ke.*

QAYKEK   Kzk. 19th c. **Qaykek** [Кайкекъ] (SOV 62).

QAYQ see **QAYÏQ**

QAYQA   Bashk. 1728 **Qayqa** [Кайка] (MIB I, 301); Bashk. 1737 **Qayqa** [Кайка Бурсуков] (MIB I, 318); Kzk. 19th c. **Qayqa-bay** [Кайкабай] (SOK 8, 82). ✧ '(Man) Walking throwing out his chest' cf. Bashk. *qayqa* 'человек, который ходит, выпячив грудь' (BRS).

QAYQA-BAS   Kzk. 19th c. **Qayqa-bas** [Кайкабасъ] (SOV 154). ⇨ **QAYQA** + **BAŠ.**

QAYQAŠ   Alt. 19th-20th c. **Qayqaš** [Кайкаш] (OjrRS 208). ✧ 'Astonishment, surprise' (Bese 13), cf. Alt. *qayqa-* 'дивиться, удивляться' (OjrRS) + suff. *-aš.*

QAYQÏ   Kzk. 19th c. **Qayqï** [Кайкы] (SOV 54); Kzk. 19th c. **Qayqï** [Май Имганъ Кайкіевъ] (Grod., Pril. 31). ✧ I. 'Anxiety, worry, longing, regret' cf. Kuman, Kzk., Tat., Turk., etc. *qayγï* 'die Trauer, Betrübniss, der Kummer' (Radl. II, 8); II. 'Bent, curved back' cf. Kzk. *qayqï* 'geriye doğru eğik' (KzTS).

QAYQŌN   Hak. 19th c. **Qayqōn** [Кайкон] (Katanov, Otč. 12).

QAYLAS   Hak. 19th-20th c. **Qaylas** [Кайлас] (Katanov, Otč. 9).

QAYLİ   Kzk. 19th c. **Qaylï** [Кайлыбай] (SOK 190); Kzk. 19th c. **Qaylï** [Кайлыбай] (AOK 94); Kzk. 19th c. **Qaylï** [Кайлыбай] (AOA 90); Kzk. 19th c. **Qaylï-bay** [Кайлибай] (SOV 54); Kzk. 19th c. **Qaylï-bay** [Кайлибай] (SODž. 10); Kzk. 19th c. **Qaylï-bay** [Кайлыбай] (SOK 190); Kzk. 19th c. **Qaylu-bay** [Кайлюбай] (SODž. 94). ✧ 'Being from the tribe Qay'? ⇨ **QAY** + suff. *-lï.*

QAYMAQ   Kzk. 19th c. **Qaymaq** [Каймакъ], from the field Qaymaq-qara-su (AOK 110); Kzk. 19th c. **Qaymaq** [Каймакъ] (SOK 56). ✧ 'Cream' cf. Kzk. *qaymaq* 'каймак, сметана' (KzRS).

QAYMAN   Kzk. 19th c. **Qayman** [Кайманъ] (AOP 30, 34); Kzk. 19th c. **Qayman** [Кайманъ] (AOP 34). ⇨ **QAY** + suff. *-man?*

QAYMATİN   Hak. 19th-20th c. **Qaymatin** [Кайматин] (HRS 349). ✧ Galaktion (R.) (Butanaev).

QAYMAZ   Bashk. 1716 **Qaymas** [Каймас Тюмкин] (MIB III, 143-44); Selj. **Qaymaz** [نصرت الـدين بسر قيماز] (Ibn Bībī IV, 178-189, 278, 280-282); Selj. **Qaymaz** [صمصام الـدين قيماز] (Ibn Bībī IV, 241, 242, 272-73, 279-282); Selj. **Qaymaz** [ناصرالـدين ارسلان بـن قيماز] (Ibn Bībī IV, 224, 226); Selj. **Qaymaz** [قـايماز كج كلاه] (Bondārī 273, 293); Selj. 11th c. -12th c. **Qaymaz** [قيماز], Tāj al-Mulūq (Usāma 24); Selj. 1103 **Qaymaz** [قيماز] (Kamāladdīn II, 146); Selj.? 1103 **Qaymaz** [قـايماز], mamluk of Alp-arslan (1063-1072), the lord of Er-Rahaba, died in 1103 (Ibn al-Athīr/Tornb. X, 249, 272, Ibn al-Athīr: RHCHor I, 214); Selj.? 1103 **Qaymaz**, Qur-buγa's governor in Rahaba (Weil, Chalif. III, 153); Selj. 1128 **Qaymaz** [قيماز / Caimaz], gorvernor of Imadeddin Zengi in Haleb (Abulfidā III, 430-31); Selj.? 1146 **Qaymaz** [قـايمازالارجوانى] (Ibn al-Athīr/Tornb. XI, 70, 96, 174); Selj. 12th c. **Qaymaz** [قـايماز] (Rāwandī 233, 267); Selj. 12th c. **Qaymaz** [سراج الـدين قيماز], from the emirs of sultan Toγrul ibn Arslan (1175-1194), Zehireddin/Dorn 77 (Rāwandī 344, 375); Selj. 12th c. **Qaymaz** [قيماز شغال] (Muh. Ibrahim 99, 100); Selj. 12th c. **Qaymaz** [Siraceddin Kaymaz], an emir in Irak (Ahbar 125, 129); Selj. 1156 **Qaymaz** قـايماز الـحـرامى] (Bondārī 228); Selj.? 1158 [جمال الـدين ايلفقشت بـن **Qaymaz** [قـايماز السلطانى] (Ibn al-Athīr/Tornb. XI, 151-52); Selj.? 1159 **Qaymaz** [قـايماز العميدى] (Ibn al-Athīr/Tornb. XI, 164, 237); Selj. 1168/69, 1182, 1190/91, 1198/99 **Qaymaz** [مـجاهدالـدين قـايماز / Modjahed ed-Dîn Kaimaz], minister of Arslan-χan, governor of Mosul (Mâwsil), then that of Arbil?, died in 1199 (Ibn al-Athīr: RHCHor I, 641, 656, Ibn al-Athīr, Atab.: RHCHor II/1, 35, II/2, 244,354, Ibn al-Athīr/Tornb. XI, 283-84, 319-21, 329-32, XII, 64-66, Abulfidā IV, 44-45, Abulfidā/Ed. 49, 76, Abulfar. 411, Abulfar./Budge I, 347); Selj. 1170/71, 1180 **Qaymaz** [قطب الـدين قـايماز / قيماز / Kotb ed-Dîn Kaïmaz], caliph Al-Mustadī's amīr al-umarā (Ibn al-Athīr, Atab.: RHCHor II/2, 273, Qazw. 367, 368, Abulfar. 403); Selj.? 1171 **Qaymaz** [قـايماز المقتفوى قطب الـدين] (Ibn al-Athīr/Tornb. XI, 236-37, 280-82); Selj.? 1173/74, 1190/91 **Qaymaz** [قـايماز الـحـرانى / Kaimaz el-Harrani], governor of Harrān (Ibn Šaddād, Nawād.:

RHCHor III, 171, Ibn al-Athīr: RHCHor I, 609, Ibn al-Athīr/Tornb. XI, 268); Selj. 1175 **Qaymaz** [قيماز / Caimaz], chief of the army(?) in Baghdad (Abulfidā IV, 24); Selj. 1187/88, 1189/90, 1192/93, 1199 **Qaymaz** [قايماز / قايمازالنجمى / صارمالـدين / Kaimaz en-Nedjmi], Saladin's (Salah ed-Dïn's) officer, emir, died in 1199 (Ibn al-Athīr/Tornb. XI, 350, 370, XII, 2, 13, Ibn al-Athīr: RHCHor I, 678, 736, Ibn Šaddād, Alep 141, 168, 260, 328, Sauvaire III, 271, IV, 278); Selj. 1191/92 **Qaymaz** [قايماز العادلى / Kaimaz el-A'deli], died in 1191/92 (Ibn Šaddād, Nawād.: RHCHor III, 261); Maml. 13th c. **Qaymaz** [قيماز] (Berchem, Jér. II, 303); Maml. 13th c. **Qaymaz** [صارم الـدين قايماز الكافرى], an emir, died in 1275 (Sobernh. I, 26); Maml. 1259 **Qaymaz** [قيماز مجاهدالـدين], commander of Hamah (Syria?) (Abulfidā IV, 580-81). ✧ 'He who won't curve; he won't recoil' (Sauvaget 52), cf. Karakh., Uyg. *qay-* 'поворачиваться; обращать внимание' (DTS), Kuman, Alt., Az., Hak., Turk. *qay- (qaï-)* '(aus)gleiten; sich zurückwenden' (Radl. II, 4). ⇨ **QAYTMAZ?**

QAYMÏŠ   Uyg. 8th c. - 12th c. **Qaymïš** (Müller, Pfahl. 12); Uyg. 12th c - 14th c. **Qaymïš-señün** [Kaymış Sängün] (Radl., USp. 141, DTS, EUTS). ✧ 'He/she veered, turned' cf. Karakh., Uyg. *qay-* 'поворачиваться; обращать внимание' (DTS), Kuman, Alt., Az., Hak., Turk. *qay- (qaï-)* '(aus)gleiten; sich zurückwenden' (Radl. II, 4). See also **BASA-QAYMÏŠ**.

QAYN see **QAYÏN**

QAYN-BULAT   Tat. 1763 **Qayn-bulat** [Каинбулатовъ] (PSZRI XVI, 323). ⇨ **QAYÏN + BULAT.**

QAYNAR   Uzb. 20th c. **Qaynar** [Қайнар] (Begmatov 1984, 207); Kzk. 19th c. **Qaynar-bay** [Кайнарбай] (SOK 40); Uzb. 20th c. **Qaynar-ĵân** [Қайнаржон] (Begmatov 1984, 207). ✧ 'Well, spring' cf. Kzk. *qaynar* 'ключ (источник)' (KzRS).

QAYR see **XAYR**

QAYR-ALAN   Kzk. 19th c. **Qayr-alan** [Кайраланъ] (AOP 46). ⇨ **XAYR + ALAN?**

QAYR-ALAP see **XAYR-ALAP**

QAYRA   Alt.(Tel.) 19th c. **Qayra-χan / Qayra-qan** [Кайра-хан], originally a hunter, called Qašqa-būrul (Verb., In. 54, Potanin IV, 327). ✧ 'Favour, bounty' cf. Shor, Tuv. *qayra* 'die Gunst, Gnade, Belohnung' (Radl. II, 21).

QAYRAQ   Kzk. 19th c. **Qayraq-pay** [Кайракпай] (SOK 18); *EN:* Kzk. 19th c. **Qayraq-pay** [Кайракпай], a clan (Potanin II, 6); *TN:* Kzk. 19th c. **Qayraq-bay** [Кайракъ-бай], a field (AOO 66). ✧ 'Hone, oilstone' cf. Chag., Kzk., Tat., Turk. *qayraq* 'der Schleifstein, Schleifriemen' (Radl. II, 21). See also

QAYÏRГAS.

QAYRAQAN   Alt. 19th c. **Qayraqan** [Кайраканъ], a hunter, whose real name was Qašqa-būrul (Potanin IV, 327). ✧ Title of respect. Cf. Alt., Hak. *qayraqqan (=qayran+qān)* 'ein Ehrenname verschiedener Gottheiten und Geister; ein Schutzengel' (Radl. II, 22).

QAYRAN I.   Kuman 1266 **Keyran** [Keyran Dominus de Cumanis de genere Borchol] (Gyárfás II, 418, ÁÚO IX, 486, Fejér IV, 3, 342-44); Maml. 1310 **Qayran / Qïran?** [قيران], an emir (Dawād. 212); Maml. 1332 **Qayran / Qïran?** [قيران السلارى] (Dawād. 365, 367); Maml. 14th c. **Qayran / Qïran?** [قيران] (Sauvaget 54). ✧ 'Showing courtesy; protector, supporter'? cf. Kipch. *kayır-* 'iltifat etmek, kayırmak' (Tuhf.), cf. also Rásonyi, KÖA 112, Rásonyi, Anthr. 142.

QAYRAN II.   Kzk. 19th c. **Qayram-bay (<Qayran-bay)** [Кайрамбай] (SODž. 90, 102); Kzk. 19th c. **Qayran** [Кайранъ] (SODž. 116); Kzk. 19th c. **Qayran** [Кайранъ] (SOK 242); Kzk. 19th c. **Qayran-bay** [Кайронбай] (SODž. 108). ✧ 'Marveling, wondering' cf. Kzk., Kirg., Tat. *qayran* (Ar.) 'erstaunt' (Radl. II, 23).

QAYRAŠ   Kzk. 19th c. **Qayraš-bay** [Кайрашбай] (SODž. 150).

QAYRÏM   Kzk. 19th c. **Qayrïm-bay (<Qayrïn-bay / Qayïrïn-bay?)** [Кайрсмбай] (SODž. 28). ✧ 'Goodness, kindness' cf. Kzk. *qayrïm* 'die Güte' (Radl. II, 25).

QAYRKE   Kzk. 19th c. **Qayrke (<Qayïrke)** [Каирке] (SODž. 162). ⇨ **XAYR** + suff. *-ke* or comp. *eke / ake.*

QAYSADU   Uyg. 12th c. - 14th c. **Qaysadu** [Kaysadu] (Radl., USp. 130-131, DTS, EUTS).

QAYSAR   Maml. 1310 **Qaysar** [قيصر], an emir (Dawād. 1310); Kzk. 19th c. **Qaysar** [Кайсаръ] (AOK 118); Kzk. 19th c. **Qaysar** [Кайсаръ] (SODž. 16); Kkalp. 1724 **Qaysar** [Апан Кайсаров] (MIKk. 181); Kzk. 18th c. **Qaysar-batïr** [Кайсаръ-Батыръ] (Nepljuev 804); Selj. 1200 **Qaysar-šah** [Mûʿiz ad-Dîn Kaisar Shâh / Muʿizuddîn Qaiseršâh], Qïlič-arslan's son (Abulfar./Budge I, 350, Aqsar./Iş. 39). ✧ 'Persistent, strong-minded' cf. Kzk. *qaysar* 'настойчивый, с твёрдой волей, упорный; решительный' (KzRS).

QAYSARA   Kzk. 18th c. **Qaysara-batïr** [Кайсара-Батыръ], envoy from Khiva (Nepljuev 813). ⇨ **QAYSAR?** + suff. *-a.*

QAYSÏDU   Uyg. 12th c. - 14th c. **Qaysïdu** [Kaysïdu] (Radl., USp. 7, Le Coq, Urkunden 455, DTS, EUTS); Uyg. 12th c. - 14th c. **Qaysïdu-tutuñ (-tutuq?)** (Radl., USp. 250, DTS).

QAYSÏM   Tat.? 1449 **Qaysïm** [Кайсымъ / Касимъ], a prince (PSRL XII, 75); Alt. 19th-20th c. **Qaysïm** [Кайсым] (OjrRS 208); Tat.? 1509 **Qaysïm-baqšï-χoĵa** [Кайсымъ-Бакшей-Хозя] (PSRL XIII, 10). ✧ Cf. Tat. PNs *Qasïym-bay / Qasïym-bek / Qasïym-ĵan*

(Sattarov). ⇨ **QASÏM.**

QAYSÏN Uyg. 12th c. -14th c. **Qaysïn** (Radl., USp. 133-134, DTS). ✧ 'May he turn!' (Bese 11), 'May he look/watch (carefully)', cf. Uyg. *qaj-* 'поворачиваться; сочувствовать' (DTS).

QAYŠÏLÏ Kzk. **Qayšïlï-qan** [Каишылы Кан], Altïnbel's son (Proben III, 63 /82/). ⇨ **KAYČÏ** + suff. *-li*?

QAYŠU Kzk. 19th c. **Qayšu-bay** [Кайшубай] (SOK 136). ⇨ **KAYČÏ?**

QAYT Kzk. 19th c. **Xayt-bay** [Хайтбай] (Grod., Pril. 158); Maml. 1475/76 **Qayt** [قيت الرحبى] (Iyās II, 162, 235, 277); Maml. 1468-1495 **Qayt-bay** [قايتباى ابو النصر], Abul Nasr Khaitbai, a sultan of Egypt (1468-1495/96) (Amari 182, 184 etc., Mehren 499, Berchem, Jér. II, 153, Berchem 47); Maml. 1489 **Qayt-bay** [السيفى قايتباى], a governor in Divrigi (CIA 3/I, 93-94); Maml. 1516 **Qayt-bay** [قايتباى] (Iyās III, 52); Maml. 1516 **Qayt-bay** [قايتباى] (Iyās III, 6); Maml. 1454 **Qayt-bay** [ابن قايتباى] (Iyās II, 45); Bashk. 1798 **Qayt-qul** [Кайткуловъ] (PSZRI XXV, 196); Kzk. 19th c. **Qayt-pek** [Кайтпекъ] (SODž. 58); Kzk. 19th c. **Qoyt-bay / Qayt-bay?** [Койтбай] (SODž. 30). ✧ 'Return; come/go back' cf. Chag., Kuman, Alt., Crm., Kzk., Kar., NUyg., Tat., Tat.(Sib.), *qayt-* 'zurückkehren, heimkehren' (Radl. II, 29), cf. also Rásonyi, Imp. 240.

QAYTAN Kzk. 19th c. **Qaytan** [Кайтанъ] (AOAtb. 58); Kzk. 19th c. **Qaytan-bay** [Кайтанбай] (SOK 90).

QAYTAR Kuman 1428 **Qaytar** [Thoma dicto Kaythor de Pabe] (Gyárfás III, 588); Kuman 1448, 1473, 1484 **Qaytar** [Kaythorzallasa, Kaythorzallas], Kumanian personal name in the name of a settlement in Hungary (Gyárfás III, 620, 673, 684); Uzb. 20th c. **Qaytar** [Кайтар] (Begmatov 1984, 207). ✧ 'He will return/come back' cf. Rásonyi, Adalékok 135, Rásonyi, KÖA 111, Rásonyi, Anthr. 142. ⇨ **QAYT.** See also **QAYTMAZ.**

QAYTASU Uyg. **Qaytasu** [Kaytasu] (Radl., USp. 128-129, DTS, EUTS).

QAYTQAN Kuman 1488 **Qaytqan** [terra Kayathkan], personal name preserved as a placename in Lesser Kumania, Hungary (Gyárfás III, 698). ✧ 'Returned, came back' (Rásonyi, KÖA 111, Rásonyi, Anthr. 141).

QAYTMAS see QAYTMAZ

QAYTMAZ Chag. **Qaytmas** [قايتماس] (Le Coq, Ind. 4); Karch., Balk.? 1822 **Qaytmas** [Сулейман Кайтмасов] (MID III, 157); 19th c. **Qaytmaz** [А. Кайтмазовъ] (ZVOIRAO VII, 352). ✧ 'He who won't return; he who keeps his word' (Le Coq). ⇨ **QAYT.** See also **QAYTAR.**

QAYTSU Uyg. 13th c. **Qaytsu-tutuñ** [Kaitsu] (DTS, EUTS).

QAYTU Kzk. 19th c. **Qaytu-bay** [Кайтубай] (SODž.

112). ✧ 'Returning'. ⇨ **QAYT.**

QAYU Bashk. 1785 **Qayu-qan?** [Каюкан Чапкинов] (MIB V, 178, 219). ⇨ **QAYÏ?**

QAYUM Kzk. 19th c. **Qayum** [Каюмъ Кумарбаевъ] (SKSO VIII, 232). ✧ Qayyum (Ar.) 'eternal, everlasting' (Ahmed), cf. also Tat. PN *Qayum* (Sattarov), Bashk. PN *Qayum / Qäyum* (Sprav. Im. 76, Kusimova).

QAYUW see QAYÏW

QAYZ see QAYÏS

QAKELLİ Trkm. 1856/57 **Qakelli** [Палван Какелли], from Khiva (MIT II, 581).

QAQ Hak. 19th-20th c. **Qaq** [Как], fem. (HRS 353); Tat.(Sib.) 1623 **Qaq-seyit** [Каксеит] (Miller, Ist. Sib. II, 293). ✧ 'Beat (him)!'? cf. Chag., Alt., Kirg., Kzk., Tat., etc. *qaq-* 'schlagen, klopfen' (Radl. I, 57). See also **AY-QAQ, TEKİR-QAQ.**

QAQ-BAŠ Tat.(Sib.) 1631 **Qaq-baš** [Аучек (Гучек, Угучек) Какбашев] (Miller, Ist. Sib. II, 383, 384). ⇨ **QAQ? + BAŠ.**

QAQ-KÜZ Kzk. 19th c. **Qaq-küz** [Карабай Каккузовъ] (Grod., Pril.). ⇨ **QAQ? + KÖZ.**

QAQ-ŠARA Tat.(Sib.) 1596 **Qaq-šara** [Какшара] (Miller, Ist. Sib. II, 148). ⇨ **QAQ + ŠARA.**

QAQA Chag. 16th c. **Qaqa** [Кака] (Ivanov 226, 227); Tat. 1624 **Qaqa** [Досай Какинъ] (Pokrovskij 70); Trkm. 1770 **Qaqa-bay** [Кака-бай], from the Yomut tribe (MIT II, 350, Sopieva 181); Trkm. **Qaqa-jan** [Какажан] (Sopieva 181); Trkm. 1879 **Qaqa-jan** [Кока-Джанъ] (Grod., Pril. 109). ✧ 'Father' cf. Trkm. *qaqa (qāqa)* 'отец' (TrkmRS), Kzk. dial. *qaqa* 'әке, мырза' (QTDS).

QAQA-GELDİ Trkm. **Qaqa-geldi** [Какагелди] (Sopieva 181). ✧ 'Father has come'. ⇨ **QAQA + KELDİ.**

QAQAČ Uyg. 13th-14th c. **Qaqač-ïnal** [Qaqač İnal], fem. (Zieme, Mat. III, 280). ✧ 'Dirt, dirty' cf. Karakh. *qaqač* 'грязь, грязный' (DTS).

QAQAY Kzk. 1846 **Qaqay** [Какай Майлиев] (MKOP 156); Kzk. 19th c. **Qaqay** [Какай] (AOA 154). ✧ I. 'Father!' (voc.); II. 'Be hard (strong), stand straight!'? cf. Kzk. *qaqay-* 'hart sein, sich gerade halten, aufrecht stehen' (Radl. II, 59). ⇨ **QAQA + voc. suff. -y.**

QAQAQ Kzk. 19th c. **Qaqaq-pay** [Какакпай] (SOK 66). ⇨ **QAQA? + suff. -q.**

QAQAMAN Kzk. 19th c. **Qaqaman** [Какаманъ] (SOK 58). ⇨ **QAQA + suff. -man.**

QAQAN Kzk. 1794 **Qaqan-bi / Qaχan** [قاقان بى / قاخان / Кахан] (MIK IV, 163).

QAQASAY Kzk. 19th c. **Qaqasay** [Какасай] (SOK 40).

QAQČÏ Turk. **Qaqčï-oγlu**, a Zeybek (Kúnos 1891, 119). ✧ 'Last (born child)' cf. Turk. dial. *kakçı* 'sonuncu (yarış, yarışma vb.)' (DS VIII).

QAQÏ Kzk. 19th c. **Qaqï-bay** [Какыбай] (AOP 42). ❖ 'Right, just; loan, duty' cf. Kzk. *kakı* 'hak; mihnet, borç' (KzTS).

QAQÏR-BAŠ Bashk. 1722 **Qaqïr-baš** [Какырбаш] (MIB I, 294). ❖ '(Clearing one's throat) hawking - head' cf. Bashk. *qaqïr-* 'харкать, отхаркивать' (BRS/Uraksin). ⇨ **BAŠ**.

QAQŠA Uyg. **Qaqša-ačqï** [qaqša ačqï / Kakşa Açǵı], P. Zieme reads it as Qarša Ačarï (Zieme, Mat. III, 280) (DTS, EUTS).

QAQTÏRQAY Kzk. **Qaqtïrqay** [Кактыркаi], a hero (Proben III, 261 /308/). ⇨ **QAQTUR** + suff. *-qay*.

QAQTUR Kzk. 19th c. **Qaqtur-bay** [Какторбай] (SOK 226).

QAL I. Uzb. 20th c. **Qâl-bây** [Қолбой] (Begmatov 1984, 207); *EN:* Yürük 1611 **Qal-jan** [كوحك اولو قلجان], a taife (tribe) (Gökçen 82, 85). ❖ I. 'Stay, remain (alive)' cf. most Trk. languages *qal-* 'bleiben' (Radl. II, 220), cf. also Pelliot 204, Pais-Rásonyi 121-124; II. 'Shameless, impertinent, reckless' Alt. *qal* 'дерзкий' (OjrRS), Hak. *qal* 'fest; grob, unverschämt' (Radl. II, 219); III. '(Good) condition, state; strength, power' cf. Kzk. *qal* 'der Zustand, Umstand', Uyg., Hak.(Sag.) *qal* 'die Kraft, Macht' (<Ar. χal) (Radl. II219), Uzb. *χâl* сила, мочь; здоровье' (UzbRS). See also **AT-QAL, BESKE-QAL? BİN-QAL, DUR-QAL, ER-QAL, EREN-QAL, QUL-QAL, ŠÄW-QAL(?)**.

QAL II. Kzk. 19th c. **Xal** [Халъ Джумабаевъ] (SKSO VIII, 221); Kzk. 19th c. **Xal** [Халъ Турдiевъ] (SKSO VIII, 224); Kzk. 19th c. **Xal** [Халъ] (SKSO VIII, 203); Kzk. 19th c. **Xal-bay** [Халбай] (SKSO VIII, 219); Kzk. 19th c. **Xal-bay** [Керимъ-кулъ Халбаевъ] (Grod., Pril. 159); Kzk. 19th c. **Xal-bay** [Халбай] (Grod., Pril. 31); Kzk. 19th c. **Xal-bay** [Халбаевъ] (SKSO VIII, 204); Uzb. 1828 **Xal-bay** [Халь-бай] (Moskal'cev 38); Uzb. 19th c. **Xal-bay** [Халбай] (SKSO VIII, 182); Uzb. 1896 **Xal-bibi** [Халь-биби], from the region of Tashkent (Sr. Az. I (11, Avg. 1896)); Kzk. **Xal-biy** [Халбiй] (Grod. 25); Kzk. 19th c. **Xal-yigit** [Хальигитъ] (SKSO VIII, 201); Kzk. 19th c. **Xal-mirza** [Халъ-Мирза] (Grod., Pril. 23); Chuv. 18th-19th c. **Kal-murza** [Калмурза] (Magn. 49); Kzk. **Qal-bay** [Кальбай] (Sb. Syr-D. IX, 54); Kzk. 19th c. **Qal-bay** [Калбай] (SOV 22); Kzk. 20th c. **Qal-bay** [Қалбай] (KkRS 774); Kzk. 1746 **Qal-bek** [Калбекъ] (Nepljuev 693); Kzk. 19th c. **Qal-bek** [Калбекъ] (AOA 66); Kzk. 19th c. **Qal-bek** [Калбекъ] (Grod., Pril. 82); Kkalp. 20th c. **Qal-biyke** [Қалбийке], fem. (KkRS 778); Kzk. 18th c. - 19th c. **Qal-bike** [Калбике], fem. (MIK IV, 240); Bashk. 1735 **Qal-čan / Qal-jan?** [Кулакай Калчановъ], a tarχan (Vel.-Zern., Bašk. 14); Bashk. 1745 **Qal-čan / Qal-jan?** [Мансур Калчанов] (MIB III, 428); Bashk. 1735 **Qal-čura** [Калчура Епановъ], a tarχan (Vel.-Zern., Bašk. 15); Bashk. 1756 **Qal-čura** [Беремкул Калчуров] (MIB IV/1, 107); Kzk. 19th c. **Qal-jan** [Кальджанъ] (SOV 154); Kzk. 19th c. **Qal-jan** [Кальджанъ] (SODž. 114); Kkalp. 20th c. **Qal-jan / Qal-žan** [Къалджан / Қалжан (Ерлепес-къызы)], fem. (Bask., Kkalp. 59 (p. 167), KkRS 778); Tat.(Sib.) 1605 **Qal-γul** [Калгул] (Miller, Ist. Sib. II, 187); Kzk. 19th c. **Qal-γul** [Калгулъ] (SOV 26); Chag. 19th c. **Qal-χan** [قال خان / Гкалъ ханъ], a Sheybanid, Eminek's son, reigned in Khiva until 1839 (Šejb. LII, Zambaur 274); Chag. 16th c. **Qal-χān** [قال خان], Yādigār-χan's descendant (Abulg./Desm. 218, 245); Kzk. 19th c. **Qal-qul** [Калкулъ] (SOV 12); Kirg. **Qal-mergen** [Калмерген] (Jud. 152); Bashk. 1798 **Qal-mulla** [Калмуллинъ] (PSZRI XXV, 197); Bashk. 1798 **Qal-murza** [Калмурза] (PSZRI XXV, 196); Kzk. 19th c. **Qal-murza** [Калмурза] (SOV 8); Kkalp. 20th c. **Qal-murza** [Қалмурза] (KkRS 774); Kzk. 19th c. **Qal-pay** [Майлыкызъ Калпаева] (TV 1876, 144). ❖ 'Birthmark, spot' cf. Kkalp. *qal* 'родинка, родимое пятно' (KkRS), Kzk. *qal* 'leke' (KzTS), Kirg. *qal* 'родинка, родимое пятнышко; пятно на лице; пятно на теле животного (чаще лошади)' (Jud.), Trkm. *χāl* 'родинка, родимое пятно' (TrkmRS), Uzb. *χâl* 'родинка, родимое пятно' (UzbRS). A birthmark on the body of the baby is considered to be a good omen among the peoples of Middle Asia (Žanuzakov). (<P. خال). See also **QALLÏ, MEŇLİ; ŠÄW-QAL(?), TÄŽİ-QAL, TURDÏ-XÂL**.

QAL-AXMET Chuv. 18th-19th c. **Kal-aχmet** [Калахметъ] (Magn. 49). ⇨ **QAL II. + AXMET**.

QAL-BARAQ Kirg. **Qal-baraq?** [Калбарак] (Jud. 745). ⇨ **QAL I. / QAL II.? + BARAQ**.

QAL-BARAN Kzk. 19th c. **Qal-baran** [Кальбаранъ Кабуловъ] (SKSO VIII, 204). ⇨ **QAL I. / QAL II.?**

QAL-BARS Khorezm. 13th c. **Qal-bars-bahadïr** [قلبرس بهادر], Jelāleddīn's (1220-1231) officer (Nasawī 85). ⇨ **QAL I. / QAL II.? + BARS**.

QAL-BAS Alt. **Qal-bas** [Калбасъ], a shaman (Nikiforov 238). ❖ 'Shameless, impertinent, reckless - head'. ⇨ **QAL I. + BAŠ**.

QAL-BERDİ Uzb. 20th c. **Xâl-berdi** [Холберди] (Begmatov 1984, 202). ⇨ **QAL I.? + BERDİ**.

QAL-BERGEN Kzk. 19th c. **Qal-bergen** [Калбергенъ] (SOK 42). ⇨ **QAL II. + BERGEN**.

QAL-BÏΓAY Tuv. 19th c. **Qal-bïγay / Qal-bïqay** [Калбыкаi / Калбыҕаi] (Proben IX, 19, 21). ❖ 'Shameless, impertinent Bïγay'. ⇨ **QAL I.**

QAL-GÜLÄT Bashk. 1732 **Qal-gülät?** [Айдел Калгулятов] (MIB III, 310). ⇨ **QAL I. / QAL II.?**

QAL-KELDİ Uzb. 20th c. **Xâl-keldi** [Холкелди] (Begmatov 1984, 203). ❖ 'Power/strength has come;

Born healthy'. ⇨ **QAL I. + KELDİ.**

QAL-QULLÏ Trkm. 1841/42 **Qal-qullï-χan** [Калкулли-хан] (MIT II, 484). ⇨ **QAL I. / QAL II.?** + **QUL** + suff. *-lï*.

QAL-MAMBET see **QAL-MUXAMED**

QAL-MAMET see **QAL-MUXAMED**

QAL-MEKEY Chuv. 18th-19th c. **Kal-mekey?** [Калмекей] (Magn. 49). ⇨ **QAL II. + MEKEY.**

QAL-MEMET see **QAL-MUXAMED**

QAL-MÏRAT see **QAL-MURAT**

QAL-MÏRZAY Kkalp. 20th c. **Qal-mïrzay** [Къалмырзай / Қалмырзай] (Bask., Kkalp. 400, KkRS 774). ⇨ **QAL I. / QAL II.?** + **MURZAY** + suff. *-y.*

QAL-MUXAMED Kzk. **Xal-maχammed** [Халмахаммедъ] (Grod. 9); Kzk. 19th c. **Xal-muχamed** [Хальмухамедъ Юлдашевъ] (SKSO VIII, 201); Uzb. 19th c. **Xal-muχamed** [Юлдашъ Халмухаммедовъ] (Sr. Az. I (1896), avg. 16); Kzk. 19th c. **Qal-maγomed?** [Калмагомедъ] (Grod., Pril. 111); Kzk. 19th c. **Qal-mambet** [Каль Мамбетъ] (Grod., Pril. 189); Kzk. 19th c. **Qal-mambet** [Калмамбетъ] (SOV 44); Tat. 1753 **Qal-mamet** [Калмаметь] (MIB IV/1, 70); Tat. 1824 **Qal-mamet** [Калмаметевъ] (PSZRI XXXIX, 266); Tat. 19th c. **Qal-mamet** [Калмаметъ Байбарисовъ] (Zolotn. 157); Kzk. 19th c. **Qal-manbet, Qal-mambet** [Калманбетъ] (SOK 68); Tat. 1779 **Qal-memet** [Калмеметь Акметев (Акмеметев)] (MIB V, 83); Kkalp. 1722 **Qal-muχamed** [Калмухамед богадыр] (MIKk. 170); Uzb. 1731 **Qalmet** [Калметевъ], from Bukhara (PSZRI VIII, 450). ✦ 'Birth-mark Mukhammad' Birth-mark was considered a good omen at the peoples of Central Asia (Žanuzakov 144). This name was taken by the Tatars from the Kazaks (Sattarov). Cf. Kzk. PNs *Qal-muχambet, Qalï-bay, Qalï-bek, Qalïmbet*, etc. (Žanuzakov 144, Žanuzakov-Esbaeva). ⇨ **QAL II. + MUXAMMED.** See also **XAL-МАГОМЕТ.**

QAL-MURAT Kzk. 19th c. **Xal-murat (Xal-murad)** [Халмурадъ Ишмурадовъ] (SKSO VIII, 203); Kzk. 19th c. **Xal-murat (Xal-murad)** [Халъ Мурадъ] (Grod., Pril. 137); Kkalp. 20th c. **Qal-mïrat** [Къалмырат] (Bask., Kkalp. 35, 37, 77, KkRS 774); Kkalp. 20th c. **Qal-murat** [Къалмурат] (Bask., Kkalp. 61, KkRS 774). ⇨ **QAL I. / QAL II.?** + **MURAT.**

QAL-NİYAZ Kkalp. 20th c. **Qal-niyaz** [Қалнияз] (KkRS 774). ⇨ **QAL I. / QAL II.?** + **NİYAZ.**

QAL-TAY Tat. 20th c. **Qal-tay** [Калтаев] (Sattarov); Tat.(Sib.) 20th c. **Qal-tay** [Калтаев] (Sattarov); Bashk. 1678 **Qal-tay** [Актанай Калтаевъ] (DAI IX, 92-93). ✦ 'Foal (child) with birthmark; lucky child' (Sattarov); II. '(Male child with) birthmark'. ⇨ **QAL II. + TAY?** or suff. *-tay(1,2).* See also **QALDAY?, QAŠ-QAL-**

TAY.

QAL-TUГAN Chuv. 18th-19th c. **Kal-tugan** [Калтуганъ] (Magn. 49). ⇨ **QAL I. / QAL II.?** + **TUГAN? I.**

QAL-TUYГAQ Hak.(Belt.) 19th-20th c. **Qal-tuyγaq** [Кал-Туйɓак] (Proben IX, 5g3). ✦ 'Strong hoof' cf. Hak. PN *Xal tuyγaχ* 'id.' (Buatanaev). ⇨ **QAL I.**

QALA Kzk. 19th c. **Qala** [Kalé], fem. (Levchine 356); Kzk. **Qala-bay** [Калабай] (Smirnov, Sultany 7); Kzk. 19th c. **Qala-bay** [Калабай] (SODž. 116, 130); Kzk. 19th c. **Qala-bay** [Калабай] (SOK 24); Kzk. 19th c. **Qala-bay** [Калабай] (AOAtb. 2, 50); Kzk. 19th c. **Qala-bay** [Калабай] (AOA 18, 78); Kzk. 19th c. **Qala-bay** [Калабай] (SOV 94); Kkalp. 20th c. **Qala-bay** [Қалабай] (KkRS 774); Tat. **Qala-bey** (Koşay: KCsA I, 324); Bashk. 1712 **Qala-biki** [Кала бикии] (MIB III, 84); Kzk. 19th c. **Qala-ĵan** [Тисанъ Каладжановъ] (Grod., Pril. 173). ✦ 'Fortress, town' cf. Tat. *qala* 'город, крепость (TatRS), Kkalp. *qala* 'город, городской базар' (KkRS). See also **NUR-QALA.**

QALAČ I. Oghuz/Trkm. 13th c. **Qalač** [قلاج اچ / qalač / Калач] (Abulg./Kon. 370, 560, DTS). ✦ 'Remainder' (Bese 13), cf. Uyg., Karakh. *qal-* 'оставаться' (DTS) + suff. *-ač.*

QALAČ II. Tat. 1375 **Qalač** [Calach], from Caffa (Jorga, Notes I, 9); Alt. **Qalaš** [Калашъ], a *qam* (shaman) (Nikiforov 149); Alt. **Qalaš** [Калаш] (Radl. I, 1103); Hak.(Sag.) 19th-20th c. **Qalās** [Калас] (Katanov, Otč. 7); Hak.(Koyb.) 19th c. **Qalās** [Калас] (Katanov, Otč. 12).

QALADAY Khorezm./Chag.? 14th c. **Qaladay** [Caladay], Timür's follower (Clavijo 42).

QALAY Chuv. 1739 **Kalay** [Чендей Калаевъ] (Alatyr. 142); Chuv. 18th-19th c. **Kalay** [Калай] (Magn. 49); Bashk. 1737 **Qalay** [Калай] (MIB I, 336); Bashk. 1761 **Qalay** [Калай Япаров] (MIB I/1, 216). ✦ 'Tin' cf. Kuman, Cr., Alt., Tat., Turk. *qalay* 'das Zinn' (Radl. II, 226), Bashk. *qalay* 'жесть' (BRS).

QALAQ-PAS Kzk. 19th c. **Qalaq-pas** [Калакпасъ] (SOV 116). ✦ 'Having spoon/ladle-like head' cf. Hak., Kzk., Tat. *qalaq* 'ein grosser Löffel' (Radl. II, 227). ⇨ **BAŠ.**

QALAQAY Kzk. 19th c. **Qalaqay** [Калакай] (SOV 54); Kzk. 19th c. **Qalaqay** [Калакай] (AOK 126). ✦ '(Stinging-)nettle' cf. Kzk. *qalaqay* 'id.' (KzTS).

QALAQSÏZ Maml. 1479 **Qalaqsïz**, governor of Syria (Sauvaire VI, 270). ✦ I. 'Without hesitation'? (Sauvaire 313: Ce nom turc signifie „sans hésitation"); II. 'Without spoon'? cf. Hak., Kzk., Tat. *qalaq* 'ein grosser Löffel' (Radl. II, 227). + suff. *-sïz.*

QALAL-DURUQ Karakh. 11th c. **Qalal-duruq** [qalalduruq / Kalalduruk] (DTS, MK/Atalay 842). ✦ '?-thin'? cf. Uyg., Karakh. *turuγ III / turuq I* 'худой, истощенный, тощий' (DTS). ⇨ **QALAL?** + **TURUQ** or dim. *-duruq?*

QALAM Turk. 13th c. **Qalam** [Καλάμης], a prince (Byz. Turc. 147).

QALAMAN Bashk. 1706 **Qalaman** [Каламан], a village (MIB III, 21).

QALAN Chuv. 18th-19th c. **Kalan** [Каланъ] (Magn. 49); Chag. 1472 **Qalan** [Khwāja Kalān] (Tar. Rashidi 94). ✧ 'Tax, duty' cf. Chag., Alt., Az., Shor *qalan* 'die abgabe, der Tribut' (Radl. II, 230). See also **BABA-QALAN**.

QALAN-TAY Tat.(GH) 1343 **Qalan-tay** [Калантай], from the Horde (PSRL III, 82). ⇨ **QALAN** + **TAY** or suff. *-tay(1,2)?*

QALANJAQ Maml. 1279 **Qalanjaq** [Kalandjak-Dāheri] (Makrīzī II, 171). ⇨ **QALAN** + suff. *-ǰaq / -ǰïq.*

QALANDAR see **QALÄNDÄR**

QALAŠ Kuman 1436 **Qalaš** [Johannes Kalas de Kalaszallasa], a person of Kuman origin in Lesser Kumania, Hungary (Gyárfás III, 228, 597); Kuman 1436 **Qalaš** [Kalaszallasa], Kalasszállása (Qalaš's settlement) in Lesser Kumania, Hungary (Gyárfás III, 228, 597); Az.? **Qalaš** [Калашевъ] (SMOK VII, 98); Kzk. 19th c. **Qalaš** [Юнусъ Калашевъ] (SKSO VIII, 206). ✧ 'Sly old fox, tricky' cf. Turk. *qalaš* 'ein schlauer Fuchs, Schurke, Schelm' (Radl. II, 232); II. 'Helpless, shiftless, orphan' cf. Chag. *qalaš* 'hilflos, ohnc Mittel zum Lebensunterhalt' (Radl. II, 232), for the more detailed etymology of Kuman *Qalaš* see Rásonyi, Kisk. 342-43, and also Rásonyi, KÖA 108, Rásonyi, Anthr. 141.

QALAŠÏ Kzk. 19th c. **Qalašï** [Калаши] (AOP 50). ✧ 'Loving going to towns' cf. Kzk. *qalašï* 'Devamlı şehre gidip gelen kimse' (KzTS). ⇨ **QALA** + suff. *-šï / -čï.*

QALAW Nog.?, Kzk.? **Qalaw** [Калау], the same as Qalu (Žirm., Epos 402).

QALĀS see **QALAŠ**

QALĀŪN Maml. 14th c. **Qalawun** [Калавун] (Tuhfa 410); Maml.? **Qalāūn** [قلاون الالفى / Saif al-Dīn Qalāūn al-Alfī] (Sīrat 85).

QALBAΓ see **QALBAQ**

QALBAΓAŠ Alt. 19th-20th c. **Qalbaγaš** [Калбагаш] (OjrRS 208). ✧ 'Little spoon' (OjrRS). ⇨ **QALBAQ** + dim. suff. *-aš.*

QALBAQ Tuv. 19th c. **Qalbaq-ōl / Qalbaγ-ōl** [Калбакъ-ол] (Proben IX, 54); Alt. 19th-20th c. **Qalbaq** [Калбак] (OjrRS 208). ✧ 'Spoon' (OjrRS) cf. Alt., Kzk. *qalbaq* 'der Löffel' (Radl. II, 270).

QALBANJÏ Tuv. 19th c. **Qalbanǰï** [Калбанцы] (Proben IX, 31).

QALBURDÏ Bashk. 1737 **Qalburdï** [Калбурди Асанов], a mulla (MIB I, 317). ✧ 'Having a sieve' cf. Crm., Turk. 'das Sieb' (Radl. II, 271). + suff. *-dï.*

QALČA Kirg. **Qalča** [Калча] (Jud. 126, 418). ✧

'Having a frightful outlook' cf. Kirg. *qalča* '(о горбоносом человеке) грозный на вид' (Jud.).

QALČI Kzk. 19th c. **Qalči** [Калчи] (SOV 6).

QALČIK Kzk. 19th c. **Qalčik-bay** [Калчикбай] (AOA 10).

QALČIM Kzk. 19th c. **Qalčim** [Калчимъ] (SOV 114).

QALČINAY Bashk. **Qalčinay** [Калчинаевъ] (PSZRI XXV, 196). ✧ 'A kind of thick shoe'? cf. Turk. *qalčin (qalčin?)* 'dicke Schuhe' (Radl. II, 266) + suff. *-ay.*

QALDA Hak. 19th-20th c. **Qalda** [Калда] (HRS 349).

QALDAY Kzk. 19th c. **Qalday** [Калдай] (SOK 88, 202, 216); Kzk. 19th c. **Qalday** [Калдай] (SODž. 14). ⇨ **QAL I./ QAL II.** + suff. *-day.* See also **XAT-QALDAY**.

QALDAQPAN Tuv. 19th c. **Qaldaqpan** [Калдакпан], from the Moňγuš tribe (Proben IX, 110). ✧ I. 'Good-for-nothing; shameless' cf. *qaltaq* (Turk.) 'lüderliche Weibsperson, die Metze', (Kuman) 'die Kupplerin', Chag. *qaltaγ / qaltaq* 'der Taugenichts' (Radl. II, 259); II. 'Having the itch, mangy, scabby; weak, incapable' + Adj. suff. *-pan.*

QALDAN see **QALDAN**

QALDAN Kzk. 1846 **Qaldan** [Байтука Калданов], a biy (MKOP 154); Alt. 19th c. **Qaldan** [Калдан] (Verb., In. 117, 119); Alt. 19th c. **Qaldan-qān** [Калданъ-Каанъ] (Verb., In. 103). ✧ 'Bald' cf. Alt. *qald'an* 'лысина; лысий' (OjrRS). See also **KEČÄL, KELEŠ, TAZ**.

QALDAN-ČERÜ Alt. 19th c. **Qaldan-čerü** [Калдан-Черю], Oyrot's son (Verb., In. 119). ✧ I. 'Bald warrior' cf. Alt. *qald'an* 'лысина; лысий' (OjrRS); II. 'Hurrying / flustered warrior' cf. Alt. *qaltañ* 'суетливый' (OjrRS). ⇨ **QALDAN / QALTAN?** + **ČERÜ**.

QALDAR Kirg. 20th c. **Qaldar** [Калдар] (Kalilov 95); Kzk. 19th c. **Qaldar-bey / Qaldar-biy** [Калдаръ-бей (-бий)], Chinggis Khan's „bey" in the Kazak tradition (IOAIÊK XIX, 133, Potanin, Pred. 50). ✧ '(Born with) Spots, Birthmarks' (Kalilov 95). ⇨ **QAL II.** + aff. plur. *-dar / -lar.*

QALDAW Kzk. 19th c. **Qaldaw** [Калдау] (SODž. 18, 118).

QALDAZÏN Tuv. 19th c. **Qaldazïn** [Калдазын] (Proben IX, 202).

QALDÏ Kzk. 19th c. **Xaldï-bay** [Ахсанъ Халдибаевъ] (Grod., Pril. 198); Kzk. 1884 **Xaldï-bay** [Баратъ Халдибаевъ] (Grod., Pril. 131); Kzk. 1884 **Xaldï-bay** [Халдибай] (Grod., Pril. 99); Chuv. 18th-19th c. **Kaldi-bay** [Калдибай] (Magn. 49); Kzk. 19th c. **Qaldï-bay / Qalda-bay (<Qaldï-bay)** [Калдабай] (SOK 192); Kzk. **Qaldï-bay** [Мамырбай Калдыбаев] (TV 1878, 186); Kzk. 1819 **Qaldï-bay** [Калдыбай] (MIK IV, 323); Kzk. 19th c. **Qaldï-bay** [Калдыбай] (SOK 30, 56, 62, 128, 194); Kzk. 19th c. **Qaldï-bay**

[Калдыбай] (AOAtb. 62); Kzk. 19th c. **Qaldï-bay** [Джанбай Калдыбаевъ] (SKSO II, 17); Kzk. 19th c. **Qaldï-bay** [Нурумбетъ Калдыбаевъ] (Grod., Pril. 142); Kuman 1361 **Qaldï-bek** [Калдибекъ], a ruler of the Horde (PSRL (Russk. Hr.) I, 411); Kzk. 1786 **Qaldu-bay** (<Qaldï-bay) [Калдубай] (MIK IV, 75); Uzb. 20th c. **Qâldï-qïz** [Қолдиқиз], fem. (Begmatov 1984, 207). ✧ I. 'Remained; survived' such names were given when a child got well after a serious illness (Sattarov); II. 'Having birth marks'. ⇨ QAL I. / QAL II.? / QALLĬ. See also QALDĬQ; DRUS-QALDĬ.

QALDĬ-BÖK Alt. 19th-20th c. **Qaldï-bök** [Калдыбӧк], fem. (OjrRS 212). ⇨ QALDĬ?

QALDĬQ Chuv. 18th-19th c. **Kalduk** [Калдукъ] (Magn. 49); Kzk. 19th c. **Qaldïq** [Сенгсалъ Калдыковъ] (Grod., Pril. 130); Tat. 1731 **Qaldïq(a)?** [Калдыка], fem. (MIB III, 284); Kzk. 19th c. **Qalduq** [Пиръ-Назаръ Калдуковъ] (Grod., Pril. 45). ✧ 'The remained (child); the rest/remainder; we stayed'. ⇨ QAL I.

QALDUQ see **QALDĬQ**

QALÄ-AYAQ Kzk. 19th c. **Qalä-ayaq** [Каляаякъ] (SOV 88). ⇨ QALA? + AYAQ.

QALÄNDAR see **QALÄNDÄR**

QALÄNDÄR Trkm. 20th c. **Ғalandar** [Galandar] (Zaj. 1971, 325); Trkm. 20th c. **Ғalandar** [Галандар / ;Каландар] (TrkmRS 145); Kzk. 19th c. **Qalandar** [Каландаръ] (Grod., Pril. 161); Uzb. 20th c. **Qalandar** [Қаландар] (UzbRS); Kzk. 19th c. **Qaländär** [Каляндаровъ] (SKSO VIII, 226); Kzk. 19th c. **Qaländär-batïr** [قلندار باطر / Каляндяръ-батыръ] (Veselovskij, Kirg. 13), Trkm. 1741 **Qaländer-bek** [Каляндер-бек], a vekil (minister?) from Merv (MIT II, 163); Uzb. 1816 **Qalendär** [Мирза Календаръ] (Moskal'cev 58); Kzk. 19th c. **Qalender** [Календеръ] (SOK 260). ✧ 'Bohemian, unconventional person; (originally) wandering mendicant dervish dervish/monk' cf. Turk. *kalender* 'id.' (TED), Turk. *qaländär* 'ein Kalender, Derwisch, Bettelmönch' (Radl. II, 236), Uzb. *qalandar* 'каландар, странствующий дерниш' (UzbRS), Trkm. *γalandar* 'странствующий дерниш; нищий, бродяга; отшельник' (TrkmRS) (//P. //Ar.). See also QARA-QALÄNDER.

QALÄNDER see **QALÄNDÄR**

QALE Kzk. **Qale** [Kale], fem. (Levšin III, 96).

QALENDAR see **QALÄNDÄR**

QALENDER see **QALÄNDÄR**

QALҒAN Chuv. 18th-19th c. **Kalgan** [Калганъ] (Magn. 49). ✧ 'He remained (survived), he is alive'. See also QALDĬ, QALDĬQ, QAL I.

QALҒĀЈĬQ Tuv. 19th c. **Qalγāǰïq** [Калвацык] (Proben IX, 82, 94).

QALĬ see **ALĬ**

QALĬM see **QALĬM II.**

QALĬMAN Bulg. **Qaliman / Qalïman?** [Καλιμᾶνος] (Byz. Turc. 147).

QALĬME Kzk. **Qalime** [Калимэ], fem. (ZIRGOGeogr. I, 440). ✧ Halima (Ar.) 'patient, tolerant', fem. of Halim (Ahmed).

QALĬN Hak. 19th-20th c. **Qalin** [Калин] (HRS 349).

QALĬS Bashk. 1735 **Qalis** [Атикей Калисевъ], a tarχan (Vel.-Zern., Bašk. 23); Kzk. 19th c. **Qalis-pay** [Калеспай] (SODž. 22). ✧ Khalis (Ar.) 'pure, true, real' (Ahmed), cf. Tat. PNs *Xalis, Ғalis, Qalis* (Sattarov).

QALĬ Bashk. 1711 **Qalï** [Калы Кусякин] (MIB III, 77); Kzk. 1817 **Qalï** [قالى / Калы] (MIK IV, 311); Kzk. 1817 **Qalï-bay** [قالى باى / Калыбай] (MIK IV, 313, 319); Kzk. 1823 **Qalï-bay** [قا لباى / Калыбай] (MIK IV, 455); Kzk. 19th c. **Qalï-bay** [Калыбай Кутыевъ] (SKSO VIII, 232); Kzk. 19th c. **Qalï-bay** [Калыбай Кутыевъ] (SODž. 98); Kzk. 19th c. **Qalï-bay** [Калыбай Кутыевъ] (SOK 56, 98); Kzk. 19th c. **Qalï-bay** [Калыбай Кутыевъ] (SOV 108); Kzk. 19th c. **Qalï-bay** [Калыбай Кутыевъ] (AOK 106); Kzk. 19th c. **Qalï-bay** [Калыбай Кутыевъ] (AOP 54); Kzk. 19th c. **Qalï-bek** [Полатъ Калыбековъ] (Grod., Pril. 174); Kzk. 19th c. **Qalï-bek** [Калыбекъ] (SOV 32); Kzk. 19th c. **Qalï-bek** [Калыбекъ] (SODž. 154); Kirg. 19th c. **Qalï-bek** [Калыбек] (Jud. 597); Kirg. 20th c. **Qalï-bek** (Kalilov 94); Kzk. 19th c. **Qalï-γul** [Калыгулъ] (SOV 16); Kzk. 19th c. **Qalï-qul** [Нурбай Калыкуловъ] (Grod., Pril. 172). ✧ I. 'Prophet Ali' (Žanuzakov-Espaeva) (<Ar.); II. '(Black) Spot, Birthmark' (Kalilov 95)? ⇨ QALĬ / ALĬ? See also BIR-QALĬ.

QALĬČ Kkalp. 1740 **Qalïč-bi** [Калыч-би], from the Mañγït tribe (MIKk. 208).

QALĬY see **ALĬY**

QALĬYMAN Kirg. **Qalïyman** [Калыйман], fem. (Jud. 70).

QALĬYPA see **XALĬFA**

QALĬQ Kzk. 19th c. **Qalik?** [Турсунбай Каликовъ] (Grod., Pril. 57); Kzk. 19th c. **Qalïq** [Калыкъ] (SOK 56, 112, 300); Kzk. 19th c. **Qalïq** [Калыкъ] (AOK 2); Kzk. 19th c. **Qalïq** [Калыкъ] (SOV 114); Kzk. 19th c. **Qalïq-pay** [Калыкпай] (SOK 200, 246); Kzk. 19th c. **Qaluq** [Калукъ] (SOV 112). ✧ Khaliq (Ar.) 'most qualified, suitable (for)' or Khāliq 'the Creator' an epithet of Allah (Ahmed). See also ÄBDĬ-QALĬQ.

QALĬQ-BERGEN see **XALĬQ-BERGÄN**

QALĬQĬM Kzk. 19th c. **Qalïqïm-bay** [Каликимбай] (SOK 244). ⇨ QALĬQ? + poss. suff. -*im*.

QALĬM I. Uyg. 12th c. -14th c. **Qalïm** [Kalım] (Radl., USp. 85, DTS, EUTS).

QALĬM II. Tat. 1791 **Qalim** [Сеит (Сагит) Калимов] (MIB V, 305); Tat. 1791 **Qalim** [Хамит

Калимов] (MIB V, 305); Kzk. 19th c. **Qalim** [Калимъ] (SOK 270); Kzk. 19th c. **Qalim-bek** [Калимбекъ] (SOV 80); Kzk. 19th c. **Qalïm** [Калымъ] (AOA 70, 74). ✧ 'Kalym (money paid by the bridegroom to the bride's family)' cf. Chag. *qalim*, Hak., Tat. *qalïm*, Alt., Hak., Kirg., Kzk. *qalïm* 'das Kaufgeld, das der Vater für die Tochter erhält' (Radl. II, 242, 247, 249).

QALÏMBET Bashk. 1798 **Qalïmbet** [Калимбетъ] (PSZRI XXV, 195); Kkalp. 20th c. **Qalïmbet** [Къалимбет / Калымбет / Қалымбет] (Bask., Kkalp. 15, 79, KkRS 774). ⇨ **QAL-MUXAMED.**

QALÏMDU Uyg. 12th c. - 14th **Qalïmdu** [Kalımtu] (Radl., USp. 98-99, Radl., Altuig. 59, DTS, EUTS); Uyg. 13th-14th c. **Qalïmdu-totoq** [Qalïmdu Totoq] (Zieme, Mat. II, 93).

QALÏMET Tat. 1496 **Qalïmet** [Калиметъ], a prince from Kazan (PSRL VI, 40-41, VIII, 231-32). ⇨ **QALÏMBET?**

QALÏN Kzk. 19th c. **Qalïn** [Каленъ] (SODž. 62); Tat. 1722 **Qalïn-bay** [Калынбай] (MIB I, 116); Bashk. 1709 **Qalïn-bay** [Юлай Калынбаев] (MIB III, 45); Selj.? 1133 **Qalïn-oγlï** [Καλλινογλῆς], a commander of the army (Byz. Turc. 147). ✧ 'Thick' cf. Uyg., Crm., Hak., Tat., Turk. *qalïn* 'dick, dicht, zahlreich' (Radl. II, 243), Kuman, Alt., Hak., Kzk. *qalïñ* 'dick, dicht' (Radl. II, 241).

QALÏÑ see **QALÏN**

QALÏÑ-QARA Uyg. **Qalïñ-qara** [Kalıng Kara] (EUTS). ✧ 'Thick-Black'. ⇨ **QALÏN + QARA?**

QALÏÑ-QARA-AČÏ Uyg. 12th c. - 14th c. **Qalïñ-qara-ačï** [qalïŋ qara ačï] (DTS). ✧ 'Thick-Black-Old-woman' cf. Karakh. *ačï* 'пожилая женщина' (DTS). ⇨ **QALÏN + QARA.**

QALÏŠ Kzk. 19th c. **Qalïš** [Калышъ] (SOK 218); Kzk. 19th c. **Qalïš** [Калышъ], fem. (Grod., Pril. 155); Kzk. 1845 **Qalïš-bay** [Джиланбаш Калышбаев] (MKOP 155); Kzk. 19th c. **Qalïš-pek** [Калышпекъ] (SOK 140). ⇨ **QALÏ, QALÏŠ?**

QALQA Kzk. 19th c. **Qalqa** [Калка] (SOV 10); Kzk. 19th c. **Qalqa** [Калка] (SODž. 94); Kzk. 19th c. **Qalqa** [Калка] (SOK 178); Kzk. 19th c. **Qalqa-bay** [Калкабай] (SODž. 8, 52, 54, 130); Kzk. 19th c. **Qalqa-bay** [Калкабай] (SOK 72, 152, 200); Kzk. 19th c. **Qalqa-bay** [Калкабай] (SOV 38, 80); Kzk. 19th c. **Qalqa-bay** [Калкабай] (AOK 22); Kzk. 19th c. **Qalqa-bek** [Калкабекъ] (SOK 34, 140). ✧ 'Defence' cf. Hak.(Kacha), Kzk. *qalqa* 'der Schutz' (Radl. II, 250), Mo. *qalqa* 'shield, protection' (Gy. Kara). ⇨ **QALQAN?**

QALQAQ Kzk. 19th c. **Qalqaq** [Калкакъ Игарбаевъ] (SKSO III, 191). ✧ 'Little defence'. ⇨ **QALQA?** + suff. *-q.*

QALQAM-BAY see **QALQAN**

QALQAMAN Tat. 20th c. **Qalqaman** [Калкаманов] (Sattarov); Bashk. 1756 **Qalqaman** [Чюрагул Калкаманов] (MIB IV/1, 128); Bashk. 1761 **Qalqaman** [Калкаман Аскаров] (MIB IV/1, 218); Bashk. 1770 **Qalqaman** [Калкаман Араптанов] (MIB IV/1, 341); Bashk. 1770, 1791 **Qalqaman** [Калкаман Бускунов] (MIB IV/1, 343, V, 313); Bashk. 1788 **Qalqaman** [Карашай Калкаманов] (MIB V, 233); Kzk. 19th c. **Qalqaman** [Калкаманъ] (Potanin II, 6); Kkalp. 20th c. **Qalqaman** [Къалкъаман] (Bask., Kkalp. 99, KkRS 774); Kirg. **Qalqaman** [Калкаманъ] (Proben V, 48 /49/, 225 /227/). ✧ 'Man with shield' (Sattarov). ⇨ **QALQA?, QALQAN?** + suff. *-man.*

QALQAN Kzk. 19th c. **Qalγan** [Калганъ] (SOK 86); Kzk. 19th c. **Qalqam-bay** (<Qalqan-bay) [Калкамбай] (SOV 4); Tat.(Lit.) 1554 **Qalqan** [Калканъ] (Kn. Metriki Lit. 103); Bashk. 1745 **Qalqan** [Калкан Араптанов] (MIB III, 426); Kzk. 19th c. **Qalqan** [Калканъ] (SODž. 118); Kzk. 19th c. **Qalqan** [Калканъ] (SOV 52); Kzk. 19th c. **Qalqan** [Калканъ] (AOAtb. 38); Kzk. 19th c. **Qalqan** [Калканъ] (AOO 46). ✧ 'Shield' cf. Crm., Kar., Tat., Turk. *qalqan* 'der Schield' (Radl. II, 151). See also **AĞÏŠ-QALQAN-AM.**

QALQAŠ Tat. 20th c. **Qalqaš** [Калкашов] (Sattarov); Bashk. 1777 **Qalqaš** [Ерлыкап (Ерлыкан) Калкашев] (MIB V, 52, 233).

QALQÏŠ Bashk. 1757 **Qalqïš** [Калкиш Стенкин] (MIB IV/1, 157).

QALLÏ see **QALLÏ**

QALLÏ Trkm. 20th c. **Xalli** [Халли] (TrkmRS 685); Trkm. 20th c. **Xalli** [Халли], fem. (TrkmRS 685); Trkm. 20th c. **Xallï** [Халлы] (Sopieva 181); Trkm. 20th c. **Xallï** [Hallï], fem. (Zaj. 1971, 341); Trkm. 20th c. **Xallï-gözel** [Hallï Gözel] (Zaj. 1971, 336); Trkm. 20th c. **Xällï** [Халли], fem. (TrkmRS 685); Trkm. 20th c. **Xollï-gözel / Xallï-gözel?** [Холлыгәзел] (Sopieva 181); Kkalp. 20th c. **Qalli** [Калли] (Bask., Kkalp. 20, 47, 53); Kkalp. **Qalli-gül** [Qalli-gül / цветок Калли], fem. (Baskakov: OSA 140); Kkalp. 20th c. **Qälli** [Кәлли] (KkRS 774); Kkalp. 20th c. **Qälli-bek** [Кәллибек] (KkRS 774); Kkalp. 20th c. **Qälli-biyke** [Кәллибийке], fem. (KkRS 778); Kkalp. 20th c. **Qälli-gül** [Кәллигүл], fem. (KkRS 778); Kkalp. 20th c. **Qälli-qïz** [Кәлликыз], fem. (KkRS 778). ✧ 'Having birthmark; born with a birthmark' cf. Trkm. *χälli* 'с родинкой, имеющий родинку' (TrkmRS). ⇨ **QAL II.** + suff. *-lï / -li.*

QALLÏQAN Kkalp. 20th c. **Qallïqan** [Къаллыкъан / Қаллыкан], fem. (Bask., Kkalp. 403, KkRS 778). ⇨ **QALLÏ** + suff. *-qan(1).*

QALMAČ see **QALMAŠ**

QALMAQAY Bashk. 1731 **Qalmaqay** [Калмакай] (MIB III, 289); Bashk. 1740 **Qalmaqay** [Калмакай Сараманов] (MIB I, 405); Bashk. 1762 **Qalmaqay** [Калмакай Уптынов] (MIB IV/2, 302); Bashk. 1772 **Qalmaqay** [Махмут Калмакаев] (MIB IV/2, 408); Bashk. 1737 **Qalmaney? / Qalmaqay?** [Калмакай / Калманей? Туккулов] (MIB I, 325, 326). ⇨ **QALMAQ** + suff. *-ay*.

QALMAQAN Kkalp. 20th c. **Qalmaqan** [Къалмакъан / Қалмақан] (Bask., Kkalp. 400, KkRS 774). ⇨ **QALMAQ?** + suff. *-an / -qan?*

QALMAQÏ Kzk. 19th c. **Qalmaqï?** [Kalmaky Bulatov / Калмакы Булатовъ (?)] (AUK 183).

QALMAN Kzk. 19th c. **Xalman** [Халманъ] (Grod., Pril. 167); Kzk. 19th c. **Xalman** [Халманъ Бекмухамедовъ] (SKSO III, 18); Uzb. 1875 **Xalman-bay** [Халъ-Манбаевъ] (Moskal'cev 48); Uzb. 19th c. **Xalmen** [Абдулкадыръ Халменов] (SKSO III, 172); Kzk. 19th c. **Xaman** [Хаманъ] (SKSO VIII, 230); Bashk. **Qalman** [Калманъ] (PSZRI XX, 736); Kzk. 19th c. **Qalman? / Qalmïn?** [Кальменъ] (SOV 146); Bashk. **Qalman-bï** [Kalman bï] (Mészáros, MH 98); Bashk. 1798 **Qalman-qul** [Калманкул] (PSZRI XXV, 196). ⇨ **QAL II.** + suff. *-man*.

QALMANEY? see **QALMAQAY**

QALMAŠ Bashk. 1728 **Qalmač** [Калмачко] (MIB I, 126); Tat. 20th c. **Qalmaš** [Калмаш (Калмыш)] (Sattarov). ⇨ **QALMÏŠ?** See also **SARÏ-QALMAŠ.**

QALMAŠ-BAŠ Bashk. 1718 **Qalmaš-baš** [Калмашбаш] (MIB III, 179). ⇨ **QALMAŠ + BAŠ.**

QALMATAY Bashk. 1812 **Qalmatay** [Калматай] (ŽS IV, 357). ⇨ **QAL I. / QAL II.** + **MATAY?**

QALMET Kzk. 18th c. **Qalmet-naq? (<Qalmet-inaq?)** [Кальметьнакъ] (Nepljuev 813). ✧ Shortened-contracted of *Qal-muχamed*, cf. Tat. PN *Qalmät* under *Qalmöχämmät* (Sattarov). ⇨ **QAL-MUXAMED.**

QALMET-NAQ see **QALMET**

QALMÏQ Trkm. 20th c. **Ғalmïq** [Galmïq] (Zaj. 1971, 325); Trkm. 20th c. **Ғalmïq** [Калмык] (TrkmRS 148); Chuv., Tat. 18th-19th c. **Kalmak / Kalmek** [Калмакъ / Калмякъ] (Magn. 49); Chuv. 18th-19th c. **Kalmïk** [Калмыкъ] (Magn. 49); Bashk. 1706 **Qalmaq** [Калмак Кулапаков] (MIB III, 25); Bashk. 1727 **Qalmaq** [Игибай Калмаков] (MIB III, 243); Bashk. 1735 **Qalmaq** [Калмакъ], a tarχan (Vel.-Zern., Bašk. 25); Bashk. 1754 **Qalmaq** [Калмак Ибрашев] (MIB IV/1, 83); Bashk. 1757 **Qalmaq** [Калмак (Калмык) Кусябяев] (MIB IV/1, 150, 153); Bashk. 1760 **Qalmaq** [Калмак Темирев] (MIB IV/1, 195); Bashk. 1772 **Qalmaq** [Танатар Калмаков] (MIB IV/2, 405); Bashk. 1789 **Qalmaq** [Калмак Бердыгулов] (MIB V, 259, 272); Bashk. 1792 **Qalmaq** [Ибрай Калмаков] (MIB V, 319); Kzk. 19th c. **Qalmaq** [Калмакъ] (AOK 102); Kzk. 19th c. **Qalmaq** [Калмакъ] (AOAtb. 62); Hak. 19th-20th c. **Qalmaq** [Калмак] (HRS 349); Kzk. 19th c. **Qalmaq-bay** [Калмакбай] (SODž. 34); Bashk. 1736 **Qalmaq-čura** [Чурюбатыр Калмакчюрин] (MIB III, 352); Bashk. 1706 **Qalmaq-qul** [Капай Калмаккулов] (MIB III, 30); Bashk. 1707 **Qalmaq-qul** [Калмаккул Апаков] (MIB III, 31); Bashk. 1778 **Qalmaq-qul** [Калмаккул Калтюков] (MIB V, 66); Bashk. 1779 **Qalmaq-qul** [Калмаккулов] (MIB V, 91); Tat. 1737 **Qalmaq-mulla** [Калмак мулла] (MIB I, 315); Bashk. 1737 **Qalmaq-mulla** [Калмак (Калмык) Явкеев] (MIB III, 360); Nog. 1802 **Qalmïq-murza** [Калмыкъ мурза Ораковъ] (Sergeev 77). ✧ 'Kalmyk' (Ethnonym) cf. Tat. *qalmïq* 'der Kalmücke, Westmongole', Turk. *qalmuq* 'id.' (Radl. II, 273), Chag., Alt.(Tel.), East.T., Kzk. *qalmaq* 'der Kalmücke der Westmongolei (die Kirgisen [=Kazaks] nennen so die Bewohner des Altai: die Altaier und die Teleuten)' (Radl. II, 272-73).

QALMÏQAN Kkalp. 20th c. **Qalmïqan** [Къалмыкъан] (Bask., Kkalp. 41). ⇨ **QALMÏQ?** + suff. *-an / -qan?*

QALMÏŠ Tat. 20th c. **Qalmïš** [Калмыш / Калмаш] (Sattarov); Bashk. 18th c. **Qalmïš** [Калмышев] (MIB V, 88). ✧ 'He remained (survived), he is alive' (Sattarov). ⇨ **QAL I.**

QALNAMAN Bashk. 1782 **Qalnaman** [Силибика Калнаманова], fem. (MIB V, 131).

QALP Bashk. 1735 **Qalp-qul** [Смаилъ Калпкуловъ] (Vel.-Zern., Bašk. 24). ✧ 'Untrue, sham; false' cf. Crm., Turk. *qalp* (Ar.) 'falsch, nechgemacht, unecht' (Radl. II, 268).

QALPAQ Trkm. 20th c. **Galpaq** [Galpaq] (Zaj. 1971, 330); Trkm. 20th c. **Galpaq** [Галпак] (TrkmRS 148); Kzk. 19th c. **Qalpaq** [Калпак] (SODž. 10); Kzk. **Qalpaq / Qolpaq?** [Колпакъ Куртаевъ] (Konšin, Po Ust'-kamenog. uezdu: Pam. kn. Semip., 1900, p. 28); Kzk. 19th c. **Qalpaq / Qolpaq?** [Колпакъ] (SOK 296). ✧ I. 'A kind of fur cap' cf. Alt.(Tel.), Crm., Kzk., Tat., Turk. *qalpaq* 'eine Art Mütze' (Radl. II, 268); II. 'Hair on the head of the child until the first cut' cf. Trkm. *γalpaq* 'волосы на голове ребенка (до первой стрижки' (TrkmRS). See also **AQ-QALPAQ.**

QALPE Kzk. 19th c. **Qalpe-bay (Qalpa-bay?)** [Кальпебай] (SOK 208). ✧ 'Master; caliph'? cf. Turk. *qalfa* (Ar.) 'Maurer master, Ladendiener' (Radl. II, 272).

QALSEK Kzk. 19th c. **Qalsek?** [Яалсекъ] (SODž. 50).

QALTAQ Oghuz/Trkm. 13th c. **Qaltaq** [قلتاق / Калтак] (Abulg./Kon. 1240). ✧ 'Good-for-nothing, shameless, layabout' cf. Kuman, Chag. *qaltaq* 'lüderliche Weibsperson, unnützes Frauenzimmer, die Metze; der Taugenichts' (Radl. II, 259).

QALTAN Kzk. 1825 **Qaltan** [قالطان / Калтан] (MIK IV, 469, 476). ✧ 'Hurrying / flustered' cf. Alt. *qaltañ* 'суетливый' (OjrRS).

QALTARAQ   Hak.(Blt.) 19th-20th c. **Qaltaraq** [Калтарак] (Proben IX, 556).

QALTÏBRAY   Kzk. 19th c. **Qaltïbray** [Калтыбрай] (SOK 200).

QALTÏRČAQ   Bashk. 1751 **Qaltïrčaq** [Калтырчак] (MIB IV/1, 43). ✧ 'Little shaky' (Rásonyi, Imp. 240).

QALTUQ   Bashk. 1778 **Qaltuq** [Калмаккул Калтюков] (MIB V, 66).

QALU see **ALİ**

QALUQ I.   Hak. 19th-20th c. **Qaluq** [Калук], fem. (HRS 353).

QALUQ II.   Kzk. 19th c. **Qaluq** [Калукъ] (SOV 112). ⇨ **QALÏQ?**

QALZAN   Tuv. 19th c. **Qalzan / Qalzaň** [Калзан / Калзаң] (Proben IX, 149, 165).

QALŽİR   Kzk. 19th c. **Qalžir-bay?** [Калжир-бай] (SODž. 64).

QAM   Kzk. 19th c. **Qam-bay** [Камбай] (SODž. 144); Uzb. 19th c. **Qam-bay** [Камбай] (SKSO III, 178); Maml. 1467/68 **Qam-bek** [قمبك الحمدى] (Iyās II, 81, 84-87); Selj. **Qam-eri** [قَمَرى / قمارى] (Āšikp. 5, Seādeddīn I, 15); Selj.? 1085 **Qam-eri?** [Καμύρης], a Turkic (Seljuk?) commander of the army, the forefather of the Ottoman dynasty? (Byz. Turc. 148); Selj.? 12th c. **Qam-eri?** [Καμύρης], a servant of Turkic (Seljuk) origin (Byz. Turc. 148); Oghuz/Trkm. 14th c. - 15th c. **Qam-ɣan / Qam-χan** [قَامْ غَان / Qam Ġān / Kam Xan / Кам-Ган] (DQorq./Rossi 100, 160, 202, DQorq. 14); Kzk. 19th c. **Qam-pek** [Кампекъ] (SODž. 158); *TN:* Hak.? 19th-20th c. **Qam-pay(skoe)** [Кампаиское], a lake or a settlement (Karta JAR IV). ✧ 'Shaman, doctor' cf. Uyg., Kuman, Alt., Hak. *qam* 'der Schaman' (Radl. II, 476); cf. also Németh, HMK 138: *Palamōn Kam.* See also **ALAŠ.**

QAM-PÜDÄGÄY   Tuv. 19th c. **Qam-püdägäy-tayǰi** [Кам-пÿдагäi], a prince (Proben IX, 164). ⇨ **QAM.**

QAMAY   Tat. 1552 **Qamay** [Камай], a murza from Kazan (PSRL VI, 306); Tat. 1624 **Qamay** [Камай Дербышевъ] (Pokrovskij 71); Tat.(Mish.) **Qamay** [Камаевъ] (IOAIÊK XIX, 143); Bashk. 1706 **Qamay** [Баймет Камаев] (MIB III, 17); Bashk. 1731 **Qamay** [Камай] (MIB III, 289); Bashk. 1757 **Qamay** [Сюлюк Камаев] (MIB IV/1, 138); Hak.(Kyz.) 1715 **Qamay** [Камай], a prince from the Qamlar tribe of the Kyzyls (Jarilov, Kyz. 10); Tat. 1552 **Qamay-murza** [Камай мурза], when taking Kazan he sided with the Russians (Zolotn. 157); Tat.(Mish.) **Qamay-murza** [Камай мурза] (IOAIÊK XIX, 143); *TN:* Chuv.? / Tat.? 18th c. **Kamay(eva)** [Камаева], a village in the district of Cheboksary (Korsakov 281). ⇨ **QAM?** + suff. -*ay.*

QAMAQ   Uyg. 1339 **Qamaq**, fem. (Chwol., Syr.-nest. 93); Hak.? 19th-20th c. **Qamaq** [Камак], fem. (Katanov, Otč. 10). ✧ 'Forehead' (Katanov) cf. Uyg.,

Alt., Hak. *qamaq* 'die Stiern' (Radl. II, 479).

QAMAQ-PER   Kzk. 19th c. **Qamaq-per** [Камакперъ] (SODž. 154). ⇨ **QAMAQ + BER?**

QAMAQAY   Bashk. 1706 **Qamaqay** [Трупберда Камакаев] (MIB III, 29); Bashk. 1706 **Qamaqay** [Камакай Беккулов] (MIB III, 25); Bashk. 1706 **Qamaqay** [Кусяк Камакаев] (MIB III, 25); Bashk. 1707 **Qamaqay** [Косяк Камакаев] (MIB III, 31); Bashk. 1740 **Qamaqay / Qamakey?** [Камакеев] (MIB III, 411, 412). ⇨ **QAMAQ?** + suff. -*ay.*

QAMAN see **QABAN**

QAMANAY   Bashk. 1735 **Qamanay** [Каманай Кошаевъ] (Vel.-Zern., Bašk. 20). ⇨ **QAMAN** + suff. -*ay.*

QAMAŇ-KÖS   Kirg. **Qamaň-kös** [Kamang Kös / Каман Köc] (Proben V, 111 /112/). ⇨ **QABAN + KÖZ.**

QAMAR   Uzb. 1918 **Qamar-ǰan** [Kamar-Djan], a Sart woman (Nazaroff 43). ✧ 'Moon' cf. Crm. *qamär* (Ar.) 'der Mond' (Radl. I, 482).

QAMAS   Bashk. 1732, 1738 **Qamas** [Урускул Камасев] (MIB III, 296, 391).

QAMAŠ   Tat. 1619 **Qamaš** [قماش / Камаш] (Jusupov 72); Kzk. 19th c. **Qamaš** [Камашъ] (SOK 266). ✧ 'Fade, weaken, fall' cf. Az., Crm., Kar., Turk. *qamaš-* 'seine Kräfte verlieren, matt werden etc.' (Radl. II, 481).

QAMAT   Hak. 19th-20th c. **Qamat** [Камат] (HRS 349). ✧ 'Praised, praiseworthy' (<Ar.) (Butanaev).

QAMAW   Kzk. 19th c. **Qamaw** [Камау] (SOK 272); Kzk. 19th c. **Qamaw-bay** [Камау бай] (SOK 278). ✧ 'Driving in, surrounding; catching, grasping'? cf. Kzk. *qamaw* 'окружить, осадить; загнать (скот) в загон' (KzRS).

QAMBAR   Bashk. 1600 **Qambar** [Мангутай Комбаров] (Miller, Ist. Sib. II, 158, 159); Kzk. **Qambar** [Камбар], Waq's (Uaq's) son, Er-kökšü's father (Proben III, 88 /112/); Kirg. **Qambar** [Камбар] (Proben V, 190); Uzb. 19th c. **Qambar-bek** [Kambar-bek], a Sart (Nalivkin-Dozon 212); Chag. / Uzb. 1507 **Qambar-bek** [Камбар-бек, Камбар-бий], an emir (MIT II, 42-44, 48, 50, 51, 54, 55); Chag. / Uzb. 1507 **Qambar-biy** [Камбар-бек, Камбар-бий], an emir (MIT II, 42-44, 48, 50, 51, 54, 55); Trkm.? 1598 **Qambar-χan** [Камбар-хан], ruler of Guriyan from the Šamlï (Šamlu) clan (MIT II, 99); Kirg. **Qambar-qan** [Камбар Кан] (Radl. I, 450); Kzk. 19th c. **Qamber-bek** [Камбербекъ] (SODž. 20); *EN:* Kzk. 18th c. - 19th c. **Qambar** [Камбар] (Tynyšp. 68). ✧ 'Servants; faithful servant; inseparable companion'? cf. Crm., Kar. *qambar,* Turk. *qanbar* 'das Hausgesinde, die Dienerschaft' (Radl. II, 131, 496), Turk. *kamber* (Ar.) 'faithful servant; inseparable companion' (TED).; ✧ 'Servant, maid' cf. Crm., Kar. *qambar = qanbar* (Radl.

II, 496), Turk. *qanbar* 'das Hausgesinde, die Dienerschaft' (Radl. II, 131).

QAMBER see **QAMBAR**

QAMBET Kzk. 19th c. **Qambet** [Турумбатъ Камбетовъ] (Grod., Pril. 141).

QAMBÏL Kzk. 19th c. **Qambïl-bay** [Камбылбай] (SODž. 92). ✧ 'Hump, hunchback' cf. Turk. *qambil* 'der Buckel' (Radl. II, 496).

QAMBÏZ Bashk. 1737 **Qambïz** [Камбыз] (MIB I, 325).

QAMBUQTU Uyg. **Qambuqdu** [Kambukdu] (EUTS); Uyg. 12th c. -14th c. **Qambuqtu-tutuň** [Qambuqdu Tutung] (Radl., USp. 85, DTS).

QAMDU Alt. 19th-20th c. **Qamdu** [Камду] (OjrRS 208). ✧ 'Otter' (OjrRS).

QAMER Turk. 1500 **Qamer-šah-ҳatun** [Kamerşâh Hatun], fem. (Gökb., Ed., 436). ✧ Qamar (Ar.) 'Moon' (Ahmed).

QAMĪ'AY see **QAMQAY**

QAMĪS Hak. 19th-20th c. **Qamis** [Камис] (HRS 349). ✧ 'Careful, provider' (<A.) (Butanaev).

QAMÏQ Yak. 1645 **Qamïq** [Камыкъ], a prince (DAI III, 36).

QAMÏN Kzk. 19th c. **Qamïn** [Камынъ] (SOK 128). ✧ 'Clutch! Cling!'? cf. Alt., Hak. *qamïn-* 'sich festhalten, sich anklammern, etwas ergreifen, um sich fest zu halten' (Radl. II, 484).

QAMÏR Tat. **Qamïr-batïr** [Камыр батыр], a hero in tales (Koşay: KCsA I, 324, TatRS 220). ✧ 'Paste, dough' cf. Kuman, Kzk., Tat. *qamïr* 'der Teig' (Radl. II, 485), Kzk. *qamïr* 'тесто' (KzRS).

QAMÏS see **QAMÏŠ**

QAMÏS-ABAQ Kzk. 19th c. **Qamïs-abaq** [Камысабакъ] (SOV 150). ⇨ **QAMÏŠ?** + **ABAQ.**

QAMÏŠ Chag. 16th c. **Qamiš** [Камиш], an emir (Ivanov 224); Chag. 16th c. **Qamiš-bahadur** [Камиш баҳадур] (Ivanov 295); Bashk. 1659 **Qamïs** [Урускилъ Камисовъ] (Vel.-Zern., Bašk. 38); Kzk. 19th c. **Qamïs-bay** [Камысбай] (AOK 54); Kkalp. 20th c. **Qamïs-bay** [Къамысбай / Қамысбай] (Bask., Kkalp. 400, KkRS 774); Kzk. 19th c. **Qamïs-pay** [Камыспай] (SODž. 82); Kzk. 19th c. **Qamïs-pay** [Камыспай] (SOK 248); Bashk. 1701 **Qamïš** [Поташ Камышев] (MIB III, 13); Bashk. 1707 **Qamïš** [Ижбулат Камышев] (MIB III, 40); Bashk. 1709 **Qamïš** [Камыш] (MIB I, 263); Kzk. 19th c. **Qamïš** [Камышъ] (SOV 104); Kzk. 19th c. **Qamïš** [Камышъ] (AOA 26); Trkm.? 1817 **Qamïš-bek** [Камыш-бек] (MIT II, 400); Kmk. 1828 **Qamïš-oҕlu** [Камыш Оглу] (MID III, 123); Kzk. 19th c. **Qams-pay** [Камыспай] (SOV 62); Kzk. 19th c. **Qams-pek** [Камыспекъ] (SODž. 152); *TN:* Kzk.? **Qamïš-bay** [Bamyš bai], a place at Lake Balkhash (Rekogn.). ✧ 'Reed' cf. Kzk. *qamïs* 'das Schilfrohr' (Radl. II, 486).

See also **YAŠ-QAMÏŠ.**

QAMÏT Kzk. **Qamït** [Камыт] (Proben III, 528 /604/); Kzk. 19th c. **Qamït-pay** [Камытпай] (SODž. 16). ✧ 'Yoke' cf. Tat. *qamït* (R.) 'das Kummet, Joch' (Radl. II, 486), <R. хомут 'id.'.

QAMQAY Kzk. 19th c. **Qamҕay** [Камгай] (SOK 90); Tat. 20th c. **Qamqay** [Камкаев] (Sattarov); Bashk. **Qamqay** [Тимир Камкаев] (MIB IV/1, 332). ✧ 'Little Shaman' cf. Tat. PN *Qamqay* (Sattarov). ⇨ **QAM** + dim. suff. *-qay.*

QAMLANČU Karakh. **Qamlančku** [Kamlançu] (MK/Atalay 842).

QAMRÏQ Kzk. 19th c. **Qamrïq** [Камрыкъ] (AOP 18). ⇨ **QAMÏR** + dim. suff. *-ïq.*

QAMUT Turk. 14th c. **Qamut** [Χαμύτης], a Turkish prince („Teilfürst") (Byz. Turc. 339).

QAMZŌL Hak.(Sag.) 19th-20th c. **Qamzōl** [Камзол] (Katanov, Otč. 8). ✧ 'Vest, waistcoat' cf. Hak.(Sag.) *qamzōl* (R.) 'ein Kamisol, eine Weste' (Radl. II, 496).

QAN Chuv. 18th-19th c. **Kan-bey** [Канбей] (Magn. 50); Chuv. 18th-19th c. **Kan-pay** [Канпай] (Magn. 50); Uyg. 12th c. - 14th c. **Qan** (DTS); Maml. 14th c. **Qan** [Кан] (Tuhfa 410); Hak.(Sag.) 19th-20th c. **Qan-arïҕ** [Кан Арыҥ / Кан Арыг], sister of the hero (Proben IX, 322, 324 etc., Radl. II, 105); Kzk. 1805 **Qan-baba** [Кан Баба], chieftain of the Nayman tribe of the Middle Horde (Orta Žüz) (MIK IV, 512); Kzk. 19th c. **Qan-baba** [Канъ-баба] (Potanin, Pred. 120); Tat. 1724 **Qan-bay** [Канбой Ишмаев] (MIB III, 228); Tat.(Sib.) 1599 **Qan-bay** [Канбай (Ханбай) Измаиловъ], a Siberian murza (AI II, 17, 22); Kzk. 19th c. **Qan-bay** [Канбай] (SOK 60); Nog. 1649 **Qan-bay** [Абла мурза Канбаевъ] (AI IV, 87); Kirg. **Qan-čoro** [Канчоро] (Jud. 38, 89, 209, 909); Bashk. 1735 **Qan-čur** [Канчуръ Теникеевъ], a tarҳān (Vel.-Zern., Bašk. 14); Tat. 1600 **Qan-čura** [Устемир Канчюрин] (MIB I, 152); Bashk. 1734, 1735 **Qan-čura** [Канчира], a tarҳān (Vel.-Zern., Bašk. 15, 20); Kkalp. 20th c. **Qan-jan** [Къанджан] (Bask., Kkalp. 98); Crm. **Qan-efendi** [Кан Äфäнди] (Proben VII, 169); Uyg. 12th c. - 14th c. **Qan-elči** [Kan elçi] (DTS, EUTS); Hak.(Sag.) 19th-20th c. **Qan-ergäk** [Кан Ергäк], a folklore hero (Proben IX, 322-27); Shor 19th-20th c. **Qan-ergek** [Qān Ergek], a „čïltïs" who was an „älïp" before (Dyrenkova 282); Kzk. 19th c. **Qan-etey** [Канетей] (SOV 22); Tat.(Sib.) 1631 **Qan-ҕulï?** [Ангилдей Кангулин] (Miller, Ist. Sib. II, 385, 391); Kzk. 19th c. **Qan-ҳoja** [Канходжа Даніяровъ] (Grod., Pril. 182); Hak. 19th-20th c. **Qan-märgän** [Кан-Мäргäн] (Radl. II, 105); Hak.(Kacha) 19th-20th c. **Qan-mergän** [Кан-Мергäн] (Radl. I, 1217); Hak.(Sag.) 19th-20th c. **Qan-mökkö** [Кан Мöккö] (Radl. I, 948); Tat. 1764 **Qan-murza** [Канмурза Атесев] (MIB IV/1, 291); Bashk. 1706 **Qan-murza** [Канмурза] (MIB III, 27); Bashk.

1735 **Qan-murza** [Канмурза Атдагуловъ] (Vel.-
Zern., Bašk. 19); Nog. 1649 **Qan-murza** [Канъ мурза
Чинъ-мурзинъ] (AI IV, 92); Uyg. **Qan-oɣlu** [Kan-
oġlu] (EUTS); Uyg. 12th c. - 14th c. **Qan-oɣul** (Radl.,
USp. 24-25, DTS); Hak. 19th-20th c. **Qan-ōlaq** (Radl.
II, 105); Hak. 19th-20th c. **Qan-pärgän** [Кан Пäргäн]
(Radl. III, 1981); Uyg. 12th c. - 14th c. **Qan-toyïn** [Kan
Toyın] (Radl., USp. 133-34, DTS, EUTS); Kzk. 19th c.
Qan-türe [Кантюре] (AOAtb. 42); Kzk. **Qan-zada-
qan** [Kansada / Канзада Кан], prince (Proben III, 133
(168)); Shor 19th-20th c. **Qān-mergen**, folklore hero
(Dyrenkova 80, 383); *TN:* Uzb. 19th c. **Qan-bay**
[Канбай] (SKSO 1902, 75). ✧ I. 'Ruler, imperor,
sovereign' (title) cf. Uyg., Kuman, Hak., Kirg., Kzk.
qan, Alt. *qān* 'der Chan, Fürst' (Radl. II, 104, 105),
according to Németh the fem. PN *Qan-arïɣ* means
'clean, fair, spotless, honest ruler' (Németh, HMK 191);
II. 'Blood' cf. all Trk. dial. *qan* 'das Blut' (Radl. II,
101); III. 'Child born on Wednesday' (Sattarov), cf.
Tat. *qan kön* 'Wednesday' (Sattarov). Used also as a
secondary component of male and female personal
names. See also **BİY-QANLARЇ, ČİY-QAN**.

QAN-АРГО Alt. 19th c. **Qan-arɣo** [Кан-Арго] (Verb.,
In. 144). ⇨ **QAN + АРГО**.

QAN-BURA Oghuz/Trkm. 14th c. - 15th c. **Qan-bura**
[Kam Büre, Kam Büre Beg, Kam Püre / Кан-Бура],
Bamsi-beyrek's father (DQorq. 32 etc.). ⇨ **QAN +
BUҐRA?**

QAN-BUTA Kzk. 19th c. **Qam-buta** < **Qan-buta**
[Камбута] (SKSO VIII, 204). ✧ 'Khan-young-camel'.
⇨ **QAN + BOTA**.

QAN-CAPPA Alt. / Tuv.? 19th c. **Qan-cappa**
[Канцаппа богатырь], a hero (Proben IX, 324-27).

QAN-ČAҐAY Kzk. 19th c. **Qan-čaɣay** [Канчагай]
(SOV 56). ⇨ **QAN + ČAҐAY?**

QAN-ČĂK Hak.(Sag.) 19th-20th c. **Qan-čăk** [Кан
Чăк] (Proben IX, 327). ✧ 'Blood-glutton' cf.
Hak.(Sag.) *čăk* 'der Fresser' (Radl. III, 1945). ⇨ **QAN**.

QAN-ČUWAR Tat.(Sib.) 1601, 1603 **Qan-čuwar /
Qan-suwar?** [Канчуваръ / Кансувар], Küčüm's son
(Andrievič, Ist. Sib. I, 102, Miller, Ist. Sib. 181, 197).
⇨ **QAN + ŠUBAR?** See also **QAN-SÜYÄR?**

QAN-JEKPEY Alt. 19th c. **Qan-jekpey** [Канъ-
Джекпей] (Potanin, Pred. 182).

QAN-DİMER see **QAN-TEMİR**

QAN-DUҐAN see **QAN-TUҐAN**

QAN-ERGÄK see **QAN**

QAN-KELDİ Kzk. 19th c. **Qan-geldї** [Кангельды]
(SOK 276); Kzk. 19th c. **Qan-geldї** [Кан-гельды]
(SOV 64); Kzk. 19th c. **Qan-geldi** [Кангельды] (SOV
64); Bashk. 1732 **Qan-gilde** [Кангильда Токмашев]
(MIB III, 302); Tat.(Sib.) 1632 **Qan-gilde(y)**
[Кангилдей Енмамаетев] (Miller, Ist. Sib., II, 398);
Kzk. 1734 **Qan-gildї** [Кангилды] (PSZRI IX, 303);

Kzk. 19th c. **Qan-gildї** [Кангильды] (Potanin II, 3);
Bashk. 1702 **Qan-gildi** [Кангильди] (MIB III, 16);
Bashk. 1707 **Qan-gildi** [Султанай Кангильдин]
(MIB III, 31); Kirg. **Qan-keldi** [Kan-Keldi / Кан-
келдi], one of Manas' comrades-in-arms (Proben V, 40
/41/). ✧ 'The Khan has come'. ⇨ **QAN + KELDİ**. See
also **XAN-KELDİ**.

QAN-KİLDİ see **QAN-KELDİ**

QAN-KÜCÜK Kzk. 19th c. **Qan-kücük** [Канкучукъ]
(SOV 82). ⇨ **QAN + KÜČÜK**.

QAN-QAYҐALAQ Hak.(Shor, Sag., Koyb.) 19th-20th
c. **Qan-qayɣalaq** (Radl. II, 371). ⇨ **QAN +
QAYҐALAҐ**.

QAN-QARTЇҐA Hak. 19th-20th c. **Qan-qartïɣa** [Кан-
Картыҕа] (Radl. II, 105). ✧ 'Khan's
hawk/kite/buzzard' cf. Hak., Kirg. *qartïɣa* 'der Habicht'
(Radl. II, 105). ⇨ **QAN + QARTЇҐA**.

QAN-QASQA Bashk. 1666 **Qan-qasqa** [Канкаска
Девлетбаевъ], a tarɣan (Vel.-Zern., Bašk. 42). ⇨
QAN + QAŠQA.

QAN-NİYAZ Kkalp. 20th c. **Qan-niyaz** [Қаннияз]
(KkRS 774). ⇨ **QAN + NİYAZ**.

QAN-PÄRGÄN see **QAN**

QAN-PURXAN Hak. 19th-20th c. **Qan-purχan** [Кан-
Пурхан] (Radl. II, 105). ⇨ **QAN + BURQAN**.

QAN-PÜDÄY Alt. **Qan-püdäy** [Кан Пÿдäi] (Radl. I,
1103); Alt. **Qān-püdäy** [Кан-Пÿдäi] (Radl. I, 1878). ⇨
QAN.

QAN-SARЇҐ Shor 19th-20th c. **Qan-sarïɣ**, fem.
(Dyrenkova 184). ✧ Khan-blond'. ⇨ **QAN + SARЇҐ**.

QAN-SORĬŠ Alt. 19th c. **Qan-soriš** [Канъ-Сорышъ]
(Potanin, Pred. 181).

QAN-SUWAR see **QAN-ČUWAR**

QAN-SÜYÄR Crm. 1557 **Xan-süwer-biyim**
[Ханъсюверъ-Биимъ], a princess from the Crimea
(Kn. Metriki Lit. 151); Tat. 1744 **Qan-süyär** [Ишим
Кансуяр] (MIB III, 415); Tat. 1777 **Qan-süyär**
[Кансуяр Муртазин] (MIB V, 60); Tat. 1777 **Qan-
süyär** [Кансуяр Еникеев] (MIB V, 60); Bashk. 1734
Qan-süyär [Аиткул Абызъ Кансуяровъ], a tarχan
(Vel.-Zern., Bašk. 11); Bashk. 1735 **Qan-süyär**
[Кансуяръ Тленчеевъ], a tarχan (Vel.-Zern., Bašk.
13); Bashk. 1749 **Qan-süyär** [Кансуяр Касыев]
(MIB III, 465); Bashk. 18th c. **Qan-süyär** [Кансуяр
султан], a sultan (MIB I, 492); Bashk. 1761 **Qan-
süyär** [Кансуяр Габдуллин] (MIB IV/1, 221); Bashk.
1761 **Qan-süyär** [Чюпан Кансуяров] (MIB IV/1,
214); Bashk. 1770 **Qan-süyär** [Нагайбак Кансуяров]
(MIB IV/1, 342); Bashk. 1789 **Qan-süyär** [Имаш
Кансуяров (Кансуляров)] (MIB V, 249); Bashk.
1789 **Qan-süyär** [Мавлюкей Кэпсуяров] (MIB V,
274); Tat. 1706 **Qan-süyer** [Кансуер] (MIB III, 24). ✧
'Khan's favourite; khan's darling'. ⇨ **QAN +**

SEWÄR.

QAN-ŠAYÏM Kkalp. 20th c. **Qan-šayïm** [Қаншайым], fem. (KkRS 778). ✧ 'My strong/nice khan'. ⇨ **QAN + ŠAYÏM.**

QAN-ŠENTÄY Kzk. **Qan-šentäy** [Кан Шентäи], a folklore hero (Proben III, 253 /297).

QAN-TÄÑÄY Hak. 19th-20th c. **Qan-täñäy** [Кан-Täнäi] (Radl. II, 105).

QAN-TEMİR Yak. 1649 **Gan-timür-ulan / Ган-timür-ulan?** [Гантимуръ-Уланъ] (AI IV, 75); Yak. 1649 **Гan-timur-ulan** [Гантимуръ-Уланъ] (AI IV, 75); Chuv. 18th-19th c. **Kan-dimer** [Кандимеръ] (Magn. 50); Maml. 14th c. **Qan-temür** [قَانْتَمُرْ] (Sauvaget 52). ✧ I. 'Blood-iron' (Sauvaget 52); II. 'Khan (ruler)-iron' (Bask., Fam. 250). ⇨ **QAN + TEMİR.**

QAN-TİMUR see **QAN-TEMİR**

QAN-TÖGÖS Hak.(Sag.) 19th-20th c. **Qan-tögös** [Кан Төгöс] (Radl. I, 981).

QAN-TUΓAN Chuv. 18th-19th c. **Kan-dugan** [Кандуганъ] (Magn. 50); Bashk. 1777 **Qan-tuγan** [Кантуган Аднашев] (MIB V, 58). ⇨ **QAN + TUΓAN I.**

QAN-TURA Kzk. 19th c. **Qan-tura** [Кантура] (AOK 2). ⇨ **QAN + TURA.**

QAN-TURALÏ Oghuz/Trkm. **Qan-turalï** [Кан-Турали], Qanlï-qoja's son (DQorq/Rossi 180, 192, DQorq. 63-72, 110, 143, 149, 189 etc.). ⇨ **QAN + TURALÏ?**

QAN-TÜK Tat.(Sib.) 1640 **Qan-tük** [Янгутай Кантюков] (Miller, Ist. Sib. II, 474). ⇨ **QAN + TÜK?**

QAN-ÜLETEY Alt.(Tuba) 19th c. **Qan-ületey** [Канъ-Улетей] (Potanin IV, 372).

QAN-ZADA see **QAN**

QANA Hak. 19th-20th c. **Qana** [Кана], fem. (HRS 353); Bashk. 1737 **Qana-bay** [Канабай] (MIB I, 326); Nog. 1632 **Qana-bey** [Канабей], a murza (Miller, Ist. Sib. II, 399); Bashk. 1690, 1696 **Qana-bek** [Канабеско / Канабечко] (Kungursk. akty 178, 237). ✧ 'Ring made of wood at the top smoke-gap; wooden wall of the tent' cf. Hak. (Sag., Blt.) *qana* 'der Holzring am Rauch loche des Filzzeltes; das Gitter, der Zaum etc.' (Radl. II, 108). See also **İLDAŠ-QANA.**

QANA-QUŠ Alt. 19th-20th c. **Qana-quš** [Канакуш] (OjrRS 208). ⇨ **QANA? + QUŠ I.**

QANAY Tat.(Sib.) 1598-1599, 1600 **Qanay** [Канай (Конай)], Küčüm's son (AI II, 3-5, 20-21, Miller, Ist. Sib. II, 156, 167, 168, 197, Andrievič, Ist. Sib. I, 100); Bashk. 1600 **Qanay** [Канай] (Miller, Ist. Sib. II, 158, 159); Bashk. 1600 **Qanay** [Канай Кудайбердеев] (MIB I, 151); Bashk. 1734 **Qanay** [Исенъ Канаевъ], a tarχan (Vel.-Zern., Bašk. 11); Bashk. 1734 **Qanay** [Юсупъ Канаевъ], a tarχan (Vel.-Zern., Bašk. 10); Bashk. 1734 **Qanay** [Етберди Канаевъ], a tarχan

(Vel.-Zern., Bašk. 10); Bashk. 1734 **Qanay** [Канай Атяшевъ], a tarχan (Vel.-Zern., Bašk. 13); Kzk. **Qanay** [Канай] (Grod. 7); Kzk. 18th c. - 19th c. **Qanay** [قاناى] (ZOOIRGO III, 377); Kzk. 19th c. **Qanay** [Канай] (SODž. 28); Kzk. 19th c. **Qanay** [Канай] (SOV 6, 50); Kzk. 19th c. **Qanay** [Канай] (AOP 18); Kzk. 19th c. **Qanay** [Канай] (SOK 212); Kzk. 19th c. **Qanay** [Канай] (AOA 10, 150); Kzk. 19th c. **Qanay** [Канай] (AOO 14, 62); Kzk. 19th c. **Qanay** [Канай] (AOK 82); Kzk. 19th c. **Qanay** [Канай] (Grod., Pril. 172); Kzk. 19th c. **Qanay** [Бiй Султанъ Канаевъ], a biy (AUK 287); Nog. 1601 **Qanay** [Канай] (Miller, Ist. Sib. II, 165); Nog. 1624 **Qanay** [Канай], a prince (DAI II, 87); Nog. 1633 **Qanay** [Канай Тинбаев] (Miller, Ist. Sib. II, 408, 409); Nog. 1649 **Qanay** [Кантемиръ? Канаевъ] (AI IV, 87); Nog.? 1614 **Qanay(-murza)** [Канай мурза], a murza (AI III, 24); Nog. 1649, 1651 **Qanay(-murza)** [Канай мурза] (AI IV, 123, PSZRI I, 248-49); Kirg. **Qanay-batïr** [Kanaï-batyr] (Rec. V. As. C. 183). ✧ 'Younger brother'? cf. Hak. *qanay* 'der jüngste Bruder' (Radl. II, 109). ⇨ **QAN / QANA** + suff. *-ay / -y.*

QANAQ Bashk. 1740 **Qanaq-bay** [Канак-бай] (MIB I, 446); Kzk. 19th c. **Qanaq-bay** [Канакбай] (AOO 58); Kzk. 19th c. **Qanaq-pay** [Канакпай] (SODž. 78). ⇨ **QAN / QANA?** + suff. *-aq / -q.*

QANAQAY Bashk. 1751 **Qanaqay** [Каразбай Канакаев] (MIB IV/1, 52); Bashk. 1751 **Qanaqay** [Сатим Канакаев] (MIB IV/1, 52); Bashk. 1761 **Qanaqay** [Канакай Аднагулов] (MIB IV/2, 224); Bashk. 1794 **Qanaqay** [Илчибай Канакаев] (MIB V, 338). ⇨ **QANA / QANAQ?** + suff. *-qay / -ay.*

QANAL-GELDİ Trkm. **Qanal-geldi** [Каналгелди] (Sopieva: OSA 182). ✧ 'The (Kara-kum) canal has come' cf. Trkm. *kanal* 'канал; Гарагум каналы - Каракумский канал' (TrkmRS) (<R.). ⇨ **KELDİ.**

QANAPİYA Kzk. 19th c. **Qanapiya** [Канапiя] (AOK 58, 86); Kzk. 19th c. **Qanapiya** [Канапiя] (AOP 102); Kzk. 19th c. **Qanapiya** [Канапiя] (AOAtb. 26). ✧ Qanafiya (<Ar.) (Žanuzakov 144).

QANAS Kzk. 19th c. **Qanas** [Байкунъ Канасовъ] (Grod., Pril. 136).

QANAT Kzk. 19th c. **Qanat** [Канатъ] (AOO 58); Kzk. 1920 **Qanat** [Konat] (Fox 149); Hak.(Sag.) 19th-20th c. **Qanat** [Канат] (Proben IX, 263); Kzk. 19th c. **Qanat-bay / Qonat-bay** [Конатбай] (AOP 106); Kzk. 19th c. **Qanat-bay / Qonat-bay** [Конатбай] (SOK 136); Kzk. 19th c. **Qanat-pay** [Канатпай] (SOK 102). ✧ 'Wing' cf. Trk. *qanat* 'id.' (Radl. II, 111). See also **AY-QANAT.**

QANAT-TİMAN Hak. 19th-20th c. **Qanat-tïman-qan** [Канаттыман-кан] (Radl., II, 105). ⇨ **QANAT.**

QANBİR Tat.(Arin) 17th c. **Qanbir**, prince of the Arïns

(Miller, Ist. Sib. II, 563); Tat. 1665 **Qanbir / Qanbïr? / Qambur?** [Куркекъ Канбиревъ] (DAI V, 39).

QANČUQ Uyg. 12th c. - 14th c. **Qančuq** [Kançuk] (DTS, EUTS). ❖ 'Little Khan' (Bese 6). ⇨ **QAN** + dim. suff. *-čuq*.

QANJİKEY Kzk. **Qanjikey** [Канджикей], a hero in a tale (ZIRGOGeogr. I, 526).

QANJÏΓALÏ Kzk. 19th c. **Qanjïγalï** [Канджигалы] (AOO 14, 42, 50). ❖ 'Having a saddle-strap' cf. Kzk., Turk. *qanjïγa* 'der Riemen hinter dem Sattel zum Anbinden leichter Sachen' (Radl. II, 130). + suff. *-lï*.

QANDA Kzk. 19th c. **Qanda-bay** [Кандабай] (SOK 22).

QANDAΓAY Kzk. 19th c. **Qandaγay** [Кандагай] (SOK 172). ⇨ **QANDA?** + suff. *-qay*.

QANDAY Kzk. 19th c. **Qanday** [Кандай] (SOV 136); Kzk. 1821 **Qandey** [Кабдей] (Dobrosm., Turg. 226); Kzk. 19th c. **Qantay** [Кантай] (AOO 50). ⇨ **QAN?** + suff. *-day / -tay*.

QANDAM Tuv. 19th c. **Qandam? / Qandamay?** [Kandam / Кандам / Кандамаі] (Proben IX, 45).

QANDAMAY Tuv. 19th c. **Qandamay / Qandam-ay?** [Кандамаі(нын)] (Proben IX, 45).

QANDAR Tat. 20th c. **Qandar** [Кандаров] (Sattarov); Tat. **Qandar-bey** [Kandar bej] (Koşay: KCsA I, 324). ❖ 'Sugar(y), sweet' (Sattarov) < P. *qandar* 'sugar-candy'.

QANDAZA Tat.? 1554 **Qandaza?** [Канъдазу царица] (PSRL XIII, 243); Kzk. 19th c. **Qandaza / Qandaza-sulu** (Ljutš 52, 53).

QANDEY see **QANDAY**

QANDÏ Kzk. **Qandï-bay** [Kandy Bai / Канды Баі] (Proben III, 47 /62/); Kzk. 19th c. **Qandï-bay** [Кандыбай] (SOK 180, 208); Kzk. 19th c. **Qandï-bay** [Кандыбай] (AOA 82); Kzk. 19th c. **Qandï-bay** [Кандыбай] (SODž. 76); Kzk. 19th c. **Qandï-bek** [Кандыбекъ] (SOV 56). ❖ 'Full-blooded; Well-kept, well-fed' cf. Kzk. *qandï* 'полнокровный, упитанный' (KzRS). See also **KÜČ-QANDÏ**.

QANDÏQČÏ Alt. 19th-20th c. **Qandïqčï** [Кандыкчы], fem. (OjrRS 212). ❖ 'He/she who gathers *qandïq*' cf. Alt., Hak. *qandïq* 'Erythronium dens canis (seine Wurzeln werden gegessen)' (Radl. II, 124). + suff. *-čï*.

QANDÏM Uzb. 20th c. **Qândïm** [Кондим], fem. (Begmatov 1984, 207); Uzb. 20th c. **Qândïm-ây** [Кондимой], fem. (Begmatov 1984, 207). ❖ 'I have been satisfied; enough of childbirth' (Begmatov) cf. Uzb. *qân-* 'удовлетворяться' (UzbRS).

QANDOT Alt. 19th c. **Qandot** [Кандот-богатырь] (Verb., In. 139, 153, 154).

QANDŌÑ Hak.(Sag.) 19th-20th c. **Qandōñ** [Кандон] (Katanov, Otč. 8, Proben IX, 227).

QANDUM Trkm. 1804 **Qandum-serdar** [Кандум-сердар] (MIT II, 361, 362, 364. 380-382); Kkalp. 1812

Qandum-serdar [Кандум-сердар] (MIKk. 122). ⇨ **QANDÏM?**

QANDÏ Kzk. 19th c. **Qandï-bay** [Акчалъ Кандыбаевъ] (Grod., Pril. 155). ❖ 'Having a khan' cf. Kzk. *qandï* 'einen Chan habend, von einem Chane regiert' (Radl. II, 124). ⇨ **QAN** + suff. *-lï*.

QANGİY Kzk. 19th c. **Qangiy** [Бекинъ Кангіевъ] (Grod., Pril. 28).

QANΓAY Kzk. 19th c. **Qanγay** [Кангай] (SOK 62, 180, 230).

QANΓALUΓ Oghuz/Trkm. 13th c. **Qanγaluγ** (DTS). ❖ 'Having a coach, possessing a car' cf. Oghuz/Trkm. *qanγa* 'повозка, телега' (DTS).

QANİKEY see **QANÏQAY**

QANÏ Bashk. 1734 **Qanï(y)? / Qani?** [Токай Каниевъ] (Vel.-Zern., Bašk. 10); Bashk. 1735 **Qanï(y)? / Qani?** [Біимбеть Каниевъ], a tarχan (Vel.-Zern., Bašk. 13); Bashk. 1735 **Qanï / Qanïy?** [Янгурчий Каныевъ], a tarχan (Vel.-Zern., Bašk. 19); Maml.? 1483 **Qanï-bay** [السيفى قانيباى], in an inscription on a copper dish (Mayer 175-76); Tat. 1783 **Qanï-bek** [Сафар Канныбеков] (MIB V, 137); Bashk. 1713 **Qanï-bek** [Деветей Канныбеков] (MIB III, 107); Bashk. 1751 **Qanï-bek** [Канныбек] (MIB IV/1, 51); Kirg. **Qanï-bek** [Канныбек] (Jud. 73, 917). ❖ 'Satisfied, contented' cf. Uyg. *qani* (<Ar.) 'zufrieden, genügsam' (Radl. II, 115).

QANÏKEY see **QANÏQAY**

QANÏQ Oghuz/Trkm. 14th c. -15th c. **Qanïq-qan** [Kapak Kan / Каньк-Кан] (DQorq. 79). ❖ 'Known; knowing' cf. Kzk. *qanïq* 'wissend, bekannt' (Radl. II, 116). ⇨ **QANÏ?** + dim. suff. *-q*.

QANÏQAY Kzk. **Xanïkey-slu** [Ханыкей-слу] (Divaev, Šura 131); Tat.(Ishim) **Kǎnikäy** [Kǎnikäi], fem. (Proben IV, 198 /243/); Kirg. **Qanïkey** [Kanykäi / Каныкей], Manas' wife (Proben V, 81, Jud. 87, 115, 319, 341, 399, 693); Bashk. 1706 **Qanïqay** [Каныкай Икустин] (MIB III, 26); Bashk. 1735 **Qanïqay** [Каныкай] (MIB III, 343). ❖ 'Princess, daughter of the khan' cf. Kirg. *qanïkey* 'дочь хана, царевна' (Jud.). Used also as a secondary component of male names. ⇨ **QANÏ?** + dim. *-qay*.

QANÏM Kkalp. 20th c. **Qanïm** [Къаным / Каным], fem. (Bask., Kkalp. 403, KkRS 778); Kzk. 19th c. **Qanïm-bay** [Канымбай] (AOO 18); Kkalp. 20th c. **Qanïm-biyke** [Канымбийке], fem. (KkRS 778); Kkalp. 20th c. **Qanïm-žan** [Канымжан], fem. (KkRS 778). ❖ I. 'Princess', female form of QAN, or variant of XANÏM; II. 'My blood'? (Sauvaget 52). ⇨ **QAN?** See also **XANÏM**.

QANÏMDU Uyg. 13th c. **Qanïmdu** [qanïmdu / Kanımudu] (DTS, EUTS).

QANÏMQAN Kkalp. 20th c. **Qanïmqan** [Къанымкъан], fem. (Bask., Kkalp. 403); Kkalp. 20th

c. **Qanïmqan** [Қанымқан], fem. (KkRS 778). ⇨ **QANÏM** + suff. -qan(1).

QANÏS see **QANÏŠ**

QANÏŠ Kzk. 19th c. **Qanïs-bek** [Kaniszbek] (Vámbéry, Vázlatok 312); Uzb. 19th c. **Qanïs-bibi** [Ханышъ-биби Юлдашбаева], a Sart woman from the region of Tashkent (Sr. Az. I, 1896, Avg. 14); Bashk. 1762 **Qanïš** [Усман Канышев] (MIB IV/1, 241); Kirg. **Qanïš-Jan** [Каныжжан], fem. (Jud. 72, 578). ✧ 'Wife of the Khan'? cf. Kirg. *qanïš* 'ханша, жена хана' (Jud.).

QANÏŠAY Kirg. **Qanïšay** [Канышай], fem. (Jud. 42). ⇨ **QANÏŠ** + suff. -ay.

QANQAY Bashk. 1783 **Qanqay** [Турабай Канкаев], from the village of Kankaevo [Kanakaevo?] (MIB V, 139); Bashk. 1783 **Qanqay** [Турсунбай Канкаев] (MIB V, 139); *TN:* Bashk. 1783 **Qanqayevo** [Канкаево], a village (MIB V, 139). ✧ I. 'Little Khan' (Sattarov); II. 'Male child who was born on Thurday' cf. Old Tat. *qan kön* 'чәршәмбе [thursday]' (Sattarov); III. 'Tall man' < Mo. *qanqai* (Sattarov); ⇨ **QAN** + suff. -qay.

QANLÏ Oghuz/Trkm. 13th c. **Qanlï** [قانلی / یاولی / Канлы], Yawlï-χan's byname (Abulg./Kon., 815); Kzk. **Qanlï-bay** [فقانلی بای / Канлы бай] (Sb. Syr-D. XI, otd. II, 18, 34); Kzk. 19th c. **Qanlï-bay** [Канлыбай] (SOV 4); Kzk. 19th c. **Qanlï-bay** [Канлыбай] (AOO 38); *EN:* Kkalp. 20th c. **Qanlï-küp** [Къанлы куьп], a Qara-noγay clan (Bask., Nog. 136, 142); Kkalp. 20th c. **Qanlï-uruw** [Къанлы урув], a Qara-noγay clan (Bask., Nog. 137). ✧ I. 'Bloody'; II. 'Having a khan'. ⇨ **QAN** + suff. -lï.

QANNADÏ Kzk. 19th c. **Qannadï** [Каннады] (AOP 74).

QANOY Hak. 19th-20th c. **Qanoy** [Каной] (HRS 349).

QANOQ Hak. 19th-20th c. **Qanoq** [Канок], fem. (HRS 353).

QANSU see **QANSUH**

QANSUH Maml. 1508 **Qansu / Qansuh?** [ابوالنصر قانصوه الغوري / Chansu el Gauri], Qansūh al-Γawrī, the Mamlūk sultan (Amari 214, 222, 226, 227, 389); Maml. 15th c. **Qansuh / Qansu?** [قانصوه الاشرفی], a governor in Divrigi at the end of the 15th c. (CIA 3/I, 95).

QANŠAW Balk. 20th c. **Qanšaw** [Qanšáu] (Pröhle, Balk. 234); Karch. **Qanšaw-biy** [Каншаубіевъ] (Sysoev 119).

QANTA-BAŠ Alt. 19th-20th c. **Qanta-baš** [Кантабаш], fem. (OjrRS 212). ⇨ **BAŠ.**

QANTAY see **QANDAY**

QANTAR Kzk. 19th c. **Qantar-bay** [Кантарбай] (SODž. 68, 118); Kzk. 19th c. **Qantar-bay** [Кантарбай] (SOV 32, 108); Kzk. 19th c. **Qantar-bay** [Кантарбай] (SOK 126); *EN:* Kzk. 18th c. - 19th c.

Qantar-bay [Кантарбай], a clan (Tynyšp. 68). ✧ 'December' cf. Kzk. *qantar* 'Ocak ayı' (KzTS).

QANTÏYKE Kkalp. 20th c. **Qantïyke** [Къантыйке], fem. (Bask., Kkalp. 403). ✧ 'Little sweet' cf. Uyg. *qant* (P.) 'der Zucker' (Radl. II, 121), Kkalp. *qant* 'сахар' (KkRS). + dim. suff. -(ï)y + -ke.

QANTÏRMÏŠ see **QANTURMÏŠ**

QANTURMÏŠ Uyg. 12th c. - 14th c. **Qantïrmïš-ïnal** (Radl., USp. 23); Uyg. 12th c. - 14th c. **Qanturmïš** [Kanturmış] (EUTS); Uyg. 13th-14th c. **Qanturmïš-šali** [Qanturmïš Šali] (Zieme, Mat. III, 271); Uyg. 12th c. - 14th c. **Qanturmuš-ïnal** [Kanturmuş İnal] (EUTS). ✧ 'Satisfied' cf. Uyg., Karakh. *qantur-* 'утолять (жажду, голод); исполнять желание' (DTS).

QANTURMÏŠ-TOQÏL Uyg. 12th c. - 14th c. **Qanturmïš-toqïl** [qanturmïš toqïl] (Radl., USp. 83, DTS). ✧ 'Fed/satisfied Toqïl(?)'. ⇨ **QANTURMÏŠ.**

QANU-GÏLDE Tat.(Sib.) 1628 **Qanu-gilde** [Канюгилдей] (Miller, Ist. Sib. II, 341).

QANUR Kzk. 19th c. **Qanur-bay** [Джансугуръ Канурбаевъ] (Grod., Pril. 89).

QANZA see **QAÑZA**

QANZADA Kkalp. 20th c. **Qanzada-qan** [Қанзада], fem. (KkRS 778). ⇨ **QAN** + suff. -zada.

QANZÄŠ Bashk. 1757 **Qanzäš?** [Канзяш Иштеряков] (MIB IV/1, 157).

QANZEY Bashk. 1758 **Qanzey** [Канзей Чюгалаев] (MIB IV/1, 168).

QANŽAL Kzk. 19th c. **Qanžal-bay / Qïnžal-bay?** [Канжалбай] (SOK 86).

QAÑΓÏL-QAQPA Tuv. 19th c. **Qañγïl-qaqpa** [Канђыл-какпа], a folklore hero (Proben IX, 131).

QAÑΓU-TAY Kzk. 19th c. **Qañγu-tay** [Кангутай] (SOV 112). ⇨ **TAY** or suff. -tay(1,2)?

QAÑQAQ Hak.(Sag.) 19th-20th c. **Qañqaq** [Канкак], fem. (Proben IX, 606). ✧ 'One holding his/her head always upright; proud?' cf. Alt.(Tel.) *qañqaq* 'immer den Kopf aufrecht haltend (von Menschen und Pferden)' (Radl. II, 82).

QAÑQÏ Kzk. 19th c. **Qañqï-bay?** [Канкыбай] (SODž. 128). ✧ 'Strolling person, loafer'? cf. Kzk. *qañγï: qañγï bas* 'rastgele dolaşan kimse' (KzTS).

QAÑQLÏ see **QAÑLÏ**

QAÑLÏ Oghuz/Trkm. 13th c. **Qañqlï** [قانتلی / Канклы] (Abulg./Kon. 265, 525, 555); Karakh. 11th c. **Qañlï** [Kanğlı] (MK/Atalay 842, DTS); Kzk. 19th c. **Qañlï-bay** [Канглыбай] (SOV 126); Kzk. 19th c. **Qañlï-bay** [Канглыбай Чилтукбаевъ] (Grod., Pril. 87); Oghuz/Trkm. 14th c - 15th c. **Qañlï-qoja** [Qanlï Qoja / Qanglï-Khoca / Канлы-Коджа (Кинглы-кожа)], Qan-turalï's father (DQorq./Rossi 180, 192, DQorq. 63-65, 68, 72, 190, 239, Togan, UTT 408); *EN:* Nog. 20th c. **Qañlï-uruwï** [Къанълы урувы], an Aq-noγay clan (Bask., Nog. 133, 142). ✧ 'Wagen; a man from the tribe *Qangli*'? cf. Chag., Uyg., Crm. *qañlï* 'ein zweirädiger Wagen'; 'der türkische Stamm der Kangly' (Radl. II, 84-85).

QAÑZA Alt. 19th c. **Qañza**, a folklore hero (Verb., In. 168); Hak. 19th c. **Qañza** [Канза], a folklore hero (Katanov, Otč. 12); Alt.(Tel.), Hak. 19th-20th c. **Qañza-bï**, a well-known folklore hero (Radl. I, 63, II, 87); Hak.(Blt., Kacha, Sag.) 19th-20th c. **Qañza-peg** [Канза-пег], a folklore hero (Proben IX, 306, 361, 385); Alt.(Tel.), Hak. 19th-20th c. **Qañza-pï**, a weel-known folklore hero (Radl. I, 63, II, 87). ✧ 'Pipe (for smoking)' cf. Alt., Hak. *qañza* (Mo.) 'die Pfeife (zum Rauchen)' (Radl. II, 87), Alt. *qañza* 'трубка (курительная)' (OjrRS).

QAÑZA-BAŠ Alt. 19th-20th c. **Qañza-baš** [Канзабаш] (OjrRS 208). ✧ 'Pipe-head'. ⇨ **QAÑZA + BAŠ.**

QAP-SAY Bashk. 1757 **Qap-say** [Капсай Султанов] (MIB IV/1, 139).

QAPA see **QABA I.**

QAPAΓAN Türk 7th c. - 8th c. **Qapaγan-qaγan** [Qapaγan], Qutluγ-qaγan' younger brother, Kül-tegin and Bilge-qaγan's uncle, ruled 691-716 (ETY I, 116, 118, 120, 128, DTS). ✧ 'Getting over / Overcoming' (Blagova 1997, 710).

QAPAY 1765 **Qapay** [Кирей Капаевъ] (PSZRI XVII, 111); Bashk. 1706 **Qapay** [Капай Калмаккулов] (MIB III, 30); Kzk. 19th c. **Qapay** [Капай] (SOK 106, 204); Kzk. 19th c. **Qapay** [Капай] (SODž. 18); Kzk. 1884 **Qapay-bay** [Капайбай Турсуновъ] (Grod., Pril. 95). ⇨ **QABAY?**

QAPAQ Bashk. 1754 **Qapaq** [Капак] (MIB IV/1, 83); Bashk. 1768 **Qapaq** [Капак Ишалин] (MIB IV/1, 332); Oghuz/Trkm. 14th - 15th **Qapaq-qan** (DQorq./Rossi 196). ✧ 'Top, cap, cover' cf. Chag., Az., Crm., Turk. *qapaq* 'der Deckel, die Schütze, Decke, der Pfropfen' (Radl. II, 405). See also **TUMAN-QAPAQ.**

QAPAQ-TİMÜR Khorezm./Chag. 14th c. **Qapaq-timür-χan** (Tar. Rashidi 36-37). ⇨ **QAPAQ + TEMİR.**

QAPAL Kzk. 19th c. **Qapal** [Капалъ] (SODž. 100); Kzk. 19th c. **Qapal** [Капалъ] (AOA 98); Kzk. 19th c. **Qapal-bay** [Капалбай] (SOK 262); Kzk. 19th c. **Qapal-bek** [Капалбекъ] (SOV 84).

QAPAN Uyg. 12th c. - 14th c. **Qapan** (Radl., USp. 7); Uyg. 14th c. **Qapan** (Le Coq, Urkunden 455); Karakh. 11th c. **Qapan** [Kapan] (DTS, MK/Atalay 842); Kzk. 18th c. - 19th c. **Qapan** [قاپان / Капанъ] (MIK IV, 309); Kzk. 19th c. **Qapan** [Капанъ] (AOAtb. 22); Kzk. 19th c. **Qapan** [Капанъ] (AOK 2, 118); Kkalp. 20th c. **Qapan** [Қапан] (KkRS 774); *EN:* Pecheneg **Qapanaq** [Kᶜapan], a tribe (Németh, HMK 45). ✧ I. Variant of the Türk title *qapɣan* (Németh, HMK 45); II. 'Boar' (Blagova 1997, 706). ⇨ **QAPAΓAN?**

QAPANAX Yak. **Qapanaχ** [Капанах (уола)] (Pek.).

QAPAR Kzk. 19th c. **Qapar** [Капаръ], a biy (Lomakin 38). ✧ I. 'Spirit'? cf. Kirg. *qapar* 'der Geist' (Radl. II, 409); II. 'Forethought; attention' cf. Kirg. *qapar* 'забота, внимание' (Jud.).

QAPČAΓAY Kzk. 19th c. **Qapčaγau** [Капчагай] (SOK 140). ✧ 'Fast, nimble' cf. Alt.(Kmd.), Hak.(Koyb.) *qapčaγay, qapšaγay* 'Schnell, flink, dünn' (Radl. II, 429, 432). ⇨ **ČAΓAU?**

QAPČAQ Oghuz/Trkm. 14th c. -15th c. **Qapčaq-melik / Qïpčaq-melik** [Qapčaq / Qïpčaq Melik] (DQorq./Rossi 144, 158).

QAPČÏQ Karg. **Qapčïq** [Капчык] (Katanov, Otč. 9); Yak. **Qapčïq** [Чюкъ Капчиковъ] (DAI VIII, 268). ✧ 'Purse' (Katanov). + dim. suff. *-čïq.*

QAPEY see **QABAY**

QAPΓAN see **QAPAΓAN**

QAPΓAN-EL-TÄRİŠ see **EL-TÄRİŠ**

QAPİYA Hak. 19th-20th c. **Qapiya** [Капия], fem. (HRS 353).

QAPÏR Kzk. 19th c. **Qapïr** [Капыръ] (Potanin II, 150).

QAPÏŠ Kzk. 1817 **Qapïš** [قاپوچ / Капыш] (MIK IV, 311, 318); Kzk. 19th c. **Qapïš** [Капышъ] (AOO 54).

QAPQAY Tat.(Mish.) 20th c. **Qapqay** [Капкаевъ] (IOAIÊK XIX, 143, 145, Sattarov); Tat.(Sib.) 20th c. **Qapqay** [Капкаев] (Sattarov). ✧ 'Little blood relative' (Sattarov) cf. Karakh. *qap* 'близкий, кровный родственник' (DTS). + dim. suff. *-qay.*

QAPQAQ see **QOPQAQ?**

QAPQAN Tat.(Mish.) 1715 **Qapqan** [Калтай Капканов] (MIB III, 127); Tat.(Sib.) 1631 **Qapqan / Qapqana?** [Капканины], a family (Miller, Ist. Sib. II, 383); *TN:* Uzb. **Qapqan-aγa** [Капкан ага], south of Samarkand (Karta JAR XIX). ✧ 'Trap, pitfall' cf. Chag., East.T., Hak., Tat. *qapqan* 'eine Falle, Schlinge' (Radl. II, 420).

QAPLAM-BAY see **QAPLAN**

QAPLAN Kirg. **Qabïlan** [Кабылан], epithet of Manas, the hero of the famous Kirghiz epic (Jud. 140); Kzk. 19th c. **Qablan** [Kablane], fem. (Levchine 356); Kzk. 19th c. **Qaplam-bay (<Qaplan-bay)** [Капламбай] (SOK 76); Turk. 16th c. **Qaplan** (Ongan, Ank. II, 1100, 1262); Turk. 1621 **Qaplan** [Kaplan] (Ün 1938, 645); Turk. 20th c. **Qaplan** [Kaplan] (Önder, Göle); Turk. 20th c. **Qaplan** [Kaplan] (Önder, Hınıs); Tat. 19th c. **Qaplan** [Каплан] (IOAIÊK XIX, 145); Tat.(Mish.) 20th c. **Qaplan** [Капланов] (Sattarov); Nog. **Qaplan** [Каплан], one of Musa's 12 sons (Žirm., Epos 400); Crm.(Tat.) 1707, 1730, 1769 **Qaplan (Qaplan-girey)**, byname of several khans in the Girey dynasty (?); Crm. 1689 **Qaplan-aγa** [قپلان اغا] (Vel.-Zern., Crim. 702, 703, 715, 719); Kzk. 19th c. **Qaplun-bay** [Капланбай] (SODž. 78); Crm. 1637 **Qaplan-mirza** [قپلان مرزه / قیچاق/] (Vel.-Zern., Crim. 179); Crm. 1689 **Qaplan-**

mïrza [قيلان مـرزه] (Vel.-Zern., Crim. 726); Turk. 1678
Qaplan-paša [Капланъ паша] (PSZRI II, 182). ✧
'Tiger, leopard' cf. Az., Tat., Turk. *qaplan* 'ein Tiger,
Leopard' (Radl. II, 423), Kzk. *qablan* 'леопард;
молодец' (KzkRS), concerning the related Old
Hungarian names see Gombocz, ÁTSz. 17. ⇨
QOBLANDÏ.

QAPLANDA Tat.(Sib.) 1638 **Qaplanda? / Qaplandï?**
[Капланда Тоскейтов (Токсейтов!)] (Miller, Ist.
Sib. II, 450); Tat.(Sib.) 1618 **Qaplandï** [Казылбай
Капляндиев] (Miller, Ist. Sib. II, 243). ⇨ **QAPLAN** +
suff. *-da/-dï* < *-lï*. See also **QOBLANDÏ?**

QAPŌT Karg. **Qapōt** (Katanov, Otč. 9). ✧ 'Cape,
garment; cowl' (Katanov) cf. R. капот 'id.', Turk.
kaput (Italian) 'die Kaputze, der Mantel' (Radl. II, 412).

QAPPÏ Tuv. 19th c. **Qappï** [Каппы / Арҕан Каппы],
fem. (Proben IX, 165).

QAPPÏLAY Hak. 19th-20th c. **Qappïlay** [Каппылаи-
пег (князь Хабулаи, Хубилаи)], an evil spirit whose
name goes back to the name of the Mongol Emperor
Kubilai (Kublai) (Proben IX, 568). ✧ 'Kubilai' (Mo.).

QAPSA Kzk. 19th c. **Qapsa** [Капса] (AOO 6). ✧ 'Box,
chest' cf. Kuman *qapsa* 'der Kasten, die Lade' (Radl.
II, 431).

QAPSALAN see **QAPSALAŇ**

QAPSALAŇ Kzk. 19th c. **Qapsalan** [Капсаланъ]
(SODž. 126); Kirg. **Qapsalaň** [Капсалаң] (Jud. 847).
✧ 'Disaster, misery' cf. Kirg. *qapsalaň* 'обильный
снегопад и буран; бада, бедствие' (Jud.).

QAPSAN Bashk. 1763 **Qapsan** [Капсан Султанов]
(MIB IV/1, 274).

QAPŠĀY Alt. 19th-20th c. **Qapšāy** [Капшаай], fem.
(OjrRS 212). ✧ 'Fast, quick' (OjrRS 212).

QAPTAҐAY Kzk. 19th c. **Qaptaγay** [Каптагай] (SOK
306); Kzk. 19th c. **Qaptaγay** [Каптагай] (Potanin II,
6). ✧ 'Wild camel' cf. Mo. *χoptaγai* 'id.' (Potanin).

QAPTAN Turk. 20th c. **Qaptan** [Kaptan] (Önder,
Göle). ✧ 'Chief, leader, captain' (<Italian) (Erol II).

QAPTAR Kzk. 19th c. **Qaptar-bay** [Каптарбай]
(SODž. 80).

QAPU-QÏRAN Yürük 1729 **Qapu-qïran** [قپو قـيران /
Kapukıran] (Su 107). ✧ 'Gate-breaker' cf. Turk. *kapı*
'door, gate' (TED). ⇨ **QÏRAN.**

QAPUDAN Turk. 20th c. **Qapudan** [Kapudan] (Önder,
Göle). ✧ 'Chief, leader, captain' (Erol II), cf. Turk.
qapudan 'der Schiffskapitän, der Chef, der Anführer'
(Radl. II, 417) (<Italian *capitano*).

QAPUSUZ Turk. **Qapusuz-oγlu**, a Zeybek (Kúnos
1891, 119). ✧ 'Not having a door; without a door
(=home?)' cf. Turk. *kapu* 'door, gate' (TED). +
suff. *-suz.*

QAR Kzk. 19th c. **Qar-bay** [Карбай] (SOK 244); Kzk.
19th c. **Qar-qul? / Qarq-ul?** [Кар кулъ] (Grod., Pril.
38); Kzk. 1826 **Qar-tikin?** [Картикинъ] (TOUAK

XXIV, 161). ✧ 'Snow' cf. Uzb. *qar* 'снег' (UzbRS).
See also **BUYAN-QAR, KÏNJÄ-QAR.**

QAR-BAS see **QARA-BAŠ**

QAR-BOL see **QARA-BOL**

QAR-JAW see **QAR-YAҐ**

QAR-JAWDÏ see **QAR-YAҐDÏ**

QAR-JAWUL Uzb. 20th c. **Qâr-Jâwul** [Коржовул]
(Begmatov 1984, 202). ✧ 'May snow be fallen' cf.
Uzb. *yâγ-* 'идти, падать' (UzbRS). ⇨ **QAR.** See also
QAR-YAҐDÏ, QAR-YAҐ.

QAR-YAҐ Tat.(Lit.) 1593 **Qar-Jaw** [Кардчавъ
Давлешевичъ] (Lit. Tat. 181); Kzk. 19th c. **Qar-Jaw**
[Карджау] (SOV 74); Kzk. 19th c. **Qar-Jaw**
[Карджау] (SOK 6); Kzk. 19th c. **Qar-Jaw-bay**
[Карджаубай] (AOA 42); Kzk. 19th c. **Qar-Jaw-bay**
[Карджаубай] (Grod., Pril. 139); Kzk. 19th c. **Qar-
Jaw-bek** [Карджаубекъ] (SODž. 148); Bashk. 1759
Qar-yaw [Карьяв Сиюндюков] (MIB IV/1, 178);
Bashk. 1777 **Qar-yaw** [Карьяу Ишимбетев] (MIB V,
60); Kzk. 19th c. **Qar-žaw-bay** [Коржаубай] (SODž.
156); Uzb. 20th c. **Qâr-yâγ** [Корёг] (Begmatov 1984,
202). ✧ 'Let the snow fall; snow-fall' cf. Kuman,
Chag., Crm., Turk. *yaγ-* 'regnen' (Radl. III, 39), Uzb.
yâγ- 'идти, падать (об атмосферных осадках)'
(UzbRS), Kzk. *žau-* 'идти (о дожде, снеге, граде)'
(KzRS). ⇨ **QAR.** See also **QAR-YAҐDÏ, QAR-
JAWUL.**

QAR-YAҐDÏ Trkm. 20th c. **Ґar-yaγdï** [Garyagdï] (Zaj.
1971, 330); Tat. 1553, 1557 **Qar-Jawdï** [Карчавъды]
(Kn. Metriki Lit. 152); Chag. 16th c. **Qar-yaγdï**
[Карягды], Jubay's son (Ivanov 153); NUyg. 19th c.
Qar-yaγdï [قار يـاغـدى / Kar yaghdi] (Le Coq, Namenl.
104); Tat.(Sib.) 1599 **Qara-yawdï? / Qar-yawdï?**
[Карѣ авдѣ], Qarmïšev's son (AI II, 23); Trkm. 19th c.
Qarï-yaγdï [Кары-Ягды] (IIRGO XXI, 8); Uzb. 20th
c. **Qâr-yâγdï** [Қорёгди / Корегди] (Begmatov 1984,
201, 202); Uzb. 20th c. **Qâr-yâγdï** [Корегди]
(Begmatov 1984, 202). ✧ 'It snowed' (Le Coq), cf.
Kuman, Chag., Crm., Turk. *yaγ-* 'regnen' (Radl. III,
39), Uzb. *yâγ-* 'идти, падать (об атмосферных
осадках)' (UzbRS), Kzk. *žau-* 'идти (о дожде,
снеге, граде)' (KzRS). ⇨ **QAR.** See also **QAR-YAҐ,
QAR-YAҐDÏ, QAR-JAWUL.**

QAR-YAMAN Kzk. 1819 **Qar-yaman** [Карьяман]
(MIK IV, 326). ⇨ **QAR / QARA? + YAMAN.**

QAR-YAT Bashk. 1756 **Qar-yat** [Теметь Карятав]
(MIB IV/1, 122); Bashk. 1756 **Qar-yat** [Умбеть
Карятов] (MIB IV/1, 122). ⇨ **QAR / QARA? + YAT.**

QAR-YAW see **QAR-YAҐ**

QAR-YAW-QUY Oghuz/Trkm. **Qar-yaw-quy** [Кар
Йав Куй], Qaraman's son (Muhamedova: OSA 170
/after Oguz-name by Salar-baba/).

QAR-ŌL see **QARA**

QAR-SÏNDÏ Trkm. 1731 **Qar-sïndï-oγlu**

[قارصندى اوغلى] (Refik, Anad. 186).

QAR-TÜGEŠ Alt. 19th c. **Qar-tügeš** [Картюгешев] (Verb., In. 23). ⇨ **QAR / QARA?** + **TÜGEŠ.**

QAR-ŽAW see **QAR-YAГ**

QARA Trkm. **Gara** [Kapa] (TrkmRS 155); Trkm. 20th c. **Gara** [Gara] (Zaj. 1971, 333); Trkm. 20th c. **Gara** [Kapa] (TrkmRS 155); Hak. 19th-20th c. **Xar-ōl** [Хароол] (HRS 352); Hak. 19th-20th c. **Xara** [Хара], fem. (HRS 355); Uyg. 762 **Xara-čur** [Ĭšbara χara-čur / Špara χaračur] (Müller, Uig. 762, Mahrnāmag 14, 39); Hak. 19th-20th c. **Xara-χïs** [Хара-Хыс], fem. (HRS 355); Uyg. 8th c. - 12th c. **Xara-qul?** [Xarâkûl Lāā Čūr] (Müller, Uig. 762, Mahrnāmag 11); Hak. 19th-20th c. **Xara-ōl** [Хара-Оол] (HRS 352); Hak. 19th-20th c. **Xara-pala** [Хара-Пала], fem. (HRS 355); Chuv. 18th-19th c. **Kara-čura** [Карачура] (Magn. 50); Chuv. 18th-19th c. **Kara-guža / Kara-χuža** [Карабузъ (Карагузъ / Карагузя / Карахузя, персидск. ходжа?)] (Magn. 50); Hak.(Sag.) 19th-20th c. **Qar-ōl** [Кар-ол] (Katanov, Otč. 7); Hak.(Kyz.) 19th-20th c. **Qar-ōl** [Кар-ол] (Katanov, Otč. 13); Türk **Qara** [Kara / Qara] (ETY II, 135); Türk? 873 **Qara** [احمد بن قرا], Aχmed, Qara's son, treasurer of Ahmed ibn Tūlūn in Egypt (Karabacek I, 105); Kuman? 1527 **Qara** [Georgii Kara], a family of Kuman (?) origin in Hungary (Gyárfás III, 760, Rásonyi, KÖA 109, Rásonyi, Anthr. 141); Karakh. 11th c. **Qara** [Kara / Qara] (MK/Atalay 842, DTS); Selj. **Qara** [Nûreddin Kara], an emir in Irak (Ahbar 125, 135); Selj. 12th c. **Qara** [نورالدين قرا], among Sultan Toγrïl's emirs, late 12th c. (Rāwandī 338); Selj.? 1197 **Qara** [ابن قرا] (Ibn al-Athīr/Tornb. XII, 82); Maml. 1309 **Qara** [قرا] (Dawād. 182); Maml. 1332 **Qara** [قرا السيفى] (Dawād. 367); Turk. 1583 **Qara** [Kara] (Ongan, Ank. I, 153, 164); Turk. 20th c. **Qara** [Kara], from Isparta, Turkey (Ün 1938, 645); Yürük 1543 **Qara** [Kara], several persons mentioned in the same source (Gökb., Rum. 184, 204, 206, 207, 211, 215, 224, 226, 229); Tat.(Lit.) 1557 **Qara** [Бойтинъ Кара] (Kn. Metriki Lit. 131); Tat. 18th c. **Qara** [Кара], a mulla (Nepljuev 599); Kzk. 1616 **Qara**, a prince (Radl., Aus Sib. I, 182); Kzk. 1621 **Qara** [Кара (Кар, Kopa)] (Miller, Ist. Sib. II, 263, 310, 317); Kzk. 19th c. **Qara** [Кара Тенгрибирдіевъ] (SKSO VIII, 201); Kzk.? 19th c. **Qara** [Кара Ураловъ] (SKSO III, 170); Kzk. 19th c. **Qara** [Кара] (SOV 152); Kkalp. 20th c. **Qara** [Къара] (Bask., Kkalp. 67); Alt. 19th-20th c. **Qara** [Кара] (OjrRS 208); Alt. 19th-20th c. **Qara** [Кара], fem. (OjrRS 212); Hak.(Kyz.) 19th-20th c. **Qara** [Кара], fem. (Katanov, Otč. 13); Hak.(Shor) 19th-20th c. **Qara** [Кара], fem. (Katanov, Otč. 11); Kzk. 1820 **Qara(-sultan)?** [Кара султанъ], a chieftain (Sib. Vest. IX, 118); Kipch. 1342 **Qara-bahadur** [قرا بهادر], Özbeg Khan's envoy to Egypt (Tizeng. I,

255, 265 /after Al-Malik An-Nāsir/); Selj. 14th c. **Qara-bahadur** [قرا بهادر], died at the beginning of the 14th c. in Yeni-šehir (Qazw. 200); Tat. 1500 **Qara-bay** [Карабай], a Tatar (or a „kazak") from the region of Azov (PSRL VI, 44, 46, 243, VIII, 238, 240, XII, 251, 253, XX, 369); Tat. 1620 **Qara-bay** [Карабай Абдаловъ] (Kurdjumov 121); Tat. 1624 **Qara-bay** [Карабай Баранчинъ] (Pokrovskij 69); Bashk. 1735 **Qara-bay** [Карабай Гаировъ], a tarχan (Vel.-Zern., Bašk. 12); Bashk. 1735 **Qara-bay** [Карабай Турумбетевъ], a prince (Vel.-Zern., Bašk. 18); Kzk. 19th c. **Qara-bay** [Карабай] (Grod., Pril. 30, 145); Kzk. 19th c. **Qara-bay** [Карабай] (AOAtb. 14); Kzk. 19th c. **Qara-bay** [Каргысчилъ Карабай] (Potanin, Pred. 104); Kkalp. 18th c. - 19th c. **Qara-bay** [Карабай хан], a khan (MIKk. 93); Kirg. 20th c. **Qara-bay** [Карабай] (Jud. 260, Kalilov 95); Uzb. 19th c. **Qara-bay** [Байкара Карабаевъ] (SKSO III, 8); Kzk. 19th c. **Qara-baqsa** [Карабакса], a biy (Lomakin 42); Kzk. 19th c. **Qara-baqsï** [Карабаксы] (SOV 24); Uyg. 12th c. - 14th c. **Qara-baqšï** [Kara Bakšï] (DTSö EUTS); Kzk. 19th c. **Qara-bala** [Карабала Чакишевъ] (Grod., Pril. 149); Kirg. 20th c. **Qara-bala** [Карабала] (Kalilov 95); Alt. 19th-20th c. **Qara-bala** [Карабала], fem. (OjrRS 212); Sib.(Tat.) **Qara-batïr** [Кара Батыр] (Proben IV, 284 /352/); Kzk. **Qara-batïr** (Vámbéry, Vázlatok 323); Kzk. 19th c. **Qara-batïr**, a bay (rich man) (Ljuts 50); Kzk. 19th c.? **Qara-batïr** (Atyns. 15); Turk. 15th c. **Qara-bäy** [Καραμπεις], a Turkish commander of arny (Byz. Turc. 152); Turk., Yürük? 1540 **Qara-beg** [Kara Beg], head of the community (cemaat) of Čödiklü (Demirtaş 49); Oghuz 947 **Qara-beh / Qara-beg?** [ابن قرا به] (Ibn al-Athīr/Tornb. VIII, 350); Uzb. 1768/69 **Qara-behadïr** [Кара-бехадыр (мирабъ)] (MIT II, 341, 363, 364, 401, 625); Kzk. 19th c. **Qara-bek** [Карабек] (Grod., Pril. 91, 99, 123, 153); Kzk. 19th c. **Qara-bek** [Мирзалъ Карабековъ] (Grod., Pril. 199); Kirg. **Qara-bek** [Карабек] (Jud. 841); Kirg. **Qara-bek** [Карабек] (Jud. 646); Maml. 1263 **Qara-bek / Qara-beg** [حسام‌الدين كره بلكا بن بركتخان] (Berchem, Jér. I, 190); Alt. **Qara-bökö** [Кара-бöкö] (Nikiforov 148, 150); Tat.(Sib.) 1599 **Qara-čan** [Карачанъ], a princess in Siberia from Küčüm's family (AI II, 18, 23); Türk **Qara-čur?** [Qar Çur] (ETY II, 134, 135); Tat. 1539/40 **Qara-čura** [قراجوره / Карачура] (Jusupov 63); Tat. 17th c. **Qara-čura** [Асанъ Карачуринъ] (IOAIÊK XXIX, 300); Bashk. 1754 **Qara-čura** [Карачуря Кулуев] (MIB IV/1, 83); Kzk. 1829 **Qara-čura** [Карачура] (MIK IV, 323); Kzk. 19th c. **Qara-ǰan** [Караджанъ] (SKSO VIII, 227); Kzk. 19th c. **Qara-ǰan** [Караджанъ] (Grod., Pril. 95); Kzk. 19th c. **Qara-ǰan** [Караджанъ] (SODž. 118); Uzb. 19th c. **Qara-ǰan**

[Караджанъ] (SKSO III, 170); Kzk. 1785 **Qara-ǰan-bahadïr** [قره‌جان بهارر], chief (aqsaqal) of the Qara-kesek tribe (MIK IV, 51, 53); Maml. 1449 **Qara-ǰan-bek** [قرا جانبك الظاهرى] (Ibn Taghrīb. VII, 166, 188, 382); Kzk. 19th c. **Qara-ǰigit** [Ходжа Бергенъ Караджигитовъ] (Grod., Pril. 171); Kzk. 19th c. **Qara-ǰigit** [Караджигитовъ] (Grod., Pril. 95); Kzk. 1794 **Qara-ǰigit / Qara-ǰīgīt** [قرا جكت ملا] (MIK IV, 165); Kzk. 1803 **Qara-ǰigit / Qara-ǰīgīt** [قرا جكت] (MIK IV, 211); Kzk. 19th c. **Qara-ǰïɣit** [Кара-Джигитъ], a hero of a tale (AUK 853); Oghuz/Trkm. 13th c. **Qara-ɣāzi-bek** [قرا غازى بيك / Кара-Гази-бек] (Abulg./Kon. 1165, 1235); Alt. 19th-20th c. **Qara-ɣïs** [Крагыс], fem. (OjrRS 212); Bashk. 1664 **Qara-ɣïz** [Иштяк Карагызов] (MIB I, 186); Selj. 11th c. - 13th c. **Qara-ɣul** [التراغول مستخنفظوا الطرق / Karaguli] (Abulfar. Or. 471); Bashk. 1735 **Qara-ɣul** [Карагулъ Чириковъ] (Vel.-Zern., Bašk. 13); Bashk. 1739 **Qara-ɣul** [Карагул Елдашев] (MIB III, 404); Bashk. 1761 **Qara-ɣul** [Кадыберда Карагулов] (MIB IV/1, 214); Bashk. 1778 **Qara-ɣul** [Баранбай Карагулов] (MIB V, 79); Kzk. 19th c.? **Qara-ɣul** [Karagul] (Atyns. 113); Kirg **Qara-ɣul** [Карагул] (Jud. 89, 537, 827); Uzb. 1722 **Qara-ɣul** [Карагулъ] (Veselovskij, Unk. 147, 154, 165); Oghuz/Trkm. 13th c. **Qara-han** [Кара-хан], Dib-baquy's son (RaD. I/1, 76); Oghuz **Qara-χan** [قرا خان], Oghuz-χan's father, the forefather of the Ottoman dynasty (Āšikp. 5); Oghuz/Trkm. 13th c. **Qara-χan** [قرا خان بن منسيك / قرا خان / Qara-Khan / Кара-хан], Mogol Khan's son in the Turkic legend of origin (Abulg./Desm. 12, Qazw. 558, Abulg./Kon. 160, 175, 195, 200, 215 etc.); Oghuz/Trkm. 13th c. **Qara-χan** [قرا خان / Кара-хан], Muryawï-χan's (?) son (Abulg./Kon. 865, 870, 875); Selj.? 1001 **Qara-χan** [احمد بن على قرا خان] (Hil. Sābī 423); Maml. 1244 **Qara-χan** [قرا خان], lord of Hims (Qalānisi); Chag.? **Qara-χan** [Qara χan] (Šejb. XXII); Turk. 20th c. **Qara-χan** [Karahan] (Önder, Göle); Trkm.? 1688 **Qara-χan** [Кара-хан-Занчендский] (MIT II, 120, 121); Trkm.? 1851 **Qara-χan** [Кара-хан] (MIT II, 283, 298, 301-304, 430); Trkm.?, Uzb.? 1846 **Qara-χan** [Кара-хан мехрем] (MIT II, 502); Selj./Khorezm. 10th c. - 11th c. **Qara-χan** [Kârâkhân], he or his son was the governor of Bukhara (Abulfar./Budge I, 186); Oghuz/Trkm. 13th c. **Qara-χoǰa** [قرا خواجه] (Abulg./Kon. 725); Uzb.? 1817/18 **Qara-χoǰa** [Кара-ходжа], Šah-murad-biy's son-in-law (MIT II, 197); Maml.? 1435/36 **Qara-χoǰa / Qara-qoǰa** [الحسنى / قرا حجا / قرا قجا] (Ibn Taghrīb., VI, 745, VII, 2, 44, 64, Weil, Chalif. II, 229, 231, Iyās); Uyg. 13th-14th c. **Qara-ïnal** [Qara İnal] (Zieme, Mat. II, 91); Kzk. 1786 **Qara-yegit? / Qara-yïkit?** [Караекит] (MIK IV,

75); Turk., Yürük? 1540 **Qara-kethudā**, head of the community (cemaat) of Čulï (Demirtaş 51); Türk 8th c. - 9th c. **Qara-qan** [qara qan / Qara qan] (DTS, ETY III, 170); Kzk. **Qara-qan** [Кара-Кан], a folklore hero mentioned together with Sarï-qan (Proben III, 221); Kkalp. 20th c. **Qara-qan** [Қарақан] (KkRS 774); Kirg. **Qara-qan** [Каракан] (Jud. 706); Alt. 19th c. **Qara-qan** [Кара-Кан-царь] (Verb., In. 161); Alt.(Tuba) 19th c. **Qara-qan** [Караканъ] (Potanin IV, 564); Hak.(Sag.) 19th-20th c. **Qara-qan** [Кара Кан], a folklore hero (Proben IX, 249, 252, 415); Shor 19th-20th c. **Qara-qan** (Dyrenkova 40); Yak. **Qara-qan** [Ала Каракан] (Pek.); Tat.(Tüm.) **Qara-qïs** [Кара Кыс], fem. (Proben IV, 503); Alt. 19th-20th c. **Qara-qïs** [Кракыс], fem. (OjrRS 212); Hak. 19th c. **Qara-qïs** [Кара-кыс], fem. (Katanov, Otč. 12); Hak.(Sag.) 19th-20th c. **Qara-qïs** [Кара-кыс], fem. (Katanov, Otč. 7); Karg. **Qara-qïs** [Кара-кыс], fem. (Katanov, Otč. 9); Selj. 12th c. **Qara-qïz** [قراقز اتابكى] (Rāwandī 375); Bashk. 1739 **Qara-qïz** [Каракыз] (MIB III, 410); Alt. 19th c. **Qara-qïz** [Кара-кыз-наложница], fem. (Verb., In. 117, 120); Chag. 15th c. **Qara-qul** [Каракулъ-Ахмедъ-мирза] (Barth., Ulugb. 87); Kzk. 19th c. **Qara-qul** [Каракуловъ] (Grod., Pril. 34); Kzk. 19th c. **Qara-qul** [Каракулъ] (SODž. 90); Kzk. 19th c. **Qara-qul** [Каракулъ Ишъ-Аліевъ] (SKSO VIII, 207); Alt. **Qara-matïr** [Кара-матыръ] (Nikiforov 228-29); Maml.? 1406/07 **Qara-melik** [قرا ملك] (Iyās I, 351, II, 19); Trkm. 1824/25 **Qara-mergen** [Кара-мерген], from the İmreli tribe (MIT II, 425); Kzk. **Qara-mergen** [Кара-Мергенъ], a folklore hero, hunter (Sb. Syr-D. IV, otd. II, 89, AUK 295); Kzk. 1832 **Qara-mergen** [Карамерген] (Konšin, Mat. V, 97, SOK 48); Kkalp. 20th c. **Qara-mïrza** [Қарамырза] (KkRS 774); Nog. 20th c. **Qara-mïrza** [Хасан Къарамырза улы Уьздоьн / Хасан Карамурзаевич Узденов], father of Baskakov's informant from the aul of Erkin-yurt (Bask., Nog. 143); Turk. 1347 **Qara-moχamet** [Καραμαχούμετ], a Turkish commander (Byz. Turc. 152); Shor 19th-20th c. **Qara-mökö** (Dyrenkova 92, 383); Kzk. 19th c. **Qara-mulda** [Карамулда] (Grod., Pril. 51); Shor 19th-20th c. **Qara-mükü** (Dyrenkova 92, 383); Shor 19th-20th c. **Qara-mükü** (Dyrenkova 92, 383); Oghuz? **Qara-oɣlan** [قرا اوغلان / قرهلو اوغلان], forefather of the Ottoman dynasty (Āšikp. 5, Nešrī, Ālī 186, Wittek 94); Yürük 1543 **Qara-oɣlan** [Karaoğlan], from the Yürüks of Kocacık, Turkey (Gökb., Rum. 103); Trkm. 1847 **Qara-oɣlan** [Кара-оглан], a corporal (onbegi) (MIT II, 240, 241); Tat. 1543 **Qara-oɣlan** [Karaoğlan] (Gökb., Rum. 240, 241, 242); Hak.(Shor) 19th-20th c. **Qara-pala** [Кара-пала], fem. (Katanov, Otč. 11); Turk. 14th c. - 16th c. **Qara-paša** [Kara Paşa] (Baştav

93); Uyg. 12th c. - 14th c. **Qara-señün** [qara señün] (DTS); Turk. 14th c. **Qara-su-bašï (Qara-subašï)** [Καρασούπασης], a commander of the army (Byz. Turc. 152); Khorezm. 1213 **Qara-šah (Qaraǰa)** [Kâra shâh (Kârâjâ) Khâs ḥâjib], a betrayer of the Khorezmshah at the time of Chinggis' invasion, in Bukhara (or Otrar?) (Abulfar./Budge I, 368); Uyg. **Qara-tägün** [Kara Tägün] (EUTS); Uyg. 12th c. - 14th c. **Qara-tegin** [Qara Tägün] (Radl., USp. 124); Oghuz 922 **Qara-tegin** [Karatekin], a general, chief of the police with the Samanids (Weil, Chalif. II, 615, 616, Qazw. 417, Ibn al-Athīr/Tornb. VIII, 59, 91, 155-57); Oghuz 988 **Qara-tegin** [قرا تكين الجهشياری] (Ibn al-Athīr/Tornb. IX, 36-37); Oghuz 989 **Qara-tegin** [Karatekin], a commander of the army of the Buyids (Weil, Chalif. III, 34); Oghuz 1040 **Qara-tegin** [Абдаллах Кaратегин], from the Salar Gazi tribe (?) (MIT I, 298); Selj. **Qara-tegin** [قرا تكين التصاب] (Bondārī 129); Selj. 11th c. - 13th c. **Qara-tegin** [Karatekin], first Turkic commander of Kangri (Gangra) under the Danishmendids (Hezârfenn - Mordtmann: ZDMG XXX, 470); Selj. 12th c. **Qara-tegin** [قرا لالا تگين] (Rāwandī 163); Uyg. 12th c. - 14th c. **Qara-tekün** [qara tekün] (DTS); Nog.?, Kmk.? 1822 **Qara-tigin?** [Каратыгин], a (first) lieutenant (MID III, 169); Uyg. 12th c. - 14th c. **Qara-toyïn** [Kara Toyın] (Radl., USp. 16-17, DTS, EUTS); Kkalp. 20th c. **Qara-žan** [Каражан] (KkRS 774); Kzk. **Qara-žan-batïr** [Каражанъ-батыръ] (IOAIÊK XX, 224); *EN:* Yürük 1602 **Qara-qoǰa** [قره قوجه / Karakoca cemaatı], a religious (ethnic) community (tribe?) (Gökçen 67); Kzk. 18th c. - 19th c. **Qara** [Кара] (Tynyšp. 65, 68, 71, 73, 74); Kzk. 18th c. - 19th c. **Qara-batïr** [Карабатыр], a clan (Tynyšp. 65, 67); Kzk. 18th c. - 19th c. **Qara-bek** [Карабек] (Tynyšp. 65); Kzk. 18th c. - 19th c. **Qara-biy** [Карабий] (Tynyšp. 65); Trkm. **Qara-qan** [Karakan oymağı], a tribe in the region of Nurhak dağı (Riza V, 51); Kzk. 18th c. - 19th c. **Qara-qul** [Каракул], a clan (Tynyšp. 67); Kzk. 18th c. - 19th c. **Qara-molda** [Карамолда], a clan (Tynyšp. 71); *TN:* Chuv. 18th c. **Kara-čurina** [Карачурина], a village in the district of Cheboksary (Korsakov 285); Crm. **Qara-bay** [Karabai], an isle in the Black Sea west of Perekop (Jervis II); Crm. **Qara-bay** [Karabai], a place north of Eski-Qïrïm (Jervis VIII); Tat. 18th c. **Qara-bay(eva)** [Карабаева], a village in the district of Tetyushinsk (Korsakov 336); Kzk. **Qara-bek** [Карабек] (Kojčubaev 119); Kzk. **Qara-mergen** [Карамерген], a place (Kojčubaev 122); Tuv. 19th c. **Qara-pay / Qara-päy** [Кара-паи / Кара-пäи], a place (Proben IX, 21, 36, 59, 80). ✧ 'Black, dark colour; (fig.) northern; evil, wicked; strong, powerful; miserable; a member of a lower classe; a foreigner; live-stock' cf. all Trk. dial. *qara*

'schwarz; schlecht, böse, unglücklich; niedriggestellt; ein anderer Mensch; ein Fremder; das Vieh' (Radl. II, 132). According to Žanuzakov in Kzk. it also means 'supporter' and 'cattle, horses, etc.' (Žanuzakov 109). E. g.: *Qara-qan* 'Northern Khan' (Blagova 1997, 704), *Qara-qoǰa* 'Black master, black lord' (Sauvaget 53). See also AƔZÏ-QARA, AYU-ГАRA, ALA-XARA, ALÏN-QARA, ALP-QARA, ALTMÏŠ-QARA, ALTUN-QARA, AS-QARA, AŠAN-QARA, BAƔLU-QARA, BAY-QARA, BAYAT-QARA, BAL-ГАRA, BAŠ-QARA I., BAŠÏ-QARA, BOZ-QARA, BUYAN-QARA, BUT-QARA, BÜRLÜK-QARA, ČEKÏM-QARA, ČER-QARA, ČET-QARA, ČÏRĀ-QARA, ǰAN-QARA, DAW-QARA, DÄW-QARA, DOST-QARA, DÜŠÜM-QARA, ÄRÄM-QARA, EYWAS-QARA, ERKE-QARA, ERÄM-QARA, ES-QARA, ESÄN-QARA, EŠ-QARA, XABÏDAL-XARA, XAǰÏ-QARA, IŠ-QARA, IT-QARA, YAMAN-QARA, YARMÏS-XARA, YÄR-QARA, YEGÄN-QARA, KENT-QARA, KET-QARA, KENČÄ-QARA, KENǰE-QARA, KÖLǰÜN-QARA, KÖNČEK-QARA, KÖRPÖ-QARA, KÜČ-QARA, QALÏÑ-QARA, QARA-QARA, QARÏS-QARA, QAŠ-QARA, QÏLÏČ-KÜČ-QARA, QÏLÏNČ-QARA, QÏSQA-QARA, QÏTÏ-QARA, QÏTAY-QARA, QUBÏQTÏ-QARA, QUL-QARA, QULUM-QARA, QULUN-QARA, QUŠ-QARA, MADAY-QARA, MAY-QARA, MÏNLÜ-QARA, MÏÑ-QARA, OYSÏL-QARA, OYSUL-QARA, ORU(URU)-QARA, ÖGRÜNČ-QARA, PATPAN-QARA, SAČÏ-QARA, SÄKÏNS-QARA, SASÏQ-QARA, SEKÏNČ-QARA, SEVÏNČ-QARA, SOYĀ-QARA, SŪQ-QARA, SUƔAN-QARA, SÜYÜN-QARA, ŠOYÏN-QARA, TAƔRÏ-BERDÏ-QARA, TAY-QARA, TAŠ-QARA, TAT-QARA, TÄWKÄL-QARA, TOƔRUL-QARA, TOPAL-QARA, TUMAN-BAY-QARA, TÖLÄK-QARA, TÜKÄL-QARA, TÜLÜK-QARA, UZUN-QARA, ÜČ-QARA, ÜKÜŠ-QARA.

QARA-AČQÏ see YETMÏŠ-QARA-AČQÏ, ÖKÜŠ-QARA-AČQÏ

QARA-AYAQ Kzk. 19th c. **Qara-ayaq** [Корааякъ] (SOK 148). ⇨ QARA + AYAQ.

QARA-ALP-ARSLAN Oghuz. 13th c. **Qara-alp-arslan** [Кара-Алп-Арслан], Qanlï-Yawlï-χan's son (Bulg./Kon. 845-855, 865). ⇨ QARA + ALP-ARSLAN.

QARA-ALTAY Kzk. 1803, 1820 **Qara-altay** [Кара Алтай / Караалтай], a leader of the Alim-ulï tribe (MIK IV, 514, Sib. Vest. IX, 115); Kzk. 1804 **Qara-altay** [Кара-Алтай], a leader of the Qulaman tribe (MIK IV, 222); Kzk. 1794, 1795, 1799 **Qara-altay / Qara-altay-bi** [قرا آلطای بی / Кара-Алтай] (MIK IV,

165, Mejer 25). ⇨ **QARA + ALTAY.**

QARA-AN Uyg. 13th-14th c. **Qara-an** [Qra An (?)], fem. (Zieme, Mat. III, 272). ✧ 'Black-?'. ⇨ **QARA.**

QARA-ARSLAN Oghuz/Trkm. 14th c. - 15th c.? **Qara-arslan** [Qara Arslān Melik] (DQorq./Rossi 133); Selj. **Qara-arslan** [ضيا الـدين قـرا ارسلان] (Ibn Bībī III, 150, 389, IV, 66, 150 etc.); Selj. 1121, 1139, 1150, 1155 **Qara-arslan** [ارسلان بـن داود / مـجيـرالـدين قـرا ارسلان ارسلان بـن داود بـن سكمان بـن ارتق فـحرالـدين / قـرا قـرا / Муджир-ад-дин Кара-Арслан ибн Дауд ибн Сукман ибн Орток], an Artukid (Ortokid) emir, Daud's son, Suqman's grandson, in 1144 became the lord of Zâîd (Qalānisi 267, 333, Kamāladdīn II, 268, 276, 297, Abulfar./Budge I, 268, Qazw. 446, Usāma 66, 115, 143); Selj. 1149, 1150 **Qara-arslan** [فـحرالـدين قـرا ارسلان / قـرا ارسلان فـحرالـدين], ruler of Hisn-Keyfa, lord of Diyarbekir (Ibn al-Athīr/Tornb. XI, 92, 185, 199, 217, Ibn al-Athīr, Atab.: RHCHor II/2, 172, 219, Ibn al-Athīr: RHCHor 537, 551); Selj. 1181 **Qara-arslan** [Kârâ 'Arslân], an Artukid (Ortokid) (Abulfar./Budge I, 310); Selj. 1292 **Qara-arslan** [Melik-Moudaffer-Kara-arslan], an Artukid (Ortokid), the lord of Māridīn, died in 1292 (Makrīzī III, 144, Weil, Chalif. I, 203); Maml.? 1298 **Qara-arslan** [Schehab-eddin-Kara-arslan] (Makrīzī IV, 60, Weil, Chalif. I, 211); Maml. 1299 **Qara-arslan** [Beha-eddin-Kara-arslan-Mansouri], governor of Damascus (Makrīzī IV, 124, Weil, Chalif. I, 221); Selj. 1067 **Qara-arslan / Qara-arslan-beg** [قـرا ارسلان / قـرا ارسلان بـك], sultan of Kirman at Alp-arslan's (1063-1072) times, bore the byname *Qawurd* (Ibn al-Athīr/Tornb. X, 36-37, Ahbar 28, Muh. Ibrahim 28). ✧ 'Black lion' (Sauvaget 52). ⇨ **QARA + ARSLAN.**

QARA-ATTÏ Alt.(Tel.) **Qara-attū-qan** (Radl. I, 472); Tuv. 19th c. **Qarattï-χan (Qara-attï)** [Каратты-ханъ] (Potanin IV, 371); Hak.(Shor) 19th-20th c. **Qarattï-pärgän (Qara-attï-pärgän)** [Каратты-Пäргäн] (Radl. II, 169); Alt. 19th c. **Qarattï-pergen (<Qara-attï-pergen)** [Каратты-Перген-богатыр], a folklore hero (Verb., In. 140-143, 145, 146, 153); Tuv. 19th c. **Qarāttï-qān (<Qara-attï)** [Каратты кан] (Proben IX, 153-164). ✧ 'With black horse'. ⇨ **QARA + AT +** suff. *-tï*.

QARA-ATTŪ see **QARA-ATTÏ**

QARA-BADÏŠ Kirg. **Qara-badïš** [Кара Бадышъ] (Proben V, 184 /186/); Kirg. **Qara-badïš** [Кара Бадыш] (Proben V, 184 (186)). ⇨ **QARA + BADÏŠ.**

QARA-ВАҒЇS Kzk. **Qara-baγïs** [Кара Баҕыс], three brothers called Kenžä, Qunan and Dönön Qara Baγïs (Proben III, 253 /297/). ⇨ **QARA + ВАҒЇS.**

QARA-BAYÏR Kirg. **Qara-bayïr** [Кара Баир] (Proben V, 40 /41/). ✧ I. 'Black hill'; II. 'A kind of (strong) horse' cf. Kirg. *qarabayïr* 'карабаир (помесь кровной лошади с простой; лошадь не чистокровная, но выносливая' (Jud.). ⇨ **QARA + BAYÏR.**

QARA-BAQAL Kzk. 19th c. **Qara-baqal** [Карабакалъ] (SOK 250). ⇨ **QARA + BAQAL.**

QARA-BAL Kzk. **Qara-bal** [Карабалъ] (Sb. Syr-D. IX, 56). ⇨ **QARA + BAL.**

QARA-BARS Türk **Qara-bars** [Qara Bars / Kara Bars], Oγul-bars's brother (ETY II, 133). ⇨ **QARA + BARS.**

QARA-BAS see **QARA-BAŠ**

QARA-BAŠ Chuv. 18th c. **Kara-baš(eva)** [Карабашева], a village in the district of Cheboksary (Korsakov 283); Chuv. 18th-19th c. **Kara-pas** [Карапасъ] (Magn. 50); Kzk. 19th c. **Qar-bas** [Карбазъ] (SOV 56); Kzk. 19th c. **Qara-bas** [Карабасъ] (AOO 30); Kzk. 1850 **Qara-bas** [Бирубай Карабасовъ] (Konšin, Mat. V, 103); Karch. **Qara-baš** [Карабашевъ] (Sysoev 126); Tat.(Sib.) 1623, 1636 **Qara-baš** [Карабашко Ишимов] (Miller, Ist. Sib. II, 300, 302, 435, 436); Bashk. 1675 **Qara-baš** [Карабаш Узюгелдин] (MIB I, 199); Bashk. ᶜ1738 **Qara-baš** [Бигишай Карабашев] (MIB III, 393); Bashk. 1738 **Qara-baš** [Кармышака Карабашев] (MIB I, 143); Bashk. 1740 **Qara-baš** [Карабаш] (MIB I, 395); Bashk. 1763 **Qara-baš** [Карабаш Ишеев] (MIB IV/1, 269); Bashk. 1792 **Qara-baš** [Зайса Карабашев] (MIB V, 328); Alt. 19th-20th c. **Qara-baš** [Карабаш] (OjrRS 208); Alt. 19th-20th c. **Qara-baš** [Карабаш], fem. (OjrRS 212); Uzb. 19th c. **Qara-baš-bay** [Карабашбай] (SKSO III, 178); Bashk. 19th c. **Qara-baš-χoджa** [قـرا باش / حواجه / Карабашъ-ходжа] (Veselovskij, Kirg. 56); Tat.(Sib.) 1634 **Qara-paš** [Карапаш] (Miller, Ist. Sib. II, 419); *TN:* Kzk. **Qara-bas** [Карабас], a place (Kojčubaev 118). ⇨ **QARA + BAŠ.**

QARA-BĀLİ Yürük 1543 **Qara-bāli** [Kara Bâli] (Gökb., Rum. 207); Yürük 1576 **Qara-bāli** [Karabali] (Gökçen 51). ⇨ **QARA + BĀLİ.**

QARA-BĂČKÄM Oghuz? 10th c. **Qara-băčkäm** [قـرابجكم / قـرا بـجكم], a fictitious person in the genealogy of the Ghaznevid Sebük-tegin (Mirch. Gasnevid.141). ✧ 'Black wolf' cf. Chag. *băčkäm* 'der Wolf, ein Türkengeschlecht' (Radl. IV, 1625). ⇨ **QARA.**

QARA-BÏŠPAN Crm. **Qara-bïšpan** [Кара Бышпан] (Proben VII, 214). ⇨ **QARA.**

QARA-BOL Kzk. 19th c. **Qar-bol (Qara-bol)** [Карболъ] (SODž. 156); Kzk. 19th c. **Qara-bol** [Караболъ] (SOV 42, 60); Kzk. 19th c. **Qara-bol** [Караболъ] (SODž. 156); Kzk. 19th c. **Qara-bul** [Карабулъ] (Grod., Pril. 155). ✧ 'Become black, be black'. ⇨ **QARA + BOL.** See also **AQ-BOL.**

QARA-BÖRÜK Kirg. **Qara-börük** [Кара Бöрÿк] (Proben V, 78 /79/). ✧ 'Black (fur) cap' cf. Kzk. *börik* 'börk, başa giyilen nesne' (KzTS), 'елтірідeн, түлкініӊ пушпағынан, не басқа аӊ терісінен істелген бас киім' (QTTS). ⇨ **QARA.**

QARA-BUDAГ see **QARA-BUDAQ**

QARA-BUDAQ   Oghuz/Trkm. 14th c. - 15th c. **Qara-budaq / Qara-budaү** [قره بُوداۋ / Qara Budaq / Qara Budaġ / Кара-Будаг (Будаг, Будак)] (DQorq./Rossi 112, 122, 127, 133, 144 etc., DQorq./Ergin 96, DQorq. 22, etc.). ⇨ **QARA + BUTAQ.**

QARA-BUГA see **QARA-BUQA**

QARA-BUГRA   Trkm.? 1454 **Qara-buɣra** [قرا بغرا] (Dorn 205); Kzk. 1794 **Qara-bura** [قرا بورا] (MIK IV, 163); Uyg. **Qara-puɣra-qan** [Кара Пуҕра кан], khan of Eastern Turkestan (Radl. II, 105, IV, 1362); *EN:* Kzk. 18th c. - 19th c. **Qara-bura** [Карабура], a clan (Tynyšp. 73, 75); *TN:* Kzk. **Qara-bura** [Кара-бура], a river (ZVOIRAO VIII, 343); Kzk. **Qara-bura** [Кара-бура], a kurgan (burial mound) (ZVOIRAO II, 225); Kzk. **Qara-bura** [Кара-бура], a mountain pass (ZVOIRAO VIII, 20); Kzk. **Qara-bura** [Кара-бура], a river (ZVOIRAO VIII, 343). ✧ 'Black stallion'. ⇨ **QARA + BUГRA.** See also **XARA-AXSÏR.**

QARA-BUQA   Hak. 19th-20th c. **Xara-puɣa** [Хара-Пуҕа] (HRS 352); Uyg. **Qara-buɣa** [Kara Buġa] (EUTS); Maml. **Qara-buɣa** [قرا بغا] (Duqmaq:RHCHor V, 20); Maml. 13th c. **Qara-buɣa** [قرا بغا الشكرى] (Zetterst. 2); Maml. 1261 **Qara-buɣa** [قرا بغا] (Iyās I, 102, 196); Maml. 1265 **Qara-buɣa** [قرا بوغا / Kârâ Boghâ], governor? of Baghdad (Abulfar. 545, Abulfar./Budge I, 445); Maml. 1346/47 **Qara-buɣa** [قرا بغا التاسمى] (Iyās I, 185, 187); Maml. 1366/67 **Qara-buɣa** [قرا بغا الصرغتمشى] (Iyās I, 219, 220); Maml. 1366/67 **Qara-buɣa** [قرا بغا البدرى] (Iyās I, 219); Maml. 1366/67 **Qara-buɣa** [قرا بغا العزى] (Iyās I, 220); Maml. 1399/1400 **Qara-buɣa** [قرا بغا مغرق] (Ibn Taghrīb. VI, 22); Maml.? 1402/3 **Qara-buɣa** [قرا بغا الا بكرى] (Iyās I, 248, 281 etc.); Uyg. 12th c. - 14th c. **Qara-buqa** [qara buqa] (Radl., USp. 21-23, Le Coq, Urkunden 458-59, DTS); *EN:* Selj.? **Qara-buqa** [قرا بو قا /قوم/], a tribe or clan (Zehireddin/Dorn 112); *TN:* Kkalp. 1810 **Qara-buqa** [Карабука], a forest (MIKk. 118). ✧ 'Black bull' cf. Sauvaget 52: *qara boga* 'taureau noir'. ⇨ **QARA + BUQA.**

QARA-BUQAY   Selj.? 1295 **Qara-buqay** [قرا بو قاى] (Dorn 137). ⇨ **QARA-BUQA** + suff. *-y.*

QARA-BUL see **QARA-BOL**

QARA-BULAQ   Kzk. 19th c. **Qara-bulaq** [Карабулакъ], a biy in Maňgïšlaq (Lomakin 33); *TN:* Uzb. **Qara-bulaq**, a place (É. Dobos, An Oghuz Dialect: AOH XXVIII, 77). ⇨ **QARA + BULAQ.**

QARA-BULAT   Tat.(GH) 1322 **Qara-bulat** [Καραπολάτ], a „Tatar" commander of the army (Byz. Turc. 152); Tat.(GH) 1322 **Qara-bulat** [Кара-Булатъ], governor of Özbek-qan in the Crimea (Smirnov, Krym. 36); Maml.? 1379/80 **Qara-bulat** [قرا بلاط الاحمدى] (Iyās I, 248); Kzk. 19th c. **Qara-bulat** [Карабулат] (AOK 2); Kzk. 19th c. **Qara-bulat** [Карабулат] (AOK 2). ✧ 'Black steel' (Sauvaget 52). ⇨ **QARA + BULAT.**

QARA-BULUQ   Türk 759 **Qara-buluq** [Qara Buluq] (ETY I, 172); Tat.(GH) 1377, 1378 **Qara-buluq** [Карабулукъ (Карабалухъ / Корбулукъ)], Mamay's prince from the Horde (PSRL IV, 74, V, 237, VIII, 33, XI, 43, XXIII, 124). ⇨ **QARA + BULUQ.** See also **BULUQ-ARSLAN.**

QARA-BULUT   Khorezm.? **Qara-bulut** [قرا بولوت] (RaD/Blochet (Appendice) 60); Chag. **Qara-bulut** (Le Coq, Ind. 4); Yürük 16th c. **Qara-bulut**, from the Yürüks of Kocacık, Turkey (Gökb., Rum. 104). ✧ 'Black cloud' (Le Coq). ⇨ **QARA + BULUT.**

QARA-BURA see **QARA-BUГRA**

QARA-BUT   Kzk. 19th c. **Qara-but** [Кара-бутъ] (Potanin II, 149). ⇨ **QARA BUT.**

QARA-BUTA   Kirg.? 19th c. **Qara-buta** [Карабутаевъ] (Grod., Pril. 95). ✧ 'Black young camel'. ⇨ **QARA + BOTA.**

QARA-BÜRÜKLÜ   Turk. 1519 **Qara-bürüklü / Qara-bürklü?** [Kara Bürüklü] (Gökb., Ed. 188). ✧ 'Having black (fur) cap'. ⇨ **QARA-BÖRÜK** + suff. *-lü.*

QARA-ČAČ   Kirg. **Qara-čač** [Карачач] (Jud. 243); Kirg. **Qara-čač** [Кара Чач], fem. (Proben V, 36 /37/); Kzk. 19th c. **Qara-čaš** [Кара-чашъ], fem. (Ibragimov 125); Crm. **Qara-šas-qanïm** [Карашас Каным (каным)], fem. (Proben VII, 214); Nog. **Qara-šaš** [Кара-шаш], fem. (Žirm., Epos 497); Kzk. **Qara-šaš / Qara-šaš-sulū** [Карашаш, Кара Шаш, Кара Шаш Сулу], fem. (Proben III, 339 /411/, 402 /476/, 414 /489/); Kzk. 19th c.? **Qara-šaš-sīlu** [Karašaš-slu], fem. (Atyns. 63); Kzk. **Qara-šaš-sulu** [Карашаш-сулу] (IOAIÊK XX, 224). ✧ 'Black hair; having black hair' cf. Kirg. *čač* 'волосы' (Jud.), Alt. *čač* 'волосы' (OjrRS). ⇨ **QARA.** See also **AQ-ČAČ, ALTUN-ŠAŠ, ČÏÑÏR-ČAČ, SULUW-ŠAŠ, UZUN-ČAŠ.**

QARA-ČAQAN   Kzk. 19th c. **Qara-čaqan** [Карачакан] (Potanin II, 149). ⇨ **QARA + ČAQAN.**

QARA-ČAQÏRČA   Uyg. 12th c. - 14th c. **Qara-čaqïrča (=Quba-caqïrča?)** (Radl., USp. 30). ⇨ **QARA + ČAQÏR** + suff. *-ča.*

QARA-ČAR   Kipch. 13th c. **Qara-čar** [Ha-la-tch'a-eul], chief of a Kipchak tribe, a dependant of Chinggis Khan (Pelliot: JA XI (S. T. XV), 161); Kipch. 1262 **Qara-ǰar / Qara-čar?** [قراجار / Караджаръ] (Baybars/Tizeng. I, 77, 99). ⇨ **QARA + ČAR.**

QARA-ČAŠ see **QARA-ČAČ**

QARA-ČÏŠQAN   Kzk. 19th c. **Qara-čïšqan** [Карачишканъ] (SOK 248). ⇨ **QARA + ČÏČQAN.**

QARA-ČOLAQ   Kzk. 19th c. **Qara-čolaq** [Карачолакъ] (SOV 10); Kzk. 19th c. **Qara-čolaq** [Карачолакъ] (SODž. 120, 144); Kzk. 19th c. **Qara-čolaq?** [Карачалакъ] (SOV 106); Kzk. 19th c. **Qara-čolaq?** [Карачалокъ] (SOV 52); Kzk. 19th c. **Qara-čulaq** [Карачулакъ] (SOK 170); Kzk. 1817 **Qara-šolaq / Qara-čolaq** [قراجولاق / Карашалак] (MIK IV, 313, 319). ⇨ **QARA + ČOLAQ.**

QARA-ČÖGÜR see **QARA-ČÜKÜR**

QARA-ČÜKÜR   Oghuz/Trkm. 14th c. - 15th c. **Qara-čükür / Qara-čögür** [Kara Cögür, Kara Çekür / Кара-Чюкюр], Qïrq-qonuq's (Qïrïq-qïnïq's?) father (DQorq./Rossi 184, DQorq. 66, 214, 237, 241). ⇨ **QARA.**

QARA-ČÜSTÜK   Hak.(Sag.) 19th-20th c. **Qara-čüstük** [Кара Чӱстӱк], daughter of the hero (Proben IX, 249). ✧ 'Black ring' cf. Alt.(Tel.) *yüstük* 'der Fingerring' (Radl. III, 616), Hak.(Sag), Shor *čüstük* 'der Fingerring' (Radl. III, 2200). ⇨ **QARA.** See also **ALTÏN-YÜSTÜK, QARA-PURBA.**

QARA-ǰAR see **QARA-ČAR**

QARA-DEMİR-DAŠ see **QARA-TEMİR-TAŠ**

QARA-DENİZ   Yürük 1543 **Qara-deniz** [Kara deniz], from the region of Filibe (Gökb., Rum. 232). ✧ 'Black sea' (from the toponym *Qara-deniz*). ⇨ **QARA + TEÑİZ.**

QARA-DERZİ   Turk. 1455 **Qara-derzi** [Kara Derzi] (Gökb., Ed. 289). ✧ 'Black-taylor' cf. Kuman, Turk. *därzi* 'der Schneider' (Radl. III, 1676). ⇨ **QARA.**

QARA-DEVLETŠAH   Turk. 15th c. **Qara-devletšah** [Kara Devletşâh] (Gökb., Ed. 23). ⇨ **QARA + DÄWLÄT + ŠAH.**

QARA-DİKEN   Turk. 1583 **Qara-diken** [قره ديكن / Karadiken] (Ongan, Ank. I, 168). ✧ 'Blackthorn' (TED), cf. Turk. *diken* 'thorn, spine' (TED). ⇨ **QARA.**

QARA-DİLENǰİ   Maml. 1349 **Qara-dilenǰi** [قرا دلنجى], Seyfeddin Dilenji, governor of Gazah (Zetterst. 219). ⇨ **QARA + DİLENǰİ.**

QARA-DON see **QARA-TON**

QARA-DOR-ATTÏ   Tuv. 19th c. **Qara-dor-attï** [Карадоръ-атты-Карадаса], byname of the hero Qaradasa in a tale (Potanin IV, 567). ✧ 'With dark-brown horse' cf. Crm., Hak.(Sag.) *tor, toru* 'braun' (Radl. III, 1180). ⇨ **QARA + AT.**

QARA-DÖ   Kirg. **Qara-dö** [Карадөө] (Jud. 71, 149, 366, 639). ✧ 'Black ogre, demon'. ⇨ **QARA + DÄW.**

QARA-GEZĀ   Maml. 1486 **Qara-gezā** [قراكزا مملوك تمراز] (Iyās II, 232); Maml. 1496/97 **Qara-gezā** [قراكزا البهلوان] (Iyās II, 325). ⇨ **QARA.**

QARA-GÖZ see **QARA-KÖZ**

QARA-GÜYÜK   Kipch. 1293 **Qara-güyük / Qara-küyük** [قراكيوك / Каракуюкъ], an emir (Baybars/Tizeng. I, 86, 109, Nuwairī 137, 158). ⇨ **QARA + KÜYÜK?**

QARA-GÜNE   Oghuz/Trkm. 14th c. - 15thc. **Qara-güne / Qara-göne** [قَرَ ه كُونَهْ / Кара-Гюне], Qara-buday's father, (Salur) Qazan-bek's brother (DQorq./Rossi 112, 122, 135, 137, DQorq./Ergin 96, DQorq. 22 etc.). ⇨ **QARA + KÜNE.**

QARA-ГUČA   Tat.(Tara) **Qara-γuča** [Караӈуча] (Proben IV, 129 /166/). ⇨ **QARA + QUČA.**

QARA-ГULA   Alt. 19th c. **Qara-γula** [Карагула-богатырь] (Verb., In. 145); Alt.(Tuba) 19th c. **Qara-γula** [Кара-Гула] (Potanin IV, 372); Tuv. 19th c. **Qara-γula** [Кара Гула] (Potanin IV, 371). ✧ 'Black/dark yellowish grey (horse)'. ⇨ **QARA + QULA.**

QARA-XAYDER   Trkm. 1531/32 **Qara-χayder** [Кара Хайдер] (MIT II, 58-59). ⇨ **QARA + XAYDAR.**

QARA-İKLİŠ   Tat. 1554, 1555 **Qara-ikliš** [Кара-Иклишъ (Иклешъ)], a prince (PSRL XIII, 143, 259). ⇨ **QARA.**

QARA-İŠ   Tat. 20th c. **Qara-iš** [Караиш] (Sattarov); *TN:* Tat. 1624 **Qara-iševa** [Караишева], a village in the county of Kazan (Pokrovskij 72). ⇨ **QARA + EŠ.**

QARA-ÏSA   Turk. 1484 **Qara-γïsa / Qara-isā?** [قره عيسا] (Āšikp. 188). ⇨ **QARA + İSA.**

QARA-ÏŠÏQ   Yürük 1543 **Qara-išïq** [Kara Işık] (Gökb., Rum. 232); Tat. 1543 **Qara-išïq** [Kara Işık] (Gökb., Rum. 232). ✧ 'Ill-willed, Ill-disposed' cf. Turk. dial. *ışık* 'hanım akrabalarına iyi niyet beslemeyen /adam/' (SDD). ⇨ **QARA.**

QARA-YAГMUR   Trkm. 1610 **Qara-yaγmur** [قره يغمور], from Syria (Refik, Anad. 62). ⇨ **QARA + YAГMUR.**

QARA-YAŠ   Maml. 1408 **Qara-yaš-bek** [قرا يشبك] (Ibn Taghrīb. VI, 198). ⇨ **QARA + YAŠ.**

QARA-YAWDÏ see **QAR-YAГDÏ**

QARA-YÏLAN   Trkm. **Qara-yïlan-bey**, a former leader of the Sarï-kečili tribe (Riza III, 35). ⇨ **QARA + YÏLAN.**

QARA-YOLTOY   Kirg. **Qara-yoltoy** [Kara Joltai / Кара Joлтoi], one of Manas' comrades-in-arms (Proben V, 40 /41/). ✧ 'Bringing bad luck' cf. Kirg. *qara ǰoltoy* 'приносящий несчастье' (Jud.). ⇨ **QARA.**

QARA-YOLU   Yürük 1543 **Qara-yolu** [قره يو لى] (Gökb., Rum. 224). ⇨ **QARA + YOL** + poss. -*u*.

QARA-YUSUF   Turk. 14th c. - 16th c. **Qara-yusuf** [Kara Yusuf] (Baştav 55, 98); Turk. 1388-1420 **Qara-yusuf** [Καρά᾿Ιουσούφ], prince of the Kara-koyunlu (Āšikp. 68, Byz. Turc. II, 150-151). ⇨ **QARA + YUSUF.**

QARA-YÜLÜK Turk. 1378-1435 **Qara-yülük** [Καραϊουλούκ], prince of the Ak-koyunlu (Byz. Turc. II, 150). ✧ 'Black-Shaven' cf. Turk. *yülük* 'shaven, smooth' (TED). ⇨ **QARA.**

QARA-KEBİR Turk. 1468 **Qara-kebir** [قرا كبر] (Iyās II, 99). ✧ 'Black-Kebir, Black-Big' cf. Turk. *Kebire, Kebir* 'Büyük, ulu; Yaşça büyük olan, yaşlı' (TED) (<Ar.). ⇨ **QARA.**

QARA-KEL-MAMET Nog.? 1614 **Qara-kel-mamet** [Кара-Келмаметъ], a murza (AI III, 421, 447). ⇨ **QARA + KEL-MAMET.**

QARA-KESEK Kipch. 1301/02 **Qara-kesek** [قراكسك] (Baybars/Tizeng. I, 94, 119); Maml. 14th c. **Qara-kesek** [Каракесек] (Tuhfa 410); Maml.? 1398/99 **Qara-kesek** [قراكسك], an emir (Ibn Taghrīb. VI, 7, 29, Weil, Chalif. I, 559); Kzk. 1785 **Qara-kisek** [قره كيسك] (MIK IV, 51); *EN:* Kzk. 18th c. - 19th c. **Qara-kesek** [Каракесек] (Tynyšp. 68, 74). ⇨ **QARA + KESEK.**

QARA-KEŠ Karch. **Qara-keš** [Каракешовъ] (Sysoev 132). ✧ 'Black sable'? ⇨ **QARA + KİŠ.**

QARA-KEŠİK Maml. 1379/80 **Qara-kešik?** [قرا كشك], a Yul-buɣāvī mamlūk (Iyās I, 238). ✧ 'Black-Guard/Watchman' cf. Chag., Az. *käšik* 'die Wache' (Radl. II, 1182). ⇨ **QARA.**

QARA-KİSEK see **QARA-KESEK**

QARA-KÖBÄK Kzk. 1785 **Qara-köbäk-biy** [قره كوبك بى / Кара Кобяк бий], chief (aqsaqal) of the Tört-qara tribe (MIK IV, 51, 53, 132); Kzk. 1787 **Qara-kübäk** [Каракубяк] (MIK IV, 100); Kzk. 1802 **Qara-kübäk** [Кара Кубек] (MIK IV, 202); Kzk. 1803 **Qara-kübek** [Каракубек бий], chieftain of Alim-ulï tribe of the Little Horde (Kiši Žüz) (MIK IV, 514). ✧ 'Black dog'. ⇨ **QARA + KÖPÄK.**

QARA-KÖKÖL Tat.(Bar.) **Qara-kököl** [Кара Кöкöл] (Proben IV, 65 /81/); Tat.(Tara) **Qara-kükül** [Кара Күкүл] (Proben IV, 85 /110/). ✧ 'Black lock'. ⇨ **QARA + KÖKÜL.**

QARA-KÖS see **QARA-KÖZ**

QARA-KÖZ Chag. 15th. **Qara-göz** [Гкарагёзъ Диванъ] (Šejb. LXVI); Turk. 1485 **Qara-göz** [قره كوز], Sultan Bayezid's (1481-1512) servant (Āšikp. 190); Turk. 16th c. **Qara-göz** [Καραγκιόζ], an Ottoman Pasha (Byz. Turc. II); Turk. 1552 **Qara-göz** [Karagöz] (Dávid); Turk. 1580 **Qara-göz** [Ferhad Karagöz] (Dávid); Turk. 1583 **Qara-göz** [Karagöz] (Ongan, Ank. I, 164); Yürük 1543 **Qara-göz** [Karagöz], from Kocacık, Turkey (Gökb., Rum. 103, 177, 185, 189, etc.); Tat. 1543 **Qara-göz** [Karagöz] (Gökb., Rum. 230); Tat. 1543 **Qara-göz** [Karagöz] (Gökb., Rum. 231, 237); Kkalp. 20th c. **Qara-göz** [Къарагёз / Қарагөз], fem. (Bask., Kkalp. 403, KkRS 778); Turk. 1503 **Qara-göz-bey** [Karagöz Bey], commander in chief of the Janissaries (yeniçeri ağası) in Kastamonu, Turkey (Gökb., Ed. 483); Turk. 1519 **Qara-göz-bey** [Karagöz Bey] (Gökb., Ed. 289); Selj. 12th c. **Qara-köz** [قراكز /قراقز], Sultan Toɣrïl's door-keeper (χaǰib), late 12th c. (Rāwandī 331, 339); Chag. **Qara-köz** [قرا كوز], a person from the Babur-name (Le Coq, Ind. 3); Oghuz (Uz) 1159 **Qara-köz** [Каракозъ Мнюзовичъ], a Berendey chief (voevoda) (PSRL II, 85, VII, 69); Kzk. **Qara-köz-sulū** [Кара Köз Сулу], fem. (Proben III, 332 /402/); Bashk. 1680 **Qara-küs** [Каракуска (Каракуз) Аканаев] (MIB I, 75-76); Kzk. 1828 **Qara-küz** [Каракузевъ] (TOUAK XXIV, 188). ✧ 'Black-eye(d)' (Sauvaget 53). ⇨ **QARA + KÖZ.**

QARA-KÜBÄK see **QARA-KÖBÄK**

QARA-KÜBEK see **QARA-KÖBÄK**

QARA-KÜČÜK Tat.(GH) 1474 **Qara-küčük** [Каракучукъ / Каракучюкъ] (PSRL III, 243, IV, 151, VI, 32, VIII, 180); Bashk. 1687 **Qara-küčük** [Каракучючка Сараязовъ] (Vel.-Zern., Bašk. 31); Bashk. 1740 **Qara-küčük** [Аликей Каракучюков] (MIB I, 378); Bashk. 1771 **Qara-küčük** [Ермак Каракучюков] (MIB IV, 358); Kzk. **Qara-küčük** [Кара-кучукъ] (Kustanaev 37); Kzk. **Qara-küčük** [Кара-кучукъ] (Kustanaev 37); Bashk. 1740 **Qara-küsük** [Кушинай Караккусюк] (MIB I, 396); Bashk. 19th c. **Qara-küsük** [Кара-Кусюкъ] (P. R.-n.: Moskovskij Telegraf, XLVIII, 261 (1832).). ✧ 'Black puppy'. ⇨ **QARA + KÜČÜK.**

QARA-KÜS see **QARA-KÖZ**

QARA-KÜSÜK see **QARA-KÜČÜK**

QARA-KÜZ see **QARA-KÖZ**

QARA-KÜKÜL see **QARA-KÖKÖL**

QARA-QAČQÏN Bashk. 1708 **Qara-qačqïn** [Каракачкин] (MIB I, 233). ⇨ **QARA + QAČQÏN.**

QARA-QALÄNDER Uzb. 1770 **Qara-qaländer** [Кара Каляндер], quš-begi (officer responsible of hunting birds, falconer) from the Qoñrat tribe (MIT II, 343). ✧ 'Black-Dervish'. ⇨ **QARA + QALÄNDÄR.**

QARA-QARA Bulg. 1000-1015 **Qara-qara** [Κρακρᾶς], a commander (Byz. Turc. 173). ⇨ **QARA + QARA?**

QARA-QAS see **QARA-QAŠ**

QARA-QASAY Nog. 1649, 1673 **Qara-qasay?** [Каракасай], a murza (AI IV, 79, 510). ⇨ **QARA + QASAY.**

QARA-QAŠ Maml. 1438/39 **Qara-qaš** [قراقاش سودون الاينالى المؤيدى] (Ibn Taghrīb. VII, 65, 117 etc.); Turk. 1570 **Qara-qaš** [Bâli Karakaş] (Gökb., Ed. 181); Kzk. **Qara-qaš-slu (Qara-qaš-sïlu)** [Каракашъ-слу], fem. (Sb. Syr-D. III, otd. II, 49); Trkm. 1833 **Qara-qaš-vekil** [Каракаш-векиль], from the Salïr (Salor) tribe (MIT II, 463); *EN:* Kzk. 18th c. - 19th c.

Qara-qas [Каракасъ], a clan (Potanin II, 2, Tynyšp. 70); Yürük **Qara-qaš** [Karakaş], a tribe living in Komalar yayla, Turkey (Şölen 16). ✧ 'Black eyebrow' (Sauvaget 52), cf. Kzk. *qas* 'бровь' (KzRS). ⇨ **QARA + QAŠ.**

QARA-QAT   Alt. 19th c. **Qara-γat-qan** [Карагатъ-канъ] (Potanin IV, 559); Alt.(Tuba) 19th c. **Qara-γat-qan** [Карагат-канъ] (Katanov, Otč. 12); Hak. 19th c. **Qara-qat** [Кара-кат], fem. (Katanov, Otč. 12). ✧ 'Blackcurrant' cf. Alt., Hak. *qaraγat* 'die schwarze Johannisbeere' (Radl. II, 151). ⇨ **QARA + QAT.** See also **BOROÑOT.**

QARA-QAVUQ   Turk. 20th c. **Qara-qavuq-oγlu**, a Zeybek (Kúnos 1891, 119). ✧ 'Black hood'. ⇨ **QARA.**

QARA-QÏS   Karg. **Qara-qïs** [Кара-кіс], fem. (Katanov, Otč. 9). ✧ 'Black felt'. ⇨ **QARA + KÏYÏZ.**

QARA-QÏLÏŠ   Shor 19th-20th c. **Qara-qïlïš** (Dyrenkova 190). ⇨ **QARA + QÏLÏČ.**

QARA-QÏZÏJAQ   Hak. 19th-20th c. **Xara-χïzïJaχ** [Хара-Хызычах], fem. (HRS 355); Hak.(Kyz.) 19th-20th c. **Qara-qïzïJaq** [Кара кызыцак], fem. (Katanov, Otč. 13); Karg. **Qara-qïzïJaq** [Кара кызыцак], fem. (Katanov, Otč. 8). ✧ 'Little black girl'. ⇨ **QARA + QÏZ** + dim. suff. -*ïJaq*?

QARA-QOČ   Turk. 16th. **Qara-qoč** [Karakoç], among the masters of the author of a Bāznāme of 15th c. (TMİB VIII/2, 181); Yürük 1543 **Qara-qoč** [Kara Koç] (Gökb., Rum. 184); *TN:* Turk. 20th c. **Qara-qoč** [Karakoç], a village in the province of Erzurum, Turkey (TMİB 346). ⇨ **QARA + QOČ.**

QARA-QOY   Hak. 19th-20th c. **Xara-χoy** [Хара-Хой], fem. (HRS 355); Tat.(Lit.) 1552 **Qara-qoy** [Каракой] (Kn. Metriki Lit. 86). ⇨ **QARA + QOY.**

QARA-QOŠ see **QARA-QUŠ**

QARA-QOZΓAL   Kzk. 19th c. **Qara-qozγal** [Кара-козгалъ] (AOAtb. 6). ⇨ **QARA-QOZΓAN?**

QARA-QOZΓAN   Kzk. 19th c. **Qara-qozγan** [Кара-козганъ] (AOAtb. 10). ⇨ **QARA + QUZΓAN.** See also **SARÏ-QOZΓAN.**

QARA-QUČA   Hak. 19th-20th c. **Xara-χuča** [Хара-Хуча] (HRS 355); Tat. 1483 **Qara-quča** [Каракуча] (PSRL VI, 285, XX, 349). ✧ 'Black ram'. ⇨ **QARA + QUČA?**

QARA-QULA   Kzk. 19th c. **Qara-qula** [Каракула] (AOP 106). ⇨ **QARA + QULA.**

QARA-QULAY   NUyg.? 1621 **Qara-qulay** [Каракулай], from the branch of Djungaria (Andrievič, Ist. Sib. I, 128). ⇨ **QARA + QULAY.**

QARA-QULAQ   Yürük 16th c. **Qara-qulaq** [قارا قولاق / Kara Kulak] (Gökb., Rum. 103). ⇨ **QARA + QULAQ.**

QARA-QULPAN   Kzk. **Qara-qulpan** [Кара Кулпан] (Proben III, 73 /95/). ⇨ **QARA + QULPAN.**

QARA-QUNAZ   Uyg. 12th c. - 14th c. **Qara-qunaz, Qara-quñaz** [qaraqunaz / Kara Kungaz / Kapa Кунгаз] (Radl., USp. 100-101, 278, DTS, EUTS). ✧ 'Black-?' (Blagova 1997, 709). ⇨ **QARA + QUNAZ.**

QARA-QUŠ   Selj. 12th c. **Qara-γuš** [قراغوش] (Muh. Ibrahim 51); Selj. 12th c. **Qara-γuš** [قراغوش], emir of Khorasan (Muh. Ibrahim 52-57); Alt. 19th c. **Qara-qoš** [Каракош], servant of the shaman (Verb., In. 68-70); Hak.(Sag.) 19th-20th c. **Qara-qus** [Кара кус] (Katanov, Otč. 8); Uyg. 12th c. - 14th c. **Qara-quš** [qara quš / Kara Kuş] (Radl., USp. 54, DTS, EUTS); Selj. 1128 **Qara-quš** [قراقوش], took part in the discord around Aleppo (Abulfidā III, 430-31); Selj. 1128 **Qara-quš** [حسن قراقوش], emir, governor of Aleppo (Ibn al-Athīr: RHCHor I, 380); Selj. 1169/70 **Qara-quš** [قراقوش بهاالدين], emir, chief of the palace („maître de palais") of the last Fatimid (Ibn al-Athīr/Tornb. XI, 228, 342-5, XII, 29, Ibn al-Athīr: RHCHor I, 568, 580); Selj. 1172/73, 1185/86 **Qara-quš** [شرق الدين قراقوش], conqueror of Tripolis and Tunis (Ibn al-Athīr: RHCHor I, 590, 669); Selj.? 1173 **Qara-quš** [قراقوش], Toγan-šah's emir (Ibn al-Athīr/Tornb. XI, 248); Selj. 1190/91 **Qara-quš** [قراقوش], emir, commander of Acre (Ibn al-Athīr: RHCHor II/1, 19, 20); Selj. 1190/91 **Qara-quš** [قراقوش] (Abū Šāma: RHCHor IV, 495, 508); Selj. 1191/92 **Qara-quš** [قرا قوش / Karakouch], Saladin's servant (Ibn Šaddād, Nawād.: RHCHor III, 210); Selj.? 1191/92 **Qara-quš** [قرا قوش / Karakouch / Kara Kush], a young eunuch of Greek origin, vizier of Saladdin (Abū Šāma: RHCHor V, 5, Abulfar. Or. 266); Khorezm.? **Qara-quš** [قراقوش], an emir (Juwaynī II, 21); Maml. **Qara-quš** [قراقوش الافرمى] (Duqmaq:RHCHor IV, 14, 79); Maml. 1294 **Qara-quš** [بها' الدين قراقوش الحبشى] (Iyās I, 70, 74, Weil, Chalif. I, 193); Maml. 1325 **Qara-quš** [قراقوش الكوندكى], envoy to Desht-i Kipchak (Zetterst. 172, 174, Tizeng. I, 257, 266 /after Al-Malik An-Nāsir/); Maml. 14th c. **Qara-quš** [قراقوش / Karakuş] (Tarj/Houtsma 88, Tarj/Toparlı 41); Tat.(Lit.) 1557 **Qara-quš** [Каракушъ] (Kn. Metriki Lit. 152); Kzk. 19th c. **Qara-quš** [Каракушъ] (SOK 110); Kzk. 19th c. **Qara-quš** [Каракушъ] (SODž. 64); Uyg. 8th c. - 9th c. **Qara-quš-tigin** [Q.raquš tigin] (Le Coq, Man. III, 46). ✧ I. '(Golden) Eagle; (astr.) the Jupiter' (Le Coq, Ind. 2: „der Adler"); 'Vulture', cf. Kzk. *qara-qus* 'стервятник' KzRS); II. 'Black-bird' (Blagova 1997, 707). ⇨ **QARA + QUŠ I.**

QARA-QUZURUQ   Hak. 19th-20th c. **Qara-quzuruq** [Кара-кузурук] (Katanov, Otč. 11). ✧ 'Ermine; (lit.) black tail'. ⇨ **QARA + QUYRUQ.**

QARA-LAČÏN   Maml. 1310, 1311, 1320 **Qara-lačïn** [حسام الدين قرا لاجين أستادار], an emir, the same as

Xisāmuddīn Lāčïn (1280)? (Dawād. 218, 219, Zetterst. 136, 156, Abulfidā V, 246-47); Maml. 1302 **Qara-lāčïn** [قرا لاجين / Kara-lâdjin] (Makrīzī IV, 211, Zetterst. 148, 157). ✧ 'Black hawk/falcon' (Sauvaget 53). ⇨ **QARA + LAČÏN.**

QARA-MAÑDAY Alt. 19th-20th c. **Qara-mañday** [Карамандай], fem. (OjrRS 212). ✧ 'Black forehead'. ⇨ **QARA + MAÑLAY.**

QARA-MAÑQA Kirg. **Qara-mañqa** [Кара Маӊка] (Jud. 517). ✧ 'Black (man) talking through his nose' (Jud.), cf. Kirg. *mañqa* 'сап' [glanders] (Jud.). ⇨ **QARA.**

QARA-MENDİ Kzk. 1820 **Qara-mendi** [Караменди], one of the chiefs of the Arɣïn tribe (Sib. Vest. IX, 103). ⇨ **QARA + MENDİ.**

QARA-MİREK Chag. 16th c. **Qara-mirek** [Кара-Мирек] (Ivanov 301). ⇨ **QARA + MİR + suff. -ek.**

QARA-MİRAD Maml.? 1421 **Qara-mïrad(-χoǰa)** [قرا مراد حجا الشعبانى الظاهرى] (Ibn Taghrīb. VI, 497, 601 etc.). ⇨ **QARA + MURAT.**

QARA-MOΓUS Alt. 19th c. **Qara-moɣus** [Кара-Moɣyc] (Verb., In. 141, 142, 154); Hak.(Sag.) 19th-20th c. **Qara-mos** [Кара-Мосъ], father of the hero (Kostrov II, 237); Alt. 19th c. **Qara-mōs** [Карамоос] (Verb., In. 152); Hak.(Kacha) 19th-20th c. **Qara-mōs** [Кара Moc], a folklore hero (Proben IX, 218, 219). ⇨ **QARA + MOΓOS?**

QARA-MOYÏN Hak. 19th-20th c. **Xara-moyïn** [Хара-Мойын] (HRS 352); Kzk. 18th c. - 19th c. **Qara-moyïn** [Карамоин], personal name preserved in the name of a clan (Tynyšp. 70). ✧ 'Black neck'. ⇨ **QARA + MOYUN.**

QARA-MOS see **QARA-MOΓUS**

QARA-MŌL Hak.(Sag.) 19th-20th c. **Qara-mōl** [Кара Мол] (Proben IX, 295-97). ⇨ **QARA + MŌL?**

QARA-MŌS see **QARA-MOΓUS**

QARA-MUXAMMAD Trkm. 14th c. **Qara-muχammad** [قرا محمد], Bayram-χoǰa's son the chief of the Türkmen, died in 1394 (Weil, Chalif. I, 546, II, 45). ⇨ **QARA + MUXAMMAT.**

QARA-MURT Kzk. **Qara-murt-ata** [قرا مورت اطا / Kara-murt-ata] (Divaev, Baksy XV, 312). ✧ 'Black moustache' cf. Kzk. *murt* 'der Schnurbart' (Radl. IV, 2194). ⇨ **QARA.**

QARA-MÜKÜ see **QARA**

QARA-MÜSÄY Maml.?, Turk.? 1481 **Qara-müsäy?** [قرا موسى] (Iyās III, 206, 221, 248). ⇨ **QARA + MÜSÄY.**

QARA-NÜÑÜL Hak.(Sag.) 19th-20th c. **Qara-nüñül** [Кара Нӱӊӱл], a folklore hero (Proben IX, 325). ⇨ **QARA.**

QARA-OQUY Uyg. 12th c. - 14th c. **Qara-oquy** [Qara Oqui / Kara-Okuy / qara oquj] (Radl., USp. 118, EUTS,
DTS). ✧ 'Black-Oquy'? ⇨ **QARA + OQUY.**

QARA-ÖYLİ Oghuz/Trkm. 13th c. **Qara-öyli / Qara-üyli?** [قرا ايولى / قرا ايولى / Кара-уйли / Кара-ӧйли], Kün-χan's son (RaD I/1, 76, Abulg./Kon. 515, 545, 590). ✧ 'With black tent; having a black tent' cf. Chag. *öy* 'das Haus, die Jurte' (Radl. I, 1171), Trkm. *öy* 'кибитка' (TrkmRS) + suff. *-li = öyli* 'having a yurt', cf. also Chag. *öylüg~öylük* 'ein Haus habend, verheirathet; der Haupt der Familie; die Frau' (Radl. I, 1176). ⇨ **QARA.**

QARA-ÖYLÜK Trkm.? **Qara-öylük** [قرا ايلوك] (Arabš. I, 534, Weil, Chalif. V, 59). ✧ 'Having a tent; living in a tent, native' (Karabacek 105), cf. Chag. *öylüg~öylük* 'ein Haus habend, verheirathet; der Haupt der Familie; die Frau' (Radl. I, 1176). ⇨ **QARA.**

QARA-PAYÏR Tuv. 19th c. **Qara-payïr** [Кара Пajыр] (Proben IX, 143). ✧ 'Black feast'? cf. Tuv. *bayïr* 'праздник, торжество' (TuvRS). ⇨ **QARA.**

QARA-PAS see **QARA-BAŠ**

QARA-PAŠ see **QARA-BAŠ**

QARA-PETİKEY Shor 19th-20th c. **Qara-petikey,** an old woman (Dyrenkova 176). ✧ 'Black Petikey'. ⇨ **QARA.**

QARA-PİLÄK Hak.(Blt.) 19th-20th c. **Qara-piläk** [Кара-пiläк Чебодаев] (Proben IX, 557). ✧ 'Black wrist' cf. Alt., Hak., Shor *piläk* 'das Handgelenk; der Unterarm' (Radl. IV, 1338). ⇨ **QARA.**

QARA-PUΓRA see **QARA-BUΓRA**

QARA-PURBA Shor 19th-20th c. **Qara-purba** (Dyrenkova 176). ✧ 'Black ring'? cf. Shor *purba* 'die Schraube; der Fingerring' (Radl. IV, 1371). ⇨ **QARA.** See also **QARA-ČÜSTÜK.**

QARA-SAY Bashk. 1744 **Qara-say** [Карасай Султанаев] (MIB III, 415); Kzk. **Qara-say** [Kapacaй] (Proben III, 134 (170)); Kzk. 19th c. **Qara-say** [Карасай] (SOV 44); Nog. **Qara-say** [Карасай] (Žirm., Epos 402); *TN:* Kzk. 19th c. **Qara-say** [Карасай], a field (SOV 110). ✧ 'Black-stream; Black reed-grass'? cf. Bashk. *say* 'речная ленточная водоросль' (BRS), Kzk. *say* 'dere, ova' (KzTS). ⇨ **QARA.**

QARA-SAYÏN Nog. 1649 **Qara-sayïn / Qara-sayin?** [Таганъ мурза Карасаинов] (AI IV, 87). ⇨ **QARA + SAYÏN.**

QARA-SAQAL Maml. 14th c. **Qara-saqal** [قرا سَنَل] (Sauvaget 52); Tat.(Sib.) 1616 **Qara-saqal** [Кара-Сакалъ] (Andrievič, Ist. Sib. I, 206); Bashk. 1740, 1741 **Qara-saqal** [Карасакалъ], leader of the rebellious Bashkirs, later took up the name *Qara-χan* (Howorth II, 644, Levšin 193, MIB I, 381-393, Valihanov, Soč. 201, Nepljuev 151, 164-174, 181, etc.); Kzk. 1817 **Qara-saqal** [قرا صاقال / Карасакалъ] (MIK IV, 311); Tuv. 1616 **Qara-saqal,** a Soyon prince (Radl., Aus Sib. I, 162). ✧ 'Black beard'. ⇨ **QARA +**

SAQAL.

QARA-SALΓÏN Shor 19th-20th c. **Qara-salɣïn** (Dyrenkova 122). ✧ 'Black (strong) wind'. ⇨ **QARA + SALQÏN.**

QARA-SANATAY Kirg. **Qara-sanatay** [Карасанатай] (Jud. 632). ✧ 'Envious, malevolent' cf. Kirg. *qarasanatay* 'ненавистник, человек, радующийся чужому несчатстью' (Jud.) < Mo. *sanātai* 'having [good or bad] intentions (Gy. Kara). ⇨ **QARA.** See also **AQ-SANATAY.**

QARA-SARÏ Kzk. **Qara-sarï** [Кара Сары] (Proben III, 47 /63/). ⇨ **QARA + SARÏ.**

QARA-SART Kzk. **Qara-sart** [Ували Карасартовъ] (Konšin, Pam. 19); Kzk. 19th c. **Qara-sart** [Карасартъ] (AOO 50). ⇨ **QARA + SART.**

QARA-SÏRT Kzk. 19th c. **Qara-sïrt** [Карасыртъ] (SOK 20). ⇨ **QARA + SÏRT.**

QARA-SOÑQUR Maml. 14th c. **Qara-soñqor / Qara-soñqur** [قراسنقر / Karasunkur] (Tarǰ/Houtsma 88, Tarǰ/Toparlı 41); Selj.? **Qara-soñqur** [قرا سنقر] سيفالدين / Seyfeddin Karasungur], Qara-tay's brother? (Ibn Bībī IV, 311, Belleten XII, 115); Selj. **Qara-soñqur** [قرا سنقر] (Bondārī 156, 165); Selj. **Qara-soñqur** [محمد قرا سنقر] (Bondārī 185); Selj. 1035 **Qara-soñqur** [قرا سنقر], ata-beg of Sultan Dawud (Čaɣri-beg), governor (lord) of Azerbaidjan (Ibn al-Athīr/Tornb. X, 480, 483, XI, 29, 30, 40, Rāwandī 227 etc.); Selj. 12th c. **Qara-soñqur** [قرا سنقر], an ata-beg (Qazw. 464-466); Selj. 1189/90 **Qara-soñqur** [قرا سنقر], Saladin's mamlūk (Ibn Šaddād, Nawād.: RHCHor III, 150); Maml.? 1208 **Qara-soñqur** [قرا سنقر علاالدين], lord of Marāgha (Ibn al-Athīr/Tornb. XII, 182); Maml. 1247 **Qara-soñqur** [علا'الدين قرا سنقر السا قي], mamluk of Eyyub's son (Abulfidā IV, 492,93); Maml. 1283, 1291, 1300/01 **Qara-soñqur** [شمسالدين قرا سنقر / Šemseddīn Qarasonqur], emir, the governor of the Sultan in Haleb (Makrīzī I, 86, III, 53, 62, Iyās I, 126, 137, 157 etc., Weil, Chalif. I, 236, Dörner-Naumann, Forschungen in Kommagene, Berlin, 1939, 98); Maml. 1299 **Qara-soñqur** [Kara-Sonkor], commander of the fort Subaybah (Makrīzī IV, 127); Maml. 1299, 1309 **Qara-soñqur** [سيفالدين قرا سنقر المنصورى], melik (lord) of the emirs (Dawād. 14, 39, 199 etc.); Maml. 14th c. **Qara-soñqur** [قرا سُنْقُرْ] (Sauvaget 52); Maml. 1438/39 **Qara-soñqur** [قرا سنقر] (Ibn Taghrīb. VII, 259); Maml.(Kipch.)? **Qara-soñqur** [قرا سنقر], an native of Dešt-i Kipčak in the service of the Caliph of Baghdad (RaD/Quatrem. 268-69); Maml. 1304 **Qara-soñqur / Qara-suñqur** [Šemseddīn Qarasunqur], an emir (Björkm. 160); *TN:* Maml. **Qara-soñqur(iya)** [المدرسة قرا سنقرية], a mosque (medrese) named after

Qara-soñqur (Makrīzī, Khit. I, 388). ⇨ **QARA + SOÑQUR.**

QARA-SOÑSUY Uyg. **Qara-soñsuy** [Kara Songsuy] (EUTS). ⇨ **QARA + SOÑSUY.**

QARA-SUÑQUR see **QARA-SOÑQUR**

QARA-ŠAŠ see **QARA-ČAČ**

QARA-ŠEBELDEY Shor 19th-20th c. **Qara-šebeldey**, a folklore hero (Dyrenkova 126). ✧ 'Black evil spirit' cf. Shor, Hak.(Kacha) *šïbäldäi* 'ein böser Geist' (Radl. IV, 1089). ⇨ **QARA.**

QARA-ŠOLAQ see **QARA-ČOLAQ**

QARA-TABÏN Bashk. **Qara-tabïn-bï**, in a legend of origin, Čolman bï's father (Mészáros, MH 99). ⇨ **QARA.**

QARA-TAΓ Chag. 1533 **Qara-taɣ** [Kará Tágh, maulánâ], took part in Mirza Haydar's expedition to Tibet (Tar. Rashidi 460, 463); Kzk. 1785, 1793 **Qara-taw** [قرا طاۇ / قره طاو], chief of the settlement (aq-saqal) (MIK IV, 52, 53, IV, 146); Kzk. 19th c. **Qara-taw** [Каратавъ] (SOK 214). ✧ 'Black mountain'. ⇨ **QARA + TAΓ.**

QARA-TAY Hak. 19th-20th c. **Xara-tay** [Харатай] (HRS 352); Selj. 1249 **Qara-tay** [Jalâl ad-Dîn Kârâtai], in the service of Sultan Alāaddīn (Abulfar./Budge I, 413); Selj. 13th c. **Qara-tay** [قرا طاى / قـرطـاى / Jalaloddin Kortaï al. Karatai], atabeg of Sultan İzzeddīn (1210-1219) (Abulfar. Or. 319, 321, 329); Maml. 1310, 1316 **Qara-tay** [شهابالـدين قـرطـاى], governor of Hims (Dawād. 221, 297, Sauvaire III, 416); Maml. 1316-1326, 1333/34 **Qara-tay** [قـرطـاى بن عبدالله], governor of Tripolis, died in 1333/34 (Inscr. Ar. Syr. N. I, 55); Maml. 14th c. **Qara-tay** [قـراطـاى / Karatay] (Tarǰ/Houtsma 88, Tarǰ/Toparlı 42); Maml.? 1376/77 **Qara-tay** [قـرطـاى الطازى / Kertai (Schihab Eddin) Attazi], governor of Haleb (Iyās I, 232, Weil, Chalif. 529-33); Maml.?, Trkm.? 1379/80 **Qara-tay** [قـرطـاى التـركمانى] (Iyās I, 246); Tat. 1601 **Qara-tay** [Базбира Каратаев] (Miller, Ist. Sib. II, 169); Tat.(Sib.) 1725 **Qara-tay** [Каратаевъ], a prince (Andrievič, Ist. Sib. II, 387); Kzk. 18th c. **Qara-tay** [Каратай], Nur-Ali Khan's (1749-1785) son, Abul Khair Khan's grand-son (Nepljuev 681); Kzk. 1797 **Qara-tay** [Karataï / Каратай], a sultan, Burali's („Pourali") son (Levšin II, 319 III, 96, Levchine 290, 356); Kzk. 1816 **Qara-tay** [Каратай] (MIK IV, 301); Kzk. 1817 **Qara-tay** [Каратай / Султанъ Каратай], a sultan of the Bay-ulï clan (Mejer 35, AUK 959); Kzk. 19th c. **Qara-tay** [Каратай] (AUK 484, 959); Kzk. 19th c. **Qara-tay** [Каратаевъ] (AUK 421); Kzk. 19th c. **Qara-tay** [Сарыджанъ Каратаевъ] (Grod., Pril. 170); Kkalp. 1724 **Qara-tay** [Каратай Сумергенев] (MIKk. 182); Kirg. **Qara-tay** [Каратай] (Jud. 291); Tat.(Mish) **Qara-tay** [Каратаевъ] (IOAIÊK XIX,

145); Trkm. 1859 **Qara-tay-šeyχ** [Каратай-шейх] (ZIRGOÊtn. I, 207); *EN:* Trkm.? 1615 **Qara-tay** [قرطای / Karatay], a tribe (cemaat) in Anatolia (Refik, Anad. 73); Kzk. 18th c. - 19th c. **Qara-tay** [Каратай], a clan (Tynyšp. 71). ✦ 'Black foal' (Sauvaget 53). ⇨ **QARA + TAY** or suff. *-tay(1,2)?*

QARA-TAL   Kzk. **Qara-tal** [Каратал] (Žirm., Epos 400); Kzk. 19th c. **Qara-tal** [Караталъ] (SOK 120, 180); Kzk. 19th c. **Qara-tal** [Караталъ] (SOV 114); Kzk. 19th c. **Qara-tal** [Караталъ] (AOO 70). ⇨ **QARA + TAL.**

QARA-TAN   Hak. 19th-20th c. **Qara-tan** [Каратан] (HRS 349). ✦ 'Black (cool?) wind' cf. Hak. *tan* 'ветерок' (HRS). ⇨ **QARA.**

QARA-TAS see **QARA-TAŠ**

QARA-TAŠ   Alt. 19th c. **Qara-tas** [Кара-Тасъ], a heroine in a legend (Verb., In. 151); Trkm. 1690 **Qara-taš** [قره طاش / Karataş] (Refik, Anad. 83). ⇨ **QARA + TAŠ.**

QARA-TÄMÜR see **QARA-TEMİR**

QARA-TEKE   Bashk. 1760 **Qara-teke** [Еркей Каратекин] (MIB IV/2, 38); Kzk. 19th c. **Qara-teke** [Каратеке] (SOK 176, 184). ⇨ **QARA + TEKE.**

QARA-TEMİR   Maml. 1325 **Qara-demir** [سيف الدين قرا دمر], emir, envoy sent to Dešt-i Kipčak (Nuwairī 149, 171); Uyg. **Qara-tämir** (Le Coq, Urkunden 456); Uyg. **Qara-tämür** [Kara Tämür] (EUTS); Maml. 1325 **Qara-temir** [قرا تمر] (Zetterst. 172, 179); Maml. 1366/67 **Qara-temir** [قرا تمر] (Iyās I, 217); Kzk. 18th c. - 19th c. **Qara-temir** [Каратемир] (Tynysp. 73); Uyg. 12th c. - 14th c. **Qara-temür** [qara temür] (DTS). ✦ 'Dark/mighty-Iron' (Blagova 1997, 705). ⇨ **QARA + TEMİR.**

QARA-TEMİR-TAŠ   Maml. 1389, 1399/1400 **Qara-demir-daš** [قرادمرداش الاحمدى / الحمدى] (Iyās I, 272, Ibn Taghrīb. VI, 145); Selj. 14th c. **Qara-temir-taš** [قره تمرتاش], beglerbeg of Anatolia under Bayezid I (1389-1402) (Nešrī 339). ✦ 'Black-iron-stone' (Sauvaget 52). ⇨ **QARA + TEMİR + TAŠ.**

QARA-TEMÜR see **QARA-TEMİR**

QARA-TİN   Hak. 19th-20th c. **Qara-tin** [Каратин], fem. (HRS 353); Maml. 1410/11 **Qara-tin-bek?** [قرا تنبك] (Ibn Taghrīb. VI, 297). ⇨ **QARA + TİN?**

QARA-TÏŠQAN   Kzk. 19th c. **Qara-tïšqan** [Каратышканъ] (SOV 142). ⇨ **QARA + TÏŠQAN.**

QARA-TOΓAN   Oghuz 897, 904 **Qara-toγan** [طوغان] [محمد بن قرا] (Kindī 242, Tabarī, Annal. III, 2241); Selj. **Qara-toγan** [قرا طغان] (Bondārī 156); Selj. **Qara-toγan** [قرا طوغان] (Zehireddin/Dorn 118, 424 etc.); Trkm.? 1290 **Qara-toγan** [قرا تغان] (Dorn 135). ⇨ **QARA + TOΓAN.**

QARA-TOΓMA   Uyg. 12th c. - 14th c. **Qara-toγma** [qara toγma / Kara Toğma] (DTS, EUTS). ✦ I. 'Black-Child'; II. 'Black-Button'? (Blagova 1997, 712). ⇨ **QARA + TOΓMA.**

QARA-TOQ   Kzk. 19th c. **Qara-toq** [Каратокъ] (SOK 102). ⇨ **QARA + TOQ?**

QARA-TOQMA   Uyg. 12th c. - 14th c. **Qara-toqma** (Radl., USp. 12-13). ⇨ **QARA + TOQMA.**

QARA-TOQO   Kirg. **Qara-toqo** [Кара Токо] (Proben V, 70 (71), Jud. 515). ⇨ **QARA + TOQO?, TOQA?**

QARA-TOL   Kzk. 19th c. **Qara-tol** [Каратолъ] (SOK 142). ⇨ **QARA + TOL.**

QARA-TON   Nog.? **Qara-don-batïr** [Карадон-батыр] (Žirm., Epos 395). ⇨ **QARA + TON.**

QARA-TORONTAY   Maml. 1299 **Qara-torontay**, among the murderers of Sultan Lājïn (Makrīzī IV, 96). ⇨ **QARA + TURUMTAY?**

QARA-TÖLÖK   Kirg. **Qara-tölök** [кара Төлөк / Кара төлök], one of Manas' comrades-in-arms, the soothsayer (Proben V, 40 (41), 151 (152)). ⇨ **QARA + TÖLEK?**

QARA-TÜKEN   Oghuz/Trkm. 14th c. - 15th c. **Qara-tüken** [Kara Tüken Melik, Qara Tekür Melik / Кара-Тюкен] (DQorq. 31, 58, 234). ⇨ **QARA.**

QARA-ÜYLİ see **QARA-ÖYLİ**

QARA-ÜLÖK   Kzk. **Qara-ülök** [Кара-улёк] (Žirm., Epos 398). ✦ 'Black camel-foal' cf. Kzk. *ülek* 'tek hörgücü olan devenin genç buğrası' (KzTS). ⇨ **QARA.**

QARABTÏ   Tuv. 19th c. **Qarabtï-χan** [Карабты-ханъ] (Potanin IV, 414). ✦ 'Having herons, with herons' cf. Alt.(Kmd.) *qarap* 'der Reiher' (Radl. II, 164) + suff. *-tï / -lï.*

QARAČ   Tat.(GH) 1368 **Qarač** [Карачь], a prince (PSRL XI, 10); Tat.(GH) 1382, 1383 **Qarač** [Карачь], envoy of Toqtamïš to Moscow (PSRL IV, 90, VI, 103, VIII, 48, XI, 82, XVI, 130, XXIII, 129); Tat.(Lit.) 1552 **Qarač** [Карачъ] (Kn. Metriki Lit. 82); Tat. 1624 **Qarač** [Карачъ Крынсымовъ] (Pokrovskij 70); Tat. 1624 **Qarač** [Янбай Карачинъ] (Pokrovskij 70); Tat.(Sib.) 1591 **Qarač** [Курманчикъ Карачевичъ] (Lit. Tat. 96); Tat.(Sib.) 1637 **Qarač** [Карачец Акбердеева], fem. (Miller, Ist. Sib. II, 444); Bashk. 1780 **Qarač** [Рясул Карачев] (MIB V, 120); Kirg. 19th c. **Qarač** [Карачъ], a manap (chieftain) of the Salmeke tribe (Valihanov, Soč. 59); Alt. 19th-20th c. **Qarač** [Карач], fem. (OjrRS 212); Kirg. 19th c. **Qarač / Čoñ-qarač** [Чонъ-Карачъ] (Valihanov, Soč. 359); Turk. 1453 **Qarač-bey** [Карачь-бей], an army commander (PSRL VIII, 137, XII, 92, PSRL (Russk. Hr.) I, 454, ZVOIRAO II, 148, 149). ✦ 'Little Black' (Bese 5), 'Black Man' (Sattarov). ⇨ **QARA + dim. suff. -č.** See also **ČOŇ-QARAČ.**

QARAČA   Tat.(GH) 1367 **Qarača** [Karacha], a distinguished representative of the Khan (Howorth II, 208); Tat.(GH) 1367 **Qarača** [Karacha], envoy of

Mamay-qan in Moscow (Howorth II, 208); Crm. 1411
Qarača [Caracha] (Jorga, Notes I, 22); Crm. 1537
Qarača [Карача-князь], a prince (PSRL XIII, 119);
Tat.(Mish.) 1737 **Qarača** [Карача] (MIB I, 309);
Tat.(Sib.) 16th c. **Qarača** [Карача (Корача, Крачей,
Koчапа)], Küčüm-qan's (1563-1598) follower (Sib.
Let. 20, 33, 78 etc.); Tat.(Tob.) 1581 **Qarača**
[Karatscha], a prince of Tobol Tatars, fought against
Yermak (Radl., Aus Sib. I, 149); Kirg. **Qarača**
[Карача] (Jud. 309); Kzk. 1817 **Qarača** / **Karaša**
[قراچه / Караша] (MIK IV, 308); Tat. 1539/40
Qaraća / **Qarač?** [قراج / Карача] (Jusupov 63);
Tat.(Bar.) **Qarača-bi** [Карача Би] (Proben IV, 141
/179/); Kirg. **Qarača-qan** [Карача Кан] (Proben V,
398 /401/); *EN:* Kzk. 18th c. - 19th c. **Qarača**
[Карача] (Tynyšp. 66, 75). ✧ 'Little Black' (Bese 5).
⇨ **QARA** + dim. duff. *-ča*.

QARAČA-BULAT   Tat. 1519 **Qarača-bulat** [Карача-
Булатъ] (PSRL XIII, 32). ⇨ **QARAČA** + **BULAT.**

QARAČAQ   Alt. 19th-20th c. **Qaračaq** [Карачак]
(OjrRS 208). ✧ 'Little Black' (Bese 5). ⇨ **QARA** +
dim. suff. *-čaq.*

QARAČÏ I.   Crm. **Qaračï** / **Qaračï-beg**, title of the
former leading chieftains in the Crimea (?); Maml. 1334
Qarašï? [الوالى سيف الدين قرشى], a governor (Dawād.);
EN: Tat. 1594 **Qaračï** / **Qarači** [Карачи Кипьчакъ],
clan of the prince in the horde (Lit. Tat. 230); *TN:* Kzk.
Qaračï-mulla / **Qarači-mulla**, a place (Karta JAR XI).
✧ 'Minister; chieftain'? Used also as a title in the
Crimea. Cf. Uyg. *qaraju* / *qaračï* 'der Minister' (Radl.
II, 162).

QARAČÏ II.   Alt. **Qaračï-qïz** [Карачы-кызъ], fem.
(Nikiforov 188). ✧ 'Smoke gap of the yurta; chimney-
pot' cf. Hak. *qaračï* 'das Raubloch der Jurte, der
Rauchfang, Schornstein'.

QARAČÏN   Chag. 15th c. **Qaračïn** / **Qaračïn-bahadur**
[قراجين بهادر / Гкарачинъ (Бахадуръ)], Hüseyn-
bahadur's byname (Šejb. LV, LXII); *TN:* Kzk.
Qaračïn [Карачинъ], mountains east of Karkaralinsk
(Karta JAR XII). ⇨ **QARA** + suff. *-čïn / -čin?*

QARAČUQ see **QARAJÏQ**

QARAJ   Oghuz/Trkm. 13th c. **Qaraj** [قراج / Карадж],
Qara-γazï-bek's father (Abulg./Kon. 1165). ⇨ **QARA**
+ suff. *-č?*

QARAJA   Oghuz **Qaraja** [قراجه], forefather of the
Ottoman dynasty (Āšikp. 5); Pecheneg?, Uz? 11th c.
Qaraja [Καρατζᾶς], a Byzantine commander of
Sauromata (Uz) or Schythian (Pecheneg) origin (Byz.
Turc. 153); Selj. **Qaraja** [قراجه جاندار] (Ibn Bībī IV,
217, 218); Selj. **Qaraja** [قراجه], Nūreddīn's father (Ibn
Bībī IV, 319); Selj. 1095, 1104 **Qaraja** [قراجه], an
emir, mamlūk/γulām of Malik Shah I (1072-1092), the
governor of Harrān (Ibn al-Athīr/Tornb. X, 168, 256,

Ibn al-Athīr: RHCHor I, 220); Selj. 1097, 1113 **Qaraja**
[قراجه الوالى] (Qalānisi 133, 183); Selj. 1111, 1119/20,
1132 **Qaraja** [قراجة الساقى/عزالدين / Karaca es-
Sâkî], an emir and commander, Nūreddīn's emir, killed
by Sultan Sandjar (Kamāladdīn 176, Ibn al-Athīr:
RHCHor I, 321, Ibn al-Athīr/Tornb. X, 387-88, 475-
477, Bondārī 123, 125, 158, 159, Ibn al-Athīr, Atab.:
RHCHor II/2, 78-81, Ahbar 63, 70, 71, 73, etc.); Selj.
1113/14 **Qaraja** [قراجه], lord of Emesa, died in
1113/14 (Ibn al-Athīr: RHCHor 288, Abulfidā/Ed. 11);
Selj. 1114, 1136 **Qaraja** [قراجه], Xayïr-χan's (Qara-
jan's) father (Kamāladdīn II, 173, 174, 181 etc., Ibn al-
Athīr/Tornb. XI, 24); Selj. 1115 **Qaraja** [قراجه]
(Kamāladdīn II, 172); Selj. 1131 **Qaraja** [Mas'ūd
Kârâjâ], the captain of the host of the Khalīfah
(Abulfar./Budge I, 256); Selj. 1131/32 **Qaraja** [Karadja
es-Saki] (Ibn al-Athīr, Atab.: RHCHor II/2, 78-81);
Selj. 1134 **Qaraja** [قراجه], lord of Umadiya? (Ibn al-
Athīr/Tornb. XI, 8); Selj. 12th c. **Qaraja** [قراجه], lord
of Fārs at the times of Sultan Mas'ūd (1134-1152)
(Qazw. 467); Selj. 12th c. **Qaraja** [قراجه] (Usāma 34,
133); Selj. 1195 **Qaraja** [قراجه زين الدين], an emir
(Ibn al-Athīr/Tornb. XII, 77, 106, 107); Khorezm. 13th
c. **Qaraja** [قراجه], an emir of Sultan J̌elāleddīn Meñgü-
berdi (J̌uwaynī II, 219-221); Khorezm. 13th c. **Qaraja**
[قراجه حاجب / Qaradja-Hâdjib], an officer of the
Khorezmshah, went over to Chinggis' side
(Abulg./Desm. 111); Khorezm. 13th c. **Qaraja**
[قراجه / قراجا], χas-χajib of Muχamed II (1200-
1220) in Otrar (J̌uwaynī I, 64, 65); Maml. **Qaraja**
[قراجه], a treasurer (Iyās II, 41); Maml. **Qaraja** [Zayn
ed-dîn Qarâdja es-Salâhy], lord of Sarkhad, his
mausoleum (türbe) is in Damascus (Sauvaire V, 252);
Maml. 1312 **Qaraja** [قراجه / Караджа], Mamlūk
envoy to the Desht-i Kipchak (Duqmaq/Tizeng. I, 316,
323); Maml. 1354 **Qaraja** [قراجه بن دلغادر] (Iyās I,
201, Weil, Chalif. I, 346); Maml. 1438/39 **Qaraja**
[قراجا] (Ibn Taghrīb. VII, 2, 21, 27, etc., VI, 636, 675,
Weil, Chalif. II, 219, 228); Maml. 1442/43 **Qaraja**
[قراجه] (Ibn Taghrīb. VII, 123, 150, 192, VI, 128, 193,
Weil, Chalif. II, 252); Maml.? 1443/44 **Qaraja**
[قراجا ابنة ارغون شاه] (Ibn Taghrīb. VII, 291);
Maml.? 1448 **Qaraja** [قراجه] (Ibn Taghrīb. VII, 24,
156, Iyās, II, 365); Maml. 1452/53 **Qaraja** [قراجه]
(Iyās II, 36); Maml. 1459 **Qaraja** [قراجه] (Ibn Taghrīb.
VII, 518, 549, Iyās II, 71, 92); Maml. 1469/70 **Qaraja**
[قراجه] (Iyās II, 115, 168, 229); Maml. 1496/97
Qaraja [قراجا] (Iyās II, 324, 357); Turk. 1478
Qaraja, a master of the horse (emir-i ahur) (Gökb., Ed.
80); Turk. 1519 **Qaraja** [قراجه بن طرابای] (Iyās III,
191, 211); Turk. 1611 **Qaraja** [Karaca] (Ün 1938, 645);

Yürük 1543 **QaraJa** [قرهجه / Karaca], from Kocacık, Turkey (Gökb., Rum. 103, 179, 192, 193, 201, 202, 225, 237, 239); Maml.(Trkm.)? 1332 **QaraJa** [قرا جا التركمانى] (Dawād. 368); Kzk. 19th c. **QaraJa-bay** [Караджабай] (Grod., Pril. 139); Turk. 1444 **QaraJa-beg** [قراجه بك], fell in the battle of Varna (Āšikp. 95); Uzb. 1538/39 **QaraJa-behadur-vekil?** [Караджа-бехадур-векиль] (MIT II, 60); Turk. **QaraJa-bey** [Karaca Bey] (Uzunçarş., Anad. 42, 43, 46); Turk. 14th c. - 16th c. **QaraJa-bey** [Karaca Bey] (Baştav 85); Turk. 1455 **QaraJa-bey** [Karaca Bey ibn Abdullah] (Gökb., Ed. 236-238); Turk. 1529 **QaraJa-bey** [Karaca Bey] (Gökb., Ed. 45); Kzk. 19th c. **QaraJa-bey** [Кокабай Караджаевъ] (Grod., Pril. 66); Crm. 1635 **QaraJa-ɣazi-bek** [قراجه غازى بك] (Vel.-Zern., Crim. 143, 168); Khorezm. 1219 **QaraJa-χan** [Караджа-ханъ], an officer of the Khorezmshah (RaD/Ber. III, 43); Uzb. 1867 **QaraJa-mehrem** [Караджа-мехрем] (MIT II, 631); Kar.(Crm.) **QaraJa-oɣlan** [Караца Оɓлан] (Proben VII, 297); Turk. 1516 **QaraJa-paša** / **QaraJa-baša** [قراجه پشا / قراجه باشا / Karaca Paşa], envoy of Sultan Selim I (1512-1520) to Egypt, then governor of Haleb (Iyās III, 40, 42, Weil, Chalif. II, 409, 410, Āšikp. 197, Baştav 121); *EN:* Yürük?, Turk.? 1554 **QaraJalar** [Karacalar cemaatı], aan ethnic group (Gökçen 36); *TN:* Trkm. **QaraJa-batïr** [Караджа батыръ], a well (Karta JAR XVIII); Turk. 20th c. **QaraJa-bey** [Kracabey], a village in the province of Bursa (TMİB 217); Turk. 20th c. **QaraJa-oɣlan** [Karacaoğlan], a village in the province of Kırklareli, Turkey (TMİB 538); Turk. 20th c. **QaraJa-oɣlu** [Karacaoğlu], a village in the province of Samsun, Turkey (TMİB 741). ✦ I. 'Blackish; somewhat black or dark' (Sauvaget 52: „en turc diminutif noir") cf. Crm., Turk. *qaraja* 'schwärzlich' (Radl. II, 162); II. 'Roe, roe deer (Capreolus capreolus)' (TED) cf. *qaraja* 'eine Art wilder Ziegen' (Radl. II, 162). See also **QULTAQ-QARAJA, SOLAQ-QARAJA.**

QARAJA-RAXMAN Turk. **QaraJa-raχman** [قرهجه رحمان] (Āšikp. 33). ⇨ **QARAJA** + **RAXMAN.**

QARAJİN Maml. 1276 **QaraJin** [Karadjin] (Makrīzī II, 135); Kzk. 19th c. **QaraJin** [Караджинъ] (SOK 190); Maml.(Kipch) 1293 **QaraJin** [قراجين / Караджинжъ] (Baybars/Tizeng. I, 86, 109, Nuwairī 137, 158). ✦ '?' (<Mo.?).

QARAJÏQ Oghuz/Trkm. 13th c. **Qaračïq / QaraJïq?** [قراجيق / Qarâtchiq / Караджик] (Abulg./Desm. 28, Abulg./Kon. 525, 555); Kuman/Tat.? **Qaračuq** [Карачюкъ], envoy (PSRL (Russk. Hr.) 1, 494); Oghuz/Trkm. 14th c. - 15th c. **Qaračuq-čoban / QaraJïq-čoban** [قرهجق چوبان] (DQorq./Ergin 97,

DQorq./Rossi 136-146). ✦ 'Little Black'. ⇨ **QARA** + dim. suff. *-jïq.*

QARADAY Tat.(Lit.) 1592 **Qaraday** [Меретъ Кородаевичъ] (Lit. Tat. 123). ⇨ **QARA** + suff. *-day.*

QARADAS Alt.(Tub.) 19th c. **Qaradas** [Карадасъ] (Potanin IV, 569). ✦ 'Black woodpecker' cf. Hak.(Sag.) *qaradas* 'der Schwarzspecht' (Radl. II, 161).

QARAFQAN Kzk. 19th c. **Qarafqan** [Карафканъ] (SOV 94).

QARAƔA Kzk. 19th c. **Qaraɣa** [Карага] (AOK 122). ⇨ **QARAƔAY?**

QARAƔAY Kzk. 19th c. **Qaraɣay** [Карагай], one of the forefathers of the Merkits (Potanin II, 5); Kzk. 19th c. **Qaraχay** [Карахай] (AOO 50). ✦ 'Larch' cf. Chag., Kzk., Tat. *qaraɣay* 'die Tanne, der Lärchenbaum' (Radl. II, 5).

QARAƔAN Trkm. **Qaraɣan** [Караганъ] (Grod., Vojna II, 147). ✦ I. '?' cf. Trkm. *garagan* 'солянка древовидная' (TrkmRS); II. 'Common service tree (Siberian); acacia-bush'? cf. Alt.(Tel.) *qaraɣan* 'robina caragana; ein Akazienstrauch' (Radl. II, 151).

QARAƔAT see **QARA-QAT**

QARAƔÏR Selj. 12th c. **Qaraɣïr** [قراغر] (Muh. Ibrahim 162).

QARAƔUT Kzk. 1846 **Qaraɣut** [Карагут Кулякеневъ] (МКОР 151).

QARAƔUZ Kzk. 19th c. **Qaraɣus / Qaraɣuz?** [Карагусъ] (AOA 66); Khorezm.? 1222 **Qaraɣuz** [ابن قراغز / Ibn Qarâghouz], from Iraq (Nasawī 70); Chag. 1485 **Qaraɣuz-begüm** [Karaguz Begum], fem. (Tar. Rashidi 114, 116). ⇨ **QARA-QUŠ?**

QARAXAY see **QARAƔAY**

QARAY Tat. 1624 **Qaray** [Чиникей Караевъ] (Pokrovskij 70); Tat. 1624 **Qaray** [Енглычъ Караевъ] (Pokrovskij 70); Tat. 18th-19th c. **Qaray** [Карай] (Magn. 50); Tat. 20th c. **Qaray** [Karaev / Карай] (Sattarov 144); Bashk. 1663 **Qaray** [Карай] (MIB I, 169); Uzb. 19th c. **Qaray** [Гурапъ Караевъ] (SKSO III, 164); *TN:* Tat. 1624 **Qaray(ev)** [деревни Караевы] (Pokrovskij 69). ✦ 'Be strong, be dreadful' (Sattarov). See also **ATA-QARAY, ATÏ-ГARAY, BOLÏ-QARAY.**

QARAYƔAN Bashk. 1777, 1787 **Qarayɣan** [Карайган Явгильдин], from the village of Karayganovo (!) (MIB V, 52, 204). ✦ 'Blacked, stained' cf. Bashk. *qaray-* 'чернеть, грязнеть, опозориться' (BRS/Uraksin).

QARAKE Kzk. 19th c. **Qarake** [Караке] (SOK 62); Kirg. **Qarake**, Qarbantay's hypocoristic shortened name (Ajtmatov). ⇨ **QARA** + dim. suff. *-ke.*

QARAQ Hak. 19th c. **Qaraq** [Каракъ] (Katanov, Otč. 12); Hak.(Blt.) 19th-20th c. **Qaraq** [Каракъ] (Katanov, Otč. 9); Hak.(Sag.) 19th-20th c. **Qaraq** [Каракъ] (Proben IX, 467, Katanov, Otč. 7); Kzk. 19th c. **Qaraq-bay** [Каракбай] (Grod., Pril. 164); Kzk. 19th c.

Qaraq-pay [Каракпай] (AOAtb. 18); Kzk. 19th c. **Qarq-pay** (<Qaraq-pay) [Каркпай] (SOV 110); *TN:* Kzk. **Qaraq-ata** [Карак-ата], a well (Karta JAR XIX). ✧ 'Eye; pupil' cf. Uyg., Chag., Hak., Tuv. *qaraq* 'der Blick, das Auge', (Kzk.) 'ein Liebeswort' (Radl. II, 147). See also **AY-QARAQ**.

QARAQ-BAQ Maml. 1313 **Qaraq-baq?** [قـراقبق], among the soldiers of Toqtay (Dawad. 275). ⇨ **QARAQ + BAQ**.

QARAQAY Tat. 1677 **Qaraqay** [Умеркъ Каракаевъ (в крещеніи Никита)] (DAI IX, 55, 56); Tat.(Sib.) 1623 **Qaraqay** [Каракай Кадеров], envoy (Miller, Ist. Sib. II, 306); Bashk. 1737 **Qaraqay** [Каракай-Чечень Сюндюков] (MIB III, 367); Bashk. 1756 **Qaraqay** [Муллакай Каракаев] (MIB IV/I, 109); Kzk. 1846 **Qaraqay** [Корагуза Каракаев], a biy (MKOP 154); Kzk. 19th c. **Qaraqay** [Каракай] (AOP 58, 70); Kzk. 19th c. **Qaraqay** [Каракай] (SOK 140). ✧ 'Somewhat black' cf. Bashk. *qaraqay* 'чёрненький' (BRS). ⇨ **QARA** + dim. suff. *-qay*.

QARAQAYČİ Kzk. 19th c. **Qaraqayči** [Каракайчи] (SOV 94). ⇨ **QARAΓAY** + suff. *-či*.

QARAQČİ Trkm. 1879 **Qaraqči** [Каракчи] (Grod., Vojna IV, Grod., Pril. 108); Kzk. 19th c. **Qaraqsï** [Караксы] (SOV 80); Kzk. 19th c. **Qaraqsï** [Караксы] (Lomakin 39); Bashk. 1740 **Qaraqši** [Чюрагул Каракшеев] (MIB I, 435). ✧ 'Robber, thief' cf. Uyg., Alt., Tat. *qaraqči* 'der Räuber, Dieb', Chag. *qaraqči* 'id.' (Radl. II, 149, 150), Kzk. *qaraqši* 'der Räuber, Dieb' (Radl. II, 150). See also **PATPAN-QARAQČİ**.

QARAQČİN Alt. 19th c. **Qaraqčin?** [Очи Каракчин], fem. (Verb., In. 154). ⇨ **QARAQ** + suff. *-čin*.

QARAQSÏ see **QARAQČİ**

QARAQŠİ see **QARAQČİ**

QARALDAY Alt. **Qaralday** [Каралъ-дай] (Nikiforov 127).

QARALİY Kzk. 19th c. **Qaraliy?** [Аманъ Каралiевъ] (Grod., Pril. 101).

QARALÏΓ Maml. 1332 **Qaralïγ / Qarlïγ?** [قرلغ], an emir (Dawād. 327). ⇨ **QARLÏQ?**

QARAMAY Tuv. 19th c. **Qaramay** [Карамаi] (Proben IX, 86).

QARAMAN Gag.? 1458 **Xaraman** [Haraman] (Wickenhauser, Moldawa I, 66); Crm. **Xaraman** [Хараман] (Proben VII, 34); Khorezm.?, Turk.? 14th c. **Qaraman** [قرمان] (Ibn Bat. II, 152); Gag.? 1434 **Qaraman** [Karaman], Berin's brother, a (Gipsy) slave of the monastery in Moldowica (Wickenhauser, Moldawa I, 18); Turk. 1540 **Qaraman** [قرهمان], head of the Şeyh Mihmadlu community (tribe) according to a defter of Diyarbekir (Demirtaş 55); Turk. 1583 **Qaraman** [Karaman] (Ongan, Ank. I, 164); Yürük 1543 **Qaraman**, among the Yürüks of Kocacık, Turkey (Gökb., Rum. 102, 193, 198, 217, 218 etc.); Crm.? 1689 **Qaraman** [Караманъ Кутлу-Баевъ], envoy of the Russians in the Crimea (Smirnov, Krym. 625); Bashk. 1744 **Qaraman** [Алишай Караманов] (MIB III, 415); Kzk. **Qaraman** [Караманъ] (Divaev, Šura 125); Kzk. 19th c. **Qaraman** [Караманъ] (Grod., Pril. 109); Kzk. 19th c. **Qaraman** [Караманъ] (AOP 126); Kzk. 19th c. **Qaraman** [Караманъ] (AOO 78); Kzk. 19th c. **Qaraman** [Караманъ] (SOK 100); Kzk. 19th c. **Qaraman** [Караманъ] (SOV 52); Uzb. 19th c. **Qaraman** [Караманъ Умырбаевъ] (SKSO III, 19); Kzk. 19th c. **Qaraman / Qaraman-batïr** [Караманъ (батыръ)] (Potanin, Pred. 73, 110); Crm. **Qaraman-batïr** [Караман Батыр] (Proben VII, 21); Turk. 1471 **Qaraman-bey**, from the Karamanoğulları dynasty (Gökb., Ed. 13); Turk. 1570 **Qaraman-bey** [Καραμάμπενς], Pasha Haydar's byname (Byz. Turc. 151, 152); Trkm.? 1598 **Qaraman-bek** [قـرامـان بيك / Караман-бек], a governor (daruγa) in Mañγïšlaq (Abulg./Kon. 1090, MIT II, 91); *EN:* Turk. **Qaraman**, a Zeybek tribe (aşiret) in the region of Tire, Turkey (Kúnos 1891, 117); *TN:* Uzb. 1851 **Qaraman** [Караманъ], a village in the region of Khiva (ZIRGO V, 116). ✧ 'Black'; Used also as a name of black dogs and horses (Moskov). ⇨ **QARA** + suff. *-man*.

QARAMEN Kzk. 19th c. **Qaramen?** [Карамень] (AOO 42). ⇨ **QARAMAN?**

QARAMÏŠ Tat. 1541 **Qaramïš** [Карамышъ] (PSRL XIII, 100); Kzk. 19th c. **Qaramïš** [Карабекъ Карамишевъ] (Grod., Pril. 153); Tat. 1552 **Qaramïš-ulan** [Карамышь-уланъ] (PSRL XIII, 172). ✧ 'He/she looked in, was born' (Sattarov), cf. Chag., Kuman, Alt., Hak., Kirg., Kzk., Tat. *qara-* 'schauen, hin sehen etc.' (Radl. II, 142).

QARAMŠAQ Bashk. 1712 **Qaramšaq** [Акзигит Карамшаков] (MIB III, 83).

QARAMUČ Uyg. 13th-14th c. **Qaramuč**, fem. (Zieme, Mat. III, 271).

QARAN Bashk. 1714 **Qaran-bay** [Каранбаева], personal name preserved in the name of a village (MIB III, 113). ✧ 'Open water-surface among ice-floes' cf. Bashk. *qaran* 'полынья' (BRS).

QARANAY Bashk. 18th c. **Qaranay** [Каранай Темеев] (MIB III, 80); Bashk. 1756 **Qaranay** [Каранай Азмеков] (MIB IV/1, 128); Bashk. 1783 **Qaranay** [Каранай Мратов] (MIB V, 143). ✧ 'Having black/dark face; serious outlook'? (Sattarov). ⇨ **QARAN?**

QARANAQ Alt. 19th-20th c. **Qaranaq** [Каранак], fem. (OjrRS 212).

QARANDAY Tat. 1708 **Qaranday** [Карандайка Итеев] (MIB I, 233). ⇨ **QARAN?** + suff. *-day*.

QARANDER Kirg. 19th c. **Qarander?** [Карандеръ Бикаліевъ] (Grod., Pril. 172).

QARAÑMAY Tuv. 19th c. **Qarañmay** [Караӊмаі] (Proben IX, 176).

QARAP Kzk. **Qarap-bay** [Карапбай] (Sb. Syr-D. IX, 52).

QARAPAN Kzk. 19th c. **Qarapan** [Карапанъ] (AOP 26).

QARAS Oghuz 1159 **Qaras** [Карасъ Кокѣй (Карасъ и Кокѣй)], chief of the Berendeys (PSRL II, 85, VII, 69); Bashk. 1710 **Qaras** [Карас Бекчюрин] (MIB III, 67); Bashk. 1731 **Qaras** [Карас] (MIB III, 289); Bashk. 1735 **Qaras** [Карясь Тахтаралиевъ], a tarχan (Vel.-Zern., Bašk. 15); Bashk. 1757 **Qaras** [Именай Карасев] (MIB IV/1, 136); Nog. 20th c. **Qaras** [Меджит Рамазан улы Къарас / Меджит Рамазанович Карасов], one of Baskakov's informants from the aul of Quban-χalq (Bask., Nog. 143); Nog. 20th c. **Qaras** [Мухаммет Иймин Ишметдин Аьфенди улы Къарас / Мухаммед-Имин Исметдин Эфенди Карасов], one of Baskakov's informants from the aul of Erkin-χalq, Cherkess Autonomous Region (Oblast') (Bask., Nog. 143, 158); Bashk. 1751 **Qaraz-bay** [Каразбай (Карасбай) Канакаев] (MIB IV/1, 52); Kzk. 19th c. **Qaraz-bay** [Каразъ] (SOK 206); *EN:* Nog. 20th c. **Qaras-uruwï** [Къарас урувы], an Aq-noγay clan from the district of Mineralovodsk (Bask., Nog. 132, 142); *TN:* Bashk. 1773 **Qaraz-bay(evo)** [Каразбаево], a village (MIB IV/2, 414). ✧ I. 'Mill'? cf. Kkalp. *qaraz* 'мельница' (KkRS); II. 'Wickedness'? cf. Bashk. *qaraz* 'злодейство' (BRS/Uraksin).

QARAS-KÖKEY Oghuz 1159 **Qaras-kökey** [Карасъ Кокѣй (Карасъ и Кокѣй)ъ Карасъ-Кокѣй], chief of the Berendeys (PSRL II, 85, VII, 69, Ipat. 343 /356/). ⇨ **QARAS + KÖKEY.**

QARASÏ Trkm. / Turk.? 14th c. **Qarasï / Qarasï-bey** [Καρασῆς / Karası Bey], a prince, founder of a Trkm. dynasty (Uzunçarş., Anad. 10, 27, 33, 34, Byz. Turc. 152). ✧ 'A kind of fish'? (Radl. II, 163).

QARASMAN Bashk. 1664 **Qarasman** [Акимбетко Карасманов] (MIB I, 193); Bashk. 1758 **Qarasman** [Алишай Карасманов] (MIB IV/1, 164). ✧ 'Somewhat black/dark' cf. Bashk. *qarasman* 'тёмненький, чёрненький' (BRS/Uraksin).

QARASTAY Alt. 19th-20th c. **Qarastay** [Карастай] (OjrRS 208). ⇨ **TAY** or suff. *-tay(1,2)?*

QARAŠ Trkm. **Qaraš** [Карашъ] (Mel'gunov 322); Bashk. 18th c. **Qaraš** [Карашев] (MIB V, 545); Kzk. 19th c. **Qaraš** [Карашъ] (SOV 6, 22); Kzk. 19th c. **Qaraš** [Карашъ] (SOK 248, 266). ✧ 'Servant, footman'? cf. Kzk. *qaraš bala* 'қызметши бала [servant boy]' (QTDS).

QARAŠAY Bashk. 1731 **Xarašay** [Харашай] (MIB III, 290); Bashk. 1757 **Xarašay** [Сюяргул Карашаев] (MIB IV/1, 145); Bashk. 1664 **Qarašay** [Карашай Кусюков] (MIB I, 193); Bashk. 1728 **Qarašay** [Карашай] (MIB I, 134); Bashk. 1757 **Qarašay** [Нылкыр Карашаев] (MIB IV/1, 157); Bashk. 1764 **Qarašay** [Аблай Карашаев] (MIB IV/1, 276); Bashk. 1788 **Qarašay** [Карашай Калкаманов] (MIB V, 233); Nog. 1649 **Qarašay** [Карашай мурза] (AI IV, 79). ⇨ **QARAŠ?** + suff. *-ay.*

QARAŠÏ see **QARAČÏ I.**

QARAŠÏT Oghuz/Trkm. 13th c. **Qarašït** [قراشيت / Карашыт], enemy of the Oghuz (Abulg./Kon. 1125, 1130).

QARAŠMAN Bashk. **Qarašman** [Аликей Карашманов] (MIB III, 472). ⇨ **QARAŠ** + suff. *-man.*

QARATTÏ see **QARA-ATTÏ**

QARATTÏ-PÄRGÄN see **QARA-ATTÏ-PERGEN**

QARATTÏ-PERGEN see **QARA-ATTÏ-PERGEN**

QARAW Kzk. 19th c. **Qaraw-bay** [Караубай] (AOA 78). ✧ 'Miser; miserly, stingy; shabby' cf. Kzk. *qarav* 'cimri, pinti' (KzTS). See also **QAS-QARAW.**

QARAWUL Tat. 1612 **Qarawul** [Алкай Карауловъ] (Nižegorod. platež. 48, 201); Tat. 1742-1748 **Qarawul** [Карауловъ], from Cheboksary (IOAIÊK XIV, 539); Bashk. 1786 **Qarawul** [Караул Дайоров] (MIB V, 198, 199); Kzk. 19th c. **Qarawul** [Караулъ] (SODž. 6, 24); Kzk. 19th c. **Qarawul** [Караулъ] (AOA 154); Kzk. 19th c. **Qarawul** [Караулъ] (AOAtb. 18); Kzk. 19th c. **Qarawul** [Караулъ] (AOO 22, 66); Kzk. 19th c. **Qarawul** [Караулъ] (SOK 82); Kzk. 19th c. **Qarawul** [Караулъ] (SOV 50); *EN:* Kzk. 18th c. - 19th c. **Qarawul** [Караул], a clan (Tynyšp. 71, 72). ✧ 'Guard, watch, post' cf. Chag. *qaraul* 'die Wache, ein Vorposten' (Radl. II, 146), Kzk. *qarawïl* 'караул, охрана' (KzRS). See also **QAYΓUL, EWEZ-QARAUL, UYTO-QAYTTÏ-QARAΓUL.**

QARAWUL-BAS Kzk. 19th c. **Qarawul-bas** [Кораулбасъ] (SOK 78). ⇨ **QARAWUL + BAŠ.**

QARAWULAN Khorezm.? 13th c. - 14th c. **Qarawulan?** [قراولان], a family in Qazwïn with members famous of their beauty (Qazw. 847).

QARAWULČÏ Kzk. 19th c. **Qarawulči** [Караульчи] (AOP 6). ✧ 'Guard' cf. Tat. *qaraulčï* 'der Wächter', Kzk. *qaraulšï* 'id.' (Radl. II, 147). ⇨ **QARAWUL.**

QARAZ see **QARAS**

QARAZAQ Kzk. 19th c. **Qarazaq** [Каразакъ] (SKSO VIII, 230).

QARĀYS Hak. 19th c. **Qarāys** [Карайс], fem. (Katanov, Otč. 12). ✧ 'Bream (type of fresh water fish of the carp family)' <R. карась (Katanov). See also **ČABAQ, ČAPAQ, TABAN.**

QARĀSÏM Hak.? 19th-20th c. **Qarāsïm** [Карасым]

(Katanov, Otč. 10). ✧ Gerasym (R. Герасымъ).

QARĀSQA Hak.(Shor) 19th-20th c. **Qarāsqa** [Караска] (Katanov, Otč. 11). ✧ Geras'ka (R. Гераська).

QARĀTTÏ see **QARA-ATTÏ**

QARBANTAY Kirg. **Qarbantay** [Карбантай], an elderly man whose hypocoristic shortened name is Qarake (Ajtmatov). ⇨ **?** + **TAY?** or suff. -tay(1,2)?

QARBÏM Kzk. **Qarbïm-bay** / **Qarbïn-bay?** [Карбымбай] (?).

QARBUZ Kzk. 19th c. **Qarbuz** [Карбозъ] (SOK 24, 292); Kzk. 19th c. **Qarbuz** [Карбузъ] (SODž. 126); Kirg. 1850 **Qarbuz** [Карбузъ], manap (nobleman) (Aristov, Opyt 50); Kzk. 19th c. **Qarïboz** [Карыбозъ] (SOV 52, 94); Kzk. 19th c. **Qarïboz** [Карибозъ] (SOV 158); Kzk. 19th c. **Qarïboz** [Карыбозъ Кантаровъ], from the Qurman tribe (Pantusov, Kirg. 22); Kirg.?, Kzk.? **Qarïbuz** [Карыбузъ], manap (nobleman) (Smirnov, Sultany 16); *EN:* Kirg. 19th c. **Qarbuz** [Карбузъ], a branch of the Sultu tribe (Aristov, Opyt 50). ✧ 'Water melone' cf. Crm., Turk. *qarpuz*, Tat. *qarbis*, Uyg. *qarbus* 'die Wassermelone' (Radl. II, 212, 214, 215), Kzk. *qarbiz* 'арбуз' (KzRS) (<Ir.).

QARČA Karch. 20th c. **Qarča** [Qʿarčá / Карча], forefather of the Karachays (SMOK III, 164, Pröhle, Kar. X, 116); Kzk. 19th c. **Qarča** [Карча] (SODž. 90). ✧ 'Swallow' cf. Chag. *qarča* 'eine kleine Schwalbe' (Radl. III, 164).

QARČAĞA see **QARČÏĞA**

QARČAR Oghuz/Trkm. 14th c. - 15th c. **Qarčar** / **Qarjar** [Delü Karcar / Карчар] (DQorq. 36-39, 150, 209 etc.). ✧ I. 'Black (child) with white head'? see QARA + ČAR; II. 'Little Black'? ⇨ **QARA** + dim. suff. -čar.

QARČÏ Tat.(Lit.) 1552 **Qarči?** [Карчие] (Kn. Metriki Lit. 36); Uzb. 19th c. **Qarči-bay** [Карчибай] (SKSO III, 182). ✧ 'Lover of snow; born when it was snowing'? ⇨ **QAR?** + suff. -či.

QARČÏĞA Bashk. 1746 **Qarčaγa?** / **Qarčïγa?** [Карчага Усеинов] (MIB III, 446); NUyg. 19th c. **Qarčïγa** [قارچىغا / Karchigha] (Le Coq, Namenl. 104); Bashk. 1709 **Qarčïγa** / **Qarčïγa?** [Карчига] (MIB III, 53); Bashk. 1728 **Qarčïγa** / **Qarčïγa?** [Сапар Карчигин] (MIB III, 256); Kzk. 19th c. **Qarčïγa** / **Qarčïγa?** [Карчига] (SOK 308); Kkalp. 20th c. **Qaršïγa** [Каршыга], fem. (KkRS 778). ✧ 'Falcon' cf. Kuman *qarčaγa (?)* 'Habicht' (CC), Alt., Crm., Tat. *qarčïγa* 'der Habicht' (Radl. II, 204), Chag., NUyg.(Tar.) *qarčïγa* 'id.' (Radl. II, 205), Kkalp. *qaršïγa* 'ястреб, сокол, охотничья ловчая птица' (KkRS). See also **KÖK-QARČÏĞA**.

QARČÏQ Hak. 19th-20th c. **Qarčïq** [Карчык] (Katanov, Otč. 10). ✧ I. 'Tick, itch' cf. Hak.(Sag., Kacha, Koyb.) *qarčïq* 'die Schafszwecke' (Radl. II,

204); II. 'Oppose!, withstand!' cf. Shor *qarčïq-* 'sich widersetzen' (Radl. II, 204).

QARJÏ Turk. **Qarjï-oγlu** [Karžy oγlu], a Zeybek (Kúnos 1891, 119). ✧ 'Seller of snow'? cf. Turk. *karcı* 'id.' (TED). ⇨ **QARČÏ?**, **QAR** + suff. -jï.

QARDAMÏŠ Bulg. 777-803 **Qardamïš** [Κάρδαμος], a prince (Byz. Turc. 153-154).

QARDAN Kzk. **Qardan** [Кардан], a folklore hero (Laptev, Materialy 27).

QARDÏ Bashk. 1722 **Qardï-γul** [Бюляк Кардыгулов] (MIB I, 289).

QARDÏĞAČ see **QARLÏĞAČ**

QAREKE Kzk. 19th c. **Qareke** [Кареке] (AOA 138). ✧ Hypocoristic and shortened form of a name beginning with the syllable(s) *Qar-* or *Qara-* + comp. *eke.*

QAREKEY Bashk. 1773 **Qarekey** [Каракей] (MIB IV/1, 369). ⇨ **QAREKE** + suff. -y.

QARFÏK Kzk. 19th c. **Qarfik** [Орасъ Магомедъ Карфиковъ] (Grod., Pril. 173); Kzk. 1879 **Qarfik** [Окули Карфиковъ] (Grod., Pril. 130).

QARĞA Kkalp. 20th c. **Ғарγа-bay** [Ғарғабай] (KkRS 773); Hak. 19th-20th c. **Xarγa** [Харға], fem. (HRS 355); Kzk. 19th c. **Qarγa** [Карга] (AOA 114); Kzk. 19th c. **Qarγa** [Карга] (SOV 22); Kzk. 19th c. **Qarγa** [Карга Бектемирзаевъ] (Grod., Pril. 147); Hak. 19th-20th c. **Qarγa** [Карҕа] (Katanov, Otč. 11); Turk. 16th c. **Qarγa-baba**, a dervish (Gökb., Ed. 36); Kzk. 19th c. **Qarγa-bay** [Карга-Бай] (AUK 501); Kzk. 19th c. **Qarγa-bay** [Каргабай] (SOV 158); Kzk. 19th c. **Qarγa-bay** [Каргабай] (SOK 144); Kzk. 19th c. **Qarγa-bay** [Каргабай] (SODž. 76, 96); Kzk. 19th c. **Qarγa-bek** [Каргабекъ] (SOK 204, 214); Kzk. 1825 **Qarqa-bay** [قارقا باى / Каркабай] (MIK IV, 473, 4777). ✧ 'Crow, rook' cf. in several Trk. languages: *qarγa* 'die Krähe' (Radl. II, 191), Kkalp. *γarγa* 'ворона' (KkRS).

QARĞA-BOYLÏ Kzk. **Qarγa-boylï** [Каргабойлы] (Žirm., Epos 395). ⇨ **QARĞA** + **BOY.**

QARĞA-MAMBET Crm. 1785 **Qarγa-mambet** [Карга-мамбет] (IAN 1928, 380). ⇨ **QARĞA** + **MAMBET.**

QARĞAJAQ Hak.(Shor) 19th-20th c. **Qarγajaq** [Карҕацак] (Katanov, Otč. 11). ✧ 'Little crow'. ⇨ **QARĞA** + dim. suff. -jaq.

QARĞAJÏ Tat.(GH)? 1313 **Qarγajï** [قرغاجى], a Moghul emir (Dawād. 274). ⇨ **QARĞA** + suff. -jï.

QARĞAN Kmk. / Balk.? 1830 **Qarγan** [Карганов], a major (MID III, 208); Kzk. 19th c. **Qarγan** [Карганъ] (SODž. 124).

QARĞANDAY Kirg., Kzk. **Qarγanday** [Карҕандаi], a Kazak hero in the Manas epic (Proben V, 184 /186/). ⇨ **QARĞAN** + suff. -day.

QARĞARDAY Kirg. **Qarγarday** [Kagardai! /

Карӊардаі] (Proben V, 151 /152/). ❖ 'Ash-grey crane'? cf. Chag., Kirg., Kzk. *qarqara* 'eine Reiherart; der Name eines Flusses' (Radl. II, 190) (<Mo.) + suff. *-day*.

QARĞAS Kzk. 19th c. **Qarɣas-pay** [Каргаспай] (SODž. 150).

QARĞÏL Kzk. 19th c. **Qarɣïl-bay** [Каргылбай] (SOV 58).

QARĞÏM Kzk. 19th c. **Qarɣïm-bay (Qarɣïn-bay?)** [Каргымбай] (AOP 46).

QARĞÏSČIL Kzk. 19th c. **Qarɣïsčil** [Каргысчилъ Карабай] (Potanin, Pred. 104). ❖ 'Cursed, blasted'? cf. Kzk. *qarɣïs* 'der Fluch' (Radl. II, 194). + suff. *-čil*.

QARĞUZ Kzk. 19th c. **Qarɣuz-pay? (<Qarɣïs-pay?)** [Каргозпай] (SODž. 98). ❖ 'Curse, anathema' cf. Kzk. *qarɣïs* 'der Fluch' (Radl. II, 194).

QARÏB see **QARÏP**

QARÏM see **KERÏM**

QARÏNA Hak. 19th-20th c. **Qarina** [Карина], fem. (HRS 353).

QARÏNÏ Uyg. **Qarini** [qarini] (DTS). ❖ (<Skr.).

QARÏP see **QARÏP**

QARÏ Trkm. 20th c. **Qarï** [Qarï] (Zaj. 1971, 333); Kzk. 19th c. **Qarï-bay** [Карыбай] (SOV 10, 54); Kzk. 19th c. **Qarï-bay** [Карыбай] (SODž. 104); Kzk. 19th c. **Qarï-bay** [Карыбай] (AOAtb. 2); Kzk. 19th c. **Qarï-bay** [Карыбай] (SOK 32); Kzk. 19th c. **Qarï-ɣïz (<Qarï-qïz)** [Карыгыз] (SOK 280); Trkm. 1598 **Qarï-χan / Qari-χan** [Кари-хан], from the Oχlu tribe (clan?) (MIT II, 96, 97). ❖ I. 'Old; old woman?' cf. Uyg., Chag., Alt., Crm. Hak., Turk. *qari* 'alt, eine Frau' (Radl. II, 167); II. 'Reader of the Qurʿan' cf. Uzb. *qāri* 'чтец Корана (занющий весь Коран наизусть)' (UzbRS).

QARÏ-ČAL Kzk. 19th c. **Qarï-čal** [Каричалъ] (SOV 98); Kzk. 19th c. **Qarï-čal** [Каричалъ] (SOK 234); Kzk. 19th c. **Qarï-čal** [Каричалъ] (SODž. 16). ⇨ **QARÏ + ČAL?**

QARÏ-YAĞDÏ see **QAR-YAĞDÏ**

QARÏBOZ see **QARBUZ**

QARÏBUZ see **QARBUZ**

QARÏKEY Bashk. 1753 **Qarïkey / Qarïkäy** [Карикей / Карекай] (MIB IV/1, 75); Bashk. 1764 **Qarïkey / Qarïkäy** [Карикей Бакиев] (MIB IV/1, 277). ⇨ **QARÏ + dim. suff. *-key*.**

QARÏQ Uyg. 12th c. - 14th c. **Qarïq** [Карık] (Radl., USp. 137, DTS, EUTS); Kzk. 19th c. **Qarïq-bay** [Карыкбай] (AOAtb. 50); Kzk. 19th c. **Qarïq-pay** [Карыкпай] (SOK 8). ❖ 'Plenty, abundance' cf. Kzk. *qarïq: qarïq bol-* 'получить что-л. в изобилии' (KzRS).

QARÏQ-BOL Kzk. 19th c. **Qarïq-bol** [Карыкболъ] (AOO 50, 66); Kzk. 19th c. **Qarïq-bol** [Карыкболъ] (AOA 60). ❖ 'Be/live in plenty' cf. Kzk. *qarïq: qarïq*

bol- 'получить что-л. в изобилии' (KzRS). ⇨ **QARÏQ + BOL.**

QARÏLAN Kzk. 19th c. **Qarïlan?** [Бака Карилановъ] (Grod., Pril. 184).

QARÏLĞAČ see **QARLÏĞAČ**

QARÏMDU see **QARÏMTU**

QARÏMÏŠ Uyg. **Qarïmïš** [Karımış] (EUTS). See also **TÏTRÄKČI-QARÏMÏŠ.**

QARÏMSAQ Kzk. 19th c. **Qarïmsaq** [Карымсакъ] (SOK 242); Kzk. 19th c. **Qarïmsaq** [Карымсакъ] (AOP 10); Kzk. 19th c. **Qarïmsaq** [Карымсакъ] (AOAtb. 10); Kzk. 19th c. **Qarïmsaq** [Карымсакъ] (AOA 82); Kzk. 19th c. **Qarïmsaq** [Карымсакъ] (SOV 80, 118); Kzk. 19th c. **Qarïmsaq** [Карымсакъ] (SODž. 8).

QARÏMTU Uyg. **Qarïmdu / Qarïmtu?** (Radl., USp. 40, 86); Uyg. 12th c. - 14th c. **Qarïmtu-tutuň** [Karımtu / qarïmtu tutuŋ] (EUTS, DTS).

QARÏN Kzk. 19th c. **Qarïn** [Карынъ] (SOV 54); Kzk. 19th c. **Qarïn** [Карынъ] (SOK 90); Kzk. 19th c. **Qarïn** [Карынъ] (SODž. 120); Kzk. 19th c. **Qarïn** [Карынъ] (AOO 6); Kzk. **Qarïn-bay** [Карын Баі] (Proben III, 755 /845/); Kzk. 19th c. **Qarïn-bay** [Карынбай] (SOV 124); Kzk. 19th c. **Qarïn-bay** [Карынбай] (AOO 66); Kzk. 19th c. **Qarïn-bay** [Карынбай] (AOA 38); Kzk. 19th c.? **Qarïn-bay** (Atyns. 118); Kzk. 19th c. **Qarïn-bay** (Ljutš 32); Kirg. **Qarïn-bay** [Карынбай] (Jud. 712); Kzk. 19th c. **Qarïn-bul** [Карынбулъ] (AOO 70); Kzk. 19th c. **Qarun-bay** [Карунбай] (AUK 105); Kzk. 19th c. **Qarun-bay** [Карунбай] (Potanin II, 151). ❖ 'Stomach, belly' cf. Uyg., Kuman, Alt., Crm., Hak., Tat., Turk., Tat. *qarïn* 'der Bauch, Magen, Leib' (Radl. II, 171), Kirg. *qarïn* 'живот, брюхо, желудок' (Jud.).

QARÏNDAŠ Alt. 19th-20th c. **Qarïndaš** [Карындаш], fem. (OjrRS 212); Selj. **Qarïndaš-χan** [قرىنداش / قراىنداشحان], Salɣur-šah's laqab (Ǧuwaynī II, 10). ❖ 'Brother or sister' cf. Alt., Az., Hak., Kirg., Kzk., Tat. etc. *qarïndaš* 'der Bruder oder die Schwester' (Radl. II, 173).

QARÏNTAY Kzk. 19th c. **Qarïntay** [Карынтай] (SOV 138). ⇨ **QARÏN + suff. *-tay(1,2)*?**

QARÏP Kzk. **Qarib-bay** [Кариббай] (Divaev, Šura 79); Kzk. 19th c. **Qarip** [Карипъ] (SOK 4); Kzk. 19th c. **Qarip-ǰan** [Карипджанъ] (SOK 44); Crm. **Qarïp** [Карыпъ] (Proben VII, 21); Kzk. 19th c. **Qarïp** [Карыпъ] (SOK 26); Kirg. **Qarïp** [Карып] (Jud. 618); *EN:* Kzk. 18th c. - 19th c. **Qarip-ǰan** [Карипджан], a clan (Tynyšp. 71). ❖ 'Alien, foreigner' cf. Kirg. *qarip* (Ar.) 'бесприютный, обездоленный, находящийся в бедственном положении' (Jud.). See also **BURALQÏ, ČÏT, YAT, TAT.**

QARÏS-QARA Kzk. **Qarïs-qara** [Карыс Кара] (Proben III, 253 /297/). ❖ 'Span-black' cf. Hak., Kzk.

qarïs 'die Spanne' (Radl. II, 177). ⇨ **QARA.**

QARQ-ABÏZ Bashk. 1715 **Qarq-abïz? / Qïrq-abïz?** [Ибрай Каркабызов] (MIB III, 120). ⇨ **QARAQ? / QÏRQ? + ABÏZ.**

QARQ-MULTUQ see **QÏRQ-MULTUQ**

QARQA see **QARГA**

QARQARUBAD Kzk. 19th c. **Qarqarubad** [Ташимъ Каркарубадовъ] (Grod., Pril. 178).

QARQÏN Oghuz/Trkm. 13th c. **Qarqïn** [قارقين / Каркын], Yulduz-χan's son (RaD I/1, 76, Abulg./Kon. 57, 520, 555, 600); Turk. 1583 **Qarqïn** (Ongan, Ank. I, 153). ✧ 'A kind of (dark) leather' cf. Turk. dial. *qarqïn* 'eine Art dunkelgefärbtes Leder' (Radl. II, 190).

QARQÏN-QONAQ Oghuz/Trkm. 13th c. **Qarqïn-qonaq-alp** [قارقين قوناق آكب / Каркын-Конак-алп] (Abulg./Kon. 1450). ⇨ **QARQÏN? + QONAQ.**

QARLA Tat. 1543 **Qarla** [Karla] (Gökb., Rum. 235). ⇨ **QARLÏ?**

QARLAГAŠ see **QARLÏГAČ**

QARLAQ Yak. 1680 **Qarlaq** [Мазара Карлакъ] (DAI VIII, 268).

QARLAM-BAY see **QARLAN**

QARLAN Kzk. 19th c. **Qarlam-bay (<Qarlan-bay)** [Карламбай] (SOK 288). ✧ 'Get angry, be furious' cf. Kzk. *qarlan-* (Ar.) 'zornig werden, sich heftig ärgern' (Radl. II, 196).

QARLAPÏN Hak. 19th-20th c. **Qarlapin** [Карлапин] (HRS 349).

QARLÏ Kuman 1353, 1359, 1368 **Qarla (<Qarlï)** [Karla], a chief (capitaneus) of the Kumans in Hungary (Gyárfás III, 488, 498, 504); Kuman 1183 **Qarlï** [Кобякъ Карлыевичъ], a Polovets prince (Ipat. 427); Turk. 1455 **Qarlï** [Karlı] (Gökb., Ed. 275); Turk. 1583 **Qarlï** [قررلى / Karlı] (Ongan, Ank. I, 164); Yürük **Qarlï** [قرر لى / Karlı] (Gökb., Rum. 105, 178, 198, 200 etc.); Turk. 1528 **Qarlï / Qarlï-bey** [Karlı / Karlı Bey], Yağınur Baba's son (Gökb., Ed. 275); Kzk. 19th c. **Qarlï-bay** [Карлыбай] (SOK 278); Trkm. 1833 **Qarlï-yüzbašï** [Карлы-юзбашы] (MIT II, 464-466, 469, 463 etc.); Trkm. 1867 **Qarlï-qul** [Карлы-куль], from the İmreli tribe (MIT II, 634); Trkm.? 1841/42 **Qarlï-mehrem** [Карлы-мехрем] (MIT II, 483); Turk. 16th c. **Qarlï-oγlu** [Abdürrezak Karlı oğlu] (Ongan, Ank. II, 1301, 1306); Selj.? 1068, 1071 **Qarlu** [قرلو] (Ibn al-Athīr/Tornb. X, 40, Qalānisi 98, Kamāladdīn II, 31); Kzk. 1825 **Qarlu-bay** [قارلوبای / Карлубай] (MIK IV, 468, 475 etc.); *TN:* Hak. 19th-20th c. **Qarlï-χan** [Карлыхан], a ridge at around the source of Abakan river (Karta JAR V); Selj. 12th c. **Qarlu** [قرلو / مسجد /], a mosque (Ibn Šaddād, Alep 75). ✧ 'Snowy, snowclad' (cf. Rásonyi, KÖA 110). ⇨ **QAR** + suff. *-lï.*

QARLÏГAČ Kirg. **Qardïγač** [Кардыӊач], Manas' sister (Proben V, 116 /117/); Kzk. 19th c. **Qarïlγač** [Карылгачъ], fem. (Potanin, Pred. 100); Alt. 19th-20th c. **Qarlaγaš** [Карлагаш] (OjrRS 208); Kzk. 19th c. **Qarlïγaš** [Карлыгашъ], fem. (Grod. I, 98); Chag. **Qarloγač** [قارلوغاج / Qarloγač] (Le Coq, Ind. 4); *EN:* Kzk. 18th c. - 19th c. **Qarlïγaš** [Карлыгаш], a clan (Tynyšp. 72). ✧ 'Swallow' cf. Chag. *qarlaγač*, Tat. *qarlïγač*, Tat.(Bar.) *qarlïγac*, Alt. *qarlaγaš, qarlïγaš*, Hak. *qarlaγas*, Alt., Hak., Kzk. *qarïlïγaš* (Radl. II, 176, 196, 197), Kirg. *qardïγač* 'стриж' (Jud.).

QARLÏQ Oghuz/Trkm. 13th c. **Qarlïq** [قارليق / Карлык] (Abulg./Kon. 350, 565).

QARMAY Bashk. 1759 **Qarmay** [Юзей Кармаев] (MIB IV/2, 24).

QARMAQ Bashk. 1754 **Qarmaq** [Бекжен Кармяков] (MIB IV/1, 88). ✧ 'Hook, fish-hook' cf. Kuman, Chag., Alt., Hak., Kirg., Kzk., Tat. etc. *qarmaq* 'der Haken, Angelhaken' (Radl. II, 216), Karch. *qᶜarmaq* 'id.' (Pröhle, Kar.).

QARMAQAY Karch. **Qarmaqay** [Кармакай] (Sysoev 135). ✧ 'Little hook, fish-hook'. ⇨ **QARMAQ** + dim. suff. *-y.*

QARMAN Bashk. 1701, 1706 **Qarman** [Карман] (MIB III, 10, 27); Bashk. 1709 **Qarman** [Карман] (MIB I, 253-56, 263); Bashk. 1748 **Qarman** [Сеит Карманов] (MIB III, 454); Bashk. 18th c. **Qarman** [Абдулла Карманов] (MIB V, 109); Bashk. 1756 **Qarman** [Карман Купеев] (MIB IV/1, 109); Bashk. 1760 **Qarman** [Юзей Карманов] (MIB IV/2, 384); Kzk. 1823 **Qarman** [قرمان / Карман] (MIK IV, 458, 462); Alt. 19th-20th c. **Qarman** [Карман] (OjrRS 208); Bashk. 1751 **Qarman-γul** [Кармангул Елдашбаев] (MIB IV/1, 52); Bashk. 1798 **Qarman-γul** [Кармангулъ] (PSZRI XXV, 196); *TN:* Bashk. 1722 **Qarmanovo** [Карманово] (MIB I, 297). ✧ 'Pocket' cf. Alt. *qarman* (R.) 'die Tasche' (Radl. II, 217). ⇨ **QARAMAN?**

QARMANAY Bashk. 1711 **Qarmanay** [Сармаш Карманаев (Корманаев)] (MIB III, 68, 70, 154). ✧ 'Little pocket'. ⇨ **QARMAN** + dim. suff. *-ay.*

QARMÏS see **QARMÏŠ**

QARMÏŠ Kzk. 19th c. **Qarmïs** [Кармысъ] (SODž. 158); Kzk. 19th c. **Qarmïs** [Кармысъ] (AOK 70); Kzk. 19th c. **Qarmïs** [Кармысъ / Кармызъ] (AOA 46, 122); Kzk. 19th c. **Qarmïs** [Кармысъ] (AOAtb. 46); Kzk. 19th c. **Qarmïs** [Кармысъ] (SOK 130, 220); Tat.(Lit.) 1545 **Qarmïš** [Кармыш] (Kn. Metriki Lit. 22); Tat.(Lit.) 1552 **Qarmïš** [Кармышъ] (Kn. Metriki Lit. 64); Bashk. 1623 **Qarmïš** [Кармыш Игилдик] (Miller, Ist. Sib. II, 300); Bashk. 1659 **Qarmïš** [Кармышка Ахтеевъ], a tarχan (Vel.-Zern., Bašk. 37); Bashk. 1664 **Qarmïš** [Акайко Кармышев] (MIB I, 192); Bashk. 1730 **Qarmïš** [Кармыш] (MIB III,

277); Bashk. 1731 **Qarmïš** [Кармыш Уразаев] (MIB III, 284); Bashk. 1734 **Qarmïš** [Тлевкей Кармышев] (MIB III, 317); Bashk. 1734 **Qarmïš** [Казыр Кармыш] (MIKk. 205); Bashk. 1735 **Qarmïš** [Кармышъ Кызыкуртовъ], a tarχan (Vel.-Zern., Bašk. 20); Bashk. 1745 **Qarmïš** [Кармыш] (MIB III, 427); Bashk. 1756 **Qarmïš** [Кармыш Биксекеев] (MIB IV/1, 119, 129); Bashk. 1756 **Qarmïš** [Кармыш Байчюрин] (MIB IV/1, 123); Bashk. 1757 **Qarmïš** [Кармыш Карагулов] (MIB IV/1, 157); Bashk. 1777 **Qarmïš** [Умер (Гумер) Кармышев] (MIB V, 52); Bashk. 1787 **Qarmïš** [Кармыш Каткашев] (MIB V, 204); Bashk. 1787 **Qarmïš** [Кармыш Кулмашев] (MIB V, 338); Bashk. 1787 **Qarmïš** [Кармыш Мамбетев] (MIB V, 683); Bashk. 1787 **Qarmïš** [Ресюль Кармышев] (MIB V, 204); Bashk. 1793 **Qarmïš** [Зюбеир Кармышев] (MIB V, 328); Bashk. 1794 **Qarmïš** [Кармыш] (MIB V, 338); Kzk. 19th c. **Qarmïš** [Кармышъ] (SKSO III, 20); Kzk. 19th c. **Qarmïš / Qarmiš?** [Буташъ Кармишевъ] (Grod., Pril. 25); Oghuz/Trkm. 13th c. **Qarmïš-bay** [بای قارمش / Кармыш-бай] (Abulg./Kon. 1445); Kzk. 19th c. **Qarmïš-pay** [Кармышпай] (SOV 114); *TN:* Bashk. 1770 **Qarmïševo** [Кармышево], a village (MIB IV/1, 341). ◆ I. Wooden paling, plank'?; II. 'A clan of the tribe Yurmatï' cf. Bashk. *qarmïš* I. 'тын из брёвен', *qarmïš* II. 'кармыш (название одного из башкирских родов племени юрматы' (BRS/Uraksin), Kzk. *qarmïs* 'a group of clans (branch)' (Kojčubaev); III. According to Sattarov it goes back to QARAMÏŠ. ⇨ **QAR?** + suff. *-mïš*.

QARMÏŠAQ   Bashk. 1623 **Qarmïšaq** [Кармышак] (Miller, Ist. Sib. II, 299, MIB I, 157); Bashk. 1623 **Qarmïšaq** [Кармышак] (MIB I, 157); Bashk. 1773 **Qarmïšaq** [Сулейман Кармышаков] (MIB IV/2, 414); Bashk. 1798 **Qarmïšaq** [Кармышакъ] (PSZRI XXV, 195). ⇨ **QARMÏŠ?** + suff. *-aq*.

QARMUT   Kzk. 19th c. **Qarmut** [Кармутъ] (AOP 94).

QARNAY   Trkm. 1858 **Qarnay-yüzbaši** [Карнай-юзбаши], from the Čawdur tribe (MIT II, 569, 570). See also **SARÏ-QARNAY**.

QARNAQ   Kzk. 19th c. **Qarnaq** [Карнакъ] (Lomakin 39).

QARNÜŠ   Alt. 19th-20th c. **Qarnüš** [Карнÿш] (OjrRS 208). ◆ Kornyusha, Korniliy (R.).

QAROLDAY   Alt. **Qarolday-mergen** [Карольдай-(Мергенъ)] (Nikiforov 111). ◆ 'Guard, watch'? cf. Alt. *qaruul* 'стража, охрана' (OjrRS) + suff. *-day*.

QARPAQ   Uyg. 12th c. - 14th c. **Qarpaq** [Karpak / qarpaq] (EUTS, DTS).

QARPÏQ   Bashk. 1737 **Qarpïq** [Карпык] (MIB I, 327); Kzk. 18th c. - 19th c. **Qarpïq** [Бекмухамсдъ Карпыковъ] (ZOOIRGO III, 26); Kzk. 1846 **Qarpïq** [Карпык Джаманкарин], a biy (MKOP 155); Kzk.

19th c. **Qarpïq** (Ljutš. 138); Kzk. 19th c. **Qarpïq** [Карпыкъ] (AOK 34); Kzk. 19th c. **Qarpïq** [Карпыкъ] (SOV 116, 134); Kzk. 19th c. **Qarpïq** [Карпыкъ] (AOO 6); Kzk. 19th c. **Qarpïq** [Карпыкъ / Карпекъ] (SODž. 12, 122); Kzk. 19th c. **Qarpïq** [Карпыковъ] (AOO 26, 46); Kzk. 19th c. **Qarpïq-bay** [Карпыкбай] (AOA 26).

QARSAQ   Chuv. 18th-19th c. **Karsak** [Карсакъ] (Magn. 50); Bashk. 1700 **Qarsaq** [Апачко Карсаковъ] (Vel.-Zern., Bašk. 35); Bashk. 1700 **Qarsaq** [Карсакъ Бюляковъ] (Vel.-Zern., Bašk. 35); Bashk. 1724 **Qarsaq** [Карсак Кутлугозин] (MIB III, 222); Kzk. 19th c. **Qarsaq** [Карсакъ] (SODž. 106); Kzk. 19th c. **Qarsaq** [Карсакъ] (AOA 22); Kzk. 19th c. **Qarsaq** [Карсакъ] (AOO 30); Kirg. **Qarsaq** [Карсак], one of Manas' comrades-in-arms (Proben V, 40-41); Hak. 19th-20th c. **Qarsaq** [Карсак] (HRS 349); Kzk. 19th c. **Qarsaq-bay** [Карсакбай] (SODž. 86); Kzk. 19th c. **Qarsaq-bay** [Карсакбай] (AOP 82); Kzk. 19th c. **Qarsaq-bay** [Карсакбай] (SOK 86, 182, 222, 302); Kzk. 19th c. **Qarsaq-bay** [Карсакбай] (SOV 114); Kzk. 19th c. **Qarsaq-bay** [Карсакпай] (SOV 54); Kkalp. 20th c. **Qarsaq-bay** [Къарсакъбай / Қарсаққбай] (Bask., Kkalp. 400, KkRS 774); Bashk. **Qarsaq-qul** [Карсаккул Пяляев] (MIB IV/1, 122); *TN:* Turk. 20th c. **Qarsaq** [Karsak], a village in the province of Bursa (TMİB 223). ◆ 'Steppe-fox' (Sauvaget 53: renard de la steppe), cf. Chag., Kirg., Kzk., Tat.(Bar.), Turk. *qarsaq* 'der Steppenfuchs' (Radl. II, 206).

QARSAN   Kzk. 19th c. **Qarsam-bay (<Qarsan-bay?)** [Карсамбай] (SOV 30); Bashk. 1756 **Qarsan** [Карсан Микеев] (MIB IV/1, 134); Bashk. 1756 **Qarsan** [Карсан Аднашев] (MIB IV/1, 126); Bashk. 1758 **Qarsan** [Карсан Султанаев] (MIB IV/1, 164). ◆ 'Eve' cf. Kzk. *qarsan* 'arefe, belli bir meselenin, bir vakanın önündeki günler' (KzTS).

QARSÏ see **QARŠI**

QARSÏDAQ   Kzk. 19th c. **Qarsïdaq** [Карсыдакъ] (SOK 56).

QARŠA   Uyg. 13th-14th c. **Qarša-[?]mïš** [Qarša []mïš] (Zieme, Mat. III, 280).

QARŠA-AČARİ   Uyg. 12th c. - 14th c. **Qarša-ačari (Qaqša-ačqï)** [qaqša ačqï / Qarša Ačari] (DTS, Zieme, Mat. III, 280). ⇨ **QARŠA.**

QARŠÏ   Kzk. 19th c. **Qarsï-bay** [Карсыбай] (SODž. 26); Uzb. 19th c. **Qarši-bay** [Каршибай Ерметовъ] (SKSO III, 166); Uzb. 19th c. **Qarši-bay** [Каршибай] (SKSO III, 172); Uzb. 19th c. **Qarši-bay** [Кумарбай Каршибаевъ] (SKSO III, 174); Uzb. 19th c. **Qarši-bay** [Каршибай Худайбердіевъ] (SKSO III, 172). ◆ 'Opposite, contrary; headstrong' cf. Kar., Kzk. *qarsï* 'das Entgegenstehende' (Radl. II, 206), Kuman, Crm., Tat., Turk. etc. *qaršï* 'gegenüberliegend, eigensinnig'

(Radl. II, 208). See also **BİKE-QARŠİ**.

QARŠİĠA see **QARČİĠA**

QARŠİĠAN Hak.(Shor) 19th-20th c. **Qaršïɣan-qan** [Каршыӊан-кан] (Radl. II, 536).

QARŠİN Kzk. 19th c. **Qaršïn-bay** [Каршинбай] (AOA 118).

QART Kzk. 19th c. **Qart** [Картъ] (SOV 26); Bashk. 1715 **Qart-batïr** [Карт-Батыр] (MIB I, 278-79); Crm. 1784 **Qart-murza** [Карт мурза] (IAN 1928, 379); Kzk. 19th c. **Qart-pay** [Картпай] (AOA 138); Kzk. 19th c. **Qart-pay** [Картпай] (SOK 120, 308); Kzk. 19th c. **Qart-pay** [Картпай] (SODž. 12, 114); Kkalp. 20th c. **Qart-pay** [Къартпай / Картпай] (Bask., Kkalp. 46, KkRS 774); Bashk. 1693 **Qartï-bay (<Qart-bay?)** [Картыбайко / Карт-бай] (MIB I, 81); Bashk. 1740 **Qartï-batïr (<Qart-batïr?)** [Картыбатырев (Юсуп)] (MIB I, 468); *EN:* Kkalp. 18th c. - 19th c. **Qart** [Карт], a clan (Tynyšp. 72); *TN:* Crm. **Qart-bey** [Kart bei], a place north-west of Evpatoria (Jervis VII). ✧ 'Old man' cf. Kuman, Crm., Kirg., Kzk., Tat. etc. *qart* 'alt (an Jahren), bejahrt' (Radl. II, 198).

QARTA Kzk. 19th c. **Qarta-bay** [Картабай] (SOK 106, 242); Kzk. 19th c. **Qarta-bay** [Картабай] (SOV 150). ✧ 'Bowel, colon; sausage made by using the colon' cf. Chag., Alt., Hak., Tat. яарта 'der Darm, Fettdarm, Mastdarm' (Radl. II, 199), Kzk. *qarta* 'колбасаъ приготовляемая изъ толстой кишки' (PKRS).

QARTAĠA Alt., Hak. 19th-20th c. **Qartaɣa-mergen** [Картаӊа-Мäргäн] (Radl. I, 1878). ✧ 'Hawk, goshawk, kite' cf. Shor *qartaɣa* 'der Habicht, Geier' (Radl. II, 200). See also **ALTÏN-QARTAĠA**.

QARTAYĠAN Kzk. 19th c. **Qartayɣan** [Картайганъ] (SOK 34). ✧ 'He/she grew old' cf. Kzk., Tat. *qartay-* 'alt werden' (Radl. II, 200).

QARTAYSAN Kzk. 19th c. **Qartaysan** [Картайсанъ] (SODž. 82). ✧ 'May he grow old / Be him longlived' cf. Kar., Kzk., Tat. *qartay-* 'alt werden' (Radl. II, 200).

QARTAMÏS Kzk. 19th c. **Qartamïs** [Картамысъ] (SODž. 64); Kzk. 19th c. **Qartamïs** [Картамысъ] (SOK 4). ✧ 'He grew old; Grown old' cf. Kar., Kzk., Tat. *qartay-* 'alt werden' (Radl. II, 200).

QARTAN Kzk. 19th c. **Qartam-bay (<Qartan-bay)** [Картамбай] (SODž. 16); Kzk. 19th c. **Qartan** [Картанъ] (SOK 244); Kzk. 19th c. **Qartan-bay** [Картанбай] (SOV 44, 104, 114). ✧ 'Oldish, elderly' cf. Kzk. *qartañ* 'староватый, пожилой' (KzRS).

QARTÏ-BAY see **QART**

QARTÏ-BATÏR see **QART**

QARTÏĠA Shor 19th-20th c. **Qartïɣa-pergen**, a folklore hero (Dyrenkova 8, 376). ✧ 'Hawk/kite/buzzard' cf. Hak., Kirg. *qartïɣa* 'der Habicht' (Radl. II, 201), Shor *qartaɣa* 'der Habicht, Geier' (Radl. II, 200). See also **ALTÏN-QARTÏĠA,**

KÜMÜŠ-QARTÏĠA, QAN-QARTÏĠA.

QARTUQ Kzk. 19th c. **Qartuq** [Картукъ] (SOK 180). ✧ 'He who sacrifices' cf. Chag. *qartuq* 'sacrificateur' (Radl. II, 201).

QARU Tat.(GH) 1339 **Qaru-qan?** / **Qarï-qan?** [Καρουκανος], a christened Tatar, died in 1339 (Byz. Turc. 155). ✧ I. 'Strength; weapon' cf. Kzk. *karuv* 'güç, kuvvet; silâh, malzeme' (KzTS); II. 'Arm' cf. Chag. *qaru* 'der Arm' (Radl. II, 187); III. 'Old man, old woman'? ⇨ **QARÏ?**

QARUN Karakh. **Qarun** [qarun] (DTS). ✧ Qarun (Ar.), a famous richman in the East (DTS).

QARZ Kzk. 19th c. **Qarz-bay** [Джуманъ Карзбаевъ] (Grod., Pril. 19). ✧ 'Debt, score' cf. Kzk., Turk. *qarz* 'die Schuld' (Radl. II, 207).

QARZÏQ Kzk. 19th c. **Qarzïq** [Сарыбашъ Карзыковъ] (Grod., Pril. 82). ⇨ **QARZ?** + suff. -*iq*.

QARŽAS Kzk. 19th c. **Qaržas** [Каржасъ] (AOO 66); Kzk. 19th c. **Qaržas-pay** [Каржаспай] (AOP 2, 126).

QAS I. see **QAZ**

QAS II. Kzk. 19th c. **Qas-bay** [Касбай] (SOK 76); Kzk. 19th c. **Qas-eke** [Касеке] (SODž. 138); Kzk. 19th c. **Qaz-eke** [Казеке] (SOV 84). ✧ I. 'Eye-brow' see **QAŠ**; II. 'Enemy' cf. Kzk. *qas II.* 'враг' (KzRS); III. 'True, real, genuine' cf. Kzk. *qas III.* 'настоящий, подлинный' (KzRS), Kzk. *qas* 'бровь, чистый, настоящий' (PKRS).

QAS-BULAT Bashk. 1712 **Qas-pulat** [Каспулат Бурсяков] (MIB III, 87); Bashk. 1713 **Qas-pulat** [Каспулатъ Бучаков] (MIB III, 94); Bashk. 1735 **Qas-pulat** [Бекбулатъ Каспулатовъ], a tarɣan (Vel.-Zern., Bašk. 25); Bashk. 1735 **Qas-pulat** [Каспулатъ Муайтмасовъ] (Vel.-Zern., Bašk. 14); Bashk. 1764 **Qas-pulat** [Каспулат Мютюков] (MIB IV, 290); Nog. 1649 **Qas-pulat** [Каспулатъ Мамаевъ], a murza (AI IV, 85); Nog. 1649 **Qas-pulat** [Сармулатъ мурза Каспулатовъ] (AI IV, 87); Nog. 1654 **Qas-pulat** [Каспулатъ] (DAI III, 538); Nog. 1654 **Qas-pulat** [Каспулатъ] (AI III, 538); Nog. 1720 **Qas-pulat** [Каспулатъ], by the Terek river (PSZRI VI, 165, 167); Bashk. 1735 **Qaš-bulat** / **Qaž-bulat** / **Qaz-bulat?** [Кажбулатъ Гауровъ], a prince (Vel.-Zern., Bašk. 12); Bashk. 1716 **Qaz-bulat** [Казбулат Бурчаков] (MIB III, 142); Bashk. 1731 **Qaz-bulat** [Казбулат Тленчи] (MIB III, 292); Bashk. 1735 **Qaz-bulat** [Казбулат Тубашев] (MIB III, 336); Bashk. 1738 **Qaz-bulat** [Мурза Козбулатов] (MIB III, 393); Bashk. 1782 **Qaz-bulat** [Казбулат (Канбулат) Каймурзин] (MIB V, 267); Bashk. 1782 **Qaz-bulat** [Казбулат Макаев] (MIB V, 262); Bashk. 1782 **Qaz-bulat** [Казбулат Мутюкаев] (MIB V, 130); Bashk. 1789 **Qaz-bulat** [Курамша Казбулатов] (MIB V, 250). ✧ 'True/genuine steel'. ⇨ **QAS II. + BULAT.**

QAS-KELDİ Kzk. 19th c. **Qas-keldï** [Каскельды]

(SOK 126); Bashk. 1759 **Qas-kildi** [Ибрай Каскильдин] (MIB IV/1, 176). ⇨ **QAZ?** + **KELDİ.**

QAS-KELEN Kzk. 19th c. **Qas-kelen** [Каскеленъ] (SOV 96, 140); Kzk. 19th c. **Qas-kelen** [Каскеленъ] (SOK 126); *TN:* Kzk. 19th c. **Qas-kelen** [Каскеленъ], a field (SOV 70). ⇨ **QAZ?** + **KELEN?**

QAS-KİLDİ see **QAS-KELDİ**

QAS-QARA see **QAŠ-QARA**

QAS-QARAW Kzk. 19th c. **Qas-qaraw** [Каскарау] (SOK 72); Kzk. 19th c. **Qasqaraw** [Каскарау] (SOV 34); Kzk. 19th c. **Qasqaraw** [Каскарау] (SOV 28). ✧ 'Nightfall' cf. Kzk. *qas: qas qarav(dı)* 'hava kararmaya başladı, geç oldu' (KzTS).

QAS-QULAQ Kzk. 19th c. **Qas-qulaq** [Каскулакъ] (SOV 84). ⇨ **QAZ** + **QULAQ.**

QAS-QULAT Kzk. 1734 **Qas-qulat?** / **Qas-qulaq?** [Жаубазаръ Каскулатовъ] (PSZRI IX, 341). ⇨ **QAZ** + **QULAQ?**

QAS-PİRA? Tat.(Sib.) 1601 **Qas-pïra?** / **Qas-pirin?** [Бухтураз Каспирин] (Miller, Ist. Sib. II, 165). ⇨ **QAZ.**

QAS-PULAT see **QAS-BULAT**

QAS-TEN Kzk. 1824 **Qas-ten?** [Кастенъ Чингильдинъ] (TOUAK XXIV, 146). ⇨ **QAS II.** + **TEN?**

QASA I. Hak. 19th-20th c. **Qasa** [Каса], fem. (HRS 353).

QASA II. Tat. 1734 **Qasa-bay** [Казай Касабаевъ], from Kungur(sk) (PSZRI IX, 339); Kzk. 19th c. **Qasa-bay** [Касабай] (SOK 90); Kzk. 19th c. **Qasa-bay** [Касабай] (SODž. 74, 104); Kzk. 19th c. **Qasa-bay** [Касабай] (SOV 26, 120). ✧ 'Penis of a stallion' cf. Kzk. *qasa* 'der Penis des Hengstes'; 'irgend ein Stoff' (Radl. II, 348), Bashk. *qaθa* 'крайняя плоть (у лошади); мошонка, яичник' (BRS/Uraksin), Alt.(Tel.) *qaza* 'der Hodensack des Hengstes' (Radl. II, 363). See also **QARA-QASAY.**

QASA-BULAT Kzk. 19th c. **Qasa-bulat** [Касабулатъ] (SODž. 64). ✧ 'Stallion-penis/genital-steel'. ⇨ **QASA II.** + **BULAT.**

QASA-BULUT Kzk. 19th c. **Qasa-bulut** [Касабулутъ] (SOK 226). ✧ 'Stallion-penis-cloud'? ⇨ **QASA II.** + **BULUT.**

QASA-QÏRBAS Kzk. **Qasa-qïrbas?** / **Qasa-qurbas?** [قاساقورباس / Каса-кирбасъ], a famous conspirator (IOAIÊK XV, 336, 339). ⇨ **QASA II.**

QASAČÏQ Tat.(GH) 1258 **Qasačïq** / **Qasačik?** [Касачикъ / Касачей] (PSRL XVI, 53); Tat.(GH) 1259 **Qasačïq** / **Qasačik?** [Касачикъ], envoy of the Horde (PSRL III, 56-57, V, 189-190, VII, 162). ⇨ **QASA II.** + dim. suff. *-čïq.*

QASAY Bashk. 1738 **Qasay** [Касай Атикесев] (MIB III, 391); Bashk. 1763 **Qasay** [Исмак Касаев] (MIB IV/2, 45); Bashk. 1786 **Qasay** [Яркей Касаев] (MIB V, 196); Kzk. 1744 **Qasay** [Касай] (Nepljuev 682); Nog. 1626 **Qasay** [Касай Исламовъ], a prince (AI III, 460); Nog. 1649 **Qasay** [Касай мурза], a murza (AI IV, 87, 123); Nog. 1802 **Qasay** [Касай мурза] (Sergeev 77); Alt. 19th-20th c. **Qazay** [Казай] (OjrRS 208). ⇨ **QASA II.** + dim. suff. *-y.* See also **QARA-QASAY.**

QASALAT Kirg. **Qasalat** [Касалат], one of Manas' comrades-in-arms (Proben V, 40 /41/).

QASAM-BAY see **QASAN**

QASAN Kzk. 19th c. **Qasam-bay (<Qasan-bay?)** [Касамбай] (SOV 44); Kzk. 19th c. **Qasam-bay (<Qasan-bay?)** [Джурабій Касамбаевъ] (TV 1876, 144); Tat. 1776 **Qasan** [Касанъ Ибраимовъ] (PSZRI XX, 456); Kzk. 19th c. **Qasan** [Касанъ] (SODž. 120). ✧ 'Unfaithful, untrustworthy'? cf. Kzk. dial. *qasañ* 'опасыз' (QTDS).

QASTAQ Hak.(Koyb.) 19th c. **Qastaq** [Кастакъ] (Katanov, Otč. II, 12-15). ✧ 'Unripe / draw privet' (Katanov).

QASEYİN Kirg. **Qaseyin** [Касейин] (Jud. 291, 646).

QASEN Bashk. 1735 **Qasen** [Якшигилди Касеневъ], a tarχan (Vel.-Zern., Bašk. 21); Kzk. 19th c. **Qasen** [Касенъ] (AOA 82); Kzk. 19th c. **Qasen** [Касенъ] (SOV 142).

QASÏQAY see **QAŠÏQAY**

QASÏM Bashk. 1776-1777 **Qasïm** [Сутай Касымбаев] (MIB V, 542-544); Kirg. **Qasïm** [Касым] (Jud. 111); Kirg. **Qasïm-χan** [Касымхан] (Jud. 298); Kirg. **Qasïm-yan** [Касым- Jан], daughter of Qas, one of the forty followers of Aq-sayqal (Proben V, 394 /397/). ✧ I. Qasim (Ar.) 'distributor, divider' (Ahmed), cf. *Kasım* (Erol II), Tat. PN *Qasïym* (Sattarov),; II. 'Beautiful, kind, graceful'? (<Ar.) *χasim* (Žanuzakov 145). See also **ÄBİL-QASİM.**

QASÏM-BERDİ Tat.(Lit.) 1681 **Qasïm-berdi** [Раина Касимбердевичовна] (Lit. Tat. 464). ⇨ **QASÏM** + **BERDİ.**

QASÏRČA-NİKE Oghuz/Trkm. **Qasïrča-nike?** / **Qïsïrja-yeñä?** [قِصِرجَه يِنْكَه / Kısırça Yinge, Kısırca Yenge / Касырча-Нике] (DQorq./Rossi 116, 129, DQorq. 34, 35, 46).

QASÏŠ Bashk. 18th c. **Qasïš** [Якупъ Касишевъ] (Nepljuev 72).

QASKEŇ Kirg. **Qaskeñ** [Каскен] (Jud. 38).

QASQA-BAS Kzk. 19th c. **Qasqa-bas** [Каскабасъ] (SODž. 8); Kzk. 19th c. **Qasqa-bas** [Каскабасъ] (SOV 38). ⇨ **QAŠQA** + **BAŠ.**

QASQAJAQ Hak.(Koyb.) 19th-20th c. **Qasqajaq** [Каскацак] (Proben IX, 432, 559). ⇨ **QAŠQA** + dim. suff. *-jaq.*

QASQAY see **QAŠQAY**

QASQAQ Kzk. 19th c. **Qasqaq-pay** [Каскакпай]

(SOK 106). ✧ 'Steep ravine' cf. Alt., Hak. *qasqaq* 'steil, ein steiler Abhang; ein mit Steingeröll und Felsen bedecktes Land' (Radl. II, 352).

QASQALDAQ Kzk. 19th c. **Qasqaldaq** [Каскалдакъ] (SOK 10). ✧ 'A kind of mallard' cf. Kzk. *qasqaldaq* 'лысуха (вид дикой утки)' (KzRS).

QASQAN see **QAŠQAN**

QASQAR Kzk. 19th c. **Qasqar** [Каскаръ] (SOV 28); Kzk. 19th c. **Qasqar-bay** [Каскарбай] (SODž. 100). ✧ 'Go against; resist (the enemy)' cf. Kzk. *qasqar-(=qasqay)* 'grade darauf losgehen, entgegen gehen' (Radl. II, 352). ⇨ **QASQÏR?**

QASQÏN see **QAČQÏN**

QASQÏR Kzk. 19th c. **Qasqïr-bay** [Каскырбай] (SOK 126). ✧ 'Wolf' cf. Kzk. *qasqïr* 'der Wolf' (Radl. II, 354).

QASLA Hak. 19th-20th c. **Qasla** [Касла], fem. (HRS 353). ✧ 'Bait for bees' cf. Shor *qasla* 'die Lockspeise für die Bienen' (Radl. II, 355).

QASMAQ Tat.(Ishim) **Qasmaq** [Касмак], a folklore hero Salar-sofi's son at the times of Küčüm and Yarmaq (Yermaq) (Proben IV, 213 /262/). ✧ 'Flake' cf. Tat.(Bar., Tara) *qasmaq* 'die Fischschuppe' (Radl. II, 359).

QASMÏŠ Uyg. 12th c. - 14th c. **Qasmïš** (Radl., USp. 139, DTS). ✧ 'Digged, excavated' (Blagova 1997, 717).

QASTÏY Alt. 19th-20th c. **Qastïy** [Кастый] (OjrRS 208). ✧ 'Goose-like'. ⇨ **QAZ** + suff. *-tïy*.

QASTÏQ Kzk. 19th c. **Qastïq-pay** [Кастыкпай] (SOV 124); Kzk. 19th c. **Qastïq-pay** [Кастекпай] (SOV 30, 44, 92, 118); Kzk. 19th c. **Qastïq-pay** [Кастекпай] (SODž. 50). ✧ 'Enmity, quarrel' cf. Kzk. *qastïq* 'враждебность' (KzRS).

QASUQ Uyg. 12th c. -14th c. **Qasuq** (Radl., USp. 7, Le Coq. Urkunden 455). ⇨ **QAŠÏQ?**

QAŠ Uyg. **Qaš** [qaš] (DTS); Chag. 1551 **Qaš** [Баба Каш] (Ivanov 313); Tat.(Mish.) 1755, 1761 **Qaš-qul** [Ижбулат (Ишпулат) Кашкулов] (MIB IV/1, 93); Bashk. 1761 **Qaš-qul** [Казак Кашкулов] (MIB IV/1, 219); Kzk. 19th c. **Qaš-qul** [Кашкулъ] (AOA 114); Kzk. 19th c. **Qaš-pay** [Кажпай] (SOK 150); Kzk. 19th c. **Qaš-pay** [Кашпай] (SOK 218). ✧ I. 'Eyebrow'? cf. Uyg., Kuman, Chag., Alt., Crm., Tat., Turk. etc. *qaš* 'die Erhebung, der Wall, Hügel, etc.; der hervorstehende Holzbogen des Sattels; die Augenbrauen' (Radl. II, 386-89); II. 'Yade-stone' (Uyg.) *qaš* 'der Jadestein' (Radl. II, 386-89), Bashk. *qaš* 'драгоценный камень' (BRS); III. 'Pilgrimage to Mecca'? cf. Kzk. *qaš* (<Ar.) 'die Pilgerfahrt nach Mekka' (Radl. II, 389). See also **AL-QAŠ, ARÏQLÏ-QAŠ, ARLÏ-QAŠ, ÏLÏ-QAŠ, YARAN-QAŠ, KÏN-QAŠ, QARA-QAŠ, QUL-QAŠ, QURT-QAŠ, QURUQ-QAŠ, MÏNÄ-QAŠ, TÏN-QAŠ, TÏNÏ-QAŠ, TOQ-QAŠ, TÜTE-QAŠ, UZUN-QAŠ.**

QAŠ-QAYA Uyg. 13th-14th c. **Qaš-qaya-tarχan** (Zieme, Mat. II, 88). ✧ 'Eyebrow-rock? Yade-rock?'. ⇨ **QAŠ + QAYA.**

QAŠ-QAL-TAY Bashk. 1724, 1734 **Qaš-qal-tay** [Муса Кашкалтаев (Кошкалтаев)] (MIB III, 222, 322). ⇨ **QAŠ? + QAL-TAY** or suff. *-tay(1,2)*?

QAŠ-QARA Tat.(Sib.) 1582 **Qas-qara** [Каскара], a prince (Sib. Let. 322); Tat. 1677, 1693, 1708 **Qaš-qara** [Эшей (Ишей) Кашкаринъ (Кошкаринъ)], from Astrakhan (DAI V, 402, VII, 264, VIII, 26, MIB I, 219). ✧ 'His/her eyebrow is black'? ⇨ **QAŠ + QARA / QAŠQAR, QOČQAR?**

QAŠ-QOŠ Kzk. 19th c. **Qaš-qoš-pay?** [Кашкошпай] (SOK 204). ⇨ **QAŠ + QOŠ I.?**

QAŠ-TEMÜR Selj. 1231 **Qaš-temür** [Jamâl ad-dîn Kashtemûr], sent to Arbil against the Mongols (Abulfar./Budge I, 397); Maml. **Qaš-temür** [الملك قَشْتِمُر], Fakhruddîn Buγday's father (Fakhrī 77); Maml. 1305 **Qaš-temür** [قشتمر / Kachetimur], Qara-soñqur's mamluk (Abulfidā/Ed. I, 173). ⇨ **QAŠ? + TEMÏR.**

QAŠAΓAN Kzk. 19th c. **Qačaγan** [Качаганъ] (SOK 58, 128); Kzk. 19th c. **Qačaγan** [Качаганъ] (SOV 62, 76); Kzk. 19th c. **Qačaγan** [Качаганъ] (AOA 106); Kzk. 19th c. **Qašaγan** [Качаганъ] (AOO 38); Kzk. 19th c. **Qašaγan** [Кашаганъ] (SOV 120). ✧ 'Stray, runaway?; burdock' cf. Kzk. *qašaγan* 'ein aus der Heerde entflohenes Vieh; die Klette' (Radl. II, 390). See also **QAČQÏN.**

QAŠAY see **QOŠAY?**

QAŠAQ Bashk. 1675 **Qašaq** [Кашак Козенбаев] (MIB I, 200). ⇨ **QACAQ?**

QAŠAQAY Kzk. 19th c. **Qašaqay** [Кашакай] (AOA 14). ⇨ **QAŠÏQAY?**

QAŠAN Kzk. **Qašan** [Кашанъ] (Laptev, Materialy 27).

QAŠAR Kzk. 19th c. **Qašar** [Кашаръ] (AOA 82). ✧ 'A two-year-old calf' cf. Kzk. *qašar: qašar sïr* 'ein zweijähriges Kalb' (Radl. II, 391). See also **BÏ-QAŠAR, TORPAQ, UT-QAŠAR.**

QAŠAW Kzk. 19th c. **Qašaw-bek** [Кашаубекъ] (SOK 6, 136). ✧ 'Chisel, engraver' cf. Kzk. *qašau* 'der Meissel' (Radl. II, 390).

QAŠΓA see **QAŠQA**

QAŠÏ Kzk. 19th c. **Qaši-γul?** [Кащигулъ] (AOP).

QAŠÏ-WAR Bashk. 1714 **Qašï-war?** [Кашевар Токаев] (MIB III, 108). ✧ 'He/she has got an eyebrow'? ⇨ **QAŠ.**

QAŠÏQ Kzk. 19th c. **Qasïq-pay** [Касыкпай] (SOK 66); Kzk. 19th c. **Qasïq-pay** [Баймирза Касыковъ] (Grod., Pril. 132); Tat.(Sib.) 1631 **Qasïq** [Кашик] (Miller, Ist. Sib. II, 568); Maml. 14th c. **Qašïq** [قاشق] (Sauvaget 51); Türk 7th c. - 9th c. **Qašuq** [qašuq] (DTS). ✧ 'Spoon' cf. Karakh. *qašuq* 'id.' (DTS),

Kuman, Crm., Tat., Turk. *qašïq* 'der Löffel' (Radl. II, 392), Bashk. *qašïq* 'поварёшка; деревянная или берестяная ложка' (BRS/Uraksin), Kzk. *qasïq* 'der Löffel' (Radl. II, 350), also Sauvaget 51, Blagova 1997, 712.

QAŠÏQAY Bashk. 1761 **Qasïqay** [Сапар Касыкаев] (MIB IV/1, 205); Kzk. 19th c. **Qasïqay / Qašïqay?** [Кашекай] (SOV 132). ⇨ **QAŠQAY / QAŠÏQ?** + dim. suff. *-ay*.

QAŠÏM Kzk. 19th c. **Qašïm-qul** [Кашимкулъ] (AOP 94). ⇨ **QAŠ?** + poss. suff. *-ïm*.

QAŠKE Kzk. 19th c. **Qaške** [Кашке] (SOK 250). ⇨ **QAŠ** + suff. *-ke*.

QAŠQA Chuv. 18th-19th c. **Kaška** [Кашка] (Magn. 50); Kzk. **Qasqa** [Каска] (Sb. Syr-D. IX, 56); Kzk. 19th c. **Qasqa-bay** [Каскабай] (SOK 78, 140); Kzk. 19th c. **Qasqa-bay** [Каскабай] (SOV 48, 122); Kzk. 19th c. **Qasqa-bay** [Каскабай] (SODž. 120); Kzk. 19th c. **Qasqa-bay** [Каскабай] (AOA 70); Oghuz/Trkm. 13th c. **Qašγa** [قاشغا / Кашга-чора], a slave's son (Abulg./Kon. 1345, 1385, 1410, 1435); Trkm. 1717 **Qašqa** [Манглай Кашка] (ZIRGO IX, 321); Bashk. 1783 **Qašqa** [Бултрюк Кашкин] (MIB V, 147); Bashk. 1783, 1789 **Qašqa** [Таймас (Тоймас) Кашкин] (MIB V, 148, 254, 311, 361); Kzk. 1680 **Qašqa** [Еренячковъ Алтыначка Кашка] (DAI VIII, 44); Kzk. 1744 **Qašqa** [Мергенъ-Кашка] (Nepljuev 682); *EN:* Kzk. 18th c. - 19th c. **Qasqa** [Каска], a clan (Tynyšp. 67, 70, 73). ✧ 'A white spot/blaze on the forehead (of animals); brilliant, gallant (in Chag.)' cf. Tat. *qašqa* 'звёздочка, белая отметина на лбу (животного)' (TatRS), Kuman, Chag., Hak., Tat. *qašqa* 'die kahle Stelle (Platte) auf dem Kopfe' (Radl. II, 394), Kzk. *qasqa* 'stark, heldenmüthig, grimmig' (Radl. II, 352), Kzk., Hak. *qasqa* 'die Blässe auf der Stirn der Pferde'; (Kzk.) 'kahlköpfig' (Radl. II, 352). See also **BAY-ΓASQA, KÖTÄLÏ-QAŠQA, KÜKÄMÄN-QASQA, QAN-QASQA, MERGEN-QAŠQA.**

QAŠQA-BŪRUL Alt.(Tel.) 19th c. **Qašqa-būrul**, Qayra-qan's former real name (Potanin IV, 327). ⇨ **QAŠQA + BURUL.**

QAŠQAY Bashk. 1781 **Qasqay** [Сапер Каскаев] (MIB V, 124); Bashk. 1715 **Qašqay** [Мырым Кашкаев] (MIB III, 124); Bashk. 1773 **Qašqay** [Ишкай Кашкаев] (MIB IV/2, 415). ⇨ **QAŠ / QAŠQA / QAŠÏQ?** + dim. suff. *-qay / -(a)y.*

QAŠQALTAY Bashk. 1721 **Qašqaltay** [Асе Кашкалтай] (MIB III, 196); Bashk. 1722 **Qašqaltay** [Муса Кашколтаев] (MIB I, 109); Bashk. 1734 **Qašqaltay** [Усей Кашкалтаев (Кошкалтаев)] (MIB III, 322); Bashk. 1734 **Qašqaltay** [Айса Кашкалтаев (Кошкалтаев)] (MIB III, 322).

QAŠQAN Tat. 1748 **Qasqan** [Касканъ] (Nepljuev 438); Bashk. 1763 **Qasqan** [Каскан Кутлыхозин] (MIB IV/1, 274); Kzk. 19th c. **Qašqan** [Кашканъ] (SODž. 70); Kzk. 19th c. **Qašqan-bay** [Кашканбай] (SOV 36); *TN:* Bashk. 1728 **Qasqanovo** [Касканово], a village (MIB III, 251). ✧ 'He escaped; fugitive; runaway' cf. Kzk. *qaš-* 'entfliehen' (Radl. II, 389). ⇨ **QAČQÏN.**

QAŠQANAY Bashk. 1709 **Qašqanay** [Расланбек Кашканаев] (MIB III, 53). ⇨ **QAŠQAN** + dim. suff. *-ay.*

QAŠQAR Bashk. 1734 **Qačqar** [Качкаровъ Акназаръ] (Vel.-Zern., Bašk. 10); Bashk. 1735 **Qačqar** [Киникъ Качкаровъ], a tarχan (Vel.-Zern., Bašk. 15); Tat.(Mish.) 20th c. **Qašqar** [Кашкарев], a family (Sattarov); Bashk., Kzk.? **Qašqar** [Кашкарово], in Kaskarovo, a settlement in the Ural (Karta JAR III); Kzk. **Qašqar** [Кашкаръ Якшибаевъ] (Êtnogr. Obozr. 1915, vyp. 3-4, 62); Kzk. 19th c. **Qašqar-mulda** [могила Кашкаръ мулды], his tomb is on the northern beach of the Caspian Sea, in the region of Tentäk-sor (IIRGO XVI). ✧ 'Wolf; dog with white forehead'? (Sattarov) cf. Bashk. *qašqar* 'белолобая собака; волк' (BRS/Uraksin), Chuv. *qašqar* 'wolf' (Sattarov). ⇨ **QOČQAR?**

QAŠQÏM-BAY see **QAČQÏN**

QAŠQÏN see **QAČQÏN**

QAŠTAQ Alt. 19th-20th c. **Qaštaq** [Каштак] (OjrRS 208). ✧ 'Basket' cf. Alt. *qaštaq* 'ein Korb' (Radl. II, 398). See also **TERGIŠ.**

QAŠTÏÑ Kzk. 1862 **Qaštïñ** [Каштынъ Саиновъ] (ZIRGOGeogr. I, 311). ✧ 'You escaped'? cf. Kzk. *qaš-* 'entfliehen' (Radl. II, 389).

QAŠUQ see **QAŠÏQ**

QAŠUQČÏ Trkm. 1824/25 **Qašuqči-qurban-serdar** [Кашукчи Курбан-сердар], from the Qaradašlï tribe (MIT II, 425). ✧ 'Maker of (wooden) spoons' cf. Turk. *qašïqčï* 'der Löffelmacher' (Radl. II, 393), Chag. *qašuq* 'ein hölzerner Löffel' (Radl. II, 394). + suff. *-čï.*

QAŠWAN Kzk. 19th c. **Qašwan?** [Кашванъ Манчаевъ] (Grod., Pril. 109).

QAT Bashk. 1675 **Qat-čura** [Катчюра Ишиметев] (MIB I, 200); Tat.(Sib.)?, Alt.? 1633 **Qat-qan / Qat-χan?** [Катканъ / Катъ-ханъ], Altïn-χan's relative (Kuznecov 1); Kzk. 19th c. **Qat-qul** [Каткулъ] (SOK 266). ✧ I. 'Currant; seed'? cf. Karakh. *qat* 'ягода, плод вообще' (DTS), Alt., Hak., Kzk. *qat* 'jede glatte, runde Beere' (Radl. II, 275); II. 'Letter'? cf. Kzk. *qat* 'die Schrift' (Radl. II, 276). See also **QARA-QAT, QÏZÏL-ΓAT, QOZÏNCÏ-QAT(?).**

QAT-KELDÏ Kzk. 19th c. **Qat-keldï** [Каткельды] (SODž. 18). ✧ 'A letter (writing) has come'? cf. Kzk. *qat* 'die Schrift' (Radl. II, 276). ⇨ **QAT + KELDÏ.**

QATA Chuv. 18th-19th c. **Kata** [Ката / Катаевъ] (Magn. 50); Kzk. 19th c. **Qata** [Ката] (SODž. 6, 104);

Kzk. 19th c. **Qata-bek** [Катабекъ] (SODž. 160). ✧
'Galoshes, overshoes' cf. Tat. *qata* 'галоши' (TatRS),
Bashk. *qata* 'глубокие, кожаные галоши; лёгкая
обувь' (BRS/Uraksin).

QATAΓAY   Kzk. 19th c. **Qataγay-bay** [Катагайбай]
(SKSO III, 18); Uzb. 19th c. **Qataγay-bay** [Юлдашъ
Катагайбаевъ] (SKSO III, 18).

QATAΓAN   Kzk. 19th c. **Qataγan** [Катаганъ] (SODž.
78, 94); *EN:* Nog. 20th c. **Qataγan-uruw** [Къатагъан
урув], an Aq-noγay clan (Bask., Nog. 133, 142). ✧ I.
'Hardened'?; II. 'Suppression, barrier'; III. Tribal
name. Cf. Chag. *qataγan* 'hart gworden; das Verbot, die
Hemmung; der Name eines stammes' (Radl. II, 279).
See also **QATÏΓAN, QATMÏŠ.**

QATAY   Chuv. 18th-19th c. **Katay** [Катаевъ] (Magn.
50); Uzb. 1740 **Qatay** [Катай] (MIB I, 436).

QATAQ   Kzk. 19th c. **Qataq-pay** [Катакпай] (AOAtb.
46).

QATAQ-TAŠ   Khorezm./ Mo.? **Qataq-taš** [قتاقتاش],
fem. (RaD/Ber. I, 152).

QATAL   Kzk. 19th c. **Qatal-bay** [Каталбай] (SOV 12).
✧ 'Merciless, hard, severe' cf. Kzk. *qatal*
'merhametsiz, sert' (KzTS).

QATAN   Kzk. 19th c. **Qatan** [Катанъ] (SODž. 82);
Hak.(Sag.) 19th-20th c. **Qatan** [Катанъ] (ZIRGOÊtn.
XXXIV, 274). ✧ 'Merciless, hard, severe' cf. Kzk.
qatan 'merhametsiz, sert' (KzTS).

QATAR   Tat. 1600 **Qatar-γul** [Катаргул (Девлетев)]
(Miller, Ist. Sib. II, 159); Tat.(Mish.) 1775 **Qatar-γul**
[Катаргул Кучюмбаев] (MIB IV/2, 417). See also
TUÑ-ΓATAR.

QATARMÏŠ   Türk 868, 883 **Qatarmïš** [خطارمش], a
commander of the army under Al-Muʿtaz (Tabarī,
Annal. III, 1694, 1828, 2037, Weil, Abbas II, 406,
Masʿūdī 369). ✧ 'Turned back, dispelled (the enemy)'?
cf. Karakh. *qatar-* 'проворачивать, прогонять'
(DTS).

QATAŠ   Kzk. 19th c. **Qataš** [Каташъ] (SOK 4); Kzk.
19th c. **Qataš** [Коташъ] (SOV 148). ⇨ **QATA** +
suff. -*š*.

QATĀY   Hak.(Shor) 19th-20th c. **Qatāy** [Катай]
(Katanov, Otč. 11); Karg. 19th-20th c. **Qatāy** [Катай],
fem. (Katanov, Otč. 10). ✧ 'Old woman' cf.
Hak.(Kacha), Tuv. *qaday* 'eine alte Frau' (Radl. II,
307), also Hak. fem. PN *Qatay* '?' (Butanaev), <R.
катай? (Katanov).

QATBAR   Kzk. 19th c. **Qatbar** [Катбаръ] (Grod., Pril.
48). ✧ 'Wrinkle, fold' cf. Kzk. *qatpar* 'складка,
морщина' (KzRS).

QATBÏS   Bashk. 1737 **Qatbïs** [Катбыс] (MIB I, 324).

QATEÑKLİ-BERDİ   Trkm. 1867 **Qateñkli-berdi**
[Катенкли-берды] (MIT II, 627). ⇨ **BERDİ.**

QATİČE   Hak. 19th-20th c. **Qatiče** [Катиче], fem.
(HRS 353). ✧ '?' cf. Hak. fem. PN *Qatiča* '?'

(Butanaev).

QATÏ   Tat. / Bashk. 1791 **Qatï** [Каты Юлдашев]
(MIB V, 679); Kzk. 19th c. **Qatï-bay** [Катыбай] (SOK
232); Karch. 20th c. **Qatū** [Qʾatʾú] (Pröhle, Kar. 117).
✧ 'Hard, strong' cf. Kuman, Tat., Turk. *qatï* 'hart'
(Radl. II, 282), Karch. *qʾatʾū* 'Kummer, Schmerz, Leid'
(Pröhle, Karch. 117).

QATÏ-YALU   Maml. 14th c. **Qatï-yalu (Qatï-yallu?)**
[قاتى‌يـالو / Katıyalu] (Tarǰ/Houtsma 88, 102,
Tarǰ/Toparlı 43). ⇨ **QATÏ.**

QATÏČ see **BAY-QATÏČ**

QATÏΓ-MOLAT   Hak.(Sag.) 19th-20th c. **Qatïγ-molat**
[Катыгъ-Молатъ], a folklore hero (Kostrov 237). ✧
'Hard, strong steel' cf. OT *qatïγ* 'fest, stark, heftig'
(Radl. II, 284). ⇨ **BULAT.**

QATÏΓAN   Kzk. 19th c. **Qatïγan** [Катыганъ] (SOK
44). ⇨ **QATAΓAN?** See also **QATMÏŠ.**

QATÏYAQ   1251 **Qatïyaq?** [Катіакъ] (PSRL X, 138).

QATÏQ   Bashk. 1713 **Qatïq** [Мамак Катыков] (MIB
III, 97); Kzk. 19th c. **Qatïq** [Катыковъ] (AOK 74);
Trkm. / Selj.? 1083 **Qatïq** [حتق التركماني] (Qalānisi
116); Kzk. 19th c. **Qatïq-pay** [Катыкпай] (SODž. 60);
Kzk. 19th c. **Qatïq-pay** [Катыкпай] (SOV 38). ✧
'Addition, extra' cf. Karakh. *qatïq* 'добавка,
добавление' (DTS), Kzk. *qatïq* 'густое кислое
молоко; приправа (к супу)' (KzRS).

QATÏMBET   Kzk. 19th c. **Qatïmbet** [Катымбетъ]
(AOAtb. 42). ✧ 'Strong Muχammed'. ⇨ **QATÏ** +
suff. -*mbet*.

QATÏR   Kzk. 19th c. **Qator-bay? / Qatïr-bay?**
[Каторбай] (SOK 208); Kzk. 19th c. **Qatur-bey**
[Катурбей] (SOK 162).

QATÏRMET see **QADÏRMET**

QATÏŠ   Bashk. 1695 **Qatïš** [Катыш Иткулов] (MIB I,
97). ✧ 'Mixed, mixture' cf. Tat. *qatïš* 'das Gemisch,
die Beimischung' (Radl. II, 288), Bashk. *qatïš*
'смешанный' (BRS). See also **AQ-QATÏŠ.**

QATÏŠAQ   Hak.(Kyz.) 1715 **Qatïšaq** [Катышакъ], a
prince (Jarilov, Kyz. 10). ⇨ **QATÏŠ?** + dim. suff. -*aq*.

QATKEY see **QATQAY**

QATQA   Bashk. 1732, 1734 **Qatqa / Qatqa-mulla**
[Катка Токатовъ / Катка-мулла Токаков], a mulla
(PSZRI IX, 339, MIB III, 302).

QATQAY   Tat. 1731 **Qatkey** [Каткей Тлевлин] (MIB
III, 293); Bashk. 1745 **Qatkey** [Каткей] (MIB III,
427); Uyg. 12th c. - 14th c. **Qatqay** [Katkay] (Radl.,
USp. 86, DTS, EUTS). ⇨ **QATÏ, QAT?** + dim.
suff. -*qay / -key*.

QATQANČILA   Alt. 19th c. **Qatqančila** [Катканчила-
богатырь] (Verb., In. 139, 162).

QATLAMÏŠ   Selj. 1078 **Qatlamïš** [Katlamish], Yabaγu-
arslan's son (Abulfar./Budge I, 226).

QATLÏ   Bashk. 1706 **Qatlï-bay** [Чюраш Катлыбай]
(MIB III, 30).

QATMÏŠ Karakh. 11th c. **Qatmïš** [Katmış / qatmïš] (MK/Atalay 843, EUTS, DTS). ✧ 'Hardened'? cf. Karakh. *qat-* 'становиться твердым; неметь' (DTS). See also **EL-QATMÏŠ, SUYUR-ГАТМÏŠ; QATAГAN, QATÏГAN.**

QATO Hak. 19th-20th c. **Qato** [Като], fem. (HRS 353).

QATOQ Hak. 19th-20th c. **Qatoq** [Каток] (HRS 353).

QATPA Kzk. 19th c. **Qatpa** [Катпа] (AOP 126); Kzk. 19th c. **Qatpa** [Катба] (AOA 38); Kzk. 19th c. **Qatpa** [Катпа] (Grod. I, 98); Kzk. 19th c. **Qatpa** [Катпа] (SOV 92); Kzk. 19th c. **Qatpa** [Катпа] (SODž. 40); Kzk. 19th c. **Qatpa** [Катпа] (SOK 146). ✧ I. 'Stunted, scraggy' cf. Kzk. *qatpa* 'худосочный ' (KzRS); II. 'Illness of camels' (Grodekov).

QATPAГAY Kzk. 19th c. **Qatpaγay** [Катпагай] (SOK 124). ⇨ **QATPA** + dim. suff. *-γay / -qay.*

QATRAN Kzk. **Qatran** [Катранъ], Qaarman's brother (Laptev, Materialy 27). ✧ I. 'Tar, pitch'? cf. Turk. *qatran* 'das Theer' (Radl. II, 297) (<Ar.); II. 'December'? cf. Bashk. *qatran* 'декабрь' (BRS/Uraksin). ⇨ **QANTAR?**

QATRAS Bashk. 1737 **Qatras** [Катрас батырь] (MIB I, 314).

QATRÏS Hak. 19th-20th c. **Qatris** [Катрис] (HRS 353).

QATŠA Kkalp. 20th c. **Qatša** [Қатша], fem. (KkRS 778). ✧ '?' cf. Kzk. fem. PN *Qatša-gül* (Žanuzakov-Esbaeva). Used also as a female component in Karakalpak (see comp. *χatša*). ⇨ **XADÏJA?**

QATTA Chag. 15th c. **Qatta-beg** [كتّه بيك] (Le Coq, Ind. 3); Kzk. 19th c. **Qatta-bek** [Иргашбай Каттабековъ] (SKSO III, 16). ✧ 'Big' (Le Coq), 'Strong'? cf. Hak. *qattïγ* 'hart, rauh, stark, streng' (Radl. II, 303). ⇨ **QATÏ?**

QATTAГAY Kzk. 19th c. **Qattaγay** [Каттагай] (SOK 12). ⇨ **QATTA** + suff. *-γay / -qay.*

QATTAY Hak. 19th-20th c. **Qattay-qan** [Каттаи-кан] (Radl. II, 105). ⇨ **QATAY?**

QATTAN Hak.(Sag.) 19th-20th c. **Qattan** [Каттан], a folklore hero (Proben IX, 434).

QATTÏГ-TEMİR Hak.(Blt.) 19th-20th c. **Qattïγ-temir** [Каттыӈ Темір], a folklore hero (Proben IX, 359-61). ✧ 'Hard iron' cf. Hak. *qattïγ* 'hart, rauh, stark, streng' (Radl. II, 303). ⇨ **TEMİR.**

QATUY Hak. 19th-20th c. **Qatuy** [Катуй] (HRS 353).

QATUYČÏ Kzk. 19th c. **Qatuyčï** [Катуйчи] (SKSO VII, 226).

QATUQ Uyg. 12th c. - 14th c. **Qatuq** [Katuk] (Radl., USp. 48, DTS, EUTS). ✧ 'Hardened; strengthened' (Bese 13), cf. Uyg., Karakh. *qat-* 'становиться твердым, твердеть' (DTS) + suff. *-uq.*

QATUN Oghuz 894 **Xatun** [خاتون] (Tabarī, Annal. I, 866, III, 2138); Selj.? 1071 **Xatun** [خاتون], fem. (Kamāladdīn II, 331); Selj.? 1071 **Xatun** [خاتون], fem. (Kamāladdīn II, 262); Selj.? 1071 **Xatun** [خاتون], Alp-arslan's sister (Kamāladdīn II, 79); Selj.? 1071 **Xatun** [خاتون], fem. (Kamāladdīn II, 147); Selj.? 1071 **Xatun** [خاتون], Melik-šah's (mid)wife (Kamāladdīn II, 105, 118); Selj.? 1071 **Xatun** [خاتون], Nizm al-Mulk's wife (Kamāladdīn II, 24); Maml. **Xatun** [خاتون], in Qalāwun's family (Duqmaq:RHCHor IV, 125); Maml. 1465/66 **Xatun** [خاتون], Aχmed ibn al-ᶜAynī's mother (Ibn Taghrīb. VII, 809); Chag. 16th c. **Xatun-bike** [Хатун-бике], fem. (Ivanov 313); Turk. 1583 **Xatun-šah** [خاتون شاه بشه] / Hatunşah Beşe), Pirce's daughter (Ongan, Ank. I, 158); Khazar 760 **Qatun**, daughter of the Qaγan *Baγatur (Golden, Khaz. 196); Karakh. **Qatun** [Katun] (MK/Atalay 843); Kirg. / Kzk.? 19th c. **Qatun-er** [Катун.рь] (Potanin II, 149). ✧ 'I. (fem. title) 'wife of a khan or prince; princess', II. (fem. comp.) 'lady, noble high-born woman; married woman, wife' (Sogd.), cf. Türk., Uyg. *qatun* 'госпожа, вельможная дама, женщина знатного происхождения; жена правителя, знатного человека' (DTS), Turk. *χatun* 'eine Dame von hohem Range, eine Prinzessin, eine Frau überhaupt' (Radl. II, 1683).

QATUN-BEŠE Turk. 16th c. **Qatun-beše** (Ongan, Ank. II); Turk. 16th c. **Qatun-beše**, fem. (Ongan, Ank. II). ⇨ **QATUN + BEŠE.**

QATUN-BULA Turk. 1485 **Xatun-bula** [Hatun Bula], Arbuz-ata's grand-daughter (Gökb., Ed. 195); Turk. 16th c. **Qatun-bula**, fem. (Ongan, Ank. II); Turk. 1584 **Qatun-bula** [قاطون بوله], fem. (Ongan, Ank. I, 164). ⇨ **QATUN + BULA I.**

QATUR see **QATÏR**

QATŪ see **QATÏ**

QATÜK Alt. 19th-20th c. **Qatük** [Катӱк], fem. (OjrRS 212). ✧ Derived from R. fem. *Katya* (OjrRS).

QAVŠUT Karakh. 11th c. **Qavšut** [Kawşut/ qavšut] (MK/Atalay 843, DTS). ✧ 'Conclusion of peace, peace-treaty' cf. Karakh. *qavšut / qawšut* 'договор о примирении, скрепленный рукопожатием двух правителей' (DTS).

QAW Oghuz 12th c. **Qaw-χan? / Quw-χan?** [قوحان] (Qazw. 493); Bulg. 11th c. **Qaw-qan / Qap-χan** [Καυκάνος], a chieftain and commander of the army (Byz. Turc. 157). ✧ 'Tinder, punk, fungus' cf. Karakh. *qav* 'трут' (DTS), Kzk., Tat.(Sib.) *qaw* 'der Feuerschwamm, Zunder' (Radl. II, 50).

QAWAN Kzk. 1846 **Qawan-bay?** [Найман Каванбаев] (MKOP 101).

QAWANDÏQ Uzb. 19th c. **Qawandïq** [Кавандыкъ Умаровъ] (SKSO III, 170).

QAWARD? see **QAWURT**

QAWČUQ Tat.(Sib.) 1631 **Qawčuq** [Бибахша Кавчуков] (Miller, Ist. Sib. II, 382). ✧ 'Little fungus' cf. Karakh. *qav* 'трут' (DTS), Kzk., Tat.(Sib.) *qaw* 'der Feuerschwamm, Zunder' (Radl. II, 50). ⇨ **QAW** + dim. suff. *-čuq*.

QAWDAN Kzk. 19th c. **Qawdan** [Кауданъ] (SOK 258). ✦ 'Dry grass/herb' cf. Kzk. *kavdan* 'kuru ot' (KzTS).

QAWГALÏ Tat.(GH) 1281, 1317, 1319 **Qawγalï / Qawγadï?** [Кавыдай / Ковадый / Кавадый / Кавьдый / Кавгады], Tatar commander and envoy of the Horde (PSRL (Russk. Hr.) I, 402, 403, PSRL X, 159, XXIII, 98-99).

QAWÏR Kzk. 1819 **Qawïr-bek** [Квирбек] (MIK IV, 324).

QAWÏS Kzk. 19th c. **Qaws-pay / Qaus-pay** [Кауспай] (SOK 252); Kzk. 19th c. **Qaws-pay / Qaus-pay** [Кауспай] (SODž. 58); Kzk. 19th c. **Qaws-pek / Qaus-pek** [Кауспекъ] (SODž. 80); Kzk. 19th c. **Qawz / Qauz** [Каузъ] (SOK 308); Kzk. 19th c. **Qawz-bay / Qauz-bay** [Каузбай] (SOV 94, 150); Kzk. 19th c. **Qawz-bay / Qauz-bay** [Каузбай] (SOK 208). ✦ 'November' (< Ar. qaws).

QAWKE Kzk. 19th c. **Qawke-bay** [Каукебай] (AOP 66). ⇨ **QAW** + dim. suff. *-ke*.

QAWQA Kzk. 19th c. **Qawqa** [Куйбай Кавкиновъ] (Grod., Pril. 48); Kzk. 19th c. **Qawqa-bay / Qauγa-bay?** [Каукабай] (SOK 148). ✦ 'Pail, bucket' cf. Kzk. *qauγa* 'ein Brunneneimer' (Radl. II, 51). ⇨ **QAW?** + dim. suff. *-qa*.

QAWQAM Kzk. 19th c. **Qawqam-bay** [Каукамбай / Наукамбай?] (SOK 128).

QAWLAN Kzk. 19th c. **Qawulam-bay (<Qawlan-bay?)** [Кауламбай] (SOK 118); Kzk. 19th c. **Qawulam-bay (<Qawlan-bay?)** [Кауламбай] (SOV 30). ✦ 'Grow up quickly!'? cf. Kzk. qawla- развиваться бурно (KzRS).

QAWM Kzk. 19th c. **Qawm-bay** [Каумбай] (SOV 112); Kzk. 19th c. **Qawm-bay** [Каумбай] (SOV 148). ✦ 'Folk, religious community' cf. Kzk. *qaum* (Ar.) 'das Volk, die Glaubensgemeinschaft' (Radl. II, 55).

QAWM-BAS Kzk. 19th c. **Qawm-bas** [Каумбасъ] (SOV 112). ✦ I. 'Leader of the folk/community'?; II. 'Opress the folk/community'? ⇨ **QAWM + BAŠ / QAWM + BAS II.**

QAWMAN Kzk. 19th c. **Qawman** [Кауманъ] (AOAtb. 42); Kzk. 19th c. **Qawmen** [Кауменъ] (SODž. 16); Kzk. 19th c. **Qawmen** [Кауменъ] (AOP 110); Kzk. 19th c. **Qawmen** [Кауменъ] (SOK 172); Kzk. 19th c. **Qawmen** [Кауменъ] (AOO 10); Kzk. 19th c. **Qawmen** [Кауменъ] (AOAtb. 18). ⇨ **QAW** + suff. *-man*.

QAWMEN see QAWMAN

QAWMET Kzk. 19th c. **Qawmet** [Кауметъ] (SOK 108). ⇨ **QAW** + suff. *-met*.

QAWNÏŠ Kzk. 19th c. **Qawnïš-pay** [Каунышпай] (SODž. 12); Kzk. 19th c. **Qawnïš-pay** [Каунышпай]

(SOV 34).

QAWS see QAWÏS

QAWSAR Trkm.? 1745 **Qawsar-χoǰa** [Каусар-ходжа] (MIT II, 173, 174).

QAWŠÏ Kzk. 19th c. **Qawšï-bay / Qawšï-bay** [Каушебай] (SODž. 40). ✦ 'Maker or seller of punk (tinder)' cf. Turk. *kavcı* 'id.' (TED). ⇨ **QAW?** + suff. *-šï*.

QAWUL Kzk. 19th c. **Qawul-bay** [Каульбай] (SOV 88).

QAWUN Kzk. 19th c. **Qawun-bek** [Каунбекъ] (SOV 102); Uzb. 19th c. **Qawun-čur?** [قاونجور / Kavoundjour] (Meyendorff). ✦ 'Muskmelon, melon' cf. Turk. *qawïn, qawun* 'die Melone' (Radl. II, 468, 470), Kzk. *qawïn* 'дыня' (KzRS).

QAWURT Selj. 1033 **Qawurt-bek** [Кавард / Кавурт-бек ибн Дауд], Čaγrï-bek's son (MIT I, 354, 373, 376).

QAWUŠTÏ Trkm. **Qawuštï-χan** [Каушты-ханъ] (Smirnov, Sultany 75). ✦ 'He joined (came to us)' cf. Uyg. *qawuš-* 'zusammenkommen, sich vereinigen' (Radl. II, 471).

QAWZ see QAWÏS

QAZ Kirg. 19th c. **Гaz-bek** [Газбекъ] (Grod., Pril. 19); Tat.(Lit.) 1593 **Xaz-bey** [Хазбей Асичъ], a prince (Lit. Tat. 179); Tat.(Lit.) 1593 **Xaz-bey / Qaz-bey?** [Хозбей Охметевичъ Адамовичъ] (Lit. Tat. 168); Chuv. 18th-19th c. **Kas-bay** [Касбай] (Magn. 50); Tat.(Tob.) 1683, 1696 **Qas-saltan** [Касъ салтанъ], a sultan, the ruler of the town Savran (DAI X, 378); Karakh. 11th c. **Qaz** [Kaz / qaz], Afrasyab's daughter (MK/Atalay 844, DTS); Kzk. **Qaz** [Казъ] (ZOOO 1870, 234); Trkm. 1803 **Qaz-bay** [Мугамедъ-ниязъ Казбаевъ] (PSZRI XXVII, 139); Kzk. 19th c. **Qaz-bala** [Казбала] (SOK 158); Kzk. **Qaz-bek** [Казбекъ] (Valihanov, Soč. 162); Kzk. **Qaz-bek** [Казбекъ] (Grod. I, 25); Kzk. **Qaz-bek** [Казбекъ] (Sb. Syr-D. IX, 44); Kzk. 1845 **Qaz-bek** [Казбек Чегенев], a biy (MKOP 153); Kzk. 19th c. **Qaz-bek** [Казбекъ] (AOK 94); Kzk. 19th c. **Qaz-bek** [Казбекъ] (AOA 70); Kzk. 19th c. **Qaz-bek** [Казбекъ Аллахбергановъ] (Grod., Pril. 185); Kzk. 19th c. **Qaz-bek** [Казбекъ] (SOV 34); Nog. 20th c. **Qaz-bek** [Казбек Джангелди увлы Елгитар / Казбек Джанкельдиев], one of Baskakov's informants from the aul of Qoyasulï (Bask., Nog. 144); Kirg. 19th c. **Qaz-bek** [Казбекъ] (Potanin II, 4); Tat.(Sib.) 1630 **Qaz-γul** [Казгул], a murza from Čat (Čatskij murza) (Miller, Ist. Sib. II, 369, 370); Oghuz **Qaz-χan** [قارا خان / قازخان] (Nešrī 186, Seādeddīn I, 15); *EN:* Kzk. 18th c. - 19th c. **Qaz-bek** [Казбек], a clan (Tynyšp. 73). ✦ 'Goose' cf. Kuman, Crm., Kirg., Kzk., Tat., Turk. etc. *qaz* 'die Gans' (Radl. II, 360), Kzk. *qaz* 'гусь (домашний)' (KzRS). See also **BAY-QAZ.**

QAZ-AYDAR   Kzk. 19th c. **Qaz-aydar** [Казайдаръ] (SOK 38). ⇨ **QAZ + AYDAR.**

QAZ-BUL   Kzk. 19th c. **Qaz-bul** [Казбулъ] (SOK 158). ✦ 'Be a goose' cf. Tat. *bul-* 'sein, werden' (Radl. IV, 1835). ⇨ **QAZ.**

QAZ-BULAT see **QAS-BULAT**

QAZ-EKE see **QAS II.**

QAZ-GÖZ   Kzk. 19th c. **Qaz-göz?** / **Qaz-köz?** [Сунбатбай Казгозовъ] (Grod., Pril. 181). ⇨ **QAZ + KÖZ?**

QAZ-MAMBET   Kzk. 19th c. **Qaz-mambet** [Казмамбетъ] (SOV 124). ⇨ **QAZ + MUXAMMED.**

QAZ-MUXAMBET   Nog. 20th c. **Qaz-muχambet** / **Qazi-muχambet** [Къазмухамбет Мулла увлы / Казимухамбет Муллаев], one of Baskakov's informants from the Sarï-awul (Bask., Nog. 144). ⇨ **QAZ / QAZÏ + MUXAMMED.**

QAZ-TÏΓAN see **QAZ-TUΓAN**

QAZ-TUΓAN   Nog. **Qaz-tuγan** [Казтуган] (Žirm., Epos 398); Nog. **Qaz-tuγan-batïr?** / **Qaz-tïγan-batïr?** [Казтыган] (Žirm., Epos 395). ✦ 'A goose (child) was born'. ⇨ **QAZ + TUΓAN I.**

QAZA   Chuv. 18th-19th c. **Kaza** [Каза] (Magn. 49); Kzk. 18th c. **Qaza-bay** [Казабай] (Nepljuev 808); Kzk. 19th c. **Qaza-bek** [Казабекъ] (SOV 116); Bashk. 1734 **Qaza-γul** [Абдулъ Казагуловъ] (PSZRI IX, 340). ✦ 'Loss, decay, damage' cf. Uyg., Az., Crm., Turk. *qaza* (Ar.) 'das Verhängnis; ein böses Schicksal, der Unglücksfall; (Kzk.) die Versäumniss einer Pflicht' (Radl. II, 362-63), Tat. *qaza* 'напасть, гибель (скота, живности); урон, утрата' (TatRS), Kzk. *qaza* 'ölim, ajal; ötelmegen, oqïlmaγan' (QTTS 16).

QAZA-BAXTÏ   Bashk. 1791 **Qaza-baχtï** [Казябахты Канферов] (MIB V, 679). ⇨ **QAZA / QAZÏ + BAQTÏ.**

QAZA-BERDİ   Bashk. 1623 **Qaza-berdi** / **Qaza-berdey?** [Казебердей] (Miller, Ist. Sib. II, 299). ⇨ **QAZA / QAZÏ + BERDİ.**

QAZAD   Tat.(Sib.) 1600 **Qazad** [Казад Енгилдеев] (Miller, Ist. Sib. II, 159).

QAZAΓAN see **QAZΓAN**

QAZAY I.   Chuv. 18th-19th c. **Kazay** [Казай] (Magn. 49); Tat. 1696 **Qazay** [Азняшко Казаевъ] (Kungursk. akty 244); Tat. 1734 **Qazay** [Казай Касабаевъ] (PSZRI IX, 339); Bashk. 1760 **Qazay** [Казай Усеев] (MIB IV/1, 187). ⇨ **QAZ** + dim. suff. *-ay.*

QAZAY II. see **QASAY**

QAZAQ   Chuv. 18th-19th c. **Kazak** [Казакъ] (Magn. 49); Oghuz 1561/62 **Qazaq** [Казак], Muhammed-χan Sarafuddïn-oγlï's son (MIT II, 63, 64); Yürük 1543 **Qazaq** (Gökb., Rum. 204); Yürük 16th c. **Qazaq** [قزاق], from the Yürüks of Kocacık, Turkey (Gökb., Rum. 102); Karch. **Qazaq** [Казакъ] (Sysoev 123);

Bashk. 1756 **Qazaq** [Казак Батлеимбаев] (MIB IV/1, 123); Bashk. 1761 **Qazaq** [Казак Кашкулов] (MIB IV/1, 219); Bashk. 1779 **Qazaq** [Казак Исенчурин] (MIB V, 101); Bashk. 1779 **Qazaq** [Казак Мукаев] (MIB V, 203); Bashk. 1787 **Qazaq** [Казак Мукашев] (MIB V, 203); Alt. 19th-20th c. **Qazaq** [Казак], fem. (OjrRS 212); Trkm. 1856 **Qazaq-bay** [Казак-бай], an išan from the Čawdur tribe (MIT II, 566, 568, 571, 585, 586); Bashk. 1777 **Qazaq-bay** [Казакбай Тюканов] (MIB V, 65); Kzk. 19th c. **Qazaq-bay** [Казакбай] (SODž. 160); Kzk. 19th c. **Qazaq-bay** [Казакбай] (Grod., Pril. 85); Kzk. 19th c. **Qazaq-bay** [Казакбай] (SODž. 18); Kzk. 19th c. **Qazaq-bay** [Казакбай] (SOV 150); Kzk. 19th c. **Qazaq-bay** [Кошпелы Казакбаевъ], a writer of articles (AUK 392); Kirg. **Qazaq-bay** [Казакбай] (Jud. 94); Uzb. 19th c. **Qazaq-bay** [Таштимир Казакбаев] (SKSO III, 170); Uzb. 19th c. **Qazaq-bay** [Казакбай] (SKSO III, 156, 164); Chag. 16th c. **Qazaq-χanum** [Казак-ханум], fem. (Ivanov 242); Bashk. 1765 **Qazaq-qul** [Казаккул Асылов] (MIB IV/1, 312); Kzk. **Qazaq-pay** [Казакпай] (Konšin, Oč. 81); Kzk. 19th c. **Qazaq-pay** [Казакпай] (SOV 14); Kzk. 19th c. **Qazaq-pay** [Казакпай] (SOK 4); Alt. 19th-20th c. **Qazaq-ül** [Казакуул] (OjrRS 208); *EN:* Kkalp. 20th c. **Qazaq-bay** [Қазақбай] (KkRS 774); Nog. 20th c. **Qazaq-uruw** [Казакъ урув], an Aq-noγay clan (Bask., Nog. 135, 142). ✦ 'Free, independent person, vagabond; Kazakh; Russian [in Alt.]' cf. *qazaq* (Chag., Crm., Tat.) 'ein freier, unabhängiger Mensch, Abenteurer, Vagabund', (Hak., Kirg., Kzk.) 'der Kirgise; Kirgis-Kaisake [Kazakh]', (Alt.) 'der Russe', (Tat.) 'ein unverheiratheter Mensch, Junggeselle' (Radl. II, 364-365), cf. also Bask., Fam. 132. See also **BAY-QAZAQ, BÏŠ-QAZAQ, SAR-ΓAZAQ.**

QAZAQ-KÜZ   Kzk. 19th c. **Qazaq-küz** [Казаккузъ] (SODž. 88). ⇨ **QAZAQ + KÖZ.**

QAZAQAY   Chuv. 18th-19th c. **Kazakay** [Казакай] (Magn. 49); Bashk. 1706 **Qazaqay** [Ахман Казакаев] (MIB III, 26); Bashk. 1723 **Qazaqay** [Маатмас Казакаев] (MIB III, 201); Bashk. 1730 **Qazaqay** [Казакай Чюрашев] (MIB III, 276); Bashk. 1754 **Qazaqay** [Казакай Килимбетев] (MIB IV/1, 84); Bashk. 1778 **Qazaqay** [Казакай Мончаков] (MIB V, 71); Bashk. 1791 **Qazaqay** [Абулхаир Казакаев] (MIB V, 310); Kzk. 1883 **Qazaqay** [Казакаевъ] (Grod., Pril. 93). ⇨ **QAZA(Q)** + dim. suff. *-qay/-ay.*

QAZAMAN   Kzk. 19th c. **Qazaman** [Казаманъ] (SOK 84). ⇨ **QAZA** + suff. *-man.*

QAZAN   Chuv. 18th-19th c. **Kazan** [Казанъ] (Magn. 49); Chuv. 18th-19th c. **Kazan-bay** [Казанбай] (Magn. 49); Uyg. 13th c. - 14th c. **Qazan**, „Scholasticus" (Chwol., Syr.-nest. (NF) 48, Kokovcov

192); Maml. **Qazan** [قازان] (Mayer 189); Trkm. 19th c. **Qazan** [Казанъ] (Volodin 53); Bashk. 1754 **Qazan** [Казян Урускулов] (MIB IV/1, 83); Bashk. 1772 **Qazan** [Кинзегул Казанов] (MIB IV/1, 363); Hak. 19th-20th c. **Qazan** [Казан] (HRS 349); Hak.(Sag.) 19th-20th c. **Qazan** [Казан] (Katanov, Otč. 8); Oghuz/Trkm. 13th c. **Qazan / Qazan-bek / Qazan-big** [قزان بيك / Han Kazan / Qazan Big / Agam Qazan / Qazan / Казан-бек], the same as Salor-qazan (Salur-qazan) (MIT I, 4, DQorq./Ergin 95, 96, DQorq./Rossi 112, 122, 127 etc., DQorq., 22 etc., Abulg./Kon. 1090); Selj. 11th c. **Qazan** [قزان], an emir (Ibn Taghrīb. II, 281, 284); Oghuz/Trkm. 13th c. **Qazan-alp** [قزان آلب / Казан-алп] (Abulg./Kon. 1070); Kmk. 1649, 1651 **Qazan-alp** [Казаналпъ Салтанъ-Маметовъ], a murza (AI IV, 102, 161, 209); Tat. 1649 **Qazan-alp** [Казаналпъ] (AI IV, 101); Nog. 1654 **Qazan-alp** [Казаналпъ], a murza (AI IV, 205); Bashk. 1745 **Qazan-bay** [Казанбай] (MIB III, 430); Bashk. 1749 **Qazan-bay** [Крус Казанбаев] (MIB III, 464); Bashk. 1773, 1776 **Qazan-bay** [Терегул Казанбаев] (MIB IV/2, 414, MIB V, 33); Bashk. 1776 **Qazan-bay** [Терегул Казанбаев] (MIB V, 33, 64, 80); Bashk. 1777 **Qazan-bay** [Казанбай Илкачев] (MIB V, 103); Bashk. 1778 **Qazan-bay** [Казанбай] (MIB V, 80); Bashk. 1780 **Qazan-bay** [Казанбай Илкачев] (MIB V, 103); Kzk. 19th c. **Qazan-bay** [Казанбай] (SOK 252); Kzk. **Qazan-bek** [Казанъ-бекъ] (ZVORIAO VIII, 204, 206-208); Bashk. 1735 **Qazan-ɣul** [Казангулъ Таникечевъ], a tarχan (Vel.-Zern., Bašk. 24); Yürük 19th c. **Qazan-oɣlu** [Kasanoglu], a chieftain of a tribe in the 1960-s of the 19th c. (Das Ausland 64: 342), Oghuz/Trkm. **Qazan-sultan** [قزان سلطان], Chaǧatay's 21st khan (Khulāset ul Akhbār?, Abulg./Desm. 158); *EN:* Kzk. 18th c. - 19th c. **Qazan-bay** [Казанбай], a clan (Tynyšp. 71). ✧ I. 'Kettle, boiler' (Sauvaget 51), cf. several Turkic languages *qazan* 'der Kessel' (Radl. II, 367); II. 'Good'? (<Ar.) (Butanaev). See also **SALÏR-QAZAN, SAMÏR-QAZAN.**

QAZAN-ГАР see **QAZAN-QAP**

QAZAN-KÜN Bashk. 1756 **Qazan-kün?** [Казанкун Яббисев] (MIB IV/1, 128). ⇨ **QAZAN + KÜN.**

QAZAN-QAF see **QAZAN-QAP**

QAZAN-QAP Kzk. 1846 **Qazan-ɣap** [Казангап Джандыров], a biy (MKOP 100); Kzk. 19th c. **Qazan-ɣap** [Казангапъ] (SOV 78); Kzk. 1878 **Qazan-qaf** [Турманбай Казанкафовъ] (Grod., Pril. 121); Kzk. 1794 **Qazan-qap** [قزان قب / Казанкап] (MIK IV, 158); Kzk. 19th c. **Qazan-qap** [Казанкапъ] (AOAtb. 66); Kzk. 19th c. **Qazan-qap** [Урталбай Казанкаповъ] (Grod., Pril. 136). ✧ 'Black-felt-bag, (lit.) Kettle-bag' (Espaeva 1984, 233), cf. Kzk. *qap*

'geniş çuval' (KzTS). ⇨ **QAZAN.**

QAZANAQ Tat.(Sib.) 1629 **Qazanaq** [Казанак] (Miller, Ist. Sib. II, 360). ⇨ **QAZAN?** + suff. *-aq.*

QAZANČA Chuv. 18th-19th c. **Kazanča** [Казанча] (Magn. 49). ⇨ **QAZAN?** + suff. *-ča.*

QAZANČİ Bashk. 1756 **Qazanči** [Казанчи Баимов] (MIB IV/1, 120). ⇨ **QAZAN** + suff. *-či.*

QAZANČİY Tat.(GH) 1316 **Qazančiy** [Казаньчïй / Казначïй / Казанчïй], envoy from the Horde (Lavr. 501, PSRL I, 229); Bashk. 1664 **Qazančiy** [Казанчейко Чекеев] (MIB I, 192). ⇨ **QAZANČİ** + R. suff. *-y?*

QAZANDAY Chuv. 18th-19th c. **Kazanday** [Казандай] (Magn. 49); Chuv. 19th c. **Kazanday** [Chasandaï] (Kronheim 96); Chuv. 18th-19th c. **Kazandey** [Казандей] (Magn. 49); Kzk. 1846 **Qazanday** [Муал Казантаев] (MKOP 101); Kzk. 19th c. **Qazanday** [Казантай] (Grod., Pril. 19). ⇨ **QAZAN** + suff. *-day.*

QAZANDEY see **QAZANDAY**

QAZANDÏQ Tuv. 19th c. **Qazandïq** [Казандык] (Proben IX, 178, 180).

QAZANƔAN Kzk. 19th c. **Qazanɣan** [Арунъ Казангановъ], prefect of the district (volost') of Karautkel (AUK 295).

QAZANQA Chuv. 18th-19th c. **Xazanka** [Хазанка] (Magn. 89); Chuv. 18th-19th c. **Kazanka** [Казанка] (Magn. 49); Tat.(Sib.) 1620 **Qazanqa** [Бекмамет Казанкин] (Miller, Ist. Sib. II, 210). ⇨ **QAZAN** + suff. *-qa.*

QAZANQAY Kzk. 19th c. **Qazanqay** [Казанкай] (SOK 180). ⇨ **QAZAN** + dim. suff. *-qay.*

QAZANQAT Kzk. 19th c. **Qazanqat** [Казанкатъ] (SOK 212).

QAZANTAY see **QAZANDAY**

QAZAR Oghuz/Trkm. 13th c. **Xazar** [خزر / Хазар], Yafet's son (Abulg./Kon. 130); Tat. 1600 **Qazar** [Казар Енгилбеев] (MIB I, 152); Bashk. 1756 **Qazar** [Казяр Ирисакав] (MIB IV/1, 123). ✧ Goes back to the ethnonym Khazar. See also **BAY-QAZAR, ČUL-QAZAR.**

QAZARMAN Bashk. 18th c. - 19th c. **Qazarman** [Казарман], a folklore hero (batïr) mentioned in several songs (ZOOIRGO III, 227).

QAZAT Tat.? 1460 **Qazat** [Казатъ (Казатулъ)], a murza from the Horde (PSRL IV, 148, VI, 184); Tat.? 15th c. **Qazat-ulan** [Казатъ Улан мурза], a murza from the Horde (PSRL V, 272).

QAZĀ Hak.(Sag.) 19th-20th c. **Qazā** [Каза] (Katanov, Otč. 7). ✧ 'Yard, courtyard' (Katanov), cf. Hak.(Sag.) *qazā* 'das Vorratshaus bei der Jurte, der Hof' (Radl. II, 363).

QAZDAQ Kzk. 19th c. **Qazdaq-pay** [Каздакпай] (SODž. 70).

QAZΓA Hak.(Kyz.) 19th-20th c. **Qazγa** [Казга], a folklore hero (Kostrov 7-8).

QAZΓAN Kzk. 19th c. **Qazγam-bay (<Qazγan-bay)** [Казгамбай] (AOK 18); Khorezm. 14th c. **Qazγan / Qazan** [قازان / قازغان / قرغن] / Казаган], Kerbende's brother was named as *Qazγan* but commonly called *Qazan* (Ibn Batuta), emir (ruled 1347-1357), defeated and killed Qazan Sultan in Māwerannahr (Abul Ghāzi) (Ibn Bat. II, 115, Abulg./Desm. 161, Barth., Ulugb. 10-15, MIT I, 512).

QAZÏ Turk. 1543 **Qadï** [Kadı], from the yürüks of Silistre (Gökb., Rum. 227); Nog. **Qazï** [Казы] (Žirm., Epos 402, 406); Kzk. 19th c. **Qazï-bay** [Казыбай] (AOK 118); Kuman/Tat.? **Qazï-bey** [Казибей], a prince from the Horde (PSRL); Kzk. **Qazï-bek** [Казибек] (IOAIÊK XX, 667); Kzk. **Qazï-bek** [Казыбекъ] (Karta JAR XI); Kkalp. 20th c. **Qazï-gül** [Қазыгүл], fem. (KkRS 778, Baskakov: OSA 140); *TN:* Kzk. **Qazï** [Казы], a settlement (Kojčubaev 112). ✧ 'Kadi (judge of Islamic canon law); governor of a *kaza*' (TED), cf. Turk. *qadï* 'id.' (Radl. II, 317-318), Uyg., Crm., Kzk., Tat., Turk. *qazï* 'der Richter' (Radl. II, 373), Uyg. *qazï* (Ar.) 'судья' (DTS), Bashk., Tat. *qazïy* 'id.' (BRS/Uraksin, TatRS), Kirg. *qazï* II. 'id.' (Jud.).

QAZÏ-BAQ? Bashk. 1789 **Qazï-baq?** [Казыбак Субхангулов] (MIB V, 241). ⇨ **QAZÏ** + **BAQ?**

QAZÏ-BERGEN Kzk. 18th c. **Qazï-bergen / Qazï-bergän** [Казибергенъ / Казиберганъ] (Nepljuev 741). ⇨ **QAZÏ** + **BERGEN.**

QAZÏ-QURT Oghuz/Trkm. 13th c. **Qazï-qurt** [قازغورت / Казыкурт] (Abulg./Kon. 525, 555). ⇨ **QAZÏ** + **QURT.**

QAZÏČ Tat.(Sib.) 1638 **Qazïč** [Казыч (Хозяинов)] (Miller, Ist. Sib. II, 450). ⇨ **QAZÏ?** + suff. -*č*.

QAZÏY Tat. 1526 **Qazïy** [Казый], a prince from Kazan (PSRL VIII, 271); Kzk. 1692 **Qazïy** [Казей], a prince of the Kazak Horde (DAI X, 387); Tat. 1555 **Qazïy-mïrza** [Казый-мырза] (PSRL XIII, 245). ⇨ **QAZÏ** + dim. suff. -*y*.

QAZÏKE Kzk. 19th c. **Qazïke** [Казыке] (AOP 90); Kzk. 19th c. **Qazïke** [Казыке] (SOV 108). ⇨ **QAZÏ?** + suff. -*ke*.

QAZÏQ Kzk. 19th c. **Qazïq-pay** [Казыкпай] (SODž. 154). ✧ 'Spike, pale, post' cf. Alt., Kirg., Kzk. *qazïq* 'der Pflock, der Pfahl' (Radl. II, 374).

QAZÏLÏQ Oghuz/Trkm. **Qazïlïq-qoJa** [قازيليق توجه / Qaziliq Qoğa / Казылык-Коджа], Yekenk's father (DQorq./Ergin 113, DQorq./Rossi 112, 144, 158, 160, DQorq. 30. 32, 58, 73 etc.). ⇨ **QAZÏ?** + suff. -*lïq*.

QAZÏMBET Kkalp. 20th c. **Qazïmbet** [Қазымбет] (KkRS 774). ⇨ **QAZ?** / **QAZÏ** + suff. *imbet* / -*mhet*.

QAZLAN Tat.(Sib.) 1629 **Qazlan-murza** [Казлан мурза] (Miller, Ist. Sib. II, 360).

QAZLÏY Kzk. 19th c. **Qazlïy?** [Казлей] (SOK 218).

QAZLÏQ Kzk. 19th c. **Qazlïq** [Казлыкъ] (AOA 126). ⇨ **QAZ** + suff. -*lïq*.

QAZLU Turk. 1540 **Qazlu-kethudā**, one of the chiefs of the Čaγïryanlu tribe (Demirtaş 58). ⇨ **QAZ** + suff. -*lu*.

QAZNA Kkalp. 20th c. **Qazna** [Қазна], fem. (KkRS 778). ✧ 'Treasure, crown' cf. Kuman. Tat. *qazna* 'der Schatz, Die Krone' (Radl. II, 385).

QAZNAČEY Alt. 19th-20th c. **Qaznačey** [Казначей] (OjrRS 208); Karg. **Qaznačey** [Казначей] (Katanov, Otč. 9). ✧ 'Treasurer' <R. *kaznačej* 'id.'.

QAZON Hak. 19th-20th c. **Qazon** [Казон] (HRS 349).

QAŽ-BULAT see **QAS-BULAT**

QAŽAΓAY Alt. 19th-20th c. **QaJaγay** [Кажагай], fem. (OjrRS 212). ✧ 'Whitish; blondish' (OjrRS). ⇨ **QAŠAQAY.**

QAŽAN Alt. 19th-20th c. **Qažan** [Кажан], fem. (OjrRS 212). ✧ 'Lazy' (OjrRS).

QAŽIK Kzk. 19th c. **Qažik** [Кажикъ], a biy (Lomakin 35).

QĀQA Alt. 19th-20th c. **Qāqa** [Каака], fem. (OjrRS 212).

QĀQAŠ Alt. 19th-20th c. **Qāqaš** [Каакаш] (OjrRS 208). ✧ 'Eggshell' (OjrRS).

QĀN-PÜDÄY see **QAN-PÜDÄY**

QĀN-SÜLÜ Hak.(Blt.) 19th-20th c. **Qān-sülü** [Кан Сүлү] (Proben IX, 355, 362, 366). ✧ 'Khan-noble'. ⇨ **QAN** + **SÏLÜ?**

QĀNČA Karg. **Qānča** (Katanov, Otč. 9). ✧ Gan'ča (R.).

QĀNQA Hak.(Sag.) 19th-20th c. **Qānqa** [Канка] (Katanov, Otč. 7, 8). ✧ Gan'ka (R.) (Katanov).

QĀRQA Hak. 19th-20th c. **Qārqa** [Каарка] (HRS 349); Hak.(Sag.) 19th-20th c. **Qārqa** [Карка] (Proben IX, 555).

QĀSA Hak.(Sag.) 19th-20th c. **Qāsa** [Каса] (Katanov, Otč. 7). ✧ 'Pulp, squash' cf. R. каша 'id.'.

QÄDÏR-NÏYAZ Kkalp. 20th c. **Qädir-niyaz** [Кәдирнияз] (KkRS 774). ⇨ **QADÏR** + **NÏYAZ.**

QÄDÏRÏMBET Kkalp. 20th c. **Qädirimbet** [Кәдиримбет] (KkRS 774).

QÄLEMPÏR Kkalp. 20th c. **Qälempir** [Кәлемпир], fem. (KkRS 778). ✧ 'Carnation' cf. Kkalp. *qalempir / qalampir* 'id.' (KkRS) (<Ar.).

QÄLLÏ see **QALLÏ**

QÄTÏYRA Kkalp. 20th c. **Qätiyra** [Кәтийра], fem. (KkRS 778). ⇨ **KÄDÏR** + fem. suff. -*a*.

QÄTÏYŠA see **XADÏJA**

QÏRÏSKÄ Hak. 19th c. **Qiriskä** [Кіріскä] (Katanov, Otč. 12). ✧ Grishka (R.) (Katanov).

QÏASAY Yak. **Qïasuy** [Кыасаі] (Pek.).

QÏBA Yak. **Qïba** [Кыба] (Pek.).

QÏBÏY-ÄRÏMÄX Yak. **Qïbïy-ärimäχ-qïs** [Кыбыі

Äpimäx кыс], fem. (Pek.).

QÏBÏR   Kzk. 19th c. **Qïbïr-bay** [Кыбырбай] (SOK 156). ✦ 'Slow movement' cf. Kzk. *qibir* 'медленное движение' (KzRS).

QÏBÏRAY   Kzk. **Qïbray** [Кыбрай] (Grod. 25); Kzk. 19th c. **Qïbray** [Кыбрай] (SOV 20, 76); Kzk. 19th c. **Qïbray** [Кыбрай] (SOV 110); Kzk. 19th c. **Qïbray** [Кыбрай] (SODž. 56); *EN:* Kzk. 18th c. - 19th c. **Qïbray-batïr** [Кыбрай-батыр], a clan (Tynyšp. 66). ⇨ **QÏBÏR** + suff. -*ay*.

QÏBRAY see **QÏBÏRAY**

QÏBRÏDU   Uyg. 12th c. - 14th c. **Qïbrïdu** (Radl., USp. 3-4).

QÏČAY   Hak. 19th-20th c. **Qïčay** [Кычай], fem. (Katanov, Otč. 11). ✦ 'Emotion, passion, eagerness, wish' cf. Alt. *qiča* 'die Leidenschaft, Begierde, der Wunsch' (Radl. II, 792). + dim. suff. -*y*.

QÏČAQ   Hak.(Sag.) 19th-20th c. **Qïčaq** [Кычакъ] (Katanov, Otč. 8). ✦ 'Emotion, passion, eagerness, wish' cf. Alt., Hak. *qičaɣ, qiča* 'die Leidenschaft, Begierde, der Wunsch' (Radl. II, 792). ⇨ **QÏČAY.**

QÏČAN   Kirg. **Qïčan** [Кычан] (Jud. 922).

QÏČČÏY   Yak. **Qïččïy** [Кыччыі] (Pek.).

QÏČORQA   Hak. 19th-20th c. **Qïčorqa** [Кычорка], fem. (HRS 353).

QÏJĀN   Hak.(Blt.) 19th-20th c. **Qïjān** [Кыцан] (Proben IX, 366).

QÏDA   Hak. 19th-20th c. **Qïda** [Кыда], fem. (HRS 353). ✦ 'Virgin' cf. Hak. fem. PN *Qïda / Xïda* (Butanaev).

QÏDAY   Yak. **Qïday-baχsï** [Кыдаи Бахсы / Кытаі Бакœы тойон], an evil spirit, chief of one of the eight clans of the underworld gods, he is believed to be the protector of the smiths; name of a legendary smith (cf. Küdäy Baχsïtay üstar), folkl. (Pek.). ✦ 'Chinese wizard'? See also **QÏTAY, KÜDÄY.**

QÏDÏQ   Kzk. 19th c. **Qïdïq** [Кыдыкъ] (SODž. 70); Kzk. 19th c. **Qïdïq** [Кыдыкъ] (SODž. 84). ✦ 'Border, frontier' cf. Uyg. *qïdïq* 'die Grenze' (Radl. II, 790).

QÏDÏR see **XÏZÏR**

QÏDÏR-ALÏ   Kzk. 1807 **Qïdr-alï-biy** / **Qïdïr-alï** [Кыдралы-бий] (Tynyšp. 71). ✦ 'Khizr Ali' cf. Kzk. PNs *Qïdïr-äli, Qïdïr-ɣali* (Žanuzakov-Esbaeva). ⇨ **XÏZÏR + ALÏ.**

QÏDÏR-NÏYAZ   Kkalp. 20th c. **Qïdïr-niyaz** [Къыдырнийаз / Қыдырнияз] (Bask., Kkalp. 401, KkRS 774). ⇨ **XÏZÏR + NÏYAZ.**

QÏDÏRÏMBET   Kkalp. 20th c. **Qïdïrïmbet** [Къыдырымбет / Қыдырымбет] (Bask., Kkalp. 4, KkRS 774). ⇨ **XÏZÏR** + suff. -*ïmbet.*

QÏDÏRMA   Kzk. 19th c. **Qïdïrma** [Кидырма] (AOK 2). ✦ 'Don't gad, prowl' cf. Kzk. *qidïr-* 'sich herumtreiben' (Radl. II, 790).

QÏDRAY   Bashk. 1729 **Qïdray** / **Qïdïray** [Баимъ-Тарханъ Кидряевъ] (PSZRI X, 982).

QÏFČAQ see **QÏPČAQ**

QÏĠAČAQ   Hak.(Shor) 19th-20th c. **Qïɣačaq** [Кыңацак] (Katanov, Otč. 11).

QÏĠAW   Kzk. 19th c. **Qïɣaw-bay** [Кигаубай] (AOA 150).

QÏĠA   **Qïɣa-χan** [Kyja-xan] (Barth., Turk. I(?), 301).

QÏĠABLAN   Kzk. 19th c. **Qïɣablan** [Кіабланъ] (SOK 266).

QÏĠAĠAN   Türk 8th c. - 9th c. **Qïɣaɣan** [qïɣaɣan / Qïɣaɣan] (DTS, ETY II, 67); Türk 750 **Qïɣaɣan-uruñu** [Qïɣaɣan Ur(u)ŋu / Qïɣaɣan Uruñu / qïɣaɣan uruŋu] (Thomsen, Stein 187, 189, ETY II, 67, DTS). See also **KÜČ-QÏĠAĠAN.**

QÏĠAXÏ   Yak. **Qïɣaχï** [Кыіахы] (Pek.).

QÏĠAL   Kzk. 19th c. **Qïɣal** [Кіялъ] (SOK 104); Kzk. 19th c. **Qïɣal** [Кіялъ] (AOK 70); Kzk. 19th c. **Qïɣal-bay** [Кыялбай] (SODž. 32); Kzk. 19th c. **Qïɣal-bek** [Кіяльбекъ] (SOK 18). ✦ I. 'Wild, disobedient, insubordinate, stubborn' cf. Kzk. *qïɣal* 'störrisch, unbändig, wild (von Thieren), eigensinnig (von Menschen)' (Radl. II, 712); II. 'Illusion, fantasy' cf. Kzk. *qïɣal* 'мечта, фантазия' (KzRS). See also **AQ-QÏĠAL, QONČ-QÏĠAL.**

QÏĠALBÏQ   Kzk. 19th c. **Qïɣalbïq** [Кыалбыкъ] (AOP 50).

QÏĠAM   Bashk. 1789 **Qïɣam-qul** [Исенгул (Исянгул) Киамкулов] (MIB V, 260). ✦ 'Respected, awaited (child)' (Kusimova), 'Rising, resurrection' (Sattarov).

QÏĠAN   Hak.(Sag.) 19th-20th c. **Qïɣan-arïɣ** [Кыіан Арыг], an evil spirit (Proben IX, 507); Kzk. 1819 **Qïɣan-bay** [Кыянбай] (MIK IV, 326). ✦ 'Far, remote' cf. Kzk. *qïɣan* 'дальний' (KzRS).

QÏĠAN-GÜČI   Oghuz/Trkm. **Qïɣan-güči, Qïɣan-küči?** [قِیَان کُوجی / Qïɣan Güči] (DQorq./Ergin 97, DQorq./Rossi 136). ⇨ **QÏĠAN + KÜČ** + suff. -*i.*

QÏĠAN-SELČÜK   Oghuz/Trkm. **Qïɣan-selčük** / **Qïɣan-seljük** [قِیَان سَلجُوك / Kayan Selçuk / Qïɣan Seljük / Кыян-Сельджук (Киян-Сельджук, Кыян)], Uruz-qoja's son, Delü Dundaz's (Dundar's?) father (DQorq./Ergin 96, Žirm., Epos 22 etc.). ⇨ **QÏĠAN + SELČÜK.**

QÏĠAS   Kirg. **Aq-qïɣas** [Ak Kyjas / Ак Кыјас], Kök-qïɣas' brother (folkl.) (Proben V, 27 /28/); Kkalp. 20th c. **Qïɣas** [Кыяс] (KkRS 774); Kirg. **Qïɣas** [Кыяз] (Jud. 89); Kkalp. 20th c. **Qïɣas-bay** [Кыясбай] (KkRS 775); Kzk. 19th c. **Qïɣas-pay** [Кіаспай] (SODž. 54); Kirg. **Qïɣaz** [Кыяз] (Jud. 474); Kirg. **Qïɣaz** [Кыяз] (Jud. 70). ✦ 'Value, price' cf. Kar.(L., T.) *qïɣas* (Ar.) 'der Preis, Werth' (Radl. II, 713). See also **AQ-QÏĠAS, KÖK-QÏĠAS.**

QÏĠAT   Kkalp. 20th c. **Qïɣat** [Қыятбай] (KkRS 775). ✦ A Mongol tribe in Jochi's empire (Erol II).

QÏĠAZ see **QÏĠAS**

QÏĠBAT see **QÏĠMAT**

QÏYBÏRDĀN Yak. **Qïybïrdān** [Ытык Кыібырдан] (Pek.).

QÏYČAQ Kzk. 19th c. **Qïyčaq-pay** [Кыйчакпай] (SODž. 18). ✧ I. 'Awry, skew (little child)' cf. Kzk. *qïysïq* 'shicf, seitwärts gebogen' (Radl. II, 699); II. '(Little) Shit/dung of a sheep' cf. Kzk. *qïy* 'der Schafmist' (Radl. II, 687) + suff. *-čïq/-šïq*. See also **ARÏQ II., BAYNAQ, BOQ, QOMUQ.**

QÏYΓAN Kzk. 19th c. **Qïyγan** [Кійганъ] (SOK 134). ✧ 'Destroyed, left; dared' cf. Kzk. *qïy-* 'vernichten, verlassen; wagen, den Muth haben' (Radl. II, 688-690); Hak. *qïyγan* 'ein Holzbrett mit zackiger Oberfläche zum Waschen des Leders' (Radl. II, 691).

QÏYΓÏR Bashk. 1780 **Qïyγïr** [Кыйгыр] (MIB V, 120); Bashk. 1780 **Qïyγïr** [Мустафа Кыйгыров] (MIB V, 120). ✧ 'A kind of falcon' cf. Bashk. *qïyγïr* 'чеглок' (BRS).

QÏYÏMDU see **QÏYÏMTU**

QÏYÏMTU Uyg. 12th c. - 14th c. **Qïyïmdu** [Q.yïmdu] (Radl., USp. 25-26); Uyg. 12th c. - 14th c. **Qïyïmdu / Qayïmtu?** [Qïjïmdu] (Radl., USp. 41, 79); Uyg. 12th c. - 14th c. **Qïyïmtu** [Qïjïmtu] (Radl., USp. 10); Uyg. 12th c. - 14th c. **Qïyïmtu** [qïyïmtu] (DTS); Uyg. **Qïymtu** [Kıymtu] (EUTS). ✧ 'Frightened' (Blagova 1997, 714).

QÏYÏNTU Uyg. 12th c. - 14th c. **Qïyïntu** [qïyïntu] (DTS). ✧ 'Convicted/punished' (Blagova 1997, 711).

QÏYÏNTU-TAYÏN Uyg. **Qïyïntu-tayïn** [Kıyıntu Tayın] (EUTS). ⇨ **QÏYÏNTU.**

QÏYQÏM Kzk. 19th c. **Qïyqïm** [Кійкымъ] (SOK 144); Kzk. 19th c. **Qïyqïm** [Кійкымъ] (AOK 122, 134); Kzk. 19th c. **Qïyqïm** [Кійкымъ] (SOK 206); Kzk. 19th c. **Qïyqïm** [Кійкымъ] (AOP 30). ✧ 'Litter, rubbish, scraps' cf. Kzk. *qïyqïm* 'etwas von einer Sache Abgebrochenes' (Radl. II, 691), 'мусоръ, объѣдки, крошки, соръ' (PKRS).

QÏYLÏ I. Kzk. 19th c. **Qïylï-bay** [Кыйлыбай] (AOA 98); Kkalp. 20th c. **Qïylï-bay** [Къыйлыбай / Қыйлыбай] (Bask., Kkalp. 401, KkRS 774); Uzb. 19th c. **Qïylï-bay / Kiyli-bay?** [Кийлибай] (SKSO III, 176); Kzk. 19th c. **Qïylï-bay /Kiyli-bay?** [Кийлибай] (SODž. 152); Kzk. 19th c. **Qïylï-bay / Kiyli-bay?** [Кийлибай] (AOK 110); Kzk. 19th c. **Qïylï-bay / Kiyli-bay / Kiylï-bay?** [Кийлыбай] (SOK 116); Kzk. 19th c. **Qïylï-bay / Kiylï-bay?** [Кийлебай] (SODž. 22, 32); Kzk. 19th c. **Qïylï-bek / Kiylï-bek / Kiylï-bek?** [Кийлыбекъ] (SOK 286). ✧ 'Shitty, mucky' cf. Kzk. *qïy* 'кизяк из овечьего помёта' (KzRS). + suff. *-lï/-li.*

QÏYLÏ II. Karch. **Qïylï / Kiylï / Kiylï?** [Кіилы] (SMOK III, 158). ✧ 'Sufferer, bearer' (Ibid.) cf. Kbalk. *qïyïnlï* 'страдалец' (KbalkRS).

QÏYMAY Kzk. 19th c. **Qïymay** [Кіймай] (SOK 16).

QÏYMAT Trkm. 20th c. **Γïmmat** [Gïmmat], fem. (Zaj. 1971, 336); Trkm. 20th c. **Γïmmat / Qïmmat** [Кыммат], fem. (TrkmRS 231); Kkalp. 20th c. **Qïybat** [Қыйбат], fem. (KkRS 778); Nog. **Qïybat** [Кыйбат], fem. (Žirm., Epos 407); Kkalp. 20th c. **Qïmbat** [Қымбат], fem. (KkRS 778). ✧ 'Valuable, precious, dear; noble; price' cf. Uyg., Kuman, Alt., Shor *qïymat* 'der Preis, Werth; theuer, prächtig, schätzenswerth' (Radl. II, 703), Kirg., Tat., Tat(Tob.) *qïybat* 'theuer, vornehm, der theuere Preis' (Radl. II, 700), Kzk. *qïmbat* 'кıymetli, pahalı; saygılı, hürmetli' (KzTS), Kzk. *qïmbat* 'theuer' (Radl. II, 854), Kkalp. *qïmbat* 'дорогой, ценный; имеющий большую цену' (KkRS), Trkm. *γïmmat* 'дорогой, ценный' (TrkmRS) (<Ar.).

QÏYRATAY Kzk. 19th c. **Qïyratay** [Кійратай] (AOP 42).

QÏYSÏ Kzk. 19th c. **Qiysï-bay / Qïysï-bay / Kiysï-bay?** [Кійсыбай] (SOV 4).

QÏYSÏQ Kzk. 1841 **Qiysïq / Qïysïq / Kiysïq?** [Кійсыкъ Тезековъ] (Konšin, Mat. V, 51); Kzk. 19th c. **Qiysïq / Qïysïq / Kiysïq?** [Кійсыкъ] (AOAtb. 14); Kzk. 19th c. **Qiysïq / Qïysïq / Kiysïq?** [Кійсыкъ] (AOAtb. 10); Kzk. 19th c. **Qiysïq / Qïysïq / Kiysïq?** [Кійсыкъ] (Grod., Pril. 90); Kzk. 19th c. **Qiysïq / Qïysïq / Kiysïq?** [Кійсыкъ] (SOV 40); Kzk. 19th c. **Qiysïq / Qïysïq / Kiysïq?** [Кійсыкъ] (AOP 70); Kzk. 19th c. **Qiysïq / Qïysïq / Kiysïq?** [Кійсыкъ] (Potanin, Pred. 100); Kzk. 19th c. **Qiysïq / Qïysïq / Kiysïq?** [Кійсыкъ] (Lomakin 39). ✧ 'Curved, hooked, slant; stubborn' cf. Kzk. *qïysïq* 'кривой, покривившийся' (KzRS), 'schief, seitwärts gebogen' (Radl. II, 699), 'кривой, упрямый, бѣдовый' (PKRS).

QÏYSÏQ-PAS Kzk. 19th c. **Qiysïq-pas / Qïysïq-pas / Kiysïq-pas?** [Кійсыкпасъ] (SOK 230). ⇨ **QÏYSÏQ + BAŠ.**

QÏYSÏN-PAS Kzk. 19th c. **Qiysïn-pas / Kiysïn-pas** [Кійсынпасъ] (SOK 156). ⇨ **? + BAŠ.**

QÏYZATAN Kzk. 19th c. **Qïyzatan** [Кыйзатанъ] (SOV 54).

QÏQAR-QALTURΓAN **Qïqar-qalturγan / Qïyar-qalturγan?** [قالتورقان قيتار / قيغار / Хыхаръ-халтурганъ] (RaD/Ber. II, 141).

QÏQÏR-ATAX Yak. **Qïqïr-ataχ** [Кыкыр атах], a shaman, who received this byname because of his limping (Pek.). ✧ 'Creaking-leg' cf. Yak. *qïqïr* 'подражание разнородному скрипу' and *ataχ* 'нога' (JRS). ⇨ **AYAQ.**

QÏL Kzk. 19th c. **Qïl-bay** [Кылбай] (SOK 216). ✧ '(Horse)hair' cf. Alt., Kirg., Kzk., Tat. etc. *qïl* 'die langen Pferdehaare' (Radl. II, 767), Kkalp., Kzk. *qïl* 'волос, волосок' (KkRS, PKRS).

QÏL-BAŠ Oghuz/Trkm.? **Qïl-baš** [قلباش / Qïlbaš] (DQorq./Rossi 166, 167, 170); *TN:* Turk. 20th c. **Qïl-baš** [Kılbaş], a village in the province of Adana, Turkey (TMİB 9). ⇨ **QÏL + BAŠ.**

QÏL-KEÑIRDEK   Kkalp. 20th c. **Qïl-kenirdek** [Къылкенъирдек] (Bask., Kkalp. 401); Kzk. 19th c. **Qïl-keñirdek** [Кылъ-Кенердекъ] (Potanin, Pred. 162); Kkalp. 20th c. **Qïl-keñirdek** [Кылкеҥирдек] (KkRS 774). ✧ 'Hair-throat; tiny throat?' cf. Kkalp., Kzk. *keñirdek* 'дыхательное горло' (KkRS, PKRS). ⇨ **QÏL.**

QÏLAΓACCÏXĀN   Yak. **Qïlaγaccïxān** [Кылаҕаччыхан] (Pek.). ✧ 'Shining, sparkling' cf. Yak. *qïlaγaččïy-* 'проблескивать' (Pek.).

QÏLAY   Yak. **Qïlay** [Кылаi] (Pek.). ✧ 'Shine, glitter' cf. Yak. *qïlay-* 'светиться, блестеть (о серебре, о солнце' (Pek.).

QÏLAL   Oghuz/Trkm. 13th c. **Qïlal** [قلال غازى / Кылал-Газы] (Abulg./Kon. 1165).

QÏLAN   Hak. 19th-20th c. **Klan** [Клан] (HRS 349); Hak. 19th-20th c. **Qlan (<Qïlan)** [Кланъ], fem. (HRS 353). ✧ Klavdij (R. fem. PN) (Butanaev). See also **AMÏN-QÏLAN, QÏSQA-QÏLAN, UZUN-QÏLAN.**; ✧ Klavdij (R. fem. PN) (Butanaev), Klava (R.) cf. Hak. PN *Qïlan* (Butanaev). See also **AMÏN-QÏLAN, QÏSQA-QÏLAN, UZUN-QÏLAN.**

QÏLAN-ARSLAN   Selj. 11th c. **Qïlan-arslan** [Qïlān Arslan], Süleyman-šah's son, I. Qïlïč-arslan's (1092-1107) brother, defeated by Tatuš at Maʿarrat an-Nuʿmān (Aqsar./Iš. 34). ✧ 'Hairy lion'? cf. Tat.(Bar.) *qïlañ* 'das Pferdehaar' (Radl. II, 768). ⇨ **QÏLAN? + ARSLAN.** See also **QÏSQA-QÏLAN, UZUN-QÏLAN.**

QÏLANČA   Hak. 19th-20th c. **Qlanča (<Qïlanča)** [Кланча] (HRS 349). ✧ I. Klavdiy (R.), cf. Hak. PN *Qïlanča (<Qïlan)* (Butanaev); II. Klava (R. fem.), cf. Hak. fem. PN *Qïlanča (<Qïlan)* (Butanaev). ⇨ **QÏLAN** + suff. *-ča*.

QÏLAS   Kzk. 19th c. **Qïlas** [Курбанъ Киласъ Ходжаевъ] (Grod., Pril. 170); Nog. 20th c. **Qïlas** [Шашлыкъан Къылас къызы / Шашлыкан Класова], father of one of Baskakov's informants from the aul of Nökis (Bask., Nog. 143); Hak.(Blt.) 19th-20th c. **Qïlas** [Кылас], fem. (Katanov, Otč. 9).

QÏLAÑ   Hak.(Kacha) 19th-20th c. **Qïlañ** [Кылаҥ] (Proben IX, 550). ✧ I. 'Horse-hair/mane' cf. Tat.(Bar.) *qïlañ* 'das Pferdehaar' (Radl. II, 768). See also **QÏSQA-QÏLAN?, UZUN-QÏLAN?**

QÏLČA   Kzk. 19th c. **Qïlča-bay** [Кылчабай] (SOK 180); Tat.(Sib.) 1634, 1625 **Qïlča-ul** [Бахтемир Килчаулов (Кинчаулов)] (Miller, Ist. Sib. II, 319, 411). ⇨ **QÏL** + suff. *-ča*.

QÏLČÏQ   Kzk. 19th c. **Qïlčik-bay** [Кылчикбай] (Pantusov, Kirg. 39); Kzk. 19th c. **Qïlčuq-pay? (Qïlčïq-pay)** [Килчукпай] (SOK 128). ✧ '(A long) Hair; Little dear hairy (child)' cf. Kzk. *qïlšïq* 'волосинка' (KzRS), *qïlšïq* 'Tübït arasïndaγï üzïn talšïq, qattï žün.' (QTTS). ⇨ **QÏL** + dim. suff. *-čïq*.

QÏLČÏR   Kzk. 1838 **Qïlčïr-bay / Qïlčir-bay** [Кылчирбай Турсунаевъ], sultan of the Middle Horde, (Orta Žüz) (Konšin, Mat. V, 15).

QÏLΓAŠ   Alt. 19th-20th c. **Qïlγaš** [Кылгаш], fem. (OjrRS 212).

QÏLÏN   Karg. 19th-20th c. **Qïlïn** (Katanov, Otč. 10). ✧ 'Chock, wedge' cf. R. клин 'id.' (Katanov).

QÏLÏ   Kzk. 19th c. **Qïlï-bay** [Кылыбай] (SOK 144); Kzk. 19th c. **Qïlï-bay** [Кылыбай] (SOV 48); Kzk. 19th c. **Qïlï-bek** [Килибекъ] (SODž. 52). ✧ 'Holder of a bucket (pail)' cf. *qïlï* 'перевесло ведра' (PKRS), 'ручка (ведра)' (KzRS).

QÏLÏČ   Trkm. 20th c. **Γïlïč** [Gïlïč] (Zaj. 1971, 331); Trkm. 20th c. **Γïlïč / Qlïč** [Клыч] (TrkmRS 231); Oghuz 999-1002 **Qïlïč** [قُلُج / قُلُج / قلج ابو النوارس] (Hil. Sābī 370, 395, 396, 463 etc.); Selj.? 1007 **Qïlïč** [قلج] (Ibn al-Athīr/Tornb. IX, 136); Selj.? 1168/69, 1185/86 **Qïlïč** [قليج / قلج غرس الدين / Ghirs ed-Dîn Kilidj / Ghars ed-Dîn Kilîdj], Asedaddīn's mamluk, Salahaddīn's envoy (Abū Šāma: RHCHor IV, 117, Ibn Šaddād, Nawād.: RHCHor III, 84, Ibn Šaddād, Alep 148); Khorezm. 13th c. **Qïlïč** [قليج] (Ǧuwaynī II, 152); Maml. 1245 **Qïlïč** [Sayf ed-dîn Qilîdj en-Noûry], an emir from Damascus, a medresse has been named after him (Sauvaire IV, 275); Maml. 1264 **Qïlïč** [Seïf-eddin-Kilidj-Bagdadi] (Makrīzī II, 13, Weil, Chalif. I, 38); Maml. 1310 **Qïlïč** [قليج البتقى], an emir (Dawād. 212); Maml. 14th c. **Qïlïč** [قليج / Kïlïč] (Tarǰ/Houtsma 92,, Tarǰ/Toparlı 42); Turk. 1570 **Qïlïč** (Dávid); Turk. 1583 **Qïlïč** [Kilids] (Velics-Kamm. II, 577); Turk. 1584 **Qïlïč** [Kılıç] (Ongan, Ank. I, 164); Turk. 20th c. **Qïlïč** [Kılıç] (Önder, Göle); Yürük 1543 **Qïlïč** [Kılıç] (Gökb., Rum. 192, 193, 216, 228); Yürük 16th c. **Qïlïč** [قليج / Kılıç], in Kocacık, Turkey (Gökb., Rum. 103, 192); Trkm. **Qïlïč** [Мухаммедъ-Ніязъ Кылычевъ] (ZIRGOÊtn. I, 32); Trkm. 19th c. **Qïlïč** [Кылычъ] (Volodin 53); Crm. 18th c. **Qïlïč** [Кылыджъ] (Smirnov, Krym. 34); NUyg. 19th c. **Qïlïč** [قليج / Kilich] (Le Coq, Namenl. 106); Kuman/Tat. 12th c. - 13th c. **Qïlïč** [Κηλήτζ], a christened Tatar (Byz. Turc. 159); Kkalp. 1740 **Qïlïč-bi** [Кылычь Би] (Hanykov, Poezdka 19); Oghuz 1598/99 **Qïlïč-χan** [قليج خان] (Dorn 358, 403); Karakh. **Qïlïč-χan** [Kılıç Xan] (MK/Atalay 844); Chag. **Qïlïǰ-bay** [Qylyǯ Bai Bahadur] (Šejb. LIV); Bashk. 1756 **Qïlïs** [Мрясь Кылысев] (MIB IV/1, 130); Alt.? **Qïlïs** [Кан Кылыс] (Proben IX, 293, 294); Bashk. 1760 **Qïlïš** [Мряк Килишев] (MIB IV/1, 191); Kzk. 19th c. **Qïlïš** [Кылышъ] (SOK 86); Kzk. 19th c. **Qïlïš** [Кылышевъ] (AOK 110); Kzk. 19th c. **Qïlïš** [Кылышъ] (AOK 26); Kkalp. 20th c. **Qïlïš-bay** [Кылышбай] (KkRS 775); Kzk. 19th c. **Qïlïš-pay** [Кылышпай] (SOV 16); Kzk. 19th c. **Qïlïš-pay** [Кылышпай] (AOP 70); Kzk. 19th c. **Qïlïš-pay** [Кылышпай] (AOK 106); Kkalp. 20th c.

Qïlïš-pay [Къылышпай] (Bask., Kkalp. 76); Chag. 16th c. **Qlïč** [Кльıч Кара-султан] (Ivanov 26); Uzb. 1816 **Qlïč-behadïr** [Клыч-бехадыр], from the Xïtay tribe (clan) (MIT II, 397); Trkm. 1597 **Qlïč-bek** [Клыч-бек] (MIT II, 90); Uzb. 1813 **Qlïč-bek** [Клыч-бек] (MIT II, 387); Trkm.? 1816 **Qlïč-biy** [Мухаммед Клыч-бий] (MIT II, 392); Trkm. 1657/58 **Qlïč-χan** [Клыч-хан], from the Talïš tribe (MIT II, 113, 114); Trkm. 1688 **Qlïč-χan** [Клыч-хан], from the Papalu tribe (MIT II, 119); Trkm. 1816 **Qlïč-χan** [Клыч-хан] (MIT II, 220, 221, 388); Trkm. 1836 **Qlïč-χan** [Клыч-хан] (MIT II, 468); Trkm. 1851 **Qlïč-χan** [Клыч-хан] (MIT II, 304); Uzb. 1804 **Qlïč-inâq** [Клыч-инак / Клыч Нияз-инак], an emir (MIT II, 359, 362-366, 368, 376, 377); Uzb. 1816 **Qlïč-yüz-bašï** [Клыч-юзбаши], from the Mañγït tribe (MIT II, 397-399, 412); Uzb. 1770 **Qlïč-nāib** [Клыч-наиб], a governor (nāᶜib), from the Nüküs tribe (MIT II, 347); Trkm. 1863 **Qlïč-oγlï** [Клыч-оглы], from the Yomut tribe (MIT II, 608, 633); Trkm. 1818/19 **Qlïč-serdar** [Клыч-сердар], from the Yomut tribe (MIT II, 413, 414); Trkm. 1821 **Qolïj / Qïlïj?** [Колиджъ] (Murav'ev: Russk. Arhiv 1888, I, 253); Kzk. 19th c. **Qulïč / Qïlïč?** [Салимъ Кулычевъ] (Grod., Pril. 184). ✧ 'Sword' (Sauvaget 53), cf. Türk, Uyg., Alt., Az., Crm., Tat. *qilič* 'das Schwert, der Säbel' (Radl. II, 776), Kkalp. *qiliš* 'кылыш, меч' (KkRS), Kzk. *qïlïš* 'id.', (Radl. II, 779), Hak. *qïlïs* 'id.' (Radl. II, 779), Bashk. *qïlïs* 'сабля, меч' (BRS/Uraksin). See also **AY-QÏLÏŠ, AQ-QÏLÏČ, AL-QÏLÏČ, ALTÏN-QÏLÏŠ, ǰAN-QÏLÏČ, DURDÏ-QÏLÏČ, YAN-QÏLÏČ, YAZ-ΓÏLÏČ, QARA-QÏLÏŠ, QÏRΓAN-QÏLÏŠ, QOWRAT-QLÏŠ?, QURBAN-QÏLÏČ, OTQA-KÖNMÏŠ-QÏLÏČ, TAXTA-QLÏJ, TÏN-QÏLÏČ, URDÏ-QLÏČ.**

QÏLÏČ-ARSLAN Selj. 11th c. - 12th c. **Qïlïč-arslan** [قلج ارسلان], Izzeddïn Qïlïč-arslan ibn Suleyman ibn Qïlïč-arslan (Ibn Bïbï III, 61-73, IV, 23-28); Selj. 1092 **Qïlïč-arslan** [قلج ارسلان / Кылыч-Арслан], Seljuk ruler in Anatolia, Qïlïč-arslan I (1092-1107), Suleyman's son (Qazw. 481, 482, RaD I/2, 102, MIT I, 47); Selj. 1094 **Qïlïč-arslan** [قلج ارسلان], Suleyman's son, died in 1094 (Ibn al-Athïr, Atab.: RHCHor II/2, 18); Selj. 1106 **Qïlïč-arslan** [قليج ارسلان / Kelej 'Arslân / Кылыч-Арслан], known under the name of Melik-šah II (Malik Shah, Shah-melik) sultan (1104-1105), Ali-χan's son (Abulfar./Budge I, 239, MIT I, 47); Selj. 1157 **Qïlïč-arslan** [قلج ارسلان], Suleyman ibn Qutlamïš' son (Qalānisi 336, 343); Selj. 1171/72, 1181, 1190/91, 1192 **Qïlïč-arslan** [قلج ارسلان / Κλιτζασ / Kelej 'Arslân], Qïlïč-arslan II (1156-1192), Masᶜūd / Mesᶜud's (1116-1156) son who was the son of Qïlïč-arslan I ibn Qutlamïš (Qutlumïš) ibn Seljuk (Bondāri 225, Ibn al-Athïr, Atab.: RHCHor II/2, 291,

Abulfar./Budge I, 275, 281, 310 etc., Ibn al-Athïr: RHCHor II/1, 22-25, 68-71); Selj. 1203, 1205 **Qïlïč-arslan** [قلج ارسلان], Rukneddïn's son (Abulfar./Budge I, 360, Ibn al-Athïr/Tornb. XII, 131); Selj.? 1228/29 **Qïlïč-arslan** [قلج ارسلان], Al-Mansur Moχammed's son, known also as Silaheddïn (Ibn al-Athïr: RHCHor II/1, 179-80); Selj. 13th c. **Qïlïč-arslan** [قلج ارسلان], Izzeddïn Qïlïč-arslan ibn Keykubād (Ibn Bïbï III, 391, IV, 151, 206, 212); Selj. 14th c. **Qïlïč-arslan** [Kılıç Arslan], ruler of Şarkî Karahisar, Anatolia (Uzunçarş., Anad. 50); Turk. 1474 **Qïlïč-aslan, Qïlïč-aslan-bey** [قلج ارسلان / Kılıç Aslan (Bey)], Âli-bey's son, the ruler of Alâiye after Lûtfi-bey, maybe that's why Ašikpašazade thought him to be Lûtfi-bey's son (Āšikp. 167-169, Uzunçarş., Anad. 55, 56); *TN:* Turk. 20th c. **Qïlïč-arslan** [Kılıçaslan], a village in the province of Amasya, Turkey (TMİB 65); Turk. 20th c. **Qïlïč-arslan** [Kılıçarslan], a village in the province of Bolu, Turkey (TMİB 187). ⇨ **QÏLÏČ + ARSLAN.**

QÏLÏČ-KEM Trkm. 1804 **Qlïč-kem** [Клыч-кем], from the „orus-qošči" (Urus-quščï) clan of the Yomut tribe (MIT II, 359, 360, 363, 364, 368, 370). ⇨ **QÏLÏČ + KEM.**

QÏLÏČ-KÜČ-QARA Türk 8th c. - 9th c. **Qïlïč-küč-(qar)a** [[Kılıç] Küç Qara / qïlïč küč (qar)a] (ETY II, 66, DTS); Uyg.? 750 **Qïlïč-küč-qara** [Qïlïč Küč Qara] (Thomsen, Stein?). ✧ 'Sword-strength-powerful' (Blagova 1997, 713). ⇨ **QÏLÏČ + KÜČ + QARA.**

QÏLÏČ-QARA Chag.? 1500 **Qïlïč-qara** [Гкыльıджъ Гкара] (Šejb. LXXVIII); Chag./Uzb. 1560 **Qïlïč-qara** [Гкылыджъ Гкара], Šeybani-χan's relative (Šejb. LXXVIII). ⇨ **QÏLÏČ + QARA.**

QÏLÏČ-NÏYAZ Trkm.? 1816 **Qlïč-niyaz / Qlïč-niyaz-bay** [Клыч Нияз-бай (бий)], a biy (MIT II, 391, 404, 405, 408). ⇨ **QÏLÏČ + NÏYAZ.**

QÏLÏČČUQ Maml. 14th c. **Qïlïččuq** [Кылыччук] (Tuhfa 410). ✧ 'Little Sword'. ⇨ **QÏLÏČ** + dim. suff. *-čuq.*

QÏLÏYAN Yak. **Qïlïyan** [Кылыјан] (Pek.). ✧ 'Leaping, springing' cf. Yak. *qilïy-* 'прыгать (скакать на одной ноге, карныкать)' (Pek.).

QÏLÏQÏNAY Yak. **Qïlïqïnay** [Кылыкынаi], a smith in a tale (Pek.).

QÏLÏN Tat.(Sib.) 1654 **Qïlïn** [Кылин] (Miller, Ist. Sib. II, 540).

QÏLÏNČ Yürük 1543 **Qïlïnč** [Kılınç] (Gökb., Rum. 239, 241). ✧ I. 'Sword' cf. Turk. *qilinč* 'das Schwert, der Säbel' (Radl. II, 776); II. 'Action'? Uyg. *qilinč* 'die Handlung, Thätigkeit, Handlungsweise' (Radl. II, 775).

QÏLÏNČ-QARA Khorezm. 13th c. **Qïlïnč-qara / Qïlïč-qara?** [Hei-lin-tch'e-ha-la], killed Sängün, the son of Oň-χan, the Kereit ruler (Pelliot: JA, Ser. XI. Tome XV, 184). ⇨ **QÏLÏNČ + QARA.**

QÏLÏŠ see **QÏLÏČ**

QÏLÏŠ see **QÏLÏČ**

QÏLQ Oghuz/Trkm. 13th c. **Qïlq-bek / Qïlïq-bek?** [قيلق بيك / Кылк-бек] (Abulg./Kon. 1090).

QÏLQA Kzk. 19th c. **Qïlqa** [Кылка] (SOK 172). ✧ 'Fur-coat' cf. Kzk. *qïlqa* 'ein Pelz mit dem Fell nach aussen' (Radl. II, 780).

QÏMAČ Oghuz/Trkm. 13th c. **Qïmač** [قيماج / Кымач], Dudal-bay's son (Abulg./Kon. 1450).

QÏMAQÏ Yak. **Qïmaqï** [Кымакы], a male, who got his name because of his height (Pek.).

QÏMĀ Alt. 19th-20th c. **Qïmā** [Кымаа] (OjrRS 209).

QÏMĀS Hak. 19th c. **Qïmās** [Кымас], fem. (Katanov, Otč. 12); Hak.(Shor) 19th-20th c. **Qïmās** [Кымас] (Katanov, Otč. 11). ✧ 'Kvas (sourish sherbet)' cf. R. квасъ (Katanov).

QÏMBAT see **QÏYMAT**

QÏMCÏN Tat.(Sib.), Alt.? 1622 **Qïmcïn** [Кымцын], a prince at the Kas river (Miller, Ist. Sib. II, 274).

QÏMÏS see **QÏMÏZ**

QÏMÏZ Alt. 19th-20th c. **Qïmïs** [Кымыс], fem. (OjrRS 212); Kzk. 19th c. **Qïmïz-bay** [Кымызбай] (SOV 24); Kzk. 19th c. **Qumïs-bek** [Кумысбекъ] (SODž. 44); Tat.(Sib.) 1599 **Qumïz / Kümis?** [Кумызъ], a Siberian princess, Küčüm's daughter (AI II, 18, 20, 23). ✧ 'Koumis, kumiss (fermented mare's milk)' cf. Karakh. *qïmïz* 'кумыс' (DTS), Uyg. *qïmïs* 'der Kumyss, ein Getränk aus gesäuerter Stutenmilch' (Radl. II, 854), Kzk., Tat. *qïmïz* 'id.' (Radl. II, 854), Alt. *qïmïs* 'квашеное кобылье молоко' (OjrRS), Hak. *qumïs* 'id.' (Radl. II, 1049). See also **SAWMAL**.

QÏMÏZAQ Hak.(Kyz.) 19th-20th c. **Qïmïzaq** [Кымызак] (Katanov, Otč. 13). ⇨ **QÏMÏZ** + dim. suff. -*aq*.

QÏMMAT see **QÏYMAT**

QÏMPÏ Kzk. 19th c. **Qïmpï-bay** [Кымпыбай] (SOK 216).

QÏMZĀR Alt. 19th-20th c. **Qïmzār** [Кымзаар], fem. (OjrRS 212).

QÏNA Uyg. 12th c. - 14th c. **Qïna** [Кына] (Radl., USp. 142, DTS, EUTS).

QÏNAMAN Kzk. 19th c. **Qïnaman** [Кынаманъ] (AOP 54). ⇨ **QÏNA?** + suff. -*man*.

QÏNAČÏ Hak.(Blt.) 19th-20th c. **Qïnāčï** [Кыначы] (Proben IX, 366). ✧ 'Scabbard, sheath' cf. Hak. PN *Xïnāčï* < *Xïnān* (Butanaev). ⇨ **QÏNĀN**.

QÏNĀN Oghuz/Trkm. 13th c. **Qïnān** [قينان / Кинан], Anuš's son (Abulg./Kon. 80); Hak.(Blt.) 19th-20th c. **Qïnān** [Кынан] (Proben IX, 366). ✧ 'Scabbard, sheath' cf. Hak. PN *Xïnān* (Butanaev). ⇨ **QÏNĀČÏ**.

QÏNČAQ Kzk. 19th c. **Qïnčaq-pay / Qïpčaq-pay?** [Кынчакпай (Кыпчакпай?)] (SOK 230).

QÏNDÏ Kzk. 19th c. **Qïndï-bay** [Кындыбай] (SOK 210).

QÏNÏQ Oghuz/Trkm. 13th c. **Qïnïq** [قنق / Кынык], Teñiz-χan's son (Abulg./Kon. 520, 565, 615); Trkm. 1719 **Qïnïq** [قنق / Kînîk] (Refik, Anad. 156); Oghuz/Trkm. 13th c. **Qïnïq-bay** [قنق باى / Кынык-бай] (Abulg./Kon. 1450); *TN:* Selj.? 12th c. **Qïnïq** [قنق], a small mosque (Ibn Šaddād, Alep 78); Turk. 20th c. **Qïnïq** [Kınık], a village in the province of Ankara (TMİB 82). ✧ 'Well; eager, greedy; wish'? cf. Turk. dial. *kınık* 'memba, kaynak; tamahkâr, aç gözlü; istek, arzu' (DS).

QÏNÏM Kzk. 19th c. **Qïnïm-bay** [Кынмбай] (AOP 42); Kzk. 19th c. **Qïnïm-qul** [Кынымкулъ Халматовъ] (SKSO VIII, 225). ✧ 'My scabbard' cf. Alt., Hak., Kzk., Tat. etc. *qïn* 'die Scheide' (Radl. II, 725). + poss. suff. -*ïm*.

QÏNÏSUN Uyg. 12th c. - 14th c. **Qïnïsun** [Кынısun] (Radl., USp. 142, DTS, EUTS).

QÏNÏŠ Kzk. 19th c. **Qïnïš-bek** [Кынышбекъ] (Lomakin 39).

QÏNNÏYATA Yak. **Qïnnïyata** [Кынныјата] (Pek.).

QÏNSUN Uyg. 12th c. - 14th c. **Qïnsun** [qïnsun] (DTS). ✧ 'May he struggle / Let him try' (Blagova 1997, 716), cf. Uyg. *qïn-maq* 'стермление, усердие, усилие' (DTS) + suff. -*sïn*.

QÏÑDAM Uyg. 12th c. - 14th c. **Qïñdam** [Qïngdam / Kıngdam] (Radl., USp. 130-131, DTS, EUTS).

QÏÑRUL Uyg. 12th c. - 14th c. **Qïñrul** [qïñrul / Kıngrul] (DTS, EUTS). See also **YEGÄN-QÏÑRUL**.

QÏPČAQ Kzk. 19th c. **Xïpčaq-bay** [Хипчакбай] (SOK 8); Tat.(Bar.) **Qïpcaq-pï** [Kyptschak Pi / Кыпцак Пі], the eldest of the 12 chieftains (Proben IV, 42); Uyg. 12th c. - 14th c. **Qïpčaq** (Radl., USp. 100-101); Oghuz/Trkm. 13th c. **Qïpčaq** [قبجاق / Кыпчак] (Abulg./Kon. 285-295, 565); Karakh. **Qïpčaq** [Kıpçak] (MK/Atalay 844, EUTS, DTS); Selj. 1139/40 **Qïpčaq** [قبجاق بن ارسلان شاه / بن الب ارسلان شهرزور], Alp-arslan's (Arslan-šah's) son (Abulfidā III, 482-83, Ibn al-Athīr: RHCHor I, 25, 437); Kzk. 19th c. **Qïpčaq** [Кыпчакъ] (AOO 78); Kzk. 19th c. **Qïpčaq** [Кипчакъ] (AOAtb. 18); Kzk. 19th c. **Qïpčaq** [Кипчакъ] (SODž. 76); Kzk. 19th c. **Qïpčaq** [Кыпчакъ] (SODž. 50); Kzk. 19th c. **Qïpčaq** [Кыпчакъ] (AOO 30); Kzk. 19th c. **Qïpčaq** [Кипчакъ] (SOK 254); Selj. 1140 **Qïpčaq / Qïfčaq** [قنجاق بن ارسلان تاش التركمانى], son of the Türkmen Arslan-taš (?), Temirek's brother (Ibn al-Athīr/Tornb. XI, 50); Selj. 12th c. **Qïpčaq / Qïfčaq** [قنجاق], governor of Azerbaidjan (Rāwandī 356, 362); Kzk. 19th c. **Qïpčaq-bay** [Кипчакбай] (Grod., Pril. 74); Kzk. 19th c. **Qïpčaq-bay** [Кыпчакбай] (Grod., Pril. 19); Kzk. 19th c. **Qïpčaq-bay** [Кыпчакпай] (SODž. 78); Kzk.? 19th c. **Qïpčaq-bay** [Кыпчакпай Айтыковъ] (Konšin, Oč. 131); Uzb. 19th c. **Qïpčaq-bay** [Кипчакбай Саитбаевъ] (SKSO III, 168);

Oghuz/Trkm. **Qïpčaq-beg** [Kıpçak Beg], in the legend of origin of the Oghuz it is Uluγ Orḍu-beg's name which was given to him by Oγuz-qaγan because he cut a passage through a forest (Oğuz K. Dest. 23); Kzk. 19th c.? **Qïpsaq** [Arγïn Küpsaq] (Atyns. 85); Kzk. 19th c. **Qïpšaq** [Kïpšak] (Ljutš 116); Kzk. 19th c. **Qïpšaq-bay** [Кипшакбаевъ] (AOO 26); Kzk. 19th c. **Qïpšaq-bay** [Кыпшакбай] (AOK 130); *EN:* Tat.(Lit.) 1594 **Qïpčaq** [Кыпчакъ Карачи], clan of the prince (Lit. Tat. 230); Nog. 20th c. **Qupšaq** [Къупшакъ], an Aq-noγay clan (Bask., Nog. 133); *TN:* Kzk. **Qïpčaq-bay** [Кипчак-бай], a place (Karta JAR XI); Uzb. 1828 **Qïpčaq-bay** [Кипчакъ-бай] (Moskal'cev 38). ✧ 'Kipchak' (Ethnonym); cf. Németh, HMK 36. See also **YÜRÜK-QÏPČAQ.**

QÏPČAQ-BAŠÏ Uzb. 18th c. **Qïpčaq-bašï** [Kiptchak-Bachi], commandant of a detachment in Ferghana (Nalivkin-Dozon 76). ✧ 'The head of the Kipchak'. ⇨ **QÏPČAQ + BAŠ + suff. -ï.**

QÏPPÏYAN Yak. **Qïppïyan** [Кыппыйан] (Pek.).

QÏPRÏDU Uyg. 12th c. - 14th c. **Qïprïdu** [qïprïdu / Kıprıdı] (DTS, EUTS).

QÏPŠAQ see QÏPČAQ

QÏR Kzk. 19th c. **Qïr-bay** [Кырбай] (SOV 70); Kzk. 19th c. **Qïr-pay** [Кырпай] (SOV 64). ✧ I. 'Field on a mountain, on the hills' (KzRS), cf. Turk. *qïr* 'die Steppe, Ebene', (Kzk.) 'die bergige Steppe zwischen Irtisch und Balkasch' (Radl. II, 732-33); II. 'Club, bludgeon' cf. Kzk. *qïr* 'die Keule' (Radl. II, 734); III. 'Grey, bay' cf. Karakh. *qïr* 'караковый' (DTS), Hak., Turk. *qïr* 'grau' (Radl. II, 734). See also **ČAPTAR, TORUQ.**

QÏR-BAS Kzk. 19th c. **Qïr-bas** [Кырбасъ] (SOK 86, 126, 140); Kzk. 19th c. **Qïr-bas** [Кырбасъ] (SOV 42, 96). ✧ 'Grey head'. ⇨ **QÏR + BAŠ.**

QÏR-ČÄČÄK see QÏR-ČEČÄK

QÏR-ČEČÄK Uyg. **Qïr-čäčäk** [Kır Çäçäk] (EUTS); Uyg. 12th c. - 14th c. **Qïr-čäčäk** (Radl., USp. 93); Uyg. 12th c. - 14th c. **Qïr-čečäk** [qïr čečäk], fem. (DTS). ✧ 'Grey flower, wild flower'. ⇨ **QÏR + ČEČÄK.**

QÏR-ÖLEÑ Shor 19th-20th c. **Qïr-öleñ** [Qyr Öleñ], a folklore hero (Dyrenkova 154, 386). ✧ 'Grey grass'. ⇨ **QÏR + ÖLEN.**

QÏRA Uyg. **Qïra** [Kıra] (EUTS). See also **BOYU-QÏRA.**

QÏRA-BÏRJAL Yak. **Qïra-bïrjal-toyon** [Кыра бырцал тојон], epithet of the spirit of the fire (Pek.). ✧ 'With white beard' (Pek.). ⇨ **QÏRA?**

QÏRAČÏ Alt. 19th-20th c. **Qïračï** [Кырачы] (OjrRS 209). ✧ 'Ploughman, farmer' (OjrRS).

QÏRAMŠA see QURAMŠA

QÏRAN Oghuz 1183 **Qïran** [Kyran], served under Tekiš (Töküš) the Khorezmshah (Belleten VII (1940), 204); *TN:* Turk. 20th c. **Qïran-šeyh / Qïran-šïh** [Kıranşeyh

(Kıranşıh)], a village in the province of Manisa, Turkey (TMİB 622). ✧ 'Breaking' cf. Turk. *kır-* 'to break' (TED). See also **AT-QÏRAN, QAPU-QÏRAN.**

QÏRAP Alt. 19th-20th c. **Qïrap** [Кырап], fem. (OjrRS 212).

QÏRÄÑ Hak.(Kacha) 19th-20th c. **Qïräñ** [Кыраң] (Proben IX, 554). ✧ 'Headland, rock, cliff' cf. Hak. *qïrañ* 'ein Vorstehender Bergvorsprung, das Kap' (Radl. II, 737).

QÏRBÏTAN Yak. **Qïrbïtan** [Чӧмчӧрӱкän Кырбытан], a legendary smith (Pek.). ✧ 'Hollowing; rummaging' cf. Yak. *qïrbïtä-* 'ковырять, скоблить' (Pek.).

QÏRČÏYAN Alt. 19th c. **Qïrčïyan-χan** [Кырчыган-хан] (Verb., In. 141).

QÏRJANAQ Hak.(Koyb.) 19th-20th c. **Qïrjanaq** [Кырцанак] (Katanov, Otč. 13). ✧ 'Fool, quarrelsome' cf. Hak. *qïrčän* 'zänkisch' (Radl. II, 758). + dim. suff. -aq.

QÏRDAN Kzk. 19th c. **Qïrdan** [Кырданъ] (Pam. kn. Turg. 61).

QÏRDASÏN Kzk. 19th c. **Qïrdasïn** [Кырдасынъ] (AOO 50).

QÏRΓA Kzk. 19th c. **Qïrγa-bek** [Кыргабекъ] (SOV 84); Kzk. 19th c. **Qïrγa-bek? / Qïrγabaq?** [Кыргабакъ / Кыргобакъ] (SOK 204).

QÏRΓAN-QÏLÏŠ Shor 19th-20th c. **Qïrγan-qïlïš** [Qyrγan Qylyš], Aq-qan's son (Dyrenkova 212). ✧ 'Broken sword' cf. Uyg., Alt., Hak., Kzk., Tat., Turk. etc. *qïr-* 'zerbrechen, vernichten, ab schlachten etc.' (Radl. II, 734-35). ⇨ **QÏLÏČ.**

QÏRΓÏČÏ Kzk. 19th c. **Qïrγïčï** [Кыргычи] (SODž. 152).

QÏRΓÏL Kirg. **Qïrγïl** [Кыргыл] (Jud. 435, 923); Kirg. **Qïrγïl** [Кырҕыл (Кырҕылды)], one of Manas' comrades-in-arms (Proben V, 39 /40-41/, 151 /152/).

QÏRΓÏN-ČAL Kirg. **Qïrγïn-čal** [Kyrgyn Tschal / Кырҕын Чал] (Proben V, 21 /22/). ✧ 'Slaughter, massacre - old man/gaffer' cf. Kzk. *qïrγïn* 'das Niedermetzeln, die Ausrottung' (Radl. II, 750-751). ⇨ **ČAL.**

QÏRΓÏZ Bashk. 1754 **Qïrγïs** [Киргис Шурановъ] (MIB IV/1, 83); Türk 568 **Qïrγïz** [Χερχίς], a girl whom the Turkic khagan presented to the Byzantine envoy (Byz. Turc. 344); Oghuz/Trkm. 13th c. **Qïrγïz** [قيرغـز / Кыргыз] (Abulg./Kon. 530); Kzk.? **Qïrγïz** [Киргызбай], a forefather of a Qara-qïrγïz clan (ZIRGO V, 140); Kzk. 19th c. **Qïrγïz** [Берди Назаръ Киргизовъ] (SKSO III, 10); Kzk. **Qïrγïz-ata** [Кыргызата], protector-spirit of all Kirghiz folk (Jud. 77); Kzk. **Qïrγïz-bay** [Кыргызбай] (Protok. Turk. IV, 51); Kzk. 19th c. **Qïrγïz-bay** [Кыргызбай] (SODž. 116); Kzk. 19th c. **Qïrγïz-bay** [Кыргызбай] (SODž. 26); Kzk. 19th c. **Qïrγïz-bay** [Киргизбай] (SODž.

132); Kzk. 19th c. **Qïrγïz-bay** [Киргызбай] (AOP 10); Kzk. 19th c. **Qïrγïz-bay** [Киргизбай] (AOK 42); Kzk. 19th c. **Qïrγïz-bay** [Кыргызбай] (AOAtb. 58); Kzk. 19th c. **Qïrγïz-pay** [Кыргызпай] (SOV 46); Uyg. 13th-14th c. **Qïrqïz-täñrim** [Qïrqïz Tängrim], fem. (Zieme, Mat. II, 93); Kirg. 19th c. **Qïrqïz** [Кыркызъ] (Potanin II, 150); *EN:* Kzk. 18th c. - 19th c. **Qïrγïz-bay** [Кыргызбай], a clan (Tynyšp. 68); *TN:* Kzk. **Qïrγïz** [Кыргыз], a settlement (Kojčubaev 162). ✧ 'Kirghiz' (Ethnonym) cf. Alt., Hak. *Qïrγïs* 'der Kirgise (jetzt werden so von den Altajern und Teleuten die Kasak-Kirgisen genannt; in alten Liedern werden sie überall als Kasak bezeichnet)' (Radl. II, 751). Cf. also Žaparov-Konkobaev 1984, 119-124.

QÏRÏQ 1694 **Qïrïq** [Кирикъ] (PSZRI III, 181); Oghuz 13th c. **Qïrïq / Qïzïq?** [Кырык / Кызык], Yulduz-χan's son (RaD I/1, 76, Abulg./Kon. 515, 550, 600); Kzk. 19th c. **Qïrïq-pay** [Кырыкпай] (AOK 66). ✧ 'Broken' cf. Kirg. *qïrïq* 'zerschlagen, zerbrochen' (Radl. II, 740).

QÏRÏQ-QÏNÏQ see **QÏRQ-QONUQ**

QÏRÏL Kzk. 1747 **Qïrïl-bay / Kiril-bay?** [Кирилбай] (Nepljuev 701).

QÏRÏLMAZ Trkm. 1610 **Qïrïlmaz** [قيريلماز], from Syria (Refik, Anad. 62). ✧ 'He won't break/die (he is hard, strong)' cf. Kuman, Alt., Crm., Hak., Kzk., Turk. *qïrïl-* 'zerbrochen werden, getödtet, vernichtet werden' (Radl. II, 742, 743).

QÏRÏM Karch. 20th c. **Qïrïm** (Pröhle, Kar. 118); Bashk. 1779 **Qïrïm** [Улемай Кырымов] (MIB V, 94); Tat. 1670 **Qrïm** [Чювашенинъ Крымко Ивашковъ] (Poliv.-Kras. 51); Maml. 1460 **Qrïm-χoǰa / Qïrïm-χoǰa** (Ibn Taghrïb., VII, 639). ✧ The Crimea (placename) (Pröhle, ibid.), cf. Kzk. *qïrïm* 'uzak diyar' [distant land!] (KzTS). Sattarov mistakenly connects the Tatar *Qïrïm* with *Qorum* (see).

QÏRÏRQUS Uyg. 12th c. - 14th c. **Qïrïrqus** [qïrïrqus] (DTS); Uyg. 12th c. - 14th c. **Qïrïrquz** (Radl., USp. 42).

QÏRÏRQUZ see **QÏRÏRQUS**

QÏRÏS Kzk. 19th c. **Qïrïs-bay** [Кырысбай] (AOA 98). ✧ 'Defective (unsound); fighting, quarrelling; angry' cf. Alt.(Tel.) *qïrïs* 'mangelhaft', (Hak.) 'der Zank, Streit, Kampf' (Radl. II, 744).

QÏRÏŠDÏRÏ Uyg. 12th c. - 14th c. **Qïrïšdïrï** [qïrïšdïrï] (DTS).

QÏRĪNYA Yak. **Qïrīnya** [Кырынja] (Pek.). ✧ Grinya (R.), dim. of R. *Grigoriy* (Pek.).

QÏRQ NUyg. 19th c. **Qïrq / Qïrïq** [قرق / قيريغ / Kirik, Kirk] (Le Coq, Namenl. 106); Kzk. 19th c. **Qïrq-bay** [Кыркбай] (SOK 160); Kzk. 19th c. **Qïrq-bay** [Кыркбай] (AOK 106); Kkalp. 20th c. **Qïrq-bay** [Қыркбай] (KkRS 775); Trkm. 19th c. **Qïrq-ǰigit** [Джайнаръ Кирк джигитовъ] (SKSO III, 178);

Trkm. 19th c. **Qïrq-ǰigit?** [Киркджигитовъ] (SKSO III, 178); Kzk. 19th c. **Qïrq-pay** [Кыркпай] (SOV 108, 156); Kzk. 19th c. **Qïrq-pay** [Кыркпай] (SODž. 30, 32, 66); Kzk. 19th c. **Qïrq-pay** [Кыркпай] (SOK 88); Kkalp. 20th c. **Qïrq-pay** [Қыркъпай] (Bask., Kkalp. 44). ✧ 'Forty' cf. Türk, Uyg., Hak., Tat., Turk. etc. *qïrq* 'vierzig' (Radl. II, 746), see also Rásonyi, Nombre 45-71.

QÏRQ-BEŠ Chag. **Qïrq-beš** [Qyrqbeš Bahram Xodža] (Šejb. LIV). ⇨ **QÏRQ + BEŠ.**

QÏRQ-QONUQ Oghuz/Trkm. **Qïrq-qonuq** [Kırk Kınık, Qïrq Qïnuq, Qïrïq Qïnïq (Qïnuq) / Кырк-Конук], Qara Čükür's (Čögür's) son (DQorq/Rossi 184, DQorq. 66, 214, 237, 241). ⇨ **QÏRQ + QONUQ.**

QÏRQ-MULTUQ Kzk. 19th c. **Qarq-multuq** (<Qïrq-multuq) [Каркмултукъ] (ZOOO 1870, 234); Kzk. **Qïrq-multuq** [Каркмултукъ] (ZOOO 1870, 234). ⇨ **QÏRQ + MÏLTÏQ.**

QÏRQAY Tat. 1619 **Qïrqay** [قرکای / Кыркай], fem. (Jusupov 72).

QÏRQAM Kzk. 19th c. **Qïrqam-bay** (<Qïrqan-bay?) [Кыркамбай] (SOV 126).

QÏRQAR Uzb. 20th c. **Qïrqar** [Қиркар] (Begmatov 1984, 207). ✧ 'He who will cut/shear' cf. Uzb. *qïrq-* 'резать, стричь' (UzbRS).

QÏRQÏ Kkalp. 1722 **Qïrqï** [Кирки Мергеневъ] (PSZRI VI, 779, MIKk. 172).

QÏRQÏM Kzk. 19th c. **Qïrqïm-bay** (<Qïrqïn-bay) [Кыркымбай], personal name preserved in the name of a field (AOP 98).

QÏRQÏZ see **QÏRĞÏZ**

QÏRQU Uyg. **Qïrqu** [Kırku] (EUTS). See also **BEGÜ-TUTUQ-QÏRQU.**

QÏRQUDU Uyg. 12th c. - 14th c. **Qïrqudu** [Kırkudu] (Radl., USp. 5, DTS, EUTS).

QÏRQUT Oghuz/Trkm. 13th c. **Qïrqut / Qïrqut-bek** [قـرقوت / قيرقوت بيك / Кыркут / Кыркут-бек], from the province (il) of Qayï (Abulg./Kon. 1055, 1060, 1070-1080).

QÏRMA Tat.(Sib.)? 1654 **Qïrma / Kïrmä?** [Кирма], prince Qoyan's son (Miller, Ist. Sib. II, 540).

QÏRMAY Bashk. 1735 **Qïrmay** [Сюлейманъ Кырмаевъ], a tarχan (Vel.-Zern., Bašk. 23).

QÏRMAQ Alt. 19th-20th c. **Qïrmaq** [Кырмак], fem. (OjrRS 212). ✧ 'Teasing, quarrelling; teaser, fussy' (OjrRS 212), cf. Alt. *qïr-* 'скоблить; уничтожать, истреблять' (OjrRS) + suff. *-maq.*

QÏRMANDAY Kzk. 19th c. **Qïrmanday** [Кырмандай] (AOP 22).

QÏRMÏŠ Maml. 14th c. **Qïrmïš** [Qirmiš] (Sauvaget 53). ✧ 'Broke; he has broken (it)' (Sauvaget 53), cf. Uyg., Alt., Hak., Kzk., Tat., Turk. etc. *qïr-* 'zerbrechen, vernichten, ab schlachten etc.' (Radl. II, 734-35).

QÏRMÏZÏ Kkalp. 20th c. **Qïrmïzï** [Қырмызы], fem.

(KkRS 778). ✦ 'Red' cf. Kuman, Kzk., Turk. *qïrmïzi* 'rot, scharlachroth' (Radl. II, 764).

QÏRNA Karg. **Qïrna** [Кырна] (Katanov, Otč. 8). ✦ 'Leather coat' cf. Shor *qïrna* 'der Ledermantel' (Radl. II, 752).

QÏRPÏČAQ Bashk. 1632 **Qïrpïčaq** [Качанако Кырпычаковъ] (Vel.-Zern., Bašk. 39).

QÏRSAĴAQ Hak.(Kyz.) 19th-20th c. **Qïrsaĵaq** [Кырсацак] (Katanov, Otč. 13). ✦ 'Little fox' cf. Alt.(Tel.), Kirg. *qïrsa* 'der Fuchs' (Radl. II, 759). + dim. suff. *-jaq*.

QÏRSAN Bashk. 1735 **Qïrsan** [Кирсанъ Чирикеевъ] (Vel.-Zern., Bašk. 13).

QÏRTAS-ÜČÜGÄY Yak. **Qïrtas-üčügäy** [Кыртас Ӱчӱгäi], sister of the folklore hero Xara Qïrčït (Pek.). ✦ 'Shining, sparkling?' cf. Yak. *qïrtas* 'блестящий' (Pek.). ⇨ **ÜČÜGÄY?**

QÏRTÏ Selj. 1140 **Qïrtï?** [قرتي بن طغان ارسلان], Toɣan-arslan's son (Qalānisi 208, 367).

QÏRUDIS Uyg. **Qïrudis** [Кырудіs] (EUTS).

QÏRŽALÏɣ Karg. **Qïržalïɣ** [Кыржалыгъ] (Katanov: ZIRGOÊtn. XVII vyp. III, 146).

QÏS see QÏZ

QÏSAQ Uyg. 12th c. - 14th c. **Qïsaq** [Кısak] (Radl., USp. 124, DTS, EUTS).

QÏSÏQ Kzk. 19th c. **Qïsïq** [Кысыковъ] (AOK 78); Kzk. 19th c. **Qïsïq** [Утемисъ Кысыковъ] (Grod., Pril. 134). ✦ 'Stubby' cf. Kzk. *qïsïq* 'приплюснутый' (KzRS).

QÏSÏM Kzk. 19th c. **Qïsïm** [Кысымъ] (AOA 98); Kzk. 19th c. **Qïsïm-bek** [Кысымбекъ] (SOK 290). ✦ 'Opressing, slight; misfortune' cf. Kzk. *qïsïm* 'die Beeinträchtigung, Beleidigung, das Unglück' (Radl. II, 807).

QÏSÏMLER Turk. 19th c. **Qïsïmlerin-oɣlu** [Kysymlerin oɣlu], Zeybek family name (Kúnos 1891, 119).

QÏSÏRĴA-YEÑÄ see QASÏRČA-NÏKE

QÏSQA Maml. 14th c. **Qïsqa** [قِصَا] (Sauvaget 53). ✦ 'Short; (animal) having short tail, curt' (Sauvaget 53), cf. Uyg., Kuman, Alt., Kirg., Kzk., Tat. etc. *qïsqa* 'kurz' (Radl. II, 807).

QÏSQA-QALAP Alt.(Leb., Tel.) **Qïsqa-qalap** [Кыска-Калап], Uzun-qalap's brother (Radl. I, 1307). ⇨ **QÏSQA.**

QÏSQA-QARA Alt. **Qïsqa-qara** [Кыска-Кара] (Nikiforov 144). ⇨ **QÏSQA + QARA.**

QÏSQA-QÏLAN Alt. 19th c. **Qïsqa-qïlan** [Кыска-Кылан], Uzun-qïlan's brother (Verb., In. 151). ✦ 'Short hair(ed), with short mane'. ⇨ **QÏSQA + QÏLAÑ.**

QÏSQAĴAQ Hak.? 19th-20th c. **Qïsqaĵaq** [Кыскацак], fem. (Katanov, Otč. 10). ✦ 'Little (dear) short (child)'. ⇨ **QÏSQA** + dim. suff. *-jaq*.

QÏSQÏYDAN Yak. **Qïsqïydan-quo** [Кыскыйдан-куо],

fem. (Pek.).

QÏSLAU Tat.(Sib.) 1630 **Qïslau** [Kyslau], a Chat (čatskij) prince (Radl., Aus Sib. I, 181). ✦ 'Winter pasture'? ⇨ **QÏSTAW?**

QÏSPÏN Karg. **Qïspïn** [Кыспін] (Katanov, Otč. 9). ✦ 'Not embarrassed / embarrassing' (Katanov).

QÏSRAWU Kzk. 1820 **Qïsrawu-batïr-χan** [Кысраву-батыръ-ханъ], sultan of the Tabuqlï tribe (Sib. Vest. IX, 110).

QÏSTAY Alt. **Qïstay-mergen** [Кыстай-Мергенъ], a hero in a tale (Nikiforov 201); Alt.(Tuba) 19th c. **Qïstay-mergen** [Кыстай-мергенъ], a hero in a tale (Potanin IV, 570); Tuv. 19th c. **Qïstay-mergen** [Кыстай-мергенъ], a hero in a tale (Potanin IV, 570). ⇨ **QÏZ?** + suff. *-tay*.

QÏSTAN Alt. 19th-20th c. **Qïstan** [Кыстан], fem. (OjrRS 212). ✦ 'Embroidery, stitching on a clothes' cf. Shor *qïstan* 'die Stickerei auf der Kleidung' (Radl. II, 814).

QÏSTANČÏ Alt. 19th-20th c. **Qïstančï** [Кыстанчы], fem. (OjrRS 212). ✦ 'Maker or seller of embroidery'. ⇨ **QÏSTĀNČA?, QÏSTAN** + suff. *-čï.*

QÏSTANČÏQ Alt. 19th-20th c. **Qïstančïq** [Кыстанчык], fem. (OjrRS 212). ✦ 'Littlre (nice) embroidery'. ⇨ **QÏSTAN** + dim. suff. *-čïq.*

QÏSTAR Hak. 19th c. **Qïstar** [Кыстар], fem. (Katanov, Otč. 12); Hak.(Shor) 19th-20th c. **Qïstar** [Кыстар], fem. (Katanov, Otč. 11); Hak.(Sag.) 19th-20th c. **Qïstār** [Кыстар], fem. (Proben IX, 265). ✦ 'Girl' (Katanov). ⇨ **QÏZ.**

QÏSTAU see QÏSTAW

QÏSTAW Kzk. 19th c. **Qïstau-bay** [Кыстаубай] (Potanin II, 3); Kzk. 19th c. **Qïstaw** [Киставбай] (Grod., Pril. 186); Kzk. 19th c. **Qïstaw** [Киставъ] (Grod., Pril. 190); Kzk. 19th c. **Qïstaw-bay** [Галбиръ Киставбаевъ] (Grod., Pril. 171). ✦ 'Winter pasture' cf. Kzk. *qïstau* 'das Winterquartier, die Stelle, wo man überwintert' (Radl. II, 814).

QÏSTĀNČA Karg. **Qïstānča** [Кыстанча], fem. (Katanov, Otč. 8). ✦ 'Littlre (nice) embroidery'. ⇨ **QÏSTAN** + dim. suff.? *-ča.*

QÏSTĀR see QÏSTAR

QÏŠ-TUɣAN Selj. 12th c. **Qïš-tuɣan** [قشطغان], his name was preserved in the name of a small mosque (Ibn Šaddād, Alep 86). ✦ 'Born in winter' cf. in most Turkic languages *qïš* 'der Winter' (Radl. II, 834). ⇨ **TUɣAN I.**

QÏŠ-TURA Kuman 1347 **Qïš-tura** [Kystre filium Japza], Taš-tura's brother, a Kuman of Hungary (Gyárfás III, 484). ✦ 'Winter-house' (Rásonyi), cf. Kuman *qïš* 'Winter' (CC), cf. also Rásonyi, NTK 106, Rásonyi, KÖA 112, Anthr. 142. ⇨ **TURA.** See also **TAŠ-TURA.**

QÏŠAN Alt. 19th-20th c. **Qïšan** [Кышан], fem. (OjrRS

212). ❖ 'Stubborn'? cf. Tat.(Tob.) *qišañ* 'eigensinnig' (Radl. II, 835).

QÏŠÏM Tat.?, Bashk.? 1675 **Qïšim-bay?** / **Qošim-bay?** / **Qašim-bay?** [Кышимбайко, Кошымбайко, Кашымбайко] (Kungursk. akty 25).

QÏŠÏN Hak. 19th-20th c. **Qïšïn-araχ** [Кышынарахъ], fem. (Titov 120). ❖ 'Clean, pure silver' (Titov). ⇨ **ARÏΓ**.

QÏŠLAT Kzk. 19th c. **Qïšlat-bay** [Борибай Кишлатбаевъ] (Grod., Pril. 60); Kzk. 19th c. **Qïšlat-bay** [Нурманъ Кишлатбаевъ] (Grod., Pril. 60).

QÏŠLÏQ Chag. 15th c. **Qïšlïq** [قىشلىق / Гкышлыкъ] (Šejb. LVIII). ❖ 'Winter; born in winter' cf. Tat., Turk. *qišlïq* 'die Winterzeit' (Radl. II, 838).

QÏŠLU Kzk.? 19th c. **Qïšlu-bay** [Ильбеги Кишлубаевъ] (Grod., Pril. 192); Kzk.? 19th c. **Qïšlu-bay** [Нурманъ Кишлубаевъ] (Grod., Pril. 192).

QÏTA Hak. 19th-20th c. **Qta / Qïta?** [Кта], fem. (HRS 353).

QÏTAY Khorezm./Chag. 1372 **Xïtay-behadur** [Хитай-бехадур] (MIT I, 516, 517); Oghuz 1156 **Xïtay-χan** [Хитай-хан], son of the Khorezmshah Atsïz (1128-1156), governor of Khorezm (MIT I, 444); Uyg. **Qïtay** [Kïtay] (EUTS); Bashk. 1750 **Qïtay** [Смаил Китаев] (MIB III, 472); Kzk. 19th c. **Qïtay** [Кытай] (AOAtb. 38); Yak. **Qïtay** [Кытаi] (Pek.); Bashk. 1698 **Qïtay?** / **Kitey?** [Китейко Манзигитовъ] (Kungursk. akty 267); Yak. **Qïtay-baχsï** [Кыдаи Бахсы / Кытаи Баксы тойон], an evil spirit, chief of one of the eight clans of the underworld gods, he is believed to be the protector of the smiths; name of a legendary smith (cf. Küdäy Baχsïtay üstar), folkl. (Pek.); Uyg. 12th c. - 14th c. **Qïtay-yalawač** (Radl., USp. 207, 249); Uyg. 13th-14th c. **Qïtay-täñrim** [Qïtay [Tn]gri[m]], fem. (Zieme, Mat. III, 280). ❖ 'China, Chinese' (Ethnonym), cf. Türk., Uyg., Tat. *Qïtay* 'China, chinesisch' (Radl. II, 786). See also **QUDUΓČÏ-ESÄN-QÏTAY**.

QÏTAY-BÖRT Uyg. 12th c. - 14th c. **Qïtay-bört** [qïtaj bört] (DTS); Uyg. 13th-14th c. **Qïtay-bört-ïnal** [Qïtay Bört Inal] (Zieme, Mat. III, 272 (after Tuguševa)); Uyg. 12th c. - 14th c. **Qïtay-bürt** [Qïtai-Bürt] (Radl., USp. 44). ❖ 'Chinese-touch/feel(?)' (Blagova 1997, 709). ⇨ **QÏTAY + BÖRT**.

QÏTAY-BUΓA see **QÏTAY-BUQA**

QÏTAY-BUQA Uyg. 12th c. - 14th c. **Qïtay-buγa** [qïtaj buγa] (DTS); Uyg. 12th c. - 14th c. **Qïtay-buqa** (Radl., USp. 48). ❖ 'Kitay/Chinese-bull' (Blagova 1997, 709). ⇨ **QÏTAY + BUQA**.

QÏTAY-BÜRT see **QÏTAY-BÖRT**

QÏTAY-QARA Uyg. 12th c. - 14th c. **Qïtay-qara** (Radl., USp. 211, 253); Uyg. 12th c. - 14th c. **Qïtay-qara** [Qïtai Qara] (Radl., USp. 211, 253). ⇨ **QÏTAY + QARA**.

QÏTARBA Yak. **Qïtarba** [Кытарба] (Pek.). ❖ 'Don't mix it up'? cf. Yak. *qïtar-* 'смешивать, соединить кого или что с кем или чем' (Рек.).

QÏTARÏ Hak. 19th-20th c. **Qïtarï** [Кытары], fem. (HRS 353).

QÏTARÏN Yak. **Qïtarïn** [Кытарын] (Рек.).

QÏTAT Yak. **Qïtat / Qïtat-baχsïnay** [Кытат, Кытат Бахсынаi] (Рек.). ❖ I. 'China, Chinese' cf. Alt.(Tel.) *Qïdat* 'China, chinesisch' (Radl. II, 790); II. 'Cotton'? cf. Tat. *qïtat* 'Baumwollengewebe' (Radl. II, 787). ⇨ **QÏTAY**.

QÏTČÏ Tuv. 19th c. **Qïtčï-qam** [Кытчы кам], a shaman (Proben IX, 198).

QÏTΓAQ Kzk. 19th c. **Qïtγaq-pay** / **Qïtqaq-pay** [Кытгакпай] (SOV 62).

QÏTÏ Kzk. 19th c. **Qïtï-bay** [Кытыбай] (AOP 82).

QÏTÏ-QARA Uyg. 12th c. - 14th c. **Qïtï-qara** [qïtï qara] (DTS). ⇨ **? + QARA**.

QÏTÏM Kzk. 19th c. **Qïtïm** [Кытымъ] (AOP 22).

QÏTÏR Alt. 19th-20th c. **Qïtïr** [Кытыр], fem. (OjrRS 212); Kzk. 19th c. **Qïtïr-bay** [Кытырбай] (SOK 154). ❖ 'Rough, rude' cf. Tat. *qïtïr* 'die Unebenheit, Rauheit der Oberfläche' (Radl. II, 788).

QÏTQÏLÏQ Karg. **Qïtqïlïq** [Кыткылыкъ] (Katanov: ZIRGOÊtn. XVII vyp. III, 214); Karg. **Qïtqïlïq** [Кыткылык] (Proben IX, 660).

QÏTQÏLÏQ see **QÏTQÏLÏQ**

QÏTLÏ Kzk. 19th c. **Qïtlï-bay** [Кытлибай] (SOK 288).

QÏTUNAY Tat. 1647 **Qïtunay?** [Китунайко Кызылбаев] (Miller, Ist. Sib. II, 523).

QÏWÏLJÏM Turk. 19th c. **QïwïlJïm-oγlu** [Kyvylǰym oγlu], a Zeybek (Kúnos 1891, 119). ❖ 'Spark' cf. Turk. *kıvılcım* 'id.' (TED).

QÏZ Uyg. Bl[?]-qïz [Bl??? Qïz], fem. (Zieme, Mat. I, 75); Hak. 19th-20th c. **Xïs-pala** [Хыс-Пала], fem. (HRS 356); Alt. 19th-20th c. **Qïs** [Кыс], fem. (OjrRS 212); Alt. **Qïs-mergen** [Кысъ-Мергенъ] (Nikiforov 202); Alt. 19th-20th c. **Qïs-pala** [Кыспала], fem. (OjrRS 212); Karg. **Qïz** [Кыс], fem. (Katanov, Otč. 9); Uyg. 1339 **Qïz-χatun** [Kiz Chatun], fem. (Chwol., Syr.-nest. (NF) 33); Selj.? **Qïz-melik** [قـز مَلِك], ruler (malike?) of Gürjistan (?) (Juwaynī I, 212, Juwaynī II, 160, 164, 261); Uyg. 1338 **Qïz-tarïm / Qïz-tärim?** [Kiz Tarim] (Chwol., Syr.-nest. (NF) 32); *TN:* Kzk. **Qïz-bay** [К. Кызбай] (Karta JAR XIX). ❖ 'Girl, daughter' cf. Türk., Az., Crm., Kirg., Kzk., Tat., Turk. *qïz* 'das Mädchen, die Tochter' (Radl. II, 818), Uyg., Alt., Hak. *qïs* 'die Tochter' (Radl. II, 800). Used also as a secondary component of female names. See also **QARA-QÏS?**

QÏZ-AŠA Uyg. 1266 **Qïz-aša** [Kiz Aša], Altun-aba's daughter (Chwol., Syr.-nest. (NF) 8); Uyg. 1327 **Qïz-aša** [Kiz Aša], fem. (Chwol., Syr.-nest. (NF) 27); Uyg. 1327 **Qïz-aša** [Kizascha], fem. (Chwol., Syr.-nest. (NF) 68, 151). ⇨ **QÏZ + AŠA**.

QÏZ-TOΓAN   Maml. 1438/39 **Qïz-toγan** [العلائى
قيز طوغان] (Ibn Taghrīb. VII, 65, 111). ⇨ **QÏZ** +
TOΓAN.

QÏZ-TURMÏŠ   Uyg. 12th c. - 14th c. **Qïz-turmïš** [Qïz
Turmïš / Kız Turmış], fem. (Radl., USp. 113, DTS,
EUTS). ✦ 'Daughter was born' (Blagova 1997, 708),
'The daughter stayed/survived'. ⇨ **QÏZ** + **TURMÏŠ.**
See also **ΓÏZ-DURDÏ.**

QÏZA   Hak. 19th-20th c. **Xïza** [Хыза], fem. (HRS 356);
Alt. 19th-20th c. **Qïza** [Кыза] (OjrRS 209). ✦ I.
'Vulture' cf. Shor *qïza* 'die Mäusegeier' (Radl. II, 820);
II. 'Hawk, buzzard (bird of prey from the family of
eagles which feeds on snakes)' cf. Hak. *χïza* 'хищная
птица из семейства орлиных (питается змеями'
(HRS).

QÏZABA   Hak. 19th-20th c. **Qïzaba** / **Qïz-aba?**
[Кызаба], fem. (HRS 353).

QÏZAY   Hak. 19th-20th c. **Xïzay** [Хызай] (HRS 352);
Kzk. 1830 **Qïzay** [Кызай] (Konšin, Mat. I-III, 56);
Kzk. 19th c. **Qïzay** [Кызай] (SOK 198); Kzk. 19th c.
Qïzay-bay [Кызайбай] (SOV 42); Kzk. 19th c. **Qïzay-
bek** [Кызайбекъ] (SOK 10). ⇨ **QÏZA** + suff. -*y*.

QÏZAQ   Tat.(Sib.) 1599 **Qïzaq** [Кызакъ], playmate in
Küčüm's family (AI II, 20). ✦ 'Playmate, lady-friend'
cf. Tat.(Bar.) *qïzaq* 'die Gespielin' (Radl. II, 820).

QÏZAM-BAY see **QÏZAN**

QÏZAN   Kzk. 19th c. **Qïzam-bay** (<Qïzan-bay)
[Кызамбай] (Lomakin 41); Kzk. 19th c. **Qïzan**
[Кызанъ] (SOK 166); Kzk. 19th c. **Qïzan-bay**
[Кызанбай] (SOK 30).

QÏZĀNČA   Hak. 19th-20th c. **Xïzanče** [Хызанче], fem.
(HRS 352); Hak. 19th c. **Qïzānča** [Кызанча], fem.
(Katanov, Otč. 12). ✦ 'Virgin'? cf. Hak. fem. PN
Xïzanča <*Xïzana* <*Xïza* <*Xïs* (Butanaev).

QÏZČÏQ   Karch. 20th c. **Qïzčïq**, fem. (Pröhle, Kar. 119).
✦ 'Little girl' (Pröhle). ⇨ **QÏZ** + dim. suff. -*čïq*.

QÏZDÏQ   Kzk. 19th c. **Qïzdïq** [Кыздыкъ] (SOV 124).

QÏZDÏR   Kzk. 19th c. **Qïzdïr** [Кыздыръ] (AOP 58).

QÏZΓÏČ   Bashk.? 1711 **Qïzγïč** [Кызгыч / Кызгич],
fem. (MIB III, 71); Kzk. 19th c. **Qïzγïč-bay?** / **Qïzïγïč-
bay?** [Кызегыцбай] (SODž. 84). ✦ 'A kind of bird
living in morasts, marshy places' cf. Kzk. *qïzγïš*
'bataklıkta, sazlıkta yaşayan bir tür kuş' (KzTS).

QÏZÏ   Kzk. 19th c. **Qïzï-bay** [Кызыбай] (SOV 40);
Alt.? 19th c. **Qïzï-bay** [Кызы-бай] (Katanov, Otč. 12);
Kzk. 19th c. **Qïzï-bek** [Кызыбекъ] (SOV 52). ✦
'Daughter of him/her' cf. Katanov's interpretation:
Qïzï-bay means „его дочь богатая" [his daughter is
rich] (loc. cit.). ⇨ **QÏZ** + poos. suff. -*ï*.

QÏZÏJAQ   Hak. 19th-20th c. **Xïzïjaχ** [Хызычах], fem.
(HRS 355); Hak.(Blt.) 19th-20th c. **Qïzïjaq**
[Кызыцак], fem. (Proben IX, 366); Hak.(Sag.) 19th-
20th c. **Qïzïjaq** [Кызыцак] (Katanov, Otč. 7);
Hak.(Sag.) 19th-20th c. **Qïzïjaq** [Кызыцак] (Katanov,

Otč. 8); Hak.(Kyz.) 19th-20th c. **Qïzïjaq** [Кызыцак],
fem. (Katanov, Otč. 13); Hak.(Shor) 19th-20th c.
Qïzïjaq [Кызыцак], fem. (Katanov, Otč. 11); Karg.
Qïzïjaq [Кызыцак] (Katanov, Otč. 9). ✦ 'Little Girl,
Little Daughter' cf. also Hak. fem. PN *Xïzičaχ*. ⇨ **QÏZ**
+ dim. suff. -*jaq*. See also **QARA-QÏZÏJAQ.**

QÏZÏQ   Oghuz/Trkm. 13th c. **Qïzïq** / **Qïrïq?** [قزيق /
Кызык / Кырык], Yulduz-χan's son (Abulg./Kon.
515, 550, 600, RaD I/1, 76); Kzk. 19th c. **Qïzïq-bay**
[Кызыкбай] (AOP 50); *EN:* Turk. 1689 **Qïzïq** [قزق /
Kızık aşireti] (Refik, Anad. 68); Turk. 1740 **Qïzïq**
[قزيق], a tribe in the region of Raka (Refik, Anad. 203,
204); Trkm. 1613 **Qïzïq** [قزق], a tribe (cemaat) in the
region of Haleb and Yenice (Refik, Anad. 69). ✦
'Amiable, nice, charming; joy, pleasure' cf. Kzk., Tat.
qïzïq 'angenehm, verlockend, reizend, wohlgefällig'
(Radl. II, 823), Kzk. *qïzïq* 'enteresan; eğlence; sevinç,
rahat' (KzTS).

QÏZÏL   Trkm. 20th c. **Gïzïl** [Gïzïl] (Zaj. 1971, 333);
Trkm. 20th c. **Gïzïl** [Кызыл] (TrkmRS 229); Hak.
19th-20th c. **Xïzïl** [Хызыл] (HRS 352); Hak. 19th-20th
c. **Xïzïl-ōl** [Хызыл-Оол] (HRS 352); Chuv. 18th-19th
c. **Kïzïl-bay** [Кызылбай] (Magn. 54); Oghuz.?, Selj.?
1160 **Qïzïl** [قزل], took part in the events in Luristan
(Qazw. 538); Oghuz/Trkm. 1030-1040 **Qïzïl** [Кызыл],
a Türkmen chief (MIT 234-35, 260, 363, 364); Selj.
Qïzïl [قزل], an emir (Bondārī); Selj.? 1129 **Qïzïl** [قزل],
an emir (Ibn al-Athīr/Tornb. X, 461, 477, 480); Selj.
1131/32 **Qïzïl** [قزل], Sultan Mesʿud's (1134-1152) emir
(Ibn al-Athīr, Atab.: RHCHor II/2, 80); Turk. 15th c.
Qïzïl [Κιζìλ Αχμέτης / Qïzïl Ahmed], a Turkish prince
from the family of İsfendiyar-oγlu (Byz. Turc.); Kzk.
19th c. **Qïzïl** [Кызылъ] (SODž. 134); Alt. 19th-20th c.
Qïzïl [Кызыл] (OjrRS 209); Hak.(Sag.) 19th-20th c.
Qïzïl [Кызыл] (Katanov, Otč. 8); Hak.(Sag.) 19th-20th
c. **Qïzïl** [Кызыл] (Proben IX, 553); Hak.(Shor) 19th-
20th c. **Qïzïl** [Кызыл] (Katanov, Otč. 11); Tat. 1601
Qïzïl-bay [Кизылбай Усенгилдеев] (Miller, Ist. Sib.
II, 169); Tat. 1647 **Qïzïl-bay** [Китунай Кызылбаев]
(Miller, Ist. Sib. II, 523); Tat. 1684 **Qïzïl-bay**
[Кызылбай] (Zolotn. 157); Tat.(Sib.) 1601 **Qïzïl-bay**
[Кызылбай] (Miller, Ist. Sib. II, 163); Tat.(Sib.) 1603
Qïzïl-bay [Кызылбай], a prince (Miller, Ist. Sib. II,
179); Tat.(Sib.) 1628 **Qïzïl-bay** [Кызылбай] (Miller,
Ist. Sib. II, 582); Tat.(Sib.) 1629 **Qïzïl-bay** [Аитикул
Кызылбаев] (Miller, Ist. Sib. II, 343, 344); Tat.(Tob.)
1699 **Qïzïl-bay** [Кызылбай] (PSZRI III, 562, 563);
Bashk.? 1675 **Qïzïl-bay** [Кизилбаевъ] (Kungursk.
akty 24); Bashk. 1754 **Qïzïl-bay** [Сеиткул
Кызылбаев] (MIB IV/1, 83); Kzk. 19th c. **Qïzïl-bay**
[Кызылбай] (Grod., Pril. 140); Kzk. 19th c. **Qïzïl-bay**
[Кызылбаевъ] (Grod., Pril. 193); Kzk. 19th c. **Qïzïl-
bay** [Таламишъ Кизылбаевъ] (Grod., Pril. 117);

Selj. **Qïzïl-bek** [قـزل بـك سيفـالـديـن] (Ibn Bībī III, 119, 208 IV, 49); Kzk. 19th c. **Qïzïl-jigit** [Кызылджигитъ] (SOK 172); Karakh. 924 **Qïzïl-tegin** [قـزل تَكيِ] (Kindī 280). ✧ 'Red' cf, Uyg., Chag., Turk. and the other Trk. languages *qïzïl* 'roth' (Radl. II, 826).

QÏZÏL-AXOR Selj. 1134/35 **Qïzïl-aχor** [قثل احـر / Kizil-Akhor], rises against Mesʿud (1134-1152) (Ibn al-Athīr, Atab.: RHCHor II/2, 88). ✧ 'Red stable/shed' cf. Turk. *ahur* 'ahır' (Özön) (<P.). ⇨ **QÏZÏL.**

QÏZÏL-ARSLAN Selj.? **Qïzïl-arslan** [Кызыл-Арслан] (RaD I/2, 102); Selj. 1100, 1107 **Qïzïl-arslan** [قزل ارسلان] (Qalānisi 137, 158); Selj. 1103 **Qïzïl-arslan** [قـزل ارسلان بـن السبع الاحمـر] (Ibn al-Athīr/Tornb. X, 247); Selj. 12th c. **Qïzïl-arslan** [Muzaffereddin Kïzïl Arslan], Pehlivan atabeg's brother under Sultan Rukneddin Toγrul III ibn Arslan-šah (1175-1194) (Ahbar 94, 98, 101, 120); Selj. 12th c. **Qïzïl-arslan** [قـزل ارسلان], İl-degiz' (İl-deñiz') son (Rāwandī 44, 293 etc., Qazw. 466, 473); Selj. 12th c. **Qïzïl-arslan** [قـزل ارسلان], an atabeg (Muh. Ibrahim 51, 135); Khorezm.? **Qïzïl-arslan** (Qazw. 466, 473). ✧ 'Red lion'. ⇨ **QÏZÏL + ARSLAN.**

QÏZÏL-BÖRİ Kzk. 19th c. **Qïzïl-böri** [Кызылборы] (SOV 74). ✧ 'Red wolf'. ⇨ **QÏZÏL + BÖRİ.**

QÏZÏL-BUΓA Oghuz **Qïzïl-buγa** [قـزل بـوغـا], forefather of the Ottoman dynasty (Āšikp. 5). ✧ 'Red-bull'. ⇨ **QÏZÏL + BUQA.**

QÏZÏL-BÜRÜK Kzk. 19th c. **Qïzïl-bürük** [Кызылбурукъ] (SODž. 10). ✧ 'Red high cap' (Bese 15). ⇨ **QÏZÏL + BÜRÜK.**

QÏZÏL-JİBEK Hak.? **Qïzïl-jibek** [Kesel Džibäk / Djibäk], fem. (Schiefner XLIV). ✧ 'Red silk' (Schiefner). ⇨ **QÏZÏL + JİBEK.**

QÏZÏL-DELÜ-BABA see **TELİ**

QÏZÏL-ΓAT Alt. 19th-20th c. **Qïzïl-γat** [Кызылгат], fem. (OjrRS 212). ✧ 'Redcurrant' Alt., Hak., Kzk. *qat* 'jede glatte, runde Beere' (Radl. II, 275). ⇨ **QÏZÏL + QAT. See also QARA-QAT.**

QÏZÏL-ΓURT see **QÏZÏL-QURT**

QÏZÏL-QURT Kirg. 19th c. **Qïzïl-γurt** [Кызыл-гуртъ], Mayqa-biy's grand-son (Potanin II, 149); Bashk. 1664 **Qïzïl-qurt** [Кызылкурт Аксаков] (MIB I, 192); Bashk. 1735 **Qïzïl-qurt** [Артыкъ Кызыкуртовъ], a tarχan (Vel.-Zern., Bašk. 20); *EN:* Kzk. 1785 **Qïzïl-qurt** [قـزل قـورت / Кызылкурт], a clan (MIK IV, 52, 54); *TN:* Kzk. **Qïzïl-qurt** [Кызылкурт], a place in western Kazakstan (Kojčubaev 161). ✧ 'Red wolf'. ⇨ **QÏZÏL + QURT.**

QÏZÏL-QUTQARMÏŠ Bashk. 1734 **Qïzïl-qutqarmïš** [Казыллъ-Куттъ-Кармышъ] (PSZRI IX, 339). ✧ 'Red rescued, saved' cf. Uyg., Kuman, Chag., Kzk. *qutqar-* 'befreien' (Radl. II, 994), Bashk. *qotqar-* 'освобождать; спасать' (BRS/Uraksin). ⇨ **QÏZÏL.**

QÏZÏL-ÖKÜZ Chag., Uzb. 1505 **Qïzïl-öküz** [عوض قـيزل اوكوز / Kizil öküz], a spy from Khiva (Abulg./Desm. 213). ✧ 'Red steer, bullock'. ⇨ **QÏZÏL + ÖKÜZ.**

QÏZÏL-SUXBAT Trkm. 1826 **Qïzïl-suχbat-serdar** [Кызыл Сухбат-сердар], from the Sarïq tribe (MIT II, 441). ✧ 'Red speech/conversation'? cf. Trkm. *söχbet* 'беседа, разговор' (TrkmRS). ⇨ **QÏZÏL.**

QÏZÏL-TAQ Hak.(Sag.) 19th-20th c. **Qïzïl-taq** [Кызылтак] (Katanov, Otč. 8). ⇨ **QÏZÏL + TAQ?**

QÏZÏL-TAS Kirg. **Qïzïl-tas** [Кызыл-Тас] (Proben V, 375-386, Radl. II, 313). ⇨ **QÏZÏL + TAZ / TAŠ?**

QÏZÏLAQ Kzk. 19th c. **Qïzïlaq** [Махмудъ Кызылаковъ] (Grod., Pril. 130).

QÏZÏLJİ NUyg. 19th c. **Qïzïlji-χanïm** [قـيزيلجى خـانيم / Kizilji Khanim], fem. (Le Coq, Namenl. 106). ⇨ **QÏZÏL?** + suff. *-jï.*

QÏZÏLXAN Kkalp. 20th c. **Qïzïlχan** [Қызылхан], fem. (KkRS 778). ⇨ **QÏZÏL** + suff. *-χan(1).*

QÏZÏM-TAS Alt. 19th c. **Qïzïm-tas** [Кызым-Тас] (Verb., In. 139). ✧ 'My daughter-bald'? ⇨ **QÏZ + TAZ.**

QÏZÏMAY Alt. 19th-20th c. **Qïzïmay** [Кызымай], fem. (OjrRS 212). ✧ 'My little daughter'. ⇨ **QÏZ. See also XÏZÏNAY.**

QÏZÏNAQ Alt. 19th-20th c. **Qïzïnaq** [Кызынак], fem. (OjrRS 212); Alt. 19th-20th c. **Qïznaq** [Кызнак] (OjrRS 209). ✧ 'Warm-hearted, kind girl' (OjrRS).

QÏZÏRΓAN Hak.(Blt.) 19th-20th c. **Qïzïrγan** [Кызырӷан], fem. (Katanov, Otč. 10). ✧ 'Diminutive'? (Katanov: „уменьшитель"), 'The withheld, repudiated child', cf. Hak. *qïzïr-* 'verkürzen, verringern', *Quday paladan qïzïrγan* 'Gott hat ihm den Kindersegen verkürzt' (Radl. II, 826).

QÏZKİNÄ Uyg. 1320 **Qïzkinä** [Kïz-Kina], fem. (Chwol., Syr.-nest. 61). ⇨ **QÏZ?** + dim. suff. *-kinä.*

QÏZLAN Tat.(Sib.)? 1629 **Qïzlan** [Кизлан (Казлан)], a murza of Chat (čatskij murza) (Miller, Ist. Sib. II, 359, 360).

QÏZLAR Kkalp. 20th c. **Qïzlar-gül** [Qyzlar-gül / Қызларгул], fem. (KkRS 778, Baskakov: OSA 140). ✧ 'Girls'. In Baskakov's opinion: *Qïzlar-gül* 'девушки цветок' [=girls-flower]. ⇨ **QÏZ** + suff. *-lar.*

QÏZLAR-BEYİ Turk. 1583, 1584 **Qïzlar-beyi** [Kızlarbeyi], fem. (Ongan, Ank. I, 164); Turk. 16th c. **Qïzlar-beyi / Qïzlar-begi?** [قـزلـر بكى / Kızlarbeyi], fem. (Ongan, Ank. II, 68). ✧ 'Lord/prince of the girls'. ⇨ **QÏZ + BEK.**

QÏZNAQ see **QÏZÏNAQ**

QÏČA Yak. **Qïča** [Кыча], fem. (Pek.).

QÏΓÏNĀN Yak. **Qïγïnān** [Кыгынан], a smith in a tale (Pek.). ✧ 'Clanging, ringing' cf. Yak. *qïγïnā-* 'звенеть, шуметь; хрипеть, сипеть' (Pek.).

QÏQÏLLĀN Yak. **Qïqïllān** [Кыкыллан], legendary

name of a shaman (shamaness) (Pek.). ✧ 'Grating, creaking, howling' cf. Yak. *qïqinä-* 'скрипеть (о двери, санях, седле; визжать; сипеть' (Pek.).

QÏLLAY Yak. **Qïllay** [Кыллаі] (Pek.). ⇨ **QÏLLÏY**.

QÏLLÏY Yak. **Qïllïy** [Кыллыі] (Pek.). ✧ 'Be(come) wild; go prowling' cf. Yak. *qïllïy* 'превращаться в зверя; отправляться бродяжить' (Pek.).

QÏRA Yak. **Qïra** [Кыра Чохчоі удаӊан], a part of the name of a shamaness (Pek.).

QÏRDA Yak. **Qïrda** [Кäӊjijäр-Кырда], a folklore hero (Pek.).

QLÏČ see **QÏLÏČ**

QLUŠ see **QULUŠ**

QOBA see **QUBA**

QOBA-ГОŠ see **QUBA-ГUŠ**

QOBAY Kzk. **Qobay** / **Köbäy?** [کوبای / Кобай, Кубай] (Miropiev / Divaev, Dem. 21, 43, 75). ⇨ **KÖBÄY?**

QOBAYÏLDA Kzk. 19th c. **Qobayïlda?** [Кобаййльда] (SOV 58).

QOBAQAY see **QUBAQAY**

QOBÏLDÏ Kzk. 19th c. **Qobïldï** [Кобылды] (AOO 14).

QOBÏZ Kzk. 19th c. **Qobïz** [Кобызъ] (SOK 180); Kzk. 19th c. **Qomïs-pay** [Комыспай] (SODž. 156); *TN:* Tat.? 18th c. **Qobïz** [Кобызово], a village in the district of Svijažsk (Korsakov 358). ✧ 'A kind of string instrument' cf. Crm., East.T., Kar., Kzk., *qobuz* 'ein musikalisches Saiteninstrument; die Kobus; die (kirgisische) Geige' (Radl. II, 662), Alt., Hak. *qomïs* 'ein Musikinstrument; die Musik' (Radl. II, 670).

QOBLAN Kkalp. 20th c. **Qoblan** [Къоблан, Коблан] (Bask., Kkalp. 75, KkRS 774); Kkalp. 20th c. **Qoblan-bay** [Кобланбай] (KkRS 774). ✧ 'Leopard; brave, strong man'? See also **QAPLAN, KOBLANDÏ**.

QOBLANDÏ Kzk. 19th c. **Qoblandï** [Кобланды] (Potanin, Pred. 73); Kkalp. 20th c. **Qoblandï** [Кобланды] (KkRS 774); Kzk. 15th c. **Qoblandï-batïr** [Кобланды батыр], from the Qara-qïpšaq tribe (Tynyšp. 70); Kzk. 19th c.? **Qoblandï-batïr** [Koblandï batïr] (Atyns. 88); Tat.(Sib.) 1646 **Qoplanda** [Копланда] (Miller, Ist. Sib. II, 512); Bashk. 1719 **Qoplanda** [Копланда] (MIB III, 182); Bashk. 1723 **Qoplanda** [Копланда] (MIB III, 210); Bashk. 1726 **Qoplanda** [Копланда Мамбетев] (MIB III, 239); Crm. **Qoplandï** [Копланды] (Proben VII, 132); Tat. 1699 **Qoplandï** [Кызылбай Копландеевъ (Капландеевъ)] (PSZRI III, 562-63); Tat. 1628 **Qoplandï(y)** [Кызылбай Копландеев] (Miller, Ist. Sib. II, 582); Kzk. **Qublanda** [Кубланда], Kazak folklore hero of the Qara-qïpšaq tribe (Proben III, 183 /222/); Kzk. **Qublanda** [Кара Кыпчак Кубланда], a folklore hero (Proben III, 200 /240/); Tat.(Ishim) **Quplandï** [Купланды], Qoblandï, the historical and folklore hero of the Qara-qïpšaq tribe of the Kazak folk

(Proben IV, 193 /238/); Bashk. 1770 **Quplandï** [Иман Купландин] (MIB IV/1, 343); Bashk. 1790 **Quplandï** [Ишкара Купландин] (MIB V, 276); Bashk. 1790 **Quplandï** [Барангул (Бурангул) Купландин] (MIB V, 283, 355); Bashk. 1793 **Quplandï** [Кузекей (Кузекай) Купландин] (MIB V, 331); *EN:* Kzk. 18th c. - 19th c. **Qoblandï** [Кобланды], a clan? (Tynyšp. 66, 70); *TN:* Bashk. 1723 **Qoplandina** [Копландина], a village (MIB III, 210). ✧ 'With leopards; brave, strong man'. ⇨ **QAPLAN** + suff. *-dï-lï*. See also **QAPLANDA**.

QOBRAT Bulg. 7th c. **Qobrat** [Κοβράτος], head of the Bulghars at the Maiotis, died in 642 (Byz. Turc. 161-162). ✧ 'Gather, raise (the nation)!' (Németh, Kobrat 440-444, Rásonyi, Imp. 240), cf. Türk *qobrat-, qubrat-* 'собирать' (DTS).

QOBUQ Crm. **Qobuq-ul** [Кобук ул] (Proben VII, 156 etc.). ✧ 'Bark' cf. Kuman, Crm., Kzk., Tat., Turk. *qabïq* 'die Rinde, die Schale' (Radl. II, 448), East.T. *qobuq* 'die Baumrinde' (Radl. II, 660).

QOBUQTÏ Kzk. 19th c. **Qobuqtï-batïr** [Кобуктыбатыръ] (Potanin, Pred. 98). ✧ 'Having bark, crusty' cf. Kzk. *qabïqtï* 'mit einer Schale, einer Rinde versehen' (Radl. II, 449). ⇨ **QOBUQ** + suff. *-tï.*

QOBUL Kzk. 19th c. **Qobul** [Кобулъ] (SOV 94). ✧ 'Fine, pretty nose' cf. Kirg. *qobul* 'fein geschnitten (von der Nase)' (Radl. II, 661).

QOČ Trkm. 20th c. Гоč [Goč] (Zaj. 1971, 331); Trkm. 20th c. Гоč [Гоч] (TrkmRS 190); Uyg. **Qoč** [Koç] (EUTS); *TN:* Turk. 20th c. **Qoč-γazi** [Koçgazi], a village in the province of Afyon, Turkey (TMİB 42). ✧ 'Ram' cf. Chag., Crm., Turk. *qoč* 'der Widder' (Radl. II, 615), Trkm. *qoč* 'баран-производитель; тур' (TrkmRS). See also **QARA-QOČ, MUBARÄK-QOČ**.

QOČ-QULAY Uzb. 1722 **Qoč-qulay** [Муратъ Кочкулаевъ], from Bukhara (Veselovskij, Unk. 170). ⇨ **QOČ** + **QULAY.**

QOČ-SEVİNDİGİ Trkm. 20th c. **Qoč-sevindigi** [Koçsevindiği], a Türkmen in Anatolia (Özbaş 13). ⇨ **QOČ** + **SEVİNDİK.**

QOČA Uyg. **Qoča** [Koça] (EUTS); Kuman? 1204 **Qoča** [Κοτζᾶς], a commander of the army of the Schythians (=Kumans) (Byz. Turc. 164); Turk. 20th c. **Qoča** [Koça] (Önder, Göle); Kuman 1190 **Qoča** / **Qočay?** [Кочаевичъ], a Polovets prince (Ipat. 451 (462)); Kzk. 19th c. **Qoča-bay** [Кочабай Минаевъ] (Grod., Pril. 196, SODž. 80); Kzk. 19th c. **Qoča-bay** [Кочабай Минаевъ] (SODž. 80); Kuman 1190 **Qočay** [Кочаевичи], princes, descendants of Qočay (Köčäy?) (PSRL II, 140, 323); *TN:* Kuman? 1369 **Qoča** [Kocha (possessio)], landed property in the county of Csanád, Hungary (Gyárfás III, 504). ⇨ **XOJA?**

QOČAY Tat.(Sib.) 1675 **Qočay** [Егалачка Кочайковъ] (AI VII, 341); Tat.(Sib.) 19th c. **Qočay**, a folklore hero from an epic (Radl., Aus Sib. I, 160).

QOČAQ Chuv. 18th-19th c. **Kočak** [Кочакъ] (Magn. 53); Yürük 1543 **Qočaq** [Koçak] (Gökb., Rum. 225); Yürük 1543 **Qočaq** [Koçak] (Gökb., Rum. 181); Yürük 1543 **Qočaq** [Koçak] (Gökb., Rum. 205); Yürük 16th c. **Qočaq** [قوجاق / Koçak], from the Yürüks of Kocacık, Turkey (Gökb., Rum. 102); Trkm. 1879-1881 **Qočaq** [Kotsak] (O'Donovan I, 222); Kzk. 1841 **Qočaq** [Кочакъ Тлемысовъ], from the Middle Horde (Orta Žüz) (Konšin, Mat. V, 22); Karg. **Qočaq** [Кочак] (Katanov, Otč. 9). ✧ 'Brave soldier, hero' cf. Turk., Chag. *qočaq* 'ein tapferer Jüngling, tapferer Soldat, der Held' (Radl. II, 616), also TMEN III, No. 1433.

QOČAQLÏ Turk. 19th c. **Qočaqlï-oɣlu** [Kočakly oɣlu], a Zeybek (Kúnos 1891, 119). ✧ 'Heroic'. ⇨ **QOČAQ** + suff. *-lï*.

QOČALÏ Kuman 1340 **Qočalï** [Petrus filius Kochola (Kachala) Comanus], among the Kumans in Hungary (Gyárfás III, 479). ✧ 'Having a shaman-mask' (Rásonyi, KÖA 113, Anthr. 142).

QOČAN Bashk. 1664 **Qočan** [Кочан] (MIB I, 192).

QOČAR Chuv. 18th-19th c. **Kočar** [Кочаръ] (Magn. 53); Kzk. 19th c. **Qočar-bay** [Кочарбай] (Grod., Pril. 81).

QOČAŠ Tat. 1631, 1634 **Qočaš** [Кочаш Танатаров] (Miller, Ist. Sib. II, 381-85, 408-414, 443, 467). ⇨ **XOJAŠ?**

QOČER Turk. 20th c. **Qočer** [Koçer] (Önder, Hınıs). ✧ I. 'Nomad' cf. Turk. dial. *koçer* 'konar göçer, göçebe, yörük' (Gülensoy, Doğu Anadolu Osmanlıcası, Ankara 1986); II. 'Ram-Man/hero' (Erol II), see QOČ + ER.

QOČÏ-SALAN? Kzk. 19th c. **Qočï-salan / Köči-salan?** [Кочисаланъ] (SODž. 146). ⇨ **QOČ / KÜČ?** + **SALAN?**

QOČÏ-TUBAY? Kzk. 19th c. **Qočï-tubay? / Köči-tubay?** [Кочитубай] (SODž. 112). ⇨ **QOČ / KÜČ?** + **TUBAY.**

QOČÏY Kuman 1103 **Qočiy / Kičiy?** [Кочiй (Кчiй)], a Kuman (Polovets) prince (Lavr. 269, Ipat. 184, PSRL VII, 19). ✧ I. 'Small, little, young'? (Bask., Im. polov. 70); II. 'Puppy'? (Bask., Im. polov. 70)? III. 'Nomad'? (cf. Sattarov: Köčey~Köčer). ⇨ **KIČI(Y)?, KÖČEY?**

QOČÏ Trkm. 20th c. **Goči** [Goči] (Zaj. 1971, 327); Trkm. 20th c. **Goči** [Гочи] (TrkmRS 191); Yürük 1543 **Qoči** [قوجى / Koçı] (Gökb., Rum. 193, 197, 203, 225, 231 etc.). ✧ 'Brave, bold, daring' cf. Trkm. *ɣoči* 'смельчак, храбрец' (TrkmRS), Turk. *küči* 'Fratze, ausgelassener Bursche, der Lotterbube; ein Liebes-Knabe' (Radl. II, 1492-1493).

QOČQA see **QONČA?**

QOČQAR Chag. 16th c. **Xučqar** [Хучкар] (Ivanov 269); Uyg. **Qočqar** [Koçkar] (EUTS); Bashk. 1735 **Qočqar** [Аккуза Кочкаров], a tarɣan (Vel.-Zern., Bask. 16); Bashk. 1735 **Qočqar** [Беккуза Кочкаров], a tarɣan (Vel.-Zern., Bask. 16); Bashk. 1735 **Qočqar** [Байгуза Кочкаров], a tarɣan (Vel.-Zern., Bašk. 16); Maml. 14th c. **Qočqar / Qïčqar?** [قِجْتار] (Sauvaget 52); Kzk. **Qočqar-ata** [قوجتار اطا / Kočkar-ata] (Divaev, Baksy 310); Uzb. 1770 **Qočqar-bek** [Кочкар-бек] (MIT II, 343); Kzk. 19th c. **Qočqor-bay** [Кочкорбай (батыръ)] (Potanin IV, 218); Kzk. 19th c.? **Qošqar** (Atyns. 19); Tat.(Tara) **Qucqar-alïp** [Куцкар алып] (Proben IV, 89 /114/); Chag. 16th c. **Qučqar** [Кучкар] (Ivanov 266); Bashk. 1761 **Qučqar** [Кулкан Кучкаров] (MIB IV/1, 221); Kzk. 19th c. **Qučqar** [Кучкарбай Буринбаевъ] (SKSO III, 15); Kzk. 19th c. **Qušqar-bay** [Kuškar-bay] (Ljutš 118). ✧ 'Ram' cf. Chag., Kar., Turk. *qočqar* 'der Widder' (Radl. II, 617), Alt. *qočqor* 'der Argali-Bock, Widder' (Radl. II, 618). See also **AQ-QOČQAR.**

QOČQOR see **QOČQAR**

QOČO-TAY Tat.(Lit.) 1548 **Qočo-tay** [Кочотай] (Kn. Metriki Lit. 45). ⇨ **?+ TAY** or suff. *-tay(1,2)?*

QOČU Chuv. 18th-19th c. **Koču-bay** [Кочубай] (Magn. 53); Turk. 20th c. **Qoču** [Koçu] (Önder, Göle); Kzk. 19th c. **Qoču-bay** [Кочубай] (SOK 74, 96); Kirg. 1847 **Qoju-bek** [Кожубекъ Таштанбековъ], a manap (Konšin, Mat. V, 104). ✧ 'A kind of wagen, coach'? cf. Crm., Turk. *qoču* 'ein grosser geschlossener Wagen, in der frühen angesehene Leute Fuhren; der Wagen, die Kutsche' (Radl. II, 617).

QOČULDAY Alt. **Qočulday-mergen** [Кочульдай-Мергенъ] (Nikiforov 111).

QOČUM Kzk. 19th c. **Qočum-bay / Köčüm-bay** [Кочумбай] (SODž. 80, 100); Kzk. 19th c. **Qočum-bay / Köčüm-bay** [Кочумбай] (AOK 74). See also **KÜČÜM?**

QOČUR Kzk. 19th c. **Qočur-bay** [Кочурбай] (AOK 98).

QOČUR-ENTEY Tat.?, Vog. 1598 **Qočur-entey** [Кочурентей] (Miller, Ist. Sib. II, 152). ⇨ **QOČUR.**

QOJ-EKE see **XOJA**

QOJA-AXMET Kkalp. 20th c. **Qoja-aqmet** [Къоджаакъмет] (Bask., Kkalp. 400); Crm. **Qoja-amet** [Коца Амäт] (Proben VII, 161); Kkalp. 20th c. **Qož-aɣmet (<Qoža-aɣmet)** [Қожахмет] (KkRS 774); Kkalp. 20th c. **Qož-amet (<Qoža-aɣmet)** [Қожамет] (KkRS 774). ⇨ **XOJA + AXMET.**

QOJA-AQMET see **QOJA-AXMET**

QOJA-AMET see **QOJA-AXMET**

QOJA-BAŠ Turk. 19th c. **Qoja-baš-oɣlu** [Koža baš oɣlu], a Zeybek (Kúnos 1891, 119); *TN:* Turk. 20th c. **Qoja-baš** [Kocabaş], a village in the province of Denizli, Turkey (TMİB 273); Turk. 20th c. **Qoja-baš** [Kocabaş], a village in the province of Ankara, Turkey (TMİB 79). ✧ 'Big-head; having big head'. ⇨ **XOJA + BAŠ.**

QOJA-BĪYĪQ   Turk. 19th c. **Qoja-bïyïq-oγlu** [Koʒa byjyk oγlu], a Zeybek (Kúnos 1891, 119). ✧ 'Big, large moustache'. ⇨ **XOJA + MĪYĪQ.**

QOJA-İRİ   Turk. 19th c. **Qoja-iri-oγlu** [Koʒa iri oγlu], a Zeybek (Kúnos 1891, 118). ✧ 'Big, large' cf. Turk. *iri* 'huge, large' (TED). ⇨ **XOJA.** See also **BOYŠAN, DÄW, DUOLANTAY, ÄLLÄY, KETTÄ, QOŽAQ, ULUΓ, ZOR.**

QOJA-QASAP   Yürük 1543 **Qoja-qasap** [Koca Kasap] (Gökb., Rum. 201). ✧ 'Old butcher, big, strong butcher' cf. Turk. *kasap* 'butcher' (TED). ⇨ **XOJA + QASAP.**

QOJA-MAJAR   Kzk. 1822 **Qoja-majar** [قوجا مجار] (MIK IV, 416). ⇨ **XOJA + MAJAR.**

QOJA-PABUČ   Turk. 19th c. **Qoja-pabuč-oγlu** [Koža pabuč oγlu], a Zeybek (Kúnos 1891, 119). ✧ 'Big slipper' cf. Turk. *pabuç* 'shoe, slipper, sandal' (TED). ⇨ **XOJA.**

QOJA-TAY   Tat.(Lit.) 1552 **Qoja-tay** [Коджатай], a prince (Kn. Metriki Lit. 64). ⇨ **XOJA + TAY** or suff. *-tay(1,2)*?

QOJAJĪQ   Maml. 14th c. **Qojajïq** [قُجَاجِق] (Sauvaget 52). ✧ 'Little master, lord' (Sauvaget 52). ⇨ **XOJA +** dim. suff. *-jïq.*

QOJAM   Kirg. 19th c. **Qojem-jar / Qojam-jar?** [Коджемджар], a sultan in the region of Kobdo river (Potanin I, 29, 49 II, 2); Bashk. 1735 **Közäm-γul** [Козямгулъ Мурзинъ], a tarγan (Vel.-Zern., Bašk. 16). ✧ 'My lord, husband'. ⇨ **XOJA.**

QOJAM-BERDİ   Kkalp. 1810 **Xojam-berdi** [Ходжам берди] (MIKk. 110); Bashk. 1623 **Közäm-berdi / Közäm-berdey?** [Козембердейко] (Miller, Ist. Sib. II, 299); Tat.(Sib.) **Közäm-berdi? / Közäm-berdey / Qožam-berdi?** [Козембердей / Кожембердей] (Miller, Ist. Sib. II, 168); Nog. 1649 **Qožam-berdi / Qožam-berdey?** [Кожем Бердѣй] (AI IV, 123); Kzk. 18th c. - 19th c. **Qožam-berli (<Qožam-berdi?)** [Кожамберлы], a clan (Tynyšp. 75); *EN:* Kzk. 18th c. - 19th c. **Qožam-berdi** [Кожамберды], a clan (Tynyšp. 66, 71). ✧ 'My lord, husband has given (the child)'. ⇨ **XOJA / QOJAM + BERDİ.**

QOJAM-BERGEN   Kkalp. 20th c. **Qožam-bergen** [Кожамберген] (KkRS 774). ✧ 'My lord, husband has given (the child)'. ⇨ **XOJA / QOJAM + BERGEN.**

QOJAMĪŠ   Yürük 1543 **Qojamïš** [Kocamış], a Yürük from Varna, Bulgaria (Gökb., Rum. 242); Bashk. 1776 **Qožamïš / Qužamïš** [Байгазя Козямышев (Кузямышев)] (MIB V, 542, 543, 547). ✧ 'He grew old'? cf. Turk. *koca-* 'to grow old' (TED).

QOJO-JAŠ   Kirg. **Qojo-jaš** [Кожожаш] (Jud. 68, 242, 650,). ⇨ **XOJA + YAŠ.**

QOJON   Kirg. **Qojon-bay** [Кожонбай] (Jud. 298).

QOJOS see **XOJAŠ**

QODAY   Hak. 19th-20th c. **Qoday** [Кодай], fem. (HRS 353).

QODAR   Kzk. 19th c. **Qodar** [Кодаръ], a groom and the chief of the captives (Potanin, Pred. 100); Kzk. 19th c. **Qodar** [Кодаръ] (SOK 166); Kzk. 19th c. **Qodar** [Кодаръ] (SODž. 50); Kzk. 19th c. **Qodar-bek** [Кодарбекъ] (SOK 124); Kzk. **Qodar-qul** [Кодар Кул] (Proben III, 227 /268/).

QODAS   Kzk. 1817 **Qodas** [قوداس / Кодас] (MIK IV, 312, 319). ✧ 'With curved, crooked legs' cf. Kzk. *qodas* 'кривоногий (ноги хомутом)' (KzRS).

QODÏR-ALİ   Tat.(Tob.) 1678 **Qodr-ali(y)? / (<Qodïr-ali)** [Кодралей] (DAI VIII, 38). ⇨ **QODÏR + ALİ.**

QODÏRLÏ   Kzk. 19th c. **Qodïrlï** [Кодырлы] (SOK 12). ✧ 'Itchy, mangy'? ⇨ **QODÏR +** suff. *-lï.*

QODOČA   Hak. 19th-20th c. **Qodoča** [Кодоча], fem. (HRS 353).

QODOS   Kzk. 19th c. **Qodos-pay** [Кодоспай] (SODž. 56). ⇨ **QODAS?**

QODUΓAN   Karg. **Qoduγan / Xoduγan** [Кодуҕан / Ходуҕан] (Proben IX, 640, 658-659).

QODUQ   Kzk.? 19th c. **Qoduq** [Кодукъ] (Grod., Pril. 52). ✧ 'Foal; foal of a donkey' cf. Kzk. *qodïq* 'жеребёнок кулана; ослёнок' (KzRS).

QOΓA   Kzk. 19th c. **Qoγa-bay** [Когабай] (SOK 8). ✧ 'Reed' cf. Kzk. *qoγa* 'eine Schilfart, der Kalmus' (Radl. II, 516).

QOΓA-TAY   Karg. **Qoγa-tay** [Коҕа-таi] (Proben IX, 660); Karg. **Qoγo-tay** [Коготай] (Katanov: ZIRGOÊtn. XVII vyp. III, 214). ⇨ **QOΓA + TAY** or suff. *-tay(1,2)*?

QOΓAY   Hak. 19th-20th c. **Qoγay** [Когай] (HRS 349). ✧ 'Little pike' cf. Hak. PN *Xoγay* (Butanaev).

QOΓAN see **QUΓAN**

QOΓDÏΓAS   Hak.(Sag.) 19th-20th c. **Qoγdïγas** [Коҕдыҕас], a folklore hero (Proben IX, 428). ✧ 'Child born from the previous marriage of the wife'? cf. Hak. PN *Xoγda* (Butanaev) + suff. *-(γ)as*?

QOΓO-TAY see **QOΓA-TAY**

QOΓON   Kzk. 19th c. **Qoγom-bay (<Qoγon-bay)** [Когомбай] (SODž. 50). ✧ 'Pursuer, persecutor; chase, pursuit' cf. Crm., Kzk. *qūγun* 'der Verfolger, die Verfolgung' (Radl. II, 899). ⇨ **QOΓAN?**

QOΓONAY   Tat.(Sib.)?, Tung.? 1639 **Qoγonay** [Котан Когонаев] (Miller, Ist. Sib. II, 453). ⇨ **QOΓON? +** suff. *-ay.*

QOΓÕÑ   Hak. 19th-20th c. **Qoγõñ** [Когоонъ] (HRS 349); Hak.(Sag.) 19th-20th c. **Qoγõñ** [Когоӊ] (Proben IX, 353, 554).

QOΓUL   Kzk. 19th c. **Qoγul** [Когулъ] (SODž. 8, 70, 138); Kzk. 19th c. **Qoγul** [Когулъ] (SOK 304). ✧ 'Pale'? cf. Kzk. *quqil* 'бледноватый' (KzRS).

QOΓUR   Kzk. 19th c. **Qoγur-bay** [Когурбай] (SOK

302); *EN:* Kuman 1315, 1385 **Qoɣur** [Koor / Kool / Koos? (genus)], a Kumanian clan in Hungary (Gyárfás III, 508). ✧ 'Little, few; scant' cf. Uyg. *qoɣur* 'wenig, gering' (Radl. II, 517), *qoɣur, qoqur* 'пустой, ничтожный, мало, незначительно' (DTS), cf. also Rásonyi, KÖA 115, Rásonyi, Anthr. 143.

QOƔUŠ NUyg. 19th c. **Qoɣuš** [قوغوش / Koghush] (Le Coq, Namenl. 106). ✧ 'Groan, sob' (Le Coq) cf. Chag. *qoɣuš* 'der Seufzer, das laute Schluchzen' (Radl. II, 519).

QOX-DEMAN Tat. 1603 **Qoχ-deman** [Кохдеман Устаянышев] (Miller, Ist. Sib. II, 179).

QOY Oghuz/Trkm. **Qoy** [قوى / Кой] (Abulg./Sabl. 25, Abulg./Desm. 28); Balk. 20th c. **Qoy-baylarï** [Qojbájlari], a former slave-family (Pröhle, Balk. 238); Alt. 19th-20th c. **Qoy-bala** [Койбала], fem. (OjrRS 212); Tat. 1675 **Qoy-murza** [Koймурзинъ] (Kungursk. akty 27); Bashk. 1739 **Qoy-sula (<Qoy-sulï)** [Койсула Мамметчюрина], fem. (MIB III, 410); Kzk. 19th c. **Quy-bay** [Куйбай] (Grod., Pril. 48). ✧ 'Sheep' cf. Türk, Uyg., Chag., Alt., Crm., Kirg., Kzk. etc. *qoy* 'das Schaf, der Hammel' (Radl. II, 499), Alt. *qoybala* 'lamb' (OjrRS). See also **QARA-QOY, TANSÏQ-QUY**.

QOY-AYDAR Kzk. 19th c. **Qoy-aydar** [Койайдаръ] (SOV 10). ⇨ **QOY + AYDAR**.

QOY-BAƔAR see **QOY-BAQAR**

QOY-BAƔÏŠ Tat.(Sib.) 1631 **Qoy-baɣïš** [Койбагыш] (Miller, Ist. Sib. II, 383). ✧ 'Sheep-herding'? ⇨ **QOY + BAƔÏŠ?**

QOY-BAYLARÏ see **QOY**

QOY-BAQ Bashk. 1740 **Qoy-baq** [Япиш Кайбаков] (MIB I, 404); Kzk. 1817 **Qoy-baq** [قويباق / Койбак] (MIK IV, 309); Kzk. 1794 **Qoy-baq-bï** [قوى باق بى / Койбак] (MIK IV, 165); Uzb. 20th c. **Qoy-bâq** [Кўйбоқ] (Begmatov 1984, 201); Bashk. 1760 **Quy-baq** [Куйбак Зеилеев] (MIB IV/2, 160); Bashk. 1776 **Quy-baq** [Куибак Жаилявов] (MIB V, 47-49); Kzk. 19th c. **Quy-baq** [Куебаковъ] (AUK 585); Kzk. 19th c. **Quy-baq** [Куйбакъ] (Grod., Pril. 78). ✧ 'Herd (the) sheep: Look after / take care of / the sheep' cf. Tat. *Quy-baɣïš* (Sattarov). ⇨ **QOY + BAQ.** See also **QOY-BAQAR**.

QOY-BAQAR Kkalp. 20th c. **Qoy-baɣar** [Қойбағар] (KkRS 774); Kzk. 1726 **Qoy-baqar** [Kaïbakar], envoy of the Kazaks (Levchine 153); Kzk. 19th c. **Qoy-baqar-bay** [Кой Бакарбай] (Grod., Pril. 123); Uzb. 20th c. **Qoy-bâqar** [Кўйбоқар] (Begmatov 1984, 201). ✧ 'Herds the sheep; he who will herd the sheep; shepherd'. ⇨ **QOY + BAQAR.** See also **QOY-BAQ**.

QOY-BAS Kzk. 19th c. **Qoy-bas** [Койбасъ] (SOV 60); Kzk. 19th c. **Qoy-bas** [Койбасъ] (SODž. 72). ✧ 'Sheep-head'? ⇨ **QOY + BAŠ.**

QOY-GELDİ see **QOY-KELDİ**

QOY-KEL Kzk. 19th c. **Qoy-kel** [Кайкель] (SOK 262); Kzk. 19th c. **Qoy-kel** [Койкель] (SOV 138). ⇨ **QOY + KEL.**

QOY-KELDİ Kzk. 19th c. **Qoy-geldi** [Кайгельды] (SOK 148); Kzk. 19th c. **Qoy-geldi** [Койгельды] (SOV 72); Kzk. 1822 **Qoy-keldi** [قوى كالدى / Койкельды] (MIK IV, 433, 435); Kzk. 19th c. **Qoy-keldi** [Койкельды] (SODž. 90); Kzk. 1824 **Quy-gilde** [Чалысъ Куйгильдинъ] (TOUAK XXIV, 146); *EN:* Kzk. 18th c. - 19th c. **Qoy-geldi** [Койгельды], a clan (Tynyšp. 66); Kzk. 18th c. - 19th c. **Qoy-geldi-batïr** [Койгельды-батыр], a clan? (Tynyšp. 66). ✧ 'Sheep has come'. ⇨ **QOY + KELDİ.**

QOY-KİY Kzk. 19th c. **Qoy-kiy? / Qoy-kiyew?** [Джалдибай Койкіевовъ] (Grod., Pril. 126). ⇨ **QOY + KİY?**

QOY-KÖZ Kzk. 19th c. **Qoy-köz** [Койкочь(!)], fem. (Ibragimov 125). ✧ 'Sheep-eye(d)' (Ibragimov). ⇨ **QOY + KÖZ.**

QOY-MURAD Kzk. 19th c. **Qoy-murad** [Коймурадъ] (SKSO VIII, 204). ⇨ **QOY + MURAT.**

QOY-SARÏ Kzk. 1794 **Qoy-sarï** [قويصارى / Койсары] (MIK IV, 158). ⇨ **QOY + SARÏ.**

QOY-SOBAQ Kzk. 19th c. **Qoy-sobaq? / Qoy-sabaq?** [Койсобакъ] (SOV 98). ⇨ **QOY + SABAQ?**

QOY-SOMAS Kzk. 19th c. **Qoy-somas?** [Койсомасъ] (SOV 98). ⇨ **QOY.**

QOY-SUÑUR 1822 **Qoy-suñur** [Койсунгур] (MID III, 155, 157). ⇨ **QOY + SOÑQUR.**

QOY-TAL Kzk. 19th c. **Qoy-tal** [Койталъ] (SOK 270). ⇨ **QOY + TAL.**

QOY-TENİS Tat. 1554 **Qoy-tenis** [Койтенисъ] (Kn. Metriki Lit. 103). ⇨ **QOY + TENİŠ?**

QOY-TLEW Kzk. 19th c. **Qoy-tlew** [Коитлеу] (SOK 186). ⇨ **QOY + TİLÄW.**

QOY-TORÏ Kzk. 19th c. **Qoy-torï** [Койторы] (AOK 34). ⇨ **QOY + TORÏ.**

QOYAM-BAY see **QOYAN**

QOYAN Kzk. 19th c. **Qoyam-bay (<Qoyan-bay)** [Коямбай] (AOK 106); Kzk. 19th c. **Qoyam-bay (<Qoyan-bay)** [Коямбай] (SODž. 28); Kzk. 19th c. **Qoyam-bay (<Qoyan-bay)** [Коянбай] (SOV 56); Kzk. 19th c. **Qoyam-bay (<Qoyan-bay)** [Коянбай] (AOK 26); Kuman 1438 **Qoyan** [Koyampalzallas], preserved in the name of a settlement (Gyárfás III, 233); Kzk. 19th c. **Qoyan** [Коян (знахаръ)], a sorcerer, clever man (AUK 133-134); Tat.(Sib.)? / Tung.? 1630 **Qoyan** [Коян (Коан, Куян)], a taysha (Miller, Ist. Sib. II, 57, 115, 580); Alt. 19th-20th c. **Qoyon** [Койон], fem. (OjrRS 212); Kzk. 19th c. **Quyan** [Куянъ] (AOA 114); Kzk. 19th c. **Quyan-bay** [Куянбай] (Grod., Pril. 78); Kzk. 19th c. **Quyan-bay**

[Куянъ-бай] (SOK 240); *TN:* Kzk. 19th c. **Qoyam-bay (<Qoyan-bay)** [Коямбай], a field (AOK 6); Bashk. 1750, 1758, 1765 **Qoyan(ovo)** [Кояново] (MIB III, 472, IV/1, 164, IV/2, 323); Kzk. **Quyan-bay** [Куян-бай], east of Awliye-ata, Kazakstan (Karta JAR XIX). ✧ 'Rabbit, hare' cf. Chag. *qoyan* 'der Hase' (Radl. II, 526), Kzk. *qoyan* 'заяц' (KzRS), cf. also Rásonyi, KÖA 116, Rásonyi, Anthr. 143, Rásonyi, Adalékok. See also **AQ-QOYAN**.

QOYAN-KÖZ Kzk. 19th c. **Quyan-güz** [Куянгузъ] (SOK 268); *TN:* Kzk. **Qoyan-köz** [Коянкöз] (Kojčubaev 152).

QOYANAQ Kzk. **Qoyanaq** [Kojanak / Коянак] (Proben III, 127 /162/). ⇨ **QOYAN** + dim. suff. *-aq*.

QOYANDÏ Kzk. 19th c. **Qoyandï** [Коянды] (SOK 59). ✧ 'With rabbit, having rabbits'. ⇨ **QOYAN** + suff. *-dï*.

QOYČÏ Kzk. 19th c. **Qoyči** [Койчи] (SOV 38); Alt. 19th-20th c. **Qoyčï** [Койчы] (OjrRS 208); Kzk. 1824 **Qoyčï-bek** [Койчибекъ] (SOV 10, 56); Kirg. 1824 **Qoyčï-bek** [Койчибекъ] (Konšin, Mat. I-III, 76); Trkm. 1826 **Qoyčï-mulla** [Койчи-Мулла], from the Sarïq tribe (MIT II, 441); Karch. **Qoyču** [Койчу] (Sysoev 120); Kzk. 19th c. **Qoyču-bay** [Койчубай] (SOV 34, 158); Kzk. 19th c. **Qoyču-bay** [Койчубай] (SODž. 92); Kzk. 19th c. **Qoyču-bek** [Койчубекъ] (SOV 106); Kzk. 19th c. **Qoyču-bek** [Койчубекъ] (SODž. 114); Kzk. 19th c. **Qoyšï** [Койше] (SOK 200); Kzk. 19th c. **Qoyšï / Qoyši** [Койши] (AOK 42); Kzk. 19th c. **Qoyšï-bay** [Койшебай] (AOP 122); Kzk. 19th c. **Qoyšï-bay / Qoyši-bay** [Койшибай] (SODž. 88); Kzk. 19th c. **Qoyšï-bay / Qoyši-bay** [Койшибай] (AOK 114); Kzk. 19th c. **Qoyšu** [Койшу] (AOO 46); Kzk. 19th c. **Qoyšu** [Койшу] (SOK 130); Kzk. 19th c. **Qoyšu-bay** [Койшубай] (SOK 166); Kzk. 19th c. **Qoyšu-bay** [Койшубай] (AOO 18); Tat.(GH) 1261 **Quyčï / Quyčï(y)** [Куичий] (PSRL II, 199); *EN:* Kuman/Kipch.? 1261 **Quyčï** [Куичия], a clan (Ipat. 563). ✧ 'Shepherd' cf. Chag., East.T. *qoyči*, Uyg. *qoyjï* 'der Schafhirt' (Radl. II, 506). See also **ČOŇ-QOYČU**.

QOYČÏMAN Kzk. 19th c. **Qoyčïman** [Койчиманъ] (SODž. 44); *TN:* Kzk. 19th c. **Qoyčuman** [Койчуманъ], a winter pasture (SODž. 24). ⇨ **QOYČÏ** + suff. *-man*.

QOYČU see **QOYČÏ**

QOYČUMAN see **QOYČÏMAN**

QOYDÏ Uzb. 20th c. **Quydï-nisâ** [Кўйдинисо], fem. (Begmatov 1984, 207). ✧ '(God) put/left him/her'? cf. Uzb. *qoy-* 'ставить, класть; бросать; пускать' (UzbRS). See also **QOYSÏN**.

QOYƔU Kzk. 19th c. **Qoyɣu-bek** [Койгубекъ] (SODž. 112).

QOYƔUL Kzk. 19th c. **Qoyɣul** [Койгулъ] (SOV 20).

QOYÏL Kzk. 19th c. **Qoyïl-bay** [Койылбай] (AOO 70).

QOYÏN Kzk. 19th c. **Qoyn-bay** [Коинбай] (SOK 46); Kzk. 19th c. **Qoyn-bay** [Ишан-Кулъ Коинбаевъ] (Grod., Pril. 81); Kzk. 19th c. **Qoyn-bay** [Мусабекъ Коинбаевъ] (Grod., Pril. 172). ✧ 'Embrace; bosom, breast' cf. Alt., Hak., Kirg., Kzk. *qoyn, qoin* die Umarmung' (Radl. II, 504).

QOYQAP Kzk. **Qoyqap** [Коiкап] (Proben III, 50 /65/).

QOYLAN Kzk. 19th c. **Qoylan?** [Койланъ] (Grod., Pril. 24).

QOYLÏ Kzk. 19th c. **Qoylï-bay** [Койлыбай] (AOK 30); Kkalp. 20th c. **Qoylï-bay** [Қойлыбай] (KkRS 774); Kzk. 19th c. **Qoylu-bay** [Койлубай] (SOK 298); Kzk. 19th c. **Qoylu-bay** [Койлюбай] (AOK 30); Kzk. 19th c. **Qoylu-bay** [Койлюбай] (SODž. 88); Kzk. 19th c. **Qoylu-bay** [Койлюбай] (AOP 50); Kzk. 19th c. **Qoylu-bay** [Койлюбай] (AOA 138); Kirg. **Qoylū-bay** [Коiлу Баi] (Proben V, 182); Kzk. 19th c. **Qoytu-bay** [Койтубай] (AOAtb. 14); Kzk. 19th c. **Qoytu-bay** [Койтубай] (AOA 142); Kzk. 19th c. **Qoytu-bay** [Койтубай] (AOP 86); Kzk. 19th c. **Quylï-bay** [Куйли-бай] (Grod., Pril. 84); *EN:* Kzk. 18th c. - 19th c. **Qoylï-bay** [Койлыбай], a clan (Tynyšp. 68, 75). ✧ 'Having sheep; with sheep'. ⇨ **QOY** + suff. *-li*.

QOYLU see **QOYLÏ**

QOYLUQ Kzk. 19th c. **Qoyluq-bay** [Койлюкбай] (SODž. 34).

QOYLUQQAY Tuv. 19th c. **Qoyluqqay** [Коiлуккаi], fem. (Proben IX, 147).

QOYMAN Kzk. 19th c. **Qoyman** [Койманъ] (AOAtb. 30); Kzk. 19th c. **Qoyman** [Койманъ] (AOP 18, 94); Kzk. 19th c. **Qoyman** [Коймановъ] (AOK 6); Kzk. 19th c. **Qoyman-bay** [Койманбай] (SOK 122); Kzk. 19th c. **Qoyman-bay** [Койманбай] (AOK 70). ⇨ **QOY** + suff. *-man*.

QOYMAS Tat.(Sib.)? 1633 **Qoymas** [Коймас], a prince, Obaq's grandson (Miller, Ist. Sib. II, 405).

QOYMASA Alt.(Tel.) 1632 **Qoymasa** [Koimasa] (Radl., Aus Sib. I, 174).

QOYN see **QOYÏN**

QOYON see **QOYAN**

QOYONČÏ Alt. 19th-20th c. **Qoyončï** [Койончы] (OjrRS 208). ✧ 'He who goes rabbiting; hunter for rabbits, hares'. ⇨ **QOYAN**.

QOYONOQ Alt. 19th-20th c. **Qoyonoq** [Койонок] (OjrRS 208). ✧ 'Little hare, rabbit'. ⇨ **QOYAN** + dim. suff. *-oq*.

QOYPA Kzk. 19th c. **Qoypa** [Койпа] (SOK 232).

QOYSA Kzk. 19th c. **Qoysa-bay** [Койсабай] (SOK 46).

QOYSAL Kzk. 1825 **Qoysal** [قويصال / Койсал] (MIK IV, 471, 476).

QOYSÏMAN Kzk. 1817 **Qoysïman** [قوى سمان / Койсыман] (MIK IV, 313, 319). ✧ 'Little sheep; like a sheep'? ⇨ **QOY** + dim. suff. *-sïman.*

QOYSÏN Uzb. 20th c. **Qoysïn** [Кӯйсин] (Begmatov 1984, 207); Uzb. 20th c. **Qoysïn** [Кӯйсин], fem. (Begmatov 1984, 207); Uzb. 20th c. **Qoysïn-ây** [Кӯйсиной], fem. (Begmatov 1984, 207); Uzb. 20th c. **Qoysïn-bây** [Кӯйсинбой] (Begmatov 1984, 207); Uzb. 20th c. **Qoysïn-χân** [Кӯйсинхон], fem. (Begmatov 1984, 207). ✧ 'Let him put; Let God leave him/her' cf. Uzb. *qoy-* 'ставить, класть; бросать; пускать' (UzbRS). See also **QOYDÏ.**

QOYŠÏ see **QOYČÏ**

QOYŠU see **QOYČÏ**

QOYŠUQ Kzk. 19th c. **Qoyšuq** [Коишукъ] (SOK 256). ✧ 'Little sheep; lamb'. ⇨ **QOY** + dim. suff. *-šuq.*

QOYŠUM Kzk. 19th c. **Qoyšum-bay / Qoyšun-bay?** [Койшумбай] (AOO 26). ✧ 'My shepherd'. ⇨ **QOYČÏ** + poss. suff. *-m.*

QOYTEK Kzk. 19th c. **Qoytek?** [Койтекъ] (SOV 112). ⇨ **QOY** + suff. *-tek.*

QOYTU see **QOYLÏ**

QOYUNLU Yürük 1543 **Qoyunlu** [Koyunlu] (Gökb., Rum. 179, 183, 199). ✧ 'Having sheep, with sheep' cf. Turk. *qoyunlu* 'Schafe habend' (Radl. II, 529). See also **BOZ-QOYUNLU.**

QOQA Alt.(Tel.) 1633 **Qoqa** [Koka], a Teleut prince (Radl., Aus Sib. I, 175); Kzk. 19th c. **Qoqa-bay** [Кокабай] (Grod., Pril. 66). ✧ 'Adam's apple' cf. Kirg. *qoqo* 'надгортанник; кадык, адамого яблоко' (Jud.). ⇨ **QAQA?**

QOQAQ Kzk. 19th c. **Qoqaq** [Джайманъ Кокаковъ] (Grod., Pril. 66). ✧ 'Fruit, growth; embryo, foetus' cf. Kirg. *qoqoq* 'название плода (в эпосе)' (Jud.).

QOQAN Kzk. 19th c. **Qoqan** [Коканъ] (AOP 26); Kzk. 19th c. **Qoqan-bay** [Коканбай] (SOV 120); Kzk. 1823 **Qoqan-murza** [قوقان مُرظا / Кокан мурза] (MIK IV, 458, 462); Kkalp.? 1697, 1699 **Qoqon-batïr** [Коконъ батыръ] (MIKk. 152, AI V, 521); *TN:* **Qoqan-bay** [Коканъ-бай], a place in the region of Namangan (Kostenka: Turk. Kraj II, 37). ✧ 'Silver coin' cf. Kirg. *qoqon* [=Khokand] 'серебряная монета Кокандского ханства двадцатикопечного достоинства' (Jud.).

QOQAŠ Kzk. 19th c. **Qoqaš-pay** [Кокашпай] (SODž. 112).

QOQČA Hak. 19th-20th c. **Qoqča** [Кокча] (HRS 349).

QOQÏŠ Kzk. 19th c. **Qoqïš** [Кокышъ] (AOK 2, 6, 122, 134); Tat.(Sib.) 1601 **Qoqus / Qoquz?** [Шугурда Кокузов] (Miller, Ist. Sib. II, 167, 168); Kzk. 19th c. **Qoquš** [Кокушъ Чингисовичъ Балихановъ] (Potanin, Pred. 73). ✧ 'Old, unnecessary, needless (thing)' cf. Kzk. *qoqïs* 'eski, lüzumsuz eşya' (KzTS), *qoqïs* 'беспорядок, хаос' (KzRS). Kzk. 19th c. **Qoquš** [Кокушъ] (Lomakin 36).

QOQQU Tuv. 19th c. **Qoqqu** [Кокку(?)] (Proben IX, 133).

QOQO Tat. 1675 **Qoqo-bay** [Кокобаевъ] (Kungursk. akty 25); Kzk. 19th c. **Qoqo-bay** [Кокобай] (SOV 62).

QOQSUP Tat. 1591 **Qoqsup** [Солкечъ Коксубовичъ] (Lit. Tat. 94).

QOQTU Kzk. 19th c. **Qoqtu-bay** [Коктубай] (SOK 160). ✧ 'Dirty, mangy' cf. Kzk. *qoqtïq* 'мусор' (KzRS).

QOQUČAN Tat.(Bar.) 1699 **Qoqučan** [Мончагутъ Кокучановъ] (PSZRI III, 563).

QOQUDAŠ Tat.(Sib.)? 1618 **Qoqudaš** [Кокудаш Кордануков], a murza (Miller, Ist. Sib. 244).

QOQUN Kzk. 19th c. **Qoqum-bek (<Qoqun-bek)** [Кокумбекъ] (SOV 18); Kzk. 19th c. **Qoqun-bek** [Кокунбекъ] (SOK 102).

QOQUS see **QOQÏŠ**

QOQUŠ see **QOQÏŠ**

QOQUZ see **QOQÏŠ**

QOL Kzk. 19th c. **Qol-bay** [Кольбай] (AOK 130); Kzk. 19th c. **Qol-bay** [Кольбай] (AOP 34); Kzk. 19th c. **Qol-bay** [Колбай] (Grod., Pril. 79); Kzk. 19th c. **Qol-bay** [Колбай] (SODž. 124, 162); Kzk. 19th c. **Qol-bay** [Колбай] (SOK 260); Kzk. 19th c. **Qol-bay** [Колбай] (SOV 36); Kzk. 19th c. **Qol-bala** [Колбала] (SOK 146); Kzk. 19th c. **Qol-bike** [Кольбике] (SOV 60); Tat. 1624 **Qol-čura** [Янгурчей Колчуринъ / Тонай Колчюринъ] (Pokrovskij 71); Tat. 1624 **Qol-čura** [Тонай Колчюринъ] (Pokrovskij 71); Bashk. 1675 **Qol-čura** [Колчюра Бексимов] (MIB I, 199); Bashk.? 1715 **Qol-čura** [Колчюра Бердыкеев] (MIB III, 124); Bashk. 1735 **Qol-čura** [Колчура Тоганашев] (MIB III, 333); Kzk. 19th c. **Qol-murza** [Колмурза] (SODž. 40); Nog. 1649 **Qol-murza** [Колъ мурза Курмашовъ] (AI IV, 87); *TN:* Chuv. 18th c. **Kol-čurino (<Kol-čura)** [Колчурино], a village in Spasskij uezd (Korsakov 197); Chuv. 18th c. **Kol-čurino (<Kol-čura)** [Колчурино], a village (Laiševskij uezd) (Korsakov 184). ✧ 'Arm; army, troop' cf. in several Trk. languages: *qol* (<Mo.) 'der Arm des Menschen, Vorderfuss der Thiere, die Hand; die Armee, Mannschaft' (Radl. II, 578-582), Uzb. *qol* 'рука; палец' (UzbRS), TMEN I, No. 307, IV, No. 1571. See also **ALTÏ-QOL.**

QOL-BAS 1798 **Qol-bas** [Петръ Колбасовъ] (PSZRI XXV, 405); Kuman 1395, 1459, 1460 **Qol-bas** [Kolbazzallasa / Kolbaz de Kolbazzallasa / possessio Kolbaz], a person and a settlement of Kuman origin in Hungary (Gyárfás III, 272, 526, 642 etc.); Kzk. 1793 **Qol-bas** [قولباس] (MIK IV, 147); Kzk. 19th c. **Qol-bas** [Колбасъ] (SOK 160). ✧ 'Defeat army-flank; Beat/opress the wing of the army' cf. Türk., Kuman, Chag., Az., Crm., Kirg., Kzk., Tat. etc. *bas-* 'drücken, pressen; unterdrücken, beherrschen' (Radl. IV, 1525). Cf. Rásonyi, Kolbászszék: MNy. 32 (1936), pp. 266-

267, Rásonyi, KÖA 114, Rásonyi, Anthr. 142. ⇨ **QOL + BAS II.**

QOL-BAŠČĬ   Kzk. 19th c. **Qol-baščĭ** [Колбаща] (SOV 158). ✧ 'Commander of a troop'. ⇨ **QOL + BAŠČĬ.**

QOL-BAT   Kzk. 19th c. **Qol-bat?** / **Qol-bas?** [Кольбатъ] (SODž. 54). ⇨ **QOL + BAT?**

QOL-BULAT   Khorezm.? **Qol-bulat** [Кол-Булат] (RaD II, 33). ✧ 'Arm-Steel'. ⇨ **QOL + BULAT.**

QOL-KÜRĒČĬ   Alt.? 19th c. **Qol-kürēči?** [Кол-куреэчи], a soothsayer (Verb., In. 45). ✧ 'Arm-Soothsayer'? ⇨ **QOL.**

QOLA-QĬRĬS see **QOLA-QĬRĬŠ**

QOLA-QĬRĬŠ   Hak.(Sag.) 19th-20th c. **Qola-qĭrĭs** [Кола Kipic] (Proben IX, 371); Alt. 19th c. **Qola-qĭrĭš-χan** [Кола-Кырыш-хан] (Verb., In. 153). ✧ 'Brass-quarrelling (man/khan)' cf. Hak., Kzk. *qola* (Mo.) 'das Messing' (Radl. II, 585). ⇨ **QĬRĬŠ.**

QOLAY   Chuv. 18th-19th c. **Kolay** [Колай] (Magn. 52); Tat. 1548 **Qolay** [Колай] (Kn. Metriki Lit. 44). ✧ 'Servant!; nice, lovely' (Sattarov). ⇨ **QUL + voc. suff. -ay.**

QOLAQŠA   Kipch.? 1096 **Qolaqša** [Колагша / Колокша] (Lavr. 231 (172)).

QOLAP   Hak. 19th c. **Qolap-pay** [Колаппай] (Katanov, Otč. 12).

QOLBĬR   Kzk. 19th c. **Qolbĭr** [Колбыръ] (SOK 22).

QOLČA   Kuman 1097 **Qolča** [Колча / Колчко], a Polovets lad, together with Ulan (Lavr. 252, 255, Ipat. 171 (176), 173 (179)); Kzk. 19th c. **Qolča-bay** [Кольчабай] (AOAtb. 18); Kzk. 19th c. **Qolža-bay** / **Qolša-bay** [Кольжабай] (SOK 52). ✧ 'Nice, beautiful' (Bask., Im. polov. 68), cf. Kzk. *qolja* 'красивый' (Budagov).

QOLČAQ   Kipch.? 1313 **Qolčaq** [قلجق], Toqtay (Toqtaγu) Khan's (1290-1312) soldier (Dawād.275); Selj. 1173 **Qolčaq** [قلجق] (Muh. Ibrahim 96-98, 103, 104); Karch. **Qolžaq** / **Qolǰaq?** [Колжаковъ] (Sysoev 126). ✧ 'Piece of plate armor for the protection of either the upper arm or the forearm; gauntlet' cf. Chag., Turk. *qolčaq* 'die Armschienen des Panzers; wollene Fausthandschiene' (Radl. II, 602).

QOLČU   Bashk. 1735 **Qolču-bay(eva)** [Колчюбаева], a village (MIB III, 335). ✧ 'Beggar, pauper' cf. Chag. *qolči* 'ein Bittender, Bettler' (Radl. II, 602). See also **KERİP, TİLENČEK, TİLENČİ.**

QOLǰAQ see **QOLČAQ**

QOLDAČĬ   **Qoldači** [Колдечи (Колдечихъ)] (PSRL II, 140, 323); Kuman 1190 **Qoldačĭ** [Колдечи], a Polovets prince (Ipat. 451 (462), PSRL II, 140, 323). ✧ I. 'Protector, defender' (Bask., Im. polov. 67-68), cf. Chag., Kzk. *qolda-* 'оказать защиту, помощь' (Budagov II, 87-88); II. 'Beggar' (Bask., Im. polov. 67-68), cf. Karakh. *qoldačy* 'Bettler' (MK/Brock.).

QOLDAY   Kzk. 19th c. **Qolday** [Колдай] (SOV 72).

QOLDAN   Kzk. 19th c. **Qoldan** [Колданъ] (SOK 260); Kzk. 19th c. **Qoldan** [Колданъ] (SOV 24). ✧ 'Use (it)!, act!' cf. Kzk. *qoldan-* 'etwas immer unter den Händen haben, ein Ding immer im Gebrauch haben' (Radl. II, 600).

QOLDAS see **QOLDAŠ**

QOLDAŠ   Kzk. 19th c. **Qoldas-pay** [Колдаспай] (SOK 108, 164); Kzk. 19th c. **Qoldas-pay** [Колдоспай] (SOK 72, 116, 166); Kzk. 19th c. **Quldas** [Джанъ Мурадъ Кулдасовъ] (Grod., Pril. 104); Chag. 16th c. **Quldaš** [Кулдаш] (Ivanov 297); Kzk. 19th c. **Quldaš** [Кулдашъ] (Grod., Pril. 118); Kzk. 19th c. **Quldaš** [Кулдашевъ] (SKSO VIII, 206); Kzk. 19th c. **Quldaš** [Кулдашъ] (Grod., Pril. 35); Kzk. 19th c. **Quldaš** [Кулдашъ] (SKSO VIII, 219); Trkm. 19th c. **Quldaš-bay** [Кулдашбай] (SKSO III, 178). ✧ 'Helper, mate, comrade' cf. Uyg., Chag. *qoldaš* 'der Helfer, Gefährte' (Radl. II, 600), Tat. *quldaš, qoldaš* 'der Gefährte, Genosse' (Radl. II, 988), Kzk. *qoldas- I* 'совместно что-л. нести' (KzRS), Kzk. PN *Qoldas* (Žanuzakov-Esbaeva). See also **YOLDAŠ.**

QOLDĬ   Kzk. 19th c. **Qoldĭ-ba(y)?** [Колдыба] (SOK 52); Kzk. 19th c. **Qoldĭ-bay** [Колдыбай] (SODž. 128); Kzk. 19th c. **Qoldĭ-bay** [Колдыбай] (AOAtb. 14); Kzk. 19th c. **Qoldĭ-bay** [Колдыбай] (SOK 70, 120, 148, 208, 264); Kzk. 19th c. **Qoldĭ-bay** [Колдыбай] (SOV 154); Kzk. 19th c. **Qoldĭ-qul** [Колдыкулъ] (SOK 244). ✧ 'Having an arm; having an army'? ⇨ **QOL + suff. -dĭ.**

QOLDĬ-ČET   Kzk. 19th c. **Qoldĭ-čet** / **Qoldĭ-šet** [Колдычетъ] (SOV 134). ⇨ **QOLDĬ.**

QOLΓOW   Bashk. 1730 **Qolγow** [Елдаш Колговов] (MIB III, 277).

QOLΓUNA   Tat. 16th c. - 17th c. **Qolγïna** [Колгына] (Sattarov); Kuman 1332 **Qolγuna** [Kolguna filius Boklow], Boqlow's son, from the Kumans of Hungary (Gyárfás III, 475); Bashk. 1761 **Qulγuna** [Кулберда Кулгунин] (MIB IV/1, 216); Bashk. 1789 **Qulγuna** [Сейфулла Кулгунин] (MIB V, 274); *TN:* Tat. 16th c. - 17th c. **Qolγïna** [Колгына], a village in the region of Apas, Tataristan (Sattarov). ✧ 'Mouse' cf. Mo. *kulkana* 'Maus' (Poppe 1099), cf. also Rásonyi, Bas., 19, Rásonyi, KÖA 114, Rásonyi, Anthr. 143; Sattarov 108.

QOLĬ see **QULĬ**

QOLĬǰ see **QĬLĬČ**

QOLĬQ   Kzk. 19th c. **Qolïq-pay** [Колыкпай] (SOK 206).

QOLĬM-BEK see **QULUN**

QOLĬMBET see **QULĬMBET**

QOLĬŠ   Kzk. 19th c. **Qolĭš** [Колышъ] (AOO 10); Kzk. 19th c. **Qolĭš-pay** [Колышъ] (AOO 38). ✧ 'Slave-mate (helper, companion, child' cf. Tat. PN *Qolïš* / *Qolĭš* (Sattarov). ⇨ **QOL + EŠ.**

QOLÏZ Tat. 1619 **Qolïz-bay** [Секизачко Колызбаевъ] (Kurdjumov 117, 120, 121).

QOLQA Alt. 19th-20th c. **Qolqa** [Колка] (OjrRS 208). ✧ Kol'ka cf. R. Колька, dim. of R. PN Николай (OjrRS 208).

QOLQAY see **QULQAY**

QOLQAL see **QUL-QAL**

QOLQAMAN Bashk.? 1785 **Qolqaman** [Колкаман Бускуновъ] (MIB V, 178).

QOLQUN Kzk. 19th c. **Qolqun** [Колкунъ] (SODž. 48). ⇨ **QULƔUN?**

QOLLU Yürük 1543 **Qollu** [Kollu] (Gökb., Rum. 230). ✧ 'Having arms'. ⇨ **QOL** + suff. /lu / -lï.

QOLMAQ Chuv. 18th-19th c. **Kolmak** [Колмакъ] (Magn. 52); Tat. 1645 **Qolmaq** [Енгилдѣйко Колмаковъ] (AI IV, 23). ✧ I. 'Hop' cf. Tat. qolmaq 'хмель (растение)' (TatRS); II. 'Kalmyk' (people).

QOLMANBET Kirg. **Qolmonbet** / **Qolmanbet?** [Kolmon Bet / Колмон Бет], one of Manas' comrades-in-arms coming from the Kazak people (Proben V, 40 /41/). ✧ 'Slave-Mukhammed'. ⇨ **QUL** + **MAMBET** + / suffixoid -bet.

QOLMONBET see **QOLMANBET**

QOLO-ŽAM-BAY see **QULÏ**

QOLODAT Tat.(Sib.) 1603 **Qolodat** [Дингузя Колодат] (Miller, Ist. Sib. II, 181).

QOLON Hak. 19th-20th c. **Qolon** [Колон] (HRS 349).

QOLOWAN Tat.(Sib.) 1631 **Qolowan** [Кутлуш Колованов] (Miller, Ist. Sib. II, 385, 386, 391).

QOLPA see **QULPA**

QOLPAQ see **QALPAQ**

QOLŠA see **QOLČA**

QOLŠAN see **QULČAŇ**

QOLŠUQ Kzk. 19th c. **Qolšuq** [Кольшукъ] (AOAtb. 42). ✧ 'Little arm'. ⇨ **QOL** + dim. suff. -šuq.

QOLTÏRČAQ Bashk. 1709 **Qoltïrčaq** [Алдакай Колтырчаков] (MIB I, 262).

QOLTUZ Kzk. 19th c. **Qoltuz** [Кольтузовъ] (AOO 26).

QOLU see **QULÏ**

QOLU-QÏSA Trkm. 1708 **Qolu-qïsa** [قولو قصه / Qoluqïsa boybeği], chief of the tribe of the Türkmen of Anatolia (Refik, Anad. 219); *TN:* Turk. 20th c. **Qolu-qïsa** [Kolukısa], a village in the province of Konya, Turkey (TMİB 578). ✧ 'His arm is short; short-armed' cf. Turk. qïsa 'kurz' (Radl. II, 803). ⇨ **QOLU**.

QOLUDÏ-BÏNTUN Uyg. 12th c. - 14th c. **Qoludï-bïntun** [qoludï bïntun] (DTS).

QOLUMBET Bashk. 18th c. **Qolumbet** [Шала Колумбетевъ] (Nepljuev 895). ⇨ **QUL** / **QOL** + suff. -umbet / -bet.

QOLUN see **QULUN**

QOLWAT Tat. 1632 **Qolwat** [Термаметко Колватов] (Miller, Ist. Sib. II, 391).

QOLŽA see **QOLČA**

QOLŽAQ see **QOLČAQ**

QOM-BAXTÏ Tat.(Sib.) 1604 **Qom-baχtï** [Исенгул Комбахта] (Miller, Ist. Sib. II, 187). ⇨ **QOM / QUM + BAQTÏ.**

QOM-BAY see **QON**

QOMA Kzk. 19th c. **Qoma-bay** [Комабай] (SOV 126); Oghuz/Trkm. 13th c. **Qoma-bek** [قمابيك / Кома-бек], ruler of Khorasan (Abulg./Kon. 1330-1345). ✧ 'Lover, helper' cf. Chag. qoma 'das Kebsweib, der Gehülfe' (Rasdl. II, 667).

QOMAQ Kzk. 19th c. **Qomaq** [Комакъ] (Grod., Pril. 187); Kzk. 19th c. **Qomaq** [Комакъ] (SOK 76); Kzk. 19th c. **Qomaq** [Комакъ] (SOV 150); Kzk. 19th c. **Qomaq** [Комакъ] (SODž. 10).

QOMAN Kzk. 19th c. **Qoman** [Команъ] (SOK 142). ⇨ **QUMAN?**

QOMAR Kzk. 19th c. **Qomar-bay** [Комарбай] (SOK 72). See also **MAY-QOMAR.**

QOMAW Kzk. 19th c. **Qomaw** [Комау] (SOK 142, 306); Kzk. 19th c. **Qomaw-bay** [Комаубай] (SOK 150).

QOMBU Tuv. 1879 **Qombu** [Комбу], Potanin's Uryankhay informant from the Balïq clan (Potanin IV, 179, 293).

QOMDEY Hak. 19th-20th c. **Qomdey-mirgän** [Komdei Mirgän] (Schiefner XLV).

QOMÏS see **QOBÏZ**

QOMNAQ Kzk. 19th c. **Qomnaq-pay** [Комнакпай] (SOK 46).

QOMOQ Hak. 19th-20th c. **Qomoq** [Комок], fem. (HRS 353). ⇨ **QOMUQ?**

QOMUQ Karakh. 11th c. **Qomuq** [Komuk / qomuq] (MK/Atalay 845, DTS). ✧ 'Shit/dung of a horse' cf. Karakh. qomuq 'конский навоз' (DTS). See also **İT-BOQ.**

QOMUŇ Hak. 19th-20th c. **Qomuň** [Комунъ] (HRS 349).

QON Kzk. 19th c. **Qom-bay** [Комбай] (SOK 16); Kzk. 19th c. **Qon-bay** [Конбай] (SOK 158); Kzk. 19th c. **Qon-ɣoža** [Конгожа] (AOO 62). ✧ 'Settle!, perch!' cf. Kuman, Kirg., Kzk. etc. qon- 'anhalten, sich niederlassen, sich aufhalten und übernachten' (Radl. II, 531).

QON-SOLAP Kzk. 19th c. **Qon-solap** [Консолапъ] (SOK 44). ⇨ **QON.**

QON-TAY Kzk. 19th c. **Qon-tay** [Контай] (SOK 16); Kzk. 19th c. **Qon-tay** [Контай] (SOV 54); Kzk. 19th c. **Qon-tay** [Контай] (AOP 6, 58); Kzk. 19th c. **Qon-tay** [Контай] (AOK 122). ⇨ **QON + TAY** or suff. -tay(1,2)?

QON-UZAQ Kzk. 19th c. **Qon-uzaq** [Конузакъ] (SOK 152). ⇨ **QON + UZAQ / QOŇUZ?** + dim. suff. -aq?

QONA Hak. 19th-20th c. **Qona** [Кона] (HRS 349);

Kzk. 1817 **Qona-bay** [قونا بای / Конабай] (MIK IV, 312, 319); Kzk. 19th c. **Qona-bay** [Конобай] (SODž. 62); Kzk. 19th c. **Qona-bay** [Конобай] (AOAtb. 14).

QONAY Tat.(Sib.) 1607 **Qonay** [Ужен Конаев] (Miller, Ist. Sib. II, 557); Tat.(Ishim) **Qonay** [Конаi] (Proben IV, 215 /265/); Bashk. 1734 **Qonay** [Нурумбетъ Конаевъ] (Vel.-Zern., Bašk. 11); Kzk. 19th c. **Qonay** [Конай] (SOV 84, 112, 120, 132); Kzk. 19th c. **Qonay** [Конай] (AOP 6); Kzk. 19th c. **Qonay** [Конай] (AOA 98); Nog. 1802 **Qonay** [Конай] (Sergeev 78); Hak. 19th-20th c. **Qonay** [Конай], fem. (HRS 353); Kzk. 1823 **Qonay-biy** [قونای بی / Конай бий] (MIK IV, 459, 462). ⇨ **QONA** + dim. suff. -*y*.

QONAQ NUyg. 19th c. **Qonaq** [قوناق / Konak] (Le Coq, Namenl. 107); Bashk. 1738 **Qonaq-bay** [Конакбай] (MIB III, 382); Bashk. 1756 **Qonaq-bay** [Казы Конакбаев] (MIB IV/1, 128); Bashk. 1762 **Qonaq-bay** [Конакбай Чирюшев] (MIB IV/1, 241); Kzk. 1803 **Qonaq-bay** [قوناق بای] (MIK IV, 212); Kzk. 19th c. **Qonaq-bay** [Конакбай] (AOP 122); Kzk. 19th c. **Qonaq-bay** [Конакбай] (AOK 82); Kzk. 19th c. **Qonaq-bay** [Конакбай] (AOK 114); Kzk. 19th c. **Qonaq-bay** [Конакбай] (SOK 68); Kzk. 19th c. **Qonaq-bay** [Конакбай] (SODž. 4); Kkalp. 20th c. **Qonaq-bay** [Конакбай] (KkRS 774); Kzk. **Qonaq-bay / Xonaq-bay?** [قوناق بای / Хонакбай] (Syzdykov 354); Kirg. **Qonoq-bay** [Конокбай] (Jud. 398); Bashk. 1753 **Qonoq-bay / Qonaq-bay** [Конокбай / Конакбай] (MIB IV/1, 75); Kzk. 19th c. **Qonoq-pay** [Конокпай] (SOK 90); Kzk. 19th c. **Qonoq-pay** [Конокпай] (AOP 130); Bashk. 1706 **Qunaq** [Кунак Падбалташев] (MIB III, 25); Bashk. 1728 **Qunaq** [Иртуган Куняков] (MIB I, 127); Kzk. 19th c. **Qunaq** [Кунакъ] (SOV 42); Kzk. 19th c. **Qunaq** [Кунакъ] (AOO 10); Kzk. 19th c. **Qunaq** [Кунакъ] (AOP 98); Kzk. 19th c. **Qunaq** [Кунакъ] (SODž. 82); Kzk. 19th c. **Qunaq** [Кунаковъ] (SKSO VIII, 204); Bashk. 1734 **Qunaq-bay** [Кунакбай], a tarχan (Vel.-Zern., Bašk. 11); Bashk. 1735 **Qunaq-bay** [Кунакбай Купаев], a tarχan (Vel.-Zern., Bašk. 17); Bashk. 18th c. **Qunaq-bay** [Кунакбаев] (MIB V, 558); Bashk. 1773 **Qunaq-bay** [Кунакбай Акметев] (MIB IV/1, 369); Bashk. 1778 **Qunaq-bay** [Ерлыкап (Ерлычап) Кунакбаев] (MIB V, 69); Bashk. 1789 **Qunaq-bay** [Кунакбай Абзанов] (MIB V, 260); Bashk. 1798 **Qunaq-bay** [Кунакбаевъ] (PSZRI XXV, 196-97); Kzk. **Qunaq-bay** [Кунакбай] (Grod. 147); Kzk. 1803 **Qunaq-bay** [Кунакбай], one of the chiefs of the Kün-delen tribe (Куделянъ!) of the Middle Horde (Orta Žüz) (Sib. Vest. IX, 106, MIK IV, 513); Kzk. 19th c. **Qunaq-bay** [Кунакбай] (AOAtb. 38); Kzk. 19th c. **Qunaq-bay** [Оразбекъ Кунакбаевъ] (Grod., Pril. 65); Chag. 16th c. **Qunaq-χoja** [Кунак ходжа] (Ivanov 224); Tat. 1541/42 **Qunaq-χoja-bay** [قوناق حوجه بای / Кунак-Ходжа-бай] (Jusupov 7); Bashk. 1742 **Qunaq-qoža** [Салтанали Кунаккозин] (MIB I, 486); Tat. 1758 **Qunaq-qul** [Кунаккул Атзитерев] (MIB IV/2, 20); Bashk. 1770 **Qunaq-qul** [Кунаккул Азмамбетев] (MIB IV/1, 343); Bashk. 1785 **Qunaq-qul** [Кунаккул (Кунапкул) Шерыпов] (MIB V, 172, 175, 241, 305, 306); Bashk. 1756 **Qunaq-quža (-küzä?)** [Аташ-мулла Кунаккузин] (MIB IV/1, 130); Bashk. 1756 **Qunaq-quža (-küzä?)** [Нурумбеть Кунаккузин] (MIB IV/1, 130); Bashk. 1756 **Qunaq-quža (-küzä?)** [Иван Кунаккузин] (MIB IV/1, 130); Kzk. 19th c. **Qunaq-pay** [Кунакпай] (SOK 30, 96, 130, 134); *EN:* Kzk. 18th c. - 19th c. **Qonaq-bay** [Конакбай], a clan (Tynyšp. 66); *TN:* Kzk. **Qunaq-bay** [Кунак-бай] (Karta JAR XIX); Bashk. **Qunaq-bay(eva)** [Кунакбаева], a village in the Ural, Southwest of Zlatoust (?); Kzk. **Qunaq-pay** [Kunakpai], a burial mound south of Ilijsk (PM Ergh. 42). ✧ I. 'Guest' cf. Kuman, Chag., East.T., Kzk. *qonaq* 'der Gast, Besuch' (Radl. II, 536), Tat. *qunaq* 'id.' (Radl. II, 909), Bashk. *qunaq* 'гость' (BRS/Uraksin), Kkalp. *qonaq* 'id.' (KkRS), Kirg. *qonoq* 'id.' (Jud.); II. 'Nimble, playful'? cf. Kzk. *qunaq* 'бодрый, игривый' (KzRS). See also **QARQÏN-QONAQ**.

QONAQ-TAY Kzk. 19th c. **Qonaq-tay** [Конактай] (SOK 140). ⇨ **QONAQ** + **TAY** or suff. -*tay(1,2)*?

QONAQAN Kzk. 19th c. **Qonaqan** [Конаканъ] (AOO 66).

QONAÑ Hak. 19th-20th c. **Qonañ** [Конанъ] (HRS 349).

QONAR Kzk. 19th c. **Qonar** [Конаръ] (SOV 94); Kzk. 19th c. **Qonar-bay** [Конарбай] (SOK 59). ⇨ **QUNAR?** See also **ÖDÄ-QONAR**.

QONAŠ Yürük 16th c. **Qonaš** [قوناش / Konaş] (Gökb., Rum. 103).

QONBAR Chag. **Qonbar-biy** [Конбар-бий] (Ivanov 23).

QONČ-QÏYAL Khorezm.? 1291 **Qonč-qïyal** [قونجتیال / Qončqïyāl], emir who fought against Keihatu il-χan helping Baidu (Aqsar./Iš. 84). ✧ '(Boot-)Leg-stubborn'? cf. Kuman *qonč* 'Bein, Wade' (CC), Chag., Alt., Turk. *qonč, qonj, qonja* 'der Stiefelschaft' (Ral. II, 547). ⇨ **QÏYAL.**

QONČA Kuman 1264 **Qonča** [Koncha Cumanus] (Gyárfás II, 416); Tat.(GH) 1318 **Qonča** [Конча (Кочка)] (PSRL I, 229 IV, 49 V, 207 VII, 188, Lavr. 502). ✧ I. 'Neighbour; bud'? (Rásonyi, KÖA 115, Rásonyi, Anthr. 143), cf. Crm., Turk. *qonja* (<P.) 'die Knospe' (Radl. II, 547); II. 'Boot-leg, boot-uppers'? cf. Chag., Turk. *qonja* 'id.' (Radl. II, 547).

QONČAGAU Kzk. 19th c. **Qončaγau** [Кончагай] (SOK 214, 270). ⇨ **QONČA** + dim. suff. -*γay / -qay*.

QONČAY Kzk. 19th c. **Qončay-bay** [Кончайбай] (SOK 256). ⇨ **QONČA** + dim. suff. *-y*.

QONČAQ Khorezm. 13th c.? **Qončaq** [Кончак] (RaD II, 10). ✧ 'Foot-armour; hip-armour' (Bask., Im. polov. 68), cf. also Chag. *qončaq* 'eine längliche Schüssel, ein Trinkgefäss' (Radl. II, 547). ⇨ **KÖNČÄK.** See also **BAY-ГОNČAQ?**

QONČAM Kzk. 19th c. **Qončam-bay / Qončan-bay?** [Кончамбай] (SOK 140).

QONČĬN Hak. 19th-20th c. **Qončĭn** [Кончін] (Katanov, Otč. 13). ✧ 'End' cf. R. *končina* 'id.' (Katanov).

QONČĬ Kzk. 19th c. **Qončĭ** [Кончи] (SOV 26); Karakh.? 1003 **Qončĭ / Qonǰĭ** [قنجى] (Ibn al-Athīr/Tornb. IX, 124); Kzk. 19th c. **Qončĭ-γul** [Кончигулъ] (Pam. kn. Turg. 58); Kzk. 19th c. **Qonču-bay** [Коньчубай] (SOV 8); Kzk. 19th c. **Qonču-γul** [Конџугулъ] (AOA 114).

QONČĬL Kzk. 19th c. **Qončĭl** [Кончилъ] (SOK 240).

QONČU see **QONČĬ**

QONČU-BUГA Maml. 1314 **Qonču-buγa / Qunǰu-buγa?** [قنجو بغا] (Dawād.). ⇨ **QONČU** + **BUQA.**

QONDA Kalm. / Mo.? 1640 **Qonda** [Конда], envoy of the çontayši (Miller, Ist. Sib. II, 456); Kzk. 19th c. **Qonda-bay / Qondĭ-bay?** [Кондабай] (SOK 144).

QONDAM Kuman 1315/1385 **Qondam / Qandam?** [Kondam et Juhpogo], from the Kool or Koor (see QOГUR) clan of the Kumans of Hungary (Gyárfás III, 508).

QONDAR Bashk.? 1718 **Qondar** [Уразай Кондаров] (MIB III, 177); Kzk. 1734 **Qondar-bi** [Кондарби] (PSZRI IX, 303).

QONDĬ Kzk. 19th c. **Qondĭ** [Конди] (Grod., Pril. 109); Oghuz/Trkm. 13th c. **Qondĭ-bay** [قوندى باى / Конды-бай] (Abulg./Kon. 1450); Kzk. 19th c. **Qondĭ-bay** [Кондыбай] (AOAtb. 42); Kzk. 19th c. **Qondĭ-bay** [Кондыбай] (SOK 66, 136, 150, 182); Kzk. 19th c. **Qondĭ-bay** [Кондыбай] (SODž. 50); Kzk. 19th c. **Qondĭ-bay / Qontĭ-bay?** [Контыбай] (AOO 14); Kzk. 19th c. **Qondu-bay** [Кондубай] (SOV 46, 80); Kzk. 19th c. **Qondu-bay** [Кондубай] (AOK 10, 122); Kzk. 19th c. **Qondu-bay** [Кондубай] (SODž. 70); Kzk. 19th c. **Qondu-bay** [Кондубай] (AOO 2); Kzk. 19th c. **Qondu-bay** [Контубай] (SOK 130); Kirg. **Qondu-bay** [Кондубай] (Jud. 354); Kirg. 19th c. **Qondu-bay** [Кондубай] (Potanin II, 3); Kzk. **Qondu-bay / Qondĭ-bay** [Kondy Bai / Кондy Баи] (Proben III, 55 /63/); Uzb.? **Qondu-sufi-χoǰa** [Kondu-Sufi-χodža] (Barth., Turk. I); *TN:* Kzk. 19th c. **Qondĭ-bay** [Кондыбай], a field (AOO 70); Kzk. 19th c. **Qondu-bay** [Кондубай], a field (AOO 2, 62). ✧ 'He settled down; stayed (for the night)' cf. Kuman, Kirg., Kzk. etc. *qon-* 'anhalten, sich niederlassen, sich aufhalten und übernachten' (Radl. II, 531). See also **BEK-QONDĬ, İL-QONDĬ, KÖČ-QONDĬ, TOÑA-BİK-QONDĬ.**

QONDĬQAR Kzk. 1825 **Qondĭqar / Qonduqar?** [قوندوكار / Кондыкар] (MIK IV, 473, 477).

QONDĬR Hak. 19th-20th c. **Xondĭr** [Хондыр] (HRS 352); Kzk. 19th c. **Qondĭr** [Кондыръ] (AOP 22); Hak. 19th-20th c. **Qondĭr** [Кондыр] (HRS 349); Hak.(Kacha) 19th-20th c. **Qondĭr** [Кондыр] (Proben IX, 555). ✧ 'Make him settle (down); make him stay (for the night)' cf. Alt., Hak., Kzk., etc. *qondĭr-, qondur-* 'übernachten lassen, Gäste empfangen' (Radl. II, 545-546), Hak. *χondĭr-* 'позволить ночевать, переночевать; позволить жить оседло' (HRS).

QONDRAT see **QOÑIRAT**

QONDU see **QONDĬ**

QONDUQ Nog.?, Crm.? 1594 **Qonduq** [Кондюкъ], envoy of the ruler of Perekop (Lit. Tat. 230); Kzk. 19th c. **Qonduq-pay** [Кондукпай] (SOK 134, 150, 282); Kzk. 19th c. **Qonduq-pay** [Кондукпай] (SOV 124). ✧ 'We settled down; stayed for the night'. ⇨ **QON.**

QONDURAW Kzk. 1796, 1825 **Qonduraw** [قوندراۋ / Кондурау султан], Nur-ali khan's son (MIK IV, 187, 261, 477).

QONГAN Kzk. 19th c. **Qonγam-bay (<Qonγan-bay)** [Конгамбай] (SOK 292). ✧ 'He who settled down; he who stayed (for the night)' cf. Kuman, Kirg., Kzk. etc. *qon-* 'anhalten, sich niederlassen, sich aufhalten und übernachten' (Radl. II, 531). See also **QONDĬ.**

QONĬ Kzk. 19th c. **Qonĭ-bay** [Коныбай] (AOK 122).

QONĬQ Kzk. 19th c. **Qonĭq-bay** [Конкбай] (AOP 52); Kzk. 19th c. **Qonĭq-pay** [Коныкпай] (SODž. 76); Kzk. 19th c. **Qonĭq-pay** [Коныкпай] (SOV 20). ⇨ **QONAQ?**

QONĬS see **QONĬŠ**

QONĬŠ Kzk. 1785 **Qonĭs-biy / Qonus-bay** [قونص باى / Конис-бий], from the Kerderi tribe (MIK IV, 52, 54); Kzk. 19th c. **Qonĭs-pay** [Коныспай] (SODž. 130); Kzk. 19th c. **Qonĭš-pay** [Конышпай] (SOK 304); Kzk. 19th c. **Qons-pay (<Qonĭs-pay)** [Конспай] (AOK 66); Kzk. 19th c. **Qonus** [Конузъ] (AOK 134); Kzk. 1823 **Qonus-biy** [قونص بى / Конус бий] (MIK IV, 458, 462); Kzk. 19th c. **Qonus-pay** [Конуспай] (SOV 30, 44, 54); Kzk. 19th c. **Qonus-pay** [Конуспай] (SODž. 70, 122, 130, 136); Kzk. 19th c. **Qonus-pay** [Конуспай] (AOA 26, 46); Kzk. 19th c. **Qonus-pay** [Конуспай] (AOK 10, 110); Kzk. 19th c. **Qonus-pay** [Конуспай] (AOO 22); Kzk. 19th c. **Qonus-pay** [Конуспаевъ] (AOO 34). ✧ 'Residence, abode; staying for the night (when on a journey)' cf. Kzk. *qonĭs* 'mekân, ikâmet edilen yer, göçerek gelip konaklanan yer' (KzTS), Kuman *qonĭš* 'der Aufenthalt' (Radl. II, 539).

QONQA Kzk. 19th c. **Qonqa** [Конка] (AOAtb. 22);

Kzk. 19th c. **Qonqa-bay** [Конкабай] (SOV 58); Kzk. 19th c. **Qonqa-bay** [Конкабай] (AOP 114); Kzk. 19th c. **Qonqa-bay** [Конкабай] (Pam. kn. Turg. 77); Tat.(Lit.) 1594 **Qunqa** [Кунка Итешовна Михайлова], fem. (Lit. Tat. 221, 232). ⇨ **QON / QUN?** + suff. -qa.

QONQAQ Kzk. 19th c. **Qonqaq** [Конкакъ] (SOV 192). ✧ 'Its centre is elevated, protuberant, bulging' cf. Kzk. *qonqaq* 'ortası yüksekçe' (KzTS).

QONQAS Bashk. 1663 **Qonqas** [Конкас Девлетбаев], a tarχan (MIB I, 164, 183, 198-199); Bashk. 1663 **Qonqas** [Конкас Ителев] (MIB I, 179); Bashk. 1743 **Qonqas** [Конкас Каскинов] (MIB III, 514); Kzk. 19th c. **Qonqas** [Конкасъ] (SODž. 62). ✧ 'Its centre is elevated, protuberant, bulging' cf. Kzk. *qonqaš = qonqaq* 'ortası yüksekçe' (KzTS).

QONQOTAN Mo.? **Qonqotan** [Конкотан], forefather of the Qonqotan tribe (RaD I/1, 167).

QONQOZ Tat.(Sib.) 1600 **Qonqoz / Qoñuz?** [Кобдевлет Конкозов] (Miller, Ist. Sib. II, 157). ⇨ **QOÑUZ?**

QONLAM Kzk. 19th c. **Qonlam-bay / Qondam-bay?** [Конламбай] (SOK 176). ⇨ **QONDAM?**

QONOKEN Kzk. 19th c. **Qonoken?** [Конокенъ] (AOK 126).

QONOQ see **QONAQ**

QONRAP Kzk. 19th c. **Qonrap / Qoñrat?** [Конрапъ] (SOK 104).

QONRAT see **QOÑÏRAT**

QONSA Kzk. 19th c. **Qonsa-bek** [Консабекъ] (SODž. 82). ✧ 'Neighbour; wretch'? cf. Kzk. *qoñsu* 'der Nachtbar; ein armer, elender Mensch' (Radl. II, 525). See also **TOQ-QONSA**.

QONSAS Kzk. 19th c. **Qonsas** [Консасъ] (AOAtb. 46).

QONSUQ Kzk. 19th c. **Qonsuq** [Консукъ] (SOV 158).

QONŠAW Karch. **Qonšaw** [Коншавъ] (Sysoev 131).

QONTAYMA Alt.? 19th c. **Qontayma** [Контайма] (Verb., In. 117-119).

QONTAR Kzk. 19th c. **Qontar-bay** [Контарбай] (SOV 96); Kzk. 19th c. **Qontar-bay** [Контарбай] (AOP 78); Kzk. 19th c. **Qontar-bay** [Контарбай] (SODž. 18); Kzk. 19th c. **Qontar-bay** [Контарбай] (SOK 180, 198); Kzk. 19th c. **Qontar-bay** [Контарбай] (AOO 42, 70); Kzk. 19th c. **Qontor-bay / Qontar-bay?** [Конторбай] (Konšin, Po Ust'-Kamenog. uezdu: Pam. kn. Semip. 1900, 30); Kzk. 19th c. **Qontor-bay / Qontar-bay?** [Конторбай] (AOP 50). ⇨ **QANTAR?**

QONTÏR Kzk. 19th c. **Qontïr-bay / Qondïr-bay?** [Контырбай] (AOAtb. 6). ⇨ **QONDÏR?**

QONTOR see **QONTAR**

QONTU Kzk. **Qontu-mulla** [Конту-мулла], a place(?) north of Lake Aral (Karta JAR XI).

QONUQ' Maml. 14th c. **Qonuq** [قُنُق] (Sauvaget 54); Kzk. **Qonuq / Qonuqa?** [Джераманъ Конукинъ] (Konšin, Pam. 26); Maml. 14th c. **Qonuq-bay** [قنبای], fem. (Sauvaget 54); Maml. 1440/41 **Qonuq-bay** [قنق بای] (Ibn Taghrīb. VII, 273). ✧ 'Guest' cf. Uyg., Chag., Turk. *qonuq* 'der Gast' (Radl. II, 540). ⇨ **QONÏQ?** See also **QÏRQ-QONUQ**.

QONUM Kzk. 19th c. **Qonum-bek** [Коньумбекъ] (AOO 18). ✧ '(Close) Relative' cf. Karakh. *qonum* 'близкий; сородич, соплеменник' (DTS).

QONUR see **QOÑUR**

QONUS see **QONÏŠ**

QONUSUP Kzk. 19th c. **Qonusup** [Конусупъ] (SODž. 138).

QONUŠ Kzk. 19th c. **Qonuš-pay** [Конушпай] (SOK 88). ⇨ **QOÑÏŠ**.

QONŽA Tat.(Sib.)? 1637 **Qonža** [Конжа], Quyši tayša's wife (Miller, Ist. Sib. II, 442).

QOÑDAYČ Alt.(Tel.) 19th c. **Qoñdayč** [Конгдайч], a Teleut khan (Verb., In. 117-119). ✧ Qontayči (Mo.) '(reining) prince (title)' (Mo. <Chin.).

QOÑÏRAT Kzk. 19th c. **Qondrat / Qoñrat?** [Кондратъ] (SODž. 52); Kzk. 19th c. **Qonrat-pay** [Конратпай] (SOK 206); Nog. 1649 **Qunrat** [Шигай Кунратовъ] (AI IV, 123); *EN:* Nog. 20th c. **Qoñïrat** [Конъырат], an Aq-noγay clan in the Cherkess autonomous region and in the region of Mineralovodsk (Bask., Nog. 133). ✧ A Kazak tribe of the Middle Horde. Cf. Mo. *Qonggirad / Onggirad*.

QOÑOŠ Kzk. 1676 **Qoñoš** [Конгошъ], a Kazak prince (DAI VII, 333, 341-43). ✧ 'Very proud' cf. Chag. *qoñoš* 'ein überaus stolzer Mensch' (Radl. II, 523).

QOÑR-ŌLÏ see **QOÑUR**

QOÑR-ŌLŪ see **QOÑUR**

QOÑRAT see **QOÑÏRAT**

QOÑUR Turk. 20th c. **Qonur** [Konur], a village in the province of İçel, Turkey (TMİB 442); Turk. 20th c. **Qonur-alp** [Konuralp Bucağı], a village in the province of Bolu, Turkey (TMİB 191); Oghuz/Trkm. **Qonur-qoja-sarï-čoban** [Конур-Коджа-Сары-Чобан] (DQorq./Rossi 193, DQorq./Gökyay 82, DQorq. 77, 226); Kzk. 19th c. **Qoñïr** [Бердіяръ Конгировъ] (Grod., Pril. 97); Kzk. 1817 **Qoñïr / Qoñïr-bay** [قونكفر بای / Коныр] (MIK IV, 311, 319); Kuman **Qoñr-olu (<Qoñur-ōlu)** [Kongrolu rétje], Kuman personal name preserved in the name of a meadow (Rásonyi, Adalékok 131 /after Pesty, Helynévtár XXII/, KÖA 115); Kirg. **Qoñr-ōlï-bay / Qoñr-ōlū / Qoñr-ōlū-bay** [Конролы Баи / Конролу / Конролу Баи] (Proben V, 184 /186/, 189 /191/); Kuman 1731, 1733 **Qoñur** [Kangur], personal name preserved in family names and bynames of families of Kuman origin in Greater Kumania (Nagykunság), Hungary (Rásonyi, Adalékok 131, Rásonyi, KÖA 115); Kzk. 19th c. **Qoñur** [Конуръ] (SOK 184); Kzk. 19th c. **Qoñur**

[Конуръ] (AOK 90); Kzk. 19th c. **Qoñur** [Конуръ] (AOO 22); Kirg. **Qoñur / Qoñur-bay** [Конур / Коңурбай / Конгурбай] (Jud. 65, 76); Turk. **Qoñur-alp** [قوكر الپ / Konuralp], Or-χan's comrade-in-arms (Āšikp. 31, 35, 37 etc., Hammer, GOR I, 70, 84 etc.); Bashk. 1675 **Qoñur-bay** [Конур-бай Козягулов] (MIB I, 199); Kzk. 19th c. **Qoñur-bay** [Конурбай] (AOK 114); Kzk. 19th c. **Qoñur-bay** [Конурбай] (SODž. 12); Kirg. **Qoñur-bay** [Коңурбаі / Коңур Баі], a folklore hero in the Manas epic, lord of the Kalmyks (Proben V, 4, 33, 64); Kzk. 1822 **Qoñur-bay / Qoñur / Qoñïr?** [قونكغور / قونكغربای / Конгурбай / Коныр] (MIK IV, 441, 442, 457); Kirg. **Qoñur-yan** [Коңур-Jан], daughter of Qoñuš, one of the forty retainers of Aq-sayqal (Proben V, 394 /397/); Hak.(Sag.) 19th c. **Qoñur-tarγa** [Kongur Targa], head of the Kirghiz (=Kazak) in a historical legend (Radl., Aus Sib. I, 185); Bashk. 1739, 1754 **Qunur** [Кунур Умиров] (MIB III, 409, IV/1, 79); Bashk. 1751 **Qunur** [Кунур Темиров] (MIB IV/1, 34); Kzk. 1830 **Quñur** [Сабекъ Кунгуровъ] (Konšin, Mat. I-III, 62); Alt.(Tuba)? 1654 **Quñur** [Кунгур], a prince („tubinskij knjaz'") (Miller, Ist. Sib. II, 540); *TN:* Turk. 20th c. **Qonur / Qonur-χajï** [Konur, Konur Насюбаsı], a village in the province of Ankara, Turkey (TMİB 83). ✧ 'Dark-brown; sunburnt; kind' cf. Karakh. *qoñur* 'рыжеватый, каштановый; коричневый; каурый' (DTS), Kirg. *qoñur* 'тёмно-бурый, смуглый; (а характере) мягкий, нежный' (Jud.), Bashk. *quñir, qoñγor* 'id.' (BRS/Uraksin). See also **TAY-QOÑUR, TÜRÄ-QOÑUR.**

QOÑUR-ATÏ-BİYİKJİ Alt.(Tuba) 19th c. **Qoñur-atï-biyikJi** [Конгураты-біикджи] (Potanin IV, 560-62). ⇨ **QOÑUR + AT.**

QOÑUR-BARAQ Kzk. 19th c. **Qoñur-baraq** [Конуръ-Баракъ] (Grod., Pril. 27). ⇨ **QOÑUR + BARAQ.**

QOÑUR-BORAQ Kzk. 19th c. **Qoñur-boraq / Qoñur-baraq?** [Конгуръ-Боракъ] (Grod., Pril. 166). ⇨ **QOÑUR + BORAQ / BARAQ?**

QOÑUZ Kzk. 19th c. **Qoñuz-bay** [Конгузбай] (SODž. 108). ✧ 'Bug, beetle' cf. Chag., East.T., Kzk. *qoñuz* 'der Käfer' (Radl. II, 523). See also **JATÏ-QOÑÏZ.**

QOP Yürük 1543 **Qop** [قوپ / Kop] (Gökb., Rum. 186, 188, 189, 201, 202 etc.).

QOPA Kzk. **Qopa** [Оспанъ Копинъ] (Konšin, Oč. 78); Kzk. 19th c. **Qopa-bay** [Копабай] (SODž. 128, 152); Kzk. 19th c. **Qopa-bay** [Копабай] (AOAtb. 38); Kzk. 19th c. **Qopo-bay** [Копобай] (SODž. 34); Kzk. 19th c. **Qopo-bay** [Копобай] (SOK 74); Kzk. 19th c. **Qopo-bay** [Копобай] (AOO 54); Kzk. 19th c. **Qupa** [Купа] (AOO 18). ✧ 'Lake (place) overgrown with reed' cf. Kzk. *qopa* 'ein dicht mit Schilf bewachsener

See' (Radl. II, 652), Kirg. *qopo* 'der am Ufer eines Sees wachsende Schilf' (Radl. II, 653).

QOPAY Bashk. 1758, 1764 **Qopay** [Елдаш (Юлдаш) Копаев] (MIB IV/1, 165, 294); **Qupay** [Кирей Купаевъ] (PSZRI XVII, 110, 111); Bashk. 1735 **Qupay** [Кунакбай Купаевъ], a tarχan (Vel.-Zern., Bašk. 17); Bashk. 1780 **Qupay** [Шайлы Купаев] (MIB V, 103). ⇨ **QOPA / QUPA** + suff. -*y*.

QOPAL Kzk. 19th c. **Qopal** [Копалъ] (SOV 158); Kzk. 19th c. **Qopal-bay** [Копалбай] (SOK 220, 260); Kzk. 19th c. **Qopal-bay** [Копальбай] (SOK 14). ✧ 'Rude, shapeless, clumsy' cf. Chag., East.T. *qopal* 'formlos, ungestaltet, grob, plump' (Radl. II, 653).

QOPAN Kzk. 19th c. **Qopan** [Копанъ] (SODž. 116); Kzk. 19th c. **Qopan** [Копанъ] (AOO 62); Kzk. 19th c. **Qoppan** [Коппанъ] (SOV 54); Kzk. 19th c. **Qoppan** [Коппанъ] (SOK 184); Bashk. 1725 **Qupan** [Купан Девлетбаев] (MIB III, 230); Bashk. 1763 **Qupan** [Исергап Купанов] (MIB IV/1, 271); Kzk. 19th c. **Qupan** [Давидъ Юнусъ Купановъ] (Grod., Pril. 65). ✧ 'Great, strong, triumphant' cf. Chag. *qopan* 'gross, siegreich etc.; hoch, rüstig' (Radl. II, 652), Turk. *qupan* 'id.' (Radl. II, 1033).

QOPAR Kzk. 19th c. **Qopar** [Копаръ] (AOA 90); Kzk. 19th c. **Qopar-bay** [Копарбай] (SOV 118). ✧ 'Rise?' cf. Chag., Crm., Kzk. etc. *qopar-* 'sich erheben, aufstehen lassen' (Radl. II, 652).

QOPARAN Yürük 1543 **Qoparan** [Koparan] (Gökb., Rum. 212). ✧ 'Plucking; breaking off; he who takes something by force' cf. Turk. *qopar-* 'to pluck; to break off; to take by force' (TED).

QOPAS Hak. 19th c. **Qopas** [Копас], fem. (Katanov, Otč. 12).

QOPČU Kzk. 19th c. **Qopču-bay** [Копчубай] (SOV 62); Kzk. 19th c. **Qopču-bay** [Копчубай] (SOK 216). ✧ 'Backbiter, liar' cf. Alt., Hak. *qopčï* 'der Verleumder' (Radl. II, 656).

QOPÏGÏ Kzk. 19th c. **Qopïγï** [Копыги] (AOO 14).

QOPÏR Bashk. 1706 **Qopïr-yan** [Тонатар Копырьянов] (MIB III, 27). ✧ 'Disdainful, arrogant' cf. Bashk. *qupïr, qupïq* 'чванливый, кичливый' (BRS/Uraksin).

QOPÏŠ Kzk. 19th c. **Qopïš** [Копышъ] (AOA 62).

QOPQAQ Kzk. 19th c. **Qopqaq / Qapqaq?** [Копкакъ] (SOV 84).

QOPLAN Tat.(Sib.) 1632 **Qoplan / Qaplan?** [Коплан] (Miller, Ist. Sib. II, 398); Uzb. 1600 **Quplan** [Куплан], from Bukhara (MIB I, 153). ⇨ **QAPLAN, QOBLAN?**

QOPLANDA see **QOBLANDÏ**

QOPLANDÏ see **QOBLANDÏ**

QOPO see **QOPA**

QOPPAN see **QOPAN**

QOPTÏ Kuman 1185 **Qoptï** [Копти (Вулашевич)], a prince from the Ulaš tribe (Ipat. 434 (447), PSRL II,

131, 320). ✧ 'He rose, got up' cf. Kuman *qop-* 'sich erheben, aufstehen' (Radl. II, 654, CC).

QOPUR Kzk. 19th c. **Qopur** [Копуръ] (SOK 240). ✧ 'Cup, saucer' cf. Chag. яопур 'die Tasse, Unterschale' (Radl. II, 654).

QOR Kzk. 19th c. **Qor-bay** [Корбай] (AOAtb. 34). ✧ 'Shame' cf. Kuman, Kzk. *qor* (P.) 'die Schande' (Radl. II, 549).

QOR-SAY Bashk. 1663 **Qor-say** [Корсай] (MIB I, 177); Bashk. 1723 **Qor-say / Qar-say?** [Кулумбеть Корсаев (Карсаев)] (MIB III, 219-20).

QORAN Kzk. 19th c. **Qoran** [Коранъ] (SODž. 40); Kzk. 19th c. **Qoran-bay** [Коранбаевъ] (Grod., Pril. 165). ✧ '(The holy) Quran' cf. Kzk. *qoran* 'der Koran' (Ar.) (Radl. II, 551).

QORAZ see **XORAZ**

QORBOZ Kzk. 19th c. **Qorboz** [Корбозъ] (SOK 204).

QORČIN Kzk. 1698 **Qorčin?** [Корчинко Ереняковъ] (Jarilov, Tel. 9).

QORJUN Kzk. 19th c. **Qoržun** [Коржунъ] (AOP 90); Kzk. 19th c. **Qoržun-bay** [Коржунбай] (SOK 12, 36, 72); Kzk. 19th c. **Qoržun-bay** [Коржунбай] (AOO 18); Kzk. 19th c. **Qoržun-bay** [Коржунбай] (AOAtb. 46); Kzk. 19th c. **Qoržun-bay** [Коржунбай] (SODž. 58, 70, 110); Kzk. 19th c. **Qoržun-bay** [Коржунбай] (SOV 12); Kzk. 19th c. **Qoržun-bay** [Коржунбай] (Pam. kn. Turg. 60); *TN:* Kzk. **Qorjum-bay (<Qorjun-bay)** [Корджумбай] (Karta JAR XI); Kzk. **Qorjun** [Korždžun], an isle in Lake Balkhash (?). ✧ 'Bags for carrying things on the horseback' cf. Kzk. *qoržun* 'куржумъ - мешочки, соединенные между собой' (PKRS).

QORDAY Kzk. 19th c. **Qorday** [Кордай] (SOV 110).

QORDANUQ Tat.(Sib.) 1618 **Qordanuq** [Кокудаш Кордануков], a murza (Miller, Ist. Sib. II, 244).

QORĠAN Kzk. 19th c. **Qorγan-bay** [Корганбай] (SOV 30, 52, 104). ✧ 'Fortress, fortification' cf. Kzk. *qorγan* 'die Befestigung, Festung' (Radl. II, 570), 'крепостная стена' (PKRS).

QORĠAS Kzk. 19th c. **Qorγas-pay** [Коргаспай] (SODž. 156); Kzk. 19th c. **Qorγas-pay** [Коргазпай] (SODž. 98); Kzk. 19th c. **Qorγaz-bay** [Коргозбай] (SODž. 100). ✧ 'Defend, save (the others and yourself)!' cf. Kzk. *qorγas-* 'sich gegenseitig schützen' (Radl. II, 571).

QORĠOLDOY Kirg. **Qorγoldoy** [Корголдой] (Jud. 921). ✧ '(He is like) muck, dung' cf. Kirg. *qorγol* 'помёт (овечий, козий, верблюжий)' (Jud.) + suff. -*doy*.

QORĠUL Kzk. 19th c. **Qorγul** [Коргулъ] (Grod., Pril. 101).

QORĠUT see **QORQUT**

QORÏM Kzk. 19th c. **Qorïm-bay** [Корымбай] (SOV 40). ✧ I. 'Soot'? cf. Kzk. *qïrïm* 'копоть, сажа'

(KzRS). ⇨ **QORUM?**

QORÏP Kzk. 19th c. **Qorïp** [Корыпъ] (SOK 202).

QORÏS Kzk. 19th c. **Qorïs** [Корысъ] (AOK 74).

QORQÏYAQ Hak.(Blt.) 19th-20th c. **Qorqïyaq** [Коркыјак] (Proben IX, 362).

QORQMAZ Selj.? **Qorqmas** [قرقماس الصغير], governor of Malata (Iyās I, 113, 128, Weil, Chalif. II, 336); Maml. 14th c. **Qorqmas / Qurqmas** (Sauvaget 53); 19th c. **Qorqmaz** [Ǧelal Korkmazov], from Dagestan (Mende 176); Turk.? 1487 **Qorqmaz** [بن ولى الدين] (Iyās II, 245, 313, III, 61, 192 etc., Weil, Chalif. II, 365); Karch. **Qorqmaz** [Коркмазовъ] (Sysoev 123); Kzk. 19th c. **Qorqpas** [Коркпасъ] (SODž. 92); Kzk. 19th c. **Qorqpas** [Коркпасъ] (SOK 270). ✧ 'Won't be afraid; isn't afraid; brave' cf. Uyg., Kuman, Chag., Crm. *qorq-* 'fürchten, sich fürchten' (Radl. II, 563), cf. also Sauvaget 53.

QORQPAS see **QORQMAZ**

QORQUD see **QORQUT**

QORQUT Oghuz 1153 **Qorγut** [Коргут ибн Абд-ал-хамид (Куркараб)], a Ghuz emir (MIT I, 323-24, 355, 357, 387, 440); Yürük 1543 **Qorqud** [Korkud] (Gökb., Rum. 203, 221, 227 etc.); Tat. 1543 **Qorqud** [Korkud] (Gökb., Rum. 234); Turk. 1503 **Qorqud / Qorqut-bey** [Korkud Bey / Korkud (Şehzade)], son of Bayezid II (1481-1512) (Gökb., Ed. 471, Baştav 30, 184, 187 etc.); Pecheneg, Turk.? **Qorqut** [Κουρκούτης] (Byz. Turc. 168); Turk. 1565 **Qorqut** [Qorqud bin Musztafa] (Dávid); Yürük 1543 **Qorqut** [Korkut] (Gökb., Rum. 225); Oghuz/Trkm. **Qorqut-ata** [Коркут-Ата] (DQorq. 11); Oghuz/Trkm. 13th c. **Qorqut-ata** [آتا قورقوت / Коркут-ата] (Abulg./Kon. 675, 680, 725-740, 750 etc.); *TN:* Turk. 20th c. **Qorqut** [Korkut], a village in the province of Amasya, Turkey (TMİB 63). ✧ 'Terrorize, intimidate, dispel (the enemy)' cf. Kuman, Chag., Kirg., Turk. *qorqut-* 'erschrecken, drohen' (Radl. II, 567), cf. Rásonyi, Imp. p. 240, Bazin, Qorqut, pp. 278-283.

QORLA Uyg. 12th c. - 14th c. **Qorla-elči** [qorla elči] (DTS).

QORMONĠON Alt. 19th c. **Qormonγon** [Кормонгон], Uzun-qara's son (Verb., In. 153).

QOROŠAY Bashk. 1716 **Qorošay** [Корошай] (MIB III, 141).

QORPÏQ Kzk. 19th c. **Qorpïq** [Корпыкъ] (AOK 122).

QORS see **QORUS**

QORSA Kzk. 19th c. **Qorsa-bay** [Корсабай] (SOV 60).

QORSÏ Kzk. 19th c. **Qorsï-bay** [Корсыбай] (SOK 146).

QORSU Kzk. 19th c. **Qorsu-bay** [Корсубай] (SOK 114).

QORSUN Kzk. **Qorsun-bay** [Корсунбай], a well (?) southwest of Tashkent preserving a personal name

(Karta JAR XIX). ❖ 'Make him smaller, neglect him' cf. Kzk. *qorsun-* 'gering machen, erniedrigen, verachten' (Radl. II, 578).

QORTAN Kzk. 19th c. **Qortan** [Кортанъ] (AOP 82); Kzk. 19th c. **Qortan** [Кортанъ] (AOA 110).

QORTQAČÏQ Bashk. 1734 **Qortqačïq** [Корткачикъ Тоймасовъ], a tarχan (Vel.-Zern., Bašk. 6, 11); Bashk. 1742 **Qurtqačïq** [Уруслу Курткачик] (MIB I, 493); Bashk. 1756 **Qurtqasïq** [Ибраким Курткасиков] (MIB IV/1, 130); Bashk. 1756 **Qurtqasïq** [Тюрзюма Курткасиков] (MIB IV/1, 130); Bashk. 1756 **Qurtqasïq** [Курткасык Чюряков] (MIB IV/1, 130). ❖ 'Little old woman; wife; witch' cf. Tat., Bashk. *qortqa* 'id.' (TatRS, BRS/Uraksin) + dim. suff. -*čïq*.

QORTUQ Kzk. 19th c. **Qortuq** [Кортукъ] (AOA 114); Kzk. 19th c. **Qortuq** [Кортукъ] (SOK 124). ❖ 'Hernia of a sheep' cf. Kzk. *qortuq* 'der Seitenbruch des Schaťes' (Radl. II, 576).

QORTULAN Karch. **Qortulan** [Кортуланъ] (Sysoev 135).

QORUBA Türk? 967 **Qoruba** [Koruba], a slave (gulām) of the Hamdanids in Haleb (Weil, Chalif. III, 38-39).

QORUQAY Tat.(Sib.)? 1635 **Qoruqay** [Корукайко Пышболдуев] (Miller, Ist. Sib. II, 423).

QORUM Uzb. 1638 **Qorum** [Корум], from Bukhara (Miller, Ist. Sib. II, 453). ❖ 'Landslide, rock-fall' cf. Uyg., Alt., Hak. *qorum* 'der Bergsturz, das Geröll' (Radl. II, 561).

QORUMČÏ Uyg. 12th c. - 14th c. **Qorumčï-oγul** [Korumçi oġul / qorumčï oγul] (EUTS, DTS). ❖ 'Worker on landslide/rock-fall' (Blagova 1997, 711). ⇨ **QORUM** + suff. -*čï*.

QORUMQA Uzb. 1639 **Qorumqa** [Корумка Абымановъ], from Bukhara (Miller, Ist. Sib. II, 453). ⇨ **QORUM** + suff. -*qa*.

QORUN Kirg. **Qorun** [Корун] (Jud. 645, 948). ❖ 'Save yourself, hide' cf. Kirg. *qorun-* 'остерегаться, искать спасения, прятаться, затаиться' (Jud.).

QORUS Kzk. 19th c. **Qors-pay** [Корспай] (AOAtb. 34); Kzk. 19th c. **Qorus-pay** [Коруспай] (AOP 122); Kzk. 19th c. **Qorus-pay** [Коруспай] (SOK 302).

QORZA-PÏRAN Kzk. **Qorza-pïran** [Korsapyran / Корзапыранъ], Qorluq's sister (Proben III, 490 /566/).

QORŽUQ Kzk. 19th c. **Qoržuq-pay** [Коржукпай] (AOP 42). ⇨ **QOR** + dim. suff. -*žuq*?

QORŽUN see **QORJUN**

QOS see **QOŠ I.**

QOS-AYAQ Kzk. 19th c. **Qos-ayaq** [Косаякъ] (SOK 88, 128). ❖ 'Rabbit' cf. Kzk. *qosayaq* 'der Springhase' (Radl. II, 623). ⇨ **QOŠ I. + AYAQ?**

QOS-AYDAR Kzk. 19th c. **Qos-aydar** [Косайдаръ] (AOO 58). ❖ II. 'He who will look after lambs'? ⇨ **QOŠ I. + AYDAR.**

QOS-AMAN Kzk. 19th c. **Qos-aman** [Косаманъ] (Grod., Pril. 78). ⇨ **QOŠ I. + AMAN.**

QOS-ASA Kzk. 19th c. **Qos-asa-bay?** [Kosasa-bay] (Ljutš 128). ⇨ **QOŠ I.**

QOS-BAΓAR Kzk. 1874 **Qos-baγar** [Кос Богар] (MIKk. 249). ❖ I. 'He who will look after the tent'? cf. Kzk. *qos* 'маленькая (походная) юрта; совокупность земледельческих орудий с рабочим скотом и рабочей силой' (KzRS), cf. also Kzk. PNs *Qos-basar, Qos-žan, Qos-nazar* (Žanuzakov-Esbaeva); II. 'He who will look after lambs'? see QOZÏ-BAΓAR. ⇨ **QOŠ I. / QOZÏ? + BAQAR?**

QOS-BARMAQ see **QOŠ-BARMAQ**

QOS-BELGE Kzk. 19th c. **Qos-belge** [Косбельге] (SOV 142). ⇨ **QOŠ I.**

QOS-BERDİ see **QOŠ-BERDİ**

QOS-BERGEN see **QOŠ-BERGEN**

QOS-JAYSAN Kzk. 19th c. **Qos-jaysan** [قوس جايسان / Косъ-джай-санъ] (Veselovskij, Kirg. 78 /122/). ⇨ **QOŠ I. + YAYSAN.**

QOS-DÄWLET Kzk. 19th c. **Qos-däwlet** [Kos-Däulet] (Altyns. 93). ⇨ **QOŠ I. + DÄWLÄT.**

QOS-KİLDÄK Bashk. 18th c. **Qos-kildäk-mulla** [Коскильдак-мулла] (MIB III, 132). ⇨ **QOŠ I. + KELDİ?**

QOS-QODAM Kzk. 19th c. **Qos-qodam / Qos-qadam?** [Коскодамъ] (AOA 18). ⇨ **QOŠ I.**

QOS-QULAQ Kzk.? **Qos-qulaq** [Умурзакъ Коскулаковъ] (?). ❖ 'Twin ears'. ⇨ **QOŠ I./İİ. + QULAQ.**

QOS-MUXAMMED see **QOŠ-MUXAMMAD**

QOS-MUXAMMET see **QOŠ-MUXAMMAD**

QOS-MURAT Kzk. 18th c. - 19th c. **Qos-murat** [Космуратъ], a clan (Tynyšp. 65). ⇨ **QOŠ I. + MURAT.**

QOS-MURZA Kzk. **Qos-murza** [Кос-мурза], a place? (Karta JAR X). ⇨ **QOŠ I. + MURZA.**

QOS-PARMAQ see **QOŠ-BARMAQ**

QOS-TAY see **QOŠ-TAY**

QOS-TAYAQ Hak. 19th c. **Qos-tayaq** [Костайак] (Katanov, Otč. 12); Karg. **Qos-tayaq** [Кос-тајак] (Katanov, Otč. 8); Karg. **Qos-tayaq** [Костаяк] (Proben IX, 626, 640, 658, 659). ❖ 'Twin/double stick' (Katanov). ⇨ **QOŠ I. + TAYAQ.**

QOS-UWAQ Kzk. 19th c. **Qos-uwaq** [Косуакъ] (SOV 94). ❖ 'Twin small/little'. ⇨ **QOŠ I. + UWAQ.**

QOSAΓAL Kzk. 19th c. **Qosaγal** [Косагалъ] (AOAtb. 42).

QOSAY see **QOŠAY**

QOSAQ Kzk. 19th c. **Qosaq-bay** [Косакбай] (AOA 74); Kzk. 19th c. **Qosaq-bay** [Косакбай] (SOK 262); Kzk. 19th c. **Qosaq-pay** [Косакпай] (SOV 72); *TN:*

Kzk. **Qosaq** [Косак], streams in the county of Karaganda (Kojčubaev 149); Kzk. **Qošaq** [Кошак], a place (Kojčubaev 151). ✧ 'A pair of animals (sheep) bound to each other; girlfriend; wife' cf. Kzk. *qosaq* 'zwei zusammen angespannte Thiere, das Gespann' (Radl. II, 623), 'подруга (жена)' (PKRS).

QOSAL Kzk. 19th c. **Qosal** [Косалъ] (SODž. 158); Kzk. 19th c. **Qosal** [Косалъ] (SOK 22, 288).

QOSAN Kzk. 19th c. **Qosan** [Косанъ] (AOK 46); Kzk. 19th c. **Qosan** [Косанъ] (AOAtb. 50).

QOSAR Kzk. 19th c. **Qosar** [Косаръ] (SOV 134); Kzk. 19th c. **Qosar-bay** [Косарбай] (AOK 10). ✧ 'Who allies; adds, who will enrich' cf. Kzk. *qos* 'vereinigen, zusammenlegen, hinzufügen' (Radl. II, 622).

QOSAWMAS Kzk. 19th c. **Qosawmas** [Косаумасъ] (SOK 292).

QOSBÏR Kzk. 19th c. **Qosbïr-bay** [Косбырбай] (SOK 34).

QOSČU Kzk. 19th c. **Qosču-bay** [Косчубай] (AOP 14). ✧ I. 'Fellow traveller, mate, companion; servant' cf. Kzk. *qosšï, qosšï bala* 'der Reisediener, der das Reisezelt aufräumt' (Radl. II, 627), *qosšï* 'сопровождающий в пути' (KzRS); II. 'Living in a temporary yurt'? ⇨ **QOŠ I.** + suff. *-čï*.

QOSÏMBET Kkalp. 20th c. **Qosïmbet** [Қосымбет] (KkRS 774). ⇨ **QOŠ I.** + suff. *-imbet*.

QOSKE see **QOŠ I.**

QOSQA Tat. 1709 **Qosqa** [Коска] (MIB III, 45). ⇨ **QUSQA?**

QOSQAL Kzk. 19th c. **Qosqal** [Коскалъ] (SOK 214).

QOSQÏR Hak.(Blt.) 19th-20th c. **Qosqïr** [Коскыр] (Proben IX, 563).

QOSQORAW Kzk. 19th c. **Qosqoraw** [Коскорау] (SOV 62).

QOSLÏ Kzk. 19th c. **Qoslï-bay** [Кослыбай] (SODž. 148). ⇨ **QOŠ I.** + suff. *-lï*.

QOSOQ Kzk. 19th c. **Qosoq / Qosaq?** [Косокъ] (SOK 146). ⇨ **QOSAQ?**

QOSPAN Kzk. 19th c. **Qospan** [Коспанъ] (AOK 126).

QOSPOQ Kzk. 19th c. **Qospoq-bay / Qospaq-bay?** [Коспокбай] (SOK 146). ✧ 'A kind of hybrid camel (a crossbreed of a Bactrian camel and a dromedary)' cf. Kzk. *qospaq* 'ein Kameel, das aus Vermischung von einem einhöckrigen Kameele [nar] mit einem zweihöckrigen [tüö] hervorgegangen ist' (Radl. II, 627).

QOSSÏN Hak. 19th-20th c. **Qossïn** [Коссын], fem. (HRS 353).

QOST Kzk. 19th c. **Qost-bay** [Костбай] (AOA 18).

QOSTA Pecheneg 10th c. **Qosta / Qošta?** [Κώστας], chief of the sixth tribe of the Pechenegs (Byz. Turc. 176).

QOSTAQ Kzk. 19th c. **Qostaq / Köstäk-bay?** [Костакбай] (SOK 162); Kzk. 19th c. **Qostaq-bay / Köstäk-bay?** [Костакбай] (AOA 82); Kzk. 19th c.

Qostaq-pay / Köstek-pay? [Костекпай] (SODž. 52).

QOSTAN Kzk. 1846 **Qostan** [Ал-Чан Костанов], a biy (MKOP 155).

QOSTÏNAÑ Hak. 19th-20th c. **Qostinañ** [Костинанъ] (HRS 349).

QOSTROQ Tat.(GH) 1377, 1378 **Qostruq / Qostroq** [Кострокъ /Острукъ], a prince of Mamay (PSRL XI, 43, XXIII, 124).

QOSTU Kzk. **Qostu-bay** [Костубай] (Sb. Syr-D. IX, 54); Kzk. 19th c. **Qostu-bay** [Костубай] (AOP 46). ✧ 'Having a temporary tent'? ⇨ **QOŠ I.** + suff. *-tu (<-lï)*.

QOSTUQ see **KÖSTÜK**

QOSU Kzk. 19th c. **Qosu-bay** [Косубай] (SOV 40).

QOSUČÏ 1689 **Qosuči / Qosučï** [Косючи Монготей] (PSZRI III, 15). ⇨ **QOSU?** + suff. *-čï*.

QOSUƔUN Kzk. 19th c. **Qosuɣun** [Косугунъ] (SODž. 116).

QOSUM Kzk. 1822 **Qosum** [Косум] (MIK IV, 433, 435). ⇨ **QOŠUM?, QOSU / QOŠU?** + poss. suff. *-m?*

QOSUN Kzk. 19th c. **Qosun** [Косунъ] (SODž. 8). ✧ 'Soldier, scout' cf. Kzk. *qosïn* 'asker, ordu; iki tarafın sınırındaki gözcü' (KzTS). ⇨ **ƔOŠUN.**

QOŠ I. Kzk. 19th c. **Qos-aba** [Косъ-аба], personal name preserved in the name of a field (AOK 62); Kzk. 1817 **Qos-eke** [قوس اكه / Косеке] (MIK IV, 311, 318); Kzk. 19th c. **Qos-pay** [Коспай] (SOK 46); Tat. 1739 **Qos-türä** [Ф. С. Костюринъ], family name of a landlord (Alatyr. 148); Kzk. 1838 **Qoske (<Qos-eke?)** [Коске Урмаковъ], from the Middle Horde (Orta Žüz) (Konšin, Mat. V, 16); Kzk. 19th c. **Qoš** [Мулла Кошевъ] (SKSO VIII, 219); Kzk. 19th c. **Qoš-bay** [Кошбай] (AOA 82); Kzk. 19th c. **Qoš-bay** [Кошбай] (AOP 90); Kzk. 19th c. **Qoš-bay** [Кошбай] (SKSO III, 18); Kzk. 19th c. **Qoš-qulï** [Кошкулы] (AOO 2); Kzk. 19th c. **Qoš-pay** [Кошпай] (SOK 190); Kzk. 19th c. **Qoš-šan (<Qoš-ǰan?)** [Кощанъ] (AOO 6); *EN:* Kzk. 18th c. - 19th c. **Qos-qul** [Коскул], a clan (Tynyšp. 73); *TN:* Tuv. 19th c. **Qoš-pay** [Košpai / Кошпаi], a stream (Proben IX, 103). ✧ I. 'Being together; pair, twin, two things' cf. Uyg., Chag., Alt., Crm., Hak., Kirg. *qoš, qos* 'zusammen sich befindend; ein Paar' (Radl. II, 635), Kzk. *qos* 'das Paar, zwei zusammengehörige Dinge' (Radl. II, 622), Bashk. *quš* 'парный; пара' (BRS/Uraksin), Tat. *quš* 'id.' (TatRS); II. 'Temporary yurt (tent), camp; household of a farmer' cf. Chag., East.T., Kirg., Kzk. *qoš / qos* das Lager, Heer etc.' (Radl. II, 635), Kzk. *qos* 'маленькая (походная) юрта; совокупность земледельческих орудий с рабочим скотом и рабочей силой' (KzRS), cf. also Kzk. PNs *Qos-basar, Qos-žan, Qos-nazar* (Žanuzakov-Esbaeva).

QOŠ II. see **QUŠ I.**

QOŠ-ABÏŠ Kirg. **Qoš-abïš** [Кош Абыш], one of Manas' comrades-in-arms (čoro), Qoñɣr-ölï-bay's son

(Proben V, 186). ⇨ **XOŠ / QOŠ I. + ABÏŠ.**

QOŠ-АГАČ Tat.(Sib.) 1680 **Qož-aɣač** (<Qoš-aɣač?) [Кожегачко] (DAI VIII, 44). ⇨ **QOŠ I. + АГАČ?**

QOŠ-ALİ Uzb. 19th c. **Qoš-ali** [Кошъ Али] (SKSO III, 162). ⇨ **XOŠ / QOŠ I. + ALİ.**

QOŠ-ASAN Kzk. 19th c. **Qož-asan? / Qoš-asan** [Кожасанъ] (SODž. 8). ⇨ **XOŠ + ASAN? (XASAN).**

QOŠ-BAXTÏ Tat.(Sib.) 1599 **Qož-baχtï** [Кожбахтый], a mirza from Siberia (AI II, 7). ⇨ **XOŠ + BAQTÏ.**

QOŠ-BAMBET Kzk. 18th c. - 19th c. **Qož-bambet /** (<Qož-mambet <Qoža-mambet?) [Кожбамбет], a clan (Tynyšp. 67, 71). ⇨ **XOŠ / QOJA + MAMBET.**

QOŠ-BARMAQ Kkalp. 20th c. **Qos-barmaq** [Қосбармак] (KkRS 774); Kzk. 1794 **Qos-barmaq / Qoš-barmaq** [قوش برمق / Косбармак] (MIK IV, 162); Kzk. 19th c. **Qos-parmaq** [Коспармакъ] (SOK 64); Kkalp. 20th c. **Qos-parmaq** [Къоспармакъ] (Bask., Kkalp. 56). ✧ 'Pair/twin fingers'. ⇨ **QOŠ I. + BARMAQ.**

QOŠ-BERDİ Bashk. 1735 **Qoš-perdi** [Кошперде] (MIB III, 334); *EN:* Kzk. 18th c. - 19th c. **Qos-berdi** [Косберды], a clan (Tynyšp. 67). ⇨ **QOŠ I. + BERDİ.**

QOŠ-BERGEN Kzk. 19th c. **Qos-bergen** [Косбергенъ] (SOK 120); Kkalp. 20th c. **Qos-bergen** [Қосберген] (KkRS 774); Kkalp. 1820 **Qoš-bergen** [Кош-берген бий] (MIKk. 107). ⇨ **QOŠ I. + BERGEN.**

QOŠ-DÄWLÄT Tat. 1632 **Qož-däwlät** [Менглыбай Кождевлетев] (Miller, Ist. Sib. II, 399, 400); Tat. 1634 **Qož-däwlät** [Мутык Кождевлетев] (Miller, Ist. Sib. II, 421); Bashk. 1714 **Qož-däwlät** [Кусюм Кождевлетев] (MIB I, 105); *EN:* Kzk. 18th c. - 19th c. **Qos-dawlet** [Косдаулет], a clan (Tynysp. 73). ⇨ **XOŠ + DÄWLÄT.**

QOŠ-KİLDİ Tat.(Sib.) 1631 **Qoš-kilde / Qoš-kildey?** [Янгул Кошкилдеев], a falconer (Miller, Ist. Sib. II, 384); Tat.(Sib.) 1632 **Qoš-kilde / Qoš-kildey?** [Кошкилдей] (Miller, Ist. Sib. II, 397); Tat.(Sib.) 1632 **Qoš-kilde / Qoš-kildey?** [Кошкилдей (Баубеков)] (Miller, Ist. Sib. II, 397); Tat. 1662 **Qoš-kildi** [Емангулька Кошкильдиевъ] (DAI IV, 286); Tat. 1662 **Qoš-kildi** [Емангулька Кошкильдиевъ] (DAI IV, 286); Kzk. 19th c. **Qož-geldi** (<Qoš-keldi) [Кожгельды] (SOK 252). ✧ 'The fellow (pair, mate) has come' cf. Tat. PN *Quš-kilde* (Sattarov); II. 'Nice/good child has come (has been born)' cf. Tat. PN *Xuš-kilde* (Sattarov). ⇨ **QOŠ I. / XOŠ + KELDİ.**

QOŠ-MAYDAN Tat.(Sib.) 1603 **Qoš-maydan / Qaš-maydan?** [Кошмаиданко / Кашмаидан] (Miller, Ist. Sib. II, 178, 179). ⇨ **QOŠ I. / XOŠ? + MAYDAN.**

QOŠ-MUXAMMAD Kzk. 19th c. **Qos-muχammed** [Космухаммедъ] (Grod., Pril. 78); Kzk. 19th c. **Qoš-muχammad** [Кошмухаммадъ] (SKSO VIII, 203). ⇨ **QOŠ I. + MUXAMMED.**

QOŠ-NAZAR Kzk. 19th c. **Qoš-nazar** [Кошназаръ] (SKSO VIII, 222). ⇨ **QOŠ I. + NAZAR.**

QOŠ-NİYAZ Kkalp. 20th c. **Qoš-niyaz** [Қошнияз] (KkRS 774). ⇨ **QOŠ I. + NİYAZ.**

QOŠ-TAY Kzk. 19th c. **Qos-tay** [Костай] (AOO 66); Kzk. 19th c. **Qoš-tay / Qoštay?** [Коштай] (AOA 82); Kzk. 19th c. **Qoš-tay / Qoštay?** [Коштаевъ] (AOO 30). ⇨ **QOŠ I. + TAY** or suff. *-tay?*

QOŠAY Tat.(GH) **Qosay** [Косай] (PSRL (Russk. Hr.) I, 528); Kzk. **Qosay** [Kocai / ер Kocai] (Proben III, 91 /116/); Kzk. 1822 **Qosay** [قوصای / Косай] (MIK IV, 433, 435); Kzk. 19th c. **Qosay** [Иръ-Косай] (Potanin, Pred. 79); Kzk. 19th c. **Qosay** [Косай] (SOK 44); Kzk. 19th c. **Qosay** [Косай] (SODž. 98); Kzk. 1794 **Qosay-mïrza** [قوصای مرضه / Косай] (MIK IV, 163); Tat. **Qošay** [Košaj] (H. Z. Koşay: KCsA I, 324); Tat. 1675 **Qošay** [Кошай / Кошайко] (Kungursk. akty 30); Tat. 1696 **Qošay** [Кошайко] (Kungursk. akty 240); Tat. 1724 **Qošay** [Кошай Тирибердеев] (MIB III, 228); Tat. 1737 **Qošay** [Кошай Нукаев] (MIB I, 315); Bashk. 1715 **Qošay** [Кошай Досметев] (MIB III, 130); Bashk. 1729 **Qošay** [Кошай Маметев] (MIB III, 264); Bashk. 1731 **Qošay** [Чюра Кошаев] (MIB III, 292); Bashk. 1735 **Qošay** [(Тахтаръ, Ишкей) Кошаевъ], a tarχan (Vel.-Zern., Bašk. 13); Bashk. 1737 **Qošay** [Ювакай Кошаев] (MIB I, 318); Bashk. 18th c. **Qošay** [Каманай Кошаевъ], a tarχan (Vel.-Zern., Bašk. 20-21); Bashk. 1756 **Qošay** [Явгуста Кошаев] (MIB IV/1, 109); Bashk. 1760 **Qošay** [Биимбеть Кошаев] (MIB IV/1, 189); Bashk. 1761 **Qošay** [Кошай Кузюмов] (MIB IV/1, 200); Bashk. 1776 **Qošay** [Митрей Кошаев] (MIB V, 44); Bashk. 1783 **Qošay** [Мамбеть Кушаев] (MIB V, 143); Tat. 1720 **Qošay / Qašay?** [Амай Кашаевъ] (PSZRI VI, 180); Tat. 1722 **Qošay / Qašay?** [Кашай] (MIB I, 293); Tat.(Sib.) 1638 **Qošay / Qašay?** [Кашайко] (Miller, Ist. Sib. II,); Tat.(Sib.) 1638 **Qošay / Qašay?** [Кашай, Кошай] (Miller, Ist. Sib. II, 452); Uzb. 19th c. **Qošay-bay** [Кошайбай] (SKSO II, 16); Tat. 1557 **Qošay-murza** [Кошай мурза] (Kn. Metriki Lit. 152); Kirg. **Qošoy** [Кошой] (Jud. 25); Kirg. **Qošoy** [Held Koschai / Ер Кошоi] (Proben V, 17 /18/); Kirg. **Qošoy** [Ер Кошоi] (Proben V, 141 /143/); Tat. 1779 **Qušay** [Максют Кушаев] (MIB V, 81, 93); Bashk. 1742 **Qušay** [Чиря Кушаев] (MIB III, 513); Bashk. 1764 **Qušay** [Кушай Ишмурзин] (MIB IV/2, 105); Bashk. 1776 **Qušay** [Кутуш Кушаев] (MIB V, 43, 44, 45); Bashk. 1776 **Qušay** [Ракай Кушаев (Кошаев)] (MIB V, 43, 44); Kzk. 19th c. **Qušay** [Кушай] (Grod., Pril. 25); Bashk. 1776 **Qušay / Qošay** [Кутуш Кушаев (Кошаев)] (MIB V, 43, 44).

⇨ **QOŠ I.** + dim. suff. *-ay/-oy*? See also **ER-QOSAY**.

QOŠAQ I.   Tat.(GH) 1357 **Qošaq** [Кошакъ], envoy of the Horde (PSRL IV, 63, V, 228, VIII, 10, X, 229 XVI, 87); Crm. **Qošaq** [Кощакъ (Кучакъ-огланъ)], a Crimean prince, thc same as Qušaq-oγlan? (PSRL XIX, 69, 70-72, 326); Crm. 1551 **Qošaq-ulan** [Кошакъ-уланъ], the same as Qošaq and Qušaq-oγlan? (PSRL XIII, 166). ✧ 'Historical song'? cf. Kuman *qošaq* 'ein historischer Gesang' (Radl. II, 638); 'Little yurt (tent)'? ⇨ **QOŠ**? + dim. suff. *-aq*?

QOŠAQ II. see **QOSAQ**

QOŠAQAY   Kzk. 19th c. **Qošaqay** [Кошакай] (AOAtb. 6). ⇨ **QOŠAQ I.** + dim. suff. *-ay*.

QOŠALAQ   Kzk. 19th c. **Qošalaq** [Кошалаковъ] (AOK 26). ✧ 'Vulture' cf. Chag. *qučalaq* 'der Geier' (Radl. II, 1009).

QOŠAR   Bashk. 1732 **Qošar** [Кошар-сотник Теуков] (MIB III, 302).

QOŠBARXAN   Tat.(Sib.) 1601 **Qošbarχan** [Болтин Кошбархан] (Miller, Ist. Sib. II, 169).

QOŠČĬ   Kzk. **Qošči-γul** [Koščegulov, Alichan] (Mende 102); Kzk. 19th c. **Qoššï-bay (<Qošči-bay?)** [Кошибаевъ] (SKSO III, 18); Kzk. 19th c. **Qoššï-bay (<Qošči-bay)** [Кощибай] (SOV 64); Kzk. 19th c. **Qoššï-bay (<Qošči-bay)** [Кощибай] (SOK 212); Kzk. 19th c. **Qoššu-bay (<Qošču-bay)** [Кощубай] (AOP 38); Kzk. 19th c. **Qoššu-bay (<Qošču-bay)** [Кощубай] (SODž. 8); Kzk. 19th c. **Qoššu-γul (<Qošču-γul)** [Кощугулъ] (AOP 26); Kzk.? 19th c. **Qošu-bay (<Qoššu-bay <Qošču-bay)** [Кошубай] (Konšin, Oč. 81); Kzk. 19th c. **Qošu-bay (<Qoššu-bay <Qošču-bay)** [Кощубай] (AOP 74); Kzk. 19th c. **Qošu-bay (<Qoššu-bay <Qošču-bay?)** [Кощубай] (AOAtb. 62). ✧ 'Travelling servant who takes care of pack-horses and tents' cf. Kzk. *qoššu (qošči)* 'ein Arbeiter, der die Packpferde zu führen und zu besorgen hat' (Radl. II, 646), Kzk. *qossï (qosči)* 'der Reisediener, der das Reisezelt aufräumt' (Radl. II, 627), Trkm. *yošči* 'охранник, сторож стана, коша; пахарь' (TrkmRS). ⇨ **QOŠ I.** + suff. *-či*. See also **ORUS-QOŠČĬ**.

QOŠČU see **QOŠČĬ**

QOŠĬ   Uzb. 19th c. **Qoši-bay** [Юлдашъ Кошибаевъ] (SKSO III, 18). ⇨ **QOŠČĬ**?

QOŠĬ-BAY see **QOŠČĬ**

QOŠĬM   Kzk. 19th c. **Qošïm** [Кошымъ] (AOAtb. 38). ⇨ **QOŠ I.** + poss. suff. *-ïm*.

QOŠQAY   Bashk. 1742 **Qošqay** [Умирбакы Кошкаев] (MIB III, 513). ⇨ **QOŠ I. / QUŠ I.**? + dim. suff. *-qay*.

QOŠQAN   Uzb. 20th c. **Qošqân** [Кушкон] (Begmatov 1984, 207). ✧ '(He/she) joined (us); Let him/her join us' (Begmatov), cf. Uzb. *qoš-* 'соединять; увеличивать; преподнести (что-л. в подарок по случа[свадьбы]' (UzbRS).

случа[свадьбы]' (UzbRS).

QOŠQAR see **QOČQAR**

QOŠQĬN   Uzb. 20th c. **Qošqïn** [Кушкин] (Begmatov 1984, 207); Uzb. 20th c. **Qošqïn-bây** [Кушкинбой] (Begmatov 1984, 207). ✧ '(He/she) joined (us); Let him/her join us' (Begmatov), cf. Uzb. *qoš-* 'соединять; увеличивать; преподнести (что-л. в подарок по случа[свадьбы]' (UzbRS) + suff. *-qïn*.

QOŠQUM-BAY (<QOŠQUN-BAY) see **QOŠQUN**

QOŠQUN   Kzk. 19th c. **Qošqum-bay (<Qošqun-bay)** [Кошкумбай] (SOV 44); Kzk. 19th c. **Qošqum-bay (<Qošqun-bay)** [Кошкумбай] (SOK 132); Kzk. 19th c. **Qošqum-bay (<Qošqun-bay)** [Кошкумбай] (AOO 50); Kzk. 19th c. **Qošqum-bay (<Qošqun-bay)** [Кошкумбай] (AOP 122).

QOŠMAN   Uzb. 19th c. **Qošman** [Хамра Кошмановъ] (SKSO III, 188). ⇨ **QOŠ I.** + suff. *-man*.

QOŠO   Kirg. **Qošo** [Kosha / Кошо], Qoñr-ölü-bay's son (Proben V, 47).

QOŠOY see **QOŠAY**

QOŠOÑ   Kirg. **Qoyon / Qošoñ**? [Kan Koschong / Кан Којоñ] (Proben V, 144 /146/).

QOŠPAN   Kzk. 19th c. **Qošpan** [Кошпанъ] (SODž. 14). ⇨ **QOŠ I.** + suff. *-pan*.

QOŠŠU see **QOŠČĬ**

QOŠTA   Tat.(Sib.) 1634 **Qošta** [Кошта] (Miller, Ist. Sib. II, 415).

QOŠTAQ   Bashk. 1713 **Qoštaq** [Коштак] (MIB III, 104, 142).

QOŠTAN   Bashk. 1712 **Qoštan** [Коштан Чюлаков] (MIB III, 44, 87).

QOŠTĬ   Kzk. 19th c. **Qoštï-bay** [Коштибай] (Grod., Pril. 81); Kzk. 19th c. **Qoštu-bay** [Коштубай] (SOK 38). ✧ 'Comrade, mate' cf. Chag. *qošti* 'der Gefährte, Genosse' (Radl. II, 646). ⇨ **QOŠ I.**? + suff. *-tï*.

QOŠTU see **QOŠTĬ**

QOŠTUR   Turk. 19th c. **Qoštur-oγlu** [Koštur oγlu], a Zeybek (Kúnos 1891, 119). ✧ 'Make him/her run' (Rásonyi, Imp. 240), vf. Turk. *qoštur-* 'id.' (Zenk.).

QOŠU I.   Türk 732 **Qošu-tutuq** [Qoşu Tutuq] (ETY I, 48); Türk **Qošu-čopan-irkin** [Ko-šu (?) čopan irkin], a chieftain of the western Türks (Ligeti, R. tör. nev. II-III 75:41); Türk **Qošu-kül-irkin** [Ko-šu kül irkin], a chieftain of the western Türks (Ligeti, R. tör. nev. II-III 75:41). See also **QOŠO**?

QOŠU II. see **QOŠČĬ**

QOŠUY   Tat.(Sib.) 1605 **Qošuy** [Кошуй], a prince (Miller, Ist. Sib. II, 189).

QOŠUM   Kzk. 19th c. **Qošum** [Кошумъ] (SOK 170); Nog. **Qošum** [Кошум] (Žirm., Epos 422); Nog. 1558 **Qošum** [Кошумъ], a Noγay mirza (MIK 29); Kzk. 19th c. **Qošum-bay** [Кошумбай] (SODž. 82); Kzk. 19th c. **Qošum-bay** [Кошумбай] (AOO 62); Kzk. 19th c. **Qošum-bay** [Кошумбай] (SOK 44); Kzk. 19th c.

Qošum-bay [Кошумбай] (AOK 30); Nog. 1533 **Qošum-murza / Köšüm-murza** [Кошумъ мурза / Кошюмъ-мурза] (PSRL VIII, 280, XIII, 65 XX, 413); Kzk. 19th c. **Qšum (<Qošum)** [Кшумъ] (AOK 122). ⇨ **QUŠUM, QOŠ I.?** + poss. suff. *-um / -m?*

QOŠUNČÏ **Qošunčï** (Byz. Turc.). ⇨ **ГOŠUN / QOSUN?** + suff. *-čï.*

QOŠUP Kipch. 1298 **Qošup / Qušub** [قوشب / Кушуб], a Kipchak chief (leader), Nogay's follower (Baybars/Tizeng. I, 88, 111).

QOŠUR Tat.(Sib.)? 1616 **Qošur** [Кошур], a taysha (tayša) (Miller, Ist. Sib. II, 235); Kzk. 19th c. **Qošur-bay** [Кошурбай] (AOK 26).

QOT see **QUT**

QOTA Kzk. 19th c. **Qota-bay** [Котабай] (SODž. 46). ⇨ **QUTA.**

QOTA-BERDİ Kzk. 19th c. **Qota-berdi** [Котаберды] (SOV 88). ⇨ **QOTA** + **BERDİ.**

QOTA-NAZAR Kzk. 19th c. **Qota-nazar** [Кота-Назаръ] (AOP 2). ⇨ **QOTA** + **NAZAR.**

QOTAQAY Bashk. 1706 **Qotaqay** [Кусяк Котакаев] (MIB III, 20). ⇨ **QOTA / QUTAQ?** + suff. *-(q)ay.* See also **QUTAQAY.**

QOTAN see **QUTAN**

QOTAN-TOГRÏ Uyg. **Qotan-toγrï** [Kotan Toğrı] (EUTS). ⇨ **TOГRÏ.**

QOTAN-TOГRÏL see **QUTAN-TOГRÏL**

QOTAŠ Kzk. 19th c. **Qotaš** [Коташъ] (SOK 144). ⇨ **QOTA** + suff. *-š.*

QOTAZ NUyg. 19th c. **Qotaz** [قوتاز / Kotaz] (Le Coq, Nam.enl. 107). ✧ 'Yak-steer' (Le Coq).

QOTBA Kzk. 19th c. **Qotba** [Котба] (AOA 118).

QOTČAQ Bashk. 1695 **Qotčaq** [Котчак] (MIB I, 90).

QOTİL Hak. 19th-20th c. **Qotil** [Котил] (HRS 349).

QOTÏ see **QUTU**

QOTÏČ see **TİBRÄNŠÏ-QOTÏČ**

QOTÏГAY Kzk. 19th c. **Qotïγay** [Котыгай] (AOP 18). ✧ 'Little box'. ⇨ **QUTU** + dim. suff. *-γay / -qay.* See also **QUTUГAY.**

QOTÏY Kipch.? 1251, 1252 **Qotïy** [Котій], a chieftain („vojevoda") of the Horde (PSRL V, 186 VII, 159).

QOTÏNBET Kzk. 19th c. **Qotïnbet / Qotïmbet?** [Котынбетъ] (SODž. 58).

QOTÏRAГ Bulg. **Qotïraγ?** [Κότραγος], Qobrat / Qubrat's son (after Teophanes) (Byz. Turc. 165).

QOTKE Kzk. 19th c. **Qotke / Qot-eke / Kötke?** [Котке] (SODž. 76).

QOTQAN Kzk. 19th c. **Qotqan-bay** [Котканбай] (AOP 82).

QOTLU see **QUTLUГ**

QOTLU-BAQ see **QUTLU-BAQ**

QOTLU-BAQAŠ Tat. 18th c. **Qotlu-baqaš** [Котлубакашевы Челны], personal name preserved

in the name of a village in the district of Laiševsk (Korsakov 187). ⇨ **QUTLUГ** + **BAQAŠ.**

QOTLUQ see **QUTLUГ**

QOTOŠ see **QUTUŠ**

QOTSU Uyg. **Qotsu** [Kotsu] (EUTS).

QOTTÏMBET see **QUTLUMBET**

QOTTU see **QUTLUГ**

QOTTUMBET see **QUTLUMBET**

QOTU see **QUTU**

QOTUM see **QUTUM**

QOTUR Trkm. 20th c. **Gotur** [Gotur] (Zaj. 1971, 333); Trkm. 20th c. **Gotur** [Готур] (TrkmRS 190); Hak.? 19th-20th c. **Qodïr** [Кодыр] (Katanov, Otč. 10); Kzk. 19th c. **Qotur** [Котуръ] (AOO 42). ✧ 'Scab, scabies, smallpox, pockmark' cf. Kzk. *qotur* 'id.' (PKRS, Radl. II, 609), Kuman, Bashk., Crm., Kzk. *qotur* 'der Schorf, Grind, Ausschlag, die Krätze' (Radl. II, 609), Trkm. *γotur* 'рябина, оспина; чесотка, парша' (TrkmRS).

QOTUR-ŠİГAL Uzb.? 1816 **Qotur-šiγal** [Котур Шигал] (MIT II, 391). ⇨ **QOTUR.**

QOTURAQ Kirg. 19th c. **Qoturaq** [Котуракъ] (Potanin II, 3). ⇨ **QOTUR?** + suff. *-aq.*

QOTUZ see **QUTUZ**

QOWADÏY Tat.(GH) 1281 **Qowadïy** [Ковадый], a Tatar (Kuman, Kipchak) chieftain of the Horde (PSRL I, 227 IV, 43 V, 199 VII, 175, XVI, 55, 308 Suzd. 498).

QOWГADÏY Tat.(GH) 1317, 1319 **Qowγadïy / Qowγadï / Qawadïy?** [Ковгадый / Ковгады / Кавадый / Кавьдый], a Tatar (Kuman/Kipchak?) chieftain (Suzd. 502, PSRL I, 229 IV, 48, V, 207-10, 212-14, VII, 188-196, XVI, 61).

QOWÏRГU Tat.(GH) 1377, 1378 **Qowïrγu / Köwergü?** [Ковергу / Ковергуй], a „Tatar" (Kuman/Kipchak?) prince of Mamay (PSRL XI, 43, XXIII, 124).

QOWÏRTA Tat.(GH) 1379 **Qowïrta / Qawïrtï?** [Коверта (Каверта)], a prince of the Horde (PSRL XVI, 106).

QOWÏT Kzk. 19th c. **Qowït-bay** [Фишджанъ Кула Ковитбаевъ] (Grod., Pril. 43).

QOWQAQ Kzk. 19th c. **Qowqaq** [Коукакъ] (SOV 100).

QOWRAT-QLÏŠ? Tat. 1554 **Qowrat-qlïš? / Qurat-qlïš?** [Коурат(Куратъ)-Клешь] (PSRL XIII, 243). ⇨ **QOBRAT? / QURAT** + **QÏLÏČ?**

QOWUY Oghuz? 1151, 1185 **Qowuy?** [Коуи / Ковуи], from the yearbooks of Kiev (PSRL II, 427-28, 638-639, 642, 644).

QOZA I. see **QOZÏ**

QOZA II. Chuv. 18th-19th c. **Koza** [Коза] (Magn. 52).

QOZAY Bashk. 1761 **Qozay** [Козай Тугашев] (MIB IV/1, 213).

QOZAQ Chuv. 18th-19th c. **Kozak** [Козакъ] (Magn. 52); Kzk. 19th c. **Qozaq** [Козакъ] (SOK 212); Kzk.

19th c. **Qozaq-pay** [Козакпай] (SOV 100). ⇨ **QAZAQ.**

QOZAQ-KİLDE   Bashk. 1734 **Qozaq-kilde** [Козаккилда] (Vel.-Zern., Bašk. 10). ⇨ **QOZAQ + KELDİ.**

QOZAQČİ   Turk. 19th c. **Qozaqčï-oγlu** [Kozakčy oγlu], a Zeybek (Kúnos 1891, 119). ✧ 'Seller of mast' cf. Turk. *qozaq* 'der Tannenzapfen; die Buchennuss' (Radl. II, 629).

QOZANΓAY   Kzk. 19th c. **Qozanγay** [Козангай] (SOK 140).

QOZDAS Kzk. 19th c. **Qozdas** [Коздасъ] (SOK 88).

QOZİ   Kuman 1185 **Qoza** [Кзичь / Романъ Кзичь], a Polovets prince (PSRL II, 131, 320); Kuman 1168 **Qoza / Qozï?** [Коза], a Polovets (Ipat. 364 (377)); Oghuz/Trkm. 13th c. **Qozï-tegin-χan** [قوزى تكين / Кузы-Тегин-хан], Boγra-χan's son (Abulg./Kon. 890-920, 930-960); Bashk. 1675 **Qozu-bay** [Иттимес Козубаев] (MIB I, 200); NUyg. 19th c. **Quzï** [قوزى / Kuse] (Le Coq, Namenl. 109); Kzk. 1826 **Quzï-bay** [Кузебаевъ] (Konšin I-III, 21); Kzk. 19th c. **Quzï-bay** [Кузыбай] (SKSO VIII, 200); Kzk. 19th c. **Quzï-bek** [Кузыбекъ] (Grod., Pril. 133); Kzk. 19th c. **Quzï-qul** [Саматъ Кузыкуловъ] (SKSO VIII, 201, 233); Bashk. 1623 **Quzu-bay** [Кузубай] (MIB I, 157); Bashk. 1623 **Quzu-bay** [Кузубай] (Miller, Ist. Sib. II, 299); Kzk. 19th c. **Quzu-bay** [Кузубай] (AOP 62); *TN:* Tat.(Sib.) 1623 **Quzu-bay(eva)** [Кузубаева], a village (Miller, Ist. Sib. II, 299). ✧ 'Lamb' cf. Karakh. *qozï* 'id.' (DTS) Uyg., Kuman, Chag. *qozï* 'das Lamm' (Radl. II, 630), Crm., Turk. *quzu* 'id.' (Radl. II, 1019). See also **AQ-QOZİ, ATA-QOZİ, BAY-QOZİ, ĴAN-QOZİ, TEL-ΓOZİ, TİN-QUZİ, TOQTA-QOZİ, TURDİ-QOZİ.**

QOZİ-BAΓAR   Kzk. 19th c. **Qoz-baγar** [Козбагаръ] (SOV 62); Kkalp. 20th c. **Qozï-baγar** [Козыбаѓар] (KkRS 774). ✧ 'He will look after lambs'. ⇨ **QOZİ + BAQAR.**

QOZİ-KÖRPÖC see **QOZİ-KÖRPÖŠ**

QOZİ-KÖRPÖŠ   Tat.(Bar.) **Qozï-körpöc** [Kosy Körpöz / Козы Көрпöц] (Proben IV, 9-20); Kzk. **Qozï-körpöš / Qozu-körpöš** [Kosy Körpösch / Козы Көрпöш / Козу Көрпöш] (Proben III, 221, 245, etc. /261-297/). ⇨ **QOZİ + KÖRPEŠ.**

QOZİKÄ   Kzk. **Qozïkä** [Козыкä], Qozï-körpöš's blandishing name (Proben III, 234, 235, 237 etc. /276-278/). ✧ Diminutive-hypocoristic form of Qozï. ⇨ **QOZİ** + dim. *-kä.*

QOZİL   Kuman 1180 **Qozïl** [Козелъ Сатановичъ / Козл Сотанович], a Polovets prince (Ipat. 421 (435), PSRL II, 623). ✧ 'Adjoin!' (Bask., Im. polov. 67), cf. Tat.(Sib.) *qozïl-* 'присоединяться' (Budagov).

QOZİNCİ-QAT   Hak.(Sag.) 19th-20th c. **Qozïncï-qat** [Козынцы-кат], a water-spirit (devil) (Proben IX, 566,

570). ⇨ **?+QAT.**

QOZLİ   Tat.(Sib.) 1626 **Qozlï-bay** [Козлыбаев (Сенизак)] (Miller, Ist. Sib. II, 329).

QOZU see **QOZİ**

QOZU-KÖRPÖŠ see **QOZİ-KÖRPÖŠ**

QOZUR Kzk. 19th c. **Qozur** [Козуръ] (AOK 58).

QOŽ-AXMET see **QOĴA-AXMET**

QOŽ-AMET see **QOĴA-AXMET**

QOŽ-BAXTİ see **QOŠ-BAXTİ**

QOŽ-EKE see **XOĴA**

QOŽ-GELDİ see **QOŠ-KİLDİ**

QOŽA see **XOĴA**

QOŽA-BASTİ   Kzk. 19th c. **Qoža-bastï** [Кожебасты] (SOV 54). ✧ 'With big head'? ⇨ **XOĴA + BAŠ?** + suff. *-tï / -lï.*

QOŽA-GELDİ see **XOĴA-KELDİ**

QOŽA-MİRAT see **XOĴA-MURAT**

QOŽA-MURAT see **XOĴA-MURAT**

QOŽA-NASİR   Kkalp. 20th c. **Qoža-nasïr** [Кожанасыр] (KkRS 774). ⇨ **XOĴA + NASİR.**

QOŽA-NAZAR   Kkalp. 20th c. **Qoža-nazar** [Кожаназар] (KkRS 774). ⇨ **XOĴA + NAZAR.**

QOŽA-NİYAZ   Kkalp. 20th c. **Qoža-niyaz** [Кожанияз] (KkRS 774). ⇨ **XOĴA + NİYAZ.**

QOŽAQ   Kzk. **Qožaq** [Koschak / Кожак] (Proben III, 127 /162/); Kzk. 19th c. **Qožaq** [Кошакъ] (SOK 6, 170). ✧ 'Big, grown-up' (Žanuzakov-Esbaeva 460). See also **BOYŠAN, DÄW, DUOLANTAY, ÄLLÄY, KETTÄ, ULUΓ, ZOR.**

QOŽAM-BERDİ see **QOĴAM-BERDİ**

QOŽAM-BERGEN see **QOĴAM-BERGEN**

QOŽAMİŠ see **QOĴAMİŠ**

QOŽAN   Kzk. 19th c. **Qožan** [Кожанъ] (AOO 30); Kkalp. 20th c. **Qožan** [Кожан] (KkRS 774).

QOŽANAY   Kzk. 19th c. **Qožanay / Qoš-anay** [Кожанай] (AOK 6). ⇨ **QOŽAN** + dim. suff. *-ay.*

QOŽAS see **XOĴAŠ**

QOŽİLDAQ   Kzk. 19th c. **Qožïldaq** [Кожилдакъ] (AOO 66).

QOŽOŇČİ   Alt. 19th-20th c. **Qožoňčï** [Кожончы], fem. (OjrRS 212). ✧ 'Singer' (OjrRS).

QOŽUQ Kzk. 19th c. **Qožuq** [Кожукъ] (SOK 138).

QOŽUR Trkm. 19th c. **Qožur** [Кожуръ] (Lomakin 39).

QOŽUT Alt. 19th-20th c. **Qožut** [Кожут] (OjrRS 208).

QŌ-KÖKŠİN   Alt. 19th c. **Qō-kökšin** [Коо-Кокшин] (Verb., In. 122). ✧ I. 'Swan-?'; II. 'Beautiful / pretty?' cf. Tel., Alt., Tuv., Shor *qū* 'der Schwan' (Radl. II, 883), Alt. *qoo* 'красивый, изящный' (OjrRS), also a secondary comp. of female names. < Mid. Mo. *qo'a.*

QŌQ   Karg. **Qōq** [Кöк] (Katanov, Otč. 9). ✧ 'Bladder' cf. Alt., Hak. *qōq* 'die Harnblase' (Radl. II, 508).

QŌR-TAS   Shor 19th-20th c. **Qōr-tas** (Dyrenkova 90). ✧ 'Dark-brown bald' cf. Hak. (Kacha, Koyb., Sag.) *qōr* 'bleich, falb' (Radl. II, 550). ⇨ **QOŇUR + TAZ.**

QŌRA Hak.(Sag.) 19th-20th c. **Qōra** [Копа] (Katanov, Otč. 7). ✧ 'A kind of fish, salmon (Salmo thymallus)' cf. Hak. *qōra* 'der Chairus, ein Fisch' (Radl. II, 550).

QŌT Hak.(Koyb.) 19th-20th c. **Qōt** [Кот] (Katanov, Otč. 13). ✧ I.'Year', II.'Cat'? cf. R. *god* 'year' or *kot* 'cat' (Katanov).

QRÏM see **QÏRÏM**

QRÏM-SARAY Tat. 1619 **Qrïm-saray** [Крымъ-Сарайко Буюргановъ] (Kurdjumov 117, 119, 120, 370); Tat.? 17th c. **Qrïm-saray** [Изенкей Крымсаревъ], a Cossack from the government of Kazan (IOAIÊK XXIX, 348). ⇨ **QÏRÏM** + **SARAY**.

QRÏSTUOS Yak. **Kiristiäs** [Кіpicтiäc] (Pek.); Yak. **Kristiäs** [Кpicтiäc] (Pek.); Yak. **Qrïstuos** [Крыс-туос] (Pek.). ✧ Hristos (R.).

QRÏMPAY Yak. **Qrïmpay** [Крымпаі] (Pek.).

QRUM see **QURUM**

QRUS Bashk. 1749 **Qrus** [Крус Казанбаев] (MIB III, 464). ⇨ **QURUS?**

QŠUM see **QOŠUM**

QTA see **QÏTA**

QU Kzk. 19th c. **Qu-bala** [Ку-бала] (Potanin, Pred. 132); Türk 735 **Qu-säñün** [Qu Säñün] (ETY I, 70). ✧ 'Foxy, tricky (boy)' (Potanin). See also **BOROLГAY-QU.**

QUB-TAY see **QUBA-TAY**

QUBA Trkm. 20th c. **Guba** [Guba] (Zaj. 1971, 336); Trkm. 20th c. **Guba** [Губа] (TrkmRS 205); Tat. 20th c. **Qoba** [Коба] (Sattarov); Kzk. 18th c. - 19th c. **Quba** [Утегенъ Кубинъ] (ZOOIRGO III, 26); Hak.(Sag.) 19th-20th c. **Quba** [Куба], an evil spirit (Proben IX, 568). ✧ 'Pale, white-grey' cf. Hak. *quba* 'bleich, weissgrau' (Radl. II, 1034), Bashk. *qoba* 'светло-бурый, коричневый; бледный' (BRS/Uraksin), Trkm. *yuba* 'золотистый (о цвете гусей и верблюдов)' (TrkmRS).

QUBA-ČAQÏRČA Uyg. 12th c. - 14th c. **Quba-čaqïrča** [quba čaqïrča / Kuba Çakïrça] (DTS, EUTS). ✧ 'White-grey hawk'. ⇨ **QUBA** + **ČAQÏRČA.**

QUBA-ГUŠ Bashk. 20th c. **Qoba-ɣoš** [Қобаҕош / Кубаҕуш] (Kusimova); Bashk. 1735 **Quba-ɣuš** [Кубаҕушъ Кушкеевъ], a tarχan (Vel.-Zern., Bašk. 23). ✧ A kind of brown bird'? ⇨ **QUBA** + **QUŠ I.?**

QUBA-TAY Kzk. **Qub-tay** (<Quba-tay?) [Кубтай] (Sb. Syr-D. IX, 52); Kzk. 19th c. **Qubatay** [Илангъ Кубатай] (Grod., Pril. 79). ⇨ **QUBA** + **TAY** or suff. *-tay?*

QUBADÏ Balk. 20th c. **Qubadï** [Qubadi] (Pröhle, Balk. 240).

QUBAQ Bashk. 1715 **Qubaq** [Рыс Кубаков] (MIB III, 126).

QUBAQAY Tat. 20th c. **Qobaqay** [Кубакай] (Sattarov); Bashk. 1790 **Qubaqay** [Кубакай Кулчуманов] (MIB IV/1, 341). ⇨ **QUBA** + dim.

suff. *-qay.*

QUBAQTÏ Bashk. 1778 **Qubaqtï / Qu-baqtï?** [Кубакты (Кубахта) Инкагузин] (MIB V, 71, 110, 269).

QUBANČA Hak.(Shor) 19th-20th c. **Qubanča** [Кубанча] (Katanov, Otč. 11). ✧ 'Fawn, blond' cf. Hak. PN *Xuban* (Butanaev) + suff. *-ča.*

QUBARSÏ Yak. **Qubarsï** [Кубарсы Уібан], a hero of the drama „Mančārī tüökün" (Pek.).

QUBAS-QUŠ Bashk. 1756 **Qubas-quš, Qu-bas-quš?** [Амир Кубаскушев] (MIB IV/1, 128). ⇨ **QUBAŠ?** + **QUŠ I.**

QUBASÏN Yak. **Qubasïn-arïɣ** [Kubasen Areg], fem. (Schiefner XLV). ✧ 'Swan(-clean)'? cf. Yak. *quba* 'Schwan' (Schiefner). ⇨ + suff. *-sïn.* See also **ARÏГ.**

QUBAŠ Tat.(Mish.) 20th c. **Qubaš** [Кубашев] (Sattarov); Kzk. 18th c. **Qubaš** [Кубашъ] (Nepljuev 762, 763); Alt.(Tuba) 19th c. **Qubaš** [Кубашъ] (Potanin IV, 574-75). ✧ 'A kind of bird' (Sattarov).

QUBAT see **QUWAT**

QUBATAN Tat.(GH) 1279, 1280 **Qubatan?** [Кубатанъ (Кубитанъ)], a chieftain (PSRL II, 208, 346, Ipat. 581 (582)).

QUBBAN Bashk. 1779 **Qubban-ɣul** [Куббангул Шерыпов] (MIB V, 89). ✧ 'Good-looking, kind' (<Ir.), cf. Kzk. PN *Quban* (Žamuzakov 146; Žanuzakov-Esbaeva).

QUBÏLAY Yürük 16th c. **Qubilay** [Kubilây] (Gökb., Rum. 103). ✧ 'Kubilai' (Mo.).

QUBÏQTÏ-QARA Bashk. **Qubïqtï-qara** [Кубыкты-Кара], a hero in a tale (Zelenin, Perm. 481). ✧ 'Ivy-black' cf. Uyg. *qobïq, qubïq* 'der Bernstein' (Radl. II, 660, 1036). ⇨ **QARA.**

QUBÏZAY Kzk. 19th c. **Qubïzay** [Куздамбай Кубизаевъ] (Grod., Pril. 89). ⇨ **QOBÏZ** + dim. suff. *-ay.*

QUBLANDA see **QOBLANDÏ**

QUBRO Hak. 19th-20th c. **Qubro** [Кубро], fem. (HRS 353).

QUBUL Tat.(Sib.) 1599 **Qubul** [Кубулъ], a Siberian princess, Küčüm's seventh wife (AI II, 17, 20, 23); Kzk. 1846 **Qubul** [Кубул Чуйгашев], a biy (MKOP 152). ✧ 'Transform yourself; change your (out)look' cf. Kzk. *qubŭl-* 'sich verwandeln; seine Gestalt verändern' (Radl. II, 1038).

QUBUNDAY Tuv. 19th c. **Qubunday** [Кубундаі] (Proben IX, 123).

QUCQAR see **QOČQAR**

QUČA Tat.(Ishim) **Quča** [Куча] (Proben IV, 193 /239/); Hak.(Koyb.) 19th-20th c. **Quča** [Куча] (Katanov, Otč. 13); Oghuz/Trkm. 1372 **Quča-melik** [Куча-мелик] (MIT I, 515). ✧ 'Sheep, ram' cf. Alt., Hak. *quča* 'der Widder, Schafbock' (Radl. II, 1007), Hak. *χuča* 'баран' (HRS). See also **QARA-QUČA.**

QUČAYA   Yak. **Qučaya** [Кучаја], fem. (Pek.). ✧ Hypocoristic name given to the beloved (favourite) daughter. (Pek.).

QUČAQ   Maml. 14th c. **Qučaq** [قُجَق] (Sauvaget 52); Bashk. 1778 **Qučaq** [Ишбай Кучаков] (MIB V, 70, 83, 84); Bashk. 1779 **Qučaq** [Ишбай Кучаков] (MIB V, 84); Kzk. **Qučaq** [Кучакъ] (Žarkov: Biblioteka dlja Čtenija CXXIV, 227); Kzk. 1748 **Qučaq** [Кучакъ], khan of the Middle Horde (Orta Žüz) (Nepljuev 715, MIKk. 220); Kzk. 1750 **Qučaq / Qučaq-bi** [Koutchak / Sultan-Koutchak-by], a sultan known also as Abul Qasïm (Levchine 222, Nalivkin-Dozon 63-64); Trkm. 1859 **Qučaq-χan** [Кучакъ-ханъ Уразгилдіевъ] (ZIRGOÊtn. I, 157); Uzb. 1804 **Qučaq-inâk?** [Кучак-инак] (MIT II, 353); Nog.? **Qučaq-oγlan** [Кучакоглан (Кощак)] (Žirm., Epos 454); Yürük 1543 **Quǰaq** [Kucak] (Gökb., Rum. 188, 198, 216); Kzk. 19th c. **Quǰaq-bay** [Куджакбай] (Grod., Pril. 174); Kzk. 1820 **Qužaq** [Кужакъ] (Sib. Vest. IX, 119). ✧ 'Lap, embrace' (Sauvaget 52), cf. Chag., Alt., Hak. *qučaq* 'id.' (Radl. II, 1007).

QUČAN   Bashk. 1689 **Qučan** [Кучанъ Зьяналыевъ], a tarχan (Vel.-Zern., Bašk. 30).

QUČAŇ   Uyg. **Qučañ** [Kuçang] (EUTS).

QUČAS   Hak.(Sag.) 19th-20th c. **Qučas** [Кучас] (Proben IX, 443). ✧ 'Little sheep, ram'? ⇨ **QUČA** + suff. -*s*.

QUČÏQAY   Bashk. 1715 **Qučïqay** [Кучыкай Тохтаров] (MIB III, 138).

QUČÏN   Kzk. 19th c. **Qučïn-bay / Qučin-bay** [Кучинбай] (Grod., Pril. 175). ✧ 'Soldier / servant' (title)? cf. Chag. *qučin* 'die zweite Klasse der Einwohner von Kaschgar, die Soldaten' (Radl. II, 1010). See also **MÏRZA-ŠAH-QUČÏN.**

QUČQAČ   NUyg. 19th c. **Qučqač / Qušqač** [قوشتاج / Kuchkach] (Le Coq, Namenl. 108). ✧ 'A small bird, sparrow' cf. East.T. *qučqač* 'id.' (Jarring).

QUČQAY   Bashk. 1757 **Qučqay** [Кучкай Аднагулов] (MIB IV/1, 157). ⇨ **QUČ** + dim. suff. -*qay*.

QUČQAN   Bashk. 1785 **Qučqan** [Кучкан] (MIB V, 170).

QUČQUN   Tat.(Lit.) 1590 **Qučqun** [Матфей Кучкунъ] (Lit. Tat. 59, 130); Tat. 1646 **Qučqun** [Кучкун] (Miller, Ist. Sib. II, 512). ✧ 'Red'? cf. Kirg. *qočqun* 'roth' (Radl. II, 618).

QUČQUNǰÏ   Chag. 16th c. **Qučqunǰi-χan** [Кучкунджи-хан] (Ivanov 24); + suff. -*ǰi*;

QUČTAR   Bashk. 1789 **Qučtar** [Имангул (Зимагул) Кучтаров] (MIB V, 267).

QUČUYUQ   Yak. **Qučuyuq** [Кучуюк] (Pek.).

QUČUŇ   Hak.(Shor) 19th-20th c. **Qučuň** [Кучуӊ] (Katanov, Otč. 11). ✧ 'Man with great strength' cf. Hak. PN *Qučïn* 'силач (Butanaev).

QUČUR   Kzk. 19th c. **Qučur-bay** [Антокъ Кучурбаевъ], born in the Inner Horde (AUK 171-172, 719). ⇨ **QOČUR?**

QUČURČA   Tat.(Sib.)? 1647 **Qučurča** [Кучурча (Кучюрча)], a taysha (tayša) (Miller, Ist. Sib. II, 520).

QUČURQA   Hak. 19th-20th c. **Qučurqa** [Кучурка], fem. (HRS 353).

QUǰAΓUŠ   Mo.? **Quǰaγuš** [Куджагуш Буюрук-хан] (RaD I/1, 113).

QUǰAY   1220 **Quǰay-tegin** [Куджай-Тегинъ] (RaD/Ber. III, 67); Khorezm. 1220 **Quǰay-tegin** [Куджай-тегин], an emir, J̌elāleddīn's officer (RaD/Ber. III, 67, MIT I, 503 /Abulg./).

QUǰAQ see **QUČAQ**

QUǰAMÏŠ   Bashk. 1737 **Quǰamïš** [Куджамыш (Куземыш, Кусямыш) Беккузин] (MIB I, 315-17).

QUǰAŠ see **XOǰAŠ**

QUǰÏQ   Oghuz/Trkm. 13th c. **Quǰïq** [قوجیق / Куджык] (Abulg./Kon. 1245).

QUDA I.   Kzk. 19th c. **Quda-bay** [Кудабай] (SOK 84); Kzk. **Quda-bay / Xuda-bay?** [Kustanaev Chudabaj], a Kazak writer (Or. Bibl. VIII, 178); Tat.(Sib.) 1634 **Quda-bek** [Кудабяков (Юзеян)] (Miller, Ist. Sib. II, 413); *TN:* Kzk. **Quda-bay** [Кудобай-чечесы], a tomb south of Karkaralinsk (ZIRGOGeogr. I). ✧ 'Friend, mate; wooer' cf. Uyg., Chag., Alt., Hak., Kirg., Kzk. *quda* 'der Freund, Genosse; der Freiwerber, Brautwerber' (Radl. II, 998), Bashk. *qoδa* 'сват' (BRS), Tat. *qoda* 'id.' (TatRS), Kzk. *qŭda* 'id.' (KzRS).

QUDA II. see **XUDAY**

QUDA-BERDEY see **XUDAY-BERDÏ**

QUDA-BERDÏ see **XUDAY-BERDÏ**

QUDA-BÏDÏN   Uyg. 12th c. - 14th c. **Quda-bïdïn** [Quda Bïdïn / Kuda Bıdın] (Radl., USp. 4-5, DTS, EUTS). ⇨ **QUDA I.**

QUDA-GEL   Kzk. 19th c. **Quda-gel** [Кудагелъ] (SOK 254). ✧ 'Come (be born) as friend'. ⇨ **QUDA I.** + **KEL.**

QUDA-GELDÏ   Kzk. 19th c. **Quda-geldi** [Кудагельды] (SOV 22). ✧ 'A mate, friend, wooer has come'. ⇨ **QUDA I. + KELDÏ.**

QUDA-MENDÏ see **XUDAY**

QUDAČÏ   Alt. 19th-20th c. **Qudačï** [Кудачы] (OjrRS 209). ✧ 'Wooer' (OjrRS). ⇨ **QUDA I.** + suff. -*čï.*

QUDAY I.   Trkm. 19th c. **Quday** [Толекъ (Мулла) Кудаевъ] (Ščeglov IV, 186); Tat.(Lit.) 1592 **Quday** [Кудай Данцевичъ] (Lit. Tat. 124); Tat. 1534 **Quday** [Кудай], a cavalier armed with a lance (PSRL VIII, 286-87); Kzk. 1807 **Quday** [Кудай Байсармышевъ] (TOUAK XXIV, 80); Tat. **Quday-ulan** [Кудай-уланъ] (PSRL XIII, 79); Tat.(Mish.) 1798 **Qudey** [Арасланъ Кудѣевъ] (Nepljuev 438); Tat.(Sib.) 1647 **Qutay** [Кутай] (Miller, Ist. Sib. II, 521); Kzk. 19th c. **Qutay** [Кутаевъ] (SKSO VIII, 230); Tat.(Tüm.) 1649 **Qutay-γul** [Кутайгулъ] (DAI III, 174-75). ✧ 'Little friend,

mate, wooer'. ⇨ **QUDA I.** + dim. suff. *-y*. See also
QUN-QUDAY.

QUDAY II. see **XUDAY**

QUDAY-BAQTÏ   Tat.(Lit.) 1557 **Quday-baqtï** [Кудай
Бакты] (Kn. Metriki Lit. 152). ✦ 'God-fortune'. ⇨
XUDAY + BAQTÏ.

QUDAY-BENDE see **XUDAY**

QUDAY-BERDİ see **XUDAY-BERDİ**

QUDAY-BERGEN see **XUDAY-BERGEN**

QUDAY-DAT see **XUDAY-DAD**

QUDAY-NAZAR see **XUDAY-NAZAR**

QUDAY-SÜGÜR see **XUDAY-ŠÜKÜR**

QUDAYQ   Tat.(Lit.) 1591 **Qudayq?** / **Qudayïq?** [Хава
Кудайковна Сувовичъ], fem. (Lit. Tat. 82). ⇨
QUDAY I. + suff. *-q*.

QUDAYMET   Bashk. 1761 **Qudaymet** [Кудайметь]
(MIB IV/1, 211). ⇨ **XUDAY** + suff. *-met*.

QUDAKE   Kirg. **Qudake** [Кудаке] (Jud. 89, 210, 479).
⇨ **QUDA I.** + dim. suff. *-ke*.

QUDAQAY   Tat. 1779 **Qudaqay** [Кудякай
Измаилов] (MIB V, 94); Bashk. 1759 **Qudaqay**
[Шерып Кудакаев] (MIB IV/2, 26); Bashk. 1802
Qudaqay [Мухтаръ Кудакаевъ] (TOUAK XXIV,
124). ⇨ **QUDA I.** + dim. suff. *-qay*.

QUDALAY   Alt. 19th-20th c. **Qudalay** [Кудалай]
(OjrRS 212).

QUDAMÏŠ   Tat. 1640 **Qudamïš** [Байтереков
Кудамышко] (Miller, Ist. Sib. II, 473); Tat. 1695
Qudamïš [Кутук Кудатышев] (MIB I, 90); Tat.(Sib.)
1635 **Qudamïš** [Кудамыш] (Miller, Ist. Sib. II, 430);
Tat.(Sib.) 1637 **Qudamïš** [Кутук Кудамышев]
(Miller, Ist. Sib. II, 443, 444); Tat.(Sib.) 1637 **Qudamïš**
[Токмамет Кудамышев] (Miller, Ist. Sib. II, 443,
444); Tat.(Sib.) 1637 **Qudamïš** [Федор Кудамышев]
(Miller, Ist. Sib. II, 443, 444).

QUDAN   Oghuz 1092 **Qudan** [Кудан], slave-soldier
(gulām) of Nizām al-Mulk, an emir, security (police)
officer (?).

QUDAR   Kzk. 19th c. **Qudar** [Кударъ Шахмурадовъ]
(Grod., Pril. 44). ⇨ **QODAR?**

QUDARKİN   Oghuz 10th c. **Qudarkin?** [Кударкин],
Ghuz chief (MIT I, 161-62 (after Ibn Fadlān)).

QUDAS see **QUDAŠ**

QUDAŠ   Kzk. 19th c. **Qudas** [Кудасъ] (AOO 30); Kzk.
19th c. **Qudas-pay** [Кудаспай] (AOA 134); Kzk. 19th
c. **Qudas-pay** [Кудаспай] (SOK 74); Chag. 15th c.
Qudaš [Kudásh], took part in Mirza Haydar's
expedition to Tibet in 1533 (Tar. Rashidi 461, 462);
Crm. 1517 **Qudaš** [Кудашъ], a murza (PSRL VI, 259
VIII, 261); Tat.(Lit.) 1592 **Qudaš** [Кудашъ
Негучучевичъ] (Lit. Tat. 123); Tat.(Lit.) 1593 **Qudaš**
[Оразъ Кудашевичъ] (Lit. Tat. 176, 177); Tat. 1624
Qudaš [Токтаръ Кудашевъ] (Pokrovskij 69); Tat.
1624 **Qudaš** [Кудашъ Тевкелевъ] (Pokrovskij 70);

Tat. 17th c. **Qudaš** [Kudašev], a Tatar prince in the
country of the Mordvins (Smyrnov 277); Tat. 1654
Qudaš [Кудашъ Ерлыгашевъ] (AI IV, 236); Tat.
1764 **Qudaš** [Утякей Кудашев] (MIB IV/1, 279);
Tat.(Mish.) **Qudaš** [Kudašev] (IOAIÊK XIX, 143);
Tat.(Mish.) 1755 **Qudaš** [Кудаш Тоймасов] (MIB
IV/1, 93); Tat.(Sib.) 1618 **Qudaš** [Кудашев
(Елекай)], a murza (Miller, Ist. Sib. II, 244); Bashk.
1709 **Qudaš** [Кудаш(ев)] (MIB I, 264); Bashk. 1712
Qudaš [Кудаш] (MIB III, 84); Bashk. 1714 **Qudaš**
[Кинзегул Кудашев] (MIB I, 105); Bashk. 1734
Qudaš [Кудашъ Куреевъ] (Vel.-Zern., Bašk. 10);
Bashk. 1734 **Qudaš** [Кудашъ] (Vel.-Zern., Bašk. 10);
Bashk. 1734 **Qudaš** [Кудашъ Апасевъ], a tarχan
(Vel.-Zern., Bašk. 11); Bashk. 1734 **Qudaš** [Кудашъ
Якшимбетевъ] (Vel.-Zern., Bašk. 11); Bashk. 1756
Qudaš [Кудаш Исламгулов] (MIB IV/1, 123);
Bashk. 1761 **Qudaš** [Илиш Кудашев] (MIB I/1, 221);
Bashk. 1761 **Qudaš** [Кудаш Азикеев] (MIB IV/1,
214); Bashk. 1780 **Qudaš** [Кудаш Баталин] (MIB V,
119); Kzk. 1785 **Qudaš** [قداش / Кудаш], aq-saqal of
the Šekti tribe (MIK IV, 51, 53, 63, 65); Kzk. 19th c.
Qudaš [Кудашъ] (SOK 114); Bashk. 1756 **Qudaš-bay**
[Кудажбай Ракаев] (MIB IV/1, 109); Kzk. 18th c.
Qudaš-bey [Кудашъ бей] (Sib. Vest. IX, 189); Crm.
1517 **Qudaš-murza** [Кудашъ-мурза] (PSRL XIII, 26).
✦ 'Little wooer; wooer's child; boy born from different
mother but the same father' (Sattarov). ⇨ **QUDA I.** +
suff. *-š*.

QUDAŠMAN   Bashk. 1675 **Qudašman** [Иткиня
Кудашманов] (MIB I, 201); Bashk. 1740 **Qudašman**
[Кудашман] (MIB I, 409); Bashk. 1740 **Qudašman**
[Кудашман Текеев] (MIB I, 421); Bashk. 1769
Qudašman [Туманча Кудашманов] (MIB IV/1,
334); Bashk. 1780 **Qudašman** [Кудашман
Адзитеров (Адзитеров)] (MIB V, 116, 275). ⇨
QUDAŠ + suff. *-man*.

QUDAT see **QUTAD**

QUDĀ see **XUDAY**

QUDELEK   Kkalp. 20th c. **Qudelek** [Куделек] (KkRS
774).

QUDLAY   Kzk. 19th c. **Qudlay** [Бай Мурза-Кудлай]
(AUK 399).

QUDRÄS   Bashk. 1740 **Qudräs?** [Кудряс Килдашев]
(MIB I, 395).

QUDRET   Trkm. 20th c. **Gudrat** [Gudrat] (Zaj. 1971,
328); Trkm. 20th c. **Gudrat** [Кудрат] (TrkmRS 206);
Kzk. 19th c. **Qudret-pay** [Кудретпай] (SOK 122);
TN: Kzk. **Qudret** [Кудрет] (Kojčubaev 152). ✦
'Power, influence' cf. Kzk. *qüdïret* 'всемогущество'
(KzRS), Turk. *qudrät* (Ar.) 'die Macht, Kraft, das
Vermögen, der Reichthum' (Radl. II, 1005), Trkm.
γudrat 'чудо, могущество' (TrkmRS) (<Ar.).

QUDRET-BERGÄN   Kzk. 19th c. **Qudret-bergän**

[Бала-Чубай Кудратъ Бергановъ] (Grod., Pril. 125).
⇨ **QUDRET + BERGEN.**

QUDRİN   Hak. 19th-20th c. **Qudrin** [Кудрин] (HRS 349).

QUDU see QUTU

QUDUƔČİ-ESÄN   Uyg. 13th c. **Quduɣči-esän** [quduɣči esän] (DTS).

QUDUƔČİ-ESÄN-QÏTAY   Uyg. 13th c. **Quduɣči-esän-qïtay** [quduɣči esän qïtaj] (DTS). ✧ 'Well-borer-healthy-Chinese' (Blagova 1997, 709). ⇨ **QUDUQ + ESÄN + QÏTAY.**

QUDUƔU-BADUR   Uyg. 12th c. - 14th c. **Quduɣu-badur / Quduqu-batur?** [Kuduġu / Quduqu Batur] (EUTS, Radl., USp. 30, DTS). ⇨ **? + BADUR.**

QUDUQ   Kzk. 19th c. **Quduq** [Кудукъ] (AOP 18); Kzk. 19th c. **Quduq** [Кудукъ] (SOK 50); Kzk. 19th c. **Quduq** [Кудукъ] (SOV 42); Kzk. 1825 **Quduq-žan** [قودوق جان / Кудукжан] (MIK IV, 471, 476); Alt. 19th-20th c. **Qutuq** [Кутук] (OjrRS 209). ✧ 'Well' cf. Kzk. *quduq* 'der Brunnen' (Radl. II, 1002), Alt. *qutuq* 'колодец' (OjrRS).

QUDUQU-BATUR see QUDUƔU-BADUR

QUDUMAN   Kzk. 19th c. **Quduman** [Кудуманъ] (AOK 126). ✧ 'Grim, raging, mad' cf. Chag. *quduman* 'wüthend, toll, verrückt' (Radl. II, 1006).

QUDUR see QUTUR

QUDURUM   Kzk. 19th c. **Qudurum** [Кудурумъ] (SOK 150).

QUDUZ see QUTUZ

QUƔADLÏ   Oghuz/Trkm. 13th c. **Quɣadlï** [قوغادلی / Кугадлы], Qïnïq-bay's daughter, Qïmač's wife (Abulg./Kon. 1450).

QUƔAY   Tat. 1696 **Quɣay** [Сапайко Кугаевъ] (Kungursk. akty 232).

QUƔAN   Kzk. 19th c. **Qoɣan-bay** [Коганбай] (SOK 120); Kzk. 19th c. **Quɣam-bay** (<Quɣan-bay) [Кугамбай] (AOO 14); Bashk. 1750 **Quɣan** [Куган Кугашин] (MIB III, 472). ✧ 'Chased, pursued' cf. Kuman, Alt., Crm., Kzk., Tat. *qū-* 'verfolgen, folgen' (Radl. II, 883).

QUƔANAY   Tat.(Sib.)? 1607 **Quɣanay** [Кугонай Турбеев], a taysha (Miller, Ist. Sib. II, 557, 558); Tat.(Sib.) 1636 **Quɣanay** [Кугоней / Куганей], a prince (Miller, Ist. Sib. II, 432). ⇨ **QUƔAN + suff. -ay.**

QUƔANČÏN   Bashk. 1788 **Quɣančïn** [Бикмурза Куганчин] (MIB V, 234). ⇨ **QUƔAN? + dim. suff. -čin(1).**

QUƔAŠ   Bashk. 1738 **Quɣaš** [Кугаш Дегашев] (MIB III, 393); Bashk. 1749 **Quɣaš** [Кусядык Кугашев] (MIB III, 462); Bashk. 1750 **Quɣaš** [Кугаш Тогашев] (MIB III, 472). ✧ 'Rush, matgrass'? cf. Bashk. *quɣa* 'кута (растение)' (BRS/Uraksin) + suff. -š.

QUƔATEK   Tat.(Bar.) 1645 **Quɣatek** [Куготек] (Miller, Ist. Sib. II, 496).

QUƔU see AƔČA-QUƔU

QUƔUL   Kzk. **Quɣul / Quɣūl?** [Kuguul] (Vámbéry, Vázlatok 310).

QUƔUM   Bashk. 1735 **Quɣum** [Курманай Кугумов] (MIB III, 341).

QUƔUNČA   Tat.(Sib.) 1609 **Quɣunča** [Кугунча] (Miller, Ist. Sib. II, 209).

QUƔUŠ   Tat. **Quɣuš** [Kugušev] (Mende 126); Nog. **Quɣuš-murza** [Кугуш Мурза], Yamɣurči's son (Žirm., Epos 430).

QUY see QOY

QUY-BAQ see QOY-BAQ

QUY-BAŠÏ   Kzk. 19th c. **Quy-bašï** [Куйбаши] (SKSO III, 19). ✧ 'Head of the sheep'. ⇨ **QOY + BAŠ.**

QUY-KİLDİ see QOY-KELDİ

QUYAQ-TAYANČ   Uyg. 12th c. - 14th c. **Quyaq-tayanč / Quywaq-tayanč** [Quy(v)aq Tayanč] (Radl., USp. 133-34). ✧ I. 'Socage - supporter/shoulder' cf. Uyg. *qujaq / quvaq* 'кувак, название трудовой повинности' (DTS), Karakh. *tajanč* 'опора' (DTS); II. 'Shell-bearer'? cf. Karakh. *qujaɣ / qujaq* 'панцирь, кольчуга' (DTS). ⇨ **TAYANČ.**

QUYALÏ   Kirg. **Quyalï** [Куялы] (Jud. 109); Kirg. **Quyalï** [Куялы], fem. (Jud. 806). ✧ 'Having bad luck; miserable, unfortunate' cf. Kirg. *quya* 'беда, напасть' (Jud.).

QUYAN see QOYAN

QUYAN-BASAR   Kzk. 19th c. **Quyan-basar** [Куянбосаръ] (SOK 220). ✧ 'Who will press (get, catch) rabbits'. ⇨ **QOYAN + BASAR.**

QUYAN-GÜZ see QOYAN-KÖZ

QUYANČÏ   Kzk. 1803, 1820 **Quyančï-taɣay? / Quyanča-taɣay?** [Куянча Тагай / Куянча-тагай], chief of the Čumïčlï (Čumučlï) tribe of the Little Horde (Kiši Žüz) (MIK IV, 514, Sib. Vest. IX, 110). ⇨ **QOYAN? + suff. -čï.**

QUYAŠ   Oghuz **Quyaš / Qubaš?** [قو باش], forefather of the Ottoman dynasty (Ālī 186). ✧ 'Sun' (Wittek, D. Islam. XIV, 94; Erol II).

QUYČİ see QOYČİ

QUYČÏ see QOYČÏ

QUYDANTUL   Kzk. 1731 **Quydantul? / Quydan-qul?** [Сеиткулъ Куйдантуловъ] (PSZRI VIII, 383, 386).

QUYƔAČÏ   Alt. 19th-20th c. **Quyɣačï** [Куйгачы], fem. (OjrRS 212). ✧ 'The egg of a lice' (OjrRS).

QUYƔUR   Yak. **Quyɣur** [Куйгур] (Pek.).

QUYQA   Alt. 19th-20th c. **Quyqa** [Куйка], fem. (OjrRS 212). ✧ 'Earring' (OjrRS).

QUYQALAQ   Kzk. 19th c. **Quyqalaq** [Куйкалакъ] (SOK 50). ✧ 'Confused, untidy' cf. Kzk. *quyqalaq* 'pek tertipli değil, karma-karışık' (KzTS).

QUYQAŇ   Alt. 19th-20th c. **Quyqaň** [Куйкан] (OjrRS 212).

QUYLAN   Kzk. 1826 **Quylan** [Куйлановъ] (TOUAR

XXIV, 168).

QUYLÏ see **QOYLÏ**

QUYLUQ Kzk. 19th c. **Quyluq** [Тезакбай Джанъ Куйлюковъ] (Grod., Pril. 172).

QUYRUQ Alt. 19th-20th c. **Quyruq** [Куйрук] (OjrRS 209); Hak.(Blt.) 19th-20th c. **Quzuruq** [Кузурук], fem. (Katanov, Otč. 10). ✧ 'Tail' (OjrRS), cf. Kuman, Chag., Alt., Kirg., Kzk., Turk., Uzb. *quyruq* 'der Schwanz, der Hintertheil' (Radl. II, 890), Hak. *quzuruq* 'der Schwanz' (Radl. II, 1020). See also **QARA-QUZURUQ**.

QUYSUNÏ Alt. 19th c. **Quysunï** [Куйсуны] (Potanin, Pred. 182).

QUYŠA Tat.(Sib.)? 1634 **Quyša** [Куйша (Кушей)], a taysha (Miller, Ist. Sib. II, 399, 412, 437, 442, 443 etc.).

QUYTTUÑ Tuv. 19th c. **Quyttuñ** [Куіттун] (Proben IX, 45).

QUQ-BAŠ Kzk. 1846 **Quq-baš** [Кукбаш Баубеков], a biy (MKOP 155). ✧ 'Bladder-head' cf. Alt., Kzk. *qūq* 'die Blase' (Radl. II, 896). ⇨ **BAŠ**.

QUQAQ Bashk. 1740 **Quqaq-bay** [Кукак-бай Икчюрин] (MIB I, 447).

QUQUM Bashk. 1759 **Ququm** [Курманай Кукумов] (MIB IV/1, 176).

QUL Trkm. 20th c. Гул [Gul] (Zaj. 1971, 325); Chuv. 18th-19th c. **Kul-bey** [Кулбей] (Magn. 53); Chuv. 19th c. **Kul-bikä** [Kulbika], fem. (Kronheim 96); Chuv. 18th-19th c. **Kul-čura** [Кулчура] (Magn. 54); Chuv. 18th-19th c. **Kul-murza?** [Крлмурза (Кулмурза?)] (Magn. 54); Uyg. 1324 **Qul** [Kul], fem. (Chwol., Syr.-nest. (NF) 24); Bashk. 1756 **Qul** [Кул Кумертев] (MIB IV/1, 120); Kuman 1183 **Qul-aba** [Кулобицкій Содвакъ (Куловицкій)], a Polovets prince (region of the Donets river) (PSRL II, 128, 319); Kzk. 18th c. **Qul-aqa-batïr** [Куляка-Батыръ] (Nepljuev 747, 748); Türk 750 **Qul-apa-uruñu** [Qul Apa Ur(u)ŋu / Qul Apa Uruñu] (Thomsen, Stein 187, 189, DTS, ETY II, 67); Bashk. 1776 **Qul-bay / Qulu-bay** [Кулбай (Кулубай) Хасанов] (MIB V, 42, 43, 96); Kzk. **Qul-bay / Kül-bay?** [Кюлбаевъ] (Grod. 166); Kzk. **Qul-bay / Kül-bay?** [Кюльбай] (Slovohotov, Narodnyj sud obyčnago prava kirgiz Maloj ordy. Orenburg 1905, 141); Kzk. **Qul-bay** [Табулбай Кулбаевъ] (TOUAK XXIV, 85); Kzk. 19th c. **Qul-bay** [Кульбай] (AOA 18); Kzk. 19th c. **Qul-bay** [Кулбай] (Grod., Pril. 146); Kzk. 19th c. **Qul-bay** [Ніязбай Кулбаевъ] (Grod., Pril. 150); Kzk. 19th c. **Qul-bay** [Кулбай] (SOK 186); Kzk. 1839 **Qul-batïr** [Kulbatyr] (AUK 57); Trkm. **Qul-batïr-sardar** [Куль-батыръ-сардаръ] (Grod., Vojna II, 143); Kzk. 19th c. **Qul-biy** [Кульбіевъ] (Grod., Pril. 177); Kzk. 19th c. **Qul-biy** [Алтибай Кулбіевъ] (Grod., Pril. 182); Tat. 1668 **Qul-bikä** [Кулпика], fem. (Kungursk. akty 10); Kzk. 19th c. **Qul-čan** (<Qul-ǰan?) [Кульчанъ] (SOK 200); Kzk. 19th c. **Qul-čan** (<Qul-

ǰan?) [Кулчанъ] (SOV 86); Nog. 1556 **Qul-čan** (<Qul-ǰan?) [Кулчанъ], envoy (PSRL XIII, 262); Tat. 1531 **Qul-čur / Qul-čura?** [Кулчюръ / Кулчюра], envoy (PSRL VIII, 277, XIII, 57); Bashk. 1735 **Qul-čura** [Назаръ-Мамутъ Кулчуринъ], a tarχan (Vel.-Zern., Bašk. 19); Bashk. 1740 **Qul-čura** [Кусюкей Кулчюрин] (MIB I, 422); Bashk. 1743 **Qul-čura** [Кулчура Таныбеков] (MIB III, 513); Kzk. 19th c. **Qul-ǰan** [Кулджанъ] (Grod., Pril. 107); Kzk. 19th c. **Qul-ǰan** [Кульджанъ] (Grod., Pril. 27); Kzk. 19th c. **Qul-ǰan-bay** [Кульджанбай] (SOV 152); Kzk. 19th c. **Qul-eke** [Кулеке] (SODž. 148); Kzk. 19th c. **Qul-eke** [Кулеке] (SOV 62); Kkalp. 20th c. **Qul-eke** [Кулеке] (KkRS 774); Kzk. **Qul-eke? / Qul-ike?** [Кулике], a sultan (ZIRGOGeogr. I, 410); Kzk. 19th c. **Qul-eke / Qul-ike?** [Куликинъ] (Grod., Pril. 98); Trkm. 19th c. **Qul-ekey** [Кулекей] (Ščeglov IV, 170); Oghuz/Trkm. 13th c. **Qul-χaǰi** [قل حاجى / Кул-хаджи] (Abulg./Kon. 1240, 1245); Kirg. **Qul-mïrza** [Кул Мырза] (Radl. I, 657); Tat. 17th. c. **Qul-sit** [Кулситко Байситовъ] (IOAIÊK XXIX, 346); Kkalp. 20th c. **Qul-žan** [Кулжан] (KkRS 774); Kirg. **Qūl-yan** [Кул-Јан], daughter of a slave (qul), one of the forty retainers of Aq-sayqal (Proben V, 394 /397/); *EN:* Kzk. 18th c. - 19th c. **Qul** [Кул], a clan (Tynyšp. 65, 75); Kzk. 19th c. **Qul-bey** [Кулбей-Джумай], a clan (AUK 389); *TN:* Kzk. **Qul-bay** [Кульбай], a well, west of Lake Aral (Karta JAR X); Bashk. 18th c. **Qul-bay(eva)** [Кулбаева], a village in the district of Čistopol (Korsakov 223). ✧ 'Slave, servant; God's slave, mate, friend' (Sattarov, Kusimova), cf. *qul* 'раб, невольник' (DTS). It is a very frequent component of male names. On the meaning of *qul* in Trkm. consider Stein's note: „bei den Jomuden *Kul* sind von einer Sclavin geboren, und haben nur Anrecht auf die Hälfte der Erbschaft; die *Is (Iz)* stammen von einer jomudischen oder ogurdschalischen Mutter" (F. v. Stein: P. Mitt. XXVI, 328). The Kuman *Qul-aba* may be interpreted as 'Slave/servant-uncle' (Bask., Im. polov. 69). See also **YANÏ-ГUL**.

QUL-APA-URUÑU see **QUL**

QUL-ARÏQ Kzk. 19th c. **Qul-arïq** [Куларыкъ] (SOV 100). ⇨ **QUL + ARÏQ**.

QUL-ARSLAN Uyg. **Qul-arslan** (TT IV, 432). ✧ 'Slave-lion'. ⇨ **QUL + ARSLAN**.

QUL-BAY-IŠ Tat. 17th c. **Qul-bay-iš** [Янчюбайко Кулбаишевъ] (IOAIÊK XXIX, 344); Tat. 17th c. **Qul-bay-iš** [Кулбаишко Атуевъ], from the government of Kazan (IOAIÊK XXIX, 344). ⇨ **QUL + BAY-IŠ**.

QUL-BARAQ Kzk. 1831 **Qul-baraq** [Кульбаракъ] (Mejer 47); Kzk. 19th c. **Qul-baraq** [Кулбаракъ] (Grod., Pril. 52); Kzk. 19th c. **Qul-baraq** [Кулбаракъ] (SOK 106). ⇨ **QUL + BARAQ**.

QUL-BARS   Maml. 14th c. **Qul-bars** [قلبرس / Kulbars] (Tarj/Houtsma 61, 92, Tarj/Toparlı 41). ⇨ **QUL + BARS.**

QUL-BAŠ   Oghuz/Trkm. **Qul-baš** [Kılbaş / Кулбаш] (DQorq. 101, 102, 104, 238); Tat.? **Qul-baš** [Петейко Кулбашевъ], a Cossack ataman in the region of Kazan (IOAIÊK XXIX, 342); Tat.(Tob.) 1654 **Qul-baš / Qulbašï(y)** [Кулбашейко Теребердѣевъ] (AI IV, 230). ⇨ **QUL + BAŠ.**

QUL-BATÏ   Kzk. 1883 **Qul-batï** [Актай Кулбатiевъ] (Grod., Pril. 90). ⇨ **QUL + BATÏ?**

QUL-BÄRT   Türk **Qul-bärt** [Qul Bärt] (ETY II, 137). ⇨ **QUL.**

QUL-BERDİ   Uzb. 20th c. **Qul-berdi** [Кулберди] (Begmatov 1984, 202). ✦ '(His / God's) slave gave him/her'. ⇨ **QUL? + BERDİ.**

QUL-BÏГDÏ   Kzk. 19th c. **Qul-bïydï** [Кулбыгды] (SOK 60). ⇨ **QUL.**

QUL-BOLDÏ   Bashk. 1755 **Qul-boldï** [Зайляу Кулбулдин] (MIB IV/1, 99); Crm. 17th c. **Qul-boldu** [Кулъ-Болду], Feth Girey I (or II?), a Crimean Khan (Smirnov, Krym. 501); Bashk. 1755 **Qul-buldï** [Зяйляу Кулбулдин] (MIB IV/1, 99); Bashk. 1757 **Qul-buldï** [Зяйлягул Кулбулдин] (MIB IV/1, 148); *EN:* Kzk. 18th c. - 19th c. **Qul-boldï** [Кулболды], a clan (Tynyšp. 68); *TN:* Kzk. **Qul-boldï** [Кулболды], a field (Kojčubaev 155); Kzk. **Qul-boldï** [Kul-buldy] (Rekogn.). ⇨ **QUL + BOLDÏ.**

QUL-BOLDU see **QUL-BOLDÏ**

QUL-BULDÏ see **QUL-BOLDÏ**

QUL-ČARA   Kzk. 19th c. **Qul-čara** [Кульчара] (AOK 10). ⇨ **QUL +?**

QUL-JÏГAČ   Kirg. **Qul-jïɣač** [Кулжыгач] (Jud. 61, 674). ✦ 'Slave/servant-tree'? cf. Kirg. *jïɣač* 'дерево' (Jud.). ⇨ **QUL.**

QUL-JUMUR   Kzk. 19th c. **Qul-jumur** [Кульджумуръ] (SOV 64). ✦ 'Slave-round' cf. Kzk. *žumïr* 'круглый' (KzRS). ⇨ **QUL.** See also **QUL-YUMRÏ.**

QUL-DELEN   Tat.(Sib.)? 1642, 1645 **Qul-delen?** [Кулделен (Кунделен, Кульделет, Кульдевлет)], a taysha (Miller, Ist. Sib. II, 485, 486, 494, 496, 509). ⇨ **QUL.**

QUL-DERBİŠ see **QUL-DERVİŠ**

QUL-DERVİŠ   Tat. 1519 **Qul-derbiš** [Кулдербышгъ], envoy from Kazan (PSRL VIII, 266, XXIII, 202); Nog. 1489 **Qul-derviš**, a baχšï in the Golden Horde (Vásáry 54). ⇨ **QUL + DERVİŠ.**

QUL-EKEN   Kzk. 1846 **Qul-äken?** [Карагут Кулякенев] (MKOP 151); Kzk. 19th c. **Qul-eken** [Кулекенъ] (AOAtb. 30). ✦ 'He was a slave'? ⇨ **QUL.**

QUL-GİLDE   Bashk. 1761 **Qul-gilde** [Кулгильда]

(MIB IV/1, 205). ⇨ **QUL + KELDİ.**

QUL-YAT   Bashk. 1756 **Qul-yat** [Кулъят Тамасов] (MIB IV/1, 120). ⇨ **QUL + YAT.**

QUL-YUMRÏ   Kkalp. 1822 **Qul-yumrï** [Кул-IОмри бий], a biy (MIKk. 127). ✦ 'Slave-Round' cf. Kzk. *žumrï / žumïrï* круглый (KkRS). ⇨ **QUL.** See also **QUL-JUMUR.**

QUL-KÜK-TAY   Bashk. 1756 **Qul-küktey? / Qul-kük-tay?** [Мурат Кулкуктеев] (MIB IV/1, 109). ⇨ **QUL+ KÖK + TAY** or suff. *-tay?*

QUL-QAYA   Uyg. 13th-14th c. **Qul-qaya** [Qul Qy-a] (Zieme, Mat. II, 92). ⇨ **QUL + QAYA.**

QUL-QAL   Tat.(Sib.) 1623 **Qolqal** [Колкал Иликов] (Miller, Ist. Sib. II, 292); Turk. 1519 **Qul-qal** [Kulkal] (Gökb., Ed. 296); Yürük 1543 **Qul-qal** [Kulkal], from the Yürüks of Kocacık, Turkey (Gökb., Rum. 103, 190, 221, 227, 228 etc.); Yürük 1543 **Qul-qal** [Kulkal] (Gökb., Rum. 181); Yürük 1543 **Qul-qal** [Kulkal Küçük] (Gökb., Rum. 206); Tat. 1543 **Qul-qal** [Kulkal] (Gökb., Rum. 242). ⇨ **QUL + QAL I.?**

QUL-QARA   Uyg. 12th c. - 14th c. **Qul-qara** [qul qara / Kula Kara] (DTS, EUTS). ✦ 'Slave-Black (Mighty)' (Blagova 1997, 711), 'Slave from North' (Blagova 1997, 704).

QUL-QAŠ   Bashk. **Qul-ɣaš** [Кулгаш Кураев] (MIB I, 326); Bashk. 1770, 1773, 1789 **Qul-qaš** [Ирясюлъ (Рясулъ / Ресюль) Кулкашевъ (Куркашевъ)] (MIB IV/1, 345, IOAIÊK XXVIII, 587, MIB V, 243); Bashk. 1789 **Qul-qaš** [Рясул (Ресюль) Кулкашев] (MIB V, 243). ⇨ **QUL + QAŠ?**

QUL-QUDA-YAR   Kkalp. 20th c. **Qul-quda-yar** [Кулкудаяр] (KkRS 774). ⇨ **QUL + QUDA-YAR.**

QUL-MAMBET   Kzk. 1860 **Qul-mambet** [Ильченъ Кульмамбетевъ] (ZIRGOGeogr. I, 272); *EN:* Kzk. 18th c. - 19th c. **Qul-mambet** [Кулмамбет], a clan (Tynyšp. 71). ⇨ **QUL + MAMBET.**

QUL-MİŠÄR   Bashk. 1776 **Qul-mišär** [Кулмышар Якунев] (MIB V, 683). ⇨ **QUL + MİŠÄR.**

QUL-MÏRAT see **QUL-MURAT**

QUL-MURAT   Kkalp. 20th c. **Qul-mïrat** [Кулмырат] (KkRS 774); Kkalp. 20th c. **Qul-murat** [Кулмурат] (KkRS 774). ⇨ **QUL + MURAT.**

QUL-SADÏQ   Kzk. 18th c. - 19th c. **Qul-sadïq** [Кулсадык], a clan (Tynyšp. 67). ⇨ **QUL + SADÏQ.**

QUL-SAR   Bashk. 1777 **Qul-sar / Kül-sar?** [Кулсар Юлдашбаев] (MIB V, 64); Tat.(Sib.) 1601 **Qul-zar / Kül-zar?** [Кульзар], a prince (Miller, Ist. Sib. II, 165). ⇨ **QUL-SARÏ?**

QUL-SARÏ   Oghuz/Trkm. 13th c. **Qul-sarï** [قل سارى / Кул-Сары], Otqan's son (Abulg./Kon. 665); Bashk. 1754 **Qul-sarï** [Кулсары Токбулатов] (MIB IV/1, 77); Kzk. 18th c. **Qul-sari** [Кулсары] (Nepljuev 747-48). ⇨ **KÜL / QUL? + SARÏ.** See also **KÜL-SARÏГ?**

QUL-ŠÄRİP Bashk. 1735 **Qul-šärip** [Кулшерипъ Сабангуловъ], a tarχan (Vel.-Zern., Bašk. 14); Bashk. 1763 **Qul-šärip** [Ярыш Кульшарыпов] (MIB IV/2, 45). ⇨ QUL.

QUL-TABAY Bashk. 1719 **Qul-tabay** [Култабай] (MIB I, 280); Kzk. 19th c. **Qul-tabay** [Илбакъ Култабаевъ] (Grod., Pril. 24). ✧ '(Little) Pan with handle' cf. Tat. *qul taba* 'die Pfanne mit Stiel' (Radl. IV, 960) + suff. *-y*.

QUL-TAY Tat., Tat.(Mish.), Tat.(Sib.) 20th c. **Qol-tay** [Колтаев] (Sattarov); Tat.(Sib.) 1632 **Qul-tay** [Култай] (Miller, Ist. Sib. II, 398, 450); Bashk. 1737 **Qul-tay** [Култай Бикимбетев] (MIB III, 376); Bashk. 18th c. **Qul-tay** [Бадран Култаев] (MIB V, 99); Bashk. 1761 **Qul-tay** [Култай] (MIB IV/1, 215); Bashk. 1770 **Qul-tay** [Бурангул Култаев] (MIB IV/1, 341); Bashk. 1770 **Qul-tay** [Култай Сафаров] (MIB IV/1, 349); Bashk. 1783 **Qul-tay** [Култай Сапаров] (MIB V, 139); Kzk. **Qul-tay** [Култай] (Divaev, Alp. 53); Kzk. 19th c. **Qul-tay** [Культай] (AOO 18); Tat. 1660 **Qul-tay-batïr** [Култай-Батыръ] (AI IV, 295); Nog. **Qul-tay-murza** [Култай Мурза] (Žirm., Epos 430). ⇨ QUL + TAY or suff. *-tay*?

QUL-TAŠ Tat. 20th c. **Qol-taš** [Колташ] (Sattarov); **Qul-taš** [قولتاش] (Qazw. 519); 1392 **Qul-taš** [سيفالدين قولتاش], an emir (Qazw. 750); Bashk. 1798 **Qul-taš** [Култашевъ] (PSZRI XXV, 196). ⇨ QUL + TAŠ.

QUL-TEKE Kzk. 19th c. **Qul-teke** [Культеке] (SOV 66). ⇨ QUL + TEKE.

QUL-TEMİR Kzk. **Qul-timir** [Культимиръ] (Sb. Syr-D. IX, 44); *EN:* Kzk. 18th c. - 19th c. **Qul-temir / Qul-temïr** [Култемыр], a clan (Tynyšp. 66). ⇨ QUL + TEMİR.

QUL-TİMİR see **QUL-TEMİR**

QUL-TUΓAN Tat. 20th c. **Qol-tuγan** [Колтуган] (Sattarov); Kzk. 19th c. **Qul-tuγan** [Культуганъ] (SODž. 124). ⇨ QUL + TUΓAN I.

QUL-TUMÏŠ Bashk. 1756 **Qul-tumïš** [Тунгун Культумышев] (MIB IV/1, 121). ✧ I. 'Slave-Saddle-horse'? cf. western Kzk. *Tomïš / Tumïš* 'arγïmaq at [=full-blooded horse]' (Žanuzakov-Esbaeva 462); II. '(God's) Slave was born'. ⇨ QUL + TOΓMÏŠ?

QULA Yürük 1543 **Qula** [Kula] (Gökb., Rum. 241); Tat. 1543 **Qula** [Kula] (Gökb., Rum. 241); Tat.(Sib.) 1634 **Qula** [Кула], a taysha (Miller, Ist. Sib. II, 412, 457, 459-61); Kzk. 19th c. **Qula** [Кула Муратовъ] (Grod., Pril. 115); Bashk. 1740 **Qula-bay** [Кула-бай] (MIB I, 381); Kzk. 19th c. **Qula-bay** [Оймаутъ Кулабаевъ] (Grod., Pril. 195); Kzk. 19th c. **Qula-bay** [Кулабай] (SOK 218); Kzk. 19th c. **Qula-ǰan** [Саниязъ Куладжанъ] (Grod., Pril. 133); Tat. 1717 **Qula-γul?** [Кулагулъ / Кудагулъ] (ZIRGO IX, 325); Kzk. 19th c. **Qula-žan** [Кулажанъ] (SOV 54); *TN:* Kzk.? **Qula-bay** [Кулабай-мулласы] (Karta JAR XI). ✧ I. 'Yellow(ish)-grey; brown' cf. Uyg., Kuman, Alt., Hak., Kzk., Turk. *qula* 'gelbgrau (braun), falb; braun (eine Pferdefarbe)' (Radl. II, 967), Hak. *χula* 'саврасый (масть лошади)' (HRS); II. 'Bucket, pail' cf. Bashk. *qula* 'ведро (для варки пищи в поле)' (BRS). See also **QARA-QULA, POLAT-QULA, TAY-QULA.**

QULA-ATTÏ Hak. 19th-20th c. **Qulatï (<Qula-attï) / Qulattuγ / Qulattïγ? (<Qula-attïγ)** [Кулаты (Кулатътогъ)], a hero („Savrasyj bogatyr na savrasom kone") (Titov 191). ✧ 'Having brown horse'. ⇨ QULA + AT + suff. *-tï/-tïγ.*

QULA-BERDİ Crm.(Tat.) 1555 **Qula-berdi** [Занебѣкъ Кулабердѣевъ] (PSRL XIII, 247); *TN:* Bashk. 18th c. **Qula-berdi(na)** [Кулабердина], a village in the district of Svijažsk (Korsakov 357). ✧ 'Yellow(ish)-grey / brown (horse?) gave him'. ⇨ QULA + BERDİ.

QULA-DOΓAN Yürük 1543 **Qula-doγan** [Kula Doğan] (Gökb., Rum. 230). ⇨ QULA + TOΓAN.

QULA-TAY Hak. 19th-20th c. **Xula-tay** [Хулатай] (HRS 352); Kzk. 18th c. - 19th c. **Qula-tay** [Кулатай] (ZOOIRGO 1881, IV, 99); Kzk. 19th c. **Qula-tay** [Кулатай] (AOO 10); Kzk. 19th c. **Qula-tay** [Магомедъ Кулатаевъ] (Grod., Pril. 100); Kzk. 19th c. **Qula-tay** [Кулатай] (SODž. 38); Kzk. 19th c. **Qula-tay** [Кулатай] (SOV 102); Alt. 19th c. **Qula-tay / (Er-)Qula-tay** [Эр-Кулатай], a folklore hero (Verb., In. 153); Kzk. 19th c. **Qula-tay-batïr** [Kulatay-batïr] (Ljutš 65). ✧ 'Yellow(ish)-grey / brown foal'. ⇨ QULA + TAY or suff. *-tay*?

QULAČ Bashk. 1734 **Qulač** [Абубакыр Кулачев] (MIB III, 325); Kzk. 1819 **Qulač** [Кулачь] (MIK IV, 326); Bashk. 1740 **Qulas** [Бабакир Куласов] (MIB I, 396); Kzk. 19th c. **Qulaš** [Кулашъ] (SOK 262). ✧ 'Fathom' cf. Uyg., Chag., Turk., Uzb. *qulač* 'der Klafter' (Radl. II, 975). See also **ALTÏ-QULAČ.**

QULAǰÏ Kzk. 1884 **Qulaǰï / Qul-aǰï?** [Куладже Актаевъ] (Grod., Pril. 93).

QULADA Tat.(Sib.)? 1629 **Qulada** [Кулада], Qara-qula taysha's brother (Miller, Ist. Sib. II, 360).

QULAΓUZ Turk. 1329 **Qulaγuz** [Κολαούζης Σαλιγγαρί], a commander of the army (Byz. Turc. 162); Turk. 1528 **Qulaγuz** [Hacı Bedreddin Mahmud bin Kulağuz] (Gökb., Ed. 53); Yürük 1543 **Qulaγuz** [قولاغوز / Kulağuz] (Gökb., Rum. 185, 213, 215, 222); Selj. **Qulawuz** [قلاوز] (Ibn Bībī IV, 315). ✧ 'Guide, leader' cf. Turk. *qulaγuz*, Uyg. *qulaγus* 'der Führer, Wegweiser' (Radl. II, 973).

QULAX see **QULAQ**

QULAY Tat. 1739 **Qulay** [Кулаевъ] (Alatyr. 146); Tat.(Mish.) 1708 **Qulay** [Келманко Кулаев] (MIB I,

225); Bashk. **Qulay** [Kulaev] (Mende 29, 173); Bashk. 1709 **Qulay** [Кулай] (MIB I, 264); Bashk. 1740 **Qulay** [Явгилда Кулаев] (MIB I, 404); Bashk. 1778 **Qulay** [Кулай Курмышев] (MIB V, 68); Bashk. 1778, 1780 **Qulay** [Кулай (Кулей) Болтасев] (MIB V, 552); Uzb. 19th c. **Qulay** [Кулай] (SKSO III, 180). ✦ I. 'Right, pleasing, suitable, capable'? cf. Tat. *qulay* 'удобный, сподручный; благоприятный; лёгкий' (TatRS); Bashk. *qulay* 'удобный, походящий' (BRS); II. 'Yellow(ish)-grey; brown' cf. Uyg., Kuman, Alt., Hak., Kzk., Turk. *qula* 'gelbgrau (braun), falb; braun (eine Pferdefarbe)' (Radl. II, 967), Hak. *χula* 'саврасый (масть лошади)' (HRS), see qula + suff. *-y*. See also **AQ-QULAY, QARA-QULAY, QOČ-QULAY.**

QULAYQAN   Alt.(Tel.) **Qulayqan** [Кулаи-кан], Ülgen's daughter (Radl. II, 968). ⇨ **QULAY** + suff. *-qan(1)*.

QULAQ   Tat.(Lit.) 1644 **Qulaq** [Мустафа Абрагимовичъ Кулаковскій] (Lit. Tat. 319-21); Bashk. 1769 **Qulaq** [Балгаир Кулаков] (MIB IV/1, 336); Kzk. 19th c. **Qulaq** [Кулакъ Актановъ] (Grod., Pril. 93); Hak. 19th c. **Qulaq** [Кулак] (Katanov, Otč. 12); Hak.(Kyz.) 19th-20th c. **Qulaq** [Кулак], fem. (Katanov, Otč. 13); Kzk. 19th c. **Qulaq-bay** [Кулакбаевъ / Кулякбаевъ] (SKSO VIII, 232). ✦ 'Ear' cf. Trk. *qulaq* 'das Ohr' (Radl. II, 967). See also **ABA-QULAQ, BAY-QULAQ, ČOYUN-ƔULAQ, DÖRT-QULAQ, İT-QULAQ, QALDÏ-QULAQ, QARA-QULAQ, QAS-QULAQ, QOS-QULAQ, QUM-QULAQ, QUŠ-QULAQ, SAQ-QULAQ, TAS-QULAQ, ÜŠ-QULAQ.**

QULAQAY   Bashk. 1735 **Qulaqay** [Кулакай Калчановъ], a tarχan (Vel.-Zern., Bašk. 14); Kzk. 19th c. **Qulaqay** [Кулакай] (SOV 12). ⇨ **QULA?** + suff. *-qay*.

QULAQJALÏ   Yürük 1543 **Qulaqjalï** [قولاقحالى / Kulakcalı] (Gökb., Rum. 206). ✦ 'Having a cap with ear-flaps' cf. Turk. *qulaqča* 'eine Mütze mit Ohrenklappen' (Radl. II, 972).

QULAQSÏZ   Maml. 14th c. **Qulaqsïz** [قلقسيز] (Sauvaget 53); Turk. 19th c. **Qulaqsïz-oγlu** [Kulaksyz oglu], a Zeybek (Kúnos 1891, 119). ✦ 'Without ear' (Sauvaget 53).

QULAM   Tat.(Sib.)? 1643 **Qulam** [Куламко], envoy (Miller, Ist. Sib. II, 491); Trkm. 1879 **Qulam-oγlï** [Махмудъ-Куламъ-оглы] (Grod., Pril. 109).

QULAN   Kzk. 19th c. **Qulam-bay** (<Qulan-bay) [Куламбай] (AOO 14); Kzk. 19th c. **Qulam-bay** (<Qulan-bay) [Найманбай Куламбаевъ] (Grod., Pril. 82); Kzk. 1860 **Qulam-bay** (<Qulan-bay) [Куламбаевъ], a yasaul, head of the Yappas clan (IOAIÊK XX, 673, ZOOIRGO 1870, 137); Uyg. 12th c. - 14th c. **Qulan** [Qulan / Kulan] (Radl., USp. 130-131,

DTS, EUTS); Kzk. **Qulan** [Куланъ], Tüle-bay's son in the tale „J̌ez-tïrnaq" (Sb. Syr-D. XI otd. II, 6); Kzk. 1819 **Qulan** [Кулан] (MIK IV, 324); Kzk. 1825 **Qulan** [كولان / Кулан] (MIK IV, 470, 476); Kzk. 1831, 1832 **Qulan** [Куланъ Адилевъ], a sultan (Konšin, Mat. I-III, 33, V, 96); Kzk. 19th c. **Qulan** [Куланъ] (AOA 154); Kzk. 19th c. **Qulan** [Куланъ] (AOAtb. 6); Kzk. 19th c. **Qulan** [Куланъ] (AOK 90); Kzk. 19th c. **Qulan** [Куланъ] (SOK 198); Kzk. 1846 **Qulan-bay** [Бермухамед Куланбаев], a biy (MKOP 156); Kzk. 19th c. **Qulan-bay** [Куланбай] (AOA 102); Kzk. 19th c. **Qulan-bay** [Аширъ-Кулъ Куланбаевъ] (Grod., Pril. 25); Kzk. 19th c. **Qulan-bay** [Куланбай] (SOK 144); Kzk. 19th c. **Qulan-bay** [Куланбай] (SOV 114, 136); Kzk. 19th c. **Qulan-bay** [Куланбай] (SOV 56); Kzk. **Qulan-biy** [Кулянъ-бій], one of the chiefs of the Quñγrat tribe of Naymans (Sib. Vest. IX, 103); Kzk. 1805 **Qulan-biy** [Кулянбий], one of the chiefs of the Nayman tribe of the Middle Horde (Orta Žüz) (MIK IV, 512); Kzk. 1859 **Qulan-biy** [Куланъ-Бій] (Moskal'cev 40); *TN:* Kzk.? **Qulam-bay** (<Qulan-bay) [С. Куламбай], a hill(?) south of Lake Teniz (Karta JAR XI); Kzk. **Qulam-bay** (<Qulan-bay) [Куломбай] (Karta JAR XI); Chag.? 15th c. **Qulan** [Куланъ] (Barth., Ulugb. 54 (after Arabš.)); Kzk. **Qulan** [Кулан], a field (Kojčubaev 154); NUyg. 19th c. **Qulan** [قولان / Kulan] (Le Coq, Namenl. 108). ✦ 'Wild horse' (Le Coq, Blagova 1997, 706), 'wild donkey', cf. *qulan* 'das Kulan, ein wildes Pferd' (Uyg.), 'der wilde Esel' (Chag., Kirg., Kzk.) (Radl. II, 974), Karakh. *qulan* 'кулан, дикий азиатский осел' (DTS). See also **BAY-QULAN.**

QULAN-AYAQ   Kzk. 19th c. **Qulan-ayaq** [Куланаякъ] (SOV 12). ✦ 'Wildhorse-leg'. ⇨ **QULAN + AYAQ.**

QULAN-SARÏQ   Kirg. **Qulan-sarïq** [Кулансарык] (Jud. 526). ⇨ **QULAN + SARÏQ.**

QULAN-TAYA   Yak. **Qulantaya** [Кулантаja Куллугур] (Pek.). ✦ 'Foal of wild-horse/donkey'. ⇨ **QULAN + TAY?**

QULANČÏ   Kzk. 19th c. **Qulančï / Qulanči** [Куланчи] (SOK 110); Kzk. 19th c. **Qulančï / Qulanči** [Куланчи] (SOV 58); Tat.(Sib.) 1640 **Qulančï / Qulanči(y)?** [Куланчейка] (Miller, Ist. Sib. II, 457-463). ⇨ **QULAN** + suff. *-čï*. See also **SARÏ-QULANČÏ.**

QULANČÏQ   Maml. 14th c. **Qulančïq** [قلنجق] (Sauvaget 53 (after Mayer 190)). ✦ 'Little wild-donkey' (Sauvaget 53). ⇨ **QULAN** + suff. *-čïq*.

QULAPAQ   Bashk. 1706 **Qulapaq** [Калмак Кулапаков] (MIB III, 25).

QULAS see **QULAČ**

QULAŠ see **QULAČ**

QULATÏ see **QULA-ATTÏ**

QULATTÏГ see QULA-ATTÏ

QULATTUГ see QULA-ATTÏ

QULAWUZ see QULAГUZ

QULĀČÏQ   Yak. **Qulāčïq** [Кулачык] (Pek.). ✧ '?' cf.
R. кулащик (Pek.).

QULBAQ   Karakh. 11th c. **Qulbaq** [qulbaq / Kulbak]
(DTS, MK/Atalay 846).

QULČA see QULŽA

QULČAQ   Kzk. 19th c. **Qulčaq** [Кульчакъ] (SOK 32).

QULČAÑ   Kzk. 1817 **Qolšan-bay / Qulčañ-bay?**
[قول‌چانکبای / Колшанбай] (MIK IV, 311, 318).

QULČÏ-ГAS see QULČU-ГAŠ

QULČU-ГAČ see QULČU-ГAŠ

QULČU-ГAŠ   Kzk. 19th c. **Qulčï-γas / Külčï-γaš
(Qulčï-qas?)** [Кульчигасъ] (SOK 308); Kzk. **Qulču-
γač / Külčü-γač** [Кульчугачъ] (Valihanov, Soč. 386);
Kzk. 19th c. **Qulču-γaš** [Кулчугашъ] (SOV 82). ⇨
KÜLČE? + QAŠ?

QULČUГAY see QULČUQAY

QULČUQ   Bashk. 1735 **Qulčuq** [Аиткулъ
Кулчуковъ] (Vel.-Zern., Bašk. 14); Kzk. 19th c.
Qulčuq [Кулчукъ] (SODž. 158); Kzk. 19th c. **Qulčuq**
[Кулчукъ] (SOV 72, 92). ✧ 'Little slave (of God)'. ⇨
QUL? + dim. suff. *-čuq*? See also **KÜLČÜK**.

QULČUQAY   Kzk. 1826 **Qulčuγay** [Кулчугай]
(TOUAK XXIV, 161); Bashk. 1790 **Qulčuqay** [Ярыш
Кулчукаев] (MIB V, 279). ⇨ **QULČÏ** + dim.
suff. *-qay / -γay*.

QULČUMA   Chuv. 1737 **Kulčuma** [Кулчюма],
Yanbetev's daughter (MIB III, 365). ✧ Female form of
Qulčum.

QULČUMAN   Kzk. 19th c. **Qulčuman** [Кулчуманъ]
(SOV 62). ⇨ **QUL + ČUMAN? / QULČU / QULČÏ?**
+ suff. *-man*.

QULŽA see QULŽA

QULDAN   Kzk. 19th c. **Quldan** [Кулдановъ] (AOP
70). ⇨ **QULTAN?**

QULDAS see QOLDAŠ

QULDEK   Tat.(Sib.)? 1648 **Quldek?** [Кулдек
(Кулцен) Абаша], a taysha (Miller, Ist. Sib. II, 527).

QULDÏŠ   Bashk. 1740 **Quldïš** [Буран Кулдышев]
(MIB I, 422).

QULDU   Kzk. 1846 **Quldu-bay** [Кулдубай Берденев]
(MKOP 155); Kzk. 19th c. **Quldu-bay** [Кулдубай]
(SOV 148); Kzk. 19th c. **Quldu-bay** [Кулдубай] (SOV
150).

QULDU-ГAČ   Kzk. 19th c. **Quldu-γač** [Кульдугачъ]
(AOK 6). ⇨ **QULDU + QAŠ?**

QULDU-QAYA   Uyg. 12th c. - 14th c. **Quldu-qaya**
[Quldu qaya / qulduqaja] (Radl., USp. 26-27, DTS). ✧
'?-rock'. ⇨ **QULDU? + QAYA.**

QULDUY   Kzk. 19th c. **Qulduy** [Кулдуй] (SOK 152).

QULГAY   Kzk. 19th c. **Qulγay** [Онгдасинъ
Кулгаевъ] (Grod., Pril. 65).

QULГAN   Bashk. 1735 **Qulγan** [Ератъ Кулгановъ], a
tarχan (Vel.-Zern., Bašk. 18); Bashk. 1789 **Qulγan**
[Кулган Алимгулов] (MIB V, 260).

QULГUN   Bashk. 1735 **Qulγun** [Кулгунъ Кунаевъ], a
tarχan (Vel.-Zern., Bašk. 14).

QULГUNA see QOLГUNA

QULГUNČA   Tat. 18th c. **Qulγunča** [Кулгунча], a
village in the district of Mamadyš (Korsakov 241). ⇨
QULГUN + suff. *-ča*.

QULÏ see QULÏ

QULÏ   Kzk. 19th c. **Qolï-bay** [Колыбай] (SOV 34);
Kzk. 19th c. **Qolï-bay** [Колыбай] (SODž. 50); Kzk.
19th c. **Qolo-žam-bay (<Qolu-žan-bay)**
[Коложамбай] (SOK 180); Bashk. 1675 **Qolu-bay**
[Иликей Колюбаев] (MIB I, 200); Kzk. 1820 **Qolu-
bay** [Колубай], one of the chiefs of the Jaγalbaylï tribe
(Sib. Vest. IX, 123); Kzk. 19th c. **Qolu-bay** [Колубай]
(SOK 180); Kzk. 19th c. **Qolu-bay** [Колубай] (SOV
42); Kzk. 19th c. **Qolu-bay** [Колюбай] (AOAtb. 14);
Kzk. 19th c. **Qolu-bay** [Колюбай] (SOK 10); Kzk.
19th c. **Qolu-bay** [Колюбай] (SOV 44); Kzk. 19th c.
Qolu-bek [Колубекъ] (AOK 82); Tat. 1468 **Qolu-pay**
[Колупай], a heroic warrior (PSRL (Russk. Hr.) I,
470); Tat. 20th c. **Quli** [Кулиев] (Sattarov); Kirg. 1788
Qulï-bek-batïr [Кулебакъ-Батыръ] (PSZRI XXII,
1086); Bashk. 1735 **Qulu-bay** [Кулубай Еликеевъ], a
tarχan (Vel.-Zern., Bašk. 15); Bashk. 1776 **Qulu-bay**
[Кулубай] (MIB V, 42); Kzk. **Qulu-bay** [Tiak-
Koulubaï], an aq-saqal (Levchine 154); Kzk. 19th c.
Qulu-bek [Кулубекъ] (AOAtb. 38); Kzk. 19th c.
Qulu-bek [Кулубековъ] (AOO 34); Kzk. 19th c.
Qulu-bek [Кулубекъ] (SOK 70); Tat.(Sib.) 1599
Qulu-bi (<Qul-bi?) [Кулуби], Küčüm's young(er)
wife (AI II, 20); Bulg. 927 **Qulu-tarqan**
[Κουλουτερκανος] (Byz. Turc. 166). ✧ 'His (Allah's)
servant' Used also as a secondary component of male
names. ⇨ **QUL** + poss. suff. *-ï*.

QULÏČ see QÏLÏČ

QULÏQ   Turk. 19th c. **Qulïq-oγlu / Qulik-oγlu?** [Kulik
oγlu], a Zeybek (Kúnos 1891, 119).

QULÏMBET   Bashk. 1735 **Qolïmbet** [Колимбеть
Бекеевъ] (Vel.-Zern., Bašk. 20); Kkalp. 20th c.
Qulïmbet [Кулымбет] (KkRS 774). ✧ 'Slave-
Mukhammad' cf. Tat. PN *Qolmöχämmät / Qolïmbet*
(Sattarov). ⇨ **QUL** + suff. *-ïmbet*.

QULÏN see QULUN

QULÏN-TAY see QULUN-TAY

QULÏNČAQ see QULUNČAQ

QULÏŠUQ   Kzk. 19th c. **Qulïšuq** [Кулышукъ] (AOO
50). ⇨ **QULÏ** + dim. *-čïq*.

QULQA   Maml.? 1514 **Qulqa** [Kulka], head of the
Markit (Merkit) tribe (Tar. Rashidi 309). ⇨ **QUL** +
suff. *-qa*?

QULQAY   Bashk. 1754 **Qolqay** [Колкай] (MIB IV/1,

83); Kzk. 19th c. **Qolqay** [Колкай] (SOK 208); Bashk. 1735 **Qulqay** [Солтангулъ Кулкаевъ], a tarχan (Vel.-Zern., Bašk. 21); Bashk. 1761 **Qulqay** [Турабай Кулкаев] (MIB IV/1, 214); Bashk. 1761 **Qulqay** [Япар Кулкаев] (MIB IV/1, 221); Kzk. 19th c. **Qulqay** [Кулкай] (AOP 22). ⇨ **QUL / QULQA?** + dim. suff. *-qay / -y*.

QULQAMÏS Kzk. 19th c. **Qulqamïs** [Кулкамысъ] (SOV 100). ⇨ **QUL + QAMÏS.**

QULQAN Bashk. 1761 **Qulqan** [Кулкан Кучкаров] (MIB IV/1, 221). ⇨ **QULΓAN?**

QULQAR Kzk. 19th c. **Qulqar** [Кулкаръ] (Grod., Pril. 38).

QULLUΓUR Yak. **Qulluγur** [Куллугур] (Pek.). ✧ 'Drooping (ear), crooked (neck)' (Pek.).

QULLUQ Chag. 15th c. **Qulluq** [انتوجی قوللوق / Атгкучи Гкуллугкъ] (Šejb. LXII). ⇨ **QUL** + suff. *-luq*.

QULMAN Trkm. 20th c. **Γulman** [Gulman / Гулман] (Zaj. 1971, 325); Tat.? 1612 **Qolman** [Колманъ Вергомасовъ] (Nižegorod. platež. 116); Tat. 1768 **Qolman** [Колманъ Иштеряковъ] (Nikol'skij 271); Tat. 20th c. **Qolman** [Колман] (Sattarov); Kzk. 19th c. **Qolman-bay** [Колманбай] (SOK 122); Bashk. 1713 **Qulman** [Кулман] (MIB III, 96); Bashk. 1755 **Qulman** [Кулман Кадышев] (MIB IV/1, 101); Kzk. 18th c. - 19th c. **Qulman** [Турумдай-кожа Кулмановъ] (ZOOIRGO IV, 99); Kzk. 1846 **Qulman** [Мурзабек Кулманов], a biy (MKOP 156); Kzk. 19th c. **Qulman** [Бахти-Тирей Кулмановъ], a sultan (AUK 917); Kzk. 19th c. **Qulman** [Кулманъ Аминъ] (Grod., Pril. 146); Kzk. 19th c. **Qulman** [Кулманъ] (Grod., Pril. 160); Kzk. 19th c. **Qulman** [Кульманъ] (Grod., Pril. 70); Kzk. 19th c. **Qulman** [Кулманъ] (SODž. 36); Kzk. 19th c. **Qulman** [Кулманъ] (SOK 88); Uzb. 19th c. **Qulman** [Норбай Кульмановъ] (SKSO III, 158); Uzb. 19th c. **Qulman** [Кульманъ Акъ Мурзаевъ] (SKSO III, 22); Kzk. 19th c. **Qulman-bay** [Кульманбай] (SODž. 162); Kkalp. 1822 **Qulman-sufi** [Кулман Суфи] (MIKk. 127); Uzb. 1887 **Qulman-sufi** [Кульманъ-Суфи] (Moskal'cev 48); *EN:* Nog. 20th c. **Qulman-uruw** [Кулман урув], a Qara-noγay clan (Bask., Nog. 137). ✧ 'Slave, servant' (Sattarov; Zaj. 1971), cf. Trkm. *γulman* 'райский юноша' (TrkmRS) (<Ar.). ⇨ **QUL** + suff. *-man*.

QULMET Tat. 1671 **Qulmet** [Еналѣевъ Кулметъ] (DAI IX, 76-78); Tat. 1724 **Qulmet** [Кулмет] (MIB III, 227). ⇨ **QUL** + suff. *-met*.

QULMÏ Oghuz/Trkm. 13th c. **Qulmï** [قلمی / Кулмы], Berdi's son (Abulg./Kon. 1240).

QULPA Kuman **Qolpa** [Kolpakorhana], a Kuman whose name is preserved in that of a burial mound in Lesser Kumania, Hungary (Gyárfás III, 499); 1359 **Qulpa** [Кульпа] (Lavr. 504); 1359 **Qulpa** [Кульпа / Кулпа] (PSRL VIII, 10, X, 231, XXIII, 168); Tat.(GH) 1359 **Qulpa** [Кулпа], a ruler of the Golden Horde (PSRL (Russk. Hr.) I, 411, PSRL VIII, 10, X, 231, XXIII, 168). ✧ 'Hut, cabin' (detailed explanation in Pelliot, Notes 107-108), cf. also Rásonyi, NTK 104-107, Rásonyi, KÖA 114-15, Rásonyi, Anthr. 143).

QULPAN Kzk. **Qulpan** [Кара Кулпан] (Proben III, 73 /95/). See also **QARA-QULPAN.**

QULTAQ Bashk. 1740 **Qultaq** [Култак] (MIB I, 396).

QULTAQ-QARAJA Oghuz/Trkm. 13th c. **Qultaq-qaraJa-mergän** / **Qïltaq-qaraJa-mergän?** [قولتاق / قلتاق / قراجه میرکان / Култак-Караджа-Мерген] (Abulg./Kon. 1340). ⇨ **QULTAQ + QARAJA.**

QULTAN Trkm. 1879 **Qultan** [Култанъ] (Grod., Pril. 108); Kzk. 19th c. **Qultan** [Култанъ] (SOK 190, 194); Kzk. **Qultan-bek** [Култанбекъ] (Protok. Turk. IV, 60).

QULU see **QULÏ**

QULUČ Karakh. 11th c. **Quluč** [quluč / Kuluç] (DTS, MK/Atalay 846).

QULUY Bashk. 1754 **Quluy** [Карачюра Кулуев] (MIB IV/1, 83); Bashk. 1764 **Quluy, Qoloy** [Кулуй (Колой) Болтасев] (MIB IV/1, 286). ⇨ **QULU** + suff. *-y*.

QULUKE Kzk. **Quluke** [Кулуке Булхаковъ] (Konšin, Pam. 17); Kzk. 19th c. **Quluke** [Кулуке] (SOK 98). ⇨ **QULÏ** + suff. *-ke* or comp. *eke?*

QULUQ Bashk. 1728 **Quluq** [Ярлогай Кулуков] (MIB I, 124); Bashk. 1754 **Quluq** [Кигикбай Кулуков] (MIB IV/1, 83); Bashk. 1754 **Quluq** [Кулук Шакаров] (MIB IV/1, 83); Bashk. 1770 **Quluq** [Кулук Уруспаев] (MIB IV/1, 342); Bashk. 1787 **Quluq** [Кулук Уразбаев] (MIB V, 219, 313). ✧ I. 'Turban' cf. Chag. *quluq* 'eine Kopfbinde, der Turban' (Radl. II, 979); II. 'Young foal' cf. Kzk. *qŭluq* 'ein junges Füllen' (Radl. II, 979).

QULUQAY Bashk. 1735 **Quluqay** [Кулукай Тлепеевъ], a tarχan (Vel.-Zern., Bašk. 16); Bashk. 1754 **Quluqay** [Мрат Кулукаев] (MIB IV/1, 83); Bashk. 1780 **Quluqay** [Кулукай (Кулакай, Кунукай) Танатаров] (MIB V, 106, 172, 241, 305); Kzk. 19th c. **Quluqay** [Косаманъ Кулукаевъ] (Grod., Pril. 78). ⇨ **QULÏ, QULUQ?** + suff. *-qay / -ay*.

QULUM Chuv. 18th-19th c. **Kulum** [Кулумъ] (Magn. 54); Kzk. 19th c. **Qulum** [Кулумъ] (SOK 268); *EN:* Kzk. 18th c. - 19th c. **Qulum-bay** [Кулумбай], a clan (Tynyšp. 75). ✧ I. 'My slave/servant'; II. 'Chicken' cf. Chag. *qulum* 'das Küchel' (Radl. II, 981). ⇨ **QUL.**

QULUM-QARA Uyg. 12th c. - 14th c. **Qulum-qara** (Radl., USp. 30-31); Alt. **Qulum-qara** [Кулум-Кара], a character in a heroic legend (AI 151). ✧ I. 'My slave/servant - black'; II. 'Chicken-black'? ⇨ **QULUM**

+ **QARA.** See also **QULUN-QARA.**

QULUM-TAY see **QULUN-TAY**

QULUMBET Bashk. 1777 **Qulumbet** [Байкай Кулумбетев] (MIB V, 57); Bashk. 1777 **Qulumbet** [Байкай Кулумбетев] (MIB V, 57); Kkalp. 20th c. **Qulumbet** [Къулумбет] (Bask., Kkalp. 50). ⇨ **QUL, QULUM?** + suff. *-umbet / -bet.*

QULUN Kzk. 19th c. **Qolïm-bek (< Qolïn-bek?)** [Колымбекъ] (SOK 204); Tat. 20th c. **Qolïn** [Колын] (Sattarov); Tat. 20th c. **Qolïn-bay** [Колынбай] (Sattarov); Bashk. 20th c. **Qolon-bay** [Колонбай / Кулунбай] (Kusimova); Kzk. 19th c. **Qolum-bek (Kölüm-bek?)** [Колюмбекъ] (SODž. 40); Pecheneg 1050 **Qulïn** [Κουλῖνος], a chieftain, Kegene's son (Byz. Turc. 166); Alt. 19th-20th c. **Qulun** [Кулун] (OjrRS 209); Hak.(Kacha) 19th c. **Qulun** [Кулунъ] (Katanov, Otč. II, 42); Hak.(Kyz.) 19th-20th c. **Qulun** [Кулун] (Katanov, Otč. 13); Kzk. 19th c. **Qulun-bay** [Кулунбай] (SOK 54); Uzb. 1717 **Qulun-bey / Qolun-bey** [Кулунъ-Бей / Колунъ-Бей], a commander of the army (ZIRGO IX, 324, 325); Kzk. 19th c. **Qulun-bek** [Кулунбекъ] (SOK 72). ✧ 'Foal' cf. Karakh. *qulun* 'id.' (DTS), Chag., Alt., Crm., Hak., Kzk. *qulun* 'ein einjähriges Füllen' (Radl. II, 979), Bashk. *qolon* 'жеребенок' (BRS), Tat. *qolin* 'id.' (TatRS).

QULUN-BAΓAR Kzk. 19th c. **Qulum-baγar (<Qulun-baγar)** [Кулумбагаръ] (SODž. 100). ✧ 'He who will take care of foals'. ⇨ **QULUN + BAQAR.**

QULUN-QARA Uyg. 12th c. - 14th c. **Qulun-qara** [Qulun Qara / Kulun Kara] (Radl., USp. 30-31, DTS, EUTS). ✧ 'Foal-black' (Blagova 1997, 706). ⇨ **QULUN + QARA.**

QULUN-SAQAL Khorezm.? **Qulun-saqal** [قولون ستل / Кулунъ-Сакалъ] (RaD/Ber. II, 5). ⇨ **QULUN + SAQAL.**

QULUN-TAY Kzk. 19th c. **Qulïn-tay** [Кулинтай] (Grod., Pril. 186); Maml. 1404/05 **Qulum-tay** [قلطاى] (Ibn Taghrīb. VI, 122); Kzk. 19th c. **Qulun-tay / Quluntay?** [Кулунтай] (AOO 22). ✧ 'Foal (under one year of age)' cf. Kzk. *Qulïn-tay* 'Kısrağın henüz bir yaşını doldurmamış yavrusu' (QzTS, QTTS). ⇨ **QULUN + TAY** or suff. *-tay?*

QULUNČAQ Kkalp. **Qulïnčaq-batïr** [Кулынчак-батыр], from the Naγaylï (Noγaylï) clan (Divaev: OOIKK III, 123); Chuv. 18th-19th c. **Kulunčak** [Кулунчакъ] (Magn. 54); Crm. **Qulunčaq-batïr** [Кулунчак Батыр] (Proben VII, 21); Chag. 1503 **Qulunǰaq** [Kulunják], governor of Balkh (Tar. Rashidi 164); Tuv. 19th c. **Qulunǰaq** [Кулунцак], from the Qŭlar tribe (Proben IX, 117, 119). ✧ 'Little foal' cf. Hak., Kzk. *qulunaq, qulunǰaq, qulunšaq* 'ein kleines Füllen; mustela sibirica' (Radl. II, 980-81).

QULUNǰAQ see **QULUNČAQ**

QULUNΓAY Chul. 1674 **Qulunγay** [Кулунгайко] (Jarilov, Tel. 8). ⇨ **QULUN** + dim. suff. *-qay.*

QULUNKEY Tat. 1624 **Qulunkey** [Усекъ Кулункѣевъ] (Pokrovskij 72). ⇨ **QULUN** + dim. suff. *-key.*

QULUŠ Bashk. 1780 **Qluš, Quluš** [Егафер Клушев (Кулушев)] (MIB V, 121); Tat. 1547 **Quluš** [Кулушь-князь], a prince (PSRL XIII, 149); Tat. 1718 **Quluš** [Илыш Кулушев] (MIB III, 168); Bashk. 1633 **Quluš** [Кулушев], a captain (MIB I, 70); Bashk. 1713 **Quluš** [Исянкул Кулушев] (MIB III, 93); Bashk. 1714 **Quluš** [Ишкара Кулушев] (MIB III, 116); Bashk. 1728 **Quluš** [Кулуш] (MIB I, 125); Bashk. 1735 **Quluš** [Унгаръ Кулушевъ] (Vel.-Zern., Bašk. 13); Bashk. 1735 **Quluš** [Кулушъ], a tarγan (Vel.-Zern., Bašk. 17); Bashk. 1740 **Quluš** [Сарбан Кулушев] (MIB I, 396); Bashk. 1740 **Quluš** [Сарбак Кулушов] (MIB I, 404); Bashk. 1740 **Quluš** [Кулуш Сеитбаев] (MIB I, 439); Bashk. 1754, 1761 **Quluš** [Айсюль Кулушев] (MIB IV/1, 83, MIB IV/1, 214); Bashk. 1758 **Quluš** [Айсюля Кулушев] (MIB IV/1, 174); Bashk. 1761 **Quluš** [Кулуш Токтаров] (MIB IV/1, 221); Kzk. 19th c. **Quluš** [Кулушъ] (Lomakin 32); *TN:* Bashk. 1756 **Quluš(evo)** [Кулушево], a village (MIB IV/1, 126). ⇨ **QOLÏŠ?**

QULUŠQA Bashk. 1666 **Qulušqa** [Кулушка Аккочкаровъ] (Vel.-Zern., Bašk. 28). ⇨ **QULUŠ** + suff. *-qa.*

QULUT-QUDAQ Tat.(Sib.) 1641 **Qulut-qudaq** [Кулуткудак] (Miller, Ist. Sib. II, 479, 480).

QULUZİN Alt. **Quluzin-qan** [Кулузинъ-канъ] (Nikiforov 34). ✧ 'Reed'? cf. Alt. *quluzun* 'das Schilf' (Radl. II, 981).

QULZİMAN Tat.(Lit.) 1582 **Qulziman / Qulsïman** [Хазбей Кульзиманобичъ] (Lit. Tat. 48, 243); Tat.(Lit.) 1591 **Qulziman / Qulsïman?** [Кульзиманъ Оразовичъ] (Lit. Tat. 98). ✧ 'Slave-like'. ⇨ **QUL** + suff. *-sïman.*

QULŽA Kzk. 1870 **Qulča** [Альменъ Кульчиновъ] (Grod., Pril. 128); Kzk. 1829 **Qulča-bay** [Кулчабай] (MIK IV, 324); Kzk. 19th c. **Qulǰa** [Османъ бекъ Кульджаевъ] (Grod., Pril. 153); Kzk. **Qulǰa / Bayqulǰa** [Bai Kuldzsa] (Prisvin, A fekete arab 38); Kzk. 19th c. **Qulǰa-bay** [Кульджабай] (AOAtb. 30); Kzk. 19th c. **Qulǰa-bay** [Кульджебай] (AOK 58); Kzk. 19th c. **Qulǰa-bay** [Кульджабай] (AOO 34); Kzk. 19th c. **Qulǰa-bay** [Кульджабай] (SOK 12); Kzk. 19th c. **Qulǰa-bay** [Кульджабай] (SOV 34); Kzk. 19th c. **Qulǰa-bay** [Кульджобай / Кульджабай] (SOV 56); Kirg. 20th c. **Qulǰa-bay** [Кулжабай] (Kalilov 92); Kzk. 1846 **Qulǰa-bay / Qulža-bay** [Кулджабай (Кулжабай) Чарабасов (Чорабасов)], a biy (MKOP 100, 154); Kzk. 19th c. **Qulža** [Кульжа] (AOK 42); Kzk. 19th c. **Qulža-bay** [Кулжабай] (AOA 66); Kzk.

19th c. **Qulža-bay** [Кульжабай] (AOK 30); Kzk. 19th c. **Qulža-bay** [Кулжабай] (AOK 86); Kzk. 19th c. **Qulža-bay** [Кульжабай] (SODž. 32); Kzk. 19th c. **Qulža-bay** [Кулжабай] (SODž. 62); Kzk. 1785, 1787, 1794 **Qulža-bay / Qulǰa-bay** [قولجابای / قلجبای / Колжабай / Кулжабай], head (aq-saqal) of the Tazlar tribe (MIK IV, 52, 53, 87, 158); *TN:* Kkalp. **Qulča-biy** [قلجه بی / Кулчабій], a village (in Širazskij tumen') (ZIRGOStat. IV). ✧ I. 'Beautiful, brave' cf. Kzk. *qulža* 'tüchtig, wacker' (Radl. II, 989); II. 'Wild goat; chamois' cf. Kirg. *qulǰa* 'die Gemse' (Radl. II, 989).

QUM   Kzk. 19th c. **Qom-ǰar** [Комджаръ Алду-Муратовъ] (Grod., Pril. 109); Kzk. 19th c. **Qom-murza** [Коммурза] (SODž. 12); Kzk. 19th c. **Qum-bay** [Кумбай] (AOP 82); Uzb. 1854 **Qum-bay** [Исламъ Кумъ-бай], son of Ay-tay-bay-oγlï (Moskal'cev 40); Maml. 1352 **Qum-äri** [قماری الحموی / Kumeri Alhamavi] (Iyās I, 196, Weil, Chalif. I, 486); Maml. 1332 **Qum-eri** [قماری الحسنی], an emir (Dawād. 366, 367); Maml. 14th c. **Qum-eri** [قماری / قماری الساقی] (Zetterst. 222); Maml. 14th c. **Qum-eri** [قماری / Kumeri] (Tarǰ/Houtsma 45, Tarǰ/Toparlı 42); Maml. 1379/80 **Qum-eri** [الخازندار / قماری] (Iyās I, 196); *TN:* Kzk. **Taš-qum-bay** [Таш-кумбай], a well at Mertvyj Kultuk (Karta JAR X). ✧ I. 'Sand' cf. most Trk. dial. *qum* 'id.' (Radl. II, 1043); II. 'Felt' cf. Bashk. *qum* 'войлок, обшитый кожей (который подкладывается под седло сверх кошмы)' (BRS).

QUM-BALAY Kzk. 19th c. **Qum-balay** [Кумбалаевъ] (SKSO VIII, 200). ⇨ **QUM** + **BALAY.**

QUM-BAS see **QUN-BAŠ**

QUM-BEL Kzk. 19th c. **Qum-bel** [Кумбель] (SOK 214); Kzk. 19th c. **Qum-bel** [Кумбель] (SOK 214). ⇨ **QUM** + **BEL?**

QUM-ER Kzk. 19th c. **Qum-er-bay / Qumïr-bay?** [Кумербай] (SOK 68). ⇨ **QUM** + **ER?**

QUM-QULAQ Kzk. 1819 **Qum-qulaq** [Кумкулак] (MIK IV, 323). ⇨ **QUM** + **QULAQ.**

QUM-TAY Kzk. 1730 **Qum-tay** [Кулумбетъ Кумтаевъ] (Dobrosm., Turg. 7). ⇨ **QUM** + **TAY** or suff. *-tay(1,2)?*

QUM-UWAQ Kzk. 1846 **Qum-uwaq?** [Кумувак Бусурмановъ] (MKOP 151). ⇨ **QUM** + **UWAQ?**

QUMA I. Kzk. 19th c. **Quma-bay** [Кумабай] (SOV 74). ✧ 'Concubine, second wife' cf. Kuman, Chag., Turk. *quma* 'das Kebsweib' (Radl. II, 1044).

QUMA II. Kzk. 19th c. **Quma** [Кума] (Samojlovič: ŽS XXIV (1915), 165). ✧ Distorted form of *Žuma* and used by women instead of it when it is a tabu-name. ⇨ **ǰUMA.**

QUMA III. Uyg. 10th c. **Quma-qatun** [quma qatun],

fem. (DTS). ✧ 'Linseed oil' (Blagova 1997, 708).

QUMAČ see **QUMAŠ**

QUMAČÏX Hak. 19th-20th c. **Qumačïχ** [Кумачых], fem. (HRS 353). ✧ 'Red cloth, textile' (HRS). See also **QUMAŠ.**

QUMAY Kzk. 19th c. **Qumay** [Кумай] (AOO 70); Kzk. 19th c. **Qumay** [Кумай] (SODž. 128); *TN:* Kzk. 19th c. **Qumay** [Кумай], a winter pasture (qïstau) (SODž. 98). ✧ 'A quiet horse; a greyhound of Turkmen breed' cf. Kzk. *qumay* 'id.' (Radl. II, 1044).

QUMAQ Bashk. 1737 **Qumaq** [Кумак Суюндюков] (MIB I, 327).

QUMAQAY Bashk. 1724 **Qumaqay** [Ака-мулла Кумакаев] (MIB III, 222); Bashk. 1728 **Qumaqay** [Ака Кумакаев] (MIB III, 252-53); Bashk. 1728 **Qumaqay** [Кусяк Кумакаев] (MIB III, 252-53). ⇨ **QUMA** + suff. *-qay?*

QUMALAQ Tat.(Lit.) 1671 **Qumalaq** [Хасенъ Кумалюкъ Яблонскій] (Lit. Tat. 417-15); Kzk. 1817 **Qumalaq** [قومالاق / Кумалак] (MIK IV, 313, 319). ✧ 'Rounded; ball-shaped excrement of sheep' cf. Chag., Kzk. *qumalaq* 'kugelförmig, die Schafmistkügelchen' (Radl. II, 1047).

QUMAN Bulg. 14th c. **Quman** [Κόμανος], a noble Bulghar (Byz. Turc. 163); Kuman 1096, 1103 **Quman** [Куманъ / Кунамъ], a Polovets (Ipat. 166, 184, Lavr. 269, PSRL VII, 20); Selj.? 1128 **Quman** [Kuman], emir, governor of Haleb (Ibn al-Athïr/Tornb. X, 457); Maml. 1298 **Quman** [Moubâriz-eddin Avlia-ben-Kouman] (Makrïzï IV, 65); Kzk. 19th c. **Quman** [Куманъ] (SOK 240); Kzk. 19th c. **Quman** [Куманъ] (SOK 246); Kzk. 19th c. **Quman-bay** [Куманбай] (SOV 26); Kzk. 19th c. **Quman-bay** [Куманбай] (SOV 80); Uzb. 1875 **Quman-bay** [Тюря-кулъ Куманбаевъ] (Moskal'cev 48); Kzk. 18th c. **Quman-χoǰa** [Куманъ-Ходжа] (Nepljuev 804). ✧ I. 'Ethnic name of Kuman (Polovets), yellowish grey' cf. Bask., Imena polov. 69; II. 'Pitcher' cf. Kzk. *quman* 'die Wasserkanne' (Radl. II, 1944). ⇨ **QUMΓAN.**

QUMANAY Bashk. 1715 **Qumanay** [Куманай Ураскин] (MIB III, 124). ⇨ **QUMAN** + suff. *-ay.*

QUMANAQ Alt. 19th-20th c. **Qumanaq** [Куманак] (OjrRS 209); Alt. **Qumanaq / Qumanaq-mergen** [Купанакъ, К.-Мергенъ] (Nikiforov 204, 207, 220 etc.). ✧ 'Hop', cf. Alt.(Kmd.) *qumanaq* 'der Hopfenzapfen' (Radl. II, 1044), Alt. *qumanaq* 'id.' (OjrRS).

QUMAR see **XUMAR**

QUMAR-ARSLAN Uyg. 8th c. - 12th c. **Qumār-arslan(-čañši)** [Qumar arslan čangši / qumar arslan] (Müller, Pfahl. 23, Radl., USp. 155, DTS). ⇨ **XUMAR** + **ARSLAN.**

QUMAR-BARS Uyg. 13th-14th c. **Qumar-bars-tarχan** (Zieme, Mat. II, 88). ✧ 'Wish(ed) panther'? ⇨

XUMAR? + BARS.

QUMARA   Bashk. 1752 **Qumara** [Кумара Токбулатов] (MIB IV/1, 64).

QUMARMÏŠ   Kipch. 13th c. **Qumarmïš-qulǰï / Qamarmïš-qulǰï / Qumur?** [قمرمیش قولجی / اویوموقومور] / Ujumuckumur / Камармышъ-Кулджи] (RaD/Ber. I, 132, RaD/Erdmann 71).

QUMARU   Uyg. 13th-14th c. **Qumaru**, fem. (Zieme, Mat. II, 93). ✧ 'Mascot, lucky charm' cf. Uyg. *qumaru* 'der Talisman, das Andenken' (Radl. II, 1045).

QUMAŠ   Selj. 1142 **Qumač** [Kumaç / Ала-ад-дин Кумач], sultan Sanjar's (1117-1157) atabek, emir, ruler of Balkh (Ahbar 66, 70, MIT I, 323, 324, 355, 356, 382-83, 387-89); Selj. 1153 **Qumač** [Ала-ад-дин Кумач], emir, governor of Balkh (MIT I, 323-24, 355-56, 387-89); Uyg. **Qumas-bay** [Kumas bay] (EUTS); Kzk. 19th c. **Qumaš** [Кумашъ] (AOK 18); Alt. 19th-20th c **Qumaš** [Кумаш], fem. (OjrRS 212); Uyg. 12th c. - 14th c. **Qumaš-bay** [Qumaš-bai] (Radl., USp. 40, DTS); Kzk. 1819 **Qumaš-bay** [Кумашбай] (MIK IV, 325); Crm. 1638 **Qumaš-mïrza** [Kumaš mïrza] (?). ✧ 'Red cloth, textile' cf. Alt., Hak., Crm., Turk. *qumaš* 'ein rothes Baumwollenzeug; die Scnittwaren' (Radl. II, 1048).

QUMČAY   Bashk. 1761 **Qumčay** [Тляугул Кумчаев] (MIB IV/1, 216).

QUMČUΓAŠ   Kzk. 19th c. **Qumčuγaš** [Кумчугашъ] (SODž. 80).

QUMDAQ   Kzk. 19th c. **Qumdaq-pay** [Кумдакпай] (SOV 122). ✧ I. 'Stock; butt' cf. Kzk. *qumdaq* 'der Gewehrschaft' (Radl. II, 1051); II. 'Sand, sandhill' cf. Kzk. *qumdaq* 'id.' (Radl. II, 1051).

QUMDUZAQ   Alt. 19th-20th c. **Qumduzaq** [Кумдузак] (OjrRS 212). ✧ 'Little Beaver (female)' (OjrRS), cf. Alt., Hak. *qumdus* 'der Biber' (Radl. II, 1051). ⇨ **QUNDUZ** + suff. *-aq*.

QUMΓA   Kzk. 19th c. **Qumγa-bay** [Кумгабай] (SOK 216).

QUMΓAM-BAY see **QUMΓAN**

QUMΓAN   Kzk. 19th c. **Qumγam-bay (<Qumγan-bay)** [Кумгамбай] (SOK 308); Kzk. 19th c. **Qumγam-bay (<Qumγan-bay)** [Кумгамбай] (SOV 152); Uyg. 10th c. **Qumγan-tuduň** [qumγan tuduŋ] (DTS). ✧ 'Pitcher' cf. Chag., Alt., Az. Crm. etc. *qumγan* 'die Wasserkanne, der Wasserkrug' (Radl. II, 1049), Kzk. *qumγan* 'чугунный или медный кувшинъ' (Potanin, Pred. 126), Kzk. *quman* 'die Wasserkanne' (Radl. II, 1944). ⇨ **QUMAN.**

QUMÏ   Oghuz/Trkm. 13th c. **Qumï** [قومی / Кумы], Oghuz Khan's descendant (Abulg./Kon. 525, 550).

QUMÏS see **QÏMÏZ**

QUMÏZ see **QÏMÏZ**

QUMLU   Yürük 1543 **Qumlu** [Kumlu] (Gökb., Rum. 197); *TN:* Turk. 16th c. **Qumlu-beg** [قوملوك / Kumlubeg], the homeland of the Kayı (Qayï) tribe (Turan: Belleten XII (1948), 604). ✧ 'Sandy' cf. Turk. *qumlu* 'sandig' (Radl. II, 1050).

QUMRAL   Yürük 1543 **Qumral** [قومرال / Kumral] (Gökb., Rum. 102, 197). ✧ 'Reddish yellow, light brown (hair); light chestnut (horse); olive (skin)' cf. Turk. *qumral* 'id.' (Radl. II, 1050).

QUMRAT   Nog. 20th c. **Qumrat** [Ибрахим Аджымахмет Къумратулы], father of one of Baskakov's informants from the aul of Üykön-χalq (Ikon-halk), Cherkess Autonomous Region (Oblast') (Bask., Nog. 143).

QUMRU   Uyg. 1339 **Qumru** [Kumru] (Chwol., Syr.-nest. 90). ✧ 'Turtledove (Streptipelia turtur); ring dove (Columba palumbus)' cf. Turk. *qumru* 'id.' (Radl. II, 1050).

QUMUQ   Karakh. **Qumuq** [Kumuk] (MK/Atalay 846); Kzk. 19th c. **Qumuq** [Журмухамедъ Кумоковъ] (Pam. kn. Turg. 59); *EN:* Nog. 20th c. **Qumuq-uruw** [Къумукъ урувъ], an Aq-noγay clan in the autonomous county of Cherkessk and the district of Mineralovodsk (Bask., Nog. 134, 141). ✧ 'Kumyk (ethnic name)'.

QUMUQ-ALİ   Crm. 1637 **Qumuq-ali-biy** [قوموقعلی بی] (Vel.-Zern., Crim 173). ⇨ **QUMUQ + ALİ.**

QUMULTÏ   Alt. 19th c. **Qumultï-čumultï** [Кумулты-Чумулты] (Potanin, Pred. 182).

QUMUM   Kzk. 19th c. **Qumum-bek / Qumun-bek?** [Кумумбекъ] (SOV 150).

QUMURSQA   Hak.(Sag.) 19th-20th c. **Qumusqa** [Кумуска] (Katanov, Otč. 7); *EN:* Kzk. 18th c. - 19th c. **Qumursqa** [Кумурска], a clan (Tynyšp. 67). ✧ 'Ant' cf. Kzk. *qumïrsqa* 'каринца' (KzTS), Hak.(Sag.) *qumusqa* 'id.' (Radl. II, 1049).

QUMUSQA see **QUMURSQA**

QUN   Bashk. 1735 **Qun** [Кунъ Кусеевъ], a tarχan (Vel.-Zern., Bašk. 18); Bashk. 1738 **Qun-bay** [Кунбай] (MIB I, 370); Kzk. 19th c. **Qun-ǰan** [Кунджанъ] (SOK 46); Bashk. 1757 **Qun-γāzï** [Кунгазы Адингулов] (MIB IV/1, 157). ✧ I. 'Value, worth' cf. Kzk. *qun* 'стоимость' (KzRS); II. 'Leather' cf. Kzk. *qun* 'кожа скотины, пропавшей летомъ' (Potanin II, 5).

QUN-AΓAČ   Uzb. 1632 **Qun-aγač** [Кунагач], from Bukhara (Miller, Ist. Sib. II, 398). ⇨ **QUN + AΓAČ?**

QUN-BAŠ   Kzk. 1846 **Qum-bas (<Qun-bas)** [Турмамбет Кумбасов] (MKOP 101); Kzk. 19th c. **Qum-bas (<Qun-bas)** [Кумбасъ] (SODž. 36); Kzk. 1846 **Qun-bas** [Илемес Кунбасов], a biy (MKOP 155); Kzk. 19th c. **Qun-bas** [Кунбасъ] (SOK 46); Kzk. 1819 **Qun-baš** [Кунбаш] (MIK IV, 325). ✧ 'Valuable, worthy head (child)'. ⇨ **QUN + BAŠ.**

QUN-BUΓAR   Tat. 1777 **Qun-buγar** [Кунбугаръ]

(PSZRI XX, 577, 579). ⇨ QUN + BUΓAR?

QUN-BULAT   Kzk. 19th c. **Qun-bulat** [Кунбулатъ] (SOK 62). ✧ 'Worth(y) steel'? ⇨ QUN + BULAT.

QUN-ČEKAN   Kirg. 19th c. **Qun-čekan-bek?** [Kun-csckan-bek], aq-saqal in the Lop region (Almásy 338). ⇨ QUN + ČAQAN?

QUN-ΓĀZÏ see QUN

QUN-QUDAY   Bashk. 1740 **Qun-quday** [Азят Кункудаев] (MIB I, 409). ⇨ QUN + XUDAY / QUDAY I.?

QUN-SADAQ   Kirg. 19th c. **Qun-sadaq** [Кунь-садакъ] (Potanin II, 5). ✧ 'Leather quiver' cf. Kzk. *qun* 'кожа скотины, пропавшей летомъ', *sadaq* 'колчанъ' (Potanin). ⇨ QUN.

QUN-SAYA   Kzk. 19th c. **Qun-saya** [Кунсая] (SODž. 108). ⇨ QUN.

QUN-SERİK   Kzk. 19th c. **Qun-serik** [Кунсерикъ] (SOK 278). ⇨ QUN + ŠERİK II.

QUNA   Tuv. 19th c. **Quna-pay** / **Qunap-pay?** [Кунаппаи] (Proben IX, 96, 128).

QUNAY   Tat. 16th c. **Qunay** [Кунай] (Sattarov); Bashk. 1734 **Qunay** [Юмакай Кунаев], a tarɣan (Vel.-Zern., Bašk. 10); Bashk. 1735 **Qunay** [Кулгунъ Кунаевъ], a tarɣan (Vel.-Zern., Bašk. 14); Bashk. 1762 **Qunay** [Кунай Назаров] (MIB IV/2, 302); Kzk. 19th c. **Qunay** [Кунай] (AOK 30). ✧ I. 'Proud, high-minded' (Sattarov); II. 'Pleasure, joy' (Sattarov).

QUNAQ see QONAQ

QUNAQ-KİLDİ   Bashk. 1777, 1784 **Qunaq-kildi** [Кунаккилды Шиганаев (Шианаев)] (MIB V, 64, 154, 196, 197, 198, 243, 244). ⇨ QONAQ + KELDİ.

QUNAQ-ŠOL-XAN   Türk 6th c. **Qunaq-šol-ɣan?** [Κουναξολάν], a prince of the Türks (Byz. Turc. 168). ⇨ QONAQ.

QUNAQAY   Kzk. 1819 **Qunaqay** [Кунакай] (MIK IV, 325). ⇨ QONAQ + dim. suff. *-ay*.

QUNAM see QUMAN

QUNAN   Kzk. **Qunan** [Кунан Кара Баҕыс], three brothers called Kenžä, Qunan and Dönön Qara Baɣïs (Proben III, 253 /297/); Kzk. 19th c. **Qunan** [Кунанъ] (Grod., Pril. 35); Kzk. 19th c. **Qunan** [Кунанъ] (SOV 32); Kzk. **Qunan-bay** [Кунан Баи] (Proben III, 47 /63/); Kzk. 19th c. **Qunan-bay** [Кунанбай] (AOA 10); Kzk. 19th c. **Qunan-bay** [Кунанбай] (SODž. 128); Kzk. 19th c. **Qunan-bay** [Кунанбай] (SODž. 146); Kzk. 19th c. **Qunan-bay** [Кунанбай] (SODž. 42); Kzk. 19th c. **Qunan-bay** [Кунанбай] (SOK 118); Kzk. 19th c. **Qunan-bay** [Кунанбай] (SOK 186); Kzk. 19th c. **Qunan-bay** (<**Qunan-bay**) [Кунамбай] (SOK 146); Kzk. 19th c. **Qunan-pay** [Кунанпай] (SOK 276); *EN:* Kzk. 18th c. - 19th c. **Qunan-bay** [Кунанбай], a clan (Tynyšp. 68). ✧ 'A three-year-old (foal, sheep, calf)' cf. Chag., Alt., Kzk. *qunan* 'id.' (Radl. II, 910), Kirg. *qunan* 'жеребёнок по третьему году, жеребёнок-

третьяк' (Jud.).

QUNAN-QARA-BAΓÏS see QARA-BAΓÏS

QUNANČÏ   Kirg. **Qunančï** [Кунанчы] (Jud. 537). ✧ 'Groom who deals with three-year-old foals'? ⇨ QUNAN + suff. *-čï*?

QUNAR   Kzk. 19th c. **Qunar** [Бай Мамбетъ Кунаровъ] (Grod., Pril. 125); Kzk. 19th c. **Qunar** [Бектасъ Кунаровъ] (Grod., Pril. 126); Kzk. 19th c. **Qunar** [Баки Кунаровъ] (Grod., Pril. 126); Kzk. 19th c. **Qunar** [Баймамбетъ Кунаровъ] (Grod., Pril. 38); *TN:* Kzk. **Qunar-bay** [Кунар-бай] (?). ✧ 'Usefulness, productivity' cf. Kzk. *qunar* 'bir şeyin verimli veya faydalı olma özelliği' (KzTS).

QUNAŠ   Kzk. 19th c. **Qunaš** [Кунашпай] (SODž. 106); Selj.? 1034/35 **Qunaš** / **Qunuš?** [Кунаш, Куфас, Кунуш, Тунаш, Тунуш], a commander (MIT I, 243, 246); Kzk. 19th c. **Qunaš-bay** [Ибрагим Кунашбаевъ] (AUK 294). ✧ 'Foal' cf. Hak. *qunaš* 'id.' (Radl. II, 911).

QUNAZ   Kzk. 19th c. **Qunaz-bay** [Куназбай] (AOA 58). See also QARA-QUNAZ.

QUNBAR   Kzk. 1819 **Qunbar** [Кунбар] (MIK IV, 325).

QUNČAY   Kzk. 19th c. **Qunčay** [Кунчай] (SOK 26).

QUNČÏQ   Tat. 1779 **Qunčïq** / **Künčik?** [Резяп Кунчиков] (MIB V, 83); Uzb.? 18th c. - 19th c.? **Qunčuq** [Kuntschug, Kundjug] (ArchKR XVIII, 367). ⇨ QUN + suff. *-čïq*.

QUNČUY   Uyg. 8th c. - 12th c. **Quynuy-täñrim!** / **Qunčuy-täñrim** [Kuinui tängrim], a princess (Müller, Pfahl. 10); Uyg. 8th c. **Qunčuy-täñrim** [Qunčui tängrin], a princess (Müller, Pfahl. 10). ✧ 'Female relative of the khan, princess, noble woman' cf. Türk *qunčuy* (Chinese) 'id.' (Radl. II, 915-16).

QUNČUY-TÄÑRİ   Uyg. 12th c. - 14th c. **Qunčuy-täñri** [qunčuj taŋri] (DTS). ✧ 'Princess-Lord'. ⇨ QUNČUY + TÄÑRİ.

QUNČUR   Kzk. 1846 **Qunčur-bay** [Кунчурбай Бутбаев] (MKOP 89).

QUNJÏ   Maml. 13th c. **Qunjï** [Кунджи] (Baybars/Tizeng. I, 93, 118).

QUNDAJÏQ   Türk 906 **Qundajïq** / **Qundāj?** [Muhammed Ibn Ishak Ibn Kundadjik / Ishāk ibn Kundāj], governor of Mosul, a commander of the army, fought against the Sarmatians, fled away from the caliphs and underwent to Xumārūyeh (Xumārawaih) of Egypt (Weil, Abbas II, 430-35, 467, Weil, Chalif. II, 528-29, Justi 166). ✧ 'Hero'? cf. (P.) *kundā* 'Weiser, Held', Pehlevi **kundāk* (Justi 166) + dim. suff. *-jik*?

QUNDAQ   Maml. 1277 **Qundaq** [Seïf-eddin-Koundek-Sâki], a cup-bearer, later a governor (Makrīzī II, 158, 171, Weil, Chalif. I, 106 etc.); Maml. 1280 **Qundaq** [Schems-eddin-Koundek-Dâheri] (Makrīzī III, 29); Kzk. 19th c. **Qundaq-bay** [Кундакбай] (AOO 54);

Kzk. 19th c. **Qundaq-bay** [Кундакбай] (SOK 244); Kzk. 19th c. **Qundaq-pay** [Кундакпай] (SOK 38, 50, 174, 194). ✧ 'Cradle'? cf. Tat.(Bar.), Kirg., Turk. etc. *qundaq* 'die Wiege' (Radl. II, 914); II. 'Hero' cf. P. *kundā* 'Weiser, Held', Pehlevi **kundāk* (Justi 166) + dim. suff. *-jik*?

QUNDĀJ see **QUNDAJÏQ**

QUNDÏ   Kzk. 19th c. **Qundï** [Бiй Оразбай Кундибаевъ], a biy (Grod., Pril. 170); Kzk. 19th c. **Qundï / Qundïy?** [Усарбай Кундiевъ] (Grod., Pril. 183); Kzk. 19th c. **Qundï-bay** [Кундибай] (Grod., Pril. 159); Kzk. 19th c. **Qundï-bay** [Кундыбай] (SODž. 148); Kzk. 19th c. **Qundu** [Кунду] (SOK 86); Kzk. **Qundu-bay** [Кундубай] (Konšin, Oč. 120); Kzk. 1819 **Qundu-bay** [Кундубай] (MIK IV, 326); Kzk. 19th c. **Qundu-bay** [Саламбай Кундубаевъ] (Grod., Pril. 110); Kzk. 19th c. **Qundu-bay** [Кундубай] (SOK 164). ✧ 'Valuable, worthy' cf. Kzk. *qŭndï* 'ценный' (KzRS).

QUNDÏ-NAR   Kzk. 1846 **Qundï-nar** [Кундынар Акбаеэ] (MKOP 153). ✧ 'Valuable/dear camel'. ⇨ **QUNDÏ + NAR I.**

QUNDÏQ   Kzk. 19th c. **Qundïq-pay** [Кундыкпай] (SODž. 34).

QUNDÏZ see **QUNDUZ**

QUNDU see **QUNDÏ**

QUNDUГUZ   Selj.? 1104/05 **Qunduγuz** [Кундугуз], an emir (MIT I, 385).

QUNDUQAR   Tat. 1675 **Qunduqar** [Кундукарко] (Kungursk. akty 25).

QUNDUR   Kzk. 1820 **Qundur** [Кундровъ], a sultan, a leader of the Čümekey tribe (Sib. Vest. IX, 117).

QUNDURГUT   Tat. 1675 **Qundurγut?** [Кундургутко] (Kungursk. akty 26).

QUNDUS-DORA   Kzk. 19th c. **Qundus-dora?** [Кундусдора] (SOK 24). ⇨ **QUNDUZ + TURA?**

QUNDUZ   Kuman 1509 **Qonduz** [Dyonisio Konduz], a person of Kuman origin from Kenchekzallasa, Hungary (Gyárfás III, 728); Kkalp. 20th c. **Qundïz** [Кундыз] (KkRS 778); Hak.(Sag.) 19th-20th c. **Qundus** [Кундус] (Katanov, Otč. 8); Kzk. 19th c. **Qundus-bay** [Кундусбаевъ] (Grod., Pril. 96); Uzb. 19th c. **Qunduz** [Мулла Абдулъ Кундузъ] (SKSO III, 17, 22); Uzb.? **Qunduz-sufi** [قندوز صوفى / Кундуз-суфи], from Šawdar-tum (ZIRGOSStat. IV); *TN:* Kzk. 19th c. **Qunduz-bay** [Кундузбай], a winter pasture (qïstaw) (SODž. 100). ✧ 'Beaver, otter, lizard' cf. Karakh. *qunduz* 'бобер' (DTS), Kkalp. *qunduz* 'id.' (KkRS), Chag., Turk. *qunduz* 'der Biber', (Kzk.) 'die Fischotter'; *qundus* Tat.(Bar.) 'der Biber', (Shor) '(grüne) Eidechse' (Radl. II, 915), cf. also Rásonyi, Adalékok 128, Rásonyi, Anthr. 143.

QUNDUZ-SİKİ   Trkm.? 1598/99 **Qunduz-siki** [قندوز سكى / Kunduz-siki], Mir Ziyāeddīn (Dorn). ⇨ **QUNDUZ + SİKİ.**

QUNÏ   Türk 712-716 **Qunï-säñün** [qunï säŋün / Qunï Säñün] (DTS, ETY I, 102).

QUNÏŠ   Kzk. 19th c. **Qunïš** [Адилъ Кунишевъ] (Grod., Pril. 175); Kzk.? 1862 **Qunïš-bay** [Кунышъбай] (Moskal'cev 46); Kzk. 19th c. **Qunus** [Мусабекъ Кунусовъ] (Grod., Pril. 171); Kzk. 19th c. **Qunus-bay** [Байбакъ Кунусбаевъ] (Grod., Pril. 28); Kzk. 19th c. **Qunuš-bay** [Кунушбай] (Grod., Pril. 65). ✧ 'Hunchbacked' cf. Kzk. *qunıs* 'arka kemiği dışa doğru çıkmış, kambur' (KzTS).

QUNQA see **QONQA**

QUNQAL   Crm. 1808 **Qunqal** [Ахметъ-Бей Кункаловъ] (PSZRI XXX, 34).

QUNQAS   Tat. 1696 **Qunqas** [Кункаско] (Kungursk. akty 238); Bashk. 1706 **Qunqas** [Кункас] (MIB III, 17).

QUNQÏR   Kzk. **Qunqïr** [Кункыръ], Kaarman's mentor (Laptev, Materialy 19).

QUNMAN   Uzb. 1875 **Qunman** [Мулла Кунманъ] (Moskal'cev 48). ⇨ **QUN** + suff. *-man*.

QUNMET   Tat. 1696 **Qunmet** [Кунметко] (Kungursk. akty 240). ⇨ **QUN** + suff. *-met*.

QUNORQA   Tat.(Lit.) 1599 **Qunorqa?** [Кунорка Итешовна], fem. (Lit. Tat. 280-81).

QUNRAT see **QOÑÏRAT**

QUNTÏBAT   Bashk. 1751 **Quntïbat** [Ялкибай Кунтыбатов] (MIB IV/1, 52).

QUNTUBAN   Crm. 1537 **Quntuban** [Кунтубанъ] (PSRL XIII, 119).

QUNTUQ   Bashk. 1713 **Quntuq** [Яналей Кунтуков (Кундуков)] (MIB III, 100). ⇨ **QUNDÏQ?**

QUNU   Kzk. 19th c. **Qunu-bek / Künü-bek?** [Кунубекъ] (SOK 96).

QUNUD   Bashk. 1740 **Qunud-bay** [Кунуд-бай Кутлугилдин] (MIB I, 383).

QUNUY   Kuman 1096 **Qunu(y) / Künü(y)?** [Кунуй], a Polovets (PSRL VII, 11, Lavr. 231).

QUNUQ   Tat. 1634 **Qunuq** [Кунюк Бекбаев] (Miller, Ist. Sib. II, 421); Kzk. 1819 **Qunuq** [Кунук] (MIK IV, 325).

QUNUR see **QOÑUR**

QUNURAČ   Bashk. 1764 **Qunurač** [Кунурач Бердыгулов] (MIB IV/1, 285). ⇨ **QOÑUR?** + suff. *-ač*?

QUNUS see **QUNÏŠ**

QUNUŠ see **QUNÏŠ**

QUÑ   Kzk. 19th c. **Quñ** [Кунг] (AOO 2); Kzk. 19th c. **Quñ-bay** [Kungbay Šokay] (Ljutš 128). ✧ 'Anus, ass' cf. Kzk. *quñ* 'der After' (Radl. II, 899).

QUÑ-BAŠ   Kzk. 19th c. **Quñ-baš** [Нурманъ Кунгбашевъ] (Grod., Pril. 120). ✧ 'As s-head'? ⇨ **QUÑ + BAŠ.**

QUÑUR-TAY   Selj.? 1276 **Quñur-tay** [Kûnghûrtâi]

(Abulfar./Budge I, 456). ⇨ **QOÑUR + TAY** or suff. *-tay(1,2)*?

QUÑURČA   Kzk. 1846 **Quñurča** [Тлямиш Кунгурчин] (MKOP 154). ⇨ **QOÑUR** + suff. *-ča*.

QUO-ČAMČAY   Yak. **Quo-čamčay-tïsï-χopčoŀɣu-ämäχsin** [Куо-Чамчаи-тысы-хопчолгу-ämäхсін], an old woman-abāsï (Pek.). ✧ 'Beautiful *Čamčay*' cf. Yak. *quo* 'красивый' (Pek.). ⇨ **ČAMČAY / ČÄMČÄY?**

QUOXALĪSA   Yak. **Quoχalïsa** [Куохалыса / Уот-Куохалыса], fem. (Pek.).

QUOLLARÏQĀN   Yak. **Quollarïqān** [Куолларыкан] (Pek.).

QUOMA   Yak. **Quoma** [Куома] (Pek.). ✧ Foma (R.).

QUONĀSQÏ   Yak. **Quonāsqï** [Куонаскы] (Pek.). ✧ 'Man who holds his head aslant' cf. Yak. *quonay-* 'о человеке: держать голову на бок' (Pek.).

QUPA see **QOPA**

QUPAY see **QOPAY**

QUPLAN see **QOPLAN**

QUPLANDÏ see **QOBLANDÏ**

QUPORŌS   Hak. 19th c. **Quporōs** [Купорос] (Katanov, Otč. 12). ✧ 'Sulphate, vitriol' cf. R. *kuporos* 'id.' (Katanov).

QUPSŪN   Yak. **Qupsūn** [Купсун] (Pek.).

QUR   Tat. 1629 Ѓur-bay [Гурбаев Бехматев] (Miller, Ist. Sib. II, 357); Kzk. 19th c. **Qur-bay** [Курбай] (SODž. 18); Kzk. 19th c. **Qur-bek** [Курбекъ] (SODž. 138, 148); *TN:* Kzk. 1867 **Qur-bay** [Курбай], a kurgan (burial mound) in the region of Vernoje (Alma-Ata?) (ZIRGOGeogr. I, 268). ✧ Possible meanings: I. 'Belt; Mate, contemporary; Weapon; Turtle' cf. Uyg., Kuman, Chag., Alt., Hak. etc. *qur* 'der Leibgurt, der Rang; der Nahestehende, Altersgenosse; die Waffe; die Schildkröte' (Radl. II, 915-18); II. 'Wool braid (string)' cf. Kkalp. *qur* 'тесьма' (KkRS); 'Some kinds of birds' cf. Kzk. *qur* 'die Feldhühner: das Auerhuhn, Birkhuhn, Rebhuhn' (Radl. II, 918); III. 'Blind' cf. Kzk. *qur* (<P.) 'id.' (Radl. II, 919).

QUR-BAŠ   Kkalp. 20th c. **Qur-baš** [Курбаш] (KkRS 774). ⇨ **QUR + BAŠ.**

QUR-MUXAMED   Kzk. 19th c. **Qur-muχamed** [Курмухамедъ Дустматовъ] (SKSO VIII, 221). ⇨ **QUR + MUXAMED.**

QUR-TAY   Kzk. **Qur-tay** [Колпакъ Куртаевъ] (Konšin, Po Ust'-kamenog. uezdu: Pam. kn. Semip., 1900, p. 28). ⇨ **QUR + TAY** or suff. *-tay(1,2)*?

QUR-TEMÜR   Khorezm.? 1298 **Qur-temür / Qur-timür** [قورتيمور امير / Kurtimur], emir, Ghazan's chief against Sulamïš (RaD/Jahn 121, Hammer, Ilch. II, 72, 146, 154). ⇨ **QUR + TEMİR.**

QURA   Kzk. 19th c. **Qura-bay** [Курабай], a baqsï (tutor, quack-doctor) (AUK 338); Kzk. 19th c. **Qura-bay** [Курабай] (SODž. 78); Kkalp. 20th c. **Qura-bay** [Къурабай] (Bask., Kkalp. 58); Kkalp. 20th c. **Qura-bay** [Курабай] (KkRS 774); Kzk. 1819 **Qura-bek** [Курабек] (MIK IV, 324); Kzk. 19th c. **Qurabay** [Байсалбай Курабаевъ] (Grod., Pril. 97). ✧ I. 'Assemble, gather, hive' cf. Kkalp. *qura-* 'составлять что-либо из отдельных кусков или из лоскутков; собирать, копить' (KkRS); II. 'Weed'? Kuman, Kar., Tat. *qūra, qura* 'das Unkraut' (Radl. II, 920).

QURA-BOLDÏ   Kzk. 19th c. **Qura-boldï** [Кураболды] (SODž. 148). ⇨ **QURA + BOLDÏ.**

QURA-KÜČÜK   Uzb. 1722 **Qura-küčük** [Кура-Кучукъ], from Bukhara (Veselovskij, Unk. 176). ⇨ **QURA + KÜČÜK.**

QURAҒAČČÏ   Yak. **Quraɣaččï-sürük** [Кураҕаччы сӱрӱк / Кураҕаччы-сӱрӱк], a forest spirit driving game to the hunters (Pek.).

QURAҒAY   Kzk. 1634 **Quraɣay** [Курагай / Буксук Курагай] (Miller, Ist. Sib. II, 410).

QURAҒAN   Hak.(Sag.) 19th-20th c. **Quraɣan** [Кураҕан], fem. (Katanov, Otč. 7); Hak.(Sag.) 19th-20th c. **Qurāɣan** [Кураҕан] (Katanov, Otč. 11); Alt. 19th-20th c. **Qurān** [Кураан], fem. (OjrRS 212). ✧ 'Lamb' (Katanov), cf. Hak., Alt.(Kmd.) *quraɣan* 'ein junges Schaf' (Radl. II, 922), Alt.(Leb.) *qurān* 'ein junges Schaf' (Radl. II, 923).

QURAҒATČÏ   Yak. **Quraɣatčï-doχsun** [Кураҕатчы-дохсун], divinity presenting the horses their fallow colour (Pek.).

QURAY   Tat.(Sib.) 1631 **Quray** [Ерманчак Кураев] (Miller, Ist. Sib. II, 386); Bashk. 1706 **Quray** [Чюра Кураев] (MIB III, 26); Bashk. 1737 **Quray** [Кулгаш Кураев] (MIB I, 326). ✧ 'A kind of flute' cf. *quray* (Kzk.) 'eine Pflanze (Heraclium sibiricum)', (Bashk.) 'eine Art Flöte (bei den Baschkieren)' (Radl. II, 921).

QURAYÏŠ   Tat.(GH) 1446 **Qurayïš?** [Курайшъ], a prince of the Horde (PSRL VI, 172 VIII, 114).

QURAQ   Kzk. 19th c. **Quraq** [Куракъ] (AOK 118); Kzk. 19th c. **Quraq** [Куракъ] (SODž. 112); Hak.(Sag.) 19th-20th c. **Quraq** [Курак] (Katanov, Otč. 7); Kzk. 19th c. **Quraq-bay** [Куракбай] (AOA 62); Kzk. 19th c. **Quraq-pay** [Куракпай] (AOK 34); Kzk. 19th c. **Quraq-pay** [Куракпай] (SODž. 110, 148); Kzk. 19th c. **Quraq-pay** [Куракпай] (SOK 256). ✧ I. 'Dry; lean' (Bask., Fam. 47-49); II. 'A thing sewn out of several smaller pieces; upper leaves of the reed' cf. Kzk. *quraq* 'Etwas, was aus kleinen Stücken zusammengenäht ist' (Radl. II, 922), Kirg., Kzk. *quraq* 'die oberen Blätter des Schilfes' (Radl. II, 922). ⇨.

QURAQ-TAY   Kzk. 19th c. **Quraq-tay** [Курактай] (SOK 120). ⇨ **QURAQ + TAY** or suff. *-tay(1,2)*?

QURAL   Kzk. 19th c. **Qural** [Куралъ Токъ Фулатовъ] (Grod., Pril. 34); Kzk.? 1884 **Qural** [Кураловъ] (Grod., Pril. 94); Kzk. **Qural-bay** [Куральбай] (Sb. Syr-D. IX, 48); Kzk. 19th c. **Qural-**

bay [Куралбай] (SODž. 82); Kzk. 19th c. **Qural-bay** [Куралбай] (SOK 300); Kzk. 19th c. **Qural-bay** [Kuralbaj] (SOV 6); Kzk.? 19th c. **Qural-bay-batïr** [قورالبای باطر / Куралбай-дадха] (Veselovskij, Kirg. 14); Kzk. 1794 **Qural-bay-biy** [قورالبای بی / Куралбай] (MIK IV, 165). ✧ 'Instrument, tool' cf. Tat.(Sib.) *qural* 'das Instrument' (Radl. II, 923).

QURALAY Yak. **Quralay-bergen** [Куралаі бäргäн] (Pek.).

QURALĬ Kzk. 19th c. **Qeralï** [Куралы] (SOK 270). ⇨ **QURA?** + suff. -*lï.*

QURALĬYA Yak. **Qeralïya** [Куралыja] (Pek.).

QURAM Kzk. **Quram** [Курам], Qošqar's son (Proben III, 26 /31/); Kzk. 19th c. **Quram-bay** [Курамбай] (SOV 4). ✧ 'Small leather pieces sewn together' cf. Kzk. *quram* 'kleine Stücke Leder oder Zeug, die man zusammennäht' (Radl. II, 924).

QURAMA Kzk. 19th c. **Qurama** [Курама] (AOA 138); Kzk. 19th c. **Qurama** [Кураминъ] (AOK 30); Kzk. 19th c. **Qurama** [Курама] (SOK 84). ✧ I. 'Cover. blanket sewn of smaller pieces' cf. Kzk. *qurama* 'eine aus Lappen zusammengenähte Decke' (Radl. II, 924); II. 'A Turkic tribe ion Turkestan' (Radl. II, 924).

QURAMŠA Tat.(Ishim) **Qïramša** [Kyramscha / Кырамша] (Proben IV, 189 /234/); Bashk. 1777, 1779 **Quram-ša** [Курамша Арасланов] (MIB V, 545); Crm. 1656 **Quramša** [Курамша Сулешевъ] (PSZRI I, 364-65); Tat. 1779 **Quramša** [Курамша Байков] (MIB V, 83); Bashk. 1789 **Quramša** [Курамша Казбулатов] (MIB V, 250). ✧ I. 'Gatherer, he who joins (the nation)' (<Mo.) (Sattarov); II. 'Shah with merry (joyful) heart' (Sattarov).

QURAN Kzk., Uzb.? **Quran-bay** [Куранбаевъ] (Sb. Syr-D. VII, 132); Kzk. 1803, 1820 **Quran-batïr** [Куранъ-батыръ], chief of the Jilder tribe, Kiši Žüz (MIK IV, 514, Sib. Vest. IX, 114). ✧ 'Weapon' cf. Chag. *quran* 'die Waffen' (Radl. II, 923). ⇨ **QURAL?**

QURANAQ Alt. **Quranaq** [Чолмошъ Куранаковъ] (Nikiforov 2). ✧ 'A two-year-old roebuck' cf. Alt. *quranaq* 'ein zweijähriger Rehbock' (Radl. II, 923). See also **SERKE**.

QURANČA Kzk. 19th c. **Quranča** [Куранча] (SOV 50). ⇨ **QURAN** + suff. -*ča?*

QURAP Kzk. 19th c. **Qurap-pay** [Кураппай] (SOV 82).

QURAPŠĬ Kzk. 19th c. **Qurapšï** [Курапшы] (AOP 94). ⇨ **QURAP** + suff. -*šï.*

QURASQA Tat. 1690 **Qurasqa** [Кураска Кучуковъ] (Kurdjumov 25).

QURAŠ Kkalp. 20th c. **Quraš** [Кураш] (KkRS 774). ✧ 'High fur cap' cf. Kkalp. *quraš* 'высокая меховая шапка' (KkRS).

QURAT Kzk. 1529 **Qurat** [Куратъ-князь], a prince

from Kazan (PSRL VIII, 272, XIII, 46); Kzk. 19th c. **Qurat** [Куратъ] (SOV 6).

QURAT-GELDİ Trkm. 1828 **Qurat-geldi** [Курат-Гельди], from the Bayrač clan (MIT II, 447). ⇨ **QURAT.**

QURAZMAN Bashk. 1746 **Qurazman** [Тогусяй Куразманов] (MIB III, 435); Bashk. 1708 **Qurazman-batïr** [Куразман батыр] (MIB I, 222). ⇨ **QURAZ** + suff. -*man.*

QURĀĠAN see **QURAĠAN**

QURĀN see **QURAĠAN**

QURBAĠA Selj.? 1090 **Qurbaɣa** [Κουρπαγάς], a prince (Byz. Turc. 169); Khorezm.? **Qurbaɣa** / **Qurbaqa** [ایلچی / قوربغا / قربغا / قربتا / Kurbuɣa], envoy (ilči) (Ǧuwaynī II); Turk. 1489 **Qurbaɣa(-reis)** [Kurbağa-reis], a chief (Gökb., Ed. 303). ✧ 'Frog' cf. Karakh. *qurbaqa* 'id.' (DTS), Turk. *qurbaɣa* 'der Frosch' (Radl. II, 961).

QURBAQA see **QURBAĠA**

QURBAN Trkm. 20th c. **Gurban** [Gurban], fem. (Zaj. 1971, 341); Trkm. 20th c. **Gurban** [Курбан], fem. (TrkmRS 211); Chag. 16th c. **Qurban** [Курбан] (Ivanov 149, 194, 214, 300, 313); Chag. 16th c. **Qurban** [Курбан маулана] (Ivanov 194); Az. **Qurban** [Mechhedi Qourban], a hero of a play (Rec.T.Trad. I, 108); Trkm. **Qurban** [Гурбан] (Sopieva 180); Trkm. 1814 **Qurban** [Курбан], from the Yomud tribe (MIT II, 217); Trkm. 19th c. **Qurban** [Курбанъ Толековъ] (Ščeglov I, 350); Tat. 1467-1479 **Qurban** [Hāǧǧī Qurban], a hāfiz in the Golden Horde (Vásáry 54); Kzk. **Qurban** [Курбанъ Бабаевъ] (Grod. 246); Kzk. 19th c. **Qurban** [Молла Курбанъ] (Grod., Pril. 166); Kzk. 19th c. **Qurban** [Курбанъ] (Grod., Pril. 73); Kzk. 19th c. **Qurban** [Курбанъ] (Grod., Pril. 94); Kzk. 19th c. **Qurban** [Курбанъ Бердыбаевъ] (SKSO IV, otd. II, 32); Kkalp. 20th c. **Qurban** [Курбан] (KkRS 774); Chag. 16th c. **Qurban-aqa** [Курбан Ака] (Ivanov 214); Kzk. 19th c. **Qurban-bay** [Ишмуратъ Курбанбаевъ] (SKSO II, 8); Kzk. 19th c. **Qurban-bay** [Курбанбай Утагановъ] (SKSO III, 7); Kkalp. 20th c. **Qurban-bay** [Къурбанбай] (Bask., Kkalp. 401); Kkalp. 20th c. **Qurban-bay** [Курбанбай] (KkRS 774); Uzb. 19th c. **Qurban-bay** [Джанузакъ Курбанбаевъ] (SKSO III, 176); Uzb. 1887 **Qurban-bay** [Курбанъ-бай] (Moskal'cev 48); Az. **Qurban-bey** [Курбан-бей] (Az. Skaz. 603); Trkm. 1821/22 **Qurban-bek** [Курбан-бек], from the Er-sarï tribe (MIT II, 421); Trkm. 1867 **Qurban-bek** [Курбан-бек], from the Toχtamïš tribe (MIT II, 310); Kzk. 19th c. **Qurban-bek** [Курбанбекъ] (SKSO VIII, 207); Kkalp. 20th c. **Qurban-bek** [Къурбанбек] (Bask., Kkalp. 41); Kkalp. 20th c. **Qurban-bek** [Курбанбек] (KkRS 774); Trkm. 1811 **Qurban-bek-biy** [Курбан-бек-бий], a biy? (MIT II, 380); Kkalp. 20th c. **Qurban-biyke** [Къурбанбийке], fem. (KkRS 778); Kzk. 19th c. **Qurban-ǰan-datχa** [Qurban J̌an Datχa], a tribal chief from the Alay-mountains (Nazaroff 86, AUK 839); Kzk. 19th c. **Qurban-ǰan-χatun** [Курбанъ-Джанъ-Хатунъ Эръ-Магомедъ-Кызы], Er-maγomed's daughter (Grod., Pril. 58); Kkalp. 20th c. **Qurban-gül** [Qurban-gül / Курбангүл], fem. (KkRS 778, Baskakov: OSA 140); Kkalp. 20th c. **Qurban-γazï** [Курбанғазы] (KkRS 774); Trkm. 1859 **Qurban-χan** [Курбанъ-ханъ] (ZIRGOÊtn. I, 173); Tat. 1819 **Qurban-qul** [Курбанкулъ Курбанбакіевъ] (PSZRI XXXVI, 29); Kzk. 1832 **Qurban-qul** [Курбанкулъ Курбанбакіевъ] (Konšin, Mat. V, 96); Kzk. 19th c. **Qurban-qul** [Курбанъ-Кулъ] (Grod., Pril. 79); Kkalp. 20th c. **Qurban-qul** [Курбанқул] (KkRS 774); Trkm. 1829 **Qurban-quli-yïzbaši** [Курбан-кули-юзбаши] (MIT II, 455); Uzb. 1770 **Qurban-quli-qazi** [Курбан-кули-кази], from the Nayman tribe (MIT II, 350, 369); Trkm. **Qurban-murad-iman** [Курбанъ-Мурадъ-Иманъ] (Voenn. Sb. CXXIX, 333); Turk.? 1580 **Qurban-sultan** [قربان سلطان روملو] (Dorn 289); Chag. 16th c. **Qurban-šeyχ** [Курбан-шейх] (Ivanov 222). ✧ 'Sacrifice; sacrificial gift' cf. Kkalp. *qurban, qurman* 'id.' (KkRs), Kuman, Kzk., Turk. *qurban* 'das Opfer, Opfergeschenk' (Radl. II, 962), Kzk. *qurman* (<Ar.) 'id.' (Radl. II, 964), Kirg. *qurman* 'id.' (Jud.). In Baskakov's interpretation *Qurban-gül* is 'Sacrifice-flower' (Baskakov, loc. cit.). See also **ANNA-ГURBAN**.

QURBAN-AY   Kkalp. 20th c. **Qurban-ay** [Къурбанай / Курбанай] (Bask., Kkalp. 401, KkRS 774). ✧ 'Qurban (Sacrifice) - Month' cf. Tat. PN *Qorbanay* (Sattarov). ⇨ **QURBAN + AY?** + voc. suff. *-ay*.

QURBAN-ALİ   Tat.(Mish.) 1785 **Kurban-γaliy** [Курбангалий / Кулбангалий Тулубаев] (MIB V, 178); Trkm. 1817/18 **Qurban-ali** [Курбан Али], a mulla from the Teke tribe (MIT II, 405); Kzk. 19th c. **Qurban-ali** [Курбанъ-Али] (SKSO VIII, 200); Trkm. 1855 **Qurban-ali-bek** [Курбан Али-бек], from Merv (MIT II, 262); Bashk. 1785 **Qurban-γali / Qurban-ali** [Курбангали (Курманали) Абдуллин] (MIB V, 166, 168, 332); Kkalp. 20th c. **Qurban-γaliy** [Курбангалий] (KkRS 774); Kzk. **Qurman-γaliy** [Курмангалій] (Konšin, Po Ust'-Kamenog. uezdu: Pam. kn. Semip. 1900, 33); *TN:* 19th c. **Qurman-alï** [Курманалы] (IIRGO XVI). ⇨ **QURBAN + ALİ**.

QURBAN-BAQÏY   Tat. 1819 **Qurban-baqïy** [Курбанкулъ Курбанбакіевъ] (PSZRI XXXVI, 29). ⇨ **QURBAN + BAQÏ** + suff. *-y*.

QURBAN-BERDİ   Trkm. **Гurban-berdi** [Гурбанберди] (Sopieva 180); Kkalp. 20th c. **Qurban-berdi** [Курбанберди] (KkRS 774). ⇨ **QURBAN + BERDİ**.

QURBAN-DURDÏ see **QURBAN-TURDÏ**

QURBAN-GELDİ   Trkm. 1820/21 **Qurban-geldi** [Курбан-Гельды], a captain from the Čawdur (Čoudor) tribe (MIT II, 417, 450); Trkm.? 1821 **Qurban-geldi** [Мулла Курбан Гельди], a mulla from the Čarïq clan of the Qayï-χan tribe (Samojlovič 1927, 41); Trkm. 1828 **Qurban-geldi** [Курбан-Гельды], from the İmreli tribe (MIT II, 447). ✧ 'Sacrifice has come (has been born)' (Sattarov). ⇨ **QURBAN + KELDİ**.

QURBAN-ГALİ see **QURBAN-ALİ**

QURBAN-QÏLÏČ   Trkm. **Qurban-qlïč** [Курбанъ-Клычъ] (Mel'gunov 322); Trkm. 1817/18 **Qurban-qlïč** [Курбан-клыч], from the Teke tribe (MIT II, 404); Trkm. 1813 **Qurban-qlïč-χan** [Курбан Клыч-хан], from the Yomud tribe (MIT II, 210, 211, 215, 219, 389). ⇨ **QURBAN + QÏLÏČ**.

QURBAN-QLÏČ see **QURBAN-QÏLÏČ**

QURBAN-NİYAZ   Trkm. 1859 **Qurban-niyaz** [Курбанъ-Ніязъ] (ZIRGOÊtn. I, 207); Kkalp. 20th c. **Qurban-niyaz** [Курбанияз] (KkRS 774). ⇨ **QURBAN + NİYAZ**.

QURBAN-SAR   Kkalp. 20th c. **Qurban-sar** [Къурбансар] (Bask., Kkalp. 26); Kkalp. 20th c. **Qurban-sar** [Курбансар] (KkRS 774). ✧ 'Sacrifice-falcon' cf. Kuman, Chag. *sar* 'der Sperber, der Geier' (Radl. IV, 312). ⇨ **QURBAN**.

QURBAN-TAY   Kkalp. 1768/69 **Qurban-tay-biy** [Курбантай-бий] (MIT II, 340); Kzk. 1803, 1820 **Qurman-tay-biy** [Курмантай-бій], a biy, the chief of the Aday tribe of Kiši-žüz (MIK IV, 515, Sib. Vest. 118); *TN:* Kzk. **Qurman-tay** [Курмантай], at the Syr-Darya river, west of the town Turkestan (Yassi) (Karta JAR XI). ⇨ **QURBAN + TAY** or suff. *-tay(1,2)*?

QURBAN-TURDÏ   Trkm. 20th c. **Гurban-durdï** [Гурбандурды] (Sopieva: OSA 180); Trkm. 1879 **Qurban-durdï** [Курбанъ-Дурды] (Grod., Pril. 109); Uzb. 20th c. **Qurbân-turdï** [Курбонтурди] (Begmatov 1984, 204). ⇨ **QURBAN + TURDÏ**.

QURBANČÏQ   NUyg. 19th c. **Qurbančïq** [قوربانچیق / Kurbanchik] (Le Coq, Namenl. 108). ✧ 'Little sacrifice' (Le Coq). ⇨ **QURBAN** + suff. *-čïq*.

QURBASUN   Kzk. 19th c. **Qurbasun** [Курбасунъ] (SOK 296).

QURBUSTUN   Alt.(Tuba) 19th c. **Qurbustun-χan** [Курбустунъ-ханъ] (Potanin IV, 372). ✧ 'The good divinity (Ülgen)' cf. Alt. *qurbustan* (Mo.) 'die gute Gottheit, die grösstenteils Uelgän genannt wird' (Radl. II, 963).

QURČA   Uyg. 12th c. - 14th c. **Qurča** [Mäkiling Qurča] (Radl., USp. 46); Bashk. 1765 **Qurča / Kürče?** [Кузян Курчин] (MIB IV/1, 310); Kzk. 19th c. **Qurča-bay** [Курчабай] (SOK 76); Kzk. 19th c. **Qurža / Qurša?** [Куржа] (AOAtb. 54). See also **MEKİLİÑ-QURČA**.

QURČAN Bashk. 1756 **Qurčan** [Усман-мулла Курчанов] (MIB IV/1, 106); Bashk. 1756 **Qurčan** [Чюра Курчанов] (MIB IV/1, 107).

QURČİ Maml. 1299 **Qurči** [Kurdji], sultan al-Mansūr Lājin's (1296-1299) killer (Makrīzī IV, 96, 114); Tat.(Sib.) 1628 **Qurči** [Курчейко] (Miller, Ist. Sib. II, 59, 60); Kzk. 1620 **Qurči** [Курчейко], a prince (Miller, Ist. Sib. II, 257, 262, 351, 373); Kzk. 19th c. **Qurči** [Пулатъ Курчиевъ] (SKSO VIII, 203); Maml. 14th c. **Qurči / Gürči?** [كُرْجِي] (Sauvaget 187); Maml. 1276 **Qurči-χatun** [Kurdji-Khatoun] (Makrīzī II, 144). ✧ I. 'Cavalier-guard of the Safavī rulers; noblemen's cavalier at the Persan court' (cf. Le Coq, Ind. 4; Radl. II, 954), 'Quarrelsome, fighting' (cf. Sauvaget 54: (<Mo.) gürči); II. 'Georgian' (Sauvaget 54).

QURJİQ Oghuz/Trkm. 13th c. **Qurjïq** [قورجق / Курджык] (Abulg./Kon. 525).

QURJU Kzk. 1845 **Qurju-bay** [Курджубай Иткаринъ] (Konšin, Mat. V, 62); Kzk. 19th c. **Qurju-bay** [Курджу-бай] (Potanin, Pred. 112); Kzk. 19th c. **Quržu-bay** [Куржубай] (AOA 82). ⇨ **QURČİ?**

QURJUГİ Kzk. 19th c. **Qurjuγï-bay** [Нуржан Курджугибаевъ] (TV 1876, 63).

QURDAN Alt. 19th-20th c. **Qurdan** [Курдан] (OjrRS 209).

QURDAŠ Alt. 19th-20th c. **Qurdaš** [Курдаш] (OjrRS 209); Kzk. 19th c. **Qurdaš-bay** [Курдашбай] (SKSO III, 17). ✧ 'Contemporary, mate, friend of childhood' cf. Kzk. qurdas 'der Altersgenosse, Jugendfreund' (Radl. II, 950), Kirg. qurdaš 'der Freund' (Radl. II, 950).

QURDİ Kzk. 19th c. **Qurdï-bek** [Курдыбекъ] (SKSO III, 16). ✧ 'Started, established (life, family)' cf. Kzk. qur- 'kurmak, yapmak' (KzTS) + suff. -dï(2). See also **QURMİŠ**.

QURDİQ Selj. 1092 **Qurdïq** [Khurdîk], slave of Melik-šah I (1072-1092) (Abulfar./Budge I, 232); Kuman 1340 **Qurduq** [Corduk], among the Kumans in Hungary (Gyárfás III, 479); Selj.? **Qurtig / Qurdïq?** [Khûrtig (Khûrdîk?)] (Abulfar./Budge I, 246). ✧ 'We set (him)'? cf. Uyg., Chag., Kuman, Crm. etc. qur- 'aufstellen, einrichten, herrichten, ausbreiten' (Radl. II, 919), cf. also Rásonyi, Adalékok 132, Rásonyi, KÖA 119, Rásonyi, Anthr. 143.

QURDİMİČ Kzk. 1621 **Qurdïmič** [Курдымеч], a prince (Miller, Ist. Sib. II, 264).

QURDUQ see **QURDİQ**

QURDUM Kzk. 19th c. **Qurdum** [Курдумъ], son of Mayqa-biy the forefather of Kazaks in Mongolia (Potanin II, 149).

QURDUM Kzk. 19th c. **Qurdum** [Курдумъ] (SOK 298).

QURDUN Alt. 19th-20th c. **Qurdun** [Курдун] (OjrRS 209).

QURDUN-UBAN Alt. 19th c. **Qurdun-uban** [Курдюн-Убан] (Verb., In. 123).

QURГAN Bashk. 1756 **Qurγan** [Балкия Курганов] (MIB IV/1, 107, 119, 122); Bashk. 1756 **Qurγan** [Усман Курганов] (MIB IV/1, 119); Kzk. 19th c. **Qurγan-bay** [Курганбай] (SOK 144). ✧ 'Fortification' cf. Chag., NUyg.(Tar.), Turk. qurγan 'die Festung, Befestigung' (Radl. II, 940).

QURГĀRAQ Hak.(Shor) 19th-20th c. **Qurγāraq** [Курђарак], fem. (Katanov, Otč. 11). ✧ 'Drier' (Katanov).

QURГONA Kuman 1320 **Qurγona?** [Kurgona cumanus], among the Kumans in Hungary (Gyárfás III, 462).

QURГUN Kzk. 19th c. **Qurγun-bay** [Байджулъ Кургунбаевъ] (Grod., Pril. 193). ✧ 'Slaughter, massacre' cf. Kzk. qirγïn 'das Niedermetzeln, die Ausrottung' (Radl. II, 750-751). See also **QÏRГĪN-ČAL**.

QURİ see **QURUQ**

QURİM see **QURUM**

QURİN Kzk. 19th c. **Qurïn-bay** [Курынбай] (SOV 114). ✧ 'In time? born in time?' cf. Chag., Kzk. qurin 'zur Zeit' (Radl. II, 931).

QURİNKEY Kzk. 19th c. **Qurïnkey** [Курынкей] (SOK 250). ⇨ **QURİN** + dim. suff. -key.

QURQ see **QURUQ**

QURQAČİQ Bashk. 1737 **Qurqačïq** [Тункатар Куркачиков] (MIB I, 309); Bashk. 1740 **Qurqačïq** [Куркачик] (MIB I, 398).

QURQUMAN Turk. 1460 **Qurquman** [Κουρκουμάν], a warrior (Byz. Turc. 168).

QURLA Uyg. **Qurla-elči** [Kurla Elçi] (EUTS).

QURLAY Tat. 1554 **Qurlay** [Курлай], from Astrakhan (PSRL XIII, 244).

QURLAQ Kzk. 19th c. **Qurlaq** [Курлакъ] (SOK 296).

QURLAŠ Kzk. 1822 **Qurlaš** [قورلاچ / Курлаш] (MIK IV, 433, 435).

QURLU I. Kzk. 19th c. **Qurlu-bay** [Курлубай] (SODž. 160); Kzk. 19th c. **Qurlu-bay** [Курлубай] (SOK 16); Kzk. 19th c. **Qurlu-bey** [Курлубей] (SODž. 148). ✧ 'Readiness' cf. Kzk. qurlū, qurilū 'das Bereitsein, Fertigsein' (Radl. II, 944).

QURLU II. Turk. 19th c. **Qurlu-oγlu**, a Zeybek (Kúnos 1891, 119). ✧ 'Querulous, always complaining (man); greedy, eager; ungrateful' cf. Turk. dial. kur 'durumundan çok yakınan (kimse); aç gözlü kimse; iyilik bilmez, nankör' (DS) + suff. -lu.

QURLUN Kirg.? **Qurlun** [Курлун], a Kirghiz (?) chief (RaD I/1, 151).

QURMA Qitay? / Mo. 1172/73 **Qurma** [Курма (Фума)], Qitay commander-in-chief (MIT I, 404-05, 445-46); Kzk. 19th c. **Qurma-bek** [Курмабекъ] (SOK 262); Kzk. **Qurma-jan(-daχta? / -datχa?)** [Kurma

dzsan-Dachta], a princess in Ferghana (Almásy 585);
Tat. 1624 **Qurma-γoĵa** [Курмагозя Савинъ]
(Pokrovskij 72). ❖ 'Date'? cf. Kzk. *qurma* 'id.' (Kzk.).

QURMAY Tat. 1779 **Qurmay** [Багат Курмаев] (MIB
V, 83); Tat. 1779 **Qurmay** [Салих Курмаев] (MIB V,
83); Tat. 1779 **Qurmay** [Курмай Салеев] (MIB V,
93). ❖ Shortened from *Qorbanay* (Sattarov). ⇨
QURBAN-AY.

QURMAQ Bashk. 1735 **Qurmaq** [Кутлушъ
Курмаковъ] (Vel.-Zern., Bašk. 25). ❖ 'Frog' cf. Chag.
qurmaq 'id.' (Radl. II, 964).

QURMAQAY Tat. 1776 **Qurmaqay** [Курмакай-
Абдуллъ Агишевъ] (PSZRI XX, 457, 462). ⇨
QURMA, QURMAQ? + suff. *-qay / -ay.*

QURMAN Tat.(Lit.) 1592 **Xurman** [Хурманъ
Тугушевичъ] (Lit. Tat. 124); Kzk. 19th c. **Qurmam-
bay (<Qurman-bay)** [Курмамбай] (SOV 14); Kuman
1323 **Qurman** [Kurman], among the Yass in Hungary
(Gyárfás III, 463); Maml. 1309 **Qurman** [قرمان]
(Dawād. 180); Maml. 1399/1400 **Qurman** [المنجكى]
[قرمان] (Ibn Taghrīb.? VI, 20); Tat.(Lit.) 1595
Qurman [Ахметъ Кургмановичъ] (Lit. Tat. 246);
Tat.(Lit.) 1598 **Qurman** [Айша Курмановна
Адамовичъ], fem. (Lit. Tat. 270, 495); Tat.(Mish.)
1775 **Qurman** [Ягшигул Курманов] (MIB IV/2,
416); Tat.(Mish.) 1775 **Qurman** [Танайгул
Курманов] (MIB IV/2, 416); Tat.(Sib.) 1700 **Qurman**
[Курманъ], a Tatar chief (Andrievič, Ist. Sib. II, 268);
Tat.(Sib.) 1722 **Qurman** [Курманъ] (PSZRI VI, 787);
Tat.(Tob.) 1695 **Qurman** [Муратко Курмановъ], a
settler (posadskij) from Tobol (DAI X, 384); Bashk.
1740 **Qurman** [Курман] (MIB I, 447); Bashk. 1756
Qurman [Кузакмет Курманов] (MIB IV/1, 128);
Bashk. 1761 **Qurman** [Курман Мрясев] (MIB IV/1,
221); Bashk. 1775 **Qurman** [Якшигул Курманов],
from the village Kurmanovo (MIB IV/2, 416); Bashk.
1796 **Qurman** [Курман Арислякеев] (MIB V, 362);
Kzk. **Qurman** [Žamanbala Kurmanov] (IOAIÊK XX,
665); Kzk. **Qurman** [Курманъ Абитовъ] (TOUAK
XXIV, 79); Kzk. **Qurman** [Курман] (Proben III, 77
/100/); Kzk. 1817 **Qurman** [قرمان / Курман] (MIK
IV, 313, 319); Kzk. 19th c. **Qurman** [Курманъ]
(AOAtb. 58); Kzk. 19th c. **Qurman** [Курманъ] (AOK
58); Kzk. 19th c. **Qurman** [Маралъ Курмановъ]
(AUK 484); Kzk. 19th c. **Qurman** [Курманъ] (Grod.,
Pril. 92); Kzk. 19th c. **Qurman** [Тенучтибай
Курмановъ] (Grod., Pril. 98); Kzk. 19th c. **Qurman**
[Курманъ] (SODž. 134); Kzk. 19th c. **Qurman**
[Курманъ] (SOK 178); Kzk. 19th c. **Qurman**
[Курманъ] (SOV 4); Kzk. 19th c. **Qurman** [Курманъ]
(SOV 50, 94); Kirg. **Qurman** [Курман] (Jud. 723);
Kzk. 19th c. **Qurman-bay** [Курманбай] (AOA 66);
Kzk. 19th c. **Qurman-bay** [Курманбай] (AUK 92);

Kzk. 19th c. **Qurman-bay** [Курманбаевъ], a writer of
articles (AUK 487); Kzk. 19th c. **Qurman-bay**
[Курманбай] (SOK 120); Kzk. 19th c. **Qurman-bay**
[Курманбай] (SOK 156); Kzk. 19th c. **Qurman-bay**
[Курманбай] (SOV 40); Kzk. 1899 **Qurman-bay**
[Курманбай] (AUK Dobavl. 7); Kzk. **Qurman-batïr**
[Курманъ-батыръ] (Smirnov, Sultany 22); Kirg.
Qurman-bek [Курманбек] (Jud. 77, 79, 676); Kirg.
19th-20th c. **Qurman-bek** [Kurmanbek], the escort
(guide) of Gyula Prinz (Prinz 28); Kzk. 1794 **Qurman-
biy** [برقن قورمن بى] (MIK IV, 163); Bashk. 1737
Qurman-γul [Курмангул Яикбаев] (MIB III, 362);
Bashk. 1791 **Qurman-γul** [Ахмер Курмангулов]
(MIB V, 313); Bashk. **Qurman-γul / Qurban-γul**
[Курмангул (Курбанкул) Шерыпов (Шарифов)]
(MIB V, 151, 172, 173, 175, 241, 242, 307, 320);
Bashk. 1793, 1784 **Qurman-γul / Qurban-γul**
[Курмангул (Курбангул) Мурзекеев] (MIB V,
329); Kzk. 1806 **Qurman-qoža(y)** [Ислемесъ
Курманкожаевъ] (PSZRI XXIX, 303); *EN:* Kzk. 18th
c. - 19th c. **Qurman** [Курман], a clan (Tynyšp. 73);
Kzk. 1846 **Qurman** [Курман], a part of the
Tapïn/Tabïn? clan (MKOP 151); *TN:* Kzk.? **Qurman**
[Курманъ] (Karta JAR III); Kzk. **Qurman** [Курман],
a field (Kojčubaev 158). ❖ I. 'Quiver' cf. Karakh.
qurman 'налучье, саадак' (DTS), cf. also Rásonyi,
Adalékok 136, Rásonyi, Bas. 9, Rásonyi, KÖA 119-20,
Anthr. 143; II. 'Sacrifice' cf. Kzk. *qurman* (<Ar.) 'id.'
(Radl. II, 964), Kirg. *qurman* 'id.' (Jud.). See also
BURQAN-QURMAN.

QURMAN-ALÏ see QURBAN-ALİ
QURMAN-ΓALİY see QURBAN-ALİ
QURMAN-TAY see QURBAN-TAY

QURMANAY Tat.(Mish.) 1757, 1764 **Qurmanay**
[Курманай Газиев (Газев)] (MIB IV/1, 135, 290,
291); Bashk. 1710 **Qurmanay** [Сармаш Курманаев]
(MIB III, 57); Bashk. 1715 **Qurmanay** [Курманай
Багаев] (MIB III, 124); Bashk. 1728 **Qurmanay**
[Курманай Текеев] (MIB I, 128); Bashk. 1735
Qurmanay [Курманай Кугумов] (MIB III, 341);
Bashk. 1738 **Qurmanay** [Курманай Зиянгулов]
(MIB I, 361); Bashk. 1756 **Qurmanay** [Курманай
Минлюшев] (MIB IV/1, 122); Bashk. 1759
Qurmanay [Курманай Кукумов] (MIB IV/1, 176);
Bashk. 1759 **Qurmanay** [Мавлют Курманаев] (MIB
IV/2, 26); Bashk. 1760 **Qurmanay** [Курманай
Темашев] (MIB IV/2, 160); Bashk. 1764 **Qurmanay**
[Курманай Мансуров] (MIB IV/1, 276); Bashk. 1767
Qurmanay [Искак Курманаев] (MIB IV/1, 324);
Bashk. 1778 **Qurmanay** [Курманаев] (MIB V, 80);
Bashk. 1788 **Qurmanay** [Курманай Алдаров] (MIB
V, 223); Bashk. 1789 **Qurmanay** [Менлигул
Курманаев] (MIB V, 252); *TN:* Tat. 18th c.

Qurmanay(eva) [Курманаева], a village in the district of Čistopol (Korsakov 218); Tat.? 1693 **Qurmanay(evo)** [Курманаево], a village (Kungursk. akty 214); Tat. 18th c. **Qurmanay(evo)** [Курманаево], a village in the district of Arsk (Korsakov 251); Tat. 18th c. **Qurmanay(evo)** [Курманаево] (Korsakov 251). ✧ 'Quiver' cf. Bashk. PN *Qormanay* (Kusimova). ⇨ **QURMAN** + suff. *-ay*.

QURMANAQ Tat. 1654 **Qurmanaq** [Курманакъ Маркашевъ] (AI IV, 236). ⇨ **QURMAN** + suff. *-aq*.

QURMANČÏQ Tat.(Lit.) 1591 **Qurmančïq** [Курманчикъ] (Lit. Tat. 96). ⇨ **QURMAN** + suff. *-čïq*.

QURMAS see QURMAŠ

QURMAŠ Bashk. 1738 **Qurmas** [Ирмяш Курмасев] (MIB I, 143); Tat.(Lit.) 1591 **Qurmaš** [Курмашъ Балдышевичъ] (Lit. Tat. 82); Tat./Bashk.? 1777 **Qurmaš** [Курмаш Арасланов], a Teptär (MIB V, 545, 546); Tat.(Sib.) 1648 **Qurmaš** [Курмашко] (Miller, Ist. Sib. II, 528); Bashk. 1706 **Qurmaš** [Курмашев], a mulla (MIB III, 17); Bashk. 1728 **Qurmaš** [Мустай Курмашев] (MIB III, 251); Bashk. 1744 **Qurmaš** [Курмаш Елдашев] (MIB III, 415); Bashk. 1754 **Qurmaš** [Курмаш Танатаров] (MIB IV/1, 83); Kzk. **Qurmaš** [Салиха Курмашева], fem. (IOAIÊK XXII, 643); Nog.? 1614 **Qurmaš** [Курмашъ], a murza (AI III, 24, IV, 87); Nog. 1649 **Qurmaš** [Дергучѣй мурза Курмашовъ] (AI IV, 87); Nog. 1649 **Qurmaš-murza** [Курмашъ мурза Канъмурзинъ] (AI IV, 87); Kzk. 19th c. **Qurmaš-pay** [Курмашпай] (SOK 110); *TN:* Tat. 18th c. **Qurmaš** [Курмашева], a village in the region of Tetjušinsk (Tetyushinsk) (Korsakov 338). ✧ 'Pulp, squash made of barley; toasted wheat' cf. *qurmač* (Alt.(Tel.)) 'die Graupe aus gedörrter Gerste', (Chag.) 'gerösteter Weizen' (Radl. II, 965), Bashk. *qurmas* 'id.' (BRS).

QURMAŠUQ Uzb. 1645 **Qurmašuq** [Курмашук], from Bukhara (Miller, Ist. Sib. II, 496). ⇨ **QURMAŠ** + suff. *-uq*.

QURMET Kzk. 19th c. **Xurmet-ay** [Хурметъ-ай], fem. (SKSO IV, otd. II, 36); Tat. 1731 **Qurmet** [Акметь Курметев] (MIB III, 293); Bashk. 1737 **Qurmet** [Курметъ Иделевъ], a Teptär (Nepljuev 427), Kzk. 19th c. **Qurmut (<Qurmet?)** [Курмутъ] (AOP 62); Bashk. 1744 **Ürmet** [Урмет] (MIB III, 415); Tat. 1675 **Ürmet / Urmet** [Урметко] (Kurdjumov 327); Tat. 1748 **Ürmet / Urmet** [Усеинъ Урметевъ] (Nepljuev 438). ✧ 'Respect, honor, dignity' cf. Kzk. *qurmet* 'почесть (KzRS), NUyg. *χürmät = hürmät* (Radl. II, 1738), Tat. *χörmät* 'почёт, уважение; угощение' (TatRS). (<Ar.).

QURMÏŠ Chuv. 18th-19th c. **Kurmuš** [Курмушъ] (Magn. 54); Bulg. 8th c. **Qormïš / Qurmïš?** [Κορμέσιος], a Bulghar prince (740-756) (Byz. Turc.

164); 1446 **Qurmïš** [Курмышъ] (PSRL XII, 66); Maml. 1294 **Qurmïš** [قرمش], a bearer of arms (Iyās I, 129, 132); Bashk. 1778 **Qurmïš** [Кулай Курмышев] (MIB V, 68); Tat. 1714 **Qurmïš / Qurmaš** [Курмыш / Курмаш] (MIB III, 113); *TN:* Tat.(Mish.) 1611 **Qurmïš** [Kurmyšskij / Курмышскій уѣздъ], a district in the county (gubernija) of Simbirsk (Letop. ZAK I (1861), 10, IOAIÊK XIX, 119); Tat.(Mish.)? 1611 **Qurmïš** [Курмышъ] (Letop. ZAK I (1861), 8-9); Tat.(Bar.) 19th c. **Qurmïš** [Kurmyš], a settlement (aul) (Radl., Aus Sib. I, 243); Uzb. **Qurmïš** [Курмышъ], east of Samarkand (Karta JAR XIX). ✧ 'Started, established (life, family)' (Sattarov).

QURMUŠ see QURMÏŠ

QURMUT see QURMET

QURNAY Bashk. 1740 **Qurnay** [Курнаевъ Аднагунъ] (PSZRI XI, 111). ✧ 'Basin' cf. Crm., Turk. *qurna* 'das Badebassin; der Winkel, die Ecke' (Radl. II, 942). + suff. *-y*.

QURNAŠ Tat.(Lit.) 1592 **Qurnaš** [Асанъ Курнашевичъ] (Lit. Tat. 124).

QUROMÏS Kzk. 19th c. **Quromïs-pay / Qurumïs-pay?** [Куромыспай] (SOK 222).

QURS see QURUS

QURS-YAW-QUY Oghuz/Trkm. **Qurs-yaw-quy** [Курс Йав Куй], Oghuz's descendant (Muhamedova: OSA 170). ⇨ **QURS.**

QURSA Kzk. 19th c. **Qursa-bay** [Курсабай] (SOV 134).

QURSAQ Kzk. 19th c. **Qursaq** [Курсакъ] (AOK 134); Kzk. 19th c. **Qursaq-pay** [Курсакпай] (SODž. 120); Kzk. 19th c. **Qursaq-pay** [Курсакпай] (SOK 40). ✧ 'Stomach' cf. most Trk. dial. *qursaq* 'id.' (Radl. II, 956).

QURŠU Kzk. 19th c. **Quršu-bay** [Куршубай] (SOK 290).

QURT Trkm. 20th c. **Гurt** [Gurt] (Zaj. 1971, 331); Trkm. 20th c. **Гurt / Qurt?** [Курт] (TrkmRS 213); Bulg. 9th c. **Qurt** [Κοῦρτος], a chief (Byz. Turc.?); Khorezm.? 1379 **Qurt** [Гияс-ад-дин Курт], ruler of Herat (MIT I, 520, 523); Maml. 1298 **Qurt** [Seïf-eddin-Kurt], emir-aχor (master of the horse) (Makrīzī IV, 69); Maml. 1299 **Qurt** [Seïf-eddin Kurt], a χājib (door-keeper), the governor of Tarabulus (Makrīzī IV, 126); Turk. 15th c. **Qurt** [Κούρτης], a commander of the army (Byz. Turc. 169); Turk. 16th c. **Qurt** [Kurd] (Ongan, Ank. II); Turk. 1580 **Qurt** [Qurd bin Xudaverdi] (Dávid); Turk. 1580 **Qurt** [Qurd bin İna-χan] (Dávid); Turk. 1583 **Qurt** [قورت] (Ongan, Ank. I, 165); Turk. 1583 **Qurt** [قورد / Kurd] (Ongan, Ank. I, 165); Turk. 1662 **Qurt** [Kürkçü Kurt], from Isparta (Ün 1938, 646); Yürük 16th c. **Qurt** [قورد / Kurd] (Gökb., Rum. 103); Tat. **Qurt** [Kurt Umer] (H. Z. Koşay: KCsA I,

324); Tat. 20th c. **Qurt** [Курт / Куртов] (Sattarov); Bashk. 1760 **Qurt** [Курт] (MIB IV/1, 195); Kzk. 19th c. **Qurt** [Джидабай Куртовъ] (Grod., Pril. 181); Turk. 1515 **Qurt** / **Qurt-köy?** [Hamza veledi Kurt/köy/] (Gökb., Ed. 82); Oghuz / Selj.? **Qurt-eri?** [قرتارى], forefather of the Ottoman dynasty (Seādeddīn I, 10, Nešrī 186); Crm. 1784 **Qurt-murza** [Курт] (IAN (Otd. gum. nauk.) 1928, 379); Turk. 1523 **Qurt-oγlu** [Κούρτουγλης], a commander of the army (Byz. Turc. 170); *TN:* Turk. 20th c. **Qurt-bey** [Kurtbey], a village in the province of Edirne, Turkey (TMİB 306); Turk. 20th c. **Qurt-šeyχ** [Kurtşeyh], a village in the province of Eskişehir, Turkey (TMİB 364). ✧ 'Wolf' cf. Az., Crm., Turk. *qurt* 'id.' (Radl. II, 945); II. 'worm, caterpillar cf. several Trk. dial. *qurt* 'id.' (Radl. II, 944). See also **BOZ-QURT, QAZÏ-QURT, QÏZÏL-QURT, İDİ-QURT, TOQTÏ-QURT.**

QURT-GELDİ   Trkm. 1826 **Qurt-geldi** [Курт-Гельды], a serdar (chief) and mir-aχur (master of the horse) of the Sarïq tribe (MIT II, 435, 440, 441). ⇨ **QURT + KELDİ.**

QURT-QAŠ   Bashk. 1756 **Qurt-qaš** [Балтагул Курткашев] (MIB IV/1, 122). ⇨ **QURT + QAŠ?**

QURTARAN   Turk. 1948 **Qurtaran** [Orhan Abdi Kurtaran], a surgeon in Ankara (L. Rásonyi's communication). ✧ 'Rescuer' cf. Turk. *kurtar-* 'to save, rescue' (TED). + suff. *-an.*

QURTĀSQÏ   Yak. **Qurtāsqï** [Куртаскы] (Pek.). ✧ 'Small stomach' cf. Yak. *qurtaχ, qurttaχ* 'желудок, чрево; пупок (птичий)' + R. dim. suff. *-ška* (Pek.).

QURTÏQ   Kuman 1103 **Qurtïq** / **Qurtuq** [Куртокъ / Куртка / Куръткка], a Kuman (Polovets) prince (Lavr. 269 (187), Ipat. 184 (189), PSRL VII, 20). ✧ 'Little wolf; little worm' (Bask., Im. polov. 69). ⇨ **QURT** + dim. suff. *-ïq.*

QURTQA   Tat.(Sib.) 1632 **Qurtqa** [Куртка Исенгилдеев] (Miller, Ist. Sib. II, 398); Bashk. 1756 **Qurtqa** [Куртка Чеккутуков] (MIB IV/1, 120); Kzk. **Qurtqa** [Куртка], a hero in a short story (Vasil'ev 39); Kzk. 19th c. **Qurtqa** [Куртка] (SODž. 94); Kzk. 19th c. **Qurtqa** [Куртка] (SOV 124); Nog. 1649 **Qurtqa-bek** [Курткабекъ], fem. (AI IV, 123). ✧ 'Old woman' cf. Uyg., Kuman, Chag. *qurtqa* 'id.' (Radl. II, 948). See also **YEDİ-QURTQA, ÜČ-QURTQA, QUTLU-QORTQA.**

QURTQAČÏQ see **QORTQAČÏQ**

QURTQASÏQ see **QORTQAČÏQ**

QURTU   Kzk. 19th c. **Qurtu-bay** [Куртубай] (SOK 120, 212, 266); Kzk. 19th c. **Qurtu-bay** [Куртубай] (SOV 52, 120).

QURTUQ see **QURTÏQ**

QURTUQA   Tat.(GH) 1318 **Qurtuqa** [قرطنا / Куртука], Özbek-χan's envoy to Egypt (Duqmaq/Tizeng. I, 318, 325, Aynī/Tizeng. I, 489,

519).

QURTULMÏŠ   Uyg. **Qurtulmïš** [Kurtulmış] (EUTS); Oghuz / Selj.? **Qurtulmïš** / **Qurtulmuš** [قورتلمش], forefather of the Ottoman dynasty (Āšikp. 5, Wittek 94). ✧ 'He escaped' cf. Chag., Turk. *qurtul-* 'sich retten, befreit werden' (Radl. II, 948).

QURTUM   Tat.(Sib.) 1645 **Qurtum** [Туруздан Куртумов] (Miller, Ist. Sib. II, 511).

QURTUZ   Kzk. 1819 **Qurtuz** [Куртуз] (MIK IV, 326).

QURU see **QURUQ**

QURU-BAŠ   Alt.(Tuba) 19th c. **Quru-baš** [Курубашъ], a hero in a tale (Potanin IV, 572-73). ⇨ **QURU + BAŠ.**

QURU-BUQA   Mo.? **Quru-buqa** [Куру-буга] (RaD/Ber. I, 117). ⇨ **QURUQ + BUQA.**

QURU-GÖT   Turk. 19th c. **Quru-göt-oγlu** [Kuru göt oγlu], a Zeybek (Kúnos 1891, 119). ✧ 'Dry ass' cf. Turk. *göt* 'der Hintern; das Hintertheil' (Radl. II, 1601). ⇨ **QURUQ.**

QURU-YASAQ-YAW-QUY   Oghuz/Trkm. **Quru-yasaq-yaw-quy** [Куру Йасакъ Йав Куй], Oghuz' descendant in the Oghuz-name by Salar-baba (Muhamedova: OSA 170). ⇨ **QURUQ.**

QURUQ   Oghuz/Trkm. **Qurï-tekin** [Куры текин], Buqra-χan's middle son in the Oghuz-näme by Salar-baba (Muhamedova: OSA 170); Kzk. 19th c. **Qurq-pay** [Куркпай] (SODž. 104); Turk. **Quru-bey** [Kuru Bey] (Uzunçarş., Anad. 20); **Quruq** / **Quruγ** [Куругъ / Курук] (RaD/Ber. II, 51, RaD II, 75); Kzk. 19th c. **Quruq-pay** [Курукпай] (SOK 208); Tuv. 1879 **Quruq-pay** [Курукпай], an Uryankhay shamaness, Potanin's informant (Potanin IV, 235). ✧ 'Dry, empty; unproductive' cf. Alt.(Tel.), Uyg., NUyg.(Tar.), Uzb. *quruq* 'trocken, leer' (Radl. II, 929), further Trk. dial. *quru* 'trocken, leer, mager' (Radl. II, 926). See also **İT-QURUQ, TİGİN-QURUQ.**

QURUQ-QAŠ   Bashk. 1756 **Quruq-qaš** [Балтагул Куруккашев] (MIB IV/1, 123). ⇨ **QURUQ + QAŠ.**

QURUQ-TAY   Kzk. 19th c. **Quruq-tay** [Куруктай] (SOK 14). ⇨ **QURUQ + TAY** or suff. *-tay(1,2)?*

QURUQČÏ   Kipch. 1304/05 **Quruqčï?** [قرقجى / Курукджи], a Kipchak envoy to Egypt (Baybars/Tizeng. I, 94, 119). ✧ I. 'Watchman' cf. Uzb.(Sart) *quruqči* 'der Wächter' (Radl. II, 930); II. 'He who uses the lasso well' cf. Kzk. *qurïqšï* 'тот, кто ловко умеет пользоваться курукум' (KzRS).

QURULÏ   Kzk. 19th c. **Qurulï-bay?** [Курулебай] (AOO 62).

QURUM   Kzk. 19th c. **Qrum** [Мустапа Крумовъ] (AOK 46); Kzk. 19th c. **Qurïm-bay** [Курымбай] (AOA 114); 1828 **Qurum** [Мустафа Курумов] (MID III, 123); Bulg. 9th c. **Qurum?** / **Qrumïš** / **Qrum?** [Κροῦμος], a Bulghar prince (803-814) (Byz. Turc. 174); Kzk. 19th c. **Qurum-bay** [Курумбай] (AOK 58); Kzk. 19th c. **Qurum-bay** [Курумбай] (Grod., Pril.

169); Kzk. 19th c. **Qurum-bay** [Курумбай] (SODž. 12); Kzk. 19th c. **Qurum-bay** [Курумбай] (SOK 10, 16, 44, 78, 150, 106); Kzk. 19th c. **Qurum-bay** [Курумбай] (SOV 42); Kzk. 1846 **Qurum-bay** (<Qurun-bay?) [Дюсембе (Дюсембек) Курумбаев (Курунбаев)] (MKOP 101); *TN:* Kzk. 19th c. **Qurum-bay-ötkel** [Курумбай-откель], a field (AOA 6). ✧ 'Soot, grime; smutty felt' cf. Kuman., Kzk., Turk. *qurum* 'der Russ; schwarzer, verbrannter, alter Filz' (Radl. II, 936).

QURUMAQ   Kzk. 19th c. **Qurumaq** [Курумакъ] (SODž. 158).

QURUMBET   Bashk. 1754 **Qurumbet** [Мазан Курумбетев] (MIB IV/1, 83); Kzk. 19th c. **Qurumbet** [Курумбетъ] (SODž. 112).

QURUN   Bulg. 927 **Qurun / Qorun?** [Κρόνος], a Bulghar chief (Byz. Turc. 174).

QURUNČAQ   Kzk. 19th c. **Qurunčaq** [Курунчакъ] (AOK 82).

QURUNDAY   Tat.(Sib.) 1675 **Qurunday** [Кабычакъ Курундаевъ] (DAI VII, 333).

QURUNKEY   Kzk. 19th c. **Qurunkey** [Курункей] (SOK 270).

QURUPČĬ   Hak. 19th c. **Qurupčĭ** [Курупчы], fem. (Katanov, Otč. 12). ✧ 'Foxglove' (Katanov), cf. Hak.(Sag.) *qurupčĭ* 'der Fingerhut' (Radl. II, 936).

QURUS   Kzk. 19th c. **Qurs-oγlï** [Курсъ-оглы] (Lomakin 32); Kzk. 19th c. **Quruz-bay** [Садибай Курузбаевъ] (Grod., Pril. 160). ✧ 'Anger, fury' cf. Kzk. *qurus* 'der Zorn, die Wuth' (Radl. II, 935).

QURUSQA   Hak. 19th c. **Qurusqa** [Куруска], fem. (Katanov, Otč. 12); Hak.(Blt.) 19th-20th c. **Qurusqa** [Куруска], fem. (Katanov, Otč. 10); Hak.(Sag.) 19th-20th c. **Qurusqa** [Куруска] (Katanov, Otč. 7). ✧ 'Lambskin, lamb-fell' (Katanov), cf. Alt. *qurusqa* 'gekräuselt; ein kleines Lammfell; ein junges Lamm' (Radl. II, 936).

QURUŠ   Tat. 1748 **Quruš** [Курушевъ] (Nepljuev 438); Kzk. 19th c. **Quruš** [Курушъ] (SODž. 114); Kzk. 19th c. **Quruš-pay** [Курушпай] (SOK 88, 210). ✧ 'White steel' cf. Kzk. *quruš* 'weisser Stahl' (Radl. II, 936).

QURUT   Alt. 19th-20th c. **Qurut** [Курут], fem. (OjrRS 212). ✧ 'Cheese' (OjrRS).

QURUZ see **QURUS**

QURŪBAY   Yak. **Qurūbay** [Курубаи Ханнах Кулун Куллустур], part of the name of a folklore hero in a tale (Pek.). ✧ 'Rude' cf. R. *grubyj* 'id.' (Pek.).

QURŪNQA   Hak.(Blt.) 19th-20th c. **Qurūnqa** [Курунка], fem. (Katanov, Otč. 10). ✧ Grun'ka (R.).

QURŽU see **QURǰU**

QURŽUQ   Kzk. 19th c. **Quržuq** [Куржукъ] (SOK 216). ⇨ **QUR?** + dim. suff. *-žuq*.

QUS see **QUŠ I.**

QUS-AMAN   Kzk. **Qus-aman** [Кусамановъ] (TOOIK

I, 76); Kzk. 19th c. **Qus-aman** [Илеусисъ Кусамановъ], a chief of an aul (Pam. kn. Turg. 39). ⇨ **QUŠ I. + AMAN.**

QUSAYİN   Kzk. 19th c. **Xuseyn / Xuseyin** [Хусейнъ Ходжа Кельдыевъ] (Grod., Pril. 115); Bashk. 1772 **Xuseyn-tarχan / Xösäyn-tarχan** [Хусейн-тархан Таймасов] (MIB IV/2, 408); Kzk. 19th c. **Qusayin** [Кусаинъ] (AOK 22); Kzk. 19th c. **Qusayin** [Кусаинъ] (AOP 98); Kirg. 19th c. **Quseyin** [Кусейин] (Jud.); Bashk. 1789 **Quseyn** [Кусейн Еканаев] (MIB V, 240); Kzk. 19th c. **Qusen** [Кусенъ] (AOK 38); Kzk. 1786 **Üsän-biy / Üsen-biy?** [Усян бий] (MIK IV, 75); Bashk. 1735 **Üsen** [Усен Мрясев], a tarχan (Vel.-Zern., Bašk. 15); Bashk. 1760, 1761 **Üsen** [Усень Дюскеев] (MIB IV/1, 195, 202); Kzk. 19th c. **Üsen** [Усенъ] (Valihanov, Soč. 318); Kzk. 19th c. **Üsen** [Усенъ] (SOV 32); Kzk. 19th c. **Üsen** [Усенъ] (SODž. 8); Kzk. 19th c. **Üsen** [Усеновъ] (Grod., Pril. 157); Kzk. 19th c. **Üsen** [Усенъ] (SOK 206); Kzk. 19th c. **Üsen** [Бакса Усенъ] (AUK 494); Kzk. 19th c.? **Üsen** [Üsen] (Atyns. 20); Kzk. 19th c. **Üsen** [Аитъ Усеновъ] (Grod., Pril. 157, 166); Kkalp. 20th c. **Üsen** [Усен] (KkRS 776); Kirg. 20th c. **Üsen** [Үсен] (Kalilov 94); Bashk. 1735 **Üsen / Ösän** [Усенъ Емамбетевъ], a tarχan (Vel.-Zern., Bašk. 18); Kzk. 19th c. **Üsen-bek** [Усенбекъ] (SOK 280). ✧ Husayn (Ar.).

QUSAN   Kzk. 19th c. **Qusan** [Кусанъ] (Grod., Pril. 95); Kzk. 18th c. **Qusan-bay-batïr** [Кусанбай-Батыръ] (Nepljuev 141).

QUSANDAQ   Bashk. 1748 **Qusandaq / Qusandïq?** [Кусандак Нугашев] (MIB III, 454).

QUSAÑ-ÄSÄN   Uyg. 12th c. - 14th c. **Qusañ-äsän** [Qusang Äsän] (Radl., USp. 133-34). ⇨ **QUSAN?** + **ESÄN.**

QUSAR   Oghuz/Trkm. 13th c. **Qusar** [قوسار / قسار / Кусар], Ögürǰik-alp's son (Abulg./Kon. 1240, 1275).

QUSBAN   Kzk. 19th c. **Qusban** [Кусбановъ] (Grod., Pril. 97).

QUSČAQ   Hak.(Kyz.) 19th-20th c. **Qusčaq** [Кусчак] (Katanov, Otč. 13). ✧ 'Little bird' cf. Hak.(Sag.) *qusčaq* 'das Vögelchen' (Radl. II, 1018). ⇨ **QUŠ I.** + dim. suff. *-čaq.*

QUSEYİN see **QUSAYİN**

QUSEYN see **QUSAYİN**

QUSEN see **QUSAYİN**

QUSÏ   Uyg. 13th c. **Qusï** [qusï] (DTS).

QUSÏQ   Karakh. 11th c. **Qusïq** [qusïq / Kusık], fem. (DTS, EUTS). ✧ 'Walnut, nut' cf. Karakh. *qusïq* 'орех' (DTS).

QUSÏM   Kzk. 19th c. **Qusïm** [Кусимъ] (Grod., Pril. 137). ✧ I. 'My bird'? II. 'Chief, leader' cf. Kzk. *kösem* 'вождь' (KzRS). ⇨ **QUŠ I.?**

QUSKE   Kirg. **Quske** [Куске] (Jud. 38). ✧ Little

Husayn (Ar.). ⇨ **QUSAYİN** + suff. *-ke* <comp. *-ake.*

QUSQA   Hak.(Sag.) 19th-20th c. **Qusqa** [Куска], fem. (Katanov, Otč. 8). ✧ 'Little bird'. ⇨ **QUŠ I.** + dim. -*qa.*

QUSQAJAQ   Hak.(Koyb.) 19th-20th c. **Qusqajaq** [Кускацак], fem. (Katanov, Otč. 13). ✧ 'Little bird' (Katanov), cf. Hak. *qusqajaq* 'das Vögelchen' (Radl. II, 1015). ⇨ **QUSQA** + dim. suff. *-jaq.*

QUSQAQ   Karg. **Qusqaq** [Кускак] (Katanov, Otč. 8).

QUSQAR   Bashk. 1773 **Qusqar** [Кускар Мякаев] (MIB IV/2, 412). ✧ 'Snail' cf. Bashk. *qusqar* 'id.' (BRS).

QUSQUN see QUZĞUN

QUSQUN-QAYRAN   Tuv. 19th c. **Qusqun-qayran** [Кускунъ-Кайранъ], Pad-padaqši's wife in a tale (Potanin IV, 426). ✧ 'Crow-kindliness, goodness' cf. Alt.(Tel.), Hak. *qayran* 'lieb, vortrefflich, gütig; die Güte, die Noth' (Radl. II, 22). ⇨ **QUZĞUN.**

QUSQUNAQ   Hak.(Sag.) 19th-20th c. **Qusqunaq** [Кускунак] (Proben IX, 458). ✧ 'Little rook, crow'. ⇨ **QUZĞUN** + dim. suff. *-aq.*

QUSLU   Tat., Nog.? 1543 **Quslu-bek-mïrza** [Куслубекъ-мырза] (PSRL XIII, 144). ⇨ **QUŠ I.** + suff. *-lu.*

QUSTA   Kzk. 1819 **Qusta-bay** [Кустабай] (MIK IV, 324).

QUSTAY see QUŠTAY

QUSTAN see QUŠTAN

QUSTAP   Hak. 19th-20th c. **Qustap** [Кустап] (HRS 349).

QUSTUQ-TARBAX   Yak. **Qustuq-tarbax** [Кустук тарбах] (Pek.).

QUSTULAQ   Kzk. 19th c. **Qustulaq** [Нуръ Мамбетъ Кустулаковъ] (Grod., Pril. 179).

QUSUQ   Uyg. 12th c. - 14th c. **Qusuq** [Kusuk] (DTS, EUTS); Uyg. 1327 **Qusuq** [Kuzuk] (Chwol., Syr.-nest. (NF) 26). ✧ 'Vomit'? (Blagova 1997, 713).

QUSUL   Kzk. 1846 **Qusul-bay** [Кусулбай Сатбалдынъ] (MKOP 155). ✧ 'Wash(ing)' cf. Kzk. *qusul* 'die Waschung, das Baden' (Radl. II, 1015) (<Ar.).

QUSUM see QUŠUM

QUSŪSQA   Hak.(Shor) 19th-20th c. **Qusūsqa** [Кусуска], fem. (Katanov, Otč. 11). ✧ 'Small brandy-bottle' cf. R. *kosuška* (косушка) 'id.' (Katanov).

QUSWAQ   Kzk. 19th c. **Quswaq** [Ахметъ-Гирей Кусваковъ] (Pam. kn. Turg. 40).

QUŠ I.   Chuv. 18th-19th c. **Kus-murza** [Кусмурза] (Magn. 54); Chuv. 18th-19th c. **Kus-patïr** [Куспатыръ] (Magn. 54); Chuv. 1670 **Kus-pey** [Куспейка] (Poliv.-Kras. 64); Kzk. **Qus-bek-sultan** [Кус Бек Султан] (Proben III, 55 /93/); Kzk. 19th c. **Qus-Jan** [Тураджанъ Кусджановъ] (Grod., Pril. 100); Kzk. 19th c. **Qus-jan** [Тораджанъ Кустжановъ] (Grod., Pril. 101); Hak.(Sag.) 19th-20th c. **Qus-pay** [Куспай] (Katanov, Otč. 8); Kzk. 19th c. **Qus-pek** [Куспекъ] (AOO 38); Kzk. 19th c. **Quš** [Кушъ] (Grod., Pril. 30); Kzk. 19th c. **Quš** [Кушъ Чутаковъ] (SKSO VIII, 221); NUyg. 19th c. **Quš** [قوش / Kush] (Le Coq, Namenl. 109); Kzk. 19th c. **Quš-atay** [Сирибашъ Кушатаевъ] (Grod., Pril. 24); Yürük 1543 **Quš-χan / Quš-Jan?** [قوشحان / Kuşhan] (Gökb., Rum. 179, 180); Kzk. 1839 **Quš-pek** [Кушпекъ Таукинъ], a sultan of the Middle Horde (Orta Žüz) (Konšin, Mat. V, 12); *EN:* Trkm. 1691 **Quš** [قوش / Kuş], an ethnic group (cemaat) of the Türkmen tribe in the region of Rakka, Syria (Refik, Anad. 97); *TN:* Kzk. **Quš-bay** [Куш-бай], a well at Mertvyj Kultuk (Karta JAR X). ✧ 'Bird' cf. Bashk. *qoš* 'id.' (BRS/Uraksin), Tat. *qoš* 'id.' (TatRS), Kzk. *qŭs* 'id.' (KzRS), East.T. *quš* 'Vogel: Beizvogel, speziell der Adler (*qara quš*)' (Le Coq, Namenl. 109), 'eagle, hunting-eagle, any large-sized bird e. g. a hawk; often used for 'bird' in general' (Jarring). See also **AYAZ-QUŠ, AQ-QUŠ, ALA-QUŠ, ALP-QUŠ, ALTUN-QUŠ, BALA-QUŠ, BAZ-QUŠ, BEREN-QUŠ, BİK-QUŠ, BOZ-QUŠ, BUR-QUŠ, BURAN-QUŠ, ČANAR-QUS, ER-QUŠ, YARÏN-QUŠ, KİN-QUŠ, QANA-QUŠ, QARA-QUŠ, QUBA-ĞUŠ, QUBAS-QUŠ, QUTLU-QUŠ, SANA-QUŠ, SARÏ-QOŠ, SİRİ-BAŠ-QUŠ, TAN-QUŠ, TAT-QUŠ.**

QUŠ II. see QOŠ I.

QUŠ-AYAQ   Kzk. 19th c. **Quš-ayaq** [Кушъ Аякъ] (Grod., Pril. 137). ✧ 'Bird-leg; pair-leg, double leg?'. ⇨ **QOŠ I. / QUŠ I.?** + **AYAQ.** See also **QOS-AYAQ.**

QUŠ-BUĞA   Khorezm.?/ Maml.? **Quš-buγa** [ارغون بن قشبغا], Arγun's(?) father (Duqmaq:RHCHor V, 10, 31). ⇨ **QUŠ I.** + **BUQA.**

QUŠ-QULAQ   Kzk. 1803, 1820 **Quš-qulaq** [Кушкулак], one of the chiefs of the Kereyit tribe of the Little Horde (Kiši Žüz) (MIK IV, 514, Sib. Vest. IX, 113). ⇨ **QUŠ I.** + **QULAQ.**

QUŠ-MANAY   Tat. 1824 **Quš-manay** [Кушманаевъ] (PSZRI XXXIX, 266). ⇨ **QUŠ II.** + **MANAY.**

QUŠ-MURAT   Kzk. 19th c. **Quš-murat** [Кушмурадъ] (SKSO VIII, 230). ⇨ **QUŠ I. / II.?** + **MURAT.**

QUŠ-TEMİR   **Quš-temir** [قشتمور], an emir of Nāsireddīn Allah (Juwaynī II, 154, 155); Maml. **Quš-temir** [قشتمر / Kuştemür] (Tarj/Houtsma 94, Tarj/Toparlı 42); Maml. 1254 **Quš-temir** [Kaschtemur Adjemi] (Makrīzī I, 50); Maml. 1305 **Quš-temir** [قشتمر / Caschtimur] (Abulfidā V, 196-97); Maml. 1305 **Quš-temir** [سيف‌الدين قشتمر المنصورى], an emir (Dawād. 131, 132); Maml. 1332 **Quš-temir** [قشتمر], an emir (Dawād. 369); Turk. 1540 **Quš-temir** [قشتمر / Kuştemir], chief of the Halilhacılu ethnic group (cemaat) in a defter from Diyarbekir, Turkey (Demirtaş 48); Trkm. 15th c.? **Quš-temir** [قوشتمر], a Türkmen settler in Çukurova, Turkey (Āšikp. 225, Sümer: DTCFD XI, 331). ⇨ **QUŠ I. + TEMİR.**

QUŠ-TUĠAN Selj., Turk. 1302 **Quš-tuɣan** [Κουστουγανης], a commander of the army (Byz. Turc. 170). ⇨ **QUŠ I. + TUĠAN I.**

QUŠ-UWAQ Kzk. 1825 **Quš-uwaq** [قوشؤاق / Кушууак] (MIK IV, 473, 477). ⇨ **QUŠ I. + UWAQ.**

QUŠAY see **QOŠAY**

QUŠAQ Kzk. 19th c. **Qušaq** [Кушакъ] (Grod., Pril. 31); Uzb. 19th c. **Qušaq** [Гура Кушаковъ] (SKSO III, 156); Uzb. 19th c. **Qušaq** [Ирманъ Кушаковъ] (SKSO III, 172). ✧ 'Fathom, embrace' cf. Kzk. qǔšaq 'объятие; обхват; охапка' (KzRS). ⇨ **QUČAQ.**

QUŠAN Kzk. 19th c. **Qušan-bay** [Сандибай Кушанбаевъ] (Grod., Pril. 50).

QUŠAT Kzk. 19th c. **Qušat** [Кушатъ] (SKSO VIII, 233).

QUŠČI see **QUŠČÏ**

QUŠČÏ Chag. 16th c. **Qušči** [Кушчи] (Ivanov 303); NUyg. 19th c. **Qušči** [قوشچی / Kushchi] (Le Coq, Nameńl. 109); Tat.(Mish.) 1775 **Quščï** [Кущигул Муксинов] (MIB IV/2, 416); Kzk. 19th c. **Quščï** [Кущиевъ] (SKSO VIII, 224); Kzk. 19th c. **Quščï-bay** [Кушчибай] (Grod., Pril. 180); Bashk. 1756 **Quščï-ɣul** [Кущигул Юлушев] (MIB IV/1, 123); Bashk. 1756 **Quščï-ɣul** [Ишмен Кущигулов] (MIB IV/1, 123); Kirg. **Qušču** [Кушчу] (Jud. 720); Kzk. 19th c. **Qušču-bay** [Кущубай] (SOK 12); Kkalp. 1723 **Qušču-bay** [Кушубай] (MIKk. 174); *EN:* Nog. 20th c. **Qussï-uruw** [Къусшы урув], a Qara-noɣay clan (Bask., Nog. 136). ✧ 'Breeder and trainer of hunting birds (e.g. falcons), falconer' cf. Kirg. qušču 'соколятник, охотник с ловчей птицей' (Jud.), East.T. qušči 'Beizjäger, der Adler zur Jagd abrichtet' (Le Coq, Nameńl. 109).

QUŠČU see **QUŠČÏ**

QUŠKEY Bashk. 1735 **Quškey** [Кубагушъ Кушкеевъ], a tarχan (Vel.-Zern., Bašk. 23); Kzk. 19th c. **Quškey** [Кушкей] (SODž. 90). ✧ I. 'Little bird'; II. 'Wish, mood' cf. Kkalp. qoškey 'id.' (KkRS). ⇨ **QUŠ I.? + dim. suff. -key.**

QUŠQAČ see **QUČQAČ**

QUŠQAR see **QOČQAR**

QUŠQUN Kzk. 19th c. **Qušqun-bay** [Кушкунбай Джантюринъ] (Grod., Pril. 131).

QUŠTAY Kzk.? 19th c. **Qustay** [Кустай] (Potanin II, 4); Kzk. 19th c. **Quštay / Quš-tay?** [Кутлумбетъ Кушташевъ (Кошташевъ)] (PSZRI VIII, 383, 386, SKSO VIII, 206); Tat.(Sib.) 1727 **Quštey** [Кукчелей Кушшеевъ], from the Tsagay (Caɣay) clan in the region of Kuzneck (PSZRI VII, 890). ⇨ **QUŠ I. / QOŠ I.? +**

TAY or suff. -tay(1,2)?

QUŠTAN Uyg. 1266 **Qustan** [Kustan] (Chwol., Syr.-nest. (NF) 9); Kzk. **Qustan** [Джаксыбай Кустановъ] (?); Kzk. 1811 **Qustan** [Таштимиръ Куштаневъ] (TOUAK XXIV, 43); *TN:* Kzk. 19th c. **Mulla-qustan** [Мулла Кустанъ], a field in Üst-yurt at Mertvyj Kultuk (Hanykov, Karta ZK).

QUŠTEY see **QUŠTAY**

QUŠTÏ Kzk. 19th c. **Quštï-bay** [Куштыбай] (AOP 26); Kzk. 19th c. **Quštu** [Кушту] (SOK 140); Kzk. 19th c. **Quštu-bay** [Куштубай] (AOK 102); Bashk. 1756 **Quštu-ɣul** [Ашмень Куштугулов] (MIB IV/1, 107). ✧ I. 'Younger brother'? cf. Bashk. PN Qustïbay (Kusimova), Bashk. qusti 'младший брат, братишка' (BRS/Uraksin); II. 'Having birds'? ⇨ **QUŠ I. + suff. -tï <-lï.**

QUŠTU see **QUŠTÏ**

QUŠU Türk 732 **Qušu-tutuq** (DTS). ✧ 'Bird of Him' (Blagova 1997, 707). See also **RUM-QUŠU.**

QUŠUĠAY Uzb. 1686 **Qušuɣay** [Маметий Кушугаевъ], from Bukhara in Tobolsk (PSZRI II, 816).

QUŠUQ Kzk. 19th c. **Qušuq** [Кушукъ] (AOA 118); Kzk. 19th c. **Qušuq** [Кушукъ] (AOO 46); Kzk.? 19th c. **Qušuq** [قوشوق / Мулла Кушукъ] (Veselovskij, Kirg. 7); Kzk. 19th c. **Qušuq-biy** [Молла Кушукъ бій] (Grod., Pril. 168); Kzk. 19th c. **Qušuq-pay** [Кушукпай] (SOK 286, 292). ⇨ **QOŠUQ / KÖŠEK?**

QUŠUM Kzk. 19th c. **Qusum-qul** [Кусумкулъ], Nurum-qul's brother (Grod., Pril. 72); Kzk. 1823 **Qušum** [قوشم / Кушум] (MIK IV, 455); Kzk. 19th c. **Qušum** [Кушумъ] (AOP 46); Bashk. 1773 **Qušum-bay (<Qušun-bay?)** [Унгар Кушумбаев] (MIB IV/2, 413). ✧ 'My bird'? ⇨ **QUŠ I. + poss. suff. -um.**

QUŠUN Bashk. 1762 **Qušun-bay** [Кушунбай Аднагулов] (MIB IV/1, 235); Bashk. 1762 **Qušun-bay** [Ишали Кушунбаев] (MIB IV/1, 235). ⇨ **ĠOŠUN?**

QUŠUŠ Kzk. 19th c. **Qušuš** [Кушушъ] (SODž. 90).

QUŠUT Kzk. 1803, 1820 **Qušut** [Кушут], one of the chiefs of the Čerkes tribe of Kiši-žüz (MIK IV, 515, Sib. Vest. IX, 118).

QUT Uyg. 762 **Xut-χatun**, fem. (Mahrnāmag 15); Kzk. 19th c. **Qot-bay** [Котбай] (SODž. 70, 136); Kzk. 19th c. **Qot-pay** [Котпай] (SOV 34); Kzk. 19th c. **Qot-pay** [Котпай] (SOK 40); Türk / Uyg. 8th c. - 9th c. **Qut** [qut] (DTS); Kzk. 19th c. **Qut-bay** [Кутбай] (AOA 114); Bashk. 1757 **Qut-čura** [Кутчюра Укменев] (MIB IV/1, 136); Bashk. 1757 **Qut-qul** [Куткул Сяферов] (MIB IV/1, 150, 153); Kzk. 19th c. **Qut-pek** [Кутпекъ] (SODž. 138); Uyg. 1323 **Qut-tegin-päg** [Kut-tägin-päg] (Chwol., Syr.-nest. 140); Uyg. 1323 **Qut-tegin-peg** [Kut-Tegin-Peg] (Chwol., Syr.-nest. 63). ✧ I. 'Soul, spirit, vitality, life' cf. Uyg. qut I. 'id.'

(DTS), Uyg. *qut* 'kut, saadet, takdis, ruh' (US), Alt.(Tel.) 'die Lebenskraft, Seele' (Radl. II, 991); II. 'Fortune, chance, luck, mercy, success' cf. Uyg. *qut II.* 'id.' (DTS), Türk, Uyg., Alt.(Tel.), Chag., East.T., Kirg., Turk. *qut* 'das Glück' (Radl. II, 990-991), Kzk. *qŭt* 'счастье' (KzRS). See also **AY-QUT, BAY-QUT, BALÏQ-QUT, BOQ-QUT, ǰAN-QUT, MÏR-QUT, SARÏ-ГUT(?).**

QUT-AČUQ Uyg. **Qut-ačuq / Qutačuq?** [Qutačuq] (Zieme, Mat. I, 78). ✧ 'Happiness-open, chance-open' (Zieme), but it may also be derived with suff. *-ačuq* forming personal names only (see Erdal 39). ⇨ **QUT + AČÏQ.**

QUT-AYAQ Kzk. 19th c. **Qut-ayaq** [Кутаякъ] (AOAtb. 54); Kzk. 19th c. **Qut-ayaq** [Кутаякъ] (SODž. 96); Kzk. 19th c. **Qut-ayaq** [Кутаякъ] (SOV 42). ✧ 'Chance - foot'. ⇨ **QUT + AYAQ.**

QUT-BAYAN Uyg. 762 **Xut-payan / Xut-puyan?** [Xutpayan], a translator (Müller, Uig. 762 Mahrnāmag 8, 12). ⇨ **QUT + BAYAN.**

QUT-BOL Kzk. 19th c. **Qut-bol-bay** [Кутьболбай / Кутболбай] (SOK 268). ✧ 'Be fortunate / be lucky!; Be successful!'. ⇨ **QUT + BOL.**

QUT-KELDİ Kzk. 19th c. **Qut-keldi / Qut-keldĭ** [Куткельды] (SODž. 64, 66, 160). ✧ 'The chance has come (has been born)' / 'A soul arrived' (Bese 22). ⇨ **QUT + KELDİ.**

QUT-ÖYÖÑÖY Yak. **Qut-öyöñöy** [Кут Öjöҥöi] (Pek.).

QUT-TÄÑRİ Uyg. 12th c. - 14th c. **Qut-täñri-χatunï** [qut täŋri χatunï], fem. (DTS). ✧ 'Happiness/mercy-sky/God' (Blagova 1997, 703).

QUTA Bashk. 1738 **Quta** [Кута Салтаев] (MIB I, 143); Kzk. 19th c. **Quta-bay** [Кутабай] (AOAtb. 38); Kzk. 19th c. **Quta-bay** [Бекигитъ Кутабаевъ] (Grod., Pril. 162); Kzk. 19th c. **Quta-bek** [Кутабекъ] (SODž. 104). ⇨ **QOTA?**

QUTAČUN Uyg. **Qutačun** [Kutaçun] (EUTS); Uyg. 12th c. - 14th c. **Qutačun** [Qutačun] (Radl., USp. 205, 247, DTS). ✧ 'May he become happy' (Bese 11), cf. Uyg. *quta-* 'становиться счастливым' (DTS) + imp. suff. *-čun.*

QUTAD Uyg. **Qudat** [Qudat] (Müller, Uig. II, 84, DTS); Uyg. 12th c. - 14th c. **Qutad** [qutad] (Müller, Uig. II, 88, DTS); Uyg. **Qut[ad?]-täñrim** [Qut??? Tängrim], fem. (Zieme, Mat. I, 75, 82). ✧ 'Be happy; make (people) happy' cf. Uyg. *qutad-* 'становиться счастливым' (DTS), *qudat-* 'glücklich machen, beglücken' (Radl. II, 1000).

QUTADA Uyg. **Qutada** [Kutada], fem. (EUTS).

QUTADMÏŠ Uyg. 8th c. **Xutadmïš** [Tai Ügä Xutadmïš] (Le Coq: Fest Thomsen 146); Uyg. 12th c. - 14th c. **Qutadmïš** (DTS); Uyg. 12th c. - 14th c. **Qutadmïš-silavanti** (Radl., USp. 144); Uyg. 13th c.

Qutadmïš-täñrim, a princess (Müller, Pfahl. 10); Uyg. 13th c. **Qutadmïš-täñrim**, fem. (Müller, Pfahl. 23); Uyg. 8th c. - 12th c. **Qutadmïš-ügän-tarχan** (Müller, Pfahl. 24). ✧ 'He/she got happy, glad; blessed' cf. Uyg. *qutad-* 'становиться счастливым' (DTS), Uyg. *qutad-* 'bahtiyar, mesud, kutlu olmak' (US). See also **İL-QUTADMÏŠ, TAY-ÜGÄ-XUTADMÏŠ.**

QUTADMÏŠ-BARS Uyg. 8th c. **Qutadmïš-bars** (DTS); Uyg. **Qutadmïš-pars** [Kutadmïş Pars] (EUTS). ✧ 'Blessed/happy-Panther' (Blagova 1997, 706). ⇨ **QUTADMÏŠ + BAŠ.**

QUTADMÏŠ-BAŠ Uyg. 13th-14th c. **Qutadmïš-baš-öz-ïnanč-totoq-bäg** [Qutadmïš Baš Öz İnanč Totoq Bäg] (Zieme, Mat. II, 93). ✧ 'Blessed/happy head (man)'. ⇨ **QUTADMÏŠ + BAŠ.**

QUTADMÏŠ-QARA Uyg. 13th c. **Qutadmïš-qara** (DTS). ✧ 'Blessed/happy-Mighty/Black' (Blagova 1997, 717). ⇨ **QUTADMÏŠ + QARA.**

QUTADMÏŠ-BÖRT Uyg. 13th-14th c. **Qutadmïš-bört** [Qutadmïš Bört], fem. (Zieme, Mat. III, 272). ✧ 'Blessed/happy?'. ⇨ **QUTADMÏŠ + BÖRT.**

QUTADMÏŠ-TOГRÏL Uyg. 13th-14th c. **Qutadmïš-toγrïl** [Qu[tad]mïš Toγrïl] (Zieme, Mat. III, 272). ✧ 'Blessed/happy falcon' (Zieme: „Gesegneter Falke"). ⇨ **QUTADMÏŠ + TOГRÏL.**

QUTAY-MENDİ see **XUDAY**

QUTAYÏN Yak. **Qutayïn** [Кутаjын] (Pek.). ✧ 'Bad egg, rogue; little naughtiness', cf. Yak. *qutayï* 'испорка' (hypochoristic nickname which mothers give to little babies when dealing with them, Pek.).

QUTAQ Kzk. 19th c. **Qutaq** [Кутакъ] (SODž. 84). ✧ 'Penis; tail'? cf. Chag., Kzk. *qotaq* 'der Penis, der Schweif' (Radl. II, 606).

QUTAQAY Kzk. 1846 **Qutaqay** [Итемген Кутакаев] (MKOP 155). ⇨ **QUTA(Q)?** + suff. *-(q)ay.* See also **QOTAQAY.**

QUTALMÏŠ see **QUTULMÏŠ**

QUTAM-BAŠ see **QUTAN-BAŠ**

QUTAN Tat.(Sib.) 1638, 1639 **Qotan** [Котан], a taysha (tayša) (Miller, Ist. Sib. II, 110, 453); Kzk. 19th c. **Qotan** [Котанъ] (SOK 252); Kzk. 19th c. **Qotan** [Котанъ] (AOK 86); Kzk. 19th c. **Qotan-bay** [Котанъ-бай], in a Kazak tradition (legend) of origin (Potanin, Pred. 54); **Qutan** [Кутан] (RaD II, 11); 1699 **Qutan** [Кутанъ Ишеевъ] (PSZRI III, 562); Karakh. 11th c. **Qutan** [Kutan] (DTS, MK/Atalay 846); Bashk. 1728 **Qutan** [Маммет Кутанов] (MIB III, 254); Bashk. 1729 **Qutan** [Кутан Кузеев] (MIB III, 260); Bashk. 1776 **Qutan** [Кутан Чураков] (MIB V, 42, 43); Kzk. 19th c. **Qutan** [Кутанъ] (AOA 34); Kzk. 19th c. **Qutan** [Кутанъ] (SOK 244). ✧ I. 'Coward, faint-hearted' cf. Kzk. *qotan* 'feige, der Feigling' (Radl. II, 607); II. 'Pen, corral, hurdle (for sheep)' cf. Kzk. *qotan* 'id.' (KzRS), Bashk. *qotan* 'плетёный хлев для овец' (BRS/Uraksin); III. 'Pelican' cf. Chag. *qotan* 'der Pelikan' (Radl. II, 607), Chag. *qutan* 'der Wiedehopf' (Radl. II, 992); IV. 'Paint, décor *qotan* 'id.' (BRS/Uraksin); V. 'Not enough, short, thin; greedy, open-mouthed' cf. *qotan* 'id.' (BRS/Uraksin); VI. 'Servant' cf. Kzk. *qutan* 'der Diener' (Radl. II, 992). ⇨ **QUTAN?**

QUTAN-BAŠ   Kzk. 1789 **Qutam-baš-derviš (<Qutan-baš)** [Кутамбаш-дервиш] (MIK IV, 126). ⇨ **QUTAN + BAŠ.**

QUTAN-TOҐRÏL   Uyg. 12th c. - 14th c. **Qutan-toɣrïl / Qotan-toɣrïl** [Qotan Toɣrïl] (Radl., USp. 113, DTS). ✧ 'Pelican-falcon/hawk'? ⇨ **QUTAN + TOҐRÏL.**

QUTAR   Kzk. 1819 **Qutar** [Кутар] (MIK IV, 324).

QUTAŠ   Uyg. 12th-14th c. **Qutaš** [Kutäš] (Chwol., Syr.-nest. 105, 139); Bashk. 1756 **Qutaš** [Куташ Исламгулов] (MIB IV/1, 120). ⇨ **QOTAŠ?**

QUTAŠÏQ   Uyg. 1316 **Qutašïq** [Kutäschek / Kutaschek] (Chwol., Syr.-nest. 57, 58). ⇨ **QOTA + suff. -šïq.**

QUTBAN see **QUTMAN**
QUTBANAY see **QUTMANAY**

QUTÏ   Kzk. 1829 **Qutï-bay** [Кутебаевъ] (Konšin, Mat. I-III, 21); Kzk. 19th c. **Qutï-bay** [Кутыбай] (AOP 106); Kzk. 19th c. **Qutï-bay** [Кутибай] (Grod., Pril. 168); Kzk. 19th c. **Qutï-bay** [Кутыбай] (SOK 12); Uzb. 1848 **Qutï-bay** [Куты-Бай] (Moskal'cev 34); Kzk. 19th c. **Qutï-bek** [Кутебекъ] (SODž. 64); Uyg. 762 **Qutï-χunčuy** [Qutï Xunčui] (Mahrnämag 14, 35); *TN:* Kzk. **Qutï-bay** [Кутебай], south of Mertvyj Kultuk (Karta JAR X). ✧ 'His/her chance, luck'. ⇨ **QUT.**

QUTÏ-BAR   Bashk.? **Qutï-bar** [Куты-баръ Итьаякоҡ] (ZVOIRAO X, 194). ✧ 'He/she has got a chance'. ⇨ **QUT, QUTÏ.**

QUTÏQ see **QUTUQ**

QUTÏMÏQ   Kzk. 19th c. **Qutïmïq** [Кутымыкъ] (SOK 216).

QUTÏR   Kzk. 18th c. **Qutïr** [Кутыръ] (Nepljuev 762, 763); Kzk. 1740 **Qutïr-batïr** [Кутырь-Батыръ] (Hanɣkov, Poezdka 15). ⇨ **QOTUR?, QUTUR?**

QUTQAN   Uyg. 12th c. - 14th c. **Qutqan** (Radl., USp. 44, DTS).

QUTLA   Chuv. 18th-19th c. **Kutla** [Кутла] (Magn. 54); Bashk. 1735 **Qutla** [Кутле Аднагуловымъ], a tarχan (Vel.-Zern., Bašk. 14); Bashk. 1735 **Qutla** [Кутла Аднагуловъ], a tarχan (Vel.-Zern., Bašk. 14); Bashk. 1784 **Qutla** [Кутла Джегаферовъ] (MIB V, 154); Bashk. 1784 **Qutla** [Кутла (Кута) Рахмангуловъ] (MIB V, 157); Bashk. 1785 **Qutla** [Кутла (Икутла) Сафаровъ] (MIB V, 166, 168); Bashk. 1788 **Qutla** [Смак Кутлин] (MIB V, 233); Bashk. 1789 **Qutla** [Кутла Ибраевъ] (MIB V, 267); Kirg. 1824 **Qutla** [Япалакъ Кутлинъ], fem. (Konšin, Mat. I-III, 72). ✧ 'Happy, lucky'? ⇨ **QUT + suff. -la<-li?** See also

QUTLUҐ.

QUTLANAY   Tat. 1779 **Qutlanay** [Кутланаев] (MIB V, 81).

QUTLİ see **QUTLUҐ**

QUTLİ-QÏNALÏ   Oghuz/Trkm. 13th c. **Qutli-qïnalï** [قتلى قنالى / قيلى قتالى]   /   Кутли-Кыналы] (Abulg./Kon. 325). ⇨ **QUTLUҐ + QÏNA + suff. -lï.**

QUTLİ see **QUTLUҐ**

QUTLİ-MİRAT see **QUTLUҐ-MURAT**
QUTLİ-ŠORA see **QUTLUҐ**
QUTLİ-TEMÜR see **QUTLUҐ-TEMİR**
QUTLU see **QUTLUҐ**

QUTLU-BAQ   Tat. 1362 **Qutlu-baq** [Кутлубакъ / Котлубакъ], a prince (PSRL II, 350). ⇨ **QUTLUҐ + BAQ.**

QUTLU-BUҐA see **QUTLUҐ-BUQA**

QUTLU-BULAT   Tat.(Lit.) 1555 **Qutlu-bolat** [Кутлу Болатъ] (Kn. Metriki Lit. 113); Tat. 1533 **Qutlu-bulat** [Кутлу Булатъ], a prince (PSRL XX, 416); Bashk. 1712 **Qutlu-bulat** [Кутлубулат Тименчюрин] (MIB III, 83); Bashk. 1735 **Qutlu-bulat** [Кутлубулатъ Усеевъ], a tarχan (Vel.-Zern., Bašk. 21, 22); Bashk. 1737 **Qutlu-bulat** [Кутлубулат] (MIB III, 357); Bashk. 1754 **Qutlu-bulat** [Кутлубулат Кутлуюлов] (MIB IV/1, 83); Bashk. 1779, 1780 **Qutlu-bulat** [Менлигул (Минлигул) Кутлубулатов] (MIB V, 87); Bashk. 1780 **Qutlu-bulat** [Минлигул Кутлубулатов] (MIB V, 111); Bashk. 1787 **Qutlu-bulat** [Кутлубулат Чурагуловъ] (MIB V, 214); Kzk. 1533 **Qutlu-bulat** [Кутлубулатъ] (PSRL XIII, 69); *EN:* Kzk. 18th c. - 19th c. **Quttï-bolat** [Куттыболат], a clan (Tynyšp. 71). ⇨ **QUTLUҐ + BULAT.**

QUTLU-DEMÜR see **QUTLUҐ-TEMİR**
QUTLU-DOMUR see **QUTLUҐ-TEMİR**

QUTLU-GİLDİ   Bashk. 1735 **Qutlu-gildi** [Кутлугилди Акинъ], a tarχan (Vel.-Zern., Bašk. 21); Bashk. 1740 **Qutlu-gildi** [Кунуд-бай Кутлугилдин] (MIB I, 383); Bashk. 1756 **Qutlu-gildi** [Кутлугильды Метеев] (MIB IV/1, 123); Bashk. 1777 **Qutlu-gildi** [Ишберда (Ишбурда) Кутлугильдин] (MIB V, 65); Bashk. 1788 **Qutlu-gildi** [Кутлугильда Кукулчюлов] (MIB V, 235). ✧ 'Lucky (son) has come (has been born)' (Sattarov). ⇨ **QUTLUҐ + KELDİ.**

QUTLU-GÜZÄ see **QUTLUҐ**

QUTLU-ҐAYA see **QUTLUҐ-QAYA**

QUTLU-ҐAZAN   Bashk. 1761 **Qutlu-ɣazan** [Кутлугазан Сиюндюков] (MIB IV/1, 218). ⇨ **QUTLUҐ + ҐAZAN.**

QUTLU-ҐUDAQ   Bashk. 1695 **Qutlu-ɣudaq** [Куземетко Кутлугудаков] (MIB I, 92). ⇨ **QUTLUҐ.**

QUTLU-ҐUŠ see **QUTLU-QUŠ**

QUTLU-XAYÏR   Maml. **Qutl-χayïr-χatun (<Qutlu-**

χayïr-χatun) [خطلخير / Khotlkhayr Khâtoûn], wife of Salāhaddīn's brother the Šāhanšāh (Sauvaire IV, 272). ✧ 'Happy/lucky blessing/wealth' cf. Ar. PN *Khayr* 'good, blessing, boon, wealth, fortune' (Ahmed). ⇨ **QUTLUΓ + XAYR.**

QUTLU-YOL see **QUTLU-YUL**

QUTLU-YUL Bashk. 1737 **Qutlu-yol?** [Кутлуел] (MIB I, 349); Bashk. 1751 **Qutlu-yol?** [Кутлуелу Калтырчаков] (MIB IV/1, 43); Bashk. 1734 **Qutlu-yul** [Кутлуюлъ Кадырчиковъ], a tarχan (Vel.-Zern., Bašk. 10); Bashk. 1735 **Qutlu-yul** [Кутлуюлъ Акинъ], a tarχan (Vel.-Zern., Bašk. 21); Bashk. 1735 **Qutlu-yul?** [Байгуза Кутлуяловъ], a tarχan (Vel.-Zern., Bašk. 23); Bashk. 1761 **Qutlu-yul** [Котлуюл Мурзин] (MIB IV/1, 209); Bashk. 1761 **Qutlu-yul** [Янчюра Кутлуюлов] (MIB IV/1, 218); Bashk. 1772 **Qutlu-yul** [Кутлуюл] (MIB IV/1, 364); Bashk. 1779 **Qutlu-yul** [Кутлуюл Масегутов / Мясягутов] (MIB V, 44, 94, 265); Tat.(Mish.) **Qutluγ-yul** [Kutlug-julov] (IOAIÊK XIX, 141). ✧ 'Let his path of life be lucky' cf. Tat. PN *Qotlï-yul / Yul-qotlï* (Sattarov), Bashk. *Yul-γotlo* (Kusimova). ⇨ **QUTLUΓ + YOL.** See also **YOL-QUTLUΓ.**

QUTLU-QADÄM see **QUTLUΓ-QADÄM**

QUTLU-QAYA see **QUTLUΓ-QAYA**

QUTLU-QORTQA Tat.(GH) 1302, 1312 **Qutlu-qortqa** [Кутлукортка], coming from the Horde (PSRL I, 228, Lavr. 501). ⇨ **QUTLUΓ + QURTQA.**

QUTLU-QUŠ Tat. 1779 **Qutlu-γuš** [Беккул (Биккул) Кутлугушев] (MIB V, 81); Tat. 1779 **Qutlu-γuš** [Кутлугуш Дюскеев (Дескеев)] (MIB V, 81, 93); Bashk. 1664 **Qutlu-γuš** [Кутлугушко Биртюков] (MIB I, 191); Bashk. 1731 **Qutlu-γuš** [Кутлугуш Чюрючеев] (MIB III, 284); Bashk. 1735 **Qutlu-γuš** [Кутлугушъ Дюсекинъ], a tarχan (Vel.-Zern., Bašk. 22); Bashk. 1762 **Qutlu-γuš** [Беккул Кутлугушев] (MIB IV/1, 249); Bashk. 1779 **Qutlu-γuš** [Кутлугуш] (MIB V, 81). ⇨ **QUTLUΓ + QUŠ I.**

QUTLU-MAMET Bashk. 1708 **Qutlu-mamet** [Кутлумаметко] (MIB I, 215). ⇨ **QUTLUΓ + MAMAET.**

QUTLU-MURAT see **QUTLUΓ-MURAT**

QUTLU-SĀT Crm. 1635 **Qutlu-sāt-beg** [قتلو ساعت بك] (Vel.-Zern., Crim. 144, 210). ⇨ **QUTLUΓ + SĀT.**

QUTLU-ŠA see **QUTLUΓ**

QUTLU-ŠİR Turk. 1380 **Qutlu-šir, Šeyχ-qutlu-šir** [شيخ قتلو شير / Šēr], an Anatolian dervish (died in 1380) who told Ahmed the Sultan of Sivas his fortune (Astarab. 84, 120, 171). ⇨ **QUTLUΓ + ŠIR.**

QUTLU-TEMÜR see **QUTLUΓ-TEMİR**

QUTLUJA see **QUTLUQČA**

QUTLUΓ Trkm. 20th c. **Γutlï** [Gutli] (Zaj. 1971, 327); Trkm. 20th c. **Γutlï** [Кутлы] (TrkmRS 215); Selj. 12th c. **Xutlu** [حساالدين محمود بن ختلو] (Ibn Šaddād, Alep 117); Khorezm. /Tat.(GH) 1282 **Xutlu-χatun** [خطلو خاتون], wife of Kipchak Khan Meñgü-temür (Qalāūn/Tizeng. I, 66); Karakh.? 934-936 **Xutluγ** [خطلغ], a door-keeper (Miskawayh 471-473, 538); Karakh.? 982 **Xutluγ** [خطلغ الحاجب] (Qalānisi 26); Kzk. 19th c. **Qottu-bay** [Коттубай] (AOK 10, 94); Kzk. 19th c. **Qottu-bay** [Коттубай] (AOO 78); Kzk. 19th c. **Qottu-bay** [Коттубай] (AOP 14); Chag. 16th c. **Qutli-yar** [Кутли Яр] (Ivanov 197); Oghuz 1039 **Qutlï** [Эмирек Кутли] (MIT I, 280); Kkalp. 20th c. **Qutlï-bay** [Кутлыбай] (KkRS 774); Kkalp. 20th c. **Qutlï-gül** [Кутлыгул], fem. (KkRS 778); Tat.(Sib.) 1631 **Qutlï-mergen (Qutlï-mergey?)** [Кутлимергей] (Miller, Ist. Sib. II, 384, 385); Trkm. 19th c. **Qutlï-šora-aji** [Уразакай Кутлышора-аджиевъ] (Ščeglov I, 355); Maml.? **Qutlu** [Sayf ed-dîn Qotloûbek châchenkîr er Roûmy], „c'est lui qui restaura le canal a Jerusalem", his mausoleum is in Damascus (Sauvaire VI, 253); Maml. **Qutlu** [قطلو], fem. (Sobernh. I, 136); Maml.? 1300 **Qutlu** [Aba-eddin Katlouberes-Adeli], an emir from „Bordj" (Makrīzī IV, 142, Weil, Chalif. I, 227); Turk. 1583 **Qutlu** [Kutlu], fem. (Ongan, Ank. I, 165); Tat. 1718 **Qutlu** [Кутлу Токташев] (MIB III, 172); Bashk. 1664 **Qutlu** [Кутлу Беляков] (MIB I, 192); Bashk. 1748 **Qutlu** [Кутлу] (PSZRI XXV, 190); Bashk. 1757 **Qutlu** [Кутлу Минеев] (MIB IV/1, 140); Bashk. 1693 **Qutlu? / Qutla?** [Афанасій Кутлин], from Ufa (MIB I, 84); Crm. 1689 **Qutlu-bay** [Караманъ Кутлу-Баевъ], envoy of the Russians in the Crimea (Smirnov, Krym. 625); Bashk. 1675 **Qutlu-bay** [Кусятерди Кутлубаев] (MIB I, 200); Bashk. 1781 **Qutlu-bay** [Кутлубай Гумеров] (MIB V, 124); Kzk. **Qutlu-bay** [Кутлубай Касимовъ] (Valihanov, Soč. 347); Kzk. 18th c. **Qutlu-bay** [Кутлубай] (Nepljuev 764); Kzk. 18th c. **Qutlu-bay** [Нуралабай Кутлубаевъ] (Nepljuev 803); Kzk. 18th c. **Qutlu-bay** [Кутлубай Давлетбаевъ] (Nepljuev 803, 804); Maml.? 1261 **Qutlu-bäg** [Kûtlû Bâg], emir of Arbil (Abulfar./Budge I, 441, 449); Tat.(GH) 13th c. **Qutlu-bäg / Qutlu-bäy** [Κουτλούπενς], a christened Tatar (Byz. Turc. 170); Turk. 14th c. **Qutlu-bäg / Qutlu-bäy** [Κουτλούπενς], emir, chief of the Akkoyunlu (Byz. Turc.); Turk. 1388 **Qutlu-bäg / Qutlu-bäy** [Κουτλούπενς], a governor (Byz. Turc. 170); Maml. 14th c. **Qutlu-bäg / Kutlu-beg** [قتلوبك / Kutluba] (Tarǰ/Houtsma 63, Tarǰ/Toparlı 42 /see facs. 31b/); Maml. 14th c. **Qutlu-bäk** [قطلو بَك] (Sauvaget 53); Turk. **Qutlu-bey** [Kutlu Bey] (Uzunçarş., Anad 63); Crm. 13th c. **Qutlu-bey** [Кутлубей] (Smirnov, Krym. 34); Maml. 1310 **Qutlu-bek** [قطبك بن الجاشنكير]

(Dawād. 216); Maml. 1311 **Qutlu-bek** [قطلوبك /
Cotlubek] (Abulfidā V, 248-49); Maml. 1335 **Qutlu-
bek** [سيف الدين قطلبك الوشاقى], an emir (Dawād.
393); Nog. 1649 **Qutlu-bek** [Кутлубекъ], fem. (AI IV,
123); Tat.(GH) 1262 **Qutlu-biy** [Кутлубий], ruler of
the Tatar (Lavr. 453, PSRL V, 190 VII, 163); Tat.
1695/96 **Qutlu-biy** [قوتلو بى / Кутлу-бий] (Jusupov
74); Bashk. 1771 **Qutlu-čura** [Кутлучура Абдуллин]
(MIB IV/1, 358); Crm. 1640 **Qutlu-čura-bahadïr**
[قتلو چوره بهادر] (Vel.-Zern., Crim. 251); Bashk. 1735
Qutlu-güzä [Кутлугузе], a tarχan (Vel.-Zern., Bašk.
24); Bashk. 1776 **Qutlu-güzä** [Иастай Кутлугузин]
(MIB V, 42); Bashk. 1779 **Qutlu-güzä** [Кутлугузя
Зиянгулов] (MIB V, 101, 255, 327); Khorezm. 14th c.
Qutlu-χan [Kothlû Khân], an emir in Transoxania (Ibn
Bat. III, 45, 337, 341); Turk. 1583 **Qutlu-χan**
[قوتلو خان / Kutluhan] (Ongan, Ank. I, 165);
Oghuz/Trkm. **Qutlu-melik** [قُوتلوُ مَلِك / Qutlu Melik /
Кутлу-Мелик], fem. (DQorq./Rossi 100, DQorq. 13);
Tat.(Sib.) 1634 **Qutlu-mergen (Qutlu-mergey?)**
[Кутлумергей Ясаулов] (Miller, Ist. Sib. II, 383,
411); Tat.(Lit.) 1557 **Qutlu-soltan** [Кутлу-Солтанъ
Ханикинъ] (Kn. Metriki Lit. 151); Crm. 1346 **Qutlu-
sultan** [قتلوسلطان], daughter of Gāzi Girey Xan (Vel.-
Zern., Crim. 134, 791); Crm. 1784 **Qutlu-ša(-murza)**
[Кутлуша мурза], a murza (IAN (Otd. gum. nauk.)
1928, 379); Khorezm. 13th c. **Qutlu-šah** [قطلوشاه /
Кутлушахъ], Ghazan Khan's beglerbeg (bekleri-bek)
(Umarī/Tizeng. I, 227, 249); Maml. 1305 **Qutlu-šah**
[ابن قطلوشاه] (Dawād.); Crm. 1670 **Qutlu-šah(-
yazuji)** [Kutlu šāh jazudži] (Vel.-Zern., Crim. 615);
Crm. 1637 **Qutlu-šah-aγa** [قتلو شاه اغا] (Vel.-Zern.,
Crim. 216, 256 etc.); Crm. 1635 **Qutlu-šah-beg** [Kutlu
šāh beg Külük ogly] (Vel.-Zern., Crim. 143); Crm.
1637 **Qutlu-šah-bĭ** [Kutlu šāh bĭ] (Vel.-Zern., Crim.
171); Crm. 1679 **Qutlu-šah-mirza** [Kutlu šāh mirza]
(Vel.-Zern., Crim. 696, 707); Maml. 14th c. **Qutlu-be /
Xutlu-be** [حُطلبا / قتلوبا / قتلوباً / chotluba /
Huṭluba / Kuṭluba] (Tarǰ/Houtsma 73, 87, Tarǰ/Toparlı
42); Türk **Qutluγ** [Kutluġ / Qutluγ], fem. (ETY I, 156);
Uyg. **Qutluγ-?** [Qutluγ ???q] (Zieme, Mat. I, 74); Uyg.
Qutluγ [Kutluġ / Qutluγ], fem. (EUTS, ETY II, 65);
Uyg.? 750 **Qutluγ** (Thomsen, Stein 186, 188); Uyg.
12th c. - 14th c. **Qutluγ** [Qutluγ], a woman who was
sold to Qutluγ-temür (Le Coq, Urkunden 458); Uyg.
12th c. - 14th c. **Qutluγ**, fem. (Radl., USp. 21-23, Le
Coq, Urkunden 1918, 458-59); Selj. **Qutluγ**
[قتلغ الرشيدى] (Bondārī 162); Selj. 1107/08 **Qutluγ**
[خطلغ / Khotlogh] (Kamāladdīn: RHCHor III, 595);
Selj. 1128 **Qutluγ** [Cotlog], he occupied Haleb
(Abulfidā III, 430-31); Selj. 1147/48 **Qutluγ** [خطلغ /
Khotlokh], Altun-taš (the lord of Sarkhad)'s brother

(Abū Šāma: RHCHor IV, 53); Selj. 12thc. **Qutluγ**
[قتلغ], Aq-soñqur's brother at the times of Arslan ibn
Togrul (1160-1175) (Qazw. 472); Selj. 12th c. **Qutluγ**
[قتلغ تشتدار] (Rāwandī 350, 351); Selj. 12th c.
Qutluγ [فخرالدين قتلغ] (Rāwandī 362, 365); Selj.?
1173-74 **Qutluγ** [البته قتلغ الكمالى / Ilbuka Kutluγ]
(Ibn al-Athīr, Atab.: RHCHor II/2, 294); Selj. 1248
Qutluγ [محمد بن بها'الدين قتلغ / Bahaeddin Kutluğ]
(Turan: Belleten XII, 99, 118); Khorezm.? 1282 **Qutluγ**
[قتلغ تركان], he rules in Kirman (Qazw. 529-531);
Tat.(GH) 1307 **Qutluγ** [Κουτλούγ], a christened Tatar,
died in 1307 (Byz. Turc. 170); Uyg. **Qutluγ / Xutluγ**,
fem. (Müller, Uig. II, 84-86, 88); Selj. 1158/59 **Qutluγ
/ Xutluχ** [خطلغ الزاهد / Khotlokh ez-Zahid], Zengi I's
mamluk (Abū Šāma: RHCHor IV, 100); Selj. 1169/70
Qutluγ / Xutluχ? [خطلغ / Khotlokh al-'Alemdar], a
standard bearer, Nūreddīn's mamluk (gulām?), the
governor of Hisn 'Akkar (Abū Šāma: RHCHor IV,
149); Selj. 1035 **Qutluγ-aba** [قتلغ ابه صارو والدين], an
emir (Ibn al-Athīr/Tornb. X, 475, 478, XI, 311); Selj.
1108, 1127 **Qutluγ-aba** (Kamāladdīn II, 152, 237);
Selj. 1108, 1127, 1128 **Qutluγ-aba** [ختلغ ابه السلطا نى]
(Kamāladdīn II, 152, 237, Qalānisi 218); Selj. 1144
Qutluγ-aba [خطلبا / Nâsirüddîn Kutluğ-aba el Bâzdâr],
an emir (a falconer?) (Ahbar 79); Selj. 12th c. **Qutluγ-
aba** [سراج الدين قتلغ ابه'] (Rāwandī 347, 349); Selj.
1182 **Qutluγ-aba** [Sārim el-Dīn Hutluba] (Ramazan
Şeşen: İslâm Tetkikleri Ensitüsü Dergisi, VI, 3-4
(1976), p. 18); Türk 7th c. - 9th c. **Qutluγ-baγa-tarqan**
[qutluγ baγa tarqan / Qutluγ Baγa tarqan] (DTS, ETY I,
156); Uyg. 12th c. - 14th c. **Qutluγ-bäg** (Radl., USp.
95-96); Uyg. 12th c. - 14th c. **Qutluγ-beg / Qutluγ-bäg**
[qutluγ beg / Kutluġ bäg] (DTS, EUTS); Türk 7th c. -
9th c. **Qutluγ-čigši** [qutluγ čigši / Qutluγ Çigşi] (DTS,
ETY III, 121); Uzb. 1846 **Qutluγ-ǰan-bay** [Кутлуг-
джан-бай] (MIT II, 504); Khorezm./Chag.? 1463
Qutluγ-derviš [Кутлуг-дервиш Илахи], ruler of
Khiva (MIT I, 540); **Qutluγ-χan** [قتلغ خان] (J̌uwaynī
II, 146); **Qutluγ-χan** [قتلغ خان], Baraq-χajib's
byname (J̌uwaynī II, 211); Khorezm. **Qutluγ-χan**
[قتلغ خان], chief of the emirs (J̌uwaynī I, 67); Trkm.
1847 **Qutluγ-χan** [Кутлуг-хан], chief of the Göklens
(MIT II, 511); Selj. 11th c. **Qutluγ-χatun** [قتلغ خاتون
نورادى], Muhammad I (1092-1094) ibn Melikshah's
wife (Rāwandī 163); Khorezm.? 13th c. **Qutluγ-χatun**
[Кутлуг-хатун], Arγun-χan's (1284-1291) elder (first)
wife (RaD I/1, 120); Uyg. 13th-14th c. **Qutluγ-ïnal**
(Zieme, Mat. III, 275); Uyg. 8th c. **Qutluγ-oγul**
[Kutluġ oġul / qutluγ oγul] (EUTS, DTS); Khoream.?
13th c. **Qutluγ-sultan** [قتلغ سلطان], Rukneddīn Xoǰa
Mubarek's byname (J̌uwaynī II, 215); Chag. 16th c.

Qutluγ-sultan-χanum [Кутлук Султан-ханум], fem. (Ivanov 130, 242); Trkm.? 1851 **Qutluγ-sultan** [Кутлуг Султан] (MIT II, 294); 14th c. **Qutluγ-ša-χatun** [كتلغ شا حاتون] (Qazw. 601); **Qutluγ-šah** [قتلغشاه], an emir (Qazw. 592, 596); Khorezm. **Qutluγ-šah** [Kûtlûg Shâh], a commander-in-chief under Ghazan Khan (1295-1304) (Abulfar./Budge II, XXVI); Khorezm. 14th c. **Qutluγ-šah** [شاه قتلغشاه], in Kirman (Qazw. 633); Crm.? 17th c. **Qutluγ-šah** [Кутлугъ-шахъ], Kantemir's brother (Smirnov, Krym. 512); **Qutluγ-šah-χatun** [كتلغ شاه حاتون / Kotlokschah-khatoun] (RaD/Quatrem. 96); Uyg. 1330 **Qutluγ-tärim** [Kutluk Terim], fem. (Chwol., Syr.-nest. 71); Uyg. 1339 **Qutluγ-tärim** [Kutluk Tarim], fem. (Chwol., Syr.-nest. 89); Uyg. 1339 **Qutluγ-tärim** [Kutluk Tarim], fem. (Chwol., Syr.-nest. (NF) 33); Uyg. 1367 **Qutluγ-tärim** [Kutluγ Tärim Koštanc], fem. (Kokovcov XVI, 198); Selj. 1073 **Qutluγ-tegin** [Rükneddevle Kutluğ Tekin], an emir, Melik-šah I (1072-1092) donated him the region of Fars (Ahbar 40); Karakh. **Qutluγ-tegin** [Kutlug tégin] (MK/Atalay 846); Uyg. 13th-14th c. **Qutluγ-tigin** [Qutluγ Tigin] (Zieme, Mat. II, 91); Karakh. **Qutluγ-tigin** [Kutluğ tigin] (MK/Atalay 846); Uyg. 12th c. - 14th c. **Qutluγ-toña** [Qutluγ Tonga / Kutluğ Tonga] (Radl., USp. 210, 252, DTS, EUTS); Uyg. 13th c. -14th c. **Qutluq** [Kutluk] (Chwol., Syr.-nest. 100, 103); Uyg. 1269 **Qutluq** [Kutluk] (Chwol., Syr.-nest. 22); Uyg. 1313 **Qutluq** [Kutluk], a priest (Chwol., Syr.-nest. 55); Uyg. 1339 **Qutluq** (Chwol., Syr.-nest. 89); Uzb. 1709 **Qutluq** [قتلق سرای], a eunuch, Qarši's hakim in Bukhara (Buchari 315); Khorezm. 1219 **Qutluq-χan** [Кутлукъ-Ханъ], officer of the Khorezmshah (RaD/Ber. III, 45); Chag. 16th c. **Qutluq-yar-aqa** [Кутлук Яр Ака] (Ivanov 167); Kzk. 19th c. **Qutluq-pay** [Куттукпай] (SOV 16); Uyg. **Qutluq-peg** [Kutluk-Peg] (Chwol., Syr.-nest. 93); Uyg. 13th c. - 14th c. **Qutluq-tärim** [Kutluk Tarim], fem. (Chwol., Syr.-nest. (NF) 42); Uyg. 1339 **Qutluq-tärim** [Kutluk Tarim], fem. (Chwol., Syr.-nest. (NF) 36); Uyg. 13th c. - 14th c. **Qutluq-terim** [Kutluk-Terim], fem. (Chwol., Syr.-nest. 107); Uyg. 13th c. - 14th c. **Qutluq-terim** [Kutluk Terim] (Chwol., Syr.-nest. (NF) 48); Uyg. 1310 **Qutluq-terim** [Kutluk Terim], daughter of Kurikus (Kyriakos) (Chwol., Syr.-nest. 54); Uyg. 1329 **Qutluq-terim?** [Kutluk], fem. (Chwol., Syr.-nest. (NF) 28); Uyg. 1318 **Qutluq-tirim** [Kūtlūk Tīrīm], fem. (Chwol., Syr. I, 16); Uyg. 1318 **Qutluq-tirim** [Kutluk Tirim], fem. (Chwol., Syr.-nest. 60); Kzk. 19th c. **Qutti-bay** [Куттыбай] (SOV 58); Kzk. 19th c. **Quttu-bay** [Куттубай] (AOA 134); Kzk. 19th c. **Quttu-bay** [Куттубай] (AOP 26), *EN:* Turk.? / Yürük? 1576 **Qutlular** [قطلولر / Kutlular], an ethnic group (cemaat)

(Gökçen 50); Kzk. 18th c. - 19th c. **Qutti-bay-biy** [Куттыбай-бий], a clan (Tynyšp. 65, 71). ❖ 'Happy, lucky, blessed, successful' cf. Türk *qutluγ* 'glücklich' (Radl. II, 996), Karakh., Uyg. *qutluγ* 'счастливый, приносящий счастье, успех, удачу; благословенный, святой' (DTS), Uyg. *qutluq* 'glücklich' (Radl. II, 996), *qutluγ* 'glücklich' TMEN III, No. 1568, Uyg. *χutluγ* 'mesut, kutlu, uğurlu' (US), Kuman, Crm., Turk. *qutlu* 'glücklich' (Radl. II, 996), Kzk. *quttu* 'id.' (Radl. II, 997), Kzk. *qŭttï* 'счастливый, благодатный' (KzRS). – A part of the title of the Uyghur Khans (Müller, Pfahl. 26). In certain cases it comes before personal names as an attribute. Cf. also Ahmarov: IOAIÊK XIX, 140-141, Németh, HMK 14, A. Bombaci, Qutluγ bolzun! A Contribution to the History of the Concept of 'Fortune' among the Turks (Part One): UAJb. XXXVI (1965), pp. 284-291, (Part Two) XXXVII (1966), pp. 13-43. In Baskakov's interpretation *Qutlï-gül* is 'Lucky rose' (Baskakov: OSA 141). ⇨ QUT + suff. *-luγ/-luq, -lïγ/-lï*. See also **AY-QUTLUГ, ALP-QUTLUГ, ANA-QUTLU, BAY-QUTLÏ, BU-QUTLUГ, ĴAN-QUTTÏ, ĴAR-QUTLU, EDGÜ-QUTLUГ, İL-QUTLUГ, YOL-QUTLUГ OLĴAY-QUTLUГ, SALÏ-QUTLUГ, TAPMÏŠ-XUTLUГ, TEMİR-QUTLUQ, TÜMÄN-QUTLUГ.**

QUTLUГ-ARSLAN Uyg. 1274 **Qutluγ-arslan / Qutluq-arslan** [Kutluk Arslan] (Chwol., Syr.-nest. 18); Uyg. 1307 **Qutluγ-arslan / Qutluq-arslan** [Kutluk Arslan] (Chwol., Syr.-nest. (NF) 16); Uyg. 1325 **Qutluγ-arslan / Qutluq-arslan** [Kutluk Arslan] (Chwol., Syr.-nest. 65). ⇨ QUTLUГ + ARSLAN.

QUTLUГ-AŠA Uyg. 1308 **Qutluγ-aša / Qutluq-aša** [Kutluk-Aša-Koštanz], fem. (Chwol., Syr.-nest.52-53). ⇨ QUTLUГ + AŠA.

QUTLUГ-AŠÏ Uyg. 1338 **Qutluγ-ašï / Qutluq-aši** [Kutluk Aschi], fem. (Chwol., Syr.-nest. (NF) 31). ⇨ QUTLUГ + AŠÏ.

QUTLUГ-BAГA Uyg. **Qutluγ-baγa-tarqan-ügä** [Kutluγ-Baγa-Tarqan-Ügä], „a title" (Ramstedt, Uig. 4-6). ⇨ QUTLUГ + BAГA II.

QUTLUГ-BAYUTMÏŠ Uyg. 8th c. - 12th c. **Qutluγ-bayutmïš** [Qutluγ bayutmïš] (Müller, Pfahl. 10, DTS).

QUTLUГ-BARS Maml. 14th c. **Qutlu-bars** [قتلوبرس / Kuṭlubars] (Tarĵ/Houtsma 61, Tarĵ/Toparlı 41); Uyg. 8th c. **Qutluγ-bars** (Müller, Pfahl. 24); Selj. **Qutluγ-bars** [مظفرالدين قتلغ برس] (Bondārī 237); Selj. 1155 **Qutluγ-bars** [Kutluğ Bars] (Ahbar 92, 93). ⇨ QUTLUГ + BARS.

QUTLUГ-BİLGÄ Uyg. **Qutluγ-bilgä-χaγan** [Qutluγ bilgä χaγan] (Müller: SBAW (1909), 729); Uyg. 1332 **Qutluq-bilgä** [Kutluk Pilga], fem. (Chwol., Syr.-nest. (NF) 28). ⇨ QUTLUT + BİLGÄ.

QUTLUГ-BUQA Kipch. 1298 **Qutlu-buγa** [قطلو بغا], a chieftain, Noγay's follower (Baybars/Tizeng. I, 88,

111); Tat.(GH) **Qutlu-buγa** [Кутлубуга], Toqtamïš's envoy to Yagaylu (Smirnov, Krym. 160); Maml. 1229 **Qutlu-buγa** [سيف الدين قطلو بغا المغربى], an emir (Dawād. 310, 314); Maml. 1320 **Qutlu-buγa** [قطلوبغا البغدادى], envoy to (Desht-i) Kipchak (Tizeng. I, 257, 266 /after Al-Malik An-Nāsir/); Maml. 1323 **Qutlu-buγa** [قطلوبغا طاز], an emir (Dawād. 31); Maml. 1332 **Qutlu-buγa** [قطلوبغا الطويل], an emir (Dawād. 368); Maml. 1367/68 **Qutlu-buγa** [سيف الدين قطلو بغا نظر الحرمين] (Berchem, Jér. II, 134); Tat.(GH) 1351 **Qutlu-buγa-inaq** [Кутлубуга Инакъ], one of the four persons who - according to tradition - are the rulers in Özbek's land; the governor of Janï-bek-qan (PSRL? 338, 348); Uyg. **Qutluγ-buγa** [Kutluġ Buġa] (EUTS); Mo.? **Qutluγ-buqa** [Кутлуг-Бука] (RaD I/1, 142); Mo.? **Qutluγ-buqa** (RaD/Ber. I, 95); Uyg. 12th c. - 14th c. **Qutluγ-buqa** (Radl., USp. 95, DTS); Uyg. 13th c. **Qutluq-buqa** [قتلوقبوقا], „Körgüz's" son in Iran (RaD/Ber. I, 117); Chag. **Qutluq-buqa** [قتلوق بوقا], a Shaybanid (Šejb. XLIX). ✧ 'Happy/lucky bull' (Sauvaget 53: heureux taureau); 'Lucky bull'; 'Bull having vitality' (Blagova 1997, 706). ⇨ QUTLUГ + BUQA.

QUTLUГ-BÜRT Uyg. 12th c. - 14th c. **Qutluγ-bürt / Qutluγ-bört** [Qutluγ Bürt / Kutluġ Bürt / qutluγ bört] (Radl., USp. 212, 253, EUTS, DTS). ✧ 'Blessed/happy-?'. ⇨ QUTLUГ + BÖRT.

QUTLUГ-ÏNANČ Selj. 1192, 1195 **Qutluγ-ïnanč / İnanč-qutluγ** [قتلغ اينانج], Muhammad ibn İl-degiz atabek's son died in 1195, mentioned in the text as *Qutluγ-inanč* or *İnanč-qutluγ*, in Zambaur as *Qutluγ-inanč* (Juwaynī II, 28-31, etc., Qazw. 475-478, 837). ⇨ QUTLUГ + ÏNANČ.

QUTLUГ-YUL see QUTLU-YUL

QUTLUГ-QABA Oghuz/Trkm.? **Qutluγ-qaba** [قتلق قبا / Qoutlouq Qabâ], from the Aq-mañγït tribe, İdikey's grand-father (Abulg./Desm. 171). ⇨ QUTLUГ + QABA.

QUTLUГ-QADÄM Bashk. 1760 **Qutlu-qadäm** [Кутлукадям Аитов] (MIB IV/2, 33); Chag. 16th c. **Qutluq-qadam** [Кутлук Кадам] (Ivanov 133, 151, 259); Kirg. 19th c. **Quttu-qadam** [Куттукаданъ] (Potanin II, 5). ✧ 'Happy/lucky step/chance' cf. Crm., Turk. *qadām* 'der Fuss; die Ankunft; das Glück; der Verdienst' (Radl. II, 317), Kzk. *qadam* 'der (langsame) Schritt' (Radl. II, 316). ⇨ QUTLUГ.

QUTLUГ-QAYA Tat.(GH) **Qutlu-γaya-bï** [Кутлуβaja бï], Toqtamïš-qan's (1382-1397) war-hostage (saqlau; Kriegsgeissel) in a tale (Proben VII, 99); Crm. **Qutlu-qaya / Qutlu-γaya-bï** [Кутлуβaja бï / Кутлу Kaja], Ädigä's father in a legend (Proben VII, 158, 162); Uyg. 12th c. - 14th c. **Qutluγ-qaya** (Radl., USp. 122); Uyg. 12th c. - 14th c. **Qutluγ-qaya** [Qutluγ Qaya] (Radl.

USp. 124). ⇨ QUTLUГ + QAYA.

QUTLUГ-MUXAMMED Tat.(Mish.) **Qutluγ-muχamet** [Kutlug-Muχamet] (IOAIÊK XIX, 140); Uzb. 1770 **Qutluγ-muχammed-inaq** [Кутлуг Мухаммед-инак] (MIT II, 343, 362, 378, 390, 393, 394, 423, 425, 428); Uzb. 1804 **Qutluγ-muχammed-bek** [Кутлуг Мумаммед-бек] (MIT II, 365, 366, 376). ⇨ QUTLUГ + MUXAMMED.

QUTLUГ-MURAD see QUTLUГ-MURAT

QUTLUГ-MURAT Kkalp. 20th c. **Qutlï-mïrat** [Кутлымырат] (KkRS 774); Uzb. 1851 **Qutlu-mrad-biy** (<Qutlu-murad-biy) [Кутлумрадъ-Бий], from Khiva (ZIRGO V, 107); Kkalp. 20th c. **Qutlu-murat** [Кутлумурат] (KkRS 774); Trkm. 1817 **Qutluγ-murad-bek** [Кутлуг Мурад-бек] (MIT II, 400, 412); Trkm. 1838 **Qutluγ-murad-yüzbašï** [Кутлуг Мурад-юзбаши] (MIT II, 473); Uzb. 1768/69 **Qutluγ-murad-inaq** [Кутлуг Мурад-инак] (MIT II, 341, 410, 412-414, 545 etc.); Uzb. 1838 **Qutluγ-murad-biy** [Кутлуг Мурад-бий], from the Qoñγrat tribe (MIT II, 473, 555, 573, 575, 584); Uzb. 1855 **Qutluγ-murat-χan** [Кутлуг Мурад-хан] (MIT II, 551-553, 556, 558, 562, 564, 567). ⇨ QUTLUГ + MURAT.

QUTLUГ-SİÑГUR Uyg. **Qutluγ-siñγur** [Qutluγ Sïngγur], Yöläk's son, aged 10, Qutluγ Sïngγur's younger brother (Zieme, Mat. I, 80); Uyg. 8th c. **Qutluγ-sïñγur** [ïγaččï Qutluγ šingγur] (Müller, Pfahl. 24). ⇨ QUTLUГ + SOÑQUR?

QUTLUГ-SİÑГUR see QUTLUГ-SİÑГUR

QUTLUГ-TAYAQ Uyg. **Qutluγ-tayaq** [Kutluġ Tayak] (EUTS). ⇨ QUTLUГ + TAYAQ.

QUTLUГ-TÄÑRİ Uyg. **Qutluγ-täñri** [Kutluġ Tängri] (EUTS). ⇨ QUTLUГ + TÄÑRİ.

QUTLUГ-TEMİR Khorezm. 14th c. **Qutlu-demür** [قطلو دمور / Kothloûdomoûr], emir of Özbek (M. Uzbec) in Khorezm (Ibn Bat. III, 4); Crm. 14th c. **Qutlu-demür** [قطلو دمور / Cothloûdomoûr], son of the governor of Eski-Qïrïm Tolaq-temür (Toloctomoûr) (Ibn Bat. II, 362); Khorezm. 14th c. **Qutlu-domur** [قطلو دُمُور / Kothloûdomoûr] (Ibn Bat. II, 73); Oghuz/Trkm. 13th c. **Qutlu-temür / Qutlï-temür** [قوتلى تيمور / Кутлу-Тимур], Yomut's son (Abulg./Kon. 1240, 1245); Tat.(GH) 1321 **Qutluγ-temir** [قطلنتمر / Кутлуктемиръ], governor of the Kipchak Özbeg Khan (Duqmaq/Tizeng. I, 321, 328); Uyg. 12th c. - 14th c. **Qutluγ-temür** [Qutluγ Tämür] (Le Coq, Urkunden 458); Uyg. 12th c. - 14th c. **Qutluγ-temür** [Qutluγ Tämür / Kutluġ Tämür] (Radl., USp. 100-101, DTS, EUTS); Kipch. 1262 **Qutluγ-temür** [قتلغ تمور / Кутлугтимуръ] (Baybars/Tizeng. I, 77, 99); Khorezm./Chag. 1391 **Qutluγ-temür** [قتلغ تيمور / Kutluγ Timür], one of Temür's lieutenants (Arabš. I, 276 etc.); Uyg. 12th c. - 14th c. **Qutluγ-temür /**

Qutluɣ-temir [Qutluɣ Tämür (Tämir)] (Radl., USp. 21-23, Le Coq, Urkunden 458-59); Chag. 16th c. **Qutluq-teymür?** / **Qutluq-temür** [Кутлук Теймур] (Ivanov 245); Maml. 1309 **Qutluq-temir** / **Qutluɣ-temür?** [سيف الدين قطلقتـمـر], an cmir (Dawād. 195, 207, 216); Maml. 1332 **Qutluq-temir** / **Qutluɣ-temür?** [قطلقتـمـر], a bearer of arms (Dawād.367); Maml. 14th c. **Qutluq-temür** [قطلـتـمـُر] (Sauvaget 53). ✦ 'Happy-Iron' (Blagova 1997, 712). ⇨ QUTLUΓ + TEMİR.

QUTLUΓ-TEMÜR-TAYAQ Uyg. **Qutluɣ-temür-tayaq** [Kutluk Temür Tajak] (?); Uyg. 12th c. - 14th c. **Qutluɣ-temür-tayaq** [Qutluɣ Tämür Tayaq] (Radl., USp. 98-99, 100-101, DTS). ✦ 'Happy-Iron-Support/shoulder' (Blagova 1997, 713). ⇨ QUTLUΓ + TEMİR + TAYAQ.

QUTLUΓ-TUΓMÏŠ Uyg. 8th c. **Qutluɣ-tuɣmïš-tigin** [Qutluɣ tuɣmïš tigin] (Müller, Pfahl. 23). ⇨ QUTLUΓ + TUΓMÏŠ.

QUTLUΓ-TURMÏŠ Uyg. 12th c. - 14th c. **Qutluɣ-turmïš, Qadïr-čigši, Časañ-tuz?** [Qutluɣ Turmïš Qadïr Čigši Časangtuz / Kutluġ Turmïš], perhaps names of different persons (cf. EUTS pp. 189, 277, 303) (Radl., USp. 155, EUTS). ⇨ QUTLUΓ + TURMÏŠ.

QUTLUΓ-TÜRK'ĀN-AΓA see TERKEN

QUTLUΓ-ZAMAN Bashk. 1787 **Qutlu-zaman** [Якмаметъ Кутлузаманов] (MIB V, 203); Crm. 15th c. **Qutluq-zeman** [Qoutlouq-Zémân], son of the Crimean Khan Haji Girey I (1426/1430-1466) (Abulg./Desm. 187). ⇨ QUTLUΓ + ZAMAN.

QUTLUΓXAN Khorezm.? 1328 **Qutluɣχan** [قتلغ حـان], Qutbeddīn Shah's daughter, Mubārizuddīn Muhammad's wife (Qazw. 625). ⇨ QUTLUΓ + suff. -χan(1).

QUTLUX-QÏZ-TOLUN Uyg. 762 **Qutluχ-qïz-tolun**, fem. (Mahrnāmag 15). ⇨ QUTLUΓ + QÏZ + TOLUN.

QUTLUKEY Bashk. 1732 **Qutlukey-mulla** [Кутлукей-мулла] (MIB III, 298). ⇨ QUTLUΓ + dim. suff. -key.

QUTLUQ see QUTLUΓ

QUTLUQ-BARAQ Selj. 12th c. **Qutluq-baraq** [قتلق بـراق] (Muh. Ibrahim 138, 200, 201). ⇨ QUTLUΓ + BARAQ.

QUTLUQ-BİLGÄ see QUTLUΓ-BİLGÄ

QUTLUQ-BUQA see QUTLUΓ-BUQA

QUTLUQ-QADAM see QUTLUΓ-QADÄM

QUTLUQ-TEMİŠ Maml. **Qutluq-temiš (Qutluq-temir?)** [Saifaddīn Qutluqtemiš], Nāsir's silāχdar (bearer of arms) (Björkm. 160). ⇨ QUTLUΓ + TEMİŠ.

QUTLUQ-TEMÜR see QUTLUΓ-TEMİR

QUTLUQAY Tat.(Mish.) **Qutluqay** [Кутлукай] (IOAIÊK XIX, 140). ⇨ QUTLUΓ + dim. suff. -qay.

QUTLUQČA Selj.? **Qutluǰa** [قتلوجـه / قتلوجـا]

[بهاالـدين] (Ibn Bībī III, 266, IV, 106, IV, 115); Turk. 15th c. **Qutluǰa** [Mustafa veled-i Kutluca] (Gökb., Ed. 77); Maml. 1357 **Qutluqča** [قطلوقـچاه], a bearer of arms (Iyās I, 200-204); Maml. 1377/78 **Qutluqča** [قطلوتـچاه] (Iyās I, 239). ✦ I. 'Lucky little (child)' (Sauvaget 53: PN *Qutluqča* is dim. of *Qutluq*); II. 'Luckily'? (Erol II). ⇨ KUTLUΓ + dim. suff. -ja.

QUTLUMBET Kzk. **Kötlömbet[!** / Kötlömbät] (IOAIÊK XIX, 140); Kzk. 19th c. **Qottïmbet** [Коттымбетъ] (AOO 50); Kzk. 19th c. **Qottumbet** [Коттумбетъ] (AOO 30); Kzk. 19th c. **Qotumbet** [Котумбетъ] (AOK 10); Bashk. 1709 **Qutlumbet** [Бикмет Кутлумбетев] (MIB I, 264); Bashk. 1734 **Qutlumbet** [Кутлумбетевъ] (Vel.-Zern., Bašk. 10); Bashk. 1735 **Qutlumbet** [Кутлумбеть Юлмашевъ], a tarχan (Vel.-Zern., Bašk. 18); Bashk. 1737 **Qutlumbet** [Кутлумбеть] (MIB III, 357); Kzk. 18th c. **Qutlumbet** [Кутлунбеть Коштаевъ] (Nepljuev 137-38); Kzk. 1822 **Qutlumbet** [Кутлумбетъ Даукаринъ] (TOUAK XXIV, 122). ⇨ QUT + suff. -lu-tï + suffixoid -mbet.

QUTLUMET Tat.(Mish.) **Qutlumet** [Кутлумет] (IOAIÊK XIX, 140); Bashk. 1735 **Qutlumet** [Килчура Кутлуметевъ], a tarχan (Vel.-Zern., Bašk. 16). ⇨ QUTLUΓ + suff. -met.

QUTLUMÏŠ see QUTULMÏŠ

QUTLUMUŠ see QUTULMÏŠ

QUTLUŠ Tat. 1631 **Qutluš** [Кутлуш Калованов] (Miller, Ist. Sib. II, 385, 386, 391); Tat.(Mish.) **Qutluš** [Кутлуш] (IOAIÊK XIX, 140); Bashk. 1735 **Qutluš** [Кутлушъ Курмаковъ], a tarχan (Vel.-Zern., Bašk. 25); Bashk. 1766 **Qutluš** [Кутлуш Рысовъ] (MIB IV/1, 320). ✦ I. 'Happy, lucky mate, friend' (Sattarov: Qotlïiš); II. 'Happy, lucky shah'?; III. 'Happy, lucky (little fellow). ⇨ QUTLUΓ + suff. -š.

QUTMAN Kzk. 19th c. **Qutban-bay** [Кутбанбай] (SOK 178); Kirg. **Qutman** [Кутман] (Jud. 810); Kzk. 19th c. **Qutpam-bay (<Qutpan-bay)** [Кутпамбай] (SODž. 56); Kzk. 19th c. **Qutpam-bay (<Qutpan-bay)** [Кутпамбай] (SOK 128); Kzk. 19th c. **Qutpan** [Кутпанъ] (AOA 82); Kzk. 19th c. **Qutpan** [Кутпанъ] (AOP 14); Kzk. 19th c. **Qutpan** [Кутпанъ] (SOK 168); Kzk. 19th c. **Qutpan** [Кутпанъ] (SOK 304); Kzk. 19th c. **Qutpan** [Кутпанъ] (SOV 16); Kzk. 19th c. **Qutpan** [Кутпанъ] (SOV 38); Kzk. 19th c. **Qutpan-bay** [Кутпанбай] (SODž. 98); Kzk. 19th c. **Qutpan-bay** [Кутпанбай] (SOK 228); Kzk. 19th c. **Qutpan-qul** [Кутпанкуль] (SOV 118). ✦ 'Chance, luck; lucky fellow' cf. Kirg. *qutman* 'das Glück' (Radl. II, 998), Kirg. *qutman* 'id.' (Jud.), Kzk. *qutpan* 'ein Glückskind' (Radl. II, 997).

QUTMANAY Kzk. 19th c. **Qutbanay** [Тулабай Кутбанаевъ] (Grod., Pril. 105); Bashk. 1762 **Qutmanay?** / **Qut-manay?** [Шарып Кутманаев]

(MIB IV/1, 249). ⇨ **QUTMAN** + dim. suff. *-ay*.

QUTNAQ   Hak. 19th-20th c. **Qutnaq** [Кутнак] (HRS 349).

QUTPAM-BAY see **QUTMAN**

QUTPAN see **QUTMAN**

QUTRULMÏŠ   Uyg. 13th c. **Qutrulmïš** [qutrulmïš] (DTS). ✧ 'He who escaped; he who was set free; he who got rid of' cf. Uyg. *qutrul-* 'спасаться, избавляться; быть спасенным' (DTS).

QUTTU see **QUTLUÏ**

QUTTU-BAŠ   Kzk. 1820 **Quttu-baš?** [Koutoubash] (MIK IV, 355). ⇨ **QUTLUÏ** + **BAŠ**.

QUTTU-GİL   Kzk. 19th c. **Quttu-gil** [Куттугиль] (AOO 6). ⇨ **QUTLUÏ** + **KEL?**

QUTTU-QADAM see **QUTLUÏ-QADÄM**

QUTU   Kzk. 19th c. **Qotï-bay (Köti-bay?)** [Котибай] (Grod., Pril. 80); Kzk. 19th c. **Qotu-bay** [Котубай] (AOAtb. 6); Kzk. 19th c. **Qotu-bek /** [Котубекъ] (SODž. 126); Kzk. 19th c. **Qotu-bek** [Котубекъ] (SOK 132); Kzk. 19th c. **Qudu-bay** [Кудубай] (SOK 166); Kzk. 19th c. **Qutu-bay** [Кутубай] (SOK 94); *TN:* **Qutu-bay** [Кутубай], south-east of Lake Aral (Karta JAR XI). ✧ '(Gun)powder-horn' cf. Kzk. *qutu* 'das Pulverhorn' (Radl. II, 997), *qotu* 'id.' (PKRS).

QUTUČ   Tat. 1638 **Qutuč** [Кутучко] (Miller, Ist. Sib. II, 448, 449); Tat. 1675 **Qutuč** [Кутючко] (Kungursk. akty 29). ⇨ **QUTU** + dim. suff. *-č*.

QUTUÏAY   Tat.(Sib.) 1582 **Qutuɣay** [Кутугай], Küčürn's follower, the envoy to Tarɣan-murza (Sib. Let. 321-22); Kzk. 19th c. **Qutuɣay** [Кутугай] (AOK 42). ⇨ **QUTU** / **QUTUQ** + dim. suff. *-ɣay* / *-ay?* See also **QOTÏÏAY**.

QUTUÏAN   Khorezm. / Tat.(GH) 1282 **Qutuɣan** [قطغان / Кутуганъ], Meñgü-temir's son (Baybars/Tizeng. I, 82, 104).

QUTUÏMÏŠ   Oghuz 1030/31 **Qutuɣmïš(-Jamedār)** [Кутугмыш-джамедар], a cloth-supervisor, commander of the army (MIT I, 234).

QUTUY   Tat. 20th c. **Qotïy** [Котыев] (Sattarov); Tat. 20th c. **Qutay / Kotay** [Котаев (Кутаев)] (Sattarov); Tat. 20th c. **Qutïy** [Кутыев] (Sattarov); Bashk. 1728 **Qutuy** [Акметь Кутуев] (MIB III, 251); Bashk. 1735 **Qutuy** [Кусяпъ Кутуевъ], a tarɣan (Vel.-Zern., Bašk. 14); Bashk. 1745 **Qutuy** [Ибраш Кутуев] (MIB III, 548); Bashk. 1748 **Qutuy** [Ибрагимъ Кутуевъ], a captain (Nepljuev 437); Bashk. 1754 **Qutuy** [Смакай Кутуев] (MIB IV/1, 83); Bashk. 1764 **Qutuy** [Кутуй Юмакаев] (MIB IV/1, 287); Bashk. 1767 **Qutuy** [Мансур Кутуев] (MIB IV/1, 324). ✧ 'Happy, lucky' (Sattarov).

QUTUYUQ   Yak. **Qutuyuq** [Кутуйук] (Pek.).

QUTUQ   Tat. 20th c. **Qotïq / Qutuq** [Котыков (Кутуков)] (Sattarov); Kzk. 19th c. **Qutïq-bay** [Кутикъ-бай] (Grod., Pril. 173); Uyg. 12th c. -14th c.

Qutuq [Kutuk], „der Scholasticus" (Chwol., Syr.-nest. 104); Uyg. 12th c. -14th c. **Qutuq** [Kutuk], fem. (Chwol., Syr.-nest. 104); Uyg. 1286 **Qutuq** [Kutuk], „(der Greise) Kirchenvisitator" (Chwol., Syr.-nest. 30); Uyg. 1313 **Qutuq** [Kutuk], fem. (Chwol., Syr.-nest. (NF) 19); Uyg. 1316 **Qutuq** [Kutuk] (Chwol., Syr.-nest. (NF) 21); Chag. **Qutuq** [قوقوق] (Šejb. LI, LXXVIII); Tat. 1637 **Qutuq** [Кутук Кудамышев] (Miller, Ist. Sib. II, 435, 443, 444); Tat. 1695 **Qutuq** [Кутук Кудамышев] (MIB I, 90); Tat. 1706 **Qutuq** [Кутюк] (MIB III, 19); Bashk. 1740 **Qutuq** [Кутук] (MIB I, 397); Bashk. 1751 **Qutuq** [Бурангул Кутуков] (MIB IV/1, 34); Bashk. 1756 **Qutuq** [Кутук Девлетенов] (MIB IV/1, 106); Bashk. 1756 **Qutuq** [Кутук Ямяшев] (MIB IV/1, 111); Bashk. 1756 **Qutuq** [Кутук Тевлетелиев] (MIB IV/1, 123); Bashk. 1770 **Qutuq** [Зюбеир Кутюков] (MIB IV/1, 347); Bashk. 1788 **Qutuq** [Суяргул (Сюяргул) Кутуков] (MIB V, 233); Kzk. 19th c. **Qutuq** [Кутукъ] (AOA 118); Kzk. 19th c. **Qutuq** [Кутукъ] (SOK 214); Nog.? 1614 **Qutuq** [Кутукъ Янараслановъ], a murza (AI III, 23, 411); Uyg. 1301 **Qutuq-χatun** [Kutuk Chatun], fem. (Chwol., Syr.-nest. 44). ✧ 'Luck, chance' (Sattarov). ⇨ **QUT** + dim. suff. *-uq?*

QUTUQ-MÄÑÜ   Uyg. 13th c. -14th c. **Qutuq-mäñü** [Kutuk Magnu] (Chwol., Syr.-nest. (NF) 48). ⇨ **QUTUQ** + **MEÑGÜ**.

QUTUQAS   Bashk. 1754 **Qutuqas** [Кутукась] (MIB IV/1, 83).

QUTULDÏ   Kzk. 19th c. **Qutuldï** [Джанъ Туганъ Кутулдіевъ] (Grod., Pril. 114). ✧ 'He/she got free; escaped' cf. Kuman, Crm., Kar., Kzk. *qutul-* 'frei werden, von etwas freikommen, entfliehen, sich befreien' (Radl. II, 994). See also **QUTULMÏŠ**.

QUTULMÏŠ   Selj. 1049, 1064, 1077 **Qutulmïš / Qutlumïš / Qutlumuš?** [قتُلمش / قتلمش / قطلومش / Κουτουλμούς / Kutulmisch / Melik Kutlumuş / Cotlumisch / Kutalmış / Кутулмыш], a prince (in Armenia?), Arslan Israil's son, Seljuk (Selčük)'s grandson, Toɣrïl-bey's nephew; Köprülü reads Kutalmış in Anīs al-Qulūb: Belleten VII, 475, 502-503 (Weil, Chalif. III, 88, Abulfidā III, 250-53, Rāwandī 92, 104, Bondārī 12, 13, 28, Ahbar 3, 12, 21, 22, 136, Byz. Turc. 171, MIT I, 352, 355, 463, F. Köprülü, Anīs al-Qulūb: Belleten VII, 475, 502-503). ✧ 'He/she got free; escaped' cf. Kuman, Crm., Kar., Kzk. *qutul-* 'frei werden, von etwas freikommen, entfliehen, sich befreien' (Radl. II, 994). See also **QUTULDÏ**.

QUTUM   Kzk. 19th c. **Qotum-bay** [Котумбай] (SOK 262); Kzk. 19th c. **Qotum-bay** [Котумбай] (AOO 18); Tat.(Sib.) 1632 **Qutum** [Кутум Баучанов] (Miller, Ist. Sib. II, 391); Tat.(Tob.) 1631 **Qutum** [Кутум Байчанов] (Miller, Ist. Sib. II, 385, 386); Bashk. 1695 **Qutum** [Кутум Аксакалов] (MIB I, 90); Kzk. 19th c.

Qutum [Кутумъ] (SOK 150); Kzk. 19th c. **Qutum** [Кутумъ] (SOV 148); Nog.? 1654 **Qutum** [Кутумовъ] (AI IV, 211); Kzk. 19th c. **Qutum-bay** [Кутумбаевъ] (AUK 585); Nog.? **Qutum-murza** [Кутум-мурза] (Žirm., Epos 431). ✧ I. 'My chance, my life'; II. 'My gun-powder-horn'? ⇨ **QUT / QUTU?** + suff. *-um / -m*.

QUTUMAN Kzk. 19th c. **Qutuman** [Кутуманъ] (SOK 182).

QUTUMBET Bashk. 1735 **Qutumbet** [Кузякъ Кутумбетевъ], a tarχan (Vel.-Zern., Bašk. 21); Kzk. 19th c. **Qutumbet** [Кутумбетъ] (SODž. 156). ⇨ **QUT? / QUTUM?** + suff. *-umbet / -bet*. See also **QUTLUMBET**.

QUTUNAČQA Tat.(Sib.) 1661 **Qutunačqa** (<**Qutunaq?** / **Qutunay**) [Кутуначка Купердин] (Miller, Ist. Sib. II, 546).

QUTUNAY Kirg. **Qutunay** [Кутунаi], Manas' comrade-in-arms (Proben V, 40 /41/).

QUTUR Maml. **Qudur?** (**Quduz?**) [سلطان قودور], the same as Qutuz (1259-1260), the sultan of Egypt (Qazw. 580); Kzk. 19th c. **Qudur-bay / Qudor-bay?** [Кудорбай] (SOV 44); Bashk. 1740 **Qutur-bay** [Кутур-бай] (MIB I, 378); Bashk. 1787 **Qutur-bay** [Кутурбай Ялмаметев] (MIB V, 203); Uyg. 1337 **Qutur-tärim** [Kutur-Tarim], fem. (Chwol., Syr.-nest. 79); Uyg.? **Qutur-tegin** [قوتر تکین] (Ǧuwaynī I, 41, 42). ✧ I. 'Rage, be mad' cf. Alt., Hak. *qudur-* 'wahnsinnig werden, rasen, wüthen' (Radl. II, 10003); II. 'A kind of wild animal (cat?); deer, stag' cf. Uyg., Chag. *qudur* 'ein wildes Thier (eine wilde Katze)' (Radl. II, 1003), Uyg. *qutur* 'благородный олень, марал (?), як (?)' (DTS); III. 'Fat; ill, weak' cf. Chag. *qutur* 'fett, dick, schwach, krank' (Radl. II, 994).

QUTUR-BAŠ Kzk. 1803 **Qutur-baš** [Кутурбаш], chief of the Ǧaγalbaylï tribe of the Little Horde (Kiši Žüz) (Sib. Vest. IX, 123, MIK IV, 516); Kzk. 1820 **Qutur-baš** [Кутурбаш] (Sib. Vest. IX, 123). ✧ 'Sick head; weak head'. ⇨ **QUTUR + BAŠ.**

QUTURΓA Yak. 1640 **Quturγa** [Кутурга], a prince (DAI II, 241).

QUTUŠ Bashk. 20th c. **Qotoš** [Котош / Кутуш] (Kusimova); Bashk. 1776 **Qušay** [Кутуш Кушаев] (MIB V, 43, 44, 45); Tat. 1706 **Qutuš** [Ижбулатъ Кутюшевъ] (Kurdjumov 342); Bashk. 1664 **Qutuš** [Кутушко Тинбаев] (MIB I, 192); Bashk. 1709 **Qutuš** [Кусяк Кутушев] (MIB III, 49); Bashk. 1751 **Qutuš** [Байряш Кутушев] (MIB IV/1, 34); Bashk. 1770 **Qutuš** [Кутуш Унгаров] (MIB IV/1, 347); Bashk. 1777 **Qutuš** [Кутуш Муртазин] (MIB V, 65); Bashk. 1778 **Qutuš** [Умитей (Умютей) Кутушев] (MIB V, 76, 97); Bashk. 1779 **Qutuš** [Умитбай (Уметбай) Кутушев] (MIB V, 101, 102, 245, 284, 327); Uzb.? 1644, 1645 **Qutuš-batïr** [Кутушъ / Кутушъ-Батыръ], a carrier (messenger) (AI III, 500, IV, 44); Trkm. 1841 **Qutuš-meχrem** [Кутуш-мехрем] (MIT II, 480). ✧ 'Happy, lucky mate, friend' (Kusimova). ⇨ **QUT + EŠ.**

QUTUZ Khorezm. / Maml. 1254, 1259 **Qotuz, Qutuz** [المظفر قُطُز / سيفالدين / المظفر قطز / قوتوز / Kotoz / Kotouz / Kōtâz / Kutuz, Kûtûz (Mamlucorum Rex)], nephew of the Khorezmshah Ǧelāleddīn Meñgüberdi (1220-1231), emir, the later sultan of Egypt, al-Muzaffar Kutuz (1259-1260) who was sold to be a mamluk from Mongol captivity (Abulfidā IV, 536-37, Abulfidā/Ed. I, 135-144, Abulfar./Budge I, 416, 437, Abulfar. Or. (325, 349, 351) 497, Ibn Šaddād, Alep 27, Sīrat 82); Uyg. 13th c. -14th c. **Quduz** [Kuduz] (Chwol., Syr.-nest. (NF) 47); Selj. **Quduz** [قوذوز / قودوز / Koudouz], an atabek (RaD/Quatrem. 344-345); Kipch. 13th c. **Quduz-χan?** / **Qotoz-χan?** / **Qutuz-χan?** [Hou-t'ou-sseu-han], a chief of a Kipchak (Qañlï?) tribe subordinated to the Mongols (Pelliot: JA XI (S. T. XV), 161); Bashk. 1754 **Qutus** [Мурсалым Кутусев] (MIB IV/1, 87); Maml. 1281 **Qutuz** [Seïfeddin Koutouz- Mansouri] (Makrīzī III, 44); Maml. 1332 **Qutuz** [قطز], an emir-i aχor (master of the horse) (Dawād. 366); Maml. 1332 **Qutuz** [قطز ساطلمش], an emir (Dawād. 367); Maml. 1332 **Qutuz** [قطز], an emir (Dawād. 368); Maml. 14th c. **Qutuz** [قُطُز] (Sauvaget 53); Türk 750 **Qutuz-uruñu** [Qutuz uruŋu / Qutuz Uruñu] (Thomsen, Stein 186, 188, DTS, ETY II, 65). ✧ I. 'Rabid, raging' cf. Karakh. *qutuz* 'бешеный' (DTS), Chag. *qutuz* 'ein toller Hund' (Radl. II, 994); II. 'A kind of wild animal, deer?, stag?' (Sauvaget 53: une des formes du nom du *yak*), cf. Karakh., Uyg. *qutuz* 'благородный олень, марал (?), як (?)' (DTS).

QUWAL Kzk. 19th c. **Quwal-bay** [Куалбай] (SOK 119).

QUWAN Kzk. 19th c. **Quwam-bay** (<**Quwan-bay**) [Куамбай] (SOK 180); Kzk. 19th c. **Quwan** [Куанъ] (AOA 82); Kzk. 19th c. **Quwan** [Куанъ] (AOO 18); Kzk. 19th c. **Quwan-bay** [Куванбай] (Grod., Pril. 23); Uzb. 19th c. **Quwan-bay** [Шаука Куванбаевъ] (SKSO III, 174); Uzb. 20th c. **Quwân** [Кувон] (Begmatov 1984, 207); Uzb. 20th c. **Quwân-bây** [Кувонбой] (Begmatov 1984, 207); Uzb. 20th c. **Quwân-ǰân** [Кувонжон] (Begmatov 1984, 207). ✧ 'Be glad! Be happy!' cf. Tat. *quwan-* 'sich freuen, fröhlich sein, sich über Etwas freuen, sich den Vergnügen hingeben' (Radl. II, 1040), Kzk. *quvan(uv)* 'sevinmek, memnun olmak' (KzTS), Uzb. *quwân-* 'радоваться, веселиться' (UzbRS). See also **KİLÄN, SEVİN.**

QUWAN-DOΓDÏ Trkm. 19th c. **Quwan-doγdï?** [Куандагдыевъ] (Ščeglov I, 356). ⇨ **QUWAN + TOΓDÏ.**

QUWANČ Trkm. 20th c. **Γuvanč** [Guvanč] (Zaj. 1971,

328); Trkm. 20th c. **Ḡuvanč** [Куванч] (TrkmRS 206); Kkalp. 1821 **Quwanč** [Куванч] (MIKk. 126); Kkalp. 1827 **Quwanč-behadïr** [Куванч бехадыр], from the Qolïdaɣlï clan (MIKk. 133); Kkalp. 1822 **Quwanč-biy** [Куванч бий] (MIKk. 127); Trkm. 1804 **Quwanïč-sufi** [Куваныч-суфи (векиль)], from the Yomut tribe (MIT II, 361, 370, 376); Kzk. 19th c. **Quwanïs-pek** [Куаныспекъ] (SOK 40); Kzk. 1817 **Quwanïš** [قۇانچ / Куаныш] (MIK IV, 311); Kzk. 19th c. **Quwanïš** [Куанышъ] (AOAtb. 18); Kzk. 19th c. **Quwanïš** [Куанышъ] (AOK 46); Kkalp. 20th c. **Quwanïš** [Куўаныш] (KkRS 774); Kzk. 19th c. **Quwanïš-bay** [Куаныш бай] (AOAtb. 58); Kkalp. 20th c. **Quwanïš-bay** [Куўанышбай] (KkRS 774); Kkalp. 20th c. **Quwanïš-bek** [Куўанышбек] (KkRS 774); Kzk. 19th c. **Quwanïš-pay** [Куанышпай] (SOV 12); Kzk. 19th c. **Quwanïš-pek** [Куанышпекъ] (AOAtb. 62). ✧ 'Joy, pleasure' cf. Tat. *quwanč* 'die Freude, Fröhlichkeit' (Radl. II, 1040), Kkalp. *quwanïš* 'id.' (KkRS), Kzk. *quwanïš* 'id.' (KzRS), Trkm. *ɣuvanč* 'гордость, радость' (TrkmRS).

QUWANČÏ Trkm. 1879 **Quwančï** [Куванчи] (Grod., Vojna IV, 109). ✧ 'Pride, joy'? ⇨ **QUWANČ**.

QUWANJUQ Kzk. 19th c. **Quwanjuq-bay** [Кувэнджукбай] (Grod., Pril. 131). ⇨ **QUWAN** + dim. suff. *-juq*.

QUWANDAY see **QUWANTAY**

QUWANDÏQ Kzk. 1846 **Quwandïq** [Кувандык Бутбаев] (MKOP 86); Kzk. 19th c. **Quwandïq** [Куандыкъ] (AOAtb. 38); Kzk. 19th c. **Quwandïq** [Куандыкъ] (AOK 34); Kzk. 19th c. **Quwandïq** [Куандыковъ] (AOK 98); Kzk. 19th c. **Quwandïq** [Куандыкъ] (AOO 58); Kzk. 19th c. **Quwandïq** [Куандыкъ] (AOP 34); Kzk. 19th c. **Quwandïq** [Кувэндыкъ] (Pam. kn. Turg. 68); Kzk. 19th c. **Quwandïq** [Байбута Кувандыковъ] (SKSO III, 10); Uzb. 19th c. **Quwandïq** [Кувандыкъ] (SKSO III, 174, 176); Uzb. 19th c. **Quwandïq** [Ташмуратъ Кувандыковъ] (SKSO III, 188); Kzk. 19th c. **Quwandïq (Quwandaq?)** [Гюлумъ Кувандаковъ] (Grod., Pril. 110); Kzk. 19th c. **Quwanduq** [Мамирбай Кувандуковъ] (Grod., Pril. 66); Kzk. 19th c. **Quwanduq** [Кувандукъ Сагировъ] (Grod., Pril. 66); Uzb. 20th c. **Quwândïq** [Кувондик] (Begmatov 1984, 207); *TN:* **Quwandïq** [Кувандыкъ], a winter pasture (ZIRGOStat. IV). ✧ 'We were glad; we were delighted (at the birth of the child)' cf. Tat. *quwan-* 'sich freuen, fröhlich sein, sich über Etwas freuen, sich den Vergnügen hingeben' (Radl. II, 1040), Kzk. *quvan-* 'Sevinmek, memnun olmak' (KzTS).

QUWANÏŠ see **QUWANČ**

QUWANSÏN Uzb. 20th c. **Quwânsïn** [Кувонсин] (Begmatov 1984, 207). ✧ 'May he/she be glad! Let him/her be happy!'. ⇨ **QUWAN** + imp. suff. *-sïn*.

QUWANTAY Kzk. 19th c. **Quwanday** [Куандай] (SOK 168); Kzk. 19th c. **Quwantay** [Куантай] (AOO 70); Kzk. 19th c. **Quwantay** [Куантай] (AOP 94); Uzb. 20th c. **Quwântây** [Кувонтой] (Begmatov 1984, 207). ⇨ **QUWAN** + **TAY?** or suff. *-tay(1,2)*. See also **QUWANDAY**.

QUWAÑ Kzk. 19th c. **Quwañ** [Куангъ] (AOA 134); Kzk. 19th c. **Quwañ-bay** [Кувангбай] (Grod., Pril. 194). ✧ 'Parched, dried up' cf. Kzk. *quwañ* 'засушливый, выгоревший (о траве)' (KzRS).

QUWAR Kzk. 19th c. **Quwar-bay** [Куарбай] (SOK 48).

QUWAŠ Kzk. 19th c. **Quwaš** [Куашъ] (AOO 50); Kzk. 19th c. **Quwaš** [Куашъ] (SOV 158).

QUWAT Kirg. **Qubat** [Кубат] (Jud. 595); Bashk. 1735 **Quwat** [Куватъ Кочкаровъ], a tarχan (Vel.-Zern., Bašk. 16); Bashk. 1761 **Quwat** [Куват Китичев] (MIB IV/1, 209); Bashk. 1780 **Quwat** [Евкей Куватов] (MIB V, 109); Bashk. 1798 **Quwat** [Куватовъ] (PSZRI XXV, 196); Kzk. 19th c. **Quwat** [Куватъ] (SKSO VIII, 219); Kkalp. 20th c. **Quwat** [Къуват] (Bask., Kkalp. 401); Kkalp. 20th c. **Quwat** [Куўат] (KkRS 774); Uzb. 1848 **Quwat-biy** [Куватъ-бий] (Moskal'cev 34); Kzk. 19th c. **Quwat-pek** [Куатпекъ] (SOK 28). ✧ 'Strength, power' cf. Kkalp. *quwat* 'id.' (KkRS), Kar. *quwat*, Chag. *quat* (<Ar.) 'die Kraft' (Radl. II, 1041), Kirg. *qubat* 'id.' (Jud.). (<Ar.). See also **ALLA-ƔUWAT, AÑ-QUWAT, IŠ-QUWAT, ES-QUWAT, KEY-QUWAT, TÏN-KOVAT**.

QUWƔUNČA Bashk. 1784 **Quwɣunča** [Кувгунча Мандыгулов] (MIB V, 155).

QUWÏN Kzk. 1823 **Quwïn-bay** / **Qufïn-bay?** [Куфынбай Бурковъ] (TOUAK XXIV, 139).

QUWORAN Kzk. 19th c. **Quworan** [Аюка Куоранов] (Grod., Pril. 169).

QUWSUN Maml. **Quwsun** [السيفى قوصون], in an inscription, without year (Mayer 120-121); Maml. 1330 **Quwsun** [قوصون السا فى / Qûsûn Saif ad-dîn Nâsiri], an enir (Berchem 119-123); Maml. 1332 **Quwsun** [سيفالسين قوصون], an emir (Dawād. 366, 381); Maml.? 1343 **Quwsun** [سيفالسين قوصون الاتابكى], an emir, died in 1343 (Zetterst. 188, 226 etc., Iyās I, 166, 167 etc., Makrīzī, Khit. I, 307, Weil, Chalif. I, 364). ✧ 'Let him chase (his enemy)!' cf. Kuman, Alt., Crm., Kzk., Tat. *qū-* 'verfolgen, folgen' (Radl. II, 883) + suff. *-sïn*.

QUWUQ Kzk. 19th c. **Quwuq** [Кувюкъ] (AOP 98). ✧ 'Urinary bladder'? cf. Kzk. *quvıq* 'sidik torbası' (KzTS).

QUZ Uyg. **Quz** [Kuz] (EUTS); Uyg. 1339 **Quz-peg** [Kuz Peg] (Chwol., Syr.-nest. (NF) 34); *TN:* Bashk. **Quz-bay(eva)** / **Küz-bay(eva)** [Кузбаева], a lake(?) in the government (gubernija) of Ufa, north of Birsk (?).

See also **BEG-TEMİR-QUZ, MİSİR-QARA-QUZ.**

QUZ-BAQ Kzk. 19th c. **Quz-baq** (<Qozï-baq) [Тасимъ Кузбаковъ] (Grod., Pril. 108). ⇨ **QOZİ** + **BAQ.** See also **QOZİ-BAҐAR.**

QUZ-BAŠ Bashk. 1788 **Quz-baš / Küð-baš?** [Кузбаш Чураков] (MIB V, 233). ⇨ **QUZ / KÖZ / QOZİ?** + **BAŠ.**

QUZ-MAMBET Kzk. **Quz-mambet** [Кузмамбетъ] (Divaev, Šura 131). ⇨ **QUZ** + **MAMBET.**

QUZ-TAYGİNE Tuv. 19th c. **Quz-taygine** [Кузъ-тайгине], fem. (Potanin IV, 427). ⇨ **QUZ** + **TAY** + suff. *-kine / -qina.*

QUZAQ Uzb. 19th c. **Quzaq-bay** [Ишманъ Кузакбаевъ] (SKSO III, 22). ✧ 'Husk'? cf. Tat. PN *Quzaq* (Sattarov).

QUZAN Kzk. 19th c. **Quzan-bay** [Кузанбай] (AOP 62).

QUZBAZAҐAR Kzk. 1822 **Quzbazaɣar** [Кузбазагаръ] (TOUAK XXIV, 130).

QUZDAM Kzk. 19th c. **Quzdan-bay** (<Quzdam-bay) [Куздамбай] (Grod., Pril. 84).

QUZDUQ Kzk. 19th c. **Quzduq-pay** [Куздукпай] (AOA 138). ✧ 'Donkey-foal' cf. Chag. *quzduq* 'das Eselsfüllen' (Radl. II, 1022).

QUZҐAN Kzk. 19th c. **Quzɣam-bay** (<Quzɣan-bay?) [Кузгамбай] (AOP 46).

QUZҐUN Alt. 19th c. **Qusqun-alïp** [Кускун-Алып-богатырь], khan of the 30th heaven (Verb., In. 139, 152); NUyg. 19th c. **Quzɣun** [قوزعون / Kuzghun] (Le Coq, Namenl. 109). ✧ 'Crow' (Le Coq) cf. Chag., Turk., Uzb. *quzɣun* 'der Rabe' (Radl. II, 1021), Uyg., Alt., Hak. *qusqun* 'id.' (Radl. II, 1016).

QUZİ see **QOZİ**

QUZİ-YAWÏ Oghuz/Trkm. 13th c. **Quzï-yawï-χan** [قوزى ياوى حان / Кузы-Йавы-хан] (Abulg./Kon. 660, 670, 680). ⇨ **QOZİ** + **YAWÏ?**

QUZİJİ Oghuz/Trkm. 13th c. **Quzïjï-bek** [قوزيجى بيك / Кузыджы-бек], from the country of Bükdez (Bükdüz?) (Abulg./Kon. 1025-1045, 1060, 1075, 1080).

QUZÏQAY Bashk. 1740 **Quzïqay** [Мустафа Кузыкаев] (MIB I, 397). ⇨ **QOZİ** + dim. suff. *-qay.*

QUZİN Uyg. 13th c. -14th c. **Quzïn** [Kuzin], fem. (Chwol., Syr.-nest. (NF) 49).

QUZQÏZ Uyg. 1288 **Quzqïz?** [Kuzkiz] (Chwol., Syr.-nest. 34).

QUZLA-GİLDİ Bashk. 1675 **Quzla-gildi** [Кузлагилди] (MIB I, 200). ⇨ **?** + **KELDİ.**

QUZU see **QOZİ**

QUZUQ Alt. 19th-20th c. **Quzuq** [Кузук], fem. (OjrRS 212). ✧ 'Nut; cedar-nut' cf. Chag., Alt., Hak., Tat.(Sib.) *quzuq* 'die Cedernnüsse' (Radl. II, 1019), Alt. *quzuq* 'орех' (OjrRS).

QUZURUQ see **QUYRUQ**

QUZAM-BERDİ see **XOJAM-BERDİ**

QUŽAMÏŠ see **QOJAMÏŠ**

QUŽAN Kzk. 19th c. **Qužan** [Ташгулъ Кужановъ] (Grod., Pril. 169).

QUŽAŠ see **XOJAŠ**

QŪ Hak. 19th-20th c. **Qū-qat** [Kukat], fem. (Schiefner, XLV); Hak.(Sag.) 19th-20th c. **Qū-qat** [Кукат], a witch (Proben IX, 248, 325, 422); Shor 19th-20th c. **Qū-qïs**, fem. (Dyrenkova 42); Kzk. 19th c. **Qū-murza?** [Кумурза] (SOK 240). ✧ 'Swan' cf. Alt., Hak., Kzk., Tat. *qū* 'der Schwan' (Radl. II, 883), Uyg., Chag. *quɣu* 'der Schwann' (Radl. II, 898), cf. also cf. Alt. *qat* 'женщина, жена' (Verb., Sl.).

QŪ-QAT see **QŪ**

QŪČÏNČÏ Alt. 19th-20th c. **Qūčïnčï** [Куучынгы], fem. (OjrRS 212). ✧ 'Talkative, chatty (woman), babbler' (OjrRS).

QŪL-YAҐAN Kirg. **Qūl-yaɣan** [Küljagan / Кулjаӊан], one of Manas' comrades-in-arms (Proben V, 40 /41/). ✧ 'Slave-Elephant'? ⇨ **QUL** + **YAҐAN.**

L

LABÏT Yak. **Labït** [Лабыт] (Pek.). ✧ David (R.).

LAČÏN Hak.(Blt.) 19th-20th c. **Ïlačïn** [Ылачын] (Katanov, Otč. 9, Radl. III, 735); Az. **Lačin** [Лачин], two sisters in a tale Lačin and Belis (Az. Skaz. 540 ff.); Tat.(Mish.) 1755 **Lačin** [Лачин Явгостин?] (MIB IV/1, 93); Bashk. 1761 **Lačin** [Лачин Ибаков] (MIB IV/1, 208); Kzk. 19th c. **Lačin** [Карабай Лачиновъ] (Grod., Pril. 34); Kzk. 19th c. **Lačin** [Лочинъ Турдіевъ] (SKSO VIII, 221); OT (Qarluq) 1158 **Lačin-bek / Lajin-bek** [Ладжин-бек], a Qarluq chieftain (MIT I, 444); Uyg. **Lačïn** (Zieme, Mat. I, 74); Karakh.? 870 **Lačïn** [لجين / لُجَين / Laჳïn?] (Tabarī, Annal. III, 1806); Selj. **Lačïn** [محمد ا بن لاجين], nephew of Salaheddin on his mothers's side (Ibn al-Athīr: RHCHor I, 77); Selj. 12th c. **Lačïn** [نجم الـدين لاجين], governor of Hamadan (Rāwandī 345); Selj. 12th c. **Lačïn** [حسام الـدين لاجين عمر بن اقبورى] (Ibn Šaddād, Alep 45); Selj. 12th c. **Lačïn** [بن عمر بن لاجين], [حسام الـدين محمد] (Ibn Šaddād, Alep 114); Selj.? 1191 **Lačïn** [لاجين], Xisāmuddīn Maχmud's grand-father (Abulfidā IV, 114,); Khorezm.? 13th c. **Lačïn** [ابن لاجين جنترجة / Ibn Lādjin Djekardja], a Turk from Irak (Nasawī 69-75); Maml.? **Lačïn** [لاجين حنائى], an emir of Nasreddin Qabača (Juwaynī II, 148); Maml. 1259 **Lačïn** [Ladjin-Schakiri] (Makrīzī I, 83); Maml. 1260 **Lačïn** [Ladjin djemdar-Sâléhi] (Makrīzī I, 90); Maml. 1260 **Lačïn** [Husāmeddīn Lačyn al-Aïntabi], governor of Haleb (Zambaur 34, Weil, Chalif. I, 22);

Maml. 1273, 1259 **Lačïn** [لاجين الدرفيـل / Hosâm-eddin-Lâdjin Aïdemuri], „dawādār" of the sultan, better known under the byname (laqab) Derfil (Makrīzī I, 83, II, 119, Iyās I, 98); Maml. 1277 **Lačïn** [Ladjin- al-Zeïni] (Makrīzī II, 158, Weil, Chalif. I, 110); Maml. 1280 **Lačïn** [حسام الدين لاجين], Xisāmuddīn Lačïn, the governor of Damascus, identical with the emir Xisāmuddīn Qara-lačïn (1311)? (Abulfidā V, 52-3); Maml. 1293 **Lačïn** [لاجين] (Abulfidā V, 114-5); Maml. 1294 **Lačïn** [لاجين جـركس] (Iyās I, 126, Makrīzī IV, 9); Maml. 1296-1298 **Lačïn** [حسام الدين لاجين الحسامى], Sultan Lačïn's follower (Zetterst. IV, 53, 170, Weil, Chalif. I, 221, 258); Maml. 1297 **Lačïn** [الرومى حسام الدين لاجين], „Haus und Domänenminister", the regent after the death of sultan Lačïn (Zetterst. I, 221, Makrīzī IV, 2 ff., 40, Iyās I, 115, 124); Maml. 1301 **Lačïn** [حسام الدين لاجين] (Dawād. 65); Maml. 1302 **Lačïn** [لاجين], an emir from Mosul (Dawād. 88); Maml.? 1303 **Lačïn** [حسام الدين لاجين], mentioned in connection with one of Ghazan's campaigns (RaD/Jahn 146); Maml. 1305 **Lačïn** المعروف بزيربـاج [لاجين الجاشنكير / لاجين العمرى الجاشنكير] (Zetterst. 156-158, Dawād. 135, 218); Maml. 1320 **Lačïn** [لاجين الابراهيمى] (Zetterst. 149); Maml. 1320 **Lačïn** [لاجين الحموى البريدى] (Zetterst. 255); Maml. 1328 **Lačïn** [حسام الدين لاجين الصغير], an emir (Dawād. 344, 353); Maml. 1332 **Lačïn** [لاجين الناصرى], an emir (Dawād. 365); Maml. 1332 **Lačïn** [لاجين], Master of the Horse (amīr-ī-aχur) (Dawād. 368); Maml. 1339 **Lačïn** [لاجين الحموى], a Mamluk envoy in the Kipchak steppe (Tizeng. I, 258, 267 /after Al-Malik An-Nāsir/); Maml. 14th c. **Lačïn** [لاجين / Laçın] (Tarj/Houtsma 101, Tarj/Toparlı 41); Maml. 14th c. **Lačïn** [Лачын] (Tuhfa 410); Maml. 1351 **Lačïn** [حسام الدين لاجين / Husâm ud-dîn Lâdjîn / Lâchîn] (Berchem (No.) 154); Maml. 1400 **Lačïn** [Ladjîn], an officer (Notes et Extr. XIX. I.); Maml. 1400 **Lačïn** [لاجين الجركسّى] (Ibn Taghrīb. VII, 60, 87, Weil, Chalif. II, 88); Maml. 1447, 1452/53, 1469/70, **Lačïn** [لاجين الظا هرى] (Iyās II, 112, 115 etc., Ibn Taghrīb. VII, 150, 213, 237); Maml. 1512 **Lačïn** [لاجين], a guard mentioned in an inscription (Mehren 513); Turk. 1382 **Lačïn** [لاچين], a cavalier of Ahmed the sultan of Sivas (Astarab. 271); Turk. 20th c. **Lačïn** [Lâçin] (Önder, Göle); Tat.? 1557 **Lačïn** [Мокѣй Лачиновъ] (PSRL XIII, 289); NUyg. 19th c. **Lačïn** [لاجين / Lachin] (Le Coq, Namenl. 109); Maml. 1279, 1297 **Lačïn / Lāčïn** [حسام الدين لاجين المنصورى / لاجين / Hosam-eddin-Ladjin / Ladjin-assaghir / Ladschin Aegypti soldanus / Lâdjîn], a bearer of arms of Manşūr, the governor of the Citadel of Damascus, later the Mamluk sultan in Egypt

al-Manşūr Lāčïn (Lājin) (1296-1299) (Makrīzī III, 11, 145, 153, IV, 40-114, Makrīzī, Khit. I, 239, Reg. Hieros., Berchem (No.) 14-16, Iyās I, 136, 137 etc., Duqmaq:RHCHor IV, 124, Weil, Chalif. I, 116, 192-219, RaD/Jahn 122, Dawād. 65, Mayer 148-49); Crm. 1637 **Lačïn-bek** [لاجين بك] (Vel.-Zern., Crim. 171, 291); OT (Qarluq) **Lačïn-bek** [لاجين بك], Qarluq chief (Juwaynī 14); Hak. 19th-20th c. **Lačïn-tayčï** [Лачинъ-Тайчи] (Kostrov 238); Crm. 1670 **Lačïn-tïlmač** [لاجين تلماچ] (Vel.-Zern., Crim. 609); *TN:* Turk. 20th c. **Lāčin** [Büyük Lâçin, Küçük Lâçin], villages in the provinces of Çorum and Eskişehir, Turkey (TMİB 258-9, 363). ✧ 'Falcon, hawk; brave man' cf. Karakh., Uyg. *lačïn* 'id.' (DTS), Karakh. *lačïn* 'yiğit adama da laçin denir' (MK/Atalay I, 410), Uyg. *lajïn* 'id.' (Radl. III, 736), Hak., Turk. *lačïn* 'id.' (Radl. III, 735), Chag., East.T. *lačïn* 'id.' (Radl. III, 735), 'Lāchïn (Elliot, Hist. of Ind. II, 397) ist der Name des Wanderfalken' (Le Coq, Ind. 2), cf. also Sauvaget 55. See also **QARA-LAČÏN.**

LAČÏN-BAYLUQ Uyg. **Lačïn-bayluq** [Laçin Bayluq] (ETY II, 66). ⇨ **LAČÏN + BAYLÏQ.**

LAGLAT Yak. **Laglat** [Лаглат] (Pek.).

LAYNA Oghuz/Trkm. 13th c. **Layna** [لاينا / Лайна] (Abulg./Kon. 1245).

LAYTEK Bashk. 20th c. **Laytek** [Алтыбай Лайтеков] (MİB IV/2, 18).

LAKİN Hak. 19th-20th c. **Lakin** [Лакин], fem. (HRS 353).

LAL Tat.(Sib.)? **Lal-totay** (<**Lal-tutay?**) [Лалтотая / Лалтатая], fem. (AI II, 20). ✧ I. 'Tulip'; II. 'Ruby' cf. Kuman, Crm., Turk. *lāl* 'der Rubin; roth' (Radl. III, 733). ⇨ **LALA? (+ TUTAY).**

LALA Oghuz/Trkm. 13th c. **Lala** [لالا / Lâlâ / Лала] (Abulg./Desm. 28, Abulg./Kon. 530, 545); Az. **Lala** [Лала], a hero in a tale, his sister is Nargis (Az. Skaz. 195); Uyg. 13th-14th c. **Lala-χatun** [Lala Xatun], fem. (Zieme, Mat. III, 272). ✧ I. 'Manservant who takes care of a child; tutor of a prince' (TED, TS), cf. Turk. *lala* 'der mit der Aufsicht über die Kinder betraute Diener, Gouverneur von Prinzen' (Radl. III, 734) (<P.); II. 'Shining, glittering' (Zieme, ibid.) (<Ar.); III. 'Tulip' (Zieme, ibid.) Turk. *lâle* 'id.' (TED, TS) (<P.).

LALUWA Karch. 20th c. **Laluwa** [Laluwá], fem. (Pröhle, Kar. 122).

LAMART Alt. **Lamart** [Ламартъ], a hero from a tale, Čumart's fellow (E. Baranov, Skazki gorsk. tatar: SMOK XXIII, otd. III, 38).

LAPPÏYÏQ Yak. **Lappïyïq** [Лаппыйык] (Pek.).

LARİK Tat.(Sib.) 1596 **Larik** [Лариков Баюрас] (Miller, Ist. Sib. II, 149, 151).

LASA Hak. 19th-20th c. **Lasa** [Ласа], fem. (HRS 353).

LAW Kzk. 19th c. **Law-bay** [Лаубай] (SOK 50); Kzk. 19th c. **Law-bay** [Лаубай] (SOV 90); Kzk. 19th c.

Law-bay [Лаубай] (SODž. 134). ✧ 'Vehicle, draught?' cf. Kzk., Tat. *lau* 'die Pflichtpferde' (Radl. III, 728) <P.<Ir.

LAWDAN   Bashk. 1746 **Lawdan?** [Исенбай Лавданов] (MIB II, 434).

LAWOR   Kuman 1185 **Lawor?** [Лаворъ], a Polovets (Ipat. 437 (450), 438 (451)).

LĀS-BALTÏSAX   Yak. **Lās-baltïsaχ** [Лас балтысах / Нас балтысах оҕонjор], one of the ten *bayanai* forest devil-protector (Pek.).

LÄGİÄNTÄY see **İLLÄKÄNTÄY**

LÄGLÄRÄ   Yak. **Läglärä** [Ляглярä, Ляглярäӈ] (Pek.). ✧ Byname meaning 'a short man'.

LÄKÄTTÄ   Yak. **Läkättä** [Лäкäття] (Pek.).

LÄKİÄNTÄY see **İLLÄKÄNTÄY**

LÄKİÄSKÄ   Yak. **Läkiäskä** [Лäкiäскä] (Pek.). ✧ Dim. of *Läkiäskä*; byname of a male child.

LÄLE   Trkm. 20th c. **Läle** [Läle], fem. (Zaj. 1971, 339); Trkm. 20th c. **Läle** [Ляле], fem. (TrkmRS 436). ✧ 'Tulip', 'Red flower of the fields' (Zaj. 1971), cf. Trkm. *läle* 'полевой цветок (алого цвета)' (TrkmRS) (<P.).

LÄÑKÄY   Yak. **Läñkäy** [Лäӈкäі] (Pek.).

LÄÑKÄSİY   Yak. **Läñkäsiy** [Лäӈкäсіі], a legendary smith (Pek.).

LÄPPÄY   Yak. **Läppäy** [Лäппäі] (Pek.).

LÄPSÄY   Yak. **Läpsäy** [Лäпсäі] (Pek.). ✧ Yevseviy (R.).

LEBAY   Kzk. 19th c. **Lebay / Le-bay?** [Лебай] (SODž. 78, SOV 94).

LEČE   Selj. 1141/42 **Leče** [لجه الترك] (Kamāladdīn: RHCHor III, 683).

LEYE   Hak. 19th-20th c. **Leye** [Лее] (HRS 349). ✧ Lev / Il'ya (R.) (Butanaev).

LEYLİ   Uyg. **Leyli-gül** (S. Kakuk, Chants ouigoures: AOH XXV, 418, 426). ✧ 'Poppy, white poppy' cf. East.T. *lejle gul* 'id.' (Jarring), Uzb. *läjli gül* 'мак' (UzbRS).

LEKER   Kzk. 1877 **Leker** [ليكر / Лекер] (MIK IV, 311, 318).

LEPES   Kzk. 1783 **Lepes** [Лепесъ] (Dobrosm., Turg.); Kkalp. 20th c. **Lepes** [Лепес] (Bask., Kkalp. 83, KkRS 775); Kzk. 19th c. **Lepes-pay** [Лепеспай] (SOV 24); Kzk. 19th c. **Lepĭš / Lepis** [Лэпышъ / Лэписъ], Merkit's son (Potanin II, 5). ✧ 'Word, speech' cf. Kzk. *lepäs* 'id.' (Radl. III, 749).

LEPİS see **LEPES**

LEPİŠ see **LEPES**

LEVEND   Yürük 1543 **Levend** [Levend] (Gökb., Rum. 184). ✧ 'Soldier; vagabond; proud, brave man' cf. Turk. *lävänd* 'ein sich freiwillig stellender Soldat, ein Franc-tireur; der Vagabund; von stolzen Aeussern, kühn' (Radl. III, 750).

LEZGİ   Turk. 20th c. **Lezgi** (Önder, Hınıs); Turk. 20th c. **Lezgi** (Önder, Göle). ✧ 'Lezgin' (Ethnical name) cf. *Läzgi* 'der Lesgine' (Radl. III, 747).

LİBEY see **EL**

LİÄBÄ   Yak. **Liäbä** [Лiäбä], fem. (Pek.). ✧ Yeva (R.).

LİÄP   Yak. **Liäp** [Лiäп] (Pek.). ✧ Lev (R.).

LİFÄS   Kzk. 19th c. **Lifäs / Lifas?** [Чуктаганъ Лифасовъ] (Grod., Pril. 100). ⇨ **LEPES**.

LİPPÄRDÄN   Yak. **Lippärdän-buχatïr** [Тiмiр Лiппäрдäн-бухатыр] (Pek.).

LİSÄ   Yak. **Lisä** [Лісä], fem. (Pek.). ✧ Liza (R.), dim. of R. Yelizaveta.

LİPPÏČÏAXA   Yak. **Lippïčïaχa-amäχsin** [Тiмiр Лыппычыаха амäхсін], Ačaraman-Čačiraman bogatyr's mother (Pek.). See also **TİMİR-LİPPÏČÏAXA**.

LİSPİRDÄN   Yak. **Lispïrdän** [Лыспырдан] (Pek.).

LOČUY   Yak. **Ločuy** [Лочуі] (Pek.).

LOČURDÄN   Yak. **Ločurdän** [Тiмiр Лочурдан] (Pek.).

LOƔUY   Yak. **Loɣuy** [Лоҕуі Уібан] (Pek.). ✧ 'Thud'? cf. Yak. *loɣuy-* 'производить звук, ударяя одно тело о другое' (Pek.).

LOQMAN see **LUQMAN**

LOLLUQ   Trkm. 20th c. **Lolluq** [Lolluq] (Zaj. 1971, 333); Trkm. 20th c. **Lolluq** [Лоллук] (TrkmRS 434). ✧ 'Fat, plump' cf. Trkm. *lolluq* 'толстый, полный, пухлый (о ребенке)' (TrkmRS).

LOPAQ   Bashk. 1664 **Lopaq** [Лопак] (MIB I, 193).

LOSOX   Yak. **Losoχ** [Лосох] (Pek.).

LOSUYUQ   Yak. **Losuyuq** [Лосуjук / Носуjук] (Pek.).

LÖGÖY   Yak. **Lögöy** [Лöгöі, Лöҕöі], head of the big clan-federation called Boroɣon (Pek.).

LÖKSÖÑÖ   Yak. **Löksöñö** [Лöксöнö] (Pek.).

LÖPPÖRÖSÖ   Yak. **Löppörösö** [Лöппöрöсö] (Pek.).

LUBAQ-TEMER see **BULAT-TEMİR**

LUƔABA   Tat.(Sib.)? 1635 **Luɣaba** [Лугабин] (Miller, Ist. Sib. II, 423).

LUXĀSQÏ   Yak. **Luχāsqï** [Лухаскы] (Pek.). ✧ 'Lukashka' (R.), dim. of Luka.

LUQMAN   Uyg. **Loqman** [Локман] (Radl. III, 253); Karch. **Loqman** [Локманъ Борлаковъ] (Sysoev 135); Nog. 20th c. **Luqman** [Аджы Лукъман увлы], father of one of Baskakov's informants from the aul of Nökis (Bask., Nog. 143); Kzk. 19th c. **Luqman-χakim** [Лукманъ-Хаким] (AUK 924). ✧ Loqman (Luqman) (Ar.), a legendary wise, leech.

LUTFİ   Turk. 1450 **Lutfi-bey** [Λουτφήμπενς], an emir from Kandelovo (Byz. Turc. 178); Turk. 1479 **Lutfi-bey** [Λουτφήμπενς], an Ottoman messenger (Byz. Turc. 178); Turk. 16th c. **Lutfi-bey** [Λουτφήμπενς], an Ottoman Great-vezīr (Byz. Turc. 178). ✧ 'Kind, friendly, courteous' (Ahmed) (<Ar.).

LŪQAP   Yak. **Lūqap** [Лукап] (Pek.). ✧ 'Lukashka'

(R.), dim. of Luka.

LÜNEK   Hak. 19th-20th c. **Lünek** [Лӱнек], fem. (HRS 353).

LÜÑKÜRDÄN   Yak. **Lüñkürdän-buχatīr** [Тіміp Лӱнкӱрдӓн-бухатыр], a bogatyr (Pek.).

LÜP   Hak. 19th-20th c. **Lüp** [Луп] (HRS 349). ✧ Lev (R.) (Butanaev).

M

MA-BERGÄN   Kzk. **Ma-bergän** [Маберганъ] (Nepljuev 762, 763). ✧ '?-gave him/her'. ⇨ **MAY?** + **BERGEN.**

MAČAY   Hak. 19th-20th c. **Mačay** [Мачай] (HRS 349).

MAČAQ   Bashk. 1725 **Mačaq-bay** [Мачакбай Пулатовъ] (ZIRGO IX, 392).

MAČĬK see **MAJĬK**

MAČĬQ see **MAJĬK**

MAČOQ   Hak. 19th-20th c. **Mačoq** [Мачок], fem. (HRS 354).

MAČOŃ   Hak. 19th-20th c. **Mačoň** [Мачонъ] (HRS 349).

MAJAN   Kzk. 1785 **Majan-bahadur** / **Mažan-bahadur?** [ماجان بهادر / Мажан бахадур] (MIK IV, 51, 53).

MAJAR   Maml. 1332 **Majar** [ماجار], an emir (Dawād. 369); Maml. 1388 **Majar (al-Majari)** [Almadjari], governor of Bireh, takes part in the revolt against Berkuk (Weil, Abbas I, 546 (after Makrīzī)); Kzk. 19th c. **Mažar** [Мажаръ] (SOV 12); Kzk. 19th c. **Mažar** [Можаръ / Мажаръ] (SOK 220, 304); *EN:* Yürük 1725 **Majar** [Macar], mentioned among the nomad Saçıkaralu, Karahacılı, Manavgat, Eski Yörük, Karaçakal and Güzelbeyli tribes in a diploma from Isparta, Turkey (Fehmi Aksu, Yılanlı Oğullarına dair Vesikalar: Ün IV (1938), 686); Crm. **Majar-qalqï** [Маҗар калкы], Hungarian people mentioned in a Crimean tale (Proben VII, 214); *TN:* Turk. 1485 **Majar** [Macar (köy)], a village (Gökb., Ed. 452); Turk. 20th c. **Majar** [Macarköy], a village in the province of Antalya (TMİB 102); Turk. 20th c. **Majar** [Gebiz (Macar)], the old name of the settlement (village) Gebiz, the centre of a district in the province of Antalya, Turkey (TMİB 107); Turk. 20th c. **Majarlar** [Macarlar], a village in the province of Bolu (TMİB 192); Turk. 20th c. **Majarlar** [Macarlar] (TMİB 137). ✧ 'Hungarian' (Pelliot), cf. Turk., Crm. *majar* 'id.', Crm. 'der Wagen' (Radl. IV, 2050). See also **QOJA-MAJAR.**

MAJĬK   Tat.(Sib.)? 1643 **Mačik** [Мачик], a prince of Kersagal'sk (Miller, Ist. Sib. II, 486, 487); Kzk. 1841

Majik [Маджикъ Кучуковъ], a sultan of the Middle Horde (Orta Žüz) (Konšin, Mat. V, 22); Alt.(Tel.) 1640 **Majik** / **Mačïq** [Madžik / Matschyk / Маджикъ], a prince (Andrievič, Ist. Sib. I, 110, Radl., Aus Sib. I, 175, 178); Kzk. 19th c. **Mažik** [Мажикъ] (AOA 146); Kzk. 19th c. **Mažĭk** [Мажекъ] (SOV 94).

MAJĬR   Karch. 20th c. **Majir** [Маʒir] (Pröhle, Kar. 246).

MAD-YAR see **MÄDĬ-YAR**

MAD-UMAR   Kzk. 19th c. **Mad-umar** [Мадумаръ Анаркуловъ] (SKSO VIII, 204). ✧ I. Component *Mad-* / *Mat-* is the shortened form of *Muχammed*; II. Component *Mad-* / *Mat-* can be derived from Ar. *madh* 'praise' cf. Kzk. PNs *Mat-žan, Mat-qarim, Mat-qasim* (Žanuzakov 149). ⇨ **UMAR.**

MADAL   Kzk. 19th c. **Madal-bek** [Мадальбекъ] (SODž. 126).

MADALĬ   Kzk. 1870 **Madali** [Исмуратъ Мадалеевъ] (Grod., Pril. 128); Uzb. 1821-1842 **Madali-χan** [Madali-Khan], khan of Kokand (Nalivkin-Dozon 148). ✧ Shortened form of (Ar.) *Muχammad-ali* (Žanuzakov).

MADAŃ   Hak. 19th-20th c. **Madañ** [Маданъ], fem. (HRS 353).

MADAR   Chag. 1551 **Madar-bike** [Мадар-бике], Omar-χoja's daughter, Xatun-bike's sister (Ivanov 313). ✧ 'Mother' cf. Chag. *madär* 'die Mutter' (Radl. IV, 2048) (<P.).

MADAT   Kzk. 19th c. **Madat** [Мадатовъ] (SKSO VIII, 203). ✧ 'Helper, supporter' cf. Turk. *mädäd* (Ar.) 'id.' (Radl. IV, 2048).

MADEN   Turk. 1583 **Maden** [معدن] (Ongan, Ank. I, 165); Yürük 1543 **Mäden** (Gökb., Rum. 211, 217). ✧ 'Mine' cf. Turk. *maden* 'das Bergwerk; das Metall' (Radl. IV, 2048).

MADĬ-YAR see **MÄDĬ-YAR**

MADIN   Hak. 19th-20th c. **Madin** [Мадин], fem. (HRS 353).

MADĬ-YAR see **MÄDĬ-YAR**

MAҒABALĬ   Uyg. **Maɣabali** [Maġabali] (EUTS).

MAҒAY   Tat.(Sib.)? 1631 **Maɣay** [Магай], a prince from Kotovsk (Miller, Ist. Sib. II, 377, 378). ✧ 'Little frog'? cf. Chul.(Küer) *maɣa* 'der Frosch' (Radl. IV, 2000). + dim. suff. *-y.*

MAҒALDAY   Tat.(Sib.)? 1640 **Maɣalday** [Магалдай] (Miller, Ist. Sib. II, 460).

MAҒANAX see **MAҒANAQ**

MAҒANAQ   Hak. 19th-20th c. **Maɣanaχ** [Мағанах] (HRS 349); Hak.(Sag) 19th-20th c. **Maɣanaq** [Маҕанак] (Proben IX, 613). ✧ '(Little) White horse; little horse having light coloured eyes; white spot on the forehead of an animal (horse, cow)' cf. Hak.(Sag.) *maɣan* 'id.' (Radl. IV, 2000), Hak. *maɣan* 'id.' (HRS).

MAҒAS see **MAҒAZ**

МАГAZ Bashk. 1782 **Maγas** [Магась Шикметев] (MIB V, 133); Bashk. 1740 **Maγaz** [Магаз] (MIB I, 384); Bashk. 1749 **Maγaz** [Магаз Султангулов] (MIB III, 465). ✧ 'Dear, beloved' (<Ar.) (Kusimova).

МАГÏRQA Hak.(Kyz.) 19th-20th c. **Maγïrqa** [Маӈырка], fem. (Katanov, Otč. 13). ✧ 'Tobacco' (<R. Mahorka 'a kind of tobacco') (Katanov).

МАГLİYAR-AMİN Uzb. 19th c. **Maγliyar-amin** [Magliar-Amin], from Khokand (Nalivkin-Dozon 108). ⇨ ? + **AMİN.**

МАГMET see MAXMED

МАГNAY Hak. 19th-20th c. **Maγnay** [Магнай], fem. (HRS 353).

МАГOMED see MAXMED

МАГTÏM see MAXTUM

МАГZÏM Kzk. 19th c. **Maγzïm-bay** [Магзымбай] (SOK 26). ✧ 'Guest, invited; guarded' (Ar.) (Žanuzakov).

MAH Chag. 16th c. **Mah-begim** [Max-Бегим], fem. (Ivanov 177, 178, 181, 182, 187, 189); Chag. 16th c. **Mah-bibi** [Max Биби], fem. (Ivanov 290); Chag. 16th c. **Mah-bike** [Max-Бике], fem. (Ivanov 176, 186). ✧ 'Moon' (the moon-like face is a symbol of women's beauty) cf. Crm., Turk. *mah* (<P.) 'der Mond' (Radl. IV, 2003), East. T. *ma:h* (<P.) 'month, moon' (Jarring), P. *māh* 'moon; month; beauty, fair lady' (PRS). See also **AY**; **АГA-MAH, AГA-MAHİM.**

MAH-ALTÏ Maml. 14th c. **Mah-altï / Māh-altï** [مهلتى / Mehaltı], fem. (Tarǰ/Houtsma 101, Tarǰ/Toparlı 43, 127). ✧ 'Moon-Six' (Toparlı: 'Ay altı'). ⇨ **MAH + ALTÏ.**

MAH-ǰİHAN Maml. 14th c. **Mā-ǰihān / Mah-ǰihan** (<**Māh-i ǰihān**) [ماهجهان / سَاجَهَان / Mācihān / Mah-ı Cihān], fem. (Tarǰ/Houtsma 101, Tarǰ/Toparlı 43, 128). ✧ 'World's Moon' (Toparlı: 'Dünya ayı'). ⇨ **MAH + ǰİHAN.**

MAH-PERİ Selj. 1239 **Mah-peri-χatun** [ماه برى خاتون], mother of Giyaseddin Keyhusrev II (1236-1246) (Uzunçarş., Küt. 75). ⇨ **MAH + PERİ.**

MAHİM Chag. 16th c. **Mahim** [Махим], fem. (Ivanov 245, 300); Chag. 16th c. **Mahim** [Махим], a χoja (Ivanov 233, 235, 241); Chag. 15th c. **Mahim-sultan** [Махим Султан] (Ivanov 197). ✧ 'My Moon, my beauty'. ⇨ **MAH** + poss. suff. *-im*. See also **АГA-MAHİM.**

MAXA Yak. **Maχa** [Maxa] (Pek.).

MAXAY Uyg. **Maχay** [Maḥay] (EUTS); Hak. 19th-20th c. **Maχay** [Махай] (HRS 349). ⇨ **MAQAY?**

MAXAMBET see MUXAMMED

MAXAMMED see MUXAMMED

MAXAS Yak. **Maχas** [Maxac] (Pek.).

MAXČAXĀN Yak. **Maχčaχün / Maχčaχān** [Махчахан], names from a riddle (Pek.).

MAXČAY Yak. **Maχčay** [Maxчаi] (Pek.).

MAXČAYAN Yak. **Maχčayan** [Махчаjан], a name in a riddle (Pek.).

MAXČAR Yak. **Maχčar** [Махчар] (Pek.). ✧ 'Having short curve legs, a large waist' cf. Yak. *maχčaγar* 'коротко и криво- ногий и широкий в поясе' (Pek.).

MAXČASAY Yak. **Maχčasay / Maχčāsay** [Махчасаi], a name in a riddle (Pek.).

MAXMED Crm. 1509 **Maγmet-ša** [Магметша] (PSRL XIII, 10); Kzk. 19th c. **Maγomed** [Бай Ола Магомедовъ] (Grod., Pril. 95); Uzb. 1840 **Maγomet** [Магометъ Киримъ], from Khiva (ZIRGOÊtn. I, 100); Nog. 20th c. **Maγomet-ulï** [Асан Магомет улы Санълыбай / Асан Магометович Санглыбаев], father of Baskakov's informant from the aul of Erkin-χalq (Bask., Nog. 143). ✧ 'Praiseworthy deed' (Žanuzakov 149) <Ar. See also **АǰÏ-MAXMET, DUZ-МАГOMET, XAL-МАГOMET, İRİK-МАГOMET, İS-MAГOMED, YAQŠÏ-МАГMED, NOR-MAXMET, ORAZ-МАГOMET, TURSUN-МАГOMET.**

MAXMUD Karakh. 11th c. **Maχmud** [Maḥmud ibnu-l-husajn ibn muhammad al-qašγari], the author of Dīvān Luγāt at-Turk (DTS); Karakh. 13th c. **Maχmud** [mahmud-i jügnäki], father of the author of Atebetu-l-Xaqāiq (MK/Atalay 847, DTS); Alt.? 19th c. **Maχmud** [Махмуд], a prince of Choros? (Verb., In. 5); Kkalp. 20th c. **Maqmut** [Макмут] (KkRS 775). ✧ Mahmud (Ar.), 'praised, praiseworthy, lauded, laudable' (Ahmed). See also **İNANČ-MAXMUD, KELDİ-MAXMUD, NUR-MAXMUD, SULTAN-MAXMUD.**

MAXMUT-DURSUN Turk. 20th c. **Maχmut-dursun** [Mahmutdursun], a village in the province of Malatya, Turkey (TMİB 604). ⇨ **MAXMUD + TURSÏN.**

MAXROŽA Tat.(GH) 1315 **Maχroža / Mar-χoža?** [Махрожа / Мархожа], envoy from the Horde (Suzd. 501).

MAXSÏN Yak. **Maχsïn** [Махсын] (Pek.). ✧ Maksim (R.).

MAXTUM Trkm. 20th c. **Maγtïm-γulï** [Магтымгулы], name given because of the respect to the great Turkmen poet Mahtumkuli (Mahdumkuli Piragi 1733-1783) (Sopieva 182); NUyg.(Tar.) 19th c. **Maχtum-sula** [ماختوم سولا / Махтумъ-сула], fem. (Pantusov, Tar. 1-10); Kkalp. 20th c. **Maqtïm-qulï** [Мактымкулы] (KkRS 775); NUyg.(Tar.) **Mäχtim-silä** [Mächtim Silä / Мäхтімсілä], fem. (Proben VI, 168 /221/). ✧ Maχdum / Maχtūm (Ar.) (Erol II), 'Lord, ruler; male child' cf. Turk. *mahdum* 'efendi, bey, hükümdar; erkek evlât' (Özön), 'Master, hodja' cf. also Tat. PN *Mäχdüm* (Sattarov) (<Ar.). See also **ARU-MAQTÏM.**

MAY Kzk. 19th c. **May-bek** [Майбекъ] (SODž. 56). ✧

'Fat, grease; butter' cf. Kzk. *may* 'id.' (KzRS), Alt., Hak., Kzk., Tat. *may* 'die Butter, das Fett' (Radl. IV, 1985). See also **AQ-MAY, AQČA-MAY, BİK-MAY, SARÏ-MAY.**

MAY-BAS Kzk. 19th c. **May-bas** [Майбасъ] (SOK 58). ✧ I. 'Press/tred on fat'; II. 'Fat-head'? ⇨ **MAY + BAS II.; MAY + BAŠ?** See also **MAY-BASAR.**

MAY-BASAR Kzk. 19th c. **May-basar** [Майбасаръ] (SODž. 116). ✧ 'Treading fat' (Bese 22). ⇨ **MAY + BASAR.** See also **MAY-BAS.**

MAY-EMER Kzk. 19th c. **May-emer** [Маемеръ] (SODž. 80); Kzk. 1817 **May-imer** / **Maymïr?** [ایمار ای ماس / Маймыр] (MIK IV, 310); *TN:* Kzk. **May-emer** [Майэмер] (Kojčubaev 165). ✧ 'Fat/grease-sucker' (Kojčubaev, 165), cf. Kzk. *em-* 'сосать' (KzRS). ⇨ **MAY.** See also **İT-EMER, İT-EMGEN, MAY-EMER, MAY-İMGEN.**

MAY-İMER see **MAY-EMER**

MAY-İMGÄN see **MAY-İMGEN**

MAY-İMGEN Kzk. 19th c. **May-imgän** [Май Имганъ] (Grod., Pril. 31); Kzk. 19th c. **May-imgen** [Майингенъ] (SOK 216). ✧ 'He/she sucked fat/grease' cf. Kzk. *em-* 'Emmek' (KzTS). ⇨ **MAY.** See also **MAY-EMER.**

MAY-KÖT Kzk. 19th c. **May-köt** [Майкотъ] (SODž. 14); Kzk. 19th c. **May-köt** [Майкотъ] (SODž. 80); Kzk. 19th c. **May-köt** [Майкотъ] (SOV 110); Kzk. 19th c. **May-küt** [Майкутъ] (Grod. I, 98); Kzk. 19th c. **May-küt** [Майкутъ] (SODž. 128); Kzk. 19th c. **May-küt** [Майкутъ] (Grod. 5); Kzk. 19th c. **May-küt** [Майкутъ] (SOK 100). ✧ 'Fat-ass' cf. Kuman, Chag., Alt., Crm., Kzk. *köt* 'die Schamtheile und der Hintern' (Radl. II, 1275). ⇨ **MAY.** See also **MAYLÏ-GÜT.**

MAY-KÜR Kirg. 1816 **May-kür** [Майкур] (MIK IV, 299) ⇨ **MAY + KÜR?**

MAY-KÜT see **MAY-KÖT**

MAY-QOMAR Kzk. 19th c. **May-qomar** [Майкомаръ] (SODž. 64). ⇨ **MAY + QOMAR.**

MAYA I. Hak. 19th-20th c. **Maya** [Мая], fem. (HRS 354).

MAYA II. Trkm. **Maya** [Мая], fem. (Sopieva 178); Trkm. 1854 **Maya** [Маяевъ] (ZIRGOÊtn. I, 158); Trkm. 20th c. **Maya** [Maya], fem. (Zaj. 1971, 338); Trkm. 20th c. **Māya** [Мая], fem. (TrkmRS 445). ✧ 'Mare of a camel; she-camel' cf. Trkm. *maya* 'id.' (Radl. IV, 2011), Trkm. *māya* 'мая (двугорбая верблюдица)' (TrkmRS).

MAYAQ Hak. 19th-20th c. **Mayaq** [Майак], fem. (HRS 353).

MAYAN Kzk. 19th c. **Mayan** [Маянъ] (SOK 54).

MAYANTÏLĀP Yak. **Mayantïlāp** [Маянтылап], Lögöy's pupil (Pek.).

MAYČÏ Kzk. 19th c. **Mayčï-bay** [Майчибай] (SOK 218); Kzk. 19th c. **Mayčï-bay** [Майчибай] (SOV 114); Kzk. 19th c. **Mayčï-bay** [Майчибай] (SOK 162); Kzk. 19th c. **Mayču-bay** [Майчубай] (SOK 110). ✧ 'Maker and/or seller of grease, butter'. ⇨ **MAY** + suff. *-čï.*

MAYČU see **MAYČÏ**

MAYJU see **MAYČÏ**

MAYDA Kzk. 19th c. **Mayda-bala** [Майда бала] (SOK 186). ✧ 'Small; soft' cf. Kzk. *mayda* 'id.' (KzRS).

MAYDAN Kzk. 19th c. **Maydan** [Майданъ] (AOA 90). ✧ 'Field, battlefield' (Žanuzakov), cf. Kuman, Kzk., Trkm., Uzb. *maydan* (Ar.) 'eine Ebene, eine freie Stelle; der Kampfplatz' (Radl. IV, 1990). See also **QOŠ-MAYDAN.**

MAYDANA Kzk. **Maydana** [Майдана], fem. (Levšin III, 96); Kzk. 19th c. **Maydana** [Maïdana], fem. (Levchine 356). ⇨ **MAYDAN?** + suff. *-a.*

MAYDU see **MAYLÏ**

MAYDUQ see **MAYLÏQ**

MAYETME-KİREY Crm. 1522 **Mayetme-kirey?** [Маетме Кирей], ruler of Perekop (Lit. Tat. 1). ⇨ **KERÄY.**

MAYƔAK Alt. 19th-20th c. **Mayɣak** [Майгак] (OjrRS 209).

MAYƔAR Kzk. 19th c. **Mayɣar** [Майгаръ] (SOK 212).

MAYƔUČ Tat. 1662 **Mayɣuč** [Майгучко] (DAI IV, 286).

MAYÏLDÏ Tuv. 19th c. **Mayïldï** [Маjылды] (Proben IX, 50). ✧ 'Got tired, weak; weakened' cf. Hak. *mayïl-* 'ermüden, schwach werden, ermatten' (Radl. IV, 2014).

MAYÏNQA Tuv. 19th-20th c. **Mayïnqa** [Майынка], fem. (OjrRS 212).

MAYÏSÏAY Yak. **Mayïsïay** [Маjысыаi] (Pek.). ✧ Moisey (R.).

MAYQA Kzk. 19th c. **Mayqa-bek** [Майкабекъ] (AOA 78); Kzk. 19th c. **Mayqa-biy** [Майкабій], legendary forefather of the Kazaks (Potanin II, 149). ✧ 'A kind of summer-shirt' cf. Kzk. *mayqa* 'id.' (KzTS).

MAYQAY Kzk. 19th c. **Mayqay** [Майкай] (AOK 58). ⇨ **MAY?** + dim. suff. *-qay.*

MAYQAN Kzk. 19th c. **Mayqan** [Майканъ] (SOK 216).

MAYQARA Kzk. 19th c. **Mayqara** [مايترا / Майкара] (Veselovskij, Kirg. 73, 118). ✧ 'A kind of plant' cf. Kzk. *mayqara* 'eine Pflanze, die wie Stöcke auf der Salzsteppe wächst' (Radl. IV, 1986).

MAYQÏ Kzk. 19th c. **Mayɣï-bay** [Майгибай] (SOK 168); Kzk. 19th c. **Mayqï-biy** [Майкы-бій], mentioned in a legend about Chinggis (Potanin, Pred. 50).

MAYLÏ Kzk. 19th c. **Maydu-bay** [Майдубай] (Grod., Pril. 66); Kzk. 1846 **Maylï** [Какай Майлиев] (MKOP 156); Kzk. 19th c. **Maylï** [Майлы] (SODž. 90); Kzk. 19th c. **Maylï-bay** [Майлы-бай] (Grod., Pril. 123);

Kzk. 19th c. **Maylĭ-bay** [Майлыбай] (AOAtb. 38);
Kzk. 19th c. **Maylĭ-bay** [Майлибай] (AOP 2); Kzk.
19th c. **Maylĭ-bay** [Майлибай] (SODž. 122); Kzk.
19th c. **Maylĭ-bay** [Майлибай] (SOV 38, 76); Uzb.
19th c. **Maylĭ-bay** [Джура Майлибаевъ] (SKSO III,
160); Kzk. 19th c. **Maylĭ-bala** [Майлибала] (SOK
152); Kzk. **Maylĭ-χoǰa** [Майлы-ходжа] (Divaev, Šura
136); Kzk. **Maylĭ-qïz** [Майлыкызъ Калпаева], fem.
(TV 1876, 144); Kzk. 19th c. **Maylĭ-qïz**
[Майлыкызъ], fem. (Grod., Pril. 53); Kzk. 19th c.
Maytï-bay [Майтыбай] (SOV 28); Kzk. 19th c.
Maytu-bay [Майтубай] (SODž. 64, 80); *EN:* Kzk.
18th c. - 19th c. **Maylï** [Майлы] (Tynyšp. 68); Kzk.
18th c. - 19th c. **Maylï-bay** [Майлыбай] (Tynyšp. 69);
Kzk. 18th c. - 19th c. **Maylï-bek** [Майлибек] (Tynyšp.
73). ✧ 'Fatty, greasy'. ⇨ MAY + suff. *-lï*.

MAYLĬ-GÜT Kzk. 19th c. **Maylĭ-güt** [Майлыгутъ]
(AOO 10). ✧ 'Fat ass' cf. Kuman, Chag., Alt., Crm.,
Kzk. *köt* 'die Schamtheile und der Hintern' (Radl. II,
1275). ⇨ **MAYLĬ**. See also **MAY-KÖT**.

MAYLĬKE Kzk. 19th c. **Maylĭke** [Майлике] (SOV
54). ⇨ MAYLĬ + suff. *-ke* or comp. *-ake*.

MAYLĬQ Kzk. 19th c. **Mayduq** [Майдукъ] (SOK
174); Kzk. 19th c. **Maylïq** [Майлыкъ] (SOV 116);
Kzk. 19th c. **Maylïq** [Майлыкъ] (SOK 232); Kzk. 19th
c. **Maylïq-pay** [Майликпай] (SOK 140); Kzk. 19th c.
Maytïq / Maytik? [Майтиковъ] (Grod., Pril. 119);
Kzk. 19th c. **Maytïq / Maytek?** [Майтекъ] (AOO 42).
✧ 'A towel for wiping hands after eating' cf. Kzk.
maylïq 'Handtuch mit den man die fettigen Hände nach
dem Essen abwischt' (Radl. IV, 1989).

MAYLĬŠ Kzk. 1803 **Maylĭš-bi** [مايلوش بى /
مايلش بى / Майлыш] (MIK IV, 212). ⇨ MAYLĬ +
suff. *-š*.

MAYMA Kirg.? 19th c. **Mayma** [Майма] (Potanin II,
4).

MAYMAQ Kzk. 19th c. **Maymaq** [Маймокъ] (SOK
224); Kzk. 19th c. **Maymaq** [Маймакъ] (AOP 58);
Kzk. 19th c. **Maymaq** [Маймакъ] (SOV 56); Kzk.
19th c. **Maymaq** [Маймакъ] (AOP 10); Kzk. 19th c.
Maymaq [Мймакъ Айбулатовъ] (AUK 865); Kzk.
19th c. **Maymaq / Maymïk?** [Маймекъ] (SOK 102).
✧ 'Having curve, crosswise legs' cf. Kzk. *maymaq*
'krummbeinig, schiefbeinig (Thiere)' (Radl. IV, 1991).

MAYMAN Kzk. 19th c. **Mayman** [Майманъ] (SOK
186); Kzk. 19th c. **Mayman** [Майманъ] (AOO 6, 66).

MAYMĬR see MAY-EMER

MAYMĬŠ Kzk. 19th c. **Maymïš** [Маймышъ] (SOK
80). ✧ 'Got tired' cf. Kzk. *may-* 'müde werden,
ermüden' (Radl. IV, 1986).

MAYNA Alt. 19th-20th c. **Mayna** [Майна], fem.
(OjrRS 212). ✧ Manya, Mariya (R.).

MAYNE Hak. 19th-20th c. **Mayne** [Майне], fem.

(HRS 353).

MAYOR Hak. 19th-20th c. **Mayor** [Майор], fem.
(HRS 353). ✧ Mayor (Colonel) cf. R. майор.

MAYR Tat. 1552 **Mayr** [Маиръ] (Kn. Metriki Lit. 86);
Kzk. 19th c. **Mayr-bek** [Маирбекъ] (SODž. 58).

MAYRA Hak. 19th-20th c. **Mayra** [Майра], fem.
(HRS 353). ✧ Mariya (R. fem.) (Butanaev).

MAYRAM see BAYRAM

MAYRĬQ Kzk. 19th c. **Mayrïq** [Отушъ Майриковъ]
(Grod., Pril. 133); Hak.(Kyz.) 1715 **Mayrïq**
[Майрыкъ], a prince (Jarilov, Kyz. 9). ✧ 'Leaning,
awry; cripple' cf. Alt., Hak., Kzk. *mayrïq* 'schief, auf
die Seite gebogen; schiefbeinig, der Krüppel' (Radl. IV,
1987).

MAYRĬN Hak. 19th c. **Mayrïn** [Майрын] (Katanov,
Otč. 12). ✧ 'Skinny, meagre, frail, perishable' cf. Chag.
mayrun 'mager, schwach, zerbrechlich' (Radl. IV,
1988).

MAYSA Trkm. **Maysa** [Майса], fem. (Sopieva 178);
Trkm. 20th c. **Maysa** [Maysa], fem. (Zaj. 1971, 339);
Trkm. 20th c. **Maysa** [Майса], fem. (TrkmRS 440);
Trkm. 20th c. **Maysa-gözel** [Майсагёзель] (Nikonov:
OSA 160); Trkm. 20th c. **Maysa-gül** [Майсагюль],
fem. (Nikonov: OSA 160). ✧ 'Field, green field of first
corn; early spring' (Sopieva: 'зелень первых
злаков'), cf. Trkm. *maysa* 'нива' (TrkmRS), cf. also
Kzk. PN *Maysa* (Žanuzakov). (<Tadj. <Ir.).

MAYT Karg. **Mayt** [Майт] (Katanov, Otč. 9). ✧
'Mother' (Katanov), cf. R. *mat'* / мать 'id.'.

MAYT-BAS Kzk. 19th c. **Mayt-bas** [Майтбасъ] (AOA
134); Kzk. 19th c. **Mayt-pas** [Майтпасъ] (SOV 80). ⇨
MAYT? + BAŠ.

MAYT-PAS see MAYT-BAS

MAYTA Hak. 19th-20th c. **Mayta** [Майта] (HRS 349).

MAYTAMAS see MAYTMAS

MAYTAS Hak.(Sag.) 19th-20th c. **Maytas** [Майтас]
(Katanov, Otč. 7).

MAYTĬ see MAYLĬ

MAYTĬQ see MAYLĬQ

MAYTĬÑ Hak. 19th-20th c. **Maytïñ** [Майтынъ] (HRS
349). ✧ 'Tail, bottom of the tail of a horse' cf. Hak. PN
Maytïn 'репица, основание хвоста лошади'
(Butanaev).

MAYTMAS Bashk. 1751 **Maytamas / Maytmas?**
[Якуп Маитамасов] (MIB IV/1, 34); Tat. 1753
Maytmas [Маитмас (Магитмас) Сарбаев] (MIB
IV/1, 67, 68); Tat.(Sib.) 1596 **Maytmas** [Майтмас]
(Miller, Ist. Sib. II, 148); Tat.(Tüm.) 1606, 1618
Maytmas [Майтмас (Матамас, Мотмас,
Майтмас)] (Miller, Ist. Sib. II, 193, 242, 243); Bashk.
1739 **Maytmas** [Маитмас Казакаев] (MIB III, 407);
Bashk. 1748 **Maytmas** [Якуп Маитмасов] (MIB III,
451); Bashk. 1758 **Maytmas** [Маитмас Аблаев]
(MIB IV/1, 169); Bashk. 1764 **Maytmas** [Маитмас

Амиров] (MIB IV/1, 277); *TN:* Tat. 1697 **Maytmasovo** [Майтмасово], a village (Kungursk. akty 246).

MAYTMASA Tat.(Sib.)? 1581 **Maytmasa** [Маитмаса], a prince (Sib. Let. 322).

MAYTU-BET Kzk. 19th c. **Maytu-bet** [Майтубетъ] (SOK 6). ✧ 'Fatty face'? ⇨ **MAYLÏ?** + **BET.**

MAYZ-BAR Kzk. 19th c. **Mayz-bar** [Майзбаръ] (SOK 210). ⇨ **BAR.**

MAKEY see **MAQAY**

MAKEN Kzk. 19th c. **Maken** [Макенъ] (SOK 306).

MAKIŠ Alt. 19th-20th c. **Makiš** [Макиш], fem. (OjrRS 212).

MAKÖN Alt. 19th-20th c. **Makön** [Макöн], fem. (OjrRS 212).

MAQ Tat.(Lit.) 1592 **Maq** [Нурумъ Макевичъ], preserved in the family-name Makevič (Lit. Tat. 118, 121); Tat.(Lit.) 1592 **Maq** [Бегимъ Макевичъ] (Lit. Tat. 118, 121); *TN:* Kzk. **Mah-bay?** [Mahbai], a kurgan (burial mound) south of Ala-kül, not far from the Chinese border (Sewerzoff-Petermann: PM Ergh. 43). ✧ 'Praise' cf. Kuman, Chag., Alt., Hak. *maq* 'das Lob' (Radl. IV, 1993).

MAQ-AČA Bashk. 1764 **Maq-ača?** [Макача Тилкзев] (MIB IV/1, 300). ⇨ **MAQ?**

MAQ-AŠA Uyg. 1339 **Maq-aša** [Mak Aša], fem. (Chwol., Syr.-nest. 90). ⇨ **MAQ** + **AŠA.**

MAQA Kzk. 19th c. **Maqa** [Мака] (AOA 102).

MAQAY Bashk. 1780 **Makey** [Макей Абдрахманов] (MIB V, 113); Tat. 1723 **Maqay** [Юлай Макаев] (MIB III, 217); Tat. 1779 **Maqay** [Макай Тулбаев] (MIB V, 94); Bashk. 1779 **Maqay** [Макай Тулабаев] (MIB V, 94); Kzk. 19th c. **Maqay** [Макай] (AOP 6); Kkalp. 20th c. **Maqay** [Макай] (KkRS 775); Hak. 19th-20th c. **Maqay** [Макай] (HRS 349). ⇨ **MAQA** + suff. -*y.* See also **KÏL-MAQAY, MAXAY?**

MAQAL Bashk. 1789 **Maqal** [Макал Смаилов] (MIB V, 250).

MAQALAN Bashk. 1785 **Maqalan** [Макалан Юнаев] (MIB V, 178); Bashk. 1785 **Maqalan** [Макалан Юнаев] (MIB V, 178).

MAQAMBET see **MAMBET**

MAQAN Kzk. **Maqan** [Маканъ] (Sb. Syr-D. Galkin, Êtn. mat.) 106); Kzk. 19th c. **Maqan** [Иръ Маканъ] (Grod., Pril. 69); Kzk. 19th c. **Maqan** [Маканъ] (AOAtb. 10); Kzk. 19th c. **Maqan** [Маканъ] (AOK 114); Kzk. 19th c. **Maqan-bay** [Макапбай] (SOV 144). See also **BAY-MAQAN.**

MAQARAČ Türk 732 **Maqarač** [Maqaraç] (ETY I, 52); Türk 8th c. **Maqarač-tamɣačï**, from the Türgeš tribe (Thomsen, Inscr. 114, DTS). ✧ 'Great king; ruler (title)' cf. Ind. *maχārāj* 'Grosskönig' (Mahrnāmag) < Skr. *mahārāja* (DTS).

MAQAS Bashk. 1756 **Maqas** [Умер Макасев] (MIB IV/1, 122).

MAQAŠ Kzk. 19th c. **Maqaš** [Макашъ] (SOV 32, 106).

MAQAT Kzk. 19th c. **Maqat** [Макат] (AUK 337); Kkalp. 1809 **Maqat-biy** [Макат бий] (MIKk. 100).

MAQATAY Kzk. 19th c. **Maqatay** [Макатай] (AOO 30).

MAQĀRQA Yak. **Maqārqa** [Макарка] (Pek.). ✧ Makarka (R.), dim. of R. Makar (Pek.).

MAQÏY Alt. 19th-20th c. **Maqïy** [Макый], fem. (OjrRS 212); Alt. 19th-20th c. **Maqïy** [Макый] (OjrRS 209).

MAQÏYLA Alt. 19th-20th c. **Maqïyla** [Макыйла] (OjrRS 209).

MAQÏL Kzk. 19th c. **Maqïl-bay** [Макылбай] (SOK 298); Kzk. 19th c. **Maqïl-bek** [Макылбекъ] (AOO 10).

MAQÏP Kzk. 19th c. **Maqïp** [Макыб] (Samojlovič: ŽS XXIV (1915), 165). ✧ Distorted form of *Žaqip* and used by women instead of it when it is a tabu-name. ⇨ **ǏAQÏP?**

MAQÏŠ Kzk. 1863 **Maqïš / Moqïš?** [Мокышъ], from the Tawke tribe (ZIRGOGeogr. I, 439); Kzk. 19th c. **Maquš / Moquš?** [Мокушъ] (AOP 58). ✧ I. Hypocoristic, contracted form of *Mamadiyar, Maχmet-yali,* etc. (Žanuzakov 148); II. 'Little praise'? ⇨ **MAQ** + suff. -*iš / -uš.*

MAQQĀǏÏQ Tuv. 19th c. **Maqqāǰïq** [Маккацык] (Proben IX, 188).

MAQLAY Bashk. 1735 **Maqlay** [Маклай Сапаровъ], a tarχan (Vel.-Zern., Bašk. 24).

MAQMUT see **MAXMUD**

MAQPA Tuv. 19th c. **Maqpa** [Макпа], fem. (Proben IX, 142).

MAQPAL Kkalp. 20th c. **Maqpal** [Макпал], fem. (KkRS 778). ✧ 'Velvet' cf. Kkalp. *maqpal* 'бархат, плюш' (KkRS 778).

MAQRÏN Hak. 19th-20th c. **Maqrin** [Макрин], fem. (HRS 353).

MAQSAT Trkm. 20th c. **Maqsat** [Maqsat], fem. (Zaj. 1971, 342); Trkm. 20th c. **Maqsat** [Максат], fem. (TrkmRS 440); Kkalp. 20th c. **Maqset** [Макрет] (KkRS 775). ✧ 'Aim, goal' cf. Trkm. *maqsat* 'цель; намерение' (TrkmRS), Kkalp. *maqsat* 'цель; намерение, желание' (KkRS) (<Ar.).

MAQSET see **MAQSAT**

MAQSÏM Kkalp. 20th c. **Maqsïm** [Максым] (KkRS 775). ✧ 'The son of the *išan*' cf. Kkalp. *maqsim* 'id.' (KkRS).

MAQŠAY Tat. 1624 **Maqšay** [Макшай Дербышевъ] (Pokrovskij 72).

MAQŠÏ see **BAQŠÏ**

MAQŠÏY Tuv. 19th c. **Maqšïy** [Макшыи] (Proben IX, 143, 175). ✧ Maksim (R.) (Katanov).

MAQTA Kzk. 19th c. **Maqta-bek** [Мактабекъ] (SODž. 70). ✦ I. 'Praise; be praised!?' cf. Kuman, Chag., Alt., Hak., Kzk., Tat. *maqta-* 'loben, preisen' (Radl. IV, 1997); II. 'Cotton; wad' cf. Kzk. *maqta* 'die Baumwolle, die Watte' (Radl. IV, 1997).

MAQTEY Bashk. 1769 **Maqtey** [Мактей Сюлюкев] (MIB IV/1, 336).

MAQTÏ Kzk. 1819 **Maqtï-bay** [Мактыбай] (MIK IV, 323); Kzk. 19th c. **Maqtï-bay** [Мактыбай] (SODž. 146); Kzk. 19th c. **Maqtï-bay** [Мактыбай] (SOK 16); Uzb. 19th c. **Maqtï-bay** [Сати Мактыбаевъ] (SKSO III, 22); Kzk. 19th c. **Maqtï-bek** [Мактыбекъ] (SOK 80); Kzk. 19th c. **Maqtï-bek** [Мактыбекъ] (SOK 80, 130); Kzk. 19th c. **Maqtï-bek** [Мактыбекъ] (SODž. 44). ✦ 'Praised'? ⇨ **MAQ** + suff. *-tï < -lï*.

MAQTÏM see MAXTUM

MAQUL Kzk. 1785 **Maqul** [متول بهادر / Макул б.], an aqsaqal (MIK IV, 52, 53); Kzk. 19th c. **Maqul** [Макулбекъ] (AOAtb. 2); Kzk. 19th c. **Maqul** [Макуловъ] (AOO 46); Kzk. 19th c. **Maqul-bay** [Макулбай] (SOK 14); Kzk. 19th c. **Maqul-bek** [Макулбекъ] (SOK 82). ✦ 'Understanding, agreement' cf. Tat., Turk. *maqul* (Ar.) 'einverstanden' (Radl. IV, 1996).

MAQUŠ Bashk. 1760 **Maquš** [Макуш Китяпов] (MIB IV/1, 184); Kzk. 19th c. **Maquš** [Макушгъ (Даумъ и М.)] (AUK 883).

MAL Kzk. 19th c. **Mal** [Малъ] (SOK 212); Maml. 1462/63 **Mal-bay** [ملباى المشرف] (Iyās III, 75); Maml.? 1468/69 **Mal-bay** [مالباى الاقطع] (Iyās II, 109); Kzk. **Mal-bek** [Мальбекъ] (Sb. Syr-D. IX, 56); Kzk. 19th c. **Mal-bek** [Мальбекъ] (AOP 78); Uzb. 1614 **Mal-qul** [Малкулъ], a khan of Bukhara (AI III, 421); *EN:* Kzk. 18th c. - 19th c. **Mal-žan** [Малжан] (Tynyšp. 75). ✦ 'Property, possession (mainly animals such as horses, sheep, goats cattle)' cf. Uyg., Alt., Crm., Az., Kirg., Kzk., etc. *mal* 'der Besitz, die Habe, die Waare' (Radl. IV, 2035). See also **AQ-MAL, SARÏ-MAL.**

MAL-AYDAR Kzk. 19th c. **Mal-aydar** [Малайдаръ] (AOQ 70). ✦ 'He will drive animals'. ⇨ **MAL + AYDAR.**

MAL-BAΓAR Kzk. 19th c. **Mal-baγar** [Малбагаръ] (AOK 10); Kzk. 19th c. **Mal-baγar** [Малбагаръ] (SOV 36); Kkalp. 20th c. **Mal-baγar** [Малбадар (Малбаҕар!)] (KkRS 775). ✦ 'He will look after livestock'. ⇨ **MAL + BAQAR.**

MAL-BERDİ Tat. 1450 **Mal-berdi** [Малберди] (Vel.-Zern., Kasim. I, 23); Tat. 1450 **Mal-berdi** [Мальбердѣй (Малымбердѣй) / Малъ бердѣй / Малберди], a prince of the Horde (PSRL VIII, 123, XII, 75, Vel.-Zern., Kasim. I, 23). ⇨ **MAL + BERDİ.**

MAL-GELDİ Kzk. 19th c. **Mal-geldi / Mal-geldï** [Малгельды] (SOV 42); *TN:* Kzk. **Mal-geldi / Mal-geldï** [Малгельды] (Kojčubaev 167); Kzk. **Mal-geldi / Mal-geldï** [Малгельды], a field (Krasovskij 380). ✦ 'Flock, herd has come'. ⇨ **MAL + KELDİ.**

MAL-TABAR Kzk. 1803 **Mal-tabar** [Малтабаровъ] (Valihanov, Soč. 523); Kzk. 1819 **Mal-tabar** [Малтабар] (MIK IV, 324); Kzk. 19th c. **Mal-tabar** [Малтабаръ] (SOK 216); Kzk. 19th c. **Mal-tabar** [Малтабаровъ] (Grod., Pril. 114); Kzk. 19th c. **Mal-tabar** [Малтабаръ] (SOK 202, 216); Kzk. 19th c. **Mal-tabar** [Малтобаръ] (SOV 138); Kzk. 19th c. **Mal-tabar** [Малтаберъ] (SOK 60). ✦ 'He will find (have, get) animals; he will be rich'. ⇨ **MAL + TABAR.**

MAL-TUΓAN Tat. 1699 **Mal-tuγan?** [Малгутанъ] (PSZRI III, 563). ⇨ **MAL + TUΓAN I.**

MALA I. Hak. 19th-20th c. **Mala** [Мала], fem. (HRS 353). ✦ 'Red, ruddy' (Butanaev).

MALA II. Kzk. 19th c. **Mala-bay** [Малабай] (SOV 110, 116); Kzk. 19th c. **Mala-bay** [Малабай] (AOP 50). ✦ I. 'Trowel, mason's trowel' cf. Kzk. *mala* 'id.' (KzTS); II. 'Drag, harrow' in southern Kirghiz (Kalilov 92).

MALAΓAN Maml. (Kipch.) 1282 **Malaγan** [مَلَغان / Малаганъ] (Baybars/Tizeng. I, 82, 104).

MALAX Kzk. 19th c. **Malaχ** [Юнусъ Малаховъ] (SKSO IV, otd. II, 13).

MALAY Tat.(Mish.) 1775 **Malay** [Малай Мансуров] (MIB IV/2, 416); Kzk. 1786 **Malay** [Малай] (MIK IV, 75); Kzk. 19th c. **Malay** [Малай] (Grod., Pril. 158); Kzk. 19th c. **Malay** [Малай] (SOV 48); Kzk. 19th c. **Malay** [Малай] (SOV 56); Kzk. 19th c. **Malay** [Малай] (SOK 54); Kzk. 19th c. **Malay** [Малай] (SOK 202); Kzk. 19th c. **Malay** [Малай] (Grod., Pril. 148); Kzk. 19th c. **Malay** [Малай] (SOK 6, 24, 106); Kzk. 19th c. **Malay** [Малай] (SOV 150); Kzk. 19th c. **Malay** [Малай] (AOK 90); Kzk. 19th c. **Malay** [Малай] (AOP 118); Kzk. 19th c. **Malay** [Малай] (AOO 66); Kzk. 19th c. **Malay** [Малай] (AOO 34); Kzk. 19th c. **Malay** [Малай] (AOK 14); Kzk. 19th c. **Malay-bay** [Малайбай] (AOA 98); Kzk. 19th c. **Malay-bek** [Малайбекъ] (SOK 176); *TN:* Kzk. **Malay** [Малай] (Kojčubaev 167). ✦ 'Boy, servant, hired man, worker' cf. Tat., Uzb. *malay* 'der Knabe, der Junge' (Radl. IV, 2037), Kzk. *malay* 'работник' (KzRS).

MALAY-SARÏ Kzk. 1785 **Malay-sarï** [ملاى سارى], from the Tana tribe (MIK IV, 52, 54); Kzk. 19th c. **Malay-sarï** [Малайсары] (SODž. 70); Kzk. 19th c. **Malay-sarï** [Малайсары] (AOAtb. 58); Kzk. 19th c. **Malay-sarï** [Малайсары] (SOV 16); *TN:* Kzk. **Malay-sarï** [Малайсары] (Kojčubaev 167). ⇨ **MALAY + SARÏ.**

MALAYQA Tat. 1662 **Malayqa** [Молойко] (DAI IV, 287). ⇨ **MALAY + suff. -qa.**

MALAQAN Kirg. **Malaqan** [Малакан] (Jud. 798).

MALAŠ Kzk. 19th c. **Malaš** [Малашъ] (SOK 150).

MALĀJĪYA Yak. **Malājïya** [Малацыја, Маланјыја], fem. (Pek.). ✦ Melaniya (R.).

MALĀNYÏYA Yak. **Malānyïya** [Маланјыја], fem. (Pek.).

MALČES Hak. 19th-20th c. **Malčes** [Малчес] (HRS 349).

MALČÏ Kzk. 19th c. **Malčï** [Малчибай] (SOK 12); Kzk. 19th c. **Malčï** [Мальчибай] (SOV 30); Alt. 19th-20th c. **Malčï** [Малчы] (OjrRS 209). ✦ 'Shepherd; stockbreeder' (OjrRS), cf. Alt., Kzk. *malčï, malšï* 'id.' (Radl. IV, 2042-43).

MALČÏQ Alt. 19th-20th c. **Malčïq** [Малчык], fem. (OjrRS 212). ✦ 'Boy' cf. R. мальчик 'id.' (OjrRS).

MALDA Kzk. 19th c. **Malda-bay** [Малдабай] (SOK 182); Kzk. 19th c. **Malda-bay** [Малдабай] (SOK 32); Kzk. 19th c. **Malda-bay** [Мелдабай] (SOV 8); Kzk. 19th c. **Malda-bek** [Малдабекъ] (SOV 22); Kzk. 19th c. **Malda-bek** [Малдабекъ] (SODž. 44). ✦ I. 'Having (livestock) property; rich in livestock' cf. Kzk. *maldï* 'id.' <*mal* 'koyun, keçi; zenginlik' (KzTS); II. 'Priest'?, distorted form of *molda* <*molla*. Cf. Kzk. PNs Molda-bay, Molda-bek, Molda-γali (Žanuzakov-Esbaeva).

MALDA-BERGEN Kzk. 19th c. **Malda-bergen** [Малдабергенъ] (SOV 62). ⇨ MALDA / MALDÏ? + BERGEN.

MALDA-QÏDAN Uyg. 13th-14th c. **Malda-qïdan** [Malda Qïdan] (Zieme, Mat. II, 92). ⇨ MALDA / MALDÏ?

MALDA-QURŽAN Kzk. 19th c. **Malda-quržan** [Малцакуржанъ] (SOV 78). ⇨ MALDA / MALDÏ?

MALDÏ Kzk. 19th c. **Maldï-bay** [Малдыбай] (SOV 124); Kzk. 19th c. **Maldï-bay** [Малдыбай] (SODž. 92); Kzk. 19th c. **Maldï-bay** [Малдыбай] (SOV 10); Kzk. 19th c. **Maldï-γul** [Малдыгулъ] (SOK 24); Kzk. 19th c. **Maldu-bay** [Парманъ Малдубаевъ] (Grod., Pril. 57); Kzk. 19th c. **Maldu-γul** [Малдугулъ] (AOK 98); *TN:* Kzk. **Maldï-bay** [Maldybai], a tomb? (Rekogn.); Kzk. **Maldï-bay(evskaya)** [Малдыбаевская], a settlement? east of Awlie-Ata (Karta JAR XIX). ✦ 'Having many animals; being rich' cf. Kzk. *maldï* 'id.' <*mal* 'koyun, keçi; zenginlik' (KzTS), Kzk. *maldï* 'viel Vieh habend' (Radl. IV, 2042). Cf. also Kzk. PN Maldï-bay (Žanuzakov-Esbaeva).

MALDÏN Kzk. 19th c. **Maldïm-bay** (<Maldïn-bay) [Малдымбай] (SOK 220).

MALDU see **MALDÏ**

MALΓAR see **MALQAR**

MALΓUN Kirg. **Malγun** [Малгун] (Jud. 514). ✦ 'Damned, blasted' (Jud.).

MALÏK Nog. 20th c. **Malik / Mälik?** [Малик Бестеней улы Огъурлы], one of Baskakov's

informant from the aul of Erkin-χalq (Bask., Nog. 143); Tat.(Lit.) 1522 **Malik-baša** [Маликъбаша] (Lit. Tat. 1); Tat.(Lit.) 1559, 1562 **Malik-baša** [Осанъ / Усеинъ Маликбашичъ] (Lit. Tat. 3); Kzk. 19th c. **Malik-batïr / Mälik-batïr** (Ljutš 155); Tat.(GH)? **Melik-čan-χoža** [Меликчанъ-хозя] (PSRL VI, 343, 353); Selj. 11th c. **Melik-šah** [Мелик-шах], Seljuk ruler (1072-1092) (MIT II, 167). ✦ 'Ruler, sovereign, emperor, king' (Sattarov, Žanuzakov) cf. Uyg., Chag., Turk. *mälik* (<Ar.) 'der König' (Radl. IV, 2100). It is also a component. See also **SÄYPÜL-MÄLİK**.

MALİK-BAŠ Tat.(Lit.) 1559 **Malik-baš** [Осанъ Малыкбашичъ] (Lit. Tat. 3). ⇨ MALİK + BAŠ.

MALÏNČA Hak.(Kyz.) 19th-20th c. **Malïnča** [Малiнча], fem. (Katanov, Otč. 13). ✦ 'Raspberry' cf. R. малинча, малина 'id.' (Katanov).

MALÏ Kzk. 18th c. **Malï-bay** [Малыбай] (Nepljuev 755, 804, 810-12); Kzk. 19th c. **Malï-bay** [Малыбай] (SOK 4, 226); Kzk. 19th c. **Malï-bay** [Малибай] (SODž. 144); Kzk. 19th c. **Malï-bay** [Малыбай] (SODž. 4, 76); Kzk. 19th c. **Malï-bay** [Малыбай] (SOV 32); Kzk. 19th c. **Malï-bek** [Малибекъ] (SOV 14); *TN:* Kzk. **Malï-bay** [Малыбай] (Kojčubaev 167). ✦ 'Possession (property) of (God?, his family, father, etc.?)'. The names *Malï-bay* and *Malï-bek* usually are regarded as real compound (or full sentence) names meaning 'His flocks, herds are rich' and 'His flocks, herds are strong'(Kojčubaev). However, they may be defective compound names with missing first component. ⇨ MAL + suff. *-ï*.

MALÏŠ Kirg. 19th c. **Malïš-bay** [Малышбаевъ] (Grod., Pril. 158); Turk. 19th c. **Malïš-oγlu**, a Zeybek (Kúnos 1891, 119). ✦ 'Sheep of Russian breed' cf. Kzk. *mäliš* 'овца (русской породы)' (KzRS), Kirg. *mäliš* 'метизованная порода овец' (Jud.). See also **AQ-MALÏŠ**.

MALKE Kzk. 19th c. **Malke** [Мальке] (SODž. 44). ⇨ MAL + dim. suff. *-ke*.

MALKENDE Kzk. 19th c. **Malkende** [Малькендинъ] (AOO 14).

MALKÏŠ Hak.(Blt.) 1727 **Malkiš** [Малкишъ Магалаковъ] (PSZRI VII, 890).

MALQAR Kzk. 19th c. **Malγar** [Малгаръ] (SOK 210); Kzk. 19th c. **Malqar** [Малкаръ] (SOK 98).

MALQARALÏ Yürük 1543 **Malqaralï** [معلتره لى / Malkaralı], from the Yürüks of Kocacık, Turkey (Gökb., Rum. 105, 199).

MALQARÏ Kzk. 19th c. **Malqarï** [Малкары] (SOK 14).

MALQOČ Turk. 15th c. **Malqoč** [Μαλεκόκης], a commander of the Sultan Muhammed II (Byz. Turc. 180); Yürük 1543 **Malqoč** [Malkoç] (Gökb., Rum. 188, 212); Turk. 1528 **Malqoč-bey** [Malkoç Bey] (Gökb., Ed. 45). ✦ 'Swindler, trickster' cf. Turk. *malkoç[oğlu]* 'id.' (TED), *malqoč* 'frühere irreguläre Reitertruppen' (Radl. IV, 2039).

MALLA   Kzk. 19th c. **Malla-bay** [Маллабай Магомедъ] (Grod., Pril. 32); NUyg.? / Kzk.? 1858 **Malla-bek** [Малла-бекъ], from Eastern Turkestan (Valihanov, Soč. 560); Kzk. **Malla-bek** / **Mallä-bek** [Маллябекъ Дуненбаевъ] (Protok. Turk. IV, 76). ⇨ **MALDA / MALDÏ / MOLLA?**

MALLA-BOL   Kzk. 19th c. **Malla-bol** [Маллаболъ] (SOV 158). ⇨ **MALLA? + BOL.**

MALMAQ   Kzk. 19th c. **Malmaq** [Малмакъ] (SODž. 62).

MALTAY   Kzk. 19th c. **Maltay** [Малтай] (SOV 82, 158). ⇨ **MAL? + TAY** or suff. *-tay(1,2)*?

MALTAYA   Yak. **Maltaya** [Ан-Малтаjа], fem. (Pek.).

MALTAYQA   Tat.(Sib.) 1625 **Maltayqa** [Малтайка] (Miller, Ist. Sib. II, 321). ⇨ **MALTAY** + suff. *-qa.*

MALTMAS   Tat.(Sib.) 1648 **Maltmas** [Мурган Малтмасов] (Miller, Ist. Sib. II, 529). ⇨ **MĀTMAS?** / **MAYTMAS?**

MAM-BAY see **MAN**

MAM-BUMAQ   Kzk. 19th c. **Mam-bumaq (<Man-bumaq?)** [Мамбумакъ] (SOK 104). ⇨ **MAN + BUMAQ.**

MAMA   Uyg. 1338 **Mama**, Bulmiš' (Bulmïš') son (Chwol., Syr.-nest. (NF) 32); Chag. 16th c. **Mama** [Мама] (Ivanov 285, 289); Turk. 16th c. **Mama**, fem. (Ongan, Ank. II, 1342); Trkm. **Mama** [Мама], fem. (Sopieva 182); Trkm. 20th c. **Mama** [Мама], fem. (Zaj. 1971, 335); Hak. 19th-20th c. **Mama** [Мама], fem. (HRS 353); Chag. 16th c. **Mama-aγa** [Мама Ага], fem. (Ivanov 250); Turk. 1519 **Mama-bey** [Mama Bey] (Gökb., Ed. 251); Trkm. **Mama-ǰan** [Мамажан], fem. (Sopieva 182); Trkm. **Mama-gözel** [Мамагөзел], fem. (Sopieva 182); Turk. 1485 **Mama-paša** [Mama Paşa], Süleyman Bey's daughter (Gökb., Ed. 452); Trkm. 20th c. **Māma** [Мама], fem. (TrkmRS 441); Trkm. 20th c. **Māma** [Мама] (TrkmRS 441). ✧ I. 'Grand-mother', also as addressing to an elder woman. Cf. Maml. *mama* 'Yaşlı kadının çağrıldığı esnade söylenen veya söylenilen kelime; İsmi has (kadın)', (AH), Trkm. 'grand-mother on mother side' (Sopieva), Tat., NUyg.(Tar.) *mama* 'die Grossmutter, ein altes Weib' (Radl. IV, 2064; II. 'Mother' cf. Turk., Kar. *mama* 'id.' (Radl. IV, 2064); III. 'Mother's breast, tit' cf. Kzk., Alt.(Tel.) *mama* 'id.' (Radl. IV, 2064), Uzb. *mämmä* 'женская грудь' (UzbRS).

MAMA-NAZAR   Kirg. **Mama-nazar** [Маманазар] (Jud. 97). ⇨ **MAMA + NAZAR.**

MAMAXAN   Chag. 16th c. **Mamaχan** [Мама-хан], fem. (Ivanov 229). ⇨ **MAMA** + suff. *-χan(1).*

MAMAY   Tat.(GH) 1361, 1370, 1374, 1375, 1380 **Mamay** [Мамай], a prince of the Horde (PSRL IV, 65, V, 229, VIII 21, 41-42, XI, 12, XVI, 89, 99, 104, Jorga,

Notes I, 8); Tat.(GH)? 1378 **Mamay** [Мамай], a prince of the Horde (Lavr. 508); Maml. 15th c. **Mamay** [السيفى مماى], chancellor, then envoy to Istanbul, died in 1497, his name was found in an inscription in the Palace of Mamay in Cairo, nowadays used as a law court (Mayer) (Mayer 153, also Iyās II, 274, 292, 315-17); Maml. 1450 **Mamay** [ماماى البيبغاوى المظفرى] (Ibn Taghrīb. VII, 183, 234); Maml. 1484 **Mamay** [ماماى الخاصكى] (Iyās II, 224, 229); Maml. 1493/94 **Mamay** [ماماى حوشن] (Iyās II, 285 ff.); Maml. 1496 **Mamay** [ماماى / Mamaj] (Berchem 362); Maml. 1516 **Mamay** [ماماى الصغير] (Iyās III, 18); Maml. 1516 **Mamay** [ماماى المحتسب] (Iyās III, 81); Maml. 1520 **Mamay** [ماماى الساقى] (Iyās III, 222); Maml. 16th c. **Mamay** [ماماى], Qanï-bay's chancellor (Iyās III, 73); Chag. 16th c. **Mamay** [Мамай Карауль-Беги] (Ivanov 206); Trkm. 19th c. **Mamay** [Мамай Хаджиевъ] (Ščeglov IV, 190); Crm. 1520 **Mamay** [Мамай], a prince (PSRL VI, 29); Crm. 1565 **Mamay** [Мамай], a prince of Širins (PSRL IV, 316); Tat. 1619 **Mamay** [مماى / Мамай] (Jusupov 72); Tat. 17th c. **Mamay** [Туткененка Мамаевъ], from the government of Kazan (ИОАІЕ̂К XXIX, 148); Tat.(Mish.) **Mamay** [Mamai] (Pelissier 25); Bashk. 1751 **Mamay** [Мамай Сармашев] (MIB IV/1, 51); Kzk. **Mamay** [Кӱлдӱр Мамаі] (Proben III, 96 /75/); Kzk. 1819 **Mamay** [Мамай] (MIK IV, 325); Kzk. 19th c. **Mamay** [Мамай] (Grod., Pril. 112); Kzk. 19th c. **Mamay** [Мамайбекъ] (Grod., Pril. 25); Kzk. 19th c. **Mamay** [Мамай] (Grod., Pril. 156); Kzk. 19th c. **Mamay** [Моминъ Мамаевъ] (Grod., Pril. 149); Kzk. 19th c. **Mamay** [Мамай] (AOA 154); Kzk. 19th c. **Mamay** [Мамай] (Pam. kn. Turg. 40); Kzk. 19th c. **Mamay** [Мамай] (AOA 78); Kkalp. 20th c. **Mamay** [Мамай] (KkRS 775); Kkalp. 20th c. **Mamay** [Мамай] (Bask., Kkalp. 63); Nog. **Mamay** [Мамай], hero of heroic poems (Farforovskij 26); Nog. 1530 **Mamay** [Мамай] (PSRL XIII, 47); Nog. 1530, 1531 **Mamay** [Мамай], a murza (PSRL VIII, 273, 277); Nog.? 1626-29 **Mamay** [Мамай Тинмаметовъ], a murza (AI III, 460, IV, 87); Nog. 1649 **Mamay** [Мамай Сююнчевъ] (AI IV, 92); Hak. 19th c. **Mamay** [Мамай], fem. (Katanov, Otč. 12); Hak. 19th-20th c. **Mamay** [Мамай] (HRS 349); Maml. (Kipch.) 1371 **Mamay** [Мамай], a Kipchak khan (Al-Muχibbī/Tizeng. I, 339, 350); Hak.(Sag.) 19th-20th c. **Mamay** / **Mamāy** [Мамаі] (Proben IX, 443, 613); Bashk. 1740 **Mamay-bay** [Мамай-бай] (MIB I, 446); Crm. **Mamay-bï** [Мамаі бі] (Proben VII, 132); Tat.(GH) **Mamay-χan** [Мамай ханъ] (Sib. Let. 358-59); Tat. 1718 **Mamay-mulla** [Мамай-мулла] (MIB III, 165); Balk. 20th c. **Mammaylarï** [Mammájları /

Мамаевъ], family-name (Pröhle, Balk. 242). ✧ I. 'Mythical being which children are frightened with' cf. Tat. *mamay* 'ein mythisches Wesen, mit dem man die Kinder erschreckt' (Radl. IV, 2064), Kirg. dial. *mamay* 'название детской игры' (Jud.); II. According to Sattarov it is the old Turkic variant of *Muχammet*; III. Dim. of *Mama*?; IV. 'Fed with breast' (for the Hak. name), cf. Hak. PN *Mamay* 'вскормленный грудью' (Butanaev). ⇨ MAMA? + dim. *-y*. See also AQ-MAMAY, ORAQ-MAMAY.

MAMAQ Oghuz/Trkm.? **Mamaq** [Mamaq] (DQorq./Rossi 195, DQorq./Gökyay 82); Tat.(GH) **Mamaq** [Мамакъ-Салтанъ], a ruler of the Horde (PSRL VII, 241); Maml.? 1390 **Mamaq** [ماـمـق] (Iyās I, 288); Chag. **Mamaq** [مـاـمـاـق / Mamak] (Šejb. L); Bashk. 1713 **Mamaq** [Мамак Катыков] (MIB III, 97); Kzk. 19th c. **Mamaq** [Мамакъ] (Grod., Pril. 27); Kzk. 19th c. **Mamaq** [Мамакъ] (AOAtb. 10). ✧ A variant of the Ar. Mukhammad (Sattarov).

MAMAL Kzk. 19th c. **Mamal-bay** [Мамалбай] (SOK 158).

MAMALAY Tat. 1555 **Mamalay** [Мамалай] (Kn. Metriki Lit. 113). ✧ '(Grand-)Mother-like'. ⇨ MAMA + suff. *-lay*.

MAMALAQ Kirg. **Mamalaq** [Мамалак] (Jud. 726). ✧ 'Calf of a yak, bear's cub' (Jud.).

MAMALÏ Turk. 18th c. **Mamalï-oγlu** [Mamalı oğlu Şemsi Bey] (Uzunçarşılı: Belleten 1974, 222). ⇨ MAMA + suff. *-lï*.

MAMAN Kzk. 19th c. **Maman-bay** [Маманъ-бай] (AUK Dobavl. 3); Kkalp. 1810 **Maman-biy** [Маманбий] (MIKk. 111); Chag. 16th c. **Maman-qïz** [Маман-кыз], fem. (Ivanov 89). ✧ 'Specialist' cf. Kzk. *maman* 'id.' (KzRS).

MAMAŠ Tat. 1764 **Mamaš** [Бигаш Мамашев] (MIB IV/1 279); Bashk. 1737 **Mamaš** [Мамаш Итыков] (MIB I, 319); Maml. 1438/39 **Mamaš** / **Mamïš** [ماـمـش الـمـؤيـدى] (Ibn Taghrīb. VII, 80). ✧ 'Little Mama'. ⇨ MAMA + dim. suff. *-š*?

MAMAT see **MAMET**

MAMAT-ČÏN Uyg. **Mamat-čin** [Mamat-Çin] (EUTS). ⇨ MAMET? + ČÏN.

MAMAT-MOÑTUL-ČÏN Uyg. 12th c. - 14th c. **Mamat-moñtul-čïn** [Mamat moŋtul čïn] (DTS). ⇨ MAMET? + ? + ČÏN.

MAMBET Kkalp. 20th c. **Maqambet** [Мақамбет] (KkRS 775); Bashk. 1735 **Mambet** [Апасъ Мамбетевъ] (Vel.-Zern., Bašk. 21); Kkalp. 20th c. **Mämbet** [Мәмбет] (KkRS 775); Kkalp. 20th c. **Mämbet-yar** [Мәмбетияр] (KkRS 775); *EN:* Kzk. 18th c. - 19th c. **Mambet** [Мамбет] (Tynyšp. 68, 71, 72, 73, 75); *TN:* Kzk. **Mambet**, a tomb? (Rekogn.); Crm. **Mambet-ulan**, a place? south-west of Karasubazar (Jervis VIII). ✧ I. Shortened of

Mukhammad / Makhammad (Ar.) (Sattarov, Kajbullaev, Kalilov); II. 'Helper, collaborator; benefactor' (Ir. / P.) (Žanuzakov). ⇨ MUXAMMED. See also AJÏ-MAMBET, AYT-MAMBET, BAQ-PANBET, ČÏL-MAMBET, JAR-MAMBET, JÏL-MAMBET, JOL-MAMBET, DOS-MAMBET, ER-MAMBET, QARГA-MAMBET, QAZ-MAMBET, QOŠ-BAMBET, QUL-MAMBET, QUZ-MAMBET, OR-MAMBET, TAŠ-MAMBET, TEL-MAMBET, TOQ-MAMBET, TUR-MAMBET, UL-MAMBET.

MAMCÏQ see **MAMJÏQ**

MAMJÏQ Maml. 1438/39 **Mamjïq** / **Mamcïq** [مـمـجـق الـنـوروزى], an emir (Ibn Taghrīb. VII, 74, 273); Maml. 1441 **Mamjïq** / **Mamčïq** [مـمـجـف الـنـدرورى] (Ibn Taghrīb. VIII, 2); Maml. 1453 **Mamjïq** / **Mamčïq** [مـمـجـق الـيـشـبـكى] (Ibn Taghrīb. VII, 412).

MAMED-DURDÏ Trkm. **Mamed-durdï(-igdïr)** [Мамедъ-дурды-Игдыръ], from the İgdïr (İgdir)? tribe (Mel'gunov 320). ⇨ MAMET + TURDÏ.

MAMET Uyg. 12th c. - 14th c. **Mamat** (DTS); Tat.(GH) 1339/40 **Mamat** [مَـمَـات / Мамат] (Jusupov 26); Tat. 19th c. **Mamat** [Šerif Mamatov] (Mende 139, 155); Tat. 20th c. **Mamat** [Маматов / Маметов] (Sattarov); Tat.(GH) 1358 **Mamat-χoža** [Мамат-хожа], a prince of the Horde (PSRL VIII, 10); Tat. 1624 **Mamet** [Маметъ Сатимовъ] (Pokrovskij 71); Tat.(Ishim) **Mämät-qul** [Мәмәт Кул] (Proben IV, 200 /245/); Bashk. 1756 **Memet** [Тисканбай Меметев] (MIB IV/1, 107); Crm. 1787 **Memet-ša(-bey)** [Меметша бей], a Crimean murza (IAN (Otd. gum. nauk) 1928, 382). ✧ I. Shortened (colloqial) form of Mukhammed (<Ar.) (Sattarov); II. 'Helper; benefactor' (<Ir.) (Žanuzakov). ⇨ MUXAMMED? See also AQSA-KEL-MAMET, AL-MAMET, ARZA-MAMET, ČEK-MAMET, JAN-MAMET, İG-MAMBET, İŠ-MAMET, YAL-MAMET, YAŠ-MEMET, KEL-MAMET, QARA-KEL-MAMET, QUTLU-MAMET, SÜYÄR-MAMET, SÜL-MAMET, ŠA-MAMET, TAL-MAMET, TER-MAMET, TÏN-MAMET, TOY-MAMET, TOQ-MAMET, TOL-MEMET, TOS-MAMET, TUR-MAMET, TURDÏ-MÄMÄT, TURSUN-MÄMÄT, UR-MAMET, URAZ-MAMET, URAZ-MEHMED, URUS-MAMET.

MAMETEK Kzk. 18th c. - 19th c. **Mametek** [Маметекъ] (ZOOIRGO IV, 99); Kzk. 1820 **Mametek** [Маметекъ], chief of the Kipchak tribe of the Middle Horde (Orta Žüz) before 1820 (Sib. Vest. IX, 105); Kzk. 19th c. **Mametek** [Маметекъ] (SODž. 124); Tat.(Lit.) 1590 **Mamtek** (<**Mametek**) [Шавдавлетъ Мамтековичъ] (Lit. Tat. 59, 130). ⇨ MAMET + dim. suff. *-ek*.

MAMГAU Kzk. 19th c. **Mamγau** [Кузыбекъ

Мамгаевъ] (Grod., Pril. 133).

MAMÏQ   Bashk. 1765 **Mamïq** [Тойгуза Мамыков] (MIB IV/1, 310); Alt.(Tel.) 19th c. **Mamïq** [Mamyk], a prince in a legend (Radl., Aus Sib. I, 177); Kzk. 19th c. **Mamïq** [Мамекъ] (Grod., Pril. 44-45); Chag. 1496 **Mamuq** [Мамукъ], a Sheybanid ruler (PSRL VI, 40, VIII, 231); Trkm. 20th c. **Pamïq** [Pamïq], fem. (Zaj. 1971, 340); Trkm. 20th c. **Pāmïq** [Памык], fem. (TrkmRS 513); *TN:* Kzk. **Mamïq** [Мамык] (Kojčubaev 167). ✧ 'Cotton; wad' cf. Kuman, Chag. *mamuq* 'die Baumwolle', Tat. *mamïq* 'Baumwolle, Watte' (Radl. IV, 2065), Trkm. *pāmïq* 'вата' (TrkmRS) (<P.). See also **AQ-MAMÏQ**.

MAMÏN   Kzk. 19th c. **Mamïn-bay** [Мамынбай] (SODž. 112). ⇨ **MOMUN.**

MAMÏR   Kirg. **Mamïr** [Мамыр] (Jud. 964); Kzk. 19th c. **Mamïr-bay** [Мамырбай] (SODž. 132); Kzk. **Mamïr-χan** [Исимъ Мамырхановъ] (ZIRGOGeogr. I (1862), 311); Kzk. 1862 **Mamïr-χan** [Даутъ Мамырхановъ] (ZIRGOGeogr. I (1862), 311). ✧ I. 'Quiet, satisfied' (Ar.) (Jud.); II. 'Spring moon months (May and April)' (Ar.) (Žanuzakov), cf. Kzk. *mamïr* 'Monatsname' (Radl. IV, 2065); III. 'Lame' cf. Kzk. *mamïr* 'hinkend, lahm' (Radl. IV, 2065).

MAMÏR-AZÏQ   Kirg. **Mamr-azïq** (<**Mamïr-azïq**) [Мамразыкъ] (Valihanov, Soč. 59). ⇨ **MAMÏR + AZÏQ.**

MAMÏS see MAMÏŠ

MAMÏŠ   Hak.(Sag.) 19th-20th c. **Mamïs** [Мамыс] (Katanov, Otč. 7); Trkm. 20th c. **Mamïš** [Mamïš], fem. (Zaj. 1971, 335); Crm. 1509 **Mamïš** [Мамышъ], a ruler in the Crimea (PSRL VI, 54, 248, XIII, 10); Tat.(Lit.) 1554 **Mamïš** [Мамышъ] (Kn. Metriki Lit. 103); Tat. 1529 **Mamïš** [Мамышъ], a prince of Kazan (PSRL VIII, 272, XIII, 46); Oghuz/Trkm. 13th c. **Mamïš-bek** [ماش بيك / Мамыш-бек], Barčïn-Salur's husband (Abulg./Kon. 1445); Crm. 1523 **Mamïš-bek** [Мамышъ-бекъ], envoy to Istanbul (Smirnov, Krym. 393); Trkm. 1836 **Mamïš-χan** [Мамыш-хан], from the Göklen tribe (MIT II, 468); Uzb. 1510 **Mamuš** [Мамуш] (MIT II, 56). ✧ 'Little Mama' (dim. of *Mama*, cf. Zaj. 1971, p. 335). ⇨ **MAMA** + dim. suff. -*ïš*. See also **TOQ-MAMÏŠ.**

MAMÏŠEY   Kuman 1277 **Mamïšey** [Мамъшѣй], a „Tatar" chieftain or/and a warrior (Ipat. 578, (579), PSRL II, 207). ⇨ **MAMÏŠ** + suff. -*ey.*

MAMÏT   Kirg. 19th c. **Mamït** [Мамытъ] (Potanin II, 3); Alt.(Tel.) 19th c. **Mamït** [Мамыт] (Verb., In. 121). ✧ Shortened of *Muχammed* (Žanuzakov 148; Žanuzakov-Esbaeva). See also **SARÏ-MAMÏT, SEYÏT-MAMÏT.**

MAMLÏ   Tat. 19th c. **Mamley / Mämle?** [S. Mamleev] (Mende 126); Tat.(GH) **Mamli** [مَملِ / Mamali / Мамли] (Jusupov 42, Epigr. Bulg. 116, 117). ⇨

MAMALÏ?

MAMR-AZÏQ see MAMÏR-AZÏQ

MAMSAQA   Bashk. 1740 **Mamsaqa** [Мамсака], fem. (MIB I, 423).

MAMUΓAY   Tat. 1646 **Mamuγay** [Мамугай] (Miller, Ist. Sib. II, 511).

MAMUQ see MAMÏQ

MAMUŠ see MAMÏŠ

MAMUTÄK   Tat.(GH) 1437, 1445, 1447, 1455, 1460-61 **Mamotäk / Mamutäk** [Мамотякъ / Мамутякъ], 4th khan in Kazan, Magomet's son, prince of the Horde (PSRL V, 267, VI, 150, 171 ff., XII, 64, Zolotn. 158, AI I, 77, 119, 497). ✧ 'Little Mahmud'. ⇨ **MAXMUD** + dim. suff. -*äk.*

MAN   Kzk. 19th c. **Mam-bay (<Man-bay)** [Мамбай] (SOK 14); Kzk. 19th c. **Man-bay** [Манбай] (AOP 26); Kzk. 19th c. **Man-bek** [Манбекъ] (SODž. 88); Kzk. 19th c. **Man-čora** [Манчора] (SOV 36); Tat. 1698 **Man-jigit** [Китейко Манзигитовъ], a captain (Kungursk. akty 267); Kzk. 19th c. **Man-qul** [Манкулъ] (AOK 126). ✧ 'Three-year-old sheep'? cf. Karakh. *mañ yašlïq qoy* 'ein über 4 Jahre altes Schaf' (MK/Brock.); Kzk. dial. *mañ* 'трехлетний баранъ овца' (Ščerbak 1961, 116).

MAN-GÏLDÏ   Kzk. 19th c. **Man-gildi** [Мангильди] (Grod., Pril. 159). ⇨ **MAN + KELDÏ.**

MAN-TABAR   Tat.(Sib.) 1681 **Man-tabar** [Мантабарко Кокбиринъ] (DAI VIII, 177). ⇨ **MAN + TABAR.**

MANA   Nog. 20th c. **Mana** [Исакей Мана Огъурлы / Исакай Манаевич Огурлиев], father of one of Baskakov's informants from the aul of Erkin-yurt (Oraγ-awul) (Bask., Nog. 143); Kzk. 19th c. **Mana-bay** [Манабай] (SOV 34, 36); Kzk. 19th c. **Mana-bay** [Манабай] (SODž. 38, 56, 88, 102, 132); Kzk. 19th c. **Mana-bay** [Манабаевъ] (Grod., Pril. 102).

MANA-BAŠ   Alt. 19th-20th c. **Mana-baš** [Манабаш] (OjrRS 209). ⇨ **MANA + BAŠ.**

MANAY see ÏMANAY

MANAQ   Türk 568 **Manaq** [Μανάχ], envoy of the Türks (Byz. Turc. 181); Kuman 1090 **Manaq** [Μανάχ], a chieftain of the Kumans (Byz. Turc. 181); Tat.(Lit.) 1548 **Manaq** [Манакъ] (Kn. Metriki Lit. 45); Tat.(Sib.) 1631 **Manaq** [Баубеков Манак] (Miller, Ist. Sib. II, 386); Kzk. 1803-1820 **Manaq** [Манакъ], a leader of the Kiräit (Kereyit) tribe of Jeti-ru, Kiši-žüz (MIK IV, 514, Sib. Vest. IX., 113); Kzk. 19th c. **Manaq** [Ташканбай Манаковъ] (Grod., Pril. 56); Kzk. 19th c. **Manaq** [Манакъ] (SODž. 152); Kzk. 19th c. **Manaq** [Манакъ] (SOK 12); Kzk. 19th c. **Manaq** [Манакъ] (SOK 170); Alt. 19th c. **Manaq** [Манак], fem. (Verb., In. 125); Alt. 19th c. **Manaq** [Манак], fem. (Verb., In. 125); Kzk. **Manaq-pay** [Манакпаевъ] (Patkanov II, 92); Kzk. 19th c. **Manaq-pay**

[Манакпай] (SODž. 46); Kzk. 19th c. **Manaq-pay** [Манакпай] (SOK 88); Kzk. 19th c. **Manaq-pay** [Манакпай] (SODž. 84). ✧ 'Chin' cf. Uzb. *manaq* 'das Kinn' (Radl. IV, 2016).

MANAQAY Bashk. 1776 **Manaqay** [Манакай Салихов] (MIB V, 49). ⇨ MANA / MANAQ? + suff. *-qay / -ay*.

MANAM-BAY see **MANAN**

MANAN Kzk. 19th c. **Manam-bay (<Manan-bay)** [Манамбай] (AOO 38); Kzk. 19th c. **Manan-bay** [Кинджакаръ Мананбаевъ] (Grod., Pril. 37); Kzk. 19th c. **Manan-bay** [Manén-Baï] (Levchine 356); *TN:* **Manam-bay** [Манам-бай] (Karta JAR XI). ✧ 'Noble, generous, open-handed' (Ar.) (Žanuzakov).

MANAP Bashk. 1779 **Manap** [Манап Шеркеев] (MIB V, 91); Kzk. 19th c. **Manap-bay** [Манапбай] (SOV 92); Kzk. **Manap-qan** [Манап Кан] (Proben III, 228 /269/); *TN:* Kzk. **Manap** [Манап], a field (Kojčubaev 167). ✧ '(Kirghiz) chieftain (of common origin); (later) aristocrat; substitute' cf. Kirg. *manap* (Ar.) 'die Stammältesten der schwarzen Kirgisen' (Radl. IV, 2017), cf. also Žanuzakov, Togan, BTT 71.

MANAR Kzk. 19th c. **Manar-bay** [Манарбай] (SOV 6). ✧ 'Lantern, lamp' cf. Tat.(Tüm.) *manar* 'die Laterne' (Radl. IV, 2016) (<R.).

MANAS Turk. 16th c. **Manas** (Ongan, Ank. II); Kzk. **Manas** [Манасъ] (Valihanov, Soč. 72); Kzk. 19th c. **Manas** [Манасъ] (SOV 44, 54); Kzk. 19th c. **Manas** [Манасъ] (SODž. 74); Kirg. **Manas** [Манас], hero of the famous Kirghiz epic (Proben V, 1); Kzk. 19th c. **Manas-bay** [Манасбай] (SOK 160); *TN:* Kzk. **Manas** [Манасъ], a well(?) east of Lake Aral (Karta JAR XI); Kirg. **Manas** [Манасъ], a tomb south-east of Aulie Ata in the valley of the Talas (Karta JAR XIX). ✧ 'The hero of the greatest Kirghiz epos, also a river and a town in Eastern Turkestan' (Erol II), cf. Bernštam, A. I., K proishoždeniju imeni Manas. In: Manas - geroičeskij êpos kirgizskogo naroda. Frunze, 1968, pp. 177-191.

MANAŠA Kzk. **Manaša** [Манаша] (Proben III, 89 /113/).

MANAŠÏ Nog. **Manašï-batïr** [Манашы-батыр] (Žirm., Epos 395).

MANAT Kzk. 19th c. **Manat** [Манатъ] (SOK 170); Kzk. 19th c. **Manat** [Ахмедъ Манатовъ] (Grod., Pril. 105). ✧ 'A kind of cloth, usually red; red shawl' (Žanuzakov), cf. Kzk., Uzb. *manat* 'rothes Tuch' (Radl. IV, 2017), in northern dial. of Kzk. 'Rubel, Money' (Žanuzakov-Esbaeva 460).

MANATAY Kkalp. 1809 **Manatay** [Манатай] (MIKk. 102); Kkalp. 20th c. **Manatay** [Манатай] (Bask., Kkalp. 28, KkRS 775). ⇨ MANAT + dim. suff. *-ay*.

MANATQAY Kzk. 19th c. **Manatqay** [Манаткай] (SOK 72). ⇨ MANAT + dim. suff. *-qay*.

MANAW Kzk. 19th c. **Manaw** [Манау] (SOK 50, 202). ✧ 'Fruit seller, vegetable man' cf. Turk. *manav* 'der Gemüse- und Fruchthändler (eine ironische Benennung der Türken von Kleinasien)' (Radl. IV, 2017).

MANČA Kzk.? 19th c. **Manča / Mančay?** [Манчаевъ] (Grod., Pril. 109).

MANČAQ Bashk. 1754 **Mančaq** [Кудайгул Манчаков] (MIB IV/1, 83).

MANČARÏ Yak. **Mančarï** [Маньчары] (Seroševskij, Razsk. 173). ✧ 'Marshy grass' (Seroševskij).

MANČÜK Uyg. **Mančük** [Mançük] (EUTS).

MANJU Kzk. 19th c. **Manju** [Манджу] (SODž. 76); Kzk. 19th c. **Manju-ɣul** [Манджугулъ] (SOK 218). ✧ Ethnonym.

MAND'Ï Alt. 19th-20th c. **Mand'ï** [Мандьы] (OjrRS 209). ✧ 'Rich fur (coat)' (OjrRS).

MAND'ÏQ Alt. 19th-20th c. **Mand'ïq** [Мандьык] (OjrRS 209).

MANDAY Kzk. 19th c. **Manday** [Мандай] (AOAtb. 6).

MANDALAY Hak. 19th-20th c. **Mandalay** [Мандалай] (HRS 349).

MANDAW Kzk. 19th c. **Mandaw-bay** [Мандаубай] (AOA 130).

MANDĀJÏQ Tuv. 19th c. **Mandājïq** [Мандацык] (Proben IX, 121).

MANDĀQA Yak. **Mandāqa** [Мандака] (Pek.).

MANDİ see **MEÑLİ**

MANDÏQ Kzk. **Mandïq** [Mandyk / Мандык], a folklore hero (Proben III, 84 /108/).

MANDRAQ Tat.(Sib.) 1642 **Mandraq** [Мандракъ], a prince of Teles (Tölös), in region of Kuznetsk at Lake Altïn-köl (R.: Teleckoe ozero) (Andrievič, Ist. Sib. I, 97, AI III, 379, Radl., Aus Sib. I, 179).

MANDULA Kuman 1270 **Mandula** [Mandula, puella Cumana], one of the Kuman concubines of the Hungarian king Ladislaus (Kun László) IV (1272-1290) (SRH I, 473); Kuman 1347 **Mandula** [Paulum dictum Chyta filium Manthula], Chyta's (Čita?) father from the Kumans of Hungary living in tents (Gyárfás III, 484). ✧ '?' < Mo. / Hung.? cf. Rásonyi, KÖA 121, Rásonyi, Anthr. 144.

MANEK Kzk. 19th c. **Manek / Manïq?** [Манекъ] (SOV 144).

MANEN Kzk. **Manen-bay** [Маненъ-бай] (Levšin III, 96). ⇨ MANAN?

MANİ Hak. 19th-20th c. **Mani** [Мани] (HRS 349).

MANİNEK Hak. 19th-20th c. **Maninek** [Манинек], fem. (HRS 353). ✧ 'Merciful, clement' (<Ar.) cf. Hak. PN *Manin / Maminek [Maninek!]* (Butanaev).

MANİT Hak. 19th-20th c. **Manit** [Манит], fem. (HRS 353); Hak.? 19th-20th c. **Manit** [Манiт], fem. (Katanov, Otč. 10). ✧ 'Silver coin, Rubel' (HRS, Butanaev), cf. R. монета 'coin' (Katanov, Otč. 10).

MANİTKE Hak. 19th-20th c. **Manitke** [Манитке], fem. (?). ❖ 'Little silver coin'. ⇨ **MANİT** + dim. suff. *-ke*.

MANİT see **MANİT**

MANÏ Kzk. 19th c. **Manï-bay** [Маныбай] (AOAtb. 66); Kzk. 19th c. **Manï-bay** [Маныбай] (SOV 44); *TN:* Kzk. 19th c. **Manï-bay** [Маныбай], a field (AOP 10).

MANÏY Hak. 19th-20th c. **Manïy** [Маный], fem. (HRS 353).

MANÏR Kzk. 19th c. **Manïr** [Маныръ] (SODž. 84).

MANKE Kzk. 1845 **Manke** [Манкэ] (Konšin, Mat. V, 68). ⇨ **MAN?** + suff. *-ke*.

MANKEBEK Maml. **Mankebek / Man-kebek? / Manke-bek?** [Mankebek], one of Qalāūn's daughters-in-law, Nuqay's daughter, her sister is „Ardekin" (Makrīzī III, 54).

MANQA Trkm. 19th c. **Manqa? / Mañqa?** [Манька] (Ščeglov IV, 178); Kzk. 1846 **Manqa? / Mañqa?** [Манка Кулов], a biy (MKOP 157).

MANQAY Kzk. 19th c. **Manqay** [Бекджа Манкаевъ] (Grod., Pril. 109); Kzk. 19th c. **Manqay** [Манкай] (AOA 82); Kzk. 19th c. **Manqay** [Манкай] (SOK 60). ⇨ **MAN** + suff. *-qay*.

MANQÏŠ Kzk. 19th c. **Manqïš / Mankiš?** [Манкишъ] (SOK 182). ⇨ **MAÑÏŠ?**

MANQÏT see **MAÑĠÏT**

MANLAY see **MAÑLAY**

MANMAN Tat.(GH)? 1243 **Manman** [Маньманъ], a Tatar(?) hero (warrior) (Ipat. 528 (532)). ⇨ **MANOMAN?**

MANMUŠ Tat. 1533 **Manmuš** [Манмушъ], from the Horde (PSRL VIII, 281).

MANO Hak. 19th-20th c. **Mano** [Мано], fem. (HRS 353).

MANOMAN Tat. 1533 **Manoman** [Маноманъ], a commander of the army (PSRL II, 180-181). ⇨ **MANMAN?**

MANRAQ Kzk. 19th c. **Manraq** [Манракъ] (SOK 238).

MANSAR Alt. 19th c. **Mansar-γan** [Мансар-ган] (Verb., In. 57). ❖ A spirit. Cf. Alt.(Tel.) *mansarγan* 'ein Geist' (Radl. IV, 2024).

MANSEY Tuv. 1653 **Mansey** [Mansei], a prince (Radl., Aus Sib. I, 176).

MANSUP Tat.(GH) 1440 **Mansup** [Мансупъ], a prince of the Horde (PSRL XII, 30).

MANSUR Oghuz 951, 1062 **Mansur** [Мансур ибн Себуктегин], Sebük-tegin's son, Ghaznevid (Ibn al-Athīr/Tornb. VIII, 360, 366, 463-8 etc., Ibn Taghrīb. II, 231, Hil. Sābī 179, MIT I, 359); Oghuz 1035/36 **Mansur** [Мансур], chief of the Ghuzz (MIT I, 364). ❖ Mansur 'Aided by God, victorious, triumphant' (Ar.) (TED, Žanuzakov, Sattarov). See also **ŠAH-MANSÏR**.

MANTA Kzk. 19th c. **Manta-bay** [Мантабай] (SODž. 52).

MANTAY Kzk. 19th c. **Manday** [Мандай] (AOAtb. 26); Kzk. 19th c. **Mantay** [Мантай] (SOV 26, 98); Kzk. 19th c. **Mantay** [Мантай] (SOK 230). ⇨ **MAN** + suff. *-tay(1,2)*.

MANTU Maml. 14th c. **Mantu** [مَنطو] (Sauvaget 56). ❖ 'Dish prepared with rolled dough, ground meat and yoghurt' (Sauvaget 56), cf. East.T. *mantu* 'id.' (Radl. IV, 2022).

MANTUKEY Bashk. 1734 **Mantukey** [Сюлей Мантокеев] (MIB III, 322).

MANTUQ Maml. 1407/08 **Mantïq** [منطوق], an emir (Ibn Taghrīb. VI, 189, 287).

MANU Kzk. 19th c. **Manu-bay** [Базаръ бигэ Манубаева] (Grod., Pril. 142).

MANŽUQ 1820 **Manžuq** [Манжукъ Бекменевъ] (PSZRI XXXI, 429).

MAÑ Uyg. 13th-14th c. **Mañ-čor** (Zieme, Mat. II, 84, 90).

MAÑ-QÏŠLAQ Tat.(GH)? **Mañ-qïšlaq-sultan** [منقشلاق سلطان / Mangischlâq-Sultan], a Jochid from Māverannāhr (Abulg./Desm. 188). ❖ Placename. The territory of the Oghuz state, cf. Karakh. *man qišlaγ* 'название местности' (DTS).

MAÑA Kzk. 19th c. **Maña-bay** [Мангабай] (AOO 18, 22); Kzk. 19th c. **Maña-bay** [Мангабай] (SODž. 126).

MAÑAN Yak. **Mañan** [Маңан Маңхалын-хотун], a part of the name of a female spirit, Ürüñ-ayï-toyōn's daughter (Pek.). See also **ĴUXXARÏ-MAÑAN**.

MAÑDAY see **MAÑLAY**

MAÑDÏ-ŠİRE Alt.(Tel.) 19th c. **Mañdï-šire** [Мангдышире-богатыръ Мандышірä] (Verb., In. 90, 91, 99, 101, 113). ❖ 'One of the first created men' (< Skr. *Manjusri*, Radl. IV, 2011).

MAÑĠÏS Tuv. 19th c. **Mañγïs** [Мангысъ] (Potanin IV, 380 etc.). ❖ 'Locust' cf. Alt. *manyïs* 'Wanderheuschrecke' (Radl. IV, 2020).

MAÑĠÏŠ Tat.(Tara) **Mañγïš** [Мангыш Султан], a hero in a tale (Proben IV, 144 /182/); 1814 **Mañγuš** [Мангушевъ], a prince (PSZRI XXXII, 805); Kipch. 1320 **Mañγuš** [منغوش / Мангушъ], Özbeg Khan's envoy to Egypt (Duqmaq/Tizeng. I, 320, 327, Aynī/Tizeng. I, 489, 519); Tat.(Bar.) **Mañγuš** [Mangusch / Мангуш Алып], Ködön Kan's son (Proben IV, 49 /61/); Bashk. 1735 **Mañγuš** [Мангушъ] (Vel.-Zern., Bašk. 14); Bashk. 1756 **Mañγuš** [Апиш Мангушев] (MIB IV/1, 107).

MAÑĠÏT Crm. 17th c. **Manqït-bey** [Манкытъ-бей] (Smirnov, Krym. 323); Tat.(Sib.) 1601 **Mañγut** [Мангут] (Miller, Ist. Sib. II, 169); *TN:* Nog. 20th c. **Mañγït** [Mangit / Манъгъыт урув] (Bask., Nog. 137). ❖ Ethnonym.

MAÑĠÏTAČ? Tat.(Sib.) 1643 **Mañγïtač?**

[Мангитачко] (Miller, Ist. Sib. II, 491).

MAÑĠÏTAY   Kzk. 19th c. **Mañɣïtay** [Мангытай] (SOV 40).

MAÑĠUŠ see **MAÑĠÏŠ**

MAÑĠUT see **MAÑĠÏT**

MAÑĠUTAY   Khorezm. 1230 **Mañɣu-tay-šah (Mäñgütäy-šah?)** [منكطوى شاه / Mankothoui], Jelāleddīn's son (Nasawī 228); Bashk. 1600 **Mañɣutay** [Мангутай (Мамготай) Комбаров] (Miller, Ist. Sib. II, 158, 159, 160, MIB I, 151).

MAÑXALÏN   Yak. **Mañχalïn-toyon** / **Mañχalyïn** [Манхалын, Манхалјын], spirit of the world, creator of the cattle (Pek.).

MAÑXARĀT   Yak. **Mañχarāt** / **Mañχarātay** [Манхарат, Манхаратаи] (Pek.).   ✧ Pankrat, Pankratiy (R.) (Pek.).

MAÑÏ   Kzk. 19th c. **Mañï-bay** / **Mañɣï-bay** [Мангыбаевъ] (AOO 34); Kzk. 19th c. **Mañï-bay** / **Mañɣï-bay** [Мангыбай] (AOP 106).

MAÑÏR   Alt. 19th-20th c. **Mañïr** [Маныр], fem. (OjrRS 212).   ✧ 'Onion / garlic'? (OjrRS: 'лук-слизун; чеснок, слизун'), cf. Alt. *mañɣïr* 'чеснок, (обл.) слизун' (OjrRS). See also **KÖBİRGÄN, SOĠAN, SOĠONOQ**.

MAÑÏRČÏ   Alt. 19th-20th c. **Mañïrčï** [Манырчы], fem. (OjrRS 212 m).   ✧ 'Who gathers onion/garlic' (OjrRS).   ⇨ **MAÑÏR** + suff. *-čï*. See also **SUĠANČÏ**.

MAÑQAŠ   Alt. 19th-20th c. **Mañqaš** [Манкаш], fem. (OjrRS 212).   ✧ 'Runner (woman)' (OjrRS).

MAÑQU   Maml. 1294 **Mañqu** [Seïf-eddin Mankou], a chancellor (Makrīzī III, 156).

MAÑLAY   Kzk. 19th c. **Manlay** [Манлай] (SOK 12); Kzk. 19th c. **Manlay** [Манлай] (SOV 132); Kzk. 19th c. **Mañday** [Кулджанъ Мангдаевъ] (Grod., Pril. 107); Kzk. 1820 **Mañday-batïr** [Мангдай-батыръ / Мангдай батырь], one of the chiefs of the Uzun (Qïpšaq) tribe of the Middle Horde (Orta Žüz) (Sib. Vest. IX, 108, MIK IV, 513); Trkm. 1717 **Mañlay** [Манглай (Мангла) Кашка] (ZIRGO IX, 321); Kkalp. 1810, 1820 **Mañlay** [Манглай] (MIKk. 115, 116, 118); Kkalp. 1820 **Mañlay** [Манглай] (MIKk. 115).   ✧ 'Forehead, brow' cf. Kuman, Chag., Crm., Tat., Trkm. *mañlay* 'die Stirn' (Radl. IV, 2009). See also **AQ-MAÑLAY, ARU-MANDAY, QARA-MAÑDAY**.

MAÑNAY   Hak. 19th-20th c. **Mañnay** [Манънай], fem. (HRS 353).   ✧ Title of a prince, cf. Hak. fem. PN *Mannay* (Butanaev).

MAÑRAŠ   Tat. 1592 **Mañraš** [Ахметъ Манграшевичъ] (Lit. Tat. 116).   ✧ 'Bleat' cf. Kuman, Chag., Hak., Kzk., Tat.(Bar.) *mañra-* 'blöken' (Radl. IV, 2008) + suff. *-š*.

MAÑREY   Kzk. 19th c. **Mañrey** [Мангрей] (AOO 62).   ✧ 'Bleats'? cf. Kuman, Chag., Hak., Kzk., Tat.(Bar.)

mañra- 'blöken' (Radl. IV, 2008).

MAÑURAS   Selj.? 1187 **Mañuras** [Mangûrâs], a slave of Salāhaddīn, died at Hattīn (Abulfar./Budge I, 323).

MAÑZÏR   Hak. 19th-20th c. **Mañzïr** [Манъзыр] (HRS 349).   ✧ 'Rush, hurry'? cf. Hak. *mañzira-* 'sich beeilen' (Radl. IV, 2011).

MAPA   Kzk. 19th c. **Mapa** [Мапа] (AOP 106).   ✧ 'Goodness, good deed' (Jud.).

MAPAQ   Kzk. 19th c. **Mapaq** [Мапакъ] (SODž. 18).   ✧ 'Soft, mellow, mild; small'? cf. Kzk. *mapa* 'yumşak, ufak' (KzTS).

MAR   Uyg. **Mar** [Mar] (EUTS).

MAR-AMU   Uyg. **Mar-amu** [Mar Amu] (EUTS).   ⇨ **MAR + AMU?**

MARAQ   Bashk. 1675 **Maraq** [Маряк Екилдяков] (MIB I, 200); Kzk. 19th c. **Maraq-bay** [Маракбай] (Grod., Pril. 145).   ✧ 'Observing point, exploration' cf. East.T. *maraq* 'der Beobachtungsposten, der Hinterhalt, die Lauer' (Radl. IV, 2025).

MARAQAY   Bashk. 1750 **Maraqay** [Маракай Девенеев] (MIB III, 476).

MARAL   Chag.? **Maral** [قوتى مرال / Maral] (Šejb. XXVII); Trkm. 20th c. **Maral** [Маралъ], very frequent name in Ashabad (Nikonov: OSA 160); Trkm. 20th c. **Maral** [Maral], fem. (Zaj. 1971, 338); Trkm. 20th c. **Maral** [Марал], fem. (TrkmRS 443); Kzk. 19th c. **Maral** [Маралъ] (AOP 58); Kzk. 19th c. **Maral** [Мараловъ] (AOO 38); Kzk. 19th c. **Maral** [Маралъ] (AOP 66); Kzk. 19th c. **Maral** [Маралъ Курмановъ] (AUK 484); Kzk. 19th c. **Maral** [Мараловъ] (Grod., Pril. 86); Kzk. 19th c. **Maral** [Маралъ] (SODž. 156); Kzk. 19th c. **Maral** [Маралъ] (SOK 230, 272); Alt. **Maral** [Старикъ Маралъ] (Nikiforov 65); Kzk. 19th c. **Maral-bay** [Маралбай] (AOK 110); Kzk. 19th c. **Maral-bay** [Маралбай] (SODž. 64, 74); Kzk. 19th c. **Maral-bay** [Маралбай] (Grod., Pril. 149); Kzk. 19th c. **Maral-bay** [Маралбай] (SODž. 24); Kzk. 19th c. **Maral-bay** [Маралбай] (SOV 72); Kzk. 19th c. **Maral-bay** [Маралбай] (SOK 90).   ✧ 'Deer, hind' cf. Uyg., Kzk. *maral* 'der Hirsch' (Radl. IV, 2025), Chag., East.T., Trkm., Uzb. *maral* 'die Hirschkuh' (Radl. IV, 2025). See also **AQ-MARAL**.

MARALČÏ   Uzb. **Maralčï** [Маралчи], from Bukhara (Veselovskij, Unk. 177).   ✧ 'Hunter of deer'.   ⇨ **MARAL** + suff. *-čï*.

MARAM-BEK see **MARAN**

MARAN   Uzb.? **Maram-bek** (<**Maran-bek**) [Марам-бек], from the Pamir-region (IRGO LV, 30); Kzk. 19th c. **Maran-bay** [Маранбай] (SOK 10).   ⇨ **MARAL?**

MARAS I.   Alt. 19th-20th c. **Maras** [Мараc], fem. (OjrRS 212).

MARAS II.   Kzk. 19th c. **Maras-ul** [Марасулъ] (SKSO VIII, 232).   ✧ 'Illness' cf. Crm., Trkm., Turk., Uzb. *maraz* 'die Krankheit' (Radl. IV, 2026).

MARAT Kzk. 19th c. **Marat-pay** [Маратпай] (SODž. 88). ✧ I. 'Sacred, saint' (<Ar.) (Kajbullaev); II. Marat (Fr.), the family-name of Jean-Paul Marat (1743-1793), the famous French revolutionary (cf. Sattarov, Kusimova, Kajbullaev).

MARAZÏQ Kzk. 19th c. **Marazïq** [Маразыкъ] (SKSO VIII, 232). ✧ 'Illness' cf. Crm., Trkm., Turk., Uzb. *maraz* 'die Krankheit' (Radl. IV, 2026). + dim. suff. -*ïq*.

MARBÏQ Yak. **Marbïq** [Марбык] (Pek.).

MARČA Hak. 19th-20th c. **Marča** [Марча], fem. (HRS 354). ✧ 'A kind of silk'? cf. Hak. fem. PN *Marča / Parča* '?' (Butanaev).

MARJALLA Yak. **Marjalla** [Марцалла] (Pek.).

MARJÏQÏN Yak. **Marjïqïn** [Марцыкын] (Pek.).

MARĞA Hak. 19th-20th c. **Marγa** [Марға], fem. (HRS 353). ✧ 'Debate; bet' (HRS).

MARĞUZ Mo.? **Marγuz** [Marguz] (RaD/Ber. I, 96); Oghuz/Trkm.? **Marγuz** [Marghouz] (Abulg./Desm. 47).

MARXA Hak. 19th-20th c. **Marχa** [Марха], fem. (HRS 354). ✧ 'Button, knob' (HRS, Butanaev).

MARİY Hak. 19th-20th c. **Mariy** [Марий], fem. (HRS 353). ✧ Mariya (R. fem.) (HRS).

MARİK Hak. 19th-20th c. **Marik** [Марик], fem. (HRS 353).

MARİN see **MARİNA**

MARİNA Hak. 19th-20th c. **Marin** [Марин], fem. (HRS 353); Tat. 20th c. **Marina** [Марина] (Sattarov); Kzk. 20th c. **Marina** [Марина] (Žanuzakov 148); Hak. 19th-20th c. **Marine** [Марине], fem. (HRS 353); Yak. **Marīna** [Марына], fem. (Pek.). ✧ Marina (R. fem.).

MARİS see **MARİŠ**

MARÏN Kzk. 19th c. **Marïm-bay (<Marïn-bay)** [Марымбай] (SODž. 78).

MARÏS Alt. 19th-20th c. **Marïs** [Марыс] (OjrRS 209). ⇨ **MARİS?**

MARÏŠ Hak. 19th-20th c. **Maris** [Марис], fem. (HRS 353); Alt. 19th-20th c. **Marïš** [Марыш], fem. (OjrRS 212). ✧ Mariša (R.), dim. of R. Marina / Mariya (OjrRS, Butanaev).

MARİNA see **MARİNA**

MARÏŅQA Yak. **Marïŋqa** [Марыӈка], fem. (Pek.). ✧ Marinka (R.), dim. of R. Marina (Pek.).

MARQA Kzk. 19th c. **Marqa** [Марка] (SKSO VIII, 204); Kzk. **Marqa-bay** [Досай Маркабаевъ], from the district of Kopal (ZIRGOGeogr. I, 309); Kzk. 1819 **Marqa-bay** [Маркабай] (MIK IV, 325); Kzk. 1846 **Marqa-bay** [Маркабай Тенебеков], a biy (MKOP 156); Kzk. 19th c. **Marqa-bay** [Маркабай] (SOV 12); Kzk. 19th c. **Marqa-bay** [Маркабай] (SOK 36); Kzk. 19th c. **Marqa-bay** [Маркабай] (SOK 120); Kzk. 19th c. **Marqa-bay** [Маркабай] (SOV 112); Kzk. 19th c. **Marqa-bay** [Маркабай] (AOK 86); Kzk. 19th c. **Marqa-bay** [Маркабай] (AOA 10). ✧ 'Lamb (born before April); premature (lamb, calf etc.)' cf. Kzk. *marqa* 'id.' (Radl. IV, 2028). See also **KÖRPEŠ**.

MARQA-TAY Kzk. 19th c. **Marqa-tay** [Маркатай] (AOO 58). ✧ 'Premature foal'. ⇨ **MARQA + TAY** or suff. -*tay(1,2)*?

MARQAŠ Kzk. 19th c. **Marqaš** [Маркашъ] (AOK, 110, 126). ✧ 'Little lamb; premature' cf. Kzk. *marqa* 'biraz büyüyen, birkaç aylık olmuş kuzu' (KzTS), Kzk. *marqa* (Radl. IV, 2028), also Kzk. PN *Marqas* (Žanuzakov-Esbaeva) + suff. -*š* / -*s*.

MARLAN Hak.(Sag.) 19th-20th c. **Marlan** [Марлан] (Katanov, Otč. 11). ⇨ **MARLEN?**

MARLEN Trkm. **Marlen** [Марлен] (Sopieva 182). ✧ Marlen (R.), derived from the first syllables of the family-ames Marx and Lenin.

MARLO Hak. 19th-20th c. **Marlo** [Марло] (HRS 349).

MARSATÏŇ Yak. **Marsatïñ** [Марсатын] (Pek.).

MARTİL Hak. 19th-20th c. **Martil** [Мартил] (HRS 349).

MARTOŇ Hak. 19th-20th c. **Martoñ** [Мартонъ] (HRS 349). ✧ 'Teacher of religion' cf. Hak. PN *Marton* 'вероучитель' derives from the Old Turkic (Butanaev).

MARTOTAY Hak. 19th-20th c. **Martotay** [Мартотай], fem. (HRS 353). ✧ '?' cf. Hak. PN *Martot* '?' (Butanaev) + suff. -*ay*.

MARU Hak. 19th-20th c. **Maru** [Мару], fem. (HRS 353).

MARZAS Kzk. 19th c. **Marzas** [Марзасъ] (SOV 94).

MARŽAN see **MERJAN**

MAS Kzk. 19th c. **Maz-bay (<Mas-bay)** [Мазбай] (AOP 110); Turk. 15th c. **Maz-oul** [Μαζούλης], a commander of the army (Byz. Turk. 180). ✧ 'Drunk; edgy, raging, fierce' cf. Kzk., Trkm., Uzb. *mas* 'der Betrunkene; erregt, wild geworden' (Radl. IV, 2051).

MASA Kzk. 19th c. **Masa-bay** [Масабай] (AOO 58); Kzk. 19th c. **Masa-bay** [Масабай] (AOK 94). ✧ 'Moskito' cf. Kzk. *masa* (P.) 'id.' (Radl. IV, 2051).

MASAY Bashk. 1714 **Masay** [Масайко Яшпулатов] (MIB I, 107). ✧ 'Hope!' cf. Tat. *masay-* 'hoffen' (Radl. IV, 2052).

MASAQ Kzk. 19th c. **Masaq** [Масакъ] (SOV 188); Kzk. 19th c. **Masaq-pay** [Масакпай] (SOK 260); Kzk. 19th c. **Masaq-pay** [Масакпай] (SOV 16, 74). ✧ 'Iron gad; cock, hammer' cf. Kzk. *masaq* 'id.' (Radl. IV, 2052).

MASAN Kzk. 19th c. **Masan-bay** [Масанбай] (SOK 238). ✧ 'A little drunk'? cf. Kzk. *masan(daw)* 'sarhoş gibi, sarhoşa yakın' (KzTS).

MASAR Oghuz **Masar** [Masar], in the Oghuz legend of origin (Oğuz K. Dest. 29, DTS, EUTS). ⇨ **MÏSÏR?**

MASATÏ Kkalp. 20th c. **Masatï** [Масаты], fem. (KkRS 778). ✧ 'Silk, velvet' (KkRS).

MASENİK Hak. 19th-20th c. **Masenik** [Масеник], fem. (HRS 354).

MASİNEK Hak. 19th-20th c. **Masinek** [Масинек], fem. (HRS 354).

MASÏ Kzk. 19th c. **Masï-bay** [Масыбай] (SOK 50).

MASÏQ Kzk. 19th c. **Masïq-pay** [Масыкпай] (SOK 254).

MASQAY Hak. 19th-20th c. **Masqay** [Маскай] (HRS 349).

MASQAR Kzk. 1785 **Masqar / Masqar-uruɣï** [مصقار اوروغى / Маскар], a clan (MIK IV, 52, 54).

MASQOV see **MOSQOV**

MASLA Hak. 19th-20th c. **Masla** [Масла] (HRS 349).

MASMADAR Uyg. 12th c. - 14th c. **Masmadar** [Masmadar] (DTS, EUTS).

MASMÏR Kzk. 19th c. **Masmïr** [Масмыръ] (AOP 66).

MASTAN Uzb. 19th c. **Mastan** [Мулла Мастанъ Бадалбаевъ], a mulla (TV 1876, 83).

MASTEY Bashk. 1754-55 **Mastey** [Мастей Абызаев] (MIB IV/1, 79, 95). ⇨ **MAS** + suff. *-tey*.

MASTÏR Hak. 19th-20th c. **Mastïr** [Мастыр], fem. (HRS 354).

MASTUR Bashk. 1745 **Mastur** [Мастюр Букаев] (MIB III, 426).

MASUME Turk. 1741 **Masume-χatun** [Masume Hatun], fem. (Gökb., Ed. 350). ✧ 'Innocent, guiltless; little child' cf. Turk. *masum* 'id.' (TED).

MASUP Kzk. 19th c. **Masup** [Масупъ Сарбасовъ] (AUK 153).

MAŠ-PARAQ Alt. 19th c. **Maš-paraq** [Машпарак-богатыръ], a hero (Verb., In. 157).

MAŠAD Trkm. 1889 **Mašad** [Машадъ] (ZIRGOEtn. I, 188). ⇨ **MAŠAT?**

MAŠAN Kzk. 19th c. **Mašan** [Машанъ] (AOA 98); Kzk.?, Kirg.? 19th c. **Mašan** [Машанъ] (Potanin II, 6).

MAŠAR Bashk. 1759 **Mašar** [Муслюм Машаров] (MIB IV/2, 22).

MAŠAT Kzk. 1846 **Mašat** [Турабай Машатов], a biy (MKOP 152). ✧ 'Well' cf. Kirg. *mašat* 'die Quelle' (Radl. IV, 2060).

MAŠÏ Uyg. **Mašï** (Radl., USp. 4-5, 113-14, DTS).

MAŠÏQ Kzk. 19th c. **Mašïq** [Машикъ] (SODž. 44). ✧ 'Master, expert' cf. Kzk. *mašïq* 'alışık, tecrübeli, belli bir şeyi iyi bilen' (KzTS).

MAŠKE Kzk. 19th c. **Maške** [Машке] (SOK 102); Kzk. 19th c. **Maške (<Mašake?)** [Машке] (SOK 200). ✧ 'Little cock, hammer' cf. Kirg., Uzb. *maša* (P.) 'id.' (Radl. IV, 2058). + dim. suff. *-ke* / comp. *-ake*.

MAT Hak.(Blt.) 19th-20th c. **Mat** [Мат] (Katanov, Otč. 9). ✧ 'Honest, righteous, faithful' cf. Alt.(Tel.) *mat* 'id.' (Radl. IV, 2043).

MAT-MURAT see **MÄT-MURAT**

MAT-NAZAR Kzk. 19th c. **Mat-nazar** [Матназаръ] (Grod., Pril. 142). ⇨ **MÄT + NAZAR.**

MATA I. Kzk. 19th c. **Mata-mergen** [Матамергенъ] (SKSO VIII, 224). ✧ 'A kind of mostly blue cotton-ware or linen' cf. Kzk., Trkm., Uzb. *mata* 'Baumwollenzeug, Leinwand (hauptsächlich blau gefärbt)' (Radl. IV, 2043). ⇨ **MATÏ.**

MATA II. Alt. 19th-20th c. **Mata** [Мата], fem. (OjrRS 212); Hak. 19th-20th c. **Mata** [Мата], fem. (HRS 354). ✧ 'Do well!, Work carefully' cf. Hak. *mata-* 'тщательно, хорошо что-л. делать' (HRS).

MATAY I. Kzk. 1742 **Matay** [Матай], fem. (MIB I, 494); Tat. 1739 **Matay** [Матяевъ] (Alatyr. 145); Kzk. **Matay** [Джулай Матаевъ] (Valihanov, Soč. 347); Kzk. **Matay** [Matay] (Divaev, Biket 5); Kzk. 1819 **Matay** [Матай] (MIK IV, 395); Kzk. 19th c. **Matay** [Матай] (SOV 8); Kzk. 19th c. **Matay** [Матай] (SOK 176, 206); Kzk. 19th c. **Matay** [Матай] (SODž. 100); Kzk. 19th c. **Matay** [Матай] (Grod., Pril. 78); Kzk. 19th c. **Matay** [Матай] (Grod., Pril. 158); Kzk. 19th c. **Matay** [Матай] (AOO 22); Kzk. 19th c. **Matay** [Матай] (AOA 146); Kzk. 19th c. **Matay** [Матай] (SOV 64); Kzk. 19th c. **Matay** [Матай] (AOP 14); Kirg. **Matay** [Матай] (Jud. 904); Kzk. 19th c. **Matay-bay** [Матайбай] (SOK 32); Kzk. 19th c. **Motay-bay / Mutay-bay?** [Мотайбай] (SOK 136); *TN:* **Matay** [Матай] (Karta JAR XI). ⇨ **MATA I.?** + dim. suff. *-y.* See also **SABRA-MATAY, TİRİM-MATAY.**

MATAY II. Hak. 19th-20th c. **Matay** [Матай] (HRS 349); Hak. 19th-20th c. **Matay** [Матай], fem. (HRS 354). ⇨ **MATA II.?** + dim. suff. *-y.*

MATAMAS Tat.(Tüm.) 1606 **Matamas** [Матамас Ачентатов] (MIB I, 154); Tat. 1638 **Matmas** [Мугел Матмасов] (Miller, Ist. Sib. II, 450); Tat.(Tüm.) 1649 **Matmas** [Кутайгулко Матмасовъ (Матмасъ)] (DAI III, 174-75); Bashk. 1675 **Matmas** [Матьмас Кушелев] (MIB I, 199). ✧ 'He will not fuss, he will not disturb' cf. Tat. *mata-* 'hindern' (Radl. IV, 2043). See also **MATAR.**

MATAR Trkm. 1690 **Matar** [مطر / Abdullah bey ibn Matar] (Refik, Anad. 80); Kzk. 19th c. **Matar** [Мадали Матаровъ] (SKSO VIII, 222). ✧ 'He who will fuss'? cf. Tat. *mata-* 'hindern' (Radl. IV, 2043). See also **MATAMAS.**

MATAS Kzk. 1841 **Matas** [Матасъ Чувашевъ], from the Middle Horde (Orta Žüz) (Konšin, Mat. V, 22).

MATEN Kzk. 1846 **Maten** [Бикташ Матенев], a biy (MKOP 157); Kzk. 19th c. **Maten** [Матенъ] (AOO 26); Kzk. 19th c. **Maten** [Беркамбай Матеневъ] (Grod., Pril. 82).

MATÏ Kzk. 19th c. **Matï** [Маты] (AOP 6); Kzk. 19th c. **Matï** [Маты] (SOV 32).

MATÏL Kzk. 19th c. **Matïl** [Матылъ] (SOK 218).

MATÏR see **MATUR**

MATÏRÏAS Yak. **Matïrïas** [Мат(ы)рыяс (Мат(ы)рыяна)], fem. (Pek.). ✧ Matryosha (R.), dim of. R. Matryona (Pek.).

MATÏŠ Kzk. 19th c. **Matïš** [Матышъ] (SOV 28).

MATQUŠ Bashk. 1745 **Matquš** [Маткуш Имилев] (MIB III, 427).

MATLÏ-BAS Kzk. 19th c. **Matlï-bas** [Матлыбасъ] (SODž. 160). ⇨ **BAŠ** + **MÄT?** + suff. -lï.

MATMAS see **MATAMAS**

MATPEY Hak. 19th-20th c. **Matpey** [Матпей] (HRS 349). ✧ Matvey (R.) (HRS).

MATPİ Hak.(Sag.) 19th-20th c. **Matpi** [Матпі] (Katanov, Otč. 7). ✧ Matvey (R.) (HRS).

MATRÏANA Yak. **Matrïana** [Матрыана], fem. (Pek.). ✧ Matryona (R.) (Pek.).

MATROQ Alt. 19th-20th c. **Matroq** [Матрок], fem. (OjrRS 212).

MATUR Kzk. 18th c. **Matïr-χenikey** [Матырь-Хеникей], Nurali-χan's daughter (Nepljuev 811); Kzk. 19th c. **Matur-bay** [Кулманъ Матурбаевъ] (Grod., Pril. 160). ✧ 'Goodlooking; pretty, nice' cf. Tat. matur 'schön (vom Ansehen)' (Radl. IV, 2045).

MAVUJA Trkm. 20th c. **Mavuja** [Мавуға], fem. (Zaj. 1971, 342); Trkm. 20th c. **Māvuja** [Мавуджа], fem. (TrkmRS 437). ✧ 'Saltyness' (Zaj. 1971), cf. Trkm. māvuja 'название некоторых солей серной кислоты, содержащихся в морской воде' (TrkmRS) (<Ar.).

MAW Kzk. 19th c. **Maw-bay** [Маубай] (AOK 38); Kzk. 19th c. **Maw-bay** [Маубай] (SODž. 6). ✧ 'Tarantula' cf. Chag. mau 'id.' (Radl. IV, 1992).

MAW-PAS Kzk. 19th c. **Maw-pas** [Маупасъ] (SOK 300). ✧ I. 'Sleepy(-head), silly(-head), dull(-head)' cf. Kzk. maubas 'schläfrig, schlafmützig, stumpf, dumm' (Radl. IV, 1993); II. 'Tarantula-head'? ⇨ **MAW?** + **BAŠ.**

MAWÏT see **MAWUT**

MAWKE Kzk. 19th c. **Mawke** [Мауке] (SOV 44). ⇨ **MAW** + dim. suff. -ke / comp. -ake.

MAWKEY Bashk. 1735 **Mawkey** [Мавкей Татыевъ], a tarχan (Vel.-Zern., Bašk. 15). ⇨ **MAW** + dim. suff. -key.

MAWQO Kzk. 19th c. **Mawqo?** [Мауко] (SOV 78). ⇨ **MAWKE?**

MAWSA Kzk. 19th c. **Mawsa-bay** [Маусабай] (SOV 12). ⇨ **MAW** + suff. -sa.

MAWSAM see **MAWSUN**

MAWSUN Kzk. 1846 **Mawsam-bay** / **Mawsun-bay?** [Бий Маусамбай (Маусунбай) Чалабаев], a biy (MKOP 100, 156); Kzk. 19th c. **Mawsun-bay** [Маусунбай] (SOK 32, 120, 126). ✧ 'Let him/her snivel/whine' (Rásonyi, Imp. 239).

MAWUT Kkalp. 20th c. **Mawït** [Маўыт], fem. (KkRS 778); Kkalp. 20th c. **Mawut** [Мавут], fem. (Bask., Kkalp. 403); Kzk. 19th c. **Mawut-bay** [Маутбай] (AOA 74, 106). ✧ 'Cloth' (KkRS), cf. Kzk., Trkm. maūt 'die beste Art von Tuch' (Radl. IV, 1993), Kkalp. mavut 'id.' (Bask., Kkalp.).

MAWZİM Bashk. 1740 **Mawzim** [Алиша Маузимовъ] (ZOOIRGO III, 225).

MAZ see **MAS**

MAZAQ Turk. 15th c. **Mazaq** [Μαζάκης], an Ottoman chief (Byz. Turk. 179).

MAZAN Tat.(Sib.) 1643 **Mazan** [Мазанко] (Miller, Ist. Sib. II, 487); Bashk. 1742 **Mazan** [Куват Мазанов] (MIB III, 513); Bashk. 1754 **Mazan** [Мазан Курумбетев] (MIB IV/1, 83); Bashk. 1754 **Mazan** [Мазан Нурумбетев] (MIB IV/1, 85); Bashk. 1763 **Mazan** [Ирмаметь Мазанов] (MIB IV/1, 267); Bashk. 1763 **Mazan** [Мазан Иманов] (MIB IV/2, 45); Bashk. 1765 **Mazan** [Мазан Сатлыков] (MIB IV/1, 313). ✧ '?' cf. Kzk. PN Masan (Žanuzakov 149). ⇨ **MASAN?**

MAZARA Yak. 1679 **Mazara** [Мазара Бозековъ], a prince (DAI VIII, 5, 10, 244).

MAZLÏMQAN Kkalp. 20th c. **Mazlïmqan** [Мазлымкъан / Мазлымкъан], fem. (Bask., Kkalp. 403, KkRS 778). ⇨ **MAZLÏM** + suff. -qan(1).

MAZMUM Kzk. **Mazmum** [Мазмумъ], fem. (Pojarkov 13).

MAŽAQ Kzk. 19th c. **Mažaq** [Мажакъ] (SOK 302); Kzk. 19th c. **Mažaq-pay** [Мажакпай] (SODž. 86). ✧ 'Ear/head of corn' cf. Alt. mažaq 'die Ähre' (Radl. IV, 2061), Chag., Crm. mašaq 'die Pfeilspitze; die Ähren' (Radl. IV, 2059).

MAŽAR Bashk. 1797 **Mažar** [Сотник Матвей Семенович Мазаров], a captain, in the region of the Ik river (MIB V, 374).

MAŽİKEY Kzk. 19th c. **Mažikey** [Мажикей] (AOK 210). ⇨ **MAJİK** + dim. suff. -ey.

MAŽİK see **MAJİK**

MĀJA Yak. **Māja** [Маца] (Pek.). ✧ The byname refers to a man whose legs form letter "o" when walking, cf. Yak. bājay, mājaγar '?' (<Buryat mayā) (Pek.).

MĀJAX Yak. **Mājaχ** [Мацах] (Pek.).

MĀJUR OT? 870-879 **Mājur** [ساجُور التركيّ] (Kindī 215, 217, 219, 220). ✧ Muhajir? (<Ar.) 'emigrant' (Ahmed).

MĀDAY Alt. **Māday** / **Māday-qara** [Мадай / Мадай-Кара] (Nikiforov 110-126 etc., 283).

MĀYA Yak. **Māya** [Maja], fem. (Pek.). ✧ Maya (R.).

MĀYAQA Yak. **Māyaqa** [Маjака], fem. (Pek.). ⇨ **MĀYA** + dim. suff. -qa (R.?).

MĀYAQASÏT Yak. **Māyaqasït** [Маjакасыт] (Pek.).

MĀYAQQA Yak. **Māyaqqa** [Маjакка], fem. (Pek.). ⇨ **MĀYA** + dim. suff. -qqa (R.?).

MĀYRA Karg. **Māyra** [Майра], fem. (Katanov, Otč. 9). ✧ Marya (Mariya) (R.) (Katanov).

MĀLQA Hak.(Sag.) 19th-20th c. **Mālqa** [Малкя], fem. (Katanov, Otč. 8); Karg. **Mālqa** [Малка] (Katanov, Otč. 8). ✧ 'Stick' cf. R. палка 'id.' (Katanov).

MĀNÏS Hak.(Blt.) 19th-20th c. **Mānïs** [Маныс]

(Proben IX, 364, 365). ❖ Child of the hero, often used in the form *Ala-manïs*, cf. Hak. PN *Manïs* (Butanaev).

MĀPA   Yak. **Māpa / Mārpa** [Мапа / Марпа], fem. (Pek.). ❖ Marfa (R.) (Pek.).

MĀRÏYA   Yak. **Mārïya** [Марыйа], fem. (Pek.). ❖ Mariya (R.) (Pek.).

MĀRPA   Yak. **Mārpa** [Марпа], fem. (Pek.). ❖ Marfa (R.).

MĀRPAJAQ   Hak.(Blt.) 19th-20th c. **Mārpajaq** [Марпацак], fem. (Katanov, Otč. 10). ❖ Marfochka (Marfočka) (R.) (Katanov). ⇨ **MĀRPA** + dim. suff. *-jaq*.

MĀRU   Alt. 19th-20th c. **Māru** [Маару], fem. (OjrRS 212). ❖ Mariya (R.) (OjrRS).

MĀSA   Hak.(Blt.) 19th-20th c. **Māsa** [Маса] (Katanov, Otč. 10); Hak.(Shor) 19th-20th c. **Māsa** [Маса], fem. (Katanov, Otč. 11); Yak. **Māsa** [Маса], fem. (Pek.). ❖ Masha (R. fem.), dim. of R. *Mariya* (Pek., Katanov).

MĀSÏNQA   Hak.? 19th-20th c. **Māsïnqa** [Масынка] (Katanov, Otč. 10). ❖ Mashenka (R. fem. Машенька) (Katanov).

MĀSQA   Hak.(Sag.) 19th-20th c. **Māsqa** [Маска], fem. (Katanov, Otč. 7); Karg. **Māsqa** [Маска], fem. (Katanov, Otč. 9). ❖ Mashka (R. fem.) (Katanov).

MĀSLA   Hak.(Sag.) 19th-20th c. **Māsla** [Масла] (Katanov, Otč. 8). ❖ 'Butter' cf. R. масло [pronounced: *māsla*] 'id.' (Katanov).

MĀTAX   Yak. **Mātax** [Кӓлтӓгӓи Матах], white shaman with half a face (Pek.).

MĀTÏR-TAS   Shor 19th-20th c. **Mātïr-tas** [Мätyr Tas], Qan-mergen's shepherd in a heroic poem (Dyrenkova 90). ⇨ **BATÏR** + **TAZ.**

MĀTQA   Hak.? 19th-20th c. **Mātqa** [Матка], fem. (Katanov, Otč. 10). ❖ 'Mother, little old woman, granny' cf. R. *mātka* / матка 'id.' (Katanov).

MĀTMAS   Bashk. 1723 **Mātmas** [Маатмас Казакаев] (MIB III, 201).

MĀVÏ   Trkm. 20th c. **Mavi** [Mavi], fem. (Zaj. 1971, 341); Trkm. 20th c. **Māvï** [Мавы], fem. (TrkmRS 437). ❖ 'Blue' cf. Trkm. *māvï* 'голубой; лазурный' (TrkmRS) (<Ar.).

MÄDİ-YAR   Kzk. 19th c. **Mad-yar (<Madi-yar)** [Мадьяръ] (SOK 58); Kzk. 19th c. **Madi-yar** [Мадіяръ] (SOV 106); Kzk. 19th c. **Madi-yar** [Мадіяръ] (SOK 274); Kzk. 19th c. **Madi-yar** [Мадіяръ] (SOK 198); Uzb. (Kipch.) 19th c. **Madi-yar-datχa** [Madiar-Datkha] (Nalivkin-Dozon 207); Kkalp. 20th c. **Madï-yar** [Мадыйар] (Bask., Kkalp. 75); Kkalp. 20th c. **Mädi-yar** [Мәдияр] (KkRS 775). ❖ 'Mähdi's friend' cf. Tat. *Mähdi* (Ar.) 'He who goes on the way shown by Allah' (Sattarov), consider the possibilty of the change *Mähdi / Mädi / Madi.* ⇨ **MÄGDİ + YAR.**

MÄDİ-REYİM   Kkalp. 20th c. **Mädi-reyim** [Мәдирейим] (KkRS 775). ❖ 'Mahdi-Rahim' (Ar.) 'Rightly guided - merciful' (Ahmed), cf. Tat. *Mähdi* (Ar.) 'He who goes on the way shown by Allah' (Sattarov), consider the possibilty of the change *Mädi / Madi < Mähdi.* ⇨ **MÄGDİ.**

MÄGDİ   Kzk. 19th c. **Maγdï-bek / Mägdi-bek?** [Магдыбекъ] (SODž. 148); Bashk. 1756 **Mägdi** [Мягди Илчюбаев] (MIB IV/1, 128). ❖ Mahdi (Ar.) 'Rightly guided' (Ahmed), cf. Tat. *Mähdi* 'He who goes on the way shown by Allah' (Sattarov).

MÄHİYDA   Kkalp. 20th c. **Mähiyda** [Мәхийда], fem. (KkRS 778). ❖ 'Moon-like' (P.) (cf. Kusimova: *Mahiðä*).

MÄXĀYLÄ   Yak. **Mäχậylä** [Мäхậйлä] (Pek.); Yak. **Mäχậlä** [Мäхậлä] (Pek.); Yak. **Mäkậlä** [Мäкậлä] (Pek.). ❖ Mihayla (R.) (Pek.).

MÄXĀLÄ see **MÄXĀYLÄ**

MÄXTİM-SİLÄ see **MAXTUM**

MÄYÄRÄM-SÜPPÜ   Yak. **Mäyäräm-süppü** [Мäйäрäм сÿппÿ], one of the forefathers of the Yakuts, Öksüsü's son (Pek.).

MÄKÄN-XUDAY-BERDİ   Uzb. 1740 **Mäkän-χuday-berdi** [Мяканъ-Худай-Берды], from Khiva (Hanykov, Poezdka 21). ❖ 'Antelope-God-given' cf. Chag. *mäkän* 'eine grosse Antilope' (Radl. IV, 2072). ⇨ **XUDAY-BERDİ.**

MÄKÄN-YARÏM-MAXRAM   Uzb. 1740 **Mäkän-yarïm-maχram** [Мяканъ-Ярымъ-Махрамъ], from Khiva (Hanykov, Poezdka 21). ❖ 'Antelope-half-?' cf. Chag. *mäkän* 'eine grosse Antilope' (Radl. IV, 2072). ⇨ **YARÏM?**

MÄKÄN-TÜRT   Uzb. 1740 **Mäkän-türt** [Мяканъ-Тюртъ], from Khiva (Hanykov, Poezdka 21). ❖ 'Antelope-?' cf. Chag. *mäkän* 'eine grosse Antilope' (Radl. IV, 2072).

MÄKĀLÄ see **MÄXĀYLÄ**

MÄKİYKĂN   Yak. **Mäkiykăn** [Мäкiiкäн] (Pek.).

MÄKİS   Bashk. 1701 **Mäkis** [Мякис Юкшиев] (MIB III, 9).

MÄQALAN   Bashk. 1770 **Mäqalan** [Мякалан Юнаев] (MIB IV/1, 342).

MÄLGÄR   Yak. **Mälgär** [Мäлгäр] (Pek.).

MÄLİK see **MALİK**

MÄLİM   Kzk. 19th c. **Mälim-bay** [Малимбай] (SODž. 98); Kzk. 19th c. **Mälim-bay** [Малимбай] (SOK 140). ❖ 'Known' cf. Kzk. *mâlim (=mälim)* 'malûm, belli' (KzTS) (<Ar.).

MÄLİN   Kzk. 19th c. **Mälin-bay** [Малинбай] (Grod., Pril. 60); Kzk. 19th c. **Mälin-bay** [Малинбай] (SODž. 156). ❖ 'Wild cat'? cf. Kzk. *mâlin (=mälin)* 'yabani kedi' (KzTS).

MÄLYÄXSİ   Yak. **Mälyäχsi / MälJäχsi** [Мäлjäхci, Мäлцäхci], fem. (Pek.).

MÄLYÄXSİN   Yak. **Mälyäχsin-ayïta** [Мäлjäхciн],

daughter of a spirit (Pek.).

MÄLTÄYÄ   Yak. **Mältäyä** [Мӓлтӓйӓ] (Pek.).

MÄMBET see MAMBET

MÄMBET-ALÏ   Kkalp. 20th c. **Mämbet-alï** [Мәмбсталы] (KkRS 775); Kkalp. 20th c. **Mämbet-qaliy** [Мәмбеткалий] (KkRS 775). ⇨ **MAMBET + ALÏ.**

MÄMBET-ĴUMA   Kkalp. 20th c. **Mämbet-ĵuma** [Мәмбетжума] (KkRS 775). ⇨ **MAMBET + ĴUMA.**

MÄMBET-MÏRAT see MÄMBET-MURAT

MÄMBET-MURAT   Kkalp. 20th c. **Mämbet-mïrat** [Мәмбетмырат] (KkRS 775); Kkalp. 20th c. **Mämbet-murat** [Мәмбетмурат] (KkRS 775). ⇨ **MAMBET + MURAT.**

MÄMBET-NAZAR   Kkalp. 20th c. **Mämbet-nazar** [Мәмбетназар] (KkRS 775). ⇨ **MAMBET + NAZAR.**

MÄMBET-NÏYAZ   Kkalp. 20th c. **Mämbet-niyaz** [Мәмбетнияз] (KkRS 775). ⇨ **MAMBET + NÏYAZ.**

MÄMÄŠ   Bashk. 1770 **Mämäš** [Мямяш Девлетбаев] (MIB IV/1, 343). ⇨ **MAMAŠ.**

MÄMÄT see MAMET

MÄMMÄ-TURDÏ   Uzb. 20th c. **Mämmä-turdï** [Мамматурди] (Begmatov 1984, 204). ⇨ **MAMA? + TURDÏ.**

MÄNDÄY see MENDEY

MÄNDÄL   Yak. **Mändäl** [Мӓндӓл] (Pek.). ✧ 'Tall and leaning backwards' cf. Yak. *mändälï* 'высокий и откинувшийся назад' (Pek.).

MÄNDÄLÄ   Tuv. 19th c. **Mändälä** [Мӓндӓлӓ] (Proben IX, 23).

MÄNDEY see MENDEY

MÄNDÏ see MENDÏ

MÄNÄLĴIMÄ   Yak. **Analĵïma-Mänälĵimä-quo** [Аналцыма Мӓнӓлцимӓ куо], fem. (Pek.).

MÄNÏ   Kkalp. 20th c. **Mäni-gül** [Мәнигул], fem. (KkRS 778). ✧ 'Sense, meaning, essence' cf. Kkalp. *mäni* 'id.' (KkRS), cf. also *Mäni-gül* 'Spiritualized rose' (Baskakov: OSA 141).

MÄNLÏ see MEÑLÏ

MÄNGÏ-BAΓ   Uyg. **Mängi-baγ-iši** [Mängi Baγ Iši], fem. (Mahrnāmag 15). ⇨ **MEÑGÜ + BAΓ.**

MÄÑKÄ   Yak. **Mäñkä** [Мӓҥкӓ] (Pek.). ✧ 'Big, tall man' (Pek.). See also **BÜYÜK, ČOÑ, EVREN, YOΓAN, KÄNDÄL.**

MÄÑLÏ see MEÑLÏ

MÄÑLÏ-ARŪ-SÏLŪ see MEÑLÏ

MÄÑLÏG see MEÑLÏ

MÄÑLÏK see MEÑLÏ

MÄÑLÏK-TÄMÜR   Uyg. 13th c. -14th c. **Mäñlik-tämür** [Miglak Tamur] (Chwol., Syr.-nest. (NF) 48). ✧ 'Iron with a birthmark'. ⇨ **MEÑLÏ + TEMÏR.**

MÄRĴAN see MERĴAN

MÄRÏYÄT   Yak. **Märiyät-märgän** [Мӓріӓт-мӓргӓн] (Pek.).

MÄRÏLÏ   Yak. **Märili-bärgän** [Мӓрілі Бӓргӓн] (Pek.).

MÄRYÄM   Kkalp. 20th c. **Märyäm** [Мәрьям], fem. (KkRS 778). ✧ Maryam (Ar.).

MÄRKÏT   Uyg. **Märkit** [Märkit] (EUTS). ✧ Ethnonym.

MÄSÄΓUT see MÄSΓUT

MÄSEΓUT see MÄSΓUT

MÄSΓUT   Bashk. 18th c. **Mäsäγut** [Мясягутъ] (Nepljuev 433); Bashk. 1734 **Mäseγut** [Масегутъ Кебесевъ], a tarχan (Vel.-Zern., Bašk. 11); Bashk. 1736 **Mäseγut** [Мясегутъ] (PSZRI IX, 743); Tat. 1776 **Mäsuγut** [Мясогутъ Юсуповъ] (PSZRI XX, 466). ✧ Masud / Mas'ūd (Ar.) 'Lucky, happy, fortunate' (Ahmed), cf. also Tat. PN *Mäsγut* (Sattarov), Bashk. *Mäsγüt* (Kusimova).

MÄSKÄY   Bashk. 1650 **Mäskäy** [Маскайко Тайдигашевъ] (Vel.-Zern., Bašk. 30); Bashk. 1779, 1780, 1782, 1787 **Mäskey** [Елдаш Мяскеев (Миксеев) / Юлдаш Маскеев (Мяскеев)], chief of "Kirgizskaja Volost'" (MIB V, 87, 111, 133, 207). ✧ 'Avid, open-mouthed, voracious' cf. Bashk. *mäskäy* 'обжора; вампир; обжорливый' (BRS/Uraksin).

MÄT   Kzk. 19th c. **Mat-bay** [Матбай] (AOA 66); Kkalp. 20th c. **Mät-ĵan** [Мәтжан] (KkRS 775); Kkalp. 20th c. **Mät-eke** [Мәтеке] (KkRS 775); Kkalp. 20th c. **Mät-seyit** [Мәтсейит] (KkRS 775). ✧ 'Praise' cf. Uyg., Crm. *mät* 'das Lob' (Radl. IV, 2102), Karakh. *mädḥ* 'хвала, восхваление' (DTS) (<Ar. *madḥ*).

MÄT-MURAT   Kzk. 19th c. **Mat-murad** [Матъ-Мурадъ], in Khiva (AUK 416); Kkalp. 20th c. **Mät-murat** [Мәтмурат] (KkRS 775). ⇨ **MÄT + MURAT.**

MÄT-NÏYAZ   Kzk. 19th c. **Mat-niyaz / Mät-niyaz** [Матъ-Ніязъ], in Khiva (AUK 416); Kkalp. 20th c. **Mät-niyaz** [Мәтнияз] (KkRS 775). ⇨ **MÄT + NÏYAZ.**

MÄT-SAPA   Kkalp. 20th c. **Mät-sapa** [Мәтсапа] (KkRS 775). ⇨ **MÄT + SAPA.**

MÄTÏ   Kkalp. 20th c. **Mäti-bay** [Мәтибай] (KkRS 775).

MÄTÏK   Bashk. 1735 **Mätik** [Мятикъ Татыевъ], a tarχan (Vel.-Zern., Bašk. 15); Bashk. 1740 **Metük** [Метюк] (MIB I, 398).

MÄTÏS   Yak. **Mätis** [Мӓтис] (Pek.).

MÄTKEY   Kzk. 19th c. **Mätkey** [Маткей] (AOP 18). ⇨ **MÄT + suff. -key.**

MÄWEŠ   Kkalp. 20th c. **Mäweš** [Мәйеш], fem. (KkRS 778).

MÄWKEY   Tat.(Mish.) 1755 **Mäwkey** [Мявкей Битыровъ] (MIB IV/1, 93).

MÄWLAN-BERDÏ   Uzb. 20th c. **Mäwlân-berdi** [Мавлонберди] (Begmatov 1984, 202); Uzb. 1770 **Mäwläm-berdi** (<**Mäwlän-berdi**) [Мавлям-берды] (MIT II, 343); Kzk. 19th c. **Mäwlän-berdi** [Маулянъ берды Муминбаевъ] (SKSO IV, otd. II, 32); Kzk. 19th c. **Mäwlän-berdi** [Маулянберды Игамбердiевъ] (SKSO II, 13). ✧ 'My Lord (Allah) has him/her given', cf. Uzb. *mäwlânâ* 'мавляна (букв. господин наш - титул мусульманских богословов и учёных)' (UzbRS), Turk. *mevlâna* (Ar.) 'Efendimiz anlamında olup bazı sarıklı ulemaya lakap' (Özön), also Tat. PN *Mäwlabirde / Mäwlambirde* 'id.' (Sattarov), Kzk. PN *Mawlen* (Žanuzakov-Esbaeva). ⇨ MEWLĀNĀ + BERDİ. See also BERDİ-MĀWLÂN.

MĀWLÂN-BERDİ see MÄWLAN-BERDİ

MÄWLÄN-BERDİ see MÄWLAN-BERDİ

MÄWLUT Tat. 1779 **Mäwlut** [Мавлют Мусин], chief (MIB V, 81, 83, 105), Bashk. 1759 **Mäwlut** [Мавлют Курманаев] (MIB IV/2, 26); Bashk. 1764 **Mäwlut** [Менлкей Мавлютов] (MIB IV/1, 285); Bashk. 1780 **Mäwlut** [Ишмет Мавлютов] (MIB V, 115); Bashk. 1784 **Mäwlut** [Мавлют Муратов] (MIB V, 152). ✧ 'New-born child, infant; festive day (Prophet Moχamed's birthday)' (Sattarov, Kusimova), cf. Turk. *mevlud, mevlût* (Ar.) 'id.', Bashk. *mäwlit* 'рождение' (BRS/Uraksin) (<Ar.).

MÄWLUTEY Bashk. 1737 **Mäwlutey** [Араслан Мавлутеев] (MIB III, 367). ✧ 'Newly born child' cf. Tat. PN *Mäülüd / Mäülüt* (Sattarov) (<Ar.). ⇨ MÄWLUT + suff. -*ey*.

MÄWLÜKEY Tat. 1763 **Mäwlükäy** [Мавлюкай] (MIB IV/1, 261); Bashk. 1732 **Mäwlükey** [Мевлюкей (Мавлюк) Утеев] (MIB III, 310); Bashk. 1784 **Mäwlükey** [Мавлюкей (Мевлюкей) Мустафин] (MIB V, 158, 160, 162, 363); Bashk. 1786 **Mäwlükey** [Мавлюкей Мухаметев] (MIB V, 188, 314). ✧ I. 'Lord' cf. Tat. PN *Mäüli* (Sattarov), cf. Ar. *Mawla* 'helper, protector' (Ahmed); II. 'Wished (child)' cf. Bashk. PN *Mäüli* (Kusimova). ⇨ MÄWLUT + dim. suff. -*key*.

MĀLİKÄ see MELİKÄ

MÄTÄK Yak. **Mätäk** [Мätäк] (Pek.).

MEJİT Nog. 20th c. **Mejit** [Меджит Рамазан улы Къарас / Меджит Рамазанович Карасов], one of Baskakov's informants from the aul of Quban-χalq (Bask., Nog. 143); Balk. 20th c. **Mežit** [Mežit] (Pröhle, Balk 243); *EN:* Nog. 20th c. **Mesit-küp** [Месит куьп], a group of the Qara Noγay clans (Bask., Nog. 136, 142). ✧ Majeed (Ar.) 'glorious, noble' (Ahmed), also Tat. PN *Mäjit* (Sattarov).

MEJNUN Trkm.? 1745 **Mejnun-bek** [Меджнун-бек], Nadir's commander? (MIT II, 172). ✧ 'Obsessed, mad, lunatic' (Erol II) (<Ar.).

MEDAR see MEDÄR

MEDÄR Kzk. 19th c. **Medar-bay / Medär-bay** [Медарбай] (SOV 94); Kzk. 19th c. **Meder-bay** [Медербай] (SOV 38). ✧ 'Aim, goal; butt, target' cf. Kirg. *medär* 'das Ziel, die Zielscheibe' (Radl. IV,

2104).

MEDEČİ Kzk. 1652 **Medeči** [Медечи] (DAI III, 382). ✧ 'Helper, supporter' cf. Kzk. *medäü* (Ar.) 'die Hülfe' (Radl. IV, 2104). + suff. -*či*.

MEDER see MEDÄR

MEDES Kzk. 19th c. **Medes-pek** [Медеспекъ] (SOK 254).

MEDET Kzk. 1794 **Medät** [ميدات / Медет] (MIK IV, 158); Kzk. 19th c. **Medet** [Медетовъ] (Grod., Pril. 63); Kkalp. 20th c. **Medet** [Медет] (KkRS 775); Kkalp. 20th c. **Medet-bay** [Медетбай] (KkRS 775); Kirg. **Medet-bek** [Медетбек] (Jud. 169); Kzk. 19th c. **Medet-pay** [Медетпай] (SOV 158); Kzk. 19th c. **Medet-pek** [Медетъпекъ] (SOV 24). ✧ 'Strength, power; help; support, inspiring' Kkalp. *medet* (Ar.) 'id.' (KkRS), Kzk. *medät* (Ar.) 'id.' (Radl. IV, 2105), Kirg. *medet* 'id.' (Jud.).

MEDEW Kzk. 19th c. **Medew** [Медеу] (SOK 278); Kzk. 19th c. **Medew-bay** [Медеубай] (SOK 14); Kzk. **Medew-biy** [Медеу-бий] (Smirnov, Sultany 18). ✧ 'Help, support, hope' cf. Kzk. *medäü* (Ar.) 'die Hülfe' (Radl. IV, 2104), Kzk. *medev* 'Ümit, güvenç, dayanak' (KzTS).

MEGE Kzk. 19th c. **Mege-bay** [Мегебай] (SOK 254).

MEGEDELEY Tat.(Sib.) 1623 **Megedeley** [Мегеделейко] (Miller, Ist. Sib. II, 298, 299).

MEGİL Kzk. 19th c. **Megil-bay** [Мегильбай] (SOK 78).

MEGİN Kzk. 19th c. **Megin-bay** [Мегинбай] (SODž. 80).

MEHRİBAN Kzk. 19th c. **Mehriban** [Молла Мехрибанъ] (Grod., Pril. 138). ✧ 'Pleasant (nice, charming) goodness (quality, habit)' (<P.).

MEYDAN Turk. 1584 **Meydan** [Meydan] (Ongan, Ank. I, 169); Trkm. 20th c. **Meydan** [Meydan] (Zaj. 1971, 330); Trkm. 20th c. **Meydan** [Мейдан] (TrkmRS 447). ✧ 'Open place; public square, field' cf. Turk. *mäydan* 'die Ebene, der Platz' (Radl. IV, 2069) (<Ar.).

MEYÄT Kzk. 19th c. **Meyät** [Меятовъ] (SKSO II, 14).

MEYERMAN Kzk. 19th c. **Meyerman** [Мейерманъ / Меерманъ] (SOV 8, 12, 100). ✧ 'Kind-hearted, charitable, generous' cf. Kzk. *meyirban* 'милосердный, доброжелательный; любезный, ласковый (KzRS).

MEYİS Kzk. 19th c. **Meyis** [Меисъ] (SODž. 132). ✧ 'Raisin, currant' cf. Kzk. *meis* 'keline getrocknete Weinbeeren' (Radl. IV, 2070).

MEYLİ Kzk. 19th c. **Meyli-bay** [Мейлибай] (SOK 18). ✧ 'Affection, love' cf. Kzk. *meyli* 'meyil' (KzTS).

MEYLİS Trkm. 20th c. **Meylis** [Meylis] (Zaj. 1971, 330); Trkm. 20th c. **Meylis** [Мейлис] (TrkmRS 447). ✧ 'Social gathering, small feast' cf. Trkm. *meylis* 'вечеринка, пирушка' (TrkmRS) (<Ar.).

MEYZÜ Kzk. 19th c. **Meyzü-bay** [Мейзюбай] (SODž.

124).

MEKE Kzk. 19th c. **Meke** [Меке] (SODž. 102); Kzk. 19th c. **Meke-bay** [Мекебай] (SOK 234); Kzk. 19th c. **Meke-bay** [Мекебай] (SODž. 46); Kzk. 19th c. **Meke-bek** [Мекебекъ] (SODž. 118). ✧ 'Inventive, smart, tricky' cf. Alt., Hak. *mäkä* 'die Erfindungsgabe, die geistige Gewandheit, die Listigkeit' (Radl. IV, 2071).

MEKEY Bashk. 1771 **Mekey** [Мекей Юсупов] (MIB IV/1, 354). See also **İL-MEKEY, QAL-MEKEY.**

MEKEŠ Kzk. 19th c. **Mekeš** [Мекешъ] (AOK 86); Kzk. 19th c. **Mekeš** [Мекешъ] (SOK 270); Alt. 19th-20th c. **Mekeš** [Мекеш] (OjrRS 209). ⇨ **MEKE** + suff. -*š*.

MEKİLİÑ-QURČA Uyg. **Mekiliñ-qurča** [Mekiliñ qurča] (Radl., USp. 46, DTS). ⇨ **QURČA.**

MEKİSKÄ Hak.(Blt.) 19th-20th c. **Mekiskä** [Мекіскä] (Katanov, Otč. 10); Hak.(Shor) 19th-20th c. **Mekiskä** [Мекіскä, Никишка] (Katanov, Otč. 11). ✧ Nikishka (R.) (Katanov).

MEKLİ-BULAT Nog. 20th c. **Mekli-bulat** [Мекли Булат Йарболды увлы], one of Baskakov's informants from the aul of Yaman-γoy, District of Ači-qulaq (Bask., Nog. 143). ⇨ **BULAT.**

MEKŌLČA Hak.(Blt.) 19th-20th c. **Mekōlča** [Меколча] (Katanov, Otč. 10). ✧ Nikolcha (R.) (Katanov).

MEKŌLKA Hak.(Blt.) 19th-20th c. **Mekōlka** [Меколка] (Katanov, Otč. 10). ✧ Nikolka (R.) (Katanov).

MEKSÄMBİ Kzk. 19th c. **Meksämbi** [Мексämбі] (Samojlovič: ŽS XXIV (1915), 165). ✧ 'Sunday' (<P.) (Samojlovič). Distorted form of *Žeksämbi* 'Sunday' and used by women when *Žeksämbi* is a tabu-name. ⇨ **YEKŠENBE.**

MEKSİZ Kzk. 19th c. **Meksiz-bay** [Мексызбай] (AOA 122).

MEKTİ Kzk. 19th c. **Mekti-bay** [Мектыбай] (SOV 50).

MELBES Tat.(Sib.) 1643 **Melbes** [Мельбес] (Miller, Ist. Sib. II, 488).

MELE Trkm. 20th c. **Mele** [Mele] (Zaj. 1971, 333); Trkm. 20th c. **Mele** [Меле] (TrkmRS 448). ✧ 'Light-brown' (Zaj. 1971), cf. Trkm. *mele* 'светло-жёлтый; смуглый' (TrkmRS).

MELEY Hak. 19th-20th c. **Meley** [Мелей], fem. (HRS 354). ✧ 'Glove' (HRS).

MELEK Yürük 1583 **Melek** [ملك], Mehmed's daughter (Ongan, Ank. I, 169); Yürük 1543 **Melek-qïzï** [ملك قيزى / Melek-kızı] (Gökb., Rum. 230). ✧ 'Angel' cf. Turk. *mäläk* 'id.' (Radl. IV, 2099).

MELENTEY Bashk. 1735 **Melentey** [Мелентей Емяковъ], a tarγan (Vel.-Zern., Bašk. 22).

MELİK see **MALİK**

MELİK-BUQA Uyg. 1333 **Melik-buqa** [Milig Buka] (Chwol., Syr.-nest. (NF) 29). ⇨ **MALİK + BUQA.**

MELİK-NİYAZ Trkm. 19th c. **Melik-niyaz** [Атай Мелитньязовъ] (Ščeglov IV, 190). ⇨ **MALİK + NİYAZ.**

MELİK-TEMİR Maml. **Melik-temir** [سيف الدين ملكتمر], a bearer of arms, in an inscription on a comb (Mayer 152); Maml.? 1335 **Melik-temir** [سيفالدين ملكتمر السرجوانى] (Zetterst. 183, 218, Weil, Chalif. I, 404); Maml. 1346/47 **Melik-temir** [ملكتمرالحجازى] (Iyās I, 185, Weil, Chalif. I, 466); Maml. 1362 **Melik-temir** [ملكتمرالمحمدى] (Iyās I, 211); Tat.(GH) (Kipch.) 1340 **Melik-temir** [ملكتمر], a Kipchak governor in the Crimea (Zetterst. 219, Tizeng. I, 260, 269 /after Al-Malik An-Nāsir/); **Melik-timür** [Мелик-Тимур] (RaD II, 168). ⇨ **MALİK + TEMİR.**

MELİK-TİMÜR see **MELİK-TEMİR**

MELİKÄ Kzk. **Mälikä** / **Mälikä-qïz** [Мäлікä / Мäлікä кыз], fem. (Proben III, 587 /667/, 615 /698/); Tat.(GH) 13th c. **Melikä** [Меликэ], [roest Antonij's daughter (Smirnov, Krym. 34); Tat.(GH) 1345 **Melikä** [Μελέκα], a christened Tatar woman (Byz. Turc.). ✧ 'Empress', female form of Ar. *Malik*. ⇨ **MALİK** + fem. suff. -*ä* (Ar.).

MEMEK NUyg.(Tar.) 19th c. **Memek** [Мемекъ] (Pantusov, Tar. 15).

MEMET see **MAMET**

MEMİŠ Selj.? **Memiš** (Giese 62).

MEN see **MEÑ**

MEN-ALİ Tat.(Sib.) 1640 **Men-ali-yar** [Янмат Меньалияров] (Miller, Ist. Sib. II, 455). ⇨ **MEN + ALİ.**

MEN-ĀTÏR Hak.(Sag.) 19th-20th c. **Men-ātïr** [Менатыр] (Proben IX, 557). ⇨ **MEN?**

MEN-BALAS Kzk. **Men-balas** [Менбаласъ] (Sb. Syr-D. IX, 50). ⇨ **MEÑ?**

MENBÄT Kzk. **Menbät** [Menbät / Менбäт] (Proben III, 88 /113/).

MENBES Tat.(Sib.) 1634 **Menbes** [Менбес] (Miller, Ist. Sib. II, 415).

MENČİK Maml. 14th c. **Menčik** [منجك اليوسفى الناصرى], emir, governor of Tripolis, then that of Damascus (1367-73), died in 1374, a medresse and a djami in Cairo was named after him (Iyās I 182, 184, 193, 259, Ibn Taghrīb. VII, 595, VI, 245, 542, Makrīzī, Khit. I, 320, Weil, Chalif. I, 522, Sauvaire IV, 286); Maml. 1361 **Menčik** [مَنجك / Mandjik], governor of Damascus, he founded a medresse in Jerusalem (Berchem, Jér. I, 285); Maml. 1368 **Menčik** [السينى منجك / Sayf ad-Dîn Mangak], a viceroy in Damascus, mentioned in an inscription of Tingiz-ǰami in Damascus (Sauvaget: BEO II, 4-5); Maml. 1374-75 **Menčik** [السينى منجك / Saifaddîn Mandjak Yûsufi-Nâsiri], an emir (Berchem 153, 532);

Maml. 1375 **Menčik** [سيفالدين منجك], a viceroy in Egypt, commander-in-chief, died in 1375, mentioned in the inscriptions of a palace, public baths and a medresse (Mayer 153-55); Uyg. **Menčük** [Menčük] (Radl., USp. 129-30, DTS). ✧ I. 'Little birthmark'; II. 'Little eficiency'. ⇨ **MEÑ** + dim. suff. -*čik*.

MENČİN   Kzk. 19th c. **Menčin-bay** [Менчинбай] (SOK 46).

MENČÜK see **MENČİK**

MENJİ   Kzk. 19th c. **Menji** [Менджи] (SOK 44).

MENJİLJİ   Turk. 19th c. **Menjilji-oγlu** [Menʒilʒi oγlu], a Zeybek (Kúnos 1891, 119). ✧ 'Postmaster, inkeeper'cf. Turk. *mänzilji* 'der Posthalter, der Gastwirth' (Radl. IV, 2089).

MENDE   Kzk. 19th c. **Mende-bay** [Мендебай] (SODž. 56, 120); Kzk. 19th c. **Mende-bay** [Мендебай] (SOK 160); Selj. 1200 **Mende-bek** [منده بيك / منده بك], an emir (Ibn Bībī III, 61, IV, 23, Seldj. Nameh 42, 82); Kzk. 19th c. **Mende-qoža** [Мендекожа] (AOK 82); *TN:* Trkm. 19th c. **Bende-pay**, a place in the Kaukasus (Dorn, Bericht über eine wiss. Reise: Bull. de l'Ac. Spbg. 1862, 353). ✧ 'Slave, servant' cf. Chag., Turk., NUyg.(Tar.) *bändä* 'Diener, Sklave' (Radl. IV, 1590), Kzk. *bende* 'pende fert, bende' (KzTs), Tat. *mändä* 'id.' (Radl. IV, 2087). <P. *bendeh*. See also **BAY-MENDE, KER-BENDE, SARAQ-MENDE.**

MENDEY   Crm.(Tat.) 1517 **Mänday** [Hāǰǰï Mänday], a ḥāfiz (baχšï) from the Golden Horde (Vásáry 54); Tat.(Mish.) 1782 **Mendey** [Мендей Тупеев] (MIB V, 130, 276, 277); Bashk. 1759 **Mendey** [Мендей Тупеев] (MIB IV/2, 24); Tat. 1779 **Mendey** / **Mändey** [Мендей (Мяндей) Сафаров] (MIB V, 93); Bashk. 1765 **Mendey** / **Mendiy** [Мендей (Мендий) Аркаев] (MIB IV/1, 311); Bashk. 1761 **Mentey** [Ментей Мусаев] (MIB IV/1, 204). ⇨ **MENDE** + suff. -*y*.

MENDEKE   Kzk. 19th c. **Mendeke** [Мендеке] (SOK 104, 286, 222); Kzk. 19th c. **Mendeke** [Мендеке] (SOV 42). ⇨ **MENDE** + dim. suff. -*ke*.

MENDEKEY   Bashk. 1795 **Mendekey** [Мендекей Аскаровъ] (IOAIÊK XXVIII, 590); Bashk. 1770 **Mendekey** / **Mendekäy** [Мендекай Евкаев] (MIB IV/1, 348). ⇨ **MENDE** + dim. suff. -*key*.

MENDELEY   Tat.(Sib.) 1630 **Mendeley** [Менделей], a prince of the Mungat, a Tatar folk living in the vicinity of the Mongols (Miller, Ist. Sib. II, 56, 368).

MENDES   Kzk. 19th c. **Mendes-pay** [Мендеспай] (SOV 108). ✧ '?' cf. Kzk. PN *Meñdeš* (Žanuzakov-Esbaeva). ⇨ **MEÑ** + suff. -*des* / -*deš*.

MENDET   Kzk. 19th c. **Mendet-pay** [Мендетпай] (Pam. kn. Turg. 68).

MENDİ   Kzk. 19th c. **Mändi** [Манди] (SOK 32); Kzk. 19th c. **Mändi-bay** [Мандибай] (Grod., Pril. 133); Bashk. 1784 **Mändi-γul** [Кувгунга (Кувгунча) Мандыгулов] (MIB V, 155); Bashk. 1740 **Mändi-γul** /

Mindi-γul [Мандигул (Миндигул)] (MIB I, 395); Uzb. 1648 **Mändi-seyit** [Мандисеитов], from Bukhara (Miller, Ist. Sib. II, 527); Kzk. 1825 **Mendi-bay** [مينتباى / Мендибай] (MIK IV, 468, 475); Kzk. **Mendi-bay** / **Meñdi-bay** [Даніяръ Мендыбаичъ] (ZIRGOGeogr. I, 452); Kzk. 19th c. **Mendi-bay** / **Meñdi-bay** [Мендыбаевъ] (AUK 861); Kzk. 19th c. **Mendi-bay** / **Meñdi-bay** [Мендыбай] (AOK 118); Kzk. 19th c. **Mendi-bay** / **Meñdi-bay** [Мендыбай] (AOAtb. 2); Kzk. 19th c. **Mendi-bay** / **Meñdi-bay** [Мендыбай] (SOK 34); Kzk.? 19th c. **Mendi-bek** [Мендибекъ] (SKSO III, 20); Kzk. 19th c. **Mendi-bek** / **Meñdi-bek** [Мендыбекъ Атонбековъ] (Grod., Pril. 72); Kzk. 1828 **Mendi-qul** / **Meñdi-qul** [Мендыкулъ], a mulla (Dobrosm., Turg. 290); *TN:* Kzk. 19th c. **Mendi-bay** / **Meñdi-bay** [Мендыбай], a field (AOA 66). ⇨ **MENDE** / **MEÑLi?** See also **JAL-MENDİ, QARA-MENDİ, QUDA-MENDİ.**

MENDİY see **MENDEY**

MENDİRMAN   Kirg. **Mendirman** [Мендирман], fem. (Jud. 424).

MENEY   Tat. 1624 **Meney** [Меней Безергановъ] (Pokrovskij 70); Bashk. 1749 **Meney** [Меней Касымов] (MIB III, 459). ⇨ **MEÑ** + suff. -*ey*.

MENET   Bashk. 1711 **Menet** [Менеть Иткинин] (MIB III, 75).

MENİKEY   Bashk. 1764 **Menikey** [Меникей Мавлютов] (MIB IV/1, 285).

MENİS   Kzk. 19th c. **Menïs-pay** / **Menis-pay** [Меныспай] (SODž. 90).

MENİŠ   Kzk. 19th c. **Meniš** [Менишъ] (AOK 10).

MENKEY   Tat.? 17th c. **Menkey** [Менкей Салтыковъ], a Cossack (of Tatar origin?) in the government of Kazan (IOAIÊK XXIX, 348). ⇨ **MENİKEY** / **MEÑ?** + suff. -*key*.

MENLİ see **MEÑLİ**

MENTEY see **MENDEY**

MENTEŠ   Yürük 1543 **Menteš** [Menteş] (Gökb., Rum. 188, 206); Yürük 1550 **Menteš** [Menteş] (Gökçen 27); *TN:* Turk. 20th c. **Menteš-bey** [Menteşbey (Gökbel)], a village in the province of Antalya, Turkey (TMİB 98). ⇨ **MENTEŠE?**

MENTEŠE   Turk. 1300-1309 **Menteše** [Μενδεσίας], a prince (Teilfürst) (Byz. Turc. 188); Turk. 1446 **Menteše** [منتشا بن مراد] (MB Qastam. 123); Turk. 1528 **Menteše** [Menteşe (Hacı Menteşe)] (Gökb., Ed. 54). ✧ I. 'Hinge' (TED), cf. Turk. *mäntäšä* 'der Thür oder Fensterriegel' (Radl. IV, 2087); II. Town "Magnesia"? (Radl. IV, 2087); III. 'Golden or silver bracelet' cf. Turk. dial. *menteşe* 'ince, altın ve gümüş bilezik' (DS).

MEÑ   Kzk. 19th c. **Men-bay** [Мусулманъ Менбаевъ] (Grod., Pril. 107); Kzk. 19th c. **Men-jan** [Менджанъ

Уразаліевъ] (AUK 865); Tat.(Sib.) 1620 **Meñ / Meñk?** [Бекмамет Менков] (Miller, Ist. Sib. II, 257, 293); Kzk. 19th c. **Meñ-ĵen / Meñ-ĵan?** [Менгдженъ] (AOO 10); Tat.(Sib.) 1603 **Meñ-güzä** [Менгузя] (Miller, Ist. Sib. II, 181); Kuman 1279 **Meñk** [dux Menk comanus] (Gyárfás II, 436); Kkalp. 20th c. **Min-ayïm** [Минайым], fem. (KkRS 778). ✧ I. 'Brain' cf. Kuman *meŋ* 'Gehirn' (CC); II. 'Birthmark' cf. Chag., Alt., Hak., Trkm. *mäñ* 'id.' (Radl. IV, 2079), Kzk. *meñ* 'id.' (KzRS), Kkalp. *meñ* 'родинка, родимое пятно; бородавка' (KkRS); Being born with a birthmark meant a peculiar fate for the child. If it appeared later, they gave such names (e. g. *Min-hïlïw, Minde-bay, Mindekäy*) as second names so that the birthmarks cannot spread on the whole body (Kusimova 1971, p. 53); III. 'Deficiency' cf. Kzk. *min (mïn)* 'недостаток, дефект' (KzRS).

MEÑ-GİREY   Crm. 1541 **Meñ-girey** [Менъ-Гирей], Safa-keräy khan's son (PSRL VIII, 296). ⇨ **MEÑ + KERÄY.**

MEÑ-TAY   Kzk. 1817 **Meñ-tay** [منكتای / Ментай] (MIK IV, 313, 319). ⇨ **MEÑ + TAY** or suff. *-tay(1,2)*?

MEÑ-TUWA   Maml. 14th c. **Meñ-tuwa** [حسام‌الدین‌حسین بن منكتوا] (Zetterst. 190). ⇨ **MEÑ + TUWA.**

MEÑDİ see **MEÑLİ**

MEÑDİ-GİREY see **MEÑLİ-GİREY**

MEÑÄY-ĴÜZÖY   Kzk. **Meñäy-ĵüzöy** [Меңгäi Цÿзöi] (Proben III, 50 /65/).

MEÑETEY   Yak. **Mäñätäy** [Мäңäтäi] (Pek.); **Meñedey** [Мэнгэдэй] (ZVOIRAO II, 205-207, 212, 218).

MEÑGİN   Kzk. 19th c. **Meñgin-bay** [Менгинбай] (SODž. 154).

MEÑGİS   Kzk. 19th c. **Meñgis** [Менгысъ] (SOV 148).

MEÑGÜ   Uyg. 8th c. - 12th c. **Meñgü** [ïγaččï Mängü] (Müller, Pfahl. 12); Uyg. 1331 **Meñgü** [Mengu] (Chwol., Syr.-nest. (NF) 28); Selj.? **Meñgü** [منگو], an emir (Zehireddin/Dorn 250, 251); Uyg. **Meñgü-bay** [منكوبای], the first ruler of the Uyghurs who was given the title *il-il-täbär* (RaD/Ber. I, 126); Kzk. 19th c. **Meñgü-bay** [Мангубай] (SOK 162); Maml. 1325 **Meñgü-ĵar** [منكجار] (Zetterst. 170); Turk. 20th c. **Meñgü-χan** [Mengühan] (Önder, Göle); Tuv. 19th c. **Meñgü-qïz** [Менгу-кызъ], fem. (Potanin IV, 347); Uyg. 1339 **Müñgä-tärim** [Munga Tarim] (Chwol., Syr.-nest. (NF), 34). ✧ 'Eternal' cf. Uyg., Karakh. *meŋgü* 'вечность, вечный' (DTS), Uyg. *meŋü* 'вечность, вечный' (DTS). See also **AY-MEÑGÜ, ARSLAN-MEÑÜ, BEK-MEÑGÜ, BERK-MEÑGÜ, İL-MEÑGÜ, İNANČČİ-MEÑÜ, QUTUQ-MÄNÜ, TAŠ-MEÑÜ, TUTA-MEÑGÜ.**

MEÑGÜ-BARS   Selj. **Meñgü-bars** [منكوبرس], an emir (Bondārī 125, 129, 172, 173); Selj.? **Meñgü-bars** [منگوبرز] (Zehireddin/Dorn 218); Selj. **Meñgü-bars** [منكوبرس], atabek (Bondārī 163, 170, 183); Selj. **Meñgü-bars** [ناصرالدین منكوبرس] (Bondārī 237-39); Selj. 1118 **Meñgü-bars** [Mengü Bars], an emir and atabeg (Ahbar 62); Selj. 1119/20 **Meñgü-bars** [Imādeddīn Mengübars], atabek of Sultan Maχmud II (1118-1131) (Ibn al-Athīr: RHCHor I, 312, 320); Selj. 1150 **Meñgü-bars** [منكوبرس], an emir (Qalānisi 311, 312); Selj. 12th c. **Meñgü-bars** [منكوبرس], Toγrïl Sultan's door-keeper (Rāwandī 208); Selj. 12th c. **Meñgü-bars** [منكبرس / منكوبرس / Mengü Bars], an emir and atabeg, the owner (ruler) of Fars in the days of Sultan Masʿūd (1134-1152) (Rāwandī 231, Ibn al-Athīr, Atab.: RHCHor II/2. 98, Ahbar 63, 71, 73, 74, 76, 77, 92, 93); Selj. 12th c. **Meñgü-bars** [منكوبرز], an atabek under Sultan Masʿūd bin Muχammad (1134-1152) (Qazw. 447, 467-465); Selj. 1155 **Meñgü-bars** [Mengü Bars], an atabeg (Ahbar 92, 93). ✧ 'Eternal tiger' (Sauvaget 56). ⇨ **MEÑGÜ + BARS.**

MEÑGÜ-BERDİ   Khorezm. 1220-1231 **Meñgü-berdi** [Джелал-ад-дин Менкубирти], the last Khorezmshah (MIT I, 39-40, 474-77, 479, 481-84, 502-04); Khorezm. 1220-1231 **Meñgü-berdi** [Jelâl al-Dîn Manjâbarnî], the last Khorezmshah (Abulfar./Budge I, 394); Khorezm. 1220-1231 **Meñgü-berdi** [منكبرتی / حلال‌الدین منكبرتی / Mangoubirti] (Nasawī 12, 55, 247 etc.). ✧ 'Given by God (by the Eternal)' (Hist. crois. I, 844). ⇨ **MEÑGÜ + BERDİ.**

MEÑGÜ-BOLMÏŠ   Uyg. 12th c. - 14th c. **Meñgü-bolmïš / Meñgü-bulmïš, Bolmïš** (!) [Mängü Bo(u)lmïš] (Radl., USp. 89). ⇨ **MEÑGÜ + BULMÏŠ.**

MEÑGÜ-KELKA   Uyg. 1339 **Meñgü-kelka** [Mangu-Kelka], Qutluq's wife (Chwol., Syr.-nest. 89). ⇨ **MEÑGÜ.**

MEÑGÜ-TAŠ   Uyg. 1169 **Meñgü-taš** [Mengkūteneš] (Chwol., Syr. I, 7-8); Uyg. 1258 **Meñgü-taš** [Mangkutaš] (Chwol., Syr.-nest. 15); Uyg. 1278 **Meñgü-taš** [Mäŋütäš], Päg's (Beg's) son (Chwol., Syr.-nest. 138); Uyg. 1332 **Meñgü-taš** [Mengu Tasch] (Chwol., Syr.-nest. (NF), 29); Uyg. 1338 **Meñgü-taš** [Mangu-taš] (Chwol., Syr.-nest. 81); Uyg. 1338 **Meñgü-taš** [Mengu Tasch] (Chwol., Syr.-nest. (NF), 32). ✧ 'Eternal stone'. ⇨ **MEÑGÜ + TAŠ.**

MEÑGÜ-TAŠ-TAY   Uyg. 1212 **Meñgü-taš-tay** [Mengutaš-tai], a „kobuzči" (musician, player) (Chwol., Syr.-nest. (NF), 19, Hvol'son, Zam. 121). ✧ 'Eternal-stone-foal'. ⇨ **MEÑGÜ + TAŠ + TAY.**

MEÑGÜ-TEMİR   Uyg. **Mängü-temür** [Mängü Temür] (EUTS); Maml. 14th c. **Mäñgü-tämür** [مَنْكوتَمُر] (Sauvaget 56); Uyg. 13th-14th c. **Mäñgü-tämür** [Mänggü Tämür] (Zieme, Mat. II, 92); Mo. / Khorezm.? 1269 **Meñgü-temir** [منكوتمر / Mangutimur], Toγan's son (Abulfidā: RHCHor I, 152, 160, 844, Abulfidā V, 26-27,); Mo. / Khorezm.? 1278 **Meñgü-temir** [Менгу Темирь], a ruler (PSRL X, 155); Maml. 1297 **Meñgü-temir** [منكوتمر] (Abulfidā V, 132); Maml. 1298/99 **Meñgü-temir** [سيف الدين منكوتمر الحسامى], a governor (Zetterst. 43, 52-59, Makrīzī IV, 46-96, Weil, Chalif. I, 207); Maml. 1320 **Meñgü-temir** [منكوتمر الطباخى] (Zetterst. 155); Maml. 1368/69 **Meñgü-temir** [منكوتمر الشيخونى] (Iyās I, 224); Uyg. 12th c. - 14th c. **Meñgü-temür** [meŋgü temür] (DTS). ✧ 'Eternal iron' (Blagova 1997, 714). ⇨ **MEÑGÜ** + **TEMİR.**

MEÑGÜ-TİMUR see **MEÑGÜ-TEMÜR**

MEÑGÜ-VİRİŠ Selj. 1181/82?, 1287 **Meñgü-viriš** [ركن الدين منكورش / خان منكورش], an emir, cup-bearer (Makrīzī, Khit. I, 93, Mayer 156). ✧ 'The Eternal (God) has given' (Sauvaget 56: 'l'Eternel a donné'). ⇨ **MEÑGÜ.**

MEÑGÜČİK Selj. **Meñgüčik** [منكوجك], an emir (Ibn Bībī IV, 2); Selj. 11th c. **Meñgüčik-γāzi** [منكوجك غازى] (Seldj. Nameh 39, 80, Ibn Bībī IV, 21, III, 57); *TN:* Kzk. **Mäñgüčäk?** [Мангучакъ], a village in the district of Kainsk (Patkanov II, 259). ⇨ **MEÑGÜ** + dim. suff. *-čik.*

MEÑGÜSER Selj. 1152 **Meñgüser** [منگسر], Sultan Masʿūd's door-keeper (Rāwandī 225).

MEÑGÜTEY Bashk. 1756 **Meñgütey** [Мангутай Тевекеев] (MIB IV/1, 123); Kirg. 1785 **Meñgütey?** [Менкетей] (MIK IV, 63). ⇨ **MEÑGÜ?** + suff. *-tey.*

MEÑLİ Yürük 1543 **Benli** (Gökb., Rum. 218); Kzk. 19th c. **Mandi-yar / Mändi-yar** [Мандіяръ] (SOK 182); Bashk. 18th c. **Mänli-bay** [Чурагулъ Манлибаевъ] (Nepljuev 882); Crm. **Mäñli-arü-sïlū / Mäñli-sïlū** [Мäнлі-Ару-Сылу / Мäнлі-Сылу], fem. (Proben VII, 169); Kzk. 19th c. **Mäñli-bay** [Бапишъ Манглибаевъ] (Grod., Pril. 165); Crm. **Mäñli-sïlu** [Мäнлі-Сылу], fem. (Proben VII, 123); Kkalp. **Mäñli-slu / Miñli-slu** [Мангли-слу / Мингли-слу] (Divaev? III, 120); Uyg. **Mäñlig-säñün** [Mänglig Sängün] (EUTS); Chag. 15th c. **Mäñlik / Mäñlik-bigim** [مينكليك بيكيم / Manlik / Mänglik-bägim], wife of the Chaghataid İsän-buγa (1434-1462) (Tar. Rashidi 6, 7, Le Coq, Ind. 3); Bashk. 1737-39 **Mendi-yar** [Мендияр (Мандар, Мандиер, Маландар)] (MIB I, 312); Bashk. 1776 **Mendi-yar** [Мендияр Аркаев] (MIB V, 35); Bashk. 1780 **Mendi-yar** [Мендияр Кубалдин (Кулбалдин)] (MIB V, 109); Bashk. 1784 **Mendi-yar** [Мендияр Бекбаев] (MIB V, 154); Bashk. 1797 **Mendi-yar** [Сейфулла Мендияров] (MIB V, 363); Kzk. **Mendi-yar** [Мендіяръ] (Levšin III, 96); Kzk. 1817 **Mendi-yar** [مندىيار] (MIK IV, 302); Kzk. 19th c. **Mendi-yar** [Мендіяръ] (SOK 284);

Kzk. 19th c. **Mendi-yar** [Мендіяръ] (SOK 142); Kzk. 19th c. **Mendi-yar** [Méndiar] (Levchine 356); Trkm. **Menli** [Менли] (Sopieva 181); Kzk. 18th c. - 19th c. **Meñdi-bay** [مينكد يباى / Мендибай] (ZOOIRGO III, 382); Kirg. **Meñdi-bay** [Mengdi Bai / Менді Баі] (Proben V, 83 /84/, 284 /286/); Kzk. 19th c. **Meñdï-bay** [Менгдыбай] (AOK 18); Selj.? 12th c. **Meñli** [منگلى], an emir in Iraq? (Rāwandī 402); Selj. 1213 **Meñli** [منكلى / Mengli], Ay-doγmïš's killer (Abulfidā IV, 250-51); Maml. 1320 **Meñli** [منكلى], a cup-bearer (Zetterst. 168); Maml. 1325 **Meñli** [منكلى] (Zetterst. 170); Maml. 1381 **Meñli** [السيفى منكلى الطرخانى], governor of Karak, mentioned in an inscription (Mayer 102); Maml. 1411/12 **Meñli** [منكلى الخليلّى] (Ibn Taghrīb. VI, 249); Turk. 1504 **Meñli** [Mengli Giray Han] (Gökb., Ed. 472, 483); Trkm. 1816 **Meñli** [Менгли Али-сердар], from the Yomud tribe (MIT II, 396, 398, 459, 461, 464, 635 etc.); Trkm. 20th c. **Meñli** [Meŋli], fem. (Zaj. 1971, 336); Trkm. 20th c. **Meñli** [Менли], fem. (TrkmRS 449); Tat.(Sib.) 1635 **Meñli** [Менглибаев] (Miller, Ist. Sib. II, 423); Bashk. 1075 **Meñli** [Менли Токпердин] (MIB I, 200); Turk.(Osm.) 1399/1400 **Meñli** [منكلى] (Ibn Taghrīb. VI, 16); Trkm. 1722 **Meñli-abïz** [Менгли Абыз] (MIKk. 173); Tat.(Sib.) 1601 **Meñli-bay** [Менглибай абыз] (Miller, Ist. Sib. II, 165); Tat.(Sib.) 1632 **Meñli-bay** [Менглыбай Кождевлетев] (Miller, Ist. Sib. II, 399, 400); Bashk. 1719 **Meñli-bay** [Айбулат Менлибаев] (MIB III, 186); Bashk. 1726 **Meñli-bay** [Янгултан Менлибаев] (MIB III, 242); Bashk. 1807 **Meñli-bay** [Менлибай Абдуловъ] (TOUAK XXIV, 171); Kzk. 1803, 1820 **Meñli-bay** [Менли-бай], one of the chiefs of the Čaqčaq tribe of the Middle Horde (Orta Žüz) (Sib. Vest. IX, 107, MIK IV, 513); Kzk. 1846 **Meñli-bay** [Менлибаевъ] (Konšin, Mat. V, 91); Kzk. 19th c. **Meñli-bay** [Менглибай] (SOK 6); Kzk. 19th c. **Meñli-bay** [Менлибай] (SODž. 80); Kzk. 19th c. **Meñli-bay?** [Менгельбай] (SODž. 94); Kzk. 19th c. **Meñli-bay** [Менглибаевъ] (SKSO VIII, 233); Kzk. 19th c. **Meñli-bay** [Менглибаевъ] (SKSO VIII, 200); Kzk. 19th c. **Meñli-bay** [Генджебай Менглибаевъ] (Grod., Pril. 130); Kzk. 19th c. **Meñli-bay** [Менлибай] (SOV 32); Kkalp. 20th c. **Meñli-bay** [Менлибай] (KkRS 775); Kirg.? 19th c. **Meñli-bay** [Менгли-бай] (Potanin II, 4); Trkm. 19th c. **Meñli-bay, Meñil-bay?** [Менгильбай Оразаньязовъ] (Ščeglov IV, 184); Selj.? **Meñli-beg** [منكله العبّاسّى] (Bondārī 237); Khorezm. 1227 **Meñli-bek** [منكلى بك طاين / Menkeli Bek Thain], Jelāl's officer (Nasawī 138); Trkm. 1829 **Meñli-bek** [Менгли-бек], from the Teke tribe (MIT II, 455); Kzk. 19th c. **Meñli-bek** [Кадыръ-бекъ Менглибековъ] (Grod., Pril. 130); Kzk. 19th c. **Meñli-**

bek [Менглибекъ Абдраимовъ] (Grod., Pril. 152); Selj. 12th c. **Meñli-bek / Meñli-tegin** [كلبنم/ منكلى بيك/ منكلى تكين / Менгли-бек (Менгли-тегин)], Sandjar-šah's (1118-1157) atabek (Ǯuwaynī II, 22-26, MIT I, 405, 446, 447); Tat. 1675 **Meñli-bič(ä)kä? (<Meñli-bičä?)** [Меглибичка] (Kungursk. akty 26); Kkalp. 20th c. **Meñli-gül** [Meŋli-gül / Меңлигул], fem. (KkRS 778, Baskakov: OSA 140); Bashk. 1779 **Meñli-ɣul** [Менлигул Кутлубулатов] (MIB V, 87); Bashk. 1789 **Meñli-ɣul** [Менлигул Курманаев] (MIB V, 252); Oghuz **Meñli-χan** [منكلىخان / Mingli-Khan] (Abulg./Desm. 29); Oghuz/Trkm. 1372 **Meñli-χoǰa** [Менгли-ходжа] (MIT I, 515); Maml. 1400 **Meñli-χoǰa** [الارغون شاوى منكلى حجا] (Ibn Taghrīb. VI, 369); Tat.(Sib.) 1640 **Meñli-yar** [Янмамет Менлияров] (Miller, Ist. Sib. II, 471, 472); Crm. **Meñli-qatun** [منكلى قاتون / Mingli-Khatoun], mother of Toɣluq-temür, khan of Kashghar (Abulg./Desm. 165-66); Kzk. 19th c. **Meñli-qul** [Менгликулъ] (Grod., Pril. 45); Trkm. 1829 **Meñli-quli-χan** [Менгли-Кули-хан], from the Ali-eli tribe (MIT II, 455); Khorezm.? 13th c. **Meñli-tigin** [منكلى تيكين], Buluɣan-χatun's mother, Arɣun-aqa's daughter (RaD/Jahn 13); Uyg. 12th c. -14th c. **Meñlig-señün** [Meñlig señün] (DTS); Tat.(Sib.) 1600 **Meñlï-bay** [Менглыбай абыз] (Miller, Ist. Sib. II, 156, 165); Tat.(Sib.) 1600 **Meñlï-bay** [Менглыбай] (Miller, Ist. Sib. II, 156); Tat.(Sib.) 1603 **Meñlï-bay** [Менлыбай] (Miller, Ist. Sib. II, 181); Tat.(Sib.) 1632 **Meñlï-bay** [Менглыбайка Кождевлетев] (Miller, Ist. Sib. II, 399); Kzk. 19th c. **Meñlï-bay** [Менглабай] (SODž. 96); Kzk. 19th c. **Meñlï-bay** [Менлыбай] (SOV 50); Kzk. 19th c. **Meñlï-bay** [Менлыбай] (SOV 64); Bashk. 1781 **Meñnä-ɣul** [Меннягул Уметеев] (MIB V, 124); Bashk. 1727 **Milli-ɣul (<Miñli-ɣul)** [Миллигуловъ] (MIB III, 244); Kzk. 19th c. **Mindi-bay** [Mindi-Baï], Arɣïm-bay's, Alčï-bay's and Altïm-bay's brother (Levchine 356); Bashk. 1737 **Minli-ɣul** [Бордыкей Минлигулов] (MIB III, 364, 365); Bashk. 18th c. **Miñde-ɣul** [Миндегулъ] (Nepljuev 165); Kzk. 1846 **Miñdi-bay** [Тлясбай Миндибаев] (MKOR 154); Bashk. 1740 **Miñdi-güzä** [Заит Миндигузин] (MIB I, 395); Bashk. 1740 **Miñdi-ɣul** [Миндигул], a leader of a revolt (MIB I, 399, 453, 487 etc.); Bashk. 1762 **Miñdü-bay** [Миндубай Арыков] (MIB IV/1, 244); Uyg. 1338 **Miñgleg-tegin / Meñlig-tegin?** [Migleg-Tegin], fem. (Chwol., Syr.-nest. 82); Bashk. 1744 **Miñiläk** [Мингиляк Тойчин] (MIB III, 415); Bashk. 1753 **Miñlï-bay** [Минлыбай Юртюкеев] (MIB IV/1, 68); Chag. 16th c. **Miñli** [Мингли] (Ivanov 214, 215); Bashk. 1738 **Miñli-bay** [Минлибай Тулумбаев] (MIB III, 387); Bashk. 1744 **Miñli-bay** [Минлибай Бигишев] (MIB III, 415); Bashk. 1755 **Miñli-bay** [Минглибай Ишменев] (MIB IV/1, 95); Bashk. 1756 **Miñli-bay** [Мряс Минлибаев] (MIB IV/1, 119); Bashk. 1761 **Miñli-bay** [Минлибай Ишменев] (MIB IV/1, 204); Bashk. 1764 **Miñli-bay** [Урманчи Минлибаев] (MIB IV/1, 284); Bashk. 1787 **Miñli-bay** [Ишкиня Минлибаев] (MIB V, 219); Bashk. 1675 **Miñli-gözä** [Келирак Минлигозин] (MIB I, 200); Bashk. 1710 **Miñli-ɣul** [Минлигул Чюманаев] (MIB III, 65); Bashk. 1740 **Miñli-ɣul** [Минлигул Зюлаев] (MIB I, 424); Bashk. 1749 **Miñli-ɣul** [Минлигул Танатаров] (MIB III, 469); Bashk. 1780 **Miñli-ɣul** [Минлигул Кутлубулатов] (MIB V, 111); Bashk. 1795 **Miñli-ɣul** [Минлигулъ] (PSZRI XXV, 195); Uzb.? 19th c. **Miñli-qul** [Мингликуловъ] (SKSO II, 17); Chag. 16th c. **Miñli-sultan** [Мингли Султан] (Ivanov 214); Kzk. 19th c. **Miñlï** [Минглы], son of Merkit who was the forefather of the Merkits (Potanin II, 5); Bashk. 1776 **Miñlü-ɣuža** [Иркабек Минглюгужин] (MIB 33, 34); Kzk. 19th c. **Miñti-bay** [Минтибай] (Grod., Pril. 91); Tat.(Mish.) 1755 **Münlü-gül / Münlü-ɣul?** [Аиткул Мюнлюгулов] (MIB IV/1, 93); *TN:* Kzk. **Miñdï-bay** [Миндыбай], a stream south of Orsk (Karta JAR III). ✧ 'Having a birthmark; born with a birthmark' cf. Karakh. *meñlig* 'id.' (DTS), Chag. *mäñlik [meñlik!]* (cf. مينكليك ibid.) (Radl. IV, 2083), Turk. *bänli* 'mit Leberflecken versehen' (Radl. IV, 1589), cf. also Kzk. PNs *Meñdi-bay, Meñdi-ɣali, Meñd-aχmet (<Meñdi-aχmet), Meñl-aχmet (<Meñli-aχmet)* (Žanuzakov-Esbaeva) and Bashk. PNs *Min-hïlïw, Minde-bay, Mindekäy* (Kusimova 1971, p. 53).

MEÑLİ-ALİ Trkm. 19th c. **Meñli-ali** [Менгли-Али] (Ščeglov I, 352); Trkm. 1867 **Meñli-ali** [Менгли Али Кафир], from the Yomut tribe (MIT II, 635); Trkm. 1816 **Meñli-ali-serdar** [Менгли Али-сердар / Менгли-Али-сердар], from the Yomut tribe (MIT II, 396, 398, 459, 461, 464, 635). ⇨ **MEÑLİ + ALİ.**

MEÑLİ-BUQA Maml. 1380 **Meñli-buɣa** [السيفى / سيف الدين / منكلى بغا الاحمدى] (Berchem, Jér. I, 292); Maml. 1387 **Meñli-buɣa** [منكلى بغا المنجكى] (Iyās I, 292); Maml. 1399 **Meñli-buɣa** [منكلى بغا الناصرى] (Iyās I, 313); Khorezm.? **Meñli-buqa** [Менгли-Бука] (RaD II, 63); Maml. 1325 **Meñli-buqa** [سيف الدين منكلى بغا] (Zetterst. 182); Maml. 1350 **Meñli-buqa** [Menkeli bogha], Minister of War (Zetterst. 199, Weil, Chalif. I, 422-23); Maml. 1363 **Meñli-buqa** [منكلىبغا الشمسى], a governor of Damascus (Iyās I, 194, 213 etc., II, 40, Ibn Taghrīb. VI, 798, 817, Weil, Chalif. I, 511); Maml. 1377/78 **Meñli-buqa** [منكلىبغا الطرحانى] (Iyās I, 239); Maml. 1395 **Meñli-buqa** [منكلىبغا الشبغاوى] (Iyās I, 303); Maml. 1399/1400 **Meñli-buqa** [منكلىبغا الصلاحى] (Ibn Taghrīb. VI, 25, 824); Maml. 1400 **Meñli-buqa**

[منكلىبغا], a governor (Ibn Taghrīb. VI, 383); Maml.?
1400 **Meñli-buqa** [منكلى بغا] (Ibn Taghrīb. VI, 368,
371); Maml. 1409/10 **Meñli-buqa**
[منكلى بغا /كاشف القبلية/] (Ibn Taghrīb. VI, 216). ✧
'Spotted/pied-bull' (Sauvaget 56). ⇨ **MEÑLİ** +
BUQA.

MEÑLİ-DÄWLÄT Trkm. 1816 **Meñli-däwlät**
[Менгли-девлет], a mulla from the Toqtamïš clan of
the Teke tribe (MIT II, 389). ⇨ **MEÑLİ** + **DÄWLÄT.**

MEÑLİ-DURDÏ Trkm. 1859 **Meñli-durdï** [Суфи
Менглыьдурдыевъ] (ZIRGOEtn. I, 157); Trkm. 1859
Meñli-durdï [Суфи Менглидурдыевъ] (ZIRGOEtn.
I, 157). ⇨ **MEÑLİ** + **TURDÏ.**

MEÑLİ-GELDİ Trkm. 1819 **Meñli-geldi** [Менгли-
гельды Ярук] (MIT II, 415). ⇨ **MEÑLİ** + **KELDİ.**

MEÑLİ-GELDİ-SAQAW Trkm. 1768/69 **Meñli-geldi-
saqaw** [Менгли Гельды Сакау], from the Yomut
tribe (MIT II, 338, 339, 341, 345, 350). ⇨ **MEÑLİ** +
KELDİ + **SAQAW.**

MEÑLİ-GİREY Crm.(Tat.) 1469, 1515 **Benli-geräy**
[Бенлы-Герай (Менгли-Герай)], Crimean Khan
Mengli Girey I (1469-1474, 1478-1515) (Smirnov,
Krym 278); Crm.(Tat.) 1502 **Menli-girey** [Менли-
Гирей], Khan Mengli Girey I (1469-1474, 1478-1515)
(PSRL XII, 256); Crm.(Tat.) 1484-85 **Menli-girey /
Men-girey / Min-girey** [Менли-Гирѣй / Менъ-
Гирѣй / Минъ-Гирѣй], Khan Mengli Girey I (1469-
1474, 1478-1515) (PSRL XXIII, 183, 184); Crm.(Tat.)
15th c. **Mendi-girey** [Mendigirei], Khan Mengli Girey
I, mentioned in a Polish source (Smirnov, Krym. 243);
Crm.(Tat.) 15th c. **Meñli-girey** [Менглы-Гирей],
Khan Mengli Girey I (1469-1474, 1478-1515) (PSRL
XIX, 31, 242); Crm.(Tat.) 1656 **Meñli-girey**
[منكلى كراى سلطان] (Bakč. Nadp. 37); Crm.(Tat.) 1739
Meñli-girey [Mengli-Girej], Crimean Khan Mengli
Girey II (1737-1739) (Bakč. Nadp. 28); Crm.(Tat.) 15th
c. **Meñli-girey / Minli-girey / Men-girey / Min-girey**
[Менгли-Гирей (Менгирѣй, Минлигирей,
Миньгирѣй) Азибаба], Khan Mengli Girey I (1469-
1474, 1478-1515) (PSRL (Russk. Hr.) I, 462-63, 493-
94, 501-02, 508-17, 534); Crm.(Tat.) 1469, 1515
Meñli-girey-χan [منكلى كراىحان / Mingli Guireï-
khan / Mengli Giray Han / Менгли-Гирей], Crimean
Khan Mengli Girey I (1469-1474, 1478-1515), a
descendant of Jochi (Abulg./Desm. 187, PSRL VIII,
178-79 VIII, 253 etc., Byz. Turc. 186, Gökb., Ed. 472,
483); Crm.(Tat.) 15th c.? **Meñli-girey-χan**, Xaji-girey-
χan's son, Khan Mengli Girey I (1469-1474, 1478-
1515) (Vel.-Zern., Crim. 261). ⇨ **MEÑLİ** + **KERÄY.**

MEÑLİ-MURAT Trkm. 1804 **Meñli-murad** [Менгли
Мурад], from the Yomut tribe (MIT II, 360). ⇨
MEÑLİ + **MURAT.**

MEÑLİ-SERDAR see **MEÑLİ-ALİ**

MEÑLİG-QAYA Uyg. 13th-14th c. **Meñlig-qaya**
[Mnglig Qaya] (Zieme, Mat. II, 88). ✧ 'Rock a with
birthmark'. ⇨ **MEÑLİ** + **QAYA.**

MEÑLİG-ŠİÑQUR Uyg. 8th c. - 12th c. **Meñlig-
šiñqur** [Mänglig Šïngqur] (Müller, Pfahl. 12). ⇨
MEÑLİ.

MEÑLİXAN Kkalp. 20th c. **Meñliχan** [Меңлихан],
fem. (KkRS 778). ⇨ **MEÑLİ** + suff. -χan(1).

MEÑLİŠ Tat.(Sib.) 1632 **Meñliš** [Менлыш Супин]
(Miller, Ist. Sib. II, 397); Bashk. 1713 **Miñliš**
[Минлиш Ишкинин] (MIB III, 103); Bashk. 1756
Miñliš [Минлиш Минлибаев] (MIB III/1, 122);
Uzb.? 1594 **Miñliš-bi** [منكليش بى دورمان / Minglisch-
Bi], a governor in Khiva (Abulg./Desm. 282). ⇨
MEÑLİ + suff. -š.

MER-DÜLÄT Crm. 1479, 1480, 1491 **Mer-dŭlät**
[Мердулатъ] (PSRL VI, 223 VIII, 205, 223 etc.). ⇨ ?
+ **DÄWLÄT.**

MERJAN Kkalp. 20th c. **Maržan** [Маржан], fem.
(KkRS 778); Bulg.? / Tat.(GH) 1339/40 **Märjan**
[مَرجان / Мäрджан], fem. (Jusupov 26); Turk. 1349
Merjan [Μερτζιάνης], a eunuch (Moravcsik 188);
Trkm. 20th c. **Merjen** [Mergen], fem. (Zaj. 1971, 338);
Trkm. 20th c. **Merjen** [Мерджен], fem. (TrkmRS
449). ✧ 'Coral' cf. Kkalp. *maržan* 'id.' (KkRS), Uyg.,
Kuman *marjan* 'die Koralle' (Radl. IV, 2033), Turk.
märjan 'id.' (Radl. IV, 2097), Trkm. *merjen* 'моллюск;
коралл' (TrkmRS) (<Ar.).

MERJİMEK Turk. 1528 **Merjimek** [Mercimek (Hacı
Mercimek)] (Gökb., Ed. 54). ✧ 'Lentil' (TED).

MERDAN Tat. 1531 **Märdän** [Мерденъ], a servant of
the khan of Kazan (PSRL VIII, 274); Oghuz/Trkm.
13th c. **Merdan** [مردان / Мердан] (Abulg./Kon. 390,
400-410). ✧ '(Brave) men; people, (heroic) men' cf.
Turk. *märd* (<P.) 'ein tüchtiger, tapferer Mann; muthig'
(Radl. IV, 2096), Turk. *märdanä* (P.) 'tapfer' (Radl. IV,
2096), Turk. *merdan* (P.) 'İnsanlar, erler, yiğitler'
(Özön). (<P.). See also **ŠAH-MERDAN.**

MEREKE Kzk. 19th c. **Mereke** [Мереке] (SODž. 8);
Kzk. 19th c. **Merke** [Мерке] (AOA 114); Kzk. 19th c.
Merke-bay [Меркебай] (SOV 14); Kzk. 19th c.
Merke-bay [Меркебай] (SODž. 34, 96); Kzk. 19th c.
Merke-bay [Меркебай] (SOV 42). ✧ 'Merry-making,
feasting, festive day' cf. Kzk. *meräkä* 'die Lustbarkeit,
der Feiertag' (Radl. IV, 2092), Kkalp. *mereke*
'вечеринка, празднество, творчество; пир'
(KkRS). See also **AY-MEREKE.**

MERET Trkm. **Meret** [Мерет] (Sopieva 179); Trkm.
20th c. **Meret** [Meret] (Zaj. 1971, 332); Trkm. 20th c.
Meret [Мерет] (TrkmRS 449); Trkm. **Meret-gül**
[Меретгул], fem. (Sopieva 179). ✧ I. 'A name of the
(8th) Ar. month Shaban' (Sopieva)' cf. Chag. *märäd*
(Ar.) 'id.' (Radl. IV, 2092); II. 'Big, frightful' cf. Turk.
märät 'gross, schrecklich, furchtbar' (Radl. IV, 2092).

MERET-DURDÏ   Trkm. **Meret-durdï** [Меретдурды] (Sopieva 179). ⇨ **MERET + DURDÏ.**

MERGEN   Hak.(Sag.) 19th-20th c. **Mergän** [Кан Мергäн], a folklore hero (Proben IX, 251-54); Mo.? **Mergen** [Мэргэн] (RaD I/2, 153); Khorezm. 13th c. **Mergen** [مرکن بن شیبانخان / Merguene], Sheyban Khan's son (Abulg./Desm. 191); Trkm. 1747 **Mergen** [Мерген-султан] (MIT II, 189); Trkm. 20th c. **Mergen** [Mergen] (Zaj. 1971, 326); Trkm. 20th c. **Mergen** [Мерген] (TrkmRS 449); Bashk. 1740 **Mergen** [Салтык Мергенев] (MIB I, 405); Kzk.? 1689 **Mergen** [Мергенъ], a Tabunut (?) chieftain (sait) (PSZRI III, 15); Kkalp. 1722 **Mergen** [Кирки Мергеневъ] (PSZRI VI, 779, MIKk. 172); Kkalp. 1810 **Mergen** [Тёл[Мерген] (MIKk. 110); Hak. 19th-20th c. **Mergen** [Мирген] (HRS 349); Uzb. 19th c. **Mergen** [Казакбай Мергеневъ] (SKSO III, 156); Uzb. 1875 **Mergen** [Мергенъ], from the settlement Teläü in the region of Tashkent (Moskal'cev 40); Uzb. 1884 **Mergen** [Ахунъ Мергенъ Алимбай Мергенъ оглы], from Tashkent (Moskal'cev 68); NUyg. **Mergen** [Ahmed Mergen] (Hedin, En färd I, 539, II, 101 etc.); Trkm. 19th c. **Mergen?, Niyaz-mergen?** [Магмедъ Ніазъ Мергенъ] (Murav'ev I, 48); Kzk. 19th c. **Mergen-bay** [Мергенбай] (SOK 170); Kzk. 19th c. **Mergen-bay** [Мергенбай] (AOK 126); Kkalp. 20th c. **Mergen-bay** [Мергенбай] (Bask., Kkalp. 7, KkRS 775); Kzk. 19th c. **Mergen-bï** [Мергенбы] (SODž. 96); Alt. **Mergen-χan** [Мергенъ-ханъ] (Nikiforov 196 ff.); Kzk. 19th c. **Mirgän** [Джумагулъ Миргановъ] (Grod., Pril. 38); Alt. 19th c. **Pergen-χan** [Пергень ханъ] (Verb., In. 139, 144, 146, 152); *TN:* Kzk. **Mergen** [Мерген], a lake and settlement (Kojčubaev 170). ✧ I. 'Sharpshooter, brave hunter' cf. Hak. *mirgen* 'меткий; ловкий, проворный' (HRS 349), Yak. *bergen* 'меткий, ловкий; молодец, удалец' (JRS). Used also as a secondary component. (<Mo.) *mergen.* II. 'Bride; wife of the elder brother' cf. Yak. *bergen* 'невестка (жена старшего деверя)' (JRS). See also **BURÏ-MERGEN.**

MERGEN-DARŠÏ   Kzk. 19th c. **Mergen-darši / Darši-mergen?** [Мергенъ-Дарыши / Дарыши-Мергенъ] (Potanin, Pred. 104). ⇨ **MERGEN.**

MERGEN-İŽENEY   Kzk. 1652 **Mergen-iženey** [Мергень-Иженей], a prince (DAI III, 379, 382). ⇨ **MERGEN + İŽENEY.**

MERGEN-QAŠQA   Kzk. 1744 **Mergen-qašqa** [Мергенъ-Кашка] (Nepljuev 682). ⇨ **MERGEN + QAŠQA.**

MERİEDİYİN-TEMENE   Alt. 19th c. **Meriediyin-temene-kö-χan** [Мерыэдіин-темэнэ-коо-ханъ] (Verb., In. 101). ⇨ **TEMENE.**

MERKE see **MEREKE**

MERKİM   Kzk. 19th c. **Merkim-bay (<Merkin-bay?)**

[Меркымбай] (SOK 100).

MERKİT   Uyg. **Merkit** [Märkit] (Le Coq, Urkunden 456); Uyg. 12th c. - 14th c. **Merkit** [Märkit] (Radl., USp. 15-16); Uyg. 12th c. - 14th c. **Merkit** (DTS); Kzk. 19th c. **Merkit** [Мэркитъ], forefather of the Merkits (Potanin II, 5). ✧ A Mongol, Kazak and Uzbek tribe.

MERKİTAY   Mo.? **Merkitay** [Меркитай] (RaD I/1, 165).

MERWERİ   Maml. 14th c. **Merweri / Merwāri** [مرواری / märwäri / Mervārī], fem. (Tarǰ/Houtsma 101, Tarǰ/Toparlı 44).

MERWERT   Kkalp. 20th c. **Merwert** [Меруерт], fem. (KkRS 778). ✧ 'Pearl' cf. Kkalp. *merüert* 'жемчуг; жемчужина' (KkRS).

MES-GİLDİ   Bashk. 1755 **Mes-gildi** [Abdulla Masgildin] (Rytschkow II, 22?). ✧ 'A leather-bottle-like child has come (= has been born)' cf. Kzk. *mes* 'ein Leder-Schlauch aus einer ganzen Schaf- oder Ziegenhaut (ohne Naht)' (Radl. IV, 2107-08). ⇨ **KELDİ.**

MESEY   Bashk. 1760 **Mesey** [Месей Юсупов] (MIB IV/2, 28); Kzk. 19th c. **Mesey** [Месей] (AOK 42). ✧ 'A kind of leather-bottle' cf. Kzk. *mes* 'ein Leder-Schlauch aus einer ganzen Schaf- oder Ziegenhaut (ohne Naht)' (Radl. IV, 2107-08). + dim. suff. -*ey.*

MESTEK   Kzk. 1817 **Mestek** [ماستاك / Местек] (MIK IV, 312, 319). ✧ 'Horse, farmer-horse' cf. Kzk. *mästäk* 'die Mähre, der Klepper, ein Bauernpferd' (Radl. IV, 2110).

MEŠEL   Kzk. 19th c. **Mešel** [Мешель] (AOK 34, 94). ✧ 'He who cannot walk; cripple, disabled' cf. Kzk. *mešäl* 'id.' (Radl. IV, 2114).

MEŠER see **MİŠÄR**

MEŠİT   Kzk. 19th c. **Mešit-pay** [Мешитпай] (SOV 76). ✧ 'Mosque' cf. Kzk. *mešit* 'die Moschee' (Radl. IV, 2115).

MEŠKER   Tat.(Sib.) 1636 **Mešker** [Абут Мешкеров] (Miller, Ist. Sib. II, 435). ✧ 'Bashkir' (ethnonym).

METE   Kzk. 19th c. **Mete-bay** [Метебай] (AOK 130). ✧ 'A kind of insect' cf. Chag. *mätä* 'ein Insekt' (Radl. IV, 2103).

METEY   Bashk. 1664 **Metey** [Копбердейко Метеев] (MIB I, 193); Bashk. 1756 **Metey** [Кутлугильды Метеев] (MIB IV/1, 123); Bashk. 1756 **Metey** [Килдияр Метеев] (MIB IV/1, 123); Kzk. 19th c. **Metey** [Метей] (AOA 54, 110); Tat.(Tob.) 1678 **Metey / Matay? / Mätäy?** [Метей (Матай) Кучюгаев] (DAI VIII, 38, MIB I, 205). ⇨ **METE + dim. suff. -*y.***

METEL   Kzk. 19th c. **Metel** [Метелъ] (SOK 260); Kzk. 19th c. **Metel-bay** [Метельбай] (SODž. 34).

METER   Uzb. 1740 **Meter** [Метеръ], from Khiva 1740 (Hanykov, Poezdka 21); Kzk. 19th c. **Meter-bay** [Метербай] (SOK 202); Kzk. 19th c. **Meter-bay**

[Метербай] (SODž. 112).

METKE Hak. 19th-20th c. **Metke** [Метке] (HRS 349).

METKEL Kzk. 19th c. **Metkel-bay** [Меткельбай] (SODž. 14).

METÜK see **MÄTİK**

MEWLĀNĀ Selj. 1383 **Mewlānā-paša**, Šeyh ᶜĀdil's successor (Astarab. 283, 412). ✧ '(Our) Lord, Master, Our Lord Supreme' (Erol II; Ahmed), cf. Turk. *mevlâna* 'Efendimiz anlamında olup bazı sarıklı ulemaya lakap' (Özön) (<Ar.). See also **BERDİ-MÄWLÂN, MAWLAN-BERDİ**.

MEZİD see **MEZİT**

MEZİT Turk. 1528 **Mezid-bey (<Mezit-bey)** [Mezid Bey] (Gökb., Ed. 44, 243, 244, 256, Baştav 74, 80). ✧ 'Whiting (a kind of fish, Gadus merlangus/euxinus)' cf. Turk. *mezit* 'id.' (TS, TED).

MEŽİT see **MEJİT**

MİDA Kzk. 19th c. **Mida-bay** [Мидабай] (Grod., Pril. 114).

MİÄKÄSTÄY see **ÜÖLÄN-ÖKSÖKÜLÄX - MİÄKÄSTÄY**

MİGRİ Kzk. 19th c. **Migri / Xoja-migri** [Ходжа-Мигри Балбанговъ] (Grod., Pril. 54).

MİHRİMAH Turk. 16th c. **Mihrimah-sultan** [Mihrimah Sultan] (Gökb., Ed. 500, 501, 524, 525). ✧ 'Sun and Moon' (<P. *mihr-i-mah*).

MİHRİNİGĀR Turk. 1609 **Mihrinigâr** [Mihrinigâr], Firuz-aγa's wife (Gökb., Ed. 52). ✧ 'Sun(-like) beautiful woman, sweetheart' (P. *mihrinigār*).

MİXA Hak. 19th-20th c. **Miχa** [Миха] (HRS 349). ✧ Mikhail (R.).

MİXAL Turk. 16th c. **Miχal-oγlu** [Mihaloğlu] (Baştav 75, 120). ✧ 'Michael'.

MİXĀS Yak. **Miχäs** [Miχäc] (Pek.). ✧ Misha (R.), dim. of R. Mikhail.

MİXLİ Kzk. 19th c. **Miχli-bay / Mïχlï-bay?** [Мамай Михлибаевъ] (Grod., Pril. 113). ⇨ **MÏQTÏ?**

MİYİR Kkalp. 20th c. **Miyir-gül** [Мийиргүл], fem. (KkRS 778); Kkalp. 20th c. **Miyir-padša** [Мийирпадша], fem. (KkRS 778). ✧ 'Careful, heedful, tender' cf. Kkalp. *miyir* 'забота; жалость, милосердие' (KkRS), Kzk. *meyĭr* 'симпатия; благосклонность' (KzRS).

MİYİR-ŠAT Kkalp. 20th c. **Miyir-šat** [Мийиршат], fem. (KkRS 778). ⇨ **MİYİR + ŠAT.**

MİYİRXAN Kkalp. 20th c. **Miyirχan** [Мийирхан], fem. (KkRS 778). ⇨ **MİYİR** + suff. *-χan(1).*

MİYİRMAN see **MİYİRMAN**

MİYİRMAN Kzk. 19th c. **Miyirman** [Міирманъ] (SOV 20); Kzk. 19th c. **Miyirman** [Міирман Балгимбаевъ] (AUK 770); Kkalp. 20th c. **Miyirman** [Мийирман] (KkRS 775). ✧ 'Charitable, hearty, pitiful, kind' cf. Kzk. *meyĭrban* 'id.' (KzRS). ⇨ **MİYİR** + suff. *-man.*

MİYİZ Kzk. 19th c. **Miyiz-gül** [Мииэгуль], fem. (Grod. I, 98); Kzk. 19th c. **Miz-bay** [Мизбай] (SODž. 58). ✧ 'Grape; raisin' cf. Kzk. *meyĭz* 'изюм, сушёный виноград' (KzRS).

MİYRİMDİ Kzk. 19th c. **Miyrimdi** [Мійрмды] (AOO 34). ✧ 'Hearty, pitiful, kind' cf. Kzk. *meyĭrĭmdĭ* 'id.' (KzRS).

MİYÜZ Oghuz (Berendey)? 1159 **Miyüz** [Каракозь Миюзовичъ] (Ipat. 343 (356), PSRL VII, 69). ✧ 'Horn' cf. Kzk. *müyüz* 'das Horn' (Radl. IV, 2221), Tuv. *müyïs* 'рог' (TuvRS). See also **XARA-MUYUZTU.**

MİKÄN see **MİKEN**

MİKE Kzk. **Mike-bay** [Микебай] (Grod. 169); Kzk. 19th c. **Mike-bay** [Микебай] (AUK 287).

MİKEY Hak. 19th-20th c. **Mikey** [Микей] (HRS 340). ✧ 'Cheat, lie, slyness'? cf. Hak. *mike* 'id.' (HRS). + dim. suff. *-y.*

MİKEN Kzk. 19th c. **Mikän** [Миканъ] (Grod., Pril. 51); Kzk. 1846 **Miken** [Мыкенбай Чигиров] (MKOP 154); Hak. 19th-20th c. **Miken** [Микен] (HRS 349); Kzk. 19th c. **Mikin (<Mike?)** [Микинъ] (Grod., Pril. 60).

MİKEŠ Bashk. 1737 **Mikeš** [Явкей Микешев] (MIB III, 360).

MİKİN see **MİKEN**

MİKİTTÄ Yak. **Mikittä** [Мікіття] (Pek.). ✧ Nikita (R.).

MİKİPÄR Yak. **Mikïpär** [Мікіпäр] (Pek.). ✧ Nikifor (R.).

MİKİS Yak. **Mikïs** [Мікіс] (Pek.). ✧ Dim. of *Mikïpär.*

MİLAY Hak. 19th-20th c. **Milay** [Милай] (HRS 349).

MİLDA Kzk.? 19th c. **Milda-bay** [Милдабай] (Grod., Pril. 100).

MİLİMİÄN Yak. **Milimiän** [Міліміän] (Pek.). ✧ Filimon (R.).

MİLLET-VİRDİ Yürük 1543 **Millet-virdi** (Gökb., Rum. 228). ✧ 'Nation (folk) gave him' cf. Turk. *millet* 'nation, people, crowd, folk' (TED), *ver- [vir-]* 'to give' (TED). ⇨ **BERDİ.**

MİLÜŠ Bashk. 1735 **Milüš** [Милюшъ Аднагуловъ], a tarχan (Vel.-Zern., Bašk. 14).

MİM-BAY see **MİÑ**

MİM-BULAT see **MİÑ-BULAT**

MİM-ΓUL see **MİÑ**

MİN I. see **MEÑ**

MİN II. see **MİÑ**

MİN-AYDAR Kzk. 19th c. **Min-aydar** [Хакимжанъ Минайдаровъ] (AUK 444). ⇨ **MEÑ / MİÑ + AYDAR.**

MİN-BAŠÏ see **MİÑ-BAŠÏ**

MİN-JAWAR Uzb. 20th c. **Min-jawar** [Минжавар] (Begmatov 1984, 202). ⇨ **MİÑ?**

MİN-TAŠ Maml. 1388 **Min-taš** [الافضلى / تمربغا

منطاش], governor of Malatya, Hamah etc., fought against Barqūq, died in 1393 (Ibn Taghrīb. VI, 40, 137, 143 VII, 243, 593, Weil, Chalif. I, 549, Astarab. 339, 343); Maml. 1467 **Min-taš** [منطاش] (Ibn Taghrīb. VIII, 617); Maml.? 1496/97 **Min-taš** [منطاش الناصرى] (Iyās II, 316). ✧ 'Thousand stones; Thousandfold-Stone' (Sauvaget 55: 'mille-pierre / mille pierres'). ⇨ **MİÑ** + **TAŠ.**

MİNAJ Bulg. / Tat.(GH)? 1352 **Minaj / Manaj / Manaji?** [منج / Минадж] (Jusupov 28, Epigr. Bulg. 88, 89). ✧ 'Way of luck' (<Ar. *minχaj*).

MİNATÏR Hak. 19th-20th c. **Minatïr** [Минатыр] (HRS 349).

MİNDÄR Yak. **Mindär-quo** [Солко-Мīндäр-куо], fem. (Pek.).

MİNDİ see **MENDİ, MEÑLİ**

MİNÄ-QAŠ Bashk. 1761 **Minä-qaš** [Минякаш Якупов] (MIB IV/1, 211). ⇨ **QAŠ.**

MİNÄŠ Tat. 1724 **Minäš** [Миняш Утемишев] (MIB III, 227); Bashk. 1745 **Minäš** [Идрис Миняшев] (MIB III, 426).

MİNE Turk. 1583 **Mine** [منه], fem. (Ongan, Ank. I, 169). ✧ 'Glaze, enamel' cf. Turk. *minä* 'id.' (Radl. IV, 2153).

MİNEY Bashk. 1707 **Miney** [Миней Тютеев] (MIB III, 32); Bashk. 1707 **Miney** [Миней Тюкеев] (MIB III, 32); Bashk. 1746 **Miney** [Атаман Минеев] (MIB III, 439); Bashk. 1757 **Miney** [Кутлу Минеев] (MIB IV/1, 140); Bashk. 1757 **Miney** [Чурагул Минеев] (MIB IV/1, 142); Bashk. 1760 **Miney** [Миней Бекбовов] (MIB IV/2, 28); Bashk. 1761 **Miney** [Миней Султуков] (MIB IV/1, 211); Bashk. 1764 **Miney** [Миней Ибраев] (MIB IV/1, 276).

MİNELİ Kzk. 1826 **Mineli-qul** [Минеликулъ] (Dobrosm., Turg. 282).

MİNİKE Kzk. 19th c. **Minike** [Минике] (Grod., Pril. 85). ⇨ **MİNKE?**

MİNİKEY see **MİNKEY**

MİNKÄ see **MİNKE**

MİNKE Tat. 1744 **Minkä** [Минка Илтутов] (MIB III, 421); Bashk. 1735 **Minke** [Субхангулъ Минкинъ], a tarχan (Vel.-Zern., Bašk. 20). ⇨ **MİÑ** + dim. suff. *-ke.*

MİNKEY Bashk. 1770 **Minikey** [Миникей Мавлютов] (MIB IV/1, 347); Bashk. 1798 **Minkey** [Минкеевъ] (PSZRI XXV, 197). ⇨ **MİÑ** + dim. suff. *-key.*

MİNLÜ-QARA Kzk. 1819 **Minlü-qara** [Минлю-кара] (MIK IV, 323). ⇨ **MEÑLİ** + **QARA.**

MİNNET Turk. 1474 **Minnet** [Hacı Minnet bin Abdülkerim] (Gökb., Ed. 347); Yürük 1543 **Minnet** (Gökb., Rum. 193). ✧ Minnat (Ar.) 'grace, kindness, gift' (Ahmed), 'Obligation, favor, taunt; praise, thanks' (TED).

MİNNİKEY Bashk. 1759 **Minnikey** [Минникей Щербенев] (MIB IV/1, 179). ⇨ **MEÑLİ** + dim. suff. *-key.*

MİNSİN Uyg. 12th c. - 14th c. **Minsin** [minsin] (DTS, EUTS).

MİNTÏQ see **MİLTÏQ**

MİÑ Kzk. 1820 **Mim-bay (<Min-bay)** [Мимбай], head (chief) of the İsen-temir tribe of the Little Horde (Kiši Žüz) (Sib. Vest. IX, 120); Bashk. 1764 **Mim-γul (<Miñ-γul)** [Сюирьгул Мимгулов] (MIB IV/1, 300); Kzk. **Min-bay** [Минбай] (Smirnov, Sultany 26); Uyg. **Miñ** [Miŋ] (DTS); Uzb.? 19th c. **Miñ-bay** [Мингбай] (SKSO III, 10); Kzk. 1823 **Miñ-bay / Min-bay** [منكباى / Минбай] (MIK IV, 456); Oghuz? 839 **Miñ-čur** [منكجورالاشروسنى] (Tabarī, Annal. III, 1301, 1302, 1305, 1315, 1577 etc., Fragm. Hist. Ar. 515, 516, 524, 525); Oghuz? 865 **Miñ-čur** [منكجور بن حدرُوسى/قدروش] (Tabarī, Annal. III, 1620, 1625); Oghuz? 874 **Miñ-čur** [منكجور], a governor in Hims (Tabarī, Annal. III, 1885); Oghuz? 876 **Miñ-čur** [Mankidjur Albucharij], in Mutamid's times (Weil, Abbas II, 458); Kzk. 19th c. **Mïm-bay (<Miñ-bay / Mïn-bay?)** [Мымбай] (SODž. 144); Kzk. 19th c. **Mïn-bay** [Мынбай] (SOK 118, 156, 176); Kzk. 19th c. **Mïn-bay** [Мынбай] (SOV 42); Kzk. 19th c. **Mïn-bay** [Мынбай] (AOK 82); Kzk. 19th c. **Mïn-bay** [Мынбай] (SODž. 160); Kzk. 19th c. **Miñ-bay** [Мынгбай] (SOV 116); Kzk. 19th c. **Miñ-bay** [Мынгбай] (AOK 50); Kzk. 19th c. **Miñ-žan** [Мынгжанъ] (AOK 130). ✧ I. 'Thousand' (Rásonyi, Nombre 69-70), cf. Kzk. *miñ* 'id.' (Radl. IV, 2139); II. 'Defective, faulty (child)'? cf. Kzk. *mïn* 'недостаток, дефект' (KzRS); Alt.(Kmd.) *miñ* 'der Mangel, die Noth' (Radl. IV, 2139). See also **ARSLAN-MİÑ.**

MİÑ-BAŠÏ Turk. 20th c. **Bin-baši** [Binbaşı] (Önder, Göle); NUyg. 19th c. **Min-baši** [Khodja Min Baschi], a courtier (Hedin, En färd I, 119); Kzk. 19th c. **Min-bašï / Min-baši?** [Халъ Сеидъ Минбаши] (Grod., Pril. 148). ✧ 'Head of one thousand (soldiers); colonel'. ⇨ **MİÑ** + **BAŠ** + poss. suff. *i.*

MİÑ-BULAT Karch. **Mim-bulat (<Min-bulat)** [Мимбулатъ] (Sysoev 126); Tat.(GH) 1432 **Min-bulat** [Минь-Булатъ], a prince of the Horde (PSRL VIII, 96, XII, 15); Khorezm.? **Miñ-fulād** [منكفولاد ايلچى] (Juwaynī I, 36); Nog. 1649 **Mïn-bulat** [Мынъ-Булатъ], a murza (AI IV, 87). ✧ 'Thousand-steel'. ⇨ **MİÑ?** + **BULAT.**

MİÑ-ČASAR see **MİÑ-JASAR**

MİÑ-JASAR Kzk. 19th c. **Miñ-časar** [Мингчасаръ] (Grod., Pril. 101); Kzk. 19th c. **Miñ-jasar** [Мингчасаръ Байкопаковъ] (Grod., Pril. 101); Kzk. 19th c. **Mïn-jasar** [Мынджасаръ] (SOK 4, 262); Kzk. 19th c. **Mïn-jasar** [Мынджасаръ] (AOK 6); Kzk. 19th

c. **Mïn-Jasar** [Мынджасаръ] (SOV 18); Kzk. 19th c. **Mïn-Jasar** [Мынджасаръ] (SODž. 150); Kzk. 19th c. **Mïn-Jasar** [Мынджасаръ] (AOO 34). ✧ 'He will live to be thousand, he will be long-lived'. ⇨ **MİÑ** + **YAŠAR.** See also **JÜZ-JASAR.**

MİÑ-FULĀD see **MİÑ-BULAT**

MİÑ-QARA Uyg. **Miñ-qara** [Miŋ qara] (DTS); Uyg. 12th c. - 14th c. **Miñ-qara** [Ming-Qara] (Radl., USp. 27-28); Uyg. **Mïñ-qara** [Mıng Kara] (EUTS). ✧ 'Thousand-black'. ⇨ **MİÑ** + **QARA.**

MİÑ-TEMÜR Uyg. **Miñ-temür** [Miŋ temür] (DTS); Chag. **Miñ-temür-χan** [مينك تيمور خان], a Sheybanid ruler (Šejb. XLIX); Uyg. **Mïng-tämür** [Mıng Tämür] (EUTS); Uyg. **Mïñ-temür** [Mïng-tämür] (Radl., USp. 1). ⇨ **MİÑ** + **TEMİR.**

MİÑİLÄK see **MEÑLİ**

MİÑLİ see **MEÑLİ**

MİÑLİŠ see **MEÑLİŠ**

MİÑLÜ see **MEÑLİ**

MİÑTİ see **MEÑLİ**

MİPİS Kzk. 19th c. **Mipis-pay** [Миписпай] (AOP 114).

MİR Uzb. **Mir-baba** [Mir-Baba] (Mozer, A travers l'Asie centrale, p. 213); Kirg. **Mir-bek** [Мирбек] (Jud. 561). ✧ 'Chief, governor; emir' (<P.).

MİR-DÄWLÄT see **DÄWLÄT**

MİR-DÖWLET see **DÄWLÄT**

MİR-QUT Kuman 1097 **Mir-qut / Mir-qot?** [Миркотъ], a Polovets prince who helped David Igorevitch to defeat the Ugry (Ugors?) (PSRL II, 284). ⇨ **MİR** + **QUT.**

MİR-TURSUN Uzb. 20th c. **Mir-tursun** [Миртурсун] (Begmatov 1984, 204). ✧ 'Let the *(e)mir* stay/live'. ⇨ **MİR** + **TURSÏN.** See also **BAY-TURSUN, BEK-TURSUN.**

MİRAS Bashk. 1731 **Mräs** [Мрясь Урмяшев] (MIB III, 294); Bashk. 1735 **Mräs** [Аллакай Мрясевъ], a tarχan (Vel.-Zern., Bašk. 15); Bashk. 1735 **Mräs?** [Усен Мрясев], a tarχan (Vel.-Zern., Bašk. 15); Bashk. 1738 **Mräs** [Мряс Елумбетев (Юлумбетев)] (MIB I, 143, 145); Bashk. 1756 **Mräs** [Туманчи Мрясов] (MIB IV/1, 109); Bashk. 1756 **Mräs** [Мрясь Кылысев] (MIB IV/1, 130); Bashk. 1779 **Mräs** [Габбас Мрясев] (MIB V, 87); Hak. 19th-20th c. **Muras** [Мурас] (HRS 350). ✧ 'Heritage' cf. Bashk. *miraθ* 'наследие, наследство' (BRS).

MİRČA Kzk.? 19th c. **Mirča** [Мирча] (Grod., Pril. 185). ⇨ **MİR** + suff. -*ča.*

MİRÄK Kzk. 19th c. **Miräk-bay** [Миракбай] (Grod., Pril. 28); Bashk. 1760 **Mräk (<Miräk)** [Мряк Килишев] (MIB IV/1, 191). ⇨ **EMİREK?**

MİRGEN see **MERGEN**

MİRİŠ Trkm. 1821 **Miriš** [Миришъ], a mulla (Russk. Arhiv I, 237); Trkm. 1859 **Miriš-bay** [Миришъ-бай] (ZIRGOÊtn. I, 190). ⇨ **MİR** + suff. -*iš.*

MİRQA Kzk. 19th c. **Mirqa** [Джулалбай Миркабаевъ] (Grod., Pril. 101); Kzk. 19th c. **Mirqa-bay** [Миркабай] (Grod., Pril. 182); Kzk. 19th c. **Mirqa-bay** [Миркабай] (Grod., Pril. 80). ⇨ **MİR** + suff. -*qa / -kä?*

MİRZA-PAYAS Uzb.? 19th c. **Mirza-payas-datχa** [Мирза-Паясъ датха] (AUK 840). ⇨ **MİRZA.**

MİRZA-TAY Kzk. 19th c. **Mirza-tay** [Мирзатаевъ] (Grod., Pril. 106). ⇨ **MİRZA** + **TAY** or suff. -*tay(1,2)?*

MİSE Hak. 19th-20th c. **Mise** [Мисе], fem. (HRS 354); Hak. 19th-20th c. **Mise** [Мисе] (HRS 349).

MİSEKŠE Kzk. 19th c. **Misekše** [Мисекше] (SOK 84).

MİSKE Hak. 19th-20th c. **Miske** [Миске] (HRS 349). ✧ 'Mushroom' cf. Hak. *miske* 'гриб; губа, гриб (твёрдый нарост на стове дерева)'.

MİŠÄR Bashk. 1778 **Mešer** [Утямыш Мещеров] (MIB V, 80, 81); Bashk. 1798 **Mešer** [Мещеровъ] (PSZRI XXV, 196); Bashk. 1756, 1757 **Mišär** [Иштуган Мишаров (Мешаров)] (MIB IV/1, 111, 150); Chuv. 18th-19th c. **Mišär-bay** [Мишарбай] (Magn. 58); Chuv. 18th-19th c. **Mišer** [Мишеръ] (Magn. 58); Bashk. 1740 **Mišer** [Мишер] (MIB I, 396); Bashk. 1779 **Mišer** [Токтамыш Мишерев] (MIB V, 90); Chuv. 18th-19th c. **Mižer-bey** [Мижербей] (Magn. 57). ✧ Misher / Mishar (Ethnonym), cf. Tat. *mišär* 'ein tatarischer Volksstamm (Tataren von Simbirs, Pensa)' (Radl. IV, 2166). See also **QUL-MİŠÄR.**

MİŠER see **MİŠÄR**

MİŠEREY Chuv. 18th-19th c. **Mišerey** [Мишерей] (Magn. 58). ⇨ **MİŠÄR** + dim. suff. -*ey.*

MİŠERKÄ Chuv. 18th-19th c. **Mišerkä?** [Мищерка] (Magn. 58). ⇨ **MİŠÄR** + suff. -*kä?*

MİŠERLÄ Chuv. 18th-19th c. **Mišerlä / Mišerkä?** [Мишерля] (Magn. 58).

MİT Kzk. **Mit-bay** [Митбай] (Sb. Syr-D. IX, 52).

MİTAN Kzk. 19th c. **Mitan** [Митанъ] (SODž. 34); Kzk. 19th c. **Mitan-bay** [Митанбай] (SKSO III, 10); Uzb. 19th c. **Mitan-bay** [Митанбай] (SKSO III, 176).

MİTİKEY Bashk. 1761 **Mitikey** [Утягул Митикеев] (MIB IV/1, 204).

MİTKE see **MİTKÄ**

MİTREY Bashk. 1757 **Mitrey** [Япар Митреев] (MIB IV/1, 142). ✧ Dmitriy (R.).

MİTSU Uyg. **Mitsu** (DTS).

MİVE Trkm. 20th c. **Mive** [Mive], fem. (Zaj. 1971, 339); Trkm. 20th c. **Mive** [Миве], fem. (TrkmRS 452). ✧ 'Fruit' cf. Trkm. *mive* 'фрукт; плод' (TrkmRS) (<P.).

MİZ see **MİYİZ**

MİŽ Nog. 20th c. **Miž** [Адимей Халил улы Миж],

one of Baskakov's informants from the aul of Adil-χalq (Bask., Nog. 143).

MİŽÄK Tat.(Bar.) **Mižäk-alïp** [Mischäk Alyp / Міжäк Алып], a character in a tale (Proben IV, 26). ✧ 'Cat' cf. Tat.(Bar.) *mižäk* 'id.' (Radl. IV, 2166).

MİŽER see **MİŠÄR**

MİSÄ Yak. **Mïsä** [Micä] (Pek.). ✧ Misha (R.), dim. of R. Mikhail.

MİSKÄ Hak.? **Mïskä** [Мicкä] (Katanov, Otč. 11). ✧ Mishka (R.) (Katanov).

MİTÄ Yak. **Mïtä** [Мітä, Мiт(ä)кä, Мітäcкі] (Pek.). ✧ Mitya (R.), dim. of R. Dmitriy.

MİTİRÄY Yak. **Mïtiräy / Mïträy** [Мітіpäi, Мітpäi] (Pek.). ✧ Dimitriy, Dmitriy (R.).

MİTİRİYÄN Yak. **Mïtiriyän / Mïträyän** [Мітіpijäн, Мітpäjäн] (Pek.). ✧ Dmitrian (R.).

MİTKÄ Hak. 19th-20th c. **Mitke** [Митке] (HRS 349); Yak. **Mïtkä** [Міткä] (Pek.). ✧ Mit'ka (R.), dim. of R. Dmitriy.

MİTRÄY Yak. **Mïträy** [Мітpäi] (Pek.). ✧ Dmitriy (R.).

MİTRÄYÄN Yak. **Mïträyän** [Мітpäjäн] (Pek.). ✧ Dmitrian (R.).

MİTRİY Alt.? 19th-20th c. **Mïtriy** [Мітpій] (Katanov, Otč. 10). ✧ Dmitriy (R.) (Katanov).

MİTTÄ Yak. **Mïttä** [Мiттä] (Pek.). ✧ Dim. of *Mikittä* coming from R. Nikita.

MİČČİLLA Yak. **Mïččïlla** [Мыччылла], a shaman (Pek.).

MİDİRAQ Hak. 19th-20th c. **Mïdïraq** [Мыдырак] (HRS 350). ✧ Ways of ritual hand positions, cf. Hak. PN *Midir / Midiraχ* (Butanaev).

MİĞİŠ Kzk. 19th c. **Mïγïš** [Мыгышъ] (AOA 110).

MİĞLAY see **MUQLAY**

MİYA-BAS Kzk. 19th c. **Mïya-bas** [Сатбай Міябасовъ] (Grod., Pril. 66). ✧ 'Sweet-tree-head'? cf. Kzk. *mïya* 'Süssholz (Glycyrrhiza)' (Radl. IV, 2139); ⇒ **BAŠ.**

MİYAČİQ Khorezm. **Mïyačïq / Mïyančïq** [ميانجق / مياجق], one of the emirs of the Khorezmshah Tekiš (Rāwandī 366, 380, Ǧuwaynī II, 32, 37, 38 etc.). ✧ 'Little sweet-tree'. ⇒ **MİYA?** + suff. *-čïq.*

MİYAQ Alt. 19th-20th c. **Mïyaq** [Мыйак] (OjrRS 209).

MİYANČİQ see **MİYAČİQ**

MİYAĞİS Hak.(Blt.) 19th-20th c. **Mïyaγïs** [Мыjaвыс] (Proben IX, 355, 362, 366). ✧ 'Dung, excrement' cf. Hak. PN *Mïyaχ / Mïyaγas* (Butanaev).

MİYİQ Maml. 1368 **Mïyïq** [ميق] (Sauvaget 56). ✧ 'Moustache' cf. Maml. (Kipch.) *mïyïq* 'id.' (Tuhfa), *byjyk* 'Schnurrbart' (Tarǧ/Houtsma), Turk. *bïyïk* 'moustache' (TED). See also **QOĴA-BÏYÏQ, SARÏ-BÏYÏQ.**

MİYTİQ Kkalp. 20th c. **Mïytïq** [Мыйтыкъ / Мыйтык̣] (Bask., Kkalp. 401, KkRS 775).

MİQ Kzk. 19th c. **Mïq-bay** [Мыкбай] (SOK 230). ✧ 'Suitable, useful' cf. Kzk. *mïq* 'tüchtig, brauchbar' (Radl. IV, 2137).

MİQÏLAY see **MUQULAY**

MİQİŠ Kzk. 19th c. **Mïqïš-pay** [Мыкышпай] (SOK 94).

MİQTİ Kzk. 19th c. **Mïqta-bay / Mïqtï-bay?** [Миканъ Миктабаев] (Grod., Pril. 51); Kzk. 1846 **Mïqtï-bay** [Мухамед Мыктыбаев], a biy (MKOP 156); Kzk. 19th c. **Mïqtï-bay** [Мыктыбай] (AOA 130); Kzk. 19th c. **Mïqtï-bay** [Мыктыбай] (SOK 38, 88); Kzk. 19th c. **Mïqtï-bek** [Мыктыбекъ] (SODž. 8); Kzk. 19th c. **Mïqtï-bek** [Мыктыбекъ] (SOK 74, 262); Kzk. 19th c. **Mïqtï-bek** [Мыктыбекъ] (SOV 116); Kzk. 19th c. **Moqtï-bek / Mïqtï-bek?** [Моктыбекъ] (SOV 148); Kzk. 19th c. **Muqtï-bay** [Муктыбай] (AOK 118); Kzk. 19th c. **Muqtu-bay** [Муктубай] (SODž. 148). ✧ 'Strong, brave' cf. Kzk. *mïqtï* 'fest, stark, furchtlos, trotzig, vorsichtig' (Radl. IV, 2137).

MİLA Hak. 19th-20th c. **Mïla** [Мыла] (HRS 350).

MİLAXSİN Yak. **Mïlaχsïn** [Ырбаiбан-Мылахсын], a lad (young man) who takes the fat off the animals (Pek.); Yak. **Mïlaχsïn-χotun** [Мылахсын-хотун], fem. (Pek.); Yak. **Mïlaχsïn-toyon** [Мылахсын-тоjoн], fem. (Pek.).

MİLAYİM Trkm. 20th c. **Mïlayïm** [Mïlayïm], fem. (Zaj. 1971, 336); Trkm. 20th c. **Mïlāyïm** [Мылайым], fem. (TrkmRS 463). ✧ 'Mild, nice' cf. Trkm. *mïlāyïm* 'приятный, мягкий, сердечный' (TrkmRS) (<Ar.).

MİLĀDAY Yak. **Mïlāday(-χotun)** [Мыладаi(хотун)], a goddess, protector of cattle (especially cows and calves) (Pek.).

MİLQİQ Trkm. 20th c. **Mïlqïq** [Mïlqïq] (Zaj. 1971, 333). ✧ 'Overripe, soft' cf. Trkm. *mïlqï* 'id.' (TrkmRS).

MİLTÄÑ Hak. 19th-20th c. **Mïltäñ** [Мылтаанъ] (HRS 350); Hak.(Sag.) 19th-20th c. **Mïltäñ** [Мылтаң] (Proben IX, 553).

MİLTİSQA Hak. 19th-20th c. **Mïltïsqa** [Мылтиска] (HRS 350).

MİLTİĞAS see **MİLTİĞAŠ**

MİLTİĞAŠ Hak.(Sag.) 19th-20th c. **Mïltïγas** [Мылтыҕас / Мылтыгас] (Proben IX, 554, 613, HRS 350); Hak.? 19th c. **Mïltïγaš** [Мылтыҕаш] (Katanov, Otč. 12); Hak.(Blt.) 19th-20th c. **Mïltïγaš** [Мылтыҕаш], fem. (Katanov, Otč. 10); Hak.(Sag.) 19th-20th c. **Mïltïγaš** [Мылтыҕаш] (Katanov, Otč. 7); Hak.(Sag.) 19th-20th c. **Mïltïγaš** [Мылтыҕаш] (Katanov, Otč. 11); Hak. 19th c. **Multïγaš** [Мултыҕаш] (Katanov, Otč. 12); Hak.(Koyb.) 19th-20th c. **Multïγaš** [Мултыҕаш] (Katanov, Otč. 13); Hak.(Kyz.) 19th-20th c. **Multïγaš** [Мултыҕаш]

(Katanov, Otč. 13); Hak.(Shor) 19th-20th c. **Multïγaš** [Мултыңаш] (Katanov, Otč. 11). ✧ I. 'Small rifle, gun' (Katanov, Butanaev); II. 'Christening; (Born on) Twelfth-day' cf. Hak. PN *Miltïχ / Miltïγas* (Butanaev). ⇨ **MÏLTÏQ** + dim. suff. *-aš*.

MÏLTÏQ   Kzk. 19th c. **Maltïq-pay / Mïltïq-pay?** [Малтыкпай] (SOK 116); Kzk. 19th c. **Mintïq-bay / Mïltïq-bay** [Батманъ Минтыкбаевъ] (Grod., Pril. 172); Karg. **Mïltïq** [Мылтык] (Katanov, Otč. 8); Kzk. 19th c. **Mintïq-bay?** [Тулягенъ Мнитыкбаевъ] (Grod., Pril. 144); Kzk. 19th c. **Moltïq-pay / Mïltïq-pay?** [Молтыкпай] (SOK 102); Kzk. 19th c. **Montïq / Mïltïq?** [Мöнтыкъ] (AOO 46); Kzk. 19th c. **Multïχ-bay** [Мултыхбай] (AOO 50); Kzk. 19th c. **Multïq-pay** [Мултыкпай] (SOK 280). ✧ 'Rifle, gun' cf. Hak., Kzk., Tat., Trkm., Uzb. *miltïq* 'das Gewehr (eigentlich das Luntengewehr)' (Radl. IV, 2144), Hak. *miltïχ* 'ружьё' (HRS), Alt., Chul.(Küer.) *multïq* 'die Flinte, das Gewehr' (Radl. IV, 2197). See also **XANAT-MÏLTÏQ, QÏRQ-MULTUQ.**

MÏLTÏQ-AŠXA   Alt. 19th c. **Mïltïq-ašχa** [Мылтык-ашха], a folklore hero (Verb., In. 121). ⇨ **MÏLTÏQ.**

MÏLTÏQ-ATQAN   Alt.(Tel.) 19th c. **Mïltïq-atqan** [Myltyk-atkan] (Radl., Aus Sib. I, 178). ✧ 'Rifle-shot; he shot from a rifle'. ⇨ **MÏLTÏQ.**

MÏM-BAY see MÏÑ

MÏMAQ   Yak. 17th c. **Mïmaq** [Мымак], a prince, leader of the revolt in 1634 (Pek.).

MÏN see MÏÑ

MÏN-AYTPAS   Kzk. 19th c. **Mïn-aytpas** [Мынайтпасъ] (SOV 22, 110). ⇨ **MÏÑ? + AYTMAS.**

MÏN-JASAR see MÏÑ-JASAR

MÏNASİP   Kzk. 19th c. **Mïnasip** [Мнасибъ] (Grod., Pril. 137). ✧ 'Right, satisfactory, fitting' cf. Crm. *minasip* (Ar.) 'das Geziemende, das Gehörende, das Rechte' (Radl. IV, 2140), Chag., Turk. *munasib* (Ar.) 'passend, geeignet, entsprechend' (Radl. IV, 2186).

MÏNDAY   Yak. **Mïnday** [Мындаі], a prince, chief in the ulus of Suntar (Pek.).

MÏNDİ   Kzk. 19th c. **Mïndï-bay** [Мындыбай] (AOO 50). ✧ 'Faulty, defective'? ⇨ **MÏÑ** + suff. *-dï.*

MÏNKE   Kzk. 19th c. **Mïnke** [Мыньке] (SOK 268); Kzk. 19th c. **Mïnke** [Мынке] (AOK 2). ⇨ **MÏÑ** + suff. *-ke.*

MÏNTAY   Kzk. 19th c. **Mïntay / Mïn-tay?** [Мынтай] (SODž. 16). ⇨ **MÏÑ** + suff. *-tay(1,2).*

MÏNTÏQ see MÏLTÏQ

MÏÑ-TEMÜR see MÏÑ-TEMÜR

MÏÑČA   Kzk. 19th c. **Mïnča** [Мынча] (AOK 78); Kzk. 19th c. **Mïñča** [Мынгча] (SOK 106). ⇨ **MÏÑ** + suff. *-ča.*

MÏÑNAN-BÜLEK   Kzk. 19th c. **Mïñnan-bülek-batïr** [Мынгнанъ-булекъ-батыръ] (Potanin, Pred. 81). ⇨ **MÏÑ? + BÜLEK.**

MÏRADÏL   Tat.(Bar.) **Mïradïl** [Мырадыл], İdägä-pi's son (Proben IV, 52).

MÏRAT see MURAT

MÏRČÏQ I.   Kkalp. 1810 **Mïrčïq** [Мырчык], a biy from the Qoldawlï (Qolda-ulï) tribe (MIKk. 109).

MÏRČÏQ II.   Alt. 19th-20th c. **Mïrčïq** [Мырчык], fem. (OjrRS 212); Alt. 19th-20th c. **Murčïq** [Мурчык], fem. (OjrRS 212). ✧ 'Pea' (OjrRS), cf. Alt.(Tuba), Shor *mirčaq* 'die Erbse' (Radl. IV, 2143), Alt.(Tel.) *mirčïq* 'die Baumknospe' (Radl. IV, 2143).

MÏRİČČİ   Yak. **Mïriččï** [Мырыччы] (Pek.).

MÏRÏY   Alt. 19th-20th c. **Mïrïy** [Мырый], fem. (OjrRS 212).

MÏRİM   Bashk. 1715 **Mïrïm** [Мырым Кашкаев] (MIB III, 124).

MÏRSA see MÏRZA

MÏRSÏQÏ   Yak. **Mïrsïqï** [Мырсыкы] (Pek.).

MÏRŠAZ   Kkalp. 20th c. **Mïršāz / Mïrša-az?** [Мыршааз] (Bask., Kkalp. 1).

MÏRTABÏL   Kzk. 19th c. **Mïrtabïl** [Мыртабыль] (SOK 56).

MÏRTAZ   Balk. 20th c. **Mïrtazlarï** [Мыртáзларı], an Özden-family (Pröhle, Balk. 243).

MÏRTAZA see MURTAZA

MÏRZA   Tat.? 19th c. **Mirza-bala** [Mirza-Bala] (Mende 16); Yak. **Mïrsa / Mïssa** [Мырса, Мысса], a well-known wrestler, one of Čhinggis' commanders (Pek.); Kkalp. 20th c. **Mïrza** [Мырза] (KkRS 775); Kkalp. 20th c. **Mïrza-bay** [Мырзабай] (KkRS 775); Kkalp. 20th c. **Mïrza-biyke** [Мырзабийке], fem. (KkRS 778); Kkalp. 20th c. **Mïrza-jan / Mïrza-žan** [Мырзажан] (KkRS 775); Kkalp. 20th c. **Mïrza-gül** [Мырзагул], fem. (KkRS 778); Kmk. 20th c. **Murza** [Kumüs Ak Murza, Bek Murza] (KSz. XIII, 141); Bashk. 1735 **Murza** [Яргушъ Мурзинъ], a tarχan (Vel.-Zern., Bašk. 15); Bashk. 1738 **Murza** [Мурза Козбулатов] (MIB III, 393); Bashk. 1757 **Murza** [Мурза Кискинин] (MIB IV/1, 140); Bashk. 1761 **Murza** [Юлдаш Мурзин] (MIB IV/1, 209); Bashk. 1772 **Murza** [Мурза Таукаев] (MIB IV/2, 408); Bashk. 1772 **Murza** [Мурза Айсин] (MIB IV/2, 410); Kkalp. 20th c. **Murza** [Мурза] (KkRS 775); Bashk. 1685 **Murza-γul** [Мурзагулъ Аканаевъ], a tarχan (Vel.-Zern., Bašk. 42); Kirg. **Murza-qul** [Мурзакул] (Jud. 687); Nog. 20th c. **Murza-uwlï** [Имам Мурза увлы], father of one of Baskakov's informants from the Sarï-awul (Bask., Nog. 144); Trkm. 20th c. **Mürze** [Mürze] (Zaj. 1971, 326). ✧ 'Rich (noble) man; son of an emir; secretary' Component of male names meaning 'gentleman, open-handed, hospitable'. Cf. Kzk., Tat. *mïrza* 'freigiebig, der Murza, der Edelmann' (Radl. IV, 2143), Kzk. *mïrza II.* 'id.' (QTTS), Kkalp. *mïrza* 'господин, барин; щедрый' (KkRS), Alt.(Tel.), Kzk. *murza* 'Würdenträger der Kalmückenchane;

freigiebig, gastfrei, wohlthätig; Herr' (Radl. IV, 2196), Trkm. *mürze* 'писарь, секретарь' (TrkmRS) (<P.). See also **AQ-MURZA, DÏN-MURZA, KELDÏ-MURZA, KON-MURZA.**

MÏRZA-GELDÏ   Kzk. 18th c. - 19th c. **Mïrza-geldi** [Мырзагельды] (Tynyšp. 66); Kzk. 1794 **Murza-geldi** [مرضه كيلدى / Мурзагельды] (MIK IV, 163); Kzk. 19th c. **Murza-geldi** [Мурзагельды] (SODž. 102, 144); Tat.(Sib.) 1628 **Murza-gilde** [Мурзагилдей Енабеков], a yasaul (commander) (Miller, Ist. Sib. II, 338); Tat.(Sib.) 1635 **Murza-gilde** [Мурзогилдей Келдебанов] (Miller, Ist. Sib. II, 430, 473); Tat. 1675 **Murza-gildi** [Мирзагилди] (Kungursk. akty 35). ⇨ **MÏRZA + KELDÏ.**

MÏRZA-ГALÏY   Kkalp. 20th c. **Mïrza-γaliy** [Мырзағалий] (KkRS 775). ⇨ **MÏRZA + ALÏ.**

MÏRZA-MÏRAT see MÏRZA-MURAT

MÏRZA-MURAT   Kkalp. 20th c. **Mïrza-mïrat** [Мырзамырат] (KkRS 775); Kkalp. 20th c. **Mïrza-murat** [Мырзамурат] (KkRS 775). ⇨ **MÏRZA + MURAT.**

MÏRZA-ŠAH-QUČÏN   Chag. **Mïrza-šah-qučïn** [ميرزا شاه قوچين / Mirza Šaḫ Qučïn] (Radl. IV, 1328). ⇨ **MÏRZA + ŠAH + QUČÏN.**

MÏRZA-TUS   Tat.(Ishim) **Mïrza-tus** [Мырза Тус] (Proben IV, 212 (168)). ✧ 'Myrza-salt; Myrza-ace?' cf. Alt., Hak. *tus* 'das Salz', Alt. *tus* (<R.) 'das Ass (im Kartenspiel)'; Alt.(Tel.) *tūs* 'eng, dicht' (Radl. III, 1499). ⇨ **MÏRZA + TUZ.**

MÏRZAMBET   Kkalp. 20th c. **Mïrzambet** [Мырзамбет] (KkRS 775). ⇨ **MÏRZA(M), MÏRZAN? + suff. -mbet / -bet.**

MÏRZAN   Kkalp. 20th c. **Mïrzan** [Мырзан] (KkRS 775).

MÏRŽÏQ   Kzk. 19th c. **Mïržïq / Mïržik?** [Мыржикъ] (AOA 62).

MÏS-BURČAQ see MUZ-BURČAQ

MÏSAN   Kzk. 19th c. **Mïsan-bay** [Карача Мысанбаевъ] (Grod., Pril. 151).

MÏSXAL-PERÏ   Kkalp. 20th c. **Mïsχal-peri** [Мысхалпери], fem. (Bask., Kklap. 41, KkRS 778). ✧ 'Small scales; silver coin (from Kokand) - fairy' cf. Crm., Kzk., Tat., Tat.(Bar.) *misqal* 'id.' (Radl. IV, 2145), Kkalp. *misqal* 'золотник (мера веса)' (KkRS). ⇨ **MÏSQAL + PERÏ.**

MÏSÏQ   Kzk. 19th c. **Mïsïq** [Мысыкъ] (AOK 74); Kzk. 19th c. **Mïsïq-bay** [Мысыкбай] (AOA 98); Kzk. 19th c. **Mïsïq-pay** [Мысыкпай] (SODž. 58); Kzk. 19th c. **Mïsïq-pay** [Мысыкпай] (SOK 56); Kzk. 19th c. **Mïsïp-pay** (<Mïsïq-pay) [Мысыппай] (SOK 138). ✧ 'Cat' cf. Kzk. *misïq*, Alt.(Tel.) *mižiq* 'id.' (Radl. IV, 2145). See also **AQ-MÏČÏQ.**

MÏSÏP-PAY see MÏSÏQ

MÏSÏR   Bashk. 1735 **Mïsïr** [Мысыръ Алдаровъ], a tarχan (Vel.-Zern., Bašk. 27); Uyg. 12th c. - 14th c. **Mïsïr / Misir / Masar?** [Misir / Mïsïr / Masar] (Radl., USp. 16-18, 25-26, EUTS, DTS); Maml. 1493/94 **Mïsïr-bay** [مصرباى على باى] (Iyās II, 286); Maml. 1496/97 **Mïsïr-bay** [مصرباى الشريفى] (Iyās II, 313); Maml. 1496/97 **Mïsïr-bay** [مصرباى التور] (Iyās II, 309); Maml. 1500/01 **Mïsïr-bay** [مصرباى], first chancellor (dawādar-i kebīr) (Iyās II, 380, 383); Uyg. **Mïžïr** (Zieme, Mat. I, 74). ✧ 'Egypt; Egyptian' (Zieme, after Pelliot, Notes on Marco Polo II. Paris 1968, 640), cf. Maml. *Mïsïr* 'id.' (Tarj/Toparlı).

MÏSÏR-QARA-QUZ   Uyg. 13th c. **Mïsïr-qara-quz** (DTS). ⇨ **MÏSÏR + QARA + QUZ?**

MÏSÏR-ŠÏLA   Uyg. **Mïsïr-sïla** [Mısır Sıla] (EUTS); Uyg. 12th c. - 14th c. **Mïsïr-šïla** [Mïsïr šïla] (DTS). ⇨ **MÏSÏR?**

MÏSÏRLARÏ   Balk. 20th c. **Mïsïrlarï** [Misirlari], an Özden family (Pröhle, Balk. 243). ⇨ **MÏSÏR + plur. suff. -lar + poss. suff. -ï.**

MÏSQAL   Kzk. 19th c. **Mïsqal** [Мыскалъ] (Potanin II, 6); Kirg. **Mïsqal** [Мыскал] (Jud. 963). ✧ 'Small scales; silver coin (from Kokand)' cf. Crm., Kzk., Tat., Tat.(Bar.) *misqal* 'id.' (Radl. IV, 2145), Kkalp. *misqal* 'золотник (мера веса)' (KkRS), Kirg. *misqal* 'id.' (Jud.). See also **BÏR-MÏSQAL.**

MÏSSA see MÏRZA

MÏŠAQ   Tat.(Sib.) 1638 **Mïšaq** (<Mïsïq?) [Уразмамет Мышаков] (Miller, Ist. Sib. II, 451). ⇨ **MÏSÏQ?**

MÏŠAN   Uyg. 13th c. **Mïšan-χan** (DTS).

MÏTAYÏR   Tat.(Ishim) **Mïtayïr** [Мытайыр], hero, mentioned together with Tayïr in a tale (Proben IV, 205 /252/).

MÏTÏ   Kzk. 19th c. **Mïtï-bay** [Мытыбай] (AOO 58).

MÏZZAQ   Turk. 19th c. **Mïzzaq-oγlu** [Myzzak oγlu], a Zeybek (Kúnos 1891, 119).

MÏŽÏR see MÏSÏR

MÏQ   Yak. **Mïq** [Мык] (Pek.).

MLUNKÏ   Uyg. 13th c. **Mlunki** (DTS).

MOČUY   Yak. **Močuy** [Мочуй], a shaman (Pek.).

MOJO   Hak. 19th-20th c. **Mojo** [Мочо], fem. (HRS 354).

MOJOY   Yak. **Mojoy** [Моцоі] (Pek.).

MOJUQĀN   Yak. **Mojuqān** [Моцукан], Onoγoy-bāy's single son; İgidäy's son (Pek.); Yak. **Mojuqān** [Моцукан], İgidäy's son (Pek.). ✧ 'Strong, mighty' cf. Yak. *moju* 'id.' (Pek.). + suff. -qan?

MODAY   Karg. **Moday** [Модай] (Katanov, Otč. 9).

MODEN   NUyg. **Moden-gül** [Модангюль], fem. (URS). ✧ Derived from Chin. *mou-tan.*

MODENXAN   NUyg. **Modenχan**, fem. (S. Kakuk, Chants ouigours: AOH XXV, 417, 426). ⇨ **MODEN + suff. -χan(1).**

MODORAQ Hak.(Sag.) 19th-20th c. **Modoraq** [Модорак] (Proben IX, 432, 559). ✧ A tirbal group of Khakas, cf. Hak. fem. PN *Modar / Modaraχ* (Butanaev).

MOΓOL see **MOΓUL**

MOΓOS Yak. **Moɣos** [Moҕoc], a rich man from a tale (Pek.); Hak. 19th-20th c. **Mūs** [Myyc] (HRS 350). ✧ I. 'Voracious; stupid; strong' cf. Yak. *moɣus* 'прожорливый; ненасытный; монгус (герой якутских сказок, сильный, прожорливый и очень глупый)' (Pek.); II. 'Warrior' cf. Hak. *moɣus (=moñus)* 'der Kämpfer' (Radl. IV, 2122). See also **ČĪLAN-MOΓUS, EKİ-MŌS, YEL-MOΓUS, QARA-MOΓUS.**

MOΓUL Chag. / Uzb.? 1510 **Moɣol-χanum** [Моголханум], Shaybani-χan's wife (MIT II, 56); Chag. 16th c. **Moɣul** [Могул], a mir (emir) (Ivanov 126, 301); Maml. 1400 **Moɣul-bay** [مغلباى], governor of Jerusalem (Ibn Taghrīb. VI, 329); Maml. 1438/39 **Moɣul-bay** [مغلباى الجتمتى] (Ibn Taghrīb. VII, 41-43, VIII, 625, 667 etc.); Maml. 1449 **Moɣul-bay** [مغلباى التنهابى] (Ibn Taghrīb. VII, 167, 398); Maml. 15th c. **Moɣul-bay** [مغلباى الاشرفى الساقى] (Ibn Taghrīb. VIII, 444); Maml.? 1452 **Moɣul-bay** [مغلباى البجاسى], an atabeg (Ibn Taghrīb. VII, 233, 463, Weil, Chalif. II, 303-04); Maml. 1454, 1463 **Moɣul-bay** [مغلباى طاز الا بونكرى] (Ibn Taghrīb. VIII, 224, 458 etc.); Maml. 1460 **Moɣul-bay** [المؤيدى مغلباى طاز الابوبكرى] (Iyās II, 48, 81, 85, Ibn Taghrīb. VI, 493, 506, 512 VII, 554, 650, Weil, Chalif. II, 319, 323); Maml. 1462 **Moɣul-bay** [مغلباى الاشرفى] (Ibn Taghrīb. VII, 700); Maml. 1467/68 **Moɣul-bay** [مغلباى المحتسب], an emir (Iyās II, 81); Maml. 1467/68 **Moɣul-bay** [مغلباى] (Iyās II, 89, 91, III, 26, 42 etc.); Maml. 1467/68 **Moɣul-bay** [مغلباى الخشتدمى], an emir (Iyās II, 88, 108, Ibn Taghrīb. VII, 744); Maml. 1467/68 **Moɣul-bay** [مغلباى الخليل الاشرفى] (Iyās II, 96); Maml. 1467/68 **Moɣul-bay** [مغلباى الظاهرى] (Ibn Taghrīb. VII, 832 etc.); Maml. 1474/75 **Moɣul-bay** [مغلباى سرق الاشرفى] (Iyās II, 155); Maml. 1483 **Moɣul-bay** [مغلباى النقيه] (Iyās II, 219); Maml. 1487 **Moɣul-bay** [مغلباى البجمتدار] (Iyās II, 242, 254); Maml. 1487 **Moɣul-bay** [الاشرفى الزدكاش بن لطويك مغلباى] (Iyās II, 246, 259 etc.); Maml. 1488 **Moɣul-bay** [مغلباى العهلوان المحمدى الاشرفى الاينالى] (Iyās II, 204); Maml. 1496/97 **Moɣul-bay** [الاشرفى برسباى مغلباى صصرق] (Iyās II, 325); Khorezm. 1220 **Moɣul-χajib** [Могул-хаджиб (Огул-хаджиб)], an emir (MIT I, 486, 490, 503, 504); Chag. 16th c. **Moɣul-χoja** [Могул ходжа], a mir (emir) (Ivanov 108); Hak. 19th-20th c. **Mōl-qan** [Мол-Кан] (Radl. II, 105); NUyg.

19th c. **Muɣal** [مغل / Mughal] (Le Coq, Nameml. 111). ✧ 'Mongol' cf. Turk. *moɣol* 'id.' (Radl. IV, 2122).

MOΓUL-ČAΓATAY Chag. 16th c. **Moɣul-čaɣatay** [Могул Чагатай] (Ivanov 261, 266). ⇨ **MOΓUL + ČAΓATAY.**

MOΓUL-TAY Maml. 1309/10 **Moɣul-tay** [مغلطاى], Master of the Horse (Oberstallmeister) of Sultan Hasan (Iyās I, 150, 151, 210, Weil, Chalif. I, 485-86); Maml. 1320-40 **Moɣul-tay** [علا'الد ين مغلطاى امير مجلس] (Zetterst. 157, 166); Maml. 1320-40 **Moɣul-tay** [علا'الدين مغلطاى بن سيفالدين بلبان الحسنى] (Zetterst. 218); Maml. 1325 **Moɣul-tay** [مغلطاى السيواسى] (Zetterst. 170); Maml. 1325 **Moɣul-tay** [مغلطاى المرتينى] (Zetterst. 209); Maml. 1340/41 **Moɣul-tay** [علا'الدين مغلطاى الجمالى], Nefsir's last vizier (Iyās I, 175, Zetterst. 148, 173, Weil, Chalif. I, 410); Maml. 14th c. **Moɣul-tay** [مغلطاى ايتغلى علاالدين] (Zetterst. 140, 170); Maml. 14th c.? **Moɣul-tay** [مغلطاى المسعودى] (Iyās I, 129, Zetterst. 158); Maml. 14th c. **Moɣul-tay** [مغلطاى / Moġaltay] (Tarǰ/Houtsma 101, Tarǰ/Toparlı 42); Maml. 1398/99 **Moɣul-tay** [ابن مغلطاى] (Ibn Taghrīb. VI, 136); Maml. 1471/72 **Moɣul-tay** [يوسف بن مغلطاى] (Iyās II, 134); Maml. 1486 **Moɣul-tay** [اميرحاج بن مغلطاى] (Iyās I, 235, 243, 268); Kuman (Kipch.) 1298 **Moɣul-tay** [مغلطاى] (Baybars/Tizeng. I, 88, 111); Maml. 1302 **Moɣul-tay / Moɣul-atay?** [Ala-eddin Moglataï-Takwi-Mansouri], died in 1302 (Makrīzī IV, 194); Maml. 1323 **Moɣul-tay / Moɣul-atay?** [مغلطاى القازنى / Ala Eddin Moglatai / Mughlatai], fought against the beduins (Zetterst. 138, Weil, Chalif. I, 331). ✧ I. 'Mongol-foal'? (Sauvaget 55); II. 'Mongol' („Moɣultay"). ⇨ **MOΓUL + TAY?** or suff. *-tay(3)* (<Mo.).

MOXOYON Yak. **Moχoyon** [Мохоjон] (Pek.). ✧ 'Rolling up, curling up'. Gerund of the Yak. Verb *moχoy-* 'съежиться, сжаться; говориться с лаской по отношени[к зайченку' (Pek.).

MOXŌTUQ Yak. **Moχōtuq** [Мохотук (оjун)], a shaman (Pek.).

MOY-MURAT Tat.(Sib.) 1598 **Moy-murat** [Моймуратъ], a Siberian prince (AI II, 3-4). ⇨ **MURAT.**

MOYAR Hak. 19th-20th c. **Moyar** [Мойар] (HRS 349). ✧ 'Landlord' cf. Hak. PN *Moyar / Poyar* 'боярин' (Butanaev).

MOYİČKİNDZE Hak. 19th-20th c. **Moyičkindze** [Моичкиндзе] (Titov 214).

MOYÏN see **MOYUN**

MOYNAΓAS see **MOYNAΓAŠ**

MOYNAΓAŠ Hak.? 19th-20th c. **Moynaɣas** [Мойнаҕас] (Katanov, Otč. 10); Karg. **Moynaɣaš** [Мойнагашевъ], a family (Katanov: ZIRGOÊtn. XVII, vyp. III, 200). ✧ 'A dog with white neck (dog name)' (Butanaev). ⇨ **BOYNAQ** + suff. *-aš*.

MOYNAQ see **BOYNAQ**

MOYOXU Yak. **Moyoχu** [Мojoxy] (Pek.).

MOYUMAS Tat. 1600 **Moyumas** [Моюмас] (MIB I, 152).

MOYUN Uyg. 8th c. **Moyun-čur**, Kül Bilge-qaɣan's son (Ramstedt, Uig. 45); Kzk. **Moyuň** [Мojyң] (Proben III, 79 /102/); *EN:* Kzk. 18th c. - 19th c. **Moyïn** [Моин] (Tynyšp. 68). ✧ 'Neck' cf. Kzk. Alt., Hak. *moin, moyïn* 'der Hals' (Radl. IV, 2119), Kzk. *moyun* 'id.' (Radl. IV, 2123). See also **ČİY-MOYÏN, QARA-MOYÏN, SARÏ-MOYUN**.

MOYUŇ see **MOYUN**

MOKİN Hak. 19th-20th c. **Mokin** [Мокин] (HRS 349).

MOQAN Kzk. 19th c. **Moqan** [Моканъ] (AOO 54). ✧ Shortened form of Mukhambet (Žanuzakov).

MOQAR Bashk. 1730 **Moqar** [Моняк Мокаров] (MIB III, 276). ✧ 'Short, not having legs'? cf. Kzk. *maqar* 'kısa boylu, bacaksız' (KzTS).

MOQOLUŠ Alt. 19th-20th c. **Moqoluš** [Моколуш] (OjrRS 209). ✧ Mikolasha (R.), dim. of Nikolay.

MOQŠA Tat. 1684 **Moqša** [Аитка Мокшин] (Zolotn. 155); Bashk. 1663 **Moqša** [Мокша] (MIB I, 119); Bashk. 1663 **Moqša** [Мокша (Мокшей)] (MIB I, 177); Bashk. 1663 **Moqša** [Мокша] (MIB I, 193); Bashk. 1706 **Moqša** [Мокша Артегенев] (MIB III, 29, 30); Bashk. 1717 **Moqša** [Мокша Тергеев] (MIB III, 152); Bashk. 1722 **Moqša** [Мокша Келчюра] (MIB I, 119); Bashk. 1761 **Moqša** [Мокша Чермышаков] (MIB IV/1, 221); Bashk. 1790 **Moqša** [Ямангул Мокшин] (MIB V, 295); Bashk. 1790 **Moqša** [Ямансур Мокшин] (MIB V, 295). ✧ 'Moksha (ethnical name, Mordvin)'?

MOQŠAY Bashk. 1706 **Moqšay** [Мокшай] (MIB III, 20). ⇨ **MOQŠA** + dim. suff. *-y*.

MOQTÏ see **MÏQTÏ**

MOQTÏ-BAS Kzk. 19th c. **Moqtï-bas** [Моктыбасъ] (AOO 82). ✧ 'Strong head'. ⇨ **MÏQTÏ** + **BAŠ**.

MOQUMAN Kzk. 19th c. **Moquman** [Мокуманъ] (SODž. 126).

MOL Kzk. 19th c. **Mol-bay** [Молбай] (SOK 150, 204). ✧ 'Much, plenty, rich' cf. Kzk. *mol* 'viel, reichlich' (Radl. IV, 2125). See also **QARA-MŌL?**

MOL-BOSÏN Kzk. 19th c. **Mol-bosïn** [Молбосынъ] (SODž. 54). ✧ 'May he be rich'. ⇨ **MOL** + **BOLSÏN**.

MOL-JİΓAY Kzk. 19th c. **Mol-ǰïɣay** [Молджигай] (SODž. 146). ⇨ **MOL**.

MOLAT see **BULAT**

MOLJOROY Yak. **Molǰoroy** [Молџороi] (Pek.).

MOLJUN Yak. **Molǰun** [Буор Молцун], a folklore hero (Pek.).

MOLDAΓA Kzk. 19th c. **Moldaɣa** (<Molda-aɣa) [Молдага] (SODž. 136). ⇨ **MULLA** + **AΓA**.

MOLDAN Kzk. 19th c. **Moldan** [Молданъ] (SOV 72). ✧ 'Swank, be capricious' cf. Kzk. *buldan-* 'sich zieren, kapriziös sein, launisch sein' (Radl. IV, 1852).

MOLDAS see **MOLDAŠ**

MOLDASAQ Kzk. 19th c. **Moldasaq** [Молдасакъ] (AOA 134).

MOLDAŠ Kzk. 19th c. **Moldas** [Молдасъ] (SOK 204); Kzk. 19th c. **Moldaš** [Молдашъ] (SODž. 40); *TN:* **Muldaš(eva)** [Мулдашева], a village south of Zlatoust in the Ural mountains (?). ✧ 'Little Mollah'. ⇨ **MULLA** + suff. *-š*.

MOLDO-JAŠ Kirg. **Moldo-ǰaš** [Молдожаш] (Jud. 680). ⇨ **MULLA** + **YAŠ**.

MOLÏT Kzk. 19th c. **Molït-qul** [Молитъ Кулъ] (Grod., Pril. 192).

MOLLA see **MULLA**

MOLLA-BOL Kzk. 19th c. **Molla-bol** [Моллаболъ] (SOV 158). ✧ 'Be/become a mullah'. ⇨ **MULLA** + **BOL**.

MOLLA-TAŠ Kzk. 19th c. **Molla-taš** [Молла-Ташъ] (Grod., Pril. 19). ⇨ **MOLLA** + **TAŠ**.

MOLLA-TİLÜ Kzk. 19th c. **Molla-tilü** [Молла-Тилу Ирасовъ] (Grod., Pril. 180). ⇨ **MULLA** + **TİLÄW**.

MOLO see **MULLA**

MOLOXTO Yak. **Moloχto** [Молохто] (Pek.).

MOLORDŪR Yak. **Molordūr** [Молордур] (Pek.).

MOLOSŌQ Yak. **Molosōq** [Молосок, Молусуок] (Pek.).

MOLOTOY-ORXON see **BOLOTOY-OXXON**

MOLTAY Kzk. 19th c. **Moltay** [Молтай] (SODž. 12). ⇨ **MOL?** + **TAY** or suff. *-tay(1,2)*?

MOLTÏQ see **MİLTÏQ**

MOLTOY see **KÜN-MOLTOY**

MOLU Kzk. 19th c. **Molu-bay** [Молубай] (AOO 62).

MOLUYUQ Yak. **Moluyuq** [Молуjук] (Pek.).

MOLUQUS Yak. **Moluqus** [Молукус] (Pek.).

MOLUSUOK Yak. **Molusuok** [Молусуок] (Pek.).

MOM Kzk. 19th c. **Mom-bay** [Момбай] (SODž. 8); Kzk. 19th c. **Mom-bay** [Момбай] (SOV 90); Kzk. 19th c. **Mom-bay** [Момбай] (AOO 50); Kzk. 19th c. **Mon-bay (=Mom-bay?)** [Монбай] (SOK 148); Kzk. 19th c. **Mon-bay (Mom-bay?)** [Монбай] (AOA 134); Kzk. 19th c. **Mum-bay** [Мумбай] (SODž. 8). ✧ 'Candle' (Žanuzakov), cf. Uyg., Chag., Crm., East.T., Trkm., Uzb. *mum* 'das Wachs, das Licht' (Radl. IV, 2216).

MOMÏNA Kzk. 1878 **Momïna** [Момина], fem. (Grod., Pril. 121). ✧ 'Open-handed, hospitable, peaceful, quiet, modest', female form of *Momïn*. ⇨ **MOMUN** + fem. suff. *-a*.

MOMUN Kzk. 19th c. **Momun-bay** [Момунбай] (Pantusov, Kirg. 23); Kirg. **Momun-ǰan** [Момунжан] (Jud. 23); Kirg. **Momun-qan** [Момун Кhан], from the Buɣu tribe (Almásy 362). ✧ 'Open-handed, hospitable, peaceful, quiet, modest; pious', cf. Kzk. *momïn* 'смирный, кроткий, тихий; скромный' (KzRS), *motun* 'gastfrei, freigiebig, der Gastgeber, der Wirth' (Radl. IV, 2129), Kirg. *motun* 'воздержанный, скромный; смирный' (Jud.).

MON-BAY see **MOM**

MONAČUQ see **MUNČUQ?**

MONAQ Kzk. 19th c. **Monaq-pay** [Монакпай] (SOK 40); Kzk. 19th c. **Monaq-pay** [Монакпай] (AOP 6); Kzk. 19th c. **Monoq-pay** [Монокпай] (SOV 58); *TN:* **Monoq** [Монокская] (Karta JAR V).

MONAS Kzk. 19th c. **Monas-pay** [Монаспай] (SOK 108, 146).

MONČAҐUT Tat.(Bar.) 1699 **Mončaγut** [Мончагутъ Кокучановъ] (PSZRI III, 563).

MONČETAY Kzk. 19th c. **Mončetay** [Мончетай] (SODž. 66). ⇨ **? + TAY** or suff. *-tay(1,2)?*

MONDAY see **MONTAY**

MONDAYAX Hak. 19th-20th c. **Mondayaχ** [Мондаях], fem. (HRS 354).

MONDÏ Kzk. 19th c. **Mondï-bay** [Мондыбай] (SOV 22).

MONÏLA Kzk. 19th c. **Monïla-bay** [Моныллабай] (SODź. 154).

MONOQ see **MONAQ**

MONRAQ Kzk. 19th c. **Monraq** [Монракъ] (SOK 266).

MONTAY **Monday** [Мондай] (PSZRI VII, 889); Kzk. 1863 **Monday** [Гафаръ Мондаевъ] (Valihanov, Soč. 524); Kzk. 19th c. **Montay** [Монтай] (AOK 34, 38); Kzk. 19th c. **Montay** [Монтай] (AOP 50). ⇨ **MON + TAY?** or suff. *-tay(1,2)?*

MONTAQ Kzk. 19th c. **Montaq** [Монтакъ] (AOP 110).

MONTÏQ see **MÏLTÏQ**

MONTU Kzk. 19th c. **Montu** [Монту] (SOK 44, 74).

MONUS-PAQAY Alt. 19th c. **Monus-paqay** [Монус-Пакай], a folklore hero (Verb., In. 147, 151). ✦ 'Strong, brave frog'? ⇨ **MOÑҐUŠ + BAQA** + suff. *-y.*

MOÑҐUŠ Tuv. 20th c. **Moñγuš** [Моңгуш] (Sprav. Im. 188); *EN:* Tuv. 19th c. **Moñγuš** [Моңɓуш] (Proben IX, 20, 46, 68, 71). ✦ 'Strong/brave man; hero, warrior' cf. Alt., Shor *moñus* 'stark, tapfer; der Held, Kämpfer; böse' (Radl. IV, 2122).

MOÑXOL Yak. **Moñχol-toyon** [Моңхол-тоjон] (Pek.). ⇨ **MAÑXAL.**

MOÑOTEY Kzk.? 1689 **Moñotey** [Косючи Монготей], a Tabunut (?) chieftain (sait) (PSZRI III, 15). ⇨ **MAÑҐUT?** + suff. *-ey.*

MOÑUL-BUQA Uyg. 12th-14th c. **Moñul-buqa** [Mongul Buγa / Mongul Buġa / moŋul buqa] (Radl., USp. 137, EUTS, DTS). ✦ 'Stupid-Bull' cf. Uyg. *moñul / muñqul* 'неразумный, глупый' (DTS). ⇨ **BUQA.**

MOÑŪDAY Yak. **Moñūday** [Моңудаi] (Pek.).

MOPAL Kzk. 19th c. **Mopal-bay** [Мопалбай] (SOK 254).

MORAÐ-BAQÏ Bashk. 1770 **Mrad-baqï** (<**Morað-baqï**) [Мрадбакы Сюлейманов] (MIB IV/1, 347). ⇨ **MURAT + BAKİ.**

MORČA Hak. 19th-20th c. **Morča** [Морча], fem. (HRS 354). ✦ 'Buttercup (Ranunculus)' (HRS).

MORJUN Yak. **Morjun** [Морцун] (Pek.).

MORXAY Hak. 19th-20th c. **Morχay** [Морхай] (HRS 349).

MORXOY Yak. **Morχoy** [Морхоi] (Pek.).

MORMO Alt. **Mormo** [Мормо], a folklore hero (AI 112).

MOROSTON Yak. **Moroston** [Моростон] (Pek.).

MORŌX Yak. **Morōχ** [Морох] (Pek.). ✦ 'He who seems big, strong' (*moroy + -oχ*), cf. Yak. *moroy-* 'бросаться в глаза своей крупной фигурой' (Pek.).

MORŌXUYA Yak. **Morōχuya** [Мороxyja] (Pek.).

MOROŠ Hak.(Sag.) 19th-20th c. **Morōs** [Морос] (Katanov, Otč. 8). ✦ 'Frost, freeze, chill' cf. R. *moroz* 'id.' (Katanov), or R. family-name Moroz.

MORTOQ Alt. 19th-20th c. **Mortoq** [Мортоκ] (OjrRS 209).

MOSXOYŪ Yak. **Mosχoyū** [Мосхоjy], a shaman (Pek.).

MOSQOV Bashk. 1685-1738 **Masqov** [Масков (Москов) Атаков] (MIB I, 77, 108, 130, 142); Bashk. 1685-1738 **Masqov** [Масков (Москов) Козелаев] (MIB I, 77, 108, 130, 142); Bashk. 1685-1738 **Masqov** [Масков (Москов) Уразаев] (MIB I, 77, 108, 130, 142); Bashk.?/Tat. 1734 **Mosqov** [Москов Бевкеев], a Teptär (MIB III, 328); Bashk. 1709 **Mosqov** [Москав Акзигитов] (MIB III, 49); Bashk. 1711 **Mosqov** [Москов Тукумбетев] (MIB III, 73); Bashk. 1761 **Mosqov** [Гумер Московов] (MIB IV/1, 200); Bashk. 1779 **Mosqov** [Москов Кадыргулов] (MIB V, 93); Bashk. 1780 **Mosqov** [Москов Чюреев] (MIB V, 113); Bashk. 1783 **Mosqov** [Москов Токметев] (MIB V, 145); Bashk. 1790 **Mosqov** [Москов Кинзебоев] (MIB V, 292, 299, 319). ✦ 'Moscow; Russian'? (R.), cf. Turk. *mosqov* 'die Stadt Moskau; russisch' (Radl. IV, 2128).

MOSOČČU Yak. **Mosočču** [Мосоччу] (Pek.).

MOSŌQQO see **BASÏQQA**

MOST Tat.(Sib.) 1608 **Most** [Боча Мостов], a prince (Miller, Ist. Sib. II, 206, 207). ✦ 'Bridge' cf. Shor *mosta* (<R. *most*) 'id.' (Radl. IV, 2128).

MOSŪQQA see **BASÏQQA**

MOTÏŠ Kzk. 19th c. **Motïš** [Мотышъ] (AOK 90).

MOTOR **Motor-baχadur** [متربهادر / Моторъ-Бахадуръ] (RaD/Ber. II, 39, 40). ⇨ **MATUR?**

MOTŌSQA Hak. 19th c. **Motōsqa** [Мотоска] (Katanov, Otč. 12). ✦ 'Bobbin, spool' cf. R. мотушка

(Katanov).

MOTRUONA   Yak. **Motruona** [Мотруона, Мотуруона, Мотуруна], fem. (Pek.). ✧ Matrena (Matryona) (R.).

MOTTAYLARÏ   Balk. 20th c. **Mottaylarï** [Mottájlari], an Özden family (Pröhle, Balk. 243).

MOTTOΓOR   Yak. **Mottoγor** [Моттоҕор] (Pek.). ✧ 'Man with fat face' cf. Yak. *mottoy* 'в отношении человека с жирным лицом' + suff. *-γor* (Pek.).

MOTTOXON   Yak. **Mottoχon** [Моттохон] (Pek.).

MOTTOYUQĀN   Yak. **Mottoyuqān** [Моттоjукан] (Pek.). ✧ 'Unimportant, petty; nobody' (Pek.).

MOTURUNA see MOTRUONA

MOZOWŠA   1451 **Mozowša** [Мозовша], a prince (PSRL XII, 76).

MŌČO   Yak. **Mōčo** [Мочо] (Pek.).

MŌL see MOΓUL

MŌLAQ   Hak.(Blt.) 19th-20th c. **Mōlaq** [Молак] (Proben IX, 362, 366). ✧ 'Mongol' Hak. PN *Mōl / Mōlaχ* (Butanaev).

MŌRT-SĀRT   Hak.(Sag.) 19th-20th c. **Mōrt-särt** [Морт Сарт] (Proben IX, 448-49, 451-53).

MŌRUOS   Yak. **Mōruos** [Моруос] (Pek.).

MŌS see EKİ-MŌS

MÖČÖN   Yak. **Möčön** [Мӧчӧн], Tïγïn's younger son (Pek.).

MÖDÜKĂN   Yak. **Mödukän** [Мӧддүкän], main part of several compound personal names such as *Batas (Bötös)-Mödükän, Ösük-Mödükän, Sarin-Mödükän* (Pek.).

MÖGÜLÜ   Yak. **Mögülü-bögö** [Мӧгүлү-бӧҕӧ] (Pek.).

MÖQSİN   Bashk. 1745 **Möqsin / Muqsin** [Муксин Бекбатырев] (MIB III, 428); Bashk. 1788 **Möqsin / Muqsin** [Султангул Муксинов] (MIB V, 223); Bashk. 1746 **Möqsün / Muqsun** [Муксун Сюлеев] (MIB III, 444). ✧ Muhsin / Mohsen / Mohsin (Ar.) 'benevolent, beneficent, charitable, humanitarian' (Ahmed); 'Kind, warm-hearted' cf. Bashk. PN Möqsin (Kusimova).

MÖQSÜN see MÖQSİN

MÖLEXAN   Karch. 20th c. **Mölexan** [Mölexán], fem. (Pröhle, Kar. 124). ⇨ **MÖLE?** + suff. *-χan(1)*.

MÖLŌRÜYÄ   Yak. **Mölōrüyä** [Мӧлӧрӱjä] (Pek.).

MÖLŌTTÜR   Yak. **Mölōttür** [Мӧлӧттүр] (Pek.).

MÖLSÜT   Yak. **Mölsüt-bögö** [Мӧлсүт-бӧҕӧ] (Pek.).

MÖMEKKEY   Karg. **Mömekkey** [Мӧмеккей] (Katanov: ZIRGOÊtn. XVII, vyp. III, 146).

MÖNDÜR   Khorezm.? **Möndür / Mündür?** [موئدور / موندور / Мондуръ] (RaD/Ber. II, 131); Tat.(Sib.), Alt.? **Möndür / Mündür** [Мондуръ (Мундуръ)], a Siberian princess (AI II, 18, 20, 23). ✧ 'Hail' cf. Uyg., Alt., Hak. *möndür* 'der Hager' (Radl. IV, 2131). See also **ERKE-MÖNDÜR**.

MÖNÄK see MÖNEK

MÖNEK   Bashk. 1730 **Mönäk** [Моняк Мокаров] (MIB III, 276); Kzk. **Mönök** [Мӧнӧк] (Proben III, 38 /48/); Kzk. 19th c. **Mönök** [Мӧнёкъ] (AOK 34).

MÖNÖK see MÖNEK

MÖÑÄJĬK   Tuv. 19th c. **Mönäjĭk** [Мӧҥгäцiк] (Proben IX, 167).

MÖÑKE   Uyg. **Mönge** [مونكا / Mounga], from the Uyghur tribe (Abulg./Desm. 205); Kzk. 19th c. **Mönke-bay** [Монкебай] (SOK 178); Kzk. 19th c. **Mönke-bay** [Монкебай] (SOV 142); Tat.(Bar.) **Mönkö** [Iästäi Möngkö / Jäctäi Мӧҥкӧ] (Proben IV, 78 /99/). ✧ 'Eternal' cf. Mo. (<Trk.) *möŋke* 'ewig' (TMEN IV, No. 1744). See also **BAY-MÖÑKE, YÄSTÄY-MÖÑKÖ, TOY-MÖÑKE**.

MÖÑKÜLEY   Alt. 19th-20th c. **Mönküley** [Мӧҥкӱлей], fem. (OjrRS 212). ✧ 'Silvery' (OjrRS).

MÖRÖY   Alt. 19th-20th c. **Möröy** [Мӧрӧй] (OjrRS 209). ✧ 'Butt, target' (OjrRS).

MÖRÖN   Alt. 19th-20th c. **Mörön** [Мӧрӧн] (OjrRS 209); Yak. **Morüön** [Мӧрӱӧн] (Pek.). ✧ Miron (R.).

MÖRÜÖN see MÖRÖN

MÖSKÖ   Yak. **Möskö** [Мӧскӧ] (Pek.).

MÖSKÖLLÖ   Yak. **Mösköllö** [Мӧскӧллӧ] (Pek.). ✧ Byname of a fat man. Gerund of Yak. *möskölün* (Pek.).

MÖSTÄQİM see MÜSTÄQİM

MÖŽEK   Kzk. 19th c. **Möžek-bay** [Можекбай] (AOP 58).

MÖJEK   Trkm. **Möjek** [Мөжек] (Sopieva 178). ✧ 'Wolf' (Sopieva).

MRADİM see MURADİM

MRÄK see EMİREK

MRÄS see MİRAS

MUAY   Bashk. 1762 **Muay** [Муай Татлыбаев] (MIB IV/1, 235, 236); Bashk. 1762 **Muay** [Муай Ишкильдин] (MIB IV/1, 235, 236).

MUAYTMAQ   Bashk. 1761 **Muaytmaq** [Якуп Муаитмаков] (MIB IV/2, 385).

MUAYTMAS   Bashk. 1735 **Muaytmas** [Муайтмасъ Якшимбетевъ], a tarχan (Vel.-Zern., Bašk. 19); Bashk. 1735 **Muaytmas** [Каспулатъ Муайтмасовъ], a tarχan (Vel.-Zern., Bašk. 14); Bashk. 1735 **Muaytmas** [Муайтмасовъ], a prince (Vel.-Zern., Bašk. 12); Bashk. 1761 **Muaytmas** [Ибрак Муаитмасов] (MIB IV/1, 221); Bashk. 1762 **Muaytmas** [Муаитмас Амиров] (MIB IV/1, 238); Bashk. 1763 **Muaytmas** [Юмак Муаитмас] (MIB IV/2, 45).

MUAL   Kzk. 1846 **Mual** [Муал Казантаев] (MKOP 101).

MUARRİF   Turk. 1528 **Muarrif-χoja** [Maruf, Muarrif Hoca] (Gökb., Ed. 44, 45, 464). ✧ 'Announcing, proclaiming' (Ar.).

MUAŠ see MUΓAČ

MUATPAS   Kzk. 19th c. **Muatpas** (<Muaytpas /

Muaytmas?) [Муатпасъ] (SOV 104). ⇨ **MUAYTMAS?**

MUBARÄK Türk / Uyg. 8th c. **Mubaräk** [مبارك التركى], a ruling caliph from 785 (Fragm. Hist. Ar. 284, EI 799); Uyg. 12th c. - 14th c. **Mubaräk** (DTS); Selj. 12th c. **Mubaräk-šā** [مباركشا], Qïlïč-arslan's (1156-1192) follower, lord (governor?) of Kayseri for a short period (Astarab. 198). ✧ 'Happy, blessed' cf. Chag., Tat., Turk., Uzb. *mubaräk* (<Ar.) 'glücklich, gesegnet; unglücklich' (Radl. IV, 2212), cf. also Ar. male PN *Mubarak* 'blessed, fortunate, lucky, auspicious' (Ahmed).

MUBARÄK-QOČ Uyg. **Mubaräk-qoč** [Mubaräk Koç] (EUTS); Uyg. 12th c. - 14th c. **Mubaräk-qoč** [Mubaräk qoč] (DTS). ✧ 'Blessed/lucky Ram'. ⇨ **MUBARÄK + QOČ.**

MUČAQ Kzk. 1819 **Mučaq** [Мучак] (MIK IV, 324).

MUČAN Alt. 19th-20th c. **Mučan** [Мучан], fem. (OjrRS 212).

MUDAY Alt.(Tel.) 19th c. **Muday** [Мудай], from the Qobaq clan (Potanin IV, 167, 193). ✧ 'Suffer, endure, bear (shortness, need) cf. Alt.(Tel.) *muda-* 'Mangel leiden' (Radl. IV, 2199).

MUΓAĆ Bashk. 1735 **Muaš** / **Muwaš?** [Аднагулъ Муашевъ], a tarχan (Vel.-Zern., Bašk. 16); Bashk. 1763, 1770 **Muaš** / **Muwaš?** [Идрись Муашев] (MIB IV/1, 271, 341); Bashk. 1770 **Muaš** / **Muwaš?** [Аллагул Муашев] (MIB IV/1, 343); Bashk. 1780 **Muaš** / **Muwaš?** [Муаш Чювашев] (MIB V, 106); Tat.(Tüm.) 1649 **Muγač** [Мугачъ] (DAI III, 174-75); Bashk. 1756 **Muγaš** [Мугаш Кизяков] (MIB IV/1, 122). ⇨ **BUΓAČ?**

MUΓAL see **MOΓUL**

MUΓAL Kzk. 19th c. **Muγal** [Мугалъ] (ZOOIRGO IV, 99); Kzk. 19th c. **Muγol** [Байходжа Муголовъ] (Grod., Pril. 70).

MUΓAŠ see **MUΓAČ**

MUΓLAY see **MUQLAY**

MUΓOL see **MOΓUL**

MUΓRALĬ Bashk. 1756 **Muγralï** [Мугралы Табашаков] (MIB IV/1, 122).

MUXAMMED Kzk. 1846 **Muχamed** [Мухамед Мыктыбаев] (MKOP 156); Tat.? **Muχammed-yar** [Šakir Muchammedjarov] (Mende 100, 106); Nog. 20th c. **Muχammed** [Мухаммед Али Алиберди / Мухаммед Алиевич Алибердиев], one of Baskakov's informants from the aul of Erkin-yurt (Oraγ-awul) (Bask., Nog. 143); Kirg. **Muqambät** [Мукамбӓт] (Radl. I, 671). ✧ Mukhammad (Ar.). Very frequently used and adapted name by the Turkic peoples. Its shortened forms *-mat / -mät* seem to have become affixe-like components (affixoids) of male-names. ⇨. See also **ARZĬ-MUXAMBET, BĬRK-MUXAMMED, ČOQ-MUXAMED, DĬN-MUXAMET, MUXAMED, MUXAMMED, MUXAMET, MUXAMMED, MUXAMED, MUXAMBET, MUXAMED, MUXAMED, MAXAMBET, MUXAMMED, MUXAMMET, MUXAMMED, GÜL-MUXAMMED, İGİ-MUXAMMET, İRİS-MUXAMMED, KELDİ-MUXAMMAD, YÄR-MÖXÄMMÄT, QARA-MUXAMMAD, QOŠ-MUXAMMAD, QUTLUΓ-MUXAMMAD, ÖTÄ-MUXAMMAD, SAY-MAΓAMBET, TAŠ-MUXAMMED, TUR-MUXAMET, TURSUN-MUXAMMED, XAL-MUXAMMED, İL-MUXAMMED, İŠİM-MUXAMMED, YAXŠĬ-MUXAMMED, QAL-MUXAMMED, QAZ-MUXAMMED, QUR-MUXAMMED, NUR-MUXAMMED, PAL-MUXAMMED, SULTAN-MUXAMMED, TİN-MUXAMMED, TURDĬ-MUXAMMED, ZAR-MUXAMET.**

MUXAMMET-EMİN Nog. 20th c. **Muχammet-iymin** / **Muχammed-imin** [Мухаммет Иймин Ишметдин Аьфенди улы Къарас / Мухаммед-Имин Исметдин Эфенди Карасов], one of Baskakov's informants from the aul of Erkin-χalq, Cherkess Autonomous Region (Oblast') (Bask., Nog. 143, 158). ⇨ **MUXAMMED + EMİN.**

MUXARREM Turk. 1583-84 **Muχarrem** [Muharrem] (Ongan, Ank. I, 169-70); Yürük 1543 **Muχarrem** [Muharrem] (Gökb., Rum. 222). ✧ 'Muharrem (Ar. name of the first month); child born in the first month' (Sattarov).

MUXLĀS Hak. 19th-20th c. **Muχlās** [Мухлаас] (HRS 350).

MUXTAR Az. **Muχtar-bek** [Мухтар-бек] (Az. Skaz. 340). ✧ 'Head man, elder (of a quarter or village)' (Ar.) (TED, Radl. IV, 2176).

MUXTEREME Turk. 1489 **Muχtereme-χatun** [Muhtereme Hatun], fem. (Gökb., Ed. 305). ✧ 'Honored, respected, esteemed (woman)' (Ar.) (TED).

MUYQAŠ Bashk. 1761 **Muyqaš** [Ижболда Муйкашев] (MIB IV/1, 211).

MUYLĬ Kzk. 19th c. **Muylï-bay** [Муилибай] (SOK 230); Kzk. 19th c. **Muylï-bay** [Муйлибай] (SOK 230).

MUYNAQ see **BOYNAQ**

MUYNUQ Mo.? **Muynuq** [Муйнук], Keyuk-baχadur's son (RaD I/1, 127).

MUYSUN Kzk. 19th c. **Muysun** [Муйсунъ], fem. (Grod., Pril. 143).

MUQAY Bashk. 1738 **Muqay** [Мукаев] (MIB III, 385); Bashk. 1745, 1760 **Muqay** [Мукай Урсаев] (MIB III, 430, IV/1, 184); Bashk. 18th c. **Muqay** [Мукай] (MIB V, 130, 161, 305); Bashk. 1765 **Muqay** [Мукай Кузянов] (MIB IV/1, 310).

MUQAYLAŠ Alt. 19th-20th c. **Muqaylaš** [Мукайлаш] (OjrRS 209). ✧ Mikhail (R.) (OjrRS).

MUQAMBÄT see **MUXAMMED**

MUQAMBET-QALİY Kkalp. 20th c. **Muqambet-qaliy** [Мукамбеткалий] (KkRS 775). ⇨ **MUXAMMED + ALİ.**

MUQAN Bashk. 1749 **Muqan** [Араптан Муканов] (MIB III, 469); Bashk. 1788 **Muqan** [Габайдулла Муканов] (MIB V, 223); Kzk. 19th c. **Muqan** [Муканъ] (AOO 30); Kzk. 19th c. **Muqan** [Муканъ] (SOK 44); Kkalp. 20th c. **Muqan** [Мукъан / Муқан] (Bask., Kkalp. 401, KkRS 775). ✧ I. Shortened form of *Muχambet* / *Muqambet* (Žanuzakov; Žanuzakov-Esbaeva); II. 'Servant' cf. Ar. *muhhān* 'id.' (Bask., Fam. 107; also Sattarov). ⇨ **MUXAMMED.** See also **AL-MUQAN, İZ-MUXAN, TÄŽİ-MUXAN.**

MUQAŠ Bashk. 1757 **Muqaš** [Мукаш Сарин] (MIB IV/1, 149); Bashk. 1787 **Muqaš** [Казак Мукашев] (MIB V, 203). ✧ Shortened hypocoristic form of *Muqa-γali, Muqambet, Muqambet-γali* (Žanuzakov). ⇨ **MUXAMMED.**

MUQATAY Kzk. 19th c. **Muqatay** [Мукатай] (SOV 150); Kzk. 19th c. **Muqatay** [Мукатай] (AOK 26).

MUQĀ Hak.(Sag.) 19th-20th c. **Muqā** [Мука] (Katanov, Otč. 11). ✧ 'Flour' cf. R. мука (Katanov).

MUQÏM Trkm. 20th c. **Muqïm** [Muqïm] (Zaj. 1971, 327); Trkm. 20th c. **Muqïm** [Мукым] (TrkmRS 458); Kzk. 19th c. **Muqum** [Мукумъ Алимбаевъ] (SKSO IV. otd. III, 12); Kzk. 19th c. **Muqum-bay** [Мукумъ-бай Тухлыбаевъ] (SKSO IV, otd. II, 36); Uzb. 19th c. **Muqum-bay** [Мукумбай] (SKSO III, 158). ✧ I. 'Diligent' cf. Trkm. *muqïm* 'прилежный, старательный' (TrkmRS); II. 'Long-lived, stable, strong' (Ar. *muqim*) (Žanuzakov), cf. Kzk., Uzb. *muqum* 'ganz und gar' (Radl. IV, 2173).

MUQQUN Yak. **Muqqun** [Муккун] (Pek.).

MUQLAY Tuv. 19th c. **Muγlay / Mïγlay?** [Мыӊлаі / Мыӊлаі (Николай Катанов!)] (Proben, IX, 9, 81, 139); Hak. 19th-20th c. **Muqlay** [Муклай] (HRS 349). ✧ Nikolay (R.) (Katanov).

MUQOLČE Hak. 19th-20th c. **Muqolče** [Муколче] (HRS 349). ✧ Nikolay (R.) cf. Hak. PN *Muqulča* <*Muqul* (Butanaev). ⇨ **MUQUL** + suff. *-če* / *-ča.*

MUQON Hak. 19th-20th c. **Muqon** [Мукон] (HRS 349).

MUQSİN see **MÖQSİN**

MUQSUN see **MÖQSİN**

MUQTÏ see **MÏQTÏ**

MUQTU see **MÏQTÏ**

MUQTUŠ Kzk. 1883 **Muqtuš-bay** [Муктушбай] (Grod., Pril. 93). ⇨ **MÏQTÏ?** + suff. *-š.*

MUQUL Hak. 19th-20th c. **Muqul** [Мукул] (HRS 349); Hak.(Kacha) 19th-20th c. **Muqūl** [Мукул] (Proben IX, 554). ✧ Nikolay (R.) cf. Hak. PN *Muqul* (Butanaev).

MUQULAY Alt. 19th-20th c. **Mïqïlay / Muqulay** [Мыкылай, Мукулай] (OjrRS 209); Kzk. 19th c. **Muqulay** [Мукулай] (AOA 110); Alt. 19th-20th c. **Muqulay** [Мукулай] (OjrRS 209); Hak.(Sag.) 19th-20th c. **Muqulay** [Мукулай] (Katanov, Otč. 8). ✧

Mikolay, Nikolay (R.) (Katanov).

MUQULQA Hak. 19th-20th c. **Muqulqa** [Мукулка] (HRS 349). ✧ Mikolka (R.). ⇨ **MUQUL** + dim. suff. *-qa.*

MUQUM see **MUQÏM**

MUQUŠ Kzk. 19th c. **Muquš** [Мукушъ] (AOK 78, 94, 126); Kzk. 19th c. **Muquš** [Мукушъ] (AOP 2); Hak. 19th-20th c. **Muquš** [Мукуш] (HRS 350); Hak.(Kacha) 19th-20th c. **Muquš** [Мукуш] (Proben IX, 555, 559). ✧ Nikolay (R.) cf. Hak. PN *Muqus* (Butanaev).

MUQŪL see **MUQUL**

MULAQ Kzk. 19th c. **Mulaq** [Мулакъ] (SOK 160).

MULDA-GELDİ see **MULLA-GİLDE**

MULDÏ Kzk. **Muldï-bay** [Мулдыбай Дерепсалыповъ] (TOUAK XXIV, 57). ⇨ **MULLA.**

MULΓA Kzk. 19th c. **Mulγa-bay** [Мулгабай] (SOV 118).

MULQAŠ Trkm.? 1524 **Mulqaš-sultan** [Мулькаш-султан], Bek-taš-χan's brother from the Ustajlu tribe (MIT II, 100).

MULQU Kzk. 19th c. **Mulqu? / Mülkü?** [Мульку] (SODž. 70); Kzk. 19th c. **Mulqu? / Mülkü?** [Мульку] (SOV 60).

MULLA Tat.(Sib.) **Molla** [Молла], Küčüm's son (AI II, 3-4, 17, 20); Kkalp. 20th c. **Molla** [Молла] (KkRS 775); Kzk. 19th c. **Molo-žigit** [Молоджигитъ / Моложигитъ] (SODž. 32); Uyg. 12th c. - 14th c. **Mulda** [mulda] (DTS); Uzb. 19th c. **Mulla-bay** [Муллабай] (SKSO III, 164); Uzb. 1868 **Mulla-bay** [Мулла-Бай Бута] (Moskal'cev 54); Uzb. 1875 **Mulla-yar-bay** [Мулла-Яръ-бай Нарманъ-баевъ] (Moskal'cev 48); Kzk. **Mulla-qul** [Мулла-кулъ Танакузовъ] (Sb. Syr-D. III otd. II, 35); Nog. 20th c. **Mulla-uwlï** [Къазмухамбет Мулла увлы / Казимухамбет Муллаев], father of one of Baskakov's informants from the Sarï-awul (Bask., Nog. 144). ✧ 'Mullah; chief judge' (a religious dignity); theological student; any literate (educated) man'. Used also as a title and/or component of names. Cf. Trkm., Turk. *molla* 'der Mulla; jeder des Lesens und Schreibens Kundige' (Radl. IV, 2126), Kzk. *molda* / *molla* 'id.' (QTTS). (<Ar.). See also **ER-MOLLA, TEKE-MOLDA.**

MULLA-BERDİ Tat. 1828 **Mulla-berdi** [Мулла Берды], from the Soqtï clan (MIT II, 447). ✧ 'Mullah has given (him/her)'. ⇨ **MULLA** + **BERDİ.**

MULLA-BUTA Kzk. 19th c. **Mulla-buta** [Муллабутаевъ] (SKSO VIII, 206). ✧ 'Mullah-young-camel'. ⇨ **MULLA** + **BOTA.**

MULLA-DURDÏ Trkm. **Mulla-durdï** [Мулла-дурды] (Mel'gunov 321). ⇨ **MULLA** + **TURDÏ.**

MULLA-GİLDE Kzk. 19th c. **Mulda-geldi** [Мулдагельды] (SODž. 154); Bashk. 1750 **Mulla-gilde** [Муллагильда Енурусов] (MIB III, 475). ✧

'Mullah has come'. ⇨ **MULLA + KELDİ.**

MULLA-SERİK   Kzk. 19th c. **Mulla-serik** [Мулласерикъ] (SOV 158). ⇨ **MULLA + ŠERİK I.**

MULLA-TAŠ   Uzb.? 19th c. **Mulla-taš-bi** [Moulla-Tach-by], from Khokand (Nalivkin-Dozon 179). ⇨ **MULLA + TAŠ.**

MULLAQAY   Bashk. 1735 **Mullaqay** [Кедрясъ Муллакаевъ], a tarχan (Vel.-Zern., Bašk. 22); Bashk. 18th c. **Mullaqay** [Муллакаевъ] (Nepljuev 373); Bashk. 1756 **Mullaqay** [Муллакай Каракаев] (MIB IV/I, 109). ✧ 'Dear Mullah (addressing)' cf. Kzk. *mullaqay* 'lieber Mulla (Anrede)' (Radl. IV, 2197). ⇨ **MULLA** + dim. suff. *-qay.*

MULTAQ   Kzk. 19th c. **Multaq-bay** [Мултакбай] (AOO 10). ✧ 'Short cut' cf. Kzk. *multaq* 'kurz abgehauen' (Radl. IV, 2197).

MULTALAP see **MUTALLİP**

MULTÏĞAŠ see **MİLTÏĞAŠ**

MULTÏX see **MİLTÏQ**

MULTÏQ see **MİLTÏQ**

MULUN   Kzk. 19th c. **Mulun-bay** [Мулунбай] (Grod., Pril. 172). ✧ 'Wild cat?' cf. East.T. *molun* 'id.' (Radl. IV, 2126).

MULUŠ   Kzk. 19th c. **Muluš** [Ике Мулушевъ] (Grod., Pril. 57).

MUM see **MOM**

MUMAŠ   Bashk. 1776 **Mumaš** [Яуша Мумашев] (MIB V, 51).

MUN   Kzk. 19th c. **Mun-bay** [Мунбай] (SOK 134); Kzk. 19th c. **Mun-bay** [Мунбай] (SOK 240); Uzb. 19th c. **Mun-bay** [Хатанъ Мунбаевъ] (SKSO III, 176); Kzk. 19th c. **Mün-bay** [Мюнбай] (AOAtb. 62). ✧ 'Trouble, sadness, sorrow, suffering' cf. Uyg., Karakh. *muŋ* 'потребность, нужда; страдание, горе' (DTS), Uyg., Alt., Hak., Kirg., Kzk., etc. *muñ* 'id.' (Radl. IV, 2178), Kzk. *mun* 'Üzüntü, evham' (KzTS).

MUN-ĴASAR   Kzk. 19th c. **Mun-ĵasar** (<**Mïn-ĵasar**) [Мунджасаръ] (SOV 72). ✧ 'He/she makes (causes) trouble' cf. Kzk. *ĵasa-* 'сделать; сотворить, создать' (KzRS). ⇨ **MUN / MİÑ?** See also **MİN-ĴASAR?**

MUNA   Kzk. 19th c. **Muna** [Муна] (AOO 10); Kzk. 1817 **Muna-bay** [مناباى / Мунабай] (MIK IV, 311, 318).

MUNAČ   Bashk. 1725 **Munač** [Аднагул Муначев] (MIB III, 232).

MUNAYTBAS   Kzk. 19th c. **Munaytbas** [Мунайтбасъ] (AOA 6). ✧ 'He will not sadden/hurt (us)' cf. Kzk. *muñayït-* 'betrüben, kränken' (Radl. IV, 2179).

MUNAL   Kzk. 19th c. **Munal-bay** [Муналбай] (SOV 56).

MUNAP   Kzk. **Munap-batïr** [Мунап батыр], Älkämän's son, a folklore hero (Proben III, 757 /848/).

MUNAT   Alt. 19th-20th c. **Munat** [Мунат] (OjrRS 209).

MUNČUQ   Shor 19th-20th c. **Munčuq-qān** (Dyrenkova 346). ✧ 'Pearl, necklace, ball, round (thing)' cf. Uyg., Karakh. *mončuq* 'бусы; драгоценность, зерно' (DTS), Mo. *montsok [mončoq?]* 'une chose un peu ronde, une balle, un globe' (Kow.), Németh, HMK 133: *Mundžuk.* See also **AL-MONČUQ, ER-MONČUQ, GEY-MUNČUQ.**

MUNDUR   Bashk. 1740 **Mundur** [Мундуров], a tarχan (MIB I, 405).

MUNYAN   Yak. **Munyan-darχan** [Мунјан-Дархан], one of the six main forefathers, descendants of Älläi (Pek.).

MUNQUŠ   Kzk. 19th c. **Munquš** [Мункушъ] (AOK 50).

MUNLUQ   Kzk. 19th c. **Munluq** [Мунлукъ] (AUK Dobavl. 12). ✧ 'Sad, suffering' cf. Uyg., Chag. *muñluq* 'betrübt, leidend, kummervoll' (Radl. IV, 2181).

MUNMÏQ   Bashk. 1728 **Munmïq** [Мунмик Токурбетев] (MIB I, 131).

MUNTEK   Kzk. 19th c. **Muntek** [Мунтекъ] (SODž. 38).

MUÑAT   Tat.(Sib.) 1634 **Muñat** [Мунгат] (Miller, Ist. Sib. II, 417); Tat.(Sib.) 1684 **Muñat** [Узечка Мунгатовъ] (DAI XI, 160).

MUÑĞAŠ   Bashk. 18th c. **Muñγaš** [Аргымбай Мунгашев] (MIB V, 154, 156); Bashk. 1756 **Muñγaš** [Мунгаш Кулумбетев] (MIB IV/1, 123).

MUÑÏŠ   Kzk. 19th c. **Muñïž-bay** [Мунгжбай] (AOAtb. 34).

MUÑSUZ   Oghuz 1256 **Bonsuz / Bunsuz** [بونسوز / Bonsuz (Karaman oğlu) / Bunsuz], an Afshar, Karaman Bey's brother (Uzunçarş., Anad. 3, Sevim-Yücel 240, 241, 377); Selj. **Bunsuz** [بونسوز] (d'Ohsson III, 491, Ibn Bībī IV, 322); Selj.? 1261 **Bunsuz / Buñsuz** [بنسوز / إبونسوز], a Turkic emir (died in 1261) (Aqsar./Iş. 55-56); Uyg. **Muñsus** [Mungsus] (EUTS); Uyg. 12th c. - 14th c. **Muñsuz** [Mungsuz] (Le Coq, Urkunden 1918, 458-59, Radl., USp. 21-23, DTS); *EN:* Kzk. 18th c. - 19th c. **Munsïz** [Мунсыз] (Tynyšp. 71). ✧ 'Not having troubles, suffering; not sad' cf. Türk *buñsuz* 'id.' (DTS), Karakh. *muñsuz* 'без забот; не ведающий забот, тягот, страданий' (DTS). ⇨ **MUN (MUÑ)** + suff. *-suz.*

MUOČAY   Yak. **Muočay** [Мyoчai], a shaman in the ulus of Boroγon (Pek.).

MUR   Kzk. 19th c. **Mur-bay** [Мурбай] (SOK 132).

MUR-YAWÏ   Oghuz/Trkm. 13th c. **Mur-yawï / Mur-yawï-χan** [مور ياوى / مور ياوى خان / Мур-Йавы-хан], Qanlï-yawlï-χan's son (Abulg./Kon. 845-855, 865, 870). ⇨ **MUR + YAWÏ.**

MUR-SALİM   Tat. 1777 **Mur-salim** [Мурсалим Мусалов] (MIB V, 60); Bashk. 1780 **Mur-salim**

[Мурсалим Муслюмов] (MIB V, 109). ✦ 'Sound emir' (P.-Ar.), cf. Tat., Bashk. *Mir-sälim* (Sattarov, Kusimova), Kzk. *Salim* (Žanuzakov). ⇨ **MĪR**.

MURADÏM   Tat.(Ishim) **Mïratïm** [Мыратым] (Proben IV, 198 /244/); Bashk. 1761 **Mradïm (<Moraðïm)** [Кумышка Мрадымов] (MIB IV/1, 211); Bashk. 1777 **Mradïm (<Moraðïm)** [Мрадым Алдаров] (MIB V, 60, 62); Bashk. 1777 **Mradïm (<Moraðïm)** [Мрадым Абдрахманов] (MIB V, 60, 62). ✦ 'My wish'. ⇨ **MURAT** + poss. suff. -*ïm*.

MURAQAY   Bashk. 1706 **Muraqay** [Муракай Киликеев] (MIB III, 26). ✦ 'Little heritage' cf. Kzk. *mura* 'die Erbschaft' (Radl. IV, 2190). + suff. -*qay*.

MURAN   Bashk. 1735 **Muran** [Муранъ], a prince (Vel.-Zern., Bašk. 12).

MURANAY   Bashk. 1757 **Muranay** [Унгар Муранаев] (MIB IV/1, 139, 274).

MURAPTAN   Bashk. 1754 **Muraptan** [Мураптан Исенгулов] (MIB IV/1, 83).

MURAS see **MÏRAS**

MURAT   Trkm. 20th c. **Mïrat** [Mïrat] (Zaj. 1971, 329); Kkalp. 20th c. **Mïrat** [Мырат] (KkRS 775); Trkm. 20th c. **Mïrāt** [Мурат] (TrkmRS 464); Bashk. 1795 **Murat** [Идильбай Муратовъ] (IOAIÊK (Dobavlenie) XXVIII, 590); Kkalp. 20th c. **Murat** [Мурат] (KkRS 775); Kkalp. 20th c. **Murat-bay** [Муратбай] (KkRS 775); Kkalp. 20th c. **Murat-bek** [Муратбек] (KkRS 775). ✦ 'Wish, aim, goal' cf. Chag., Crm., Trkm., Turk., Uzb. *murad* 'id.' (Radl. IV, 2191). Its colloquial form is *Mïrat* in Karakalpak. Cf. also the Ar. PN *Murad* 'will, intended, aimed at' (Ahmed). See also **AY-MURAT, AYT-MURAT, ADAŠ-MURAT, AL-MURAT, ALDAN-MURAD, ALLA-MURAT, AŠ-MURAT, ATA-MURAT, BEK-MURAT, BERDİ-MURAT, DÄWLET-MURAT, DOST-MURAT, ÄBDİ-MURAT, EL-MURAT, EŠ-MURAT, GENJE-MURAT, XAL-MURAT, XOJA-MURAT, İYMA-MURAT, YAQŠÏ-MURAD, KELDİ-MURAT, KÖČKÄN-MURAT, QAL-MURAT, QARA-MÏRAD, QOY-MURAD, QOS-MURAT, QOŽA-MURAT, QUL-MURAT, QUŠ-MURAT, QUTLUГ-MURAT, MÄMBET-MURAT, MÄT-MURAT, MEÑLİ-MURAT, MÏRZA-MURAT, MOY-MURAT, ORAZ-MURAD, OWĀZ-MURAD, ÖTÄ-MURAT, PAL-MURAT, SOLTAN-MURAT, ŠA-MURAT, ŠAD-MURAT, TAJİ-MURAT, TAГAY-MURAT, TAŠ-MURAT, TAW-MURAT, TÄŽİ-MURAT, TİLÄW-MURAT, TİLE-MURAT, TOYDÏ-MURÂD, TOГAY-MURAD, TOXTA-MURAT, TÖRE-MURAT, TURDÏ-MURAT, TURSÏN-MURAT, TÜGÄL-MURAT, ŽAQSÏ-MURAT, ŽÏYE-MURAT, ŽUMA-MURAT.**

MURČÏQ see **MÏRČÏQ II.**

MURDA   Uzb. 19th c. **Murda** [Mourda], from Khokand

(Nalivkin-Dozon 126). ✦ 'Dead, lifeless' cf. Tadj. *murda* 'id.' (TadžRS).

MURDAR   Kuman 1280 **Mordar / Murdar?** [Mordar], among the Kumans of Hungary (ÁÚO XII, 323-324). ✦ 'Perished, depraved' cf. Kuman *murdar* (P.) 'faul, verfault (vom Geruch); Hure' (CC), Kuman, Crm., Kzk., Trkm., Turk., Uzb. *murdar* 'schmutzig, unrein; schlecht, böse' (Radl. IV, 2195), also Rásonyi, KÖA 122.

MURDAŠUY   Oghuz/Trkm. 13th c. **Murdašuy** [مرده شوی / Мурдашуй] (Abulg./Kon. 530, 550).

MURГAN   Tat.(Sib.) 1648 **Murɣan** [Мурган Малтмасов] (Miller, Ist. Sib. II, 529); Kzk. 19th c. **Murɣan** [Мурганъ] (Samojlovič: ŽS, XXIV (1915), 165). ✦ Distorted form of *Turɣan* and used by women instead of it when it is a tabu-name.

MURİ   Kzk. 19th c. **Muri-bay** [Мурибай Джанбануровъ] (Grod., Pril. 161). ✦ 'Pipe, downpipe' cf. Chag., East.T. *muri* 'id.' (Radl. IV, 2193).

MUROMA   Uzb. 1600 **Muroma** [Мурома Амаллыков], from Bukhara (MIB I, 153).

MURSUN   Kzk. 19th c. **Mursun** [Мурсунъ] (Samojlovič: ŽS XXIV (1915), 165). ✦ Distorted form of *Tursun* and used by women instead of it when it is a tabu-name. ⇨ **TURSÏN.**

MURTAГ see **OMURTAГ**

MURTAY   Bashk. 1772 **Murtay** [Муртай] (MIB IV/1, 364). ✦ 'Leather bottle with narrow mouth' cf. Bashk. *murtay* 'узкогорлый мешочек из кожи животного; бурдюк' (BRS/Uraksin).

MURTANDÏ   Kzk. 19th c. **Murtandï** [Муртанды] (SODž. 160).

MURTAZ-ALİ   Nog.? 1692 **Murtaz-ali (<Murtaza-ali)** [Муртозалей], a murza (AI V, 370, 402). ⇨ **MURTAZA + ALİ.**

MURTAZA   Kkalp. 20th c. **Mïrtaza** [Мыртаза] (KkRS 775); Tat.(GH) 1471 **Murtaza** [Муртоза], a prince of Kazan (PSRL VIII, 216 etc.); Tat.(GH) 1485 **Murtaza** [Муртоза], a prince of the Horde (PSRL VIII, 216 etc.); Bashk. 1759 **Murtaza** [Муртаза Мустаев] (MIB IV/2, 26); Turk. 1397 **Murtaza-bey** [Murtaza Bey] (Gökb., Ed. 23). ✦ Murtaza (Ar.) 'chosen, approved', an epithet of Muhammad (Ahmed); 'The Elect, The Pleased (the ephitet of Caliph Ali)' (Özön).

MURUM-BAY see **BURUN**

MURUN see **BURUN**

MURUNČAQ   Kzk. 19th c. **Murunčaq** [Мурунчакъ] (SOK 64). ⇨ **BURUN** + suff. -*čaq*.

MURUNDÏQ see **BURUNDUQ**

MURUTLUQ   Uyg. 13th-14th c. **Murutluq / Murutluɣ** [Muru[t]luɣ / Murutluq?] (Zieme, Mat. III, 271).

MURZA see **MÏRZA**

MURZA-BERGEN   Kkalp. 1750 **Murza-bergen**

[Мурза Берген], from the Quñrat tribe (MIKk. 221). ⇨ **MĪRZA + BERGEN.**

MURZA-BULAT   Kzk. 19th c. **Murza-bulat** [Мурзабулатъ] (AOO 18, 26). ⇨ **MĪRZA + BULAT.**

MURZA-GELDİ see **MĪRZA-GELDİ**

MURZA-GİLDE see **MĪRZA-GELDİ**

MURZA-GİLDİ see **MĪRZA-GELDİ**

MURZA-TAY   Kzk. 18th c. **Murza-tay-batïr** [Мурзатай-Батыръ] (Nepljuev 764, 767, 826). ⇨ **MĪRZA + TAY** or suff. *-tay(1,2)*?

MURZAY   Chuv. 18th-19th c. **Murzay** [Мурзай] (Magn. 59). ✧ Hypocoristic form of *Murza*. ⇨ **MĪRZA** + suff. *-ay / -y*. See also **QAL-MĪRZAY.**

MURZAKE   Kzk. 19th c. **Murzake** [Мурзаке] (SODž. 84). ✧ 'Little Murza' (hypoc.). ⇨ **MĪRZA** + suff. *-ke* or comp. *-ake*.

MURZAQAY   Bashk. 18th c. **Murzaqay** [Мурзакай], several persons in the 18th c. (MIB V, 60, 259, 360); Bashk. 1763 **Murzaqay** [Мурзакай Каспулатов] (MIB IV/1, 270). ✧ Hypocoristic form of *Murza*. ⇨ **MĪRZA** + suff. *-qay*.

MURZAŠ   Tat. 1780 **Murzaš** [Мурзаш Юсупов] (MIB V, 116); Bashk. 1726 **Murzaš** [Мурзаш Илчюрин] (MIB III, 240); Bashk. 1790 **Murzaš** [Мурзаш Туйсин] (MIB V, 279); Kzk. 1825 **Murzaš** [مرزاش / Мурзаш] (MIK IV, 469, 476); Crm. 17th c. **Murzaš-aɣa** [مرزاش اغا / Мурзашъ-ага] (Smirnov, Krym. 585). ✧ 'Little Murza' (hypoc.). ⇨ **MĪRZA** + suff. *-š.*

MUS-BURČAQ see **MUZ-BURČAQ**

MUSA   Bashk. 1734 **Musa** [Кудаменди Мусинъ] (Vel.-Zern., Bašk. 27); Bashk. 1734 **Musa** [Ушкилди Мусинъ], a tarχan (Vel.-Zern., Bašk. 27); Kkalp. 20th c. **Musa** [Муса] (KkRS 775); Nog. 20th c. **Musa** [Муса Батал улы Ахметджан / Муса Беталович Ахметджанов], one of Baskakov's informants from the aul of Qañlï (Bask., Nog. 143); Yürük 16th c. **Musa-jellād** [موسى جلاد / Musa-cellâd] (Gökb., Rum. 104). Oghuz 11th c. **Musa-yabɣu** [موسى يبغو], one of Seljük's three sons (Köprülü, Arūs al-Qulūb: Belleten VII, 475, 502); *EN:* Kzk. 18th c. - 19th c. **Musa-bay** [Мусабай] (Tynyšp. 68). ✧ 'Moses' (Ar.-Hebr.).

MUSAY   Kkalp. 20th c. **Musay** [Мусай] (KkRS 775). ⇨ **MUSA** + suff. *-y.*

MUSAQ   Kzk. 1823 **Musaq-bay** [مصاقبای / Мусакбай] (MIK IV, 455).

MUSAN   Bashk. 1735 **Musan** [Мусанъ Теперысовъ], a tarχan (Vel.-Zern., Bašk. 20).

MUSQA   Hak. 19th-20th c. **Musqa** [Муска], fem. (HRS 354).

MUSLİM   Nog. 20th c. **Muslim** [Муслим Йалакъай увлы / Муслим Ялкаев], one of Baskakov's informants from the aul of Qoyasulï (Bask., Nog. 144);

Bashk. 1734 **Müslüm** [Муслюмъ Савельевъ] (PSZRI IX, 340); Bashk. 1746 **Müslüm** [Муслюм Тогучев (Тогусев] (MIB III, 439, 444); Bashk. 1746 **Müslüm** [Муслюм Акчюрин] (MIB III, 440); Bashk. 1759 **Müslüm** [Муслюм Машаров] (MIB IV/2, 22). ✧ 'Muslim, Mohammedan' (Ar.) '(male) follower of the Islam' (Ahmed).

MUSTAFA   Tat.(GH) 1443 **Mustafa** [Мустофа], a prince from the Horde (PSRL VIII, 111 etc.). ✧ Mustafa (Ar.) 'chosen, selected, preferred' (Ahmed).

MUSTAY   Bashk. 1714 **Mustay** [Мустай Тугибаев] (MIB III, 113); Bashk. 1728 **Mustay** [Мустай Курмашев] (MIB III, 251); Bashk. 1735 **Mustay** [Енаберда Мустаев] (MIB III, 334); Bashk. 1738 **Mustay** [Мустай Сабанчин] (MIB I, 143); Bashk. 1750 **Mustay** [Мустай Янурусов] (MIB III, 475); Bashk. 1757 **Mustay** [Мустай Кинзин] (MIB IV/1, 156); Bashk. 1759 **Mustay** [Муртаза Мустаев] (MIB IV/2, 26); Bashk. 1761 **Mustay** [Мустай Юсупкулов] (MIB IV/1, 204); Bashk. 1761 **Mustay** [Муртаза Мустаев] (MIB IV/1, 204); Bashk. 1778 **Mustay** [Мустаев] (MIB V, 79); Bashk. 1780 **Mustay** [Ижбулда Мустаев] (MIB V, 109); Bashk. 1798 **Mustay** [Мустай] (PSZRI XXV, 195); Kzk.? 1807 **Mustay** [Мустай Ильмурзинъ], a Cossack from Orenburg (TOUAK XXIV, 76). ⇨ **BUZ?** + suff. *-tay*. See also **MUŠTAY.**

MUSTAQAY   Bashk. 1776 **Mustaqay** [Чангыз Мустакаев] (MIB V, 38).

MUSTÏKEY   Tat.(Mish.) 1757 **Mustïkey** [Мустыкей Сюлейманов] (MIB IV/2, 380).

MUSTÏQ   Kzk. 19th c. **Mustïq-pay** [Мустыкпай] (SOK 192).

MUSUQ   Balk. 20th c. **Musuqlarï** [Musuqlari], an Özden family (Pröhle, Balk. 244).

MUSULMAN   Bashk. 1737 **Busluman / Buslüman?** [Буслюман Мулканаев] (MIB I, 337); Kzk. 19th c. **Musulman** [Байкопакъ Мусулманов] (Grod., Pril. 126); Kzk. 1803, 1820 **Musulman-biy** [مسلمان می / Мусулманъ бий], a chieftain (Sib. Vest. IX, 116, MIK IV, 211); Uzb. (Kipch.) 1853 **Musulman-oul** [Moussoulman-Qoul], a Kipchak warrior in Khokand (Rec. V. As. C. 198). ✧ 'Muslim, Mohammedan' cf. Kzk., Tat., Trkm., Uzb. *musulman* 'id.' (Radl. IV, 2205).

MUSUN   Kzk. 1819 **Musun-bay** [Мусюнбай] (MIK IV, 325).

MUSUR   Nog. 20th c. **Musur-biy / Musor-biy** [Мусурбий Аджатур увлы / Мусорбий Аджатуров], one of Baskakov's informants from the aul of Nökis (Bask., Nog. 143).

MUŠ-WEREN   Az. **Muš-weren** [Мушверен], Šahraban's brother (Az. Skaz. 319).

MUŠAL   Bashk. 1756 **Mušal** [Ягуда Мушалев] (MIB

IV/1, 130).

MUŠTAY   Bashk. 1737 **Muštay** [Муштай] (MIB I, 350); Bashk. 1737 **Muštay-mulla** [Муштай] (MIB I, 307). ✧ '?' cf. Kzk. PN Moštay (Žanuzakov-Esbaeva). ⇨ **MUSTAY?**

MUŠTUM   Bashk. 1757 **Muštum** [Исерган Муштумов] (MIB IV/1, 157).

MUTA   Bashk. 1756 **Muta-bay** [Мутабай Чюрагулов] (MIB IV/1, 107).

MUTAČ   Bashk. 1770 **Mutač** [Асылгузя Мутачев] (MIB IV/1, 342).

MUTAY   1801 **Mutay** [Мутай], Qara-qaytaχ (MID III, 75); Bashk. 1754 **Mutay** [Мутай Аиткулов] (MIB IV/1, 89); Bashk. 1756 **Mutay** [Мутай] (MIB IV/1, 123); Bashk. 1756 **Mutay** [Мутай Чюрагулов] (MIB IV/1, 107); Bashk. 1756, 1757, 1761, 1763 **Mutay** [Мутай Аиткулов] (MIB IV/1, 121, 134, 215, MIB IV/2, 45); Bashk. 1783 **Mutay** [Бектемир Мутаев] (MIB V, 143). ✧ 'Sly, wily; tricky' cf. Bashk. *mut* 'хитрый, шаловливый, озорной' (BRS/Uraksin) + suff. *-ay*.

MUTALLAP see **MUTALLİP**

MUTALLİP   Bashk. 1737 **Multalap** [Мулталап Салтанаев] (MIB III, 367); Bashk. 1761 **Mutallap** [Муталлап Ишмакулов] (MIB IV/1, 214); Bashk. 1768 **Mutallap** [Багындык Муталлапов] (MIB IV/1, 332); Bashk. 1770 **Mutallip** [Абыкай Муталлыпов] (MIB IV/1, 342). ✧ Muttalib (Ar.) 'Seeker' (Ahmed); 'Searching, investigator, spotter, applicant, demanding'.

MUTİQAY   Bashk. 1761 **Mutiqay** [Утя Мутикаев] (MIB IV/1, 200). ✧ 'Obedient, he who surrenders' (Ar.) (Kusimova, Sattarov), hypoc. form. ⇨ **MUTU** + suff. *-qay*.

MUTTUQ   Yak. **Muttuq** [Муттук], a shaman (Pek.).

MUTU   Bashk. 1747, 1751 **Mutu / Mütü?** [Мут[Янурусов] (MIB III, 447 MIB IV/1, 50); Bashk. 1747, 1751 **Mutü / Mütü?** [Темир Мутюев (Мутин)] (MIB III, 447 MIB IV/1, 39, 50). ✧ 'Obedient, he who surrenders' (Ar.) (Kusimova, Sattarov).

MUWAŠ? see **MUΓAČ**

MUZ-BURČAQ   Kirg. **Mïs-burčaq** [Мыс Бурчак], prince of Ōγan (Proben V, 145 /147/); Kirg. **Mus-burčaq / Muz-burčaq** [Мус Бурчак / Музбурчак], an Afghan [Ōγan?] prince in the Manas epic (Proben V, 223 /225/, Jud. 825). ✧ 'Ice-pea; hail, hailstone' cf. Kuman, Az., Crm., Kar., Trkm., Turk. *buz* 'das Eis' (Radl. IV, 1866), Uyg., Alt. *mus* 'das Eis' (Radl. IV, 2202), Chag., Kzk., Kirg., Uzb. etc. *muz* 'id.' (Radl. IV, 2207). ⇨ **BUZ + BURČAQ.**

MUZDİ   Kzk. 19th c. **Muzdï-bay** [Муздыбай] (SOK 138, 154, 238, 280); Kzk. 19th c. **Muzdu-bay** [Муздубай] (SOK 172); Kzk. 19th c. **Muzdu-bay** [Муздубай] (AOP 122). ✧ 'With ice, icy'. ⇨ **BUZ +**

suff. *-dï.*

MUZDU see **MUZDİ**

MUŽAQ   Kzk. 19th c. **Mužaq-pay** [Мужакпай] (AOP 18).

MUŽİK   Kzk. 19th c. **Mužik** [Тыржанъ Мужиковъ] (AOK 110); Kzk. 19th c. **Mužik-pay** [Мужикпай] (AOO 78). ✧ 'Villager, peasant' cf. Tat. *mužik* 'der Kerl, der gemine Mann' (Radl. IV, 2211) (<R.mužik).

MUŽİQAY   Kzk. 19th c. **Mužiqay** [Мужикай] (AOK 42). ⇨ **MUŽİK** + suff. *-ay.*

MŪCUY   Yak. **Mūčuy** [Мучуй] (Pek.).

MŪDAS   Khorezm./Chag. 14th c. **Mūdas-aγa** [Mūdasaga], one of Temūr's (Timur's) wives (Clavijo 52).

MŪS see **MOΓOS**

MŪS-SALÏANYAY   Yak. **Mūs-salïanyay** [Муссалыанjai], Xaγdan-būray-toyon's wife (Pek.).

MÜBÄRÄK-KÖR   Uyg. 12th c. - 14th c. **Mübäräk-kör** (DTS). ✧ 'Happy, successful - blind' cf. Ar. PN *Mubarak* 'blessed, fortunate, lucky, auspicious' (Ahmed). ⇨ **KÖR.**

MÜBÄRÄK-KÜČ   Uyg. **Mübäräk-küč** [Мӱбäрäк Куч] (?). ✧ 'Happy, successful' cf. Ar. PN *Mubarak* 'blessed, fortunate, lucky, auspicious' (Ahmed). ⇨ **KÜČ.**

MÜDÜR   Turk. 20th c. **Müdür** (Önder, Göle). ✧ 'Director, official' (Ar.) (TED).

MÜGEL   Tat.(Sib.) 1638 **Mügel?** [Мугел Матмасов] (Miller, Ist. Sib. II, 450).

MÜHİMLİK   Selj. 11th c. **Mühimlik-χatun** [مملك خاتون], Melik-šah's (1072-1092) daughter (Rāwandī 14); Selj. 12th c. **Mühimlik-χatun** [مملك خاتون], Sultan Sandjar's (1117-1157) daughter (Rāwandī 205).

MÜKMEN   Tat.(Mish.) 1760 **Mükmen** [Мукмень Уткин] (MIB IV/2, 37); Tat.(Mish.) 1765 **Mükmen** [Ибрагим Мукмен(ев)] (MIB IV/1, 311); Bashk. 1719 **Mükmen** [Мукмень Токумбетев] (MIB III, 188); Bashk. 1728 **Mükmen** [Мукмень Тонкобетев] (MIB I, 128); Bashk. 1757 **Mükmen** [Мукмень Кулеев] (MIB IV/2, 19); Bashk. 1760 **Mükmen** [Масегут Мукменев] (MIB IV/1, 193); Bashk. 1760 **Mükmen** [Мукмень Юзеев] (MIB IV/2, 28); Bashk. 1789 **Mükmen** [Нурей Мукменев] (MIB V, 274).

MÜLĀZİM   Turk. 20th c. **Mülāzim** [Mülâzim] (Önder, Göle). ✧ 'Lieutenant' (Ar.) (TED).

MÜLEŠ   Kzk. 19th c. **Müleš** [Мулешъ] (SOV 150). ✧ 'Stupid'? cf. Chag. *mülä* 'ein Dummkopf, ein Tölpel' (Radl. IV, 2223) + suff. *-š.*

MÜLK   Trkm. 20th c. **Mülk** [Mülk] (Zaj. 1971, 329); Trkm. 20th c. **Mülk** [Мюлк] (TrkmRS 460). ✧ 'Possession/wealth' cf. Uyg., Chag., Kïrg., Turk. *mulk* 'die Herrschaft, das Königreich; der Besitz, der Reichtum' (Radl. IV, 2223), Trkm. *mülk* 'имущество, имение; страна' (TrkmRS). (<Ar.).

MÜLK-AMAN Tat.(Lit.) 1595 **Mil-qaman / Mil-qoman?** [Милкаманъ Корлачевичъ] (Lit. Tat. 238-40); Kzk. 19th c. **Mil-qaman / Mil-qoman?** [Милькаманъ] (SOV 50); Tat.(Lit.) 1590 **Mil-quman / Mülk-aman?** [Милкуманъ Алеевичъ] (Lit. Tat. 64); Bashk. 1784 **Mülk-aman** [Мулкаман Тавлянов] (MIB V, 154); Kzk. 19th c. **Mülk-aman** [Мулькаманъ] (AOO 66); Uzb. 1816 **Mülk-aman** [Мульк-аман] (MIT II, 392). ✧ 'Possession/wealth-Sound'. ⇨ **MÜLK + AMAN.**

MÜLÜKAY Bashk. 1740 **Mülükay / Mülükäy?** [Мулюкай] (MIB I, 395). ✧ '(Little) Possession/wealth; movable property' cf. Uyg., Chag., Kirg., Turk. *mülk* (Ar.) 'die Herrschaft, das Königreich; der Besitz, der Reichtum' (Radl. IV, 2223), Uyg., Kzk. *mülük* 'die bewegliche Habe' (Radl. IV, 2223). + suff. *-ay*.

MÜLÜRÜS Yak. **Mülürüs** [Мүлүрүс] (Pek.).

MÜN-BAY see **MUN**

MÜNČÜ Türk 992 **Münčü-tegin** [بنحو تكين الوالي] (Qalānisi 40); Türk 992 **Münčü-tegin / Bengü-tegin / Münǰü-tegin?** [منحو تكين / بنحو تكين التركى,] slave-soldier (gulām) (Kamāladdīn I, 185). ⇨ **MÜN / MUN + suff. -čü.**

MÜNČÜK Selj. 1085 **Münčük / Menčik?** [ابن منجك] (Kamāladdīn II, 87); Maml. 1293 **Münčük / Menčik?** [منجك / Мунджукъ], father of Taz (Noγay's son-in-law) (Baybars/Tizeng. I, 86, 109, Nuwairī 137, 158, Aynī/Tizeng. I, 486, 516). ⇨ **MUNČUQ?, MÜN, MUN? + suff. -čük.**

MÜNÄK Bashk. 1727 **Münäk** [Балта (Болта) Муняков] (MIB III, 165, 245); Bashk. 1738 **Münäk** [Муняк Тюкелев] (MIB III, 391).

MÜNKE Kzk. 19th c. **Münke** [Мюнке] (SOK 206). ⇨ **MÜN + suff. -ke.**

MÜNLÜ see **MEÑLİ**

MÜNTÜŠ-AYDÏ Alt. 19th c. **Müntüš-aydï** [Мунтюшайды], Taryïn-nama's wife (Verb., In. 93, 94).

MÜRKÜTEY see **ÜRKÜTEY-MÜRKÜTEY**

MÜRRÜK Trkm. 20th c. **Mürrük** [Mürrük] (Zaj. 1971, 333); Trkm. 20th c. **Mürrük / Mürrik** [Мюррик] (TrkmRS 461). ✧ 'Haggard, skinny, wrinkled' cf. Trkm. *mürrük* 'сухой, сморщенный' (TrkmRS).

MÜRSEL Turk. 1455 **Mürsel** [Hacı Mürsel] (Gökb., Ed. 171); *TN:* Turk. 20th c. **Mürsel-oγlu** [Mürseloğlu], a village in the province of Adana (TMİB 9). ✧ 'Sent with a message or mission, messenger, apostle' (Ar.) (TED, Zenk.).

MÜSÄY Tat. 1739 **Müsä / Müsäy?** [Мюсяевъ] (Alatyr. 146). ⇨ **MUSA, MUSAY.** See also **QARA-MÜSÄY.**

MÜSÄKÄW Crm. **Müsäkäw-bay** [Мүсäкäÿ Баі] (Proben VII, 214). ⇨ **MOSQOV.**

MÜSİR Kkalp. 20th c. **Müsir** [Мусир] (KkRS 775). ⇨ **MÜŠİR?**

MÜSİREP Kkalp. 20th c. **Müsirep** [Мусиреп] (KkRS 775).

MÜSLÜM see **MUSLİM**

MÜSTÄKİM Bashk. 1770 **Müstäkim / Möstäqim** [Мустаким Абутаков] (MIB IV/1, 345); Bashk. 1775 **Müstäkim / Möstäqim** [Мустаким Муслюмов] (MIB IV/1, 376). ✧ 'Right, frank, honest' (Ar.), cf. Bashk. *möstäqim* 'id.' (BRS/Uraksin), also Tat. PN Möstäqïym (Sattarov).

MÜŠİR Turk. 20th c. **Müşir** [Müşir] (Önder, Göle). ✧ 'Field-Marshall' cf. Turk. *müşir* (Ar.) 'der Feldmarschall; der Generalfeldmarschall' (HŞ).

MÜTÜ Bashk. 1751 **Mütü / Mutü** [Мют[(Мутю) Янурусов] (MIB IV/1, 34, 69, 75, 96, 276, 392); Bashk. 1759 **Mütü-γul** [Бякир Мютюгулов] (MIB IV/2, 26).

MÜTÜK Bashk. 1758 **Mutük** [Суюндук Мутюков] (MIB IV/1, 163); Bashk. 1775 **Mutük** [Егафер Мутюков] (MIB IV/1, 376); Bashk. 1775 **Mutük? / Mütün?** [Каспулат Мутюнов] (MIB IV/1, 376); Bashk. 1764 **Mütük** [Каспулат Мютюков] (MIB IV/1, 290). ⇨ **MUTU, MÜTÜ + suff. -k.**

MÜTÜKÄY Bashk. 1735 **Mütükäy** [Мутюкай Якчюрин] (MIB III, 336).

MÜZÜRET Kirg. **Müzüret** [Мүзүрет] (Jud. 200); Kirg. **Müzüret-bek** [Мүзүретбек] (Jud. 190, 778).

N

NABAT Trkm. 20th c. **Nabat** [Nabat], fem. (Zaj. 1971, 336); Trkm. 20th c. **Nabāt** [Набат], fem. (TrkmRS 467). ✧ 'A kind of crystallized candy' cf. Trkm. *nabāt* 'набат (сорт леденцов)' (TrkmRS) (<Ar.). See also **AQ-NABAT, OΓUL-NABAT.**

NABÏZ Alt. 19th c. **Nabïz-qam** [Набыз-кам] (Verb., In. 77). ✧ 'Pulse, pulsation'? (Ar.) (TED).

NAČAQ Alt. 19th-20th c. **Načaq** [Начак], fem. (OjrRS 212).

NAČČÏL Karg. **Naččïl** [Наччыл], fem. (Katanov, Otč. 8).

NAD'OS Hak. 19th-20th c. **Nad'os** [Надёс], fem. (HRS 354). ✧ Nadezhda (R.fem.).

NADA Hak. 19th-20th c. **Nada** [Нада], fem. (HRS 354).

NADE NUyg.(Tar.) 19th c. **Nade-χan** [ناده خان / Наде-ханъ] (Pantusov, Tar. 42, 135).

NADÏR Trkm.? 1682 **Nadïr-mergen** [Надырь-

Мергень], tayša, envoy to Moscow (DAI X, 370). ✧ 'Rare, extraordinary; unusual' (Ar.) (Sattarov, Kusimova), cf. Uzb. *nodir [nâdir]* 'редкий' (UzbRS), Turk. *nadir* 'rare, unusual' (TED).

NADÏŠ Tat.(Tüm.) 1649 **Nadïš** [Надышъ Матмасовъ] (DAI III, 174-75).

NAFAS see **NEFES**

NAΓAČAQ Hak.(Sag.) 19th-20th c. **Naγačaq** [Нагачак], fem. (Katanov, Otč. 7). ✧ 'Little child' cf. Shor *naγas* 'ein kleines Kind' (Radl. III, 640). + dim. suff. *-čaq / -aq*.

NAΓAY see **NOΓAY**

NAΓAYBAQ see **NOΓAYBAQ**

NAΓAL Uzb. 19th c. **Naγal-bay** [Нагальбай] (SKSO III, 170). ✧ 'Heel-piece' cf. Uzb. *naγal* 'id.' (UzbRS).

NAΓAŠ-PAY see **NAΓAŠÏ**

NAΓAŠÏ Kzk. 19th c. **Naγaš-pay(<Naγašï-pay)** [Нагашпай] (SOV 114); Kkalp. 20th c. **Naγašï-bay** [Нагашыбай] (KkRS 775); Kzk. 19th c. **Naγašï-pek** [Нагашипекъ] (SOV 72). ✧ 'In-laws (father-, mother-, brother-, etc. -in-law)' cf. Kzk. *naγašï, naγaš-ata, naγaš-ana* 'id.' (Radl. III, 640), Kkalp. *naγašï* 'id.' (KkRS).

NAΓAZUR Bashk. 1687 **Naγazur** [Нагазурко Бакировъ] (Vel.-Zern., Bašk. 45).

NAΓÏY Kkalp. 20th c. **Naγïy** [Нағый] (KkRS 775).

NAΓÏM Kkalp. 20th c. **Naγïm** [Нағым] (KkRS 775).

NAΓÏS Kzk. 19th c. **Naγïs-pek** [Нагыспекъ] (SODž. 142). ✧ 'Hard, tight, strong' cf. Kzk. *naγïs* 'festgeklemmt, fest' (Radl. III, 641).

NAÏL Kzk. **Nail-bay / Naïl-bay** [Наельбай Кайтановъ] (TV 1876, 78). ✧ 'Present, gift, heritage' (Kusimova, Sattarov) (Ar.).

NAYMAN Kzk. **Nayman** [Тюленбай Наймановъ] (Konšin, Mat. I-III, 49); Kzk. 1846 **Nayman** [Найман Каванбаев] (MKOP 101); Kzk. 19th c. **Nayman** [Найманъ] (AOO 26); Kzk. 19th c. **Nayman-bay** [Найманбай] (SOV 90); Kzk. 19th c. **Nayman-bay** [Найманбай] (SOV 38); Kzk. 19th c. **Nayman-bay** [Найманбай] (Grod., Pril. 82); Uzb. 19th c. **Nayman-bay** [Бурибай Найманбаевъ] (SKSO III, 176); *EN:* Nog. 20th c. **Nayman** [Nayman küp / Найман куьп] (Bask., Nog. 137); Nog. 20th c. **Nayman-uruw** [Найман урув], an Aq-noγay clan (Bask., Nog. 133, 141); Nog. 20th c. **Nayman-uruwï** [Найман], an Aq-noγay clan in the autonomous region of Cherkessk (Bask., Nog. 132, 141). ✧ 'Nayman' (A Turkic/Mongol tribe or clan existing at several Turkic peoples).

NAYMAN-TAY Kzk. 19th c. **Nayman-tay** [Наймантай] (AOK 38); Kzk. 19th c. **Nayman-tay** [Наймантай] (AOP 58). ⇨ **NAYMAN + TAY?** or suff. *-tay(1,2)*.

NAYPÏR Alt. 19th-20th c. **Naypïr** [Найпыр], fem. (OjrRS 212).

NAYRA Kzk. 19th c. **Nayra-bay** [Найрабай] (SOK 22). ✧ '?' (< Mo.?).

NAYTAQ Alt. 19th-20th c. **Naytaq** [Найтак], fem. (OjrRS 212).

NAYZA Kkalp. 20th c. **Nayza-bay** [Найзабай] (KkRS 775). ✧ 'Lance' cf. Kzk. *nayza* (P.) 'id.' (Radl. III, 635), Kkalp. *nayza* 'id.' (KkRS).

NAQÏS Kzk. 19th c. **Naqïs-pay** [Накыспай] (SODž. 66); Kzk. 19th c. **Naqïs-pek** [Накыспекъ] (SODž. 6, 58); Kzk. 19th c. **Naqïz-bek** [Накызбекъ] (SODž. 44). ✧ 'Defect (at speaking)' cf. Kzk. *naqïs* 'das Gebrechen, der Fehler (beim Sprechen); das Verdeckende' (Radl. III, 637).

NAQÏZ-BEK see **NAQÏS**

NAL Kzk. **Nal-bay** [Нальбай] (Tr. Syr-D. OSK 1888, 12); Nog. 1649 **Nal-bek** [Налбекъ], fem. (AI IV, 123); Nog. 1649 **Nal-bikä** [Налбика], fem. (AI 122); Nog. 1649 **Nal-tutay** [Налъ-Тутай], fem. (AI IV, 122). ✧ 'Sole, woodden sole, horse-shoe' cf. Kuman, Crm., Tat., Turk. *nal* 'id.' (Radl. III, 651).

NALÏM Karg. 19th-20th c. **Nalïm** [Налім] (Katanov, Otč. 10). ✧ 'A kind of fish' cf. R. *nalim* (Katanov).

NAMAQ Hak.(Koyb.) 19th-20th c. **Namaq** [Намак] (Katanov, Otč. 13).

NAMART Kzk. 19th c. **Namart-pay** [Намартпай] (SOK 46). ✧ 'Monster, brute' cf. Crm. *namärt* (P.) 'ein Unmensch' (Radl. III, 664).

NAMAZ Turk. 20th c. **Namaz** (Önder, Göle); Kzk. 19th c. **Namaz** [Намазъ] (SODž. 12); Kzk. 19th c. **Namaz** [Намазъ] (SOV 98); Kzk. 19th c. **Namaz-bay** [Намазбай] (SOV 44); Kzk. 19th c. **Namaz-bay** [Намазбай] (SODž. 12); Kzk. 19th c. **Namaz-bay** [Намазбаевъ] (SKSO VIII, 220); Kzk. 19th c. **Namaz-bek** [Намазбекъ] (SODž. 42). ✧ 'Ritual worship; prayer, namaz' cf. Crm., Kzk., Turk. *namaz* (Ar.) 'Gebet' (Radl. III, 663).

NAMAZA Kzk. 18th c. **Namaza** [Намаза] (Nepljuev 718). ⇨ **NAMAZ** + suff. *-a*.

NAMÏAY Yak. **Namïay** [Намыаі] (Pek.).

NAMÏN Yak. **Namïn** [Намын / Номун] (Pek.); Yak. **Nomūn** [Номун / Намын] (Pek.). ✧ Naum (R.).

NAMNAXA Yak. **Namnaχa** [Намнаха], fem. (Pek.).

NAMNĀYÏ Yak. **Namnāyï** [Намнаjы], Är-älläy's grandson (Pek.).

NAMRA Hak. 19th-20th c. **Namra** [Намра], fem. (Katanov, Otč. 11). ✧ '?' cf. Hak. fem. PN *Namira* '?' (Butanaev).

NANA Hak. 19th-20th c. **Nana** [Нана], fem. (HRS 354).

NANAY Kzk. 19th c. **Nanay** [Нанай Рустамовъ] (Grod., Pril. 188).

NANİ Hak. 19th-20th c. **Nani** [Нани], fem. (HRS 354).

NANQO Hak. 19th-20th c. **Nanqo** [Нанко], fem. (HRS 354).

NANNA Hak. 19th-20th c. **Nanna** [Нанна], fem. (HRS 354).

NAPÏQĀ Yak. **Napïqā** [Напыка] (Pek.).

NAPTA Nog. 20th c. **Napta-uwlï / Nafta-uwlï** [Ибрайим Нафта увлы / Ибраим Наптаев (!)], father of one of Baskakov's informants from the aul of Qoyasulï (Bask., Nog. 144).

NAR I. Kzk. 19th c. **Nar** [Наръ] (AOA 114); Kzk. 19th c. **Nar-bay** [Нарбай] (SODž. 116); Kzk. 19th c. **Nar-bay** [Нарбай] (SOV 8); Kzk. 19th c. **Nar-bay** [Нарбай] (Grod., Pril. 95); Kzk. 19th c. **Nar-bay** [Нарбай] (SOK 290); Kkalp. 20th c. **Nar-bay** [Нарбай] (Bask., Kkalp. 96, KkRS 775); Kzk. 19th c. **Nar-bek** [Нарбекъ] (Grod., Pril. 31); Kkalp. 20th c. **Nar-jan** [Наржан], fem. (KkRS 778); Kzk. **Nar-igit** (<**Nar-yigit**) [Наръ-игитъ] (Tr. Syr-D. OSK 1888, 12); Kzk. 19th c. **Nar-pay** [Нарпай] (AOO 54). ✧ '(Arabian) camel, dromedary; (fig.) brave, heroic; noble' cf. Kzk. *nar* 'das einhöckrige Kameel (Dromedar)' (Radl. III, 647), Kkalp. *nar* 'одногорбый верблюд; мужественный, храбрый; благородный' (KkRS), Uzb. *nâr* 'одногорбый верблюд; верблюд-самец' (UzbRS). See also **QUNDÏ-NAR**.

NAR II. Trkm. 20th c. **Nar** [Nar], fem. (Zaj. 1971, 341); Uzb. 1848 **Nar-bibi (Nâr-bibi?)** [Наръ-Биби], fem. (Moskal'cev 34); Kkalp. 20th c. **Nar-jan-gül** [Наржангүл] (KkRS 778, Baskakov: OSA 139); Trkm. **Nar-gözel** [Наргөзел], fem. (Sopieva 181); Kkalp. 20th c. **Nar-gül** [Наргүл], fem. (KkRS 778, Baskakov: OSA 139, 141); Kzk. 19th c. **Nar-kül** [Наркуль Умыровъ] (SKSO IV, otd. III, 13); Trkm. 20th c. **Nār** [Нар], fem. (TrkmRS 470). ✧ I. 'Birthmark' cf. Uzb. *nor (nâr)* 'id.' (UzbRS); II. 'Pomegranate (Punica granatum)' cf. Trkm. *nār I.* 'гранат' (TrkmRS), Uzb. *nor / nâr* 'id.' (UzbRS) (<P.). See also **GÜL-NAR**.

NAR-BOL Kzk. 19th c. **Nar-bol** [Нарболъ] (SOK 294). ✧ 'Be dromedary (=brave, heroic man)'. ⇨ **NAR I. + BOL.** See also **NAR-BOL**.

NAR-BOTA Kzk. 19th c. **Nar-bota** [Нарбота] (AOP 106); Kzk. 19th c. **Nar-bota** [Нарбота] (SOV 32, 72); Bashk. 1789 **Nar-buta** [Нарбута Чангушев] (MIB V, 271); Kzk., Uzb.? **Nar-buta-bek** [Narbutabekov] (Mende 147); Uzb. 1868 **Nâr-buta** [Норъ-Бута] (Moskal'cev 54); Uzb. 1885 **Nâr-buta** [Норъ-Бута] (Moskal'cev 34). ✧ 'Camel-foal'. ⇨ **NAR I. + BOTA.** See also **NAR TAYLAQ, TURUM**.

NAR-BULAT Bashk. 1764 **Nar-bulat** [Нарбулатов] (MIB IV/2, 105). ⇨ **NAR I. + BULAT.**

NAR-BUTA see **NAR-BOTA**

NAR-KEL Uzb. 20th c. **Nâr-kel** [Норкел] (Begmatov 1984, 202). ✧ 'Come/be born (as brave) a dromedary!'. ⇨ **NAR I. + KEL.**

NAR-KELDİ Uzb. 20th c. **Nâr-keldi** [Норкелди] (Begmatov 1984, 202). ✧ 'Dromedary (brave, heroic man) has come/been born'. ⇨ **NAR I. + KELDİ.**

NAR-TAYLAQ Kzk. 19th c. **Nar-taylaq** [Нартайлякъ] (SODž. 80); Kzk. 19th c. **Nar-taylaq**, a baqsï (tutor, quack-doctor) (AOK 338). ✧ 'Camel-foal on the 2nd year of age'. ⇨ **NAR I. + TAYLAQ.** See also **TURUM**.

NAR-TURSUN Uzb. 20th c. **Nâr-tursun** [Нортурсун] (Begmatov 1984, 204). ✧ 'Let the dromedary (brave, heroic man) stay/live/be healthy'. ⇨ **NAR I. + TURSÏN.**

NARAҐLÏY Kzk. 18th c. **Naraɣliy / Nar-ɣaliy?** [Нараглій] (Nepljuev 718). ⇨ **NAR I. + ALİ?**

NARAXA Yak. **Naraχa** [Нараха], a shaman in a tale (Pek.).

NARAN see **NARAÑ**

NARAÑ Kzk. **Naran-sulū** [Наран Сулу], fem. (Proben III, 270 /321/); Hak. 19th-20th c. **Narañ** [Наранъ], fem. (HRS 354). ✧ 'Sun' (<Mo.) cf. Hak. fem. PN *Naran* (Butanaev).

NARČA Kzk. 19th c. **Narča-ɣul** [Нарчагулъ] (Grod., Pril. 66). ✧ 'Young dromedary' cf. Kirg. *narča* (Ir.) 'молодой одногорбий верблюд' (Jud.). ⇨ **NAR I. + suff. -ča.**

NARDAN Az. **Nardan-χanum** [Нардан-ханум], fem. (Az. Skaz. 297 ff.). ✧ 'Pomegranate (Punica granatum)' cf. Kuman *nardan* 'id.' (Radl. III, 651). ⇨ **NAR II. + suff. -dan.**

NAREK see **NARİK**

NARGİLÄ Kzk. 19th c. **Nargilä** [Наргила] (Grod., Pril. 155). ✧ 'Water-pipe, hookah, narghile, hubble-bubble' cf. Turk. *nargilä* (P.) 'id.', Crm. *nargälä* 'id.' (Radl. III, 651).

NARGİS Az. **Nargis** [Наргис], fem. (Az. Skaz. 194). ✧ I. 'A kind of flower' cf. Trkm. *narɣiz* 'штейнбергия жёлтая' (TrkmRS); II. 'Crossing flame-fire'? cf. Tat. PN *Nargiz* 'ут-ялкын кичүче' (Sattarov) (<Ar.-P.).

NARİK Kzk. **Narek / Narik?**, a folklore hero (Vámbéry, Vázlatok 323); Kzk. 19th c. **Narik-bay** [Нарикбай] (Ljutš.); Kkalp. **Narik-batïr** [Нарик-Батыр] (Divaev, Biket?); Crm. **Nârik** [Нârик] (Proben VII). ✧ 'Price, value, worth, honour'? cf. Kirg. *narïq, narq* (Ir.) 'id.' (Jud.). ⇨ **NAR I., NAR II.?** + suff. *-ik / -ïq?*

NARÏAY Yak. **Narïay-χotun / Narey-χotun** [Нарыаи-хотун / Нарей-хотун], a mighty, rich and pious spirit, the protector of domestic animals (Pek.).

NARÏM-BAY see **NARÏN**

NARÏM-BEK see **NARÏN**

NARÏMBET Kkalp. 20th c. **Narïmbet** [Нарымбет] (KkRS 775). ⇨ **NAR I. / NARÏN** + suff. *-bet / -ïmbet.*

NARÏN Kzk. 19th c. **Narïm-bay** (<**Narïn-bay**) [Нарымбай] (AOA 146); Kzk. 19th c. **Narïm-bay**

(<**Narïn-bay**) [Нарымбай] (SOV 88); Kzk. 19th c.
Narïm-bek (<**Narïn-bek**) [Нарымбекъ] (SODž. 50);
Kzk. 1828 **Narïn-bay** [Нарынбаевъ] (Dobrosm., Turg.
289); Kzk. 19th c. **Narïn-bay** [Нарынбай] (AOP 86,
122); Kzk. 19th c. **Narum-bay** (<**Narun-bay**)
[Нарумбай] (SOK 172); *EN:* Kzk. 18th c. - 19th c.
Narïn-bay-biy [Нарынбай-бий], a clan (Tynyšp. 71).
✧ I. 'Strength, power' (P.) (Kusimova); II. 'Slender,
slim, delicate, tender'? cf. Turk. *narin* (P.) 'id.' (Radl.
III, 649, TED); III. 'A kind of meal made of minced
meat slightly doused with soup' cf. Kzk., Kirg. *narin*
'id.' (KzRS, Jud.).

NARÏŠ   Kzk. 19th c. **Narïš-pay** [Нарышпай] (SOK
52).

NARÏT   Kzk. 19th c. **Narït-bay** [Нарытбай] (SODž. 4);
Kzk. 19th c. **Narït-bay** [Нарытбай] (SOV 84).

NARLÏ   Yürük 1543 **Narlï** [Narlı] (Gökb., Rum. 226);
Trkm. **Narlï** [Нарлы], fem. (Sopieva 181). ✧ 'Having
a red birthmark on the body' (Sopieva 181). ⇨ **NAR II.**
+ suff. -*lï*.

NARMAN   Uzb. 1875 **Narman-bay** [Нарманъ-бай]
(Moskal'cev 48). ✧ 'Strong, brave, heroic (warrior)'
(<P.) (Kusimova, Sattarov, Žanuzakov).

NARMEN   Alt. 19th-20th c. **Narmen** [Нармен], fem.
(OjrRS 212). ⇨ **NARMAN?**

NARPOZ   Kzk. 19th c. **Narpoz** [Нарпозъ] (SOK 150).
✧ 'Peel, husk of the fruit of pomegranate (used for
making yellow paint)' cf. Kirg. *narpos* (Ir.) 'id.' (Jud.).

NART   Kzk. 19th c. **Nart** [Нартъ] (SOK 70, 216).

NARTEČ   Trkm. **Nartеč** [Нартэч] (Sopieva 181). ⇨
NARLÏ.

NARUM-BAY see **NARÏN**

NARUMBET   Kzk. 19th c. **Narumbet** (<**Narunbet**)
[Окабасъ Нарумбетовъ] (Grod., Pril. 101). ⇨ **NAR
I./II. / NARÏN?** + suff. -*umbet / -bet*?

NARUN see **NARÏN**

NAS-BALTÏSAX-OΓONYOR   Yak. **Nas-baltïsaχ-
oγonyor** [Нас балтысах оӊонjор] (Pek.).

NASĀR   Yak. **Nasār** [Насар] (Pek.). ✧ Nazar (R.).

NASÏR   Kkalp. 20th c. **Nasïr** [Насыр] (KkRS 775). ✧
'Helper, supporter' (Ar.) (Kusimova, Sattarov,
Žanuzakov). See also **QOŽA-NASÏR.**

NASTA   Hak. 19th c. **Nastā** [Наста], fem. (Katanov,
Otč. 12); Hak. 19th-20th c. **Nastā** [Настаа], fem. (HRS
354); Yak. **Nastā** [Наста], fem. (Pek.); Yak. **Nāsta**
[Наста], fem. (Pek.). ✧ Nastya (R. fem.), hypoc. of
Anastasiya (Katanov), cf. Hak. fem. PN *Nastas*
(Butanaev).

NASTAŇ   Alt. 19th-20th c. **Nastañ** [Настаӈ] (OjrRS
209).

NASTĀ see **NASTA**

NASTĀČČÏYA   Yak. **Nastāččïya** [Настаччыйа], fem.
(Pek.). ✧ Nastasya, Anastasiya (R.) (Pek.).

NASTÏAXA   Yak. **Nastïaχa** [Настыыаха, Настыыаха-

удаӊан], a shamaness (Pek.). ✧ Nastyuha (R.), dim. of
R. fem. *Anastasiya.*

NATAΓALJÏN   Yak. **Nataγalǰïn-χotun** [Натаӊалцын-
хотун], fem. (Pek.).

NATĀ   Yak. **Natā** [Ната], fem. (Pek.). ✧ Shortened of
Natāsha.

NATĀLÏYA   Yak. **Natālïya** [Наталыjа / Таjахтах
Наталыjа], a „christened" spirit (Pek.). ✧ Nataliya (R.)
(Pek.).

NATĀSA   Yak. **Natāsa** [Натаса/Ната], fem. (Pek.). ✧
Natasha (R.), dim. of R. fem. Nataliya (Pek.).

NATRUS   Alt.(Tel.) **Natrūs** [Натрус] (Radl. III, 1010);
Hak.? 19th-20th c. **Natrūs** [Натрус] (Katanov, Otč.
10). ✧ 'Holder of gunpowder' cf. R. *natruska*
(Katanov).

NAURUS see **NAWRUZ**

NAWRUS see **NAWRUZ**

NAWRUZ   Trkm. 20th c. **Navruz** [Навруз] (TrkmRS
475); Kkalp. 20th c. **Nawrïz** [Наўрыз] (KkRS 775);
Bashk. 1709 **Nawrus** [Наурус] (MIB III, 44); Bashk.
1726 **Nawrus** [Наурус Багозин] (MIB III, 239);
Tat.(GH) 1359, 1360 **Nawrus / Naurus / Narus**
[Наврусъ (Нарусъ / Наурусь / Наоуроусъ)], a
ruler (prince) of the Horde (Lavr. 504, PSRL (Russk.
Hr.) I, 411, PSRL VIII, 10-11, X, 231, XXIII, 168);
Kzk. **Nawrus-bay** [Наурус Баи] (Proben III, 72 /93/);
Nawruz [Nawrûz], a persecutor (Abulfar./Budge II,
XXVI); 1295 **Nawruz** [نوروز], an emir (Qazw. 591,
593); Selj.? 1282 **Nawruz** [نوروز], a messenger of Rūm
(Aqsarāyī 140, Aqsar./Iş. 78); Selj. 1283 **Nawruz**
[Naurouz], an atabek in Khorasan (Makrīzī III, 61);
Khorezm.? 1295 **Nawruz?**, an emir, Ghazan's (1295-
1304) attendant (Qazw. 591, 593); Maml. 1330
Nawruz [نوروز] (Zetterst. 190); Maml. 1332 **Nawruz**
[نوروز], an emir (Dawād. 368); Maml. 1332 **Nawruz**
[نوروزأمير طبلخانه], an emir (Dawād. 366); Maml.
1398, 1414 **Nawruz** [نوروزالحافظى], Master of the
Horse, Berqūq's son-in-law, the governor of Syria
(Damascus, 1406/07) several times, died in 1414/15
(Iyās I, 304, 308, 312, Weil, Chalif. II, 13, 75, 86, 133,
Ibn Taghrīb. VI, 12, 23, 25, VII, 59, 269 etc., Mayer
172-74); Maml.? 1448 **Nawruz** [نوروز الخضرى] (Ibn
Taghrīb. VII, 321); Maml. 1461 **Nawruz**
[نوروز الاسحاقى] (Ibn Taghrīb. VII, 697); Maml. 1463
Nawruz [نوروز], emir, the Master of the Horse (Ibn
Taghrīb. VIII, 463); Maml. 1468/69 **Nawruz**
[نوروز الدوادار الاشرفى] (Iyās II, 111); Tat. 1776
Nawruz [Енаберда Наурузов] (MIB V, 544); Bashk.
1714 **Nawruz** [Наурузъ Атаков] (MIB I, 107); Bashk.
1735 **Nawruz** [Наурузъ Нуркеевъ], a tarγan (Vel.-
Zern., Bašk. 22); Bashk. 1764 **Nawruz** [Наурузъ
Зиянов] (MIB IV/1, 277); Bashk. 1773 **Nawruz**
[Ишбулды Наурузов] (MIB IV/2, 130); Nog.? 1629

Nawruz [Наврузъ Касаевъ], a murza (AI III, 460);
Nog. 1649 **Nawruz** [Наврузъ], a murza (AI IV, 78);
Nog. 1649 **Nawruz** [Белекъ мурза Наврузовъ] (AI
IV, 87); Nog. 1689 **Nawruz** [Наврузъ], a murza (DAI
XII, 276); Bashk. 1791 **Nawruz-bay** [Науразбай
Сатыбаев] (MIB V, 301); Kzk. 1794 **Nawruz-bay**
[نوروز باى] (MIK IV, 164); Kzk. 19th c. **Nawruz-bay**
[Наурузбай] (SOV 34, 36); Kzk. 19th c. **Nawruz-bay**
[Наурузбай] (SOK 114); Kzk. 19th c. **Nawruz-bay**
[Наурузбай Кенджабаевъ] (SKSO VIII, 230, 232);
Kzk. 19th c. **Nawruz-bay** [Наурузбай] (SODž. 118);
Kzk. 19th c. **Nawruz-bay** [Наурузбай] (AOK 46);
Kzk. 19th c. **Nawruz-bay** [Наурузба] (AOP 46); Kzk.
19th c. **Nawruz-bay / Nowruz-bay?** [Новрузбай]
(Grod., Pril. 161); Kzk. 19th c. **Nawruz-bek**
[Наврузбекъ] (AOO 26); Tat.(Sib.) 1599 **Nawruz-
bekä** [Наврузбека], a Siberian princess from Küčüm's
family (AI II, 18, 20, 23); Uzb. 1811 **Nawruz-ǯan**
[Наврузжановъ], from Bukhara (TOUAK XXIV, 44);
Trkm. 1814 **Nawruz-χoǯa** [Навруз-ходжа], the same
as Mir Döwlet-išan?, from the Ǯafar-bay tribe (MIT II,
215); Bashk. 1728 **Näwruz** [Нявруз Атаков] (MIB I,
124); Turk. 1472 **Nevruz** [Nevruz binti Abdullah], fem.
(Gökb., Ed. 352); Tat.(Sib.) 1629 **Newrus** [Невруско
Евгаштин] (Miller, Ist. Sib. II., 358, 447); Trkm. 20th
c. **Novruz** [Novruz] (Zaj. 1971, 332); *EN:* Kzk. 18th c.
- 19th c. **Nawruz** [Науруз], a clan (Tynyšp. 73, 74);
Karch. **Nawruz(ovï)** [Наурузовы], a clan (Sysoev
123). ✧ 'New Year; first day of a new year' (P.), cf.
Kkalp. *nawrïz* 'id.' (KkRS). See also **BABA-
NOWRUZ.**

NAWRUZ-ŠIKEL   Maml. 1468/69 **Nawruz-šikel?**
[نوروز شكال بن تغرى بردى], Taγrï-berdi's son (Iyās
II, 111). ⇨ **NAWRUZ.**

NAWRUZ-TEMIR   Maml. 1468/69 **Nawruz-temir**
[نوروزتمر] (Iyās II, 111). ⇨ **NAWRUZ + TEMİR.**

NAWRUZÏQ   Kzk. 19th c. **Nawruzïq / Nawruzïq?**
[Наурузекъ] (SOV 68). ⇨ **NAWRUZ** + suff. *-ïq / -q.*

NAZ   Kkalp. 20th c. **Naz-biyke** [Назбийке], fem.
(KkRS 778); Kzk.?, Kirg.? 19th c. **Naz-bike** [Назъ-
бикэ], her brother is called Dawlet-bike (!) (Potanin II,
4). ✧ 'Flirtation, coquetry, whims; temptation' cf.
Kkalp. *naz* 'жеманство, кокетство; капризы'
(KkRS).

NAZAR   Trkm. 20th c. **Nazar** [Nazar] (Zaj. 1971, 330);
Trkm. 20th c. **Nazar** [Назар] (TrkmRS 468); Chuv.
18th-19th c. **Nazar** [Назаръ] (Magn. 60); Kkalp. 20th
c. **Nazar** [Назар] (KkRS 775); Kirg. 19th c. **Nazar**
[Назаръ] (Potanin II, 4); Trkm. 1764/65 **Nazar-atalïq**
[Назар-аталык] (MIT II, 339, 349); Trkm. 1841
Nazar-bay [Назар-бай] (MIT II, 480, 484); Kkalp.
20th c. **Nazar-bay** [Назарбай] (KkRS 775); Uzb. 1867
Nazar-bay [Назар-бай] (MIT II, 631); Kkalp. 20th c.

Nazar-bek [Назарбек] (KkRS 775); Bashk. 1735
Nazar-γul [Девлеткулъ Назаргуловъ], a tarχan
(Vel.-Zern., Bašk. 15); *EN:* Kzk. 18th c. - 19th c.
Nazar-biy [Назар-бий], a clan (Tynyšp. 68); Kzk.
18th c. - 19th c. **Nazar-qul** [Назаркул], a clan
(Tynyšp. 75); *TN:* Kzk. 18th c. - 19th c. **Nazar**
[Назар], a clan (Tynyšp. 66). ✧ 'Look, glance, sight;
evil eye; someone sacrificing himself to God'
(Kusimova, Sattarov, Žanuzakov) cf. Crm., Kzk., Turk.
nazar (Ar.) 'der Blick; das böse Auge; das Individuum'
(Radl. III, 658). See also **AY-NAZAR, AYT-NAZAR,
AQ-NAZAR, ALLA-NAZAR, ATA-NAZAR, BAY-
NAZAR, BEK-NAZAR, BERDİ-NAZAR, BİY-
NAZAR, BİR-NAZAR, ǮUMA-NAZAR, DÄWLET-
NAZAR, DOS-NAZAR, ER-NAZAR, EŠ-NAZAR,
XUDAY-NAZAR, İL-NAZAR, YAN-NAZAR,
QAY-NAZAR, QAYÏP-NAZAR, QOŠ-NAZAR,
QOTA-NAZAR, QOŽA-NAZAR, MAMA-NAZAR,
MAT-NAZAR, MÄMBET-NAZAR, ÖTÄ-NAZAR,
PAL-NAZAR, PİR-NAZAR, SAYÏP-NAZAR,
SEYİT-NAZAR, ŠA-NAZAR, TOXTA-NAZAR,
UL-NAZAR.**

NAZAR-ALÏ   Kzk. 18th c. - 19th c. **Nazar-alï**
[Назаралы], a clan (Tynyšp. 75). ⇨ **NAZAR + ALİ.**

NAZARKA   Chuv. 18th-19th c. **Nazarka** [Назарка]
(Magn. 60). ⇨ **NAZAR** + suff. *-ka<-qa.*

NAZİK   Türk? 7th-8th c. **Nazik-tarχan** [Назик-Тархан
/ Низак-Тархан (Незак-тархан, Тархан)], Türk
(Qarluq) or Heftalite ruler of Bagdis, murdered in 709
(MIT I, 62, 74, 81, 94-95, etc.).

NAZÏLQAN   Kkalp. 20th c. **Nazïlqan / Nazlïqan?**
[Назылкъан], fem. (Bask., Kkalp. 403). ⇨ **NAZÏL** +
suff. *-qan(1).*

NAZÏM   Kkalp. 20th c. **Nazïm** [Назым], fem. (KkRS
778). ✧ I. 'Who arranges, who puts things in order'
(Ar.) (Kusimova, Sattarov); II. 'Beautiful, nice' in
Western Kazakistan (Žanuzakov-Esbaeva).

NAZÏMXAN   Kkalp. 20th c. **Nazïmχan** [Назымхан],
fem. (KkRS 778). ⇨ **NAZÏM** + suff. *-χan(1).*

NAZLÏ   Az. **Nazdï-χatun** [Назды-Хатун], fem. (Az.
Skaz. 273). ✧ 'Coquettish' (Mirzäjev). ⇨ **NAZ** +
suff. *-lï.*

NAZLÏXAN   Kkalp. 20th c. **Nazlïχan** [Назлыхан],
fem. (KkRS 778). ⇨ **NAZLÏ** + suff. *-χan(1).*

NĀXÏRÏQĀN   Yak. **Nāχïrïqān** [Нахырыкан / Кöбöл-
Нахырыкан], fem. (Pek.). ✧ '?' cf. Yak. *nāχira* (Pek.)
+ fem. suff. *-qan(1).*

NĀS   Hak. 19th c. **Nās** [Нас] (Katanov, Otč. 12). ✧ 'Our
(child?), ours' cf. R. *naš* 'id.' (Katanov).

NĀSTA see **NASTA**

NĀTÏQ   Yak. **Nātïq-märgän** [Натык-märгän] (Pek.).

NĀZMAN   Türk? 887 **Nāzman** [Nāzmān], eunuch,
captain of the host of the Arabs (Abulfar./Budge I,
151).

NÄBİ Uzb. 20th c. **Näbi** [Наби] (UzbRS); Kkalp. 20th c. **Näbiy** [Нәбий] (KkRS 775); Trkm. 1855 **Nebi-bay** [Неби-бай] (MIT II, 547). ✦ 'Prophet, messenger' (Ar.) (Kusimova, Mirzäjev, Sattarov). See also **BERDİ-NÄBİ**.

NÄBİY see **NÄBİ**

NÄBİYRA see **NÄBİRÄ**

NÄBİRÄ Kkalp. 20th c. **Näbiyra** [Нәбийра], fem. (KkRS 778); Uzb. 20th c. **Näbirä** [Набира] (UzbRS). ✦ 'Grand-daughter' cf. Uzb. *näbirä* 'внук, внучка' (UzbRS).

NÄJİM Kkalp. 20th c. **Näjim** [Нәжим] (KkRS 775). ✦ Najm (Ar.) 'star' (Ahmed), cf. also Crm. PN Неайм (Kajbullaev).

NÄGMET Kkalp. 20th c. **Nägmet** [Нәгмет] (KkRS 775). ✦ 'Happy life, richess'. ⇨ **NİGMET?**

NÄĠÏYMA Kkalp. 20th c. **Näγïyma** [Нәғыйма], fem. (KkRS 778). ✦ 'Happiness, luck; joy; happy, soft-hearted' (Ar.) (Kusimova, Sattarov).

NÄXÄN Yak. **Näχän** [Нәхән] (Pek.).

NÄKÄBİL Yak. **Näkäbil** [Ӱрӱҥ Нäкäбiл-äмäхсiн], fem. (Pek.).

NÄLBÄGÄLJİN Yak. **Nälbägäljin** [Нäлбäгäлцiн], fem. (Pek.). ✦ 'Wide'? cf. Yak. *nälbägäy* 'широкий; часть тела в области лобковой кости' (Pek.).

NÄLBÄY Yak. **Nälbäy** [Нäлбäi], fem. (Pek.). ✦ 'Corpulent, portly' cf. Yak. *nälbäy-* 'широко распуститься, разсесться' (Pek.).

NÄLBÄN Yak. **Nälbän** [Нäлбäн], fem. (Pek.). ✦ 'Eat; eating' cf. Yak. *nälbän-* 'подъедать, поедать, вылизывать' (Pek.).

NÄLÄGÄLJİN Yak. **Nälägäljin** / **Nälägälyin** [Нäлäгäлцiн, Нäлäгäлјiн, Нäлäмäiцiн] (Pek.).

NÄLÄSÄY Yak. **Nälǎsäy** [Нäлäцäi] (Pek.).

NÄMÄ Kzk. 19th c. **Nemä** [Немä], a Kazak prince in Siberia (Radl., Aus Sib.). ✦ 'Something' cf. Uyg., Kuman, Chag., Alt. *nämä* 'irgend etwas, ein Ding' (Radl. III, 690).

NÄMİRİYÄ Yak. **Nämiriyä** / **Nämäriyä** [Нäмiпiјä, Нäмäпiјä], a young woman who got mad and became an evil spirit (Pek.).

NÄMTÄLİKÄN Yak. **Nämtälikän** [Нäмтäлiкäн] (Pek.). ✦ 'Short man who walks faltering' (Pek.).

NÄMTǍKÄN Yak. **Nämtǎkän** [Нäмтäкäн] (Pek.).

NÄÑ Türk 732 **Näñ-säñün** / **Nek-señün?** [Näñ Säñün] (ETY I, 52).

NÄSTÄ Yak. **Nästä** [Нäстä] (Pek.). ✦ Nastya (R. fem.).

NÄWKE Kkalp. 20th c. **Näwke** [Нәӱке] (KkRS 775). ✦ 'The little young (new-born child)'? cf. P. *new, now* 'new'. + suff. *-ke*.

NÄWŠE Kkalp. 20th c. **Näwše** [Нәӱше], fem. (KkRS 778). ✦ 'The young'? cf. P. *new, now* 'new'. + suff. *-še*.

NÄZ-BERGEN Kkalp. 20th c. **Näz-bergen** [Нәзберген] (KkRS 775). ⇨ **NAZ + BERGEN**.

NÄZİ Kkalp. 20th c. **Näzi-gül** [Нәзигул], fem. (KkRS 778). ✦ 'Affectionate (gentle, kind, perishable) rose' (P.) (Baskakov: OSA 140, Kusimova, Sattarov). ⇨ **NAZ**.

NÄZİYRA Kkalp. 20th c. **Näziyra** [Нәзийра], fem. (KkRS 778). ✦ 'Joyful, kind, smiling face; beautiful' (Kusimova, Sattarov) <Ar.

NÄZİK Trkm. 20th c. **Näzik** [Näzik], fem. (Zaj. 1971, 336); Trkm. 20th c. **Näzik-Jemal** [Näzikǧemal], fem. (Zaj. 1971, 336); Trkm. 20th c. **Näzik** [Нязик], fem. (TrkmRS 477). ✦ 'Kind, nice, charming' cf. Trkm. *näzik* 'нежный, тонкий, обидчивый' (TrkmRS) (<P.). See also **GÖL-NÄZİK**.

NÄXÄLÄ Yak. **Näχälä-buqatïr** [Нäхäлä, Нäхäллä, Нäххäллä букатыр], a folklore hero, prince of the western country (Pek.).

NĀRİK see **NARİK**

NEBİ see **NÄBİ**

NEBİLSA Tat.(Sib.) 1601 **Nebilsa** [Небылса Юлаев] (Miller, Ist. Sib. II, 169).

NEJ Selj. 1094 **Nej-tegin** / **Neč-tekin** [نجتكين / Nedjtékîn], governor of Baghdad (Kamäladdïn: RHCHor III, 716).

NEDİR Trkm. 20th c. **Nedir** [Недир] (TrkmRS 471); Trkm. 20th c. **Nedir** [Nedir] (Zaj. 1971, 327). ✦ 'Rare, infrequent' cf. Trkm. *nedir* 'редкий, редкостный' (TrkmRS) (<Ar.).

NEFES Uzb. 1876 **Nafas-biy** [Нафасъ-бiй] (Moskal'cev 38); Turk. 1583 **Nefes** [نفس] (Ongan, Ank. I, 173); Kkalp. 1827 **Nefes** [Нефес], from the Hendekli clan (MIKk. 133); Trkm. 20th c. **Nepes** [Nepes] (Zaj. 1971, 329); Trkm. 20th c. **Nepes** [Непес] (TrkmRS 472). ✦ 'Breath, a breathing; a moment' (<Ar.) cf. Uzb. *nafas* 'id.' (UzbRS), Kuman, Turk. *näfäs* 'der Athem' (Radl. III, 689).

NEYÄN Kzk. 1826 **Neyän** [Буккара Неяновъ] (TOUAK XXIV, 162).

NEK Türk 8th c. **Nek-señün** (DTS). ✦ 'Crocodile' cf. Karakh. *nek* 'id.' (DTS) (<P.).

NEKEÑ Hak. 19th-20th c. **Nekeñ** [Некенъ], fem. (HRS 354).

NELEK Kzk. 1630 **Nelek** [Нелек, Иченей Нелеков], a prince (Miller, Ist. Sib. II, 374).

NELÜK? Tat.(Sib.)? / Vogul? 1609 **Nelük?** [Нелук] (Miller, Ist. Sib. II, 210).

NEMEK Kzk. 1675 **Nemek** [Немекъ], a prince (Spafarij, Putešestvie: ZIRGOÊtn. X, vyp. I, 9); Bashk. 1653 **Nemik** [Немикъ], a tarχan (Vel.-Zern., Bašk. 43).

NEMEL Kzk. 19th c. **Nemel-bay** [Нсмсльбай] (SOK 34, 122).

NEMERE Kzk. 19th c. **Nemere-bay** [Немербай]

(SOK 224); Kzk. 19th c. **Nemere-bay** [Немеребай] (SOK 260); Kzk. 19th c. **Nimere-bay** [Нимеребай] (SOK 174). ✧ 'Grand-son' cf. Kzk. *nemere* 'id.' (KzRS).

NEMİK see **NEMEK**

NENE Hak. 19th-20th c. **Nene** [Нене], fem. (HRS 354).

NENEKE Tat.(GH) 1437 **Neneke-ǰan-χanïm** [ننكه جانخانم / Ненеке-Джанъ-ханымъ], Toqtamïš-qan's (1382-1397) daughter (Smirnov, Krym. 107, Bakč. Nadp. 41). ✧ 'Little mother, nurse' (hypoc.), cf. Crm., Turk. *nänä* 'das Mütterchen' (Radl. III, 678). + suff. *-ke*.

NES Kzk. 19th c. **Nes-pay** [Неспай] (SODž. 58).

NESİBELİ Kkalp. 20th c. **Nesibeli** [Несибели], fem. (KkRS 778). ✧ 'Lucky' cf. Kkalp. *nesiybeli* 'удачливый, тот, кому везёт в жизни' (KkRS). (<Ar.) ⇨ **NESİP.**

NESİP Kkalp. 20th c. **Nesip-bay** [Несипбай] (KkRS 775). ✧ 'Fate, fortune' (<Ar.) cf. Kkalp. *nesip* 'id.' (KkRS).

NEWBAHAR Maml. 14th c. **Newbahar** [نوبهار / näwbähär / Nevbahār], fem. (Tarǰ/Houtsma 102, Tarǰ/Toparlı 44); Turk. 1489 **Newbahar** [Nevbahar binti Abdullah], fem. (Gökb., Ed. 466); Turk. 1487 **Newbahar-χatun** [Nevbahar Hatun], fem. (Gökb., Ed. 205); Trkm. 20th c. **Nōbahar** [Nobahar], fem. (Zaj. 1971, 336); Trkm. 20th c. **Nōbahar** [Нобахар], fem. (TrkmRS 474).

NEWRUS see **NAWRUZ**

NEZAK Türk? 7th-8th c. **Nezak-tarχan** [Назик-Тархан / Низак-Тархан (Незак-тархан, Тархан)], Türk (Qarluq) or Heftalite ruler of Bagdis, murdered in 709 (MIT I, 62, 74, 81, 94-95, etc.).

NEZNAYKA Alt. 19th c. **Neznayka** [Незнайка] (Verb., In. 143, 146). ✧ 'I don't know it' cf. R. *neznajka* (Verbickij).

NĒZAQ Türk 7th c. **Nēzaq-tarχan** [Nēzak], a chief of the Türks died in 671 (Justi 229 after Ibn Khordādbeh and Ṭabarī). ✧ 'Lance' (Pehl. *nēzak*, NP *nīzeh*, Ar. *naizak*) (Justi). ⇨ **NAYZA** + suff. *-q*.

NİBASA Bashk. 1717 **Nibasa** [Нибаса (Нибоса) Ильчигулов] (MIB III, 161).

NİGARXAN Kkalp. 20th c. **Nigarχan** [Нигархан], fem. (KkRS 778). ⇨ **NİGĀR** + suff. *-χan(1).*

NİGĀR Chag. 1505 **Nigār-χanïm / Qutluγ-nigār-χanïm** [Kutluk Nigár Khánim, Kutlugh Turkán Aghá] (Tar. Rashidi 43, 94, 96, 117 etc., Justi 169, IOAIÊK XIX, 141); Oghuz? 1290 **Nigār-aqa** [نكار اقا] (Dorn 171); Turk. 1508 **Nigār-χatun** [Nigâr Hatun], fem. (Gökb., Ed. 467). ✧ 'Beautiful woman, sweetheart; beauty' (TED), Kkalp. *nigar* 'любимый, милый' (KkRS), (P. *nigār*). See also **XUSN-NİGĀR; GÜZEL, HÄSEN, KÜRKLİ, KÖRKLÄ, KÖRTLÄ, SİLİГ, ZİFA.**

NİГMÄTULLA Tat. 1764 **Nigmätulla** [Нигмер-улле Ягоферов] (MIB IV/1, 279). ✧ Nigmatullah (Ar.) 'Blessing of Allah' (Ahmed). ⇨ **ALLA.**

NİYAZ Bashk. 1777 **Niyaz** [Нияз (Нилзь) Увакаев] (MIB V, 54, 89, 91, 92, 106, 151, 172, 173); Kkalp. 20th c. **Niyaz** [Нияз] (KkRS 775); Kkalp. 20th c. **Niyaz-bay** [Ниязбай] (KkRS 775); Kkalp. 20th c. **Niyaz-bek** [Ниязбек] (KkRS 775); Kzk. 19th c. **Niyaz-bibi** [Нiязъ-биби Нiязъ-Магомедова], fem. (SKSO IV, otd. II, 34); Trkm. 20th c. **Nïyaz** [Ныяз] (TrkmRS 477); Trkm. 20th c. **Nïyaz** [Nïyaz] (Zaj. 1971, 329); *EN:* Kzk. 18th c. - 19th c. **Niyaz** [Нияз], a clan (Tynyšp. 67); Kzk. 18th c. - 19th c. **Niyaz-bek-batïr** [Ниязбек-батыр], a clan (Tynyšp. 66); *TN:* Kzk. **Niyaz** [Нияз], a huge mountain (Kojčubaev 179-80). ✧ 'Need; begging; alms, gift' (Kusimova, Sattarov, Žanuzakov), cf. Kirg. *niyaz* 'милостыня; добродетель' (Jud.), Trkm. *nïyāz* 'милостыня, пожертвования' (TrkmRS) (<P.). See also **ALLA-NİYAZ, AMAN-NİYAZ, ATA-NİYAZ, BABA-NİYAZ, BAY-NİYAZ, BAL-NİYAZ, BEK-NİYAZ, BERDİ-NİYAZ, ǰUMA-NİYAZ, DOS-NİYAZ, ÄŽİ-NİYAZ, EŠ-NİYAZ, XÄKİM-NİYAZ, İMAN-NİYAZ, İR-NİYAZ, KÄDİR-NİYAZ, QAL-NİYAZ, QAN-NİYAZ, QÏDÏR-NİYAZ, QÏLİČ-NİYAZ, QOŠ-NİYAZ, QOŽA-NİYAZ, QURBAN-NİYAZ, MÄMBET-NİYAZ, MÄT-NİYAZ, MELİK-NİYAZ, OGUL-NÏYAZ, ORA-NÏYAZ, ORAZA-NÏYAZ, ÖMİR-NÏYAZ, ÖTE-NÏYAZ, PALWAN-NÏYAZ, PİR-NÏYAZ, SAN-NÏYAZ, SAPAR-NÏYAZ, SEYİT-NÏYAZ, ŠİR-NÏYAZ, TAǰÏ-NÏYAZ, TAГAN-NÏYAZ, TÄŽİ-NÏYAZ, TİLEW-NÏYAZ, TOXTA-NÏYAZ, TÖRÄ-NÏYAZ, TUR-NÏYAZ, TURDÏ-NÏYAZ, USTA-NÏYAZ, ÜBBİ-NÏYAZ.**

NİYAZ-BERDİ Uzb. 20th c. **Niyâz-berdi** [Ниёзберди] (Begmatov 1984, 202). ⇨ **NİYAZ + BERDİ.**

NİYAZ-DURDÏ Trkm. **Niyaz-durdï** [Нiязъ-дурды] (Mel'gunov 322). ⇨ **NİYAZ + TURDÏ.**

NİYAZÏMBET Kkalp. 20th c. **Niyazïmbet** [Ниязымбет] (KkRS 775). ✧ 'Muhammed's gift' (P.-Ar.) cf. Kzk. *Niyaz-muχambet* (Žanuzakov), Tat. *Niyaz-möχämmät* (Sattarov). ⇨ **NİYAZ** + suff. *-ïmbet.*

NİYET Kkalp. 20th c. **Niyet-bay** [Нийетбай] (KkRS 775). ✧ 'Wish, aim' cf. Kkalp. *niyet* (Ar.) 'id.' (KkRS).

NİYETULLA Kkalp. 20th c. **Niyetulla** [Нийетулла] (KkRS 775). ✧ 'Allah's wish/aim' (Ar.). ⇨ **NİYET + ALLA.**

NİKÜ Uyg. **Nikü** [Nikü] (EUTS).

NİLÜFER Turk. 14th c. **Lulufer-χatun / Nilüfer-χatun** [نيلوفر / لولوفر خاتون / Lûlûfer-hâtûn / Nilüfer Hatun], Ur-χan's / Orhan Gazi's (1281-1362) wife, Yarhisar Tekfur's daughter (Nešrī XIII, 204, Erol II, 299). ✧ 'Water lily' cf. Turk. *nilüfer* 'id.' (TED).

NİMERE see **NEMERE**

NİSAN Kzk. 19th c. **Nisan-bek** [Нисанбекъ] (Grod., Pril. 126); Bashk. 1735 **Nizan-γul / Nisan-γul?** [Низангулъ Умутбаевъ], a tarχan (Vel.-Zern., Bašk. 16); Kkalp. 20th c. **Nïsan-bay** [Нысанбай] (KkRS 775). ✧ 'April' (Erol II). See also **SÄÜRÄ, TOBA-AY.**

NİSE Hak. 19th-20th c. **Nise** [Нисе], fem. (HRS 354).

NİŠAN Kirg. 19th-20th c. **Nišan-bay** [Нишанбай] (Kallilov 94); Uzb. **Nišan-bay** [Нишанбай Рахимбековъ] (Sr. Az. I, 1896, Avg. 15). ✧ 'Mark, sign; Designated (child)' (Kalilov 94), (Ar.), cf. Chag., Turk. *nišan* 'id.' (Radl. III, 701).

NİZA Hak. 19th-20th c. **Niza** [Низа], fem. (HRS 354).

NİZAK Türk? 7th-8th c. **Nizak-tarχan** [Назик-Тархан / Низак-Тархан (Незак-тархан, Тархан)], Türk (Qarluq) or Heftalite ruler of Bagdis, murdered in 709 (MIT I, 62, 74, 81, 94-95, etc.).

NİJAQ Hak.(Kyz.) 19th-20th c. **Nïjaq** [Ныцак] (Katanov, Otč. 13).

NİYAZ see **NİYAZ**

NİLDİ Kzk. 19th c. **Nïldï-bay** [Ныльдыбай] (SOV 124).

NİLQÏR Bashk. 1757 **Nïlqïr** [Нылкыр Карашаев] (MIB IV/1, 157).

NİSAN see **NİSAN**

NİSİQ Kzk. 19th c. **Nïsïq-pay** [Нысыкпай] (SOK 54).

NİSİRİQÏ Yak. **Nïsïrïqï** [Нысырыкы] (Pek.). ✧ 'Carrying heavy load on his shoulders' cf. Yak. *nïsïrïy-* 'взять на плечи много громоздких вещей, нагромоздить на себя' + -*qï* (Pek.).

NİZAM Kkalp. 20th c. **Nïzam** [Нызам] (KkRS 775). ✧ 'Rule, law, order' (Ar.) (Sattarov, Kusimova), cf. Kkalp. *nïzam* 'закон' (KkRS).

NYAXA Yak. **Nyaχa** [Нjаха-Харахсын-Нjырылын-куо], protector-spirit of home (yurta) (Pek.).

NYAQQÏ Yak. **Nyaqqï** [Нjаккы] (Pek.).

NYALBARÏYA Yak. **Nyalbarïya** [Нjалбарыjа] (Pek.).

NYALÏAP Yak. **Nyalïap** [Нjалыап] (Pek.).

NYARΓÏY Yak. **Nyarγïy** [Нjаргыı / Царгыı] (Pek.).

NYĀJAY Yak. **Nyājay** [Нjацаı, Цацаı], a goddess (Pek.).

NYĀJÏ Yak. **Nyājï-jañχa** [Нjацы-Цанха], a hostess (spirit) of the stable (Pek.); Yak. **Nyājï-χotun** [Нjацы-хотун / Нjацы-дархан-хотун], protector-spirit of cattle, Ulū-toyon's daughter, a good spirit (Pek.). ✧ 'Friend' (Pek.).

NYÄLBİČİK Yak. **Nyälbičik** [Нjälбiчiк] (Pek.).

NYĂPİT Yak. **Nyăpit** [Нjâпит] (Pek.). ✧ Neofit (R.) (Pek.).

NYĀSTĂR Yak. **Nyăstăr** [Нjăстăр] (Pek.). ✧ Nestor (R.) (Pek.).

NYİRGİYÄ Yak. **Nyirgiyä-bay-toyon** [Нjiргijä-баı-тоjон] (Pek.). ✧ 'Having strong voice' cf. Yak. *nyirgiy-* 'звучать издали' + suff. -*ä* (Pek.).

NYİRİLİJÄ Yak. **Nyirilijä-bāy-χotun / Nyirilijär-bāy-χotun** [Нjiрiлijä-баі-хотун, Нjiрiлijäр-баі-хотун], fem. (Pek.). ✧ 'Man with strong voice' cf. Yak. *nyirilä-* 'гулко звучать, грохотать' (Pek.).

NYİČİLLĀN Yak. **Nyïčïllān-buχatïr** [Tiмip Нjычыллан бухатыр] (Pek.).

NYİΓÏL Yak. **Nyïγïl-bōtur / Nyïγïl-buχatïr** [Нjыгыл-ботур / Tiмip-Нjыгыл бухатыр] (Pek.). ✧ 'Hard, strong, stubby' (Pek).

NYİQÏ Yak. **Nyïqï-χaraχsïn-qïs** [Нjыкы Харахсын кыс], fem. (Pek.). ✧ 'Spoilt' cf. Yak. *nyïqā* (Pek.).

NYİQQA Yak. **Nyïqqa** [Нjыкка] (Pek.). ✧ Nilka (R.) dim. of R. Nil (Pek.). ⇨ **NYİL.**

NYİL Yak. **Nyïl** [Нjыл] (Pek.). ✧ Nil (R.) (Pek.).

NYİLAXSÏN Yak. **Nyïlaχsïn-uol** [Нjылахсын], spirit of the trees (Pek.). ✧ '(Boy) with smooth, slick face' (Pek.).

NYİLBÏQ Yak. **Nyïlbïq** [Нjылбык] (Pek.). ✧ 'Thin; walking quietly' cf. Yak. *nyïlbïy-* 'спадать с тела, худеть; тихо, скрытно ходить' + suff. -*q* (Pek.).

NYİMARÏS Yak. **Nyïmarïs** [Нjымарыс] (Pek.).

NYİRΓĀYÏ Yak. **Nyïrγāyï-bōtur** [Нjырβаjы Ботур], an ancient male name (Pek.).

NYİRİLİN Yak. **Nyïrïlïn** [Нjырылын], fem. (Pek.).

NYİXAN Yak. **Nyïχan** [Нjыхан] (Pek.). ✧ Nikon (R.) (Pek.).

NYOXČOR Yak. **Nyoχčor** [Нjохчор] (Pek.). ✧ 'With curved back' cf. Yak. *nyoχčoy-* 'пригибать спину' + suff. -*r* (P.).

NYOXČŌSOY Yak. **Nyoχčōχōn** [Нjохчохон] (Pek.); Yak. **Nyoχčōsoy** [Нjохчосоı] (Pek.).

NYOLŌX Yak. **Nyolōχ** [Нjолох Уибан] (Pek.). ✧ 'Having long (oval?) face' (Pek.), cf. Yak. *nyoloy-* '(об узком лице) выдаваться, вытягиваться' + suff. -*ōχ* (Pek.).

NYONTUOQ Yak. **Nyontuoq** [Нjонтуок] (Pek.).

NYOPPUROSAY Yak. **Nyoppuruosay** [Нjоппуруоcaı] (Pek.). ✧ Amvrosij (R.).

NYŌČUR Yak. **Nyōčur** [Нjочуор] (Pek.).

NYŌM Yak. **Nyōm** [Нjом], (nick)name of a boy (Pek.).

NYŌSPU Yak. **Nyōspu** [Нjоспу] (Pek.).

NYUQUYĀX Yak. **Nyuquyāχ / Nyuquyāq** [Нjукуjах / Нукуjак] (Pek.). ✧ Nikolay (R.)?

NYUQULAY Yak. **Nyuqulay** [Нjукулаı] (Pek.). ✧ Nikolka (R.), dim. of R. Nikolay (Pek.).

NYUQULĀSQÏ Yak. **Nyuqulāsqï** [Нjукуласкы] (Pek.). ✧ Nikolashka (R.), dim. of R. Nikolay (Pek.).

NYUQŪ Yak. **Nyuqū** [Нjуку] (Pek.). ✧ Nikolka (R.), dim. of R. Nikolay (Pek.).

NYUQŪQA Yak. **Nyuqūqa / Nyuqūlqa** [Нjукука, Нjукулка] (Pek.). ✧ Nikolka (R.), dim. of R. Nikolay (Pek.).

NYUQŪLQA Yak. **Nyuqūlqa** [Нjукулка] (Pek.). ✧

Nikolka (R.), dim. of R. Nikolay (Pek.).

NYUQŪS Yak. **Nyuqūs / Nyuqūsa** [Нјукус, Нјукуса] (Pek.). ✧ Nikushka (R.), dim. of R. Nikolay (Pek.).

NYULAUÑA Yak. **Nyulauña** [Нјулауңа], fem. (Pek.).

NYULĠUY Yak. **Nyulġuy-χalġïy** [Нјулгу(і)-халгыі], a shaman (Pek.). ✧ 'Arrow?' cf. Tung. *nyulgi* 'стрела' (Pek.).

NYUORALJÏN see **NYURAΓALJÏN**

NYURAΓALJÏN Yak. **NyuraγalJïn-χotun / Nyuoralʒïn-χotun** [Ајы Нјураңалцын (Нјуоралцын) хотун], a woman living in the sky (heaven), Ajiña-siär-toyon's wife (Pek.).

NYURΓUSTAY Yak. **Nyurγustay / Nurγustay** [Нјургустаі / Нургустаі], a part of the names of shamanesses (Pek.). ✧ 'Elected, the select' (Pek.).

NYŪČČAQĀN Yak. **Nyūččaqān** [Нјуччакан/Нуччакан] (Pek.). ✧ 'Russian' cf. Yak. *nyuča, nyūča, nyučča, nyūčča* 'id.' + suff. *-qān?* (Pek.).

NYŪČČAQÏY Yak. **Nyūččaqïy / Nūččaqïy** [Нјуччакыі / Нуччакыі] (Pek.). ✧ 'Russian' cf. Yak. *nyuča, nyūča, nyučča, nyūčča* 'id.' + suff. *-qïy?* (Pek.).

NYŪNYALÏR Yak. **Nyūnyalïr** [Нјунјалыр] (Pek.).

NYŪSÄR Yak. **Nyūsär** [Нјўсäр], a folklore hero (Pek.). ✧ 'Clumsy, sluggish' cf. Yak. *nüsär* 'id.' (Pek.).

NOČAQ Hak.(Sag.) 19th-20th c. **Nočaq / Načaq?** [Ночак] (Katanov, Otč. 7).

NOJÏΓ Hak. 19th-20th c. **NoJïγ** [Ночыг] (HRS 350).

NOΓAY Bashk. 1779 **aoγay** [Нагай Сулейманов] (MIB V, 83); Tat. 1534 **Naγay** [Нагай Тулешевъ] (PSRL XIII, 84); Tat. 1624 **Naγay** [Уразнай Нагаевъ] (Pokrovskij 71); Tat. 18th-19th c. **Naγay** [Нагай / Нагайчеринъ / Нагайчуринъ] (Magn. 60); Bashk. 1787 **Naγay** [Нагай Урсумбетев] (MIB V, 203); Tat. 18th-19th c. **Naγay-čura** [Нагайчуринъ] (Magn. 60); Bashk. 1734 **Naγay-čura** [Нагайчуре], a tarχan (Vel.-Zern., Bašk. 10); Bashk. 1735 **Naγay-čura** [Юлумбетъ Нагайчуринъ], a prince (Vel.-Zern., Bašk. 12); Chuv. 18th-19th c. **Nogay** [Ногай] (Magn. 60); Tat.(GH), Kipch.? **Noγay** [نوغاى] (Qalāūn/Tizeng. I, 64); Maml. **Noγay** [Nougaï], one of the murderers of Sultan Khalil (Makrīzī III, 153, Weil, Chalif. I, 192); Maml. 1298 **Noγay** [سيفالدين نوكاى], an emir (Dawād. 13); Trkm. 19th c. **Noγay** [Ногай Толековъ] (Ščeglov IV, 174); Bashk. 1715 **Noγay** [Минли Ногаев] (MIB III, 132); Bashk. 1715 **Noγay** [Уразай Ногаев] (MIB III, 132); Bashk. 1729 **Noγay** [Ногай Кодраев (Кадраев)] (MIB III, 269); Bashk. 1745 **Noγay** [Ибрай Ногаев] (MIB III, 428); Bashk. 1776 **Noγay** [Ногаев Илья Васильев] (MIB V, 31, 32, 35, 37, 45); Bashk. 1776 **Noγay** [Ногаев Кирилл Яковлев] (MIB V, 31, 32); Bashk. 1794 **Noγay / Naγay** [Ногаев (Нагаев) Андрей] (MIB V, 486, 550); Kzk. 19th c. **Noγay-bay** [Ногайбай] (AOAtb. 2, 42); Kzk. 19th c. **Noγay-bay** [Ногайбай] (AOP 10); Kzk. 19th c. **Noγay-bay** [Ногайбай] (SODž. 40, 102); Kzk. 19th c. **Noγay-bay** [Ногайбай] (SOV 6); Kzk. 19th c. **Noγay-bay** [Ногайбай] (AOK 66); Crm. 1638 **Noγay-bek** [دبـغـا ى بك], Bayram-aγa's son (Vel.-Zern., Crim. 174); Bashk. 1711 **Noγay-bikä** [Ногайбика Бимашева], fem. (MIB III, 71); Bashk. 1779 **Noγay-čura** [Ногайчюра? Салдатов] (MIB V, 81); Kzk. 19th c. **Noγay-mïrza** [Nogay-Mïrza] (Ljutš 114); Crm. 1652 **Noγay-oγlï** [نوغـا اوغلى] (Vel.-Zern., Crim. 458, 461); Kzk. 19th c. **Noqay** [Нокай] (AOO 46); Maml. 1299 **Nuγay** [Seïf-eddin-Nougai], one of the murderers of Sultan Lājin (1296-1299) (Makrīzī IV, 96, Weil, Chalif. I, 217); *EN:* Kzk. 18th c. - 19th c. **Noγay** [Ногай], a clan (Tynyšp. 66, 69, 75); *TN:* Kzk.? **Nuγay** [نوغى اتا / Нугай-ата], a settlement and canal in the region of Sugut (Sugutskij tumen') (ZIRGOStat. 2). ✧ I. 'Dog' (Mo.) child born in the 11th year of the animal calendar (Sattarov); II. 'Tatar' ancient Turkic ethnical name (Kusimova, Sattarov, Ahmetzjanov), cf. Crm. *noγay* 'Nogaier (in der Krym und im Kaukasus), Kzk. *noγay* 'in Ostrussland lebender Tatar, kasanischer Tatar' (Radl. III, 693). Cf. also Žaparov-Konkobaev 1984, p. 124-127. See also **KÖZEY-NOΓAU.**

NOΓAYBAQ Bashk. 18th c. **Naγaybaq** [Нагайбакъ] (Nepljuev 440); Bashk. 1770 **Naγaybaq** [Нагайбак Кансуяров] (MIB IV/1, 342); Bashk. 1789 **Naγaybaq** [Нагайбак Хасанов] (MIB V, 252); Bashk. 1789 **Naγaybaq** [Курманай Нагайбаков] (MIB V, 250); Bashk. 1735 **Noγaybaq** [Якишгулъ Ногайбаковъ], a tarχan (Vel.-Zern., Bašk. 20); Bashk. 1775 **Noγaybaq** [Ногайбак Асанов] (MIB IV/1, 376); Bashk. 1782 **Noγaybaq** [Ногайбак Кансуяров] (MIB V, 135); Bashk. **Noγaybaq / Naγaybaq** [Ногайбак (Нагайбак) Асанов (Исанов)] (MIB 29, 130, 250, 252); Bashk. 1715 **Noγaybaq? / Noγay-bäk?** [Ногойбак Текеляков] (MIB III, 124). ✧ 'Noghaybak, Naghaybak' (ethnical name).

NOXA Hak. 19th-20th c. **Noχa** [Hoxa], fem. (HRS 354).

NOYAN Tat.(Sib.)? 1633 **Noyan** [Бектен Ноянов] (Miller, Ist. Sib. II, 407, 422). ✧ I. 'Chief, commander (of ten thousand warriors), noble man' (Mo.) (Žanuzakov), II. 'Young man, lad, chap, brave man, hero', cf. Yak. *noyon* 'молодой человек, парень, парнишка; молодец, удалец' (Pek). Used also as secondary component of names.

NOYOXU Yak. **Noyoχu** [Hojoxy] (Pek.).

NOYONNŪR Yak. **Noyonnūr** [Нојоннур] (Pek.). ✧ Dim. of *Noyon* (Pek.). ⇨ **NOYAN** + dim. suff. *-nūr.*

NOYOTTON Yak. **Noyotton** [Нојоттон] (Pek.).

NOQAY see **NOΓAY**

NOQTA Kzk. 19th c. **Noqta-bay** [Ноктабай] (SOV 40). ✧ 'Halter, hobble' cf. Kuman, Chag., Hak., Kzk. *noqta* 'die Halfter' (Radl. III, 693).

NOM Tat.(Sib.) 1629 **Nom** [Ном], Küçüm's great-grandson (Miller, Ist. Sib. II, 361); Uyg. 13th c. **Nom-qulï / Nom-quli** [Nom Quli / Nom-Kulı / nom qulï] (Radl., USp. 2-3, 34, Le Coq, Urkunden 1918, 454, EUTS, DTS). ✦ 'Book, law' cf. Uyg., Alt.(Tel.) *nom* 'das Buch, die Schrift; das Gesetz' (Radl. III, 695).

NOMDAŠ Uyg. 12th c. -14th c. **Nomdaš** (DTS). ✦ 'Book-fellow' (Radlov: Büchergefährte). ⇨ **NOM** + suff. *-daš.*

NOMÍK Hak. 19th-20th c. **Nomik** [Номик] (HRS 350).

NOMŪN see **NAMÏN**

NONAQ Hak. 19th c. **Nonaq** [Нонак] (Katanov, Otč. 12). ✦ 'Black bilberry' cf. Hak.(Sag.) *nonaɣ* 'die Blaubeere, Schwarzbeere' (Radl. III, 694).

NONQA Hak. 19th-20th c. **Nonqa** [Нонка], fem. (HRS 354).

NOÑNOYO Yak. **Noñnoyo** [Ноҥнojo] (Pek.). ✦ 'Chubby' cf. Yak. *noñnoɣ-* 'ласкательное слово, относится к маленьким, толстеньким детям' + Ger. *-a* (Pek.).

NOÑSOLUN Yak. **Noñsolun** [Ноҥсолун] (Pek.).

NOR Kzk. 19th c. **Nor-bay / Nur-bay?** [Нормахметъ Норбаевъ] (SKSO VIII, 233). ✦ 'Saint/sacred (man)' cf. Tat. *nor* 'ein Heiliger' (Radl. III, 694).

NOR-BAŠÏ Kzk. 1820 **Nor-baša? (<Nor-bašï)** [Норбаша] (Sib. Vest. IX, 3, 81?). ✦ 'Head of the sacred'? ⇨ **NOR** + **BAŠ** + poss. suff. *-ï.*

NOR-ČÏLAN Hak.(Kyz.) 19th-20th c. **Nor-čïlan** [Норчылан] (Katanov, Otč.). ✦ 'Saint/sacred (man) - snake'? cf. Tat. *nor* 'ein Heiliger' (Radl. III, 694). ⇨ **YÏLAN.**

NOR-MAXMET Kzk. 19th c. **Nor-maχmet / Nur-maχmet?** [Нормахметъ Норбаевъ] (SKSO VIII, 233). ✦ I. 'Saint/sacred Mukhammad'; II. 'Mukhammad's brightness'. ⇨ **NOR/NUR** + **MUXAMMED.** See also **NURÏMBET, NURMET.**

NORMAT see **NURMAT**

NOROXU Yak. **Noroχu** [Нороху] (Pek.).

NORULUYA Yak. **Noruluya** [Норулуjа / Норулуjа Iäjäxciт], a goddess, the protector of the reproduction of dogs (Pek.). ✦ 'Drag, lugging' cf. Yak. *noruluɣ-* 'волочиться (о длинной одежде)' + aff. *-a* (Pek.).

NOSTULARÏ Balk. 20th c. **Nostularï** [Nostúlari], a former qul (slave, servant) family (Pröhle, Balk. 245).

NOSUYUQ Yak. **Nosuyuq** [Носуjук / Лосуjук] (Pek.).

NOSUOQ Yak. **Nosuoq** [Носуок] (Pek.).

NOTÏY Hak. 19th-20th c. **Notïy** [Нотый], fem. (HRS 354).

NOV Trkm. 20th c. **Nov-gül** [Novgül], fem. (Zaj. 1971, 340). ✦ 'New, fresh' (<P.new/now), *Nov-gül* 'Fresh flower' (Zaj. 1971).

NŌBAHAR see **NEWBAHAR**

NŌBAT Trkm. 20th c. **Nobat** [Nobat] (Zaj. 1971, 330); Trkm. 20th c. **Nōbat** [Нобат] (TrkmRS 474). ✦ 'Row, line, cue' cf. Trkm. *nōbat* 'очередь' (TrkmRS) (<Ar.).

NŌBAT-GELDÍ Trkm. 20th c. **Nōbat-geldi** [Nobatgeldi] (Zaj. 1971, 334). ✦ 'The row has come' (Zaj. 1971). ⇨ **NŌBAT + KELDÍ.**

NŌNNŪR Yak. **Nōnnūr** [Ноннур] (Pek.).

NŌTOY Yak. **Nōtoy-buɣatïr** [Нотоi-буҕатыр] (Pek.). ✦ 'Short-legged'? (Pek.).

NÖGER see **NÖKER**

NÖGÜR see **NÖKER**

NÖXČÖR Yak. **Nöχčör** [Нöхчöр] (Pek.). ✦ 'Sitting about, lounging with bent back' cf. Yak. *nöχčöy-* 'скорчиться в присядку' + aff. *-r* (Pek.).

NÖKER Kzk. 19th c. **Nöger-bek** [Ногербекъ] (AOA 62); Kzk. 19th c. **Nögür-bek** [Ногурбекъ] (AOK 18, 90); Trkm. 20th c. **Nöker** [Nöker] (Zaj. 1971, 326). ✦ 'Helper, fellow; soldier, servant, footman' cf. Kuman *nöger* 'Genosse, Kamerad' (CC), Chag. *nökär* 'der Gehülfe, Gefährte, Klient, Diener, der Soldat, der Beamte', Alt. *nökör* 'der Gefährte', Kzk. *nögör* 'der Diener, Gefährte' (Radl. III, 695), Trkm. *nöker* 'нукер, дружинник' (TrkmRS), cf. also Trk. *nökär*, Mo. *nökör* 'Gefährte' (TMEN I, No. 388). It may also be used as a secondary component of male names. (<P.<Mo.). See also **AL-NÖKÜR.**

NÖRMÖNBET Kzk. **Nörmönbet** [Нöрмöн Бет], a khan in a tale having two daughters called *Tünüköy* and *Künüköy* (Proben III, 101 /129/). ⇨ **NOR-MAXMET?, NURÏMBET, NURMET.**

NÖTÜS Hak. 19th-20th c. **Nötüs** [Нöтÿc], fem. (HRS 354).

NUČÏƔAŠ Hak.(Shor) 19th-20th c. **Nučïɣaš** [Нучыҕаш] (Katanov, Otč. 11).

NUČUMAN Kzk. 19th c. **Nučuman** [Нучуманъ] (SOK 26).

NUFULLĀN Yak. **Nufullān-quo** [Нуфуллан-куо], fem. (Pek.).

NUX Karakh. **Nuχ** [Nuh / nuḥ] (MK/Atalay 848, DTS); Nog. 20th c. **Nuχ** [Нух Огъурлы улы / Нух Огурлиев], one of Baskakov's informants from the aul of Erkin-yurt (Oraɣ-awul) (Bask., Nog. 143); Selj. 1200 **Nuχ-alp** [نوح الب / Nouh Alp] (Ibn Bībī III, 61 IV, 23, Seldj. Nameh 42, 82). ✦ 'Noah' (Prophet) (Ar.-Hebr.) (Sattarov, Kusimova), cf. Karakh. *nuḥ* (DTS).

NUXA Hak. 19th-20th c. **Nuχa** [Нуха], fem. (HRS 354).

NUQUYĀQ Yak. **Nuquyāq / Nuquyāχ** [Нукуjак / Hjукуjax Уiбан] (Pek.). ✦ 'Moving enervated, loose' cf. Yak. *nuquy-* 'двигаться вяло' (Pek.).

NUOY Yak. **Nuoy** [Hyoi] (Pek.). ✦ Noy (R.) (Pek.). ⇨ **NUX.**

NUONA Yak. **Nuona** [Нуона] (Pek.).

NUORALYÏN Yak. **Nuoralyïn** [Тiмiр Нуоралjын], a demonic folklore hero (Pek.).

NUORULLĀN   Yak. **Nuorullān** [Нуоруллан], fem. (Pek.); Yak. **Nuorullān-quo** [Ытык-Нуоруллан-куо], fem. (Pek.). ❖ 'Kind-hearted (beauty)' (Pek.).

NUR   Nog. 20th c. **Nur-aqay** [Нуракъай Йакъуп увлы], one of Baskakov's informants from the aul of Qara-töbe (Bask., Nog. 143); Kkalp. 20th c. **Nur-bay** [Нурбай] (KkRS 775); Kkalp. 20th c. **Nur-bay** [Нурбай] (KkRS 775); Trkm. 20th c. **Nur-ǰan** [Nurğan] (Zaj. 1971, 329); Kkalp. 20th c. **Nur-ǰan** [Нуржан] (KkRS 775); Kzk. 19th c.? **Nur-ǰan-biy** [Nurʒan-biy] (Atyns. 82); Turk.? 1482 **Nur-χatun** [نور حاتون], Xaji Xamza's daughter, mentioned in an inscription (Berchem, Perg. 16); Trkm. 20th c. **Nur-soltan** [Nursoltan], fem. (Zaj. 1971, 337); Kkalp. 20th c. **Nur-sultan** [Нурсултан] (KkRS 775); Karakh. 1038 **Nur-tegin** [نور تكين / Нур-тегин], enemy of the Ghaznavid Masʿūd, attacked Balkh in 1038, Alp-tegin's son (Mirch. Gasnevid. 106, 107, MIT I, 243); *EN:* Kzk. 18th c. - 19th c. **Nur-bay** [Нурбай], a clan (Tynyšp. 68); Kzk. 18th c. - 19th c. **Nur-χoǰa** [Нурходжа], a clan (Tynyšp. 72). ❖ 'Light, shine, brightness; beauty' cf. Uyg., Kuman, Chag., Kzk., Tat., Turk. *nur* (Ar.) 'das Licht, der Glanz, die Schönheit' (Radl. III, 705), Kkalp. *nur* 'id.' (KkRS). In Trkm. rain and snow figuratively is called *nur* (Muhamedova 1957, 36). See also **AY-NURA, BİYBİ-NUR, YAZ-NUR.**

NUR-ALİ   Kzk. 1750 **Nur-ali** [Nourali] (Levchine 220, 223, 280). ⇨ **NUR + ALİ.**

NUR-ALLĀN   Yak. **Nur-allān** [Нураллан], fem. (Pek.).

NUR-BERDİ   Uzb. 20th c. **Nur-berdi** [Нурберди] (Begmatov 1984, 202); Trkm. 1859 **Nur-berdï** [Нуръ-Берды] (ZIRGOEtn. I, 209); Trkm. 20th c. **Nur-berdï** [Nurberdï] (Zaj. 1971, 334); Trkm. 19th c. **Nur-berdï-χan** [Noor Berdi Khan], chief of the Tekke tribe (O'Donovan I, 363, II, 261). ⇨ **NUR + BERDİ.**

NUR-BOLDÏ   Kzk. 19th c. **Nur-boldï** [Нулбольды] (SOV 80). ⇨ **NUR + BOLDÏ.**

NUR-BOTA   Uzb. 1885 **Nur-bota** [Нурбота] (SOK 38). ❖ 'Light (fig. beautiful) - young camel'. ⇨ **NUR + BOTA.**

NUR-BOZ   Kzk. 19th c. **Nur-boz** [Нурбозъ] (SOK 20). ⇨ **NUR + BOZ.**

NUR-BULҐAN   Kzk. 19th c. **Nur-bulɣan** [Нурбулганъ] (SOK 252). ⇨ **NUR + BOLҐAN.**

NUR-ǮAHAN   Trkm. 20th c. **Nur-jahan** [Nurğahan], fem. (Zaj. 1971, 336). ❖ 'Light/shine-(of the)-world'. ⇨ **NUR + ǰIHAN.**

NUR-ǰÂW   Uzb. 20th c. **Nur-ǰâw** [Нуржов] (Begmatov 1984, 202). ❖ 'Let the light fall (on him/her)! Light-fall!' cf. Kuman, Chag., Crm., Turk. *yaγ-* 'regnen' (Radl. III, 39), Uzb. *yâγ-* 'идти, падать (об атмосферных осадках)' (UzbRS), Kzk. *žau-* 'идти (о дожде, снеге, граде)' (KzRS). ⇨ **NUR, NUR-YAҐDÏ.**

NUR-GELDİ see **NUR-KELDİ**

NUR-YAҐDÏ   Uzb. 20th c. **Nur-yâγdï** [Нурёгди] (Begmatov 1984, 202). ❖ 'Light/beauty fell (on him/her)' cf. Kuman, Chag., Crm., Turk. *yaγ-* 'regnen' (Radl. III, 39), Uzb. *yâγ-* 'идти, падать (об атмосферных осадках)' (UzbRS), Kzk. *žau-* 'идти (о дожде, снеге, граде)' (KzRS). ⇨ **NUR.** See also **NUR-ǰÂW.**

NUR-KELDİ   Trkm. 1880 **Nur-geldi** [Нургельды Худай-Бердiевъ] (Grod., Vojna IV, 39); Uzb. 20th c. **Nur-keldi** [Нуркелди] (Begmatov 1984, 202). ❖ 'Light/beauty has come/been born', 'Bright (child) has come (been born)'. ⇨ **NUR + KELDİ.**

NUR-QAČQA   Bashk. 1701 **Nur-qačqa** [Нуркачка Тяькинъ], a tarχan (Vel.-Zern., Bašk. 29). ⇨ **NUR + QAŠQA?**

NUR-QALA   Kzk. 1884 **Nur-qala** [Нуркала Аллахбековъ] (Grod., Pril. 93). ⇨ **NUR + QALA?**

NUR-MAXAMBET see **NUR-MUXAMED**

NUR-MAXAN   Kkalp. 20th c. **Nur-maχan** [Нурмахан] (KkRS 775). ⇨ **NUR.**

NUR-MAXMUD   Chag. **Nur-maχmud-sultan** [نور محمد], a Sheybanid sultan (Šejb. L, LXXVIII). ⇨ **NUR + MAXMUD.**

NUR-MUXAMED   Kkalp. 20th c. **Nur-maχambet** [Нурмахамбет] (KkRS 775); *EN:* Kzk. 18th c. - 19th c. **Nur-muχamed** [Нурмухамед], a clan (Tynyšp. 74).

NUR-SALTANA   Crm. 1509, 1512 **Nur-saltana / Nur-sultana?** [Нурсалтана], a Crimean empress, Meñli-girey-χan's wife (PSRL IV, 137, VI, 137, 252, 249, VIII, 252 etc.). ❖ Female form of *Nur-saltan/Nur-sultan.* ⇨ **NUR + SULTAN.**

NUR-TAY   Kkalp. 20th c. **Nur-tay** [Нуртай] (KkRS 775); Kkalp. 1810 **Nur-tay-biy** [Нуртай бий] (MIKk. 109). ⇨ **NUR + TAY** or suff. *-tay(1,2)?*

NUR-TUҐAN   Kzk. **Nur-tuγan** [Нуртуган] (Žirm., Epos 403). ⇨ **NUR + TUҐAN I.**

NURAQ   Trkm. 19th c. **Nuraq** [Шарай Нураковъ] (Ščeglov IV, 188); Kzk. 19th c. **Nuraq** [Нуракъ] (SOK 102, 128); Kzk. 19th c. **Nuraq** [Нуракъ] (SODž. 98, 118). ❖ 'Little shine; little beauty'? cf. Kzk. PNs *Nuraq / Nurek* (Žanuzakov-Esbaeva). ⇨ **NUR + suff. *-aq / -ek.***

NURALÏ   Yak. **Nuralï** [Ытык Нуралы], a beauty in tales, Saχa Sārïn Toyōn's daughter (Pek.).

NURČA   Kzk. 19th c. **Nurča** [Нурча] (Grod., Pril. 86); Turk. 15th c. **Nurǰa** [Nurca], fem. (Gökb., Ed. 172); Kzk. 19th c. **Nurša-bay** [Нуршабай] (SOV 62). ❖ 'Little light, shine, beauty'. ⇨ **NUR + dim. suff. *-ča.***

NURǰA see **NURČA**

NURǰAY   Kzk. 19th c. **Nurǰay** [Нурджай] (Grod., Pril. 24).

NURET Trkm. 19th c. **Nuret** [Нуретъ Орокаевъ] (Ščeglov IV, 175).

NURГUГUS Yak. **Nurɣuɣus** [Нургугус] (Pek.). ✧ 'Looking downwards' cf. Yak. *nurɣuy-* 'id.' + suff. *-ɣus.* + suff. *-ɣus.*

NURГUSTAY Yak. **Nurɣustay / Nyurɣustay** [Нургустаі / Нjургустаі] (Pek.). ✧ 'Debauched, lewd, coward' (Pek.). ⇨ **NYURГUSTAY.**

NURİ Trkm. **Nuri-bay** [Нури-бай] (Mel'gunov 321); Bashk. 18th c. **Nurïy** [Нурей Баскуновъ] (Nepljuev 882); Bashk. 1789 **Nurïy** [Нурей Мукменев] (MIB V, 274). ✧ 'Bright (face), light; beautiful' (Ar.) (Kusimova, Žanuzakov).

NURİMAN Bashk. **Nuriman** [Nurimanov Bagau] (Mende 138). ✧ 'Strong, brave, heroic' (P.) (Kusimova), 'The light (brightness) of faith, religion' (Sattarov).

NURÏY see **NURİ**

NURÏMBET Kkalp. 20th c. **Nurïmbet** [Нурымбет] (KkRS 775); Bashk. 1734 **Nurumbet** [Нурумбет[Конаеву] (Vel.-Zern., Bašk. 11); *EN:* Kzk. 18th c. - 19th c. **Nurumbet** [Нурумбет], a clan (Tynyšp. 74). ✧ 'Muhammad's light (brightness)' (Ar.) (Kusimova, Sattarov, Žanuzakov). ⇨ **NUR + MUXAMMED** + suffixoid *-ïmbet.*

NURÏŠ see **NURUŠ**

NURKEY Bashk. 1735 **Nurkey** [Наурузъ Нуркеевъ], a tarχan (Vel.-Zern., Bašk. 22); Bashk. 1729 **Nurkey / Nurkäy?** [Тохтар Нуркеев] (MIB III, 269). ⇨ **NUR** + dim. suff. *-key / -käy.*

NURLAN Kzk. 19th c. **Nurlan** [Нурланъ] (SOK 134). ✧ 'Be bright, shiny' (Sattarov, Žanuzakov), cf. Tat., Turk. *nurlan-* 'glänzen, scheinen' (Radl. III, 706).

NURLÏ Trkm. 20th c. **Nurlï** [Nurlï] (Zaj. 1971, 327); Bashk. 1759 **Nurlï** [Нурли Нурметев] (MIB IV/2, 26); Yürük 16th c. **Nurlu** [نورلى / Nurlu], from the Yürüks of Kocacık, Turkey (Gökb., Rum. 105); Trkm. 20th c. **Nūrlï** [Нурлы] (TrkmRS 476); *TN:* Kzk. **Nurlï-bay** [Нурлыбай], a place (Karta JAR XI); Kzk.? **Nurlu-bay** [Нурлубай], a place (Karta JAR XI). ✧ 'Bright, shiny; beautiful' (Sattarov), cf. Tat. *nurlï* 'id.' (Radl. III, 706). ⇨ **NUR** + suff. *-lï.*

NURLU see **NURLÏ**

NURMAN Kzk. 1846 **Nurman** [Нурман Джаманбаев] (MKOP 152); Kzk. 19th c. **Nurman** [Нурманъ] (SOV 74, 84); Kzk. 19th c. **Nurman** [Нурманъ] (SODž. 10, 20, 126, 140); Kzk. 19th c. **Nurman** [Нурманъ] (SOK 150); Kzk. 1850 **Nurman** [Нурманъ] (Konšin, Mat. V, 103); Kzk.? 19th c. **Nurman** [Нурманъ] (Grod., Pril. 81); Kzk. 19th c. **Nurman** [Нурманъ] (Grod., Pril. 163); Kzk. 19th c. **Nurman** [Нурманъ] (Grod., Pril. 120); Kzk. 19th c. **Nurman** [Нурманъ Кишлатбаевъ] (Grod., Pril. 60); Kzk. 19th c. **Nurman** [Нурманъ] (AOA 114); Kkalp. 20th c. **Nurman** [Нурман] (KkRS 775); Kkalp. 20th c. **Nurman** [Нурман] (Bask., Kkalp. 401); Kzk. 19th c. **Nurman-bek** [Нурманъ бекъ Саричаевъ] (Grod., Pril. 112). ⇨ **NURİMAN / NUR** + suff. *-man?*

NURMANČİL Kzk. 19th c. **Nurmančïl / Numančil?** [Хумбатъ Нурманчиловъ] (Grod., Pril. 112). ⇨ **NURMAN + ČİL?** + suff. *-čïl?*

NURMÄŠ Tat. 1748 **Nurmäš** [Нурмяшевъ] (Nepljuev 438). ✧ Shortened-contracted of Tat. *Nur-möχämmät* (Sattarov)? + suff. *-(ä)š.*

NURMET Kzk. 19th c. **Normat / Nurmat?** [Норматъ Ирматовъ] (SKSO VIII, 232); Bashk. 1715 **Nurmet** [Нурмет Кинзибаев] (MIB III, 123); Kzk.? **Nurmet** [Нурметъ Иганъ- Бердыевъ] (TV 1876, 132). ⇨ **NOR/NUR?** + suff. *-mat / -met.*

NURŠA see **NURČA**

NURTEK Kzk. 19th c. **Nurtek** [Нуртекъ] (SODž. 12). ⇨ **NUR** + suff. *-tek.*

NURUM Tat.(Lit.) 1592 **Nurum** [Нурумъ] (Lit. Tat. 118, 121); Kzk. 1817 **Nurum** [نوروم / Нурум], a Kazak sultan (MIK IV, 307); Kzk. 19th c. **Nurum-bay** [Нурумбай Султановъ] (SKSO III, 190); Kzk. 19th c. **Nurum-qul**, Qusum-qul's brother (Grod., Pril. 72). ✧ 'My brightness; my beauty'. ⇨ **NUR** + poss. suff. *-um.*

NURUMBET see **NURÏMBET**

NURUŠ Kkalp. 20th c. **Nurïš** [Нурыш] (KkRS 775); Bashk. 1732 **Nuruš** [Нуруш Уркашев] (MIB III, 297); Bashk. 1735 **Nuruš** [Нурушъ Иткининъ], a tarχan (Vel.-Zern., Bašk. 25); Bashk. 1739 **Nuruš** [Нурушъ Кинзекіевъ] (PSZRI X, 983); Bashk. 1770 **Nuruš** [Тоймас Нурушев] (MIB IV/1, 343); Bashk. 1795 **Nuruš** [Таймас Нурушев] (MIB V, 275); Bashk. 1798 **Nuruš** [Нурушевъ] (PSZRI XXV, 196); Kzk. 19th c. **Nuruš** [Нурушъ] (AOAtb. 10). ⇨ **NUR, NURİ?** + suff. *-uš / -š?*

NUSUQ Kzk. 19th c. **Nusuq-pay** [Нусукпай] (SODž. 84); Kzk. 19th c. **Nusuq-pay** [Нусукпай] (SOK 124).

NUZURUX Hak. 19th-20th c. **Nuzuruχ** [Нузурух] (HRS 350). ✧ 'Fist' (HRS).

NŪČČAQĀN Yak. **Nūččaqān** [Нуччакан] (Pek.). ⇨ **NYŪČČAQĀN.**

NŪČČAQÏY Yak. **Nūččaqïy** [Нуччакыі / Нjуччакыі] (Pek.). ⇨ **NYŪČČAQÏY.**

NŪRAY Yak. **Nūray** [Сöкö (Сöкü) Нураі] (Pek.). ✧ 'Drowsy, sleeper' cf. Yak. *nūray-* 'дремать, задремывать, засыпать' (Pek.).

NŪRAQÏ Yak. **Nūraqï** [Нуракы] (Pek.). ✧ 'Slumbering, drowsing' cf. Yak. *nūray-* 'дремать, задремывать, засыпать' + aff. *-qï* (Pek.). ⇨ **NŪRAY.**

NŪRULDĀN Yak. **Nūruldān-quo** [Нурулдан, Нуруллан / Нуоруллан, Нjурулан], epithet of modest girls (Pek.). ✧ 'Kind, Beautiful, modest, honest girl', became an epithet (Pek.).

NŪRULLĀN   Yak. **Nūrullān-quo** [Нуруллан-куо], a legendary girl (shamaness) (Pek.).

NÜGERBEN   Kzk. 19th c. **Nügerben** [Нугербенъ] (AOO 70).

NÜÖRÄLJİN   Yak. **Nüörälin-χotun / Nüörälyin-χotun** [Нүөрäлцiн-хотун, Нүөрäлjiн], fem. (Pek.).

NÜÖRÜKTĀYİ   Yak. **Nüörüktäyi-toyon** [Н(ÿ)öрÿктäji-тойон] (Pek.).

NÜSTÄP   Yak. **Nüstäp** [Нÿстäр] (Pek.).

NÜSÜP   Kzk. 19th c. **Nüsüp** [Нюсупъ] (SOV 48). ✧ Nusip (Ar. form of Hebr. Yosif).

O

OBAS   Hak. 19th-20th c. **Obas** [Обас], fem. (HRS 354).

OBDO   Hak. 19th-20th c. **Obdo** [Обдо] (HRS 354). ✧ Avdot'ya (R. fem.) (HRS), Yevdokiya (R. fem.) (Butanaev).

OBDOTAY   Hak. 19th-20th c. **Obdotay** [Обдотай], fem. (HRS 354). ✧ Avdot'ya (R.) (HRS). ⇨ **OBDO** + suff. -tay.

OBİLČA   Kzk. 19th c. **Obïlča** [Обыльча] (SOK 156).

OBLOS   Alt. 19th c. **Oblos-χan** [Облос-хан] (Verb., In. 139).

OBOY   Yak. **Oboy-toyon** [Обоi-тojон] (Pek.). ✧ 'Fat, plump'.

OBOQŪM   Yak. **Oboqūm / Oboqūn** [Обокум, Обокун] (Pek.). ✧ Avvakum (R.) (Pek.).

OBRAY   Kzk. 19th c. **Obray** [Обрай] (AOO 62). ✧ 'Piggy, open-mouthed' cf. Kzk. *obïr* 'обжора; ненасытный' (KzRS).

OBRİN   Hak. 19th-20th c. **Obrin** [Обрин], fem. (HRS 354); Hak.(Sag.) 19th-20th c. **Obrïn** [Обрiн] (Proben IX, 557). ✧ Aver'yan (R.) cf. Hak. PN *Obïrin* (Butanaev).

OBUX   Tat. 1600 **Obuχ** [Обух Безбергенев] (MIB I, 152).

OČAQ   Chuv. 18th-19th c. **Očak** [Очакъ] (Magn. 64); Hak.(Kyz.) 19th-20th c. **Očïq** [Очык], fem. (Katanov, Otč. 13); Kzk. 19th c. **Ošaq-pay** [Ошакпай] (SOK 10, 90, 118, 126, 170, 190, 200); Kzk. 19th c. **Ošaq-pay** [Ошакпай] (SODž. 70, 110); Kzk. 19th c. **Ošaq-pay** [Ошакпай] (SOV 36); Kzk. 19th c. **Ošoq-pay** [Ошокпай] (SOK 120, 212,). ✧ 'Tripod' cf. Chag., NUyg.(Tar.) *očaq* 'der Dreifuss', Hak.(Sag.) *očïq* 'id.' (Radl. I, 1134, 1135), Kzk. *ošaq* 'id.' (Radl. I, 1149), Alt. *očoq* 'таган; очаг в айыле' (OjrRS).

OČAŇ   Hak. 19th-20th c. **Očaň** [Очанъ], fem. (HRS 354).

OČČİ-TAY   Karg. **Očči-tay** [Оччы-тай], fem. (Katanov, Otč. 8). ✧ 'Middle aged foal' (Katanov). ⇨ OČİ + TAY or suff. -tay(1,2)?

OČČŌX   Yak. **Očč̄ōχ** [Оччох] (Pek.). ✧ 'Cross-eyed' cf. Yak. *oččoy-* 'косить, рознить глазами, косоглазить' (Pek.).

OČİ   Alt. 19th-20th c. **Oči / Ōčïy** [Очы / Оочый] (OjrRS 209). ✧ 'Younger (child)' (HRS).

OČİ-QARAQČİN   Alt. 19th c. **Očï-qaraqčïn** [Очи-Каракчин], fem. (Verb., In. 154-155). ✧ 'Younger Qaraqčïn'. ⇨ OČİ + QARAQČİN.

OČİQ see **OČAQ**

OČOĠOČŌN   Yak. **Očoγočōn-čuo-χān / Očoχočōn-čuo-χān** [Очоҕочон (Очохочон)-чуо-хан] (Pek.).

OČOQŪN   Yak. **Očoqūn** [Очокун] (Pek.).

OČORBOY   Yak. **Očorboy / Očorγoy** [Очорбоi (Очорγоi) Хосун] (Pek.).

OČULLĀN-ČOČULLĀN   Yak. **Očullān-čočullān** [Очуллан-Чочуллан], a folklore hero (Pek.).

OČUMAY   Alt. 19th-20th c. **Očumay** [Очумай] (OjrRS 209).

OJAQČİ   Turk. 19th c. **Ojaqčï-oγlu** [Оджакčу], a Zeybek (Kúnos 1891, 119). ✧ 'Chimneysweep; stoker' cf. Turk. *ocakçı* 'id.' (TED).

OJAN   Kzk. 1817 **Ojan** [اوجان / Ожан] (MIK IV, 304).

OJAR   Trkm. 20th c. **Ojar** [Oğar] (Zaj. 1971, 332); Trkm. 20th c. **Ojar** [Оджар] (TrkmRS 484). ✧ 'Saksaul (a special tree of Middle Asian wasteland' cf. Trkm. *ojar* 'саксаул' (TrkmRS). See also **SAZAQ**.

OJAS   NUyg.(Tar.) **Ojas** [Odschas / Оцас] (Proben VI, 64 /84/).

ODABAŠ   Yürük 1543 **Odabaš** [اوده باش / Odabaş] (Gökb., Rum. 195); Crm. **Odabaš** (Mende 175). ✧ 'Janitor' cf. Turk. *odabaşı* 'janitor in a large establishment; man in charge of the rooms of an inn' (TED), 'der Zimmervermieter in einem "han"' (HŞ).

ODĠURMİŠ   Karakh. 11th c. **Odγurmïš / Otqurmïš** [odγurmïš / Откурмыш / Октурмыш] (Radl. I, 1111, II, 110, DTS). ✧ I. 'Impassioned' (Blagova 1997, 717); II. 'Originator, maker, evoked' (Radl. I, 1112), cf. Uyg. *odγur-*, Karakh. *oðγur-* 'будить' (DTS).

ODİR   Kzk. 19th c. **Odïr-bay** [Одырбай] (SODž. 26).

ODİRİN   Kzk. 19th c. **Odïrïn** [Одырынъ] (SOK 250).

ODOQ   Hak. 19th-20th c. **Odoq** [Одок], fem. (HRS 354).

ODON see **OTUN**

ODONOVAN   Trkm. 1879-1881 **Odonovan-bahadur** [O'Donovan Bahadur] (O'Donovan II, 411); Trkm. 1879-1881 **Odonovan-beg** [O'Donovan Beg] (O'Donovan II, 411); Trkm. 1879-1881 **Odonovan-χan** [O'Donovan Khan] (O'Donovan II, 411). ✧ 'O'Donovan' (Edmond), the Irish traveler whom several children were named after and he explained the reason as follows: „I asked, why these babies were brought to my house, and what was the reason of this general presentation. It turned out that among the

Tekke's newly born children are, as a rule, called after any distinguished strangers who may be in the oasis at the time of the births or have resided there a short time previously, or after some event intimately connected with the tribe" (O'Donovan II, 411).

ODOT   Hak. 19th-20th c. **Odot** [Одот], fem. (HRS 354).

ODUBĀR   Yak. **Odubār** [Одубар, Одугар] (Pek.). ✧ Eduard (R.) (Pek.).

ODUY   Yak. **Oduy** [Одуй], a shaman (Pek.).

ODUM-BEY see **OTUN**

ODUN see **OTUN**

ODUNA   Yak. **Oduna-bärgän** [Одуна Бäргäн], a folklore hero in a tale (Pek.).

ODUNČA   Yak. **Odunča** [Одунча], a Tunguz hero in a tale (Pek.). ✧ 'Strong, cruel' cf. Yak. *odun* 'id.' (Pek.).

ODURUY   Yak. **Oduruy** [Одуруй] (Pek.).

ODǴURMĬŠ see **ODǴURMĬŠ**

OGREPEN   Hak. 19th-20th c. **Ogrepen** [Огрепен], fem. (HRS 354). ✧ Agrippina (R.) (HRS).

OҐAY   Hak. 19th-20th c. **Oγay** [Огай], fem. (HRS 354). ✧ Agaf'ya (R. fem.) (HRS, Butanaev).

OҐAN   Uyg. **Oγan** [Oğan] (EUTS); Maml. **Oγan** [عزالدين اوغان] / Izz-al-dīn Awghān al- Ruknī (Sīrat 85); Yürük 1543 **Oγan** [اوغان] / Oğan] (Gökb., Rum. 219); Kzk. 19th c. **Oγan** [Дустанъ Огановъ] (Grod., Pril. 152). ✧ 'God' cf. Karakh. *oγan* 'Gott' (MK)., Uyg., Chag. *oγan* 'Gott' (Radl. I, 1007).

OҐAN-BERDİ   Chag.? **Oγan-berdi** [Oγan bärdi] (Le Coq, Ind. 3). ✧ 'God has given him/her'. ⇨ **OҐAN + BERDİ.**

OҐAS   Hak. 19th-20th c. **Oγas** [Огас], fem. (HRS 354). ✧ Agaf'ya (R. fem.) (HRS, Butanaev).

OҐĀN-TORJU   Tuv. 19th c. **Oγān-torǰu** [Оҕан Торду (Аван-Доржи)] (Proben IX, 131).

OҐDOLŪSA   Yak. **Oγdolūsa** [Огдолуса] (Pek.). ✧ 'Prowler, vagabond' cf. Yak. *oγdoluy-* 'убираться, уходить прочь' etc. + aff. *ūsa* (Pek.).

OҐĬL-KELDİ   Uzb. 20th c. **Oγĭl-keldi** [Угилкелди], fem. (Begmatov 1984, 203). ✧ 'Son has come/been born'. ⇨ **OҐUL + KELDİ.**

OҐĬRLĬ see **OҐURLU**

OҐLAQ   Kzk. 19th c. **Laq** [Лакъ] (SOK 138); Kzk. 19th c. **Oγlaq-pay** [Оглакпай] (SODž. 156); Trkm. 20th c. **Ovlaq** [Ovlaq], fem. (Zaj. 1971, 338); Trkm. 20th c. **Ovlaq** [Овлак], fem. (TrkmRS 481); Kzk. 19th c. **Ulaq** [Улакъ] (SOK 150). ✧ 'Kid; boy, young man' cf. Uyg., Chag., Crm., Hak. *oγlaq* 'der Knabe, ein junger Mensch' (Hak), 'das Zicklein' (Uyg., Kuman, Chag., Crm., Turk.) (Radl. I, 1022), Trkm. *ovlaq* 'козлёнок' (TrkmRS), Kzk. *laq* 'das Zücklein' (Radl. III, 728).

OҐLAN   Türk **Oγlan-ču̇r** [Oγlan Çur] (ETY II, 136); Trkm. 1816 **Oγlan-išan** [Оглан-ишан] (MIT II, 393,

415). ✧ 'Boy; young man' cf. Kuman, Az., Hak., Turk. *oγlan* 'id.' (Radl. I, 1022). Used also as a secondary component of male names. See also **AҐĬR-OҐLAN.**

OҐLANLĬ   Yürük 1543 **Oγlanlĭ** [Oğlanlı] (Gökb., Rum. 228); Yürük 1543 **Oγulanlĭ** [اوغولنلى / Oğulanlı] (Gökb., Rum. 228). ✧ 'Having a boy; with boy'. ⇨ **OҐLAN** + suff. *-lĭ*.

OҐLĬ see **OҐUL**

OҐONYORUQĀN   Yak. **Oγonyoruqān** [Оҕонјорукан] (Pek.). ✧ 'Old man' cf. Yak. *oγonyor* 'старый человек, старик; медведь' + aff. *qān* (Pek.).

OҐRAQ   Khorezm. 13th c. **Oγraq** [سيف الدين اغراق,] an emir of Sultan Meñgü-berdi (1220-1231) (J̌uwaynī I, 106, 109, II, 135, 137, 193, 195).

OҐRAMĬŠ   Türk **Oγramĭš** [Oγramĭş], fem. (ETY II, 137).

OҐŠUQ   Trkm. **Oγšuq** [Огшук] (Sopieva 178); Trkm. 20th c. **Ogšuq** [Ogšuq] (Zaj. 1971, 331); Trkm. 20th c. **Ogšuq** [Огшук] (TrkmRS 483). ✧ 'One-year-old camel' (Sopieva), 'Camel-foal' (Zaj. 1971), cf. Trkm. *oγšuq* 'верблюжонок (от года до двух лет)' (TrkmRS). See also **BOTA, KÖŠEK, TAYLAQ, TURUM.**

OҐUČUYAR   Yak. **Oγučuyar** [Оҕучујар] (Pek.).

OҐUL   Uyg. **Oγĭl** [Oğıl] (EUTS); Uyg. **Oγul** [Oğul] (EUTS); Uyg. 12th c. - 14th c. **Oγul** (Radl., USp. 115-16); Selj. **Oγul-beg** [اوغول بك / اغلبك], Master of the Horse (Ibn Bībī III, 193, 194, IV, 87); Selj.? 1135 **Oγul-beg** [اغلبك], an emir (Ibn al-Athīr/Tornb. XI, 11,15); Oghuz 1156 **Oγul-beg** / **Oγlĭ-bek** [الغل بَك / اغلبك / Оглы-бек], Süleyman-šah's (son of Atsïz) atabeg, executed in 1156 (MIT I, 444); Selj. 1157/58 **Oγul-beg** / **Oγlĭ-bek** [اوغلبك / Aghlebec] (Ibn al-Athīr, Atab.: RHCHor II/2, 201); Turk. 1583 **Oγul-bey** [اوغل بك / Oğulbey] (Ongan, Ank. I, 167); Turk. 1583 **Oγul-bey** [اوغل بك / Oğulbey] (Ongan, Ank. I, 173); Trkm. 20th c. **Oγul-bek**, in a modern short story (?); Trkm. 20th c. **Oγul-bike**, in a modern short story (?); Trkm. 20th c. **Oγul-bike** [Ogulbike], fem. (Zaj. 1971, 335); Trkm. 20th c. **Oγul-gözel** [Ogulgözel], fem. (Zaj. 1971, 335); Khorezm. **Oγul-χaǰib** [اغول / حاجب / اغل], an emir of Muχammed Khorezmshah (J̌uwaynī I, 97, 114, II, 131); Khorezm. 1220 **Oγul-χaǰib** [Могул-хаджиб (Огул-хаджиб)], an emir, commander (MIT I, 486, 490, 503, 504); Uyg. 8th c. - 12th c. **Oγul-ĭnal-ügä** [Oγul ĭnal ügä qanmĭš] (Müller, Pfahl. 23); Uyg. **Oγul-qunčuy-täñrim** [Oγul Qunčuy Tängrim], fem. (Zieme, Mat. I, 74, 80); Oghuz 12th c. **Oγul-melik** [اغول ملك], Qutb al-Dīn Khorezmshah's (1097-1128) son (Qazw.); Oghuz 12th c. **Oγul-melik**, an emir of the Khorezmshah (J̌uwaynī II, 202);

Khorezm. 1220 **Oγul-saχib** [Огулъ-Сахибъ], Ǯelāleddïn Meñgü-berdi's (1220-1231) officer (RaD/Ber. III, 67); Trkm. 20th c. **Oγul-soltan** [Ogulsoltan], fem. (Zaj. 1971, 340); Chag. 16th c. **Oγul-sultan-bikeč** [Огуль Султан-бикеч], fem. (Ivanov 141); Türk 732 **Oγul-tarqan** [Oγul Tarqan] (DTS, ETY I, 52); Uyg. 12th c. - 14th c. **Oγul-tegin** [Oγul Tegin] (Radl., USp. 12-13, DTS); Khorezm.? **Oγul-tekin-χatun** [Огул-Текин-хатун] (RaD II, 202); Uyg. **Oγul-tigin** [Oġul-Tigin] (EUTS); Hak. 19th-20th c. **Ōl** [Оол] (HRS 350); Kkalp. 20th c. **Uγïl** [Уғыл], fem. (KkRS 778); Kkalp. 20th c. **Uγïl-ǰan** [Уғылжан], fem. (KkRS 778); Chag. 16th c. **Uγul-sultan** [Угуль-Султан] (Ivanov 116); Kkalp. 20th c. **Ul-biy** [Улбий], fem. (KkRS 778); Kkalp. 20th c. **Ul-biyke** [Улбийке], fem. (KkRS 778); Kzk. 19th c. **Ul-ǰan** [Улджанъ], fem. (Grod., Pril. 120); Kkalp. 20th c. **Ul-ǰan** [Улджан], fem. (Bask., Kkalp. 404); Kkalp. 20th c. **Ul-žan** [Улжан], fem. (KkRS 778); *EN:* Trkm. 1540 **Oγul-beglü** [Ogulbeglü], an ethnic community (cemaat) in the region of Diyarbekir, Turkey (Demirtaş 47); Trkm. 1614 **Oγul-beyli** [Oğulbeyli], an ethnic community (cemaat) in the region of Diyarbekir, Turkey (Refik, Anad. 67). ✧ 'Son, boy, young man' cf. Uyg., Kuman, Az., Crm., Turk. *oγul* 'der Sohn; der Knabe, Jüngling' (Radl. I, 1015), Uzb. *oγïl* 'сын' (UzbRS), Tuv. *ōl* [оол] 'сын, мальчик, детёныш' (TuvRS), Hak *ōl* 'молодой человек, парень' (HRS), Kzk., Tat. *ul* 'der Sohn' (Radl. I, 1675), Alt.(Tel.), Tat.(Bar.) *ūl* 'der Sohn, Knabe' (Radl. I, 1674). Used also as a secondary component of male names (mainly in possessive forms *-oγlï, -oγlu*). It is frequently used as a component of female names (e. g. in Turkmen) as well. See also **TÜÖRT-ÜGÜL, ZÏMAQ-ULLARÏ**.

OΓUL-ARSLAN   Uyg. 13th-14th c. **Oγul-arslan-tarχan** [Oγul Arslan Ta[rχa]n] (Zieme, Mat. II, 88). ✧ 'Son-lion'. ⇨ OΓUL + ARSLAN.

OΓUL-ASUΓ   Türk **Oγul-asuγ** [Oγul Asuγ] (ETY II, 135). ⇨ OΓUL + ASUΓ.

OΓUL-AŠUNMÏŠ   Uyg. 13th-14th c. **Oγul-ašunmïš-täñrim** [Oγul [A]šunmïš [Tngri]m], fem. (Zieme, Mat. III, 273). ✧ 'Son-surpassed (enough of sons?)' cf. Karakh. *ašun-* 'опережать, перейти; превосходить' (DTS). ⇨ OΓUL.

OΓUL-BAYRAM   Trkm.   **Oγul-bayram** [Огульбайрам], fem. (Sopieva: OSA 180). ⇨ OΓUL + BAYRAM.

OΓUL-BARS   OT? **Oγul-bars** (Németh, HMK 133 /taken from KCsA II, p. 135/); Türk **Oγul-bars** [Oγul Bars] (ETY II, 133). ✧ 'Boy/son-panther'. ⇨ OΓUL + BARS.

OΓUL-BOSSAN   Trkm. 20th c. **Oγul-bossan** [Ogulbossan], fem. (Zaj. 1971, 340). ✧ 'Son-garden'. ⇨ OΓUL + BOSTAN.

OΓUL-DURSUN   Trkm. 20th c. **Oγul-dursun** [Oguldursun], fem. (Zaj. 1971, 335). ✧ 'May the son stay/remain/survive'; 'A son must be born' (Zaj. 1971). ⇨ OΓUL + TURSÏN.

OΓUL-GEREK   Trkm. 20th c. **Oγul-gerek** [Ogulgerek], fem. (Zaj. 1971, 340). ✧ 'A son is needed' (Zaj. 1971). ⇨ OΓUL + KEREK. See also **OΓUL-XAǮAT, OΓUL-NÏYAZ**.

OΓUL-XAǮAT   Trkm. 20th c. **Oγul-χaǰat** [Ogulhağat], fem. (Zaj. 1971, 340). ✧ 'A son is needed' (Zaj. 1971). ⇨ OΓUL + XAǮAT. See also **OΓUL-GEREK, OΓUL-NÏYAZ**.

OΓUL-ÏNANČ   Uyg. 8th c. - 9th c. **Oγul-ïnanč** [Oγul ïnanč tiräk känč] (Haneda 3). ⇨ OΓUL + ÏNANČ.

OΓUL-YÏTMÏŠ   Uyg. 13th c. - 14th c. **Oγul-yitmiš** [Oγul Yitmiš], fem. (Zieme, Mat. III, 271); Uyg. 13th-14th c. **Oγul-yitmiš** [Oγul Yitmiš [Tängrim?]], fem. (Zieme, Mat. III, 271). ✧ '(A) son is lost' (Zieme), cf. Uyg., Karakh. *jit-* 'исчезать, теряться' (DTS). ⇨ OΓUL.

OΓUL-YÏΓMÏŠ   Uyg. 13th-14th c. **Oγul-yïγmiš** [Oγul Yïγmiš] (Zieme, Mat. II, 93). ⇨ OΓUL + YÏΓMÏŠ.

OΓUL-NABAT   Trkm. 20th c. **Oγul-nabat** [Ogulnabat], fem. (Zaj. 1971, 340). ✧ 'Son-sugar-candy'. ⇨ OΓUL + NABAT.

OΓUL-NÏYAZ   Trkm. 20th c. **Oγul-nïyaz** [Ogulnïyaz], fem. (Zaj. 1971, 340).

OΓUL-SAPAR   Trkm. 20th c. **Oγul-sapar** [Ogulsapar], fem. (Zaj. 1971, 340). ✧ 'Son-travelling/trip' (Zaj. 1971), 'Son-Sapar-month'. ⇨ OΓUL + SAFAR.

OΓUL-TAČ   Trkm. 20th c. **Oγul-tač** [Ogultač], fem. (Zaj. 1971, 335). ✧ 'Son-crown'; 'Son-beauty-mark' (Zaj. 1971). ⇨ OΓUL + TAǮ.

OΓUL-TOÑA   Uyg. 12th c. - 14th c. **Oγul-toña** [Oγul Tonga] (Radl., USp. 206, 248, DTS). ✧ 'Son-Panther' (Blagova 1997, 706). ⇨ OΓUL + TOÑA.

OΓUL-TUWAQ   Trkm. **Oγul-tuwaq** [Огултувак] (Sopieva 181). ⇨ OΓUL + TUWAQ.

OΓUL-UMDU   Uyg. 13th-14th c. **Oγul-umdu-täñrim** [[O]γul Umdu Tngrim], fem. (Zieme, Mat. III, 274). ✧ '(S)he hoped for a son; (S)he expected a son' (Zieme), cf. Karakh. *um-* 'надеяться; ожидать' (DTS). ⇨ OΓUL.

OΓULANLÏ see OΓLANLÏ

OΓULČAQ   Karakh. 893 **Oγulčaq / Oγulǰaq** [Ogulcak / Ogulçak], a Karakhanid ruler, Satuq Boγra-χan's uncle on mother side, better known by his byname Tabyač (Toğan, UTT 59, 81). ✧ 'Little son, little boy' (Erol II). ⇨ OΓUL + suff. *-čaq / -ǰaq*.

OΓULMÏŠ   Maml. 1262 **Oγulmïš** [اغلمش / ناصرالـدين] Oghulmish], a bearer of arms (Sïrat 145). ✧ 'Being rubbed and pressed' cf. *Oğulmuş* 'Sıkı sıkı el gezdirilip basılmış ve sıkılmış' (Erol II).

OΓURLÏ see OΓURLU

OҐURLU Nog. 20th c. **Oɣurlï** [Малик Бестеней улы Огъурлы / Малик Бестенеевич Огурлиев], Baskakov's informant from the aul of Erkin-χalq (Bask., Nog. 143); Nog. 20th c. **Oɣurlï** [Исакей Мана Огъурлы / Исакай Манаевич Огурлиев], one of Baskakov's informants from the aul of Erkin-yurt (Oraɣ-awul) (Bask., Nog. 143); Nog. 20th c. **Oɣurlï** [Нух Огъурлы улы / Нух Огурлиев], father of one of Baskakov's informants from the aul of Erkin-yurt (Oraɣ-awul) (Bask., Nog. 143); Karch. **Oɣurlu** [Огурлу Токовъ] (Sysoev 120); Trkm. 1593 **Oɣurlu-sultan** [Огурлю-султан], from the Bayat tribe (MIT II, 83, 103, 106); Selj. **Uɣurlu** [آغرلو / Muzafferuddīn Ugurlū], Master of the Horse (Aqsarāyī 46, 70, 75, Aqsar./Iş. 47, 54, 58); Selj. 1248 **Uɣurlu** [اغرلو بن ايلك / Uğurlu ibn İlig], İlig's son (Turan: Belleten XII, 100, 119); Turk. 16th c. **Uɣurlu** [Uğurlu] (Ongan, Ank. II, 386, 749, 1304); Turk. 1583 **Uɣurlu** [Uğurlu] (Ongan, Ank. I, 178); Yürük 1543 **Uɣurlu** [اوغورلى / Uğurlu], from the Yürüks of Kocacık, Turkey (Gökb., Rum. 105, 196, 197, 204, 207, 227); Turk. 1540 **Uɣurlu-kethudā** [Uğurlu kethudā], chief of the ethnic community Gündüzlü cemaat (Demirtaş 50). ✧ 'Lucky, bringing good luck, having good chance; having good/happy omen' cf. Crm., Turk. *oɣurlu* 'glücklich, von glücklicher Vorbedeutung' (Radl. I, 1013).

OҐURUODAY Yak. **Oɣuruoday** [Уот Оҕуруодаі], a legendary abāsï (Pek.).

OҐURUOLĀX Yak. **Oɣuruolāχ-oyūn** [Оҕуруолах ojун], a shaman (Pek.). ✧ 'Glass beads' cf. Yak. *oɣuruo* 'мелкие бусы, корольки, бисер; стеклярус' (Pek.). + suff. *-lāχ*.

OҐUTAQQÏ Yak. **Oɣutaqqï** [Оҕутаккы] (Pek.). ✧ 'Arqan (=rope with sling made of horsehair)' cf. Yak. *oɣūr* 'шест с веревочной петлей на конце, укрюк, аркан' (Pek.).

OҐUZ Selj.? 13th c. **Oɣuz** [شمس‌الدين اوغوز], son of the ruler of Amasya Tuɣraq-bek (died in 1235) (Hakkı, Ves. I); Yürük 1543 **Oɣuz** [Oğuz] (Gökb., Rum. 215); Oghuz/Trkm. 13th c. **Oɣuz / Oɣuz-χan** [اوغوزخان / Огуз / Огуз-хан], Qara-χan's son in the Turkic legend of origin, forefather of the Ottoman dynasty (Qazw. 558, 559, 561, Āšikp. 50, Nešrī XIII, 187, Šejb. XXII, RaD I/1, 76, Abulg./Desm. 13, Abulg./Kon. 165, 180-195, 205-215, 225-265, 275-295, 330-345 etc.); Oghuz 13th c. **Oɣuz-alp** [Ογουζάλπης], prince of the Oghuz, Gündüz-alp's son, Er-toɣrul's father (Byz. Turc. 213); Türk 8th c. **Oɣuz-bilgä-tamɣačï** [oɣuz bilgä tamɣačï] (DTS); Oghuz **Oɣuz-qaɣan / Oɣus-qaɣan** [Oğuz Kağan / oɣuz qaɣan / Оҕус-Каҕан] (Radl. I, 1017, II, 72, Oğuz K. Dest. 11, DTS); Selj. 1139 **Oɣuz-oɣlï / Oɣuz-oɣlu?** [غزغلى/غزغلى / Oğuz oğlu], an emir (Ahbar 78). ✧ I. 'Oghuz (ethnical name)'; II. 'Rude, rough, simple, silly' cf. Chag., Turk. *oɣuz* 'ungeschliffen, grob; thöricht, dumm; einfach' (Radl. I, 1017).

OҐUZ-BİLGÄ Türk 732 **Oɣuz-bilgä** [Oɣuz Bilgä] (ETY I, 52). ⇨ **OҐUZ** + **BİLGÄ**.

OҐUZ-BİLGÄ-ТАМҐAČÏ see **OҐUZ**

OҐUZLU Tat. 1543 **Oɣuzlu** [Oğuzlu] (Gökb., Rum. 241). ⇨ **OҐUZ** + suff. *-lu*.

OXAT Chuv. 18th-19th c. **Oχat** [Охатъ] (Magn. 64). ⇨ **OXOT?**

OXATČI Chuv. 18th-19th c. **Oχatči** [Охатчи] (Magn. 64). ⇨ **OXAT** + suff. *-či*. See also **OXOTČI**.

OXATDER Chuv. 18th-19th c. **Oχatder** [Охатдеръ] (Magn. 64).

OXATEY Chuv. 18th-19th c. **Oχatey** [Охатей] (Magn. 64).

OXATKA Chuv. 18th-19th c. **Oχatka** [Охатка] (Magn. 64); Chuv. 18th-19th c. **Oχotka** [Охотка] (Magn. 64).

OXATNİK see **OXOTNİK**

OXATTİ Chuv. 18th-19th c. **Oχatti** [Охатти] (Magn. 64).

OXČÏN Hak. 19th-20th c. **Oχčïn** [Охчын] (HRS 350). ✧ 'Warrior, fighter' (Butanaev).

OXONŌS Yak. **Oχonōs** [Охонос] (Pek.); Yak. **Oqonōs** [Оконос] (Pek.). ✧ Dim. of Yak. *Oχ(q)onōsoi* 'Afanasiy' (R.) (Pek.).

OXONŌSOY Yak. **Oχonōsoy** [Охоносои, Оконосои] (Pek.). ✧ Afanasiy (R.) (Pek.). See also **ANPANÏS**.

OXOT Chuv. 18th-19th c. **Oχot** [Охотъ / Охоть] (Magn. 64); Chuv. 18th-19th c. **Oχotey** [Охотей] (Magn. 64). ⇨ **OXAT**.

OXOTČI Chuv. 18th-19th c. **Oχotči** [Охотчи] (Magn. 64). ⇨ **OXOT** + suff. *-čï*. See also **OXATČI**.

OXOTÄ Chuv. 18th-19th c. **Oχotä** [Охотя] (Magn. 64); Chuv. 18th-19th c. **Oχottä** [Охоття] (Magn. 64). ✧ 'Hunting' cf. Chuv. *uxata / oxata / uxuta* 'охота' (Ashmarin III, 342, 343) <R. *ohota* 'id.'.

OXOTKA see **OXATKA**

OXOTNİK Chuv. 18th-19th c. **Oχatnik** [Охатникъ] (Magn. 64); Chuv. 18th-19th c. **Oχotnik** [Охотникъ] (Magn. 64). ✧ 'Hunter' cf. R. *ohotnik* 'id.'.

OXOTRİ Chuv. 18th-19th c. **Oχotri** [Охотри] (Magn. 64).

OXOTTÄ see **OXOTÄ**

OXŌN Yak. (Dolgan) **Oχōn** [Охон] (Pek.). ✧ 'Arrow' cf. Yak. *oq* 'стрела' + aff. *-ōn*? (Pek.). ⇨ **OQ**.

OXŌNNŪR Yak. **Oχōnnūr** [Охоннур] (Pek.). ✧ Derived from Yak. *Oχōn* + dim. aff. *-lūr* (Pek.). ⇨ **OXŌN**.

OXSUN Bulg. 814-831 **Oχsun** (Byz. Turc. 239).

OY Hak. 19th-20th c. **Oy-χan** [Ойханъ] (HRS 350). ✧ 'Reason, mind, sense; advice' cf. Chag., Alt., Kirg., Kzk., Shor, etc. *oy* (Radl. I. 969).

OY-ČUWAQ Kzk. 19th c. **Oy-čuwaq** [Ойчуакъ]

(SODž. 98). ✧ 'Moon-beam' cf. Tat. dial. *čuaq* 'погожий, ясный' (TatRS), Kirg. *čubaq* 'луч (солнца)' (Jud.), Kzk. *šuaq* 'солнечный луч' (KzRS), Kzk. *šuaq (čōq)* 'der Glanz, der Strahl' (Radl. IV, 1095). ⇨ **OY.**

OY-MOLOT   Alt. 19th c. **Oy-molot** [Ой-Молот-богатырь], a folklore hero (Verb., In. 139). ⇨ **OY + BULAT.**

OYAN   Karg. **Oyan** [Ойан] (Katanov, Otč. 8). ✧ 'Nice, kind' (Butanaev).

OYAÑ   Hak. 19th-20th c. **Oyañ** [Оянъ] (HRS 350). ⇨ **OYAN?**

OYĞU   Kzk. 19th c. **Oyγu** [Ойгу] (SOK 300).

OYÏNČÏ   Alt. 19th-20th c. **Oyïnči** [Ойынчы], fem. (OjrRS 212). ✧ 'Player, playful' (OjrRS).

OYÏNQAY   Kzk. 19th c. **Oynqay-bek** [Ойнкайбекъ] (SODž. 30). ✧ 'Little toy; play; joke, fun' cf. Kzk. *oyïn* 'игра, шалость, шутка'. + dim. suff. *-qay.*

OYQA   Hak. 19th-20th c. **Oyqa** [Ойка] (HRS 350).

OYQUĞA   Tat. 1288 **Oyquγa** [?] (Moravcsik 216).

OYQUĞAČ   Kuman 1288 **Oyquγač**, a christened „Tatar" (woman) (Byz. Turc. 216).

OYLA   Hak. 19th-20th c. **Oyla** [Ойла], fem. (HRS 354). ✧ I. 'Run!' (HRS); II. Ol'ga (R. fem.) (Butanaev), Olya (R. fem.)?

OYLAMAY   Alt. 19th-20th c. **Oylamay** [Ойламай] (OjrRS 207). ✧ 'S/He doesn't run (away), He/She won't escape' cf. Hak. *oyla-* 'laufen, entlaufen' (Radl. I, 981).

OYLAWUQ   Kzk. 19th c. **Oylawuq / Öyläük?** [Ойляукъ] (SOK 54).

OYMAWUT   Kzk. 19th c. **Oymawut** [Оймаутъ] (Grod., Pril. 195); Kzk. 19th c. **Oymawut** [Оймаутъ] (SODž. 152). ✧ An Uzbek tribe (ethnical/tribal name).

OYMÏŠ   Kzk. 19th c. **Oymïš** [Оймышъ] (AOA 142). ✧ 'Digged (out), thought over'? cf. Chag., Alt., Hak., Kzk. *oy-* 'herausgraben, ausmeisseln; durchstossen; genau bedenken' (Radl. I, 970).

OYMOQ   Alt. 19th-20th c. **Oymoq** [Оймок], fem. (OjrRS 212). ✧ 'Thimble' (OjrRS).

OYMON   Alt.(Tel.) **Oymon-qadïn** [Оймон Кадын], mother of fire (Radl. I, 1076).

OYNA   Hak. 19th-20th c. **Oyna** [Ойна], fem. (HRS 354). ✧ 'Play, have some fun!' (HRS).

OYNAQ   Kzk. 19th c. **Oynaq** [Бори-Ойнаковъ] (Grod., Pril. 164). ✧ 'Toy; playground; player, dancer' cf. Chag., Crm., Alt., Hak. *oynaq* 'id.' (Radl. I, 974-75). See also **AT-OYNAQ, BÖRİ-OYNAQ.**

OYNQAY see **OYÏNQAY**

OYNOŠ   Alt. 19th-20th c. **Oynoš** [Ойнош] (OjrRS 209). ✧ 'Lover, sweetheart' (OjrRS).

OYROŠ   Alt. 19th-20th c. **Oyroš** [Ойрош], fem. (OjrRS 212).

OYROT   Alt. 19th-20th c. **Oyrot** [Ойрот] (OjrRS 209); Alt. 19th c. **Oyrot-χan** [Ойрот-царь / Ойрот-хан] (Verb., In. 119, 122, 123). ✧ 'Oyrot (Altay Turk)' (ethnical name).

OYSÏL-QARA   Kzk. 19th c. **Oysïl-qara** [Oysïl-Kara] (Ljutš 151); Kzk. 19th c.? **Oysul-qara** [Oysulkara / Ойсулъ-кара], forefather (and protector) of camels in tales (Potanin II, 152, 153, Atyns. 118, Potanin, Pred. 114). ✧ 'Protector of camels; camel' cf. Kkalp. *oysïl qara* 'покровитель верблюдов; (перен.) верблюд' (KkRS). ⇨ **QARA** + suff. *-sïl / -sul / -čïl?* See also **WAYSÏL-ATA.**

OYSUL-ATA see **WAYSÏL-ATA**

OYSUL-QARA see **OYSÏL-QARA**

OYZÏP   Hak.(Kyz.) 19th-20th c. **Oyzïp** [Ойзып] (Katanov, Otč. 13). ✧ Osip (R.) (Katanov).

OKOČU   Chuv. 18th-19th c. **Okoču** [Окочубай] (Magn. 61). ✧ 'Pupil, scholar, schoolboy' cf. Tat. *uqučï* 'id.' (TatRS).

OKTAY   Tat.(Mish) **Oktay** [Октаевъ], a family (IOAIÊK XIX, 143).

OQ   Selj. **Oq** [Atsïz ibn Ok] (?); Shor 19th-20th c. **Oq** [Külüg Altïn Oq] (Dyrenkova 144); Kzk. 1871 **Oq-ulï? / Oqulï?** [Окули] (Grod., Pril. 130); Kzk. 19th c. **Uq-bay** [Тинъ-кузы Укбаевъ] (Grod., Pril. 37); Kzk. 19th c. **Uq-bay** [Укбай] (AOO 58). ✧ 'Arrow' cf. most of Turkic languages *oq* 'id.' (Radl. I, 988). See also **ALTÏN-OQ, ÜČ-OQ.**

OQ-TEMİR   Chuv. 18th-19th c. **Ok-temir** [Октемиръ] (Magn. 61); Chuv. 18th-19th c. **Ok-timer** [Октимеръ] (Magn. 61); Khorezm.? 13th c. **Oq-temür** [Oqtémour], Qazan-sultan's grandfather (Abulg./Desm. 160); *EN:* Kzk. 18th c. - 19th c. **Oq-temĭr** [Октемр], a clan (Tynyšp. 68). ⇨ **OQ + TEMİR.**

OQ-TEMÜR see **OQ-TEMİR**

OQ-TİMER see **OQ-TEMİR**

OQABAS   Kzk. 19th c. **Oqabas / Oqa-bas?** [Окабасъ] (Grod., Pril. 101).

OQAQA   Hak. 19th-20th c. **Oqaqa** [Окака] (HRS 350).

OQČĀ   Hak. 19th-20th c. **Oqčā** [Окча], fem. (Katanov, Otč. 10). ✧ 'Bow and arrows' (Katanov), '(Martial) Bow' cf. Hak. PN *Oχčā* (Butanaev). See also **YAY, SADAQ.**

OQČÏ   Oghuz/Trkm.? **Oqčï** (DQorq./Rossi 170); Oghuz/Trkm. **Oqčï / Oqči** [Oqčï / Окчи (Окчи-Козан-Сары)], Eksek-qoja's (Ense-qoja's?) son (DQorq./Rossi 170, DQorq. 105, 238, 240, 241); Turk. 19th c. **Oqču-oγlu**, a Zeybek (Kúnos 1891, 119). ✧ 'Archer; maker of arrows' cf. Uyg. *oqčï*, Turk. *oqču* 'id.' (Radl. I, 1001).

OQČU see **OQČÏ**

OQLİS   Hak. 19th-20th c. **Oqlis** [Оклис], fem. (HRS 354).

OQLÏ   Oghuz/Trkm. 13th c. **Oqlï** [اوقلى / Оклы] (Abulg./Kon. 525). ✧ 'Having arrows; with arrows'. ⇨

OQ + suff. -*lï*.

OQO see **OQU**

OQOLDÏ   Kzk. 19th c. **Oqoldï-bay / Oquldï-bay?** [Околдыбай] (SOK 86).

OQONŌS see **OXONŌS**

OQONŌSOY see **OXONŌSOY**

OQSAN   Hak. 19th-20th c. **Oqsan** [Оксан] (HRS 350). ✧ 'Kiss' cf. Hak. *oqsan-* 'id.' (Radl. I, 1002).

OQSÏN   Hak. 19th-20th c. **Oqsin** [Оксин], fem. (HRS 354); Hak.(Blt.) 19th-20th c. **Oqsïn** [Оксін], fem. (Katanov, Otč. 10). ✧ Aksin'ya (R.) (HRS).

OQSÏN see **OQSÏN**

OQSÏQ   Kzk. 19th c. **Oqsïq-pay** [Оксыкпай] (SODž. 40).

OQŠAW   Kzk. 19th c. **Oqšaw-bay** [Окшаубай Айчуваковъ] (AUK 452). ✧ 'Similarity, resemblance' cf. Uyg., Kuman *oqša-* 'ähnlich sein, gleich sein' (Radl. I, 1002). + suff. -*w* / -*u*.

OQTA   Selj. **Oqta** [اوقتا ولد شكتور / Oktä Weled-i-Sīktūr], Šik-tur / Šük-tur's son (Aqsarāyī 305, Aqsar./Iš. 112). ✧ 'Shooting with an arrow' cf. Karakh. *oqta* 'Pfeilschuss' (MK).

OQTUΓAN   Alt. 19th c. **Oqtuɣan** [Окту-ган] (Verb., In. 59). ✧ The name of a spirit (Radl. I, 1001).

OQU   Kzk. 19th c. **Oqo-bay** [Окобай] (SOK 218); Kzk. 19th c. **Oqu-bay** [Окубай] (SODž. 56); Kzk. 19th c. **Oqu-bay** [Окубай] (AOAtb. 14); Kkalp. 1811 **Oqu-bay** [Окубай, Окюбай] (MIKk. 121). ✧ 'Call, invite, shout' cf. Kuman, Chag., Crm., Kirg., Kzk., Turk. *oqu-* 'rufen, einladen, schreien' (Radl. I, 994). ⇨ UQU?

OQUY   Uyg. **Oquy** [Oqui] (Radl., USp. 51, DTS). ✧ I. 'Little arrow?' II. 'Little *Oqu*'. ⇨ OQ / OQU? + dim. suff. -*y*. See also QARA-OQUY.

OQULÏ see **OQ**

OQUM   Kzk. 19th c. **Oqum** [Окумъ] (SOK 32). ✧ 'My little arrow'? ⇨ OQ / OQU? + poss. suff. -*m*.

OQUNČUQ   Kzk. 19th c. **Oqunčuq** [Окунчукъ] (AOK 122).

OQUŠ   Kzk. 19th c. **Oquš** [Окушъ] (SOK 28). ✧ 'Reading; knowledge' cf. Chag. *oquš* 'das Lesen, die Belesenheit, Bildung' (Radl. I, 998).

OLAQ see **ŌLAQ**

OLAQA I.   Kuman 1367 **Olaqa** [Olaka / Oloka], from the Čertan clan of the Kumans of Hungary (Gyárfás III, 503). ✧ '?' (Rásonyi, KÖA 122).

OLAQA II.   Hak. 19th-20th c. **Olaqa** [Олака] (HRS 350).

Kzk. **Olalay** [Олалаі Кан] (Proben III, 134 /169/).

OLAÑ   Hak. 19th-20th c. **Olañ** [Оланъ] (HRS 350). ✧ 'Little lad, boy' cf. Hak. PN *Ōlan* (Butanaev).

OLČA   Hak. 19th-20th c. **Olča** [Олча] (HRS 350); Hak.(Sag.) 19th-20th c. **Ōlča** [Олча] (Proben IX, 613). ✧ 'Little boy'. ⇨ OΓUL + dim. suff. -*ča*?

OLČAY   Hak. 19th-20th c. **Olčay** [Олчай] (HRS 350). ✧ 'Little boy'? ⇨ OLČA + suff. -*y*.

OLǮA   Kzk. 19th c. **Olǯa-bay** [Олджабай] (SOK 280); Kzk. 19th c. **Olǯa-bay** [Олджабай] (SOV 58, 80, 112, 148); Kzk. 19th c. **Olǯa-bay** [Ольджабай] (SOK 44, 280); Kzk. 19th c. **Olǯa-bay** [Олджабай] (SODž. 144); Kzk. 19th c. **Olǯa-bay** [Олджабай] (AOAtb. 30); Kzk. 19th c. **Olǯa-bay** [Ольджабай] (AOA 154); Kzk. 19th c. **Olǯa-bay** [Ольджабай] (AOP 102); Kzk. 19th c. **Olǯa-bay** [Олджабай] (AOK 98); Kzk. 19th c. **Olǯa-bay** [Ольжабай] (AOO 46); Kzk. 19th c. **Olǯa-ɣul** [Олджагулъ] (AOP 18); Kirg. **Olǯo** [Олжо] (Jud. 369); Kirg. **Olǯo-bay** [Олжобай] (Jud. 139); Kirg. **Olǯo-bay** [Олжобай] (Jud. 28); Kzk. 19th c. **Olǯu-bay** [Ольджубай] (SODž. 48); Kirg. 1824 **Ulǯa-bay** [Акимбекъ Ульджебаевъ] (Konšin, Mat. I-III, 70); Kzk. 1846 **Ulža-bay** [Улжабай Сагындыков] (MKOP 155); *TN:* Kzk.? **Olǯa-bay** [Oldža-bai], an isle north-east of Lake Balkhash (IRGO XL). ✧ 'Booty, trophy; prisoner of war' cf. Chag. *olǯa* (Mo.) 'id.' (Radl. I, 1094), Kzk. *olža* 'die Beute, der Erwerb' (Radl. I, 1095), Kirg. *olžo* 'добыча, трофей (на войне, на охоте)' (Jud.), Mo. *olǯa* 'Beute' (TMEN I, No. 27).

OLǮA-GELDI   Kzk. 19th c. **Olǯa-geldi** [Ольджагельды?] (SODž. 154). ✧ 'A booty/trophy has come (has been born); Came as booty'. ⇨ OLǮA + KELDI.

OLǮAY-QUTLUΓ   Khorezm. / Mo.? 13th c. - 14th c. **Olǯay-qutluɣ** [اولجای قتلغ], Ghazan Ilkhan's (1295-1304) and Bulughan Khatun's daughter (RaD/Jahn 105, 107, 150). ⇨ OLǮAY + QUTLUΓ.

OLǮAN   Kzk. 19th c. **Olǯan** [Ирніязъ Олджановъ] (Grod., Pril. 91); Kzk. 19th c. **Olǯan** [Олджанъ] (SOV 126); Kzk. 19th c. **Olǯan** [Олджанъ], fem. (Grod., Pril. 117).

OLǮEKE   Kzk. 19th c. **Olǯeke** [Ольджеке] (SOK 116); Kzk. 19th c. **Ulǯeke** [Ульджеке] (SOK 116).

OLǮO see **OLǮA**

OLǮU see **OLǮA**

OLǮUN   Kzk. 19th c. **Olǯun / Ölǯün?** [Геньджа Олджунова], fem. (Grod., Pril. 192). ⇨ ÖLǮIN?

OLDAŠ   Bashk. 1731 **Oldaš / Yoldaš?** [Усянчи Олдашев] (MIB III, 287); Bashk. 1737 **Oldaš / Yoldaš?** [Олдашев] (MIB I, 344). ⇨ YOLDAŠ?

OLEŠKA   Chuv. 18th-19th c. **Oleška** [Олешка] (Magn. 61). ✧ Alyoshka (R.).

OLGUDEK   Alt. 19th c. **Olgudek** [Ольгудек-богатырь], a folklore hero (Verb., In. 132).

OLΓAR   Bashk. 1754 **Olɣar** [Олгар Якупов] (MIB IV/1, 77).

OLIGUN   Uyg. 1252 **Oligun** [Givargis Oligun] (Chwol., Syr.-nest. (NF) 6).

OLKÏ   Hak. 19th-20th c. **Olkï** [Олки] (HRS 350).

OLODU   Yak. **Olodu-bärgän** [Олоду-бäргäн], a folklore hero (Pek.).

OLON-DOLON   Yak. **Olon-dolon** [Олон-долон] (Pek.).

OLONČU-PAGEN   Alt. 19th c. **Olonču-pagen** [Олончу-Паген] (Verb., In. 140).

OLONČU-PAΓAY   Alt. 19th c. **Olonču-paγay-χan** [Олончу-Пагай-хан] (Verb., In. 145).   ⇨ **BAQA** + suff. -*y*.

OLONQO   Alt. 19th c. **Olonqo** [Олонко] (Potanin IV, 174). ✧ Oloñχō. Heroic poem of the Yakuts.

OLOÑXOLŌN   Yak. **Oloñχolōn** [Олонхолон-бургу], a folklore hero (Pek.). ✧ 'Telling of Oloñχō (the heroic poem of the Yakuts)' cf. Yak. *oloñχolō-* 'излагать героическую поему' + Ger. -*n* (Pek.).

OLOPOČČUYA   Yak. **Olopoččuya** [Олопоччуја] (Pek.).

OLORBO   Yak. **Olorbo** [Олорбо] (Pek.). ✧ 'Seeing badly' (Pek.), cf. *oloy-* 'пучить или таращить глаза, строить глупое лицо' + -*rbo* (Pek.).

OLŌDO   Yak. **Olōdo** [Олодо], a singer, storyteller and quack-doctor (Pek.).

OLŌXŌN   Yak. **Olōχōn** [Олохон] (Pek.).

OLŌN-DOLŌN   Yak. **Olōn-dolōn** [Олон-Долон] (Pek.).

OLTAY   Kzk. 19th c. **Oltay** [Олтай] (SOK 40).

OLTŌQ   Hak. 19th-20th c. **Oltōq** [Олтоок] (HRS 350); Hak.(Sag.) 19th-20th c. **Oltōq** [Олток] (Proben IX, 487, 556, 559).

OLTUQ see **ARTÏQ**

OLTUSUP   Kzk. 19th c. **Oltusup** [Олтусупъ] (SODž. 48).

OLUTAQU   Uyg. 1317 **Olutaqu**, priest Yūχanan's son (Chwol., Syr.-nest. 60).

OM-BAY see **ON**

OM-BES see **ON-BES**

OMAQ   Kzk. 19th c. **Omaq** [Омакъ] (SODž. 70). ✧ 'Lively, nimble' cf. Chag., Hak. *omaq* 'flink, munter, hurtig, leichtfüssig' (Radl. I, 1166).

OMAL   Kzk. 19th c. **Omal-bay** [Омалбай] (SODž. 12).

OMAR   Uyg. 13th c. **Omar** ['omar] (DTS, EUTS); Kzk. 19th c. **Omar** [Eldes Omarov] (Mende 145); Nog. 20th c. **Omar** [Омар Рамазан улы], one of Baskakov's informants from the aul of Qañlï (Bask., Nog. 143); Uyg. **Omar-oγul** [Омар-огул], the idi-qut's envoy sent to Chinggis Khan (RaD I/1, 148); Kirg. **Omor** [Омор] (Jud. 578); Kirg. **Omor** [Омор] (Jud. 650). ✧ Omar (Ar.) (Žanuzakov).

OMBET see **ONBET**

OMÏRT   Kzk. 19th c. **Omïrt-pay** [Омыртпай] (SOV 48).

OMÏRTAY see **OMURTAY**

OMÏŠ   Kzk. 19th c. **Omïš** [Омышъ] (SOK 202); Kzk. 19th c. **Omïš-pay** [Омышпай] (SOV 36).

OMÏT   Kzk. 19th c. **Omït-bay** [Омытбай] (AOP 122).

OMOΓOY   Yak. **Omoγoy-bāy** [Омоҕой-бай], a hero, the great forefather of the Yakut folk; one of Xayarañ's two sons (Pek.).

OMOΓON   Yak. **Omoγon** [Омоҕон (Омоҕoi, Оноҕoi)], the first Yakut who settled down in the place which is now Yakutsk, all important events there were ascribed to his days (Pek.).

OMOLLON   Yak. **Omollon** / **Omollōn** [Омоллон, Омоллон] (Pek.).

OMOLON   Yak. **Omolon** [Омолон], forefather of the ulus of Boturusk who introduced *yasaq* in his ulus (Pek.).

OMONUMA   Yak. **Omonuma** [Омонума], a „scribe of the sky" (Pek.).

OMOR see **OMAR**

OMUQČĀN   Yak. **Omuqčan** [Омукчан], a child (Pek.).

OMUNNUQ   Yak. **Omunnuq** [Омуннук] (Pek.). ✧ Derived from Yak. *omunnā расплошать*' + suff. -*uq* (Pek.).

OMUOČA   Yak. **Omuoča** [Омуоча], a well-known robber (Pek.).

OMUOS   Yak. **Omuos** [Омуос] (Pek.). ✧ Amos (R.) (Pek.).

OMURTAΓ   Bulg. **Murtaγ** [Муртагъ Болгарскій] (PSRL (Russk. Hr.) I, 336); Bulg. 9th c. **Omurtaγ**, Bulghar prince (814-831) (Byz. Turc. 217-218).

OMURTAY   Kzk. 19th c. **Omïrtay** [Омыртай] (SOV 94, 138); Kzk. 19th c. **Omurtay** [Омуртай] (SOK 160); Kzk. 19th c. **Omurtay** [Омуртай] (AOP 114); Kzk. 19th c. **Omurtay** [Омиртай] (AOK 122). ⇨ **OMUR** + **TAY?** or suff. -*tay(1,2)*?

OMURTAQ   Kzk. 19th c. **Omurtaq** [Омуртакъ] (AOAtb. 42).

OMURUYA   Yak. **Omuruya-kinǎs** [Омуруја кінǎс] (Pek.). ✧ 'Resting, taking a break' cf. Yak. *omuruy-* 'делать перерыв в работе для отдыха и еды' (Pek.).

ON   Kzk. 1850 **Om-bay** (<**On-bay**) [Омбаевъ], a sultan (Konšin, Mat. V, 103); Kzk. 19th c. **On-bay** [Онбай] (SOK 138, 176, 222); Kzk. 19th c. **On-bay** [Онбай] (SODž. 86, 88); Kzk. 19th c. **On-bay** [Онбай] (SOV 122, 126); Kzk. 19th c. **On-bay** [Онбай] (Grod., Pril. 80); Kzk. 19th c. **On-bay** [Онбай] (Lomakin 33); Kzk. 1792 **On-bay(-biy)** [اونباى بى / Онбай], a biy (MIK IV, 149); Uyg. 762 **On-čur** [Ončur Yīšöʿyān 'Āsag Tūlīš Yināl Tamgāntarχān] (Mahrnāmag 11); Kzk. 1792 **Un-bay** [Унбай] (MIK IV, 142); *EN:* Kzk. 18th c. - 19th c. **On-bay** [Онбай], a clan (Tynyšp. 67). ✧ 'Ten' cf. several Turkic languages *on* 'ten' (Radl. I, 1042).

ON-BES   Kzk. 19th c. **Om-bes-pay** (<**On-bes-pay**) [Омбеспай] (SODž. 114). ✧ 'Fifteen; the fifteenth child?'. ⇨ **ON** + **BEŠ**.

ON-BOTA   Kzk. 19th c. **On-bota** [Онбота] (SODž.

102). ✧ 'Ten-camel'. ⇨ **ON + BOTA.**

ON-İKEY   Tat.? 18th-19th c. **On-ikey** [Оникей] (Magn. 62). ✧ 'Twelve'? cf. Tat. *unike* 'id.' (TatRS). ⇨ **ON** + suff. *-y.*

ON-TİLÜ   Kzk. 19th c. **On-tilü / On-tilüy?** [Онтилуевъ] (Grod., Pril. 153). ⇨ **ON** + **TİLÜ / TİLÄW.**

ON-TOΓAR   Kzk. 19th c. **On-taγar / On-toγar?** [Онтогаръ] (SOV 122); Kzk. 19th c. **On-toγar** (SOV 122); Kzk. 19th c. **On-toγar / On-taγar?** [Онтагаръ] (SOV 18). ⇨ **ON + TUΓAR?**

ON-TOΓOR   Kzk. 19th c. **On-toγor** [Онтогоръ] (SODž. 60). ⇨ **ON + TUΓUR.** See also **ON-TOΓAR.**

ONAY   Kzk. 19th c. **Onay-bay** [Онайбай] (AOP 42). ⇨ **ON?** + dim. suff. *-ay.*

ONAL see **OÑAL**

ONANAY   Hak. 19th-20th c. **Onanay** [Онанай] (HRS 350). ✧ Ananiy (R.) (HRS).

ONAÑ   Hak. 19th-20th c. **Onañ** [Онанъ] (HRS 350). ✧ Anan? (R.), shortened of Ananiy, cf. Hak. PN *Onan* (Butanaev).

ONĀQ   Hak. 19th-20th c. **Onāq** [Онаак] (HRS 350); Hak.(Sag.) 19th-20th c. **Onāq** [Онак] (Proben IX, 556).

ONBAR   Kzk. 19th c. **Onbar** [Онбаръ] (Grod., Pril. 196).

ONBET   Kzk. 19th c. **Ombet-pek (<Onbet-pek)** [Омбетпекъ] (SODž. 158). ⇨ **ON** + suff. *-bet.*

ONBÏYAQ see **ONPÏYAQ**

ONBÏYAQ   Hak.(Blt.) 19th-20th c. **Onbïyaq / Qän-onbïyaq** [Кан Онбыйак], khan Pespiyäk's and Qosqar's brother (Proben IX, 355, 356, 362). ✧ '(The)-Tenth (child)' cf. Hak. PN *Onpïy / Onpïyaχ* 'десятый' (Butanaev).

ONČA   Kzk. 19th c. **Onča** [Онча] (SOK 88). ⇨ **ON** + dim. suff. *-ča.*

ONČOLŪN   Yak. **Ončolūn-toyon** [Ончолун-тойон] (Pek.).

ONČU   Kzk. 19th c. **Onču-bay** [Ончубай] (SODž. 82).

ONDAS   Kzk. 19th c. **Ondas-pay** [Ондаспай] (SOK 110).

ONDÏ   Kzk. 19th c. **Ondï-bay** [Ондыбай] (AOA 2); Tat. 1635 **Ondï-yar** [Ондеяр], a prince (Miller, Ist. Sib. II, 426). ⇨ **ON** + suff. *-dï.*

ONDÏQ   Hak. 19th-20th c. **Ondïq** [Ондык] (HRS 350). ⇨ **ON** + suff. *-dïq?*

ONDÏQAN   Hak. 19th-20th c. **Ondïqan** [Ондыкан] (HRS 350).

ONDÏRAY   Hak.(Sag.) 19th-20th c. **Ondïray** [Ондырай] (Katanov, Otč. 11); Tuv. 19th c. **Ondïray** [Ондыраi (Андрей Павловичъ Сафьяновъ)], a Russian merchant (Proben IX, 74, 84). ✧ Andrey (R.) (Katanov).

ONDŌ   Yak. **Ondō** [Ондо] (Pek./).

ONDUR   Hak.? 19th-20th c. **Ondur** [Ондур] (Katanov, Otč. 10).

ONIS   Hak. 19th-20th c. **Onis** [Онис] (HRS 350).

ONÏR   Kzk. 19th c. **Onïr-bay** [Онырбай] (SOK 190).

ONYŌXOY   Yak. **Onyōχoy** [Ытык Онjoxoi], fem. (Pek.).

ONYUSAX   Yak. **Onyusaχ** [Онjусах] (Pek.).

ONQUŠ see **OÑQÏŠ**

ONOΓOY   Yak. **Onoγoy / Onoχoy** [Оноβoi, Онохoi], forefather of the Yakuts, Ĵuγun's son (Pek.); Yak. **Onoχoy** [Онохoi] (Pek.). ✧ 'Understanding, appreciation' cf. Mo. *onoqui* 'id.' (Pek.).

ONOXOY see **ONOΓOY**

ONOS   Hak. 19th-20th c. **Onos** [Онос], fem. (HRS 354).

ONŌPUL   Yak. **Onōpul / Onōpur** [Онопул, Онопур] (Pek.). ✧ Onufriy (R.) (Pek.).

ONŌPUR see **ONŌPUL**

ONPÏYAQ   Hak.(Blt.) 19th-20th c. **Onbïyaq** [Он Быйак] (Proben IX, 357-58); Hak.(Blt.) 19th-20th c. **Onpïyaq** [Он пiйак] (Proben IX, 563). ✧ 'The tenth (child)' cf. Hak. PN *Onpïyaχ* (Butanaev). See also **PESPÏYAQ.**

ONPÏYAQ see **ONPÏYAQ**

ONTOLŌN   Yak. **Ontolōn** [Онтолон] (Pek.).

ONTŌN   Yak. **Ontōn** [Онтон] (Pek.). ✧ Anton (R.) (Pek.).

ONTŌRUS   Yak. **Ontōrus** [Онторус] (Pek.).

ONUQ   Karg. **Onuq** [Онук], fem. (Katanov, Otč. 9). ✧ 'The tenth (child)' cf. Hak. *Onoq* (Butanaev).

OÑ   Türk 732 **Oñ-tutuq** [Oñ Tutuq] (ETY I, 44, 60). ✧ I. 'Prince' (Ecsedy), cf. *oŋ* 'Fürst' (TMEN II, 623); II. 'Right; fair, righteous' cf. Uyg., Karakh. *oñ* 'правый; правдивый' (DTS), *oŋ* 'rechts' (TMEN II, 623), Alt., Tat. *uñ* 'recht; das Gute, Richtige' (Radl. I, 1623); III. 'Light, easy; suitable, proper' Karakh. *oŋ* 'легкий; удобный' (DTS).

OÑAY   Kkalp. 20th c. **Oñay** [Оңай] (KkRS 775); Kzk. 19th c. **Oñay-bek** [Оңгайбекъ] (AOP 78); Kkalp. 20th c. **Oñay-bek** [Оңайбек] (KkRS 775). ✧ 'Likely, fitting, agreeable, easy' cf. Uyg., Alt.(Leb.), Kzk., NUyg.(Tar.) *oñay* 'leicht, ohne Schwierigkeit, umgänglich' (Radl. I, 1027), Kkalp. *oñay* 'id.' (KkRS).

OÑAL   Kzk. 19th c. **Oñal-bay** [Оналбай] (SOK 282); Kzk. 19th c. **Oñal** [Онгалъ] (AOK 6); Uzb. 20th c. **Oñal** [Ўнгал], fem. (Begmatov 1984, 206); Uzb. 20th c. **Oñal-ây** [Ўнгалой], fem. (Begmatov 1984, 206); Kzk. 19th c. **Oñal-bay** [Оналбай] (SOV 122); Kzk. 19th c. **Oñal-bay** [Онгалбай] (SOV 120); Kzk. 19th c. **Oñal-bay** [Онгалбай] (SODž. 70). ✧ 'Be better, be healthy' cf. Chag., Kzk. *oñal-* 'sich verbessern, gesund werden, genesen, gedeihen' (Radl. I, 1028).

OÑAR see **OÑΓAR**

OÑAR-BAY-BUTA   Kzk. 19th c. **Oñar-bay-buta** [Онгарбай-Бута Караевъ] (Grod., Pril. 73). ⇨

OÑAR + BAY + BUTA.

OÑARSÏN Uzb. 20th c. **Oñarsïn** [Ӯнгарсин], fem. (Begmatov 1984, 206). ✧ 'Let him make (things) better! Let him make (people) happy/successful!' cf. Uyg., Chag., Crm., Kzk. *oñar- / oñɣar-* 'richtig machen, verbessern, heilen, glücklich machen, gelingen machen' (Radl. I, 1027, 1030), Uzb. *oñɣar-* 'налаживать, поправлять, направлять' (UzbRS).

OÑDASÏN Kzk. 19th c. **Oñdasïn** [Онгдасинъ] (Grod., Pril. 65); Kzk. 19th c. **Oñdasïn** [Онгдасын] (Grod., Pril. 65). ✧ 'Let him make it better, let him correct it' cf. Kzk. *oñda-* 'bessern, verbessern, ausbessern' (Radl. I, 1032).; ✧ 'Let him/her improve!' (Rásonyi, Imp. 239), cf. Kzk. *oñda-* 'bessern, verbessern' (Radl. I, 1032).

OÑGAN Kzk. 19th c. **Oñɣan-χatun** [Онганъ-Хатунъ], fem. (Grod., Pril. 126). ✧ 'Succeeded (gifted, talented) child' cf. Kzk. *oñ-* 'gelingen, gerathen' (Radl. I, 1026).

OÑGAR Kzk. 19th c. **Oñar** [Онгаръ] (SOK 34); Kzk. 19th c. **Oñar** [Онгаръ] (SODž. 50); Uzb. 20th c. **Oñar** [Ӯнгар] (Begmatov 1984, 206); Uzb. 20th c. **Oñar-bây** [Ӯнгарбой] (Begmatov 1984, 206); Kkalp. 20th c. **Oñɣar** [Онгар] (KkRS 775); Kzk. 19th c. **Oñɣar-bay** [Онгар-бай] (Grod., Pril. 23); Kzk. 19th c. **Oñɣar-bay** [Онгарбай] (SOV 20); Kzk. 19th c. **Oñɣar-bay** [Онгарбай] (SOV 10); Kzk. 19th c. **Oñɣar-bay** [Онгарбай] (SOV 80); Kzk. 19th c. **Oñɣar-bay** [Онгарбай] (SOK 116); Kzk. 19th c. **Oñɣar-bay** [Онгарбай] (SOK 216); Kzk. 19th c. **Oñɣar-bay** [Онгарбай] (SOV 30); Kkalp. 20th c. **Oñɣar-bay** [Онгарбай] (KkRS 775); Bashk. 1723 **Uñɣar** [Унгар Елумбетев] (MIB III, 219-20); Bashk. 1735 **Uñɣar** [Унгаръ Кулушевъ], a tarχan (?) (Vel.-Zern., Bašk. 13); Bashk. 1740 **Uñɣar** [Унгар Тургаев] (MIB I, 397); Bashk. 18th c. **Uñɣar** [Абдулла Унгаров] (MIB V, 415); Bashk. 1754 **Uñɣar** [Унгар Рыскулов] (MIB IV/1, 84); Bashk. 1754 **Uñɣar** [Унгар Буракаев] (MIB IV/1, 90); Bashk. 1754 **Uñɣar** [Еман Унгаров] (MIB IV/1, 83); Bashk. 1755 **Uñɣar** [Иштан Унгаров] (MIB IV/1, 101); Bashk. 1756 **Uñɣar** [Емангул Унгаров] (MIB IV/1, 121); Bashk. 1757 **Uñɣar** [Унгар Муранаев] (MIB IV/1, 139, 274); Bashk. 1761 **Uñɣar** [Назаргул Унгаров] (MIB IV/1, 218); Bashk. 1761, 1762 **Uñɣar** [Ярыш Унгаров] (MIB IV/1, 205, 251); Bashk. 1770 **Uñɣar** [Илтуган Унгаров] (MIB IV/1); Bashk. 1770 **Uñɣar** [Сыртлан Унгаров] (MIB IV/1, 343); Bashk. 1773 **Uñɣar** [Унгар Кушумбаев] (MIB IV/2, 413); Bashk. 1793 **Uñɣar** [Унгар Смагилов] (MIB V, 328); Kzk. 1819 **Uñɣar** [Унгар] (MIK IV, 325); Kzk. 19th c. **Uñɣar** [Ункарбай] (SODž. 160); Kzk. 19th c. **Uñɣar** [Унгорбай] (SOK 64); Kzk. 19th c. **Uñɣar-bay** [Унгорбай] (SOK 64); *EN:* Crm. 1638 **Otuz Oñɣar (u)ruɣ** [غور انغار اوتوز], clan of the Thirty Oñɣars

(Vel.-Zern., Crim. 227); *TN:* Kzk. **Uñɣar** [Унгаръ], a village in the region of the Ču river (Vyšnegorskij: Tr. Syr-D. OSK 16). ✧ I. 'He will succeed; he will be successful' cf. Kzk. *oñ-* 'gelingen, gerathen' (Radl. I, 1026), Kkalp. *oñ-* 'быть удачным; быть удачливым; налаживаться' (KkRS), Uzb. *ong-* 'удаваться, оправиться' (UzbRS); II. 'Make (him) happy, make (him) successful; make (him/it) better; heal (him)' cf. Uyg., Chag., Crm., Kzk. *oñar- / oñɣar-* 'richtig machen, verbessern, heilen, glücklich machen, gelingen machen' (Radl. I, 1027, 1030). See also **ALLA-OÑAR.**

OÑQAQ Hak.(Koyb.) 19th c. **Oñqaq** [Онгкакъ], fem. (Katanov, Otč. II, 12-15). ✧ 'Snub nosed' (Katanov), cf. Hak. PN *Onχaχ* (Butanaev).

OÑQÏŠ Kzk. 19th c. **Oñqïš / Onqïš?** [Онкышъ] (SODž. 136); Kzk. 19th c. **Oñquš-pay / Onquš-pay?** [Онкушпай] (SOK 182).

OÑLA Kzk. 19th c. **Oñla-bay** [Онлабай] (SOK 46); Kzk. 19th c. **Oñla-bay / Onla-bay** [Онлабай] (SOK 286). ✧ 'Make him/it better (right), correct him/it, heal him' cf. Chag., NUyg.(Tar.), *oñla-* 'auf den rechten Weg führen, zurechtweisen, belehren, verbessern' (Radl. I, 1031), Kzk. *oñda-* 'bessern, verbessern, ausbessern' (Radl. I, 1032).

OÑOGOSTŌN-ČUOQAN Yak. **Oñoɣostōn-čuoqan** [Оноѳостон-Чуокан], a person in a tale (Pek.).

OÑUR Kzk. 19th c. **Oñur-bay** [Онгурбай] (SOK 298); Kzk. 19th c. **Oñur-bay** [Онгурбай] (SOK 304); Kzk. 19th c. **Oñur-bay** [Онгурбай] (SOK 308); Kzk. 19th c. **Uñur-bay** [Унгурбай] (SOK 66). ✧ 'Make (him) happy, make (him) successful; make (him/it) better; heal (him)' cf. Uyg., Chag., Crm., Kzk. *oñar-, oñur-* 'richtig machen, verbessern, heilen, glücklich machen, gelingen machen' (Radl. I, 1027). ⇨ **OÑGAR.**

OPČÏN see **OVČÏN**

OPČÏN see **OVČÏN**

OPONČA Hak. 19th-20th c. **Oponča** [Опонча] (HRS 350). ✧ Afon'ša (R.) (Butanaev).

OPONQA Hak. 19th-20th c. **Oponqa** [Опонка] (HRS 350); Hak.(Sag.) 19th-20th c. **Opōnqa** [Опонка] (Proben IX, 460-62). ✧ Afon'ka (R.) (Katanov), cf. Hak. PN *Opan* 'Афанасий' (Butanaev).

OPORUOS see **OPURUOS**

OPPAYNĀ Tuv. 19th c. **Oppaynā** [Оррайпа] (Proben IX, 42). ✧ Afonya (R.) (Katanov).

OPPOY Yak. **Oppoy** [Оппоі] (Pek.). ✧ 'Throw lips out' cf. Yak. *oppoy-* 'вытянуть губы настолько, что.то другим бросается в глаза' (Pek.).

OPPOYO Yak. **Oppoyo** [Оппоjо] (Pek.). ✧ 'Throwing his/her lips out' cf. Yak. *oppoy-* 'вытянуть губы настолько, что.то другим бросается в глаза' + aff. -*a* (Pek.).

OPPUONYA Yak. **Oppuonya** [Оппуоnja], fem. (Pek.). ✧ Afanasiya (R.) (Pek.). ⇨ **OPUONA.**

OPPURUOSA Yak. **Oppuruosa** [Оппуруоса], fem. (Pek.). ✧ Evfrosiniya (R.) (Pek.). See also **OPRAS, OPROSİN, OPURUOS.**

OPRAS Hak. 19th-20th c. **Opras** [Опрас], fem. (HRS 354). ✧ Efrosin'ya (R. fem.) (HRS), cf. Hak. fem. PN *Opïras* 'Ефросинья (Butanaev).

OPROSİN Hak. 19th-20th c. **Oprosin** [Опросин], fem. (HRS 354); Hak. 19th-20th c. **Oprosïn** [Опросін] (Katanov, Otč. 13). ✧ Efrosin'ya (R. fem.)? ⇨ **OPRAS?**

OPROSİN see **OPROSİN**

OPUONA Yak. **Opuona** [Опуона], fem. (Pek.). ✧ Afonya (R.), dim. of R. *Afanasiya* (Pek.). ⇨ **OPPUONYA.**

OPURUOS Yak. **Oporuos** [Опоруос], fem. (Pek.); Yak. **Opuruos** [Опуруос], fem. (Pek.). ✧ Frosya (R.) (Pek.). See also **OPRAS, OPROSİN, OPPURUOSA.**

OR Kkalp. 20th c. **Or-jan** [Оржан] (KkRS 775); Oghuz.? **Or-χan** [Ор-хан], Dib-yaquy's son (RaD I/1, 76); Khorezm. 13th c. **Or-χan** [اور خــان / Urchan dux / Орхан], one of Sultan Meñgü-berdi's (1220-1231) emirs (Ĵuwaynī II, 14, 148, 163, Abulfar. Or. 308, MIT I, 483); Turk. **Or-χan** [Ορχάνης] (Byz. Turc. 221-222); Turk. 1394 **Or-χan** [اورخـان / Orhan Beǧ], an emir in Asia Minor yielded to Timur (Timür) in 1394, Saruhanoǧlu İshak Beǧ's son, died in 1402 (Astarab., Erol II); Khorezm. 13th c. **Or-χan / Ur-χan?** [ارخـان], Ĵelāl's emir (Nasawī 88); Turk. 1430 **Or-χan-beg** [بك اورخـان], Ibrahim-beg's son, an Isfendiarid (MB Qastam. 73); Turk. 15th c. **Or-χan-bey** [Orhan Bey] (Gökb., Ed. 6, 161, 162); Selj. / Turk. 14th c. **Or-χan-γāzi** [اورخـان غـازی / Orhan Gazi], a ruler of the Ottoman dynasty (1324-1362), Osman's son, Murad I's father (Āšikp. 3, 5, 19, 22, Nešrī 190, Togan, UTT 317, 318, 323 etc.); Turk. 1489 **Or-χan-kātib** [Orhan Kâtib] (Gökb., Ed. 156); Uyg. **Or-tegin** [اور تـكيـن] (Ĵuwaynī I, 41); Kzk. 19th c. **Or-žan** [Оржанъ] (SODž. 112); Türk 7th-9th c. **Ur** [Ur] (ETY III, 135); Kzk. 19th c. **Ur-bay** [Урбай] (AOAtb. 66); Türk 7th-9th c. **Ur-beg** [Ur Beg / Ur Bäg] (ETY III, 133); Oghuz/Trkm. 13th c. **Ur-χan** [اور حــان / Ур-хан], Moγol-χan's son (Abulg./Kon. 160, 205, 215); Kzk. 19th c. **Ur-χan** [Урханъ] (SOK 162); *TN:* Turk. 20th c. **Orχanlï** [Orhanlı], a village in Turkey (TMİB 457). ✧ I. 'Dike, trench, pit; earthwork (fort) protected by a ditch' cf. Kuman, Chag., Crm., Kzk., Turk. *or* 'id.' (Radl. I, 1046); II. 'Neither dark nor light (of colours of animals), greyish' cf. Kzk., Alt.(Tel.) *or* 'nicht dunkel und nicht hell (von Pferden); grau' (Radl. I, 1047). Gordlevskij (1913, p. 131) derived the name *Or-χan / Ur-χan* from the verb stem *ur-/vur-* interpreting it as „Khan, beat (it)!".

OR-MAMBET Kzk. 1817 **Or-mambet** (MIK IV, 308); Nog. / Kzk. 19th c. **Ur-manbet** [Урманбетъ], a Noγay biy in a Kazak legend of origin (Potanin, Pred. 54-55). ⇨ **OR + MAMBET.**

ORA Trkm. 1859 **Ora-išan** [Ора-ишан], from the Yomut tribe (MIT II, 598).

ORA-NİYAZ Trkm. 19th c. **Ora-nyaz / Ora-niyaz / Oran-niyaz?** [Ораньязъ Сафаргельдіевъ] (Ščeglov IV, 183). ⇨ **ORA/ORAN + NİYAZ?**

ORAQ Chuv. 18th-19th c. **Orak** [Оракъ] (Magn. 62); Kzk. 19th c. **Oraq** [Оракъ] (Potanin, Pred. 100); Kzk. 19th c. **Oraq** [Оракъ] (SOV 126); Kzk. 19th c. **Oraq** [Оракъ] (AOP 110); Kkalp. 20th c. **Oraq** [Орақ] (Bask., Kkalp. 63, KkRS 775); Nog. 1909 **Oraq** [Оракъ], Mamay's mythical nephew, a hero of the Noghay epic (Farforovskij 26); Kzk. 19th c. **Oraq-bay** [Оракбай] (SODž. 58); Kkalp. 20th c. **Oraq-bay** [Орақбай] (KkRS 775); Kzk. 19th c.? **Oraq-batïr** [Orak], a folklore hero, Ali-bek's father (Atyns. 78); Kkalp. 1822 **Oraq-biy** [Орак бий], from the Qañlï tribe (MIKk. 127); Crm. 1629 **Oraq-mïrza** [اوراق ميـرزا] (Vel.-Zern., Crim. 40); Crm. 1642 **Oraq-oγlï** [اوراق اوغلى] (Vel.-Zern., Crim. 321, 496); Kzk. 19th c. **Oraq-pay** [Оракпай] (SOV 88); Kzk. 19th c. **Oraq-pay** [Оракпай] (SOK 54, 88, 158, 180); Kirg. 20th c. **Oroq-bay** [Орокбай], from Southern Kirghizia (Kalilov 92); Tat. 1496, 1499, 1500 **Uraq** [Уракъ], a prince from Kazan (PSRL VI, 40, 44, VIII, 231, 237, XII, 250, XX, 369, PSRL (Russk. Hr.) I, 514); Tat. 1673 **Uraq** [Дивѣй мурза Ураковъ] (AI IV, 506); Tat. 1717 **Uraq** [Урак Яныбеков] (MIB III, 152); Tat. 1738 **Uraq** [Кил-Мухаммедь Ураков] (MIB I, 144); Tat.(Mish.)? 1549 **Uraq** [Уракъ] (PSRL (Russk. Hr.) I, 529); Bashk. 1706 **Uraq** [Урак Аныбеков] (MIB III, 30); Bashk. 1708 **Uraq** [Уряк Чукалев] (MIB I, 234); Bashk. 1753 **Uraq** [Урак Абдулин] (MIB IV/2, 426); Bashk. 1760 **Uraq** [Урак Абдулов] (MIB IV/1, 195); Bashk. 1778-1790 **Uraq** [Урак / Ураков] (MIB V, 71-392); Bashk. 1791 **Uraq** [Алибай Ураков] (MIB V, 309); Kzk.? 1496 **Uraq** [Уракъ] (PSRL XII, 242); Kzk. 1785 **Uraq** [Урак] (MIK IV, 63); Kzk. 1819 **Uraq** [Урак] (MIK IV, 326); Kzk. 19th c. **Uraq** [Уракъ] (AOK 118); Kzk. 19th c. **Uraq** [Уракъ] (SOV 52); Crm.? 17th c. **Uraq-murza** [Уракъ-мурза], Qan-temir's brother (Smirnov, Krym. 512); Nog.? 1626, 1649 **Uraq-murza** [Уракъ Шихимовъ] (AI III, 460, IV, 79); Nog. 1649 **Uraq-murza** [Уракъ Шигимовъ] (AI IV, 79); Nog. 1649 **Uraq-murza** [Уракъ] (AI IV, 87); Kzk. 19th c. **Uraq-pay** [Уракпай] (SODž. 100); *EN:* Nog. 20th c. **Oraq** [Оракъ], an Aq-noγay clan in the district of Mineralovodsk, county of Cherkessk (Bask., Nog. 133, 142). ✧ 'Sickle, hook, scythe; harvest' cf. Chag., Az., Crm., Kar., Kzk., Tat., Turk. *oraq, uraq* 'id.' (Radl. I, 1049, 1651), Kkalp. *oraq* 'id.' (KkRS).

ORAQ-GELDİ Trkm. 20th c. **Oraq-geldi-aγa**, a person in a modern short story (?). ⇨ **ORAQ + KELDİ.**

ORAQ-MAMAY Crm. **Oraq-mamay-mïrza** [Орак Мамаі Мырза] (Proben VII, 194-95). ⇨ **ORAQ + MAMAY.**

ORAQČÏ see **ORAQČÏ**

ORAQČÏ Kuman (Crm.) 13th c. **Oraqči** [Оракчи] (Smirnov, Krym. 34); Tat.(GH) 14th c. **Oraqčï** [Ορακτζή], a christened Tatar (Byz. Turc.); Tat. 1601 **Uraqčï** [Уракчей (Буранчеев)] (Miller, Ist. Sib. II, 165). ✧ 'Mower, harvester' cf. Turk. *oraqčï* 'id.' (Radl. I, 1050), Tat. *uraqčï* 'der Schnitter, der Mäher' (Radl. IV, 1651). ⇨ **ORAQ** + suff. *-čï*.

ORAQTAY Kzk. 19th c. **Oraqtay** [Орактай] (SOK 140). ⇨ **ORAQ + TAY?** + suff. *-tay(1,2)?*

ORAL Kzk. 19th c. **Oral** [Оралъ] (SOV 80, 114); Kzk. 19th c. **Oral** [Оралъ] (Grod., Pril. 35); Kzk. 19th c. **Oral** [Оралъ] (AOO 10); Kzk. 19th c. **Oral** [Оралъ] (AOAtb. 6, 50); Kkalp. 20th c. **Oral** [Орал] (KkRS 775); Kkalp. 20th c. **Oral** [Орал], fem. (KkRS 778); Kzk. 19th c. **Oral-bay** [Оралбай] (AOK 134); Kzk. 19th c. **Oral-bay** [Оралбай] (SODž. 60, 70, 136); Kzk. 19th c. **Oral-bay** [Оралбай] (SOK 84, 88, 104, 164, 202); Kzk. 19th c. **Oral-bek** [Оралбекъ] (AOO 58); Kzk. 19th c. **Oral-bek** [Оралбекъ] (SOV 58); Kkalp. 20th c. **Oral-biyke** [Оралбийке], fem. (KkRS 778). ✧ I. 'Wrap yourself in; be winded' cf. Alt., Hak., Kzk. *oral-* 'id.' (Radl. I, 1051); II. 'Satisfaction, being satisfied' cf. Kzk. *oral* 'id.' (Radl. I, 1051).

ORAMAL Kzk. 19th c. **Oramal** [Орамалъ] (SODž. 46). ✧ 'Kerchief, diaper; towel' cf. Kzk. *oramal* (P. romal) 'id.' (Radl. I, 1052).

ORAMAN Hak. 19th-20th c. **Oraman** [Ораман] (HRS 350). ✧ Roman (R.) (HRS).

ORAN Kzk. 19th c. **Oran** [Оранъ] (AOO 30); Kzk. 19th c. **Oran-bay** [Оранбай] (Grod., Pril. 159); Kzk. 19th c. **Oran-bay** [Оранбай] (SOK 244). ⇨ **ORAL?**

ORANTAY Kzk. 19th c. **Orantay** [Орантай] (SODž. 80). ⇨ **ORAN +TAY?** + suff. *-tay(1,2).*

ORAP Kzk. 19th c. **Orap-pay** [Ораппай] (SOV 44).

ORAPİS Hak. 19th-20th c. **Orapis** [Орапис] (HRS 350). ✧ Arefiy (R.) (Butanaev) <Ar. *ḥarata.*

ORAS see **ORAZ**

ORASQA see **URAZQA**

ORAZ Chuv. 18th-19th c. **Aras** [Арасъ] (Magn. 24, 29); Kzk. 1732 **Aras** [Арасъ] (Dobrosm., Turg. 10); Kzk. 19th c. **Aras-bay** [Арасбай] (SOK 160); Kzk. 1734 **Aras-batïr** [Арасъ Батыръ] (PSZRI IX, 303); Trkm. (Yomud) **Araz** [Араз], from the Yomud tribe (Sopieva: OSA 179); Trkm. (Yomud) **Araz-bibi** [Аразбиби], fem. (Sopieva: OSA 179); Trkm. (Yomud) **Araz-gözel**, fem. (Sopieva: OSA 179); Trkm. (Yomud) **Araz-gül**, fem. (Sopieva: OSA 179); Chuv. 18th-19th c. **Oras** [Орасъ] (Magn. 62); Kzk. 19th c. **Oras** [Орасъ] (Grod., Pril. 143); Hak. 19th c. **Oras** [Орас] (Katanov, Otč. 12); Chuv. 18th-19th c. **Oras-pay** [Ораспай] (Magn. 62); Trkm. **Oraz** [Ораз], fem. (Sopieva 179); Trkm. 20th c. **Oraz** [Oraz] (Zaj. 1971, 332); Tat.(Lit.) 1593 **Oraz** [Оразъ Кудашевичъ] (Lit. Tat. 176, 177); Kzk. 18th c. - 19th c. **Oraz** [Ораз] (Tynyšp. 70, 74, 75); Kzk. 19th c. **Oraz** [Оразъ] (Grod., Pril. 118, 177, 185, 196); Kkalp. 20th c. **Oraz** [Ораз] (KkRS 775); Trkm. 19th c. **Oraz-bay** [Oraz-Bai] (Mende 149); Kzk. 19th c. **Oraz-bay** [Исджанъ Оразбаевъ] (Grod., Pril. 50); Kzk. 19th c. **Oraz-bay** [Оразбай] (SODž. 36); Kzk. 19th c. **Oraz-bay** [Оразбай] (Grod., Pril. 35, 145, 163); Kzk. 19th c. **Oraz-bay** [Оразбай] (SOK 38); Kzk. 19th c. **Oraz-bay** [Дусджанъ Оразбаевъ], İs-jan Oraz-bayev's brother (Grod., Pril. 50); Kzk. 19th c. **Oraz-bay** [Моллабай Оразбаевъ] (Grod., Pril. 100); Kzk. 19th c. **Oraz-bay** [Оразбай Мурадовъ] (Grod., Pril. 104); Kzk. 1879 **Oraz-bay** [Калдарбекъ Оразбаевъ] (Grod., Pril. 129); Kzk. 1884 **Oraz-bay** [Алнокуръ Оразбаевъ] (Grod., Pril. 94); Kkalp. 20th c. **Oraz-bay** [Оразбай] (KkRS 775); Kkalp. 20th c. **Oraz-bay** [Оразбай] (Bask., Kkalp. 77); Trkm. **Oraz-bibi** [Оразбиби], fem. (Sopieva 179); Uzb. 1628 **Oraz-biy / Oraz-beχadur** [Ораз-бий / Ораз-бехадур] (MIT II, 108, 109); Kkalp. 20th c. **Oraz-biyke** [Оразбийке], fem. (KkRS 778); Tat.(Lit.) 1592 **Oraz-Jan** [Ораждчанъ Гурповичъ] (Lit. Tat. 124); Trkm. 20th c. **Oraz-gül** [Orazgül], fem. (Zaj. 1971, 340); Kkalp. 20th c. **Oraz-gül** [Oraz-gül / Оразгюл / Оразгул], fem. (Bask., Kkalp. 403, KkRS 778, Baskakov: OSA 140); Trkm. 1847 **Oraz-χan** [Ораз-хан], an aqsaqal (MIT II, 241-242, 249, 253-255, 262, 264, 268, 307, 309); Kzk. 19th c. **Oraz-qul** [Оразъ-Кулъ Иръ Магомедовъ] (Grod., Pril. 91); Trkm. 1918 **Oraz-sardar** [Oraz-Sardar], commander of the „white" troops in Turkestan (Castagné 23); Trkm. 19th c. **Oraz-serdar** [Oraz-Serdar] (Mende 149); Chuv. 18th-19th c. **Uras** [Урасъ] (Magn. 89); Bashk. 1687 **Uras** [Урасъ Тлевбердеевъ] (Vel.-Zern., Bašk. 34); Tat. 1600 **Uras-qul** [Ураскул / Ураксул] (Miller, Ist. Sib. II, 156); Chuv. 18th-19th c. **Uras-pay** [Ураспай] (Magn. 89); Chuv. 18th-19th c. **Uras-patïr** [Ураспатыръ] (Magn. 89); Tat. 1768 **Uraz** [Уразъ], from Tambov (Nikol'skij 274); Tat. 18th-19th c. **Uraz** [Уразъ] (Magn. 89); Bashk. 1734 **Uraz** [Гулъ Уразовъ] (PSZRI IX, 336); Bashk. 1735 **Uraz** [Уразъ Тюринъ], a tarχan (Vel.-Zern., Bašk. 23); Bashk. 1735 **Uraz** [Теликешъ Уразовъ], a tarχan (Vel.-Zern., Bašk. 13); Bashk. 1735 **Uraz** [Биімбеть Уразовъ] (Vel.-Zern., Bašk. 13); Kzk. **Uraz** [Уразъ Араповъ] (ZIRGOOrenb. III, 26); Kzk. 19th c. **Uraz** [Уразъ] (Grod., Pril. 132); Kzk. 19th c. **Uraz** [Чалабай Уразовъ] (SKSO III, 19); Bashk. / Tadj.? 1735 **Uraz**

[Якупъ Уразовъ] (Vel.-Zern., Bašk. 25); Trkm. 19th c. **Uraz-bay** [Уразбай Джулдыбаевъ] (SKSO III, 178); Chuv. 18th-19th c. **Uraz-bay** [Уразбай] (Magn. 89); Bashk. 1735 **Uraz-bay** [Уразбай Куреевъ], a tarχan (Vel.-Zern., Bašk. 23); Bashk. 18th c. **Uraz-bay** [Уразбай / Уразбаев] (MIB V, 415); Bashk. 1762 **Uraz-bay** [Уразбай Сапаров] (MIB IV/1, 238); Bashk. 1787 **Uraz-bay** [Кулук Уразбаев] (MIB V, 219, 313); Kzk. 19th c. **Uraz-bay** [Уразбай] (Grod., Pril. 84); Uzb. 1704 **Uraz-behadïr** [اوراز بهادر], from the Nayman in Bukhara tribe (Buchari 274); Bashk. 1735 **Uraz-γul** [Уразгулъ Акчувашевъ], a tarχan (Vel.-Zern., Bašk. 16); Bashk. 1756 **Uraz-γul** [Тиментей Уразгулов] (MIB IV/1, 123); Bashk. 1756 **Uraz-γul** [Алиш Уразгулов] (MIB IV/1, 119); Kzk. 19th c. **Uraz-χoja** [Уразъ Ходжа / Уразъ-Ходжа] (Grod., Pril. 87, 116); Nog. 1542 **Uraz-mïrza** [Уразъ-мырза] (PSRL XIII, 140); *TN:* Kzk.? **Aras-pay-kül** [Араспай-куль], a lake (Karta JAR III); 19th c. **Araz-mula (-mulla?)** [Аразъ-мула], a tomb north of the Caspian sea? (IIRGO XVI); Kzk.? **Uraz-χan** [Уразханъ] (Karta JAR XX). ✧ I. 'The ninth month of the Muslim lunar year when the feast *Oraza* is celebrated' (Sopieva 179), '(Month of) Fast' (Baskakov: OSA 140), Muhamedova (1957, 40) derives it from *Oraza*; II. 'Chance, luck' (Zaj. 1971, Sattarov), cf. Chag., Tat. *uraz* 'das Glück, die glückliche Vorbedeutung' (Radl. I, 1655), Bashk. *uraδ* 'счастье, талан' (BRS/Uraksin) (<P.); III. 'Angry, cross with sb.'? cf. Kzk. *araz* 'zornig, uneinig' (Radl. I, 260) (<Ar.). See also **BAY-URAZ, BUXT-URAZ, KELDİ-URAZ.**

ORAZ-ALİ   Uzb. 1779 **Oraz-ali** [Ораз Али, Башмак], from the Mañγït tribe (MIT II, 352); Kkalp. 20th c. **Oraz-γaliy** [Оразғалий] (KkRS 775); Kzk. 19th c. **Ors-alï (<Oras-alï?)** [Орсалы] (SODž. 78); Kzk. 1820 **Uraz-ali** [Уразали], a chieftain (Sib. Vest. IX, 120); Kzk. 19th c. **Uraz-ali** [Торабай Оразалиевъ] (Grod., Pril. 98); Kzk. 19th c. **Uraz-ali** [Менджанъ Уразалиевъ] (AUK 865); Kzk. 19th c. **Uraz-alï** [Уразалы] (SOK 32); Kzk. 1920 **Uraz-alï / Oraz-alï?** [Ursala(!)] (Fox 172); *TN:* Kkalp. 19th c. **Uraz-ali** [اورازعلی / Уразъ Али], a settlement (qïšlaq) in the tümen of Šeraz (Širazskij tumen') named after the aqsaqal (ZIRGOStat. IV). ✧ 'Lucky Ali' cf. Kzk. PN *Oraz-alï* (Žanuzakov 153, Žanuzakov-Esbaeva), Tat. PN *Uraz-γali / Uraz-ali* (Sattarov). ➪ **ORAZ(A) + ALİ.**

ORAZ-ALÏ see ORAZ-ALİ

ORAZ-BERDİ   Trkm. **Oraz-berdi** [Оразберди] (Sopieva 179). ✧ 'The Oraz-month has given him; born in the Oraz-Month'. ➪ **ORAZ + BERDİ.**

ORAZ-ГALİY see ORAZ-ALİ

ORAZ-KELDİ   Uzb. 20th c. **Orâz-keldi** [Ўрозкелди] (Begmatov 1984, 203); Kzk. 19th c. **Ras-keldi (<Uras-keldi)** [Раскельды] (SOK 164); Chuv. 18th-19th c. **Ras-kilde (<Uras-kilde)** [Раскилда (Ураскильтъ?)] (Magn. 70); Tat.? 1612 **Roz-gildey / Raz-gildey** [Яшкильдѣй Розгильдѣевъ / Разгильдѣевъ] (Nižegorod. platež. 199, 201); Chuv. 18th-19th c. **Uras-kilde** [Ураскилда] (Magn. 89); Nog. 1649 **Uraz-geldi** [Уразъ-Гелдѣй Токумбетевъ] (AI IV, 123); Tat. 18th-19th c. **Uraz-gilde** [Уразгилда] (Magn. 89); Bashk. 1761 **Uraz-gilde** [Уразгильда Кузайгулов] (MIB IV/1, 218); Trkm. 1859 **Uraz-gildi** [Кучакъханъ Уразгильдіевъ] (ZIRGOEtn. I, 157); Tat. 19th c.? **Uraz-gildi** [Уразгильди] (IOAIÊK XIX, 141); Bashk. 1735 **Uraz-gildi** [Уразгильди Куреевъ], a tarχan (Vel.-Zern., Bašk. 23); Bashk. 1738 **Uraz-gildi** [Уразгилды Тентяков] (MIB I, 143); Bashk. 1742 **Uraz-gildi** [Уразгильды Талтиков] (MIB III, 513); Bashk. 1756 **Uraz-gildi** [Жиянак Уразгильдин] (MIB IV/1, 109); Tat.(Mish) 19th c. **Uraz-keldi** [Уразгильди] (Ahmarov: IOAIÊK XIX, 141); *EN:* Kzk. 18th c. - 19th c. **Oraz-geldi** [Оразгельды] (Tynušр. 68, 74); *TN:* Chuv. 1738 **Uras-keldinï** [Ураксильдины(!)], a village (Alatyr. 138). ✧ 'Fortune, luck has come (has been born)' (Ahmarov, Sattarov). ➪ **ORAZ + KELDİ.**

ORAZ-МАГОМЕТ   Kzk. 19th c. **Oras-maγomed** [Орасъ Магомедъ] (Grod., Pril. 173). ➪ **ORAZ + MAXMED.**

ORAZ-MURAD   Trkm. 1881 **Oraz-murad-usta** [Оразъ-Мурадъ-Уста] (Grod., Vojna IV, 18). ➪ **ORAZ + MURAT.**

ORAZ-TUWAQ   Trkm. **Oraz-tuwaq** [Оразтувак], fem. (Sopieva 179). ➪ **ORAZ + TUWAQ.**

ORAZA   Kzk. 19th c. **Oraza-bay** [Оразабай] (SOK 44); Chuv. 18th-19th c. **Orza (<Oraza)** [Орза] (Magn. 62); Chuv. 18th-19th c. **Orza-bay (<Oraza-bay)** [Орзабай] (Magn. 62); Chuv. 18th-19th c. **Uraza** [Ураза] (Magn. 89). ✧ 'Fast(ing)' cf. Hak. *oraza* (P.) 'die Fasten' (Radl. I, 1052), Kirg. *orozo* 'пост у мусульман в течение месяца' (Jud.), Kzk. *oraza* 'пост' (RKzS), Tat. *uraza* 'id.' (Radl. I, 1655) (<P.)

ORAZA-NİYAZ   Trkm. 19th c. **Oraza-niyaz** [Менгильбай Оразаньязовъ] (Ščeglov IV, 184). ➪ **ORAZA + NİYAZ.**

ORAZAY   Karch. 20th c. **Orazay** [Orazáj] (Pröhle, Kar. 126); Chuv. 18th-19th c. **Orazay** [Оразай] (Magn. 62); Kirg. **Orozoy** [Орозой] (Jud. 135, 700); Chuv. 18th-19th c. **Orzay (<Orazay)** [Орзай] (Magn. 62); 1683 **Urazay** [Уразайка Чичкановъ] (DAI X, 378); Tat. **Urazay** [Тлевъ Уразаевъ] (AI V, 402); Tat.? 1695 **Urazay** [Уразай], an interpreter (DAI X, 381); Tat. 1698 **Urazay** [Уразайко Буталинъ], a captain (Kungursk. akty 267), Tat. 1780, 1796 **Urazay** [Аюхан Уразаев] (MIB V, 103, 104, 362, 363); Tat. 18th-19th c. **Urazay** [Уразай] (Magn. 89); Bashk. 1686 **Urazay**

[Шекерка Уразаевъ], a tarχan (Vel.-Zern., Bašk. 40);
Bashk. 1709 **Urazay** [Юразай] (MIB I, 264); Bashk.
1709 **Urazay** [Уразай] (MIB I, 255); Bashk. 1714
Urazay [Уразай Тюлянов] (MIB I, 105); Bashk. 1735
Urazay [Теушъ Уразаевъ], a tarχan (Vel.-Zern.,
Bašk. 13); Bashk. 1743 **Urazay** [Юзей Уразаев]
(MIB III, 540); Bashk. 18th c. **Urazay** [Уразай]
(Nepljuev 181); Bashk. 1781 **Urazay** [Сеит (Сагит)
Уразаев] (MIB V, 125, 126, 299); Kzk. 19th c. **Urazay**
[Уразай] (SOK 26); Kzk. 19th c. **Urazay** [Уразай]
(SOK 248). ⇨ **ORAZA** + dim. suff. *y*.

ORAZÏMBET Kkalp. 20th c. **Orazïmbet** [Оразымбет]
(KkRS 775); Kkalp. 20th c. **Orazïmbet** [Оразымбет]
(Bask., Kkalp. 94). ⇨ **ORAZ** + suff. *-ïmbet*. See also
URAZ-MAMET, URAZÏMBET.

ORAZLA Chuv. 18th-19th c. **Orazla** [Оразла] (Magn.
62). ✧ 'Happy, lucky'. ⇨ **URAZLÏ.**

ORBAY Hak. 19th-20th c. **Orbay** [Орбай] (HRS 350).
✧ 'Shaman's drumstick (=shaman's successor)'
(Butanaev), cf. Shor *orba* 'der Schlägel, mit dem der
Schaman seine Trommel schlägt' (Radl. I, 1077), Hak.
orba 'колотушка для шаманского бубна' (HRS).
+ dim. suff. *-y*.

ORBOČİ Alt. 19th-20th c. **Orboči** [Орбочы] (OjrRS
209). ✧ 'He who makes (or carries) the shaman's
drumstick; the shaman's successor?' cf. Alt. *orbo*
'колотушка для шаманского бубна' (OjrRS). +
suff. *-čï*.

ORBOY Yak. **Orboy-udaγan** [Орбой-удаҕан], fem.
(Pek.). ✧ 'Throw your lips out' cf. Yak. *orboy-*
'выставлять, вытягивать (губы)' (Pek.).

ORBOLJUN Yak. **Orboljun-udaγan** [Орболцун-
удаҕан], a shamaness (Pek.). ✧ 'Throwing her lips out'
cf. Yak. *orboy-* 'выставлять, вытягивать (губы)' +
aff. *-ljuy* + *-n* (Pek.). See also **ORBOY.**

ORČA Kzk. 19th c. **Orča-bay** [Орчабай] (SODž. 26).
✧ 'Neither dark nor light (of colours of animals),
greyish' cf. Kzk., Alt.(Tel.) *or* 'id.' (Radl. I, 1047). ⇨
OR + suff. *-ča*.

ORDA Chuv. 18th-19th c. **Orda** [Орда] (Magn. 62);
Kzk. **Orda-bay** [Орда Баі] (Proben III, 32 /39/); Kzk.
19th c. **Orda-bay** [Ордабай] (AOK 94); Kzk. 19th c.
Orda-bay [Ордабай] (SOK 14); Kzk. 19th c. **Orda-
bay** [Ордабай] (SOV 28); Kkalp. 20th c. **Orda-bay**
[Ордабай] (KkRS 775); Kkalp. 20th c. **Orda-bay**
[Ордабай] (Bask., Kkalp. 401); Kzk. 19th c. **Orda-γul**
[Ордагулъ] (SOK 64); Kzk. 19th c. **Orda-χan**
[Ордаханъ] (SOK 262); Khorezm.? **Orda-tikin**
[Орда-Тикин] (RaD II, 70); Kzk. 19th c. **Ordo-bay**
[Ордобай] (SOV 28, 116); Kzk. 19th c. **Ordo-bay**
[Ордобай] (AOK 14); Kzk. 19th c. **Ordo-bay**
[Ордобай] (AOO 66); Kirg. **Ordo-bay** [Ордобай]
(Jud. 251, 398); Kzk. 19th c. **Urda-bay** [Урдабай]
(SKSO III, 10); *TN:* Kzk. 1862 **Ordo-bay** [Ордобай],

a field in the district of Kopal (ZIRGOGeogr. I, 314). ✧
'Tent of the ruler, the khans dwelling place, court,
palace' cf. Kuman *orda* 'Rathaus?, Hoflager?, curia'
(CC), Chag., Az., Kzk. etc. *orda* (Mo.) 'der Palast; das
Zelt des Sultans' (Radl. I, 1072), Kkalp. *orda* 'ханская
ставка; ставка знатного лица; богатая юрта
знатного лица' (KkRS), Kirg. *ordo* 'id.' (Jud.).

ORDİK Hak. 19th-20th c. **Ordik** [Ордик] (HRS 350).

ORDİÑ Hak. 19th-20th c. **Ordiñ** [Ординъ] (HRS 350).

ORDİS Hak. 19th-20th c. **Ordis** [Ордис] (HRS 350).

ORDO see **ORDA**

ORDŌXŌN Yak. **Ordōχōn** [Ордохон] (Pek.). ✧
'Crying, boasting' cf. Yak. *ordōtō* 'кричать (о
шамане); бодреть (хорохориться)' (Pek.).

ORDU Kzk. 19th c. **Ordï-bay** [Ордыбай] (AOK 74);
Kzk. 19th c. **Ordu-bay** [Ходжаханъ Ордубаевъ]
(Grod., Pril. 158); Maml.? 1422 **Ordu-bay / Ordï-bay**
[ارد باى/الست/] (Ibn Taghrīb. VI, 554, 556); Maml.?
1449 **Ordu-bay / Ordï-bay?** [ارد باى] (Ibn Taghrīb.
VIII, 44); Uyg. **Ordu-beg** [Ordu beg] (EUTS); Oghuz?
Ordu-χan [اوردو / Ordou-khan], great-grandson of
„Tatar khan" in a legend of origin (Abulg./Desm. 11);
Turk. 1380 **Ordu-šah** [اوردو شاه], governor of Erzurum
(Astarab. 167). ✧ 'The khan's tent; palace, the camp of
the khan' cf. Uyg., Chag. *ordu* 'id.' (Radl. I, 1072). ⇨
ORDA.

ORDU-BAŠÏ Maml. 1472/73 **Ordu-bašï** [ورد بش/],
governor of Beyrut (Iyās II, 141); Maml. 1474/75
Ordu-bašï [ورد بش] (Iyās II, 151, 201); Maml. 1478
Ordu-bašï [ورد بش الظاهرى] (Iyās II, 182); Maml.
1484 **Ordu-bašï** [ورد بش], governor of Haleb (Iyās II,
224); Maml. 1518 **Ordu-bašï** [ورد بش], governor of
Tripolis, chancellor (Iyās III, 186). ✧ 'The head of an
Ordu; butler' cf. Karakh. *ordu bašy* 'fürstlicher
Kammerdiener' (MK/Brock.), *ordu baši* 'дворецкий'
(DTS). ⇨ **ORDU** + **BAŠ.**

ORDU-BUΓA Maml. 1421 **Ordu-buγa** [ارد بغا] (Ibn
Taghrīb. VI, 331, 499). ⇨ **ORDU** + **BUQA.**

ORDUJA Khorezm. 14th c. **Orduja** [اردجا /
Ourdoudjâ], Mohammed Özbek's fourth wife (Ibn Bat.
II, 395). ⇨ **ORDU** + suff. *-ja.*

ORDUΓA NUyg.(Tar.) **Orduγa** [Orduga Bai / Ордуҕа
Баі] (Proben VI, 152 /202/).

ORDUQ Uyg. **Orduq** [Orduk] (EUTS).

ORΓAY Kzk. 19th c. **Orγay-bay** [Оргайбай] (SODž.
20).

ORΓAM-BAY see **ORΓAN**

ORΓAN Kzk. 19th c. **Orγam-bay** (<Orγan-bay)
[Оргамбай] (SOV 148); Kzk. 19th c. **Orγan-bay**
[Органбай] (SOV 120).

ORXON Chuv. 18th-19th c. **Orχon** [Орхонъ] (Magn.
63).

ORİNE Hak. 19th-20th c. **Orine** [Орине], fem. (HRS

354). ✧ Irina (R.).

ORĬNČA Hak.(Kyz.) 19th-20th c. **Orĭnča** [Орiнча], fem. (Katanov, Otč. 13). ✧ Orinča (R. fem.), dim. of R. fem. PN *Irina*.

ORĬM-BAY see **ORUN**

ORĬMBET Kkalp. 20th c. **Orĭmbet** [Орымбет] (KkRS 775); Kzk. 19th c. **Orumbet** [Орумбетъ] (SOV 40, 72); Kkalp. 20th c. **Orumbet** [Орумбет] (Bask., Kkalp. 68, 91). ⇨ **OR** + suff. *-ĭmbet*.

ORĬN-BÂSAR Uzb. 20th c. **Orĭn-bâsar** [Уринбосар] (Begmatov 1984, 201). ✧ 'Deputy, substitute' cf. Uzb. *orïnbâsar* 'id.' (UzbRS). ⇨ **BASAR**.

ORĬNŠA Kkalp. 20th c. **Orĭnša** [Орынша], fem. (KkRS 778). ⇨ **ORUN** + suff. *-ša*.

ORQAY Hak. 19th-20th c. **Orqay** [Оркай] (HRS 350).

ORQUM-BAY see **ORQUN**

ORQUN Kzk. 19th c. **Orqum-bay (<Orqun-bay)** [Оркумбай] (SOK 264).

ORLO Hak.(Shor) 1630 **Orlo** [Орло] (Miller, Ist. Sib. II, 368).

ORMAQ Kzk. 19th c. **Ormaq** [Ормакъ] (SOK 34, 130); Kzk. 19th c. **Ormaq** [Ормакъ] (AOP 30).

ORMAM-BEK see **ORMAN**

ORMAN Kzk. 19th c. **Ormam-bek (<Orman-bek)** [Ормамбекъ] (SODž. 78); Kzk. 19th c. **Ormam-bek (<Orman-bek)** [Ормамбекъ] (SOV 70); Kzk. 19th c. **Orman** [Орманъ] (AOA 134); Kzk. 19th c. **Orman** [Орманъ] (SOV 4, 34); Kzk. 19th c. **Orman** [Орманъ] (SODž. 116); Kzk. 19th c. **Orman** [Орманъ] (SOK 20, 52); Kzk. 19th c. **Orman** [Орманъ] (SODž. 36, 58); Kzk. 19th c. **Orman** [Орманъ] (SOV 106, 134); Kirg. 1845 **Orman** [Орманъ Нiазбековъ] (Konšin, Mat. V, 72); Kzk. 19th c. **Orman-bay** [Орманбай] (AOA 6); Kkalp. 20th c. **Orman-bay** [Орманбай] (KkRS 775); Kkalp. 20th c. **Orman-bay** [Орманбай] (Bask., Kkalp. 99); Kzk. 1809, 1823 **Orman-saltan** [اورمان سلطان] (MIK IV, 242, 454); Kirg. 19th-20th c. **Ormon**, from the region of Narin (Prinz 328); Chuv. 18th-19th c. **Urman** [Урманъ] (Magn. 89); Bashk. 1709 **Urman** [Урман Байсарыев] (MIB I, 264); Bashk. 1714 **Urman** [Урман Семенов] (MIB III, 108); Bashk. 1738 **Urman** [Урман Семенов] (MIB III/1, 387); Bashk. 1750 **Urman** [Ишкильда Урманов] (MIB III, 472); Bashk. 1755 **Urman** [Урман Кукин] (MIB IV/1, 101); Kzk. 1801 **Urman** [Урманъ] (Dobrosm., Turg. 232); Kzk. 1805 **Urman** [Урманъ Нуралiевъ] (Dobrosm., Turg. 241); Kzk. 1822 **Urman** [Чингалiй Урмановъ] (TOUAK XXIV, 132); Kzk. 19th c. **Urman** [Урманъ] (Grod., Pril. 101); Kzk. 19th c. **Urman** [Урманъ] (SOK 150); Kzk. 19th c. **Urman** [Урманъ] (Veselovskij, Kirg. 65); Kzk. 19th c. **Urman** [Урманъ] (Grod., Pril. 130); Kirg. 1847, 1851 **Urman** [Урманъ], head (manap) who yielded to the Russians in 1847 (Smirnov, Sultany 16, Archiv W. K. Russl. IX, 403, Konšin, Mat. V, 105, ZIRGO V, 141); Kzk. 19th c. **Urman-biy** [Урманбiй] (Grod., Pril. 162); Bashk. 1780 **Urman-ɣul** [Урмангул Биганов] (MIB V, 105); Kzk. 1820 **Urman-sultan** [Урманъ], a chieftain (Sib. Vest. IX, 121). ✧ 'Forest, wood' cf. Chag., Crm., Kzk., Turk. *orman* 'der Wald' (Radl. I, 1077).

ORMANČA see **ORMANČĬ**

ORMANČĬ Chuv. 18th-19th c. **Ormanča** [Орманча] (Magn. 62); Bashk. 1781 **Urmanča / Urmančĭ?** [Урманча Юмакаев] (MIB V, 128); Bashk. 1675 **Urmančey** [Урманчейко] (MIB I, 204); Tat. 18th c. **Urmančeyeva** [Урманчеева], a village in the district of Mamadyš (Korsakov 243); Bashk. 1734 **Urmančĭ** [Урманчи Илбахтын], a tarχan (Vel.-Zern., Bašk. 10); Bashk. 1740 **Urmančĭ** [Урманчи Бигеев] (MIB I, 427); Bashk. 1758 **Urmančĭ** [Урманчи Минлибаев] (MIB IV/2, 20); Bashk. 1764 **Urmančĭ** [Урманчи Минлибаев] (MIB IV/1, 284); Bashk. 1780 **Urmančĭ** [Измаил (Смаил) Урмачин] (MIB V, 113); Kzk. 19th c. **Urmančĭ** [Урманчи] (AOAtb. 58); Tat. 1650 **Urmančĭ / Urmančey** [Урманчеевъ] (Zolotn. 159); Bashk. 1765 **Urmančĭ / Urmančey** [Урманчи / Урманчей] (MIB IV/1, 316); Tat. 1624 **Urmančĭ / Urmančiy** [Урманчей Калчюринъ] (Pokrovskij 71); Bashk. 1739 **Urmančĭ / Urmančiy** [Урманчей Аккушева], fem. (MIB III, 406); Bashk. 1664 **Urmansĭ** [Урмансы (Юрманчи, Урманчей)] (MIB I, 192); Chuv. 1737 **Vurmanču** [Вурманчу] (Alatyr. 136); *EN*: Kzk. 18th c. - 19th c. **Ormančĭ** [Орманчы], a clan (Tynyšp. 68); Nog. 20th c. **Ormanšĭ-uruw** [Орманшы урув], a Qara-noɣay clan (Bask., Nog. 136, 1429). ✧ 'Forester, woodman' cf. Tat. *urmančĭ* 'der Waldwächter' (Radl. I, 1673), Bashk. *urmansĭ* 'id.' (BRS). ⇨ **ORMAN** + suff. *-čĭ*.

ORMANŠĬ see **ORMANČĬ**

ORMANTAY Kzk. 19th c. **Ormantay** [Ормантай] (SOV 120). ✧ 'Wooded; owner of a wood' cf. Sattarov: *Urmantay / Urmanday*. ⇨ **ORMAN** + suff. *-tay(1,2)*?

ORMATAY Kzk. 19th c. **Ormatay** [Орматай] (SOV 96); Kirg. **Ormotoy** [Ормотой] (Jud. 21). ⇨ **ORMANTAY?** + suff. *-tay(1,2)*?

ORMOQAY Kzk. 19th c. **Ormoqay** [Ормокай] (SOV 106); Kzk. 19th c. **Ormoqay** [Ормокай] (SOK 76).

ORMON see **ORMAN**

ORNUQ Kzk. 19th c. **Ornuq-pay** [Орнукпай] (SOK 114).

OROJUMAN Yak. **Orojuman** [Ороцуман] (Pek.). ✧ Radivon, Rodion (R.) (Pek.).

OROY Alt. 19th-20th c. **Oroy** [Орой] (OjrRS 209). ✧ 'The little; child born last in the family' (OjrRS), cf. Alt. *oroy* 'spät' (Radl. I, 1053).

OROY-BŪRAY Yak. **Oroy-bŭray** [Орои-бураi Ор(Уор?)-Цасын], Thundergod (Pek.).

OROYQO-DOXSUN Yak. **Oroyqo-doχsun / Oroyqo-bōtur** [Оройко Дохсун / Оройко-Ботур], a folklore hero (Pek.).

OROYOQO-MOROYOQO Yak. **Oroyoqo-moroyoqo** [Оройоко-Моройоко] (Pek.). ✧ 'Shameless cheek (=man, nose, lips)' (Riddle). ⇨ **OROYQO.**

OROQ see **ORAQ**

OROQAY Trkm. 19th c. **Oroqay** [Нуретъ Орокаевъ] (Ščeglov IV, 175).

OROM-BAY see **ORUN**

ORON see **ORUN**

ORON-TAY see **ORUN-TAY**

OROÑO see **URUÑU**

OROZMAT Kirg. 20th c. **Orozmat** (Aytmatov). ⇨ **ORAZ** + suff. -*mat*. See also **ORAZĪMBET, ORAZ-МАΓОМЕТ.**

OROZOЎ see **ORAZAY**

ORS-ALİ see **ORAZ-ALİ**

ORSULAY Uyg. 12th c. - 14th c. **Orsulay** [Orsulay] (DTS, EUTS).

ORTA Kzk. 19th c. **Orta-bay** [Ортабай] (SOV 124). ✧ 'Middle (child)' (Sattarov: Urta), cf. in several Trk. languages: *orta* 'die Mitte, die Hälfte' (Radl. I, 1064).

ORTAQ Türk 865 **Ortaq-čur / Ornat-čur?** (Tabarī, Annal. III, 1543, 1544).

ORTAM Kzk. 19th c. **Ortam-bay / Ortan-bay?** [Ортамбай] (SOK 180).

ORTŌYUQ Yak. **Ortōyuq** [Ортоjук] (Pek.).

ORU Kzk. 19th c. **Oru-bay** [Орубай] (SOV 50); Uyg. 8th c. - 12th c. **Oru-χara / Uru-χara** [Oru / Uru χara] (Müller, Pfahl. 12). ✧ 'Harvest, cutting' cf. Uyg., Chag., Alt., Kirg., Kzk. *or-* 'mähen, ernten; schneiden' (Radl. I, 1047). + dev. suff. -*u*.

ORUČ Turk.?, Maml.? 1421 **Oruč** [اوروج], Temür-taš' son (Āšikp. 86, 92, 95, 96); Yürük 1543 **Oruč** [اوروج / Oruç], from the Yürüks of Kocacık, Turkey (Gökb., Rum. 180, 182, 197, 199 206, 225, 229); Yürük 16th c. **Oruč** [Oruç] (Gökb., Rum. 101, 180, 182, 193, 197, 198, 199, 229, 240 etc.); Tat. 1543 **Oruč** [Oruç] (Gökb., Rum. 238, 240); Maml. 1315, 1316 **Oruč / Uruč?** [سيف الدين ارج / اروج / Уруджъ], emir, envoy to (Desht-i) Kipchak (Nuwairī 145, 167, Duqmaq/Tizeng. I, 317, 324); Turk. 15th c. **Oruč-beg (Oruč-bey)** [Οροὺτζπεγις], a commander of the army (Byz. Turc. 220); Turk. **Oruč-bey** [Oruç Bey] (Uzunçarş., Anad. 54); Turk. 1489 **Oruč-χan** [Oruçhan] (Gökb., Ed. 156); Yürük 1543 **Oruč-χan** [اوروج حان / Oruçhan] (Gökb., Rum. 104); Yürük 16th c. **Oruč-χan** [Oruç-han] (Gökb., Rum. 104); Turk. 1485 **Oruč-paša** [Oruç Paşa] (Gökb., Ed. 246, 247); Turk. 16th c. **OruJ** [Oruc] (Ongan, Ank. II); Turk. 1583 **OruJ** [Oruc] (Ongan, Ank. I, 173); Turk. 16th c. **UruJ** [Uruc] (Baştav 63, 66, 75, 76, 90); Turk. 1552, 1565, 1570 **UruJ** [Uruj]

(Dávid); Turk. 1580 **UruJ** [Uruj bin Hamza] (Dávid); Turk. 1580 **UruJ** [Pir Ali bin Uruj] (Dávid); Turk. 1590 **UruJ-aγa** [Urudzs aga], an „ulûfeci" (clerk/secretary of Janissary guards, or palace servants) from Lippa (Velics-Kamm. I, 379); *TN:* Turk. 20th c. **Oruč** [Oruç], a village in the province of Samsun, Turkey (TMİB 750); Turk. 20th c. **Oruč-bey** [Oruçbey], a village in the province of Adana, Turkey (TMİB 13); Turk. 20th c. **Oruč-bey** [Oruçbey], a village in the province of Giresun, Turkey (TMİB 389); Turk. 20th c. **Oruč-γazi** [Oruçgazi], a village in the province of Adana, Turkey (TMİB 18). ✧ 'Fast(ing)' cf. Az., Crm., Turk. *oruč* (P.) 'das Fasten' (Radl. I, 1059).

ORUČMAN Yürük 1543 **Oručman** [Oruçman] (Gökb., Rum. 224); Tat. 1543 **Oručman** [اورجمان / Oruçman] (Gökb., Rum. 234, 236); Yürük 1543 **OruJman** [اورجمان / Orucman] (Gökb., Rum. 176). ⇨ **ORUČ** + suff. -*man*.

ORUJ see **ORUČ**

ORUJMAN see **ORUČMAN**

ORUQ Kzk. 19th c. **Oruq-pay** [Орукпай] (SODž. 126). ⇨ **ARUQ.**

ORULUOS-DOXSUN Yak. **Oruluos-doχsun** [Орулуос дохсун] (Pek.). ✧ 'A kind of duck (Fuligula clangula), mallard - harsh (coarse, rude)' (Pek.), cf. Yak. *oruluos* 'гоголь (род нырка)' and *doχsun (kihi)* 'дерзкий, нахальный, резкий человек' (JRS).

ORUM-BAY see **ORUN**

ORUMBET see **ORÏMBET**

ORUN Kzk. 19th c. **Orïm-bay (<Orïn-bay)** [Орымбай] (AOA 50); Kkalp. 20th c. **Orïn-bay** [Орынбай] (KkRS 775); Kkalp. 20th c. **Orïn-bek** [Орынбек] (KkRS 775); Kkalp. 20th c. **Orïn-biyke** [Орынбийке], fem. (KkRS 778); Kkalp. 20th c. **Orïn-gül** [Орынгул], fem. (KkRS 778); Kzk. 19th c. **Orom-bay (<Orum-bay <Orun-bay)** [Оромбай] (AOA 102); Kzk. 19th c. **Orum-bay (<Orun-bay)** [Орумбай] (SOK 82, 162); Kzk. 19th c. **Orum-bay (<Orun-bay)** [Орумбай] (SODž. 106, 158); Kzk. 19th c. **Orum-bay (<Orun-bay)** [Орумбай] (AOK 26); Kzk. 19th c. **Orum-bay (<Orun-bay)** [Орумбай] (AOO 14, 58); Kzk. **Orun** [Orun Bai / Орун Баи], a singer on the side of Sultan Turdu-bek (Proben III, 43 /55/); Kzk. 19th c. **Orun-bay** [Orunbay] (Ljutš 124); Kzk. 19th c.? **Orun-bay** [Orunbay] (Atyns. 83); Kzk. 19th c. **Orun-bay** [Орунбай] (AOA 22); Kkalp. 1806 **Orun-bay** [Орунбай], a biy (MIKk. 98, 109 etc.); Kkalp. 1810 **Orun-bay** [Орунбай] (MIKk. 110, 111 etc.). ✧ 'Place, location, position' cf. in several Trk. languages: *orin, orun* 'Stelle, Ort, Platz' (Radl. I, 1055, 1057), Karakh. *orun* 'id.' (DTS), Kkalp. *orin* 'место, местность; должность; служба, пост; постель' (KkRS), Kkalp. fem. *Orin-gül* 'разумная роза [=intelligent, clever rose]' (Baskakov: OSA 141).

ORUN-TAY Kzk. 19th c. **Oron-tay** [Оронтай] (SODž. 14, 52); Kzk. 19th c. **Orun-tay** [Орунтай] (SOK 138); Kzk. 19th c. **Orun-tay** [Орунтай] (SOV 46, 80). ⇨ **ORUN** + **TAY** + suff. *-tay(1,2)*?

ORUÑU see **URUÑU**

ORUÑU-YARAMÏŠ Uyg. 8th c. - 12th c. **Oruñu-yaramïš** [Orungu Yaramïš] (Mahrnāmag 10). ⇨ **URUÑU** + **YARAMÏŠ.**

ORUS see **URUS**

ORUS-QOŠČİ Uzb. 1804 **Orus-qošči-behadïr** [Орус-кошчи-бехадыр], from the Qïyat clan (MIT II, 365, 372). ⇨ **URUS** + **QOŠČİ.**

ORUSKE Tat. 1552 **Oruske** [Оруске] (Kn. Metriki Lit. 85). ⇨ **URUS** + suff. *-ke* <comp. *-ake.*

ORUZ I. Uyg. 12th c.- 14th c. **Oruz / Orus** [oruz / Orus] (Radl., USp., 127, 114-15, DTS, EUTS). ⇨ **ORAZ?**

ORUZ II. Yürük 1543 **Oruz** (Gökb., Rum. 212); Turk. 1568 **Oruz-χatun** [Oruz Hatun], fem. (Gökb., Ed. 321); *TN:* Turk. 1528 **Oruz** [Oruz (Köy)], a village (Gökb., Ed. 328); Turk. 1530 **Oruz** [Oruzlu (Köy)], a village (Gökb., Ed. 78, 375). ✧ 'Idea, thought' cf. Turk. dial. *oruz* 'Fikir, düşünce' (DS).

ORUZ III. Kirg. **Oruz-bay (Orus-bay?)** [Орузбай] (Jud. 187). ✧ I. 'Russian'; II. 'Fast' cf. Chag. *oruz* 'das Fasten' (Radl. I, 1060). ⇨ **ORAZ / URUS?**

ORZA see **ORAZA**

ORZAY see **ORAZAY**

ORZAQAY see **URAZAQAY**

OS-KİLDİ Bashk. 1735 **Os-kildi** [Оскилди Уруспаевъ], a tarχan (Vel.-Zern., Bašk. 20). ⇨ **UZ** + **KELDİ.**

OSAL Kzk. 19th c. **Osal** [Осалъ] (SOV 138). ✧ 'Weak, not hard' cf. Kzk. *osal* 'слабый, некрепкий, непрочный' (KzRS).

OSAM-BAY see **OSAN**

OSAN Kzk. 19th c. **Osam-bay (<Osan-bay)** [Осамбай Исантайлаковъ] (Grod., Pril. 48).

OSQA Kkalp. 1735 **Osqa** [Оска Уразметов] (MIKk. 207); Hak.(Sag.) 19th-20th c. **Osqa** [Оска] (Katanov, Otč. 7).

OSMAN Bashk. 1749 **Гusman / Гosman** [Гусман Якупов] (MIB III, 465); Oghuz/Trkm. **Osman** [Осман] (DQorq. 11); Oghuz/Trkm. **Osman** [Осман], Affan's son (DQorq. 12); Oghuz/Trkm. 13th c. **Osman** [عثمان / Осман-хан], İl-tegin-χan's son (Abulg./Kon. 1005, 1010); Karakh. **Osman** [osman] (DTS); Nog. 20th c. **Osman** [Осман Халил улы Доьрмен / Осман Халилович Дурменов], one of Baskakov's informants from the aul of Adil-χalq (Bask., Nog. 143); NUyg.? 19th c. **Osman-bek** [Osman Bek] (Hedin, En färd I, 165); Kirg. **Osmon** [Осмон] (Jud. 324, 595); Kzk. 19th c. **Ospan** [Ospan] (AUK 697); Kkalp. 20th c.

Ospan [Оспан] (KkRS 775); Kzk. 19th c. **Ospan-bay** [Оспанбай] (SOV 20); Kzk. **Ospan-qan** [Оспан Кан] (Proben III, 30 /36/); Kzk. 19th c. **Span < Ospan** [Сспанъ] (SOV 94); Kzk. 19th c. **Span-bek < Ospan-bek** [Спанбекъ] (SOV 32); Bashk. 1756 **Usman** [Беккине / Беккиня Усманов] (MIB IV/1, 134); Kzk. **Uspan** [Успанъ] (PKTO 40); *TN:* **Osman-bay** [Осман-бай], a well south-west of Cherchen (Karta JAR XX). ✧ Osman (Othman) (Ar.), the name of the third Caliph (Ahmed).

OSMANJÏQ Turk. **Osmanjïq-beg** [Osmandschik Beg] (Hezarfenn-Mordtmann: ZDMG XXX, 470). ✧ 'Little Osman'. ⇨ **OSMAN** + dim. suff. *-jïq.*

OSMÏŠ see **OZMÏŠ-TOГRÏL**

OSMON see **OSMAN**

OSPAN see **OSMAN**

OSPAR Kzk. 19th c. **Ospar-bay** [Оспарбай] (SOK 202).

OSTĀP Hak.(Blt.) 19th-20th c. **Ostāp** [Остап], fem. (Katanov, Otč. 9). ✧ Ostap(ka) (R.), dim. of R. *Evstafiy.*

OSTÏ Kzk. 19th c. **Ostï-bay** [Остыбай] (SOK 82).

OSU Kzk. 19th c. **Oso-bay** [Особай] (SODž. 28); *TN:* Kzk.? **Osu-bay** [Osu bai], a bay of Lake Balkhash (Rekogn.).

OSUQ Uyg. 12th c. - 14th c. **Osuq** (DTS).

OSUM Turk. 1475 **Osum-bey** [Osum-Bey (köy)], a village (Gökb., Ed. 276).

OŠAR Kzk. 19th c. **Ošar** [Ошаръ] (AOO 14). ⇨ **USAR?**

OŠÏM Kzk. 19th c. **Ošïm-bek** [Ошимбекъ] (SOV 80).

OŠOQ see **OČAQ**

OŠUR NUyg.? 19th c. **Ošur-bek** [Oschur Bek] (Hedin, En färd I, 236, 251).

OT Hak.(Sag.) 19th-20th c. **Ot** [От], a folklore hero (Proben IX, 220); Tat.(GH) 13th c. **Ot-aba?** [Οτάβας], a christened Tatar (Byz. Turc. 222); Kzk. 1823 **Ot-bay** [اوتبای / Отбай] (MIK IV, 457); Oghuz/Trkm. 13th c. **Ot-qan** [اوتکان / Откан], Enkeš' son (Abulg./Kon. 665); Hak.(Sag.) 19th-20th c. **Ot-qan** [От Кан] (Proben IX, 450-51); Chuv. 18th-19th c. **Ot-murza** [Отмурза] (Magn. 63); Kzk. 19th c. **Ot-pay** [Отпай] (SOV 6); Kzk. 19th c. **Ut-bay** [Утбай] (SKSO II, 14); Bashk. 1758 **Ut-qul** [Уткул Сабанаев] (MIB IV/1, 168); Kzk. 19th c. **Ut-qul-bay** [Уткульбай] (SOK 60); Kzk. 19th c. **Ut-qul-bay** [Уткюльбай] (SOK 32). ✧ 'Fire', cf. in several Trk. languages: *ot* 'das Feuer' (Radl. I, 1096). See also **TÖDÖ-OT.**

OT-BAS Uzb. 20th c. **Ot-bâs** [Утбос] (Begmatov 1984, 201). ✧ 'Opress (conquer) the fire'? ⇨ **OT** + **BAS II.** See also **OT-BASAR.**

OT-BASAR Uzb. 20th c. **Ot-bâsar** [Утбосар] (Begmatov 1984, 201). ✧ 'He who opresses (conquers?) the fire'? ⇨ OT + BASAR. See also OT-BAS.

OT-ČAPAR   Uzb. 20th c. **Ot-čâpar** [Ўтчопар] (Begmatov 1984, 206). ✧ 'Maker/layer of fire' (Begmatov), cf. Uzb. *čap- II.* 'рубить; окучивать (растения)' (UzbRS). ⇨ OT.

OT-SÜLİ   Kzk. 19th c. **Ot-sülï** [Отсули] (SOV 80). ⇨ OT + SÜLİ?

OTAY   Hak. 19th-20th c. **Otay** [Отай] (HRS 350); Kzk. 19th c. **Otay-bek** [Отайбекъ] (SODž. 74); Nog.? 1551 **Otay-mïrza** [Отай-мырза] (PSRL XIII, 161); Kzk. **Utay-bay** [Утайбай] (Sb. Syr-D. IX, 44). ✧ 'Gathering; destroying' (Bese 14).

OTAQ   Kzk. 19th c. **Otaq-pay** [Отакпай] (SOK 78, 290, 298). ✧ 'Shanty, hut, tent' cf. Chag., East.T., NUyg., Turk. *otaq* 'eine Hütte aus Zweigen, das Zelt, der Pavillon' (Radl. I, 1104).

OTAMÏŠ   Karakh. 11th c. **Otamïš** [Otamış] (MK/Atalay 848, DTS); Kzk. 19th c. **Otamïš** [Ханъ-Кути Отамишевъ] (Grod., Pril. 136, 137); Kzk. 19th c. **Otamïš-bek** [Отамишъ Бекъ] (Grod., Pril. 29). ✧ 'Healed; cured' cf. Uyg., Karakh. *ota-* 'лечить' (DTS).

OTAN   Kzk. 1817 **Otan** [اوتان] (MIK IV, 308). ✧ 'Country, fatherland' cf. Kzk. *otan* 'родина, отечество' (KzRS).

OTANBET   Kzk. 19th c. **Otambet (<Otanbet)** [Отамбетъ] (Grod., Pril. 112). ✧ 'Country/home' cf. Kzk. *otan* 'родина, отечество' (KzRS). + suff. *-bet.*

OTAR   Kzk. 1817 **Otar** [اوطار] (MIK IV, 311, 318); Kzk. 19th c. **Otar** [Нуръ Сеидъ Отаровъ] (Grod., Pril. 159); Kkalp. 20th c. **Otar** [Отар] (Bask., Kkalp. 51); Kkalp. 20th c. **Otar** [Отар] (KkRS 775); Kzk.? **Otar-bay** [Отарбай] (Karta JAR XI); Kzk. 1794 **Otar-bay** [اوطار بای] (MIK IV, 160); Kzk. 19th c. **Otar-bay** [Отарбай] (AOP 42); Kzk. 19th c. **Otar-bay** [Отарбай] (SOV 84); Kzk. 19th c. **Otar-bay** [Отарбай] (SODž. 46); Kzk. 19th c. **Otar-bay** [Отарбай] (SOK 20, 120, 150); Kkalp. 20th c. **Otar-bay** [Отарбай] (KkRS 775); Kzk. 19th c. **Otar-bek** [Отарбекъ] (SOK 168); Kzk. 19th c. **Otar-bek** [Отарбекъ] (SOV 50); Kkalp. 20th c. **Otar-biyke** [Отарбийке], fem. (KkRS 778); Kzk. **Utar** [Утаръ] (Sb. Syr-D. IX, 58); *TN:* Kuman 1451 **Otar(halma)** [Otarhalma], Otar's hill in Lesser Kumania, Hungary (Gyárfás III, 626, Rásonyi, KÖA 92, Rásonyi, NTK 89); Kzk.? **Utar-bay(eva)** [Утарбаева], a village in the Ural Mountains (Karta JAR III). ✧ 'Pasture' cf. Crm., Kzk. *otar* 'die Weide; ein vom Aule entfernter Weideplatz' (Radl. I, 1105), Kkalp. *otar* 'отдалённое от аула пастбище' (KkRS).

OTAR-ALİ   Kzk. 1823 **Otar-ali** [اوطارعلی / Отар-Али] (MIK IV, 424, 429); Kkalp. 20th c. **Otar-alï** [Отаралы] (KkRS 775). ⇨ OTAR + ALİ.

OTAR-ALÏ see **OTAR-ALİ**

OTARČÏ   Maml. 1320 **Otarčï** [سيف الدين أطرجی], an emir (Dawād. 302, Zetterst. 169, 173); Maml. 1325 **Otarčï** (Zetterst. 149); Maml. 1332 **Otarčï** [أطرجی] (Dawād. 368); Kzk. 19th c. **Otarčï** [Отарчи] (SOK 4). ✧ 'Herd, shepherd'. ⇨ OTAR + suff. *-čï.*

OTČİ   Uyg. **Odčï-buyruq** [Odçı Buyruk] (EUTS); Tat.(Sib.)? 19th c. **Otčï-arï** [Отче-ары], fem. (Potanin IV, 618); Uyg. 12th c. - 14th c. **Otčï-buyruq-beg** [otčï bujruq beg] (DTS). ✧ 'Doctor, leech' cf. Uyg. *otčï* 'der Artzt' (Radl. I, 1119).

OTÏNČİ see **OTUNČİ**

OTÏŠ see **OTUŠ**

OTQA-KÖNMÏŠ-QÏLÏČ   Türk 750 **Otqa-könmiš-qïlïč** [Otqa Könmiš Qïlïč] (Thomsen, Stein 186). ✧ 'Sword steeled in fire' cf. Karakh. *kön-* 'гореть' (DTS). From Thomsen's days it is cosidered a personal name but according to the list of the source, it is only one of the inherited items (ETY II, 256). ⇨ OT + QÏLÏČ.

OTQUN   Kzk. 19th c. **Otqum-bay (Otqun-bay)** [Откумбай] (SOK 304).

OTQURMÏŠ see **ODΓURMÏŠ**

OTQUTQA   Hak.(Kyz.) 1685 **Otqutqa** [Откутка] (Kuznecov 59-60).

OTOY   Hak. 19th-20th c. **Otoy** [Отой] (HRS 350).

OTOY-GİLDE   Chuv. 18th-19th c. **Otoy-gilde?** [Отойгилда] (Magn. 63). ⇨ ATAY + KELDİ.

OTON   Alt. 19th-20th c. **Oton** [Отон], fem. (OjrRS 212).

OTOR see **OTUR**

OTOŠ see **OTUŠ**

OTRAQ   Kuman 1068, 1107, 1201? **Otraq / Otroq / Atraq?** [Отрокъ], a Polovets prince, Šaruqan's son (PSRL II, 155). ✧ 'Camp, dwelling place, station' (Bask., Im. polov. 71).

OTROQ see **OTRAQ**

OTUČ   Tat. 1533 **Otuč / Otun?** [Отучъ (Отунъ)], a commander (voyevoda) in Kazan (PSRL XIII, 69, XIX, 35, 249).

OTUN   Kirg. **Odon** (Almásy 296); Kirg. 19th-20th c. **Odum-bey (<Odun-bey?)** [Ódummbej, Bódummbej], a guide (Prinz 170); Kzk. 19th c. **Otum-bay (<Otun-bay?)** [Отумбай] (AOP 10); Kzk. **Utïm-bay** [Утымъбай] (Êtnogr. Obozr. 1915 vyp. 3-4, 62). ✧ 'Firewood' cf. Chag., Az., Kzk. etc. *otun* 'das Brennholz' (Radl. I, 1106), Kirg. *otun* 'дрова, топливо' (Jud.).

OTUNČ-TEMİR   Uyg. 12th c. - 14th c. **Otunč-temir / Ötünč-temir?** (DTS). ⇨ TEMİR.

OTÜNČİ see **OTUNČİ**

OTUNČİ   Kzk. 19th c. **Otïnči** [Отынчи] (SOV 64); Kzk. 19th c. **Otunči** [Отунчи] (SOV 64); Kzk. 19th c. **Otunči** [Джеттибай Отунчиевъ] (Grod., Pril. 34); Kzk. 19th c. **Otunči** [Отунчи] (AOP 2); Kzk. 19th c. **Otunči** [Отунче] (AOP 6); Kzk. 1822 **Otunčï / Otunšï**

[اوطونچی / Отуншы] (MIK IV, 433, 435); Kzk. 19th c. **Otunši** [Отунши] (AOP 54). ✧ 'Seller of firewood, woodcutter' cf. Chag., Az., Kzk. etc. *otun* 'das Brennholz' (Radl. I, 1106). ⇨ OTUN + suff. *-či*.

OTUNŠÏ see **OTUNČÏ**

OTUR Kzk. 19th c. **Otor-bay** [Оторбай] (SOV 48); Kzk. 19th c. **Otor-bay** [Оторбай] (SODž. 72); Kzk. 19th c. **Otur-bay** [Отурбай] (SOK 34); Kzk. 19th c. **Otur-bay** [Отурбай] (AOA 130); Kzk. 19th c. **Otur-bay** [Отурбай] (AOAtb. 38); *TN:* Kzk. 19th c. **Otur-bay-čoqosï** [Отурбай чокосы], a field (AOK 42); Kzk. **Utur-χan** [Утурханъ], a field (Krasovskij 383). ✧ 'Sit, stay, live (somewhere)' cf. Az., Crm., Kzk., Turk. *otur-* 'id.' (Radl. I, 1107).

OTUŠ Kzk. 19th c. **Otïš** [Отышъ] (SODž. 18); Kzk. 19th c. **Otoš-pay** [Отошпай] (SOK 86); Kzk. 19th c. **Otuš** [Байджанъ Отушовъ] (Grod., Pril. 133). ⇨ OT? + dim. suff. *-uš*.

OTUZ Uyg. 12th c. - 14th c. **Otuz** (Radl., USp. 125, DTS); Kzk. 19th c. **Otuz-bay** [Отузбай] (AOK 118); Kzk. 19th c. **Otuz-bay** [Отузбай] (AOAtb. 14); Kzk. 19th c. **Otuz-bay** [Отузбай] (SOK 110); Kzk. 19th c. **Otuz-bay** [Отузбай] (SODž. 160); Türk **Otuz-oγlan** [Otuz Oγlan] (ETY II, 136); *EN:* Crm. 1638 **Otuz-(u)ruγ** [اوتوز/روغ] (Vel.-Zern., Crim.); *TN:* Crm. **Otuz**, a village (and ruins) southwest of Kefe (Jervis IX). ✧ 'Thirty' cf. Kuman, Az., Crm., Kzk., Turk. *otuz* 'id.' (Radl. I, 1110).

OVČÏN Hak. 19th-20th c. **Opčin** [Опчин] (HRS 350); Hak.(Kyz.) 19th-20th c. **Opčin** [Опчин] (Katanov, Otč. 13); Hak.(Sag.) 19th-20th c. **Opčïn** [Опчін] (Proben IX, 613); Hak. 19th-20th c. **Ovčin** [Овчин] (HRS 350); Hak.(Sag.) 19th-20th c. **Ovčin** [Овчинъ] (Proben IX, 613). ✧ 'Lambskin, sheepskin' < R. *ovčina* 'id.' (Katanov).

OWĀZ-DURDÏ see **AWAZ-TURDÏ**

OWĀZ-MURAD Trkm. 1879 **Owāz-murad** [Овазъ-Мурадъ] (Grod., Vojna 121, Grod., Pril. 108). ✧ 'Famous Murat' Chag., Az., Tat. *auaz / awaz* 'Stimme, Ton, Klang, Echo, Ruf, Gerücht' (Radl. I, 68), Trkm. *owāz* 'голос, звук; мелодия' (TrkmRS) (<P.). ⇨ MURAT.

OZ Kzk. 19th c. **Oz-bay** [Озбай] (AOO 46). ✧ 'Be the first, overtake (the others); get free, escape' cf. Chag., Kzk. *oz-* 'vorausgehen, übertreffen (im Wettlauf)' (Radl. I, 1143), Uyg. *oz-* 'спасаться, освобождаться', Karakh. *oz-* 'опережать' (DTS). See also **OZAR, OZMÏŠ**.

OZAY Kzk. 19th c. **Ozay** [Озай] (SOV 22); Hak.? 19th c. **Ozay** [Озай], fem. (Katanov, Otč. 12).

OZAR Uzb.? 14th c. **Ozar**, a robber from the Qangli tribe (Barth., G. Ch. M. A. 63); **Ozar-χan** [اوزارخان المالیغ / اوزارخان] (Juwaynī I, 21, 48, 57 etc.). ✧ 'He who will be the first, he who overtakes the others' cf.

Chag., Kzk. *oz-* 'vorausgehen, übertreffen (im Wettlauf)' (Radl. I, 1143). ⇨ **OZMÏŠ**. See also **OZ, OZMÏŠ**.

OZLAΓ see **OZLAQ**

OZLAQ Khorezm. 1220 **Ozlaq-sultan / Ozlaγ-šah** [Ozlak schah, filius Alayeddin Mahommed / Озлаг-шах, Кутб-ад-дин (Озлак-султан)], son of the Khorezmshah Muχammed II (1200-1220) (Sin. Fr. 113, MIT I, 476, 477, 503, 504, RaD I/2, 214); Khorezm.? 13th c. **Uzlaq-sultan** [Узлакъ-Султанъ] (RaD/Ber. III, 67, 88). ✧ 'Evening prayer' cf. Chag. *ozlaq (namazï)* 'id.' (Budagov I, 133).

OZMÏŠ Uyg. 12th c. - 14th c. **Ozmïš** [ozmïš / Ozmış] (DTS, EUTS); Türk / Uyg. 8th c. **Ozmïš-qaγan** [Ou-sou-mi-che Kagan], the last Türk ruler of the Türk dynasty, the same as Ozmïš-tegin, died in 743 (Chavannes 86); Türk / Uyg. 8th c. **Ozmïš-tegin / Ozmïš-tigin** [Ozmyš tigin / Ozmış tegin], the last Türk ruler of the Türk dynasty, died in 743 (Ramstedt, Uig. 15, 46, Radl., USp. 44, DTS, ETY I, 166). ✧ 'Escaped, got rid of' (Blagova 1997, 717), 'Became first; overtook (the others), escaped'. See also **OZ, OZAR**.

OZMÏŠ-TOΓRÏL Uyg. 12th c. - 14th c. **Ozmïš-toγrïl** [Ozmïš Toγrïl / ozmïš toγrïl] (Radl., USp. 202, 204-205, 244, 246-47, DTS). ✧ 'Escaped-Falcon' (Blagova 1997, 717). ⇨ OZMÏŠ + TOΓRÏL.

OZOČÏ Alt. 19th-20th c. **Ozočï** [Озочы] (OjrRS 209). ✧ 'Ancestor, predecessor; forerunner' (OjrRS).

OZOY Alt. 19th-20th c. **Ozoy** [Озой] (OjrRS 209).

OŽAR Nog. 1649 **Ožar** [Ожаръ] (AI IV, 124). ✧ 'Shameless, rude' cf. Kzk. *ožar* 'дерзкий, грубый' (KzRS).

Ō

ŌČÏY Alt. 19th-20th c. **Ōčïy / Očï** [Оочый / Очы] (OjrRS 209).

ŌQOY Alt. 19th-20th c. **Ōqoy** [Оокой] (OjrRS 209); Alt. 19th-20th c. **Ōköy** [Ööкöй] (OjrRS 209). ✧ 'Little, small; wolf (in women's speech)' (OjrRS), cf. Alt. *ōqoy* 'волк' (OjrRS).

ŌL see **OΓUL**

ŌLAX see **ŌLAQ**

ŌLAQ Alt. **Olaq** [Олак], Olγudek's brother (AI 133); Alt. 19th c. **Olaq** [Олак] (Verb., In. 133); Hak. 19th-20th c. **Ōlaχ** [Оолах] (HRS 350); Hak. 19th c. **Ōlaq** [Олак] (Katanov, Otč. 12); Hak.(Sag.) 19th-20th c. **Ōlaq** [Олак] (Katanov, Otč. 11); Hak.(Kacha) 19th-20th c. **Ōlaq** [Олак] (Proben IX, 536); Hak.(Kyz.) 19th-20th c. **Ōlaq** [Олак] (Katanov, Otč. 13). ✧ '(Little) boy' (HRS, Butanaev), cf. Alt.(Leb.), Hak.

ōlaq 'ein Knabe, jünger Mensch' (Radl. I, 1084), also Hak. PN *Ōlaχ* 'id.' (Butanaev). + suff. *-aq*.

ŌLAS Hak. 19th-20th c. **Ōlas** [Оолас] (HRS 350). ✧ 'Little boy'? ⇨ OΓUL + suff. *-as*.

ŌLČA see **OLČA**

ŌMAS Hak.(Blt.) 19th-20th c. **Ōmas** [Омас], fem. (Katanov, Otč. 10). ✧ 'Silly, stupid' (Katanov).

ŌZÏQ Alt. 19th-20th c. **Ōzïq** [Оозык], fem. (OjrRS 212). ✧ 'Hoe, hack' (OjrRS).

Ö

ÖBDŌTTÏYÄ Hak.(Sag.) 19th-20th c. **Öbdŏttiyä** [360 / Öбдӧггijä], fem. (Katanov, Otč. 7). ✧ Avdot'ya (R. fem.) (Katanov).

ÖBÖY Alt. 19th-20th c. **Öböy** [Öбöй], fem. (OjrRS 213).

ÖBÜČÜK Yak. **Öbüčük** [Öбÿчÿк] (Pek.). ✧ 'Little penis' cf. Yak. *öbüs* 'мужеский детородный уд; мужской половой орган' (Pek.).

ÖČÖKÜN Yak. **Öčökün** [Öчöкÿн], one of the well-known wrestlers from the ulus of Nam (Pek.).

ÖČÜKEN Mo.? **Öčüken** (Vladimircov: DAN 1929, 135).

ÖJÄÑ Hak.(Sag.) 19th-20th c. **Öjäñ-peg** [Öцäñ-пег], a folklor hero (Proben IX, 469-70, 488). ✧ 'Ruler, emperor' (<Mo.).

ÖDÄ-QONAR Tuv. 19th c. **Ödä-qonar** [Öдä-конар], another name of Qōmu/Qombu (Proben IX, 147). ⇨ ?+ **QONAR?**

ÖDEMIŠ see **ÖTÄMIŠ**

ÖDER Kzk. 19th c. **Öder-bay** [Одербай] (SODž. 48). ✧ 'He will achieve; he will be successful; he will pay' cf. Uyg., Turk. *ödä-, ötä-* 'erfüllen, ausführen; bezahlen' (Radl. I, 1276), Kzk. *öte-* 'compensate' (Bese 4).

ÖDEREP Kzk. 19th c. **Öderep** [Одерепъ] (SOV 60). ⇨ **ÖDER?**

ÖDÜŠ Uyg. 13th-14th c. **Ödüš**, fem. (Zieme, Mat. III, 272); Uyg. 13th-14th c. **Ödüš-ïnal** [Ödüš Ïnal] (Zieme, Mat. III, 272 (after Tuguševa)); Uyg. **Ödüš-täñrim** [Ödüš Tängrim], fem. (Zieme, Mat. I, 75). ✧ 'Compensation'. ⇨ **ÖDER.**

ÖDÜŠ-IKIR Uyg. 12th c. - 14th c. **Ödüš-ikir / Üdüš-igir** [Üdüš Igir / Ödüš Ikir / ödüš ikir] (Radl., USp. 253, 212, DTS). ⇨ **ÖDÜŠ.**

ÖG Türk 7th-9th c. **Ög?-alp** [Öğ()in alp / Öğd()in Alp?] (ETY III, 189).

ÖGDÄM Türk 7th c. - 9th c. **Ögdäm-ïnal** [Ögdämïnal] (DTS). ✧ 'Proud, high-minded' cf. Karakh. *ögdäm, öktem* 'id.' (DTS).

ÖGDÜLMIŠ Karakh. 11th c. **Ögdülmiš / Öktülmiš** (Radl. I, 9, DTS). ✧ 'Blessed, praised' cf. Karakh. *ögdil-* 'быть восхваляемым, прославляемым' (DTS).

ÖGÄ Khorezm./Chag. 1404 **Ögä-begüm / Ögä-biki** [Öгэ-бегÿмъ], Ulug-beg's (1393-1449) first wife (Barth., Ulugb. 115); Türk 8th - 9th c. **Ügä** [Ügä] (Thomsen, Stein 188). ✧ 'Wise(man)', also used as a title (of respect), supreme councillor' (DTS), cf. Karakh. *ögä* 'мудрый, мудрец' (DTS), Uyg. *ögä* 'die Ehre' (Radl. I, 1192). Used also as a secondary component of male names. See also **IL-ÖGÄSI.**

ÖGÄ-TERKEN Chag. 15th c. **Ögä-terken-šah** [Öгэ-турканъ-Шахъ], Ulug-beg's (1393-1449) daughter, the same as Tuγa-terken (?) (Barth., Ulugb. 116). ⇨ **ÖGÄ + TERKEN.**

ÖGÄČI Khorezm. 1282 **Ögäči** [أوكجى], Meñgü-temür-qan's brother (Qalāūn/Tizeng. I, 65). ⇨ **ÖGÄ + suff. -či?**

ÖGÄČÜK Uyg. 12th c. - 14th c. **Ögäčük** [Ögäçük] (DTS, EUTS). ✧ 'Little wiseman'. ⇨ **ÖGÄ + dim. suff. -čük / -čik.** See also **TURUQ-ÖGÄČÜK.**

ÖGÄDÄY Uyg. **Ögädäy** [Ögädäy] (EUTS); Khorezm.? 1303 **Ögötäy-tarχan?** [اغوتاى تـرخـان], a dignitary executed by Ghazan Khan (1295-1304) in 1303 (RaD/Jahn); Kuman 1333 **Ügüdäy** [Tatar filio Ugudey], among the Kumans of Hungary (Gyárfás III, 476). ✧ 'Ögödei'? (Mo.), concerning the Kuman names cf. Rásonyi, KÖA 136, Rásonyi, Anthr. 146.

ÖGRENČI Turk. 1540 **Ögrenči-kethudā** [Örgençi], chief of the ethnic community (cemaat) Dalguç (Demirtaş 57). ✧ 'Pupil, student' cf. Turk. *öğrenci* 'id.' (TED).

ÖGRETMIŠ Türk 903 **Ögretmiš** [Igritmisch], governor of Rei (Weil, Chalif. II, 519); Türk 902 **Ögretmiš / Ögretmüš** [أوكرتمش / اوكرتمش / اكرتمش] (Tabarī, Annal. III, 2208, 2215). ✧ 'Tought, suggested, instructed' cf. Karakh. *ögrät-* 'учить, обучать' (DTS), Turk. *öğret-* 'id.' (TED).

ÖGRÖPŪNÄ Yak. **Ögröpŭnä** [Öгрöпÿнä] (Pek.). ✧ Agrippina (R.) (Pek.).

ÖGRÜNČ Uyg. 12th c. - 14th c. **Ögrünč-täñrim**, a princess (Müller, Uig. II, 93, DTS); Uyg. **Ökrünč** [Ökrünç] (EUTS). ✧ 'Joy, pleasure, gladness' cf. Uyg. *ögrünč* 'id.' (DTS).

ÖGRÜNČ-QARA Uyg. 12th c. - 14th c. **Ögrünč-qara** [Ögrünč Qara] (Radl., USp. 44, DTS). ✧ 'Gladness-black' (Bese 18), 'Gladness-Great' (Blagova 1997, 705). ⇨ **ÖGRÜNČ + QARA.**

ÖGRÜNČÄ Uyg. **Ögrünčä** [Ögrünçä] (EUTS); Uyg. 12th c. - 14th c. **Ögrünčä** (Radl., USp. 95-96).

ÖGÜN Türk 7th c. - 9th c. **Ögün-tutuq** [Öqün (!) tutuq] (DTS). ✧ 'Clever, meaningful' cf. Karakh. *ögün* 'толково, с умом' (DTS).

ÖGÜNČ   Uyg. **Ögünč** [اوكنج], ruler of the Uyghurs (J̌uwaynī I, 38, 39). ✧ 'Glory, kudos' cf. Karakh. *ögünč* 'восхваление, слава' (DTS).

ÖGÜRǰIK see **SALOR-ÖGÜRǰIK**

ÖGÜZ   Kzk. 19th c. **Ögüz-bay** [Огузбай] (SODž. 76, 108); Kzk. 19th c. **Ögüz-bay** [Огузбай] (SOK 284). ✧ 'Steer, bullock' cf. Chag., Kuman, Karch., Kzk. *ögüz* 'der Ochs, Stier' (Radl. I, 1200).

ÖYGE   Kzk. 19th c. **Öyge** [Ойге] (SOK 296). ✧ 'Pairing period of cattle, sheep and horses' cf. Chag. *öygä* 'die Brunstzeit der Rinder, Schafe und Pferde' (Radl. I, 1173).

ÖYÜÖRGEN   Yak. **Öyüörgen** [Öjyöргäн], fem. (Pek.). ✧ 'Helper, supporter' cf. Yak. *öyȫ (öyüö)* 'поддерживать (падающего, слабого), подпирать; помогать, содействовать' (Pek.).

ÖKER   Kzk. 19th c. **Öker-bay** [Окербай] (SOK 188).

ÖKILINČÄ   Hak.(Kyz.) 19th-20th c. **Ökïlinčä** [Öкiлiнчä], fem. (Katanov, Otč. 13). ✧ Akulincha (R.) (Katanov).

ÖKKÜYNÄ   Tuv. 19th c. **Ökküynä** [Öккÿинä] (Proben IX, 45).

ÖKÖM-BOLOT   Kirg. **Ököm-bolot** [Oeköm Bolot / Öкöм Болот], Yoloy's son (Proben V, 184). ✧ 'Vehement, hot-tempered, impatient steel' cf. Kirg. *öküm* 'несдержанный, вспыльчивый; нетерпеливый, торопливый' (Jud.). ⇨ **BULAT.**

ÖKPE   Kzk. 19th c. **Ökpe** [Öкпе] (SOK 222). ✧ 'Lung' cf. Alt., Kzk. *ökpö* 'id.' (Radl. I, 1191-92).

ÖKRÜNČ see **ÖGRÜNČ**

ÖKRÜŠ-TEMIR   Uyg. **Ökrüs-tämir** [Ökrüs Tämir] (EUTS); Uyg. 13th c. **Ökrüš-temir** (DTS). ✧ '?-Iron'. ⇨ **TEMIR.**

ÖKSEK   Kzk. 19th c. **Öksek-pay** [Оксекпай] (SOV 110). ✧ 'Tall, high' cf. Chag. *öksäk* 'hoch, erhoben, erhaben' (Radl. I, 1187).

ÖKSEL   Kzk. 19th c. **Öksel-bay** [Оксельбай] (SOV 140). ✧ 'Rise, Grow up!' cf. Chag. *öksäl-* 'erwachsen' (Radl. I, 1187).

ÖKSIZÄK   Hak.(Blt.) 19th-20th c. **Öksizäk** [Öксiзäк], a motherless child (Proben IX, 365, 366).

ÖKSIZEK   Alt. 19th-20th c. **Ösküzek** [Öскÿзек] (OjrRS 213).

ÖKSIN   Hak.? 19th-20th c. **Öksin** [Öксiн] (Katanov, Otč. 10). ✧ Aksin'ya (R.) (Katanov).

ÖKSÖN   Yak. **Öksön** [Öксöн] (Pek.). ✧ Short form of *Ölöksȫndrö*. ⇨ **ÖLÖKSÖNDRÖ.**

ÖKSÜK see **EKSIK**

ÖKSÜSÜ   Yak. **Öksüsü** [Öксÿсÿ], Mäyäräm Süppü's father, forefather of the Yakuts from the times when they lived together with the Kirghiz and Buryats (Pek.).

ÖKSÜZ   Turk. 1558 **Öksüz**, cemaat (Gökçen 38); *TN:* Turk. 20th c. **Öksüzler** [Öksüzler], a village (TMİB 597). ✧ 'Orphan' Chag., Crm., Kar., Turk. *öksüz*, Hak.

öksüs 'die Waise' (Radl. I, 1190), Alt. *ösküs* 'сирота' (OjrRS).

ÖKŠE   Tat.(Sib.)? 1609 **Ökše / Ökšey?** [Юзеим Окшеев] (Miller, Ist. Sib. II, 210); Kkalp. 20th c. **Ökše-bay** [Öкшебай] (KkRS 775). ✧ 'Heel of a shoe' (KkRS), cf. Kzk. *ökšö* 'die Ferse, der Hacken, der Schuhabsatz' (Radl. I, 1191).

ÖKTĒS   Hak. 19th-20th c. **Öktēs** [Öктеес] (HRS 350); Hak.(Sag.) 19th-20th c. **Öktēs** [Öктäс] (Proben IX, 613). ✧ 'Brother (on mother side)' cf. Hak. PN *Öktes* (Butanaev).

ÖKTÜLMIŠ see **ÖGDÜLMIŠ**

ÖKÜLÜNÄ see **ÄKILINÄ**

ÖKÜLÜNÄ see **ÄKILINÄ**

ÖKÜLÜS   Yak. **Ökülüs** [Öкÿлÿс], fem. (Pek.). ✧ Diminutive of *Ökülünä*. ⇨ **ÄKILINÄ.**

ÖKÜŠ-QARA see **ÜKÜŠ-QARA**

ÖKÜŠ-QARA-AČQÏ see **ÜKÜŠ-QARA- AČQÏ**

ÖKÜZ   Trkm. **Öküz-bey** [Öкюзъ-бей] (Mel'gunov 321). ✧ 'Bullock, steer, ox' cf. Turk. *öküz* 'der Ochs' (Radl. I, 1180). See also **QÏZÏL-ÖKÜZ.**

ÖKÜZ-TOƔRÏL   Uyg. 12th c. - 14th c. **Öküz-toγrïl** [Öküz Toγrïl] (Radl., USp. 208, 250). ⇨ **ÖKÜZ +TOƔRÏL.**

ÖKÜZ-UƔRÏSÏ   Turk. 1583 **Öküz-uγrïsï / Öküz-oγrïsï** [اوكوز اوغـريسى / Öküz uğrïsï], a byname (Ongan, Ank. I, 173). ✧ 'Rustler, thief of oxes' cf. Turk. *uγru, oγrï* 'der Dieb, Räuber' (Radl. I, 1622). ⇨ **ÖKÜZ.**

ÖLBES see **ÖLMEZ**

ÖLBÖT-BÄRGÄN   Yak. **Ölböt-bärgän-oburγu** [Öлбöт-Бäргäн-обургу] (Pek.).

ÖLBÖZÖK   Alt. 19th-20th c. **Ölbözök** [Öлбöзöк], fem. (OjrRS 213). ✧ 'She won't die; deathless' + suff. *-ök*.

ÖLǰIN   Kzk. 19th c. **Ölǰin** [Ольджинъ] (AOO 14).

ÖLDIR   Kzk. 19th c. **Öldir-bay** [Олдербай] (SOK 230). ✧ 'Kill (the enemy?)' cf. Kzk. *öltïr-* 'убить; умертвить' (KzRS).

ÖLÄKŠIY   Tat.(Sib.) 1632 **Öläkšiy / Öläkšey?** [Янгозя Олякшеев] (Miller, Ist. Sib. II, 397). ✧ Aleksey (R.)? See also **ÖLÖKSÖY.**

ÖLEKŠIN   Alt. **Ölekšin** [Олекшинъ] (Nikiforov 269); Alt. **Ölökšin** [Олöкшинъ] (Nikiforov 31). ✧ Aleksey (R.)? See also **ILEKSEŇ.**

ÖLEN   Kzk. 19th c. **Ölen-bay** [Оленбай] (SODž. 152). ✧ 'Grass' cf. Kzk. *öleň* 'id.' (KzRS), Alt., Kzk. *ölöň* 'die Pflanze, das Grass, Heu' (Radl. I, 1247). See also **AQ-ÖLEŇ, QÏR-ÖLEŇ, SÏR-ÖLEŇ.**

ÖLEŇ-TAYČÏ   Shor 1834 **Öleň-tayčï**, a folklore hero (Dyrenkova 72). ⇨ **ÖLEN + TAYČÏ.**

ÖLER   Kzk. 19th c. **Öler-bek** [Олербекъ] (SOK 114); Kzk. 19th c. **Öler-bek** [Олербекъ] (AOP 22). ✧ 'He/she will die' cf. Kzk. *öl-* 'умереть, пасть' (KzRS).

ÖLEŠ   Chuv. 18th-19th c. **Öleš** [Олешъ] (Magn. 61). ✧

'Part, share, portion' cf. Tat. *öleš* 'id.' (TatRS).

ÖLEŠEN Chuv. 18th-19th c. **Ölešen** [Олешенъ] (Magn. 61).

ÖLKE Kzk. 19th c. **Ölke** [Ольке] (SODž. 64). ✧ 'Region, territory' cf. Kzk. *ölke* 'id.' (KzRS).

ÖLKEN Kzk. 19th c. **Ölkem-bay (<Ölken-bay?)** [Олькембай] (SOV 94). ✧ 'Big; elder; experienced' cf. Kzk. *ülken* 'büyük, yaşı büyük, tecrübeli' (KzTS).

ÖLMÄS see **ÖLMEZ**

ÖLMESEK Kzk. 19th c. **Ölmesek** [Ольмесекъ] (AOO 62). ✧ 'If we didn't die' cf. Kzk. *öl-* 'умереть, пасть' (KzRS).

ÖLMEZ Kirg. 19th c. **Ölbes** (Kalilov 95); Maml. 1333 **Ölmäs** [السينى الماس], an emir (emir-i χājib) of the door-keepers, the governor (viceroy) of Egypt, mentioned in an inscription on a glass lamp (Mayer 241, Zetterst. 147, 166, 187, 226); Uzb. 20th c. **Ölmäs** [Ӱлмас] (Begmatov 1984, 206); Uzb. 20th c. **Ölmäs** [Ӱлмас], fem. (Begmatov 1984, 206); Maml./Turk.? 1467 **Ölmäs** [السينى الماس], an atabek of Aleppo, mentioned in an inscription on a copper basin and bowl, died in 1467 (Mayer 242); Uzb. 20th c. **Ölmäs-ây** [Ӱлмасой], fem. (Begmatov 1984, 206); Uzb. 20th c. **Ölmäs-bây** [Ӱлмасбой] (Begmatov 1984, 206); Uzb. 20th c. **Ölmäs-jân** [Ӱлмасжон] (Begmatov 1984, 206); Uzb. 20th c. **Ölmäs-χân** [Ӱлмасхон], fem. (Begmatov 1984, 206); Tat.(GH) 14th c. **Ölmäz** [Ολμάσης], a christened „Tatar" (Byz. Turc. 216); Türk **Ölmes** [الماس / Almas / Ölmâs] (Weil, Chalif. IV, 377, Karabacek I, 105, II-III, 272); Trkm. 20th c. **Ölmez** [Ölmez], fem. (Zaj. 1971, 341); Tat. **Ülmäs** [Улмяс] (Katanov, Star. Kaz.: 297); Tat. 1765 **Ülmäs** [Ульмяс (Ульмяс) Султанова], fem. (MIB IV/1, 314); Bashk. 1725 **Ülmäs** [Улмас Телясев] (MIB III, 235); Bashk. 1795 **Ülmäs** [Ульмясъ Курмангуловъ] (IOAIÈK XXVIII, 589); Bashk. 1740 **Ülmäs-qul** [Улмяскул Саранчин] (MIB I, 397); Bashk. 1740 **Ülmäs-qul** [Улмяскул] (MIB I, 396); Bashk. 1742 **Ülmäs-qul** [Яныш Улмяскулов] (MIB I, 486); Chuv. 18th-19th c. **Ülmes** [Улмесь] (Magn. 88); Bashk. 1664 **Ülmes** [Уразай Ульмесов] (MIB I, 192); Tat. 1611 **Ülmâs** [اولماس / Ӱлмâс] (Jusupov 71). ✧ 'He/she won't die; (the child) will be healthy, long-lived; immortal' (Sauvaget 38, Kusimova, Sattarov). See also **ÖLER**.

ÖLÖKSÖY Yak. **Ölöksöy** [Ӫлӫксӫй] (Pek.). ✧ Aleksey (R.) (Pek.).

ÖLÖKSÖN Alt. **Ölöksön** [Олоксонъ] (Nikiforov 279). ✧ Aleksey (R.)? See also **ÖLEKŠIN**.

ÖLÖKSÕNDRÖ Yak. **Ölöksõndrö** [Ӫлӫксӫндрӫ], fem. (Pek.); Yak. **Ölöksõnnörö** [Ӫлӫксӫннӫрӫ] (Pek.). ✧ Aleksandr / Aleksandra (R.) (Pek.).

ÖLÖKSÕNNÖRÖ see **ÖLÖKSÕNDRÖ**

ÖLÖKSÕSÖ Yak. **Ölöksös** [Ӫлӫксӫс] (Pek.); Yak. **Ölöksõsö** [Ӫлӫксӫсӫ] (Pek.). ✧ Aleksasha (R.), dim. of R. Aleksandr.

ÖLÖKŠIN see **ÖLEKŠIN**

ÖLÖNBİR Alt. **Ölönbir** [Ӫлӫнбиръ] (Nikiforov 107).

ÖLÖŇČİ Alt. 19th-20th c. **Ölöňči** [Ӫлӫнчи], fem. (OjrRS 213). ✧ 'Grass-collector/seller' cf. Kzk. *öleň* 'id.' (KzRS), Alt., Kzk. *ölöň* 'die Pflanze, das Grass, Heu' (Radl. I, 1247). + suff. -*či*.

ÖLÕN Hak.(Sag.) 19th-20th c. **Ölõn** [Ӫлӫн], fem. (Katanov, Otč. 8). ✧ Elena (R.) (Katanov).

ÖLÕNČÜK Yak. **Ölõnčük** [Ӫлӫнчӱк], fem. (Pek.). ⇨ **ÖLÕN(Ö)** + dim. suff. -*čük*.

ÖLÕNÖ Yak. **Ölõnö** [Ӫлӫнӫ], fem. (Pek.). ✧ Olyona, Elena (R.) (Pek.). ⇨ **ÖLÕN**.

ÖLÕSKÖ Yak. **Ölõskö** [Ӫлӫскӫ] (Pek.). ✧ Alyoshka (R.), dim. of R. Aleksey (Pek.).

ÖLÕSÖ Yak. **Ölõsö** [Ӫлӫсӫ] (Pek.). ✧ Alyosha (R.), dim. of R. Aleksey (Pek.).

ÖLTİ Kzk. 19th c. **Ölti-bay** [Ольтебай] (AOK 122). ✧ 'Died, dead'? See also **ÖLER, ÖLMEZ**.

ÖLÜM Trkm. 1538/39 **Ölüm-χan** [Олюм-хан] (MIT II, 59). ✧ 'Death' cf. most Trk. languages *ölüm* 'id.' (Radl. I, 1251).

ÖLÜÖSKÄ Yak. **Ölüöskä** [Ӫлӱӫскä] (Pek.). ✧ Alyoshka (R.), dim. of R. Aleksey (Pek.).

ÖLÜ-ÜÖDÜLBÄ Yak. **Ölü-üödülbä** [Ӫлӱ-Ӱӫдӱлбä], a folklore hero also known as *Ān-adilγa, Känyiyär-qïrda* (Pek.). ✧ 'Miserable/sickly - accreation/growth'? cf. Yak. *ölü* 'смерть, болезнь, беда, несчастие' (JRS) and *üödüy-* 'пускать ростки (побеги), расти' + aff. -*bä* (Pek.).

ÖMİR see **ÖMÜR**

ÖMİR-NİYAZ Kkalp. 20th c. **Ömir-niyaz** [Ӫмирнияз] (KkRS 775). ⇨ **ÖMÜR + NİYAZ.**

ÖMİR-ZAQ see **ÖMÜR-UZAQ**

ÖMÜR Tat. 18th c. **Ğumer** [Гумеръ] (Nepljuev 824-25); Tat. 1764 **Ğumer** [Гумер Салихов] (MIB IV/1, 284); Bashk. 18th c. **Ğumer** [Гумеров] (MIB V, 203); Bashk. 1754 **Ğumer** [Гумер Курюндюков] (MIB IV/1, 83); Bashk. 1761 **Ğumer** [Гумер Московов] (MIB IV/1, 200); Bashk. 1770 **Ğumer** [Гумер Бектемиров] (MIB IV/1, 350); Bashk. 1777 **Ğumer** [Гумер Кармышев] (MIB V, 52); Bashk. 1798 **Ğumer** [Гумеровъ] (PSZRI XXV, 196); Kzk. 1819 **Ğumer** [Гумер] (MIK IV, 324); Uzb. 18th c. **Ğumer-bay** [Гумербай], from Khiva (Nepljuev 803); Kzk. 18th c. **Ömir** [Умиръ] (Nepljuev 741, 747); Kzk. 19th c. **Ömir-bek** [Омирбекъ] (SODž. 100); Kzk. 19th c. **Ömir-qan** [Омирканъ] (SODž. 122); Kzk. **Ömür** [Ӫмӱр], Sebän's father (Proben III, 134 /170/); Kkalp. 20th c. **Ömir-bay** [Ӫмирбай] (KkRS 775); Kzk. 1794 **Ömür-batïr** [اومور باطير] (MIK IV, 158); Kzk. 18th c. - 19th c. **Ömür-bek** [عمر بك / Омурбек] (MIK IV, 309); Kirg. **Ömür-bek** [Ӫмӱрбек] (Jud. 603, 692);

Bashk. 1735 **Ümer** [Умеръ Умешевъ], a tarχan (Vel.-Zern., Bašk. 16); Tat. 18th c. **Ümer / Gümer** [Умер (Гумер) Беккулов] (MIB V, 550); Tat. 18th c. **Ümer / Gümer** [Умер (Гумер) Исмаилов] (MIB V, 94); Bashk. 18th c. **Ümer / Gümer** [Умер (Гумер) Аминев] (MIB V, 87, 111); Bashk. 18th c. **Ümer / Gümer** [Умер (Гумер) Асанов] (MIB V, 60); Bashk. 18th c. **Ümer / Gümer** [Умер (Гумер) Бектемиров] (MIB V,63); Bashk. 18th c. **Ümer / Gümer** [Умер (Гумер) Ишалин (Ишалиев)] (MIB V, 311); Bashk. 18th c. **Ümer / Gümer** [Умер (Гумер) Кармышев] (MIB V, 52); Bashk. 18th c. **Ümer / Gümer** [Умер (Гумер) Кучуков] (MIB V,328); Bashk. 18th c. **Ümer / Gümer** [Умер (Гумер) Мусин] (MIB V, 65); Bashk. 18th c. **Ümer / Gümer** [Умер (Гумер) Рянгулов] (MIB V, 157); Bashk. 18th c. **Ümer / Gümer** [Умер (Гумер) Усманов] (MIB V, 559); Bashk. 18th c. **Ümir** [Умиръ Тахторовъ] (Nepljuev 151); Kzk. 19th c. **Ömir-bay** [Умырбай Албаевъ] (SKSO III, 18). ✧ I. 'Life, living; lively' cf. Tat. PNs Гомер, Гомäр, Гумär; Tat.(Mish.) Omar, Umar, Ümär(kä); Tat.(Sib.) Ömär, Kümär (Sattarov); II. 'Long-lived' cf. Bashk. PN Гöмär (Kusimova), cf. also Kzk. *ömür* 'das Leben, die Ewigkeit, ewig' (Radl. I, 1314), Kzk. *ömir* 'жизнь' (KzRS), Kzk. PNs *Ömir / Ömir-bay* (Žanuzakov-Esbaeva), Kkalp. *ömir* 'жизнь' (KkRS), Kirg. *ömür* 'жизнь' (Jud.), Tat. *γomer*, Bashk. *γümer* 'id.'. <Ar. Umar / Āmir <*umr* 'life' (Ahmed). See also **BAY-ГOMÏR**.

ÖMÜR-UZAQ Kzk. 1825 **Ömir-zaq** [اومـرزاق / Омрзак] (MIK IV, 469, 476); Kzk. 19th c. **Ömir-zaq** [Омырзакъ] (SODž. 4); Kzk. 19th c. **Ömir-zaq** [Омырзакъ] (SOK 190); Kzk. 19th c. **Ömir-zaq** [Омырзакъ] (AOO 6); Kzk. 19th c. **Ömir-zaq** [Омырзакъ] (AOAtb. 2, 22); Kkalp. 20th c. **Ömir-zaq** [Өмирзақ] (KkRS 775); Kzk. 19th c. **Ömir-zaq** [Омурзакъ] (SOK 4, 200); Kzk. 19th c. **Ömir-zaq** [Омурзакъ] (AOP 78); Kzk. 19th c. **Ömir-zaq** [Омурзакъ] (AOO 46); Kzk. 19th c. **Ömir-zaq** [Омурзакъ] (AOA 14); Kzk. 19th c. **Ömir-zaq** [Омюрзакъ] (AOP 50); Kirg. 19th c. **Ömir-zaq** [Өмурзак] (Kalilov 95); Bashk. 1757 **Ümir-zaq** [Бурагул Умирзаков] (MIB IV/1, 145); Trkm. 1859 **Ümr-uzaq** (<**Ümir-uzaq**) / **Umr-uzaq** (<**Umir-uzaq**) [Умрузакъ] (ZIRGOÊtn. I, 187); Trkm. 1859 **Ümr-uzaq** (<**Ümir-uzaq**) / **Umr-uzaq** (<**Umir-uzaq**) [Умрузокъ Сарыповъ] (ZIRGOÊtn. I, 210); Kzk. 1793 **Ümür-zaq / Ömür-zaq?** [اومورزاق] (MIK IV); Kzk. 19th c. **Ümür-zaq / Ömür-zaq?** [Умурзаковъ] (SKSO VIII, 225); Kzk. 19th c. **Ümür-zaq / Ömür-zaq?** [Рустемъ Умырзаковъ] (SKSO IV, otd. III, 13); Kzk. 19th c. **Ümür-zaq / Ömür-zaq?** [Умурзакъ] (Grod., Pril. 119); Kzk. 19th c. **Ümür-zaq / Ömür-zaq?** [Умурзакъ Баратъ] (SKSO III, 6); Kzk. 19th c. **Ümür-zaq / Ömür-zaq?** [Умурзакъ] (SOK 154); Kzk. 19th c. **Ümür-zaq / Ömür-zaq?** [Умурзакъ] (Grod., Pril. 143); Kzk. 19th c. **Ümür-zaq / Ömür-zaq?** [Умурзакъ] (Grod., Pril. 90); Kzk. 19th c. **Ümür-zaq / Ömür-zaq?** [Акмантай Умурзаковъ] (Grod., Pril. 162); Kzk. 1890 **Ümür-zaq / Ömür-zaq** [Аякишъ Умурзаковъ], a sultan from the Inner Horde (AUK 235); Kzk. 18th c. **Ümür-zaq / Ömür-zaq** [Умурзакъ] (Nepljuev 755); Kzk. 19th c. **Ümür-zaq / Ömür-zaq** [Умурзакъ Коскулаковъ] (AUK 879). ✧ 'Long life (lit. life-long); be long-lived'! cf. also Tat. PN *Umïrzaq (Γomerozaq)* (Sattarov). ⇨ **ÖMÜR + UZAQ.** See also **BAY-UZAQ, ĴAN-UZAQ.**

ÖN-TEMÜR Crm. 1700 **Ön-timür** [Öнъ-Тимуръ / Öн-тимуръ], leader of a livā (district) from the Širin tribe (Smirnov, Krym. 651). ✧ 'The first (best) Temür' cf. Turk. *ön* 'der Vordertheil' (Radl. I, 1213). ⇨ **TEMIR.**

ÖNDÖLÜKÜ-BÖKÖNÖ Yak. **Öndölükü-bökönö** [Öндöлÿкÿ бöкöнö] (Pek.).

ÖNDÜRÄY Yak. **Öndüräy** [Öндÿräi] (Pek.). ✧ Andrey (R.).

ÖNDÜRÜS Yak. **Öndürüs** [Öндÿрÿс] (Pek.). ✧ Andryusha (R.), dim. of R. Andrey (Pek.).

ÖNDÜRÜSKÄ Yak. **Öndürüskä** [Öндÿрÿcкä] (Pek.). ✧ Andryushka (R.), dim. of R. Andrey (Pek.).

ÖNER Selj. 1134, 1148, 1149 **Öner / Önär?** [انـر / انُـر / انَـر / Anar / Onar Mo'în ed-Dîn / Muʿīnuddīn Ünär], governor of Damascus, died in 1149 (Ibn al-Athīr: RHCHor I, 405, 420, 470, 760, 785, Pelliot 180); Selj. 1100 **Öner / Üner** [انَـر / انـر / Üner], an emir, commander-in-chief (sipehsalar) in Berk-yaruq's days (Rāwandī 141, 145, Ahbar 53, 93); Selj. 1142 **Üner** [Ömer ibn Üner], an emir, died in 1142 (Ahbar 66). ✧ I. 'He/she will grow up' cf. Karakh. *ön-* 'wachsen; weggehn' (MK/Brock.); II. 'He who comes to the fore, he who takes the lead' (Erol II).

ÖNÖK Yak. **Önök** [Öнöк], one of At-küsänäy' four sons (Pek.).

ÖNSÄKÄY Bashk. 1714 **Önsäkäy?** [Онзекей Токаев] (MIB I, 105). ✧ 'Little Woman' cf. Tat. fem. PN *Önsä* (Sattarov) (<Ar) + dim. suff. -*käy*.

ÖNÜKÄ Yak. **Önükä** [Öнÿкä], prince Qutuyaχ's younger son (Pek.).

ÖÑÜ Uyg. 12th c. - 14th c. **Öñü** [Öngü] (Radl., USp. 153-54, DTS, EUTS).

ÖPPÖNÜYÄ Yak. **Öppönüyä** [Öппöнÿjä], fem. (Pek.). ✧ Evfimiya (R.) (Pek.).

ÖRDÄK Chuv. 18th-19th c. **Ördäk** [Ордякъ] (Magn. 62); Turk. 20th c. **Ördek**, fem. (Önder, Hınıs). ✧ 'Duck' cf. Uyg., Chag., Az., Crm., Turk *ördäk* 'id.' (Radl. I, 1237).

ÖRDEK see ÖRDÄK

ÖRDEN Kzk. 19th c. **Örden** [Орденевъ] (AOO 26).

ÖRÄ-BÖRT Türk 8th c. - 9th c. **Örä-bört-tutuq** [Örä bört tutuq / Örä Bört Tutuq] (Runic Mss. 219, DTS, ETY II, 96). ⇨ **BÖRT.**

ÖRÄKÄN Hak. 19th-20th c. **Öräkän** [Öpäкäн], fem. (Katanov, Otč. 10). ✧ 'Old woman' (Katanov), cf. Hak. *öräkkän* 'eine Alte, ein altes Mütterchen' (Radl. I, 1219).

ÖRÄMÄ Hak.(Koyb.) 19th-20th c. **Örämä** [Öpäмä], fem. (Katanov, Otč. 13). ✧ 'Cream' (Katanov), cf. Tuv. *örömä* 'die Sahne, der Schmant' (Radl. I, 1222).

ÖRE Trkm. 20th c. **Öre** [Öre] (Zaj. 1971, 331); Trkm. 20th c. **Öre** [Ope] (TrkmRS 505). ✧ 'Brace, support(er)' cf. Trkm. *öre* 'подпорка (кибитки)' (TrkmRS).

ÖRGÖS Yak. **Örgös** [Öpröc], a shaman (Pek.). ✧ 'Someone who acts bravely/boldly, decidedly' cf. Yak. *örgöy-* / *joryoy-* 'проявлять смелую, решите.льну[деятельность' + aff. -s (Pek.).

ÖRİK see **ÜRÜK**

ÖRKEM-BAY see **ÖRKEN**

ÖRKEN Kzk. 19th c. **Örkem-bay** (<**Örken-bay**) [Оркембай] (SODž. 96). ✧ I. 'Descendant(s)' cf. Kzk. *örken* 'потомство' (KzRS); II. 'Maker of ropes'? cf. Crm., Kar. *örkän* (Radl. I, 1227).

ÖRKENČİ Kzk. 19th c. **Örkenči** [Оркенчи] (SOV 80); + aff. -*či*.; ⇨ **ÖRKEN?** + suff. -*či*.

ÖRKER Kzk. 19th c. **Örker** [Оркеръ] (SOV 90). ✧ 'The Pleiades'? cf. Kzk. *ürker* 'Yıldız topu' (KzTS).

ÖRMÖNBET Kzk. **Örmönbet-qan** [Öрмöн Бет Кан] (Proben III, 88 /112/).

ÖRÖPŪNÄ Yak. **Öröpünä** [Öpöпÿнä], fem. (Pek.). ✧ Agrippina (R.) (Pek.). See also **KÜN-ÖRÖPŪNÄ.**

ÖRÖS-KÜÖL-JUL-Jİ̈YİN Yak. **Örös-küöl-jul-jï̈yin** [Öpöc Кÿöл Цул-Цыгын], one of the ancestors of the Yakuts, Ayal's son, Omoγoy's great-grand father (Pek.).

ÖRTEMİŠ Maml. 1368 **Örtemiš** [ارْتامِش] (Sauvaget 35).

ÖRTÜK Chuv. 18th-19th c. **Örtük** [Ортюкъ] (Magn. 63). ✧ 'Cover, blanket' cf. Chag. *örtük* 'id.' (Radl. I, 1236).

ÖRÜNČÄ Yak. **Örünčä** [Öpÿнчä], a Tunguz folklore hero from the past times (Pek.).

ÖRÜÑ-BOΓA Maml. 14th c. **Örüñ-boγa** [ارُنْبُغا] (Sauvaget 36). ✧ 'White bull or stallion' (Sauvaget 36). ⇨ **BUQA.**

ÖRÜNÄ Yak. **Örünä** [Öpÿнä], fem. (Pek.). ✧ Irina (R.) (Pek.).

ÖS-TEMİR see **ÖZ-TEMİR**

ÖSÄN see **QUSAYİN**

ÖSÄR see **ÖSER**

ÖSÄR-ALİ Uzb. 20th c. **Ösär-ali** [Ÿсарали] (Begmatov 1984, 206). ⇨ **ÖSER + ALİ.**

ÖSÄR-TAY Uzb. 20th c. **Ösär-tây** [Ÿсартой] (Begmatov 1984, 206). ✧ 'Growing-up-foal' cf. Kzk. *ös-* 'расти' (KzRS), Uzb. *ös-* 'расти' (UzbRS). ⇨ **ÖSER + TAY** + suff. -*tay(1,2)*?

ÖSEK Kzk. 19th c. **Ösek-pay** [Осекпай] (SODž. 142); Kzk. 19th c. **Ösik-pay / Ösĭk-pay?** [Осыкпай] (SOK 112). ✧ 'Lie, aspersion' cf. Kzk. *ösök* 'die Rederei, das Geschwätz, die Lüge, Verleumdung' (Radl. I, 1293).

ÖSER Uzb. 20th c. **Ösär** [Ÿсар] (Begmatov 1984, 206); Uzb. 20th c. **Ösär-qul** [Ÿсарқул] (Begmatov 1984, 206); Kzk. 19th c. **Öser-bay** [Осербай] (SOV 28); Kzk. 19th c. **Ösir-bay** [Осиръ-бай] (Grod., Pril. 129); Kzk. 19th c. **Üser-bay** [Усербай] (SOK 48, 126, 150, 162); Kzk. 19th c. **Üser-bay** [Усербай] (Grod., Pril 23, 128); Kzk. 1864 **Üser-bay** [Усербай] (Valihanov, Soč. 506); *TN:* Kzk. 19th c. **Öser-bay** [Осербай], a winter pasture, field (AOP 130). ✧ 'He will grow up; He/she won't die' cf. Kzk. *ös-* 'расти' (KzRS), Uzb. *ös-* 'расти' (UzbRS).

ÖSİR see **ÖSER**

ÖSKÄN-TAY Uzb. 20th c. **Öskän-tây** [Ÿскантой] (Begmatov 1984, 206). ✧ 'Grown-up-foal'. ⇨ **ÖSKEN + TAY** + suff. -*tay(1,2)*?

ÖSKEN Uzb. 20th c. **Öskän** [Ÿскан] (Begmatov 1984, 206); Uzb. 20th c. **Öskän-jân** [Ÿсканжон] (Begmatov 1984, 206); Uzb. 20th c. **Öskän-mirza** [Ÿсканмирза] (Begmatov 1984, 206); Kzk. 19th c. **Öskem-bay** (<**Ösken-bay**) [Оскембай] (SODž. 24); Kzk. 19th c. **Öskem-bay** (<**Ösken-bay**) [Оскембай] (SOV 8); Kzk. 19th c. **Ösken-bay** [Оськенбай] (SOV 150); Kirg. **Öskön-bay** [Öскöнбай] (Jud. 642); Kzk. **Öskün-bay** (<**Öskün-bay**) [Ösküm Bai / Öскÿм Баi] (Proben III, 53 /68/); Kzk. 19th c. **Öskün-bay** (<**Öskün-bay**) [Оскумбай] (AOA 2); Kzk. 19th c. **Üskem-bay** (<**Üsken-bay**) [Ускембай] (Konšin, Oč. 105); Kzk. 19th c. **Üskem-bay** (<**Üsken-bay**) [Ускембай] (SODž. 48); Kzk. 19th c. **Üskem-bay** (<**Üsken-bay**) [Усекембай] (SOV 56); Kzk. 19th c. **Üsken-bay** [Ускенбай] (SOK 48, 68, 72); Kzk. 19th c. **Üskön** [Усконовъ] (AOK 102); Kzk. 19th c. **Üsküm-bay** (<**Üskün-bay**) [Ускумбай] (SOK 78); Kzk. 19th c. **Üsküm-bay** (<**Üskün-bay**) [Ускумбай] (SOK 20); Kzk. 19th c. **Üsküm-bay** (<**Üskün-bay**) [Торамуратъ Ускумбаевъ] (Grod., Pril. 98). ✧ 'Grown up' cf. Kzk. *ös-* 'расти' (KzRS), Uzb. *ös-* 'расти' (UzbRS).

ÖSKİ Hak. 19th-20th c. **Öski** [Öскi], fem. (HRS 354). ✧ '(He/she-)goat' (HRS, Butanaev).

ÖSKİLÄÑ Tuv. 19th c. **Öskīläñ** [Öскiläн], from the Tülüš tribe (Proben IX, 110, 130); Tuv. 19th c. **Ösküläñ** [Öскÿläн] (Proben IX, 110, 130).

ÖSKÖN see **ÖSKEN**

ÖSKÜLÄÑ see **ÖSKİLÄÑ**

ÖSKÜM-BAY see **ÖSKEN**

ÖSKÜN see **ÖSKEN**

ÖSKÜZEK see **ÖKSİZÄK**

ÖSMEY Tat.(Sib.) 1598 **Ösmey** [Осмѣй], a prince from Küčüm's family (AI II, 3). ✧ 'He doesn't (won't) grow up' cf. Kzk. *ös-* 'расти' (KzRS).

ÖSÖYÖ Yak. **Ösöyö** [Öcöjö] (Pek.). ✧ 'Silent, lazy man' (Pek.).

ÖSSİN Uzb. 20th c. **Ossin** [Ўссин] (Begmatov 1984, 206). ✧ 'May he grow up!' cf. Kzk. *ös-* 'расти' (KzRS), Uzb. *ös-* 'расти' (UzbRS) + imp. suff. *-sin*.

ÖSTEM Kzk. 19th c. **Östem-bay** [Остембай] (SOK 204). ✧ 'Superior, dominant, high' cf. Kzk. *üstem* 'üstün, hüküm edici, yukarı' (KzTS), also Kzk. PN *Üstem* (Žanuzakov-Esbaeva).

ÖSTİ Kzk. 19th c. **Östi-bay** [Остебай] (SODž. 128). ✧ 'He grew up' cf. Kzk. *ös-* 'расти' (KzRS). See also **ÖSER, ÖSKEN, ÖSSİN.**

ÖTÄ Kzk. 19th c. **Ötä-bay** [Урманъ Отабаевъ] (Grod., Pril. 101); Kzk. 19th c. **Ötä-čan / Ötä-ǰan** [Отачанъ] (Grod., Pril. 186); Bashk. 1761 **Ötä-γul** [Утягул Митикеев] (MIB IV/1, 204); Uzb. 20th c. **Ötä-yâr** [Ўтаёр] (Begmatov 1984, 207); Kzk. 18th c. **Ötä-ulï** [Утявли] (Nepljuev 806); Kzk. 18th c. **Ötä-ulï-batïr** [Утявли-Батыръ] (Nepljuev 820); Kkalp. 20th c. **Öte-biyke** [Өтебийке], fem. (KkRS 778); Kkalp. 20th c. **Öte-ǰan** [Ётеджан] (Bask., Kkalp. 400); Kzk. 1749 **Öte-γul / Ötä-γul?** [اوتاغول / Отегул] (MIK IV, 163); Kzk. 1794 **Öte-ul / Öte-ulu** [اوتولو / Отеул] (MIK IV, 163); Kzk. 1794 **Öte-ul / Öte-wul?** [اوتاؤل / Отеул] (MIK IV, 159); Kkalp. 20th c. **Öte-žan / Öte-ǰan** [Өтежан] (KkRS 775); Kzk. 1785 **Ötewli-biy / Öte-ulï?** [اوتاو لى بى / Отевли бий], a chief (aqsaqal) of the Alaša tribe (MIK IV, 52, 53); Kzk. **Ötö-ülü? / Ötöwlü?** [Öтöÿлÿ] (Proben III, 47 /62/); Bashk. 1761 **Ütä** [Утя Мутикаев] (MIB IV/1, 200); Bashk. 1756 **Ütä-bay** [Утябай] (MIB IV/1, 123); Kzk. 1846 **Ütä-bay** [Утябай Санкибаев], a biy (MKOP 152); Kzk. 1742 **Ütä-bi** [Утяби] (MIB I, 490); Tat. 1702 **Ütä-γul** [Утягулко Тенебековъ], from Kungursk (Letop. ZAK II, 7); Bashk. 1735 **Ütä-γul** [Утегулъ Кошаевъ], a tarχan (Vel.-Zern., Bašk. 20); Bashk. 1789 **Ütä-γul** [Субхангул Утягулов] (MIB V, 260); Kzk. 19th c. **Ütä-qïz** [Утакызъ], fem. (Grod., Pril. 58); Kzk. 18th c. - 19th c. **Üte-bay** [Утебай], a clan (Tynyšp. 71); Kzk. 19th c. **Üte-bay** [Аткильтаръ Утебаевъ] (AUK 570); Kzk. 19th c. **Üte-bay** [Утебай Карамсиновъ] (AUK 537); Kzk. 19th c. **Üte-bay** [Хайралапъ Утебаевъ] (Grod., Pril. 129); Nog. 1649 **Üte-bay** [Утебайко] (AI IV, 96); Kzk. **Üte-ulï** [Исен Утеулиев] (TOOIK III, 182); Kzk. 19th c. **Üte-ulï** [Утеуле] (SOK 160); Kzk. 19th c. **Üte-ulï** [Утевли] (Pam. kn. Turg. 60); *EN:* Kzk. 18th c. - 19th c. **Öte-bay** [Отебай], a clan (Tynyšp. 73, 74); Kzk. 18th c. - 19th c. **Öte-ulï** [Отеулы], a clan (Tynyšp. 65, 73); *TN:* Kzk. 19th c. **Ütä-bay** [Утабай],

a place (?) on the norhtern beach of the Caspian Sea (IIRGO XVI). ✧ I. 'Fulfil (it)!, achieve (it)!' cf. Karakh. *ötä-* 'выполнять; отплачивать' (DTS), Maml. *öte-* 'borç ödetmek' (İM), Tat. *ütä-* 'ausführen, vollbringen' (Radl. I, 1863), Tat. *ütä-* 'исполнять; удовлетворять' (TatRS), Chag., East.T. *ötä-* 'erfüllen, ausführen, bezahlen' (Radl. I, 1264), Uzb. *ötä-* 'исполнять, выполнять; служить' (UzbRS); II. 'Over, too, quite, super; exaggerated, extreme' (Kusimova, Sattarov, Žanuzakov), cf. Bashk. *ütä* 'слишком, крайне' (BRS/Uraksin), Tat. *ütä* 'слишком, очень, крайне' (TatRS), Kzk. *öte* 'очень, слишком, совсем' (KzRS), Kkalp. *öte* 'очень' (KkRS). Cf. also Bashk. PNs *Ütä-bay, Ütä-γol* (Kusimova), Tat. PNs *Ütä-bay, Ütä-bikä, Ütä-γali* (Sattarov), Kzk. PNs *Öte-bay Üte-bay, Öte-žan, Öte-γali / Üte-gali, Öte-maγambet / Üte-maγambet / Üte-muχambet* (Žanuzakov 160, Žanuzakov-Esbaeva). See also **ÖTÄGÄN, ÖTÄMİŠ.**

ÖTÄ-BAS see **ÖTÄ-BAŠ**

ÖTÄ-BAŠ Kzk. 1785 **Ötä-bas-biy / Öte-baš-bi, Ütä-baš-bey** [اوتاباش بى / Утябашъ бей / Отябас бий], a biy, the chief (aqsaqal) of the Tört-qara clan (Sib. Vest. IX, 189, MIK IV, 51, 53). ⇨ **ÖTÄ + BAŠ.**

ÖTÄ-MUXAMMAD Uzb. 20th c. **Ötä-muχammad** [Ўтамухаммад] (Begmatov 1984, 207). ⇨ **ÖTÄ + MUXAMMED.**

ÖTÄ-MURAT Uzb. 20th c. **Ötä-murâd** [Ўтамурод] (Begmatov 1984, 207); Kkalp. 20th c. **Öte-mïrat** [Өтемырат], colloquial (unformal) variant (KkRS 775); Kkalp. 20th c. **Öte-murat** [Ётемурат] (Bask., Kkalp. 55, 93); Kkalp. 20th c. **Öte-murat** [Өтемурат] (KkRS 775). ⇨ **ÖTÄ + MURAT.**

ÖTÄ-NAZAR Uzb. 20th c. **Ötä-nazar / Ötän** [Ўтаназар (Утан)] (Begmatov 1984, 207). ⇨ **ÖTÄ + NAZAR.**

ÖTÄB see **ÖTEP**

ÖTÄGÄY Kzk. 19th c. **Ötägäy** [Отагай] (AOK 14).

ÖTÄGÄN Kzk. 19th c. **Ötägän** [Отаганъ] (Grod., Pril. 150); Kzk. 19th c. **Ötägän** [Отегенъ] (AOO 22); Kzk. 19th c. **Ötägän** [Отегенъ] (AOP 2); Kzk. 19th c. **Ötägän** [Отегенъ] (AOAtb. 50); Uzb. 20th c. **Ötägän** [Утаган] (Begmatov 1984, 207); Uzb. 20th c. **Ötägän-χoǰa** [Утаганхужа] (Begmatov 1984, 207); Kzk. 19th c. **Ötegen** [Отегенъ] (SODž. 112); Kkalp. 20th c. **Ötegen** [Өтеген] (KkRS 775); Kkalp. 20th c. **Ötegen** [Ётеген] (Bask., Kkalp. 30, 36); Kzk. 1817 **Ötegen / Ötägän?** [اوتاكان / Отеген] (MIK IV, 310, 311); Tat. 1715 **Ütägän** [Утеган] (MIB III, 135); Tat. 1747 **Ütägän** [Утяганъ Ехчуринъ] (PSZRI XII, 668); Tat. 1760 **Ütägän** [Утеган Бигашев] (MIB IV/1, 200); Tat. 1764 **Ütägän** [Иштеряк Утеганов] (MIB IV/2, 106); Tat. 1767 **Ütägän** [Утяганъ Уразметевъ] (PSZRI XVIII, 142 XX, 456); Tat. 1777 **Ütägän**

[Утяганъ] (PSZRI XX, 577); Bashk. 1709 **Ütägän** [Утяган] (MIB I, 264); Bashk. 1749 **Ütägän** [Утеган Басланов] (MIB III, 465); Bashk. 1751 **Ütägän** [Акбез Утяганов] (MIB IV/1, 34); Bashk. 1751 **Ütägän** [Утеган Агышев] (MIB IV/1, 57); Bashk. 1760 **Ütägän** [Утяган Алакаев] (MIB IV/1, 187); Bashk. 1762 **Ütägän** [Давыд Утяганов] (MIB IV/2, 302); Bashk. 1763 **Ütägän** [Агабез Утяганов] (MIB IV/1, 269); Bashk. 1771 **Ütägän** [Ашир Утяганов] (MIB IV/1, 358); Bashk. 1774 **Ütägän** [Утеган] (MIB V, 81, 551); Bashk. 1790 **Ütägän** [Абзан Утеганов] (MIB V, 295); Kzk. 18th c. **Ütägän** [Утяганъ] (Nepljuev 812); Kzk. 1819 **Ütägän** [Утяган] (MIK IV, 325); Kzk. 1826 **Ütägän** [Бакабашъ Утягановъ] (TOUAK XXIV, 167); Kzk. 19th c. **Ütägän** [Курбанбай Утаганов] (SKSO III, 7); Bashk. 1738 **Ütegen** [Утегень Биметев] (MIB III, 394); Kzk. 18th c. - 19th c. **Ütegen** [Утегенъ Кубинъ] (ZOOIRGO III, 26); Kzk. 19th c. **Ütegen** [Утегенъ] (SOK 182); Kzk. 19th c. **Ütegen** [Утегенъ] (AOP 38); Kzk. 19th c. **Ütegen** [Несипбай Утегеновъ] (Pam. kn. Turg. 60); Kzk. 19th c. **Ütegen** [Утегенъ] (Pam. kn. Turg. 76); Uzb. 19th c. **Ütegen** [Санакулъ Утегеневъ] (SKSO III, 150); Uzb. 19th c. **Ütegen** [Джумабай Утегеневъ] (SKSO III, 172); Uzb. 19th c. **Ütegen** [Утегенъ] (SKSO III, 176); Kzk. 19th c. **Ütügen** [Утюгенъ] (SOK 16); *TN:* Kzk. **Ötägän** [Өтегень (Утегень)], a hill (Kojčubaev 185). ✧ 'Fulfilled, achieved (wish)' (Sattarov), cf. Karakh. *ötä-* 'выполнять; отплачивать' (DTS), Maml. *öte-* 'borç ödetmek' (İM), Chag., East.T. *ötä-* 'erfüllen, ausführen, bezahlen' (Radl. I, 1264), Turk. *öde-* 'zahlen, bezahlen, einzahlen, einlösen' (HŞ), Tat. *ütä-* 'ausführen, vollbringen' (Radl. I, 1863), Tat. *ütä-* 'исполнять; удовлетворять' (TatRS). See also **ÖTÄ (I.), ÖTÄMIŠ**.

ÖTÄLSIN Uzb. 20th c. **Ötälsin** [Ўталсин] (Begmatov 1984, 207). ✧ 'Let it be fulfilled!'. ⇨ **ÖTEL.**

ÖTÄMIŠ Turk. 1583 **Ödemiš** [Ödemiş] (Ongan, Ank. I, 171); Kzk. 19th c. **Ötemis** [Өтемисъ] (SODž. 46); Kzk. 19th c. **Ötemis** [Отемисъ] (AOA 26); Türk **Ötemiš** [اتامش / Atamech], „un turc affranchi" (Ibn Khaldūn/Quatrem. I, 331); Türk 843 **Ötemiš** [اتامس] (Ibn al-Athīr/Tornb. VII, 62, 76, 80, 108); Türk? 862 **Ötemiš** [أتُامش / اوتامش / اتامش / Utamiš], a vezir who helped caliph al-Mustaʿīn to get the throne (Tabarī, Annal. III, 150, Weil, Abbas II, 378, Björkm. 61); Türk? 862-866, 879 **Ötemiš** [ابا موسى اوتامش / موسى بن أوُتامش / Abou Mouça Outamich] (Masʿūdī, Prairies VII, 324, Tabarī, Annal. III, 1458, 1874, 1930, 1931 etc.); Türk 864 **Ötemiš** [اوتامش] (Fragm. Hist. Ar. 555, 562, 564, 566); Maml. 1300 **Ötemiš** [اتامش بن عبدلله], mamluk of Sultan Šihab ad-Dīn al-Ġūrī (Zetterst. 82, 96, 108); Maml. 1322 **Ötemiš**

[اتامش الناصرى / Atamisch] (Abulfidā V, 350-51); Tat.(Lit.) 1554 **Ötemiš** [Отемышъ] (Kn. Metriki Lit. 103); Türk? **Ütämiš** [اوتامش غلام الواثق / Outamich page de Watik] (Masʿūdī, Prairies VII, 273); Chuv. 18th-19th c. **Ütämiš** [Утемишъ] (Magn. 89); Tat. 1600 **Ütämiš** [Утемыш] (MIB I, 151); Tat. 1624 **Ütämiš** [Утемышъ Темешевъ] (Pokrovskij 71); Tat. 1624 **Ütämiš** [Сюндюк Утемышинъ] (Zolotn. 159); Tat. 1724 **Ütämiš** [Миняш Утемишев] (MIB III, 227); Tat. 1809 **Ütämiš** [Утямышевъ] (PSZRI XXX, 969); Tat.(Sib.) 1600, 1601 **Ütämiš** [Утемыш] (Miller, Ist. Sib. II, 156, 159, 166, 167); Bashk. 1730 **Ütämiš** [Утемыш] (MIB III, 283); Bashk. 1746, 1753 **Ütämiš** [Утемыш Акчюрин] (MIB III, 440, IV/1, 68); Bashk. 1757 **Ütämiš** [Бокча Утемышев] (MIB IV/1, 136); Bashk. 1760 **Ütämiš** [Утямыш Акчюрин] (MIB IV/1, 191, 236); Bashk. 1761 **Ütämiš** [Ракай Утемышев] (MIB IV/1, 200); Bashk. 1777 **Ütämiš** [Утямыш Бизиков] (MIB V, 62, 66); Bashk. 1777 **Ütämiš** [Утямыш Мещеров] (MIB V, 80, 81); Bashk. 1777 **Ütämiš** [Утямыш Муртакаев] (MIB V, 295); Bashk. 1790 **Ütämiš** [Ракай Утямышев] (MIB V, 288); Kzk. 1829 **Ütämiš** [Утямыш] (MIK IV, 324); Kzk. 1846 **Ütämiš** [Утямиш Табулдин], a biy (MKOP 155); Kzk. 19th c. **Ütämiš** [Утямышевъ], a merchant from Mamadyš (AUK 232); Tat.(Mish.) 1708 **Ütämiš / Ütesmiš?** [Елдаш Утесмышев / Утямышев] (MIB I, 233); Kzk. 1820 **Ütämiš-batïr** [Утямышъ батыръ], one of the chiefs of the Nayman tribe (Sib. Vest. IX, 109); Kzk. 19th c. **Ütemis** [Утемисъ] (Grod., Pril. 134); Kzk. 19th c. **Ütemis** [Утелисъ] (AOP 26); Kzk. 19th c. **Ütemis** [Утемысъ] (SODž. 34); *EN:* Trkm. **Ötämiš**, a clan (Németh, HMK 67); *TN:* Turk. 20th c. **Ödemiš** [Ödemiş], a village in the province of İzmir (TMİB 476); Turk. 20th c. **Ötemiš** [Ödemiş], a village in the province of Çankırı (TMİB 248); Tat. 18th c. **Ütämiš(eva)** [Утямышева], a village in the district of Tetyushinsk (Korsakov 337); Crm. **Ütemiš-eli** [Utemisch eli], a place (?) north of Eski-Qïrïm (Jervis VIII). ✧ 'Fulfilled, achieved (wish), child being paid for' (Kusimova, Sattarov), cf. Karakh. *ötä-* 'выполнять; отплачивать' (DTS), Maml. *öte-* 'borç ödetmek' (İM), Chag., East.T. *ötä-* 'erfüllen, ausführen, bezahlen' (Radl. I, 1264), Turk. *öde-* 'zahlen, bezahlen, einzahlen, einlösen' (HŞ), Turk. *öde-* 'zahlen, bezahlen, einzahlen, einlösen' (HŞ), Tat. *ütä-* 'ausführen, vollbringen' (Radl. I, 1863), Tat. *ütä-* 'исполнять; удовлетворять' (TatRS), also Németh, HMK 67, Rásonyi, KÖA 123. See also **ÖTÄ (I.), ÖTÄGÄN**.

ÖTÄR see **ÖTER**

ÖTÄŠ see **ÖTEŠ**

ÖTÄW Kzk. 19th c. **Ötäw** [Отавъ] (Grod., Pril. 189); Kzk. 19th c. **Ütäw** [Тюлебекъ Утауевъ] (Grod., Pril. 154). ✧ 'Payment' cf. Kzk. *ötew* 'ödemek, karşılığını vermek' (KzTS).

ÖTÄWLİ   Kzk. 19th c. **Ötäwli** [Отавли] (Grod., Pril. 35). ❖ 'Paid'. ⇨ **ÖTÄW** + suff. -*li*.

ÖTE see **ÖTÄ**

ÖTE-NİYAZ   Kkalp. 20th c. **Öte-niyaz** [Ётенийяз] (Bask., Kkalp. 15, 44, 73); Kkalp. 20th c. **Öte-niyaz** [Өтенияз] (KkRS 775). ⇨ **ÖTÄ** + **NİYAZ.**

ÖTE-TİLÄW   Kzk. 19th c. **Öte-tlew** / **Öte-tïlew** [Отетлеу] (SODž. 58); Kzk. 19th c. **Öte-tïlew** (<**Öte-tilew?**) [Отлеу] (AOA 102); Kzk. 18th c. **Ütä-tïliw-biy** / **Ütä-tïläw-bey** [Утятливъ-Бій / Утятлявъ], a tarχan (Nepljuev 767, 778, Sib. Vest. IX, 189). ❖ '(Child) Wished, asked for very much' (Žanuzakov). ⇨ **ÖTÄ** + **TİLÄW.**

ÖTE-TİLEW see **ÖTE-TİLÄW**

ÖTE-TİLEW   Kzk. 19th c. **Öte-tïlew** [Отетлеу] (SOK 114).

ÖTEXAN see **ÖTEQAN**

ÖTEY   Kzk. 19th c. **Ötey** [Отей] (SODž. 20); Kzk. 19th c. **Ötey** [Отей] (AOA 126); Kzk. 19th c. **Ötey-bay** [Отейбай] (AOP 114); Kzk. 19th c. **Ötey-bek** [Отейбекъ] (SOV 96); Kzk. **Ütäy** [Утяй] (Žarkov, Bibl. dlja čtenija CXXIV, 231); Kkalp. 1740 **Ütäy-bi** [Утяй-би] (MIKk. 208); Bashk. 1663 **Ütey** [Карабаш Утеев] (MIB I, 175); Bashk. 1701 **Ütey** [Утей Васильев] (MIB III, 13); Bashk. 1732 **Ütey** [Мевлюкей Утеев] (MIB III, 310); Bashk. 1748 **Ütey** [Утей Юнусов] (MIB III, 456); Bashk. 1756 **Ütey** [Утей Чюрагулов] (MIB IV/1, 106); Bashk. 1772 **Ütey** [Утей Ярабкулов] (MIB IV/2, 403); Bashk. 1793 **Ütey** [Утей Ишбердин] (MIB V, 329); Kzk. 19th c. **Ütey** [Утей] (AOAtb. 50). ❖ 'Wished, asked (from God)' (Sattarov). ⇨ **ÖTÄ** + dim. suff. -*y*.

ÖTEY-BAS   Kzk. 19th c. **Ötey-bas** [Отейбасъ] (SOV 26). ⇨ **ÖTÄ** / **ÖTEY?** + **BAŠ**. See also **ÖTÄ-BAŠ.**

ÖTEK   Kzk. 19th c. **Ötek** [Отекъ] (SOV 136); Kzk. 1785 **Ötek-bahadïr** [باهادر اوتك / Отек б.], chief (aqsaqal) (MIK IV, 52, 53); Bashk. 1709 **Ütäk** [Утяк] (MIB III, 44); Bashk. 1735 **Ütäk** [Утякъ Назаровъ], a tarχan (Vel.-Zern., Bašk. 20); Bashk. 1749 **Ütäk** [Максют Утяков] (MIB III, 465); Bashk. 1751 **Ütäk** [Максют Утяков] (MIB IV/1, 57); Bashk. 1754 **Ütäk** [Бурангул Утяков] (MIB IV/1, 84); Kzk. 19th c. **Ütek** [Утекъ] (Lomakin 32). ❖ I. 'Traveller passing through; alien, foreigner' cf. Chag. *ötäk* 'vorübergehend, fremd' (Radl. I, 1264); II. 'Fulfilled, (Son) Wished, asked (from God)' (Sattarov: *Ütäk*). ⇨ **ÖTÄ?** + suff. -*k*.

ÖTEKE   Kzk. 19th c. **Öteke?** [Отекинъ] (AOO 54). ⇨ **ÖTÄ** + dim. suff. -*ke*.

ÖTEQAN   Kkalp. 20th c. **Öteχan** [Өтехан], fem. (KkRS 778); Kkalp. 20th c. **Öteqan** [Ётекъан], fem. (Bask., Kkalp. 71). ⇨ **ÖTÄ** + suff. -*qan(1)*.

ÖTEL   Kzk. 19th c. **Ötel-bay** [Отельбай] (AOP 86); Kzk. 19th c. **Ötel-bay** [Отелбай] (SOK 140, 214, 300); Kzk. 19th c. **Ötel-bay** [Отельбай] (SOV 138, 142); Kzk. 19th c. **Ötöl-bay** [Отольбай] (SOK 260); Kzk. 1846 **Ütäl** [Утял Сагындыков], a biy (MKOP 157); Kzk. 19th c. **Ütel-bay** [Утельбай] (SOK 34); Kzk. 19th c. **Ütel-bek** [Утельбекъ] (SOK 38). ❖ 'Be paid for; be recuperated' cf. Kzk. *ötel-* 'быть возмещённым; быть выплаченным' (KzRS). See also **TÖLEN.**

ÖTEMİS see **ÖTÄMİS**

ÖTEN   Kzk. 19th c. **Öten** [Отенъ] (AOP 70); Kzk. 19th c. **Öten** [Отеновъ] (AOK 98); Kzk. 19th c. **Üten** [Утенъ] (AOA 82).

ÖTENČİ   Kzk. 19th c. **Ötenči** [Отенчи] (SODž. 110). ⇨ **ÖTEN** + suff. -*či*.

ÖTEP   Kzk. 19th c. **Ötäb** [Халъ Назаръ Отабовъ] (Grod., Pril. 158, 167); Kzk. 19th c. **Ötäb** [Джузайбай Отабовъ] (Grod., Pril. 161); Kzk. 19th c. **Ötäb** [Отабъ] (Grod., Pril. 31); Uzb. 20th c. **Ötäb** [Ўтаб] (Begmatov 1984, 207); Uzb. 20th c. **Ötäb-bây** [Ўтаббой] (Begmatov 1984, 207); Uzb. 20th c. **Ötäb-bek** [Ўтаббек] (Begmatov 1984, 207); Kzk. 19th c. **Ötep** [Отепъ] (AOAtb. 18); Kzk. 19th c. **Ötep** [Отепъ] (AOK 14); Kzk. 19th c. **Ötep-pay** [Отеппай] (SODž. 52); Kzk. 19th c. **Ötep-pay** [Отеппай] (SOV 18); Bashk. 1754 **Ütäp** [Утяп] (MIB IV/1, 84); Kzk. 1819 **Ütäp** [Утяп] (MIK IV, 323); Kkalp. 1740 **Ütäp-bi** [Утяпъ-Би] (Hanykov, Poezdka 19); Kzk. 19th c. **Ütep** [Утепъ] (SOK 150); Kzk. 19th c. **Ütep** [Утепъ] (Grod., Pril. 78). ❖ I. 'Wished, asked (child); Compensating (given by God)'; II. 'Passed by'? ⇨ **ÖTÄ.**

ÖTEP-BERGEN   Kkalp. 20th c. **Ötep-bergen** [Өтепберген] (KkRS 775). ⇨ **ÖTEP** + **BERGEN.**

ÖTER   Tat. 1706 **Ötär-γul** [Отяргул] (MIB III, 19); Kzk. 19th c. **Öter-bay** [Отербай] (SODž. 52). ❖ 'He who will fulfil, achieve (his goal); He will compensate'. ⇨ **ÖTÄ?**

ÖTEŠ   Kzk. 19th c. **Ötäš** [Оташъ] (Grod., Pril. 64); Kzk. 19th c. **Ötäš** [Оташъ] (SODž. 6); Kzk. 19th c. **Öteš** [Отешъ] (AOO 70); Kzk. 19th c. **Öteš** [Отешъ] (AOP 130); Kkalp. 20th c. **Öteš** [Өтеш] (KkRS 775); Kzk. 19th c. **Öteš-pay** [Отешпай] (SOK 216); Tat.(Mish.) 1755, 1761 **Ütäš** [Утяш Игимбетев] (MIB IV/1, 93, 219); Bashk. 1777 **Ütäš** [Утяш Байгулов] (MIB V, 301); Bashk. 1777 **Ütäš** [Утяш Каипов] (MIB V, 57, 153); Tat. 1446 **Üteš** [Утешъ], a prince (PSRL VI, 172, VIII, 114, XII, 66, XX, 259); Tat. 1624 **Üteš** [Утешъ Кобяковъ] (Pokrovskij 72); Bashk. 1675 **Üteš** [Капей Утешев] (MIB I, 201); Bashk. 1731 **Üteš** [Якуп Утешев] (MIB III, 292); Bashk. 1732 **Üteš** [Азангул Утешев] (MIB III, 298); Bashk. 1740 **Üteš** [Утеш] (MIB I, 404); Nog. 1649 **Üteš** [Уразъ-Девлетъ Утешевъ] (AI IV, 122); Bashk.

1735 **Üteš / Ütäš?** [Утеш (Утяш) Кисеев] (MIB III,
331); Kzk. 19th c. **Üteš-pay** [Утешпай] (SOK 172). ❖
I. '(Son) Wished, asked (from God)' (Sattarov: *Ütäš*);
II. 'Compensating' derived from Kzk. *öte-*
'compensate' (Bese 4). ⇨ **ÖTÄ** + suff. *-š*.

ÖTEWLİ see **ÖTÄ**

ÖTKÄN   Uzb. 1704 **Ötkän** [اوتکان / Otkan-i Juz], from
the Yüz tribe, fought efficiently against Sultan
Ubaydullah in Bukhara (Buchari 263, 271). ❖ 'He went
away; passed, went by' cf. Uyg., Kuman, Chag., Alt.,
Kirg., Kzk. etc. *öt-* 'hindurchgehen, durchsickern;
vergehen, verleben' (Radl. I, 1260).

ÖTKEL   Kzk. 19th c. **Ötkel-bay** [Откельбай] (SOK
168, 202); Kzk. 19th c. **Ötköl-bay** [Откольбай] (SOK
102, 300). ❖ 'Ford, shallow' cf. Kzk. *ötkel* 'id.'
(KzRS), Kirg. *ötköl* 'die Furt' (Radl. I, 1269).

ÖTKÖL see **ÖTKEL**

ÖTKÜZLİ-URUS   Oghuz/Trkm. 13th c. **Ötküzli-urus**
[اوتکوزلی اورس / Öтküзли-Урус] (Abulg./Kon. 1165).
⇨ **? + URUS.**

ÖTLEW see **ÖTE-TİLÄW**

ÖTÖ-GÜN   Kzk. 19th c. **Ötö-gün** [Отёгунъ] (AOK
114). ⇨ **ÖTÄ + KÜN?**

ÖTÖ-ÜLÜ see **ÖTÄ**

ÖTÖL see **ÖTEL**

ÖTRÄT see **ÜTRÄT**

ÖTÜKÄN   Uyg. 13th-14th c. **Ötükän / Ödükän**
[Ödükän] (Zieme, Mat. III, 271). ❖ Toponym. See also
İL-ÖTÜKÄN.

ÖTÜKÄN-TEMÜR   Uyg. 12th c. - 14th c. **Ötükän-
temür / Ötükän-temir** [ötükän temür / Ötükän Tämir]
(DTS/USp., Zieme, Mat. III, 271 (after Yamada, who
mistakenly reads it as *Ötünč*)). ❖ 'Ötükän-Iron', 'Iron
from Ötükän'? ⇨ **TEMİR.**

ÖTÜNČ-TEMÜR   Uyg. 12th-14th c. **Ötünč-temür /
Otunč-temir?** [ötünč temür / otunč temir / Ötünç
Tämür / Otunč Tämir] (DTS, EUTS, Radl., USp. 137).
❖ I. 'Appeal/wish-Iron' cf. Türk *ötünč I* 'просьба'
(DTS); II. 'Loan-Iron' cf. Karakh. *ötünč II* 'ссуда,
заем' (DTS). ⇨ **TEMİR.**

ÖTÜR   Uyg.? **Ötür-buyla-tarχan** [Ötür Buila Tarχan]
(Fest. Thomsen 211); Uyg. 762 **Ötür-ügä** [Ötür Ügä]
(Mahrnāmag 9). ❖ 'Indigestion, flux, diarrhoea' cf.
Uyg. *ötür* 'id.' (DTS).

ÖVELEK   Trkm. 20th c. **Övelek** [Övelek] (Zaj. 1971,
333); Trkm. 20th c. **Övelek** [Овелек] (TrkmRS 496).
❖ 'Tomfool, simpleton' cf. Trkm. *övelek* 'разиня (о
ребёнке)' (TrkmRS).

ÖVEZ   Trkm. 20th c. **Övez** [Övez] (Zaj. 1971, 329);
Trkm. 20th c. **Övez** [Овез] (TrkmRS 496). ❖
'Compensation' cf. Trkm. *övez* 'возмещение'
(TrkmRS) (<Ar.).

ÖZ   Türk 8th - 9th c. **Öz** (DTS); Maml. 1325 **Öz**
[از بك / يوزبك] (Zetterst. 161-174, 181, 200, 221);

Selj. 12th c. **Öz-aba / Öz-apa?** [از ابه], Qïzïl-arslan
atabeg's slave (mamluk) (Rāwandī 347); Türk 8th c. -
9th c. **Öz-apa-tutuq** [Öz Apa Tutuq] (Thomsen, Stein
219, DTS, ETY II, 96); Uyg. 13th-14th c. **Öz-bäg** [Öz
Bg] (Zieme, Mat. III, 272); Selj. 1198 **Öz-beg? / Öz-
aba?** [از به], ruler of Balχ (Balkh) (Ibn al-Athīr/Tornb.
XII, 88); Selj.? 12th c. **Öz-bek** [اٌز بك], brother of the
atabeg Abubekir (Rāwandī 388-393 etc.); Selj. 1194
Öz-bek [ازبك], ruler of Azerbaijan (Abulfidā/Ed. I, 71,
100); Selj. 1224 **Öz-bek** [از بك / Vzbek], ruler of
Tawrīz, yielded to the Tatars [Mongols] (Abulfidā IV,
320-21); Khorezm. 13th c. **Öz-bek** [ازبك باين /
Ouzbek Bâin], one of the officers of J̌elāleddīn Meñgü-
berdi (1220-1231) (Nasawī 90); Maml. 1325 **Öz-bek**
[از بك العنتابى] (Zetterst. 170); Maml. 1332 **Öz-bek**
[أزبك الفلخرى], an emir (Dawād. 365); Maml. 1332
Öz-bek [أزبك الجرمكى] (Dawād. 368); Maml. 1398/99,
1400 **Öz-bek** [از بك الرمضانى] (Iyās I, 321, Ibn
Taghrīb. VI, 25, 160); Maml. 1400/01 **Öz-bek** [از بك],
a chancellor (Ibn Taghrīb. VI, 93, 182); Maml. 1401/02
Öz-bek [از بك الاشتر] (Ibn Taghrīb. VI, 97); Maml.
1404/05 **Öz-bek** [از بك الاهيمى] (Ibn Taghrīb. VI, 128,
131); Maml. 1421 **Öz-bek** [أزبك المحمّدىّ الظاهرىّ]
(Ibn Taghrīb. VI, 512, 529, etc.); Maml. 1422 **Öz-bek**
[از بك المحمودى] (Iyās II, 16); Maml. 1451, 1453,
1464, 1468/69, 1471/72, 1475, 1499 **Öz-bek**
[اليوسفى / ازبك السيفى / ازبك من ططخ / السيفى/
ازبك / Uzbek min Tuṭukh], viceroy of Syria, then
commander-in-chief, an atabeg of the emir-i kebir,
treasurer, died in 1499, mentioned in the inscription of a
copper dish (bronze dish), sword and mosque as well
(Ibn Taghrīb. VIII, 411, 497 etc., Iyās II, 10, 100, 101,
206, 282, 355 etc. III, 9, 23, 160, Weil, Chalif. V, 256,
300, 348, 374, Berchem 307, 316, Mayer 244-247);
Maml. 1453 **Öz-bek** [از بك بن ططر] (Iyās II, 43);
Maml. 1456 **Öz-bek** [از بك الششمانى] (Ibn Taghrīb.
VIII, 378); Maml. 1467/68 **Öz-bek** [از بك], governor of
Tripolis (Iyās II, 96); Maml. 1475/76 **Öz-bek** [جتمق
از بك قشق الظاهرى] (Iyās II, 159, 316); Maml. 1479
Öz-bek [ازبك الخا صكى أبوريد الاينالى] (Iyās II, 191,
225, 349); Maml. 1486 **Öz-bek** [از بك قنص] (Iyās II,
238, 289, 361); Maml. 1487 **Öz-bek** [از بك الاشرفى]
(Iyās II, 247); Maml. 1489 **Öz-bek** [از بك النصرانى]
(Iyās II, 259); Maml. 1493/94 **Öz-bek** [السيفى جانيبك]
(Iyās II, 317); Maml. 1500/01 **Öz-bek**
[از بك النصراوى] (Iyās II, 382); Maml.? 1516 **Öz-bek**
[از بك العجمى] (Iyās III, 52); Maml. / Turk.? 1498/99
Öz-bek [از بك المكحل بن طراباى] (Iyās II, 352, III, 3,
26, 97); Maml.? / Turk. 1516 **Öz-bek** [از بك السوفى]
(Iyās III, 62); Tat.(GH) 1311, 1313, 1316, 1340 **Öz-bek**

/ **Öz-bäk** / **Üz-bek** [Οὐζπέχ / Озбякъ / Азбякъ / Возбякъ / Узбекъ], Giyaseddin Muhammed, the Mongol (Kipchak?) ruler of the Golden (Blue?) Horde (1312-1340) (Nuwairī 145 ff., 166 ff., Lavr. 501, PSRL I, 229, IV, 55, V, 205, X, 178 etc., PSRL (Russk. Hr.) I, 403, 409, Byz. Turc. 229); Selj. 1220/21, 1221, 1224 **Öz-bek** / **Üz-bek** [از بك / اوزبك / Ouzbek / Vzbek / Uzbec / Узбекъ Атабекъ], an atabeg (prince) of Azerbaijan, the enemy of Ǧelāleddīn Meñgü-berdi (1220-1231), the ruler of Tawrīz who yielded to the Tatars [Mongols] (Ibn al-Athīr: RHCHor II/1, 154-55, Qazw. 496, 501, Nasawī 77 etc., RaD/Ber. ﭑ, 90, Abulfidā IV, 320-21); Selj.? **Öz-bek-aγa** [الزبك،غا] (Āšikp. 109, 110); Maml. 1321 **Öz-bek-χan** [از بك خان], ruler of Mosul (Iyās I, 161); Maml. 1432 **Öz-bek-χoǰa** [از بك حجا] (Ibn Taghrīb. VI, 704); Khorezm. 13th c. **Öz-bek-pehlivān** [از بك پهلوان], a deputy of Ǧelāleddīn Meñgü-berdi (1220-1231) in India (Qazw. 500, 501); Chag. / Uzb. 1500 **Öz-bek-sultan** / **Üz-bek-sultan** [Узбекъ Султанъ], relative of Sheybani, the Uzbek Khan (Šejb. LXXVIII); Uyg. 8th c. **Öz-bilgä** (DTS); Uyg.? **Öz-čigši** [Ǯägän öz čigši] (Fest. Thomsen 211); Karakh.? 868 **Öz-čur** [ار جُور / از جُور] (Kindī 208-212); Oghuz/Trkm. **Öz-χan** [اوز خان], Mogol-khan's son in the Turkic legend of origin (Abulg./Desm. 12); Türk/Uyg. 8th c. - 9th c. **Öz-qatun**, fem. (Le Coq, Man. III, 46); Oghuz 1043 **Öz-tegin** [ازسكين حاجب], Mawdūd's (1041-1048) supreme commander against the Seljuks (Mirch. Gasnevid. 253); Selj. 1132 **Üz-bek** [حسين اوزبك / Hoçein Uzbec], an emir in the service of Sultan Mas‘ūd ibn Muχammad (1134-1152), died in 1132 (Ibn al-Athīr, Atab.: RHCHor II/2, 80); Tat.(GH) 14th c. **Üz-bek** [Узбек] (RaD II, 76); Maml.? 13th c. **Üz-bek** [ازبك] (Ibn al-Athīr: RHCHor I, 862); Tat.(Mish.) **Üz-bek** [Üzbek] (IOAIÊK XIX, 142); Bashk. 1754 **Üz-bek** [Узбек Буляновъ] (MIB IV/1, 84); Kzk. 19th c. **Üz-bek** [Узбекъ] (SODž. 64); Kzk. 19th c. **Üz-bek** [Узбекъ] (SODž. 138); Trkm. 1855 **Üz-bek** (<**Üz-bek-qlīč**) [Узбек Клыч] (MIT II, 261); Kzk. **Üz-pök** [Üzpök] (Almásy 479); Selj.? 1299 **Üzbek** [ازبك / Saremeddīn Uzbec] (Abulfidā/Ed. I, 171, 180); Oghuz/Trkm. 13th c. **Üzbek-χan** [اوزبك خان / Узбек-хан] (Abulg./Kon. 1295, 1395); Tat.(GH) 14th c. **Üzbek-χan** [Узбек-хан], a ruler of the Golden Horde (1312-1340) (MIT I, 17, 516); *EN:* Kzk. 18th c. - 19th c. **Öz-bek** [Озбек], a clan (Tynyšp. 72); *TN:* Turk. 20th c. **Öz-bey Yeniköy** [Özbey Yeniköy], a village in the province of Aydın, Turkey (TMİB 130); Turk. 20th c. **Öz-beyli** [Özbeyli], a village in the province of Uşak, Turkey (TMİB 880). ✧ 'Self, inner part, heart, life, the best (of something)' cf. Türk, Uyg., Karakh. *öz* 'id.' (DTS), Kuman, Chag., Az., Crm., Kirg., Kzk. etc. *öz* /

ös 'id.' (Radl. I, 1299), also Pelliot 92: 'maître de [sa] personne', Sauvaget 36, H. Eren, Türk Onomastique'i hakkında 127-129, Žaparov-Konkobaev 1984, p. 127-128, Blagova 1997, 708. Concerning the names *Öz-bek* / *Üz-bek* consider the interpretation: 'Perfect Lord (bey)' („le bey accompli") in Ibn al-Athīr: RHCHor I, 862. See also **ALT-ÖZ, BUYAN-ÖZ, İN-ÖZ, İNAL-ÖZ.**

ÖZ-APA-TUTUQ see **ÖZ**

ÖZ-BİLGÄ-BÜNYİN Uyg. 759 **Öz-bilgä-bünyin** / **Öz-bilgä-büyin** [Öz Bilgä Bünyin / Öz Bilgä Büyin] (ETY I, 182). ⇨ **ÖZ** + **BİLGÄ.**

ÖZ-ǮANÏ-BEK Kzk. **Öz-ǰanï-bek** [Öз Цаны Бек] (Proben III, 68 /89/). ⇨ **ÖZ** + **ǮANÏ-BEK.**

ÖZ-DEMİR see **ÖZ-TEMİR**

ÖZ-ER Trkm. **Öz-er** [اوزر] (Āšikp. 225, Sümer: DTCFD XI, 331). ✧ 'He himself is brave' (Erol II). ⇨ **ÖZ** + **ER.**

ÖZ-YİGÄN-ALP-TURAN Türk 7th-9th c. **Öz-yigän-alp-turan** [Öz Yiğen Alp Turan / Öz Yigän Alp Turan] (ETY III, 61). ⇨ **ÖZ** + **YİGÄN** + **ALP** + **TURAN?**

ÖZ-TAY Crm. 1679 **Ös-tay-mirza** [اوستای ميرزا] (Vel.-Zern., Crim. 673, 682). ⇨ **ÖZ** + **TAY** + suff. *-tay(1,2)*?

ÖZ-TEMİR Turk.? 1488, 1503 **Ös-demir?** / **Us-tamïr?** [اصطمر / Astimur], a leader of a caravan of pilgrims (Iyās II, 249, 260, 394, Weil, Chalif. II, 390); Crm. 1641 **Ös-temir** [اوستمر بن جانتمور بی], Ǯan-temür's son (Vel.-Zern., Crim. 284); Kzk. 19th c. **Ös-temir** [Остемиръ] (SODž. 138); Kzk. 19th c. **Ös-temir** [Остемиръ] (SODž. 138); Maml. 14th c. **Öz-dämür** [الاَزْدمُرْ], an emir coming from Circassia (Sauvaget 36); Selj. 12th c. **Öz-demir** [ازد مر], police chief in Isfahan (Rāwandī); Maml. **Öz-demir** [ازد مر], slave of the emir Seyfeddīn Beštek (?) (Zetterst. 211); Maml. 1253 **Öz-demir** [Izz-eddin Ezdemur] (Makrīzī I, 39); Maml. 1282/83 **Öz-demir** [ازد مر العلائی] (Iyās I, 115); Maml. 1300 **Öz-demir** [حسام الدين ازد مرالمجمری] (Zetterst. 98, 130); Maml. 1301 **Öz-demir** [ازدمر المخيری / حسام‌الدين], an emir (Dawād.); Maml. 1349/50 **Öz-demir** [ازدمر العمری الناصری] (Iyās I, 196-225); Maml. 1377/78 **Öz-demir** [ازدمر الشمسی] (Iyās I, 169); Maml. 1393 **Öz-demir** [ازدمر الساقی] (Iyās I, 300, Weil, Chalif. II, 48); Maml.? 1398/99 **Öz-demir** [عزّالدين ازدمر], Inal al-Yūsufī's brother (Ibn Taghrīb. VI, 12, 21 etc.); Maml. 1421 **Öz-demir** [ازدمر الناصرّی / Azdimur] (Ibn Taghrīb. VI, 416, 488, Weil, Chalif. II, 161); Maml. 1421 **Öz-demir** [السيفی ازد مر امير عشروت] (Mayer 247-48); Maml. 1422 **Öz-demir** [ازد مر] (Ibn Taghrīb. VI, 557); Maml.? 1429 **Öz-demir** [ازد مر الساقی], among

Taghrī-birdī's mamluks (Ibn Taghrīb. VI, 654); Maml. 1460/61 **Öz-demir** [ازدمر الطويل الابرهيمى] (Iyās II, 71, 93, 124, 149, 197, Weil, Chalif. II, 257); Maml. 1463, 1467 **Öz-demir** [الابراهيمى الاشرفى الاينالى] [ازدمر] (Ibn Taghrīb. VIII, 445, 622, 633 etc.); Maml. 1467 **Öz-demir** [ازدمر تمساح الظاهرى] (Ibn Taghrīb. VIII, 609); Maml. 1468/69 **Öz-demir** [ازد مر], an emir (Iyās II, 102, 182, 224, 348); Maml. 1470/71 **Öz-demir** [ازد مر الاستادار] (Iyās II, 127); Maml. 1472/73 **Öz-demir** [ازدمر الصغير الابرهيمى] (Iyās II, 135); Maml. 1475 **Öz-demir** [ازدمر بن مزيد] (Iyās II, 156-281); Maml. 1475/76 **Öz-demir** [ازدمر المسرطن] (Iyās II, 158, 203, 281); Maml. 1478 **Öz-demir** [ازدمر الاشرفى], governor of Tripolis (Sobernh. I, 57); Maml. 1478 **Öz-demir** [السيفى ازد مر], governor of Tripolis (Sauvaget: BEO XII (1948), 51); Maml. 1479 **Öz-demir** [ازد مر], governor of Hamah (Iyās II, 190); Maml. 1480 **Öz-demir** [ازدمر بن ازبك] (Iyās II, 194); Maml. 1482 **Öz-demir** [ازدمر تمساح] (Iyās II, 203-286); Maml. 1483 **Öz-demir** [ازدمر الاشتر] (Iyās II, 218); Maml. 1484 **Öz-demir** [ازد مر], emir of the mejlis (Iyās II, 225, 231); Maml. 1487 **Öz-demir** [ازدمر الاشرفى برسباى] (Iyās II, 245); Maml. 1489 **Öz-demir** [ازد مر النقيه] (Iyās II, 260, 375); Maml. 1494/95 **Öz-demir** [ازدمر بن مرادخجا] (Iyās II, 288); Maml. 1496/97 **Öz-demir** [ازدمر], a treasurer (Iyās II, 314, 317); Maml. 1498/99 **Öz-demir** [بن على باى ازدمر] (Iyās II, 353-379, III, 61, 68); Maml. 1498/99 **Öz-demir** [ازد مر] (Iyās II, 346); Maml. 1516 **Öz-demir** [ازدمر المهمندار] (Iyās III, 3, 7, 73); Maml. 1516 **Öz-demir** [ازد مر], a chancellor (Iyās III, 82, 214, 295); Turk. 1546 **Öz-demir**, a pasha, the conquerer of Yemen (EI III, 156); Maml. 1254 **Öz-demür** [Ezdemur-Bawaschki] (Makrīzī I, 50); Kzk. **Öz-temir** [Öз Темір] (Proben III, 101 /129/); Crm. 1636 **Öz-temür-mirza** [اوزتمور ميرزا] (Vel.-Zern., Crim. 143, 209); Uzb. 1701, 1707 **Öz-timür-bi** [اوز تيمور بى / Oez-Timur Bi-i Qatafân], nobleman from Bukhara, the governor (hākim) of Nasaf, then a „dīvānbigi" in 1707 (Buchari 258-59, 265, 286-87); Kzk. 19th c. **Üs-tämir** [Устамиръ] (SOK 216); Kzk. 19th c. **Üs-tämir? / Us-tamir?** [Устамыръ] (SOK 216); Tat. 1600 **Üs-temir** [Устемир] (MIB I, 151); Tat. 1600 **Üs-temir** [Устемир Канчюрин] (MIB I, 152); Tat.(Sib.) 1600 **Üs-temir** [Устемир] (Miller, Ist. Sib. II, 156); Bashk. 1690 **Üs-temir** [Тленчекъ Устемировъ] (Vel.-Zern., Bašk. 39); Kzk. 19th c. **Üs-temir** [Устемиръ] (SODž. 42); Kzk. 19th c. **Üs-temir** [Устемиръ] (SOV 50); Kzk. 19th c. **Üs-temir** [Устемиръ] (SODž. 42); Kzk. 19th c. **Üs-temir** [Устемиръ] (SOV 50, 52); Tat.(Sib.) 1600 **Üs-timir** [Устимир Канчурин] (Miller, Ist. Sib. II, 156, 159); *EN:* Kzk. 18th c. - 19th c. **Ös-temĭr** [Остемр], a clan (Tynyšp. 74); *TN:* Turk. 20th c. **Öz-demir** [Özdemir], a village in the province of Antalya, Turkey (TMİB 101); Kzk. **Üs-temir** [Устемиръ], a village in the region of Chu river (Vyšnegorskij: Tr. Syr-D. OSK 1888, 14). ✧ I. 'The best or better quality iron' (Sauvaget 36), 'Pure iron' (Bese 15); II. 'Man with strong, iron-like heart' (Gafurov 42). ⇨ **ÖZ + TEMİR.**

ÖZ-TEMÜR see **ÖZ-TEMİR**

ÖZDEN   Kzk. 19th c. **Özdem-bay (<Özden-bay)** [Оздембай] (AOAtb. 6); Kzk. 19th c. **Özden-bay** [Озденбай] (AOO 60); Tat. 1624 **Üzden** [Узденъ Сарымовъ] (Pokrovskij 70); Kzk. 19th c. **Üzden-bay** [Узденбай] (AOK 2); Kzk. 19th c. **Üzden-bay** [Узденбай] (AOP 14); Nog. 20th c. **Üzdön** [Хасан Къарамырза улы Уьздоьн / Хасан Карамурзаевич Узденов], Baskakov's informant from the aul of Erkin-yurt (Bask., Nog. 143).

ÖZEN   Chuv. 18th-19th c. **Özen** [Озенъ] (Magn. 61); Kzk. 19th c. **Özen-bay** [Озенбай] (SOK 88). ✧ 'Stubborn'? cf. Kuman *özäñ* 'widerspenstig' (Radl. I, 1301).

ÖZEN-BAŠLĬ   Crm. 19th c. **Özen-bašlĭ** [A. Özenbašly] (Mende 140, 141). ✧ 'Person coming from (or born in) *Özen-baš* (village)'. ⇨ **ÖZEN? + BAŠ** + suff. *-li.*

ÖZENKÄ   Chuv. 18th-19th c. **Özenkä** [Озенка] (Magn. 61). ⇨ **ÖZEN** + dim. suff. *-kä.*

ÖZLİ-TEMÜR   Oghuz/Trkm. 13th c. **Özli-temür** [اوزلى تيمور / Özli-Тимур], Yomut's son (Abulg./Kon. 1240). ⇨ **ÖZ + TEMİR** + suff. *-li.*

ÖZÖK   Alt. 19th-20th c. **Özök** [Öзöк], fem. (OjrRS 213). ✧ 'The inner part; heart; kernel' cf. Alt., Kirg., Kzk. *özök* 'das Innere eines Dinges, der Kern etc.' (Radl. IV, 1301); II. 'Brook, stream; valley' cf. Alt., Kzk. *özök* 'der Fluss, Bach; das Thal' (Radl. IV, 1302).

ÖZÜ-BEK   Crm. **Özü-bäk** [Öзÿ Бäк] (Proben VII, 161); Tat.(Mish.) 1759 **Üzü-bek** [Усман Юзюбеков] (MIB IV/1, 183); Bashk. 1787 **Üzü-bek** [Юзубек] (MIB V, 219). ✧ 'He-himself-(is)-violent / He-himself-(is)-healthy' (Eren 1953, pp. 127-129), cf. also Pelliot 92-94. ⇨ **ÖZ? + BEK.**

ÖZÜT-UГDĬ   Türk 7th c. - 9th c. **Özüt-uүdĭ / Özüt-oүdĭ** [Özüt Oүdĭ / özüt uүdĭ] (ETY III, 97, DTS). ✧ 'Essence-Uүdĭ'? (Blagova 1997, 713).

ÖKÖY see **ŌQOY**

P

PA-MURZA see **BAY**

PABAQ   Karg. **Pabaq** [Пабак] (Katanov, Otč. 9). ❖ 'Father' cf. Hak. *paba* 'id.' (HRS). + dim. suff. *-q*.

PABİN   Hak. 19th-20th c. **Pabin** [Пабин] (HRS 350).

PABÏR   Hak.(Sag.) 19th-20th c. **Pabïr** [Пабыр] (Katanov, Otč. 7).

PABLUSQA   Hak. 19th-20th c. **Pablusqa** [Паблуска], fem. (HRS 354). ❖ Pavlushka (<Pavel) (R.).

PAČAY   Hak. 19th-20th c. **Pačay** [Пачай] (HRS 350).

PAČAQ   Hak.(Blt.) 19th-20th c. **Pačaq** [Пачак], fem. (Katanov, Otč. 9). ❖ 'Little child, baby' cf. Hak. PN *Pačaχ* (Butanaev).

PAČAQOÑ   Hak. 19th-20th c. **Pačaqoñ** [Пачаконъ] (HRS 350); Hak. 19th-20th c. **Paǰaqoñ** [Пачаконъ] (HRS 350).

PAČANAX   Hak. 19th-20th c. **Pačanaχ** [Пачанах] (HRS 350). ❖ 'Brother-in-law' (Butanaev). ⇨ **PAČAN** + dim. suff. *-aχ*.

PAČQA   Hak. 19th-20th c. **Pačqa** [Пачка] (HRS 350); Hak.(Sag.) 19th-20th c. **Pāčqa** [Пачка], fem. (Katanov, Otč. 8). ❖ 'Parcel, bunch, bundle' < R. *pačka* (Katanov).

PAČQOY   Hak. 19th-20th c. **Pačqoy** [Пачкой], fem. (HRS 354).

PAČOSQA   Hak. 19th-20th c. **Pačosqa** [Пачоска], fem. (HRS 354).

PAǰAQOÑ see **PAČAQOÑ**

PAǰAÑ   Hak. 19th-20th c. **Paǰañ** [Пачанъ] (HRS 350). ❖ 'Brother-in-law' cf. Hak. PN *Pačan* (Butanaev).

PAǰAT   Hak. 19th-20th c. **Paǰat** [Пачат] (HRS 350).

PAD-PADAQŠİ   Tuv. 19th c. **Pad-padaqši** [Падъ-падакши] (Potanin IV, 426).

PADA   Hak. 19th-20th c. **Pada** [Пада] (HRS 350). ❖ 'Hard' (Mo.) (Butanaev).

PADAX   Hak. 19th-20th c. **Padaχ** [Падах], fem. (HRS 354). ❖ 'Having big belly; portly; corpulent'. ⇨ **PADAQ?**

PADAQ   Hak.(Sag.) 19th-20th c. **Padaq** [Падак], fem. (Katanov, Otč. 11); Karg. **Padaq** [Падак] (Katanov, Otč. 8). ❖ 'Ability of eloquence; talkative'? cf. Alt.(Leb.) *padaq* 'die Beredtsamkeit' (Radl. IV, 1181). ⇨ **PADAX?**

PADBALTAŠ   Bashk. 1706 **Padbaltaš** [Кунак Падбалташев] (MIB III, 25). ⇨ **BALTAČ, BALTAS?**

PADÏ-KEREDE   Alt. 19th c. **Padï-kerede** [Пады-Кереде богатырь], a folklore hero (Verb., In. 139, 141, 145). ⇨ **KEREDE.**

PADYÏAY   Yak. **Padyïay** [Падјыаі] (Pek.). ❖ Faddey (R.).

PAΓA see **BAQA**

PAHLEVAN see **PALWAN**

PAXRAS   Alt. 19th c. **Paχras** [Пахрас], an informant (teller of tales) (Potanin IV, 279). ❖ 'Copper; small cup made of cast iron'? cf. Alt.(Tel.) *paqras* 'das Kupfer;

eine kleine gusseiserne Schale' (Radl. IV, 1130).

PAY see **BAY**

PAY-BAXTA see **BAY-BAQTÏ**

PAY-BULAT see **BAY-BULAT**

PAY-DEMİR see **BAY-TEMİR**

PAY-DİMER see **BAY-TEMİR**

PAY-GİLDİ see **BAY-GELDİ**

PAY-KİLDİ see **BAY-GELDİ**

PAY-TUΓAN see **BAY-TUΓAN**

PAY-TÜLÜŠ   Tuv. 19th c. **Pay-tülüš** [Паи-Түлүш] (Proben IX, 44). ⇨ **BAY.**

PAYADÏY   Hak. 19th-20th c. **Payadïy** [Паядый] (HRS 350).

PAYAN see **BAYAN**

PAYANDÏ   Tuv. 19th c. **Payandï** [Пајанды] (Proben IX, 170).

PAYAÑ see **BAYAN**

PAYAPAN   Hak. 19th-20th c. **Payapan** [Пайапан] (HRS 350). ❖ Feofan (R.) (Butanaev).

PAYDAÑ   Hak. 19th-20th c. **Paydañ** [Пайданъ], fem. (HRS 354); Hak.(Kyz.) 19th-20th c. **Paydañ** [Пайдан] (Katanov, Otč. 13).

PAYDÏM   Hak. 19th-20th c. **Paydïm** [Пайдым], fem. (HRS 354).

PAYENDE   Chag. 16th c. **Payende** [Пайендэ], a mir (emir) (Ivanov 175-77); Chag. 16th c. - 17th c. **Payende-bike** [Пайенде], fem. (Ivanov 353-54); Chag. 16th c. - 17th c. **Payende-χoǰa** [Пайенде] (Ivanov 353-54); Chag. 16th c. - 17th c. **Payende-mirza** [Пайенде] (Ivanov 353-54); Chag. 16th c. **Payende-sultan** [Пайендэ Султан] (Ivanov 149, 229). ❖ 'Eternal, constant, hard, firm; helper, supporter' cf. Turk. *payändä* (P.) 'fest, solid, ausdauernd; die Stütze, die Hülfe' (Radl. IV, 1139).

PAYENDE-ČİHRE   Chag. 16th c. - 17th c. **Payende-čihre** [Пайенде Чихре] (Ivanov 353-54). ⇨ **PAYENDE + ČİHRE.**

PAYİÑ see **BAYAN**

PAYÏL   Hak.(Sag.) 19th-20th c. **Payïl** [Паи Пајыл] (Proben IX, 432).

PAYQA   Hak. 19th-20th c. **Payqa** [Пайка] (HRS 350).

PAYOQA   Hak. 19th-20th c. **Payoqa** [Пайока], fem. (HRS 354). ❖ 'Rich' cf. Hak. PN *Payo* (Butanaev), or variant of Hak. fem. PN *Payaχo* 'Rich Beauty' (Butanaev)? + fem. suff. *-qa*.

PAYS   Hak. 19th-20th c. **Pays** [Пайс], fem. (HRS 354).

PAYŠAQ   Bashk. 1751 **Payšaq** [Байгильда Паишаков] (MIB IV/1, 52).

PAYZULLA   Kkalp. 20th c. **Payzulla** [Пайзулла] (KkRS 775). ❖ Faizullah (Ar.).

PAQTAY   Hak.(Kyz.) 19th-20th c. **Paqtay** [Пактай] (Katanov, Otč. 13). ❖ 'Lucky, fortunate' cf. Hak. PN *Paχtay* (Butanaev). ⇨ **BAQTÏ** + suff. *-y*.

PAQTAN   Hak.(Shor) 19th-20th c. **Paqtan** [Пактан]

(Katanov, Otč. 11). ✧ 'Be praised; boast' cf. Alt.(Leb.), Shor *paqtan-* 'sich rühmen, sich prahlen' (Radl. IV, 1131).

PAL I.   Kkalp. 20th c. **Pal-zada** [Палзада], fem. (KkRS 778). ✧ 'Spell; fortune, fate, destiny; telling fortunes, soothsaying' cf. Kkalp. *pal I.* 'ворожба; гадание' (KkRS) (<Ar. *fāl*). See also **BOS-PAL**.

PAL II. see **BAL**

PAL-MAXAMBET   Kkalp. 20th c. **Pal-maxambet** [Палмахамбет] (KkRS 775). ⇨ **PAL I./II.?** + **MUXAMMED.**

PAL-MÏRAT see **PAL-MURAT**

PAL-MURAT   Kkalp. 20th c. **Pal-mïrat** [Палмырат] (KkRS 775); Kkalp. 20th c. **Pal-murat** [Палмурат] (KkRS 775). ⇨ **PAL I./II.?** + **MURAT.**

PAL-NAZAR   Kkalp. 20th c. **Pal-nazar** [Палназар] (KkRS 775). ⇨ **PAL I.** + **NAZAR.**

PALA see **BALA**

PALAQ   Uzb. 1770 **Palaq** [Палак] (MIT II, 347). ✧ 'Rotten, tainted, spoiled' cf. Trkm. *palaq* 'тухлый' (TrkmRS).

PALAMŌN   Tuv.? **Balamon-qam** (Németh, HMK 138 /taken from Potanin, Oč. II, 56/); Alt.? **Palamōn-qam** [Palamōn Kam] (Németh, HMK 138 /after Katanov/). ✧ Filamon? (R.).

PALASTAY   Hak. 19th-20th c. **Palastay** [Паластай] (HRS 350).

PALAW   Kkalp. 20th c. **Palaw** [Палав / Палаў], fem. (Bask., Kkalp. 404, KkRS 778). ✧ 'Pilaf' cf. Kkalp. *palav* 'id.' (Bask., Kkalp.).

PALBÏГAR   Tuv. 19th c. **Palbïɣar** [Палбыңар] (Proben IX, 65).

PALDÏR-PÄJÏK   Tuv. 19th c. **Paldïr-päjïk** [Палдыр-пăцiк], a folklore hero (Proben IX, 159-60). ✧ 'Calf (of) leg, shank - ?' cf. Alt.(Tel.), Hak.(Sag.), Tat.(Bar.) *paldïr, paltïr* 'die Wade; der Schenkel' (Radl. IV, 1171), Tuv. *baldïr* 'id.' (TuvRS).

PALDÏŠ see **BALDÏŠ**

PALÏQĀR   Yak. **Palïqar** [Палыкар] (Pek.). ✧ 'Polikarp' (R.) (Pek.).

PALÏM   Kkalp. 20th c. **Palïm** [Палым] (Bask., Kkalp. 78, KkRS 775). ✧ 'My honey, my sweetheart; my darling'; Dialectal variant of *Balïm* (Žanuzakov-Esbaeva 460). ⇨ **BAL?** + poss. suff. *-im.*

PALÏMBET   Kkalp. 20th c. **Palïmbet** [Палымбет] (KkRS 775); Kkalp. 20th c. **Palïmbet** [Палымбет] (Bask., Kkalp. 78). ⇨ **BAL(ÏM) / PALÏM?** + suff. *-ïmbet / -mbet.*

PALÏWAN see **PALWAN**

PALTA-POLAT   Trkm. 19th c. **Palta-polat** [Палта-полатъ] (Volodin 53). ✧ 'Axe-steel; Steel Axe' (Volodin: stal'noj topor). ⇨ **BALTA + BULAT.**

PALTAY see **BALTAY**

PALTAN   Hak. 19th-20th c. **Paltan** [Палтан] (Katanov,

Otč. 10). ✧ Platon (R.) cf. Hak. *Palton* (Butanaev).

PALTÏJAX   Hak. 19th-20th c. **Paltïjaɣ** [Палтыǯах] (HRS 350). ✧ 'Small axe'. ⇨ **BALTA** + dim. suff. *-jaɣ.*

PALWAN   Bashk. 1744, 1755, 1764 **Balwan** [Аит Болванов] (MIB III, 417, IV/1, 97, 276, 298); Kzk. 19th c. **Balwan** [Балванъ] (SOK 128); Kzk. 19th c. **Balwan** [Болванъ] (SOK 184); Chag. 16th c. **Pahlevan** [Пахлеван] (Ivanov 172, 173, 316); Kkalp. 20th c. **Palïwan** [Палыван] (Bask., Kkalp. 76); Trkm. 1856/57 **Palwan** [Палван Какелли], from Khiva (MIT II, 581); Kkalp. 20th c. **Palwan** [Палўан] (KkRS 775); NUyg. 19th c. **Palwan** [پهلوان] (Le Coq, Namenl. 113); Uzb. 19th c. **Palwan-qul** [Сатаркулъ Палванкуловъ] (SKSO III, 160); Crm. **Palwan-sultan** [Палван-султан], a prince, Batïr-ɣan's brother (Žirm., Epos 443); Selj. 1160 **Pehlivan** [Nusretüddîn Pehlivan ibn İl-Deniz], lord of Rey (Ahbar 103, 105, 119 etc.). ✧ 'Brave man, wrestler, hero' (P.) cf. Turk. *pählivan / pählävan* 'der Ringer, der Atleht; der Tapfere, der Held' (Radl. IV, 1221), Kkalp. *palwan* 'id.' (KkRS), Kzk. *palwan* 'der Ringer, ein starker Mann, ein Held' (Radl. IV, 1169).

PALWAN-NİYAZ   Kkalp. 20th c. **Palwan-niyaz** [Палўанияз / Палваннийаз] (Bask., Kkalp. 401, KkRS 775). ⇨ **PALWAN + NİYAZ.**

PANA   Hak. 19th-20th c. **Pana** [Пана] (HRS 350).

PANČİKİ   Uyg. **Pančiki** [Pançiki] (EUTS).

PANYUTİN   Tat.(Tob.) 1646 **Panyutin** [Панютинъ], an ataman (DAI III, 76). ✧ Panyutin (R.), family-name coming from R. *Panyuta*, dim. of *Pavel.*

PANOJAX   Hak. 19th-20th c. **Panojaɣ** [Паночах] (HRS 350). ✧ Epifan (R.)? cf. Hak. PN *Paničaɣ* (Butanaev).

PANOQ   Hak. 19th-20th c. **Panoq** [Панок] (HRS 350).

PANPİL   Hak. 19th-20th c. **Panpil** [Панпил] (HRS 350). ✧ Panfil (R.).

PAÑ I.   Hak. 19th-20th c. **Pañ** [Панъ], fem. (HRS 354). ✧ Fan (shortened of R. Epifan)? cf. Hak. PN *Pan* (Butanaev).

PAÑ II.   Kkalp. 20th c. **Pañ** [Паң], fem. (KkRS 778). ✧ 'Proud; disdainful, lordly, haughty' cf. Kkalp. *pañ* 'id.' (KkRS).

PAPAY   Kzk. 1739 **Papay** [Papaï / Папай], Abul Khair Khan's wife (Levchine 188, 356, Levšin III, 96, Hanykov and Nepljuev mention her as Pupay (see)).

PAPUS   Hak. 19th-20th c. **Papus** [Папус] (HRS 350).

PAR see **BAR**

PARAXAT see **BEREKET**

PARAS   Hak. 19th-20th c. **Paras** [Парас], fem. (HRS 354). ✧ Praskov'ya (R.).

PARASXÏR   Hak. 19th-20th c. **Parasɣïr** [Парасхыр] (HRS 350).

PARASİN   Hak. 19th-20th c. **Parasin** [Парасин] (HRS

354). ❖ Praskov'ya (R.).

PARĀN Hak. 19th-20th c. **Parān** [Паран] (Katanov, Otč. 11). ❖ I. 'Furniture; outfit of a house (yurt); shelf' (Butanaev), cf. Hak.(Kyz.) *parān* 'место, где стоят сундуки (в юрте); полка'; II. 'Widder; sheep' cf. R. *baran* (Katanov).

PARĀNAX Hak. 19th-20th c. **Parānaχ** [Параанах] (HRS 350); Hak.(Blt.) 19th-20th c. **Parānaq** [Паранак] (Proben IX, 613). ⇨ **PARĀN** + dim. suff. -*aχ*?

PARĀNAQ see **PARĀNAX**

PARBARA Yak. **Balbārï** [Балбары], fem. (Pek.); Hak. 19th-20th c. **Parbara** [Парбара], fem. (HRS 354). ❖ Varvara (R.).

PARBĬČE Hak. 19th-20th c. **Parbiče** (<**Parbinče**) [Парбиче], fem. (HRS 354). ❖ Parfeniya (R.).

PARČA Hak.(Kyz.) 19th-20th c. **Parča** [Парча], fem. (Katanov, Otč. 13); Karg. **Parča** [Парча], fem. (Katanov, Otč. 8); Hak. 19th c. **Parčā** [Парча] (Katanov, Otč. 12); Kkalp. 20th c. **Parša-gül** [Паршагул], fem. (KkRS 778). ❖ 'A kind of silk' cf. R. *parča* (< Trk. < P.), Kirg., Kzk. *barča / barša* 'ein Seidenzeug' (Radl. IV, 1487, 1488), Kkalp. fem. *Parša-gül* 'парчовый цветок' [=silk(y) flower] (Baskakov: OSA 139). See also **AY-PARČA**.

PARČAJAX Hak. 19th-20th c. **ParčaJaχ** [Парчачах], fem. (HRS 354). ⇨ **PARČA** + dim. suff. -*Jaχ*.

PARČĀ see **PARČA**

PARČÏX see **PARČÏQ**

PARČÏQ Hak. 19th-20th c. **Parčïχ** [Парчых], fem. (HRS 354); Hak. 19th c. **Parčïq** [Парчык] (Katanov, Otč. 12); Hak.(Sag.) 19th-20th c. **Parčïq** [Парчык] (Katanov, Otč. 7). ❖ 'Starling' (Katanov), cf. Alt.(Tel.) *pārčïq, qara pārčïq* 'der Staar' (Radl. IV, 1158).

PARDA see **PERDE**

PARDÏ see **BARLÏ**

PARDO Hak. 19th-20th c. **Pardo** [Пардо] (HRS 350). ❖ 'Rich, substantial, well-to-do' (Butanaev).

PARÏS see **BARS**

PARLAQ Hak. 19th c. **Parlaq** [Парлак] (Katanov, Otč. 12). ❖ 'Thrush' cf. Shor *parlaq* 'die Drossel' (Radl. IV, 1155).

PARLAS Hak.(Sag.) 19th-20th c. **Parlas** [Парлас] (Katanov, Otč. 8). ❖ 'Starling, thrush' (Butanaev). See also **XARA-PARLAS**.

PARLĀSQA Hak. 19th c. **Parlāsqa** [Парласка] (Katanov, Otč. 12); Hak. 19th c. **Parlāsqa** [Парласка] (Katanov, Otč. 12); Hak.(Sag.) 19th-20th c. **Parlāsqa** [Парласка] (Katanov, Otč. 7); Karg. **Parlāsqa** [Парласка] (Katanov, Otč. 9). ❖ 'Varlashka' (Katanov).

PARMAQSÏZ Turk. 20th c. **Parmaqsïz** [Parmaksız], a village in the province of Yozgat, Turkey (TMİB 901). ❖ 'Without fingers'.

PARMAN see **FERMAN**

PARNİ Uzb. 1885 **Parni-bay** [Парнибай] (Moskal'cev 34).

PARS-BUQA see **BARS-BUQA**

PARŠA see **PARČA**

PAS see **BAŠ**

PASA Hak. 19th-20th c. **Pasa** [Паса] (HRS 350). ❖ Vasya (R.)? cf. Hak. PN *Paysa* (Butanaev).

PASÏNQA Hak.(Sag.) 19th-20th c. **Pasïnqa** [Пасынка] (Katanov, Otč. 11). ❖ Vasyn'ka (R.) (Katanov).

PASKİR Hak. 19th-20th c. **Paskir** [Паскир] (HRS 350). ❖ Bashkir (<R.) (Butanaev).

PASQA Hak. 19th-20th c. **Pasqa** [Паска] (HRS 350); Hak. 19th-20th c. **Pasqa** [Паска] (Katanov, Otč. 10); Hak.(Koyb.) 19th c. **Pasqa** [Паска] (Katanov, Otč. II, 12). ❖ 'Hammer, mallet' (Katanov), cf. Alt.(Tel.), Hak.(Sag.), Shor *pasqa* 'ein grosser Hammer' (Radl. IV, 1188).

PASQAJAQ Hak.(Kyz.) 19th-20th c. **Pasqajaq** [Паскацак], fem. (Katanov, Otč. 13); Hak.(Kacha) 19th c. **Pasqajaq / Pasqaljaq (?)** [Паскалджакъ (!)] (Katanov, Otč. II, 42). ❖ 'Small hammer' (Katanov). ⇨ **PASQA** + dim. suff. -*jaq*.

PASLÏSKE Hak. 19th-20th c. **Pasliske** [Паслиске], fem. (HRS 354). ❖ Vasiliska (R.).

PASTAY Hak.(Sag.) 19th-20th c. **Pastay** [Пастай] (Katanov, Otč. 11). ❖ 'Head'? cf. Hak.(Sag., Koyb.) *pas* 'der Kopf' (Radl. IV, 1185). ⇨ **POSTAY?** / **BAŠ** + suff. -*tay(1,2)*?

PASTĀNJA Hak. 19th-20th c. **Pastānja** [Пастанца], fem. (Katanov, Otč. 10). ❖ 'Until he began' (Katanov).

PASTÏΓAS Hak. 19th-20th c. **Pastïγas** [Пастыгас] (HRS 350). ❖ 'Leader, chief (of a clan)' cf. Hak.(Sag.) *pastïq* 'der Führer, der Geschlechtsälteste' (Radl. IV, 1192). + dim. suff. -*as*.

PASTŪQ Hak. 19th-20th c. **Pastūq** [Пастук], fem. (Katanov, Otč. 13); Hak.(Sag.) 19th-20th c. **Pastūq** [Пастук] (Katanov, Otč. 8). ❖ 'Shepherd' cf. R. *pastuh* (Katanov).

PAŠA Turk. 20th c. **Paša** [Paşa] (Önder, Göle); Yürük 16th c. **Paša** [پاشا / Paşa] (Gökb., Rum. 103); Turk. 1583 **Paša? / Peše?** [پا شا / پشه] (Ongan, Ank. I, 174); Yürük 16th c. **Paša-alp** [پاشا الب / Paşa-alp], from the Yürüks of Kocacık, Turkey (Gökb., Rum. 105); Turk. 1422 **Paša-beg** [پاشا بك] (Āšikp. 94, 114); Yürük 1543 **Paša-yigit** [Paşa Jiğit] (Gökb., Rum. 188); Yürük 16th c. **Paša-yigit** [Paşa-yiğit], from the Yürüks of Kocacık, Turkey (Gökb., Rum. 103); Turk. 1422 **Paša-kireJe?** [پاشا كرجه], Germiyanoğlu Ya'qub-beg's khatun (wife) (Āšikp.). ❖ 'Pasha (the highest title of civil and military officials; Minister)' Used also as a secondary component expressing respect or/and love when addressing. Cf. Crm., Turk. *paša* 'der Pascha (früher nur ein Militär-Titel); der Titel eines Ministers' (Radl.

IV, 1200).

PAŠAČÏQ　Turk. 1383 **Pašačïq-aγa** [پاشاچق اغا]
(Āšikp. 54). ✧ 'Little Pasha'. ⇨ **PAŠA** + suff. -*čïq*.

PAŠAQ see **BAČAQ**

PAŠŠA see **PATŠA**

PATANOÑ　Hak. 19th-20th c. **Patanoñ** [Патанонъ]
(HRS 350).

PATÏYMA see **FATİMA**

PATÏLLA　Kkalp. 20th c. **Patïlla** [Патылла] (KkRS
775).

PATÏR see **BATÏR**

PATPA see **FATİMA**

PATPAN-QARA　Kzk. 19th c. **Patpan-qara** [Патпан-
кара / Патпан-каракчи] (Verb., In. 91). ⇨
BATPAN + QARA.

PATPAN-QARAQČI　Kzk. 19th c. **Patpan-qaraqči**
[Патпан-кара / Патпан-каракчи] (Verb., In. 91). ⇨
BATPAN + QARAQČI.

PATRAQ see **BATRAQ**

PATSAYÏ　Kkalp. 20th c. **Patsayï** [Патсайы], fem.
(KkRS 778). ✧ 'A kind of silk-web' cf. Kzk. *patsayı*
'ipekli kumaşın bir çeşidi' (KzTS).

PATŠA　Kkalp. 20th c. **Pašša** [Пашша] (KkRS 778);
Kkalp. 20th c. **Patša** [Патша], fem. (KkRS 778);
Kkalp. 20th c. **Patša-gül** [Патшагул], fem. (KkRS
778). ✧ 'Ruler, imperor, sovereign (title)' A secondary
component of personal names as well. Cf. Uyg., Tat.,
NUyg.(Tar.) *patša* 'id.' (Radl. IV, 1180), Kkalp. fem.
Patša-gül 'царский цветок' (Baskakov: OSA 140).

PATŠAXAN　Kkalp. 20th c. **Patšaχan** [Патшахан],
fem. (KkRS 778). ⇨ **PATŠA** + suff. -*χan(1)*.

PATULLA　Kkalp. 20th c. **Patulla** [Патулла] (KkRS
775). ✧ 'Allah's house; Kaaba' cf. Tat. PNs *Bäytulla /
Bqtulla / Batulla* (Sattarov), also *Beytullah* (Erol II)
(<Ar.). ⇨ **ALLA.**

PAZAQ see **BAZAQ**

PAZAR　Hak.(Sag.) 19th-20th c. **Pazar** [Пазар] (Proben
IX, 236, 259); Tuv. 19th c. **Pāzar** [Пазар] (Proben, IX,
131). ✧ I. 'Diamond' (<Mo.) (Butanaev); II.
'Market(place)' cf. Uyg., Alt., Shor, Turk. *pazar* 'der
Markt, Jahrmarkt' (Radl. IV, 1193). See also **ALMAZ.**

PAZARLÏ　Yürük 1543 **Pazarlï** [Pazarlı], from the
Yürüks of Kocacık, Turkey (Gökb., Rum. 105, 187). ✧
'Born on market-day; coming from a settlement called
Pazar'. ⇨ **PAZAR** + suff. -*lï.*

PĀBİL　Hak. 19th c. **Pābïl** [Пабіл] (Katanov, Otč. 12).
✧ Pavel (R.) (Katanov).

PĀBÏY　Tuv. 19th c. **Pābïy** [Пабыи] (Proben IX, 137).
✧ Pavel (R.).

PĀČQA see **PAČQA**

PĀDÏ　Tuv. 19th c. **Pādï** [Пады] (Proben IX, 138).

PĀΓ-ALÏN see **PĀQ-ALÏN**

PĀYSA　Hak. 19th-20th c. **Pāysa** [Пайса] (Katanov,
Otč. 10); Hak.(Sag.) 19th-20th c. **Pāysa** [Пайса]

(Katanov, Otč. 7); Hak.(Kacha) 19th c. **Pājsa** [Пайса]
(Katanov, Otč. II, 42); Hak.(Shor) 19th-20th c. **Pāysa**
[Пайса] (Katanov, Otč. 11). ✧ Vasja (R.) (Katanov,
Butanaev).

PĀQ-ALÏN　Tat.(GH) 1345 **Pāγ-alïn** (<**Pāq-alïn**)
[Παγαλίν], a christened Tatar woman, died in 1345
(Byz. Turc. 239); Turk. 20th c. **Pāq-alïn** [Mehmet Zeki
Pakalın] (Resimli Yeni Lûgat ve Ansiklopedi). ✧
'Clear/clean forehead' cf. P. *pāk* + Trk. *alïn* 'forehead'.
⇨ **ALÏN.** See also **ARU-MANDAY.**

PĀQA　Hak. 19th-20th c. **Pāqa** [Паака] (HRS 350).

PĀNQA　Yak. **Bāñqa** [Баҥка] (Pek.); Hak.(Shor) 19th-
20th c. **Pānqa** [Панка] (Katanov, Otč. 11); Karg.
Pānqa [Панка] (Katanov, Otč. 9). ✧ Van'ka (dim. of
R. Ivan) (Katanov).

PĀRA　Hak. 19th-20th c. **Pāra** [Паара], fem. (HRS
354). ✧ Varvara (R.).

PĀSQA　Yak. **Bāsqa** [Баска] (Pek.); Hak.(Sag.) 19th-
20th c. **Pāsqa** [Паска] (Katanov, Otč. 7); Karg. **Pāsqa**
[Паска] (Katanov, Otč. 9). ✧ Vas'ka (R.), dim. of R.
Vasiliy.

PĀZAQ　Tuv. 19th c. **Pāzaq** [Пазак] (Proben IX, 14).

PĀZAÑ　Tuv. 19th c. **Pāzañ** [Пазан] (Proben IX, 71).

PĀZAR see **PAZAR**

PÄLÄK see **UQQUN-PÄLÄK**

PÄRİYDA　Kkalp. 20th c. **Päriyda** [Пәрийда], fem.
(KkRS 778). ✧ Farida (Ar. fem.) 'unique, matchless'
(Ahmed).

PÄRWAZ　Kkalp. 20th c. **Pärwaz** [Пәрўаз], fem.
(KkRS 778). ✧ 'Elation, elevated spirits; love' cf.
Kkalp. *pärwaz* 'приподнятое настроение;
влюблённость' (KkRS).

PÄTĀR　Karg. 19th-20th c. **Pätăr** [Пäтăр] (Katanov,
Otč. 10). ✧ 'Flat, housing' cf. R. *kvartira* (Katanov).

PÄTRŌ　Karg. **Pätrō** [Пäтро] (Katanov, Otč. 8). ✧
Petr/Pyotr (R.).

PÄTRŪQA　Karg. **Pätrūqa** [Пäтрука] (Katanov, Otč.
9). ✧ Petruha (R.), dim.-hypoc. of R. Pyotr.

PÄTTŪQ see **PETÜK**

PÄRES see **PERES**

PÄTİR　Hak.(Sag.) 19th-20th c. **Pătir** [Пăтiр], fem.
(Katanov, Otč. 11). ✧ 'Wind' cf. R. *veter* (ветерь) 'id.'
(Katanov).

PÄTKÄ　Karg. **Pătkä** [Пăткä] (Katanov, Otč. 9). ✧
Pet'ka (R.), dim. of R. Pyotr.

PEČETTİ　Alt. 19th c. **Pečetti-χan** [Печетти-хан]
(Verb., In. 141, 146). ✧ 'Having a seal; sealed' cf.
Hak.(Kacha) *pečättīg* 'versiegelt, mit Siegel versehen'
(Radl. IV, 1252) (<R. *pečat'* 'seal, signet').

PEDĀ　Hak.(Sag.) 19th-20th c. **Pedā** [Педа], fem.
(Katanov, Otč. 7). ✧ 'Misery, mishap' cf. R. *beda*
(Katanov).

PEDE　Hak. 19th-20th c. **Pede** [Педе] (HRS 350). ✧
Petya (hypocoristic of Pyotr) (R.).

PEDEY Hak. 19th-20th c. **Pedey** [Педей] (HRS 350). ⇨ **PEDE?** + dim. suff. *-y*.

PEDOS Hak. 19th-20th c. **Pedos** [Педос], fem. (HRS 354). ✧ Fedos'ya (R.).

PEHLİVAN see **PALWAN**

PEHTEMEY Chuv. 17th c. **Pehtemey** [Пехтемейко Ахтубаевъ], a tarχan (IOAIÊK XXIX, 341).

PEKE Hak. 19th-20th c. **Peke** [Пеке] (HRS 350).

PEKİN Hak.(Sag.) 19th-20th c. **Pekin** [Пекинъ] (Katanov, Otč. 7). ✧ Vikentiy (R.) (Butanaev).

PEKLİSKE Hak. 19th-20th c. **Pekliske** [Пеклиске], fem. (HRS). ✧ Fjokla (R.) or Fektistka (R.), dim.-hypoc. of R. fem. *Feoktista* or that of Hak. *Peklĭs* (see above). ⇨ **PEKLĬS** + suff. *-ke* < comp. *-ake*.

PEKLĬS Hak. 19th-20th c. **Peklĭs** [Пäкліс] (Katanov, Otč. 10). ✧ Feoktist (R.), dim.-hypoc. of R. fem. *Feoktista*.

PEKTŌR see **PİKTOR**

PELEŇ I. Trkm. 20th c. **Peleň** [Peleŋ] (Zaj. 1971, 331). ✧ 'Tiger' (Zaj. 1971), 'Lion' (Muhamedova 1957), cf. Trkm. *peleň* 'тигр' (TrkmRS) (<P.).

PELEŇ II. Hak. 19th-20th c. **Peleň** [Пеленъ], fem. (HRS 354). ✧ Pelageya (R. fem.) cf. Hak. fem. PN *Pelen* (Butanaev).

PEN Nog. 1607 **Pen** [Пен], a murza (Miller, Ist. Sib. II, 197).

PENA Trkm. 20th c. **Pena** [Pena] (Zaj. 1971, 329); Kkalp. 1822 **Pena-behadïr** [Пена бехадыр] (MIKk. 127); Trkm. 20th c. **Penā** [Пена] (TrkmRS 522). ✧ 'Refuge, shelter' cf. Trkm. *penā* 'укрытие, защита, покровительство' (TrkmRS) (<P.).

PENE Hak. 19th-20th c. **Pene** [Пене], fem. (HRS 354). ✧ Penya (Fenya?) (R. fem.), hypoc. of R. fem. PN *Epistima*.

PERČUK Hak.(Sag.) 19th-20th c. **Perčük** [Перчӱк] (Proben IX, 547).

PERDE Uzb. 19th c. **Parda-bay** [Пардабай Турсуновъ] (SKSO III, 174); Kkalp. 20th c. **Perde** [Перде], fem. (KkRS 778); Kkalp. 20th c. **Perde-bay** [Пердебай] (KkRS 775); Kkalp. 20th c. **Perde-gül** [Пердегул], fem. (KkRS 778). ✧ 'Curtain, valance, gauze' cf. Kkalp. *perde* 'id.' (KkRS), fem. *Perde-gül* 'вуалевый цветок' [=gauze/veil-flower] (Baskakov: OSA 139).

PERDİ see **BERDİ**

PERE Hak. 19th-20th c. **Pere** [Пере], fem. (HRS 354). ✧ Vera (R. fem.).

PERES Hak.(Sag.) 19th-20th c. **Päres** [Пäрäс], fem. (Katanov, Otč. 8); Hak. 19th-20th c. **Peres** [Перес], fem. (HRS 354). ✧ 'Pepper' cf. R. *perec* 'id.' (Katanov).

PERGEN I. see **BERGEN**

PERGEN II. see MERGEN

PERİ Kkalp. 20th c. **Peri-gül** [Перигул], fem. (KkRS 778). ✧ 'Fairy; demon' cf. Kkalp. *peri* 'id.' (KkRS), Tat., Turk. *päri* 'ein Peri, (Tat.) ein böser Geist' (Radl. IV, 1280) (<P.). See also **MAH-PERİ, MĬSXAL-PERİ**.

PERİ-ZAT Kkalp. 20th c. **Peri-zat** [Перизат], fem. (KkRS 778); Az. **Peri-zat-χanum** [Перизад-ханум], a person in a tale (Az. Skaz. 45). ✧ 'Fairy-thing; fairy-son' cf. Kkalp. *zat* 'вещь, предмет' (KkRS). ⇨ **PERİ**.

PERİXAN Kkalp. 20th c. **Perixan** [Перихан], fem. (KkRS 778). ⇨ **PERİ** + suff. *-χan(1)*.

PERİYZA Kkalp. 20th c. **Periyza** [Перийза], fem. (KkRS 778). ✧ 'Beautiful, fairy-like; (lit. born by a fairy)' cf. Kkalp. *periyzat* 'рождённый от пери; красавица (подобная фее)' (KkRS). See also **HÄSEN, KÜRKLİ, KÖRKLÄ, KÖRTLÄ, NİGĀR, SİLİГ, ZİFA**.

PERİKEY Trkm. 19th c. **Perikey** [Кочекъ Перикеевъ] (Ščeglov IV, 180). ⇨ **PERİ** + suff. *-key?*

PERİM Uzb. 1740 **Perim-atalïq** [Перимъ-Аталыкъ], from a Kipchak tribe (Hanykov, Poezdka 20).

PERİMAN Kzk. 19th c. **Periman-qul** [Перыманкулъ] (SOV 100).

PERMAN see **FERMAN**

PERMÄK Chuv. 18th-19th c. **Permäk** [Пермякъ] (Magn. 66).

PERSŌK Hak.(Sag.) 19th-20th c. **Persōk** [Персок] (Katanov, Otč. 8). ✧ 'Inch' cf. R. *veršok* 'id.' (Katanov).

PERŠE Kkalp. 20th c. **Perše** [Перше], fem. (KkRS 778).

PERUZA Kkalp. 20th c. **Peruza** [Перуза], fem. (KkRS 778). ✧ Firuza (P. fem.) 'turqoise, a bright greenish-blue colour' (Ahmed).

PERVANE Turk. 20th c. **Pervane** (Önder, Göle). ✧ 'Night butterfly' cf. Turk. *pärvanä* (P.) 'id.' (Radl. IV, 1241).

PESİN see **BESİN**

PESPİYAQ Hak.(Blt.) 19th-20th c. **Pespiyäk / Qān-pespiyäk** [Кан Песпіјäк], khan Onbïyaq's and Qosqar's brother (Proben IX, 355, 356, 362); Hak.(Blt.) 19th-20th c. **Pespĭyaq / Pespĭyäk** [Песпіјак / Песпіjäк] (Proben IX, 357-58). ✧ '(The) Fifth child' cf. Hak. *pes* 'fünf</i> (Radl. IV, 1253). See also **ONBÏYAQ**.

PETRİPĀN Hak. 19th-20th c. **Petripān** [Петрипан] (Katanov, Otč. 10). ✧ Mitrofan (R.).

PETROPĀNČA Hak. 19th c. **Petropānča** [Петропанча] (Katanov, Otč. 12). ✧ Mitrofan (R.).

PETŬK Alt. 19th-20th c. **Bötük** (OjrRS 208); Hak.(Sag.) 19th-20th c. **Pättük** [Пäттук] (Katanov, Otč. 8); Hak.(Sag.) 19th-20th c. **Petük** [Петӱк] (Katanov, Otč. 7). ✧ 'Cock' cf. R. *petuh* 'id.' (Katanov), Alt. *bötük* (<R.) *petuh* 'петух' (OjrRS 208).

Pİ-BARÏS see **BAY-BARS**

Pİ-BARS see **BAY-BARS**

Pİ-BOLDÏ see **Bİ-BOLDÏ**

Pİ-BULAT see **BİY-BULAT**

Pİ-BULDÏ see **Bİ-BOLDÏ**

Pİ-ČURA see **BEK**

Pİ-DEMİR see **BEK-TEMİR**

PİČÄKÄY Tuv. 19th c. **Pičäkäy / Pičäkkäy** [Пічäкäі / Пічäккäі], fem. (Proben IX, 88, 98, 140). ✧ 'Aunt, elder sister' cf. *pičä* Alt.(Tel.) 'die Tante', Hak.(Sag.) 'die ältere Schwester' (Radl. IV, 1348).

PİČÄKKÄY see **PİČÄKÄY**

PİČİK see **BİČİK**

PİDES Hak. 19th-20th c. **Pides** [Пидес] (HRS 350).

PİDİK Hak. 19th-20th c. **Pidik** [Пидик] (HRS 350).

PİҐĀQ Hak. 19th-20th c. **Piɣāq** [Пигаак] (HRS 350).

PİX see **BEK**

PİX-BARS see **BEK-BARS**

PİX-BULAT see **BEK-BULAT**

PİX-PARS see **BEG-BARS**

PİX-PULAT see **BEK-BULAT**

PİX-TEMİR see **BEK-TEMİR**

PİX-TUҐAN see **BEK-TUҐAN**

PİK see **BEK**

PİK-BARÏS see **BEK-BARS**

PİK-BARÏS see **BEK-BARS**

PİK-BARS see **BEK-BARS**

PİK-BULAT see **BEK-BULAT**

PİK-TEMİR see **BEK-TEMİR**

PİK-TUҐAN see **BEK-TUҐAN**

PİKSEN Hak. 19th-20th c. **Piksen** [Пиксен] (HRS 350). ✧ 'Strong' (Butanaev).

PİKTOR Yak. **Bïktär** [Біктäр] (Pek.); Karg. **Pektōr** [Пектор] (Katanov, Otč. 9); Hak. 19th-20th c. **Piktor** [Пиктор] (HRS 350). ✧ Viktor (R.).

PİKUN Hak. 19th-20th c. **Pikun** [Пикун] (HRS 350).

PİLASOP Hak. 19th-20th c. **Pilasop** [Пиласоп] (HRS 350). ✧ Filosof (R.).

PİLİP Karg. **Pilïp** [Піліп] (Katanov, Otč. 8). ✧ Filipp (R.).

PİLİS Hak.(Sag.) 19th-20th c. **Pilïs** [Піліс] (Katanov, Otč. 7). ✧ 'Velvety textile' cf. R. *plis* (Katanov).

PİNAČEK Hak. 19th-20th c. **Pinaček** [Пиначек], fem. (HRS 354).

PİNAY Bashk. 1709 **Pinay / Pinäy?** [Пинай Тленчеев] (MIB III, 48).

PİNKE Hak. 19th-20th c. **Pinke** [Пинке] (HRS 350).

PİÑGİLTAQ NUyg.(Tar.) **Piñgiltaq** [Pingiltak / Піңгілтак], Šiñgiltaq's counterpart in the tale (Proben VI, 166 /219/).

PİR Kkalp. 20th c. **Pir-jan** [Пиржан] (KkRS 775); Turk. 1583 **Pir-qulu** [Pirkulu] (Ongan, Ank. I, 174); *TN:* Turk. 20th c. **Pir-oɣlu** [Piroğlu], a village in the province of Bolu, Turkey (TMİB 188). ✧ 'Old man, (religious) teacher; leader, chief (of an order)' Used also as a prepositive component of personal names. Cf. Az., Crm., Kar.(L.), Turk. *pir* (P.) 'der Alte, der Heilige; der Herrscher, der Befehlshaber' (Radl. IV, 1331), Kkalp. *pir* 'id.' (KkRS), Kirg. *pir* 'id.' (Jud.).

PİR-ALİ Kzk. 1750 **Pir-ali** [Pirali] (Levchine 219); Kzk. 1784 **Pir-ali** [Pirali / Пирали], Nur-ali's son, a khan of Turkestan (Levšin II, 310, Levchine 285). ⇨ **PİR + ALİ.**

PİR-BERDİ Trkm. 1840 **Pir-berdi** [Пиръ-Берды] (ZIRGOÊtn. I, 105). ⇨ **PİR + BERDİ.**

PİR-BOLDÏ Turk. 1397 **Pir-boldï** [پیـر بولـدی], in the region of Karaman and Kayseri (Astarab. 527). ⇨ **PİR + BOLDÏ.**

PİR-NAZAR Kkalp. 20th c. **Pir-nazar** [Пирназар] (KkRS 775). ⇨ **PİR + NAZAR.**

PİR-NİYAZ Kkalp. 20th c. **Pir-niyaz** [Пирнияз] (KkRS 775). ⇨ **PİR + NİYAZ.**

PİRAT Uzb. 19th c. **Pirat-bay** [Пиратбаевъ] (SKSO II, 13 III, 19).

PİRJE Turk. 1583 **Pirje** [پیـرجـه / Pirce] (Ongan, Ank. I, 153). ✧ 'Pir-like; worthy of a pir' cf. *Pirce* (Erol II). ⇨ **PİR** + suff. *-če.*

PİRXLE Kzk. 1846 **Pirχle** [Пирхле] (MKOP 86).

PİRİ Turk. 1580 **Piri** (Dávid); Turk. 1580 **Piri** [Piri bin Dur Ali] (Dávid). ✧ 'Old-age; old-aged' cf. Turk. *pîrî* (P.) 'Greisenalter' (Zenker).

PİRİM Uzb. 19th c. **Pirim** [Пиримъ Тлеубаевъ] (SKSO III, 150); Kkalp. 20th c. **Pirim-bay** [Пиримбай] (KkRS 775); Kzk. 19th c. **Pirim-qul** [Пиримкуловъ] (SKSO VIII, 233); Kirg. **Pirim-qul** [Пиримкул] (Jud. 18); Chag. 1558 **Pirim-sultan** [Пирим Султан] (Ivanov 210); Chag. 1554 **Pirim-šeyχ** [Пирим-шейх] (Ivanov 140, 145). ⇨ **PİR** + poss. suff. *-im.* See also **AWČİ-PİRİM.**

PİRİMBET Kzk. 19th c. **Pirimbet** [Пиримбетъ] (Grod., Pril. 84). ⇨ **PİR / PİRİM?** + suff. *-imbet / -mbet.*

PİRKÄSİK Hak. 19th c. **Pirkäsik** [Піркäсик] (Katanov, Otč. 12). ✧ 'Commander; captain' cf. R. *prikaščik* 'id.' (Katanov).

PİRLİ Turk. 1583 **Pirli** (Ongan, Ank. I, 174). ⇨ **PİR** + suff. *-li.*

PİROLA Hak. 19th-20th c. **Pirola** [Пирола] (HRS 350).

PİSON Hak. 19th-20th c. **Pison** [Писон] (HRS 350).

PİSPEK Kzk. 19th c. **Pispek-bay** [Писпекъ-бай], according to a Kazak legend of origin he is Qanjïɣalï's grand-father on mother side (Potanin, Pred. 57). ✧ 'A stick for stirring kumys' cf. Kzk. *piskäk* 'Stock zum Mischen des Kumiss in der Saba' (Radl. IV, 1352).

PİSTA Kzk. 19th c. **Pista-gül** [Пистагуль], fem. (Grod. I, 98). ✧ 'Pistachio (nut)' cf. NUyg.(Tar.) *pistä* 'die Pistacie' (Radl. IV, 1352).

PİSTİG Hak.(Sag.) 19th-20th c. **Pistig** [Пістіг]

(Katanov, Otč. 11). ✧ 'Sharp, pointed' (Katanov).

PÏŠEN Kzk. **Pišen-bay** [Пишенбай], preserved in a placename (Kojčubaev 186). ✧ 'Hay' cf. Kzk. *p(i)šän* 'das Heu' (Radl. IV, 1354).

PÏŠÏM Kzk. 19th c. **Pišim-bay** [Пишимбай Худаяровъ] (Grod., Pril. 80). ✧ 'My prince' cf. Chag. *piš* 'der Herrscher, der Fürst' (Radl. IV, 1353). + poss. suff. *-im*.

PÏTÄK Tat. 1723 **Pitäk** [Питяк] (MIB III, 201).

PÏTPAQ-ŠARAB Tat.(Sib.) **Bitpaq-šarab** [Бітпак Шараб] (Proben IV, 189 /235/). ⇨ **ŠARAP.**

PÏTRONČA Hak. 19th-20th c. **Pitronča** [Питрончa] (HRS 350). ✧ Petroncha (R.).

PÏ see **BEK**

PÏČAN Hak. 19th-20th c. **Pïčan** [Пычан], fem. (HRS 354). ✧ 'Hay'? cf. Alt.(Kmd.) *pičan* 'das Heu' (Radl. IV, 1317). ⇨ **PÏŠEN?**

PÏČÏRO Hak. 19th-20th c. **Pïčïro** [Пычыро] (HRS 351).

PÏČQAQ-XOJAP Kzk. 18th c. **Pïčqaq-χoJap** [Пичкак-Ходжапъ] (Nepljuev 784).

PÏJÏŃ Hak. 19th-20th c. **Pïjïń** [Пычынъ] (HRS 351); Hak.(Kacha) 19th-20th c. **Pïjïń** [Пыцынъ] (Proben IX, 555-56).

PÏYOS Hak.(Sag.) 19th-20th c. **Pïyos / Pïyōs** [Пыйос / Пыjос] (Proben IX, 384, 556, 559, HRS 351).

PÏYŌS see **PÏYOS**

PÏLĀQA Karg. **Pïlāqa** [Пылака] (Katanov, Otč. 9). ✧ 'Block, log, chunk' cf. R. *plaha* 'id.' (Katanov).

PÏLĀSQAŃ Hak.(Blt.) 19th-20th c. **Pïlāsqań** [Пылаасканъ] (Proben IX, 366, 555, HRS 351). ✧ 'Taken away (from the evil spirits)' (cf. Butanaev: *Pïlasχan*), cf. Alt.(Tel.), Hak.(Sag., Koyb.) *pïlās / pïlāš* 'die Räuberei' (Radl. IV, 1314).

PÏNARLÏ Yürük. 16th c. **Pïnarlï** [پیکارلی / Pınarlı], from the Yürüks of Kocacık, Turkey (Gökb., Rum. 105). ✧ 'Being born or dwelling at/near a well (spring or source)' cf. Turk. *pınar* 'die Quelle, die Fontaine, der Brunnen' (Radl. IV, 1309).

PÏRQO Hak. 19th-20th c. **Pïrqo** [Пырко], fem. (HRS 354).

PÏRŌQ see **PROK**

PÏRŌNČA see **PRONČA**

PÏRŌNQA Hak.(Sag.) 19th-20th c. **Pïrōnqa** [Пыронка] (Katanov, Otč. 7). ✧ Pronka (<R. Пронька) (Katanov).

PÏRŌS Hak. 19th-20th c. **Pïrōs** [Пырос] (Katanov, Otč. 13). ✧ '?' cf. R. *prost* '?' (Katanov).

PÏRŌSQA Hak. 19th c. **Pïrōsqa** [Пыроска] (Katanov, Otč. 12); Hak. 19th-20th c. **Pïrōsqa** [Пыроска] (Katanov, Otč. 10). ✧ Proshka (R.) (Katanov).

PÏSTARA Hak. 19th-20th c. **Pïstara** [Пыстара], fem. (HRS 354). ✧ 'Cat' (Butanaev).

PÏŠ-BOLDU Tat.(sib.)? 1635 **Pïš-boldu** [Корукайко

Пышболдуев / Пышлободуев] (Miller, Ist. Sib. II, 423). ⇨ **BOLDÏ.**

PÏŠAQ see **BÏČAQ**

PÏTAQ Hak.(Blt.) 19th-20th c. **Pïtaq** [Пытак] (Katanov, Otč. 9).

PÏTAŃ Hak.(Blt.) 19th-20th c. **Pïtaň / Pïtāň** [Пытаң] (Proben IX, 366, 555).

PÏZAJAQ Hak.(Shor) 19th-20th c. **Pïzajaq** [Пызацак], fem. (Katanov, Otč. 11). ✧ 'Little calf' cf. Hak. PN *Pïzočaχ* (Butanaev), cf. also Alt. *bïza* 'телёнок' (OjrRS). ⇨ **BUZAƔU** + dim. suff. *-jaq*.

PLÏK Hak. 19th-20th c. **Plik** [Плик], fem. (HRS 354).

PLOY Hak. 19th-20th c. **Ploy** [Плой], fem. (HRS 354).

POBÏY Hak. 19th-20th c. **Pobiy** [Побий] (HRS 354).

POČAROQ Hak. 19th-20th c. **Počaroq** [Почарок] (HRS 351).

POČQA Hak. 19th-20th c. **Počqa** [Почка] (HRS 351).

POČUQ Alt. 19th c. **Počuq** [Почукъ], a christened tale-teller (Potanin IV, 190).

POJAX Hak. 19th-20th c. **Pojaχ** [Почах], fem. (HRS 354).

POJAŃ Hak. 19th-20th c. **Pojań** [Почанъ] (HRS 351); Hak.(Kacha) 19th-20th c. **Pojań** [Поцаң] (Proben IX, 557).

POJAR Hak. 19th-20th c. **Pojar** [Почар], fem. (HRS 354).

POJÏLAY Hak.(Koyb.) 19th c. **Pojïlay** [Поджылай], fem. (Katanov, Otč. II, 12-15). ✧ 'Dregs / sediment of ayran' (Katanov).

POXLAX Hak. 19th-20th c. **Poχlaχ** [Похлах] (HRS 351).

POY-BOLDÏ see **BAY-BOLDÏ**

POYAN Hak. 19th-20th c. **Poyan** [Поян] (HRS 351).

POYAN-GÏLDE Chuv. 18th-19th c. **Poyan-gilde / Puyan-gilde?** [Поянгилда] (Magn. 69). ⇨ **BAYAN + KELDÏ.**

POYANDAY Chuv. 18th-19th c. **Poyanday / Puyanday?** [Пояндай] (Magn. 69). ⇨ **BAYAN +** suff. *-day*.

POYAŃ Hak. 19th-20th c. **Poyań** [Поянъ] (HRS 351).

POYBA Tuv. 19th c. **Poyba** [Поiба] (Proben IX, 157).

POYRAZ Yürük 1543 **Poyraz** [پویراز], a Yürük from Yanbolu, Turkey (Gökb., Rum. 235). ✧ 'North wind' cf. Turk. *poyraz* 'der Nordwind' (Radl. IV, 1263).

POQA Hak. 19th-20th c. **Poqa** [Пока] (HRS 350). ✧ Foka (R.).

POQAY-SARÏƔ Shor 19th-20th c. **Poqay-sarïγ** [Poqaj Saryğ], Qolazï-qan's wife (Dyrenkova 174). ✧ 'Excrement/shit-yellow' cf. Uyg., Alt., Hak. *poq* 'Excremente, Unrath, Dung, Mist' (Radl. IV, 1264). ⇨ **BOQAY + SARÏƔ.**

POQTAŃ Hak.(Sag.) 19th-20th c. **Poqtań / Poqtāń** [Поктанъ] (Proben IX, 558, HRS 350).

POQTUƔ-KÏRÏŠ Shor 19th-20th c. **Poqtuγ-kiriš**

[Poktuǧ Kiriš], fem. (Dyrenkova 176). ❖ 'Stretched bowstring' cf. Hak. PN from the folkl. *Poχtï Kïrïs* 'id.' (Butanaev). ⇨ **KİRİŠ I.** See also **TEMİR-KİRİS.**

POQUYAÑ Karg. **Poquyañ** [Покујаӈ] (Proben IX, 659).

POLAD see **BULAT**

POLAT see **BULAT**

POLAT-QULA 1673 **Polat-qula** [Полатъ-Кула], envoy (DAI VI, 254-55). ⇨ **BULAT + QULA.**

POLİT Hak. 19th-20th c. **Polit** [Полит] (HRS 350). ❖ Ippolit (R.) (Butanaev).

POLİTQA Hak.(Blt.) 19th-20th c. **Politqa** [Політка] (Katanov, Otč. 10); Hak.(Sag.) 19th-20th c. **Politqa** [Політка] (Katanov, Otč. 8). ❖ Ippolitka, Politka (R.) (Katanov).

POLİN Hak.(Sag.) 19th-20th c. **Polin** [Полін] (Katanov, Otč. 8). ❖ Pavlin (R.) (Katanov).

POLİTQA see **POLİTQA**

POLQŌY Karg. **Polqōy** [Полкоi] (Proben IX, 658, 659).

POLŌS Karg. **Polōs** [Полос] (Katanov, Otč. 9). ❖ 'Runner of sleigh' cf. R. *poloz* 'id.' (Katanov).

PONOÑ Hak. 19th-20th c. **Ponoñ** [Пононъ] (HRS 350).

POR Tuv. 19th c. **Por-aqa / Poraqa?** [Порака] (Proben IX, 62, 76). ⇨ **BORA?**

PORA see **BORA**

PORBAY Karg. **Porbay** [Порбай] (Katanov, Otč. 9); Hak.(Kacha) 19th-20th c. **Porbāy** [Порбаi] (Proben IX, 536). ❖ 'Stuck-up, capricious' (Butanaev).

PORBAK Hak. 19th c. **Porbak** [Порбак], fem. (Katanov, Otč. 12). ❖ I. 'Earrings (pendants) of girls made of feathers' (cf. Butanaev: fem. *Porbaχ*); II. 'Stuck-up, capricious' (Butanaev). See also **PORBAY.**

PORBAN Hak.? 19th-20th c. **Porban** [Порбан], fem. (Katanov, Otč. 10).

PORBĀY see **PORBAY**

PORČO Hak. 19th-20th c. **Porčo** [Порчо], fem. (HRS 354); Hak.(Koyb.) 19th-20th c. **Porčō** [Порчо], fem. (Katanov, Otč. 13). ❖ 'Flower' (Butanaev), cf. Hak.(Sag., Koyb.) *porča / portya* 'eine Blume' (Radl. IV, 1271, 1272).

PORČŌ see **PORČO**

PORİS Chuv. 1772 **Poris** [Порис (Яков Григорьев)] (MIB IV/1, 361). ❖ Boris (R.)?

PORLAX Hak. 19th-20th c. **Porlaχ** [Порлах] (HRS 351).

PORLOT Hak. 19th-20th c. **Porlot** [Порлот] (HRS 351).

PORSÏ Trkm. 20th c. **Porsï** [Porsï] (Zaj. 1971, 333); Trkm. 20th c. **Porsï** [Порсы] (TrkmRS 532). ❖ 'Stinking' cf. Trkm. *porsï* 'вонючий' (TrkmRS).

POS see **BOZ**

POS-KİLDE Chuv. 18th-19th c. **Pos-kilde** [Поскилда]

(Magn. 69). ⇨ **BOZ + KELDİ.**

POS-TUGAN Chuv. 18th-19th c. **Pos-tugan** [Постуганъ] (Magn. 69). ⇨ **BOZ + TUΓAN I.**

POS-TUΓAN see **BOZ-DOΓAN**

POSTAY Hak. 19th-20th c. **Postay** [Постай], fem. (HRS 354); Hak.(Sag.) 19th-20th c. **Postay** [Постай], fem. (Katanov, Otč. 7); Hak.(Kacha) 19th c. **Postay** [Постай], fem. (Katanov, Otč. II, 42). ❖ 'Independent, self-reliant' (Butanaev 91), cf. Alt.(Tel.) *pos* 'eigensinnig, halsstarrig, eigenwillig', Hak.(Koyb., Sag.) *pos* 'leer, lose, frei' (Radl. IV, 1288). Katanov mistakenly interprets it as 'Halt! Stop!' from R. *postoj* (Katanov, Otč. II, 42) + suff. *-tay(1,2)*?

POTAŠ Bashk. 1701 **Potaš** [Поташ Камышев] (MIB III, 13). ❖ 'Ash-grease'? (<R.) *potaš* 'id.'; II. 'Young camel'. ⇨ **BOTAŠ?**

POTĀP Karg. **Potāp** [Потап] (Katanov, Otč. 9). ❖ Potap (R.).

POZÏRAQ Hak. 19th c. **Pozïraq** [Позырак] (Katanov, Otč. 12); Hak.(Sag.) 19th-20th c. **Pozïraq** [Позырак], fem. (Katanov, Otč. 8); Hak.(Koyb.) 19th-20th c. **Pozïraq** [Позырак], fem. (Katanov, Otč. 13); Hak. 19th-20th c. **Pozraχ** [Позрах] (HRS 350). ❖ I. 'Sunday' (Butanaev), cf. Hak. *pozraχ* 'id.' (HRS), Hak.(Kacha) *pozraq (kün)* (R.) 'der Sonntag' (Radl. IV, 1294); II. 'Red' (Katanov), cf. Hak.(Sag.) *pozraq* 'der Fuchs (Pferdefarbe)' (Radl. IV, 1294), Hak. *pozraχ* 'id.' (HRS).

POZÏRAÑ Hak. 19th-20th c. **Pozïrāñ** [Позыраанъ] (HRS 350); Hak.(Kacha) 19th-20th c. **Pozïrañ** [Позыраӈ] (Proben IX, 553); Hak.(Koyb.) 19th-20th c. **Pozïrañ** [Позыраӈ], fem. (Katanov, Otč. 13). ⇨ **POZÏRAQ?**

POZRAX see **POZÏRAQ**

PŌČQA see **BOČQA**

PŌSQA Hak. 19th-20th c. **Pōsqa** [Пооска] (HRS 350); Hak.(Sag.) 19th-20th c. **Pōsqa** [Поска] (Proben IX, 613). ❖ '(Cow, mare) with young, pregnant' cf. Hak. *pōs* 'стельная (о корове); жерёбая (о лошади); подвязка' (HRS). + suff. *-qa.*

PÖČÖK Alt. 19th c. **Pöčök** [Пöчöк] (Potanin IV, 170).

PÖDİR Karg. **Pödir** [Пöдiр] (Katanov, Otč. 9); Hak.(Sag.) 19th-20th c. **Pōdir** [Пöдiр] (Proben IX, 265); Hak.(Shor) 19th-20th c. **Pōdir** [Пöдiр] (Katanov, Otč. 11). ❖ Fedor (R.) (Katanov).

PÖKKÄ Karg. **Pökkä** [Пöккä] (Proben IX, 658).

PÖKLE Hak. 19th-20th c. **Pökle** [Пöкле], fem. (HRS 354). ❖ Fyokla (R.).

PÖP-PÜRÄ Tuv. 19th c. **Pöp-pürä-qam** [Пöп-пÿрä-кам], a shaman (Proben IX, 210).

PÖPÖGÖTÖY Kzk. **Pöpögötöy** [Пöпöгöтöi] (Proben III, 68 /89/).

PÖSSÄLJİK Karg. **Pössäljik** [Пöссäлжiк] (Proben IX, 658).

PŎTÜR Yak. **Pŏtür / Bŏtür / Büötür** [Пöтÿр / Бöтÿр, Бÿöтÿр] (Pek.). ✧ Pyotr (R.) (Pek.).

PRAČET Hak. 19th-20th c. **Pračet** [Прачет], fem. (HRS 354).

PRÏK-TLEMÏŠ Bashk. 1675 **Prïk-tlemïš** [Прыктлемишев] (MIB I, 199). ✧ '?-Wished (child)'. ⇨ **TÏLEMÏŠ.**

PROK Karg. **Pïrŏq** [Пырок] (Katanov, Otč. 9); Hak. 19th-20th c. **Prok** [Прок] (HRS 351). ✧ Prokopiy, Prokl (R.).

PRONČA Hak.(Sag.) 19th-20th c. **Pïrŏnča** [Пыронча] (Katanov, Otč. 8); Hak.(Kacha) 19th-20th c. **Pïrŏnča / Pronča** [Пыронча / Пронча] (Proben IX, 535); Hak. 19th-20th c. **Pronča** [Пронча] (HRS 351). ✧ Proncha, Pronya (R.) (Katanov), cf. Hak. *Pïronča* (Butanaev) (<R. PN *Pronya, Pron'ča* / Проньча). + suff. *-ča.*

PRŎBUYAP Yak. **Prŏbuyap** [Пробујап], a folklore hero in a Yakut legend (Pek.).

PRUSTAY Hak. 19th-20th c. **Prustay** [Прустай] (HRS 351).

PŠAQ see **BÏČAQ**

PŠLÏK Kzk. 19th c. **Pšlik** [Пшликъ] (SOK 268).

PUDAQ see **BUTAQ**

PUDORA Hak. 19th-20th c. **Pudora** [Пудора], fem. (HRS 354). ✧ Fedora (R.).

PUDŬ-KÄÜČ Tat.(Bar.) **Pudŭ-käüč** [Пудў Кäÿч], Qara-kököl's sister (Proben IV, 66 /81/). ✧ '(Her) legs-galoshes' cf. Alt., Hak. *put* 'das Bein, die Weiche' (Radl. IV, 1379), Tat.(Bar.) *käüc* 'die Galoschen' (Radl. II, 1057).

PUҐA see **BUQA**

PUҐAÑ Hak. 19th-20th c. **Puҕañ** [Пуҕанъ] (HRS 351).

PUYAN see **BAYAN**

PULAD see **BULAT**

PULAY Hak. 19th-20th c. **Pulay-qan** [Пулаи-кан] (Radl. 105). ⇨ **BULAY?** See also **ÏŠ-PULAY.**

PULAT see **BULAT**

PULAT-BUҐA see **BULAT-BUҐA**

PULAT-TÏMÏR see **TEMÏR-BULAT**

PULDÏ-SAQ Uyg. 1339 **Puldï-saq? / Poldï-čaq?** [Puldi-Sak], fem. (Chwol., Syr.-nest. 90). ⇨ **BOLDÏ + SAQ.**

PULҐUNJAQ Hak.(Blt.) 19th-20th c. **Pulҕunjaq** [Пулҕунцак], fem. (Katanov, Otč. 9). ✧ I. 'Stirrer' (Katanov); II. 'Leather pot, vessel' cf. Hak. PN *Pulχunčaχ* (Butanaev).

PULPAČ see **BOLPAŠ**

PUPAY Kzk. 1740 **Pupay / Pupay-χanša** [Пупай], Abul Khair Khan's wife (Hanykov, Poezdka 8, Nepljuev 687, 715, 717, etc., Levchine mentions her as *Papay* (see)). ⇨ **PAPAY?**

PURAŠ Hak. 19th c. **Puraš** [Пураш] (Katanov, Otč. 12).

PURBA see **KÖK-PURBA, QARA-PURBA**

PURČIS Hak. 19th-20th c. **Purčis** [Пурчис], fem. (HRS 354).

PURČUQ see **KÖGÖY-PÜRČUK**

PURLAÑ Hak. 19th-20th c. **Purlañ** [Пурланъ] (HRS 351).

PURTAL Turk. 19th c. **Purtal-oҕlu** [Purtal oҕlu], a Zeybek (Kúnos 1891, 119).

PUSAM-BAY see **PUSAN**

PUSAN Kzk. 19th c. **Pusam-bay (<Pusan-bay)** [Пусамбай] (AOP 74).

PUSČU Bashk. 1756 **Pusču-ҕul / Pušču-ҕul?** [Пущугул Юлушев] (MIB IV/1, 106).

PUŠUQ Kzk. 19th c. **Pušuq** [Пушукъ] (SOV 120). ✧ 'Snub-nosed' cf. Kzk. *pušïq* 'id.' (KzRS).

PŪN Hak.(Sag.) 19th-20th c. **Pūn** [Пун], fem. (Katanov, Otč. 8). ✧ 'Pound' cf. R. *funt* 'id.' (Katanov).

PÜČÜRÖ Hak.(Koyb.) 19th c. **Püčürö** [Пючюрё], fem. (Katanov, Otč. II, 12-15). ✧ 'Cheese' (Katanov).

PÜDEY Alt. 19th c. **Püdey-χan** [Пюдей-хан] (Verb., In. 139, 140, 146, 150-52).

PÜDREK Hak. 19th-20th c. **Püdrek** [Пiдрек] (HRS 354).

PÜDÜKKÄY Karg. **Püdükkäy** [Пÿдÿккäй], fem. (Katanov, Otč. 9). ✧ 'Slit-eyed' cf. Hak. fem. *Püdük* 'узкоглазая' (Butanaev). + dim. suff. *-käy.*

PÜLÜKKÄY Tuv. 19th c. **Pülükkäy** [Пÿлÿккäi] (Proben IX, 128).

PÜRČUK see **KÖGÖY-PÜRČUK**

PÜRGÜN Kzk. 19th c. **Pürgüm-bek (<Pürgün-bek)** [Пюргумбекъ] (AOA 150). ⇨ **BÜRGÜN?**

PÜRÜK Karg. **Pürük** [Пÿрÿк] (Katanov, Otč. 8). ✧ 'Cap' (Katanov), cf. Alt.(Leb.) *pürük / pörük* 'die Mütze' (Radl. IV, 1302, 1397).

PÜRÜÑGÄY Karg. **Pürüñgäy** [Пÿрÿҥгäi] (Proben IX, 626).

PÜTKE Hak. 19th-20th c. **Pütke** [Пÿтке] (HRS 351).

PÜTRÜK Uyg. **Pütrük** [Pütrük] (EUTS).

PŪREK Hak. 19th-20th c. **Pŭrek** [Пÿÿрек], fem. (HRS 354). ✧ 'Little wolf (cub)' cf. Hak. *pŭr* 'волк' (HRS). + dim. suff. *-ek.*

PŪT Hak. 19th-20th c. **Pŭt** [Пÿÿт] (HRS 351).

R

RABAY Kkalp. 20th c. **Rabay** [Рабай] (KkRS 775). ✧ 'Circumstances, events, happenings' (KkRS).

RAJAB Kzk. 1888 **Rajab-bay** [Раджабъ-бай] (Nalivkin 8); Uzb. 19th c. **Rajab-bay** [Раджаббай] (SKSO III, 152); Trkm. 20th c. **Rejep** [Reǧep] (Zaj. 1971, 332); Trkm. 20th c. **Rejep** [Реджеп] (TrkmRS

547). ✧ The seventh month of the Arabic (Islamic) calendar. 'Awesome, great' (<Ar.).

RAXMAN   Trkm. 20th c. **Raχman** [Rahman] (Zaj. 1971, 327); Tat. 18th c. **Raχman** [Рахман Бермалиев] (MIB V, 83); Tat. 18th c. **Raχman** [Рахман Султанов] (MIB V, 83); Bashk. 18th c. **Raχman** [Рахман], several persons (MIB V, 83,); Bashk. 18th c. **Raχman-γul** [Рахмангул], several persons (MIB V, 60, 165, 328, etc.); Bashk. 18th c. **Raχman-γul** [Рахмангул Абдуллин] (MIB V, 328); Bashk. 1780 **Raχman-γul** [Рахмангул Иртуганов] (MIB V, 109); Nog.? 1635 **Raχman-γul** [Рахмангулъ], a murza of Yedi-san (DAI II, 150-51); Bashk. 18th c. **Raχman-γul / Raχman-qul** [Рахмангул (Рахманкул) Субханкулов (Суханкулов)] (MIB V, 259); Tat. 19th c. **Raχman-qul** [Rachmankulov] (Mende 99); Trkm. 1628 **Raχman-quli-sultan** [Рахман-кули-султан] (MIT II, 104, 105); Trkm. 1824/25 **Raχman-quli-töre** [Рахман-кули-тöре (инак)] (MIT II, 222-224, 427, 429 etc.). ✧ 'Rahman; Compassionate, All-Compassionate (Allah's epithet)' (Sattarov, Kusimova), *Raχman-quli* 'Slave of the All-Compassionate (Allah)' <Ar. See also **QARAJA-RAXMAN.**

RAXMAN-BERDİ   Trkm. 1818 **Raχman-berdi-biy** [Рахман-берды-бий], from the Xïtay(?) tribe (MIT II, 412); Trkm. 1826, 1856 **Raχman-berdi-bay** [Рахман-берды-бай], from the Sarïq tribe (MIT II, 435, 437, 555, 558, etc.); Trkm. 19th c. **Raχman-berdi** [Рахман-берды], from the Sarïq tribe (MIT II, 520, 521); Kzk. 19th c. **Raχman-berdi** [Рахманъ-берды] (Nalivkin 8); Kzk. 19th c. **Raχman-berdi** [Рахманберды], a biy (Lomakin 33); Kzk. 19th c. **Raχman-berdi** [Рахманберды] (SKSO VIII, 200); Uzb. 1838 **Raχman-berdi** [Рахман-берды-парваначи], nobleman (high dignitary) from the region of Merv (MIT II, 470); Uzb. 1851 **Raχman-berdi-biy** [Рахманъ-Берды-Бий], from Khiva (ZIRGO V, 105); Uzb. 1887 **Raχman-berdi-bay** [Рахманъ-Берды-Бай] (Moskal'cev 52); Uzb. 20th c. **Rahmân-berdi** [Рахмонберди] (Begmatov 1984, 202). ✧ 'The All-Compassionate (Allah) has given him/her'. ⇨ **RAXMAN + BERDİ.**

RAXMAN-BERGEN   Trkm. 19th c. **Raχman-bergen** [Рахман-берген], ešik-aγasï (MIT II, 638).

RAXMAN-QULİ-QARAMAŠ   Trkm. 1628 **Raχman-quli-qaramaš** [Рахман-кули-карамаш] (MIT II, 104, 105). ✧ 'Qaramaš The Slave of The All-Compassionate (Allah)'. ⇨ **RAXMAN + QUL** + poss. *-i*.

RAXMET   Nog. 20th c. **Raχmet** [Рахмет Йакъуп улы Сыйкъаллы / Рахмет Якубович Сыйкалиев], one of Baskakov's informants from the aul of Üykön-χalq (Ikon-halk), Cherkess Autonomous Region (Oblast') (Bask., Nog. 143). ✧ Rahmat (Ar.)

'mercy, compassion, kindness' (Ahmed).

RAY   Kzk. 19th c. **Ray** [Рай] (AOO 42). ✧ 'Upright, honest, frank, brave' (Ar.) (Žanuzakov), cf. Kkalp. *ray* 'внешний вид; насторение' (KkRS).

RAYXAN   Kkalp. 20th c. **Rayχan** [Райхан], fem. (KkRS 778). ✧ 'A kind of flower, (sweet) basil?' (Ar.) (Žanuzakov, Sattarov, Kusimova).

RAYKE   Kzk. 19th c. **Rayke** [Райке] (SOV 152). ⇨ **RAY** + suff. *-ke* <comp. *-ake*.

RAYMAN   Bashk. 1770 **Rayman** [Таир Райманов] (MIB IV/1, 349). ⇨ **RAY** + suff. *-man.*

RAQAY   Bashk. 1761 **Raqay** [Ракай Утемышев] (MIB IV/1, 200). ⇨ **URAQAY?**

RAQÏYĀJ   Bulg. / Tat.? 1351/52 **Raqïyāj** [رقیاج / Riqyāj / Ракийадж] (Jusupov 27).

RAQÏM see **RĀHİM**

RAQÏM-BERDİ see **RĀHİM-BERDİ**

RAMAZAN   Bulg. 1323 **Ramazan** [رَمَضَان / Рамазан] (Jusupov 23); Maml. 1320 **Ramazan** [سیف‌الدین رمضان] (Dawād. 300); Turk. **Ramazan** [رمضان محمد بن محمود], in an inscription of a tomb in Amasya, Turkey (Hakkı, Ves. I, 139); Turk. 1497 **Ramazan** [Hacı Ramazan] (Gökb., Ed. 82); Turk. 1515 **Ramazan** [Mehmed bin Hacı Ramazan] (Gökb., Ed. 82); Turk. 1519 **Ramazan** [Ramazan] (Gökb., Ed. 188); Turk. 1528 **Ramazan** [Ramazan bin Durmuş] (Gökb., Ed. 296); Turk. 1543 **Ramazan** [Ramazán Mohammed] (Velics-Kamm. I, 8); Turk. 1583-84 **Ramazan** [Ramazan] (Ongan, Ank. I, 175); Yürük 1543 **Ramazan** [Ramazan] (Gökb., Rum. 177, 179, 181, 183, 200 etc.); Trkm.? 1740 **Ramazan** [Рамазанъ Султанъ], Šahseven (PSZRI VIII, 278); Crm. 1350 **Ramazan** [زین‌الدین رمضان / Зейнеддинъ Рамазанъ], a Crimean ruler (Al-Muχibbī/Tizeng. I, 340, Al-Qalqašandī/Tizeng. I, 401, 413); Tat. 1614 **Ramazan** [Рамазанъ / Ромазанъ], from Astrakhan (AI III, 30); Tat. 1654 **Ramazan** [Келимбетъ Ромозановъ] (AI IV, 236); Tat. 1774 **Ramazan** [Рамазан Абтиков] (MIB V, 544, 683); Tat. 1779 **Ramazan** [Рамазан Юсупов] (MIB V, 83); Bashk. 1754 **Ramazan** [Рамазан Кичкитаев] (MIB IV/1, 86); Kzk. **Ramazan** [Ажимовъ Рамазанъ] (TOOIK III, 182); Kzk. 19th c. **Ramazan** [Рамазанъ] (AOP 70, 122); Kzk. 19th c. **Ramazan** [Рамазанъ] (SOK 128); Kzk. 19th c. **Ramazan** [Рамазанъ] (SODž. 64); Kzk. 19th c. **Ramazan** [Рамазанъ] (AOK 54, 130); Nog. 20th c. **Ramazan** [Меджит Рамазан улы Къарас / Меджит Рамазанович Карасов], father of one of Baskakov's informants from the aul of Quban-χalq (Bask., Nog. 143); Nog. 20th c. **Ramazan** [Омар Рамазан улы], father of one of Baskakov's informants from the aul of Qañlï (Bask., Nog. 143); Tat.(Mish.) 1775 **Ramazan / Rämäzan** [Рямязан Гаитов] (MIB

IV/2, 417); Turk. 1552 **Ramazan-aγa** [Ramazán aga] (Velics-Kamm. I, 75); Turk. 1519 **Ramazan-čelebi** [Ramazan Çelebi] (Gökb., Ed. 249, 250); Trkm. 20th c. **Remezan** [Remezan] (Zaj. 1971, 332); Trkm. 20th c. **Remezān** [Рамазан] (TrkmRS 548). ✧ '*Ramazan*, the ninth month of the year during which Muslims fast between dawn and sunset' (Ar.) (TED), child born in this month (Sattarov, Žanuzakov).

RAMEÑLİ   Tat.(Tüm.)   1651   **Rameñli-bay** [Раменглыбаевъ] (DAI III, 330).

RAN Kzk. 19th c. **Ran** [Ранъ] (SOV 58). ⇨ **URAN?**

RAS Kzk. 19th c. **Ras-bek** [Разбекъ] (SOK 32); Chuv. 18th-19th c. **Ras-pay** [Распай] (Magn. 70); Kzk. 19th c. **Raz-bay** [Разбай] (SOK 44). ✧ 'Right, good, satisfactory' cf. Crm., Kzk. *ras* (<P.) 'geziemend, richtig, den Anforderungen entsprechend' (Radl. III, 712). ⇨ **ORAZ?**

RAS-KİLDE see **ORAZ-KELDİ**

RAS-TUΓAN see **URAZ-TUΓAN**

RASLAN see **ARSLAN**

RASTA Tat. 1531 **Rasta** [Раста], a prince from Kazan (PSRL VIII, 277).

RASUL Selj. 11th c. **Rasul-tegin** (Ibn al-Athīr/Tornb. IX, 436-437); Bashk. 1777 **Rasul / Räsul** [Расул (Рясулъ) Иджимасов] (Vel.-Zern., Bašk. 3, MIB V, 545). ✧ Rasul (Ar.) 'Messenger of Allah (God); Prophet' (Ahmed); '(Prophet) Mukhammad' (Erol II). See also **BERDİ-RASUL, ÄBDİ-RÄSUL.**

RAWİYA Kkalp. 20th c. **Rawiya** [Раўия], fem. (KkRS 778).

RAZ-BERGEN see **URAZ-BERGEN**

RAZ-DAWLET see **URAZ-DÄWLÄT**

RAZ-GİLDEY see **ORAZ-KELDİ**

RAZÏYA Kkalp. 20th c. **Razïya** [Разыя], fem. (KkRS 778). ✧ 'Sweet-tempered, kind, satisfied' (Ar.) (Žanuzakov).

RÂZÏQ-BERDİ Kzk. 19th c. **Razïq-berdi** [Халыкъ-Берды Разыкбердыевъ] (SKSO IV, otd., III, 13); Uzb. 20th c. **Râziq-berdi** [Розикберди] (Begmatov 1984, 202). ✧ '?-gave him/her'. ⇨ **BERDİ.**

RÄ Kkalp. 20th c. **Rä-biybi** [Рәбийби], fem. (KkRS 778).

RÄHİYMA Kkalp. 20th c. **Rähiyma** [Рәхийма], fem. (KkRS 778); Kkalp. 20th c. **Räyima** [Рәйима], fem. (KkRS 778). ✧ Rahima (Ar. fem. of Rahim) 'kind, compassionate' (Ahmed); 'Kind, pious, warm-hearted' (Žanuzakov, Sattarov), cf. Tat. fem. PN *Räimä* (Sattarov).

RÄHİM Kzk. 19th c. **Raqïm-bay** [Или-бай Рахимбаевъ] (Grod., Pril. 58); Uzb. 1793 **Rähim-bay** [Rachimbai Dostmuratow] (ArchKR XVIII, 352); Uzb. **Rähim-bek** [Нишанбай Рахимбековъ] (Sr. Az. I, 1896, Avg. 15). ✧ 'Rahim (Ar.), Merciful, compassionate, kind (Allah's epithet)' (Ahmed), cf.

also Uzb. *rähim* 'милосердный, милостивый (один из.питетов бога)' (UzbRS). See also **BERDİ-RÄHİM, ÄBDİ-RÄYİM.**

RÄHİM-BERDİ Kzk. 19th c. **Rahim-berdi** [Рахимъ Берди Тилуевъ] (Grod., Pril. 40); Kzk. 19th c. **Raim-berdi** [Раимъ Берди] (Grod., Pril. 110); Kzk. 19th c. **Raim-berdi / Ram-berdi** [Раимберды / Рамберды], a biy (Lomakin 34, 35); Uzb. 1764 **Rähim-berdi** [Рахимъ Берди Тилуевъ], a Kipchak (MIT II, 338); Uzb. 20th c. **Rähim-berdi** [Рахимберди] (Begmatov 1984, 202); Uzb. 1855 **Rähim-berdi-biy** [Рахимъ Берди Тилуевъ], a commander from Khiva (MIT II, 553). ✧ 'The gracious/merciful (God) gave him/her'. ⇨ **RÄHİM + BERDİ.**

RÄHİM-BERGEN   Kzk. 19th c. **Raim-bergen** [Раимбергенъ] (SODž. 58); Uzb. 20th c. **Rähim-bergän** [Рахимберган] (Begmatov 1984, 202); Kkalp. 20th c. **Räyim-bergen** [Рәйимберген] (KkRS 775). ✧ 'The Merciful (God) gave (him/her); (The) Kind, warm-hearted gave (him/her)', 'The Merciful's gift' (Jankowski 1998, p. 14), cf. also Sattarov: Tat. *Räim* (<Ar.) Rahim. ⇨ **RÄHİM + BERGEN.** See also **RÄHİM-BERDİ.**

RÄHMÂN-BERGÄN Uzb. 20th c. **Rähmân-bergän** [Рахмонберган] (Begmatov 1984, 202). ✧ 'The All-Compassionate (Allah) has given him/her'. ⇨ **RAXMAN + BERGEN.**

RÄYİM-BERGEN see **RÄHİM-BERGEN**

RÄYİMA see **RÄHİYMA**

RÄSUL see **RASUL**

RÄSUL-BERDİ   Uzb. 20th c. **Räsul-berdi** [Расулберди] (Begmatov 1984, 202). ✧ 'Prophet has him/her given'. ⇨ **RÄSUL + BERDİ.** See also **BERDİ-RASUL.**

RÄWŠAN Kkalp. 20th c. **Räwšan** [Рәўшан], fem. (KkRS 778). ✧ 'Bright, shiny, light' (P.) (Žanuzakov, Sattarov).

RÄZZÂQ-BERDİ   Uzb. 20th c. **Räzzâq-berdi** [Раззокберди] (Begmatov 1984, 202). ✧ 'Bread-giver/provider (God) gave him/her' cf. Uzb. *räzzâq* 'дающий хлеб насущный, кормилец (эпитет бога)' (UzbRS) (<Ar.) ⇨ **BERDİ.**

RÄZZÂQ-BERGÄN Uzb. 20th c. **Räzzâq-bergän** [Раззокберган] (Begmatov 1984, 202). ✧ 'Bread-giver/provider (God) gave him/her' cf. Uzb. *räzzâq* 'дающий хлеб насущный, кормилец (эпитет бога)' (UzbRS) (<Ar.) ⇨ **BERGEN.**

REBİŠ Turk. 19th c. **Rebiš-oγlu** [Rebiš oγlu], a Zeybek (Kúnos 1891, 119).

REHBER Yürük 1543 **Rehber** [Rehber] (Gökb., Rum. 211). ✧ 'Guide; leader' (TED).

REYXAN Yürük 16th c. **Reyχan** [ريحان / Rey han] (Gökb., Rum. 104). ✧ 'Ease, fragrant herb, sweet basil (Ocimum basilicum)' (Ahmed; Erol II) (<Ar.).

RΓA   Kzk. 19th c. **Rγa-bay** (<**Ĭrγa-bay?**) [Ргабай] (SOV 144). ⇨ **ĬRGE?**

RΓÏZ   Kzk. 1730-1750 **Rγïz-bay** (<**Ĭrgiz-bay**) [Ргызбай], born on the İrgiz river (Tynyšp. 68). ✧ '(Born on the river) *Irgiz*' (Tynyšp.).

RĬŠĬM   Kzk. 19th c. **Rišĭm-bek** (<**İrišim-bek?**) [Ришымбекъ] (SOK 12). ⇨ **İRĬS?** + poss. suff. *-im*.

RĬQAY   Bashk. 1760 **Rĭqay** [Рыкай Биганов] (MIB IV/2, 28).

RĬMČĬ   Alt. 19th c. **Rĭmči** [Рымчи] (Verb., In. 45). ✧ 'Soothsayer, diviner' cf. Alt. *irïmčï* 'id.' (OjrRS).

RĬS see **İRĬS**

RĬS-KELDİ   Kzk. 18th c. - 19th c. **Rĭs-keldi** [Рыскельды] (Tynyšp. 67). ⇨ **RĬS** + **KELDİ.**

RĬS-MELDİ   Kzk. 19th c. **Rĭs-meldi?** / **Rĭs-keldi?** [Рысмелды] (SODž. 14). ⇨ **RĬS** + **KELDİ?**

RĬSAY   Chuv. 1764 **Rĭsay** [Ишпулай Рысаев] (MIB IV/2, 103). ⇨ **İRĬS** + suff. *-ay*.

RĬSLĬ   Nog. 1649 **Rĭslï** [Рыслы] (AI IV, 123). ✧ 'Lucky'. ⇨ **RĬS** + suff. *-lï*.

RĬSMÄŠ   Bashk. 1741 **Rĭsmäš** [Рысмяш Сеитов] (MIB III, 505, 507).

RĬSMET   Tat. 1760 **Rĭsmet** [Рысметь Уразметь] (MIB IV/2, 36). ⇨ **İRĬS** + suff. *-met*.

ROBEGEN   Kzk. 19th c. **Robegen** [Робегенъ] (SOK 140).

RODYUMĀN   Yak. **Rodyumān** [Роӊӱман / Ороӊӱман, Уруоӊӱман] (Pek.).

RODMAN   Pecheneg 1001 **Rodman** [Родманъ], a prince (PSRL IX, 68).

ROPA   Khorezm./Chag. 14th c. **Ropa?** [Ropa Arbaraga], one of Timur's wives (Clavijo 52).

ROS   Tat. 1680 **Ros-pay?** / **Ras-pay?** [Токманко Роспаевъ] (DAI VIII, 272-73). ⇨ **ORAZ?**

ROZ-GİLDEY see **ORAZ-KELDİ**

ROZMA-GİLDEY   Tat. 1675 **Rozma-gildey** [Розмагилдѣйко] (Kungursk. akty 36). ⇨ **KELDİ.**

RÖVŠEN   Trkm. 20th c. **Rövšen** [Rövšen] (Zaj. 1971, 327); Trkm. 20th c. **Rövšen** [Ровшен] (TrkmRS 552). ✧ 'Shining, sparkling; excellent; happy' cf. Trkm. *rövšen* 'блестящий; светлый, радостный, счастливый' (TrkmRS) (<P.).

RUM   Karakh. **Rum** [Rum] (MK/Atalay 849); Maml. 14th c. **Rum-eri** [رومرى / **Rūmeri**] (Tarǰ/Houtsma 45, Tarǰ/Toparlı 42). ✧ cf. Turk. *Rum* 'the Byzantines; Asia Minor; the Ottoman Empire' (TED).

RUM-QUŠU   Turk. 1489 **Rum-qušu** [Muslihiddin veled-i Rumkuşu] (Gökb., Ed. 156). ✧ 'Bird of Rum'. ⇨ **RUM** + **QUŠ I.** + poss. suff. *-u*.

RUMİ   Turk. 20th c. **Rumi** [Rumi] (Önder, Hınıs). ✧ 'Greek or one being/coming from Lesser Asia' cf. Turk. *rum* 'römisch, griechisch' (Radl. III, 724), Turk. *Rum* 'the Byzantines; Asia Minor; the Ottoman Empire' (TED). ⇨ **RUM** + .Ar. adj. suff. *-ī*.

RUS see **URUS**

RUSTEM see **RÜSTEM**

RÜSTÄM see **RÜSTEM**

RÜSTEM   Karakh. **Rüstäm** [rüstäm] (DTS); Kkalp. 20th c. **Rüstem** [Рустем] (KkRS 776); Kzk. 19th c. **Urustem** (<**Rustem**) [Урустемъ] (AOK 18); Kirg. **Urüstüm** [Sultan Urüstüm] (?). ✧ Rustam (P.), the name of a king of Iran (867-95) (Ahmed); 'Very big, strong, mighty, heroic' (Žanuzakov, Sattarov).

RZAMBET   Kkalp. 20th c. **Rzambet** [Рзамбет] (KkRS 776). ⇨ **URAZĬMBET?**

S

SA-TEMİR   Kzk. 19th c. **Sa-temir** [Сатемиръ] (SOV 62); Kkalp. 20th c. **Sa-temir-qan** [Сатемир-къан] (Bask., Kkalp. 73); Kzk. **Sa-temir-qan** (<**Sat-temir-qan?**) [Satemir-kan] (Altyns. 2). ⇨ **SAT?** + **TEMİR.**

SABA I.   Alt. 19th-20th c. **Saba** [Саба] (OjrRS 209); Alt. 19th-20th c. **Sāba** [Сааба] (OjrRS 209); Yak. **Sāba** [Саба] (Pek.). ✧ I. 'Pot made of birch-rind' (OjrRS); II. 'Leather-bag/sack' cf. also Shor, Kzk., Tat. *saba* 'ein Ledersack zum Bereiten des Kumiss, ein Lederschlauch; (Shor) grosses Birkenrindengefäss, welches bei der Opferung eines Pferdes am Opferfeiertage zur Frühlingszeit für das Getränk verwendet wird' (Radl. IV, 411), Tat. *saba* 'саба (большой бурдюк для приготовления и хранения кумыса)' (TatRS). See also **BAD-SABA, SANA-SABA, TOQ-SABA.**

SABA II.   Hak. 19th-20th c. **Saba** [Саба], fem. (HRS 354). ✧ 'Wrong, improper' (HRS).

SABADEY   Chuv. 18th-19th c. **Sabadey** [Сабадей] (Magn. 70). ✧ 'Like a leather bottle' cf. Tat. *saba* 'саба (большой бурдюк для приготовления и хранения кумыса)' (TatRS) + suff. *-dey*.

SABAΓALDAY   Tuv. 19th c. **Sabaγalday** [Сабаӊалдаи], fem. (Proben IX, 47).

SABAY   Tat. 1780 **Sabay** [Сабай Михайлов] (MIB V, 116); Bashk. 1706 **Sabay** [Сабай] (MIB III, 21); Bashk. 1735 **Sabay** [Сабай Беккуловъ], a tarχan (Vel.-Zern., Bašk. 19); Bashk. 1746 **Sabay** [Балтай Сабаев] (MIB III, 444); Kzk. 19th c. **Sabay** [Сабай] (SOV 54); Kzk. 19th c. **Sabay** [Сабай] (SODž. 22). ✧ 'Small leather bottle' + dim. suff. *-y*. See also **ČAN-SABAY, TOQ-SABAY.**

SABAQ   Bashk. 1754 **Sabaq** [Даут Сабаков] (MIB IV/1, 83). ⇨ **ČABAQ?** See also **QOY-SOBAQ?**

SABAN I.   Kzk. 18th c. - 19th c. **Saban-qul** [Сабанкул] (Tynyšp. 74); *EN:* Kzk. 18th c. - 19th c. **Saban** [Сабан] (Tynyšp. 67). ✧ 'Plough' cf. Kuman, Kzk.,

Tat., Turk., etc. *saban* 'der Pflug; das Ackerfeld' (Radl. IV, 414), Tat. PN *Saban* (Sattarov), Tat. *saban* 'плуг; пахота' (TatRS). See also **İL-SABAN**.

SABAN II. Hak.(Koyb.) 19th-20th c. **Saban** [Сабан кадка], fem. (Katanov, Otč. 13). ✧ 'Grouse' cf. Hak.(Sag., Koyb.) *saban, qara saban* 'der Auerhahn' (Radl. IV, 415).

SABAN-AY Chuv. 18th-19th c. **Saban-ay** [Сабаней] (Magn. 70); Chuv. 18th-19th c. **Saban-ay** [Сабанай] (Magn. 70); Tat. 1716 **Saban-ay** [Алимбет Сабанаев] (MIB III, 138); Bashk. 1706 **Saban-ay** [Сабанай Яшимиров] (MIB III, 27); Bashk. 1710 **Saban-ay** [Емекей Сабанаев] (MIB III, 67); Bashk. 1711 **Saban-ay** [Сабанай Айбахтин] (MIB III, 71); Bashk. 1754 **Saban-ay** [Сабанай / Сабакай] (MIB IV/1, 92); Bashk. 1758 **Saban-ay** [Тойчибай Сабанаев] (MIB IV/1, 167); Bashk. 1758 **Saban-ay** [Уткул Сабанаев] (MIB IV/1, 167); Bashk. 1787 **Saban-ay** [Сабанай Аллагулов] (MIB V, 211). ✧ 'May, month of Saban, plough-month; child born in the plough-month (in May, in spring)' (Sattarov), cf. Tat. *saban ayï* 'der Monat Mai' (Radl. IV, 415). ⇨ **SABAN I. + AY.**

SABANAQ Bashk. 1742 **Sabanaq** [Сабанак Чюрюкеев] (MIB III, 513); Bashk. 1756 **Sabanaq** [Сабаняк Бикчювашев / Бекчювашев] (MIB IV/1, 130). ✧ 'Little plough; child born at the time of plough in winter' (Sattarov), cf. Kuman, Kzk., Tat., Turk., etc. *saban* 'der Pflug; das Ackerfeld' (Radl. IV, 414) + dim. suff. -*aq*.

SABANČA see **SABANČÏ**

SABANČÏ Chuv. 18th-19th c. **Sabanča** [Сабанча] (Magn. 70); Bashk. 1738 **Sabanča** [Мустай Сабанчин] (MIB I, 143, 145); Karch. **Sabanči** [Сабанчи] (Sysoev 120); Tat. 1738 **Sabanči** [Алдакай Сабанчеев] (MIB III, 400); Bashk. 1732 **Sabanči** [Сабанчи Кошеваров] (MIB III, 302); Kzk. 19th c. **Sabanči** [Сабанчи] (SOK 234); Kzk. 19th c. **Sabanči** [Сабанчи] (SODž. 6). ✧ 'Farmer, ploughman, peasant' cf. Crm., Tat., *sabanči* 'der Ackerbauer, Ackerarbeiter' (Radl. IV, 415).

SABANKA Chuv. 18th-19th c. **Sabanka** [Сабанка] (Magn. 70). ⇨ **SABAN I. + suff. -*qa*.

SABAR Bulg. 1291 **Sabar-ilči** [صبر ايلجى / Сабар-илчи], Buraš-bek's daughter (Jusupov 4, Epigr. Bulg. 4). ✧ 'Finger / toe' cf. Alt. *sabar* 'der Finger, Zeh' (Radl. IV, 416). See also **AY-SABAR, YETİ-SABAR, KÜN-SABAR.**

SABARĀYQA Yak. **Sabarāyqa** [Сабараiка] (Pek.).

SABARTA see **SABATTA**

SABAS see **SABAZ**

SABAŠ Bashk. 1754 **Sabaš** [Игисяк Сабашев] (MIB IV/1, 83). ✧ 'Little leather bottle' cf. Tat. *saba* 'саба (большой бурдюк для приготовления и хранения кумыса)' (TatRS) + dim. suff. -*š*.

SABATA Kzk. 19th c. **Sabata** [Сабата] (SOV 42).

SABATTA Yak. **Sabatta** / **Sabarta** [Сабатта / Сабарта] (Pek.).

SABAZ Kzk. 19th c. **Sabas** [Сабасъ] (SOK 256); Kzk. **Sabaz** [Сабазъ] (ZIRGOGeogr. I, 444); Kzk. 19th c. **Sabaz** [Сабазъ] (SOK 240). ✧ 'Smart, right-handed' cf. Kzk. *sabaz* 'ein tüchtiger Mann' (Radl. IV, 416).

SABDAR Bashk. 1790 **Sabdar** [Сабдар Алакаев] (MIB V, 292). ⇨ **ŠABDAR?**

SABDEN Kzk. 19th c. **Sabden** [Сабденъ] (SOV 142); Kzk. 19th c. **Sabden-bay** [Сабденбай] (SOK 14).

SABİČKA Chuv. 1670 **Sabička** [Сабичка Тимирева], fem. (Poliv.-Kras. 64).

SABİKE Kzk. 19th c. **Sabike** [Сабике] (AOK 74). ✧ Sabiha (Ar. fem.) 'morning' (Ahmed), Kzk. PN *Sabiga / Säbiyya* 'freshness; beautiful' (Žanuzakov 155, Žanuzakov-Esbaeva), Tat. PN *Säbiyya* 'id.' (Sattarov).

SABİR see **SABÏR**

SABÏR-KÖR Trkm. 1863 **Sabir-kör** [Сабир Köр], from the Čawdar (Čoudor) tribe (MIT II, 608). ⇨ **SABÏR + KÖR.**

SABİT Kzk. 19th c. **Sabit** [Сабит] (AOO 2); Kzk. 19th c. **Sabit-pay** [Сабитпай] (SOK 26); Kzk. 19th c. **Sabit-pay** [Сабетпай] (SODž. 78); Kzk. 19th c. **Sabut** [Нурманъ Сабутовъ] (Grod., Pril. 81). ✧ 'Hard, strong, steady; faithful' (Ar.) (Žanuzakov, Sattarov, Kusimova), cf. Turk. *sabit* 'beständig, standhaft' (Radl. IV, 420).

SABÏ-BUQA Uyg. **Sabï-buɣa** [Sabı Buġa] (EUTS); Uyg. 12th c. - 14th c. **Sabï-buqa** (Radl., USp. 98-99, DTS). ✧ 'Sabï-Bull'. ⇨ **BUQA.**

SABÏYA Yak. **Sabïya-bāy-toyon** [Сабыjа-баi-тоjон] (Pek.).

SABÏYĀJÏQ Tuv. 19th c. **Sabïyājïq** [Сабыjацык], fem. (Proben IX, 170).

SABÏYÏQ Yak. **Sabïyïq-bāy-χotun** [Сабыjык-баi-хотун], Sabïya-bāy-toyon's wife (Pek.).

SABÏQ-BASAR Türk **Sabïq-basar** [Sabyq basar] (Radl., Inschr. 339, DTS). ✧ '?-presser; ?-opresser'. ⇨ **BASAR.**

SABÏN-SATÏ Uyg. 12th c. - 14th c. **Sabïn-satï** / **Sabïn-sadï** [Sabïn Sadï / sabïn satï / Sabın Satı] (Radl., USp. 122, DTS, EUTS). ⇨ **SATÏ.**

SABÏR Trkm. 20th c. **Sabïr** [Sabïr], fem. (Zaj. 1971, 342); Trkm. 20th c. **Sabïr** [Сабыр], fem. (TrkmRS 554); Tat. 1543 **Sabïr** (Gökb., Rum. 237); Kzk. **Sabir** [Сабир Капин] (TOOIK I, 61); Kzk. 19th c. **Sabïr** [Сабыръ] (SOK 222); Kzk. 19th c. **Sabïr** [Сабыръ] (SOK 138); Kkalp. 20th c. **Sabïr** [Сабыр] (KkRS 776); Kirg. **Sabïr** [Сабыр] (Jud. 26, 650); Kzk. 1840 **Sabïr-bay** [Еспергенъ Сабырбаевъ] (Konšin, Mat. V, 25); Kzk. 1845 **Sabïr-bay** [Испергенъ Сабырбаевъ] (Konšin, Mat. V, 63); Kzk. 19th c. **Sabïr-bay**

[Сабырбай] (SOV 36); Trkm. 1856 **Sabïr-išan** [Сабир-ишан] (MIT II, 575); Kzk. 19th c. **Sabïr-qul** [Сабыркуль] (SOV 92); Yürük 1543 **Sabur** [Sabur] (Gökb., Rum. 237); Kzk.? 19th c. **Säbir / Sabïr?** [Сябыръ], in the genealogy of the Kazaks (Potanin IV, 15). ❖ 'Patience; steadiness; strength' cf. Crm. *sabur* 'die Geduld' (Radl. IV, 421), Kuman, Kzk., Tat. *sabïr* (Ar.) 'die Geduld; geduldig' (Radl. IV, 418), Kkalp., Kirg. *sabïr* 'терпение; сдержанность' (KkRS, Jud.) (<Ar.). See also **AY-SABÏR, KÜN-SABÏR.**

SABÏRT Hak. 19th-20th c. **Sabïrt** [Сабырт] (HRS 351). ❖ 'Hard, steady' (Ar.) (Butanaev).

SABÏŠ Bashk. 1785 **Sabïš** [Сабыш (Сабыт) Кусяшев] (MIB V, 170); Bashk. 1783 **Sabïš / Sapïš / Sapuš** [Сабыш (Сапыш, Сапуш) Араслангулов] (MIB V, 147, 234, 259). ❖ 'Running; horse racing' cf. Bashk. *sabïš* 'бега; скачки' (BRS/Uraksin).

SABÏT Nog. 20th c. **Sabït** [Абдырахман Сабыт увлы / Абдырахман Сабитов], father of one of Baskakov's informants from the aul of Ïrγaqlï (Bask., Nog. 143). ❖ Sabit (ar.) 'strong, well established, certain, sure' (Ahmed).

SABÏTAY Bashk. 1756 **Sabïtay** [Сабытай Тугульбаев] (MIB IV/1, 132). ⇨ **SABÏT** + suff. -*ay.*

SABOT Hak. 19th-20th c. **Sabot** [Сабот] (HRS 351).

SABRA Türk / Uyg.? **Sabra** (Inschr. II, 277a, 389); Türk 731 **Sabra-tamγan-čur** [sabra tamγan čur] (DTS); Türk 731 **Sabra-tamγan-tarqan** [sabra tamγan tarqan] (DTS); Türk 731 **Sabra-tarqan** [sabra tarqan] (DTS).

SABRA-MATAY Uyg. 13th c. - 14th c. **Sabra-matay / Sabramatï?** [Sabra Matai] (Chwol., Syr.-nest. (NF) 48). ⇨ **SABRA + MATAY.**

SABUR see **SABÏR**

SABUTU Uyg. 12th c. - 14th c. **Sabutu** [sabutu] (DTS, EUTS).

SABUWAQAS Kzk. 19th c. **Sabuwaqas** [Сабуакасъ] (AOO 46). ❖ 'Lucky(?)-warrior' It may be the result of contraction of the Arabic *Saʿad ibn Abu Waqqas*, the name of the well-known sahaabi (Ahmed), cf. also Osm. (Turk.) *saʿd / saad* 'kutluluk, uğur getiren şey, uğur', and *vakkas* 'savaşçı' (Özön) (<Ar.). See also **SADWAQAS.**

SABÜRBEY Hak. 19th-20th c. **Sabürbey** [Сабÿрбей] (HRS 351).

SAČA Pecheneg? 1086 **Sača** [Σατζᾶς], a Scythian (Pecheneg?) chief (Byz. Turc. 270).

SAČIU see **SAČU**

SAČÏ-QARA Turk. 1714 **Sačï-qara** [صاجى قره / Saçıkara cemaati], forefather or chief of a clan in the Yürükân tribe (tayife) (Refik, Anad. 148). ❖ 'Black-haired' cf. Türk, Uyg., Chag., Crm., Turk. *sač* 'die Haare' (Radl. IV, 389). ⇨ **QARA.**

SAČÏ-QARALÏ Turk. 19th c. **Sačï-qaralï-oγlu** [Saçy Karaly oγlu], a Zeybek (Kúnos 1891, 119). ❖ 'Black-haired' cf. Türk, Uyg., Chag., Crm., Turk. *sač* 'die Haare' (Radl. IV, 389). ⇨ **SAČÏ-QARA** + suff. -*li.*

SAČÏQ Turk. 1583 **Sačïq** [صاجـك / Saçık] (Ongan, Ank. I, 175). ❖ 'Scattered, untidy, messy' cf. Turk. *sačiq* 'ausgestreut, in Unordnung' (Radl. IV, 391), 'zerstreut, verstreut' (Zenker II, 558), Chag. *sačiq* 'kleine Münze, die man über das Haupt der Neuvermählten ausstreut, als Zeichen des Glückes' (Radl. IV, 391).

SAČLÏ Kzk. 19th c. **Čaštï-qïz** [Чашты-кызъ], fem. (Sozontov 7); Turk. 16th c. **Sačlï-qoǰa** [Saçlıkoca] (Ün 3(1936), 359). ❖ 'Haired, hairy' cf. Crm., Turk. *sačli* 'mit Haaren versehen, behaart' (Radl. IV, 392), also Alt. *čač* 'volosy' (OjrRS), Shor, Kzk. *šaš* 'die Haare' (Radl. IV, 973) + suff. -*li / -ti.*

SAČU Uyg. **Sačiu / Saču?** [Saçiu] (EUTS); Uyg. 8th c. **Saču** [Saçu], byname (EUTS); Uyg. 12th-14th c. **Saču** [Saçu] (EUTS); Uyg. 12th c. - 14th c. **Saču-señün** [sačuseñün] (DTS). ❖ 'Fringe/flounce (of a clothing)' cf. Karakh. *sačuʿid.*' (DTS). See also **ÏNANČ-SAČU.**

SAJÏR Kzk. 19th c. **Sajïr-bay** [Акмантай Саджирбаевъ] (Grod., Pril. 159).

SAJÏS Hak.(Kacha) 1684 **Sajïs** [Сажиско Сабукинъ] (DAI XI, 161).

SAD-BEK see **SAT**

SADA Uyg. 12th c. - 14th c. **Sada** [sada] (DTS); Kzk. 19th c. **Sada-bay** [Садабай] (Grod., Pril. 113).

SADAГAY Alt. 19th c. **Sadaγay** [Садагай-богатырь], a folklore hero (Verb., In. 129). ⇨ **SADAQ?** + dim. suff. -*ay.*

SADAQ Khorezm.? 1302 **Sadaq** [ساداق], Ghazan's (1295-1304) emir (RaD/Jahn 140); Kzk. 19th c. **Sadaq-pay** [Садакпай] (SODž. 56); Khorezm.? 1289 **Sadaq-tarχan** [ساداق تـرخان / Садак-тархан], from the Uryauts; Ghazan Khan's (1295-1304) envoy to Nevrūz (RaD/Ber. I, 166, II, 212, RaD/Jahn 16, 17, RaD I/1, 171); Alt. 19th-20th c. **Sādaq** [Саадак] (OjrRS 209). ❖ 'Bow-armament' cf. Chag., Alt., Hak., Kzk. *sadaq* 'der Bogen mit allem Schiessgeräthe' (Radl. IV, 383), Alt. *sādaq* 'лук и колчан' (OjrRS). See also **QUN-SADAQ; YAY, OQČĀ.**

SADAQA Chuv. 18th-19th c. **Sadaka** (<Sadaqa) [Садака] (Magn. 72). ❖ 'Alms, pittance, charity' cf. Crm., Kar., Turk. *sadaqa* (Ar.) 'die Almosen' (Radl. IV, 384). See also **BUŠÏ.**

SADAP Trkm. **Sadap** [Садап], fem. (Sopieva 177); Trkm. 20th c. **Sadap** [Sadap], fem. (Zaj. 1971, 338); Trkm. 20th c. **Sadap** [Садап], fem. (TrkmRS 556). ❖ 'Pearl' (Sopieva) cf. Trkm. *sadap* 'перламутр' (TrkmRS) (<Ar.).

SADAR Hak. 19th-20th c. **Sadar** [Садар] (HRS 351). ❖ 'Sold' (Butanaev).

SADAГЇS Hak.(Blt.) 19th-20th c. **Sadaγïs** [Садаɓыс] (Proben IX, 358).

SADBAN   Kzk. 19th c. **Sadban-bek** [Садбанбекъ] (SOK 282); Kzk. 19th c. **Sadben** [Садбенъ] (SOV 104, 106); Kzk. 19th c. **Sadben** [Садбенъ] (SOK 220).

SADBEN see **SADBAN**

SADEK   Nog. 20th c. **Sadek / Sadeχ / Saden** [Мустафа Садех увлы / Мустафа Саденов (?)], father of one of Baskakov's informants from the aul of Abram-töbe (Bask., Nog. 144). ⇨ **SADÏQ?**

SADİKA   Chuv. 18th-19th c. **Sadika** [Садика] (Magn. 72).

SADÏ   Alt. 19th-20th c. **Sadï-bay** [Садыбай] (OjrRS 209). ✧ 'Clean, neat, spotless; simple' (Ir.) (Žanuzakov).

SADÏYĀJÏQ   Tuv. 19th c. **Sadïyājïq** [Садыjацык] (Proben IX, 126).

SADÏQ   Karakh. 13th c. **Sadïq** [sadïq] (DTS); Tat.(GH) 13th c. **Sadïq** [Σαδώκ], a christened Tatar (Byz. Turc. 263); Trkm. 20th c. **Sadïq** [Sadïq] (Zaj. 1971, 328); Bashk. 1792 **Sadïq** [Садык Ишалин] (MIB V, 315); Kzk. 19th c. **Sadïq** [Садыкъ], Kenisara Kasimov's son (AUK 287); Kkalp. 20th c. **Sadïq** [Садык] (KkRS 776); Uzb. 1818 **Sadïq-bek** [Садык-бек], from the Qïyat tribe (MIT II, 407, 656 etc.); Uzb. 18th c. **Sadïq-bi** [Sadïq-by] (Nalivkin-Dozon 76); Trkm. 20th c. **Sādïq** [Садык] (TrkmRS 556). ✧ 'Frank, outright, faithful' cf. Turk. *sadïq* 'wahr, aufrichtig' (Radl. IV, 387), Kkalp. *sadïq* 'верный, преданный; правдивый, искренний, чистосердечный' (KkRS) (<Ar.). See also **QUL-SADÏQ**.

SADÏR   Selj. 1094 **Sadïr** [صادر], an emir (Qalānisi 128); Trkm. 1717 **Sadïr** [Садыръ] (ZIRGO IX, 319); Kirg. **Sadïr** [Садыр] (Jud. 346); Kzk. **Sadïr-bay** [Sadyr Bai / Садыр Баи] (Proben III, 32 /39/); Kzk. 1840 **Sadïr-bay** [Эспергенъ Садырбаевъ] (Konšin, Mat. V, 25); Kzk. 1788 **Sadïr-bek** [Sadyrbek] (Levchine 280); Kirg. **Sadïr-qul** [Садыркул] (Jud. 680); *EN:* Kzk. 18th c. - 19th c. **Sadïr** [Садыр] (Tynyšp. 71); Kzk. 18th c. - 19th c. **Sadïr-bay** [Садырбай] (Tynyšp. 71). ✧ 'Chief, head; heart' (Ar.) (Žanuzakov).

SADRİMEN   Kzk. 19th c. **Sadrimen** [Садрименъ] (SOK 246). ⇨ **SADÏR?** + suff. *-men*.

SADWAQAS   Kzk. 19th c. **Sadwaqas** [Садвакасъ] (SOK 286); Kzk. 19th c. **Saγiduwaqas** [Сагидувакасъ] (AOK 46). ✧ 'Good luck - warrior'? cf. Ar. PN *Saᶜad* 'good luck, good fortune, success, happiness, prosperity; lucky'; *Saᶜad ibn Abu Waqqas*, a well-known sahaabi (Ahmed), Kzk. PN *Sagit* (<Ar.) (Žanuzakov 155), Turk. *sa'd / saad* 'kutluluk, uğur getiren şey, uğur', and *vakkas* 'savaşçı' (Özön) (<Ar.). See also **SABUWAQAS**.

SAFA-KİREY   Tat. 1532 **Safa-kirey** [Сафа-Кирѣй], a ruler (PSRL XIII, 56). ✧ 'Cleanness/honesty-Kirey' (Sattarov) cf. Tat. *safa* 'наслаждение, блаженство' (TatRS), Turk. *safa* (Ar.) 'die Reinheit, die Freude'

(Radl. IV, 422). ⇨ **KERÄY.**

SAFAR   Bashk. 1778 **Safar** [Даут Сафаров] (MIB V, 78); Kzk. 19th c. **Safar** [Сафаръ Хуніевъ] (Grod., Pril. 126); Uzb. **Safar-bay** [Сафарбай] (SKSO III, 162); Trkm. 20th c. **Sapar** [Sapar] (Zaj. 1971, 330); Trkm. 20th c. **Sapar** [Sapar] (Zaj. 1971, 332); Trkm. 20th c. **Sapar** [Сапар] (TrkmRS 565); Bashk. 1707 **Sapar** [Сапар Киндибяков] (MIB III, 35); Bashk. 1735 **Sapar** [Сапаръ Емайкинъ], a tarχan (Vel.-Zern., Bašk. 23); Bashk. 1735 **Sapar** [Сапаръ Бютюковъ], a tarχan (Vel.-Zern., Bašk. 24); Bashk. 1735 **Sapar** [Сапаръ Теперысовъ], a tarχan (Vel.-Zern., Bašk. 20); Bashk. 1735 **Sapar** [Сапаръ Емайкинъ], a tarχan (Vel.-Zern., Bašk. 23); Bashk. 1756 **Sapar** [Султыкай Сапаров] (MIB IV/1, 109); Bashk. 1762 **Sapar** [Уразбай Сапаров] (MIB IV/1, 238); Bashk. 1771 **Sapar** [Аблай Сапаров] (MIB IV/1, 354); Kzk. 18th c. - 19th c. **Sapar** [Сапар] (Tynyšp. 69); Kzk. 19th c. **Sapar** [Сапаръ] (SOV 50); Kkalp. 20th c. **Sapar** [Сапар] (KkRS 776); Kirg. **Sapar** [Сапар] (Jud. 693); Kzk. 19th c. **Sapar-bay** [Сапарбай] (SODž. 100); Kkalp. 20th c. **Sapar-bay** [Сапарбай] (KkRS 776); Kirg. **Sapar-bay** [Сапарбай] (Jud. 88); Kkalp. 20th c. **Sapar-biyke** [Сапарбийке], fem. (KkRS 778); Kkalp. 20th c. **Sapar-gül** [Сапаргул / Сапаргюл], fem. (Bask., Kkalp. 404, KkRS 778); Bashk. 1734 **Sapar-γul** [Сапаргулъ Ахтаевъ], a tarχan (Vel.-Zern., Bašk. 10); Kirg. **Sapar-kül** [Сапаркюль], fem. (?); Chuv. 18th-19th c. **Saper / Sapar** [Саперъ] (Magn. 73); Kzk. 19th c. **Sappar** [Саппаръ] (SODž. 142); Turk. 1583 **Sefer** [Sefer] (Ongan, Ank. I, 175-176); Yürük 1526 **Sefer-šah** [سنفر شاه / Seferşah] (Su 7); Yürük 1543 **Sefer-šah** [Seferşah] (Gökb., Rum. 190); Chuv. 18th-19th c. **Seper** [Сеперъ] (Magn. 75); *TN:* Bashk. 1770 **Saparovo** [Сапарово], a village (MIB IV/1, 349). ✧ I. 'Travelling, journey, trip; traveller' A name given to the children whose father was on the road at the time of birth. (cf. Kuman *safar* 'die Reise' (Radl. IV, 422), Crm., Tat., Turk. *säfär* 'die Reise, die Expedition' (Radl. IV, 503), Turk. *sefer* 'Reise, Zug, Feldzug, Krieg; Abzug, Fortzug' (Zenker), Kirg., Kzk. *sapar* (<P.<Ar.) 'der Weg, die Reise; der Reisende' (Radl. IV, 404), Kkalp. *sapar* 'id.' (KkRS), Kirg. *sapar* 'путешествие, дальний путь; последний путь' (Jud.) (<Ar.); II. 'The second month of the Arabic (Islamic) calendar' cf. Trkm. *sapar III* 'id.' (TrkmRS) (<Ar.). See also **OΓUL-SAPAR.**

SAFAR-GELDİ   Trkm. **Safar-geldi** [Ораньязъ Сафаргельдіевъ] (Ščeglov IV, 183); Trkm. **Sapar-geldi** [Сапаргелди] (Sopieva 179). ⇨ **SAFAR + KELDİ.**

SAFARAQ   Trkm. 1855 **Safaraq** [Сафарак] (MIT II, 261, 262).

SAGALDA   Chuv. 18th-19th c. **Sagalda** [Сагалда] (Magn. 71).

SAGİ   Kzk. 19th c. **Sagi** [Сагибай Тылбековъ] (SOK 252); Kzk. 19th c. **Sagi-bay** [Сагибай Тылбековъ] (SKSO III, 19). ✦ 'Happy, lucky; generous' (Ar.) (Žanuzakov).

SAΓAY I.   Kzk. **Saγay** [Сагай Даутпаев] (TV 1878, 116); Kzk. 19th c. **Saγay** [Сагаевъ] (Pam. kn. Turg. 42).

SAΓAY II.   Hak. 19th-20th c. **Saγay** [Сағай] (HRS 351). ✦ 'Saghay (a Hakas ethnic group)' (Butanaev).

SAΓAYDÏQ see **SAΓÏYDÏQ**

SAΓAQ   Kzk. 19th c. **Saγaq** [Сагаковъ] (Grod., Pril. 71). ✦ 'Neck, throat' cf. Kzk. *saγaq* 'boyun, boğaz kısım' (KzTS).

SAΓALAČ   Tat.(Sib.) 1629 **Saγalač** [Сагалач], Küčüm's grand-son (Miller, Ist. Sib. II, 361).

SAΓAN   Kzk. 19th c. **Saγan** [Саганъ] (AOA 150); Kzk. 19th c. **Saγan-bay** [Саганбай] (AOA 102). ✦ 'Bowl'.

SAΓANAY   Kzk. 19th c. **Saγanay** [Саганай] (AOA 102); Kzk. 19th c. **Saγanay** [Саганай] (AOK 130); Kzk. 19th c. **Saγanay** [Саганай] (Pam. kn. Turg. 71); Bashk. 1737 **Saγanaya (<Saγanay?)** [Саганая Мустафина], fem. (MIB III, 354). ⇨ **SAΓAN?** + suff. *-ay*.

SAΓANDAY see **SAΓANTAY**

SAΓANDÏQ see **SAΓÏNDÏQ**

SAΓANTAY   Kzk. 19th c. **Saγanday** [Сагандай] (SOV 96, 110); Kzk. 19th c. **Saγantay** [Сагантай] (AOO 42). ⇨ **SAΓAN** + suff. *-tay(1,2)*.

SAΓAP   Kzk. 19th c. **Saγap** [Сагапъ] (AOO 62).

SAΓAŠTU   Tuv. 19th c. **Saγaštu-χan** [Сагашту-ханъ], a folklore hero (Potanin IV, 417).

SAΓĀN   Karg. **Saγān** [Саҧан], a family (Proben IX, 659). ⇨ **SAΓAN?**

SAΓDÏ   Kzk. 19th c. **Saγdï** [Сагды] (AOK 2); Kzk. 19th c. **Saγdï-bay** [Сагдыбай] (SOK 250). ✦ Saᶜdi (Ar.) 'happy, lucky, blissful fortunate' (Ahmed), cf. Kzk. PN *Saγdi* (Žanuzakov-Esbaeva).

SAΓÏDUWAQAS see **SADWAQAS**

SAΓÏT   Tat. 1768 **Sayit** [Сагитъ Халфинъ] (Nikol'skij 272). ✦ Saeed (Ar.) 'happy, lucky' (Ahmed); 'Lucky, successful' cf. Kzk. PN *Sagit / Sayit* (Žanuzakov; Žanuzakov 155).

SAΓÏYDA see **SAYDA**

SAΓÏYDÏQ   Bashk. 1779 **Saγïydïq / Saγaydïq** [Сагыйдык (Сагайдык) Сагыйдыков] (MIB V, 97). ⇨ **SAΓÏNDÏQ?**

SAΓÏYDULLA   Kkalp. 20th c. **Saγïydulla** [Сағыйдулла] (KkRS 776). ✦ 'Lucky son of God (Allah)' (Ar.). ⇨ **ALLA.**

SAΓÏMBET   Kzk. 19th c. **Sayïmbet** [Сагымбетъ] (SODž. 52).

SAΓÏN   Kzk. 19th c. **Sayïm-bay (<Sayïn-bay)** [Сагымбай] (AOAtb. 42); Kzk. 19th c. **Sayïm-bek (<Sayïn-bek)** [Сагымбекъ] (SODž. 118, 156); Kzk. 19th c. **Sayïm-bek (<Sayïn-bek)** [Сагымбекъ] (SOV 106); Kzk. 19th c. **Sayïm-bek (<Sayïn-bek)** [Сагымбекъ] (SODž. 124); Tat. 20th c. **Sayïn-bay** [Сагынбай] (Sattarov); Bashk. 1779 **Sayïn-bay** [Мезит Сагынбаев] (MIB V, 91); Bashk. 20th c. **Sayïn-bay** [Сагынбай] (Kusimova); Kirg. **Sayïn-bek** [Сагынбек] (Jud. 905); Uzb. 20th c. **Sâγïn** [Соғин] (Begmatov 1984, 203); Uzb. 20th c. **Sâγïn-bek** [Соғинбек] (Begmatov 1984, 203). ✦ I. 'A kind of deer' (Kusimova); II. 'Awaited, wished child' (Sattarov, Begmatov), cf. Uzb. *sâγïn-* 'скучать, желать, хотеть' (UzbRS). See also **SAΓÏNDÏQ.**

SAΓÏNAY   Kzk. 19th c. **Saγïnay** [Сагынай] (AOO 30). ⇨ **SAΓÏN** + dim. suff. *-ay*.

SAΓÏNDÏQ   Trkm. 19th c. **Saγandïq** [Сагандыковъ] (Ščeglov I, 357); Bashk. 1757, 1761 **Saγandïq** [Сагындык Телдеев] (MIB IV/1, 156, 204); Bashk. 1761 **Saγandïq** [Сагандык Мусин] (MIB IV/1, 200); Bashk. 1762 **Saγandïq** [Сагандык Кузмекеев] (MIB IV/1, 235); Kzk. 19th c. **Saγandïq** [Сагандыкъ] (AOP 34); Kzk. 19th c. **Saγandïq** [Сагандыкъ] (SOK 184, 286); Kzk. 19th c. **Saγandïq** [Сагандыковъ] (TOUAK XXIV, 47); Kzk. 19th c. **Saγandïq** [Сагандыкъ] (AOP 34); Tat. 20th c. **Sayïndïq** [Сагындыков] (Sattarov); Bashk. 1764 **Sayïndïq** [Сагындык Айдагулов] (MIB IV/1, 298); Kzk. 1803 **Sayïndïq** [صاغندوق بی] (MIK IV, 211); Kzk. 1846 **Sayïndïq** [Улжабай Сагындыков], a biy (MKOP 155); Kzk. 1846 **Sayïndïq** [Утял Сагындыков], a biy (MKOP 157); Kzk. 19th c. **Sayïndïq** [Сагындыкъ] (SOK 40, 152, 242, 286); Kzk. 19th c. **Sayïndïq** [Сагындыкъ] (SOV 60, 76, 92, 114); Kzk. 19th c. **Sayïndïq** [Сагындыкъ] (SODž. 92); Kzk. 19th c. **Sayïndïq** [Сагындыковъ] (Grod. IV); Kzk. 19th c. **Sayïndïq** [Сагындыкъ] (AOA 102); Kzk. 19th c. **Sayïndïq** [Сагындыкъ] (AOK 10, 42, 54); Kzk. 19th c. **Sayïndïq** [Сагындыкъ] (AOO 58); Kzk. 19th c. **Sayïndïq** [Сагындыкъ] (AOP 2); Bashk. 1783, 1792 **Sayïndïq / Saγandïq** [Сююндок Сагындыков / Сагандыков] (MIB V, 137, 329); Kzk. 1794 **Sayïndïq-bi** [صاغندوق بی / Сагандык] (MIK IV, 163); Kzk. 19th c. **Sayunduq** [Ахмедъ Сагундуковъ] (Grod., Pril. 47); Kzk. 19th c. **Sayunduq** [Мирзали Сагундуковъ] (Grod., Pril. 92); Tat. 1768 **Saχandïq** [Сахандыкъ Базѣевъ] (Nikol'skij 273); Uzb. 20th c. **Sâγïndïq** [Соғиндик] (Begmatov 1984, 203). ✦ 'Awaited, wanted, wished (child)' (Sattarov), cf. Karakh. *sayïn-* 'желать, хотеть' (DTS), Uyg., Kuman, Alt., Hak., Kar., Kzk., Tat. *sayïn-* 'denken; sich sehnen' (Radl. IV, 265).

SAΓÏNDÏM   Uzb. 20th c. **Sâγïndïm** [Соғиндим] (Begmatov 1984, 203). ✦ 'I awaited / wanted / wished (the child)' cf. Karakh. *sayïn-* 'желать, хотеть' (DTS), Uyg., Kuman, Alt., Hak., Kar., Kzk., Tat. *sayïn-* 'denken; sich sehnen' (Radl. IV, 265). ⇨ SAΓÏN. See also SAΓÏNDÏQ.

SAΓÏR Bashk. 1742 **Sayïr** [Сагыр Чювашев] (MIB I, 486); Kzk. 19th c. **Sayïr** [Хусеинбай Сагыровъ] (Grod., Pril. 172); Kzk. 19th c. **Sayïr** [Сагыръ] (SOK 228); Kzk. 1820 **Sayïr** / **Sayïr-ulan** [Сагырь Уланъ] (Sib. Vest. IX, 122); Kzk. **Sayur-χan** [Sagur-chan], a hero in a tale (Krist, Allein durchs verbotene Land 102). ✧ 'Young orphan; little child' (Ar.) (Sattarov), cf. Kirg. *sayïr* 'малолетний сирота; ребёнок, дитя' (Jud.). See also KÜK-SAΓÏR.

SAΓÏZ Kzk. 1827 **Sayïz** [Тугазъ Сагизбаевъ] (TOUAK XXIV, 181). ✧ 'Resin; pitch' cf. Kzk., Tat. *sayïs / sayïz* 'der Theer, das Harz' (Radl. IV, 270).

SAΓLÏQ Uyg. 8th c. **Sayliq** [Saǧlık] (EUTS); Uyg. **Sayliq-sañun** (Müller, Pfahl. 23). ✧ 'Health' cf. Kuman, Crm., Turk. *sayliq* 'die Gesundheit' (Radl. IV, 278).

SAΓON Hak. 19th-20th c. **Sayon** [Сагон], fem. (HRS 354).

SAΓRAΓU NUyg. 19th c. **Sayrayu** [ساغراغو / Saghraghu] (Le Coq, Namenl. 113). ✧ 'Deaf' (Le Coq).

SAΓRÏN Kzk. 19th c. **Sayrïn-bay** [Сагрынбай] (AOP 50).

SAΓU Türk **Sayu** [Sayu] (ETY II, 134).

SAΓUN Karakh. **Sayun** [Sagun] (MK/Atalay 849).

SAΓUNDUQ see SAΓÏNDÏQ

SAΓUR see SAΓÏR

SAXANDÏQ see SAΓÏNDÏQ

SAXĀBÏT Yak. **Saχābït** [Сахабыт] (Pek.).

SAXĀR Yak. **Saχār** [Сахар] (Pek.). ✧ Zahar (R.) (Pek.).

SAXÏN Kzk. 19th c. **Saχin** [Ишбула Сахиновъ] (Grod., Pril. 65). ⇨ ŠAHÏN / SAYÏN?

SAXÏ Trkm. 20th c. **Sahï** [Sahï] (Zaj. 1971, 328); Trkm. 20th c. **Sahï** [Сахы] (TrkmRS 568). ✧ 'Generous, open-handed' cf. Trkm. *saχï* 'щедрый' (TrkmRS). See also XATAM.

SAXMÄT Kzk. 19th c. **Saχmät** [Сахмäт] (Samojlovič: ŽS XXIV (1915), 165).

SAXSALÏYA Yak. **Saχsalïya** [Сахсалыja] (Pek.). ✧ 'Dry, weaken'? cf. Yak. *saχsay-* 'разсыхаться; осушаться, ослаблятьcя' (Pek.).

SAXT-ALÏ Nog. 20th c. **Saχtalï** [Сахшалы (!) Насыр увлы / Сахталы Насыров], one of Baskakov's informants from the aul of Ïryaqlï (Bask., Nog. 143). ✧ 'Lucky Ali'. ⇨ SAΓÏT + ALÏ. See also SAYD-ALÏ.

SAÏB-GÏREY see SĀHÏB-GÏREY

SAÏP-GÏREY see SĀHÏB-GÏREY

SAY Maml. 1466/67 **Say-bay** [سيباى الظاهرى / Sibai Assaghir], governor of Damascus (Ibn Taghrīb. VII, 744 etc., Weil, Chalif. II, 391etc.); Kzk. 19th c. **Say-bek** [Сайбекъ] (SODž. 98); Kzk. 19th c. **Say-bek** [Сайбекъ] (SOV 6); Kzk. 19th c. **Say-bek** [Сайбекъ] (SOK 110); Kzk. 19th c. **Say-bek** [Бузбай Сайбековъ] (Grod., Pril. 19); Khorezm. 13th c. **Say-yan** [سايغان اقتاجى] (RaD/Jahn 31, Hammer, Ilch. II, 17); Khorezm.? 13th c. **Say-yan** [امير هزاره / سايغان مولاجو], an emir in the days of Ghazan (1295-1304) (RaD/Jahn 91); Khorezm.? 1303 **Say-yan** / **San-yan?** [سايغان / سانغان], envoy from Khorasan (RaD/Jahn 148); Kuman 1255 **Say-χan** [Zeyhan(us)], prince (dux) of the Kumans in Hungary (Györffy, Kun. 255); Chuv. 18th-19th c. **Say-murza** [Саймурза] (Magn. 72). ✧ 'Good, handsome, nice', cf. Hak.(Kyz.) *say* 'jung' (Radl. IV, 219), Kzk. *say* 'uygun, layık, tam' (KzTS), Kkalp. *say* 'подходящий' (KkRS), also Tat. PN *Sayχan / Sayqan* (Sattarov) (<Mo.).

SAY-BUQA Uyg. 12th c. - 14th c. **Say-buya** [Sai-Buǧa / saj buya] (EUTS, DTS); Uyg. 12th c. - 14th c. **Say-buqa** [Sai Buqa] (Radl., USp. 30). ⇨ SAY + BUQA.

SAY-BULAQ Kzk. 1830 **Say-bulaq** [Сугуръ Сайбулаковъ] (Konšin, Mat. I-III, 62). ⇨ SAY + BULAQ.

SAY-BULAT Kzk. 19th c. **Say-bulat** [Сайбулатъ] (SODž. 100). ⇨ SAY + BULAT.

SAY-MAΓAMBET Nog.? **Say-mayambet** [Саймагамбет] (Žirm., Epos 400). ⇨ SAY + MUXAMMED.

SAY-MURUQ Kzk. 19th c. **Saymuruq** [Саимурукъ] (SOK 146). ⇨ SAY.

SAY-MURZA see SAY

SAY-SAR I. Yak. **Say-sar** [Cai-cap (?)], the Kirghiz Sara-bay-toyon's wife, originally a Tatar woman, after her husband's death coming from the south and settling down to the place where nowadays Yakutsk is situated at the branch of Lena called Say-sarï (!) (Pek.). ⇨ SAY + SARÏ?

SAY-SAR II. Uyg. 1339 **Say-sar (?)** [Saisar] (Chwol., Syr.-nest. 90). ⇨ SAY.

SAY-SEKE Kzk. 19th c. **Say-seke** / **Sayïs-eke?** [Сайсеке] (SOK 290). ✧ 'Struggle, fight, competition' cf. Kzk. *sayïs* 'id.' (KzTS). ⇨ SAY + SEKE? or comp. *eke*?

SAY-TOL Uzb. 20th c. **Sây-tol** [Сойтўл] (Begmatov 1984, 205). ⇨ SAY + TOL.

SAY-TOLDÏ Uzb. 20th c. **Sây-toldï** [Сойтўлди] (Begmatov 1984, 205). ⇨ SAY + TOLDÏ.

SAYAQ Kzk. 19th c. **Sayaq** [Саякъ] (SODž. 98); Kzk. 19th c. **Sayaq** [Саякъ] (SOK 198); Kzk. 19th c. **Sayaq-pay** [Саякпай] (SOK 74, 138, 192, 230); *EN:* Kirg. 19th c. **Sayaq** [Саякъ], a tribe (Valihanov, Soč. 128). ✧ 'Male horses excluded from the stud' cf. Kzk. *sayaq* 'die männlichen Pferde, die nicht in der Tabune gehalten werden' (Radl. IV, 289).

SAYANDÏQ Trkm. **Sayandïq** [Курбанъ Саяндыковъ] (Ščeglov I, 352).

SAYATXAN see **SAYATQAN**

SAYATQAN Kkalp. 20th c. **Sayatχan** [Саятхан], fem. (KkRS 778); Kkalp. 20th c. **Sayatqan** [Сайаткъан], fem. (Bask., Kkalp. 78). ⇨ **SAYÏT?** + suff. *-χan(1)*.

SAYBAQ Kzk. 1817 **Saybaq** [صايباق / Сайбак] (MIK IV, 307); Kzk. 19th c. **Saybaq** [Сайбакъ] (Grod., Pril. 81).

SAYBALAY Kzk. 19th c. **Saybalay** [Сайбалай] (SODž 144).

SAYBÏRAQ Hak.(Blt.) 19th-20th c. **Saybïraq** [Саибьрак] (Proben IX, 358). ✧ 'Hack (horse that ables)' (Butanaev).

SAYČAR Alt. 19th c. **Sayčar** [Сайчар-богатырь], a folklore hero (Verb., In. 146).

SAYJAR Kzk. 19th c. **Sayjar** [Саиджаръ] (SOK 296).

SAYD-ALİ Trkm. 1717 **Sayd-ali** (<Sayid-ali) [Сайдали-Салтанъ] (ZIRGO IX, 319). ✧ 'Said-Ali' (Ar.); 'Lucky/happy Ali'. ⇨ **SAĞİT + ALİ.** See also **SAXT-ALİ.**

SAYDA Kkalp. 20th c. **Sayïyda** [Сағыйда], fem. (KkRS 778); Uyg. **Sayda** [Saida] (EUTS); Uyg. 12th c. - 14th c. **Sayda** [Saida] (Radl., USp. 16-17, DTS); Tat. 1781 **Sayda** [Саида Усманова] (MIB V, 126). ✧ 'Happy, lucky; generous (lady)' (Ar.) (Žanuzakov, Sattarov, Kusimova).

SAYDAQ Tat.(Mish.) 1755 **Saydaq** [Сайдак Игибаевъ] (MIB IV/1, 93); Tat.(Sib.) 1584-1588 **Saydaq-qan** [Saidak], from the region of Tobol (Radl., Aus Sib. I, 150). ⇨ **SAYTAQ?**

SAYDAN Kzk. 19th c. **Saydan** [Сайданъ] (AOA 78).

SAYDÏ Kzk. 19th c. **Saydï-bay** [Сайдыбай] (AOO 58). ⇨ **SAYLÏ?**

SAYDÏT Alt. 19th-20th c. **Saydït** [Сайдыт] (OjrRS 209).

SAYDU Alt. 19th-20th c. **Saydu** [Сайду] (OjrRS 209).

SAYXAN Alt. 19th c. **Sayχan** [Сайханъ-сангиабахай], fem. (Potanin II, 179). ⇨ **SAY** + suff. *-χan(1)*.

SAYİNÄK Tat. 1600 **Sayinäk** [Саиняк Келментаевъ] (MIB I, 152). ⇨ **SAYÏN** + dim. suff. *-äk*.

SAYÏQ Uyg. 12th c. - 14th c. **Sayïq** [sajïq] (DTS).

SAYÏLĞAN Oghuz/Trkm. 13th c. **Sayïlγan** [سايلغان], Shayban Khan's son (Abulg./Desm. 191 /182/). ✧ 'Respected, experienced' cf. Karakh. *etilgen sayïlgan* 'bir çok işlere giren, çıkan' (MK/Atalay IV, 202), Turk. *sayïl-* 'geehrt sein, einflussreich sein' (Radl. IV, 292).

SAYÏM Kzk. 19th c. **Sayïm / Saim** [Саимъ Бекмирзаевъ] (Grod., Pril. 194). ✧ I. 'He who fasts' cf. Tat. *Saim* (Ar.) (Sattarov); II. 'My good, handsome (son)'. ⇨ **SAY** + poss. suff. *-im*.

SAYÏM-BÜLÜK Kzk. 19th c. **Sayïm-bülük** (<Sayïn-bülük) [Саимбулюкъ] (SOV 6). ⇨ **SAYÏN** + **BÜLÜK.**

SAYÏMBET Kkalp. 20th c. **Sayïmbet** [Сайымбет] (KkRS 776); Kkalp. 20th c. **Sayïmbet** [Сайымбет] (Bask., Kkalp. 10). ✧ 'Good (Mukhammet) / Fasting (Mukhammet'. ⇨ **SAY/SAYÏM** + suff. *-ïmbet /-bet*.

SAYÏN Kzk.? 1689 **Sayin** [Саинъ Окинъ], a Tabunut (?) chieftain (sait) (PSZRI III, 15); Kzk. 19th c.? **Sayin** [Хаидубекъ Саиновъ] (?); Kzk. 19th c. **Sayin** [Каштынъ Саиновъ] (?); Kzk. 19th c. **Sayin** [Елемисъ Саиновъ] (?); Kzk. 19th c. **Sayin** [Саинъ] (AOA 140); Kzk. 19th c. **Sayin** [Джангубекъ Саиновъ] (?); Kzk. **Sayïn-batïr** [Саін Батыр] (Proben III, 205 (166)); Nog. 1649 **Sayïn-murza** [Саинъ мурза] (AI IV, 78, 87); Nog. 1649 **Sayïn-murza** [Саинъ мурза Иштерековъ] (AI IV, 79); Kzk. 1822 **Sayun** [صايون / Саюн] (MIK IV, 433, 435). ✧ 'Very good; famed, celebrated, glorious (epithet of Eastern sovereigns)' (Sattarov), cf. Chag. *sayin* 'gut, tüchtig' (Radl. IV, 294) (<Mo. *sain*). See also **QARA-SAYÏN.**

SAYÏN-BUL Kzk. 19th c. **Sayïn-bul / Sain-bul?** [Саинбулъ] (SODž. 78). ✧ 'Be good, famed, celebrated, glorious'. ⇨ **SAYÏN** + **BOL.**

SAYÏN-BULAT Tat. 1572 **Sayïn-bulat** [Саинбулатъ (Саинбулай Санбулай)], a prince (PSRL III, 168). ✧ 'Good steel'. ⇨ **SAYÏN** + **BULAT.**

SAYÏNKÄ Kzk.? 1689 **Sayïnkä** [Саинкя Сотулай], a Tabunut chieftain (sait) (PSZRI III, 15). ⇨ **SAYÏN** + dim. suff. *-kä*.

SAYÏP-NAZAR Kkalp. 20th c. **Sayïp-nazar** [Сайыпназар] (KkRS 776). ✧ 'Lord-Nazar'? cf. Crm.(Tat.) *saip* 'хозяин, владелец' (KrmRS), Turk. *sahib* (Ar.) 'der Besitzer, der Wirth, der Herr' (Radl. IV, 285), cf. also Kzk. *sayıp kıran* 'kahraman, bahadır' (KzTS). ⇨ **NAZAR.**

SAYÏR Oghuz/Trkm. 13th c. **Sayïr** [سايـر / Sâir / Сайыр], an Oghuzid (Abulg./Desm. 28, Abulg./Kon. 530). ✧ 'Sair (=goer, traveller)' (Ar.) (Sattarov).

SAYÏT Hak.(Kacha) 19th-20th c. **Sayït-qan** [Сајытхан], an evil spirit (Proben IX, 582, 583). ✧ 'Courtier, nobleman' cf. Shor *sayit* 'ein Hofmann, ein Adliger' (Radl. IV, 293).

SAYKA Chuv. 18th-19th c. **Sayka** [Сайка] (Magn. 72). ✧ 'A kind of bread roll' cf. Chuv. *sayka* 'сайка (булка)' (ČRS/Skvor.).

SAYQAL Kirg. **Sayqal / Aq-sayqal** [Аңгычал кысы ак Саікал / Аңгычалдын Ак Саікал / Аңгычал кысы Саікал], Aňγičal's daughter, Yoloy-qan's wife (Proben V, 193 /194/, 393 /397/ etc.); Kirg. **Sayqal** [Сайкал], fem. (Jud. 426, 876). ✧ 'Glance, shine, brightness' cf. Kirg. *sayqal* (Ar.) 'полировка' (Jud.). See also **AQ-SAYQAL.**

SAYLAW Trkm. **Saylaw** [Сайлав] (Sopieva 182). ❖ 'Elections' (Sopieva).

SAYLÏ Kzk. 19th c. **Saylï-bay** [Саилы-бай] (Grod., Pril. 108); Kzk. 19th c. **Saylï-bay** [Саилы-бай] (SOV 44); Kzk. 19th c. **Saylï-bay** [Саилы-бай] (SOK 88); Kzk. 19th c. **Saylï-bay** [Сайлибай] (SOV 18); Kzk. 19th c. **Saylï-bay** [Сайлибай] (SOK 150); Kzk. 19th c. **Saylï-bek** [Сайлыбекъ] (SODž. 158); Kzk. 19th c. **Saylï-bek** [Сайлыбекъ] (SOK 200); Kzk. 19th c. **Saylu-bay** [Сайлюбай] (SOK 226); Kzk. 19th c. **Saylŭ-bay** [Сайлобай] (SOK 178). ❖ 'Ready; fulfilled; well done' cf. Kzk. *saylï* 'fertig, ausgeführt; gut gefertigt' (Radl. IV, 229).

SAYLÏQ Tuv. 19th c. **Saylïq** [Саілык], fem. (Proben IX, 119). ❖ 'Unlucky, miserable' cf. Hak.(Sag.) *saylïγ* 'unglücklich, ein Unglückspilz' (Radl. IV, 229).

SAYLU see SAYLÏ

SAYLUK Chuv. 1739 **Sayluk** [Сайлукъ] (Alatyr. 142). ❖ I. 'Shallow, shoal'; II. 'A kind of fish' cf. Tat. *saylïq* 'das Seichtsein; die Schleihe' (Radl. IV, 229).

SAYMAN Kzk. 19th c. **Sayman** [Сайманъ], Čokan Čingisovič Valihanov's great-grand father (Protok. Turk. IV, 51). ❖ 'Tool, household utensil' cf. Kzk. *sayman* 'das Geräth, das Haus geräth' (Radl. IV, 232).

SAYMAŠ Alt. 19th-20th c. **Saymaš** [Саймаш], fem. (OjrRS 213). ❖ 'Little ornament, décor' (OjrRS).

SAYMU Alt. 19th-20th c. **Saymu** [Сайму] (OjrRS 209).

SAYPAQ Kzk. 19th c. **Saypaq** [Сайпакъ] (SODž. 28).

SAYPÄŠ Bashk. 1760 **Saypäš** [Байзигит Сайпяшев] (MIB IV/1, 193).

SAYRAN Kzk. 19th c. **Sayram-bay (<Sayran-bay)** [Сайрамбай] (SOK 270); Kzk. 19th c. **Sayram-bay <Sayran-bay)** [Сайрамбай] (SODž. 134); Bashk. 1777 **Sayran** [Сайран Сеитов] (MIB V, 52, 88, 204, 205, 206, 233, 279); Bashk. 1742 **Sayran / Sayrän?** [Саирян Смаилов] (MIB III, 513). ❖ 'Feasting, amusement; feast, holiday' (Ar.) (Kusimova, Sattarov), cf. Crm. *sayran* 'die Feierlichkeit; das Fest' (Radl. IV, 226). See also **SAWSQAN-SAYRAN**.

SAYSA Yürük 1543 **Saysa** (Gökb., Rum. 214).

SAYTAQ Bashk. 1740 **Saytaq** [Сайтак Кашаев] (MIB I, 439). ⇨ **SAYDAQ?**

SAYTÄŠ Bashk. 1756 **Saytäš** [Икберда Сайтяшев] (MIB IV/1, 106).

SAQ Bashk. 1731 **Saq** [Саков] (MIB III, 289); Bashk. 1765 **Saq** [Абизяр Сакбаев] (MIB IV/1, 313); Bashk. 1770 **Saq** [Саков Мурзаев] (MIB IV/1, 342); Kzk. **Saq** [Сакъ Каримкуловъ] (SKSO VIII, 222); Nog. 1649 **Saq** [Еналѣй Саковъ] (AI IV, 123); Kzk. 19th c. **Saq-bay** [Сакбай] (AOAtb. 34); Kzk. 19th c. **Saq-mulla** [Сакмулла] (SOK 28); Kzk. 19th c. **Saq-pay** [Сакпай] (SOV 50, 114); Kzk. 19th c. **Saq-pay** [Сакпай] (SOK 120). ❖ 'Watchful, careful' cf. Uyg.,

Kuman, Alt., Hak., Kzk., Tat. etc. *saq* 'wachsam, vorsichtig' (Radl. IV, 239). See also **PULDÏ-SAQ**.

SAQ-QULAQ Kzk. 18th c. - 19th c. **Saq-qulaq-biy** [Саккулак-бий] (Tynyšp. 68). ❖ 'Watchful-ear'. ⇨ **SAQ + QULAQ.**

SAQA Kzk. 19th c. **Saqa-bay** [Сакабай] (SODž. 66). ❖ 'Column, support(er)' cf. Chag., Kzk. *saqa* 'das untere Ende der Schneide des Beiles; das Wurfstück beim Knöchelspiele; der Pfosten, der Pfahl' (Radl. IV, 241).

SAQAY Bashk. 1737 **Saqay** [Искак (Искяк) Сакаев] (MIB III, 374); Kzk. 19th c. **Saqay** [Сакай] (SOV 40); Kzk. 19th c. **Saqay** [Сакай] (SOK 256). ⇨ **SAQA** + dim. suff. -*y*.

SAQAQ see ISHAQ

SAQAL Kzk. 1839 **Saγal** [Чибинтай Сагаловъ] (Konšin, Mat. V, 42); Kzk. 19th c. **Saγal** [Сагалъ] (AOO 62); Kzk. 19th c. **Saγal-bay** [Сагалбай] (AOO 18); Kzk. 19th c. **Saγal-bek** [Сагальбекъ] (AOO 22); Kzk. 19th c. **Saqal** [Сакалъ] (SOV 14); *EN:* Turk. 1554-1558 **Saqal** [Sakal cemaatı] (Gökçen 37). ❖ 'Beard' cf. Chag., Kuman, Kzk., Tat., etc. *saqal* 'id.' (Radl. IV, 244-45), Uyg., Alt., Hak. *saγal* 'id.' (Radl. IV, 263). See also **AQ-SAQAL, BAY-SAQAL, BUYRA-SAQAL, JAN-SAQAL, QABA-SAQAL, QARA-SAQAL, QULUN-SAQAL, UZUN-SAQAL.**

SAQAL-TUTAN Trkm. 1610 **Saqal-tutan**, a Turkmen tribe in Syria (Gökçen 62). ⇨ **SAQAL + TUTAN.**

SAQALAQ Kzk. 19th c. **Saqalaq** [Коргулъ Сакалаковъ] (Grod., Pril. 101). ❖ 'Little beard' cf. Alt.(Tel.) *saqalaq* 'ein kleiner Bart, ein Bärtchen' (Radl. IV, 245).

SAQALSÏZ Maml. 14th c. **Saqalsïz** [سقلسيز / صقلسز] (Sauvaget 48-49). ❖ 'Without beard'. ⇨ **SAQAL** + suff. -*sïz*.

SAQAN Kzk. 19th c. **Saqan** [Саканъ] (SOK 44); Kzk. 19th c. **Saqan** [Саканъ] (AOO 42).

SAQAR Trkm. 20th c. **Saqar**, in a contemporary short story (?); *EN:* Trkm. 16th - 17th c. **Saqar** [Сакар], a tribe (Ivanov, Vosstanie 43). ❖ 'White strip on the forhead of a horse; having white forehead; bald' cf. Chag., Turk. *saqar* (Radl. IV, 243), Trkm. *saqar* 'с белой отметиной, со звёздочкой на лбу (о животных); белолобый; лысый' (TrkmRS).

SAQAŠ Alt. 19th-20th c. **Saqaš** [Сакаш] (OjrRS 209).

SAQAW Kzk. 19th c. **Saqaw** [Сакау] (Potanin II, 5); Kzk. 19th c. **Saqaw** [Сакау] (SODž. 20, 26, 66); Kzk. 19th c. **Saqaw** [Сакау] (AOP 110). ❖ 'Dumb; stutterer, stammerer' cf. Chag., Kuman, Kzk., Tat. *saqau* 'stumm, schwerfällig sprechend, schlecht aussprechend' (Radl. IV, 242). See also **MEÑLÏ-GELDÏ-SAQAW.**

SAQĀR Yak. **Saqār** [Сакар] (Pek.). ❖ Zahar (R.).

SAQDÏQ Kzk. 19th c. **Saqdïq / Saqtïq?** [Сакдыкъ]

(SODž. 156); Kzk. 19th c. **Saqdïq / Saqtïq?** [Сакдыкъ] (AOP 34). ⇨ **SAQ** + suff. *-tïq?*

SAQÏ Kzk. 19th c. **Saqï-bek** [Сакыбекъ] (SODž. 130).

SAQÏL Alt. 19th-20th c. **Saqïl** [Сакыл] (OjrRS 209). ✧ 'Squirrel, chipmunk' (OjrRS). See also **ČAQČAQ, SANZÄP, TİYEN.**

SAQÏP Kzk. 19th c. **Saqïp** [Sakïp] (Altyns. 53). ✧ 'Fellow-traveller, mate, friend' (Ar.), cf. Kzk. *Sakip* (Žanuzakov).

SAQÏP-ĴAMAN Kzk. **Saqïp-ĵaman** [Sakyp Dschaman / Сакып Џаман], fem. (Proben III, 742 (742)). ⇨ **SAQÏP + YAMAN.**

SAQÏŠ Alt. 19th-20th c. **Saqïš** [Сакыш] (OjrRS 209). ✧ 'Waiting, expectation' (OjrRS).

SAQÏZ Kuman 1096 **Saqïz** [Сакзь], a Polovets (?) prince captured by Vladimir (PSRL I, 103); Kzk. 19th c. **Saqïz-bay / Saqqïz-bay** [Тикаръ Саккизбаевъ (Сакизбаевъ)] (Grod., Pril. 171). ✧ 'Rosin, resin' cf. Kirg., Tat. *saɣïz* 'der Theer, das Harz' (Radl. IV, 270).

SAQLAQ Kzk. 19th c. **Saqlaq** [Каргулъ Саклаковъ] (Grod., Pril. 38).

SAQMAQ 1554 **Saqmaq** [Сакъмакъ] (PSRL XIII, 241).

SAQŌN Hak. 19th-20th c. **Saqon** [Сакон] (HRS 351); Hak.? 19th-20th c. **Saqōn** [Сакон] (Katanov, Otč. 10); Hak.(Sag.) 19th-20th c. **Saqōn** [Сакон], fem. (Katanov, Otč. 8, Proben IX, 557). ✧ 'Law, canon' (Katanov), cf. R. *saqón* 'das Gesetz' (Radl. IV, 247).

SAQSAN Kzk.? **Saqsan** [Саксанбаевъ] (SKSO VIII, 221); Kzk. 1884 **Saqsan** [Эльфисъ-бай Саксанбаевъ] (Grod., Pril. 94).

SAQSAUL Kzk. 19th c. **Saqsaul** [Саксаулъ] (Grod., Pril. 48). ✧ 'A kind of tree (Salsola arbustris)' cf. Chag. *saqsaul* 'id.' (Radl. IV, 257).

SAQSÏS see **SAQSÏZ**

SAQSÏZ Kzk. 19th c. **Saqsïs-bay (<Saqsïz-bay)** [Саксысбай] (SODž. 152). ✧ I. 'Careless, rash' cf. Tat. *saqsïz* 'id.' (Radl. IV, 258); II. 'Weak' cf. Kuman *saqsïz* 'id.' (Radl. IV, 258). ⇨ **SAQ** + suff. *-sïz.*

SAQTA Bashk. 1740 **Saqta-ɣul** [Рыс Сактагулов] (MIB I, 397). ✧ 'Protecte, guarde; awaite' cf. Alt., Hak., Kirg., Kzk. *saqta-* 'bewachen, behüten, bewahren; warten, zögern; erwarten, auflauern' (Radl. IV, 255).

SAQTAɣAN Kzk. 19th c. **Saqtaɣan** [Сактаганъ] (AOP 22); Kzk. 19th c. **Saqtaɣan** [Сактаганъ] (AOK 6, 10). ✧ 'Protected, guarded; awaited (child)' cf. Alt., Hak., Kirg., Kzk. *saqta-* 'bewachen, behüten, bewahren; warten, zögern; erwarten, auflauern' (Radl. IV, 255).

SAQTAN Alt. 19th-20th c. **Saqtan** [Сактан] (OjrRS 209); Kzk. 19th c. **Saqtan-bay** [Сактанбай] (SODž. 96). ✧ 'Be protected, defend yourself, be guarded; be awaited; be careful' cf. Alt., Hak., Kirg., Kzk. *saqta-* 'bewachen, behüten, bewahren; warten, zögern;

erwarten, auflauern' (Radl. IV, 255), Alt. *saqta-* 'ждать, ожидать; хранить, сохранять' (OjrRS).

SAQU Uyg. 1298 **Saqu-tärim** [Saku Tarim] (Chwol., Syr.-nest. (NF) 13).

SAQUN Uyg. 12th c. - 13th c. **Saqun / Saquz?** [ايغور / ساقون / ساقوز / ازامرا·], an emir (Ĵuwaynī I, 34, 39). ✧ I. 'Be protected, defend yourself, be careful; be cautious' cf. Uyg., Karakh. *saqïn-* 'остерегаться, беречься' (DTS); II. 'Title of noblemen at the Karluks' cf. Karakh. *saɣun* 'id.' (DTS).

SAQUR see **SUɣAR**

SAL Chuv. 18th-19th c. **Sal-bay** [Салбай] (Magn. 72); Oghuz/Trkm. 14th c. - 15th c. **Sal-ĵan-χatun** [Salĵan Hātūn] (DQorq./Rossi 185-92). ✧ 'Raft, float' cf. Alt., Hak., Kzk., Tat. etc. *sal* 'id.' (Radl. IV, 343). See also **BİR-ĴAN-SAL, KÖK-SAL, SEÑ-SAL.**

SAL-DİMER Chuv. 18th-19th c. **Sal-dimer** [Салдимеръ] (Magn. 72); Chuv. 18th-19th c. **Sal-dimer / Sal-dimer** [Салдымеръ] (Magn. 72). ⇨ **SAL + TEMİR.**

SAL-KEREY Chuv. 18th-19th c. **Sal-kerey** [Салкерей] (Magn. 72). ⇨ **SAL + KEREY.**

SAL-TUɣAN Chuv. 18th-19th c. **Sal-tïɣan** [Салтыганъ] (Magn. 72); Tat. 1491 **Sal-tïɣan / Satïlɣan?** [Салтыганъ] (PSRL IV, 159 VI, 38 VIII, 223); Chuv. 18th-19th c. **Sal-tugan** [Салтуганъ] (Magn. 72); *TN:* Tat. 18th c. **Sal-tuɣan** [Салтуганъ], a village in the district of Mamadysh (Korsakov 235). ⇨ **SAL? + TUɣAN.**

SALA Chuv. 18th-19th c. **Sala-ba (<Sala-bay)** [Салаба] (Magn. 72); Chuv. 18th-19th c. **Sala-bay** [Салабай] (Magn. 72). ✧ 'Russian village, settlement' cf. Chuv. *sala* (R. *selo*) 'русское селение, село' (ČRS).

SALA-BA see **SALA**

SALAY Chuv. 18th-19th c. **Salay** [Салай] (Magn. 72). ⇨ **SALA?** + dim. suff. *-y.*

SALAYDAY Chuv. 18th-19th c. **Salayday** [Салайдай] (Magn. 72). ⇨ **SALAY** + suff. *-day.*

SALAQ Kzk. 19th c. **Salaq** [Салакъ] (SOV 40); Kzk. 19th c. **Salaq-bay** (AUK 189); Kkalp. 1811 **Salaq-serdar** [Салак сердат] (MIKk. 120). ✧ 'Neglectful, careless, lazy' cf. Kzk. *salaq* 'unbesorgt, abgestümpft, faul' (Radl. IV, 350).

SALAM Trkm. 20th c. **Salam** [Salam] (Zaj. 1971, 329); Chuv. 18th-19th c. **Salam** [Салам] (Magn. 72); Kzk. 19th c. **Salam** [Саламъ], fem. (Grod., Pril. 119); Kzk. 19th c. **Salam-bay** [Саламбай] (Grod., Pril. 110); Trkm. 20th c. **Salām** [Салам] (TrkmRS 559). ✧ 'Greeting, peace' cf. Kuman, Tat., etc. *salam* 'der Gruss' (Radl. IV, 353), Trkm. *salām* 'привет, поклон' (TrkmRS), Chuv. *salam* 'привет, поклон' (ČRS) (<Ar.). See also **ALTAYÏN-SAYÏN-SALAM.**

SALAM-BERDİ Tat. 1686 **Salam-berdi**

[Саламбердеевъ] (Kungursk. akty 120); Uzb. 20th c. **Sälâm-berdi** [Саломберди] (Begmatov 1984, 202). ✧ 'Peace gave him/her; the All-peaceable (Allah) has given him/her' cf. Uzb. *sälâm* 'привет, поклон' (UzbRS), cf. Ar. PN *Salam* 'peace, safety, security' (Ahmed). ⇨ **SALAM + BERDİ.**

SALAMAT Tat.(GH)? 1296 **Salamat** [Σαλαμάτης] (Byz. Turc. 264); Trkm. 20th c. **Salamat** [Salamat], fem. (Zaj. 1971, 336); Chuv. 18th-19th c. **Salamat** [Саламатъ] (Magn. 72); Tat. 1654 **Salamat** [Темиръ Саламатовъ] (Katanov IV, 236); Crm. 1689 **Selamet-girey-χan** [خان كراى سلامت / Selāmet], a Crimean sultan, Selim-girey-χan's son (Vel.-Zern., Crim. 777); Crm.(Tat.) 1631 **Selamet-girey** [سلامت كراى سلطان], a Crimean sultan, Devlet-girey-χan's son (Vel.-Zern., Crim. 11). ✧ 'Healthy' cf. Uyg., Kuman, Tat. *salamat* (Ar.) 'gesund, die Gesundheit' (Radl. IV, 353), Tat. *salämät* 'gesund, unbeschädigt, unversehrt' (Radl. IV, 354), < Ar. PN *Salamat* 'Safety, security, soundness, integrity' (Ahmed).

SALAMÏŠ Maml. 1298 **Salamïš** [بن باجوا / سلامش بن باكبوا / باكوا] (Dawād. 8, 9 etc.); Maml. 1340 **Salamïš** [طرخان بن بدرالدين بيسرى الشمسى] 1340; Maml. 1299 [سيف الدين سلامش بن سلاح الدين] (Zetterst. 220); Maml. 1299 **Selamïš** [Selâmesch], a (Mongolian?) governor of Rum, son of Afal (Makrīzī IV, 130, Weil, Chalif. I, 223, Jorga, Notes XIII, 342-43 /Mesalekalabsar/); Maml. 1404/05 **Selamïš** [سلامش حاجب] (Ibn Taghrīb. VI, 126, 174); Maml. 1278, 1279/80 **Selamïš / Salamïš** [بدرالدين سلامش / Selamech / Salamesch], son of Beybars I., moves to Constantinople in 1291 (Iyās I, 111, 136, Abulfidā/Ed. I, 157, 161, Weil, Chalif. I, 111-14, 160, 218, Makrīzī III, 139).

SALAMQA Alt. 19th-20th c. **Salamqa** [Саламка], fem. (OjrRS 213). ✧ 'A kind of salty cake (long and thin)' cf. R. *solomka* 'batonsale [bâton salé]' (RTurkS).

SALAN Kzk. 19th c. **Salan-bay** [Саланбай] (SODž. 150). See also **KÖP-SALAN, QAY-SALAN, QOČI-SALAN?**

SALANDÏ Uyg. **Salandï** [سالندى], ruler of the Uyghurs (J̌uwaynī I, 34).

SALAR 998 **Salar** (Qazw. 430); 1043 **Salar** [سلار الطرم] (Ibn al-Athīr/Tornb. IX, 348); Karakh.? 942 **Salar** [سلار بن وشمكير] (Ibn al-Athīr/Tornb. VIII, 292); Selj. **Salar** [كمال الدين حوايج سالار] (Ibn Bībī IV, 278, 279); Selj.? 1235 **Salar** [سيف الدين سلار], Toγraq-bek's (?) [طغراق بك] son, from Amasya (Uzunçarş., Küt. I, 946); Selj.? 1073/74 **Salar** [سلار العجمى] (Ibn Taghrīb. II, 154); Maml. **Salar** [سلار], an emir (Duqmaq:RHCHor IV, 42, 71); Maml. 1264 **Salar** [Schems-eddin-Sellar-Bagdadi], an emir (Makrīzī II, 13, Weil, Chalif. I, 37 etc.); Maml. 1310 **Salar** [سيف الدين سلار عبد الله], mamlūk of Seljuk origin, governor, mentioned in the inscription of a shrine, died in 1310 (Zetterst. 40, 54, 81, 96, 144-146, Makrīzī IV, 55, 114, 126, Weil, Chalif. I(IV?), 206-207, 221, 258 etc., Iyās I, 139, 155, Mayer 196-197); Maml. 1340 **Salar** [سلار القرمى] (Zetterst. 202, 219); Maml. 14th c. **Salar** [سلار] (Sauvaget 48); Uzb. 1851 **Salar** [Салар], a commander from Khiva (MIT II, 526, 527); Selj. 1077 **Salar / Aqsaq-salar?** [Oksok-Salār], a chief (feudataire de Holwan) who fought in Bahrein (De Goeje: JA 1895, V, 14); Oghuz 16th c. **Salar-baba** [Салар Баба], author of an Oghuz-nāme variant (Muhamedova: OSA 169); 13th c. **Salar-bek** [Саларбек], Xandučaq's brother (RaD I/1, 100); Chag. 1554 **Salar-χoǰa** [Салар] (Ivanov 124); Trkm. 1823/24 **Salar-yüzbaši** [Салар-юзбаши] (MIT II, 423); *EN:* Trkm. 1724 **Salarlu** [Salârlu] (Refik, Anad. 167). ✧ 'Prince, commander of army, chief' (Sauvaget 48), cf. P. Sālār (//sardār) 'Fürst, Heerführer' (Justi 280).

SALAR-TÜRK'ĀN Selj. 11th c. **Salar-türk'ān** [سالار توركان] (Qazw. 437). ⇨ **SALAR + TERKEN.**

SALAT Chuv. 18th-19th c. **Salat** [Салатъ] (Magn. 72). ✧ 'Salad' cf. Chuv. *salat* (R.) 'id.' (ČRS).

SALAWAY Alt. 19th-20th c. **Salaway** [Салавай] (OjrRS 209).

SALAWAT Bashk. 18th c. **Salawat** [Салават Юлаев], one of Pugachev's brigadiers (MIB V, 678, AUK 370); Bashk. 18th c. **Salawat** [Салават Аимбетев] (MIB V, 683). ✧ 'Prayer' cf. Crm., Tat., Turk. *salavat* (Ar.) 'das Gebet' (Radl. IV, 352-53).

SALBAR Bashk. 1616 **Salbar** [Салбар Карашин], a participant of the Bashkir revolt of 1737-1739 (MIB I, 376). ✧ 'Baggy trousers, shalwar' cf. Bashk. *salbar* 'шаровары, брюки' (BRS).

SALBEN Kzk. 19th c. **Salben** [Сальбенъ] (SODž. 4, 44).

SALBÏR Hak.(Blt.) 19th-20th c. **Salbïr** [Салбыр] (Katanov, Otč. 9).

SALČÏ Tat.(GH) 1375 **Salčï** [Салчѣй / Салчей / Сальчей / Сальчий / Салчеи], a prince from Astrakhan (PSRL III, 231 IV, 72 V, 235 VIII, 24, XVI, 102, XXIII, 120); Turk. 19th c. **Salǰïlarïn-oγlu** [Salǯylaryn oγlu], a Zeybek (son of raftsmen) (Kúnos 1891, 119). ✧ 'Raftsman; maker of rafts/floats' cf. Turk. *salǰï* 'Jemand, der Flösse baut' (Radl. IV, 372). ⇨ **SAL + suff. -*čï*.**

SALČUQ see **SELČÜK**

SALǰAR Yak. **Salǰar** [Салцар] (Pek.).

SALǰÏLARÏN-OΓLU see **SALČÏ**

SALǰUDAY Kipch. 1300 **Salǰuday** [صلجوداى / Салджудай] (Baybars/Tizeng. I, 90, 113).

SALǰUQ see **SELČÜK**

SALDA see **SALDÏ**

SALDAY see **SALTAY**

SALDAK   Chuv. 18th-19th c. **Saldak** [Салдакъ] (Magn. 72). ✧ 'Soldier' cf. Chuv. *saltak* 'солдат' (R.) (ČRS). See also **SALDAT**.

SALDAKAY   Chuv. 18th-19th c. **Saldakay** [Салдакай] (Magn. 72). ✧ 'Little soldier'. ⇨ **SALDAQ** + dim. suff. *-qay / -ay*.

SALDAT   Bashk. 1779 **Saldat** [Ногайчюра / Ногайчура Салдатов] (MIB V, 81); Bashk. 1779 **Saldat** [Ногайчюра Салдатов] (MIB V, 81); Chuv. 1670 **Saldatko** [Салдатко] (Poliv.-Kras. 64). ✧ 'Soldier' cf. Tat. *saldat* (<R.) 'der Soldat' (Radl. IV, 370).

SALDÏ   Kzk. **Salda-bay / Sald-bay** [Салдабай / Салдбай] (Sb. Syr-D. IX, 46, 56); Chuv. 18th-19th c. **Salda-bay** (<**Saldï-bay**) [Салдабай] (Magn. 72); Bashk. 1728 **Saldï-bay** [Алманта Салдыбаев] (MIB I, 127); Bashk. 1781 **Saldï-bay** [Уразбай Салдыбаев] (MIB V, 122); Bashk. 1781 **Saldï-bay** [Урузбай Салдыбаев] (MIB V, 122); Kzk. 19th c. **Saldï-bay** [Салдыбай] (SODž. 54); Chuv. 18th-19th c. **Saldu-bay** [Салдубай] (Magn. 72); Kzk. 19th c. **Saldu-bay** [Салдубай] (Grod., Pril. 149); Kzk. 19th c. **Saldu-bay** [Салдубай] (Grod., Pril. 149); Kzk. 19th c. **Saltï-bay** [Салтыбай] (SOK 182); Chuv. 18th-19th c. **Saltu-bay** [Салтубай] (Magn. 72); *TN:* Kzk. 19th c. **Saldï** [P. Карымъ Салды Тургай], a river in the system of Turgay (Hanykov, Karta ZK); Kzk. 19th c. **Saldï-bay** [Салдь Бай], a tomb on the territory of the Bukeev-Horde, between the Volga and the Ural, at *Hanskaja stavka* (the khan's headquarters) (Hanykov, Karta ZK); Uzb.? **Saltu-bay** [Салтобай], a well (?), Southwest of Tashkent (KartaJAR XIX).

SALDU see **SALDÏ**

SALEY   Bashk. 1762 **Saley** [Салей Бускумов] (MIB IV/2, 300-01); Uzb. 1645 **Saley-batïr** [Салей-Батыръ], envoy from Bukhara (AI IV, 44).

SALEM   Kzk. 18th c. - 19th c. **Salem / Salim?** [Салем] (Tynyšp. 68). ✧ Salem / Saalim (Ar.) 'safe, secure, perfect, complete' (Ahmed).

SALGAN   Chuv. 18th-19th c. **Salgan** [Салганъ] (Magn. 72). ⇨ **SALDÏ?**

SALΓAY   Kipch. 1298 **Salγay** [صلغاى / Салгай], a chieftain, Noγay's follower (Baybars/Tizeng. I, 88, 111). ✧ 'Nettle' cf. Hak.(Kyz.) *salγay* 'die Nessel' (Radl. IV, 364).

SALΓAR   Uyg. **Salγar** [Salġar] (EUTS).

SALΓUR   Oghuz/Trkm. 12th c. **Salγur** [سلغر], forefather of the Salghurïds (of the race of طاق خان) (Qazw. 503); Oghuz/Trkm. 1363 **Salγur-šah** [سلغرشاه تركمان بنكاولى امير], an emir (Qazw. 691, 696, etc.); Selj. 13th c. **Salγur-šah** [بن زنكى سلغرشاه / سلغورشاه بن اتابك سعد], fought against the Mongols in Luristan in the days of Keihatu-ilkhan

(1291-1295) (J̌uwaynī II, 150, Qazw. 544, 545). ✧ 'Making an attack' (Erol II), 'Make an attack! Rush upon!'; 'He who will beat/fight' (according to Pelliot it is an aorist form, see Pelliot, Notes 229), cf. Uyg., Karakh. *sal-* 'класть, бросать; бить, ударять' (DTS). See also **SALÏR**.

SALİ I.   Uyg. **Sali** [Sali] (EUTS); Uyg. 12th c. - 14th c. **Sali** (Müller, Uig. II, 80).

SALİ II.   Chuv. 18th-19th c. **Sali** [Сали] (Magn. 72); Kzk. 19th c. **Sali** [Салі] (Samojlovič: ŽS, XXIV (1915), 165); Kzk. 19th c. **Sali** [Сали] (Grod., Pril. 199); Chuv. 18th-19th c. **Sali-bay** [Салибай] (Magn. 72).

SALİX   Bashk. 1777 **Salïχ** [Салих Азигулов] (MIB V, 58); Crm.(Tat.) 1499, 1500 **Salïχ / Salïχda / Salïγda?** [Салыхда Алакозъ (Алыкозъ / Алакузъ) / Салых Алакузъ / Салыхда (Салыгда) Оларко], envoy from the sultan of Caffa, Crimea (PSRL XII, 250, XX, 369). ✧ Salih (Ar.) 'Pious, righteous, upright, just, virtous, devoted' (Ahmed). ⇨ **SALÏQ?**

SALİYXA   Kkalp. 20th c. **Salïγχa** [Салийха], fem. (KkRS 778). ✧ 'Good, kind, warm-hearted' (<Ar. fem. *Salikha*).

SALİK see **SALÏQ**

SALİKEY see **SALÏQAY**

SALİN   Hak. 19th-20th c. **Salin** [Салин] (HRS 351).

SALÏ   Turk. 1583 **Salï** [Salı] (Ongan, Ank. I, 154); Yürük 1543 **Salï** [Salı] (Gökb., Rum. 217); Yürük 1543 **Salï** [Sâlî] (Gökb., Rum. 186, 217, 218, 229 etc.); Tat. 1543 **Salï** [Salı] (Gökb., Rum. 231); Turk. 1540 **Salï-beg** [صالى], chief of the Şehkovanlu tribe (cemaat), mentioned in the defter of Diyarbekir (Demirtaş 49); Kzk. 19th c. **Salï-pay** [Салыпай] (SOK 90). ✧ 'Tuesday' cf. Turk. *salï* 'id.' (Radl. IV, 355).

SALÏ-QUTLUΓ   Uyg. **Salï-qutluγ** [Salı Kutluġ] (EUTS). ⇨ **SALÏ?** + **QUTLUΓ**.

SALÏANYAY   Yak. **Salïanyay / Soluonyay** [Салыанjai / Солуонjai], fem. (Pek.); Yak. **Soluonyay / Salïanyay** [Ытык-Солуонйаi / Салыанйаi], an abāsï-woman (Pek.). See also **MŪS-SALÏANYAY**.

SALÏΓDA see **SALİX**

SALÏX see **SALİX**

SALÏXDA see **SALİX**

SALÏY   Kkalp. 20th c. **Salïy** [Салый] (KkRS 776); Kirg. **Salïy** [Салый] (Jud. 65).

SALÏQ   Kzk. 19th c. **Salik** [Саликъ Раисовъ] (Grod., Pril. 192); Kzk. 19th c. **Salïq** [Салыкъ] (SODž. 80); Kkalp. 20th c. **Salïq** [Салык] (KkRS 776); Maml. 1471/72 **Salïq / Saluq?** [قانى بك صلق], (Iyās II, 132, 135); Kzk. 19th c. **Salïq-bay** [Салыкбаевъ] (Grod., Pril. 184); Kzk. 19th c. **Salïq-bek** [Салыкбекъ] (AOA 114); Kzk. 19th c. **Salïq-pay** [Салыкпай] (SOK 200, 262); Kzk. 19th c. **Salïq-pay** [Салыкпай] (SODž. 16, 100, 122); Kzk. 19th c. **Salïq-pay** [Салыкпай] (SOV

100); Kzk. 19th c. **Salïq-pay** [Салыкпай] (AOAtb. 18); Kzk. 19th c. **Salq-pay** (<**Salïq-pay**) [Салкпай] (SOK 204); 913-914 **Saluq** (Weil, Chalif. II, 613-14); 923-924 **Saluq** [Ahmed Ibn Ali Saluk], under Al-Muqtadir (Weil, Chalif. II, 624). ✧ 'Good, kind, warm-hearted; honest' (Žanuzakov), (<Ar.) *Salikh.* See also **AY-SALÏQ, BAY-SALÏQ.**

SALÏQ-PAŠ Kzk. 19th c. **Salïq-paš** [Салыкпашъ] (SOK 142). ⇨ **SALÏQ + BAŠ.**

SALÏQAY Kzk. 19th c. **Salikey** [Саликей] (SOK 18); Kzk. 19th c. **Salïqay** [Салыкай] (SOV 74). ⇨ **SALÏQ?** + suff. *-ay.*

SALÏN Kzk. 19th c. **Salïn-bay** / **Salim-bay?** [Салинбай] (SOK 40).

SALÏNDÏ Uyg. 13th c. **Salïndï** [سالـندى / Салынди], *ïduq-qut* (RaD/Ber. I, 128, RaD I/1, 149).

SALÏNDÏQ Kzk. 19th c. **Salindïq** [Салендыкъ] (AOO 54); Kzk. 19th c. **Salïndïq** [Салындыкъ] (SOV 118).

SALÏR Oghuz/Trkm. 13th c. **Salor** [سالور / Салор] (Abulg./Kon. 1170); Oghuz/Trkm. 13th c. **Salor** [Салор], Oghuz Khan's grand-son (DQorq. 82, 176); Oghuz/Trkm. 13th c. **Salor / Salïr?** [سالور / Салор / Салыр], Taq-χan's / Таγ-χan's son (RaD I/1, 76, Abulg./Kon. 520, 560, 605); Selj.? 1261 **Salor-bek** [سالوربـك], an emir, who fought against the Mongols and was captured (Aqsarāyī 71, Aqsar/İş. 55). ✧ I. Ethnonym, a Turkmen tribe (Kononov: DQorq. 176, Abulg./Kon. p. 93, Toğan, UTT 216, 245, etc.); II. 'He who will beat/fight' (Erol II: *Salur* 'Nereye varsa kılıç ve çomağı iş görür'), according to Pelliot *Salur* [and *Salïr*?] is a shortened form of *Salγur* which is an aorist-form (Pelliot, Notes 229), cf. Uyg., Karakh. *sal-* 'класть, бросать; бить, ударять' (DTS). See also **SALΓUR; BARČÏN-SALOR.**

SALÏR-QAZAN Tat.(Tara) **Salïr-qazan** [Salyr Kasan / Салыр Казан] (Proben IV, 150 /190/); Oghuz/Trkm. 13th c. **Salor-qazan-alp** [سالور قـزان آلـب / Салор-Казан-алп / Казан-Салор / Казан-алп] (Abulg./Kon. 705, 1185-1195, 1190-1205, 1255, 1260); Oghuz/Trkm. 14th c. - 15th c. **Salor-qazan / Salur-qazan / Qazan / Qazan-bek** [Ulaş-oğlı Salur Kazan / Салор-Казан (хан Казан, Казан-бек)] (DQorq. 22, 23, 24, etc.). ⇨ **SALÏR + QAZAN.**

SALÏS Kzk. 19th c. **Salïs-pay** [Салыспай] (SODž. 54). ✧ 'Argue, quarrel!' cf. Kzk. *salïs-* 'sich zanken' (Radl. IV, 358).

SALÏŠ Bashk. 1744 **Salïš / Sališ?** [Салиш Ишимов] (MIB III, 415); Bashk. 18th c. **Salïš / Sališ?** [Салишев] (MIB V, 559); Bashk. 1757 **Salïš / Sališ?** [Салиш Агбезов] (MIB IV/1, 142); Bashk. 1763 **Salïš / Sališ?** [Салиш Тлекеев] (MIB IV/1, 267). ✧ 'Bent, crooked, lean'? cf. Bashk. *sališ* 'косой, кривой' (BRS/Uraksin).

SALQ-AWUZ Kzk. 19th c. **Salq-awuz** (<**Salïq-awuz?**) [Салкаузъ] (SODž. 118). ✧ 'Good mouth'. ⇨ **SALÏQ + AWÏZ.**

SALQA Kzk. 19th c. **Salqa-bay** [Салкабай] (SOK 118).

SALQAY Kzk. 19th c. **Salkey?** [Салкей] (AOK 30); Tat. 1686 **Salqay** [Кусекайко Салкаевъ] (Kungursk. akty 118); Bashk. 1735 **Salqay** [Салкай] (MIB III, 343). ✧ 'Hard, strong' (Sattarov), cf. also Kzk. *sal* 'ein zänkischer, unbändiger Mensch' (Radl. IV, 344).

SALQÏM-BAY see **SALQÏN**

SALQÏN Kzk. 19th c. **Salqïn-bay / Salqïm-bay** [Салкынбай / Салкымбай] (SODž. 94). ✧ 'Strong/cool wind; cool' cf. Kzk. *salqïn* 'Luftzug bei grosser Hitze; kühl' (Radl. IV, 361), Shor, Alt.(Leb.) *salγïn* 'der Wind', Tat.(Tob.) 'kalt, kühl' (Radl. II, 364). See also **QARA-SALΓÏN.**

SALQÏR Kzk. 19th c. **Salqïr-bay** [Салкырбай] (AOK 70).

SALMAQ Kzk. 19th c. **Salmaq** [Салмакъ] (SODž. 146); Kzk. 19th c. **Salmaq-pay** [Салмакпай] (SOV 22). ✧ 'Support(er)' cf. Kzk. *salmaq* 'die Stütze' (Radl. IV, 374).

SALMAN Tat. 1739 **Salman** [М. П. Салманов], a farmer (Alatyr. 144); Kzk. 19th c. **Salman** [Салманъ] (SOV 110); Kzk. **Selmän-bay** [Селмän Баі] (Proben III, 77 /100/); *TN:* Tat. 18th c. **Salman** [Салман], a village in Spasskij uezd (district) (Korsakov 203); Tat. 18th c. **Salmanka** [Салманка], a river in Spasski uezd (Korsakov 203). ✧ Salman (Ar.) 'safe' (Ahmed). ⇨ **SAL** + suff. *-man.*

SALMEKE Kzk. 19th c. **Salmeke** [Сальмеке] (SODž. 16).

SALNÄN Tat. 1600 **Salnän** [Сальнян Келментаев] (Miller, Ist. Sib. II, 159).

SALOR-QAZAN see **SALÏR-QAZAN**

SALOR-ÖGÜRJIK Oghuz/Trkm. 13th c. **Salor-ögürjik-alp** [سالور اوكورجيق آلـب / Салор-Öгÿрджик-алп] (Abulg./Kon. 1160-1180, 1210, 1220, etc.); Oghuz/Trkm. 13th c. **Salor-ögürjik-alp** [Салор-Огурджик-алп], Uruz-bek's descendant (DQorq. 177). ⇨ **SALÏR.**

SALPAΓAR Karch. **Salpaγar** [Салпагаровъ] (Sysoev 119); Karch. 20th c. **Salpaγarla** (<**Salpaγarlar**) [Salp'aγarla], family-name (Pröhle, Kar.130).

SALPAΓARLA see **SALPAΓAR**

SALPAQU Kzk. 19th c. **Salpaqu** [Салпаку] (SOK 294).

SALPAN Kzk. 19th c. **Salpan** [Салпанъ] (SODž. 16). ✧ 'Hanging down' cf. Kzk. *salpañ* 'herabhängend' (Radl. IV, 372).

SALPÏQ Kzk. 1819 **Salpïq** [Салпык] (MIK IV, 326); Kzk. 19th c. **Salpïq** [Салпыкъ] (AOP 10); Kzk. 19th c. **Salpïq-pay** [Салпыкпай] (SOV 102). ✧ '(With lips) hanging down' cf. Kzk. *salpï-* 'herabhängen (von den

Lippen)' (Radl. IV, 373) + suff. *-q*.

SALTAY Chuv. 18th-19th c. **Salday** [Салдай] (Magn. 72); Bashk. 1738 **Saltay** [Кута Салтаев] (MIB I, 143). ✧ 'Strong, healthy' (Sattarov). ⇨ **SAL?** + suff. *-tay(1,2)*.

SALTAQ see **SALTÏQ**

SALTAN see **SULTAN**

SALTANAY Tat. 1633 **Saltanay** [Салтанай], a murza from Altaul (Miller, Ist. Sib. II, 408, 409); Nog. 1649 **Saltanay** / **Saltanay-murza** [Салтанай мурза], a murza (AI IV, 87). ⇨ **SULTAN** + dim. suff. *ay*.

SALTANAQ Tat. 1690 **Saltanaq** [Бийметко Салтанаковъ] (Kungursk. akty 178); Kzk. 19th c. **Saltanaq** [Салтанакъ] (SODž. 52). ⇨ **SULTAN** + dim. suff. *aq*.

SALTANAŠ Nog. 1649 **Saltanaš-murza** [Салтанашъ мурза Аксаковъ] (AI IV, 78-79). ⇨ **SULTAN** + suff. *-aš*.

SALTANAT Kzk. 19th c. **Saltanat** [Салтанатъ], fem. (Grod. I, 98); Kzk. 19th c. **Saltanat-bibi** [Салтанатъ биби], fem. (Grod., Pril. 193); Nog.? **Saltanat-murza** [Салтанат-мурза] (Žirm., Epos 431). ✧ 'Nobility, honour; splendour, glance' cf. Kzk. *saltanat* 'das Ansehen, die Würde, der Glanz; eine schöne häusliche Einrichtung, das bewegliche Vermögen, das Hausgeräth' (Radl. IV, 370).

SALTANÏM Tat.(Sib.) 1599 **Saltanïm** [Салтанымъ], Küčüm-qan's wife (AI II, 20, 22). ✧ 'My sovereign, my ruler'. ⇨ **SULTAN** + poss. suff. *-ïm*.

SALTAŠ Bashk. 1735 **Saltaš** [Салташъ Мамбетевъ] (Vel.-Zern., Bašk. 21). ⇨ **SAL** + **TAŠ.**

SALTEN-BER Kzk. 19th c. **Salten-ber** [Салтенберъ] (SODž. 58). ⇨ **SULTAN?** + **BER.**

SALTÏ see **SALDÏ**

SALTÏQ Selj. 1154, 1162 **Saltïq** [سلتق غرالدين], ruler of Arzan (Qalānisi 324, 328); Turk. 1583 **Saltïq** [صالتق / Saltuk] (Ongan, Ank. I, 175); Yürük 1543 **Saltïq** [صالتق / Saltïk], from the Yürüks of Kocacık (Gökb., Rum. 180, 186, 193, 201 etc.); Bashk. 1719 **Saltïq** [Юнай Салтыков] (MIB III, 188); Bashk. 1740 **Saltïq** [Салтык Мергенев] (MIB I, 405); Bashk. 1756 **Saltïq** [Салтык Елдашев] (MIB IV/1, 119); Bashk. 1788 **Saltïq** [Чинбурза Салтыков] (MIB V, 231); Kzk. 19th c. **Saltïq** [Салтык] (AOP 74); Uzb. **Saltïq** [Шкульметъ Салтыковъ], from Bukhara (Veselovskij, Unk. 170); Selj.? 1154/55, 1161, 1200 **Saltïq** / **Saltuq** / **Saltaq?** [سلتق بن علی / Saltâk], a prince, Ali's son; „in Arzân ar-Rûm -- there was in it a son of Mâlik Mâhamâd, the son of Saltâk; now they belonged to a very old family, and had ruled over 'Arzân ar-Rûm for a very long time" (Ibn al-Athīr: RHCHor I, 491, 522, Abulfar./Budge I, 350); Turk. 1481 **Saltïq-bey** / **Saltuq-bey** [Saltuk (Saltïk) Bey] (Gökb., Ed. 229); Bashk. 1722 **Saltïq-bek** [Салтык-

бек] (MIB I, 297); Crm. 1679 **Saltïq-bi** [صالتق بی] (Vel.-Zern., Crim.); Selj. 1153-1160 **Saltuq** [Σάλτουχος / Σαλτοῦχος], Izzeddin Salduk, the Turkic ruler (1153-1160) of Erzerum (Moravcsik 265); Selj. **Saltuq-alp** [صَلتُق الپ], at the time of Oñ-χan (Āšikp.); *TN:* Turk. 20th c. **Saltïq** [Saltïk], a village in the province of Afyon, Turkey (TMİB 42); Tat. 18th c. **Saltïq(i)** [Салтыки], a village in the district of Tetyushinsk (Korsakov 332); Tat. 18th c. **Saltïq(ova)** [Салтыкова], a village in the distrikt of Mamadysh (Korsakov 241); Turk. 1485 **Saltuqlu** [Saltuklû (Köy)], a village (Gökb., Ed. 69, 70, 413). ✧ I. 'Lame' (Bask., Fam. 86; Sattarov), Kzk. *saltaq* 'die Beschmutzung; ein wenig lahm' (Radl. IV, 369); II. 'Right, honest, correct' (Bask., Fam. 86; Sattarov). See also **SARÏ-SALTÏQ.**

SALTÏM Kzk. 19th c. **Saltïm-bek** [Салтымбекъ] (SOK 134, 158).

SALTÏR Hak.? 19th c. **Saltïr** [Салтыр] (Katanov, Otč. 12).

SALTU see **SALDÏ**

SALTUQ see **SALTÏQ**

SALU Uyg. **Salu** [Salu] (EUTS).

SALUQ see **SALÏQ**

SALUR-QAZAN see **SALÏR-QAZAN**

SAM Kzk. 19th c. **Sam** [Самъ] (SODž. 136); Trkm.? 1688 **Sam-bek** (<**San-bek?**) [/ Сам-бек], vekil (ruler of a tribe) of the Kurd Čemškezek tribe (MIT II, 121); Trkm. 1847 **Sam-χan** [Сам-хан], an ilkhanid, from the Zafaranlu clan (MIT II, 242-244, 246, 249, 252 etc.). ✧ 'Babbler'? cf. Trkm. *sam-sam* 'болтливый' (TrkmRS). ⇨ **SAN?**

SAM-BURUN Kzk. 19th c. **Sam-burun** [Самбурунъ] (SOK 122). ⇨ **SAM** + **BURUN.**

SAMA Kirg. **Sama-yan** [Сама-Jан], one of the forty followers of Aq-sayqal (Proben V, 394 /397/). ✧ 'Esssence of tea' cf. Kzk. *sama* 'der Theegrund' (Radl. IV, 432).

SAMAČAQ Alt. 19th-20th c. **Samačaq** [/ Самачак] (OjrRS 209).

SAMAČÏ Alt. 19th-20th c. **Samačï** [Самачы], fem. (OjrRS 213).

SAMAҐAYĀN Yak. **Samaγayān** [Самаҕајан] (Pek.).

SAMAY Kzk. 1846 **Samay** [Самай] (MKOP 152); Kzk. 19th c. **Samay** [Самай] (SOK 272); Kzk. 19th c. **Samay** [Самай] (SOV 148); Kzk. 19th c. **Samay** [Самай] (AOAtb. 10); Kzk. 19th c. **Samay** [Самай] (AOP 2, 58, 82); Kzk. 19th c. **Samay** [Самай] (AOA 10); Kzk. 19th c. **Samay** [Самай] (AOK 118, 134); Alt. 19th-20th c. **Samay** [Самай] (OjrRS 209); Tuv. 19th c. **Samay** [Самаi] (Proben IX, 48, 49, 51). ✧ 'Temple, hair on the temple' cf. Alt., Kzk. *samay* 'id.' (Radl. IV, 432).

SAMAQ Kzk. 19th c. **Samaq-pay** [Самакпай] (SOK 126).

SAMAQAR Tat.(GH)? 1417 **Samaqar-oγlï** [تاتار صَمَقَر اوغلى] (Āšikp. 80).

SAMAL Kzk. **Samal** [Самал], fem. (Proben III, 481 /556/). ✧ 'Light wind' cf. Kzk. *samal* 'ein leiser Windzug' (Radl. IV, 433); II. 'Nightfall' cf. Kzk. *samal* 'die Dämmerung' (Radl. IV, 433).

SAMALΓUN Uzb. 1696 **Samalγun / Samayγun** [Самалгунъ], khan of Bukhara (DAI X, 384).

SAMALÏQ Kzk. 1819 **Samalïq** [Самалык] (MIK IV, 323); Kzk. 19th c. **Samalïq** [Шаирбекъ / Чаиръ бекъ Самалыковъ] (Grod., Pril. 56, 1ö9). ✧ 'Teapot for holding tea-essence'. ⇨ **SAMA** + suff. *-lïq*.

SAMALTÏR Kzk. 19th c. **Samaltïr** [Самалтыръ] (SOK 206).

SAMAM-BAY see **SAMAN**

SAMAMBET Kirg. 19th c. **Samambet** (<Samanbet?) [Самамбетъ] (Potanin II, 3). ⇨ **SAMAN?** + suffixoid *-bet*.

SAMAN Kzk. 19th c. **Samam-bay** (<Saman-bay) [Самамбай] (SOV 50); Bulg. **Saman** [سَمَان / Саман] (Jusupov 35); Chuv. 18th-19th c. **Saman** [Саманъ] (Magn. 72); Kzk. 19th c. **Saman** [Саманъ] (AOAtb. 14); Kzk. 19th c. **Saman** [Саманъ] (AOAtb. 54); Tuv. 19th c. **Saman-ōl** [Саман-ол] (Proben IX, 59); *TN:* Kzk.? **Saman-batïr** [Саман-батыръ], a well or/and tomb? south of Čalqar-teñgiz (KartaJAR XI). ✧ 'Straw' cf. Uyg., Crm., Turk. *saman* 'das Stroh' (Radl. IV, 432), Kirg. *saman* 'солома' (Jud.). See also **AQ-SAMAN, ÏT-SAMAN, SARÏΓ-SAMAN.**

SAMANJÏ Turk. 19th c. **Samanǰï-oγlu** [Samanǯу oγlu], a Zeybek (Kúnos 1891, 119). ✧ 'Seller of straw'. ⇨ **SAMAN** + suff. *-ǰï*.

SAMANDAY Chuv. 18th-19th c. **Samanday** [Самандай] (Magn. 72); Chuv. 18th-19th c. **Samandey** [Самандей] (Magn. 72); Chuv. 1764 **Samandey** [Самандей Ирдемеевъ] (MIB IV/1, 275). ⇨ **SAMAN** + suff. *-day*.

SAMANDAR Trkm. 19th c. **Samandar** [Ачильды Самандаровъ] (SKSO III, 178); Uzb.? **Samandar** [Самандаръ Ильмуратовъ] (SKSO III, 15); Uzb. **Samandar** [Самандаръ Шарифовъ] (SKSO III, 186); Uzb. **Samandar** [Кошъ Али Самандаровъ] (SKSO III, 162); Chuv. 18th-19th c. **Samander** [Самандеръ] (Magn. 72); Chuv. 18th-19th c. **Semender** [Семендеръ] (Magn. 75). ✧ 'Salamander' cf. Uzb. *samandar* 'id.' (UzbRS), Turk. *sämändär* 'der Salamander' (Radl. IV, 508) (<P.).

SAMANDEY see **SAMANDAY**

SAMANDER see **SAMANDAR**

SAMAR Bashk. 1754, 1764 **Samar** [Каскин Самаровъ] (MIB IV/1, 83, 300); Bashk. 1761 **Samar** [Качкун Самаровъ] (MIB IV/1, 215); Bashk. 1763 **Samar** [Качкун Самаровъ] (MIB IV/2, 45); Bashk. 1777 **Samar** [Качкин Самаровъ] (MIB V, 65); Kzk.

19th c. **Samar-bay** [Самарбай] (AOK 34); Kzk. **Samar-qul** [Самаркуль] (Sb. Syr-D. IX, 48). ✧ 'Large (wooden) bowl; trough' cf. Chag., Kzk. *samar* 'das Becken, die Kanne; ein sehr grosser Holznapf' (Radl. IV, 434).

SAMARDİN Kzk. 1823 **Samardin** [Туманчій Самардиновъ] (TOUAK XXIV, 137).

SAMARQAN Kzk. 19th c. **Samarqan** [Саморконъ] (SOK 114); Kirg. 19th c. **Samarqan / Samar-qan?** [Самарканъ], a sultan from the region of Kobdo river (Potanin II, 2). ⇨ **SAMAR?** + suff. *-qan* or comp. *qan?*

SAMAT Kzk. 19th c. **Samat** [Саматъ Кузыкуловъ] (SKSO VIII, 201, 233). ✧ I. Samad (Ar.) 'eternal' (Ahmed), cf. also Kzk., Tat. PN *Samat* (Sattarov, Žanuzakov 155); II. 'Listening; hearing'? (Kusimova) (<Ar.).

SAMATAY Kzk. 19th c. **Samatay** [Саматай] (AOP 114). ⇨ **SAMAT** + suff. *-ay.*

SAMBAZ Kzk. 19th c. **Sambaz** [Самбазъ] (SOK 114).

SAMBET Kzk. 19th c. **Sambet** [Самбätъ] (Samojlovič: ŽS XXIV (1915), 165); Kzk. 19th c. **Sambet** [Кулджанъ Самбетовъ] (Grod., Pril. 61).

SAMBODU Uyg. **Sambodu (Samboqtu?)** [Sambodu] (EUTS).

SAMBUN Uyg. 12th c. - 14th c. **Sambun** [Sambun] (Radl., USp. 130-31, DTS, EUTS).

SAMDAR Karg. **Samdar** [Самдар] (Katanov, Otč. 8). ✧ 'Colour of a horse' (Katanov: *igrenij*). ⇨ **ŠABDAR.**

SAMÄ Bashk. 1734 **Samä** [Самя Тавлин] (MIB III, 322). ⇨ **SAMA?**

SAMEN Kzk. 18th c. - 19th c. **Samen** [Самен] (Tynyšp. 68); Kzk. 19th c. **Samen** [Саменъ] (SOV 116); Kzk. 1798 **Samen-batïr** [Самен-батыр], chief of the branch Bot-bay (Tynyšp. 65). ⇨ **SAMAN?**

SAMİT Bashk. 1735 **Samit / Sämit?** [Самитъ Ешляповъ], a tarχan (Vel.-Zern., Bašk. 24). ✧ 'Hard, firm' cf. Tat. PN *Sämit* (Sattarov) (<Ar.).

SAMÏYĀ Tuv. 19th c. **Samïyā** [Самыja], fem. (Proben IX, 138).

SAMÏLTÏR Kzk. 19th c. **Samïltïr** [Самылтыръ] (SOV 116).

SAMÏR-QAZAN Tat.(Bar.) **Samïr-qazan** [Samyr Kasan / Самыр Казан] (Proben IV, 48 /60/). ⇨ **SAMUR?** + **QAZAN.**

SAMOΓUR Kuman 1202 **Samoγur / Samγur?** [Сомогуръ Сутоевичъ], a Polovets prince (Ipat. 481 /488/, PSRL II, 156). ✧ 'Sable' (Bask., Im. polov. 71), cf. Crm., Turk. *samur* 'der Zobel' (Radl. IV, 434).

SAMOY Hak. 19th-20th c. **Samoy** [Самой] (HRS 351); Hak.(Kacha) 19th-20th c. **Samōy** [Самоi] (Proben IX, 558). ✧ Samuil (R.) (Butanaev).

SAMOLAY Hak. 19th-20th c. **Samolay** [Самолай], fem. (HRS 354).

SAMORŌTQA Hak.(Shor) 19th-20th c. **Samorōtqa**

[Саморотка] (Katanov, Otč. 11). ❖ '(Undiscovered) talent'? (<R.) самородок (Katanov).

SAMPA Kzk. 19th c. **Sampa-bay** [Сампабай] (SODž. 112).

SAMPİR Hak. 19th-20th c. **Sampir** [Сампир] (HRS 351); Hak.(Sag.) 19th-20th c. **Sampïr** [Сампір] (Proben IX, 432, 542).

SAMSAY Karg. **Samsay** [Самсай] (Katanov, Otč. 8).

SAMSAQ see **SARÏMSAQ**

SAMSALÏ Kzk. 1850 **Samsalï-biy** [Самсалы бiй] (Valihanov, Soč. 363). ❖ 'Having a kind of pastry filled with meat' cf. Kzk. *samsa* 'id.' (KzTS), Kzk. *samsa* 'пирожок' (KzRS) + suff. *-lï*.

SAMSAM Trkm. 1835/36 **Samsam-ɣan** [Самсам-хан] (MIT II, 231). ⇨ **SAMSA** + poss. suff. *-m*.

SAMSAR Alt. 19th-20th c. **Samsar** [Самсар] (OjrRS 209); Hak.(Sag.) 19th-20th c. **Samsar** [Самсар] (Katanov, Otč. 7).

SAMTAM Kzk. 19th c. **Samtam-bek (<Samtan-bek?)** [Самтамбекъ] (SOV 52).

SAMTÏR Kzk. 1814 **Samtïr** [Нурбекъ Самтыровъ] (TOUAK XXIV, 56); Kzk. 19th c. **Samtïr** [Самтыръ] (SODž. 52); Kirg. **Samtïr** [Самтыр], earlier he was called *Sarï-qul* (Jud. 25, 154). ❖ 'Tatterdemalion, ragamuffin' cf. Kirg. *samtïr* 'оборвыш, оборванец' (Jud.).

SAMTSO Uyg. **Samtso** [Samtso] (EUTS).

SAMUQ Selj.? 1056 **Samuq** [Σαμούχης], a commander of the army (Byz. Turc. 266); Selj.? 1138 **Samuq** [Σαμούχης], a commander of the army (Byz. Turc. 266).

SAMUNŠÏ Uyg. 12th c. - 14th c. **Samunšï** [Samunşı] (Radl., USp. 128, DTS, EUTS); Uyg. 12th c. - 14th c. **Samunšu** (Radl., USp. 128, DTS). ❖ 'Maker or/and seller of soap' cf. Alt., Kirg. *samïn* 'die Seife' (Radl. IV, 434).

SAMUNŠU see **SAMUNŠÏ**

SAN Chuv. 18th-19th c. **Sam-bay (<San-bay?)** [Самбай] (Magn. 73); Kzk. 19th c. **Sam-bay (<San-bay?)** [Самбай] (SOK 64); Kzk. 19th c. **Sam-bay (<San-bay?)** [Самбай] (SOV 142); Tuv. 19th c. **Sam-bay-dägine? (<San-bay?)** [Самбай-дагине] (Potanin IV, 373); Kzk. 1823 **San-bay** [Санбай Чанчигитовъ] (TOUAK XXIV, 139); Kzk. 1846 **San-bay** [Тляубай Санбаев] (MKOP 151); Bashk. 1777 **San-qul** [Сафар Санкуловъ] (MIB V, 546); Kzk. 19th c. **San-mïrza** [Санмырза] (AOP 122). ❖ I. 'Hip, haunch' cf. Kzk. *san I.* 'бедро, ляжка' (KzRS); II. 'Splendour, pomp, grace(fulness)' cf. Kkalp. *sän* 'роскошь, изящество, укращение' (KkRS) <Ar. *sana* 'блескъ сияние' (ArRS). See also **AQ-SAN, BAY-SAN, BAQT-SAN, SANA-SAN**.

SAN-BEKE Kzk. 19th c. **San-beke / Sän-beke?** [Санбеке] (SODž. 76). ⇨ **ESÄN / SAN + BEKE.**

SAN-BUҐA Maml. 1399 **San-buɣa / Sän-boɣa? (<Esän-boɣa?)** [اسنبغا] (Iyās I, 317). ⇨ **ESÄN / SAN + BUQA.**

SAN-BULAT Chuv. 18th-19th c. **San-bulat** [Санбулатъ] (Magn. 73). ❖ 'Strong / hard steel, steel-like' (Sattarov). ⇨ **ESÄN / SAN? + BULAT.** See also **SAN-DEMİR**.

SAN-DEMİR Chuv. 18th-19th c. **San-demir** [Сандемиръ] (Magn. 73); Chuv. 18th-19th c. **San-dimer** [Сандимеръ] (Magn. 73). ❖ 'Strong/healthy iron'. ⇨ **ESÄN / SAN? + TEMİR.** See also **SAN-BULAT**.

SAN-DERYOQ-AQ Uyg. 1334 **San-deryoq-aq?** [San-Derjok-Ak] (Chwol., Syr.-nest. 75). ⇨ **SAN + ? + AQ?**

SAN-DİMER see **SAN-DEMİR**

SAN-GEL Trkm.? **San-gel** [Сангельбаевъ Хамрабай], a merchant in Andijan (Turk. Kraj 1912: 5). ⇨ **ESÄN / SAN? + KEL.**

SAN-NİYAZ Kzk. 19th c. **Sa-niyaz (<San-niyaz?)** [Санiязъ] (Grod., Pril. 133); Kzk. 19th c. **Sa-niyaz (<San-niyaz?)** [Джубай Санiязовъ] (Grod., Pril. 172); Kzk. 19th c. **Sa-niyaz (<San-niyaz?)** [Санязъ] (SOK 222). ⇨ **ESÄN / SAN? + NİYAZ.**

SAN-TARҐÏN Karg. **San-tarɣin** [Санъ-Таргынъ], a fatty man (Katanov: ZIRGOÊtn. XVII, vyp. III, 175); Karg. 19th-20th c. **San-tarɣïn** [Сан Тарвын], a folklore hero (Proben IX, 637). ⇨ **ESÄN / SAN? + TARҐÏN.**

SAN-TÜZ Kuman 1159, 1160 **San-tüz? / Sïnï-tüz?** [Сантузъ], a Polovets prince (PSRL VII, 71, Ipat. 346 (358)). ❖ I. 'Prove your honour' (Bask., Im. polov. 72), cf. Uyg., Chag., Kuman etc. *san* 'die Zahl; die Ehre, die Reputation' (Radl. IV, 296), *tüz-* 'строй, настрой' (Budagov I, 391); II. 'Having straight, slim figure' (Bask., Im. polov. 72), cf. Uyg., Kuman etc. *sin* 'das Aeussere, die Gestalt' (Radl. IV, 628), Chag., Tat. *tüz* 'прямой, прямостоящий' (Budagov I, 391). Cf. also Rásonyi, KÖA 123. ⇨ **ESÄN / SAN?**

SANA see **SANĀ**

SANA-QUŠ Alt. 19th-20th c. **Sana-quš** [Санакуш] (OjrRS 209). ❖ I. 'Sparing/cautious - Mind' cf. Hak. PN *Sana-bay* 'расчетливый бай' (Butanaev); II. 'Mind/reason?-Bird' cf. Kzk. *sana* 'сознание, мысль, дума' (KzRS). ⇨ **QUŠ I.**

SANA-SABA Kzk. 1788 **Sana-saba** [Санасаба] (MIK IV, 104). ❖ 'Mind/reason? - Leather bag' cf. Kzk. *sana* 'сознание, мысль, дума' (KzRS). ⇨ **SABA I.**

SANA-SAN Kzk. 1822 **Sana-san** [صنه صان صاتى اوعلى / Засап Сатыулы] (MIK IV, 409, 410). ❖ 'Mind/reason?-Hip' cf. Kzk. *sana* 'сознание, мысль, дума' (KzRS). ⇨ **SAN.**

SANA-SAP Kzk. 1819 **Sana-sap / Sana-san?** [Санасап] (MIK IV, 324). ❖ 'Mind/reason - Stock'? cf. Kzk. *sana* 'сознание, мысль, дума' (KzRS). ⇨

SAP.

SANABÏR Alt. 19th-20th c. **Sanabïr** [Санабыр] (OjrRS 209). ✧ 'Rhubarb' (OjrRS).

SANAY I. Alt. 19th-20th c. **Sanay** [Санай] (OjrRS 209). ⇨ **SANĀ** + dim. suff. -*y*.

SANAY II. Kzk. 19th c. **Sanay** [Санай] (SOK 52); Kzk. 19th c. **Sanay** [Санай] (AOA 74). ⇨ **SAN** + dim. suff. -*ay*.

SANAQ Kzk. 19th c. **Sanaq** [Санакъ] (SODž. 82). ✧ 'Census, listing' cf. Chag. *sanaq* 'die Rechnung' (Radl. IV, 298), Kzk. *sanaq* 'статистика; перепись' (KzRS).

SANAQAY Bashk. 1759 **Sanaqay** [Санакай Карачюрин] (MIB IV/2, 188). ⇨ **SANAQ** + dim. suff. -*ay*.

SANAL Yürük 1543 **Sanal** [سانال] (Gökb., Rum. 190).

SANAM Uzb. 19th c. **Sanam-bibi** [Санамъ-биби Раджаббаева] (Sr. Az. I, 1896, 15); Kkalp. 20th c. **Sänem** [Сәнем], fem. (KkRS 778). ✧ 'My beloved darling' (Sattarov), cf. Kkalp. *sän* 'роскошь, изящество, украшение' (KkRS) < Ar. *sana* 'блескъ сийание' (ArRS). See also **AY-SÄNEM, BÏYBÏ-SÄNEM.**

SANAMAS Kzk. 1817 **Sanamas** [صناماس] (MIK IV, 303). ✧ '(He/she) doesn't count/matter' cf. Kzk., Tat., Turk. etc. *sana-* 'zählen, schätzen' (Radl. IV, 297) + suff. -*mas*.

SANARÏY Alt. 19th-20th c. **Sanariy** [Санарий] (OjrRS 209).

SANASÏS Kzk. 1819 **Sanasïs-bay** [Санасысбай] (MIK IV, 325). ✧ 'Insensible, senseless, unreasonable, foolish'. ⇨ **SANA** + suff. -*sïz*.

SANAŠ Kzk. / Kirg.? 19th c. **Sanaš** [Санашъ Алтащъ] (Potanin IV, 291); Alt. 19th c. **Sanaš** [Санаш] (Potanin IV, 288); Alt. 19th c. **Sanaš** [Санашъ], an informant (Potanin IV, 173, 178, 194, 288, 291); Alt. 19th-20th c. **Sanaš** [Санаш] (OjrRS 209). ✧ 'Wish, aim, intention' (OjrRS).

SANAT I. Alt. 19th-20th c. **Sanat** [Санат] (OjrRS 209).

SANAT II. Kzk. 19th c. **Sanat-bay** [Санатбай Джанъ Узаковъ] (Grod., Pril. 48); Kzk. 19th c. **Sanat-bay** [Санатбай] (Grod., Pril. 48). ✧ 'Thought, idea, reason; memory' cf. Kzk. *sanat* 'der Verstand, Sinn, die Erinnerung, das Gedächtniss' (Radl. IV, 300). ⇨ **SANĀ.**

SANĀ Alt. 19th-20th c. **Sana** [Сана] (OjrRS 209); Alt. 19th-20th c. **Sana** [Сана], fem. (OjrRS 213); Hak. 19th-20th c. **Sana** [Сана], fem. (HRS 354); Alt. 19th-20th c. **Sana-bay** [Санабай] (OjrRS 209); Uzb. **Sana-qul** [Санакулъ Гаджибаевъ] (SKSO III, 184); Uzb. **Sana-qul** [Санакулъ] (SKSO III, 150, 172); Uzb. **Sana-qul** [Санакулъ] (SKSO III, 150); Alt. 19th-20th c. **Sanā** [Санаа] (OjrRS 213). ✧ 'Thought, idea, reason; sorrow; temper, mood' cf. Alt. *sanaa*

'сознание, мысль; печаль; дух, настроение' (OjrRS), Kzk. *sana* 'сознание; мысль; дума' (KzRS). ⇨ **SANAT II.** See also **AMÏR-SANĀ.**

SANČA Hak. 19th-20th c. **Sanča** [Санча] (HRS 351).

SANČAR see SANJAR

SANČÏ Alt. 19th-20th c. **Sančï** [Санчы] (OjrRS 209). ✧ Hypocoristic form of R. *Aleksandr* (OjrRS).

SANČMÏŠ Uyg. **Sančmïš** [Санчмыш] (EUTS). ✧ 'Stabbed' cf. Karakh. *sanč-* 'колоть, вонзать; побеждать' (DTS). See also **ER-SANČMÏŠ.**

SANJAQ Maml. 1280 **Sanjaq** [Bedr-eddin-Sandjak-Bagdâdi] (Makrīzī III, 20); Maml. 1389 **Sanjaq** [سنجق الحسنى] (Iyās I, 276). ✧ 'Banner, flag' cf. Turk. *sanjaq* 'id.' (Radl. IV, 310).

SANJAR Kzk. 1819 **Sančar** [Санчар] (MIK IV, 325); Oghuz 12th c. **Sanjar** [سنجر سلطان], byname (laqab) of Muhammad Khorezmshah (Juwaynī II, 79); Selj. **Sanjar** [Санджар] (RaD I/2, 159); Selj. **Sanjar** [ملك سنجر], Sultan Suleyman's (?) son (Rāwandī 338, 363 etc.); Selj. **Sanjar** [سنجرمَلِك], governor of Bukhara (Juwaynī II, 74); Selj. 1114, 1118, 1160 **Sanjar** [سنجر سلطان / سنجر بن ملكشاه معزّالـدين] Санджар ибн Меликшах ибн Алп-арсланъ Муиз-ад-динъ Абу-л-Харис], Sultan Sandjar (1117-1157), Melik-šah's son from the Qïnïq tribe, died in 1160 (Ibn al-Athīr/Tornb. IX, 213, X, 180-83 etc., XI, 16-18 etc., XII, 198, 295, Ibn al-Athīr: RHCHor I, 318, 381-82, Abulfidā III, 256-57, 432-33 etc., Abulfidā/Ed. 32, Qazw. 404, 444, Aqsarāyī 9, 10, 22, 31, Aqsar/Iš. 27, 30, 35-36, Juwaynī I, 119, II, 3-5, 12-14, Rāwandī 21,38, 85 etc., Qalānisi 147, 210 etc., Mirch. Gasnevid. 129, Ahbar 60, Abulfar. Or. (242-43, 251-52), 369-70, Abulfar./Budge I, 256, Arūs al-Qulūb: Belleten VII, 507, 514, MIT I, 45, 46, 48, 183, 194 etc.); Selj.? 1206 **Sanjar** [بن مهارش امير عبادة بالعراق] [سنجر بن مقلد بن سليمان] (Ibn al-Athīr/Tornb. XII, 160); Selj.? 13th c. **Sanjar** [Alámo'ddin Senjar], from Mosul (Abulfar. Or. (353, 354), 541); Selj. 1254, 1265/66 **Sanjar** [علم الـدين سنجـر الباشـتردئّ / Alem-eddin Sandjār-Bashkirdi], emir, governor of Emesa (Makrīzī I, 50, Aynī: RHCHor II/1, 223); Maml. **Sanjar** [Alem-eddin - Sandjar-al-gatmi], governor of Rahabah (Makrīzī IV?, Weil, Chalif. I, 256); Maml.? 1206 **Sanjar** [سنجر قطب الـدين مملوك الـناصرالـدين الله] (Ibn al-Athīr/Tornb. XII, 160, 170, 190); Maml. 1254 **Sanjar** [سنجر], from Egypt (Abulfidā IV, 536-37); Maml. 1254 **Sanjar** [Sandjār-Bedri] (Makrīzī I, 50); Maml. 1259 **Sanjar** [Sandjar-Masoudi] (Makrīzī I, 83); Maml. 1260 **Sanjar** [سنجـر الحلبى], governor of Damascus under Kutuz (1259-1260) (Iyās I, 97, 100, Weil, Chalif. I, 17 etc.); Maml. 1264, 1300 **Sanjar** [علم الـدين سنجر الصالحى], made numerous foundations in Damascus and Syria, died in 1300 (Makrīzī II, 13, Sauvaire III, 297); Maml. 1279 **Sanjar** [Sandjar-Tardadj], an emir (Makrīzī II, 170); Maml. 1280 **Sanjar** [Alem-eddin-Sandjar-Arbeli], died at Hims in 1280 (Makrīzī III, 39); Maml. 1280 **Sanjar** [Alem-eddin-Sandjar-Tekriti] (Makrīzī II/1, 18); Maml. 1280 **Sanjar** [علم‌الدين سنجر الباشقردى], governor of Haleb (Abulfidā V, 52-53); Maml. 1280/81 **Sanjar** [علم‌الدين سنجر الشجاعى], governor of Syria (Iyās I, 115, 121, 130 etc., Weil, Chalif. I, 171, 176, 178); Maml. 1295, 1296 **Sanjar** [سنجر الدوادارى الصالحى / Alam eddin Sandjar al-déwadâri], governor of the Citadel of Damascus (Berchem, Jér. I, 214, Makrīzī IV, 29, Weil, Chalif. I, 114); Maml. 1298 **Sanjar** [Alem-eddin-Sandjar-Taksaba], an emir, died in 1298 (Makrīzī IV, 81); Maml. 1299, 1304 **Sanjar** [علم‌الدين سنجر الجاولى / علم‌الدين سنجر الجولى / Sandjar-Djâouli], an emir (Dawād. 125, 180 etc., Makrīzī I, 126, IV, 126, Iyās I, 93, 155, Weil, Chalif. I, 303, 370); Maml. 1300 **Sanjar** [علم‌الدين سنجر], a sultan (Dawād. 59); Maml. 1300 **Sanjar** [Alem-eddin-Sandjar-Mesrouri], governor of Cairo, died in 1300 (Makrīzī IV, 140); Maml. 1302 **Sanjar** [علم‌الدين سنجر ارجواش / Alem-eddin-Sandjar-Ardjewasch-Mansauri], governor of the Citadel of Damascus, died in 1302 (Makrīzī IV, 192, Zetterst. 46, Weil, Chalif. I, 182, 236); Maml. 1305 **Sanjar** [علم‌الدين سنجر] (Dawād. 133); Maml. 1310 **Sanjar** [علم‌الدين سنجر الخازن], an emir (Dawād. 212, 221); Maml. 1310, 1315 **Sanjar** [سنجر الاحمدى] (Dawād. 212, 299,); Maml. 1310, 1320 **Sanjar** [علم‌الدين سنجر الجمقدار], an emir (Dawād. 213, 309, Zetterst. 136, 153, Iyās I, 161); Maml. 1325 **Sanjar** [علم‌الدين سنجر الاحمدى], an emir (Zetterst. 169); Maml. 1325, 1335 **Sanjar** [علم‌الدين سنجر الحمصى], an emir (Zetterst. 193, Dawād. 400); Maml. 1345 **Sanjar** [سنجر الجماق‌دار نائب السلطنة بحصن عكار], a governor (?) (Sobern. I, 10); Maml. 14th c. **Sanjar** [سنجر البرونى] (Zetterst. 170); Maml. 14th c. **Sanjar** [سنجر الخازن] (Zetterst. 151, 175); Maml. 14th c. **Sanjar** [سنجر الدميترى] (Zetterst. 165); Maml. 14th c. **Sanjar** [سنجر / Sançar] (Tarǰ/Houtsma 80, Tarǰ/Toparlı 42); Maml. 1350/51 **Sanjar** (Iyās I, 193); Chag. 1459 **Sanjar** [Султан-Санджар / Муиз-ад-дин Санджар], the Timurid ruler (mirza) of Merv, poet (MIT I, 534-537); Chag. 1571 **Sanjar** [سنجر سلطان], Ali-sultan's son in Khiva, died in 1571 (Abulg./Desm. 265 /248/); Trkm. **Sanjar** [Санджаръ] (Mel'gunov 320); Khorezm./Chag.? 15th c. - 16th c. **Sanjar-sultan** [سنجر سلطان] (Šejb. L, LI, LXXVII); Selj. 12th c. **Sanjar-šah** [سنجر شاه], a Seljukid from Asia Minor, Qïlïč-arslan II's (1156-1192) son (Aqsarāyī 29, 30, Aqsar/Iş. 39-40, Qazw. 482); Selj.? 1181 **Sanjar-šah** [Moezzo'ddin Sanjar Shah, Ebn Saifo'ddin] (Abulfar. Or. (270), 411); Selj. 1202? **Sanjar-šah** [سنجرشاه بن طغانشاه بن مؤيّد اى ابه / Санджаршах], Tuγan-šah's son, ruler (emir) of Nishapur (Ibn al-Athīr/Tornb. IX, 249, XII, 116, J̌uwaynī II, 22, 23, 32, Rāwandī 387, MIT I, 405, 446, 447); *TN:* Turk. 1543 **Sanjar** [سنجار / Sencar (Köy)], a village (Gökb., Ed. 72); Turk. 20th c. **Sanjar** [Sancar], a village in the province of Eskişehir, Turkey (TMİB 363); Turk. 20th c. **Sanjar** [Sancar], a village in the province of Çankırı, Turkey (TMİB 250). ✧ 'He who will stab/thrust; stabber' cf. Maml. *sanj- / sanč-* (صانج / سنج) 'stechen' (Tarǰ/Houtsma 78, 80), cf. also Pelliot 176, 180, Sauvaget 48, Justi 283.

SANJAR-MĀZĪ Selj. 1117-1160 **Sanjar-māzī** [سنجرماضى / Sandjar-Mâzi / Санджар-Мази / Санджар Мазы], the great Seljuk Sultan Sandjar (1117-1157), died in 1160 (Abulg./Desm. 51, Abulg./Kon. 1100, 1145, MIT II, 129, 154, 256 etc.). ✧ 'Stabbing/thrusting sharp (sword, knife)' cf. Ar. *māḍī* (ماضى) 'durchgehend, durchschneidend, scharf (Säbel, Messer u. dgl.)' (Zenker). ⇨ **SANJAR.**

SANJĪ Kipch. 1262 **Sanjī** [صنجى / Санджи] (Baybars/Tizeng. I, 78, 100). ✧ 'Stomach ache, colic; spiky stick'? cf. Turk. *sanjī* 'das Stechen in den Eingeweiden, die Kolik; ein Stock mit einem Stachel (zum Anspornen der Thiere)' (Radl. IV, 311).

SANJĪ-ČAÑĪ Tuv. 19th c. **Sanjī-čañγï** [Санцы-чанҕы], a clerk (Proben IX, 98).

SANDA Kzk. 19th c. **Sanda-bay / Sandï-bay?** [Сандабай] (SODž. 70).

SANDAY I. Chuv. 18th-19th c. **Sanday** [Сандай] (Magn. 73); Chuv. 18th-19th c. **Sandey** [Сандей] (Magn. 73).

SANDAY II. Hak. 19th-20th c. **Sanday** [Сандай] (HRS 351).

SANDAL I. Maml. 14th c. **Sandal** [سَنْدَل] (Sauvaget 49); Maml.? 1463 **Sandal** [صندل الظاهرى] (Ibn Taghrīb. VII, 716,); Kkalp. 1821 **Sandal** [Сандал] (MIKk. 126). ✧ I. 'Ark, boat' (Sauvaget 49) cf. Crm., Turk. *sandal* 'ein breites Boot' (Radl. IV, 304); II. 'Block for holding the anvil; anvil' cf. Chag., Kzk., Tat. *sandal* 'id.' (Radl. IV, 305), Kkalp. *sandal* 'наковальня' (KkRS). See also **SUNU-SANDAL.**

SANDAL II. Hak.? 19th c. **Sandal** [Сандал] (Katanov. Otč. 12). ✧ 'Candlestick' cf. R. *sandal* 'id.' (Katanov).

SANDAŠ Hak.(Shor) 19th-20th c. **Sandaš** [Сандаш] (Katanov, Otč. 11).

SANDĀR Yak. **Sandār-toyon** [Сандар Тойон], an old man (Pek.). ✧ 'Shine, sparkle' cf. Yak. *sandār-* 'распространять яркий светъ, сиять, освещать (о солнце)' (Pek.).

SANDĀRÏSQAY   Yak. **Sandārïsqay** [Сандарыскаі Дарыja], female byname (Pek.). ⇨ **SANDĀR.**

SANDEY see **SANDAY I.**

SANDÏ   Kzk. 1860 **Sandï** [Ерденъ Сандыбаевъ] (Konšin, Mat. V, 102); Kzk. 19th c. **Sandï-bay** [Сандыбай] (AOA 102); Kzk. 19th c. **Sandï-bay** [Сандыбай] (AOAtb. 2); Kzk. 19th c. **Sandï-bay** [Сандыбай] (AOK 6, 18, 78, 106, 110); Kzk. 19th c. **Sandï-bay** [Сандыбай] (AOA 150); Kzk. 19th c. **Sandï-bay** [Сандыбай] (SOK 26, 108, 110, 116, 190, 236); Kzk. 19th c. **Sandï-bay** [Сандыбай] (Grod., Pril. 50); Kzk. 19th c. **Sandï-bay** [Сандыбай] (SODž. 102); Uzb.? **Sandï-bay** [Сандыбай] (SKSO III, 20); Kzk. **Sandï-bek** [Сандыбекъ Турсунбаевъ] (SKSO II, 15); Kzk. 1846 **Sandï-bek** [Бикмурза Сандыбеков] (MKOP 157); *TN:* Kzk.? **Sandï-bay** [Сандыбай], a kurgan (burial mound) (KartaJAR XI); Kzk. 19th c. **Sandï-bay-qatïn** [Сандыбай-катынъ], a burial mound north of Caspian Sea (IIRGO XVII (Karta ur. Tentjaksor)). ⇨ **SAN** + suff. -*dï*.

SANDÏQ   Bashk. 1738 **Sandïq** [Иман Сандыков] (MIB III, 394); Oghuz? 11th c. - 12th c. **Sanduq** [صندوق], mamlūk/gulām (slave) of Usāma's family (Usāma 104); Selj. 1070, 1078 **Sanduq** [صندق التركى] (Kamāladdīn II, 16, 25, 56). ✧ 'Chest, box' cf. Crm., Kzk., Tat., Turk. *sandïq* 'der Kasten' (Radl. IV, 306).

SANDUQ see **SANDÏQ**

SANDUQAS   Chuv. 18th-19th c. **Sanduqas** [Сандукась] (Magn. 73). ✧ 'Nightingale' cf. Chag. *sanduγač* 'id.' (Radl. IV, 308).

SANGOR see **SOÑQUR**

SANΓAY   Kipch. 1298 **Sanγay** [صنغى], a chieftain (Baybars/Tizeng. I, 88, 111); Kzk. 19th c. **Sanγay** [Сангай] (AOK 6).

SANİK   Hak. 19th-20th c. **Sanik** [Саник], fem. (HRS 354).

SANÏ   Kzk. 19th c. **Sanï-bek** [Саныбекъ] (SOV 64); *TN:* Kzk.? **Sanï-bay** [Саныбай], a well? (KartaJAR X).

SANÏYAČ   Uyg. 12th c. - 14th c. **Sanïyač** [Sanïy(ï)nč] (Radl., USp. 57, DTS).

SANÏYÏNČ   Uyg. **Sanïyïnč** [Sanıyınç] (EUTS).

SANÏQ   Hak.(Sag.) 19th-20th c. **Sanïq** [Саныk] (Katanov, Otč. 11).

SANÏOT   Nog. 20th c. **Sanïot** [Аджымамбет Сапыот (!) увлы / Ажимамбет Сануотова], father of one of Baskakov's informants from Sarï-awul (Bask., Nog. 144).

SANKE   Kzk. 19th c. **Sanke** [Санке] (SOV 16). ⇨ **SAN** + suff. -*ke* <comp. -*ake*.

SANKEY   Kzk. 19th c. **Sankey** [Санкей] (AOA 98). ⇨ **SAN** + suff. -*key*.

SANKLÏ-SİN   Oghuz/Trkm. 13th c. **Sanklï-sin** [سانقلى سين] / Санклы-Син], Ǯanï-bek's envoy sent to the Türkmen (Abulg./Kon. 1300-1315).

SANQ see **SAÑΓ**

SANQÏ   Kzk. 1846 **Sanqï-bay** [Утябай Санкибаев], a biy (MKOP 152); Kzk. 19th c. **Sanqï-bay** [Санкибай] (Grod., Pril. 78); *TN:* Kzk.? 19th c. **Sanqï-bay** [Санкыбай / Санкибай], a lake on the plateau of Turgay (ZOOO 1870, 240, AUK 753).

SANQOR   Kzk. 19th c. **Sanqor-bay? / Soñqor-bay?** [Санкорбай] (AOA 126). ✧ 'Wonderment' cf. Chag. *sanqur* 'das Staunen, die Verwunderung' (Radl. IV, 302). ⇨ **SOÑQUR?**

SANMAR   Selj. 12th c. **Sanmar? / Sanamaz?** [عزيزالدين صنمار] (Muh. Ibrahim 51).

SANMÏŠ   Uyg. **Sanmïš** [Sanmış] (EUTS); Uyg. 8th c. - 12th c. **Sanmïš-qunčuy**, fem. (Müller, Pfahl. 23).

SANNALÏΓ   Karg. **Sannalïγ** [Санналыгъ] (Katanov: ZIRGOÊtn. XVII, vyp. III, 194). ✧ 'Clever, judicious' cf. Alt.(Leb.) *sanālïγ* / *sanālū* 'klug, einsichtsvoll' (Radl. IV, 300).

SANOP   Alt. 19th-20th c. **Sanop** [Саноп] (OjrRS 209).

SANOSQA   Hak. 19th-20th c. **Sanosqa** [Саноска] (HRS 351).

SANPİR   Hak. 19th-20th c. **Sanpir** [Санпир] (HRS 351).

SANRÏQ see **SAÑΓÏRÏQ**

SANSÏ   Kzk. 19th c. **Sansï-bay** [Сансыбай] (AOK 10).

SANSÏZ   Uyg. 1339 **Sansïs** [Sansis] (Chwol., Syr.-nest. (NF) 36); Khorezm.? 14th c. **Sansïs** [سانسز / Emir Sansis], Abaqa's (1265-1282) commander (Wassaf 102); Kzk.? **Sansïs-bay** [Сансыс-бай], a kurgan (burial mound) north of Lake Aral (KartaJAR XI); Kzk. 19th c. **Sansïs-bay** [Исымъ Сансысбаевъ] (Grod., Pril. 144); Uyg. 13th c. - 14th c. **Sansiz** [Sansiz] (Chwol., Syr.-nest. 98); Uyg. 1313 **Sansïz** (Chwol., Syr.-nest. (NF), 19); Kzk. 19th c. **Sansïz** [Сансызъ] (SOV 8, 158); Kirg. **Sansïz** [Сансыз] (Jud. 96, 780); Uyg. 762 **Sansïz / Sansïz-pačaγ?** [Türlüg Apa Sansïz Pačaq] (Mahrnāmag 10); Kzk. 1817 **Sansïz-bay** [صانسزباى / Сансыз] (MIK IV, 311, 318); Kzk. 19th c. **Sansïz-bay** [Самсызбай] (SODž. 4); Kzk. 19th c. **Sansïz-bay** [Сансызбай] (AOP 26); Kzk. 19th c. **Sansïz-bay** [Сансызбай] (Pam. kn. Turg. 60); Kkalp. 20th c. **Sansïz-bay** [Сансызбай] (KkRS 776); *TN:* Kzk. **Sansïs-bay** [Сансыс-бай], a field(?) at the Lake Aral (KartaJAR XI); Trkm. **Sansïz** [Сансызъ], a well (KartaJAR XVIII). ✧ 'Countless, innumerable' cf. Uyg., Kuman, Kzk., Tat. *sansïz* 'zahllos' (Radl. IV, 312). ⇨ **SAN?** + suff. -*sïz*.

SANT   Maml. 1428 **Sant-bay** [سنطباى الاشرفىّ] (Ibn Taghrīb. VI, 635); Maml. 1461 **Sant-bay** [ام سنطباى الظاهرى] (Ibn Taghrīb. VIII, 792); Maml. 1469/70 **Sant-bay** [سنطباى] (Iyās II, 116); Maml. 1483

Sant-bay [سنطباى العلا ئى الظاهـرى] (Iyās II, 220);
Maml. 1500/01 **Sant-bay** [الشيخ صنطباى], a šeyχ (Iyās
II, 377); Maml. 1458, 1461 **Sant-bay-qara**
[سنطباى قـرا الظاهـرى] / Suntbai] (Ibn Taghrīb. VIII,
323, Ibn Taghrīb. VII, 390, 430, Weil, Chalif. II, 283).
✥ 'Pastry board; anvil' cf. Maml. *sant* (<Ar.? سَنت)
(Unbekannt) 'Nudelbrett' (Tarǰ/Houtsma?), cf. also
Turk. *sant* 'die Akazie' (Radl. IV, 304), Chag. *sand*
(<P.) 'der Ambos' (Radl. IV, 304).

SANTAY Kzk. 19th c. **Santay** [Сантай] (AOK 6). ✥
'Hip, haunch'? cf. Kzk. PNs *San-bay* / *San-gerey*
(Žanuzakov-Esbaeva). ⇨ **SAN** + **TAY** +
suff. *-tay(1,2)*?

SANTÏQ Kzk. 19th c. **Santïq-pay** [Сантыкпай] (SOK
170). ⇨ **SANDÏQ?**

SANUQ Alt. 19th-20th c. **Sanuq** [Санук], fem. (OjrRS
213). ✥ Hypocoristic shortened form of R. fem.
Aleksandra (OjrRS).

SANZÄP Bashk. 1763 **Sanzäp** [Санзяп Аднагулов]
(MIB IV/1, 268); Bashk. 1764 **Sanzäp** [Санзяп
Алакаев] (MIB IV/1, 290); Bashk. 1776 **Sanzäp**
[Сююндюк Санзяпов] (MIB V, 44). ✥ 'Squirrel' cf.
Tat. PN *Sänjap* (Sattarov), Turk. *sinjab* 'das
Eichhörnchen' (Radl. IV, 699) (<Ar.). See also
ČAQČAQ, SAQÏL, TÏYEN.

SAÑAS Hak. 19th-20th c. **Sañas** [Санъас], fem. (HRS
354).

SAÑГ Kuman 1451, 1465 **Sanq** [Scancsalasa /
Zankzallasa], Szankszállása, a settlement of a man
called Sanq in Lesser Kumania, Hungary (Gyárfás III,
626, 651, for further data see Rásonyi, KÖA 123 and
Rásonyi, NTK 129); Kzk. 19th c. **Sañγ** [Сангъ] (AOO
50). ✥ 'Excrement of birds' cf. Karakh. *saŋ* 'птичий
помет' (DTS), Turk. *sanq* 'der Mist von Raubvögeln'
(Radl. IV, 302), cf. also Rásonyi, KÖA 123, NTK 129,
Anthr. 144.

SAÑГÏ Uzb. **Sañγï-bay** [Сангибай] (SKSO III, 23). ✥
'Wondering, surprised' cf. Chag. *sanγï* 'erstaunt, in die
Höhe fahrend' (Radl. IV, 302).

SAÑГÏL Kzk. 19th c. **Sañγïl** [Сангылъ] (SOK 274).

SAÑГÏRÏQ Kzk. 1714 **Sanrïq** / **Sañγïruq-batïr**
[صانكـروق بـاطر / Санрык] (MIK IV, 163); Kzk. 1725
Sanrïq-batïr [Санрык-батыр], thrashed the Kalmyks
in south-west of Turgay (Tynyšp. 67); Kzk. 1817
Sañγïrïq [صانكغـرق / Сангырык] (MIK IV, 309). ✥
'Dirt of a bird; guano' cf. Kzk. *sanγïrïq* 'kuşun pisliği'
(KzTS).

SAÑГÏRUQ see **SAÑГÏRÏQ**

SAÑQA Tat.(Sib.)? 1601 **Sañq** / **Sañqa?** [Юртъ
Санкинъ] (Andrievič, Ist. Sib. I, 52). ⇨ **SAÑГ?** +
suff. *-a/-qa*.

SAÑLÏ Nog. 20th c. **Sañlï-bay** [Асан Магомет улы
Санълыбай / Асан Магометович Санглыбаев],
Baskakov's informant from the aul of Erkin-χalq

(Bask., Nog. 143). ⇨ **SAÑГ** + suff. *-lï.*

SAÑNÄLÏГ Karg. **Sañnälïγ** [Санналыг] (Proben IX,
659).

SAÑUŠ Bashk. 1787 **Sañuš** [Иткучюк Сангушев]
(MIB V, 214, 215).

SAP Trkm. 20th c. **Sap-ǰan** [Sapǧan] (Zaj. 1971, 328);
Kzk. 19th c. **Sap-pay** [Саппай] (SOK 296). ✥ 'Clean,
pure, spotless' (Zaj. 1971), cf. Uyg. *sap* 'rein (von
Metallen)' (Radl. IV, 401), Kzk. *sap* 'чистый (без
примеси)' (RKzS), Trkm. *sāp* 'чистый;
возвышенный, нравственно безупречный'
(TrkmRS) (<P.<Ar.). See also **BAY-SAP, SANA-SAP.**

SAP-KÏREY Chuv. 18th-19th c. **Sap-kerey?**
[Сапкарей] (Magn. 73); Chuv. 18th-19th c. **Sap-kerey**
[Сапкерей] (Magn. 73); Chuv. 18th-19th c. **Sap-kirey**
[Сапкирей] (Magn. 73). ⇨ **SAP** + **KERÄY.**

SAP-POLAT Kzk. 19th c. **Sap-polat** [Сапполатъ]
(SOV 138). ✥ 'Pure steel'. ⇨ **SAP** + **BULAT.**

SAP-TAZA Kzk. 19th c. **Sap-taza** [Саптаза] (SOV
58). ✥ 'Clean-fresh'. ⇨ **SAP** + **TAZA.**

SAPA Trkm. 20th c. **Sapa** [Sapa] (Zaj. 1971, 329);
Trkm. 20th c. **Sapa** [Сапа] (TrkmRS 564); Kkalp. 20th
c. **Sapa** [Сапа] (KkRS 776); Kzk. 19th c. **Sapa-bay**
[Сапабай] (SODž. 66). ✥ I. 'Happiness, joy' (Zaj.
1971), cf. Trkm. *sapā* 'блаженство; блаженный,
довольный, умиротворенный' (TrkmRS) (<Ar.); II.
'Clearness, cleanness, righteousness' (Žanuzakov), cf.
Kzk. *sapa* 'качество' (KzRS), Kkalp. *sapa* 'id.'
(KkRS) (<Ar.). See also **MÄT-SAPA.**

SAPA-TAY Kzk. 19th c. **Sapa-tay** [Сапатай] (SOV 10,
14); Kzk. 19th c. **Sapa-tay** [Сапатай] (SODž. 30). ⇨
SAPA + **TAY?** + suff. *-tay(1,2)*? See also **SÏPA-TAY.**

SAPAY Bashk. 1723 **Sapay** [Сапай Бердишев] (MIB
III, 201); Bashk. 1735 **Sapay** [Сатлыкъ Сапаевъ], a
tarχan (Vel.-Zern., 24); Tat. 1696 **Sapay(ko)** [Сапайко
Кугаевъ] (Kungursk. akty 232); Bashk. **Sapey** [Сапей
Лавлиновъ], a tarχan (Vel.-Zern., Bašk. 21). ⇨
SAPA? + suff. *-y.*

SAPAQ I. Kzk. 1785 **Sapaq** [Сапак] (MIK IV); Kzk.
1794 **Sapaq** [صنق / Сапак] (MIK IV, 158); Kzk. 1803
Sapaq, chieftain of the Kerderi tribe, Little Horde (Kiši
Žüz) (MIK IV, 515); Kzk. 1817 **Sapaq** [صابـاق /
Сапак] (MIK IV, 311); Kzk. 19th c. **Sapaq** [Сапакъ]
(Lomakin 32); Kzk. 19th c. **Sapaq** [Сапакъ] (AOAtb.
34); Kzk. 19th c. **Sapaq** [Сапакъ] (AOA 126); Kzk.
19th c. **Sapaq** [Сапакъ] (AOK 2); Kzk. 19th c. **Sapaq**
[Сапакъ] (Protok. Turk. IV, 77); Kzk. 19th c. **Sapaq**
[Сапакъ] (SOK 38); Kzk. 19th c. **Sapaq** [Сапакъ]
(SODž. 24, 76); Kzk. 19th c. **Sapaq** [Сапакъ] (SOV
46, 72, 76); Kzk. 19th c. **Sapaq-bay** [Сапакбай] (SOK
276); Kzk. 19th c. **Sapaq-bay** [Сапакбай] (AOK 14).
✥ I. 'Stock, handle' cf. Chag. *sapaq* 'der Stiel, der
Stengel' (Radl. IV, 403); II. 'Thread, wire; stem, stalk'

cf. Chag., Alt., Hak., Kzk. *sabaq* 'der Zwirn, der Nähfaden, der Halm, der Stengel, die Knopföse' (Radl. IV, 412), East.T. *sapaq* 'die Knopföse' (Radl. IV, 403); III. 'Little cleanness, righteousness'. ⇨ **SAPA?** + suff. *-q*.

SAPAQ II.   Chuv. 18th-19th c. **Sapak** [Сацакъ (Сапак)] (Magn. 73). ✧ 'Cluster, bunch' cf. Chuv. *sabak* 'traube (von beeren), büschel' (Paas.).

SAPAQ-PAS   Kzk. 19th c. **Sapaq-pas** [Сапакпасъ] (AOK 38). ⇨ **SAPAQ I.** + **BAŠ.**

SAPAQAY   Bashk. **Sapaqay** [Сапакай Смаиловъ], a tarχan (Vel.-Zern., Bašk. 18). ⇨ **SAPA(Q) I.** + suff. *-(q)ay.*

SAPAR see **SAFAR**

SAPAR-ALÏ   Kzk. 19th c. **Sapar-alï** [Сапаралы] (AOK 18); Kkalp. 20th c. **Sapar-γaliy** [Сапарғалий] (KkRS 776). ⇨ **SAFAR** + **ALİ.**

SAPAR-GELDİ see **SAFAR-GELDİ**

SAPAR-ГАLİY see **SAPAR-ALİ**

SAPAR-NİYAZ   Kkalp. 20th c. **Sapar-niyaz** [Сапарнияз] (KkRS 776). ⇨ **SAFAR** + **NİYAZ.**

SAPÏ   Kzk. **Sapï** [Сапы] (Radl. I, 457); Kzk. 1823 **Sapï-bay** [صاپی‌بای / Сапибай] (MIK IV, 455). ✧ I. 'A kind of sword' cf. Kzk. *sapï* 'eine Art Dolch, Säbel' (Radl. IV, 404); II. '(The) chosen' (Ar.) (Žanuzakov).

SAPÏR   Alt. 19th-20th c. **Sapïr** [Сапыр] (OjrRS 209); Kzk. 19th c. **Sapïr-bay** [Сапирбай] (SOK 34).

SAPÏŠ see **SABÏŠ**

SAPÏŠ I.   Kzk. 19th c. **Sapïš** [Сапышъ] (SOV 36). ⇨ **SAP(Ï)?** + suff. *-ïš / -š.*

SAPÏŠ II.   Alt. 19th-20th c. **Sapïš** [Сапыш] (OjrRS 209).

SAPPAR see **SAFAR**

SAPRA   Nog.? **Sapra** [Сапра] (Žirm., Epos 410).

SAPROQ   Alt. 19th-20th c. **Saproq** [Сапрок] (OjrRS 209).

SAPRON   Hak. 19th-20th c. **Sapron** [Сапрон] (HRS 351). ✧ Sofron (R.) (HRS).

SAPUŠ see **SABÏŠ**

SAPŪQ   Hak.(Sag.) 19th-20th c. **Sapūq** [Сапук] (Katanov, Otč. 7); Alt. **Sopoq** [Сопок] (ORS 210). ✧ 'Boots' cf. R. *sapog* 'id.' (Katanov; OjrRS).

SAR see **SARÏ?**

SAR-ALTÏN   Alt. 19th c. **Sar-altïn** (<Sara-altïn?) [Сар-Алтын] (Verb., In. 154, 155); Alt. **Sar-altïn** (<Sarï-altïn) [Сар-Алтын] (Verb., In. 154). ✧ 'Pure (yellow?) gold'. ⇨ **SARA I.** / **SARÏ** + **ALTÏN.**

SAR-BAQ   Bashk. 1740 **Sar-baq** [Сарбак Кулушов] (MIB I, 404); Kzk. **Sar-baq** [Сарбакъ] (SKSO VIII, 222). ✧ 'Pure (yellow?)-Luck'? ⇨ **SARA I.** / **SARÏ** + **BAQ?**

SAR-BALTA   Chuv. 18th-19th c. **Sar-balta** (<Sarï-balta) [Сарбалта] (Magn. 73). ⇨ **SARÏ** + **BALTA.**

SAR-BAS see **SARÏ-BAŠ**

SAR-BAŠLARÏ see **SARÏ-BAŠ**

SAR-BUГA see **SARÏ-BUГA**

SAR-BULA   Kzk. 1846 **Sar-bula** [Сары Гуджи Сарбулин] (MKOP 153). ⇨ **SARÏ** + **BULA?**

SAR-BULAT see **SARÏ-BULAT**

SAR-ČOLAN   Kzk. 19th c. **Sar-čolan** (<Sarï-čolan) [Сарчоланъ] (SOK 58). ⇨ **SARÏ?**

SAR-ESKEY   Kzk. 19th c. **Sar-eskey** [Сарескей] (AOP 46). ⇨ **SARÏ?** + **ESKEY.**

SAR-ESTEK   Kzk. 19th c. **Sar-estek** [Сарестекъ] (AOA 14). ⇨ **SARÏ?** + **ESTEK.**

SAR-FUFAY   Kzk. 19th c. **Sar-fufay** [Берсокаръ Сарфуфаевъ] (Grod., Pril. 74). ⇨ **SARÏ.**

SAR-ГAZAQ   Kzk. 19th c. **Sar-γazaq** (<Sarï-qazaq?) [Саргазаковъ] (AOO 30). ⇨ **SARÏ** + **QAZAQ.**

SAR-ГİLDAQ   Kzk. 19th c. **Sar-γïldaq** [Саргылдак], forefather of the Qara-tay clan (Potanin II, 7). ⇨ **SARÏ.**

SAR-ÏZAQ   Kzk. 19th c. **Sar-ïzaq** (<Sarï-uzaq) [Сарызаковъ] (AOK 62). ⇨ **SARÏ** + **UZAQ?**

SAR-ÏŽAQ   Kzk. **Sar-ïžaq** (<Sarïǰaq?) [Сарыжакъ] (Valihanov, Soč. 386). ⇨ **SARÏ** + **UZAQ?** See also **SAR-ÏZAQ?**

SAR-KÖPEY   Kzk. 19th c. **Sar-köpey** (<Sarï-köpey) [Саркопей] (AOK 6). ⇨ **SARÏ.**

SAR-MAL see **SARÏ-MAL**

SAR-ŌLAX see **SARÏ**

SAR-SÄLİ   Kzk. 19th c. **Sar-säli** (<Sarïs-äli?) [Сарсали] (SOK 140); Kzk. 19th c. **Sar-seli** (<Sarïs-äli?) [Сарселы] (SOK 46). ⇨ **SARÏ** + **SALİ II.?**

SAR-SEKEY   Kzk. 19th c. **Sar-sekey** (Sarïs-ekey?) [Сарсекей] (AOP 98). ⇨ **SARÏ** + **SEKE?** + suff. *-y.*

SAR-TAY see **SARÏ-TAY**

SARA I.   Kzk.?, Uzb.? 1691 **Sara** [Сара], a murza from Turkestan (DAI X, 376, 386); Kkalp. 20th c. **Sara** [Сара], fem. (Bask., Kkalp. 404); Kkalp. 20th c. **Sara** [Сара], fem. (KkRS 778); Bashk. 1695 **Sara-bay** [Сара-бай Елубаев] (MIB I, 92); Uzb. 19th c. **Sara-bibi** [Сарабиби], fem. (Sr. Az. I, 1896, avg. 15); Tat.(Sib.) 1607 **Sara-gil / Sara-γul?** [Сарагил] (Miller, Ist. Sib. II, 204); Kkalp. 20th c. **Sara-gül / Sere-gül,** fem. (Baskakov: OSA 141); Tat.(Sib.) 1600 **Sara-γul** [Бегов Сарагул] (Miller, Ist. Sib. II, 159); Bashk. 1710 **Sara-γul** [Сююш Сарагулов] (MIB III, 60); Tat. 1600 **Sara-γul-beg** [Есаул Сарагулбегов] (MIB I, 152); Kzk. 1898 **Sara-qïz** [Сара-кызъ], from the Nayman tribe, the heroine of قصة برجان صال (Kazan 1898) (AUK Dobavl. 3). ✧ I. 'True, real, genuine; pure, clean' cf. Chag. *sara* 'echt, rein' (Radl. IV, 314), Kkalp. *sara~sere* (P.) 'лучший, отборный' (Baskakov: OSA 141); II. 'Manliness, strength' cf. Chag. *sara* 'der Muth, die Kraft' (Radl. IV, 314); III. 'Moon' cf. Mo. *sara* 'id.' (Poppe). See also **D'AMAN-SARA, GÜL-SARA, TAY-SARA, TAL-SARA,**

TOK-SARA, TOL-SARA, TOP-SARA.

SARA II.   Yak. **Sara-bay-toyon** [Сарабаі-тojoн], a Kirghiz from whom, according to tradition, the Yakuts originate (Pek.).

SARA-BİL   Kzk. **Sara-bil** [Найда Сарабилевъ] (SKSO III, 26). ⇨ **SARA I. + BİL.**

SARA-YAZ   Bashk. 1697 **Sara-yaz** [Каракучючка Сараязовъ] (Vel.-Zern., Bašk. 31); Bashk. 1735 **Sara-yaz** [Тлевкей Сараязовъ], a tarχan (Vel.-Zern., Bašk. 18). ⇨ **SARA I. + YAZ.**

SARA-TAY see SARÏ-TAY

SARA-TOZ   Tat.(Sib.) 1637 **Sara-toz** [Саратоз], fem. (Miller, Ist. Sib. II, 444). ⇨ **SARA I. + TUZ?**

SARAЈ   Turk. 19th c. **SaraЈ** [Saraȝ], a Zeybek tribe (āširet) in the region of Aydın, Turkey (Kúnos 1891, 117). ✧ 'Leather worker; saddler' cf. Turk. *saraǰ* 'der Lederarbeiter, der Sattler' (Radl. IV, 318) (<Ar.).

SARAXAN   NUyg.(Tar.) 19th c. **Saraχan** [ساره خان / Сара-ханъ], fem. (Pantusov, Pesni 105, Pantusov, Tar. 165). ⇨ **SARA I. + suff. -χan(1).**

SARAY   Tat.(GH) 1408, 1409 **Saray** [Сараи Усаховъ сынъ / Сарай], a prince of the Horde (PSRL VI, 136, XI, 205, XXIII, 142); Maml. 1379/80 **Saray** [صراى الرحبى لطوبى] (Iyās I, 246); Trkm. 20th c. **Saray** [Saray] (Zaj. 1971, 330); Chuv. 18th-19th c. **Saray** [Сарай] (Magn. 73); Bashk. 1742 **Saray** [Биган Сараев] (MIB III, 513); Tat.(Mish) 19th c. **Saray-χan** [Saraiχan] (Pelissier 25); Tat.(GH) 1374, 1375 **Sarayko** [Сарайко], a murza of the Horde (PSRL VIII, 21-22, XI, 20); *EN:* Nog. 20th c. **Saray-küp** [Сарай куьп], a Qara-noγay tribe (Bask., Nog. 137); Nog. 20th c. **Sarayli̇-uruw** [Сарайлы урув], a Qara-noγay clan (Bask., Nog. 136). ✧ 'Palast' cf. Uyg., Kuman, Kzk., Tat. etc. *saray* 'das Haus, das Schloss, die Karavansarai, der Stall, der Wagenremise' (Radl. IV, 315). See also **İL-SARAY, KİL-SARAY, QRÏM-SARAY.**

SARAY-ВUГА   Kipch. 1282, 1283, 1291 **Saray-buγa** [صَرَاى بغا / Saraiboga / Сарайбуга], Mengü-temür's son (Baybars/Tizeng. I, 82, 104, Nuwairī/Tizeng. I, 134, 155, Abulfidā V, 100-01). ✧ 'Palace-bull' (Bese 17). ⇨ **SARAY + BUQA.**

SARAY-TEMİR   Maml. 14th c. **Saray-tämür** [صَرَانْ تَمُرْ] (Sauvaget 49); Kipch. 1313/14 **Saray-temir** [صراى تمر] (Aynī/Tizeng. I, 486, 515); Maml. 1376/77, 1390 **Saray-temir** [صراى تمر المحمدى], an emir (Iyās I, 231, 286, Weil, Chalif. I, 528, 566); Maml. 1399/400 **Saray-temir** [صراى تمر الناصرَى], atabeg of Haleb (Ibn Taghrīb. VI, 33, Weil, Chalif. II, 77). ⇨ **SARAY + TEMİR.**

SARAYBA see ÜRÄYBÄ-SARAYBA

SARAQ   Kzk. 19th c. **Saraq-mende** [Саракменде] (SOK 102); Kzk. 19th c. **Saraq-pay** [Саракпай] (SOV 4, 134). ⇨ **SARÏQ?**

SARALDAY   Alt. **Saralday** [Саральдай] (Nikiforov 127).

SARALÏMA   Yak. **Saralïma** [Сырдык-Саралыма-Ытык-Тумалыма], part of the name of a fabulous shamaness (Pek.).

SARAM-BAY see SARAÑ

SARAMAN   Bashk. 1740 **Saraman** [Калмакай Сараманов] (MIB I, 405). ⇨ **SARA / SARÏ? + suff. -man.**

SARAN see SARAÑ

SARAN-BALTA   Chuv. 18th-19th c. **Saran-balta** [Саранбалта] (Magn. 73). ⇨ **SARAÑ? + BALTA.**

SARAN-DÏLDA   Kzk. **Saran-dïlda** [Sarandylda / Сарандылда], a khan (Proben III, 592 /673/). ✧ 'Miserly coin'? ⇨ **SARAÑ + TİLLA.**

SARANČA   Bashk. 1740 **Saranča** [Муртаза Саранчин] (MIB I, 397). ⇨ **SARAÑ + suff. -ča.**

SARANČÏ   Kzk. 19th c. **Sarančï** [Саранчи] (SOK 134). ⇨ **SARAÑ + suff. -čï.**

SARANČUQ   Tat.(GH) 1333 **Sarančuq / Sarayčuq?** [Саранчюкъ], envoy of the Tatar (PSRL X, 206). ⇨ **SARAÑ + suff. -čïq.**

SARANDAY   Chuv. 18th-19th c. **Saranday** [Сарандай] (Magn. 73); Chuv. 18th-19th c. **Sarandey** [Сарандей] (Magn. 73). ⇨ **SARAÑ? + suff. -day.**

SARANDEY see SARANDAY

SARAÑ   Kzk. 1816 **Saram-bay < Saraň-bay** [Сарамбай Буринъ] (TOUAK XXIV, 74); Chuv. 18th-19th c. **Saran** [Саранъ] (Magn. 73); Chuv. 18th-19th c. **Saran-bay** [Саранбай] (Magn. 73); Maml.? 1395 **Saraň-χan / Sara-bek-χan?** [سَارَ نْك خان] (Ibn Taghrīb. VI, 78). ✧ 'Parsimonious, miserly; weak, sickly; imbecil, stupid' cf. Alt., Hak., Kzk., NUyg.(Tar.), Tat., etc. *saraň* 'geizig; schwach, kränklich, wenig Speise zu sich nehmend, wahnsinnig, blödsinnig, schwachsinnig, verdreht' (Radl. IV, 316-317), Uyg., Alt., Tat. *saran* 'geizig' (Radl. IV, 317).

SARAÑUČ   Uyg. 12th c. - 14th c. **Saraňuč** (Radl., USp. 3-4, DTS). ✧ 'Little niggard/miser' (Bese 5), cf. Uyg. *saran* 'id.' (DTS), Kirg. *saraň* 'id.' (Jud.) + dim. suff. -uč.

SARAPANAY   Yak. **Sarapanay-χotun** [Ан-Сарапанаі-хотун], fem. (Pek.).

SARAS   Alt. 19th-20th c. **Saras** [Capac] (OjrRS 209). ✧ 'Siberian mink (Mustela sibirica)' cf. Alt. *saras* 'колонок' (OjrRS).

SARAW   Nog.? **Saraw** [Capay] (Žirm., Epos 402).

SARBA   Bashk. 1732 **Sarba** [Сарба Зиянов] (MIB III, 302).

SARBAN   Bashk. 1740 **Sarban** [Сарбан Кулушев] (MIB I, 396); Kirg. **Sarban** [Сарбан], a servant (qul) (Proben V, 527 /531/). ✧ 'Wog' cf. Turk. *sarban* (<P.) 'der Kameeltreiber' (Radl. IV, 342). See also

SAWRAN?

SARČ-AYAQ see **SARIČ-AYAQ**

SARČA   Kzk. 19th c. **Sarča** [Нурманъ Сарчиновъ] (Grod. 161); Kzk. 19th c. **Sarča < Sariča?** [Сарча] (SOV 26); Kzk. 19th c. **Sarče** [Сарче] (SOV 48). ✧ 'An old kind of bow' cf. Kzk. *sarža* 'ein Bogen mit Knocheninkrustationen' (Radl. IV, 339), *sarja* 'mit Horn ausgelegter Bogen' (Radl. IV, 337), *sarca* [=*sarja*] 'eski zamandaki yayın bir çeşidi' (KzTS).

SARČE see **SARIČA**

SARČIK   Chuv. 18th-19th c. **Sarčik** [Сарчикъ] (Magn. 74). ⇨ **SARI?** + suff. *-čiq*.

SARJĀNA   Yak. **Sarjāna-bātïr** [Сарцана батыр] (Pek.).

SARDAÑA-ČĀN   Yak. **Sardaña-čan** [Сарданачан], fem. (Pek.). ✧ 'Shine-smoke/boiler?' cf. Yak. *sardaña* 'сияние (солнца, луны или молнии)ъ блистание, яркий свет, луч; заря' + *čān* 'чад, дым; большой котёл' (Pek).

SARɣAČÏQ   Tat.(Sib.) 1581 **Sarγačïq** [Саргачикъ], a ruler from Ishim (Sib. Let. 318, 342). ✧ 'Small wooden vessel' cf. Alt., Hak. *sarγas, sarγaš* 'ein halbrundes Gefäss mit dünnen Boden und Wänden' (Radl. IV, 332-33).

SARɣALDAQ   Kzk. 18th c. - 19th c. **Sarγaldaq** [Саргалдак] (Tynyšp. 71); Kzk. 19th c. **Sarγaldaq** [Саргалдакъ] (AOAtb. 42). ✧ 'Tulip' cf. Kzk. *sarγaldaq* 'id.' (KzkRS).

SARɣALTAY   Kzk. 19th c. **Sarγaltay** [Саргалтай], according to Kazak traditions he is Chinggis Khan's son (Potanin II, 149); Kzk. 19th c. **Sarγaltay** [Саргалтай] (Potanin II, 149).

SARɣÏTMÏŠ   Maml. 1351, 1356, 1358 **Sarγïtmïš** [السيفى صرغتمس / Sargitmich], an emir, chief of the Corps of Mamluks from 1351, died in 1358 (Mayer 208-209, Iyās I, 196, 200, 202 etc., Berchem No. 161-62); Maml. 1467 **Sarγïtmïš** [صرغتمس] (Ibn Taghrīb. VIII, 612). ✧ 'Suspended; dropped to the ground?' cf. Sauvaget 49: 'il a pendu, été suspendu', 'il est tombé a terre', 'il a dégoutte'; „le nom insolite doit se justifier par quelque incident ayant marqué le début de la né de l'enfant". Cf. also Crm., Turk. *sarqit-* 'herablassen, sich herabstürzen' (Radl. IV, 330-31), Tat. *sarqit-* 'herabtröpfeln lassen, tropfenweise ausgiessen' (Radl. IV, 331).

SARɣUČ   Tat.(Sib.) 1643 **Sarγuč** [Саргуч] (Miller, Ist. Sib. II, 487).

SARXÏT see **SARQÏT**

SARIJEK   Hak. 19th-20th c. **Sarijek** [Саричек], fem. (HRS 354). ✧ 'Little Blond' cf. Hak. fem. PN *Sari* 'светлая (Butanaev). ⇨ **SARI** + dim. *-jek*.

SARI   Bashk. 1738 **Sar-bay (<Sarï-bay)** [Сарбай Атиев] (MIB III, 394); Bashk. 1783 **Sar-bay (<Sarï-bay)** [Сарбай Бекембетев] (MIB V, 143); Bashk. 1783 **Sar-bay (<Sarï-bay)** [Сарбай Бекембетев] (MIB V, 143); Kzk. 19th c. **Sar-bay (<Sarï-bay)** [Сарбай (бакса)] (AUK 494); Kzk. 19th c. **Sar-bay (<Sarï-bay)** [Сарбай] (AOK 6); Kzk. 19th c. **Sar-bay (<Sarï-bay)** [Сарбай] (AOO 74); Kzk. 19th c. **Sar-bay (<Sarï-bay)** [Моллаханъ Сарбаевъ] (Grod., Pril. 149); Kzk. 19th c. **Sar-bay (<Sarï-bay)** [Сарбай] (SOK 244); Kzk. 19th c. **Sar-bay (<Sarï-bay)** [Сарбай Тулесовъ,] (AUK 877); Kzk. 19th c. **Sar-biy (<Sarï-biy)** [Сарбій] (AOAtb. 10); Kzk. **Sar-jigit (<Sarï-jigit)** [Сарджигитъ] (Sov 26); Kzk. 19th c. **Sar-jigit (<Sarï-jigit)** [Сарджигитъ] (SOV 26); Bashk. 1740 **Sar-yan (<Sarï-yan?)** [Сарьян] (MIB I, 423); Kzk. 18th c. - 19th c. **Sar-mïrza** [Сармырза] (Tynyšp. 66); Hak. 19th-20th c. **Sar-ōlaχ** [Сароолах] (HRS 351); Bashk. 1798 **Sar-pay (<Sarï-pay)** [Сарбаевъ] (PSZRI XXV, 196); Kzk. 19th c. **Sar-pay (<Sarï-pay)** [Сарпай] (SOK 268); Kzk. 19th c. **Sar-pek (<Sarï-pek)** [Сарпекъ] (SODž. 100); Kzk. **Sar-žan (<Sarï-žan)** [Sarshan / Саржан], Äl-žän's brother (Proben III, 78 /100/); Kzk. 1845 **Sar-žan (<Sarï-žan)** [Иржанъ Саржановъ] (Konšin, Mat. V, 62); Uyg. 1283 **Sari?** [Sari'] (Chwol., Syr.-nest. (NF) 10); Yürük 1543 **Sarï** [Sarı] (Gökb., Rum. 240); Yürük 1543 **Sarï** [Sarı] (Gökb., Rum. 216, 226); Trkm. 20th c. **Sari** [Sarï] (Zaj. 1971, 333); Bashk. 1714 **Sarï** [Байрамили Сарыев] (MIB I, 105); Kzk. **Sarï** [Сары Махмедовъ] (SKSO VIII, 200); Kzk. **Sarï** [Сары Итемгеневъ] (Valihanov, Soč. 347); Kzk. **Sarï** [Сары] (SKSO VIII, 206); Kzk. 18th c. - 19th c. **Sarï** [Сары], forefather of several clans (Tynyšp. 65, 67, 68, 69, 71 etc.); Kzk. 1817 **Sarï** [صارى / Сары] (MIK IV, 311); Kzk. 19th c. **Sarï** [Сары] (AOK 70); Kzk. 1879 **Sarï** [Иркэ Сарыевъ] (Grod., Pril. 130); Kzk. 1879 **Sarï** [Сари] (Grod., Pril. 182); Kzk. 1879 **Sarï** [Малай Саріевъ] (Grod., Pril. 126); Kkalp. 20th c. **Sarï** [Сары] (Bask., Kkalp. 401); Kkalp. 20th c. **Sarï** [Сары] (KkRS 776); Alt. 19th-20th c. **Sarï** [Сары], fem. (OjrRS 213); Bashk. 1757 **Sarï / Sara?** [Мукаш Сарин] (MIB IV/1, 149); Trkm. 20th c. **Sarï-bay** [Sarïbay] (Zaj. 1971, 333); Tat.(Sib.) 1654 **Sarï-bay** [Сарыбай] (AI IV, 229); Kzk. **Sarï-bay** [Сарыбай] (SKSO VIII, 200); Kzk. **Sarï-bay** [Sary Bai / Сары Байы] (Proben III, 47 /62/); Kzk. 1820 **Sarï-bay** [Сарыбай] (Sib. Vest. XI, 16); Kzk. 19th c. **Sarï-bay** [Сарыбай] (AOAtb. 6); Kzk. 19th c. **Sarï-bay** [Сарибай] (Grod., Pril. 188); Kkalp. 20th c. **Sarï-bay** [Сарыбай] (Bask., Kkalp. 75); Kkalp. 20th c. **Sarï-bay** [Сарыбай] (KkRS 776); Kirg. **Sarï-bay** [Сарыбай] (Jud. 94, 571, 691); Uzb. **Sarï-bay** [Сарыбай] (SKSO III, 162); Kzk. 19th c. **Sarï-bala** [Сарыбала] (SOV 112); Alt. 19th-20th c. **Sarï-bala** [Сарыбала], fem. (OjrRS 213); Crm. **Sarï-batïr** [Сары Батыръ] (Proben VII, 21); Kzk. 1805 **Sarï-**

batïr [Сарыбатырь], a leader of the Greater Horde (Ulu Žüz) (MIK IV, 512); Kzk. 1820 **Sarï-batïr** [Сары-батыръ], sultan of Sara-usun of the Ǯalayïr clan (Sib. Vest. IX, 101); Kirg. 19th c. **Sarï-batïr** [Сары Батыровъ] (AUK 338); Crm. **Sarï-bäk** [Сары Бäк] (Proben VII, 212); Trkm. 1802 **Sarï-bek** [Кусабъ-Батыръ Сарыбековъ] (PSZRI XXVII, 139); Kzk. **Sarï-bï / Aq-sarï-bï** [Ak Sary Bï / Ак Сары Бï], often mentioned only as *Sarï-bï* (Proben III, 94 /120/); Tat. 1545 **Sarï-čora** [Саричора] (Kn. Metriki Lit. 22); Kzk. 19th c. **Sarï-jan** [Сарыджан] (Grod., Pril. 170); Alt. 19th-20th c. **Sarï-γïs** [Сарыгыс], fem. (OjrRS 213); Bashk. 1777, 1779 **Sarï-γul** [Сарыгул Жанымов] (MIB V, 96); Bashk. 1777, 1779 **Sarï-γul** [Сарыгул Иштаκов] (MIB V, 57); Kkalp. 20th c. **Sarï-γül** [Сарыгул], fem. (KkRS 778, Baskakov: OSA 141); Trkm. 1844 **Sarï-χaji** [Сары-хаджи] (MIT II, 494); Trkm. 19th c. **Sarï-χan** [Сары-ханъ] (IIRGO XXI, 9); Tat.(GH) 1370, 1371 **Sarï-χoža** [Сары хожа], envoy of the Horde (PSRL VIII, 17, XI, 15); Trkm. 1838 **Sarï-yüzbašï** [Мухаммед Сары-юзбаши] (MIT II, 473); Kzk. **Sarï-qan-bay** [Сары-кан-баи] (Proben III, 221); Crm. **Sarï-qanïm** [Сары Каным], fem. (Proben VII, 129); Alt. 19th-20th c. **Sarï-qïs (<Sarï-qïz)** [Сарыкыс], fem. (OjrRS 213); Kzk. 19th c. **Sarï-qïz** [Сарыкызъ] (SOK 94); Kzk. 19th c. **Sarï-qïz** [Сарыкызъ], fem. (Grod. I, 98); Kzk. **Sarï-qul** [Сарыкулъ] (SKSO VIII, 203, 207); Kzk. 18th c. - 19th c. **Sarï-qul** [Сарыкул] (Tynyšp. 71, 73); Kzk. 19th c. **Sarï-qul** [Сарыкулъ] (Lomakin 33); Kirg. **Sarï-qul** [Сарыкул] (Jud. 25); Bashk. 1663 **Sarï-mergen** [Сарымерген] (MIB I, 161); Uzb. 1594 **Sarï-oγlan** [ساری اوغلان / Sâri-Oghlân], governor in Urgench under Abdullah, the Khan of Bukhara (Abulg./Desm. 282 /263, 267/); Kzk. 19th c. **Sarï-pek** [Сарыпекъ] (SODž. 80); Trkm. 1867 **Sarï-serdar** [Сары-сердар], from the Yomut tribe (MIT II, 633, 634, 635, 636 etc.); Alt. 19th-20th c. **Sarï-ül** [Сары-уул] (OjrRS 209); Uyg. 12th c. - 14th c. **Sarïγ** (Radl., USp. 124); Uyg. 12th c. - 14th c. **Sarïγ** [sarïγ / Sarïg] (DTS, EUTS); Hak. 19th-20th c. **Sarïγ** [Сарығ] (HRS 351); Hak.(Blt.) 19th-20th c. **Sarïγ** [Сарыҥ] (Proben IX, 362, 366); Hak.(Sag.) 19th-20th c. **Sarïγ** [Сарыҥ] (Katanov, Otč. 7); Hak. 19th-20th c. **Sarïγ-χïs** [Сарыг-Хыс], fem. (HRS 354); Hak. 19th-20th c. **Sarïγ-ōl** [Сарыг-Оол] (HRS 351); Uyg. 12th c. - 14th c. **Sarïq-toyïn** (Radl., USp. 208, 250); Uyg. 12th c. - 14th c. **Sarïq-toyïn / Sarïγ-toyïn** [Sarïq Toyïn / sarïγ tojïn] (Radl., USp. 208, 250, DTS); Yürük 1543 **Saru** [Saru] (Gökb., Rum. 219); Crm. 14th c. **Saru-bek** [صارو بك / Sârôu bec], Qutlu-demür's brother, Toluq/Toγluq-temür's son (Ibn Bat. II, 362); Turk. 1385 **Saru-χan** [صاروخان / Sârôu khân], lord (sultan) of Magnisia (Manisa), Turkey

(Āšikp. 52, 56, 61, Ibn Bat. II, 313, Jorga, Notes XIII, 339); Turk.?, Maml.? 1400? **Saru-χan** [صاروخان] (Ibn Taghrīb. VI, 385); Yürük 1543 **Saru-χan** [Saruhan] (Gökb., Rum. 193, 214); Yürük 1543 **Saru-χan** [صارو خان / Saru-han] (Gökb., Rum. 104, 193, 214); Trkm. 1745 **Saru-χan** [Сару-хан], from the Qaraχlu (?) tribe (MIT II, 173-177, 181); Tat. 1543 **Saru-χan** [Saruhan] (Gökb., Rum. 241, 242); Turk. 14th c. **Saru-χan / Sar-χan** [Σαρχάνης / Saruhan Bey], a prince from the dynasty of Saruhan-oğulları (1300-1345) (Moravcsik 269-270, Uzunçarş., Anad. 10, 27, 28, 31, 84, Baştav 78); Turk. 15th c. **Saru-χatun** [صارو خاتون], in the days of Mohamed (Muhammmad) I (Āšikp. 153); Tat.(Tüm.) 1639 **Saru-ol** [Саруоль Якшеев] (Miller, Ist. Sib. II, 453); Trkm. 20th c. **Sārï** [Сары] (TrkmRS 567); *EN:* Turk. 1554 **Saru-χan(iler)** [Saruhaniler cemaatı], a (Yürük?) tribe (Gökčen 37); *TN:* Bashk. 1715 **Sarï-bay** [Сарыбай], a river (MIB III, 123); Kzk. **Sarï-bay** [Сарыбай], a well (Karta JAR XIX); Turk. 20th c. **Sarï-beyli** [Sarıbeyli], a village in the province of Sakarya, Turkey (TMİB 733); Turk. 20th c. **Sarï-qïz** [Sarıkız], a village in the province of Malatya, Turkey (TMİB 609); Turk. 20th c. **Sarï-qïz** [Sarıkız], a village in the province of Konya, Turkey (TMİB 566); Turk. 20th c. **Sarï-oγlan-palas** [Sarıoğlan], a village in the province of Kayseri, Turkey (TMİB 529). ✧ 'Blond, fair; red' cf. Karakh., Uyg. *sarïγ* 'желтый; бледный; соловый (о масти лошади)' (DTS), Hak. *sarïγ* 'жёлтый; русый; блондин' (HRS), Trk. *sarïγ* 'gelb' (TMEN III, No. 1207), Kuman, Alt., Kirg., Kzk., Tat., Turk. etc. *sarï* 'gelb, bleich' (Radl. IV, 320). – E. g. *Sarï-bala* 'Blond child; child with light-coloured hair'. See also **AY-SARÏ, AQ-SARÏ, ALP-SARÏ, ALTÏN-SARÏ, ATA-SARÏ, BAY-SARÏ, BABA-SARÏ, ČEL-SARÏ, ǮAN-SARÏ, ǮAÑQ-SARÏ, ER-SARÏ, ERKÄ-SARÏ, GÜL-SARÏ, İR-SARÏ, YAMAN-SARÏ, YAVLAQ-SARÏΓ, KENE-SARÏ, KÜL-SARÏΓ, QAN-SARÏΓ, QARA-SARÏ, QOY-SARÏ, QUL-SARÏ, MALAY-SARÏ, POQAY-SARÏΓ, SUΓAN-SARÏ, TABA-SARÏ, TADA-SARÏ, TUΓAY-SARÏ, UZUN-SARÏ.**

SARÏ-ALTAY Kzk. 1792 **Sarï-altay** [Сарыалтай] (MIK IV, 139); Kzk. 1799, 1803, 1820 **Sarï-altay** [Сары-Алтай / Сары Алтай / Сарыалтай], one of the chieftains of the Alim-ulï tribe (Mejer 25, MIK IV, 514, Sib. Vest. IX, 115); Kzk. 1804 **Sarï-altay** [Сары Алтай], chieftain of the Qulaman tribe (MIK IV, 222). ⇨ **SARÏ + ALTAY.**

SARÏ-ASLAN Trkm. 1835 **Sarï-aslan** [Хасан-хан Сары Аслан] (MIT II, 231, 233). ⇨ **SARÏ + ARSLAN.**

SARÏ-BAΓÏS Kzk. 19th c. **Sarï-baγïs** [Сарбагысъ] (SOV 106); Kzk. 19th c. **Sarï-baγïz** [Сарыбагызъ] (SOK 276). ⇨ **SARÏ + BAΓÏS.**

SARÏ-BAГÏZ see **SARÏ-BAГÏS**

SARÏ-BAQAL   Uzb.? **Sarï-baqal** [Сарыбакаловъ Мамутчанъ], a merchant from Khazaraz (Turk. Kraj 1912, 14). ⇨ **SARÏ** + **BAQAL**.

SARÏ-BAS see **SARÏ-BAŠ**

SARÏ-BAŠ   Kzk. **Sar-bas** (<**Sarï-bas**) [ﺻﺎﺭﺑﺎﺱ / Сарбасъ] (Syzdykov 354); Kzk. 19th c. **Sar-bas** (<**Sarï-bas**) [Сарбасъ] (Potanin II, 5); Kzk. 19th c. **Sar-bas** (<**Sarï-bas**) [Масупъ Сарбасовъ] (AUK 153); Kzk. 19th c. **Sar-bas** (<**Sarï-bas**) [Сарбасъ] (AOAtb. 50); Kzk. 19th c. **Sar-bas** (<**Sarï-bas**) [Сарбасъ] (Grod., Pril. 152); Kzk. 19th c. **Sar-bas** (<**Sarï-bas**) [Сарбасъ] (SOK 168); Bashk. 1670 **Sar-baš** (<**Sarï-baš**) [Сарбашевъ] (Vel.-Zern., Bašk. 37); Bashk. 1727 **Sar-baš** (<**Sarï-baš**) [Сарбаш Тиулин] (MIB III, 245); Bashk. 1740 **Sar-baš** (<**Sarï-baš**) [Чермыш Сарбашев] (MIB I, 392); Bashk. 1746 **Sar-baš** (<**Sarï-baš**) [Сарбаш Бекчюрин] (MIB III, 435); Bashk. 1764 **Sar-baš** (<**Sarï-baš**) [Солтан-мрат Сарбашев] (MIB IV/1, 298); Balk. 20th c. **Sar-bašlarï** (<**Sarï-bašlarï**) [Sarbášları], an Özden-family (Pröhle, Balk. 250); Kzk. 18th c. - 19th c. **Sarï-bas** [Сарыбас] (Tynyšp. 74); Kzk. 19th c. **Sarï-bas** [Сарыбасъ] (SOK 22); Kzk. 1742 **Sarï-baš** [Сарыбаш] (MIB I, 486); Kzk. 19th c. **Sarï-baš** [Сарыбашъ] (Grod., Pril. 82); Kirg. **Sarï-baš** [Сарыбаш] (Jud. 876); Alt. 19th-20th c. **Sarï-baš** [Сарыбаш], fem. (OjrRS 213); Alt. 19th-20th c. **Sarï-baš** [Сарыбаш] (OjrRS 209); Chag. **Sarïγ-baš** [ﺳﺎﺭﻳﻐﺒﺎﺵ] (Le Coq, Ind. 3); Uyg. **Sarïγ-baš-tarχan** (Müller, Pfahl. 10); Hak. 19th-20th c. **Sarïγ-pas** [Сарығ-Пас], fem. (HRS 354); *TN:* Kzk.? **Sarï-baš** [Сары басъ] (KartaJAR XI). ✧ 'Yellow(ish) head; light-coloured head; flaxen'. ⇨ **SARÏ** + **BAŠ**.

SARÏ-BÏYÏQ   Turk. 20th c. **Sarï-bïyïq** [Sarıbıyık], a village in the province of Ağrı, Turkey (TMİB 52). ✧ 'Yellow moustache' cf. Turk. *bıyık* 'moustache' (TED), Maml. (Kipch.) *byjyk* 'Schnurrbart' (Tarj/Houtsma). ⇨ **SARÏ** + **MÏYÏQ**.

SARÏ-BUГA   Khorezm.? **Sar-buγa** (<**Sarï-buγa**) [Sár Bughá], an emir, Temür's officer (Tar. Rashidi 32, 49); Maml. 1390 **Sar-buγa** (<**Sarï-buγa**) [ﺻﺮ ﺑﻐﺎ ﺍﻟﻨﺎﺻﺮﻯ] (Iyās I, 292); Maml. 1406 **Sar-buγa?** (<**Sarï-buγa**) [ﺳﺮ ﺑﻐﺎ], a Master of the Horse (Ibn Taghrīb. VI, 186); Chag. **Sar-buγa** (<**Sarï-buγa**) [Сарбуга], grand-father of one of Uluγ-beg's concubines (Mihr-sultan) (Barth., Ulugb. 116); Khorezm./Chag.? 1376/77 **Sarï-buγa** [Сары-Буга], an emir (MIT I, 516, 517 (after Qazwīnī)); Maml. 1313 **Saru-buγa** [ﺻﺎﺭﻭ ﺑﻐﺎ ﻣﻦ ﺗﻜﻼﻥ ﻣﻦ ﻋﺴﻜﺮ ﻃﻐﺘﺎﻯ] (Dawād. 272, 275 etc.). ✧ 'Yellow-bull'. ⇨ **SARÏ** + **BUQA**.

SARÏ-BULAT   Chuv. 18th-19th c. **Sar-bulat** (<**Sarï-bulat**) [Сарбулатъ] (Magn. 73); Tat. 1624 **Sar-bulat** (<**Sarï-bulat**) [Сарбулатъ Сарауловъ] (Pokrovskij

70); Nog. 1649 **Sar-pulat** (<**Sarï-pulat**) [Сарпулатъ] (AI IV, 87). ⇨ **SARÏ** + **BULAT**.

SARÏ-BÜNÄ   Kzk. 1846 **Sarï-bünä** [Сары-Буня Кинжегарин], a biy (MKOP 152). ⇨ **SARÏ**.

SARÏ-ČAL   Kzk. 19th c. **Sarï-čal** [Сарычалъ] (SOK 258). ⇨ **SARÏ** + **ČAL**.

SARÏ-ČÄLBÄGÄN   Hak.(Shor) 19th-20th c. **Sarï-čälbägän** [Сары-Чälбäгäн] (Radl. II, 648). ⇨ **SARÏ** + **YÄLBÄГÄN**.

SARÏ-ČİČÄN   Tat.(Bar.) **Sarï-čičän** [Сары Чічäн], fem. (Proben IV, 66 /81/). ⇨ **SARÏ** + **ČEČEN**.

SARÏ-ČOBAN see **QOÑUR-QOJA**

SARÏ-JALA   Kzk. 1785 **Sarï-jala-bahadïr** [ﺳﺎﺭﻯﺟﻼ ﺑﻬﺎﺩﺭ] (MIK IV, 52, 54). ⇨ **SARÏ** + **ČALA**.

SARÏ-DÏWANA   Kzk. **Sarï-diwana** [Сарыдиванаевъ] (SKSO VIII, 230). ✧ 'Yellow/blond beggar' cf. Chag., East.T. *divanä* 'ein verrückter, ein Bettler, ein Derwisch' (Radl. III, 1779). ⇨ **SARÏ**.

SARÏ-ГUT   Kzk. 19th c. **Sarï-γut** [Мамабетъ Али Саригутовъ] (Grod., Pril. 98). ⇨ **SARÏ** + **QUT**.

SARÏ-YATÏ   Selj. 13th c. **Sarï-yatï / Saru-yatï?** [ﺻﺎﺭﻭﻳﺎﺗﻰ / Sary jaty], Er-toγrul's son, Osmān's brother [Gündüz-alp], in Jihān-numā always mentioned as *Sarï-bāli* (ﺻﺎﺭﻯ ﺑﺎﻟﻰ), in other sources *Saru-bati* (Nešrī XIII, 196). ⇨ **SARÏ**.

SARÏ-YUSUN   Kzk. 19th c. **Sarï-ysum-bay** (<**Sarï-yusum-bay**<**Sarï-yusun-bay**) [Сарийсюмбай] (SOK 228); Kzk. 19th c. **Sarï-yusun / Sarï-uysun** [Сары-Юсунъ (Уйсун)], forefather of the Kirey tribe of the Kazaks (Potanin II, 3). ⇨ **SARÏ** + **YUSUN**.

SARÏ-KÜČÜK   Kzk. 19th c. **Sarï-küčük** [Сарыкучукъ] (SOK 246). ⇨ **SARÏ** + **KÜČÜK**.

SARÏ-QALMAŠ   Oghuz/Trkm. 14th c. - 15th c. **Sarï-qalmaš / Sarï-qulmas / Sarï-qulmaš?** [ﺻَﺎﺭﻯْ ﻗُﻠْﻤَﺎﺵْ / Sarı Kulmas / Sarï Qulmaš / Сары-Калмаш], İlik-(Elig- / Eylik)-qoja's son (DQorq./Ergin 96, DQorq./Rossi 136, DQorq. 23, etc.). ⇨ **SARÏ** + **QALMAŠ**.

SARÏ-QARNAY   Trkm. 1817 **Sarï-qarnay-serdar** [Сары Карнай-сердар], from the Yomut tribe (MIT II, 400, 411, 412, 415 etc.). ⇨ **SARÏ** + **QARNAY**.

SARÏ-QOŠ   Kzk. 19th c. **Sarï-qoš** [Сарыкошъ] (AOP 46). ⇨ **SARÏ** + **QUŠ I**.

SARÏ-QOZГAL   Kzk. 19th c. **Sarï-qozγal** [Сарыкозгалъ] (AOAtb. 6). ⇨ **SARÏ**. See also **SARÏ-QOZГAN?**

SARÏ-QOZГAN   Kzk. 19th c. **Sarï-qozγan** [Сарыкозганъ] (AOAtb. 10). ⇨ **SARÏ** + **QUZГAN**.

SARÏ-QULANČİ   Oghuz/Trkm. 1360/61 **Sarï-qulanči / Sarïq-qulanči** [Сары-куланчи / Сарык-куланчи], Timur's guide (MIT I, 513). ⇨ **SARÏ** + **QULANČİ**.

SARÏ-QULMAS see **SARÏ-QALMAŠ**

SARÏ-MAY   Kzk. 1787 **Sarï-may-bey** [Сарымай]

(MIK IV, 100). ⇨ **SARÏ** + **MAY.**

SARÏ-MAL Kzk. 19th c. **Sar-mal (<Sarï-mal)** [Сармалъ] (SOK 304). ⇨ **SARÏ** + **MAL.**

SARÏ-MAMÏT Kirg. **Sarï-mamït** [Сары Мамыт] (Jud. 844). ⇨ **SARÏ** + **MAMÏT.**

SARÏ-MOYUN Kzk. 19th c. **Sarï-moyun** [Сары-Моюнъ] (AUK 421). ⇨ **SARÏ** + **MOYUN.**

SARÏ-OΓLAN-PALAS Selj. 1247 **Sarï-oγlan-palas** [صارى اوغلان بلاس], mentioned in a vakfiye (Turan: Belleten XII, 100, 120). ✧ 'Yellow-boy-rag?' cf. Chag. *palas* 'ein kleiner Teppich' (Radl. IV, 1165), Turk. *palas* (P.) 'coarse textile; rag' (TED). ⇨ **SARÏ** + **OΓLAN.**

SARÏ-SALTÏQ Selj. / Turk.? 1263 **Sarï-saltïq** [Sarı Saltık] (Uzunçarş., Anad. 33). ⇨ **SARÏ** + **SALTÏQ.**

SARÏ-SÏY Kzk. 19th c. **Sarï-sïy** [Сарысый] (SOK 216). ✧ 'Yellow/blond - gift/present' cf. Kzk. *sïy* 'подарок, награда, премия', *sïy qonaq* 'почётный гость' (KzRS). ⇨ **SARÏ** + **SÏY.**

SARÏ-SOÑQUR Selj.? 1195 **Sarï-soñqur? / Sara-soñqur?** [سراسنقر], an emir (Ibn al-Athīr/Tornb. XII, 77, 84). ⇨ **SARÏ / SARA I.?** + **SOÑQUR.**

SARÏ-TAY Bashk. **Sar-tay (<Sarï-tay)** [Енаберде Сартаевъ], a tarχan (Vel.-Zern., Bašk. 11); Kzk. 1817 **Sar-tay (<Sarï-tay)** [Сартай] (MIK IV, 308); Kzk. 1846 **Sar-tay (<Sarï-tay)** [Сартай] (MKOP 86); Tat. 18th-19th c. **Sara-tay** [Саратай] (Magn. 73); Kzk. 1788 **Sarï-tay-bey** [Sarytaï-bey] (Levchine 280); Kzk. 19th c. **Sarï-tay** [Sarïtay] (AChr. 82); Nog. 19th c. **Sarï-tay** [Сары-тай], from the Qara-Noγays (Anan'ev 49). ✧ 'Yellow foal', 'Red foal' (Anan'ev). ⇨ **SARÏ** + **TAY** + suff. *-tay(1,2)*?

SARÏ-TAL Kzk. 19th c. **Sar-tal (<Sarï-tal)** [Сарталъ] (SOV 26). ⇨ **SARÏ** + **TAL.**

SARÏ-TÏRMAŠ Kzk. 19th c. **Sarï-tïrmaš** [Сары Тырмаш], (great/first) shaman of the Qayraqan tribe (Potanin IV, 328). ⇨ **SARÏ** + **TURMAŠ?**

SARÏ-TOQOY Kirg. 19th c. **Sarï-toqoy** [Сарытокой], an ancestor of the J̌as-tabans (Potanin II, 5). ✧ 'Yellow forest' cf. Kirg. *toqoy* 'лес; тугай' (Jud.). ⇨ **SARÏ.**

SARÏ-TOQTAY Maml. 14th c. **Sar-toqtay (<Sarï-toqtay)** [سرطقطاى] (Zetterst. 194, 208). ⇨ **SARÏ** + **TOQTAY.**

SARÏ-UYSUM see **SARÏ-YUSUN**

SARÏ-UYSUN see **SARÏ-YUSUN**

SARÏ-ZEYBEK Turk. 19th c. **Sarï-zeybek** [Szári-zejbek], a hero of Zeybek songs (Kúnos 1891, 116). ✧ 'Yellow/blond Zeybek' cf. Turk. *zeybek* 'Turk from southwestern Anatolia in traditional costume' (TED). ⇨ **SARÏ.**

SARÏBAN Kzk. 19th c. **Sarïban** [Сарыбанъ] (SOK 182). ⇨ **SARBAN?**

SARÏBAR Kirg. **Sarïbar** [Джунусъ Сарыбаровъ]

(Pojarkov 14).

SARÏČ Tat. 1601 **Sarïč** [Ишмамет Сарычев] (Miller, Ist. Sib. II, 165); Tat. 1633 **Sarïč** [Саричъ / Сарычъ] (Kuznecov 1). ✧ 'A kind of kite' (Sattarov) cf. Tat. *sarïč* (TatRS).

SARÏČ-AYAQ Kzk. 19th c. **Sarč-ayaq** [Сарчаякъ] (SOV 68). ⇨ **SARÏČ** + **AYAQ.**

SARÏČA Kzk. 19th c. **Sarïča** [Сарыча] (SOK 190); Kzk. 19th c. **Sarïča** [Сарычаевъ] (Grod., Pril. 112). ✧ I. 'Yellowish'? cf. Kzk. *sarïša* 'gelblich' (Radl. IV, 325); II. 'A kind of bow'? ⇨ **SARČA?**

SARÏČEY Bashk. 1734 **Sarïčey / Sarïča?** [Аликей Сарычеев] (MIB III, 325). ⇨ **SARÏČA.**

SARÏJA Maml. 1310 **Sarïja** [شهاب الدين صاروجه المظفرى الحسامى] (Dawād. 211, 257); Yürük 1543 **Sarïja** [صارى/جه/ / Sarıca] (Gökb., Rum. 102, 214 etc.); Khorezm.? 14th c. **Saruja** [ساروجة الصغير / Sâroûdjah Assaghîr], an emir (Ibn Bat. II, 444); Maml. 1332 **Saruja** [شهان الدين صاروجه النخرى النقيب], an emir (Dawād. 365, 367 etc.); Maml. 14th c. **Saruja** [صاروجه] (Sauvaget 48); Maml. 14th c. **Saruja** [صاروجه الحسامى] (Zetterst. 155, 160); Turk. 15th c. **Saruja** [Σαρουτζᾶς], an Ottoman grand vizier (Byz. Turc. 269); Turk. 1457 **Saruja** [Saruca bin Abdullah] (Gökb., Ed. 352); Yürük 1543 **Saruja** [Saruca] (Gökb., Rum. 181, 184, 213 etc.); Tat. 1543 **Saruja** [Saruca] (Gökb., Rum. 232, 235, 236, 237, 238); Turk. 1451 **Saruja-paša** [صاروجه پاشا] (Āšikp. 129, 197); Turk. 16th c. **Saruja-paša** [Saruca Paşa] (Gökb., Ed. 234, 247); *EN:* Yürük 1611 **Sarïjalar** [Sarıcalar], a tribe (cemaat) (Gökçen 82); *TN:* Turk. 20th c. **Sarïjalar** [Sarıcalar], a village in the province of Konya, Turkey (TMİB 565); Selj.? 12th c. **Saruja(-mesjit)** [صاروجا /مسجد/], a small mosque (Ibn Šaddād, Alep. 86). ✧ 'Little yellow, little blond' (Sauvaget 48), cf. Turk. *sarïča, sarïja* 'gelblich; irregulare Truppen' (Radl. IV, 325), Kzk. *sarïša* 'id.' (Radl. IV, 325); II. 'A kind of bird of prey with yellow back' cf. Chag. *sarïča* 'ein kleiner Raubvogel mit gelben Rücken; eine Krankheit der Pferde' (Radl. IV, 328).

SARÏΓ see **SARÏ**

SARÏΓ-ADAY Hak. 19th-20th c. **Sarïγ-aday** [Сарыг-Адай] (HRS 351). ✧ 'Yellow dog'. ⇨ **SARÏ** + **ADAY I.**

SARÏΓ-BAŠ see **SARÏ-BAŠ**

SARÏΓ-PAS see **SARÏ-BAŠ**

SARÏΓ-ČÏR Türk 750 **Sarïγ-čïr** [Sarïγčïr / sarïγčïr] (Thomsen, Stein 186, 188, ETY II, 65, DTS). ✧ 'Yellow-?'. ⇨ **SARÏ.**

SARÏΓ-SAMAN Uyg. 12th c. - 14th c. **Sarïγ-saman** [] (Radl., USp. 213, 254, DTS). ✧ 'Yellow Straw' (Blagova 1997, 705). ⇨ **SARÏ** + **SAMAN.**

SARÏГ-TARBA   Karg. **Sarïγ-tarba** [Сарыгъ Тарба] (Katanov: ZIRGOÊtn. XVII vyp. III, 164); Karg. **Sarïγ-tarba** [Сарыгъ Тарба богатыръ] (Proben IX, 630). ✧ 'Yellow wizardry/incantation' cf. Alt., Hak. *tarba* 'die Verhexung, die Besprechung' (Radl. IV, 871). ⇨ **SARÏ**. See also **TARBA-KİNJİ**.

SARÏY   Tat. 1553 **Sarïy** [Сарый-богатырь] (PSRL XIII, 230); Bashk. 1735 **Sarïy** [Сарый Кадралинъ], a tarχan (Vel.-Zern., Bašk. 21); Kzk. 1826 **Sarïy** [Сарый Баубековъ] (TOUAK XXIV, 162); Nog. 20th c. **Sarïy** [Базархан Сарый къызы], father of Bazar-χan, one of Baskakov's informants from Sarï-awul (Bask., Nog. 144); Kzk. 1846 **Sarïy / Sarï?** [Бий Темир Сарыев] (MKOP 86). ✧ Sari (Ar.)? 'known, famous, valuable; noble' (Žanuzakov 156).

SARÏQ see **SARÏ**

SARÏQ   Kzk. 19th c. **Sariq-pay** [Сарекпай] (SOK 160); Tat.(Sib.) 1637 **Sarïq** [Сарык] (Miller, Ist. Sib. II, 443, 444); Kzk. 19th c. **Sarïq** [Сарыкъ] (SOK 104); Kzk. 19th c. **Sarïq** [Сарикъ] (SODž. 162); Kzk. 19th c. **Sarïq-bay** [Сарыкбай] (SODž. 144); Kzk. 19th c. **Sarïq-bay** [Сарыкбай] (SOK 262). ✧ 'Sheep' cf. Kzk., Tat. *sarïq* 'das Schaf; das russische Schaf' (Radl. IV, 322). See also **ALÏM-SARÏQ, QULAN-SARÏQ**.

SARÏM   Tat. 1624 **Sarïm** [Узбенъ Сарымовъ] (Pokrovskij 70); Kzk. 1846 **Sarïm** [Казы Сарымов], a biy (MKOP 152); Kzk. 19th c. **Sarïm** [Сарымъ] (AOK 14); Kzk. **Sarïm-bay** [Сарымбай] (Konšin, Oč. 81); Kzk. 19th c. **Sarïm-bay** [Сарымбай] (SODž. 44); Chag. 15th c. - 16th c. **Sarïm-sultan** [سايم سلطان], a Sheybanid (Šejb. LII); *EN:* Kzk. 1846 **Sarïm** [Сарым], a branch, part of Čümekey (MKOP 86); *TN:* Turk. 20th c. **Sarïm-bey** [Sarımbey], a village in the admionistrative province of Yozgat, Turkey (TMİB 899). ✧ 'Sharp sword / sabre' cf. Turk. *sarïm* 'ein scharfer Säbel; ein schwerer, befehlshaberischer Charakter' (Radl. IV, 326).

SARÏMBET   Tat. 1819 **Sarïmbet** [Сарымбетъ Унтагаровъ] (PSZRI XXXVI, 29); Kzk. 18th c. - 19th c. **Sarïmbet** [Сарымбет] (Tynyšp. 67). ⇨ **SARÏ** + suff. *-(i)mbet*.

SARÏMSAQ   NUyg. 19th c. **Samsaq / Sāmsaq** (Le Coq, Namenl. 114); 1758 **Sarïmsaq** [Sarymsak], from Eastern Turkestan (ArchKR XXII, 71); Kzk. 19th c. **Sarïmsaq** [Сарымсаковъ] (Grod., Pril. 117); Kzk. 19th c. **Sarïmsaq** [Сарымсакъ] (Nalivkin 16); Kzk. 19th c. **Sarïmsaq** [Сарымсакъ] (SKSO VIII, 201-33); Uzb. 1839 **Sarïmsaq** [Сарымсакъ Азаматовъ], from Tashkent (Konšin, Mat. V, 20); Uzb. 19th c. **Sarïmsaq** [Sarymsak], Šir-ali-χan's son (Nalivkin-Dozon 178, 182); Uzb. 19th c. **Sarïmsaq** [Сарымсак] (TV 1878, 144); Uzb. 19th c. **Sarïmsaq** [Сарымсакъ Хайталиевъ] (SKSO III, 168); Kzk. 1862 **Sarïmsaq-bay** [Sarymsak-baï], from (a place? called) Talaq of the

Nayman tribe (Nalivkin-Dozon 240); Uzb. 1848 **Sarïmsaq-murza** [Сарымсакъ Мурза] (Moskal'cev 34); Kzk. 19th c. **Sarmsaq (<Sarïmsaq)** [Джалкиши Сармсакбаевъ] (Grod., Pril. 60). ✧ 'Garlic' cf. Kuman, Crm., Kzk., Tat. *sarïmsaq* 'der Lauch, der Knoblauch' (Radl. IV, 326).

SARÏN   NUyg.? / Kzk.? 1864 **Sarïn-bek** [Сарынбекъ], from Eastern Turkestan (Valihanov, Soč. 515). ⇨ **SARÏM?**

SARÏÑQ   Kzk. 19th c. **Sarïñq-pay** [Сарынкпай] (SOK 172).

SARÏŠ   Kzk. **Sarïš** [Sarysch / Сарыш] (Proben III, 47 /62/).

SARÏT   Kzk. 19th c. **Sarït** [Джорунбай Сарытовъ] (Grod., Pril. 58); Kzk. 19th c. **Sarït-pay (<Sart-pay?)** [Сарытпай] (SOK 82).

SARKE   Kzk. 18th c. - 19th c. **Sarke** [Сарке] (Tynyšp. 75); Kzk. 19th c. **Sarke** [Сарке] (AOK 94); Kzk. 19th c. **Sarke** [Сарке] (SOK 128). ⇨ **SARÏ** + suff. *-ke*. See also **BAY-SARKE**.

SARQA   Hak. 19th-20th c. **Sarqa** [Сарка] (HRS 351). ⇨ **SARKE?** See also **YAN-SARQA**.

SARQAM-BAY see **SARQAN**

SARQAN   Kzk. 19th c. **Sarqam-bay (<Sarqan-bay?)** [Саркамбай] (SOV 50); Kzk. 19th c. **Sarqam-bay (<Sarqan-bay?)** [Саркамбай] (SOK 178).

SARQÏL   Yak. **Sarqïl-χotun** [Кÿн Цöлöрÿмä Саркыл-хотун], foremother of the evil spirit Altan Sabaray-toyon and all his family (Pek.).

SARQÏL-BAŠ   Oghuz **Sarqïl-baš** [Саркылбаш], a commander in the Oghuz-name by Salar-baba (Muhamedova: OSA 171). ⇨ **SARQÏL + BAŠ.**

SARQÏM-BEK see **SARQÏN**

SARQÏN   Kzk. 19th c. **Sarqïm-bek (<Sarqïn-bek)** [Саркымбекъ] (AOA 2). ✧ 'He who fell behind; last (child)'? cf. Kzk. *sarkın* 'arta kalan, son damla, son lokma' (KzTS).

SARQÏNDÏ   Trkm. 1731 **Sarqïndï-oγlï** [سرقندى اوغلى محمد], from Anatolia (Refik, Anad. 186).

SARQÏT   Kzk. 19th c. **Sarqït** [Саркытъ] (SOV 40); Kzk. 19th c. **Sarqït-pay** [Саркытпай] (SOK 66); Kzk. 1822 **Sarqït / Sarχït?** [صرقت / Сархыт] (MIK IV, 416); Kzk. 19th c. **Sarqït-bay** [Саркытбай] (AOO 18); Kzk. 1823 **Sarqït-bay / Sarχït-bay** [صارقطباى / Сархытбай] (MIK IV, 459). ✧ '(The) rest/end, remainder; alms' cf. Kzk. *sarqït* 'die Ueberbleibsel vom Essen und Trinken, die man den Weibern und Niedrigstehenden giebt' (Radl. IV, 331).

SARQÏTMÏŠ   Maml. 1352 **Sarqïtmïš** [صرغتمش] (Iyās I, 196, 200, 208); Maml. 1376/77 **Sarqïtmïš** [صرغتمش الاشرفى] (Iyās I, 231); Maml. 1399 **Sarqïtmïš** [صرغتمش لمحمدى] (Iyās I, 313); Maml.

1412/13 **Sarqïtmïš** [صرغتمش القلمطاوىّ] (Ibn Taghrīb. VI, 315); Maml. 1421 **Sarqïtmïš** [صرغتمش الناصرى] (Iyās II, 10). ✧ '(He) let (him) down' cf. Crm., Turk. *sarqït-* 'herablassen, sich herabstürzen' (Radl. IV, 330).

SARQOWOY Alt. **Sarqowoy?** [Сарковой] (OrjRS 209).

SARLÏ Bashk. 18th c. **Sarlï-bay** [Сарлыбай] (Nepljuev 896-97); Kzk. 19th c. **Sarlï-bay** [Сарлыбай] (AOP 10); Kzk. 19th c. **Sarlï-bay** [Сарлыбай] (Pam. kn. Turg. 76); Kzk. 19th c. **Sarlï-bay** [Сарлыбай] (AOP 66); Kzk. 19th c. **Sarlï-bay** [Сарлыбай] (AOAtb. 46); Kzk. 19th c. **Sarlï-bay** [Сарлыбай] (SOV 110); Kzk. 19th c. **Sarlï-bay** [Сарлыбай] (SOK 12). ✧ 'Powerful, strong' cf. Kirg. *sār* 'die Gewalt, der innere Gehalt, die Gestalt' (Radl. IV, 313) + suff. *-lï.*

SARMAKAY Chuv. 18th-19th c. **Sarmakay** [Сармакай] (Magn. 73). ⇨ **SARMAQ?** + suff. *-ay.*

SARMAQ Chuv. 18th-19th c. **Sarmak** [Сармакъ] (Magn. 73); Kzk. 1828 **Sarmaq** [Сармакъ] (Dobrosm., Turg. 354); *TN:* Bashk. 1752 **Sarmaq(ovo)** [Сармаково], a village (MIB IV/1, 59).

SARMAN Tat.(Mish.) 1737 **Sarman** [Сарман Ермеев] (MIB I, 315); Bashk. 1744 **Sarman** [Бигим Сарманов] (MIB III, 415); Bashk. 1777 **Sarman** [Тумачи (Туманчи / Тумача) Сарманов] (MIB V, 57); Kzk. **Sarman** [Аулъ Сармановъ] (Patkanov II, 92); Kzk. 19th c. **Sarman** [Сарманъ] (SODž. 36); Kzk. 19th c. **Sarman** [Сарманъ] (SOV 52); Kzk. 19th c. **Sarman** [Сарманъ] (SOK 272); Kzk. 19th c. **Sarman** [Сарманъ] (Grod., Pril. 104, 134); Kzk. 19th c. **Sarman** [Сарманъ] (AOAtb. 14); Kzk. 19th c. **Sarman** [Сарманъ] (AOO 66); Kzk. 19th c. **Sarman** [Сарманъ] (AOK 70); Kkalp. 20th c. **Sarman** [Сарман] (KkRS 776); Kzk. 19th c. **Sarman-bay** [Илеу Сарманбаевъ] (Grod., Pril. 62); Uzb. **Sarman-bay** [Сарманбай] (SKSO III, 8); Kkalp. 1822 **Sarman-behadïr** [Сарман бехадыр] (MIKk. 127); *EN:* Kzk. 19th c. **Sarman-ili** [Utalmay Sarman ili] (Ljutš 135). ✧ I. 'Moonlit' cf. Mo. *sar* 'луна' + suff. *-man* (Žanuzakov); II. '(The) Moon rose' cf. Mo. *sar* 'ay [Moon]' + Mo. *mandaw* 'čïqtï [rose / has risen]' (Sattarov); III. 'Yellow, blond' (Sattarov). ⇨ **SARÏ?** + suff. *-man.*

SARMAN-TAY Kzk. **Sarman-tay** [Сармантаi] (Proben III, 79 /102/). ⇨ **SARMAN** + **TAY** or suff. *-tay.*

SARMANAY Tat. 1704 **Sarmanay** [Мрекай Сарманаевъ] (Kurdjumov 341-42). ⇨ **SARMAN** + suff. *-ay.*

SARMANDAY Chuv. 1739 **Sarmanday** [Иванъ Сармандаевъ] (Nikol'skij 70). ⇨ **SARMAN** + suff. *-day.*

SARMAS Chuv. 18th-19th c. **Sarmas** [Сармасъ] (Magn. 73).

SARMAŠ Bashk. 1710 **Sarmaš** [Сармаш Курманаев] (MIB III, 57); Bashk. 1711 **Sarmaš** [Сармаш Карманаев] (MIB III, 68); Bashk. 1744, 1752, 1755 **Sarmaš** [Сармаш Ураев] (MIB III, 416, MIB IV/1, 64, 97); Bashk. 1751 **Sarmaš** [Мамай Сармашев] (MIB IV/1, 51).

SARMSAQ see **SARÏMSAQ**

SARNAQAY Kzk. 19th c. **Sarnaqay** [Сарнакай] (SOV 50).

SARP-ATUN Uyg. 12th c. - 14th c. **Sarp-atun** [sarp atun] (DTS).

SARSA Kzk. 19th c. **Sarsa-bek** [Сарсабекъ] (SOK 212); Kzk. 19th c. **Sarse** [Сарсе] (SODž. 26, 28); Kzk. 19th c. **Sarse-bay** [Сарсебай] (SOV 44).

SARSE see **SARSA**

SARSEY Nog. 20th c. **Sarsey** [Согъан Сарсей увлы / Согон Сарсеев], father of one of Baskakov's informants from the settlement Terekli-mektep (Bask., Nog. 144). ⇨ **SARSE** + suff. *-y.*

SARSEM-BAY see **SARSEN**

SARSEN Kzk. 19th c. **Sarsem-bay (<Sarsen-bay)** [Сарсембай] (AOAtb. 38); Kzk. 19th c. **Sarsem-bay (<Sarsen-bay)** [Сарсембай] (AOO 42); Kzk. 19th c. **Sarsem-bay (<Sarsen-bay)** [Сарсембай] (AOK 70); Kzk. 19th c. **Sarsem-bay (<Sarsen-bay)** [Сарсембай] (SOV 16, 50); Kzk. 19th c. **Sarsen** [Сарсенъ] (AOK 46); Kzk. 19th c. **Sarsen** [Сарсенъ] (AOO 30); Kkalp. 20th c. **Sarsen** [Сарсен] (Bask, Kpk. 401); Kzk. 19th c. **Sarsen-bay** [Сарсенбай] (AOK 6); Kzk. 19th c. **Sarsen-bay** [Сарсенбай] (AOA 126); Kzk. 19th c. **Sarsen-bay** [Сарсенбай] (AOAtb. 2); Kkalp. 20th c. **Sarsen-bay** [Сарсенбай Нуржан-улы] (Bask, Kpk. 48); Kzk. 19th c. **Sarsïm-bay** [Сарсымбай] (AOK 62). ✧ 'Thursday; child born on Thursday' (Žanuzakov 156) (<Ir.).

SARSÏ Kzk. 19th c. **Sarsï-bay** [Сарсыбай] (AOO 58).

SARSÏГ Kipch. **Sarsïγ** [Сарсыг-хан] (RaD I/2, 208); Kipch. **Sarsïγ** [سرسيغ خان], served to the sultan of Samarkand (Juwaynī I, 90); Kipch. 1219 **Sarsïγ-χan** [Сарсыг-Ханъ], from the Qañlï tribe (RaD/Ber. III, 58).

SARSÏM-BAY see **SARSEN**

SART Bashk. 1712 **Sart** [Аслан Сартов] (MIB III, 85); Kzk. 1817 **Sart** [صارت / Сарт] (MIK IV, 311); Bashk. 1780 **Sart-bay** [Бигиш Сартбаев] (MIB V, 103); Tat.(Sib.) 1629 **Sart-qul** [Сарткул], a murza (Miller, Ist. Sib. II, 360); Kzk. 19th c. **Sart-pay** [Сартпай] (SOK 4); *TN:* Bashk. 1717 **Sart(ova)** [Сартова], a village (in Nogajskie dorogi) (MIB III, 161). ✧ 'Sart (ethnic name); merchant; urban inhabitant' cf. Uyg., Chag., Alt., Kzk., Turk. *Sart* 'der Sarte (der türkisch sprechende Städtebewohner Mittelasiens); der Kaufman; ein Geschlechsname der Altajer; alle Städtebewohner Mittelasiens (Kzk.)' (Radl. IV, 335).

See also **ADAM-SART, AQ-SART, ǰUL-SART, QARA-SART**.

SART-APAY   Kzk. 19th c. **Sart-apay** [Сартапай] (SODž. 80). ⇨ **SART + APAY**.

SART-ČAN   Kzk. 19th c. **Sart-čan** [Сартчань] (SOV 120). ⇨ **SART + ǰAN +** / suff. *-čan*.

SARTAQ-TAY   Alt. **Sartaq-tay** [Сартакпай / Сартактай] (ZSOIRGO XXXVIII, 145); Alt. **Sartaq-tay** [Сартактай] (Nikiforov 242); Alt. 19th c. **Sartaq-tay** [Сартактай] (Potanin, Pred. 188); Alt. 1879 **Sartaq-tay** [Сартактай], a character in a tale (Potanin IV, 285). ✧ 'Iranian; Sart (urban Uzbek)' (Sattarov). ⇨ **TAY** or suff. *-tay(1,2)*.

SARTAN   Tat.(Mish.) 1739 **Sartan** [мещеряк Сартан Бильмеев] (MIB I, 373); Kzk. 1846 **Sartan** [Сасык Сартанов], a biy (MKOP 155).

SARTÏQ   Bashk. 1749 **Sartïq** [Чаптар Сартыков] (MIB III, 460). ✧ 'Iranian; Sart (urban Uzbek)'?

SARTÏQ-TAY   Alt. **Sartïq-tay** [Сартыктай] (Nikiforov 244). ✧ 'Iranian; Sart (urban Uzbek)'? ⇨ **?** + **TAY** or suff. *-tay(1,2)*. See also **SARTAQ-TAY**.

SARTÏMBET   Kzk. 19th c. **Sartïmbet** [Сартымберъ(!)] (AOO 66); Kzk. 19th c. **Sartïmbet** [Сартымбетъ] (AOO 50). ⇨ **SART** + suffixoid *-ïmbet*.

SARTLAN   Bashk. 1728 **Sartlan** [Сартлан] (MIB I, 301).

SARTU   Bashk. 1740 **Sartu-bay / Sartqu-bay?** [Сарту-бай / Сартку-бай] (MIB I, 442).

SARU see **SARÏ**

SARUǰ   Bulg. **Saruǰ / Saruǰi?** [Саруджи] (Jusupov 32, Epigr. Bulg. 96, 97).

SARUǰA see **SARÏJA**

SARUǰÏ see **SARUǰ**

SARUMBE   Kzk. 19th c. **Sarum-be / Sar-umbet?** [Саромбе] (SOK 52). ⇨ **SARÏM?**

SAS   Kzk. 19th c. **Sas-bay** [Сасбай] (AOK 74); Uyg. 1320 **Sas-tärim** [Sas Tarim], fem. (Chwol., Syr.-nest. (NF) 22). ✧ 'Hurry up' cf. Kzk. *sas-* 'in Verlegenheit sein; sich beeilen' (Radl. IV, 394). See also **KERMESEN-SAS, ŠAYUN-SAS**.

SAS-EL   Kzk. 19th c. **Sas-el-bay** [Сасельбай] (SOK 164). ⇨ **SAS + EL?**

SAS-QUL see **SASÏ**

SASA   Turk. 1495 **Sasa-bey** [Sasa bey] (Uzunçarşılı: Belleten 1939, 394, Uzunçarş., Anad. 27).

SASAY   Kzk. 1794 **Sasay** [صاصاى / Сасай] (MIK IV, 159); Kzk. 19th c. **Sasay** [Тостанбекъ Сасаевъ] (Grod., Pril. 173).

SASAQ   Kzk. 1820 **Sasaq-biy** [Сасакъ-бій], a chief of the Kiši Žüz (Sib. Vest. IX, 110). ⇨ **SASÏQ?**

SASAM-BAY see **SAZAN**

SASAN see **SAZAN**

SASÏQ see **SASÏQ**

SASÏ   Kzk. 19th c. **Sas-qul (<Sasï-qul)** [Саскулъ] (Grod., Pril. 172); Bashk. 1740 **Sasï-qul** [Сасыкул Тоймасев] (MIB I, 382); Kzk. 19th c. **Sasï-qul** [Сасыкулъ] (AOP 6). ✧ 'Stinking' cf. Kuman, Crm., Tat., Turk. *sasï* 'faul, übelriechend' (Radl. IV, 395).

SASÏ-BUQA   Khorezm.? 14th. c. **Sasï-buqa** [Сасы-Бука], an Uzbekid (Barth., Ulugb. 85). ✧ 'Stinking bull'. ⇨ **SASÏ + BUQA**.

SASÏQ   Kzk. 19th c. **Sasiq / Sasïq** [Джаджабекъ Сасиковъ] (Grod., Pril. 69); Khorezm.? **Sasïq** [Сасык] (RaD II, 76); Kzk. 18th c. - 19th c. **Sasïq** [Сасык] (Tynyšp. 69, 72); Kzk. 1819 **Sasïq** [Сасык] (MIK IV, 325); Kzk. 1846 **Sasïq** [Сасык Сартанов], a biy (MKOP 155); Kzk. 19th c. **Sasïq** [Сасыкъ] (AOAtb. 50); Kzk. 19th c. **Sasïq** [Сасыкъ] (AOK 2, 82, 134); Kzk. 19th c. **Sasïq** [Сасыкъ] (Pantusov, Kirg. 39); Kzk. 19th c. **Sasïq** [Сасыкъ] (SOK 262); Kzk. 19th c. **Sasïq** [Сасыкъ] (SOV 14, 90); Kzk. 1876 **Sasïq** [Сасыкъ], from the district (uezd) of Čimkent (TV 1876, 63); Kzk. 1825 **Sasïq / Sasuq?** [صاصوق / Сасык] (MIK IV 470, 476); Bashk. 20th c. **Sasïq-bay** [Сасыкъбай] (Bask., Kkalp. 401); Kzk. 18th c. - 19th c. **Sasïq-bay** [Сасыкъбай] (Tynyšp. 74); Kzk. 1785 **Sasïq-bay** [صاصيق باى], from the Esen-temir tribe (MIK IV, 52, 54).

SASÏQ   Kzk. 19th c. **Sasïq-bay** [Каракасъ Сасыкбаевъ] (Grod., Pril. 57).

SASÏQ   Kirg. **Sasïq-bay** [Сасыкъбай] (Jud. 896).

SASÏQ   Kzk. 19th c. **Sasïq-pay** [Сасыкпай] (SOK 140, 202); Kzk. 19th c. **Sasïq-pay** [Сасыкпай] (SOV 24, 56); Kzk. 19th c. **Sasïq-pay** [Сасыкпай] (SODž. 76).

SASÏQ   Kzk. 19th c. **Sasïq-pay** [Сасыкпай] (AOO 42).

SASÏQ-QARA   Kzk. **Sasïq-qara** [Sasyk Kara / Сасык Кара] (Proben III, 263 /312/). ⇨ **SASÏQ + QARA**.

SASÏQ-URUS   Kzk. **Sasïq-urus** [Сасыкъ Урусъ] (Valihanov, Soč. 386). ✧ 'Stinking Russian'. ⇨ **SASÏQ + URUS**.

SASÏM   Kzk. 19th c. **Sasïm** [Сасымъ] (AOA 142).

SASLAN   Maml. 1378/9 **Saslan / Sasïlan?** [صصلان الجمالى] (Iyās I, 244, 245).

SASMAN   Kzk. **Sasman** [Сасман], chief of the Uysun tribe (MIK IV, 75).

SASPAQ   Kzk. 19th c. **Saspaq** [Саспакъ] (AOK 106, 114); Kzk. 19th c. **Saspaq** [Саспакъ] (SOV 26).

SASPAN   Kzk. 19th c. **Saspan** [Саспанъ] (AOA 10); Kzk. 19th c. **Saspan** [Саспанъ] (AOP 42).

SASTU   Kzk. 19th c. **Sastu-bek** [Састубекъ] (SOK 160).

SAŠQA   Alt. **Sašqa** [Сашка], fem. (ORS 213). ✧ 'Sashka' Hypoc. form of R. fem. *Aleksandra* (OjrRS).

SAŠWAN   Kzk. 19th c. **Sašwan** [Савкумъ Сашвановъ] (Grod., Pril. 109).

SAT   Kzk. 1785 **Sad-bek** [Садбек (тюленгут)] (MIK

IV, 47); Chuv. 18th-19th c. **Sat** [Сатъ] (Magn. 74); Kzk. 19th c. **Sat** [Сатъ] (SOK 200); Kzk. 19th c. **Sat** [Сатъ] (SOV 4, 60); Kzk. 19th c. **Sat** [Сатъ] (AOAtb. 34); Kzk. 19th c. **Sat** [Сатъ] (AOK 62); Kzk. 19th c. **Sat** [Сатъ] (AOP 114, 126); Kzk. 19th c. **Sat** [Бикатай Сатовъ] (Grod., Pril. 74); Kzk. 19th c. **Sat** [Сатъ] (SODž 96); Hak. 19th-20th c. **Sat** [Сат] (HRS 351); Tat. 1792 **Sat-bay** [Сатбай Понамаревъ] (MIK IV, 141); Kzk. 19th c. **Sat-bay** [Сатбай] (AOA 22, 86); Kzk. 19th c. **Sat-bay** [Сатбай] (AOP 102); Kzk. 19th c. **Sat-bay** [Сатбай] (Grod., Pril. 66, 195); Kzk. 19th c. **Sat-bay** [Сатбаевъ] (AUK 433); Kzk. **Sat-qul** [Алимкуль Саткуловъ] (SKSO VIII, 260); Chuv. 18th-19th c. **Sat-murza** [Сатмурза] (Magn. 74); Kzk. **Sat-pay** [Сатпай Чуртуковъ] (Konsin, Pam. 19); Kzk. 19th c. **Sat-pay** [Сатпай] (AOK 38, 82); Kzk. 19th c **Sat-pay** [Сатпай] (SOV 22, 28); Kzk. 19th c. **Sat-pay** [Сатпай] (SOK 12, 16, 44, 200, 216, 284); Kzk. 19th c. **Sat-pek** [Сатпекъ] (SOV 32); Kzk. 19th c. **Sat-pek** [Сатпекъ] (SODž. 58). ❖ I. 'Luck, fortune' (Ar.) (Žanuzakov); II. 'Sell (him/her)' cf. Uyg., Chag., Alt., Crm., Kzk., Tat. etc. *sat-* 'verkaufen, handeln' (Radl. IV, 375), also Rásonyi, Imp. 240. See also **IŠ-SAT, KENE-SAT, SATQÏL, SATQÏN.**

SAT-BURUN   Kzk. 19th c. **Sat-burun** [Сатбурунъ] (SOK 120). ⇨ **SAT + BURUN.**

SAT-KEREY   Chuv. 18th-19th c. **Sat-kerey** [Саткэрей] (Magn. 74). ⇨ **SAT + KERÄY.**

SAT-PAQ   Kzk. 19th c. **Sat-paq** [Сатпакь] (SODž 134). ⇨ **SAT + BAQ?**

SATA   Kzk. 19th c. **Sata-bay** [Сатабай] (SOV 34); Kzk. 19th c. **Sata-bay** [Сатабай] (AOK 46). ❖ 'Credulous' cf. Tat.(Tob.), Tat. *sata* 'leichtgläubig, phantasirend' (Radl. IV, 376).

SATAΓAY   Kzk. **Sataɣay** [Сатагай Куйбакаровъ], from the Kipchak ethnic group (SKSO III, 191).

SATAΓAN   Tat.(Sib.)? 1654 **Satayan** [Сатаган], a prince (Miller, Ist. Sib. II, 540).

SATAXA   Yak. **Sataχa** [Сатаха] (Pek.).

SATAY   Kzk. 1834 **Satay-batïr** [Сатай Батыръ] (PSZRI IX, 303); Maml. 1300 **Satay** [ستای] (Zetterst. 55); Chuv. 18th-19th c. **Satay** [Сатай] (Magn. 74); Tat. **Satay** [Sataj Kulajev], a mirza in the Mordva country (Smyrnov 279); Bashk. 1738 **Satay** [Сатай] (MIB III, 381); Bashk. 1767 **Satay** [Сатай Солтанбеков] (MIB IV/1, 324); Kzk. 19th c. **Satay** [Сатай] (SOV 36, 52, 72); Kzk. 19th c. **Satay** [Сатай] (SOK 10, 204); Kzk. 19th c. **Satay** [Сатай] (SODž. 158); Kzk. 19th c. **Satay** [Джутаякъ Сатаевъ] (Grod., Pril. 186); Kzk. 19th c. **Satay** [Сатай] (AOO 54); Kzk. 19th c. **Satay** [Сатай] (AOP 114); Kirg. **Satay** [Сатай] (Jud. 943); Kirg. 1848 **Satay** [Сатай] (Konšin, Mat. V, 109); Bashk. 1736 **Sedey** [Бекчюра Седеевъ] (MIB III, 344); Chuv.

18th-19th c. **Setey** [Сетей] (Magn. 76); Bashk. 1740 **Setey** [Сетей Аркаев] (MIB I, 397). ❖ 'Darling, favourite; close relative' (Mo.) (Žanuzakov, Sattarov).

SATAQAY   Kzk. 1803 **Sataqay** [Сатакай], chief of the Berč tribe of Kiši Žüz (MIK IV, 515). ⇨ **SATA** + suff. *-qay.*

SATAL   Crm. 1542 **Satal-qul-ulan / Sat-al-qul-ulan?** [Саталъкулъ-уланъ] (PSRL XIII, 143).

SATAM   Kzk. 19th c. **Satam-bay (<Satan-bay?)** [Сатамбай] (SODž. 12).

SATAN   Kzk. 1819 **Satan** [Сатан] (MIK IV, 326); Kzk. 19th c. **Satan** [Сатанъ] (SODž 70); Kzk. 19th c. **Satan** [Сатанъ] (SOV 94). ❖ 'Leg, hind leg; calf' cf. *satan* (Chag.) 'das Bein', (Turk) 'die Waden' (Radl. IV, 377), Turk. *satan* 'leg (in man); hind leg (of an animal); straddle' (TED).

SATANAY   Kzk. 19th c. **Satanay** [Сатанай] (SOK 4). ⇨ **SATAN** + suff. *-ay.*

SATAR   Kzk. 19th c. **Satar** [Сатар] (AOO 14); Kzk. 19th c. **Satar** [Сатар] (SOK 254); Kzk. 19th c. **Satar-bay** [Сатарбай] (SOK 146); Uzb. **Satar-qul** [Сатаркуловъ] (SKSO III, 154, 160). ❖ '(He) will sell, trade; seller' cf. several Trk. dial. *sat-* 'verkaufen, handeln' (Radl. IV, 375).

SATĀYÏN   Yak. **Satāyïn** [Сатајын] (Pek.).

SATĀYQA   Yak. **Satāyqa** [Сатаіка] (Pek.).

SATB-ALDÏ see **SATÏP-ALDÏ**

SATBEN   Kzk. 19th c. **Satben** [Сатбенъ] (SOK 50, 62).

SATÏ see **SATÏ**

SATÏQ   Hak. 19th-20th c. **Satiq** [Сатик] (HRS 351). ❖ 'Righteous, fair' (Ar.) (Butanaev).

SATÏ   Uzb. **Sati** [Сати] (SKSO III, 22); Uyg. **Satï** [Satı] (EUTS); Maml. 1302, 1310 **Satï** [سيف الدين ساطى], an emir (Dawād. 158, 211); Maml. 1435 **Satï** [Saty], Hasan's father (Berchem, Perg. 10); Turk. 1436, 1439 **Satï** [Satı bin Hacı Zekeriyâ] (Gökb., Ed. 172); Yürük 1603 **Satï** [Satï] (Su 25); Bashk. 1761 **Satï** [Саты Якупов] (MIB IV/1, 200); Kzk. 1823 **Satï** [ساطى / Саты] (MIK IV, 424); Kzk. 19th c. **Satï** [Саты] (SODž 128, 132); Nog.? 1649 **Satï** [Алѣй мурза Сатыевъ сынъ] (AI IV, 87); Khorezm. 1363 **Satï -bahadur** [ساتى بهادر], an emir (Qazv. 691); Uyg. 12th c. - 14th c. **Satï / Sadï** [Sadï] (Radl., USp. 114-115); Bashk. 1791 **Satï-bay** [Наурзбай Сатыбаев] (MIB V, 301); Kzk. 18th c. - 19th c. **Satï-bay** [Сатыбай] (Tynyšp. 66); Kzk. 19th c. **Satï-bay** [Сатыбай] (SOK 272); Kzk. 19th c. **Satï-bay** [Сатыбай] (SODž. 46, 80, 112); Kzk. 19th c. **Satï-bay** [Сатыбай] (AOA 78); Kzk. 19th c. **Satï-bay** [Сатыбай] (AOO 2, 46); Kzk. 1878 **Satï-bay** [Сатыбай Куваничев] (TV 116); Kzk. 19th c. **Satï-bek** [Сатыбекъ] (AOA 102); Uzb. **Satï-qul** [Тангрыберды Сатыкуловъ] (SKSO III, 23); Uzb.?

Satï-qul [Саты-куль], from the Kipchak ethnic group in Khokand (Valihanov, Soč. 145); Kzk. 1822 **Satï-ulï** [Sanasan Satyuly] (MIK 409, 410); Kzk. 1786 **Satu-bay** [Сатубай] (MIK IV, 75); *TN:* Kzk. 19th c. **Satï-baba** [Саты Баба], a well in Üst-yurt (Hanykov, Karta ZK). ✧ I. 'Selling, sale' cf. Turk. *satï* 'der Verkauf' (Radl. IV, 378); II. 'Ladder' cf. Kzk. *satï* 'die Leiter' (Radl. IV, 378). It may be a protective name (Noyan 11). See also **SABÏN-SATÏ, SATÏŠ**.

SATÏB-AL   Kzk. 19th c. **Satïb-al** (<**Satïp-al**) [Сатыбаль] (SODž. 154). ✧ 'Buy (it/him)!, take (it/him)!'; 'Taken, bought child' (Sattarov). ⇨ **SAT + AL**. See also **SATÏP-ALDÏ**.

SATÏB-ALDÏ see SATÏP-ALDÏ

SATÏY Bashk. 1752 **Satïy** (<**Satï?**) [Сатый Урмекеев] (MIB IV/1, 59); Nog.? 1614 **Satïy** (<**Satï?**) [Сатый], a murza (AI III, 411). ⇨ **SATAY / SATÏ?** + suff. *-y?*

SATÏQ Kzk. 19th c. **Satïq** [Сатыкъ] (AOA 134); Kzk. **Satïq-bay** [Сатыкбай] (SKSO VIII, 224); Kzk. 19th c. **Satïq-bay** [Сатыкбай] (SOK 202); Chag. 1554 **Satuq** [Сатук], son of Ĵutuš (Ivanov 145); Chag. **Satuq-χan** [Sátuk Khán], Ulugh Khan's chieftain (Tar. Rashidi 71, 73); Chag. 15th. c. **Satuq-χan** [Сатукь-хань] (Barth., Ulugb. 72, 87, 89). ✧ 'Sold' Protective name (Noyan 11). ⇨ **SAT / SATÏ** + suff. *-ïq / -q*.

SATÏQAY Bashk. 18th. c. **Satïqay** [Сатыкаев] (MIB V, 329); Bashk. 1778, 1792 **Satïqay** [Сатыкай Таминеев /Тимкеев/] (MIB V, 76, 97, 329). ⇨ **SATÏ / SATÏQ?** + suff. *-qay / -ay*.

SATÏL Kzk. 19th c. **Satïl** [Сатыль] (SODž 40); Kzk. 19th c. **Satïl-bay** [Сатылбай] (SOV 88); Kzk. 19th c. **Satïl-bay** [Сатылбай] (SOK 186); Uzb. 20th c. **Sâtïl** [Сотил] (Begmatov 1984, 203); Uzb. 20th c. **Sâtïl-bây** [Сотилбой] (Begmatov 1984, 203); Uzb. 20th c. **Sâtïl-mirza** [Сотилмирза] (Begmatov 1984, 203). ✧ 'Be sold' cf. Kar., Kzk., Tat., Turk. *satïl-* 'verkauft werden, gangbar sein ' (Radl. IV, 378). ⇨ **SATÏLSAN, SATÏLMÏŠ, SATÏN**.

SATÏLČAQ   Kzk. 19th c. **Satïlčaq** [Сатылчакъ Симиновъ] (Grod., Pril. 25). ⇨ **SATÏL** + suff. *-čaq*.

SATÏLƔAN   Tat.(GH) 1491, 1503 **Satïlƴan** [Сатылганъ], a prince (PSRL XII, 228, Smirnov, Krym. 288); Bashk. 1701 **Satïlƴan** [Сатылган Бердыкеев] (MIB III, 11); Bashk. 1732 **Satïlƴan** [Арыкбай Сатлыганов] (MIB III, 302); Kzk. 19th c. **Satïlƴan** [Сатылганъ] (SOV 54, 76); Kzk. 19th c. **Satïlƴan** [Сатылганъ] (SOK 118); Kzk. 19th c. **Satïlƴan** [Сатылганъ] (SODž. 14); Kzk. 19th c. **Satïlƴan** [Урманъ Сатилгановъ] (Grod., Pril. 130); Tat.(Kasim.) 1496-1506 **Satïlƴan-qan** [Satilgan khan] (Howorth II/2, 432); *TN:* Tat. **Satlïƴan** (<**Satïlƴan**) [Сатлыганъ], settlements in the districts of Tetyushinsk, Laishevsk and Mamadysh (IOAIÊK XIX, 137). ✧ 'Sold (child)' cf. Kar., Kzk., Tat., Turk. *satïl-* 'verkauft werden, gangbar sein' (Radl. IV, 378) + suff. *-ƴan*. See also **SATÏL, SATÏLMÏŠ**.

SATÏLÏ Kzk. 19th c. **Satïlï** [Сатылы] (SODž 40). ⇨ **SATÏ?** + suff. *-lï*.

SATÏLMÏŠ   Bulg. 1322 **Satïlmïš** [صطلمش / Сатылмыш] (Jusupov 17); Maml. 1279 **Satïlmïš?** [Satlemes] (Makrīzī II, 171); Maml. 1280 **Satïlmïš** [Satilmisch] (Makrīzī III, 29); Maml. 1294 **Satïlmïš** [Seïf-eddin-Satelmesch], an emir (Makrīzī IV, 1294); Maml. 1310 **Satïlmïš** [ساطلمش الكريمى], an emir (Dawād. 212); Maml. 1332 **Satïlmïš** [ساطلمش] (Dawād. 367); Maml. 1332 **Satïlmïš** [ساطلمش الجلالى], an emir (Dawād. 367); Maml. 14th c. **Satïlmïš** [صطلمش / Satilmïş] (Tarǰ/Houtsma 75, Tarǰ/Toparlı 43); Turk. 1540 **Satïlmïš** [Satïlmïş], a kethuda from the Bozulus tribe in the region of Diyarbekir, Turkey (Demirtaş 54); Turk. 16th c. **Satïlmïš** [Satılmış] (Ongan, Ank. II); Turk. 1583 **Satïlmïš** [Satılmış] (Ongan, Ank. I, 149, 175); Yürük 974/1566 **Satïlmïš** [Satïlmïş] (Gökçen 42); Yürük 1543 **Satïlmïš** [Satılmış] (Gökb., Rum. 193, 222, 225); Yürük? 1553 **Satïlmïš** [Satïlmïş] (Gökçen 35); Yürük 1606 **Satïlmïš** [Himmet bin Satïlmïş] (Gökçen 74); Yürük 1701 **Satïlmïš** [صاتلمش] (Refik, Anad. 132); Trkm. 1102, 1691 **Satïlmïš** [صاتلمش], a kethuda in the region of Rakka, Syria (Refik, Anad. 101); Tat. 1543 **Satïlmïš** [Satılmış] (Gökb., Rum. 231, 235, 236, 241); Khorezm.? 1293 **Satïlmïš-bek** [ستلميش بيك], an emir (Dorn 133, 136); Chag. 15th c. **Satïlmïš-χatun** [ساتلمش خاتون / Satilmitch-Khatoun / Sátilmish Khátun], wife of Isän-buƴa-χan (Isan Bugha = Ïl-χoǰa), the Khan of Kashghar (Abulg./Desm. 165 /100, 104/, Tar. Rashidi 6); *TN:* Selj.? 12th c. **Satïlmïš**, a masǰid (small mosque) (Ibn Šaddād, Alep 84). ✧ 'Sold / disposed of (child)' cf. Kar., Kzk., Tat., Turk. *satïl-* 'verkauft werden, gangbar sein' (Radl. IV, 378), also Sauvaget 48-49: صطلمش / ساطلمش 'il a été vendu', Gordlevskij 1913, p. 132. According to A. Schimmel, the Turkish name, and its feminine version *Satı*, points to a vow which the parents had made at a saint's tomb, promising that they would „sell" the hoped-for child to the saint, that is, donate it or its services to the shrine (p. 37). It is a beloved protective name. See also **SATÏL, SATÏLƔAN**.

SATÏM Uzb. 1722 **Satim** [Сатимъ], from Bukhara (Veselovskij, Unk. 63-4, 72-4); Tat. 1624 **Satïm** [Байгора Сатымовъ] (Pokrovskij 70); Tat. 1624 **Satïm** [Маметъ Сатимовъ] (Pokrovskij 71); Kzk. 19th c. **Satïm-bay** [Сатымбай] (SODž 26); Kzk. 19th c. **Satïm-bay** [Сатымбай Хамытовъ] (AUK 452); Kzk. 19th c. **Satïm-bek** [Сатымбекъ] (SOV 4); Kzk. 19th c. **Satïm-qul** [Сатым кулъ] (SOK 44). ✧ 'Selling; sold (child)' cf. Crm., Turk. *satim* 'der Verkauf, der Handel' (Radl. IV, 379). See also **SATÏL**,

SATÏŠ.

SATÏM-QOLU Uzb.? 20th c. **Satïm-qolu-bay / Satïm-qulu-bay?** [Сатымколубаевъ], a merchant (Turk. Kraj 1912, 15). ⇨ **SATÏM + QUL** + poss. -*u*.

SATÏMĞAN Kzk. 19th c. **Satïmɣan / Satïlɣan?** [Сатымганъ] (AOA 110). ⇨ **SATÏLĞAN?**

SATÏN Kzk. **Satïn / Säten?** [Сатеновъ] (SKSO III, 190); Kzk. 19th c. **Satïn-bay** [Сатынбай] (SODž 98). ✧ 'Sell! Be sold!' cf. Kzk. *satïn*- 'seine eigene verkaufen' (Radl. IV, 378). See also **SATÏL.**

SATÏP Bashk. 1756 **Satïp** [Сатып Итзимесов] (MIB IV/1, 107).

SATÏP-ALDÏ Kzk. **Satb-aldï (<Satïb-aldï)** [Кусулбай Сатбалдын] (MKOP 155); Uzb. 1945-47 **Satib-aldi** [Сатиболди], in the Zerafshan-region (Erohina-Ramazanova: OSA 201); NUyg. **Satip-aldi** [Satip Aldi] (Stein 93, 111); Kzk. 1846 **Satïb-aldï** [Сатыбалды Юнгутин], a biy (MKOP 158); Kzk. 19th c. **Satïb-aldï** [Сатыбалды Сартова] (AOK 851); Kzk. 19th c. **Satïb-aldï** [Сатыбалды] (SOV 12); Kzk. 19th c. **Satïb-aldï** [Сатыбалды] (AOK 42, 102); Kkalp. 20th c. **Satïb-aldï** [Сатыбалды] (KkRS 776); Kirg. **Satïb-aldï** [Сатыбалды] (Jud. 741); Kzk. 19th c. **Satïb-aldï / Satib-aldi?** [Сатибалди] (Grod., Pril. 177); Kzk. 1817 **Satïb-aldï / Satub-aldï** [صاتوب الدى / Сатыбалды] (MIK IV, 310); Kkalp. 20th c. **Satïb-aldï-ulï** [Бёленбай Жахъайым Сатыбалды-улы] (Bask., Kkalp. 77); Kirg. 19th c. **Satïw-aldï** [Сатывалды] (Kalilov 93); Kzk. 19th c. **Satub-alda (<Satub-aldï)** [Сатубалда] (Grod., Pril. 30); Bashk. 1756 **Satub-aldï** [Сатубалды Идзимясов] (MIB IV/1, 123); Kzk. **Satub-aldï** [Сатубалды Вайбулатовъ] (SKSO III, 190); Kzk. **Satub-aldï** [Бутабекъ Сатубалдіевъ] (SKSO VIII, 221); Kzk. **Satub-aldï** [Сатубалды Тулябаевъ] (SKSO VIII, 221); Kzk. **Satub-aldï** [Атабай Сатубалдіевъ] (SKSO VIII, 223); Kzk. 1822 **Satub-aldï** [صاتوب الدى / Сатубалды] (MIK IV, 432, 434); Kzk. 19th c. **Satub-aldï** [Сатубалды] (Grod., Pril. 185); Kzk. 19th c. **Satub-aldï** [Сатубалдіев,] (SKSO VIII, 201-233); Kzk. 19th c. **Satub-aldï** [Сатубалды] (SKSO VIII, 201-233); Kzk. **Satw-aldï (<Satïw-aldï <Satïp-aldï)** [Сатвальтъ / Сатвальдъ] (Sb. Syr-D. IX, 54, 58); Uzb. 20th c. **Sâtïb-âldï** [Сотиболди] (Begmatov 1984, 203); *TN:* Kzk.? **Satïb-aldï** [Saty-baldy] (PM Ergh. 43 /Table/); Kirg. 1888 **Satub-aldï** [Сатубалды], a village in the region of the Chu river (Vyšnegorszkij: Tr. Syr-D. OSK 1888, 22). ✧ 'Taken, bought (child)' (Sattarov). ⇨ **SAT + AL.**

SATÏR Hak. 19th-20th c. **Satïr** [Сатыр] (HRS 351).

SATÏRÏQ Tat.(GH) 1278 **Satïrïq** [Сатирикъ], a christened Tatar in the Crimea (Smirnov, Krym. 34). ✧ 'Knife' cf. Crm., Turk. *satïr* 'ein grosses Fleischermesser' (Radl. IV, 378).

SATÏRQAN Kzk. 19th c. **Satïrqan** [Сатырканъ] (SOK 104).

SATÏŠ Bashk. 1710 **Satïš** [Сатыш] (MIB III, 57); Bashk. 1710, 1711 **Satïš** [Сатыш Бостанаев] (MIB III, 57, 68); Bashk. 1735 **Satïš** [Сатышь Кулушевъ], a tarɣan (Vel.-Zern., Bašk. 17); Bashk. 1761 **Satïš** [Райман Сатышев] (MIB IV/1, 216); *TN:* Tat. **Satïš** [Сатышъ], a settlement in the district of Mamadysh (IOAIÊK XIX, 137); Chuv. 18th. c. **Satïš(eva)** [Сатышева], a village in the district of Cheboksary (Korsakov 287). ✧ 'Selling; help with trade!' cf. Tat. *satïš*- 'Handel treiben, handeln; beim Handel Beistand leisten' (Radl. IV, 379), Turk. *satïš* 'der Verkauf' (Radl. IV, 379).

SATKE Kzk. 19th c. **Satke** [Сатке] (SOV 76). ⇨ **SAT** + suff. -*ke*.

SATQAY Kzk. 19th c. **Satqay** [Саткай] (SOK 216). ⇨ **SAT** + dim. suff. -*qay*.

SATQAM-BAY see **SATQAN**

SATQAN Chuv. 18th-19th c. **Satkan** [Сатканъ] (Magn. 74); Kzk. 19th c. **Satqam-bay (<Satqan-bay)** [Саткамбай] (SODž. 150). ✧ 'Sold' cf. Uyg., Chag., Kuman, Alt., Hak., Kzk., etc. *sat*- 'verkaufen, handeln' (Radl. IV, 375). See also **SATÏLĞAN, SATMÏŠ.**

SATQÏL Uzb. 20th c. **Sâtqil** [Соткил] (Begmatov 1984, 203). ✧ 'Sell him/her!' cf. Uzb. *sât*- 'продавать' (UzbRS) + imp. suff. 2nd P. sing. -*qil*. See also **SAT, SATQÏN.**

SATQÏN Kzk. 19th c. **Satqïm-bay (<Satqïn-bay)** [Саткымбай] (SOK 218); Kzk. 19th c. **Satqïn** [Саткынъ] (SODž 50); Kzk. 19th c. **Satqïn** [Саткынъ] (SOV 30, 130); Kzk. 19th c. **Satqïn** [Саткынъ] (AOA 2); Kzk. 19th c. **Satqïn** [Саткынъ] (AOO 26); Kzk. 19th c. **Satqïn-bay** [Саткынбай] (SOK 98, 116); Uzb. 20th c. **Sâtqïn** [Соткин] (Begmatov 1984, 203); Uzb. 20th c. **Sâtqïn-ây** [Соткиной], fem. (Begmatov 1984, 203); Uzb. 20th c. **Sâtqïn-bây** [Соткинбой] (Begmatov 1984, 203); Uzb. 20th c. **Sâtqïn-Jân** [Соткинжон] (Begmatov 1984, 203). ✧ I. 'Selling, trade; on sale, to be sold' cf. Chag. *satqun* 'der Handel' (Radl. IV, 381), *sâtqin* 'продажный' (UzbRS); II. 'Sell him/her' (Begmatov), cf. Uzb. *sât*- 'продавать' (UzbRS) + imp. suff. 2nd P. sing. -*qin*. See also **SAT, SATQÏL.**

SATLÏĞAN see SATÏLĞAN

SATLÏQ Tat. 1731 **Satlïq** [Сатлык] (MIB III, 284); Bashk. 1711 **Satlïq** [Сатлык Кузеев] (MIB III, 78); Bashk. 1713 **Satlïq** [Сатлык Кузеев] (MIB III, 90); Bashk. 1713 **Satlïq** [Сатлык Кузеев] (MIB III, 90); Bashk. 1735 **Satlïq** [Сатлыкъ Сапаевъ], a tarɣan (Vel.-Zern., Bašk. 24); Bashk. 1742 **Satlïq** [Сатлык Ишметев] (MIB III, 513); Bashk. 1751 **Satlïq** [Сатлык] (MIB IV/1, 45); Bashk. 1754 **Satlïq** [Сатлык Евкеев] (MIB IV/1, 83); Bashk. 1755 **Satlïq**

[Satlyk], mentioned in connection of the revolt of Batïrša (Rytschkow II, 27); Bashk. 1756 **Satlïq** [Сатлык Букчюбаев] (MIB IV/1, 128); Bashk. 1760 **Satlïq** [Мазан Сатлыков] (MIB IV/1, 313); Bashk. 1761 **Satlïq** [Юлдаш Сатлыков] (MIB IV/1, 221); Bashk. 1761 **Satlïq** [Сатлык Ибаков] (MIB IV/1, 202, 208); Bashk. 1770 **Satlïq** [Сатлук Мурзакаев] (MIB IV/1, 347); Bashk. 1776 **Satlïq** [Сатлык Кирилов] (MIB V, 89, 106); Bashk. 1776 **Satlïq** [Сатлык Янеев] (MIB V, 39-41); Bashk. 1779 **Satlïq** [Сатлык] (MIB V, 89); Bashk. 1779 **Satlïq** [Сатлык] (MIB V, 101); Bashk. 1789 **Satlïq** [Сейдоулла Сатлыков] (MIB V, 255, 284, 327); Kzk. 1823 **Satlïq** [Сатлык], a biy (MIK IV, 447); Kirg. 1876 **Sattïq-bek** [Саттыкъ-беѣъ], a manap (TV 1876, 183). ✦ '(Child) on sale, to be sold' cf. Tat. *satlïq* 'verkäuflich' (Radl. IV, 382).

SATMA   Chuv. 18th-19th c. **Satma** [Сатма] (Magn. 74). ✦ 'Don't sell (him/her)' cf. Uyg., Chag., Alt., Crm., Kzk., Tat. etc. *sat-* 'verkaufen, handeln' (Radl. IV, 375). ⇨ **SAT.**

SATMAZ   Kipch. 1159 **Satmaz** [Тудоръ Сатмазовичь Берендай] (Ipat. 343 /356/); Kipch. 1162 **Satmaz** [Затмазовичи], father of several Polovets princes (Ipat. 356 /369/, PSRL VII, 76); Selj. **Satmaz** [صطماز] (Bondârî 164); Selj. 1160, 1675 **Satmaz** [عزالـديـن ستمـاز / Emir Izzeddin Satmaz ibn Kaymaz el-Harânî], an emir of Sultan Suleyman (Bondârî 243, 248, 253, 286, Ahbar 102, 110, Râwandî 275, 277, 343, 345 etc.); Maml. 14th c. **Satmaz** [صطماز / Satmaz] (Tarǰ/Houtsma 75, Tarǰ/Toparlı 43). ✦ 'He who is not to be sold or can't be sold' (Tarǰ/Houtsma). ⇨ **SAT +** suff. *-maz.*

SATMÏR   Kzk. 1822 **Satmïr** [ستمـر / Сатмыр] (MIK IV, 47, 416).

SATMÏŠ   Uyg. **Satmïš** [Satmış] (EUTS); Uyg. 8th c. - 9th c. **Satmïš-tarχan** [Satmiš] (Müller, Pfahl. 12); *TN:* Tat.(Mish.) **Satmïš** [Сатмыш / Сатламышева], a settlement in the district of Sviyažsk (IOAIÊK XIX, 137). ✦ 'Sold' cf. Uyg., Chag., Kuman, Alt., Hak., Kzk., etc. *sat-* 'verkaufen, handeln' (Radl. IV, 375). See also **SATÏLΓAN, SATÏLMÏŠ, SATTÏ, SATQAN.**

SATODA   Uyg. **Satoda** [Satoda] (EUTS).

SATTAR   Trkm.? 1813/14 **Sattar-quli-aqa** [Саттар-кули-ака (и- Кахрамани)] (MIT II, 387, 389, 400). ✦ Sattar (Ar.) 'Veiler (of sin)', Al-Sattar 'the veiler of sin (one of the names of Allah)' (Ahmed).

SATTAR-BERDİ   Trkm. 1817/18 **Sattar-berdi-arbab** [Саттар-берды-арбаб] (MIT II, 406). ✦ 'The veiler of sin (=Allah) gave him/her'. ⇨ **SATTAR + BERDİ.**

SATTÏ   Chuv. 18th-19th c. **Sattï** [Сатти] (Magn. 74); Kzk. 19th c. **Sattï-bay** [Саттыбай] (SOK 36, 114); Kzk. 19th c. **Sattï-bay** [Саттыбай] (AOP 94); Kzk. 19th c. **Sattï-bay** [Саттыбай] (AOA 154); Uzb. 20th c.

Sâttï [Сотти] (Begmatov 1984, 203); Uzb. 20th c. **Sâttï** [Сотти], fem. (Begmatov 1984, 203); Uzb. 20th c. **Sâttï-bây** [Соттибой] (Begmatov 1984, 203); Uzb. 20th c. **Sâttï-χân** [Соттихон], fem. (Begmatov 1984, 203). ✦ '(He) Sold (it)'. ⇨ **SAT?** + suff. *-tï.* See also **SATÏLMÏŠ, SATMÏŠ.**

SATTÏQ see **SATLÏQ**

SATU see **SATÏ**

SATUB-ALDÏ see **SATÏP-ALDÏ**

SATUQ see **SATÏQ**

SAV   Uyg. **Sav** [Sav] (EUTS).

SAV-DEMEN   Chuv. 18th-19th c. **Sav-demen** [Савдеменъ] (Magn. 71). ⇨ **SAW?**

SAV-DİMER   Chuv. 18th-19th c. **Sav-dimer** [Савдимеръ] (Magn. 71). ⇨ **SAW + TEMİR.**

SAV-GALEY   Chuv. 18th-19th c. **Sa-galey (<Sav-gali?)** [Сагалей] (Magn. 71); Chuv. 1670 **Sav-aley(ko) (<Sav-gali?)** [Савалѣйко Ахметевъ] (Poliv.-Kras. 64). ✦ 'Healthy Ali'. ⇨ **SAW + ALİ.**

SAV-KELDİ   Chuv. 18th-19th c. **Sav-gildä** [Савгилда] (Magn. 71); Chuv. 18th-19th c. **Sav-keldä** [Савкелда] (Magn. 71); Chuv. 18th-19th c. **Sav-gäldä / Sav-galda (<Saw-qaldï?)** [Савгалда] (Magn. 71). ⇨ **SAW + KELDİ.**

SAV-KİREY   Chuv. 18th-19th c. **Sav-kirey** [Савгирей] (Magn. 71); Chuv. 18th-19th c. **Sav-kirey** [Савкирей] (Magn. 71). ⇨ **SAW + KERÄY.**

SAVAŠ   Chuv. 18th-19th c. **Savaš** [Савашъ] (Magn. 71). ✦ 'Fight, battle' cf. Chag., Crm., Turk. *savaš / sawaš* 'der Kampf, die Schlacht' (Radl. IV, 426).

SAVLİK   Chuv. 18th-19th c. **Savlik** [Савликъ] (Magn. 71).

SAVNE   Chuv. 1670 **Savne-bey?** [Савнебейка] (Poliv.-Kras. 64).

SAW   Chuv. 18th-19th c. **Sav-batïr** [Савбатыръ] (Magn. 71); Chuv. 18th-19th c. **Sav-čura** [Савчура] (Magn. 71); Chuv. 18th-19th c. **Sav-murza** [Савмурза] (Magn. 71); Kzk. 19th c. **Saw-qulï** [Савкули] (Grod., Pril. 124); Selj.? 1062 **Saw-tegin** [سَرْهَنْك سَاوتكين / ساوتكين سـرهـنك] (Ibn al-Athîr/Tornb. X, 14, 63 etc., Bondârî 18, 49, 61, 77); Selj.? 1095, 1096 **Saw-tegin** [ساوتكين الخـادم / Sautegin] (Ibn al-Athîr/Tornb. X, 169, Abulfidâ III, 300-301, Qalânisi 130, 131); Selj.? 1097 **Saw-tegin** [Savtekin], governor of Diyarbekir (Weil, Chalif. III, 150); Maml.? 13th c. **Saw-tegin** [ساودكين / Saoutikîn / Savdik] (Ibn al-Athîr: RHCHor I, 855). ✦ 'Healthy' cf. Crm., Kar. *saw* 'gesund' (Radl. IV, 424). See also **BAY-SAU.**

SAWAΓ   Uyg. 762 **Sawaγ-tutuγ** [Savag Tutuγ] (Mahrnâmag 9).

SAWAYAN   Bashk. 1714 **Sawayan** [Саваян Гуразов] (MIB I, 105).

SAWAR Karakh. 862 **Sawar-tegin** [صولار تكين / صوار تكين] (Ṭabarī, Annal. III, 1460); Karakh. 906, 907, 909 **Sawar-tegin** [وصيف بـن صَوَار / سوار تكين] / Wasif Ibn Suwartekin], a general (commander of Caliph Muqtafī (Ṭabarī, Annal. III, 2262, 2275, 2278, Arīb 12, 17, 18, 26, Masʿūdī 375, 376, Hil. Sābī 88, Miskawayh V, 48, 56, 64, Weil, Chalif. II, 530).

SAWAŽAN Bashk. 1730 **Sawažan-qul** [Саважанкул Сафаров] (MIB III, 280).

SAWČĬ Bashk. 1756 **Sawčï-ɣul** [Савчегул Текеев] (MIB IV/1, 122). ❖ 'Prophet, messenger' cf. Uyg. *savčï* 'id.' (Radl. IV, 431), Karakh., Uyg. *savčï / sawčï* 'пророк, посланник; сват' (DTS).

SAWČĬ-BUГA Uyg. 762 **Sawčï-buɣa** [Savcï Buɣa Tarkan Ügä] (Mahrnāmag 7, 9, 39). ⇨ **SAWČĬ + BUQA.**

SAWJĬ Turk. 1486 **Sawjï** [Savcı], an architect (Gökb., Ed. 221, 222); Turk. 16th c. **Sawjï** [Savci], an Ottoman prince (Baştav 32, 48, 49, 93). ❖ 'Advocate, spokesman'? cf. Turk. *savcı* 'attorney general' (TED), or perhaps Turk. *savacı* '(archaic) bringer of good tidings, harbinger; messenger' (TED).

SAWDA Kzk. 19th c. **Sawda-bay** [Саудабай] (SODž 146); Kzk. 19th c. **Sawda-bay** [Саудабай] (SOK 232); Kzk. 19th c. **Sawda-bay** [Саудабай] (SODž. 92); Kzk. 19th c. **Sawda-bay** [Савдабай] (Grod., Pril. 29); Kzk. 19th c. **Sawda-bek** [Саудабекъ] (SODž. 44); *TN:* Kzk. 19th c. **Sawda-bay-qstau** [Саудобай кстау], a (settlement) winter pasture (SODž. 60). ❖ 'Trade' cf. Kzk. *sawda* 'торговля' (KzRS).

SAWDĬГĬR Kzk. 19th c. **Sawdïɣïr** [Саудыгыръ] (SOV 40).

SAWELEY Bashk. 1756 **Saweley / Saw-ali?** [Бакта Савелеев] (MIB IV/1, 127).

SAWГAN Kzk. 19th c. **Sawɣan** [Tura keldi Savgan] (Hedin, En färd I, 166, 167). ❖ 'Milked' cf. Kar., Tat. *sav-* 'melken' (Radl. IV, 425).

SAWĬQ Kzk. 19th c. **Sauq / Sawq (<Sawïq)** [Саукъ] (SOK 212, 256). ❖ 'Amusement' cf. Kzk. *sawïq* 'увеселение' (KzRS).

SAWĬM Kzk. 19th c. **Saum-bay / Sawm-bay (<Sawïm-bay)** [Саумбай] (AOO 74). ❖ 'Milking (time), born at milking time' cf. Kzk. *sawïm* 'доение, удой (промежуток между думя дойками' (KzRS).

SAWĬN Tat. 1624 **Sawïn / Sawa?** [Курмагозя Савинъ] (Pokrovskij 72).

SAWĬR Kzk. 19th c. **Sawïr-bek** [Савирбекъ] (Grod., Pril. 195); Kzk. 18th c. - 19th c. **Sawr-bay (<Sawïr-bay)** [Саурбай] (Tynyšp. 75); Kzk. 19th c. **Sawr-bay (<Sawïr-bay)** [Саурбай] (AOA 98); Kzk. 19th c. **Sawr-bay (<Sawïr-bay)** [Саурбай] (SODž. 58, 60); Kzk. 19th c. **Sawr-bay (<Sawïr-bay)** [Саурбай] (SOK 20, 234, 124); Kzk. 19th c. **Sawr-bay (<Sawïr-bay)** [Саурбай] (AOK 130); Kzk. 19th c. **Sawr-bay (<Sawïr-bay)** [Саурбай] (AOO 14, 58); Kzk. 19th c. **Sawr-bay (<Sawïr-bay)** [Саурбай] (AOP 122). ❖ 'Rump, backside' cf. Kzk. *sawïr* 'круп' (KzRS).

SAWQA Bashk. 1776 **Sawqa-bay** [Савкабай Кучеляков] (MIB V, 42, 43, 544). ❖ 'Gift from the booty' cf. Kzk. *sawɣa* 'подарок из военной или охотничьей добычи' (KzRS). ⇨ **SAW?** + suff. *-qa.*

SAWQAT Kzk. 19th c. **Sawqat** [Буменъ Саукатовъ] (SKSO III, 20); Nog. 20th c. **Sawqat** [Савкъат Тилек увлы / Саукат Тилеков], one of Baskakov's informants from the aul of Qaraɣas (Bask., Nog. 144). ❖ 'Gift, reward' cf. Chag. *sauɣat / savɣat* 'ein Geschenk, eine Gabe, eine Belohnung' (Radl. IV, 234, 431).

SAWQUM Kzk. 1845 **Sawqum** [Савкумъ] (Grod., Pril. 109); Kzk. 1845 **Sawqum-bay** [Саукумбай Тазовъ] (Konšin, Mat. V 62). ⇨ **SAWUQ II.?** + poss. suff. *-um.*

SAWMAL Kzk. 19th c. **Sawmal-bay** [Саумалбай] (SOV 148). ❖ 'Koumis, kumiss (fresh, not entirely fermented mare's milk)' cf. Kzk. *sawmal* 'молодой (ещё не перебродивший) кумыс' (KzRS). See also **QĬMĬZ.**

SAWRAN Kzk. 19th c. **Sawram-bay (<Sawran-bay)** [Саурамбай] (SODž. 116); Kzk. 19th c. **Sawram-bay (<Sawran-bay)** [Саврамбай] (SOK 6); Kzk. 19th c. **Sawran** [Сауранъ] (SOK 282); Kzk. **Sawran-bay** [Сауранбаевъ] (Sb. Syr-D. VII, 130); Kzk. 19th c. **Sawran-bay** [Сауранбай] (SODž 38); *TN:* Kzk. **Sawram-bay (<Sawran-bay)** [Саврамбай], a kurgan (burial mound) south-east of Lake Aral (Karta JAR XI). ❖ I. 'Second month of the lunar calender' (Žanuzakov 156); II. 'Gift, reward' (Žanuzakov 156); III. 'Wog'? cf. Turk. *sarban / savran* 'der Kameeltreiber' (Radl. IV, 342). See also **SAWQAT?**

SAWRAŠ Kzk. 19th c. **Sawraš-bay** [Саурашбай] (SODž. 100).

SAWRĬQ Kzk. 19th c. **Sawrïq** [Саурыкъ] (Grod., Pril. 59); Kzk. **Sawrïq-batïr** [Саурыкъ-батыръ] (Smirnov, Sultany 14); Kzk. 19th c. **Sawruq** [Саурукъ] (SOK 38, 50, 114); Kzk. 19th c. **Sawruq** [Саурукъ] (SOV 40); Kzk. 19th c. **Sawruq** [Саурукъ] (SODž 10, 18, 64, 112); Kzk. 19th c. **Sawruq** [Саурыкъ] (SOK 10); Kzk. 1864 **Sawruq** [Саурукъ] (?); Kzk. 18th c. - 19th c. **Sawruq-batïr** [Саурук-батыр] (Tynyšp. 66); Kzk. 19th c. **Sawruq-pay** [Саурукпай] (SOV 152); Kzk. 19th c. **Sawruq-pay** [Саурукпай] (SOK 172). ⇨ **SAWĬR / SAWRĬ / SAWRU?** + dim. suff. *-ïq / -q.*

SAWRĬM-BAY see **SAWRUN**

SAWRU Kzk. 19th c. **Sawru-bay** [Саврубай] (AOK 130); Kzk. 19th c. **Sawru-bay** [Саврубай] (AOP 86). ❖ 'Rump, backside' cf. Kirg. *sooru* 'круп' (Jud.).

SAWRUQ see **SAWRÏQ**

SAWRUN   Kzk. 19th c. **Sawrïm-bay** (<**Sawrïn-bay**) [Савримбай] (SOK 44); Kzk. 19th c. **Sawrum-bay** (<**Sawrun-bay?**) [Саурумбай] (AOAtb. 6); Kzk. 19th c. **Sawrum-bay** (<**Sawrun-bay**) [Саурумбай] (SOV 32); Kzk. 19th c. **Sawrun-bay** [Саурунбай] (SOV 46); Kzk. 19th c. **Sawrun-bay** [Саурунбай] (SODž. 62, 66). ✧ 'Part of booty or quarry' cf. Kirg. *soorun* 'часть военной или охотничьей добычи' (Jud.).

SAWSQAN   Tat.(Sib.) 1582 **Sawsqan** [Саусканъ], a Siberian ruler (Sib. Let. (Rem.) 319); Kzk. 19th c. **Sawsqan** [Саусканъ] (AOK 98, 126). ✧ 'Magpie' cf. Uyg., Alt., Hak. *sayïsqan* 'die Elster' (Radl. IV, 269).

SAWSQAN-SAYRAN   Tuv. 19th c. **Sawsqan-sayran** [Саусканъ-сайранъ], one of Pad-padaqši's wives, the other one was called Qusqun-qayran (Potanin IV, 426). ⇨ **SAWSQAN + SAYRAN.**

SAWT   Kzk. **Sawt-bay** [Саутбай Тлемисовъ] (ZIRGO III, 26); Kzk. 19th c. **Sawt-bek** [Саутбекъ] (AOAtb. 14). ✧ 'Vessels, pots' cf. Chag., Kar., Tat. *sawït / savut / sawut* 'das Gefäss' (Radl. IV, 430).

SAWTÏSQ   Kzk. 19th c. **Sawtïsq** [Саутыскъ] (AOAtb. 42).

SAWUQ I.   Chuv. 18th-19th c. **Savuk** [Савукъ] (Magn. 71). ✧ 'Throwing / spreading shovel' cf. Chuv. *sawuq* 'совок' (ČRS), *savǝk* 'kleine schaufel um korn od. mehl aus- und einzuschütten' (Paas.).

SAWUQ II.   Kuman 1096 **Sawq** (<**Sawuq**) [Саукъ], a Polovets prince (PSRL I, 103). ✧ I. 'Be healthy' (Bask., Im. polov. 72), cf. Kkalp. *sawïq-* 'выздоравливать, поправляться' (KkRS); II. 'Cold' (Bask., Im. polov. 72), cf. Kuman *savuq / savuχ* 'kalt, Kälte' (CC).

SAZ   Kzk. **Saz-bay** [Сазбай] (Sb. Syr-D. IX, 48). ✧ 'Morass; loam, clay' cf. Kuman, Chag., Kirg., Kzk. *saz* 'id.' (Radl. IV, 397).

SAZA   Kzk. 19th c. **Saza** [Саза] (SOV 122); Kzk. 19th c. **Saza-bay** [Сазабай] (Grod., Pril. 147). ✧ 'Punishment' cf. East.T. *saza* (P.) 'die Strafe' (Radl. IV, 397).

SAZAQ   Trkm. 20th c. **Sazaq** [Sazaq] (Zaj. 1971, 332); Trkm. 20th c. **Sazaq** [Sazak] (TrkmRS 556); Kzk. 19th c. **Sazaq** [Сазакъ] (SOK 78); Kzk. 19th c. **Sazaq-pay** [Сазакпай] (SOK 134). ✧ 'Saksaul (a special tree of Middle Asian wasteland' cf. Trkm. *säzaq* 'саксаул' (TrkmRS). See also **OJAR.**

SAZAM   Kirg. **Sazam(-batïr)** [Sasam / Сазам батыр], one of Manas' comrades-in-arms (Proben V, 40). ✧ 'A kind of fish' cf. Kirg. *sasam* 'ein Fisch' (Radl. IV, 395).

SAZAN   Kzk. 19th c. **Sasam-bay** (<**Sasan-bay**) [Сасамбай] (SODž 132); Turk.? 14th. c. **Sasan** [Σασᾶν / Sasan], an emir (Byz. Turc. 270); Kzk. **Sasan** [Сасанъ] (Konšin: ZSOIRGO II, 117); Kzk. 1819 **Sasan** [Засан] (MIK IV, 323); Kzk. 19th c. **Sasan** [Сасан(овъ)] (SOK 14); Kzk. 19th c. **Sasan** [Сасанъ] (AOA 146); Kzk. 19th c. **Sasan-bay** [Сасанбай Баркіевъ] (Grod., Pril. 93); Kzk. 19th c. **Sasan-bay** [Сасанбай] (SOK 146); Chuv. 18th-19th c. **Sazan** [Сазанъ] (Magn. 72); Kzk. 19th c. **Sazan** [Сазанъ] (SOV 70); Kzk. 19th c. **Sazan** [Сазанъ] (AOA 82); Kzk. 19th c. **Sazan** [Сазанъ] (AOP 74); Alt. **Sazan** [Сазан] (ORS 209); Kzk. 19th c. **Sazan-bay** [Сазанбай] (SOK 40, 98, 186); Kzk. 19th c. **Sazan-bay** [Сазанбай] (SOV 56, 132); *EN:* Kzk. **Sazan** [Сазанъ], a subdivision of the Ĵaɣalbaylï tribe (Aristov 111); *TN:* Kzk.? **Sazan-bay** [Сазанбай], a lake (Karta JAR III); Kzk. 19th c. **Sazan-bay** [Сазанъбай], a well at the Ĵïlančïq river (Hanykov, Karta ZK). ✧ 'Carp' cf. Kzk., Turk. *sazan* 'der Sasan, der Karpfen' (Radl. IV, 398), Chuv. *sazan* 'сазан' (ČRS), also Šipova 270.

SAZANAQ   Hak.(Sag.) 19th-20th c. **Sazanaq** [Сазанак] (Katanov, Otč. 7). ⇨ **SAZAN?** + dim. suff. *-aq.*

SAZANΓAY   Bashk. 1740 **Sazanɣay** [Сазангай Тангирбаев] (MIB I, 443). ⇨ **SAZAN** + dim. suff. *-qay.*

SAZANŠAÑ   Kirg. **Sazanšañ** [Сазаншаң] (Jud. 92).

SAZDÏ   Kzk. 19th c. **Sazdï-bay** [Саздыбай] (SODž 132). ✧ 'Marshy, boggy; reeds, rushes' cf. Turk. *sazlï* 'mit Schilf, Röhricht bewachsen; sumpfig' (Radl. IV, 399). ⇨ **SAZ** + suff. *-dï.*

SAZÏM   Kzk. 19th c. **Sazïm-bay** [Сазымбай] (SOV 50). ⇨ **SAZ** + poss. suff. *-ïm.*

SAZÏMAY   Tuv. 19th c. **Sazïmay** [Сазымаi] (Proben IX,122).

SAZNAY   Alt. **Saznay** [Сазнай] (ORS 209).

SĀBÏSQA   Yak. **Sābïsqa** [Сабыска] (Pek.). ✧ Savvuška (R.), dim. of R. Savva (Pek.).

SĀDA   Kirg. **Sāda-bay** [Саадабай] (Jud. 520). ✧ 'Fearful, coward' cf. Kirg. *zāda, sāda* (Ir.) 'запуганный, пугливый, трусливый' (Jud.).

SĀDAQ see **SADAQ**

SĀDAT   Maml.? 1421 **Sādat** [سعادات بنت صرغتمس], fem. (Ibn Taghrīb. VI, 397, 477, 507); Kirg. **Sādat** [Саадат] (Jud. 35, 632); Trkm.? 1813 **Sādat-quli-χan** [Садат-кули-хан], from the Buɣairlï (бугаирлы) clan (MIT II, 213); Trkm.? 1813 **Sādet-quli-χan** (**Saadet-quli-χan**) [Саадет-кули-хан], governor of Bam (MIT II, 386); Kzk. **Sādät-qan** [Sädät / Сäдäт кан] (Proben III, 39). ✧ 'Happiness, prosperity, felicity' cf. Turk. *saadet* (Ar.) 'id.' (TED).

SĀDET see **SĀDAT**

SĀDET-GÏREY   Crm. 1689 **Sādet-girey-χan** [سعادت كراى خان], Crimean Khan (1691), Qïrïm-girey-sultan's son (Vel.-Zern., Crim. 763, 767); Crm. 1532 **Sädet-girey** (<**Saydet-girey**) [Сайдетъ-Гирей], Crimean Khan (1524-1532) (PSRL VIII, 279). ⇨

SĀDAT + KERÄY.

SĀDU Alt. 19th-20th c. **Sādu** [Сааду] (OjrRS 209). ✧ 'Trading' cf. Alt. *sādu* 'id.' (OjrRS).

SĀFİ Yürük 1543 **Sāfi** [Sâfî] (Gökb., Rum. 186). ✧ 'Clear, pure, sincere' (Ar.) (Kusimova, Sattarov), cf. Turk. *safi* 'die Reinheit' (Radl. IV, 423).

SĀHİB-GİREY Kzk. 19th c. **Sahib-kirey / Sahib-girey** [Sahibkirey / Sahib Girey], Jihangir Khan's son, died in 1849 (Toğan, BTT 246,); Crm.(Tat.) 1510 **Sāhib-girey-χan / Saib-girey / Saip-girey** [Sâhib Girey Han / Саибъ Гирей / Саипгирей], a Crimean Khan (1532-1551), Meñli-girey's son (Toğan, BTT 132). ✧ I. 'Lord-giant'; II. 'Friend/companion - Kirey / Friend/companion - follower'(<Ar.-P) (Kusimova), cf. Crm.(Tat.) *saip* 'хозяин, владелец' (KrmRS), Turk. *sahib* (Ar.) 'der Besitzer, der Wirth, der Herr' (Radl. IV, 285). ⇨ **KERÄY.**

SĀQÏNYÏQ Yak. **Sāqïnyïq / Sāχïnyïq** [Сакынjык, Сахынjык] (Pek.).

SĀL Kzk. 19th c. **Sāl-bay** [Саалбай] (SODž. 38). ⇨ **SAQAL?**

SĀLÏY Hak.(Sag.) 19th-20th c. **Sālïy** [Салыі богатыръ] (Proben IX, 327).

SĀM Hak.? 19th-20th c. **Sām** [Сам], fem. (Katanov, Otč. 13). ✧ 'He himself' cf. R. *sam* 'id.' (Katanov).

SĀMSAQ see **SARÏMSAQ**

SĀNA Hak.(Sag.) 19th-20th c. **Sāna** [Сана] (Katanov, Otč. 8). ✧ Sanya cf. R. Саня (Katanov).

SĀNČA Tuv. 19th c. **Sanja** [Санца] (Proben IX, 149); Hak.? 19th c. **Sānča** [Санча] (Katanov, Otč. 12); Hak.? 19th-20th c. **Sānča** [Санча], fem. (Katanov, Otč. 13); Karg. **Sānča** [Санча], fem. (Katanov, Otč. 9); Hak.(Sag.) 19th-20th c. **Sānča / Sanča** [Санча, Саньча] (Proben IX, 553). ✧ Sancha (R.), cf. R. *San'ča* (Саньча) (Katanov).

SĀNQA Hak.? 19th c. **Sānqa** [Санка] (Katanov, Otč. 12). ✧ Sanka (R.), cf. R. *San'ka* (Санька) (Katanov).

SĀNU Alt. 19th-20th c. **Sānu** [Саану] (OjrRS 209); Alt. 19th-20th c. **Sānu** [Саану], fem. (OjrRS 213).

SĀR-BAS Kzk. 19th c. **Sār-bas** [Саарбасъ] (SOK 64). ✧ 'Strong head?' cf. Kirg. *sār* 'die Gewalt, der innere Gehalt, die Gestalt' (Radl. IV, 313). ⇨ **SARÏ? + BAŠ.**

SĀRΓÏR Yak. **Sārγïr** [Саргыр], Ojolūn's younger son (Pek.).

SĀSXAN Hak. 19th-20th c. **Sāsχan** [Саасхан], fem. (HRS 354). ✧ 'Magpie' (HRS, Butanaev).

SĀSQA Hak.(Shor) 19th-20th c. **Sāsqa** [Саска] (Katanov, Otč. 11).

SĀT Yürük 1543 **Sāt** [ساعت / Saat] (Gökb., Rum. 221, 222, 226, 229). ✧ 'Hour; clock' cf. Turk. *sa'at* (Ar.) 'id.' (Radl. IV, 218), *sāt* (Alt.) 'lange Zeit, spät', (Tat., Turk.) 'die Stunde' (Radl. IV, 376). See also **YÏPAR-ΓAZAN-SĀT, QUTLU-SĀT.**

SĀBÄNDÄY Tuv. 19th c. **Sābändäy** [Сäбäндäі]

(Proben IX, 69).

SÄBİN-TÜBÄ Bashk. 1761 **Säbin-tübä** [Сябын-тюба] (MIB IV/1, 225).

SÄDÄY Yak. **Sädäy** [Сäдäі (ус)], byname of a smith (Pek.). ⇨ **SATAY?**

SÄGÄYÄN Yak. **Sägäyǎn** [Сäгäjäн] (Pek.).

SÄXET Trkm. 20th c. **Säχet** [Sähet] (Zaj. 1971, 332); Trkm. 20th c. **Säχet** [Сахат] (TrkmRS 610). ✧ 'Day favorable for a feast or wedding' (Zaj. 1971), cf. Trkm. *säχet* 'день, счияемый удачным для проведения тоя, свадьбы' (TrkmRS) (<Ar. *saîd*).

SÄXET-DURDÏ Trkm. 20th c. **Säχet-durdï** [Sähetdurdï] (Zaj. 1971, 334). ✧ 'Lucky day - remained/survived' cf. Trkm. *säχet* 'день, считаемый удачным для проведения тоя, свадьбы и т. п.' (TrkmRS) (<Ar. *saîd*). ⇨ **TURDÏ.**

SÄXRA Trkm. 20th c. **Säχrā / Saχrā** [Сахра], fem. (TrkmRS 610); Trkm. 20th c. **Säχra** [Sähra], fem. (Zaj. 1971, 336). ✧ 'Steppe, desert' cf. Trkm. *säχrā* 'пустыня; степь' (TrkmRS) (<Ar.). See also **DALA, YABAN, ŠÖLKEY, TÏS.**

SÄİL Uyg. **Säil** [Säil] (EUTS).

SÄYİK Uyg. 12th c. - 14th c. **Säyik-buyruq** [Säiik Buiruq] (Radl., USp. 249).

SÄYMÄLJİN-UDAΓAN Yak. **Säymäljin-udaγan** [Сäімälцін-удаɓан], Ürgäl-toyon's daughter (Pek.).

SÄYPÜL-MĀLİK Kzk. **Säypül-mǎlik** [Сäіпӱл Мǎлік] (Proben III, 521 /597/). ✧ Sayf-ul-Malik (Ar.) 'Sword of the King (sovereign)', cf. Ar. comp. of names *Sayf-* 'sword' (Ahmed). ⇨ **MELİK.**

SÄYTÄ Bulg. 1323 **Säytä** [سَيتَ / Сäйтä], Ramazān's daughter (Jusupov 23).

SÄKEN Kzk. 19th c. **Säken** [Сакенъ] (AOK 26); Kkalp. 20th c. **Säken** [Сакен], fem. (Bask., Kkalp. 404); Kkalp. 20th c. **Säken** [Сәкен] (KkRS 778); Kzk. 19th c. **Seken / Säken?** [Секенъ] (AOK 14). ✧ I. 'Quiet, peaceful' (Ar.), cf. Tat. *Säkin* (Sattarov), Kzk. *Seken* (Žanuzakov-Esbaeva); II. Shortened form of *Sädwaqas* (<Ar. Sa'ad Waqqas; see SADWAQAS above) in Kazak (Žanuzakov-Esbaeva 458), cf. Kzk. PN *Säken* (Žanuzakov-Esbaeva). See also **BİY-SEKEN.**

SÄKİM Kzk. 19th c. **Säkim-bay (<Säkin-bay?)** [Сакимбай] (Grod., Pril. 182). ⇨ **SÄKEN.**

SÄKİNČ-QARA Uyg. **Säkins-qara**[!] / Säkins Kara] (EUTS); Uyg. 12th - 14th c. **Sävinč-qara**[!] (Radl., USp. 5?); Uyg. 12th c. - 14th c. **Sekinč-qara** [Säkinč Qara / sekinč qara] (Radl., USp. 6, DTS). ✧ 'Säkinč (Sävinč?) the Black' cf. Uyg. *sekin* 'секин, вид подати (DTS). ⇨ **SEVİNČ + QARA.**

SÄKİR Bashk. 1761 **Säkir** [Иликей Сякиров] (MIB IV/1, 218). ✧ 'Jump, dance!' cf. Kuman., Alt., Hak. *säkir-*, Kirg., Kzk. *sekir-* 'springen, hüpfen, tanzen' (Radl. IV, 441-42).

SÄKRİÄTÄM Yak. **Säkriätäm** [Сäкриäтäм], empress in a story (Pek.).

SÄLÂM-BERGEN Uzb. 20th c. **Sälâm-bergän** [Саломберган] (Begmatov 1984, 202). ✧ 'Peace gave him/her; the All-peaceable (Allah) has given him/her' cf. Uzb. *sälâm* 'привет, поклон' (UzbRS), cf. Ar. PN *Salam* 'peace, safety, security' (Ahmed). ⇨ **SALAM + BERGEN.**

SÄLÄÑÄ Yak. **Säläñä** [Сäлäңä] (Pek.). ✧ 'Man with irrepressible/lax character' (Pek.).

SÄLÄÑÄDÄY Yak. **Säläñädäy-udaγan** [Сäлäңäдäй], a legendary shamaness (Pek.). ⇨ **SÄLÄÑÄ +** suff. *-däy.*

SÄLİ Uyg. **Säli** [Säli] (EUTS). See also **SAR-SÄLİ.**

SÄLİYMA Kkalp. 20th c. **Säliyma** [Сәлийма], fem. (KkRS 778). ✧ Salima / Sälima (Ar.), fem. form of Ar. Salim (Žanuzakov).

SÄLİM Bashk. 1777 **Sälim** [Салим Аитов] (MIB V, 59); Bashk. 1778 **Sälim** [Тюкей Салимов] (MIB V, 70); Kzk. 19th c. **Sälim** [Салимъ Кулычевъ] (Grod., Pril. 184); Nog. 20th c. **Sälim** [Салим Йантувгъан увлы], Baskakov's informant from the aul of İrγaqlï (Bask., Nog. 143); Tat.(Lit.) 1585 **Selim** [Селимъ Ямбековичъ] (Lit. Tat. 50-53); Bashk. 1756 **Selim** [Селим Елдашев] (MIB IV/1, 207). ✧ Salim (Ar.) 'sound, perfect, complete, safe, secure' (Ahmed), cf. Uzb. *sälim* 'здравомыслящий человек' (UzbRS), also Kzk. PN *Sälim* (Žanuzakov-Esbaeva).

SÄLİM-BERDİ Uzb. 20th c. **Sälim-berdi** [Салимберди] (Begmatov 1984, 202). ✧ 'Sound/perfect gave him/her; Reasonable thinking (man) gave him/her'. ⇨ **SÄLİM + BERDİ.**

SÄLİPİÄN Yak. **Sälipiän / Silipiän / Silippiän** [Сäліпіäн / Сіліп(п)іäн] (Pek.). ✧ Ksenofont (R.).

SÄLLİKTÄY Yak. **Sälliktäy** [Сäлліктäі] (Pek.). ✧ 'Consumptive, miserable (man)' (= R. Čahotnik) (Pek.).

SÄLMEN Kkalp. 20th c. **Sälmen** [Сәлмен] (KkRS 776). ⇨ **SALMAN?**

SÄMBİL Tuv. 19th c. **Sämbïl** [Сämбіл] (Proben IX, 149).

SÄMÄČČİK see **SÄMÄNČİK**

SÄMÄN Yak. **Sämän** [Сämäн] (Pek.). ✧ Semen (Semyon) (R.) (Pek.).

SÄMÄNČİK Yak. **Sämänčik / Sämäččik** [Сämäнчік, Сämäччік] (Pek.). ✧ Dim. of R. *Semen (Semyon)* (Pek.). ⇨ **SÄMÄN + dim. suff.** *-čik.*

SÄMEKİ Kkalp. 20th c. **Sämeki** [Сәмеки] (KkRS 776).

SÄMİČÄ Uyg. **Sämiçä** [Sämiçä] (EUTS); Uyg. 12th c. - 14th c. **Sämičä** (Radl., USp. 130-131).

SÄMİŠ Uyg. **Sämiš** [Sämiş] (EUTS).

SÄNEM see **SANAM**

SÄÑÄ Uyg. **Säñä** [Sängä] (EUTS). See also **İNČ-SÄÑÄ.**

SÄÑÄKDÄZ see **SEÑÄKTÄZ**

SÄÑÄKTÄS see **SEÑÄKTÄZ**

SÄÑÄTÄZ see **SEÑÄKTÄZ**

SÄPİNLİG Türk 8th-9th c. **Säpinlig** [Säpinlig] (ETY II, 146).

SÄRGÄY Yak. **Särgäy** [Сäргäі] (Pek.); Karg. **Särkäy** [Сäркäй] (Katanov, Otč. 9). ✧ Sergey (R.) (Pek., Katanov).

SÄRİN Khorezm./Chag. 14th c. **Särin-beg**, Miranshah's wife at the end of the 14th c. (Barth., Ulugb. 30).

SÄRKÄ see **SERKE**

SÄRKÄY see **SÄRGÄY**

SÄRQAN Kkalp. 1750 **Särqan-batïr / Sär-qan-batïr?** [Сяркан батыр] (MIKk. 222).

SÄRMİŠ Uyg. 13th-14th c. **Särmiš-täñrim**, fem. (Zieme, Mat. II, 91). ✧ '(S)he endured/tolerated' cf. Karakh. *ser-* 'терпеть, выносить' (DTS).

SÄRSÄN see **SÄRSEN**

SÄRSEN Kkalp. 20th c. **Särsän** [Сäрсäн] (Bask., Kkalp. 401); Kkalp. 20th c. **Särsen** [Сәрсен] (KkRS 776); Kkalp. 20th c. **Särsen-bay** [Сәрсенбай] (KkRS 776); Kzk. 19th c. **Sersen-bay** [Серсенбай] (SOK 46). ✧ 'Dried; wet'? cf. Kkalp. *särsem* 'вяленый; мокрый, невысохший' (KkRS).

SÄT see **SET**

SÄTÄRČİ NUyg.(Tar.) **Sätärči** [Sätärgi [!] / Сätäрчі], from Kashgar (Proben VI, 12 /15/). ✧ 'Player of *sätär* (a three-stringed instrument)' cf. NUyg.(Tar.) *sätärči* 'der Seterspieler' (Radl. IV, 483).

SÄTİ Oghuz/Trkm. 11th c. **Säti** [Сати ибн Алтунташ], son of the Khorezmshah Altun-taš (MIT I, 340). ✧ 'Happy, lucky'? cf. Kzk. *sättï* 'glücklich' (Radl. IV, 484), *sättï* 'удачливый, успешный; удачный, счастливый' (KzRS).

SÄÜRÄ Tat.(Tob.) **Säürä** [Сäÿpä], fem. (Proben IV, 275 /341/). ✧ 'April; born in April' (Sattarov) (<Ar.). See also **NİSAN, TOBA-AY.**

SÄVİG see **SÄWÜK**

SÄVİK see **SÄWÜK**

SÄVİNÄ Uyg. 13th-14th c. **Sävinä**, fem. (Zieme, Mat. II, 88). ✧ 'Oh, rejoice! Oh, be delighted!' (Vocative form). ⇨ **SEVİN + voc. suff.** *-ä / -a.*

SÄVİNÄK Uyg. **Sävinäk** (Zieme, Mat. I, 74, 80). ✧ 'Little joy' cf. Uyg., Karakh. *sevin-* 'радоваться' (DTS). ⇨ **SEVİN + suff.** *-äk.* See also **SEVİNÜG.**

SÄWKÄ Bashk. 1777 **Säwkä-bay** [Сявкабай Кучеляков] (MIB V, 544, 545). ✧ 'Jackdaw' cf. Bashk. *säükä* 'галка' (BRS/Uraksin). See also **TÄN.**

SÄWLE Kkalp. 20th c. **Säwle** [Сäвле / Сәўле], fem. (Bask., Kkalp. 404, KkRS 778). ✧ 'Beam, gleam' cf. Kkalp. *säwle* 'луч, отражение' (KkRS).

SÄWÜK Uyg. **Säük-buyruq / Säwük-buyruq** [Säük Buiruq] (Radl., USp. 249); Uyg. 13th-14th c. **Sävig-täñrim**, fem. (Zieme, Mat. III, 274 (after Tuguseva));

Uyg. **Sävik** [Sävik] (EUTS); Turk. 16th c. **Sevik** (Ongan, Ank. II /Num. 481/). ✦ 'Beloved, loving, kind' cf. Uyg., Karakh. *sevüg / sewüg* 'любимый, любящий, милый' (DTS), Chag. *säwik* 'geliebt' (Radl. IV, 505). See also **DİLBER, SÜYÜM, SÜYÜŠ**.

SĀDÄT see **SĀDAT**

SĀTİ Kzk. **Sāti-bay** [Sāti Bai / Cāти Баи] (Proben III, 80 /103/).

SEBÄN Kzk. **Sebän / Sïban** [Себäн / Сыбан] (Proben III, 134 /170/, 163 /202/).

SEBE Kzk. 19th c. **Sebe** [Себе] (SOK 238).

SEBEK Tuv. 19th c. **Sebek** [Сäбäк] (Proben IX, 215, 216); Kzk. 19th c. **Sebek-pay** [Себекпай] (SODž 72).

SEBENĊ see **SEVİNČ**

SEBİNČ see **SEVİNČ**

SEBÜK Oghuz **Sävük-tigin / Sävük-täkin / Sävük-tägin** [Sävük tigin (t(ä)kin / t(ä)gin)] (Le Coq, Ind. 1); Uyg. 1337 **Sebüg** [Sebug], fem. (Chwol., Syr.-nest. (NF) 31); Oghuz 923, 924 **Sebük** [سُبُك / سبك المنلحى / Sebük] (Hil. Sābī 276, Miskawayh 190, Arīb 111); Oghuz 908-932, 949 **Sebük? / Sebük-tekin** [Sabak / Sebüktekin], a liberated (slave), commander, died in 949 (Weil, Chalif. II, 324, III, 23); Oghuz 917, 923 **Sebük / Sübük** [سبك / سَبك / سُبُك], a slave (γulām) (Miskawayh 118, 163); Uyg. 1325 **Sebük-tärim**, fem. (Chwol., Syr.-nest. (NF) 25); Oghuz 924 **Sebük-tegin** [ناصرالـدين سبكتكين / Sebüktegin] (Mirch. Gasnevid. 4, Muh. Ibrahim 28); Oghuz 964 **Sebük-tegin** [العجمى سبكتكين] (Ibn al-Athīr/Tornb. VIII, 409-10, 434); Oghuz 975 **Sebük-tegin** [سبكتكين المعزّي] (Qalānisi 11); Oghuz/Trkm. 974, 977, 997 **Sebük-tegin** [سبكتكين / سبكتكِين / سبكتـكِّين / سبنتكين / Soboctegin / Sabûktakîn / Sebegtegin / Subukteghin / Sebüktekin / Себÿкгегин / Себуктегин], (977-997), the founder of the Ghaznavid dynasty, the Khorezmshah Mahmud's (998-1030) father (Abulfidā III, 74-5, Ibn al-Athīr/Tornb. VIII, 503-6, IX, 75-7, X, 4, Juwaynī II, 2, Qazw. 388, 424, Abulfar. 219, 317, Abulfar./Budge I, 186, Jorga, Notes XIII, 256 /Mesalekalabsar/, Muh. Ibrahim 28, Mirch. Bujeh 27, 28, Weil, Chalif. III, 60, Arūs al-Qulūb: Belleten VII, 497, Abulg./Kon. 700, MIT I, 29, 228, 350, etc.); Oghuz 951, 1062 **Sebük-tegin / Sübük-tegin** [ابو مـنصور / سُبكتكين], Manṣur's father (Ibn al-Athīr/Tornb. VIII, 360, 366, 463-8 etc., Ibn Taghrīb. II, 231, Hil. Sābī 179, MIT I, 359); Oghuz 11th c. **Sebük-tegin / Sübük-tegin?** [بن سبكتكن / سُبُكتَكِين] (Bondārī 5, 6, 8); Oghuz 10th c. **Sebük-tegin / Sübük-tegin?** [سبكتكين / سُبُكتَكِين] (Fakhrī 390); Khorezm. **Sebük-tegin / Sübük-tegin** [محمود بن سبكتكين / محمود بن سبكتكين / يمين الـدولة / Subukteghin] (Abulfar./Budge I, 186,

Muh. Ibrahim 28, Ibn Bībī III, 217, IV, 93); Oghuz 902 **Sübük** [سبك الـد يلمى] (Miskawayh 31, 32); Oghuz? 919 **Sübük** [سبك الطولونى], a Tulunid (Arīb 75-76); Oghuz? 920 **Sübük** [سُبُك غلام ابى الساج], a slave (γulām) (Arīb 77); Oghuz? 927 **Sübük** [سبك], a slave (γulām) of Caliph al-Muktafī (902-908) (Arīb 133). ✦ I. 'Light(-headed), fast, not being quiet (moderate)' (<P.) (Erol II); II. 'Sinew, tendon (of foot); heel' cf. Chag. sübük = der Sehne des Fusses (Radl. IV, 850), also PN *Sübük* 'Ferse Fuss' (Tarj/Houtsma 29); III. 'Beloved, love, loving, kind'? cf. Chwol., Syr.-nest. (NF) p. 61: Trk. *säbük* 'Liebe'. ⇨ **SĀWÜK**.

SEBÜNČ see **SEVİNČ**

SEDEY see **SATAY**

SEDENKEY Alt. 19th c. **Sedenkey** [Седенкей] (Verb., In. 151).

SEDİK Nog. 20th c. **Sedik** [Седик Быйаш увлы / Седик Бияшев], one of Baskakov's informants from the aul of Abram-töbe (Bask., Nog. 144). ✦ I. 'Toothless'? cf. Kzk. *setik* 'zahnlos' (Radl. IV, 483); II. 'Torn out'? cf. Kzk. *setik* 'setilen, sökülen' (KzTS).

SEGEZ see **SEKİZ**

SEGİS see **SEKİZ**

SEGİZ see **SEKİZ**

SEGREK Oghuz/Trkm. 14th c. - 15th c. **Segrek** (DQorq./Rossi 211-219). ✦ 'Flax seed; intelligent, wide awake' cf. Turk. *seğrek* 'keten tohumu, zeyrek' (Tar. Sözl.).

SEYAN see **ZİYAN**

SEYDEK Tat.(Sib.)? **Seydek / Seydäk / Zeydäk / Sedäk / Sendäk** [Сейдекъ / Зейдякъ / Седякъ / Сейдякъ / Сендякъ], son of prince Bikbulatov (Sib. Let. 19, 28, 41-43, 155-159 etc.).

SEYİL Uyg. 12th c. - 14th c. **Säyil?** [Säil] (Radl., USp. 291); Kzk. 19th c. **Seyil** [Сеиль] (SODž 134); Kzk. 19th c. **Seyil** [Сеиль] (SOV 88); Kzk. 1788 **Seyil-χan** [Сеиль-Хань] (Konšin, Mat. V, 100); Kzk. 1846 **Seyil-χan** [Сеильхань] (Konšin, Mat. V, 98); Kzk. 1846 **Seyil-χan** [Сеильхань Джолтабаровъ] (Konšin, Mat. V, 92); Kkalp. 20th c. **Seyil-χan** [Сейилхан] (KkRS 776). ✦ 'Excursion, travel; amusement' cf. Kkalp. (<Ar.) *seyil* 'гулянье, прогулка; народное гулянье, праздничное гулянье; пирушка' (KkRS), Kzk. *seyil* 'der Spaziergang, die Belustigung' (Radl. IV, 438).

SEYİN Kzk. 19th c. **Seyn-bay / Seyin-bay** [Уилди Сеинбаевъ] (Grod., Pril. 90).

SEYİR Tat. 1770 **Seyr-ul / Seyir-ul** [Сеирул Салеев] (MIB IV/2, 398). ✦ 'Excursion, walking' Crm., Tat., Turk. (<Ar.) *säir* 'der Gang, die Promenade' (Radl. IV, 437).

SEYİT Nog. 20th c. **Sayit** [Сайит Еракли увлы / Саит Еракиев], one of Baskakov's informants from the aul of Abram-töbe (Bask., Nog. 144); Kkalp. 20th c. **Seyit** [Сейит] (KkRS 776); Kirg. **Seyit** [Сейит] (Jud.

906); Kkalp. 20th c. **Seyit-žan** [Сейитжан] (KkRS 776); Kzk. 1770-1830 **Sent-qul** [Сентъ-Кулъ], a Kipchak from the Kitaba-Turayɣïr branch of the subdivision Qara (AUK 751); Kzk. **Sent-qul / Seyt-qul?** [Sentkul] (Atyns. 37); NUyg.(Tar.) **Sït-bay** [Sit Bai / Сіт баі] (Proben VI, 113 /149/). ✧ I. Seyyid (Ar.), descendant of the Prophet (TED, Radl. IV, 451, Jud.); II. (Comp.) 'Master, gentleman, (land)lord, aristocrat, chief; ruler, chieftain, leader' (Kusimova, Sattarov). Originally one born in the clan of the Prophet *Muhammed.* Cf. Uyg. *säyid* 'сейид, почетный (мусульманский титул)' (DTS). As a secondary component originally comes before the main component of the name (Cafer., Ağa 90).

SEYİT-ASAN   Tat. 1446 **Seyit-asan** [Сеитъ-Асанъ (Сеусанъ)], a prince from Kazan (PSRL VI, 172, VIII, 114). ⇨ SEYİT + XASAN.

SEYİT-BATTAL   Tat.(Mish.) 1765 **Seyit-battal** [Сеитбаттал Батыршын] (MIB IV/1, 308); Bashk. 1780 **Seyit-battal** [Бекберда Сеитьатталов] (MIB V, 110, 111, 145). ⇨ SEYİT + BATTAL.

SEYİT-ГALİY   Kkalp. 20th c. **Seyit-ɣaliy** [Сейитгалий] (KkRS 776); Tat.(GH) 1408 **Seyt-ali-biy** [/ Снитялибъ / Сейтялибій] (PSRL VI, 136, VIII, 82-83). ⇨ SEYİT + ALİ.

SEYİT-KÄMAL   Kkalp. 20th c. **Seyit-kämal** [Сейиткәмал] (KkRS 776). ⇨ SEYİT+ KEMAL.

SEYİT-MAMÏT   Kkalp. 20th c. **Seyit-mamït** [Сейитмамыт] (KkRS 776). ⇨ SEYİT + MAMÏT.

SEYİT-NAZAR   Kkalp. 20th c. **Seyit-nazar** [Сейитназар] (KkRS 776). ⇨ SEYİT + NAZAR.

SEYİT-NİYAZ   Kkalp. 20th c. **Seyit-niyaz** [Сейитнияз] (KkRS 776). ⇨ SEYİT + NİYAZ.

SEYKİM-BAY see SEYKİN

SEYKİN   Kzk. 19th c. **Seyken-bay** [Сейкенбай] (SOK 234); Kzk. 19th c. **Seykim-bay** [Умурзакъ Сейкымбаевъ] (Grod., Pril. 143); Kzk. 19th c. **Seykim-bay** [Сейкымбай] (Grod., Pril. 143); Kzk. 19th c. **Seykim-bay** [Сейкымбай] (SOK 104); Kzk. 19th c. **Siykim-bay (<Siykin-bay)** [Сикимбай] (Grod., Pril. 122); Kzk. 19th c. **Siykim-bay (<Siykin-bay)** [Сикимъ-бай Байтилаевъ] (Grod., Pril. 199); Kzk. 19th c. **Siykim-bay (<Siykin-bay)** [Сикимбай] (SOK 302).

SEYMSAN   Tat.(GH) 1472 **Seymsan** [Сеимъсань], a Tatar ruler (PSRL (Russk. Hr.) I, 490).

SEYPİL   Kzk. 19th c. **Seypil / Sïypïl?** [Сейпылъ] (AOO 42).

SEYREK-BASAN   Turk. 19th c. **Seyrek-basan-oɣlu**, a Zeybek (Kúnos 1891, 119). ✧ 'Taking thinly steps' cf. Turk. *seyrek* 'few and far between; rare(ly)' (TED). ⇨ BASAN.

SEYREKLİ   Turk. 19th c. **Seyrekli-oɣlu**, a Zeybek (Kúnos 1891, 119). ✧ 'Wide apart, open; rare(ly)' cf. Turk. *seyrek* 'id.' (TED) + suff. *-li.*

SEYSE   Kzk. 19th c. **Seyse-bay** [Сейсебай] (SODž 28).

SEYSEKE   Kzk. 19th c. **Seyseke / Seys-eke?** [Сейсеке] (AOA 114).

SEYSEN   Kzk. 19th c. **Seysen-bay** [Сейсенбай] (SOK 162); Kkalp. 20th c. **Siysen** [Сийсен] (KkRS 776). ✧ 'Child born on the third day of the lunar calendar' (Žanuzakov 156) (<Ir.).

SEYSENBİ   Kzk. 19th c. **Seysenbi** [Сейсенбы] (SOK 142). ✧ 'Tuesday' cf. Kzk. *seysenbi* 'id.' (KzTS).

SEYTÄK see SEYTEK

SEYTE   Kzk. 19th c. **Seyte-bay** [Сейтебай] (SODž. 24).

SEYTEK   Bashk. 1763 **Seytäk** [Исенаман Сейтяков] (MIB IV/2, 45); Kzk. 19th c. **Seytek** [Сейтекь] (AOAtb. 10); Kirg. **Seytek** [Сейтек] (Jud. 79, 190). ⇨ SEYİT + suff. *-ek?*

SEYTEN   Kzk. 19th c. **Seyten** [Сейтенъ] (AOK 90); Kzk. 19th c. **Seyten** [Сейтеновъ] (AOO 46).

SEYTİMBET   Kkalp. 20th c. **Seytimbet** [Сейтимбет] (KkRS 776). ⇨ SEYİT + suff. *-imbet.*

SEYÜRÜK   Kzk. 19th c. **Seyürük-bay** [Бикай Сеюрукбаевъ] (Grod., Pril. 69).

SEYÜŠ   Tat. 1624 **Seyüš** [Сеюшъ Арыковъ] (Pokrovskij 72).

SEK   Kzk. 19th c. **Sek-pay** [Секпай] (SOK 70, 228, 240). ✧ 'Sheep in the second spring' cf. Kzk. *sek* 'ein Hammel im zweiten Frühling' (Radl. IV, 441).

SEKE see SEKİ

SEKEL   Kzk. / Kirg.? 19th c. **Sekel** [Сэкэль] (Potanin II, 3).

SEKEN I.   Maml. 1250 **Seken** [سكن] (Iyās I, 91). ✧ 'Jump, dance!' cf. Chag. *säkän-*, Kuman., Alt., Hak. *säkir-*, Kirg., Kzk. *sekir-* 'springen, hüpfen, tanzen' (Radl. IV, 441-42).

SEKEN II. see SÄKEN

SEKER see ŠEKER

SEKİ   Bashk. 1729 **Seke** [Секе Иркенеев] (MIB III, 264); Tat.(GH) 13th c. **Sekke / Seki?** [Σεκκέ / Секке], a christened Tatar from the Crimea (Byz. Turc. 272, Smirnov, Krym. 34); Bashk. 1757 **Siki** [Сики Сююндюков] (MIB IV/1, 157, 171). ✧ 'Banch' cf. Tat., Turk. *säkï / sikï* 'der erhöhte Sitzplatz im Hause' (Radl. IV, 442, 681). See also **BAY-SEKE, SAY-SEKE, İNČ-SEKÄ.**

SEKİČÜN   Uyg. 13th c. **Sekičün** [sekičün] (DTS).

SEKİZ   Kzk. 19th c. **Segez-bay** [Сегезбай] (SODž. 68, 158); Kzk. 19th c. **Segez-bay** [Сегезбай] (AOK 34); Kzk. 19th c. **Segis-bay** [Сегисбай] (SOK 180); Kzk. 1803, 1820 **Segiz-bay** [Сегизбай], chief of the Masqar tribe of the Little Horde (Kiši Žüz) (MIK IV, 515, Sib. Vest. IX, 119); Kzk. 1820 **Segiz-bay** [Сегизбай], one of the chiefs of the Tazlar tribe (Sib. Vest. IX, 120); Kzk. 19th c. **Segiz-bay** [Сегизбай] (AOO 70); Kzk.

19th c. **Segiz-bay** [Сегызбай] (AOA 78); Kzk. 19th c. **Segiz-bay** [Сегизбай] (SOK 59, 104, 106, 286, 300); Kzk. 19th c. **Segiz-bay** [Сегизбай] (SODž. 36, 102, 134); Kzk. 19th c. **Segiz-bay** [Сегизбай] (SOV 38, 140); Turk. 1540 **Sekiz** [سكز], a kethudâ, chief of the Haydarlu of Bozulus tribe (cemaat) (Demirtaş 49); Kzk. 1794 **Sigez-bay / Sikiz-bay?** [سیکز بای] (MIK IV, 163); Kzk. 18th. c. **Sigiz-bay** [Сигизбай] (Sib. Vest. IX, 189); Kzk. 1789 **Sigiz-bay** [Сигизбай бей], a biy (MIK IV, 117); Kzk. 19th c.? **Sigiz-bay** [Сигизъ бай] (Voenn. Sb. L, 105); Kzk. 19th c. **Sigiz-bay** [Сигизбай] (SOV 122); Kzk. 1785 **Sikiz-bay** [Сикизбай] (MIK IV, 63); Kzk. 1785 **Sikiz-bay** [سكز بای], the aqsaqal of the Šekti tribe (جكتی) (MIK IV, 51, 53 etc.); *TN:* Kzk. **Sekiz-χan** [Секиз-хань], a well at Qara-buγaz (Karta JAR X.). ✧ 'Eight' cf. Türk, Uyg. *segiz / sekiz* 'восемь' (DTS), Kuman, Chag., Crm., Kar., Turk. *säkiz* 'acht' (Radl. IV, 443), Kirg., Kzk. *segiz* 'id.' (Radl. IV, 446), Tat. *sigĭz* 'id.' (Radl. IV, 685).

SEKİZEK   Tat. 1619 **Sekizäk** [Секизачко Колызбаевъ] (Kurdjumov 117, 120, 121); Tat. 1708 **Sekizek** [Секисечка Калчегулов] (MIB I, 233). ✧ 'Little eight; eighth (child)' (Sattarov), cf. Türk, Kuman, Chag., Crm., Kar., Turk. *säkiz* 'acht' (Radl. IV, 443). ⇨ SEKİZ + dim. suff. -ek.

SEKREK   Oghuz/Trkm. 14th c. - 15th c. **Sekrek / Segreg / Segrek** [Segrek, Segreg / Секрек], Ušun-qoĭa's younger son (DQorq. 89, 90, 94, 111, 113, 140 etc.).

SEKSEM-BAY see SEKSEN

SEKSEN   Kzk. 1884 **Säksän-bay** [Эльфисъ-бай Саксанбаевъ] (Grod., Pril. 94); Kzk. **Säksen-bay** [Усербай Саксенбаевъ] (Grod., Pril. 23); Kzk. 1803, 1820 **Säksen-bay** [Саксенбай], one of the chiefs of the Čar-žitim of Orta Žüz tribe (MIK IV, 513, Sib. Vest. IX, 106); NUyg. 19th c. **Seksan** [سكسان / Seksan] (Le Coq, Namenl. 114); Kzk. **Seksän-batïr** [Seksän Batyr / Сексäн батыр] (Proben III, 74 /96/); Kzk. **Seksän-batïr** [Сексäн Батыр] (Proben III, 74 /96/); Kzk. 19th c. **Seksem-bay** [Сексембай] (AOK 46); Kzk. 19th c. **Seksem-bay** [Сексембай] (AOK 106); Kzk. 19th c. **Seksem-bay** [Сексембай] (SOK 110, 182); Kzk. 19th c. **Seksem-bay** [Сексембай] (SODž. 116); Kzk. 19th c. **Seksem-bay** [Сексембай] (AOO 26); Kzk. 19th c. **Seksem-bay** [Сексембай] (SOV 4, 56); Kzk. 19th c. **Seksem-bay** [Сексембай] (SODž. 34, 144); Maml. 14th c. **Seksen** [سكسن] (Sauvaget 48); Kzk. 18th c. - 19th c. **Seksen** [Сексен] (Tynyšp. 71, 74); Kzk. 19th c. **Seksen** [Сексенъ] (AOK 42, 82); Kzk. 19th c. **Seksen** [Сексеновъ] (AOO 46); Kzk. 19th c. **Seksen** [Сексенъ] (SOK 204); Kzk. 19th c. **Seksen** [Сексенъ] (SODž. 154); Kzk. 19th c. **Seksen** [Сексенъ] (SOV 22,

104); Kzk. 1870 **Seksen** [Сексенъ] (Lomakin 39); Kzk. 19th c. **Seksen-bay** [Сексенбай] (AOP 10, 82, 110); Kzk. 19th c. **Seksen-bay** [Сексенбай] (SOK 130, 264); Kirg. **Seksen-bay** [Сексенбай] (Jud. 597); Kzk. 1817 **Seksen-bay / Seksän-bay** [سیکسا نبای / Сексенбай] (MIK IV, 311); Kzk. 19th c. **Siksen** [Бора Сиксеновъ] (Pam. kn. Turg. 71). ✧ 'Eighty' cf. Karakh. *seksün* 'восемьдесят' (DTS), Chag., Kuman, Crm., Turk. *säksän* 'achtzig' (Radl. IV, 444), Kirg., Kzk. *seksän* 'id.' (Radl. IV, 444).

SEL   Chuv. 18th-19th c. **Sel-murza** [Селмурза] (Magn. 75).

SELAMÏŠ see SALAMÏŠ

SELBE   Kzk. 19th c. **Selbe** [Селбе] (SOK 264). ⇨ **SELBİ?**

SELBİ   Trkm. 20th c. **Selbi** [Selbi], fem. (Zaj. 1971, 340); Trkm. 20th c. **Selbi** [Селби], fem. (TrkmRS 571). ✧ 'Cypress'; 'Willow' (Zaj. 1971), cf. Trkm. *selbi* 'ива' (TrkmRS).

SELČÄ   Pecheneg 1057 **Selčä** [Σελτέ], a chieftain (Byz. Turc. 272); Kirg. 1624 **Selčä** [Сельча], a prince, Qara's brother (Miller, Ist. Sib. II, 316, 317).

SELČUQ see SELČUK

SELČUQİ-XOWAND   Selj. 1292 **Selčuqi-χowand?** [سلجوقی خواند], Qïlïč-arslan's daughter, mentioned in an inscription of Tokat, Turkey (Hakkı, Ves. I, 12).

SELČUK   Selj. 12th. c. **Selčuq** [سالجوق], Muχammed-šah's (1105-1118) son (Ibn Taghrïb. II, 369); Turk. 16th c. **Selčuq** [سلجوق / Selçuk], fem. (Ongan, Ank. II /Num. 1439/); Khorezm.? 1333 **Selčuq** [سلجق], among the soldiers of Toqtay (Dawād. 276); Turk. 1459 **Selčuq-hatun** [Selçuk Hatun], daughter of Abdullah (Hoşkadem azadlısı) (Gökb., Ed. 352); Turk. 1503, 1509, 1528 **Selčuq-hatun** [Selçuk Hatun], Mehmet Çelebi's daughter (Gökb., Ed. 47, 467, 475); Turk. 1508, 1530 **Selčuq-hatun** [Selçuk Hatun], daughter of Bâyezid II (1480-1512) (Gökb., Ed. 388, 389); Turk. 1519 **Selčuq-hatun** [Selçuk Hatun], wife of Şeyh Seyyid Abdi Paşa (Gökb., Ed. 389); Turk. 1528 **Selčuq-hatun** [Selçuk Hatun], Mürsel's daughter (Gökb., Ed. 50); Turk. 14th c. **Selčuq-χatun** [سالجوق خاتون], in the family of Kadı Burhaneddin, proprietor of Sivas (Nafiz-Hakkı 154); Turk.? 1446/47 **Selčuq-χatun** [سلجق خاتون / Saldjuq khatun], Sultan Burhan's daughter (?) (CIA 3/I, 50); Khorezm.? 1280 **Selčuq-χatun** [سالجوق خاتون], mentioned in connection with Abaqa Ilkhan (RaD/Jahn 10); Selj. **Selčuq-šah** [سلجوقشاه بن سعد بن زنگی] (Qazw. 508-509); Karakh. **Selčük** [Selçük] (MK/Atalay 850); Turk. 1402 **Selčük-χatun** [سلجوك خاتون], Saruja-beg's daughter (MG Ank. 23); Turk. 1430 **Selčük-paša** [سلجوك پاشا], İzzeddin-čelebi's daughter, mentioned in a tomb inscription in Tokat, Turkey (Hakkı, Ves. I, 53);

Oghuz/Trkm. 10th c. **Selĵuq / Selčuq / Salĵuq?**
[سلجوق بن لقمان / Amîr Saljûk / Сельджук ибн
Дукак (Тукак) / Сельджук ибн Лукман], an emir,
Toqaq Temir Yalïɣ's (Tuqaq's / Duqaq's) son,
forefather of the Seljuks from the Qïnïq tribe of the
Oghuz (Abulfar./Budge I, 195, Qazw. 434, Rāwandī 87,
88, 479, Abulfidā III, 102-103, MIT I, 246, 312, 320,
344, 345 etc.); Oghuz/Trkm. 13th c. **Selĵuq-bay /
Selčuq-bay** [سلجوق بای / Сельджук-бай]
(Abulg./Kon. 1135); Oghuz? **Selĵuq-šah** [سلجوقشاه /
Сельджук-шах] (Qazw. 434, RaD II, 199); Oghuz
11th c. **Selĵük-sü-baši** [selǯük sü baši], forefather of
the Seljuk dynasty (DTS); *TN:* Turk. 20th c. **Selčik**
[Selçik], a village in the province of Afyon, Turkey
(TMİB 42). ✧ 'Little stream, flood' cf. Crm., Kirg.,
Turk. *säl* 'der Strom, die Strömung, die
Ueberschwemmung' (Radl. IV, 476), cf. also Rásonyi:
Selçük adının menşeine dair: Belleten III (1939), pp.
377-384. See also **QÏYAN-SELČÜK**.

SELĴAN Oghuz/Trkm. 14th c. - 15th c. **Selĵan-χatun /
Salĵan-χatun / Selĵen-χatun** [Salcan Xatun, Selcen
Hātūn / Сельджан-хатун] (DQorq. 65-72, 196, 239,
245).

SELÄN Chuv. 19th c. **Selän** [Selän], fem. (Kronheim
96).

SELE Kzk. 19th c. **Sele-bay / Sili-bay?** [Селебай]
(SOK 76). ⇨ **SİLÜ?**

SELENDEY Chuv. 19th c. **Selendey** [Selendeï]
(Kronheim 96).

SELENKE Kzk. (<R.?) 19th c. **Selenkin (<Selenke?)**
[Бедырденъ Селенкинъ] (AOK 66).

SELEPES Kzk. 19th c. **Selepes** [Селепесовъ] (AOK
98).

SELİ Kzk. 19th c. **Seli-bay** [Селибай] (SOK 258);
Kkalp. 20th c. **Seli-χan** [Сели-хан] (KkRS 776). ✧
'Seli-Blessed-Rock' (Blagova 1997, 704). See also
SİÑQU-SELİ.

SELİ-QUTLUɢ-QAYA Uyg. 12th c. - 14th c. **Seli-
qutluɣ-qaya** (DTS). ⇨ **SELİ** + **QUTLUɢ** + **QAYA**.

SELİM see **SÄLİM**

SELİMŠA Tat.(Lit.) 1593 **Selimša** [Селимша
Муступинъ Куминовичъ] (Lit. Tat. 168). ⇨ **SÄLİM**
+ suff. -*ša* or comp. *šah?*

SELİS Kzk. 19th c. **Selis-pay** [Селизпай] (SOV 134);
Kzk. 19th c. **Seliz-bay** [Селизбай] (SOK 38).

SELKEY Bashk. 1756 **Selkey** [Селкей Тевеков]
(MIB IV/1, 128). ⇨ **SEL** + suff. -*key*.

SELMÄN see **SALMAN**

SELTÄŠ Bashk. 1754, 1759 **Seltäš** [Селтяж (Селташ)
Нуркеев] (MIB IV/1, 83, IV/2, 20, 24); Bashk. 1763
Seltäš [Селтяш Нуркеев] (MIB IV/2, 45); Bashk.
1764 **Seltäš** [Иткуста Селтяшев] (MIB IV/1, 279).

SELÜK Selj.? 1290 **Selük** [سالوك], Salar's brother
(Dorn 147, 153). ⇨ **SEL?** + suff. -*ük*.

SEM-BAY see **ESÄN**

SEM-BEY see **ESÄN**

SEM-BEK see **ESÄN**

SEMBİ Kzk. 19th c. **Sembe** [Сембе] (SODž. 8); Kzk.
19th c. **Sembi** [Сембы] (SOV 18). ✧ 'Saturday (child
born on Saturday)' (Žanuzakov), cf. Kzk. *sembi* 'der
Sonnabend' (Radl. IV, 512), Kzk. *senbi* 'суббота'
(KzRS) (<Ir.). See also **SUBBŌTA**.

SEMÄTÄY see **SEMETEY**

SEMEY Tat. 1675 **Semey** [Семейко Араслановъ
(Арысланов / Яраслановъ)] (Kungursk. akty 25, 27);
Kzk. 19th c. **Semey-bay** [Семейбай] (AOP 103). ✧
'High ranked, great; dear' cf. Bashk., Kzk., Tat. PN
Sämiy (Kusimova, Sattarov, Žanuzakov-Esbaeva)
(<Ar.).

SEMEYKE Bashk. 1740 **Semeyke** [Семейке] (MIB I,
398). ⇨ **SEMEY** + suff. -*ke*.

SEMEK Kzk. 19th c. **Semek** [Семекъ] (AOP 86);
Maml. 1308 **Semek / Šemek** [Seïf-eddin-Semek /
Schemek], a vice-roy, Salar's brother (Makrīzī IV, 274,
/ Weil, Chalif. I, 287). ✧ 'Flabby (lymphatic), parched'
cf. Kzk. *semik* 'дряблый, отсохший' (KzRS), Kzk.
semik 'welk, mürbe, vertrocknet (Fuss oder Hand)'
(Radl. IV, 509).

SEMEN Tat. 1558 **Semen-murza** [Семенъ-мурза]
(PSRL XIII, 281).

SEMENDER see **SAMANDAR**

SEMENDRE Turk. 1552 **Semendre** [Ferruh Semendre]
(G. Dávid's communication). ⇨ **SEMENDER?**

SEMENTEY Tat. 1704 **Sementey** [Сементей
Иментеев] (Kurdjumov 338).

SEMEŇ Kirg. **Semeň** [Семең] (Jud. 114). ⇨
SEMETEY.

SEMERÄ Chuv. 18th-19th c. **Semerä** [Семеря] (Magn.
75).

SEMETEY Kirg. **Semetey / Semätäy** [Семӓтӓi /
Семетей], Manas' son (Proben V, 280 /282/, Jud. 20);
Kirg. **Sümötöy** [Сӱмöтöi], Manas' son? (Radl. I, 19).

SEMİČ Kzk. 19th c. **Semič** [Семычъ] (SOK 250).

SEMİČÄ Uyg. 12th c. - 14th c. **Semičä** [semičä] (DTS).

SEMİLTİR Kzk. 19th c. **Semiltir** [Семильтверь]
(SOK 142).

SEMİLTİR Kzk. 19th c. **Semiltir / Sïmïltïr?**
[Семылтыръ] (SOK 262).

SEMİLTİR Kzk. 19th c. **Sumïltïr / Semiltir?**
[Сомылтыръ] (SOK 142).

SEMİŠ Uyg. 12th c. - 14th c. **Semiš** [Semiš] (Radl.,
USp. 55, 201, DTS). See also **İT-SEMİŠ**.

SEMİZ Kzk. 19th c. **Semis-bay** [Семисбай] (AOA 26);
Maml. 14th c. **Semiz** [سميز] (Sauvaget 48); Kzk. 19th c.
Semiz [Семизъ] (SOK 38, 104); Kirg. **Semiz-bala**
[Семиз бала] (Jud. 245). ✧ 'Fat' cf. Kuman, Turk.
sämiz 'fett, gemästet', Uyg., Alt. *sämis* 'fett', Kzk.
semiz 'id.' (Radl. IV, 510), Tat. *simez* 'жирный,

упитанный, полный, тучный' (TatRS). See also **İT-SEMİŠ**.

SEMPİR   Kzk. 19th c. **Sempir** [Семпыръ] (SOK 196).

SEMSİBÄ   Uyg. 12th c. - 14th c. **Sämsibä / Semsibä** [Sämsibä] (Radl., USp. 112-113, DTS, EUTS).

SEN   Chuv. 18th-19th c. **Sen** [Сень] (Magn. 75). ⇨ **ESÄN**.

SEN-BAXTA see **ESÄN-BAXTÏ**

SEN-EXMET   Chuv. 19th c. **Sen-exmet** (<İsän-axmet) [Сенехметь] (Magn.). ⇨ **ESÄN + AXMET**.

SEN-GEREY see **ESÄN-GİREY**

SEN-GİLDE see **ESÄN-KELDİ**

SEN-GİLDİ see **ESÄN-KELDİ**

SEN-GİREY see **ESÄN-GİREY**

SENDEL   Turk. 1519, 1528 **Sendel-bey / Sündül-bey** [Sende: Bey / Sündül Bey] (Gökb., Ed. 297).

SENEY   Nog., Kkalp.? 1678 **Seney-aγa** [Сеней ага] (DAI VII, 217).

SENEK   Kkalp. 20th c. **Senek / Seneke-ulï** [Селихъан Сенекe-улы / Сенек], an informant, aged 58 (Bask., Kkalp. 47). ✧ 'A kind of fork' cf. Kzk. *senek* 'вилы с двумя зубьями на длинном шесте' (KzRS).

SENİSLİ   Tat. 1648 **Senisli-bay** [Айдар Сенислыбаев] (Miller, Ist. Sib. II, 529).

SENİZÄK   Tat. 1626 **Senizäk** [Сенизак] (Miller, Ist. Sib. II, 329).

SENKE see **SENKİ**

SENKİ   Kzk. 19th c. **Senke-bay** [Сенкебай] (SOK 204, 210); Kzk. 19th c. **Senke-bay** [Сенкебай] (SOV 100); Kzk. 19th c. **Senke-bay** [Сенкебай] (AOAtb. 66); Kzk. 19th c **Senke-bay** [Сенкебай] (AOP 110); Kzk. 19th c. **Senki-bay** [Сенкибай] (SODž. 12); Kzk. 19th c. **Senki-bay** [Сенкибай] (AOP 42, 82); Kzk. 19th c. **Senki-bay** [Сенкыбай] (AOK 74); *TN:* Kirg. 1862 **Senki-bay** [Сенкибай], a stream in the district of Kopal (ZIRGOGeogr. I, 310). ✧ 'Hard, firm, stony' cf. Crm. *sängi* 'hart, schwer, steinern' (Radl. IV, 449) (<P. سنكى).

SENKÜ   Tat. 1553 **Senkü** [Сенку Тугаевъ] (PSRL XIII, 232). ⇨ **SENKİ?**

SENT-AXMET   Kzk. **Sent-axmet** (<Seyt-axmet?) (Altyns. 81). ⇨ **SEYİT + AXMET**.

SENT-QUL see **SEYİT**

SENTE   Kzk. 19th c. **Sente-bay** [Сентебай] (AOP 122). ✧ 'Anvil' cf. East.T.(Tar.) *sändä* 'der Ambos' (Radl. IV, 455). ⇨ **SANT?**

SENTİK   Kzk. 19th c. **Sentik** [Сентыкъ] (AOK 18).

SENZEK   1453 **Senzek-bey** [Сензекъбѣй], envoy (PSRL (Russk. Hr.) 458). ⇨ **SANJAQ?**

SEÑ-KELDİ see **ESÄN-KELDİ**

SEÑ-SAL   Kzk. 19th c. **Señ-sal** [Сенгсалъ] (Grod., Pril. 130). ⇨ **ESÄN? + SAL**.

SEÑÄ   Uyg. 12th c. - 14th c. **Säñä** [Sängä] (Radl., USp.

51, 54); Uyg. 12th c. - 14th c. **Säñä / Señä** [Sängä / Seŋä] (Radl., USp. 11-12, DTS); Alt. 19th c. **Señä** [Сенгэ] (Verb., In. 119).

SEÑÄKTÄZ   Uyg. 12th c. - 14th c. **Säñäktäs-aγa / Säñäkdäz-aγa** [Sängäktäs-Aγa / Sängäkdäz-Aγa] (Radl., USp. 100-101); Uyg. **Säñätäz** [Sängätäz] (EUTS); Uyg. **Señäktäz** [Sengektes / seŋäktäz / Сäҥгäктäс], an early Uyghur name (Radl., Altuig. 65, DTS). ✧ Sangadaz / Samghadāsa (Skr.) (cf. Zieme, Samb. p. 125).

SEÑGİR   Kzk. 19th c. **Señgir-bay** [Сенгырбай] (SOK 86); Kzk. 19th c. **Señkir** [Сенкиръ] (SODž. 40). ✧ 'Huge, high' cf. Kzk. *zeñgïr* 'громадный, высокий, огромный' (KzRS), Uyg., Karakh. *señir* 'мыс горы; конец стены' (DTS). See also **BAY-SEÑGİR; BOYŠAN, DÄW, DUOLANTAY, KETTÄ, QOŽAQ, ULUΓ, ZOR**.

SEÑİKEY   Kzk. 1679 **Señikey** [Шалдыкъ (Шалдычко) Сенгикѣевъ] (DAI VIII, 44-45).

SEÑİPŌN   Hak.(Blt.) 19th-20th c. **Señipōn** [Сеніпон] (Katanov, Otč. 10).

SEÑKÄ   Uyg. 12th c. - 14th c. **Señkä** [Sängkä] (Radl., USp. 8, DTS).

SEÑKİR see **SEÑGİR**

SEÑMEN   Selj.? **Señmen** [قطب الدين سنغمان] (Qazw. 446).

SEÑÜY   Uyg. **Säñgüy** [Sänggüi] (EUTS); Uyg. **Säñüy-tutuñ** [Sängüi Tutung] (EUTS); Uyg. 12th c. - 14th c. **Señüy** [seŋüj] (DTS); Uyg. 12th c. - 14th c. **Señüy-tutuñ** [seŋüj tutuŋ] (DTS).

SEÑÜY-ARA   Uyg. 12th c. - 14th c. **Señüy-ara** [seŋüj ara] (DTS); Uyg. **Señüy-ara / Säñüy-ara** [Sängüi Ara / señüj ara] (EUTS, DTS).

SEÑÜN   Uyg. **Sañun** [Sañun] (ETY II, 66); Uyg. **Säñün** [Sängün] (EUTS); Türk 7th-9th c. **Šañun** [!] / **Sañun** [Çocuk Böri Şangun / Çocuq Böri Sañun] (ETY III, 53, 144). ✧ 'General' (Chin.), cf. Türk *säñün* 'General' (Gabain), *seŋün / saŋun* (title) (DTS), *säñün* 'ein Beamtenwürde' (Radl. IV, 449).

SEP   Kzk. 19th c. **Sep-pay** [Сеппай] (SOV 156). ✧ 'Help, supporter' cf. Kzk. *sep* 'yardım, destek' (KzTS).

SEPER see **SAFAR**

SER I.   Kzk. 19th c. **Ser-bay** [Сербай] (SODž. 104); Kzk. 19th c. **Ser-bay** [Сербай] (Pam. kn. Turg. 39); Kzk. 19th c. **Ser-bek** [Сербекъ] (AOP 46); Kkalp. 20th c. **Ser-γazï** [Сергазы] (KkRS 776); Chag. 16th c.? **Ser-χoja** [سيرحواجه] (Šejb. LIV); Kkalp. 20th c. **Ser-žan** [Сержан] (KkRS 776). ✧ I. 'Head, chief' cf. Crm., Turk. *sär* (P.) 'der Kopf, das Haupt, der Anführer' (Radl. IV, 456); II. 'Gold' cf. Kirg. *ser / zer* 'золото' (Jud.).

SER II.   Chuv. 18th-19th c. **Ser-bey** [Сербей] (Magn. 75). ✧ 'Hundred' cf. Chuv. *s'ĕr* 'id.' (ČRS).

SER-ALİ see **ŠER-ALİ**

SER-ALİ see **ŠER-ALİ**

SERBAN Khorezm.? **Serban** [ساربان], an emir (RaD/Jahn 127, 140, 193).

SERBİ Chuv. **Serbİ**, a pagan female name (Mészáros 231). ✧ 'Cypress'? cf. Tat. PN *Särwiy / Särbiy* (Sattarov) (<Ar.).

SERČE Turk. 19th c. **Serče-oγlu**, a Zeybek (Kúnos 1891, 119). ✧ 'Sparrow' cf. Crm., Turk. *serčä* 'der Sperling' (Radl. IV, 470). See also **EWĀZ-DURDİ-SERČE**.

SERDAN Kkalp. 20th c. **Serdan** [Сердан] (KkRS 776).

SERDĀR Trkm. 20th c. **Serdar** [Serdar] (Zaj. 1971, 326). ✧ 'Chief; supreme military commander; (lit.) 'holding or possessing the head' cf. Trkm. *serdār* 'вождь' (TrkmRS) (<P.<Ar. *sirdār*).

SERÄK Kirg. **Seräk** [Серäк], one of Manas' comrades-in-arms (Proben V, 39 /41/). ✧ 'Standing upright' cf. Kzk. *seräk* 'aufrechtstehend' (Radl. IV, 459). ⇨ **SEREK I.?**

SERÄZAN Kzk. 19th c. **Seräzan** [Серязанъ] (SOK 48).

SERE Kkalp. 20th c. **Sere-gül** [Серегул], fem. (KkRS 778). ✧ 'Chosen, high quality' cf. Kkalp. *sere* 'отборный, высокого качества' (KkRS).

SEREY Chuv. 18th-19th c. **Serey** [Серей] (Magn. 75).

SEREK I. Kzk. 19th c. **Serek** [Серекъ] (SODž. 100); Kzk. 19th c. **Serek-bay** [Серекбай] (SODž. 40, 92); Kzk. 19th c. **Serek-pay** [Серекпай] (SOV 8, 14, 18, 28, 32, 52); Kzk. 19th c. **Serek-pay** [Серекпай] (AOAtb. 38); Kzk. 19th c. **Serek-pay** [Серекпай] (SODž. 14). ✧ 'Lively, vivid; alert, careful' cf. Kzk. *serek* 'Açıkgöz, hareketli, dikkatli' (KzTS), Kzk. *serek II* 'сергек, сақ' (QTTS). See also **AY-SEREK**.

SEREK II. Kirg. **Serek** [Серек] (Jud. 725). ✧ 'Dog' cf. Kirg. *serek* 'дворняга, пёс' (Jud.).

SERELİ Kzk. 19th c. **Sereli** [Серелы] (SOK 256).

SEREM-BAY see **SEREN I.**

SEREN I. Kzk. 19th c. **Serem-bay** [Серембай] (SOV 92); Kzk. 19th c. **Seren** [Серенъ] (SOK 246); Kzk. 19th c. **Seren** [Серенъ] (SODž. 6); Kzk. 19th c. **Seren-bay** [Серенбай] (SOK 244).

SEREN II. Chuv. 18th-19th c. **Seren** [Серенъ] (Magn. 75). ✧ 'Feast before Eastern' cf. Chuv. *səren* 'id.' (Paas.).

SERENDEY Chuv. 18th-19th c. **Serendey** [Серендей] (Magn. 75).

SERENEY Chuv. 18th-19th c. **Sereney** [Сереней] (Magn. 75).

SERENEK Bashk. 1737 **Serenek** [Кусюк Серенеков] (MIB I, 354).

SERENGEY Chuv. 18th-19th c. **Serengey** [Серенгей] (Magn. 75).

SERENKA Chuv. 18th-19th c. **Serenka** [Серенка] (Magn. 75). ⇨ **SEREN II.** + suff. *-ka*.

SEREŇK Oghuz/Trkm. 13th c. **Sereňk** [سرنك / Серенк-хан], Arslan-χan's son (Abulg./Kon. 1120, 1130, 1135, 1155).

SEREŠKA Bashk. 1693 **Sereška** [Серешка Шигаев] (MIB I, 84). ✧ Seryoshka (R.)?

SERGE Kzk. 19th c. **Serge-bay** [Сергебай] (SOV 56); Kzk. 19th c. **Serge-bay** [Сергебай] (SOK 256); Kzk. 19th c. **Serge-bay** [Сергебай] (SODž. 78, 144). ✧ 'A fork-shaped piece of wood impeding the calf to suckle milk' cf. Kzk. *sergä* 'ein gabelförmiges Holz, welches dem Kalbe über das Maul gebunden wird, damit es nicht bei der Mutter saugen kann' (Radl. IV, 466).

SERGE-TAY Kzk. 19th c. **Serge-tay** [Сергетай] (SOK 190). ⇨ **SERGE** + **TAY** or suff. *-tay(1,2)*.

SERİ Kzk. 19th c. **Seri-bay** [Серыбай] (SODž. 4); Kzk. 19th c. **Seri-bay** [Серыбай] (AOK 90). ✧ 'Knight, cavalier' cf. Kzk. *seri* 'рыцарь' (KzRS).

SERİK I. see **ŠERİK II.**

SERİK II. Chuv. 18th-19th c. **Serik** [Серикъ] (Magn. 76). ✧ 'Sickly' cf. Chuv. *sĕrĕχ* 'хилый, болезненный (о человеке)' (ČRS).

SERİK-POL Kzk. 19th c. **Serik-pol** [Серикполъ] (SOK 26). ✧ 'Be a friend/mate'; a name given to boys born second, meaning: 'Be the mate (of the first-born)' (Torma, 1999, 44), also Kzk. PN *Serik-bol* (Žanuzakov-Esbaeva). ⇨ **ŠERİK II.** + **BOL**.

SERİKČİ Kzk. 19th c. **Serikči** [Серикчи] (SOK 62). ⇨ **ŠERİK I./II.?** + suff. *-či*.

SERİMBET Kzk. **Serimbet** [Серымбетъ] (Valihanov, Soč. 313); Kkalp. 20th c. **Serimbet** [Серимбет] (KkRS 776). ⇨ **SER I.** / **ŠER?** + suff. *-imbet*. See also **ŠERİMBET**.

SERKÄ see **SERKE**

SERKE Kzk. 18 th. c. **Särkä-bey** [Сярка бей] (Sib. Vest. IX, 189); Kzk. 19th c. **Särke** [Сарке] (AOK 94); Bashk. 1776 **Serkä / Serke?** [Серка Акмычыков] (MIB V, 33); Kzk. 18 th. c. **Serkä-batïr** [Серка Батырь] (Nepljuev 763, 764, 780); Kzk. 19th c. **Serke** [Серке] (SOK 204); Kzk. 19th c. **Serke-bay** [Серкебай] (AOA 70); Kzk. 19th c. **Serke-bay** [Серкебай] (AOP 10); Kzk. 19th c. **Serke-bay** [Серкебай] (SOK 130, 222); Kzk. 1794 **Serke-bay / Serkä-bay** [سيركا باى / Серкебай] (MIK IV, 158, 160); Kzk. 19th c. **Serke-bala** [Серкебала] (SODž. 44); Kzk. 19th c. **Sirke-bay** [Сиркебай] (Grod., Pril. 117); *TN:* Kzk. 19th c. **Serke-bay-qara-su** [Серкебай-кара-су], a field (AOA 146). ✧ 'A two-year-old he-goat' cf. Kzk. *serkä* 'ein zweijähriger Bock', Alt.(Tel.) *särkä* 'ein Ziegenbock im dritten Jahre, ein kastrierter Ziegenbock' (Radl. IV, 465). See also **AQ-SERKE, BAY-SERKE; QURANAQ**.

SERKEČ Kzk. 19th c. **Serkeč** [Серкечъ] (AOK 18). ⇨ **SERKE** + suff. *-č*.

SERMEK Chuv. 18th-19th c. **Sermik** [Сермикъ]

(Magn. 76); Kzk. 19th c. **Sermek** [Сермекъ] (SOK 18).

SERMEN   Kzk. 19th c. **Sermen-bay** [Серменбай] (SOK 242).

SERMİŠ   Khorezm. 1289 **Sermiš** [سرميش] (RaD/Jahn 15).

SERNÄK   Bashk. 1737 **Sernäk** [Кучюк Серняков] (MIB I, 320).

SERSE   Kzk. 19th c. **Serse-bay** [Серсебай] (AOP 18).

SERSEK   Kzk. 19th c. **Sersek / Särsek?** [Серсекъ] (SOV 14).

SERT   Kzk. 19th c. **Sert-pay** [Сертпай] (SOV 40). ✧ I. 'Faith, promise; oath' cf. Kzk., Hak. *sert* 'das Versprechen; der Eid, der Schwur' (Radl. IV, 468), Kzk. *sert* 'клятва, обет' (KzRS); II. 'Ugly' cf. East.T. *sert* 'id.' (Jarring).

SERTAY   Kzk. 1785 **Sertay-bi / Sert-tay-bi?** [سردلاى بى], an aq-saqal (MIK IV, 51). ✧ '?' cf. Kzk. PN *Sartay* (Žanuzakov-Esbaeva). See also **SARİ-TAY?**

SET   Kkalp. 20th c. **Sät-emir-χan** [Сэтемирхан] (KkRS 776); Tuv. 19th c. **Sät-päy** [Сätпäi] (Proben IX, 145); Kzk. 19th c. **Set-pay (<Sert-pay?)** [Сетпай] (SODž. 106). ✧ I. 'Success; suitable moment' cf. Kzk. *sät* 'удача; удобный момент' (KzRS); II. 'Ugly' cf. NUyg. *sät* 'id.' (URS 1961, 171). ⇨ **SERT?**

SETEY see **SATAY**

SETER   Kzk. 19th c. **Seter-bay** [Сетербай] (SODž. 22). ✧ 'A three-stringed instrument' cf. East.T.(Tar.) *sätär* 'ein Saiteninstrument (mit drei Saiten)' (Radl. IV, 483).

SETKA   Chuv. 18th-19th c. **Setka / Setkä?** [Сетка] (Magn. 76).

SEVDİ   Maml. 14th c. **Sevdi** [سَوْدِي] (Sauvaget 48); Uzb. 20th c. **Süydi** [Суйди], fem. (Begmatov 1984, 204); Uzb. 20th c. **Süydi-bânu** [Суйдибону], fem. (Begmatov 1984, 204); Uzb. 20th c. **Süydi-bibi** [Суйдибиби], fem. (Begmatov 1984, 204); Uzb. 20th c. **Süydi-bu** [Суйдибу], fem. (Begmatov 1984, 204); Uzb. 20th c. **Süydi-χân** [Суйдихон], fem. (Begmatov 1984, 204); Tat.(Sib.) 1599 **Süydü-Jan** [Сюйдюджанъ], a Siberian princess, Küčüm's wife (AI II. 17, 20, 23). ✧ '(S/he) loved (him/her)' cf. Uyg., Chag., Turk. *säv-* 'lieben', Crm. *säw-* 'id.' (Radl. IV, 504), Kzk. *süy-* 'lieben, küssen' (Radl. IV, 796), Chag. *söy-* 'gern haben, lieben; küssen' (Radl. IV, 566).

SEVİK see **SÄWÜK**

SEVİN   Bulg. 765-767 **Sevin** [Σαβινος / Sevin], a prince (Byz. Turc. 262, Rásonyi, Ortaçağda Erdelde Türklüğün İzleri, pp. 12-13); Khorezm. / Tat.(GH)? 14th. c. **Sevin-beg / Söyün-bek** [Севинъ Бегъ / Союн-бек Ханд-задэ (Ханзадэ)], Özbeg Khan's (Uzbek's) grand-daughter, Miranšah's wife in Samarkand (Barth., Ulugb. 30, MIT I, 516, 517); Uzb.

20th c. **Sewin** [Севин] (Begmatov 1984, 203); Uzb. 20th c. **Sewin-bây** [Севинбой] (Begmatov 1984, 203); Trkm. 1826 **Söyün-bay** [Союн-бай], from the tribe Sarïq (MIT II, 435, 440); Trkm. 1816 **Söyün-behadïr / Süyün-behadïr** [/ Союн-бехадыр / Суюн-бехадыр] (MIT II, 397, 420, 439, 447, 450); Uzb. 1816 **Söyün-biy** [Союн-бий], from the Qïyat tribe (MIT II, 390-392, 398, 400 etc.); Kzk. **Süyen-bay** [Сюенбай] (AOK 138); Kzk. **Süyin-bay** [Сюинбай] (AOAtb. 62); Kzk. **Süyün** [Сююнъ] (AOAtb. 34); Kzk. **Süyün** [Суйюнъ] (AOK 90); Nog. 1649 **Süyün** [Сююнъ] (AI IV, 87); Uzb. 20th c. **Süyün** [Суюн] (Begmatov 1984, 203); Kzk. **Süyün-bay** [Сююнбай] (SOV 12); Uzb. 20th c. **Süyün-bây** [Сююнбой] (Begmatov 1984, 204); Uzb. 20th c. **Süyün-bek** [Сююнбек] (Begmatov 1984, 203); Tat. 1551, 1552 **Süyün-bek / Sün-bek** [Сююнъбекъ-царица / Сюнбекъ-царица], a princess (PSRL XIII, 168, 184); Kkalp. 1809, 1811 **Süyün-biy** [Сююн бий] (MIKk. 103, 120, 132); Tat. 1551 **Süyün-bikä** [Сююнбукъ-царица], a princess (PSRL XIII, 167); Kzk. **Süyün-bikä** [Сююнъ-бике] (PSRL XIX 69, 320, 393, etc.); Tat. 1535, 1552 **Süyün-bikä / Süyün-bike** [Сююн-бикя / Сююнбека / Сююнъ-бике (Самбекъ, Сумбѣкъ, Симбекъ)] (Katanov: IOAIÊK XXX, 295, AI I, 287, PSRL XIX 69, 320, 393 etc.); Uzb. 20th c. **Süyün-jân** [Сююнжон] (Begmatov 1984, 204); Bashk. 1710 **Süyün-γul** [Кузей Сююнгулов] (MIB III, 64); Uzb. 20th c. **Süyün-χoJa** [Сююнхўжа] (Begmatov 1984, 204); Uzb. 20th c. **Süyün-qul** [Сююнкул] (Begmatov 1984, 204); Kzk. **Sün** [Сюнъ] (SOK 268); Tat.(Mish.) 1764 **Sün-bay (<Süyün-bay)** [Абляз Сюнбаев] (MIB IV/1, 281); Bashk. 1706 **Sün-bay (<Süyün-bay)** [Сунбай / Сюнбай] (MIB III, 27); *TN:* Turk. 20th c. **Büyük Sevin**, a village in the province of Maraş, Turkey (TMİB 636). ✧ 'Be glad, be happy' cf. Uyg., Karakh. *sevin-* 'радоваться' (DTS), Chag., Turk. *sevin-* 'sich freuen, glücklich sein' (Radl. IV, 505), Trkm. *söyün-* 'радоваться' (TrkmRS), Rásonyi 1938, 116-117, Byz. Turc. II, 262. See also **QUWAN, KİLÄN.**

SEVİNČ   Uyg. 1338 **Sebinč-tärim** [Sebinz Tarim], fem. (Chwol., Syr.-nest. (NF) 32); Uyg. 13th. c. **Sebünč** [Sebunz], fem. (Chwol., Syr.-nest. (NF) 49); Uyg. 1307 **Sebünč-tirim** [Sebunz Tirim], fem. (Chwol., Syr.-nest. (NF) 17); Oghuz? 12th c. **Sevinč** [سونج], mamlūk/gulām (slave) of Usāma's family (Usāma 113); Selj. **Sevinč** [سونج], the ancestor of Ahmed, sultan of Sivas from the Salur tribe (Astarab. 42); Selj. 992 **Sevinč** [سونج النظامى / Sevinč] (Bondārī 293, 294); Selj. 11th c. - 12th c. **Sevinč** [سونج / Simes (!)], Artuq's (Ortok) father (Abulfar. Or. 369 /243/); Selj. 1128, 1130, 1136 **Sevinč** [سونج بها الدين بن بورى بورى / سونج بن], governor of Hamah, died in 1133/34

(Abulfidā III, 434-5, Qalānisi 228, 253, Ibn al-Athīr: RHCHor I, 386-7, 402,),); Selj. 1221 **Sevinč** [ملك سونج] (Muh. Ibrahim 201); Selj. 1229 **Sevinč** [بن تاج الملوك سونج بهاالدين / Sevinč] (Kamāladdīn II, 243, 245); Khorezm.? 13th c. - 14th c. **Sevinč** [سونج], an emir, served under Öljeitü (1304-1316) (Qazw. 596, 603); Turk. 1485 **Sevinč** [Sevinç (Gazi ibn Sevinç)] (Gökb., Ed. 452); Turk. **Sevinč / Sevünč** [سونج / ساونج / Sevindž], forefather of the Ottoman dynasty (Āšikp. 50, Seādeddīn I, 15); Turk. 1393 **Sevinč-bek**, an emir in Anatolia (Astarab. 433); Khorezm. **Sevinč-χan** [سونج خان / Sevindž χan], an emir of Muhammad Khorezmshah (Ǧuwaynī I, 80); Chag. 15th c. - 16th c. **Sevinč-χoǰa-sultan / Sevinč-χoǰa-χan / Sevinič-χoǰa** [سيونيج خوجه سلطان / خان / Sevindž], Abul Khair Khan's son (Šejb. L, LI, LVII, LXXI, LXXVIII); Chag. 15th c. - 16th c. **Sevinč-sultan** [سيونج سلطان], Sheybani Khan's son (Šejb. L); Maml. 1206 **Sewinč** [سونج مملوك شهاب الدين] (Ibn al-Athīr/Tornb. XII, 144, 146); Maml. (Trkm.) 1230 **Sewinč** [التركمانى سونج قشيالو شمس‌الدين] (Ibn al-Athīr/Tornb. XII, 322); Kuman 1151 **Sewinč(ä) / Sebenč(ä)?** [Себенча Боняковичъ], Bönäk's son (Ipat. 299 /310/, PSRL II, 432, VII, 13); Kuman 1151 **Sewinč / Sewenč?** [Севенчъ Боняковичъ], a Polovets prince, Bönäk's son (PSRL VII, 53, Bask., Im. polov. 72); Uyg. 1316 **Sibünč-tegin** [Sibunz Tegin] (Chwol., Syr.-nest. (NF) 21); Khorezm. 1219 **Siyünč-χan** [سيونج خان بيك / Soïounoutch-khan / Сіюнчъ-ханъ], an officer in Bukhara at the time of Chinggis' assault (RaD/Ber.III 53, 57, Abulg./Desm. 109); Uzb. 15th c. - 16th c. **Siyünč-sultan** [Мухаммедъ Сіюнджъ-Султан], Šeybani-χan's son (Šejb. 77); Chag. **Siyünič-χan** [سيونيج / Сіюниджъ / Сіюниджъ ханъ], a Sheybanid ruler, Šeyban's great-grand-son (Šejb. XLIX, XXVI); Trkm. 1817/18 **Söyünič-bek** [Союнич-бек] (MIT II, 405); Maml. 1283 **Söwünč / Söwünǰi?** [Nedjim-eddin-Soundji], commander of Jerusalem (Makrīzī III, 62); Nog.? **Süyniš / Süyiniš** [Süyiniš / Суйниш] (Žirm., 395); Nog. 1649 **Süyünč** [Сююнчъ мурза] (AI IV, 87); Nog. 1649 **Süyünč** [Мамай мурза Сююнчевъ] (AI IV, 92); Nog.? 1654 **Süyünč** [Сююнчъ мурза], from Astrakhan (DAI III, 538); Chag. 16th c. **Süyünč-χan / Süyünčük-χan** [/ Сююнчъ (Сююнчукъ)-ханъ], a Timurid ruler in Samarkand (Barth., Ulugb. 102, 116); Chag.? 1511 **Süyünč-χoǰa-χan** [Suyundj Khwája Khán] (Tar. Rashidi 133); Khorezm.? 14th c. **Süyünič / Siyünč?** [مينكتيمور خان / Souyounitch], Sheyban Khan's descendant (Abulg./Desm. 192); Trkm. 1814/15 **Süyünič-bay** [Сюнич-бай] (MIT II, 388(?)); Chag. 16th c. **Süyünič-biy** [Сююнич-бий] (Ivanov 70);

Trkm. 1554/55 **Süyünič-biy** [Сююнич-бий] (MIT II, 70); Oghuz/Trkm. **Süyünič-χan** [سونجخان بن بايدوخان / Suïunitch Khan], Tatar-khan's decendant in a legend of origin (Abulg./Desm. 11, 29-30); Trkm. 1595 **Süyünüč** [Сююнудж Мухаммед-бий] (MIT II, 85); *TN:* Turk. 20th c. **Sevinč-bey** [Sevinçbey], a village in the province of Isparta, Turkey (TMİB 430). ✧ 'Joy, pleasure, gladness' (Rásonyi, KÖA 125, Bask., Im. polov. 72), cf. Uyg., Karakh. *sevinč* 'радость, веселье' (DTS), Uyg. *säbinč* 'die Freude' (Radl. IV, 500), Turk. *sävinǰ* 'die Freude, die Fröhlichkeit', Crm. *säwinč* 'die Freude' (Radl. IV, 505), Kuman *sövünč* 'Freude' (CC), Trkm. *söyünč* 'радость; отрада' (TrkmRS), Kzk. *süyiniš* 'радость, восторг' (KzRS).

SEVİNČEK Khorezm. 1295 **Sevinček** [سونجاق] (RaD/Jahn 91); Chag.? **Sevinček** [سيونجك / Säwingäk] (Le Coq, Ind. 4); Az.?, Trkm.? 1403 **Sevinček-behadïr** [سونجك بهادر], an emir (Dorn 136, 182). ✧ 'Joy, pleasure'. ⇨ SEVİNČ + suff. -ek.

SEVİNDİ Uyg. **Sävindi** (Zieme, Mat. I, 74); Yürük 1543 **Sevindi** (Gökb., Rum. 186); Chuv. 18th-19th c. **Sündü-bay** [Сюндюбай] (Magn. 79). ✧ 'He/she rejoiced, he is pleased' cf. Uyg., Karakh. *sevin-* 'радоваться' (DTS).

SEVİNDİK Turk. 1528 **Sevindik** [Sevindik Fakih] (Gökb., Ed. 30, 50); Turk. 16th c. **Sevindik** (Ongan, Ank. II /Num. 1395, 1584, 1717); Turk. 16th. c. **Sevindik** [Şeyh Sevindik (Koğacı Dede)] (Gökb., Ed. 490); Turk. 16th. c. **Sevindik** [Sevindik ibn Mustafa], in the region of Tarsus, Turkey (Sümer: DTCFD XI, 336); Turk. 1583 **Sevindik** [سوندك] (Ongan, Ank. I, 151, 176); Yürük 1543 **Sevindik** (Gökb., Rum. 103, 200, 204); Yürük 1702 **Sevindik** [سوندك] (Refik, Anad. 131); Selj. 1248 **Sevindük** [جعفر بن سوندك] (Turan: Belleten XII, 100, 119); Chag. **Sevindük** [Säwindük] (Le Coq, Ind. 4); Yürük 1543 **Sevindük** (Gökb., Rum. 220); Uzb. 20th c. **Sewindik** [Севиндик] (Begmatov 1984, 203); Bashk. 1759 **Siyündük** [Муллакай Сиюндюков] (MIB IV/1, 176); Bashk. 1759 **Siyündük** [Исман Сиюндюков] (MIB IV/1, 176); Bashk. 1759 **Siyündük** [Абубякир Сиюндюков] (MIB IV/1, 176); Bashk. 1759 **Siyündük** [Даутай Сиюндюков] (MIB IV/1, 176); Bashk. 1795 **Siyündük? / Seyündük** [Сеюндюковъ] (IOAIÊK XXVIII, 591); Crm.(Tat.) 1558 **Söyündük** [Ссоюндюкъ Тулусуповъ], a prince from the Crimea (PSRL XIII, 287); Kzk. **Süyindik** [Сюиндыкъ] (AOAtb. 62); Kzk. **Süyindik** [Сююндикъ] (AOO 26); Uzb. 20th c. **Süyündik** [Сюндик] (Begmatov 1984, 203); Trkm. **Süyündük** [Кышикъ Сююндюковъ] (Ščeglov IV, 163); Trkm. 19th c. **Süyündük** [Кышикъ Сююндюковъ] (Ščeglov IV, 163); Tat. 1538 **Süyündük** [Сюундюкъ]

(PSRL XIII, 124); Tat. 1552 **Süyündük** [Сююндюкъ] (Kn. Metriki Lit. 82); Tat. 1614 **Süyündük** [Сююндюкъ], chief of the Tabun tribe in Astrakhan (AI III, 30, 436, 439); Bashk. 1709 **Süyündük** [Сюундюк] (MIB I, 262); Bashk. 1717 **Süyündük** [Чапкин Суюндуков] (MIB III, 161); Bashk. 1719 **Süyündük** [Сюундюк] (MIB III, 182); Bashk. 1735 **Süyündük** [Сююндюкъ Тевекеевъ], a tarχan (Vel.-Zern., Bašk. 23); Bashk. 1735 **Süyündük** [Сюярымбетъ Сююндюковъ], a tarχan (Vel.-Zern., Bašk. 24); Bashk. 1735 **Süyündük** [Атыкъ Сююндюковъ], a tarχan (Vel.-Zern., Bašk. 24); Bashk. 1737 **Süyündük** [Аиткул Сююндюков] (MIB I, 346); Bashk. 1737 **Süyündük** [Кумак Суюндюков] (MIB I, 327); Bashk. 1740 **Süyündük** [Сююндюк Балтаев (Болтаєв)] (MIB I, 393, 403); Bashk. 1745 **Süyündük** [Сююндук Телдеев] (MIB III, 432); Bashk. 1749 **Süyündük** [Сююндук Телдеев] (MIB III, 464); Bashk. 1749 **Süyündük** [Сююндук Сюрметев] (MIB III, 464); Bashk. 18th c. **Süyündük** [Сююндюков] (MIB V, 329); Bashk. 1751 **Süyündük** [Алкаш Сююндюков] (MIB IV/1, 43); Bashk. 1754 **Süyündük** [Барак Сюндюков] (MIB IV/1, 90); Bashk. 1756 **Süyündük** [Сююндюк Абликов] (MIB IV/1, 128); Bashk. 1760 **Süyündük** [Сююндюк Токбаев] (MIB IV/2, 35); Bashk. 1761 **Süyündük** [Барак Сююндюков] (MIB IV/1, 215); Bashk. 1761 **Süyündük** [Кутлугазан Сиюндюков] (MIK IV/1, 218); Bashk. 1761 **Süyündük** [Кинзекей Сююндюков] (MIK IV/1, 218); Bashk. 1763 **Süyündük** [Сююндюк Уразаев] (MIB IV/1, 267); Bashk. 1776 **Süyündük** [Сююндюк Санзяпов] (MIB V, 44); Bashk. 1776 **Süyündük** [/ Суюндук (Сююндюк) Сагандыков] (MIB V 76, 137, 329); Bashk. 1776 **Süyündük** [Суюндук (Сююндюк) Санзялов] (MIB V, 43-45, 265); Bashk. 1783 **Süyündük** [Суюндук (Сююндюк) Сагындыков (Сагандыков)] (MIB V, 76, 137, 329); Bashk. 1783 **Süyündük** [Суюндук (Сююндюк) Каскинов] (MIB V, 139); Bashk. 1787 **Süyündük** [Юлдаш Сююндюков] (MIB V, 204); Bashk. 1787 **Süyündük** [Юлдиш Сююндюков] (MIB V, 204); Bashk. 1788 **Süyündük** [Кусекей Сююндюков] (MIB V, 234); Bashk. 1789 **Süyündük** [Мурзагул Сююндюков] (MIB V, 249); Kzk. **Süyündük** [Суюндукъ] (AOK 70); Kzk. **Süyündük** [Суюндукъ] (AOK 14); Kzk. **Süyündük** [Суюндукъ] (Patkanov II, 92); Kzk. **Süyündük** [Сюундукъ] (Potanin II, 6); Kzk. 1785 **Süyündük** [Сююндюк] (MIK IV, 60); Kzk. 1803 **Süyündük** [Суюндук], chief of the Little Horde (Kiši Žüz) (MIK IV, 514); Kzk. 1829 **Süyündük** [Сююндюкъ Буланбаев] (Konšin, Mat. V, 77); Bashk. 1789 **Süyündük** / **Siyündük** [Суюндук (Сеундюк) Пулатов] (MIB V, 267); Bashk. 1730 **Süyündük** /

Sündük [Сюяндюк (Сюндюк)] (MIB III, 273); Bashk. 1779 **Süyündük** / **Sündük** [Суюндук (Сюндюк) Абдулов] (MIB V, 83); Kkalp. 1740 **Süyündük-batïr** [Сююндюкъ-Батыръ], from the Qoñyrat tribe (Hanykov, Poezdka 19, MIKk. 208); Kzk. 1820 **Süyündük-biy** [Суюндукъ-бій], one of the chiefs of the Alim-ulï-Qara-saqal tribe (Sib. Vest. IX, 113); Bashk. 1734 **Sündik** [Алкешъ Сюндековъ], a tarχan (Vel.-Zern., Bašk. 11); Tat. 1624 **Sündük** [Сюндюк Утемышинъ] (Zolotn. 159); Bashk. 1723 **Sündük** [Сюндюк Ашаров] (MIB III, 203); Bashk. 1738 **Sündük** [Сюндюк Кинкашев] (MIB III, 380); Bashk. 1738 **Sündük** / **Sunduq?** [Уракай Сундюков] (MIB III, 379); Chuv. 18th-19th c. **Sündük** (<**Süyündük**) [Сюндюкъ] (Magn. 79); Kzk. **Sündük** [Sündük / Сÿндÿк] (Proben III, 24 /28/); *EN:* Nog. 20th c. **Süyündik-uruwï** [Суьйуьндик урувы], an Aq-noγay clan in the district of Mineralovodsk and the autonomous region of Cherkessk (Bask., Nog. 135, 142). ✧ 'We rejoiced, we are pleased' cf. Uyg., Karakh. *sevin-* 'радоваться' (DTS), Turk. *sevin-* 'to be glad, to be pleased; to be happy, to rejoice' (TED). See also **QOČ-SEVİNDİGİ.**

SEVİNDÜK see **SEVİNDİK**

SEVİNİČ see **SEVİNČ**

SEVİNÜG Pecheneg? **Sevinüg-bičä**, fem. (Németh, Inschr. 29). ✧ 'Little joy' cf. Uyg., Karakh. *sevin-* 'радоваться' (DTS) + suff. *-üg.*

SEWÄR Uyg. 13th-14th c. **Sävär-täñgrim** [[Sä]vär Tngrim], fem. (Zieme, Mat. III, 274); **Sewär** [سِوَار بـن الاشعـر المـازنى] (Fragm. Hist. Ar. 108); **Sewär** [سوَار بـن عبدالله العنيرى] (Fragm. Hist. Ar. 251); Selj.? 1129, 1148 **Sewär** [مسعود] (Qalānisi 225, 240, 288); Selj. 1130 **Sewär** [سيفالـدين سوار / سوار بـن ايتكين] / Sawar Seïf ed-Dīn ibn Aïtékin], emir, Zengi's (officer) governor in Aleppo (Usāma 105, 106, Kamāladdīn: RHCHor 659, 672-76, Kamāladdīn II, 245, 247, 251-154 etc.); Selj.? 1132, 1133 **Sewär** [اسوار / سوار], an emir (in Aleppo) (Ibn al-Athīr/Tornb. X, 482, XI, 4, 25, 37, Zambaur 34); Selj.? 1190 **Sewär** [Siwar], an emir, died at Akka in 1190/91 (Abū Šāma: RHCHor IV, 522); Maml. 1467/68 **Sewär** [شاه سوار بـن دلغادر] (Iyās II, 92); Uzb. 20th c. **Sewär** [Севар] (Begmatov 1984, 204); Uzb. 20th c. **Sewär** [Севар], fem. (Begmatov 1984, 204); Karakh.? 865 **Sewär** / **Süwer** [سُور / سُور], took part in the rioting between Baghdad and Samarra (Tabarī, Annal. III, 1591); Maml. 13th c. **Sewär-bay** [خونـد سوار بـاى], under the Eyūbid Nasreddīn, then under Qutuz (1259-1260) (Iyās I, 80, 81, 95); Maml. 1448, 1465/66 **Sewär-bay** [سوارباى الـجاركسية], of Cherkess origin (Ibn Taghrīb. VII, 738, VIII, 31, 144); Uzb. 20th c. **Sewär-bây** [Севарбой] (Begmatov 1984,

204); Uzb. 20th c. **Sewär-χân** [Севархон], fem. (Begmatov 1984, 204); Tat. 1620 **Sewer-gözä** [Сюкей Севергозинъ] (Zolotn. 159); Tat.(Mish.) 1773 **Süyä-γul (<Süyär-γul?)** [Суягул Гумеров] (MIB IV/2 417); Bashk. 1735 **Süyär** [Сюяръ] (Vel.-Zern., Bašk. 12); Bashk. 1742 **Süyär** [Муса Суяров] (MIB III, 513); Bashk. 1761 **Süyär** [Сюяр Габдуллин] (MIB IV/1, 221); Bashk. 1762 **Süyär** [Сюяр Султангулов] (MIB IV/1, 233); Uzb. **Süyär** [Астакъ Суяровъ] (SKSO III, 166); Uzb. **Süyär** [Суяръ] (SKSO III, 174); Uzb. 20th c. **Süyär** [Суяр] (Begmatov 1984, 204); Bashk. 1751 **Süyär / Süyer?** [Сюер] (MIB IV/1, 45); Bashk. 1770 **Süyär-bay** [Сюярбай] (MIB IV/1, 350); Kzk. **Süyär-bay** [Суярбай] (Grod., Pril. 189); Uzb. 20th c. **Süyär-bây** [Суярбой] (Begmatov 1984, 204); Tat.(Mish.) 1755 **Süyär-γul** [Яныберди Сюяргулов] (MIB IV/1, 93); Tat.(Mish.) 1755 **Süyär-γul** [Муртаза Сюяргулов] (MIB IV/1, 93); Bashk. 1709 **Süyär-γul** [Суяргул] (MIB I, 270); Bashk. 1740 **Süyär-γul** [Сюяргул Чюекин] (MIB I, 381); Bashk. 1740 **Süyär-γul** [Суяргул Юргунов] (MIB I, 404); Bashk. 1761 **Süyär-γul** [Сюяргул Сюярметев] (MIB IV/1, 227); Bashk. 1779 **Süyär-γul** [Байрямгул (Байремгул) Сюяргулов] (MIB V, 86); Bashk. 1788 **Süyär-γul** [Сюяргул Кутюков] (MIB V, 233); Bashk. 1788 **Süyär-γul** [Суяргул Кусяпкулов] (MIB V, 310); Bashk. 1788 **Süyär-γul** [Суяргул (Сюяргул) Кутуков] (MIB V, 233); Bashk. 1790 **Süyär-γul** [Суяргул (Сюяргул) Бекчурин] (MIB V, 284, 327); Bashk. 1791 **Süyär-γul** [Суяргул Якшимбетев] (MIB V, 301); Uzb. 20th c. **Süyär-χoJa** [Суярхўжа] (Begmatov 1984, 204); Kzk. **Süyär-qul** [Байгази Суяркуловъ] (Grod., Pril. 114); Uzb. **Süyär-qul** [Суяркулъ] (SKSO III, 168); Uzb. 20th c. **Süyär-qul** [Суяркул] (Begmatov 1984, 204); Kzk. **Süyer-bay** [Сюербай] (SODž. 58); Bashk. 1675 **Süyer-γul** [Сюергул Еметов] (MIB I, 200); Bashk. 1715 **Süyer-γul** [Сюергул Терегулов] (MIB III, 120); Bashk. 1721 **Süyer-γul** [Сюергул] (MIB III, 194); Bashk. 1728 **Süyer-γul** [Суергул] (MIB I, 301); Bashk. 1764 **Süyir-γul** [Сюирьгул Мимгулов] (MIB IV/1, 300); Kzk. **Süyür** [Сююръ] (AOP 38); Bashk. 1740 **Süyür-γul** [Сююргул Шургунов] (MIB I, 395); **Süwär / Suwar?** [عُبَيْدة بن سُوَار] (Fragm. Hist. Ar. 164, 165). ✧ 'He/she will love; Loving (child)/lover' (Sattarov), cf. Chag. *söy-* 'gern haben, lieben; küssen' (Radl. IV, 566), Tat. *söy-* 'lieben, liebkosen, streicheln' (Radl. IV, 592), Kzk. *süy-* 'lieben, küssen' (Radl. IV, 796), Uzb. *sew-* 'любить' (UzbRS). See also **YAN-SÜYÄR, QAN-SÜYÄR**.

SEWÄRÄ   Uzb. 20th c. **Sewärä** [Севара], fem. (Begmatov 1984, 204). ✧ 'She will love; Loving (child)/lover' cf. Uzb. *sew-* 'любить' (UzbRS). ⇨

SEWÄR + suff. *-ä*.

SEWERGÜN   Bashk. 1667 **Sewergün** [Севергунко Горлаковъ] (AI IV, 373).

SEWGİL   Uzb. 20th c. **Sewgil** [Севгил], fem. (Begmatov 1984, 204). ✧ 'Love (him/her)' cf. Uzb. *sew-* 'любить' (UzbRS) + suff. *-gil*.

SEWİL   Uzb. 20th c. **Sewil** [Севил], fem. (Begmatov 1984, 204). ✧ 'Be loved' cf. Karakh. *sevül-* 'быть любимым' (DTS), Uzb. *sew-* 'любить' (UzbRS). See also **AMRAN, EMREN**.

SEWİNČ see **SEVİNČ**

SEWİNČ-BUΓA   Maml. 1399/1400 **Sewinč-buγa** [سَونْخِبغا] (Ibn Taghrīb. VI, 12, 245); Maml. 1449, 1453, 1468 **Sewinč-buγa** [سونخبغا اليونسى الناصرى] (Ibn Taghrīb. VII, 127, 130, 824 etc., VIII, 42, 74, 86 etc., Iyās II, 42, Weil, Chalif. II, 254); Tat.(GH) 1322 **Sewinč-buγa / Sewenč-buγa?** [Севенчьбуга], envoy of the Tatars (PSRL X, 188). ✧ 'Joy-bull' (Sauvaget 48). ⇨ **SEVİNČ** + **BUQA**.

SEWKİN   Bashk. 1756 **Sewkin-bay** [Севкинбай Куземгулов] (MIB IV/1, 120).

SEWÜNČ-TEMÜR   Tat.(GH) 1357 **Sevünč-temür / Sewünč-temür**, a mir-baχšï (Vásáry 54). ⇨ **SEVİNČ** + **TEMİR**.

Sİ-BULAT   Chuv. 18th-19th c. **Si-bulat** [Сибулатъ] (Magn. 76). ⇨ **SİY** + **BULAT**.

SİBAN   Kzk. 19th c. **Siban-bay** [Сибанбай] (AOP 82). ⇨ **ŠİBAN?**

SİBÄKČİN   Hak.(Sag.) 19th-20th c. **Sïbäkčïn / Sibäkčin** [Сібäкчін], fem. (Proben IX, 468-69). ✧ 'Female servant, maid' (Butanaev), cf. Hak.(Sag.) *sibäkči* 'der Diener' (Radl. IV, 731) (<Mo.).

SİBENEY   Chuv. 18th-19th c. **Sibeney** [Сибеней] (Magn.).

SİBİJEK   Hak. 19th-20th c. **Sibijek** [Сибичек] (HRS 351). ✧ '(Little) Lily-onion' cf. Hak. *sip* 'саранка (растение из семейства лилейных)' (HRS) + dim. suff. *-ijek*.

SİBİR   Hak.(Blt.) 19th-20th c. **Sibir / Sïbïr?** [Сібір] (Katanov, Otč. 9.). ✧ 'Skilful, masterly; careful' cf. Hak. *Siber* (Butanaev), Hak.(Sag.) *sibär* 'sparsam, sauber, vorsichtig' (Radl. IV, 731).

SİBOČA   Hak. 19th-20th c. **Siboča** [Сибоча] (HRS 351). ✧ Simon (R.) (Butanaev).

SİBREK   Hak. 19th-20th c. **Sibrek (<Sibirek)** [Сибрек] (HRS 351). ✧ 'Curly' (Butanaev).

SİBÜNČ see **SEVİNČ**

SİJİR-TAY   Kzk. 19th c. **Sijir-tay** [Акмантай Сиджиртаевъ] (Grod., Pril. 165). ⇨ **?** + **TAY** or suff. *-tay(1,2)*.

SİDİ   Tat. 1521 **Sidi** [Сиди], a cavalry-man armed with a lance (=ulanus) of Kazan (PSRL VI, 263); Tat. 1449 **Sidi / Sedi / Sidä** [Сиди (Сидя, Седи, Сѣди, Кичи) Ахметъ (Ахматъ)], a Tatar khan (PSRL VIII, 122 stb.). ⇨ **SEYİT.**

SİDLEK Chuv. 18th-19th c. **Sidlek** [Сидлекъ] (Magn. 76).

SİÄKİLÄČĀN Yak. **Siäkiläčăn** [Сіäкіläчăн], fem. (Pek.). ✧ 'Loving mirrors' cf. Yak. *siäkilä* (R.) 'зеркало' (Pek.) + suff. *-čăn.*

SİÄNČÄ Yak. **Siänčä** [Сіäнчä] (Pek.).

SİFİLA Kzk. 19th c. **Sifila** [Сифила] (Grod., Pril. 142). ✧ Seyfulla (Ar.).

SİGEZ see **SEKİZ**

SİGİDİKİ Yak. **Sigidiki** [Сігідікі], fem. (Pek.). ✧ 'Mass'? cf. Yak. *sigidi* 'масса' (Pek.) + suff. *-ki.*

SİGİZ see **SEKİZ**

SİY Maml. 1505 **Si-bay / Siy-bay** [سيباى السينى / Sībāy b. Bukht Ĵukhā], viceroy of Damascus, Syria (1505-1516), fell in 1516, mentioned in an inscription of a copper dish (Mayer 207-208, Iyās II, 247, 261, 391, III, 18, 40, 43, Sauvaget: BEO II, 48); Chuv. 18th-19th c. **Si-bay / Siy-bay** (<Sïy-bay?) [Сибай] (Magn. 76); Chuv. 18th-19th c. **Si-batïr** (<Siy-batïr) [Сибатыръ] (Magn. 76); Maml. 18th-19th c. **Si-bey / Siy-bey?** [Сибей] (Magn. 76); Kzk. 1817 **Si-pay / Sipay?** [سناى / Сипай] (MIK IV, 308). ✧ 'Gift, present; respect; entertainment' cf. Kuman, Alt., Hak., Kzk., Tat. *sī / siy* 'das Geschenk, die Bewirthung; die Ehrerbietung, die Ehrenbezeugung' (Radl. IV, 677). See also **AQ-SİY, SARĪ-SİY.**

SİYAVUŠ Karakh. 11th c. **Siyavuš / Sïyavuš** [Siyavuş (Sıyavuş) / sijavuš] (MK/Atalay 851, DTS).

SİYINDÏQ Kzk. 19th c. **Siyindïq** [Сіиндыкъ] (SOK 178). ✧ 'We hoped; we solicited' cf. Kzk. *siyïn-* 'уповать, надеяться; прибегать к защите' (KzRS).

SİYİR see **SİĜİR I.**

SİYİRČİ see **SİYİRČİ**

SİYİRČİ Kzk. 19th c. **Siyirči** [Сіирчи] (SOK 50); Kzk. 19th c. **Siyirči** [Сіирчи] (SOV 48, 122); Kzk. 19th c. **Siyirči / Siyirčī** [Сіирче] (SOK 160). ✧ 'Cowherd' cf. Alt.(Tel.) *sïrči* 'der Kuhhirt', Kzk. *sïrši* 'id.' (Radl. IV, 708). ⇨ **SİĜİR** + suff. *-či.*

SİYKİN see **SEYKİN**

SİYQİM Kzk. 19th c. **Siyqïm** [Сійкымъ] (SOK 206); Kzk. 19th c. **Siyqïm-bay** [Сійкембай] (SODž. 94); Kzk. 19th c. **Siyqïm-bay** [Сійкымбай] (SOV 22); Kzk. 19th c. **Sïyqïn-bay** (<Sïyqïm-bay) [Сыйкинбай] (AOK 122); Kzk. 1822 **Sïqïm** (<Siyqïm <Sïyqum?) [صيتوم / Сыким] (MIK IV, 433, 435); Kzk. 19th c. **Sïqïm-bay** [Sïkïmbay] (Ljutš 109). ✧ 'Dandy, swell, masher' cf. Kzk. dial. *sïyqïm(soq)* 'сылкым (щеголь, щеголиха, кокетка)' (Amanž. 405).

SİYPÏM Kzk. 19th c. **Siypïm** [Сійпымъ] (SOK 290).

SİYSEN see **SEYSEN**

SİYÜNČ see **SEVİNČ**

SİYÜNDÜK see **SEVİNDİK**

SİYÜŠ see **SÜYÜŠ**

SİKİ see **SEKİ**

SİKİZ see **SEKİZ**

SİKSÄN-ČOQ Kzk. **Siksän-čoq** [Сиксань-чокъ] (IOAIÊK XV. 328-330). ✧ 'Eighty-Feast', expressing a wish for a long life? ⇨ **SEKSEN? + ČOQ.**

SİKSEN see **SEKSEN**

SİKSİRİYÄ Yak. **Siksiriyä-udaγan** [Сіксірійä], fem. (Pek.).

SİL-DİMER Chuv. 18th-19th c. **Sil-dimer** [Силдимеръ] (Magn. 77). ✧ 'Honour-Iron'? cf. Chuv. *sil-* 'id.', first comp. of fem. names, mainly (Fedotov 107). ⇨ **SEL? + TEMİR.**

SİLAVANTÏ Uyg. 12th c. - 14th c. **Silavantï** (EUTS). ✧ 'Leader of a religious community' cf. Uyg. *silavanti / šilavanti* (Skr.) 'духовное лицо религиозной общины' (DTS).

SİLÄWSİN Bashk. 1735 **Slewsin** [Слевсинъ Аккуловъ], a tarγan (Vel.-Zern., Bašk. 13). ✧ 'Lynx' cf. Tat. *siläwsïn* 'der Luchs' (Radl. IV, 741).

SİLĂPÄ Karg. 19th-20th c. **Silăpä** [Сіläпä] (Katanov, Otč. 10). ✧ 'Hat' cf. R. *šljapa* 'id.' (Katanov).

SİLEKE Hak. 19th-20th c. **Sileke** [Сілеке] (HRS 351). ✧ 'Castrated sheep' cf. Hak. *sileke* 'холощёный баран' (HRS), *siläkä / siläkkä* 'der Hammel' (Radl. IV, 711).

SİLEN Hak. 19th-20th c. **Silen** [Силенъ] (HRS 351). ✧ Silan, Silantiy (R.) (Butanaev).

SİLİPTÄN Yak. **Siliptăn** [Сіліптäн], mentioned in a riddle (Pek.).

SİLİRBÄY Yak. **Silirbäy-ämăχsin** [Тіміp Сілірбäі-ämäxciн], fem. (Pek.). ✧ 'Dowdy, smudgy' (Pek.).

SİLİRDÄN Yak. **Silirdăn** [Сілірдäн], a shamaness (Pek.).

SİLİRİKÄN Yak. **Silirikăn-amăχsin** [Сілірікäн-амäxciн], a character in a tale (Pek.).

SİLİP Yak. **Silĭp** [Сіліп] (Pek.). ✧ Filipp (R.) (Pek.).

SİLİPGÄN Yak. **Silĭpgăn** [Сіліпгäн] (Pek.). ✧ 'Little Filipp'. ⇨ **SİLİP** + dim. suff. *-găn.*

SİLMEN Chuv. 19th c. **Silmen** [Sil'm'en'] (Mészáros 215).

SİLÜ Uyg. 12th c. - 14th c. **Silü** [silü / Silü] (DTS, EUTS). ✧ 'Clean, noble' cf. Türk, Karakh. *silig/silik* 'чистый, благородный' (DTS). See also **QĀN-SÜLÜ, TÜZÜN-SİLİK.**

SİM Chuv. 18th-19th c. **Sim** [Симъ] (Magn. 77). ✧ 'Honeyed drink' cf. Chuv. *sim* 'медовый напиток' (ČRS).

SİM-BULA Tat.(Sib.) 16th c. **Sim-bula** [Симбула], one of Küčüm's wives (Sib. Let.). ⇨ **SİM + BULA?**

SİMĀ Türk 9th c. **Simā** [Sīmā], doorkeeper of Caliph Muᶜtasim (833-842) (Justi 301); Türk 9th c. **Simā** [ابراهيم بن سيما / Sīmā] (Tabarī, Annal. III, 1894, Weil, Abbas II, 440, 441, 455).

SİMEY Chuv. 18th-19th c. **Simey** [Симей] (Magn. 77). ⇨ **SİM** + suff. *-ey*.

SİMİZEY Chuv. 18th-19th c. **Simizey** [Симизей] (Magn. 77). ✧ I. '(Little) Green' cf. Chuv. *simĕs* 'id.' (ČRS); II. '(Little) Fat'. ⇨ **SEMİZ** + suff. *-ey*.

SİN Chag. 15th c. - 16th c. **Sin-bay-bahadur** [بهادر سینبای / Синбай Бахадуръ] (Šejb. LII). ✧ 'Tomb' cf. Chag. *sin* 'das Grab, das Grabmal' (Radl. IV, 692). See also **SANKLÏ-SİN**.

SİN-QARALÏ Kzk. 1823 **Sin-qaralï / Sïn-qaralï?** [Синкаралы] (MIK IV, 457).

SİN-ÖYÜZ Kzk. 19th c. **Sin-öyüz** [Синöюзовъ] (AOO 26).

SİNAY Kzk. 19th c. **Sinay** [Бекъ Магомедъ Синаевъ] (Grod., Pril. 91).

SİNAN Uyg. **Sinan** [Sinan] (EUTS). ✧ Sinan (Ar.) 'spear' (Ahmed).

SİNİ Uyg. **Sini-är** [Sini är] (EUTS).

SİÑNÄYÄ Yak. **Siñnäyä** [Cip-уола-Сиҥнӓйä], a demonic hero (bogatyr) (Pek.). ✧ 'Landslip' (Pek.).

SİPAWČİ Az., Trkm.? 1300 **Sipawči** [سپاوچی], an emir (Dorn 143, 152).

SİPEHSALAR Maml. 14th c. **Sipehsalar** [سپهسلار / Sipehsalär] (Tarǰ/Houtsma 76, Tarǰ/Toparlı 43). ✧ 'Commander-in-chief' cf. Uyg. *siba salar* 'der Obergeneral' (Radl. IV, 670), Turk. *sipehsalâr* 'başkomutan' (Özön) (<P.).

SİPERGÜ Uzb.? 19th c. **Sipergü-bek** [Сыпергу-бекъ] (Valihanov, Soč. 150). ✧ 'Broom' cf. East.T. *sipürgi* 'der Besen' (Radl. IV, 729).

SİR-SİRÄBİL Yak. **Sir-siräbil** [Cip Cipäбiл], fem. (Pek.).

SİRA Kzk. 19th c. **Sira-bay** [Сирабай Имамбаевъ] (Grod., Pril. 182). ✧ 'Beer' cf. Kzk. *sira* 'id.' (Radl. IV, 637).

SİRAQ Kzk. 19th c. **Siraq-pay** [Сиракпай] (SOK 96). ✧ 'Long-legged' cf. Kzk. *siraq* 'langbeinig, von hohen Wuchse (Pferd)' (Radl. IV, 639).

SİRAQČİN Khorezm.? 13th c. **Siraqčin / Sïraqčïn?** [سیراقچین], envoy (J̌uwaynī II, 244). ✧ I. 'Long-legged woman/girl'?; II. 'Yellow/blond (woman/girl)', cf. Mo. *šira* (<Trk.) + fem. suff. *-qčin* forming nouns meaning colours of horses (after G. Kara). ⇨ **SİRAQ** + suff. *-čïn*.

SİRAŽADDİN Kkalp. 20th c. **Siražaddin** [Сиражатдин] (KkRS 776). ✧ Siraj-ud-Din (Ar.) 'Lamp of the religion (Islam)' (Ahmed); 'Torch of religion / brightness of religion' (Žanuzakov, Sattarov), cf. also comp. *addin* 'of the religion'.

SİRBEK Hak. 19th-20th c. **Sirbek** [Сирбек], fem. (HRS 354).

SİRÄK Kzk. 19th c. **Siräk-pay** [Сирякпай] (SOV 18); Kzk. 19th c. **Sirek-pay** [Сирекпай], a literate Kirghiz (=Kazak) (AUK 697). ✧ I. 'Sparing' cf. Kuman, Crm.,

Kzk. *siräk* 'dünn besetzt, sparsam' (Radl. IV, 701); II. 'Wide apart, open; rare(ly)' cf. Turk. *seyrek* 'id.' (TED).

SİREK see **SİRÄK**

SİRGEÑ Hak. 19th-20th c. **Sirgeñ** [Сиргенъ] (HRS 351, Proben IX, 557).

SİRΓLÏ Kzk. 19th c. **Sirγlï-bay (<Sïrïqlï-bay?)** [Сирглыбай] (Grod., Pril. 66). ⇨ **SÏRLÏ?**

SİRİ Kzk. 19th c. **Siri-bay** [Миракбай Сирибаевъ] (Grod., Pril. 28); Kzk. 19th c. **Siri-bay** [Сирибай] (Grod., Pril. 121); Kzk. 19th c. **Siri-bay** [Сирибай] (Grod., Pril. 158); Kzk. 19th c. **Siri-bay** [Бай Батуръ Сирибаевъ] (Grod., Pril. 162, 164). ✧ 'Leather of boot heel' cf. Kzk. *siri* 'das Hackenleder' (Radl. IV, 703).

SİRİ-BAŠ Kzk. 19th c. **Siri-baš** [Сирибашъ] (Grod., Pril. 24). ⇨ **SİRİ** + **BAŠ**.

SİRİ-BAŠ-QUŠ Kzk. 19th c. **Siri-baš-quš** [Сирибашъ-Кушъ Ніязовъ] (Grod., Pril. 146). ⇨ **SİRİ** + **BAŠ** + **QUŠ I.**

SİRİ-TAY Kzk. 19th c. **Siri-tay** [Джанъ Тилу Сиритаевъ] (Grod., Pril. 164). ⇨ **SİRİ** + **TAY** or suff. *-tay(1,2)*?

SİRİL Kzk. 19th c. **Siril-bay** [Гезданбай Сирилбаевъ] (Grod., Pril. 144).

SİRİSTİ Uyg. **Siristi** [Siristi] (EUTS).

SİRİŠ-BAYN Uyg. 12th c. - 14th c. **S(i)riš-bayn** [s(i)riš bajn] (DTS).

SİRKÄ-BAY-ŠAL Kzk. **Sirkä-bay-šal** (Proben III). ⇨ **SERKE** + **BAY** + **ŠAL**.

SİRKE see **SERKE**

SİRKEY Kzk. 19th c. **Sirkey** [Кулъ-баба Сиркеевъ] (Grod., Pril. 130). ✧ 'Little he-goat'. ⇨ **SERKE** + suff. *-y*.

SİRLÏ see **SÏRLÏ**

SİRMİR Bashk. 1693 **Sirmir** [Сирмир (Чирмур) Засатаев], from Ufa (MIB I, 84).

SİRTOQ Hak. 19th-20th c. **Sirtoq** [Сирток] (HRS 351).

SİRÜY Bashk. 1744 **Sirüy** [Кабан Сирюев] (MIB III, 416).

SİRÜM Kzk. 19th c. **Sirüm** [Сайлы-бай Сирумовъ] (Grod., Pril. 108). ⇨ **SÏRÏM?**

SİŠ-UR Uyg. **Siš-ur** [Siş Ur] (EUTS). ⇨ **UR.**

SİŠİ Uyg. **Siši** [Sişi] (EUTS). ✧ ? (<Chin.?).

SİTA Kzk. 19th c. **Sita-bay** [Ситабай] (Grod., Pril. 108).

SİTAN Kzk. 19th c. **Sitan-bay** [Ситанбай] (Grod., Pril. 171).

SİTKE Tat. 1724 **Sitke** [Ситке] (MIB III, 228). ⇨ **SEYİT** + suff. *-ke*.

SİWAN Kzk. **Siwan-qul** [Siwankul] (ArchKR XIV, 98).

SĬDÄR Yak. **Sĭdär** [Сiдäр] (Pek.). ✧ Sidor (R.) (Pek.).

SĬLÄP Yak. **Sĭläp** [Сiлäп] (Pek.). ✧ Sila (R.) (Pek.).

SÏMÄN Yak. **Sïmän** [Сімäн] (Pek.). ✧ Simon (R.) (Pek.).

SÏPÏY Hak. 19th c. **Sïpiy** [Сіпій] (Katanov, Otč. 12). ✧ 'Grey, bluish-grey' cf. R. *sivyj* 'id.' (Katanov). See also **BORA, KÖK**.

SÏATAÑNÏR Yak. **Sïatañnïr** [Сыатаңныр], fem. (Pek.).

SÏBAK Chuv. 18th-19th c. **Sïbak** [Сыбакъ] (Magn. 79).

SÏBAKA Chuv. 18th-19th c. **Sïbaka** [Сыбака] (Magn. 79).

SÏBAN Kzk. **Sïban** [Сыбан], Ömür's son (Proben III, 163 /202/); Kzk. 19th c. **Sïban** [Сыбанъ] (Samojlovič: ŽS XXIV (1915), 167); Kzk. 19th c. **Sïpan** [Сыпанъ] (AOP 34). ✧ I. 'Turn up (sleeves)!' (Samojlovič), cf. Kumarı, Kirg., Kzk. *sïban-* 'die Aermel aufstreifen' (Radl. IV, 670); II. Sheyban(i)?

SÏBAS Shor 19th-20th c. **Sïbas** [Сыбас] (Dyrenkova 186 etc.); Hak. 19th-20th c. **Sïbos** [Сыбос] (HRS 351). ✧ 'Sevast'yan' cf. Hak. PN *Sïbïs* '(<R.) Севастьян' (Butanaev).

SÏBÏRГA Uzb. 1722 **Sibirgä** / **Sïbïrɣa?** [Сибирга], from Bukhara (Veselovskij, Unk. 175).

SÏČQANČÏ Uyg. 12th c. - 14th c. **Sïčqančï** [Sïčqančï / Sıçkarçı] (Radl., USp. 153-154, EUTS). ✧ 'Mouser (title/dignity?)' cf. Uyg. *sıçkan* 'Sıçan, fâre; 12'li hayvan takviminin bir yılı' (EUTS) + suff. *-čï*.

SÏDÏBÏL Yak. **Sïdïbïl** [Сыдыбыл], a shaman (Pek.).

SÏDÏQ see **SÏTDÏQ**

SÏDÏÑ Alt. **Sïdïñ** [Сыдың] (ORS 210).

SÏDRAŠ Alt. **Sïdraš** [Сыдраш], fem. (ORS 213).

SÏГAY Kzk. 19th c. **Sïɣay-bay** [Сыгайбай] (Grod., Pril. 62).

SÏГAM-BAY see **SÏГAN**

SÏГAN Kzk. 19th c. **Sïɣam-bay** [Сыгамбай] (SOV 58); Hak. 19th-20th c. **Sïɣan** [Сыған] (HRS 351).

SÏГDA Hak. 19th-20th c. **Sïɣda** [Сыгда] (HRS 351).

SÏГÏB Kzk. 19th c. **Sïɣïb** [Сыгыбъ] (SOK 246).

SÏГÏR I. Kzk. 19th c. **Siyir-bay** [Сиирбай] (Potanin II, 147, 148); Kzk. 19th c. **Siyir-bay** [Сіирбай] (AOK 46); Kzk. 19th c. **Siyir-bay** [Сіирбай] (AOK 70); Uyg. 8th c. **Sïɣïr-tarχan** [Sïɣïr t(a)rχan] (Müller, Pfahl. 23). ✧ 'Cow; bullock'? cf. Karakh. *sïɣïr* 'корова' (DTS), Turk. *sïɣïr* 'eine erwachsene Kuh, ein Ochs' (Radl. IV, 618), Kzk. *sïɣïr* 'корова' (KzRS), Kuman, Kzk., Kar. *sïr* 'die Kuh' (Radl. IV, 700).

SÏГÏR II. Alt. **Sïɣïr** [Сыгыр] (ORS 210). ✧ 'Whistle!' cf. Alt. *sïɣïr-* 'свистеть' (OjrRS).

SÏYADAT Kirg. **Sïyadat** [Сыядат] (Jud. 173, 680).

SÏYDAQ Nog.? **Sïydaq** [Сыйдак] (Žirm., Epos 400).

SÏYÏN Kzk. 1822 **Sïyin** / **Sïyïn?** [صيون / Сыин] (MIK IV, 432, 434).

SÏYQÏN-BAY see **SÏYQÏM**

SÏYLÏ Kzk. 19th c. **Sïyli-bay** / **Sïyli-bay?** [Сейлибай] (SOK 104); Kzk. 19th c. **Sïyli-bay** [Сейлебай] (SODž. 46); Karch. 20th c. **Sïyli-qïz**, fem. (Pröhle, Kar. 131). ✧ 'Reverend, respectable; beloved, darling' cf. Kzk. *sïyli* 'Hürmetli, saygılı' (KzTS), Karch. *sïjlï* 'lieb, geliebt, teuer' (Pröhle, Karch. 131).

SÏYLÏXAN Karch. 20th c. **Sïylïχan**, fem. (Pröhle, Kar. 131). ⇨ **SÏYLÏ** + suff. *-χan(1)*.

SÏYMUŠ Karch. 19th c. **Siymuš** / **Sïymuš?** [Сіймушъ] (SMOK III, 162).

SÏQ Uyg. **Sïq** [Sık] (EUTS).

SÏQÏM see **SÏYQÏM**

SÏQÏM-BERGEN Kzk. 19th c. **Sïqïm-bergen** [Сыкымбергенъ] (SOK 104). ⇨ **SÏYQÏM** + **BERGEN**.

SÏQÏR Kzk. 19th c. **Sïqir-bay** [Сыкырбай] (SOK 92). ✧ 'Creak, squeak' cf. Kzk. *sïqir* 'скрип' (KzRS).

SÏQQÏ Tuv.? 19th c. **Sïqqï-qam** / **Sïqqïñ-qam** [Сыккы-кам], a shaman (Proben IX, 198, 202).

SÏQQÏÑ-QAM see **SÏQQÏ**

SÏQMAS Selj. 1156 **Sïqmas** / **Soqmas?** [ستمس بن قايماز الحرمى], an emir, Qaymaz's son (Ibn al-Athir/Tornb. XI, 142).

SÏLAÑ Uyg. **Sïlañ** [Sılang], fem. (EUTS); Yak. **Sïlañ** [Сылаң] (Pek.). ✧ 'Snake' (Pek.). ⇨ **YÏLAN?**

SÏLDÏ Bashk. 1711 **Sïldï-bay** [Сылдыбаевская мельница], preserved in the name of a settlement (MIB III, 74). See also **AQ-SÏLDÏ**.

SÏLÏГ Bashk. 1782 **Sili-bikä** [Силибика Калнаманова], fem. (MIB V, 131); Uyg. **Sïlïɣ** [Sılıg] (EUTS); Uyg. 12th c. - 14th c. **Sïlïɣ-tegin** [Sılıg / silïɣ tegin] (EUTS, DTS); Kzk. 19th c. **Sïlu-bige** [Силубигэ], fem. (Grod., Pril. 125); Turk. **Sulu** [صولو / Sulu Hacı] (Gökb., Ed. 18, 19, 235, 237, 264, 437); Tat. **Sulu**, fem. (Košay: KCsA I, 324); Kzk. 19th c. **Sulu-bala** [Сулубала] (SOK 192). ✧ 'Beautiful, nice, pretty' cf. Uyg. *sïlïɣ körklä* 'величественный' (DTS), Alt., Tat. *sïlū* 'schön, ansehnlich', Hak. *sïlïɣ* 'id.' (Radl. IV, 653), Kzk., Tat.(Tob.), Uzb. *sulū* 'schön, von schöner Gestalt (von Menschen)' (Radl. IV, 775), Kkalp. *suluw* 'красавица' (KkRS). Used also as a secondary component of female names. See also **HÄSEN, KÜRKLÏ, KÖRKLÄ, KÖRTLÄ, NÏGÄR, ZÏFA**.

SÏLQA Uyg. **Sïlqa** [Sılka] (EUTS).

SÏLLÄNÏQ Yak. **Sïllänïq** [Сылланык] (Pek.).

SÏM Kzk. 19th c. **Sïm-bek** (<Sïn-bek?) [Сымбекъ] (SOV 8). ✧ I. 'Baggy trousers, shalwar' cf. Kzk. dial. *sïm* 'шалбар' (Amanž. 405); II. 'Wire'? cf. Kzk. *sïm* 'der Draht' (Radl. IV, 675).

SÏMAČUQ Uyg. 13th-14th c. **Sïmačuq**, fem. (Zieme, Mat. III, 271).

SÏMAN Kzk. 19th c. **Sïman-bay** [Сыманбай] (SOK 258). See also **QAY-SÏMAN**.

SÏMDAX Hak. 19th-20th c. **Sïmdaχ** [Сымдах], fem.

(HRS 355). ✧ 'Obedient; hard-working' (HRS), cf. Hak.(Sag., Koyb.) *sïmdaq* 'flink, hurtig' (Radl. IV, 676).

SĪMÏQĀN Yak. **Sïmïqān-udaγan** [Уҷалах Чуораннах Сымыкан удаҕан], a most famous and dangerous *üör*-woman (Pek.).

SĪMÏRČÏQ Kzk. 18th c. - 19th c. **Sïmïrčïq** [Сымырчык] (Tynyšp. 67).

SĪMTÏ Kzk. 19th c. **Sïmtï-bay** [Сымтыбай] (SOV 126).

SĪMTÏQ Kzk. 19th c. **Sïmtïq** [Сымтыкъ] (AOP 10, 50, 106); Kzk. 19th c. **Sïmtïïq** [Сымтыкъ] (SOV 72).

SÏN-TEMÏR see **ČÏN-TEMÏR**

SÏNALÏQAY Yak. **Sïnalïqay-χotun / Sïñalïqay-χotun** [Ыатыктыр-муҥ-Сыналыкаi-хотун / Ыатыктыр-муҥ-Сыналыкаi-хотун], fem. (Pek.). ✧ 'Shouting, crying, groaning (because of pains of childbirth)' cf. Yak. *sïnalïy-* 'кричать от родовых мук и вообще; стонать' (Pek.).

SÏNALÏQÏ Yak. **Sïnalïqï-χotun** [Муҥнах Сыналыкы-хотун], fem. (Pek.). ✧ 'Groaning (because of pains of childbirth)' cf. Yak. *sïnalïqï* 'стонущий' (Pek.).

SÏNAN Uyg. 8th c. **Sïnan-sañun** [Sinan sangun] (Müller, Pfahl. 23). ✧ 'Be proved!' cf. Uyg. *sïnan-* 'erprobt, erfahren sein' (Radl. IV, 631).

SÏNARU Alt. **Sïnaru** [Сынару], fem. (ORS 213).

SÏNĀYQA Karg. **Sïnāyqa** [Сынайка] (Katanov, Otč. 9). ✧ 'Know-all' cf. R. знайка (Katanov).

SÏNJAQAN Khorezm. 1221 **Sïnjaqan-χan** [سنجتان خان / Sindjaqân khân], Jelāl's officer (Nasawī 88).

SÏNDÏ Kzk. 1870 **Sindï-γul / Sïndï-γul?** [Чаузабекъ Синдыгуловъ] (Grod., Pril. 129). ✧ 'Handsome, good-looking' (Žanuzakov), cf. Kzk. *sïn* 'фигура, внешний вид' (KzRS) + suff. -*dï*. See also **QAR-SÏNDÏ**.

SÏNÏQAY Bashk. 1778 **Sïnïqay** [Сыныкай Емашев] (MIB V, 69). ✧ I. 'Nice outlook'? cf. Kzk. *sïn* 'фигура, внешний вид' (KzRS); II. 'Little cup/glass'? ⇒ **ČÏNÏ** + suff. -*qay*. See also **ČÏNÏQAY?**

SÏNMA Alt. **Sïnma** [Сынма], fem. (ORS 213).

SÏÑÏR Hak. 19th-20th c. **Sïñïr** [Сынъыр], fem. (HRS 355).

SÏÑÏRÏA Yak. **Sïñïrïa** [Сыҥырыа] (Pek.).

SÏÑQU-SELÏ-TUTUÑ see **ŠÏÑQU-SELÏ**

SÏPA-TAY Kzk. **Sïpa-tay** [Сыпатай] (Smirnov, Sultany 18); Kzk. 18th c. - 19th c. **Sïpa-tay-batïr** [Сыпатай-батыр] (Tynyšp. 65); Kzk. 19th c. **Sopa-tay** [Sopatai] (Ljutš 115); Kzk. 19th c. **Sopa-tay-batïr** [(Botpay) Sopatay batïr] (Ljutš 110); Kzk. **Supa-tay** [Супатай] (SOV 94); Kirg. 1847 **Supa-tay** [Супотай] (Konšin, Mat. V, 106). ✧ 'Soldier-foal; noble-foal' cf. NUyg.(Tar.) *sipa* 'der Beamte, der Herr' (Radl. IV, 726), East.T. *sipa:* (P.) 'soldier' (Jarring), Kirg. *sipā* (P.) 'воин, чиновник; благородный,

благовоспитанный; утончённо-вежливый' (Jud.). ⇒ **TAY** or suff. -*tay (1,2)*.

SÏPAN see **SÏBAN**

SÏPÏR Kzk. 19th c. **Sïpïr** [Сыпыръ] (SODž 128). ✧ 'Sweep!' cf. Kzk. *sïpïr-* 'fegen' (Radl. IV, 668).

SÏPPAR Yak. **Sïppar** [Сыппар] (Pek.). ✧ 'He who drinks up (to the bottom)' cf. Yak. *sïpparïy-* 'выпивать до дна' (Pek.).

SÏPRA-JÏRAU Kzk. **Sïpra-jïrau** [Сыпра Џырау] (Proben III, 162 /201/). ✧ I. '(Leather) table-cloth-singer'; II. 'Richess-singer, Wealth-singer'?, cf. Kzk. dial. *sïpïra* 'нанныҥ астына салатын тері дастархан (кожаная скатерть); мал-мүлік (живое и неживое имущество)' (Amanž. 406), and Kzk. *jïrau* 'der Sänger' (Radl. IV, 120). See also **SUPRA**.

SÏR Kzk. 19th c. **Sïr-bay / Sïr-boy?** [Сырбой] (SOV 62). ✧ I. 'Ochre (paint); red, spotted' cf. Alt., Kzk., Tat. *sïr* 'die Farbe; der Zinnober; roth, bunt' (Radl. IV, 636); II. 'Secret' cf. Crm., Kzk., Tat. *sïr* 'das Geheimniss' (Radl. IV, 636).

SÏR-AT Kzk. 19th c. **Sïr-at-bay / Sïrat-bay?** [Миркабай Сиратбаевъ] (Grod., Pril. 182). ⇒ **SÏR** + **AT**. See also **SÏR-TAY**.

SÏR-BANAY Kzk. 19th c. **Sïr-banay / Sïr-bonay?** [Сырбонай] (SOK 50). ⇒ **SÏR** + **BANAY.**

SÏR-ÖLEÑ Shor 19th-20th c. **Sïr-öleñ- qïs** [Syr Öleŋ qys] (Dyrenkova 192). ✧ 'Colourful plants (gras)'. ⇒ **SÏR** + **ÖLEN.**

SÏR-TAY Kzk. 19th c. **Sïr-tay?** [Сыртай] (SOK 48). ⇒ **SÏR** + **TAY?** or suff. -*tay (1,2)*. See also **SÏR-AT.**

SÏRĀNA-KÜLÜK Yak. **Sïrāna-külük / Sïrānda-külük** [Сырана (Сыранда) күлүк], one of nine or ten evil-brothers of forests who is considered to be the spirit of fish (Pek.).

SÏRĀNAY Yak. **Sïrānay(-oyūn)** [Сыранаi (ойын)], a shaman (Pek.).

SÏRĀNDA-SÜRÜK Yak. **Sïrānda-sürük** [Сыранда Сүрүк], Bāy Bayanay's name or epithet (Pek.).

SÏRJEK Hak. 19th-20th c. **Sïrjek** [Сырчек], fem. (HRS 355). ⇒ **SÏR** + suff. -*jek.*

SÏRDAR Kzk. 19th c. **Sïrdar-bek** [Сырдарбекъ] (SOV 106). ⇒ **SERDAR?**

SÏRGA Hak. 19th-20th c. **Ïzïrγa** [Ызырға], fem. (HRS 356); Karg. **Ïzïrγa**, fem. (Katanov, Otč. 8, 9); Kkalp. 20th c. **Sïrγa** [Сырғъа / Сырға], fem. (Bask., Kkalp. 404, KkRS 778); Alt. **Sïrγa** [Сырга], fem. (ORS 213); Kzk. **Sïrγa-bay** [Сыргабай] (Protok. Turk. IV, 51); Kzk. 19th c. **Sïrγa-bay** [Сыргабай] (SODž. 116); Kzk. 19th c. **Sïrγa-bay** [Сыргабай] (SOK 100, 154, 236); Kirg. 20th c. **Sïrγa-bay** [Сыргабай] (Kalilov 94); Kkalp. 20th c. **Sïrγa-gül** [Syrγa-gül / Сырғагул], fem. (KkRS 778, Baskakov: OSA, 140); Kirg. **Sïrγa-yan** [Сырға-Jaн], one of the forty followers of Aq-sayqal

(Proben V, 394 /397/); Kirg. **Sïrγa-yan** [Сырҕа Jaн] (Proben V); Tuv. 19th c. **Sïrγa-pay** [Сырҕа-паі] (Proben IX, 155); Kzk. **Surγa-bay** [Сургабай] (SOV 148). ❖ 'Earrings', child born with „earrings" round the ears (Kalilov), cf. Alt., Hak., Kar., Kzk., Tat. *sïrγa* 'die Ohrringe' (Radl. IV, 643), Hak.(Sag.) *izirγa* 'der Ohrring' (Radl. I, 1398).

SÏRΓAČÏ   Alt. **Sïrγačï** [Сыргачы], fem. (ORS 213). ➪ **SÏRΓA** + suff. *-čï.*

SÏRΓAY   Hak.(Sag.) 19th-20th c. **Sïrγay** [Сырҕаі] (Proben IX, 457-58). ❖ 'A kind of bird' cf. Hak.(Sag.) *sïrγay* 'ein Vogel' (Radl. IV, 644).

SÏRΓAQ   Kirg. **Sïrγaq** [Сырҕак / Сыргак], one of Manas' comrades-in-arms (Proben V, 39 /41/, 70 /71/, Jud. 78); Kirg. **Sïrγaq** [Syrgak / Сырҕак] (Proben V, 39 /40/, 71, 152). ❖ 'A kind of eagle' cf. Kirg. *sïrγaq* 'вид беркута; (имя одного из положительных героев эпоса "Манас")' (Jud.). See also **KÖK-SÏRΓAQ.**

SÏRΓĀŽÏQ   Karg. **Sïrγāžïq** [Сырҕажык] (Proben IX, 658). ❖ 'Tiny earrings'. ➪ **SÏRΓA** + suff. *-žïq.*

SÏRΓÏ   Kzk. 19th c. **Sïrγi-bay** [Сыргебай] (SODž. 70); Kzk. 19th c. **Sïrγï-bay** [Сыргыбай] (SOK 228); Kzk. 19th c. **Sïrγï-bay** [Сыргыбай] (SOK 300). ➪ **SÏRΓA?**

SÏRÏQ   Kzk. 19th c. **Sïrïq** [Сырыкъ] (SOK 14). ❖ 'Pole, post; support, comforter' cf. Alt., Crm., Kzk. *sïrïq* 'die Stange' (Radl. IV, 640).

SÏRÏL   Kzk.? 19th c. **Sïrïl-bay** [Aftaheddin Syrylbaev] (Mende 136).

SÏRÏM   Tat. 1716 **Sïrïm** [Сырым Карин] (MIB III, 144); Bashk. 1712, 1738 **Sïrïm** [Сырым Кинзекеев / Кинзикеев] (MIB III, 88, 393); Bashk. 1714 **Sïrïm** [Сырым Бисубин] (MIB I, 105); Bashk. 1738 **Sïrïm** [Якычай Сырымов] (MIB I, 143); Bashk. 1749 **Sïrïm** [Сырым] (MIB III, 461-62); Bashk. 1751 **Sïrïm** [Юнусай Сырымов] (MIB IV/1, 34); Kzk. 18th c. **Sïrïm** [Сырымъ] (Sib. Vest. IX, 189); Kzk. 19th c. **Sïrïm** [Сырымъ] (AOP 86); Kzk. 1785, 1805 **Sïrïm** / **Srïm-bahadïr** [صريم بهادر / Сырым / Срым Дат улы], a hero (batïr) of the Bay-baqtï clan (MIK IV, 45, 47-49, 52, 63-65, 72-74, 103-5 etc.); Kzk. 19th c. **Sïrïm-bay** [Сырымбай] (SODž.78); Kzk. 19th c. **Srïm** [Срымъ] (AOO 50); Kzk. 1784 **Srïm-batïr** [Syrym Batyr / Срым-батыр], a well-known biy of the Dats of the Bay-ulï tribe (Tynyšp. 73, Levchine 267, 280). ❖ 'Deliberation, discussion' cf. Kzk. *sirim* 'die Berathung, die Besprechung' (Radl. IV, 642-43).

SÏRÏMBET   Bashk. 1735 **Sïrïmbet** [Сырымбетъ Кутлумбетевъ], a tarχan (Vel.-Zern., Bašk. 24); Kzk. 18th c. **Sïrïmbet** [Сырымбеть] (Nepljuev 716, 718); Bashk.? Tadj.? 1735 **Sïrïmbet** [Сырымбетъ Дюскинъ (тезикъ)] (Vel.-Zern., Bašk. 25); Kzk. 19th c. **Sïrmbet** [Сырмбетъ] (SODž. 30); *TN:* Kzk. **Sïrïmbet** [Сырымбет], a settlement (Kojčubaev 201).

➪ **SÏR / SÏRÏM?** + suff. *-ïmbet /-bet.*

SÏRÏN   Kzk. 19th c. **Sïrïn** [Сырынъ] (AOK 130).

SÏRYAN   Tat.(Sib.) 1647 **Sïryan(ka)** [Сырянка] (Miller, Ist. Sib. II, 522). ❖ From the Vogul PN *Sïr-yan.*

SÏRQA   Kzk. 19th c. **Sïrke-bay?** [Сыркебай] (SOK 270); Kzk. 19th c. **Sïrqa-bay** [Сыркабай] (SODž. 42); *TN:* Kzk. 19th c. **Sïrke-bay** [Сырке-Бай], a well (?) in Üst-yurt (Hanykov, Karta ZK). ❖ 'Be sick!' cf. Kzk., Tat. *sïrqa-* 'krank sein, schmerzen' (Radl. IV, 643).

SÏRLÏ   Kzk. 19th c. **Sirlï-bay** [Сирлыбай] (Grod., Pril. 95); Kzk. 19th c. **Sïrlï-bay** [Сырлыбай] (SODž. 122); Kzk. 19th c. **Sïrlï-bay** [Сырлыбай] (SOV 156); Kzk. 19th c. **Sïrlï-bay** [Сырлыбай] (SOK 62, 72); Kirg. 19th c. **Sïrlï-bek** [Сырлы-бекъ] (AUK Dobavl. 5). ❖ 'Painted, colourful' cf. Kzk. *sïrlï* 'крашеный' (KzRS).

SÏRMA   Turk. 16th c. **Sïrma** [Sirma], fem. (Ongan, Ank. II /Num. 68/). ❖ 'Golden hair(ed)' cf. Turk. *sïrma* 'lace or embroidery of silver or silver gilt thread; golden (hair)' (TED).

SÏRMAQAY   Bashk. 1776 **Sïrmaqay** [Сырмакай Илтякбаев] (MIB V, 47-49). ➪ **SÏRMA** + dim. suff. *-qay.*

SÏRMAN   Kzk. 1794 **Sïrman** / **Sïrman-batïr** [سرمن باطر / Sïrman / Сырман] (MIK IV, 165). ❖ 'Stitched (down)'? cf. Kuman *sïrman* 'gesteppt' (Radl. IV, 651).

SÏRMANAQ   Kzk. 19th c. **Sïrmanaq** [Сырманакъ] (SOK 186). ➪ **SÏRMAN** + suff. *-aq.*

SÏRMBET see **SÏRÏMBET**

SÏRMET   Bashk. 1735 **Sïrmet** [Нурумбетъ Сырметевъ], a tarχan (Vel.-Zern., Bašk. 22). ➪ **SÏR** + suff. *-met.*

SÏRT   Kirg. **Sïrt-bay** [Сыртбай] (Abramzon-Sulejmanov); *TN:* Turk. 20th c. **Sïrt-bey** [Sırtbey], a village in the province of Tekirdağ, Turkey (TMİB 810). ❖ '(Mountain) ridge, crest; hill' cf. Alt., Crm., Hak., Kzk., Tat., Turk. *sïrt* 'der Hinterseite, der Rücken; die Erhöhung, der Hügel' (Radl. IV, 646-47). See also **JAN-SÏRT, QARA-SÏRT.**

SÏRT-ASLAN   Kzk. 19th c. **Sïrt-slan** [Сыртсланъ] (SOK 32). ➪ **SÏRT?** + **ARSLAN.**

SÏRT-SLAN see **SÏRT-ASLAN**

SÏRTLAN   Tat.(Mish.) 19th c. **Sïrtlan** [صرتلان / Сыртланъ] (IOAIÊK XIX, 145); Bashk. 1732 **Sïrtlan** [Сыртлан Тленчеев] (MIB III, 298); Bashk. 1757 **Sïrtlan** [Сыртлан Яушев] (MIB IV/1, 142); Bashk. 1759 **Sïrtlan** [Баши Сыртланов] (MIB IV/2, 24); Bashk. 1761 **Sïrtlan** [Сыртлан Танатаров] (MIB IV/1, 204); Bashk. 1761 **Sïrtlan** [Сыртлан Нурметев] (MIB IV/1, 220); Bashk. 1764 **Sïrtlan** [Сыртлан Аитов] (MIB IV/1, 277); Bashk. 1765 **Sïrtlan** [Девлекей Сыртланов] (MIB IV/1, 312); Bashk. 1770 **Sïrtlan** [Сыртлан Унгаров] (MIB IV/1, 343);

Bashk. 1777 **Sïrtlan** [Сыртлан Аиткулов] (MIB V, 60); Bashk. 1789 **Sïrtlan** [Сыртлан Юсупов] (MIB V, 252); Bashk. 19th c.? **Sïrtlan** [Šah-Chaidar Syrtlanov] (Mende 38, 95, 99, 102, 103); Bashk. 19th c.? **Sïrtlan** [Ali-Asgar Syrtlanov] (Mende 38, 95, 98); Nog. 1649 **Sïrtlan** [Сыртланъ] (AI IV, 122); Bashk. 1777, 1789 **Sïrtlan** (/**Sïrtlaq** / **Sïrtlïq**) [Сыртлан (Сыртлак, Сыртлык) Айсин] (MIB V, 249). ✧ 'Hyena' cf. Tat. *sirtlan* 'id.' (TatRS), Turk. *sirtlan* 'die Hyäne' (Radl. IV, 648).

SÏRTUŠ-YEGEN-APA   Uyg. 762 **Sïrtuš-yegen-apa** [Beg Künki Taisangun Sïrtuš Yägän Apa] (Mahrnāmag 10). ⇨ **YEGÄN + APA**.

SÏRZA   Alt. **Sïrza** [Сырза], fem. (ORS 213).

SÏS   Kzk. 19th c. **Sïs-pay** [Сыспай] (AOP 50).

SÏSÏDU   Uyg. 12th c. - 14th c. **Sïsïdu** [Sïsïdu / Sısıdu] (Radl., USp. 142, DTS, EUTS).

SÏSÏR   Uyg. **Sïsïr** [Sısır] (EUTS); Uyg. 12th c. - 14th c. **Sïsïr** [Sïsïr] (Radl., USp. 153-154).

SÏTAQ   Kzk. 19th c. **Sïtaq** / **Sitaq** [Джузбай Ситаковъ] (Grod., Pril. 188).

SÏTDÏQ   Kzk. **Sïdïq** [Сыдыкъ Бургонбай] (Konsin, Pam. 26); Kzk. 19th c. **Sïdïq** [Сыдыкъ] (SOV 32); Kkalp. 20th c. **Sïdïq** [Сыдык] (KkRS 776); Kzk. 19th c. **Sïdïq-bek** [Сыдыкбекъ] (SODž. 162); Kzk. 19th c. **Sïtdïq** [Сытдыкъ] (AOAtb. 38). ✧ Siddiq (Ar.) 'Righteous, very truthful, honest', epithet of Egyptian Prophet Joseph (Yusuf), Prophet Ibrahim and Prophet Idris (Ahmed)' (<Ar.), cf. Turk. صدیق 'id.' (Zenker), Uyg. *sidïq* (Ar.) 'das Epipheton des Abu Bekr' (Radl. IV, 657).

SÏTÏY   Bashk. 1750 **Sïtïy** [Аптыкей Сытыев] (MIB III, 475).

SÏTÏ-JÏPPÏALA   Yak. **Sïtï-Jïppïala** [Сыты Цыппыала] (Pek.). ✧ 'Stubborn Sïtï' (Pek.).

SÏTTU   Kzk. 19th c. **Sïttu-bay** [Сыттубай] (SOV 64).

SÏWAN   Kzk. 1830 **Sïwan-qul** / **Siwan-qul?** [Сиванкулъ] (Konšin, Mat., I-III, 8).

SÏZAM   Kzk. 19th c. **Sïzam-bay** / **Sizam-bay?** [Сизамбай] (AOP 46).

SÏZDÏQ   Kzk. 19th c. **Sïzdïq** [Сыздыкъ] (AOK 6, 42, 86); Kzk. 19th c. **Sïzdïq** [Сыздыкъ] (AOO 42, 54); Kzk. 19th c. **Sïzdïq** [Сыздыкъ] (SOK 52); Kzk. 19th c. **Sïzdïq-pay** [Сыздыкпай] (SOK 66). ✧ 'Edge, fringe' cf. Kzk. *sizdïq* 'рант' (KzRS).

SÏZÏQ   Kzk. 19th c. **Sïzïq** [Сызыкъ] (SOK 154, 198); Kzk. 18th c. - 19th c. **Sïzïq-bay** [Сызыкбай] (Tynyšp. 66). ✧ 'Line, mark' cf. Kzk. *sizïq* 'черта, линия' (KzRS).

SQAQ see **ÏSHAQ**

SLENKE   Kzk. 19th c. **Slenke** [Сленке] (AOA 74).

SMAYL see **ÏSMAÏL**

SMÏKEY   Bashk. 1735 **Smikey** [Смикей Бекзяновъ], a tarχan (Vel.-Zern., Bašk. 14).

SMÏRKA   Chuv. 18th-19th c. **Smirka** [Смирка] (Magn. 78).

SNA   Alt. 19th c. **Sna-batïr** [Сна-батыр] (Verb., In. 120).

SOBAS   Hak. 19th c. **Sobas** [Собас] (Katanov, Otč. 12).

SOBET   Alt. **Sobet** [Собет] (ORS 209). ✧ 'Council, assembly' cf. R. *sovet* 'id.'.

SOBÏÑ   Hak. 19th-20th c. **Sobïñ** [Собынъ], fem. (HRS 354).

SODAÑ   Hak.(Sag.) 19th-20th c. **Sodañ** [Содаӊ] (Katanov, Otč. 8); Hak.(Sag.) 19th-20th c. **Sodañ** [Содаӊ] (Proben IX, 259); Hak.(Shor) 19th-20th c. **Sodañ** [Содаӊ], fem. (Katanov, Otč. 11). ✧ 'Short, curt; having bob taail' (Katanov, Butanaev).

SODAS   Hak. 19th-20th c. **Sodas** [Содас] (HRS 351).

SODOY-BAŠ   Alt. **Sodoy-baš** [Содойбаш] (ORS 209). ✧ 'Consolation - head'? cf. Alt. *sōt* 'der Trost, der Genuss, die Ergötzung' (Radl. IV, 556). ⇨ **BAŠ**.

SOFÏ   Yürük 16th c. **Sofi** [صوفى / Sofï], from the Yürüks of Kocacık, Turkey (Gökb., Rum. 102); Turk. 20th c. **Sofular** [Sofular] (TMİB 608); Trkm. 20th c. **Sōpï** [Sopï] (Zaj. 1971, 326); *TN:* Turk. 20th c. **Sofu** [Sofu], a village in the province of Kütahya, Turkey (TMİB 589). ✧ 'Mystic, philosopher; ascetic' cf. Turk. *sofu* (Greek) 'ein Philosoph, ein Mystiker, der Ascet, der Fanatiker' (Radl. IV, 560), Turk. *sofi / sufi* 'mystisch' (HŞ), Trkm. *sōpï* 'суфий' (TrkmRS) (<Ar.). Used also as a secondary component of male PN.

SOFÏ-SANDAL-MELİK see **SUNU-SANDAL**

SOҒA-TAY   Kzk. 19th c. **Soγa-tay** / **Soγat-ay?** [Согатай] (AOO 14). ✧ 'Gift-foal / Little gift'? cf. Chag. *soγa* 'Geschenk' (Radl. IV, 527). ⇨ **SOҒA(T) + (T)AY?** + dim. suff. *-ay* or *-tay(1,2)*.

SOҒAN   Nog. 20th c. **Soγan** [Согъан Сарсей увлы / Согон Сарсеев], one of Baskakov's informants from the settlement Terekli-mektep (Bask., Nog. 144). ✧ 'Onion' cf. Kuman, Chag., Crm., Turk. *soγan* 'die Zwiebel' (Radl. IV, 528). See also **KÖBÏRGÄN, MAÑÏR, SOҒONOQ**.

SOҒAN-SARÏ see **SUҒAN-SARÏ**

SOҒAN-SARU see **SUҒAN-SARÏ**

SOҒAT   Karg. **Soγat-pay** [Соӊат-паi / Согатъ-пай] (Proben IX, 659, Katanov: ZIRGOÊtn. XVII, vyp. III, 186, 187). ✧ 'Present, gift' cf. Uyg., Chag., Az. *soγat* 'das Geschenk' (Radl. IV, 529).

SOҒÏN   Hak. 19th-20th c. **Soγïn** [Соғын], fem. (HRS 355). ✧ 'Not beautiful; unsympathetic' (HRS).

SOҒO   Yak. **Soγo-toyon** [Соҕо (Сото) тойон], a legendary person (Pek.).

SOҒONOQ   Alt. **Soγonoq** [Согонок] (ORS 209). ✧ 'Onion' (OjrRS), cf. Alt. *soγono* 'die Zwiebel' (Radl. IV, 529) + suff. *-q*. See also **KÖBÏRGÄN, SOҒAN, MAÑÏR**.

SOҒUY   Yak. **Soγuy** [Соҕyi] (Pek.).

SOΓUYĀ Tuv. 19th c. **Soγuyā** [Соɓуja], fem. (Proben IX, 33).

SOΓUNČAQ Khorezm.? 1257 **Soγunčaq / Suγunčaq?** [Sughundschak], an Ilkhanid commander against Baghdad (Wassaf 41, 59).

SOΓUR see **SUΓUR**

SOΓUR-TUΓAN Tuv. 19th c. **Soγur-tuγan** [Согуръ-туганъ], a character in a tale (Potanin IV, 389). ✧ 'Blind brother/falcon?; born blind?' cf. Alt., Hak. *soγïr* 'blind' (Radl. IV, 529). ⇨ **TUΓAN I.**

SOXSO Yak. **Soχso-ärkin** [Cохсо (Сохсон?) äркін] (Pek.).

SOYA Kzk. 19th c. **Soya-bay** [Соябай] (AOP 126).

SOYAΓ Hak.(Sag.) 19th-20th c. **Soyaγ** [Сойаɓ] (Proben IX, 46⁷).

SOYAQA Hak. 19th-20th c. **Soyaqa** [Сояка], fem. (HRS 355).

SOYAN I. Uyg. 12th c. - 14th c. **Soyan-tutuγ / Soyan-tutuq** [Soyan (Süän, Suyan?) Tutuγ / sojan tutuq] (Radl., USp. 204, 246, EUTS, DTS). ✧ 'Flayer (the skin)' (Blagova 1997, 716).

SOYAN II. Hak. 19th-20th c. **Soyan** [Соян] (HRS 351); Hak.(Blt.) 19th-20th c. **Soyan** [Сойан] (Katanov, Otč. 9i; Hak.(Kacha) 19th c. **Soyan** [Соянъ] (Katanov, Otč. II, 42); Hak.(Kacha) 19th-20th c. **Soyan** [Сойан], a folklore hero (bogatyr) (Proben IX, 217-219); Alt. **Soyoñ** [Сойон], fem. (ORS 213). ✧ 'Tuvinian, Sayan' cf. Hak. PN *Soyan* 'тувинец' (Butanaev), 'Tuvinian (woman)' (OjrRS).

SOYANČE Hak. 19th-20th c. **Soyanče** [Соянче] (HRS 351). ⇨ **SOYAN** + suff. *-ča / -če?*

SOYAR Uyg. 12th c. - 14th c. **Soyar** [sojar / Soyar] (DTS, EUTS). ✧ 'He who flays; Skinner' (Blagova 1997, 716).

SOYĀ-QARA Tuv. 19th c. **Soyā-qara-madïr** [Coja-Кара-Мадыр], a folklore hero (bogatyr) (Proben IX, 132). ✧ 'Tuva-Black(-hero)' cf. Hak. PN *Soyan* 'тувинец' (Butanaev), Hak.(Sag., Koyb.) *soyan (soyañ) ürkäzï* 'das Murmelthier' (Radl. I, 1836, IV, 535). ⇨ **QARA.**

SOYÏNJA Hak.(Blt.) **Soyïnja** [Сойынца] (Proben IX, 366). ✧ 'Cast iron'? cf. Hak.(Sag.) *soyïn* 'das Gusseisen' (Radl. IV, 535). ⇨ **SOYANČE?**

SOYQA Chuv. 18th-19th c. **Soyka** [Сойка] (Magn. 78). ✧ Soyka (R. hypoc. of *Psoy, Sisoy*).

SOYNAX Hak. 19th-20th c. **Soynaχ** [Сойнах] (HRS 355).

SOYOÑ see **SOYAN II.**

SOYRÏMAS Kzk. 19th c. **Soyrïmas (<Sayramaz?)** [Сойрымасъ] (AOO 38). ✧ 'He/she won't sing' cf. Kzk. *sayra-* 'ötmek, şarkı söylemek' (KzTS) + suff. *-mas.*

SOYSEY Kzk. 19th c. **Soysey-bay** [Сойсейбай] (SOK 274).

SOKE Kirg. **Soke** [Соке] (Jud. 214).

SOQA Hak. 19th-20th c. **Soqa** [Сока], fem. (HRS 355).

SOQÏČÏ Alt. **Soqïčï** [Сокычы], fem. (ORS 213). ✧ 'Mortar; pestle' (OjrRS).

SOQMAN Oghuz/Trkm. 13th c. **Soqman** [سوقمان / Сокман], İnal-γāzi's son (Abulg./Kon. 1250); Selj. **Soqman** [سُكمان] (Bondārī 179, 185); Selj. 1091, 1096, 1108 **Soqman** [سكمان بن ارتق / سكمان بن ارتق / ستمان] / Sokman Ebn Ortok], Artuq's son (Abulfidā III, 350-51, Abulfar. Or. 369 /242-43/, Qalānisi 132-138, 158, Ibn Taghrïb. II, 304, 315, Ibn al-Athïr, Atab.: RHCHor II/2, 31, Abulfidā III, 350-51); Selj. 1110 **Soqman** [سكمان القطبى] / Sokmān el-Kotbï], prince of Khelat (Kamāladdïn: RHCHor III, 595); Selj. 1111/12 **Soqman** [سكمان القطبى] / Socmân el-Kotbî], lord of Tebriz (Ibn al-Athïr, Atab.: RHCHor II/2, 34); Selj. 12th. c. **Soqman** [ناصر الدين سكمان], lord of Khelat (Rāwandï 299); Selj. 1185 **Soqman** [Kûtab ad-Dïn Sokmân], lord of Âmid (Abulfar./Budge I, 318); Selj. 1124, 1136 **Soqman / Sökmen?** [سكمان / داود بن ستمان] (Kamāladdïn II, 220, 353, 260). ✧ 'Half boots made of leather' cf. Chag., Turk. *soqman* 'Halbstiefel aus Leder oder Safian, die auf dem blossen Fuss getragen werden' (Radl. IV, 527).

SOQOÑ Alt. **Soqoñ** [Сокон] (ORS 210).

SOQSUR Kzk. 19th c. **Soqsur** [Соксуръ], fem. (Potanin II, 4). ✧ 'A kind of duck' cf. Kzk. *soqsur ördök* 'eine Entenart' (Radl. IV, 526).

SOQTA Uyg. 12th c. - 14th c. **Soqta** [soqta / Sokta] (DTS, EUTS). ✧ I. 'Sausage, black pudding' cf. Kuman, East.T., Kzk. *soqta* 'eine mit Blut gefüllte Wurst' (Radl. IV, 525); II. 'Student' cf. Crm. *soqta* 'der Student, der in Medresse wohnt' (Radl. IV, 525) (<P.). ⇨ **SOQTU.**

SOQTU Uyg. **Soqtu-älči** [Soktu älçi] (EUTS). ✧ 'Sausage, black pudding' cf. Karakh. *soqtu* 'колбаса-казы' (DTS). ⇨ **SOQTA.**

SOQUR Kzk. 1817 **Soqur** [Сокур] (MIK IV, 313, 329); Kzk. 19th c. **Soqur** [Сокуръ] (AOO 54); Kzk. 19th c. **Soqur** [Сокуръ] (SOV 30); Kzk. 19th c. **Soqur** [Милдабай Сокуровъ] (Grod., Pril. 100); Kzk. **Soqur-abïz** [Kara-Kerey Sokur-abïz] (Atyns. 18); Kzk. 19th c. **Suqur-bay** [Сукурбай] (Grod., Pril. 87). ✧ 'Blind' cf. Kzk. *soqur* 'blind; einäugig, einen Fehler im Auge habend' (Radl. IV, 521).

SOL Oghuz? **Sol(-dihqan) / Sul?** [صول دهتان قهستان] (Ibn al-Athïr/Tornb. V, 20-23, 64); Türk? **Sol / Sul?** [صُول / Sol], at the time of Caliph Abdulmalik (Fragm. Hist. Ar. 21, 22); Chuv. 18th-19th c. **Sol-bay** [Солбай] (Magn. 78); Türk? 836, 840 **Sol-er-tegin** [صول ارتكين] (Ibn al-Athïr/Tornb. VI, 324, 368); Türk? 6th c. **Sol-χan** [Σολχάνης], governor of Nisibis (of Turkic

origin?) (Byz. Turc. 284); Türk? 836, 840 **Sol-tegin /
Sol-er-tegin** [صول تكين / صول ارتكين] (Tabarī, Annal.
III, 1194, 1313); Türk 8th c. **Sul** [صول / صُول / Сул
(Сул-тюрк)], Turkic lord of Dihistan(?) (Tabarī, Annal.
II, 1320, 1322-1325, 1327, MIT I, 63, 64, 92, 107-110,
165, 338); Türk 10th c. - 12th c. **Sul** [Сул], Nizaq-
tarχan's nephew (MIT I, 106); Türk 8th c. **Sul-tarχan**
[صول طرخان / Сул-тархан], the khalif of the Türks
(Qarluqs) (Ibn al-Athīr/Tornb. IV, 436, MIT I, 106). ✧
'Left (side); left (wing of the army?)' cf. Uyg., Kuman,
Alt., Crm., Kzk., Turk. etc. *sol* 'link, links' (Radl. IV,
548).

SOLAҒAY Hak. 19th-20th c. **Solaγay** [Солаҕай] (HRS
351); Hak. 19th-20th c. **Solaγay** [Солаӊai], an evil
spirit (Proben IX, 584). ✧ 'Left-handed' cf. Kuman,
East.T. *solaγay*, Kzk., East.T. *solaqay* 'die Linkhand'
(Radl. IV, 551). See also **SOLAQ**.

SOLAQ Turk. 1471 **Solaq** [Solak /Yayabaşı/] (Gökb.,
Ed.); Trkm. **Solaq** [صلاق جولى / Şolak culĭ], in Syria
(Refik, Anad. 62); Turk. 16th c. **Solaq-zade**
[Solakzade] (Baştav 50, 64, 65); *EN:* Trkm. **Solaq-
muslĭ** [صلاق مصلى / Solak Muslĭ], a tribe (cemaat) in
Syria (Refik, Anad. 62); *TN:* Turk. 20th c. **Solaqlar**
[Solaklar], a village in the province of Kayseri, Turkey
(TMİB 527). ✧ 'Left-handed; unlucky' cf. Chag.,
Turk. *solaq* 'die Linkshand; unglücklich' (Radl. IV,
550). See also **SOLAҒAY**.

SOLAQ-QARAJA Turk. 1398 **Solaq-qaraja**
[صولق قرهجه / صولاق قرجه], a warrior of Bayezid I in
the battle of Angora (Nešrī 364, Āšikp. 70). ⇨ **SOLAQ
+ QARAJA.**

SOLĀN Hak.(Sag.) 19th-20th c. **Solān** [Солан] (Proben
IX, 542).

SOLDA Uyg. 12th c. - 14th c. **Solda** [solda] (DTS,
EUTS); Uyg. 12th c. - 14th c. **Solda-bay** [Solda Bai /
solda baj / Solda Bay] (Radl., USp. 15, DTS, EUTS). ⇨
SOLTO?

SOLҒAT Maml. 1340 **Solγat** [سيفالدين صلغات /
Сейфеддинъ Солгатъ] (Zetterst. 219, Tizeng. I, 260,
269 /after Al-Malik An-Nāsir/).

SOLÏҒAN Kzk. 19th c. **Solïγan-qul** [Солиганкулъ]
(SODž. 6).

SOLÏM Tat.(Bar.) **Solïm / Änä-solïm** [Änä Solym /
Änä Солым], fem. (Proben IV, 74 /93/). ✧ 'Unknown;
alien; stranger' cf. Hak. *solïm*, Alt. (Leb., Tel.) *sōlin*
'unbekannt, fremd, neu' (Radl. IV, 552). See also
ÄNÄ-SOLÏM.

SOLÏN Kzk. 19th c. **Solïm-bay (<Solïn-bay?)**
[Солимбай] (SOK 158).

SOLÏNDÏQ Kzk. 19th c. **Solïndïq** [Солындыкъ] (SOV
70).

SOLKEČ Tat.(Lit.) 1591 **Solkeč?** [Солкечъ
Коксубовичъ] (Lit. Tat. 94).

SOLLONTOY Yak. **Sollontoy** [Кыс Соллонтоi], a
shamaness (Pek.). ✧ 'Glutton, voracious' cf. Yak.
sollon 'червь-нутряк, возбуждающий постоянное
ощущение голода даже при хорошем питании;
алчность, чрезмерная жадность' (Pek.) + suff. *-toy*.

SOLLU Turk. 19th c. **Sollu-oγlu**, a Zeybek (Kúnos
1891, 119). ✧ 'Left' cf. Turk. *sollu* 'links befindlich'
(Radl. IV, 554).

SOLMAN Karch. 20th c. **Solman** [Solman] (Pröhle,
Kar. 132). ⇨ **SOL** + suff. *-man.*

SOLMAZ Trkm. 20th c. **Solmaz** [Solmaz], fem. (Zaj.
1971, 341). ✧ '(S)he won't fade (=die)' cf. Trkm. *sol-*
'линять; вянуть' (TrkmRS).

SOLOQO Hak. 19th-20th c. **Soloqo** [Солоко] (HRS
351).

SOLOMUON Yak. **Solomuon** [Соломуон] (Pek.). ✧
Solomon (R.) (Pek.).

SOLOTNĬK Karg. **Solotnik** [Солотнiк] (Katanov, Otč.
9). ✧ 'A Russian measure of weight (=4.25 gr)' cf. R.
zolotnik (Katanov).

SOLTA see **SOLTO**

SOLTAQAY Bashk. 1754 **Soltaqay** [Солтакай
Янбеков] (MIB IV/1, 84). ⇨ **SOLTO** + dim.
suff. *-qay.*

SOLTAN see **SULTAN**

SOLTAN-ALİ Bashk. 1735 **Soltan-ali** [Солтанали
Идзимясовъ], a tarχan (Vel.-Zern., Bašk. 20). ⇨
SULTAN + ALİ.

SOLTAN-GİLDİ see **SULTAN-GELDİ**

SOLTAN-MURAT Bashk. 1735 **Soltan-mrat
(<Soltan-mïrat?)** [Солтанмрать Мрясевъ], a tarχan
(Vel.-Zern., Bašk. 15); Bashk. 1764 **Soltan-mrat
(<Soltan-mïrat?)** [Солтан-Мрат Сарбашев] (MIB
IV/1, 298); Bashk. 1735 **Soltan-murat**
[Солтанмурать Муайтмасовъ], a prince (Vel.-Zern.,
Bašk. 12). ⇨ **SULTAN + MURAT.**

SOLTANGİN Bashk. 1675 **Soltangin** [Солтангин
Дейдертякеев] (MIB I, 200).

SOLTĬ see **SOLTO**

SOLTĬR Hak.(Shor) 19th-20th c. **Soltïr** [Солтыр], fem.
(Katanov, Otč. 11).

SOLTO Kzk. 1838 **Solta-bay** [Солтабай Бопинъ], a
Sultan (Konšin, Mat. V, 41); Kzk. 19th c. **Solta-bek**
[Солтабекъ] (SOK 220); Kzk. 19th c. **Soltï** [Солты]
(SODž. 6, 80); Kzk. 19th c. **Soltï** [Солты] (SOK 136);
Kzk. 19th c. **Soltï-bay** [Солтыбай] (SOV 44); Kzk.
19th c. **Soltï-bay** [Солтыбай] (SODž. 110); Kzk. 1846
Solto-bay [Солтобай] (Konšin, Mat. V, 98); Kirg.
Solto-bay [Солтобай] (Jud. 61). ✧ 'Strength; power'
cf. Kzk. *Soltïbay* <Ar. *soldo* 'id.' (Žanuzakov).

SOLTONAY see **SULTANAY**

SOLUQ Trkm. **Soluq** [Гуль Мугаметъ Солуковъ]
(Ščeglov IV, 191); Nog. 1649 **Soluq** [Солукъ] (AI IV,
123); Kuman 1127, 1128 **Soluq? / Selük?** [Селукъ

(Селелукъ, Оселукъ)], a Polovets prince (Lavr. 281 /196/, Ipat. 209 /214/, PSRL VII, 26-27); Kuman 1183, 1185 **Soluq / Suluq? / Sulaq?** [Осалукъ / Осолукъ / Осулукъ / Сулакъ / Осокульф], a Polovets prince (Burčevič) (Ipat. 427 /440/, 454 /464/, Lavr. 375 /267/, PSRL I, 167, II, 128, 142, 319, 323, XV, 271). ✦ 'Breath'? (Rásonyi, KÖA 125); cf. Turk., Kzk. *soluq* 'das Aufathmen, der Athem; matt, bleich' (Turk.), 'die Athemlosigkeit' (Radl. IV, 553). Baskakov gives five possible etimons and quite different meanings: *osuluq* 'judicious, modest'; *osalluq* 'laziness'; *syjlyk* 'right, honest'; *suuluq* 'bit, curb'; *sayly / sawlyq* 'sheep' (Bask., Im. polov. 70-71).

SOLUONYAY see **SALÏANYAY**

SOM Kzk. 19th c. **Som-bay** [Сомбай] (SOV 48); Kzk. **Som-temür** [صوم تيمور / Сомъ-Темуръ] (Divaev, Dem. 9, 29). ✦ 'Figure, form; stake, pole' cf. Tel., Alt., Sag. *som* 'die Form, die Gestalt'; Tel., Alt. *som* 'die zur Ehre der Gottheit aufgestellten Birkenstangen' (Radl. IV, 562).

SOMA Uyg. 12th c. - 14th c. **Soma / Suma** [Soma] (Radl., USp. 100-101, DTS, EUTS).

SOMAČÏ Uyg. 12th c. - 14th c. **Somačï** [Somačï / Somačı] (Radl., USp. 114-115, DTS, EUTS).

SOMOΓOLLOY Yak. **Somoγolloy** [Сомоҕоллоі] (Pek.).

SOMOΓOTTO Yak. **Somoγotto** [Сомоҕотто] (Pek.).

SOMSOYŪN Yak. **Somsoyūn** [Сомсојун] (Pek.).

SOMSŪN Yak. **Somsūn** [Сомсун] (Pek.). ✦ Samson (R.) (Pek.).

SOMUR Crm. **Somur-aγa** [سمور اغا] (Vel.-Zern., Crim. 11). ✦ 'Grave, morose' cf. Crm.(Tat.) *somur* 'хмурый; ворчливый' (KrmRS).

SON Kzk. 19th c. **Son-pay** [Сонпай] (SOK 144). ✦ 'Last (child)' cf. Kuman, Kzk. *son* 'nachher, später' (Radl. IV, 533).

SONA Trkm. **Sona** [Сона], fem. (Sopieva 178); Trkm. 20th c. **Sona** [Sona], fem. (Zaj. 1971, 338); Trkm. 20th c. **Sona** [Сона], fem. (TrkmRS 584). ✦ 'Mallard; beautiful, belle' (Zaj. 1971, Sopieva), cf. Trkm. *sona* 'кряква (самка)' (TrkmRS).

SONČA Kzk. 19th c. **Sonča** [Сонча] (SOK 286).

SONÏ Kzk. 19th c. **Sonï** [Соны] (SODž. 156).

SONQUR-DÏRĀZ Selj. 1108/09, 1128 **Sonqur-diraz** [سنقر دراز / Sonkor-Diraz], prince of the lands watered by Khabur (Ibn al-Athīr: RHCHor I, 266, 290, 380); Selj. 1109 **Sonqur-dirāz** [سنقر دراز] (Ibn al-Athīr/Tornb X, 326, 352); Selj. 1115 **Sonqur-dirāz** [Senkûr Dhê-râz], Aq-soñqur's envoy (Abulfar./Budge I, 247); Selj. 1116 **Sonqur-dirāz** [سنقر دراز] (Usāma 54); Selj. 1128 **Sonqur-dirāz** [سنقر دراز / Sonkor-Diraz], an emir (Kamāladdīn II, 241, Kamāladdīn: RHCHor III, 657). ✦'Soñqur, the long' cf. P. *dirāz* 'lang' (Zenker). ⇨ **SOÑQUR.**

SONQURAQ Selj. 12th c. **Sonquraq** [بدرالدين سنقرآق] (Muh. Ibrahim 175). ⇨ **SOÑQUR** + suff. -*aq*.

SONQURČA Maml. 1258 **Sonqurča** [سنقرجاه / Singur Jāh el-Gharsī] (Sīrat 88); Maml. 14th c. **Sonqurča / Sunqurča** [سنقرجا / Sunkurça] (Tarĵ/Houtsma 31, Tarĵ/Toparlı 42); Selj. 1095 **Sonqurĵa** [سُنْتُورْجَاه] (Ibn Taghrīb. II, 312); Selj.? 1102 **Sonqurĵa** [سنقرجه], emir of Kerbogha (Ker-boγa / Ker-buγa) in Mosul (Ibn al-Athīr: RHCHor I, 209); Selj.? 1102 **Sonqurĵa** [سنقرجه] (Ibn al-Athīr/Tornb. X, 233); Selj. 1226 **Sonqurĵa** [سنقرجه], mamluk (dawādār, Master of the Horse) of atabek „Ouzbek" (Nasawī 126); Selj. 1264 **Sonqurĵa** [Schems-eddin-Sonkordjah], page of atabek Saad from Shiraz (Makrīzī I, 238). ✦ 'Little falcon, little white falcon'. ⇨ **SOÑQUR** + suff. -*ča / -ĵa*.

SONQURĴA see **SONQURČA**

SONOM-RABTAN Alt. 19th c. **Sonom-rabtan** [Соном-Рабтан] (Verb., In. 119).

SONOR see **SOÑQUR**

SONTŌYUQ Yak. **Sontōyuq** [Сонтоjук] (Pek.). ✦ 'Big-nosed' cf. Yak. *sontoy-* 'выдаваться вперед (о большом носе)' (Pek.) + suff. -*uq*.

SOÑQUR Selj. **Sonqur** [سنقرالعزيرى / Sonkur] (Bondārī 225); Selj. **Sonqur** [سُنْثُر / سنقر], lord of Zanjan (Bondārī 170); Selj. **Sonqur** [سنقرالمملوك / Sonkur] (Bondārī 271-273); Selj. **Sonqur** [سنقر الهمذانى / Sonkur] (Bondārī 239); Selj. 1105 **Sonqur** [سنقر البرسقى قسيم الدولة] (Ibn al-Athīr/Tornb. X, 272); Selj. 1118 **Sonqur** [الجكرمشي / سنقرا الجكرمش / Sonkor el-Djekermichy] (Kamāladdīn II, 178, Kamāladdīn: RHCHor III, 611, 729); Selj. 1119 **Sonqur** [سنقر نورالدولة] (Ibn al-Athīr/Tornb. X, 393); Selj. 1119 **Sonqur** [سنقر البياتى] (Ibn al-Athīr/Tornb. X, 393); Selj. 1119/20 **Sonqur** [سنقر البخارى / Sonkor el-Bokhari], an emir of Sultan Mahmud II(?) (Ibn al-Athīr/Tornb. X, 387, Ibn al-Athīr: RHCHor I, 321); Selj. 1134/1135 **Sonqur** [سنقر الخمارتكين / Sonkor el-Khomartekînî], governor of Hamadān (Ibn al-Athīr/Tornb. XI, 14, 30, 188, Ibn al-Athīr, Atab.: RHCHor II/2, 88-89); Selj. 1136 **Sonqur** [سنقور الحاجب / Sonkur] (Qalānisi 253, 257); Selj. 1144 **Sonqur** [سنقر صلاحالدين], one of Sultan Sandjar's (1118-1157) emirs (Ibn al-Athīr/Tornb. XI, 63, 206); Selj. 1145 **Sonqur** [نصرالدين سنقر], Zengi I's chieftain, died in 1145 (Usāma 116); Selj. 12th c. **Sonqur** [قطبالدين بن سنقر] (Muh. Ibrahim 111); Selj. 12th c. **Sonqur** [سنقر], governor of Hamadān (Rāwandī 285); Selj. 12th c. **Sonqur** [سنقر طويل / Sonkur], shahne (security inspector) of Isfahan (Rāwandī 381); Selj. 12th c. **Sonqur**

[سنترحاه النوري /خانتاه/] (Ibn Šaddād, Alep); Selj. 1157 **Sonqur** [سنقر العزيزى] (Ibn al-Athīr/Tornb. XI, 149-50); Selj.? 1190/91 **Sonqur** [سنقر الحلبى / Sonkor el-Halebi], a commander of the army in Egypt (Ibn Šaddād, Nawād.: RHCHor III, 169); Selj. 1191/92 **Sonqur** [سنقر الوشاقى / Sonkor el-Ouchaki / Sonkor Alouichâky], Salaheddin's emir (Ibn al-Athīr/Tornb. XII, 43, Ibn al-Athīr: RHCHor II/1, 45, Ibn Šaddād, Nawād.: RHCHor III, 233); Selj. 1195 **Sonqur** [سنقر الكبير], an emir (Ibn al-Athīr/Tornb. XII, 77); Selj. 1207 **Sonqur** [سنقر مظفرالدين] (Ibn al-Athīr/Tornb. XII, 171, 200, 277); Selj.? 13th c. **Sonqur** [سنقر الخلاطى / الاخلاطى / Sonkor el-Khalâtî] (Ibn Šaddād, Nawād.: RHCHor III, 16-18, Iyās I, 72); Selj. 13th c.? **Sonqur** [سنقور], forefather of the Ottoman dynasty (Āšikp. 5); Tat.(GH) 13th c. **Sonqur** [Сонкуръ] (Smirnov, Krym. 35); Tat.(GH) 1267/68 **Sonqur** [سنقر / Sonkor], a Tatar chief (Aynī: RHCHor II/1, 235-36); Maml. **Sonqur** [شمس‌الدين سنقور الغُتْمى / Sonkur], emir, envoy sent to (Desht-i-) Kipchak (Qalāūn/Tizeng. I, 65); Maml. 13th c. **Sonqur** [شمس‌الدين سُنقر الغُتْمى], emir, Qalāūn's (1279-1290) envoy to Meñgü-temür (Makrīzī III, 165); Maml. 13th c. **Sonqur** [شمس‌الدين سنقر القشتمرى] (Zetterst. 44); Maml. 1254 **Sonqur** [Sonkor-Habischi Alkebir] (Makrīzī I, 50); Maml. 1254 **Sonqur** [Sonkor-Djubaïli] (Makrīzī I, 50); Maml. 1277 **Sonqur** [شمس‌الدين سنقر الرومى], died in 1277 (Iyās I, 90, 276, Makrīzī I, 389, Ibn Taghrīb. VI, 228, Weil, Chalif. I, 31, 102); Maml. 1279 **Sonqur** [Sonkor-Tekriti], emir, viceroy (ostadar) (Makrīzī II, 169); Maml. 1279, 1280 **Sonqur** [سنقور الاشقر], governor of Damascus (Makrīzī II, 10, 169, Iyās I, 91, 115, Zetterst. 2, 21, Ibn Taghrīb. VI, 347, Weil, Chalif. I, 36, 115); Maml. 1280 **Sonqur** [Schems-eddin Sonkor-Arsi], died at Hims in 1280 (Makrīzī III, 39); Maml. 1280 **Sonqur** [سنقر جركس] (Iyās I, 115); Maml. 1296, 1298, 1301 **Sonqur** [شمس‌الدين سنقر الاعسر], an emir (Dawād. 12, 41, 64 etc., Zetterst. 1, 39, 43, Weil, Chalif. I, 207, Marīzī IV, 127); Maml. 1298, 1301, 1312 **Sonqur** [شمس‌الدين سنقر الكمالى], emir, commander of Haleb (Dawād. 7, 41, 72, 109 etc., Zetterst. 147, 167, Weil, Chalif., I, 308); Maml. 1302 **Sonqur** [سنقر الكافرى] (Dawād. 88, Zetterst. 118); Maml. 1304 **Sonqur** [عزالدين سنقر الكمالى], an emir (Dawād. 118); Maml. 1309 **Sonqur** [شمس‌الدين سنقر], an emir (Dawād. 200); Maml. 1309 **Sonqur** [سنقر الرومى] (Dawād. 243); Maml. 1320 **Sonqur** [سنقر الكمالى الصغير] (Dawād. 299); Maml. 1320, 1332 **Sonqur** [سنقر المرزوقى], an emir (Zetterst. 167, Dawād. 368); Maml. 1327 **Sonqur** [ابراهيم بن سنقر], a sheykh (Dawād. 331, 332); Maml.

1327 **Sonqur** [سيف‌الدين سنقر الطويل], an emir (Dawād. 342, Zetterst. 2); Maml. 1332 **Sonqur** [سنقر الخازن], an emir (Dawād. 365); Maml. 1332 **Sonqur** [سنقر تارى النتيب] (Dawād. 367); Maml. 14th c.? **Sonqur** [سنقر الاشقر / Sankar al-Ashkar], a chieftain (Abulfar. Or. (356-57), 546); Maml. 1389 **Sonqur** [سنقور], governor of Sis (Iyās I, 271); Maml. 1410 **Sonqur** [سنقر], governor (nā‘ib) of Marqab (?) (Ibn Taghrīb. VI, 382, 409); Maml. 1428 **Sonqur** [سنقور], the emir of the security guards (Ibn Taghrīb. VI, 629); Maml. 1430 **Sonqur** [سنقور], Taγrī-berdī's chancellor (dawādār) (Ibn Taghrīb. VI, 654); Maml. 1434 **Sonqur** [سنقر العزّى الناصرىّ] (Ibn Taghrīb. VI, 728, VII, 571); Maml. 1447, 1453 **Sonqur** [سنقر الظاهرى] (Ibn Taghrīb. VII, 148, 238); Maml. 1448 **Sonqur** [سنقورالحعيدى العائق / Sonkor Alaik], the chief Master of the Horse (Ibn Taghrīb. VII, 163, 174, Weil, Chalif. II, 260); Maml. 1450 **Sonqur** [سنقر السيفى جارقطلو] (Ibn Taghrīb. VIII, 77); Maml. 1450 **Sonqur** [سنقر الرومى] (Ibn Taghrīb. VIII, 85); Maml. 1451 **Sonqur** [سنقور بن وبير بن نخبار] (Ibn Taghrīb. VII, 360); Maml. 1453 **Sonqur** [سنقر الظاهرى] (Ibn Taghrīb. VIII. 170, 172); Maml. 1453 **Sonqur** [سنقور] (Iyās II, 40); Maml. 1454, 1462 **Sonqur** [سنقر قرق شبق الزردكاش الاشقر] (Ibn Taghrīb. VII, 464, 700 etc., VIII. 205, 241, 250 etc., Iyās II, 56, 58, 73); Selj. 1120 **Sonqur-alp** (Ibn al-Athīr/Tornb. X, 393); Selj. **Sonqur / Sonγur** [سلغرى] [سنقر / سنغر بن مودود] (Qazw. 365, 528); Khorezm. 1227 **Sonqur-χan** [سنقر خان], an emir called „Ketsonkor Malik" who was given this title by Jelāl (Nasawī 139); Maml. 1299 **Sonqur-šah** [سنقرشاه الحسامى المملوك] (Dawād. 37); Maml. 1309 **Sonqur-šah** [سنقر شاه اظاهرى] (Dawād. 175); Uyg. **Sonqur-tegin** [سنقر / سنقورتكين / Sonkur tegin] (Ĵuwaynī I, 41, 42); Selj. 13th c. **Sonqur-tegin** [سنقور تكين], Er-toγrul's brother (Nešrī 190); Selj. 13th c. **Sonqur-tegin** [سنقور تكين], Süleyman-šah's son (Āšikp. 6); Kzk. 19th c. **Sonor-bay** [Сонорбай] (SOK 164); Tat.(GH) 1278 **Soñγur** [Σογγούρ], a christened Tatar, died in 1278 (Byz. Turc. 283-84); Tat.(GH) 1316 **Soñγur** [Σογγούρ / Sonqur /Songur], a christened Tatar, died in 1316 (Byz. Turc. 283-84); Oghuz / Selj.? **Soñγur-inanč** [سنغر اينانج] (Zehireddin/Dorn 246); Maml. 14th c. **Soñqur / Suñqur** [سنقر / sonkor / Sunkur] (Tarǰ/Houtsma 78, Tarǰ/Toparlı 41); Kuman 1250 **Sunγur / Soñγur** [Сънъгуруви / Соногур / Сънъгур], a man of prince Yaroslav Vsevolodovich (Ipat. 536 /539/, PSRL II, 184); Kzk. 19th c. **Sunqar** [Сункаръ] (SOK 232);

Selj. 1137 **Sunqur** [Sunkur], lord of Zenjan (Ahbar 66, 77, 102); Maml. 13th c. **Sunqur** [Sunkur] (Tarj./Toparlı); Maml. 1325, 1328 **Sunqur** [شمس‌الدين سنقر السعدى / Sunqur as-Saʿdī], army inspector (naqīb al-jaiš), died in 1328, mentioned in an inscription on a glass lamp (Zetterst. 136, Iyās I, 164, Mayer 213); Maml. 14th c. **Sunqur** [Сункур] (Tuhfa 410); Crm. 13th. c. **Sunqur** [Сункуръ], from the Crimea (Smirnov, Krym. 34); Turk. 1488 **Suñγur** [سنقور / Sungur], chief (dizdar) of Sis-kale (Gökb., Ed. 212); Yürük 1543 **Suñγur** [صنغور / Sungur], from the Yürüks of Kocacık, Turkey (Gökb., Rum. 103, 208, 229, 237); Tat. 1543 **Suñγur** [Sungur], from Rumelia (Gökb., Rum. 237, 242); Oghuz/Trkm. 1163/64 **Suñqar** [Салах-ад-дин Сункар], emir, one of Sanjar's slaves (mamluks) (MIT I, 403); Bashk. 1828 **Suñur** [Сунгуровъ] (TOUAK XXIV, 185); Uyg. **Šinqur** [Şinkur] (EUTS); Uyg. **Šiñγur** [Şınggur] (EUTS); Bashk. 1757 **Šumqar** [Шумкар Янтуганов] (MIB IV/1, 150); Bashk. 1765 **Šunqar** [Апир Шункаров] (MIB IV/1, 313); Bashk. 1770 **Šunqar** [Шункар Назаров] (MIB IV/1, 349); Bashk. 1782 **Šunqar** [Шункар Абзаев] (MIB V, 130); Bashk. 1782 **Šunqar** [Шункар Уразаков] (MIB V, 243); Bashk. 1794 **Šunqar** [Чирюбай Шункаров] (MIB V, 338); Bashk. 1795 **Šunqar** [Шинкаръ (!) Уразаковъ] (IOAIÊK XXVIII, 589); Kzk. 19th c. **Šunqur** [Шункуръ] (AOAtb. 42); *TN:* Tat. **Suñγurovo** [Сунгурово], a village (Korsakov 249). ✧ 'Falcon, white falcon' cf. Uyg., Karakh. *soñqur / suñqur* 'id.' (DTS); Uyg. *soñqur* 'der Falke' (Radl. IV, 534), Oghuz/Trkm.? *šuñqar* 'id.' (DTS); Kuman *soñur* 'ein Vogel, der Falke (pielfalchus CC 130)' (Radl. IV, 534), Maml. *songor* [سنقر] 'eine Art Falke' (Tarj/Houtsma), Maml. *sunkur* 'akdoğan, aksungur' (Tarj./Toparlı), Chag. *suñqur* 'id.' (Radl. IV, 761), Chag. *suñγar* 'id.' (Radl. IV, 761), Kzk. *suñqar* 'der Falke' (Radl. IV, 760), TMEN I, No. 237, III, No. 1273: *soñqor* 'Gerfalke'; Uyg., East.T. *šuñqar* 'der Falke' (Radl. IV, 1098), Alt. *šoñqor* 'id.', (Radl. IV, 1026), Trk. (<Mo.<Trk.) *šoñqar* 'Gerfalke' (TMEN I, No. 237), NUyg.(Tar.) *šumqar* 'der weisse Falke' (Radl. IV, 1106). For a detailed explanation see Makrīzī I, 90-95. Toparlı interprets the Maml. *Sunqur* as *Aksungur* [=white falcon] (Tarj./Toparlı, p. 140). See also **AYT-SUÑQAR, AQ-SOÑQUR, ALP-ŠIÑQUR, BAY-SOÑQUR, BUYAN-SÏÑΓUR, QARA-SOÑQUR, QOY-SUÑUR, QUTLUΓ-SÏÑΓUR, MEÑLİG-ŠÏÑQUR, SARÏ-SOÑQUR, TOΓAN-SOÑQUR.**

SOÑQURČA see **SONQURČA**

SOÑQURJA see **SONQURČA**

SOÑSUY Uyg. **Soñsuy** [Songsuy] (EUTS). See also **QARA-SOÑSUY.**

SOPA-TAY see **SÏPA-TAY**

SOPAQ Kzk. 1846 **Sopaq** [Сопак], a biy (MKOP 157). ✧ 'Oval' cf. Kzk. *sopaq* 'ein langer Cylinder mit einem spitzen Ende; oval' (Radl. IV, 558).

SOPAN Kzk. 19th c. **Sopan** [Сопанъ] (SOK 14).

SOPČÏ Hak.(Kyz.) 19th-20th c. **Sopčï** [Сопчы] (Katanov, Otč. 13). ✧ 'A small species of diurnal owl' cf. Hak.(Sag.) *sopčï* 'der Kauz, die Eule' (Radl. IV, 559).

SOPOQ see **SAPŪQ**

SOPPOX Yak. **Soppoχ** [Соппох] (Pek.).

SOPPURUON see **SOPURUON**

SOPURUON Yak. **Soppuruon** [Соппуруон / Сопуруон] (Pek.); Yak. **Sopuruon** [Соппуруон / Сопуруон] (Pek.). ✧ Sofron (R.) (Pek.).

SOR-BAS Kzk. 19th c. **Sor-bas** [Сорбасъ] (SOV 138). ✧ 'Unlucky (misfortunate) head (man)' cf. Kzk. *sor* 'das Unglück, das böse Schicksal, das den Menschen verfolgt, der Unglücksstern' (Radl. IV, 541). ⇨ **BAŠ.**

SOR-TAY Kzk. 19th c. **Sor-tay** [Сортай] (SOK 132). ✧ 'Misfortunate foal (child)' cf. Kzk. *sor* 'das Unglück, das böse Schicksal, das den Menschen verfolgt, der Unglücksstern' (Radl. IV, 541). ⇨ **TAY** or suff. *-tay (1,2)?*

SORAΓAN Maml. 1264 **Soraγan** [Sârem-eddin-Soragan-Tatari], an emir (Makrīzī II, 14); Maml. (Kipch.) 1262 **Soraγan / Suraγan?** [صُراغان / Сураганъ] (Baybars/Tizeng. I, 78); Kzk. 19th c. **Sraγan** (<**Šŭraγan**) [Сраганъ] (AOP 26); Kzk. 19th c. **Sraγan** (<**Šŭraγan**) [Сраганъ] (AOAtb. 42); Kzk. **Suraγan** [Сураганъ] (AOK 30). ✧ 'Wished/asked (child)' cf. Kuman, Crm., Turk. *sor-/sora-* 'fragen' (Radl. IV, 542-543), Kzk. *sŭra-* 'спрашивать, спросить' (KzRS). See also **SURAMÏS, TİLEGEN, TİLEMİŠ.**

SORAX Hak. 19th-20th c. **Soraχ** [Сорах] (HRS 351); Hak.(Sag.) 19th-20th c. **Soraq** [Сорак] (Katanov, Otč. 7). ✧ 'Conic, lengthy' (Katanov), cf. Hak. *soraχ* 'конусообразный, остроконечный; продолговатый' (HRS).

SORAY Hak. 19th-20th c. **Soray** [Сорай] (HRS 351).

SORAQ see **SORAX**

SORAL Hak.(Koyb.) 19th c. **Soral** [Соралъ] (Katanov, Otč. II, 12-15). ✧ 'Pipestem' (Katanov).

SORAN I. Turk. 19th c. **Soran-oγlu**, a Zeybek (Kúnos 1891, 119).

SORAN II. Kzk. 19th c. **Soran** [Соранъ] (Grod., Pril. 145). ✧ 'A kind of grass grown in salty ground' cf. Kzk. *sorañ* 'трава (растущая на солончаковой почве)' (KzRS), Kzk. *sorañ* 'mit Salzflächen bedeckt' (Radl. IV, 543).

SORAÑ Hak. 19th-20th c. **Sorañ** [Соранъ] (HRS 351).

SORBÏY Hak.(Sag.) 19th-20th c. **Sorbïy** [Сорбый] (Katanov, Otč. 11).

SORBÏYAQ Hak.(Shor) 19th-20th c. **Sorbïyaq**

[Сорбыйак] (Katanov, Otč. 11).

SORBÏQ   Hak.(Sag.) 19th-20th c. **Sorbïq** [Сорбык] (Proben IX, 542).

SORČAN   Kuman 1068, 1101, 1107 **Sorčan / Sïrčan** [Сорчанъ (Сърчанъ, Сырьчанъ)], a Polovets prince, Šaru-qan's son, Otraq's brother, Bönäk's uncle (PSRL II, 155, 716, Bask., Im. polov. 73).

SORDŌQ   Hak.(Koyb.) 19th-20th c. **Sordōq** [Сордок], fem. (Katanov, Otč. 13).

SORQÏ   Oghuz/Trkm. 13th c. **Sorqï / Sorχï** [سرخی / Сорқы / Сорхы] (Abulg./Kon. 525, 545).

SORQO   Alt. **Sorqo** [Сорко] (ORS 210); Hak. 19th-20th c. **Sorqo** [Сорко] (HRS 351). ✧ 'Foresight' (OjrRS 210), cf. Alt. *sorqo* 'полка кремнёвого ружья, куда насыпается порох' (OjrRS).

SORMAZ   Oghuz? 1094 **Sormaz** [سرمز بلكابك], emir, chief of the police in Isfahan (Ibn al-Athīr/Tornb. X, 163, 198, 220).

SOROQ   Alt. **Soroq** [Сорок] (ORS 210); Hak. 19th-20th c. **Soroq** [Сорок] (HRS 351). ⇨ **SORQO.**

SOROQAY   Hak. 19th-20th c. **Soroqay** [Сорокай], fem. (HRS 355). ⇨ **SOROQ** + suff. -*ay*.

SOROLOY   Yak. **Soroloy (Nikolay)** [Соролоі Hjукулаі] (Pek.). ✧ 'Itchy, dirty' (Pek.).

SOROT   Hak. 19th-20th c. **Sorot** [Сорот] (HRS 351).

SORPA   Kzk. 19th c. **Sorpa-bay** [Сорпабай] (AOK 102). ✧ 'Broth' cf. Kzk. *sorpa* 'die Fleischbrühe, der Bouillon' (Radl. IV, 547).

SORTANAX   Hak. 19th-20th c. **Sortanaχ** [Сортанах] (HRS 351). ✧ 'Little pike' (Butanaev), cf. Hak.(Koyb., Sag.) *sortan* 'der Hecht' + suff. -*aχ*.

SOSAQ   Kzk. 19th c. **Sosaq-pay** [Сосакпай] (AOP 30). ✧ 'Wooden scoop' cf. Chag. *susaq* 'die hölzerne Schöpfkelle' (Radl. IV, 782).

SOSİN   Hak. 19th-20th c. **Sosin** [Сосин] (HRS 351).

SOSQA see **ČOČQO**

SOSRAN   Karch. **Sosran** [Сосрановъ], a family name (Sysoev 119); Karch. 20th c. **Sosran** [Sosrán] (Pröhle, Kar. 132).

SOTAY   Kzk. 19th c. **Sotay-bay** [Сотайбай] (SOV 70).

SOTAQAY   Kzk. 1820 **Sotaqay** [Сотакай], a chieftain (Sib. Vest. IX, 118). ✧ 'Mug, dumbhead' cf. Uzb. *sŭtaq* 'недотепа, растяпа, простофиля, простак' (UzbRS) + suff. -*ay*.

SOTAN   Kuman 1180 **Sotan** [Козл Сотановичъ], a Polovets prince (Ipat. 421 /435/, PSRL II, 623). ✧ 'Fire-eater, naughty' (Bask., Im. polov. 72).

SOTİN-GİLDİ   Bashk. 1737 **Sotin-gildi** [Макшигул Сотингилдин] (MIB I, 349). ⇨ **KELDİ.**

SOTQA   Hak. 19th-20th c. **Sotqa** [Сотка] (HRS 351).

SOTQAN   Hak. 19th-20th c. **Sotqan** [Сотканъ], fem. (HRS 355); Hak.(Koyb.) 19th-20th c. **Sotqāñ** [Соткан] (Proben IX, 553).

SOTQĀÑ see **SOTQAN**

SOTNİK   Chuv. 18th-19th c. **Sotnik** [Сотникъ] (Magn. 78). ✧ 'Captain' cf. R. *sotnik* 'id.'.

SOTPA-MĀRÄÑ   Tuv. 19th c. **Sotpa-märäñ** [Сотпа-märäñ], a clerk (Proben IX, 46).

SOTRAQ   Hak. 19th-20th c. **Sotraq** [Сотрак] (HRS 351).

SOTRAÑ   Hak. 19th-20th c. **Sotrañ** [Сотранъ] (HRS 351).

SOTTİ   Kzk. 19th c. **Sottï-bay** [Соттыбай] (SODž. 148).

SOVET   Trkm. **Sovet / Savet?** [Совет] (Sopieva 182). ✧ Soviet cf. R. *sovet.*

SOVETA   Hak. 19th-20th c. **Soveta / Saveta** [Совета], fem. (HRS 355). ✧ 'Soviet (woman)', female form of *Sovet.* ⇨ **SOVET** + fem. suff. -*a.*

SOWUQ   Kzk. 19th c. **Sowuq / Souq** [Соукъ] (SODž. 8); Kzk. 19th c. **Sowuq-bay** [Соукбай] (Grod., Pril. 140); Kzk. **Suwuq-pay** [Суукпай] (SODž. 154). ✧ 'Cold' cf. Turk. *souq* 'kalt, die Kälte' (Radl. IV, 516), Kzk. *suwïq* 'id.' (RKzS), Alt.(Tel.), Kzk., Tat. *sūq* 'kalt, die Kälte' (Radl. IV, 751). ⇨ **SAWUQ II.**

SOZAQ   Kzk. 19th c. **Sozaq-bay** [Созакбай] (AOP 102).

SŌN   Alt. **Sōn** [Соон], fem. (ORS 213). ✧ Sofiya (R.).

SŌRON   Kirg. **Sōron-bay** [Сооронбай] (Jud. 646). ✧ 'Be quiet, be consoled' cf. Kirg. *sōron-* 'успокаиваться, утешаться' (Jud.). See also **BASÏL.**

SŌRUNČU   Kirg. **Sōrunču** [Сорунчу], a hero (*čoro*) in Manas epic (Proben V, 116 /117/). ✧ 'Messenger, who gets *sōrun*, a share of booty (prey) for telling the good news first' cf. Kirg. *sōrunču* 'тот, кто имеет право на соорун (часть добычи); гость прибывший на поминки' (Jud.).

SÖBÄYTÄ see **ZİBAYDA**

SÖDÜÖRÄ   Yak. **Södüörä** [Сöдÿöпä], fem. (Pek.). ✧ Feodora (R.) (Pek.). See also **SÖDÖR.**

SÖGÜYÄN   Yak. **Sögüyän** [Тіmір Бытык Сöгÿjän] (Pek.).

SÖGÜN   Turk. 1485 **Sögün-oγlu** [سكون اوعلی / Sögün-oğlu] (Gökb., Ed. 332, 333, 364).

SÖYNÖ   Kirg. **Söynö-yan** [Сöінö-Jан], one of the forty followers of Aq-sayqal (Proben V, 394 /397/).

SÖYÜN see **SEVİN**

SÖYÜNDÜK see **SEVİNDİK**

SÖYÜNİČ see **SEVİNČ**

SÖKLİ see **ŠÜKLİ**

SÖKMÄZ   Khorezm.? **Sökmäz** [سكمان / سلمان / عزالـدیـن سكماز / سكمار] (Juwaynī II, 151-152). ✧ 'He who won't separate'? cf. Türk, Chag., Alt., Crm., Hak., Kzk., Turk. *sök-* 'theilen, trennen' (Radl. IV, 570) + suff. -*mez.*

SÖKMEN   Karakh. **Sökmen** [Sökmen] (MK/Atalay 851). ✧ 'He who breaks through the enemy's lines' (Erol II), cf. Türk, Chag., Alt., Crm., Hak., Kzk., Turk.

sök- 'theilen, trennen' (Radl. IV, 570) + suff. *-men.*

SÖLLÖBÜT   Yak. **Söllöbüt** [Сӧллӧбӱт] (Pek.).

SÖLMÜŠ see **SÜLEMÍŠ**

SÖLÖN   Yak. **Sölön-udaɣan** [Кӱӧх Сӧлӧн-удаҕан], a shamaness (Pek.). ✦ 'Kind, soft, weak' cf. Bur. *zölön* 'мягкий, нежный, Mo. *cögelen* 'мягкий, нежный, слабый, бабий, глупый' (Pek.).

SÖLTÖS   Yak. **Söltös** [Сӧлтӧс] (Pek.).

SÖMÖNČÄ   Hak. 19th-20th c. **Sömönčä** [Сӧмӧнчӓ] (Katanov, Otč. 11). ✦ Semyoncha (R.) (Katanov).

SÖNTÖ   Yak. **Söntö** [Сӧнтӧ] (Pek.).

SÖÑÖR   Yak. **Söñör** [Сӧҥӧр] (Pek.).

SÖÑÜ   Uyg. **Söñü** [Söngü] (EUTS); Uyg. **Söñü-ïnal** [Söngü ïnal] (Müller, Pfahl. 24); Kzk. 1823 **Süñi-bay** [سنكباى / Сынгибай] (MIK IV, 457); Maml. 14th c. **Süñü** [سنكو] (Sauvaget 48). ✦ 'Pike, lance' (Müller, Pfahl. 35), cf. Uyg., Karakh. *süñü* 'копье' (DTS), Kzk. *süñgï* 'пика, копьё' (KzRS).

SÖPTEY   Hak. 19th-20th c. **Söptey** [Сӧптей] (HRS 351). ✦ 'Rubbish-like, garbage-like'? cf. Hak. *söp* 'der Kehricht' (Radl. IV, 589) + suff. *-tey.*

SÖRÖNNÜÖXÄY   Yak. **Sörönnüöxäy** [Алып Сӧрӧннӱӧхӓи Уот Усутума], spirit of the fiery sea (Pek.).

SÖDÖR   Yak. **Södör** [Сӧдӧр] (Pek.); Yak. **Süödär** [Сӱӧдӓр] (Pek.). ✦ Fedor (R.) (Pek.). See also **SÖDÜÖRÄ.**

SÖMČÄ   Hak. 19th c. **Sömčä** [Сӧмчӓ] (Katanov, Otč. 12); Karg. **Sömčä** [Сӧмчӓ] (Katanov, Otč. 8). ✦ Syomcha (R. Сёмча) (Katanov).

SPAN see **OSMAN**

SPÍR   Bashk. 1738 **Spir** [Спир Азанов] (MIB III, 378).

SRAɣAN see **SORAɣAN**

SRAX   Hak. 19th-20th c. **Srax** (<Sïrax?) [Срах] (HRS 351). ✦ 'Arse, ass (anus)' (cf. Butanaev: *Sïrax*).

SRÍM see **SÍRÍM**

SROK   Hak. 19th-20th c. **Srok** [Срок] (HRS 351).

SRTÏZ   Kzk. 19th c. **Srtïz** [Сртызъ] (SOV 94).

STABAN see **ÍSTABAN**

STAM   Kzk. 19th c. **Stam-bek** [Стамбекъ] (SOV 14, 140); Kzk. 19th c. **Stam-bek** [Стамбекъ] (SODž. 82); Bashk. 1740 **Stam-ɣul?** [Стамгул Елдашев] (MIB I, 398).

STAPAN   Alt. **Stapan** [Стапан] (ORS 210). ✦ Stepan (R.) (OjrRS).

STAR   Kzk. 19th c. **Star-bek** [Старбекъ] (AOA 134).

STEN   Kuman 1125 **Sten** [Стень (Стѣнь)], a Polovets prince who was defeated by the Russian prince Yaropolk Vladimirovich (PSRL VII, 26).

STÍNA   Hak. 19th-20th c. **Stina** [Стина], fem. (HRS 355). ✦ Stina (R.), dim.-hypoc. form of Favstina or Hristina.

STÏQ   Kzk. 19th c. **Stïq-bay** [Стыкбай] (SODž. 34).

STRAMDUS   Alt. 19th c. **Stramdus** [Страмдус-

богатыръ], a folklore hero (Verb., In. 155, 156).

SU-BAŠÏ see **SÜ-BAŠÏ**

SUBAY   Bashk. 1788 **Subay** [Субай Смакаев] (MIB V, 223); Tat. 1684 **Subay / Sübay?** [Сюлкей Сюбаевъ] (Zolotn. 159); Bashk. 1709 **Subay / Sübay** [Сюбай] (MIB I, 264); Kkalp. 1740 **Subay-batïr** [Субай-Батыръ / Субай-батырь], from the Qoñɣrat tribe (Hanykov, Poezdka 19, MIKk. 208); Tat. 1779 **Sübiy** [Сюбий Сюлякаев] (MIB V, 94). ✦ 'Light cavalier; good looking man' (Sattarov), cf. Az., Turk. *subay* 'ein leichter Reiter; der Hagestolz' (Radl. IV, 789). See also **AQ-SUBAY.**

SUBAY-PÖDÄK   Uyg. 1305 **Subay-pödäk** [Subai Pögak] (Chwol., Syr.-nest. (NF) 16). ⇨ **SUBAY.**

SUBAQ   Yürük 1543 **Subaq** [صوباق / Subak] (Gökb., Rum. 229); Bashk. 1757 **Subaq** [Субак Утюнбетев] (MIB IV/1, 151); Bashk. 1759 **Subaq** [Девлекей Субаков] (MIB IV/2, 26); *TN:* Chuv. 18th c. **Bay-subak(ovo)** [Байсубаково], a village in the district of Yadrinsk (Korsakov 307).

SUBAQTÏ   Yürük 1543 **Subaqtï / Subaqdï** [صوباقدى / Subaktı / Subakdı] (Gökb., Rum. 104, 185, 190, 200, 224, 226).

SUBBŌTA   Hak.(Koyb.) 19th c. **Subbōta** [Суббота] (Katanov, Otč. II, 12-15); Karg. 19th-20th c. **Subōt** [Субот] (Katanov, Otč. 10). ✦ 'Saturday' cf. R. *subbota* (Katanov). See also **SEMBÍ.**

SUBHÂN-BERDÍ   Uzb. 20th c. **Subhân-berdi** [Субхонберди] (Begmatov 1984, 202). ⇨ **SUBXAN + BERDÍ.**

SUBXAN   Tat. 1783 **Sap-xan-qul** (<Subxan-ɣul?) [Сапханкуловъ] (Korsakov 97); Bashk. 1782 **Subxan-ɣul** [Субхангул Аитов] (MIB V, 133); Bashk. 1783 **Subxan-ɣul** [Субхангул Кильдикеев] (MIB V, 143). ✦ Subhan (Ar.), 'Praise, glory' (Ahmed), 'Fame, reputation', cf. Bashk. *Sobxan* (Kusimova), Tat. *Söbxan* (Sattarov).

SUBXAN-BERDÍ   Trkm. 1881 **Subxan-berdi** [Субханъ-Берды] (Grod., Vojna IV, Pril. 19). ⇨ **SUBXAN + BERDÍ.**

SUBORÏSQAY   Karg. **Suborïsqay** [Суборыскай] (Katanov: ZIRGOEtn. XVII, vyp. III, 187).

SUBŌT see **SUBBŌTA**

SUČLÏ   Oghuz/Trkm. 13th c. **Sučlï** [سوچلى / Сучлы] (Abulg./Kon. 525); Oghuz/Trkm. 13th c. **Suclï / Sücli?** [سوچلى / Soutchli / Сючли], an Oghuzid (Abulg./Rom. 18, Abulg./Sabl. 25, Abulg./Desm. 28). ✦ 'Guilty, sinner' cf. Turk. *sučlu* 'schuldig' (Radl. IV, 780).

SUJUD   Tat.(Lit.) 1610 **Sujud?** [Ахметъ Афендеевичъ Судзюдъ] (Lit. Tat. 293).

SUDAK   Chuv. 18th-19th c. **Sudak** [Судакъ] (Magn. 79). ✦ 'A kind of fish (bass?)' cf. R. *sudak* (Šipova), Chag. *sudaq* 'ein Fisch (der Zander?)' (Radl. IV, 778, Budagov I, 642).

SUDAKAY   Chuv. 18th-19th c. **Sudakay** [Судакай] (Magn. 79). ✧ 'Little fish (bass)'. ⇨ **SUDAQ** + suff. -*ay*.

SUDAQ   Kipch. / Maml. 1293 **Sudaq** [Sudak] (Baybars/Tizeng. I, 86, 109). ✧ I. Toponym; a town on the south coast of the Crimea; II. 'A kind of fish'? cf. Chag. *sudaq* 'ein Fisch (der Zander?)' (Radl. IV, 778).

SUDBAQ   Uyg. 12th c. - 14th c. **Sudbaq / Sudmaq** [Sud(t)baq] (Radl., USp. 169). ✧ 'Spitting (croaking)' cf. Uyg. *sudmaq* 'харканье' (DTS).

SUDUN   Maml. 1298 **Sudun** [سُدُن], a Kipchak chieftain (Baybars/Tizeng. I, 88, 111); Maml. 1399, 1455? **Sudun** [سودون طاز], first (chief) Master of the Horse (Ibn Taghrīb. VII, 579, Weil, Chalif. II, 73-75, 101); Maml. 1438/39, 1450, 1454 **Sudun** [المؤيدى قراقاش / سودون الاينالى] (Ibn Taghrīb. VII, 65, 117 etc., VIII, 70, 183, 224 etc.); Maml. 1439/40 **Sudun** [المؤيدى / سودون اتمكجى المحمدى] (Ibn Taghrīb. VII, 108, 167, 174 etc.); Maml. 1444 **Sudun** [سودون الطوغانى] (Ibn Taghrīb. VIII, 12); Maml. 15th c. **Sudun** [سودون العجمى / Sūdūn b. Ǧānibek al-ʿAjamī], a commander-in-chief, died in 1516 (Mayer 210-211, Iyās II, 380, III, 2, 25, 52, IV, 40); Maml. 15th c. **Sudun** [سودون المؤيدى / Sūdūn al-mu'ayyadī], an emir in Aleppo, the governor of Hama (Mayer 117, Nujūm VII, 107, 229, 767); Maml. 15th c. **Sudun** [سودون التصرووه / Sūdūn al Qasrawī], died in 1469 (Mayer 212, Iyās II, 103, III, 115); Maml. 15th c. **Sudun** [السيفى سودون اليشبكى], commander of Damascus, died in 1464, mentioned in an inscription on a copper plate (Mayer 212-213); Maml. 1450 **Sudun** [سودون], Master of the Horse (Ibn Taghrīb. VIII, 88, 238); Maml. 1453 **Sudun** [سودون يكرك] (Ibn Taghrīb. VII, 383); Maml. 1455 **Sudun** [سودون الجكمى] (Ibn Taghrīb. VIII, 361); Maml. 1461 **Sudun** [سودون], governor of Damascus (Ibn Taghrīb. VIII, 414); Maml. (Trkm.) 1453 **Sudun** [سودون القرمائى] (Ibn Taghrīb. VIII, 199); Maml. (Trkm.) 1462 **Sudun** [سودون قندورة التركمائى] (Ibn Taghrīb. VII, 705, 797, VIII, 482 stb.). ✧ '?' (<Mo.?).

SUFĪ-SANDAL-MELĪK see **SUNU-SANDAL**

SUҐA   Tat.(GH) **SuҐa / Sügä?** [Сюга], from the Horde (PSRL VII, 200, XXIII, 102).

SUҐAN-QARA   Kzk. 1831 **SuҐan-qara / SuҐon-qara?** [Сугонкара] (Mejer 47). ✧ 'Onion-black'? ⇨ **SOҐAN** + **QARA**. See also **SUҐAN-SARЇ?**

SUҐAN-SARЇ   Oghuz/Trkm. 14th c. - 15th c. **SuҐan-sarï / SoҐan-sarï / SoҐan-saru** [صُوغَنْ صَرُو / Soğan Sarı / Soğan Saru / Суган-Сары] (DQorq./Gökyay 78, DQorq./Rossi 162, DQorq./Ergin 201, DQorq. 74, 237). ✧ 'Onion-yellow'? ⇨ **SOҐAN** + **SARЇ**. See also **SUҐAN-QARA?**

SUҐANČЇ   Kzk. 18th c. - 19th c. **SuҐančï** [Суганчы] (Tynyšp. 68). ✧ 'Seller of onions'. ⇨ **SOҐAN** + suff. -*čï*. See also **MAÑĬRČĬ**.

SUҐAR   Oghuz **SuҐar / Saqur?** [ساقور / سوغار / Sakur], forefather of the Ottoman dynasty (Āšikp. 5, Nešrī 186, Seādeddīn I, 15, Wittek 94).

SUҐRALЇ   Kzk. 19th c. **SuҐralï** [Сугралы] (AOP 10).

SUҐUR   Türk 7th-9th c. **SoҐur** [SoҐur] (ETY III, 96); Kuman 1107 **SuҐr** (<SuҐur?) [Сугр], a Polovets prince, Šaru-qan's brother (Ipat. 187 /191/, PSRL I, 120, 282, VII, 21); Kzk. 1726 **SuҐur** [Sougour] (Levchine 154); Kzk. 1830 **SuҐur** [Сугуръ Сайбулаковъ] (Konšin, Mat. I-III, 62); Kzk. 19th c. **SuҐur** [Сугуровъ] (AOK 86); Kzk. 19th c. **SuҐur** [Сугуръ] (SODž. 82); Kzk. 19th c. **SuҐur-bay** [Сугурбай] (Pam. kn. Turg. 65); Kzk. 19th c. **SuҐur-bay** [Сугурбай] (AOA 2); Kzk. 19th c. **SuҐur-bay** [Сугурбай] (SODž. 32); Kzk. 19th c. **SuҐur-bek** [Сугурбекъ] (SODž. 66); *TN:* Kuman 1112 **SuҐrov** [Сугровъ], a town named after SuҐur (Lavr. 275 /191/). ✧ I. 'Marmot, mole' (Bask., Im. polov. 72), cf. Karakh. *soҐur* 'сурок (?)' (DTS), Kzk. *sūr* 'das Murmelthier' (Radl. IV, 764), Kirg. *sūr* 'сурок' (Jud.); II. 'Bucket' ? (Rásonyi, KÖA 126), cf. Chag. *suҐur* 'der Eimer, das Wassergefäss' (Radl. IV, 758). See also **ABDĬ-SUҐUR**.

SUYARЈЇ   Tat. 1543 **SuyarЈï** [Suyarcı] (Gökb., Rum. 233). ✧ 'Hunter for grouses'? cf. Tat. *suyar* 'der Birkhan' (Radl. IV, 761) + suff. -*čï*.

SUYARLĬ-AZNABA   Bulg. 1322 **Suyarli-aznaba / Suyarlï-asnaba-awlï / Süyerli-asnaba-awlï?** [سويار لِ اَصنَبَ اول / Sūyārli / suyarlı asnaba awli / Суйарли Азнаба] (Jusupov 17, Epigr. Bulg. 13, Tekin 13).

SUYTA   Kzk. 19th c. **Suyta** [Суйта] (Grod., Pril. 174).

SUYULLĀ   Yak. **Suyullā-buxatīr** [Ытык Суjулла-бухатыр] (Pek.).

SUYUR-ҐATMĬŠ   Khorezm.? **Suyur-Ґatmïš** [Джелал-ад-дин Суюргатмыш] (RaD II, 198); Chag. 15th c. **Suyur-Ґatmïš** [سيورغتمش], 29th khan of Chaghatay (after Khulāset ul-Akhbār) (Abulg./Desm. 158); Khorezm./Chag. 15th c. **Suyur-Ґatmïš** [Суюргатмышъ], Miranshah's (1405-1408) servant (?) (Barth., Ulugb. 129); Khorezm./Chag. 15th c. **Suyur-Ґatmïš** [Суюргатмышъ с. Шахруха], Shahruh's (1405-1447) servant (?) (Barth., Ulugb. 92); Khorezm./Chag. 15th c. **Suyur-Ґatmïš** [Суюргатмышъ-ханъ] (Barth., Ulugb. 17, 22); Khorezm./Chag. 1369-1388 **Suyur-Ґatmïš / Süyur-Ґutmuš?** [Suyurgátmish Khán / SüyurҐutmuş / Суюргатмыш], a Chaghatayid khan (1370-1388) (Tar. Rashidi 83, MIT I, 514, 516, 522, Toğan, UTT 63, 64). ⇨ **? + QATMĬŠ**.

SUQ   Türk 712-716 **Suq** [suq / Suq] (DTS, ETY I, 116). ✧ 'Eager, greedy; envious' cf. Türk *suq*, Uyg., Karakh.

soq 'жадный, завистливый' (DTS).

SUQAY   Kzk. 19th c. **Suqay** [Сукай] (SODž. 68). ✧ '(Little) Wooden plough' cf. Kzk. *soqa* 'coxa' (KzRS).

SUQNAQ   Khorezm.? 1219 **Suqnaq-tegin** [Сукнакъ-Тегинъ], lord of Almalïq (RaD/Ber. III, 43).

SUQRUN   Bashk. 1765 **Suqrun-bay** [Сукрунбай] (MIB I, 200).

SUQSU   Bashk. 1761 **Suqsu** [Суксу Абдул Рамгулов] (MIB IV/1, 220).

SUQUR see **SOQUR**

SUL see **SOL**

SULA   Yürük 1543 **Sula** [Sula] (Gökb., Rum. 184, 185); Tat. 1543 **Sula** [Sula] (Gökb., Rum. 235, 237). ✧ 'Aloe' cf. Turk. *sula* 'die Aloe' (Radl. IV, 772).

SULAY   Kirg. **Sulay** [Сулай], fem. (Jud. 222). See also **TOR-SULAY**.

SULAYMAN   Kirg. **Sulayman** [Сулайман] (Jud. 396); Crm. **Süläymän** [Сӱläiмäн] (Radl. IV, 831). ✧ Sulaiman (Ar.). See also **TAQ-SULEYMAN**.

SULAQ   Yürük 1543 **Sulaq** [سولاق / Sulâk] (Gökb., Rum. 192). ✧ 'Wet, abounding in water' cf. Turk. *sulaq* 'nass, wässerig; Überfluss an Wasser' (Radl. IV, 773).

SULBU   Kirg. **Sulbu-yan** [Сулбу-Jан], one of the forty followers of Aq-sayqal (Proben V, 394 /397/).

SULČU   Pecheneg 1050 **Sulču** [Σουλτζοῦς], a commander of the army (Byz. Turc. 289).

SULİ   Turk. 14th c. **Suli-bey / Süli-bey / Šaban-süli-bey** [Şaban Süli Bey / Dulkadıroğlu Suli Bey], from the Dulgadırlıs (Uzunçarş., Anad. 43, Sevim-Yücel II, 191); Karakh. **Süli** [Süli] (MK/Atalay 851). ⇨ **ŠABAN + SÜLİ?**

SULİX   Kzk. 19th c. **Suliχ-biy** [Сулихъ-бій] (Grod., Pril. 194). ✧ I. 'Quiet, peaceful' cf. Turk. *sulχ* (Ar.) 'der Friede' (Radl. IV, 777); II. 'Still, motionless' cf. Kzk. *süliq žat-* 'лежать совершенно неподвижно' (KzRS).

SULLİ   Tat.(Mish.) 1748 **Sulli** [Абдулла Суллѣевъ] (Nepljuev 438).

SULTA   Kzk. 19th c. **Sulta / Sultay?** [Джангузъ Султаевъ] (Grod., Pril. 198).

SULTAN   Tat. 1454, 1455 **Saltan** [Салтанъ], a prince (PSRL IV, 147 VI, 180); Bashk. **Saltan-γul** [Салтангул Урускулов] (MIB III, 29); Bashk. 1706 **Saltan-γul** [Салтангул Урускулов] (MIB III, 29); Crm. 1533 **Saltan-yar** [Салтаньяръ], a prince (PSRL VIII, 283); Tat.(Sib.) 1634 **Saltan-qul** [Салтанкул] (Miller, Ist. Sib. II, 419); Trkm. 20th c. **Soltan** [Soltan], fem. (Zaj. 1971, 342); Balk. 20th c. **Soltan** [Soltán] (Pröhle, Balk. 253); Bashk. 1715 **Soltan** [Солтан Терикеев] (MIB III, 123); Bashk. 1747 **Soltan** [Килей Солтанов] (MIB III, 450); Bashk. 1753, 1757, 1760 **Soltan** [Солтан Агишев] (MIB IV/1, 68, 140, 191); Bashk. 1754 **Soltan** [Солтан Сюянгулов] (MIB IV/1, 79); Kzk. 18th c. - 19th c. **Soltan** [Солтан] (Tynyšp. 74); Kzk. 18th c. - 19th c. **Soltan-bay** [Солтанбай] (Tynyšp. 73); Bashk. 1735 **Soltan-γul** [Солтангулъ Кулкаевъ], a tarχan (Vel.-Zern., Bašk. 21); Selj. 1072/73-1083/84 **Soltan-šah** [Solthân-châh ben Qâverd], 2nd Seljukid prince of Kerman (Qazw. 325); Trkm. 20th c. **Soltān** [Soltan], fem. (TrkmRS 584); Oghuz 12th c. **Sultan** [Sultan], the title of the Khorezmshah Tekiš (1172-1200) and Meñgü-berdi (1220-1231) (Ǐuwaynī I, 60-65, 78, 97, 110, 117 etc.); Tat.(GH) 1278 **Sultan** [Султанъ], a christened Tatar(?) of the Crimea (Smirnov, Krym. 34); Tat.(GH) 1321 **Sultan** [Σολτάν], a christened Tatar, died in 1321 (Byz. Turc. 284); Chag. 16th c. - 17th c. **Sultan** [Султан] (Ivanov 355); Turk. 14th c. **Sultan** [سلطان خاتون], Germiyan oğlu Süleyman's daughter, Yıldırım Bayezit's (1389-1402) wife (Qalāūn/Tizeng. I, 66, Āšikp. 52); Turk. 20th c. **Sultan** (Önder, Göle); Yürük 1543 **Sultan** (Gökb., Rum. 187); Bashk. 1756 **Sultan** [Султан Агишев] (MIB IV/1, 127); Bashk. 1761 **Sultan** [Султан Суангулов] (MIB IV/1, 204); Bashk. 1773 **Sultan** [Султан Кирбязгулов] (MIB IV/2, 412); Bashk. 1779 **Sultan** [Тайгильда Султанов] (MIB V, 101); Kzk. **Sultan** [Султань Тулябаевъ] (SKSO VIII, 221); Kzk. **Sultan** [Султанъ] (SKSO VIII, 204); Kzk. **Sultan** [Султанъ] (SKSO VIII, 202); Kkalp. 20th c. **Sultan** [Султан] (KkRS 776); Kkalp. 20th c. **Sultan** [Султан] (Bask., Kkalp. 84); Kirg. **Sultan** [Султан] (Jud. 290); Uzb. **Sultan** [Нурумбай Султановъ] (SKSO III, 190); Uzb. **Sultan-bay** [Султанбай] (SKSO III, 23); Chag. 16th c. **Sultan-begim** [Султан-бегим], fem. (Ivanov 355); Chag. / Uzb. 1507/08 **Sultan-begüm** [Султан бегум], Hüseyn-mirza's (Bay-qara's) wife (MIT II, 42); Kkalp. 1822 **Sultan-behadïr** [Султан бахадыр] (MIKk. 127); Kkalp. 1822 **Sultan-behadïr** [Султан бехадыр] (MIKk. 127); Tat.(Mish.) 19th c. **Sultan-bek** (IOAIÊK XIX, 142); Kzk. 1867 **Sultan-bek** [Султанбекъ Джангыровъ], sultan of the Seykim tribe (ZIRGOGeogr. I, 268); Tat. 1695/96 **Sultan-biy** [سولطن‌بى / Султан-бий] (Jusupov 74); Chag. 16th c. **Sultan-bike** [Султан-бикэ], fem. (Ivanov 355); Chag. 16th c. **Sultan-bikeč** [Султан-бикеч], fem. (Ivanov 355); Trkm. 1816 **Sultan-χan** [Султан-хан], from the Göklen tribe (MIT II, 389-391 etc.); Khorezm. **Sultan-χanïm / Sultan-sultanïm** [Khán Sultán Khánim / Khán Sultán Sultánim], daughter of Dughlatid „Sániz Mirzá", sister of „Abá Bákr" (Tar. Rashidi 88, 258); Chag. 16th c. **Sultan-χatun** [Султан-хатун], fem. (Ivanov 355); Khorezm. / Tat.(GH) 1282 **Sultan-χatun** [سلطان خاتون], Meñgü Temür (1266-1280) Kipchak Khan's wife (Makrīzī III, 165, 200, Qalāūn/Tizeng. I, 66); Kzk. 18th c. - 19th c. **Sultan-qul** [Султанкул]

(Tynyšp. 66, 71); *EN:* Yürük **Sultan-šeyχli** [Sultan Seyhli cemaati], a tribe (cemaat) (Refik, Anad. 76); *TN:* Kzk.? **Sultan** [Султан-бай], a well (Karta JAR XIX); Bashk. 13th c. **Sultan-bay** [Sultan-baj], a lake in the district of Belebey (Munkácsi 168-169); Bashk. 13th c. **Sultan-bayeva** [Sultan-bajeva], a mountain in the district of Belebey (Munkácsi 168-169). ✧ 'Sultan, ruler, sovereign (title); lord, master, chief (title of respect or affection, also secondary component of male names); woman originating from the family of the sovereign; daughter or wife of the sovereign (used as a secondary component of female names, e. g. in Chag.)' cf. Kuman *soltan* 'der Sultan', Turk. *sultan* (<Ar.) 'id.' (Radl. IV, 555, 777), in southern Yomud dial. of Trkm. is pronounced as *saltan* (Muhamedova 1957, 36) probably under Russian influence as is seen in Old Russian sources, see some more details in Néneth, HMK 290-91, Bask., Fam. 16, 246. See also **AQ-SULTAN, YAZ-SOLTAN.**

SULTAN-BAYAZİD   Chag. 16th c. **Sultan-bayazid** [Султан Баязид], a hodja (Ivanov 175, 177, 179, 184). ⇨ **SULTAN + BAYAZİT.**

SULTAN-BOL   Uzb. 20th c. **Sultân-bol** [Султонбӳл] (Begmatov 1984, 201). ✧ 'Be a sultan!'. ⇨ **SULTAN + BOL.**

SULTAN-GELDİ   Kzk. **Soltan-geldi** (SOV 112); Bashk. 1772 **Soltan-gildi** [Солтангильди] (MIB IV/1, 364); Kzk. 19th c. **Sultan-geldi** [Сылтан гельды] (AOK 6). ✧ 'Sultan has come'. ⇨ **SULTAN + KELDİ.**

SULTAN-MAXMUD   Chag. 16th c. - 17th c. **Sultan-maχmud** [Султан-Махмуд], a mulla (Ivanov 65). ⇨ **SULTAN + MAXMUD.**

SULTAN-MUXAMMED   Chag. 16th c. - 17th c. **Sultan-muχammed** [Султан Мухаммед] (Ivanov 355). ⇨ **SULTAN + MUXAMMED.**

SULTANAY   Bashk. 1731 **Soltonay** [Илчи Солтонаев] (MIB III, 292); Bashk. 1700 **Sultanay** [Карасай Султанаев] (MIB III, 415). ⇨ **SULTAN + suff. -*ay*.**

SULTANAQ   Tat. 1764 **Sultanaq** [Султанак Азнетев] (MIB IV/1, 279). ⇨ **SULTAN + suff. -*aq*.**

SULTANJUQ   Khorezm. **Sultanjuq** [سلطان جق / Sultan-Djouk], a man of Khorezmian origin among the Mongol scouts (RaD/Quatrem. 268-69). ⇨ **SULTAN + dim. suff. -*juq*.**

SULTANİM   Kzk. 18th c. - 19th c. **Sultanim** [Султаным] (Tynyšp. 67). ✧ 'My Sultan' (blandishing). ⇨ **SULTAN + suff. -*im*.**

SULTANLİ   Oghuz/Trkm. 13th c. **Sultanlï** [سلطانلی / Sultânli], an Oghuzid (Abulg./Desm. 28). ⇨ **SULTAN + suff. -*lï*.**

SULTÂN-BOL see **SULTAN-BOL**

SULTİ   Bashk. 1752 **Sultï** [Султы (Султи) Усеинов]

(MIB IV/1, 58).

SULTİY   Bashk. 1784 **Sultïy** [Султый Юмагулов] (MIB V, 151). ⇨ **SULTİ + suff. -*y*.**

SULTİQAY   Bashk. 1756 **Sultïqay** [Султыкай Сапаров] (MIB IV/1, 109). ⇨ **SULTİ + suff. -*qay*.**

SULTUQ   Bashk. 1715 **Sultuq** [Султуков] (MIB III, 124); Bashk. 1724 **Sultuq** [Мряк-мулла Султуков] (MIB III, 222); Bashk. 1724 **Sultuq** [Бухар-мулла Султуков] (MIB III, 222); Bashk. 1761, 1777 **Sultuq** [Миней Султуков] (MIB IV/1, 211, V, 60); Bashk. 1777 **Sultuq** [Миней Султуков] (MIB V, 60).

SULUQ   Kzk. 19th c. **Suluq-pay** [Сулукпай] (AOAtb. 50). ✧ I. 'Towel' cf. Kzk. *sülüq* 'das Handtuch' (Radl. IV, 776); II. 'Curb-bit, snaffle, bridle' cf. Alt., Kzk. *suluq* 'das Pferdegebiss, die Trense' (Radl. IV, 776).

SULUM   Bashk. 1740 **Sulum** [Исергап Сулумов] (MIB I, 400).

SULUMĀT   Yak. **Sulumāt** [Сулумат] (Pek.). ✧ 'Lonesome, nacked; single, bachelor' cf. Yak. *sulumaχ* 'одиночный, голый; одинокий, холостой, неженатый' (Pek.).

SULUR   Yak. **Sulur-bātïr** [Сулур-батыр] (Pek.).

SULUW-ŠAŠ   Kkalp. 20th c. **Suluw-šaš** [Сулуӱшаш], fem. (KkRS 778). ✧ 'Beautiful hair' cf. Shor, Kzk. *šaš* 'die Haare' (Radl. IV, 973). ⇨ **SİLİG.**

SUM   Kzk. 19th c. **Sum-bay** [Сумбай] (SODž. 104); *TN:* Kzk. **Sum-bay** [Сумбай], a well west of Lake Aral (Karta JAR X.). ✧ 'Tricky, sly, bad, wicked' cf. Kzk. *sum* 'schlau, ränkesüchtig, schlecht, böse' (Radl. IV, 792).

SUMAY   Kzk. 19th c. **Sumay-bay** [Сумайбай] (SODž. 112). ✧ I. 'Little Tricky/Sly'; II. 'Vegetable oil'? cf. Kzk. dial. *sumay* 'id.' (QTDS). ⇨ **SUM?** + dim. suff. -*ay*.

SUMAY-TOSPAÑAY   Tuv. 19th c. **Sumay-tospañay** [Сумаi-Тоспаӊаi] (Proben IX, 187). ⇨ **SUMAY.**

SUMAQ   Bashk. 1761 **Sumaq** [Ярыш Сумаков] (MIB IV/1, 221); Kuman 1493, 1690 **Sumaq / Somaq** [Zomokzallasa], personal name preserved in the name of a settlement of Lesser Kumania, Hungary (Gyárfás III, 335, 709); Kzk. 19th c. **Sumaq-pay** [Сумокпай] (SOV 48). ✧ 'Waterskin, leather water bag; leather milk bag' cf. Turk. *sumak* 'kırba, meşinden yapılan su kabı' (Tar. Sözl.), cf. also Rásonyi, Kisk. 352, KÖA 126, Anthr. 145.

SUMBUR   Alt. 19th c. **Sumbur-ul** [Сумбуръ-Улъ] (Potanin IV, 555).

SUNA   Uzb. 19th c. **Suna-ayïm** [Souna-aïm], Yarqïn-ayïm's sister from Khokand (Nalivkin-Dozon 178); Kzk. 1742 **Suna-batïr** [Суна батыр] (MIB I, 489). ✧ 'Hornet, horse-fly, gadfly'? cf. Kzk. *sona* 'at sineği' (KzTS). See also **SUNAQ.**

SUNAQ   Kzk. **Sunaq-ata** [سوناق اطا] (Divaev, Baksy 316, 332); Kzk. 19th c. **Sunaq-pay** [Сунакпай] (SOK

114). ✧ 'Horsefly, gadfly' cf. Chag. *sunaq* 'die Bremse' (Radl. IV, 763). See also **SUNA**.

SUNARČA   Bashk. 1787 **Sunarča** [Сунарча Елумбетев] (MIB V, 214). ✧ 'Hunter' cf. Tat. *sunarči* 'охотник, ловец; зверолов' (TatRS).

SUNBAR   Trkm. 1816 **Sunbar-serdar** [Сунбар-сердар], from the Yomut tribe (MIT II, 396-398, 410, 411).

SUNJAQ   Trkm.? 1536/37 **Sunjaq** [Сунджак Мухаммед-султан], Mukhammed Sultan's byname (MIT II, 59).

SUNJUQ   Uzb.? **Sunjuq** [Sundšuk], a descendant of the Özbek dynasty (Hammer, GOR I, 820).

SUNDAŇ   Trkm. 1521 **Sundaň-bek** [Сунданг-бек], from the Afšar tribe (MIT II, 57).

SUNDUГAŠ   Hak. 19th c. **Sunduγaš** [Сундуҕаш] (Katanov, Otč. 12). ✧ 'Small chest, case' (Katanov), cf. Kar. *sunduq* (<R.<Trk.) 'der Kasten' (Radl. IV, 763) + dim. suff. *-aš(1)*.

SUNDUK   Chuv. 18th-19th c. **Sunduk** [Сундукъ] (Magn. 79). ✧ 'Chest, case' cf. R.(<Trk.) *sunduk* 'id.'.

SUNDUQPAN   Tuv. 19th c. **Sunduqpan** [Сундукпан] (Proben IX, 45).

SUNDUN   Oghuz/Trkm. 13th c. **Sundun-bay** [سوندون باى] / Сундун-бай] (Abulg./Kon. 1440).

SUNİ-SANDAL-MELİK see **SUNU-SANDAL**

SUNÏŠ   Balk. **Sunïš** [Суншевъ], a Balkar tau-biy-family (Karaulov 52).

SUNU   Hak.(Koyb.) 19th-20th c. **Sunu** [Суну] (Radl.I, 657).

SUNU-SANDAL   Oghuz/Trkm. 14th c. - 15th c. **Sunu-sandal / Suni-sandal-melik / Sofi-sandal-melik / Sufi-sandal-melik?** [Suni Sandal Melik / Sūfī Sandal Melik / Sofi Sandal Melik / Суну-Сандал] (DQorq./Gökyay 23, DQorq./Rossi 145, DQorq./Ergin 113, DQorq. 30, 237).

SUŇГAT   Kzk. 19th c. **Suňγat** [Сунгатъ] (AOK 94).

SUŇГUR see **SOŇQUR**

SUŇQAR see **SOŇQUR**

SUŇQUR see **SOŇQUR**

SUOJAN   Yak. **Suojan-ärkin** [Суоҵан äркін] (Pek.).

SUOYUN   Yak. **Suoyun-ärkin** [Суојун äркін] (Pek.).

SUOPUYA   Yak. **Suopuya** [Суопуја], fem. (Pek.). ✧ Sofya (R.) (Pek.).

SUORDĀYÏ   Yak. **Suordāyï** [Суордајы] (Pek.). ✧ Matches to the R. PN *Voronec* (Pek.), cf. Yak. *suor* 'ворон, ворона (Corvus corax; Corvus Sibiricus)' + suff. *-dāyï* (Pek.).

SUORDUYA   Yak. **Suorduya-buχātïr** [Тімір Суордуја бухатыр] (Pek.). ✧ 'Raven-?' cf. Yak. *suor* 'ворон, ворона (Corvus corax; Corvus Sibiricus)' + suff. *duy* + suff. *-a* (Pek.).

SUPA   Kirg. **Supa-χan** [Супахан] (Jud. 511). ✧ I. 'Dawn, daybreak' cf. Kirg. *supa* 'рассветъ утренняя заря' (Jud.); II. 'Respectable, influential man' cf. Kirg. (Pamir dial.) *supa* 'человек, пользующийся авторитетом и имеющий власть в своей среде' (Jud.).

SUPA-TAY see **SÏPA-TAY**

SUPRA   Tat.(Tara) **Supra** [Супра], Suryanday's son (Proben IV.129 /166/, 202 /248/). ✧ 'Pastry, pasteboard; table-cloth' cf. Kzk. *supura* 'подстилка для теста (Katarinskij), Uyg. *supra* 'подстилка для разделывания теста' (URS). See also **SÏPRA-JÏRAU**.

SUPTUQU   Yak. **Suptuqu** [Суптуку] (Pek.). ✧ 'Small, lessened (man)' cf. Yak. *suptuy-* 'снизу стесываться, сниматься, умаляться, уже делаться' + suff. *-qu* (Pek.).

SUR   Kzk. **Sur-bay** [Сурбай] (SOK 236); Kzk. 1819 **Sur-bay** [Сурбай] (MIK IV. 323). ✧ I. 'Unlucky (misfortunate) (man)' cf. Kzk. *sor* 'das Unglück, das böse Schicksal, das den Menschen verfolgt, der Unglücksstern' (Radl. IV, 541); II. 'Marmot, mole'? cf. Kzk. *sūr* 'das Murmelthier' (Radl. IV, 764); III. 'Blaze, spark' cf. Alt.(Tel.) *sur* 'das Flimmern, der Funke' (Radl. IV, 764); IV. 'Greyish blue' cf. Alt.(Tel.) *sur* 'blaugrau' (Radl. IV, 764). ⇨ **SUГUR?**

SURA I.   Hak. 19th-20th c. **Sura** [Сура] (HRS 351).

SURA II.   Kzk. **Sura** [Сура] (SODž. 56). ✧ 'Ask, wish(!)' cf. Kzk. *sŭra-* 'спрашивать, спросить' (KzRS). See also **SORAГAN**.

SURAJÏQ   Oghuz/Trkm. 13th c. **Surajïq** [سوراجيق / Сураджик] (Abulg./Kon. 525). ✧ 'Little *Sura*'? cf. Tat. names *Sorančiq / Soračiq* '(Little child) wished from God' (Sattarov). ⇨ **SURA I./II.?** + suff. *-jïq*.

SURAГAN see **SORAГAN**

SURAY see **ČURAY**

SURAMÏS   Kzk. **Suramïs** [Сурамысъ] (AOP 54). ✧ 'The wished/asked (child)' cf. Kuman, Crm., Turk. *sor-/sora-* 'fragen' (Radl. IV, 542-543), Kzk. *sŭra-* 'спрашивать, спросить' (KzRS) + suff. *-mïs*. See also **SORAГAN, TİLEGEN, TİLEMİŠ**.

SURAN   Kzk. **Suran-bay** [Суранбай] (Grod., Pril. 91); Turk. 19th c. **Suran-oγlu**, a Zeybek (Kúnos 1891, 118). ✧ '(Child) wished/asked from God' cf. Tat. PN *Soran* 'id.' (Sattarov). See also **SORAГAN**.

SURANČÏ   Kzk. **Suranči** [Суранчи] (SOK 34); Kzk. **Suranči** [Суранчи] (SOK 276); Kirg. 1822 **Suranči** [Суранчи], *manap* (head) of Čon-baγïš (Valihanov, Soč. 128). ✧ '(Child) wished/asked for' cf. Tat. PNS *Sorančiq / Soračiq* '(Little child) wished from God' (Sattarov). ⇨ **SURAN** + suff. *-či*.

SURAP-ALDÏ   Kzk. 19th c. **Surab-aldï** [Сураболды] (SODž. 112); Kirg. 20th c. **Suraw-aldï** [Суравалды] (Kalilov 93). ✧ 'Wished-taken (child)' cf. Kzk., Kirg. *sura-* 'fragen, bitten' (Radl. IV, 765). ⇨ **ALDÏ**. See also **TİLEP-ALDÏ**.

SURAS   Alt. **Suraz-bay** [Суразбай] (ORS 210). ✧ 'Bastard' cf. Alt. *suras* 'незаконнорождённый' (OjRS).

SURASQA   Alt. **Surasqa** [Сураска], fem. (ORS 213). ✧ 'Little bastard'. ⇨ **SURAS** + suff. *-qa*.

SURAT   Trkm. 20th c. **Surat** [Surat], fem. (Zaj. 1971, 336); Trkm. 20th c. **Sŭrat** [Сурат], fem. (TrkmRS 594). ✧ 'Picture, figur (=beautiful girl)' cf. Trkm. *sŭrat* 'рисунок, картина; портрет, фотография' (TrkmRS) (<Ar.).

SURAW   Kzk. **Suraw-bay** [Суравбай] (AOP 22); Kzk. **Suraw-ĵan** [Сурауджанъ] (SOV 104). ✧ 'Wish; wished child'? cf. Kzk. *surav* 'sormak; istek, dilek' (KzTS).

SURAW-ALDÏ see **SURAP-ALDÏ**

SURAZ-BAY see **SURAS**

SURĴAX   Hak. 19th-20th c. **Surĵax** [Сурчах], fem. (HRS 355). ✧ '(Small) Bead, choker, pendant' cf. Hak. *sur* 'бусы' (HRS) + dim. suff. *-ĵax*.

SURΓA see **SÏRΓA**

SURΓAN I.   Kzk. **Surɣan** [Сурганъ] (AOP 22). ✧ '(The child) sucked'? cf. Uyg., Chag., Alt., Crm., Kirg., Kzk. etc. *sor-* 'saugen, aussaugen, einschlürfen' (Radl. IV, 542) + suff. *-ɣan*.

SURΓANDAY   Tat.(Tara) **Surɣanday** [Сурѣандаі] (Proben IV 129 /166/, 202 /248/).

SURÏ   Uyg. **Surï** [Surı] (EUTS).

SURÏ-BAR   Kuman 1103 **Surï-bar / Süre-ber?** [Сурьбарь / Сурьдбаръ], a Polovets prince (Lavr. 187 /269/, Ipat. 184 /189/, PSRL I, 119, II, 286, VII, 20). ✧ I. 'Having good outlook' (Bask., Im. polov. 72); II. [Süre-ber?] 'Chase it!; follow it (e. g. the enemy)' (Bask., Im. polov. 72). ⇨ **SURÏ + BAR?**

SURÏY   Uyg. **Surïy** [Surıy] (EUTS).

SURÏY-AŠÏRÏ   Uyg. **Surïy-ašïrï** [Surıy Aşırı] (Radl., USp. 26-27, DTS, EUTS).

SURYA   Uyg. 12th c. - 14th c. **Surya** [surja / Surya] (DTS, EUTS).

SURLAY   Alt. **Surlay** [Сурлай], fem. (ORS 213). ✧ 'Shines, sparkles, glitters' cf. Alt.(Tel.) *surla-* 'glänzen, flimmern' (Radl. IV, 771).

SURMAQAN   Kirg. **Surmaqan** [Сурмакан], fem. (Jud. 937). ⇨ **SÏRMA?** + suff. *-qan(1)*.

SURMAN   Kzk. **Surman** [Сурманъ] (SOK 22); Kzk. **Surman** [Сурманъ] (SODž. 136); Kzk. **Surman** [Сурманъ] (SOV 14). ✧ I. 'Dark blue, grey' cf. Kirg. *sur* '(о масти лошади) голубой; тёмно-голубой, серый' (Jud.); II. 'Unlucky, misfortunate'. ⇨ **SUR?** + suff. *-man*. See also **ALAMAN, QARAMAN**.

SURMAŠ   Kirg. **Surmaš** [Сурмаш], fem. (Jud. 633). ⇨ **SÏRMA?** + suff. *-š*.

SURS   Hak. 19th-20th c. **Surs** [Сурс] (HRS 351).

SURUQ   Alt. **Suruq** [Сурук], fem. (ORS 213). ✧ 'Demand, request' (OjrRS 213). See also **TOÑ-SURUQ**.

SURUM   Tat.(Tara) **Surum-qan** [Сурумкан], Čiñɣïs' father (Proben IV 132 /170/).

SURUN   Kzk. **Surun-bay** [Сурунбай] (SODž. 108).

SUSAÑ   Uyg. **Susañ** [Susang] (Radl., USp. 90); Uyg. **Susañ** [Susang] (EUTS).

SUSAR   Kuman **Susar** [Czuczarkut, Czuczar sziget], preserved in placenames (near Kunszentmiklós and Tatárszentgyörgy) in Lesser Kumania, Hungary (Rásonyi, NTK 101 (after Pesty)); Bashk. 1744 **Susar** [Умюдбай Сусаров] (MIB III, 426); Tat.(Sib.) 1622 **Susar(ko)** [Сусарко (басагар)] (Miller, Ist. Sib. II, 289). ✧ 'Marten, weasel' cf. Chag., Tat., Kzk. *susar* 'der Marder' (Radl. IV, 782), cf. also Rásonyi, NTK 101, KÖA 126, Anthr. 139.

SUSÏN see **SUSUN**

SUSQ   Kzk. **Susq-pay** (<Susïq-pay?) [Сускпай] (AOP 46).

SUSQUČAQ   Alt. 19th-20th c. **Susqučaq** [Сускучак], fem. (OjrRS 213). ✧ 'Small ladle, skimmer, scoop' (OjrRS), cf. Alt. *susqŭ* 'die Schöpfkelle' (Radl. IV, 784) + dim. suff. *-čaq*.

SUSPAN   Tat.? 1744 **Suspan** [Суспанов] (Alatyr. 171).

SUSTAY   Hak. 19th c. **Sustay** [Сустай] (Katanov, Otč. 12). ✧ 'Ray/beam of orbs having vitality/life' (Butanaev), cf. Hak. *sus* 'der Sonnenstrahl' (Radl. IV, 780) + suff. *-tay(1,2)*.

SUSUN   Kzk. **Susïn** [Сусынъ] (AOK 14); Maml. 1332 **Susun** [سيفالـدين صوصون], an emir (Dawād.); Maml. 14th c. **Susun** [صوصون] (Sauvaget 49). ✧ 'Drink, beverage; thirstiness' cf. Kuman *susun* 'Getränk' (CC), Kzk. *susun* 'der Durst, die Buttermilch (Chag.)' (Radl. IV, 783), Kzk. *susïn* 'напиток' (KzRS), Kzk. *susun* 'жажда' (Katarinskij).

SUTA   Kzk. **Suta-bay** [Сутабай] (SOK 220).

SUTAY   Bashk. 1776-1777 **Sutay** [Сутай Касымбаев] (MIB V, 542-544); Khorezm.? 1289, 1298, 1299, 1320 **Sutay / Suday** [سوتای احتاجی / سوتای / سنتای / سودای], Ghazan's (1295-1304) emir who arranged Baidu's execution, a commander of a tümän in Čoban's campaign against Sülemiš in Asia Minor (RaD/Jahn 19, 28, 35, 93 etc., Dawād. 9, 230, Aqsarāyï 245, 247, 253-255, Aqsar/Iş. 101, 103-104, 113, 115, Qazw. 594); Kuman 1202, 1223 **Sutay / Süttöy?** [Котян / Котяк Сутоевичъ] (PSRL I, 216, II, 156, III, 39-40, VII, 129-30 etc., Ipat. 481 /488/, 498 /504/, Lavr. 478 etc.).

SUTAMTAN   Kzk. **Sutamtan / Süt-ämgän?** [Тирликбай Сутамтановъ] (Grod., Pril. 142). ✧ ? ⇨ **SÜT-EMGEN?**

SUTAŠ   Oghuz 12th c. **Sutaš** [صوتاش], an emir from Khorezm (Rāwandī 366).

SUTMAQ   Uyg. **Sutmaq** [Sutmak] (EUTS).

SUTPAQ   Uyg. **Sutpaq** [Sutpak] (EUTS).

SUVÄRČA   Chuv. 19th c. **Svärča** (<Suvärča?)

[Swärtscha], fem. (Kronheim 96).

SUW   Tat.(Lit.) 1591 **Suw?** [Хава Кудайковна Сувовичь], fem. (Lit. Tat. 82).

SUWAQ   Uzb. **Suwaq** [Сувакъ] (SKSO III, 166).

SUWAN   Kzk. **Suwam-bay** [Суамбай] (SODž. 58); Kzk. **Suwan** [Суанъ] (SOK 50, 214); Kzk. **Suwan** [Суанъ] (SOV 16, 148); Kzk. **Suwan-bay** [Суанбай] (SODž. 82, 104); Kzk. **Suwan-bay** [Суанбай] (SOK 98); Kzk. **Suwan-bek** [Суанбекъ] (SOV 34); Uzb. **Suwan-qul** [Суанкулъ] (SKSO III 158). ✦ 'Liar, swindler' cf. Kzk. *suvan* 'Yalancı' (KzTS). See also **JAN-SUWAN**.

SUWANDÏQ   Uzb. **Suwandïq** [Суандыкъ] (SKSO III, 156).

SUWAR   Oghuz/Trkm. 13th c. **Suwar** [سوار / Сувар], Arslan Khan's inaq (Abulg./Kon. 965-1000); Trkm. 1855 **Suwar-χan** [Хан Сувар-хан Хезаре], from the Salïr tribe (MIT II, 266, 312); Oghuz? 906 **Suwar-tegin** [وصيف بن صواريـتـكـين] (Ibn al-Athīr/Tornb.VII. 376, 380, 382, VIII. 9, 10, 13). ✦ 'Cavalier, knight' cf. P. *suwār / sewār* 'Ritter' (Justi 46).

SUWARJÏQ   Oghuz/Trkm. 13th c. **Suwarjïq / Suwarjik** [سوارجيق / Суварджик], Ögürjik-alp's brother (Abulg./Kon. 1235, 1275). ✦ 'Little cavalier/knight'. ⇨ **SUWAR** + dim. suff. *-jïq*.

SUWAT   Kzk. **Suwat-pay** [Суатпай] (SOK 168). ✦ I. 'Place for drinking/watering (animals)' cf. Kzk. *suvat* 'Su alacak, hayvana su içirilecek yer' (KzTS); II. 'Edge' cf. Kzk. *suwat* 'лезвие' (KzRS).

SUWUQ see **SOWUQ**

SUWUN   Kzk. **Suwun-bay** [Суунбай] (SOK 20). ✦ 'Get cool, be quiet' cf. Kzk. *suwïn- / suwun-* 'охладеть, остывать' (KzRS).

SUZΓUN   Tat.(Sib.) 1580 **Suzγa / Suzγun** [Сузга / Сузгунъ], one of Küčüm's wives whose name has been preserved in placenames (Sib. Let. (Rem.) 320). ✦ 'Pheasant' cf. Tat. fem. PN *Suzγïn* (Sattarov).

SÜRAΓAN see **SORAΓAN**

SÜCU see **ALTÏN-SÜCU**

SŪQ-QARA   Tuv. 19th c. **Sūq-qara** [Сук-кара], fem. (Proben IX, 62). ✦ I. 'Cold-black'?; II. 'Straight/smooth-black'? cf. Tuv. *sūq* 'жидкий; плавный; прямой' (TuvRS). ⇨ **SOWUQ + QARA.**

SŪRQA   Hak.(Sag.) 19th-20th c. **Sūrqa** [Сурка] (Katanov, Otč. 7). ✦ 'Shurka', hypoc. of R. *Aleksandr* (Katanov).

SŪS   Bulg. **Sūs** (<Suwas?) / **Süs?** [سوس / Сус], fem. (Jusupov 38, Epigr. Bulg. 108, 109, Tekin 33 /106/).

SÜ   Selj. 11th c. **Sü-tegin** [Emir Sutekin kaid], Alp-arslan (1063-1072) Sultan's emir (Ahbar 21, 30, 40, 43); Selj. 1125, 1139 **Sü-tegin** [سوتكين الـكـرجى / Soutékîn el-Kordjy] (Kamāladdīn II, 231, 271, Kamāladdīn: RHCHor 651, 680). ✦ 'Army' cf. Türk, Uyg. *sü* 'das Heer' (Radl. IV, 794). See also **ČERİ I.**,

ΓOŠUN, ZURUM.

SÜ-BAŠÏ   Oghuz? 1000 **Sü-baši** [ابوطاهـر سباشي السعيد] (Hil. Sābī 377, 403); Oghuz 1038 **Sü-baši** [سباشى / Сюбаши], the Ghaznavid Sultan Masʿud's (1130-1040) doorman (χajib) and commander of the army (Ibn al-Athīr/Tornb. IX 311, 314, 327-29, MIT I, 233, 242, 244, 247, 248 etc.); Maml. 14th c. **Sü-baši** [سوبـاشى / Sübaşı] (Tarj/Houtsma 78, Tarj/Toparlı 43); Karakh. 1006 **Sü-baši-tegin** [سباشى تـكـيـن / Сюбаши-тегин], lord of Jish? (جيش), İlek-χan's commander of the army (Ibn al-Athīr/Tornb. IX, 133-134, MIT I, 226, 227, 229, 360, 361); *TN:* Kzk. **Su-basï** [Субасы] (Kojčubaev 197). ✦ 'Commander of army' cf. Karakh. *sü-baši* 'военачальник' (DTS), Chag. *su-baši* 'der Polizeimeister' (Radl. IV, 789), Turk. *su-baši* 'der Armeekommandeur' (Radl. IV, 789). ⇨ **SÜ + BAŠÏ.**

SÜBEYTE see **ZİBAYDA**

SÜBELÄK   Bashk. 1730 **Sübeläk** [Сюбеляк Абдуллин] (MIB III, 273).

SÜBİY see **SUBAY**

SÜBÜK see **SEBÜK**

SÜČELEY   Tat.? **Süčeley-saltan / Süč-eli-saltan?** [Сючелей-салтан Ибаков] (MIB I 492).

SÜČİGÄN   Kuman 13th c. **Süčigän** [Συτζιγάν], a great (high) Kuman (Byz. Turc. 294).

SÜČÜR   Türk 750 **Süčür** [Süçür] (Thomsen, Stein 186, 188, DTS, ETY II, 65).

SÜDÄY   Hak.(Sag.) 19th-20th c. **Südäy-mergän** [Сӱдӓи Мергӓн] (Radl.III, 1260).

SÜDENEY   Tat.(Sib.) 1684 **Südeney** [Сюденейко] (DAI XI, 160).

SÜDEÑ   Alt. **Südeñ** [Сӱден], fem. (ORS 213).

SÜDÜÖ   Yak. **Südüö-buχatïr** [Сӱдӱö-бухатыр (ботур)], a hero in a epic song (Pek.). ✦ 'Dignified, serious, sober-minded (man)' cf. Yak. *südü* 'важный (человек, скотина, вещ), степенный' (Pek.).

SÜGİRÄLİ   Kkalp. 20th c. **Sügiräli** [Сугирэли] (KkRS 776).

SÜYDÜ see **SEVDİ**

SÜYDÜM   Kzk. **Süydüm-bek** [Суйдумбекъ] (SODž. 154). ✦ 'I loved him/her'. ⇨ **SEVDİ.**

SÜYÄK see **SÜYEK**

SÜYÄN   Tat.(Mish.) 1741 **Süyän-γul** [Сюянгул Аккучюков] (MIB III, 503). ✦ 'Joy, pleasure' cf. Tat. *Söyen-γol* (Sattarov), Tat. *söyen-* 'радоваться, обрадоваться' (TatRS).

SÜYÄR see **SEWÄR**

SÜYÄR-MAMET   Tat. 1632 **Süyär-mamet** [Сюярмамет Изятеров] (Miller, Ist. Sib. II, 397). ⇨ **SEWÄR + MAMET.** See also **SÜYÄRİMBET, SÜYÄRMET.**

SÜYÄRİMBET   Bashk. 1735 **Süyärimbet**

[Сюярымбет Сююндюков], a tarχan (Vel.-Zern., Bašk. 24); Bashk. 1737 **Süyärimbet** [Сюярымбеть Кузмин] (MIB III, 358); Bashk. 1740 **Süyärimbet** [Сюярымбет] (MIB I, 381); Bashk. 1777 **Süyärimbet** [Итбаш Сюярымбетев] (MIB V, 52). ⇨ **SEWÄR** + suff. *-imbet*. See also **SÜYÄR-MAMET, SÜYÄRMET**.

SÜYÄRMET　　Bashk. 1761 **Süyärmet** [Сюяргул Сюярметев] (MIB IV/1, 227). ⇨ **SEWÄR** + suff. *-met*. See also **SÜYÄR-MAMET, SÜYÄRİMBET**.

SÜYEK　　Tat. 1675 **Süyäk** [Ябалакъ Сюаковъ] (Kungursk. akty 32); Kzk. **Süyek-pay** [Сюекпай] (SOK 162); Kzk. **Süyük** [Сююкъ] (SOV 100). ❖ 'Bone' cf. Kzk. *süyek* 'кость' (KzRS), Kzk. *süyök / süök* 'der Knochen; die Abstammung, das Geschlecht'.

SÜYEN-ГАРАN　　Kzk. 1823 **Süyen-γaran** [Суенгаран] (MIK IV, 443).

SÜYER see **SEWÄR**

SÜYGİN　　Uzb. 20th c. **Süygin** [Суйгин] (Begmatov 1984, 204); Uzb. 20th c. **Süygin-bây** [Суйгинбой] (Begmatov 1984, 204); Uzb. 20th c. **Süygin-ĵân** [Суйгинжон] (Begmatov 1984, 204). ❖ 'Love him/her' cf. Chag. *söy-* 'gern haben, lieben; küssen' (Radl. IV, 566), Kzk. *süy-* 'lieben, küssen' (Radl. IV, 796), Uzb. *süy-* '1. севмоқ; 2. ласкать' (UzbRS) + imp. suff. *-gin*.

SÜYİN see **SEVİN**

SÜYİNİŠ see **SEVİNČ**

SÜYİR see **SEWÄR**

SÜYMES　　Kzk. **Süymes** [Сюймесъ] (AOAtb. 30). ❖ 'He/she won't love' cf. Chag. *söy-* 'gern haben, lieben; küssen' (Radl. IV, 566), Kzk. *süy-* 'lieben, küssen' (Radl. IV, 796).

SÜYNİŠ see **SEVİNČ**

SÜYRE　　Kzk. **Süyre-bay** [Сюйребай] (AOK 126); Kkalp. 1809 **Süyri-biy** [Сюйри бий] (MIK 104). ❖ 'Pointed, spiky, conical (head?)' cf. Kzk. *süyrü* 'zugespitzt, kegelförmig' (Radl. IV, 796).

SÜYRİ see **SÜYRE**

SÜYSİN　　Uzb. 20th c. **Süysin** [Суйсин], fem. (Begmatov 1984, 204); Uzb. 20th c. **Süysin-ây** [Суйсиной], fem. (Begmatov 1984, 204); Uzb. 20th c. **Süysin-χân** [Суйсинхон] (Begmatov 1984, 204). ❖ 'May he love!' cf. Chag. *söy-* 'gern haben, lieben; küssen' (Radl. IV, 566), Kzk. *süy-* 'lieben, küssen' (Radl. IV, 796), Uzb. *süy-* '1. севмоқ; 2. ласкать' (UzbRS).

SÜYÜ　　Tat.(Tüm.) 1654 **Süyü-bay** [Маметко Сююбаевъ] (AI IV, 230); Kzk. **Süyü-bek** [Сюубекъ] (SODž. 148). ❖ 'Love, loving' cf. Tat. PNs *Söyükäy, Söyüle* (Sattarov), Tat. *söyü* 'любить; ласкать' (TatRS).

SÜYÜK see **SÜYEK**

SÜYÜKEY　　Bashk. 1763 **Süyükey** [Темиркей Сююкеев] (MIB IV/1, 271). ❖ 'Love, affection; beloved little child' cf. Tat. *Söyükäy* (Sattarov).

SÜYÜLTÜR　　Kzk. 1825 **Süyültür / Suyultur?** [سویولتور] / Суюлтур] (MIK IV, 470, 476).

SÜYÜM　　Kzk. 19th c. **Süyüm-bay (<Süyün-bay?)** [Сююмбай] (AOA 34, 102); Kzk. 19th c. **Süyüm-bay (<Süyün-bay?)** [Сююмбай] (AOK 90); Kzk. 19th c. **Süyüm-bay (<Süyün-bay?)** [Сююмбай] (SODž. 54); Kzk. 19th c. **Süyüm-bay (<Süyün-bay?)** [Сююмбай] (SOV 74). ❖ 'Beloved, kind, darling' cf. Tat. *Söyem* (Sattarov), Kzk. fem. *Süyüm-χan* (Žanuzakov). See also **DİLBER, SÄWÜK, SÜYÜŠ**.

SÜYÜMQAN　　Kirg. **Süyümqan** [Сюмкан], fem. (Jud. 214, 596). ⇨ **SÜYÜM** + suff. *-qan*.

SÜYÜN see **SEVİN**

SÜYÜN-QARA　　Kzk. **Süyün-qara** [Сююнкара], a chief (ZIRGOÊtn. I, 96). ⇨ **SEVİN** + **QARA.**

SÜYÜN-OГURĴALİ　　Trkm. **Süyün-oγurĵalï** [Сююнъ-Огурджали] (Mel'gunov 321). ⇨ **SEVİN.**

SÜYÜN-TAY　　Uzb. 20th c. **Süyün-tây** [Суюнтой] (Begmatov 1984, 204). ❖ 'Be-glad-foal!'. ⇨ **SEVİN** + **TAY** or suff. *-tay(1,2)*.

SÜYÜNČ see **SEVİNČ**

SÜYÜNČ-ALİ　　Bashk. 1795 **Süyünč-ali** [Еллай Суюнчалинъ] (IOAIÊK XXVIII, 591); 1614 **Sünč-aley / Süyünč-ali(y)** [Сунчалей Янглычевъ], a murza (AI III, 21, 411); Bashk. 1710 **Sünč-aley / Süyünč-ali(y)** [Сюнчалей] (MIB III, 64); Bashk. 1718 **Sünč-aley / Süyünč-ali(y)** [Сунчалей / Сунчилей] (MIB III, 178); Bashk. 1759 **Sünč-aley / Süyünč-ali(y)** [Сюнчалей Ишметев] (MIB IV/2 26); Bashk. / Tat.? 1748 **Sünč-ali** [Бактемиръ Сунчалинъ], a Teptär (Nepljuev 438); Bashk. 1735 **Sünč-ali(y)** [Сюнчалий Идзимясовъ], a tarχan (Vel.-Zern., Bašk. 20); Tat. 1552 **Sünč-äläy** [Сюнчелѣй-багатырь] (PSRL XIII, 206). ⇨ **SEVİNČ** + **ALİ / ALEY.**

SÜYÜNČE　　Nog. 1649 **Süyünče** [Тоганъ мурза Сююнчѣевъ] (AI IV, 87); Nog.? 1670 **Süyünče-murza** [Сююнча мурза Елмаметевъ] (AI IV, 405). ❖ 'Good news; gift for glad tidings' cf. Tat. *söyenče* 'id.' (TatRS).

SÜYÜNČEK　　Chag. 16th c. **Süyünč-χan / Süyünčük-χan** [/ Сюнчъ (Сюнчукъ)-ханъ], a Timurid ruler in Samarkand (Barth., Ulugb. 102, 116); Tat.(GH) 1278 **Süyünčük** [τζουντζκ / Сююнчукъ], a Christian woman in the Crimea, pope Antipa's wife (Smirnov, Krym. 34); Chag. **Süyünĵük-sultan** [Suyunjuk Sultán], Sheybani's follower (Shāhi Beg) (Tar. Rashidi 159, 243); Tat.(Sib.) 1635 **Süyünzük / Süyünĵük?** [Суюнзук(ов)] (Miller, Ist. Sib.II 423); Tat.(Lit.) 1593 **Sünček** [Абрагимъ Сюнчековичъ] (Lit. Tat. 146-47); *TN:* Bashk. 1723 **Sünčük(ovo)** [Сюнчюково], a village (MIB III, 211). ❖ 'Good news; little gift (hypoc.)'. ⇨ **SÜYÜNČE** + suff. -*k*.

SÜYÜNČUK see **SÜYÜNČEK**

SÜYÜNJUK see **SÜYÜNČEK**

SÜYÜNIČ see **SEVINČ**

SÜYÜR see **SEWÄR**

SÜYÜR-BAŠ   Kzk. 1819 **Süyür-baš** [Суюрьбаш] (MIK IV, 325). ⇨ **SEWÄR + BAŠ.**

SÜYÜR-ГALI   Bashk. 1760 **Süyür-ɣali** [Суюгалей Сурметев] (MIB V, 678). ✤ 'Loving Ali' cf. Tat. PN *Söyär-ɣali* (Sattarov). ⇨ **SEWÄR + ALI.**

SÜYÜRMET   Bashk. 1742 **Süyürmet** [Елдаш Сююрметев] (MIB I, 482). ⇨ **SEWÄR** + suff. -*met*.

SÜYÜŠ   Tat.(Mish.) 1755, 1761 **Süyüš** [Сююш Тоймасов] (MIB IV/1, 93, 218); Bashk. 1710 **Süyüš** [Сююш Сарагулов] (MIB III, 60); Bashk. 1739 **Süyüš** [Сююш Тойгилдин] (MIB III, 408); Bashk. 1747 **Süyüš** [Сююшъ Абзяковъ] (Nepljuev 426, 428); Bashk. 1749 **Süyüš** [Сююш Султанов] (MIB III, 465); Bashk. 18th c. **Süyüš** [Сююшев] (MIB V, 157); Bashk. 1750 **Süyüš** [Сююш Ишметев] (MIB III, 473); Bashk. 18th c. **Süyüš** [Бекбов Сююшев] (MIB V, 126, 128); Bashk. 1763 **Süyüš** [Сююш Беккинин] (MIB IV/1, 270); Bashk. 1770 **Süyüš** [Сююш Дюсенов] (MIB IV/1, 350); Bashk. 1780 **Süyüš** [Кинзекей Сююшев] (MIB V, 119); Bashk. 1791 **Süyüš** [Рафик Сююшев] (MIB V, 309); Kzk. 18th c. - 19th c. **Süyüš** [Сююш] (Tynyšp. 67); Bashk. 1723 **Süyüš(ä)?** [Сююша Исенеев] (MIB III, 201); Bashk. 1756 **Süyüš / Siyüš** [Чермыш Сююшев (Сеюш)] (MIB IV/1, 125). ✤ 'Beloved (child)' (Sattarov: *Söyeš*), cf. Tat. *söyeš-* 'любить друг друга' (TatRS), Kzk. *süyis-* 'любить друг друга, целоваться' (KzRS). See also **DILBER, SÄWÜK, SÜYÜM.**

SÜYÜŠ-BATWAN   Bashk. 1737 **Süyüš-batwan** [Сююш-Батван Тлекеев] (MIB III, 367). ⇨ **SÜYÜŠ + BATMAN?**

SÜYÜTTÜK   Kzk. **Süyüttük** [Суюттукъ] (SOV 28).

SÜYÜTÜK   Kzk. 1819 **Süyütük** [Суютук] (MIK IV, 325).

SÜK   Kzk. 1841 **Sük** [Сабекъ Сюковъ] (Konšin, Mat. V, 50). ✤ 'Oat' cf. Chag., Kzk. *sök* 'die von Hülsen gereinigte Hirse' (Radl. IV, 569). See also **SÜLE.**

SÜKEY   Tat. 1620 **Sükey** [Сюкей Севергозинъ], from the district of Svijažsk at the Klyara (?) river (Zolotn. 159). ✤ 'Love, loving', variant of Tat. PN *Söyükäy* (Sattarov), Tat. *söyü* 'любить; ласкать' (TatRS) + suff. -*key* / -*käy*.

SÜKENEY   Tat. 1731 **Sükeney** [Аит Сюкенеев] (MIB III, 293).

SÜKIN   Kzk. **Sükin-bay** [Сукинбай] (Grod., Pril. 15); Kzk. **Sükin-bay** [Сукинбай] (Grod., Pril. 80).

SÜKLI   Bashk. 1756 **Sükli** [Темиргуз Сюклеев] (MIB IV/1, 122).

SÜKLIM   Tat.(Sib.)? 1581 **Süklim / Süklem?**

[Суклемъ] (Sib. Let. 337).

SÜKTIKI   Uyg. 8th c. - 9th c. **Süktiki-sañyun** [Süktiki sangun] (Müller, Pfahl. 23).

SÜL-MAMET   Tat. 1625 **Sül-mamet** [Сюлмаметь] (Miller, Ist. Sib. II 329). ⇨ **? + MAMET.**

SÜLÄYMÄN see **SULAYMAN**

SÜLÄK   Bashk. 1716 **Süläk** [Коштак Сюлаков] (MIB III, 142); Bashk. 1760 **Süläk** [Булак Суляков] (MIB IV/2, 160).

SÜLÄKÄY   Tat. 1779 **Süläkäy** [Сюбий Сюлякаев] (MIB V, 94); Bashk. 1749 **Süläkäy** [Сюлякай Ишелеев] (MIB III, 460); Bashk. 1756 **Süläkäy** [Сюлякай Ишалеев] (MIB IV/1, 126); Tat. 1684 **Sülkey** [Сюлкей Сюбаевъ] (Zolotn. 159). ⇨ **SÜLE?** + suff. -*käy*.

SÜLE   Turk. 1378 **Süle-čawuš** [سُوله چاوش] (Āšikp. 53); Turk. 1528 **Süle-čelebi** [Süle Çelebi] (Gökb., Ed. 64). ✤ 'Oat' cf. Tat. *solï* 'овес' (TatRS). ⇨ **SULI.** See also **SÜK.**

SÜLEY   Tat. 1739 **Süläy** [Салѣй Суляевъ] (Alatyr. 141); Tat. 1764 **Süley** [Кусекей Сюлеев] (MIB IV/1, 283); Bashk. 1709 **Süley** [Сулей] (MIB III, 48); Bashk. 1734 **Süley** [Сюлей Мантокеев] (MIB III, 322); Bashk. 1746 **Süley** [Муксун Сюлеев] (MIB III, 444). ⇨ **SÜLE?** + suff. -*y*.

SÜLEMIŠ   Turk. 16th c. **Sülemiš / Sölmüš** [سولمش / Sülemiş / Sölmüş] (Gökb., Ed. 179, 181, 182). ✤ 'He directed an army' (Erol II), cf. Türk *sülä-* 'mit einem Heere gehen, einen Heereszug führen, Krieg führen' (Radl. IV, 830).

SÜLEŠ   Crm.(Tat.) 1656 **Süleš** [Курамша Сулешевъ] (PSZRI I, 364); Crm.(Tat.) 1656 **Süleš** [Чумашъ Сулешевъ] (PSZRI I, 364); Crm.(Tat.) 1656, 1670 **Süleš** [Алжитимиръ Сулешевъ] (PSZRI I, 801); Crm.(Tat.) 1656, 1670 **Süleš** [Маметъ Сулешевъ] (PSZRI I, 364); Crm.(Tat.) 1670 **Süleš** [Велишъ Сулешевъ] (PSZRI II, 359); Tat.(Lit.) 1557 **Süleš** [Сюлешъ] (Kn. Metriki Lit. 152); Crm.(Tat.) 1539, 1541 **Süleš-mïrza** [Сулешь-мырза] (PSRL XIII, 128, 133). ✤ Shortened-contracted form (dialectal variant in Sattarov's opinion) of *Süleyman*. ⇨ **SULAYMAN** + suff. -*eš*.

SÜLGÜN   Trkm. **Sülgün** [Сүлгүн], fem. (Sopieva 177); Trkm. 20th c. **Sülgün** [Sülgün], fem. (Zaj. 1971, 338); Trkm. 20th c. **Sülgün** [Сюльгун], fem. (TrkmRS 598). ✤ 'Pheasant' cf. Trkm. *sülgün* 'id.' (TrkmRS).

SÜLI see **SULI**

SÜLIPAQ   Tat.(Sib.) 16th c. **Sülipaq-qanïm / Sülipaq-qanïš? / Silü-bäg?** [Sülipak kanym], one of „Közüm"-qan's (Köcüm/Küčüm-qan's?) wives (Radl., Aus Sib. I, 147).

SÜLKÄY see **SÜLÄKÄY**

SÜLLÜYÜK   Yak. **Süllüyük** [Сүллүјүк Уйбан] (Pek.). ✤ 'Tattered, paltry, shabby' (Pek.).

SÜLÜK   Tat. 1779 **Sülük** [Сюлюк Югяев] (MIB V, 82); Bashk. 1737 **Sülük** [Сюлюк Акшибурдин] (MIB I, 316); Bashk. 1738 **Sülük** [Сюлюк Салтыковы] (MIB III, 394); Bashk. 1744 **Sülük** [Сюлюк Рысаев] (MIB III, 415); Bashk. 1749, 1751, 1763, 1764 **Sülük** [Аднагул Сюлюков] (MIB III, 468, IV/1, 34, 268, 292); Bashk. 1757, 1761 **Sülük** [Сюлюк Камаев] (MIB IV/1, 138, 220); Bashk. 1760 **Sülük** [Сюлюк Юзеев] (MIB IV/1, 197); Bashk. 1761 **Sülük** [Якшигул Сюлюков] (MIB IV/1, 211). ✧ 'Leech' cf. Chag., Turk., Tat.(Bar.) *sülük* 'der Blutegel' (Radl. IV, 832), Tat. *sülek* 'пиявка' (TatRS). See also **GÖÇER-SÜLÜK**.

SÜLÜM   Bashk. 1740 **Sülüm** [Исергап Сюлюмов] (MIB I, 434); Bashk. 1761 **Sülüm** [Усман Сюлюмов] (MIB IV/1, 218).

SÜLÜMÄDIRÄ   Yak. **Sülümädirä-buχatīr** [Сүлүмäдірä-бухатыр], a folklore hero (Pek.).

SÜMÄ Uyg. **Sümä** [Сӱмä] (Radl., Altuig. 65).

SÜMEKEY   Bashk. 1796 **Sümekey** [Сюмекей Тевеев] (MIB V, 362).

SÜMÖTÖY see **SEMETEY**

SÜN see **SEVIN**

SÜNBÜL   Turk. 1434 **Sünbül-χatun** [سنبل حاتون] (MG Ank. 47). ✧ 'Hyacinth (Hyacinthus orientalis); (poet.) curly locks and ringlets of a beauty' (TED), cf. also PNs *Sümbül / Sünbül (Zümbül)* (Erol II) <P.

SÜNÇÜLEY   Tat. 1552 **Sünçüley (<Süyünč-aley?)** [Сюнчулей], a hero killed in the battle at Kazan (Zolotn. 159). ⇨ **SÜYÜNČ-ALI**.

SÜNDET   Kzk. 19th c. **Sündät-bay?** [Сундатбай] (Grod., Pril. 181); Bashk. 20th c. **Sündet-bay** [Сюндетбай] (Bask., Kkalp. 401); Bashk. 1711 **Sünlet** [Сюнлеть] (MIB III, 74). ✧ 'Ritual circumcision (feast)' cf. Kzk. *sündet* (Ar.) 'Sünnet' (KzTS).

SÜNDIK see **SEVINDIK**

SÜNDÜ see **SEVINDI**

SÜNDÜK see **SEVINDIK**

SÜNDÜL   Osm. 1519, 1528 **Sündül-bey** (Gökb., Ed. 297).

SÜNE Kzk. **Süne-bay** [Сунебай] (SODž. 84).

SÜNEY Bashk. 1749 **Süney** [Сюней Драгишев] (MIB III, 464).

SÜNLET see **SÜNDET**

SÜÑGÜ   Maml. 14th c. **Süñgü** [سنكو / Süngü] (Tarǰ/Houtsma 78, Tarǰ/Toparlı 4). ✧ 'Lance, spear, pike' cf. Turk. *süngü* 'die Lanze' (Radl. IV, 806).

SÜÑI see **SÖÑÜ**

SÜÑÜŠ   Karakh. **Süñiš** [Süngiş] (MK/Atalay 851); Karakh. 11th c. **Süñüš** [Süngüş / süŋüš] (MK/Atalay 851, DTS). ✧ 'Fight, row' cf. Karakh. *süŋüš* 'id.' (DTS).

SÜÖDÄR see **SÖDÖR**

SÜÖDÄRKÄN   Yak. **Süödärkän** [Сӱöдäркäн] (Pek.).

✧ Hypoc.-dim. of *Süödär* originates from R. *Feden'ka* (Pek.). ⇨ **SÜÖDÄR** + dim. hypoc. suff. *-kän*.

SÜÖKÜLÄ   Yak. **Süökülä** [Сӱöкӱлä], fem. (Pek.). ✧ Fyokla (R. fem.) (Pek.).

SÜPIKU Kzk. **Süpiku-bay?** [Сюпикубай] (SOV 58).

SÜRDÄK   Bashk. 1750 **Sürdäk** [Сюрдяк Бигишев] (MIB III, 472).

SÜRDÄX-DÜPSÜN   Yak. **Sürdäχ-düpsün** [Сӱрдäх Дӱпсӱн], one of Däli-darχan's two sons (Pek.).

SÜRES   Alt. 19th-20th c. **Süres** [Сӱрес], fem. (OjrRS 213).

SÜRKEY   Bashk. 1745 **Sürkey** [Сюркей Кадырметев] (MIB III, 433).

SÜRMÄK   Tat. 1724 **Sürmäk** [Сюрмяк] (MIB III, 228).

SÜRMEY   Bashk. 1710 **Sürmey** [Сюрмей Алышев] (MIB III, 63).

SÜRMELI   Turk. **Sürmeli** (Önder, Hınıs). ✧ '(Eyelids) Tinged with kohl' cf. Turk. *sürmäli* 'mit Antimon geschwärzt' (Radl. IV, 830).

SÜRMES   Hak. 19th-20th c. **Sürmes** [Сӱрмес], fem. (HRS 355). ✧ 'Small tufts/locks (of a girl)' cf. Hak. *sürmes* 'мелкие косички (у девушки)' (HRS).

SÜRMET   Chuv. 18th-19th c. **Sürmet** [Сюрметъ / Сюрметь] (Magn. 79); Bashk. 1764 **Sürmet** [Сюрметь Тулчумов] (MIB IV/1, 277).

SÜRT Kzk. **Sürt** [Сюртъ] (SOK 106).

SÜRTI Kzk. **Sürtī / Surtī?** [Сюрты] (SOK 154).

SÜRÜ   Selj. 12th c. **Sürü** [سيف الدين سورى ملك غور] (Rāwandī 175).

SÜRÜÑ   Tuv. 19th c. **Sürüñ** [Сӱрӱн] (Proben IX, 98).

SÜSPIČ   Chuv. 1670 **Süspič** [Сюспичка Автѣева], fem. (Poliv.-Kras. 64).

SÜT   Alt. 19th-20th c. **Süt** [Сӱт], fem. (OjrRS 213); Kzk. **Süt-pay** [Сутпай] (SOK 246). ✧ 'Milk' (OjrRS) cf. Uyg., Chag., Alt., Kzk., Turk. etc. *süt* 'die Milch' (Radl. IV, 834).

SÜT-EMGEN   Kzk. **Süt-emgen** [Сутемгенъ] (AOK 2); Kzk. **Süt-emgen** [Сютенгенов] (AOK 6); Kzk. **Süt-emgen** [Сютемгенъ] (AOO 46); Kzk. **Süt-emgen** [Сютемгенъ] (AOO 46); Kzk. 18th c. - 19th c. **Süt-emgen** [Сутемген] (Tunyšp. 68, 72). ✧ '(The baby) sucked milk'; 'Milk sucking' cf. Kzk. *em-* 'Emmek' (KzTS). ⇨ **SÜT**. See also **AT-EMGEN, IT-EMGEN, TAT-EMGEN**.

SÜTČI   Alt. 19th-20th c. **Sütči** [Сӱтчи], fem. (OjrRS 213). ✧ 'Nurse (maid)' (OjrRS.

SÜTÄK   Bashk. 1740 **Sütäk** [Сютяк] (MIB I, 435); Kzk. **Sütek** [Сютекъ] (SOV 106).

SÜTEN Kzk. **Süten** [Сютенъ] (SODž. 26).

SÜTTER Kzk. **Sütter-bay** [Суттербай] (AOK 2).

SÜTTI Kzk. **Sütti-bay / Sütti-bay** [Сюттыбай] (AOP 46); Kzk. **Sütti-bay / Sütti-bay** [Сюттыбай] (SOV 144); Kzk. **Süttü-bay** [Суттубай] (AOK 14); Kzk.

Süttü-bay [Сюттубай] (AOP 6); Kzk. **Süttü-bay** [Сюттубай] (SOK 16, 64); Kzk. **Süttü-bay** [Сюттубай] (SOV 30); Kzk. **Süttü-bay** [Сюттюбай] (SOK 34); *TN:* Kzk. **Sütü-bay < Süttü-bay** [Сютюбай], a lake near the Irtish river, west of Pavlodar (Karta JAR IV).

SÜTÜK Bashk. 1756 **Sütük** [Сутюк Маметев] (MIB IV/1, 107).

SÜVASKEY Chuv. 18th-19th c. **Süvaskey** [Сюваскей] (Magn. 79).

SÜZENIČ Khorezm.? **Süzenič-sultan** [سوزنیج سلطان / Сузениджъ Султанъ], a Sheybanid (Šejb. XLIX).

SÜZGÜ Kzk. **Süzgü-bay** [Сусгубай] (SOK 150). ✧ 'Sieve, sifter' cf. East.T., Kzk., Turk. *süzgü* 'ein feines Sieb, Durchschlag' (Radl. IV, 847).

SÜNDÜK see **SEVİNDİK**

SÜRÄK Hak.(Sag.) 19th-20th c. **Sürȧk** [Сӱрӓк], fem. (Proben IX, 263). ✧ 'Spurned, expelled' (Butanaev).

SVİYAGA Chuv. 18th-19th c. **Sviyaga** [Свіяга] (Magn. 74). ✧ Toponym.

SWİNTİK Kzk. **Swintik-pay?** [Свинтыкпай] (SOK 90).

Š

Š-PEK see **EŠ**

ŠA see **ŠAH**

ŠA-MAMET Nog. 1649 **Ša-mamet** [Шамаметъ] (AI IV, 123). ⇨ **ŠAH + MUXAMMED.**

ŠA-MİRAT see **ŠA-MURAT**

ŠA-MURAT Kkalp. 20th c. **Ša-mïrat** [Шамырат] (KkRS 776); Kkalp. 20th c. **Ša-murat** [Шамурат] (KkRS 776). ⇨ **ŠAH + MURAT.**

ŠA-NAZAR Kkalp. 20th c. **Ša-nazar** [Шаназар] (KkRS 776). ⇨ **ŠAH + NAZAR.**

ŠA-TEMİR see **ŠAH-TEMİR**

ŠA-ÜSEYN Tat. 1512 **Ša-üseyn-seyit** [Шаусейнъ-сеитъ], a prince of Kazan (PSRL VIII, 252 etc.). ✧ 'Shah-Husain' (<P.-Ar.). ⇨ **ŠAH.**

ŠABAY Trkm. **Šabay** [Шабаевъ] (Ščeglov IV, 190); Tat. 1712 **Šabay** [Шабай] (MIB III, 84); Bashk. 1717 **Šabay** [Шабай Игичеков] (MIB III, 154); Bashk. 18th c. **Šabay** [Шабай(ев)] (MIB V, 328); Bashk. 1759 **Šabay** [Шабай Яковлев] (MIB IV/2, 26). ✧ 'Young fellow, lad; adolescent' (Ar.) (Sattarov).

ŠABALAT Tat. 1541 **Šabalat** [Шабалатъ] (PSRL XIII, 100).

ŠABALDA Tat. 1670 **Šabalda** [Шабалда], settlement (?) of the Khan of Astrakhan (DAI VI, 13).

ŠABAN Turk. 1583 **Šaban** [Şaban] (Ongan, Ank. I, 173, 177); Yürük 1543 **Šaban** [Şaban] (Gökb., Rum. 225, 226, 240); Tat.(Lit.) 1582 **Šaban** [Хадичъ Шабановичъ] (Lit. Tat. 44); Tat. 1543 **Šaban** [Şaban] (Gökb., Rum. 240); Bashk. 1709 **Šaban** [Тюбяч Шабанов] (MIB I, 264); Kzk. 19th c. **Šaban** [Шабанъ] (AOA 146); Kzk. 19th c. **Šaban-bay** [Шабанбай] (AOO 60); Turk. 1491 **Šaban-dede** [Şaban Dede bin Halil] (Gökb., Ed. 467). ✧ I. 'Fool, stupid' cf. Turk. *šaban* 'einfältig, albern; versteinert, erstarrt' (Radl. IV, 987); II. 'Lazy' cf. Kzk. *šaban* 'faul (vom Pferde)' (Radl. IV, 987; III. 'Nutty, amorous' cf. *šaban* 'verliebt' (Radl. IV, 987); IV. 'The tenth month of the Arabian lunar calendar' (Ar.) (Sattarov).

ŠABAN-AY Kzk. 19th c. **Šaban-ay** [Шабанай] (AOK 118). ⇨ **ŠABAN + AY.**

ŠABAN-SÜLİ see **SÜLİ**

ŠABAS see **ŠABAZ**

ŠABAŠ Kzk. 19th c. **Šabaš** [Шабашъ] (AOP 54). ✧ 'Bravo!, Well done!' cf. Kzk. *šabaz* 'id.' (Radl. IV, 988), Turk. *šabaš* (P.) 'Beğenme. „Aferin!" deme' (Özön).

ŠABATAL Tat.(Lit.) 1590 **Šabatal** [Шабаталъ Абрагимовичъ] (Lit. Tat. 66-72).

ŠABATΪ Oghuz/Trkm. 13th c. **Šabatï** [شاباتى / Шабаты], Qayï-bay's daughter, Čawuldur Bala-alp's wife (Abulg./Kon. 1445).

ŠABAZ Tat. 1541, 1551-15552 **Šabaz / Šabas** [Шабазъ / Шабасъ-князь / Шабаса-князь], a prince (PSRL XIII, 100, 169, 171); *EN:* Nog. 20th c. **Šabbaz-mïrza-uruw** [Шаббаз-мырза урув], an Aq-noγay clan (Bask., Nog. 133).

ŠABBAZ see **ŠABAZ**

ŠABΪR Kirg. **Šabïr** [Шабыр] (Jud. 291). ✧ 'Reed' cf. Kirg. *šabïr* 'мелкий камыш растущий на болотистых местах' (Jud.).

ŠAD Maml. 1434 **Šad-bek** [شاد بك الجكمى] (Ibn Taghrīb. VI, 715, 742); Maml. 1450 **Šad-bek** [السينى شاد بك], governor of Hama (?), died in Jerusalem in 1450, mentioned in an inscription on a copper dish (Mayer 199-200); Maml. 1454, 1460 **Šad-bek** [شاد بك الجلبانى] (Ibn Taghrīb. VIII, 224, 400, etc.); Maml. 1457 **Šad-bek** [شاد بك الصارمى] (Ibn Taghrīb. VII, 473, 520); Maml. 1459 **Šad-bek** [شاد بك طاز] (Ibn Taghrīb. VIII, 332); Maml. 1463 **Šad-bek** [شاد بك الجلبانى الصغير] (Ibn Taghrīb. VII, 714); Maml. 1464 **Šad-bek** [شادبك بشق الاشرفى] (Ibn Taghrīb. VIII, 339, 505); Maml. 1468/69 **Šad-bek** [شاد بك الحسنى] (Iyās II, 111); Maml. 1479 **Šad-bek** [شاد بك] (Iyās II, 190, 336); Maml. 1483 **Šad-bek** [شاد بك], Master of the Horse (Iyās II, 220, Weil, Chalif. II, 361, 431). ✧ I. 'Vice-Kaghan (title)' (Radl. IV, 971, DTS, Golden, Khaz. 206-208); II. 'Member of the khan's dynasty (comp.)' (Golden, Khaz. 206-208); III. 'The khan's younger brother or son (comp.)'

(Ligeti, R. tör. nev. II-III, 39). According to Sauvaget (p. 48) *Šad-bek* would mean „émir joie" [emir-joy / joyful emir]. (< Ir.).

ŠAD-GELDİ   Turk. 1377, 1381 **Šad-geldi / Šad-geldi-paša** [شاد كلدى باشا / الحاج شاد كلدى / Šādgeldi / Hacı Şadgeldi Paşa], emir of Amasya at the end of 14th c. (Astarab. 101, 232 etc., Uzunçarş., Küt. I, 103, 106, 109, Uzunçarş., Anad. 50, 51, 84, 85, 94). ⇨ **ŠAD + KELDİ.**

ŠAD-MURAT   Kkalp. 20th c. **Šad-murat** [Шадмурат] (KkRS 776). ✧ 'Joyful/happy Murat' cf. Kkalp. *šad* (P.) 'весёлый, радостный, довольный' (KkRS). ⇨ **ŠAD + MURAT.**

ŠADAY   Shor 19th-20th c. **Šaday**, a folklore hero (*alïp*) (Dyrenkova 124). ⇨ **ŠATAY?**

ŠADAM-AY   Kzk. **Šadam-ay** [Шадамъ-ай] (SKSO IV, 38).

ŠADAN   Uyg. 14th c. **Šadan** (Radl., USp. 15, Le Coq, Urkunden 456-457).

ŠADİ   Uyg. 1275 **Šadi** (Chwol., Syr.-nest. (NF) 9); Uyg.? 1339 **Šadi** (Chwol., Syr.-nest. (NF) 33); Kzk. 19th c. **Šadi-bek / Šadi-bek / Ǯanï-bek?** [Шадыбекъ] (AUK 556); Uyg. 1339, 1341 **Šadi-qam** [Schadikam] (Chwol., Syr.-nest. (NF) 34, 39); Uyg. 1323 **Šadi-päg / Šadï-päg?** [Šady-päg], Qut-tägin-päg's son (Chwol., Syr.-nest. 140). ✧ 'Pleasure, joy' (P.) (Sattarov).

ŠADMAN   Uzb. **Šadman** [Шадманъ-ходжа] (Smirnov, Sultany 70); Uzb. 1704 **Šadman** [Šādmān-i Jābū], from Bukhara (Buchari 276); Uzb. 1852 **Šadman-bek** [Шадманъ Бекъ] (Moskal'cev 78); Uzb. 19th c. **Šadman-χoǰa** [Chadman-hodja], fought against the Russians in Farghana (Nalivkin-Dozon 225). ✧ 'Joyful, happy' cf. Turk. *šadman* 'fröhlich, froh, glücklich' (Radl. IV, 971).

ŠAFİ   Bashk. 1792 **Šafi** [Шафи Бибков] (MIB V, 559). ✧ 'Kind, gentle, generous' (Ar.) (Kusimova).

ŠAΓAY   Tat. 1709 **Šaγay** [Шагай Ижбулатов] (MIB I, 268); Tat.(Sib.) 1599 **Šaγay** [Шагай], a Siberian prince from Küčüm's family (AI II, 17, 22); Kzk. 19th c. **Šaγay** [Шагай] (AOA 66). ⇨ **ČAΓAY?**

ŠAΓAYČÏ   Alt. 19th-20th c. **Šaγayčï** [Шагайчы] (OjrRS 210). ⇨ **ŠAΓAY** + suff. *-čï.*

ŠAΓAL see ČAQAL

ŠAΓALAQ   Kzk. 18th c. - 19th c. **Šaγalaq** [Шагалак] (Tynyšp. 68, 73). ✧ 'Clout' cf. Chag. *šaγalaq* 'die Ohrfeige' (Radl. IV, 937).

ŠAΓALAT   Uzb. 1629 **Šaγalat** [Ермамбет Шагалатов], from Bukhara (Miller, Ist. Sib. II, 361).

ŠAΓANAY   Bashk. 18th c. **Šaγanay** [Шаганай Бурчаков] (MIB V, 672, 676, 677).

ŠAΓAR see ČAΓAR

ŠAΓARBAN   Bashk. 1764 **Šaγarban** [Шагарбан Сеитова] (MIB IV/1, 281).

ŠAΓATAY see ČAΓATAY

ŠAΓATČÏ   Tuv. 19th c. **Šaγatčï** [Шаӷатчы] (Proben IX, 23).

ŠAΓÏR see ČAΓÏR

ŠAΓÏR-BUΓA   Kzk. 19th c. **Šaγïr-buγa** [Шагирбуга] (AOAtb. 30). ⇨ **ČAΓÏR + BUQA.**

ŠAΓRAY   Kzk. 19th c. **Šaγray** [Шаграй] (AOK 90). ✧ 'Little grey-eyed'. ⇨ **ČAΓÏR** + dim. suff. *-ay.*

ŠAH   Kirg. 19th-20th c. **Ša-pey?** [Šápej] (Prinz 329); Kkalp. 20th c. **Ša-zada** [Шазада], fem. (KkRS 779); Chuv. 18th-19th c. **Šah-čura** [Шахчура] (Magn. 94); Turk. 1583 **Šah-qatun** [شاه قاطون / Şahkatun], fem. (Ongan, Ank. I, 177); Trkm. 1740 **Šah-quli-bek** [Шах-кули-бек], from the Qajar tribe in Merv (MIT II, 151, 162, 163, 168, 171, 177-179, 180, 182-189); Turk. 1583 **Šah-qulu** [Şahkulu] (Ongan, Ank. I, 177); Yürük 1543 **Šah-qulu** [Şahkulu] (Gökb., Rum. 185, 204, 206, 212, 229); Chuv. 18th-19th c. **Šah-murza** [Шахмурза] (Magn. 94); Oghuz? 1020 **Šah-tegin / Ša-tegin** [شاحكن / شاحتكين], governor of Damascus (Ibn Taghrīb.II, 121, 123, Qalānisi 69, 70); Trkm. 1539 **Šah-veli** [Şahveli] (Özbaş 4); Tat. 1543 **Šah-veli** [Şah Veli] (Gökb., Rum. 237); Trkm. 20th c. **Ša-durdï** [Шадурды] (TrkmRS 749); Trkm. 20th c. **Ša-geldi** [Шагельды] (TrkmRS 749); Trkm. 20th c. **Ša-soltan** [Шасолтан] (TrkmRS 749); Trkm. 20th c. **Ša-soltan** [Šāsoltan] (Zaj. 1971, 326); *TN:* Chuv. 18th c. **Šah-čurina** (<**Šah-čura**) [Шахчурина], a village in the district of Cheboksary (Korsakov 286). ✧ 'Shah; king, monarch, ruler, imperor' cf. Turk. *şah* 'id.' (TED), Trkm. *šā / šāh* 'шах' (TrkmRS). Title used also as a secondary component of male names.

ŠAH-BERDİ   Trkm.? 1536 **Šah-verdi** [Šāhwirdī] (Justi 279); Trkm. 1550 **Šah-verdi** [Шах-верды-бек] (MIT II, 68); Trkm. 1580 **Šah-verdi** [Šahverdi] (Dorn); Trkm. 1593 **Šah-verdi(-χan)** [Шах-верды (хан)] (MIT II, 83); Trkm. 1550 **Šah-verdi-bek** [Шах-берды-бек], from the Keňkerlü tribe (MIT II, 68); Trkm. 1580 **Šah-verdi-bek / Šah-verdi-sultan** [ويـردى سلطان / شاه / شاه ويـردى بيك], / Шах-верды бек Качаль: Шах-верды-султан], Ǯelāl's son, from the Ustajlu tribe (Dorn 253, 254, 255, 289, MIT II, 60, 61, 69, 70); Trkm. 1726/27 **Šah-verdi-χan** [Шах-верды-хан], from the Šeyχvanlu tribe (MIT II, 128, 129); Turk. 1540 **Šah-virdi-kethudā** [Şahvirdi kethudâ], chief of the Döger tribe (cemaat), according to a defter of Diyarbakır, Turkey (Demirtaş 49); Uzb. 20th c. **Šâ-berdi** (<**Šâh-berdi?**) [Шоберди] (Begmatov 1984, 202); Uzb. 20th c. **Šâh-berdi** [Шохберди] (Begmatov 1984, 202). ✧ 'Shah gave him' Some more persons are known by Justi (p. 279). ⇨ **ŠAH + BERDİ.**

ŠAH-BERGEN   Uzb. 20th c. **Šâh-bergän** [Шохберган] (Begmatov 1984, 202). ✧ 'Shah gave him/her'. ⇨ **ŠAH + BERGEN.**

ŠAH-BUDAQ   Chag. 15th c. **Šah-budaɣ-sultan / Šah-budaq-sultan** [بوداغ سلطان / شاه] / Šāh Budak / Châh-Boudâq-Sultan], Abul Khair Khan's son, Mukhammed Sheybani's father (Abulg./Desm. 192, Šejb. L, LV, LXXVII). ⇨ **ŠAH + BUTAQ.**

ŠAH-BULA   Turk. 1583 **Šah-bula** [Şahbula], Seferşah's daughter (Ongan, Ank. I, 178). ⇨ **ŠAH + BULA.**

ŠAH-KELDİ   Trkm. 20th c. **Šā-geldi** [Šágeldi] (Zaj. 1971, 334); Uzb. 20th c. **Šâh-keldi** [Шохкелди] (Begmatov 1984, 203). ✧ 'Shah has come / has been born'. ⇨ **ŠAH + KELDİ.**

ŠAH-QALAQ   Tat.(Lit.) 1552 **Šah-qalaq** [Шахкалакъ] (Kn. Metriki Lit. 86). ✧ 'Shah-spoon' cf. Hak., Kzk., Tat. *qalaq* 'ein grosser Löffel' (Radl. II, 227). ⇨ **ŠAH.**

ŠAH-MANSÏR   Crm. 1554 **Šah-mansïr-ulan (<Šahi-mansïr-ulan)** [Шагманъсыр-уланъ], a Crimean envoy (PSRL XIII, 237). ✧ 'Great victor/triumphant' (P.-Ar.) cf. Tat. *Šahi* (Sattarov), Turk. *şahi* 'royal, imperial; kingship' (TED). ⇨ **MANSUR.**

ŠAH-MARDAN see **ŠAH-MERDAN**

ŠAH-MERDAN   Kzk. 19th c. **Čay-merden** [Чаймерденъ] (AOA 102); Kkalp. 20th c. **Šah-mardan (<Šahi-mardan)** [Шахмардан] (KkRS 776); Kzk. 19th c. **Šay-merden** [Шаймерденъ] (AOO 66); Bashk. 1744 **Še-mardan** [Шемардан Сырымов] (MIB III, 415); Tat. 1557 **Še-merdän** [Шемераденъ] (Kn. Metriki Lit. 157); Kzk. 1529 **Še-merden** [Шемердень-князь], prince Čuračikov, who was sent from Kazan to Moscow as one of the envoys in 1529 (PSRL XIII, 46, Zolotn. 160); *TN:* Tat. 1737 **Še-merdän(ovï)** [Шемердяновы], a village (Alatyr. 136, 139); Chuv. 18th c. **Še-merdän(ovo)** [Шемердяново], a village (R. Troitskoe) in the district of Yadrinsk (Korsakov 303). ✧ 'Shah of brave heroes' (Sattarov), 'The greatest man, the most eminent man' (Kusimova). ⇨ **ŠAH + MERDAN.**

ŠAH-PULAD see **BULAT**

ŠAH-RUZ   Turk. 1474 **Šah-ruz** [شاهروز بنت براق بك], Baraq-beg's daughter, in an inscription of Amasya, Turkey (Uzunçarş., Küt. I, 120). ✧ 'Shah-day(-time)' cf. Turk. *ruz* (P.) 'Gün, gündüz' (Özön). ⇨ **ŠAH.**

ŠAH-SİNÄ   Crm. **Šah-sinä** [Шах-Сінä] (Radl. II, 1103). ✧ 'Shah-heart' cf. Turk. *sine* (A.) 'Göğüs; iç, yürek' (Özön), also Tat. *Sinä* (Sattarov). ⇨ **ŠAH.**

ŠAH-ŠOŇƔAR   Az. **Šah-šoňyar** [Шах-Шонгар] (Az. Skaz. 348). ✧ 'Shah-falcon'? cf. Uyg. *šuňqar* 'der Falke' (Radl. IV, 1098). ⇨ **ŠAH + SOŇQUR.**

ŠAH-TEMİR   Nog. 1649 **Ša-temir** [Шатемиръ мурза Мамметевъ] (AI IV, 78); Trkm. 1735 **Šah-temir** [Шах Темир], a khan of Aral (MIT II, 333); Nog. 20th c. **Šah-temir-ᵪan** [Шахтемир-хан] (Bask., Nog. 227); Kzk. 19th c. **Šah-temür-biy** [Шахъ-Темурбій] (Grod., Pril. 161); Crm.(Tat.) 1668 **Šah-timür** [شاه تيمور اتالق] (Vel.-Zern., Crim. 580, 591); Crm. 1637 **Šah-timür-bi** [شاه تيمور بى] (Vel.-Zern., Crim. 158, 169); Crm. 1655 **Šah-timür-mirza** [تيمور ميرزا / شاه] (Vel.-Zern., Crim. 498). ✧ 'The best/strongest iron' (Sattarov). ⇨ **ŠAH + TEMİR.**

ŠAH-TİMÜR see **ŠAH-TEMİR**

ŠAH-TURDÏ   Trkm. 20th c. **Šā-durdï** [Šādurdï] (Zaj. 1971, 334); Uzb. 20th c. **Šâ-turdï** [Шотурди] (Begmatov 1984, 204). ✧ 'Shah stayed / remained / survived'. ⇨ **ŠAH + TURDÏ.**

ŠAH-VERDİ see **ŠAH-BERDİ**

ŠAH-VİRDİ see **ŠAH-BERDİ**

ŠAHARMAN   Selj. 1181 **Šaharman** [Shâharmân], lord of Khālāt (Abulfar./Budge I, 313).

ŠAHBAZ-GEREY   Tat.? **Šahbaz-gerey** [Шагбаз-герей] (IOAIÊK XIX, 145). ✧ 'Falcon/hero-nobleman' cf. Tat., Bashk. *Šahbaz* (P.) '(Sattarov, Kusimova). ⇨ **KERÄY.**

ŠAHİ-MARDAN see **ŠAH-MERDAN**

ŠAHİM   Chag. 16th c. **Šahim** [Шахим] (Ivanov 261, 262, 266-269); Chag. 16th c. **Šahim-aɣa** [Шахим Аɣа], fem. (Ivanov 215, 294); Chag. 16th c. **Šahim-quli** [Шахим-кули] (Ivanov 184, 186, 187); Chag. 16th c. **Šahim-quli** [Шахим-кули маулана] (Ivanov 179); Chag. 16th c. **Šahim-šeyᵪ** [Шахим-шеих] (Ivanov 262-67, 270-74). ✧ 'My shah'. ⇨ **ŠAH** + poss. suff. *-im.*

ŠAHİN   Maml. 1398/99 **Šahin** [شاهين كتك] (Ibn Taghrīb. VI, 4); Maml. 1400 **Šahin** [شاهين] (Berchem, Jér. I, 230); Maml. 1410/11 **Šahin** [شاهين الزرد كاش], governor of Tripolis at around 1420 (Ibn Taghrīb. VI, 230, 231, Weil, Chalif. II, 321); Maml. 1411/12 **Šahin** [شاهين], an emir (امير طبلحاناة) (Ibn Taghrīb. VI, 245); Maml. 1419 **Šahin** [شاهين الايدكارىّ الناصرىّ], governor of Tarsus (Ibn Taghrīb. VI, 367, 740, Weil, Chalif. II, 144, 145); Maml. 1443 **Šahin** [شاهين الطوغانى الاشقر] (Ibn Taghrīb. VIII, 10, 31); Maml. 1448 **Šahin** [شاهين الطوغانى الطويل] (Ibn Taghrīb. VII, 158, 319); Maml. 15th c. **Šahin** [شاهين الظاهرى الساقى الرومى] (Ibn Taghrīb. VIII, 77, 211 etc.); Maml. 1454 **Šahin** [شاهين التاجى] (Ibn Taghrīb. VIII, 210, 211); Maml. 1463 **Šahin** [شاهين الاشرفى] (Ibn Taghrīb. VIII, 463); Turk. 14th c. **Šahin** [Σαΐνης], a Turkish (Ottoman) commander (Byz. Turc. 263); Turk. 1451 **Šahin** [Σιαχήν], an Ottoman vizier (minister) (Byz. Turc. 274); Turk. 1482 **Šahin** [Σαΐνης], a Turkish envoy (Byz. Turc. 263); Turk. 1552 **Šahin** [Musztafa bin Sáhin] (Dávid); Yürük 1543 **Šahin** [Şahin] (Gökb., Rum. 178, 189); Yürük 1543 **Šahin** [ساهين / Şahin] (Gökb., Rum. 103, 178); Trkm. 1610 **Šahin** [شاهين / Şahin], from Syria (Refik, Anad. 62); Tat. 1543 **Šahin** [Şâhin] (Gökb., Rum. 242);

Turk. 1757 **Šahin-aγa** [Şahin ağa] (Unat 12); Trkm. 1690 **Šahin-beg** [شاهين بك / Şahin beğ] (Refik, Anad. 84); Turk. 1483 **Šahin-šaχ-čelebi** [شاهنشاه چلبى] (Āšikp. 186); Turk. 1486 **Šāhin** [Şâhin (Mchmcd Bey adamı)] (Gökb., Ed. 129); *TN:* Turk. 20th c. **Šahin-bey** [Şahinbey], a village in the province of Gaziantep, Turkey (TMİB 372). ✧ 'Falcon' cf. P. *šāhīn* 'faucon pélerin' (Sauvaget, 48), Turk. *šahin* 'der Königsfalke' (Radl. IV, 941), see also P. names *Šāhēn* at Justi, p. 275. See also **DELÜ-ŠAHİN**.

ŠAHİN-ČAQÏR Turk. 1560 **Šahin-čaqïr** [Šáhin Čâkir], a Janissary of Székesfehérvár, Hungary (Velics-Kamm. I, 127). ✧ 'Grey-blue-eyed falcon'. ⇨ **ŠAHİN + ČAQÏR.**

ŠAHİN-GİREY Crm.(Tat.) 1624 **Šahin-girey-sultan** [شاهين كراى سلطان], Mohammed Girey Khan's (1623-1624) brother (Vel.-Zern., Crim. 22, 27, 32 etc.); Crm.(Tat.) 1634 **Šahin-girey-sultan** [كراى سلطان شاهين], İnayet-girey Khan's (1635-1637) son (Vel.-Zern., Crim. 124, 126, 790 etc.); Kkalp. **Šan-gerey-χan** [Шангерей-хан] (Divaev: TOOIK III, 121 ff.). ✧ I. 'Falcon-nobleman'; II. 'Shah's wish' cf. Tat. *Šahin-gäräy* (Sattarov). ⇨ **ŠAHİN + KERÄY.**

ŠAHİNAY Bashk. 1759 **Šahinay** [Шагинай Бурчаков] (MIB IV/2, 167). ✧ 'Little falcon'? ⇨ **ŠAHİN** + suff. *-ay*?

ŠAHRABAN Az. **Šahraban** [Шахрабан], Muš-veren's elder brother (Az. Skaz. 319).

ŠAXANLARÏ Balk. 20th c. **Šaχanlarï**, a family (Pröhle, Balk. 254). ⇨ **ŠAHİN?** + plur. suff. *-lar*, poss. *-ï*.

ŠAİM Tat.(Sib.) 1598-1599 **Šaim** [Шаимъ], a Siberian prince from Küčüm's family (AI II, 17, 22-24); Bashk. 1733 **Šaim** [Таймасъ Батырь Шаимовъ] (Vel.-Zern., Bašk. 5); Bashk. 1790 **Šaim** [Таймас Шаимов] (MIB V, 680); Kzk. 19th c. **Šaim** [Шаимъ] (AOAtb. 6); Nog. 1649 **Šaim-murza** [Шаимъ мурза Янаевъ] (AI IV, 87). ✧ 'My silk; my darling' (P.) (Sattarov, Žanuzakov).

ŠAİR Kzk. 19th c. **Šair-bek** [Шаирбекъ] (Grod., Pril. 56). ✧ 'Resin, rosin' cf. Kzk. *šair* 'der Holztheer' (Radl. IV, 927), Kzk. *šayïr* 'das Harz' (Radl. IV, 946).

ŠAY Kirg. 20th c. **Šay-bek** [Шаибеков], a writer (Hudožniki Sov. Kirgizii. M., 1951); Chuv. 18th-19th c. **Šay-čura** [Шайчуринъ] (Magn. 94); Chuv. 18th-19th c. **Šay-murza** [Шаймурза] (Magn. 94); *TN:* Bashk. 1760 **Šayčurino** (< **Šay-čura**) [Шайчюрино], a village (MIB IV/2, 28). ✧ I. 'Strong, brave' cf. Chag. *šay* 'stark, tapfer, tüchtig' (Radl. IV, 926); II. 'Nice like silk' cf. Kzk. *šay-gül* (Žanuzakov); III. 'Shah's; great or good of its kind; the best, the greatest' (Sattarov).

ŠAY-BULAT Chuv. 18th-19th c. **Šay-bulat** [Шайбулатъ] (Magn. 94). ✧ 'Strong steel'. ⇨ **ŠAY + BULAT.**

ŠAY-MERDEN see **ŠAH-MERDAN**

ŠAY-TEREK Tat. 1614 **Šay-terek** [Шайтерекъ], a murza from the region of Astrakhan (AI III, 22). ⇨ **ŠAY + TERÄK.**

ŠAYΓLAN Uzb. 1624 **Šayγlan** [Шаиглан], from Bukhatra (Miller, Ist. Sib. II, 316).

ŠAYXUN Maml. 15th c. **Šayχun / Šayχu** [Σειχοῦν], an emir (Byz. Turc. 271).

ŠAYÏMBET Kirg. **Šayïmbet** [Шайымбет] (Jud. 69, 598). ⇨ **ŠAY** + suff. *-ïmbet*.

ŠAYÏN-MÄRAN Crm. **Šayïn-märan** [Шайын Мäран] (Proben VII, 37). ⇨ **ŠAHİN + MARAN?**

ŠAYÏRQAY Kzk. **Šayïrqay** [Шайыркаi], a folklore hero (Proben III, 308 /261/). ⇨ **ŠAİR** + dim. suff. *-qay*.

ŠAYQUM Bashk. 1778 **Šayqum** [Ягафер Шаикумов] (MIB V, 79).

ŠAYLA Bashk. 1754 **Šayla** [Шайла Кулумбетев] (MIB IV/1, 83).

ŠAYLÏ Bashk. 1780 **Šaylï** [Шайлы Купаев] (MIB V, 103).

ŠAYMAQAN Kkalp. 20th c. **Šaymaqan** [Шаймакъан / Шаймақан] (Bask., Kkalp. 402, KkRS 776).

ŠAYMAN Chuv. 18th-19th c. **Šayman** [Шайманъ] (Magn. 94); Uzb. **Šayman** [Джамантура Шаймановъ] (SKSO III, 158); Uzb. **Šayman** [Балтабай Шаймановъ] (SKSO III, 166). ⇨ **ŠAY** + suff. *-man*.

ŠAYMET Chuv. 18th-19th c. **Šaymet** [Шайметь] (Magn. 94). ⇨ **ŠAY** + suff. *-met*. See also **ŠAYÏMBET**.

ŠAYNA Chuv. 18th-19th c. **Šayna** [Шайна] (Magn. 94).

ŠAYSUP Tat. 1519 **Šaysup** [Шаисупъ] (PSRL XIII, 32).

ŠAYUN-SAS Alt. 19th c. **Šayun-sas** [Шайун-Сас-богатыри], folklore heroes (Verb., In. 154). ✧ '?-hair/morass'. ⇨ **SAZ?**

ŠAKEY Tat.(Sib.) 1600 **Šakey / Šaki?** [Кебяк Шакеев] (Miller, Ist. Sib. II, 156).

ŠAKİ see **ŠAQÏ**

ŠAKİR Bashk. 1793 **Šakir** [Кузей Шакиров] (MIB V, 332); Kkalp. 20th c. **Šäkir** [Шəкир] (KkRS 776). ✧ 'Thankful, grateful, quiet' (Ar.) (Sattarov, Kusimova).

ŠAQ see **ČAQ**

ŠAQA see **ČAQA**

ŠAQAY Tat. 1714 **Šaqay** [Шакай] (MIB III, 118); Bashk. 1756 **Šaqay** [Шакай Исяков] (MIB IV/1, 122). ⇨ **ČAQA** + dim. suff. *-y*. See also **ŠİR-ŠAQAY.**

ŠAQAMAN Kzk. 19th c. **Šaqaman** [Шакаманъ], a field (AOO 38); *TN:* Kzk. 19th c. **Šaqaman** [Шакаманъ], a field (AOA 66). ✧ 'Young boy, little child' cf. Kzk. PN *Šaqa-bay* (Žanuzakov-Esbaeva). ⇨ **ČAQA** + suff. *-man.*

ŠAQAN see **ČAQAN**

ŠAQAR Khorezm./Chag. / Tat.(GH) 14th c. **Šaqar-bek** [Шакарбек], Özbeg Khan's (1312-1341) daughter (MIT I, 516). ✧ 'Brave, heroic, nimble' cf. Kzk. *šaqar* 'tapfer, brav, kühn, durchtrieben' (Radl. IV, 931), *šaqar* 'бедовый; отчаянный' (KzRS).

ŠAQARÏMBET Bashk. 1754 **Šaqarïmbet** [Иней Шакарымбетев] (MIB IV/1, 85). ⇨ **ŠAQAR** + suff. *-ïmbet.*

ŠAQÏ Kzk. 19th c. **Šaqï-bay / Šaki-bay?** [Шакыбай / Шакибай] (AOK 90, 94).

ŠAQÏR Alt. 19th-20th c. **Šaqïr** [Шакыр], fem. (OjrRS 214). ⇨ **ČAГÏR?**

ŠAQMAN Balk. **Šaqman** [Шакмановъ], a prince from a *taubiy* family (Karaulov 52); Bashk. 1756 **Šaqman** [Шакман Юсупов] (MIB IV/1, 122). ✧ 'Heroism' cf. Bashk. *Šaqman* 'батырлык дәрәжәhe' (Kusimova).

ŠAQPÏN see **ALTÏN-ŠAQPÏN**

ŠAQŠA Kzk. **Šaqša** [Schakscha / Шакша], Ǧanï-bek's father (Proben III, 47 /62/). ✧ 'Tobacco case; nickname of the Tatars' cf. Kzk. *šaqša* 'das Horn zum Aufbewahren des Schnupftabaks', *šaqša bas* 'Spottnamen für Tataren' (Radl. IV, 935).

ŠAQTÏ Kirg. 20th c. **Šaqtï-gül** [Шактыгюль], fem. (Abramzon-Sulejmanov). ✧ 'Mine' cf. Kirg. *šaqtï* (R.) 'шахта' (Jud.).

ŠAQUM Kzk. 19th c. **Šaqum** [Шакумъ] (AOP 10).

ŠAL see **ČAL**

ŠALA see **ČALA**

ŠALDÏ see **ČALDÏ**

ŠALDÏQ see **ČALDÏQ**

ŠALГÏM-BAY see **ŠALГÏN**

ŠALГÏN Kzk. 19th c. **Šalγïm-bay** [Шалгымбай] (SOK 24); Kzk. 19th c. **Šalγïn-bay** [Сулейманъ Шалгынбаевъ] (Pam. kn. Turg. 59); Kzk. 19th c. **Šalγïn-bay** [Шалгынбай] (AOK 6). ✧ 'High green grass' cf. Kzk. *šalγïn* 'hohes grünes Gras, welches zum Mähen tauglich ist, bei dem man die Füllen zum Abweiden anbindet' (Radl. IV, 965).

ŠALÏ Trkm. 20th c. **Šalï** [Šalï] (Zaj. 1971, 332); Bashk. 1754 **Šalï** [Шали Чагирчин] (MIB IV/1, 83); Trkm. 20th c. **Šālï** [Шалы] (TrkmRS 751). ✧ 'Rice' cf. Trkm. *šālï* 'рис' (TrkmRS), Kzk. *şalı* 'kabuğundan temizlenmemiş pirinç, çeltik' (KzTS).

ŠALÏKEY Bashk. 1706 **Šalïkey** [Келмекей Шаликеев] (MIB III, 27). ✧ '(Small) Grain of rough rice'? ⇨ **ŠALÏ** + suff. *-key.*

ŠALÏP Kzk. 19th c. **Šalïp** [Шалиппай] (SOK 74).

ŠALQAR Kzk. 19th c. **Šalqar** [Шалкарбай] (AOK 42); Kzk. 19th c. **Šalqar** [Шалкарбай] (AOO 54). ✧ 'A large lake' cf. Kzk. *šalqar* 'ein grosser See' (Radl. IV, 963).

ŠALQÏM Maml. 1311 **Šalqïm** [شلتم الامير الكرجى], an emir (Dawād. 255).

ŠALTA Kzk. 19th c. **Šalta** [Шалтабай] (SODž. 48).

ŠALTAY Kzk. 19th c. **Šaltay** [Шалтай] (AOAtb. 2); *TN:* Kzk. **Šaltay** [Šaltaj / Шалтай], a tomb (Karta JAR XI,).

ŠALTAQ Kzk. 1822 **Šaltaq-batïr** [چالطاق باطر / Шалтак батыр] (MIK IV, 458, 462). ✧ 'Debauched' cf. East.T. *šaltaq* 'verführt' (Radl. IV, 965).

ŠALTAN Alt. **Šaltan** [Шалтанъ и Алтанъ] (Nikiforov 4).

ŠALTÏQ Kzk. 19th c. **Šaltïq** [Шалтыкъ] (AOP 70); Kzk. 19th c. **Šaltïq** [Шалтыкъ] (AOK 22); Bashk. 1722 **Šaltïq-abïz** [Шалтык-Абыз] (MIB I, 113); *TN:* Bashk. / Tat.? 1719 **Šaltïq** [Шалтыкъ], a village (MIB III, 163).

ŠALTÏRAQ Alt. 19th-20th c. **Šaltïraq** [Шалтырак], fem. (OjrRS 214); Alt. 19th-20th c. **Šaltïraq** [Шалтырак] (OjrRS 210). ✧ 'Light-hearted, neglectful' (OjrRS).

ŠAM Kzk. **Šam-pay** [Шампай] (PKTO 40). ✧ 'Light, candle' cf. Chag., East.T., Kzk., Tat. *šam* 'das Licht, die Kerze' (Radl. IV, 991).

ŠAMA Kzk. 19th c. **Šama** [Баламбетъ Шаминовъ] (Grod., Pril. 101); Kzk. **Šama-törö** [Шама Төрö] (Proben III, 70 /91/). ✧ I. 'Strength' cf. Kzk. *šama* 'die Kraft, die nötig ist um etwas auszuführen' (Radl. IV, 991); II. 'Residue/sludge of tea' cf. Chag., Kzk. etc. *šama* 'der Theegrund' (Radl. IV, 991), Bashk. *šama* 'остаток заваренного чая' (BRS).

ŠAMAГANA Bashk. 1792, 1793 **Šamaγana** [Шамагана Идильбеев / Идельбеев] (MIB V, 328). ⇨ **ŠAMA?** + suff. *-γana.*

ŠAMAY Nog.? **Šamay** [Шамай] (Žirm., Epos 400). ⇨ **ŠAMA** + suff. *-y.*

ŠAMAQ Bashk. 1783 **Šamaq** [Имангул Шамаков] (MIB V, 139, 199); Kzk. 19th c. **Šamaq** [Шамакъ] (AOP 42); Kzk. 19th c. **Šamaq-pay** [Шамакпай] (SODž. 56). ⇨ **ŠAMA** + suff. *-q.*

ŠAMAQAY Kzk. 19th c. **Šamaqay** [Шамакай] (AOK 66). ⇨ **ŠAMA** + suff. *-qay.*

ŠAMBET Kirg. **Šambet** [Шамбет] (Jud. 96, 288); Bashk. 1712 **Šembet** [Шембет Илишев] (MIB III, 86). ⇨ **ŠAM / ŠAÏM?** + suff. *-bet.*

ŠAMÏR Kirg. **Šamïr-bek** [Шамырбек] (Jud. 150, 708).

ŠAMÏŠ Kzk. 19th c. **Šamïš** [Шамыш] (AOO 46).

ŠAMÏT Kzk. 19th c. **Šamït** [Шамитъ] (Grod., Pril. 190).

ŠAMÏZ-TAYÏŠMA Uyg. 12th c. - 14th c. **Šamïz-tayïšma** [Şamız Tayışma] (Radl., USp. 121, DTS, EUTS). ⇨ **TAYÏŠMA.**

ŠAMŠAQAN Yak.? / Tung.? 1649 **Šamšaqan** [Шамшаканъ] (AI IV, 76).

ŠAMWAN Kzk. 19th c. **Šamwan** [Довлатъ Шамвановъ] (Grod., Pril. 193).

ŠAN Kzk. **Šan** [Шанъ] (AOA 142).

ŠAN-GEREY see **ŠAHİN-GEREY**

ŠANDA Kzk. 1679 **Šanda** [Шанда] (DAI VIII, 47).

ŠANKİ Kzk. 19th c. **Šanki-bay** [Шанкибай] (AOK 122).

ŠAÑ see **ČAÑ**

ŠAÑ-DAYAQ Kzk. **Šañ-dayaq** [Шандайак] (Proben III, 50 /65/). ⇨ **ŠAHİN + TAYAQ?**

ŠAÑ-DİMÏ Alt. 19th c. **Šañ-dimï / Mañ-dimï?** [Шанг-дімы / Манг-димы] (Verb., In. 94).

ŠAÑΓARA Kzk. 19th c. **Šañγara** [Шангара] (AOP 34).

ŠAÑLÏ Nog. 20th c. **Šañlï-bay** [Шанълыбай], a chief (?) whose name was given to the Aq-noγay clan (Bask., Nog. 132). ⇨ **ČAÑ + suff. -lï.**

ŠAÑMAQ Alt. 19th-20th c. **Šañmaq** [Шанмак], fem. (OjrRS 214).

ŠAPAQ Kzk. 1785 **Šapaq-batïr** [Шапак батыр] (MIK IV, 60). ✧ I. 'Horizon, skyline' cf. Kzk. *šapaq* 'der Horizont' (Radl. IV, 982); II. 'Gum of eyes'? ⇨ **ČAPAQ.**

ŠAPŠAQ Nog. 20th c. **Šapšaq** [Шапшакъ], husband of one of Baskakov's informants from the Sarï-awul (Bask., Nog. 144). ✧ 'Impure, untidy' cf. Tat. *šapšaq* 'unreinlich, unsauber, unordentlich' (Radl. IV, 985).

ŠAR Bashk. 1755 **Šar** [Ижпулда Шаров] (MIB IV/1, 101). ✧ I. 'Hone, oilstone' cf. Shor *šar* 'der Schleifstein' (Radl. IV, 950); II. 'Chaff' cf. Kzk. *šār* 'die Spreu' (Radl. IV, 950).

ŠAR-ŽETİM Kzk. 19th c. **Šar-žetim** [Шаржетымъ] (AOP 82). ⇨ **ŠAR + YETİM.**

ŠARA Kzk. 19th c. **Šara** [Шара] (AOO 58); Kzk. 19th c. **Šara** [Шара] (AOA 154). ✧ I. 'Eyehole' (Žanuzakov); II. 'Measure' (Žanuzakov) cf. Kzk. *šara* 'die Möglichkeit, der Wille, das Hilfsmittel' (Radl. IV, 951); III. 'A large wooden' cf. Shor, Kzk. *šara* 'eine grosse Holzschüssel, auf die man das gekochte Fleisch legt' (Radl. IV, 951). See also **QAQ-ŠARA.**

ŠARAY Trkm. **Šaray** [Шарай Нураковъ] (Ščeglov IV, 188).

ŠARALDAY Kirg. **Šaralday** [Шаралдай] (Jud. 520).

ŠARANAY Alt. **Šaranay** [Шаранай и Аранай], Aranay's brother (Nikiforov 3).

ŠARAP Kkalp. 20th c. **Šarap** [Шарап] (KkRS 776); Tat.(Ishim) **Šarap-qul** [Бітпак Шарап кул] (Proben IV, 189 /235/). ✧ 'Wine' cf. Uyg., Chag., Crm., Turk. *šarap* 'ein Getränk, der Wein' (Radl. IV, 951). See also **PİTPAQ-ŠARAB.**

ŠARAPAT Kirg. **Šarapat** [Шарапат] (Jud. 260). ✧ 'Nobleness, honesty, honour' cf. Kirg. *šarapat* (Ar.) 'благородство; честь' (Jud.).

ŠARBAQ Kzk. 19th c. **Šarbaq-pay** [Шарбакпай] (AOP 42). ✧ 'Fence; courtyard' cf. Kzk. *šarbaq* 'der Zaun, die Hecke, der Hof' (Radl. IV, 959).

ŠARDAM Kzk. 19th c. **Šardam-bay / Šardan-bay?**

[Шардамбай] (AOP 94).

ŠARDÏ Bashk. 1735-1737 **Šardï-bay** [Беккул Шардыбаев] (MIB III, 341, 375).

ŠAREY Tat. 18th c. **Šarey** (<**Šarï?**) [Шарей Сайдашевъ] (Nepljuev 825). ⇨ **ŠARAY?**

ŠARÏQ see **ČARÏQ**

ŠARÏQAY Bashk. 1739 **Šarïqay** [Шарыкай / Шурыкай] (MIB I, 375). ⇨ **ČARÏQ + suff. -ay.**

ŠARİP see **ŠERİF**

ŠARQ Maml. 14th c. **Šarq-eri** [شرقرى / Şarkeri] (Tarǰ/Houtsma 45, Tarǰ/Toparlı 42). ✧ 'East(ern)'? cf. Turk. *šarq* 'der Osten, östlich' (Radl. IV, 953) (<Ar.).

ŠARQAY Kzk. **Šarqay** [Шаркай], a folklore hero (Proben III, 261 /308/). ⇨ **ŠAR + suff. -qay.**

ŠARQAR Kzk. 19th c. **Šarqar-bay** [Шаркарбай] (AOO 10).

ŠARMAN Kzk. 19th c. **Šarman** [Шарманъ] (AOO 2).

ŠARŠE Kirg. **Šarše** [Шарше] (Jud. 36, 642, 896). ✧ 'A kind of tree' cf. Kirg. *šarše* 'название дикорастущего дерева' (Jud.).

ŠARTÏM Kzk. 19th c. **Šartïm-bay** [Шартымбай] (AOP 42).

ŠARUQAN Kuman 1096, 1107, 1117 **Šaruqan** [Шаруканъ / Шуруканъ], a Polovets prince, Atraq's father (Ipat. 186 /191/, 187 /191/, Lavr. 241(164), 271(189), 272, PSRL VII, 20-21). ✧ I. 'Dragon' (Baskakov); II. 'Šora-χan' (Baskakov).

ŠAŠAY Kzk. 19th c. **Šašay** [Шашай] (AOA 62).

ŠAŠİM-BAY see **ŠAŠİN**

ŠAŠİN Kzk. 19th c. **Šašim-bay** [Шашимбай] (AOP 70); Kzk. 19th c. **Šašin-bay** [Тажибай Шашинбаевъ] (AUK 865).

ŠAŠKE Kzk. 19th c. **Šaške** [Шашке] (AOK 114). ✧ 'Little hair' cf. Shor, Kzk. *šaš* 'die Haare' (Radl. IV, 973) + suff. -*ke.*

ŠAŠLÏ see **SAČLÏ**

ŠAŠLÏQAN Nog. 20th c. **Šašlïqan** [Шашлыкъан Къылас къызы / Шашлыкан Класова], one of Baskakov's informants from the aul of Nökis (Bask., Nog. 143). ⇨ **SAČLÏ + fem. suff. -qan(1).**

ŠATAY Bashk. 1735 **Šatay** [Шатай Кызыкуртовъ], a tarχan (Vel.-Zern., Bašk. 20). ⇨ **ŠADAY?**

ŠATAQ Kzk. 19th c. **Šataq** [Шатакъ] (AOA 142). ✧ 'Confused (affair); scandal' cf. Kzk. *šataq* 'запутанное дело, скандал' (KzRS).

ŠATÏR Trkm. 1550 **Šatïr-bek** [Шатыр-бек], governor (daruγa) (MIT II, 61,70). ✧ 'Groom, stirrup-holder, henchman' cf. Trkm. *šatïr* 'стремянный' (TrkmRS).

ŠATUN Türk 7th c. - 9th c. **Šatun-tarqan** [šatun tarqan] (DTS).

ŠAULUXLARÏ Balk. 20th c. **Šauluχlarï**, a former qul-family (Pröhle, Balk. XV, 255). ✧ '(One of) one's horses of noble race' cf. Balk. *šauluχ* 'ein Pferd edler Rasse von grösserem Wuchs' (Pröhle, Balk. 255) +

poss. suff. *-larï*.

ŠAW-BATA Uzb. **Šaw-bata** [Шаубата] (SKSO III, 182). ⇨ BATA I.?

ŠAWÏP-KEL Kzk. 19th c. **Šawïp-kel** [Шаубкелъ] (AOK 22); Kzk. 19th c. **Šawïp-kel** [Шаукпель (!)] (AOK 2); Kzk. 19th c. **Šawïp-kel** [Шаупкель] (AOK 34). ✧ 'Come riding at full speed' cf. Kzk. *şabuv [şap- / şab-]* 'atla koşturmak, atla hızlı gitmek, atla hamle yapmak' (KzTS). ⇨ KEL.

ŠAWQA Uzb. **Šawqa** [Шаука] (SKSO III, 174). ✧ 'Lazy, idle; slow'? cf. Kzk. *şav* 'tembel, yavaş' (KzTS) + suff. *-qa*.

ŠAWQÏR Kzk. 19th c. **Šawqïr** [Шаукыръ] (AOK 110); Kzk. 19th c. **Šawqïr** [Шаукыръ] (AOP 58).

ŠAWQUN Tat. 1698 **Šawqun** [Иванъ Шавкуновъ], „kungurets" (a man coming from Kungur) (Kungursk. akty 272). ✧ I. 'Ghost' cf. Tat. *šawqïn* 'ein Wesen, das dem Menschen im Walde, auf dem Felde, bei Kirchhöfen und ganz besonders dort erscheint, wo sich Jemand erhängt oder ertränkt hat' (Radl. IV, 929); II. Chag. *šawqun/šawqum* 'das Geräusch, der Tumult' (Radl. IV, 929).

ŠABAL Kzk. **Šabal** [Шабал] (Proben III, 586 /667/); Kzk. **Šäbäl** [Шäбäл] (Proben III, 622 /705/). ✧ 'The tenth month of the Arabian lunar calendar' (Ar.) (Žanuzakov).

ŠADÏƔAY Alt. 19th c. **Šadïɣay-qō** [Шаадыгай-коо], fem. (Verb., In. 101).

ŠAH-RUX Khorezm./Chag. 1405-1447 **Šāh-ruχ** [شاهر / Σιαχρούχ / Шахрух], the Timurid sultan (1405-1447) of Khorasan (Ibn Taghrīb. VIII, 59, 136, Byz. Turc. 274, MIT I, 56-59, 525, 526, 530 etc.); Turk. 1540 **Šah-ruχ** [Şāhruh], chief of a tribe (cemaat) in Diyarbakır, Turkey (Demirtaş 51). ✧ 'Shah's hero' cf. P. *ruχ* 'Recke, Thurm im Schachspiel' (Justi 277). ⇨ ŠAH.

ŠARÏP see **ŠARÏP**

ŠÄHER Trkm. 20th c. **Šäher** [Šäher] (Zaj. 1971, 330); Trkm. 20th c. **Šäher** [Шэхер] (TrkmRS 766). ✧ 'Town' cf. Trkm. *šäher* 'город' (TrkmRS) (<P.).

ŠÄKÏR see **ŠAKÏR**

ŠÄL Tuv. 19th c. **Šäl-ɣan** [Шялъ-ганъ], a hero of a tale (Potanin IV, 424-427).

ŠÄRÏ Kkalp. 20th c. **Šäri-bay** [Шәрибай] (KkRS 776); Kkalp. 20th c. **Šäri-gül** [Шәригул], fem. (KkRS 779, Baskakov: OSA 141); Kkalp. 20th c. **Šäri-χan / Šeri-χan** [Шерихан] (KkRS 779). ✧ 'Sad' (Baskakov), cf. Kkalp. *šer* 'печаль, тоска' (KkRS).

ŠÄRÏYPA Kkalp. 20th c. **Šäriypa** [Шәрийпа], fem. (KkRS 779). ✧ 'Famous, respeted; merciful, saint' cf. Tat. fem. *Šärifä* (Ar.) 'id.' (Sattarov). ⇨ ŠERÏF + fem. suff. *-a/-e*.

ŠÄW-DÄWLET Tat.(Lit.) 1590 **Šäw-däwlet / Šaw-dawlet?** [Шавдавлетъ Мамтековичъ] (Lit. Tat. 66).

⇨ ? + DÄWLÄT.

ŠÄW-QAL Tat. 1537 **Šäw-qal** [Шавкалъ] (PSRL XIII, 116); Tat.(GH) **Šew-qal** [Шевкалъ / Щолканъ / Щелканъ Дуденевичъ], envoy of the Horde (PSRL XVI, 65). ⇨ QAL I. / II.?

ŠÄBÄL see **ŠABAL**

ŠÄR-BÄNÜ Kzk. **Šär-bänü** [Шәрбәнÿ], fem. (Proben III, 620 /702/). ⇨ ŠER / ŠÏR + BANÏ.

ŠÄRÜŠ-ŠÄBÄL Kzk. **Šärüš-šäbäl** [Schärüsch Schübül (!) / Шäрÿш Шäбäл] (Proben III, 468 /543/, 490 /566/).

ŠE-MARDAN see **ŠAHÏ-MERDAN**

ŠE-MERDÄN see **ŠAHÏ-MERDAN**

ŠEGÄNÄY Bashk. 1740, 1742 **Šegänäy / Šigänäy** [Шеганай Бурчаков / Шиганай Барсуков / Шеганай Бурчаков] (MIB I, 378, III, 513).

ŠEGE Kzk. 18th c. - 19th c. **Šege** [Шеге] (Tynyšp. 71); Kzk. 19th c. **Šege-bay** [Шегебай] (AOA 30); Kzk. 19th c. **Šege-bay** [Шегебай] (AOK 130); Kzk. 19th c. **Šege-bay** [Шегебай] (AOO 18); Kkalp. 20th c. **Šege-bay** [Шегебай] (KkRS 776); Kzk. 19th c. **Šegi-bay** [Шегибай] (AOK 38). ✧ I. 'Temple' cf. *šegä* 'die Stelle oberhalb der Schläfen; die Schädelhöhle (die Stelle, wo sich das Gehirn befindet' (Radl. IV, 997), Kzk. *šeke* 'висок' (KzRS); II. 'Nail' (wishing the child be healthy - Žanuzakov), cf. Kzk. *šegä* 'der Nadel' (Radl. IV, 999). ⇨ ŠEKE.

ŠEGEY Chuv. 18th-19th c. **Šegey** [Шегей] (Magn. 94).

ŠEGEM-BAY see **ŠEGEN**

ŠEGEN Kzk. 19th c. **Šegem-bay** [Шегембай] (AOO 46); Kzk. 1817 **Šegen** [چکن / Шеген] (MIK IV, 312, 319); Kzk. 1842 **Šegen** [Шегень] (Dobrosm., Turg. 353, 399); Kzk. 19th c. **Šegen** [Шегенъ] (AOAtb. 14); Kzk. 19th c. **Šegen** [Шегенъ] (AOK 122); Kkalp. 20th c. **Šegen** [Шеген] (KkRS 776); Kzk. 19th c. **Šegen-bay** [Шегенбай] (AOA 90); Kzk. 1817 **Šekin** [چکن / Шекн] (MIK IV, 317). ✧ Hypoc.-shortened form of *Šege* (Žanuzakov).

ŠEGER see **ŠEGÏR**

ŠEGEREK Kzk. 18th c. - 19th c. **Šegerek** [Шегерек] (Tynyšp. 66). ⇨ ŠEGÏR? + dim. suff. *-ek*.

ŠEGÏ see **ŠEGE**

ŠEGÏR Kzk. 19th c. **Šeger / Šegir** [Шегеръ] (AOA 34); Kzk. 18th c. - 19th c. **Šegir** [Шегр] (Tynyšp. 67). ✧ 'Grey(-eyed)' cf. Kzk. *šegir* 'серый (о глазах человека)' (KzRS). See also ČAQÏR.

ŠEHER Chuv. **Šeher-Jan** [Šĕχĕrdž'ĕn'], fem. (Mészáros 215). ✧ 'Very famous/celebrated' cf. Tat. *Šähir* 'id.' (Ar.) (Sattarov), Bashk. fem. *Šähär* 'id.; town' (P.) (Kusimova).

ŠEHERČÄK Chuv. 19th c. **Šeherčäk** [Schechertschak], fem. (Kronheim 96). ✧ 'Very famous/celebrated (little child)' cf. Tat. *Šähir* 'id.' (Ar.) (Sattarov), Bashk. fem. *Šähär* 'id.; town' (P.) (Kusimova).

ŠEYBAN Oghuz/Trkm. 13th c. **Šeyban** [شبان / Шейбан-хан], Esli-χan's son (Abulg./Kon. 1010).

ŠEYBANİ Khorezm./Chag.? 15th c. **Šeybani-χan** [محمد / شيبانى خان] / / Šejbāni], Muhammad Sheybani, Abul Khair Khan's grand-son (Šejb. L, LI ff.).

ŠEYDAYÏ Trkm. 20th c. **Šeydayï** [Šeydayï] (Zaj. 1971, 328); Trkm. 20th c. **Šeydāyï** [Шейдайы] (TrkmRS 755). ❖ 'Passionately loving/amorous' cf. Trkm. *šeydāyï* 'страстно влюбленный' (TrkmRS) (<P.).

ŠEYX Tat. **Šik-čura**, a Tatar prince in Mordvin lands (Smyrnov 279); Trkm. 20th c. **Šïχ** [Šïh] (Zaj. 1971, 326); Trkm. 20th c. **Šïχ** [Шых] (TrkmRS 765). ❖ Sheikh / Shaykh (Ar.), 'chief, head, old man' (Ahmed). Cf. Trkm. *šïχ* 'id.' (TrkmRS). Title, used also as a secondary component of male names. The name of a Trkm. tribe (*Šïh*).

ŠEYX-QUTLU-ŠİR see **QUTLU-ŠİR**

ŠEYXİM Chag. 16th c. **Šeyχim** [Шейхим] (Ivanov 178, 180, 181, 183, 185-188, 250); Chag. 16th c. **Šeyχim** [Шейхим], an emir (Ivanov 178, 201, 207); Khorezm./Chag. **Šeyχim-sultan** [شيخيم سلطان], a Sheybanid (Šejb. LII.). ❖ 'My Sheykh' (Ar.). ⇨ **ŠEYX** + poss. suff. -*im*.

ŠEKÄR see **ŠEKER**

ŠEKE Kzk. 1817 **Šeke** [چاكى / Шеке] (MIK IV, 312, 319). ❖ I. 'Temple' cf. *šegä* 'die Stelle oberhalb der Schläfen; die Schädelhöhle (die Stelle, wo sich das Gehirn befindet)' (Radl. IV, 997), Kzk. *šeke* 'висок' (KzRS); II. 'Nail' (wishing the child be healthy - Žanuzakov), cf. Kzk. *šegä* 'der Nadel' (Radl. IV, 999). ⇨ **ŠEGE**.

ŠEKEY Chuv. 18th-19th c. **Šekey** [Шекей] (Magn. 95); Bashk. 1787 **Šekey** [Шекей] (MIB V, 208). ⇨ **ŠEKE** + suff. -*y*.

ŠEKER Kzk. 19th c. **Čikir-bay** [Чикирбай] (SODž. 132); Kzk. 19th c. **Seker** [Секеръ] (SOK 194); Maml. 1389 **Seker-bay** [سكر باى الخاصكى] (Iyās I, 273); Tat. 1731 **Šekär** [Шекар] (MIB III, 291); Kirg. **Šekär-yan** [Шекäр Jан], one of the forty followers of Aq-sayqal (Proben V, 394 /397/); Maml. 1254 **Šeker** [Seïf-eddin Scheker] (Makrīzī I, 53); Turk. 16th c. **Šeker** [Şeker], fem. (Ongan, Ank. II.); Yürük 1543 **Šeker** [Şeker] (Gökb., Rum. 177, 192); Yürük 1543 **Šeker** [Şeker] (Gökb., Rum. 177, 192); Trkm. 20th c. **Šeker** [Şeker], fem. (Zaj. 1971, 337); Trkm. 20th c. **Šeker** [Шекер], fem. (TrkmRS 755); Tat. 1543 **Šeker** [Şeker] (Gökb., Rum. 230); Bashk. 1686 **Šeker** [Шекерка Уразаевъ], a tarχan (Vel.-Zern., Bašk. 40); Bashk. 1735 **Šeker** [Шекеръ Уразаевъ], a tarχan (Vel.-Zern., Bašk. 13); Kkalp. 20th c. **Šeker** [Шекер], fem. (Bask., Kkalp. 404, KkRS 779); Maml. 1464 **Šeker-bay** [شكر باى الاحمدية] (Ibn Taghrib. VIII, 481, 485, 584). ❖ 'Sugar; sweet (child); darling' cf. Kuman, Turk.

688

šäkär (P.) 'der Zucker' (Radl. IV, 997), Bashk. *šäkär* 'сахар' (BRS), Kkalp. dial. *šäkär/šäker* 'сахар' (Bask., Kkalp. 394), Kzk. dial. *seker* 'шекер' (Amanž. 404), Alt. *čikir* (P.) 'der Zucker' (Radl. III, 2112) (<Mo.) dial. *čiχir* (<P.) See also **BAL-ŠEKER**.

ŠEKER-BAQÏY Bashk. 1735 **Šeker-baqïy** [Шекербакый Тымыковъ] (Vel.-Zern., Bašk. 13). ⇨ **ŠEKER + BAQÏ(Y)**.

ŠEKERMAT Turk. **Šekermat-mulla** [Shekermat Mullaning Saiye], personal name preserved in a placename south-east of Yangi-Hissar, Eastern Turkestan (Stein, Serindia Maps, Sh. No. 7). ⇨ **ŠEKER** + suff. -*mat*.

ŠEKİL Trkm. 20th c. **Šekil** [Šekil], fem. (Zaj. 1971, 337); Trkm. 20th c. **Šekil** [Шекил], fem. (TrkmRS 756). ❖ 'Form, figur' cf. Trkm. *šekil* 'форма; фигурка' (TrkmRS) (<Ar.).

ŠEKİN see **ŠEGEN**

ŠEKLİ see **ŠEKTİ**

ŠEKTİ Kzk. **Šekti-bay** (Atyns. 113); Kzk. 1794 **Šekti-bay** [چيكتى باى / Шектыбай] (MIK IV, 164); Kzk. 19th c. **Šekti-bay** [Шектыбай] (AOP 114); Kkalp. 20th c. **Šekti-bay** [Шектибай] (KkRS 776); Kzk. 1787 **Šekti-bay / Šekli-bay** [چيكلى باى / Шектыбай] (MIK IV, 95); *EN:* Kzk. 1785 **Šekti / Šekti-uruγï** [چكتى اوروغى / Шекты], a clan (MIK IV, 51). ❖ 'Last (child); suspicious?' cf. Kzk. *šekti* 'ограниченный, конечный; сомнительный, подозрительный' (KzRS).

ŠELDA Kzk. 1673 **Šelda / Šeldi?** [Шелда] (DAI VI, 316, 318).

ŠELİ Bashk. 1742 **Šeli-tarχan** [Шелы-тархан Колумбетев] (MIB III, 513).

ŠELMES Tat.(Sib.)? 1598 **Šelmes** [Шелмес Шевоев] (Miller, Ist. Sib. II, 152).

ŠELTİK Bashk. 1712, 1714 **Šeltik** [Юнай Шелтыков] (MIB III, 90, 116); Bashk. 1718 **Šeltik** [Шелтык Козяшев] (MIB III, 164).

ŠELTİN Bashk. 1737 **Šeltin** [Юнай-бай Шелтынов] (MIB III, 367).

ŠEMA Tat.(Arin) 1629 **Šema / Šama** [Шема (Шама)] (Miller, Ist. Sib. II, 345). ⇨ **ŠAMA?**

ŠEMBET see **ŠAMBET**

ŠEMÄK Bashk. 1744 **Šemäk** [Шемяк Тютюков] (MIB III, 415).

ŠEMÄKÄ Bashk. 1731 **Šemäkä** [Шемяка] (MIB III, 289-290).

ŠEMERDEY Tat.(Lit.) 1592 **Šemerdi / Šemerdey?** [Янсуба Шемердеевичъ] (Lit. Tat. 124).

ŠEMSÜDDİN-YAMAN-ĴANDAR see **YAMAN-ĴANDAR**

ŠENE Kzk. 19th c. **Šene-bay** [Шенебай] (AOAtb. 22). See also **GÜL-ŠENE**.

ŠENLİK Yürük 1543 **Šenlik** [Şenlik] (Gökb., Rum.

221). ✧ 'Joy, cheer, festivity' cf. Turk. *šänlik* 'die Freudigkeit, die Fröhlichkeit; ein öffentliches Fest mit Illumination und Feuerwerk' (Radl. IV, 1004).

ŠEPE Kzk. 19th c. **Šepe** [Шепе] (AOP 110).

ŠEPEL Bashk. 1776 **Šepel** [Шепелев Дементий] (MIB V, 216); Bashk. 1776 **Šepel** [Шепелев Василий] (MIB V, 45).

ŠER Kirg. **Šer-yan** [Шер Jан], one of the forty followers of Aq-sayqal (Proben V, 394 /397/); Trkm. 20th c. **Šir** [Šir] (Zaj. 1971, 331); Kzk. 1812 **Šir-ɣazï** [Chirghazy / Šïrgisi / Ширгазы], khan of the Little Horde (Kiši Žüz) (Levšin II, 331, Levchine 297, Radl., Aus Sib. I, 198); Uzb. 1725 **Šir-ɣazï-χan** [Scirgasi Han] (ZIRGO IX, 404); Trkm. 20th c. **Šïr** [Шир] (TrkmRS 759). ✧ Sher (P.) 'lion', an epithet of Khalifa Ali (Ahmed), cf. Kirg. *šer* (Ir.) 'лев (эпитет богатыря)' (Jud.), Turk. *şîr* (P.) 'Aslan' (Özön), also Tat. PN *Šir-ɣazi* (<P.-Ar.) (Sattarov).

ŠER-ALİ Kkalp. **Ser-alï** [Сералы] (KkRS 776); Kzk. 1845 **Ser-alï / Ser-ali?** [Аджибай Сералинь] (Konšin, Mat. V, 72); Kirg. **Šer-alï-qan / Šer-ālï-qan?** [Шераалыкан / Шералыкан] (Jud. 798); Kkalp. **Šir-ali-batïr** [Ширалей-батырь] (Hanykov, Poezdka 19). ✧ 'Lion Ali' (Žanuzakov), 'Hero-Ali', cf. Kirg. *šer* (<Ir.) 'лев (эпитет богатыря)' (Jud.), Kzk. dial. *šer* 'ер, ержүрек, қайратты [=man, brave man, hero, courageous]' (QTDS), Turk. *şîr* (<P.) 'Aslan' (Özön), also Tat. *Šir-ɣali* (Sattarov), Bashk. *Šir-ɣäli* (Kusimova), Kzk. *Šer-ɣali* (Žanuzakov-Esbaeva) (<P., Ar.). ⇨ **ALİ.**

ŠERBEN Bashk. 1759 **Šerben** [Минникей Шербенев] (MIB IV/1, 179).

ŠERDİ Bashk. 1711 **Šerdi-bay** [Шердыбай Чоптин] (MIB III, 78).

ŠEREY Tat. 17th c. **Šerey** [Ахтумерко Шереевъ], from the county of Kazan (IOAIÊK XXIX, 344).

ŠEREN Uzb. 1740 **Šerem-bay** (<**Šeren-bay**) [Шерембай], from Khiva (Hanykov, Poezdka 21). ✧ 'Nimble, brisk' cf. East.T. *šärän* 'flink' (Radl. IV, 1005).

ŠEREN-UBAN Alt. 19th c. **Šeren-uban** [Шерен-убан] (Verb., In. 123). ⇨ **ŠEREN + UBAN.**

ŠEREP Trkm. 1859 **Šereb** [Шеребъ] (ZIRGOÊtn. I, 174); Trkm. **Šerep** [Шерепъ] (Mel'gunov 320). ✧ Sharaf (Ar.) 'nobility, high rank, eminence, honour' (Ahmed), cf. Tat. PN *Šäräf / Šäräp* (Sattarov).

ŠERİF Karg. **Šarïp** [Шарыпъ] (Katanov: ZIRGOÊtn. XVII, vyp. III, 186); Bashk. 1772 **Šarïp-qul** [Устюкай Шарыбкулов] (MIB IV/2, 405); Karg. **Šārïp** [Шарып] (Proben IX, 659); Trkm. 20th c. **Šerif** [Šerif] (Zaj. 1971, 328); Trkm. **Šerif** [Шериф] (TrkmRS 757); Bashk. 1760 **Šerip-qul** [Шерыпкул Илкин] (MIB IV/2, 28). ✧ Sharif (Ar.) 'noble, honourable, highborn' (Ahmed); 'Famous, respeted; merciful, saint' (Žanuzakov), cf. Trkm. *šerif* 'благородный; святой,

почитаеный' (TrkmRS), also Bashk., Tat. PN *Šärip* 'id.' (Kusimova, Sattarov).

ŠERİK I. Tat.(GH) 1318 **Šerik** [شريك / Шерикъ], a commander of a tümän, Özbeg's the Kipchak Khan's envoy in Egypt (Duqmaq/Tizeng. I, 318, 325). ✧ 'Soldier; army' (Žanuzakov), cf. Karakh. *çeriğ* 'asker, asker dizisi, ordu' (MK/Atalay), *čerig* 'id.' (DTS), Kirg. *čerik* 'солдат (главным обр. китайский)' (Jud.) <Skr.

ŠERİK II. Kkalp. 20th c. **Serik** [Серик] (KkRS 776); Kkalp. 20th c. **Serik** [Серик] (Bask., Kkalp. 401); Kzk. **Serik-bay** [Серік Баи] (Proben III, 71 /55/); Kzk. 18th c. - 19th c. **Serik-bay** [Серикбай] (Tynyšp. 71); Kzk. 19th c. **Serik-bay / Serük-bay?** [Серокбай] (AOK 74); Kzk. 19th c. **Serik-pay** [Серикпай] (AOAtb. 18); Kzk. 19th c. **Serik-pay** [Серыкпай] (AOO 38); Kzk. 19th c. **Serik-pay** [Серикпай] (SOK 56, 90, 114, 146, 148, 306); Kzk. 19th c. **Serik-pay** [Серикпай] (SOV 100); Kzk. 19th c. **Serik-pay** [Серикпай] (SOK 14, 168); Kzk. 19th c. **Serik-pay** [Серыкпай] (SOK 176, 196); Kzk. 19th c. **Serik-pay** [Серикпай] (Konšin, Oč. 76); Kzk. 19th c. **Serik-pay** [Серыкпай] (AOAtb. 2); Chuv. 18th-19th c. **Šerik** [Шерикъ] (Magn. 95); *TN:* Kzk. **Serik-bay** [Серик-бай] (Karta JAR XI.). ✧ 'Fellow, mate' cf. Turk. *šärik* 'der Genosse, der Gefährte' (Radl. IV, 1006-7), Tat. *šärik* 'одноклассник' (TatRS), Uzb. *šerik* 'id.' (UzbRS), Kzk. *serik* 'der Genosse, der Theilnehmer' (Radl. IV, 460), Kkalp. *serik* 'компаньон, соучастник' (Bask., Kkalp. 378) (<Ar.), cf. also Kzk. PNs *Serik, Serik-bay, Serik-bek, Serik-žan* (Žanuzakov-Esbaeva). See also **BAY-SERİK, JAY-SERİK, QUN-SERİK, MULLA-SERİK.**

ŠERİMBET Kkalp. 20th c. **Serimbet** [Шеримбет] (KkRS 776). ⇨ **ŠER** + suff. -*imbet.*

ŠERİÑ Chag.? **Šeriñ-χan** [شرنك خان], commander of India (Arabš I, 460).

ŠERİP see **ŠERİF**

ŠERKEY Bashk. 1779 **Šerkey** [Манап Шеркеев] (MIB V, 91). ✧ 'Little fellow / mate'. ⇨ **ŠERİK II.** + dim. suff. -*ey.*

ŠERMÄK Chuv. 18th-19th c. **Šermäk** [Шермякъ] (Magn. 95).

ŠERMÄKEY Chuv. 18th-19th c. **Šermäkey** [Шермякей] (Magn. 95). ⇨ **ŠERMÄK** + suff. -*ey.*

ŠERÜ see **ČERİ I.**

ŠETKE Kzk. 19th c. **Šetke** [Шетке] (AOP 18).

ŠEVERDEN Tat.(Lit.) 1592 **Ševerden** [Шеверденъ Чютуровичъ] (Lit. Tat. 123).

ŠEWLELİ Tat.(Sib.) 1599 **Šewleli** [Шевлели], one of Küčüm's wives (AI II, 17, 21).

ŠEMŠAT Trkm. 20th c. **Šemšat** [Šemšat], fem. (Zaj. 1971, 340); Trkm. 20th c. **Šemšāt** [Шемшат], fem. (TrkmRS 757). ✧ 'Boxwood (Buxus sempervivens)' cf. Trkm. *šemšāt* 'самшит вечнозелёный, букс, кавказская пальма' (TrkmRS) (<P.).

ŠĪ Kzk. 19th c. **Ši-bay** [Шибай] (AOP 74); Kzk. 1819 **Ši-bek** [Шибек] (MIK IV, 324); Az. / Trkm.? 1508 **Ši-bek-χan** [شيبك خان] (Dorn 455). ✧ 'A kind of high grass' cf. Kzk. *šī* 'hartes Steppengrass; Matten aus diesem Grase, welche man von aussen um das Jurtengitter befestigt' (Radl. IV, 1066), Kkalp. dial. *šiy* 'чий (вид болотного растения из которого изготовляются цыновки)' (Bask., Kkalp.) (<R.) *čij* (<Trk.) *čiy / čī* (Šipova).

ŠĪ-BUT Alt. 19th c. **Ši-but** [Ши-бутъ] (Potanin, Pred. 162). ✧ 'Grass-leg/thigh' (Potanin). ⇨ **ŠĪ + BUT.**

ŠĪ-ГALE Tat. 1514, 1519, 1541 **Ši-γale / Šiχ-ali** (<**Šeyh-ali**) [Шигалей / Шигалѣй / Шигъ-Алей / Шиголей / Шаалей, Шихалей], a ruler of Kazan (PSRL VI, 263, VIII, 266, 298 etc., XIII, 32). ✧ Shaykh-Ali (Ar.), cf. Tat. PN *Šäyχe-γali* (Sattarov). ⇨ **ŠEYX + ALİ.**

ŠĪ-ŽELEK Hak.(Shor) 1629 **Ši-želek** [Шижелек], a Mator prince (Miller, Ist. Sib. II, 355, 367, 368). ⇨ **ŠĪ?**

ŠİDÄK Nog. 1534 **Šidäk** [Шидякъ-князь], a prince (PSRL XIII, 84).

ŠİGİM Bashk. 1754, 1761 **Šigim** [Юзей Шигимов] (MIB IV/1, 79, 220); Bashk. 1761 **Šigim** [Юзей Шигимов] (MIB IV/1, 220).

ŠİГAY Tat.? 1555 **Šiγay** [Шигай-богатырь Антуловъ] (PSRL XIII, 245); Bashk. 1735 **Šiγay** [Келмекей Шигаевъ], a tarχan (Vel.-Zern., Bašk. 22); Bashk. 1738 **Šiγay** [Шигай Ишимов] (MIB III, 378); Bashk. 1749 **Šiγay** [Шигай Сепеев] (MIB III, 460); Kzk. 18th c. **Šiγay** [Шигай] (Nepljuev 716, 720); Nog. 1649 **Šiγay** [Шигай Кунратовъ] (AI IV, 123); Tat. 1710 **Šiγay / Šiχay** [Шигай, Шихай] (MIB III, 60); Kzk. 19th c. **Šiγay-bay** [Šgajbaj], a hero in a tale (AUK 82); Kirg. **Šīγay** [Шыгай] (Jud. 20, 946); Kzk. 16th c. **Šīγay-qan** [Šyγai kan], a prince (Radl., Aus Sib. I, 147). ✧ 'Poor' (Ar.) (Žanuzakov, Sattarov), cf. Chag. *čiγay / čïγay* 'arm' (Radl. III, 2109).

ŠİГANAY Bashk. 1745 **Šiγanay** [Шиганай Бурчаков] (MIB III, 548); Bashk. 18th c. **Šiγanay** [Шиганай] (Nepljuev 194); Bashk. 1752 **Šiγanay** [Шиганай Бурчаковъ] (Nepljuev 615); Bashk. 1762 **Šiγanay** [Рысбай Шиганаев] (MIB IV/1, 246); Bashk. 1777 **Šiγanay** [Кунаккилды Шиганаев] (MIB V, 64); Bashk. 1784 **Šiγanay** [Кунаккилды Шиганаев] (MIB V, 154); Bashk. 1786 **Šiγanay** [Кунаккильды Шиганаев], a principal (MIB V, 196); Bashk. 1786 **Šiγanay** [Кунаккилды Шиганаев], a principal (MIB V, 197, 198); Bashk. 1789 **Šiγanay** [Кунаккильды Шиганаев], a principal (MIB V, 243, 244).

ŠİXAY see **ŠİГAY**

ŠİXMÄT Tat.(GH) 1382, 1389 **Šiχmät** [Шихматъ / Шихоматъ] (PSRL IV, 89, VI, 103, VIII, 47, 60); Bashk. 1728 **Šiχmät** [Шихметь] (MIB III, 252). ✧ I. 'Šeyχ Aχmet'; II. 'Šah Ahmet' cf. Tat. PNs *Šäyäχmät / Šäyχmät* (Sattarov). ⇨ **ŠEYX?** + suff. *-mät*.

ŠİY-AYAQ Kkalp. 20th c. **Šiy-ayaq** [Шийайакъ] (Bask., Kkalp. 402). ⇨ **ŠĪ + AYAQ.**

ŠİYRİN see **ŠİRİN**

ŠİK see **ŠEYX**

ŠİK-BİRMEZ Kzk. 19th c. **Šik-birmes**, a character in a tale (AUK 82). ⇨ **ŠEYX + BERMES.**

ŠİK-TİMÜR Khorezm.? 1289 **Šik-timür-aqa** [شيكتيمور اقا], an emir (RaD/Jahn 23). ⇨ **ŠEYX?** + **TEMİR.**

ŠİLAQAY Uyg. 13th-14th c. **Šilaqay-ïnal-älik** (Zieme, Mat. II, 93).

ŠİLAZİN Uyg. **Šilazin** [Şilazin] (EUTS).

ŠİLDE Kzk. 19th c. **Šilde-bay** [Шильдебай] (AOK 62); Kirg. **Šilde-bay** (Atyns. 82). ✧ 'The forty hottest days of the summer' cf. Kzk. *šildä* 'die vierzig heissesten Tage des Sommers' (Radl. IV, 1079).

ŠİLDİK Kzk. 19th c. **Šildik / Šildïq?** [Шилдыкъ] (AOAtb. 26); Bashk. 1713 **Šiltik / Šiltïq?** [Шилтык] (MIB III, 97).

ŠİLGİNEY Yak.? / Tung.? 1649 **Šilginey** [Шилгинѣй], a prince (AI IV, 75).

ŠİLİK Kzk. 19th c. **Šilik-pay** [Шиликпай] (AOAtb. 26); Kzk. 19th c. **Šilik-pay** [Шиликпай] (AOP 6); Kzk. 19th c. **Šilik-pay** [Шиликпай] (AOA 142). ✧ 'A kind of plant used as firewood' cf. Kzk. *šilik* 'eine als Brennholz verwandte Pflanze' (Radl. IV, 1078).

ŠİLİMBET Kkalp. 20th c. **Šilimbet** [Шилимбет] (KkRS 776). ✧ 'Ruffled grouse; francolin' cf. Kzk. *šil* 'das Haselhuhn' (Radl. IV, 1076) + suff. *-imbet*.

ŠİLTEY Trkm. **Šiltey** [Шилтей Оразакаевъ] (Ščeglov IV, 189). ✧ 'A small pillow/cushion'? cf. Turk. *šiltä* 'ein kleines Kissen' (Radl. IV, 1079).

ŠİLTİK see **ŠİLDİK**

ŠİMA Bashk. 1734 **Šima-batïr** [Шима Батырь Кадырчиковъ], a tarχan (Vel.-Zern., Bašk. 9). ✧ 'Smooth' cf. Chag. *šima* 'glatt, poliert' (Radl. IV, 1091).

ŠİMAY Bashk. 1735 **Šimay** [Шимай Аслаевъ], a tarχan (Vel.-Zern., Bašk. 18). ⇨ **ŠİMA** + suff. *-y.*

ŠİNİT Kzk. 19th c. **Šinit-pay** [Шинитпай] (AOP 30).

ŠİNQUR see **SOÑQUR**

ŠİÑGİLTAQ NUyg.(Tar.) **Šiñgiltaq** [Schingiltak / Шиңгілтак], rival of Piñgiltaq in the tale (Proben VI, 219).

ŠİÑГUR-ÄRDÄM Uyg. 8th c. - 9th c. **Šiñγur-ärdäm** (Müller, Pfahl. 23). ⇨ **SOÑQUR? + ERDÄM.**

ŠİÑİLDEK see **ŠİÑKİLDEK.**

ŠİÑİS see **ČİÑİZ**

ŠİÑKİLDEK Kzk. 19th c. **Šiñïldek** [Шингылдекъ] (AOP 106); Kkalp. 20th c. **Šiñkildek** [Шиңкилдек]

(KkRS 776). ✧ '(Having) High, thin/piping (voice); whining, whimpering (child)' cf. Kkalp. *šiñkildek* 'id.' (KkRS), Kzk. *šiqïldaq* 'пискун' (KzRS), Kzk. *šiñïlda-* 'издавать звон, звякать' (KzRS).

ŠĪR see **ŠER**

ŠĪR-ALİ see **ŠER-ALİ**

ŠĪR-BULAT Chuv. 18th-19th c. **Šïr-bulat** [Ширбулатъ] (Magn. 95). ✧ 'Lion-steel'. ⇨ **ŠER + BULAT.**

ŠĪR-ŠAQAY Bashk. 1756 **Šïr-šaqay** [Гайса Ширшакаев] (MIB IV/1, 122); Bashk. 1756 **Šïr-šaqay** [Кусюк Ширшакаев] (MIB IV/1, 122). ⇨ **ŠER + ŠAQAY.**

ŠİRAN Oghuz/Trkm. 13th c. **Širan** [شيران / Ширан], ruler of the Qalač tribe (Abulg./Kon. 390).

ŠİRDAY Kzk. 19th c. **Širday** [Ширдай] (AOP 98). ⇨ **ŠER?** + suff. *-day.*

ŠİRÄY Bashk. 1762 **Širäy** [Максим Ширяев] (MIB IV/2, 302).

ŠİRE Khorezm. 14th c. **Šire-oɣul** [Schire-oghoul], khan of Kashghar, Toɣluq-temür's (1348-1363) stepfather (Abulg./Desm. 165-166). ✧ 'Fruit juice' cf. Chag., East.T., Turk. *širä* 'Fruchtsaft, Weinsaft' (Radl. IV, 1071). See also **MAÑDÏ-ŠİRE.**

ŠİREKİ Mo.? **Šireki** [Ширеки] (RaD II, 168).

ŠİRİY Bashk. 1735 **Širiy** [Ширий Девлетбаевъ], a tarɣan (Vel.-Zern., Bašk. 16).

ŠİRİM Bashk. 1763 **Širim** [Ширим Илишев] (MIB IV/2, 45); Kzk. 19th c. **Širim-ay** [Ширимъ-ай Тухлыбаева], fem. (SKSO 32); Bashk. 1760 **Širïm** [Ширым Илишев] (MIB IV/1, 191). ✧ I. 'My lion'; II. 'Sweat'? ⇨ **ŠER / ŠİRİN?**

ŠİRİN Trkm. 20th c. **Širin** [Širin], fem. (Zaj. 1971, 337); Trkm. 20th c. **Širin** [Ширин], fem. (TrkmRS 759); Crm.(Tat.) 1773 **Širin-bey** [Ширинъ-Бей] (PSZRI XIX, 709, 710); *EN:* Crm.(Tat.) **Širin** [Ширинъ], a Crimean Tatar tribe (PSRL VI, 287). ✧ 'Sweet (child); darling' cf. Az., Crm., Kar., Turk. *širin* 'süss, angenehm, lieblich' (Radl. IV, 1073), Kkalp., *šiyrin* 'сладкий, вкусный' (KkRS).

ŠİRİN-TEGİNÄ Tat.(GH)? 1408, 1432 **Širin-teginä / Teginä** [Ширинъ-Тегиня / Ширинъ-Тягиня], a prince of the Horde (PSRL VI, 136, VIII, 82, 96, PSRL XII, 15). ⇨ **ŠİRİN + TEGİNÄ.**

ŠİRİNXAN Kkalp. 20th c. **Šiyrinxan** [Шийринхан], fem. (KkRS 779). ⇨ **ŠİRİN** + suff. *-xan(I).*

ŠİRKİN see **ČİRKİN**

ŠİRMAN Kzk. 19th c. **Širman** [Ширманъ Дустъ Магомедовъ] (Grod., Pril. 106). ✧ 'Rosy, plump (of face)' cf. Uzb. *širmân (širmon) / sirmây(i) (širmoyi)* 'сдобная лепёшка; румяный и полный, пышный' (UzbRS).

ŠİŠ Uyg. **Šiš** [Şiş] (EUTS); Oghuz 12th c. **Šiš** [Абу-л-Аббас Шиш], a Ghurid hero, commander-in-chief

(MIT I, 441). ✧ 'Swelling, lump' cf. Shor, Turk. *šiš* 'die Geschwulst, angeschwollen' (Radl. IV, 1082), Uzb. *šiš* 'опухоль, шишка, отёк, вздутие' (UzbRS).

ŠİŠAR Bashk. 1740 **Šišar / Šišär?** [Шишар Тарханов] (MIB I, 397).

ŠİŠİK Turk. 19th c. **Šišik-oɣlu**, a Zeybek (Kúnos 1891, 119). ✧ 'A two-year-old sheep' cf. Turk. *šišik* 'ein zweijähriges Schaf, das fett zu werden beginnt' (Radl. IV, 1084). See also **TUSAQ.**

ŠİŠQAT Selj. 12th c. **Šišqat** [شيشتاط], an emir of Atabeg Abubekir (Rāwandī 391).

ŠİŠMAN Kuman 1330/31 **Šišman** [Σίσμανος / Ivan Stephan Schischman], a Bulgarian sovereign (1330/31) of Kuman origin (Byz. Turc. 277); Kuman 1371-1393 **Šišman** [Σίσμανος / Schischman], a Bulgarian sovereign (1371-1393) (Byz. Turc. 277); Maml. 1423, 1425, 1439/40 **Šišman** [ششمان / اينال الششماني] (Ibn Taghrīb. VI, 569, 593, VII, 87, 102). ✧ 'Fat, corpulent, obese' (Sauvaget 48), cf. Turk. *šišman* 'dick und fett, korpulent' (Radl. IV, 1086).

ŠİTAS Kzk. 1794 **Šitas-batïr** [شيتاس باطر / Шитас] (MIK IV, 165).

ŠĪR-MERD Yürük 1543 **Šïr-merd** [Şîrmerd] (Gökb., Rum. 187, 188). ✧ 'Lion-hero' cf. Turk. *şïr* (<P.) 'Aslan' (Özön), Turk. *merd* (<P.) 'Adam, insan; erkek; yiğit' (Özön). ⇨ **ŠER.**

ŠÏBAČÏ Alt. 19th-20th c. **Šïbačï** [Шыбачы] (OjrRS 210). ✧ 'Plastering, bedaubing, smudging' (OjrRS).

ŠÏBÏŠQÏN Tuv. 19th c. **Šïbïšqïn** [Шібішкін] (Proben IX, 152).

ŠÏDAQ Bashk. 1770 **Šïdaq** [Касым Шыдаков] (MIB IV/1, 341).

ŠÏΓAY see **ŠİΓAY**

ŠÏX see **ŠEYX**

ŠÏQAYLİK Alt. 19th-20th c. **Šïqaylik** [Шыкайлик] (OjrRS 210). ✧ 'Brandy-glass' cf. R. *škalik* 'id.'.

ŠÏQAR Nog. 20th c. **Šïqar / Šïqïr** [Şikar / Шыкъар (!) Амеш (!) къызы / Шыкыр Амитова], one of Baskakov's informants from the aul of Nökis (Bask., Nog. 143); Kzk. 19th c. **Šïqar-bek** [Шикарбекъ] (AOO 42).

ŠÏQARİDUQ Kzk. 19th c. **Šïqariduq?** [Шкаридукъ] (AOO 62).

ŠÏLÏMBET Kkalp. 20th c. **Šïlïmbet** [Шылымбет] (KkRS 776). ✧ 'Tools (pipe) for smoking' cf. Kkalp. *šilïm* 'чилим, кальян (прибор для курения)' (KkRS), Kzk. *šilïm* 'die Tabakspfeife, das Räuchergefäss, die Cigarette' (Radl. IV, 1056). ⇨ **ČİLİM?** + suff. *-bet.*

ŠÏM Kkalp. 20th c. **Šïm-bay** [Шымбай] (KkRS 776). ✧ 'Clean, untainted' cf. Kzk. *šim* 'rein, unverfälscht' (Radl. IV, 1064).

ŠÏM-TÖMÜR see **ČİN-TEMİR**

ŠÏMAN Kkalp. 20th c. **Šïman** [Шыман] (KkRS 776);

Nog.? **Šïmon-batïr** [Шымон-батыр] (Žirm., Epos 395).

ŠİMAWXA   Karch. 20th c. **Šïmawχa** [Šimauχá] (Pröhle, Kar. 134).

ŠİMÏR   Kzk. 19th c. **Šïmïr / Šimir?** [Бахтибай Шимировъ] (Grod., Pril. 34). ✧ 'Quick, nimble' cf. Kzk. *šïmïr* 'бойкий' (KzRS).

ŠİMON see **ŠİMAN**

ŠİN see **ČİN**

ŠİN-BAS   Nog.? **Šïn-bas-batïr** [Шынбас-батыр] (Žirm., Epos 395). ✧ 'True/right-head' cf. Kkalp. *šïn* 'истина, правда; правдивый' (KkRS). ⇨ **ČİN + BAŠ.**

ŠİN-DAWLET   Kzk. 19th c. **Šïn-dawlet / Šin-dawlet?** [Šïn-däwlät / Шиндаулетъ] (AOP 78). ⇨ **ČİN + DÄWLÄT.**

ŠİN-GÜMİS   Kkalp. 20th c. **Šïn-gümis** [Шынгумис], fem. (KkRS 779). ✧ 'True/genuine silver'. ⇨ **ČİN + KÜMÜŠ.**

ŠİN-TEMİR see **ČİN-TEMİR**

ŠİNÏ I.   Kkalp. 20th c. **Šïnï-gül** [Шыныгул], fem. (KkRS 779). ✧ 'True, real' cf. Kkalp. *šïnï* 'настоящий, действительный, реальный' (KkRS). ⇨ **ČİN.**

ŠİNÏ II. see **ČİNÏ**

ŠİNÏKE   Kzk. 19th c. **Šïnïke** [Шыныке] (AOP 42). ⇨ **ČİNÏ** + suff. *-ke.*

ŠİŇΓUR see **SOÑQUR**

ŠİÑQU-SELİ   Uyg. 10th c. **Šïñqu-seli-tutuñ / Šïñqu-seli-tutuñ**, Uyghur translator of Altun Yaruq „Golden Beam Sutra" (DTS). ⇨ **SELİ.**

ŠİR-NİYAZ   Kzk. **Šïr-niyaz** [شیر نیاز / Šir-nijāz], fem. (Divaev, Biket 5, 21). ⇨ **ŠİR + NİYAZ.**

ŠİRAY see **ČİRAY**

ŠİRDAQ   Kirg. 19th-20th c. **Šïrdaq-bek** [Sirdak-bek], a manap (Prinz 323). ✧ 'A large ornate felt; sweat-cloth' cf. Kirg. *šïrdaq* 'текимет (шитый в два слоя орнаментированный войлок); (южн.) потник' (Jud.), Mo. *sirdeg*. See also **TOΓÏM.**

ŠİRİN-AΓİŠ   Crm.(Tat.) 1517 **Širin-aγiš** [Шыринъ-Агишъ] (PSRL XIII, 26). ⇨ **ŠİRİN + AΓİŠ.**

ŠİRÏŠPAN   Karg. **Šïrïšpan** [Шырышпанъ] (Katanov: ZIRGOÊtn. XVII, vyp. III, 171). ✧ 'Juice; juicy'? cf. Kzk. *širiš* 'der Frucht- oder Pflanzensaft' (Radl. IV, 1052) + suff. *-pan(1).*

ŠİX see **ŠEYX**

ŠQAP   Alt. 19th-20th c. **Šqap** [Шкап] (OjrRS 210). ✧ 'Chest, cupboard' cf. R. *škaf* 'id.'.

ŠOBAQ   Kzk. 19th c. **Šobaq** [Шобак] (AOA 150); Kzk. 19th c. **Šobaq-pay** [Шобакпай] (AOA 46).

ŠOΓA   Kzk. 19th c. **Šoγa** [Шога] (AOP 126).

ŠOΓAY see **ŠUQAY**

ŠOΓUR   Türk 7th c. - 9th c. **Šoγur** [šoγur] (DTS).

ŠOYÏN-QARA   Kzk. 1794 **Šoyïn-qara** [چوینکارى / Шоинкара] (MIK V, 163). ✧ '(Cast) Iron-Black'. ⇨ **ČOYÏN + QARA.**

ŠOYTA   Kzk. 19th c. **Šoyta** [Шойта] (AOK 30).

ŠOYTAS   Kzk. 19th c. **Šoytas** [Шойтасъ] (AOK 130).

ŠOYUNTAY   Kzk. 19th c. **Šoyuntay** [Шоюнтай] (AOP 90). ✧ 'Iron-like' cf. Kzk. *šoyïn* 'чугун' (KzRS) + suff. *-tay(1,2)*?

ŠOQAY see **ČOQAY**

ŠOQAR-AY   Kzk. 19th c. **Šoqar-ay** [Шокаръ-ай] (SKSO IV, otd. II, 32). ✧ ? ⇨ **AY.**

ŠOQAT   Kzk. 19th c. **Šoqat** [Шокатъ] (AOK 2).

ŠOQU   Kzk. 19th c. **Šoqu-bay** [Шокубай] (AOK 118); Kzk. 19th c. **Šuqu-bay** [Шукубай] (AOO 54). ✧ 'Pike, hunch/hump' cf. Kzk. *šoqu* 'ein vereinzelt stehender Bergkegel' (Radl. IV, 1023).

ŠOLAQ see **ČOLAQ**

ŠOLAN   Kzk. 19th c. **Šolan** [Шоланъ] (AOP 42, 114). ✧ 'Kitchen' cf. Kzk. *šolan* 'mutfak' (KzTS).

ŠOLDAN   Kzk. 19th c. **Šoldan** [Шолданъ] (AOP 22).

ŠOLQAN   Tat. 1327 **Šolqan** [Щолканъ] (PSRL XXIII, 102).

ŠOLO   Kzk. 19th c. **Šolo-pay** [Шолопай] (AOP 42).

ŠOLPAN see **ČOLPAN**

ŠOMAQ see **ČOMAQ**

ŠOMATÏŠ   Kzk. 19th c. **Šomatïš** [Шоматышъ] (AOK 106).

ŠONA   Kzk. 19th c. **Šona-bay** [Шонабай] (AOK 102, 106). ✧ 'Wolf' (<Mo.) (Žanuzakov). See also **BÖRİ, QASQÏR, QAŠQAR, QURT, MÖJEK.**

ŠONAY   Kzk. 19th c. **Šonay** [Шонай] (AOP 10); Kzk. 19th c. **Šunay** [Шунай] (AOK 94). ✧ 'Little wolf'. ⇨ **ŠONA** + suff. *-y.*

ŠONDA   Kzk. 19th c. **Šonda** [Шонда] (AOK 10).

ŠONQA   Kzk. 19th c. **Šonqa-bay** [Шонкабай] (AOP 126). ✧ I. 'Mighty/great! (voc.)'; II. 'Little wolf'? + dim./voc. suff. *-qa* or comp. *-ake*?

ŠONŠA   Kzk. 19th c. **Šonša** [Шонша] (AOO 50).

ŠONTÏ   Kzk. 19th c. **Šontï** [Шонты] (AOP 50); Kzk. 19th c. **Šontu-bay** [Шонтубай] (AOA 110).

ŠONTU see **ŠONTÏ**

ŠONU   Kzk. 19th c. **Šonu-bay** [Шонубай] (AOAtb. 54).

ŠOÑÑURLARÏ   Balk. 20th c. **Šoññurlarï** [Šoŋŋúrlarï], an Özden-family (Pröhle, Balk. 255). ⇨ **SOÑQUR?** + suff. *-larï.*

ŠOPAN see **ČOBAN**

ŠORA see **ČURA**

ŠORAQ see **ČURAQ**

ŠORATAY   Kkalp. 20th c. **Šoratay** [Шоратай] (Bask., Kkalp. 402, KkRS 776). ✧ I. 'Little slave; little friend'?; II. 'He who wets the bed'? cf. Kzk. *šora* 'der Bettpisser' (Radl. IV, 1027). ⇨ **ČURA?** + hypoc. suff. *-tay(2).*

ŠORQAY   Kzk. 19th c. **Šorqay** [Шоркай] (AOK 30).

⇨ **ČUR(A)** + suff. *-qay*.

ŠORLAR   Tuv. 19th c. **Šorlar** [Шорлар] (Proben IX, 171).

ŠORMAN   Kzk. **Šorman** [Шорман] (Proben III, 39 /50/); Kzk. 19th c. **Šorman** [Шорманъ] (AOK 50); Kzk. 19th c. **Šorman** [Шорманъ] (AOP 46); Kzk. 19th c. **Šorman** [Шорманъ] (AOK 122); Kzk. 19th c. **Šorman** [Шормановъ] (AOK 6). ⇨ **ČURAMAN?**

ŠORŠUT   Kzk. 19th c. **Šoršut** [Шоршутъ] (AOO 42).

ŠORTAN see **ČORTAN**

ŠORTÏQ   Kzk. 19th c. **Šortïq-qan** [Шортыкканъ] (AOK 2); Kzk. 19th c. **Šortuq-bay** [Шортукбай] (AOP 62).

ŠORTU   Kzk. 19th c. **Šortu-bay** [Шортубай] (AOP 118). ✧ 'Quite fat'? cf. Kzk. *šortuy* 'ziemlich dick' (Radl. IV, 1029).

ŠORTUQ see **ŠORTÏQ**

ŠORUQ   Kirg. **Šoruq** [Шорук], Aqïlay's father (Proben V, 78 /79/); Kirg. **Šoruq** [Шорук] (Proben V, 77 /79/).

ŠOSAN   Kzk. 19th c. **Šošan** [Шошанъ] (AOP 46). ✧ 'Flighty, spoiled, impertinent' cf. Kzk. *şoşan-şoşan et-* 'zıplamak, fırlamak, şımarıkça hareket etmek', *şoşanda-* 'şımarıkça hareketlerde bulunarak koşmak, konuşmak' (KzTS).

ŠOT   Kzk. 19th c. **Šot** [Шотъ] (AOA 82); *EN:* Shor 19th-20th c. **Šot** (Dyrenkova 308). ✧ I. 'Engraver, chisel' cf. Kzk. *šot* 'ein Kelt, eine Hacke (für Holzarbeiten)' (Radl. IV, 1031). According to Žanuzakov (p. 163) the name would remind an ancient custom when the umbilical cord was cut with a sharp tool.; II. 'A special kind of calculator' cf. Shor, Kzk. *šot* (R.) 'die Rechenmaschine' (Radl. IV, 1031).

ŠOTA   Kzk. 19th c. **Šota** [Шота] (AOK 130). ✧ 'Side of a cart' cf. Kzk. *šota* 'die Leiter des Wagens' (Radl. IV, 1031).

ŠOTAY   Kzk. 19th c. **Šotay** [Шотай] (AOA 22). ⇨ **ŠOTA** + suff. *-y*.

ŠOTAN   Kzk. 18th c. - 19th c. **Šotan** [Шотан] (Tynyšp. 67); Kzk. 1785 **Šotan-bahadur** [شوتان بهادر / Шотан бахадур] (MIK IV, 52, 54).

ŠOTÏ   Kzk. 19th c. **Šotï-bay** [Шотыбай] (AOAtb. 38).

ŠOTMANDAY   Kzk. 19th c. **Šotmanday** [Шотмандай] (AOP 118). ⇨ **ŠOT?** + suff. *-man* + *-day*.

ŠŌJA   Tuv. 19th c. **Šōja** [Шоџа], fem. (Proben IX, 131).

ŠŌJÏT   Tuv. 19th c. **Šōjït-pï** [Шоџыт-пі] (Proben IX, 11).

ŠÖHRĀT   Trkm. 20th c. **Šöhrāt** [Шохрат] (TrkmRS 761); Trkm. 20th c. **Šöhrät** [Šöhrät] (Zaj. 1971, 329); Trkm. **Šöχrat** [Шөхрат] (Sopieva 182). ✧ 'Fame, respect' (Sopieva), cf. Trkm. *šöhrāt* 'слава, известность' (TrkmRS) (<Ar.).

ŠÖHRÄT see **ŠÖHRĀT**

ŠÖXRAT see **ŠÖHRĀT**

ŠÖKEMEN see **ČÖKEMEN**

ŠÖKET   Kzk. 19th c. **Šöket** [Шокетъ] (AOAtb. 6).

ŠÖKLİ see **ŠÜKLİ**

ŠÖLKEY   Kzk. 1794 **Šölkey-batïr** [شولكاى باطر / Шолькей] (MIK IV, 165). ✧ 'Desert (tract), dry land' cf. Shor, Kzk. *šöl* 'die Steppe, die Wüstenei (ohne Wasser); der Durst' (Radl. IV, 1037). See also **YABAN, SÄXRA, TÏS.**

ŠÖMEK   Kzk. 19th c. **Šömek** [Шомекъ] (AOO 66).

ŠÖN   Kzk. 19th c. **Šön-bi** [Шönъ-би], a hero in a tale, Idyge's son (Potanin IV, 404).

ŠÖREK   Kzk. 19th c. **Šörek** [Шорекъ] (AOA 98).

ŠÖVKET   Trkm. 20th c. **Šövket** [Šövket] (Zaj. 1971, 329); Trkm. 20th c. **Šövket** [Шовкет] (TrkmRS 761). ✧ 'Strength, might' (Zaj. 1971), 'Fame' cf. Trkm. *šövket* 'слава' (TrkmRS) (<Ar.).

ŠÄŇGÄ   Uyg. **Šäŋgä** [Šänggä / Sängä] (Zieme, Mat. I, 76). ✧ 'Lion'? (<Tib. <Skr.) (Zieme, Mat. I, 76-77).

ŠU   Karakh. **Šu** [Şu] (MK/Atalay 852).

ŠUBAY   Kzk. 1742 **Šubay** [Choubaï] (Levchine 158). ⇨ **ČUBAY / JUBAY?**

ŠUBAR see **ČOBAR**

ŠUBÏRTBALÏ   Kzk. 19th c. **Šubïrtbalï** [Шубыртбалы] (AOAtb. 22). ✧ 'Having a necklace/collar' cf. Kzk. *šuburtpa* 'der Lügner; das Halsband' (Radl. IV, 1106) + suff. *-lï*.

ŠUΓLAQ   Chag. 16th c. **Šuγlaq** [Шуглак] (Ivanov 230).

ŠUΓULAY   Tat.(Sib.) 1684 **Šuγulay** [Шугулайка] (DAI XI, 160).

ŠUYA   Kzk. 19th c. **Šuya / Šüyä?** [Шуябай] (Grod., Pril. 84).

ŠUQAY   Karch. **Šoγay** [Шогай] (Sysoev 131); Bashk. 1764 **Šuqay** [Шукай Усманов] (MIB IV/1, 276, 277); Bashk. 1798 **Šuqay** [Шукай] (PSZRI XXV, 195). ✧ 'Brave man' cf. Kzk. *šuqay* 'tapfer' (Radl. IV, 1096). See also **ČUΓA.**

ŠUQU see **ŠOQU**

ŠUL   Shor 19th-20th c. **Šul-bay** [Šulbaj] (Dyrenkova 310). ✧ 'River' cf. Hak.(Sag.) *čul* 'der Fluss' (Radl. III, 2175).

ŠULAQ see **ČOLAQ**

ŠULAM   Kzk. **Šulam-bay** [Шуламбай] (Karta JAR XI).

ŠULΓAW   Kzk. 19th c. **Šulγaw** [Шульгау] (AOP 78); Kzk. 19th c. **Šulγaw-bay** [Шулгаубай] (AOAtb. 6). ✧ 'Foot clout' cf. Kzk. *šulγau* 'die Fusslappen' (Radl. IV, 1103).

ŠULXÏ   Karakh.? 922 **Šulχi?** [Шулхи], Almuš' father (MIT I, 163).

ŠULPAN see **ČOLPAN**

ŠULU   Crm. **Šulu-bay** [Шулубаи] (Proben VII, 154).

ŠULUN   Alt. 19th-20th c. **Šulun** [Шулун] (OjrRS 210).

ŠUM   Crm. **Šum-bey** [Schumbei], at Salgir river? (Jervis III). ✧ 'Unlucky; tricky; evil' cf. East.T., Turk., Uzb.

šum 'unglücklich, schlau, gewandt, böse' (Radl. IV, 1106).

ŠUMAQ I.   Uyg. **Šumaq**, fem. (Zieme, Mat. I, 75); Uyg. 1362 **Šumaq**, Atay-buqa's wife (Zieme, Mat. I, 83 (after Cleaves, The Sino-Mongolian Inscription of 1362: HJAs. 12 (1949), p. 87)). ⇨ **ČOMAQ?**

ŠUMAQ II. see **ČOMAQ**

ŠUMAN see **ČUMAN**

ŠUMQAR see **SOÑQUR**

ŠUMŠÏVAŠ   Chuv. 1739 **Šumšïvaš** [Шумшевашъ] (Alatyr. 146).

ŠUNAY see **ŠONAY**

ŠUNAQ   Kzk. 1794 **Šunaq-mïrza / Šunuq-mïrza?** [شونوق مرضه / Шунак] (MIK IV, 164); Tat. 1552 **Šunaq-murza** [Шунакъ-мурза] (PSRL XIII, 202). ✧ 'Having short ears; without ears' cf. Kzk. *šunaq* 'mit kurzen Ohren; ein Schimpfwort' (Radl. IV, 1098).

ŠUNČİLEY   Tat.(Lit.) **Šunčiley / Šunčuley?** [Szunczulei / Шунчилей] (Lit. Tat. 390).

ŠUNQÏLDÏQ   Kzk. 19th c. **Šunqïldïq?** [Шункыльдекъ] (AOA 114).

ŠUÑQAR see **SOÑQUR**

ŠUÑQAT   Chag. **Šuñqat** [شونتات / Шунгкатъ] (Šejb. LV.).

ŠUÑQUR see **SOÑQUR**

ŠUR see **ČOR**

ŠURA see **ČURA**

ŠURAN   Bashk. 1754 **Šuran** [Киргис Шурановъ] (MIB IV/1, 83).

ŠURҐUN   Bashk. 1740 **Šurɣun** [Сююргул Шургуновъ] (MIB I, 395).

ŠURMÏN   Kzk. 19th c. **Šurmïn / Šurma?** [Искакъ Шурмынъ] (AOAtb. 22).

ŠUŠA   Kzk. 19th c. **Šuša** [Шуша] (AOA 130).

ŠUŠALA   Kzk.? 18th c. - 19th c. **Šušala** [Шушала Хан гельдинъ], a mulla (ZOOIRGO IV, 99).

ŠUWALDAQ   Kzk. 18th c. - 19th c. **Šuwaldaq** [Шууалдак] (Tynyšp. 65, 67, 75). ✧ 'Rousing, uproarious, noisy' cf. Kzk. *šuwïldaq* 'шумливый' (KzRS), Kzk. *šuwïldaq* 'Gürültücü, hep bağıran-çağıran' (KzTS).

ŠUWAN   Kzk. 19th c. **Šuwan** [Шуанъ] (AOP 34).

ŠUWAÑ   Kzk. 19th c. **Šuwañ** [Шуангъ] (AOP 102).

ŠUWAŠ see **ČUWAŠ**

ŠŪT   Kirg. **Šūt** [Шут], one of Manas' comrades-in-arms (Proben V, 40).

ŠÜBÜTKÄY   Kipch. 1298 **Šübütkäy / Šubutqay?** [شبتكای / Шубуткай] (Baybars/Tizeng. I, 88, 111).

ŠÜGÜR   Tat.(Tüm.) 1649 **Šügür** [Шугуръ] (DAI III, 174-175); Bashk. 1735 **Šügür** [Шугуръ Рахмангуловъ], a tarɣan (Vel.-Zern., Bašk. 15); Bashk. 1766 **Šügür** [Елдаш Шугуровъ] (MIB IV/1, 320). ✧ 'Mind, reason' (Ar.) cf. Tat. *Šögur / Šöger* (Sattarov). See also **ALLA-ŠÜGÜR, KÖZÄM-**

ŠÜGÜR.

ŠÜGÜR-DÄWLÄT   Tat.(Sib.) 1601 **Šuɣur-däwlät** [Шугурдевлет] (Miller, Ist. Sib. II, 165). ⇨ **ŠÜGÜR / ŠÜKÜR + DÄWLÄT.**

ŠÜGÜRÄ   Tat. 1601 **Šügürä** [Шугура (Шугурда) Кокузов] (Miller, Ist. Sib. II, 167-168). ⇨ **ŠÜGÜR + suff. -ä.**

ŠÜYKÄ   Kzk. 19th c. **Šüykä-bay** [Шюйкабай] (AOK 106). ✧ 'Wool, ball (of wool, string)' cf. Kzk. *şüyke* 'Yün, yumak' (KzTS).

ŠÜK-TUR   Selj. 13th c. **Šük-tur / Šik-tur** [شیکتور / شکتور], Oqta's father from Asia Minor (Aqsar/Tur. 305, Aqsar/Iş. 112, Shaikh Uwais 39, 137). ✧ 'Be/remain silent! Be quiet!' cf. Karakh. *šük (tur)* 'schweige still' (MK/Brock.), *šük tur* 'успокойся!' (DTS), cf. also Rásonyi, Imp. 242. ⇨ **TUR.**

ŠÜKİR see **ŠÜKÜR**

ŠÜKLİ   Oghuz/Trkm. 14th c. - 15th c. **Sökli-melik / Šökli-melik** [Sökli Melik] (DQorq./Rossi 133, 135, 136, 143, 145, 151, 206); Oghuz/Trkm. **Šükli-melik / Šökli-melik** [Şökli Melik / Sökli Melik / Шюкли], a ruler of the giaours (unbelievers); A Türkmen emir called Šökli lived in Syria at the end of the 11th c. (M. Halil, Türkiye Tarihi. Selçuklular Devri, p. 58). According to F. Demirtaş he is a Pecheneg or Qangli-Kipchak chieftain (Ankara Dergisi VII, 355) (DQorq./Rossi 133, 135, 136 etc., DQorq. 22, 23, 27 etc.).

ŠÜKÜR   Kkalp. 20th c. **Šükir / Šükür** [Шукир], fem. (KkRS 779); Kkalp. 20th c. **Šükir-bek / Šükür-bek** [Шукирбек] (KkRS 776); Trkm. 20th c. **Šükür** [Şükür] (Zaj. 1971, 329); Trkm. 20th c. **Šükür** [Шукур] (TrkmRS 763); Bashk. 1772 **Šükür** [Шукур Абзанов] (MIB IV/2, 405); Bashk. 1786 **Šükür** [Шукур Шиганаев] (MIB V, 196); Bashk. 1827 **Šükür** [Алтынбай Шукуровъ] (TOUAK XXIV, 182); Alt.(Tel.) 1824 **Šükür** [Уйсунбай Шукуровъ] (Konšin, Mat. V, 70); Kzk. 19th c. **Šükür-bay** [Шукурбай] (Grod., Pril. 99); Kzk. 19th c. **Šükür-bay** [Кусимъ Шукурбаевъ] (Grod., Pril. 137); Kzk. 19th c. **Šükür-bek** [Шукурбекъ] (Grod., Pril. 73); Kzk. 19th c. **Šükür-bek** [Шукуръ-бекъ] (Grod., Pril. 147); Kzk. 19th c. **Šükür-bek** [Шукуръ-Бекъ] (Grod., Pril. 140). ✧ 'Gratefulness, thankfulness' cf. Kuman, Kar., Kzk. *šükür* (Ar.) 'der Dank' (Radl. IV, 1108), Kkalp. *šükir* 'благодарность, признательность' (KkRS), Bashk. *šökör* 'благодарение, благодарность, признательность' (BRS/Uraksin). See also **ALLA-ŠÜGÜR?, BERDİ-ŠÜKÜR, XOJAM-ŠÜKÜR?, XUDAY-ŠÜKÜR.**

ŠÜKÜR-ALİ   Kzk. 1788 **Šükür-ali-biy** [Choucourali-bey / Шукурали Бий] (Levšin II, 301, Levchine 280). ⇨ **ŠÜKÜR + ALİ.**

ŠÜKÜR-BERDİ   Uzb. 20th c. **Šükür-berdi**

[Шукурберди] (Begmatov 1984, 202); Trkm. 1859 **Šükür-berdi-šeyχ** [Шукур-берды-шейх] (MIT II, 597, 598, 599, 633); *TN:* Trkm. **Šükür-berdi** [Шукур-берды], a well (Karta JAR XVIII). ✧ 'Thankfulness gave him/her'. ⇨ **ŠÜKÜR-BERDİ.**

ŠÜKÜRLİ   Kzk. 19th c. **Šükürli-biy** [Шукурли-бий] (Grod., Pril. 154). ✧ 'With greatfulness/thankfulness'. ⇨ **ŠÜKÜR** + suff. *-li.*

ŠÜLEM   Kzk. 19th c. **Šülem-bay** [Шулембай] (AOO 54); Kzk. 19th c. **Šülim-bay / Šülöm-bay?** [Шулёмбай] (AOK 30). ✧ 'Helm, helmet' cf. Kzk. *šülem* 'Başı kurşundan korumak için askerlerin savaşta başına giydiği miğfer' (KzTS) (<R.) *šlem* 'id.' 680.

ŠÜRTÜK   Kzk. 19th c. **Šürtük** [Шюртукъ] (AOO 10).

ŠÜNİ   Alt. 20th c. **Šüni** [Шÿÿни] (OjrRS 210).

T

TAB-ALDÏ see TABÏP-ALDÏ

TABA-SARÏ   Kzk. 19th c. **Taba-sarï** [Табасары] (AOO 74). ⇨ **SARÏ.**

TABAY I.   Tat. 1529-1533 **Tabay** [Табай / Табаи], a prince from Kazan (PSRL VIII, 272, 273, 276-77, 282, XIII, 46, XXIII, 204, XX 416); Bashk. 1717 **Tabay** [Табай Ибыкеев] (MIB III, 148); Kzk. 19th c. **Tabay** [Табай] (AOP 50); Kzk. 19th c. **Tabay** [Табай] (Pam. kn. Turg. 68). ✧ 'Pan, casserole' cf. Kzk., Tat., Turk. *taba* (P.) 'die Pfanne' (Radl. III, 960) + dim. suff. *-y.* See also **QUL-TABAY.**

TABAY II.   Hak. 19th-20th c. **Tabay** [Табай] (HRS 351); Hak.(Koyb.) 19th c. **Tabay** [Табай], fem. (Katanov, Otč. II, 12-15); Hak.? 19th-20th c. **Tabāy** [Табаӣ] (Katanov, Otč. 10); Hak.(Sag.) 19th-20th c. **Tabāy** [Табаи] (Proben IX, 613). ✧ 'Come along! Come on! Hurry up!, Now then!, Go on!' (<R.) *davaj* 'id.' (Katanov).

TABAYΓU   Türk? 870 **Tabayγu** [ارتکین, طبایغوا / طبایغو بن صول], Sol (Sul) Er-tegin's son (Tabarī, Annal. III, 1313).

TABAQ   Chuv. 17th c. **Tabak** [Табакъ] (IOAIÊK XXIX, 343); Oghuz/Trkm. 13th c. **Tabaq** [تباق / Табак (Батак)] (Abulg./Kon. 665); Hak.(Sag.) 19th-20th c. **Tabaq** [Табак], fem. (Katanov, Otč. 8.). ✧ 'Dish, bowl; plate' cf. Alt., Hak., Kzk., Tat., Turk. *tabaq* 'die Schüssel, die Schale' (Radl. III, 961).

TABALDÏ see TABÏLDÏ

TABAN   Chuv. 18th-19th c. **Taban** [Табанъ] (Magn. 79); Tat.(Sib.) 1629 **Taban / Tabanko?** [Табанко] (Miller, Ist. Sib. II, 357); Khorezm./Chag.? 1381 **Taban-behadur** [Табан-бехадур], governor (daruγa) (MIT I, 520, 524); *TN:* Kzk. **Taban** [Табан], a

settlement (Kojčubaev 202). ✧ I. 'Bream (type of fresh water fish of the carp family)' cf. Kzk., Tat., Tat.(Tob.) *taban* 'der Blei, Karausse' (Radl. III, 964); II. 'Sole, bottom'? cf. Kuman, Alt., Crm., Hak., Kzk., Tat. *taban* 'die Sohle; der untere Theil' (Radl. III, 963). See also **ČABAQ, ČAPAQ, QARĀYS**

TABANAY   Bashk. 1714 **Tabanay** [Мустафа Табанаев] (MIB III, 117); Bashk. 1737 **Tabanay** [Табанай] (MIB I, 326); Bashk. 1738 **Tabanay** [Баряс Табанаев] (MIB I, 143); Bashk. 1738 **Tabanay** [Мряс Табанаев] (MIB I, 145); Bashk. 1744 **Tabanay** [Юрты Табанаев] (MIB III, 415). ⇨ **TABAN** + suff. *-ay.*

TABANAYQA   Tat. 1675 **Tabanayqa / Tabanayka?** [Табанайка] (Kungursk. akty 27). ⇨ **TABANAY** + suff. *-qa* / (R.) *-ka?*

TABANKA   Chuv. 18th-19th c. **Tabanka** [Табанка] (Magn. 79). ⇨ **TABAN** + (R.?) suff. *-ka.*

TABAR   Kzk. 19th c. **Tabar** [Табаръ] (SODž. 24). ✧ 'He/she will find/acquire' / 'He/she will be found/born' (Butanaev), cf. Uyg., Chag., Alt., Kzk., Tat. etc. *tap-* 'finden, erhalten, erwerben' (Radl. III, 947). See also **ĴAY-TABAR, MAL-TABAR, MAN-TABAR.**

TABARAX   Hak. 19th-20th c. **Tabaraχ** [Табарах], fem. (HRS 355). ✧ I. 'Quick, nimble' cf. Hak. *tabraχ* 'быстрый, скорый' (HRS); II. Dim.-hypoc. of *Tabar*? ⇨ **TABAR?** + dim. suff. *-aχ.*

TABAS   Hak.(Sag.) 19th-20th c. **Tabas** [Табас], fem. (Katanov, Otč. 8). ✧ 'Sole, palm, hand' cf. Alt., Shor *tabaš* 'die Sohle, die Handfläche, ein Handvoll' (Radl. III, 968), Tat.(Bar.) *tabac* 'die Handfläche' (Radl. III, 968).

TABAŠA   Hak. 19th-20th c. **Tabaša** [Табаша], fem. (HRS 355).

TABAŠAQ   Bashk. 1756 **Tabašaq** [Мугралы Табашаков] (MIB IV/1, 122).

TABĀČ   Bulg. 13th c. - 14th c. **Tabāč / Taqač / Toqač?** [طباج / طُعَاج / Taqāǰ / ṭokac / Tokaç / Табач] (Jusupov 34, Epigr. Bulg. 100-101, Tekin 102).

TABĀY see TABAY II.

ТАВГАЧ   Karakh. 893 **Tabγač-χan / Tafγač-qaγan / Oγulčaq-χan** [Tafgaç Kağan / Tabgaç Ogulçak Han], a Karakhanid ruler, also known as Oγulčaq or Oγuljaq (Toğan, UTT 59, 81); Karakh. / Selj.? 11th c. - 12th c. **Tafγač / Tafqač** [شمس الملک تکین بن طنتاج / طنغاج] (Bondārī 46); Karakh.? / Selj.? 1018 **Tafγač-χan** [طنغاج خان ابوالمظفر ابراهیم] (Ibn al-Athīr/Tornb. IX, 211, 212); Oghuz 1155 / 1192? **Tamγač** [طمغاج / Tamγač / Тамгадж], an emir, commander of the Khorezmshah Tekiš (Ĵuwaynī II, 29, 30, Rāwandī 366, MIT I, 447); Karakh.? / Selj.? 11th c. **Tamγač / Tamγač-χan / Tabγač-χan?** [طمغاج خان بن محمد], ruler of Mawarannahr at the time of Melik Shah I (1072-1092) (Ĵuwaynī II, 4, Ibn al-Athīr/Tornb. XI,

133, Rāwandī 133); Karakh. **Tawγač** [Tawgaç] (MK/Atalay 853). ✧ 'Chinese of Tan-dynasty' cf. Türk *tabγač / tapqač* (<Chinese?) 'id.' (Radl. III, 980).

TABÏB Chag. 16th c. **Tabib** [Табиб], a χoĵa (Ivanov 105). ✧ 'Doctor, leech' (Ar.) (Kusimova, Sattarov).

TABÏQ Kzk. 19th c. **Tabïq** [Табыкъ] (AOP 58, 86). ✧ 'Duty, service' cf. Kuman *tabïq* 'der Dienst' (Radl. III, 970).

TABÏQAY Bashk. 1798 **Tabïqay** [Табыкайъ] (PSZRI XXV, 195). ⇨ **TABÏQ** + suff. *-ay*.

TABÏL Alt. 19th-20th c. **Tabïl** [Табыл] (OjrRS 210); Uzb. 20th c. **Tâpïl** [Топил] (Begmatov 1984, 205); Uzb. 20th c. **Tâpïl-bây** [Топилбой] (Begmatov 1984, 205). ✧ 'Be found' (OjrRS). See also **TABÏN**.

TABÏLDÏ Kzk. 19th c. **Tabïldï** [Табылды] (SOV 38); Kirg. **Tabïldï** [Табылды] (Jud. 35, 474); Kzk. 18th c. - 19th c. **Tabulda** (<**Tabuldï**) [Жайсанъ Табулдинъ] (ZOOIRGO IV, 99); Kzk. 19th c. **Tabulda** (<**Tabuldï**) [Табулда] (AOK 126); Bashk. 1779 **Tabuldï** [Джиянгул Табулдин] (MIB V, 83, 84); Bashk. 1788 **Tabuldï** [Зиянгул Табулдин] (MIB V, 233); Kzk. 1846 **Tabuldï** [Утямыш Табулдин], a biy (MKOP 155); Kzk. 19th c. **Tabuldï** [Табульдиновъ] (AOO 58); Kzk. 19th c. **Tabuldï** [Табулды] (AOP 78); Kzk. 19th c. **Tabuldï** [Тапулди Бекбуевъ] (Grod., Pril. 164); Kzk. 19th c. **Tapïldï** [Тапильди Исановъ] (Grod., Pril. 70); Kzk. 19th c. **Tawïldï** [Тавилди] (Grod., Pril. 17); Uzb. 20th c. **Tâpïldï** [Топилди] (Begmatov 1984, 205); *TN:* Kzk.? **Tabuldï** [Табулды], a winter pasture (Karta JAR XI); Kzk.? **Tabuldï** [Тобулды] (Karta JAR XI). ✧ 'Found (child)' cf. Uyg., Alt., Hak., Kzk., Tat. *tabïl-* 'gefunden werden, sich finden, sich befinden' (Radl. III, 971). See also **TABÏL, TABÏN**.

TABÏN Hak. 19th-20th c. **Tabïn** [Табынъ], fem. (HRS 355); *EN:* Kzk. 1785 **Tabïn-uruγï** [تابين اوروغى / Табын] (MIK IV, 52, 54); Kzk. 1629 **Tabun** [Табун] (Miller, Ist. Sib. II, 351, 374). ✧ 'Be found' (Butanaev). See also **BAY-TABÏN, QARA-TABÏN, TABÏL**.

TABÏN-SAXAL Tuv. 19th c. **Tabïn-saxal** [Табынъ сахалъ], a shaman and an informant from Kobdo (Potanin IV, 295). ⇨ **TABÏN** + **SAQAL?**

TABÏN-TARAΓAY Yak. **Tabïn-taraγay** [Табын Тараҕаi түöкÿн] (Pek.).

TABÏP-ALDÏ Tat. 1675 **Tab-aldï** [Табалдынъ] (Kungursk. akty 35); Kzk. 19th c. **Tab-aldï** [Табалды] (SOK 160); Kzk. 19th c. **Tawb-aldï / Tawïb-aldï** [Таубалды] (SOV 52); Kzk. 19th c. **Tawb-aldï / Tawïb-aldï** [Таубалды] (SOV 92); Kirg. 20th c. **Tāb-aldï** [Таабалды] (Kalilov 93); Uzb. 20th c. **Tâpïb-âldï** [Топиболди] (Begmatov 1984, 205). ✧ '(He/she) found/obtained (the child), (He/she) found and took (the child)' cf. Uyg. *tap-* 'находить, получать'

(DTS), Uyg., Chag., Alt., Kzk., Tat. etc. *tap-* 'finden, erhalten, erwerben' (Radl. III, 947), Kzk. *tawïp al-* 'находить, приобрести' (KzRS). ⇨ **ALDÏ**.

TABÏRDÏ see **TABÏRTÏ**

TABÏRTÏ Uyg. 12th c. - 14th c. **Tabïrdï** [Tabïrdrï] (Radl., USp. 127-8); Uyg. **Tabïrtï** [Tabırtı] (EUTS).

TABÏS Bashk. 1710 **Tabïs** [Иман Табысев] (MIB III, 64); Kzk. 19th c. **Tabïs-pay** [Табыспай] (SODž. 70); Kzk. 19th c. **Tabïs-pay** [Табызпай] (SOK 150). ✧ 'Benefit, purchase, gain' cf. Kzk. *tabïs* 'das, was man gefunden hat, der Vortheil, der Verdienst' (Radl. III, 972).

TABÏT Alt. 19th-20th c. **Tabït** [Табыт] (OjrRS 210). ✧ 'David' cf. R. *Davyd* (OjrRS).

TABLAQ Chag. 16th c. **Tablaq-aqa** [Таблак Ака] (Ivanov 230).

TABU-ΓAŠTÏ Bashk. 1762 **Tabu-γaštï / Tabun-γaštï?** [Табугашты] (MIB IV/1, 245).

TABUQ Tat.(GH)? 13th c. **Tabuq** [Табукъ], Berke (1257-1266) khan's governor in the Crimea (Smirnov, Krym. 38). ✧ 'Service, duty' cf. Uyg. *tabuq* 'der Dienst' (Radl. III, 977).

TABULDA see **TABÏLDÏ**

TABULDAY Kirg. 1817 **Tabulday** [Табулдай Кулбаевъ] (TOUAK XXIV, 85). ⇨ **TABÏLDÏ?**

TABULDÏ see **TABÏLDÏ**

TABURČAQ Chag. 1697 **Taburčaq-sultan** [Табурчак-султан], from Khiva (DAI X, 384).

TABUT-BÜYÜK Crm. **Tabut-büyük** [Табут Бÿjÿк] (Proben VII, 31). ⇨ **BÜYÜK**.

TAČADAN Uyg. 12th c. - 14th c. **Tačadan** [Tačadan / Taçadan] (Radl., USp. 121, DTS, EUTS).

TAČAM Türk 731 **Tačam** [Taçam] (DTS, ETY I, 130 II, 114). See also **BÏLGÄ-TAČAM**.

TAČČÏL Karg. 19th-20th c. **Taččïl** [Таччыл] (Katanov, Otč. 8).

TAČÏΓAS Hak. 19th-20th c. **Tačïγas** [Тачыгас] (HRS 351).

TAČKENT Kzk. 19th c. **Tačkent** [Тачкентъ Довлаевъ] (Grod., Pril. 110). ✧ Tashkent (city)?

TAČQA Hak. 19th-20th c. **Tačqa** [Тачка] (HRS 351).

TAĴ Kirg. **Taĵ-bay** [Таджбай] (Sb. Syr-D. IX, 52); Kzk. 19th c. **Taž-bek?** [Тожбекъ] (SODž. 104). ✧ 'Crown' cf. Kuman, Chag., Az., Kar., Turk. *taĵ* 'die Krone' (Radl. III, 913), Kzk. *taž* 'корона' (KzRS). See also **OΓUL-TAČ**.

TAĴÏ Kzk. 19th c. **Taĵi-bay** [Таджибай] (Grod., Pril. 177); Kzk. 19th c. **Taĵi-bay** [Таджибай] (Grod., Pril. 69); Kzk. 19th c. **Taĵi-bay** [Таджибай Кусбановъ] (Grod., Pril. 97); Uzb. 19th c. **Taĵi-bay** [Таджибай] (SKSO III, 184); Kzk. 19th c. **Taĵi-bek** [Таджибекъ], fem. (Grod., Pril. 141); Uzb. 1768/69 **Taĵi-biy** [Таджи бий], from the Qïyat tribe (MIT II, 342, 352); Kzk. 19th c. **Taĵi-gül** [Таджи-Гуль], fem. (Grod., Pril. 119);

Kkalp. 20th c. **Taǰi-gül** [Таджигюл], fem. (Bask., Kkalp. 404, Baskakov: OSA 139); Kzk. 1860 **Taǰi-χan-χoǰa** [Таджи-ханъ-ходжа] (ZIRGOGeogr. I, 271); Kkalp. 20th c. **Taǰï-bay** [Таджыбай] (Bask., Kkalp. 6); Nog. 20th c. **Taǰï-bay** [Таджыбай Илийас увлы / Таджибай Илиясов], one of Baskakov's informants from the settlement Terekli-mektep (Bask., Nog. 144); Kzk. 19th c. **Taži-bay** [Тажибай Шашинбаевъ] (AUK 865); Kkalp. 20th c. **Täži** [Тэжи] (KkRS 776); Kkalp. 20th c. **Täži-bay** [Тэжибай] (KkRS 776); Kkalp. 20th c. **Täži-bek** [Тэжибек] (KkRS 776); Kkalp. 20th c. **Täži-biyke** [Тэжибийке], fem. (KkRS 778); Kkalp. 20th c. **Täži-gül** [Тэжигул], fem. (KkRS 778). ✧ 'Crowned' (Sattarov), 'Crown' (Žanuzakov) (<Ar.) See also **ALTÏN-TAǰI, KÜMÜŠ-TAǰI.**

TAǰI-MURAT Kkalp. 20th c. **Taǰi-mïrat** [Таджы мырат] (Bask., Kkalp. 401); Kkalp. 20th c. **Taǰï-murat** [Таджы мурат] (Bask., Kkalp. 44 /118/). ⇨ **TAǰÏ + MURAT.**

TAǰIK Kzk. 19th c. **Taǰik** [Баймаканъ Таджиковъ] (Grod., Pril. 106); Bashk. 1777 **Täžik** [Юлай Тяжиков] (MIB V, 57). ✧ 'Tadjik' cf. Csag., Turk. *taǰik* 'die Tadschik' (Radl. III, 913).

TAǰÏ see TAǰI

TAǰÏ-NÏYAZ Kkalp. 20th c. **Taǰï-niyaz** [Таджы нийаз] (Bask., Kkalp. 401). ⇨ **TAǰÏ + NÏYAZ.**

TADA Hak. 19th-20th c. **Tada** [Тада], fem. (HRS 355).

TADA-SARÏ Kzk. 19th c. **Tada-sarï** [Тадасары] (AOO 74). ✧ ? ⇨ **SARÏ?**

TADAГAN Hak.(Kacha) 19th-20th c. **Tadaγan** [Тадаван] (Proben IX, 386). ✧ 'Eyebrow (in children's language)' (Radloff).

TADAQOS Hak. 19th-20th c. **Tadaqos** [Тадакос], fem. (HRS 355).

TADAN Hak. 19th-20th c. **Tadan** [Тадан] (HRS 351).

TADAR Tuv. 19th c. **Tadar-oγlu** [Тадар-оғлу], nickname of the Abakan-Tatars (Proben IX, 41). ✧ 'Tatar'?

TADEY Chuv. 18th-19th c. **Tadey** [Тадей] (Magn. 79).

TADÏǰAQ Hak.? 19th-20th c. **Tadïǰaq** [Тадыцак], fem. (Katanov, Otč. 10). ⇨ **TADA? + suff. -iǰaq / -ǰaq?**

TADÏQ Türk 732 **Tadïq-čur** [Tadïqïk Çur / Tadïq Çur] (ETY I, 44).

TADÏN Alt. 19th-20th c. **Tadïn** [Тадын] (OjrRS 210); Alt. 19th-20th c. **Tädïn** [Таадын] (OjrRS 210). ✧ 'Taste!' (OjrRS).

TADÏÑAY Alt. 19th-20th c. **Tadïñay** [Тадынай] (OjrRS 210).

TADÏRT Hak. 19th-20th c. **Tadïrt** [Тадырт] (HRS 351).

TADOY Hak. 19th-20th c. **Tadoy** [Тадой], fem. (HRS 355).

TAFAY Kzk. 19th c. **Tafay-bay** [Тафайбай] (SODž. 108); Kzk. 19th c. **Tafay-bay** [Тафайбай] (SODž

108). ⇨ **TABAY?**

TAFГAČ see TABГAČ

TAFQAČ see TABГAČ

TAГ Oghuz/Trkm. 13th c. **Taγ / Taγ-χan / Taq-χan** [تاغ / تاغ / Tâgh / Tağ / Таг-хан], Oghuz Khan's son in the legend of origin (Abulg./Desm. 23, Oğuz K. Dest. 15, Abulg./Kon. 430, 510, 520, 560, 1170, Šejb. XXIII, DTS); Kzk. 19th c. **Taw** [Тау] (AOA 70); Kzk. 19th c. **Taw-bay** [Таубай] (AOO 22, 94); Kzk. 19th c. **Taw-bay** [Ходжабай Тавбаевъ] (Grod., Pril. 73); Kzk. 19th c. **Taw-bay** [Таубай] (SOK 130); Kkalp. 20th c. **Taw-bay** [Таўбай] (KkRS 776); Tat. **Taw-batïr** [Tav Batyr], a character in a tale (Košay: KCsA I, 324); Kzk. 19th c. **Taw-bek** [Таубекъ] (AOK 18); Kzk. 19th c. **Taw-bek** [Таубекъ] (SODž. 74); Kzk. 19th c. **Taw-bek** [Тоубекъ] (SOV 82); Tat.(Lit.) 1672 **Taw-digin?** [Towdginowna] (Lit. Tat. 426). ✧ 'Mountain' cf. Türk, Kuman, Chag. *taγ* 'der Berg' (Radl. III, 795), Kuman, Kzk., Tat. *tau* 'der Berg, das Gebirge' (Radl. III, 772), Uyg. *taq* 'der Berg' (Radl. III, 777). See also **AHRAM-DAГ, AQ-TAW, BAY-TAW, BEK-TAW, BES-TAW, BÏK-TAW, ǰAN-TAW, QARA-TAГ.**

TAГ-ARSLAN Uyg. 1337 **Taγ-arslan** [Tag-arslan] (Chwol., Syr.-nest. 140); Uyg. 1323 **Taq-arslan** [Tak Arslan], a leader of a church, Agusak's son (Chwol., Syr.-nest. 62). ✧ 'Mountain-lion' (Radloff, ibid. p. 153). ⇨ **TAГ + ARSLAN.** See also **TAQ-ARSLAN.**

TAГ-ASAR Kzk. 19th c. **Tuw-asar / Taw-asar** [Туасаръ /Тауасаръ?/] (AOO 6).

TAГ-AŠAR Kzk. 19th c. **Taw-asar** [Тауасар] (Potanin II, 4); Kzk. 19th c. **Taw-asar** [Таосаръ] (SODž. 46); Kzk. 19th c. **Taw-asar** [Тауасаръ] (SOV 66); Uzb. 20th c. **Tâγ-âšar** [Тоғошар] (Begmatov 1984, 203); Uzb. 20th c. **Tâw-ašar** [Товашар] (Begmatov 1984, 203). ✧ 'He will pass over mountains' cf. Uyg., Kuman, Chag., Alt., Az., Crm., Tat., Turk., etc. *aš-* 'über etwas hinübersteigen; steigen; über etwas hervorragen, etwas übertreffen' (Radl. I, 586), Kzk. *as-* 'перевалить, пройти, проехать' (KzRS). ⇨ **TAГ.** See also **BEL-ASAR, TAŠ-AŠAR.**

TAГ-VERMÏŠ Maml. 1439 **Taγ-vermiš** [Taghvermich], "grand-écuyer", the governor of Egypt, then the governor of Haleb, his mausoleum (türbe) is in Damascus (?). ⇨ **TAГ + BERMÏŠ.**

TAГA Uyg. 1339 **Taγa** [Taga] (Chwol., Syr.-nest. (NF) 36); Tat.(Sib.)? 1582 **Taγa** [Сеибахта Тагинъ] (Sib. Let. 27, 73, 107, 300, 338). ✧ 'Relative on mother's side' cf. East.T. *taγa* 'der Verwandte von Mutterseite' (Radl. III, 795).

TAГAY Mo.? **Taγay** [Тагай] (RaD I/1, 100); Tat.(GH) 14th c. **Taγay** [Тагаи] (PSRL XXIII, 113); Tat.(GH) 1365 **Taγay** [Тагай], a prince of the Horde (PSRL XI, 5, XVI, 91); Bashk. 1757 **Taγay** [Тагаш Тагаев]

(MIB IV/1, 18); Kzk. **Taɣay** [Тагай-ханъ] (Sb. Syr.-D. III, otd. II, 70); Kzk. 19th c. **Taɣay** [Тагаевъ] (SKSO VIII, 200, 223); Kzk. 19th c. **Taɣay** [Дустъ Тагаевъ] (SKSO VIII, 206); Kirg. **Taɣay** [Тагай] (Jud. 807); Uzb. 19th c. **Taɣay** [Кувандыкъ Тагаевъ] (SKSO III, 174); Uzb. 20th c. **Taɣay** [Tagaï Hal Djïguitov], a basmačï from Bukhara (Castagné 79); Tat.(GH) 1361, 1365 **Taɣay / Täɣay** [Тагай (Тягай)], a prince of the Horde (PSRL IV, 65, V, 230, VIII, 11, 13); Kzk. 19th c. **Taɣay-bay** [Тагайбай] (AOK 18); Kzk. 19th c. **Taɣay-bay** [Тагайбай] (Grod., Pril. 89, 132); Kzk. 19th c. **Taɣay-bay** [Тагайбай] (SKSO III, 10); Nog.? **Taɣay-batïr** [Тагай-батыр] (Žirm., Epos 404); Kzk. 19th c. **Taɣay-bek** [Тагайбекъ] (SKSO VIII, 204); Trkm. 1828 **Taɣay-mirab** [Тагай-мирабъ] (MIT II, 451, 453, 488, 506 etc.); Uyg. 8th c. - 9th c. **Taɣay-toña-säñün** [Taɣai-Tonga-Sangun] (Müller, Uig. II, 81); *TN:* Kzk.? 19th c. **Taɣay-bek** [طغای بیك / Тагай-Бекъ], a settlement (qïšlaq) in the district (tümem) of Katta Kurgan (ZIRGOStat. IV). ✧ 'Uncle (on mother side)' (Žanuzakov), cf. Kuman, Chag. *tayai* 'der Onkel von Mutterseite' (Radl. III, 795), Chag. *taġai* 'Mutterbruder' (Le Coq, Ind. 3). See also **ĴAMAN-TAҐAY**.

TAҐAY-BUQA Khorezm./Chag. 1405 **Taɣay-buqa** [Rustem-Tagaï-bouka] (Matla-assaadeïn 23). ⇨ **TAҐAY + BUQA**.

TAҐAY-MURAT Kzk. 19th c. **Taɣay-murat** [Тагаймуратовъ] (SKSO VIII, 221); Kzk. 19th c. **Taɣay-murat** [Тагаймурадъ] (SKSO VIII, 233). ⇨ **TAҐAY + MURAT**.

TAҐALDÏY Crm. 1541 **Taɣaldïy** [Тагалдый-князь], envoy from the Crimea (PSRL VIII, 296, XIII, 100); Crm. 1540 **Taɣaldïy-mïrza** [Тагалдый мырза] (PSRL XIII, 132).

TAҐAM-BAY see TAҐAN

TAҐAN Kzk. 19th c. **Taɣam-bay** [Тагамбай] (SODž. 112); Trkm. 19th c. **Taɣan** [Таганъ Пиреевъ] (Ščeglov I, 358); Trkm. 19th c. **Taɣan** [Kasy Mahmed Taghan / Кази Магмедъ Таганъ] (Murav'ev I, 41, ArchKR III, 239); Trkm. 20th c. **Tagan** [Tagan], fem. (Zaj. 1971, 341); Chuv. 18th-19th c. **Taɣan** [Таганъ] (Magn. 79); Nog. 1649 **Taɣan** [Таганъ] (AI IV, 87); Hak.(Sag.) 19th-20th c. **Taɣan** [Паi Таңан], an evil spirit (Proben IX, 509); Kzk. 19th c. **Taɣan-atay** [Таганатай], according to Kazak tradition he is Chinggis' half-brother (Potanin, Pred. 50); Uzb. 19th c. **Taɣan-gül** [Тагангуль], fem. (SKSO III, 176); Trkm. 1859 **Taɣan-qāzï** [Таганъ-Казы] (ZIRGOÊtn. I, 200); Trkm. 20th c. **Tāɣan** [Таган], fem. (TrkmRS 611). ✧ 'Hanger, tripod' cf. Tat. *tayan* 'Ständer, Böcke zum Aufhängen' (Radl. III, 795).

TAҐAN-DURDÏ Trkm. 19th c. **Taɣan-durdï** [Генендыкъ Тагандурдыевъ] (Ščeglov I, 354);

Trkm. 19th c. **Taɣan-durdï** [Таганъ-дурды] (Volodin 53); Trkm. 1859 **Taɣan-durdï-šeyχ** [Тоганъ-Дурды-шейхъ] (ZIRGOÊtn. I, 195). ✧ 'Tripod-stood; tripod was standing' (Volodin). ⇨ **TAҐAN + TURDÏ**.

TAҐAN-NÏYAZ Trkm. 1819-1820 **Taɣan-niyas** [Таганъ-Ніясъ] (Murav'ev I, 48); Trkm. 1821 **Taɣan-niyas** [Таганъ-Ніясъ] (Russk. Arhiv 1888, I, 244); Trkm. 1803 **Taɣan-niyaz** [Кулъ-Мугамедъ Таганіязъ Батыровъ] (PSZRI XXVII, 139). ⇨ **TAҐAN + NÏYAZ**.

TAҐANAY Tat.(Sib.) 1629 **Taɣanay** [Таганай Яугилдеевъ] (Miller, Ist. Sib. II, 357); Bashk. 1786 **Taɣanay** [Таганаев Михаил] (MIB V, 201, 202, 237); Bashk. 1787 **Taɣanay** [Андрей Таганаев], from Ufa (MIB V, 202); Bashk. 1787 **Taɣanay** [Иван Таганаев] (MIB V, 202). ⇨ **TAҐAN + suff. -ay**.

TAҐANAQ Hak.(Sag.) 19th-20th c. **Taɣanaq-matïr** [Таганакъ-Матыръ Костровъ], a folklore hero (Trudy AS IV, II, 237).

TAҐARMÏY Uyg. **Taɣarmïy** [Taġarmıy] (EUTS).

TAҐAŠ Bashk. 1757 **Taɣaš** [Тагаш Тагаев] (MIB IV/2, 18); Kzk. 19th c. **Taɣaš** [Тагашъ] (SOV 84). ✧ 'Small horseshoe' cf. Kzk. *taya* 'das Hufeisen' (Radl. III, 795) + suff. -š.

TAҐAŠÏ Kzk. 18th c. - 19th c. **Taɣaši** [Тагашы] (Tynyšp. 73). ✧ 'Shoeing-smith' cf. Kzk. *taya* 'das Hufeisen' (Radl. III, 795) + suff. -šï.

TAҐBA Tuv. 19th c. **Taɣba** [Таңба] (Proben IX, 114, 164).

TAҐĴÏ Kzk. 18th c. - 19th c. **Taɣči** [Тагчи] (ZOOO 1870, 234); Maml. 1294 **Taɣĵï** [Tagdji], emir, murderer of Sultan Lâdjin (Makrīzī IV, 95, 114); Kkalp. 20th c. **Tawše-χan** [Таўшехан] (KkRS 776); Kkalp. 20th c. **Tawše-qan** [Тавше-къан] (Bask., Kkalp. 58); 19th c. **Towču-bek** [Тоучубекъ], a fortification upon the stream Keskelen, named after a man (ZIRGOGeogr.I, 257). ✧ 'Mountaineer'? ⇨ **TAҐ + suff. -či**.

TAҐÏ Az. 19th c. **Taɣï** [Tagiev] (Mende 69); Trkm. **Taɣï-bay** [Тагы-бай] (Mel'gunov 321); Trkm. 1803/04 **Taɣï-χan** [Мухаммед Тагы-хан (Лисан-уль-мульк, Сипихр)], a mirza, an historien (MIT II, 18-19, 205, 213); Trkm. 1825 **Taɣï-χan** [Таги-хан] (MIT II, 431, 432); Trkm. 1851 **Taɣï-χan** [Тагы-хан], emir-i-nizām (MIT II, 305); Trkm. 1856/57 **Taɣï-χan** [Мухаммед Тагы-хан], commander of Shahsevens and Afshars (MIT II, 278); Khorezm.? 14th c. **Taɣï-χatun** [Thaghy khâtoûn], from Iraq (Ibn Bat. II, 118); Trkm. 19th c. **Taɣu-bay** [Тагу-бай] (SOK 10). ✧ 'Wild, cross (man)' cf. Kzk. *tayï / tayï adam* 'дикий; нелюдимый человек (KzRS).

TAҐÏL Kzk.? **Taɣïl-bay** [Тагыл-бай], a well? (Karta JAR X).

TAҐÏŠ Kzk. 19th c. **Taɣïš** [Тагышъ] (AOO 50).

TAҐMA-YABU Uzb. 1704 **Taɣma-yabu** [طغمه یابو],

Taɣma of the Yābū tribe from Bukhara (Buchari 276).

TAΓRÏ-BERDİ see **TÄÑRİ-BERDİ**

TAΓRÏ-BERDİ-QARA Maml. 1398/99 **Taɣrï-berdi-qara** [تغرى بردى قرا] (Ibn Taghrīb. VI, 4). ⇨ **TÄÑRİ-BERDİ + QARA.**

TAΓRÏ-BERMİŠ see **TÄÑRİ-BERMİŠ**

TAX-KİSİ Yak. **Taχ-kisi** [Tax кici] (Pek.). ✧ 'Small/little man' (Pek.).

TAXA Hak. 19th-20th c. **Taχa** [Taxa], fem. (HRS 355). ✧ 'Heel' (HRS).

TAXDU Hak.(Kyz.) 1585 **Taχdu** [Taxдy] (Jarilov, Kyz. 6).

TAXMASP Trkm. 1688 **Taχmasp-quli-xan / Taχmasp-bek / Taχmasp-xan** [Тахмасп-кули-хан / Тахмасп-бек / Тахмасп-хан], a „vekil" (ruler of a tribe) from the Jalayïr tribe (MIT II, 120, 135-138, 141, 142). ✧ Tahmasp (1513-1576), a Safavid shah of Iran.

TAXTA-QLÏJ Az. **Taχta-qlïj** [Тахта-Клыдж] (Az. Skaz. 140). ✧ 'Board-sword' cf. East.T., Kar., Turk. *taχta* 'das Brett' (Radl. III, 802). ⇨ **QÏLİČ.**

TAXTAMÏŠ see **TOQTAMÏŠ**

TAXTAR see **TOQTAR**

TAXTAR-ALİ Bashk. 1735 **Taχtar-ali** [Тахтар-али Рахмангуловъ] (Vel.-Zern., Bašk. 15). ⇨ **TOQTAR + ALİ.**

TAİR Tat.(Mish.) 1743 **Tair** [Таир Акбулат] (MIB III, 539); Bashk. 1770 **Tair** [Таир Райманов] (MIB IV/1, 349); Bashk. 1779 **Tair** [Ялтей (Ялти) Таиров] (MIB V, 91); Bashk. 1789 **Tair** [Буляк Таиров] (MIB V, 250, 252); Kzk. 19th c. **Tair** [Бабакулъ Таировъ] (Grod., Pril. 291); Kzk. 19th c. **Tair** [Таиръ Даукеровъ] (SKSO III, 190); Uzb. 19th c. **Tair** [Джурабай Таировъ] (SKSO III, 152); Kzk. / NUyg.? 1864 **Tair** [Бекъ Таиръ] (Valihanov, Soč. 515); Tat.(Ishim) **Tayïr** [Тайыр], a prince in a tale (Proben IV, /204 /250/, 274 /341/); Bashk. 1735 **Toir** (<Tair <Tahir?) [Тоиръ Каскаевъ], a tarχan (Vel.-Zern., Bašk. 17). ✧ 'Flying (bird)' (Ar.) (Kusimova, Sattarov, Žanuzakov).

TAİR-BUΓA Maml. 1302/03, 1325 **Tair-buɣa** [طايـر بغا] (Zetterst. 177, Iyās I, 166); Maml. 1330 **Tair-buɣa** [سيفالـدين طايـر بغا] (Zetterst. 196); Maml.? 1332 **Tair-buɣa** [سيفالـدين طايـر بغا], an emir (Dawād.). ⇨ **TAİR + BUQA.**

TAY Uyg. **Tay** [Tai] (EUTS); Khorezm./Chag. 1372 **Tay** [Тай-ходжа] (MIT I, 515); Trkm. 20th c. **Tay** [Tay] (Zaj. 1971, 331); Trkm. 20th c. **Tay** [Тай] (TrkmRS 612); Kzk. 19th c. **Tay** [Тай] (AOAtb. 2); Kzk. 19th c. **Tay** [Тай] (SOV 16); Chuv. 18th-19th c. **Tay-aba / Toy-aba?** [Тояба (Таяба)] (Magn. 87); Kzk. 19th c. **Tay-baba** [Тайбаба] (SODž. 100); Kzk. 19th c. **Tay-bača** [Тайбача] (SODž. 112); Kzk. 19th c. **Tay-bay** [Тайбай] (AOK 34); Kzk. 19th c. **Tay-bay** [Тайбай] (SOK 86, 136); Kzk. 19th c. **Tay-bay** [Тайбай] (SOV 6, 48, 120); Kzk. 19th c. **Tay-bala** [Тайбала] (SOK 46); Uyg. 12th c. - 14th c. **Tay-beg** [Tai Bäg] (Radl., USp. 120, DTS); Kzk. 19th c. **Tay-bek** [Тайбекъ] (AOK 38); Kzk. 19th c. **Tay-bek** [Тайбекъ] (Grod., Pril. 182); Uzb. 19th c. **Tay-bek** [Тайбекъ] (SKSO III, 168); Kzk. 1822 **Tay-jan** [طاى جان] (MIK IV, 433, 435); Kzk. 19th c. **Tay-jigit** [Тайджигитъ] (SOV 80); Kzk. 19th c. **Tay-eke** [Taeкe] (SOK 294); Bashk. 1754 **Tay-ɣul** [Тайгул Кыльдыгулов] (MIB IV/1, 83); Khorezm.? 1313 **Tay-inal** [طينال], an emir of the „Moghuls" (Dawād. 274); Khorezm.? 1314 **Tay-inal** [سيفالـد يـن طينـال الحـاجـب], an emir and doorkeeper (Dawād.); Khorezm.? 1324 **Tay-inal** [سيفالـد يـن طينـال / Tinal], an emir (Abulfidā V, 360-361); Maml. 1326-41 **Tay-inal** [السيفى طينـال], governor of Tripolis, founder of a mosque (Sobern. I, 87-88); Maml. 1340 **Tay-inal** [الساقى سيفالـد يـن طينـال] (Zetterst. 147, 193, Weil, Chalif. I, 441, 453); Uyg. **Tay-ügä** [Tai ügä / Tay Ügä] (EUTS, ETY II, 67); Kzk. 19th c. **Tay-žan** [Тайжанъ] (AOO 46); *TN:* Kzk. **Tay** [Тай], a settlement (Kojčubaev 203); Chuv. 18th c. **Tay-aba** [Таяба], a village in the district of Tetyushinsk (Korsakov 346); Chuv. **Tayabā** [TajaBā] (Mészáros II, 48). ✧ I. 'Foal'; 'Stallion' (Zaj. 1971), cf. Uyg., Chag., Alt., Crm., Hak.(Sag.), Shor, Kirg., Kzk., Tat., Turk. *tai* 'ein junges Pferd; das einjährige Pferd' (Radl. III, 765), Trkm. *tay* 'жеребец' (TrkmRS); II. 'Uncle on mother-side' cf. Alt., Hak.(Sag.) *tai* (Radl. III, 765). See also **AΓA-TAY, AY-TAY, AQ-TAY, AQ-JOL-TAY, AQA-TAY, AQMAN-TAY, AQU-TAY, ALA-TAY, ALAQ-TAY, ALTÏN-TAY, ARΓU-TAY, ARÏQ-TAY, ASPAN-TAY, ATAN-TAY, ATÏM-TAY, ATÏP-TAY, BAQ-TAY, BALA-TAY, BAŽÏN-TAY, BİYMEN-TAY, BİKİ-TAY, BOTAN-TAY, BOZ-TAY, BUQPAN-TAY, BUR-TAY, BURAN-TAY, BURΓUL-TAY, ČÏRAN-TAY, ČÏMÄN-TAY, ČÏN-TAY, JAN-TAY, JON-TAY, JUL-TAY, JUMAN-TAY, JURUN-TAY, JÜRÜP-TAY, EL-TAY, ER-QULA-TAY, ES-TAY, İR-TAY, İŠAN-TAY, YALMAN-TAY, YURUN-TAY, YUSUF-TAY, KEBE-TAY, KENJE-TAY, KER-TAY, KİČKİ-TAY, KÖK-TAY, KÖRPE-TAY, KÖTEN-TAY, KÜBEN-TAY, KÜČ-TAY, KÜK-TAY, QAL-TAY, QALAN-TAY, QAÑΓU-TAY, QARA-TAY, QOČO-TAY, QOJA-TAY, QOΓA-TAY, QON-TAY, QONAQ-TAY, QOŠ-TAY, QUBA-TAY, QUL-TAY, QULA-TAY, QULUN-TAY, QUM-TAY, QUÑUR-TAY, QUR-TAY, QURAQ-TAY, QURBAN-TAY, QURUQ-TAY, MARQA-TAY, MEÑ-TAY, MEÑGÜ-TAŠ-TAY, MURZA-TAY, MOΓUL-TAY,**

NAYMAN-TAY, NUR-TAY, OČČĬ-TAY, ORUN-TAY, ÖSÄR-TAY, ÖSKÄN-TAY, ÖZ-TAY, SAPA-TAY, SARĬ-TAY, SARMAN-TAY, SARTAQ-TAY, SARTĬQ-TAY, SERGE-TAY, SĬJĬR-TAY, SĬRĬ-TAY, SĬPA-TAY, SĬR-TAY, SOΓA-TAY, SOR-TAY, SÜYÜN-TAY, TALĬN-TAY, TARΓĬL-TAY, TASKĬN-TAY, TEL-TAY, TĬREN-TAY, TOLAŠ-TAY, TORĬ-TAY, TUΓUL-TAY, TUQUM-TAY, TUL-TAY, TÜBEK-TAY, TÜLE-TAY, TÜLEN-TAY, TÜRĬ-TAY, TÜRK-TAY, URUP-TAY, ÜMBET-TAY, ŽUMA-TAY.

TAY-BAČA see **TAY**

TAY-BAΓAR Kzk. 19th c. **Tay-baγar** [Тайбагаръ] (SODž. 108). ✧ 'He will look after foals'. ⇨ **TAY + BAQAR.**

TAY-BARS Maml. 1260, 1261, 1262, 1270 **Tay-bars** [علاٴالدين طيبرس / Alā al-dīn Taibars al-wazīrī], emir, governor of Damascus, a medresse in Cairo bears his name (Duqmaq:RHCHor IV, 27, 36 etc., Sīrat 122, 154, Zetterst. 57, 81, 110, Weil, Chalif. I, 31, 46, 74, Malrīzī, Khit. I, 383, 426, Makrīzī I, 83, 178, III, 37); Maml. 1261 **Tay-bars** [طيبرس / Tajbars], from Egypt (Abulfidā IV, 632); Maml. 1303, 1309 **Tay-bars** [علاٴالدين طيبرس الخزندارى], an emir (Dawād. 41, 109, 195 etc.); Maml. 14th c. **Tay-bars** [طيبرس / Taybars] (Tarǰ/Houtsma 61, Tarǰ/Toparlı 41); Maml. 14th c. - 15th c. **Tay-bars** [السيفى طيبرس العلاٴى راش نوبة الجمدارية], mentioned without date in an inscription of a lamp (Mayer 227); Maml. 1422 **Tay-bars** [طيبرس / احو تنبك اليخياوى] (Ibn Taghrīb.VI, 554). ✧ 'Foal-tiger/panther' (Sauvaget 51, Németh, HMK 133, Sattarov). ⇨ **TAY + BARS.**

TAY-BASAR Kzk. 19th c. **Tay-basar** [Тайбасаръ] (SOK 292). ✧ 'Who will press (get, catch) foals'. ⇨ **TAY + BASAR.**

TAY-BATAR Kzk. 19th c. **Tay-batar** [Тайбатаръ] (AOAtb. 54). ✧ ? ⇨ **TAY + BATAR?** See also **ČĬΓ-BATAR.**

TAY-BĬLGÄ Uyg. 759 **Tay-bilgä-tutuq** [Taj Bilgä-Tutuq / taj bilgä tutuq], a „yabγu" (Ramstedt, Uig. 16-17, 20-21, 48, DTS, ETY I, 170). ✧ I. 'Chief/first-Wise(-Commander), cf. comp. *tay-sañun* 'great/chief general'; II. 'Foal-Wise(-Commander)' (Blagova 1997, 706, 710). ⇨ **TAY + BĬLGÄ.**

TAY-BOLAT see **TAY-BULAT**

TAY-BOLDĬ Kzk. 19th c. **Tay-boldï** [Тайболды] (SOV 76). ✧ 'A foal (boy) came / was born; born as foal'. ⇨ **TAY + BOLDĬ.**

TAY-BUΓA Selj. 12th c. **Tay-buγa** [حان طٮٮغا], a khan (Ibn Šaddād, Alep 91); Selj. 12th c. **Tay-buγa** [طيبغا علاٴالدين] (Ibn Šaddād, Alep 94); Maml.? **Tay-buγa** [طابوغا] (Ibn Bībī IV, 333); Maml. 1310 **Tay-buγa** [طيبغا الحموى] (Dawād. 215); Maml. 1313/14 **Tay-buγa** [طيبغا الكرفونى / الكرمونى / Тайбога Элькарафуни], envoy sent to Özbek Khan in (Desht-i) Kipchak in 1314 (Zetterst. 121, Aynī/Tizeng. I, 485, 515, Aynī: RHCHor II/1, 256, 265); Maml. 1332 **Tay-buγa** [طيبغا الها شمى], an emir (Dawād. 368); Maml. 1340 **Tay-buγa** [علاالدين طيبغا المجد ى] (Zetterst. 196, 197, 202, Weil, Chalif. I, 456); Maml. 1363/64 **Tay-buγa** [طيبغا العلا ئى], chief of the doormen (Iyās I, 213, 219); Maml. 1390, 1452 **Tay-buγa** [طيبغا الطويل] (Iyās I, 219, 325, Ibn Taghrīb. VII, 225, 284); Maml. 1398/99 **Tay-buγa** [طيبغا الحسنىّ] (Ibn Taghrīb. VI, 136); Maml.? 1399/1400 **Tay-buγa** [طيبغا الطولوتمرى] (Ibn Taghrīb. VI, 25); Tat.(Sib.) 1581 **Tay-buγa** [Тайбуга (Дайбуга, Тайбуганъ)], a Siberian prince, the son of the ruler (Sib. Let. 18, 113, 273 etc.); Kzk. 19th c. **Tay-buγa** [Тайбуга] (SODž. 114); Uyg. 762 **Tay-buγa-tarχan-ügä** [Tai Buya Tarχan Ügä] (Mahrnāmag 10). ✧ 'Foal-bull' (Sauvaget 51), 'Colt/foal-bull' (Bese 17). ⇨ **TAY + BUQA.**

TAY-BULAQ Kzk. 19th c. **Tay-bulaq** [Азирбай Тайбулаковъ] (Grod., Pril. 142). ⇨ **TAY + BULAQ.**

TAY-BULAT Kzk. 19th c. **Tay-bolat** [Тайболатъ] (SOV 74); Kzk. 19th c. **Tay-bulat** [Tay-bulat / Тайбулатъ] (AOK 2). ⇨ **TAY +BULAT.**

TAY-BŪRUL Kzk. 19th c.? **Tay-būrul** [Tay-Burul] (Atyns. 93). ⇨ **TAY + BURUL.**

TAY-ČABAR Kzk. 19th c. **Tay-čabar** [Тайчабаръ] (SODž. 6); Kzk. 19th c. **Tay-čabar** [Тайчабаръ] (SOV 24). ✧ 'Foal-galloper', 'He who will ride foals'. ⇨ **TAY + ČAPAR.** See also **AT-ČABAR.**

TAY-DEMĬR see **TAY-TEMĬR**

TAY-DEMÜR see **TAY-TEMĬR**

TAY-GELDĬ Kzk. 19th c. **Tay-geldi** [Тайгельды] (SODž. 70); Bashk. 1779 **Tay-gilde** [Тайгильда Султанов] (MIB V, 101). ✧ 'A foal/child has come / has been born'. ⇨ **TAY + KELDĬ.**

TAY-XAN Uyg. 8th c. - 9th c. **Tay-χan** [tajχan] (Müller, Uig. II, 80, DTS); Uyg. 8th c. - 9th c. **Tay-χan-χan / Tay-χañ-χan?** [Taichanghan / Tavghan chan? / tajχan] (Müller, Uig. II, 80, DTS). ✧ 'Great-Khan'? (<Chin. *ta<d'âi* 'great, high', cf. comp. *tay-sañun, tay-ügä*). ⇨ **XAN.**

TAY-KELTĬR Kzk. 18th c. - 19th c. **Tay-keltir** [Тайкельтр] (Tynyšp. 73); Kzk. 18th c. - 19th c. **Tay-keltir-biy** [Тайкельтр-бий] (Tynyšp. 68). ✧ 'Bring/lead a foal' cf. Kzk. *keltïr-* 'приводить' (KzRS). ⇨ **TAY.**

TAY-QARA Tat. 1624 **Tay-qara** [Тайкара Тевкелевъ] (Pokrovskij 71); Kzk. 19th c. **Tay-qara** [Тайкара] (SOK 4). ⇨ **TAY + QARA.**

TAY-QOÑUR Kzk.? 1696 **Tay-qoñur** [Тайкомуръ / Такомуръ Аталыковъ], envoy from Turkestan (DAI

X, 375, 376). ⇨ **TAY + QOÑUR.**

TAY-QULA Kzk. 19th c. **Tay-qula** [Tay-kula], a horse (Ljutš 78). ⇨ **TAY + QULA.**

TAY-SARA Kzk. 1823 **Tay-sara** [Тай Сара] (Syn Otečestva CXXXVI, 348). ⇨ **TAY + SARA I.**

TAY-TANA Kzk. 19th c. **Tay-tana** [Тайтана] (SOK 106). ⇨ **TAY + TANA I.?**

TAY-TELE Kzk. 19th c. **Tay-tele** [Тайтеле] (SODž. 28); Kzk. 19th c. **Tay-tele** [Тайтеле] (SODž. 28); Kzk. 19th c. **Tay-tele** [Тайтеле] (SOV 90). ⇨ **TAY + TELİ.**

TAY-TELEY Tat.(Sib.) 1628, 1635 **Tay-teley** [Тайтелей] (Miller, Ist. Sib. II, 338, 430, 473). ⇨ **TAY-TELE + suff. -y.**

TAY-TEMİR Maml. 1315 **Tay-demir** [طيدمر / Taidemor] (Abulfidā V, 296, 297); Maml. 1320 **Tay-demir** [طيدمر الجمدار], a cup-bearer (Zetterst.163); Maml. 1332 **Tay-demir** [طيدمر الساقى], an emir (Dawäd. 366); Maml. 1260 **Tay-demür** [Bedreddin-Taïdemour alakhout] (Makrīzī I, 100); Maml. 1298 **Tay-demür** [Taïdemur-Badjakbasch] (Makrīzī IV, 55); Tat.(GH) 1315 **Tay-temir** [Тайтемерь], envoy of the Horde (Suzd. 501, PSRL III, 71, IV, 48, V, 206, VII, 187, XVI, 60); Trkm. 1583 **Tay-temür / Tay-timür** [تاى نيمور / Taytimür], from Anatolia (Refik, Anad. 49). ⇨ **TAY + TEMİR.**

TAY-TEMÜR see **TAY-TEMİR**

TAY-TİMÜR see **TAY-TEMİR**

TAY-TOΓLÏ Tat.(GH) 14th c. **Tay-toγlï** [طيطغلى / Thäithoghly], a Kipchak woman, one of Özbek's wives (Ibn Bat. II, 383-84, 389 etc., Pelliot 101-103). ⇨ **TAY + TOQLÏ.**

TAY-ÜGÄ-XUTADMÏŠ Uyg. 8th c. **Tay-ügä-χutadmïš** (Le Coq, Buch-Fragm. 146). ⇨ **TAY + ÜGÄ + XUTADMÏŠ.**

TAYAQ Kzk. 19th c. **Tayaq** [Таякъ] (SOK 190); Karg. 19th-20th c. **Tayaq** [Кос-тајак] (Katanov, Otč. 8). ✧ 'Stick, staff' cf. Uyg., Chag., Alt., Kar., Kirg., Kzk. etc. *tayaq* 'der Stock, der Stab' (Radl. III, 816). See also **JUWAN-TAYAQ, QOS-TAYAQ, QUTLUΓ-TAYAQ, QUTLUΓ-TEMÜR-TAYAQ.**

TAYALÏ Kzk. 19th c. **Tayalï** [Таялы] (SOK 198).

TAYAN Bashk. 1764 **Tayan** (<Tayanqa) [Кусекей Таянкин] (MIB IV/1, 300); Kzk. 19th c. **Tayan-bay** [Tajanbay] (Ljutš 243).

TAYANČ Uyg. **Tayanč** [Tayanç] (EUTS). ✧ 'Supporter/shoulder' cf. Karakh. *tajanč* 'опора' (DTS). See also **QUYAQ-TAYANČ.**

TAYANČAR Tat.(GH) 1321 **Tayančar** [Таянчаръ] (PSRL X, 187).

TAYANÏŠ Kzk. 19th c. **Tayanïš-pay** [Таянышпай] (SOV 42, 56). ✧ 'Support(er)' cf. Kzk. *tayanïš* 'die Stütze, der Thürpfosten' (Radl. III, 818).

TAYBAQ Kzk. 19th c. **Taybaq** [Ходжа-Бай Тайбаковъ] (Grod., Pril. 175).

TAYBÏN Hak.(Blt.) 19th-20th c. **Taybïn** [Таібын] (Proben IX, 362); Yak. **Taybïn** [Таібын] (Pek.).

TAYBÏR Yak. **Taybïr / Taybïr** [Таібыр] (Pek.). ✧ ? See also **AYÏ-TAYBÏR, ĀN-TAYBÏR.**

TAYBU Uyg. **Taybu** [Taibu] (EUTS).

TAYČA Trkm. 20th c. **Tayča** [Tayča] (Zaj. 1971, 331); Trkm. 20th c. **Tayča** [Тайча] (TrkmRS 613); Kzk. 19th c. **Tayča** (<Taycï?) [Тайча] (Grod., Pril. 187); Kzk. 19th c. **Tayča** (<Taycï?) [Тайча] (SOV 130). ✧ 'Foal' (Zaj. 1971), cf. Trkm. *tayča* 'жеребёночек' (TrkmRS), also *tai(ča)* 'Füllen' (TMEN II, Nos. 863, 865). ⇨ **TAY + dim. suff. -ča.**

TAYČAQ see **TAYČÏQ**

TAYČÏ-TULUN Uyg. **Tayči-tulun** [Taiçi-tulun] (EUTS). ⇨ **TAYČÏ + TOLUN?**

TAYČIK see **TAYČÏQ**

TAYČİN Bashk. 1787 **Tayčin** [Мунасып Тайчинов] (MIB V, 207); Bashk. 1787 **Tayčin** [Салих Тайчинов] (MIB V, 207); Kzk. 19th c. **Tayčin** [Тайчиновъ] (SKSO III, 18). ✧ Ethnonym? Cf. Mo. *Tayčin tabun* in 1634 (Andrievič, Ist. Sib. I, 120).

TAYČÏ Kzk. 19th c. **Tayči** [Турганбай Тайчіевъ] (Grod., Pril. 54); Kzk. 19th c. **Tayči** [Тайчи] (SOV 22, 54); Kzk. **Tayči-bek** [Тайчибекъ] (Smirnov, Sultany 18); Kzk. 19th c. **Tayči-bay** [Тайчебай] (SOK 180); Kzk. 19th c. **Tayču-bay** [Тайчубай] (SOK 54); Kzk. 19th c. **Tayču-bek** [Тайчубекъ] (SOK 26); Kzk. 19th c. **Tayču-bek** [Тайчубекъ] (SOV 106); Kzk. 19th c. **Tayši** [Тайше] (AOP 82); Kzk. 19th c. **Tayši** [Тайше] (SOK 216); Kzk. 19th c. **Tayži-bay** [Тайжбай] (SODž. 154). ✧ 'Heir of the throne; prince; (a Mongol) noble man' (Mo.). Used also as a secondary component of personal names. See also **ÖLEÑ-TAYČÏ.**

TAYČÏQ Kzk. 19th c. **Tayčaq** (<Taycïq?) [Джунусъ Тайчаковъ] (Grod., Pril. 77); Kzk. **Tayčik** [Султанъ юнусъ Тайчиковъ] (Sb. Syr-D. II, 69); Kzk. **Tayčik** [Тайчикъ], Kenisara's son (Smirnov, Sultany 25); Kzk. 19th c. **Tayčik** [Бухарбай Тайчиковъ] (Grod., Pril. 66); Kzk. 19th c. **Tayšïq** [Тайшикъ] (AOK 106, 134). ⇨ **TAY + suff. -čïq.**

TAYČU see **TAYČÏ**

TAYJAP Tuv. 19th c. **Tayjap** [Таіцап] (Proben IX, 143, 161).

TAYDALA see **TAYDULA**

TAYDAÑ Hak. 19th-20th c. **Taydañ** [Тайданъ] (HRS 351).

TAYDÏΓAŠ Bashk. 1650 **Taydïγaš** [Маскайко Тайдигашевъ] (Vel.-Zern., Bašk. 30).

TAYDÏQ Uyg. 12th c. - 14th c. **Taydïq-ilči** (Radl., USp. 30-31); Uyg. 12th c. - 14th c. **Taytïq** (DTS); Kzk. 19th c. **Taytïq** [Тайтыкъ] (AOO 78). ✧ 'We slipped' (Bese 12), cf. Uyg., Karakh. *tay-* 'поскользнуться, упасть' (DTS).

TAYDÏQ-ALČİ   Uyg. **Taydïq-alči** [Taidık-Alçi] (EUTS). ⇨ **TAYDÏQ** + **ALČİ.**

TAYDULA   Tat.(GH) / Mo.? 1357, 1378 **Taydala / Taydula?** [Таидала / Тайдала / Тайдула], Janï-bek's wife (PSRL II, 350, VII, 220, VIII, 10, X, 229, XI, 32). ✧ Mongol fem. PN? Cf. Mo. *Taytula* in RaD.

TAYDULUY   Nog. 1649 **Tayduluy** (<**Taydula?**) [Тайдулуй], fem. (AI IV,123).

TAYFANQ   Kzk. 19th c. **Tayfanq** [Тайфанкъ] (Grod., Pril. 114).

TAYGİ   Uzb. 1873 **Taygi-bay** [Тайгибай] (Moskal'cev 36).

TAYГA   Kzk. 19th c. **Tayγa** [Тайга Алла Яровъ] (SKSO III, 18); Kzk. 19th c. **Tayγa-bay** [Тайго бай] (SOK 34). ✧ 'Tayga' cf. Alt., Hak. *tayγa* 'das Felsengebirge' (Radl. III, 767).

TAYГAQ   Kzk. 19th c. **Tayγaq** [Тайгакъ] (SOK 228). ✧ 'Greasy, slippery' cf. Alt., Kzk., Tat. *tayγaq* 'schlüpfrig' (Radl. III, 767).

TAYГAM-BEK see **TAYГAN**

TAYГAN   Kzk. 19th c. **Tayγam-bay** [Тайгомбай] (SOV 72); Kzk. 19th c. **Tayγam-bek** [Тайгамбекъ] (SOV 6); Kzk. 19th c. **Tayγan** [Тилле Тайгановъ] (Grod., Pril. 158). ✧ 'Greyhound' cf. Chag., Alt., East.T. *tayγan* 'der Windhund' (Radl. III, 768).

TAYГUN   Bashk. 1769 **Tayγun** [Тайгун Угяшев] (MIB IV/1, 335); Bashk. 1777 **Tayγun** [Тайгун] (MIB V, 54); Bashk. 1789 **Tayγun** [Тляп Тайгунов] (MIB V, 241).

TAYXAR   Kkalp. 20th c. **Tayχar-bay** [Тайхъарбай] (Bask., Kkalp. 5).

TAYÏAXA   Yak. **Tayïaχa** [Тајыаха] (Pek.).

TAYÏN-İRKÄ   Kzk. 1676 **Tayïn-irkä** [Таинъ-Ирка], a prince (DAI VII, 341). ⇨ **ERKE.**

TAYÏNČAQ   Uyg. **Tayïnčaq** [Tayınçak] (EUTS); Uyg. 12th c. - 14th c. **Tayïnčaq-tarqan** (Radl., USp. 121, DTS).

TAYÏR see **TAİR**

TAYÏŠ   Bashk. 1742, 1761 **Tayïš** [Таиш Иткинин] (MIB III, 513, MIB IV/1, 200); Bashk. 1789 **Tayïš** [Таиш Зиянгулов] (MIB V, 255); Tat. 1543 **Tayuš** [Таюшъ Токъсубинъ / Таютъ Тосубинь], from Astrakhan (PSRL XIII, 144). ✧ 'Bandy-legged' cf. Bashk. *tayïš* 'косолапый' (BRS/Uraksin).

TAYÏŠMA   Uyg. **Tayïšma** [Tayışma] (EUTS). See also **ŠAMÏZ-TAYÏŠMA.**

TAYÏLA   Yak. **Tayïla** [Тајыла] (Pek.). ✧ Danilo (R.).

TAYÏLALÏR   Yak. **Tayïlalïr** [Тајылалыр / Тајыла лыр] (Pek.). ⇨ **TAYÏLA** + dim. suff. *-lïr.*

TAYYÏBE   Turk. 1440 **Tayyibe-χatun** [طيبه خاتون] (MG Ank. 23). ✧ 'Good, nice, beautiful' (Erol II), cf. Turk. *tayyip* 'gut, richtig, ausgezeichnet' (HŞ) (<Ar.).

TAYKE   Kzk. 19th c. **Tayke** [Тайке] (SOK 154). ⇨

TAY + dim. suff. *-ke.*

TAYQANA   Kzk. 1635 **Tayqana** [Тайкана], a prince (Miller, Ist. Sib. II, 424). ✧ 'Little foal'. ⇨ **TAY** + suff. *-qana.*

TAYQAR   Kkalp. 20th c. **Tayqar-bay** [Тайқарбай] (KkRS 776). ✧ 'Eatable bulbous plant' cf. Kzk. *tayqar* 'Pflanze, deren Wurzel gegessen werden' (Radl. III, 767).

TAYQUQ   Bashk. 1756 **Tayquq** [Кинзягул Тайкуков] (MIB IV/1, 128).

TAYLAQ   Tat.(Sib.) 1599 **Taylaq** [Тойлакъ] (AI II, 18); Bashk. 1789 **Taylaq** [Каип Тайлаков] (MIB V, 271); Bashk. 1789 **Taylaq** [Каип Тайлаков] (MIB V, 271); Kzk. 18th c. - 19th c. **Taylaq** [Тайлак] (Tynyšp. 65); Kzk. 1820 **Taylaq** (MIK IV, 354); Kzk. 1823 **Taylaq** [طايلاق] (MIK IV, 459, 462); Kzk. 19th c. **Taylaq** [Тайлакпай] (AOAtb. 42); Kzk. 19th c. **Taylaq** [Тайлякъ] (AOP 6); Kzk. 19th c. **Taylaq** [Тайлакъ] (Grod., Pril. 110, 157); Kzk. 19th c. **Taylaq** [Тайлякъ] (SKSO VIII, 204); Kzk. 19th c. **Taylaq** [Тайлякъ] (SKSO VIII, 221); Kzk. 19th c. **Taylaq** [Тайлякъ] (SOK 130); Kirg. **Taylaq** [Тайлак] (Jud. 404, Kalilov 92); Kirg. **Taylaq** [Таiлак] (Proben V, 70 /71/, 151 /152/); Kirg. 1827 **Taylaq** [Тайлакъ] (Konšin, Mat. I-III, 113); Kirg. 19th c. **Taylaq** [Тайлякъ] (Potanin II, 3); Kirg. 19th c. **Taylaq** [Тайлакъ], from the Sayaq tribe (Valihanov, Soč. 128); Kzk. **Taylaq-bï** [Tailak Bï / Таiлак бi] (Proben III, 226 /267/); Kzk. 19th c. **Taylaq-pay** [Тайлякпай] (SOV 8); Kzk. 19th c. **Taylaq-pay** [Тайлакпай] (SOV 82). ✧ 'A two-year-old camel' Kzk. *taylaq* 'zweijähriges Kameel' (Radl. III, 769), Kzk. *taylaq* 'годовалый верблюжонок' (KzRS). See also **AQ-TAYLAQ, BAY-TAYLAQ, BOZ-TAYLAQ, JAN-TAYLAQ, KER-TAYLAQ, NAR-TAYLAQ, TURUM.**

TAYLAM-BAY see **TAYLAN**

TAYLAN   Kzk. 19th c. **Taylam-bay** [Тайламбай] (AOP 118); Kzk. 19th c. **Taylam-bay** [Тайламбай] (SOV 80); Kzk. 19th c. **Taylan** [Тайланъ] (Lomakin 33); Uzb. 19th c. **Taylan-bay** [Тайлянбай] (SKSO III, 166).

TAYLAR   Tat.(Sib.) 1684 **Taylar** [Корочинъ Тайларовъ] (DAI XI, 160).

TAYLE   Hak. 19th-20th c. **Tayle** [Тайле], fem. (HRS 355).

TAYLÏ   Trkm. 20th c. **Taylï** [Taylï] (Zaj. 1971, 331); Trkm. 20th c. **Taylï** [Тайлы] (TrkmRS 613); Kzk. 19th c. **Taylï-bay** [Тайлибай] (Grod. 254); Kzk. 19th c. **Taylï-bay** [Умбатбай Тайлибаевъ] (Grod., Pril. 185); Kzk. 19th c. **Taylï-bay** [Тайлибай] (SOV 14); Kzk. 19th c. **Taylï-bek** [Тайлибекъ] (SODž. 156); Selj. **Taylu** [طيلو], one of the first Danishmendid rulers

(Mordtmann: ZDMG XXX, 474); Selj. 12th c. **Taylu?** [علاالـدیـن بـن طیلو], a name preserved in the name of a mosque (Ibn Šaddād, Alep). ❖ 'Having a foal' (Zaj. 1971), cf. Trkm. *taylï* 'с жеребёнком, имеющий жеребёнка' (TrkmRS), Kzk. *tailï* 'einen Füllen habend' (Radl. III, 769). ⇨ **TAY** + suff. *-lï.*

TAYLÏMBET Kzk. 1732 **Taylïmbet** [Тайлымбетъ] (Dobrosm., Turg. 10). ⇨ **TAYLÏ** + suff. *-mbet.*

TAYMAN Kzk. 19th c. **Tayman** [Тайманъ] (AOA 86); Kzk. 19th c. **Tayman** [Исетай Таймановъ] (AUK 897); Kzk. 19th c. **Tayman** [Тайманъ] (SOK 300). ⇨ **TAY?** + suff. *-man.*

TAYMANKE Kzk. 19th c. **Taymanke?** [Таймонке] (SOK 74); Kzk. 19th c. **Taymenke?** [Тайменке] (SOK 130). ⇨ **TAYMAN** + suff. *-ke* or comp. *-ake.*

TAYMARÏN Yak. **Taymarïn-χotun / Kün-taymarïn-χotun** [Кюн Таімарын хотун], fem. (Pek.).

TAYMAZ Bashk. 18th c. **Taymas** [Таймасов] (MIB V, 147, 234, 254, 259 etc.); Bashk. 18th c. **Taymas** [Таймасъ] (Nepljuev 137); Bashk. 1763 **Taymas** [Таймас Кутлин] (MIB IV/2, 45); Bashk. 1772 **Taymas** [Хусейн-тархан Таймасов] (MIB IV/2, 408); Bashk. 1776, 1777, 1779 **Taymas** [Ялтыр Таймасов / Ялтыр-тархан Таймасов] (MIB V, 41, 64, 85); Bashk. 1777 **Taymas** [Ялтътыръ Таймасовъ] (Vel.-Zern., Bašk. 3-4); Bashk. 1779 **Taymas** [Ялтыр-тархан Таймасов] (MIB V, 85]; Bashk. 1783 **Taymas** [Алишей Таймасов] (MIB V, 147); Bashk. 1789 **Taymas** [Таймас Кашкин] (MIB V, 254, 259); Bashk. 1789 **Taymas** [Таймас Егаферов] (MIB V, 269); Bashk. 1790 **Taymas** [Таймас Нурушев] (MIB V, 275); Bashk. 1790 **Taymas** [Таймас Шаимов] (MIB V, 680); Kzk. 1732 **Taymas** [Batyr Taimas], a forefather of the Bashkirs (Levchine 169); Kzk. 18th c. - 19th c. **Taymas** [Таймас] (Tynyšp. 73); Kzk. 1817 **Taymas** [طایماس / Таймас] (MIK IV, 313, 319); Kzk. 19th c.? **Taymas** [Ханъ Таймасъ], a hero in a legend (Vasil'ev 1); Kzk. 19th c. **Taymas** [Таймасъ] (AOAtb. 42); Kzk. 19th c. **Taymas** [Таймасъ] (AOK 82); Kzk. 19th c. **Taymas** [Таймасъ] (AOO 38); Kzk. 19th c. **Taymas** [Таймасъ] (AOP 92); Kzk. 19th c. **Taymas** [Курумбай Таймасовъ] (Grod., Pril. 169); Kzk. 19th c. **Taymas,** Dubal-bas' son (Ljutš 54); Kzk. 19th c. **Taymas** [Таймасъ] (SOK 196); Bashk. 1711, 1733, 1734, 1740, 1760 **Taymas / Taymas-batïr / Taymas-tarχan** [Таймасъ Шаимовъ / Таймасъ Батыръ Шаимовъ / Таймасъ Батыръ / Таймасъ-Тарханъ / Таймас-тархан Шаимов], a tarχan (MIB III, 80, MIB I, 309, 317 etc., Vel.-Zern., Bašk. 5, 28, PSZRI IX, 311, PSZRI XI, 311, Nepljuev 134, 136, 159, 458, MIB IV/2, 160); Bashk. 1783 **Taymas / Toymas** [Таймас (Тоймас) Кашкин] (MIB V, 148, 254, 311, 361); Bashk. 1783, 1789 **Taymas / Toymas?** [Алишей /

Алишай Таймасов] (MIB V, 147, 254); Kmk.? 1807 **Taymaz** [Кучук Таймазов] (MID III, 143). ❖ 'He doesn't slide/come down; he won't die' (Sattarov), 'He won't slide; he won't make a mistake' (Kusimova), cf. Alt., Chag., Hak., Kar. *tay-* 'ausgleiten' (Radl. III, 766), Kzk. *tayï-* 'скользить, оступаться' (PKRS) + suff. *-maz.*

TAYMÄK Bashk. 18th c. **Taymäk / Taylaq?** [Акзигит Таймяков (Таиляков)] (MIB V, 259, 295).

TAYMENKE see **TAYMANKE**

TAYMUR Kzk. 19th c. **Taymur-bek** [Таймуръбекъ] (Grod., Pril. 193).

TAYRAN Chag. 15th c. **Tayran-bahadur** [طیران بـهادر / Tajran / Ттайранъ Баhадуръ], Sheybani's follower (Šejb. LXV).

TAYSA Hak. 19th-20th c. **Taysa** [Тайса], fem. (HRS 355). ❖ Taisiya (R.) (HRS).

TAYSAT Kzk. 19th c. **Taysat** [Джума Таисатовъ] (Grod., Pril. 69).

TAYSÏ Uyg. **Taysi** [Taisi] (EUTS). ⇨ **TAYŠÏ?**

TAYSÏR Bashk. 1785 **Taysïr** [Тайсыр Тенишев] (MIB V, 178).

TAYŠA Kzk. **Tayša-χan** [تایشه خان / Тайша] (Divaev, Alp. 45); Kzk. **Tayša-qalmaq** [Tayša-kalmak] (Divaev, Alp. 47). ❖ 'Heir of the throne; (Mongol) noble man' see comp. *tayči* (<Mo.<Chin.).

TAYŠÏ Uyg. **Tayši** [Taişi] (EUTS). ❖ 'Scribe, writer' cf. Chag., East.(Tar.) *taiši* 'der Schreiber, Schriftsteller' (Radl. III, 770), used also as a title or secondary component of names. (<Mo.<Chin.).

TAYŠÏN Oghuz 10th c. - 11th c. **Tayšin-oγul** [Tischin-oγul] (Mirch. Gasnevid.?).

TAYŠÏŇ Uyg. **Tayšing-du** (<**Tayšing-Tutuň**) [Tayšingdu] (Zieme, Mat. I, 75, 83). ❖ 'Large vehicle of transport' (Zieme: 'Grosse Fahrzeug') (<Chin.).

TAYŠÏQ see **TAYČÏQ**

TAYTA Tat.(GH) 1300 **Tayta** [طیطا / Тайта], a Kipchak who went over from Noγay to Toqtamïš (Baybars/Tizeng. I, 90, 113, Veselovskij, Nog. 48). ❖ 'Grand-father on mother's side' cf. Alt., Hak. *tayda* 'der Grossvater von Mutterseite' (Radl. III, 770).

TAYTAX see **TAYTAQ**

TAYTAQ Yak. **Taytaχ** [Taitax], a popular shaman of the district of Vilyuysk (Pek.); Kzk. 19th c. **Taytaq** [Тайтакъ] (AOAtb. 22). ❖ 'Grand-father on mother's side'? cf. Alt., Hak. *tayda / taydaq* 'der Grossvater von Mutterseite' (Radl. III, 770).

TAYTAL Tat.(Sib.)? 1632 **Taytal(ko)** [Тайталко] (Miller, Ist. Sib. II, 395).

TAYTALA Kzk. 19th c. **Taytala** [Тайталинъ] (SOV 94).

TAYTAN Tat.(Sib.) 1632 **Taytan** [Тайтанъ] (Miller, Ist. Sib. II, 397); Kzk. **Taytan** [Нурмухамедъ Тайтановъ] (Sb. Syr-D. III., otd. II, 65); Kzk. 1846

Taytan [Тайтанъ] (Konšin, Mat. V, 101). ❖ 'Knock-kneed, bandy-legged' cf. Kzk. *taytanda-* 'paytak paytak koşmak' (KzTS).

TAYTAR Tat. 1776 **Taytar** [Ахметъ Тайтаровъ] (PSZRI XX, 456).

TAYTARČÏN Uyg. 13th-14th c. **Taydarčïn-täñrim** [Taydarčïn Tngrim], fem. (Zieme, Mat. III, 280 (after Tuguševa)); Uyg. 13th-14th c. **Taytarčïn**, fem. (Zieme, Mat. III, 280).

TAYTĀRÏSA Yak. **Taytārïsa** [Таітарыса], fem. (Pek.).

TAYTÏBET Kzk. 19th c. **Taytïbet** [Тайтыбетъ] (SOV 84). ⇨ **TAYLÏ?** + suff. *-bet*.

TAYTÏQ see **TAYDÏQ**

TAYTÏQAR Kzk. 1624 **Taytïqar** [Тайтыкар] (Miller, Ist. Sib. II, 317).

TAYTUL Tat.(Sib.)/Mo.? 1654 **Taytul** [Тайтул Икычей] (Miller, Ist. Sib. II, 540). See also **TAYDULA**.

TAYUŠ see **TAYÏŠ**

TAKİ see **TAQÏ**

TAKİM see **TAQÏM**

TAQ Oghuz **Taq-χan** [طاق خان / Tak χān / Так-хан], Oghuz Khan's son, the legendary forefather of the Salɣurids (Qazw. 503, RaD I/1, 76); Kzk. 19th c. **Taq-pay** [Такпай] (SOK 144). ❖ 'Lonesome'? (Sattarov), cf. Uyg., Kuman, Chag., Kirg., Tat. *taq* 'ungrade, unpaar, der Einzelne' (Radl. III, 777). ⇨ **ТАГ?** See also **ALTUN-TAQ, QÏZÏL-TAQ**.

TAQ-ARSLAN see **ТАГ-ARSLAN**

TAQ-KEZ Kzk. 19th c. **Taq-kez** [Таккезъ] (SOK 216).

TAQ-SABA see **TOQ-SABA**

TAQ-SULEYMAN Kzk. **Taq-suleyman** [Такъ-Сулейманъ] (Pojarkov 12). ⇨ **TAQ + SULAYMAN**.

TAQ-ТОГА Maml.? 1291 **Taq-toɣa / Toq-toɣa?** [Tactoga] (Abulfidā V, 100-101). ⇨ **TAQ / TOQ?** + **TOQA**.

TAQA Kzk. 1819 **Taqa-bay** [Такабай] (MIK IV, 324); *TN:* Kzk.? **Taqa** [Такабай], a well south-east of Lake Aral (Karta JAR XI); Uzb.? **Taqa-bay** [Така-бай], south-west of Tashkent (Karta JAR XIX). ❖ 'Shoe heel; horseshoe' cf. Kzk. *taqa* 'der Hacken' (Radl. III, 780), Chag. *taqa* 'das Hufeisen' (Radl. III, 779).

TAQAY Bashk. 1751 **Taqay** [Акынчин Такаев] (MIB IV/1, 43); Bashk. 1760 **Taqay** [Чюнай Такаев] (MIB IV/2, 28); Kzk. 19th c. **Taqay** [Такай] (AOK 46). ❖ 'Male relative, uncle' (Sattarov). ⇨ **ТАГАУ?**

TAQANAY Tat. 1764 **Taqanay** [Таканай Уразметев] (MIB IV/2, 105).

TAQANAQ Kzk. 19th c. **Taqanaq** [Таканакъ] (AOP 18).

TAQANAN Yak. **Taqanan-üs** [Таканан-ус], a smith (Pek.).

TAQAR Tat.(GH) 14th c. **Taqar** [Τάκαρ], a christened Tatar (Byz. Turc. 296). ❖ 'Big needle'? cf. Chag. *taqar* 'eine grosse Nadel' (Radl. III, 780). See also **TEBEN, TEMENE, TEMENEY, TEBENEYKA**.

TAQAŠ Kzk. 19th c. **Taqaš** [Такашъ] (SOK 86); Kzk. 19th c. **Taqaš-pay** [Такашпай] (SOK 152). ⇨ **TAQA?** + suff. *-š*.

TAQAWUN Kzk. 19th c. **Taqawun** [Такаунъ] (AOK 22).

TAQÏ Bashk. 1757 **Taki** [Таки Мишаров] (MIB IV/1, 150, 153); Bashk. 1761 **Taki** [Ильяс Такиев] (MIB IV/1, 214); Trkm. 1745 **Taqï-χan** [Такы-хан] (MIT II, 172); Trkm. 1817/18 **Taqï-qul** [Такы-кул] (MIT II, 407). ❖ Taqi (Ar.) 'Godfearing, devout, pious' (Ahmed).

TAQÏČUQ Uyg. 12th c. - 14th c. **Taqïčuq** [Takıçuk] (Radl., USp. 209, 251, DTS, EUTS). ⇨ **TAQÏ** + suff. *-čuq*.

TAQÏX Kirg. 19th c. **Taqïχ** [Саскулъ Такихъ] (Grod., Pril. 172).

TAQÏM Kzk. 19th c. **Takim** [Такимъ] (Grod., Pril. 107); Kzk. 19th c. **Taqïm-bay** [Такымбай] (AOP 18). ❖ 'A part of the thigh near the knee' cf. Chag., Kzk. *takim / taqïm* 'der untere Theil des Oberschenkels des Kniees' (Radl. III, 788).

TAQÏR-BAS Kzk. 19th c. **Taqïr-bas** [Такырбасъ] (SOK 170); Kzk. 19th c. **Taqïr-bas** [Такырбасъ] (SOV 36). ❖ 'Bald-head(ed)' cf. Alt., Kzk., Kirg., Tat. *taqïr* 'glatt, eben, ohne Haar, ohne Grass, kahl' (Radl. III, 783). ⇨ **BAŠ**.

TAQÏŠ Kzk. 19th c. **Taqïš** [Такышъ] (AOAtb. 46).

TAQLÏ Uzb. 1886 **Taqlï-pählewan** [Таклы Пахлеванъ] (Moskal'cev 66).

TAQMAN Kzk. 19th c. **Taqman** [Такманъ] (AOO 70).

TAQŌ Hak.(Kyz.) 19th-20th c. **Taqō** [Тако] (Katanov, Otč. 13).

TAQPAYČÏ Alt. 19th-20th c. **Taqpayčï** [Такпайчы], fem. (OjrRS 213). ❖ 'Gatherer of chips/cuttings' (OjrRS), cf. Alt., Hak. *taqpay* 'der Spahn' (Radl. III, 798).

TAQSİM Bashk. 1756 **Taqsim** [Таксим Каракшиев] (MIB IV/1, 128). ❖ 'Division, partition' cf. Turk. *taksim* 'id.' (TED) (<Ar.).

TAQSÏR Bashk. 1737 **Taqsïr** [Актюш Таксыров] (MIB I, 325); Bashk. 1789 **Taqsïr** [Таксыр Тянышев] (MIB V, 263). ❖ 'Majesty (respectful addressing to a Kazakh sultan)' cf. Kirg., Kzk. *taqsïr* 'id.' (Radl. III, 793).

TAQTAQ Turk. 19th c. **Taqtaq** [Taktak asan oɣlu], nickname of a Zeybek (Kúnos 1891, 119). ❖ 'Rap-rap (noise); woodpecker?' cf. Turk. *taktak* 'стук, грохот' (TRS), Kzk. *taktak* 'der Specht' (Radl. III, 791).

TAQTAM Tat.(Lit.) 1595 **Taqtam** [Ордюшко

Тактамовичъ] (Lit. Tat. 229, 230).

TAQTAMÏŠ see **TOQTAMÏŠ**

TAQTÏ Bashk. 18th c. **Taqtï-bay** [Такты-бай] (MIB I, 399).

TAL Kzk. 1676 **Tal-bäk** [Талбачка] (DAI VII, 343); Kzk. 1684 **Tal-bäk?** [Талбакъ], a prince (DAI XI, 160); Chuv. 18th-19th c. **Tal-murza** [Талмурза] (Magn. 80); Kzk. 19th c. **Tal-žan** [Тальжанъ] (AOA 138). ✧ 'Willow' cf. Alt., Hak., Kirg., Kzk., Tat. etc. *tal* 'die Weide' (Radl. III, 875). See also **ÏR-TAL, QARA-TAL, QOY-TAL, SARÏ-TAL.**

TAL-MAMET Tat. 1629 **Tal-mamet** [Талмамет] (Miller, Ist. Sib. II, 357). ⇨ **TAL + MAMET.**

TAL-SARA Tat. 1675 **Tal-sara / Tal-sarï?** [Талсаринъ] (Kungursk. akty 29, 30). ⇨ **TAL + SARA I.**

TAL-SU Kzk. 19th c. **Tal-su?** [Талсу] (AOP 106).

TALA I. Chuv. 18th-19th c. **Tala** [Тала] (Magn. 80).

TALA II. Hak. 19th-20th c. **Tala** [Тала], fem. (HRS 355).

TALAY Kzk. 1622, 1643 **Talay** [Талай], a prince (Miller, Ist. Sib. II, 289, 410, 411, 429, Kuznecov 8, 10); Shor 19th-20th c. **Talay** [Talaj] (Dyrenkova 208); Alt. 19th c. **Talay-χan** [Талай-хан] (Verb., In. 123); Hak.(Koyb.) 19th-20th c. **Talay-qan** [Талаi Кан] (Radl. I, 1080). ✧ 'Sea, large lake' cf. Chag. *dalai* 'das Meer; der Verlust' (Radl. III, 1633), Alt., Hak. *talai* 'das Meer, ein grosser See' (Radl. III, 878). See also **AY-DALAY.**

TALAQ Bashk. 1735 **Talaq** [Талякъ Илбахтинъ], a tarχan (Vel.-Zern., Bašk. 17); NUyg. 19th c. **Talaq** [طلاق / Talak] (Le Coq, Namenl. 116); Kkalp. 18th c. - 19th c. **Talaq-behadïr** [Талак бехадыр] (MIKk. 118); Kzk. 19th c. **Talaq-pay** [Талакпай] (SOK 206). ✧ I. 'Divorce of a wife by her husband' cf. Kzk., Tat., Turk. *talaq* (Ar.) 'die Lösung der Ehe, die Ehescheidung' (Radl. III, 880); II. 'Robbery' cf. Chag. *talaq* 'der Raub' (Radl. III, 880); III. 'Milt, spleen' cf. Kzk., Tat. *talaq* 'die Milz' (Radl. III, 880). See also **BAY-TALAQ, TALAN.**

TALAN Kzk. 19th c. **Talan-bay** [Таланбай] (SOK 244). ✧ I. 'Robbery; booty' cf. Chag. *talan* 'die Räuberei', der Raub, die Plünderung, die Beute' (Radl. III, 881); II. 'Seventy' (Mo.) (Sattarov). See also **TALAQ.**

TALAÑ Alt. 19th-20th c. **Talañ** [Талаҥ], fem. (OjrRS 213). ✧ 'A kind of bird; skylark' cf. Alt. *talañ / talañ-γälän* 'ein kleiner Vogel' (Radl. III, 881), *talañ-kileñ* 'жаворонок' (OjrRS).

TALAS Kzk. 19th c. **Talas** [Таласпай] (AOK 22); Kzk. 19th c. **Talas** [Таласъ Ходжиевъ] (Grod., Pril. 169); Kzk. 19th c. **Talas** [Таласпай] (SOK 84, 104, 128, 132); Kzk. 19th c. **Talas-bay** [Таласбай] (SODž. 60, 122); Kzk. 19th c. **Talas-bay** [Таласбай] (SOK 160); Kzk. 19th c. **Talas-bay** [Таласбай] (SOV 102); Kirg. **Talas-bay** [Таласбай] (Jud. 270); Kzk. 19th c. **Talas-biy** [Тасбау Таласбыевъ] (Grod., Pril. 134); Kzk. 19th c. **Talas-pay** [Таласпай] (SODž. 148); Kzk. 19th c. **Talas-pay-mergen** [Талас-пай мерген], Qoblandï's son, Qaraman (Potanin, Pred. 73, Žirm., Epos 389); Kzk. 19th c. **Talas-pek** [Таласпекъ] (SOK 24). ✧ I. 'Quarrel, brawl; wish, hope, aim, goal' cf. Hak., Kzk. *talas* 'der Streit, der Zank' (Radl. III, 882), Kzk. *talas* 'айтыс, тартыс; талап, үміт, дәме' (QTTS); II. Talas (toponym, mountain chain and river in Kirghizistan). See also **BAY-TALAS, TOQ-TALAS.**

TALAT Kzk. 19th c. **Talat-bay** [Талатбай] (AOP 58). ✧ 'Face; beauty; grace' (Ar.), cf. Kzk. PN *Talγat* 'id.' (Žanuzakov).

TALBÏTAQ Bashk. 1779 **Talbïtaq** [Талбытак Исенчурин] (MIB V, 101).

TALČU Kzk. 19th c. **Talču-bay** [Талчубай] (SOK 36).

TALDA Hak. 19th-20th c. **Talda** [Талда] (HRS 351).

TALDABAS Alt. 19th-20th c. **Taldabas** [Талдабас] (OjrRS 210). ✧ 'Modest, frugal' (OjrRS).

TALEP-BERDİ Kzk. 19th c. **Talep-berdi** [Талепберды] (SODž. 50). ✧ 'Wish-given (child); He/she wished (the child)' cf. Crm., Kzk., Tat. *talap* (Ar.) 'der Wunsch, die Sehnsucht, das Streben' (Radl. III, 885). ⇨ **BERDİ.**

TALΓAJAQ Hak.(Kacha) 19th-20th c. **Talγajaq** [Талңацак] (Proben IX, 318).

TALΓAM-BAY see **TALΓAN**

TALΓAN Kzk. 19th c. **Talγam-bay** [Талгамбай] (AOAtb. 22). ✧ 'Voraciousness (of pregnant women)' cf. Kzk. *talγan* 'die Esslust schwangerer Frauen' (Radl. III, 891).

TALΓAR Kzk. 19th c. **Talγar-bay** [Талгарбай] (SODž. 130); Kzk. 19th c. **Talγar-bek** [Талгарбекъ] (SOK 268). ✧ 'Choosy; capricious' cf. Chag., Kzk. *talγa-* 'wählig, wählerisch im Essen sein' (Radl. III, 891).

TALΓÏDAN Karg. 19th-20th c. **Talγïdan / Talγïdan** [Талңыданъ / Талгыданъ] (Proben IX, 659, Katanov: ZIRGOÊtn. XVII, vyp. III, 164).

TALİQAY Bashk. 1798 **Taliqay** [Таликай] (PSZRI XXV, 195).

TALİM Kzk. 19th c. **Talim-bay** [Талимбай] (SOV 114). ✧ Talim (Ar.) 'education, instruction' (Ahmed).

TALİP Kzk. 19th c. **Talip** [Талибъ] (SOK 246); Kzk. 19th c. **Talip-bay** [Талипбай] (SODž. 22); Trkm. 20th c. **Talïb** [Talïb] (Zaj. 1971, 329); Trkm. 20th c. **Tālïb** [Талиб] (TrkmRS 616). ✧ 'Seeking/searching knowledge; pupil' (Kusimova, Sattarov, Žanuzakov), cf. Trkm. *tālïp* 'студент, учащийся (в медресе)' (TrkmRS) (<Ar.).

TALÏ Kzk. 19th c. **Talï-bay** [Талыбай] (SOV 90). ✧ 'Fortune, destiny' cf. *Tâlih* (Erol II); 'Kader, kısmet, baht' (<Ar.). See also **BAY-TALĬ.**

TALĬČ Tat.(GH) 1410 **Talĭč** [Талычъ], a prince of the Horde (PSRL V, 258, VI, 139, VIII, 85).

TALĬM Kzk. **Talĭm-qĭz** [Talym Kys / Талым кыз], fem. (Proben III, 322 /389/).

TALĬMBET Kzk. 1734 **Talĭmbet-batĭr / Tatlĭmbet-batĭr?** [Талымбетъ-Батыръ / Татлымбетъ] (PSZRI IX, 303, 304).

TALĬN-TAY Tuv. 19th c. **Talĭn-tay** [Талын-таi] (Proben IX, 128). ⇨ **TAY?** or suff. -tay(1,2).

TALĬNJĬ Turk. 19th c. **Talĭnjĭ-oγlu** [Talynǯy oγlu], a Zeybek (Kúnos 1891, 119).

TALĬS Kzk. 19th c. **Talĭs-pay** [Талыспай] (SODž. 94). ✧ 'Small bag/sack' cf. Kzk. talĭs 'eine kleine Tasche zum Aufbewahren der Ahle und der Schuhmacher-Werkzeuge, das Täschchen, der Beutel' (Radl. III, 887).

TALĬŠ Selj. **Talĭš** [طالش چوپانى] (Zehireddin/Dorn 97); Bashk. 1695 **Talĭš / Talĭš?** [Талиш (Туиш, Тоиш) Иткулов] (MIB I, 85); Kzk. 19th c. **Talĭš-pay** [Талышпай] (SOK 256).

TALĬŠĬ Kzk. 19th c. **Talĭšĭ** [Талышы] (AOP 18).

TALĬŠMAN Crm. 1554 **Talĭšman-atalïq** [Талышманъ-Аталыкъ], a messenger (PSRL XIII, 234).

TALKE Kzk. 19th c. **Talke** [Тальке] (AOK 94). ⇨ **TAL** + suff. -ke.

TALQ-TAMĬR Maml. 13th c. **Talq-tamir / Talq-tamïr?** [Talktamir], an emir at Qalāūn's (1279-1290) time (Björkm. 161).

TALQAM-BAY see **TALQAN**

TALQAN Kzk. 19th c. **Talqam-bay** [Талкамбай] (SODž.72); Kzk. 19th c. **Talqam-bay** [Талкамбай] (SOK 88, 300); Kzk. 19th c. **Talqam-bay** [Талкамбай] (SOV 12, 42, 54); Kzk. 19th c. **Talqam-bay (<Talqan-bay)** [Толкамбай] (SOK 200); Trkm. 1841/42 **Talqan-baba / Talχatan-baba?** [Талкан-баба / Талхатан-баба] (MIT II, 481, 484); Kzk. 19th c. **Talqan-bay** [Талканбай] (SOV 150); Kzk. 19th c. **Talqam-bay (<Talqan-bay)** [Толкамбай] (SODž. 54, 128); Kzk. 1820 **Talqan-batïr** [Талканъ-батыръ], one of the chiefs of the Nayman-Quñyrat tribe of the Middle Horde (Orta Žüz) (Sib. Vest. IX, 103, MIK IV, 512); Kzk. 19th c. **Talqan-bek** [Талканбекъ] (SOV 18). ✧ 'Pulp, squash' Kzk. talqan 'крупа' (KzRS), Chag., Hak. talγan 'geröstetes Gerstenmehl; eine aus geröstetem Gerstenmehl bereitete Speise' (Radl. III, 891), Alt., Kzk., Tat. talqan 'geröstete kleine gestossene Gerste; ein Gericht aus geröstetem Gerstenmehl und Butter' (Radl. III, 889).

TALQANČĬ Alt. 19th-20th c. **Talqančĭ** [Талканчы], fem. (OjrRS 213). ✧ 'Maker of talqan'. ⇨ **TALQAN** + suff. -čĭ.

TALQAŠ Kzk. 19th c. **Talqaš** [Талкашъ] (SODž.[154).

TALQĬ Kzk. 19th c. **Talqĭ-bay** [Талкыбай] (SODž. 100). ✧ 'A tool for tanning' cf. Kzk., Tat. talqĭ 'Instrument zum Gerben des Leders; das Gerben' (Radl. III, 890).

TALMA Türk 865-870-880 **Talma-čür?** [طلمجور / طلمَجُور] (Tabarī, Annal. III, 1545, 1723, 1786, 1790 etc.); Kzk. 19th c. **Talma-χatun** [Талма Хатунъ], fem. (Grod., Pril. 44). ✧ 'Taste (it)!' cf. Kzk. talma- 'пробовать вкусь' (PKRS).

TALPAQ Kzk. 1846 **Talpaq** [Талпак Язырбаев], a biy (MKOP 100). ✧ 'Stocky, stumpy, squat; short' cf. Kzk. talpaq 'коренастый, низкого роста (человек)' (KzRS).

TALTAQ Kzk. 1787 **Taltaq** [Талтак] (MIK IV, 95). ✧ 'Split/torn into two' cf. Kzk. taltaq 'in zwei Theile gespalten' (Radl. III, 893).

TALTAQAY Kzk. 19th c. **Taltaqay** [Талтакай] (AOK 34, 90). ⇨ **TALTAQ** + suff. -ay.

TALTAN Kzk. 19th c. **Taltan** [Талтанъ] (SODž. 114). ✧ 'With sprawled legs' cf. Kzk. taltañ 'mit gespreizten Beinen' (Radl. III, 893).

TALTĬK Bashk. 1742 **Taltik** [Уразгильды Талтиков] (MIB III, 513).

TALU Kzk. 19th c. **Talu-bay** [Талубай] (SOK 176). ✧ I. 'Beauty, goodness'? cf. Uyg. talu 'trefflich' (Radl. III, 888); II. 'Faint, blackout'? cf. Kzk. taluw 'падать в обморок, потерять сознание' (KzRS).

TALUM Kzk. 19th c. **Talum-bek** [Талумбекъ] (SOK 12). ✧ 'Arm, weapon' cf. Uyg. talum 'die Waffe' (Radl. III, 889).

TAM-BAY see **TAÑ**

TAM-BALTA Kzk. 19th c. **Tam-balta (<Tañ-balta?)** [Тамбалта] (Grod., Pril. 25). ✧ ? ⇨ **TAÑ?** + **BALTA.**

TAM-BEK see **TAÑ**

TAM-FULAT see **TAÑ-BOLAT**

TAMA Kzk. 19th c. **Tama** [Тама] (AOO 42); Kzk. 19th c. **Tama-bay** [Тамабай] (SODž. 134); Kzk. 19th c. **Tama-bay** [Тамабай] (SOV 62); Kzk. **Tama-batïr** [Тама-батыр] (Vámbéry, Vázlatok 323, Žirm., Epos 395); *EN:* Kzk. 1785 **Tama-uruγï** [اوروغى / Род Тама], a clan (MIK IV, 52, 54); *TN:* Uzb.? **Tama-qanĭn-musï** [Тама-канын-мусы], a tomb south of Lake Aral (Karta JAR X). ✧ Ethnonym.

TAMAČA 1542 **Tamača** [Тамача / Гамача] (PSRL XIII, 143).

TAMAΓ-ĬDUQ Türk 732, 735 **Tamaγ-ĭduq** [Tamaγ ïduq] (ETY I, 48, 62).

TAMAYA Yak. **Tamaya-oγonyor** [Тамаja] (Pek.). ✧ 'Walking with knees raised high' cf. Yak. tamay- 'при хотьбе высоко поднимать колени' (Pek.) + suff. -a.

TAMAYAN Yak. **Tamayan** [Тамаjан] (Pek.). ✧ 'Walking with knees raised high' cf. Yak. tamay- 'при хотьбе высоко поднимать колени' (Pek.) + suff. -an.

TAMAQ Bashk. 1737-1739 **Tamaq** [Тамак Мустуев] (MIB I, 324, 370). ✦ 'Food' cf. Alt., Hak., Kzk., Tat. etc. *tamaq* 'die Speise; die Kehle' (Radl. III, 993).

TAMAN I. Maml. 1259 **Taman** (Makrīzī I, 83); Tat.(Mish.) 1775 **Taman** [Блакты Таманов] (MIB IV/2, 417); Tat.(Mish.) 1775 **Taman** [Лип Таманов] (MIB IV/2, 417); Tat.(Mish.) 1775 **Taman** [Табалил (?) Таманов] (MIB IV/2, 417); Kzk. 19th c. **Taman** [Таманъ] (AOK 10); Türk 735 **Taman-tarqan** [Taman tarqan], one of Bilge-qaγan's titles (ETY I, 72). ✦ I. 'A title' cf. Türk *taman* 'eine Würde' (Radl. III, 996); II. '(Born) in time' cf. Kzk., Tat. *taman* 'zur rechter Zeit, in rechtem Verhältnisse' (Radl. III, 995). ⇨ **ТАМГAN.**

TAMAN II. Alt. 19th-20th c. **Taman** [Таман], fem. (OjrRS 213). ✦ 'Heel' cf. Alt. *taman* 'id.' (OjrRS).

TAMANAY Kzk. 19th c. **Tamanay** [Таманай] (AOO 42). ⇨ **TAMAN I.** + suff. *-ay*.

TAMAR **Tamar-mulla** [Тамар-мулла] (Karta JAR XI).

TAMAS Bashk. 1756 **Tamas** [Кульят Тамасов] (MIB IV/1, 120).

TAMAŠ Karch. **Tamaš** [Тамашъ Текеевъ] (Sysoev 129); Tat.(Sib.) 1634 **Tamaš** [Тамаш Иткулов] (Miller, Ist. Sib. II, 411).

TAMAŠA Kzk. 19th c. **Tomača / Tamaša?** [Томача] (Valihanov, Soč. 317).

TAMBA Tuv. 19th c. **Tamba** [Тамба] (Proben IX, 13).

TAMBAL Chag. 16th c. **Tambal / Tämbäl?** [Тамбал] (Ivanov 160). ✦ I. 'Underpants'? cf. East.T., Kzk. *tambal* 'die Unterhosen' (Radl. III, 1008); II. 'Layabout, lazy' cf. Uzb. *tambal / tanbal* 'лентяй; ленивец' (UzbRS).

TAMBÏJĀ Tuv. 19th c. **Tambïjā** [Тамбыца], fem. (Proben IX, 110).

TAMBUL Kzk. 19th c. **Tambul-bay** [Тамбулбай] (SODž. 97).

TAMČİ Kzk. 19th c. **Tamči-bay** [Тамчибай] (SOK 54, 78). ✦ 'Drop' cf. Alt., Kar., Tat. *tamčï* 'der Tropfen' (Radl. III, 1006).

TAMJÏDAQ Tuv. 19th c. **Tamjïdaq** [Тамцыдак] (Proben IX, 15).

TAMDÏÑ Tuv. 19th c. **Tamdïñ-qam** [Тамдың-кам], a shaman (Proben IX, 199).

TAMEKE Kzk. 19th c. **Tameke** [Тамеке] (SODž. 12, 102); Kzk. 19th c. **Tameke** [Тамеке] (SOK 34); Kzk. 19th c. **Tameke** [Тамеке] (SOV 118). ⇨ **TAMA** + comp. *eke / ake*.

TAMEN Kzk. 19th c. **Tamen?** [Таменъ] (AOP 78).

ТАМГAČ see **ТАВГAČ**

ТАМГAČÏ-TARÏQ Uyg. 12th c. - 14th c. **Tamγačï-tarïq** [Tamġaç Tarık] (DTS, EUTS). ✦ 'Keeper of the seal - corn/grain' (Blagova 1997, 711), cf. Türk, Karakh. *tamγačï* 'хранитель печати' (DTS). ⇨ **TARÏQ.**

ТАМГAN Khazar 9th c. **Tamγan** [Ταμγάν], a christened Khazar (Byz. Turc. 297, Golden, Khaz. 254); Türk **Tamγan-čor** [Išbara tamγan čor], in Chinese transcription (Ligeti, R. tör. nev. II-III, 41); Türk 731 **Tamγan-čur / Išbara-tamγan-čur?** [Išbara Tamγan Çur] (ETY I, 128); Uyg. 8th c. - 9th c. **Tamγan-tarχan / Tamγan-tarqan** [Tamgântarχân / altun Tamgan Tarkan] (Mahrnāmag 11, DTS, ETY II, 122). ✦ A title (dignity) (DTS). ⇨ **TAMAN.**

ТАМГUT-AŠİR Bashk. 1740 **Tamγut-ašir** [Тамгут-Ашер] (MIB I, 398).

TAMİNEY Bashk. 1778 **Taminey?** [Сатыкай Таминеев (Тимкеев)] (MIB V, 76, 97).

TAMÏJAP Tuv. 19th c. **Tamïjap** [Тамыцап] (Proben IX, 72).

TAMÏLČA Kzk. 19th c. **Tamïlča** [Тамыльча] (SOV 38).

TAMLÏ **Tamlï-bay** [Тамлы-бай] (Karta JAR X); *TN:* **Tamlï** [Чулан-тамъ] (Karta JAR X).

TAMPÏČ Kzk. 1846 **Tampïč** [Тампыч] (MKOP 86).

TAMU **Tamu-tarχan** [Tamu-tarchan] (Byz. Turc. 297).

TAMU-GELDİ Tat.(Sib.) 1629 **Tamu-geldi** [Тмугелдей Мучнев] (Miller, Ist. Sib. II, 356). ⇨ **KELDİ.**

TAN Uyg. **Tan** [Tan] (EUTS). ✦ 'Daw' cf. Alt.(Tel.), Hak.(Shor, Sag., Koyb.) *tan* 'die Dohle' (Radl, III, 822), Hak. *tān* [таан] 'галка (Coleus monedula)' (HRS). See also **AQ-TĀN, EŠ-TAN, QARA-TAN; SÄÜKÄ.**

TAN-AT see **TAÑ-AT**

TAN-ATQAN see **TAÑ-ATQAN**

TAN-BERDİ Tat. 18th c. **Tam-berdi** [Бикей Тамбердинъ] (Nepljuev 598); Tat.(Sib.) 1634 **Tan-birde** [Танбирдей] (Miller, Ist. Sib. II, 417). ✦ 'The dawn gave him/her; born at daybreak'. ⇨ **TAÑ + BERDİ.**

TAN-BİRDE see **TAN-BERDİ**

TAN-EKE see **TANÏ**

TAN-QUŠ Maml. 14th c. **Tan-quš** [طنـتوش / Tankuş] (Tarǰ/Houtsma 94, Tarǰ/Toparlı 43, 142). ✦ 'Dawn-bird / morning-bird' (Tarǰ/Toparlı 142). ⇨ **TAÑ + QUŠ I.**

TAN-TELE Kzk. 19th c. **Tan-tele** [Тантеле] (SODž. 114); Kzk. 19th c. **Tan-tele** [Тантеле] (SODž. 114). ⇨ **TAÑ + TELİ?**

TANA I. Karch. 20th c. **Tana** [Tᶜana], fem. (Pröhle, Kar. 136); Kzk. 18th c. - 19th c. **Tana** [Тана] (Tynyšp. 73); Kzk. 1817 **Tana** [طاناہ / Тана] (MIK IV, 313, 319); Kzk. 19th c. **Tana** [Тана] (AOA 70); Kzk. 19th c. **Tana** [Таня] (AOK 34); Kzk. 1863 **Tana** [Тана (Тлемисовъ)], Potanin's guide (follower) (ZIRGOGeogr. I, 363); Kzk. 18th c. -19th c. **Tana-bay** [Утюпъ Танабаевъ] (ZOOIRGO III, 26); Kzk. 19th c.

Tana-bay [Танабай] (AOA 18); Kzk. 19th c. **Tana-bay** [Танабай] (AOAtb. 18); Kzk. 19th c. **Tana-bay**, a folklore hero (AUK 108); Kzk. 19th c. **Tana-bay** [Танабай] (AUK 449); Kzk. 19th c. **Tana-bay** [Акташъ Танабаевъ] (Grod., Pril. 152); Kzk. 19th c. **Tana-bay** [Танабай] (Lomakin 32); Kzk. 19th c. **Tana-bay** [Джусуп Танабаевъ], a mulla (Pam. kn. Semip. 1898, III, 43.); Kzk. 19th c. **Tana-bay** [Танабай] (SODž. 28, 78); Kzk. 19th c. **Tana-bay** [Танабай] (SOK 226); Kzk. 19th c. **Tana-bay** [Танабай] (SOV 46, 58, 158); Kkalp. 20th c. **Tana-bay** [Танабай] (KkRS 776); Kzk. / Nog.? **Tana-batïr** [Тана-батыр] (Žirm., Epos 395); Bashk. 1735 **Tana-γul** [Танагулъ Адагуловъ], a tarγan (Vel.-Zern., Bašk. 19); *EN:* Kzk. 1785 **Tana-uruγï** [طانه اوروغى / Тана], a clan (MIK IV, 52, 54); *TN:* Crm. **Tana-bay** [Tanabaï], a village (Jervis? II.). ✧ 'Calf' cf. Chag., Crm., Kar., Tat. *tana* 'eine junge Kuh, die Ferse, ein einjähriges Kalb' (Radl. III, 822), Kzk. *tana* 'dana, bir yaşına gelmiş sığır' (KzTS), Kzk. *tana* 'id.' (QTTS). See also **AQ-TANA, BAY-TANA, TAY-TANA, TOQ-TANA.**

TANA II. Alt. 19th c. **Tana** [Тана-богатырь], a folklore hero (Verb., In. 139, 141, 142, 145); Alt. 19th-20th c. **Tana** [Тана], fem. (OjrRS 213); Hak. 19th-20th c. **Tana** [Тана], fem. (HRS 355). ✧ 'Pearl, pearly button, button' (OjrRS) cf. Alt., Hak., Kzk. *tana* 'Perlmutter, die Perle; jeder flache Knopf' (Radl. III, 823), Alt. *tana* 'перламутр; пуговица, которая привязывается к концу женской косы' (OjrRS), Hak. Alt. *tana* 'крупная перламутровая пуговица' (HRS). See also **ALTÏN-TANA.**

TANA-BUГA see **TANA-BUQA**

TANA-BUQA Maml. 1352 **Tana-buγa** [طنيفا الاحانى] (Iyās I, 197); Maml. 1364/65 **Tana-buγa** [الطويل طنيفا] (Iyās I, 213, Weil, Chalif. 502, 517); Kzk. 19th c.? **Tana-buγa** [Tanabuga eline] (Atyns. 82); Kzk. 18th c. - 19th c. **Tana-buqa** [Танабука] (Tynyšр. 70). ✧ 'Calf-bull'. ⇨ **TANA I. + BUQA.**

TANA-GEREL Tuv. 19th c. **Tana-gerel** [Тана-Герель], in a tale (Potanin IV, 424); Tuv. 19th c. **Tanā-kärāl** [Тана-кäрäл], fem. (Proben IX, 160). ⇨ **TANA II.**

TANA-KÜZ Kzk. **Tana-küz?** [Мулла-кулъ Танакузовъ] (Sb. Syr-D. III, otd. II, 35). ✧ 'Calf-eye(d)'. ⇨ **TANA I. + KÖZ?**

TANAČAQ Alt. 19th-20th c. **Tanačaq** [Таначак], fem. (OjrRS 213). ✧ 'Small button' (OjrRS). ⇨ **TANA II. +** dim. suff. *-čaq.*

TANAČÏ Alt. 19th-20th c. **Tanačï** [Таначы] (OjrRS 210). ✧ 'Small button' (OjrRS). ⇨ **TANA II. +** dim. suff. *-čï.*

TANAY I. Tat. 1764 **Tanay** [Танай Зюмаев] (MIB IV/1, 292); Bashk. 1716 **Tanay** [Танай] (MIB I, 216, 217, 226); Tat.(Mish.) 1775 **Tanay-γul** [Танайгул Курманов] (MIB IV/2, 416). ✧ 'Little calf'. ⇨ **TANA I. +** dim. suff. *-y.* See also **AQ-TANAY, BOS-TANAY, TOX-TANAY, ŽUL-TANAY.**

TANAY II. Alt. 19th-20th c. **Tanay II.** [Танай], fem. (OjrRS 213). ✧ Little pearly button' (OjrRS). ⇨ **TANA II. +** dim. suff. *-y?*

TANAQ Hak.(Shor) 19th-20th c. **Tanaq** [Танак] (Katanov, Otč. 11); Bashk. 17th c. **Tanaq / Tanäk?** [Таняк] (MIB I, 76); Tat. 1690 **Tanaq-bay** [Танакбаевъ] (Kungursk. akty 174). See also **TÜ-DANAQ(?).**

TANALDÏ Kzk. 1862 **Tanaldï** [Tanaldy], a chief (Nalivkin-Dozon 243).

TANAR Kzk. 19th c. **Tanar** [Танаръ] (SOK 218).

TANAŠ Kzk. 19th c. **Tanaš** [Tanašev] (Mende 145); Kzk. 19th c. **Tanaš** [Танашъ] (SOV 88); Alt. 19th-20th c. **Tanaš** [Танаш], fem. (OjrRS 213). ✧ 'Pearly button' (OjrRS). ⇨ **TANA II. +** suff. *-š.*

TANĀ-KÄRÄL see **TANA-GEREL**

TANČA Hak. 19th-20th c. **Tanča** [Танча], fem. (HRS 355). ✧ Tatyana (R.) (HRS).

TANČÏ Kzk. 19th c. **Tanči-bay** [Танчибай] (AOAtb. 2).

TANČÏŠ Chuv. 1737 **Tančiš? / Tančit?** [Танчишевъ] (Alatyr. 136).

TANČÏT Chuv. 18th c. **Tančit / Tančiš?** [Баландай Танчитевъ] (Nikol'skij 97).

TANЈЇQ Hak.? 19th-20th c. **Tanјïq** [Танцык] (Katanov, Otč. 10).

TANDAR Tuv. 19th c. **Tandar** [Тандар] (Proben IX, 17).

TANDÏQ see **TANÏDÏQ**

TANDU Balk. 20th c. **Tandu** [Tandú] (Pröhle, Balk. 256).

TANİ see **TANÏ**

TANİK Hak. 19th-20th c. **Tanik** [Таник], fem. (HRS 355).

TANİKE Hak. 19th-20th c. **Tanike** [Танике], fem. (HRS 355).

TANİKEČ Bashk. 1735 **Tanikeč** [Казангулъ Таникечевъ], a tarγan (Vel.-Zern., Bašk. 24).

TANİS Hak. 19th-20th c. **Tanis** [Танис], fem. (HRS 355). ✧ Taisiya (R.) (HRS).

TANİLA Hak.(Sag.) 19th-20th c. **Tanïla** [Таніла] (Katanov, Otč. 8). ✧ Daniil (R.) (Katanov).

TANÏ Kzk. 19th c. **Tan-eke (<Tanï-eke?)** [Ясимбекъ Танекинъ / Таникинъ] (ZIRGOGeogr. I, 311); Kzk. 19th c. **Tan-eke (<Tanï-eke?)** [Танеке] (SOV 64); Kzk. 18th c. - 19th c. **Tan-eke-batïr (<Tanï-eke-batïr?)** [Танеке-батыр] (Tynyšр. 71); Kzk. 19th c. **Tani-bek** [Танибэкъ] (Potanin II, 3); Chuv. 1658 **Tani-bek / Tanï-bek?** [Танибек Урмаевъ] (Zolotn.

159); Maml. 1422 **Tanï / Tanï-bäk** [تاني الملكى السيفى /
Tânî Bak], governor of Aleppo (Sauvaget: BEO III,
15); Kzk. 19th c. **Tanï-bay** (AOAtb. 42); Kzk. 19th c.
Tanï-bay [Таныбай] (AOK 90); Maml. 14th c. - 15th
c. **Tanï-bek** [تاني بك السيفى], an emir, mentioned in an
inscription of a copper bowl (Mayer 217); Maml. 1352
Tanï-bek [تانى بك اليحياوى] (Iyās I, 197, Ibn Taghrïb.
VI, 443); Maml. 1424, 1452/53 **Tanï-bek** [البردبكى
تنبك / تانى بك] (Iyās II, 39, Ibn Taghrïb. VI, 581,
692); Maml. 1431 **Tanï-bek** [تانى بك], Bars-bay's
father, mentioned in an inscription (Berchem 252);
Maml. 1457 **Tanï-bek** [تنبك / تانى بك الصغير] (Iyās
II, 57, Ibn Taghrïb. VII, 497, 708); Maml. 1460/61
Tanï-bek [تانىبك السيفى الظهرى] (Iyās II, 65, 96);
Maml. 1460/61 **Tanï-bek** [تانى بك قرا الاينالى] (Iyās
II, 71, 175); Maml. 1467/68 **Tanï-bek** [تانى بك المعلم]
(Iyās II, 95, 100, 123, Ibn Taghrïb. VII, 453, 705,
1455); Maml. 1468/69 **Tanï-bek** [تانى بك الظهرى]
(Iyās II, 111); Maml. 1472/73 **Tanï-bek**
[تانى بك الشرفى السيفى الماس] (Iyās II, 136, III, 73);
Maml. 1474/75 **Tanï-bek** [تانى بك الازدمرى], a
doorkeeper (Iyās II, 155); Maml. 1476/77, 1503 **Tanï-
bek** [تانى بك الجمالى], died in 1503 (Iyās II, 167, Weil,
Chalif. II, 348, 391); Maml. 1480 **Tanï-bek**
[تانى بك الاشتر المحمدى] (Iyās II, 192); Maml. 1488
Tanï-bek [تانى بك الابناسى] (Iyās II, 249); Maml. 1489
Tanï-bek [تانى بك الحمدى الاينالى] (Iyās II, 260, 336);
Maml. 1492/93 **Tanï-bek** [تانى بك الابح] (Iyās II, 278,
380, Weil, Chalif. II, 380); Maml. 1493/94-1521 **Tanï-
bek** [تانى بك بن يشبك لمعروف] (Iyās II, 284, III, 21,
265); Maml. 1496/97 **Tanï-bek** [تانىبك أبوشامه] (Iyās
II, 317); Maml. 1496/97 **Tanï-bek** [تانىبك الشريفى]
(Iyās II, 324); Maml. 1497/98 **Tanï-bek** [بن حميد
تانىبك] (Iyās II, 336); Maml. 1516 **Tanï-bek**
[تانى بك النجمى] (Iyās III, 3, 111); Maml. 1517 **Tanï-
bek** [السيفى تانى بك], an emir and treasurer, mentioned
in an inscription of a copper dish, he very likely is
identical with the colonel (chiliarch) who was executed
by Sultan Selim in 1517 (Iyās, II, 371, III, 3, 29, 111,
Mayer 21); Bashk. 1743 **Tanï-bek** [Кулчура
Таныбеков] (MIB III, 513); Kzk. 19th c. **Tanï-bek**
[Таныбекъ] (AOO 14); Kzk. 19th c. **Tanï-bek**
[Таныбекъ] (SODž. 96, 148); Maml. / Turk.? 1516
Tanï-bek / Tanï-beg? [تانى بك العثمانى] (Iyās III, 62).
❖ 'Friend, acquaintance' cf. Turk. *tani* 'Freund,
Bekannter' (Radl. III, 825).

TANÏ-BERDÏ   Maml. 1484 **Tanï-berdi**
[تانى بردى الاينالى] (Iyās II, 222). ⇨ **TANÏ + BERDÏ.**

TANÏDÏQ Turk. 1681 **Tandïq-aγa** [Тандыкъ] (DAI X,
212). ❖ 'Acquaintance' cf. Turk. *tanıdık* 'id.' (TED).

See also **TANÏŠ.**

TANÏKEY   Bashk. 1682 **Tanïkey** [Акинчишко
Таникеев (Таняк, Тиняк)], a tarγan (MIB I, 76);
Kzk. **Tanïkey** [Таныкей], fem. (Divaev, Šura 125). ⇨
TANÏ + suff. *-key.*

TANÏQ   Kzk. 19th c. **Tanïq** [Таныкъ] (SOK 160);
Maml. 1405/06 **Tanïq-bay** [تنق باى] (Iyās I, 349);
Chuv. 18th-19th c. **Tanuk** [Танукъ] (Magn. 80). ❖
'Witness, acquaintance' cf. Kuman, Tat., Turk. *tanïq*
'der Zeuge; bekannt, wissend' (Radl. III, 826).

TANÏQTAČÏ Uyg. 12th c. - 14th c. **Tanïqtačï** (Radl.,
USp. 82, DTS).

TANÏM   Kzk. 19th c. **Tanïm** [Танымъ] (AOAtb. 38);
Kkalp. 20th c. **Tanïm-bay** [Танымбай] (Bask., Kkalp.
97, KkRS 776).

TANÏR see **TÄÑRÏ**

TANÏR-BERDÏ see **TÄÑRÏ-BERDÏ**

TANÏRÏQ Maml. 1353 **Tanïrïq** [السيفى طانيرق], in an
inscription of Hama (Sauvaget: BEO XII (1948), 36).

TANÏSTAM   Kzk. 19th c. **Tanïstam** [Таныстамъ]
(SOV 108).

TANÏŠ Tat.(GH)? **Tanïš** [تنيش / Tanisch], a Jochid ruler
of the Kazaks (Abulg./Desm. 188); Bashk. 1770 **Tanïš**
[Таныш Зиянов] (MIB IV/1, 347); Alt. 19th-20th c.
Tanïš [Таныш] (OjrRS 210); Kzk. 19th c. **Tanïš-pay**
[Танышпай] (SOK 184, 204); Kzk. 19th c. **Tanus-
qoža** [Танус-кожа] (SODž. 130); Alt. 19th-20th c.
Tānïš [Тааныш] (OjrRS 210); Kzk. 19th c. **Tonïš-pay**
[Тонышпай] (SOK 200). ❖ 'Friend, acquaintance' cf.
Kuman, Alt., Crm., Kar., Kirg., Tat., *tanïš* 'Freund,
Bekannter' (Radl. III, 825), East.T., NUyg.(Tar.) *tonuš*
'der Bekannte, die Bekanntschaft' (Radl. III, 1177). ⇨
TANÏ + suff. *-š.*

TANKE Kzk. 19th c. **Tanke** [Танке] (SOK 52); Kzk.
19th c. **Tanke-bay** [Танкебай] (SODž. 66). ⇨ **TAÑ?**
+ suff. *-ke.*

TANKEY Kzk. 19th c. **Tankey** [Танкей] (AOP 30). ⇨
TANKE + suff. *-y.*

TANQA Kzk. 19th c. **Tanqa-bay** [Танкабай] (SOV
152). ⇨ **TAÑ?** + suff. *-qa.*

TANQÏ Kzk. 19th c. **Tanqï-bay** [Танкыбай] (AOAtb.
62); Kzk. 19th c. **Tanqï-bay** [Танкибай] (AOK 74);
Kzk. 19th c. **Tanqï-bay** [Танкибай] (AOP 106); Kzk.
19th c. **Tanqï-bay** [Танкыбай] (SOK 18); Kzk. 19th c.
Tanqu-bay [Танкубай] (SODž. 126). ❖ 'Having a
pug-nose, snub-nosed' cf. Kzk. *tañqï / tañqanai* 'mit
aufgestülpter Nase' (Radl. III, 808).

TANQU see **TANQÏ**

TANLÏ   Bashk. 1729 **Tanlï-bay** [Нияз Танлыбаев]
(MIB III, 271).

TANRÏ-BERDÏ see **TÄÑRÏ-BERDÏ**

TANRÏ-VERMÏŠ see **TÄÑRÏ-BERMÏŠ**

TANSÏQ Kzk. 19th c. **Tansïq** [Тансыкъ] (SODž. 48);

Kzk. 19th c. **Tansïq** [Тансыкъ] (SOV 106); Kzk. 19th c. **Tansïq-bay** [Тансыкбай] (AOK 114); Kzk. 1794 **Tansïq-χoja** [طانصق حوجه] (MIK IV, 160); Kzk. 19th c. **Tansïq-pay** [Тансыкпай] (SOK 164). ✧ 'Wonderful, imposing; rare'; 'Wished, awated (child)' (Sattarov, Kusimova), cf. Kzk. *tañsïq* 'удивительный, редкий' (PKRS), Kzk. *tañsïq* 'sich wundernd, vor Freude erregt, wunderbar, merkwürdig, selten' (Radl. III, 813).

TANSÏQ-QUY Kzk. 19th c. **Tansïq-quy** [Тансыкъкуй Алмамбетовъ] (Grod., Pril. 80). ⇨ TANSÏQ + QOY?

TANTA Kzk. 19th c. **Tanta-bek** [Тантабек] (SOV 66); Kzk. 19th c. **Tanta-bek** [Тантабекъ] (SOV 66).

TANTAY Bashk. 18th c. **Tantay** [Тантай] (MIB I, 281); Kzk. 19th c. **Tantay** [Тантай] (SODž. 18); Kzk. 19th c. **Tantay** [Тантай] (SODž. 18, 84); Hak.(Kyz.) 19th-20th c. **Tantay** [Тантай] (Katanov, Otč. 13). ✧ 'Dawn, daybreak'? ⇨ TAÑ + suff. voc./dim. *-tay(2)*?

TANTÏ Kzk. 19th c. **Tantï-bay** [Тантыбай] (AOK 6).

TANTÏQ Tat.(Sib.) 1599 **Tantïq** [Тантык], a woman from Kücüm's family (AI II, 20).

TANU Kzk. 19th c. **Tanu** [Тану], fem. (Grod., Pril. 129). ⇨ TANÏ?

TANUQ see **TANÏQ**

TANUMBET Kzk. 19th c. **Tanumbet** [Сарибай Танумбетовъ] (Grod., Pril. 188). ⇨ TANÏ / TANU + suff. *-mbet*.

TANUŠ-BUГA Tat.(GH) 1262 **Tanuš-buγa** / **Tanušuq-buγa** [تنش بغق / تَنُشُق بُغَا / Танушбуга / Танушукбуга], a Kipchak (Baybars/Tizeng. I, 77, 99). ⇨ TANÏŠ + BUQA.

TANÜS Hak. 19th-20th c. **Tanüs** [Танӱс], fem. (HRS 355).

TANVASÏN Uyg. **Tanvasin** [tanvasin] (DTS). ✧ (<Skr.?).

TAÑ Kzk.? **Tan!-bay-murza** [Танбай-мурза] (Žirm., Epos 475); Kzk. 19th c. **Tam-bay** [Тамбай] (SOK 124); Kzk. **Tam-bek** [Тамбекъ] (Sb. Syr-D. IX, 58); Karch. **Tam-biy** [Тамбіевъ] (Sysoev 123); Kzk. 19th c. **Tan** [Тань] (AOK 50); Maml. 1433 **Tan-bäk?** [Tanbak], a governor, died in 1433, his mausoleum is in Damascus (Sauvaire VI, 234); Kzk. 19th c. **Tan-qul** [Умурзакъ Танкуловъ] (Grod., Pril. 90); Kzk. 19th c. **Tañ-bay** [Тангбай] (AOA 26); Kzk. 19th c. **Tañ-bay** [Баршинъ Тангбаевъ] (Pam. kn. Turg. 78); Kzk. 1817 **Tañ-bay** / **Tan-bay?** [طانكباى / Танбай] (MIK IV, 310); *TN:* Kzk. **Tan-bay** [Танбай], a lake in Siberia (Karta JAR IV). ✧ 'Dawn, daybreak' cf. Türk., Uyg., Chag., Alt., Kzk., Tat. etc. *tañ* 'die Morgenröthe, Morgendämmerung' (Radl. III, 804), Maml. *tan* 'seher vakti, tan' (Tarj/Toparlı 142). See also **AQ-TAÑ**.

TAÑ-ARSLAN Uyg. 8th c. - 12th c. **Tañ-arslan-sañun** [Tang arslan] (Müller, Pfahl. 10). ✧ 'Light-lion' (Müller ibid. p. 16: Licht-Löwe). ⇨ TAÑ + ARSLAN.

TAÑ-AT Kzk. 19th c. **Tan-at** [Танатовъ] (AOK 106); Kzk. 19th c. **Tan-at** [Танатъ] (AOK 6, 46); Kzk. 19th c. **Tan-at** [Алписбай Танатовъ] (Grod., Pril. 117); Kzk. 19th c. **Tan-at** [Танатъ] (SOV 12, 18); Kzk. 19th c. **Tan-at-pay** [Танатпай] (SOV 40); Kzk. 19th c. **Tann-at?** / **Tañ-at** [Тоннатъ] (SOK 166); Kzk. 19th c. **Tañ-at** [Тангатъ] (AOK 18); Kzk. 19th c. **Tañ-at** / **Tan-at** [تانكات / Танатъ] (Veselovskij, Kirg. 78). ✧ 'Dawn!' cf. Trk. *at-* 'werfen, schleudern; schiessen; anbrechen, aufleuchten' (Radl. I, 445-449). ⇨ TAÑ. See also **BAY-TAÑ-AT, TAÑ-ATAR, TAÑ-ATQAN**.

TAÑ-ATAR Tat. 1555 **Tan-atar** [Тонатаръ], envoy from Astrakhan (PSRL XIII, 258); Tat. 1624 **Tan-atar** [Тонатаръ Собакинъ] (Pokrovskij 70); Tat. 1780 **Tan-atar** [Салиш Танатаров] (MIB V, 116); Tat.(Sib.) 1631, 1634 **Tan-atar** [Кочаш Танатаров] (Miller, Ist. Sib. II, 381, 414, 467); Bashk. 1706 **Tan-atar** [Тонатар] (MIB III, 27); Bashk. 1706 **Tan-atar** [Тонатар Копырьянов] (MIB III, 27); Bashk. 18th c. **Tan-atar** [Танатаров (Тонатаров)] (MIB V, 54, 88, 101, 102 etc.); Bashk. 1752 **Tan-atar** [Танатар Кайгильдин] (MIB IV/1, 64); Bashk. 1754 **Tan-atar** [Курмаш Танатаров] (MIB IV/1, 83); Bashk. 1761 **Tan-atar** [Сыртлан Танатаров] (MIB IV/1, 204); Bashk. 1764 **Tan-atar** [Танатар Айдагулов] (MIB IV/1, 276); Bashk. 1772 **Tan-atar** [Танатар Калмаков] (MIB IV/2, 405); Bashk. 1780 **Tan-atar** [Кулукай (Кулакай, Кунукай) Танатаров] (MIB V, 106, 172, 241, 305); Kzk. 18th c. - 19th c. **Tan-atar** [Танатар] (Tynyšp. 66, 70, 71); Kzk. 19th c. **Tan-atar** [Танатаръ] (AOK 122); Kzk. 19th c. **Tan-atar** [Танатаръ] (Grod., Pril. 143); Kzk. 19th c. **Tan-atar** [Танатаръ] (Lomakin 33); Nog. 1649 **Tan-atar** [Танатаръ Тукумбетевъ] (AI IV, 123); Kzk. 19th c. **Tan-atar-bay** [Танъ Атарбай Довлатовъ] (Grod., Pril. 74); Trkm. 19th c. **Tañ-atar** [Тангатаровъ] (Ščeglov IV, 191); Trkm. 19th c. **Tañ-atar** [Якшелыкъ Тангатаровъ] (SKSO III, 178); Bashk. 18th c. **Tañ-atar** [Тангатар (Тунгатар) Сарыгулов] (MIB V, 42, 43, 544, 545); Bashk. 1776 **Tañ-atar** [Тангатар] (MIB V, 33); Bashk. 1776 **Tañ-atar** [Тангатар Лякаев] (MIB V, 33, 34, 79); Bashk. 1778 **Tañ-atar** [Тангатар] (MIB V, 79); Kzk. 19th c. **Tañ-atar** [Тангатаръ] (Grod., Pril. 130); Kzk.? 19th c. **Tañ-atar** [Тангатаръ Бергенбаевъ] (SKSO III, 19); Kkalp. 20th c. **Tañ-atar** [Таңатар] (Bask., Kkalp. 401, KkRS 776); Uzb. 19th c. **Tañ-atar** [Тангатаръ Хыдыровъ] (SKSO III, 166); Uzb. 19th c. **Tañ-atar** [Ярлакачъ Тангатаровъ] (SKSO III, 180); Tat. 1779 **Tañ-atar** / **Tan-atar** [Тангатар (Танатар) Абдуллов] (MIB V, 81); Uzb. 20th c. **Tâñ-âtar**

[Тонготар] (Begmatov 1984, 203). ✧ 'It will dawn; Born at daybreak' (Sattarov, Kusimova), cf. Trk. dial. *at-* 'werfen, schleudern;schiessen; anbrechen, aufleuchten' (Radl. I, 445-449), Kzk. *tañ attï* 'рассвело' (KzRS). See also **TAÑ-AT, TAÑ-ATQAN, TUÑ-ATAR.**

TAÑ-ATQAN   Kzk. 1846 **Tan-atqan** [Танаткан Самаев] (MKOP 156); Kzk. 19th c. **Tañ-aqan** (<**Tañ-atqan?**) [Узунъ-Ата Тангаканъ] (Grod., Pril. 80). ✧ 'Dawned' cf. almost every Trk. dial. *at-* 'werfen, schleudern;schiessen; anbrechen, aufleuchten' (Radl. I, 445-449). ⇨ **TAÑ.**

TAÑ-BOLAT   Kzk. 19th c. **Tam-fulat** [Тамфулатъ] (Grod., Pril. 156); Nog. **Tañ-bolat** [Тангъ-болатъ], a Qara-noγay person (SMOK XX, 49). ✧ 'Good steel' (Anan'ev), 'Dawn-steel' (Sattarov, Kusimova). ⇨ **TAÑ + BULAT.**

TAÑ-YARÏQ   Maml. 14th c. **Tañ-yarïq** [طانيرق] (Sauvaget 50). ✧ 'Dawn-light' (Sauvaget 50). ⇨ **TAÑ + YARUQ.**

TAÑXAR   Yak. **Tañχar** [Таңхар] (Pek.).

TAÑÏŠ   Kzk. 19th c. **Tañïš-pay** [Тангышпай] (SOK 82); Kzk. 19th c. **Toñïš / Tañïš?** [Тонгышъ] (SOV 124); Kzk. 19th c. **Toñïš-bay / Tañïš-bay?** [Тонгышбай] (Grod., Pril. 19). ✧ 'Band' cf. Kzk. *tañïš* 'das Band, mit dem die einzelnen Theile des Jurtengitters zusammengebunden werden' (Radl. III, 807).

TAÑÏZÏQ   Kzk. **Tañïzïq** [Schangysyk (!) / Таңызык], sister-in-law of Qozï Körpöš, the legendary folklore hero (Proben III, 252 /297/).

TAÑRÏ see **TÄÑRÏ**

TAÑRÏ see **TÄÑRÏ**

TAÑRÏQ   Kzk. 19th c. **Tañrïq** [Кадырбай Тангриковъ] (Grod., Pril. 115); Bashk. 1776 **Tañruq** [Батюк Тангруков] (MIB V, 33).

TAÑRUQ see **TAÑRÏQ**

TAÑŠÏ   Kzk. 19th c. **Tañšï** [Танкши] (SOV 92). ✧ '(Child) born at daybreak' cf. Tat. *Tañčï* 'id.' (Sattarov).

TAÑUT   Uyg. 12th c. - 14th c. **Tañut** [Tangut / Tanġut] (Radl., USp. 204, 246, DTS, EUTS). ✧ Tangut (ethnonym), cf. Türk., Uyg., Chag. *Tañut* 'der Tangute' (Radl. III, 808).

TAÑZA   Alt. 19th-20th c. **Tañza** [Танза] (OjrRS 210). ✧ 'Leap, jump, play!' (OjrRS).

TAÑZÏN   Tuv. 19th c. **Tañzïn** [Таңзын] (Proben IX, 56, 61).

TAP   Uyg. 1313 **Tap-tirim** [Tap Tirim Kuštanz] (Chwol., Syr.-nest. (NF) 19).

TAP-AŠA   Uyg. 1331 **Tap-aša** [Tapaša Koštanz], fem. (Chwol., Syr.-nest. 72). ⇨ **TAP + AŠA?**

TAPAQ   Uyg. 1339 **Tapaq** [Tapak], fem. (Chwol., Syr.-nest. (NF) 36); Kzk. 19th c. **Tapaq** [Тапакъ] (SODž.

22).

TAPAR   Karakh. **Tapar** [Tapar] (DTS, MK/Atalay 852); Selj. 11th c. **Tapar** [Ταπάρης], byname of the Seljuk Sultan Melikshah (1072-1092) (Byz. Turc. 298); Kzk. 19th c. **Tapar-bay** [Тапарбай] (SOV 36). ✧ 'He will find/get (fame/richess)' cf. several Trk. dial. *tap-* 'finden, erwerben' (Radl. III, 947) + suff. *-ar*.

TAPDU   Karakh. 11th c. **Tapdu** [tapdu / Tapdu] (DTS, MK/Atalay 852); Uyg. 8th c. - 12th c. **Tapdu-tiräk** (Müller, Pfahl. 12). ✧ I. 'He/she found' (Bese 11); II. It is perhaps of Chinese origin (Müller, Pfahl. 16).

TAPEY   Kzk. 19th c. **Tapey** [Тапей] (SODž. 4).

TAPİLE   Hak. 19th-20th c. **Tapile** [Тапиле], fem. (HRS 355).

TAPÏΓLÏΓ   Uyg. 762 **Tapïγlïγ-sañun** [Tapïγlïγ Sangun] (Mahrnāmag 10). ✧ 'Worthy, excellent, respectable' cf. Karakh. *tapiγluγ* 'заслуженный, имеющий заслуги' (DTS).

TAPÏLDÏ see **TABÏLDÏ**

TAPQAY   Kzk. 19th c. **Tapqay** [Тапкай] (AOK 74).

TAPMÏŠ   Uyg. **Tapmïš** [Xutluγ ičräki Tapmyš] (Fest. Thomsen 211); Uyg. 762 **Tapmïš** [Tapmïš] (Mahrnāmag 11); Uyg. 12th c. - 14th c. **Tapmïš** [Tapmïş] (Radl., USp. 42, DTS, EUTS); Uyg. 762 **Tapmïš-tarχan** [Tapmïš Tarχan] (Mahrnāmag 10). ✧ I. '(He who) Found; (He who was) Found' (Blagova 1997, 716), '(A child) was found; (He who) Found (a child)' cf. Uyg. *tap-* 'находить, получать' (DTS) + suff. *-mïš*. See also **UYΓUR-TAPMÏŠ, ÜN-TAPMÏŠ, TAPTÏQ.**

TAPMÏŠ-XUTLUΓ   Uyg. **Tapmïš-χutluγ-tutuχ** (Fest. Thomsen 211). ⇨ **TAPMÏŠ + QUTLUΓ.**

TAPPAY   Hak. 19th c. **Tappay** [Таппай] (Katanov, Otč. 12).

TAPPAS   Hak.(Koyb.) 19th c. **Tappas** [Таппас] (Katanov, Otč. II, 12-15). ✧ 'He will not find (it)' (Katanov).

TAPPĀN   Hak.(Sag.) 19th-20th c. **Tappān** [Таппӑн] (Katanov, Otč. 11). ✧ 'Not found; (he/she) did not find' (Katanov).

TAPRAΓ   Oghuz 12th c. **Tapraγ** [Tapragh], king of the Khazârâyê, father of Tûrkân Khâtûn (Abulfar./Budge I, 232).

TAPRĀSAY   Yak. **Taprāsay** [Тапрасаi] (Pek.).

TAPSAY   Bashk. 1740 **Tapsay** [Тапсай Алкалин] (MIB I, 439).

TAPTAY   Hak.(Kyz.) 19th-20th c. **Taptay** [Таптай] (Katanov, Otč. 13).

TAPTÏQ   Turk. 1583 **Taptïq** [طابدق / Tapdık (Kaya oğlu)] (Ongan, Ank. I, 178); Turk. 20th c. **Taptïq** [Taptık] (Önder, Göle); Yürük 1543 **Taptïq** [Tapdık] (Gökb., Rum. 182, 186, 189, 191etc.); Yürük 1543 **Taptïq** [Taptık] (Gökb., Rum. 225, 226, 229); Tat. 1543 **Taptïq** [Tapdık] (Gökb., Rum. 231, 232, 243);

Bashk. 1787 **Taptïq** [Таптыков Ефим Захарович] (MIB V, 219, 256, 257, 258). ✧ 'Found, born (child); (we) found (him/her)' cf. Uyg. *tap-* 'находить, получать' (DTS), Uyg., Chag., Alt., Kzk., Tat. etc. *tap-* 'finden, erhalten, erwerben' (Radl. III, 947). For the R. *Taptykov* see Bask., Fam. 189. + suff. *-tïq*. See also **TAPMÏŠ**.

TAPTÏQ-EMRE   Selj./ Turk.? **Taptïq-emre** [Taptık Emre] (Uzunçarş., Anad. 82). ✧ 'Found-Emre', cf. Turk. PN *Emre* 'âşık, düşkün, müptelâ' (Erol II). ⇨ **TAPTÏQ**.

TAPTÏL   Hak. 19th-20th c. **Taptïl** [Таптыл], fem. (HRS 355).

TAR   Kzk. 19th c. **Tar-bay** [Тарбай] (SOV 62).

TAR-VERDİ see **TÄÑRİ-BERDİ**

TARA   Uyg. **Tara** [Tara] (EUTS); Chuv. 18th-19th c. **Tara** [Тара] (Magn. 80).

TARA-BERDE see **TÄÑRİ-BERDİ**

TARAΓAY   Kzk. 19th c. **Taraγay** [Тарагай] (AOK 110). ✧ 'Kite, hawk, buzzard' cf. Chag. *taraγay* 'der Habicht' (Radl. III, 840). See also **TABÏN-TARAΓAY**.

TARAQ   Kzk. 19th c. **Taraq** [Таракъ] (SOK 198, 218). ✧ 'Comb' cf. Chag., Alt., Kzk., Tat., Turk. *taraq* 'der Kamm' (Radl. III, 838). See also **BAY-TARAQ, UL-TARAQ**.

TARAQAN   Hak. 19th c. **Taraqan** [Таракан] (Katanov, Otč. 12). ✧ 'Cockroach' (Katanov), cf. R. *tarakan* 'id.'.

TARAQČÏ   Turk. 19th c. **Taraqčï-oγlu** [Taraqčy-oγlu], a Zeybek (Kúnos 1891, 119). ✧ 'Maker or seller of combs' cf. Turk. *taraqčï* 'der Kammmacher' (Radl. III, 840).

TARAQTÏ   Kzk. 19th c. **Taraqtï** [Таракты] (AOA 106). ✧ 'Having combs, with combs' cf. Chag., Alt., Kzk., Tat., Turk. *taraq* 'der Kamm' (Radl. III, 838) + suff. *-tï*.

TARAN   Alt.(Tel.) 19th c. **Taran** [Таран], a Telengit shaman at the Chuya river, and teller of tales (Potanin IV, 179, 215, 235, 328). ✧ 'Millet' cf. Alt.(Tel.) *tarān* 'die Hirse' (Radl. III, 841).

TARANEY   Yak. 1680 **Taraney** [Таранѣй Чевелгинъ] (DAI VIII, 268).

TARAÑGÏ   Selj.? 1071 **Tarañγï?** [Ταράγγης], a commander of the army (Byz. Turc. 298). ✧ 'Tamarisk'? cf. Chag. *tarañgu* 'die Tamarinde' (Radl. III, 841).

TARAÑÏŠ   Alt. 19th-20th c. **Tarañïš** [Тараныш] (OjrRS 210).

TARAŠ   Trkm. 20th c. **Taraš** [Taraš] (Zaj. 1971, 330); Trkm. 20th c. **Taraš** [Тараш] (TrkmRS 621). ✧ 'Cleaning of the watering network system' cf. Trkm. *taraš* 'id.' (TrkmRS).

TARBA-KİNJİ   Hak.(Kuyb.) 19th-20th c. **Tarba-kinji** [Тарба Кінџі], Talay-qan's son (Radl. I, 1080). ✧ 'Conjuring, incantation - chain'? cf. Alt., Hak. *tarba*

'die Verhexung, die Besprechung' (Radl. III, 871) and Hak.(Kacha) *kinjï* 'die Kette' (Radl. II, 1349).

TARBAΓATAY   Kzk. 19th c. **Tarbaγatay** [Тарбагатай], Dombaul's son in a legend (Potanin, Pred. 47). ✧ Tarbagatay (mountains), cf. Kzk. *tarbaγadai* 'das Tarbagataigebirge' (Radl. III, 872).

TARBAQ   Kzk. 19th c. **Tarbaq** [Тарбакъ] (AOA 6); Kzk. 19th c. **Tarbaq** [Тарбакъ] (AOP 50); Kzk. 19th c. **Tarbaq** [Тарбакъ] (SODž. 32); Kzk. 19th c. **Tarbaq** [Тарбакъ] (SOV 18). ✧ 'Short, thick fingers' cf. Kzk. *tarbaq* 'kurze dicke Finger' (Radl. III, 872). See also **QUSTUQ-TARBAX**.

TARJİÑ   Hak. 19th-20th c. **Tarjïñ** [Тарчынъ] (HRS 351).

TARDANAQ   Alt. **Tardanaq** [Тарданак] (Radl. I, 927); Alt. 19th c. **Tardanaq** [Тарданак-богатырь] (Verb., In. 156, 157).

TARDÄÑ   Tuv.? 19th c. **Tardäñ** [Тардаҥ], fem. (Proben IX, 463).

TARDUŠ   Türk / Uyg. 8th c. **Tarduš-ïnanču-čor** [Tarduš ïnanču čor] (Ligeti, R. tör. nev. II-III, 41); *EN:* 9th c. - 10th c. **Tarduš** [Tarduš] (Tabarī, Annal. II, 1337); Uyg. 12th c. - 14th c. **Tarduš** [Tardyš] (Radl., USp. 12); Türk? 576 **Tarduš** [? / Tardu, Tarduš] (Byz. Turc. 299); Türk / Uyg. 8th c. **Tarduš** [Tarduš šad] (Ligeti, R. tör. nev. II-III, 41). ✧ Ethnonym, one of the main tribes of the Türks (Radl. III, 869).

TARGİG   Uyg. 1338 **Targig-tigin** [Targig Tigin], fem. (Chwol., Syr.-nest. (NF) 32).

TARΓ   Kuman 12th c. **Tarγ / Tarχ?** [Таргъ (Тархъ)] (PSRL II, 128, 319, I, 167); *EN:* Kuman 1185 **Tarγ-ōlu / Tarïγ-ulï?** [Тарголове (Таргаломве)], a Polovets clan (PSRL II, 131, 320).

TARΓALTAY   Kzk. 19th c. **Tarγaltay** [Таргалтай], Dombaul's son in a legend (Potanin, Pred. 47).

TARΓAP   Kzk. 19th c. **Tarγap-pay** [Таргаппай] (SOV 96).

TARΓÏΓ   Uyg. 1338 **Tarγïγ-tigin** [Targig Tigin], fem. (Chwol., Syr.-nest. (NF) 32).

TARΓÏL   Crm. **Tarγïl / Är-tarγïl** [Тарԑыл / Äр Тарԑыл], a folklore hero (Proben VII, 201). ✧ 'Piebald (red and black) cow' cf. Kzk. *tarγïl* 'eine Farbe der Kühe (roth mit schwarzen Flecken)' (Radl. III, 854).

TARΓÏL-TAY   Alt. 19th c. **Tarγïl-tay** [Таргылтай] (Potanin, Pred. 50). ⇨ **TARΓÏL + TAY** or suff. *-tay(1,2)*?

TARΓÏL-TAS   Kirg. **Tarγïl-tas** [Тарԑыл Тас] (Proben V, 196 /198/). ⇨ **TARΓÏL + TAZ**.

TARΓÏN   Kzk. 19th c. **Tarγïn / Tarγïn-batïr** [ايـر طـارغـن] / Er Tarγyn / Тарԑын / Ер Тарԑын/ Тарԑын батыр / Еръ-Таргынъ], hero of the Kazak epic Er-tarγïn (Kazan, 1862) (Proben III, 120 /153/, 133 /168/, AUK Dobavl. 12); Alt. 19th c. **Tarγïn-nama** [Таргын-Нама], a hero in a legend (Verb., In. 93, 94,

97). ❖ I. 'Tarkhan (title)' (Žanuzakov); II. 'Fretful, angry' cf. Turk. *taryïn* 'zornig, erzürnt' (Radl. III, 854); III. 'Fat, gross' cf. Chag. *taryun* 'dick, fett' (Radl. III, 854). See also **SAN-TARΓÏN**.

TARΓÏN-NAMA see **TARΓÏN**

TARΓÏT Avar 560-580 **Taryït** (Byz. Turc. 299).

TARXAN see **TARQAN**

TARİJEK Hak. 19th-20th c. **Tarijek** [Таричек], fem. (HRS 355).

TARİKE Hak. 19th-20th c. **Tarike** [Тарике], fem. (HRS 355). ❖ 'Spring-Goddess' (Mo.) (Butanaev).

TARİNE Hak. 19th-20th c. **Tarine** [Тарине], fem. (HRS 355).

TARÏ Kzk. 18th c. - 19th c. **Tarï** [Тары] (Tynyšp. 70); Kzk. 18th c. - 19th c. **Tarï-bay** [Тарыбай] (Tynyšp. 74); Kzk. 19th c. **Tarï-bay** [Таробай] (SODž. 144); Kzk. 19th c. **Tarï-bay** [Тарыбай] (SOK 106, 108); Kzk. 19th c. **Tarï-bek** [Тарюбекъ] (AOP 74). ❖ 'Millet' cf. Kuman, Kzk., Tat. *tarï* 'die Hirse' (Radl. III, 846).

TARÏ-BERDE see **TÄÑRİ-BERDİ**

TARÏΓ Kuman 1183, 1185 **Tarïχ** / **Tarïγ** [Тархъ / Таргъ], a Polovets prince (Ipat. 427 /440/, Lavr. 375 /267/, PSRL I, 167, II, 128, 319). ❖ 'Blood-relative / one's own flesh and blood; core, seed' (Bask., Im. plov. 73), Uyg., Karakh. *tarïγ* 'зерно, злаки, хлеб; просо' (DTS).

TARÏYMA Tuv. 19th c. **Tarïyma** [Тарыіма], fem. (Proben IX, 165, 168).

TARÏQ Uyg. **Tarïq** [Tарık] (EUTS); Uyg. 12th c. - 14th c. **Tarïq** (Radl., USp. 117). ❖ 'Field' cf. Uyg. *tarïq* 'das Ackerland' (Radl. III, 846). See also **TAMΓAČÏ-TARÏQ**.

TARÏQČÏ Uyg. 12th c. - 14th c. **Tarïqčï** [tarïqčï] (DTS); Uyg. **Tarïqčï-bäg** [Tarıkçı bäg] (EUTS). ❖ 'Peasant, ploughman' cf. Karakh. *tarïγčï / tarïqčï* 'id.' (DTS).

TARÏM Uyg. **Tarïm** [Tarım] (EUTS); Uyg. **Tarïm** [Tarım] (EUTS); Uyg. 1336 **Tärim** [Tarim] (Chwol., Syr.-nest. 77, DTS). ❖ I. 'prince; princess; title of the women and children from the khan's clan; an official of the subordinate states', used as secondary component (comp.) of male and female names; cf. Karakh. *tarim* 'титул, присоединяемый к именам женщин или детей ханского рода' (DTS); II. 'Feeder of a river' cf. Karakh. *tarim* 'рукав, приток реки' (DTS).

TARÏN Kzk. 19th c. **Tarïn-bay** [Тарынбай] (SODž. 78).

TARQA Kzk. 19th c. **Tarqa-bay** [Таркабай] (SODž. 144).

TARQAN Türk? 7th-8th c. **Tarχan** [Назик-Тархан / Низак-Тархан (Незак-тархан, Тархан)], Türk (Qarluq) or Heftalite ruler of Bagdis, murdered in 709 (MIT I, 62, 74, 81, 94-95, etc.); Türk? 746/47 **Tarχan** [Тархан ал-Джаммала] (MIT I, 122); Oghuz? 836

Tarχan [طرخان / Tarchan], one of Babek's generals (Tabarī, Annal. III, 1179, 1193, Weil, Abbas II, 300); Oghuz 10th c. **Tarχan** [Тархан], Ghuz chief (MIT I, 163); Karakh. **Tarχan** [Tarxan] (MK/Atalay 852); Selj. 1126 **Tarχan** [طرخان بن محمد الشيباني / Tarχan] (Qalānisi 216); Selj. 1126 **Tarχan** [Nâser ed-dauleh Tarkhân], an emir in Damascus, died in 1126 (Sauvaire IV, 266); Maml.? 1310 **Tarχan** [طرخان بن اليسرى] (Dawād. 212); Trkm. 20th c. **Tarhan** [Tarhan] (Zaj. 1971, 328); Trkm. 20th c. **Tarχan** [Тархан] (TrkmRS 622); Bashk. 1740 **Tarχan** [Мишер Тарханов] (MIB I, 396); Karakh. / Khazar? 917 **Tarχan** [بن كنداجيق / طرخان بن محمد بن اسحاق], Maχmud's son, a descendant of Kündečik (Arīb 63); Nog. / Tat.? 1468 **Tarχan** [Тарханъ] (PSRL XII, 120); Turk.? 1474 **Tarχan-beg** [طرخان بك] (Āšikp. 175); Nog. / Tat.? 1580 **Tarχan-murza** [Тарханъ мурза] (Sib. Let. 321); 1180 **Tarqan** [Tarcanus] (Reg. Hieros. 37); Uyg. **Tarqan** [Tarkan] (EUTS); *TN:* Crm. **Tarχan** [Tarkhan], a peninsula of the Crimea in the west (?); Crm. **Tarχan** [Tarkhan], a cape on the western part of Tarkhan peninsula (Jervis I.); Bashk. 1763 **Tarχan(ka)** [Тарханке] (MIB IV/2, 100); Crm. **Tarqan**, a village south-east of Perekop (Jervis II.); Crm. **Tarqan** [Tarkan] (Jervis III.); Crm. **Tarqan** [Tarkan], north-east of Simferopol' (Jervis VII.). ❖ I. 'Vice-roy (a title at ancient Turks); collector of taxes; noble man (at Mongol times)' cf. Türk *tarqan* 'der Tarhan, eine Würde' (Radl. III, 851), Chag., Turk. *tarχan* 'der Tarchan, der privilegierte Stand; ein dschagataischer Volksstamm; der Bestandtheil eines Eigennamens' (Radl. III, 854), Uyg. *tarqan* 'титул', Karakh. *tarχan* 'титул правителя' (DTS), cf. also Gombocz, ÁTSz. 48-49, Golden, Khaz. 210-213. Used also as a secondary component (originally a title) in compound names. II. 'Spoiled/pampered' (Zaj. 1971), cf. Trkm. *tarχan* 'избалованный' (TrkmRS). See also **İŠBARA-TARQAN**.

TARQAP Hak. 19th-20th c. **Tarqap** [Таркап] (HRS 351).

TARQOP Hak. 19th-20th c. **Tarqop** [Таркоп] (HRS 351).

TARLAW Tat.(Sib.) 1617, 1621, 1629, -1645 **Tarlaw** [Tarlau / Тарлавъ], a Chat (?) prince from Siberia (Miller, Ist. Sib. II, 263, 359, 363, 368, 504, Andrievič, Ist. Sib. I, 104, Radl., Aus Sib. I, 174, 181); Kzk. 19th c. **Tarlu-bay** (<**Tarlaw-bay**) [Тарлубай] (SOK 18). ❖ 'Field' cf. Kuman, Kzk., Tat. *tarlau* 'der Acker, ein frischgepflegtes Feld' (Radl. III, 856).

TARLÏ Trkm. 20th c. **Tarlï** [Tarlï], fem. (Zaj. 1971, 337); Trkm. 20th c. **Tärlï** [Тарлы], fem. (TrkmRS 621). ❖ 'Stringed' cf. Trkm. *tärlï* 'струнный' (TrkmRS).

TARLÏQ Kzk. 19th c. **Tarlïq-pay** [Тарликпай] (SOK

106); Uyg. 12th c. - 14th c. **Tarlïq-tutuñ** [Tarlïq Tutung] (Radl., USp. 203).

TARMA Khorezm. / Mo.? **Tarma-bala** [Тармабала] (RaD II, 10). ✧ 'Rake'? cf. Chag. *tarma* 'die Harke' (Radl. III, 873).

TARMAN Kzk. 1819 **Tarman** [Тарман] (MIK IV, 324). ✧ 'White with yellow apples (horse-colour)' cf. Kzk. *tarman* 'Pferdefarbe (weiss mit gelben Aepfeln)' (Radl. III, 874).

TARPAN Bashk. / R.? 1700 **Tarpan** [Тарпановъ] (Letop. ZAK II, 3); Bashk. 1722 **Tarpan** [Тарпан] (MIB I, 120); Kzk. 19th c. **Tarpan** [Тарпанъ] (SOK 186); Kzk. 19th c. **Tarpan** [Тарпанъ] (SOV 74); Kzk. 19th c. **Tarpan-bay** [Тарпанбай] (SODž. 58). ✧ 'Wild horse' cf. Kzk. *tarpan* 'das wilde Pferd (equus Przevalski)' (Radl. III, 871).

TARSUM Kzk. 19th c. **Tarsum-bek** [Тарсумбекъ] (SOK 178).

TART Hak. 19th c. **Tart** [Тарт] (Katanov, Otč. 12). ✧ 'Pull (it), drag (it)!' (Katanov), cf. all Trk. dial. *tart-* 'ziehen, fortziehen, schleppen' (Radl. III, 857).

TARTAL Kzk. 19th c. **Tartal-bay** [Тарталбай] (SOK 200).

TARTAN Hak.(Shor) 19th-20th c. **Tartan** [Тартан] (Katanov, Otč. 11).

TARTÏQ Maml.? 1331 **Tartïq** [/الامـيـر الـكـرجـى / طرطق] (Dawād. 255). ✧ 'Awry, sloping; evasive, insincere' cf. Alt., Tat. *tartïq* 'schief, verzogen, sich widersetzend, ausweichend' (Radl. III, 861).

TARTÏN Kzk. **Tartïm-bay** (<Tartïn-bay?) [Тартым Бай] (Proben III, 83 /106/). ✧ 'Abstain / hesitate!' cf. Kuman, Alt., Kzk., Tat. *tartïn-* 'an sich ziehen; sich gegen Etwas stämmen, sich widersetzen' (Radl. III, 861).

TARTÏŠ I. Uyg. 12th c. - 14th c. **Tartïš** (DTS). ✧ A tribe (clan) (DTS, Blagova 1997, 709), belonging or coming from the tribe (clan) Tartïš.

TARTÏŠ II. Bashk. 1794 **Tartïš** [Тартыш Кулшерыпов] (MIB V, 338). ✧ 'Fight, struggle, quarrel!' cf. Türk., Alt., Tat., Turk. *tartïš-* 'sich ziehen, ringen, streiten' (Radl. III, 863).

TARUČ Maml. 1264 **Taruč** [Alem-eddin-Taroudj-Amidi] (Makrïzï II, 14). ⇨ **TARUŠ?**

TARUMBET Kzk. 19th c. **Tarumbet (Tar-umbet)** [Сарбасъ Тарумбетовъ] (Grod., Pril. 152). ⇨ **TAR + MUXAMMED0.**

TARUŠ Kzk. 19th c. **Taruš** [Тарушъ] (SOK 306). ⇨ **TARUČ?**

TARŽÏQAY Kzk. 19th c. **Taržïqay / Taržiqay** [Таржикай] (AOO 14).

TAS see **TAŠ**

TAS-BAYMAT Kirg. **Tas-baymat** [Тас Баімат] (Radl., Altuig. I, 710 Proben V, 70 /71/, 152). ⇨ **TAZ + BAYMAT?**

TAS-BAU Kzk. 19th c. **Tas-bau** [Тасбау Таласбыевъ] (Grod., Pril. 134). ⇨ **TAŠ? + ВАГ.**

TAS-BAWUR Kzk. 19th c. **Tas-bawur** [Тасбауръ] (SODž. 18); Kzk. 19th c. **Tas-pawur** [Таспауръ] (SOK 184). ✧ 'Stone-liver (stony, senseless man)' cf. Kzk. *tas-bawïr* 'чёрствый человек' (KzRS). ⇨ **TAŠ + ВАГÏR.** See also **TAŠ-YÜRÄK.**

TAS-BOLAT see **TAŠ-BULAT**

TAS-BULAT see **TAŠ-BULAT**

TAS-ČİREK see **TAŠ-YÜRÄK**

TAS-ČÜRÜK see **TAŠ-YÜRÄK**

TAS-KÜÑ Uyg. 12th c. - 14th c. **Tas-küñ / Taq-küñ?** [Taš] (Radl., USp. 206, 248).

TAS-QARA see **TAŠ-QARA**

TAS-QULAQ Kzk. 19th c. **Tas-qulaq?** [Таксулакъ] (SODž. 128). ✧ 'Stone-ear'. ⇨ **TAŠ + QULAQ.** See also **TAS-BAWUR, TAŠ-YÜRÄK.**

TAS-MUXAMED see **TAŠ-MUXAMMED**

TAS-MUXAMMET see **TAŠ-MUXAMMED**

TAS-PALAY Kzk. 19th c. **Tas-palay** [Таспалай] (SOV 124). ⇨ **TAZ / TAŠ? + BALA + dim. suff. -y.**

TAS-PAŠ Alt. 19th-20th c. **Tas-paš** [Таспаш], fem. (OjrRS 213). ✧ 'Bald-head(ed)' (OjrRS), 'Tadpole' cf. Kzk. *taspaš* 'der Kaulbars, die Kaulquappe' (Radl. III, 924). ⇨ **TAZ + BAŠ.**

TAS-PAWUR see **TAS-BAWUR**

TAS-POLAT see **TAŠ-BULAT**

TAS-PULAT see **TAŠ-BULAT**

TAS-T'ÜREK see **TAŠ-YÜRÄK**

TAS-TELEK Kzk. 19th c. **Tas-telek / Tas-tilik?** [Тастелекъ] (SOV 98). ⇨ **TAZ / TAŠ + TİLEK.**

TAS-TEMİR see **TAŠ-TEMİR**

TAS-ŽÜREK see **TAŠ-YÜRÄK**

TASA Kzk. 19th c. **Tasa-bay** [Тасабай] (SOK 168); *TN:* Kzk. 19th c. **Tasa-bay** [Тасабай], a tomb on the northern coast of the Caspian Sea (IIRGO XVI (Karta ur. Tentjak-sor)). ✧ 'Missing, invisible, unseen; lair, nest' cf. Kzk. *tasa* 'unsichtbar, verschwunden' (Radl. III, 917), Kzk. *tasa* 'заслон, прикрытие' (KzRS).

TASAN Kzk. 19th c. **Tasan** [Тасанъ] (AOO 46); Kzk. **Tasan-mirza** [Тасанъ-мирза] (Divaev, Šura 80); Kzk. 19th c. **Tašan** [Ташанъ] (SOV 140).

TASBAN see **TASPAN**

TASBİN Kzk. 19th c. **Tasbin** [Мамбетъ Тасбиновъ] (Grod., Pril. 140).

TASÏ Kzk. 19th c. **Tasï-bay** [Тасыбай] (AOA 134); Kzk. 19th c. **Tasï-bay** [Давбай Тасибаевъ] (Grod., Pril. 131); Kzk. 19th c. **Tasï-bay** [Тасыбай] (SOK 256); Kzk. 19th c. **Tasï-bek** [Тасыбекъ] (AOP 22); Kzk. 19th c. **Tasï-bek** [Тасыбекъ] (AOP 50); Kzk. 19th c. **Tasï-bek** [Тасыбекъ Чинкиновъ] (Grod., Pril. 157); Kzk. 19th c. **Tasï-bek** [Тасыбекъ] (Grod., Pril. 78, 154); Kzk. 19th c. **Tasï-γul** [Тасыгулъ] (SOV

110); Kzk. 19th c. **Taši-bay** [Ташибай] (SOV 96); Kkalp. 20th c. **Taši-bay** [Ташибай] (KkRS 776).

TASÏL Kzk. 19th c. **Tasïl-bay** [Оразъ Тасилбаевъ] (Grod., Pril. 185).

TASÏM Bashk. 18th c. **Tasïm** [Измаил Тасимов] (MIB V, 682, 683); Bashk. 1800 **Tasïm** [Тасим Майметев (Мамеревъ)] (MIB V, 582); Kzk. 19th c. **Tasïm** [Тасимъ] (AOAtb. 42); Kzk. 19th c. **Tasïm** [Тасимъ] (Grod., Pril. 108).

TASÏMBET Kkalp. 20th c. **Tasïmbet** [Тасымбет] (KkRS 776). ⇨ **TAŠ-MUXAMMET; TAŠ** + suffixoid *-ïmbet.*

TASÏN-QURBAY Yak. **Tasïn-qurbay** [Тасын Курбаи̇], one of Bayanay's daughters (Pek.). ✧ 'Cantankereous, thoughtless, rash' (Pek.).

TASÏR Kzk. 19th c. **Tasïr-bay** [Тасырбай] (SOV 72). ✧ 'Show-off, disdainful, lofty'? cf. Kzk. *tasïr* 'грохот, топот', *tasïr adam* 'чванливый человек' (KzRS).

TASYAN Uyg. **Tasyan-ïnal / Tašyan-ïnal** [Tasyan / Tašyan'' Ïnal] (Zieme, Mat. I, 74, 79).

TASKÏN-TAY Kzk. 19th c. **Taskïn-tay** [Таскентай] (SOV 56). ⇨ **TAŠQÏN + TAY?** or suff. *-tay(1,2).*

TASQA Kzk. 19th c. **Tasqa** [Таска] (SODž. 82). ⇨ **TAŠ?** + suff. *-qa* or comp. *ake.*

TASQAQ Alt. 19th c. **Tasqaq** [Таскак] (Verb., In. 50). ✧ 'Sacrificial altar' (Verbickij) cf. Alt. *tasqaq* 'Holzgestell, auf dem die Stange mit dem Felle des Opferthieres ruht' (Radl. III, 919).

TASQÏN see **TAŠQÏN**

TASQÏR Bashk. 1770 **Tasqïr** [Таскыр Тенисевъ] (MIB IV/1, 342).

TASQUM see **TAŠQÏN**

TASPAN Kzk. 19th c. **Tasban** [Тасбанъ Юсуповъ] (Grod., Pril. 86); Kzk. 19th c. **Taspan** [Таспанъ] (SOK 40). ⇨ **TAŠMAN?**

TASPAR Kzk. 19th c. **Taspar-bay** [Таспарбай] (SODž. 138).

TASPEN Kkalp. 20th c. **Taspen** [Таспен] (KkRS 776). ⇨ **TASPAN?**

TASTAM-BEK see **TASTAN**

TASTAN Kzk. **Tastam-bek** [Тастамбекъ] (Protok. Turk. IV, 62); Kzk. 18th c. - 19th c. **Tastam-bek** [Тастамбек] (Tynyšp. 65); Kzk. 19th c. **Tastan** [Тастанъ] (AOA 2); Kzk. 19th c. **Tastan** [Тастанъ] (AOK 34, 130); Kzk. 19th c. **Tastan** [Тастанъ] (AOP 14, 98); Kzk. 19th c. **Tastan** [Тастанъ] (SOK 56); Kzk. 19th c. **Tastan** [Тастанъ] (SOV 50); Kzk. 19th c. **Tastan-bek** [Tastanbek] (Ljutš 115); Kzk. 19th c. **Tastan-bek** [Тастанбекъ] (SOK 12); Kzk. 1898 **Tastan-bek** [Тастанъ-бекъ] (AUK Dobavl. 3). ✧ '(Made) of stone; hard, strong'. ⇨ **TAŠ.**

TASTAR Alt. **Tastar-aqay** [Тастаракаi] (Radl. I, 1256); Alt.(Tuba) 19th c. **Tastar-aqay** [Тастаракай], a hero in a tale (Potanin IV, 372). ✧ Tastar (ethnonym)

cf. Alt.(Kmd.) *Tastar* 'ein Tatarengeschlecht, das an der Bija wohnt' (Radl. III, 922).

TASTÏ see **TAŠLÏ**

TASTÏQ see **TAŠTÏQ**

TASTÏM-BEK see **TASTÏN**

TASTÏN Kzk. 19th c. **Tastim-bay** [Тастембай] (SODž. 102); Kzk. 19th c. **Tastim-bek?** [Тастембекъ] (AOAtb. 6); Kzk. 19th c. **Tastim-bek?** [Тастембекъ] (SODž 58); Kzk. 19th c. **Tastim-bek?** [Тастембекъ] (SOV 106, 116); Kzk. 19th c. **Tastïm-bek** [Тастымбекъ] (AOK 126); Kzk. 19th c. **Tastïn-bek** [Тастынбекъ] (AOO 10).

TASTU see **TAŠLÏ**

TASU Kzk. 19th c. **Tasu-bay** [Тасубай] (SODž. 92). ✧ 'Flush, flooding' cf. Kzk. *tasïw* 'выходить из береговъ; выливаться через край' (KzRS).

TASU-BERDI Kzk. 1875 **Tasu-berdi** [Султанкулъ Тасубердинъ], from the district of Vernyj (TV 1875, 194). ✧ 'Fload gave (him/her)'. ⇨ **TASU + BERDI.**

TAŠ Maml. 14th c. **Daš** [ضاش] (Sauvaget 49); Kzk. 19th c. **Daš** [Дашъ] (SOK 28); Nog.? 1517 **Daš-murza** [Дашь мурза] (PSRL XX, 392); Kzk. 18th c. - 19th c. **Tas** [Тас] (Tynyšp. 67); Kzk. 19th c. **Tas** [Тасъ] (AOK 90); Hak.(Kacha) 19th-20th c. **Tas** [Тас богатырь], a folklore hero (Proben IX, 218); Kzk. 19th c. **Tas-jan / Tas-čan** [Тасчанъ] (SOK 146); Kzk. **Tas-mergen** [Тасъ-Мергенъ] (Divaev, Šura 112); Uyg. 8th c. - 9th c. **Taš** (Müller, Pfahl. 19); Uyg. 12th c. - 14th c. **Taš** [Taš] (Radl., USp. 216, 258); Kuman 1127 **Taš** [Ташъ (Ствашъ)], a Polovets prince (Lavr. 281 /196/, PSRL VII, 26, 27); Selj. **Taš** [تاش / Taš], an emir (Zehireddin/Dorn 186, 187, 189); Yürük 1543 **Taš** [Taş] (Gökb., Rum. 192); Tat.(Lit.) 1646 **Taš** [Хава Ташовна Алеевичъ] (Lit. Tat. 335-336); Tat.(Bar.) **Taš** [Таш Кан], a character in a tale (Proben IV, 87 /69/); Kzk. 19th c. **Taš** [Ташевъ] (Grod., Pril. 115); Kzk. 19th c. **Taš** [Ташевъ] (SKSO VIII, 203, 204); Kzk. 19th c. **Taš** [Ташъ Бирковъ] (SKSO VIII, 224); Kzk. 19th c. **Taš** [Тасъ] (SOK 54); Kzk. 19th c. **Taš-bay** [Исанбай Ташбаевъ] (Grod., Pril. 174); Kzk. 19th c. **Taš-biy** [Ташбіевъ] (SKSO VIII, 232); Kzk. 19th c. **Taš-γul** [Ташгулъ] (Grod., Pril. 169); Khorezm. 14th c. **Taš-χatun** [طاش خاتون / Thâch khâtoûn], a princess from Shiraz (Ibn Bat. II, 67); Uyg. **Taš-qan** [Taş kan] (EUTS); Uyg. 12th c. - 14th c. **Taš-qan** [Taš-qan] (Radl., USp. 248); Selj.? 1171, 1205 **Taš-tegin** [طاشتكين مجيرالـديـن الامـير المستنجدى], an emir (Ibn al-Athīr/Tornb. XI, 241, 370, XII, 159-160, 170, Abulfidā IV, 218-219); Selj.? 1175 **Taš-tegin** [امـيـر الـحـاج العراقي طشتـكين], emir who took Mecca in 1175 (Abulfidā IV, 27); Selj.? 1188/89 **Taš-tegin** [طشتـكين / Tachtikîn], chief of pilgrims leader (Ibn Šaddād, Nawād.: RHCHor III, 104); Uyg. 13th c. - 14th

c. **Taš-tärim** / **Taš-tarïm** [Tasch Tarim], fem. (Chwol., Syr.-nest. (NF) 47); Uyg. 1338 **Taš-tärim** / **Taš-tarïm** [Taš-Tarim], fem. (Chwol., Syr.-nest. 82,); *TN:* Kzk. **Tas** [Тас], a field (Kojčubaev 211); Turk. 20th c. **Taš-oγlu** [Taşoğlu], a village in the province of Çankırı, Turkey (TMİB 251). ✧ 'Stone' cf. Türk., Uyg., Kuman, Chag., Alt., Hak.(Kacha), Shor, Tat., Turk. *taš* 'der Stein, steinern' (Radl. III, 931), Hak.(Sag., Koyb.), Kzk. *tas* 'der Stein' (Radl. III, 916). „The 'stone' means not only health and power, but also strong marriage for the young bride." (Torma 1992, 363) See also Karabacek: M. S. Pap. Rainer I, 105-106. See also АГА-ТАŠ, AY-TAŠ, AQ-TAŠ, ALAQ-TAŠ, ALP-TAŠ, ALTUN-TAŠ, ARSLAN-TAŠ, BAL-TAŠ, BALA-TAŠ, BAY-TAŠ, BEK-TAŠ, BUYAN-KÜKEL-TAŠ, ČÏN-TAŠ, ČUY-TAŠ, ǰAN-TAS, ǰETİ-TAS, ǰULUW-TAŠ, DÖNÖLEK-TAS, ÄR-TAŠ, EL-TAŠ, ER-TAŠ, GÄWHÄR-TAŠ, XAL-TAŠ, XUMAR-TAŠ, İL-TAŠ, İR-TAŠ, YALAÑ-TAŠ, YANÏQ-TAŠ, YARUQ-TAŠ, YAW-TAŠ, YURUL-TAŠ, KÄD-TAŠ, KED-TAŠ, KÖK-TAŠ, KÜKEL-TAŠ, KÜMİŠ-TAŠ, QAMAR-TAŠ?, QARA-TAŠ, QARA-TEMİR-TAŠ, QATAQ-TAŠ?, QÏZÏL-TAS, QÏZÏM-TAS, QUL-TAŠ, MĀTÏR-TAS, MEÑGÜ-TAŠ, MİN-TAŠ, MULLA-TAŠ, SU-TAŠ, ТАРГÏL-TAS, TEGİN-TAŠ, TEMİR-TAS, ТОГАY-TEMİR-TAŠ, TOQ-TAŠ, TURSUN-TAŠ, TÜRČİ-ALP-TAŠ, ÜREÑ-TAŠ.

TAŠ-AŠAR   Uzb. 20th c. **Tâš-âšar** [Тошошар] (Begmatov 1984, 203); Uzb. 20th c. **Tâš-âšar** [Тошошар], fem. (Begmatov 1984, 203). ✧ 'He will pass over stone(=mountains)' cf. Uyg., Kuman, Chag., Alt., Az., Crm., Tat., Turk., etc. *aš-* 'über etwas hinübersteigen; steigen; über etwas hervorragen, etwas übertreffen' (Radl. I, 586), Kzk. *as-* 'перевалить, пройти, проехать' (KzRS). ⇨ TAŠ. See also BEL-ASAR, ТАГ-AŠAR.

TAŠ-AŠUR   Uzb. 1875 **Taš-ašur** [Ташъ-ашуръ] (Moskal'cev 40). ⇨ TAŠ + AŠUR / AŠÏR.

TAŠ-BERGEN   Kkalp. 20th c. **Tas-bergen** [Тасберген] (KkRS 776); Kzk. 19th c. **Taš-bergen** [Ташбергенъ Кашкинобъ] (Grod., Pril. 89). ✧ 'Stone (hard/strong man) gave (him/her)'. ⇨ TAŠ + BERGEN.

TAŠ-BOL   Uzb. 20th c. **Tâš-bol** [Тошбўл] (Begmatov 1984, 201). ✧ 'Be/become a stone (hard/strong man)'. ⇨ TAŠ + BOL.

TAŠ-BUΓA   Maml. 1332 **Taš-buγa** [طشبغا], an emir (Dawād. 367); Maml. 1390 **Taš-buγa** [طشبغا السيفى تمر باى] (Iyās I, 292, Weil, Chalif. I, 528). ✧ 'Stone-bull / bull of stone' (Sauvaget 50). ⇨ TAŠ + BUQA.

TAŠ-BULAT   Kzk. 19th c. **Tas-bolat** [Тасболатъ] (AOO 50); Kzk. 19th c. **Tas-bolat** [Тасболатъ] (SOV 38); Kzk. 19th c. **Tas-bulat** [Тасбулатъ] (SOK 214); Kkalp. 20th c. **Tas-bulat** [Таспулат] (Bask., Kkalp. 5); Kkalp. 20th c. **Tas-polat** [Тасполат] (KkRS 776); Bashk. 1779 **Taš-bulat** [Тажбулат Тусыев] (MIB V, 101); Bashk. 1795 **Taš-bulat** [Ташбулатъ Махмутовъ] (IOAIÊK XXVIII, 590); Kzk. 18th c. - 19th c. **Tas-bulat** [Тасболат] (Tynyšp. 72); Uzb. 19th c. **Taš-bulat** [Ташбулатъ] (SKSO III, 182); Uzb. 1770 **Taš-pulad** [Таш Пулад], a Nayman (MIT II, 343); Kzk. 19th c. **Taš-pulat** [Ташпулатъ Умаровъ] (SKSO VIII, 219). ✧ 'Stone-steel'. ⇨ TAŠ + BULAT.

TAŠ-DEMİR see **TAŠ-TEMİR**

TAŠ-YÜRÄK   Kzk. 19th c. **Tas-čirek** [Тасчирекъ] (SOK 288); Kzk. 19th c. **Tas-čürük** [Тасчурукъ] (SOV 142); Alt. **Tas-t'ürek** [Tas Tjürek] (Radl. II, 223); Kzk. 18th c. - 19th c. **Tas-žurek** [Тасжурек] (Tynyšp. 67); Bashk. 1751 **Taš-yüräk** [Байслан Ташюреков] (MIB IV/1, 43); *TN:* Kzk. **Tas-čürek** [Tas-Čürek], south-east of lake Balkhash (?). ✧ 'Stone-heart(ed); brave, not afraid of anything' cf. Türk, Uyg., Karakh. *jüräk/ǰüräk* 'сердце' (DTS), Kuman, Chag., Alt., Turk. etc. *yüräk* 'das Herz' (Radl. III, 600), Bashk. *yöräk* 'сердце' (BRS), Kzk. *žürek* 'сердце' (KzRS), Kzk. *tas cürek* 'таш kalb, hiç bir şeyden korkmayan' (KzTS), Alt. *d'ürek* 'сердце' (OjrRS), Tuv. *čürek* 'сердце' (TuvRS). ⇨ TAŠ.

TAŠ-KEMİR   Kzk. 1820 **Taš-kemir** [Ташкемиръ], chief of the Kündelän (Kündelen) clan/branch of the Kipchak tribe of the Middle Horde (Orta Žüz) (Sib. Vest. IX, 106). ✧ I. 'Stone-belt'?; II. 'Stone-coal (=hard coal)'? cf. Kzk. *tas kömir* 'таş kömür' (KzTS). ⇨ TAŠ + KEMİR?

TAŠ-QARA   Kzk. 19th c. **Tas-qara** [Таскара] (AOO 50); Alt. 19th-20th c. **Tas-qara** [Таскара] (OjrRS 210); Kzk. 19th c. **Taš-qara** [Ташкараевъ] (SKSO VIII, 207); Kzk. / Uzb.? **Taš-qara** [Ташъ-Кара], a hakim (Smirnov, Sultany 73); Uzb. 19th c. **Tâš-qara** / **Toš-qara** [Мамуръ Точкараевъ] (SKSO III, 182). ⇨ TAŠ + QARA.

TAŠ-MAMBET   Kzk. 1867 **Taš-mambet** [Ташмамбетъ], a kurgan (burial mound) at Vernoje (!) (Alma-Ata?) (ZIRGOGeogr. I, 268). ⇨ TAŠ + MAMBET.

TAŠ-MEÑÜ   Uyg. 13th c. - 14th c. **Taš-meñü** [Taïš-Mingku] (Chwol., Syr.-nest. 98); Khorezm.? 1295 **Taš-meñü** [طاشمنكو قوشچى] (RaD/Jahn 97, 98). ⇨ TAŠ + MEÑGÜ.

TAŠ-MUXAMMÄD see **TAŠ-MUXAMMED**

TAŠ-MUXAMMED   Kzk. 19th c. **Tas-muxamed** [Тасмухамедъ] (Grod., Pril. 116); Kzk. 19th c. **Taš-muxammäd** / **Taž-muxammäd** [Taš-muxammäd / Таж-мухаммäд] (Samojlovič: ŽS XXIV (1915), 167); Trkm.? 1738/39 **Taš-muxammed** [Таш Мухаммед Кефир], a quš-begi (master of birds) (MIT II, 139). ⇨ TAŠ + MUXAMMED.

TAŠ-MURAT Uzb. 19th c. **Taš-murat** [Ташмуратъ Кувандыковъ] (SKSO III, 188). ⇨ **TAŠ** + **MURAT**.

TAŠ-PULAT see **TAŠ-BULAT**

TAŠ-SVÏT-BARS Uyg. 13th-14th c. **Taš-svit-bars-tarχan** [Taš Svit Bars Tarχan] (Zieme, Mat. II, 88). ⇨ **TAŠ** + ? + **BARS**.

TAŠ-TEMİR Kkalp. 20th c. **Tas-temir** [Тастемир] (KkRS 776); Karg. 19th-20th c. **Tas-temir** [Тас-темір] (Katanov, Otč. 8); Trkm. 20th c. **Taš-demir** [Taşdemir], a folk poet (Özbaş 35); Maml. 14th c. **Taš-tämür** [طَشتَمُرْ] (Sauvaget 50); 870-875 **Taš-temir** [دلاشتمر] (Tabarī, Annal. III, 1830, 1868, 1878, 1879, 1888); 873 **Taš-temir** [طاشتمر] (Ibn al-Athīr/Tornb. VII, 179, 189); Maml. 1295 **Taš-temir** [المحمدى] (Iyās I, 132); Maml. 1327 **Taš-temir** [الساقى] طشتمر], an emir (Dawād. 343); Maml. [سيفالدين طشتمر 1327, 1341, 1342 **Taš-temir** [بحمص أخضر] طشتمر حمّص اخضر / طشتمر المعروف], governor of Haleb (Aleppo) in 1341, viceroy of Egypt, died in 1342, „nicknamed *Green Pea* (ḥimmis akhḍar) because of his predilection for this vegetable" (Iyās I, 164, 178, 180, Ibn Taghrīb. VI, 288, Weil, Chalif. I, 359, 419 etc., Zetterst. 178); Maml. 1334 **Taš-temir** (Mayer 226-227); Maml. 1335 **Taš-temir** [طشتمر أخو بتجاص] (Dawād. 393); Maml. 1335 **Taš-temir** [طشتمر / Taschtemir], a cup-bearer of Melik an-Nāsir died in 1335, mentioned in an epitaph (Mehren 516); Maml. 14th c. **Taš-temir** [طشتمر] (Dawād. 211); Maml. 1352 **Taš-temir** [طشتمر القاسمى] (Iyās I, 196, 211, Weil, Chalif. I, 502); Maml. 1370, 1372, 1382/83, 1384, 1407/08 **Taš-temir** [سيفالدين / طشتمر العلائى / [طشتمر العلائّ / السينى], viceroy of Egypt in 1370, viceroy of Syria in 1377 (died in 1384), mentioned in inscriptions (Iyās I, 227, 231, 235, Ibn Taghrīb. VI, 284, 739, Berchem, Jér. I, 295, Mayer 225); Maml. 1376/77 **Taš-temir** [طشتمر الصالحى] (Iyās I, 232); Maml. 1463 **Taš-temir** [طشتمر] (Ibn Taghrīb. VIII, 584); Kzk. 1803 **Taš-temir** [Таштемир], head of the Kündelen tribe of the Middle Horde (Orta Žüz) (MIK IV, 513); Kirg.? 19th c. **Taš-temir** [Таштемировъ] (SKSO VIII, 223); 1329 **Taš-temür** [طاشتمور], died in 1329, executed by Abū Saīd (Qazw.); Oghuz? 874 **Taš-temür** [Taschtimar], one of Mutamīd's generals (Weil, Abbas II, 440); Khorezm.? **Taš-temür** [Tasch-Timour], Ĵoči's descendant on Toqa(y)-temür's line (Abulg./Desm. 187); Khorezm.? 15th c. **Taš-temür** [Tásh Timur], İsän-buγa's (1434-1462) follower (Tar. Rashidi 8); Khorezm./Chag. 15th c. **Taš-temür** [Ташъ-Тимуръ] (Barth., Ulugb. 114); Khorezm.? 1292, 1299 **Taš-temür / Taš-temir** [خطايى / طاشتمور طاشتيمور / Taštemir Haṭāyī], lord of Rūm in 1292

(Aqsarāyī 180, 246, RaD/Jahn 123); Khorezm. 14th c. **Taš-temür / Taš-timür** [طاش تمور / تيمور], follower of Toghluk Timur, the khan of Kashgar (Abulg./Desm. 165); Trkm. 1829 **Taš-temür-arbab** [Таш-Тимур-арбаб], from the Ali-eli tribe (MIT II, 454-456); Kzk. 1811 **Taš-timir** [Таштимиръ Куштановъ] (TOUAK XXIV, 42); Uzb. 19th c. **Taš-timir** [Таштымиръ] (SKSO III, 172); *TN:* Kzk. 19th c. **Tas-temir** [Тасъ-темиръ], a tomb? north of the Caspian Sea (IIRGO XVI (Karta ur. Tentjak-sor)). ✧ 'Stony iron' (Katanov), 'Stone-iron' (Sauvaget 50, Bese 15). ⇨ **TAŠ** + **TEMİR**.

TAŠ-TEMÜR see **TAŠ-TEMİR**

TAŠ-TURA Kuman 1347 **Taš-tïra / Taš-tura?** [Tastra], mentioned among the Kumans of Hungary together with his brother Kystre (Qïš-tura), Japza's son („duodecim Comanos filtreas domus habentes videlicet -Kystre filium Japza, Tastra filium eiusdem Japza" (Gyárfás III, 484). ✧ 'Stone house' (Rásonyi, NTK 106, Erol). ⇨ **TAŠ** + **TURA**. See also **QÏŠ-TURA**.

TAŠ-TURΓUN Uzb. 20th c. **Tâs-turγun** [Тоштурғун] (Begmatov 1984, 204). ✧ 'Stone-resident/indigenous (people)'? ⇨ **TAŠ** + **TURΓUN**.

TAŠAN see **TASAN**

TAŠET Kzk. 19th c. **Tašet** [Ташетъ] (AOP 82).

TAŠÏ see **TASÏ**

TAŠÏQ Uyg. 12th c. - 14th c. **Tašïq** [Tasïq] (Radl., USp. 48, DTS); Kzk. 19th c. **Tašïq** [Ташикъ] (SOK 152); Kzk. 19th c. **Tašïq** [Ташикъ] (SOV 74); Kzk. 19th c. **Tošuq / Tašuq?** [Тошукъ] (SOV 100). ✧ 'Overflowed, flood'? cf. Crm., Turk. *tašïq* 'die Ueberschwemmung', Chag. *tašiq* 'überlaufend, über die Ufer tretend (von Flüssen)' (Radl. III, 936, 937).

TAŠÏQ-TEMİR Maml. 1365 **Tašïq-temir** [طشتمر الماردينى] (Iyās I, 214). ⇨ **TAŠÏQ** + **TEMİR**.

TAŠÏM Kzk. 19th c. **Tašïm** [Ташимъ] (Grod., Pril. 178, AOA 62).

TAŠKE Kzk. 19th c. **Taške** [Ташке] (SODž. 136). ⇨ **TAŠ** + suff. -*ke*.

TAŠQAN Uyg. 12th c. - 14th c. **Tašqan** (DTS); Kzk. 19th c. **Tašqan-bay** [Ташканбай] (AOO 46); Kzk. 19th c. **Tašqan-bay** [Ташканбай] (Grod., Pril. 56). ⇨ **TAŠQÏN?**

TAŠQÏN Kzk. 19th c. **Tasqïm-bay** [Таскымбай] (AOO 58); Kzk. 19th c. **Tasqïm-bay / Tasqam-bay?** [Таскамбай] (SOK 286); Kzk. 19th c. **Tasqïn?** [Тоскынъ] (SOV 114); Kzk. 19th c. **Tasqïn-pay** [Таскенпай] (SOK 14, 34, 114); Kzk. 19th c. **Tasqum-bay?** [Тоскумбай] (AOAtb. 22); Kzk. 19th c. **Tasqum-bay** [Таскумбай] (AOK 138); Chuv. 18th-19th c. **Taškin?** [Ташкинъ] (Magn. 80); Kzk. 19th c. **Tašqïm-bay** [Ташкембай] (SODž. 80); Bashk. 1734 **Tašqin** [Ташкенъ Мурзагуловъ], a tarχan (Vel.-Zern., Bašk. 11); Kzk. 19th c. **Tašqïn** [Ташкенъ]

(AOA 86); Kzk. 19th c. **Tašqïn-bay** [Тошкымбай] (AOK 78); *EN:* Trkm. 1729 **Tašqïn-oɣullarï** [طاشقين اوغللرى / Taşkïn], a Türkmen clan in Anatolia (Refik, Anad. 180); *TN:* Turk. 20th c. **Tašqïn-paša** [Taşkınpaşa], a village in the province of Nevşehir, Turkey (TMİB 688). ✧ 'Floading; hot tempered' cf. Alt., Shor, Kar., Turk. *tašqïn* 'überlaufend; hervorragend; heftiger Charakter' (Radl. III, 938), Hak.(Sag., Koyb., Kacha), Kzk. *tasqïn* 'der hohe Wasserstand' (Radl. III, 919), Bashk. *tašqïn* 'половодье; пылкий, пламенный' (BRS/Uraksin).

TAŠLAN   Bashk. 1756 **Tašlan-ɣul** [Ташлангул Мансуров] (MIB IV/1, 120). ✧ 'Fall upon (the enemy)!' cf. Bashk. *tašlan-* 'набрасываться, нападать' (BRS/Uraksin).

TAŠLÏ   Kzk. 19th c. **Tastï-bay** [Тастыбай] (AOA 154); Kzk. 19th c. **Tastu-bay** [Тастубай] (Grod., Pril. 37); Turk. 19th c. **Tašlï-oɣlu**, a Zeybek (Kúnos 1891, 118); Kzk. 19th c. **Taštï-bay** [Таштыбай] (AOA 6). ✧ 'Stony, rocky' cf. Kar., Tat., Turk. *tašlï* 'steinern, steinig, felsig' (Radl. III, 941).

TAŠMAN   Kzk. 1819 **Tašman** [Ташман] (MIK IV, 325).

TAŠMAT   Kirg. **Tašmat** [Ташмат] (Jud. 619); Kirg.? 19th c. **Tašmat** [Ташматовъ] (SKSO VIII, 221); Uzb. 19th c. **Tašmet** [Ташметъ] (SKSO III, 172). ⇨ **TAŠ** + suff. *-mat*.

TAŠMET see **TAŠMAT**

TAŠŠA   Kirg. **Tašša-bek** [Taschta Bek (!) / Ташша Бек], one of Manas' grooms (Proben V, 213 /215/). ✧ 'Eczematous, having tinea; itchy, scabby' cf. Kzk. *tašša* 'der Grindkopf' (Radl. III, 944).

TAŠTAƔAN   Alt. 19th-20th c. **Taštaɣan** [Таштаган] (OjrRS 210). ✧ 'Left, dismissed (child)' (OjrRS).

TAŠTAL   Alt. 19th-20th c. **Taštal** [Таштал] (OjrRS 210). ✧ 'Be left/dismissed!' cf. Alt., Hak., Kirg. *taštal-* 'sich werfen, geworfen werden, verziehen werden' (Radl. III, 943), Alt. *taštal-* 'быть брошенным, оставленным, броситься, кинуться' (OjrRS). ⇨ **TAŠTAN.**

TAŠTAL-BAQ   Kzk. 1819 **Taštal-baq** [Таштталбак] (MIK IV, 323). ⇨ **TAŠTAL** + **BAQ.**

TAŠTAN   Turk. 20th c. **Taštan** [Taştan] (Önder, Göle); Kzk. 19th c. **Taštan** [Таштанъ] (SKSO VIII, 224); Kzk. 19th c. **Taštan-bay** [Таштанбаевъ] (SKSO VIII, 207); Kirg. 1847 **Taštan-bek** [Кожубекъ Таштанбековъ], a manap (Konšin, Mat. V, 104); Kirg. 20th c. **Taštan-bek** [Таштанбек] (Ajtmatov). ✧ 'Be left/dismissed!' Be hard/strong like stone!; 'Stay, survive!' (Erol II), cf. the Kirg./Kzk. variant of the Passive *tašlan-* versteinern; geworfen werden; verlassen werden' (Radl. III, 940), cf. also Alt., Kirg. *tašta-* 'werfen, ablassen', and *taštal-* 'sich werfen, geworfen werden' (Radl. III, 943). ⇨ **TAŠTAL.**

TAŠTÏ see **TAŠLÏ**

TAŠTÏQ   Kzk. 19th c. **Tastïq-bay** [Тастыкбай] (SODž. 104); Kzk. 19th c. **Taštïq** [Таштыкъ] (AOO 50). ✧ 'Stony (place)'? ⇨ **TAŠ** + suff. *-lïq.*

TAŠURAQ   Kzk. 19th c. **Tašuraq** [Ташурак(овъ)] (Grod., Pril. 23).

TAT   Karakh. **Tat** [Tat] (MK/Atalay 853); Uyg. 13th c. **Tat-eri / Tat-äri?** [تاتاى / Tatari / Татари], envoy of Barčuq ïduq-qut's to Chinggis Khan (RaD/Ber. I, 127, RaD/Erdmann 67); Turk. 1583 **Tat-qïz** [طاتقز / Tatkız], fem. (Ongan, Ank. I, 178); Tat.(GH) 1423 **Tat-ol-bey** (<**Tat-ul-bey?**) [Tatol-bei], from Caffa, Crimea, the same as Tat-eri/Tatari at Rašid ad-Din? (Jorga, Notes I, 30). ✧ 'Alien, foreigner; poor, miserable' cf. Chag., Crm., Turk. *tat* 'Leute die sich von ihrem Volke getrennt haben, in Folge dessen in Abhängigkeit gerathen, armer Sünder'; *Tat*, surnom donné au population d'origine paersan ou Lourde dans le Turkestan; - au fig. pauvre, misérable, d'humble condition' (Radl. III, 899). See also **BURALQÏ, ČIT, QARÏP.**

TAT-EMGEN   Kzk. 19th c. **Tat-emgen** [Татемгенъ] (SODž. 44). ✧ '(He) sucked (some) sweetness'? cf. Chag., Crm., Kzk., Tat. etc. *tat* 'der Geschmack, die Süssigkeit' (Radl. III, 898) and Kzk. *em-* 'Emmek', (KzTS). ⇨ **TAT?** See also **AT-EMGEN, İT-EMGEN, MAY-İMGEN, SÜT-EMGEN.**

TAT-QARA   Tat.(GH)? 12th c. - 13th c. **Tat-qara?** [Τάτκαρα], a christened Tatar (Byz. Turc. 302). ⇨ **TAT** + **QARA?**

TAT-QUŠ   Kzk. 19th c. **Tat-quš-pay?** [Таткушпай] (SOK 84). ⇨ **TAT** + **QUŠ I.**

TATA   Tat.(Sib.) 1629 **Tata** [Тата] (Miller, Ist. Sib. II, 343); Kirg. 19th c. **Tata** [Манапъ Тата], a manap (TV 1876, 183).

TATAM-BAY see **TATAN**

TATAN   Kzk. 19th c. **Tatam-bay** [Татамбай] (SODž. 4); Kzk. 19th c. **Tatam-bay** [Татамбай] (SOV 14); Kzk. 1792 **Tatan** [Татанъ] (MIK IV, 142, 149); Kzk. 19th c. **Tatan** [Татанъ], one of the forefathers of the Merkits (Potanin II, 5).

TATAR   12th c. **Tatar** [تتار الطغرلى الاميرى] (Ibn al-Athīr/Tornb. XI, 59, 77); Bulg. 1334? **Tatar** [تطى / تطر / تطر / Taṭar (?) / Тотай] (Jusupov 31, Epigr. Bulg.94, 95, Tekin 98); Uyg.? 13th c. **Tatar** [Татар], envoy of the Uyghur(?) „idi-qut" to Chinggis Khan (RaD I/1, 148); Oghuz/Trkm. **Tatar**, sixth descendant of Türk in a legend (Abulg./Desm. 10); Oghuz/Trkm. 14th c. - 15th c. **Tatar** (DQorq./Rossi 220); Kuman 1333 **Tatar** [Tatar filio Vgudey], Ügüdey's son among the Kumans of Hungary (Gyárfás III, 4760); Kuman 14th c. **Tatar** [Tatar, dux Cunorum], a prince of the Kumans in Hungary (SRH I, 444); Selj.

11th c. - 12th c. **Tatar** [الامير الحاجب تتار], an emir, door-keeper (Bondārī 165, 187, 218, 222); Selj. 1139, 1149 **Tatar** [تتر المسعودى], an emir, doorkeeper, Masʿūd's (Mesʿud) follower (Ibn al-Athīr/Tornb. XI, 87, Ahbar 78); Selj.? 1182 **Tatar** [تتر الامير همام الدين], an emir (Ibn al-Athīr/Tornb. XI, 314, 377); Tat.(GH) **Tatar** [Татаръ], a prince of the Horde (PSRL X, 159); Maml. 14th c. **Tatar** [تَتَر / طَطَر] (Sauvaget 50); Maml. 1414 **Tatar** [تتر], an emir (Iyās II, 4, 13, 28); Maml. 1421 **Tatar** [ططر ططر الملك الظاهر / السلطان الملك الظاهر أبو الفتح / سيف الدين / طَطَر المظفّرى /], Mamlūk sultan (Makrīzi, Khit. I, 243, Ibn Taghrīb. VI, 89, etc., Berchem, Jér. II, 145, Uzunçarş., Anad. 6); Turk. 16th c. **Tatar** (Ongan, Ank. II.); Yürük 1543 **Tatar** [تاتار / Tatar] (Gökb., Rum. 104, 196, 214 etc.); Yürük 1543 **Tatar** (Gökb., Rum. 181); Uzb. 19th c. **Tatar** [Татаръ Тохтамышевъ] (SKSO III, 178); Uyg. 762 **Tatar-apategin** [Tatar Apa Tegin] (Mahrnāmag 9); Kzk. 19th c. **Tatar-bay** [Татарбай] (SOK 18); Chuv. 18th-19th c. **Tatar-bey / Tatar-bay** [Татарбей (Татарбай?)] (Magn. 80); Yürük 1543 **Tatar-χan**, from the Yürüks of Kocacık, Turkey (Gökb., Rum. 104, 221); 1732 **Tatar-χan-bek** [Татарханъ-Бекъ], a Kabard nobleman (?) (PSZRI VIII, 883); Oghuz/Trkm. 14th c. - 15th c. **Tatar-oγlï** [Tatar-Oğli] (DQorq./Rossi 154); Kzk. / Kmk.? 20th c. **Tatar-oγlï** [Daγestanli Tatar oγlï] (KSz. XIII, 152); Uyg. 13th-14th c. **Tatar-täñrim** [Tatar Tngrim], fem. (Zieme, Mat. III, 280 (after Ögel)); *TN:* Kkalp. 19th c. **Tatar** [تاتار / Татаръ], a village (qïšlaq) in the tümen of Seraz (Širazskij tumen') (ZIRGO/Stat.?). ✧ Ethnonym (TMEN II, No. 850), cf. also Türk, Chag., Tat., Turk. *tatar* (Türk) 'der Name eines Volkes wahrscheinlich di am Onon wohnenden Mongolen'; (Tat.) 'die Bewohner der Gegend im Norden von China'; (Turk.) 'der Courrier, die Estafette, der Vorreiter' (Radl. III, 901), also Rásonyi, KÖA 128, Anthr. 128.

TATAR-BÄLTÖK see **TATAR-BELTÜK**

TATAR-BELTÜK Bulg. 13th c. - 14th c. **Tatar-bältök / Tatar-beltük** [طط بلتك / Tatar Beltük / Татар-Бälтök] (Jusupov 41, Epigr. Bulg. 114, 115, Tekin 36). ⇨ **TATAR.**

TATARĪN Chuv. 18th-19th c. **Tatarin** [Тбтаринъ (Татаринъ!)] (Magn. 80). ✧ 'Tatar (man)' cf. R. *tatarin* 'id.'.

TATARKA Chuv. 18th-19th c. **Tatarka** [Татарка] (Magn. 80). ⇨ **TATAR** + dim. suff. *-ka*.

TATIČE Hak. 19th-20th c. **Tatiče** [Татиче] (HRS 351).

TATĪS Hak. 19th-20th c. **Tatis** [Татис], fem. (HRS 355).

TATÏ see **TATU**

TATÏQ Yak. **Tatïq-bärgän** [Татык-бäргäн] (Pek.);

TATÏM Bashk. 1714 **Tatïm** [Масягут Татимов] (MIB I, 135); Kzk. 19th c. **Tatïm** [Татимъ] (AOO 30).

TATÏN Kzk. 19th c. **Tatïn-bek** [Татынбекъ] (SOV 12).

TATÏŠ Kzk. 19th c. **Tatïš** [Татишевъ] (AOO 26); Hak.(Kacha) 1621, 1629 **Tatuš / Tatïš** [Татуш], a prince (Miller, Ist. Sib. II, 260, 274, 289, 292, 342).

TATYA Hak. 19th-20th c. **Tatya** [Татья], fem. (HRS 355). ✧ Tatya (R.), hypoc. of R. fem. *Tatyana* (HRS).

TATKEY Kzk. 19th c. **Tatkey** [Таткей] (AOO 66). ⇨ **TAT** + dim. suff. *-key.*

TATQA Hak. 19th-20th c. **Tatqa** [Татка], fem. (HRS 355).

TATQON Hak. 19th-20th c. **Tatqon** [Таткон], fem. (HRS 355). ✧ Derived from Tatyana (R. fem.) (Butanaev).

TATLA see **TATLÏ**

TATLÏ Kzk. 19th c. **Tatla-bay / Tatlï-bay** [Татлабай] (SODž. 32); Yürük 1543 **Tatlï** [طاتلى / Tatlı], from the yürüks of Kocacık, Turkey (Gökb., Rum. 104, 189); Yürük 1543 **Tatlï** [Tatlı] (Gökb., Rum. 189); Tat.(Lit.) 1591 **Tatlï** [Дчаншукъ Татлыгодичъ] (Lit. Tat. 93); Bashk. 1709 **Tatlï** [Каскын Татлыев] (MIB III, 51); Bashk. 1740 **Tatlï** [Татлы Япашев] (MIB I, 404); Bashk. 1740 **Tatlï** [Татлы] (MIB I, 423); Bashk. 1757 **Tatlï** [Алимбеть Татлин] (MIB IV/1, 157); Bashk. 1663 **Tatlï-bay** [Татлы-бай] (MIB I, 180); Bashk. 1675 **Tatlï-bay** [Юлай Татлыбаев] (MIB I, 201); Bashk. 1714 **Tatlï-bay** [Татлы-бай Кокбашев] (MIB I, 105, 106); Bashk. 1718 **Tatlï-bay** [Юлай Татлыбаев] (MIB III, 176); Bashk. 1735 **Tatlï-bay** [Аласъ Татлыбаевъ], a tarχan (Vel.-Zern., Bašk. 25); Bashk. 1736 **Tatlï-bay** [Татлыбай Тюгульбаев] (MIB III, 344); Bashk. 1753 **Tatlï-bay** [Мрат Татлыбаев] (MIB IV/1, 68); Bashk. 1757 **Tatlï-bay** [Мрат Татлыбаев] (MIB IV/1, 140); Bashk. 1762 **Tatlï-bay** [Муай Татлыбаев] (MIB IV/1, 235); Bashk. 1790 **Tatlï-bay** [Юзекей Татлыбаев] (MIB V, 288); Bashk. 1812 **Tatlï-bay** [Татлыбаевъ] (TOUAK XXIV, 45); Kzk. 18th c. **Tatlï-bay** [Татлыбай] (Nepljuev 762-763); Kzk. 1819 **Tatlï-bay** [Татлыбай] (MIK IV, 325); Bashk. 1664 **Tatlu-bay** [Усенька Татлубаев] (MIB I, 187); Kzk. 18th c. - 19th c. **Tatti-bay** [Таттыбай] (Tynyšp. 66); Kzk. 1794 **Tattï-bay** [تاتتى باى] (MIK IV, 162); Kzk. 19th c. **Tattï-bay** [Таттыбай] (AOK 10, 118); Kzk. 19th c. **Tattï-bay** [Таттебай] (SODž. 160); Kzk. 19th c. **Tattï-bay** [Таттыбай] (SOV 38); Kirg. 19th c. **Tattï-bay** [Таттыбай], İsen-tay's younger son (Potanin II, 3); Kzk. 18th c. - 19th c. **Tattï-bay-batïr** [Таттыбай-батыр] (Tynyšp. 68); Kzk. 19th c. **Tattï-bek** [Таттыбекъ] (Potanin, Pred. 94). ✧ 'Tasty, sweet, pleasant' cf. Turk. *tatlï* 'id.' (Radl. III, 907).

TATLÏJAQ Turk. 20th c. **Tatlïjaq** [Tatlıcak], a village in the province of Sivas, Turkey (TMİB 783). ⇨ **TATLÏ** + suff. *-jaq*.

TATLÏQ NUyg. 19th c. **Tatlïq / Tatlik** [تادلیق / Tatlik] (Le Coq, Namenl. 117). ✧ 'Sweet' (Le Coq).

TATLÏMBET Bashk. 1710 **Tatlïmbet** [Каскын Татлымбетев] (MIB III, 64); Bashk. 1755, 1757 **Tatlïmbet** [Татлымбеть Алымбетев] (MIB IV/1, 98, 151); Kzk. 1734 **Tatlïmbet-batïr** [Tatlymbet-Batyr] (Levchine 180). ⇨ **TATLÏ** + suff. *-mbet*.

TATRAN Pecheneg? 1090 **Tatran** [Τατράνης], a refugee (Byz. Turc. 302).

TATTÏ see **TATLÏ**

TATTÏ-BOLAT Kzk. 18th c. - 19th c. **Tattï-bolat** [Таттыболат] (Tynyšp. 71). ⇨ **TATLÏ** + **BULAT.**

TATU Bashk. 1735 **Tatï** [Бурангулъ Татыевъ], a tarχan (Vel.-Zern., Bašk. 12, 15); Tat.(Mish.) / Bashk.? 1755 **Tatï** [Таты Баркин] (MIB IV/1, 93); Kzk. 19th c. **Tatï-bay** [Татыбай] (AOO 42); Kzk. 19th c. **Tatï-bay** [Татыбай] (SODž. 80); Kzk. 19th c. **Tatï-bay** [Татыбай] (SOK 14); Kzk. 19th c. **Tatï-bek / Tatïl-bek?** [Татыльбекъ] (SOV 74); Pecheneg 1070 **Tatu** [Τατούς], a commander of the „Scythians" (Pechenegs) (Byz. Turc. 302); 19th c. **Tatu-bay** [Худай Бергенъ Татубаевъ] (Zobnin, K voprosu o tjulengutah 42). ✧ I. 'Peaceful, friendly' (Sattarov) cf. Chag., Hak.(Sag.), Kirg., Kzk. *tatū* 'die Einigkeit, die Freundschaft, der Friede, das Bündniss; einig, friedlich' (Radl. III, 906), Tat. *tatu* 'дружный, мирный, согласный' (TatRS); II. 'Horse of medium height, of strong build' (Radl. III, 906).

TATUΓA Tat.(Sib.) 1634 **Tatuγa?** [Татюга] (Miller, Ist. Sib. II, 417).

TATUY Tat.(Lit.) 1557 **Tatuy** [Татуй] (Kn. Metriki Lit. 152); Tat.(Sib.) 1640 **Tatuy** [Татуй Кадышев Ясачный] (Miller, Ist. Sib. II, 463). ⇨ **TATU** + dim. suff. *-y*.

TATUQ Kzk. 19th c. **Tatuq-pay** [Татукпай] (SOV 32).

TATULA-SUQAR Oghuz/Trkm. 13th c. **Tatula-suqar** [تاتوله سوقار / Tatoula Souqar / Тайтула-Сухаръ], *bek* of the „Toumât" [Tumat / Tymät?] tribe at Chinggis' times (RaD/Bedr. I, 88, Abulg./Desm. 46).

TAUŠ see **TAWÏŠ**

TAVUS Trkm. 20th c. **Tavus** [Tavus], fem. (Zaj. 1971, 338); Trkm. 20th c. **Tāvus** [Тавус], fem. (TrkmRS 611). ✧ 'Peafowl; peacock / peahen' cf. Trkm. *tāvus* 'павлин' (TrkmRS) (<Ar.).

TAW see **TAΓ**

TAW-ASAR see **TAΓ-AŠAR**

TAW-BAS Kzk. 19th c. **Taw-bas** [Таубас] (SOV 114). ⇨ **TAΓ** + **BAS İİ.**

TAW-ČAL Kzk. 1846 **Taw-čal** [Таучал], a branch of a Tabïn clan (MKOP 89). ⇨ **TAΓ** + **ČAL.**

TAW-ČAN Kzk. 1846 **Taw-čan** [Тавчан отделения Табынского], a branch of a Tabïn clan (MKOP 157). ⇨ **TAΓ** + **ĴAN.**

TAW-ČAR Uzb. 19th c. **Taw-čar** [Таучаръ] (SKSO III, 178). ⇨ **TAΓ** + **ČAR.**

TAW-DİGİN see **TAΓ**

TAW-KENİ Kzk. 19th c. **Taw-keni** [Таукены] (SODž. 8). ⇨ **TAΓ?**

TAW-KESÄL Tat. 1692 **Taw-kesäl** [Таукесалъ Талбековна], a princess from Astrakhan (AI V, 370). ⇨ **TAΓ?**

TAW-MÏRAT see **TAW-MURAT**

TAW-MURAT Kkalp. 20th c. **Taw-mïrat** [Таўмырат] (KkRS 776); Kkalp. 20th c. **Taw-murat** [Таўмурат] (KkRS 776). ⇨ **TAΓ** + **MURAT.**

TAW-MURΓUN Kzk. 19th c. **Taw-murγun** [Таумургунъ] (SOV 44). ⇨ **TAΓ** + **BURUN.**

TAWAQAN Kzk. 1819 **Tawaqan** [Тавакан] (MIK IV, 324).

TAWAN Kzk. 1819 **Tawan** [Таван] (MIK IV, 324). ✧ 'Patience, steadiness' cf. Kzk. *tawan* 'die Geduld' (Radl. III, 773).

TAWAR Alt. 19th-20th c. **Tawar** [Тавар (Товар)] (OjrRS 210). ✧ 'Produce, ware' cf. R. *tovar [=tavar]* 'id.' (OjrRS). See also **EWEZ-BERDİ-TAWAR.**

TAWB-ALDÏ see **TABÏP-ALDÏ**

TAWČUQ Tat.(Lit.) 1592 **Tawčuq** [Тавчукъ Салтаневичъ] (Lit. Tat. 124). ✧ 'Little mountain'. ⇨ **TAΓ** + dim. suff. *-čuq*.

TAWΓAČ see **TABΓAČ**

TAWÏB-ALDÏ see **TABÏP-ALDÏ**

TAWÏLDÏ see **TABÏLDÏ**

TAWÏM Kzk. 19th c. **Tawm-bay / Tawïm-bay** (<**Tawïn-bay?**) [Таумбай] (AOP 114).

TAWÏN Kzk. 19th c. **Tawïn-bek** [Тауенбекъ] (SOV 54).

TAWÏR Kzk. 19th c. **Tawr-bay** [Таурбай] (AOA 118); Kzk. 19th c. **Tawr-bay** [Таурбай] (AOP 90); Kzk. 19th c. **Tawr-bay** [Таурбай] (SODž 78, 122); Kzk. 19th c. **Tawr-bay** [Таурбай] (SOK 42, 270); Kzk. 19th c. **Tawr-bay** [Таурбай] (SOV 112).

TAWÏRČÏ Kzk. 19th c. **Tawrčï** [Таурчи] (SOV 150). ⇨ **TAWÏR** + suff. *-čï*.

TAWÏŠ 1684 **Tawš / Tauš** [Таушко Чичкановъ] (DAI X, 384-385); Bashk. 1756 **Tawš / Tauš** [Тауш Ухтеев] (MIB IV/1, 109); Kzk. 19th c. **Tawš / Tauš** [Таушъ] (SODž. 16). ✧ 'Voice, noise' cf. Tat. *tauš*, Kzk. *taus* 'die Stimme, der Ton, der Laut, das Geräusch' (Radl. III, 774-775).

TAWÏŠQAN 1661 **Tawšqan / Taušqan** [Осип Таушкановъ], an interpreter (AI IV, 290). ✧ 'Hare, rabbit' cf. Chag., East.T. *taušqan* 'der Hase' (Radl. III, 776).

TAWKE Kzk. 1839 **Tawke** [Кушпекъ Таукинъ],

sultan of the Middle Horde (Orta Žüz) (Konšin, Mat. V, 12); Kzk. 19th c. **Tawke** [Тауке] (AOO 54); Kzk. 19th c. **Tawke** [Тауке] (SOK 152); Kzk. 19th c. **Tawke** [Таукинъ] (SOK 264); Kzk. 19th c. **Tawke** [Тауке] (SOV 16); Kzk. 19th c. **Tawke-bay** [Таукебай] (SODž. 100); Kzk. 19th c. **Tawke-bay** [Таукебай] (SOK 12); Kzk. 19th c. **Tawke-bay** [Таукебай] (SOV 114); Kmk. 1692 **Tawqa** [Таука Салтанбековна] (AI V, 370). ⇨ **TAГ** + dim. suff. *-ke.*

TAWKEY Nog. 1649 **Tawkey?** [Таукея], fem. (AI IV, 122); Bashk. 1772 **Tawqay** [Мурза Таукаев] (MIB IV/2, 408). ⇨ **TAГ** + dim. suff. *-key.*

TAWQA see **TAWKE**

TAWQAẎ see **TAWKEY**

TAWQAṘ Kzk. 19th c. **Tawqar** [Таукаръ] (SOK 114).

TAWLA see **TAWLÏ**

TAWLAȚİM Tat. 1662 **Tawlatim?** [Тавлатимко] (DAI IV, 285).

TAWLÏ Bashk. 1757 **Tawla** [Тавла Юлумбетев] (MIB IV/1, 157); Bashk. 1757 **Tawla** [Тавла Ачин] (MIB IV/1, 157); Bashk. 1740 **Tawlï** [Нурыш Тауленев] (MIB I, 397); Bashk. 1762 **Tawlï** [Тавлы Канмурзин] (MIB IV/1, 233); Bashk. 1726 **Tawlï / Tawla?** [Явгильда Таулин] (MIB III, 237); Bashk. 1734 **Tawlï / Tawla?** [Самя Тавлин] (MIB III, 322); Bashk. 1790 **Tawlï / Tawla** [Тавлы (Тавля) Бикишев] (MIB V, 291, 300); Bashk. 1788 **Tawlï-bay** [Тавлыбай Кусяпов] (MIB V, 233); Bashk. 1734 **Tawlu** [Тавлу Кукеев] (MIB III, 322); Bashk. 1745 **Tawlu** [Тавлу Аканов] (MIB III, 426); Bashk. 1756 **Tawlu-bay** [Тавлубай Мукасев] (MIB IV/1, 109). ✧ 'With mountains; born/living in the mountains; argumentative' cf. Tat. *taulï* 'Berge habend, bergig' (Radl. III, 774), Bashk. *taulï* 'гористый; горец' (BRS/Uraksin), Bashk. *taulï* 'streitig' (Radl. III, 774).

TAWLU see **TAWLÏ**

TAWLUQAY Bashk. 1760, 1761 **Tawluqay** [Тавлукай Енелеев] (MIB IV/1, 189, 221). ⇨ **TAWLÏ** + dim. suff. *-qay.*

TAWMAN Kzk. 19th c. **Tawman** [Байгадыль Таумановъ] (AUK 611); Kkalp. 20th c. **Tawman** [Тавман / Тауман] (Bask., Kkalp. 401, KkRS 776). ⇨ **TAГ** + suff. *-man.*

TAWNÏQAY Kzk. 19th c. **Tawnïqay** [Тауныкай] (SOK 92).

TAWSAГAR Kzk. 19th c. **Tawsaγar** [Таусагаръ] (SOV 40). ✧ 'Very strong hero; defeatist, good-for-nothing' cf. Kzk. *tavsoğar* 'hayali hikayenin kahramanı; yaramaz, bozguncu, aksi' (KzTS).

TAWSAÑAR Kzk. 19th c. **Tawsañar** [Таусангаръ] (SOV 98). ⇨ **TAWSAГAR.**

TAWSİR Kzk. 19th c. **Tawsir** [Назаръ Тавсировъ] (Grod., Pril. 131).

TAWŠ see **TAWÏŠ**

TAWŠAN Kzk. 18th c. - 19th c. **Tawšan** [Таушан] (Tynyšp. 75); Trkm. 20th c. **Tovšan** [Tovšan], fem. (Zaj. 1971, 338); Trkm. 20th c. **Tovšan** [Товшан], fem. (TrkmRS 636); *TN:* Kzk.? **Tawšan** [Таушанъ] (Karta JAR XIX). ✧ 'Hare, rabbit' cf. Kkalp. *tawšan* 'заяц' (KkRS).

TAWŠE see **TAГJÏ**

TAWTA Kzk. 19th c. **Tawta-bay** [Тавтабай] (AOK 122).

TAWUQ Trkm. 1823/24 **Tawuq / Xuday-berdi-tawuq** [Худай-берды Таук] (MIT II, 423); Bashk. 1727 **Tawuq** [Токташ Тауков] (MIB III, 246); Kzk. 19th c. **Tawuq** [Тяукъ], a khan (AUK 247); Kzk. 19th c. **Towuq-bay / Tawuq-bay?** [Бердинъ Товукбаевъ] (Grod., Pril. 70); *TN:* Crm. **Tawuq** [Tauk] (Jervis III.). ✧ 'Hen, dame' cf. Chag., Kuman, Kirg., Kzk., Tat. etc. *tauq* 'das Huhn' (Radl. III, 773).

TAWUQ-BERGÄN Kzk. 19th c. **Tawuq-bergän** [Товукъ Берганъ] (Grod., Pril. 122). ✧ 'Given by a hen'. ⇨ **TAWUQ** + **BERGEN.**

TAWUQ-BULAT Kzk. 19th c. **Tawuq-bulat / Towuq-bulat?** [Мамрагимъ Товукбулатовъ] (Grod., Pril. 181). ⇨ **TAWUQ** + **BULAT?**

TAWZAQ Tat.(Sib.) **Tawzaq / Tawzan?** [Таузакъ (Таусинъ, Таузанъ)], one of Küčüm's men (Sib. Let. 16, 126, 244, 297).

TAWZAR Kzk. 19th c. **Tawzar** [Таузаръ] (AOP 54).

TAZ Az. **Daz-γïz** [Дазгыз], a character in a tale, her brother was called „kečal Ašïr" (=bald Ašïr) (Az. Skaz. 3); Uyg. 8th c. - 12th c. **Taz** [Taz] (TT IV, 432, 442-445, DTS, EUTS); Kuman 1107 **Taz** [Тазъ / Таазъ / Таязъ], a Polovets prince, Bönäk's brother or Bönäk's byname (Bask., Im. polov. 73) (Lavr. 271 /189/, Ipat. 187 /191/, PSRL VII, 21); Maml. 1293 **Taz**, a Kipchak, Noγay's son-in-law (Baybars/Tizeng. I, 86, 109, Duqmaq/Tizeng. I, 316, 323); Maml. 14th c. **Taz** [السيفى طاز / طاز أمير الحاج الناصرى], emir, originally Qalāūn's mamluk, „Grand Davādār" then governor of Haleb in 1354, died in 1361/62 (Iyās I, 193, 194, 205 etc., Weil, Chalif. I, 500, IV, 475-507, Mayer 228, Berchem, Jér. I, 286); Maml. 1399, 1455? **Taz** [سودون طاز], first (chief) Master of the Horse (Ibn Taghrīb. VII, 579, Weil, Chalif. II, 73-75, 101); Kzk. 1842 **Taz** [Джаркымбай Тазовъ] (Konšin, Mat. V, 27); Kzk. 19th c. **Taz** [Тазъ] (AOP 38); Kzk. 19th c. **Taz** [Саукумбай Тазовъ] (Konšin, Mat. V, 62); Kzk. 19th c. **Taz** [Тазъ] (SOV 74); Kzk. 1877 **Taz** [طاز] (MIK IV, 311, 319); Uyg. 8th c. - 12th c. **Taz-ïnal** [Taz] (Müller, Pfahl. 23); *EN:* Kzk. 1785 **Tazlar-uruγï** [Тазлар], a clan (MIK IV, 52); Kzk. 18th c. - 19th c. **Taz** [Таз] (Tynyšp. 68, 70, 73). ✧ 'Bald, itchy, scabby, dirty' cf. Alt., Hak.(Sag., Koyb.), Shor *tas* 'glatt, kahl, unbehart, kahlköpfig' (Radl. III, 915), Chag., Kuman, Crm., Kzk., Tat. *taz* 'abgerieben, kahl,

haarlos, kahl in der Folge des Grindes)' (Radl. III, 925).
See also **AQ-TAZ, ALTĬN-TAS, BAYRAQLĬ-TAZ, YĬQMĬŠ-TAZ, QŌR-TAS, MĀTĬR-TAS, TARГĬL-TAS; QALDAN, KEČÄL, KELEŠ.**

TAZ-AT Uyg. 8th c. - 9th c. **Taz-at-bay** [Tazat bai] (Müller, Pfahl. 24). ✧ 'Itchy/mangy horse' cf. Karakh. *taz at* 'шелудивый лошадь' (DTS). ⇨ **TAZ + AT.**

TAZ-BULAT Kzk. 19th c. **Taz-bulat** [Тазбулатъ] (SODž. 14); Kzk. 19th c. **Taz-bulat** [Тазбулатъ] (SOV 56). ⇨ **TAZ + BULAT.**

TAZA Hak. 19th-20th c. **Taza-bay** [Тазабай] (HRS 351); Kzk. **Taza-bek** [Тазабекъ] (Sb. Syr-D. IX, 44); Kzk. 19th c. **Taza-bek** [Тазабекъ] (SOK 82); Kkalp. 20th c. **Taza-gül** [Taza-gül / Тазагул], fem. (KkRS 778, Baskakov: OSA 141); Trkm. 20th c. **Täze** [Täze], fem. (Zaj. 1971, 337); Trkm. 20th c. **Tăze** [Тезе], fem. (TrkmRS 653). ✧ 'Clean, fresh, new, untouched' cf. Uyg., Kzk., Tat. *taza* 'rein, unverletzt, in gutem Zustande, fest, dauerhaft, gesund, frisch' (Radl. III, 925), Kkalp. *taza* 'чистый, опрятный' (KkRS), Trkm. *tăze* 'новый, свежий; молодой (<P.). See also **SAP-TAZA.**

TAZAN Tat.(Sib.)? 1629 **Tazan** [Тазан], a Chat (?) murza (Miller, Ist. Sib. II, 359).

TAZĬ Tat. 1822 **Tazi(y)** [Тазей Салиховъ] (TOUAK XXIV, 124); Kzk. 19th c. **Tazï-bek** [Тазыбекъ] (SOV 44). ✧ 'Greyhound' cf. Kzk., Turk. *tazi* 'der Windhund' (Radl. III, 928), Chag., East.T. *tazi* 'der Jagdhund, der Windhund' (Radl. III, 930).

TAZĬLAS Hak.(Koyb.) 19th c. **Tazïlas** [Тазылас] (Katanov, Otč. II, 12-15). ✧ 'Fusillade' (Katanov).

TAZOY Hak. 19th-20th c. **Tazoy** [Тазой] (HRS 351).

TAZŠA Kzk. 19th c. **Tazša** [Тазша], in a tale (TOOIK III, 160); Kzk. 19th c.? **Tazša-bala**, in a tale (Atyns. 68). ⇨ **TAZ + suff. -ša.**

TAŽ-MUXAMMÄD see **TAŠ-MUXAMMED**

TAŽĬ-BAY see **TAJĬ**

TĀB-ALDĬ see **TABĬP-ALDĬ**

TĀBĬY Alt. 19th-20th c. **Tābïy** [Таабый] (OjrRS 210).

TĀDĬN see **TADĬN**

TĀLA Hak. 19th-20th c. **Tāla** [Таала], fem. (HRS 355).

TĀLMĬŠ Tat. 1628 **Tālmïš** [Таалмыш Енмаметев] (Miller, Ist. Sib. II, 341).

TĀN Hak.(Shor) 19th-20th c. **Tān** [Тан] (Katanov, Otč. 11). ✧ 'Jackdaw' (Katanov), cf. Alt., Hak. *tān* 'die Dohle' (Radl. III, 822). See also **SÄÜKÄ.**

TĀNĬŠ see **TANĬŠ**

TĀT Alt. 19th-20th c. **Tāt** [Таат], fem. (OjrRS 213).

TÂM-TURDĬ Uzb. 20th c. **Tâm-urdï / Tâm-turdï?** [Томурди (Томтурди?)] (Begmatov 1984, 204). ⇨ ? **+ TURDĬ.**

TÂPĬB-ÂLDĬ see **TABĬP-ALDĬ**

TÄBÄNÄ-QŌГA Tat.(Bar.) **Täbänä-qōγa** [Täbänä Koga / Täбäнä Koва] (Proben IV, 24 /31/). ⇨

TEMENE.

TÄBÄX Yak. **Täbăχ** [Täбäх], fem. (Pek.).

TÄBRÄNŠI Uyg. 12th c. - 14th c. **Täbränši / Tibränši?** (Radl., USp. 120).

TÄČ Trkm. 20th c. **Täč** [Täč], fem. (Zaj. 1971, 337); Trkm. 20th c. **Täč** [Täč], fem. (Zaj. 1971, 341); Trkm. 20th c. **Täčgül** [Täčgül], fem. (Zaj. 1971, 339); Trkm. 20th c. **Tăč** [Тач], fem. (TrkmRS 654). ✧ 'Birthmark' cf. Trkm. *tăč* 'родинка' (TrkmRS). See also **QAL II.**

TÄČLĬ Trkm. 20th c. **Täčli** [Täčli], fem. (Zaj. 1971, 341); Trkm. 20th c. **Tăčli** [Тачли], fem. (TrkmRS 654). ✧ 'Having a birthmark'. ⇨ **TÄČ + suff. -li.**

TÄDMĬLĬG Uyg. **Tädmilig** [Tädmilig] (EUTS).

TÄGAY see **TAГAY**

TÄGÄLĬ Uyg. **Tägäli** [Tägäli] (EUTS).

TÄYGÄLÄK Yak. **Täygäläk** [Täiгäläk] (Pek.).

TÄYĬ Turk.? **Täyi-paša** [Täji Pascha] (Proben VI, 237).

TÄYLÄKDÜ Uyg. **Täyläkdü** [Täiläkdü] (EUTS).

TÄKÄN Uyg. **Täkän** [Täkän] (EUTS).

TÄKEL Uyg. 1339 **Täkel-tärim** [Täkel Tarim Kuschtanz], fem. (Chwol., Syr.-nest. (NF) 33).

TÄKEŠ see **TEKEŠ**

TÄKĬS see **TEGĬZ**

TÄKTEY Bashk. 1761 **Täktey** [Тяктей Бикеев] (MIB IV/1, 221).

TÄLBĬSTÄY Yak. **Tälbistäy-quo** [Тälбiстäi-куо], fem. (Pek.).

TÄLÄBĬS Yak. **Täläbis** [Тäläбiс, Тäлiбiс] (Pek.); Yak. **Tälibis** [Тäлiбiс] (Pek.).

TÄLÄR Yak. **Tälär** [Тäläп] (Pek.).

TÄLÄSÄY Yak. **Tälăsäy** [Тäläcäi], mentioned in a proverb (Pek.).

TÄLĬBĬS see **TÄLÄBĬS**

TÄLLÄX-TÄLĬÄRĬMÄ Yak. **Tälläχ-täliärimä** [Тäлläх Тäлiäрiмä], fem. (Pek.).

TÄMĀ-TÜRÜN Alt. 19th c. **Tämā-türün** [Тямаа-Тюрун] (Verb., In. 101).

TÄMÄ Chuv. 18th-19th c. **Tämä** [Тямя] (Magn. 88).

TÄMÄY Bashk. 1738 **Tämäy** [Тамай Тюткеев] (MIB I, 370); Tat.(Sib.) 1632 **Tämäy-murza** [Тамаймурзын Едыгер] (Miller, Ist. Sib. II, 387-89); Tat. 1728 **Temey** [Тохтар Темеев] (MIB III, 251); Bashk. 1706 **Temey** [Смаил Темеев] (MIB III, 17); Bashk. 1711 **Temey** [Каранай Темеев] (MIB III, 80). ✧ 'Joker, jester, nimble, skilful, tricky' cf. Tat. PN *Tämäy* (Sattarov), also Alt.(Kyz.) *tämäy* 'flink, hastig, gewandt' (Radl. III, 1129).

TÄMÄK Chuv. 18th-19th c. **Tämäk** [Тямякъ] (Magn. 88). ✧ 'Tobacco'? cf. Tat. *tämäki* 'der Taback' (Radl. III, 1130).

TÄMĬR-QAYA Crm. **Tämir-qaya** [Тäмiр Kaja], Ädigä's (Edige's) ancestor in the legend (Proben VII, 161). ⇨ **TEMĬR + QAYA.**

TÄMÜR-BOГA see **TEMĬR-BUГA**

TÄMÜR-YASTUQ Uyg. 12th c. - 14th c. **Tämür-yastuq** [Tämür Jastuq-ï] (Radl., USp. 56). ✧ 'Iron Yastuq; iron coin' cf. Uyg. *yastuq* 'мера серебра, серебранная монета' (DTS). ⇨ **TEMİR.**

TÄNAR Alt. 19th c. **Tänar / Tänär?** [Тянар] (Verb., In. 104).

TÄÑÄRÄ Alt. 19th c. **Täñärä** [Тянгара], the first priest (shaman) (Verb., In. 103); Alt. 19th c. **Teñere-χan** [Тенгере-хан] (Verb., In. 150, 151). ✧ 'Sky, heaven' cf. Alt.(Tel.) *täñärä* 'der Himmel, die oberen Welten' (Radl. III, 1043).

TÄÑIR Bashk. 1740 **Täñir-bay** [Сазангай Тангирбаев] (MIB I, 443). ✧ 'God, Allah, the omnipotence (of God)' cf. Kzk. *täñir* 'id.' (QTTS). See also **TÄÑRİ.**

TÄÑIR-BERDİ Kzk. **Täñir-berdi** [Танирберды], a character from the epic „Put' Abaja" by M. O. Auezov (Espaeva 1984, 231); Kzk. 18th c. - 19th c. **Täñir-berdi** [Танырберды] (Tynyšp. 68, 75). ✧ 'God gave (him/her)'; 'Sky gave (him/her)' (M. Auezov, cf. Espaeva 1984, p. 231). ⇨ **TÄÑIR + BERDİ.** See also **TÄÑIR-BERGEN.**

TÄÑIR-BERGEN Kzk. 18th c. - 19th c. **Täñir-bergen** [Танырберген] (Tynyšp. 68, 71); Kzk. 19th c. **Täñir-bergen** [Танырбергенъ], a biy (Lomakin 37); Kzk. 19th c. **Täñir-bergen** [Танырбергенъ] (SODž. 118); Kzk. 19th c. **Täñir-bergen** [Такырбергенъ / Танырбергенъ?] (SODž. 78); *TN:* Kzk. **Täñir-bergen** [Таныр-бергенъ], in lat. 50 N and long 68 E (Karta JAR XI). ✧ 'God gave (him/her), (Child) given by God'. ⇨ **TÄÑIR + BERGEN.** See also **TÄÑIR-BERDİ.**

TÄÑLİG Uyg. **Täñlig-apa** [Täñlig Apa] (ETY II, 65); Uyg. 750 **Täñlig-apa** [T(ä)nglig Apa] (Thomsen, Stein 186, 188).

TÄÑRİ Kzk. 18th c. - 19th c. **Tanïr-qul** [Таныркул] (Tynyšp. 66, 71); Chag. 16th c. **Tañri-quli / Täñri-quli** [Тангри-кули] (Ivanov 327); Chag. 16th c. **Tañri-quli / Täñri-quli?** [Тангри-кули] (Ivanov 327); Chag. 1597 **Tañrï-yar / Täñri-yar** [Tangry-Yar], Babur's younger son (Nalivkin-Dozon 269); Kzk. 19th c. **Tañrï-qul / Täñri-qul?** [Тангри-Кулъ] (Grod., Pril. 127); Kzk. 19th c. **Tañrï-qul / Täñri-qul?** [Тангрикуловъ] (SKSO III, 14); Kzk. 18th c. **Täñri-qul** [Тянгрикулъ] (Nepljuev 755, 762); Chag. 16th c. **Täñri-quli** [Тенгри-кули] (Ivanov 151, 164, 303, 310); Trkm. 1804 **Teñri-yar-bek** [Тенгри Яр-бек], Xudaybergen's father (MIT II, 365, 366). ✧ 'God (only as a part of compound names), Lord; sky; divine; ruler, lord' cf. Uyg., Karakh. *täñri* 'небо; бог, божество; божественный; повелитель, господин' (DTS). Examples: *Täñri-yar* 'God's friend', *Täñri-qul(i)* 'God's slave'. See also **AY-TÄÑRİ, QUNČUY-TÄÑRİ, QUT-TÄÑRİ, QUTLUГ-TÄÑRİ, UZ-**

TÄÑRİ.
TÄÑRİ-BERDİ Maml. 1395 **Taγrï-berdi** [تغرى بـردى بن يشبغا] (Iyās I, 303, 328); Maml. 1398/99 **Taγrï-berdi** [تغرى بـردى البيدمـرىّ] (Ibn Taghrīb. VI, 16); Maml. 1398 1438/39 **Taγrï-berdi** [تغرى بـردى البشبغاوى], historiographer Abû-l-Mahasin ibn Taghrî Birdî's son (Ibn Taghrīb. VI, 11, 13, 14, VII, 35, 68); Maml. 1399 **Taγrï-berdi** [الجلبانى] [تغرى بـردى] (Iyās I, 313, Ibn Taghrīb. VI, 16); Maml. 1399 **Taγrï-berdi** [تغرى بـردى أمير سلاح] (Iyās I, 314); Maml. 1399 **Taγrï-berdi** [تغرى بـردى] (Iyās I, 318, 319, 353, II, 60); Maml. 1404/05 **Taγrï-berdi** [تغرى بـردى التجتارىّ] (Ibn Taghrīb. VI, 118); Maml. 1408/09 **Taγrï-berdi** [تغرى بـردى السيّدى الصغير] (Ibn Taghrīb. VI, 201, 210, 232); Maml. 1421 **Taγrï-berdi** [تغرى بـردى مـن آقفا] (Ibn Taghrīb. VI, 482, 502); Maml. 1421 **Taγrï-berdi** [تغرى بـردى قصروه], governor of Behesna (Iyās II, 11, Ibn Taghrīb. VII, 688, Weil, Chalif. II, 169); Maml. 1425, 1439 **Taγrï-berdi** [تغرى بـردى المحمودىّ النـاصـرى], commander of the expedition to Cyprus (Weil, Chalif. II, 173, Ibn Taghrīb. VI, 493, 505, VII, 266, 311); Maml. 1439 **Taγrï-berdi** [تغرى بـردى البكلمشى المؤيدى] (Iyās II, 25, Ibn Taghrīb. VI, 691, VII, 2, 9, etc.); Maml. 1439 **Taγrï-berdi** [تغرى بـردى المؤزى] (Iyās II, 26, 39); Maml. 15th c. **Taγrï-berdi** [السيفى تغرى بـردى] / Saif ad-Dîn Tagri-bardi Rūmi], Sultan Čaqmaq's (1438-1452) dawādār (chancellor) (Berchem 257); Maml. 1451 **Taγrï-berdi** [تغرى بـردى التردمى] (Ibn Taghrīb. VII, 364); Maml. 1452/53 **Taγrï-berdi** [التلادى / التلاوى] [تغرى بـردى] (Iyās II, 42, 258, Ibn Taghrīb. VII, 231); Maml. 1458, 1469/70 **Taγrï-berdi** [يونس] [تغرى بـردى بن] (Ibn Taghrīb. VII, 495, 708, Iyās II, 114, 305); Maml. 1459 **Taγrï-berdi** [تغرى بـردى الاشرفى] (Ibn Taghrīb. VII, 518, 524); Maml.? 1459 **Taγrï-berdi** [تغرى بـردى الطيارى], Sultan Inal's page (Ibn Taghrīb. VII, 521, 537, Weil, Chalif. II, 270-71); Maml. 1463, 1472/73 **Taγrï-berdi** [تغرى بـردى ططر] (Ibn Taghrīb. VII, 717, 852, Iyās II, 135, 258); Maml. 1468/69 **Taγrï-berdi** [تغرى بـردى الارمنى المنصورى] (Iyās II, 111); Maml. 1476/77 **Taγrï-berdi** [تغرى بـردى المؤيدى] (Iyās II, 163, Weil, Chalif. II, 221); Maml. 1481 **Taγrï-berdi** [تغرى بـردى بن بلباى الظاهـرى] (Iyās II, 202); Maml. 1481 **Taγrï-berdi** [تغرى بـردى الاستـادار] (Iyās II, 204, 381, III, 182, 249); Maml. 1484 **Taγrï-berdi** [تغرى بـردى بن محمد بن قـاسم] (Iyās II, 224); Maml. 1486 **Taγrï-berdi** [تغرى بـردى بن بلباى القادرى] (Iyās II, 233, III, 61); Maml. 1507, 1508 **Taγrï-berdi / Tañrï-verdi?** [Tanghalavardi / Tangraverdi], envoy

(and interpreter) of Sultan Qansu in Venice; „El signor admiraglo nostro turcimanno Tangraverdi" (ibid. p. 388) (Amari 219, 387, 388); Tat.(Lit.) 1591 **Tanrï-berdi** [Ораска Танды бердовна Цербазоровичъ], fem. (Lit. Tat. 82); Turk. 1583 **Tanrï-verdi** [ویــردی / تــکری / Tanrıverdi] (Ongan, Ank. I, 178); Turk. 1540 **Tanrï-verdi-kethudā** [Tanrï Verdi kethuda], one of the chiefs of the Çağırganlu tribe (cemaat), in a defter of Diyarbekir, Turkey (Demirtaş 58); Turk. 1426 **Tañrï-berdi?** [Τακριβὲρ Μεχαμέτ], a commander of the army (Byz. Turc. 296); Kzk. 19th c. **Tañrï-berdi** [Тангры берди] (Grod., Pril. 109); Uzb. 19th c. **Tañrï-berdi** [Тангрыберды Сатыкуловъ] (SKSO III, 23); Tat.(Mish.) 1775 **Tañrï-berdi / Täñri-berdi?** [Тангриберды Гаитов] (MIB IV/2, 317); Uzb. 1740 **Tañrï-berdi / Täñri-berdi?** [Тангрибердій-Инакъ], from khiva (Hanykov, Poezdka 29); Az. **Tar-verdi (< Tanrï-verdi)** [تــارویــردی], a character in „L'ours et le voleur" by Barbier de Meynard (PÉLOV S. III, t. V, p. 108); Tat. 1662 **Tara-berde (<Tarï-berde?)** [Ендыбачъ Тарабердѣевъ] (DAI IV, 306); Tat. 1545 **Täñri-birdi** [تـنـکری بـردی] / Тянгри-Бирди] (Jusupov 9); Crm. 1532 **Tägri-berde / Tägri-berdäy?** [Тягри-Бердяй] (PSRL XIII, 62); Tat.? 1532 **Tägri-berdi** [Тягри Бердѣй] (PSRL XX, 413); Tat.(Lit.) 1595 **Tänri-berde(y)** [Тянрибердей Селимшичъ] (Lit. Tat. 236-237); Uzb. 20th c. **Täñri-berdi** [Тангриберди] (Begmatov 1984, 202); Tat.(Lit.) 1594 **Täri-berdi / Täri-berdey?** [Фатьма Тарибердеевна Мухаремова], fem. (Lit. Tat. 194-195); Tat.(Lit.) 1594 **Täri-berdi / Täri-berdey?** [Тарибердеевичъ] (Lit. Tat. 695); Tat.(GH) 1408, 1409 **Tegri-berdi(y)** [Тегриберди / Тегрибердій], a prince of the Horde (PSRL XI, 205, XXIII, 142); Chag. 16th c. **Teñri-berdi** [Тенгри-берды] (Ivanov 112, 116); Chag. 16th c. **Teñri-berdi** [Тенгри-берды Суфи] (Ivanov 190); Chag. 16th c. **Teñri-berdi** [Тенгри-берды], an emir (Ivanov 311); Chag. 16th c. **Teñri-berdi** [Тенгри-берды] (Ivanov 311); Maml. 1436 **Teñri-berdi / Teñri-bermiš** [Tengri Berdi (~ Bermiš)], governor of Haleb (Weil, Chalif. II, 173, 203, 233); Khorezm./Chag. 14th c. **Teñri-berdi / Teñri-birdi** [تـنـکری بــیـردی], Timur's (Temür's) commander of the army (Arabš. II, 454); Trkm. 1852 **Teñri-berdi-bek** [Тенгри-берды-бек], from the Alaš clan of the Sarïq tribe (MIT II, 528, 530, 532, 537); Uzb. 1804 **Teñri-berdi-bek** [Тенгри-берды-бек], ruler of the city of Ket (Kät) (MIT II, 357, 358, 363, 385); Trkm. 1836 **Teñri-berdi-ešik-aga-baši** [Тенгри-берды-Эшик-агабаши], from the Er-sari tribe (MIT II, 469); Chag. 16th c. **Teñri-berdi-oγlan** [Тенгри-Берды-оглан] (Ivanov 198, 199, 201); Kzk. 19th c. **Teñri-birdi** [Тенгрибирдіевъ] (SKSO VIII, 201); Yürük 16th c.

Teñri-virdi, from the Yürüks of Kocacık, Turkey (Gökb., Rum. 101); Tat. 1624 **Tere-berdi** [Батракъ Теребердѣевъ] (Pokrovskij 72); Tat.(Tob.) 1654 **Tere-berdi** [Кулбашейко Теребердѣевъ] (AI IV, 230); Tat.(Sib.) 1682 **Tere-berdi(y) / Tere-berde(y)** [Будайко Теребердѣевъ] (DAI XIII, 177); Tat.(Sib.) 1601 **Tere-berdi / Tere-berdey?** [Теребердей] (Miller, Ist. Sib. II, 163); *TN:* Turk. 20th c. **Tanrï-verdi** [Tanrıverdi], a village (Mollahüdayda) in the province of Ağrı, Turkey (TMİB 55); Chuv. 18th c. **Tär-berdi(na)**, a village in the district of Tsivilsk (Korsakov 324); Tat. 1738 **Tär-birdi(na)** [Тярбирдины], a village (Alatyr. 141). ❖ 'God (Allah) gave him/her; God-given' Such names were given (as protective names) if there were no children, they were sickly or did not survive in the family before (Noyan 6-7, 11). Cf. Sauvaget 44: „Dieudonné", Sattarov: Tat. *Täñrebirde*, also Rásonyi, Categ. 330, P. Categ. 217. ⇨ **TÄÑRİ + BERDİ.** See also **XUDAY-BERDİ, TÄÑIR-BERDİ, TÄÑIR-BERGEN, TÄÑIR-BERMİŠ, TÄÑRİ-BERGEN.**

TÄÑRİ-BERGEN Kzk. 19th c. **Tañrï-bergen / Taqrï-bergen?** [Такрыбергенъ] (AOO 50); Kirg. 19th c. **Tañrï-bergen / Täñri-bergen?** [Тангри-бергенъ], Chinggis Khan's father in the Kirghiz folklore (Potanin, Pred. 49); Uzb. 20th c. **Täñri-bergän** [Тангриберган] (Begmatov 1984, 202); Kzk. 1794 **Teñri-bergän** [تـنـکری بـیـرکان] (MIK IV, 162); *TN:* Kzk. 19th c. **Tañrï-bergen / Tañra-bergen?** [Тангра-Бергенъ], a river (ZIRGOÊtn. I, 73). ❖ '(Child) given by God' cf. Tat. *Täñrebirgän* 'id.' (Sattarov). ⇨ **TÄÑRİ + BERGEN.** See also **XUDAY-BERDİ, TÄÑIR-BERDI, TÄÑIR-BERGEN, TÄÑRİ-BERDİ, TÄÑRİ-BERMİŠ.**

TÄÑRİ-BERMİŠ Selj. 1100 **Taγrï-bermiš** [Ταγγριπερμῆς], a commander (Byz. Turc. 295); Maml. 1377/78 **Taγrï-bermiš** [تـغری بـرمش العلا ئی] (Iyās I, 242); Maml. 1408/09 **Taγrï-bermiš** [تـغری بـرمش] (Ibn Taghrïb. VI, 200, 216); Maml. 1437/38, 1450 **Taγrï-bermiš** [تـغری بـرمش الیشبکی] (Ibn Taghrïb. VII, 2, 112, 121); Maml. 1438/39 **Taγrï-bermiš** [تـغری بـرمش الصغیـر] (Ibn Taghrïb. VII, 260); Maml. 1442/43 **Taγrï-bermiš** [تـغری بـرمش الجلالی المویـدی النقیه] (Ibn Taghrïb. VII, 126, 132 etc.); Maml. 1442 **Taγrï-bermiš** [تـغری بـرمش التـرکمانی] (Ibn Taghrïb. VIII, 6, 10); Maml. 1444 **Taγrï-bermiš** [تـغری بـرمش], a chancellor (Ibn Taghrïb. VIII, 14); Maml. 1462 **Taγrï-bermiš** [تـغری بـرمش الخاصکی] (Ibn Taghrïb. VIII, 436); Maml. 1466 **Taγrï-bermiš** [تـغری بـرمش القرا حـحا ئی] (Ibn Taghrïb. VII, 814); Maml. 1479 **Taγrï-bermiš** [تـغری بـرمش] (Iyās II, 191, III, 61); Maml. 1494/95

Taγrï-bermiš [تعرى بـرمش الاينالى] (Iyās II, 288);
Turk. 1489 **Tanrï-vermiš** [Tanrıvermiş / Hamza veledi
Tanrıvermiş] (Gökb., Ed. 99); Turk. 1491 **Tanrï-
vermiš** [Tanrıvermiş bin Abdullah] (Gökb., Ed. 113,
280); Turk. 16th c. **Tanrï-vermiš** [Tanrıvermiş]
(Ongan, Ank. II.); Turk. 1583 **Tanrï-vermiš**
[Tanrıvermiş] (Ongan, Ank. I, 175, 178); 1403/04
Täñri-bermiš [حوجه/ تنكرى بـرمش/] (Dorn 178);
Uyg. **Täñri-birmiš** [Tängribirmiş] (EUTS); *TN:* Turk.
1528 **Tanrï-vermiš** [Tanrı-vermiş] (Gökb., Ed. 45,
413); Turk. 20th c. **Tanrï-vermiš** [Tanrıvermiş], a
village in the province of Çorum, Turkey (TMİB 264).
✧ 'God-given' (Sauvaget, 44). ⇨ **TÄNRİ** + **BERMİŠ**.
See also **XUDAY-BERDİ, TÄÑİR-BERDI, TÄÑİR-
BERGEN, TÄÑRİ-BERDİ.**

TÄÑRİ-BİLGÄ   Uyg. 804-805 **Täñri-bilgä-qaγan**
(Ligeti, R. tör. nev. II-III, 42). ✧ 'God-wise'. ⇨
TÄÑRİ + **BİLGÄ.**

TÄÑRİ-BİRDİ see **TÄÑRİ-BERDİ**

TÄÑRİ-TUΓMİŠ   Uyg. 8th c. - 9th c. **Täñri-tuγmïš /
Täñri-tuγmïs?** [Tängri tuγmïš], a prince (Müller,
Pfahl. 19). ✧ '(Divine) ruler was born'. ⇨ **TÄÑRİ** +
TOΓMİŠ.

TÄÑRİKÄN   Uyg. **Täñrikän** [T(ä)ngrikän / Tngrikän]
(EUTS); Uyg. **Täñrikän** [T(ä)ngrikän / Tngrikän]
(EUTS). ✧ Title of respect meaning 'divine' in
majestic names (Radl. III, 1048, DTS). ⇨ **TANRİ** +
suff. *-kän?* See also **BAΓA-TÄÑRİKÄN.**

TÄPÄRİS see **TEPERIS**

TÄPPÄL Yak. **Täppäl** [Тӓппӓл] (Pek.).

TÄRÄNTÄY   Yak. **Täräntäy** [Тӓрӓнтӓi] (Pek.). ✧
Tereniy (R.) (Pek.).

TÄRÄZİNTÄY   Tuv. 19th c. **Täräzïntäy (<Täräzïn-
tay?)** [Тӓрӓзінтӓi / Тӓрӓзін-таi] (Proben IX, 93).

TÄRÄÑČÄ   Hak.? 19th c. **Täräñčä** [Тӓрӓнчӓ]
(Katanov, Otč. 12); Hak.(Sag.) 19th-20th c. **Teräñčï /
Teренča** [Терӓнчи, Теренча] (Proben IX, 554). ✧
Teren'cha (R.) (Katanov).

TÄRGÄLİTTİ   Tuv. 19th c. **Tärgälïttï / Tergelittï**
[Тӓргӓлітті / Тергелитты], a folklore hero (Proben
IX, 637, Katanov: ZIRGOÊtn. III, 175).

TÄRİ Uyg. **Täri** [Täri], fem. (EUTS).

TÄRİPÄN   Yak. **Täripän / Täripiän** [Тӓріпӓн,
Тӓрiпiӓн] (Pek.). ✧ Trifon (R.) (Pek.).

TÄRKÄN Uyg. **Tärkän** [Tärkän] (EUTS).

TÄSÄK Uyg. **Täsäk** [Täsäk] (EUTS). ⇨ **TEZEK?** See
also **TESÄK-TURMİŠ.**

TÄV-GİLDİ   Chuv. 18th c. **Täv-gildi(na)**
[Тявгилдина], a village in the district of Tetyushinsk
(Korsakov 340). ✧ 'Come/Born first' cf. Tat. PN *Täw-
gilde* (Sattarov). ⇨ **KELDİ.**

TÄW-QABİL Bashk. 1735 **Täw-qabïl** [/ Тевкабылъ
Тевекеевъ], a tarχan (Vel.-Zern., Bašk. 23).

TÄWÄKKÄL see **TÄWÄKKÜL**

TÄWÄKKÜL   Tat. 1531 **Täwäkäl / Tiwekel**
[Тевекелъ / Тивекелъ], a prince (PSRL XIII, 54);
Bulg. / Tat.? 13th c. - 14th c. **Täwäkkäl** [Тӓвӓккӓл]
(Jusupov 53); Khorezm./Chag. 14th c. **Täwäkkül-
χanïm** [Tavakkul Khánim], one of Temür-χan's wife
(Tar. Rashidi 52); Trkm. 1595 **Tewekkül-χan**
[Тевеккуль-хан] (MIT II, 87); Tat.(Lit.) 1592 **Tiwekel**
[Тивекелъ], fem. (Lit. Tat. 122). ✧ I. 'Trust in God'
(Ar.) cf. Turk. *tevekkül* 'das Vertrauen auf Gott; das
Gottvertrauen; die Resignation' (HŞ); II. 'Courage,
determination' cf. Tat. *Täwäkkäl* (Sattarov).

TÄWGE   Tat.(Ishim) **Täwge** [Тӓyрӓ], a folklore hero
(Proben IV, 189 /235/). ✧ 'First (child), first born' cf.
Tat. *Täüge* (Sattarov), Tat. *täwge* 'первый,
первичный' (TatRS), Bashk. *täwge*
'первоначальный, первый' (BRS/Uraksin).

TÄWKÄ   Tat.(Tob.) **Täwkä** [Тӓyкӓ], a folklore hero
(batïr) (Proben IV, 338 /272/); Bashk. 1770 **Täwkä**
[Тивляш Тявкин] (MIB IV/1, 343); Kzk. 1719
Täwkä [Тӓüкӓ], a prince from the branch J̌adïq (Radl.,
Aus Sib. I, 194); Tat.(Sib.) 1637 **Tewkä** [Тевка], a
prince, İšim's son (Miller, Ist. Sib. II, 447). ✧ 'Little
first (child)' cf. Tat. dial. *täü/täw* 'berenče [=first]'
(TTDS), Bashk. *täü* 'впервые, в первый раз'
(BRS/Uraksin) + dim. suff. *-kä.*

TÄWKÄY   Tat.(Sib.) 18th c. **Täwkäy** [Тевкей], a
Siberian prince (Nepljuev 127, 373); Bashk. 1735
Täwkäy [Явгилде Тевкееву], a tarχan (Vel.-Zern.,
Bašk. 12). ✧ 'First born child' cf. Tat. PNs *Täw-gilde,
Täwey, Täwge-bay* (Sattarov), Bashk. *täü* 'впервые, в
первый раз' (BRS/Uraksin) + suff. *-käy.*

TÄWKÄL-QARA   Khorezm. **Täwkäl-qara /
Täwäkkäl-qara?** [توكال قرا امير نوروز], an emir
(RaD/Jahn). ⇨ **TÄWKÄL** + **QARA.**

TÄWKEL Khorezm. 13th c. - 14th c. **Täwkel** [توكال],
an emir (RaD/Jahn 61, 64, 71 etc.); Chag. 15th c.
Täwkel [Тевкел], one of Uluγ-beg's fathers-in-law
(Barth., Ulugb. 116); Tat. 1554 **Täwkel** [Тевкель], a
princess (PSRL XIII, 243); Tat. 1624 **Täwkel** [Кудашъ
Тевкелевъ] (Pokrovskij 70); Tat. 1624 **Täwkel**
[Тайкара Тевкелевъ] (Pokrovskij 71); Bashk. 1783
Täwkel [Тевкелев Осип Алексеев] (MIB V, 141,
163, 164); Bashk. 1795 **Täwkel** [Гумеръ Тевкелевъ]
(IOAIÊK XXVIII, 590); Kzk. 1571 **Täwkel** [Тевкель],
a khan (AI I, 341); Kzk. 1594 **Täwkel** [Tevkel /
Тевкелъ], a khan (Dobrosm., Turg. 5, Levchine 141);
Kzk. 1734 **Täwkel** [Mourza Mahmet Tevkelef], a
colonel (chiliarch) (Levchine 179-180). ✧ I. 'Resigned;
resignation, confidence' (Erol II); II. 'One who leaves
things to chance; daring' cf. Kzk. *tâvekel<i>* 'tevekkel'
(KzTS), *<i>täwekel* 'риск' (KzRS) (<Ar.).

TÄWLÄKÄY   Bashk. 1735 **Täwläkäy** [Тевлекей
Улеевъ] (Vel.-Zern., Bašk. 24); Bashk. 1789 **Täwläkäy**

[Тевлекей Тюкеев] (MIB V, 263); Chuv. 18th-19th c. **Tivlekey** [Тивлекей] (Magn. 81).

TÄWLÄT see **DÄWLÄT**

TÄWLÄTLİ see **DÄWLÄTLİ**

TÄWLES Bashk. 1761 **Täwles-čura** [Тевлесчюра Назарымбетев] (MIB IV/1, 218).

TÄWŠ Bashk. 1735 **Täwš / Täüš** [Теушъ Уразаевъ], a tarɣan (Vel.-Zern., Bašk. 13). ✧ 'First/next (child)' cf. Tat.(Bar.) *täüš* 'die Reihenfolge, das Zukommende' (Radl. III, 1014), or Bashk. *täü* 'впервые, в первый раз' (BRS/Uraksin) + dim. suff. -*š*.

TÄWŠE Kkalp. 20th c. **Täwše-qan** [Тәвшекъан] (Bask., Kkalp. 58).

TÄZÄK-TURMÏŠ **Täzäk-turmïš** [Täsäk Turmïš tanuq] (Grünwedel, Berichte 182); Uyg. 12th c. - 14th c. **Täzäk-turmïš** [Täzäk-turmïš] (Radl., USp. 1). ⇨ **TEZEK + TURMÏŠ.**

TÄZE see **TAZA**

TÄŽETDİN Kkalp. 20th c. **Täžetdin** [Тәжетдин] (KkRS 776). ✧ 'Crown of faith' (Ar.).

TÄŽİ see **TAЈİ**

TÄŽİ-AXMET Kkalp. 20th c. **Täži-aχmet** [Тәжиахмет] (KkRS 776). ⇨ **TAЈİ + AXMET.**

TÄŽİ-QAL Kkalp. 20th c. **Täži-qal** [Тәжиқал], fem. (KkRS 778). ⇨ **TAЈİ + QAL II.**

TÄŽİ-MÏRAT see **TÄŽİ-MURAT**

TÄŽİ-MUXAN Kkalp. 20th c. **Täži-muχan** [Тәжимухан] (KkRS 776). ⇨ **TAЈİ + MUQAN.**

TÄŽİ-MURAT Kkalp. 20th c. **Täži-mïrat** [Тәжимырат] (KkRS 776); Kkalp. 20th c. **Täži-murat** [Тәжимурат] (KkRS 776). ⇨ **TAЈİ + MURAT.**

TÄŽİ-NİYAZ Kkalp. 20th c. **Täži-niyaz** [Тәжинияз] (KkRS 776). ⇨ **TAЈİ + NİYAZ.**

TÄŽİXAN Kkalp. 20th c. **Täžiχan** [Тәжихан], fem. (KkRS 778). ⇨ **TAЈİ + suff. -χan(1).**

TÄŽİK see **TAЈİK**

TÄŽİMBET Kkalp. 20th c. **Täžimbet** [Тәжимбет] (KkRS 776). ⇨ **TAЈİ + suff. -mbet.**

TÄK Hak.(Sag.) 19th-20th c. **Tăk-mergän** [Тäк Мергäн], a folklore hero (Proben IX, 327-29); Alt. **Tăk-mögä** [Тăк-мöрä] (Proben IX, 160). ✧ '(Iron) hook' cf. Alt.(Tel.) *tăk* 'der eiserne Haken' (Radl. III, 1016).

TÄN Karg. 19th-20th c. **Tăn** [Тäн] (Katanov, Otč. 9). ✧ 'Shadow / day' cf. R. *ten' / den'* (Katanov).

TÄRİ-PÄŠ see **TERİ-BAŠ**

TÄTİ Kzk. **Tătĭ** [Тăтĭ / Тäтɪ] (Proben III, 24, 26 /28, 31/). ✧ 'Sweet, tasty, pleasant' cf. Kzk. *tăttĭ* 'süss, angenehm, wohlschmeckend' (Radl. III, 1094).

TÄZE see **TAZA**

TEBAY Bashk. 1740 **Tebay** [Тебай] (MIB I, 404).

TEBÄNÄ see **TEMENE**

TEBEY Kzk. 19th c. **Tebey** [Тебей] (SODž. 94).

TEBEK Kzk. 19th c. **Tebek-bay** [Тебекбай] (SOK 126).

TEBEN Chuv. 18th-19th c. **Teben** [Тебень] (Magn. 80). ✧ 'Big needle' cf. Chag., East.T. *täbän* 'eine grosse Nadel, Packnadel' (Radl. III, 1119). See also **İL-TEBEN, TAQAR, TEMENE, TEMENEY, TEBENEYKA.**

TEBENEY see **TEMENEY**

TEBENEYKA Chuv. 1670 **Tebeneyka** [Тебенѣйка] (Poliv.-Kras. 64). ✧ 'Big needle'. ⇨ **TEMENEY + suff. -ka.** See also **TAQAR, TEBEN, TEMENE, TEMENEY.**

TEBENEK Chuv. 18th-19th c. **Tebenäk** [Тебенякъ] (Magn. 80); Kzk. 18th c. - 19th c. **Tebenek** [Тебенек] (Tynyšp. 73); Tat. 1541 **Tebenek-ulan** [Тебенекъуланъ], from Kazan (PSRL XIII, 113). ✧ 'Short' cf. Bashk., Tat. *täbänäk* 'niedrig' (Radl. III, 1119).

TEBER Selj. 1148 **Teber** [تبر], an emir (Qalānisi 295); Selj. 1167/68 **Teber** [تبر], an emir (Ibn al-Athīr, Atab.: RHCHor II/2, 242); Tat.(Sib.) 1621 **Teber** [Зоеня Теберов] (Miller, Ist. Sib. II, 259). ✧ 'Axe'? cf. Tat. PN *Täbär* (Sattarov) (<P.). See also **AQ-TEBER, EL-TÄBÄR; BALTA, BALTU, KESER, TEŠE.**

TEBERČİK Kzk. 19th c. **Teberčik** [Теберчикъ] (SOK 62). ⇨ **TEBER + suff. -čik.**

TEBERİK Kzk. 19th c. **Teberik** [Теберикъ] (SOK 174, 214); Kzk. 19th c. **Teberik** [Теберекъ] (SOV 6). ⇨ **TEBER? + suff. -ik.**

TEBİR see **TEMİR**

TEBİR-QÏRÏŠ Alt. 19th c. **Tebir-qïrïš-χan** [Тебир-Кырыш-хан] (Verb., In. 153). ✧ 'Iron-quarrel/fight' cf. Alt., Shor *qïrïš* 'der Zank, Streit, Kampf' (Radl. II, 744). ⇨ **TEMİR.**

TEBİR-ŠİBELDEY Shor 19th-20th c. **Tebir-šibeldey** (Dyrenkova 20). ✧ 'Iron-evil spirit living under the earth' cf. Hak.(Kacha), Shor *šibäldäi* 'ein böser Geist, der unter der Erde wohnt, die Schwanfrau' (Radl. IV, 1089). ⇨ **TEMİR.**

TEBİŠ Uyg. **Täpiš** [Täpiş] (EUTS); Uyg. 12th c. - 14th c. **Tebiš / Tepiš** [Täbiš / Täpiš] (Radl., USp. 95, DTS). ✧ I. 'Enemy' cf. Uyg. *täbis* der Feind' (Radl. III, 1122); II. 'Fight!' cf. Karakh. *tepiš-* 'драться' (DTS).

TEЈEN Trkm. 20th c. **TeЈen** [Тежен] (Sopieva 180). ✧ Tejen (a river and town in Türkmenistan).

TEDİY Alt.(Tel.) **Tediy** [Тедий-богатырь], a folklore hero (Kalačev VI, 492). ✧ 'Clever'. ⇨ **TEDİK?**

TEDİK Hak. 19th-20th c. **Tedik** [Тедик] (HRS 351). ✧ 'Clever' cf. Alt., Shor *tädig / tädü* 'klug, weise, munter, flink' (Radl. III, 1095).

TEGDİGÄS Hak.(Sag.) 19th-20th c. **Tegdïgäs** [Тегдігäс] (Proben IX, 361, 386, 428). ⇨ **TEGDİK + suff. -gäs?**

TEGDİK Alt.(Belt.) **Tegdĭk** [Тегдік] (Proben IX, 361, 660).

TEGÄK Kuman 1253 **Tegäk / Tïɣaq?** [Тѣгакъ], a

Polovets prince (Ipat. 543 /546/).

TEGEL Chuv. 18th-19th c. **Tegel** [Тегель] (Magn. 80); Bashk. 1721 **Tegel-bay** [Тегелбай Кулушяев] (MIB III, 197).

TEGERİK Alt. 19th-20th c. **Tegerik** [Тегерик], fem. (OjrRS 213). ✧ 'Circle; ring; hoop of shaman-drum' cf. Alt. *tegerik* 'круг, круглый; обод шаманского бубна' (OjrRS).

TEGEZ see **TEGİZ**

TEGİČÄK Tat.(GH) 1277 **Tegičäk** [Тегичакъ], envoy of the Horde (PSRL II, 207).

TEGİN 947 **Tegin** [تكين الشرازى], from Shiraz (Ibn al-Athīr/Tornb. VIII, 350-51); Türk? 750 **Tegin** [Tigin] (Thomsen, Stein 186, 188); Türk 10th c. **Tegin** [تكين التركى / Такин ат-Турки (Тегин ат-Турки)], slave-soldier (gulām) at the times of Kumāravaih (Iyās I, 42, MIT I, 156, 158); Uyg. 1222 **Tegin** [Tekin] (Chwol., Syr. I, 8); Uyg. 13th c. - 14th c. **Tegin** [Tekin] (Chwol., Syr.-nest. (NF) 53); Uyg. 1325 **Tegin** [Takin], a priest (Chwol., Syr.-nest. (NF) 25); Uyg. 1338 **Tegin** [Tekir], fem. (Chwol., Syr.-nest. (NF) 32); Karakh. **Tegin** [Tégin] (MK/Atalay 854); Karakh.? 870 **Tegin** [عبدالله بن تكين / Tegin] (Tabarī, Annal. III, 1820, 1826, 1827); Karakh.? 870-880 **Tegin** [تكين البخارى] (Tabarī, Annal. III, 1874, 1917-20, 1937 etc.); Karakh.? 873 **Tegin** [تكين / ولى الرى /] (Tabarī, Annal. III, 1880); Karakh.? 876 **Tegin** [Tekin al Buchārī], under Chalif Mutamid (Weil, Chalif. II, 458, 459); Karakh.? 909-915, 914, 933 **Tegin** [مصر / تكين الخاصة / تكين الخاصة عامل] (Arīb 30, 34, 51, Tabarī, Annal. III, 2291, Ibn al-Athīr/Tornb. VIII, 203, Miskawayh V, 71, 410, Hil. Sābī 138, 208, 319); Karakh.? 911, 932 **Tegin** [تكين الخادم] (Ibn al-Athīr/Tornb. VIII, 45, Ibn Saʿīd IV, 32, Arīb 176); Karakh.? 913/14 **Tegin** [Tekin], governor of Egypt (Weil, Chalif. II, 594, 596); Karakh. 919 **Tegin** [تكين بن عبدالله الحربى] (Kamāladdīn I, 94); Karakh. 931 **Tegin** [تكين الخاقانى], at the time of the Ikhshids (Ibn Saʿīd IV, 7, 8, 9, 10, 13, 15, 164, Arīb 163); Karakh.? 933 **Tegin** [محمد بن تكين], Maχmud's father (Miskawayh V, 410, 411); Karakh.? 938 **Tegin** [تكين الترك] (Miskawayh V, 557); Selj. 11th c. - 12th c. **Tegin** [شمس الملك تكين بن صنقاج] (Bondārī 46); Khorezm.? 1229 **Tegin** [تكين] (Nasawī 206); Oghuz? 10th c. **Tegin / Beg-tegin** [تكين / بكتكين التركى], governor of Damascus (Ibn Taghrīb. II, 3, 4, 39); Uyg. 1339 **Tegin-beg** [Juchanan Tegin Peg], a commander of the army (Chwol., Syr.-nest. (NF) 37); Karakh. 999-1001 **Tegin-χan** [Тегин-хан], İlek-χan's governor of Samarkand (MIT I, 224); Khorezm. 1220 **Tegin-melik** [Тегин-мелик], a commander of the army (MIT I, 479); Karakh. **Tekin** [Tekin] (MK/Atalay 854); Uyg.

1398 **Tigin** [Tigin] (Chwol., Syr.-nest. 87); Karakh. **Tigin** [Tigin] (MK/Atalay 854, EUTS); Uyg. **Tigin-ügä** [Tigin-ügä] (EUTS); Oghuz/Trkm. 13th c. **Tikin** [تكان / Тикин] (Abulg./Kon. 530, 560); Yak. **Tïγïn / Tïγïñ / Tïγïn-bōtur** [Тыгын(н), Тыгын-ботур], Är Älläy's son, strong and powerful ruler fighting with the Russians, later captured and hanged (Pek.); *TN:* Tat.? **Tägin** [Тягинъ], a town on the Dneper river (Smirnov, Krym. 341). ✧ 'Prince (title), male relative(s) of the Türk khan' (cf. DTS, TMEN II, No. 922, Golden, Khaz. 186, etc.), 'the closest male relatives of the khan' (F. László), 'heir of the throne' (Gumilev; Golden, Khaz. 186), 'high and old title' (Ligeti, R. tör. nev. 39). A folk-etymology of this title has been recorded by Qašγarī, see MK/Atalay I, 413. As a title, it is a frequently used part of compound names.

TEGİN-BOLAT Kzk. 18th c. - 19th c. **Tegin-bolat** [Тегынболат] (Tynyšp. 74). ⇨ **TEGİN** + **BULAT.**

TEGİN-TAŠ 1355 **Tegin-taš** [تاج الدين تكين تاش], under the Muzaffarid Mubārizuddin (Qazw. 672). ⇨ **TEGİN** + **TAŠ.**

TEGİNÄ Khorezm. / Mo. 1288 **Teginä** [تكنه], an emir of Arghun Ilkhan who was sent to Gahazan in Khorasan (RaD/Jahn 15, 16, 17, 22); Tat.(GH) 1409 **Teginä** [Тегиня], a Tatar (Mongol?) prince (PSRL XI, 205); Tat.(GH)? 1458 **Teginä** [Тегиня Шиковъ сынъ] (PSRL XXIII, 142). ⇨ **TEGİN** + suff. *-ä / -e*. See also **ŠİRİN-TEGİNÄ.**

TEGİNEK Karakh.? 941 **Teginek** [تكينك] (Ibn al-Athīr/Tornb. VIII, 278, 280); Karakh.? 942 **Teginek** [كورتكين و تكينك / تكينك التركى] (Hil. Sābī 317). ⇨ **TEGİN** + suff. *-ek.*

TEGİRČİ Uyg. 12th c. - 14th c. **Tegirči / Tekirči** [Täkirči (Tägirči)] (Radl., USp. 215, 257, DTS).

TEGİS see **TEGİZ**

TEGİZ Bashk. 1714 **Täkis** [Тякис Асанов] (MIB I, 105); Kzk. 19th c. **Tegez-pay / Tegiz-pay** [Тегезпай] (SOV 26); Kzk. 19th c. **Tegis-pay** [Тегиспай] (SOV 124); Kzk. 19th c. **Tegiz-pay** [Тегизпай] (SOK 226); Kzk. 19th c. **Tekes-pay / Tekis-pay** [Текеспай] (SODž. 74, 90, 94). ✧ 'Even, smooth' cf. Kzk. *tegiz* 'flach, eben' (Radl. III, 1035), East.T. *täkis* 'glatt, eben' (Radl. III, 1021).

TEGMİLİK Uyg. 12th c. - 14th c. **Tegmilik** (DTS).

TEGRÄNČ Uyg. **Tegränč** [Tägränç] (EUTS).

TEGRÄNČ-YEKÄ Uyg. 12th c. - 14th c. **Tegränč-yekä** (Radl., USp. 138, DTS). ✧ ? ⇨ **TEGRÄNČ** + **YEKÄ.**

TEXPİL Kzk. 19th c. **Teχpil-bay** [Техпельбай] (SOK 124).

TEYÄR-YAŇİ Alt. 19th c. **Teyär-yañï?** [Теэрь-Янгы] (Verb., In. 104). ⇨ **?+YAŇİ.**

TEYKEY Bashk. 1735 **Teykey / Täwkey?** [Теикей

Зиямбетевъ (Тяукей)] (Vel.-Zern., Bašk. 17). ⇨ **TÄWKÄY?**

TEYLİ Kzk. 19th c. **Teyli-bay** [Тейлибай] (SOK 256); Kzk. 19th c. **Teyli-bay** [Тейлыбай] (SOK 284).

TEYLİK Kzk. 19th c. **Teylik-pay** [Тейликпай] (SOV 50).

TEYÜZ Kzk. 19th c. **Teyüz-bay** [Теюзбай] (SOK 246).

TEK Kzk. 18th c. **Täk-qulï-bay** [Tiak-Koulybaï] (Levchine 154); Trkm. 1768 **Tek-beg / Tek-bey** [تكبك / Tekbeğ], a chieftain (boy beği) in Anatolia (Refik, Anad.); Kzk. 19th c. **Tek-pay** [Текпай] (SOV 104); Chuv. 18th-19th c. **Tik-murza** [Тикмурза] (Magn. 82). ✧ 'Unwanted, unneeded; quiet, calm, silent' cf. Kuman, Chag., Alt. *täk* 'vergeblich, ohne Amt und Würde; ruhig, ohne Bewegung; ohne Geräusch' (Radl. III, 1014), Kzk., Hak. *tek* 'id.' (Radl. III, 1015), Tat. *tik* 'id.' (Radl. III, 1347). See also **BEŠ-TEK.**

TEK-TEMÜR Yürük 1543 **Tek-temür** [تكتمور / Tektemür] (Gökb., Rum. 175); Chuv. 18th-19th c. **Tïχ-temir** [Тихтемиръ] (Magn. 82); Chuv. 18th-19th c. **Tik-temir** [Тиктемиръ] (Magn. 82). ⇨ **TEK + TEMİR.**

TEK-TENEŠ Chuv. 1670 **Tek-teneš** [Тектенешъ Байчюрашева], fem. (Poliv.-Kras. 64). ⇨ **TEK.**

TEK-TURMAS Kzk. **Tek-turmas-ata** [تيك تورماس اطا / Tek-turmas-ata] (Divaev, Baksy 310); Tat. **Tik-turmas-patša**, a character in a tale (Kúnos, Volksmärchen); *TN:* Kzk. **Tek-turmas** [Tekturmas], mountains (?). ✧ 'Wriggly, fire-eater, fidgety' cf. Tat. *tiktormas* 'непоседа, вертун, бедокур, шалун' (TatRS). ⇨ **TEK.**

TEKČENKÄ Tat. 1658 **Tekčenkä / Tekčenqa?** [Текченка Тенбиреевъ] (Kuznecov 20).

TEKÄČİ see **TEKEČİ**

TEKÄŠ see **TEKEŠ**

TEKE Uyg. 12th c. - 14th c. **Täkä-baχšï / Tägä-baχšï / Tekä-baqšï** [Täkä (Tägä) Baχšï / tekä baqšï] (Radl., USp. 41, DTS); Maml.? 1293 **Tegä / Tekä?** [تكا / Teka], a Kipchak, Noγay's son (Baybars/Tizeng. I, 86, 109); Maml. 1377/78 **Tekä** [تكا الشمسى] (Iyās I, 239); Maml. 1390 **Tekä** [تكا الاشرفى / Teka] (Iyās I, 284, 285, Weil, Chalif. I, 566-569); Maml. 1309 **Teke** [تكا] (Dawād. 180, 203); Turk. 14th c. **Teke** [Τεκίης], a prince (Teilfürst) from the family Tekke-Oglu (Byz. Turc. 303); Bashk. 1713 **Teke** [Уразмет Текин] (MIB III, 102); Bashk. 1756 **Teke** [Бакиш Тякин] (MIB IV/1, 123); Kzk. 19th c. **Teke** [Теке] (SODž. 18); Kzk. 19th c. **Teke** [Теке] (SOV 114); Kzk. 1794 **Teke-bay** [تاكه بى / Текебай] (MIK IV, 162); Kzk. 19th c. **Teke-bay** [Текебай] (AOA 10); Kzk. 19th c. **Teke-bay** [Текебай] (SODž. 64); Kzk. 19th c. **Teke-bay** [Текебай] (SOK 24, 84, 138); Kirg. 20th c. **Teke-bay**

[Текебай] (Kalilov 92); Yürük 13th c. - 15th c. **Teke-oγlu** (Giese 89); *TN:* Kzk. **Teke** [Teke], a hill, near the mouth of the Ili river at Lake Balkhash (?); Kzk. **Teke** [Теке], a lake south-west of Omsk (Karta JAR IV); Kzk. **Teke** [Teke] (PM Ergh. 43); Kzk. **Teke-bay** [Текебай], a place east of Lake Aral (Karta JAR XI); Turk. 14th c. **Teke-ili** [تكه ايلى], „Teke's land" (outskirts of Antalya) in Asia Minor (Nešrī 336). ✧ 'He-goat, ram' cf. Uyg., Kuman, Shor, Alt.(Leb.) *tägä* 'der Bock, der Steinbock' (Radl. III, 1029), Maml. *tägä* 'Ziegenbock' (Tarǰ/Houtsma), Uyg., Karakh. *tekä* 'козел' (DTS), Chag., Az., Alt., East.T., Turk. *täkä* 'der Bock' (Radl. III, 1016), Bashk. *täkä* 'название самцов мелкого рогатого скота' (BRS/Uraksin), Tat. *täkä* 'id.' (TatRS). See also **BUČAŇ-TEKÄ, İČ-TÄKÄ, QARA-TEKE, QUL-TEKE.**

TEKE-BATTAL Turk. 16th c. **Teke-battal** [Tekebattal] (Ün 3 (1936), 358). ⇨ **TEKE + BATTAL.**

TEKE-MOLDA Kzk. 19th c. **Teke-molda** [Текемолда] (AOA 118). ⇨ **TEKE + MULLA.**

TEKEČİ Kirg. **Tekäči** [Tekätschi / Текäчi] (Proben V, 33); Kirg. **Tekeči / Tekeči-χan** [Текечи] (Jud. 59). ✧ 'Breeder of goats'? ⇨ **TEKE** + dim.? suff. *-či.*

TEKEY Karch. **Tekey** [Тамашъ Текеевъ] (Sysoev 129); Bashk. 1719 **Tekey** [Курманай Текей] (MIB III, 189); Bashk. 1728 **Tekey** [Курманай Текеев] (MIB I, 128); Bashk. 1731 **Tekey** [Текей] (MIB III, 289); Bashk. 1737 **Tekey** [Усейн Текеев] (MIB I, 347); Bashk. 1740 **Tekey** [Кудашман Текеев] (MIB I, 421); Bashk. 1756 **Tekey** [Бигиш Текеев] (MIB IV/1, 107); Bashk. 1756 **Tekey** [Савчегул Текеев] (MIB IV/1, 122); Bashk. 1756 **Tekey** [Яумбеть Текеев] (MIB IV/1, 122); Bashk. 1773 **Tekey** [Абдршит Текеев] (MIB IV/1, 371); Kzk. 19th c. **Tekey** [Текей] (AOAtb. 50); Kzk. 19th c. **Tekey** [Текей] (AOK 122); Kzk. 19th c. **Tekey** [Текей] (AOO 50); Kzk. 19th c. **Tekey-bay** [Текейбай] (SOK 228). ⇨ **TEKE** + suff. *-y.* See also **DEYDER-TÄKEY, İŠ-TEKEY.**

TEKELÄK Bashk. 1715 **Tekeläk** [Ногойбак Текеляков] (MIB III, 124).

TEKELİ Uyg. 12th c. - 14th c. **Tekäli** [Tägäli / Tekäli] (Radl., USp. 124, DTS); Turk. 1511 **Tekeli / Baba-tekeli** [Τεκλες / Baba Tekeli / Şahkulu Karabıyıklıoğlu], Shah Ismail's ally (By. Turc. 304, Sevim-Yücel II, 225). ✧ 'Having a he-goat' (Blagova 1997, 707).

TEKELİK Kzk. 19th c. **Tekelik** [Текеликъ] (SOV 196). ⇨ **TEKE** + suff. *-lik.*

TEKEN see **TİKÄN**

TEKERLEK Trkm. 1840 **Tekerlek-bey**, one of the chiefs of the Bahşiş tribe (aşiret) (Riza II, 45). ✧ 'Wheel (of vehicle)' (TED).

TEKES see **TEGİZ**

TEKEŠ Türk **Täkäš** [Täkäş] (ETY II, 121); Kkalp. 20th c. **Täkeš** [Тәкеш] (KkRS 776); Türk 8th c. - 9th c. **Tekäš-qul-tudun** (DTS); Khorezm.? 13th c. **Tekeš**, emir, security (police) officer of Qazwīn (Qazw. 849); Oghuz 1171, 1193 **Tekeš / Tekiš** [تكش بن ايل‌ارسلان] / علاءالدين / **'Alâ ad-Dîn Tâkîsh / Tacasche / Ala'ddin Tocush / Töküš /** Ала-ад-дин Текеш ибн Иль-Арслан], the Khorezmshah Alā al-Dīn Tekeš (1172-1200), defeats Sultan Tuγrïl at Rei (Ibn al-Athīr/Tornb. XI, 247-9, XII, 88-92 etc., Qazw. 478-486, 787, Abulfar. 405-406, Abulfar./Budge I, 345, Ǔuwaynī I, 127, II, 1, 17-23 etc., Muh. Ibrahim 136, 201, Aqsarāyī 26, Abulg./Desm. 50, MIT I, 45, 384, 404-408, 442 etc., Köprülü: Belleten VII (1943), 232); Selj. 1073, 1078, 1081, 1084/85 **Tekeš / Tekiš** [تكش بن الب ارسلان / تَكِش / تنش / شهادءالدين / تكش] / Tanasch / Tucuch / tekiš / Текеш ибн Алп-Арслан], a Seljukid prince, the brother of Melik Shah I (1072-1092), Alp-arslan Sultan's (1063-1072) son (Ibn al-Athïr/Tornb. X, 61, 64, 87-9, 241, Abulfidā III, 246-47, Bondārī 47, 71, Ibn al-Athïr, Atab.: RHCHor II/2, 14, Kamāladdïn II, 103, MIT I, 376-378, DTS); Khorezm.? **Tekeš-χan** [تكش خان سلغورى] (Qazw. 368, 409); Khorezm.? **Tekeš-χan** [محمّد تكش خان قطم‌الدين], the Khorezmshah (Qazw. 494-498); Karaḥ. **Tekiš** [Tekiş] (MK/Atalay 854). ✧ 'Little wild goat; Little ram' (Bese 5, Sattarov, Blagova 1997, 707), *Tekäš-qul* may be interpreted as 'Little he-goat-slave' (Blagova 1997, 707); M. F. Köprülü reads *Tekeš* as *Töküš* (Türk onomastique'i hakkında, p. 222, footnote 2), but H. Bayur considers it false (Belleten XIV (1950), pp. 589-594). ⇨ **TEKE** + dim. hypoc. suff. -š.

TEKEŠ-YARUQ Khorezm. 1222 **Tekeš-yaruq** [Takachiaroq Djenkéchi], Jelâl's emir (Nasawī 88 etc). ⇨ **TEKEŠ + YARUQ.**

TEKİN see **TEGİN**

TEKİR Yürük 1543 **Tekir** (Gökb., Rum. 177). ✧ 'Tiger-streaked/striped; mottled, freckled' cf. Turk. *täkir* 'getigert, mit unregelmässigen runden Flecken' (Radl. III, 1020).

TEKİR-QAQ Kzk. 19th c. **Tekir-qaq** [Текркак] (AOO 70). ✧ 'Hit hard/strongly!' cf. Kirg. *tekir* 'gross, mächtig' (Radl. III, 1020), Chag., Alt., Kirg., Kzk., Tat. etc. *qaq-* 'schlagen, klopfen' (Radl. I, 57). ⇨ **TEKİR?** + QAQ.

TEKİRČİ see **TEGİRČİ**

TEKİŠ see **TEKEŠ**

TEKLEN Maml. 1297 **Teklen** [Teklan l'Adeli] (Makrīzī IV, 39); Maml. 1332 **Teklen** [تكلان], an emir (Dawâd. 368).

TEKLİŠ Bashk. 1735 **Tekliš** [Теклишъ Беккуловъ], a tarχan (Vel.-Zern., Bašk. 19).

TEKNEJİ-XİZİR Yürük 16th c. **Tekneji-χizir** [تكنه‌جى خضر / Tekneci-Hızır] (Gökb., Rum. 104). ✧ 'Xïzïr the maker/seller of troughs' cf. Chag., Crm., Turk. *täknä* 'ein grosser, aus einem Holzstück ausgehöhlter Trog' (Radl. III, 1022). ⇨ **XİZİR.**

TEKTEBEY Alt. 19th c. **Tektebey-mergen** [Тектебей-мерген], a folklore hero (Verb., In. 143).

TEKTİ Kzk. 19th c. **Tekti-bay** [Тектыбай] (SOV 42). ✧ 'Of good origin/ancestry' cf. Kzk. *tektī* 'von guter Herkunft' (Radl. III, 1024).

TEL Kzk. 19th c. **Tel-bay** [Тельбай] (SOK 274); Kzk. 19th c. **Tel-bay** [Тельбай] (SOV 100); Kzk. 19th c. **Tel-eke** [Телеке] (AOA 110); Kzk. 19th c. **Tel-eke** [Телеке] (AOK 62); Kzk. 19th c. **Tel-eke** [Телеке] (SOV 104). ✧ 'Young animal sucking two dams; growing up free (without mother), lonely' cf. Kzk. *tel* 'ein junes Thier, welches von der Mutter fortgenommen ist und bei einem anderen Thiere saugt; in Freiheit aufgewachsen' (Radl. III, 1081), Kzk. *tel* 'единственный; выросший на свободе' (PKRS), *tel* 'молодое животное, сосущее и свою, и чужую мать' (KzRS). See also **AY-TEL.**

TEL-AГЇS Kzk.? / Nog.? **Tel-aγïs-batïr** [Тел-Агыс-батыр] (Žirm., Epos 395). ⇨ **TEL + AГЇS.**

TEL-ГOZЇ Kzk. 19th c. **Tel-γozï** [Тельгозы] (SOK 138); Kzk. 19th c. **Til-quzï(y)?** [Тилкузіевъ] (Grod., Pril. 184); Kzk. 19th c. **Til-quzï(y)?** [Бесбекъ Тилкузіевъ] (Grod., Pril. 95). ⇨ **TEL + QOZЇ.**

TEL-MAMBET Kzk. 19th c. **Tel-membet** [Тельмембетъ] (SOV 38); Bashk. 1770 **Til-mambet** [Тилмамбеть Канбулатов] (MIB IV/1, 343); Kzk. 18th c. - 19th c. **Til-mambet** [Тильмамбей] (Tynyšp. 66); Kzk. 19th c. **Til-mambet** [Тыльмамбетъ] (SOK 18). ⇨ **TEL + MAMBET.**

TEL-MEMBET see **TEL-MAMBET**

TEL-MEREK Kzk. 19th c. **Tel-merek** [Тельмерекъ] (SOV 150). ⇨ **TEL + MEREKE?**

TEL-TAY Kzk. 19th c. **Tel-tay** [Тельтай] (SOV 88, 150). ⇨ **TEL + TAY** or suff. -tay(1,2).

TELDEY Bashk. 1745 **Teldey** [Сююндук Телдеев] (MIB III, 432); Bashk. 1745, 1749, 1754 **Teldey** [Сююндук Телдеев] (MIB III, 432, 464, IV/1, 79); Bashk. 1757, 1761 **Teldey** [Сагындык (Сагандык) Телдеев] (MIB IV/1, 156, 204); Bashk. 1675 **Teldey / Teldi?** [Телдей] (MIB I, 199); *TN:* Bashk. 1749 **Teldey(evo)** [Телдеево], a village (MIB III, 464). ⇨ **TELDİ?** + suff. -y? (R.).

TELDİ Kzk. 19th c. **Teldi-bay** [Тельдебай] (SODž. 120). ⇨ **TEL?** + suff. -di.

TELÄ see **TİLÄ**

TELÄČ Tat. 1702 **Teläč / Teläš?** [Телячко Узеевъ], from Kungur (Letop. ZAK II, 7-8).

TELÄG Hak.(Kacha, Sag.) 19th-20th c. **Teläg** [Теляг], an evil spirit (Proben IX, 424, 593, 597).

TELÄGÄY Hak.(Kacha) 19th-20th c. **Telägäy**

[Теläräi], an evil spirit (Proben IX, 585); Kzk. **Telägäy-alïp** [Теläräi алып], head of the unbelievers (Proben III, 132 /104/); Alt. 19th-20th c. **Telegey / Telekey** [Телегей / Телекей], fem. (OjrRS 213). ✧ I. 'Large water, ocean' cf. Kzk. *telegey* 'büyük ve her tarafı kaplayan su, okyanus' (KzTS); II. 'World, universe, surroundings' cf. Kirg., Kzk. *telägäi* 'das Umgebende, die Umgebung' (Radl. III, 1082), Alt. *telekey* 'мир, вселенная, природа' (OjrRS); III. 'A Kokand-type cap' cf. Kzk. *telägäi* 'ein kokander Hut' (Radl. III, 1082). ⇨ **TELÄG?** / **TELEKEY?** + suff. *-äy* / *-ey*.

TELÄK see **TİLEK**

TELÄK-BERDE   Bashk. 1742 **Tläk-berdi / Teläk-berde** [Абдулла Тлякбердин] (MIB I, 481). ✧ 'Wish-gave (the child)' cf. Tat. *Teläk-birde* (Sattarov). ⇨ **TİLEK + BERDİ.**

TELÄKÄY see **TİLEKEY**

TELÄS see **TİLÄS**

TELÄT   Bashk. 1761 **Telät** [Асей Телятев] (MIB IV/1, 204).

TELE-BUҐA   Nog. 1628 **Te-buɣa** (<Tele-buɣa?) [Тебуга] (AI III, 262); Tat.(GH) 1316, 1317, 1318 **Tele-buɣa** [لغا بلا / Талабуга / Телебухъ], Özbek Kipchak Khan's envoy to Egypt, then to Novgorod (PSRL III, 72, IV, 48, V, 207, VII, 188, XVI, 61, Duqmaq/Tizeng. I, 317, 324). ✧ 'Debt / payment - bull'? Pelliot noted in connection with the name: „*Tölä* n'offre pas de sens en mongol; il y a au contraire en mongol un mot *tölǟ* (< *tölä'ä*) 'dette', 'paiement'. Je suis donc d'avis de transcrire finalement *Tölǟ-Buɣa / Tölȫ-Buɣa* (<*Töläbuqa*)." (p. 65-66). ⇨ **TELE / TELİ / TÖLE?** + **BUQA.**

TELEGEY see **TELÄGÄY**

TELEKEY see **TELÄGÄY**

TELEM   Kzk. 19th c. **Telem-bay** [Телембай] (SOK 240). ✧ '(Share of) spoil, booty' cf. Kzk. *telim* 'die Kriegsbeute, die die Theilnehmer nach der Theilung erhalten'.

TELEMES see **TİLEMİŠ**

TELEMİS see **TİLEMİŠ**

TELEN see **TİLÄN**

TELENČİ see **TİLENČİ**

TELEÑGÜR   Kzk. 19th c. **Teleñgür** [Теленгуръ] (AOK 94). ✧ 'Tin'? cf. Alt.(Tel.) *täläñïr / täläñär* 'das Zinn' (Radl. III, 1082).

TELEÑGUT   Kzk. 1734 **Teleñyut** [Бабетъ Теленгутъ] (PSZRI IX, 304); Kzk. 19th c. **Teleñyut** [Теленгутъ] (AOP 126). ✧ Ethnonym. Cf. Alt.(Tel.) *Täläñït / Täläñät* 'der Teleute' (Radl. III, 1082, 1083).

TELERİG   Bulg. 772/73-777 **Telerig** [Τελέριγος] (Byz. Turc. 304).

TELES see **TİLÄS**

TELEŠ see **TİLÄS**

TELEÜ see **TİLÄW**

TELEÜLE see **TİLÄWLİ**

TELGÖČİ   Alt. 19th c. **Telgöči** [Тельгочи] (Verb., In. 45). ✧ 'Soothsayer' (Verbickij), cf. Alt.(Tel.) *tölgöčï* 'der Wahrsager, Arzt' (Radl. III, 1263), Alt. *tölgöči* 'ворожея' (OjrRS).

TELİ   Kkalp. 20th c. **Däli** [Дәли] (KkRS 773); Kkalp. 1819 **Däli-biy** [Дёли бий] (MIKk. 127); Yürük **Deli-molla** (Giese 87, 89); Turk. 1593 **Delü-baba / Qïzïl-delü-baba** [Кızıl Delü Baba], a dervish (Gökb., Ed. 185); Kzk. 19th c. **Tele** [Теле] (SOV 40); Kzk. 19th c. **Tele-bay** [Телебай] (SODž. 54, 82, 120, 130); Kzk. 19th c. **Tele-bay** [Телебай] (SOK 36, 212, 214); Kzk. 19th c. **Tele-bay** [Телебай] (SOV 14, 34, 140); Kzk. 19th c. **Teli** [Теле] (SODž. 82); Kzk. 19th c. **Teli-bay** [Телыбай] (SOK 126); Kzk. 19th c. **Teli-bay** [Телибай] (SOK 94); Kirg. **Teli-bay** [Телибай] (Jud. 723); Kzk. 19th c. **Telü-bay** [Телюбай] (SODž. 36). ✧ I. 'Foolish; brave; ridiculous, strange; queer fish' cf. Karakh. *telü* 'дурак, слабоумный; безумный' (DTS), Kuman, Alt., Kar. *täli* 'unverständig, thöricht, dumm, närrisch, der Narr' (Radl. IV, 1083), Kirg. *teli* 'название болезни лошадей (от которой скрючивает корпус и лошадь крутится); (о человеке) помешанный; ненормальный' (Jud.), Chag., Crm., Turk. *däli* 'der Narr, der Dummkopf; kühn, tapfer' (Radl. III, 1678), Kkalp. *däli* 'смешной, чудаковатый; чудак' (KkRS), also Sauvaget 44; II. 'A young (of an animal) which sucks another dam'? cf. Kzk. *teli-* 'ein Junges daran gewöhnen bei einem fremden Thiere zu saugen' (Radl. III, 1084). See also **BAY-TELİ, ĴAN-TELE, TAY-TELE, TAN-TELE.**

TELİK   Uyg. **Tälik** [Tälik] (EUTS); Uyg. 12th c. - 14th c. **Telik** (Radl., USp. 124, DTS).

TELİKEŠ   Bashk. 1735 **Telikeš** [Теликешъ Уразовъ] (Vel.-Zern., Bašk. 13).

TELMÜR   Kzk. 19th c. **Telmür** [Тельмуръ] (SODž. 110). ✧ 'Stare! Gaze!' cf. Uyg., Chag. *telmür-* 'zu sehen wünschen, mit Ungeduld erwarten, kummervoll dastehen' (Radl. III, 1091), Kzk. *telmïr-* 'scharf ansehen; bittend ansehen, anflehen' (Radl. III, 1091).

TELPÄK   Tat. 1606 **Telpäk / Terpäk** [Телпяк / Терпяк] (MIB I, 154); Kzk. 19th c. **Telpek** [Тельпекъ] (AOA 154); Kzk. 19th c. **Telpek-pay** [Тельпекпай] (AOAtb. 22). ✧ 'Fur cap; tatar-style cap' cf. Kirg., Kzk. *telpäk* 'eine Pelzmütze; ein Tatarenkäpsel' (Radl. III, 1090).

TELPEK see **TELPÄK**

TELŽİK   Kzk. 19th c. **Telžik** [Тельжекъ] (SOK 34). ⇨ **TEL** + dim. suff. *-žik.*

TEMAM   Turk. 1583, 1584 **Temam**, fem. (Ongan, Ank. I, 178). ✧ 'Ready, perfect' cf. Kuman, Chag., Kzk., Tat., etc. *tamam* (Ar.) 'ganz und gar, im Ganzen, fertig, vollendet' (Radl. III, 997), Turk. *tamam / temam* 'tamam, bitme, bitirme, son' (Özön).

TEMDEK Alt. 19th-20th c. **Temdek** [Темдек] (OjrRS 210). ✧ 'Sign, mark' (OjrRS).

TEMÄK Bashk. 1706 **Temäk** [Темяк] (MIB III, 27).

TEMÄS Bashk. 1764 **Temäs** [Темяс Мратов] (MIB IV/1, 276). ⇨ **TİMÄŠ / TEMEŠ?**

TEMEČEY Bashk. 1742 **Temečey** [Темечей Калумбетев] (MIB III, 513). ⇨ **TEMİŠ?** + suff. *-ey*.

TEMEY see **TÄMÄY**

TEMEKEY Bashk. 1708 **Temekey** [Темекей Бунгузин] (MIB I, 237); Bashk. 1760 **Temekey** [Солтангул Темекеев] (MIB IV/1, 197); Bashk. 1785 **Timikäy** [Тимикай Яхшигулов] (MIB V, 178). ✧ 'Tobacco'? cf. Tat. *tämäkī* 'der Taback' (Radl. III, 1130), Bashk. *tämäke* 'табак' (BRS) + dim. suff. *-y*.

TEMEL Turk. 1621 **Temel**, from Isparta (Ün 1938, 645); Turk. 20th c. **Temel** (Önder, Göle); Turk. 20th c. **Temel** (Önder, Hınıs). ✧ 'Base; support(er) (?)' cf. Crm., Turk. *tämäl* (<Greek) 'das Fundament, die Basis, Grundlage' (Radl. III, 1130).

TEMENE Hak.(Sag.) 19th-20th c. **Tebän-arïγ** (<Tebänä-arïγ) [Тебäн Арыɦ], hero's sister (Proben IX, 324, 326); Alt. 19th c. **Temen-oqo / Temene-qō?** [Темен-око], a mythical being (Verb., In. 150); Alt. **Temene-qō** [Темене-коо], fem. (Nikiforov 2 ff.); Alt. 19th c. **Temene-qō** [Темене-ко], in the tale „Altay-buči" (Potanin, Pred. 181). ✧ 'Big needle' cf. Alt.(Tel.) *tämänä* 'eine grosse Nadel' (Radl. III, 1130), Chag., East.T. *täbän*, Kzk. *tebän: tebän ïnä* 'eine grosse Nadel, Packnadel', Hak. *täbänä*, Chag. *tebänä* 'grosse Nadel' (Radl. III, 1119). See also **MERİEDİYİN-TEMENE, TÄBÄNÄ-QŌГА; İYNE, TAQAR, TEBEN, TEMENEY, TEBENEYKA.**

TEMENEY Chuv. 18th-19th c. **Tebeney** [Тебеней] (Magn. 80); Tat. 1675 **Tebeney(ko)** [Тебенейко] (Kungursk. akty 29); Tat. 1779 **Temeney** [Султангул Теменеев] (MIB V, 93); Bashk. 1735 **Temeney** [Теменей Байметевъ], a tarχan (Vel.-Zern., Bašk. 21); Bashk. 1762 **Temeney** [Султангул Теменеев] (MIB IV/1, 249); Bashk. 1778 **Timiney** [Сеит (Сагит) Тиминеев] (MIB V, 76). ✧ 'Big needle' cf. Kuman, Chag. *tämän* 'eine grosse Nadel' (Radl. III, 1130), Chag., East.T. *täbän* 'eine grosse Nadel, Packnadel' (Radl. III, 1119) + suff. *-ey /-y*. See also **TAQAR, TEBEN, TEMENE, TEBENEYKA.**

TEMER see **TEMİR**

TEMERŠİK Tat. 18th c. **Temeršik** [Темершик], a village (Korsakov 237). ⇨ **TEMİR** + dim. suff. *-šik*.

TEMEŠ Crm.(Tat.) 1477 **Temeš** [Темешъ], envoy sent to Janï-bek (Smirnov, Krym. 273); Tat.(Lit.) 1596 **Temeš** [Щасный Темешевичъ] (Lit. Tat. 253); Tat. **Temeš** [Темешъ] (PSRL IV, 161, VI, 39, VIII, 224-225); Tat. 1492 **Temeš?** [Темешень], a Tatar chief (PSRL (Russk. Hr.) I, 509); Tat. 1552 **Temeš** [Темешъ] (Kn. Metriki Lit. 64); Tat. 1624 **Temeš** [Утемышъ Темешевъ] (Pokrovskij 71); Bashk. 1678 **Temeš** [Утенѣй Темешовъ] (DAI IX, 93); Kzk. 1533 **Temeš** [Темешъ Кадышевъ] (PSRL VIII, 281, XIII, 67, XX, 415); Kzk. 19th c. **Temeš** [Темешъ] (AOP 90); Crm. 1534, 1535 **Temeš / Temeš-kitay** [Темешь-князь Китай / Темешъ-Китай], a prince from the Crimea (PSRL VIII, 289, XIII, 84); *TN:* Crm. **Temeš** [Temesch], a place (?) on the northern side of the Kerch peninsula (Jervis IV.); Bashk. 1728 **Temeš(evo)** [Темешево], a lake (MIB I, 127). ✧ 'Helper, supporter'? cf. Alt. *tämäš* 'der Theilnehmer, der Gehilfe' (Radl. III, 1132).

TEMEŠ-KİTAY see **TEMEŠ**

TEMET Bashk. 1756 **Temet** [Теметь Карятав] (MIB IV/1, 122); Bashk. 1776 **Temet** [Адулбай Теметов / Абдулай Теметев] (MIB V, 39).

TEMGİL Kzk. 19th c. **Temgil** [Темгилъ] (SOK 162).

TEMİČİ Alt.(Tuba) 19th c. **Demiči-eren (<Demirči-eren?)** [Демичи Еренъ] (Potanin IV, 369); Uyg. 12th c. - 14th c. **Temiči** [Tämiči] (Radl., USp. 2-3, Le Coq, Urkunden 1918, 453, DTS). ✧ '(Title) vice Zaisan (chief of the clan)' cf. Alt. *tämičī* 'der zweite Beamte nach dem Saissan (Geschlechtsältester)' (Radl. III, 1134).

TEMİNDAR Turk. 20th c. **Temindar** [Temindar] (Önder, Göle). ✧ 'Assuring, ensuring, securing (child)' cf. Turk. *temin* (Ar.) 'assurance; confidence' (TED) + suff. *-dar* (P.).

TEMİR Turk. 14th c. **Demir-χan** [Demirhan], Karasioğlu's (Karesioğlu's) son (Uzunçarş., Anad. 33, 34, 35, Jorga, Notes XIII, 365, Mesalek alabsar / Quatrem.: Notes. Extr. XIII, 365); Turk.? 14th c. **Demür-χan** [دمورخان / Domoûr khân], sultan of Balıkesir (Ibn Bat. II, 317); Turk. 1485 ʿ**Demür-oγlu** [Demür-oğlu] (Gökb., Ed. 242); Uyg. **Tämir** [Tämir] (EUTS); Tat.(GH) **Tämir-qan** [Тäмір кан], a character in a tale, mentioned together with Toqtamïš-qan (1382-1397) (Proben VII, 100); Uyg. 8th c. - 12th c. **Tämir-tiräk-tigin** [Tämir tiräk tigin], an Uyghur tarqan (Müller, Pfahl. 23); Uyg. **Tämür** [Tämür] (EUTS); Shor 19th-20th c. **Tebir-ālïp** [Tebir Ālyp] (Dyrenkova 96); Kzk. 19th c. **Temer-qul** [Темеркулъ] (AOO 2); Uyg. 12th c. - 14th c. **Temir** [Temir] (Radl., USp. 84); Tat.(GH)? 1460, 1485 **Temir** [Темиръ (Темирь)], a prince of the Horde (PSRL V, 272, VI, 182, 237, VIII, 216); Tat.(GH) 1471 **Temir** [Темиръ], a Tatar prince (PSRL (Russk. Hr.) I, 474); Maml. 1309 **Temir** [سيف الدين تمر الساقى], an emir (Dawād. 174, 243); Maml. 1309/10 **Temir** [تمر الساقى] (Iyās I, 152); Maml. 1331 **Temir** [سيف الدين تمر], from Mosul (Dawād. 357, 366); Maml. 1332 **Temir** [سيف الدين تمر], an emir, a cup-bearer (Dawād. 365); Maml. 1332 **Temir** [تمر الموسوى] (Iyās I, 166, Weil,

Chalif. I, 471); Maml. 14th c. **Temir** [تمر الساقى]
(Zetterst. 157, 159); Maml. 1398/99 **Temir**
[تمر الساقى] (Ibn Taghrīb. VI, 9, 25, 128); Maml.
1400/401 **Temir** [تمر البريدى] (Iyās I, 337); Maml.
1453 **Temir** [تمر الاشرفى] (Ibn Taghrīb. VII, 383);
Maml. 1461/62 **Temir** [تمر الظاهرى] (Iyās II, 74, 384);
Maml. 1466/67 **Temir** [تمر المحمودى] (Ibn Taghrīb.
VII, 743, 826); Maml.? 1467 **Temir** (Ibn Taghrīb. VIII,
625, 644); Maml. 1467/68 **Temir** [تمر] (Iyās II, 92,
142, III, 111); Maml. 1467/68 **Temir** [حاجب الحجاب]
(Iyās II, 95, 149); Maml. 1475/76 **Temir** [الظاهرى]
[تمر بن محمد شاه] (Iyās II, 158); Maml. 1493/94
Temir [تمر التصير الزردكاش] (Iyās II, 283); Maml.
1499/500 **Temir** [تمر بن جانم الظاهرى] (Iyās II, 367);
Maml. 1499/1500 **Temir** [تمر قريب الظاهر قانصوه]
(Iyās II, 371); Maml. 1516 **Temir** [بالزردكاش]
[تمر الحسنى المعروف] (Iyās III, 3, 25, 57, 106); Maml.
1516 **Temir** [تمر رأس نوبة النوب] (Iyās III, 92); Trkm.
19th c. **Temir** [Темиръ Хаджикараевъ] (Ščeglov IV,
173); Tat. 1654 **Temir** [Темиръ] (AI IV, 236); Bashk.
1738 **Temir** [Темир Ирмяков] (MIB I, 366); Kzk.
18th c. - 19th c. **Temir** [Темр] (Tynyšp. 66); Kzk. 19th
c. **Temir** [Темиръ] (Grod., Pril. 161); Nog. 1649
Temir [Темиръ Саламатовъ] (AI IV, 102); Kirg.
Temir [Темир] (Jud. 17, 479); Kirg. 19th-20th c.
Temir (Prinz 22); Alt. 19th-20th c. **Temir** [Темир]
(OjrRS 210); Hak.(Sag.) 19th-20th c. **Temir** [Темир
Кан], an evil spirit (Proben IX, 610); Kzk./Nog.?
Temir [Темир Князь] (Žirm., Epos 430); Maml.
1378/79 **Temir-bay** [تمرباى الدمرداشى] (Iyās I, 242,
262, Weil, Chalif. I, 538); Maml. 1378/79 **Temir-bay**
[تمرباى الحسنى] (Iyās I, 242, 276, Weil, Chalif. I,
559); Maml. 1421 **Temir-bay** [تمرباى اليوسنى] (Ibn
Taghrīb. VI, 419, 493 etc.); Maml. 1428, 1444 **Temir-
bay** [تمرباى التمربغاوى], chief emir (Ibn Taghrīb. VI,
627, 634, VII, 2, 8, 24, VIII, 1, 15, Weil, Chalif. II,
229-31); Maml. 1433 **Temir-bay** [تمرباى الختمتى] (Ibn
Taghrīb. VI, 704); Maml. 1444 **Temir-bay** [تمرباى]
(Ibn Taghrīb. VIII, 1, 15, etc.); Maml. 1455 **Temir-bay**
[تمرباى من حمزة / ططر الناصرى/] (Ibn Taghrīb.
VII, 464); Maml. 1461/62 **Temir-bay** [تمرباى العادلى]
(Iyās III, 73, 150, 166); Maml. 1462, 1467 **Temir-bay**
[تمر باى الظاهرى], a bearer of arms (Ibn Taghrīb. VII,
707, 715, VIII, 625, 644); Maml. 1463/64 **Temir-bay**
[تمرباى الساقى الاشرفى] (Iyās II, 76); Maml. 1467/68
Temir-bay [تمرباى], mihmandar (official guide) (Ibn
Taghrīb. VII, 533); Maml. 1467/68 **Temir-bay**
[تمرباى ططر] (Iyās II, 83); Maml. 1467/68 **Temir-bay**
[تمرباى] (Iyās II, 93, 394); Maml. 1467/68 **Temir-bay**

[تمرباى قزل الظاهرى] (Iyās II, 96); Maml. 1467/68,
1469/70 **Temir-bay** [تمرباى التمرازى] (Iyās II, 115,
Ibn Taghrīb. VII, 833); Maml. 1468/69 **Temir-bay**
[تمرباى الجلبانى] (Iyās II, 111); Maml. 1469/70
Temir-bay [تمرباى السيفى] (Iyās II, 112); Maml.
1476/77 **Temir-bay** [تمرباى الجلب] (Iyās II, 170);
Maml. 1496/97 **Temir-bay** [الحمدى كاشف الشرقية]
[تمرباى] (Iyās II, 314, 317); Maml. 1500/1501 **Temir-
bay** [تمرباى], treasurer of Tuman-bay emir (Iyās II,
375, 381, III, 61); Maml. 1500/501 **Temir-bay**
[تمرباى الطويل] (Iyās II, 383); Bashk. 1789 **Temir-
bay** [Темирбай Токтаров] (MIB V, 263); Bashk.
1791 **Temir-bay** [Темирбай Илдашев] (MIB V,
309); Bashk. 1798 **Temir-bay** [Темирбаевъ] (PSZRI
XXV, 195); Kirg. **Temir-bala** [Темір Бала] (Proben
V, 144 /145/); Crm. 1642 **Temir-behadïr** [تمر بهادر]
(Vel.-Zern., Crim. 284); Kzk. 19th-20th c. **Temir-bey**
[Temir-bej], from the Pamir Mountains (Prinz 253);
Oghuz/Trkm. **Temir-bek** [Темиръ-бек] (Radl. III, 506
(taken from the Babur-name)); Kkalp. 20th c. **Temir-
bek** [Темирбек] (Bask., Kkalp. 11, KkRS 776); NUyg.
19th c. **Temir-bek** [Temir Bek], a courtier (Hedin, En
färd II, 163); Crm. 1047 **Temir-bek-mïrza**
[تمر بك ميرزا] (Vel.-Zern., Crim.); Alt. 19th c. **Temir-
bökö** [Темиръ-бöкö / Темиръ-Боко], a character in
a tale (Nikiforov 76, 274, Potanin IV, 173); Kzk. 19th c.
Temir-ǰan [Темиръ-джанъ] (Valihanov, Soč. 317);
Nog. 20th c. **Temir-ǰan** [Хисаметдин Темирджан
улы Баисов], father of Baskakov's informant from the
aul of Üykön-χalq (Ikon-halk), Cherkess Autonomous
Region (Oblast') (Bask., Nog. 143); Uyg. 12th c. - 14th
c. **Temir-elči** (DTS); Alt. **Temir-ergek** [Темиръ-
эргэкъ] (Nikiforov 81, 89); Bashk. 1779 **Temir-ɣaza /
Temir-ɣazi?** [Темиргаза (Темиргазей) Асеев]
(MIB V, 83); Tat. 1788 **Temir-ɣaza / Timir-ɣaza?**
[Темиргаза (Тимиргаза) Ахметев] (MIB V, 231);
Crm. 1635 **Temir-ɣāzi** [تمر غازى] (Vel.-Zern., Crim.
143, 144); Turk.? 14th c. **Temir-χan** [Ταμηρχάνης /
Temir-χan] (Byz. Turc. 297); Maml. 14th c. **Temir-χan
/ Tämür-χan** [تمرخان / Temürḫan] (Tarǰ/Houtsma 68,
Tarǰ/Toparlı 43); Tat.(GH) 1351, 1361 **Temir-χoǰa /
Temir-χoža / Temir-qoža** [Темиръ Ходжа /
Темирьхожинъ / Темирькоза / Темирьхозя], a
ruler of the Horde, Kidar's son (PSRL XVI, 89, PSRL
(Russk. Hr.) I, 411); Tat.(GH) 1361 **Temir-χoža**
[Темиръ (Темирь)-Хожа (Хожинъ / Хозя /
Козя)], ruler of the Golden Horde (PSRL IV, 64, V,
229, VIII, 11 etc.); Kirg. **Temir-qan** [Темиркан] (Jud.
399); Tat.(GH) 1380 **Temir-murza** [Темирь-мурза], a
Tatar hero (bohgatyr) (PSRL XI, 60); Tat./Nog.? 1551
Temir-murza [Темиръ мурза] (PSRL (Russk. Hr.) I,
532); Uzb. 1725 **Temir-sultan** [Sciah Temir Sultan],

from Khiva (Popov, Snoš. 398); Bashk. 1675 **Temir-zän** [Чердяк Темирзянов] (MIB I, 95); Hak.(Sag.) 19th-20th c. **Temïr-mökä** [Темір Мöкä богатырь] (Proben IX, 324-327); Uyg. 12th c. - 14th c. **Temür** [Tämür] (Radl., USp. 10-11, DTS); Selj.? 1235 **Temür** [تیمور, حسام‌الدین], Toγraq-bek's (?) (طغراق بك) son, died in Amasya in 1235 (Uzunçarş., Küt. I, 94); Khorezm. 14th c. **Temür** [الملك تمور / Témoûr], a ruler (Ibn Bat. III, 351); Khorezm./Chag. 14th c. **Temür** [T.-Aksak], Temür-aqsaq or Aqsaq-temür (1370-1405), a. k. a. Timurlenk (CIA 3/I, 16); Yürük 1611 **Temür** [تمور / Hasan bin Temur] (Gökçen 84); Oghuz 11th c. **Temür-balïγ** [تیمور بالیغ], byname of the forefather of the Seljuks (Budagov I, 378; Blagova interprets it as *Timir-balïγ* (Blagova 1997, 707)); Crm. 1637 **Temür-γāzi-kethudā** [تمر غازی کتخدا / Temür] (Vel.-Zern., Crim. 173); Turk. 1378 **Temür-χan** [تمور خان چاوش] (Āšikp. 53); Yürük 16th c. **Temür-χan** [تمور خان / Temür han], from the Yürüks of Kocacık, Turkey (Gökb., Rum. 103, 104); Crm. 1666 **Temür-mirza** [حاجی تمور میرزا], a χaji (Vel.-Zern., Crim. 570, 608); Chuv. 18th-19th c. **Timir** [Тимиръ] (Magn. 82); Hak. 19th-20th c. **Timir** [Тимір] (HRS 351); Uzb. 19th c. **Timir** [Тимиръ] (SKSO III, 174); Bashk. 1765 **Timir-bay** [Тимирбай Рангулов] (MIB IV/1,2, 313); Kzk. 1860 **Timir-bek** [Джайнакъ Тимиръ-бековъ] (ZIRGOGeogr. I, 271); Turk. 1543 **Timur** [Timur Jussuf], a byname (Velics-Kamm. I, 8); Yürük 1543 **Timur** [تیمور / Timur], from the Yürüks of Kocacık, Turkey (Gökb., Rum. 103, 198, 204 etc.); Turk. 1552 **Timur / Temür?** [Timur Rejeb] (G. Dávid's communication); Turk. 16th c. **Timur-χan** [Timurhan Şeyh] (Gökb., Ed. 172); Turk. 1552 **Timur-χan** [Timurkhán] (Velics-Kamm. I, 85); Yürük 1543 **Timur-χan** [Timurhan] (Gökb., Rum. 199); Turk. 1552, 1565 **Timur-χan / Temür-χan?** [Timur-χan İnebegi] (G. Dávid's communication); Turk. 1552, 1565 **Timur-χan / Temür-χan?** [Murad bin Timur-χan] (G. Dávid's communication); Oghuz/Trkm. 13th c. **Timür** [تیمور / Тимур], Salor's son (Abulg./Kon. 1170); Chag. 15th c. - 16th c. **Timür** [تیمور / Timür] (Šejb. XLIX.); Khorezm./Chag. 1462 **Timür / Šeyχ-timür** [Шейх-Тимур], one of Abu Saʿid's commanders (MIT I, 540); Khorezm./Chag. 1370 **Timür / Timür-leng** [تیمور / تیمور کورکان / Тимур (Тимурленг) / Тимур (Сахиб-кыран)], emir of Samarkand then the well-known khan (1370-1405) of Iran, Irak and Afghanistan (Abulg./Kon. 1370, Qazw. 646, 730, Astarab. 448, MIT I, 7, 9, 15, 40, 54 etc.); Khorezm./Chag. 1388 **Timür-beχadur** [Шейх-Тимур-бехадур] (MIT I, 523); Uzb. 1845 **Timür-biy** [Тимуръ-бій], Pulat-biy's father (Moskal'cev 34);

Khorezm./Chag. 1410/11 **Timür-χan** [Тимур-хан], Timür-qutluγ-χan's son, a Jochid (MIT I, 531, 532); Chag. 15th - 16th c. **Timür-χan** [محمد تیمورخان] (Šejb. L, LXV, LXX); Yürük 1543 **Timür-χan** [Timurhan] (Gökb., Rum. 216); Trkm. 1690 **Timür-χan** [Хаджи Тимур-хан], a Qïzïlbaš (MIT II, 116); 10th c. - 13th c. **Timür-ilči** [تیمور ایلچی] (Ǧuwaynī II, 231, 232); Khorezm.? **Timür-qān** [Тимур-каан] (RaD II, 154); Khorezm. 13th c. **Timür-melik** [تیمور ملك / Тимуръ-Меликъ], one of the emirs of the Khorezmshah Muhammad II (1200-1220), the commander of Khojand, the officer of Jelāladdīn (1220-1231) (Ǧuwaynī II, 131, Abulg./Desm. 114-116, RaD/Ber. III, 67, MIT I, 503); Khorezm. 16th c. **Timür-sultan** [تیمور سلطان بن اقاطای خان / Timour], Aqatay-χan's son (Abulg./Desm. 250); Chag. 1500, 1510 **Timür-sultan** [Мухаммедъ Тимуръ Султанъ / Тимур-султан (Мужаммед Тимур Султан)], Sheybani Khan's son (Šejb. LXXVI., MIT II, 55, 56, 57); Chag.? **Timür-šah** [تیمورشاه / Timüršāh] (Abulg./Desm. 158); Chag. 15th c. - 16th c. **Timür-šeyχ** [تیمور شیخ / Timür] (Šejb. LI); *TN:* Trkm. **Demir-Jan** [Демирджонъ], a well near Qïzïl-Arwat (Karta JAR XVIII); Kzk. **Temir-bay** [Темир-бай], a well? (Karta JAR XIX); **Temir-χan-šura** [Темир-хан-шура], a town in the Caucasus (Karta JAR IX); Kzk. **Temirlan** [Темирлан], a settlement called after Timurlenk (Kojčubaev 216). ❖ 'Iron' cf. Türk, Kuman, Alt., Kar. *tämir* 'das Eisen' (Radl. III, 1133), Hak., Kirg., Kzk. *temir* 'id.' (Radl. III, 1133), NUyg.(Tar.) *tömür* 'id.' (Radl. III, 1274), Alt.(Leb.), Shor *täbïr* 'das Eisen' (Radl. III, 1121), Maml. تَمُر *tämür* 'id.' (Sauvaget 44). Concerning the form *Timur* widely used throughout the old and new historical literature, P. B. Golden writes as follows: „*Temür* is the proper Turkic form. The adjectival „*Timurid*" (<Arabo-Pers. Tîmûr), long in use in European languages, has been retained, rather then the less familiar *Temürid*" (Golden 309, footnote 1). See also **ABJÏ-TEMİR, AY-TEMİR, AQ-TEMÜR, AL-TEMİR, ALΓÏN-TİMÜR, ARA-TEMÜR, ASAN-TÄMÜR, AŠAQ-TEMÜR, AŠAN-TEMÜR, ВАГА-ТЕМİR, BAY-TEMİR, BASA-TEMİR, BEK-TEMİR, BİLİG-TEMİR, Bİ-MELİK-TEMİR, BUYAN-TEMÜR, BULA-TEMÜR, BULAT-TEMİR, BÜRİ-TEMÜR, ČÄRİ-DÄMÜR, ČÄRİK-TÄMÜR, ČIY-TEMİR, ČİN-TEMİR, ǰAN-TEMİR, DUWA-TEMÜR, EDGÜ-TEMÜR, EL-TEMİR, ELİK-TEMÜR, ES-TEMİR, ESÄN-TEMİR, EŠEK-TEMİR, XAYR-TEMÜR, İG-TEMÜR, İN-TEMİR, İŠ-TİMER, İŠÏQ-TEMÜR, YAŠ-TEMİR, YÜZ-TEMİR, KEY-TEMİR, KİL-DEMİR, KİN-TİMÜR, KÖK-TEMİR, KÜČ-TEMÜR, KÜČÜK-TEMÜR, QAYA-TEMİR, QAN-**

TEMİR, QAPAQ-TİMÜR, QARA-TEMİR, QAŠ-TEMÜR, QATTÏΓ-TEMİR, KAZ-DİMER, QUL-TEMİR, QUR-TEMÜR, QUŠ-TEMİR, QUTLUΓ-TEMİR, MÄÑLİK-TÄMÜR, MELİK-TEMİR, MEÑGÜ-TEMİR, MİÑ-TEMÜR, NAWRUZ-TEMİR, OQ-TEMİR, OTUNČ-TEMİR, ÖKRÜŠ-TEMİR, ÖN-TEMÜR, ÖTÜKÄN-TEMÜR, ÖTÜNČ-TEMÜR, ÖZ-TEMİR, ÖZLİ-TEMİR, SA-TEMİR, SAL-DİMER, SAN-DEMİR, SARAY-TEMİR, SAV-DİMER, SEWÜNČ-TEMİR, SİL-DİMER, ŠAH-TEMİR, ŠİK-TİMÜR, TAY-TEMİR, TAŠ-TEMİR, TAŠÏQ-TEMİR, TEK-TEMÜR, TÏS-TEMİR, TOΓAY-TEMİR, TOQLUQ-TEMİR, TOQUZ-TEMİR, TOY-TEMİR, TOL-DİMER, TOLAQ-TEMİR, TON-DEMİR, TÖLEK-TEMİR, TULU-TÄMÜR, TUMAN-TEMİR, TUR-TEMİR, TURA-TEMİR, TURAY-TEMİR, TURMÏŠ-TEMÜR, TÜLÄK-TEMİR, TÜMÄN-TEMİR, ULA-TEMİR.

TEMİR-AQSAQ Bashk. 1735 **Temir-aqsaq** [Темиръ-Аксакъ Каскаевъ], a prince (Vel.-Zern., Bašk. 17); Khorezm./Chag. 1370, 1390-1401 **Temir-aqsaq** [Темиръ-Аксакъ / Темирь / Тамерланъ], emir of Samarkand then the well-known khan (1370-1405) of Iran, Irak and Afghanistan (PSRL (Russk. Hr.) I, 419-26, PSRL IV, 97, V, 245, VI, 127-128, VIII, 75 etc.). ⇨ **TEMİR + AQSAQ.**

TEMİR-AL Tat. 1777 **Temir-al** [Темиралъ Буранчинъ] (PSZRI XX, 577, 579). ⇨ **TEMİR + AL.**

TEMİR-ASAQ Uyg. 12th c. - 14th c. **Temir-asaq** [Tämir-asaq] (Radl., USp. 93, DTS). ✦ 'Iron-Asaq' (Blagova 1997, 712). ⇨ **TEMİR + ASAQ.**

TEMİR-BEKE Kzk. 19th c. **Temer-beke** [Темербеке] (SOK 72). ⇨ **TEMİR + BEKE / BİKE?**

TEMİR-BUΓA Maml. 14th c. **Tämür-boγa** [تَمُرْ بُغَا] (Sauvaget 45); Khorezm. 1325, 1328, 1329 **Temir-buγa** [الرسول المغلى رسول ابى سعيد / تمربغا / تمربغا], Abu Said's envoy in Cairo in 1328 (Zetterst. 180, Dawād. 351); Maml. 1332, 1340 **Temir-buγa** [تمربغا العقيلى] (Dawād. 367, Zetterst. 210); Maml. 1377/78 **Temir-buγa** [تمربغا البدرى] (Iyās I, 239); Maml. 1379/80 **Temir-buγa** [تمربغا الشمسى] (Iyās I, 248); Maml. 1385, 1388 **Temir-buγa** [بمنطاش تمربغا الافضلى المعروف], governor of Hamah (Iyās I, 262, Weil, Chalif. I, 546, 549); Maml. 1389 **Temir-buγa** [تمربغا الفخارى السواق] (Iyās I, 271); Maml. 1389, 1398/99 **Temir-buγa** [تمربغا المنجكى] (Iyās I, 273, 337, Weil, Chalif. I, 552, Ibn Taghrīb. VI, 5, 6, 9, 29 etc.); Maml. 1399 **Temir-buγa** [تمربغا باشاه] (Iyās I, 313, 339); Maml. 1400/401 **Temir-buγa** [تمربغا المشطوب] (Iyās I, 338, 345, Weil, Chalif. II, 112-116, Ibn Taghrīb. VI, 87, 90, 93 etc., VII, 337); Maml. 1401/402 **Temir-buγa** [تمربغا الطرنطاى] (Iyās I, 345); Maml. 1407 **Temir-buγa** [السيفى تمربغا الناصرى], governor of Haleb, mentioned in an inscription of Damascus (Sauvaget: BEO III, 14); Maml. 1449 **Temir-buγa** [تمربغا الظاهرى] (Ibn Taghrīb. VIII, 47, 61 etc.); Maml. 1452/53 **Temir-buγa** [تمربغا], an emir (Iyās II, 37, 84); Maml. 1467 **Temir-buγa** [تمربغا الافضلى منطاش] (Ibn Taghrīb. VIII, 617); Maml. 1467 **Temir-buγa** [تمربغا الظاهرى قـزل] (Ibn Taghrīb. VIII, 668); Maml. 1467 **Temir-buγa** [تمربغا الظاهر], Mamlūk sultan (1467-1468), died in 1475 (Iyās II, 40, 86, 92, 97, 185, 382, Weil, Chalif. II, 320-332, Ibn Taghrīb. VII, 133, 145, 740 etc., Makrīzī, Khit. I, 244); Maml. 1467/68 **Temir-buγa** [تمربغا الوالى] (Iyās II, 82, 88); Maml. 1476/77 **Temir-buγa** [تمربغا كاشف الشرقية] (Iyās II, 168); Maml. 1484 **Temir-buγa** [تمربغا مملوك الاتّابكى أزبـك] (Iyās II, 225); Maml. 1496/97 **Temir-buγa** [تمربغا الترجمان], an interpreter (Iyās II, 327); Uyg. 12th c. - 14th c. **Temür-buγa** [Tämür Buqa (Buγa)] (Radl., USp. 10-11, 19-20, 50, DTS); Turk. 1461 **Timur-boγa** [Timur-Boğa] (Gökb., Ed. 344, 345); Selj.? 1300 **Timür-buqa** [تموربوقـا], security (police) officer of Kirman (Qazw. 533); Khorezm.? **Timür-buqa** [Тимур-Бука] (RaD II, 71); Khorezm./Chag. 14th c. **Timür-buqa** [تيموربوقـا], an emir (hadji), an officer of Timurlenk (Qazw. 75); *TN:* Turk. 1461 **Timur-boγa-mahallesi** [Timur-Boğa mahallesi], a district (Gökb., Ed. 344, 345). ✦ 'Iron-bull' (Sauvaget 45). ⇨ **TEMİR + BUQA.**

TEMİR-BULAT Tat. 1777 **Temir-bulat** [Темирбулат Слакаев] (MIB V, 60); Bashk. 1712, 1715 **Temir-bulat** [Тоганаш (Туганаш) Темирбулатов] (MIB III, 82, 137); Kzk. 1801 **Temir-bulat** [Темирбулатъ], from Orenburg (TOUAK XXIV, 4); Tat.(Lit.) 1784 **Timir-bulat** [Jachis Tymirbulatowicz / Яхисъ Тымирбулатовичъ], a prince (Lit. Tat. 544); Tat.(GH) 14th c. **Timir-pulat / Pulat-timir** [Тимиръ-Пуладъ / Пуладъ-Тимиръ], mentioned in one of Toqtamïš's yarlïqs and on his coins (Smirnov, Krym. 140); Crm. 1700 **Timür-bulat** [Тимуръ-Булатъ], an emir (Smirnov, Krym. 670); *TN:* Crm. **Demir-bulat** [Demir bulat], a village (Jervis II). ✦ 'Iron-steel'. ⇨ **TEMİR + BULAT.**

TEMİR-GENDİK Kzk. 19th c. **Temir-gendik** [Темиръ-гендикъ] (Potanin, Pred. 142). ✦ 'Iron-navel' (Potanin). ⇨ **TEMİR + KİNDİK.**

TEMİR-GÜZ Bashk. 1756 **Temir-güz** [Темиргуз Сюклеев] (MIB IV/1, 122). ⇨ **TEMİR + KÖZ.**

TEMİR-YALÏΓ Oghuz/Trkm. **Temir-yalïγ**, byname (laqab) of *Toqaq* (see), forefather of the Seljuks; „because of his strength, was called *Temûryâlig*, that is to say 'Iron Bow'. There was born to this man and he was called by the name of *Saljûk*" (Budge); (Abulfar./Budge I, 195). ✧ 'Iron bow/arrow' (Budge, Golden). ⇨ **TEMİR**.

TEMİR-KİRİS   Hak.(Sag.) 19th-20th c. **Temir-kiris** [Temip Kipic] (Proben IX, 371). ✧ 'Iron catgut/bowstring' cf. Hak. PN *Timır Kırıs* 'id.' (Butanaev). ⇨ **TEMİR + KİRİŠ I.** See also **POQTUΓ-KİRİŠ.**

TEMİR-QUTLUΓ   Tat.(GH) 1389, 1395, 1396, 1399 **Temir-qutlu** [تمرقتلو / Темиръ-Котлуй / Темиръ-Кутлуй], Temür-qutluγ (1397-1399/1400), the ruler of the Golden Horde, the Kipchak Toqtamiš-qan's successor (PSRL (Russk. Hr.) I, 422-424, PSRL IV, 142, VI, 130, VIII, 60, XI, 167, XXIII, 136, Asqalanī/Tizeng. I, 451, 454,); Tat.(GH) 1398 **Temir-qutluq** [Темирь Кутлукъ], Temür-qutluγ (1397-1399/1400), the Kipchak ruler of the Golden Horde, Toqtamiš-qan's successor (PSRL XVI, 45, 50, 144, 145, 150); Khorezm./Chag. 15th c. **Timür-qutluγ** [Тимуръ Кутлугъ] (Barth., Ulugb. 114); Khorezm./Chag. 1388 **Timür-qutluγ-χan** [Тимур-Кутлуг-оглан / Тимур-Кутлуг-хан], a Jochid commander (MIT I, 523, 531); Khorezm./Chag. 1400 **Timür-qutluγ-qan** [Timour-Qoutlouq-Khan], Timur-bek-oγlan's son, İdikey's father (Abulg./Desm. 171). ✧ 'Iron-happy/lucky'. ⇨ **TEMİR + QUTLUΓ.**

TEMİR-QUTLUQ see **TEMİR-QUTLUΓ**

TEMİR-MİZE   Alt. **Temir-mize** [Темиръ-мизе] (Nikiforov 136 ff.). ✧ 'Iron blade / Temir's blade' cf. Alt.(Tel., Kmd.) *mis* 'die Schneide' (Radl. IV, 2162). ⇨ **TEMİR.**

TEMİR-TAŠ   Maml. 1377/78 **Demir-daš** [دمرداش التمان دمرى] (Iyās I, 242); Maml. 1378/79 **Demir-daš** [دمرداش] (Iyās I, 243, 246, III, 123); Maml. 1386 **Demir-daš** [دمرداش اليوسفى] (Iyās I, 239, Weil, Chalf. I, 549); Maml. 1393 **Demir-daš** [السيفى دمرداش الظاهرى], governor of Tarābulūs (Tripoli) (Jamine Sourdel-Thomine: BEO XIV(1954), 62); Maml. 1398/99, 1401/02, 1408/09, 1415 **Demir-daš** [السيفى دمرداش الناصرى], governor of Aleppo, then that of Syria, died in 1415 (Ibn Taghrīb. VI, 3, 12, 39, 100, 131 etc., Iyās I, 322, 334, 341, 342 etc., Weil, Chalif. II, 78, 102-124, Mayer 114-115); Maml. 1438/39 **Demir-daš** [دمرداش الحسنى الظاهرى] (Ibn Taghrīb. VII, 21); Maml. 1438/39 **Demir-daš** [الاشرفى / دمرداش الاشرفى / السيفى دمرداش الملكى], mentioned in an inscription on a copper dish (Ibn Taghrīb. VII, 8, 24, Mayer 113-114); Maml. 1439/40 **Demir-daš** [دمرداش المحمدى] (Ibn Taghrīb. VII, 264); Maml. 1449 **Demir-daš** [دمرداش كاشف الشرقية] (Ibn Taghrīb. VIII, 52); Maml. 1457 **Demir-daš** [دمرداش الطويل] (Ibn Taghrīb. VII, 492); Maml. 1463 **Demir-daš** [دمرداش], a governor (Ibn Taghrīb. VIII, 450, 531); Maml. 1466/67

Demir-daš [دمرداش الغرى بردائى] (Ibn Taghrīb. VII, 744); Turk. 1467/68 **Demir-daš** [دمرداش العثمانى] (Ibn Taghrīb. VII, 855, VIII, 626, Iyās II, 94, 117); Maml. **Demir-taš** [دمرتاش غلام ظهيرالـدين] (Ibn Bībī IV, 232); Khorezm.? 1325, 1326/27 **Demir-taš / Demür-taš / Temür-taš?** [تمورتاش نوين بن جوبان / دَ مُرطاش / الامير المغلى دمرداش / Ταμουρτάσης / Demur Thâch / Demir Taş / Demirtaş / Timurtaş], an emir and ruler (1318-1327), the Ilkhanid (Moghul) Čoban emir's son, the governor of Asia Minor (Anatolia), in the days of Abū Saʿīd Ilkhan; the same as Taš-temür? (Ibn Bat. II, 121, Dawād. 289, 345, Zetterst. 179, 192, Weil, Chalif. I, 328, 329, Uzunçarş., Anad. 5, 13, 14, 15, 16, 17, 36, 49, Aqsarāyī 4, 312-321, Aqsar/Iş. 115, Byz. Turc. 297-98); Trkm.? **Demir-taš-bey** [Demirtaş bey], head of the Sarıkeçili tribe in the past (Riza III, 35); Maml.? 14th c. **Demür-taš** [دُمرطاش / Domourthâch], Qara-soñqur's son (Ibn Bat, I, 172); Kzk. 19th c. **Temer-tas** [Темертасовъ] (AOO 26); Karakh.? 991 **Temir-taš** [تمرتاش قايد شرف الدولة] (Ibn al-Athīr/Tornb. IX, 58); Selj. 1152/53 **Temir-taš** [حسام الـدين تمرتاش / Hosâm ed-Dîn Timurtach], lord of Nisibe, then that of Maridīn, died in 1152/53 (Ibn al-Athīr, Atab.: RHCHor II/2, 67, 141, 188, Bondārī 244); Selj. 1191/92 **Temir-taš** [تمرتاش ابن الجاولى / حسام الـدين / Housam ed-Dîn Timourtach ibn Djaweli] (Abū Šāma: RHCHor V, 20-21); Maml. 14th c. **Temir-taš / Tämür-taš** [تمرتاش / Temürtaş] (Tarj/Houtsma 68, 83, Tarj/Toparlı 43); Selj. 1117, 1118, 1122, 1141, 1206 **Temir-taš / Temir-daš / Temür-taš** [تمرداش / حسام الـدين / تمرداش بن ايلغازى بن ارتق / تمرتاش بن ايلغازى / Temûrtâsh], İl-γazi's governor in Damascus, the lord of Mardin, then that of Haleb (Abulfidā III, 390-391, Kamāladdīn II, 180, 209, 218, Ibn al-Athīr/Tornb. X, 373, 467, XI, 92, 115, Ibn Taghrīb. II, 378, Zambaur 228-230, Qalānisi 199, 274-276, Arabš I, 596 ff., Abulfar./Budge I, 251, 362); Chag.? **Temür-taš** [Tämürtaš] (Le Coq, Ind. 4); Turk. 14th c. **Temür-taš** [Ταμουρτάσης], a commander of the army (Byz. Turc. 297-298); Yürük 1543 **Timur-taš** [Timurtaş] (Gökb., Rum. 205); Turk. 1485 **Timur-taš / Timur-taš-paša** [Timurtaş Paşa (Kara Timurtaş)] (Gökb., Ed. 6, 14, 201); Turk. 15th c.? **Timur-taš-bey** [Timurtaş Bey] (Baştav 61); Turk. 1485 **Timur-taš-bey** [Timurtaş Bey] (Gökb., Ed. 200, 201, 203); Khorezm. 14th c. **Timür-taš** [تيمور تاش / تمور تاش / Timour-Tasch / Timour Tâsch], Čoban's (Ĵuban's?) son, died in 1328 (Jorga, Notes XIII, 350 /Mesalekalabsar/, Qazw. 606, 609, Abulg./Desm. 175); Trkm. 1836 **Timür-taš** [Тимурташ] (MIT II, 233); *TN:* Turk. 20th c. **Demir-taš** [Demirtaş], a village in the province of Elâzığ, Turkey (TMİB 316). ✧ 'Iron-stone' (Sauvaget 47). ⇨ **TEMİR + TAŠ.** See also **QARA-DEMİR-DAŠ,**

QARA-TEMİR-TAŠ, ТОГАУ-TEMİR-TAŠ.

TEMİRBET Kkalp. 1722 **Temirbet-murza** (PSZRI VI, 778). ⇨ **TEMİR** + suffixoid *-met*.

TEMİRČİ Yürük 16th c. **Demirji-dede / Timürči-dede?** [تیمورجی دهده / Demirci dede] (Gökb., Rum. 101); Tat. 1686 **Temerči** [Темерчи] (Kungursk. akty 119); Yürük 16th c. **TemürJi-χaJï** [تمورجی حاجی / Temürci-hacı], from the Yürüks of Kocacık, Turkey (Gökb., Rum. 104); Yürük 1543 **Timurji** [Timurci] (Gökb., Rum. 198); *EN:* Yürük 1618 **TimurJu** [Timurcu naam cemaat], a tribe (cemaat) (Gökçen 90). ✧ 'Smith' cf. Crm. *tämirJï* 'der Schmied', Kzk. *temiršï* 'id.' (Radl. III, 1134), Turk. *dämirji* 'der Schlosser, der Scmied' (Radl. III, 1700).

TEMİRÄK Bashk. 1708 **Temeräk** [Темеряк Тюкалев] (MIB I, 234); Selj. 1073 **Temiräk / Temir-el?** [تمیرال / تمراك / Emir Temirel ibn Ferruhşah] (Ahbar 39); Selj. 1116 **Temirek** [تمیرك] (Usāma 54); Selj.? 1182/83 **Temirek** [تمیرك الـدین حسام / Husām ad-Dīn Temirek ibn Junus], police chief in Aleppo/Haleb (Abū Šāma: RHCHor IV, 237-238); Selj. 1106, 1113 **Temirek / Temiräk** [صاحب سنجار], son [تمیراك بن ارسلان تاش / تمیرك احو ارسلان تاش], of Arslan-taš, Qïfčaq's (Qïpčaq's) brother (Ibn al-Athīr/Tornb. X, 281, 351, Qalānisi 185); Bashk. 1780 **Timräk** [Тюлкубай Тимряков] (MIB V, 120). ⇨ **TEMİR** + dim. suff. *-äk / -ek*.

TEMİRÄZ Selj.? 1453 **Temiräz** [الشمسى], [الاتابکى تمراز], an atabek (Iyās II, 38, Weil, Chalif. II, 256, 335 etc.); Tat.(GH)? 1408 **Temiräz** [Ибрагимъ Темирязевъ сынъ] (PSRL VI, 136, VIII, 82); Maml. 1399, 1400 **Temiräz** [تمراز الناصرى] (Iyās I, 313, 328, Weil, Chalif. II, 75, 104, Ibn Taghrīb. VI, 6, 23, 25 etc., VII, 264, 442); Maml. 1422, 1428, 1437/38, 1439, 1447 **Temiräz** [تمراز القرمشى] (Ibn Taghrīb. VI, 554, 634 etc., VII, 2, 8, 21 etc., VIII, 1, 22, 43 etc., Iyās II, 25, Weil, Chalif. II, 219); Maml. 1424, 1439 **Temiräz** [تمراز المویّدى] (Ibn Taghrīb. VI, 574, 728, VII, 107, 109); Maml. 1444/45, 1462 **Temiräz** [تعریص] [تمراز النوروزى] (Ibn Taghrīb. VII, 133, VIII, 140); Maml. 1450, 1452/53 **Temiräz** [تمراز الاینالى الاشرفى], governor of Safed (Ibn Taghrīb. VII, 187, 344, 412, Iyās II, 40, 75, III, 62, Weil, Chalif. II, 282-297); Maml. 1467/68 **Temiräz** [تمراز الاشرفى الساقى] (Ibn Taghrīb. VII, 846, 854); Maml. 1469/70 **Temiräz** [تمراز] (Iyās II, 114, 173, 303, III, 20); Maml. 1470/71 **Temiräz** [تمراز التمشى] (Iyās II, 124, 232, III, 260); Maml. 1475/76 **Temiräz** [تمراز رأس نوبة النوب] (Iyās II, 159, 172); Maml. 1477 **Temiräz** [السیفى تمراز] / S. a. d. Timrâc Ahmadi], an emir (Berchem 293-294); Maml. 1484 **Temiräz** [تمراز حشیش بن حشاش الاینالى] (Iyās II, 224); Maml. 1485 **Temiräz** [تمراز أمیرسلاح] (Iyās II, 231, 257); Maml. 1496/97 **Temiräz** [تمراز أمیر کبیر], great (first) emir (Iyās II, 306); Maml. 1496/97 **Temiräz** [تمراز جوشن] (Iyās II, 306, 392); Maml. 1496/97 **Temiräz** [تمراز الشیخ] (Iyās II, 314); Maml. 1497/98 **Temiräz** [تمراز الـزردکاش] (Iyās II, 332, 380, III, 13, 64); Maml. 1516 **Temiräz** [تمراز الاشرفى], governor of Tarabulus (Iyās III, 3, 51). ✧ Shortened-contracted of *Temir-yazi* (Bask., Fam. 214), cf. also Tat. PN *Timer-yazi / Timeryaz (= Timeräz)* (Sattarov).

TEMİREK see **TEMİRÄK**

TEMİRKEY Bashk. 1763 **Temirkey** [Темиркей Сююкеев] (MIB IV/1, 271); Bashk. 1770 **Temirkey** [Темиркей Юлдашев] (MIB IV/1, 350); Bashk. 1760 **Timirkey** [Тимиркей Ирмекеев] (MIB IV/2, 28). ⇨ **TEMİR** + dim. hypoc. suff. *-key*.

TEMİRTAY Kzk. 19th c. **Temirtay** [Темиртай] (SOK 114); Yak. **Timirdäy** [Тімірдäі] (Pek.); Khorezm.? **Timurtay** [Тимуртай] (RaD II, 75). ✧ 'Iron-foal', 'Iron(-boy)'? ⇨ **TEMİR** + **TAY?** or suff. *-tay(1,2)*.

TEMİRTEK Kzk. 19th c. **Temirtek** [Темиртекъ] (SOK 280). ✧ 'Iron-like'? ⇨ **TEMİR** + suff. *-teg/-tek*.

TEMİS see **TEMİŠ**

TEMİŠ Bashk. 1742 **Temis** [Темисъ Илкеев] (MIB III, 513); Kzk. 19th c. **Temis** [Темисъ] (SOK 264); Chag. 16th c. **Temiš** [Темиш], a mir (emir) (Ivanov 149); Kzk. 19th c. **Temiš** [Темишъ] (AOA 102); Kzk. 19th c. **Temiš** [Темишъ] (AOAtb. 30); Kzk. 19th c. **Temiš-pay** [Темышпай] (AOAtb. 42); *TN:* Crm. **Temiš** [Temisch], a place (village) east of Yevpatoriya (Jervis VII.). ✧ 'He spoke, he said'? (Erol II). See also **BAY-TEMİŠ, QUTLUQ-TEMİŠ.**

TEMİZ Oghuz? 1070 **Tämis** [Ταμίς / Tämiz], an Uz (?) commander of the army (Byz. Turc. 297). ✧ 'Clean, pure; neat; honest' cf. Az., Crm., Turk. *tämiz* 'rein, fleckenlos; tugendhaft, von gutem Rufe' (Radl. III, 1134). See also **ES-TEMİZ.**

TEMNİK Tat.(GH) 1237 **Temnik** [Темникъ], a Tatar prince (Ipat. 520 /525/). ✧ 'Tatar commander of a *tümen* (army of ten thousand warriors) (Šipova). A dignity. (<R.).

TEMREY Kzk. 19th c. **Temrey** [Темрей] (AOA 82). ✧ 'Dear little Iron' cf. Tat. PN *Timräy* (Sattarov). ⇨ **TEMİR** + dim. suff. *-ey*.

TEMSENEK Tat.(Sib.)? 1629, 1631 **Temsenek / Temsänik?** [Темсенек / Тесеник / Темсяник], a prince (Miller, Ist. Sib. II, 345, 366, 377).

TEMSİK Kzk. 19th c. **Temsik-pay** [Темсыкпай] (SOK 116).

TEMTİ Kzk. 19th c. **Temti-bay** [Темтыбай] (AOA 82).

TEMÜKÄ Uyg. **Tämükä** [Tämükä] (EUTS); Uyg. 12th c. - 14th c. **Temükä** [Tämükä] (Radl., USp. 30, DTS).

TEMÜR-ALTÏ Khorezm. 14th c. **Temür-altï** [تمورالطى / Tomoûralthi], in Khorassan (Ibn Bat. III, 71-73). ⇨ **TEMİR + ALTÏ.**

TEMÜR-BUΓA see **TEMİR-BUΓA**

TEMÜR-TURMÏ!Š Uyg. 12th c. - 14th c. **Temür-turmiš** [Tämür Turmïš] (Radl., USp. 51,).

TEN Chuv. 18th-19th c. **Tän-bäk** [Тянбякъ] (Magn. 88); Chuv. 18th-19th c. **Tän-bek** [Тянбекъ] (Magn. 88); Kzk. 19th c. **Ten-bay** [Тенбай] (AOA 150); Kzk. 19th c. **Ten-bay** [Тенбай] (SOV 60); Nog. **Ten-bay / Ten-bay-murza / Tin-bay** [Тен-Бай Мурза (Тинбай)] (Žirm., Epos 430); Maml. 1394 **Ten-bek** [تنبك لحسنى الظاهرى], viceroy (governor) of Syria (Mayer 216-217); Maml. 1398/99 **Ten-bek** [الظاهرى تنبك الحسنى] (Ibn Taghrīb. VI, 3, 7, 11 etc.); Maml. 1400 **Ten-bek** [تنبك/ دوادار قانى باى/] (Ibn Taghrīb. VI, 349); Maml. 1400 **Ten-bek** [تنبك], governor of Tarsus (Ibn Taghrīb. VI, 409); Maml. 1400 **Ten-bek** [تنبك القاضى] (Ibn Taghrīb. VI, 469); Maml. 1402/03 **Ten-bek** [تنبك] (Ibn Taghrīb. VI, 106); Maml. 1414 **Ten-bek** [تنبك البجاسىّ], governor of Hama (Ibn Taghrīb. VI, 329, 339, 560, 786, 855, Weil, Chalif. II, 134); Maml. 1418 **Ten-bek** [تنبك ميق العلائى], governor of Damascus (Ibn Taghrīb. VI, 341, 375, VII, 579, Weil, Chalif. II, 140); Maml. 1433 **Ten-bek** [تنبك من سيّدى بك الناصرىّ المدارى] (Ibn Taghrīb. VI, 423, 750); Maml. 1438 **Ten-bek** [الجتمقى الخضرى تنبك النوروزى] (Ibn Taghrīb. VII, 2, 15, 23); Maml. 1438/39 **Ten-bek** [تنبك النيسى الينالى] (Ibn Taghrīb. VII, 23, 104); Maml. 1450 **Ten-bek** [تنبك المؤيّدىّ] (Ibn Taghrīb. VI, 354, 453); Maml. 1460 **Ten-bek** [تنبك], an interpreter (Ibn Taghrīb. VIII, 348); Maml. 1461 **Ten-bek** [الاشرفى حنيكات القصير] (Ibn Taghrīb. VII, 554, 702); Maml. 1461 **Ten-bek** [تنبك الاشرفى المعلم] (Ibn Taghrīb. VIII, 416, 544); Maml. 1463 **Ten-bek** [تنبك الجانبكى] (Ibn Taghrīb. VII, 715); Maml. 1467 **Ten-bek** [تنبك الساقى] (Ibn Taghrīb. VIII, 625); Kkalp. 1740 **Ten-bek-bi** [Тенбекъ-Би / Тенбек-би] (Hanykov, Poezdka 19, MIKk. 208); Chuv. 18th-19th c. **Ten-čura** [Тенчуринъ] (Magn. 81); Bashk. 1664 **Ten-čura** [Асылай Тенчюрин] (MIB I, 193). ❖ 'Body' cf. Uyg., Kuman, Chag., Az., Tat., etc. *tän* P. 'der Körper, der Rumpf' (Radl. III, 1051), Turk. *tän* 'ein grosser Fluss; der Fluss Don' (Radl. III, 1052), Kzk. *den* 'der Körper' (Radl. III, 1666). See also **AY-TEN, QAS-TEN; BOY, DENE, TULΓA.**

TEN-AXMAT see **TEN-AXMET**

TEN-AXMET Nog. 1599 **Ten-aχmat** [Тенъ-Ахматъ], a prince (AI II, 20); Chuv. 18th-19th c. **Ten-eχmet** [Тенехметь] (Magn. 81); Nog. 18th c. **Tin-aχmat /**

Tin-aχmet [Тинахматъ / Тинахметъ], a prince (AI IV, 105, Nepljuev 283); Nog. 1678 **Tin-aχmet** [Тинокпатовъ] (DAI VIII, 25). ⇨ **TEN + AXMET.**

TEN-BEČEK Kzk. 1676 **Ten-beček** [Тенбечекъ] (DAI VII, 343). ⇨ **TEN + BİČİK.**

TEN-BEGEY Alt. 19th c. **Ten-begey** [Тен-бегей], a folklore hero (Verb., In. 173). ⇨ **TEN + BEGEY?**

TEN-BİREY Tat. 1658 **Ten-birey** [Текченка Тенбиреевъ] (Kuznecov 20).

TEN-SUBUY Nog. **Ten-subuy?** [Тенсубуй Князь] (Žirm., Epos 430).

TENBEL 9th c. **Tenbel**, ruler of Kabul (Qazw. 374). ⇨ **TAMBAL?**

TENÄK Bashk. 1701 **Tenäk** [Султанай Теняков] (MIB III, 12). ⇨ **TENEK I./II.?**

TENE see **TENİ**

TENEY Tat. 1779 **Teney** [Теней Янгалаев] (MIB V, 43); Tat.(Sib.) 17th c. **Teney** [Теней Утеевъ] (Miller, Ist. Sib. II, 453); Bashk. 1717 **Teney** [Албек Тенеев] (MIB III, 157); Bashk. 1754 **Teney** [Асикай Тенеев] (MIB IV/1, 83); Kzk. 19th c. **Teney** [Теней] (SOV 4); Uzb. 1697 **Teney** [Тенейко Аиткулов (Анткулов!)], a man from Bukhara in Tobolsk (PSZRI III, 355, Andrievič, Ist. Sib. II, 22); *TN:* Chuv. 18th c. **Teney(eva)** [Тенеева], a village in the district of Tsivilsk (Korsakov 321). ❖ 'Little boy'? cf. Tat. *Teni/Tenäy* (Sattarov). ⇨ **TENİ** + suff. *-y.*

TENEK I. Tuv. 19th c. **Tänäk-qam** [Тänäk-кам], a shaman (Proben IX, 146); Alt. 19th-20th c. **Tenek** [Тенек] (OjrRS 210). ❖ 'Stupid, foolish' (OjrRS).

TENEK II. Kkalp. 1827 **Tenek-bay** [Тенекбай] (MIKk. 131); Uzb. 1804 **Tenek-behadïr** [تَنَك بهادر / Тенек-бехадыр] (MIT II, 366).

TENEKE Kzk. 19th c. **Teneke** [Тенеке] (AOK 2); Kzk. 19th c. **Teneke** [Тенеке] (AOO 66); Kzk. 19th c. **Teneke-bay** [Тенекебай] (SOK 182).

TENEKEY see **TENİKEY**

TENESPİM Kzk. 19th c. **Tenespim** [Тенеспымъ] (SOV 52).

TENİ Crm. **Täni-bäk** [Тäнi Бäк] (Proben VII, 161); Kzk. 19th c. **Tene-bay / Teni-bay?** [Тенебай] (SOV 140); Tat.(GH) 1342 **Tene-bek** [Тенебек], Čanï-bek's / Janï-bek's brother (PSRL XXIII, 106); Tat. 1702 **Tene-bek** [Утягулко Тенебековъ], from Kungur (Letop. ZAK II, 7); Kzk. 1846 **Tene-bek** [Маркабай Тенебеков], a biy (MKOP 156); Kzk. 19th c. **Tenï-bek** [Теныбекъ] (AOA 62); Kzk. 19th c. **Tene-bek** (AOK 38); Kzk. 19th c. **Tene-bek** [Тенебекъ] (AOO 54); Kzk. 19th c. **Tene-bek** [Тенебекъ] (SOV 32, 66); Kzk. 1822 **Teni-bahadur / Tene-batïr** [تنى بهادور / Тенебатыр] (MIK IV, 432, 434); Karch. **Teni-bek** [Тенибекъ] (Sysoev 124); Kzk. 19th c. **Teni-bek** [Теныбекъ] (SODž. 144); Chuv. 18th-19th c. **Teni-bek**

/ **Täni-bek** [Тенибекъ / Тянибекъ] (Magn. 81, 88); Chuv. 18th-19th c. **Tini-bäk** [Тинибякъ] (Magn. 82); Kzk. 19th c. **Tinĭ-bek** [Тныбекъ] (AOAtb. 6). ✧ 'Child, son'? (Sattarov); II. 'Body' cf. Kirg. *tene / dene* (Ir.) 'корпус, тело' (Jud.). ⇨ **TANÏ?, TÏNÏ.**

TENİGEY see **TENİKEY**

TENİKEY   Kzk. 19th c. **Tenekey** [Тенекей] (AOK 126); Kzk. 19th c. **Tenekey** [Тенекей], a biy (Lomakin 36); Tat. 1662 **Tenigey** [Тенигейка Тозаев] (MIB I, 161); Bashk. 1729 **Tenikey** [Имангул Теникеев] (MIB III, 260); Bashk. 1735 **Tenikey** [Канчуръ Теникеевъ], a tarχan (Vel.-Zern., Bašk. 14); Bashk. 1735 **Tenikey** [Канчуръ Теникеевъ], a tarχan (Vel.-Zern., Bašk. 14); Bashk. 1735 **Tenikey** [Иманъ Теникеевъ], a tarχan (Vel.-Zern., Bašk. 16); Bashk. 1735 **Tenikey** [Умиръ Теникеевъ], a tarχan (Vel.-Zern., Bašk. 16); Bashk. 1735 **Tenikey** [Теникей Черкаринъ], a tarχan (Vel.-Zern., Bašk. 24); Bashk. 1756 **Tenikey** [Илимгул Теникеев] (MIB IV/1, 122); Bashk. 1740 **Tenikey / Tinikey** [Теникей (Тиникей) Текелев] (MIB I, 423); Bashk. 1670 **Tinikey** [Акилничка Тиникеевъ] (Vel.-Zern., Bašk. 36); Bashk. 1735 **Tinikey** [Теникей Мурзинъ], a tarχan (Vel.-Zern., Bašk. 15); Nog. 1649 **Tinikey** [Тиникѣевъ] (AI IV, 87). ⇨ **TENİ** + suff. *-key.*

TENİKEŠ   Chuv. 1728 **Tenikeš** [Тетейке Теникешев] (MIB I, 128).

TENİŠ   Bashk. 1779 **Täniš** [Кусти Тянишев] (MIB V, 94); Bashk. 1789 **Täniš** [Таксыр Тянышев] (MIB V, 263); Bashk. 1779 **Tenič** [Teniš / Тенич Диянов] (MIB V, 89); Bashk. 1770 **Tenis** [Таскыр Тенисев] (MIB IV/1, 342); Tat.(GH) 14th c. **Teniš**, a murza in the country of the Mordvins (Smyrnov 276); Tat. 1624 **Teniš** [Тетяй Тенишевъ] (Zolotn. 159); Tat. 17th c.? **Teniš** [Тениш], a prince from Astrakhan (Zolotn. 159); Tat.(Mish.) 19th c. **Teniš** [Тенишевъ] (IOAIÊK XIX, 143); Bashk. 1764 **Teniš** [Тениш Зиянов] (MIB IV/1, 285); Chag. 16th c. **Tiniš** [Тиниш], a mirza (Ivanov 178, 183, 187, 188); Chag. 16th c. **Tiniš-aγa** [Тиниш-Ага] (Ivanov 145); Chag. 16th c. **Tiniš-biy** [Тиниш-бий], an emir (Ivanov 220); Chag. 16th c. **Tiniš-χoǰa** [Тиниш-ходжа] (Ivanov 88, 90); *TN:* Tat. 18th c. **Teniš(evo)** [Тенишево], a village in Spasskij uezd (district?) (Korsakov 193). ✧ I. 'Little child; child/son-mate' (Sattarov 178); II. 'Quiet, calm; born at peaceful times' (Ibid. after Baskakov), see TïnïŠ.

TENİZEK   Kzk. 19th c. **Tenizek** [Тенызекъ] (AOK 6); Kzk. 19th c. **Tenizek** [Игберъ Тенызековъ] (AOK 6). ⇨ **TEÑIZ?** + suff. *-ek.*

TENKEY   Tat. 1675 **Tenkey / Teñkey?** [Тенкеевъ] (Kungursk. akty 27). ⇨ **TEN / TEÑ?** + dim. suff. *-key.*

TENLES   Kzk. 19th c. **Tenles-pay** [Тенлеспай] (SOK 114).

TENSEL   Kzk. 19th c. **Tensel-bay** [Тенсельбай] (SOK

224). ✧ 'Move hither an thither!' cf. Kzk. *teñsäl-* 'sich hin und her bewegen, schaukeln, wackeln' (Radl. III, 1049).

TENTÄK see **TENTEK**

TENTE   Kzk. 19th c. **Tente-bay** [Тентебай] (SOK 186).

TENTEK   Bashk. 1738 **Tentäk** [Уразгилды Тентяков] (MIB I, 143); Kzk. 19th c. **Tentek** [Тентекъ] (AOAtb. 22); Kzk. 19th c. **Tentek** [Тентекъ] (SOK 208); Kzk. 19th c. **Tentek-bala** [Тентекъ-бала] (Ibragimov 125); Kzk. 19th c. **Tentek-pay** [Тентекпай] (SOK 8). ✧ 'Stupid, silly; sinner' cf. Chag., Crm., Kar. *täntäk* 'dumm, närrisch; schlau, gewandt', Kzk. *tentäk* 'verdreht, thöricht; schuldig' (Radl. III, 1056), Kzk. *tentek* 'шалун, озорник; дурень' (KzRS).

TENTEKÄY   Tat. 1739 **Tentekäy** [Тентекай] (MIB I, 374-75); Bashk. 1675 **Tentikey** [Тентикей Итихбатин] (MIB I, 202). ⇨ **TENTÄK** + suff. *-äy / -ey.*

TENTÜK   Tat. 1628, 1635 **Tentük** [Тайтелей Тентюков] (Miller, Ist. Sib. II, 338, 340, 430, 473); Tat.(Sib.) 1620 **Tentük** [Ишмамет Тентюков] (Miller, Ist. Sib. II, 251, 254, 475). ⇨ **TENTÄK(?).**

TEÑGE   Kzk. 19th c. **Teñge-bay** [Бекъ Ходжа Тенгебаевъ] (Grod., Pril. 58); Kzk. 19th c. **Teñge-bay** [Тенгебай] (SODž. 14). ✧ 'Money, (silver) coin' cf. Kzk. *teñgä* 'Geld, Silbergeld' (Radl. III, 1046).

TEÑIZ   Yürük 1543 **Deniz** [دكز], from the Yürüks of Koсаcık, Turkey (Gökb., Rum. 177, 183, 188 etc.); Trkm. 1826 **Deñiz-bek** [Денгиз-бек], from the Salïr tribe (MIT II, 435, 440); Trkm. 1817/18 **Deñiz-χalife** [Денгиз-халифе] (MIT II, 403, 404, 410, 436, 438); Oghuz/Trkm. 13th c. **Deñiz-χan / Diñiz-χan / Teñiz / Tiñiz / Tiñiz-χan** [دينكيز / تكر / تينكز / Tinguiz / Tingiz χan / Tengiz / teñiz / Денгиз-хан / Дингизъ-ханъ / Тенгиз-хан], Oghuz Khan's son in the Turkic legend of origin (RaD I/1, 76, Abulg./Desm. 23, Abulg./Kon. 430, 510, 520, 560, Oğuz K. Dest. 15, Šejb. XXIII, DTS); Kzk. 19th c. **Diñiz-pay** [Дынгизпай] (SOK 22); Uyg. **Täñiz** [Тängiz] (EUTS); Kzk. 19th c. **Tenes-bay** [Тенесбай] (SOV 24); Kzk. 19th c. **Tenez-bay** [Тенезбай] (Pam. kn. Turg. 42); Kzk. 19th c. **Tenez-bay** [Тенезбай] (SODž. 22); Chuv. 18th-19th c. **Tenges** [Тенгесь] (Magn. 81); Kzk. 19th c. **Tenis-bay** [Тенисбай] (AOK 106); Kzk.? 19th c. **Tenis-bay** [Тэнисъ-бай] (Potanin II, 3); Kzk. 19th c. **Tenis-bay** [Тенисбай] (SOK 4, 180); Kzk. **Teniz-bay** [Байтулакъ Тенизбаевъ] (Konšin 59); Kzk. 19th c. **Teniz-bay** [Тенизбай] (SOK 190); Kzk. 19th c. **Teniz-bay** [Тенызбай] (SOK 282); Kzk. 19th c. **Teniz-bay** [Тенизбай] (SOK 4, 190); Kzk. 19th c. **Teñis-bay** [Тенгисъ-бай / Тэнгисъ-бай] (Potanin II, 3, 163); NUyg. 19th c. **Teñis-bay** [Tengis-baj], a pass in Eastern

Turkestan (Hedin, En färd I, 91, 100 etc.); Alt. **Teñis-bi** [Тенгисъ-би], a divinity (Nikiforov 128 ff.); Selj. 1132 **Teñiz** [تنكز الحاجب] (Ibn al-Athīr/Tornb. X, 483); Selj.? 1163 **Teñiz** [تنكز] سيف الدين / سيف الدين تنكز مملوك المويد ايابه / Сейф-ад-дин Тенгиз], emir Al-Muayyid Ay-aba's slave (mamluk) (Ibn al-Athīr/Tornb. XI, 192, 206, 208, Muh. Ibrahim 48); Maml. 1254 **Teñiz** [Tenkez] (Makrīzī I, 48); Maml. 1260 **Teñiz** [Seïf-eddin-Tenkez] (Makrīzī I, 90); Maml. 1312, 1315/16, 1325, 1328/29, 1339 **Teñiz** الناصرى / المقر الاشرف السيفى تنكز الحسامى] تنكز/ السيفى تنكز الملك الناصرى / تنكز الدين سيف / الحسامى تنكز سيف الدين /], emir, governor of Damascus, Syria (1312-1340), founder of a medresse, died in 1339 (Abulfidā V, 270-71, Abulfidā/Ed. I, 177, 180, Zetterst. 158, 210-212, Dawād. 242, 247, 264, Berchem, Jér. I, 256, II, 128, Sauvaire III, 285, Duqmaq:RHCHor IV, 40, Iyās I, 157-59, 166, 172, Makrīzī, Khit. II, 54, Weil, Chalif. I, 310, 392); Maml. 1342 **Teñiz** [Sayf ed-dîn Tenkez], governor of Syria, died in 1342, his mausoleum is in Damascus (Sauvaire VI, 226); Maml. 14th c. **Teñiz** [تكيز / Tenkīz] (Ibn Bat. I, 219); Maml. 1455 **Teñiz** [تنكز الناصرى] (Ibn Taghrīb. VII, 580); Turk. 1379/80 **Teñiz** [تنكز العثمانى] (Iyās I, 248); Maml. 1434 **Teñiz** / **Deñiz** [تنكز / بنكز] (Ibn Taghrīb. VI, 830); Kzk. 19th c. **Teñiz-bay** [Тенизбай] (AOP 30); Kzk. 19th c. **Teñiz-bay** [Айбала Тенгизбаевъ] (Grod., Pril. 194); Kzk. 19th c. **Teñiz-bay** [Тенгызбай] (SOK 226); *TN:* Chuv. 18th c. **Tengeseva** [Тенгесева], a village in the district of Cheboksary (Korsakov 282); Kzk. 19th c. **Teñiz-bay** [Тенизъ-бай], a tomb north of the Caspian Sea (IIRGO XVI (Karta ur. Tentjak-sor)); Kzk. 19th c. **Teñiz-bay** [Тенизъ-бай], a kurgan (burial mound) north of the Caspian Sea (IIRGO XVI (Karta ur. Tentjak-sor)); Kzk. **Teñiz-bay** [Тенгиз-бай], a place (?) in the Alay mountains south-west of Osh (Karta JAR XIX). ✧ 'Sea' cf. Kzk. *teñiz* 'das Meer' (Radl. III, 1045), cf. also Trkm. „tenkis" [*teñkis*] 'sudden storm; violent storms from the wetward' (O'Donovan I, 218). See also **AY-DEÑIZ, İL-DEÑIZ, KÜN-DEÑIZ, QARA-DENİZ.**

TEÑİZ-BUΓA Türk? 8th c. **Teñiz-buγa** [تنكز بغا] (Mehren 514); Maml. 1360 **Teñiz-buγa** [تنكز بغا المارديني / Tankiz bugâ], emir of Maridīn (Iyās I, 207, Berchem 173); Maml. 1379/80 **Teñiz-buγa** [تنكز بغا السيفى] (Iyās I, 249); Maml. 1389 **Teñiz-buγa** [تنكزبغا اليلغاوى] (Iyās I, 278); Maml. 1450 **Teñiz-buγa** [تنكزبغا الحططى] (Ibn Taghrīb. VI, 9, 16, 23, 73, Iyās I, 337). ✧ 'Sea-bull' (Sauvaget 45). ⇨ **TEÑİZ + BUQA.**

TEPE-GÖZ see **DEPE-GÖZ**

TEPEY Bashk. 1715 **Tepey** [Арык Тепеев] (MIB III, 132); Bashk. 1787 **Tipey** [Салих Типеев] (MIB V, 207). ✧ 'Trap' cf. Tat. *täpäi* 'die Falle' (Radl. III, 1110).

TEPEK Bashk. 1737 **Tepek-mulla** [Тепек мулла Кушаев] (MIB I, 309).

TEPER Tat.(Sib.) 1623 **Teper** [Беня Теперов], a taxpayer (payer of yasaq) (Miller, Ist. Sib. II, 292); Kzk. 18th c. - 19th c. **Teper** [Тепер] (Tunyšp. 74); Hak. 19th-20th c. **Teper** [Тепер] (HRS 351). ✧ 'Kicking (animal/man), trampling, scraping out' cf. Hak. *tep-* 'пинать (о человеке); лягаться (о лошади)' (HRS), Kirg., Kzk. *tep-* 'das Futter unter dem Schnee hervorscharren' (Radl. III, 1109), Chag., Alt., Hak.(Schor), Turk. *täp-* 'mit den Füssen stossen, stampfen, dreschen, treten' (Radl. III, 1108).

TEPERIS Bashk. 1693 **Täpäris** [Тяпариско Тлебердеевъ], a tarγan (Vel.-Zern., Bašk. 34); Bashk. 1735 **Teperis** [Сапар Теперысовъ], a tarγan (Vel.-Zern., Bašk. 20); Bashk. 1735, 1740 **Teperis / Teperiš** [Юнусъ Теперисовъ / Юнус Тепиришев], a tarγan (Vel.-Zern., Bašk. 11, MIB I, 439). ✧ 'Fun, amusement, cheer' cf. Kzk. *tepäriš* (Ar.) 'das Vergnügen, die Belustigung' (Radl. III, 1110).

TEPERİŠ see **TEPERİS**

TEPİŠ see **TEBİŠ**

TEPLÄK Tat. 1606 **Tepläk** [Тепляк] (Miller, Ist. Sib. II, 193); Bashk. 1701 **Tepläk** [Бииш Тепляков] (MIB III, 14).

TEPREMEZ Kuman 1280 **Tepremez** [Teprez Cumano / Tepremez], from Hungary (Gyárfás II, 445, ÁUO XII, 313-314); *TN:* Kuman 1346, 1347 **Tepremez** [Possessio Thepremez / Tepermez / Tepremez], a village in the county of Bodrog, Hungary, preserving the name of its Kuman owner (Csánki II, 200, 211). ✧ I. 'He won't move' (Rásonyi, KÖA 130, Anthr. 145); II. 'True-blue, strong, steady' nearly the same as Latin „Constantinus" (Gombocz, ÁTSz. 28).

TEPSE Kuman 1521 **Tepse** [Osvaldo Thepse], from Greater Kumania, Hungary (Gyárfás III, 754). ✧ I. '(Small) tray' (Rásonyi, KÖA 130, Anthr. 145), cf. Kuman, Chag., Crm., Turk. *täpsi* 'kleine Schüssel, Teller' (Radl. III, 1116); II. 'Saddle-pad'? cf. Mad. *täpsä* 'das Sattelkissen' (Radl. III, 1115).

TEPSİN Kzk. 19th c. **Tepsin?** [Тепсонъ] (AOO 14).

TER Tuv. 19th c. **Ter-χan** [Терь-ханъ] (Potanin IV, 375-381). See also **AYT-TER, DÖWLET-TER.**

TER-BERDİ see **TERE-BERDİ**

TER-MAMET Tat.(Sib.) 1632 **Ter-mamet** [Термамет Колватов] (Miller, Ist. Sib. II, 391). ✧ 'Live Mukhammed'. ⇨ **TERE + MAMET.**

TERBİ Uyg. **Tärbi-inal** [Tärbi-İnal] (EUTS); Uyg. 12th c. - 14th c. **Terbi-ïnal / Terbi-inäl** (DTS). ✧ 'Terbi-(the)-high-born' (Blagova 1997, 710).

TERBUS Trkm. 1690 **Terbus** [تربوس اوغلو محمد قزق] (Iyās I,

/ Kızık Mehmedoğlu Terbus], from Anatolia (Refik, Anad. 83).

TERJÜMAN   Yürük 1543 **Terjüman** [Tercüman] (Gökb., Rum. 225). ✧ 'Interpreter' cf. Turk. *tärjüman* 'der Uebersetzer, der Dragoman' (Radl. III, 1074).

TERDEY   Tat.(Sib.) 1632 **Terdey** [Тердей Ишеев] (Miller, Ist. Sib. II, 397).

TERÄK   Uyg. **Täräk** [Täräk] (EUTS); Chuv. 18th-19th c. **Terek** [Терекъ] (Magn. 81); Kzk. 19th c. **Terek-pay** [Терекпай] (AOP 26); Kzk. 19th c. **Terek-pay** [Терекпай] (SODž. 54); Kzk. 19th c. **Terek-pay** [Терекпай] (SOV 116). ✧ 'Poplar', in OT considered a sacred tree (Sattarov); cf. Karakh. *teräk* 'тополь' (DTS), Kuman, Chag., Alt., Shor *täräk* 'die Pappel' (Radl. III, 1061), Hak.(Sag., Koyb.), Kirg., Kzk. *teräk* 'die Pappel' (Radl. III, 1062), Kzk. *terek* 'тополь, дерево' (KzRS), Bashk., Tat. *tiräk* 'тополь' (BRS/Uraksin, TatRS). See also **AY-TERÄK, BAY-TERÄK, BOZ-TEREK, İŠ-TERÄK, YABDU-TERÄK, YAŠ-TERÄK, ŠAY-TEREK.**

TERÄKÄY   Bashk. 1740 **Teräkäy** [Мемедели Тракаев] (MIB I, 383); Chuv. 18th-19th c. **Terekey** [Терекей] (Magn. 81); Alt. 19th-20th c. **Terekey** [Терекей] (OjrRS 210); Tat. 1729 **Tirekey** [Резяп Тирекеев] (MIB III, 266). ✧ 'Little poplar; Little healthy (child)'. ⇨ **TERÄK** + dim. suff. *-ey*.

TERÄNČİ see **TÄRÄNČÄ**

TERE   Kzk. 19th c. **Tere-bay** [Теребай] (SOK 84, 118, 120); Kzk. 19th c. **Tere-bay** [Теребай] (SOV 158); Tat. 1620 **Tere-ɣul** [Турсунбай Терегуловъ] (Kurdjumov 121); Tat. 1777 **Tere-ɣul** [Терегулов Илбек] (MIB V, 60); Bashk. 1776 **Tere-ɣul** [Терегул Казанбаев] (MIB V, 33, 64, 80); Tat. 1547 **Tere-ul** [Тереулъ] (PSRL XIII, 149); Bashk. 1763 **Teri-ɣul** [Térigoulof], envoy to the Middle Horde (Orta Žüz) (Levchine 245); OT **Tiri** [Tiri] (EUTS); Kuman 1183, 1185 **Tiri** / **Tiriy** [Глѣбъ Тиріевичъ / Глѣбъ Тирьевич], a prince (Ipat. 424 / 437/, Lavr. 375 /267/, Bask., Im. polov. 74). ✧ 'Live, healthy, lively; alive' cf. Türk, Uyg., Karakh. *tirig* 'живой' (TDS), Kuman, Kzk., Kar. *tiri* 'lebendig, lebend, belebt' (Radl. III, 1367), Tat., Bashk. *tere* 'живой' (TatRS, BRS), also Tat. PN *Tere* (Sattarov).

TERE-BERDİ   Bashk. 1779 **Ter-berdi** / **Ter-berdiy?** [Тербердиев] (MIB V, 83); Tat. 1724 **Tiri-berde** / **Tiri-berdey?** [Кошай Тирибердеев] (MIB III, 228). ✧ 'Live-given; born alive/healthy'. ⇨ **TERE** + **BERDİ.**

TERE-GİLDİ   Kzk. 19th c. **Tere-gildi** [Терегильди] (AOO 6). ✧ '(He/she) came alive / was born alive'. ⇨ **TERE** + **KELDİ.**

TERE-KERELTİ   Alt. 19th c. **Tere-kerelti** [Тере Керельты] (Verb., In. 104). ⇨ **TERE.**

TEREYENČİ   Hak. 19th-20th c. **Tereyenči?** / **Terēnči?** [Тереенчі] (HRS 351).

TEREKEY see **TERÄKÄY**

TEREMKA   Chuv. 18th-19th c. **Teremka** [Теремка] (Magn. 81).

TERENČA see **TÄRÄNČÄ**

TERENDEY   Chuv. 1738 **Terendey** [Терендѣевъ] (Alatyr. 137).

TERES see **TİRİS**

TERGEY   Bashk. 1717 **Tergey** [Мокша Тергеев] (MIB III, 152). ⇨ **TEREKEY?**

TERGEW   Kzk. 19th c. **Tergew** [Тергеу / Терчеу] (SOK 66, 128). ✧ 'Searching, questing' cf. Kzk. *tergäü* 'die Untersuchung, die Erforschung' (Radl. III, 1070).

TERGEWSİZ   Kzk. 19th c. **Tergewsis** [Тергеусысъ] (SODž. 6, 128); Kzk. 19th c. **Tergewsis** [Тергеусысъ] (SOV 16); Kzk. 19th c. **Tergewsiz** [Тергеусызъ] (SOV 130). ✧ 'Without searching, questing'. ⇨ **TERGEW** + suff. *-siz.*

TERGİN   Alt. 19th-20th c. **Tergin** [Тергин], fem. (OjrRS 213).

TERGİŠ   Alt. 19th-20th c. **Tergiš** [Тергиш] (OjrRS 210). ✧ 'Basket' cf. Alt. *tergiš* 'корзина, кузов' (OjrRS). See also **QAŠTAQ.**

TERGÜG see **EL-TERGÜG**

TERİ I.   Kzk. 19th c. **Teri-bay** [Терибай] (SOV 136). ✧ 'Leather' cf. Kzk. *teri* 'die Haut, das Leder, das Fell' (Radl. III, 1065).

TERİ II.   Alt. 19th-20th c. **Teri** [Тери] (OjrRS 210).

TERİ-BAŠ   Karg. **Tärï-päš** [Täpi-пäш] (Proben IX, 637); Karg. 19th-20th c. **Teri-baš** [Терибашъ] (Katanov: ZIRGOÊtn. XVII, vyp. III, 167). ⇨ **TERİ I.** / **TERİ II. ? + BAŠ.**

TERİ-ŽAL   Kzk. 19th c. **Teri-žal** [Терыжалъ] (AOK 30). ⇨ **TERİ** + **YAL I.**

TERİG   Bashk. 1712, 1713 **Terig** [Тергов Килеев] (MIB III, 84, 98); Bashk. 1730 **Terig** [Алей Тергов(ов)?] (MIB III, 277). ✧ 'Healthy, sound' cf. Tat. PN *Terek* (Sattarov). ⇨ **TİRİG.**

TERİKEY   Bashk. 1715 **Terikey** [Салтан Терикеев] (MIB III, 123); Kzk. 19th c. **Terkey** [Теркей] (AOK 114). ⇨ **TİRİ** + suff. *-key.*

TERİM   Uyg. 1339 **Tärim**, fem. (Chwol., Syr.-nest. (NF) 35); Uyg. 12th c. - 14th c. **Tärim-bäg** / **Tarïm-bäg** [Tärim Bäg / Tarïm Bäg] (Radl., USp. 201, 209); Uyg. 1286 **Terim** [Terim chinesin], the Uyghur name of a Chinese (Chwol., Syr.-nest. (NF) 11). ✧ 'Highborn (noble) woman (title)' (Thúry, Behdset), used as a secondary component (comp.) of female names; it probably originates from *teñrim* 'id.' (Clauson).

TERİW   Kzk. 19th c. **Teriw-bay** [Териу бай] (SOK 14).

TERKEY see **TERİKEY**

TERKEN   Khorezm. 13th c. **Terken** [ترکان], J̌elāleddīn Meñgü-berdi's daughter (J̌uwaynī II, 201); Maml.?

1352/53 **Terken** [کاتون ترکان], Toq-tay emir's daughter, died in 1352/53 (Berchem, Jér. I, 273); Chag. 16th c. **Terken** [Туркан], fem. (Ivanov 109); Oghuz 12th c. **Terken / Turqan?** [Туркан], İl-arslan's (1156-1172) wife, Sultan-šah's (1172-1193) mother (MIT I, 445, Ǧuw. II, 17, Qazw. 491, 492); Khorezm. 14th c. **Terken-aγa / Qutluγ-terken-aγa** [Kutlug Turkan Aga / Кутлуг-Туркан-ага], Aqsaq-temür's (1370-1405) sister (Barth., Ulugb. 16, 18, 116, MIT I, 520); Oghuz 11th c. **Terken-χatun** [خاتون ترکان], Baraq-χaǰib's daughter, wife (or mother?) of Qutbeddīn Sultan Muhammed I (1098-1128) (Ǧuwaynī II, 217); Selj. 1092 **Terken-χatun** [خاتون ترکان / Tûrkân Khâtûn / Turcâr-Khatun / Türkân Hatun / Terken hatun], Sultan Melik-šah's (1072-1092) wife, *Abïš-χatun* in other sources; „she was descended from 'Apdâsyâb, the first king of the Huns. Her father was Tapragh, king of the Khazârâyê" (Abulfaraǰ) (Rāwandī 132, 133 etc., Abulfar./Budge I, 232, Ahbar 51, Ibn al-Athīr, Atab.: RHCHor II/2, 24, RaD/Erdmann 801, O. Turan: Türk Hukuk Mecm. I, Toğan, UTT 198, 432, Sevim-Yücel 69); Selj. 12th c. **Terken-χatun** [خاتون ترکان / Terken], İl-arslan's (1156-1172) daughter (?), Sultan Sanǰar's (1118-1157) wife (Rāwandī 174, Ahbar 64, 66); Khorezm. 13th c. **Terken-χatun** [خاتون ترکان], wife of the Khorezmshah Muhammed II (ibn Tekiš, 1200-1220) (Ǧuwaynī II, 72, 81, 90 etc.); Chag. 16th c. **Terken-χatun** [Туркан-хатун], fem. (Ivanov 313); Oghuz 11th c. **Terken-χatun / Turqan-χatun?** [خاتون ترکان / Туркан-хатун], from the Bayat (Bayaut) tribe, the wife of the Khorezmshah Muhammed I (1098-1128) (Ǧuwaynī I, 65, 97, MIT I, 449, 471, 486, 504); Khorezm.? 13th c. **Terken-χatun / Uluγ-terken-χatun** [خاتون ترکان], her byname was *Uluγ* (Great) (Nasawī 25, 42); Khorezm. 1220 **Terken-sultan** [سلطان ترکان], daughter of Muhammed II (1200-1220), Türk'ān-χatun's grand-daughter (Nasawī 41); Oghuz? 11th c. **Terken-šah** [Turkān-šāh / Туркан-шах], the Ghaznavid Ibrahim's (1058--1099) son (RaD I/2, 103, Justi 330). ✧ I. 'Princess' (Erol); II. 'Beautiful girl' (Erol), III. 'Governor of a county (title)' cf. Karakh. *terkän / terkin* 'титул, даваемый правителям областей' (DTS), *tärkän* 'ein Titel' (TMEN II, 889); IV. 'Cart' cf. Mo. *terken* 'телега' (RaD/Ber. I, 298), Karakh. *tergän* 'id.' (DTS). Earlier the name was interpreted as *Türk'ān* which proved to be false (cf. O. Turan, Türkân Değil, Terken: Türk Hukuk Dergisi I, Ankara, 1944). See also **İLEK-TÜRK'ĀN, ÖGÄ-TERKEN, SALAR-TÜRK'ĀN, TUΓA-TERKEN.**

TERKEN-ARLAT Khorezm.? 1375 **Terken-arlat** [Turkán Arlát / Туркен-арлат], Aqsaq-temür's enemy (Tar. Rashidi 43-45, MIT I, 817). ⇨ **TERKEN + Ethnonym.**

TERLEN Kzk. 19th c. **Terlen-bay** [Терленбай] (SOK 244).

TERLİK Kzk. 19th c. **Terlik** [Терликъ] (SODž. 116); Kzk. 19th c. **Terlik** [Терлыкъ] (SOK 108); Kzk. 19th c. **Terlik-pay** [Терлыкпай] (SODž. 78); Kzk. 19th c. **Terlik-pay** [Терликпай] (SOK 70, 118); Kzk. 19th c. **Terlik-pay** [Терликпай] (SOV 22, 24, 36, 54); Kzk. 19th c. **Terlik-pay** [Терлыкпай] (SOV 50); Kzk. 19th c. **Tirlik-bay** [Тирликбай] (Grod., Pril. 142). ✧ 'A sheet of felt under the saddle-cover' cf. Kzk. *terlik* 'die Filzdecke unter der Schabracke' (Radl. III, 1072), Kzk. *terlĭk* 'потник' (KzRS).

TERMİ-YAQŠİ Bashk. 1780 **Termi-yaqši** [Термы Якши Рахмангулов] (MIB V, 116). ⇨ **? + YAQŠİ.**

TERMİŠ Tat. 1742-48 **Termiš** [Термишевъ], from Cheboksary (IOAIÊK XIV, 539).

TERMİŽEK Alt. 19th-20th c. **Termižek** [Термижек], fem. (OjrRS 213).

TERPEY Hak. 19th-20th c. **Terpey** [Терпей], fem. (HRS 355).

TERS-UZAMÏŠ Oghuz/Trkm. 14th c. - 15th c. **Ters-uzamïš** [Ters Uzamïš / Терс-Узамыш], Oghuz cavalryman (DQorq./Rossi 170, 211, DQorq. 89, 105, 238, 241). ✧ 'Spread inversely' (Kononov: „протянувшийся наизнанку, навыворот"), cf. Kuman, Chag., Alt., Turk. *tärs* 'verquer, umgekehrt, feindlich, widrig' (Radl. III, 1075), Chag., Alt., Az., Turk. etc. *uza-* 'lange währen, sich ausdehnen' (Radl. I, 1755).

TERSÄK Tat.(Sib.) 1648 **Tersäk** [Денмет Терсяк] (Miller, Ist. Sib. II, 527). ✧ 'Supporter, helper' (Sattarov), cf. Tat. *tersäk* 'локоть' (TatRS).

TERSE Kzk. 19th c. **Terse-bay** [Терсебай] (SODž. 40).

TERSTÄN Kzk. **Terstän-bala** [Terstän Bala / Терстäн Бала], a tribe (Proben III, 48 /63/).

TES-BULAQ Kzk. 19th c. **Tes-bulaq** [Тесбулакъ] (SOK 256). ⇨ **TEZ + BULAQ.**

TESÄK-TURMÏŠ Uyg. 12th c. - 14th c. **Tesäk-turmïš** [tesäk turmïš] (DTS). ✧ 'Peat/turf-Stayed (was born)'? (Blagova 1997, 713). ⇨ **TÄSÄK / TEZEK? + TURMÏŠ.**

TESİKİ-ARA Uyg. 12th c. - 14th c. **Tesiki-ara** (DTS).

TESTİK Kzk. 19th c. **Testik-pay** [Тестыкпай] (SOK 192).

TEŠE Kirg. 20th c. **Teše-bay** [Тешебай], in Southern Kirghizia (Kalilov 92). ✧ 'Axe (a special kind of axe)' (Kalilov 92). See also **BALTA, BALTU, KESER, TEBER.**

TEŠTER Alt. 19th-20th c. **Tešter** [Тештер] (OjrRS 210).

TETAR Nog. **Tetar / Toχtar? / Tatar?** [Тетар Мурза (Тохтар)] (Žirm., Epos 430).

TETÄ Crm. 1549 **Tetä** [Тетя] (PSRL (Russk. Hr.) I,

530). ✧ 'The next (child)' cf. Kzk. *tetä* 'der folgende' (Radl. III, 1091).

TETÄK Tat.(GH) 1380 **Tetäk** [Тетякъ / Ентякъ], byname(?) of Mamay-χan, ruler of the Golden Horde (PSRL VI, 94, VIII, 38, XI, 64).

TETÄK-YEDİ Crm. 1537 **Tetäk-yedi-ulan / Tetäk-edi-ulan?** [Тетякъ-Еди-уланъ] (PSRL XIII, 115). ⇨ **TETÄK.**

TETEY Tat. 1624 **Tetäy** [Тетяй Тенишевъ] (Zolotn. 159); Tat. 1624 **Tetey** [Тетей Тахтамышевъ] (Pokrovskij 71); Bashk. 1664 **Tetey** [Абезайко Тетеев] (MIB I, 193); Bashk. 1734 **Tetey** [Апасъ Тетѣевъ] (PSZRI IX, 336). ✧ 'Elder sister' cf. Tat. *tätäi* 'die ältere Schwester' (Radl. III, 1092). See also **TÜTÄY.**

TETEYKE Chuv. 1728 **Teteyke** [Тетейке Теникешев] (MIB I, 128). ✧ 'Dear little sister'. ⇨ **TETEY** + suff. *-ke.*

TETELČİ Bashk. 1740 **Tetelči** [Тетелчи Тляубердин] (MIB I, 395).

TETEMİK Kzk. 19th c. **Tetemik** [Тетемикъ] (AOP 50).

TETEŠ-BULAQ Tat.(Tob.) 1643 **Teteš-bulaq** [Тетеш Булак] (Miller, Ist. Sib. II, 486). ⇨ **? + BULAQ.**

TETİY Kuman 1185 **Tetiy** [Тѣтий] (Lavr. 375). ✧ 'The next, the younger (child)' (Bask., Im. polov. 74). ⇨ **TETÄ** + dim. suff. *-y.*

TETİK Maml. 1340 **Tetik** [تتك بن شَيْخُو] (Zetterst. 206); Bashk. 1664 **Tetik** [Тетик] (MIB I, 193); Kzk. 19th c. **Tetük-pay** [Тетукпай] (SOK 214); Karakh.? 870 **Titek / Tetik?** [تيتك], slave-soldier (gulām) of Abu Nasr (Tabarī, Annal. III, 1826). ✧ 'Quick, sharp-witted, clever' cf. Kuman, Chag. *tätik* 'flink, schnell; scharfsinnig, klug, einsichtsvoll' (Radl. III, 1092).

TETİMBET Kzk. 19th c. **Tetimbet** [Тетимбетъ] (Lomakin 32).

TETİZ Kzk. 19th c. **Tetiz-bay** [Тетзбай] (SOK 116).

TETLÄYİN-BERDEY-DUWAN Crm. **Tetläyin-berdey-duwan** [Тетлаинъ-Бердѣй-Дуванъ], envoy from the Crimea (PSRL XII, 259). ⇨ **? + BERDİ + DUWAN.**

TETMİLİK Uyg. 12th c. - 14th c. **Tetmilik-qara-buqa** [Tädmilig] (Radl., USp. 21-23, Le Coq, Urkunden 458-59, DTS). ✧ '?-Black-Bull'. ⇨ **QARA + BUQA.**

TETÜY Hak.(Kacha) 1636 **Tetüy / Tütey?** [Тетюйко / Тютей] (Miller, Ist. Sib. II, 439). ⇨ **TETİY?**

TETÜK see **TETİK**

TEVER Chuv. 1771 **Tever-bi** [Теверби], fem. (MIB IV/1, 361).

TEWEY see **TEVEY**

TEWEK Bashk. 1710 **Tewek** [Елкычюра Тевеков] (MIB III, 66); Bashk. 1710 **Tewek** [Елкы чюра Тевеков] (MIB III, 66); Bashk. 1756 **Tewek** [Селкей Тевеков] (MIB IV/1, 128).

TEWEKEY Bashk. 1735 **Tewekey** [Сююндюкъ Тевекеевъ], a tarχan (Vel.-Zern., Bašk. 23); Bashk. 1735 **Tewekey** [/ Тевкабылъ Тевекеевъ], a tarχan (Vel.-Zern., Bašk. 23); Bashk. 1756 **Tewekey** [Мангутай Тевекеев] (MIB IV/1, 123).

TEWEL Tat. **Tewel-baqši** [Тевель-бокшей], envoy from Kazan (PSRL VIII, 271).

TEWEN Bashk. 1722 **Tewen** [Тевень] (MIB I, 120); Bashk. 1762 **Tewen** [Тевень Бугазиев] (MIB IV/1, 233). ✧ 'Strength, power' (P.) cf. Tat. *Täwan* (Sattarov).

TEWENEY Bashk. 1762 **Tewen** [Кузяк Товенеев] (MIB IV/1, 233); Bashk. 1663 **Teweney** [Тевеней Девлембаев] (MIB I, 176); Bashk. 1738 **Teweney** [Тевеней Урсаев] (MIB III, 387). ⇨ **TEWEN** + dim. suff. *-ey.*

TEWKİ 1674 **Tewki-qan** [Тевкиканъ], a khan of Turkestan (DAI VI, 294, X, 375-390). ⇨ **TÄWGE?, TÄWKÄ.**

TEZ Bashk. 1714 **Tez-bay** [Тезбай] (MIB I, 105). ✧ 'Quick' cf. Kzk. *tez* 'schnell, plötzlich, unerwartet' (Radl. III, 1102). See also **AY-TES, BAY-TEZ.**

TEZ-BULA Turk. 16th c. **Tez-bula** [Tezbula], fem. (Ongan, Ank. II.); Turk. 1583 **Tez-bula** [تـزبو له / Tezbula], fem. (Ongan, Ank. I, 178). ⇨ **TEZ + BULA.**

TEZEK Kzk. 19th c. **Tezäk-bay** [Тезакбай] (Grod., Pril. 172); Kzk. 18th c. **Tezek** [Тезекъ] (Nepljuev 752); Kzk. 19th c. **Tezek** [Tezek] (AUK 159); Kzk. 19th c. **Tezek** [Тезекъ] (SODž. 38); Kzk. 19th c. **Tezek** [Тезекъ] (SOK 244); Kzk. 19th c. **Tezek-bay** [Тезекбай] (AOA 10, 58, 134); Kzk. 19th c. **Tezek-bay** [Тезекбай] (AOK 114); Kzk. 19th c. **Tezek-bay** [Тезекбай] (AOO 42); Kzk. 19th c. **Tezek-bay** [Тезекбай] (SOK 132); Kzk. 19th c. **Tezek-pay** [Тезекпай] (AOAtb. 50); Kzk. 19th c. **Tezek-pay** [Тезекпай] (AOO 22); Kzk. 19th c. **Tezek-pay** [Тезекпай] (Konšin, Oč. 94); Kzk. 19th c. **Tezek-pay** [Тезекпай] (SODž. 64); Kzk. 19th c. **Tezek-pay** [Тезекпай] (SOK 82, 106, 180, 232); Kzk. 19th c. **Tezek-pay** [Тезекпай] (SOV 14, 44, 50, 98). ✧ 'Peat, turf' cf. Chag., Alt., Az., Crm., Hak., etc. *täzäk* 'der trockene Mist, der Mist', Kirg., Kzk. *tezäk* 'id.' (Radl. III, 1103).

TEZGENČ Kuman 1284, 1322 **Tezgenč / Teskenč** [Tescench quidam alter Cumanus frater oredicti Kuchmeg / Biter filius Teschench] (ÁÚO IX, 105, Gyárfás III, 462, 463). ✧ 'Turn, spinning round' cf. Kuman *tezgin-* 'sich drehen' (CC), see also Melich, HM, 202, Gombocz: MNy.XI, 151, Gombocz, ÁTSz. 31, Rásonyi, KÖA 130, Rásonyi, Anthr. 145 + suff. *-č.*

TİBA Chuv. 19th c. **Tiba-χan** [Tibachan] (Kronheim 96).

TİBČON Hak. 19th-20th c. **Tibčon** [Тибчон], fem. (HRS 355).

TİBÄS Hak.(Blt.) 19th-20th c. **Tibäs** [Тібäс] (Proben IX, 548).

TİBEK Kzk. 19th c. **Tibek-pay** [Тибекпай] (SOK 120).

TİBERİK Kzk. 19th c. **Tiberik / Tïbirïq?** [Тыберыкъ] (SOK 142).

TİBİN Uyg. 12th c. - 14th c. **Tibin** [Tibin] (Radl., USp. 131-132, DTS, EUTS).

TİBRÄNŠİ-QOTÏČ Uyg. 12th c. - 14th c. **Tibränši-qotïč** (Radl., USp. 120, DTS).

TİJAY Kzk. 19th c. **TiJay / TiJäy?** [Кусанъ Тиджаевъ] (Grod., Pril. 95).

TİÄXÄN Yak. **Tiäχän** [Тіäхäн] (Pek.). ✧ Tihon (R.) (Pek.).

TİGÄN Bashk. 1718 **Tigän** [Азикей Тиганов] (MIB III, 179, 180); Oghuz/Trkm. **Tigän? / Tikin?** [تيكان / Tekân], an Oghuzid (Abulg./Rom. 18, Abulg./Desm. 28). ⇨ **TİKÄN?**

TİGİN see **TEGİN**

TİGİN-QURUQ Uyg. **Tigin-quruq** [Tigin Quruq] (Zieme, Mat. I, 75). ✧ 'Prince-empty' (Zieme: 'Prinz-Leer'). ⇨ **TEGİN + QURUQ.**

TİGTİ Kzk. 19th c. **Tigti-bay** [Тигтыбай] (SODž. 58). ✧ I. 'Leather/felt sack' cf. Chag. *tigdi* 'ein Sack aus Leder oder aus Filz' (Radl. III, 1355); II. 'Felt shoes' cf. Chag. *tikti* 'Filzschuhe' (Radl. III, 1351).

TİGÜ Uyg. **Tigü** [Tigü] (EUTS).

TİX-TEMİR see **TİK-TEMİR**

TİYEN Bashk. 1742 **Tiyim-bay** [Тиим-бай Иткинин] (MIB I, 486); Kzk. 19th c. **Tiyim-bay (<Tiyin-bay)** [Тiембай] (SODž. 58); Hak.(Blt.) 19th-20th c. **Tïn** [Тін] (Katanov, Otč. 9). ✧ 'Squirrel' cf. Kzk. *tiyïn* 'белка' (KzRS), Tat. *tiyen* 'id.' (TatRS), Bashk. *teyen* 'id.' (BRS/Uraksin), Uyg., Kuman, Chag., Hak. *tïn* 'das Eichhörnchen' (Radl. III, 1360). See also **ČAQČAQ, SAQÏL, SANZÄP.**

TİYİK Bashk. 1740 **Tiyik-bay** [Тиикбай] (MIB I, 404).

TİYİM-BAY see **TİYEN**

TİYİŠ Bashk. 1735 **Tiyiš** [Тиишъ Беккуловъ], a tarχan (Vel.-Zern., Bašk. 19); Kzk. 19th c. **Tiyiš-bay** [Тиишбай] (AOP 82).

TİYTİ Kzk. 19th c. **Tiyti** [Тийте] (AOP 86).

TİK see **TEK**

TİK-MİYÜZ Kzk. 1803, 1820 **Tik-miyüz / Tik-miyüs** [Тикмиюз / Тикмiюсъ], a leader of the Alim-ulï tribe of Little Horde (Kiši Žüz) (MIK IV, 514, Sib. Vest. IX, 115). ✧ 'Straight horn' cf. Kuman, Chag., Kirg., Kzk. *tik* 'aufrechtstehend, gerade, steil; klar, offen' (Radl. III, 1347). ⇨ **MİYÜZ.**

TİK-TEMİR see **TEK-TEMÜR**

TİKÄ Kzk. 19th c. **Tikä-bay** [Тикабай] (Grod., Pril. 131). ✧ 'A small piece'? cf. Az., East.T., Kirg., Turk. *tikä* 'ein kleines Stückchen' (Radl. III, 1349).

TİKÄY Chuv. 1737 **Tikäy** [Тикѣевъ] (Alatyr. 135).

TİKÄR Kzk. 19th c. **Tikär** [Тикаръ] (Grod., Pril. 171).

TİKEY Kzk. 19th c. **Tikey** [Тыкей] (AOAtb. 58). ✧ 'Straight, right (man)' cf. Kzk. *tike* 'прямой' (KzRS) + dim. suff. -*y*.

TİKEN Bashk. 1709 **Tekän** [Илик Текянов] (MIB III, 49); Kzk. 19th c. **Teken** [Текенъ] (AOP 122); Kzk. 19th c. **Tiken** [Тыкенъ] (SOK 194). ✧ 'Thorn' cf. Chag., East.T., Kzk. *tikän* 'der Dorn, der Strauch mit Dornen' (Radl. III, 1349) 'Thorn' cf. Uyg., Karakh. *tikän* 'шип, колючка' (DTS), Chag., East.T., Kzk. *tikän* 'der Dorn, der Strauch mit Dornen' (Radl. III, 1349), cf. *dikän* 'der Dorn, die Nadel' (Radl. III, 1753). See also **AQ-TİKEN, QARA-DİKEN.**

TİKİN see **TEGİN**

TİKİS Kzk. 19th c. **Tikis-bay** [Тикисбай] (Grod., Pril. 25).

TİL Kzk. 19th c. **Til-äkä?** [Тилакинъ] (Grod., Pril. 98); Chag. 16th c. **Til-χoJa** [Тиль-ходжа] (Ivanov 154, 157); Kzk. 1863 **Til-χoJa-batïr** [Тиль-ходжа-батыръ] (Smirnov, Sultany 32-33); Chuv. 18th-19th c. **Til-murza** [Тилмурза] (Magn. 82); Kzk. 19th c. **Til-žan** [Тильжанъ] (AOO 14); Chuv. 18th-19th c. **Tïl-bay** [Тылбай] (Magn. 87); Kzk. / Uzb.? 19th c. **Tïl-bek** [Тылбековъ] (SKSO III, 19). ✧ 'Language; tongue' cf. Uyg., Kuman, Chag., Alt., Hak., Kirg., Kzk., etc. *til* 'die Zunge, die Sprache' (Radl. III, 1379).

TİL-AXMED Kzk. 19th c. **Til-aχmed** [Тилъ-Ахмедъ] (Grod., Pril. 83); Kzk. 19th c. **Tïl-aχmed** [Тыльахметъ] (SODž. 14). ⇨ **DİL + AXMED.**

TİL-AMAN Kzk. 19th c. **Til-aman** [Иставлетъ Тиламановъ] (Grod., Pril. 66). ⇨ **TİL + AMAN?**

TİL-QUZÏ see **TEL-ГOZÏ**

TİL-MAMBET see **TEL-MAMBET**

TİLDİ Bashk. 1664 **Tildi-ɣul** [Игибайко Тилдигулов] (MIB I, 192); Kzk. 19th c. **Tilti-bay / Tïltï-bay?** [Тылтыбай] (AOP 62). ⇨ **DİLDİ?**

TİLÄ Kzk. 1734 **Telä-bi / Telä-biy** [Телябiй / Теляби] (PSZRI IX, 303, Nepljuev 721, 722); Kirg. 18th c. **Telä-biy** [Телябiй] (Nepljuev 721, 722); Kzk. 19th c. **Tilä-bay** [Авизъ Тилабаевъ] (Grod., Pril. 98); NUyg. 19th c. **Tilä-bay** [Tila Bai], a pony-man (Stein 257, 424); Uzb. 19th c. **Tilä-qul** [Тилякулъ] (SKSO III, 182). ✧ 'Please!, Wish!' cf. Türk, Uyg., Kuman, Chag., Hak., Kzk. *tilä-* 'bitten, wünschen, wollen' (Radl. III, 1381), Bashk. *telä-* 'желать, хотеть' (BRS), Kzk. *tile-/tïle-* 'желать, просить' (KzRS), Uzb. *tilä-* 'желать, просить, клянчить' (UzbRS).

TİLÄB-BAY see **TİLÄP**

TİLÄB-BERGÄN see **TİLEP-BERGEN**

TİLÄGÄN see **TİLEGEN**

TİLÄY see **AYГU-TİLÄY**

TİLÄN Kzk. 19th c. **Telen** [Теленъ] (AOAtb. 38); Alt. **Tilän-qō** [Тиланъ-коо], fem. (Nikiforov 174, 175). ✧

'Wish (for yourself); scrounge!' cf. Türk, Hak.(Sag.), Chag., Kzk. *tilän*- 'für sich bitten, für sich wünschen, betteln' (Radl. III, 1383), Kzk. *tĭlen*- 'id.' (KzRS).

TİLÄNČÄ see **TİLENČİ**
TİLÄNČİ see **TİLENČİ**
TİLÄNŠİ see **TİLENČİ**

TİLÄP   Uzb. 20th c. **Tiläb** [Тилаб] (Begmatov 1984, 204); Kzk. 19th c. **Tiläb-bay** [Тилаббай] (Grod., Pril. 53); Uzb. 20th c. **Tiläb-ĵân** [Тилабжон] (Begmatov 1984, 204); Uzb. 20th c. **Tiläb-χoĵa** [Тилабхўжа] (Begmatov 1984, 204); Uzb. 20th c. **Tiläb-qul** [Тилабкул] (Begmatov 1984, 204); Uzb. 20th c. **Tiläp-bây** [Тилаббой] (Begmatov 1984, 204); Kzk. 19th c. **Tilep** [Телеповъ] (AOO 50); Kzk. 19th c. **Tilep** [Телепъ] (SOK 194); Tat. 1783 **Tläp** [Тляп Каныбеков] (MIB V, 138); Bashk. 1731 **Tläp** [Тляп Кусякеев] (MIB III, 287); Bashk. 1763 **Tläp** [Тляп Тюркеев] (MIB IV/1, 273); Bashk. 1789 **Tläp** [Тляп Тайгунов] (MIB V, 241, 320); Bashk. 1789 **Tläp** [Тляп Тайгунов] (MIB V, 241, 320); Kzk. 1714 **Tlep-biy** (<Tilep-biy) [تلاب بی / Тлеп бий] (MIK IV, 159). ✧ 'Wished / wishing' cf. Bashk. *teläp* 'охотно, с охотой' (BRS). ⇨ TİLÄ.

TİLÄP-BERDİ   Uzb. 20th c. **Tiläb-berdi** [Тилабберди] (Begmatov 1984, 202); Bashk. 1740 **Tläb-berdi** [Бикмен Тляббердин] (MIB I, 379); Bashk. 1693 **Tlep-perde** [Тяпариско Тлепердеевъ], a tarχan (Vel.-Zern., Bašk. 34). ✧ 'Wished-given'. ⇨ TİLÄP + BERDİ. See also TİLEP-BERGEN.

TİLÄP-QURBAS   Kzk. 1793 **Tiläp-qurbas-uγlï** [تیلاب قورباس اوغلی] (MIK IV, 147, 150, 168, 170, 201). ⇨ TİLÄP.

TİLÄS see **TİLÄŠ**

TİLÄŠ   Bashk. 1725 **Teläs** [Улмас Телясев] (MIB III, 235); Bashk. 1707, 1729 **Teles** [Рыс Телесев] (MIB III, 34, 270); Tat.? 1535 **Teleš** [Телешъ-богатырь], a messenger (PSRL XIII, 96); Kzk. 19th c. **Teleš** [Телешъ] (SOV 60); Tuv. 19th c. **Teleš** [Телешъ] (Potanin IV, 207); Tat.(Mish.) 19th c. **Teleš-murza** [Teleš murza Kut(t)eĭĕf] (Pelissier 27); Kzk. 19th c. **Tiläs** [Джигабай Тиласовъ] (Grod., Pril. 185); Kzk. 19th c. **Tiläs-bay** [Садабай Тиласбаевъ] (Grod., Pril. 113); Tat.(Lit.) 1548 **Tiläš** [Тилешъ] (Kn. Metriki Lit. 44); Tat. 1784/85 **Tiläš** [تلاش / Тиляш] (Jusupov 76); Tat.(Sib.) 1632 **Tiläš** [Исенгул Тлешев] (Miller, Ist. Sib. II, 397); Kzk. 19th c. **Tiläš** [Тилашъ], fem. (Grod., Pril. 28); Kzk. 19th c. **Tiläš** [Тилашъ], fem. (Grod., Pril. 28); Kzk. 19th c. **Tiläš-bay** [Тилашбаевъ] (Grod., Pril. 166); Kzk. 19th c. **Tileš** [Тылешъ] (SOK 264); Kzk. 1808 **Tläs** [Тляс] (MIK IV, 240); Kzk. 1846 **Tläs-bay** [Тлясбай Миндибаев], a biy (MKOP 154); Tat. 1640 **Tläš** [Авес Тлешев] (Miller, Ist. Sib. II, 467, 470); Bashk. 1695 **Tläš** [Исенгул Тлешев] (MIB I,

90); Bashk. 1780 **Tläš** [Тлеш Мустаев] (MIB V, 109); Kzk. 18th c. - 19th c. **Tles** [Тлес] (Tynyšp. 68, 73); Kzk. 19th c. **Tles-pay** [Тлеспай] (AOP 42); Kzk. 19th c. **Tles-pay** [Тлеспай] (SOK 40); Kzk. 19th c. **Tleš** [Тлешъ] (SOV 16); *TN:* Tat. 1739 **Teleš(eva)** [Телешева], a village (Alatyr. 144). ✧ 'Wished-awaited (child)' (Sattarov), cf. Türk., Uyg., Kuman, Chag., Hak., Kzk. *tilä*- 'bitten, suchen, wünschen' (Radl. III, 1381), Tat. *telä*- 'желать, хотеть' (TatRS), Bashk. *telä*- 'id.' (BRS/Uraksin) + dev. suff. *-s(2)*. See also AY-TELÄŠ, BAY-TELES, BAY-TİLÄŠ, YAN-TELÄŠ.

TİLÄW   Kzk. **Teläü** [Теляỹ] (Proben III, 230 /272/, etc.); Kzk. 19th c. **Teleü** [Телеу] (AOK 90); Kzk. 19th c. **Teleü** [Телеу] (SODž. 128); Kzk. 19th c. **Teleü** [Телеу] (SOV 44); Kzk. 19th c. **Teleü-bay** [Телеубай] (SOK 162); Uzb. 20th c. **Tilâw** [Тилов] (Begmatov 1984, 204); Uzb. 20th c. **Tilâw-bek** [Тиловбек] (Begmatov 1984, 204); Uzb. 20th c. **Tilâw-χuĵa** [Тиловхўжа] (Begmatov 1984, 204); Uzb. 20th c. **Tilâw-qul** [Тиловкул] (Begmatov 1984, 204); Uzb. 20th c. **Tilâw-mirza** [Тиловмирза] (Begmatov 1984, 204); Kzk. 1794 **Tiläw** (MIK IV, 158); Kzk. 19th c. **Tiläw** [Тонгышбай Тилауевъ] (Grod., Pril. 19); Chag. 16th c. **Tiläw-biy** [Тилау-бий Кипчак] (Ivanov 240); Chag. 16th c. **Tiläw-biy** [Тилау-бий Кушчи] (Ivanov 290); Kkalp. 20th c. **Tilew** [Тилеỹ] (KkRS 776); Kkalp. 20th c. **Tilew-bay** [Тилеỹбай] (KkRS 776); Kkalp. 20th c. **Tilew-biyke** [Тилеỹбийке], fem. (KkRS 778); Tat. 1693 **Tlew** [Тлевъ Уразаевъ] (AI V, 402); Kzk. 18th c. - 19th c. **Tlew** [Тлеу] (Tynyšp. 66, 67, 74, 75); Kzk. 19th c. **Tlew** [Кийсыкъ Тлеуфъ] (Grod., Pril. 90); Kzk. 18th c. - 19th c. **Tlew-bay** [Тлеубай] (Tynyšp. 74); Kzk. 1822 **Tlew-bay** [تلاؤ بای] (MIK IV, 416); Kzk. 19th c. **Tlew-bay** [Тлеубай] (AOA 154); Kzk. 19th c. **Tlew-bay** [Тлеубай Байдалиевъ] (Grod., Pril. 85); Kzk. 19th c. **Tlew-bay** [Тлеубай Кунтугановъ] (Pam. kn. Turg. 78); Kzk. 19th c. **Tlew-bay** [Тлеубай] (SODž. 96); Kzk. 19th c. **Tlew-bay** [Тлеубай] (SOK 16); Kzk. 19th c. **Tlew-bay** [Тлеубай] (SOV 26); Kzk. 1860 **Tlew-bay** [Тлегучулъ Тлеубаевъ], a biy (ZIRGOGeogr. I, 272); Uzb. 19th c. **Tlew-bay** [Тлеубаевъ] (SKSO III, 150); Kzk. 18th c. - 19th c. **Tlew-qul** [Тлеукул] (Tynyšp. 66); *TN:* Kzk.? **Tläw-bay** [Тляубай] (Karta JAR XI). ✧ I. 'Wish, desire; wished (child)' (Sattarov, Kusimova), cf. Kzk. *tiläü* 'das Bitten' (Radl. III, 1382), Kzk. *tilev* 'Dilemek' (KzTS), Uzb. *tilâw* 'желание, просьба' (Begmatov 1984, 204); II. 'Brave' cf. Chag. *tiläü* 'tapfer' (Radl. III, 1382), cf. also Kzk. PNs beginning with *Tilew*- e. g. *Tilewbay, Tilewžan, Tilewmurat, Tilewχan* (Žanuzakov-Esbaeva). See also AY-TELEÜ, BAY-TLEW, ĴAN-TİLEW, İS-TİLÄW, QOY-TLEW, ÖTE-TİLEW.

TİLÄW-BERDİ Uzb. 20th c. **Tilâw-berdi** [Тиловберди (Тилавберди?)] (Begmatov 1984, 202); Uzb. 20th c. **Tilâw-berdi** [Тиловберди (Тилавберди?)] (Begmatov 1984, 204); Kzk. 19th c. **Tiläw-berdi** [Tileuberdi] (Ljutš 109); Tat.(Tob.) **Tiläw-birdi** [Тіläÿ Бірді] (Proben IV, 227 /279/); Bashk. 1687 **Tläw-berde** [Урасъ Тлевбердеевъ] (Vel.-Zern., Bašk. 34); Bashk. 1735 **Tläw-berdi** [Раманъ Тлевбердинъ], a tarχan (Vel.-Zern., Bašk. 21); Tat.(Sib.) 1609 **Tlew-berdi** [Клеубердый] (Miller, Ist. Sib. II, 212); Kzk. 1826 **Tlew-berdi** [Тлеуберды Кузебаевъ] (Konšin, Mat. I-III, 21); Kzk. 19th c. **Tlew-berdi** [Тлеуберды] (AOAtb. 58); Kzk. 19th c. **Tlew-berdi** [Тлеуберды] (AOO 2); Kzk. 1860 **Tlew-berdi** [Тлеуберды Иськельдинъ], head of the Siyirči clan of the Jalayïr tribe (ZIRGOGeogr. I, 272); Kzk. 18th c. - 19th c. **Tlew-berli** [Тлеуберлы] (Tynyšp. 75); Bashk. 1756 **Tliw-berdi** [Илиш Тливбердин] (MIB IV/1, 122). ✧ 'Wish-gave (the child)' (Sattarov, Kusimova). ⇨ TİLÄW + BERDİ. See also TİLÄW-BERGEN.

TİLÄW-BERGEN Uzb. 20th c. **Tiläw-bergän** [Тиловберган] (Begmatov 1984, 202); Kzk. 19th c. **Tiläw-bergen** [Тилавбергенъ] (Grod., Pril. 139, 144). ✧ 'Wish-gave (the child)'. ⇨ TİLÄW + BERGEN. See also TİLÄW-BERDİ.

TİLÄW-DURSÏQ Kzk. 19th c. **Tiläw-dursïq** [Тиловдурсикъ] (Grod., Pril. 66). ⇨ TİLÄW + TURSUQ.

TİLÄW-MURAT Uzb. 20th c. **Tilâw-murâd** [Тиловмурод] (Begmatov 1984, 204); Kkalp. 20th c. **Tilew-mïrat** [Тилеӳмырат] (KkRS 776); Kkalp. 20th c. **Tilew-murat** [Тилеӳмурат] (KkRS 776). ✧ 'Wish-Murat, Wished Murat'. ⇨ TİLÄW + MURAT.

TİLÄWÄY Kzk. 19th c. **Tiläwäy** [Кузабузаръ Тиловаевъ] (Grod., Pril. 189). ⇨ TİLÄW + suff. -äy?

TİLÄWLİ Bashk. 1709 **Teläwle** [Алкаш Телявлеев] (MIB I, 264); Kzk. 19th c. **Teleüle** [Телеуле] (SOV 48); Kzk. 19th c. **Tiläwli** [Соукбай Тиловлиевъ] (Grod., Pril. 140); Kzk. 19th c. **Tiläwli** [Тилавли] (Grod., Pril. 150); Kzk. 19th c. **Tiläwli** [Сукурбай Тиляуліевъ] (Grod., Pril. 87); Bashk. 1695 **Tläwle** [Исембетка Тлевлинъ] (Vel.-Zern., Bašk. 32); Kzk. 19th c. **Tlewli** [Тлеули] (AOO 34); Kzk. 19th c. **Tlewli** [Тлеулы], chief of a clan (Potanin II, 2). ✧ 'Wished child'? cf. Kzk. PN *Tilewli* (Žanuzakov-Esbaeva). ⇨ TİLÄW + suff. -li.

TİLÄWMBET Kzk. 19th c. **Tiläwmbet** [Тишкакъ Тилаумбетовъ] (Grod., Pril. 152); 18th c. **Tläwmbet** [Тляумбетъ] (Nepljuev 861); Tat. 1731 **Tläwmbet** [Тлеумбет] (MIB III, 293). ⇨ TİLÄW + suff. -mbet.

TİLÄWMÄT Tat.(Ishim) **Tiläwmät** [Тіläÿмäт] (Proben IV, 215 /265/). ⇨ TİLÄW + suff. -mät.

TİLE-MURAT Kkalp. 20th c. **Tile-murat** [Тилемурат] (Bask., Kkalp. 38). ⇨ TİLÄW? + MURAT.

TİLEGEN Kzk. **Tilägän** [Тілäгäн], Menbät's son (Proben III, 88 /113/); Kzk. 19th c. **Tilägän** [Тилаганъ] (Grod., Pril. 102); Kzk. 19th c. **Tilägän** [Айкази Тилодневъ] (Grod., Pril. 180); Kzk. 19th c. **Tilägän** [Тилагановъ] (Grod., Pril. 187); Kzk. 19th c. **Tilägän? / Tilügen?** [Отавъ Тилугеновъ] (Grod., Pril. 189); Kzk. 19th c. **Tiläkän? / Tilä-qan?** [Тилаканъ] (Grod., Pril. 168); Kzk. 19th c. **Tilegen** [Телегень] (AOAtb. 42); Kzk. 19th c. **Tilegen** [Телегенъ] (SOK 108, 130, 246); Kkalp. 20th c. **Tilegen** [Тилеген] (KkRS 776); Bashk. 1754 **Tläkän** [Тлякань] (MIB IV/1, 83); Bashk. 1756 **Tläkän-bay** [Тлеканбай] (MIB IV/1, 107); Kzk. 19th c. **Tlegen / Tilegen** [Тлегенъ] (AOAtb. 14); Kzk. 19th c. **Tlegen / Tilegen** [Тлегенъ] (AOK 2, 10, 34); Kzk. 19th c. **Tlegen / Tilegen** [Тлегенъ] (AOO 18); Kzk. 19th c. **Tlegen / Tilegen** [Тлегенъ] (Lomakin 42). ✧ 'Wished (child)' cf. Türk., Uyg., Kuman, Chag., Hak., Kzk. *tilä-* 'bitten, wünschen, wollen' (Radl. III, 1381), Kzk. *tile-/tïle-* 'желать, просить' (KzRS) + suff. *-γan/-gän*. See also SORAΓAN, TİLEMİŠ.

TİLEK Tat.? 1551 **Teyläk? / Taylaq?** [Тейлякъ-мырза] (PSRL XIII, 161); Oghuz 1035 **Telek** [Телек], a commander (MIT I, 256); Kzk. 19th c. **Telek** [Телековъ] (AOO 46); Kzk. 19th c. **Telek** [Телекъ] (SOK 164); Kzk. 19th c. **Telek -pay** [Телекпай] (SODž. 66); Kzk. 19th c. **Telek -pay** [Телекпай] (SOK 194, 208); Oghuz 1035 **Telek-tegin** [Телек-тегин], a doorkeeper (MIT I, 245); Kzk. 19th c. **Tilek** [Сукинбай Тилековъ] (Grod., Pril. 15, 80); Kkalp. 20th c. **Tilek** [Тилек] (Bask., Kkalp. 70, KkRS 776); Nog. 20th c. **Tilek** [Савкъат Тилек увлы / Саукат Тилеков], father of one of Baskakov's informants from the aul of Qaraγas (Bask., Nog. 144); Tat. 1731 **Tläk / Teläk** [Юмакай Тлекев] (MIB III, 293). ✧ 'Wish; Aim; Wished (child)' cf. Kzk. *tilek* 'желание, просьба; намерение' (KzTS), cf. Türk, Uyg., Kuman, Chag., Hak., Kzk. *tilä-* 'bitten, wünschen, wollen' (Radl. III, 1381), Bashk. *telä-* 'желать, хотеть' (BRS). See also BAY-TİLEK, İZ-TELEK, TAS-TELEK.

TİLEK-ALİ Trkm. 19th c. **Tlek-ali** [Тлекъ-Алиевъ] (Ščeglov I, 357). ⇨ TİLEK + ALİ.

TİLEKE Kzk. 1817 **Tleke / Tileke** [تلكە / Тлеке] (MIK IV, 309); Kzk. 19th c. **Tleke / Tileke** [Тлеке] (Potanin, Pred. II, 4); Kzk. 19th c. **Tleke / Tileke** [Тлеке] (SOV 34); Kzk. 1785 **Tleke-bahadïr / Tileke-bahadïr** [تلكه بهادر], from the Žappas tribe (MIK IV, 52, 54). ⇨ TİLE + dim. suff. -ke?

TİLEKEY Bashk. 1709 **Teläkäy** [Телякай Учкаев]

(MIB I, 264); Bashk. 1732 **Tläkäy** [Тлекей] (MIB III, 302); Bashk. 1737 **Tläkäy** [Тлекеев] (MIB III, 367); Bashk. 1763 **Tläkäy** [Салиш Тлекеев] (MIB IV/1, 267); Bashk. 1764 **Tläkäy** [Султанай Тлекеев] (MIB IV/1, 276); Trkm. 19th c. **Tlekey** [Тлекей] (Ščeglov I, 354). ⇨ **TİLEK** + dim. suff. *-ey / -äy.*

TİLEM Kzk. 19th c. **Tlem-bay** [Тлембай] (AOK 6). ◈ 'Piece' cf. Kuman, Alt., Kzk. *tilĭm* 'ein abgeschnittenes Stück, der Streifen, der Fetzen' (Radl. III, 1385).

TİLEME Kzk. 1794 **Tileme** [تلامه / Тлеме] (MIK IV, 162). ◈ 'Wish'. ⇨ **TİLE** + suff. *-me.*

TİLEMİŠ Kzk. 19th c. **Telemes** [Телемесъ] (AOO 2); Kzk. 19th c. **Telemis** [Телемисовъ] (AOK 102); Kzk. 19th c. **Telemis** [Телемисъ] (AOK 42, 90); Kzk. 19th c. **Telemis** [Телемисовъ] (AOO 10); Kzk. 19th c. **Telemis** [Телемисъ] (SOK 56, 202, 256); Kzk. 1819 **Tlämiš** [Тлямыш] (MIK IV, 323); Kzk. 1846 **Tlämiš** [Тлямиш Купгурчим (Кунгурчин?)] (MKOP 154); Kzk. 1842 **Tlemis** [Кочакъ Тлемысовъ], from the Middle Horde (Orta Žüz) (Konšin, Mat. V, 22); Kzk. 19th c. **Tlemis** [Тлемисъ] (SOK 186); Kzk. 19th c. **Tlemis** [Тлемисъ] (SOV 58); Kzk. 19th c. **Tlemis** [Тлемисъ] (ZOOIRGO III, 26). ◈ 'Wished (child)' cf. Türk., Uyg., Kuman, Chag., Hak., Kzk. *tilä-* 'bitten, wünschen, wollen' (Radl. III, 1381), Kzk. *tile-/tĭle-* 'желать, просить' (KzRS) + suff. *-mis / -miš.* See also **PRİK-TLEMİŠ, SORAЃAN, TİLEGEN.**

TİLENČÄ see **TİLENČİ**

TİLENČEK Bashk. 1690 **Tlenček** [Тленчекъ Устемировъ] (Vel.-Zern., Bašk. 39). ◈ 'Beggar' cf. Hak.(Sag.) *tilänčik* 'der Bettler' (Radl. III, 183). See also **KERİP, QOLČU, TİLENČEK, TİLENČİ.**

TİLENČİ Maml. 1349 **Dilenĵi** [Seifeddin Dilindji], governor of Gazah (Weil, Chalif. I, 484); Kzk. 18th c. - 19th c. **Telenči** [Теленчи] (MIK IV, 47); Kzk. 19th c. **Telenči** [Теленчи] (SOV 92); Kzk. 1805, 1820 **Tilänčä-biy / Tilenčä-biy** [Тилянча бий / Тиленча-бій], a leader of the Aryïn tribe, of the Middle Horde (Orta Žüz) (MIK IV, 512, Sib. Vest. IX, 102); Kzk. 18th c. - 19th c. **Tilänči** [Тилянчи] (MIK IV, 150); Kzk. 19th c. **Tilänči** [Тыланчи] (SOK 78); Kzk. **Tilänši** [Тиläнши] (Proben III, 4 /5/); Kzk. 1785 **Tilenči-bahadïr / Tlenšä** [تلانچی بهادر / Тленша], from the Tabun tribe (MIK IV, 52, 54); Kzk. 1794 **Tilenči-batïr** [تلانچی باطر] (MIK IV, 159); Kzk. 1822 **Tilenči-tarχan** [تلانچی طارخان] (MIK IV, 430, 433); Tat.(Mish.) 1755 **Tlänče** [Чирюбай Тлянчин] (MIB IV/1, 93); Kzk. 19th c. **Tlemši** [Тлемши] (AOA 82); Bashk. 1701 **Tlenče** [Явгилдка Тленчеевъ] (Vel.-Zern., Bašk. 29); Bashk. 1735 **Tlenče** [Муса Тленчеевъ], a tarχan (Vel.-Zern., Bašk. 13); Bashk. 1731 **Tlenči** [Казбулат Тленчи] (MIB III, 292); Kzk. 19th c. **Tlenči** [Тленчи] (AOA 102); Kzk. 1860 **Tlenči**

[Тленчи Балпыновъ], a biy, head of the branch Andas of the Ĵalayïr tribe (ZIRGOGeogr. I, 271); Bashk. 1701 **Tlenči** (<Tilenči) [Явгилдка Тленчеевъ], a tarχan (Vel.-Zern., Bašk. 29); Kzk. 18th c. **Tlenči-biy** [Тленчи], from the Qara-kisek tribe (Valihanov, Soč. 162); Bashk. 1709 **Tlenči(y)** [Козяк Тленчеев] (MIB III, 48); Bashk. 1711 **Tlenči(y)** [Абдула Тленчеев] (MIB III, 71); Bashk. 1664 **Tlenči(yqo)** [Тленчейко Байзигитов] (MIB I, 191); Kzk. 19th c. **Tlenši** [Тленши] (AOO 42); Kzk. 1793, 1794 **Tlenši / Tlänči** [طارخان تلانچی بونباى اوغلى / تلانچى Тленши Бокенбай / Тлянчий Буканбаев], leader („glavnyj staršina", tarχan) of the Žeti-ruw clan (MIK IV, 54, 63-64, 67, 75, 142, 157, 169-172, 177); *TN:* Kzk. **Telenči** [Теленчи] (Karta JAR XI). ◈ 'Beggar' cf. Chag., Hak.(Sag.), East.T. *tilänči* 'der Bettler' (Radl. III, 1383), Kzk. *tĭlenšĭ* 'нищий' (KzRS), Turk. *dilänĵi* 'id.' (Radl. III, 1767). See also **QARA-DİLENĴİ; KERİP, QOLČU, TİLENČEK.**

TİLENDİ Kzk. 19th c. **Tlendi / Tilendï** [Тленды] (SODž. 54). ◈ 'Wished/asked (child)' cf. Türk., Chag., Kzk. *tilän-* 'für sich bitten, für sich wünschen' (Radl. III, 1383).

TİLENMET Bashk. 1735 **Tlenmet** [Ахымбеть Тленметев] (MIB III, 336). ⇨ **TİLEN** + suff. *-met.*

TİLENŠİ see **TİLENČİ**

TİLEP-ALDİ Uzb. 20th c. **Tiläb-âldï** [Тилаболди] (Begmatov 1984, 204); Kirg. 20th c. **Tilew-aldï** [Тилевалды] (Kalilov 93); Kzk. 19th c. **Tleb-aldï** [Тлебалды] (AOO 6). ◈ 'Wished-taken (child)'. ⇨ **TİLÄP** + **ALDİ.** See also **SURAP-ALDÏ.**

TİLEP-BERGEN Uzb. 20th c. **Tiläb-bergän** [Тилабберган] (Begmatov 1984, 202); Kzk. 19th c. **Tlep-bergen** [Тлепбергенъ] (SOV 70); Kzk. 19th c. **Tlep-pergen** [Тлеппергенъ] (SOV 100). ◈ 'Wished-given'. ⇨ **TİLÄP** + **BERGEN.** See also **TİLÄP-BERDİ.**

TİLEP-UŠAR Bashk. 1735 **Tlep-ušar** [Тлепушаръ Чингырчинъ], a tarχan (Vel.-Zern., Bašk. 17). ⇨ **TİLÄP** + **UŠAR.**

TİLEPEY Bashk. 1735 **Tlepey** [Кулукай Тлепеевъ] (Vel.-Zern., Bašk. 16). ⇨ **TİLEP** + dim. suff. *-ey.*

TİLESTER Tat. 1670 **Tlester-bek** [Тлестербековъ], a mïrza (DAI VI, 26).

TİLEW see **TİLÄW**

TİLEW-ALDİ see **TİLEP-ALDİ**

TİLEW-MURAT see **TİLÄW-MURAT**

TİLEW-NİYAZ Kkalp. 20th c. **Tilew-niyaz** [Тилеўнияз] (KkRS 776). ⇨ **TİLÄW** + **NİYAZ.**

TİLİMBET Kkalp. 20th c. **Tilimbet** [Тилимбет] (KkRS 776). ⇨ **TİL** + suff. *-imbet.*

TİLKÄ Kzk. 19th c. **Tilkä-bay** [Тилкобаевъ] (Grod., Pril. 158). ⇨ **TİL** + suff. *-kä.*

TİLKÄY Bashk. 1764 **Tilkäy** [Макача Тилкаев]

(MIB IV/1, 300). ⇨ TİL + suff. *-käy.*

TİLLA   Kzk. 19th c. **Dïlda-bek** [Дылдабекъ] (SOK 258); Kzk. 19th c. **Tilla** [Тилла], fem. (Kazancev 80); Kzk. 19th c. **Tillä** [Тиллэ] (Grod., Pril. 158); Kzk. 19th c. **Tillä** [Тиллэ] (Grod., Pril. 158); Kirg. 19th c. **Tillä** [Тилля Ташевъ] (SKSO VIII, 223); Uzb. 19th c. **Tillä-bay** [Султанбай Тиллябаевъ] (SKSO III, 23); NUyg. 1850 **Tillä-χan** [Тилля-ханъ] (Valihanov, Soč. 143); Trkm. 20th c. **Tïlla** [Тылла], fem. (Sopieva 181); Trkm. 20th c. **Tïlla** [Tïlla], fem. (Zaj. 1971, 338); Trkm. 20th c. **Tïlla** [Тылла], fem. (TrkmRS 652); Kzk. 19th c. **Tïllä-bay** [Тиллябаевъ] (SKSO VIII, 202). ✧ 'Gold' (Sopieva), 'Treasure, jewel' (Kazancev), 'Gold, golden coin; money' cf. NUyg.(Tar.) *tilla* 'eine kokandische Goldmünze' (Radl. III, 1386), Trkm. *tïllā* 'золотс, золотой' (TrkmRS), Kzk. *dïlda* 'eine Bucharische Geldmünze' (Rad. III, 1747), Kzk. *dïldâ* 'dilda' (KzTS), *dilda / dildä* 'алтын ақша' [golden coin] (QTTS), (<Ar.). Cf. also Kzk. PN *Dilda-bek* (Žanuzakov-Esbaeva). See also **BAY-DİLDA, BEK-DİLLÄ, SARAN-DİLDA, UWAY-DİLDA.**

TİLLÄ see **TİLLA**

TİLLÄK   Kzk. 19th c. **Tilläk** [Тиллякъ] (SKSO VIII, 206).

TİLTİ see **TİLDİ**

TİLÜ   Kzk. 19th c. **Tilü** [Хаитъ Тилуевъ] (Grod., Pril. 40); Kzk. 19th c. **Tilü** [Рахимъ Берди Тилуевъ] (Grod., Pril. 40). ✧ 'Wish'? ⇨ **TİLÄW?** See also **ATA-TİLÜ, MOLLA-TİLÜ, ON-TİLÜ.**

TİMÄČ see **TİMÄŠ**

TİMÄPİÄY see **TİMÄPİY**

TİMÄPİY   Yak. **Timäpiäy** [Тімäпіäі] (Pek.); Yak. **Timäpiy** [Тімäпіі] (Pek.). ✧ Timofey (R.) (Pek.).

TİMÄŠ   Bashk. 1760 **Temäš** [Курманай Темашев] (MIB IV/2, 160); Tat. 1662 **Timäč** [Тимячь] (DAI IV, 284); Tat. 1675 **Timäč / Timäk?** [Тимякъ / Тимячко] (Kungursk. akty 31); Tat. 1716 **Timäš** [Тимяш Шеккулов] (MIB III, 144); Bashk. 1710 **Timäš** [Тимяш Киндикеев] (MIB III, 67); Bashk. 1770 **Timäš / Timäč?** [Азнай Тимашев] (MIB IV/1, 349).

TİMEY   Tat. 1764, 1777, 1789 **Timey** [Тимей Мавлютов] (MIB IV/1, 285, V, 54, 245, 320 etc.); Tat. 1777 **Timey** [Тимей (Тюней) Маитисев (Матисов, Мятисев)] (MIB V, 54, 245 etc.); Tat. 1790 **Timey** [Ахмер Тимеев] (MIB V, 282, 548, 549); Bashk. 1764 **Timey** [Тимей Мавлютов] (MIB IV/1, 285); Bashk. 1779 **Timey** [Тимей] (MIB V, 91).

TİMEKEY I.   Bashk. 1747 **Timekey** [Дюмей Тимекеев] (MIB III, 447); Bashk. 1764 **Timekey** [Аит Тимекеев] (MIB IV/1, 276).

TİMEKEY II.   Alt. 19th-20th c. **Timekey** [Тимекей (Тимофей)] (OjrRS 210). ✧ Timofey (R.) (OjrRS).

TİMENTEY see **TÜMÄNDÄY**

TİMİKÄY see **TEMEKEY**

TİMİNEY see **TEMENEY**

TİMİR see **TEMİR**

TİMİR-BÜKÜSTÄY   Yak. **Timir-büküstäy-oburγu** [Тіміp Бӱкӱстäі-обургу] (Pek.). ✧ 'Iron-Büküstäy'. ⇨ **TEMİR.**

TİMİR-ČASQÏY   Yak. **Timir-časqïy** [Тіміp Часкыі], a demonic shamaness (Pek.). ✧ 'Resounding iron' (Pek.), cf. Yak. *časqïy-* 'звучно кричать' (Pek.). ⇨ **TEMİR.**

TİMİR-JÄBİDİYÄ   Yak. **Timir-jäbidiyä** [Тіміp Цäбідіjä], a demonic hero (Pek.). ✧ 'Rusting iron' (Pek.), cf. Yak. *jäbidiy-* 'ржаветь, изоржаветь' (Pek.). ⇨ **TEMİR.**

TİMİR-JÄSİNÄ   Yak. **Timir-jäsinä-buqatïr** [Тіміp Цäсінä-букатыр], an *abāsï*-bogatyr (Pek.). ⇨ **TEMİR.**

TİMİR-JİÄSİNTÄY   Yak. **Timir-jiäsintäy** [Тіміp Ціäсінтäі], a bogatyr in a tale (Pek.). ⇨ **TEMİR.**

TİMİR-JOYON   Yak. **Timir-joyon-ämäχsin** [Тіміp Цоjон-äмäхсін], a fabulous *abāsï* (old) woman (Pek.). ⇨ **TEMİR.**

TİMİR-JOYOSTON   Yak. **Timir-joyoston-ämäχsin** [Тіміp-Цоjостон-äмäхсін], a fabulous *abāsï* (old) woman (Pek.). ⇨ **TEMİR.**

TİMİR-DÏBÏLİÑSA   Yak. **Timir-dïbïliñsa** [Тіміp Дыбылыңса] (Pek.). ✧ 'Iron Dïbïliñsa'. ⇨ **TEMİR +** **DÏBÏLİÑSA.**

TİMİR-DÏBÏRDĀN   Yak. **Timir-dïbïrdān** [Тіміp Дыбырдан], an *abāsï*-bogatyr (Pek.). ⇨ **TEMİR.**

TİMİR-DYÄSİNTÄY   Yak. **Timir-dyäsintäy**, a hero in a tale (Pek.). ⇨ **TİMİR-JİÄSİNTÄY.**

TİMİR-DOΓDORUQĀN   Yak. **Timir-doγdoruqān**, a hero in a tale (Pek.). ⇨ **TEMİR.**

TİMİR-DOLONUQSA   Yak. **Timir-dolonuqsa-buχatïr** [Тіміp-Долонукса-бухатыр], a hero in a tale (Pek.). ⇨ **TEMİR.**

TİMİR-XALXALÏMA   Yak. **Timir-χalχalïma** [Тіміp Халхалыма], a demonic hero (Pek.). ⇨ **TEMİR.**

TİMİR-LÏPPÏČÏAXA   Yak. **Timir-lïppïčïaχa-oburγu** [Тіміp Лыппычыаха-обургу] (Pek.). ⇨ **TEMİR.**

TİMİR-PULAT see **TEMİR-BULAT**

TİMİRDÄY see **TEMİRTAY**

TİMİRDĀYİ   Yak. **Timirdāyi** [Тімірдäji] (Pek.). ⇨ **TİMİRDÄY.**

TİMİRÄK see **TEMİRÄK**

TİMİRGÄNDİK   Tat.(Tüm.) **Timirgändik** [Тіміргäндік], a hero of a tale (Proben IV, 319 /397/).

TİMİRKEY see **TEMİRKEY**

TİMKE I.   Hak. 19th-20th c. **Timke** [Тимке] (HRS 351).

TİMKE II.   Bashk. 1713 **Timke-murza** [Тимке-мурза] (MIB III, 100). ⇨ **TİN?** + suff. *-ke.*

TİMKEY   Bashk. 1778 **Timkey** [Сатыкай Таминеев

(Тимкеев)] (MIB V, 76, 197). ⇨ **TİN**? + suff. *-key*.

TİMMET   Tat. 1753 **Timmet** [Беккине Тимметев] (MIB IV/1, 70).

TİMUR see **TEMİR**

TİMUR-BAŠ   Yürük 1543 **Timur-baš** [تمورباش / Timurbaş] (Gökb., Rum. 187). ✧ 'Iron-head'. ⇨ **TEMİR + BAŠ.**

TİMUR-BOГA see **TEMİR-BUГA**

TİMUR-SALAR   Trkm. 1409/10 **Timur-salar** [Тимур-салар], a chieftain (MIT I, 530). ⇨ **TEMİR + SALAR.**

TİMUR-TAŠ see **TEMİR-TAŠ**

TİMURЈİ see **TEMİRČİ**

TİMÜR-BUQA see **TEMİR-BUГA**

TİMÜR-BULAT see **TEMİR-BULAT**

TİMÜR-TOГLЇ   Oghuz/Trkm. 13th c. **Timür-toγlï-χan** [تيمور توغلى خان / Тимур-Тоглы-хан], from the Salor tribe (Abulg./Kon. 1285). ⇨ **TEMİR + TOQLЇ.**

TİN   Bashk. 1790 **Tim-bay** (<Tin-bay) [Байгул Тимбаев] (MIB V, 275); 1814 **Tim-bek** (<Tin-bek) [Тимбековъ] (PSZRI XXXII, 806); Chuv. 18th-19th c. **Tin-bay** [Тинбай] (Magn. 82); Tat. 1717 **Tin-bay** [Булатъ-мурза-Тинбаевъ] (ZIRGO IX, 330); Bashk. 1664 **Tin-bay** [Кутушко Тинбаев] (MIB I, 192); Bashk. 1770 **Tin-bay** [Тинбай Юсупов] (MIB IV/1, 342); Kkalp. 1714 **Tin-bay** [Чебага Тинбаев], a murza (MIKk. 164); Nog. 1649 **Tin-bay** [Тинбай] (AI IV, 83); Nog. 1649 **Tin-bay** [Абла мурза Тинбаевъ] (AI IV, 87); Nog. 1633 **Tin-bay / Tan-bay?** [Канай Тинбаевъ (Танбаевъ)], a prince (Miller, Ist. Sib. II, 408, 409); Chuv. 18th-19th c. **Tin-bey** [Тинбей] (Magn. 82); Tat.(GH) 1342 **Tin-bek** [Тинбекъ], a prince (PSRL VII, 207); Chuv. 18th-19th c. **Tin-bik** [Тинбикъ] (Magn. 82); Chuv. 18th-19th c. **Tin-čura** [Тинчура] (Magn. 82); Chuv. 18th-19th c. **Tin-murza** [Тинмурза] (Magn. 82); Chag. 16th c. **Tin-sufi** [Тин-Суфи] (Ivanov 107); Chuv. 18th-19th c. **Tïn-murza** [Тынмурза] (Magn. 87); *TN:* Tat. 18th c. **Tin-čurino** (<Tin-čura) [Тинчурино], a village in the district of Tetyushinsk (Korsakov 337). ✧ I. 'Pair, mate; equal' (Sattarov), cf. Uyg., Karakh. *tiñ / teñ* 'одинаковый, равный' (DTS); II. 'Body'? cf. Maml. *tin (~tän)* 'тело, туловище' (Tuhfa 381). See also **QARA-TİN.**

TİN-AXMAT see **TEN-AXMET**

TİN-AXMET see **TEN-AXMET**

TİN-ALЇ see **TЇN-ALİ**

TİN-BAXTA   Chuv. 18th-19th c. **Tin-baχta** [Тинбахта] (Magn. 82). ✧ I. 'Friend/mate-fortune'; II. 'A mate/pair was born; male child was born' cf. Tat. *Tiñ-baqtï* (Sattarov). ⇨ **TİN + BAQTЇ.**

TİN-BARS   Chuv. 18th-19th c. **Tin-bas** (<Tin-bars?) [Тинбасъ] (Magn. 82). ✧ 'Mate/pair-panther' cf. Tat. *Tiñ-bars* (Sattarov). ⇨ **TİN + BARS.**

TİN-BAŠ   Chuv. 18th-19th c. **Tin-baš** [Тинбашъ]

(Magn. 82). ⇨ **TİN + BAŠ.**

TİN-BUГA   Chuv. 18th-19th c. **Tin-bua** (<Tin-buγa) [Тинбуа] (Magn. 82). ⇨ **TİN + BUQA.**

TİN-BULAT   Chuv. 18th-19th c. **Tin-bulat** [Тинбулатъ] (Magn. 82); Tat. 1555 **Tin-bulat** [Тинбулатъ], from Astrakhan (PSRL XIII, 245). ✧ '(Be) Steel-like'? cf. Tat. *Tiñ-bulat* (Sattarov). ⇨ **TİN + BULAT.**

TİN-GİLDE   Chuv. 18th-19th c. **Tin-gilde** [Тингилда] (Magn. 82). ✧ 'Mate/pair came (was born)' cf. Tat. PN *Tiñ-kilde* (Sattarov). ⇨ **TİN + KELDİ.**

TİN-KOVAT   Chuv. 18th c. **Tin-govat(ova)** [Тинговатова], a village in the district of Cheboksary (Korsakov 287). ✧ 'Mate-strength / Fellow-strength' cf. Tat. PN *Tiñ-quwät* (Sattarov). ⇨ **TİN + QUWAT.**

TİN-QAŠ   Bashk. 1754 **Tin-qaš** [Ильяс Тинкашев] (MIB IV/1, 84). ⇨ **TİN + QAŠ.**

TİN-QЇLİČ   Chag. 16th c. **Tin-qlïč** [Тинклыч] (Ivanov 87, 111); Chag. 16th c. **Tin-qlïč-biy** [Тинклыч-бий], an emir (Ivanov 328). ✧ 'Healthy/strong sword'. ⇨ **TİN + QЇLİČ.**

TİN-QLЇČ see **TİN-QЇLİČ**

TİN-QUZЇ   Kzk. 19th c. **Tin-quzï** [Тинъ-кузы] (Grod., Pril. 37). ⇨ **TİN + QOZЇ.**

TİN-MAMET   Tat. 1649 **Tin-mamet** [Кейкуватъ Янмаметъ мурза Тинмаметевъ], a murza from Astrakhan (AI IV, 77); Nog.? 1626-29 **Tin-mamet** [Мамай Тинмаметевъ], a mirza (AI III, 460, IV, 87); Nog. 1633, 1649 **Tin-mamet** [Тинмаметъ] (Miller, Ist. Sib. II, 408, AI IV, 79); Nog. 1649 **Tin-mamet** [Джанъ-Маметъ мурза Тинмаметев], a murza (AI IV, 84). ⇨ **TİN + MAMET.**

TİN-MUXAMMET   Chag. 15th c. - 16th c. **Tin-muχammet-χan?** [تين محمد خان], a Shaybanid (Šejb. LII). ⇨ **TİN + MUXAMMED.**

TİNAY   Kzk. 19th c. **Tinay** [Сиръ Назаръ Тинаевъ] (Grod., Pril. 173).

TİNČA   Bashk. 1706 **Tinča?** [Тинтча Аиткулов] (MIB III, 29).

TİNÄXPİ   Chuv. 18th-19th c. **Tinäχpi / Tinäk-pi?** [Тиняхпи] (Magn. 82).

TİNÄPPÄY   Hak.(Sag.) 19th-20th c. **Tinäppäy** [Тинäппäй] (Katanov, Otč. 7). ✧ Timofey (R.) (Katanov).

TİNEY   Nog. 1649 **Tiney** [Тинѣй Бай-токташбаевъ] (AI IV, 123); Kzk. 19th c. **Tney / Tiney** [/ Тней] (AOA 2); Kzk. 19th c. **Tney / Tiney** [/ Тней] (AOAtb. 6). ⇨ **TİN + suff. -ey.**

TİNEK   Hak. 19th-20th c. **Tinek** [Тинек] (HRS 351).

TİNGEŠ   Kzk. 19th c. **Tingeš?** [Тынгешъ] (AOK 46).

TİNİ see **TENİ**

TİNİ-QAŠ   Bashk. 1762 **Tini-qaš** [Измаил Тиникашев] (MIB IV/1, 251). ⇨ **TENİ? + QAŠ.**

TİNİG-AČAQ   Tuv. 19th c. **Tinig-ačaq** [Тинигъ-ачакъ] (Potanin IV, 591). ✧ 'Spoiled-old man / husband' cf. Tuv. *tenek* 'баловник; озорник; дурак', *ašaq* 'пожилой мужчина; старик, муж' (TuvRS).

TİNİKEY see **TENİKEY**

TİNİŠ see **TENİŠ**

TİNKİ   Uyg. 12th c. - 14th c. **Tinki**, a demon (DTS).

TİNTİBEY   Alt. 19th-20th c. **Tintibey** [Тинтибей], fem. (OjrRS 213).

TİÑİKĀN   Yak. **Tiñikăn-bögö** [Тиҥікăн-бöҕö], forefather of the branches of İgideys and Žeχsogons (Pek.).

TİÑİZ see **TEÑİZ**

TİPEY see **TEPEY**

TİPSEK   Hak. 19th-20th c. **Tipsek** [Типсек] (HRS 351). ✧ '(Little)Saddle-pad'? cf. Mad. *täpsä* 'das Sattelkissen' (Radl. III, 1115) + dim. suff. *-k*.

TİR   Kzk. 19th c. **Tir / Tir?** [Тыръ] (SODž. 110); Kzk. 19th c. **Tir-žan** [Тиржанъ] (AOK 94).

TİR-TOŇ   Hak. 19th-20th c. **Tir-toň** [Тиртонъ] (HRS 351). ✧ 'Working-coat' (Butanaev). ⇨ **TİR?+TON.**

TİRBİŠ   Bashk. 1740 **Tirbiš** [Тойсур Тирбышев] (MIB I, 455).

TİRÄK   Uyg. **Tiräk** [Tiräk] (EUTS); Uyg. 13th-14th c. **Tiräk** [Tirä[k]], fem. (Zieme, Mat. III, 268); Kzk. 19th c. **Tiräk** [Тиракъ-бай Насыровъ] (Grod., Pril. 117). ✧ 'Support(er), helper' cf. Karakh. *tirä-* 'подпирать', *tirägü* 'столб; подпорка' (DTS), Kzk. *tĭrek* 'подпорка, опора' (KzRS). See also **BAL-DİRÄK, BURYUQ-TİRÄK, ĴAN-TİRÄK, İNANČ-TİRÄK.**

TİREKEY see **TERÄKÄY**

TİREN-TAY   Kzk. 19th c. **Tiren-tay / Tirentay?** [Тирентай] (SOK 92). ⇨ ? + **TAY?** or suff. *-tay(1,2)?*

TİRGÜG   Uyg. 8-9th c. **Tirgüg** [Tirgüg] (EUTS). ✧ 'Supporter'? cf. Türk / Uyg. *tirgük, tirägük* 'direk' [=column, pillar] (Gabain /1988/), *tiragük* (sic!) 'id.' (EUTS, taken from Gabain). See also **EL-TERGÜG.**

TİRİ see **TERE**

TİRİD   Turk. 15th c. **Tirid-baba-ĵamii** [Tirid Baba-Camii], preserved in the name of a mosque (Gökb., Ed. 29). ✧ 'Feeble old man' cf. Turk. *tirit* 'bread soaked in gravy; feeble old man' (TED).

TİRİG   Türk 7th-9th c. **Tirig** [Köni Tirig] (ETY III, 39, 62). ✧ 'Alive'. See also **KÜLÜG-TİRİG, KÜNİ-TİRİG, ÜČÜN-KÜLÜG-TİRİG.**

TİRİG-ÄLTMİŠÄ   Uyg. **Tirig-ältmišä** (Zieme, Mat. I, 77 (after Ramstedt, Four Uigurian Documents. In: C. G. Mannerheim: Accross Asia from West to East 1906-1908. Helsinki 1940; N. Yamada: Uighur Documents of Slaves and Adopted Sons. In: Memoirs of the Faculty of Letters, Osaka University, Vol. 16, March 1972, 250)). ✧ 'Oh, (s)he has been born alive!', „Oh! Sie ist zur Welt gebracht!" (Zieme, after Tezcan), cf. Türk, Uyg., Karakh. *elt-* 'нести, тащить; вынести' (DTS).

⇨ **TİRİG.**

TİRİŸ see **TERE**

TİRİM   Kzk. 19th c. **Trim-bay** (<Tirim-bay?) [Тримбай] (AOA 54). ✧ 'My lively/healthy (baby)'? ⇨ **TERE?** + poss. suff. *-m*.

TİRİM-MATAY   Uyg. 1306 **Tirim-matay** [Tirim-Matai] (Chwol., Syr.-nest. II, 50). ⇨ **TİRİM** + **MATAY.**

TİRİS   Bashk. 1714 **Tiris / Teres** [Иликей Тирисевъ / Иликей Тересев] (MIB I, 107, MIB III, 119). ✧ 'Dung, excrement' cf. Bashk. *tireθ* 'навоз' (BRS/Uraksin).

TİRKÄŠ   Uzb. 20th c. **Tirkäš** [Тиркаш] (Begmatov 1984, 205); Uzb. 20th c. **Tirkäš-ây** [Тиркашой], fem. (Begmatov 1984, 205); Uzb. 20th c. **Tirkäš-ĵân** [Тиркашжон] (Begmatov 1984, 205); Uzb. 20th c. **Tirkäš-χân** [Тиркашхон], fem. (Begmatov 1984, 205); Uzb. 20th c. **Tirkäš-χoĵa** [Тиркашхўжа] (Begmatov 1984, 205). ✧ 'Clutch!, Cling!; Do not die! Be alive!' (Begmatov), cf. Uzb. *tirkä-* 'прицеплять, зацеплять' (UzbRS).

TİRKE   Tat. 1764 **Tirke** [Килей Тиркин] (MIB IV/2, 105).

TİRKİ   Uyg. 12th c. - 14th c. **Tirki**, a demon (DTS).

TİRKİŠ   Trkm. 20th c. **Tirkiš** [Tirkiš] (Zaj. 1971, 330); Trkm. 20th c. **Tirkiš** [Тиркиш] (TrkmRS 634). ✧ 'Chain, train' cf. Trkm. *tirkiš* 'id.' (TrkmRS).

TİRLİK see **TERLİK**

TİRMİŠ   Uyg. 13th-14th c. **Tirmiš**, fem. (Zieme, Mat. II, 91). ✧ '(S)he gathered' cf. Uyg., Karakh. *ter-* ' Türk, Uyg., Chag. *tär-* 'sammeln' (Radl. III, 1060). See also **İL-TİRMİŠ.**

TİRŠEK   Selj. 1092, 1102 **Tiršek / Teršek?** [ترشك الصوابى], emir who conquered Yemen for Melik-shah (IA X, 229, XI, 125, 175, Ahbar 50).

TİS see **TİŠ**

TİSÄGÄN   Tat. 1791 **Tisägän** [Тисаган Кулауметов] (MIB V, 305).

TİSÄN   Kzk. 19th c. **Tisän** [Тисанъ] (Grod., Pril. 173).

TİSİ   Kzk. 19th c. **Tisi-bay** [Булень Тисыбаевъ], a biy, the chief of the Balγalï clan (of the Ĵalayïr tribe) (ZIRGOGeogr. I, 272).

TİSİKTÄY   Yak. **Tisiktäy** [Тісіктäі] (Pek.). ✧ '(Little) rope' cf. Yak. *tisik* 'веревка' (Pek.) + dim. hypoc. suff. *-täy*.

TİSTİ see **TİŠTİ**

TİSÜ   Kzk. 19th c. **Tisü-bay** [Тисубай] (SOK 92).

TİŠ   Kzk. 19th c. **Tis-bek** [Тисбекъ] (SOV 106); Kzk. 19th c. **Tiš-bay** [Тишбай] (AOP 110); Kirg. 19th c. **Tiš-bay / Tĭš-bay?** [Тишбай Джангозинъ] (Konsin, Pam. 26). See also **AQ-TİŠ.**

TİŠEŠ   Tat.(Lit.) 1555 **Tišeš** [Тишешъ] (Kn. Metriki Lit. 113).

TİŠKEY   Tat.(Lit.) 1608, 1609 **Tiškey / Kiškey?**

[Самуилъ Тишкѣевичь (Кишкѣевичь, Кишкѣевъ)] (AI II, 127, 199-200, 287).

TİŠTİ Kzk. 19th c. **Tisti-bay / Tïstï-bay?** [Тыстыбай] (SOK 126); Kzk. 19th c. **Tišti-bay** [Тиштыбай] (AOA 126). ✧ 'Having teeth; with teeth'. ⇨ **TİŠ** + suff. -*ti*.

TİŠTÏ see **TİŠTİ**

TİT Chuv. 18th-19th c. **Tit-murza** [Титмурза] (Magn. 82).

TİTÄM Tat.(GH) 1262 **Titäm** [Титямъ], envoy (PSRL I, 204, VII, 163); Bashk. 1728 **Titäm** [Титямов] (MIB I, 123). ✧ 'My next child'. ⇨ **TETÄ?** + poss. suff. -*m*.

TİTÄP Yak. **Titäp** [Титäп] (Pek.). ✧ Tit (R.) (Pek.).

TİTE Kzk. 19th c. **Tite-bek** [Титебекъ] (AOK 138).

TİTO Turk. 20th c. **Tito** (Önder, Hınıs).

TİTRÄKČİ-QARÏMÏŠ Uyg. 12th c. - 14th c. **Titräkči-qarïmïš** [titräkči qarïmïš] (DTS). ✧ 'Quivering-Qarïmïš' cf. Uyg. *titrä*- 'дрожать, трепетать' (DTS). ⇨ **QARÏMÏŠ.**

TİTU see **D'İTU**

TİWÄKÄL see **TÄWÄKKÜL**

TİWEKEL see **TÄWÄKKÜL**

TİWLÄŠ Bashk. 1770 **Tiwläš** [Тивляш Тявкин] (MIB IV/1, 343).

TİWLEKEY see **TÄWLÄKÄY**

TİZ Kzk. 1783, 1784 **Tiz / Tiz** [Tyz / Тызъ], a sultan (Dobrosm., Turg. 174, Levšin II, 273, Levchine 265); Khorezm. 1224/25 **Tiz-šah** [تیز شاه / Tiz-Chah Ghîath ed-Dîn], son of Sultan Alāaddîn Mohamed II (1200-1220), the sultan of Kerman (Kirman) (Abulfidā/Ed. I, 99). ⇨ **TEZ?**

TİZEK Chag. 16th c. **Tizek** [Тизек], a khodja (Ivanov 181, 188). ⇨ **TİZ** + suff. -*ek*.

TİZGEN Kzk. 19th c. **Tizgem-bay** (<Tizgen-bay) [Тызгембай] (SOK 192). ✧ 'Rein' cf. Kuman, Chag., Kzk. *tizgin* 'der Zügel' (Radl. III, 1399).

TİN see **TİYEN**

TİÑÄY Yak. **Tïñäy** [Тиӊäi] (Pek.).

TİT Yak. **Tït** [Тıт] (Pek.). ✧ Tit (R.) (Pek.).

TÏAQARAY Yak. **Tïaqaray** [Тыакараi] (Pek.).

TÏASĀNÏ-UDAҒAN Yak. **Tïasānï-udaγan** [Тыасаны-удаӊан], one of Tïyïn's daughters (Pek.).

TÏBAY Bashk. 1715 **Tïbay / Tïy-bay?** [Кельмесь Тыбаев] (MIB III, 124); Kzk. 19th c. **Tïbay / Tïy-bay?** [Тыбай] (SOK 264).

TÏBAN Tuv.? 19th c. **Tïban / Pay-tïban** [Паi Тыбан], a shaman (Proben IX, 613).

TÏBİL see **TUҒİL**

TÏBÏR Hak. 19th-20th c. **Tïbïr** [Тыбыр] (HRS 352).

TÏBİSTAY Kzk. 19th c. **Tïbstay / Tïbistay** [Тыбстай] (AOO 58). ⇨ **?** + **TAY** or suff. -*tay(1,2)*.

TÏBÏŠ Kzk. 19th c. **Tïbïš** [Тыбышъ] (SOK 16).

TÏBUTAY Kzk. 19th c. **Tïbutay** [Тыбутай] (AOK 30). ⇨ **?** + **TAY** or suff. -*tay(1,2)*.

TÏҒA-BÏTÏRÏS Yak. **Tïγa-bïtïrïs** [Тыга бытырыс] (Pek.).

TÏҒAMBET Bashk. 1722 **Tïγambet** [Тыгамбеть] (MIB I, 122).

TÏҒÏČ 865 **Tïγïč** [طیغج] (Tabarī, Annal. III, 1543).

TÏҒİLASTAY Yak. **Tïγïlastay-kuo** [Ытык-Тыгыластаi-куо], fem. (Pek.). ✧ 'Breathing in an interrupted (spasmodic) way' cf. Yak. *tïyïlastā*- 'вздыхать и выдыхать учащенно' (Pek.).

TÏҒÏN see **TEGİN**

TÏҒÏNA Yak. 1680 **Tïγïna** [Мазара Тыгининъ] (DAI VIII, 268).

TÏҒÏT Kzk. 19th c. **Tïγït-pay / Tigit-pay?** [Тыгытпай] (SOV 18).

TÏY Kzk. 19th c. **Tïy-bay / Tiy-bay?** [Тыйбай] (AOP 50).

TÏQAY Kzk. 19th c. **Tïqay** [Тыкай] (SODž. 130).

TÏQAM-BAY see **TÏQAN**

TÏQAN Kzk. 19th c. **Tïqam-bay** (<Tïqan-bay?) [Тыкамбай] (SOV 134).

TÏQÏ I. Kzk. 19th c. **Tïqï-bay** [Тыкыбаевъ] (AOO 34).

TÏQÏ II. Yak. **Tïqï** [Тыкы], a Boroγon shaman (Pek.).

TÏQMA Trkm. 1881 **Tïqma** [Тыкма] (Grod., Vojna II, 143).

TÏLALĀX Yak. **Tïlalāχ** [Тылалах] (Pek.).

TÏLBİČEK 1727 **Tïlbiček** [Каштыменъ Тылбичековъ], from the Tsagay (Caγay) clan in the region of Kuznetsk (PSZRI VII, 890).

TÏLÏ Kzk. 19th c. **Tïlï-bay** [Тылыбай] (SOK 131).

TÏLÏQAN Kzk. 19th c. **Tïlïqam-bay** (<Tïlïqan-bay) [Тылыкамбай] (SODž. 162).

TÏLLA see **TİLLA**

TÏLTÏ see **TİLDİ**

TÏMAQ see **TUMAQ**

TÏMAN see **TUMAN**

TÏMBAS see **TÏNBAS**

TÏMҒAN Bashk. 1719 **Tïmγan (Timgän?)** [Азикей Тимганов] (MIB III, 189); Kzk. 1747 **Tïmγan (Timgän?)** [Тимганъ] (Nepljuev 705). ✧ 'He/she got quiet, calmed down' cf. Kzk. *tïm*- 'still werden' (Radl. III, 1342).

TÏMÏQ Bashk. 1735 **Tïmïq** [Качкынъ Тымыковъ] (Vel.-Zern., Bašk. 13). ✧ 'Quiet, still' cf. Alt., Kzk. *tïmïq* 'still, ruhig, schweigend' (Radl. III, 1343).

TÏMÏRSQA Kzk. 18th c. - 19th c. **Tïmïrsqa** [Тымырска] (Tynyšp. 68).

TÏN Kzk. 19th c. **Tïm-bay** (<Tïn-bay) [Тымбай] (SOK 44); Chuv. 18th-19th c. **Tïn-bay** [Тынбай] (Magn. 87); Kzk. 19th c. **Tïn-bay** [Тынбай] (AOK 94); Kzk. 19th c. **Tïn-bay / Tïnday?** [Тындай (?)] (SOK 132). ✧ I. 'Breath, soul' cf.Uyg., Kuman, Alt., Hak., Tat. *tïn* 'der Athem, der Hauch, das Leben, die Seele, der Geist' (Radl. III, 1312), Maml. *tïn* 'Ruh, can' (İM); II. 'Quiet, calm' cf. Kuman *tïn* 'still, ruhig' (CC), Tat. *tïn* 'тихий,

спокойный, бесшумный; дыхание' (TatRS); III. 'Healthy, strong' (Sattarov); IV. 'Be quiet! Stop! Don't move!' cf. Karakh. *tin* 'дышать; отдыхать; успокаиваться; останавливаться, прекращаться' (DTS), Maml. *tïn-* 'sich beruhigen' (Tarǰ./Houtsma), 'Durmak, kımıldamamak; Dinlenmek, istirahat etmek' (Tarǰ./Toparlı), Kzk. *tïn-* 'сделать остановку, затихать' (KzRS).

TÏN-ALÏ Kzk. 19th c. **Tin-alï** [Теналы] (AOK 86); Kzk. 19th c. **Tïn-ali** [Тынали] (SODž. 18, 62); Kzk. 1846 **Tïn-alï** [Тиналы] (Konšin, Mat. V, 91); Kzk. 19th c. **Tïn-alï** [Тыналы] (AOA 82). ⇨ TÏN + ALÏ.

TÏN-BARÏS see TÏN-BARS

TÏN-BARS Chuv. 18th-19th c. **Tïn-barïs** [Тынбарысъ] (Magn. 87); Chuv. 18th-19th c. **Tïn-bars** [Тинбарсъ / Тынбарсъ] (Magn. 82, 87). ✧ 'Strong/healthy panther'. ⇨ TÏN + BARS.

TÏN-BUҐA Maml. 14th c. - 15th c. **Tïn-buγa** [العلائى طنبغا حاجّى الساقى], in the inscription of a dish (Mayer 217). ✧ 'Strong/healthy bull'. ⇨ TÏN + BUQA.

TÏNBAS Kzk. 19th c. **Tïmbas** < **Tïnbas** [Тымбасъ] (SOV 130). ✧ 'He who won't stop; He who won't be tired' cf. Kzk. *tïn-* 'сделать остановку, затихать' (KzRS). ⇨ TÏN + suff. *-bas/-mas*.

TÏNČAR Uzb. 20th c. **Tïnčar** [Тинчар] (Begmatov 1984, 205). ✧ 'He/she will calm down' cf. Uzb. *tïnčï-* 'успокаиваться, утихать' (UzbRS).

TÏNČÏ Uzb. 20th c. **Tïnčï** [Тинчи] (Begmatov 1984, 205); Uzb. 20th c. **Tïnčï-bây** [Тинчибой] (Begmatov 1984, 205). ✧ 'Calm down!, Quiet!' cf. Uzb. *tïnčï-* 'успокаиваться, утихать' (UzbRS).

TÏNDÏM Kzk. 19th c. **Tïndïm** [Тындымъ] (SOK 46).

TÏNÏ-BEK Kzk. 18th c. - 19th c. **Tïnï-bek** [Тныбек] (Tynyšp. 68, 70); Kzk. 19th c. **Tïnï-bek** [Тыныбекъ] (SODž. 54, 128); Kzk. 19th c. **Tïnï-bek** [Тыныбекъ] (SOK 292); Kzk. 19th c. **Tïnï-bek** [Тыныбекъ] (SOV 18, 143); Tat.(GH) 1341 **Tïnï-bek / Tini-bek / Tin-bek?** [تينّ ـك / Тинбѣкъ / Тинибѣкъ], Özbeg's (1313-1341) son, a ruler of the Horde (1341-1342), J̌anï-bek's elder brother (Ibn Bat. II, 397, PSRL X, 213); Kzk. 19th c. **Tïnï-bek / Tïniy-bek?** [Тынийбекъ] (SOV 6). ✧ '(His) soul-(is)-strong'; Defrémery about the names *Tini-bek* and *J̌ani-bek*: „L'aîné s'appelle *Tina bec*; *bec* a le sens d'émir, et *tîn* (ten) celui de corps; c'est donc comme s'il se nommait 'émir du corps'. Le nom de son frère est *Djâni bec*. *Djân* signifie l'âme; c'est comme s'il s'appelait 'émir de l'âme'." (Ibn Bat. II, 397); P. Pelliot was slightly of different opinion: „a coté de l'emprunt persan *jân* 'âme', il y a, pour désigner l'„âme", un mot indigène turc très répandu, attesté entre autres en coman, qui est *tin*; *Tini-* est à *tin* exactement ce que *J̌ani-* est à *jân*, et je suis convaincu que les noms des deux frères sont strictement synonyms. Le nom de

leur père *Özbeg*, formé avec *öz* la „personne", le „soi", n'en est pas lui-même bien éloigné" (Pelliot 97-98); cf. also H. Eren, Türk Onomastique'i hakkında: Köprülü Arm., 127-129, Türk Dili 495 (1993), 232-233. ⇨ TÏN / TEN / TÏN? + BEK.

TÏNÏQ Kzk. 19th c. **Tïniq** [Тынекъ] (SOK 248); *TN:* Kzk. 19th c. **Tïniq-bay-qara-su** [Тыныкбай-кара-су], a field (AOAtb. 14). ✧ 'Relax!, Be quiet!' cf. Kzk. *tïniq-* 'sich ausruhen, sich erholen' (Radl. III, 1316).

TÏNÏLÏ Kzk. 19th c. **Tïnïlï** [Тынылы] (AOA 118).

TÏNÏM Maml. 1438/39, 1461/62 **Tïnïm** [تنم المؤيـدى] (Ibn Taghrīb. VII, 80, 92, Iyās II, 73, 281); Maml. 1454, 1459 **Tïnïm** [تنم الحسينى الاشرفى / الاشرفى] (Ibn Taghrīb. VII, 433, 550, 551, 761, Ibn Taghrīb. VIII, 337, 433, 504); Maml. 1461 **Tïnïm** [تنم الفقيه الابوبكرى المؤيـدى] (Ibn Taghrīb. VII, 650, 715); Maml. 1463 **Tïnïm** [تنم بن عبدالرزاق], governor of Damascus (Iyās II, 140, Ibn Taghrīb. VII, 38, 64, Weil, Chalif. II, 242, 295); Maml. 1463 **Tïnïm** [تنم رصاص بخشايش الظاهـرى], governor of Cairo (Iyās II, 271, 277, Ibn Taghrīb. VII, 211, 387, Weil, Chalif. II, 297-298); Maml. 1467 **Tïnïm** [تنم الحسينى], governor of Sham (Tripolis) (Ibn Taghrīb. VII, 322, VIII, 651, Weil, Chalif. II, 73, Iyās I, 298, 356); Maml. 1467/68 **Tïnïm** [تنم الاجرود الظاهـرى] (Ibn Taghrīb. VII, 865); Maml. 1468 **Tïnïm** (Ibn Taghrīb. VIII, 733); Maml. 1472/73 **Tïnïm** [تنم الضبع] (Iyās II, 138, 295); Maml. 1474/75 **Tïnïm** [تنم العجمى بن ططع الظاهـرى] (Iyās II, 151); Maml. 1475/76 **Tïnïm** [تنم الفقيه الابوبكرى] (Iyās II, 163); Maml. 1483 **Tïnïm** [السيفى تنم / S. a. d. Tanam Muayaddi], an emir (Berchem 360); Maml. 1491 **Tïnïm** [الاشـرفى السيفى تنم], colonel, mentioned in an inscription of Damascus (Mayer 215); Maml. 1516 **Tïnïm** [تنم السيفى مغلباى الساقى] (Iyās III, 73); Maml. 1516 **Tïnïm** [تنم], governor opf Alexandria (Iyās III, 75); Maml. 1520 **Tïnïm** [الناصر محمد بن قايتباى تنم خازنـدار] (Iyās III, 212, 263); Maml. 1520 **Tïnïm** [تنم] (Iyās III, 214, 301); Kzk. 19th c. **Tïnïm** [Тынымъ] (AOK 98); Maml. 1393, 1423 **Tïnïm / Tanïm?** [السيفى تنم / Sayf ad-Dīn Tanam], governor of Damascus (Sauvaget: BEO II, 12); Kzk. 19th c. **Tïnïm-bay** [Тынынбай] (AOA 10); Kzk. 19th c. **Tïnïm-bay** [Тынымбай] (AOAtb. 38); Kzk. 19th c. **Tïnïm-bay** [Тынымбай] (SOV 144); Kzk. 1820 **Tïnïm-χan** [Tönum-khan], the Kazak Arun-γazï (see) sultan's byname which - according to Baron Meyendorf's record - means „khan pacificateur" (=peacemaker khan) (MIK IV, 357). ✧ 'Rest, relaxation, quietness; peace' cf. Kzk. *tïnïm* 'das Ausruhen, die Ruhr' (Radl. III, 1318). ⇨ TANÏ / TENÏ? + poss. suff. *-m*.

TÏNÏS Kzk. 18th c. - 19th c. **Tinïs** [Тныс] (Tynyšp. 73); Kzk. 19th c. **Tïnïs** [Тынысъ] (AOP 82). ✧ 'Breath; pause, interval' (Žanuzakov), cf. Hak., Kzk. *tïnïs* 'der Athem'.

TÏNÏSTAN Kzk. 19th c. **Tinïstan** [Тныстанъ] (SOV 106).

TÏNÏŠ Kzk. 19th c. **Tïnč-bik** (<**Tïnïč-bik?**) [Тенджбикъ], fem. (Grod., Pril. 66); Kzk. 19th c. **Tinïš** [Тынышъ] (AOP 34); Kzk. 19th c. **Tinïš** [Тынышъ] (SODž. 134); Kzk. 18th c. - 19th c. **Tïnïš-bay** [Тынышбай] (Tynyšp. 72); Kzk. 19th c. **Tïnïš-pay** [Тынышпай] (AOK 94); Kzk. 19th c. **Tïnïš-pay** [Тынышпай] (SOK 128); Kzk. 19th c. **Tïnïš-pay** [Тынышпай] (SOV 136). ✧ 'Calm, quiet, peaceful' cf. Kzk. *tïnïš* 'ruhig, friedlich' (Radl. III, 1317).

TÏNÏŠTÏ Kzk. 19th c. **Tenüčti-bay?** [Тенучтибай] (Grod., Pril. 98); Kzk. 19th c. **Tïnïšti** [Тынышты] (AOO 42); Kzk. 19th c. **Tïnïšti-bay** [Тыныштыбай] (SODž. 132). ✧ 'Calm, quiet, peaceful' cf. Kzk. *tïnïš* 'ruhig, friedlich' (Radl. III, 1317) + suff. *-ti*.

TÏNÏŠTÏQ Kzk. 19th c. **Tïnïštïq** [Тыныштыкъ] (AOO 46); Kzk. 19th c. **Tïnïštïq-pay** [Тыныштыкпай] (SOK 114); Kzk. 19th c. **Tïnštïq / Tïnčtïq?** [Тынчтыкъ] (AOK 6); Kzk. 19th c. **Tïnštïq-bay** [Тынштыкбай] (AOK 30); Kzk. 19th c. **Tïnštïq-pay** [Тынштыкпай] (AOP 18, 42). ✧ 'Calmness, quietness, peacefulness' cf. Kzk. *tïnïš* 'ruhig, friedlich' (Radl. III, 1317) + suff. *-tïq*.

TÏNQAR Kzk. 19th c. **Tïnqar / Tïñqar** [Тынкаръ] (AOAtb. 62).

TÏNMÏŠ Uyg. 12th c. - 14th c. **Tïnmïš** [Tınmış] (DTS, EUTS); Uyg. 13th-14th c. **Tïnmïš** (Zieme, Mat. II, 92). ✧ 'Steaded, quietened' cf. Karakh. *tïn-* 'успокаиваться, обретать покой' (DTS).

TÏNŠÏDU Uyg. 12th c. - 14th c. **Tïnšïdu** [Tinšidu / tïnšïdu / Tınşıdu] (Radl., USp. 119, DTS, EUTS).

TÏNŠTÏQ see **TÏNÏŠTÏQ**

TÏNTÏQ Kzk. 19th c. **Tïntïq** [Тынтыкъ] (AOK 6). ⇨ **TÏN** + suff. *-tïq*.

TÏŇGİ Bashk. 1722 **Tïñgi** [Айсай Тынгибаев] (MIB III, 198).

TÏŇİL Yak. **Tïñïl** [Тыңыл] (Pek.). ⇨ **TÏGİN**.

TÏŇİZ Uyg. 12th c. - 14th c. **Tïñïz** [Tiŋïz / Tıngız] (Radl., USp. 127, DTS, EUTS).

TÏŇQÏY Yak. **Tïñqïy** [Тынкыі] (Pek.).

TÏPAR Kzk. 19th c. **Tïpar** [Тыпаръ] (SOK 288).

TÏPEY Kzk. 19th c. **Tïpey / Tipey?** [Тыпей] (SOK 144).

TÏPÏ Kzk. 19th c. **Tïpï-bek** [Тыпыбекъ] (SOK 142).

TÏPÏČ Bashk. 1728 **Tïpïč** [Тыпыч Сеитов] (MIB I, 130).

TÏPLA Hak. 19th-20th c. **Tïpla** [Тыпла], fem. (HRS 355).

TÏRA Nog.? **Tïra-χan-batïr** [Тырахан-батыр] (Žirm., Epos 395).

TÏRAQ Hak.(Sag.) 19th-20th c. **Tïraq** [Тырак] (Proben IX, 567).

TÏRANQA Hak. 19th-20th c. **Tïranqa** [Тыранка] (HRS 352).

TÏRAŠ Kzk. 19th c. **Traš / Tïraš** [Трашъ] (SOV 84); Kzk. 19th c. **Traš-pek / Tïraš-pek** [Трашпекъ] (SOV 48). ✧ 'Willing to help, co-operative' cf. Kzk. *tïraš* 'готовый оказать услугу' (KzRS).

TÏRBAN Kzk. 19th c. **Tïrban** [Тырбанъ] (SODž. 74). ✧ 'Struggle!, aspire!' cf. Kzk. *tïrban-* 'талпыну, тырысу, ұмтылу' (QTTS).

TÏRBÏY Hak.(Kacha) 19th c. **Tïrbïy** [Тырбый], fem. (Katanov, Otč. II, 42). ✧ 'Scraping, scratching' (Katanov).

TÏRDAQ Hak. 19th c. **Tïrdaq** [Тырдак] (Katanov, Otč. 12); Hak.(Shor) 19th-20th c. **Tïrdaq** [Тырдак] (Katanov, Otč. 11). ✧ 'Dither, trembling' cf. Shor *tïrlaq* 'das Zittern, das Beben' (Radl. III, 1327).

TÏRXAN Yak. **Tïrχan-buχatïr** [Ан-Тырхан-бухатыр] (Pek.). ✧ 'Pompous, self-important' cf. Yak. *tïrχay-* 'высокомерничать, надмеваться' (Pek.).

TÏRÏY Alt. 19th-20th c. **Tïrïy** [Тырый] (OjrRS 210).

TÏRMAQ see **TÏRNAQ**

TÏRMAŠ Hak.? 19th c. **Tïrmaš** [Тырмашъ] (Potanin IV, 880). ✧ 'Rake' cf. Hak. *tïrbāš/tïrbās* 'die Harke, die Egge' (Radl. III, 1330). See also **SARÏ-TÏRMAŠ**.

TÏRNA see **TURNA**

TÏRNAQ Alt. 19th-20th c. **Tïrmaq** [Тырмак] (OjrRS 210); Kzk. 19th c. **Tïrnaq** [Тырнакъ] (AOK 78, 110). ✧ 'Nail' cf. Uyg., Kuman, Kzk., Tat., Turk. *tïrnaq* 'der Nagel, die Kralle' (Radl. III, 1326). See also **JEZ-TÏRNAQ**.

TÏRTA Kzk. 19th c. **Tïrta** [Тырта] (SODž. 54).

TÏS Kzk. 1784 **Tïs** [Tys], sultan of the Middle Horde (Orta Žüz) (Radl., Aus Sib. I, 200). ✧ 'Steppe; exterior, outside' cf. Kzk. *tïs* 'das Aeussere, das Oberzeug des Kleides' (Radl. III, 1336). See also **DALA, YABAN, SÄXRA, ŠÖLKEY**.

TÏS-TEMİR Kirg. 19th c. **Tïs-temir** [Тыстемиръ], a biy (Lomakin 40). ⇨ **TÏS** + **TEMİR**.

TÏSAQ Uyg. 13th c. **Tïsaq** [Tısak] (DTS, EUTS).

TÏSAWBAN Kzk. 19th c. **Tisawban / Tïsawban** [Тсаубанъ] (AOP 46). ✧ 'Fetter, hobble'? cf. Kzk. *tïšaw* 'die Fussfesseln der Pferde' (Radl. III, 1338) + suff. *-ban*?

TÏSÏMBET Kzk. 19th c. **Tïsïmbet** [Тысымбетъ] (AOK 78). ⇨ **TÏS** + suff. *-imbet*.

TÏSÏR Kzk. 19th c. **Tïsïr** [Тысыровъ] (AOK 7o). ✧ 'Noise, rattle' cf. Kzk. *tïsïr* 'шорох, треск, звук' (KzRS).

TÏSQAN see **TÏŠQAN**

TÏŠ-PERGEN Kzk. 19th c. **Tïš-pergen** [Тышпергенъ] (SOK 176). ⇨ **TÏŠ** + **BERGEN**.

TÏŠAQ Kzk. 19th c. **Tšaq (<Tïšaq / Tïšäk?)** [Тшакъ] (AOP 86).

TÏŠAN Kzk. 19th c. **Tšan (<Tïšan)** [Тшановъ] (AOK 110).

TÏŠAT Kzk. 19th c. **Tšat-bay (<Tïšat-bay)** [Тшатбай] (AOP 34).

TÏŠQAQ Kzk. 19th c. **Tïšqaq** [Тишкакъ] (Grod., Pril. 152). ✧ 'Flux, diarrhoea' cf. Kzk. *tïšqaq* 'der Durchfall' (Radl. III, 1338).

TÏŠQAN Bashk. 1756 **Tisqan-bay / Tïsqan-bay?** [Тисканбай / Тиксанбай Маметев] (MIB IV/1, 106-107); Kzk. 19th c. **Tïsqan / Tïsqan?** [Джукбаръ Тишкановъ] (Grod., Pril. 66); Bashk. 1751 **Tïsqan** [Тыскан] (MIB IV/1, 43); Kzk. 19th c. **Tïšqam-bay (<Tïšqan-bay)** [Тышкамбай] (Grod., Pril. 74); Kzk. 19th c. **Tïšqam-bay (<Tïšqan-bay)** [Тышкамбай] (SODž. 110, 144); Kzk. 19th c. **Tïšqam-bay (<Tïšqan-bay)** [Тышкамбай] (SOK 86); Kzk. 19th c. **Tïšqan** [Тышканъ] (AOK 70); Kzk. 19th c. **Tïšqan** [Тышкановъ] (AOO 34); Kzk. 19th c. **Tïšqan** [Назаръ Тышкановъ] (Grod., Pril. 189); Kzk. 19th c. **Tïšqan-bay** [Тышканбай] (AOA 6); Kzk. 19th c. **Tïšqan-bay** [Джіянбай Тышканбаевъ] (Grod., Pril. 167); Kzk. 19th c. **Tïšqan-bay** [Тишканбай] (Grod., Pril. 193); Kzk. 19th c. **Tïšqan-bay** [Тышканбай] (SODž. 100); Kzk. 19th c. **Tïšqam-bay (<Tïšqan-bay)** [Тшкамбай] (SODž. 24); Kzk. 19th c. **Tïšqan** [Тышканъ] (AOA 14); Kzk. 19th c. **Tïšqan** [Тшканъ] (AOK 34, 54, 114); Kzk. 19th c. **Tïšqan** [Тшканъ] (SOV 20, 76); Kzk. 1817 **Tïšqan-bay / Tušqan-bay?** [طوجنان باى / Тшканбай] (MIK IV, 308); Bashk. 1762 **Tošqan? / Tïšqan** [Тошкан / Тышкан Дербышев] (MIB IV/2, 300); Kzk. 19th c. **Tušqan** [Ведилъ Тушкановъ] (Grod., Pril. 158); *TN:* Bashk. **Tušqan** [Тушканъ], a place (?) north of Birsk (Karta JAR III). ✧ 'Mouse' cf. Kzk. *tïšqan* 'die Maus' (Radl. III, 1338). See also **QARA-TÏŠQAN**.

TÏŠQAN-GÖZ Kzk. 19th c. **Tïšqan-göz** [Тшкангозъ] (SOK 34). ✧ 'Mouse-eye(d)'. ⇨ **TÏŠQAN + KÖZ.**

TÏŠQÏN Kzk. 19th c. **Tïšqïm-bay? (<Tïšqïn-bay? / Tïšqan-bay?)** [Тышкымбай] (SODž. 14).

TÏŠTÏ Kzk. 19th c. **Tišti-bay** [Тштыбай] (SODž. 88); Kzk. 19th c. **Tišti-bay** [Тштыбай] (SOV 34); Kzk. 19th c. **Tišti-bek** [Тштыбекъ] (SOV 100); Kzk. 19th c. **Tišti-bay** [Тыштыбай] (SODž. 70); Kzk. 19th c. **Tišti-γul** [Тыштыгулъ] (AOK 50). ⇨ **TÏŠ / TÏŠ?** + suff. *-tï.*

TÏŠTÏQ Kzk. 19th c. **Tištiq / Tištïq?** [Тиштык] (AOK 86); Kzk. 19th c. **Tištïq-pay** [Тштыкпай] (SODž. 96); Kzk. 19th c. **Tištïq-pay** [Тштыкпай] (SOV 18); Kzk. 19th c. **Tištïq?** [Тыштекъ] (AOK 22); Kzk. 19th c. **Tištiq-bay** [Тыштекбай] (AOK 106); Kzk. 19th c. **Tištïq** [Тыштыкъ] (AOP 34). ⇨ **TÏŠ / TÏŠ?** + suff. *-tïq.*

TÏTANAX Hak. 19th-20th c. **Tïtanaχ** [Тытанах] (HRS 352).

TÏTÏ Kzk. 19th c. **Tïtï-bay(-arnasï)** [Тытыбай-арнасы], a field (AOK 90).

TÏTSU Uyg. 13th c. **Tïtsu** [tïtsu / Tıtsu] (DTS, EUTS). ✧ 'May he restrain / may he hold [sb?] back' (Blagova 1997, 716).

TÏTSU-ŠÏLA Uyg. 12th c. - 14th c. **Tïtsu-šïla** [Titsu Sila / tïtsu šïla] (Radl., USp. 138, DTS). ✧ 'May he restrain - šila / May he hold [sb?] back - šila' (Blagova 1997, 716).

TÏZÏRQO Hak. 19th-20th c. **Tïzïrqo** [Тызырко] (HRS 352).

TÏLEGEN see **TÏLEGEN**

TÏLEP see **TÏLÄP**

TLÄB-BERDÏ see **TÏLÄP-BERDÏ**

TLÄKÄY see **TÏLEKEY**

TLÄKÄN see **TÏLEGEN**

TLÄMÏŠ see **TÏLEMÏŠ**

TLÄNČE see **TÏLENČÏ**

TLÄNČÏ see **TÏLENČÏ**

TLÄP see **TÏLÄP**

TLÄW-ГABÏL see **TLÄW-QABÏL**

TLÄW-QABÏL Kzk. 19th c. **Tläw-γabïl** [Тлеугобылъ] (SOK 110); Kzk. 19th c. **Tläw-γabïl** [Тлеугабылъ] (SOV 66); Kzk. 18th c. - 19th c. **Tläw-qabïl** [Тлеукабыл] (Tynyšp. 65, 67). ✧ 'Wish - (was) accepted' (Sattarov). ⇨ **TÏLÄW + QABUL.**

TLÄWBET Bashk. 1754 **Tläwbet** [Бюляк Тлявбетев] (MIB IV/1, 83). ⇨ **TÏLÄW** + suff. *-bet.* See also **TÏLÄWMÄT.**

TLÄWKÄY see **TLEWKÄY**

TLÄWKEY see **TLEWKÄY**

TLEB-ALDÏ see **TÏLEP-ALDÏ**

TLEGEN see **TÏLEGEN**

TLEK-ALÏ see **TÏLEK-ALÏ**

TLEKE see **TÏLEKE**

TLEKEY see **TÏLEKEY**

TLEKEY see **TLEWKÄY**

TLEM see **TÏLEM**

TLEMÏS see **TÏLEMÏŠ**

TLEMŠÏ see **TÏLENČÏ**

TLENČE see **TÏLENČÏ**

TLENČÏ see **TÏLENČÏ**

TLENDÏ see **TÏLENDÏ**

TLENMET see **TÏLENMET**

TLENŠÄ see **TÏLENČÏ**

TLEP-BERGEN see **TÏLEP-BERGEN**

TLEP-PERDE see **TÏLÄP-BERDÏ**

TLEP-PERGEN see **TÏLEP-BERGEN**

TLEPEY see **TÏLEPEY**

TLEŠ see **TÏLÄŠ**

TLEW see **TÏLÄW**

TLEW-BERLİ see **TİLÄW-BERDİ**

TLEWBEN Kzk. 19th c. **Tlewben** [Тлеубен] (SOK 168). ⇨ **TİLÄW** + suff. *-ben*?

TLEWKÄ Kzk. 19th c. **Tleke / Tlewke** [Тлеке] (AOO 78); Kzk. 19th c. **Tlewkä** [Тлеука] (SODž. 18); Kzk. 19th c. **Tlewke** [Тлеуке] (SOV 110). ⇨ **TİLÄW** + dim. suff. *-kä*.

TLEWKÄY Tat. 1780 **Tläwkey / Tläwkäy?** [Тлавкей (Тлявкей) Акбулатов] (MIB V, 551, 552); Kzk. 19th c. **Tlekey / Tlewkey** [Тлекей] (AOO 10); Tat. 1731 **Tlewkey / Tläwkäy** [Тлевкей] (MIB III, 293); Bashk. 1734 **Tlewkey / Tläwkäy** [Тлевкей Кармышев] (MIB III, 317); Bashk. 1735 **Tlewkey / Tläwkäy** [Бердыгулъ Тлевкеевъ], a tarχan (Vel.-Zern., Bašk. 15); Bashk. 1735 **Tlewkey / Tläwkäy?** [Тлевкей Сараязовъ], a tarχan (Vel.-Zern., Bašk. 18); Bashk. 1740 **Tlewkey / Tläwkäy** [Тлевкей Володимеров] (MIB I, 421, 468). ⇨ **TİLÄW** + dim. suff. *-käy*.

TLEWKE see **TLEWKÄ**

TLEWKEY see **TLEWKÄY**

TLEWLEYKÄ Bashk. 1616 **Tlewleykä / Tläwleykä** [Тлевлейка], a murza (Miller, Ist. Sib. II, 235). ⇨ **TİLÄWLİ** + suff. *-y* + *-kä*.

TLEWLİ see **TİLÄWLİ**

TNEY see **TİNEY**

TOBA Kzk. 19th c. **Toba** [Тоба] (SOK 170); Kzk. 19th c. **Toba-žan** [Тобожонъ] (SODž. 10); Kzk. 19th c. **Toba-žan** [Тобожанъ] (SODž. 64). ✧ 'Repentance, penitence' (Ar.) cf. Uyg., Kuman, Kzk. *toba* 'die Reue' (Radl. III, 1231).

TOBA-AY Kuman 1419 **Tobay** (<Toba-ay) [Jacobus Tobay], a chief (capitaneus) of the Kumans of Hungary (Gyárfás III, 566); Kzk. 1737 **Tobay** (<Toba-ay) [Тобай Сабаев] (MIB I, 349). ✧ 'April (month of repentance)' (Rásonyi, KÖA 131, Anthr. 145), cf. Kuman *tob-aj* 'Reuemonat, aprilis' (CC). ⇨ **TOBA** + **AY**. See also **NİSAN, SÄÜRÄ**.

TOBA-AYAQ Nog.? **Tobayaq** [Тобаяк] (Žirm., Epos 403). ✧ 'Lame' cf. Tat.(Tüm.) *tobayaq* 'der Beine hat, die nur bis zum Knie reichen' (Radl. III, 1232). ⇨ **AYAQ**.

TOBA-QABİL Kzk. 19th c. **Toba-qabïl** [Тобакабылъ] (SOK 302). ⇨ **TOBA** + **QABUL**.

TOBAY see **TOBA-AY**

TOBAYAQ see **TOBA-AYAQ**

TOBALAQ see **TOMALAQ**

TOBAR Khorezm./Chag. 14th c. **Tobar / Toban?** [Homar Tobar], Timür's retainer (Clavijo 42, 64).

TOBİČAQ Kzk. 19th c. **Tobïčaq** [Тобычакъ] (AOK 2); Kzk. 19th c. **Tobïčaq** [Тобычакъ] (SOK 64). ✧ 'A kind of race-horse' cf. Uyg. *tobïčaq* 'ein grosses Pferd aus dem Westen', Kirg. *toburčaq* 'ein Racepferd' (Radl. III, 1233).

TOBİQ Bashk. 1738 **Tobïq** [Бекметь Тобикова], fem. (MIB III, 401); Kzk. 1838 **Tobuq** [Тобукъ] (Konšin, Mat. V, 57); Kzk. 19th c. **Topïq?** [Топекъ] (SOV 100); Tat.(GH)? 1284 **Topïq / Topuq?** [Τώπαχ], a christened Tatar, died in 1284 (Byz. Turc. 330); Kzk. 19th c. **Towuq-bay** [Товукбай] (Grod., Pril. 107); *TN:* Kzk. **Topuq-bay** [Топук-бай], a place south-east of Lake Aral (Karta JAR XI). ✧ 'Knee; hoof' cf. Hak. *tobïq*, Kzk. *tobuq* 'die Kniescheibe, das Knie' (Radl. III, 1232, 1233), Turk. *tobuq* 'der Knöchel am Fusse' (Radl. III, 1224), Bashk. *tubïq* 'колено' (BRS), Chag. *tofuq* 'rund, kugelförmig' (Radl. III, 1234). See also **TOPAY**.

TOBİQTİ see **TOBUQLİ**

TOBİL see **TOBUL**

TOBİLAY Karg. **Tobïlay / Tobïl-ay?** [Тобылаi] (Proben IX, 632). ⇨ **TOBİL** + suff. *-ay*?

TOBOLDAY Tat.(Sib.) 1605 **Tobolday** [Тоболдай], a prince (Ist., Sib. II, 189). ⇨ **TOBİL** + suff. *-day*.

TOBUQ see **TOBİQ**

TOBUQLİ Kzk. 18th c. - 19th c. **Tobïqtï** [Тобыкты] (Tynyšp. 68); Kzk. 19th c. **Tobuqlï** [Тобуклы], forefather of the Kazak (Potanin IV, 15). ✧ 'With knees'. ⇨ **TOBİQ** + suff. *-tï*.

TOBUL Kzk. 19th c. **Tobïl-bay** [Тобылбай] (AOP 54); Kzk. 1794 **Tobul** [توبـل / Тобул] (MIK IV, 165); Kzk. 19th c. **Tobul-bay** [Тобулбай] (AOK 134); Kzk. 19th c. **Tobul-bay** [Тобулбай] (AOP 82). ✧ I. 'Tobol (river)'? cf. Kzk. *Tobul* 'der Fluss Tobol' (Radl. III, 1233); II. 'Tall; grand, majestic' cf. Alt.(Tel.) *tobïl* 'hoch, erhaben' (Radl. III, 1233). ⇨ **TOBİL**.

TOBULA Uyg. 12th c. - 14th c. **Tobula** [Tobula] (Radl., USp. 209, 251, DTS, EUTS).

TOČA see **TOJA**

TOČAX Hak. 19th-20th c. **Točaχ** [Точах] (HRS 352). ⇨ **TOČAQ?**

TOČAY Kzk. 19th c. **Točay** [Точай] (AOP 70).

TOČAQ Hak.(Kacha) 19th-20th c. **Točaq** [Точак] (Proben IX, 545). ✧ The name of the Tuva-clan (Butanaev).

TOČİ Hak.(Koyb.) 19th c. **Točï** [Точы] (Katanov, Otč. II, 12-15); Bashk. 1729 **Točï-bay** [Точибай Якшиметев] (MIB III, 260).

TOČİY Hak.(Sag.) 19th-20th c. **Točïy** [Точый] (Katanov, Otč. 11).

TOČQİ see **TOČQO**

TOČQO Alt. 19th-20th c. **Točqï** [Точкы], fem. (OjrRS 213); Alt. 19th-20th c. **Točqo** [Точко], fem. (OjrRS 213). ✧ 'Daughter' cf. R. *dočka* 'id.' (OjrRS).

TOJA Hak.(Sag.) 19th-20th c. **Toča** [Точа] (Katanov, Otč. 11); Hak. 19th-20th c. **Toja** [Точа], fem. (HRS 355).

TODA Hak.? 19th-20th c. **Toda** [Тода] (Katanov, Otč. 10); Karg. 19th-20th c. **Toda** [Тода] (Katanov, Otč. 8).

TODAX see **TŌDAQ**

TODAŇ Hak. 19th-20th c. **Todañ** [Тоданъ] (HRS 351).

TODÏLDAY Alt. 19th-20th c. **Todïlday** [Тодылдай], fem. (OjrRS 213).

TODÏS Hak. 19th-20th c. **Todïs** [Тодыс], fem. (HRS 355).

TODO Hak. 19th-20th c. **Todo** [Тодо], fem. (HRS 355).

TODOY Hak. 19th-20th c. **Todoy** [Тодой], fem. (HRS 355).

TODOQ Hak. 19th-20th c. **Todoq** [Тодок] (HRS 352).

TODOQAY Hak. 19th-20th c. **Todoqay** [Тодокай], fem. (HRS 355).

TODURQA Tat.(Lit.) 1548 **Todurqa** [Тодурка] (Kn. Metriki Lit. 45).

TOFUNJAQ Kzk. 19th c. **Tofunjaq** [Хадиджа-биби Тофунджакова], fem. (Grod., Pril. 118).

TOГ Tuv. 19th c. **Toγ** [Тоҕ], fem. (Proben IX, 209). ✧ 'Barren, effete' cf. Hak.(Sag.), Shor *toy* 'gelt (die noch nicht geboren hat)' (Radl. III, 1157).

TOГ-ARSTAN see **TOQ-ARSTAN**

TOГ-ORSTAN see **TOQ-ARSTAN**

TOГA-TERKEN see **TUГA-TERKEN**

TOГAY Chuv. 18th-19th c. **Togay** [Тогай] (Magn. 83); Tat.(GH) 1361 **Toγay** [Тогай], a prince of the Horde (PSRL X, 233); Maml. 1310 **Toγay** [الجاشنكير / سيف الدين طغاى / طوغاى], an emir (Dawād. 239, 348); Maml. 1318 **Toγay** [طغاى الناصرى], an emir (Dawād. 293); Maml. 1320 **Toγay** [خوند طغاى] (Iyās I, 161, Zetterst. 171, 202); Maml. 1347 **Toγay** [طغاى / سيف الدين / Togay], governor of Diyarbekir (Zetterst. 165, 168, Weil, Chalif. I, 342); Maml. 14th c. **Toγay** [خانقاه طغاى النجمى] (Makrīzī, Khit. I, 425); Maml. 1372 **Toγay** [طغاى], an emir (Iyās I, 267); Bashk. 1714 **Toγay** [Тогай Козембаев] (MIB I, 105); Kzk. 19th c. **Toγay** [Тогай] (SODž. 42); Kirg. 19th c. **Toγay** [Тогай], forefather of the Kirghiz (ZIRGO V, 140); Hak. 19th-20th c. **Toγay** [Тоҕай] (HRS 351); Maml.? 1321 **Toγay-baχši** [طغاى بخشى / Тогайбахши] (Duqmaq/Tizeng. I, 321, 328); Kzk. 19th c. **Toγay-bay** [Тогайбай] (Konšin, Oč. 128); Kzk. 19th c. **Toγay-bay** [Тогайбай] (SODž. 100, 106); Kzk. 19th c. **Toγay-bay** [Тогайбай] (SODž. 46); Kzk. 19th c. **Toγay-bay** [Тогайбай] (SOK 118, 286); Kzk. 19th c. **Toγay-bay** [Тогайбай] (SOK 14); Kzk. 19th c. **Toγay-bay** / **Tuγay-bay** [Тогайбай (Тугайбай)] (Grod., Pril. 118); Kkalp. 1822 **Toγay-behadïr** [Тогай бехадыр] (MIKk. 127); Kzk. 19th c. **Toγay-bek** [Тогайбекъ] (SODž. 134); Kzk. 19th c. **Toγay-bek** [Тогайбекъ] (SOV 30); Kipch.? 10th c. - 13th c. **Toγay-χan** [تغاى خان], from Samarkand (Juwaynī I, 90); Kipch. 1219 **Toγay-χan** [Тогай-Ханъ], from the Qañlï tribe (RaD/Ber. III, 58); Kzk. 1826 **Toγay-χan** [طغى خان قزاق / Toghaï-khan le

Kazak], from Bukhara (Vel.-Zern., Haïder 280-282); Crm. 1641 **Toγay-mirza** [طوغاى مرزه] (Vel.-Zern., Crim. 275); OT / Mo.? **Tuγay** [طغاى / Тугай], a Kereit (RaD/Ber. II, 110 /178/); Tat. 1553 **Tuγay** [Сенку Тугаевъ] (PSRL XIII, 232); Kzk. 1819 **Tuγay** [Тугай] (MIK IV, 326); Kzk. 19th c. **Tuγay** [Тугай Бабаевъ] (Grod., Pril. 23); Kzk. 19th c. **Tuγay** [Калбекъ Тугаевъ] (Grod., Pril. 82); Kzk. 19th c. **Tuγay-bay** [Тугайбаевъ] (AUK 585); *EN:* Trkm. **Toγay-šeyχlü** [طغى شيخلو], a tribe (taife) in the region of Rakka, Syria (Refik., Anad. 96); *TN:* Chuv.? 18th. c. **Tugayeva** [Тугаева], a village in the district of Tsivil'sk (Korsakov 315). ✧ 'Field, flat with a forest' cf. Chag., East.T., Kzk., Tat.(Sib.) *toγay* 'eine Wiese, Niederung, die mit Wald bewachsen ist; die Flusswindungen; der Wald, das Waldland' (Radl. III, 1158), Chag. *toqay* 'id.' (Radl. III, 1147), Tat. *tuγay* 'извив, излучина (реки) пойма; тугай' (TatRS), Bashk. *tuγay* 'кустарник в поймах рек, урема; пойменный луг' (BRS/Uraksin). See also **YAN-TUГAY; TOQAY**.

TOГAY-MURAD Uzb. 1707 **Toγay-murad** [طغاى مراد اوچى / Tagaj Murād-i Qungrāt], from Bukhara (Buchari 291). ⇨ **TOГAY + MURAT.**

TOГAY-TEMİR Maml. 14th c. **Toγay-demir** [طغيدمر السيفى], a bearer of arms (Mayer 232); Maml. 1332 **Toγay-temir** [سيف الدين طغاى تمر], an emir (Dawād. 366); Maml. 1347 **Toγay-temir** [النجمى الدودار السيفى طغيتمر], great chancellor, mentioned in inscriptions of glass lamps (Mayer 232-33, Weil, Chalif. IV, 473); Maml. 1347 **Toγay-temir** [النجمى طغاى تمر], an emir and treasurer of state (Weil, Chalif. I, 473); Maml. 14th c. - 15th c. **Toγay-temir** [السيفى طغاى تمر الساقى], mentioned in an inscription oo a box (Mayer 234); Maml. 1366/67 **Toγay-temir** [طغيتمر النظامى] (Iyās I, 220); Maml.? 1389 **Toγay-temir** [طغيتمر القيلاوى] (Iyās I, 271); Maml. 1398/99 **Toγay-temir** [طغاى تمر] (Ibn Taghrīb. VI, 8, 34); Khorezm.? 14th c. **Toγay-temür** [طغيتمور / تغاتيمور بن نوشى بن چنگيزخان / Toghaïtomoûr], emir, owner of a part of Khorasan (Ibn Bat. II, 124, III, 66, Juwaynī I, 145, 205). ⇨ **TOГAY + TEMİR.**

TOГAY-TEMİR-TAŠ Crm. 1328 **Toγay-temir-taš** [طغاى تمرتاش] (Aynī/Tizeng. I, 496, 527). ⇨ **TOГAY + TEMİR + TAŠ.**

TOГAY-TEMÜR see **TOГAY-TEMİR**

TOГAL see **TOQAL**

TOГALAQ Kzk. 19th c. **Doγalaq** [Доголакъ] (AOK 78); Kzk. 19th c. **Toγalaq** [Тогалакъ] (SOK 200); Kzk. 19th c. **Tuγalaq** [Тугалакъ] (SODž. 74). ✧ 'Roundish' cf. Chag. *toγalaq* 'abgerundet' (Radl. III, 1160), Kzk. *doγalaq* 'rund; das Rad' (Radl. III, 1706).

TOГAN Turk. 1436-1439 **Doγan** [Doğan bin Abdullah]

(Gökb., Ed. 173); Turk. 1611 **Doγan** [Doğan], from Isparta, Turkey (Ün 1938, 645); Yürük 1543 **Doγan** [Doğan] (Gökb., Rum. 219); Yürük 1543 **Doγan** [Doğan] (Gökb., Rum. 226); Yürük 16th c. **Doγan** [طوغان / Doğan], from the Yürüks of Kocacık (Gökb., Rum. 103); Tat. 1543 **Doγan** [Doğan] (Gökb., Rum. 240); Turk. 1413 **Doγan-aγa** [Hacı Doğan Ağa] (Gökb., Ed. 21); Turk. 20th c. **Doγan-baba** [Doğanbaba], a village in the province of Burdur, Turkey (TMİB 206); Trkm. 1690 **Doγan-beg** [دوغان بك / Doğan beğ] (Refik., Anad. 82); Turk. 1485 **Doγan-bey** [Doğan Bey (Kurtçu/Korucu)] (Gökb., Ed. 224-225); Chuv. 18th-19th c. **Togan** [Тоганъ] (Magn. 83); Kzk. 19th c. **Toγam-bay** (<Toγan-bay) [Тогамбай] (SODž. 134); 882/83 **Toγan** [طغان] (Tabarī Annal. III, 2028); 10th c. - 13th c. **Toγan** [طغان تاج‌الدين], governor of the fortress of Qarun (?) (Ǧuwaynī II, 113); 13th c. **Toγan** [طغان], an emir (Qazw. 589); Türk **Toγan** [طغان], an emir, slave-soldier (gulām) (Ibn Bībī IV, 218); Türk 7th-9th c. **Toγan** [Toγan] (ETY III, 31); Karakh.? 946 **Toγan** [ابوحرب طغان], a door-keeper (Ibn al-Athīr/Tornb. VIII, 346, 509, IX, 37); Karakh.? 966 **Toγan** [بن طغان] (Ibn al-Athīr/Tornb. VIII, 419); Karakh. 977 **Toγan** [طغان / طوغان صاحب بست], commander of Bust before the Ghaznavids (Ibn al-Athīr/Tornb. VIII, 509, Mirch. Gasnevid. 5-7); Maml. 1290 **Toγan** [المنصوری سيف‌الدين طوغان], inspector of the councils of Syria (Zetterst. 170, Makrīzī III, 116); Maml. 1298 **Toγan** [سيف‌الدين طوغان], an emir (Dawād. 8, 42, 209); Maml. 1299 **Toγan** [طوغان من أهل دمشق] (Dawād. 34); Maml. 1328, 1333, 1340 **Toγan** [طوغان الشمسى سيف‌الدين], an emir (Dawād. 342, 378, Zetterst. 216); Maml. 1332 **Toγan** [طوغان], an emir (Dawād. 368); Maml. 14th c. **Toγan** [Toğan] (Tarǰ/Houtsma 84, Tarǰ/Toparlı 41); Maml. 14th c. **Toγan** [Тоган] (Tuhfa 191, 410); Maml. 1377/78 **Toγan** [طوغان العمرى], a chess-player (Iyās I,); Maml. 1400 **Toγan** [طوغان], governor of the fortress of Rūm (Ibn Taghrīb. VI, 340); Maml. 1414 **Toγan** [طوغان الحسنى], chancellor of state (Iyās I 354, Ibn Taghrīb. VI, 193, 201, VII, 319, Weil, Chalif. II, 132); Maml. 1414, 1461 **Toγan** [طوغان امير آخور المؤيّد], a master of the horse (supervisor of the horses) (Ibn Taghrīb. VI, 328, 377, 488, 498, 789, VIII, 562, Weil, Chalif. II, 132); Maml. 1422 **Toγan** [طوغان الدقماقى] (Ibn Taghrīb. VI, 555); Maml. 1426 **Toγan** [طوغان], chancellor of Sultan Taghrī-berdi (Ibn Taghrīb. VI, 601, 615); Maml. 1438/39 **Toγan** [طوغان الاقبردائى المنقار] (Ibn Taghrīb. VII, 56, 224, VIII, 66, 162); Maml. 1438/39,

1457 **Toγan** [طوغان الاشرفى الزردكاش] (Ibn Taghrīb. VII, 71, 82, VIII, 371); Maml. 1443/44 **Toγan** [Thoûghân en-Nâséry], an emir, died in Safad in 1443/44, his mausoleum is in Damascus (Sauvaire VI, 245); Maml. 1457 **Toγan** [طوغان السيفى] (Ibn Taghrīb. VIII, 334); Maml. 1460 **Toγan** [طوغان قلق سير التركمانى] (Ibn Taghrīb. VII, 633); Maml. 1468/69 **Toγan** [طوغان ميق المؤيدى العمرى] (Iyās II, 99, Ibn Taghrīb. VII, 854); Maml. 1475/76 **Toγan** [العلا ئى على طوغان] (Iyās III, 162); Maml. 1476/77 **Toγan** [طوغان المحمدى الاشرفى] (Iyās II, 168); Maml.? 1485 **Toγan** [طوغان], envoy (Iyās II, 229); Chag.? 17th c.? **Toγan** (Le Coq, Ind. 2); Turk. 1438/39, 1441 **Toγan** [طوغان العثمانى], governor of Jerusalem (Ibn Taghrīb. VII, 5, 65, 68, VIII, 3, 8, 147, Weil, Chalif. II, 227, 231); Turk. 1447 **Toγan** [طوغان / مرتكلور/] (Āšikp. 124); Bashk. 1735 **Toγan** [Тоганъ Кучуковъ], a tarχan (Vel.-Zern., Bašk. 16); Bashk. 1735 **Toγan** [Тоганъ], a tarχan (Vel.-Zern., Bašk. 16); Kzk. 1822 **Toγan** [طوغان / Тоган] (MIK IV, 416, 417); Nog. 1649 **Toγan** [Тоганъ], a murza (AI IV, 123); Nog. 1649 **Toγan** [Тоганъ] (AI IV, 87); Turk. 1437 **Toγan** / **Qïlïč-toγan** [قلج طوغان / طوغان / قلجى/] (Āšikp. 114); Karakh. 994, 1010, 1018 **Toγan** / **Toγan-χan** [طغان ملك الترك / طغان صاحب بها الدولة / طغان خان بن قراخان / Tagan Chan], ruler of the Türks (of Turkestan) under Al-Qadir Billāhi, İlek-χan's companion (brother?) (Ibn Taghrīb. II, 56, 117, Ibn Al-Athīr/Tornb. IX, 73, 78, 156, 209, 210, 213, Mirch. Gasnevid. 38, 46, Weil, Chalif. III, 47, Abulfidā III, 4-5, 18, 44-45, Qazw. 398); Maml. 1453, 1455 **Toγan** / **Toγan-šeyχ** [طوغان الاشرفى / شيخ /] (Ibn Taghrīb. VII, 465, VIII, 189, 340); Maml. 1493/94 **Toγan-bay** [طوغان باى الثور] (Iyās II, 283); Kzk. 18th c. - 19th c. **Toγan-bay-biy** [Тоганбай-бий] (Tynyšp. 66); Nog. **Toγan-batïr** [Тоган-батыр] (Žirm., Epos 395); Selj. 12th c. **Toγan-beg** [تغان بك / ولصّواب تغاربك/], vizier of Sultan Sanjar (1118-1157) from Kashgar (Rāwandī); Karakh. 1018 **Toγan-χan** [طغان خان بن طنفاج خان], Tafγač-χan's son (?) (Ibn al-Athīr/Tornb. IX, 212); Khorezm.? 1218 **Toγan-χan** [طغانخان], a Khorezmshahid (Nasawī 34); Maml. 14th c. **Toγan-qïz** (Sauvaget 51); Karakh.? 1173 **Toγan-šah** [طغان شاه ابوبكر المويد] (Ibn al-Athīr/Tornb. XI, 247-49, 253); Khorezm. 1300 **Toγan-šaχ-χatun**, daughter of Mubarek Shah, died in 1300 (RaD/Jahn 132, Hammer, Ilch. II, 107); 923 **Toγan-tegin** [طغانتكين] (Ibn al-Athīr/Tornb. VIII, 97); Karakh. **Toγan-tegin** [Nizameddin İsrafil Togan Tégin / Nizameddin İsrafil Togan Tigin], a chief (MK/Atalay 848); Selj. 12th c.

Toγan-tegin / Tuγan-tegin? [تـغـيـن تغان بـدرالـديـن] (Muh. Ibrahim 197); Karakh. **Toγan-tigin** [Nizameddin İsrafil Togan Tigin] (MK/Atalay 848); Khorezm. 14th c. **Tuγan / Toγan-χan** [طغان خان حاكم فـرغـانـه / طـوغـان الفـرغـا نـيّ Thoûghân alferghâny], an emir of the town of Ferghana (Ibn Bat. III, 311, Ǧuwaynī I, 232); Selj. 1172 **Tuγan-šah** [طغنشاه بـن مـوّيَّـد ايـبـه/ طغنشـاه بـن مـلـك مـويـد] / Туган-шах / Туганшах ибн ал-Муайид Ай-Аба / Туганшах Абу-Бекр], ruler of Nishapur (Ǧuwaynī II, 19, 21, 22, RaD I/1, 103, MIT I, 404, 405, 407, 408, 445, 446, Muh. Ibrahim 111, 119, 142); *EN:* Turk. 19th c. **Toγan**, a Zeybek āširet (tribe) in the region of Tire (Kúnos 1891, 117); *TN:* Turk. 20th c. **Doγan-bey** [Doğanbey], a village in the province of Aydın, Turkey (TMİB 131); Turk. 20th c. **Doγan-bey** [Doğanbey], a village in the province of Konya, Turkey (TMİB 568); Turk. 20th c. **Doγan-beyli** [Doğanbeyli], a village in the province of Adana, Turkey (TMİB 20); Turk. 15th c. **Xaji-Toγan** [حـاجـى طـوغـان], an old mosque (mescit) in Ankara (MG Ank. 33); Kzk. **Toγam-bay?** (<**Toγan-bay**) [Тогомбай] (Karta JAR XI). ❖ 'Falcon' (Sauvaget 51), cf. Maml. *toγan* 'сокол; ворона' (Tuhfa), Turk. *doγan* 'der Falke' (Radl. III, 1706). See also **AQ-TUΓAN, BARS-TOΓAN, BOZ-DOΓAN, EL-TOΓAN, ER-TOΓAN, KİŠ-TOΓAN, QARA-TOΓAN, QÏZ-TOΓAN, QULA-DOΓAN.**

TOΓAN-ARSLAN Selj. 1119, 1120 **Doγan-arslan / Toγan-arslan?** [طُغـان ارسـلان بـن دمـلاج] / Doghân-Arslân] (Kamāladdīn: RHCHor III, 618-621, Kamāladdīn II, 189, 191, 192); Selj. 1119/20, 1123/24 **Toγan-arslan** [طغان ارسلان] / Toghân-Arslân] (Ibn al-Athīr: RHCHor I, 324, 354); Selj. 1120 **Toγan-arslan** [طغان ارسلان بـن المـكـر] (Ibn al-Athīr/Tornb. X, 389, 436, XI, 43, XII, 321); Selj. 1121 **Toγan-arslan** [شمس الـدولـة الاحـد بـا بـن حـسام الـدولـة تـمـتـكـيـن طغان ارسلان] (Qalānisi 205, 267); Selj. 1124, 1140 **Toγan-arslan** [قـرتـى طغان ارسـلان], Qïrtï's (?) father (Qalānisi 208, 367); *TN:* Turk. 1455 **Doγan-arslan-mahallesi** [Doğan-Arslan (mahallesi)], district of Doγan-arslan (Gökb., Ed. 163). ⇨ **TOΓAN + ARSLAN.**

TOΓAN-BAS Kzk. 19th c. **Toγan-bas** [Тоганбасъ] (SOK 168). ⇨ **TOΓAN + BAŠ.**

TOΓAN-BERK Selj. 11th c. **Toγan-berk?** [طغان بـرك], a door-keeper of Sultan Maχmud and Berk-yaruq (Rāwandī 139, 203). ❖ 'Falcon-strong/healthy' cf. Trkm. *berk* 'прочный, крепкий; здоровый' (TrkmRS). ⇨ **TOΓAN.**

TOΓAN-DURDÏ Trkm. 1859 **Toγan-durdï-šeyχ** [Тоганъ-Дурды-шейхъ] (ZIRGOÊtn. I, 195). ⇨ **TOΓAN + TURDÏ.**

TOΓAN-SOÑQUR Khorezm. 1230 **Toγan-soñqur /**

Tuγan-suñqur? [تغان سـنـتـور] / يغان سـنـتـور / لـعـان سـنـتـور] / Ighan Sonkor / Туган-Сункур], an emir in Khorassan (Ǧuwajnī II, 219, Nasawī 221, RaD II, 33). ⇨ **TOΓAN + SOÑQUR.**

TOΓANA Uyg. **Toγana**, fem. (Zieme, Mat. I, 74). ❖ 'Falcon!' (Vocative form). ⇨ **TOΓAN** + voc. suff. *-a.*

TOΓANAY Chuv. 18th-19th c. **Toganey** [Тоганей] (Magn. 83); Bashk. 1788 **Toγanay** [Иван Тоганаев], from Ufa (MIB V, 237); Tat.(Sib. 1633 **Toγanay** [Инбердей Тоганаев] (Miller, Ist. Sib. II, 402). ⇨ **TOΓAN** + dim. suff. *-ay?*

TOΓANAS see **TOΓANAŠ**

TOΓANAŠ Kzk. 1817 **Toγanas** [طـوغـانـاس] / Тоганас] (MIK IV, 309); Kzk. 19th c. **Toγanas** [Тоганасъ] (AOO 62); Bashk. 1712 **Toγanaš** [Тоганаш Темирбулат] (MIB III, 82); Bashk. 1735 **Toγanaš** [Колчура Тоганашев] (MIB III, 333); *TN:* Chuv. 1738 **Toganaš(evy)** [Тоганашевы], a village (Alatyr. 138). ❖ I. 'Little falcon'?; II. 'Brother-friend/mate' (Sattarov), cf. TUΓAN + İŠ. ⇨ **TOΓAN?** + suff. *-aš?*

TOΓANAŠQA Bashk. 1647 **Toγanašqa?** [Тогонашка] (Miller, Ist. Sib. II, 523). ⇨ **TOΓANAŠ** + suff. *-qa.*

TOΓANČÏQ Maml. 1332 **Toγančïq**, an emir (Dawād. 367); 1297 **Toγančuq**, wife of emir Newrūz (RaD/Jahn 54, 111); Oghuz/Trkm. 1004 **Toγančuq** [Туганчук], ruler of Serahs (?) (MIT I, 226). ⇨ **TOΓAN** + dim. suff. *-čïq.*

TOΓANEY see **TOΓANAY**

TOΓAŠ Bashk. 1750 **Toγaš** [Кугаш Тогашев] (MIB III, 472); Nog. 1649 **Toγaš** [Тогашъ] (AI IV, 81); Tat. 1543 **Tuγaš** [تـوعـاش] / Тугаш] (Jusupov 65); Bashk. 1761 **Tuγaš** [Козай Тугашев / Тургашев] (MIB IV/1, 213). ❖ I. 'Full/sated mate' cf. Tat. PN *Tuγaš* <*tuq* + *aš* <*iš* (Sattarov); II. 'A kind of pastry'? ⇨ **TOQ + EŠ / TOQAŠ?**

TOΓÏM Kzk. 19th c. **Toγïm** [Тогымъ] (AOO 14). ❖ 'Sweat-cloth' cf. Kzk. *toqïm* 'id.' (KzTS). See also **ŠİRDAQ.**

TOΓÏMBET Kzk. 18th c. - 19th c. **Toγïmbet** [Тогымбет] (Tynyšp. 68, 70). ⇨ **TOQ** + suff. *-imbet.*

TOΓÏŠ-PAY see **TOQÏŠ**

TOΓÏZAQ Kzk. 18th c. - 19th c. **Toγïzaq** [Тогызак] (Tynyšp. 71). ⇨ **TOQUZ** + suff. *-aq.*

TOΓLAX Hak. 19th-20th c. **Toγlaχ** [Тоғлах] (HRS 351). ❖ 'Round(ish), ball-like; hank' (HRS).

TOΓLÏQ-TEMÜR see **TOQLUQ-TEMÜR**

TOΓMA Uyg. 12th c. - 14th c. **Toγma** [toγma / Toğma] (DTS); Uzb. 1705, 1707 **Toγma-sultan** [طغمه سلطان], a high-ranked person in Bukhara (Buchari 280, 295). ❖ I. 'Child; slave' cf. Chag., Crm., Uzb. *toγma* 'das Kind; die Kinder eines Sklaven, Leibeigenen; der Sklave' (Radl. III, 1168); II. 'Button'? (Blagova 1997, 712). See also **BELÄ-TUΓMA, QARA-TOΓMA.**

ТОГМӤŠ 1289 Toɣmiš [تغميش] (RaD/Jahn 2); Selj.?
Toɣmïš / Toɣmuš [طوغمش / Toɣmuš], forefather of the
Ottoman-dynasty (Ncšrï 186, Seădeddïn I, 15, Wittek
94); Uyg. 13th-14th c. Tuɣmïš, fem. (Zieme, Mat. II,
90). ✧ '(He) Was born; (Sun/Moon) rose' cf. Türk,
Kuman, Chag. *toɣ*- 'geboren werden; aufgehen (von
Sonne); ersteigen' (Radl. III, 1158) + suff. *-miš*. See
also **AY-ТОГМӤŠ, AQ-DOГMUŠ, ARSLAN-
ТОГМӤŠ, BARČA-ТОГМӤŠ, ER-ТОГМӤŠ,
YARUQ-ТUГМӤŠ, KÄD-ТUГМӤŠ, KENČ-
ТОГМӤŠ, KİN-ТОГМӤŠ, KÜN-ТОГМӤŠ,
QUTLUГ-ТUГМӤŠ, TÄÑRİ-ТUГМӤŠ.**

ТОГOS-ČAYAČİ Tuv. 19th c. Toɣos-čayači [Тогосъ-
чаячи], a man in a Soyŏt tale (Potanin IV, 572). ✧
'Nine-creator; nine-fire' cf. Hak., Tuv. *čayačï* 'der
Schöpfer' (Radl. III, 1853), Tuv. *čayaačï* 'огонь (как
предмет культа)' (TuvRS). ⇨ **TOQUZ.**

ТОГOSOLUQ Yak. Toɣosoluq [Тоҕосолук] (Pek.).

ТОГOSOR-ŪS Yak. Toɣosor-ūs [Тоҕосор Ус],
Omoɣoy's son, Ayî Taybîr's father (Pek.).

ТОГRAQ Trkm. 1410, 1434 Toɣraq [بن دلغادر],
[طغرق بن داؤد بن ابراهيم], an emir (Ibn Taghrïb. VI,
369, 728). ✧ 'A kind of poplar' cf. East.T. *toɣraq* 'eine
Art Pappel' (Radl. III, 1167).

ТОГRӤ Maml. 1315 Toɣrï-bek [طغربك الانصاري] /
Togribek Ansaricus] (Abulfidā V, 300-301). ✧ 'Right,
straight' cf. Uyg. *toɣru* 'прямой; правильный,
справедливый' (DTS), Kuman *toɣru* 'grade', Chag.,
East.T. *toɣri* 'gegenüberstehend, gegenüber, grade,
wahr' (Radl. III, 1167), Az. *doɣrï*, Crm. *doɣru* 'recht,
richtig, grade, rechtschaffen' (Radl. III, 1708), Turk.
doğru 'straight, right, true, honest, loyal' (TED). See
also **QOTAN-ТОГRӤ.**

ТОГRӤL 12th c. Toɣrïl [طغرل بن اُربك] (Rāwandï
393); Uyg. Toɣrïl-[bäg? / Toɣrïl ???] (Zieme, Mat. I,
75); Uyg. Toɣrïl [Toğrıl] (EUTS); Oghuz? 990/91
Toɣrïl [طغريل بن محمّد بن جعفر ابوالقاسم الشاهد]
(Ibn Taghrïb. II, 46); Oghuz? 1282 Toɣrïl
[طغريل الايغانى] (Iyās I, 110); Selj. 10th c. - 13th c.
Toɣrïl [طغرل], a sultan (Ǧuwaynï II, 28-32 etc.); Selj.
1052 Toɣrïl [طغرل حاجب مودود الغزنوى], a
doorkeeper (Ibn al-Athïr/Tornb. IX, 399, 400); Selj.?
1089 Toɣrïl [طغرل بن ينال] (Ibn al-Athïr/Tornb. X,
115, 116); Selj.? 1131 Toɣrïl [طغرل بن برسق], the
same as Toɣrïl II (1131-1134)? (Ibn al-Athïr/Tornb. X,
480); Selj. 12th c. Toɣrïl [بن ارسلان / طُغْرُلَ بن ارسَلان
طغرل], Sultan Toɣrïl III (1175-1194), executed by
Turk'ān-ɣatun in 1220 (Qazw. 473-479, Fakhrï 435,
436, Ibn al-Athïr/Tornb. XI, 130, 295, XII, 15, 49 etc.,
Nasawï 39, Bondārï 301-04, Muh. Ibrahim 135,
Rawandï 41-43); Selj.? 1170 Toɣrïl
[طغرل بن قاورت بك], Qawurt-beg's son (Ibn al-

Athïr/Tornb. XI, 235); Selj. 1191/92 Toɣrïl [طغريل] /
Toghrïl], Saladin's mamluk and bearer of sword (Ibn
Šaddād, Nawād.: RHCHor III, 277); Selj. 1192 Toɣrïl
[طغرل], Nasireddin's mamlūk (gulām) (Ibn al-
Athïr/Tornb. XII, 52, 76); Selj.? 1203 Toɣrïl [بن مودود
طغرل بن سنقر], an atabeg in Fars till 1203 (Qazw. 369,
506); Selj.? 1218/19 Toɣrïl [شهاب الدين طغرل /
Chihâb-eddyn Toghril], an emir, a Greek (?) eunuch,
atabeg of Alazyz (Ibn al-Athïr: RHCHor II/1, 144-47);
Khorezm.? 13th c. Toɣrïl [عزّالدين طغرل], courtier of
Sultan Jelāleddïn (1220-1231) (Nasawï 31); Khorezm.?
1262/63, 1264 Toɣrïl [شجاع الدين طغريل الشبلىّ /
Chodja-eddin Toghril Achchibly / Schodja-eddin-
Togril-Schebli], an emir and host (official guide) (Aynï:
RHCHor II/1, 218, Makrïzï II, 14); Karakh. / Selj.?
1017 Toɣrïl-qara-ɣan [طغرل قراخان] (Ibn al-
Athïr/Tornb. IX, 212); Selj. 1118, 1121, 1134/35, 1145
Toɣrïl / Toɣrïl-šah [طغرل ركن الدين / بن محمد
طغرلشاه بن محمد شاه / طغريل بن محمد / طغرل
Toɣηρίλης], ruler of Kirmān, Iraq, Toɣrïl II / Tuɣrïl II
(1131-1134) (Qazw. 479, Ibn al-Athïr: RHCHor I, 316-
18, 331, 403, Ibn al-Athïr/Tornb. X, 383-4, 441-443
etc., Bondārï 4, 119 etc., Qazw. 458, Muh. Ibrahim 34-
38, Rāwandï 67, 85, Byz. Turc. 315, Qalānisi 83, 87-91,
205, 238, 282 etc.); Khorezm.? 13th c. Toɣrïl / Toɣrul-
ɣan [طغرلخان بن منكوتيمور / طغرل بن منكوتمور /
Toghroul-Khan], a Chinggisid, Özbeg Khan's father
(Abulg./Desm. 183, Qazw. 576); Tat.(GH)? 1380
Toɣrïl-beg [طغرل بك], member of the Ǧalayïr tribe,
uncle of Ali-beg, the sultan of Sivas (Astarab. 165, 245,
247, 253); Selj. 1012, 1036 Toɣrïl-beg / Toɣrul /
Toɣrul-beg / Tuɣrïl-beg / Tuɣrul-beg [طغرليبك /
طغرلبك محمد بن ميكاييل بن سلجوق /
Ταγγρολίπηξ / Tûghrel Bâg / Tuğrul Beg / Тогрул /
Тогрул-бек Мухаммед ибн Микаил ибн
Сельджук / Рукн-ад-дин Абу-Талиб / Рукн-ад-
дауле / Тогрул Туркменский], Seljuk sultan (1038-
1063), Seljuk's grand-son (Ibn al-Athïr/Tornb. IX, 165
etc. X, 4-6 etc. XI, 227, Abulfar./Budge I, 196, Byz.
Turc. 295, Ahbar 13-15, Mirch. Gasnevid. 105, 117-
118, Muh. Ibrahim 12, Rāwandï 65, 75 etc., Abulfidā
III, 102-103, Abulg./Kon. 1145, MIT I, 47-48, 231-33,
246, 248 etc.); Selj.? 1017 Toɣrïl-ɣan
[طغرلخان بن يوسف قدرخان] (Ibn al-Athïr/Tornb.
213); Selj.? 1095 Toɣrïl-yinal-bek [طغرل ينال بك]
(Ibn al-Athïr/Tornb. X, 166); Selj. 12th c. Toɣrïl-šah
[تركانشاه بن طغرلشاه], Terken-šah's / Türkan-šah's
(?) father (Muh. Ibrahim 35, 38, 40, 48, 50); Selj. 12th
c. Toɣrïl-šah [توانشاه بن طغرلشاه], Turan-šah's (?)
father (Muh. Ibrahim 35, 38, 40 etc.); Selj. 1204/05
Toɣrïl-šah [طغرلشاه], Qïlïč-arslan's (1257-1263) son
(Ibn al-Athïr/Tornb. XII, 134, 295, 312); Selj.? 1017

Toγrïl-tegin [طغرلتكين], Toγrïl-beg I (1038-1063) in his youth? (Ibn al-Athīr/Tornb. IX, 213); Selj. 11th c. - 12th c. **Toγrïl-tegin** [طغرلتكين اياز] (Bondārī 297); Selj. 1164 **Toγrïl-tegin** [طغرلتكين بن يرنتش النلكى / Тогрул-тегин Барнакаш ал-Аллаки], ruler of the country of Ghur (Ibn al-Athīr/Tornb. XI, 206, MIT I, 403); Uyg. **Toγrul** [Toğrul] (EUTS); Oghuz/Trkm. 13th c. **Toγrul** [طغرل / Тогрул-онбеги], a ruler (χan), Toγurmïš' son (Abulg./Kon. 1070-1085, 1110); Oghuz 1097 **Toγrul-tegin** [طغرلتكين بن اكنخى / Тогрул-тегин ибн Икинджи], the Khorezmshah İkinǰi's son (Ibn al-Athīr/Tornb. X, 183, 191, MIT I, 384); Tat.(GH) 1240 **Towrul** [Товруль / Товрулъ / Таврулъ] (Ipat. 522 /527/, PSRL II, 177, IV, 36, V, 175, VII, 145); Tat.(GH)? 1240 **Towrul** [Таврулъ] (PSRL X, 116). ✧ 'A kind of bird of prey; falcon, hawk?' cf. Karakh. *toγrïl/toγrul* 'хищная птица' (DTS), Chag. *toγrul* 'eine Art Jagdvogel; ein Eigenname' (Radl. III, 1167). See also **ADAM-TOΓRÏL, ALP-TOΓRÏL, ARSLAN-TOΓRÏL, ARSLAN-SÏQ-TOΓRUL, AŠAN-TOΓRÏL, BASA-TOΓRÏL, BEŠE-TOΓRÏL, EDGÜ-TOΓRÏL, ER-TOΓRUL, YAP-TOΓRÏL, QUTADMÏŠ-TOΓRÏL, QUTAN-TOΓRÏL, OZMÏŠ-TOΓRÏL, ÖKÜZ-TOΓRÏL, TOLUN-TOΓRÏL, TURUQ-EDGÜ-TOΓRÏL, ÜRK-TOΓRÏL.**

TOΓRÏL-ARSLAN Selj. 13th c. **Toγrïl-arslan** [Tûghⵏel 'Arslân], Qïlïč-arslan's (1257-1263) son (Abulfar./Budge I, 243). ⇨ **TOΓRÏL + ARSLAN.**

TOΓRÏLČA Tat.(GH)? 1282 **Toγrulǰa / Toγrïlča?** [Тогрулджа], the Kipchak Meñgü-temür-χan's son (Nuwairī/Tizeng. I, 134, 155, Tar. Beyb./Tizeng. I, 82, 104); Khorezm.? 13th c. **Tuγrïlča** [Тугрылча] (RaD II, 73). ✧ 'Little Gerfalcon' (Bese 5). ⇨ **TOΓRÏL** + dim. suff. *-ča*.

TOΓRUL see **TOΓRÏL**

TOΓRULǰA see **TOΓRÏLČA**

TOΓUČ Bashk. 1746 **Toγuč** [Муслюм Тогучев] (MIB III, 439); Bashk. 1757 **Tuquč** [Исенбай Тукучев] (MIB IV/1, 157); Bashk. 1762 **Tuquč** [Муллагул Тукучев] (MIB IV/1, 232); Kzk. 1846 **Tuquč** [Джумур Тукучев] (MKOP 154). ✧ 'Stirrer, wooden spoon' cf. Chag. *toγuč* 'der Quirl, Rührlöffel' (Radl. III, 1164), Tat.(Tob.) *tuγūč* 'der Quirl' (Radl. III, 1432).

TOΓUĆA Bashk. 1745 **Toγuča / Toγučay?** [Тогуча / Тогучай Мряков] (MIB III, 428). ⇨ **TOΓUČ?** + suff. *-a*.

TOΓUČAY Bashk. 1748, 1756 **Toγučay / Toγuča?** [Тогучай / Тогуча Мряков] (MIB III, 452, IV/1, 105); Bashk. 1761 **Toγušay** [Аяз Тогушаев] (MIB IV/1, 205). ⇨ **TOΓUĆA** + suff. *-y*.

TOΓUČUQ Bashk. 1756 **Toγučuq** [Азнакай Тогучюков] (MIB IV/1, 120). ⇨ **TOΓUČ?** + suff. *-uq*.

TOΓUL see **TUΓÏL**

TOΓULΓA Trkm. **Toγulγa** [Тогульга Кара Багадуръ] (PSZRI XXVII, 542).

TOΓUN Kzk. 19th c. **Toγun-bay** [Тогунбай] (SOK 102, 176); Bashk. 1740 **Tuγun** [Атамгула Тугунов] (MIB I, 416); Kzk. 19th c. **Tuγun-bay** [Тугунбай] (SOV 118). ✧ 'Flange / fringe of the smoke-gap' cf. Kzk. *toγun* 'der Rand des Rauchloches' (Radl. III, 1163).

TOΓURMÏŠ Oghuz/Trkm. 13th c. **Toγurmïš** [طغورمش / Тогурмыш], Keranǰe-χoǰa's son, Toγrul-χan's father (Abulg./Kon. 1065, 1070). ✧ '(She) bore' cf. Chag. *toγur-* 'gebären; aufgehen lassen' (Radl. III, 1163).

TOΓURTAQ Kuman 1094, 1096, 1113 **Toγurtaq / Toγrutaq-qan? / Tuγorqan?** [Тоγорта́к / Тугорканъ / Тугъртъканъ / Тугорканъ / Тугъртъканъ / Тугторованъ / Тмутаракань], a Polovets prince, commander of the army (Ipat. 161 (167), Lavr. 218, 223, 224, PSRL I, 96, II, 4, 279, VII, 7, VII, 23-24, Biz. Turc. 316). ✧ I. 'Flicker, woodpecker'? (Bask., Im. polov. 75), cf. Tat.(Bar.) *toγurtqu* 'der Specht' (Radl. III, 1164); II. 'Correcting Khan'? <*toγrutaq-qan* <*toγrut-* 'исправлять, выправлять' + suff. (nom. agent.) *-aq* + *qan* (Bask., Im. polov. 75).

TOΓUS-AY see **TOΓUZ-AY**

TOΓUŠAY see **TOΓUČAY**

TOΓUT Kzk. 19th c. **Toγut-bek** [Тогутбекъ] (SODž. 160). ✧ 'Water-basin (pond) where sheep are bathed' cf. Kzk. *toγït* 'водохранилище (в проточной воде), где летом купают баранов' (KzRS).

TOΓUZ see **TOQUZ**

TOΓUZ-AY Bashk. 1746 **Toγus-ay** [Тогусяй Куразманов] (MIB III, 435); Bashk. 1749 **Toγus-ay** [Тогусяй Мряков] (MIB III, 468); Kzk. 19th c. **Toγus-ay** [Тогусай] (AOK 18); Kzk. 19th c. **Toγuz-ay** [Тогузаевъ] (Pam. kn. Turg. 68). ✧ I. 'Nine' [Long live!], cf. Tat. *Tuγïzay* (Sattarov); II. 'Nine months'? ⇨ **TOQUZ (+ AY?) / TOΓUČAY?**

TOΓUZ-TOÑQULDAQ Kzk. 19th c. **Toγuz-toñquldaq** [Toguz-tonkuldak χem Šalgïz-kankïldak], a character in a tale (Ljutš 42).

TOΓUZAQ Bashk. 1708, 1710 **Toγuzaq** [Нурка Тогузаков / Нуркай Тогузяков] (MIB III, 42, 64); Bashk. 1750 **Toγuzaq** [Едигар Тогузаков] (MIB III, 474); Kirg. **Toγuzaq** [Тогузак] (Jud. 741); Kzk. 1794 **Toqzaq-batïr** [توقزاق باطر / Токзак] (MIK IV, 161); Bashk. 1695 **Tuγuzaq** [Тугузачко] (MIB I, 85); Kzk. 19th c. **Tuγuzaq** [Тюребекъ Тугузаковъ] (Pam. kn. Turg. 41); Chag. 16th c. **Tuquzaq-bahadur** [Тукузак-бахадур] (Ivanov 232); *TN:* Kzk. **Toγuzaq** [Тогузак], a field (Kojčubaev 218). ✧ I. '(Bought for) nine (things)' (Jud. 741, Žanuzakov); II. 'Bustard; heron'? cf. Tat. *Tuγzaq* (Sattarov), Bashk. *Tuγïðaq* (Kusimova). ⇨ **TOQUZ?** + suff. *-aq*? See also **TŌDAQ.**

TOX see **TOQ**

TOX-BULAT see **TOQ-BULAT**

TOX-TANAY   Bashk. 1713 Toχ-tanay? [Козяк Тохтанаев] (MIB III, 102). ⇨ **TOQ-TANA** + suff. *-y.*

TOX-TAŠ see **TOQ-TAŠ**

TOXAY see **TOQAY**

TOXLU see **TOQLÏ**

TOXMAT see **TOQMET**

TOXMET see **TOQMET**

TOXPAŇ Hak. 19th-20th c. Toχpaň [Тохпанъ] (HRS 352). ✧ 'Full, satisfied' (Butanaev).

TOXŠÏ   Karakh.? 870, 879 Toχšï [طخشّي بن بلبرد] (Kindī 215-17, 219-20, 224).

TOXTA see **TOQTA**

TOXTA-ALİ   Uzb. 20th c. Toχta-ali [Тӯхтаали] (Begmatov 1984, 205). ⇨ **TOQTA** + **ALİ.**

TOXTA-BUL see **TOQTA-BUL**

TOXTA-KÜČÜK   Nog. 1649 Toχta-küčük [Акъ мурза Тохтакучуковъ] (AI IV, 87). ⇨ **TOQTA** + **KÜČÜK.**

TOXTA-MAXMED   Kzk. 19th c. Toχta-maχmed [Тохта-махмедовъ] (SKSO VIII, 232). ⇨ **TOQTA** + **МАГМЕТ.**

TOXTA-MANJU see **TOQTA**

TOXTA-MRAT see **TOXTA-MURAT**

TOXTA-MURAT   Uzb. 19th c. Toχta-mrat [Тохта мратъ Бигменевъ] (SKSO III, 178); Uzb. 20th c. Toχta-murâd [Тӯхтамурод] (Begmatov 1984, 205). ⇨ **TOQTA** + **MURAT.**

TOXTA-NAZAR   Kzk. 19th c. Toχta-nazar [Тохтаназаръ] (SKSO VIII, 225); Uzb. 20th c. Toχta-nazar [Тӯхтаназар] (Begmatov 1984, 205). ⇨ **TOQTA** + **NAZAR.**

TOXTA-NİYAZ   Trkm. 19th c. Toχta-niyaz [Тохтаньязъ] (Ščeglov I, 358). ⇨ **TOQTA** + **NİYAZ.**

TOX-TAY see **TOQTAY**

TOXTAMAN   Chuv. 19th c. Toχtaman [Tochtaman] (Kronheim 96). ⇨ **TOQTA** + suff. *-man.*

TOXTAMÏS see **TOQTAMÏŠ**

TOXTAR see **TOQTAR**

TOXTASÏN see **TOQTASÏN**

TOXTAUL see **TOQTAUL**

TOXTÏ see **TOQLÏ**

TOXTO see **TOQTA**

TOXUM-MEXTUM   Trkm. 1821 Toχum-meχtum [Тохумъ-Мехтумъ] (Murav'ev: Russk. Arhiv 1888, I, 404). ✧ 'Offspring-Maχdum / Maχtüm' (Ar.) (Erol II), cf. Trkm. *toχum* 'семена; порода; потомство, потомок' (TrkmRS).

TOİK see **TOYÏQ**

TOY   Chuv. 18th-19th c. To-čura (<Toy-čura) [Точура] (Magn. 86); Kzk. 19th c. Toy-bay [Тойбай] (SOV 10, 30, 114, 152); Chuv. 18th-19th c. Toy-batïr [Тойбатыръ] (Magn. 83); Kzk. 19th c. Toy-bek [Тойбекъ] (SOV 28); Kzk. 18th c. **Toy-bigä** [Тойбигя], fem. (Levšin III, 96); Kzk. 19th c. **Toy-bike-Janum** / (<-Janïm) [Toï-Bihia-Tchonoum], fem. (Levchine 356); Chuv. 18th-19th c. **Toy-čura** [Тойчура] (Magn. 84); Trkm. 20th c. **Toy-jan** [Тойӷан] (Zaj. 1971, 329); Bashk. 1765 **Toy-güzä** [Тойгузя Мамыков] (MIB IV/1, 310); Kzk. 19th c. **Toy-γul** [Тойгулъ] (SOV 66); Kzk. 19th c. **Toy-γulï** [Тойгулы] (AOK 6); Kzk. 19th c. **Toy-γulï** [Тойгулы] (AOO 42); Kzk. 18th c. - 19th c. **Toy-χoja** [Тойходжа] (Tynyšp. 74); Kzk. 19th c. **Toy-quli** [Тайфанкъ Тойкуліевъ] (Grod., Pril. 114); Kzk. 19th c. **Toy-žan?** [Тожанъ] (SOV 48). ✧ 'Feast, treat; wedding' cf. Kuman, Chag., Alt., Hak., Kirg., Kzk., Turk. *toy* 'das Gastmahl, die Zecherei, die Hochzeit' (Radl. III, 1141), Alt. *toy* 'пир, пиршество, свадьба, свадебный пир, празднество' (OjrRS). See also **DAN-TOY.**

TOY-ALİ   Kirg. Toy-alï [Тоялы] (Jud. 842). ⇨ **TOY** + **ALİ?**

TOY-BARS   Chuv. 18th-19th c. **To-bars** (<Toy-bars) [Тобарсъ] (Magn. 83); Chuv. 18th-19th c. **Toy-baris** [Тойбарисъ] (Magn. 83); Chuv. 18th-19th c. **Toy-baris** [Тойбарисъ] (Magn. 83); Chuv. 18th-19th c. **Toy-bars** [Тойбарсъ] (Magn. 83); Chuv. 18th-19th c. **Toy-bars?** / **Toymas?** [Тойбасъ] (Magn. 83). ✧ 'Panther (child, bringing) feast/treat' (Sattarov). ⇨ **TOY** + **BARS.**

TOY-BOL   Kzk. 19th c. **Toy-bol** [Тойболъ] (SODž. 132); Kzk. 19th c. **Toy-bul** [Тойбулъ] (SODž. 62). ✧ 'Be feast/treat (joy)!'. ⇨ **TOY** + **BOL.**

TOY-BOLDİ see **TOY-BOLDÏ**

TOY-BOLDÏ   NUyg. 19th c. **Toy-boldi** [توی بولدی / Toi boldi] (Le Coq, Namenl. 118); Kzk. 19th c. **Toy-boldï** [Тойболды] (Konsin, Pam. 21); Kzk. 19th c. **Toy-boldï** [Тойболды] (SODž. 60, 114); Chuv. 18th-19th c. **Toy-bulda** (<Toy-buldï) [Тойбулда] (Magn. 83); Kzk. 19th c. **Toy-buldï** [Тойбулды Куменевъ (Кушеневъ)] (Konsin, Pam. 21). ✧ '(It) was feast/joy' cf. Tat. *Tuy-buldï* (Sattarov); cf. also Le Coq's interpretation in East. T. „(hier) wurde das (Hochzeits) Fest begangen" (Le Coq). ⇨ **TOY** + **BOLDÏ.**

TOY-BUL see **TOY-BOL**

TOY-BULAT   Chuv. 18th-19th c. **To-bulat** (<Toy-bulat) [Тобулатъ] (Magn. 83); Chuv. 18th-19th c. **Toy-blat** [Тойблатъ] (Magn. 83); Chuv. 18th-19th c. **Toy-bulat** [Тойбулатъ] (Magn. 83); Chuv. 18th-19th c. **Tuy-bulat** [Туйбулатъ] (Magn. 87). ⇨ **TOY** + **BULAT. See also TOY-TEMİR.**

TOY-BULDÏ see **TOY-BOLDÏ**

TOY-ČEREY   Chuv. 18th-19th c. **Toy-čerey** [Тойчерей] (Magn. 84).

TOY-DEMİR see **TOY-TEMİR**

TOY-DİMER see **TOY-TEMİR**

TOY-GİLDE   Chuv. 18th-19th c. **Toy-gilde** [Тогилда] (Magn. 83); Tat. 1686 **Toy-gilde** [Тойгилдинъ] (Kungursk. akty 68); Tat. 18th-19th c. **Toy-gilde** [Тойгилда] (Magn. 83); Bashk. 1682 **Toy-gilde** [Белекейко Тойголдинъ] (AI V, 139); Bashk. 1709 **Toy-gilde** [Тойгильди] (MIB III, 52); Bashk. 1710 **Toy-gilde** [Чюрагул-мулла Тойгильдин] (MIB III, 67); Bashk. 1712 **Toy-gilde** [Тойгильде Симкин] (MIB III, 87); Bashk. 1716 **Toy-gilde** [Тойгильде] (MIB III, 142); Bashk. 1723 **Toy-gilde** [Буря Тойгильдин] (MIB III, 209-210); Bashk. 1727 **Toy-gilde** [Юнус Тойгильдин] (MIB III, 247); Bashk. 1739 **Toy-gilde** [Сююш Тойгильдин] (MIB III, 408); Bashk. 1760 **Toy-gilde** [Тойгильда Абдуллин] (MIB IV/1, 193); Bashk. 1770 **Toy-gilde** [Тойгильда Балтачев] (MIB IV/1, 350); Tat. 1742 **Toy-gildi** [Тойгильды Тотиков] (MIB III, 511); Bashk. 1710 **Toy-gildi** [Той гильди] (MIB III, 67); Bashk. 1715 **Toy-gildi** [Тойгильди(н)] (MIB III, 122); Bashk. 1779 **Toy-gildi** [Тойгильди] (MIB V, 101); Chuv. 18th-19th c. **Toy-kilde** [Тойкилда] (Magn. 84); Tat. 1620 **Toy-kilde(y)** [Токильдѣйко] (Kurdjumov 119, 121); *TN:* Bashk. 18th c. **Toy-gildina** [Тоигилдина (Тяьгилдино)], a village in the district of Tetyushinsk (Korsakov 341). ✧ 'Feast has come; born at feast' (Sattarov, Kusimova). ⇨ **TOY + KELDİ.**

TOY-GİLDİ see **TOY-GİLDE**

TOY-GİREY   Chuv. 18th-19th c. **Toy-girey** [Тойгэрей] (Magn. 83). ⇨ **TOY + KERÄY.**

TOY-İŠ   Bashk. 1714 **Toy-iš** [Тоиш Арыков] (MIB I, 105); Bashk. 1735 **Toy-iš** [Башер Тоишев] (MIB III, 333); Tat. 1554 **Tuy-iš** [Байбер[Туишевъ] (PSRL XIII, 239); Bashk. 1764 **Tuy-uš** (<**Tuy-iš**) [Туюш Танатаров] (MIB IV/1, 298). ✧ 'Born at the time of a feast/treat; child bringing feast/treat' cf. Tat. *Tuyiš / Tuiš* (Sattarov), Bashk. *Tuyïš* (Kusimova). ⇨ **TOY + EŠ.**

TOY-KİLDE see **TOY-GİLDE**

TOY-MAMET   Trkm. 20th c. **Toy-mamed** [Toymamed] (Zaj. 1971, 329); Tat. 1675 **Toy-mamet** [Тоймаметевъ] (Kungursk. akty 35). ✧ 'Mamet in the feast' (Zaj. 1971). ⇨ **TOY + MAMET.**

TOY-MÖŃKE   Kzk. 19th c. **Toy-möñke** [Тоймонке] (SOV 82). ⇨ **TOY + MÖŃKE.** See also **BAY-MÖŃKE.**

TOY-TEMİR   Chuv. 18th-19th c. **Toy-demir** [Тойдемиръ] (Magn. 83); Chuv. 18th-19th c. **Toy-demir** [Тодемиръ] (Magn. 83); Tat. 17th c. **Toy-demir** [Атайко Тойдемировъ] (IOAK XXIX, 344); Chuv. 18th-19th c. **Toy-dimer** [Тодимеръ] (Magn. 83); Chuv. 18th-19th c. **Toy-temir** [Тойтемиръ] (Magn. 84). ⇨ **TOY + TEMİR.** See also **TOY-BULAT.**

TOY-TEMİRKA   Chuv. 18th-19th c. **Toy-temirka?** [Тотемирка] (Magn. 86). ⇨ **TOY + TEMİR** + dim. suff. *-ka / -qa.*

TOY-TUGAN   Chuv. 18th-19th c. **To-dugan** (<**Toy-dugan**) [Тодуганъ] (Magn. 83); Chuv. 18th-19th c. **Toy-tugan** [Тойтуганъ] (Magn. 84). ✧ 'Feast/treat was born; (male child bringing) feast/joy was born' (Sattarov). ⇨ **TOY + TUĞAN I.**

TOY-TUTMAZ   Oghuz/Trkm. 13th c. **Toy-tutmaz** [طوى دوتماز / Той-Тутмаз] (Abulg./Kon. 1295). ⇨ **TOY.**

TOYAN   Tat.(Sib.)? 1611 **Toyan** [Тоян], a prince from Evshtinsk (?) (Miller, Ist. Sib. II, 220, 272); Bashk. 1735 **Toyan** [Тоианъ Яныгуловъ], a tarχan (Vel.-Zern., Bašk. 25).

TOYANĞAŠKO   Tat.(Sib.) 1675 **Toyanγaško** (<**Toyan-qaš?**) [Тоянгашко Бойтоковъ] (DAI VII, 332).

TOYBAN   Hak. 19th-20th c. **Toyban** [Тойбан] (HRS 352); Alt. 19th c. **Toybon-qān / Toybon-χan** [Тойбонъ-каанъ бий / Тойбонъ-ханъ], a biy (Nikiforov 31, Potanin IV, 427). ✧ 'With stumpy horns' (Butanaev). See also **TOQAL.**

TOYBON see **TOYBAN**

TOYČİ   Trkm. 20th c. **Toyči** [Тойчи] (Zaj. 1971, 326); Trkm. 20th c. **Toyči** [Тойчы] (TrkmRS 638); Bashk. 1754 **Toyči** [Тойчи Кулумбетев] (MIB IV/1, 83); Kzk. 18th c. - 19th c. **Toyči** [Тойчы] (Tynyšp. 65); Kzk. 19th c. **Toyči** [Тойчи] (Nalivkin 12); Kzk. 19th c. **Toyči** [Тойчи] (SOV 88); Bashk. 1758 **Toyči-bay** [Тойчибай Сабанаев] (MIB IV/1, 168); Kzk. 19th c. **Toyči-bay** [Тойчибай] (SOK 218); Uzb. 19th c. **Toyči-bay** [Тойчибай] (SKSO III, 23); Kzk. 19th c. **Toyču-bek** [Тойчубекъ] (SODž. 8, 80); Kzk. 19th c. **Toyšu-bay** [Тойшубай] (SOK 136); Bashk. 1788 **Tuyči** [Рямгул Туйчин] (MIB V, 230); Kzk. 19th c. **Tuyči** [Туйчи Джанбутаевъ] (SKSO VIII, 206); Kzk. 19th c. **Tuyči** [Туйчіевъ] (SKSO VIII, 232); Kzk. 19th c. **Tuyči-bay** [Туйчибай] (SKSO VIII, 222); *TN:* Bashk. 1757 **Toyči** [Тойчи], a village (MIB IV/1, 146). ✧ '(Male) child born at the time of a feast' (Sattarov), cf. Tat. *Tuyči*; 'Guest / partaker in a feast' (Zaj. 1971), cf. Trkm. *toyči* 'участник тоя' (TrkmRS). ⇨ **TOY** + suff. *-či.*

TOYČİQ   Kzk. 19th c. **Toyčik / Toyčaq?** [Тойчакъ] (AOAtb. 34); Kzk. 19th c. **Toyčïk** [Тойчекъ] (SOK 300); Tat.(Lit.) 1594 **Toyčuq** [Сафьянъ Тойчуковичъ] (Lit. Tat. 210, 214). ⇨ **TOY** + dim. suff. *-čïq.*

TOYČİN   Tat.(Mish.) 18th c. **Toyčin** [Тойчинъ-Абдуллинъ] (Nepljuev 890); Bashk. 1744 **Toyčin** [Мингиляк Тойчин] (MIB III, 415); Bashk. 1750 **Toyčin** [Тойчин Айметев] (MIB III, 473); Bashk. 1750 **Toyčin** [Бухар Тойчин] (MIB III, 473). ⇨

TOYČÏ.

TOYČU see **TOYČÏ**

TOYČUQ see **TOYČÏQ**

TOYDÏ Uzb. 20th c. **Toydï** [Туйди] (Begmatov 1984, 205); Uzb. 20th c. **Toydï-bây** [Туйдибой] (Begmatov 1984, 205). ❖ '(He/she) Got full/satisfied' cf. Kkalp. *toy-* 'наедаться, насыщаться' (KkRS) + suff. *-dï*. See also **TOYDÏ**, **TOYΓAN**.

TOYDÏ-MURÂD Uzb. 20th c. **Toydï-murâd** [Туйдимурод] (Begmatov 1984, 205). ⇨ **TOYDÏ** + **MURAT**.

TOYDÏQ Kkalp. 20th c. **Toydïq** [Тойдык], fem. (KkRS 778). ❖ '(We) Got full/satisfied' cf. Kkalp. *toy-* 'наедаться, насыщаться' (KkRS) + suff. *-dïq*. See also **TOYDÏ**, **TOYΓAN**.

TOYΓAN Kzk. 19th c. **Toyγam-bay** (<Toyγan-bay) [Тойгамбай] (SOK 126); Uzb. 20th c. **Toyγân** [Туйғон] (Begmatov 1984, 205); Uzb. 20th c. **Toyγân-bây** [Туйғонбой] (Begmatov 1984, 205); Bashk. 1764 **Tuyγan** [Кусяп Туйганов] (MIB IV/1, 285). ❖ '(We) Got full/satisfied' cf. Kzk. *toy-* 'надоесть, насыщаться' (KzRS), Bashk. *tuy-* 'наедаться, насыщаться' (BRS) + suff. *-γan*. See also **TOYDÏ**, **TOYDÏQ**, **TOYMÏŠ**.

TOYΓÏZ Kzk. 19th c. **Toyγïz-bay** [Тойгызбай] (AOP 46). ❖ 'Sate/satiate (him)!' cf. Kzk. *toyγïz-* 'накормить досыта' (KzRS).

TOYΓU Kzk. 19th c. **Toyγu-bek** [Тойгубекъ] (SODž. 30).

TOYΓUNUR Bashk. 1715 **Toyγunur-batïr /Toγunur-batïr?** [Тойгунур / Тогунур батыр] (MIB I, 278-79).

TOYÏŠKO Tat. 17th c. **Toyïško** [Тоишко Атаевъ], in the region of Kazan (IOAK XXIX, 344). ⇨ **TOYÏŠ** + suff. *-ko*.

TOYÏQ Hak. 19th-20th c. **Toik** [Тоик], fem. (HRS 355); Alt. 19th-20th c. **Toyïq** [Тойык] (OjrRS 210).

TOYÏM Bashk. 1732 **Toyïm** [Зьяш Тоимбаев] (MIB III, 300); Kzk. 19th c. **Toyïm-bay** [Тоимбай] (SODž. 54); Bashk. 1776, 1778 **Tuyïm / Tuyum** [Туим / Тюм Пичиккулов] (MIB V, 33, 34, 79). ❖ 'My pleasure/feast' cf. Tat. *Tuyïm* (Sattarov). ⇨ **TOY** + poss. suff. *-ïm*.

TOYÏMBET Bashk. 1653 **Toymbetka / Toyïmbetka** [Тойибетка Янбаевъ] (Vel.-Zern., Bašk. 43). ⇨ **TOY/TOYÏM** + suff. *-ïmbet /-bet*.

TOYÏN Uyg. **Toyïn** (Le Coq, Urkunden 458); Uyg. 12th c. - 14th c. **Toyïn** [Toyïn / Toyın] (Radl., USp. 142, DTS, EUTS); Uyg. 12th c. - 14th c. **Toyïn-qulï** [Toyïn Quli] (Radl., USp. 23-24, DTS); Uyg. **Toyïn-qulï-ïnal** [Quanši-im Toyïn Quli Ïnal] (Zieme, Mat. I, 74, 79); Uyg. 12th c. - 14th c. **Toyïn-qulï-šila** (DTS); Uyg. 12th c. - 14th c. **Toyïn-qulï-tutuγ** [Toyïn Quli Tutuγ] (Radl., USp. 248); Uyg. 12th c. - 14th c. **Toyïn-silavanti** [Toyïn Silavanti] (Radl., USp. 144). ❖ 'Buddhist monk; priest' (DTS); „Buddhapriester" (Radl., USp.), *Quanši-im Toyïn* „Avalokitesvara-Mönch" (Zieme).

TOYÏN-ČOQ Uyg. 12th c. - 14th c. **Toyïn-čoq** (Radl., USp. 125, DTS). ❖ 'Monk/priest-Čoq?'.

TOYÏNAQ Uyg. 12th c. - 14th c. **Toyïnaq** [Toyınak / Toinak / Toin ak / tojïnaq] (EUTS, Radl., USp. 124, DTS). ❖ 'Little monk/priest'. ⇨ **TOYÏN** + dim. suff. *-aq?*

TOYQA Bashk. 1770 **Toyqa** [Араслан Тойкин] (MIB IV/1, 345); Bashk. 1773 **Toyqa** [Арасланъ Тойкинъ] (IOAK XXVIII, 587); Bashk. 1773 **Toyqa** [Араслан Тойкин] (MIB IV/1, 371); Hak. 19th-20th c. **Toyqa** [Тоика], fem. (HRS 355); Hak. 19th-20th c. **Toyqa** [Тойка], fem. (HRS 355). ❖ 'Feast/wedding' cf. Tat. *Tuyqay, Tuyqa* (Sattarov). ⇨ **TOY?** + dim. hypoc. suff. *-qa?*

TOYQAÑ Hak. 19th-20th c. **Toyqañ** [Тойканъ] (HRS 355).

TOYLA Kzk. 19th c. **Toyla-bay** [Тойлабай] (SOK 128). ❖ 'Amuse/enjoy yourself!' cf. Hak., Kzk. *toyla-* 'ein Gastmahl ausrichten; schmausen, zechen' (Radl. III, 1142).

TOYLÏ Kzk. 19th c. **Toylï-bay** [Тойлибай] (SOV 20); Kzk. 19th c. **Toylï-bek** [Тойлибекъ] (SODž. 120); Alt. 19th-20th c. **Toylu** [Тойлу], fem. (OjrRS 213); Kzk. 19th c. **Toylu-bay** [Тойлюбай] (SODž. 150); Kzk. 19th c. **Toylu-bay** [Тойлюбай] (SOV 112). ⇨ **TOY** + suff. *-lï*.

TOYLOÑ Alt. 19th-20th c. **Toyloñ** [Тойлоӈ], fem. (OjrRS 213). ❖ 'Your celebrating' (Bese 110). ⇨ **TOY** + dev. suff. *-lo/-la* + poss. suff. *-ñ*.

TOYLU see **TOYLÏ**

TOYLUQ Bashk. 1754 **Toyluq** [Тойлук Кулыев] (MIB IV/1, 84). ❖ 'Wedding-present; present for feast' cf. Chag. *toyluq* 'das Brautgeschenk, Festgeschenk; Preis beim Wettrennen, beim Spielen (bei Festen)' (Radl. III, 1143), Bashk. *tuylïq* 'свадебный; предназначенный для свадьбы (о скотине, пище, средствах)' (BRS/Uraksin).

TOYMA Kzk. 19th c. **Toyma-bay** [Тоймабай] (SOK 202); Kzk. 19th c. **Tuyma** [Туйма Аксакалъ] (SKSO III, 6).

TOYMADUQ Oghuz/Trkm. 13th c. **Toymaduq** [طویمادوق / Тоймадук], ruler of the country of Bečene (Abulg./Kon. 705, 1255). ❖ 'We did not eat our fill, we didn't have enough' cf. Chag., Alt., Kar., Kirg., Kzk. *toy-* 'satt werden' (Radl. III, 1142). See also **TOYDÏ**, **TOYDÏQ**.

TOYMAQ Chuv. 18th-19th c. **Toymak** [Тоймакъ] (Magn. 84); Kzk. 19th c. **Toymaq** [Тоймакъ] (SODž. 12).

TOYMAN Uzb. 19th c. **Toyman** [Тойманъ

Юлдашевъ] (SKSO III, 8). ⇨ **TOY** + suff. *-man.*

TOYMAS   Chuv. 18th-19th c. **Toymas** [Тоймасъ] (Magn. 84); Tat. 1717 **Toymas** [Тоймасъ] (ZIRGO IX, 319); Tat.(Mish.) 1755 **Toymas** [Сююш Тоймасов] (MIB IV/1, 93); Tat.(Mish.) 1755 **Toymas** [Кудаш Тоймасов] (MIB IV/1, 93); Bashk. 1706 **Toymas** [Тоймас Шаимов] (MIB III, 20); Bashk. 1735 **Toymas** [Кадырбакъ Тоймасовъ], a tarχan (Vel.-Zern., Bašk. 19); Bashk. 1736 **Toymas** [Тоймас] (MIB III, 352); Bashk. 1738, 1776 **Toymas** [Илчигул Тоймасов] (MIB III, 387, V, 43, 45); Bashk. 1740 **Toymas** [Сасыкул Тоймасев] (MIB I, 382); Bashk. 1745 **Toymas** [Юламан Тоймасов] (MIB III, 426); Bashk. 1751 **Toymas** [Ишкуат Тоймасов] (MIB IV/1, 34); Bashk. 1755 **Toymas** [Каскин Тоймасов] (MIB IV/1, 93); Bashk. 1755 **Toymas** [Бикул Тоймасов] (MIB IV/1, 93); Bashk. 1759 **Toymas** [Тоймас Кошкин] (MIB IV/1, 180); Bashk. 1761 **Toymas** [Сююш Тоймасов] (MIB IV/1, 218); Bashk. 1770 **Toymas** [Тоймас Нурушев] (MIB IV/1, 343); Bashk. 1775 **Toymas** [Тоймас Нурушев] (MIB IV/1, 378); Bashk. 1789 **Toymas** [Бекташ Тоймасов] (MIB V, 272); Bashk. 1789 **Toymas** [Кинзебай Тоймасов] (MIB V, 272); Bashk. 1777 **Toymas / Taymas?** [Монсуръ Тоймасовъ] (Vel.-Zern., Bašk. 6); Bashk. 1779 **Toymas / Taymas?** [Бакир Тоймасов (Таймасов)] (MIB V, 94, 104, 152 etc.); Bashk. 1789 **Toymas / Taymas?** [Алишей Тоймасов] (MIB V, 259). ❖ 'Voracious, insatiable, open-mouthed' cf. Tat. *tuymas* 'ненасытный, прожорливый' (TatRS), Bashk. *tuymaθ* 'ненасытный, прожорливый' (BRS/Uraksin) + suff. *-mas.* See also **TOYDÏQ, TOYΓAN, TOYΓÏZ.**

TOYMÏŠ   Turk. 20th c. **Doymuš** [Doymuş], a village in the province of Giresun, Turkey (TMİB 392); Chuv. 18th-19th c. **Toymïš** [Тоймышъ] (Magn. 84). ❖ 'Full, satisfied; He ate his fill; he had enough' cf. Tat. *tuy-* 'наедаться, насыщаться' (TatRS). See also **TOYΓAN.**

TOYNA I.   Tat.(Mish.) 1755 **Toyna** [Тойна Юлуков] (MIB IV/1, 93). ❖ 'He/she eates; gets full/satisfied' cf. Tat. *tuyïn-* 'питаться, насыщаться' (TatRS).

TOYNA II.   Hak. 19th-20th c. **Toyna** [Тойна], fem. (HRS 355). ❖ Tonya (R. hуpoc.) (Butanaev).

TOYNAŠ   Bashk. 1785 **Tuynaš / Toynaš** [Егафер Туиняшев (Тойняшев)] (MIB V, 170). ⇨ **TOYNA?** + suff. *-š.*

TOYON-KİNÄS   Yak. **Toyon-kinäs** [Тойон Кінäс], an evil spirit (Pek.). ⇨ **TOYOÑ** + **KİNÄS.**

TOYOÑ   Hak. 19th-20th c. **Toyoñ** [Тоёнъ] (HRS 352). ❖ 'Prince' (Butanaev), cf. Yak. *toyon* 'господин; глава семьи; начальник' (JRS), Used also as a component of personal names.

TOYPÏNAQ   Alt. 19th-20th c. **Toypïnaq** [Тойпынак]

(OjrRS 210).

TOYSÏN   Chuv. 18th-19th c. **Toysïn** [Тойсинъ] (Magn. 84). ❖ 'Let him/her get full/satisfied' cf. cf. Tat. *tuy-* 'наедаться, насыщаться' (TatRS) + suff. *-sïn.* See also **TOYUN.**

TOYŠU see **TOYČÏ**

TOYTA   Kzk. 19th c. **Toyta-bay** [Ишъ-Магомедъ Тойтабаевъ] (Grod., Pril. 172). ⇨ **TOY** + suff. *-ta?* See also **TOYTÏ.**

TOYTAN   Kzk. 19th c. **Toytan** [Тойтанъ] (AOP 30); Kkalp. 20th c. **Toytan** [Тойтан], fem. (KkRS 778).

TOYTÏ   Kzk. 19th c. **Toytï-bay** [Тойтибай] (SOK 88). ⇨ **TOY** + suff. *-ti?* See also **TOYTA.**

TOYTONNŪR   Yak. **Toytonnūr** [Тоітоннур] (Pek.).

TOYUN   Kzk. 19th c. **Toyun-bek** [Тоюнбекъ] (SOK 49). ❖ 'Get full/satisfied!' cf. Kzk. *toyun-* 'sich satt essen, sich mästen, körperlich zunehmen' (Radl. III, 1175). See also **TOYSÏN.**

TOYZU   Alt. 19th-20th c. **Toyzu** [Тойзу], fem. (OjrRS 213).

TOK-SARA   Chuv. 18th-19th c. **Tok-sara** [Токсара] (Magn. 84). ⇨ **TOQ** + **SARÏ / SARA I.?**

TOKGAČ   Chuv. 18th-19th c. **Tokgač** [Токгачъ] (Magn. 84).

TOQ   1734 **Taq-čara / Toq-čura?** [Такчара], a mulla (PSZRI IX, 338); Kkalp. 20th c. **Toγ-žan** [Тоғжан] (KkRS 776); Chuv. 18th-19th c. **Toχ-čura** [Тохчура] (Magn. 86); Chuv. 18th-19th c. **Toχ-pay** [Тохпай] (Magn. 86); Bashk. 1734 **Toχ-türä** [Тохтюра мулла], a mulla (PSZRI IX, 340); Chuv. 18th-19th c. **Tok-murza** [Токмурза] (Magn. 84); Uyg. **Toq** [Tok / Toq] (EUTS, ETY III, 180); Karch. **Toq** [Токовъ] (Sysoev 120); Kzk. 1829 **Toq** [Брали Токовъ], a sultan (Konsin, Mat. I-III, 21); NUyg. 19th c. **Toq** [توق / Tok] (Le Coq, Namenl. 119); Tat. 1756 **Toq-bay** [Токбай Тохтаров] (MIB IV/1, 113); Tat.(Mish.) 1748 **Toq-bay** [Еней Токбаевъ] (Nepljuev 438); Tat.(Mish.) 18th c. **Toq-bay** [Еней Токбаевъ] (Nepljuev 430); Bashk. 1600 **Toq-bay** [Токбай] (Miller, Ist. Sib. II, 160); Bashk. 1760 **Toq-bay** [Сююндюк Токбаев] (MIB IV/2, 35); Bashk. 1762 **Toq-bay** [Токбай Бекбаев] (MIB IV/1, 238); Bashk. 1778 **Toq-bay** [Токбай Байрямов] (MIB V, 69); Kzk. 19th c. **Toq-bay** [Токбай] (SKSO III, 11); Kzk. 19th c. **Toq-bala** [Токбала] (AOO 30); Kzk. 19th c. **Toq-bala** [Токбала] (SOK 254); Bashk. 1738 **Toq-čura** [Токчюра] (MIB I, 361); Bashk. 1740 **Toq-čura** [Токчура Тютин] (MIB I, 40); Bashk. 18th c. **Toq-čura** [Токчура] (Nepljuev 141); Kkalp. 20th c. **Toq-jan** [Токъджан] (Bask., Kkalp. 402); Kzk. 19th c. **Toq-jigit** [Токджигитъ] (SOV 24); Bashk. 1633 **Toq-közä (<Toq-xoja?)** [Токозя], a captain (MIB I, 71, 90, 92); Bashk. 1734 **Toq-qoza? / Toq-közä?** [Смаил

Токкозин] (MIB III, 325); Kzk. 18th c. - 19th c. **Toq-qoža** [Токкожа] (Tynyšp. 74); Kzk. 19th c. **Toq-molda** [Токмолда] (SODž. 34); Kzk. 19th c. **Toq-molda** [Токмолда] (SOK 264); Kzk. 19th c. **Toq-murza / Toq-murzay?** [Тикабай Тукмурзаевъ] (Grod., Pril. 131); Kzk. 19th c. **Toq-pay** [Токпай] (SOV 14, 110); Kzk. 19th c. **Toq-pay** [Токпай] (SOV 14, 24); Kzk. 19th c. **Toq-pay-bay** [Ток-пай-бай] (Potanin, Pred. 89); Tat. 1638 **Toq-seyt** [Капланда Тоскейтов (Токсейтов!)] (Miller, Ist. Sib. II, 450); Kzk. 18th c. - 19th c. **Toq-seyt** [Токсейт] (Tynyšp. 74); Tat.(Sib.) 1643 **Toq-sultan** [Токсултан], fem. (Miller, Ist. Sib. II, 490); Kkalp. 20th c. **Toq-suluw** [Токсулуў], fem. (KkRS 778); Yürük 1543 **Toq-šah** [Tokşah] (Gökb., Rum. 206); Kzk. 19th c. **Toq-šan / Toq-žan** [Токшанъ] (SOK 220); Bashk. 1706 **Toq-šeyk** [Кучюк Токшеиков] (MIB III, 26); Bashk. 1709 **Toq-šiχ** [Токших] (MIB I, 258); Selj. 1063/64, 1094, 1129 **Toq-tegin / Toγ-tegin / Tuγ-tekin?** [ابو المنصور / طغدكين / طغتكين / طغركين / طُغتِكين بن عبدالله Togtacin / Tuğtekin / Tûghtakîn / Тогтегин], Salahaddīn's brother, Duqaq's atabeg, governor of Damascus, died in 1129 (Abulfidā/Ed. I, 45, 74, Ibn al-Athīr/Tornb. I, 617, X, 25, 211-12, 341-44, 435-38 etc., Ibn al-Athīr: RHCHor I, 194, 205-6, 230, 269, 354, 383, Ibn al-Athīr, Atab.: RHCHor II/2, 33-34, 70, Ibn Taghrīb. II, 304, 336 etc., Abulfar. Or. 246, Abulfar./Budge I, 244, 249, 346, Ahbar 24, Sevim-Yücel I, 40, 162, 165, 168, ZVOIRAO V, 127); Selj. 11th c. - 12th c. **Toq-tegin / Toγ-tekin?** [طنتكين / Toγtegin] (Bondārī 173); Selj.? 1095, 1097 **Toq-tegin / Toγ-tekin?** [طغتكين / Emir Toghtekin], an emir (Abulfidā III, 300-301, Weil, Chalif. III, 150); Selj.? 12th c. **Toq-tegin / Toγ-tikin / Tuγ-tegin?** [Toghtikîn] (Ibn al-Athīr: RHCHor I, 861); Selj. 1000 **Toq-tegin / Toχ-tekin?** [تختكين ابو الهيجا الجرجاني] (Hil. Sābī 377, 403); Kzk. 19th c. **Toq-žan**, a blind singer (AUK 93); Tat.(Lit.) 1672 **Tow-degin / Toγ-degin?** [„panieu Doroty Towdginowny Marcinowey Sienkiewiczowey"] (Lit. Tat. 426); Selj.? 1182 **Tuγ-tegin** [Tuğtegîn] (Ramazan Şeşen: İslâm Tetkikleri Enstitüsü Dergisi VI, 3-4 (1976), p. 18); Kzk. 19th c. **Tuq-bay** [Тукбай] (Grod., Pril. 179); Kzk. 1820 **Tuq-bay-biy** [Тукбай-бій], a leader of the heads of the Čümekey tribe (Sib. Vest. IX, 116); *TN:* NUyg. 19th c. **Toq** [Tok] (Hedin, S. Tib. IX, 119); Kzk. 19th c. **Toq-bay** [Токбай], a field (AOK 38); NUyg. 19th c. **Toq-bay** [Tokbai] (Hedin, S. Tib. VIII, 363); Turk. 20th c. **Toqlar** [Toklar], a village in the province of Kayseri, Turkey (TMİB 930). ✧ 'Full, satisified, sated' cf. Türk., Uyg., Chag., Alt., Crm., Kirg., Kzk., Turk. *toq* 'satt, gesättigt; angefüllt; sättigend' (Radl. III, 114). See also **BAY-TOQ, İL-TOQ, QARA-TOQ, URUÑU-KÜLÜG-**

TOQ.

TOQ-ARSTAN Kzk. 18th c. - 19th c. **Toγ-arstan** [Тогарстан] (Tynyšp. 66); Kzk. 19th c. **Toγ-arstan / Toγ-orstan?** [Tok arslan / Тогорстанъ] (SOK 204); Kzk. 19th c. **Toγ-orstan** [Тогорстанъ] (SOK 204); Kzk. 19th c. **Toq-arustan** [Токъ-Арустанъ] (AUK 443); Kzk. 19th c. **Toq-arustan** [Токарустанъ] (SOV 68). ⇨ **TOQ + ARSLAN.**

TOQ-ARUSTAN see **TOQ-ARSTAN**

TOQ-BAS Kzk. 18th c. - 19th c. **Toq-bas** [Токбас] (Tynyšp. 73). ⇨ **TOQ + BAŠ.**

TOQ-BAWLU Kzk. 19th c. **Toq-bawlu** [Токбаулу] (SOV 156). ✧ 'Having full garden'? cf. Kzk. *baw* 'сад' (KzRS). ⇨ **TOQ + BAW?** + suff. *-lu.*

TOQ-BERDİ Bashk. 1709 **Toq-berdi** [Токберди] (MIB I, 264); Nog. 1649 **Toq-berdi(y)** [Утебайко Токбердѣевъ] (AI IV, 96); Bashk. 1675 **Toq-perdi** [Менли Токпердин] (MIB I, 200); Bashk. 1706 **Toq-perdi** [Бюстреть Токпердин] (MIB III, 26); Bashk. 1664 **Toq-perdi(y)** [Илчибай Токпердеев] (MIB I, 193); Chag. 16th c. **Tuq-berdi** [Тук-берды хафиз] (Ivanov 215, 298 etc.). ✧ 'Healthy, staisfied (child) was born' cf. Tat. *Tuq-birde* (Sattarov). ⇨ **TOQ + BERDİ.** See also **TOQ-BERGEN.**

TOQ-BERGEN Kzk. 19th c. **Toq-pergen** [Токпергенъ] (SOK 302); Kkalp. **Toq-pergen** [Баимбетъ Токбергеневъ] (Protok. Turk. IV, 76). ✧ 'Healthy, staisfied (child) was born'. ⇨ **TOQ + BERGEN.** See also **TOQ-BERDİ.**

TOQ-BOQ Kzk. 19th c. **Toq-boq** [Такбокъ], from the district of Kopalsk (Maev I, 160). ⇨ **TOQ + BOQ.**

TOQ-BOLAQ Kzk. 19th c. **Toq-bolaq** [Токболакъ] (SODž. 122). ⇨ **TOQ + BULAQ?**

TOQ-BÖGÜT Uyg. 12th c. - 14th c. **Toq-bögüt** [Toq-bögüt] (DTS). ✧ 'Satiated/satisfied-Wise' (Blagova 1997, 714). ⇨ **TOQ + BÖGÜ.**

TOQ-BUΓA Tat.(GH)? 1320, 1332 **Toq-buγa** [طقبغا / Тукбуга], emir, Özbeg Kipchak Khan's envoy to Egypt (Aynī/Tizeng. I, 489, 519, Duqmaq/Tizeng. I, 320, 327, Dawād. 366); Turk.? 1361 **Toq-buγa** [طقبغا صاروق] (Iyās I, 208). ✧ 'Full/sated bull'. ⇨ **TOQ + BUQA.**

TOQ-BULAT Chuv. 18th-19th c. **Toχ-bulat** [Тохбулатъ] (Magn. 86); Bashk. 1752 **Toq-bulat** [Токбулатов] (MIB IV/1, 64); Kzk. **Toq-fulat** [Мулла Кубей Токфулатовъ] (Sb. Syr-D. XII, 11, 17); Kirg. **Toq-fulat** [توقفولات / Токъ-Фулатъ] (Divaev, Dem. 21, 43); *TN:* Bashk. / Cher.? 18th c. **Toχ-bulat(ova)** [Тохбулатова], a village in the district of Tsarevokokshinsk (Korsakov 268); Kzk.? **Toq-bulat** [Ток-булатъ] (Karta JAR XI). ⇨ **TOQ + BULAT.** See also **TOQ-TEMİR.**

TOQ-BURA Kzk. 19th c. **Toq-bura** [Токбура] (SOK 292). ⇨ **TOQ + BURA.**

TOQ-ČULUQ Kirg. **Toq-čuluq** [Токчулук] (Jud. 183). ✧ 'Full/satisfied (child) with short ears' cf. Kirg. *čuluq* '(об овце, ягнёнке) короткоухий' (Jud.). ⇨ **TOQ.**

TOQ-JİGÄR Kzk. 19th c. **Toq-jigär** [Токджигаръ] (SOK 4). ✧ 'Full/satisfied liver (=darling child)'. ⇨ **TOQ + JİGER.**

TOQ-FULAT see **TOQ-BULAT**

TOQ-GÜZÄN Tat.(Lit.) 1557 **Toq-güzän** [Токгузанъ] (Kn. Metriki Lit. 152). ⇨ **TOQ + KÜZÄN.**

TOQ-KİYİK Kzk. 19th c. **Toq-kiyk-bay / Toq-kiyik-bay** [Токійкбай] (AOA 2); Kzk. 19th c. **Toq-kiyk-bay / Toq-kiyik-bay** [Токійкбай] (AOA 2). ⇨ **TOQ + KİYİK.**

TOQ-KİYK see **TOQ-KİYİK**

TOQ-QAŠ Tat.(Sib.)? 1598 **Toq-qaš** [Токкашъ], a Siberian prince (AI II, 7). ⇨ **TOQ + QAŠ.**

TOQ-QONSA Kzk. 19th c. **Toq-qonsa** [Токконса] (AOAıb. 42). ⇨ **TOQ + QONSA.**

TOQ-MAMBET Kzk. 18th c. - 19th c. **Toq-mambet** [Tokmambet] (Tynyšp. 75); Kzk. 19th c. **Toq-mambet** [Tokmambet] (Ljtuš 153). ⇨ **TOQ + MAMBET.**

TOQ-MAMET Chuv. 1663 **Tok-mametko** [Токмаметко Байзыгитовъ] (AI IV, 336); Tat. 1600 **Toq-mamet** [Токмаметь Келдеман] (MIB I, 152). ⇨ **TOQ + MAMET.**

TOQ-MAMİŠ Bashk. 1788 **Toq-mamiš** [Субхангул Токмамышев] (MIB V, 223). ⇨ **TOQ + MAMİŠ.**

TOQ-PASAR Kzk. 19th c. **Toq-pasar** [Токпасаръ] (SOK 80). ⇨ **TOQ + BASAR.**

TOQ-PERDİ see **TOQ-BERDİ**

TOQ-PERGEN see **TOQ-BERGEN**

TOQ-SABA Maml. 1298 **Toq-saba** [Alem-eddin-Sandjar-Taksaba], an emir died in 1298 (Makrīzī IV, 81); Maml. 1304 **Toq-saba** [طنصبا], a commander (Abulfidā V, 194-195); Maml. 1313, 1319 **Toq-saba** [الحسامى طنصبا سيف الدين / الوالى طنصبا / سيف الدين], governor of Kos, Upper Egypt, then commander in Western Afrika (Dawād. 266, Zetterst. 174, Weil, Chalif. I, 313, 340, Abulfidā V, 282-3); Kzk. 19th c. **Toq-saba** [Токсаба] (SODž. 100, 156); Kzk. 19th c. **Toq-saba** [Токсаба] (SOK 216); Kzk. 19th c. **Toq-saba** [Токсаба] (SOV 38, 76); Kzk. 19th c. **Toq-saba** [Азим Мамын Таксабын], a mulla in the region of Osh (TV 1878, 120); Nog. **Toq-saba** [Токъ-Саба], according to Noɣay-Tatar tradition, she is one of the foremothers of Noɣays (Smirnov, Krym. 77); Uzb. **Toq-saba** [Токсаба], an official (Mirza Šems-Grigor'ev, Sobyt. v Buhare, 2); Uzb. 1704 **Toq-saba** [توقسابه / Toksabah], a banner bearer from Bukhara (Buchari 279); Uzb. 20th c. **Toq-saba** [Achour Toqçaba], a basmačī leader (Castagné 76); Maml. 1279, 1297 **Toq-saba / Toq-sabay?** [طنصبا لناصرى] / Seïf-eddin Taksebaï-Nâseri / Seïf-eddin-

Taksaba-Nâseri] (Makrīzī II, 1, 7, IV, 43, Zetterst. 41, 45); Maml. 1321, 1322/23, 1325 **Toq-saba / Toq-soba?** [طنصبا / سيف الدين طنصبا الظاهرى / Токсоба Эззахири], emir, an envoy to (Desht-i) Kipchak (Nuwairī/Tizeng. I, 148, 170, Aynī/Tizeng. I, 492, 522, Tizeng. I, 257, 266 /after Al-Malik An-Nāsir/, Duqmaq/Tizeng. I, 321, 328, Dawād. 368, Zetterst. 170, 185); Maml.? 1282/83 **Toq-sawa** [طنصوا] (Iyās I, 115, 124); Tat. 1543 **Toq-suba** [Токъсубинъ], from Astrakhan (PSRL XIII, 144); *EN:* Kuman 1147, 1152, 1185 **Toq-saba / Toq-soba?** [Токсобичи / Токсобицъ Колобичъ], a Polovets tribal federation (PSRL VII, 39, 58, Ipat. 432 /445/, PSRL II, 131, also Bask., Im. polov. 74); *TN:* Crm. **Toq-saba** [Toksaba], two villages in the Crimea (Jervis II). ✧ I. 'Full / satisfied / plump leather bottle (skin made into a bag)' (Rásonyi, KÖA 133, Sattarov: *Tuqsaba*, Bese 15), cf. Shor, Kzk., Tat. *saba* 'ein Ledersack zum Bereiten des Kumiss, ein Lederschlauch; (Shor) grosses Birkenrindengefäss' (Radl. IV, 411); II. 'Nine-clan(s), Nine-forefathers'? (ethnical name), cf. Kuman (Polovets) *Toqs-oba* <*toqus/toquz* '9' + *oba* 'clan, tribe' (Bask., Im. polov. 74), Tat. *Tuqsaba* 'nine-father(s)'? (Sattarov); According to Sauvaget (p. 51) the Maml. surname طنصبا [toqus-bā] goes back to the ethnical name of the Kipchaks *Toqsuba*; III. 'Bearer of banner (title); colonel (?)' cf. Chag. *toqsabay* 'eine Würde in Bukhara' (Radl. III, 1155), *tuqsaba / tuqsabay* 'der Oberst, der Feldoberst' (Radl. III, 1429). ⇨ **TOQ / TOQUZ? + SABA I.** See also **ASTANA-QUL-TOQSABA?**

TOQ-SABAY Kzk. 19th c. **Toq-sabay** [Токсабай] (SOK 188); Kzk. 19th c. **Toq-sabay** [Токсабай] (SOV 87); Kzk. 19th c. **Toq-sabay, Toq-subay?** [Таксубай] (SOK 108). ⇨ **TOQ + SABAY.** See also **TOQ-SABA.**

TOQ-SAWA see **TOQ-SABA**

TOQ-SOBA see **TOQ-SABA**

TOQ-SUBA see **TOQ-SABA**

TOQ-ŠAN see **TOQ**

TOQ-TALAS Kzk. 19th c. **Toq-talas** [Токталасъ] (SOK 284). ⇨ **TOQ + TALAS.** See also **BAY-TALAS.**

TOQ-TANA Tat.(GH)? 1288 **Toq-tana?** [Tuctane], a „Tatar" princess (regina) (Reg. Hieros. 385). ✧ 'Full/sated calf' cf. Chag., Crm., Kar., Tat. *tana* 'eine junge Kuh, die Ferse, ein einjähriges Kalb' (Radl. III, 822). ⇨ **TOQ + TANA I.** See also **TOQ-TAY.**

TOQ-TAŠ Tat. 1624 **Toχ-taš** [Тохташ] (Zolotn. 159); NUyg. 20th c. **Toχ-taš** [Tochtasch], a Muslim Turk (Mughal) imam from India (Le Coq, Von Land und Leuten in Ostturkistan. Leipzig, 1928, p. 40); Chuv. 1738 **Tok-taš** [Токташевъ] (Letop. ZAK III, 139); Kzk. 19th c. **Toq-tas** [Токтасъ] (AOO 10); Bulg. **Toq-taš** [Toqtaš] (Byz. Turc. 316); Bulg. 8th c. **Toq-taš**

[Τόκτος], a prince (767-772) (Byz. Turc. 316); Tat. 1779 **Toq-taš** [Токташев], a widespread family-name (MIB V, 81-84); Tat.(Sib.) 1601 **Toq-taš** [Токташев] (Miller, Ist. Sib. II, 169); Tat.(Lit.) 1592 **Toq-taš / Taq-taš?** [Сулейманъ Такташевичъ] (Lit. Tat. 123); Nog. 1649 **Toq-taš-bay** [Тинѣй Бай-токташбаевъ (Тинѣй Бай Токташбаевъ?)] (AI IV, 123). ✧ 'Being halted, stopped; let the death or birth of children stop' (Sattarov) or. ⇨ **TOQ + TAŠ?**

TOQ-TEMİR Uyg. 12th c. - 14th c. **Toq-dämir** [Toq-dämir] (Radl., USp. 9); Maml. 14th c. **Toq-tämür** [طنتمر] (Sauvaget 50); Türk 7th c. - 9th c. **Toq-temir** [toq temir] (DTS); Uyg. / Karakh.? 895 **Toq-temir** [تكتمر], Taš-temir's son (Ibn al-Athīr/Tornb. VII, 327); Khorezm.? 1313 **Toq-temir** [طتتمر بن بولاى بهادر], a Moghul emir (Dawād. 273, 277); Tat.(GH) 1320 **Toq-temir** [Токτεμήρ], a christened Tatar, died in 1320 (Byz. Turc. 316); Tat.(GH) 1320 **Toq-temir** [Токтемиръ] (Veselovskij, Zametki po ist. Zolotoj ordy: IIAN, 1916, 14); Maml.? 1331, 1332 **Toq-temir** [سيفالدين طتتمر الخازن], an emir (Iyās I, 166, Dawād. 358, 366); Maml. 1332 **Toq-temir** [طتتمر اليوسفى], an emir (Dawād. 367); Maml. 1332 **Toq-temir** [طتتمر الاحمدى], an emir (Dawād. 367, Zetterst. 208, 224); Maml. 1332 **Toq-temir** [طتتمر الساقى] (Dawād. 368); Maml.? 1332, 1343 **Toq-temir** [سيفالدين طتتمر الصلاحى] (Dawād. 367, Iyās I, 180, 181, Zetterst. 211); Maml. 14th c. **Toq-temir** [سيفالدين طتتمر الدمشقى] (Zetterst. 164); Maml. 14th c. **Toq-temir** [سيفالدين طتتمر], a terasurer (Zetterst. 208); Maml. 14th c. **Toq-temir** [سيفالدين طتتمر الشهابى] (Zetterst. 224); Maml. 1452 **Toq-temir** [طتتمر البارزى الناصرى] (Ibn Taghrīb. VII, 233, 412); **Toq-temür** [توق تَمُرُ], forefather of the Ottoman dynasty (Āšikp. 5); *EN:* Trkm. 1693 **Toχ-temürlü** [توحتمورلى / Kīzīl Ali Tohtemürlü], a Türkmen tribe in the region of Hama and Humus of Anatolia (Refik., Anad. 107). ✧ 'Full/satisfied-iron, solid/compact iron'. ⇨ **TOQ + TEMİR.** See also **TOQ-BULAT.**

TOQ-TEMÜR see TOQ-TEMİR

TOQ-TUƳAN Khorezm.? 13th c. **Toq-tuγan** [توق تغان / توق توغان], a Merkit emir (Ǧuwaynī I, 46, 47, 51 etc.); Khorezm.? 13th c. **Toq-tuγan** [توق دغان], a Moghul soldier (Ǧuwaynī II, 101). ✧ 'Born full/satisfied'. ⇨ **TOQ + TUƳAN I.**

TOQ-TUƳUR Kzk. 19th c. **Toq-tuγur** [Токтугуръ] (SODž. 72). ✧ 'Sated horse of medium worth'. ⇨ **TOQ + TUƳUR.**

TOQ-TUMAQ Kzk. 19th c. **Toq-tumaq** [Токтумакъ] (SODž. 160). ⇨ **TOQ + TUMAQ.**

TOQA I. Uyg. 12th c. - 14th c. **Toqa** [To(u)qa / Toka] (Radl., USp. 210, 252, DTS, EUTS); Tat.(Sib.) 1599 **Toqa** [Тока Козяковъ], a Siberian murza (AI II, 18, 21, 23); Kzk. 19th c. **Toqa** [Тока] (SODž. 104); Kirg. 19th c. **Toqa** [Тока] (Potanin II, 7); Kzk. 19th c.? **Toqa-bay** (Atyns. 127); Kzk. 19th c. **Toqa-pay** [Токапай] (SODž. 142); Kzk. 1829 **Tuqa** [Тука] (MIK IV, 324); Kzk.? 1812 **Tuqa-bay** [Гильза Тукабаевъ] (TOUAK XXIV, 46); Kzk. 19th c. **Tuqa-bay** [Тутхушбай Тукабаевъ] (Grod., Pril. 93); Kzk. 19th c. **Tuqa-bay** [Аймамбатъ Тукабаевъ] (Grod., Pril. 94); Kzk. 1883 **Tuqa-bay** [Муктушбай Тукабаевъ] (Grod., Pril. 93). ✧ 'Full, satisfied' cf. Chag. *toqa* 'gesättigt, voll' (Radl. III, 1146); See also **TOQ.**

TOQA II. Hak. 19th-20th c. **Toqa** [Тока], fem. (HRS 355); Hak.(Koyb.) 19th-20th c. **Toqa** [Тока] (Katanov, Otč. 13). ✧ 'Clasp, buckle' cf. Chag., Turk. *toqa* 'die Schnalle' (Radl. III, 1146). ⇨ **TUƳA.** See also **TOQALİS.**

TOQAČ Bashk. 1761 **Toqač** [Бексентей Токачев] (MIB IV/1, 204); Bashk. 1791 **Tuqač** [Бакир Тукачев] (MIB V, 310); Kzk. 19th c. **Tuqač / Tuqaš?** [Тукачъ] (Grod., Pril. 114). ✧ I. 'A kind of bread; round pretzel' cf. Chag. *toqač* 'eine Art Brod oder Pastete' (Radl. III, 1148), Kzk. *tuγaš* 'runde Kringel (Gebäck)' (Radl. III, 1431), Kzk. *toqaš/toγaš* 'сушки; крендель; баранка' (KzRS); II. 'Wooden stocks/pillory of criminals' cf. Chag. *toqač* 'das Brett, das den Verbrechern um den Hals gelegt wird' (Radl. III, 1148).

TOQAY Bashk. 1713 **Toqay** [Токай Игимметев] (MIB III, 96); Bashk. 1714 **Toqay** [Кашевар Токаев] (MIB III, 108); Bashk. 1722 **Toqay** [Алабаш Токаев] (MIB I, 115); Bashk. 1732 **Toqay** [Толбай Токаев] (MIB III, 302); Bashk. 1734 **Toqay** [Токай Каниевъ], a tarχan (Vel.-Zern., Bašk. 10); Bashk. 1734 **Toqay** [Токай Бурашевъ], a tarχan (Vel.-Zern., Bašk. 10); Bashk. 1740 **Toqay** [Токай Сабаев] (MIB I, 427); Bashk. 1746 **Toqay** [Утекей Токаев] (MIB III, 435); Bashk. 1750 **Toqay** [Токай Бекбаев] (MIB III, 473); Bashk. 1754, 1755 **Toqay** [Токай Бекбаев] (MIB IV/1, 77, 97); Bashk. 1757 **Toqay** [Бексентей Токаев] (MIB IV/1, 138); Bashk. 1761 **Toqay** [Абызай Токаев] (MIB IV/1, 220); Bashk. 1761 **Toqay** [Абызай Токаев] (MIB IV/1, 220); Bashk. 1764 **Toqay** [Токай Бикбаев] (MIB IV/1, 298); Kzk. **Toqay** [Токай] (Sb. Syr-D. IX, 58); Kzk. 1823 **Toqay** [Токай] (MIK IV, 443); Kzk. 19th c. **Toqay** [Токай] (AOA 82); Kzk. 19th c. **Toqay** [Токай] (AOO 58); Kzk. 19th c. **Toqay** [Токай] (AOP 50); Kzk. 19th c. **Toqay** [Токай] (SOK 108); Bashk. 1728 **Toqay(eva)** [Токаева], a village (MIB III, 258); Tat. 19th c. **Tuqay** [Abdullah Tukai], the famous Kazan Tatar poet (1886-1913) (Mende 106, 108, 178); *TN:* Chuv. 18th c.

Tokay(eva) [Токаева], a village in the district of Tsivilsk (Korsakov 323). ⇨ ТОГАУ? See also **BOQAY-TOQAY, ÏŠ-TUQAY.**

TOQAQ Selj. 1097-1104 **Doqaq** [تتش بن ابونصر / دقاق شمس‌الملوق / Dokak / Ducac / Ducath / Doccac], Tutuš's son, the prince of Damascus (Qalānisi 130-140, Reg. Hieros. 1, Kamāladdīn: RHCHor III, 591-93, Ibn al-Athīr: RHCHor I, 204, 214, 223, Abulfidā III, 102-103); Oghuz 10th c. **Doqaq / Duqaq / Toqaq /Tuqaq** [Tûkâk / Дукак (Tукак)], Seljuk's father, thus the forefather of the Seljuks, known also by his byname (laqab) *Temir-yaliγ* (see); „because of his strength, was called *Temûryâlig*, that is to say 'Iron Bow'. There was born to this man and he was called by the name of *Saljûk*" (Budge); (Abulfar./Budge I, 195, MIT I, 365, 450, Toğan, UTT 183, 184, Türk Dünyası El Kitabı I, 247-248, 458); Uyg. 12th c. - 14th c. **Toqaq** [Tokak] (Radl., USp. 128, DTS, EUTS); Selj. 1041 **Toqaq** [تتاق] (Ibn al-Athīr/Tornb. 321, 322); Kzk. 19th c. **Toqaq** [Tокакъ] (SOV 110); Bashk. 1732, 1734 **Toqaq / Toqat?** [Катка Токаковъ (Токатовъ) / Катка-мулла Токаков] (MIB III, 302, PSZRI IX, 336, 339). ✧ 'He who goes straight for something' (Golden 217).

TOQAL Kzk. 19th c. **Toγal-bay** [Toгалбай] (SOV 62); Karch. **Toqal** [Токалъ] (Sysoev 120); Bashk. 1663 **Toqal** [Токалов] (MIB I, 175); Bashk. 1757 **Toqal** [Чавбура Токалов] (MIB IV/1, 157); Kzk. 19th c. **Toqal** [Токалъ] (SOK 300). ✧ I. 'With stumpy/broken horns; not having horns' cf. Chag., Kzk. *toqal* 'stumpf, mit abgebrochener Spitze; ohne Hörner' (Radl. III, 1147). Bashk. *tuqal* 'комолый, безрогий (о корове, козе и т. д.)' (BRS); II. 'Younger wife' cf. Chag., Kzk. *toqal* 'die jüngere Frau (da sie der älteren gegenüber sich nicht vertheidigen kann' (Radl. III, 1147).

TOQALÏS Hak. 19th-20th c. **Toqalis** [Токалис] (HRS 352). ⇨ **TOQA II.**

TOQAN Chuv. 18th-19th c. **Tokan** [Токанъ] (Magn. 84); Tat.(Lit.) 1552 **Toqan** [Токанъ] (Kn. Metriki Lit. 82); Bashk. 1675 **Toqan** [Токан Актуганов] (MIB I, 200); Kzk. 19th c. **Toqan** [Токанъ Онгаръ бекъ] (Grod., Pril. 161); Kzk. 19th c. **Toqan** [Токанъ] (SODž. 12, 46); Kzk. 19th c. **Toqan** [Токанъ] (SOK 168); Khorezm.? **Toqan-tarχan** (RaD/Ber. II, 212); Bashk. 1757 **Tuqan** [Тюкан Балтасев] (MIB IV/1, 139); Bashk. 1757 **Tuqan** [Юлай Туканов] (MIB IV/1, 139); Bashk. 1761 **Tuqan** [Илчимбеть Туканов] (MIB IV/1, 215); Bashk. 1763 **Tuqan** [Юлан Туканов] (MIB IV/1, 274); Bashk. 1770 **Tuqan** [Тюкан Солтанаев] (MIB IV/1, 347); *TN:* Kzk.? **Toχan-mulla** [Тохан-мулла] (Karta JAR XI). ✧ I. 'Knot, loop' cf. Bashk. *toqan* 'узел, петля' (BRS); II. 'Sated!' cf. Tat. *Tuqan* <*tuq* + voc. suff. *-an*

(Sattarov). See also **BES-TOQAN.**

TOQANAY Bashk. 1763 **Tuqanay** [Туканай] (MIB IV/1, 273). ⇨ **TOQAN** + suff. *-ay.*

TOQAÑ Hak. 19th-20th c. **Toqañ** [Токанъ] (HRS 352).

TOQAŠ Bashk. 1756 **Toqaš** [Токаш Девлетов] (MIB IV/1, 132); Kzk. 19th c. **Toqaš** [Токашъ] (AOK 2); Kzk. 19th c. **Toqaš-pay** [Токашпай] (SOV 18); Kzk. 19th c. **Tuqaš** [Тукашъ], fem. (Grod., Pril. 31); Kzk. 1883 **Tuqaš** [Тилакинъ Тукашевъ] (Grod., Pril. 98). ✧ 'Pieces of sour or sweet pastry fried in oil', in northern dial. of Kzk. (Žanuzakov-Esbaeva 460), it is the same as *bawïrsaq* 'баурсак (куски кислого или пресного теста, жаренные в масле, цале' (KzRS). ⇨ ТОГАŠ?

TOQAT Oghuz/Trkm. 13th c. **Toqat** [توقات / توتات / Токат], Toγurmïš's son (Abulg./Kon. 1070); Kirg. 18th c. **Toqat-batïr** [Токатъ-Батырь] (Nepljuev 689). ✧ 'Full/sated horse'? ⇨ **TOQ + AT.**

TOQČA Yürük 1543 **Toqča** (Gökb., Rum. 225). ⇨ **TOQ** + dim. suff. *-ča.*

TOQČAQ Kzk. 19th c. **Toqčaq** [Токчакъ] (SODž 110); Kzk. 19th c. **Toqĵaq** [Токджакъ Ходжа] (Grod., Pril. 147). ⇨ **TOQ** + dim. suff. *-čaq?*

TOQČÏN Crm. 1699 **Toqčin-oγlu / Toqčïn-oγlu?** [Токчинъ-оглу] (Smirnov. Krym. 670); Selj.? **Toqčin** [توقچین] (Qazw. 476); Hak. 19th-20th c. **Toqsïn** [Токсын] (HRS 352); NUyg.(Tar.) 19th c. **Toqsun** [توقسون / Токсунъ] (Pantusov, Tar. 104); Alt. 19th-20th c. **Toqšun** [Токшун] (OjrRS 210). ✧ I. 'Wild, uncontrolled' cf. Alt., Hak. *toqšin* 'wild, grausam, unbändig' (Radl. III, 1155); II. 'Prince' cf. Hak. PN *Toχsin / Toχčin* 'князь' (Butanaev) (<Mo.). See also **ER-TOQSÏN, TOQČÏN?**

TOQĴAQ see **TOQČAQ**

TOQÏL see **QANTURMÏŠ-TOQÏL**

TOQÏÑ Hak. 19th-20th c. **Toqïñ** [Токынъ] (HRS 352).

TOQÏŠ Kzk. 19th c. **Toγïš-pay** [Тогышпай] (AOA 118); Karakh. 11th c. **Toqïš** [toqïš / Токыş] (DTS, MK/Atalay 855); Kzk. 19th c. **Toqïš** [Токышъ] (AOK 14, 134); Kzk. 19th c. **Toqïš** [Токышъ] (AOK 90); Kzk. 19th c. **Toqïš** [Токышъ] (AOP 110); Kzk. 19th c. **Toqïš** [Токышъ] (AOP 74); Kzk. 1850 **Toqïš** [Токышъ] (Valihanov, Soč. 319); Kzk. 19th c. **Toqoš-pay** [Токошпай] (SOK 116); Kzk. 19th c. **Toquš** [Нурушъ Токушевъ] (AOK 22); Kzk. 19th c. **Toquš** [Токушъ] (AOO 62); Kzk. 19th c. **Toquš** [Токушъ] (AOP 122); Kzk. 19th c. **Toquš** [Токушъ] (SODž. 138); Kzk. 19th c. **Toquš** [Токушъ] (SOK 110); Kzk. 19th c. **Toquš** [Токушъ] (SOK 110, 204); Kzk. 19th c. **Toquš** [Токушъ] (SOK 214); Kzk. 19th c. **Tuγuš-pay** [Тугушпай] (SOK 200); Kzk. 19th c. **Tuqïš** [Тилаганъ Тукишевъ] (Grod., Pril. 102); Chag. 16th

c. **Tuquš-bahadur** [Тукуш-бахадур] (Ivanov 230, 234). ❖ 'Fight, rowdiness; service' cf. Chag. *toquš* 'der Kampf, die Prügelei; der Dienst, die Erklärung der Ergebenheit' (Radl. III, 1151). See also **ER-TOQUŠ**.

TOQKE Kzk. 19th c. **Toqke**? [Токке] (AOO 58). ⇨ **TOQ** + dim. suff. *-ke*.

TOQQA Trkm. 20th c. **Toqqa** [Toqqa], fem. (Zaj. 1971, 341); Trkm. 20th c. **Toqqa** [Токга], fem. (TrkmRS 638). ❖ 'Piece, ball' cf. Trkm. *toqɣa* 'кусок, ком' (TrkmRS).

TOQLÏ Turk.? 1363 **Toɣlï** [حوند طغلى] (Iyās I, 212); Kuman 1169, 1185 **Toɣlï(y)** / **Towlï(y)** / **Tuwlï(y)** [/ Тоглій (Толгый) Давыдовыч / Тоглый (Толгый / Товлый / Тувлій)], a Polovets prince, Boqmïš' brother (Lavr. 342, 375, Ipat. 381 (395), 450 (460), PSRL I, 154, VII, 86, 98, see also Bask., Im. polov. 74); Selj. 12th c. **Toɣlu** [عماد الدين طغلوا], governor of Hamadān (Rāwandī 381); Kkalp.? / Uzb.? 20th c. **Toχlu-bay** [Тохлюбаевъ], a merchant from Assake (Turk. Kraj 1912, 9); Tat.(Sib.) 1623 **Toχlu-bay(ko)** [Тохлубайко] (Miller, Ist. Sib. II, 293); Kzk. 18th c. - 19th c. **Toχtï** [Тохты] (Tynyšp. 66); Trkm.? 19th c. **Toqlï-bay** [Токлыбай] (TV 1878, 112); Bashk. 1714 **Toqlï-bay** [Токлыбай] (MIB I, 105); Kzk. 19th c. **Toqtu-bay** [Токтубай] (AOAtb. 66); Tat.(GH) 1293 **Toqtu-beg** [Toktubeg], the same as Toq-temir (Tochtamir) who appears on his coins as Toqtu-beg (Hammer 268); Kzk. 19th c. **Tuqtï-bay** [Туктыбай] (Grod., Pril. 32); Kzk. 19th c. **Tuqtï-bay** [Туктыбай] (SOV 150); *TN*: Kzk. **Toqtï-bay(eva)** [Токтыбаева / Токтыбай], a village (?) west of Chelyabinsk (?); Kirg.? / Kzk.? **Toqtu-bay** [Toktubai], a burial mound west of Ala-kul (PM Ergh. 43). ❖ 'A one-year-old lamb' cf. Maml. *tokly* 'einjähriges Lamm' (Tarǰ/Houtsma), *tohlï/toklï* 'bir yıllık koyun yavrusu' (İM), Chag. *toqli* 'ein drei Monate altes Lamm', Turk. *toqlu* 'id' (Radl. III, 1153), Trkm. *toqlï* 'годовалый барашек' (TrkmRS), Kirg., Kzk. *toqtu* 'ein Lamm am Endes des ersten Lebensjahres' (Radl. III, 1155), Kzk. *toqtï* 'ягнёнок, которому больше шести месяцев' (KzRS). See also **AY-TOΓLÏ, TİMÜR-TOΓLÏ.**

TOQLÏJÏ Maml. 1399 **Toqlïjï** [طقلجى السيفى يلبغا] (Iyās I, 318). ⇨ **TOQLÏ** + suff. *-jï.*

TOQLUQ Karakh.? 870 **Toɣluɣ** [طغلغ/طغلَغ] (Kindī 215, 216); Chag. 15th c. - 16th c. **Toɣluq-χaǰi** [حاجى توغلوق], a Sheybanid (Šejb. LI.); Uyg. 1341 **Toqluq** [Tuglug] (Chwol., Syr.-nest. (NF) 39); Maml.? 1325 **Toqluq** [طغلق] (Zetterst. 152, 190); Maml.? 1335 **Toqluq** [طغلق] (Iyās I, 168); Crm. **Toqluq** [Tokluk], north of Sudak (Jervis VIII.). ❖ 'Repletion, satiety; abundance, plenty' cf. Uyg., Kuman, Crm., Kar., Turk. *toqluq* 'das Gesättigtsein, Sattsein; die Fülle, das Ueberfluss' (Radl. III, 1153).

TOQLUQ-TEMİR Uyg. 12th c. - 14th c. **Toqluq-temür** [toqluq temür / Tokluk Tämür] (DTS, EUTS). ⇨ **TOQLUQ + TEMİR.**

TOQLUQ-TEMÜR Khorezm. 1360 **Toɣlïq-temür** / **Tuɣluq-temür** / **Tuqluq-temür?** [بن يلخواجه / توغليقتيمور خان / Toqluq Tämür / Туклукъ-Тимуръ-ханъ / Туглук-Тимур], 25th khan of Chaghatay's ulus (1348-1363), İl-χoǰa's son, the ruler of Eastern Turkestan (Abulg./Desm. 158, Radl., USp. 30, Barth., Ulugb. 12, 27, MIT I, 511, 512). ❖ 'Flag/banner-bearer iron'? cf. Chag., East.T. *tuɣluq* 'der Fahnenträger' (Radl. III, 1433), Chag. *tuɣlïq, tuɣlaq* 'mit der Yakschwanzfahne versehener Mann, der Fahnentrager' (Le Coq, Ind. 2). ⇨ **TEMİR.**

TOQMA Khorezm.? **Toqma** [Токма] (RaD II/10); Trkm. 1879-1881 **Toqma-serdar** [Tokmé Serdar] (O'Donovan II, 117). ⇨ **TOΓMA?** See also **QARA-TOQMA.**

TOQMAČ Tat. 1668 **Toqmač** [Василій Токмачевъ], from Astrakhan (AI IV, 436); Tat.(Sib.) 1600 **Toqmaš** [Токмаш Кенетмановъ] (Miller, Ist. Sib. II, 154); Bashk. 1732 **Toqmaš** [Кангилда Токмашев] (MIB III, 302); Bashk. 1732 **Toqmaš** [Кангильда Токмашев] (MIB III, 302); Kzk. 19th c. **Toqmaš** [Токмашъ] (AOP 46); Alt. 19th c. **Toqmaš** [Токмаш] (Verb., In. 134). ❖ 'Vermicelli' cf. Tat. *toqmač* 'лапша' (TatRS).

TOQMAQ Maml. 1401-1403 **Doqmaq** [دقماق المحمدى], governor (nā'ib) of Haleb (Iyās I, 303, 342, Weil, Chalif. II, 78, Ibn Taghrīb. VI, 10, 18 etc.); Maml. 1405 **Doqmaq** [السيفى دقماق], governor of Haleb then that of Hama, died in 1405 (the name was found in an inscription on one of the gates of Haleb (Mayer 116, Ibn Taghrīb. VI, 10, 23, 42, 90); Maml. 1449 **Doqmaq** [دقماق المحمدى] (Ibn Taghrīb. VII, 330); Maml. 1450 **Doqmaq** [دقماق اليشبكى] (Ibn Taghrīb. VII, 213, 549); Maml. 1472/73 **Doqmaq** [دقماق الاشرفى الاينـال لى] (Iyās II, 140); Maml. 1488 **Doqmaq** [السيفى اينال الاشتر] (Iyās II, 248); Maml. 1490 **Doqmaq** [دماق نايب القدس ا لشريف] (Iyās II, 265); Yürük 1543 **Toqmaq** [Tokmak] (Gökb., Rum. 221); Yürük 1543 **Toqmaq** [طوقماق / Tokmak] (Gökb., Rum. 221); Karch. **Toqmaq** [Токмакъ] (Sysoev 123); Karch. 20th c. **Toqmaq** [Toqmaq] (Pröhle, Karch. 139); Tat.(Sib.) 16th c.? **Toqmaq** [Токмакъ], Yermak's (Yermäk's) byname (Sib. Let. (Esipovsk. let.) 275); Kzk. 1846 **Toqmaq** [Токмак Изербаев], a biy (MKOP 154); Turk. 16th c. **Toqmaq-oɣlu** [Abdullah Tokmak oğlu] (Ongan, Ank. II.); Kzk. 18th c. - 19th c. **Toqpaq** [Токпак] (Tynyšp. 71); Kzk. 19th c. **Toqpaq** [Токпакъ] (SOK 298). ❖ 'Mallet; Wooden hammer' cf. Chag., East.T., NUyg.(Tar.), Turk. *toqmaq* 'der hölzerne Hammer, der Schlägel'

(Radl. III, 1156), Tat. *tuqmaq* 'колотушка, деревянный молоток' (TatRS), Kzk. *toqpaq* 'колотушка' (KzRS), also Sauvaget 47.

TOQMAN   Kzk. 1817 **Toqman** [طوقمان] (MIK IV, 303); Kzk. 1827 **Toqman** [Юмартъ Токмановъ], a sultan (Mejer 35); Kzk. 19th c. **Toqman** [Токпанъ] (AOO 18, 62); Tat. 1680 **Toqman(ko)** [Токманко Роспаевъ] (DAI VIII, 272); Kzk. 19th c. **Toqpan** [Токпанъ] (SOK 26, 130, 208); Kzk. 19th c. **Tuqban** [Сифила Тукбановъ] (Grod., Pril. 142); Kzk. 1803, 1820 **Tuqman** [Тукман / Тукманъ], a leader of the Alim-ulï (Qara-kisek?) tribe of the Little Horde (Kiši Žüz) (MIK IV, 515, Sib. Vest. IX, 116); Kzk. 19th c. **Tuquban** [Тукубанъ] (AOK 134); Kzk. 19th c. **Tuquban** [Тукубанъ] (Grod., Pril. 106); Kzk. 19th c. **Tuquman** [Тукуманъ] (SOK 134); *EN:* **Toqman** [Tokman], a place in Turkestan (Or. Bibl. XVI, 59); Kzk. 1820 **Toqman** [Токман], a Kazak tribe (MIK IV, 356); Kzk. **Tuqman(skaya)**, a village east of Čeljabinsk (?). ❖ 'Full, satisfied'. ⇨ **TOQ** + suff. *-man*. See also **AQ-TUQMAN**.

TOQMANAY   Chuv. 18th-19th c. **Tokmaney** [Токманей] (Magn. 84); Tat.(Sib.) 1596 **Toqmanay** [Токманаевъ Дмитрий], an interpreter (Miller, Ist. Sib. II, 148, 287). ⇨ **TOQMAN** + dim. suff. *-ay*.

TOQMAR   Kzk. 19th c. **Toqmar** [Токмаръ] (SOV 110). ❖ 'Light (wooden?) arrow without iron arrow-head' cf. Chag. *toqmar* 'id.' (Radl. III, 1157).

TOQMAŠ see **TOQMAČ**

TOQMET   Chuv. 18th-19th c. **Toχmat** [Тохмать] (Magn. 86); Chuv. 18th-19th c. **Toχmet** [Тохметь] (Magn. 86); Bashk. 1755 **Toqmet** [Токметь] (MIB IV/1, 105); Bashk. 1757 **Toqmet** [Токметев] (MIB IV/1, 142); Bashk. 1757 **Toqmet** [Токметев] (MIB IV/1, 142); Bashk. 1783 **Toqmet** [Москов Токметев] (MIB V, 145). ⇨ **TOQ** + suff. *-met*.

TOQMÏŠ   Tat. **Toqmïš-šiχzada** [Таоқмыш-Шихтзяда] (PSRL XIII, 239); Tat.? 1686 **Toqpïs** [Токпысевъ] (Kungursk. akty 98).

TOQO   Kirg. **Toqo** [Токо] (Jud. 99, 550); Kirg. **Toqo** [Kara Toko / Кара Токо] (Proben V, 70 /71/); Alt. 19th-20th c. **Toqo** [Токо] (OjrRS 210); Tat. 1675 **Toqo-bay** [Токобаевъ] (Kungursk. akty 24); Kzk. **Toqo-bay** [Tokobai] (PM Ergh. 43); Kirg.? **Toqo-bay** [Токобай], a well (Karta JAR XI). ⇨ **TOQA I.?** / **TOQA II.?** See also **QARA-TOQO**.

TOQOY   Yak. **Toqoy** / **Toqoy-toboroy** [Токоi / Токоi-Тобороi] (Pek.). See also **SARÏ-TOQOY**.

TOQOLDÏS   Kzk. 19th c. **Toqoldïs** [Токолдысъ] (SODž. 8).

TOQOMON   Kirg. **Toqomon** [Токомон] (Proben V, 48 (49), 225 (227)). ⇨ **TOQMAN?** / **TOQO** + suff. *-mon?*

TOQPAQ see **TOQMAQ**

TOQPAN see **TOQMAN**

TOQPÏS see **TOQMÏŠ**

TOQSAN   Kzk. **Toqsan** [Toksan] (Laptev, Materialy 47); Kzk. 19th c. **Toqsan** [Токсанъ] (AOAtb. 30); Kzk. 19th c. **Toqsan** [Токсанъ] (AOK 30, 106); Kzk. 19th c. **Toqsan** [Токсанъ] (AOP 22); Kzk. 19th c. **Toqsan** [Джанадилъ Токсановъ] (SKSO III, 19); Bashk. 1794 **Toqsan-bay** [Токсанбай Араптанов] (MIB V, 338); Kzk. 1794 **Toqsan-bay** [طوقصان بای] (MIK IV, 158); Kzk. 19th c. **Toqsan-bay** [Токсанбай] (AOAtb. 50); Kzk. 19th c. **Toqsan-bay** [Токсанбай] (AOK 78); Kzk. 19th c. **Toqsan-bay** [Токсанъ-бай Бекбергановъ] (Grod., Pril. 189); Kzk. 19th c. **Toqsan-bay** [Токсанбай] (Grod., Pril. 78); Kzk. 19th c. **Toqsan-bay** [Таксанбай], a biy (Lomakin 37); Kzk. 19th c. **Toqsan-bay** [Токсанбай] (SODž. 70); Kzk. 19th c. **Toqsan-bay** [Токсанбай] (SOV 36); Uzb. 19th c. **Toqsan-bay** [Базарбай Токсанбаевъ] (SKSO III, 176); *TN:* Kzk. **Toqsan-bay** [Таксанбай], a field (Karta JAR X); Kzk. **Toqsom-bay** / **Toqsam-bay** (<Toqsan-bay?) [Toksombai], a burial mound (PM Ergh. 43). ❖ 'Ninety' cf. Kzk. Chag., East.T., Kar. *toqsan* 'neunzig' (Radl. III, 1155); 'Ninety; three winter months' (Žanuzakov), 'Let him live to be ninety / child of a ninety-year-old father [!]' (Sattarov); In the Kirg. folk calendar *toqson* means the three winter months: December, January and February (Kalilov 94).

TOQSÏN see **TOQČÏN**

TOQSUN see **TOQČÏN**

TOQSUŠ   Uyg. 12th c. - 14th c. **Toqsuš** [Toksuş] (Radl., USp. 128, DTS, EUTS).

TOQŠU   Kzk. 19th c. **Toqšu-bay** [Токшубай] (SOK 276). ❖ 'Full/satisfied, rich?' cf. Kzk. *toqšu(lüq)* 'die Sattheit, Ueberfluss von Mundvorrath' (Radl. III, 1155). ⇨ **TOQ?**

TOQTA   Kzk. 19th c. **Toχta** [Тохта] (Grod. I, 98); Kzk. 19th c. **Toχta** [Тохта] (SKSO VIII, 219); Kkalp. 20th c. **Toχta** [Тохта], fem. (KkRS 778); Uzb. 20th c. **Toχta** [Тўхта] (Begmatov 1984, 205); Uzb. 20th c. **Toχta** [Тўхта], fem. (Begmatov 1984, 205); Uzb. 20th c. **Toχta-aχun** [Халбаевъ Тохта Ахунъ] (Turk. Kraj 1912, 5); Uzb. 20th c. **Toχta-bek** [Тўхтабек] (Begmatov 1984, 205); Uzb. 20th c. **Toχta-bibi** [Тўхтабиби], fem. (Begmatov 1984, 205); Bashk. 1734 **Toχta-γul** [Тохтагулов] (MIB III, 322); Uzb. 20th c. **Toχta-γul** [Тўхтагул], fem. (Begmatov 1984, 205); Uzb. 20th c. **Toχta-χân** [Тўхтахон], fem. (Begmatov 1984, 205); Kzk. 19th c. **Toχta-qul** [Тохтакуловъ] (SKSO VIII, 219); Uzb. 20th c. **Toχta-qul** [Тўхтакул] (Begmatov 1984, 205); NUyg. 19th c. **Toχta-manǰu** [Тохта-Манджу], from Aksu (Valihanov, Soč. 145); Chag. 16th c. **Toχta-mirza** [Тохта-мирза] (Ivanov 224); Uzb. 20th c. **Toχta-mirza** [Тўхтамирза]

(Begmatov 1984, 205); Uzb. 20th c. **Toχta-nisâ** [Тӯхтанисо], fem. (Begmatov 1984, 205); Kirg. 19th c. **Toχto-γul** [Тохтогулъ], a mergen (hunter) (Potanin II, 4, 151); Chuv. 19th c. **Tokta-bi** [Toktabi], fem. (Kronheim 96); Chuv. 19th c. **Tokto-kal** [Togtokal] (Kronheim 96); 870/71 **Toqta** [طغتـا / طُغْتـا] (Tabarī, Annal. III, 1790, 1841); 876 **Toqta** [محمد طغتا التركى] (Tabarī, Annal. III, 1894); Kzk. 19th c. **Toqta / Toγda?** [Togda Muhammed Bek] (Hedin, En färd I, 235); Kzk. 19th c. **Toqta / Toγda?** [Togda Muhammed Baj], a courtier (Hedin, En färd I, 370); Tat.(GH) 1282, 1290, 1312, 1313 **Toqta / Toqtay** [طغطـاى / طقطـا / طقطـاى / تـوقتـوقـا / Токта / Тогта / Тохта / Тахта / Токтатай / Токтакай / Туктука], Kipchak/Tatar Khan of the Horde (1291-1312), Meñgü-temür's (1267-1280) son, died in 1312 (Tizeng. I, 174, Baybars/Tizeng. I, 82, 104, Ibn Khaldūn/Tizeng. I, 377, 394, Duqmaq/Tizeng. I, 316, 323, Nuwairī/Tizeng. I, 134, 137, 155, 158, Al-Mufaḍḍal/Tizeng. I, 184, 196, Suzd. 499, PSRL I, 227, III, 129, IV, 44, V, 201, 205, VII, 186, 241 etc., PSRL (Russk. Hr.) I, 403); Tat.(GH)? **Toqta / Totqa?** (Byz. Turc. 317); NUyg. 1910 **Toqta-alun** [Tokta Alun], Aurel Stein's guide (Stein?); Maml.? 1389 **Toqta-bay** [طـتطبـاى الطشتمـرى] (Iyās I, 273); Maml. 1484 **Toqta-bay** [طـتطبـاى المحمـدى الاشـرفى] (Iyās II, 224); Maml.? 1496/97 **Toqta-bay** [طـتطبـاى بـن بـرد بـك الـدوادار] (Iyās II, 306); Kzk. 19th c. **Toqta-bay** [Токтабай] (AOK 18); Kzk. 19th c. **Toqta-bay** [Досмагилъ Токтабаевъ], a writer of articles (AUK 853); Kzk. 19th c. **Toqta-bay** [Токтабай] (SOK 14); Maml.? / Turk.? 1495/96 **Toqta-bay** [طـتطبـاى مـن طبـة الاربعيـن] (Iyās II, 292); Maml.? / Turk.? 1500/501 **Toqta-bay** [طـتطبـاى] (Iyās II, 377, 394); Maml.? / Turk.? 1516 **Toqta-bay** [طـتطبـاى العلا ئـى], a governor (Iyās III, 3, 26, 57); Maml.? / Turk.? 1516 **Toqta-bay** [طـتطبـاى بـن ولى الـديـن] (Iyās III, 61); Kzk. 19th c. **Toqta-bay / Toγda-bay?** [Togda Baj], a herdsman (Hedin, En färd I, 311); Kzk. 19th c. **Toqta-bay-bek / Toγda-bay-bek?** [Togda Baj Bek], a courtier (Hedin, En färd I, 298); Kzk. 19th c. **Toqta-bek / Toγda-bek** [Muhammed Togda Bek], a courtier (Hedin, En färd I, 370); Kzk. 19th c. **Toqta-bek / Toγda-bek?** [Togda Bek], a courtier (Hedin, En färd II, 226); Kzk. 19th c. **Toqta-bul** [Токтабулъ] (SOK 226); Tat. 1817 **Toqta-γul** [Тактагуловъ], a merchant (PSZRI XXXIV, 753-54); Bashk. 1764 **Toqta-γul** [Токтагул Токбаев] (MIB IV/1, 298); Bashk. 1784 **Toqta-γul** [Токтагул Курусев] (MIB V, 152); Kzk. **Toqta-γul** [Toktagul Mergän / Токтаҕул Мергäн] (Proben III, 64 /84/); Kzk. 1817 **Toqta-γul** [طوقتـاغـول], chief of the Šiñgilli چيـكلى(?) tribe (MIK IV, 309); Kzk. 19th c. **Toqta-γul**

[Toktagul] (Ljutš 114); Uzb. 19th c. **Toqta-χan** [Токтахан] (TV 1875, 94); Kzk. 19th c. **Toqta-qoǰa** [Токта-коджа], forefather of the Bay-ǰigits (Potanin II, 6); Kirg. 19th c. **Toqta-qoǰa-bay-suqur** [Tochto-Khodzsa-bai-szukur] (Almásy 301); Kirg. 19th/20th c. **Toqto-bübü** [Токто-бӱбӱ], fem. (Abramzon, Rožd.); Kirg. **Toqto-γul** [Токтогул] (Jud. 89, 698); Kirg. 19th c. **Toqto-γul** [Токтогулъ] (Potanin II, 6). ✧ 'Halt, stop!; enough!' cf. Tat. *Tuqta-bay / Tuqta-bikä* etc., such names were given when several babies died in the family or too many children were born (Sattarov); Kuman, Chag., Hak., Kirg., Kzk. *toqta-* 'anhalten, halten; sich niederlassen' (Radl. III, 1153). A name wishing the newborn health and long life (Grod. I, 98), or wishing to stop the birth of girls (Abramzon, Rožd.). Cf. also Rásonyi, Imp. 241. See also **AY-TOXTA, BAY-TOXTA, EŠ-TOXTA.**

TOQTA-BUL Kzk. 19th c. **Toχta-bul** [Тохтабулъ] (SODž. 114). ⇨ **TOQTA + BOL / BUL?**

TOQTA-BULAT Kzk. 19th c. **Toqta-bulat** [Токта-булатъ] (Grod., Pril. 15); Kkalp. 18th c. - 19th c. **Toqta-pulad(-biy)** [Токта-Пулад бий] (MIKk. 110); *TN:* Kzk.? **Toχta-bulat** [М. Тохта-булатъ], in the Pamir-region (Karta JAR XIX). ⇨ **TOQTA + BULAT.**

TOQTA-QOZÏ Uzb. 20th c. **Toχta-qozï** [Тӯхтакӱзи] (Begmatov 1984, 205). ⇨ **TOQTA + QOZÏ.**

TOQTA-PULAD see TOQTA-BULAT

TOQTAΓAN Kzk. 19th c. **Toqtaγan** [Савкули Токтагановъ] (Grod., Pril. 124). ✧ 'Halted; stopped' cf. Kuman, Chag., Hak., Kirg., Kzk. *toqta-* 'anhalten, halten; sich niederlassen' (Radl. III, 1153). ⇨ **TOQTA.** See also **TOQTAY, TOQTAMÏŠ, TURΓAN, TURMÏŠ.**

TOQTAY Chuv. 18th-19th c. **Toχtay** [Тохтай] (Magn. 86); Maml. 14th c. **Toq-tay** [Tokṭay] (Tarǰ/Houtsma 85, Tarǰ/Toparlı 42); Maml.? 1294 **Toqtay** [Izz-eddin Taktaï] (Makrīzī III, 156); Maml.? 1310, 1316 **Toqtay** [سيفالـديـن طنطـاى / Sayf-ed-dîn Toqtâî en-Nâsery], an emir, the governor of Qaraq (Dawād. 223, 224, Sauvaire III, 416, Zetterst. 136); Maml.? 1320 **Toqtay** [طنطـاى السـاقـى] (Zetterst. 154). ✧ I. 'Toqtäi (Toqtō)' (Mo.) <*Toqta'ai* <*Toqtaγai*, it is the exact equivalent to Turkic *Toqtamïš* (Pelliot, 70-71); II. 'Full/satisfied (male child)' cf. Tat. *Tuqtay* <*Tuq* + Mo. suff. *-tay* (Sattarov); III. 'Full/satisfied foal' (Toparlı, loc. cit.). ⇨ **TOQ + TAY?** + suff. *-tay(2,3).* See also **TOQTAMÏŠ, TOQ-TANA?, SARÏ-TOQTAY.**

TOQTALÏN Kzk. 19th c. **Toqtalïn** [Токталынъ] (SODž. 8).

TOQTAMAT Uzb. 20th c. **Toxtamat** [Tokhtamat Pansat], a basmačï (Castagné 88). ⇨ **TOQTA** + suff. *-mat.*

TOQTAMÏŠ Trkm. 1701 **Toγdamïš** [طغدمـش] (Refik., Anad. 131); Kzk. 19th c. **Toχtamïs** [Тохтамысъ]

(SOK 102); Turk. 1489 **Toχtamïš** [Tohtamış (kâtib)]
(Gökb., Ed. 156); Tat. 1543 **Toχtamïš** [Tohtamış],
from Varna (Gökb., Rum. 242); Tat. 1624 **Toχtamïš**
[Тетей Тахтамышевъ] (Pokrovskij 71); Tat.(Sib.)
1632 **Toχtamïš** [Тохтамышев] (Miller, Ist. Sib. II,
398); Nog. **Toχtamïš** [Тохтамышъ], hero of the
Noγay heroic poems and epics (Farforovskij 26); Uzb.
19th c. **Toχtamïš** [Татаръ Тохтамышевъ] (SKSO III,
178); Tat.(Lit.) 1592 **Toχtamïš / Taχtamïš?**
[Тахтамышъ Болексуповичъ] (Lit. Tat. 124); Kzk.
1860 **Toχtamïš / Taχtamïš?** [Тахтамышъ
Айкумбаевъ] (ZIRGOGeogr. I, 272); Crm. 1689
Toχtamïš-aγa [توختمش اغا] (Vel.-Zern., Crim. 865);
Crm. 1637 **Toχtamïš-atalïq** [توختامش اتالق] (Vel.-
Zern., Crim. 192, 194); Trkm. 1817/18 **Toχtamïš-biy**
[Тохтамыш-бий], from the Mañγït tribe (MIT II, 196,
197); Chuv. 1739 **Toktamïš** [Тохтамышъ] (Alatyr.
146); Kzk. 18th c. - 19th c. **Toqtamïs** [Тохтамыс]
(Tynyšp. 66); Kzk. 18th c. - 19th c. **Toqtamïs**
[Токтамыс] (Tynyšp. 75); Kzk. 19th c. **Toqtamïs**
[Токтамысъ] (AOP 110); Kzk. 19th c. **Toqtamïs**
[Товукь Берганъ Токтамисевъ] (Grod., Pril. 122);
Kzk. 19th c. **Toqtamïs** [Токтамысъ] (SOV 54); Uyg.
12th c. - 14th c. **Toqtamïs** [Toktamış] (Radl., USp.
100-101, DTS, EUTS); Maml. 1377/78 **Toqtamïš**
[طقتمش السيفى] (Iyās I, I, 239); Maml. 1378 **Toqtamïš**
[طقتمش البلغاوى] (Iyās I, 242); Maml. 15th c.
Toqtamïš [السيفى طقطمش], chancellor of Ǯan-bulat,
mentioned in an inscription of a copper bowl (Mayer
234); Maml. 1468/69 **Toqtamïš** [برسباى
الاشرفى المحمدى] [طقتمش (Iyās II, 111); Maml. 1480
Toqtamïš [طقتمش الخشتدمى] (Iyās II, 199); Yürük.
1543 **Toqtamïš** [طوقدمش] / Toktamış], from the Yürüks
of Koсaсık, Turkey (Gökb., Rum. 104); Crm. **Toqtamïš**
[Токтамыш], a khan (qan) in a tale (Proben VII, 99);
Crm. 1651 **Toqtamïš** [توقتامش / چاپتون] (Vel.-Zern.,
Crim. 456, 503, 545); Tat. 1559 **Toqtamïš**
[Токтамышъ], a prince („služilyj carevič") (PSRL IV,
311); Tat. 1697 **Toqtamïš** [Коктамышевъ]
(Kungursk. akty 247); Tat. 1783 **Toqtamïš** [Абдулъ-
Тази Токтамышебъ Бурашовъ] (Korsakov 113);
Bashk. 1748 **Toqtamïš** [Токтамыш Ишеев] (MIB III,
454); Bashk. 1768 **Toqtamïš** [Токтамышъ
Ижбулатовъ] (Nikol'skij 275); Bashk. 1777 **Toqtamïš**
[Токтамыш Ижбулатов] (MIB V, 58, 672, 684);
Bashk. 1779 **Toqtamïš** [Токтамыш Мищерев] (MIB
V, 90); Kzk. 1819 **Toqtamïš** [Токтамыш] (MIK IV,
325); Kzk. 19th c. **Toqtamïš** [Токтамышъ] (AOK 50);
Kzk. 19th c. **Toqtamïš** [Токтамышъ] (Grod., Pril.
138); Kzk. 19th c. **Toqtamïš** [Токтамыкъ] (SOV 22);
Tat.(GH) 1372, 1380, 1382, 1398 **Toqtamïš /
Toχtamïš-χan** [توقتاميش] / خان / توقتميش خان] /
توقمش خان / تقتمش خان] / Ταχταμύσης / Τοχταμ /
Emperador Totamix / Toqtâmysch / Токтамыш /
Тохтамышъ / Тахтамышъ / Тахтомышъ /
Тактамышь / Тартаныш / Тохтамыш-хан], Jochid
khan (1378-1395) of the Golden Horde, died in 1406
(Ibn Taghrīb. VI, 76, Iyās I, 302, Arabš. I, 358,
Abulg./Desm. 187, al-Askalanī/Tizeng. I, 451, 454,
Clavijo 43v, 60r, Suzd. 508, PSRL (Russk. Hr.) I, 415,
421-25, 488, 522, PSRL (Russk. Hr.) II, 195, PSRL IV,
82-3, VI, 97, VIII, 41, PSRL VI, 130, VIII, 71, XI, 69,
XVI, 118-130, XIX, 7, 201, XXIII, 127, MIT I, 523,
532, Zambaur 246, Vel.-Zern., Crim. 3, Byz. Turc. 296,
329); Bashk. 1765 **Toqtamïš / Toktomïš?**
[Токтомыш] (MIB IV/1, 315); Kzk.? 1820 **Toqtamïš-
batir** [Тактамышъ-батыръ], one of the chiefs of the
Baγanalï tribe (Sib. Vest. IX, 109); Crm. 1642
Toqtamïš-bek [توقتمش بك] (Vel.-Zern., Crim. 275);
Crm. 1520 **Toqtamïš-χan?** [توقمش خان] (Vel.-Zern.,
Crim. 3); *EN:* Trkm. **Toqtamïš**, a clan (Németh, HMK
67); *TN:* Turk. 20th c. **Toqtamïš** [Toktamış], a village
in the province of Adana, Turkey (TMİB 11); Tat. 18th
c. **Toqtamïš** [Токтамышъ], a village in the district of
Ar(sk)? (Korsakov 250); Trkm.? / Uzb.? **Toqtamïš**
[Токтамышъ], a place (?) on the Sir-Darya river,
north-west of the town of Turkestan (Karta JAR XI). ✧
'Halted, stopped; death or birth of children stopped'
(Sattarov), cf. Kuman, Chag., Hak., Kirg., Kzk. *toqta*-
'anhalten, halten; sich niederlassen' (Radl. III, 1153);
II. 'Stable, strong, firm' (Sauvaget 51) + suff. *-mïš*. See
also **TOQTAΓAN, TOQTAY.**

TOQTAMÏŠ-KİREY   Crm. 1597-1608, 1681?, 1741?
**Toqtamïš-girey / Toqtamïš-kiräy-sultan / Toχtamïš-
kiräy-sultan / Toχtamïš** [توختمش كراى سلطان] /
نورالدين تقتمش كراى سلطان] / Тактамышъ-Гирей /
Тохтамыш], Crimean ruler, the son of Gāzi Girey II
(1588-1596, 1597-1608) (PSZRI II, 359-61, PSRL
XIX, 113, Vel.-Zern., Crim. 19, Bakč. Nadp. 30); Crm.
1630 **Toqtamïš-kiräy-sultan** [توقتمش كراى سلطان]
(Vel.-Zern., Crim. 640, 641, 644). ⇨ **TOQTAMÏŠ +
KERÄY.**

TOQTAR   Tat. 1728 **Toχtar** [Тохтар Темеев] (MIB
III, 251); Bashk. 1712 **Toχtar** [Тохтар] (MIB III, 85);
Bashk. 1729 **Toχtar** [Тохтар Нуркеев] (MIB III,
269); Bashk. 1735 **Toχtar** [Тахтаръ Кошаевъ], a
tarχan (Vel-Zern., Bašk. 13); Bashk. 1741 **Toχtar**
[Тохтар Нуркеев] (MIB III, 505); Nog. 1649 **Toχtar**
[Мамбетъ-Казы мурза Тохтаровъ], a murza (AI IV,
87); Uzb.? 1857 **Toχtar** [Тохтаръ] (Valihanov, Soč.
145, 396); Uzb. 20th c. **Toχtar** [Тўхтар] (Begmatov
1984, 205); Kzk. 19th c. **Toχtar-bay** [Тохтарбай]
(SODž. 150); Kzk. 1864 **Toχtar-bay** [Тохтарбай
Кемебаевъ] (Valihanov 507); Uzb. 20th c. **Toχtar-jân**
[Тўхтаржон] (Begmatov 1984, 205); Crm.(Tat.) 1505
Toqtar, a baχšï in the Golden Horde (Vásáry 54); Tat.

1624 **Toqtar** [Токтаръ / Тактаръ Кудашевъ] (Pokrovskij 69, 70); Bashk. 1734 **Toqtar** [Токтаръ] (Vel-Zern., Bašk. 11); Bashk. 1735 **Toqtar** [Токтаръ Тугановъ], a tarγan (Vel-Zern., Bašk. 20); Bashk. 1740 **Toqtar** [Бабак Токтаров] (MIB I, 427); Bashk. 18th c. **Toqtar** [Токтаров] (MIB V, 141); Bashk. 1751 **Toqtar** [Токтар] (MIB IV/1, 34); Bashk. 1776 **Toqtar** [Токтар] (MIB V, 51); Bashk. 1777 **Toqtar** [Илчимбеть Токтаров] (MIB V, 51); Bashk. 1781 **Toqtar** [Токтар] (MIB V, 125); Bashk. 1789 **Toqtar** [Темирбай Токтаров] (MIB V, 263); Kzk. 19th c. **Toqtar** [Токтаръ] (AOK 74); Kzk. 19th c. **Toqtar** [Токтаръ] (AOO 10); Bashk. 1791 **Toqtar / Tuqtar** [Кадыргул Токтаров (Туктаров)] (MIB V, 311); Kzk. 19th c. **Toqtar-bay** [Токтарбай] (SODž. 122); Kzk. 19th c. **Toqtar-bay** [Токтарбай] (SOV 4, 98); Kzk. 19th c. **Toqtar-bek** [Токтарбекъ] (SOK 28); Bulg. 1357 **Tuqtar** [توقطار / Tw Qatār / Туктар] (Jusupov 30, Epigr. Bulg. 92, 93, Tekin 96); Tat. 19th c. **Tuqtar** [Fuad Tuktarov], from Kazan (Mende 100, 105, 106); Kzk. 19th c. **Tuqtar** [Туктаровъ] (SKSO VIII, 203); *TN:* Kzk.? **Toqtar** (PM Ergh. 43). ✦ 'Death or birth of children will stop' (Sattarov, Žanuzakov), '(He/she) Will stay, will not die' (Kusimova), cf. Kuman, Chag., Hak., Kirg., Kzk. *toqta-* 'anhalten, halten; sich niederlassen' (Radl. III, 1153), Bashk. *tuqta-* 'остановиться, перестать' (BRS), Tat. *tuqta-* 'остановиться, прекратить, перестать, затихать' (TatRS).

TOQTARAQ   Hak.(Kyz.) 19th-20th c. **Toqtaraq** [Токтарак] (Katanov, Otč. 13).

TOQTASÏN   Kzk. 19th c. **Toχtasïn** [Тохтасынъ] (SODž. 100); Kzk. 19th c. **Toqtasïn** [Токтасынъ] (SODž. 4); Kzk. 19th c. **Toqtasïn-beg? / Toγdasin-beg?** [Togdasin Bek], a courtier (Hedin, En färd I, 172, 178, 180, 230); NUyg. 19th c. **Toqtasïn-beg? / Toγdasin-beg?** [Togdasin Beg] (Stein 85); Kzk. 19th c. **Toqtasun** [Токтасунъ] (SOK 46). ✦ 'Let the death or birth of children stop, let the child (long)live / let him survive' (Žanuzakov) cf. Kuman, Chag., Hak., Kirg., Kzk. *toqta-* 'anhalten, halten; sich niederlassen' (Radl. III, 1153), Bashk. *tuqta-* 'остановиться, перестать' (BRS), Tat. *tuqta-* 'остановиться, прекратить, перестать, затихать' (TatRS) + suff. *-sïn.* See also **BEK-SULTAN-TOXTŌSUN, TURSÏN.**

TOQTASUN see **TOQTASÏN**

TOQTAUL   Tat. 1632 **Toχtaul** [Тохтаулов] (Miller, Ist. Sib. II, 398); Kzk. 18th c. - 19th c. **Toqtaul** [Токтаул] (Tynyšp. 67); Kzk. 19th c. **Toqtaul** [Токтаулъ] (AOK 94); Kzk. 19th c. **Toqtaul / Taqtaul?** [Тактаулъ] (AOAtb. 50); Kzk. 19th c. **Toqtaul / Taqtaul?** [Тактаулъ] (AOO 58); *TN:* Kzk.? **Toχtaul** [Тохтаулъ] (Karta JAR XI). ✦ 'Ploiceman' cf. Chag. *toqtaul* 'der Polizist' (Radl. III, 1153).

TOQTAUŠ   Kzk. 19th c. **Toqtauš** [Токтаушъ] (SOV 126). ✦ 'Being halted, stopped; alive' cf. Kzk. *toqtaw* 'остановиться, стать' (KzRS) + suff. *-š.*

TOQTAWČUQ   Kzk. 1830 **Toqtawčuq** [Токтаучукъ] (Konšin, Mat. I-III, 56). ✦ 'Being halted, stopped; alive' cf. Kzk. *toqtaw* 'остановиться, стать' (KzRS) + dim. suff. *-čuq.*

TOQTÏ I. see **TUΓDÏ**

TOQTÏ II. see **TOQLÏ**

TOQTÏ-BOLAT   Kzk. 18th c. - 19th c. **Toqtï-bolat** [Токтыболат] (Tynyšp. 66). ⇨ **TOQLÏ + BULAT.**

TOQTÏ-BUL   Kzk. 19th c. **Toqtï-bul** [Токтыбулъ] (SOK 12). ⇨ **TOQLÏ + BOL?**

TOQTÏ-QURT   Kzk. 18th c. - 19th c. **Toqtï-qurt** [Токтыкурт] (Tynyšp. 66); Kzk. 19th c. **Tuqtu-γurt?** [Туктугуртъ] (SOK 100). ⇨ **TOQLÏ + QURT.**

TOQTO see **TOQTA**

TOQTO-ČUR   Alt. **Toqto-čur** [Токточуръ], a mythical bird (?). ⇨ **TOQTA + ČOR?**

TOQTOR   Kzk. 19th c. **Toqtïr-bay** [Токтырбай] (SOK 184); Kzk. 19th c. **Toqtor-bay** [Токторбай] (SODž. 8, 70, 46, 96); Kzk. 19th c. **Toqtor-bay** [Токторбай] (SOK 308); Kzk. 19th c. **Toqtor-bay** [Токторбай] (SOV 8, 44, 136); *TN:* Kzk. 19th c. **Toqtor-bay** [Токторбай], a field in the region of Kegen, in the district of Ĵarkent (SODž. 70). ✦ 'Doctor' (R.)?

TOQTOUX   Kzk. 19th c. **Toqtouχ / Toqtowuq?** [Токтоухъ] (AOO 14).

TOQTU see **TOQLÏ**

TOQTUČAQ   Kzk. 19th c. **Toqtučaq** [Токтучакъ] (AOO 62). ✦ 'Darling-lamb' cf. Kzk. *toqtïšaq* 'ласкательное к токты' (KzRS). ⇨ **TOQLÏ** + dim. hypoc. suff. *-čaq.*

TOQTUΓUĴA   NUyg.(Tar.) 19th c. **Toqtuγuĵa** [Toktugutscha / Токтуӷӱ̈џ̌а] (Proben VI, 12 /15/).

TOQTUM   Kzk. 19th c. **Toqtum-bay** [Токтумбай] (AOAtb. 10). ✦ 'My lamb'. ⇨ **TOQLÏ** + poss. suff. *-m.*

TOQU   Kzk. 19th c. **Toqu-bay** [Токубай] (AOA 114); Kzk. 19th c. **Toqu-bay** [Токубай] (AOO 66, 74); Kzk. 19th c. **Toqu-bay** [Токубай] (TV 1878, 82); Kirg.? / Kzk.? 19th c. **Toqu-bay** [Токубай] (Potanin II, 3); Kzk. 1846 **Tuqu** [Туку Джапаков] (MKOP 101); **Tuqu? / Toqu-aγa** [توقو / توقو اغا] (Ibn Bībī IV, 314-17, 319, 332). ✦ Tuqu (Mo.)?

TOQUY   Kzk. 19th c. **Toquy** [Токуй] (SOK 48). ⇨ **TOQU** + suff. *-y?*

TOQUYUTTA   Yak. **Toquyutta** [Токуjутта] (Pek.).

TOQUM   Kzk. 1827 **Toγum** [Алтынсары Тогумовъ] (Konšin, Mat. I-III, 56); Kzk. 19th c. **Toγum** [Тогумъ] (AOA 6); Bashk. 1687 **Toγum / Tuγum?** [Тогум / Тагум / Тугум Ялбяев] (MIB I, 79); Kzk. 19th c. **Toqum** [Токумъ] (AOA 106); Kzk. 19th c. **Toqum** [Токумъ] (SOV 110); Kzk. 19th c. **Toqum-bay**

[Токумбай] (SOK 176); Kzk. 19th c. **Toqum-bay** [Токумбай] (SOV 150); Bashk. 1728 **Tuγum** [Тугум] (MIB I, 129); Kzk. 1777, 1778, 1793 **Tuγum** [Tougoume / Тугумъ], a sultan of the Greater Horde (Ulu Žüz) (Levchine 165, 261, Dobrosm., Turg. 154); Kzk. 19th c. **Tuγum-bay** [Тугумбай] (SODž. 76); Kzk. 19th c. **Tuqum-bay** [Тукумбай] (SOK 42); *TN:* Kzk. Toqum-bay [Токумбай], a mountain south-west of Karkaralinsk (Karta JAR XII.). ✧ I. 'A felt cover/spread under the saddle' cf. Chag., Alt., Kirg., Kzk. etc. *toqïm / toqum* 'eine Filzschicht die unter den Sattel auf den Rücken des Pferdes gelegt wird' (Radl. III, 1151), Tat.(Bar.) *toγum* 'die Sattelunterlage' (Radl. III, 1166); II. I. 'Core, seed; descendant, child'? cf. Kzk. *tuqum* 'der Saamen, das Satkorn; die Familie, das Geschlecht' (Radl. III, 1426); Tat.(Bar.) *tuγum* 'die Nachkommenschaft, die Verwandschaft, die Sippe' (Radl. III, 1432). ⇨ **TOΓUM?** See also **TERLİK.**;

TOQUMBET Bashk. 1735 **Toqumbet** [Токумбетъ Кашаевъ], a tarχan (Vel.-Zern., Bašk. 13); Nog. 1649 **Toqumbet** [Уразъ-Гелдѣй Токумбетевъ] (AI IV, 123); Kkalp. 18th c. **Toqumbet-biy** [Tokumbetbii / Токумбетъ], a chief (Rytschkow I, 129, Nepljuev 677); Bashk. 1711 **Tuqumbet** [Москов Тукумбетев] (MIB III, 73); Nog. 1649? **Tuqumbet** [Танатаръ Тукумбетевъ] (AI IV, 123). ⇨ **TOQ** + suff. *-umbet.* See also **TOQMET.**

TOQUNA Alt. 19th-20th c. **Toquna** [Токуна] (OjrRS 210). ✧ 'Calm down; be quiet!' (OjrRS).

TOQURA Kzk. 19th c. **Toqura** [Токура] (AOAtb. 34).

TOQURBET Bashk. 1728 **Toqurbet** [Мунмик Токурбетев] (MIB I, 131). ✧ 'Short and thick, stubby' cf. Bashk. *toqor* 'толстый и короткий' (BRS/Uraksin). ⇨ **TUQUR** + suff. *-bet.*

TOQURÏ Kzk. 19th c. **Toqurï** [Токуры] (AOAtb. 34).

TOQUZ Trkm. 1577 **Doquz / Toquz** [طقوز / Dokuz], a Türkmen tribe (cemaat) in the region of Adana (Refik., Anad 30); Trkm. 1729 **Doquz / Toquz** [طقوز / Dokuz cemaati], a Türkmen tribe (cemaat) in the region of Rakka (Refik., Anad. 171); Kzk. 18th c. - 19th c. **Toγïz-bay** [Тогызбай] (Tynyšp. 73); Kzk. 19th c. **Toγus-pay** [Тогуспай] (SOK 18, 46); Kzk. 1817 **Toγuz** [طوغز / Тогуз] (MIK IV, 313, 319); Kzk. 19th c. **Toγuz** [Тогузъ] (Potanin II, 6); Kzk. 18th c. - 19th c. **Toγuz-bay** [Тогузбай] (Tynyšp. 67); Kzk. 1846 **Toγuz-bay** [Тогузбай Джанабаев] (МКОР 157); Kzk. 19th c. **Toγuz-bay** [Крыкпай Тогузбаевъ] (Konsin, Pam. 26); Kzk. 19th c. **Toγuz-bay** [Тогузбай], a biy (Lomakin 33); Kzk. 19th c. **Toγuz-bay** [Тогузбай] (SODž. 70, 140); Kzk. 19th c. **Toγuz-bay** [Тогузбай] (SOK 230); Kzk. 19th c. **Toγuz-bay** [Тогузбай] (SOK 86); Kzk. 19th c. **Toγuz-bay** [Тогузбай] (SOV 88, 140); Bashk. 1761 **Toqus** [Мурсалым Токусев] (MIB IV/1, 221); Bashk. 1761

Toqus [Абызан Токусев] (MIB IV/1, 221); Kzk. 19th c. **Toqus-bay** [Токусбай] (Grod., Pril. 57); Maml. 1428 **Toquz** [طقز الطاهرى الجـركسى], of Cherkess origin (Ibn Taghrīb. VI, 635); Kzk. 19th c. **Toquz** [Токузъ Зариревъ] (Grod., Pril. 148); Nog. 1649 **Toquz** [Ожарекъ Токузовъ] (AI IV, 100); NUyg. 19th c. **Toquz** [تـوقوز / Tokuz] (Le Coq, Namenl. 119); Uyg. 13th c. - 14th c. **Toquz / Tuquz?** [Tukuz] (Chwol., Syr. nest. (NF) 42); Kzk. 19th c. **Toquz-bay** [Тогузбай] (AOA 90, 134); Maml.? / Kipch. 1262 **Toquz-oγul / Tuquz-oγul?** [تتوزغول] (Baybars/Tizeng. I, 77, 99); Kzk. 19th c. **Tuγus** [Тугусъ] (AOK 118); Kzk. 18th c. **Tuγuz** [Тугузъ] (Nepljuev 764); *EN:* Yürük 1609 **Doquz / Toquz** [طقوز], a tribe (cemaat) (Gökçen 76); *TN:* Bashk. 1761 **Toγus-qïz** [Тогускыз], a brook (MIB IV/1, 212); Kzk. **Toγuz** [Тогузъ], a field near the Irtish river, north-west of Pavlodar (Karta JAR IV); Kzk. **Toγuz** [Тогуз], a settlement (awul) (Kojčubaev 218); **Toγuz-bay** [Тогузбай], a lake east of Troitsk (Karta JAR III); **Toγuz-bay** [Тогуз-бай], a place (?) east of Perovsk (Karta JAR XI); **Toγuz-bay** [Тогуз-бай] (Karta JAR XI); Kzk. 19th c. **Toquz-bay** [Токуз-бай], a settlement (aul) in the district of Kuraminsk (Grod., Pril. 138); Kzk. 19th c. **Tuqus-mulla** [Тукусъ-Мулла], a tomb (Hanykov, Karta ZK). ✧ 'Nine; very much; ninth child in the family' (Le Coq, Sattarov), number nine had a sacred character with the Turkic peoples (RaD/Desm. 12, Sattarov), cf. Türk, Uyg. *toquz* 'девять' (DTS), Chag., East.T. *toquz* 'neun' (Radl. III, 1150), Kzk. *toγïz* 'девять' (KzRS), Tat. *tuγïz* 'девять' (TatRS), Bashk. *tuγïδ* 'девять' (BRS).

TOQUZ-DEMİR see **TOQUZ-TEMİR**

TOQUZ-DEMÜR see **TOQUZ-TEMİR**

TOQUZ-TEMİR Alt. 19th c. **Toγos-temür-χan** [Тогос-Темур-хан] (Verb., In. 5); Maml. 1309, 1332, 1340, 1345 **Toquz-temir / Toquz-demir / Toquz-demür** [السيفى طقز تمر الساقى / سيفالـبـين تُكُز دُمُور / سيفـالـبـين طقزتـمـر /دمـر / طقزدمـر / Tagoztimur / Seïf eddîn Tokoûz Domoûr], Abul Fidā's slave (mamlūk) who was given to Muhamed (I.) al-Nāsir ibn Qalāūn (1293-1294, 1299-1309, 1310-1341) by Abul Fidā himself; then he became an emir and governor (viceroy) of Hamah, Haleb and Damascus in 1345, died in the same year (Abulfidā V, 216-217, Dawād. 365, 366, Zetterst. 179, Weil, Chalif. I, 440, 453, 463, Makrīzī, Khit. I, 116, Iyās I, 166, 177, 178 etc., Ibn Bat. I, 86, II, 152, Mayer 235-239). ✧ 'Nine-iron (=much iron)' (Le Coq, Ind. 2: „Vieleisen"; Sauvaget 44, 51). ⇨ **TOQUZ + TEMİR.**

TOQUZAN Crm. 1517 **Toquzan-murza / Toqsan-murza?** [Toqsan / Токузанъ-мурза / Токазань / Токузакъ], a murza (PSRL VI, 259, VIII, 261, XIII, 26, XX, 391).

TOQZAQ see **TOГUZAQ**

TOL Türk 9th c. - 10th c. **Tol-aba / Dul-aba?** [Dūlabā] (JRAS 1915, 675); Chuv. 18th-19th c. **Tol-bay** [Толбай] (Magn. 84); Bashk. 1732 **Tol-bay** [Толбай Токеев] (MIB III, 302); Bashk. 1753 **Tol-bay** [Смаил Толбаев] (MIB IV/1, 70); Kzk. 19th c. **Tol-bay** [Толбай] (SOV 4); Hak.(Blt.) 19th-20th c. **Tol-bay** [Толбай] (Katanov, Otč. 9); Chuv. 18th-19th c. **Tol-pay** [Толпай] (Magn. 85); Tat. 1779 **Tul-bay** [Макай Тулбаев] (MIB V, 94); Bashk. 1756 **Tul-bay** [Тулбай Курнябаев] (MIB IV/1, 132); Kzk. 19th c. **Tul-bay / Tül-bay / Töl-bay?** [Тульбай] (SODž. 16); Kzk. 19th c. **Tul-bay / Tül-bay / Töl-bay?** [Тульбай] (SOV 68); *TN:* Tat. 18th c. **Tol-bay(eva)** [Толбаева], a village in the district of Mamadysh (Korsakov 233). ❖ I. 'Full, complete, satisfied (healthy child)' cf. Tat. *Tul-bay / Tuli-bay* (Sattarov); II. 'Be satisfied!' cf. Uyg., Kuman, Chag., Alt., Hak., Kar., Kirg., Kzk. *tol-* 'voll sein' (Radl. III, 1191), Tat. *tul-* 'sich füllen, voll werden' (Radl. III, 1466), cf. also Rásonyi, Imp. 241. See also **AY-DOL, QARA-TOL, SAY-TOL; TOLU.**

TOL-ĴINAR Tuv. 19th c. **Tol-ĵinar** [Тольджинаръ] (Potanin IV, 425). ⇨ **TÜL / TOL + ČĪNAR?**

TOL-DİMER Chuv. 18th-19th c. **Tol-dimer** [Толдимеръ] (Magn. 84). ⇨ **TOL? + TEMİR.**

TOL-KİLDE Chuv. 18th-19th c. **Tol-kilde** [Толкилда] (Magn. 84). ⇨ **TOL + KELDİ.**

TOL-MEMET Chuv. 18th-19th c. **Tol-memet** [Толмеметь] (Magn. 85). ⇨ **TOL + MEMET.**

TOL-SARA Tat. 1624 **Tol-sara** [Толсара / Талсара Урусаевъ] (Pokrovskij 69). ⇨ **TOL + SARA I.**

TOL-ŽANAY Karg. 19th-20th c. **Tol-žanay** [Толжанаі / Толжанай], a folklore hero (Proben IX, 637, Katanov: ZIRGOÊtn. XVII, vyp. III, 1175). ⇨ **TOL + ĴANAY.**

TOLA Kzk. 19th c. **Tola-bay** [Толабай] (Grod., Pril. 119); Kzk. 19th c. **Tola-bay** [Джиранбай Толабаевъ] (Grod., Pril. 175). ⇨ **TULA?**

TOLAГAY Nog. **Tolaγay** [Толагай] (Žirm., Epos 402).

TOLAY I. Tat.(GH) 14th c. **Tolay** [Τολαία], a Christened Tatar (Byz. Turc. 316); Tat. 1624 **Tulay** [Тулай Крымчеевъ] (Pokrovskij 69); Uzb. 1883 **Tulay-bibi** [Тулай-биби], fem. (Moskal'cev 50). ❖ I. 'Full Moon' (Sattarov); II. '(Sun/Moon) Rises'? ⇨ **TOLU + AY. / TOL / TOLA?** See also **AY-DOLAY, AY-TOLÏY.**

TOLAY II. Hak. 19th-20th c. **Tolay** [Толай] (HRS 352); Hak. 19th-20th c. **Tolay** [Толай], fem. (HRS 355); Karg. 19th-20th c. **Tulay** [Тулай] (Katanov: ZIRGOÊtn. XVII, III, 153). ❖ 'Hare, rabbit' (<Mo.) (Butanaev), cf. Hak. *tolay* 'der Hase' (Radl. III, 1192), Alt.(Tel.) *tulay* 'der langschwänzige Hase' (Radl. III, 1467).

TOLAQ see **TULAQ**

TOLAQ-TEMİR Tat.(GH) 14th c. **Tolaq-temir** [Толакъ-Темиръ], Özbek's governor in the Crimea (Smirnov, Krym. 36). ⇨ **TULAQ + TEMİR.**

TOLAN see **TULAN**

TOLAŠ-TAY Karg. 19th-20th c. **Tolaš-tay** [Толаштай] (Katanov: ZIRGOÊtn. XVII, vyp. III, 200). ⇨ **TAY?** or suff. *-tay(1,2).*

TOLBAĴAP Tuv. 19th c. **Tolbaĵap** [Толбацап], fem. (Proben IX, 155).

TOLBAM-BAY see **TOLBAN**

TOLBAN Kzk. 19th c. **Tolbam-bay** (<Tolban-bay) [Толбамбай] (SODž. 160); Kzk. 19th c. **Tolpam-bay** (<Tolpan-bay) [Толпамбай] (SOK 304).

TOLČAX Hak. 19th-20th c. **Tolčax** [Толчах] (HRS 352).

TOLČU Bashk. 1787 **Tolču-bay** [Толчу-бай] (MIB I, 314).

TOLDÏ Uzb. 20th c. **Toldï** [Тўлди] (Begmatov 1984, 205); Uzb. 20th c. **Toldï-bây** [Тўлдибой] (Begmatov 1984, 205); Uzb. 20th c. **Toldï-χân** [Тўлдихон], fem. (Begmatov 1984, 205); Uzb. 20th c. **Toldï-χoĵa** [Тўлдихўжа] (Begmatov 1984, 205); Chuv. 18th-19th c. **Toldu-bay** [Толдубай] (Magn. 84); Bashk. 1753 **Tuldï** [Явда Тюлдин] (MIB IV/2, 426); Bashk. 1791 **Tuldï** [Ягуда Тулдин] (MIB V, 309). ❖ '(The child) got full/sated; (the Moon) got full' cf. Uyg., Chag., Hak., Kirg., Kzk. etc. *tol-* 'voll sein, gefüllt sein, sich füllen' (Radl. III, 1191), *tol-* 'наполняться; становиться полной (о луне)' (DTS). See also **AY-TOLDÏ, SAY-TOLDÏ, TOLDÏQ, TOLDÏM, TOLГAN, TOLMÏŠ.**

TOLDÏQ Chuv. 18th-19th c. **Toldïk** [Толдыкъ] (Magn. 84); Kzk. 19th c. **Toldïq-pay** [Толдыкпай] (AOAtb. 34). ❖ 'We got full/sated' cf. Uyg., Chag., Hak., Kirg., Kzk. etc. *tol-* 'voll sein, gefüllt sein, sich füllen' (Radl. III, 1191). See also **TOLDÏ, TOLDÏM, TOLГAN, TOLMÏŠ.**

TOLDÏM Kzk. 19th c. **Toldïm-bek** [Толдымбекъ] (SOK 230). ❖ 'I got full/sated' cf. Uyg., Chag., Hak., Kirg., Kzk. etc. *tol-* 'voll sein, gefüllt sein, sich füllen' (Radl. III, 1191). See also **TOLDÏ, TOLDÏQ, TOLГAN, TOLMÏŠ.**

TOLDOY Alt. 19th c. **Toldoy** [Толдой] (Potanin, Pred. 187).

TOLГAN Kzk. 19th c. **Tolγam-bay** (<Tolγan-bay) [Толгамбай] (SODž. 142); Kzk. 19th c. **Tolγam-bay** (<Tolγan-bay) [Толгамбай] (SOV 150); Kzk. 19th c. **Tolγam-bay** (<Tolγan-bay) [Тольгамбай] (SOV 40); Uzb. 20th c. **Tolγân** [Тўлгон], fem. (Begmatov 1984, 205); Uzb. 20th c. **Tolγân-ây** [Тўлгоной], fem. (Begmatov 1984, 205), Uzb. 20th c. **Tolγân-bibi** [Тўлгонбиби], fem. (Begmatov 1984, 205). ❖ '(He/she) got full/sated; (the Moon) got full' cf. Uyg.,

Chag., Hak., Kirg., Kzk. etc. *tol-* 'voll sein, gefüllt sein, sich füllen' (Radl. III, 1191). See also **TOLDÏ, TOLDÏQ, TOLDÏM, TOLMÏŠ.**

TOLΓON-AY see **TULΓUN-AY**

TOLİN Hak. 19th-20th c. **Tolin** [Толин] (HRS 352). ❖ 'Tolin' Hypoc. of R. *Anatoliy* (Butanaev).

TOLİNA Hak.? 19th-20th c. **Tolïna** [Толiна], fem. (Katanov, Otč. 10). ❖ I. 'Tolina' Hypoc. of R. fem. *Anatoliya / Evstoliya.* ⇨ **TOLİN.**

TOLÏ see **TOLU**

TOLÏ-KERE Alt. 19th c. **Tolï-kere** [Толы-Кере] (Verb., In. 150). ⇨ **TOLU + KERE?**

TOLÏJAQ Hak.(Koyb.) 19th-20th c. **Tolïjaq** [Тольщак] (Katanov, Otč. 13). ⇨ **TOLU + dim. suff. -ʲaq.**

TOLÏM-BEK see **TOLUN**

TOLÏN see **TOLUN**

TOLÏŠ Alt. 19th-20th c. **Tolïš** [Толыш] (OjrRS 210). ❖ '(Ex)changed (child)' cf. Alt.(Tel.) *tolïš-* 'austauschen, wechseln' (Radl. III, 1196).

TOLQU Kzk. 19th c. **Tolqu-bay** [Толкубай] (AOAtb. 30); Kzk. 19th c. **Tolqu-bay** [Толькубай] (AOP 38); Kzk. 19th c. **Tolqu-bay** [Толькубай] (SOK 82).

TOLQUN Kzk. 19th c. **Tolqum-bek** (<Tolqun-bek) [Толкумбекъ] (AOAtb. 22); Kzk. 19th c. **Tolqun** [Толкунъ] (SOV 62); Kzk. **Tulqum-bay** (<Tulqun-bay) [Садыкъ Тулкумбаевъ] (Sb. Syr-D. IV, otd. II, 147); Kzk. 19th c. **Tulqun-bay** [Тулкунбай] (Grod., Pril. 60). ❖ 'Wave, surge (wish to be good-looking)' (Žanuzakov), cf. Kzk. *tolqun* 'die Welle' (Radl. III, 1199).

TOLMET Chuv. 18th-19th c. **Tolmet** [Толметь] (Magn. 85). ⇨ **TOL + suff. -met.**

TOLMÏŠ Türk 7th-9th c. **Tolmïš** [Tolmïş] (ETY III, 57); Uyg. 12th c. - 14th c. **Tolmïš** (Radl., USp. 19-20, 211, 219, 253). ❖ '(The Moon?) Got/became full' cf. Uyg. *tol-* 'наполняться; становиться полной (о луне)' (DTS). See also **TOLDÏ, TOLDÏQ, TOLDÏM, TOLΓAN.**

TOLON-ARÏQ Alt. 19th c. **Tolon-arïq-darχan** [Толонъ-Арыкъ-Дарханъ], a smith in a tale (Potanin IV, 609). ⇨ **TOLUN + ARÏQ I.**

TOLOS see **TOLUS**

TOLŌX Hak. 19th-20th c. **Tolōχ** [Толоох] (HRS 352).

TOLPAN see **TOLBAN**

TOLSTAX Hak. 19th-20th c. **Tolstaχ** [Толстах] (HRS 352).

TOLŠAX Chuv. 18th-19th c. **Tolšaχ** [Толшахъ] (Magn. 85).

TOLTÏ Alt. 19th c. **Toltï-χan** [Тольты ханъ], a Buryat character in the tale (Potanin IV, 329).

TOLTOY Kirg. **Toltoy** [Толтой] (Jud. 883). ❖ '(Little) Ring, hoop' cf. Kirg. *tolto* 'колечко, которое скрепляет лезвие ножа и рукоятку' (Jud.) + dim. suff. -*y*. See also **TOLTOQ.**

TOLTOQ Alt. 19th-20th c. **Toltoq** [Толток] (OjrRS 210); Alt. 19th-20th c. **Toltoq** [Толток], fem. (OjrRS 213). ❖ '(Little) Ring, hoop' cf. Alt. *tolto* 'Rand von Metall oder Schraubenmutter, durch die die Klinge an das Heft des Messers befestigt wird' (Radl. III, 1204) + dim. suff. -*q*. See also **TOLTOY.**

TOLTU Kzk. 19th c. **Toltu-bay** [Толтубай] (SOK 236). ❖ 'Ring, hoop'? cf. Kirg. *tolto* 'колечко, которое скрепляет лезвие ножа и рукоятку' (Jud.), Alt. *tolto* 'Rand von Metall oder Schraubenmutter, durch die die Klinge an das Heft des Messers befestigt wird' (Radl. III, 1204). See also **TOLTOY, TOLTOQ.**

TOLTUR Kzk. 1825 **Toltur** [طولطور / Толтур] (MIK IV, 473, 477). ❖ 'Full, fat, corpulent' cf. Kzk. *toltŭr* 'voll, fett, corpulent' (Radl. III, 1204). See also **TOLUQ.**

TOLU Kzk. 1794 **Tolï-bay** [طولباى بى / Толы-бай], a biy (MIK IV, 160, 162); Kzk. 19th c. **Tolï-bay** [Толыбай] (SOK 16); Kkalp. 20th c. **Tolï-bay** [Толыбай] (KkRS 776); Uyg. 12th c. - 14th c. **Tolu** [Tolu] (Radl., USp. 84, DTS, EUTS); Maml. 1363 **Tolu** [حوند طولو زوجة الناصر حسن], fem. (Iyās I, 211); Maml. 1376/77 **Tolu** [طولو] (Iyās I, 233); Maml. 1393 **Tolu** [طولو بن على شاه] (Iyās I, 299, 337); Maml. 1377 **Tolu / Tulu?** [طولو تمنو الاحمدى] (Iyās I, 247); Maml. 1398/99 **Tolu / Tulu?** [طولو راس نوبة], a chief of Nūbiya (Ibn Taghrīb. VI, 6, 112); Kzk. 19th c. **Tolu-bay** [Толубай] (AOO 74); Kzk. 19th c. **Tolu-bay** [Tolubay] (AUK 133); Kzk. 19th c. **Tolu-bay** [Толубай] (SODž. 42, 134); Kzk. 19th c. **Tolu-bay** [Толубай] (SOV 60, 116, 148); Kirg. **Tolu-bay** [Толубай] (Jud. 94, 681); Kirg. / Kzk.? 19th c. **Tolu-bay** [Толубай] (Potanin II, 3); Bashk. 1600 **Toulu-bay** [Токбай Тулубаев] (Miller, Ist. Sib. II, 160); Kzk. 1792 **Tulï-bay** [Тулыбай] (MIK IV, 139); Kzk. 19th c. **Tulï-bay** [Тулыбай] (SOK 232); Tat.(Lit.) 1592 **Tulu-bay** [Мисюкъ Тулубаевичъ] (Lit. Tat. 123); Tat. 16th c. -17th c. **Tulu-bay** [Тул(у)бай] (Iznoskov 142); Tat. 1557 **Tulu-bay** [Тулубай] (Kn. Metriki Lit. 153); Tat. 1600 **Tulu-bay** [Тулубай] (MIB I, 153); Tat. 1624 **Tulu-bay** [Тулубай Абызовъ] (Pokrovskij 69); Tat.(Mish.) 1785 **Tulu-bay** [Курбангалий / Кулбангалий Тулубаев] (MIB V, 178); Tat.(Sib.) 1625 **Tulu-bay** [Тулубай] (Miller, Ist. Sib. II, 321); Tat.(Sib.) 1648 **Tulu-bay** [Тулубаев] (Miller, Ist. Sib. II, 527); Bashk. 1695 **Tulu-bay** [Аблу Тулубаев] (MIB I, 90); Kzk. 19th c. **Tulu-bay** [Тулубай] (AOAtb. 46); Kzk. 19th c. **Tulu-bay** [Тулубай] (SOK 8); Kzk. 19th c. **Tulu-bay** [Тулубай] (SOV 28); Tat. 1737 **Tulu-bay / Tulï-bay** [Тулу-бай (Тулы-бай)] (MIB I, 330, 338); Kzk. 19th c. **Tulu-bek** [Аяпъ

Тулубековъ] (Grod., Pril. 129); Crm. **Tülï-bay / Tulu-bay** [Тулы баі / Тулубаі] (Proben VII, 186, 188); *TN:* Kzk.? 19th c. **Tulu-bay** [Тулубай], a field (Hanykov, Karta ZK). ✧ I. 'Full, whole', 'Full (Moon)' (Blagova 1997, 716), cf. Uyg., Kuman, Kzk. *tolu* 'die Fülle, voll' (Radl. III, 1197), Kirg. *tolu* 'полный, полно' (Jud.), Kkalp. *tolï* 'полный; целый' (KkRS), Tat. *tuli* 'voll, völlig' (Radl. III, 1468); II. 'He who has a banner (sanjaq)' (Sauvaget 51); III. 'Mirror'? <Mo. *toli/tuli* (Sauvaget 51). See also AY-TOLU, ALTÏN-TOLU, İSTÄK-TOLU.

TOLUQ Kzk. 19th c.? **Toluq-pay** [Tolukpay] (Atyns. 104); Khorezm.? 1220 **Tuluq** [Тулук ибн Инанджхан / Тулук ибн Инанч-хан], a commander of the army (MIT I, 483, 484); Kzk. 19th c. **Tuluq-pay** [Тулукпай] (SOK 106); Kzk. 19th c. **Tuluq-pay** [Тулукпай] (SOK 214). ✧ 'Full, fat' cf. Kzk. *toluq* 'voll, fett' (Radl. III, 1197).

TOLUQ-TÜKÄ Uyg. **Toluq-tügä** [Toluk Tügä] (EUTS); Uyg. 12th c. - 14th c. **Toluq-tükä** [Toluq Tükä] (Radl., USp. 122, DTS). ✧ I. 'Fulfilled-heifer' (Bese 15); II. 'Full-Moon-Ends' (Blagova 1997, 716). ⇨ TOLUQ + TÜKÄ.

TOLUQAN Yak. 1680 **Toluqan** [Толуканъ], a shaman (DAI VIII, 268).

TOLUM-BAY see TOLUN

TOLUM-BEK see TOLUN

TOLUN Kzk. 19th c. **Tolïm-bek (<Tolïn-bek)** [Тольımбекъ] (SOK 80, 262); Kzk. 19th c. **Tolïm-bek (<Tolïn-bek)** [Тольımбекъ] (SOV 20, 44); Tat.(Lit.) 1548 **Tolom-bek (<Tulun-bek?)** [Толомъ Бекъ], a princess (Kn. Metriki Lit. 44); Kuman 1279 **Tolon / Tulun?** [Tolon], a chief of the Kumans of Hungary (Gyárfás II, 433); Bashk. 1600 **Tolon-gözä** [Толонгозя] (Miller, Ist. Sib. II, 160); Bashk. 1675 **Tolon-gözä** [Аювчи Толонгозин] (MIB I, 200); Kzk. 19th c. **Tolum-bay (<Tolun-bay)** [Толумбай] (SOK 298); Kzk. 19th c. **Tolum-bek (<Tolun-bek)** [Толумбекъ] (SODž. 12, 102, 158); Kzk. 19th c. **Tolum-bek (<Tolun-bek)** [Толумбекъ] (SOK 102, 158); Kzk. 19th c. **Tolum-χoJa / Tolun-χoJa** [Толумъгоджа], legendary forefather of the Merkits (Potanin II, 5); Uyg. 762 **Tolun / Qutluχ-qïz-tolun** [Qutluχ Qïz Tolun], fem. (Mahrnāmag 15); Oghuz (Toquz-oghuz) 816, 904 **Tolun / Tulun** [بنو طولُون / بنو طولون / ابن طولون / ال طولون / beni Tulun / Tulun Turca], a slave, captured in Ferghana in 816, then presented to Caliph Mamun („servus al-Mamunis"), and was trained to be a soldier, is known as the forefather of the Tulunids, died in 855 (Ibn Saʿīd IV, 6, 95, 163, Masʿūdī 328, Miskawayh 36, Arïb 8, Kindī 223, 248, 251-253, Abulfar. Or. 175, Weil, Abbas II, 405, Toğan, UTT 175); Oghuz 9th c. **Tolun / Tulun** [عبيد بن طولون] (Ibn Saʿīd IV, 7, 21); Oghuz (Toquz-oghuz) 866, 873, 879

Tolun / Tulun [احمد بن طولون / احمد بن طولُون Ahmed Ibn Tulun], Ahmad ibn Tulun/Tolun an Abbasid emir, founder of the Tulunid dynasty (868-905), the first Turkic dynasty of Egypt (Ibn Saʿīd IV, 4-5, 15-17, Berchem 28, Kindī 208-232 etc., Weil, Abbas II, 398, Karabacek I, 105); Oghuz (Toquz-oghuz) **Tolun / Tulun** [طولون بن احمد والد طولون], son of the founder of the Tulunid dynasty (Iyās I, 37); Uyg. 762 **Tolun-apa** [Tlūnāpā] (Mahrnāmag 14, 39); Bashk. 1753, 1757, 1762 **Tolon-bay / Tulun-bay** [Кинзибай Толунбаев / Тулунбаев / Тюлюнбай] (MIB IV/1, 68, 140, 236); Kzk. 19th c. **Tolon-bek** [Толунбекъ] (SOV 94); Chag. 16th c.? **Tolun-χoJa** [تولون خوجه / Толун-Ходжа] (Radl. I, 1075); Tat.(GH)? 1320 **Tulun-bay / Tulun-biy** [Хатунь Тулунбай / Дулунба / Тулунбій], wife of Özbeg Khan? (Makrīzī/Tizeng. I, 425, 426, 438, 439); Tat.(GH) 14th c. **Tulun-bek**, a khan (?) in Desht-i Kipchak (IOAIÊK XIII, 101); Tat.(Sib.) 1599 **Tulun-bikä** [Тулунбека], a Siberian princess, Küčüm's daughter (AI II, 18, 20, 23); Uyg. 1339 **Tulun-tegin** [Tulun Tekin], fem. (Chwol., Syr.-nest. (NF) 35); *TN:* Crm. **Tolum-bey (<Tolun-bey)** [Tolumbei], north-east of Sevastopol' (Jervis VII). ✧ I. 'Full moon' (Sattarov), Uyg. *tolun* 'полный (о луне)' (DTS), Uyg., Alt. *tolun* 'die Fülle' (Radl. III, 1197), for the Kuman name cf. also Mahrnāmag 15, Gombocz, ÁTSz. 33, Rásonyi, KÖA 132-133, Rásonyi, Anthr. 146; II. 'Temporal portion of the skull, temple'? cf. Karakh. *tulun* 'висок, височная кость (у животных)' (DTS), Maml. *tulun* 'şakak' (IM), Turk. *tolun* 'die Schläfe' (Radl. III, 1198). See also TULUM, AY-TOLUM, AQ-TOLUN, QUTLUX-QÏZ-TOLUN, TAYČÏ-TULUN(?), TÖKEJÜK-TOLUN.

TOLUN-TOΓRÏL Uyg. **Tolun-toγrïl-ïnal** [Tolun Toγrïl Ïnal] (Zieme, Mat. I, 75). ✧ 'Full Moon-Falcon' (Zieme). ⇨ TOLUN + TOΓRÏL.

TOLUS Kzk. 19th c. **Tolos-pay** [Толоспай] (SOK 80); Kzk. 19th c. **Tolos-pay?** [Толоспай] (SOK 80, 182); Kzk. 19th c. **Tolus-pay** [Толуспай] (SOK 166, 298). ✧ 'Be full/fat!' cf. Kzk. *tolŭs-* 'voll werden, dick werden' (Radl. III, 1198), Kzk. *tolïs-* 'полнеть, становиться полным; созревать (о зерне)' (KzRS).

TOLUŠ Kzk. 19th c. **Toluš-pay** [Толушпай] (SOK 204); Bashk. 1777 **Tuluš** [Якуш Тулушев] (MIB V, 64). ⇨ TOLUS? / TOLU + suff. -š.

TOM-BAY see TON

TOMAY Tat. 1624 **Tomay** [Томай Янбаевъ] (Pokrovskij 72). ⇨ TUMA?

TOMAKAY Chuv. 18th-19th c. **Tomakay** [Томакай] (Magn. 85); Chuv. 18th-19th c. **Tomakey?** [Томакей] (Magn. 85). ⇨ TUMAQ? + suff. -ay.

TOMAQ Chuv. 18th-19th c. **Tomak** [Томакъ] (Magn. 85); Tat.(Lit.) 1548 **Tomaq** [Томакъ] (Kn. Metriki Lit. 44); Kzk. 1643 **Tomaq** [Томакъ], a prince (Kuznecov

8). ✧ I. 'Wooden ball; mace' cf. Turk. *tomaq* 'die Holzkugel; Schuhwerk, früher von Reitern getragen; eine Waffe (Morgenstern) mit schwerem Kopfe' (Radl. III, 1235); II. 'A kind of toy (pipe made of leather with a ball at the end)' cf. Chag. *tomaq* 'langer lederner Schlauch mit einer Kugel aus Wolle oder Baumwolle zum Spielen' (Radl. III, 1235). ⇨ **TUMAQ?**

TOMAQAY Kzk. 19th c. **Tomaqay** [Томакай] (SODž. 128). ⇨ **TOMAQ?** + suff. *-ay*.

TOMALAY Crm. **Tomalay-arū / Tumalay-arū** [Томалаi Ару / Тумалаi Ару], fem. (Proben VII, 154). ✧ 'Round(ish); plump' cf. Crm.(Tat.) *tomala(čïq)* 'кругленький, кругляшка' (KrmRS) + dim. suff. *-y*.

TOMALAQ Chuv. 18th-19th c. **Tobalaq** [Тобалакъ] (Magn. 83); Kzk. 1819, 1824 **Tumalaq / Tomalaq?** [Тумалак] (MIK IV, 326, 463). ✧ 'Round; thick; ball; hank' cf. Chag., Kzk. *tomalaq* 'rund, kugelrund; die Kugel, der Ball; dick, ramassirt' (Radl. III, 1236), Chag. *tobalaq*, Turk. *topalaq* 'rund, abgerundet, dick, ramassirt' (Radl. III, 1222).

TOMAN see **TUMAN**

TOMANDEY Chuv. 18th-19th c. **Tomandey** [Томандей] (Magn. 85). ⇨ **TUMAN** + suff. *-dey*.

TOMAR Yürük 1543 **Tomar** (Gökb., Rum. 217). ✧ I. 'Pillow-case' cf. Turk. dial. *tomar* 'Yastık ya da minder üzerine gerilen kalın kumaş' (SDD); II. 'A kind of dog' cf. Turk. dial. *tomar* 'Kaba, parlak tüylü köpek' (SDD).

TOMAS Hak. 19th-20th c. **Tomas** [Томас] (HRS 352).

TOMET Bashk. 1728 **Tomet** [Бакы Тометев] (MIB III, 250).

TOMİKA Hak. 19th-20th c. **Tomika** [Томика], fem. (HRS 355).

TOMKA Chuv. 18th-19th c. **Tomka** [Томка] (Magn. 85).

TOMNA Hak.(Kacha) 19th c. **Tomna** [Томна], fem. (Katanov, Otč. II, 42). ✧ 'Domna' (Katanov), hypoc. of R. fem. Domnika or Domnina.

TOMO Kirg. **Tomo** [Томо] (Jud. 765). ✧ 'Stem/bottom (?) of a horn' cf. Kirg. *tomo* 'комель рога' (Jud.).

TOMON Alt. 19th-20th c. **Tomon** [Томон], fem. (OjrRS 213). ✧ 'Barley-flour' cf. Alt. *tomon* 'мука из непорушенного ячменя' (OjrRS).

TOMPAQ Kzk. 19th c. **Tompaq** [Томпакъ] (AOP 46). ✧ 'Bloated, puffy, fatty' cf. Kzk. *tompaq* 'aufgeblasen, angeschwollen, die Geschwulst; Erhöhung, Hügel' (Radl. III, 1240).

TOMPAQAY Kzk. 19th c. **Tompaqay** [Томпокай] (AOP 14). ⇨ **TOMPAQ** + suff. *-ay*.

TOMUR Uyg. 12th c. - 14th c. **Tomur / Tumur** [Tumur] (Radl., USp. 55, DTS); Uyg. **Tumur** [Tumur] (EUTS).

TON Yürük 16th c. **Don** [دون], from the Yürüks of Kocacık, Turkey (Gökb., Rum. 103); Kzk. 19th c. **Don-bay** [Донбай] (SODž. 128); Kzk. 19th c. **Tom-bay**

(<**Ton-bay**) [Томбай] (SODž. 122); Kzk. 19th c. **Ton-bay** [Тонбай] (AOA 26); Kzk. 19th c. **Ton-bay** [Томбай] (AOP 54); *TN:* Kzk. 19th c. **Ton-bay** [Тонбай], a field (AOP 66). ✧ 'Upper clothes; fur coat; (archaic) clothing; trousers' cf. most Trk. languages *ton* 'das obere Kleid, das Kleid; der Pelz' (Radl. III, 1176), Turk. *don* 'das Kleid, die Hosen' (Radl. III, 1710), *don* 'coat, color (of a horse), (archaic) clothing, garment' (TED). See also **AQ-DON, QARA-TON, TİR-TOŃ**.

TON-BAXTA Chuv. 18th-19th c. **Ton-baχta** [Тонбахта] (Magn. 85). ⇨ **TON + BAQTÏ**.

TON-BARÏS Chuv. 18th-19th c. **Ton-barïs** [Тонбарисъ] (Magn. 85). ⇨ **TON + BARS**.

TON-BULAT Chuv. 18th-19th c. **Ton-bulat** [Тонбулатъ] (Magn. 85). ⇨ **TON + BULAT**. See also **TON-DEMİR**.

TON-ČERČEK Hak. 19th-20th c. **Ton-čerček** [Тончерчек] (HRS 352). ⇨ **TON**.

TON-DEMİR Chuv. 18th-19th c. **Ton-demir** [Тондемиръ] (Magn. 85). ⇨ **TON?** + **TEMİR**. See also **TON-BULAT**.

TON-GİLDE Chuv. 18th-19th c. **Ton-gilde** [Тонгилда] (Magn. 85). ⇨ **TON + KELDİ**.

TON-ŽUWAN Alt. 19th c. **Ton-žuwan** [Тонжуанъ], one of Adam's nine sons (Potanin IV, 220). ⇨ **TON**.

TONAY Tat. 1624 **Tonay** [Тонай Колчюринъ] (Pokrovskij 71); Kzk. 19th c. **Tonay** [Тонай] (AOA 78). ⇨ **TON?** + suff. *-ay*.

TONBAS see **TOŃMAS**

TONČÏ Kzk. 19th c. **Tončï-bay** [Тончибай] (SOK 158). ✧ 'Furrier' cf. Kuman *tončï* 'der Kürschner' (Radl. III, 1179). ⇨ **TON** + suff. *-čï*.

TONDÏQ Alt. 19th c. **Tondïq** [Тондыкъ] (Potanin IV, 547). ✧ 'Fur/fell (enough for a furcoat)' cf. Alt.(Tel.) *tondïq* 'das Mass eines Pelzes, das zu einem Pelze nöthige Zeug' (Radl. III, 1178).

TONГA Karakh. **Tonγa** [Tonğa] (MK/Atalay 855).

TONÏM Kzk. 19th c. **Tonïm-bay** [Тонымбай] (AOP 126). ⇨ **TANÏM?** / **TON?** + poss. suff. *-ïm*.

TONÏŠ see **TANÏŠ**

TONYUQUQ Türk 8th c. **Tonyuquq / Toñuquq** [Tonyuχ(uq) / Tonyukuk], a counselor of the Kagans in the Eastern Empire of the Türks (Le Coq, Buch-Fragm. 147, DTS, EUTS); Türk 8th c. **Toñuquq-boyla-baγa-tarqan** (Ligeti, R. tör. nev. II-III, 41). See also **BİLGÄ-TONYUQUQ, ČÏQAN-TONYUQUQ**.

TONKE Kzk. 19th c. **Tonke** [Тонке] (AOP 26). ⇨ **TON** + suff. *-ke* <comp. *-ake*.

TONQA Alt. 19th-20th c. **Tonqa** [Тонка], fem. (OjrRS 213). ⇨ **TONKE?**

TONQOBET Bashk. 1728 **Tonqobet** [Мукмен Тонкобетев] (MIB I, 128).

TONUŠAQ Kzk. 19th c. **Tonušaq** [Тонушакъ] (SOV

156). ✧ 'Little acquaintance'. ⇨ **TANÏŠ** + suff. *-aq.*

TOŇ-DORÖLJUN Yak. **Toň-doröljun / Toň-dorölyun** [Тоң Доролцун (Доролјун) бухатыр], a folklore hero (Pek.).

TOŇ-SURUQ Yak. **Toň-suruq** [Тоңсурук] (Pek.).

TOŇA Karakh. **Tonqa** [Tonka] (MK/Atalay 855); Uyg. **Toňa** [Tonga] (EUTS); Uyg. **Toňa** [Tonga] (EUTS); Uyg. 1264 **Toňa** [Tunga] (Chwol., Syr.-nest. (NF) 7, 45); Karakh. 11th c. **Toňa** [toŋa] (DTS); Uyg. 12th c. - 14th c. **Toňa-sañun** [toŋa saŋun] (DTS); Türk 732, 735 **Toňa-tegin** [Toňa tegin] (ETY I, 50, 62); Karakh. 11th c.? **Toňa-tigin** [Tonga tigin] (DTS, Ligeti, R. tör. nev. II-III, 41). ✧ 'Panther, leopard; hero'; 'Brave soldier' (Haneda); Trk. *tonga* <Chin. *t'ong-ngo* <*d'ung-ngâ* (Haneda 4, 8), cf. Karakh., Uyg. *toňa* 'леопард; герой' (DTS). Used also as a title (secondary component) of personal names. E. g. *Toña-alp-er* 'Panther-hero-man' (Blagova 1997, 706). See also **ALP-ER-TOŇA, ER-TOŇA, OΓUL-TOŇA.**

TOŇA-ALP Karakh. 11th c. **Toňa-alp-er** [toŋa alp er], Turkic byname of the legendary ruler Afrasyab (DTS). ✧ 'Brave, courageous, glorious'; '(lit.) Leopard-hero' (Blagova 1997, 706), cf. Karakh. *toňa alp* 'храбрый, доблестный' (DTS). ⇨ **TOŇA** + **ALP.**

TOŇA-ARSLAN Uyg. 13th c. - 14th c. **Toňa-arslan** [Tunga Arslan] (Chwol., Syr.-nest. (NF) 46). ⇨ **TOŇA** + **ARSLAN.**

TOŇA-BİK-QONDÏ Oghuz/Trkm. 14th c. **Tuňa-bik-qundï?** [Tounka-Bik-Qoundi] (Abulg./Desm. 192). ✧ ? ⇨ **TOŇA** + **BEK?** + **QONDÏ.**

TOŇA-YÏLAN Uyg. 1341 **Toňa-yïlan** [Tunga Jilan] (Chwol., Syr.-Nest. (NF) 39); Uyg. 1341 **Toňa-yïlan** [Tunga Jilan] (Chwol., Syr.-nest. (NF) 39). ⇨ **TOŇA** + **YÏLAN.**

TOŇAČ Kzk. 1832 **Toňač** [Тонгачевъ] (Konšin, Mat. V, 34).

TOŇÏŠ Kzk. 19th c. **Toňuš-pay / Tañuš-pay?** [Тонгушпай] (SOV 74). ⇨ **TANÏŠ?**

TOŇÏTÏ Uyg. **Toňïtï** [Tongïtï] (EUTS); Uyg. 12th c. - 14th c. **Toňïtï-tutuq** [toŋïtï tutuq] (DTS).

TOŇQÏLDAQ Kkalp. 20th c. **Toňqïldaq** [Тонъкъылдакъ / Тоңқылдақ] (Bask., Kkalp. 99, KkRS 776). ✧ 'Morose, gruff, nagging' cf. Kkalp. *toňqïldaq* 'ворчливый, брюзгливый' (KkRS).

TOŇQUR Alt. 19th-20th c. **Toňqur** [Тонкур] (OjrRS 210); Alt. 19th-20th c. **Toňqur** [Тонкур], fem. (OjrRS 213). ✧ 'With stumpy horns; not having horns; bob, not having tail' (OjrRS), cf. also Alt.(Tel.) *toňqur* 'ohne Hörner, ohne Schwanz' (Radl. III, 1173).

TOŇMA Uyg. **Toňma** [Tongma] (EUTS); Uyg. 12th c. - 14th c. **Toňma-baqšï / Toňma-baχšï** [Tongma Baχši / Tongma baχsï] (Radl., USp. 21-23, Le Coq, Urkunden 458-59, DTS).

TOŇMAS Chuv. 18th-19th c. **Tonbas** [Тонбасъ]

(Magn. 85); Hak.(Sag.) 19th-20th c. **Toňmas** [Тоңмас] (Proben IX, 542). ✧ 'He will not freeze (to death)' cf. Alt., Kuman, Kirg., Kzk., etc. *toň-* 'gefrieren, frieren' (Radl. III, 1170), Tat. *tuň-* 'frieren' (Radl. III, 1434) + suff. *-mas.*

TOŇRA-SEM Türk 712-716 **Toňra-sem** [toŋra sem / tonra semiğ / Toňra Sämig [!]] (DTS, ETY I, 102). ✧ 'Sem (?) from the tribe Toňra' (Blagova 1997, 709).

TOŇUQUQ see **TONYUQUQ**

TOŇUZ Kzk. 19th c. **Doňγus-bay** [Кожамратъ Донгусбаевъ] (Pam. kn. Turg. 69); Tat.(GH)? 10th c. - 13th c. **Toňuz** [تنوز], envoy (Ǧuwaynī II, 230, 231); Tat.(GH) 1298, 1301 **Toňuz** [طنغز بن قجان / Тунгузъ], a Kipchak (?) chief, Noγay's follower (Baybars/Tizeng. I, 88, 92, 111, 116, Nuwairī 139, 160, Duqmaq/Tizeng. I, 316, 323, Aynī/Tizeng. I, 486, 518, Veselovskij, Nog. 45 ff.); Maml. 1340 **Toňuz / Tuňuz?** [Tunkuz], a governor of Damascus (Björkm. 68, 158); Khorezm./Chag. 14th c. **Toňuz-χan** [Тонгузъ-ханъ], lit. „Hog-ruler", nickname of the Chinese emperor in Timur's (Temür's) history (Barth., Ulugb. 42); Kzk. 1858/59 **Tuňuz** [Баба Тунгузъ] (Valihanov, Soč. 500). ✧ 'Swine, sow, hog, pig' cf. Uyg., Karakh. *toňuz* 'дикая свинья; кабан, свинья' (DTS), Chag., Kuman *toňuz* 'das Schwein' (Radl. III, 1172).

TOP-PERGEN Kzk. 19th c. **Top-pergen** [Топпергенъ] (SOV 88). ✧ 'Plenty?-given' cf. Crm., East.T., Kar., Kzk., Turk. *top* 'die Haufe, die Menge, die Versammlung, die Gesammtheit' (Radl. III, 1219). ⇨ **BERGEN.**

TOP-SARA Chuv. 18th-19th c. **Top-sara** [Топсара] (Magn. 85). ✧ 'Plenty-(of) strength'? cf. Crm., East.T., Kar., Kzk., Turk. *top* 'die Haufe, die Menge, die Versammlung, die Gesammtheit' (Radl. III, 1219). ⇨ **SARA I.**

TOPA Kzk. 19th c. **Topa** [Топа] (SOV 58).

TOPAČ Bashk. 1701 **Topač** [Топач / Топачев] (MIB III, 9, 272). ✧ 'Ball-like, round(ish) child' cf. Tat. *Tupač* <*tup* [ball] + suff. *-ač* (Sattarov), also Turk. *topač* 'dick, untersetzt' (Radl. III, 1223).

TOPAY Bashk. 1737 **Topay** [Топай] (MIB I, 330); Kzk. 19th c. **Topay** [Топай] (AOP 38); Kzk. **Topay-qul** [Топаi Кул], a slave (Proben III, 108 (138)); Bashk. 1760 **Tupay** [Тупай Ишалин] (MIB IV/1, 187); Bashk. 1798 **Tupay** [Тупай] (PSZRI XXV, 195); Kzk. 19th c. **Tupay** [Тупаевъ] (SKSO III, 190). ✧ 'Hoof of a horse or camel' cf. Kzk. *topay* 'Knöchel des Pferdes oder Kameels' (Radl. III, 1221), Bashk. dial. *tupay* 'альчик, бабка' (BRS/Uraksin). See also **TOBÏQ.**

TOPAYAQ Tuv. 19th c. **Topayaq** [Топајак] (Proben IX, 77).

TOPAL Yürük 1543 **Topal** (Gökb., Rum. 194). ✧ 'Lame' cf. Crm., Turk. *topal* 'hinkend, lahm, mit

verrenktem Fusse' (Radl. III, 1222). See also
DURMUŠ-TOPAL.

TOPAL-QARA Yürük 1576 **Topal-qara** [Topal kara]
(Gökçen 51). ⇨ **TOPAL + QARA.**

TOPALAY Crm. **Topalay-arū** [Топалаі-Ару], fem.
(Proben VII, 154).

TOPAN Bashk. 1737 **Topan** [Муллагул Топанов]
(MIB III, 359); Kzk. 19th c. **Topan** [Топанъ], a biy
(Potanin I, 29); Kzk. 19th c. **Topan-bay** [Топанбай]
(SOK 132). ✧ 'Float, flooding' cf. Kzk. *topan* (Ar.)
'die Sündfluth' (Radl. III, 1221).

TOPAR Kzk. 19th c. **Topar** [Топаръ] (SOK 116, 138).

TOPAŠ Kzk. 19th c. **Topaš** [Топашъ] (AOP 34);
Bashk. 1735 **Tubaš** [Казбулат Тубашев] (MIB III,
336). ✧ 'Fool, dumb, dull, blunt; rude' cf. Kzk. *topas*
'тупой' (KzRS), Bashk. *tupaθ* 'тупой; грубый,
невежливый' (BRS/Uraksin).

TOPČĀN Hak.(Sag.) 19th-20th c. **Topčān** [Топчан], a
shaman (Proben IX, 309-311, Katanov: ZIRGOÊtn.
XXXIV, 275).

TOPČÏ I. Tat.(GH) 13th c. **Topčï / Topči?** [Топζί /
Топчи], a christened Tatar (By. Turc. 317, Smirnov,
Krym. 34); Kzk. 19th c. **Tupčï** [Тупчи] (SKSO VIII,
200). ✧ 'Artilleryman, gunner' cf. Turk. *topču* 'der
Kanonier, Artillerist', East.T. *topči* 'id.' (Radl. III,
1230). Kirg. *topču* 'пушкарь' (Jud.).

TOPČÏ II. Alt. 19th-20th c. **Topčï** [Топчы], fem.
(OjrRS 213). ✧ 'Button, knob' (OjrRS), cf. Alt., Hak.
topči 'der Knopf' (Radl. III, 1230), Kirg. *topču*
'пуговица' (Jud.).

TOPČÏ-BAŠ Az. 19th c. **Topčï-baš** [Ali-Merdan
Topčibašev], a lawyer born in Tiflis (Mende 99, 100,
102, 103, 122 etc.). ⇨ **TOPČÏ I. + BAŠ.**

TOPČÏLAY Alt. 19th-20th c. **Topčïlay** [Топчылай]
(OjrRS 210); Alt. 19th-20th c. **Topčïlay** [Топчылай],
fem. (OjrRS 213). ✧ 'Little button, knob' (OjrRS). ⇨
TOPČÏ II. + suff. -lay.

TOPČU Kirg. **Topču-bay** [Топчубай] (Jud. 462). ⇨
TOPČÏ I. / TOPČÏ II.?

TOPČUN Tuv. 19th c. **Topčun-öl** [Топчун-ол] (Proben
IX, 42, 44).

TOPÏQ see **TOBÏQ**

TOPÏŠ Kzk. 19th c. **Topïš** [Топышъ] (SOK 56); Kzk.
19th c. **Topïš** [Топышъ] (SOV 44).

TOPQAY Kzk. 19th c. **Topqay** [Топкай] (AOP 30).

TOPQAN Kzk. 19th c. **Topqan** [Топканъ] (SOK 24).

TOPLİ Chuv. 18th-19th c. **Topli** [Топли] (Magn. 85).
⇨ **TOPTÏ.**

TOPLUQ Bashk. 1730 **Topluq** [Бекмурза Топлуков]
(MIB III, 277).

TOPPO Yak. **Toppo** [Топпо] (Pek.). ✧ 'With bloated,
puffy, fatty face' (Pek.). See also **TOMPAQ.**

TOPPOY Yak. **Toppoy** [Топпоі] (Pek.). ✧ 'With
bloated, puffy, fatty face' (Pek.), cf. Yak. *toppoy-*

'выпячиваться' (Pek). ⇨ **TOPPO.**

TOPPŌXU Yak. **Toppōχu** [Топпохy] (Pek.). ✧ 'With
bloated, puffy, fatty face' (Pek.). ⇨ **TOPPOY.**

TOPPŌS Hak.(Kacha) 19th-20th c. **Toppōs** [Топпос]
(Proben IX, 390).

TOPRAQ Yürük 16th c. **Topraq** [طوپـراق / Toprak],
from the Yürüks of Kocacık, Turkey (Gökb., Rum.
102). ✧ 'Earth, land' cf. Chag., Kuman, Crm., Kzk.,
Turk. *topraq* 'die Erde, das Land' (Radl. III, 1226).

TOPRİ Chuv. 18th-19th c. **Topri** [Топри] (Magn. 85).

TOPŠUQ Bashk. 1756 **Topšuq** [Абузали Топшуков]
(MIB IV/1, 123). ✧ 'Little ball/hank' cf. Bashk. *tup*
'мяч, мячик' (BRS/Uraksin) + dim. suff. -*šuq.*

TOPTAXAY Hak. 19th-20th c. **Toptaχay** [Топтахай]
(HRS 352).

TOPTAÑ Tuv. 19th c. **Toptañ** [Топтан] (Proben IX,
193, 213).

TOPTÏ Kzk. 19th c. **Toptï-bay** [Топтыбай] (SOK
108). ⇨ **TOPLÏ?**

TOPUČUQ Az. **Topučuq** [Топучукъ] (SMOK XXIII,
otd. III, 3).

TOPUYAÑ Tuv. 19th c. **Topuyañ** [Топујан] (Proben
IX, 60).

TOPUQ see **TOBÏQ**

TOPULҐAN Uyg. **Topulγan** (Zieme, Mat. I, 76). ✧
'(S)He reached her/his goal' cf. *topul-* 'durchdringen'
(Zieme, loc. cit.), also *tupul-* (Clauson).

TOR-AYҐÏR see **TORÏ-AYҐÏR**

TOR-BALÏҐ Uyg. 12th c. - 14th c. **Tor-balïγ**
[Torbalyγ / Torbalığ] (Radl., USp. 153, 154, DTS,
EUTS). ✧ 'Net/web-fish' (Blagova 1997, 707), cf.
Uyg., Chag., Az., Kzk., Turk. *tor* 'das Fischernetz, das
Netz' (Radl. III, 1179). ⇨ **BALÏQ.**

TOR-SULAY Alt.(Tel.) **Tor-sulay-märgän** [Торсулаі
Мäргäн] (Radl. I, 654). ⇨ **TORÏ? / + SULAY?**

TOR-TAY see **TORÏ-TAY**

TORAY Kzk. 19th c. **Toray** [Торай] (AOK 70);
Tat.(GH) 1293 **Turay** [طراى / Турай], a Kipchak,
Nogay's son (Baybars/Tizeng. I, 86, 109, Veselovskij,
Nog. 57); Bashk. 1730 **Turay** [Турай Шебалаков]
(MIB III, 272); Kzk. 19th c. **Turay** [Турай] (SOK
264); *TN:* Chuv. 1738 **Toray(evy)** [Тораевы], a
village (Alatyr. 139). ✧ 'Young wildswine, pig' cf. Tat.
Turay (Sattarov), Kzk. *toray* 'ein junges Wildschwein'
(Radl. III, 1180) <Mo. *torai/toroi* 'marcassin, cochon
de lait' (Pelliot 81-82). See also **XÏS-TORAY.**

TORAMAN Yürük 1543 **Toraman** [Toraman] (Gökb.,
Rum. 180). ✧ 'Silly, rude, young, wild, rough' cf.
Turk. *toraman* 'unwissend, thöricht, jung, wild,
unbändig' (Radl. III, 1181).

TORBA Chuv. 18th-19th c. **Torba** [Торба] (Magn. 85).

TORBALÏ Yürük 1582 **Torbalï** [Torbalï] (Su 21). ✧
'Having a bag; bloated' cf. Turk. *torbalï* 'einen Sack
habend; der Bettler' (Radl. III, 1190), Az., Crm., Turk.

torba 'der Sack, der Ranzen; eine Geschwulst am Körper' (Radl. III, 1189).

TORČÏ Uyg. 13th-14th c. **Torči-taruɣači** (Zieme, Mat. III, 283); Uyg. 12th c. - 14th c. **Torčï** [torčï] (DTS/USp.); Tat.? 1551 **Torči / Torči?** [Торчи-князь-богатырь], a hero-prince (PSRL XIII, 166); Tat.(GH) 1320 **Torči / Torči / Torji?** [طرجى / Тарджи], Kipchak Khan, Özbeg's envoy to Egypt (Duqmaq/Tizeng. I, 320, 327, Aynī/Tizeng. I, 489, 519). ✧ I. 'User of mesh or fishing net' (Blagova 1997, 711) cf. Uyg. *torči* (DTS); II. Dordji (<Tib. *Rdo-rje*) (Zieme). ⇨ **TOR** + suff. *-čï*.

TORČON Hak. 19th-20th c. **Torčon** [Торчон] (HRS 352).

TORD'Ï Alt. 19th-20th c. **Tord'ï** [Тордьы], fem. (OjrRS 213).

TORDAY Hak. 19th-20th c. **Torday** [Тордай] (HRS 352). ⇨ **TORDOY?**

TORDAQ Hak.? 19th c. **Tordaq** [Тордак] (Katanov, Otč. 12).

TORDOY Alt. 19th-20th c. **Tordoy** [Тордой] (OjrRS 210). ✧ 'Residue of butter' (OjrRS), cf. Alt. *tordo* 'der Niederschlag, Absatz' (Radl. III, 1187).

TORDU Kzk. 1864 **Tordu-bek** [Тордубекъ Абдрахмановъ] (Valihanov, Soč. 507).

TORGANDEY Chuv. 18th-19th c. **Torgandey** [Торгандей] (Magn. 86). ⇨ **TURGAN** + suff. *-dey*.

TORGANEY Chuv. 18th-19th c. **Torganey** [Торганей] (Magn. 86). ⇨ **TURGAN** + suff. *-ey*.

TORGA Nog.? **Torɣa-murza** [Торга Мурза] (Žirm., Epos 430). ⇨ **TORQA?**

TORGAY Chuv. 18th-19th c. **Torgay** [Торгай] (Magn. 86); 1297 **Torɣay** [توغـای و جمجـای], an emir in the campaign of Qutluɣ-šah to Herat (RaD/Jahn 113); Maml. 1332 **Torɣay** [سيفالـدين طرغـای الجاشنكيـر], an emir (Dawād. 355, 367); Kzk. **Torɣay** [Торгай] (Grod., Vojna IV); Kzk. 18th c. - 19th c. **Torɣay** [Торгай] (Tynyšp. 68); Kzk. 19th c. **Torɣay** [Торгай] (AUK 287); Kzk. 19th c. **Torɣay** [Торгай] (AUK 287); Kzk. 19th c. **Torɣay** [Торгай] (SODž. 140); Kzk. 19th c. **Torɣay** [Торгай] (SOK 82); Kzk. 19th c. **Torɣay** [Торгай] (SOV 80); Hak. 19th-20th c. **Torɣay** [Торғай], fem. (HRS 355); Hak.(Blt.) 19th-20th c. **Torɣay** [Торҕай], fem. (Katanov, Otč. 10); 1361 **Turɣay** [محمد بن طرغـای] (Iyās I, 21); Maml. 1300 **Turɣay** [طرغـای] (Zetterst. 38, 102); Maml. 14th c. **Turɣay** [سيفالـدين طرغـای الجاشنكيـر] (Zetterst. 162, 199, 214); Bashk. 1740 **Turɣay** [Унгар Тургаев] (MIB I, 397); Kzk. 1820 **Turɣay** [Тургай] (Sib. Vest. IX/3, 81); Kzk. 19th c. **Turɣay** [Тургай] (SOK 226); Kzk. 19th c. **Turɣay** [Байкара Тургаевъ] (TOUAK XXIV, 57); Kzk. 19th c. **Turɣay-bay / Tirɣay-bay?** [Тергайбай] (SODž. 162). ✧ 'A kind of little bird: sparrow, skylark' (Sauvaget 50: 'passereau, alouette, moineau'), cf. Kuman, Chag., Kzk. *torɣay* 'kleiner Vogel' (Radl. III, 1184), Kzk. *torğay* 'serçe' (KzTS); 'Lark, skylark' (Katanov), as male and female names as well (Butanaev), cf. Hak. *torɣay* 'жаворонок' (HRS).

TORGAN see **TURGAN**

TORGAUT see **TURGAUT**

TORGÏ see **TORQA**

TORGÏJAX Hak. 19th-20th c. **Torɣïjaχ** [Торғычах], fem. (HRS 355). ⇨ **TORQA** + dim. suff. *-jaχ*.

TORGÏL Maml. 1488 **Torɣïl?** [ابن طرغـل], governor of Hama (Iyās II, 654); Kzk. 19th c. **Torɣïl-bay** [Торгылбай] (SOK 92); Türk **Torɣul** (DTS); Türk **Turɣul** [Turɣul] (ETY II, 122); Kzk. 19th c. **Turɣul** [Тургулъ] (AOP 50).

TORGUD see **TURGUT**

TORGUQ see **TORÏG**

TORGUL see **TORGÏL**

TORGUNČAQ Tuv. 19th c. **Torɣunčaq** [Торҕунчак] (Proben IX, 84). ✧ 'Little silk' cf. Kzk. fem. PN *Torɣïn* 'вид дорогого шелка' (Žanuzakov), Kzk. *torɣun* 'die Seide' (Radl. III, 1185) + dim. suff. *-čaq*. See also **TORQA**.

TORGUNDAY Tuv. 19th c. **Torɣunday** [Торҕундаі] (Proben IX, 77). ✧ 'Silk-like' cf. Kzk. fem. *Torɣïn* 'вид дорогого шелка' (Žanuzakov), Kzk. *torɣun* 'die Seide' (Radl. III, 1185) + dim. suff. *-day*? See also **TORQA**.

TORXAN Chuv. 19th c. **Torχan** [Торъ-ханъ], „Назадъ тому около тысячи лѣтъ жили среди чувашей Торханы; Торъ-ханъ значитъ великий, степенный, праведный человѣкъ" [About thousand years ago, there lived Torkhans among the Chuvash; Tor-khan means great, dignified, true-hearted man] (IOAIÊK III, 285). ✧ 'Great, just person'.

TORINA Hak. 19th-20th c. **Torina** [Торина], fem. (HRS 355); Hak. 19th-20th c. **Torine** [Торине], fem. (HRS 355). ✧ Hypoc., short form of R. Viktorina (Butanaev).

TORINE see **TORINA**

TORÏ Kzk. 19th c. **Torï-bay** [Торыбай] (AOP 50); Tat. 1629 **Turu-bay** [Чекмамет Турубаев] (Miller, Ist. Sib. II, 356); Nog. 1649 **Turu-bek** [Турубекъ], Bi-murza's or Qasay-murza's daughter (AI IV, 123); *TN:* Kzk.? **Turï-bay** [Туры-бай] (Karta JAR XI). ✧ 'Red-brown, bay (horse)'; 'Tanned' (Kalilov); cf. Kzk. *torï* 'гнедой' (KzRS), Kzk. *toru* 'rothbraun' (Radl. III, 1182), Kirg. *toru* 'гнедой' (Jud.), Crm., Hak.(Sag.) *tor* 'braun' (Radl. III, 1180). See also **ČAPTAR, QÏR, TORÏG; ALTÏN-TORÏ, ATAQTÏ-TORU, BAY-TURU, QOY-TORÏ**.

TORÏ-AYGÏR Kzk. **Tor-ayɣïr** (<Torï-ayɣïr) [Tor Aigyr / Top' Aiɓyr] (Proben III, 47 (62)); Kzk. 19th c. **Tor-ayɣïr** (<Torï-ayɣïr) [Торайгыръ] (AOO 38); Kzk. 19th c. **Tor-ayɣïr** (<Torï-ayɣïr) [Торайгыръ]

(SOV 24). ✧ 'Red-brown stallion' cf. Crm., Hak.(Sag.) *tor* 'braun' (Radl. III, 1180), Kzk. *tori* 'гнедой' (KzRS), Kzk. *toru* 'rothbraun' (Radl. III, 1182). ⇨ **TORÏ** + **AYΓÏR**. See also **TORÏ-TAY**.

TORÏ-TAY Kzk. 19th c. **Tor-tay** [Тортай] (SOK 132); Kzk. 19th c. **Tor-tay** [Тортай] (SOK 174); Kzk. 19th c. **Toru-tay** [Торутай] (SOV 92). ✧ 'Red-brown, bay foal'. ⇨ **TORÏ** + **TAY** or suff. *-tay(1,2)*? See also **TORÏ-AYΓÏR**.

TORÏΓ Hak. 19th-20th c. **Torïγ** [Торыг] (HRS 352); Hak.(Kyz.) 19th-20th c. **Torïγ** [Торыӈ], fem. (Katanov, Otč. 13); NUyg. 19th c. **Toruq / Torγuq** [توغروق / نوروق / Toruk] (Le Coq, Namenl. 120). ✧ 'Red-brown, bay (horse)' (Katanov, Butanaev); Le Coq: „braun - von Pferden", cf. East.T. *toroγ / toroq / toruγ* 'bay' (Jarring), Hak. *torïγ* 'гнедой' (HRS). See also **ČAPTAR, QÏR, TORÏ**.

TORÏX Hak. 19th-20th c. **Torïχ** [Торых], fem. (HRS 355). ✧ Doroha (R.), hypoc. short form of R. Dorofey (Butanaev).

TORÏN Chuv. 18th-19th c. **Torïn** [Торынъ] (Magn. 86); Chuv. 18th-19th c. **Torïn-bay / Tōrïn-bay?** [Тоорынбай] (Magn. 86).

TORÏSQAY Hak. 19th-20th c. **Torïsqay** [Торыскай] (HRS 352). ✧ 'Healthy, strong, bouncing' cf. Hak. *Torïs/Torïsχay* (Butanaev) + dim. suff. *-qay*.

TORKE Kzk. 19th c. **Torke** [Торке] (AOP 42). ⇨ **TOR**? + suff. *-ke* <comp. *-ake*.

TORQA Hak. 19th-20th c. **Torγï** [Торғы], fem. (HRS 355); Alt. 19th-20th c. **Torqo** [Торко] (OjrRS 210); Alt. 19th-20th c. **Torqo** [Торко], fem. (OjrRS 213); Hak.(Blt.) 19th-20th c. **Tōrqa** [Торка] (Katanov, Otč. 9); Kzk. 1846 **Turqa-bay** [Туркабай Джурунбаев], a biy (MKOP 155); Uzb. 19th c. **Turqa-bay** [Байбулатъ Туркабаевъ] (SKSO III, 180). ✧ 'Silk' cf. Chag., Hak., Kzk. *torqa* 'die Seide, der Seidenstoff' (Radl. III, 1183), Alt. *torqo / torγo* 'id.' (Radl. III, 1183-85, OjrRS), Hak. *torγï* 'id.' (Radl. III, 1185, HRS), Kzk. *torqa* 'самый драгоценный шёлк' (KzRS).

TORQO see **TORQA**

TORQOČÏ Alt. 19th-20th c. **Torqočï** [Торкочы], fem. (OjrRS 213). ✧ 'Silk-thread' (OjrRS). ⇨ **TORQA/TORQO** + suff. *-čï*.

TORQOY Yak. **Torqoy** [Торкоi], shaman Xabïllaγasoyūn (Pek.).

TORLAQ Kzk. 19th c. **Torlaq** [Торлакъ] (SOK 208); Tat.(GH) **Turlaq** [Турлакъ], from the Horde (PSRL XVI, 309, 312). ✧ I. 'Ruffled grouse (Bonasa), francolin (Francolinus)'? cf. Hak. *Torlaγï* 'id.' (Butanaev), Tuv. *torlaq* 'рябчик' (Potanin IV, 588); II. 'Ball, hank'? cf. NUyg.(Tar.) *torlaq* 'das Knäuel' (Radl. III, 1186); III. 'Attentive, thoughtful' cf. Uyg. *turlaq* 'aufmerksam' (Radl. III, 1460). ⇨ **TORLĀ?**

TORLAQQAY Tuv. 19th c. **Torlaqqay** [Торлаккаi],

fem. (Proben IX, 98). ⇨ **TORLAQ** + dim. suff. *-qay*.

TORLĀ Tuv. 19th c. **Torlā** [Торла], fem. (Proben IX, 140). ✧ '(Grey) partridge' cf. Turv. *torlā (torlaa)* 'куропатка (серая)' (TuvRS). See also **ČIL**.

TORLÏ Trkm. 20th c. **Torlï** [Torlï] (Zaj. 1971, 330); Trkm. 20th c. **Torlï** [Торлы] (TrkmRS 641). ✧ 'Trellised, grated (of a pattern)' cf. Trkm. *torlï* 'покрытый сетчатым узором (о дыне)' (TrkmRS).

TORLÏQ see **TURLUQ**

TORLŌX see **TORLŌQ**

TORLŌQ Hak. 19th-20th c. **Torlōχ** [Торлоох], fem. (HRS 355); Hak.(Sag.) 19th-20th c. **Torlōq** [Торлок] (Proben IX, 553, 556, 559). ⇨ **TORLAQ?**

TORLŌN Karg. 19th-20th c. **Torlōn** [Торлон] (Katanov, Otč. 9).

TORLU Kzk. 19th c. **Torlu-bek** [Торлубекъ] (SOK 306); Kzk. 19th c. **Torlu-γul** [Торлугулъ] (SODž. 98); *TN:* Kzk. **Torlu-bek** [Торлубекъ] (Karta JAR XI). ✧ 'Having a (fishing) net' cf. Uyg., Chag., Az., Kzk., Turk. *tor* 'das Fischernetz, das Netz' (Radl. III, 1179).

TORMAY Kzk. 19th c. **Tormay** [Тормай] (SODž. 144). ✧ 'Rough, crude, rude'? cf. Kzk. *torpay* 'grob' (Radl. III, 1189); 'Valuable scarf'? cf. Chag. *torma / tormay* 'ein kostbarer Schawl' (Radl. III, 1190). See also **TORAMAN**.

TORMANDEY Chuv. 18th-19th c. **Tormandey** [Тормандей] (Magn. 86). ⇨ **TURMAN?** + suff. *-dey*.

TORMANEY Chuv. 18th-19th c. **Tormaney** [Тормансй] (Magn. 86). ⇨ **TURMAN?** + suff. *-ey*.

TORMELDİ Kzk. 19th c. **Tormeldi (<Töre-keldi?)** [Тормельды] (SOK 148).

TOROYO Yak. **Toroyo** [Топоjо] (Pek.). ✧ 'Slanting' cf. Yak. *toroy-* 'быть в несколько наклонном положении противу отвеса' (Pek.).

TOROPEY Hak. 19th-20th c. **Toropey** [Торопей] (HRS 352). ✧ Dorofey (R.), cf. Hak. *Toropay* (Butanaev).

TORŌLYUN Yak. **Torōlyun-buχatïr** [Тоӈ Торолjунбухатыр], a folklore hero (Pek.). ⇨ **DORŌLYUN.**

TORPAQ Kzk. 19th c. **Torpaq** [Торпакъ] (AOO 22); Kzk. 19th c. **Torpaq-bay** [Торпакбай] (SOV 62). ✧ 'A two-year-old calf' cf. Kzk. *torpaq* 'ein zweijähriges Kalb' (Radl. III, 1189). See also **AQ-TORPAQ, QAŠAR.**

TORPAN Kzk. 19th c. **Torpan / Tarpan?** [Торпанъ] (SOV 124).

TORPOLOY Alt. 19th-20th c. **Torpoloy** [Торполой], fem. (OjrRS 13).

TORSAY Kkalp. 1740 **Torsay-bi** [Торсай-Би], from the Qoñrat tribe (Hanykov, Poezdka 19, MIKk. 208).

TORSUQ Kuman 1183, 1185 **Tarsuq / Torsuq?** [Тарсукъ], a Polovets prince (Ipat 427 (440), Lavr. 375 (267), Bask., Im. polov. 73); Kuman 1277 **Torsuq**

[Thorzok Cumanus], among the Kumans of Hungary (Gyárfás II, 429); Kzk. 19th c. **Torsuq-pay** [Торсукпай] (SOK 236); Kzk. 19th c. **Tursuq** [Турсукъ] (AOA 154); Kzk. 19th c. **Tursuq** [Турсукъ] (SODž. 110); Kzk. 19th c. **Tursuq** [Турсукъ] (SOK 14). ✧ I. 'Leather bottle' (Rásonyi, Baskakov), cf. Hak.(Sag.), Kzk. *torsuq* 'Lederflasche zum Aufbewahren der Milch', Hak.(Sag.) *torsïq* 'id.' (Radl. III, 1189), Kzk. *torsïq* 'посуда из козлиной шкуры (обычно для кумыса)' (KzRS), Kirg. *torsuk* 1. 'турсук, бурдюк для хранения и перевозки жидкостей (гл. обр. кумыса)' (Jud.), Tat. *tursïq* 'ein kirgisischer [=Kazak] Lederschlauch, in dem man Flüssigkeiten aufbewahrt' (Radl. III, 1462), also Rásonyi, KÖA 133, Anthr. 146, Bask., Im. polov. 73; II. 'Shrimp, scrub (of a child)' cf. Kirg. *torsuk* 2. *fig.* '(о малыше) клоп' (Jud.). See also **TULUM, BES-TORSUQ.**

TORTAN Kzk. 1838 **Tortan** [Тортанъ Урмаковъ], from the Middle Horde (Orta Žüz) (Konšin, Mat. V, 16).

TORTU Kzk. 19th c. **Tortu** [Торту] (Grod., Pril. 119).

TORTUOXAYAN Yak. **Tortuoχayan** [Тортуохајан] (Pek.).

TORU see **TORÏ**

TORUQ see **TORÏĞ**

TORULĀN Yak. **Torulān** [Торулан] (Pek.). ✧ 'Squawking' cf. Yak. *torulā-* 'о дятеле: кричать, шуметь' (Pek.) + suff. *-n.*

TORUM see **TURUM**

TORUMBET Kzk. 19th c. **Torumbet** [Торумбетъ] (AOK 14); Kkalp. 20th c. **Turïmbet** [Турымбет] (KkRS 776). ⇨ **TOR?** / **TORÏ?** + suff. *-(u)mbet.*

TORUN Yürük 1543 **Torun** [Torun] (Gökb., Rum. 177, 207); *TN:* Turk. 20th c. **Torun**, a village in the province of Hatay (TMİB 422). ✧ 'Grandchild' cf. Turk. *torun* 'id.' (TED). See also **KER-TORUN.**

TORUS see **TURÏS**

TOS Kzk. 19th c. **Tos-pay** [Тоспай] (AOP 38).

TOS-KİLDE Chuv. 18th-19th c. **Tos-kilde** [Тоскилда] (Magn. 86). ⇨ **TOS?** + **KELDİ.**

TOS-MAMET Uzb. 1632 **Tos-mamet** [Тосмамет], from Bukhara (Miller, Ist. Sib. II, 398). ⇨ **TOS** + **MAMAET.**

TOSAN Kzk. 19th c. **Tosan** [Сырлыбай Тосановъ] (Grod., Pril. 195). ✧ 'Deaf' cf. Kzk. *tosañ* 'глуховатый' (KzRS).

TOSÏM see **TOSUN**

TOSQA Karg. 19th-20th c. **Tosqa** [Тоска] (Katanov, Otč. 9). ✧ 'Board' cf. R. *doska* (Katanov).

TOSQU Bashk. 1735 **Tosqu-bay?** [Тоскубай Янымбетев] (MIB III, 336).

TOSOĞOR-ŪS Yak. **Tosoγor-ūs** [Тосоҕор-ус], Omoγoy's son (Pek.).

TOSPAN Tuv. 19th c. **Tospan** [Тоспан] (Proben IX, 114). ⇨ **TOS?** + suff. *-pan.*

TOSTAN Kzk. 19th c. **Tostan** [Тостанъ] (SOK 162); Kzk. 19th c. **Tostan-bek** [Тостанбекъ] (Grod., Pril. 172).

TOSTOĞOŠ Alt. 19th c. **Tostoγoš** [Тостогошъ], a shaman in a tale (Potanin IV, 290); Alt.(Tel.) 19th c. **Tostoγoš** [Абысъ-Тостогошъ], a priest (*abïs!*) (Potanin IV, 293).

TOSTU-BAŠ Alt. 19th c. **Tostu-baš** [Тостубашъ] (Potanin IV, 289). ✧ 'Birch-rind-head'? cf. Alt., Hak. *tos* 'die Birkenrinde' (Radl. III, 1207) + Adj. suff. *-tu.* ⇨ **BAŠ.**

TOSUYA Yak. **Tosuya** [Тосуја] (Pek.). ✧ 'Coming towards (us); waiting' cf. Yak. *tosuy-* 'итти или выходить кому навстречу встречать; предварять; упреждать' (Pek.) + suff. *-a.*

TOSUM see **TOSUN**

TOSUN Kzk. 19th c. **Tosïm-bek** [Тосымбекъ] (AOO 62); Kzk. 19th c. **Tosum-bay** [Тосумбай] (AOAtb. 54); Yürük 1543 **Tosun** [توسون] (Gökb., Rum. 234); Kzk. 19th c. **Tusum-bay (<Tusun-bay)** [Тусумбай] (AOO 30); Kzk. 19th c. **Tusum-bay (<Tusun-bay)** [Тусумбай] (SOK 240); NUyg. 19th c. **Tusun** [Tusun] (Hedin, En färd II, 210); Chag. 16th c. **Tuzum-biy (<Tuzun-biy?)** [Тузум-бий], an emir (Ivanov 260). ✧ 'Wild, boisterous' cf. Kzk. *tosun* 'wild, noch nicht abgerichtet (von Hausthieren)' (Radl. III, 1209); 'Young, strong man; three-year-old bull' cf. Turk. *tosun* 'dreijähriger Ochs; jung; eintüchtiger, prächtiger junger Mensch' (Radl. III, 1209).

TOŠMAN Kuman 1169 **Tošman / Tušman? / Tašman?** [Тошманъ Чагровичъ / Тягрович], a Polovets prince (PSRL II, 310, VII, 81); Tat.(Lit.) 1552 **Tošman / Tušman? / Tašman?** [Тошманъ Бувановъ] (Kn. Metriki Lit. 86); Tat.(Lit.) 1557 **Tošman / Tušman? / Tašman?** [Тошманъ Дуян] (Kn. Metriki Lit. 153). ⇨ **TAŠMAN?**

TOT Kzk. 19th c. **Tot-pay** [Тотпай] (SOV 148). ✧ 'Rust' cf. Chag., Kzk. *tot* 'der Rost' (Radl. III, 1205).

TOT-KİLDE Chuv. 18th-19th c. **Tot-kilde** [Тоткилда] (Magn. 86). ⇨ **TOT?** + **KELDİ.**

TOTAY see **TUTAY**

TOTAQ **Totaq / Toyaq?** [توتاق/توياق / Тотакъ] (RaD/Ber. II, 93).

TOTAM see **TUTAN**

TOTAR see **TUTAR**

TOTARAK Chuv. 18th-19th c. **Totarak** [Тотаракъ] (Magn. 86).

TOTARİN Chuv. 18th-19th c. **Totarin (<Tatarin?)** [Тотаринъ] (Magn. 86). ⇨ **TATAR** + R. suff. *-in?*

TOTARKA Chuv. 18th-19th c. **Totarka / Tatarka?** [Тотарка] (Magn. 86). ⇨ **TATAR** + R. suff. *-ka?*

TOTAW Kzk. 19th c. **Totaw** [Тотау] (AOP 66).

TOTENİS Hak. 19th-20th c. **Totenis** [Тотенис] (HRS 352).

TOTİČ Hak.(Kacha) 1684 **Totič(ko)** [Тотичко Бетликовъ] (DAI XI, 161).

TOTÏ Turk. 16th c. **Dudu**, fem. (Ongan, Ank. II); Turk. 1583 **Dudu** [طوطى / Dudu], fem. (Ongan, Ank. I, 155); Chag. 16th c. **Dudu-bibi**, fem. (Gülbeden 246); Trkm. 20th c. **Totï** [Тотï], fem. (Zaj. 1971, 338); Kzk. 19th c. **Totï-bay / Tottï-bay?** [Тоттыбай] (SOV 46); Kzk. 19th c. **Totu** [Тоту] (AOA 150); Kirg. **Totu** [Тоту], fem. (Jud. 753); Trkm. 20th c. **Tōtï** [Тоты], fem. (TrkmRS 641); Kzk. 19th c. **Tuti-bay / Tutï-bay** [Тутебай] (SOV 54); Selj. 11th c. - 12th c. **Tutï-beg** [طوصى بك] (Bondārī 281, 284); Selj. 12th c. **Tutï-beg** [طوطى بك / Tüty bäg], one of the „Ghuzz" emirs (Rāwandī 183); Chag. 16th c. **Tuti-begim** [Тути-бегим], fem. (Ivanov 313, 314, 316); Turk. 1474 **Tutï-χatun** [Tuti Hatun binti Abdullah] (Gökb., Ed. 356). ✧ I. 'Parrot (let him/her speak like a parrot); elder sister; woman' (Erol II; Zaj. 1971; Žanuzakov), cf. Hak. PN fem. *Totïy* 'Parrot' (Butanaev), Kirg. *totu* 'попугай' (Jud.), Uzb. *totï* 'попугай' (UzbRS), East.T. *totï* 'der Papagei' (Radl. III, 1205), Trkm. *tōtï* 'попугай' (TrkmRS), Tat. *tuti* 'der Papagei' (Radl. III, 1481), Turk., Crm. *dudu* 'der Papagei; der ältere Sister; eine armenische oder griechische Dame' (Radl. III, 1794), Alt.(Tel.) *tōdï / totï* 'der Pfau; der Papagei?' (Radl. III, 1206). Parrot is the symbol of the nice speech and nice voice in the eastern countries (Muhamedova 1957, 39). II. 'Pea'? cf. Kzk. *totï* 'павлин' (KzRS), Alt.(Tel.) *tōdï / totï* 'der Pfau; der Papagei?' (Radl. III, 1206). (<P.).

TOTÏҒ Hak. 19th-20th c. **Totïy** [Тотыҕ], fem. (HRS 355).

TOTÏM Alt. 19th-20th c. **Totïm** [Тотым], fem. (OjrRS 213). ✧ 'My pea/parrot'. ⇨ **TOTÏ** + poss. suff. -*m*.

TOTÏR Kzk. 19th c. **Totïr** [Тотыръ] (AOP 50).

TOTQA Hak. 19th-20th c. **Totqa** [Тотка] (HRS 352); Hak.? 19th c. **Tōtqa** [Тотка], fem. (Katanov, Otč. 12). ✧ 'Aunt' cf. R. *tjotka* 'id.' (Katanov).

TOTQAY Kzk. 19th c. **Totqay** [Тоткай] (AOK 98). ⇨ **TOT** + suff. -*qay*.

TOTQÏŠ see **TUTQUŠ**

TOTQUM see **TUTQUM**

TOTQUŠ see **TUTQUŠ**

TOTOY Alt.(Tel.) 19th c. **Totoy** [Тотой Теленгутка], fem. (Potanin IV, 177, 188).

TOTOQ-BASMÏL Uyg. 13th-14th c. **Totoq-basmïl** (Zieme, Mat. II, 93). ⇨ **TUTUQ.**

TOTU see **TOTÏ**

TOTUY Tat.(GH) 1349, 1350 **Totuy** [Тотуй], envoy of the (Golden) Horde (PSRL IV, 59, V, 226, VII, 215, XVI, 82). ⇨ **TOTÏ?** + suff. -*y* (R.).

TOTUŠ Nog. 1649 **Totuš** [Тотушъ], fem. (AI IV, 123). ⇨ **TOTÏ** + dim. suff. -*š*?

TOVAR Chuv. 18th-19th c. **Tovar-murza** [Товармурза] (Magn. 83). ⇨ **TOWAR?**

TOW-DEGİN see **TOQ**

TOWAR 19th c. **Towar-bek** [Товарбекъ], a glacier (IIRGO XLII, 40).

TOWČU see **ТАГЈÏ**

TOWRUL see **ТОГРÏL**

TOWTAR Kzk. 19th c. **Towtar-bay** [Тоутарбай] (SODž. 118).

TOWUQ I. see **TOBÏQ**

TOWUQ II. see **TAWUQ**

TOZUR Tuv. 19th c. **Tozur-ōl** [Тозур-ол] (Proben IX, 155). ✧ 'Pitted'? cf. Alt.(Kmd.) *tozïr* 'pockennarbig' (Radl. III, 1215).

TŌ Hak. 19th-20th c. **Tō** [Too], fem. (HRS 355); Hak.(Kacha) 19th-20th c. **Tō** [To], fem. (Proben IX, 554). ✧ 'Buckthorn (Rhamnus catharticus)' (HRS), cf. Hak.(Sag.), Shor *tō* 'der Weissdorn' (Radl. III, 1140).

TŌČQA Karg. 19th-20th c. **Tōčqa** [Точка] (Katanov, Otč. 9). ✧ 'Point, dot' cf. R. *točka* 'id.' (Katanov).

TŌDAQ Hak. 19th-20th c. **Todaχ** [Тодах] (HRS 351); Hak.(Kyz.) 19th-20th c. **Tōdaq** [Тодак], fem. (Katanov, Otč. 13); Hak.(Shor) 19th-20th c. **Tōdaq** [Тодак], fem. (Katanov, Otč. 11). ✧ 'Bustard; heron' cf. Bashk Hak. *todaχ* 'дрофа (степная птица)' (HRS), Hak. *tōdaq* 'das Feldhuhn', Kirg. *tōdaq* 'die Trappe' (Radl. III, 1206), Kzk. *duadaq* 'дрофа, дрохва' (RKzS). See also **ТОГUZAQ.**

TŌDAŠTAY Karg. **Tōdaštay** [Тодаштаi] (Proben IX, 660).

TŌDOT Alt. 19th-20th c. **Tōdot** [Тоодот] (OjrRS 210).

TŌQO Yak. **Tōqo** [Токо] (Pek.).

TŌLÏSTAY Karg. 19th-20th c. **Tōlïstay** [Толыстай] (Kattanov, Otč. 9). ✧ 'Fat, thick' cf. R. *tolstyj* 'id.' (Katanov).

TŌRČUQ Alt. 19th-20th c. **Tōrčuq** [Тоорчук], fem. (OjrRS 213). ✧ 'Cone of cembra pine' (OjrRS).

TŌRQA see **TORQA**

TŌS Shor 19th-20th c. **Tōs-mergen** [Qan Tōs Mergen], a khan (Dyrenkova 112).

TŌSQAN Hak.(Blt.) 19th-20th c. **Tōsqan** [Тоскан] (Katanov, Otč. 9).

TŌTQA see **TOTQA**

TŌTOQ Yak. **Tōtoq** [Тоток] (Pek.).

TŌTTAY Karg. **Tōttay** [Тоттаi] (Proben IX, 660); Karg. 19th-20th c. **Tōttay** [Тоттай] (Katanov: ZIRGOÊtn. XVII, vyp. III, 194).

TŌZÏY Alt. 19th-20th c. **Tōzïy** [Тоозый], fem. (OjrRS 213).

TÖBEK see **TÖBÖK**

TÖBERKEN Kzk. 19th c. **Töberken** [Тоберкенъ] (SOK 236).

TÖBET Kzk. 1794 **Töbet** [توبات / Тобет] (MIK IV, 159); Kzk. 1817 **Töbet** [توباة / Тобет] (MIK IV, 311,

318); Kzk. 19th c. **Töbet** [Тöбетъ] (AOO 34); Kzk. 19th c. **Tübet** [Тюбетъ] (SOV 44); Kzk. 1817 **Tübet-murza** [Тюбетъ Мурза] (Mejer 35). ✧ 'A kind of big dog; male dog; shepherd dog, sheep-dog' cf. Kzk. *töbet* 'кобель' (KzRS), Kzk. *töböt* 'eine Art grosser Hunde, Schäferhund' (Radl. III, 1272).

TÖBÖK Kzk. 19th c. **Töbek-pay** [Тобекпай] (SOK 182); Kzk. **Töbök** [Тöбöк], a singer (Proben III, 29 (34)). ✧ 'Chamber-pot for kinder' cf. Kzk. *töbök* 'das Uringefäss der Kinder' (Radl. III, 1271).

TÖDÄÑ Tuv. 19th c. **Tödäñ-qam** [Тöдäң-кам], a shaman (Proben IX, 205).

TÖDÖ-OT Alt. 19th c. **Tödö-ot?** [Тёдёот] (Verb., In. 123). ⇨ **OT.**

TÖGEY Kzk. 19th c. **Tögey?** [Тогей], fem. (SODž. 92).

TÖGEŠ Bashk. 1663 **Tögeš** [Тогеш Токалов] (MIB I, 175). ⇨ **TÜGEŠ?**

TÖGEŠEY Bashk. 1664 **Tögešey** [Тогешей] (MIB I, 193). ⇨ **TÜGEŠ** + suff. *-ey.*

TÖGÜNČİ Alt. 19th-20th c. **Tögünči** [Тöгÿнчи] (OjrRS 210). ✧ 'Cheat, swindler' (OjrRS), 'Liar' cf. Alt.(Tel.) *tögünči* 'der Lügner' (Radl. III, 1245).

TÖGÜREK Kzk. 19th c. **Tögürek** [Тогурекъ] (SODž. 20). ✧ 'Round' cf. Kirg. *tögürök* 'rund' (Radl. III, 1245).

TÖKE Kzk. 19th c. **Töke** [Токе] (SOV 46). ✧ Shortened-contracted form of a name beginning with *Tö-* + suffixoid *-ke* <comp. *ake.*

TÖKEJÜK-TOLUN Chag. 15th c. - 16th c. **Tökejük-tolun-χoĵa** [توكاجوك تولون حواجه / Tökedžük Tolun] (Šejb. LIV). ⇨ **TÖKE / TÜKÄ?** + **TOLUN** + dim. suff. *-jük / -jik.*

TÖKEY Bashk. 1734 **Tökey** [Илиш Токеев] (MIB III, 322). ⇨ **TÖKE?** + suff. *-y.*

TÖKEN Kzk. 19th c. **Töken** [Токенъ] (AOO 46). ✧ Hypochoristic contracted form of one of such names as *Tölep-bergen, Tölem-bay, Tölendi,* etc. (Žanuzakov) + hypoc. suff. *-ken.*

TÖKKÄJĬK Tuv. 19th c. **Tökkäĵĭk** [Тöккäцiк], fem. (Proben IX, 88, 95).

TÖKMİŠ Uyg. 10th c. - 13th c. **Tökmiš** [تكميس / تكمش], an emir, slave-soldier (gulām) in the caliphate (Ĵuwaynī I, 35, 39).

TÖKMİŠ-BUQA Uyg. 10th c. - 13th c. **Tökmiš-buqa** [تكمس / توكميش / بوقا], an emir in the caliphate (Ĵuwaynī I, 34, 37). ⇨ **TÖKMİŠ** + **BUQA.**

TÖKÖÑ Kzk. **Tököñ-qïz** [Тöкöng / Тöкöң кыз], fem. (Proben III, 53 (69)).

TÖKÖR Kirg. **Tökör-usta** [Тöкör / Тöкöр], gunsmith Bölök-bay's byname in the Manas-epics (Proben V, 188 /190/). ✧ 'Lame' cf. Kirg. *tökör* 'хромой' (Jud.).

TÖKPÄJÄK Tuv. 19th c. **Tökpäjäk** [Тöкпäцäк], fem. (Proben IX, 127).

TÖKÜLTİ Uyg. 8th c. - 9th c. **Tökülti** (Müller, Uig. II, 79, DTS). ✧ 'Being poured out' (Blagova 1997, 714).

TÖKÜŠ see **TEKEŠ**

TÖKÜZ **Töküz-bik** [Тукузъ-бикъ] (RaD/Ber. II, Text 180). ✧ I. 'Full, perfect' cf. Chag. *töküz* 'voll, vollständig' (Radl. III, 1243).

TÖLDÖK Alt. 19th-20th c. **Töldök** [Тöлдöк] (OjrRS 210); Hak.(Blt.) 19th-20th c. **Tüldük** [Тÿлдÿк] (Proben IX, 362). ✧ 'Fertile, having descendants' cf. Hak.(Sag.) *töllĭg* 'id.', Alt. *töldǖ* 'id.' (Radl. III, 1263). ⇨ **TÜL** + suff. *-dök.*

TÖLÄ-BUГA see **TELE-BUГA**

TÖLÄB-BERGÄN see **TÖLEP-BERGEN**

TÖLÄČİ Bulg. 762-765 **Töläči** [Τελέτζης], a prince (Byz. Turc. 304). ⇨ **TÖLE** + suff. *-či.*

TÖLÄGÄN see **TÖLEGEN**

TÖLÄK Uyg. **Töläk** [Töläk] (EUTS); Uyg. 13th-14th c. **Töläk** (Zieme, Mat. II, 92); Uyg. 13th-14th c. **Töläk-qïz-täñrim** [Töläk Qïz Tngrim], fem. (Zieme, Mat. II, 92); Uyg. 13th-14th c. **Töläk-täñrim**, fem. (Zieme, Mat. II, 91). ✧ 'Inactive, quiet' cf. Karakh. *töläk* 'бездеятельный, спокойный' (DTS).

TÖLÄK-QARA Uyg. 13th-14th c. **Töläk-qara** [Töläk Qara] (Zieme, Mat. II, 92). ⇨ **TÖLÄK** + **QARA.**

TÖLÄK-TÄMÜR see **TÖLÄK-TEMİR**

TÖLÄK-TEMİR Uyg. 13th c. **Töläk-temür** [töläk temür] (DTS); Uyg. 12th c. - 14th c. **Tüläk-tämür / Tüläk-temür** [Tüläk Tämür / tüläk temür] (Radl., USp. 19-20, DTS). ✧ 'Quiet/inactive-iron' (Blagova 1997, 712). ⇨ **TÖLÄK / TÜLÄK** + **TEMİR.** See also **TÖLEK-TEMİR.**

TÖLÄŠ-BİLGÄ Türk 7th c. - 9th c. **Töläš-bilgä** [töläš bilgä] (DTS). ✧ 'Pay-wise' (Blagova 1997, 712N+Adj). ⇨ **TÖLE** + **BİLGÄ** + suff. *-š.*

TÖLE Kzk. 18th c. - 19th c. **Töle-bay** [Толебай] (Tynyšp. 68, 75); Kzk. 1794 **Töle-bay** [توله باى / Толыбай (!)] (MIK IV, 160); Kzk. 19th c. **Töle-bay** [Толебай] (AOP 74); Kzk. 19th c. **Töle-bay** [Толебай] (SOK 8); Kzk. 19th c. **Töle-bay** [Толебай] (SOK 8); Kzk. 19th c. **Töle-bay** [Тöлебай] (SOK 86); Kkalp. 20th c. **Töle-bay** [Төлебай] (KkRS 776); Kzk. 18th c. - 19th c. **Töle-biy** [Толе-бий] (Tynyšp. 66); Kzk. 18th c. - 19th c. **Töle-biy** [Толе-бий] (Tynyšp. 66); Kzk. 19th c. **Tülä-bay** [Тулябаевъ] (SKSO VIII, 221); Kzk. 19th c. **Tülä-bay / Tüle-bay?** [Тулебай] (SODž. 28); Kzk. 19th c. **Tülä-bey** [Тюлабей Каукановъ] (TV 1876, 158); Kzk. 19th c. **Tüle** [Тулэ] (Grod., Pril. 127); Kzk. 19th c. **Tüle / Tülä** [Туле / Тюля] (Grod., Pril. 25); Kzk. **Tüle-bay** [Тюлебай] (Sb. Syr-D. XI, otd. II, 3); Kzk. 18th c. **Tüle-bay** [Тюлебай] (Nepljuev 762-63); Kzk. 19th c. **Tüle-bay** [Тулебай] (AOK 74); Kzk. 19th c. **Tüle-bay** [Тулебай] (SKSO VIII, 206); Kzk. 19th c. **Tüle-bek** [Тюлебекъ] (AOAtb. 2); Kzk. 19th c. **Tüle-**

bek [Тюлебекъ] (Grod., Pril. 154); Bashk. 1740 **Tüle-biy** [Тюле-бий] (MIB I, 436); Kzk. 18th c. **Tüle-biy** [Тулебій], a biy (judge) of the Greater Horde (Ulu Žüz) (Valihanov, Soč. 163); Kzk. 19th c. **Tüli-bay** [Тулибаевъ] (SKSO VIII, 222). ✧ 'Pay! Compensate!' (Bese 11), 'Paid' (Žanuzakov) cf. Uyg. *tölä-* 'платить, уплачивать' (DTS), Kuman, Chag., Hak. *tölä-* 'bezahlen' (Radl. III, 1260), Kzk. *töle-* 'платить, уплатить' (KzRS).

TÖLEGEN   Kzk. 19th c. **Tölägän** [Байджанъ Толагановъ] (Grod., Pril. 94); Uzb. 20th c. **Tölägän** [Тӱлаган] (Begmatov 1984, 205); Uzb. 20th c. **Tölägän** [Тӱлаган], fem. (Begmatov 1984, 205); Uzb. 20th c. **Tölägän-ây** [Тӱлаганой], fem. (Begmatov 1984, 205); Uzb. 20th c. **Tölägän-χoja** [Тӱлаганхӱжа] (Begmatov 1984, 205); Uzb. 20th c. **Tölägän-mirza** [Тӱлаганмирза] (Begmatov 1984, 205); Kzk. **Tölegen** [تولاگان / Тölегенъ] (Syzdykov 354); Kzk. 19th c. **Tölegen** [Толегёнъ] (AOK 46); Kzk. 19th c. **Tölegen** [Тулегенъ], a folklore hero (Grod., Pril. 56); Kzk. 19th c. **Tölegen** [Тулегенъ] (SODž. 52); Kzk. 19th c. **Tölegen** [Тулегенъ] (SOK 308); Kzk. 1896 **Tölegen** [Тöлегенъ], hero in a legend (poem) (AUK Dobavl. 5); Kzk. 1794 **Tölegen-bi** [تولاکن بی / Толеген] (MIK IV, 164); Kkalp. 1826 **Tölegen-yüzbaši** [Толеген-юзбаши / Тёлеген], from the Qañγlï tribe (MIT II, 400, 420, MIKk. 128); Kzk. 1805 **Tülägän-batïr** [Тюлаган батырь], one of the chiefs of the Little Horde (Kiši Žüz) (MIK IV, 512); Kzk. 1820 **Tülägän-batïr** [Тюлаганъ-батыръ / Тюлеганъ], one of the chiefs of the Tana-buγa tribe of the Middle Horde (Orta Žüz) (Sib. Vest. IX, 104, 105); Kzk. 19th c. **Tülegen** [Тулагенъ] (Grod., Pril. 144); Kzk. 19th c. **Tülegen** [Тюлегенъ] (Lomakin 40); Kzk. 19th c. **Tülegen** [Тулагенъ] (SKSO III, 190); Kzk. 19th c. **Tülegen** [Тулагенъ] (SODž. 92); Kzk. 19th c. **Tülegen** [Тулагенъ] (SOK 216); Kzk. 19th c. **Tülegen** [Тулегенъ] (SOV 152); Kzk. 19th c. **Tülügön** [Тюлюгонъ] (AOK 102); Kzk. 19th c. **Tülügün** [Тюлюгунъ] (ZIRGOGeogr. I, 482); *TN:* Kzk. 19th c. **Tülägän** [Тулаганская волость], district of Tülägän (AUK 796). ✧ 'Paid / bought / bought off / redeemed (child)'; Such names were given after several children died in the family (Žanuzakov 1971p. 101). Cf. Uyg. *tölä-* 'платить, уплачивать' (DTS), Kuman, Chag., Hak. *tölä-* 'bezahlen' (Radl. III, 1260), Kzk. *töle-* 'платить, уплатить' (KzRS). ⇨ **TÖLEMİŠ.**

TÖLEK   Trkm. 19th c. **Tölek** [Курбанъ Толековъ] (Ščeglov I, 350); Trkm. 19th c. **Tölek** [Ногай Толековъ] (Ščeglov IV, 174); Kzk. 18th c. - 19th c. **Tölek** [Толек] (Tynyšp. 73); Trkm. 19th c. **Tölek-mulla** [Толекъ Мулла Кубаевъ] (Ščeglov IV, 186); Kzk. 19th c. **Tölek-pay** [Толекпай] (AOO 14); Kzk. 19th c. **Tölek-pay** [Толекпай] (SOK 120); Kzk. 19th c.

Tölek-pay [Толекпай] (SOV 74). ✧ 'Payment, indemnity (for the lost/died child)' cf. Chag. *tölök* 'die Bezahlung' (Radl. III, 1261), Trkm. *töleg* 'плата, платёж, уплата; возмещение' (TrkmRS). ⇨ **TÜLEK?** See also **QARA-TÖLÖK.**

TÖLEK-TEMİR   Tat.(GH) 1300 **Tölek-temir / Tölök-temir / Töläk-temir?** [تلك تمر / Толактемӣр / Толактемíр / Толоктемиръ], emir, Toqta's follower when fighting against Noγay (Baybars/Tizeng. I, 90, 113, also Veselovskij 48); Tat.(GH) 1322-1340 **Tölek-temür / Tölök-tömür / Töläk-temir?** [تلکتمور / Толактемӣр / Toloctomoûr], a Tatar commander of the army, governor in Kiram (Eski-Qïrïm) (Byz. Turc. 316, Ibn Bat. II, 359); Maml.? 1389 **Tüläk-temir,** „oberster Emir unter Schaban" (Iyās I, 169, Weil, Chalif. I, 521); Maml. 1325 **Tülek-temir** [تلك تمر الابراهیمی] (Zetterst. 176). ✧ 'Payment-Iron'? ⇨ **TÖLEK / TÜLEK? + TEMİR.** See also **TÖLÄK-TEMİR.**

TÖLEK-TEMÜR see **TÖLEK-TEMİR**

TÖLEKE   Kzk. 19th c. **Töleke** [Тöлеке] (AOO 50); Kzk. 19th c. **Töleke** [Тöлеке] (AOP 130); Kzk. 19th c. **Tüleke** [Тулеке] (AOK 130); Kzk. 19th c. **Tüleke** [Тулеке] (AOP 6). ⇨ **TÖL / TÖLE / TÖLEK? +** comp. *eke* / suff. *-ke* / dim. suff. *-e?*

TÖLEMES   Kzk. 1794 **Tölemes** [تولامص / Толемес] (MIK IV, 164). ✧ 'He will not pay'? ⇨ **TÖLE +** suff. *-mes.*

TÖLEMİS see **TÖLEMİŠ**

TÖLEMİŠ   Kzk. 19th c. **Tölämiš** [Толамишъ] (Grod., Pril. 193); Kzk. 19th c. **Tölemis** [Толемисъ] (SOV 60); Kzk. 1825 **Tülämiš?** [تولامش / Туламыш] (MIK IV, 473, 477); Kzk. 19th c. **Tülemis** [Тюлемысовъ] (Grod., Pril. 56); Kzk. 19th c. **Tülemis** [Тюлемисъ] (Konšin, Oč. 120); Kzk. 19th c. **Tülemis** [Тюлемисъ], a biy (Lomakin 37); Kzk. 19th c. **Tülemis** [Тулемисъ] (SODž. 24). ✧ 'Paid / bought child'. ⇨ **TÖLE, TÖLEGEN +** suff. *-miš.*

TÖLEN   Kzk. 18th c. - 19th c. **Tölen-χoja** [Толенходжа] (Tynyšp. 68); Bashk. 1714 **Tülän** [Уразай Тюлянов] (MIB I, 105); Kzk. 1807 **Tülän** [Тюлянъ] (TOUAK XXIV, 84); Kzk. **Tülen-bay** [Исы Тюленбаевъ], from Mañγïšlaq (Zap. Kavk. Otd. IRGO VIII, 10:29); Kzk. 19th c. **Tülen-bay** [Тюленбай Наймановъ] (Konšin, Mat. I-III, 49); *TN:* Kzk. **Tülen-bay** [К. Тюленбай] (Karta JAR XIX). ✧ 'Be paid for! / be bought!' cf. Chag., Crm. *tölän-* 'bezahlt werden' (Radl. III, 1261), Alt., Kzk. *tölön-* 'id.' (Radl. III, 1262), Kzk. *tölen-* 'id.' (QTTS). See also **ÖTEL.**

TÖLENDİ   Kzk. 18th c. - 19th c. **Tölendi** [Толенды] (Tynyšp. 75); Kzk. 19th c. **Tölendi** [Толенды] (SODž. 108); *TN:* Kzk. **Tülendi** [Tulendi], a tomb (Rekogn.). ✧ 'He was paid for; he was bought, compensated' cf.

Chag., Crm. *tölän-* 'bezahlt werden' (Radl. III, 1261), Kzk. *tölen-* 'id.' (QTTS). See also **TÖLEMİŠ**.

TÖLEÑÜT   Kzk. 19th c. **Töleñüt** [Тöленгутъ] (AOK 134); Kzk. 19th c. **Töleñüt** [Тöленгутъ] (AOP 54); Kzk. 19th c. **Töleñüt** [Толенгутъ] (SODž. 124); Kzk. 19th c. **Tüleñüt** [Туленгутъ] (SODž. 6). ✧ 'Serf, bond man of the sultan; Telengüt (?)' cf. Kzk. *tölöñüt* 'die Leibeigenen der Sultane (wahrscheinlich ursprünglich die Kriegsgefangenen Teleuten)' (Radl. III, 1262).

TÖLEP-BERGEN   Kzk. 19th c. **Töläb-bergän** [Толабъ Берганъ] (Grod., Pril. 170); Kzk. 19th c. **Tölep-pergen** [Толеппергенъ] (AOO 18); Kzk. 19th c. **Tölep-pergen** [Толейпергенъ] (SOK 298); Kzk. 19th c. **Tölep-pergen** [Толппергенъ] (SOV 106); Kzk. 19th c. **Tölep-pergen** [Толеппергенъ] (SOV 66); Kzk. 19th c. **Tülep-pergen** [Тулеппергенъ] (SOK 72, 76, 240). ✧ 'Bought child / child paid for'. ⇨ **TÖLE + BERGEN.**

TÖLEP-PERGEN see **TÖLEP-BERGEN**

TÖLES   Kzk. 19th c. **Töles** [Толесъ] (AOP 106); Kzk. 19th c. **Töles** [Толесъ] (SODž. 4); Kzk. 19th c. **Töles-pay** [Толеспай] (SOV 100); Kzk. 19th c. **Tüles** [Сарбай Тулесовъ] (AUK 877); Tat. 1534 **Tüleš** [Нагай Тулешевъ] (PSRL XIII, 84); Kzk. 19th c. **Tüleš** [Тулешъ] (AOAtb. 42); Kzk. 19th c. **Tüleš** [Тулешъ] (AOK 10); Kzk. 19th c. **Tüleš** [Тюлешъ] (AOK 50). ✧ 'Payment' cf. Uyg. *tölä-* 'платить, уплачивать' (DTS), Kuman, Chag., Hak. *tölä-* 'bezahlen' (Radl. III, 1260), Kzk. *töle-* 'платить, уплатить' (KzRS). ⇨ **TÖLE** + suff. *-s /-š.*

TÖLİŠ   Uyg. 8th c. - 12th c. **Töliš-yinäl** [Töliš (Tüliš) Yīnäl Tamgāntarχān] (Mahrnāmag 11). ⇨ **TÜLEŠ?**

TÖLÖK-TÖMÜR see **TÖLEK-TEMİR**

TÖLÜ   Kkalp. 1810 **Tölü-mergen** [Тöл[Мерген] (MIKk. 110). ✧ 'Payment' cf. Kkalp. *tölew* 'плата, уплата, выплата' (KkRS).

TÖMÜRTÜ-QAΓUL   Oghuz/Trkm. 13th c. **Tömürtü-qaγul / Tömürdü-qaγul?** [Tömürdü Kağul / tömürtü qaγul] (Oğuz K. Dest. 25, DTS).

TÖNÄŠ   Bashk. 1712 **Tönäš** [Тоняш Чикеев] (MIB III, 83); Bashk. 1737 **Tönäš** [Акманай Тоняшев] (MIB III, 364).

TÖNÖGÜYÄ   Yak. **Tönögüyä** [Тöнöӈ̄йjä] (Pek.).

TÖÑGÜR   Tuv. 19th c. **Töñgür-öl** [Тöнгÿр-ол] (Proben IX, 111, 127, 155). ✧ 'Shaman-drums'? cf. Türk, Chag., Alt., Hak. *tüñür* 'die Shamanentrommel' (Radl. III, 1543).

TÖPÖ   Alt. 19th-20th c. **Töpö** [Тöпö], fem. (OjrRS 213).

TÖRBÖT   Alt. 19th-20th c. **Törböt** [Тöрбöт] (OjrRS 210). ✧ Ethnonym.

TÖRÄ-MURAT see **TÖRE-MURAT**

TÖRÄ-NİYAZ   Kkalp. 20th c. **Töre-niyaz** [Тöренияз] (KkRS 776). ⇨ **TÖRE + NİYAZ.**

TÖRÄTÜ   Uyg. **Törädü** [Törädü] (EUTS); Uyg. 12th c. - 14th c. **Törätü** [törätü] (DTS). ✧ 'Law-abiding'? (Blagova 1997, 711).

TÖRE   Kzk. 19th c. **Törä-ǰan?** [Тораджанъ] (Grod., Pril. 101); Kkalp. 20th c. **Töre** [Тöре] (KkRS 776); Kkalp. 20th c. **Töre-bay** [Тöребай / Тöребай] (Bask., Kkalp. 78, KkRS 776); Trkm.? 1851 **Töre-bay-χanum / Töre-baχt-χanum** [Тöре-Бай-ханум / Тöре-Бахт-ханум], Qutluγ-sultan's daughter (MIT II, 294); Khorezm. 14th c. **Töre-bek** [ترابك / Torâbec], princess (χatun), Qutlu-temür's wife in Khorezm (Ibn Bat. II, 73, III, 9); Kkalp. 1810 **Töre-bek** [Тöре бек] (MIKk. 110); Kkalp. 1821 **Töre-bek** [Тöре-бек-юзбаши], a captain (MIT II, 420); Trkm. 1858 **Töre-mergen** [Тöре Мерген], from the Yomut tribe (MIT II, 586); Kirg. **Törö-bek** [Тöпö Бек] (Proben V, 182 (184)); Bashk. 1735 **Türä** [Уразъ Тюринъ], a tarχan (Vel.-Zern., Bašk. 23); Uzb. 1851 **Türä-atalïq** [Тюря-Аталыкъ], lord of the town Shakh-Abat (Šaχ-abat) (ZIRGO V, 114); Kzk. 19th c. **Türä-bek** [Тюрабекъ] (Grod., Pril. 197); Uzb. 1875 **Türä-qul-biy** [Тюря-Кулъ-бiй] (Moskal'cev 40); Kzk. 19th c. **Türe** [Тагайбай Тюринъ] (Grod., Pril. 132); Kkalp. 20th c. **Türe** [Тюре] (Bask., Kkalp. 64); Kzk. 19th c. **Türe-bay** [Тюребай] (SOK 44); Kzk. 19th c. **Türe-ǰan** [Тлеубергенъ Тюреджановъ] (Grod., Pril.); Turk. 1540 **Türe-χan** [توره خان / Türehân], chief of the Şeyhlü tribe, Diyarbekir (Demirtaş 47); Bashk. 1770 **Türi** [Тюри Ишалин] (MIB IV/1, 342); Tat.(Sib.) 1608 **Türü-bay** [Тюрюбай] (Miller, Ist. Sib. II, 207); Kzk. 19th c. **Türü-žan** [Тюрюжанъ] (AOO 2); *TN:* Kzk.? **Türä-bay** [Тюря-бай] (Karta JAR XI); Kzk. **Türü-bay** [Тюрюбай] (Karta JAR XI). ✧ 'Lord, nobleman, chief, clerk' cf. Kkalp. *töre* 'господин, барин; чиновник; сановник' (KkRS), Kirg. *törö* '(в эпосе) господин (эпитет властительного богатыря); господин (так киргизы называли всех царских чиновников)' (Jud.), Bashk. *türä* 'начальник; чиновник' (BRS), Tat. *türä* 'начальник, чиновник; сановник' (TatRS).

TÖRE-GELDİ see **TÖRE-KELDİ**

TÖRE-KELDİ   Uzb. 20th c. **Törä-keldi** [Тÿракелди] (Begmatov 1984, 202); Kzk. 19th c. **Töre-geldi** [Торегельды] (SODž. 120); Kzk. 19th c. **Töre-keldi / Töre-keldi?** [Торекельды] (SOV 58); Kirg. **Törö-geldi** [Тöрöгелди] (Jud. 68); Kzk. 19th c. **Türe-geldi** [Тюрегельды] (AOK 10); Kzk. 19th c. **Türe-geldi** [Турегельды] (SODž. 26); Kzk. 19th c. **Türe-geldi** [Турегельды] (SOK 58). ✧ 'A lord arrived'. ⇨ **TÖRE + KELDİ.**

TÖRE-MİRAT see **TÖRE-MURAT**

TÖRE-MURAD see **TÖRE-MURAT**

TÖRE-MURAT   Kzk. 19th c. **Törä-murat**

[Торамуратъ] (Grod., Pril. 98); Kkalp. 20th c. **Töre-mïrat** [Тѳремырат / Тѳремырат] (Bask.,Kkalp. 402, KkRS 776); Trkm.? 1817 **Töre-murad-atalïq** [Тöпе Мурад-аталык] (MIT II, 400, 401, 451, 467, 492 etc.); Kkalp. 20th c. **Töre-murat** [Тѳремурат] (KkRS 776). ⇨ **TÖRE + MURAT.**

TÖREŠ   Kkalp. 20th c. **Töreš** [Тѳреш] (KkRS 776); Kkalp. 20th c. **Türeš** [Туреш] (Bask., Kkalp. 86). ⇨ **TÖRE** + suff. -š.

TÖRÖ see **TÖRE**

TÖRÖ-GELDİ see **TÖRE-KELDİ**

TÖRÖÑÖ   Alt.(Tel.) **Töröñö / Töröñöy?** [Тöрöнö / Тöрöнöi] (Radl. I, 726, III, 1253). ✧ 'The first man's name' (Radl. III, 1253).

TÖRÖÑÖY see **TÖRÖÑÖ**

TÖRPÄ   Türk 7th c. - 9th c. **Törpä** [törpä] (DTS); Uyg. 13th c. **Törpä** [törpä] (DTS); Türk 7th-9th c. **Törpä-ičreki** [Tör Apa içreki] (ETY III, 71). ✧ 'Gift, present'? cf. East.T. *törpä* 'ein Geschenk, das man mit der Absicht darbringt, ein noch werthvolleres Geschenk zu erhalten' (Radl. III, 1259).

TÖRT   Kzk. 19th c. **Tört-bay** [Тортбай] (SODž. 96, 108), Kzk. 19th c. **Tört-ül** [Тортуулъ] (AOAtb. 66); Kzk. 1865 **Türt-bay-datχa** [Туртбай-датха] (Smirnov, Sultany 49); Kzk. 19th c. **Türt-pay** [Туртпай] (AOP 82); Kzk. 19th c. **Türt-ul** [Туртулъ] (AOA 106); Kuman 1290 **Türt-ul / Türt-ulï** [Turtule / Turtul / Turtel], one of the murderers of King Kun László IV (1272-1290), his name is preserved in placenames (e. g. Therthelzallasa [=Törtel's settlement]) and family-names in Hungary (Gyárfás III, 596, 676, Fekete: MNy. XXX(l934), 50) (SRH I, 474, cf. also Rásonyi, KÖA 134, Anthr. 146). ✧ 'Four' cf. Türk., Uyg., Alt., Hak., Kirg., Kzk. *tört* 'vier' (Radl. III, 1257), also Rásonyi, Nombre 53-54.

TÖSÄK see **TÖSÄK**

TÖSEKEY   Kzk. 19th c. **Tösekey** [Тосекей] (AOA 134). ✧ 'Bed, couch' cf. Kzk. *tösek* 'постель; перина; подстилка' (KzRS), Kzk. *tösek* 'yatak' (KzTS). ⇨ **TÖSÄK** + suff. -ey.

TÖSTÜK see **TÖŠTÜK**

TÖSÄK   Kzk. 19th c. **Tösäk?** [Тосакъ] (AOP 46); Kzk. 19th c. **Tösäk?** [Амалбай Тосаковъ] (Konsin, Pam. 26); Kzk. 19th c. **Tösek-pay** [Тоссекпай] (SODž. 22); Kzk. 19th c. **Tösek-pay** [Тосекпай] (SOV 22); Türk **Töšäk** [Töşäk] (ETY II, 171); Alt. 19th-20th c. **Tözök** [Töжöк] (OjrRS 210). ✧ 'Bed, couch' cf. Alt. *tözök* 'id.' (OjrRS), Tat. *tüšäk* 'der Bettpfühl, die Matratze' (Radl. III, 1589), Kzk. *tösek* 'yatak' (KzTS). See also **AÑQAS-TÖSÄK.**

TÖŠTÜK   Kzk. 19th c. **Töstük** [Тостукъ] (SODž. 92); Kzk. **Töstük-batïr** [Тöстÿк Батыр] (Proben III, 314 (378)); Kirg. **Töštük** [Тöштÿк / Тѳштук] (Proben V, 143 (144), Jud. 109, 488). ✧ 'Breast with fat and

leather for frying' cf. Kzk. *töstük* 'der Bruststück zum Braten; der Brustlatz auf dem Frauenhemde)' (Radl. III, 1266), Kirg. *töstük* 'нагрудник (нагрудный панцирь воина)' (Jud.); Kzk. *tüstük?* 'eine halbe Tagereise; was sich auf den Mittag (Süden) bezieht' (Radl. III, 1580). See also **ER-TÜSTÜK.**

TÖTŎ   Yak. **Tötŏ** [Тöтö] (Pek.).

TRON   Hak. 19th-20th c. **Tron** [Трон] (HRS 352).

TROÑ   Hak. 19th-20th c. **Troñ** [Тронъ] (HRS 352).

TRUXMEN see **TÜRKMEN**

TRUP-BERDİ see **TURUP-BERDİ**

TRUS see **TURÏS**

TU   Kzk. 19th c. **Tu-murza** [Тумурза] (AOK 130).

TUBAY   Tat.(Mish.). 1709 **Tubay** [Муртаза Тубаев] (MIB III, 52); Kzk. 19th c. **Tubay** [Тубай] (SOV 68). ⇨ **TOBA?** + suff. -y. See also **AQ-TUBAY, BAY-TUBAY, QOČİ-TUBAY?**

TUBANÏŠ   Kzk. 19th c. **Tubanïš** [Тубаньшъ] (AOK 38).

TUBAŠ see **TOPAŠ**

TUBİNA   Kzk. 1811 **Tubina / Tübinä?** [Тубина Бирюбаевъ] (Dobrosm., Turg. 252).

TUBUN   Kzk. 1628 **Tubun**, a Kazak prince in Siberia (Radl., Aus Sib. I, 183).

TUBURČUQ   Tat.(Lit.) 1592 **Tuburčuq** [Тубурчикъ Кермешевич] (Lit. Tat. 124); Kkalp. 1695, 1709 **Tuburčuq / Toburčuq / Taburčaq-sultan?** [Табурчак Султан / Тубурчюкъ / Тобурчюкъ], a sultan, Qaip Saltan's son (DAI X, 384, MIKk. 150, 159). ✧ 'Cone (=good-looking man)' cf. Tat. *tubirčiq* 'der Zapfen' (Radl. III, 1515).

TUČA   Hak. 19th-20th c. **Tuča** [Туча], fem. (HRS 355).

TUČAYAN   Türk 7th-9th c. **Tučayan** [Tuçayan] (DTS, ETY II, 134).

TUDAY   Balk. 19th c. **Tuday** [Тудаевъ] (Karaulov 67).

TUDAR   Oghuz? 1159 **Tudar / Tudor?** [Тудоръ Сатмазовичъ], chief of the Berendeys (PSRL II, 85, VII, 69).

TUDARÏQ   Nog. 1649 **Tudarïq / Tudarïq-murza / Dudarïq-murza** [Тударыкъ мурза / Дударыкъ мурза], Bi-murza's son (AI IV, 89, 99, 123). ⇨ **TUDAR?** + suff. -ïq.

TUDUMJAQ   Hak.? 19th c. **Tudumjaq** [Тудумцак] (Katanov, Otč. 12). ✧ '(Hollow of the) Hand' (Katanov), cf. Chag., Turk. *tutum* 'was man mit der Hand fassen kann; vier Finger breit; der Henkel' (Radl. III, 1486) + suff. -jaq.

TUDUN   Türk **Tudun** [Tudun] (ETY II, 122); Uyg. 8th c. - 12th c. **Tudun-čigši** [Tudun Čigši] (Müller, Hofstaat 211). ✧ 'Commander' (a title) cf. also Golden, Khaz. 215-216.

TUDUN-YAMTAR   Türk 735 **Tudun-yamatar** [Tudun Yamatar] (ETY I, 66); Türk 735 **Tudun-yamtar** [tudun jamtar] (DTS). ✧ 'Governor-Yamtar'? ⇨ **TUDUN +**

YAMTAR.

TUFAN   Chag. 16th c. **Tufan** [Туфан], a mulla (Ivanov 130); Chag. 16th c. **Tufan** [Туфан] (Ivanov 182, 192); Turk. 20th c. **Tufan** (Önder, Göle); Turk. 20th c. **Tufan** (Önder, Hınıs); Trkm. 1729/30 **Tufan** [Туфан], from the Qajar tribe (MIT II, 131); Turk. 20th c. **Tufan-beyli** [Tufanbeyli], a district (ilce) in the province of Adana, Turkey (TMİB 19). ✧ 'Flood, storm' cf. Az. *tufan* 'die Ueberschwemmung' (Radl. III, 1516), Turk. *tufan* 'потоп, буря, ураган' (TRS).

TUΓ-TEKİN see **TOQ**

TUΓA   Kzk. 19th c. **Tuγa** [Туга] (Grod., Pril. 80); Kzk. 19th c. **Tuγa-bay** [Тугабай] (Grod., Pril. 151); Selj.? 1044 **Tuγa-χan** [طغاخان] (Ibn al-Athīr/Tornb. IX, 356). ✧ 'Clasp, buckle' cf. *toya* 'die Schnalle' (Radl. III, 1158). ⇨ **TOQA II.**

TUΓA-TERKEN   Chag. 15th c. **Tuγa-terken / Toγa-terken?** [Туга-Турканъ], Ulug-beg's (1393-1449) daughter, the same as Ögä-terken-šah? (Barth., Ulugb. 116). ⇨ **TUΓA + TERKEN.**

TUΓAY see **TOΓAY**

TUΓAY-BUQA   Khorezm./Chag. 1362 **Tuγay-buγa(-barlas)** [Тугайбуга-барлас], Temür's comrade-in-arms (MIT I, 512); Khorezm./Chag.? 1403/04 **Tuγay-buqa** [طغاى بوقا] (Dorn 172). ⇨ **TOΓAY + BUQA.**

TUΓAY-SARÏ   Uzb. 20th c. **Tuγay-sarï** [Tougaï-Sary], a basmačï leader (Castagné 88). ⇨ **TOΓAY + SARÏ.**

TUΓAQA   Tat.(Sib.) 1600 **Tuγaqa / Tuγ-aqa?** [Тугака Келементеев] (Miller, Ist. Sib. II, 159).

TUΓALAQ see **TOΓALAQ**

TUΓAN I.   Chuv. 18th-19th c. **Tugan** [Туганъ] (Magn. 87); Kzk. 19th c. **Tuγam-bay (<Tuγan-bay)** [Tugambay] (Ljutš 108); Trkm. 1836 **Tuγan** [Туган], a judge from the Yomut tribe (MIT II, 468); Karch. **Tuγan** [Туганъ Карабашевъ] (Sysoev 132); Bashk. 1735 **Tuγan** [Токтаръ Тугановъ], a tarχan (Vel.-Zern., Bašk. 20); Bashk. 1745 **Tuγan** [Туган Азнаев] (MIB III, 426); Bashk. 1751 **Tuγan** [Туган Ксюков] (MIB IV/1, 43); Kzk. **Tuγan** [Туßан] (Proben III, 758 /848/); Kkalp. 1724 **Tuγan** [Атбай Туганов] (MIKk. 182); Trkm. 1814 **Tuγan / Tuγan-χan** [Туган Нияз-хан], a Khan from the Yaχmur tribe (MIT II, 215); Trkm. 1809 **Tuγan / Tuγan-niyaz-behadïr** [Туган Нияз-бехадыр], from the Abdal clan of the Turkmen of Mangyshlak (MIT II, 376, 385, 406); Kzk. 19th c. **Tuγan-bay** [Туганбай] (SOK 112, 118, 172, 178, 192, 264); Kzk. 19th c. **Tuγan-bay** [Туганбай] (SOV 144); Kzk. 1820 **Tuγan-biy** [Туганъ-бій], one of the chiefs of the Altïn tribe (Sib. Vest. IX, 112). ✧ 'Brother; male relative' cf. Trkm. *doγan* 'брат; друг' (TrkmRS), Tat. *tuγan* 'родственник, родной' (TatRS), Bashk. *tuγan* 'родственник; брат или сестра; близкий друг; родной' (BaRS/Uraksin), Karch.-Balk. *tūγan* 'родной' (RKarBalkS), Kzk. *tūγan* 'der Verwandte' (Radl. III,

1431), Kkalp. *tuwγan* 'родственник, родич' (KkRS). See also **AY-TUΓAN, AL-TUΓAN, AN-TUGAN, AR-TUGAN, AT-TUΓAN, BAY-TUΓAN, BEK-TUΓAN, BİY-TUΓAN, ČİN-TUΓAN, ǰAN-TUΓAN, İŠ-TUΓAN, YAQ-TUΓAN, YAŠ-TUGAN, KİL-DUΓAN, KÜN-TUΓAN, QAL-TUΓAN, QAN-TUΓAN, QAZ-TUΓAN, QÏŠ-TUΓAN, QUL-TUΓAN, QUŠ-TUΓAN, MAL-TUΓAN, NUR-TUΓAN, POS-TUGAN, SAL-TUΓAN, SOΓUR-TUΓAN, TOY-TUGAN, TOQ-TUΓAN, UL-TUWΓAN, URAS-TUGAN, URAZ-TUΓAN, ŽAY-TUWΓAN.**

TUΓAN II. see **TOΓAN**

TUΓAN-SUÑQUR see **TOΓAN-SOÑQUR**

TUΓANAY   Bashk. 1714 **Tuγanay** [Кусяляк (Косяляк / Каселяк) Туганаев] (MIB III, 118); Bashk. 1725 **Tuγanay** [Кусюляк Туганаев] (MIB III, 232); Bashk. 1756 **Tuγanay** [Кускульда Туганаев] (MIB IV/1, 130); Bashk. 1756 **Tuγanay** [Алдар Туганаев] (MIB IV/1, 130). ⇨ **TUΓAN I.** + dim. suff. *-ay?*

TUΓANAS see **TUΓANAŠ**

TUΓANAŠ   Kzk. 1819 **Tuγanas** [Туганас] (MIK IV, 323); Bashk. 1716 **Tuγanaš** [Туганаш Темирбулатов] (MIB III, 137). ✧ I. 'Little dear brother'; II. 'Brother-friend/mate (=male child)' [cf. TUΓAN + EŠ] (Sattarov). ⇨ **TUΓAN I.** + suff. *-aš?*

TUΓANČUQ see **TOΓANČÏQ**

TUΓANǰÏ   Turk. 20th c. **Doqanǰï-oγlu**, a Zeybek (Kúnos 1891, 119); Maml.? 1395, 1398/99 **Tuγanǰï / Toγančï** [طغنجى] (Iyās I, 303, Ibn Taghrīb. VI, 6, 29); Selj.? / Turk. 14th c. **Tuγanǰï / Tuγanǰïq** [طوغانحق / طوغانجو] / Tougan-Djou / Tougan-Djak], prince/ruler of a statelet west of Trapezunt (Trebisonde) (Jorga, Notes XIII, 350, 361 /Mesalek-alabsar/). ✧ 'Falconier?; Little falcon?' cf. Turk. *doγanǰï* 'der Falkonier' (Radl. III, 1706). ⇨ **TOΓAN** + suff. *-ǰï.* See also **TOΓANČÏQ.**

TUΓANDÏQ   Uzb. 19th c. **Tuγandïq** [Тугандыкъ] (SKSO III, 176).

TUΓAR   Bashk. 1757 **Tuγar** [Али Тюгарев] (MIB IV/1, 136); Tuv. 19th c. **Tuγar** [Туßар] (Proben IX, 155). ✧ 'Being born; rising' cf. Türk, Kuman, Chag. *toγ-* 'geboren werden; aufgehen (von Sonne); ersteigen' (Radl. III, 1158). See also **AY-TUWAR, AQ-TUWAR, KÜN-TUΓAR, ON-TOΓAR(?).**

TUΓAŠ see **TOΓAŠ**

TUΓAZ   Kirg. 1827 **Tuγaz** [Тугазъ Сагизбаевъ] (TOUAK XXIV, 181).

TUΓČÏ   Oghuz? 10th c. **Tuγčï** [محمد بن طغج], founder of the Ikhshīd dynasty (Ibn Saʿīd 4-18, 23-48); Maml. 14th c. **Tuγčï** [طغجى] (Sauvaget 50); 1379/80 **Tuwǰï / Tuwčï?** [طوجى الحسنى] (Iyās I, 248); 1379/80

Tuwǰï / Tuwčï? [طوجى العلائى] (Iyās I, 249). ✧ 'Bearer of banners' (Sauvaget 50).

TUҐDÏ Uyg. **Toqtï** [Toktı] (EUTS); Uyg. **Tuɣdï-čor** (Zieme, Mat. I, 81). ✧ '(S)he was (has been) born' cf. Uyg. *toɣ-* 'рождаться, возникать, появляться; восходить (о светилах)' (DTS), Uyg. *toq-* 'geboren werden' (Radl. III, 1145). See also **AY-TOҐDÏ, BEK-TOҐDÏ, EL-TOҐDÏ, ER-TOҐDÏ, ER-BUTÏ-BÜK-TOҐDÏ, KEY-DOҐDÏ, KÏŠ-TOҐDÏ, KÜČ-DOҐDÏ, KÜN-TOҐDÏ, QUWAN-DOҐDÏ.**

TUҐÏL Alt. 19th-20th c. **Tïbïl** [Тыбыл], fem. (OjrRS 213); Bashk. 1717 **Toɣul-bay** [Чермыш Тогулбаевъ] (MIB III, 154); Kzk. 19th c. **Toɣul-bay** [Тогулбай] (SODž. 100); Uzb. 20th c. **Tuɣïl** [Туғил] (Begmatov 1984, 205); Uzb. 20th c. **Tuɣïl-bây** [Туғилбой] (Begmatov 1984, 205); Uzb. 20th c. **Tuɣïl-ǰân** [Туғилжон] (Begmatov 1984, 205); Kzk. 19th c. **Tuɣul** [Тугулъ] (AOK 18); Kzk. 19th c. **Tuɣul-bay** [Tugul Baj], a courtier (Hedin, En färd I, 266); Kzk. 19th c. **Tuɣul-bay** [Тугулбай] (SOK 68); Kzk. **Tuɣul-bek** [Тугулбек] (Kojčubaev 225); Kzk. **Tuɣul** [Тугул], a field (Kojčubaev 225). ✧ 'Be born!' cf. Shor *toɣïl-*, Chag. *toɣul-* 'geboren werden' (Radl. III, 1164), Uzb. *tuɣïl-* 'рождаться, появляться' (UzbRS), also *tïvïl-* 'to arise, be born' (Bese 11).

TUҐÏŠ Kzk. 19th c. **Tuɣïš** [Тугишъ] (Grod., Pril. 108); Tat. 1500 **Tuwïš** [Тувешъ Татаринъ] (PSRL XII, 266). ✧ 'Rise; birth' cf. Turk. *doğuş* 'birth' (TED). See also **BEK-TUҐUŠ, KÜN-DOҐUŠ.**

TUҐLUQ-TEMÜR see TOQLUQ-TEMÜR

TUҐONA Bashk. 1600 **Tuɣona** [Тугона Келментеевь] (MIB I, 152). ⇨ **TUҐAN I.?** + suff. *-a.*

TUҐRA Oghuz / Trkm. **Tuɣra** [طغرا / توغار], forefather of the Ottoman dynasty (Āšikp. 5, Nešrī 186, Seādeddīn 15, Wittek 94). ✧ 'Monogram of the sultan'? cf. Turk. *tuɣra* 'id.' (Radl. III, 1432).

TUҐRÏLČA see TOҐRÏLČA

TUҐRUL see TOҐRÏL

TUҐRUL-NAZAN Selj. 12th c. **Tuɣrul-nazan** [نزان / Tuğrul Nazân], a Ghaznavid slave who became the commander of the Seljukids (Ahbar 11). ⇨ **TOҐRÏL.**

TUҐU Crm. 1750 **Tuɣu-šaχ-bikeč** [طوغوشاه بيكج], Abdulraχman's daughter (Bakč. Nadp. 31).

TUҐUČ Türk? 893, 896, 902/03 **Tuɣuč** [طغج بن جُفّ /] Toghodj ibn Haf [=J̌uff]], Ibn Tūlūnī's governor of Damascus, Syria (Tabarī, Annal. III, 2132, 2140, 2151, 2217 etc., Miskawayh V, 30-33, Ibn Saʿīd 4-7, 18, Kindī 242, 246, 247, Weil, Chalif. II, 506, 654); Türk? 896, 936-938 **Tuɣuč** [محمد بن طغج], governor of Halab (Aleppo) (Arīb 159, 169, Miskawayh 508, 553, 577,). ⇨ **TOҐUČ?**

TUҐUČAY Bashk. 1754 **Tuɣučay** [Тугучай Мряков] (MIB IV/1, 77).

TUҐUL see TUҐÏL

TUҐUL-TAY Kzk. 19th c. **Tuɣul-tay** [Тугултай] (AOO 2). ⇨ **TUҐÏL?** + **TAY?** or suff. *-tay(1,2)?*

TUҐULČÏ Kzk. 19th c. **Tuɣulčï** [Тугулчи] (SOV 122). ⇨ **TUҐÏL** + suff. *-čï.*

TUҐULǰA Tat.(GH) 1293 **Tuɣulǰa** [Тугулджа], Noɣay's daughter (Baybars/Tizeng. I, 86, 109, Nuwairī/Tizeng. I, 137, 158, Veselovskij, Nog. 56).

TUҐULǰU Karg. 19th-20th c. **Tuɣulǰu** [Тугулджу] (Katanov: ZIRGOEtn. XVII, vyp. III, 164); Karg. 19th-20th c. **Tuɣulǰu** [Туҕулжу / Тугулджу], a folklore hero (bogatyr) (Proben IX, 630, 631, Katanov: ZIRGOEtn. XVII, vyp. III, 164).

TUҐUM see TOQUM

TUҐUN see TOҐUN

TUҐUR Kzk. 19th c. **Tuɣur-bek** [Тугурбекъ] (SODž. 144). ✧ I. 'A doe which will not foal any more' cf. Kzk. *tuɣur* 'ein Weibchen, das zu gebären aufgehört hat' (Radl. III, 1432); II. 'A horse of medium worth' cf. Kzk. *tuɣur* 'ein Pferd von mittelmässigem Werthe' (Radl. III, 1432); III. 'Stand for a hunting bird' cf. Kzk. *tuɣur* 'der Ständer für den Jagdvogel' (Radl. III, 1432). See also **ON-TOҐOR(?), TOQ-TUҐUR.**

TUҐUS see TOQUZ

TUҐUŠ I. Tat.(Lit.) 1592 **Tuɣuš** [Хурманъ Тугушевичъ] (Lit. Tat. 124); Tat. 1776 **Tuɣuš** [Бахтей Тугушевъ] (PSZRI XX, 457). ✧ Dialectal variant of *Tuɣaš < Tuq + Ïš* 'Sated friend, child' (Sattarov). ⇨ **TUҐAŠ.**

TUҐUŠ II. see TOQÏŠ

TUҐUZ see TOQUZ

TUҐUZAQ see TOҐUZAQ

TUXŠÏ Türk? 883 **Tuχšï** [طخشى] (Tabarī, Annal. III, 2028).

TUY see TOY

TUY-BUҐA Khorezm./Chag. 1376/77 **Tuy-buɣa** [Туй-буга] (MIT I, 518). ⇨ **TOY** + **BUQA?**

TUY-BULAT see TOY-BULAT

TUYAX see TUYAQ

TUYAQ Kzk. **Tuyaχ-bay** [Тюахбай] (Sb. Syr-D. IX, 48); Kzk. 19th c. **Tuyaq** [Туякбай] (AOA 102); Kzk. 19th c. **Tuyaq** [Тюякъ] (AOA 18); Kzk. 19th c. **Tuyaq** [Тюякъ] (AOK 130); Kzk. 19th c. **Tuyaq** [Тюякъ] (AOO 54); Kzk. 19th c. **Tuyaq** [Туякъ] (AOP 86); Kzk. 19th c. **Tuyaq** [Молла Туякъ] (Grod., Pril. 123); Kzk. 19th c. **Tuyaq** [Кубей Туяковъ] (Grod., Pril. 169); Kzk. 19th c. **Tuyaq** [Карабекъ Туяковъ] (Grod., Pril. 91); Kzk. 19th c. **Tuyaq** [Туякъ] (SODž. 80); Kzk. 19th c. **Tuyaq** [Туякъ] (SOK 164, 214); Kzk. 19th c. **Tuyaq** [Туякъ] (SOV 62); Kzk. 19th c. **Tuyaq-bay** [Туякбай] (AOK 10, 122); Kzk. 19th c. **Tuyaq-bay** [Туякбай] (Grod., Pril. 123); Kzk. 19th c. **Tuyaq-bay** [Туякбай Оразовъ] (Grod., Pril. 28); Nog. **Tuyaq-bay(-batïr)** [Туякбай-батыр] (Žirm., Epos

395); Kzk. 19th c. **Tuyaq-pay** [Тюякпай] (AOA 82); Kzk. 19th c. **Tuyaq-pay** [Тюякпай] (SODž. 78); Kzk. 19th c. **Tuyaq-pay** [Тюякпай] (SOK 130, 154); Kzk. 19th c. **Tuyaq-pay** [Туякпай] (SOK 74); Kzk. 19th c. **Tuyaq-pay** [Туякпай] (SOV 62); Kzk. 19th c. **Tuyaq-pay** [Тюякпай] (SOV 84). ✧ 'Hoof; descendant' cf. East.T., Kirg., Kzk. *tuyaq* 'der Huf' (Radl. III, 1435), Kirg. *tuyaq* 'копыто; потомство (мужское)' (Jud.). See also **QAL-TUYƔAQ, TUYNAQ**.

TUYAN-BAQ   Kzk. 1819 **Tuyan-baq?** [Туянбак] (MIK IV, 325). ⇨ **TOYAN?** + **BAQ**.

TUYČA   Uzb. 19th c. **Tuyča** / **Tuyčay?** [Артыкбай Туйчаевъ] (SKSO III, 174). ⇨ **TOYČÏ?**

TUYČÏ see **TOYČÏ**

TUYFAZ   Kzk. 19th c. **Tuyfaz** [Туйфазъ Магомедовъ] (Grod., Pril. 36).

TUYƔAN see **TOYƔAN**

TUYƔÏN see **TUYƔUN**

TUYƔUN   Bashk. 1761 **Toyɣun** [Туйгун Мусин] (MIB IV/1, 216); Kzk. 19th c. **Tuyɣïn** [Туйгыновъ] (AOK 106). ✧ '(White) gerfalcon; hawk, kite' cf. Chag. *toyɣun* 'id.' (Radl. III, 1142), Chag., Kzk., Tat.(Bar.) *tuyɣun* 'der weisse Falke' (Radl. III, 1424), Bashk. *toyɣon* 'кречет белый' (BRS), Kzk. *tüyɣïn* 'ястреб-стервятник' (KzRS). See also **TOƔAN**.

TUYÏM / TUYUM see **TOYÏM**

TUYMA see **TOYMA**

TUYNAQ   Uyg. **Tuynaq** [Tuynak] (EUTS); Uyg. 13th c. **Tuynaq-šilavanti** [tujnaq šilavanti] (DTS). ✧ 'Hoof' cf. Chag., Turk. *tuynaq* / *tuyyaq* 'der Huf des Pferdes' (Radl. III, 1424). ⇨ **TUYAQ**.

TUYNAŠ see **TOYNAŠ**

TUYUM see **TOYÏM**

TUQ see **TOQ**

TUQ-BERDÏ see **TOQ-BERDÏ**

TUQ-MURZA see **TOQ**

TUQA see **TOQA I.**

TUQA-TEMÜR see **TOQ-TEMÏR**

TUQAČ see **TOQAČ**

TUQAY see **TOQAY**

TUQAQ see **TOQAQ**

TUQAMBET   Kkalp. 1740 **Tuqambet-bi** [Тукамбетъ-Би] (Hanykov, Poezdka 19, MIKk. 208). ⇨ **TOQ / TOQAN?** + suff. *-ïmbet / -bet*. See also **TOƔÏMBET, TOQ-MAMBET, TOQUMBET, TUQUMBET**.

TUQAN see **TOQAN**

TUQAR   Kzk. 19th c. **Tuqar** [Бильяшаръ Тукаровъ] (SKSO VIII, 229).

TUQAŠ see **TOQAŠ**

TUQBAN see **TOQMAN**

TUQDUQ-BUQA   Uyg. 13th c. - 14th c. **Tuqduq-buqa** [Tukduk Puka] (Chwol., Syr.-nest. (NF) 42). ⇨ **TOQLUQ?** + **BUQA**.

TUQLUJA   Khorezm.? **Tuqluja** [Туклуджа] (RaD II, 76). ⇨ **TOQLÏJÏ?**

TUQLUQ see **TOQLUQ**

TUQLUQ-TEMÜR see **TOQLUQ-TEMÜR**

TUQMAN see **TOQMAN**

TUQSÏR   Kzk. 19th c. **Tuqsir-bay?** / **Tükser-bay?** [Туксербай] (SOK 268).

TUQSUQ   Kzk. 19th c. **Tuqsuq** [Туксуковъ] (AOO 30).

TUQTA see **TOQTA**

TUQTAR see **TOQTAR**

TUQTÏ see **TOQLÏ**

TUQTU-ƔURT see **TOQTÏ-QURT**

TUQU see **TOQU**

TUQUBAN see **TOQMAN**

TUQUČ see **TOƔUČ**

TUQUM see **TOQUM**

TUQUM-TAY   Kzk. 19th c. **Tuqum-tay** [Байджанъ Тукумтаевъ] (Grod., Pril. 98). ⇨ **TOQUM** + **TAY** or suff. *-tay(1,2)*?

TUQUMAN see **TOQMAN**

TUQUMBET see **TOQUMBET**

TUQUR   **Tuqur-bay** [Тукуръ-Бай], a mountain? in the Pamir-region (Semenov, Rossia XIX, 717). ✧ 'Short and thick, stubby' cf. Bashk. *toqor* 'толстый и короткий' (BRS/Uraksin) <Mo. *Tuqur*?

TUQUŠ see **TOQÏŠ**

TUQUZ see **TOQUZ**

TUQUZAQ see **TOƔUZAQ**

TUL see **TOL**

TUL-AYT   Kzk. 19th c. **Tul-ayt?** [Гасанъ Тулаитовъ] (Grod., Pril. 172). ⇨ **TOL** + **AYT?**

TUL-AZÏ   Tat. 1468 **Tul-azi** (<**Tul-χaǰi?**) [Тулазій / Тулазѣй], prince Tarχan's son (PSRL (Russk. Hr.) I, 470, PSRL VI, 188, VIII, 154). ⇨ **TOL** + **ХАǰÏ?**

TUL-TAY   Kzk. 19th c. **Tul-tay** [Тултай] (SKSO VIII, 223). ⇨ **TOL?** + **TAY** or suff. *-tay(1,2)*?

TULA   Bashk. 1779 **Tula-bay** [Макай Тулабаев] (MIB V, 94); Kzk. 19th c. **Tula-bay** [Тулабай] (Grod., Pril. 105); Kzk. 19th c. **Tula-bay** [Тулабай Джанбаевъ] (Grod., Pril. 123); Kzk. 19th c. **Tula-bay** [Кушай Тулабаевъ] (Grod., Pril. 25). ⇨ **TOLA?**

TULA-BUQA see **TELE-BUƔA**

TULAY see **TOLAY I./II.**

TULAQ   Kzk. 19th c. **Tolaq** [Толакъ Гайдаровъ] (Grod., Pril. 30); Kzk. 19th c. **Tolaq** [Тилъ-Ахмедъ Толаковъ] (Grod., Pril. 83); Kzk. 19th c. **Tulaq** [Тулакъ] (AOK 86); Kzk. 19th c. **Tulaq** [Тулакъ] (AOP 110); Kzk. 19th c. **Tulaq** [Малай Шарифъ Тулаковъ] (Grod., Pril. 148); Kirg. 1820 **Tulaq-batïr** [Тулакъ-батыръ] (Sib. Vest. IX, 109); Kzk. 19th c. **Tulaq-pay** [Тулакпай] (SODž. 110); Kzk. 19th c. **Tulaq-pay** [Тулакпай] (SOK 22, 104); Kzk. 19th c.

Tulaq-pay [Тулакпай] (SOK 48, 72). ✧ 'Leather spread/cover' cf. Alt., Kzk. *tulaq* 'kahles, abgeriebenes Fell; ein Fell, das auf dem Boden ausgebreitet ist, auf dem man sitzt' (Radl. III, 1467). See also **BAY-TULAQ**.

TULAN Kzk. 1822 **Tolan / Tulan?** [دولان / Толан] (MIK IV, 432, 434); Trkm. 1803 **Tulan** [Туланъ Ирназаровъ] (PSZRI XXVII, 139). ✧ I. 'A month (of full Moon)' cf. Alt. (Tel.) *tulan* 'ein Monatsname (nach Werbizki: Februar, März, April november, er tritt dann ein, wenn das Sternbild der Plejaden beim Monde am achten Tage nach dem Vollmonde vorbeigeht)' (Radl. III, 1468); II. 'A five-year-old horse'? cf. Chag. *tolan* 'ein Pferd im fünften Jahre' (Radl. III, 1192); III. 'Be impetuous, be fierce, be angry!' cf. Kzk. *tulan* 'erregt sein, zornig sein' (Radl. III, 1468). See also **AY-TOLAN**.

TULAS Kzk. 19th c. **Tulas-bek** [Туласъ бекъ Басбабековъ] (Grod., Pril. 152). ✧ 'Stopped, ceased' cf. Kzk. *tolas* 'перестать идти, лить (о дожде)' (KzRS).

TULAT Uyg. 12th c. - 14th c. **Tulat** [Tulat / Tolat], a woman slave (Radl., Altuig. 59, Radl., USp. 98-99, DTS, EUTS); Kzk. 19th c. **Tulat-bay** [Тулатбай] (AOAtb. 50).

TULČİ Uzb. 1875 **Tulči** [Тулчи], a guardian (Moskal'cev 40).

TULDÄN Hak.(Blt.) 19th-20th c. **Tuldän** [Тулдäн] (Proben IX, 362).

TULDÏ see **TOLDÏ**

TULΓA Kzk. 19th c. **Tulγa-bay** [Тулгабай] (SOK 170); Kirg. 18th c. **Tulγa-bek** [Тулгабекъ] (Nepljuev 813). ✧ 'Body; lord, chief, important person' cf. Kzk. *tulγa* 'die Figur, Gestalt, der Körper; der Herr, der Befehlshaber, einflussreiche Persönlichkeit' (Radl. III, 1473). See also **BOY, DENE, TEN**.

TULΓANLİ Kzk. 19th c. **Tulγanli-χatun** [Тулганъ-Ли-Хатунъ] (Grod., Pril. 146).

TULΓUN-AY Kirg. 20th c. **Tolγon-ay**, fem. (Nikonov: OSA 161); Kzk. 19th c. **Tulγun-ay** [Тулгунъ-ай], fem. (Grod., Pril. 136). ✧ 'Full moon' (Nikonov, loc. cit.). ⇨ **TOL / TOLΓAN?** + **AY** + suff. *-γun/-γïn*.

TULÏ see **TOLU**

TULÏŠ Uyg. **Tulïš** [Tulïş] (EUTS).

TULKE Kzk. 19th c. **Tulke / Tülke?** [Тульке] (SOV 60). ⇨ **TUL** + suff. *-ke*.

TULQUN see **TOLQUN**

TULQUS Bashk. 1740 **Tulqus** [Бурсей Тулкусев] (MIB I, 435).

TULLAŇ Yak. **Tullaň** [Туллаң] (Pek.).

TULPAR Trkm. 20th c. **Tulpar** [Tulpar], fem. (Zaj. 1971, 338); Trkm. 20th c. **Tulpar** [Тулпар], fem. (TrkmRS 644); Bashk. 1779 **Tulpar** [Тулпар Белекеев] (MIB V, 101); Kzk. 18th c. - 19th c. **Tulpar** [Тулпар] (Тynуšр. 68); Kzk. 19th c. **Tulpar** [Тулпаръ] (SOK 232); Kzk. 19th c. **Tulpar-bek** [Тулпарбек] (SODž. 104). ✧ 'War-horse' cf. Kirg., Kzk. *tulpar* 'das Schlachtross' (Radl. III, 1475), Trkm. *tulpar* 'Тулпар (сказочный конь)' (TrkmRS).

TULTUQ Kzk. 19th c. **Tultuq** [Тультукъ] (SOK 200). ✧ 'Widowhood' cf. Kzk. *tuldŭq* 'die Wittwenschaft' (Radl. III, 1475).

TULU see **TOLU**

TULU-TÄMÜR Maml. 14th c. **Tulu-tämür** [طولو تَمُر] (Sauvaget 51). ✧ I. 'Iron with banner'; II. 'Mirror-iron' cf. Mo. *toli/tuli* 'miroir' (Sauvaget 51). ⇨ **TEMİR**.

TULUY Kzk. 1538 **Tuluy-γoža? / Tuluy-gözä?** [Барашъ Тулуигозинъ] (PSRL XIII, 120). ⇨ **TOLU?**

TULUQ see **TOLUQ**

TULUM Bashk. 1714 **Tulum-bay** [Тулумбай Токаев] (MIB III, 108); Kzk. 1819 **Tulum-bay** [Тулумбай] (MIK IV, 325); Tat. 1557 **Tulum-bek** [Тулумъ-Бекъ Ханикинъ], a princess in the Crimea (Kn. Metriki Lit. 151); Chag. 16th c. **Tulum-beki** [Тулум-беки], fem. (Ivanov 212, 240); Kzk. 19th c. **Tulum-bay** [Мысъ Тулумбай], a cape at the entry of Mertvyj Kultuk (Hanykov, Karta ZK). ✧ I. 'Mop or tussock (of hair), plait (on the temple)' cf. Kuman, Chag., Kzk., Tat.(Bar.) *tulum* 'die Haarflechte', die Haarbüschel über den Schläfen, die man bei den Knaben reicher Leute nicht abrasiert' (Radl. III, 1470, 1471), Kzk., Nog. *tlum, tulum* 'id.' (Budagov I, 752), Bashk. *tolom* 'коса' (BRS/Uraksin); II. 'Leather bottle' cf. Turk. *tulum* 'ein gegorbenes Fell; ein Lederschlauch' (Radl. III, 1470), *tulum* 'id.' (Räs.).

TULUM-BUZAN Tat. 1624 **Tulum-buzan** [Тулумбузан] (Zolotn. 157). ⇨ **TULUM + BUZAN**.

TULUMBET Kzk. 1708 **Tulumbet / Tulum-bek?** [Тюлюмбет / Тюлюмбек?] (MIB I, 239); Kzk. 19th c. **Tulumbet (<Tulunbet?)** [Тулумбетъ-Китты], a field at the entry of Mertvyj Kultuk (Hanykov, Karta ZK). ⇨ **TULUM?** + suffixoid *-bet*.

TULUN see **TOLUN**

TULUS Hak. 19th-20th c. **Tulus** [Тулус] (HRS 352).

TULUSUP Crm. 1558 **Tulusup** [Ссоюндюкъ Тулусуповъ] (PSRL XIII, 287).

TULUŠ see **TOLUŠ**

TUM Kzk. 19th c. **Tum-bay** [Тумбай] (SOK 96).

TUMA Kzk. 19th c. **Tuma** [Тума] (SOK 80); Kzk. 19th c. **Tuma-bay** [Тумабай] (SODž. 104, 150); Kzk. 19th c. **Tuma-bay** [Тумабай] (SOV 60). ✧ 'Offspring'? cf. Tat. *tūma* 'der Nachkomme' (Radl. III, 1517). See also **BAY-TUMA**.

TUMAQ Tat.(Sib.) 1629 **Tїmaq** [Тымак], a prince from Kotov (Miller, Ist. Sib. II, 345, 353, 366, 377); Kzk. 18th c. - 19th c. **Tumaq** [Тумак] (Тynуšр. 74); Kzk. 19th c. **Tumaq-bay** [Тумакбай] (SOV 62); Kzk. 19th c. **Tumaq-pay** [Тумакпай] (SOK 56, 228). ✧ 'A kind of winter cap made of felt' cf. Uyg., Kuman, Chag., Kzk., Tat.(Tüm) *tïmaq / tumaq / tumaχ* 'eine Wintermütze mit Ohrenklappen' (Radl. III, 1342, 1517); II. 'Illegitimate, bastard' (Tat.) (Sattarov). See also **BÏ-TUMAQ, ČOQ-TUMAQ, TOQ-TUMAQ.**

TUMALAY see **TOMALAY**

TUMALÏMA Yak. **Tumalïma** [Тумалыма], a part of the name of a legendary shamaness (Pek.).

TUMAN Kzk. 19th c. **Tïman-bay** [Тыманбай] (SOK 240); Kuman 1419 **Toman** [Jacobum dictum Toman], among the Kumans of Hungary (Gyárfás III, 566); Chuv. 18th-19th c. **Toman** [Томань / Томанъ] (Magn. 85); Chuv. 18th-19th c. **Toman / Tomanka?** [Томанка] (Magn. 85); 10th c. - 13th c. **Tuman** [تومن] (Juwaynï II, 237); 1320 **Tuman** [تومان / Tuman] (Qazw.); Uyg. **Tuman** [Tuman] (EUTS); Selj. 1126, 1127 **Tuman** [تومان / Touman / Koumân? / Koumaz? / Toûmân], an emir (Kamāladdïn II, 236, 237 III, 655, Sauvaire V, 380); Khorezm.? **Tuman** [Туман] (RaD II, 70); Maml. 1309 **Tuman** [طومان] (Dawād. 180, 203); Chag. 16th c. **Tuman** [Мухаммед Туман], an emir (Ivanov 136, 299); Turk. 1330 **Tuman** [الفتى احى طومان / Akhy Thoûmân], from Asia Minor (Ibn Bat. II, 273, 274); Chuv. 18th-19th c. **Tuman** [Томанъ] (Magn. 85); Kzk. 1817, 1819 **Tuman** [تومان / Туман] (MIK IV, 311, 319, 325); Kzk. 19th c. **Tuman** [Томанъ] (AOK 42); Kzk. 19th c. **Tuman** [Туманъ] (AOO 78); Uzb. **Tuman** [Туманъ], a Kipchak Uzbeg (Smirnov, Sultany 41); Selj. 1184 **Tuman / Taman?** [طمان الياروقى], an emir of Imadeddin Zengi (Ibn al-Athïr/Tornb. XI, 327, Ibn al-Athïr: RHCHor I, 661); Selj.? 1187/88 **Tuman / Taman?** [حسام الدين طمان النورى / حسام الدين طمان] / Housam ed-Dîn Thaman] (Abū Šāma: RHCHor IV, 343, 411); Khorezm. /Chag. 1366, 1375 **Tuman-aγa** [Tumán Aghá / Tuman-Aga / Tumanga / Туман-ага], one of Temür's wife (Tar. Rashidi 42, 50, Clavijo 52, Barth., Ulugb. 28, 38, 60, 61, 68, 69, MIT I, 523); Khorezm.? 14th c. **Tuman-bahadur(-qalučï)** [Tumán Bahadur Kaluchi], follower of the Dughlatid Sultan Said (Tar. Rashidi 309); Maml. 1462, 1463, 1469/70 **Tuman-bay** [طومان باى الظاهرى] (Ibn Taghrïb. VII, 706, 708, VIII, 456, 459, 460, Iyās II, 113); Maml. 1496/97 **Tuman-bay** [طومان باى الشريفى] (Iyās II, 365); Maml. 1496/97 **Tuman-bay** [لخاصكى] طومان باى] (Iyās II, 365); Maml. 1496/97 **Tuman-bay** [طومان باى نائب البهسا], governor of Al-Behisā (?) (Iyās II, 366); Maml. 1500 **Tuman-bay** [طومان باى ابوالنصر / Toumanbay], first the mamlūk of Qayt-bay, then a treasurer, later a sultan (Weil, Chalif. II, 379-81, Makrïzï, Khit. I, 244, Iyās III, 28, 72, 257, Mehren XVI, 511, BEO II, 46-47); Maml. 1517 **Tuman-bay**

[طومان باى بن قانصوه], the last Mamlūk sultan, died in 1517 (Iyās II, 269, 332, 369 etc., III, 4, 9, 22 etc., Weil, Chalif. II, 418-31); Kzk. 19th c. **Tuman-bay** [Туманбай] (SODž. 78); **Tuman-tarχan** [ترخان / Туманъ-Тарханъ] (RaD/Ber. II, 131); Khorezm./Chag. 15th. **Tuman-uγlan** [Caruo Toman Vlglan], Clavijo's guide, Temür's retainer (Clavijo 57); Kzk. **Tuman** [Tuman], a village in the Caucasus, near the Northern Kuma (PM Ergh. 117). ✦ I. 'Fog, mist'? (Sattarov), cf. Chag., Kuman, Alt., Kirg., Kzk. etc. *tuman* 'der Nebel, die Finsterniss' (Radl. III, 1518), for the Kuman name see also Rásonyi, KÖA 134, Anthr. 146, Bas. 14; II. 'Ten thousand warriors (tümen)'? See also **BEK-TUMAN, ÏŠ.**

TUMAN-BAY-QARA Maml. 1516 **Tuman-bay-qara** [طومان باى قرا] (Iyās III, 3, 73). ➪ **TUMAN + BAY + QARA.**

TUMAN-BUΓAY Khorezm. 14th c. **Tuman-buγay(-salduz)** [Tumán Bughái Salduz], Temür's officer (Tar. Rashidi 36). ➪ **TUMAN + BUΓAY.**

TUMAN-ÏÑÜL Uyg. 12th c. - 14th c. **Tuman-iñül** [Tuman (Tümän)] (Radl., USp. 130-131, DTS). ✦ 'Fog/mist-Ïñül' (Blagova 1997, 704).

TUMAN-QAPAQ Khorezm./Chag. 14th c. **Tuman-qapaq-χan** [Tumán Kapak Khán], Temür's officer (Tar. Rashidi 36). ➪ **TUMAN + QAPAQ?**

TUMAN-TEMÏR Maml.? 1398/99 **Tuman-temir** [تمان تمر الاشتتمرى] (Ibn Taghrïb. VI, 10, 16, 72); Maml. 1405/06 **Tuman-temir** [تمان تمر النا صرى] (Ibn Taghrïb. VI, 130, 245); Maml. 1410 **Tuman-temir** [تمان تمر اليوسفى] (Ibn Taghrïb. VI, 341, 343, 353 etc.); Turk.? 1361 **Tuman-temir** [تمان تمر العمرى] (Iyās I, 209); Turk. 1378/79 **Tuman-temir** [تمان تمر العثمانى] (Iyās I, 244). ➪ **TUMAN + TEMÏR.**

TUMANČA Bashk. 1769 **Tumanča** [Туманча Кудашманов] (MIB IV/1, 334); Bashk. 1778 **Tumanča** [Туманча Ювашкин (Ювашка)] (MIB V, 68, 107, 154); Bashk. 1798 **Tumanča** [Туманчинъ] (PSZRI XXV, 196); Kzk. 19th c. **Tumanča** [Туманча] (SOK 184). ➪ **TUMAN + suff. -ča.**

TUMANČÏ Bashk. 1756 **Tumančï** [Туманчи Мрясов] (MIB IV/1, 109); Kzk. 19th c. **Tumančï** [Туманчи] (SOK 108, 272); Kirg. 1823 **Tumančï(у)** [Туманчий Самардиновъ] (TOUAK XXIV, 137). ➪ **TUMAN + suff. -čï.**

TUMAR Trkm. 20th c. **Tumar** [Tumar], fem. (Zaj. 1971, 338); Trkm. 20th c. **Tumar** [Тумар], fem. (TrkmRS 645); Kzk. 19th c. **Tumar-bay** [Тумарбай] (SOK 156); Trkm. **Tumar-eǰe**, fem. (?); Kirg. **Tumar-yan** [Тумар-Jaн], one of the forty followers of Aq-sayqal (Proben V, 394 /397/). ✦ 'Charm' cf. Chag., Kzk. *tumar* 'ein Amulett, ein Talisman' (Radl. III,

1519), Trkm. *tumar* 'украшение в форме большого треугольника, надеваемое женщинами через плечо; амулет, талисман' (TrkmRS).

TUMAR-BAS   Kzk. 19th c. **Tumar-bas** (Ljutš 74). ⇨ **TUMAR + BAŠ.**

TUMAS   Bashk. 1740 **Tumas** [Кинзягул Тумасов] (MIB I, 397). ⇨ **TUMA?** + suff. *-s*.

TUMAT   Kzk. 19th c. **Tumat** [Туматъ] (AOK 90).

TUMATAY   Kzk. 19th c. **Tumatay** [Туматай] (SOV 80). ⇨ **TUMA** + suff. *-tay.*

TUMĀ   Hak.(Sag.) 19th-20th c. **Tumā** [Тума], an evil spirit (Proben IX, 611). ✧ I. '(Hakas) Fetish, idol' (Butanaev); II. 'Epidemic, fever'? cf. Shor *tuma* 'die Seuche, das Fieber' (Radl. III, 1517).

TUMČAY   Bashk. 1758 **Tumčay** [Тумчай Кулумбетев] (MIB IV/1, 173).

TUMDUR see **TUMTUR**

TUMΓAN   **Tumγan** [تومغان / Toumghan], a Chingisid (Abulg./Desm. 188).

TUMSUQ   Kzk. 19th c. **Tumsuq** [Тумсукъ] (SODž. 64). ✧ 'Beak' cf. Kzk. *tumsuq* 'der Schnabel; das Vorgebirge' (Radl. III, 1526).

TUMTUR   Uyg. 12th c. - 14th c. **Tumtur / Tumdur** [Tumdur / Tumtur] (Radl., USp. 213, 249, 255, DTS, EUTS).

TUN-QATAR see **TUÑ-ΓATAR**

TUN-QOΓAT   Uzb. 1887 **Tun-qoγat** [Тункогатъ] (Moskal'cev 34).

TUN-ZAQ   Kzk. 1819 **Tun-zaq / Tün-zaq?** [Тунзак] (MIK IV, 324). ✧ I. 'Coat-long'; II. 'Night-long'? cf. Kzk. *tün* 'gece, karanlık vakit' (KzTS). ⇨ **TON + UZAQ?**

TUNA   Turk. 16th c. **Tuna** [طونه], fem. (Ongan, Ank. II). ✧ 'Danube' cf. Turk. *tuna* 'die Donau' (Radl. III, 1439, 1440).

TUNAČİ   Kirg. 18th c. **Tunačï-batïr** [Туначи-Батыръ] (Neрjuev 804).

TUNAΓAŠ   Hak. 19th c. **Tunaγaš** [Тунаҕаш] (Katanov, Otč. 12).

TUNALİ   Kzk. 1809 **Tunalï-sultan** [تناُلی سلطان] (MIK IV, 242).

TUNALİÑSA   Yak. **Tunalïñsa / Tunalïqsa** [Туналыӈса / Туналыкса], fem. (Pek.). ✧ 'Bright, shining' (Pek.).

TUNAN   Kzk. 1819 **Tunan** [Тунан] (MIK IV, 325).

TUNDAR see **DELÜ-DUNDAR**

TUNΓUN   Bashk. 1756 **Tunγun** [Тунгун Культмышев] (MIB IV/1, 121); Bashk. 1762 **Tunγun** [Тунгун Япаров] (MIB IV/1, 251); Bashk. 1790 **Tunγun** [Тунгун Мурзакаев] (MIB V, 284).

TUNİSE   Hak. 19th-20th c. **Tunise** [Тунисе], fem. (HRS 355).

TUNNUQ   Bashk. 1756 **Tunnuq** [Туннук Аллагузин] (MIB IV/1, 109). ✧ 'Fur, enough for a furcoat' cf. Tat.

tunnïq, tunlïq 'genug für einen Pelz' (Radl. III, 1441).

TUNU   Crm. **Tunu-bäk** [Туну Бäк] (Proben VII, 160). ⇨ **TİNİ?**

TUÑ-ATAR see **TUÑ-ΓATAR**

TUÑ-ΓATAR   Kzk. 19th c. **Tun-atar** [Джаманъ-Сари Тунатаровъ] (Grod., Pril. 45); Bashk. 1737 **Tun-qatar** [Тункатар Куркачиков] (MIB I, 309); Uzb. 19th c. **Tun-qatar** [Mad-Youssouf-Tounkatar] (Nalivkin-Dozon 151); Bashk. 1794 **Tuñ-atar** [Тунгатар Абезгильдин] (MIB V, 154); Kzk. 19th c. **Tuñ-atar** [Тунгатаръ] (AOA 110, 154); Kzk. 19th c. **Tuñ-atar** [Тунгатаръ] (AOK 6); Kzk. 19th c. **Tuñ-atar** [Тунгатаръ] (SOV 26). ✧ I. 'He who will travel/ride by night' cf. Kzk. *tuñqat-* <*tuñ-qat-* <*tün+qat-* 'die Nach durch reiten' (Radl. III, 1435), consider Kzk. PN *Tuñγatar* (Žanuzakov - Esbaeva); II. 'Night is coming'? cf. Türk., Uyg., Kuman, Alt., Kirg., Kzk., etc. *tün* 'die Nacht' (Radl. III, 1548) and PNs *Tañ-atar*.

TUÑ-QARATTÏ   Tuv. 19th c. **Tuñ-qarattï-χan** (<**Tuñ-qara-attï-χan**) [Тунгъ Каратты ханъ], a character in a tale mentioned also as Qarattï-χan or Qarättï-qān (Potanin IV, 373). ✧ 'Tuñ(?) having a black horse'. ⇨ **QARA-ATTÏ.**

TUÑ-QAT   Kzk. **Tuñ-qat** [Tunkat / Туӈкат], from the Jaγal-bay tribe (Proben III, 47 (62)). ✧ 'Travel/ride by night!'.

TUÑA-YÏLAN see **TOÑA-YÏLAN**

TUÑALİ   Maml.? 14th c. **Tuñali? / Deñkli?** [طنكلی] (Zetterst. 240, 241). ⇨ **TUNALİ?**

TUÑAŠA   Kzk. 19th c. **Tuñaša / Tuñača** [Кочарбай Тунгачаевъ] (Grod., Pril. 81); Kzk. 1794, 1817 **Tuñaša / Tuñaša-sultan / Tuñača-sultan** [طونكاچه / طونكاچه سلطان / Тунгаша / Тунгача], a sultan of the Kirey tribe of Middle Horde (Orta Žüz) (MIK IV, 307, Sib. Vest. IX, 105). ⇨ **TOÑA** + dim. suff. *-ša.*

TUÑUSÄY   Bashk. 1756 **Tuñusäy** [Янаберды Тунгусяев] (MIB IV/1, 132). + suff. *-äy.*

TUÑUŠ   Kzk. 19th c. **Tuñuš-pay** [Тункушпай] (SODž. 76); Kzk. 19th c. **Tuñuš-pay** [Тунгушпай] (SOK 130, 284, 290). ✧ 'The first-born son' cf. Chag., Kar. *tunγuč* 'der erstgeborene Sohn' (Radl. III, 1441).

TUÑUZ see **TOÑUZ**

TUOQAYĀN   Yak. **Tuoqayān** [Туокајан] (Pek.).

TUOÑXĀNÏ   Yak. **Tuoñχānï** [Туоӈханы], a fabulous hero (Pek.).

TUORALJÏN   Yak. **Tuoraljïn** [Туоралцын], fem. (Pek.). ✧ 'Resisting, disagreeing' cf. Yak. *tuora* 'поперечный; противоположный, противный' + suff. *-ljïn* (Pek.).

TUOSAYA   Yak. **Tuosaya** [Туоcаја] (Pek.).

TUPA   Uyg. **Tupa** [Tupa] (EUTS).

TUPAY see **TOPAY**

TUPALİ   Uyg. 12th c. - 14th c. **Tupali** [tupali], a demon (DTS). ⇨ **TUPA?** + suff. *-li / -lï.*

TUPČĬ see **TOPČĬ I.**

TUR Yürük 1543 **Dur** [Dur] (Gökb., Rum. 102); Yürük 1543 **Dur** [طور / Dur], from the Yürüks of Kocacık, Turkey (Gökb., Rum. 102, 184, 222 etc.); Kzk. 19th c. **Dur** [Дуръ] (SODž. 122); Turk. 1532 **Dur-aγa** [Dur aga], an „ulûfeci" (clerk/secretary of Janissary guards, or palace servants) among the Turks in Szolnok, Hungary (Velics-Kamm. I, 74); Yürük 1543 **Dur-baba** [طور بابا / Durbaba], from the Yürüks of Kocacık, Turkey (Gökb., Rum. 102, 186, 188); Kzk. 19th c. **Dur-bay** [Отавли Дурбаевъ] (Grod., Pril. 35); Yürük 1543 **Dur-beg** [Dur Beg] (Gökb., Rum. 194, 202, 222); Yürük 1543 **Dur-begi** [طور بكی / Durbeği], from the Yürüks of Kocacık, Turkey (Gökb., Rum. 103, 206); Yürük 1543 **Dur-bey** [طور بك / Durbey] (Gökb., Rum. 102); Yürük 16th c. **Dur-χan** [طور خان / Dur-han], from the Yürüks of Kocacık, Turkey (Gökb., Rum. 104); Yürük 1543 **Dur-χoĭa** [Dur Hoca] (Gökb., Rum. 192); Yürük 1543 **Dur-qul** [Durkul] (Gökb., Rum. 102, 189, 193, 208, 210, 225, 239,); Turk. 1467 **Dur-melek** [Dur Melek], Abdallah's son (Gökb., Ed. 345); Selj. 1332 **Dur-melik** [دور ملك], Mīr Arslan's daughter (Uzunçarş., Küt. I, 92); Turk. 1485 **Dur-paša-χatun** [Dur Paşa Hatun] (Gökb., Ed. 241); Yürük 1543 **Dur-šah** [طورشاه / Durşah], from the Yürüks of Kocacık, Türkey (Gökb., Rum. 101, 190, 205, 206); Kzk. **Tur-bek** [Турбек], a character from the epic „Put' Abaja" by M. O. Auezov (Espaeva 1984, 231); Chuv. 18th-19th c. **Tor-bay** [Торбай] (Magn. 85); Kzk. 19th c. **Tor-bay** [Торбай] (AOA 114); Kzk. 19th c. **Tor-bay** [Торбай] (SODž. 150); Kzk. 19th c. **Tor-bay** [Торбай] (SOK 234); Chuv. 18th-19th c. **Tor-batïr** [Торбатыръ] (Magn. 86); Tat. **Tor-χan** / **Salam-tor-χan** [صالام تورخان / Салам-Торхан], a character in a tale (Nasyrov-Poljakov 5); Kzk. **Tor-sulü** / **Tor-sülü?** [Торсулю Дихановъ], fem. (Sb. Syr-D. IX, 48); Uyg. **Tur-bay** [Turbay] (EUTS); Uyg. 12th c. - 14th c. **Tur-bay** [Turbai] (Radl., USp. 10, DTS); Maml. 1433/34, 1434, 1438/39, 1457 **Tur-bay** [طرباى الظاهرى], a governor of Tripolis (Ibn Taghrīb. VI, 59, 87, 700, 836 VII, 36, 593, Weil, Chalif. II, 192); Maml. 1461 **Tur-bay** [طرباى الظاهرى], a governor (Ibn Taghrīb. VIII, 428); Maml. 1467 **Tur-bay** [طرباى الظاهرى البواب], a janitor (Ibn Taghrīb. VII, 827, 832 etc., VIII, 605, 620); Kzk. **Tur-bay** [Турбай] (Sb. Syr-D. IX, 58); Kzk. 19th c. **Tur-bay** [Турбай] (SOV 28); Turk. 1587 **Tur-bāli** [Tur Bali], an „ulûfeci" (clerk/secretary of Janissary guards, or palace servants) among the Turks in Szolnok, Hungary (Velics-Kamm. I, 74); Kzk. 19th c. **Tur-bek / Tur-pek?** [Турпекъ] (SODž. 100); Yürük 1551 **Tur-χoĭa / Dur-χoĭa?** [طور خواجه بن طورمش / Turhoca ibn Turmuş] (Gökçen 28); Uyg. 1331 **Tur-qatun** [Tur-Katun], fem. (Chwol., Syr.-nest. II, 72); Yürük 1543 **Tur-qul** [Turkul] (Gökb., Rum. 215); Uyg. 12th c. - 14th c. **Tur-pay?** [turpaj] (DTS); Uyg. 1336, 1339 **Tur-terim / Tur-tärim** [Tur-Terim / Tur-Tarim], fem. (Chwol., Syr.-nest. II, 78, 90); Kzk. 19th c. **Tur-žan** [Туржанъ] (SODž. 46); Kzk. 19th c. **Tur-žan** [Туржанъ] (SOK 92); Bashk. 1756 **Tor** [Top], tributary of the Nugush river (MIB IV/1, 93, 118); Tat. 18th c. **Tur-bek / Tübäk?** [Турбякъ (Тюбякъ)], a village in the district of Arsk (Korsakov). ✧ 'Be alive!, Stay (with us)!, Survive!; Stop! Enough!; Live long!' (Espaeva 1984, 231). Such names were given when babies died in the family earlier. Cf. Alt., Hak., Kirg., Kzk. etc. *tur-* 'stehen, aufstehen; stehen bleiben, anhalten, leben, wohnen' (Radl. IV, 1442), Crm., Turk. *dur-* 'id.' (Radl. IV, 1787). See also **BEK-TUR, EL-TUR, İSÄN-TUR, ŠÜK-TUR.**

TUR-ALİ Turk. 1478 **Dur-ali** [Dur Ali] (Gökb., Ed. 136); Turk. 1491 **Dur-ali** [Dur Ali bin Mehmed] (Gökb., Ed. 103); Turk. 1543 **Dur-ali** [Dur Ali] (Velics-Kamm. I, 17); Turk. 1580 **Dur-ali** [Dur Ali] (Dávid); Yürük 1453 **Dur-ali** [Dur Ali] (Gökb., Rum. 179, 192, 202); Tat. 1543 **Dur-ali** [Durali] (Gökb., Rum. 234); Turk. 16th c. **Dur-ali-bey** [Dur Ali Bey] (Gökb., Ed. 556); Maml.? 1400 **Tur-ali** [طر على] (Ibn Taghrīb. VI, 370); Yürük 1575 **Tur-ali** [Turali] (Gökçen 49); Kkalp. 20th c. **Tur-γaliy** [Турғалий] (KkRS 776). ⇨ **TUR + ALİ.**

TUR-BĀLİ Yürük 1543 **Dur-bāli** [Dur Bâli] (Gökb., Rum. 196); Tat. 1543 **Dur-bāli** [Durbâli] (Gökb., Rum. 242); Yürük 1543 **Tur-bāli** [Turbâli] (Gökb., Rum. 178); Yürük 1543 **Tur-bāli** [Turbâli] (Gökb., Rum. 188). ⇨ **TUR + BĀLİ.**

TUR-BEKEY Kzk. 19th c. **Tur-bekey / Tur-pekey?** [Турпекей] (AOK 126).

TUR-GEL Kzk. 19th c. **Tur-gel** [Тургель] (SOK 216). ⇨ **TUR + KEL.**

TUR-GELDİ Kzk. 19th c. **Tur-geldi** [Тургельды] (Valihanov, Soč. 393). ⇨ **TUR/TÖRE? + KELDİ.**

TUR-ГALİY see **TUR-ALİ**

TUR-MAMBET Kzk. 1846 **Tur-mambet** [Турмамбет Кумбасов] (MKOP 101); Kirg. 18th c. **Tur-mambet** [Турмамбетъ] (Nepljuev 809). ⇨ **TUR? + MAMBET.**

TUR-MAMET Bashk. 1777 **Tur-mamet** [Турмаметъ] (Vel.-Zern., Bašk. 4). ⇨ **TUR? + MAMET.**

TUR-MUXAMET Kzk. 1809 **Tur-muχamet** [Бекмухаметъ Турмухаметовъ] (TOUAK XXIV, 37). ⇨ **TUR + MUXAMMED.**

TUR-NİYAZ Kzk. 19th c. **Tur-niyaz** [Турніязъ] (AOO 62). ⇨ **TUR + NİYAZ.**

TUR-TEMİR Crm. 17th c. **Tur-temir-murza** [Туръ-темиръ-мурза], Kantemir's son (Smirnov, Krym. 521).

⇨ TUR + TEMİR.

TURA Uyg. **Tura** [Tura] (EUTS); Tat. 1707 **Tura** [Юнус Турабаев] (MIB III, 32); Uzb. 19th c. **Tura** [Тура] (SKSO III, 156); NUyg. 19th c. **Tura** [Hakim Khan Tura] (Hedin, En färd I, 367); 1484 **Tura-bay** [طرباى الاشتر الابرهيمى الاينالى] (Iyās II, 224, III, 275, Weil II, 368, 390); Maml. 1287/88 **Tura-bay** [طرباى الظاهرى الخشقدمى] (Iyās II, 117); Maml.? 1400/01 **Tura-bay** [طرباى بن عبد الله] (Iyās I, 330); Maml. 1421 **Tura-bay** [طرباى الظاهرى] (Iyās II, 14); Maml. 1495/96, 1516 **Tura-bay** [طرباى الشريفى] (Iyās II, 305, 332, 371 etc., III, 52); Maml. 1516 **Tura-bay** [صرباى], governor of Safad (Iyās III, 16, 39); Maml. 1520 **Tura-bay** [طرباى بن قراجا] (Iyās III, 244); Tat. 1707 **Tura-bay** [Турабаев] (MIB III, 32); Bashk. 1761 **Tura-bay** [Турабай Кулкаев] (MIB IV/1, 214); Kzk. 1846 **Tura-bay** [Турабай Машатов], a biy (MKOP 152); Kzk. 19th c. **Tura-bay** [Турабай] (AOAtb. 62); Kzk. 19th c. **Tura-bay** [Турабай] (SKSO VIII, 202); Uzb. 20th c. **Tura-bay** [Toura-bay], a basmačï leader (Castagné 88); Maml. 1516 **Tura-bay(-qara)** [طرباى قرا] (Iyās III, 52); Kzk. 19th c. **Tura-ǰan** [Тураджанъ] (Grod., Pril. 100); Turk. 16th c. **Tura-χan** [Turahan] (Ongan, Ank. II); Turk. 1439, 1456 **Tura-χan-bey** [طور خان بك / Τουραχάνης / Turahan Bey], a commander and governor, died in 1456 (Āšikp. 115, 115, 122, 172, Baştav 73, 74, 81, 84, 88 etc., Byz. Turc. 319); Kzk. 19th c. **Tura-qul / Turaq-ul?** [Туракулъ] (Grod., Pril. 160); Uyg. 12th c. - 14th c. **Tura-tutuq** [Tura tutuq] (Radl., USp. 299, DTS); *TN:* Kzk. 19th c. **Tura-bay** [Турабай], a tomb east of the Caspian Sea (IIRGO XVI). ✧ 'Fortress' (Blagova 1997, 710), resort, refuge; house; shield(!)' cf. Uyg. *tura* 'укрепленное жилище крепость' (DTS), Uyg., Alt., Hak. *tura* 'das Haus, das Gebäude, der Wohnort' (Radl. II, 1446), Chag. 'das Schild, die Barrikade, die Bustwehr' (Radl. III, 1447), cf. also *tura* 'vermögend, stark' <Skr. *tura* (Justi 328, 329). See also **ǰAMAN-TURA, ǰAN-TURA, QAN-TURA, QÏŠ-TURA, TAŠ-TURA.**

TURA-KELDİ Kzk. 19th c. **Tura-keldi** [Tura Keldi Savgan] (Hedin, En färd I, 166, 167). ✧ 'Shield (=defender) came'? ⇨ **TURA + KELDİ.**

TURA-KELSÄ Kzk. **Tura-kelsä** [Туракелься Койпабаевъ] (Sb. Syr-D. 48).

TURA-QÏLNAP Uyg. 13th c. - 14th c. **Tura-qïlnap / Tura-kilnäp?** [Tura Kilnap], fem. (Chwol., Syr.-nest. (NF) 51). ⇨ **TURA.**

TURA-TEMİR see **TURAY-TEMİR**

TURA-TEMİR Tat.(GH) **Tura-temir** [Туратемеръ] (PSRL XVI, 55); Tat.(GH)? 13th c. **Tura-temir** [طراتمر / Туратемиръ], a Kipchak emir (Baybars/Tizeng. I, 86, 109); Tat.(GH) 1482 **Tura-temir** [Туратемиръ] (PSRL (Russk. Hr.) I, 402); Tat.(GH)? **Tura-temür / Tura-timür?** [Тура-Тимур] (RaD II, 69). ✧ 'Shield/Fortress-iron'. ⇨ **TURA + TEMİR.**

TURA-TEMÜR see **TURAY-TEMİR**

TURAB see **TURAP**

TURAǰAQ Hak.(Blt.) 19th-20th c. **Turaǰaq** [Турацак] (Proben IX, 362). ✧ 'A small house, building' (Butanaev), cf. Hak.(Sag.) *turaǰaq*, Alt.(Tel.) *turačaq* 'ein kleines Häuschen' (Radl. III, 1450). ⇨ **TURA +** dim. suff. *-ǰaq / -čaq.*

TURAY see **TORAY**

TURAY-TEMİR Tat.(GH)? 1282 **Turay-temir** [Тurайтемиръ], a commander of the Horde (PSRL X, 160). ⇨ **TORAY + TEMİR.**

TURAYQA Tat. 1675, 1686 **Turayqa** [Турайка / Турайко Байгозинъ] (Kurdjumov 3, Kungursk. akty 24, 121). ⇨ **TORAY + suff. -qa.**

TURAQ I. Turk. 1483 **Duraq** [Durak bin Temirtaş] (Gökb., Ed. 96); Turk. 1540 **Duraq** [Durak], chief of the Uzunlar tribe according to a defter of Diyarbekir, Turkey (Demirtaş 58); Turk. 1552, 1565 **Duraq** (Dávid); Turk. 1583 **Duraq** [طوراق / Durak] (Ongan, Ank. I, 155); Turk. 20th c. **Duraq** [Durak] (Önder, Hınıs); Yürük 1543 **Duraq** [Durak] (Gökb., Rum. 188, 191, 196, 197, 200 etc.); Tat. 1543 **Duraq** [Durak] (Gökb., Rum. 233); Turk. 15th c. **Duraq-čelebi** [Durak Çelebi] (Gökb., Ed. 82); Chuv. 18th-19th c. **Turak** [Туракъ] (Magn. 87); Pecheneg 1050 **Turaq** [Τυράχ], a commander of the army (Byz. Turc. 330); Turk. 1563 **Turaq** [Turak], a spahi (cavalry soldier) in the region of Pápa, Hungary (Velics-Kamm. II, 300); Kzk. 19th c. **Turaq** [Туракъ] (AOP 46); Turk. 1561 **Turaq-aγa** [Turak aga], an officer in Esztergom, Hungary (Velics-Kamm. I, 129); Oghuz / Selj.? **Tuzaq / Turaq?** [تنوزاق / توراق], forefather of the Ottoman dynasty (Āšikp. 5, Nešrī). ✧ 'Dwelling (place); stationary; he who will live/survive' cf. Crm., Turk. *durak* 'Ort, wo man sich aufhält, steht, der Wohnort; unbeweglich, stagnirend' (Radl. III, 1787), Maml. *turaq* 'koyulaşmış süt; durak' (AH), Chag. *turaq* [dwelling place, location, event, state] (Radl. III, 1448). See also **AQ-TURAQ.**

TURAQ II. Hak. 19th-20th c. **Turaq** [Турак] (HRS 352); Hak.(Sag.) 19th-20th c. **Turaq** [Турак] (Katanov, Otč. 8); Hak.(Sag.) 19th-20th c. **Turāq / Duraq** [Турак / Дурак] (Proben IX, 432). ✧ 'Fool' (Katanov) cf. R. *durak* 'id.'.

TURAL Kzk. 19th c. **Tural** [Туралъ] (Grod., Pril. 23); Kzk. 19th c. **Tural** [Караджанъ Тураловъ] (Grod., Pril. 95); Kzk. 19th c. **Tural-bay** [Туралбай] (Grod., Pril. 164). ✧ 'Recover, recuperate, fatten! cf. Kzk. *toral-* 'поправляться, полнеть' (KzRS).

TURALÏ Kzk. 19th c. **Turalï** [Туралы] (AOK 138);

Turk. 15th c. **Turalï-bäy / Tur-ali-bey?** [Τουραλίπεης], an Ottoman commander of the army (Byz. Turc. 319); Trkm. 1348 **Turalï-bäy / Tur-ali-bey?** [Τουραλίπεης], a commander of the army (Byz. Turc. 319). ⇨ **TURA** + suff. *-lï*. See also **QAN-TURALÏ**.

TURALÏQ Tat.(GH) 1327 **Turalïq** [Туралыкъ], prince of the Horde, commander of ten thousand soldiers (PSRL VII, 200, X, 194, XXIII, 102). ⇨ **TURA?** + suff. *-lïq*.

TURAN I. Oghuz/Trkm. 14th c. - 15th c. **Duran** [Düren / Düzen / Дуран], Alp-Rustem's father (DQorq. 78, 88, 100, 240); Turk. 1583 **Duran** [طوران / Duran], fem. (Ongan, Ank. I, 155); Kzk. 19th c. **Toran** [Торанъ] (AOP 38); Yürük 1543 **Turan** [Turan] (Gökb., Rum. 205). ❖ 'Existing, living, standing' (Bese 13, Erol II.), 'Living, surviving' cf. Uyg., Alt., Hak., Kirg., Kzk. etc. *tur-* 'stehen, aufstehen; stehen bleiben, anhalten; leben, wohnen' (Radl. III, 1442), Crm., Turk. *dur-* 'stehen, anhalten; wohnen, bleiben' (Radl. III, 1787). ⇨ **TUR** + dev. n. suff. *-an*. See also **TURΓAN, BEK-TURAN, ÖZ-YİGÄN-ALP-TURAN**.

TURAN II. Kzk. 19th c. **Tran** (<Turan) [Транъ] (AOA 142); Kzk. 19th c. **Tran** (<Turan) [Транъ] (SODž. 36); Kzk. 19th c. **Tran-bay** (<Turan-bay) [Транбай] (AOP 118); Kzk. 19th c. **Turam-bay** (<Turan-bay) [Турамбай] (SOK 36); Türk 7th-9th c. **Turan** [Turan] (ETY III, 61); Selj. 11th c. - 12th c. **Turan** [عماد الدولة توران / Turan] (Qazw. 446); Kzk. 19th c. **Turan** [Назаръ Турановъ], a biy (Grod., Pril. 25); Kzk. 19th c. **Turan** [Туранъ Алиевъ] (SKSO VIII, 206); Kzk. 19th c. **Turan** [Туранъ Атамухамедовъ] (SKSO VIII, 206); Kzk. 19th c. **Turan** [Туранъ] (SOV 138); Kzk. 19th c. **Turan** [Туранъ] (SOV 76); Kzk. 19th c. **Turan-bay** [Туранбай] (AOA 154); Oghuz? 1228 **Turan-melik**, a Menguchekid (Mengücek) princess, mentioned in an inscription of Divrigi (CIA 3/I, 77-78); Oghuz 11th c. **Turan-šah** [Tūrānšāh], the Ghaznavid Ibrahim's (1058-1099) son (Justi 330); Selj. 11th c. **Turan-šah** [Туран-шах] (RaD I/2, 103); Selj. 1085 **Turan-šah** [بن قاورد تورانشاه / Turanšāh], Qawurd's (Qara-arslan-beg's) son, the sultan of Kirman (1085-1097) (Qazw. 479, Justi 330); Selj. 1169/70, 1173, 1175 **Turan-šah** [شمس الدولة تورانشاه / تورانشاه بن أيوب / Tourân-Chah], Saladin's (Salāḫ ed-Dīn's) brother, died in 1180 (Ibn al-Athīr, Atab.: RHCHor II/2, 258, Kamāladdīn II, 339, 340, Abulfidā IV, 26, Justi 330); Selj. 1183 **Turan-šah** [تورانشاه / Turanšāh], Toyrul-šah's son from Kirman, died in 1183 (Qazw. 479, Justi 330); Maml. 1249 **Turan-šah** [Turanschah], the Ayyubid Malik al-'Ādil's grand-son from Egypt, died in 1250 (Reg. Hieros. 309, Justi 330); Maml. 1335 **Turan-šah**

[توران شاه بن الملك الصالح], an Ayyūbīd (Dawād. 387, Iyās I, 85-98); Chag. 16th c. **Turan-šah** [Тураншах] (Ivanov 198, 202, 204, 205, 209). ❖ 'Turan' (Toponym), cf. Uyg. *Turan* 'die turanische Tiefebene' (Radl. III, 1448). „(*Tūrān šāh*) Ce nom veut dire *roi d'orient*. L'orient a été appelé *Toûrân*, parce que c'est le pays des Turcs et que les Persans nomment les Turcs *Tourkân*; puis ils ont altéré ce mot et ont prononcé *Toûrân*." (Ibn Khallikān, cited by Sauvaire 407-408).

TURAP Trkm. 1825 **Turab-biy** [Тураб-бий] (MIT II, 223); Kzk. 19th c. **Turap** [Турабъ] (Grod., Pril. 168); Kzk. 19th c. **Turap** [Турапъ] (SKSO VIII, 222); Kzk. 19th c. **Turap** [Турапъ] (SODž. 150); Kzk. 19th c. **Turap** [Турапъ] (SOV 138); Uzb. 19th c. **Turap** [Турапъ Таджіевъ] (SKSO III, 158); Uzb. 19th c. **Turap** [Турапъ] (SKSO III, 164); Uzb. 19th c. **Turap** [Суяркулъ Тураповъ] (SKSO III, 168); Uzb. 1706 **Turāb-bi** [تراب بى / Turāb Bi] (Buchari 288). ❖ 'Horse radish' (Ar.) (Žanuzakov).

TURAR Kzk. 19th c. **Trar / Turar** [Траръ] (SOK 230); Kzk. 19th c. **Turar-bek** [Турарбекъ] (SODž. 64). ❖ 'Stays, remains, survives' cf. cf. Uyg., Alt., Hak., Kirg., Kzk. etc. *tur-* 'stehen, aufstehen; stehen bleiben, anhalten; leben wohnen' (Radl. III, 1442).

TURARMAN Kzk. 19th c. **Turarman** [Турарманъ] (SOV 28). ⇨ **TURAR** + suff. *-man*.

TURAŠ Kzk. 19th c. **Turaš** [Турашъ] (SODž. 4). ⇨ **TURA** + suff. *-š*.

TURAT Kzk. 19th c. **Turat** [Туратъ] (SODž. 50).

TURĀXAYDĀN Yak. **Turāχaydān** [Ытык Турахаідан], a spirit of the upper world (Pek.).

TURĀQ see **TURAQ II**.

TURBATLÏ Oghuz/Trkm.? **Turbatlï** [Tourbatli] (Abulg./Desm.); Oghuz/Trkm. 13th c. **Turbatlï** [توربـاتلى / Tourbatli / Турбатлы] (Abulg./Desm. 18, 28, Abulg./Kon. 525). ❖ 'With good (outward) looks/appearance'? cf. Kzk. *turpat* 'der Anstand, die gute Haltung; das schöne Aussere (der Menschen und der Thiere)' (Radl. III, 1463) + suff. *-lï*.

TURČA Kzk. 19th c. **Turča** [Турча] (SODž. 94). ⇨ **TUR?** + dim. suff. *-ča*.

TURČÏ Uyg. 12th c. - 14th c. **Turčï** [Turčï / Turçı] (Radl., USp. 5, 21-23, 130-131, 169-70, Le Coq, Urkunden 458-59, DTS, EUTS); Maml. 1320, 1323 **Turčï** [سيف الدين طرجى], an emir of the assembly (Iyās I, 161, Dawād. 309); Uyg. 12th c. - 14th c. **Turčï-baqšï** (DTS); Tat.(GH)? **Turϊ / Turčï?** [Турджи] (RaD II, 75). ❖ 'Stand! Stay! May He Live!'. ⇨ **TUR** + fut. optative suff. *-čï*.

TURD-ALİ see **TURDÏ-ALİ**

TURDÏ Turk. 1580 **Durdï** (Dávid); Trkm. 1859 **Durdï** [Дурды] (ZIRGOÊtn. I, 208); Trkm. 1879-1881 **Durdï** [Dourdi] (O'Donovan I, 208); Trkm. 20th c. **Durdï**

[Durdï] (Zaj. 1971, 334); Trkm. 1745 **Durdï-behadïr** [Дурды-бехадыр], from the Yomut tribe (MIT II, 175); Turk. 15th c. **Durdï-bey** [Durdı Bey] (Gökb., Ed. 344); Trkm. 1851 **Durdï-quli-χan** [Дурды-кули-хан], from the Yomut tribe (MIT II, 298); Turk. 1583 **Durdu** [طوردى] (Ongan, Ank. I, 155); Yürük 1543 **Durdu** [Durdu] (Gökb., Rum. 208); Tat. 1543 **Durdu** (Gökb., Rum. 235); Turk. 1456 **Durdu-χan** [Durdu Han], a dervish (Gökb., Ed. 194); Chag. 16th c. **Turdï** [Турды Тиргер] (Ivanov 290, 292); Kzk. 19th c. **Turdï** [Турди] (Grod., Pril. 153); Kzk. 19th c. **Turdï** [Турды, Турдіевъ] (SKSO VIII, 206); Kzk. 1914 **Turdï** (Nazaroff 181); Kkalp. 20th c. **Turdï** [Турды] (KkRS 776); Uzb. 19th c. **Turdï** [Караджанъ Турдыевъ] (SKSO III, 170); Uzb. 20th c. **Turdï** [Турди] (Begmatov 1984, 200, 204); Uzb. 20th c. **Turdï-ali** [Турдиали] (Begmatov 1984, 204); Uzb. 20th c. **Turdï-ây** [Турдиой], fem. (Begmatov 1984, 204); Kkalp. 1722 **Turdï-bay** [Турдыбай богадыр / Турдибай-Калмухамедъ-Богадыръ] (PSZRI VI, 777, MIKk 170); Kkalp. 20th c. **Turdï-bay** [Турдыбай] (KkRS 776); Uzb. 19th c. **Turdï-bay** [Турдыбай] (SKSO III, 22); Uzb. 19th c. **Turdï-bay** [Шукурбай Турдыбаевъ], a Sart (TV 154); Uzb. 1875 **Turdï-bay-sufi** [Турды-бай-суфи] (Moskal'cev 40); Uzb. 20th c. **Turdï-bây** [Турдибой] (Begmatov 1984, 204); Uzb. 20th c. **Turdï-bek** [Турдибек] (Begmatov 1984, 204); Chag. 16th c. **Turdï-bike** [Турды-бикэ], fem. (Ivanov 230); Uzb. 20th c. **Turdï-er / Turdï-yâr?** [Турдиер] (Begmatov 1984, 204); Kkalp. 20th c. **Turdï-gül** [Турдыгул], fem. (KkRS 778, Baskakov: OSA 141); Uzb. 20th c. **Turdï-γul** [Турдигул], fem. (Begmatov 1984, 204); Uzb. 20th c. **Turdï-χân** [Турдихон], fem. (Begmatov 1984, 204); Uzb. 20th c. **Turdï-χoĵa** [Турдихўжа] (Begmatov 1984, 204); NUyg. 19th c. **Turdï-χoĵa** [Turdi Khwoja], Aurel Stein's attendant in Eastern Turkestan (Stein 247, 271, 277); Trkm. **Turdï-kethudâ / Durdï-kethudâ** [كتخدا طوردى / Turdı (Durdı)] (Refik, Anad. 107); Kzk. 19th c. **Turdï-qul** [Турдыкулъ Ширматовъ] (SKSO VIII, 219); Kzk. 19th c. **Turdï-qul** [Турдыкулъ] (SKSO VIII, 233); Uzb. 20th c. **Turdï-qul** [Турдикул] (Begmatov 1984, 204); Uzb. 20th c. **Turdï-mâmâ** [Турдимомо], fem. (Begmatov 1984, 204); Uzb. 20th c. **Turdï-nisâ** [Турдинисо], fem. (Begmatov 1984, 204); Uzb. 20th c. **Turdï-pâ** [Турдипо] (Begmatov 1984, 204); Uzb. 20th c. **Turdï-pâ** [Турдипо], fem. (Begmatov 1984, 204); Chag. 16th c. **Turdï-sultan** [Турды Султан] (Ivanov 187); Chag. 16th c. **Turdï-sultan** [Турды Султан], fem. (Ivanov 187); Kzk. 19th c. **Turdu** [Muhammed Turdu] (Hedin, En färd I, 352); Kirg. 20th c. **Turdu** [Турду] (Kalilov 93 (after Abramzon)); Kirg. **Turdu-bay** [Турдубай] (Jud. 847); Kzk. **Turdu-bek** [Турдў Бек / Турду Бек], a sultan (Proben III, 43 (55), 47 (62)); Kzk. 19th c. **Turdu-bek** [Турдубекъ] (AOO 22); Kirg. 20th c. **Turdu-bek** [Kalilov 93 (after Abramzon)); Kzk. 19th c. **Turdu-γul** [Турдугулъ] (SODž. 136); Kzk. 19th c. **Turdu-γul** [Турдугулъ] (SOV 4). ✧ 'Stayed, remained, survived' (Samojlovič: ŽS 1911, 297, Zaj. 1971, Žanuzakov), cf. Uyg., Alt., Hak., Kirg., Kzk. etc. *tur-* 'stehen, aufstehen; stehen bleiben, anhalten; leben wohnen' (Radl. III, 1442). ⇨ **TURLÏ.** See also **AMAN-TURDÏ, ANNA-TURDÏ, ARAZ-DURDÏ, AWAZ-TURDÏ, BEK-TURDÏ, ČÏN-TURDÏ, ĴUMA-TURDÏ, DÄWLÄT-DURDÏ, ER-ALİ-DURDÏ, ГÏLİČ-DURDÏ, ГÏZ-DURDÏ, XÂL-TURDÏ, QURBAN-TURDÏ, MAMED-DURDÏ, MÄMMÄ-TURDÏ, MEÑLİ-DURDÏ, MERET-DURDÏ, MULLA-DURDÏ, NÏYAZ-DURDÏ, SÄXET-DURDÏ, ŠAH-TURDÏ, ТАГAN-DURDÏ, TÂM-TURDÏ, ТОГAN-DURDÏ; TURSÏN.**

TURDÏ-AY Kzk. 19th c. **Turdï-ay** [Турды-ай Адинаева], fem. (SKSO IV, otd. II, 32). ⇨ **TURDÏ + AY.**

TURDÏ-ALİ Kzk. 19th c. **Turd-ali / Turdï-ali** [Турдали] (Sb. Syr-D. IX, 52); Kirg. 1820 **Turd-ali / Turdï-ali** [Турдали], a chieftain (Sib. Vest. IX, 122); *TN:* Kzk. 18th c. **Turd-ali / Turdï-ali** [Турдалы], a lake on the territory of the Inner Horde (Haruzin, Buk. O., II, Prilož. 15). ⇨ **TURDÏ + ALİ.**

TURDÏ-BAQÏ NUyg.(Tar.) 19th c. **Turdï-baqï** [Турдыбакы], from the region of Qulja (TV 1876, 135). ⇨ **TURDÏ + BAKİ / BAQİ.**

TURDÏ-XÂL Uzb. 20th c. **Turdï-χâl** [Турдихол], fem. (Begmatov 1984, 204). ✧ 'Stayed/survived birthmark'. ⇨ **TURDÏ + QAL II.** See also **XÂL-TURDÏ.**

TURDÏ-QOZÏ Uzb. 20th c. **Turdï-qozï** [Турдикўзи] (Begmatov 1984, 204). ⇨ **TURDÏ + QOZÏ.**

TURDÏ-MÄMÄT Uzb. 20th c. **Turdï-mämät** [Турдимамат] (Begmatov 1984, 204). ⇨ **TURDÏ + MAMET.**

TURDÏ-MEXMED see **TURDÏ-MUXAMMED**

TURDÏ-MÏRAT see **TURDÏ-MURAT**

TURDÏ-MUXAMMAD see **TURDÏ-MUXAMMED**

TURDÏ-MUXAMMED Chag. 15th c. - 16th c. **Turdï-meχmed** [ترردى محمد] (Šejb. XLIX); Uzb. 20th c. **Turdï-muχammad** [Турдимухаммад] (Begmatov 1984, 204); Chag. 16th c. **Turdï-muχammed** [Турды-Мухаммед], frequently used name in Bukhara in the 16-17th c. (Ivanov 356). ⇨ **TURDÏ + MUXAMMED.**

TURDÏ-MURAT Trkm. 1818 **Durdï-murad-behadïr** [Дурды Мурад-бехадыр], from the İkdïr (İgdir?) tribe (MIT II, 412); Kkalp. 20th c. **Turdï-mïrat** [Турдымырат] (KkRS 776); Kkalp. 20th c. **Turdï-murat** [Турдымурат] (KkRS 776); Uzb. 20th c. **Turdï-murâd** [Турдимурод] (Begmatov 1984, 204).

⇨ **TURDÏ** + **MURAT.**

TURDÏ-NÏYAZ Uzb. 20th c. **Turdï-niyâz?** [Турдиниев (?)] (Begmatov 1984, 204). ⇨ **TURDÏ** + **NÏYAZ.**

TURDÏ-TÂP Uzb. 20th c. **Turdï-tâp** [Турдитоп] (Begmatov 1984, 204). ✧ 'Stayed/survived-health; Born healthy' cf. Uzb. *tâp* 'здоровье, зрелость, желание, терпение' (UzbRS). ⇨ **TURDÏ.**

TURDÏMAT Uzb. 20th c. **Turdïmat** [Турдимат] (Begmatov 1984, 204). ⇨ **TURDÏ** + suffixoid *-mat.*

TURDÏMBET Kzk. 18th c. - 19th c. **Turdïmbet** [Турдымбет] (Tynyšp. 66). ⇨ **TURDÏ** + suff. *-mbet.*

TURDU see **TURDÏ**

TURDUKE Kirg. 19th c. **Turduke** [Турдуке] (Valihanov, Soč. 386). ⇨ **TURDÏ** + dim. suff. *-ke.*

TURGÏL Kzk. 19th c. **Turgil** [Тургилъ] (SOK 216). ⇨ **TUR?** + imp. suff. *-gil.*

TURГAY see **TORГAY**

TURГAN Chuv. 18th-19th c. **Torgan** [Торганъ] (Magn. 86); Kkalp. 20th c. **Turɣan** [Тургъан / Турған], fem. (Bask., Kkalp. 29, KkRS 778); Kkalp. 20th c. **Turɣan-bay** [Турғанбай] (KkRS 776); Uzb. 20th c. **Turɣân** [Турғон], fem. (Begmatov 1984, 204); Uzb. 20th c. **Turɣân-ây** [Турғоной], fem. (Begmatov 1984, 204); Uzb. 20th c. **Turɣân-bibi** [Турғонбиби], fem. (Begmatov 1984, 204); Uzb. 20th c. **Turɣân-χân** [Турғонхон], fem. (Begmatov 1984, 204). ✧ I. 'Halted, stopped, survived; death or birth of children stopped' cf. Uyg., Alt., Hak., Kirg., Kzk. etc. *tur-* 'stehen, aufstehen; stehen bleiben, anhalten; leben wohnen' (Radl. III, 1442); II. 'Turghan' (Ethn., tribe), cf. Chag. *Turɣan* 'ein Türkengeschlecht' (Radl. III, 1457); III. 'Guard' cf. Chag. *turɣan* 'der Wächter' (Radl. III, 1457). See also **BEK-TURГAN, ÏK-TURГAN, TOQTAГAN, TOQTAMÏŠ, TURMÏŠ.**

TURГAUT Kzk. 19th c. **Torɣaut** [Торгаутъ] (AOA 22); Kzk. 19th c. **Torɣaut** [Торгаутъ] (SOK 59, 236); Kzk. 19th c. **Turɣaut** [Тургаутъ] (Grod., Pril. 159, 165); Kzk. 19th c. **Turɣaut** [Тургаутъ] (SOV 42). ✧ Ethnonym.

TURГO see **TURГU**

TURГU Kzk. 19th c. **Turɣo-bay** [Тургобай] (SOK 180); Kzk. **Turɣu-bay** [Тургубай] (Sb. Syr-D. IX, 46). ✧ I. 'Silk'?; II. 'Sparrow'?, cf. Uyg., Chag. *torɣu* 'die Seide'; eine Art kleiner Bergsperlinges' (Radl. III, 1185). ⇨ **TORQA?**

TURГUD see **TURГUT**

TURГUL see **TORГÏL**

TURГUN Kzk. 19th c. **Turɣon-bay** [Тургонбай] (SODž. 36); Kzk. 19th c. **Turɣon-bay** [Тургонбай] (SOK 20, 160); Kzk. 19th c. **Turɣon-bay** [Тургонбай] (SOV 26, 38, 88); Kzk. 19th c. **Turɣum-bay** (<Turɣun-bay) [Тургумбай] (AOA 42); Kzk. 19th c. **Turɣum-bay** (<Turɣun-bay) [Тургумбай] (AOK 106); Kzk. 19th c. **Turɣum-bay** (<Turɣun-bay) [Тургумбай] (AOP 126); Kzk. 19th c. **Turɣum-bay** (<Turɣun-bay) [Тургумбай] (SOV 6); Kirg. 19th c. **Turɣum-bek** (<Turɣun-bek) [Тургумбек / Тургунбек], a man born in 1887 (Abramzon, Êtn. 93, Kalilov 93); Kzk. 1816 **Turɣun** [Тургун] (MIK IV, 299); Kzk. 1816 **Turɣun** [Тургун] (MIK IV, 299); Kzk. 19th c. **Turɣun** [Тургун Тулябаев] (SKSO VIII, 232); Uzb. 20th c. **Turɣun** [Турғун] (Begmatov 1984, 204); Uzb. 20th c. **Turɣun** [Турғун], fem. (Begmatov 1984, 204); Uzb. 20th c. **Turɣun-ây** [Турғуной], fem. (Begmatov 1984, 204); Kzk. 19th c. **Turɣun-bay** [Тургумбай] (AOA 42); Kzk. 19th c. **Turɣun-bay** [Тургумбай] (AOK 106, etc.); Kzk. 19th c. **Turɣun-bay** [Тургунбай] (AOP 126); Kzk. 19th c. **Turɣun-bay** [Уразали Тургунбаевъ] (Grod., Pril. 130); Kzk. 19th c. **Turɣun-bay** [Тургумбай] (Grod., Pril. 130, 160); Kzk. 19th c. **Turɣun-bay** [Тургунбай Довлатовъ] (Grod., Pril. 160); Kzk. 19th c. **Turɣun-bay** [Тургумбай] (SOV 6); Uzb. 20th c. **Turɣun-bây** [Турғунбой] (Begmatov 1984, 204); Kirg. 20th c. **Turɣun-bek** [Тургунбек] (Kalilov 93 (after Abramzon)); Uzb. 20th c. **Turɣun-bibi** [Турғунбиби], fem. (Begmatov 1984, 204); Uzb. 20th c. **Turɣun-bu** [Турғунбу], fem. (Begmatov 1984, 204); Uzb. 20th c. **Turɣun-büwi** [Турғунбуви], fem. (Begmatov 1984, 204); Uzb. 20th c. **Turɣun-jân** [Турғунжон] (Begmatov 1984, 204); Uzb. 20th c. **Turɣun-χoĵa** [Турғунхўжа] (Begmatov 1984, 204); Uzb. 20th c. **Turɣun-mirza** [Турғунмирза] (Begmatov 1984, 204). ✧ 'Native, indigenous (people); May he/she stand/stay alive; may he not die' (Begmatov), cf. Kzk. *turɣün* 'der Standort' (Radl. III, 1458), Kzk. *türɣin* 'жергілікті халық' (QTTS), Uzb. *turɣun* 'постоянно живущий (где-л.); устойчивый, постоянный' (UzbRS). See also **BEK-TURГUN, TAŠ-TURГUN.**

TURГUN-ALÏ Uzb. 20th c. **Turɣun-ali** [Турғунали] (Begmatov 1984, 204). ⇨ **TURГUN** + **ALÏ.**

TURГUNA Uzb. 20th c. **Turɣuna** [Турғуна], fem. (Begmatov 1984, 204). ⇨ **TURГUN** + suff. *-a(2).*

TURГUNČA Uzb. 20th c. **Turɣunča** [Турғунча], fem. (Begmatov 1984, 204); Uzb. 20th c. **Turɣunča-χân** [Турғунчахон], fem. (Begmatov 1984, 204). ⇨ **TURГUN** + suff. *-ča(3).*

TURГUT Turk. 1552 **Durɣud** [Musztafa bin Durgud], a Janissary in Endréd, Hungary (Velics-Kamm. I, 79); Trkm.? / Turk.? 13th c. **Torɣud-alp** [طورغود الب / Torgud Alp] (Nešrî 203, 211); Turk. 1457 **Turɣud** [Turgud binti Hızır], fem. (Gökb., Ed. 356); Turk. 1528 **Turɣud** [Turgud Bazirgân] (Gökb., Ed. 47); Turk. 1565, 1570 **Turɣud** [Turɣud bin Qasïm] (Dávid); Turk. 1568 **Turɣud** [Bâli bin Turgud], a muezzin (Gökb., Ed. 281); Turk. 1587 **Turɣud** [Turgud], a spahi (cavalry soldier) in the region of Heves, Hungary (Velics-Kamm. I, 366); Yürük 1543 **Turɣud** [طورغود / Turgud], among the Yürüks of Kocacık, Turkey (Gökb., Rum. 195, 199, 200, 201 etc.); Yürük 1543 **Turɣud** [Turgud] (Gökb., Rum. 226, 227); Tat. 1543 **Turɣud** [Turgud], several persons (Gökb., Rum. 233, 236, 239 etc.); Turk 1549 **Turɣud-aɣa** [Turgud aga], a spahi (cavalry soldier) in Esztergom, Hungary (Velics-Kamm. II); Turk. 14th c. **Turɣut** [Τουργούτης / Turɣut], a reigning prince (Byz. Turc. 319); Turk. 15th c. **Turɣut** [Τουργούτης / Turɣut], son of Sultan Bayezid II (1481-1512 (Byz. Turc. 319, Baştav 175); Oghuz / Trkm. **Turɣut-alp** / **Turɣud-alp** [طورقوت الپ / طورغود الپ], Osman's comrade-in-arms (Āšikp. 18, 22, 32, Nešrī XIII, 203, 211]; *TN:* Turk. 1528 **Turɣud-mahallesi** [Turgud Mahallesi], a district founded by Turgud Bazirgân (Gökb., Ed. 47); Turk. 20th c. **Turɣut** [Turgut], a village (small town) in the province of Muğla, Turkey (TMİB 670); Turk. 20th c. **Turɣutlar** [Turgutlar], a village in the province of Muğla, Turkey (TMİB 670). ✧ I. 'Turgut' (Ethn.), a tribe of Mongol or Kipchak origin, which came to Anatolia together with the Mongols, later was mixed with the Türkmens and counted among them (Toğan, UTT 318, Sevim-Yücel I, 377); The ethnonym *turɣut / turɣawut* is probably the plural of *turɣawul / turɣaq* 'gündüz nevbetçisi [=day guard]' Toğan, UTT 484); II. 'Dwelling place' (Erol). See also **TURGAN, TURAQ I.**

TURXAN   Turk. 1552 **Durχan** [Dur-χan] (Dávid); Turk. 1565 **Durχan** [Dur-χan] (Dávid); Oghuz **Turχan** [Тур-хан], Dib-yaquy's son (RaD I/1, 76); Selj.? 1340 **Turχan** [صلاح الدين طرخان] (Zetterst. 220); Turk. 1472 **Turχan** [ترخان] (Āšikp. 171); Turk. 1485 **Turχan** [Turhan] (Gökb., Ed. 184); Yürük 1543 **Turχan** [Turhan] (Gökb., Rum. 185, 226, 227); Tat. 1543 **Turχan** [Turhan] (Gökb., Rum. 240); Maml.? / Turk.? 1457 **Turχan** [ابن طرخان] (Ibn Taghrīb. VII, 486); Turk. 1543 **Turχan-aɣa** [Turkhán aga], a commander (Velics-Kamm. I, 16); Turk. 1485 **Turχan-bey** [Turhan Bey] (Gökb., Ed. 340-342); *TN:* Turk. 15th c. **Turχan-bey** [Turhan Bey], several villages in the province of Edirne (Gökb., Ed. 340-342). ✧ 'Aristocrat, nobleman, chieftain, prince' cf. Turk. *turhan* 'аристократ, дворянин; вождь (племени), князь' (TRS), 'Nobleman, respected man (who doesn't pay taxes)', used also as a title (Erol II), 'Great, dignified, true-hearted man' (IOAIÊK III, 285).

TURXANJA   Yürük 1543 **Turχanja** [Turhanca], several persons in the district (nâhiye) of Silistire (Gökb., Rum. 185, 222, 224, 227). ⇨ **TURXAN** + suff. *-ja.*

TURÏ 1.   Uyg. 12th c. - 14th c. **Turï** [Turı] (Radl., USp. 5, 48. DTS, EUTS); Uyg. 12th c. - 14th c. **Turï-baqšï** /

Turï-baχšï [Turï Baqšï (Baχšï) / Turï-bakšï] (Radl., USp. 1, 33, DTS). ✧ I. 'Unsociable; quarrelsome' cf. Karakh. *turï kiši* 'человек с трудным характером; неуживчивый' (DTS); II. 'Enemy' cf. Karakh. *turï* 'der Feind' (Radl. III, 1452; DTS).

TURÏ II. see TORÏ

TURÏMBET see TORUMBET

TURÏS   Kzk. 19th c. **Torus-bek** [Ханъ Магоммедъ Торусбековъ], a khan (Grod., Pril. 184); Kzk. 18th c. - 19th c. **Trus-bek** [Трусбекъ] (Tynyšp. 71); Kzk. 19th c. **Trus-pek** [Труспекъ] (SODž. 26); Kzk. 19th c. **Trus-pek** [Труспекъ] (SOV 84); Kzk. 18th c. - 19th c. **Turïs-biy** [Турыс-бий] (Tynyšp. 65); Kzk. 19th c. **Turus-bay** [Турусбай] (SOK 50); Kzk. 19th c. **Turus-bek** [Тилаганъ Турусбековъ] (Grod., Pril. 42); Kzk. 19th c. **Turus-pek** [Туруспекъ] (SODž. 52, 126, 152); Kzk. 19th c. **Turus-pek** [Туруспекъ] (SOK 22). ✧ 'True, real, honest' (P.) cf. Kzk., Tat.(Bar.) *turus* 'richtig, wahrhaft' (Radl. III, 1454), Kzk. *düris* 'верный' (RKzS).

TURQA see TORQA

TURQAY   Bashk. 1756 **Turqay** [Халил Туркаев] (MIB IV/1, 128). ⇨ **TORQA?** + suff. *-y.*

TURQAN   Hak. 19th-20th c. **Turqan** [Туркан], fem. (HRS 355). ✧ 'Turkan / Turukhansk' (Top.), the place where the Hakas were exiled (Butanaev). See also **ULJAY-TURQAN.**

TURQAR   Chag. 16th c. **Turqar** [Туркар] (Ivanov 248).

TURQSÏ   Kzk. 19th c. **Turqsï-bay** [Турксыбай] (SODž. 56).

TURQŠÏ   Türk? 9th c. - 10th c. **Türkši / Turqšï?** [التـرقشى / التـركشى], sovereign of the Turks (Tabarī, Annal. II, 1613).

TURQUT see TURGUT

TURLAQ see TORLAQ

TURLÏ   Kzk. 19th c. **Turlï** [Турлы] (AOAtb. 46); Kzk. 18th c. - 19th c. **Turlï-bek** [Турлыбек] (Tynyšp. 71); Kzk. 1846 **Turlu-bay** [Турлубай Айжуваров] (MKOP 154); Kzk. 19th c. **Turlu-bay** [Турлубай] (AOA 6, 22); Kzk. 19th c. **Turlu-bay** [Турлубай] (AOK 14, 42, 122); Kzk. 19th c. **Turlu-bay** [Турлубай] (AOP 22); Kzk. 19th c. **Turlu-bay** [Turlubaj] (Ljutš 108); Kzk. 19th c. **Turlu-bay** [Турлубай] (SODž. 38); Kzk. 19th c. **Turlu-bay** [Турлубай] (SOK 168); Kzk. 19th c. **Turlu-bay** [Турлубай] (SOK 258); Kzk. 19th c. **Turlu-bay** [Турлубай] (SOV 26, 38, 74, 106); Kzk. 19th c. **Turlu-bay-tal? / Turlu-baytal?** [Турлубай-талъ] (AOP 42); Kzk. 18th c. - 19th c. **Turlu-bek** [Турлубек] (Tynyšp. 68); Kzk. 1819 **Turlu-bek** [Турлубек] (MIK IV, 324); Kzk. 19th c. **Turlu-bek** [Турлубекъ] (AOAtb. 50); Kzk. 19th c. **Turlu-bek** [Турлубекъ] (AOK 26); Kzk. 19th c. **Turlu-bek** [Турлубекъ] (AOO 50); Kzk. 19th

c. **Turlu-bek** [Турлубекъ] (AOP 6); Kzk. 19th c. **Turlu-bek** [Турлубекъ] (AOP 90); Kzk. 19th c. **Turlu-bek** [Турлубекъ] (SOK 34, 54, 190); Kzk. 19th c. **Turlu-ɣul** [Турлугулъ] (AOAtb. 42). ❖ 'Stayed, remained, survived' (Žanuzakov). ⇨ **TURDÏ?** See also **BİK-TURLÏ.**

TURLU I. see **TURLÏ**

TURLU II.   Yürük 1543 **Turlu** [طورلى / Turlu] (Gökb., Rum. 188).

TURLUƔUY   Kzk. 19th c. **Turluɣuy / Turlu-ɣul?** [Турлугуй] (SOK 236).

TURLUQ   Kzk. 19th c. **Torlïq-pay** [Торликпай] (SOK 180); Kzk. 19th c. **Turluq-pay** [Турлукпай] (SOK 280). ❖ 'Felt-cover' cf. Kzk. *türlüq* 'die Filzdecken, mit denen der ubtere Theil der Jurte Bedeckt ist' (Radl. III, 1460).

TURLUM   Kzk. 19th c. **Turlum-bey** [Турлумбей] (SODž. 74).

TURLUMAN   Yürük 1543 **Turluman** [طورلومان / Turluman] (Gökb., Rum. 215). ⇨ **TURLU II.?** + suff. *-man.*

TURLUMBET   Kzk. 19th c. **Turlumbet** [Турлумбетъ] (AOO 78). ⇨ **TURLU I.?** + suff. *-umbet / -bet?*

TURLUW   Kmk. 1828 **Turlu? / Turluw?** [Кучук Турлув] (MID III, 123).

TURMA   Kzk. 19th c. **Turma-bek** [Турмабекъ] (SOK 232).

TURMAN I.   Kkalp. 20th c. **Turman** [Турман] (Bask., Kkalp., 88, KkRS 776). ❖ 'Harness' cf. Kkalp. *turman* 'сбруя' (Bask., Kkalp.).

TURMAN II.   Turk. 1543 **Turman / Toraman?** [طورمان] (Gökb., Rum. 180); *EN:* Yürük 1617 **Turman** [تورمان / Turman taifesi], Turman's tribe (Gökçen 89). ⇨ **TORAMAN?**

TURMAŠ   Kzk. 19th c. **Turmaš** [Турмашъ] (AOK 118). ⇨ **TURMÏŠ?**

TURMÏŠ   Turk. 1552 **Durmïš** [Durmïš, Durmuš] (Dávid); Turk. 1565 **Durmïš** [Ibrahim bin Durmuš] (Dávid); Turk. 1570 **Durmïš** [Ibrahim Durmuš] (Dávid); Trkm. 1525/26 **Durmïš-χan** [Дурмиш-хан] (MIT II, 58); Turk. 1517 **Durmuš** [Durmuş], from the Qayï (Qayï) tribe, in the region of Menteşe, Turkey (Turan: Belleten XII(1948), 609); Turk. 1546 **Durmuš** [Szkender Durmus], a chief of a squadron in Tomašin (Velics-Kamm. I, 55); Turk. 1583 **Durmuš** [Durmuş] (Ongan, Ank. I, 155); Turk. 1606 **Durmuš** [Durmuş], from Isparta, Turkey (Ün 1938, 645); Yürük 1543 **Durmuš** [طورمش / Durmuş], lots of persons in the source (Gökb., Rum. 179, 185, 190, 200, 201 etc.); Yürük 1579 **Durmuš** [طورموش / Durmuş] (Refik, Anad. 31); Tat. 1543 **Durmuš** [طورمش / Durmuş] (Gökb., Rum. 230, 232, 233, 236 etc.); Turk. 13th c. - 15th c. **Durmuš-čawuš** [Durmuš čauš (Bozgirli)]

(Giese 70); Turk. 1526 **Durmuš-χan** [دورميش خان] (Dorn 248, 401); Chuv. 18th-19th c. **Tormïš** [Тормышъ] (Magn. 86); Uyg. 8th c. - 9th c. **Turmïš** [Turmïš] (Müller, Uig. II, 88); Uyg. 12th c. - 14th c. **Turmïš** [Turmïš] (Radl., USp. 90); Uyg. 12th c. - 14th c. **Turmïš** [Turmïš / Turmïş], a miller (Radl., USp. 169, 214, 255, DTS, EUTS); Uyg. 13th-14th c. **Turmïš** (Zieme, Mat. II, 92); Khorezm.? 1375 **Turmïš** [Turmish], brother of Turkan Arlat, Temür's enemy (Tar. Rashidi 44-45); Khorezm.? 1376/77 **Turmïš** [Турмыш], Türken's brother (RaD II, 193, MIT I, 517); Turk. 1585 **Turmïš** [مصلح الدين بن طورمش] (MB Qastam. 162); Chuv. 18th-19th c. **Turmïš** [Турмышъ] (Magn. 87); Tat. 1629 **Turmïš** [Турмышко Инбаев] (Miller, Ist. Sib. II, 357); Oghuz/Trkm. **Turmïš / Turtmïš?** [طورتمش / طورمش], forefther of the Ottoman dynasty, Noah's great-grand-son (Āšikp. 5, Seādeddīn I, 15, Nešrī, Ālī 186, Wittek 94); Uyg. 8th c. - 9th c. **Turmïš-χatun-tañrim** [Turmïš χatun tängrim] (Müller, Pfahl. 10); Uyg. 12th c. - 14th c. **Turmïš-tutuñ** [Turmïš Tutung] (Radl., USp. 95, 203, 245, DTS); Turk. 1543 **Turmuš** [Turmus kiája], the second-in-command in Zombor, Hungary (Velics-Kamm. I, 23); Turk. 1546 **Turmuš** [Turmus Kászim], a Janissary chief of a squadron in Székesfehérvár, Hungary (Velics-Kamm. I, 56); Turk. 1546 **Turmuš** [Ali Turmus / Ali bin Turmus], a chief of a squadron (serbölük) in Székesfehérvár, Hungary (Velics-Kamm. II, 46-47); Yürük 1551 **Turmuš** [طور خواجه بن طورمش / Turhoca ibn Turmuş] (Gökçen 28); Yürük 1551 **Turmuš** [Turmuş], several persons (Gökçen 30-31); Yürük 1576 **Turmuš** [Turmuş] (Gökçen 46); Turk. 1634 **Turmuš-aɣa** [Turmus aga], a Janissary from Székesfehérvár, Hungary (Velics-Kamm. I, 458); *TN:* Chuv. 18th c. **Turmïš** [Большой Турмышъ / Малой Турмышъ], villages of christened Chuvash in the district of Tsivilsk by the stream *Turmïška* (Korsakov 320). ❖ 'Stayed, remained, survived; halted, stopped' (Sauvaget 50), 'Got up, Arose (=Was born)' (Blagova 1997, 715), cf. Uyg., Alt., Hak., Kirg., Kzk. etc. *tur-* 'stehen, aufstehen; stehen bleiben, anhalten; leben wohnen' (Radl. III, 1442), Crm., Turk. *dur-* 'stehen, anhalten; wohnen, bleiben' (Radl. III, 1787). See also **ALP-TURMÏŠ, BABA-TURMUŠ, BARČA-TURMÏŠ, BARQ-TURMÏŠ, BEG-TURMÏŠ, BERK-TURMÏŠ, EL-TURMÏŠ, KÄNČ-TURMÏŠ, QÏZ-TURMÏŠ, QUTLUƔ-TURMÏŠ, TÄZÄK-TURMÏŠ, TEMÜR-TURMÏŠ, TESÄK-TURMÏŠ; TOQTAY, TOQTAMÏŠ, TURDÏ, TURƔAN.**

TURMÏŠ-TEGİRMÄNČİ   Uyg. 12th c. - 14th c. **Turmïš-tegirmänči** [turmïš tegirmänči] (DTS). ❖ 'Stayed/remained-miller' cf. Uyg. *tegirmänči* 'мельник' (DTS). ⇨ **TURMÏŠ.**

TURMÏŠ-TEMÜR Uyg. 12th c. - 14th c. **Turmïš-temür** [Turmïš Tämür / Turmiš Tämür] (Radl., USp. 15, 27-28, Le Coq, Urkunden 1918, 456, 457, DTS). ✧ 'Got-up-Iron, Arose-(=Was born)-Iron' (Blagova 1997, 715), 'Stayed/survived iron'. ⇨ **TURMÏŠ** + **TEMÏR.**

TURMUŠ see **TURMÏŠ**

TURNA Maml. 14th c. **Turna** [طُرْنا] (Sauvaget 50); Maml. 1300-1325 **Turna** / **Tarna?** [سيف الدين بلبان طرنه / Balbân Tarna] (Zetterst. 82, 177, Makrīzī), Hak. 19th-20th c. **Tïrna** [Тырна] (HRS 352). ✧ 'Crane' (Sauvaget 50), cf. Uyg., Kuman, Alt., Hak., Turk. *turna* 'der Kranich' (Radl. III, 1459), Kzk., Turk. *tïrna* 'der Kranich' (Radl. III, 1326).

TURNALÏ Turk. 1333 **Turnalï-beg** [طورنالى بك] (MB Qastam. 117). ✧ 'With cranes'. ⇨ **TURNA** + suff. -*lï.*

TUROY Alt. 19th c. **Turoy-χan** / **Türoy-χan?** [Тюрой-хан] (Verb., In. 143).

TURON Kzk. 19th c. **Turon** [Туронъ] (AOA 78).

TURSANAY Bashk. 1663 **Tursanay** (<Tursïn-ay?) [Турсанай] (MIB I, 177).

TURSÏN Turk. 1519 **Dursun** (Gökb., Ed. 392); Turk. 16th c. **Dursun**, several persons in the source (Ongan, Ank. II); Turk. 1552, 1565 **Dursun** (Dávid); Turk. 1553 **Dursun** [Dursun Daúd], an „ulûfeci" (clerk/secretary of Janissary guards, or palace servants) among the Turks in Veszprém, Hungary (Velics-Kamm. I, 88); Turk. 1583 **Dursun** (Ongan, Ank. I, 155); Yürük 1543 **Dursun** [طورسون] (Gökb., Rum. 102, 181, 186, 191 etc.); Trkm. 20th c. **Dursun** [Dursun], fem. (Zaj. 1971, 340); Tat. 1543 **Dursun** (Gökb., Rum. 233, 234, 236); Turk. 1485 **Dursun-bey** [Edhem Çelebi bin Dursun Bey] (Gökb., Ed. 452); Kkalp. 20th c. **Tursïn** [Турсын] (KkRS 776); Tat. 1699 **Tursïn?** / **Tur-senäk?** [Турсенячка Алыбаевъ] (AI V, 521); Kzk. 18th c. - 19th c. **Tursïn-bay** [Турсынбай] (Tynyšp. 66); Kkalp. 20th c. **Tursïn-bek** [Турсынбек] (KkRS 776); Uzb. 20th c. **Tursïn-bibi** [Турсунбиби], fem. (Begmatov 1984, 204); Uzb. 20th c. **Tursïn-büwi** [Турсунбуви], fem. (Begmatov 1984, 204); Kkalp. 20th c. **Tursïn-gül** [Tursyn-gül / Турсынгул], fem. (KkRS 778, Baskakov: OSA 141); Uzb. 20th c. **Tursïn-qul** [Турсункул] (Begmatov 1984, 204); Kzk. 19th c. **Tursum-bay** (<Tursun-bay) [Турсумбай] (AOA 78); Kzk. 19th c. **Tursum-bay** (<Tursun-bay) [Турсумбай] (AOK 82); Kzk. 19th c. **Tursum-bay** (<Tursun-bay) [Турсумбай] (SOK 150); Kzk. 1914 **Tursum-bay** (<Tursun-bay) [Tursum Bai] (Nazaroff 292); Uzb. 19th c. **Tursum-bay** (<Tursun-bay) [Toursoum-Bay] (H. Moser, A travers l'Asie centrale 212); Kzk. 1794 **Tursum-bek** (<Tursun-bek) [طورسمبك / Турсмбекъ] (MIK IV, 160); Kzk. 19th c. **Tursum-bek** (<Tursun-bek) [Турсумбекъ] (SODž. 84, 162); 1817 **Tursun** [Турсунъ] (Bukej 7); Chag. 16th c. **Tursun** [Турсун]

(Ivanov 151, 153, 192 etc.); Turk. 1549 **Tursun**, a Janissary from the county of Nógrád, Hungary (Velics-Kamm. II, 83); Trkm. **Tursun** [Дурсунъ], Mustafakuli's daughter (Samojlovič: ŽS 1911, 297); Trkm. 1623 **Tursun** [Турсун], a Khan (MIT II, 326, 335); Kzk. 18th c. - 19th c. **Tursun** [Турсун] (Tynyšp. 66); Kzk. 1752 **Tursun** [Аджа Магометъ Турсуновъ], a mulla (Nepljuev 77); Kzk. 1839 **Tursun** [Турсунъ Чингисовъ], a sultan of the Middle Horde (Orta Žüz) (Konšin, Mat. V, 12); Kzk. 19th c. **Tursun** [Турсунъ] (AOK 102); Kzk. 19th c. **Tursun** [Икамъ Бердибекъ Турсуновъ] (Grod., Pril. 158); Kzk. 19th c. **Tursun** [Турсунъ] (Grod., Pril. 36); Kzk. 19th c. **Tursun** [Капай Турсуновъ] (Grod., Pril. 95); Kzk. 19th c. **Tursun** [Турсунъ] (Grod. I, 98); Kzk. 19th c. **Tursun** [Турсун] (Potanin IV, 404); Kzk. 19th c. **Tursun** [Турсунъ] (SODž. 134); Kkalp. 20th c. **Tursun** [Турсун] (Bask., Kkalp. 402); Kirg. 20th c. **Tursun** [Турсун] (Kalilov 93); Uzb. 1945-47 **Tursun** [Турсун] (Erohina-Ramazanova: OSA 201); Uzb. 20th c. **Tursun** [Турсун] (Begmatov 1984, 200, 204); Uzb. 20th c. **Tursun** [Турсун], fem. (Begmatov 1984, 204); Trkm. 1598 **Tursun** / **Tursun-muχammed-sultan** [Турсун Мухаммед-султан] (MIT II, 92); Uzb. 20th c. **Tursun-ây** [Турсуной] (Begmatov 1984, 204); Uzb. 20th c. **Tursun-ây** [Турсуной], fem. (Begmatov 1984, 204); Tat. 1620 **Tursun-bay** [Турсунбай] (Kurdjumov 121); Bashk. 1714 **Tursun-bay** [Турсунбаев] (MIB I, 105); Bashk. 1783 **Tursun-bay** [Турсунбай Канкаев] (MIB V, 139); Kzk. **Tursun-bay** [Турсунбай], a well (Karta JAR XIX); Kzk. 18th c. - 19th c. **Tursun-bay** [Турсунбай] (Tynyšp. 70); Kzk. 1827 **Tursun-bay** [Турсунбай Исетевъ] (TOUAK XXIV, 173); Kzk. 19th c. **Tursun-bay** [Турсунбай] (Grod., Pril. 37, 130, 167); Kzk. 19th c. **Tursun-bay** [Турсунбай / Турсунбаевъ] (SKSO III, 1-52, 150-190); Kzk. 19th c. **Tursun-bay** [Турсунбай] (SOV, 30); Uzb. 1882 **Tursun-bay** [Турсунъ-бай] (Moskal'cev 48); Turk. **Tursun-beg** [طرسون بك] (Āšikp. 41); Turk. **Tursun-bey** [Tursun Bey (Karası oğlu)] (Uzunçarş., Anad. 33, 35); Yürük 1575 **Tursun-bey** [Tursun Bey] (Gökçen 49); Uzb. 20th c. **Tursun-bek** [Турсунбек] (Begmatov 1984, 204); Kzk. 19th c. **Tursun-bibi** [Турсунъ биби], fem. (Grod., Pril. 117); Kzk. 19th c. **Tursun-bibi** [Турсунъ-биби], fem. (SKSO IV, otd. II, 34); Uzb. 19th c. **Tursun-bibi** [Турсунъ биби], a Sart woman (Sr. Az. I, 1896 avg. 15); Uzb. 20th c. **Tursun-jân** [Турсунжон], fem. (Begmatov 1984, 204); Turk. 14th c. **Tursun-fakih** [طورسون فتيه / طرسون فتيه / Tursun fakih], Osman's (1280-1324) imam (Āšikp. 20, 199, Nešrī 209); Kzk. 19th c. **Tursun-gül** [Турсунгуль], fem. (Grod. I, 98); Bashk.? 18th c. **Tursun-χan** [Tursun Khan] (Howorth II, 639); Kzk.?

1630 **Tursun-χan** [Toursoune-khan] (Levchine 146); Kzk. 1630 **Tursun-χan** / **Tursun-meχmed-sultan** [سلطان مهدی بن سلطان محمد تـرسون / Toursoun-Khan], khan (sultan) of the Kazaks (Abulg./Desm. 328); Uzb. 20th c. **Tursun-χân** [Турсунхон], fem. (Begmatov 1984, 204); Uzb. 20th c. **Tursun-mâmâ** [Турсунмомо], fem. (Begmatov 1984, 204); Khorezm./Chag. 15th - 16th c. **Tursun-meχmed** [محمد تـرسون / Tursun] (Šejb.); Uzb. 20th c. **Tursun-mirza** [Турсунмирза] (Begmatov 1984, 204); *TN:* Turk. 20th c. **Dursun-bey** [Dursunbey], a village in the province of Balıkesir, Turkey (TMİB 142); Trkm. **Dursun-bek** [Дурсун-бек], ruins (Karta JAR XVIII); Kzk. **Tursun**, a burial mound in Semirečie (PM Ergh. 43); Kzk. **Tursun-bay** [Турсун-бай], a well (Karta JAR XI); Kzk.? 19th c. **Tursun-χoja** [خواجه تـرسون / Турсунъ-Ходжа], a settlement (qïšlaq) in the region of Katta Kurgan (ZIRGOStat. IV). ✧ 'May (s)he stay/live; may (s)he long-live; let him/her be healthy' (Sattarov, Žanuzakov), cf. Uyg., Alt., Hak., Kirg., Kzk. etc. *tur-* 'stehen, aufstehen; stehen bleiben, anhalten; leben wohnen' (Radl. III, 1442), Crm., Turk. *dur-* 'stehen, anhalten; wohnen, bleiben' (Radl. III, 1787). See also Grod., Vojna I, 98, Gordlevskij: Êtnogr. Obozr. 1910, vyp. 3-4, 168: „пусть он уцелет", Samojlovič: ŽS 1911, 297: „пусть остается - т. е. не умираетъ", also Rásonyi, Imp. 233. See also **ARAZ-DURSUN, BAY-TURSUN, BEK-TURSÏN, BİYİK-TURSUN, JAN-TURSUN, GÜL-TURSÏN, MAXMUT-DURSUN, MİR-TURSUN, NAR-TURSUN, OΓUL-DURSUN; TOQTASÏN.**

TURSÏN-MÏRAT see **TURSÏN-MURAT**

TURSÏN-MURAT Kkalp. 20th c. **Tursïn-mïrat** [Турсынмырат] (KkRS 776); Kkalp. 20th c. **Tursïn-murat** [Турсынмурат] (KkRS 776); Kkalp. 20th c. **Tursun-murat** [Турсунмурат] (Bask., Kkalp. 72); Uzb. 20th c. **Tursun-murâd** [Турсунмурод] (Begmatov 1984, 204). ⇨ **TURSÏN + MURAT.**

TURSUQ see **TORSUQ**

TURSUN see **TURSÏN**

TURSUN-ALİ Uzb. 20th c. **Tursun-ali** [Турсунали] (Begmatov 1984, 204). ⇨ **TURSÏN + ALİ.**

TURSUN-KÜPÄK Uzb. 19th c. **Tursum-küpäk-diwân-begi / Tursun-köpäk-diwân-begi?** [Toursoum-Koupak-Divanbégui], from the Yüz tribe (Nalivkin-Dozon 145). ⇨ **TURSÏN + KÖPÄK.**

TURSUN-MAΓOMED Kzk. 19th c. **Tursun-maγomed** [Турсунъ-Магомедъ] (SKSO IV, otd. II, 34).

TURSUN-MÄMÄT Uzb. 20th c. **Tursun-mämät** [Турсунмамат] (Begmatov 1984, 204). ⇨ **TURSÏN + MAMET.**

TURṢUN-MUHÄMMÄD see **TURSUN-MUXAMMED**

TURSUN-MUXAMMED Uzb. 20th c. **Tursun-muhämmäd** [Турсунмухаммад] (Begmatov 1984, 200); Khorezm./Chag. 17th c. **Tursun-muχammed** / **Tursun-moχammed** [محمد تورشون / Toursoun-Mohammed], relative of Abulγazi (1603-1664) (Abulg./Desm. 257). ⇨ **TURSÏN + MUXAMMED.**

TURSUN-MURAT see **TURSÏN-MURAT**

TURSUN-PULAT Uzb. 20th c. **Tursun-pulat** [Турсунпулат] (Begmatov 1984, 204). ⇨ **TURSÏN + BULAT.**

TURSUN-TAŠ Kzk. 19th c. **Tursun-taš** [Турсунъ Ташъ] (SKSO III, 10); Uzb. 19th c. **Tursun-taš** [Турсунташъ Нарбутаевъ] (SKSO III, 162). ⇨ **TURSÏN + TAŠ.**

TURSUN-TÂP Uzb. 20th c. **Tursun-tâp** [Турсунтоп] (Begmatov 1984, 204); Uzb. 20th c. **Tursun-tâp** [Турсунтоп], fem. (Begmatov 1984, 204). ✧ 'Let him/her stay/survive healthy!; May he/she be born healthy!' cf. Uzb. *tâp* 'здоровье, зрелость, желание, терпение' (UzbRS). ⇨ **TURSÏN.**

TURSUNMAT Kzk. 19th c. **Tursunmat** [Турсунъматъ] (Nalivkin 12); Uzb. 20th c. **Tursunmat** [Турсунмат] (Begmatov 1984, 204). ⇨ **TURSÏN + suff. -mat.**

TURTU Trkm. 19th c. **Turtu-bay** [Магометъ-Туртубай] (Grod., Vojna IV, (Prilož.) 18). ✧ 'Sediment, residue; last child'? cf. Turk. *turtu / turta* 'der Bodensatz beim Schmelzen der Butter' (Radl. III, 1460).

TURTU-KİL Kzk. 1794 **Turtu-kil-mïrza?** / **Turt-kil-mïrza?** / **Türt-kel-mïrza?** [مـرضه تـورتوكيل / Туртькель] (MIK IV, 160).

TURU see **TORÏ**

TURUQ Uyg. **Turuq** [Turuk] (EUTS); Kzk. 19th c. **Turuq-pay** [Турукпай] (SODž. 12, 72, 86); Kzk. 19th c. **Turuq-pay** [Турукпай] (SOV 64). ✧ 'Lean, thin' cf. Uyg., Karakh. *turuγ III / turuq I* 'худой, истощенный, тощий' (DTS); II. 'Clean, neat' cf. Uyg. *turuq* 'чистый' (DTS). See also **QALAL-DURUQ.**

TURUQ-EDGÜ-TOΓRÏL Uyg. 12th c. - 14th c. **Turuq-edgü-toγrïl** [turuq edgü toγrïl] (DTS). ✧ 'Clean-good-falcon' (Blagova 1997, 707). ⇨ **TURUQ + EDGÜ + TOΓRÏL.**

TURUQ-ÖGÄČÜK Uyg. 12th c. - 14th c. **Turuq-ögäčük** [Turuq Ögäčük (Ügäčük)] (Radl., USp. 55, 95, 96, DTS). ✧ I. 'Meagre/skinny little councillor'; II. 'Clean, clear, neat Ögäčük' (Blagova 1997, 715). ⇨ **TURUQ + ÖGÄ + comp. ügä.**

TURUM Trkm. 20th c. **Torum** [Торум] (Sopieva 178); Turk. 1583 **Turum** [طورم] (Ongan, Ank. I, 173); Kzk. 19th c. **Turum-bay (<Turun-bay?)** [Турумбай] (AOP

122); Kirg. **Turum-bek** (<Turun-bek?) [Турумбек] (Jud. 971); Chag. 16th c. **Turum-biy** [Турум-бий] (Ivanov 162, 180, 184, etc.); Kzk. 1819 **Turun-bay** [Турунбай] (MIK IV, 325); *TN:* Kzk.? **Torom-bay?** / **Turum-bay** (<Turun-bay?) [Торомбай] (Karta JAR XI). ✧ I. 'A two-year-old camel; camel-foal' (Sopieva), 'Camel-foal separated from its mother' (Muhamedova 1957), cf. Karakh. *turum* 'Kamelffüllen, dessen Mutter schon wieder trächtig ist' (MK/Brock.), Karakh. *torum* / *turum* 'верблюжонок' (DTS), Maml. *turum* 'memeden kesilmiş deve yavrusu; dördüncü yaşına giren deve' (İM), Chag. *turum* 'ein zweijähriges Füllen' (Radl. III, 1456), Trkm. *tōrum* 'Camel-foal separated from its mother' (Muhamedova 1957, 39), Turk. *torun* 'ein junges Kameelsfüllen' (Radl. III, 1183), Turk. *dorum*, (dial.) *torum* 'deve yavrusu' (Eren, TDES); II. 'Firmness, steadiness, reliability' cf. Kzk. *turum* 'der Verlass, die Festigkeit' (Radl. III, 1456), Kirg. *turum* 'дверной шарнир; выдержка, постоянство' (Jud.). See also **TAYLAQ**.

TURUMBET   Bashk. 1735 **Turumbet** [Карабай Турумбетевъ], a prince (Vel.-Zern., Bašk. 18); Bashk. 18th c. **Turumbet** [Турумбетевъ], a tarχan (Nepljuev 386); Bashk. 1760 **Turumbet** [Турумбеть Урусбаевъ] (MIB IV/1, 199); Kzk. 1794 **Turumbet** [طورومبت / Турумбет] (MIK IV, 160); Kzk. 19th c. **Turumbet?** [Турумбатъ] (Grod., Pril. 141); Kkalp. 20th c. **Turumbet** [Турумбет] (Bask., Kkalp. 19). ⇨ **TURUM** + suff. *-bet*.

TURUMČÏ see TURUMJÏ

TURUMJÏ   Oghuz/Trkm. 13th c. **Turumčï** [تورمجى / Турумчи] (Abulg./Kon. 525, 550); Trkm. 16th c. **Turumjï** / **Turumji?** [تورمجى / Touroumdji], from Merv (Abulg./Rom. 18, Abulg./Desm. 28, 257); Trkm. 16th c. **Turumjï-biy** [Турумджи-бий] (MIT II, 34). ⇨ **TURUM?** + suff. *-jï / -čï*.

TURUMTAY   Kzk. 18th c. - 19th c. **Turumday-qoža** [Турумдай-кожа Кулмановъ] (ZOOIRGO IV, 99); Karakh. 11th c. **Turumtay** [Turumtai / Turumtaj / Turumtay], a slave (MK/Brock., 250, DTS, MK/Atalay 855); Selj.? 12th c. **Turumtay** [طرمطاى / Turumtai] (Muh. Ibrahim 59-61, 64-66, 93); Uzb. 1701 **Turumtay** [طرمتاى حاجى قلماق / Tarymtaj Hâggî-Qalmaq], follower of Sultan ʿUbaydullâh from Bukhara (Buchari 360); Maml.? **Turumtay** / **Turuntay?** [طرنطاى / سيفالدين طرمطاى] (Ibn Bîbî IV, 267-269, 282, 288 etc.); Kuman 1185 **Turunday** / **Turuntay** [Турундай], a Polovets prince (Lavr. 375, PSRL XV, 271, Bask., Im. polov. 75); Selj. 1136 **Turuntay** [طرنطاى / Torontaï], governor of „Ouacet" (Ibn al-Athīr, Atab.: RHCHor II/2, 94); Selj. 12th c. **Turuntay** [حسامالدين طُرُنْطاي العزيرِيّ] (Ibn Šaddād, Alep 135); Selj. 1192/93 **Turuntay** [طرنطاى / Torontaï], Saladīn's

envoy (Ibn Šaddād, Nawād.: RHCHor III, 343-44); Maml. 13th c. - 14th c. **Turuntay** [طرنطاى], an emir (Duqmaq:RHCHor IV, 70, 120); Maml. 1260, 1279/80, 1286, 1299 **Turuntay** [حسامالدين طرنطاي / Hosameddin Tarantaï], an emir and governor (Makrīzī, Khit. I, 386, Makrīzī I, 100, III, 6, 29, 113, Dawād. 37, Zetterst. 148, Abulfidā V, 86-87, 95-96, Weil, Chalif. I, 160, 275, also Gombocz: MNy. X(1914), 296)); Maml. 1283 **Turuntay** [طرنطاى] (Iyās I, 115, 116, 117); Maml. 1294 **Turuntay** [طرنطاى الساقى], one of the murderers of Sultan Khalil (Zetterst. 29, Makrīzī III, 153, Weil, Chalif. I, 192); Maml. 1310 **Turuntay** [طرنطاى جرمشى], an emir (Dawād. 212); Maml. 1330 **Turuntay** [طرنطاى المحمدى] (Zetterst. 194); Maml. 14th c. **Turuntay** [طرنطاى], a doorkeeper (χajib) in Damascus (Iyās I, 149); Maml. 14th c. **Turuntay** [طرنطاى البشمقدار] (Zetterst. 158); Maml. 14th c. - 15th c. **Turuntay** [طرنطاى الطبّاخى / Turunṭāy aṭ-Ṭabbākhī] (Mayer 240-241); Maml. 1410 **Turuntay** [طرنطاى الظاهرى] (Ibn Taghrīb. VI, 363); Maml. 1482 **Turuntay** [طرنطاى المحمودى] (Ibn Taghrīb. II, 216); Chuv. 18th-19th c. **Turuntay** [Турундай] (Magn. 87); Tat. 1633 **Turuntay** [Илчмаметко Турунтаев] (Miller, Ist. Sib. II, 402); Tat.? 1668 **Turuntay** [Трошка Туринтаевъ], a soldier (Kungursk. akty 10); Kzk. 19th c. **Turuntay** [Турунтай] (AOP 66); Kirg.? 19th c. **Turuntay** [Турунтай] (Potanin II, 5); Maml. 14th c. **Turuntay** / **Turunta** [طُرُنطا / طُرُنطاي] (Sauvaget 50); *TN:* 1750 **Turuntay(eva)** [Турунтаева], a village in the county of Tomsk (VIRGO XXIX, II, 229). ✧ 'A species of bird of prey: sparrow-hawk, buzzard, kite, falcon, shrike, merlin' cf. Karakh. *turumtai* 'ein Raubvogel, daher Männername' (MK/Brock.), *turumtaj* 'дербник (Falco Columlarius)' (DTS), Chag., Kzk. *turumtay* 'ein kleiner Raubvogel, der Neuntödter' (Radl. III, 1456), Maml. *ṭurunṭaj* 'espèce d'autour, oiseau de proie' (BM), Maml. *ṭorunṭay* 'ястреб' (Tuhfa), also Ross, Polyglot List No. 76, Ligeti: Pais Eml. (1956), 336-346, TMEN II, No. 896, Gombocz: MNy. X(1914), 296, Rásonyi, Val.-Turc. 3. See also **QARA-TORONTAY**.

TURUN I. see TURUM

TURUN II.   Yak. **Turun** [Турун] (Pek.).

TURUN-BUƔA   Chag. 1566 **Turun-buγa** [Турун Буга] (Ivanov 318). ⇨ **TURUM** + **BUQA**.

TURUNTA see TURUMTAY

TURUNTAY see TURUMTAY

TURUP-BERDİ   Bashk. 1706, 1707 **Turup-berdi** / **Trup-berdi** [Турупберда / Трупберда Камакаевъ / Трупберды Камакаев] (MIB III, 29, 31). ✧ ? ⇨ **TURUP?** + **BERDİ.**

TURUS see TURÏS

TURUŠ I.   1670 **Turuš** [Казычка Турушевъ] (DAI

VI, 26); Uyg. 12th c. - 14th c. **Turuš-qatun** [turuš qatun], fem. (DTS). ✧ 'Resistance; debate' (Blagova 1997, 716) cf. Uyg. *turušči* 'участник спора; противник' (DTS). See also **TURUM**.

TURUŠ II.   Alt. 19th-20th c. **Turuš** [Туруш] (OjrRS 210). ✧ 'Firmness, steadiness, reliability; constancy' (OjrRS), cf. Alt., Hak. *turüš-* 'für etwas einstehen, sich für jemand stellen, bürgen; werth sein' (Radl. III, 1455).

TURUZDAN   Tat. 1645 **Turuzdan** [Туруздан Куртумов] (Miller, Ist. Sib. II, 511).

TUSAQ   Kzk. 19th c. **Tusaq-pay** [Тусакпай] (SOK 294). ✧ 'A two-year-old sheep' cf. Kzk. *tusaq* 'ein junges Schaf vom zweiten Frühlinge (nach der Geburt)' (Radl. III, 1500). See also **ŠIŠIK**.

TUSÏY   Bashk. 1779 **Tusïy** [Тажбулат Тусыев] (MIB V, 101).

TUSTUQ   Kzk. 19th c. **Tustuq** [Тузтукъ] (SOK 42, 208); Kzk. 19th c. **Tustuq-pay** [Тустукпай] (SODž. 54). ✧ 'A kind of salty soup' cf. Kzk. *tuzdüq* 'die Salzbrühe, mit der das Fleisch genossen wird' (Radl. III, 1508).

TUSUM-BAY see **TOSUN**

TUSUN see **TOSUN**

TUSUP   Kzk. 19th c. **Tusup-pek** [Тусуппекъ] (SOK 90).

TUŠ   Chuv. 18th-19th c. **Tuš** [Тушъ] (Magn. 87). See also **BAY-TUŠ, YALAÑ-TUŠ**.

TUŠKA   Chuv. 18th-19th c. **Tuška** [Тушка] (Magn. 87). ⇨ **TUŠ** + suff. *-qa*.

TUŠKEY   Chuv. 18th-19th c. **Tuškey** [Тушкей] (Magn. 87). ⇨ **TUŠ?** + suff. *-key*.

TUŠQAN see **TÏSQAN**

TUŠQANČÏQ   Kzk. 19th c. **Tušqančïq** [Тушканчикъ] (Potanin IV, 180). ✧ I. 'Little mouse'; II. 'A little animal which sucks the cows at night' (Potanin). ⇨ **TÏSQAN** + dim. suff. *-čïq*.

TUT-KERÄY   Crm. 1635 **Tut-keräy-aγa** [توتکرای اغا] (Vel.-Zern., Crim. 144, 211). ⇨ **TUT + KERÄY.**

TUTA   Nog. **Tuta-arï** [Тута-Ары], one of the foremothers of the Nogays (Smirnov, Krym. 77); Nog. **Tuta-murza** (Žirm., Epos 431). ✧ 'Elder sister, aunt (on father's side)' cf. Tat. *tuta* 'die ältere Schwester, die Tante (die ältere Schwester des Vaters)' (Radl. III, 1479), <R. тётя 'Tante' (Räs.).

TUTA-MEÑGÜ   Tat.(GH)? 1282 **Tuta-meñgü** [توتامنکو], brother of the Kipchak Meñgü-temür (Biogr. Kalavun 66). ⇨ **TUTA + MEÑGÜ.**

TUTAY   Tat.(Lit.) 1548, 1555 **Totay** [Тотай] (Kn. Metriki Lit. 45, 113); Tat. 1624 **Totay** [Тотай Янбаевъ] (Pokrovskij 71); Kzk. 19th c. **Totay** [Тотай] (AOP 30); Crm. 1558 **Tutay** [Тутай], a messenger (PSRL XIII, 287); Bashk. 18th c. **Tutay** [Тутаев Абдулкаримъ] (MIB V, 83); Bashk. 1754 **Tutay** [Тутай Сеитовъ] (MIB IV/1, 83); Bashk. 1756 **Tutay** [Муслюм Тутаевъ] (MIB IV/1, 128); Bashk. 1756 **Tutay** [Юсуп Тутаевъ] (MIB IV/1, 128); Bashk. 1776 **Tutay** [Тутай Ибраевъ] (MIB V, 33, 34); Kzk. 19th c. **Tutay** [Тутай Ирназаровъ] (SKSO IV, otd. III, 13); Kzk. 1785 **Tutay-bahadïr** [توتای بهادر], from the Jaγalbaylï tribe (MIK IV, 52, 53); Kzk. 1792 **Tutay-batïr** [Тутай батыр] (MIK IV, 140). ✧ I. '(Elder) brother and/or sister' cf. Tat.(Tara) *tutay* 'die Geschwister', Bashk. dial. *tutay* 'старшая сестра; тётка, тётя; мачеха' (BRS/Uraksin), used also as a secondary component; II. 'Camel-foal'? (in the Crimea) (Sattarov). ⇨ **TUTA** + dim. suff. *-y.*

TUTAQ   Selj.? 1040 **Tutaq** [Τουτάχ], a commander (Byz. Turc. 328); Khorezm.? **Tutaq** [Тутак] (RaD II, 12); Maml. 15th c. **Tutaq** [بیبرس الاشرفی بن ططغ] (Iyās II, 53, 156); *TN:* Uzb. **Tutaq-ata** [Тутак ата], a place (?) south of Samarkand (Karta JAR XIX). ✧ 'Hostage' cf. Chag., Turk. *tutaq* 'die Kriegsgeissel' (Radl. III, 1479).

TUTAL   Maml.? 13th c. **Tutal** [Schehab-eddin-Toutal-Schehrizouri], died at Hims in 1280 (?); Kzk. 1621, 1622 **Tutal** [Тутал], a prince of the Chulym-region (Miller, Ist. Sib. II, 289, 562).

TUTAM   Kzk. 19th c. **Totam-bay / Tutam-bay** [Тотамбай] (IOAIÊK XX, 228). ✧ 'Pinch, small handful; bunch, sheaf'? cf. Tat. *totam* 'пук; клок; мера длины равная ширине ладони' (TatRS), Kzk. *tutam* 'tutam' (KzTS).

TUTAN   Trkm. 1386 **Tutan** (Weil, Chalif. II, 29). See also **SAQAL-TUTAN.**

TUTAR   Chuv. 18th-19th c. **Totar** [Тотаръ] (Magn. 86); Chuv. 18th-19th c. **Totar-bay** [Тотарбай] (Magn. 86). See also **EL-TUTAR.**

TUTÏM   Uzb. 19th c. **Tutïm** [Иргашъ Тутымъ Джауліевъ] (SKSO III, 160). ✧ 'My parrot'. ⇨ **TUTÏ** + poss. suff. *-m.*

TUTKE   Kzk. 19th c. **Tutke** [Тутке] (AOP 42). ⇨ **TUTQA / TUT?** + suff. *-ke* <comp. *-ake?*

TUTKENENKÄ   Tat. 17th c. **Tutkenenkä** [Туткененка Мамаевъ], from the government of Kazan (IOAIÊK XXIX, 348).

TUTQA   Kzk. 19th c. **Tutqa-bay** [Туткабай] (SKSO II, 14, III, 20); Kzk. 19th c. **Tutqa-bay** [Туткобай] (SOK 26); Kzk. 19th c. **Tutqa-bek** [Туткабекъ] (SODž. 134). ✧ 'Crank, holder, handle' cf. Chag., Alt., Kzk. *tutqa* 'der Griff, der Stiel (der Pfanne), die Handhabe, die Klinke' (Radl. III, 1486).

TUTQUM   Kzk. 19th c. **Totqum** [Тоткумъ] (SOK 18); Kzk. 19th c. **Tutqum** [Халманъ Туткумовъ] (Grod., Pril 167). ✧ I. 'My crank, holder, handle'? cf. Chag. *tutqu* 'der Griff, der Stiel (der Pfanne), die Handhabe, die Klinke' (Radl. III, 1489); II. 'Captive' cf. Uyg.,

Kuman, Chag., Turk. *tutqun* 'gefasst; der Gefangene' (Radl. III, 1489), Kzk. *tŭtqïn* 'пленник' (KzRS). See also **TUTQA, TUTQUŠ**.

TUTQUNAQ Hak.(Koyb.) 19th c. **Tutqunaq** [Туткунакъ], fem. (Katanov, Otč. II, 12-15). ✧ 'Abducted' (Katanov).

TUTQUŠ Kzk. 19th c. **Totqïš** [Тоткишъ] (AOK 118); Kzk. 19th c. **Totqoš / Tutquš?** [Тоткошъ] (AOAtb. 46); Kzk. 19th c. **Totquš** [Тоткушъ] (AOA 114); Kzk. 19th c. **Totquš** [Тоткушъ] (SOV 58); Kzk. 19th c. **Totquš-pay** [Тоткушпай] (SOK 162); Kzk. 19th c. **Tutχuš-bay** [Тутхушбай] (Grod., Pril. 93); Kzk. 19th c. **Tutquš** [Туткушъ] (AOK 90); Kzk. 19th c. **Tutquš** [Туткушъ] (AOP 114); Kzk. 19th c. **Tutquš** [Туткушъ] (SOK 44); Kzk. 19th c. **Tutquš-pay** [Туткушпай] (AOO 42); Kzk. 19th c. **Tutquš-pay** [Туткушпай] (SOK 120, 200). ✧ 'Crank, holder, handle' cf. Alt., Kzk. *tutquš* 'griff, Henkel, Stiel, Istrument zum Herausnehmen heisser Töpfe aus der Tiefe des Ofens; ein Lappen oder Filzstück, mit dem man heisse Gegenstände mit der Hand anfasst' (Radl. III, 1491).

TUTMUQ Trkm. 1881 **Tutmuq** [Тутмукъ] (Grod., Vojna IV, 19).

TUTUГUŠ Bashk. 1764 **Tutuγuš** [Тутугуш Сеитова] (MIB IV/1, 281).

TUTUQ Türk? **Tutuq** [توتك / Toutouk], Türk's son, Yafet's grand-son (Abulg./Desm. 9); Karakh. 11th c. **Tutuq** [Tutuk / tutuq] (MK/Atalay 855, EUTS, DTS); Khorezm.? 14th c. **Tutuq-χanïm** [Tutuk Khánim], the Dughlatid Maχmud-χan's daughter (Tar. Rashidi 251). ✧ 'Military leader/commander (of a district)' cf. Uyg., Karakh. *tutuq II.* 'id.' (DTS) (<Chin.). As a secondary components (title) it is frequently used in personal names.

TUTUQA Yak. **Tutuqa-bātïr** [Тутука-батыр], a hero (Pek.). ⇨ **TUTUQ**.

TUTUŇ Uyg. **Tutuñ** [Tutung] (EUTS); Uyg. **Tutuñ** [Tutung] (EUTS).

TUTUŚ Khorezm./ Mo.? **Tutuǰ / Tutuč** [Тутудж] (RaD II, 73); Karakh. 11th c. **Tutuš** [tutuš / Tutuş] (DTS, MK/Atalay 855); Selj. 1079, 1085, 1095 **Tutuš** [تتش / تُتُش / تُتُش / Τουτούσης / Tatâsh / Tutuch / Тадж-ад-даула Тутуш / Тутуш ибн Алп-Арслан], Alp-arslan's (1063-1072) son, paternal uncle of Berk-yaruq (1094-1104), the lord of Damascus in 1079 and 1085, died in 1095 (Ibn al-Athīr/Tornb. IX, 165, X, 96-98, 149-151 etc., Ibn al-Athīr, Atab.: RHCHor II/2, 16, 29, Bondārī 47, 70, 84, 85, Rāwandī 142, Qazw. 446, 480, Abulfar./Budge I, 232, RaD/Quatrem. 225, Ahbar 38, 49, 52, Aqsarāyi 20, 21, Aqsar/Iş. 34, Rašīduddīn/Erdmann: ZDMG IX, 804-05, Ibn al-Athīr: RHCHor I, 862, Weil, Abbas III, 126, Byz. Turc. 328, MIT I, 376, 381). ✧ 'Strong, hard, massive' cf. Chag. *tutuš* 'fest, solide, massiv' (Radl. III, 1485).

TUVAN Chuv. 18th-19th c. **Tuvan** [Туванъ] (Magn. 87). ⇨ **TUГAN?** See also **AQ-TUWAN**.

TUVAN-GİLDE Chuv. 18th-19th c. **Tuvan-gilde** [Тувангилда] (Magn. 87). ⇨ **TUVAN + KELDİ**.

TUVANDEY Chuv. 18th-19th c. **Tuvandey** [Тувандей] (Magn. 87). ⇨ **TUVAN +** suff. *-dey*.

TUVГAN-QOZ Türk / Uyg. 8th c. - 9th c. **Tuvγan-qoz** [tuvγan qoz] (DTS). ⇨ **TUГAN I**.

TUW Kzk. 19th c. **Tuw-murza (<Tū-murza?)** [Тумурза] (AOAtb. 46); *EN:* Kzk. 18th c. - 19th c. **Tuw-ata?** [طواطا / Туата], a part (division) of a tribe (MIK IV, 432, 434). ✧ I. 'Banner, flag' cf. Kzk. *tū* 'die Fahne, das Banner' (Radl. III, 1421); II. 'Be born!' cf. Kuman, Alt., Hak., Kirg., Kzk., Tat. *tū-* 'gebären; geboren werden' (Radl. III, 1422). See also **KÜN-TUW, UL-TUW**.

TUWA 14th c. **Tuwa-χan** [Тува-ханъ], a Chinggisid (after Qazw. Barth., Ulugb. 8). See also **MEŇ-TUWA**.

TUWAQ Trkm. 20th c. **Tuwaq** [Тувак] (Sopieva 181). ✧ I. 'Born in „shirt" [caul?]' (Sopieva)'; II. 'Hoof'? cf. Chag. *tuwaγ/tuwaq* 'der Huf' (Radl. III, 1516). See also **AY-TUWAQ, ANNA-TUWAQ, ARAZ-TUWAQ, OГUL-TUWAQ, ORAZ-TUWAQ**.

TUWAŠ Kzk. 19th c. **Tuwaš-pay** [Туашпай] (SOK 126).

TUWČÏ see **TUГČÏ**

TUWJÏ see **TUГČÏ**

TUWLU Tat.(GH) 1340 **Tuwlu-bi** [Тувлуби / Товлуби / Товлубiи] (PSRL XXIII, 105). ⇨ **TUW +** suff. *-lu*.

TUZ Kzk. 19th c. **Tuz-bay** [Тузбай] (SOK 116); Selj./Trkm. 13th c. - 14th c. **Tuz-beg** [توز بك / توز بيك / Tuz Beg], an emir (Ibn Bībī III, 61); Uyg. 1339 **Tuz-tärim** [Tuz Tarim], fem. (Chwol., Syr.-nest. (NF) 35); Uyg. 1269 **Tuz-tirim** [Tuz-Tirim-Koštanz] (Chwol., Syr.-nest. II, 23); *TN:* Kzk. 19th c. **Tuz-mula** [Тузъ-мула], a tomb North of the Caspian Sea (IIRGO XVI (Karta ur. Ten'tjak-sor)). ✧ 'Salt'? cf. Chag., Kuman, East.T., Kirg., Kzk. etc. *tuz* 'id.' (Radl. III, 1502), Trkm. *duz (dūz)* 'соль' (TrkmRS). See also **BAY-TUZ, MÏRZA-TUS**.

TUZ-AYA Uyg. 1274 **Tuz-aya** [Tuzaja Kostanz] (Chwol., Syr.-nest. II, 25). ⇨ **TUZ?**

TUZ-AŠA Uyg. 1320 **Tuz-aša** [Tuz Aša], fem. (Chwol., Syr.-nest. (NF) 22). ⇨ **TUZ + AŠA**.

TUZ-AŠLAN Uyg. 13th c. -14th c. **Tuz-ašlan / Tuz-ačlan** [Tuz Achlan] (Chwol., Syr.-nest. (NF) 43). ⇨ **TUZ**.

TUZ-BİLGÄ Uyg. 1323 **Tuz-bilgä?** [Tuz Pelga], fem. (Chwol., Syr.-nest. (NF) 23). ⇨ **TUZ + BİLGÄ**.

TUZAГAŠ Alt. 19th c. **Tuzaγaš** [Тузагашъ] (Potanin, Pred. 187).

TUZANA Bashk. 1760 **Tuzana-bik(ovo)**

[Тузанабиково], a village (MIB IV/2, 28).

TUZJALÏ Turk. 19th c. **Tuzjalï-oγlu** [Tuzǯaly oγlu], a Zeybek (Kúnos 1891, 119). ✧ 'Coming/being from Tuzja'.

TUZU Kzk. 19th c. **Tuzu-bay** [Тузубаевъ] (Grod., Pril. 153); Kzk. 19th c. **Tuzu-bay** [Тузюбай] (SOK 40).

TUZUM-BÏY see **TOSUN**

TUZUN see **TOSUN**

TUŽAÑQA Alt. 19th-20th c. **Tužañqa** [Тужанка], fem. (OjrRS 213).

TŪ see **TUW**

TŪLAYÏMA Yak. **Tūlayïma** [Тулајыма] (Pek.). ✧ 'Overturning, overturner' cf. Yak. *tūlay-* 'буйствовать, переворачивать (что вверх дном)' (Pek.).

TŪNČA Hak. 19th-20th c. **Tūnča** [Тунча], fem. (Katanov, Otč. 11). ✧ Duncha (R.) (Katanov), hypoc. of R. fem. Yevdokiya or Yazdundokta.

TŪNQA Hak. 19th c. **Tūnqa** [Тунка] (Katanov, Otč. 12). ✧ Dunka (R.) (Katanov), hypoc. of R. fem. Yevdokiya or Yazdundokta.

TŪSTAYAN Yak. **Tūstayan** [Тустајан] (Pek.).

TŪ-DANAQ Alt. **Tü-danaq-bökö** [Тӱданакъ-бӧкӧ / Тӱнадакъ-бӧкӧ], hero, mentioned together with Köldenek-böko (Nikiforov 79, 85).

TÜBÄČ Bashk. 1709 **Tübäč** [Тюбяч Шабанов] (MIB I, 264).

TÜBÄK Chuv. 18th-19th c. **Tübäk** [Тюбякъ] (Magn. 87).

TÜBÄN Yak. **Tübän-bögö** [Тӱбän-бӧҕӧ], one of Älläy's sons (Pek.).

TÜBÄNČÜK Uyg. 12th c. - 14th c. **Tübänčük** [tübänčük] (DTS). ✧ 'Short (man)' cf. Chag., Kuman, Hak., etc. *töbän* 'unten, herab' (Radl. III, 1271), Tat. *tübän* 'unten befindlich, in der Niederung befindlich, unten, unterhalb' (Radl. III, 1597).

TÜBÄNDÄY see **TÜMÄNDÄY**

TÜBE-GELDİ Kzk. 19th c. **Tübe-geldi** [Тюбегельды] (SOK 176). ⇨ **TÜBE + KELDİ.**

TÜBEK Kzk. 19th c. **Tübäk-pay** [Тубакпай] (SOK 32); Kzk. 19th c. **Tübek** [Тюбекъ] (AOAtb. 50); Kzk. 19th c. **Tübek** [Тубекъ] (AOO 58); Kzk. 19th c. **Tübek-pay** [Тубекпай] (SOK 104, 124, 262); Kzk. 19th c. **Tübek-pay** [Тубекпай] (SOV 74, 136). ⇨ **TÖBÖK?**

TÜBEK-TAY Kzk. 19th c. **Tübek-tay** [Тюбектай] (SOK 120). ⇨ **TÖBÖK + TAY?** or suff. *-tay(1,2).*

TÜBEN Chuv. 18th-19th c. **Tüben** [Тюбень] (Magn. 87). ✧ 'Below, underfoot, underneath' cf. Tat. *tübän* 'unten befindlich, in der Niederung befindlich, unten, unterhalb' (Radl. III, 1597).

TÜBET see **TÖBET**

TÜČAL Bashk. 1756 **Tüčal / Tüčäl? / Tüšäl?** [Али Тючалев] (MIB IV/1, 108).

TÜČEY Kzk. 19th c. **Tüčey** [Тучей] (AOA 134).

TÜDEY Alt. 19th c. **Tüdey-χan** [Тюдей-хан] (Verb., In. 144, 147).

TÜGDENES Hak. 19th-20th c. **Tügdenes** [Тӱгденес] (HRS 352).

TÜGÄL see **TÜKÄL**

TÜGÄL-MURAT Uzb. 20th c. **Tügäl-murâd** [Тугалмурод] (Begmatov 1984, 205). ⇨ **TÜKÄL + MURAT.**

TÜGEY Chuv. 1728 **Tügey** [Досайка Тюгеев] (MIB I, 128); Chuv. 18th-19th c. **Tügey** [Тюгей] (Magn. 88); Tat. 1731 **Tügey** [Тюгей] (MIB III, 293). ⇨ **TÖKEY?** See also **BAY-TÜGEY.**

TÜGENEŠ Chuv. 18th-19th c. **Tügeneš** [Тюгенешъ] (Magn. 88). ✧ 'End; enough' cf. Chag. *tügäniš* 'die Beendigung, das Ende' (Radl. III, 1535).

TÜGEŠ Chuv. 18th-19th c. **Tügeš** [Тюгешъ] (Magn. 88). ⇨ **TÖGEŠ / TUΓUŠ I.?** See also **QAR-TÜGEŠ.**

TÜGİZ Kzk. 19th c. **Tügiz-bay** [Тюгизбай] (SOK 114). ✧ 'Full, perfect'? cf. Chag. *tököz* 'voll, vollständig' (Radl. III, 1243).

TÜGME Chag. 16th c. **Tügme-atalïq** [Тугмэ-аталык] (Ivanov 320); Tat.(Lit.)? 1277, 1281 **Tüymä / Tuyma?** [Туйма (Тюима)] (PSRL II, 207, 209, 211); Kzk. 19th c. **Tüymö-sulu** [Тüimö-sulu], fem. (IOAIÊK XXIV, 434-36). ✧ 'Knob' cf. Karakh. *tügmä* 'пуговица (завязка)' (DTS), Chag., East.T. *tügmä* 'der Knopf' (Radl. III, 1541), Kuman *tŭmä* 'id.' (Radl. III, 1602), Turk. *tüymä* 'id.' (Radl. III, 1529), Kzk. *tüymö* 'id.' (Radl. III, 1530).

TÜGÖL see **TÜKÄL**

TÜGRİN Hak. 19th-20th c. **Tügrin** [Тӱгрiн], fem. (HRS 355).

TÜGÜBÄ Kzk. 1742 **Tügübä** [Тюгуба] (MIB I, 486).

TÜGÜL Kzk. 19th c. **Tögül-bay** [Тогульбай] (SOV 78); Kzk. 19th c. **Tügöl-bay** [Тугольбай] (SOV 18); Kzk. 19th c. **Tügül** [Тугуль] (SODž. 134); Bashk. 1756 **Tügül-bay** [Сабытай Тугульбаев] (MIB IV/1, 132); Kzk. 19th c. **Tügül-bay** [Тугульбай] (SODž. 12, 62); Kzk. 19th c. **Tügül-bay** [Тугульбай] (SODž. 12, 62); Kzk. 19th c. **Tüwül-bay** [Туульбай] (SODž. 82). ✧ 'All, whole' (Žanuzakov 159), 'His every limb is sound' (Sattarov), cf. Tat. *tögäl* 'полный, сполна' (TatRS), Kzk. *tügel* 'весь, целиком, сполна' (KzRS). See also **BAY-TÜGEL.**

TÜYEŠİ Kzk. 19th c. **Tüyeši** [Туеши] (AOA 86). ✧ 'Herdsman/breeder of camels'. ⇨ **DEVE** + suff. *-ši.*

TÜYMÖ see **TÜGME**

TÜYTE Kzk. 19th c. **Tüyte-bay** [Тюйтебай] (SODž. 24); Kzk. 19th c. **Tüyte-bek** [Тюйтебекъ] (AOK 2); Kzk. 19th c. **Tüyte-bek** [Тюйтебекъ] (SODž. 124).

TÜYÜ Bashk.? 1675 **Tüyü-čura** [Тюючюра / Тевтюячира Токпердин] (MIB I, 202).

TÜYÜNČEK Kzk. 19th c. **Tüyünček** [Тююнчекъ] (SODž. 122, 124). ✧ 'Knot, loop' cf. Kzk. *tüyünšök* 'das Bündel' (Radl. III, 1547), Kzk. *tüyüm* 'узел'

TÜK Hak.(Sag.) 19th-20th c. **Tük** [Түк] (Katanov, Otč. 8); Kzk. 1785 **Tük-bay-behadïr** [توکبای بهادر / Тилбай (!) бахадур], an „aq-saqal" (chief of a settlement) (MIK IV, 51, 53); Chuv. 18th-19th c. **Tük-murza** [Тюкмурза] (Magn. 88). ✧ 'Hair, fur, wool, fleece' (Katanov), Uyg., Alt., Chag., Hak., Kirg., Kzk. *tük* 'das Thierhaar, die Haare am Körper des Menschen' (Radl. III, 1530). See also **QAN-TÜK**.

TÜKÄ Uyg. **Tügä** [Tügä] (EUTS); Maml. 1293 **Tükä** [تكا], a Kipchak? (Baybars/Tizeng. I, 86, 109); Kzk. 1819 **Tükä-bay** [Тюкабай] (MIK IV, 323); Kzk. 19th c. **Tüke-bay** [Сиркебай Тукебаевъ] (Grod., Pril. 117); Kzk. 19th c. **Tüki-bay** [Тукибай Баймирзаевъ] (Grod., Pril. 45); Kzk. 19th c. **Tüki-bay** [Ахмедъ Тукибаевъ] (Grod., Pril. 95). ⇨ **TÖKE?** See also **TOLUQ-TÜKÄ**.

TÜKÄDİ Uyg. 12th c. - 14th c. **Tükädi-tutuq** [Tükädi Tutuq] (Radl., USp. 127, 236).

TÜKÄL Uyg. **Tökäl** [Tökäl] (EUTS); Uyg. 12th c. - 14th c. **Tügäl** [Tügäl] (Radl., USp. 204, 246); Uzb. 20th c. **Tügäl** [Тугал] (Begmatov 1984, 205); Uzb. 20th c. **Tügäl** [Тугал], fem. (Begmatov 1984, 205); Uzb. 20th c. **Tügäl-ây** [Тугалой], fem. (Begmatov 1984, 205); Uzb. 20th c. **Tügäl-bây** [Тугалбой] (Begmatov 1984, 205); Uzb. 20th c. **Tügäl-bek** [Тугалбек] (Begmatov 1984, 205); Uzb. 20th c. **Tügäl-ĵân** [Тугалжон] (Begmatov 1984, 205); Chag. 15th c. - 16th c. **Tügäl-χoĵa / Tükäl-χoĵa?** [توکل خواجه] (Šejb. XLIX); Uzb. 20th c. **Tügäl-mirza** [Тугалмирза] (Begmatov 1984, 205); Kzk. 18th c. - 19th c. **Tügel** [Тугель] (Tynyšp. 66); Kzk. 19th c. **Tügel** [Тугелъ] (AOO 78); Kzk. 18th c. - 19th c. **Tügel-bay** [Тугельбай] (Tynyšp. 72); Kzk. 19th c. **Tügel-bay** [Тугельбай] (SODž. 38); Kzk. 19th c. **Tügel-bay** [Тугельбай] (SOV 108); Kzk. 19th c. **Tügöl** [Тугёлъ] (AOK 42); Kzk. 19th c. **Tügöl** [Тугёлъ] (AOO 2, 62); Kzk. 19th c. **Tügöl-bay** [Тугольбай] (SOV 42); 1403/04 **Tükäl** [توکل باورجی] (Dorn); Uyg. 12th c. - 14th c. **Tükäl** [Tükäl / Tögäl] (Radl., USp. 202, 244, DTS); Khorezm./Chag. 1360 **Tükäl** [Тукель], emir of Khiva (MIT I, 512); Bashk. 1708 **Tükäl** [Темеряк Тюкалев] (MIB I, 234); Bashk. 1738 **Tükäl** [Муняк Тюкелев] (MIB III, 391); Crm. 1644 **Tükäl-oγlu** [توکل اوغلو] (Vel.-Zern., Crim. 346); Uyg. 10th c. - 13th c. **Tükäl-tegin** [توکال دکین / Tükäl-tegin] (Ĵuwaynī I, 41, 42). ✧ I. 'Full, perfect, innocent'; 'Be finished (=enough of births! no more children!)' (Begmatov); II. 'All, whole' (Žanuzakov 159), 'His every limb is sound' (Sattarov), cf. Uyg., Karakh. *tükäl* 'полный, совершенный' (DTS), Uyg., Chag., Kuman *tügäl* 'ganz, alle; vollkommen, unschuldig' (Radl. III, 1536), Chag. *tükäl* 'id.' (Radl. III, 1531), Uzb. *tügäl* 'законченный, окончательный, полный' (UzbRS),

Tat. *tögäl* 'полный, сполна' (TatRS), Kzk. *tügel* 'весь, целиком, сполна' (KzRS).

TÜKÄL-QARA Uyg. 12th c. - 14th c. **Tükäl-qara** [Tökäl-qara / Tükäl-qara] (Radl., USp. 27-28, DTS). ✧ 'Perfect-black' (Bese 19, Blagova 1997, 715). ⇨ **TÜKÄL + QARA.**

TÜKÄLÄ Uyg. **Tükälä**, fem. (Zieme, Mat. I, 75). ✧ 'Oh, (You,) perfect!' (Zieme). ⇨ **TÜKÄL** + voc. suff. -*ä*.

TÜKÄLEY Kzk. 19th c. **Tükäley / Tük-ali(y)?** [Тюкалей] (AOP 26).

TÜKÄN Bashk. 18th c. **Tükän** [Тюканъ] (Valihanov, Soč. 205); Bashk. 1751, 1754 **Tükän** [Тюкан Балтасев / Болтасев] (MIB IV/1, 45, 83); Bashk. 1754 **Tüken** [Юлай Тюкенев] (MIB IV/1, 83).

TÜKE-TUZÏ- Kzk. 19th c. **Tüke-tuzï** [Тукетузы] (SOV 108).

TÜKEY Bashk. 1778 **Tükey** [Тюкей Салимов] (MIB V, 70); Bashk. 1789 **Tükey** [Тюкей Султанов] (MIB V, 245, 284); Bashk. 1789 **Tükey** [Тевлекей Тюкеев] (MIB V, 263); Kzk. 19th c. **Tükey** [Тукей] (SOV 112). ⇨ **TÖKE / TÜKE?** + suff. -*ey*.

TÜKEŠ Alt. 19th-20th c. **Tükeš** [Түкеш], fem. (OjrRS 213).

TÜKKÄY Hak.(Sag.) 19th-20th c. **Tükkäy** [Түккäi] (Proben IX, 236); Tuv. 19th c. **Tükkäy** [Түккäi] (Proben IX, 95, 116).

TÜKÖ Kirg. **Tükö** [Тукө] (Jud. 38). ✧ Hypochoristic contracted form of hte name *Tügöl-bay* (Jud. 38) + suff. -*kö* <comp. -*ake*.

TÜKÖÑ Kirg. **Tüköñ** [Тукөӈ] (Jud. 38). ✧ Informal-humorous form of *Tükö*. ⇨ **TÜKÖ** + poss. suff. -*ñ*.

TÜKPÄY Hak.(Sag.) 19th-20th c. **Tükpäy** [Түкпäй] (Katanov, Otč. 8). ✧ 'Hairy, bristly, woolly, fleecy' (Butanaev). ⇨ **TÜK.**

TÜKRÜNČ Uyg. **Tükrünč** [Tükrünç] (EUTS).

TÜKRÜNČ-BUQA Uyg. 12th c. - 14th c. **Tükrünč-buqa** [Tü(ö)krünč Buqa / Tökrünč Buqa] (Radl., USp. 48-49). ⇨ **TÜKRÜNČ + BUQA.**

TÜKTÏSKÄ Karg. 19th-20th c. **Tüktïskä** [Түктіскä], fem. (Katanov, Otč. 8).

TÜKTÜ Alt. 19th-20th c. **Tüktü** [Түктÿ] (OjrRS 210); Hak.(Koyb.) 19th-20th c. **Tüktü-bằy** [Түктÿбäй] (Katanov., Otč. 13). ✧ 'Hairy, bristly, woolly, fleecy' (OjrRS). ⇨ **TÜK** + suff. -*tü*. See also **TÜKPÄY**.

TÜKÜ Kzk. 1820 **Tükü-bay / Toqu-bay?** [Тюкубай], a chieftain (Sib. Vest. IX, 122).

TÜKÜM-TÜÖKÄY Yak. **Tüküm-tüökäy** [Түкÿм Тÿöкäi] (Pek.).

TÜKÜN Uyg. **Tükün** [Tükün] (EUTS). See also **ALTMÏŠ-TÜKÜN**.

TÜKÜREK Kzk. 19th c. **Tükürek** [Тукурекъ] (SOK 210). ✧ 'Spit, spittle' cf. Alt., Kirg., Kzk. etc. *tükürük* 'id.' (Radl. III, 1532).

TÜL   Kzk. **Tül-ayïm** [Тұлайым], fem. (Jud. 36); Kzk. 1740 **Tül-biy?** [Tioul-Biü] (Levchine 158); Kzk. 19th c. **Tül-χan** [Тюлханъ] (AOO 66). ✧ 'Successor, descendant; child' cf. Karakh. *töl* 'момент родов; детеныш' (DTS), Alt., Hak., Kzk. *töl* 'die Nachkommenschaft' (Radl. III, 1260).

TÜLDÜK see **TÖLDÖK**

TÜLÄ see **TÖLE**

TÜLÄ-BERGÄN see **TÜLE-BERGEN**

TÜLÄGÄN see **TÖLEGEN**

TÜLÄY see **TÜLEY**

TÜLÄK   Uyg. 13th c. **Tüläk** [tüläk] (DTS, EUTS). ✧ I. 'Modest, quiet'? cf. Maml. *tülek* (تلك) 'sükûn, barışıklık' (IM), Chag. *tüläk* 'bescheiden, zurückhaltend' (Radl. III, 1568); II. '(Time/period of) moulting' cf. Karakh. *tüläk* 'линька' (DTS), Chag. *tüläk* 'das Mausern' (Radl. III, 1568), also TMEN II, 982; III. 'Blind' cf. Maml. *tüläk* (تُولَك) 'kör' (AH), *täwlük* (تَوْلَك) 'blind' (Tarj/Houtsma). ⇨ **TÖLÄK?**

TÜLÄK-TEMİR see **TÖLEK-TEMİR**

TÜLÄMİŠ see **TÖLEMİŠ**

TÜLÄN see **TÖLEN**

TÜLÄW   Bashk. 1783 **Tüläw-bay** [Тюлявбай Бербишев] (MIB V, 139, 140). ✧ 'Payment, paying' cf. Bashk. *tüläw* 'id.' (BRS).

TÜLE see **TÖLE**

TÜLE-BERGEN   Kzk. 1792 **Tülä-bergän (Tüläb-bergän <Tüläp-bergän?)** [Тюляберган] (MIK IV, 141); Kzk. 19th c. **Tüle-bergen (Tüleb-bergen <Tülep-bergen?)** [Тюлебергенъ] (SODž. 8). ✧ 'Paid-given (child)' cf. Kzk. *Tülep-bergen* (Žanuzakov). ⇨ **TÖLE + BERGEN**. See also **TÖLEP-BERGEN**.

TÜLE-TAY   Kzk. 19th c. **Tüle-tay** [Тулетай] (AUK 960). ⇨ **TÖLE + TAY** or suff. *-tay (1,2)*.

TÜLEGÄN see **TÖLEGEN**

TÜLEY   Tat. 1675 **Tüläy** [Урметко Тюляевъ] (Kurdjumov 327); Chuv. 18th-19th c. **Tüley** [Тюлей] (Magn. 88); Tat. 1702 **Tüley** [Тюлейко Ильбаевъ] (Letop. ZAK II, 8); Kzk. 19th c. **Tüley** [Тулей] (SODž. 34). ✧ 'Pay! Compensate!'? cf. Tat. *Tüläbay* (Sattarov). ⇨ **TÖLE + dim. suff. -y.**

TÜLEK   Kzk. 1817 **Tölek** [تولك / Толек] (MIK IV, 312, 319); Bashk. 1756 **Tüläk** [Туляк Ябукгулов] (MIB IV/1, 120); Kzk. 1819 **Tüläk** [Тюляк] (MIK IV, 323); Kzk. 1826 **Tüläk** [Тюлякъ] (Dobrosm., Turg. 282); Bashk. 1751 **Tüläk / Teläk** [Тюляк / Теляк Кюлюев] (MIB IV/1, 45, 46); Kzk. 1788 **Tüläk-batyr** [Тюлякъ-Батыръ] (PSZRI XXII, 1086); Kzk. 1785 **Tüläk-χoja** [Тюляк Ходжа] (MIK IV, 63); Chag. 16th c. **Tülek** [Тулек] (Ivanov 130); Chag. 16th c. **Tülek** [Тулек] (Ivanov 130); Chag. 16th c. **Tülek** [Мухаммед Тулек] (Ivanov 323); Bashk. 1729 **Tülek** [Шерып Тюляков] (MIB III, 269); Bashk. 1737

Tülek [Тулек] (MIB I, 336); Kzk. 19th c. **Tülek** [Тулекъ] (SOV 48); Chag. 16th c. **Tülek-aqa** [Тулек-Ака] (Ivanov 123); Kzk. 19th c. **Tülek-bay** [Тюлекбай] (AOK 114); Kzk. 19th c. **Tülek-bay** [Тулекбай], a biy (Lomakin 36); Kzk. 19th c. **Tülek-batïr** [تولاك باطير] (Veselovskij, Kirg. 118); Chag. 16th c. **Tülek-mirza** [Тулек-мирза] (Ivanov 88, 328); 1059 **Tülek-tegin** [تلك تكين] (Dorn 129); Kzk. 19th c. **Tülik** [Туликъ] (AOA 82); Uyg. **Tülük** [Tülük] (EUTS); Kzk. 1841 **Tülük** [Тюлюкъ Турсуновъ], from the Middle Horde (Orta Žüz) (Orta Žüz) (Konšin, Mat. V, 21). ✧ 'Newly born child' cf. Kzk. *tülök* 'ein neugeborenes Kind' (Radl. III, 1569). ⇨ **TÖLEK?** See also **BAY-TÜLEK, JAS-TÜLÜK.**

TÜLEK-TEMİR see **TÖLEK-TEMİR**

TÜLEKE   Kzk. 1850 **Tüleke** [Тюлеке Турсуновъ] (Konšin, Mat. V, 102). ⇨ **TÖLE + suff. -ke <comp. -ake.**

TÜLEMEN   Kzk. 19th c. **Tülemen** [Тулеменъ] (AOA 22). ⇨ **TÖLE?** + suff. *-men.*

TÜLEMİS see **TÖLEMİŠ**

TÜLEN see **TÖLEN**

TÜLEN-TAY   Kzk. 19th c. **Tülen-tay** [Тулентай] (SOK 216). ⇨ **TÖLEN + TAY** or suff. *-tay (1,2)*.

TÜLEÑÜT see **TÖLEÑÜT**

TÜLEP   Kzk. 19th c. **Tülep-pek** [Тулеппекъ] (SOK 40); Kzk. **Tülüp** [Тюлюпъ] (Patkanov II, 92). ✧ 'Paid, paying'? cf. Kuman, Chag., Hak. *tölä-* 'bezahlen' (Radl. III, 1260), Kzk. *töle-* 'платить, уплатить' (KzRS).

TÜLEP-PERGEN see **TÖLEP-BERGEN**

TÜLERÜ   Kzk. 19th c. **Tülerü** [Тюлерю] (SOV 116).

TÜLES see **TÖLES**

TÜLEŠ see **TÖLES**

TÜLGÜ see **TÜLKÜ**

TÜLİ see **TÖLE**

TÜLKE see **TÜLKÜ**

TÜLKİ see **TÜLKÜ**

TÜLKİ-BASÏ   Kzk. 19th c. **Tülki-basï** [تولكى باسى] (IOAIÊK XV, 310). ✧ 'Fox-head'. ⇨ **TÜLKÜ + BAŠ + poss. suff. -ï.**

TÜLKÜ   Hak. 19th-20th c. **Tülgü** [Түлгү], fem. (HRS 355); Tat.(Sib.) 1632 **Tülke** [Тюлькин] (Miller, Ist. Sib. II, 398); Kzk. 19th c. **Tülke** [Тульке] (SODž. 154); Kzk. 1819 **Tülke-bay** [Тулкебай] (MIK IV, 324); Kzk. 19th c. **Tülke-bay** [Тулькебай] (SODž. 86, 96); Kzk. 19th c. **Tülke-bay** [Тулькебай] (SOK 38); Kzk. 19th c. **Tülki** [Tjulki] (Ljutš 58); Kzk. 19th c. **Tülki-bay** [Тюлькибай] (Grod., Pril. 174); Kzk. 19th c. **Tülkö-bay** [Тулкобай] (SOV 48); Kirg. 19th c. **Tülkü** [Түлкү] (Jud. 213, 959, Kalilov 93); Bashk. 1777, 1781 **Tülkü-bay** [Тюлкубай / Тюлькубай Алменев] (MIB V, 63, 64, 124); Bashk. 1780 **Tülkü-**

bay [Тюлкубай Тимиряков] (MIB V, 120); Kzk. 19th c. **Tülkü-bay** [Тулькубай] (AOO 58); Kzk. 19th c. **Tülkü-bay** [Тулькубай] (AOP 118); Kzk. 19th c. **Tülkü-bay** [Тулькубай] (Pam. kn. Turg. 71); Kzk. 19th c. **Tülkü-bay** [Тулькубай] (SODž. 102); Kzk. 19th c. **Tülkü-bay** [Тулькубай] (SODž. 94); Kzk. 19th c. **Tülkü-bay** [Тулькубай] (SOK 162); Kzk. 19th c. **Tülkü-bay** [Тулкудай (!)] (SOK 6); Bashk. 1737-39 **Tülkü-čura** [Тульку-чура / Тюльку-чура] (MIB I, 311); *TN:* Chuv. 18th c. **Tülgü-bay** [Тюлгубаева], a village in the region of Spassk (?) (Korsakov 202); Kzk. **Tülkü-bay** [К. Тюлкубай], a well? (Karta JAR XIX). ✦ 'Fox, file, foxy' cf. Uyg., Chag. *tülki* 'der Fuchs', Kuman, Alt., Hak., Kzk. *tülkü* 'id.' (Radl. III, 1570), Kzk. *tülki* 'лиса; хитрый, плутоватый' (KzRS), Kzk. *tülkö* 'лисица' (PKRS), Bashk. *tölkö* 'лиса, лисица' (BRS), Tat. *tölke* 'id.' (TatRS). See also **ALTÏN-TÜLGÖ**.

TÜLKÜ-BAS   Kzk. **Tülkü-bas** [Тюлькубас], a settlement (Kojčubaev 228). ✦ 'Fox-head'. ⇨ **TÜLKÜ + BAŠ**.

TÜLPÜ   Kzk. 19th c. **Tülpü-biy** [Тюльпу бий] (Lomakin 33).

TÜLÜČÜN   Kzk. 19th c. **Tülüčün / Tülükčin?** [Тюлючуновъ] (AOK 126). ✦ 'Little child'? ⇨ **TÜLEK?** + suff. *-čün / -čin.*

TÜLÜGÖN see **TÖLEGEN**

TÜLÜGÜN see **TÖLEGEN**

TÜLÜK see **TÜLEK**

TÜLÜK-QARA Uyg. 12th - 14th c. **Tülük-qara** (Radl., USp. 12-14); Uyg. 12th c. - 14th c. **Tülük-qara** [Tülük-Qara] (Radl., USp. 12, 14, DTS). ✦ 'Colour-Black' (Blagova 1997, 705), 'Hairy-Black'. ⇨ **TÜLEK?** + **QARA**.

TÜLÜKČIN   Tuv. 19th c. **Tülükčin** [Тулюкчинъ] (Potanin IV, 425).

TÜLÜP see **TÜLEP**

TÜLÜŠ see **PAY-TÜLÜŠ**

TÜM Kzk. 19th c. **Tüm** [Тюмъ] (Lomakin 32).

TÜMÄK Bashk. 1732 **Tümäk** [Имекей Тюмяков] (MIB III, 310); Bashk. 1762 **Tümäk** [Арлай Тюмяков] (MIB IV/2, 302). ⇨ **TUMAQ?**

TÜMÄN Uyg. **Tümän** [Tümän] (EUTS); Maml. 1389 **Tümän** [تمان الاشرفى] (Iyās I, 279, 292); Maml. 1500 **Tümän** [تمان الاشرفى] (Iyās II, 388); Tat. 1696 **Tümän-bek** [Тюмянбечко Чайкинъ] (Kungursk. akty 237); Kzk. 19th c. **Tümem-bay (<Tümen-bay)** [Тумембай] (SOV 26); Kzk. 18th c. - 19th c. **Tümen** [Тумень] (Tynyšр. 73); Kzk. 1817 **Tümen** [تومن / Тюмен] (MIK IV, 311, 319); Kzk. 19th c. **Tümen** [Тюменъ] (SODž. 118); Kzk. 19th c. **Tümen** [Тюменъ] (SOV 68); Kzk. 18th c. - 19th c. **Tümen-bay** [Туменбай] (Tynyšр. 73); Kzk. 19th c. **Tümen-bay** [Тюменбай] (AOA 110); Kzk. 19th c. **Tümen-bay** [Тюменбай] (SOK 200); Kzk. 19th c. **Tümen-bay** [Тюменбай] (SOV 92, 150); Kkalp. 1822 **Tümen-biy** [Тюмен бий] (MIKk. 127); Bashk. 1664 **Tümen-čura** [Кусякейко Тюменчюрин] (MIB I, 192); *TN:* Kzk. **Tümen-bay** [Тюменбай], a well (Karta JAR XIX). ✦ 'Ten thousand (soldiers); very many' (Sattarov, Žanuzakov), wishing the child a long life (Sattarov), cf. Türk, Uyg., Alt. *tümän* 'zehn tausend, sehr viel; ein Heerhaufen von zehntausend Mann' (Radl. III, 1602), Bashk. *tömän* 'тысяцкий (начальник военного ополчения)' (BRS/Uraksin), Tat. *tömän* 'десять тысяч' (TatRS), also TMEN II, 983. See also **YÜRÜK-TÜMÄN, ÜLČİ-TÜMÄN**.

TÜMÄN-GİLDE   Chuv. 18th-19th c. **Tümän-gilde** [Тюменгилда] (Magn. 88). ⇨ **TÜMÄN + KELDİ**.

TÜMÄN-QUTLUГ   Khorezm. 14th c. **Tümen-qutluɣ** [Tümen-Kutlug], Qaykhusrau's wife (Barth., Ulugb. 17). ⇨ **TÜMÄN + QUTLUГ**.

TÜMÄN-TEMİR   Maml. 1363 **Tümän-tämür / Tuman-tämür?** [تُمانْتَمُرْ / Tumāntamur al-ʿUmarī], governor of Ghaza, died in 1363 (Iyās I, 209, Wiet 111, Sauvaget 44); Maml. 1390 **Tümän-tämür / Tuman-tämür?** [تُمانْتَمُرْ / Saif ad-dīn Tumāntamur, Ashrafī], died in 1390 (Iyās I, 279, 292, Wiet 111, Sauvaget 44). ✦ 'Ten-thousand-iron' (Sauvaget 44: 'dix mille fers'). ⇨ **TÜMÄN + TEMİR**.

TÜMÄNDÄY   Bashk. 1756 **Timentey** [Тиментей Уразгулов] (MIB IV/1, 123); Tuv. 19th c. **Tübändäy** [Тÿбäндäi] (Proben IX, 11); Chuv. 18th-19th c. **Tümändey / Tümendey** [Тюмяндей / Тюмендей] (Magn. 88); Alt. 19th c. **Tümendey** [Тюмендей] (Potanin IV, 341). ⇨ **TÜMÄN** + suff. *-däy / -tay.*

TÜMÄNDEY see **TÜMÄNDÄY**

TÜMÄNÄY   Bashk. 1738 **Tümänäy** [Мустапа Тумянеев] (MIB I, 370). ⇨ **TÜMÄN** + suff. *-äy.*

TÜMÄNŠİK see **TÜMENŠİK**

TÜMÄNÜK   Tat.(Lit.) 1548 **Tümänük** [Тюманюкъ] (Kn. Metriki Lit. 45). ⇨ **TÜMÄN** + suff. *-ük.*

TÜMÄS Bashk. 1764 **Tümäs** [Тюмясь Мратов] (MIB IV/1, 277).

TÜMÄTİ Yak. **Tümäti** [Тÿмäти] (Pek.).

TÜMEY Tat. 1675 **Tümey** [Тюмейко] (Kungursk. akty 26); Tat. 18th-19th c. **Tümey** [Тюмей] (Magn. 88); Bashk. 1789 **Tümey** [Тюмей Мятисов] (MIB V, 245). ⇨ **TÜM?** + suff. *-ey.* See also **DÜMEY**.

TÜMEKEY   Tat. 18th-19th c. **Tümekey** [Тюмекей] (Magn. 88); Bashk. 1758 **Tümekey** [Тюмекей Килмекеев] (MIB IV/1, 160). ✦ 'Small button'? cf. Kuman, Tat.(Bar.) *tümä* 'der Knopf' (Radl. III, 1602) + suff. *-käy.*

TÜMELMİ   Crm.(Tat.) / Tat.(Lit.) 1557 **Tümelmi-biyim / Tünelbi- biyim** [Тюмелми-Биимъ / Тюнелби Биимъ], a princess (Kn. Metriki Lit. 151,

152).

TÜMEN see **TÜMÄN**

TÜMEN-ASTÏ-EDEN-POUDO Alt. 19th c. **Tümen-astï-eden-poudo** [Тюмень-асты-Эдень-поудо] (Verb., In. 101). ✦ 'Chinese imperor' (Verbickij). ⇨ **TÜMÄN.**

TÜMENDEY see **TÜMÄNDÄY**

TÜMENŠÏ Chuv. 18th-19th c. **Tümenši** [Тюменши] (Magn. 88). ⇨ **TÜMÄN** + suff. -ši.

TÜMENŠÏX see **TÜMENŠÏK**

TÜMENŠÏK Chuv. 18th-19th c. **Tümänšik** [Тюмянщикъ] (Magn. 88); Chuv. 18th-19th c. **Tümenšiχ** [Тюменшихъ] (Magn. 88). ⇨ **TÜMÄN** + suff. -šik.

TÜMEŠKÄ Tat.(Sib.) 1661 **Tümeškä** [Тюмешка] (Milller, Ist. Sib. II, 546).

TÜMKÄ Bashk. 1716 **Tümkä?** [Кйамас Тюмкин] (MIB III, 143). ⇨ **TÜM?** + suff. -kä.

TÜNÄK Kzk. 1819 **Tünäk** [Тюняк] (MIK IV, 324).

TÜNÄN Kzk. 1819 **Tünän** [Тюнян] (MIK IV, 323). ✦ 'Torch' cf. Chag. tünän 'eine Fackel aus Ruthen' (Radl. III, 1550).

TÜNE Kzk. 19th c. **Tüne** [Туне] (SOV 54).

TÜNEY Bashk. 1777, 1779 **Tüney** [Тюней Мятисев / Матисев] (MIB V, 54, 101).

TÜNEKÄY Bashk. 1751 **Tünekäy** [Барзанай Тюнекаев] (MIB IV/1, 52).

TÜNELBÏ see **TÜMELMÏ**

TÜNKÄ Bashk. 1659 **Tünkä / Tünkeykä / Tünkekä?** [Тюнка / Тюнкейка / Тюнкека Ахтеевъ] (Vel.-Zern., Bašk. 37, 38).

TÜNLÜK Kzk. 19th c. **Tünlük-pay** [Тунлюкпай] (SODž. 100). ✦ 'Window, smoke-gap' cf. Uyg., Chag., Crm. tünlük 'das Fenster, das Rauchloch' (Radl. III, 1554), Crm. tündük 'id.', Hak., Kzk. tündük 'das Rauchloch, die Rauchlochdecke' (Radl. III, 1555).

TÜNRÄK Kuman 1146 **Tünräk / Türnäk / Tärnäk?** [Тюнракъ (Тюрнякъ, Тярнякъ) Осолуковичъ / Осулоковицъ], a prince (Ipat. 237 (243), PSRL II, 27, VII, 37); Kzk. 19th c. **Tünrek-pay** [Тунрекпай] (SOV 18).

TÜNSÄK Uyg. 12th c. - 14th c. **Tünsäk** (Radl., USp. 127, DTS). ✦ 'Lover of night' (Blagova 1997, 704).

TÜNTÄY Hak.(Sag.) 19th-20th c. **Tüntäy** [Тÿнтäй] (Katanov, Otč. 7).

TÜNTÜK Bashk. 1784 **Tüntük** [Тюнтюк] (MIB V, 154). ⇨ **TÜNLÜK?**

TÜNÜLDÜK Bashk. 1770 **Tünüldük** [Тюнюлдюк Метисев] (MIB IV/1, 347).

TÜÑKÄLÄY Yak. **Tüñkäläy** [Тÿҥкäläi] (Pek.).

TÜÑKÜNÄN Yak. **Tüñkünän-oyun** [Тÿҥкÿнäн], a shaman of the upper world (Pek.).

TÜÑÑÏ Trkm. 20th c. **Tüññi** [Тÿҥҥi] (Zaj. 1971, 333); Trkm. 20th c. **Tüññi** [Тунги] (TrkmRS 650). ✦

'Humpbacked, crooked' cf. Trkm. tüññi 'выпуклый, горбатый' (TrkmRS).

TÜÖKÄÑ-KÄLÏR Yak. **Tüökäñ-kälïr** [Тÿöкäҥкäлiр] (Pek.).

TÜÖNÄL Yak. **Tüönäl-oyun** [Тÿöнäл-оjун], spirit of the forests (Pek.).

TÜÖRÄ Yak. **Tüörä** [Тÿöпä] (Pek.).

TÜÖRÄ-TÜMÄRÄ Yak. **Tüörä-tümärä** [Тÿöпä-Тÿмäпä] (Pek.).

TÜÖRT-ÜGÜL Yak. **Tüört-ügül** [Тÿöртÿгÿл], one of the forefathers of the Yakuts, Örös Küöl J̌ul-jügün's son, Xayarañ's father (Pek.). ✦ 'Four sons' (Pek.). ⇨ **TÖRT + OƒUL.**

TÜPEY Bashk. 1759 **Tüpey** [Мендей Тупеев] (MIB IV/2, 24); Kzk. 1828 **Tüpey** [Тупей] (Dobrosm., Turg. 288); Bashk. 1756 **Tüpiy** [Япан Тупиев] (MIB IV/1, 105).

TÜPIŠ Kzk. 19th c. **Tüpiš** [Тупишъ Мамбетовъ] (Pam. kn. Turg. 70).

TÜPKEY Bashk. 1763 **Tübkey / Tüpkey?** [Мустафа Тубкеев] (MIB IV/1, 264).

TÜPPÜLÄY Hak.(Sag.) 19th-20th c. **Tüppüläy** [Тÿппÿläi], an evil spirit (Proben IX, 568).

TÜPTÏSKE Hak. 19th-20th c. **Tüptiske** [Тÿптиске] (HRS 352); Hak.(Sag.) 19th-20th c. **Tüptïskä** [Тÿптïскä] (Proben IX, 552).

TÜPTÏSKÄ see **TÜPTÏSKE**

TÜRČÏ Uyg. **Türči** [Türçi] (EUTS).

TÜRČÏ-ALP-TAŠ Uyg. 12th c. - 14th c. **Türči-alp-taš** [Türči Alptaš] (Radl., USp. 53, DTS). ✦ 'Türči?-hero(ic)-stone' (Blagova 1997, 711). ⇨ **ALP + TAŠ.**

TÜRÄ see **TÖRE**

TÜRÄ-QOÑUR Trkm. **Türä-qoñur** [Тюря-Конгуръ] (Voenn. Sb. CXXIX, 333). ⇨ **TÖRE + QOÑUR.**

TÜRÄDÜ Uyg. 12th c. - 14th c. **Türädü** [Türädü] (Radl., USp. 21-23, Le Coq, Urkunden 458-59).

TÜRÄM NUyg.(Tar.) 19th c. **Türäm / Xan-türäm** [تورم / Тюрямъ], fem. (Pantusov, Tar. 106). ⇨ **TÖRE** + poss. suff. -m.

TÜRÄPPÄY Hak.(Blt.) 19th-20th c. **Türäppäy** [Тÿräппäi] (Proben IX, 366).

TÜRE see **TÖRE**

TÜRE-GELDÏ see **TÖRE-KELDÏ**

TÜREY Chuv. 18th-19th c. **Türey** [Тюрей] (Magn. 88); Bashk. 1790 **Türey** [Тюрей Ишалин] (MIB V, 275); Nog. 1759 **Türey / Türe?** [Турей], a khan (Nepljuev 67). ⇨ **TÖRE** + suff. -y?

TÜREKEY Chuv. 18th-19th c. **Türekey** [Тюрекей] (Magn. 88); Bashk. 1761 **Türükey** [Айса Тюрюкеев] (MIB IV/1, 221). ⇨ **TÖRE** + suff. -key.

TÜREN I. Kzk. 19th c. **Türen-bay** [Туренбай] (SOK 104). ✦ 'Fin, rake, harrow, drug hook'? cf. Kzk. türen 'sabanın yeri tırmıklayan demir ucu' (KzTS).

TÜREN II. Hak. 19th-20th c. **Türen** [Тÿрен] (HRS

352). ✧ 'Skinny, thin, meagre' cf/ Hak. *türeñ* 'id.' (HRS).

TÜRENEY   Chuv. 18th-19th c. **Türeney** [Тюреней] (Magn. 88).

TÜREŠ see **TÖREŠ**

TÜRETEY   Chuv. 18th-19th c. **Türetey** [Тюретей] (Magn. 88). ⇨ **TÖRE** + suff. *-tey.*

TÜRGÄN-ČOΓUY   Yak. **Türgän-čoγuy** [Түргäн Чоɓуй] (Pek.).

TÜRGÄNJİ   Hak.(Blt.) 19th-20th c. **Türgänji** [Түргäнџi] (Proben IX, 306).

TÜRGÄŠ   9th c. - 10th c. **Türgäš** [تـركشة / تـركش بـن احـمـد] (Tabarī, Annal. III, 1790, 1892); Uzb. 1701 **Türgäš? / Türgüš / Turakuš?** [طورهكش / طوركش بى جوشن قلماق], from Bukhara (Buchari 260-261).

TÜRGEN   Kzk. 19th c. **Türgem-bay (<Türgen-bay)** [Турɪембай] (SODž. 102); Kzk. 19th c. **Türgen-bay** [Турɪенбай] (SOV 84); *TN:* 1685 **Türgin** [Турɪиново], a village (DAI XII, 15). ✧ 'Quick, hot-tempered' cf. Alt. *türγän* 'eilig, flink, schnell laufend, reissend (von einem Flusse)' (Radl. III, 1562) < Mo.

TÜRGİŠ   Türk **Türgiš-qaγan** (Ligeti, R. tör. nev. II-III, 75:41).

TÜRGİŠ-QARA-Šİ   Türk **Türgiš-qara-ši-čor**, a chieftain in the east (Ligeti, R. tör. nev. II-III, 75:41). ⇨ **TÜRGİŠ + QARA.**

TÜRİ-TAY   Kzk. 19th c. **Türi-tay** [Гаибъ Тюритаевъ] (Grod., Pril. 167). ⇨ **TÖRE + TAY** or suff. *-tay(1,2).*

TÜRK   Uyg. 762 **Türk** (Mahrnāmag 10); Uyg. 1292 **Türk**, fem. (Chwol., Syr. I, 13, Chwol., Syr.-nest. II, 38); Oghuz/Trkm. 13th c. **Türk** [تـرك / Тюрк], Yafet's son, the legendary ancestor of the Turks and Mongols (Abulg./Desm. 8-9, Abulg./Kon. 130, 135); Karakh. **Türk** [Türk] (MK/Atalay 855); Selj.? **Türk** [أنـسـز بـن تـرك], Atsïz' father (Kamāladdīn II, 201); Khorezm.? **Türk** [تـرك] (RaD/Jahn 78, 86, 161); Maml. 13th c. **Türk** [Hass Turk] (Björkm. 168); Chag. 16th c. **Türk** [Турк] (Ivanov 179); Chag. 16th c. **Türk** [Джа'фар Тюрк] (Ivanov 196); Tat.(GH) 1298 **Türk-eri?** [تـركرى / Türkeri / Теркери], a „Kipchak" chieftain (Baybars/Tizeng. I, 88, 111); Maml. 14th c. **Türk-eri** [تـركرى / Türkeri] (Tarj/Houtsma 45, Tarj/Toparlı 42); Kzk. 19th c. **Türk-pay** [Туркпай] (SODž. 64); Kzk. 19th c. **Türk-pay** [Туркпай] (SOK 224); Türk? 576 **Türk-šad** [Τούρξα→ος] (Byz. Turc. 328, Németh, HMK 83 /after Menandros/); Oghuz / Selj.? **Türk-tegin** [تـرك تـگـیـن] (Zehireddin/Dorn 279); Kzk. 19th c. **Türük** [Турюкъ] (SOK 174); *TN:* 19th c. **Türk** [Тюркъ], a village (ZIRGOStat. IV). ✧ I. 'Turk (Ethn.)' (DTS); II. 'Strong, powerful' cf. Uyg., Karakh. *türk* 'сильный, могучий; самый обильный' (DTS).

TÜRK'ĀN see **TERKEN**

TÜRK-YARUQ see **BERK-YARUQ**

TÜRK-TAY   Khorezm.? **Türk-tay-bek** [Turktaï], Meñgü-temür's commander (Abulg./Desm. 182). ⇨ **TÜRK + TAY** or suff. *-tay(1,2).*

TÜRKBEN see **TÜRKMEN**

TÜRKČE   Karakh.? 1040 **Türkče-χajib** [Туркче-хаджиб] (MIT I, 298).

TÜRKÄTİR   Oghuz/Trkm. 15th c. **Türk(ä)tir** [Τουργατήρ], a ruler of the Türkmen (Byz. Turc. 319).

TÜRKE   Kzk. 19th c. **Türke** [Тюрке] (SOK 138); Kzk. 19th c. **Türke** [Турке] (SOK 188); Kzk. 19th c. **Türke** [Турке] (SOV 32); Kzk. 19th c. **Türke** [Турке] (SOV 54); Kzk. 19th c. **Türke-bay** [Бозай Туркебаевъ] (AUK 851); Kzk. 19th c. **Türke-bay** [Туркебай] (SODž. 22, 64); Kzk. 1803 **Türke-biy** [تـوركه بى] (MIK IV, 211); Kzk. 19th c. **Türki-bay** [Бий Магомедь Туркибаевъ] (Grod., Pril. 44); 1692 **Türkü-biy** [Тюркубій], a murza from Turkestan (DAI X, 387). ✧ 'Turki' (Žanuzakov). ⇨ **TÜRK** + suff. *-e?*

TÜRKEY   Bashk. 1744 **Türkey** [Чюракай Тюркеев] (MIB III, 426); Bashk. 1763 **Türkey** [Тюркеев Тляп] (MIB IV/1, 273); Bashk. 1789 **Türkey** [Туркей Бикметов] (MIB V, 264); Bashk. 1792, 1793 **Türkey** [Тюркей Егоферов / Егаферов] (MIB V, 329). ⇨ **TÜREKEY?**

TÜRKEN   Oghuz/Trkm. 10th c. **Türken / Terken?** [Туркен], Seljuk's son (MIT I, 439); Kzk. 19th c. **Türken-bay** [Туркенбай] (SKSO III, 19).

TÜRKİ see **TÜRKE**

TÜRKİŠ   Kzk. 1819 **Türkiš** [Туркиш] (MIK IV, 324).

TÜRKMEN   Kzk. 1820 **Truχmen-bay-biy** [Трухменъ-бай-бий], from the Baγanalï tribe (Sib., Vest. IX, 109); Kkalp. 20th c. **Türkben-bay** [Туркбенбай] (KkRS 776); Selj. 1088 **Türkmän** [تـركمـان التـركى] (Kamāladdīn II, 61, 62, 64); Selj. 12th c. **Türkmän** [تـركمـان], an emir, mentioned in the name of a mosque (Ibn Šaddād, Nawād.: RHCHor III,); Uzb. 19th c. **Türkmän-bay** [Мукумбай Туркманбаевъ] (SKSO III, 158); Chag. 16th c. **Türkmän-mirza** [Туркман мирза] (Ivanov 211); Tat.(GH) 1318 **Türkmen** [Τουρκμάν], a christened Tatar, died in 1318 (Byz. Turc. 320); Kzk. 19th c. **Türkpen** [Туркпенъ] (SOK 82); Kzk. 19th c. **Türkpen** [Туркпенъ] (SOV 10, 54); Kzk. 19th c. **Türükpen** [Турукпенъ] (SOK 260). ✧ 'Türkmen / Turkoman (Ethn.)' cf. Karakh. *türkmän* 'одно из тюркских племен' (DTS). See also **BAY-TÜRKMEN, İLEK-TÜRKMEN.**

TÜRKMEN-ALİ   Kzk. 1794 **Türkmen-ali / Türkmen-ulï?** [تـركمـان على] (MIK IV, 159). ⇨ **TÜRKMEN + ALİ.**

TÜRKPEN see **TÜRKMEN**

TÜRKÜ see **TÜRKE**

TÜRKÜNÄ   Tat. 1738 **Türkünä** [Тюркуня Алдакаева], fem. (MIB III, 400).

TÜRLÜ see **TÜRLÜG**

TÜRLÜG Kzk. **Türlü-bek** [Türlü Bek / Түрлү Бек] (Proben III, 48 (63)); Uyg. **Türlüg** [Türlüg] (EUTS); Uyg. 762 **Türlüg-apa** [Türlüg Apa Sansïz Pačag] (Mahrnāmag 10). ✧ 'Different'? cf. Uyg., Chag. *türlük*, Chag. *türlüg*, Kuman, Kzk. *türlü* 'verschieden(artig)' (Radl. III, 1564).

TÜRSÜN Kirg. **Türsün / Dürsün** [Түрсүн / Дүрсүн], one of Manas' comrades-in-arms, always mentioned together with Taylaq (Proben V, 70 (71), 151 (152)).

TÜRT see **TÖRT**

TÜRTÜM Kzk. 19th c. **Türtüm** [Тюрьтюмъ] (AOO 38).

TÜRÜ see **TÖRE**

TÜRÜK see **TÜRK**

TÜRÜKEY see **TÜREKEY**

TÜRÜKPEN see **TÜRKMEN**

TÜRÜM Bashk. 1735 **Türüm** [Тюрюмъ Ешляповъ], a tarχan (Vel.-Zern., Bašk. 24). ✧ 'My prince/lord'. ⇨ **TÖRE** + poss. suff. *-m*.

TÜRÜN-MUZÏQAY Alt. 19th c. **Türün-muzïqay** [Тюрун-Музыкай] (Verb., In. 101).

TÜRZÜMÄ Bashk. 1756 **Türzümä?** [Тюрзюма Курткашков] (MIB IV/1, 130).

TÜSÄK Uyg. **Tüsäk** [Tüsäk] (EUTS). ⇨ **TÖŠÄK?**

TÜSİN Kzk. 19th c. **Tüsin** [Тюсенъ] (AOK 10); Kzk. 19th c. **Tüsün-pay** [Тусюнпай] (SOK 288); Kzk. 19th c. **Tüsün-pay** [Тусюнпай] (SOK 288). ✧ 'Think!, Listen! Guess!' cf. Kzk. *t(ü)sün-* 'nachdenken, verstehen, verspüren' (Radl. III, 1578), *tüsïn-* 'понять; усвоить; осмыслить' (KzRS).

TÜSKENÄ Kzk. 1819 **Tüskenä** [Тюскеня] (MIK IV, 325). ✧ 'Strong little camel' cf. Kzk. *tüs* 'Kameel, das von einem einhöckrigen Hengste und einer zweihöckrigen Stute herstammt; diese Kameele gelten als sehr stark' (Radl. III, 1577), + dim. suff. *-kenä*.

TÜSTÜK see **D'ÜSTÜK**

TÜSÜK Kzk. 19th c. **Tüsük-pay** [Тюсюкпай] (SOK 226). ✧ 'A kind of little (short) horse' cf. Kzk. *tüsük* 'ein Pferd mit niedrigen Schultern' (Radl. III, 1578).

TÜSÜMÄL Yak. **Tüsümäl** [Түсүмäл], a famous shaman (Pek.). ✧ 'Clerk, official' cf. Mo. *tüsimel* 'id.' (Pek.).

TÜSÜMÄN Uyg. **Tüsümän** [Tüsümän] (EUTS).

TÜSÜN see **TÜSİN**

TÜŠEKČİ Trkm. 1817 **Tüšekči** [Тушекчи] (MIT II, 400). ✧ 'Maker or seller of beds/couches' cf. also Turk. *düšäkči* 'der im Bette zu liegen liebt, der Frauenjäger' (Radl. III, 1818). ⇨ **TÖŠÄK** + suff. *-či*.

TÜTÄY Bashk. 1731 **Tütäy** [Тютей] (MIB III, 286); Bashk. 1707 **Tütäy / Tükäy?** [Миней Тютеев / Тюкеев] (MIB III, 32). ✧ 'Little sister, aunty' cf. Tat. *tütäy* 'Schwesterchen, Tantchen' (Radl. III, 1572). See also **TETEY**.

TÜTÄK Bashk. 1760 **Tütäk** [Абдрей Тютяков] (MIB IV/1, 193). ✧ 'Shepherd-cornet/horn' cf. Az. *tütäk* 'die Schalmei' (Radl. III, 1572).

TÜTE Bashk. 1740 **Tüte** [Токчура Тютин] (MIB I, 40); Kzk. 19th c. **Tüte-bay** [Тютебай] (AOO 58); Kzk. 1749 **Tütö-bi** [Tütö-Bi], Kazak ruler of Tashkent from the Greater Horde (Ulu Žüz) (Radl., Aus Sib.I, 196). ✧ 'Reel, spool; shepherd-cornet/horn' cf. Chag. *tütä* 'Rolle, auf die man den Zwiern aufwickelt; die Schalmei' (Radl. III, 1571).

TÜTE-QAŠ Tat.(GH) 1368 **Tüte-qaš / Tüme-qaš?** [Тютекашь / Тюмекашь] (PSRL XI, 10). ⇨ **TÜTE + QAŠ?**

TÜTEK Oghuz/Trkm. 13th c. **Tütek** [دوتك / Тутек], Türk's son, Yafes' grand-son (Abulg./Kon. 135). ⇨ **TÜTÜK?**

TÜTEL Maml. **Tütel** [Tütäl] (AH); Chuv. 18th-19th c. **Tütel** [Тютель] (Magn. 88).

TÜTEM Kzk. 19th c. **Tütem-bay (<Tüten-bay?)** [Тютембай] (AOO 22); Bashk. 1739 **Tütüm** [Тютюм] (MIB III, 410).

TÜTKEY Chuv. 18th-19th c. **Tütkey** [Тюткей] (Magn. 88); Bashk. 1738 **Tütkey** [Тамай Тюткеев] (MIB I, 370). ⇨ **TÜTE / TÜTÄK?** + dim. suff. *-key*.

TÜTÖ see **TÜTE**

TÜTÜK Bashk. 1744 **Tütük** [Шемяк Тютюков] (MIB III, 415); Bashk. 1758 **Tütük** [Деум Тютюков] (MIB IV/1, 163); Kzk. 19th c. **Tütük** [Тютюкъ] (AOK 30). ✧ 'Reed, cane, pipe' cf. Kzk. *tütük* 'das Schilfrohr, das Rohr, die Röhre' (Radl. III, 1572). See also **TÜTEK**.

TÜTÜM see **TÜTEM**

TÜWE see **DEVE**

TÜWEL Kkalp. 20th c. **Tüwel-bay** [Түүелбай] (KkRS 776). ✧ 'Present, perfect, full (=healthy)' cf. Kkalp. *tüwel* 'налицо; весь, целиком, сполна' (KkRS). See also **TÜZEY**.

TÜWÜL see **TÜGÜL**

TÜZ-BAY-KÜČ-BARS-KÜLÜG Türk 7th c. - 9th c. **Tüz-bay-küč-bars-külüg** [Tüz Bay Küç Bars Külüg / tüz baj küč bars külüg] (ETY III, 119, DTS). ✧ 'Equal/even-rich-strength-tiger-famous' (Blagova 1997, 711). ⇨ **+ BAY + KÜČ + BARS + KÜLÜG.**

TÜZEY Bashk. 1785 **Tüzey** [Баислан Тюзеев] (MIB V, 558). ✧ 'Present, perfect, full (=healthy); true, right' cf. Tat. *Töz-bay, Töz-bäk* etc. (Sattarov), Tat. *töz*, Bashk. *töδ* 'прямой, меткий; верный, правильный' (TatRS, BRS/Uraksin) + suff. *-ey*.

TÜZEK see **TÜZÜK**

TÜZEL Uzb. 20th c. **Tüzäl** [Тузал] (Begmatov 1984, 205); Kzk. 19th c. **Tüzäl-bay** [Тузалбаевъ] (Grod., Pril. 64); Uzb. 20th c. **Tüzäl-bây** [Тузалбой] (Begmatov 1984, 205); Uzb. 20th c. **Tüzäl-χoja** [Тузалхўжа] (Begmatov 1984, 205); Uzb. 20th c.

Tüzäl-mirza [Тузалмирза] (Begmatov 1984, 205);
Kzk. 19th c. **Tüzel** [Тузель] (SOK 194); Kzk. 1825
Tüzel-bay [توزالبای] (MIK IV, 469, 476); Kzk. 19th c.
Tüzel-bay [Тузельбай] (SODž. 74, 108). ✧ 'Get
better! Get well!' cf. Kzk. *tüzel-* 'исправиться,
поправиться' (KzRS), *tüzöl-* 'id.' (PKRS).

TÜZER Chuv. 19th c. **Tüzer** [Tuzer] (Kronheim 96). ✧
I. 'He who will arrange (sth), he who fixes (sth)' cf.
Karakh. *tüz-* 'приводить в порядок; наводить
порядок, устрават, улаживать' (DTS); II. 'He who
will stand, bear, sustain (everything)' cf. Tat. *tüz-*
'dulden, erdulden, ertragen' (Radl. III, 1581). See also
EL-TÜZER, İL-TEZER.

TÜZLÜG Uyg. **Tüzlüg** [Tüzlüg] (EUTS); Uyg.
Tüzlüg-bäg [Tüzlüg bäg] (Le Coq, Man. III, 43). ✧
'Orderliness; comfort' cf. Chag. *tüzlük* 'das Ebensein;
das Hergerichtetsein' (Radl. III, 1586).

TÜZMİŠ Türk 8th c. **Tüzmiš** [Tüzmiş] (Thomsen, Stein
187, 189, DTS, ETY II, 67, EUTS); Uyg. 13th-14th c.
Tüzmiš (Zieme, Mat. II, 85 (after TT IV)). ✧
'Composed, marshalled' cf. Karakh. *tüz-* 'приводить в
порядок; устраивать, улаживать' (DTS). See also
İL-TÜZMİŠ.

TÜZÜK Uyg. 1291 **Tüzek** [Tuzek], fem. (Chwol., Syr.-
nest. (NF) 12); Uyg. 12th c. - 14th c. **Tüzük** [Tüzük]
(Radl., USp. 203). ✧ 'Right, true, truthful' cf. Karakh.
tüzük 'правильный, верный' (DTS).

TÜZÜN 935 **Tüzün** [توزون] (Ibn al-Athīr/Tornb. VIII,
225, 296-99, 310-15 etc.); Türk? **Tüzün** [تُوزُون /
Touzoun] (Masʿūdī 399, Masʿūdī, Prairies VIII, 346);
Uyg. 8th c. - 12th c. **Tüzün** (TT IV, 432); Oghuz 932
Tüzün, a γulām (Qazw. 410); Oghuz 934 **Tüzün**
[توزون] (Miskawayh V, 467, 531); Oghuz 942 **Tüzün**
[توزون / تُوزُون / Tuzun] (Fakhrī 385-87, Abulfar. Or.
(201-04) 305-07); Oghuz (Toquz-oghuz) 944 **Tüzün**
[توزون التـركى ابوالوفـا] / Tûzōn], an emir in Baghdad;
„a certain captain of the host obtained great power in
Baghdad" (Ibn Saʿīd 40, 41, Abulfar./Budge I, 163);
Oghuz? 944, 945 **Tüzün** [توزون], an emir of the emirs
(Qazw. 345, 347, 348, Mirch. Bujeh 20, 21); Oghuz
1021 **Tüzün** [توزون], a γulām (Kamāladdīn I, 219,
220); Karakh.? 999 **Tüzün / Bek-tüzün** [غلام بنى سامـان
توزون / بكتـوزون] (Hil. Sābī 372, 374). ✧ 'Smooth,
flat, even; suitable, right' cf. Uyg., Chag. *tüzün* 'glatt,
gleichmässig, schicklich' (Radl. III, 1584), Karakh.
tözün 'сдержанный, скромный' (DTS). See also
BEK-TÜZÜN.

TÜZÜN-BİLGÄ Uyg. 1301 **Tüzün-bilgä** [Tusun Pilga]
(Chwol., Syr.-nest.(NF) 13); Uyg. 1301 **Tüzün-bilgä**
[Tusun Pilga] (Chwol., Syr.-nest. (NF) 13); Uyg. 762
Tüzün-bilgä-χunčuy, fem. (Mahrnāmag 14, 35); Uyg.
762 **Tüzün-bilgä-χunčuy** [Tüzün Bilkä Xunčui], fem.
(Mahrnāmag 14, 35). ✧ 'Noble-wise' (Müller). ⇨

TÜZÜN + BİLGÄ.

TÜZÜN-MAYİ Uyg. 1286 **Tüzün-mayi** [Tuzun-Maji],
fem. (Chwol., Syr.-nest. II, 28). ⇨ **TÜZÜN.**

TÜZÜN-SİLİK Uyg. 762 **Tüzün-silik-χunčuy** [Tüzün
Silik Xunčui], fem. (Mahrnāmag 14, 35). ✧ 'Noble-
clean/neat/spotless' cf. Türk, Karakh. *silik* 'чистый;
благородный; изящный' (DTS). ⇨ **TÜZÜN +
SİLÜ.**

TÜŽÜMET Alt. 19th-20th c. **Tüžümet** [Тӱжӱмет]
(OjrRS 210). ✧ 'Clever, intelligent, smart' (OjrRS).

TÜNÜL Yak. **Tünül-bögö** [Тӱнӱл Бӧҕӧ], spirit of the
sacred fire of home (Pek.).

U

UBAY Alt. 19th-20th c. **Ubay** [Убай] (OjrRS 210).

UBALİ Kzk.? **Ubali-χoJa** [Убали ходжа] (Karta JAR
XI).

UBAN Chag. 16th c. **Uban** [Убан], a χoja (Ivanov 144).
See also **QURDUN-UBAN, ŠEREN-UBAN.**

UBİR Kzk. 19th c. **Ubïr-bay** [Убербай] (SOK 76). ✧
'Greedy; gluttonous' cf. Kzk. *obïr* 'Obur' (KzTS).

UČ Maml. 14th c. **Uč-eri** [اوجـرى / Uçeri]
(Tarǰ/Houtsma 45, Tarǰ/Toparlı 42). ✧ 'Point, tip (of a
sword/ lance, etc.)'? cf. Uyg., Chag., Alt., Crm., Hak.
uč 'das spitze Ende; das vordere Ende, der Anfang'
(Radl. I, 1719).

UČİ Alt. 19th-20th c. **Uči** [Учы] (OjrRS 210).

UČQAY Bashk. 1709 **Učqay** [Телякай Учкаев] (MIB
I, 264). ✧ 'Small palm; hand(ful)'? cf. Tat. *uč* 'ладонь;
горсть' (TatRS) + suff. *-qay*.

UČMAN Yürük 1543 **Učman** [اوچمان / Uçman]
(Gökb., Rum. 189). ⇨ **UČ** + suff. *-man*.

UČUΓAN Kuman 1288 **Učuγan / Učuγam?** [Vchugam
/ Vchugan], son of Keyran from the Borchol [<Borč-
ul(ï)] clan (Gyárfás II, 456).

UČUR Alt. 19th-20th c. **Učur** [Учур] (OjrRS 210). ✧
'Reason, substance' (OjrRS).

UČURAL Alt. 19th-20th c. **Učural** [Учурал] (OjrRS
210). ✧ '(First?) passer-by' (OjrRS).

UČURTİY Kzk. 1819 **Učurtïy** [Учуртый] (MIK IV,
325).

UJAQČİ Chag. 16th c. **UJaqčï** [Уджакчи] (Ivanov
310). ⇨ **OJAQČİ?**

UDAΓAN Alt. 19th-20th c. **Udaγan** [Удаган] (OjrRS
210). ✧ 'Vacillating, sluggish' (OjrRS) <Mo. *udaγan*
'slow'. See also **İÑALİ-UDAΓAN, SÄYMÄLJİN-
UDAΓAN, TÏASĀNİ-UDAΓAN.**

UDAR Türk 8th c. **Udar-sänün** [udar sänün] (DTS);
Türk 732 **Udar-señün** [Udar Sengün / Udar Sänün]
(ETY I, 52). See also **BALX-UDAR.**

UDÏMEŠ Chuv. 18th-19th c. **Udïmeš?** [Удымешъ] (Magn. 88). ⇨ **ÖTÄMÏŠ?**

UDMÏŠ Uyg. 12th c. - 14th c. **Udmïš** [udmïš / Udmïş] (DTS, EUTS); Uyg. 13th-14th c. **Uđmïš** [Uđmïš] (Zieme, Mat. II, 92). ✧ 'Joined; followed'? cf. Karakh. *uđ-/ud-* 'следовать, присоединяться', *udmïš kiši* 'примкнувшие люди' (DTS).

UDUN Türk **Udun** [Udun] (ETY II, 133). ✧ I. 'Coarse; decay, bad, horrid' cf. Karakh. *udun* 'грубый, порочный, скверный' (DTS); II. Toponym, one of the names of Khotan (DTS).

UDUR Türk 7th c. - 9th c. **Udur-čigši** [udur čigši / Udur Çigşi] (DTS, ETY III, 90).

UDURUM Kzk. 19th c. **Udurum** [Удурумъ] (SOK 150).

UĐMÏŠ see **UDMÏŠ**

UĠÄLÄχ Yak. **Uġäläχ** [Логлоjо Угалах], the elder of Sārγïr's two sons (Pek.). ✧ 'Slow, lazy' (Pek.).

UĠÏL see **OĠUL**

UĠÏNČÏN Bashk. 1714 **Uγïnčïn** [Угынчин] (MIB I, 105).

UĠLAR Kzk. 19th c. **Uγlar-bay** [Угларбай] (Sb. Syr-D. IX, 50).

UĠLÏ-YAL Bashk. 1740 **Uγlï-yal?** [Карабашъ Углеяловъ] (Nepljuev 172). ⇨ **YAL.**

UĠRAČ Türk 7th c. - 9th c. **Uγrač** [Uγraç] (ETY III, 123). See also **ÏNAÑ-UĠRAČ.**

UĠUL see **OĠUL**

UĠUR Az. **Uγur** [Угур], a ruler in a tale, girl Alta's father (Az. Skaz. 276); Kzk. 1828 **Uγur-usta** [Угуръ Уста] (Dobrosm., Turg. 290). ✧ 'Chance, good chance, luck, good/happy sign (omen)' cf. Chag., Az., Crm., Turk. *oγur / uγur* 'der Zufall, ein glücklicher Zufall, das Glück, ein gutes Zeichen' (Radl. I, 1010-1011).

UĠUR-GELDİ Turk. 20th c. **Uγur-geldi** [Uğurgeldi] (TMİB 399). ✧ 'Chance has come'. ⇨ **UĠUR + KELDİ.**

UĠURLU see **OĠURLU**

UĠUZ see **OĠUZ**

UXANDER Chuv. 1777 **Uχander** [Ухандер], christened (novokreščen) Fedor Andreev (MIB V, 63).

UXANWAY Kzk. **Uχanway** [Уханвай], fem. (Sb. Syr-D. IX, 52).

UXTİYAR Chuv. 18th-19th c. **Uχtiyar** [Ухтіяръ] (Magn. 89).

UYADAŠ Nog. 1502 **Uyadaš** [Уядашь] (PSRL VI, 47, 243, VIII, 24); Bashk. 1787 **Uyađaš / Uyazäš?** [Уязяш] (MIB V, 204). ✧ 'Fellow/mate in the nest (den, lie); brother' cf. Chag., Alt., Hak., Kzk. *uya* 'das Nest der Vögel; die Höhle der Thiere' (Radl. I, 1628), Bashk. *oya* 'гнездо' (BRS/Uraksin) + suff. *-daš*.

UYAĐAŠ see **UYADAŠ**

UYALQA Alt. 19th-20th c. **Uyalqa** [Уялка] (OjrRS 210).

UYANÏQ Turk. 20th c. **Uyanïq** [Uyanık], a village in the province of Denizli, Turkey (TMİB 279). ✧ 'Awake, vigilant; smart, quick' cf. Turk. *uyanık* 'id.' (TED).

UYBAN Yak. **Uyban / Uybān** [Уiбан] (Pck.). ✧ Ivan (R.).

UYBĀN see **UYBAN**

UYBĀNČÏQ Yak. **Uybānčïq** [Уiбанчык] (Pek.). ✧ Ivanchik (R.).

UYBĀNNĬR Yak. **Uybānnĭr** [Уibanныр] (Pek.). ✧ Ivanushka (R.) (Pek.). ⇨ **UYBAN** + hypoc. suff. *-nĭr*.

UYBĀTA Yak. **Uybāta** [Уiбата] (Pek.).

UYĠUR Uyg. 13th c. **Uyγur-bay** [اویغور بای / Уйгуръ-бай], grand-son of the Uyghur Körgüz(?) in Iran (RaD/Ber. I, 117); Uyg.? **Uyγur-eltäbär** [Uyγur eltäbär] (Ligeti, R. tör. nev. II-III, 41 (after T. Tekin)); *TN:* Turk. 20th c. **Uyγur** [Uygur], a village in the province of Amasya, Turkey (TMİB 61). ✧ I. 'Obedient, accommodating, ally' cf. Chag. *uyγur* 'nachgiebig, gehorsam; der Anhänger, Verbündete' (Radl. I, 1598); II. 'Uyghur (ethnonym)'.

UYĠUR-TAPMÏŠ Uyg. 762 **Uyγur-tapmïš** [Uiγur Tapmïš] (Mahrnāmag 11). ⇨ **UYĠUR + TAPMÏŠ.**

UYQAS Kzk. 19th c. **Uyqas-pay / Uyqos-pay?** [Уйкоспай] (SODž. 42). ✧ 'Suitable, appropriate' cf. Kzk. *uyqas* 'соответствующий; соразмерный, складный' (KzRS).

UYQU Trk./Mo.? **Uyqu** [Уйку] (RaD I/1, 131).

UYQUČÏ Alt. 19th-20th c. **Uyqučï** [Уйкучы] (OjrRS 210); Alt. 19th-20th c. **Uyqučï** [Уйкучы], fem. (OjrRS 213). ✧ 'Sleepy, drowsy' (OjrRS).

UYNAQ Kzk. 1807 **Uynaq** [Илекбай Уйнаковъ] (TOUAK XXIV, 178). ✧ 'Open space (outside) for playing games' cf. Kzk. *oynaq* 'открытое место, где происходят игры, развлечения' (KzRS).

UYSAL Yürük 1543 **Uysal** [اویسال] (Gökb., Rum. 103, 178, 181). ✧ 'Satisfied, obedient, accommodating' cf. Turk. *uysal* 'einwilligend, einverstanden, gehorsam' (Radl. I, 1604).

UYSÏM-BAY see **UYSÏN**

UYSÏN Kzk. 19th c. **Uysïm-bay** (<Uysïn-bay) [Уйсымбай] (AOK 110); Kzk. 19th c. **Uysïn** [Юсунъ-батыръ] (Potanin, Pred. 55-59); Kzk. 19th c. **Uysum-bay** (<Uysun-bay) [Дусмурадъ Уйсумбаевъ] (Grod., Pril. 39); Kzk. 19th c. **Uysun** [Уйсунъ] (AOAtb. 34); Alt.(Tel.) 1824 **Uysun-bay** [Уйсунбай Шукуровъ] (Konšin, Mat. I-III, 70); Kzk. 19th c. **Uysun-bay / Üysün-bay?** [Уйсюнбай] (SOV 110). ✧ 'Uysun (ethnonym)'? ⇨ **YUSUN.** See also **SARÏ-YUSUN.**

UYSUM-BAY see **UYSÏN**

UYSUN see **UYSÏN**

UYTO-QAYTTÏ-QARAĠUL Alt. 19th c. **Uyto-qayttï-qaraγul** [Уйто-кайтты-Карагул] (Verb., In. 119, 120). ⇨ **QARAWUL.**

UYULDÏ Kzk. 19th c. **Uyuldï** [Уилди] (Grod., Pril. 90). ❖ 'Turned (of milk), soured' cf. Chag. *uyuq-* / *uyul-* 'gerinnen (von der Milch)' (Radl. I, 1634, 1636).

UQ see **OQ**

UQA Tat.(Sib.) 1638 **Uqa** [Укин] (Miller, Ist. Sib. II, 451); Kzk. 19th c. **Uqa** [Баки Укинъ] (Konsin, Pam. 13). ❖ 'Golden/silver braid; small, tiny, nice' (Sattarov, Kusimova), cf. Kzk., Tat. *uqa* 'eine silberne oder goldene Tresse' (Radl. I, 1608), Bashk. *uqa* 'позумент' (BRS).

UQAY Bashk. 1734 **Uqay** [Укай Кедышев] (MIB III, 322). ❖ 'Small nice golden/silver braid'. ⇨ **UQA** + dim. hypoc. suff. *-y*.

UQAZÏX Tat. 1647 **Uqazïχ** [Укозых] (Miller, Ist. Sib. II, 521). ❖ 'Small nice golden/silver braid (tassel, fringe)' cf. Tat. *uqačïq* 'goldene Troddeln' (Radl. I, 1609). ⇨ **UQA** + dim. suff. *-zïχ <-čïq*?

Tat.(Bar.) **Uqqun-päläk** [Ukkun Päläk / Уккун Пäляк], fem. (Proben IV, 73 /93/).

UQMAN Kzk. 19th c. **Uqman** [Укманъ] (Grod., Pril. 75); Bashk. 1757 **Uqmen** / **Uqman?** [Кутчюра Укменев] (MIB IV/1, 136). ⇨ **OQ** / **UQ** + suff. *-man*.

UQMEN see **UQMAN**

UQMÏŚ Uyg. 13th-14th c. **Uqmïš-ïnal** [Uqmïš Ïnal] (Zieme, Mat. II, 93).

UQTA Kzk.? 19th c. **Uqta-bay** [Уктабай (Мог.)], name of a tomb (IIRGO XVI); Alt. 19th-20th c. **Uqta-bay** [Уктабай] (OjrRS 210). ❖ 'Make the clan live; have descendants' cf. Alt. *uqta-* 'производить потомство, продолжать род' (OjrRS).

UQTUR Karg. **Uqtur-pay** [Уктуръ-пай] (Katanov: ZIRGOEtn. XVII, vyp. III, 194).

UQU Kzk. 1838 **Uqu-bay** [Укубай Найзобековъ], from the Middle Horde (Orta Žüz) (Konšin, Mat. V, 9); Kzk. 19th c. **Uqu-bay** [Укубай] (AOK 74); Kzk. 19th c. **Uqu-bay** [Укубай] (AOA 6); Kzk. 19th c. **Uqu-bay** [Укубай] (AOO 42). ❖ 'Literate (man)'? cf. Tat. *uqū* 'das Lesen, die Lektion, die Kenntniss des Lesens' (Radl. I, 1612).

UQU-BAS Kzk. 19th c. **Uqu-bas** [Укубасъ] (SOK 94). ⇨ **UQU** + **BAŠ?**

UQULAN Yak. **Uqulan** / **Uqulan-toyon** [Укулан / Укулан-тojон], god of the waters, protector of the fishermen (Pek.).

UL see **OĞUL**

UL-ALMÏŠ see **EL-ALMÏŠ**

UL-BASAR Kzk. 19th c. **Ul-basar** [Улбосаръ] (SOK 220). ⇨ **OĞUL** + **BASAR.**

UL-BERGE Tuv. 19th c. **Ul-berge** / **Ul-bergen?** [Ульберге] (Potanin IV, 412). ⇨ **OĞUL** + **BERGEN** / **MERGEN?**

UL-BOLĞAN Kkalp. 20th c. **Ul-bolɣan** / **Ul-bolɣan** [Улбоған (!)], fem. (KkRS 778); Uzb. 20th c. **Ul-bolɣân** [Улбулгон] (Begmatov 1984, 202). ❖ '(He/she) became a son; a son was born'. ⇨ **OĞUL** + **BULĞAN.** See also **UL-BOLŠÏN.**

UL-BOLSÏN Kkalp. 20th c. **Ul-bolsïn** [Улболсын], fem. (KkRS 778); Uzb. 20th c. **Ul-bolsïn** [Улбўлсин], fem. (Begmatov 1984, 201). ❖ 'Let (him/her) be a son'. ⇨ **OĞUL** + **BOLSÏN.** See also **UL-BOLĞAN.**

UL-BÜLÜK Kzk. 19th c. **Ul-bülük** [Ульбулюкъ] (SOV 16). ⇨ **OĞUL** + **BÜLÜK.**

UL-BÜRČEK Kzk. 19th c. **Ul-bürček** [Ульбурчекъ] (SOV 16). ❖ 'Son-(hair)lock; boy with curly hair' cf. Chag. *bürček* 'die Locke, das gekräuselte Haar' (Radl. IV, 1892). ⇨ **OĞUL.**

UL-MAMBET Kzk. 19th c. **Ulmambet** [Улмамбетъ] (Grod., Pril. 99). ⇨ **OĞUL** + **MAMBET.**

UL-MEKEN Kkalp. 20th c. **Ul-meken** [Улмекен], fem. (KkRS 778). ❖ 'Is (the baby) a boy?'. ⇨ **OĞUL.**

UL-NAZAR Kzk. 19th c. **Ul-nazar** [Улназаръ] (SODž. 158). ⇨ **OĞUL** + **NAZAR.**

UL-TARAQ Kzk. 19th c. **Ul-taraq** [Ултараковъ] (Grod., Pril. 154); *TN:* Kzk. 19th c. **Ul-taraq** [Ултаракъ], a place on the southern beach of Zaysan-nor, named after the person who herded there in autumns (ZIRGOGeogr. I, 438). ❖ 'Son-comb'. ⇨ **OĞUL** + **TARAQ.**

UL-TUW Uzb. 20th c. **Ul-tuw** [Ултув], fem. (Begmatov 1984, 205). ❖ 'Bear a boy!' cf. Türk, Kuman, Chag. *toɣ-* 'geboren werden; aufgehen (von Sonne); ersteigen' (Radl. III, 1158), Uzb. *tuɣ-* 'рождать; рожать' (UzbRS). ⇨ **OĞUL.** See also **UL-TUWĞAN.**

UL-TUWĞAN Kkalp. 20th c. **Ul-tuwɣan** [Ултуўған], fem. (KkRS 778); Uzb. 20th c. **Ul-tuwɣân** [Ултувғон], fem. (Begmatov 1984, 205). ❖ 'A boy has been born; Born as son'. ⇨ **OĞUL** + **TUĞAN I.** See also **UL-TUW.**

ULA-TEMÍR Bashk. 1740 **Ula-temir** / **Ulï-temir?** [Тлевкей Улатемиров / Володимеров], one of the leaders of the revolt of 1740 (MIB I, 421, 468). ⇨ **ULU?** + **TEMÍR.**

ULAČÏ Alt. 19th-20th c. **Ulačï** [Улачы] (OjrRS 210). ❖ 'Carman, driver' (OjrRS), cf. Alt. *ulā* / *ulaɣ* 'das Pflichtgespann' (Radl. I, 1675). ⇨ **ULAQ** / **ULAW** + suff. *-čï*. See also **ULAQŠÏN.**

ULAĞ see **ULAQ**

ULAY Alt. 19th-20th c. **Ulay** [Улай] (OjrRS 210); Uzb. 20th c. **Ulay** [Улай] (Begmatov 1984, 205). ❖ 'He/she joins (us)' (Begmatov), cf. Uzb. passive of *ula-* 'соединять; связывать' (UzbRS).

ULAQ Kipch. 1219 **Ulaɣ-χan** / **Ulaq-χan** [Улагъ-Ханъ], from the Qañɣlï tribe (RaD/Ber. III, 58); Yürük 1543 **Ulaq** [اولاق / Ulak] (Gökb., Rum. 104, 178, 179, 184); Kipch.? **Ulaq-χan** [اولاغ‌خان / Ulaɣ χan] (Juwaynī I, 95). ❖ 'Draught animal' cf. Kuman, Chag., Turk., NUyg.(Tar.) *ulaq* 'ein Lastthier, Saumthier' (Radl. I,

1679).

ULAQŠÏN Alt. 19th c. **Ulaqšïn** [Улакшинъ] (Potanin IV, 427). ✧ 'A groom, taking care of the post-horses' <Mo. *ulaᶜačin*. ⇨ **ULAQ**. See also **ULAČÏ**.

ULAN I. Kuman? 1097 **Ulan** [Уланъ], a princely offspring(?) („knjažeskij otrok") (Lavr. 252, 255, Ipat. 171 (176), PSRL I, 111-12); Tat.(GH) 1390 **Ulan** [Уланъ], prince, envoy of the Horde (PSRL IV, 97, V, 244, VIII, 61); Tat.(GH)? 1431 **Ulan** [Мансыръ-Уланъ], a prince of the Horde (PSRL V, 264, VI, 148, VIII, 96); Tat.(GH) 1450 **Ulan** [Уланъ] (PSRL XII, 75). ✧ 'Young man, lad, chap; child' cf. *ulan* (Kar., Tat.) 'ein junger Mensch, ein Kind', (Kzk.) 'gross, erwachsen' (Radl. I, 1681). Cf. also Sattarov, Kusimova, Bask., Im. polov. 76. See also **OΓLAN**.

ULAN II. Uzb. 20th c. **Ulan** [Улан] (Begmatov 1984, 205); Uzb. 20th c. **Ulan** [Улан], fem. (Begmatov 1984, 205); Uzb. 20th c. **Ulan** [Ўлан (?)], fem. (Begmatov 1984, 205); Uzb. 20th c. **Ulan-ây** [Уланой], fem. (Begmatov 1984, 205); Uzb. 20th c. **Ulan-ǰân** [Уланжон], fem. (Begmatov 1984, 205); Uzb. 20th c. **Ulan-γul** [Улангул], fem. (Begmatov 1984, 205). ✧ 'Join (us)' (Begmatov), cf. Uzb. passive *ulan* of *ula*- 'соединять; связывать' (UzbRS). See also **ULANSÏN**.

ULANČÏ Kuman / Tat.(GH)? 1256 **Ulančï / Ulančïy?** [Уланчiй], a chief (commander) (PSRL XV, 401). ⇨ **ULAN I.?** + suff. *-čï*.

ULANSÏN Uzb. 20th c. **Ulansïn** [Улансин] (Begmatov 1984, 205); Uzb. 20th c. **Ulansïn** [Улансин], fem. (Begmatov 1984, 205). ✧ 'May he/she join (us)' (Begmatov), cf. Uzb. passive *ulan-* of *ula-* 'соединять; связывать' (UzbRS). See also **ULAN II**.

ULAŠ I. Oghuz/Trkm. 14th c. - 15th c. **Ulaš** [Улаш], Qazan's father (DQorq. 22 etc.); Yürük 1543 **Ulaš** [Ulaş] (Gökb., Rum. 184); *EN:* Kuman 1328-1329 **Ulaš** [Olaas], a clan of the Kumans of Hungary (Gyárfás III, 470); Turk. **Ulaš** [Ulaş], a tribe (boy) of the Bayındır taife (Sümer: DTCFD XI, 336-337); Turk. 1735 **Ulašlu** [اولاشلو / Ulaşlu cemaatı], a religious (ethnic) community (cemaat) (Refik, Anad. 201); Trkm. 1691 **Ulašlu** [Ulaşlu], a clan (cemaat) (Refik, Anad. 100); *TN:* Turk. 20th c. **Ulaš** [Ulaş], a village in the province of Ankara (TMİB 84). ✧ 'Joining, attached; close (relative)', cf. Maml. *ulaş* 'müttasıl, karip' (AH), Cf. Rásonyi, Kisk., 344-344, Rásonyi, KÖA 135-136, Rásonyi, Anthr. 144.

ULAŠ II. Uzb. 20th c. **Ulaš** [Улаш] (Begmatov 1984, 205); Uzb. 20th c. **Ulaš** [Улаш], fem. (Begmatov 1984, 205); Uzb. 20th c. **Ulaš-ây** [Улашой], fem. (Begmatov 1984, 205); Uzb. 20th c. **Ulaš-bek** [Улашбек] (Begmatov 1984, 205); Uzb. 20th c. **Ulaš-bibi** [Улашбиби], fem. (Begmatov 1984, 205); Uzb. 20th c. **Ulaš-χân** [Улашхон], fem. (Begmatov 1984, 205). ✧

'Join (us)' (Begmatov), cf. Uzb. reciprocal *ulaš-* of *ula-* 'соединять; связывать' (UzbRS). See also **ULAN II**.

ULAW Kzk. 19th c. **Ulaw / Ulau** [Улау] (SOK 152). ✧ 'Draught, vehicle' cf. Kzk. *ulau* 'das Pflichtgespann' (Radl. I, 1678).

ULBET Kzk. 19th c. **Ulbet** [Ульбетъ] (AOAtb. 14). ⇨ **OΓUL** + suff. *-bet*.

ULBO Tuv. 19th c. **Ulbo / Ülbö?** [Ульбо], an informant, tale-teller (Potanin IV, 225).

ULČUΓAČ Hak.(Kyz.) 1770, 19th c. **Ulčuγač / Ulčïγač?** [Учугачефъ (Ульчегачевъ)] (Jarilov, Kyz. 13). ✧ 'Little boy, little son' cf. Alt.(Tel.) *ülčaγaš* 'das Söhnchen, Knäblein' (Radl. I, 1701).

ULǰA see **OLǰA**

ULǰA-BULAT Kzk. **Ulǰa-bulat** [اولجه بولاط / Улджа-Булатъ], in the epic song about Kene-sarï (ZIRGOOrenb. III, 391). ⇨ **OLǰA** + **BULAT**.

ULǰAY Oghuz/Trkm. 16th c. **Ulǰay-χan** [Улджай-хан], Yafet's name in the „Oghuz-name" by Salor-baba, Rašïd ud-Dïn calls him as Abulǰa-χan (Muhamedova: OSA 169). ⇨ **OLǰA?** + suff. *-y*.

ULǰAY-TURQAN Khorezm./Chag. 14th c. **Ulǰay-turqan-aγa / Ulǰay-türk'ān-aγa?** [Улджай-туркан-ага], Timur's (Temür's) wife (MIT I, 512-514). ✧ 'Happiness-Turqan' cf. Mo. *ölǰei* 'happiness' (Gy. Kara). ⇨ **TERKEN**.

ULǰEKE see **OLǰEKE**

ULDAY Kkalp. 20th c. **Ulday** [Улдай] (KkRS 778). ⇨ **OΓUL?** + suff. *-day*.

ULDAR Kzk. 19th c. **Uldar-bek** [Улдарбекъ] (SODž. 4).

ULΓAY Uzb. 20th c. **Ulγay** [Улғай] (Begmatov 1984, 205); Uzb. 20th c. **Ulγay** [Улғай], fem. (Begmatov 1984, 205); Uzb. 20th c. **Ulγay-ǰân** [Улғайжон] (Begmatov 1984, 205); Uzb. 20th c. **Ulγay-ǰân** [Улғайжон], fem. (Begmatov 1984, 205). ✧ 'Grow up! (=Do not die!)' (Begmatov), cf. Uzb. *ulγay-* 'вырастать; становиться большим, взрослым' (UzbRS).

ULΓAYSÏN Uzb. 20th c. **Ulγaysïn** [Улғайсин] (Begmatov 1984, 205); Uzb. 20th c. **Ulγaysïn** [Улғайсин], fem. (Begmatov 1984, 205). ✧ 'May he/she grow up! (=Let him/her not die!)' (Begmatov), cf. Uzb. *ulγay-* 'вырастать; становиться большим, взрослым' (UzbRS).

ULÏMAY Tat. 1779 **Ulïmay / Ülemäy?** [Улемай Кырымов] (MIB V, 94).

ULÏŠ Kkalp. 20th c. **Ulïš** [Улыш], fem. (KkRS 778); Nog. 1601 **Ulïš-ayim / Ulïš-ayïm?** [Алта Улишаим], a murza (Miller, Ist. Sib. II, 169).

ULQĀBÏY Hak.(Sag.) 19th-20th c. **Ulqābïy** [Улкабый] (Katanov, Otč. 7, 9). ✧ 'Tricky, foxy' cf. R. *lukavyj* 'id.' (Katanov).

ULLAQAY Bashk. 1735 **Ullaqay** [Уллакай

Каныевъ], a tarχan (Vel.-Zern., Bašk. 19).

ULMET Bashk. 1735 **Ulmet** [Улметъ Янбердинъ], a tarχan (Vel.-Zern., Bašk. 23). ⇨ **OΓUL** + suff. *-met*. See also **UL-MAMBET**.

ULMETEK Bashk. 1735 **Ulmetek** / **Ülmätäk?** [Улмятякъ Улеевъ], a tarχan (Vel.-Zern., Bašk. 24). ⇨ **ULMET** + suff. *-ek*.

ULTAM-BAY see **ULTAN**

ULTAM-BEK see **ULTAN**

ULTAN Kzk. 19th c. **Ultam-bay** (<Ultan-bay) [Ултамбай] (AOK 34); Kzk. 19th c. **Ultam-bek** (<Ultan-bek) [Ултамбекъ] (SODž. 62); Kzk. 19th c. **Ultam-bek** (<Ultan-bek) [Ултамбекъ] (SOV 4). ❖ 'Sole' cf. Kzk. *ultan* 'id.' (KzRS, Radl. I, 1700).

ULTARAQ Kzk. 19th c. **Ultaraq** [Ультаракъ] (SOV 124). ❖ '(Cork/felt) insole' cf. Kzk. *ultaraq* 'стелька (из кожи или войлока)' (KzRS).

ULTAW Kzk. 19th c. **Ultaw-bay** [Ултаубай] (SOK 260).

ULU see **ULUΓ**

ULUΓ Bashk. 1735 **Ulu-bay** [Улубай], a tarχan (Vel.-Zern., Bašk. 24); Turk. 14th c. **Ulu-bey** [Ulu Bey], title of Aydın oğlu Mehmed Bey (died in 1333) (Uzunçarş., Anad. 27); Turk. 16th c. **Ulu-bey** [Ulubey] (Ongan, Ank. II); Kzk. **Ulu-bikä** / **Ul-bikä** [Ulu Bikä / Ul Bikä / Улу Бікä / Ул Бікä], fem., mostly as Ul-bikä (Proben III, 41 (33)); Turk. 1583 **Ulu-qatun** [اولو قاطون / Ulukatun], fem. (Ongan, Ank. I, 178); Selj.? 1183 **Uluγ** [الغ بدرالدين], in an inscription of Niksär (Uzunçarş., Küt. I, 62-63); Trkm.? 1851 **Uluγ-baba** [Улуг-баба (Лукман ибн Мухаммед)] (MIT II, 295, 438); Khorezm./Chag. 1434/35, 1449 **Uluγ-beg** [الغ بك / الوغ بك / Ulugh Beg / Улугбек], Timur Lenk's grand-son, Shāhrūkh's son, Uzbek ruler and astronomer (1394-1449) (Ibn Taghrīb. VI, 837, Bartholomäi: Bull. Hist. AI XIV, 390, MIT I, 530, II, 108, 356); Chag. 16th c. **Uluγ-bek** [Улугбек], a mirza (emirzade) (Ivanov 127, 159, 317); Chag. 16th c. **Uluγ-bek-tarχan** [Улугбек Тархан], a mirza (Ivanov 316); Türk 732 **Uluγ-erkin** [Ulug Erkin], chief of the Yïrbayïqu people (ETY I, 45); Khorezm. 1229 **Uluγ-χan** [والغ-خان], Jelāl's officer (Nasawī 190); Trkm. 1595 **Uluγ-χan** [Улуг-хан] (MIT II, 85); Hak.(Sag.) 19th-20th c. **Uluγ-irgäk** [Улуҕ Ргäк] (Proben IX, 415-16, 421, 424); Uzb. 1598 **Uluγ-mirza** [Улуг-мирза] (MIT II, 91); Oghuz 13th c. **Uluγ-ordu-beg** [Uluğ Ordu Beg] (Oğuz K. Dest. 23, DTS). ❖ 'Big, great' cf. Chag., Alt., Hak. *uluγ*, Uyg., Chag. *uluq*, Kuman, Alt.(Tel.), Az., Crm., Hak., Kirg., Kzk., Turk. *ulu* 'gross, erhaben' (Radl. I, 1692-95). Different interpretations: *Uluγ-ordu-beg* 'Prince of the great palace / Prince of the great headquarters' (Blagova 1997, 714). See also **ERÄN-ULUΓ; BOYŠAN, DÄW, DUOLANTAY, ÄLLÄY,**

KETTÄ, QOŽAQ, ZOR.

ULUΓ-PAŠTÏΓ Tuv. 19th c. **Uluγ-paštïγ** [Улуҕ-паштыҕ] (Proben IX, 36). ❖ 'Having big head, with big head'. ⇨ **ULUΓ** + **BAŠ** + suff. *-tïγ, -lïγ*.

ULUΓ-TÜPÄ Oghuz/Trkm. 13th c. **Uluγ-tüpä** [توپه اولغ / Улуг-тÿпä] (Abulg./Kon. 1250). ⇨ **ULUΓ**.

ULUΓ-TÜRK'ĀN-XATUN see **TERKEN**

ULUΓ-TÜRÜK Oghuz 13th c. **Uluγ-türük** [Uluğ Türük] (Oğuz K. Dest. 29, DTS). ❖ 'Big/great-Türük' (Blagova 1997, 714). ⇨ **ULUΓ**.

ULUΓAN Kzk. 19th c. **Uluγan** [Улуганъ] (SOK 154). ❖ 'Howling; howled' cf. Kuman, Alt., Kzk. *ulu-* (Mo.) 'heulen' (Radl. I, 1693).

ULUQMAN Kirg. **Uluqman** [Улукман] (Jud. 742). ❖ 'Lukman' (Ar.-P.).

ULUMBET Bashk. 1735 **Ulumbet** [Улумбеть Юлмашевъ], a tarχan (Vel.-Zern., Bašk. 18). ⇨ **ULU** + suff. *-mbet*.

ULUMJU Kzk. 19th c. **Ulumju** [Улюмджу] (AUK Dobavl. 12).

ULUÑ Türk 7th-9th c. **Uluñ** [Uluñ] (ETY III, 117); Türk 7th c. - 9th c. **Uluñ-šad** [uluŋ šad] (DTS).

ULUS Yürük 1543 **Ulus** [Hacı Ulus] (Gökb., Rum. 194); Nog. **Ulus** [Улусъ], according to the legend of origin he is the forefather of the Nogay-Tatars" (Smirnov, Krym. 77); Tat.(Sib.)? 1643 **Ulus-pay** [Улуспай] (Miller, Ist. Sib. II, 488); Chag. **Ulus-sultan** [Ulus Sultán], son of Rashid Sultan (Tar. Rashidi (Introd.) 122). ❖ 'Folk' cf. Uyg., Kuman, Chag., Alt., Az., Kar., Turk. *ulus* 'das Volk' (Radl. I, 1696-97).

ULUZUÑ Karg. **Uluzuñ-χān** [Улузун-хан], a hero-ruler (Proben IX, 629).

ULWUQ? Kzk. 19th c. **Ulwuq?** [Ульвукъ], fem. (Kazancev 82). ❖ 'Exemplary' (Kazancev).

ULŽA see **OLJA**

UM-BAY see **UN**

UMA Uyg. 12th c. - 14th c. **Uma** [uma] (DTS). ❖ 'Guest, passenger' cf. Karakh. *uma* 'id.' (DTS).

UMAY Türk. / Uyg. / Karakh. 12th c. - 14th c. **Umay** [Umai / Umay], a goddess (Radl., USp. 5, DTS, EUTS, ETY I, 44, 112 II, 161 III, 101). ❖ 'Umay', a godess, a good spirit, the protector of babies who is prayed to at birth and in case of illness (Abramzon, Rožd.; Kalilov), cf. Shor *umai* 'ein guter Schutzgeist der Kinder; der Geist, der die Seelen der Verstorbenen fortführt' (Radl. I, 1788).

UMAQ-AY Kzk. 19th c. **Umaq-ay** [Умокъ-ай] (SKSO IV, otd. II, 36). ❖ 'Tribe/clan-Moon'? cf. Uyg., Chag. *umaq* 'das Geschlecht, die Familie, der Stamm' (Radl. I, 1788). ⇨ **AY**.

UMAN Turk. 19th c. **Uman-oγlu** [Uman oγlu], a Zeybek (Kúnos 1891, 119). ❖ 'He who is hoping, having hope' cf. Uyg., Crm., Turk. *um-* 'hoffen, erwarten' (Radl. I, 1787) + suff. *-an*.

UMAR Bulg. 767 **Umar / Umor?** [Οὔμαρος], a prince (Byz. Turc. 230);

UMBET-ALA Kirg. 1863 **Umbet-ala / Umbet-ali?**, head (manap) of the Sarï-baγïš tribe (Almásy 95). ❖ 'Ummat (=folk, crowd, nation) Ali' (Ar.) (Žanuzakov), cf. Turk. *ümmet* 'Religionsgemeinschaft; Nation' (HŞ). ⇨ **ÜMBET + ALİ.**

UMČÏ Alt. 19th-20th c. **Umčï** [Умчы], fem. (OjrRS 213). ❖ 'Dummy' (OjrRS), cf. Alt.(Tel.) *umčï*, Hak.(Sag.), Shor *umju* 'ein Saughorn für Kinder' (Radl. I, 1796-97).

UMJUJAQ Karg. **UmJuJaq** [Умцуцак], fem. (Katanov, Otč. 8). ❖ 'Little dummy' (Katanov). ⇨ **UMČÏ** + dim. suff. *-jaq.*

UMÏČÏ Uyg. **Umïčï** [Umıçı] (EUTS); Uyg. 12th c. - 14th c. **Umïčï** [Umiči / umïčï] (Radl., USp. 130-31, DTS).

UMÏNČÏ Uyg. 13th-14th c. **Umïnčï** (Zieme, Mat. II, 92).

UMSÏN Kkalp. 20th c. **Umsïn-gül** [Умсингюл / Умсынгүл], fem. (Bask., Kkalp. 404, KkRS 778). ❖ I. 'Hope!; Be hopeful!' cf. Chag. *umsun-* 'hoffen' (Radl. I, 1797), Kirg. *umsun-* 'id.' (Jud.); II. 'Let him/her hope; let him/her be hopeful' cf. Uyg., Crm., Turk. *um-* 'hoffen, erwarten' (Radl. I, 1787).

UMSUN-AY Kirg. **Umsun-ay** [Умсунай], fem. (Jud. 372); Kirg. **Umsun-ay** [Умсунай], fem. (Jud. 903). ⇨ **UMSÏN + AY** or suff. *-ay(1).*

UMUL Kuman 1367 **Umul?** [Umul], from the Čertan clan of the Kumans of Hungary (Gyárfás III, 503).

UMUR Turk. 16th c. **Umur** [Umur] (Ongan, Ank. II); Yürük 1543 **Umur** [Umur] (Gökb., Rum. 181, 202); Yürük 16th c. **Umur** [اومور / Umur], from the Yürüks of Kocacık, Turkey (Gökb., Rum. 103); Kzk. 1820 **Umur** [Умуръ], one of the chiefs of the İsaq-kirey tribe (Sib. Vest. IX, 103); Kzk. 19th c. **Umur** [Кадыръ Умуровъ] (Grod., Pril. 120); Kzk. 19th c. **Umur** [Алда Бергинъ Умуровъ] (Grod., Pril. 147); Kzk. 19th c. **Umur-bay** [Умурбай] (SKSO III, 6); Turk. 1390, 1395 **Umur-beg / Umur-bey** [اوموربك / Umur Bei], son of (Qara) Temir-taš (Āšikp. 61, 86, 114, Nešrī XIII, 348); Turk. **Umur-bey** [Umur Bey Aydın Oğlu], governor (vali) of İzmir, Turkey (Uzunçarş., Anad. 27-29, 31, 34, 71); Turk. 1528 **Umur-bey** [Umur Bey], Timurtaş Paşa's son („Kara" oğlusu) (Gökb., Ed. 29, 56); Turk. 1568 **Umur-bey** [Umur Bey], Saruca Paşa's son (Gökb., Ed. 14-16, 261-265); Kzk. 19th c. **Umur-bek** [Умуръ-бекъ] (Grod., Pril. 83); *TN:* Turk. 16th c. **Umur-bey(-köy)** [Umur Bey (köy)], a village in the province of Edirne (Gökb., Ed. 29, 56). ❖ 'Task, duty'? (Erol II: "önemsenen iş, vazife"), cf. Turk. *umur* 'matter of importance, concern' (TED) (<Ar.).

UMUR-KEK Kzk. 19th c. **Umur-kek / Ümürkek?** [Умуркекъ] (Grod., Pril. 173). ⇨ **UMUR.**

UMUR-ZAQ see **ÖMÜR-UZAQ**

UMURAT Tat.(GH) **Umurat** [Умуратъ], a ruler of the Horde in Saray (PSRL XXIII, 168).

UMUTČAQ Kzk. 19th c. **Umutčaq** [Умутчакъ] (SOK 102). ❖ 'Forgetful, absent-minded' cf. Kzk. *umutšaq (<umut+čaq)* 'vergesslich' (Radl. I, 1794).

UMUZ Turk. 1544 **Umuz** [Umuz bin Mohamed], a commander in Esztergom, Hungary (Velics-Kamm. II, 29). ❖ 'Shoulder' cf. Turk. *omuz* 'id.' (TED).

UN Trkm. / Uzb.? 1818/19 **Um-bay-bek (<Un-bay-bek)** [Умбай-бек] (MIT II, 412); Trkm. 1649 **Um-bay-inaq (<Un-bay-inaq)** [Умбай-инак] (MIT II, 329, 587); Kzk. 1819 **Un-bay** [Унбай] (MIK IV, 326); Kzk. 19th c. **Un-bay** [Унбаевъ] (Grod., Pril. 86); Kzk. 19th c. **Un-bay** [Ахмедъ Унбаевъ] (Grod., Pril. 58); Kzk. 19th c. **Un-bay** [Унбай] (SOK 184); *TN:* Kzk. **Um-bay (<Un-bay)** [Умбай], a well west of Lake Aral (Karta JAR X). ❖ I. 'Flour' cf. Kuman, Chag., Alt., Crm., Hak., Kirg., Kzk. *un* 'das Mehl' (Radl. I, 1639); II. 'Ten'? ⇨ **ON?**

UN-TAΓAR Tat. 1819 **Un-taγar?** [Сарымбетъ Унтагаровъ] (PSZRI XXXVI, 29). ⇨ **UN + TAQAR?**

UNAΓAN Türk 8th c. - 9th c. **Unaγan-čur** [Unaγan čur / unaγan čur / Unagan Çur] (Thomsen, Stein 186, DTS, ETY II, 64). ❖ I. 'Foal' (Mo.?) (Poppe); II. 'Consented/aggreed' (Blagova 1997, 717).

UNAY Kzk. 19th c. **Unay** [Унай] (AOA 38). ❖ 'He/she is satisfied, he/she is obedient' cf. Uyg., Chag., Kuman, Crm., Kirg., Kzk. *una-* 'annehmen, auf etwas eingehen, einverstanden sein, folgsam sein etc.' (Radl. I, 1640). ⇨ **ONAY?**

UNAR Selj. 1096/97 **Unar** [Унар], an emir (MIT I, 383); Uzb. 20th c. **Unar** [Унар] (Begmatov 1984, 206); Uzb. 20th c. **Unar-jân** [Унаржон] (Begmatov 1984, 206); Uzb. 20th c. **Unar-mirza** [Унармирза] (Begmatov 1984, 206). ❖ 'He will grow up; He won't die; He will be healthy' (Begmatov), cf. Uzb. *un-* 'расти' (UzbRS).

UNDAD Bashk. 1776 **Undad** [Итжимяс Ундадов] (MIB V, 39).

UNDAY Bashk. 1795 **Unday** [Ундай Уразаковъ] (IOAIÊK XXVIII, 589).

UNDOS Kzk. 19th c. **Undos-pay / Un-dos-pay?** [Ундоспай] (SOK 159).

UNDURČÏ Tat.(Lit.) 1548 **Undurči / Undïrči?** [Уньдурчь, Унъдырчь] (Kn. Metriki Lit. 44). ❖ I. 'Worker (of a field)' cf. Tat. *indïrči* 'работник, работающий на гумне' (TatRS); II. 'Boy born in autumn in the month of İndïr (that is when they threshed the corn)' (Sattarov).

UNSUN Uzb. 20th c. **Unsun** [Унсун] (Begmatov 1984, 205); Uzb. 20th c. **Unsun** [Унсун], fem. (Begmatov 1984, 205); Uzb. 20th c. **Unsun-ây** [Унсуной], fem. (Begmatov 1984, 205); Uzb. 20th c. **Unsun-bibi**

[Унсунбиби], fem. (Begmatov 1984, 205). ✧ 'May he/she grow up; Let him/her multiply' (Begmatov), cf. Uzb. *un-* 'расти' (UzbRS).

UNUT   Alt. 19th-20th c. **Unut** [Унут], fem. (OjrRS 213). ✧ 'Forget (it)!' (OjrRS).

UNUTPAS   Alt. 19th-20th c. **Unutpas** [Унутпас] (OjrRS 210). ✧ 'He/she won't forget (it)' cf. Uyg., Kuman., Alt., Hak., Turk. etc. *unut-* 'vergessen' (Radl. I, 1643).

UÑARA   Bashk. 1792 **Uñara** [Унгара Смагилов] (MIB V, 328).

UÑUL   Kzk. 19th c. **Uñul-bay** [Унгульбай] (SOK 82). ✧ 'Get well, be healthy, cure' cf. Chag. *oñul-* 'id.' (Radl. I, 1030).

UÑUM   Kzk. 19th c. **Uñum-bay** (<**Uñun-bay**) [Унгумбай] (SOK 160). ⇨ **OÑ** + poss. suff. *-m*.

UÑUN-BAY see **UÑUM**

UÑUR see **OÑUR**

UOLA I.   Yak. **Uola-χān** [Уола-хан], one of the names of the god of thundering (Pek.).

UOLA II.   Yak. **Uola** [Уола], fem. (Pek.). ✧ Olya (R.), dim. of R. fem. *Ol'ga* (Pek.).

UORALAY-ČUTČUT   Yak. **Uoralay-čutčut** [Уоралаі Чутчут], one of Bayanay's two sons living in the deep forests and giving the hunters precious wild animals (Pek.).

UORDAX-JÖSÖGÖY   Yak. **Uordaχ-Jösögöy** [Уордах Цöсöгöі], tutelary deity of particular persons (Pek.).

UORDAX-JÜSÜGÄY-AYĬ   Yak. **Uordaχ-Jüsägäy-ayĭ** [Уордах Цÿсÿгäi-аjы], one of the secondary male gods (oro juttar) who gives people brave men, good horses and bulls (Pek.).

UORUQU-SUORUQU   Yak. **Uoruqu-suoruqu** [Уоруку-Суоруку], slave of the heavenly hero Xardayastay (Pek.); Yak. **Uoruqu-suoruqu** [Уоруку-Суоруку], a shamaness (Pek.).

UOSUQ   Yak. **Uosuq** [Уосук] (Pek.). ✧ Osip (R.).

UOT-JURĀSTAY-OBURGU   Yak. **Uot-Jurāstay-oburgu** [Уот-Цурастаі-обургу] (Pek.).

UPAY   Uzb.? 20th c. **Upay / U-pay?** [Oupaï], a basmačï leader (Castagné 86).

UPTÏN   Bashk. 1762 **Uptïn** [Калмакай Уптынов] (MIB IV/2, 302).

UR see **OR**

UR-BĬYE   Kzk. 19th c. **Ur-bïye** [Урбіэ], fem. (Grod., Pril. 141). ✧ 'Grey(ish) mare' cf. Kzk. *biye* 'кобыла' (KzRS). ⇨ **OR**.

UR-MAMBET   Kzk. 19th c. **Ur-mambet** [Аяганъ Урмамбетовъ] (Grod., Pril. 157); Kzk. 19th c. **Ur-mambet-qan** [Urmambet-Kan] (Ljutš 47). ⇨ **OR** + **MAMBET.**

UR-MAMET   Tat. 1776 **Ur-mamet** [Заидъ Урмаметевъ] (PSZRI XX, 457); Nog. 1649, 1651 **Ur-mamet** [Урмаметъ] (AI IV, 87, PSZRI I, 248). ⇨ **OR**

+ **MAMET?**

URA   Kzk. 19th c. **Ura-bay** [Урабай] (SODž. 56); Kkalp. 20th c. **Ura-bay** [Урабай] (KkRS 776). ✧ 'Nub, hunch' cf. Kzk. *ŭra* 'нарост, шишка (на теле)' (KzRS).

URAГAN   Kzk. **Uraγan** [Ураганъ] (Sb. Syr-D. IX, 50, 56). ✧ 'Gale, hurricane' cf. R. *uragan* 'id.' <French <Spanish (Šipova).

URAY   Tat. 1731 **Uray** [Урай] (MIB III, 293); Bashk. 1749 **Uray** [Урай Деумов] (MIB III, 465); Bashk. 1752 **Uray** [Сармаш Ураев] (MIB IV/1, 64, 97); Bashk. 1795 **Uray** [Урай Ильсикеевъ] (IOAIÊK XXVIII, 590); *TN:* Chuv. 18th c. **Urayeva** [Ураева], a village in the district of Cheboksary (Korsakov 281). ✧ 'Hair-braid'? cf. Kzk. *oray* 'завиток волос (на голове)' (KzRS).

URAQ see **ORAQ**

URAQAY   Tat. 1624 **Uraqay** [Уракай] (Pokrovskij 72); Bashk. 1695 **Uraqay** [Уракайко] (MIB I, 97); Bashk. 1708 **Uraqay** [Уракай] (MIB I, 249); Bashk. 1738 **Uraqay** [Уракай Сундюков] (MIB III, 379); Bashk. 1792 **Uraqay** [Уракай] (MIB V, 329); Bashk. 1793 **Uraqay** [Уракай Егаферов] (MIB V, 329). ⇨ **URA / ORAQ?** + dim. suff. *-qay / -ay*.

URAQČĬ see **ORAQČĬ**

URAL   Kzk. **Ural** [Уралъ] (Sb. Syr-D. IX, 56); Kzk. **Ural** [Махмуд Ураловъ] (TOOIK I, 53); Kzk. 19th c. **Ural** [Уралъ] (SOK 18, 22, 110); Kzk. 19th c. **Ural** [Уралъ] (SKSO III, 10); Uzb. 19th c. **Ural** [Кара Ураловъ] (SKSO III, 170); Kzk. 19th c. **Ural-bay** [Уралбай] (Grod., Pril. 60, 184). ✧ 'Ural (mountains)' (Kusimova, Sattarov).

URALTAY   Kzk. 19th c. **Uraltay / Ural-tay?** [Уралтай Мамыръ-ханъ] (Potanin II, 149). ⇨ **?** + **TAY** or suff. *-tay(1,2)*?

URAN   Kipch. 19th c. **Uran** [Alp Kara Uran], a Kipchak chief (Barth., Turk. II, 365, Köprülü: Belleten VII (1943), 235); Maml. 14th c. **Uran** [اوُران] (Sauvaget 39); Kzk. 19th c. **Uran-bay** [Ираджанъ Уранбаевъ] (SKSO III, 19). ✧ 'Battle cry (of a tribe)' (Sauvaget 39), cf. Chag., Alt., Kzk. *urān* 'das Geschrei; das Kriegsgeschrei' (Radl. I, 1653).

URANAY-TŪTČUT   Yak. **Uranay-tūtčut** [Ураnaі Тутчут], a spirit of the wild deer, able to give even children (Pek.).

URANГAY   Kzk. 1819 **Uranγay** [Урангай] (MIK IV, 326). ⇨ **URAN** + dim. suff. *-γay*.

URANĬQĀN-OГONYOR   Yak. **Uranïqān-oγonyor** [Ураныкан-оҕонjор], a character from a tale (Pek.).

URANQAY   Kzk. 19th c. **Uranqay** [Уранкай] (SOK 26). ⇨ **URAN** + dim. suff. *-qay*.

URAS see **ORAZ**

URAS-PULAT   Chuv. 18th-19th c. **Uras-pulat** [Ураспулатъ] (Magn. 89). ⇨ **ORAZ** + **BULAT.**

URAS-TUGAN see URAZ-TUΓAN
URAS-TUΓAN see URAZ-TUΓAN
URASQA see URAZQA
URASLA see URAZLÏ
URASLAN Chuv. 18th-19th c. **Uraslan** [Урасланъ] (Magn. 89).
URASMET see URAZMET
URAT Tat. 1748 **Urat-bay** [Касканъ Уратбаевъ] (Nepljuev 438).
URAZ see ORAZ
URAZ-AYDAČI Uzb. 1740 **Uraz-aydači** [Уразъ-Айдачи] (Hanykov, Poezdka 21). ✦ I. 'Chance - drover'? cf. Alt. *aydači / aydayči* 'Treiber, Viehtreiber', Crm. *aydayǰï* 'id.' (Radl. I, 49); II. 'Chance - teller'? cf. Alt. *aydači* 'Schwätzer, Sprecher, Erzähler, Sänger' (Radl. I, 50). ⇨ ORAZ.
URAZ-ALÏ see ORAZ-ALÏ
URAZ-ALÏ see ORAZ-ALÏ
URAZ-BAΓA Tat.(Mish.) 19th c. **Uraz-baγa** [Уразбага] (Ahmarov: IOAK XIX, 141). ✦ 'Fortune is looking at him/her' (Ahmarov), 'Fortune (that is a boy) is being born' (Sattarov). ⇨ ORAZ + BAΓA?
URAZ-BAXTÏ see URAZ-BAQTÏ
URAZ-BAQTÏ Tat.(Sib.) 1623 **Uraz-baχtï** [Уразбахта Уразлиев] (Miller, Ist. Sib. II, 304); Bashk. 1756 **Uraz-baχtï** [Уразбахта Аднагулов] (MIB IV/1, 132); Bashk. 1763 **Uraz-baχtï** [Уразбахта Азаматов] (MIB IV/1, 256); Tat.? 19th c. **Uraz-baqtï** [Уразбакты] (Ahmarov: IOAIÊK XIX, 141); Bashk.? / Tadj.? 1735 **Uraz-baqtï** [Акмянай Уразбактинъ] (Vel.-Zern., Bašk. 25). ✦ I. 'Chance-lucky; Fortune has looked at him/her' (Ahmarov), II. Less convincing is: 'Fortune looked in (was born)' (Sattarov). ⇨ ORAZ + BAQTÏ.
URAZ-BALTA Chuv. 18th-19th c. **Uraz-balta** [Уразбалта] (Magn. 89). ⇨ ORAZ + BALTA.
URAZ-BERGEN Kkalp. 20th c. **Raz-bergen** [Разберген] (KkRS 775). ⇨ ORAZ + BERGEN.
URAZ-DÄWLÄT Kzk. 19th c. **Raz-dawlet** [Раздаулетъ] (SOV 56); Nog. 1649 **Uraz-dewlet** [Уразъ-Девлетъ] (AI IV, 122). ⇨ ORAZ + DÄWLÄT.
URAZ-MAMET Tat. 18th-19th c. **Uraz-mamet** [Уразмаметъ] (Magn. 89). ⇨ ORAZ + MAMET.
URAZ-MEHMED Crm. 16th c.? **Uraz-mehmed** [اوراز محمد] (Vel.-Zern., Crim. 78). ✦ 'Chance - Mehmed (<Mukhammed)'. ⇨ ORAZ + MUXAMMED.
URAZ-MURAD-KÜR Trkm. 1859 **Uraz-murad-kür** [Уразь-Мурадъ-Кюръ] (ZIRGOÊtn. I, 195). ⇨ ORAZ + MURAT + KÜR.
URAZ-TUΓAN Chuv. 18th-19th c. **Ras-tugan** [Растуганъ] (Magn. 70); Chuv. 18th-19th c. **Uras-tugan** [Урастуганъ] (Magn. 89). ✦ 'Fortune, chance (that is a boy) has been born'. ⇨ ORAZ + TUΓAN I.

URAZA see ORAZA
URAZAY see ORAZAY
URAZAQ Bashk. 1760 **Urazaq** [Илкей Уразаков] (MIB IV/2, 35); Bashk. 1795 **Urazaq** [Ундай Уразаковъ] (IOAIÊK XXVIII, 589); Bashk. 1795 **Urazaq** [Шинкаръ (Шункаръ!) Уразаковъ] (IOAIÊK XXVIII, 589); Kzk. 1846 **Urazaq / Orazaq?** [Джанылич Уразаков], a biy (MKOR 157); Kkalp. 1740 **Urazaq-bi** [Уразакъ-Би] (Hanykov, Poezdka 20); Uzb. 1809 **Urazaq-biy** [Уразак-бий], from the Qaŋγlï tribe (MIT II, 376). ⇨ ORAZ + suff. *-aq*. See also ORAZAY.
URAZAQA Bashk. 1702 **Urazaqa / Uraz-aqa?** [Уразака Ишметевъ] (Vel.-Zern., Bašk. 44). ⇨ ORAZ / ORAZA? + suff. *-qa*.
URAZAQAY Chuv. 18th-19th c. **Orzakay (<Orazakay?)** [Орзакай] (Magn. 62); Trkm. 19th c. **Urazaqay / Uraz-aqay?** [Уразакай Кутлышора-аджиевъ] (Ščeglov I, 355). ⇨ ORAZA + dim. suff. *-qay*.
URAZAN Kkalp. 1722 **Urazan-batïr** [Urasan Batyr / Уразанъ-Батырь], a chief (PSZRI VI, 778, Nepljuev 677, Rytschkow I, 129).
URAZČA Chuv. 18th-19th c. **Urazča** [Уразча] (Magn. 89). ⇨ ORAZ + suff. *-ča*.
URAZÏMBET Bashk. 1756 **Urazïmbet** [Уразымбеть Бекимбетев] (MIB IV/1, 122). ⇨ ORAZ + suff. *-ïmbet*.
URAZQA Tat.(Lit.) 1591 **Orasqa** [Ораска], fem. (Lit. Tat. 82); Chuv. 18th-19th c. **Uraska** [Ураска] (Magn. 89); Tat. 1690 **Urazqa** [Уразка Байбиринъ] (Vel.-Zern., Bašk. 46). ⇨ ORAZ + suff. *-qa*.
URAZLÏ Chuv. 18th-19th c. **Urasla** [Урасла] (Magn. 89); Tat. 18th-19th c. **Urazlay (<Urazlï?)** [Уразлай, Уразлей] (Magn. 89); Tat. 1558 **Urazlï** [Уразлы-князь], a prince (PSRL XIII, 289); Tat. 1623 **Urazlï** [Уразбохта Уразлиев] (Miller, Ist. Sib. II, 304); Tat. 1719 **Urazlï** [Юзяшар Уразлин] (MIB III, 189); Tat. 1719 **Urazlï** [Юзяшар Уразлин] (MIB III, 189); Bashk. 1707 **Urazlï** [Уразле / Уразлы Акчанов] (MIB III, 39); Bashk. 1763 **Urazlï** [Уразлы Киязев] (MIB IV/1, 270); Bashk. 1793 **Urazlï** [Сейфулла Уразлин] (MIB V, 331); Nog. 1649 **Urazlï** [Уразлы], fem. (AI IV, 122); Chuv. 18th-19th c. **Urazlï / Urazla** [Уразла] (Magn. 89); Tat. 1624 **Urazlï / Urazla?** [Уразла Арыковъ] (Pokrovskij 72); Tat. 1551 **Urazlï-mïrza** [Уразлый-мырза] (PSRL XIII, 161); Nog. 1654 **Urazlï-murza** [Уразлы мурза Кутумовъ] (AI IV, 211). ✦ 'Lucky, having chance' (Sattarov), cf. Tat. *urazlï* 'id.' (Radl. I, 1655). ⇨ ORAZ + suff. *-lï*.
URAZMAQ Karch. **Urazmaq / Urïzmek** [Уразмакъ / Урызмекъ], a folklore hero (Sysoev 136, SMOK III, 145).
URAZMAN Bashk. 1708 **Urazman** [Уразманко]

(MIB I, 215); Bashk. 1754 **Urazman** [Уразман Уразаев] (MIB IV/1, 79); Bashk. 1754 **Urazman** [Кучюккул Уразманов] (MIB IV/1, 83); Bashk. 1761 **Urazman** [Уразман Азаматов] (MIB IV/1, 227); Bashk. 1770 **Urazman** [Абиш Уразманов] (MIB IV/1, 350). ❖ 'Lucky, having chance' (Sattarov). ⇨ **ORAZ** + suff. *-man*.

URAZMET Chuv. 18th-19th c. **Urasmet** [Урасметь] (Magn. 89); Chuv. 18th-19th c. **Urazmet** [Уразметъ] (Magn. 89); Tat. 1706 **Urazmet** [Уразметевъ] (Letop. ZAK II, 22); Tat. 1752 **Urazmet** [Курдай Бердей Уразметевь] (PSZRI XIII, 737); Tat. 1760 **Urazmet** [Рысметь Уразметь] (MIB IV/2, 36); Tat. 1764 **Urazmet** [Уразметь Буханов] (MIB IV/2, 105); Tat. 1783 **Urazmet** [Бикметъ Уразметевъ] (Korsakov 97); Tat.(Mish.) 1735 **Urazmet** [Оска Уразметев] (MIK̕k. 207); Bashk. 1783 **Urazmet** [Измаил Уразметев] (MIB V, 137); Kzk. 1717 **Urazmet** [Уразметь Ахметевъ], from the region of the Yaik river (ZIRGO IX, 336). ⇨ **ORAZ** + suff. *-met*.

URAZNAY Tat. 1624 **Uraznay** (<Urazlay <Urazlï?) [Уразнай Нагаевъ] (Pokrovskij 71). ⇨ **URAZLÏ?**

URČA Oghuz/Trkm. 13th c. **Urča-χan** / **Urja-χan** [اورجه خان / Урджа-хан] (Abulg./Kon. 870).

URČAƔAN Trk./Mo.? **Určaɣan** [اورجغان / Урчаганъ] (RaD/Ber. II, 81, 82 Text 135). ⇨ **URČA** + suff. *-qan*.

URDA see **ORDA**

URDA-BAQ Kzk. **Urda-baq** [Урда-бакъ], a place south of Yarkend (Karta JAR XX). ⇨ **ORDA** + **BAQ.**

URDÏ-QLÏČ Trkm. 1740 **Urdï-qlïč-yesaul** [Урды-Клычь-Есаулъ] (Hanykov, Poezdka 21). ⇨ **ORDU** + **QÏLÏČ.**

URDU Kuman? 1240 **Urdu** / **Urduy** [Урдюй], a „Tatar" commander (PSRL II, 177, 339, IV, 36, V, 175, VII, 145, X, 116, Ipat. 522 (527)); Tat.(Sib.) 1605 **Urdu-bay** [Урдубай] (Miller, Ist. Sib. II, 189); Trkm.? 1514 **Urdu-šah** [Мухаммед Урду-шах], an emir (MIT II, 47). ⇨ **ORDU?**

URƔANAQ Bashk. 1735 **Urɣanaq** [Урганакъ Ердеевъ], a tarχan (Vel.-Zern., Bašk. 18).

URƔAŠAY Bashk. 1737 **Urɣašay** / **Urɣašïy?** [Урɢашай] (MIB I, 334). ❖ 'Woman, lady'? cf. Kzk. *urğaşı* 'hanım' (KzTS) + suff. *-y?*

URIN Hak. 19th-20th c. **Urin** [Урин], fem. (HRS 355).

URÏSLÏ see **URUSLÏ**

URQAL Yürük 1543 **Urqal** [اورقال / Urkal], from the Yürüks of Kocacık, Turkey (Gökb., Rum.103).

URQAN Bulg. 6th c. - 7th c. **Urqan** [Οργανᾶς], Qobrat's uncle (Moravcsik 220).

URQAŠ Bashk. 1738 **Urqaš** [Нуруш Уркашев] (MIB III, 297).

URLA **Urla** [Урла] (RaD II, 202).

URLÏYQA Kkalp. 20th c. **Urlïyqa** [Урлыйқа], fem.

(KkRS 778).

URMAY Chuv. 1658 **Urmay** [Танибек Урмаевъ] (Zolotn. 159); Tat.(Mish.) 1737 **Urmay** [Урмаев] (MIB I, 308); *TN:* Chuv. 18th c. **Urmay(eva)** [Урмаева], a village in the district of Tsivilsk (Korsakov 323). ❖ 'Little buble?' *urma* 'eine kleine Blase' (Radl. I, 1673); II. 'Wood/forest-Month' (Sattarov) + dim. suff. *-y.* See also **URMANAY**.

URMALČIK Tat. 1662 **Urmalčik** / **Urmančik?** [Урмалчикъ] (DAI IV, 292).

URMAN see **ORMAN**

URMAN-AY Bashk. 1753, 1785 **Urmanay** [Урманай Уразаев] (MIB IV/2, 426, V, 185). ❖ 'Wood/forest-Month', child born in the month when wood was cut (Sattarov). ⇨ **URMAN** + **AY.**

URMANČÏ see **ORMANČÏ**

URMANSÏ see **ORMANČÏ**

URMAŠ Kzk. 19th c. **Urmaš** [Рысъ Урмашевъ] (SKSO VIII, 224).

URMAT Alt. 19th-20th c. **Urmat** [Урмат], fem. (OjrRS 213). ❖ 'Luck, fortune' (OjrRS).

URMET see **QURMET**

URNAQAY Tat.(Sib.) 1676 **Urnaqay** [Урнакайко] (DAI VII, 343).

URSAY Bashk. 1709 **Ursay** [Дюскей Урсаев] (MIB I, 263); Bashk. 1731 **Ursay** [Урсай] (MIB III, 284); Bashk. 1738 **Ursay** [Урсай Баскунов] (MIB III, 387); Bashk. 1738 **Ursay** [Тевенеи Урсаев] (MIB III, 387); Bashk. 1745, 1760 **Ursay** [Мукай Урсаев] (MIB III, 431, IV/1, 184); Bashk. 1748 **Ursay** [Бекмет Урсаев] (MIB III, 454). ⇨ **URUSAY?**

URSAQ Bashk. 1735 **Ursaq** [Урсакъ Мурзинъ] (Vel.-Zern., Bašk. 15).

URSUMBET Bashk. 1787 **Ursumbet?** / **Ursunbet?** [Нагай Урсумбетев] (MIB V, 203). ⇨ **URUS** + suffixoid *-umbet.*

URŠÏ Uyg. 12th c. - 14th c. **Uršï** [uršï / Urşı] (DTS, EUTS).

URU Uyg. **Uru** [uru] (DTS, EUTS); Kzk. 19th c. **Uru-bala** [Уру-бала] (Ibragimov 125). ❖ 'Thief, robber' cf. Kzk. *ŭrï* 'вор' (RKzS), Turk. *uɣru, oɣrï* 'der Dieb, Räuber' (Radl. I, 1622).

URUJ see **ORUČ**

URUDEY Tat.(Sib.) 1603 **Urudey-murza?** / **Urdï-murza?** [Урудей] (Miller, Ist. Sib. II, 180). ⇨ **URU?** + suff. *-day.*

URUƔ Uyg. 1327 **Uruɣ** [Urug] (Chwol., Syr.-nest. (NF) 26); Uyg. 1348 **Uruɣ** [Urug], fem. (Chwol., Syr.-nest. 85); Bashk. 1718 **Uruq** [Урук Илчикеев] (MIB III, 168). ❖ 'Corn, seed, kernel; clan, relatives' cf. Uyg., Karakh. *uruɣ* 'id.' (DTS), Uyg., Kuman, Chag., NUyg.(Tar.) *uruq* 'der Samen; die Nachkommenschaft, Verwandschaft; das Geschlecht' (Radl. I, 1658).

URUƔ-TAMUR Uyg. 13th c. -14th c. **Uruɣ-tamur**

[Уруг Тамуръ] (Kokovcov: ZVOIRAO XVI, 197). ⇨
URUГ + TEMİR?

URUQ see URUГ

URUM Oghuz/Trkm. 13th c. **Urum** [Urum / Rum?], Uruz's brother (Oğuz K. Dest. 17); Kzk.? **Urum-bay** [Имбек Урумбаев] (TV (1878), 144); Kzk. 19th c. **Urum-bay** [Урумбай] (AOK 14); Kzk. 19th c. **Urum-bay** [Урумбай] (AOP 6); Kzk. 19th c. **Urum-bay** [Урумбай] (SOK 246); Kzk. 19th c. **Urum-bay** [Урумбай] (AOK 82); Kzk. 19th c. **Urum-bay** [Урумбай] (SOK 14); Kzk. 19th c. **Urum-bay** [Урумбай] (AOP 2); Kzk. 19th c. **Urum-bay** [Урумбай] (AUK 404-409); Kzk. 19th c. **Urum-bay** [Уромбай] (SOV 20); Maml. 13th c. **Urum-buγa** [اُرُم بُكَا] (Zetterst. 83); Oghuz 13th c. **Urum-qaγan** [urum qaγan] (DTS); Kirg. **Urum-qan** [Урумкан] (Jud. 36). ✧ 'Hitting; beating; the art of fighting' cf. Chag. *urum* 'id.' (Radl. I, 1665), Kirg. *urum* 'удар; потомство; легендарная страна' (Jud.).

URUN Kzk. 1796 **Urun** [Урун], wife (χanša) of Khan Nur-ali (MIK IV, 187-88); Kzk. 19th c. **Urun** [Урунъ], Buldur-bay's widow (Grod., Pril. 37); Kzk. 1846 **Urun-bay** [Урунбай Айтуганов] (MKOP 155); Kzk. 19th c. **Urun-bay** [Урунбай] (SKSO II, 16); Kzk. 19th c. **Urun-bay** [Урунбай] (SKSO III, 8, 20); Kzk. 19th c. **Urun-bay** [Маматъ Урунбаевъ] (SKSO VIII, 226); Kzk. 19th c. **Urun-bay** [Калмагомедъ Урунбаевъ] (Grod., Pril. 111); Chag.? 15th c. **Urun-sultan-χanïm / Uzun-sultan-χanïm?** [Uzun Sultán Khánim / Urun Sultán Khánim], wife of the Dughlatid Sayyïd Ali (Tar. Rashidi 64, 88); *TN:* Kzk. 19th c. **Urun-bay-qurγan** [Урунбай Курганъ] (Grod., Pril. 167, 168). ⇨ **ORUN?**

URUÑU Kirg. **Oroño** [Orongo / Оронго], fem. (Proben V, 180 /182/); Türk 7th-9th c. **Uruñu** [Uruñu] (ETY III, 119, 180); Uyg. **Uruñu** [Uruñu] (ETY II, 66); Türk 750 **Uruñu-sañun** [Urungu Sangun / uruŋu saŋun / Uruñu Sañun] (Thomsen, Stein 186, 188, DTS, ETY II, 65); Uyg. **Uruñu-tigin** [urungu tigin] (Haneda 3); Türk 750 **Uruñu-tudun-čigši** [Uruŋu Tudun Čigši / uruŋu tudun čigši / Uruñu Tudun Çigşi] (Thomsen, Stein 186, DTS, ETY II, 64). ✧ 'Flag, banner; ensign (as rank or title); combatant, warrior, fighter (as title)' cf. Uyg. *urungu* 'savaşçı, muharip' (EUTS). Used also as a secondary component of male names. See also **İNČÜ-URUÑU.**

URUÑU-KÜLÜG-TOQ Türk 7th-9th c. **Uruñu-külüg-toq** [urunu külüg tok / Urungu Körüg Tok / Uruñu Külüg Toq [!]] (ETY III, 180, 181). ⇨ **URUÑU + KÜLÜG + TOQ.**

URUP-TAY Kzk. 19th c. **Urup-tay** [Уруптай] (SOK 298). ⇨ **?+ TAY** or suff. *-tay(1,2)*?

URUS Yürük 1543 **Orus**, from the district (nāhiye) of Pravad (Gökb., Rum. 240); Trkm. 1841/42 **Orus** [Худай-берген-юзбаши / Худай-берген Орус], from the Yomut tribe (MIT II, 482, 498, 566); Tat. 1543 **Orus** (Gökb., Rum. 240); Kirg. / Kzk.? 19th c. **Orus** [Орусъ] (Potanin II, 3); Kzk. 19th c. **Orus-bay** [Орусбай] (Grod. I, 98); Kirg. **Orus-bek** [Орусбек] (Jud. 731); Selj.? 12th c. **Rus** [روس / Rus], Atabeg Pehlivān's mamluk (Rāwandī 340 etc., Ahbar 122, 123); Bashk. 1757 **Rus-qul** [Рускул Русаев] (MIB IV/1, 148); Kuman 1096, 1103 **Urup / Uruba (<Urus-aba?)** [Урубъ / Урусоба / Уруба / Русоба], a Polovets prince (Ipat. 183 (188), Lavr. 241, 268, 269, PSRL I, 118, II, 140, 323, 286, VII, 19); Khorezm.? 1319 **Urus**, one of the emirs who revolted against Abu Saʿïd Ilkhan (Hammer, Ilch. II, 277); Tat.(GH) 1360 **Urus** [Урусъ], envoy (PSRL X, 232); Maml. 14th c. **Urus** [اُرُس] (Sauvaget 35); Chag. 16th c. **Urus** [Урус] (Ivanov 147, 204, 209, 223); Trkm. 1649 **Urus** [Урус], an officer (on-begi) (MIT II, 329); Chuv. 18th-19th c. **Urus** [Урусъ] (Magn. 89); Tat. 1686 **Urus** [Уруско] (Kungursk. akty 69); Tat. 1708 **Urus** [Урус], from Astrakhan (MIB I, 219); Tat.(Sib.) 1632 **Urus** [Урус Тохтамышев] (Miller, Ist. Sib. II, 398); Nog. 1598 **Urus** [Урусъ], a prince (AI II, 3-5, IV, 105); Nog. 1601 **Urus** [Урус] (Miller, Ist. Sib. II, 169, 179, 181, 207); Nog. 1601 **Urus** [Урусъ], a murza (Andrievič, Ist. Sib. I, 101); Nog. 1649 **Urus** [Батырша мурза Урусовъ] (AI IV, 85); Nog. 1558, 1601 **Urus / Urus-murza** [Урус / Урусъ-мурза] (PSRL XIII, 285, Miller, Ist. Sib. II, 169, 179, 181, 207); Chag. 1491 **Urus-baγatïr** [Урусъ Багатыръ], envoy (PSRL IV, 158. Vi, 38, VIII, 220); Chag. 16th c. **Urus-bahadur** [Урус-бахадур] (Ivanov 358); Chag. 16th c. **Urus-biy** [Урус-бий] (Ivanov 184, 202, 216 etc.); Chag. 16th c. **Urus-biy** [Урус-бий] (Ivanov 358); Balk. **Urus-biy** [Урусбіевъ], a prince (Karaulov 52); Uyg. 1338 **Urus-buqa** [Urus Puka] (Chwol., Syr.-nest. (NF) 32); Chag. 16th c. **Urus-emir** [Урус эмир] (Ivanov 358); Oghuz/Trkm. 13th c. **Urus-χan** [اوروس حان / Ourous-Khan], a Jochid who ruled the Kazaks (Abulg./Desm. 187); Khorezm.? 14th c. **Urus-χan** [Урусъ-ханъ], a Jochid (Uzbekid) ruler (Barth., Ulugb. 75, 85); Khorezm./Chag. / Tat.(GH)? 1376/77 **Urus-χan** [Урус-хан], a Jochid (MIT I, 517); Chag.? **Urus-χan** [Urus Khán] (Tar. Rashidi 45, 50); Kmk. 1653 **Urus-χan** [Кумыкъ Урусъ-ханъ Янсоховъ мурза] (AI IV, 188); Kirg.? 13th c. **Urus-inal** [اوروس اينال / Ourous-Khan], a ruler of the Kirghiz of the region Yedi-uran(?) in Chingis' days (RaD/Ber. I, 131, Abulg./Desm. 43); Bashk. 1756 **Urus-küzä** [Урускузя Яншигулов] (MIB IV/1, 123); Tat.(Mish.) 18th c. **Urus-qul** [Урускулъ] (Nepljuev 882); Bashk. 1706 **Urus-qul** [Салтангул Урускулов] (MIB III, 29); Bashk. 1735 **Urus-qul** [Урускулъ Камасовъ], a tarχan (Vel.-Zern.,

Bašk. 25); Bashk. 1735 **Urus-qul** [Урускулъ Камасовъ], a tarχan (Vel.-Zern., Bašk. 25); Bashk. 1738 **Urus-qul** [Урускул Камасев] (MIB III, 391); Bashk. 1754 **Urus-qul** [Аблай Урускулов] (MIB IV/1, 83); Bashk. 1754 **Urus-qul** [Девлеть Урускулов] (MIB IV/1, 84); Bashk. 1785 **Urus-qul** [Урускул Биганов (Биканов)] (MIB V, 175, 307); Kkalp. 18th c. **Urus-qul** [Урускулъ] (Nepljuev 679, 680); Chag. 15th c. **Urus-mirza** [اوروس ميرزا / Урусъ Мирза] (Šejb. LXII); Nog. 1649 **Urus-murza** [Урусъ мурза] (AI IV, 79, 85); Bashk. 1735 **Urus-pay** [Оскилди Уруспаевъ], a tarχan (Vel.-Zern., Bašk. 20); Kzk. 19th c. **Urus-pay** [Уруспай] (SOV 24); Chag. 16th c. **Urus-sufi** [Урус-Суфи] (Ivanov 358); Oghuz/Trkm. 14th c. - 15th c. **Uruz** [Han Uruz], Salurqazan's son (DQorq./Ergin 95); Oghuz/Trkm. 14th c. - 15th c. **Uruz / Uruz-bek / Uruz-χan** [Уруз (Уруз-бек, Уруз-хан)], Qazan's son (DQorq. 22); Bashk. 1781 **Uruz-bay** [Урузбай Салдыбаев] (MIB V, 122); Oghuz 13th c. **Uruz-beg** [uruz beg] (DTS); Oghuz/Trkm. 13th c. **Uruz-beg** [Uruz Beg], Urum's brother in the Oghuz legend (Oğuz K. Dest. 21); Oghuz/Trkm. 14th c. - 15th c. **Uruz-qoja** [اوروز قوجه / Uruz Qoja] (DQorq./Rossi 112, 127-28, 135, 139, 144, 146-156, 167-71, 223-29); Chuv. 18th-19th c. **Vïrus-pay** [Выруспай] (Magn. 36); *EN:* Kzk. 18th c. - 19th c. **Orïs** [Орыс], a clan (Tynyšp. 70, 74, 75); Kzk. 18th c. - 19th c. **Orus** [Орус], a clan (Tynyšp. 66, 71); *TN:* Kzk. **Urus-bay** [Урус-бай], a tomb south-west of Omsk (Karta JAR IV). ✧ I. 'Russian' (Pelliot 109), cf. Sauvaget, 35: „nom d'une tribu tatare dans le Nord, dans le sixième climat", Alt., Kzk. *orus*, Tat. *urïs*, Turk. *urus* 'der Russe' (Radl. I, 1059, 1657, 1663); II. 'Battle, blow, fight'? (Bask., Im. polov. 76), cf. Kzk. *urïs* 'harp, savaş; kavga, dövüş' (KzTS); III. 'Chance, share'? (Bask., Im. polov. 76), cf. Kzk. *irïs* 'devlet, zenginlik, nasip' (KzTS). See also **YAN-URUS, KEM-URUS, ÖTKÜZLİ-URUS, SASÏQ-URUS.**

URUS-DURMAN Uzb. 1510 **Urus-durman** [Urus Durman], an emir (Tar. Rashidi 237). ⇨ **URUS + DORMAN.**

URUS-KİL Bashk. 1659 **Urus-kil** [Урускилъ Камисовъ] (Vel.-Zern., Bašk. 38). ⇨ **URUS + KEL.**

URUS-MAMET Tat.(Tüm.) 1633 **Rus-mamet (<Urus-mamet)** [Русмамет] (Miller, Ist. Sib. II, 402). ⇨ **URUS + MAMET.**

URUSAX Tat.(GH) 1408 **Urusaχ / Urusaq** [Урусахъ], a prince of the Horde (PSRL VI, 136). ⇨ **URUS? +** suff. *-aχ / -aq.*

URUSAY Tat. 1624 **Urusay** [Толсара Урусаевъ] (Pokrovskij 69); Bashk. 1731 **Urusay** [Урусай Боскулов] (MIB III, 287); Kzk. 1675 **Uruzay** [Урузай] (DAI VII, 333). ⇨ **URUS +** suff. *-ay.*

URUSLAN see **İRUSLAN**

URUSLÏ Bashk. 1713, 1718 **Uruslï / Urïslï** [Урусла (Урыслы) Багарин] (MIB III, 105, 167); Bashk. 1742 **Uruslu** [Уруслу Курткачик] (MIB I, 493); Nog. 1569, 1577 **Uruzlï** [Uruzli], a murza, Ismail's son, Edige's (Edegü's) descendant (Vel.-Zern., Haïder II, 323). ⇨ **URUS +** suff. *-lï.*

URUSLU see **URUSLÏ**

URUSMANDÏ Tat.(GH) 1364 **Urusmandï** [Урусманды] (PSRL VIII, 13).

URUSMET Bashk. 1756 **Urusmet** [Урусмет] (MIB IV/1, 111); Bashk. 1764 **Urusmet** [Ахметь Урусметев] (MIB IV/1, 277); Bashk. 1764 **Urusmet** [Абдусалим Урусметев] (MIB IV/1, 277); Bashk. 1764 **Urusmet** [Кари Урусметев] (MIB IV/1, 277). ⇨ **URUS +** suff. *-met.* See also **URUS-MAMET.**

URUSTAY Maml.? 1398/99 **Urustay** [ارسطاى من فجاعلى] (Ibn Taghrīb. VI, 3, 5, 6, 9 etc.); Chuv. 18th-19th c. **Vïrïstay** [Вырыстай] (Magn. 36); Chuv. 18th-19th c. **Vurustay** [Вурустай] (Magn. 36). ⇨ **URUS + TAY? / URUS +** suff. *-tay(2,3)?*

URUSTEM see **RÜSTEM**

URUZ see **URUS**

URUZAČ Tat.(Sib.) 1675 **Uruzač** [Урузачко] (DAI VII, 333); Hak.(Kyz.) 1680 **Uruzač** [Урузачко] (Jarilov, Kyz. 5). ⇨ **URUS +** dim. suff. *-ač?*

URUZAY see **URUSAY**

URUZLÏ see **URUSLÏ**

US see **UZ**

US-KİLDE Bashk. 1757 **Us-kilde** [Ускильда Килекеев] (MIB IV/1, 136). ✧ 'Reason, wisedom has come (has been born)'. ⇨ **UZ + KELDİ.**

USAQ Kzk. 16th c. - 17th c. **Usaq** [Usak], a prince (Radl., Aus Sib. I, 193); Kkalp. 20th c. **Usaq** [Усақ] (KkRS 776); Uyg. 13th c. - 14th c. **Usaq-tärim** [Osak-Tarim] (Chwol., Syr.-nest. 94); Kkalp. 20th c. **Usaq-ulï** [Йымсамыт Усакъ-улы] (Bask., Kkalp. 21 (52)). ✧ 'Fine, tiny, nice' cf. Kzk. *usaq* 'fein, kleinkornig, fein zermahlen' (Radl. I, 1743), Kkalp. *usaq* 'мелочь; мелкий (некрупный)' (KkRS).

USAN Kzk. **Usan-bay** [Усанбай] (Sb. Syr-D. IX, 54). ✧ 'Boring, dull; lazy' cf. Chag., Tat., Turk. *usan* 'langweilig, überdrüssig; faul' (Radl. I, 1743).

USAR Kzk. 19th c. **Usar** [Усаръ Сарымсаковъ] (SKSO VIII, 221); Uzb. 19th c. **Usar** [Усаръ Хусановъ] (SKSO III, 178); Kzk. 19th c. **Usar-bay** [Усарбай] (Grod., Pril. 183); Kzk. 19th c. **Usar-bay** [Усаръ-бай], a χajï, Quwaniš' son (AUK Dobavl. 2); Uzb. 19th c. **Usar-bay** [Усарбай] (SKSO III, 174). ✧ 'He/she resembles / takes after' cf. Kzk. *usa-* 'ähnlich sein' (Radl. I, 1743).

USÏQÏ Uyg. 12th c. - 14th c. **Usïqï** [usïqï / Usıkı] (DTS, EUTS).

USMA Tat.(GH) 13th c. **Usma** [Οὐζμά], a Christened Tatar (Byz. Turc. 228).

USMAN see **OSMAN**

USPAN see **OSMAN**

USRA   Oghuz/Trkm. **Usra-χan** [Усра-хан], Ayïna-χan's son (Muhamedova: OSA 170 /after Oguz-name by Salar-baba/).

USTA   Kzk. 19th c. **Usta-bay** [Устабай] (SOK 168); *TN:* Kzk. **Usta** [Уста], a place in the region of the Nura river in cntral Kazakstan (Kojčubaev 235). ✧ 'Master, smith' cf. Chag., Alt., Kzk., Turk. etc. *usta* 'der Handwerker, der Meister; der Scmied' (Radl. I, 1749).

USTA-YAN-ÏŠ   Tat.(Sib.) 1603 **Usta-yan-ïš** [Кохдеман Устаянышев] (Miller, Ist. Sib. II, 179). ⇨ **USTA + YAN-ÏŠ.**

USTA-NİYAZ   Uzb. 1881 **Usta-niyaz** [Уста Ніязъ] (Moskal'cev 44). ⇨ **USTA + NİYAZ.**

USTA-TANGEY   Trkm. 19th c. **Usta-tangey?** [Хайтымбай Устатангеевъ] (SKSO III, 178). ⇨ **USTA.**

USTAN   Hak. 19th-20th c. **Ustan** [Устан] (HRS 352). ✧ 'Water-rat' (HRS, Butanaev)).

USTAW   Kzk. 19th c. **Ustaw** [Устау] (SOK 292).

USTUГ   Hak. 19th c. **Ustuγ** [Устуђ] (Katanov, Otč. 12). ✧ 'Sharp, pointed' (Katanov).

USTUQAY   Bashk. 1772, 1773 **Ustuqay / Üstükäy?** [Устюкай / Устукая Шарыбкулов / Шарыпкулов] (MIB IV/2, 405, 413).

USTUQAYA   Bashk. 1773 **Ustuqaya** [Устукая Шарыпкулов] (MIB IV/2, 413).

USUQ   Uyg. 12th c. - 14th c. **Usuq** [Usuq / Usuk] (Radl., USp. 124, DTS, EUTS).

USUL   Yürük 1543 **Usul** [Usul] (Gökb., Rum. 200); Yürük 1543 **Usul-begi / Usul-beyi** [اوصولبكی / Usulbeği], from the Yürüks of Kocacık, Turkey (Gökb., Rum. 196). ✧ 'Quiet, friendship, kindness; skilfulness' cf. Crm., Turk. *usul* 'die Ruhe, Freundlichkeit, Höflichkeit, das Wohlwollen; die Geschicklichkeit, eine leichte Methode' (Radl. I, 1747).

USUN   Uyg. **Usun** [Usun] (EUTS).

USURAN   Kzk. 19th c. **Usuran** [Усуранъ] (AOO 42).

USŪTUMA   Yak. **Usūtuma** [Алып Сёрённюёхäи Уот Усутума], spirit of the burning-hot sea (Pek.).

UŠ-KİLDİ see **XOŠ-KELDİ**

UŠA   Kzk. 19th c. **Uša-bay** [Ушабай] (SOK 44).

UŠAQ   Trkm. 1580 **Ušaq** [عشاق / Ušak] (Refik, Anad. 41); Tat. 1685 **Ušaq** [Ушакъ] (Kungursk. akty 55); Tat. 1698 **Ušaq** [Тимошка Ушаковъ] (Kungursk. akty 275); Tat.? 1710 **Ušaq** [Максимъ Ушаковъ], from Tobolsk (Letop. ZAK II, 25); NUyg. 19th c. **Ušaq** [اوشاق / Ushak] (Le Coq, Namenl. 121); Kzk. 19th c. **Ušaq-pay** [Ушакпай] (SOK 18). ✧ 'Fine, nice; small, short; child, boy, young footman' cf. Kuman, Chag., Az., Crm., Turk. *ušaq* 'id.' (Radl. I, 1773), East.T. *ušaq* 'klein; kleine Kinder; Diener' (Le Coq, Namenl. 121), also Bask., Fam. 70. See also **BİK-UŠAQ.**

UŠAR   Kzk. 19th c. **Ušar** [Ушаръ], a biy (Lomakin 41). ⇨ **OŠAR?** See also **TİLEP-UŠAR.**

UŠAT   Kzk. 19th c. **Ušat** [Мирзакулъ Ушатовъ] (Grod., Pril. 136).

UŠÏГA   Kkalp. 20th c. **Ušïγa** [Ушыға], fem. (KkRS 778); Kkalp. 20th c. **Ušuγa** [Ушугъа], fem. (Bask., Kkalp. 404). ✧ 'Linen, chintz; dear velvet' cf. Kkalp. *ušïγa* 'сукно' (KkRS), 'ценный бархат' (Bask., Kkalp. 391).

UŠUГA see **UŠÏГA**

UŠUN   Oghuz/Trkm. 14th c. - 15th c. **Ušun-qoJa** [Ušun Qoja / Ушун-Коджа], Ekrek's (İgrek's) and Sekrek's (Segrek's) father (DQorq./Rossi 195, 211-19, DQorq. 78, 89, 90, 94 etc.).

UT I.   Türk 8th - 9th c. **Ut-sañun** [Ut saŋun / Ut Sañun] (Thomsen, Stein 187, 189, DTS, ETY II, 67). ✧ 'Overcome!, Win!' cf. Uyg., Chag., Alt., Az., Crm., Kzk. etc. *ut-* 'besiegen, gewinnen' (Radl. I, 1703).

UT II. see **OT**

UT-QAŠAR   Chuv. 1779 **Ut-qašar** [Борис Андреев Уткашар] (MIB V, 88-90, 136). ⇨ **OT + QAŠAR / QAČAR?**

UTAD   Kzk. 19th c. **Utad-bay / Ustad-bay?** [Утадъ-бай] (Grod., Pril. 117).

UTAГAP   Kzk. **Utaγap** [Утагапъ] (Sb. Syr-D. IX, 58).

UTAY see **OTAY**

UTAM   Kzk. 19th c. **Utam-bay** [Утамбай] (SKSO VIII, 223); Kzk. 19th c. **Utam-χoJa** [Утамъ Ходжа] (Grod., Pril. 116). ⇨ **OTA?** + poss. suff. *-m.*

UTANČÏ   Kzk. 1822 **Utančï / Otančï** [Утанчи] (TOUAK XXIV, 130). ⇨ **OTAN?** + suff. *-čï.*

UTAR I.   Karakh. 11th c. **Utar** [utar / Utar] (DTS, MK/Atalay 857). ✧ I. 'He will win; winner' (Bese 12), cf. Uyg., Karakh. *ut-* 'побеждать, выигрывать' (DTS); II. 'He will follow (his enemy)' cf. Karakh. *ut-* 'следовать' (DTS) + aor. suff. *-ar.*

UTAR II. see **OTAR**

UTÏM-BAY see **OTUN**

UTQA   Hak. 19th-20th c. **Utqa** [Утка], fem. (HRS 355). ✧ 'Duck'? <R. *utka* 'id.'.

UTQUR   Trkm. 1817/18 **Utqur-sufi** [Уткур Суфи], a qušbegi (master of birds) (MIT II, 201).

UTUГUN   Kzk. 19th c. **Utuγun** [Утугунъ] (AOO 78).

UTUMÏŠ   Bashk. 1601 **Utumïš** [Утумыш], from the Tabïn tribe (Miller, Ist. Sib. II, 165).

UTUNBET   Bashk. 1757 **Utunbet** [Субак Утюнбетев] (MIB IV/1, 151). ⇨ **OTUN** + suff. *-bet.*

UTUP   Kzk. **Utup / Ütüp?** [Утюпъ Танабаевъ] (ZIRGOOrenb. III, 26). ⇨ **ÖTEP?**

UTUR see **OTUR**

UTUŠ   Karakh. **Utuš** [Utuş] (MK/Atalay 857); Karakh. 11th c. **Utuš** [utuš] (DTS). ✧ 'Prize, gain' cf. Karakh. *utuš* 'id.' (DTS).

UWAY-DİLDA   Kzk. 19th c. **Uway-dilda** [Уайдильда]

(AOP 2). ✧ '?- golden coin'? cf. Kzk. PN *Dilda-bek* (Žanuzakov-Esbaeva). ⇨ **TİLLA?**

UWAQ Kzk. **Uwaq** [Уак], Qambar's father (Proben III, 112 (88)); Kirg. 19th c. **Uwaq** [Уакъ], fem. (Potanin II, 159); Kzk. 19th c. **Uwaq-bay** [Увакбай] (AOO 10); Kzk. 19th c. **Uwaq-bay** [Уакбай] (SOK 16, 26); Kzk. 19th c. **Uwaq-bay** [Уакбай] (AOK 30, 78); Kzk. 19th c. **Uwaq-bay** [Уакбай] (SOK 262); Kzk. 19th c. **Uwaq-pay** [Уакпай] (SOK 178); Kzk. 19th c. **Uwaq-pay** [Уакпай] (AOK 10). ✧ 'Small, tiny; young' cf. Tat.(Bar., Tob.) *uaq (uwaq)* 'id.' (Radl. I, 1592), Kzk. *uwaq* 'мелкий, мелочь' (KzRS), Bashk. *waq* 'мелкий; маленький, малолетний (BRS/Uraksin). See also **QOS-UWAQ, QUM-UWAQ, QUŠ-UWAQ.**

UWAQAY Bashk. 18th c. **Uwaqay** [Увакаев], several persons in the source (MIB 54, 88, 91, 92, 106 etc.); Bashk. 1764 **Uwaqay** [Нияз Увакаев] (MIB IV/1, 285); Bashk. 1777 **Uwaqay** [Увакай] (MIB V, 54); Bashk. 1777 **Uwaqay** [Нияз /Ниязь Увакаев] (MIB 54, 89, 91, 92, 106 etc.); Bashk. 1780 **Uwaqay** [Увакай] (MIB V, 106); Bashk. 1789 **Uwaqay** [Рафик Увакаев] (MIB V, 255); Bashk. 1789, 1792 **Uwaqay** [Девлеть Увакаев] (MIB V, 255, 327); Bashk. 1792 **Uwaqay** [Убрак Увакаев] (MIB V, 327); Bashk. 1793 **Uwaqay** [Ибрай / Ибрак Увакаев] (MIB V, 327). ⇨ **UWAQ** + dim. suff. *-qay.*

UWAQPAN Kzk. 19th c. **Uwaqpan** [Уакпанъ] (SOK 186); Kzk. 19th c. **Uwaqpan** [Уакпанъ] (AOP 54). ⇨ **UWAQ** + suff. *-pan.*

UWAL Nog.? **Uwal-bek** [Уалбекъ] (DAI VI, 26).

UWALDA Kzk. 19th c. **Uwalda / Uwaldï?** [Уальда] (AOK 54).

UWALÏ Kzk. 19th c. **Uwalï** [Уали] (SODž. 42); Kzk. 19th c. **Uwalï** [Ували Карасартовъ] (Konsin, Pam. 19).

UWALÏČE Kzk. 19th c. **Uwalïče** [Уаличе] (AOK 54). ⇨ **UWALÏ** + suff. *-če.*

UWATAY Kzk. 19th c. **Uwatay** [Уатай] (AOAtb. 22).

UZ Maml. 1466/67 **Us-bay** [اصباى البواب الخوشقدمى] (Ibn Taghrïb. VII, 745, 833, Iyās II, 92); Maml. 1487 **Us-bay** [اصباى السيفى قرقماس] (Iyās II, 241); Maml. 1500/01 **Us-bay** [اصباى الاشرفى قايتباى] (Iyās II, 379); Maml. 1500/01 **Us-bay** [اصباى], an emir (Iyās II, 375); Kzk. 19th c. **Us-bay** [Усьбай] (AOAtb. 58); Türk 7th-9th c. **Uz** [Uz] (ETY III, 143). ✧ 'Smart, able, skilful; reason, wisdom' cf. Chag., Turk. *uz* gewandt, geschickt, fähig' (Radl. I, 1754), Uyg., Kuman, Alt., Hak. *us* 'die Geschicklichkeit, Kunst' (Radl. I, 1742), Uyg., Kuman, Chag., Az., Turk. *us* 'der Verstand, der Geist, Sinn, die Weiseheit' (Radl. I, 1741). See also **UZ-BİLGÄ-ČAÑSÏ-UZ.**

UZ-BİLGÄ-ČAÑSÏ-UZ Türk 7th-9th c. **Uz-bilgä-čañsï-uz** [Uz Bilgä Çansï Uz (?) / Uz Bilge Çangsı Uz

(?)] (ETY III, 143). ⇨ **UZ + BİLGÄ + ? + UZ.**

UZ-TÄÑRİ Uyg. 12th c. - 14th c. **Uz-täñri** [uz täŋri] (DTS). ✧ 'Smart/able God' (Blagova 1997, 703). ⇨ **UZ + TÄÑRİ.**

UZAQ Kzk. 19th c. **Usaq-pay** [Усакпай] (SOK 186); Kzk. 19th c. **Uzaq** [Кайке Узаковъ] (Grod., Pril. 62); Kzk. 19th c. **Uzaq** [Узакъ] (SKSO II, 14); Kzk. 19th c. **Uzaq** [Узакъ] (AOP 38); Kzk. 19th c. **Uzaq** [Узакъ] (SODž. 134); Kzk. 19th c. **Uzaq** [Узакъ] (SOK 18); Kkalp. 20th c. **Uzaq** [Узак] (KkRS 776); Kzk. 19th c. **Uzaq-bay** [Узакбай] (SOK 154); Kzk. 19th c. **Uzaq-bay** [Узакбай] (SODž. 64); Kkalp. 20th c. **Uzaq-bay** [Узакбай] (KkRS 776); Uzb. 1848 **Uzaq-biy** [Бай Узакъ-Бий], a rich (noble) man (Moskal'cev 34); Kzk. 19th c. **Uzaq-pay** [Узакпай] (SOV 62); Kzk. 19th c. **Uzaq-pay** [Узакпай] (SOK 48, 120, 132, 282); Kzk. 19th c. **Zaq-pay** [Закпай] (SOK 88). ✧ 'Far, lasting; (as a wish) long (life!)' (Žanuzakov), cf. Uyg., Kuman, Chag., Alt., Kzk. etc. *uzaq* 'lang, spät, weit' (Radl. I, 1757), Kzk., Kirg. *-zaq / -saq <uzaq* 'long' (Žanuzakov, Kalilov). See also **BAY-UZAQ, JAN-UZAQ, QON-UZAQ (KÖN-UZAQ?), ÖMÜR-UZAQ, TUN-ZAQ (TÜN-ZAQ?).**

UZAM-PEK see UZAN

UZAN Kzk. 19th c. **Uzam-pek < Uzan-pek** [Узампекъ] (SODž. 56); Kzk. 1819 **Uzan** [Узан] (MIK IV, 323); Kzk. 19th c. **Uzan** [Шукуръ-бекъ Бай Узановъ] (Grod., Pril. 147); Kzk. 1825 **Uzan-bay** [اوزانباى / Узанбай] (MIK 475, 468). ✧ 'Stretch yourself' cf. Uyg., Crm., Turk. *uzan-* 'sich ausstrecken, sich dehnen' (Radl. I, 1759).

UZEČKA Tat.(Sib.) 1684 **Uzečka?** [Узечка Мунгатовъ] (DAI XI, 160).

UZUM-BAY see UZUN

UZUN Kzk. 19th c. **Uzum-bay < Uzun-bay** [Узумбай] (SOV 32); Kzk. 19th c. **Uzun** [Узунъ] (SOV 76); Kzk. 1885 **Uzun-bay** [Исламисъ Узунбаевъ] (Grod., Pril. 124); Kzk. 19th c. **Uzun-ɣul** [Узунгулъ] (AOK 10); *TN:* 15th c. **Uzun-ata** [Узунъ-Ата] (Barth., Ulugb. 64); Kzk. **Uzun-bay(eva)** [Узунбаева], a village North-west of Orsk in the Ural Mountains (Karta JAR III). ✧ 'Long' cf. Uyg., Kuman, Chag., Alt., Kzk. etc. *uzun* 'id.' (Radl. I, 1768).

UZUN-AČAQ Tuv. 19th c. **Uzun-ačaq** [Узунъ-ачакъ] (Potanin IV, 591). ✧ 'Long (tall?) old man' (Potanin: *ačaq = apšaq* 'старик'). ⇨ **UZUN.**

UZUN-ASAN Trkm.? **Uzun-asan-bek** [Узунъ-Асанъбекъ / Узуосанбекъ / Узуосанбѣгъ], a prince of Shiraz (PSRL VI, 341, 352, 357, XX, 310). ⇨ **UZUN + XASAN.**

UZUN-BURUN Yürük 16th c. **Uzun-burun** [اوزون بورون / Uzunburun], from the Yürüks of Kocacık, Turkey (Gökb., Rum. 103). ⇨ **UZUN +

BURUN.

UZUN-ČAŠ   Kzk. 19th c. **Uzun-čaš** [Узунъ-чашъ], fem. (Ibragimov 125). ✧ 'Long hair(ed), (fig.) woman' cf. Kirg. *čač: uzun čač* 'длинные волосы, (перен.) женщина' (Jud.), Alt. *čač* 'волосы' (OjrRS), Shor, Kzk. *šaš* 'die Haare' (Radl. IV, 973). ⇨ UZUN.

UZUN-QALAP   Alt.(Tel., Leb.) **Uzun-qalap** [Узун-Калап] (Radl. I, 1307). ✧ 'Long (tall?)-(unmerciful) predator' cf. Alt. *qalap* 'хищный, жестокий' (OjrRS). ⇨ UZUN.

UZUN-QARA   Alt. 19th c. **Uzun-qara** [Узун-Кара-богатырь], a folklore hero in a heroic legend (Verb., In. 139, 153). ⇨ UZUN + QARA.

UZUN-QAŠ   Sclj. 1207 **Uzun-qaš** [ازنتش / Moubariz Eddin Ouzounqach] (Seldj. Nameh 56). ⇨ UZUN + QAŠ.

UZUN-QÏLAN   Alt. 19th c. **Uzun-qïlan** [Узун-Кылан-богатыр], Qïsqa-qïlan's brother (Verb., In. 151). ✧ 'Long hair(ed), with long mane'. ⇨ UZUN + QÏLĀÑ. See also **QÏSQA-QÏLAN.**

UZUN-MURT   Kzk. 19th c. **Uzun-murt** [Узунмуртъ] (SOK 280); Kzk. 19th c. **Uzun-murt** [Узунмуртъ] (SOV 30). ✧ 'Long moustache' cf. Kzk. *murt* 'Schnurbart' (Radl. IV, 2194). ⇨ UZUN.

UZUN-SAQAL   Chag. 15th c. **Uzun-saqal** [Uzun Sakal Tufta Kuli], follower of the Dughlatid Sultan Said (Tar. Rashidi 309). ✧ 'Long-bearded'. ⇨ UZUN + SAQAL.

UZUN-SARÏ   Kzk. **Uzun-sarï-alïp** [Узун Сары Алып], a folklore hero (Proben III, 321 (270)). ⇨ UZUN + SARÏ.

UZUN-SULTAN-XANÏM see URUN

UZUR   Kuman 1279 **Uzur** [Uzur], a noble man among the Kumans of Hungary (Gyárfás II, 438); Turk. 1475 **Uzur** [اُزر] (Āšikp. 188); *TN:* Turk. 1489 **Uzur-obasï** [Uzur-obası (Kırk-Kilise)], Uzur's field (Gökb., Ed. 303, 310).

ŪQUN   Yak. **Ūqun** [Укун], spirit of the water, Ū-Čoñqurūn's son (Pek.).

ÜBBİ-NİYAZ   Kkalp. 20th c. **Übbi-niyaz** [Уббинияз] (KkRS 776). ⇨ NİYAZ.

ÜBEK   Bashk. 1675 **Übek** [Бекбайба Убеков] (MIB I, 202).

ÜBİŠ   Kkalp. 1724 **Übiš / Ubïš?** [Чихантай Убишев] (MIKk. 182).

ÜBRES   Hak. 19th-20th c. **Übres** [Ӱбрес] (HRS 352).

ÜČ-GÖZ   Trkm. 20th c. **Üč-göz-oɣlu** [Üçgöz oğlu], among the Avshars in the Anatolian Türkmen folklore (Özbaş 15). ✧ 'Three-eye(d)' cf. in several Trk. languages: *üč / üš / üs / öč / üc / ic* 'drei' (Radl. I, 1872). ⇨ KÖZ.

ÜČ-KEMPİR   Kzk. **Üč-kempir / Üč-kämpir** [Utch-Kampyr] (Nalivkin-Dozon 640); Kzk. 19th c. **Üš-kempir** [Ушкемпиръ] (SOK 12); Kzk. 19th c. **Üš-kempir** [Ушкемперъ] (SOV 50); Kzk. 19th c. **Üš-kempir** [Ушкемпыръ] (SOV 10). ✧ 'Three old women' cf. in several Trk. languages: *üč / üš / üs / öč / üc / ic* 'drei' (Radl. I, 1872). ⇨ KEMPİR. See also **ÜČ-QURTQA.**

ÜČ-QARA   Khorezm./Chag. 1388, 1406/07 **Üč-qara** [قرا اوج السين شمس / Учкара-бехадур], an emir (Dorn 185, 190, MIT I, 524). ✧ 'Three-black(-man)' cf. in several Trk. languages: *üč / üš / üs / öč / üc / ic* 'drei' (Radl. I, 1872). ⇨ QARA.

ÜČ-QURQA see **ÜČ-QURTQA**

ÜČ-QURTQA   Kipch. 1262 **Üč-qurqa (<Üč-qurtqa)** [اجترقا / Уджкурка] (Baybars/Tizeng. I, 78, 100). ✧ 'Three old women' cf. in several Trk. languages: *üč / üš / üs / öč / üc / ic* 'drei' (Radl. I, 1872). ⇨ QURTQA. See also **ÜČ-KEMPİR.**

ÜČ-OQ   Turk. 1484 **Üč-oq-oɣlï** [اوچ اوقك اوغلى يُوركر] (Āšikp. 188). ✧ 'Three arrows' cf. in several Trk. languages: *üč / üš / üs / öč / üc / ic* 'drei' (Radl. I, 1872). ⇨ OQ.

ÜČEM-BAY see **ÜČEN**

ÜČEN   Kzk. 19th c. **Üčem-bay (<Üčen-bay)** [Учембай] (AOP 102).

ÜČİN   Kzk. 1832 **Üčin / Üče?** [Ишимъ Ючинъ] (Konšin, Mat. I-III, 34).

ÜČKÜNDÜR   Crm. **Üčkündür** [Ӱчкӱндӱр] (Proben VII, 1). ✧ 'Beetroot' cf. Crm. *üčkündür* 'die rote Rübe' (Radl. I, 1875).

ÜČÜN-KÜLÜG-TİRİG   Türk 7th c. - 9th c. **Üčün-külüg-tirig** [üčün külüg tirig / Üçin külüg tirig] (DTS, ETY III, 39). ✧ 'Üčün-Famous-Alive' (Blagova 1997, 714). ⇨ ? + KÜLÜG + TİRİG.

ÜJÜYÄN   Yak. **Üjüyän** [Ӱдӱ̈гäi Ӱдӱ̈jän], a folklore hero (Pek.).

ÜDRÄTMİŠ   Uyg. 13th-14th c. **Üdrätmiš**, fem. (Zieme, Mat. III, 280).

ÜDÜYÄ   Yak. **Üdüyä** [Ӱстäх Ӱдӱ̈jä], one of the daughters of Quoχtuya abāsï (Pek.).

ÜDÜŠ-İGİR see **ÖDÜŠ-İKİR**

ÜGBEK   Hak.(Kacha) 19th-20th c. **Ügbäk** [Ӱгбäк] (Proben IX, 558, 559); Hak. 19th-20th c. **Ügbek** [Ӱгбек] (HRS 352). ✧ 'Fuzzy' (HRS).

ÜGÄ see **ÖGÄ**

ÜGÄ-PĒRŌZ   Uyg. 762 **Ügä-pērōz-tegin** [Ügä Pērōz Tegin] (Mahrnāmag 9). ✧ 'Wise-triumph' cf. *Pērōz* 'Sieg' (Mahrnāmag 32). ⇨ ÜGÄ.

ÜGÄŠ   Bashk. 1769 **Ügäš** [Тайгун Угяшев] (MIB IV/1, 335). ⇨ ÖGÄ? + suff. -š.

ÜGÜČEK   Tat.(Sib.)? 1631 **Ügüček** [Угучек

Какбашев] (Miller, Ist. Sib. II, 383, 384); Hak.(Kyz.) 1716 **Ügüček** [Агучекъ / Угучекъ] (Jarilov, Kyz. 9); Hak.(Kyz.) 19th c. **Ügüžek** / **Ügüjek** [Угужековъ], name of a few families (Jarilov, Kyz. 9). ✧ 'Little owl' cf. Hak. fem. PN *Ügü* (Butanaev) + dim. *-ček.*

ÜGÜDÄY see **ÖGÄDÄY**

ÜGÜLİ Kuman 1359 **Ügüli** [Vgulehomoka], personal name preserved in a toponym in Lesser Kumania, Hubgary (Gyárfás III, 499). ✧ 'Having owls; with owls' cf. Chag., Crm., Hak. *ügü* 'die Eule, der Uhu' (Radl. I, 1810), Rásonyi, NTK 120-121, Rásonyi, KÖA 136 + suff. *-li.*

ÜYDEM Crm. 1517 **Üydem** / **Üydem-murza** [Уидемъ-мурза / Удеимъ-мурза], a murza from the Crimea (PSRL VI, 259, VIII, 261, XIII, 26).

ÜYÄDÄM Nog. 1502 **Üyädäm** / **Üydem?** [Уядамъ], envoy (PSRL XII, 254).

ÜKÄYDÃN Yak. **Ükäydän** / **Üökäydän** [Ÿкäідäн / Ÿöкäідäн], fem. (Pek.).

ÜKÄR NUyg. 20th c. **Ükär-qïz** [Ükär qïz], a woman in Qara-χočo (Le Coq's letter to J. Németh). ✧ 'Evening star'? ⇨ **ÜLKER.**

ÜKEY Bashk. 1731 **Ükey** [Кинзегул Укеев] (MIB III, 294).

ÜKÜN Alt. **Ükün** / **Yükün** [Юкюнъ] (Nikiforov 36, 37).

ÜKÜŠ-QARA Uyg. **Öküš-qara** [Öküş Kara] (EUTS). ⇨ **QARA.**

ÜKÜŠ-QARA-AČQÏ Uyg. 12th c. - 14th c. **Öküš-qara-ačqï** [Öküš-Qara-Ačqï / üküš qara ačqï] (Radl., USp. 44, DTS). ✧ 'Much-Black/mighty-Ačqï' (Blagova 1997, 705), cf. Uyg. *öküš, üküš* 'много' (DTS). ⇨ **QARA + AČQÏ.** See also **YETMİŠ-QARA-AČQÏ.**

ÜL-JÖMÖL Kzk. **Ül-Jömöl** [Bädi Ülshömöl / Бäді Ÿлжöмöл], Säypül Mälik's friend (Proben III, 664 (583)).

ÜLČİ-TÜMÄN Uyg. 12th c. - 14th c. **Ülči-tümän** [ülči tümän] (DTS). ⇨ **TÜMÄN.**

ÜLJEKE Kzk. 19th c. **Üljeke (<Ulja-eke?)** [Ульджеке] (SOK 116). ⇨ **OLJA?** + comp. *eke.*

ÜLÄGÜR Uyg. **Ülägür** [Ülägür] (EUTS); Uyg. 13th c. **Ülägür-elči** [ülägür elči] (DTS).

ÜLÄM Uyg. 12th c. - 14th c. **Üläm** [Üläm / Üläm] (Radl., USp. 52, DTS, EUTS).

ÜLEY Tat. 18th c. **Üley** [Гумеръ Улѣевъ] (Nepljuev 824-25); Tat. 1764 **Üley** [Улей Баймаков] (MIB IV/1, 102, 279); Bashk. 1735 **Üley** [Улмятякъ Улеевъ], a tarχan (Vel.-Zern., Bašk. 24).

ÜLEKEY Bashk. 1709 **Üläkäy** [Янай Улякеев] (MIB I, 264); Bashk. 1764 **Ülekey** [Араптан Улекеев] (MIB IV/1, 277); Bashk. 1796 **Ülekey** [Улекей Раткин] (MIB V, 361).

ÜLEŠ Tat.(Sib.) 1648 **Üleš** [Ешко Улешев] (Miller,

Ist. Sib. II, 528). ✧ 'Share, dole' cf. Chag., Alt., Hak. *üläš* 'der Theil, zukommende Theil, Antheil' (Radl. I, 1847).

ÜLGEN see **ÜLKÜN**

ÜLKÄRČÄ Hak. 19th-20th c. **Ülkärčä** [Ÿлкäрчä] (Katanov, Otč. 10). ✧ 'Lukercha' (Katanov), dim. of R. Glikeriya.

ÜLKER Az. **Ülker** [Улькер], daughter of the ruler in a tale (Az. Skaz. 54). ✧ 'Evening star' cf. Alt.(Tel.) *ülkär* 'die Plejaden' (Radl. I, 1855), Chag., Kzk. *ürkär / ürkör* 'die Plejaden' (Radl. I, 1837).

ÜLKÜM-BAY see **ÜLKÜN**

ÜLKÜN Kzk. 19th c. **Ülgen-bay** [Улгенбай], a singer (AUK 362, 639); Kzk. 19th c. **Ülküm-bay (<Ülkün-bay)** [Ульküмбай] (SOK 122); Kzk. 19th c. **Ülkün-bay** [Улкунбай] (SKSO III, 19). ✧ 'Tall, big; great' cf. Kzk. *ülkön* 'id.' (Radl. I, 1856).

ÜLMÄS see **ÖLMEZ**

ÜLMÄZ see **ÖLMEZ**

ÜLTÜK Bashk. 1758 **Ültük** [Алдар Ултюков] (MIB IV/2, 20). ✧ 'Fuzzy, shaggy; hearty' cf. Bashk. *öltök* 'торчащий пучком, всклокоченный, лохматый; услужливый, радушный' (BRS/Uraksin).

ÜLÜGDÜ Uyg. 13th c. **Ülügdü** [ülügdü] (DTS, EUTS).

ÜMBET Kkalp. 20th c. **Ümbet** [Умбет] (KkRS 776). ✧ 'Ummat (=folk, crowd, nation)' (<Ar.) (Žanuzakov), cf. Turk. *ümmet* 'Religionsgemeinschaft; Nation' (HŞ).

ÜMBET-TAY Kzk. 19th c. **Ümbet-tay** [Умбетай] (SODž. 108); Kzk. 19th c. **Ümbet-tay** [Унбеттай] (SODž. 6). ✧ 'Ummat (=folk, crowd, nation)' (Ar.) (Žanuzakov), cf. Turk. *ümmet* 'Religionsgemeinschaft; Nation' (HŞ). ⇨ **ÜMBET + TAY?** or suff. *-tay(1,2).*

ÜMÄŠ Tat. 1748 **Ümäš** [Умяшъ] (Nepljuev 437); Bashk. 1735 **Ümäš** [Умеръ Умешевъ], a tarχan (Vel.-Zern., Bašk. 16). ✧ 'Little (child born on the day of the) collective work' cf. Bashk. *ömä* 'коллективная помощь (обычно в сельской местности)' (BRS/Uraksin). ⇨ **ÜMÄ** + dim. suff. *-š.*

ÜMEKEY Bashk. 1706 **Ümekey** [Умекей Бугаев] (MIB III, 20). ✧ '(Born on the day of the) collective work' cf. Bashk. *ömä* 'коллективная помощь (обычно в сельской местности)' (BRS/Uraksin) + dim. suff. *-key.*

ÜMER see **ÖMÜR**

ÜMET see **ÜMİT**

ÜMİD see **ÜMİT**

ÜMİR see **ÖMÜR**

ÜMİR-ZAQ see **ÖMÜR-UZAQ**

ÜMİRÄK Kzk. 19th c. **Ümiräk** [Умиракъ Аскаръ Ходжаевъ] (Grod., Pril. 198); Tat. 1724 **Ümräk (<Ümiräk)** [Умряк Алмяшев] (MIB III, 227); Bashk. 1740 **Ümräk (<Ümiräk)** [Иликей Умряков] (MIB I, 392). ⇨ **ÖMÜR** + dim. suff. *-äk.*

ÜMİRÄS Bashk. 1779 **Ümräs (< Ömiräs)** [Бякян

Умрясов] (MIB V, 96). ⇨ **ÖMÜR** + suff. *-äs*.

ÜMİS   Kzk. 19th c. **Ümis** [Умисъ Бекбаевъ] (Grod., Pril. 170).

ÜMİT   Trkm. 20th c. **Umït** [Umït], fem. (Zaj. 1971, 337); Trkm. 20th c. **Umīt** [Умыт], fem. (TrkmRS 661); Turk. 16th c. **Ümid** [امید / Ümid] (Ongan, Ank. II); Turk. 20th c. **Ümit** [Ümit] (Önder, Göle); Bashk. 1781 **Ümit** [Умит Алматеев] (MIB V, 124); Kkalp. 20th c. **Ümit** [Умит], fem. (KkRS 779); Kkalp. 20th c. **Ümit** [Умит] (KkRS 776); Bashk. 1735 **Ümit-bay** [Умитбай Еликеевъ], a tarχan (Vel.-Zern., Bašk. 16); Bashk. 1735 **Ümit-bay** [Умитбай Аблаевъ], a tarχan (Vel.-Zern., Bašk. 17); Bashk. 18th c. **Ümit-bay** [Умитбай] (MIB V, 559); Bashk. 1777 **Ümit-bay** [Умитбай Арасланбеков] (MIB V, 52); Bashk. 1779 **Ümit-bay** [Умитбай (Уметбай) Кутушев] (MIB V, 101, 102, 245, 284 etc.); Bashk. 1779 **Ümit-bay** [Юлукай Умитбаев] (MIB V, 96); Trkm. 1565/1566 **Ümit-bek** [Умет-бек], from the Ustaǰlu tribe (MIT II, 74); Kirg. **Ümöt** [Uemöt / Ӳмӧт] (Proben V, 151 /153/); Bashk. 1744 **Ümüd-bay** [Умюдбай Сусаров] (MIB III, 426); Bashk. 1751 **Ümüt** [Умют Янекеев] (MIB IV/1, 43); Bashk. 1735 **Ümüt-bay** [Умутбай Кунаевъ], a tarχan (Vel.-Zern., Bašk. 14); Bashk. 1735 **Ümüt-bay** [Бердыгулъ Умутбаевъ], a tarχan (Vel.-Zern., Bašk. 16). ✧ 'Hope' cf. Turk. *ümüd* (P.), Kzk. *ümüt* (P.) 'die Hoffnung' (Radl. I, 1912), Kkalp. *ümit* 'надежда, упование, чаяние' (KkRS), Trkm. *umīt* 'надежда' (TrkmRS).

ÜMİTÄK   Bashk. 1706 **Ümitäk** [Умитяк Акелов] (MIB III, 30). ⇨ **ÜMİT** + dim. suff. *-äk*.

ÜMİTEY   Bashk. 1735 **Ümitey** [Кутей Умитеевъ], a tarχan (Vel.-Zern., Bašk. 22); Bashk. 1770 **Ümitey** [Уметей Адзитерев] (MIB IV/1, 342); Bashk. 1780 **Ümitey** [Умитей Адзитаров (Азитаров)] (MIB V, 116, 131, 178); Bashk. 1781 **Ümitey** [Меннягул Уметеев] (MIB V, 124); Bashk. 1778 **Ümitey** / **Ümütey** [Умитей (Умютей) Кутушев] (MIB V, 76, 97). ⇨ **ÜMİT** + dim. suff. *-ey*.

ÜMRÄK see **ÜMİRÄK**

ÜMRÄS see **ÜMİRÄS**

ÜMÜD see **ÜMİT**

ÜMÜK   Bashk. 1762 **Ümük** [Умюк Бинлибаев] (MIB IV/2, 300); Bashk. 1776 **Ümük?** [Сафар / Сафер Умюков / Умуков] (MIB V, 33, 34).

ÜMÜR-ZAQ see **ÖMÜR-UZAQ**

ÜMÜT see **ÜMİT**

ÜN-TAPMÏŠ   Uyg. 13th-14th c. **Ün-tapmïš-šäli** [[Ü]n Tapmïš Šäli] (Zieme, Mat. III,). ✧ 'Voice-found; (s)he found/made a name / repute' cf. Uyg., Karakh. *ün* 'голос' (DTS). ⇨ **TAPMÏŠ.**

ÜNEGEČ   Tat.(Sib.) 1675 **Ünegeč** [Унегечко] (DAI VII, 333). ✧ 'Young dog, puppy' cf. Shor *ünägäš* 'ein junger Hund' (Radl. I, 1820).

ÜNER see **ÖNER**

ÜNGÜR   Khorezm.? **Üngür** [ایلکور / السکور / السکور / انکور / انککور / Унгуръ] (RaD/Ber. II, 95 (Text 153), III, 27, 28, 141, 169).

ÜÖJÜYÄN   Yak. **Üöjüyän-bögö** [Ӳӧцӳйäн / Ӳӧдӳйäн / Бӧҕӧ], a folklore hero (Pek.).

ÜÖDÜYÄ   Yak. **Üödüyä** [Ӳстäх Ӳӧдӳйä], Quoχtuya-χotun's daughter (Pek.).

ÜÖDÜYÄN   Yak. **Üödüyän-oγonyor** [Ӳӧдӳйäн оҕонjор] (Pek.).

ÜÖRGÜ-JÜÖRGÜ-ÜGÜGÄY   Yak. **Üörgü-jüörgü-ügügäy** [Ӳӧргӳ Цӳӧргӳ Ӳгӳгäi], fem. (Pek.).

ÜÖRÜKTÄY   Yak. **Üörüktäy** [Ӳӧрӳктäi Тiмiр Бӧҕӳлӳк äмäхсiн], fem. (Pek.). ✧ 'Like a tangle, matting; shaggy' cf. Yak. *üörük* 'куст густых ветвей на лиственницъ ком или клубок сплотившихся (перепутавшихся) волос в хвосте или гриве лошади' (Pek.) + suff. *-täy*.

ÜPÖL   Kirg. **Üpöl** [Упӧл], fem. (Jud. 943).

ÜPSEK   Hak. 19th-20th c. **Üpsek** [Ӳпсек] (HRS 352).

ÜRBÜ   Kirg. **Ürbü** [Ӳрбӳ], Köküm's son (Proben V, 143 /145/).

ÜRÄYBÄ-SARAYBA   Yak. **Üräybä-sarayba** [Ӳräiбä-Сараiба Разброса-Сараiба] (Pek.). ✧ 'Distributing/distributor of meat' (Pek.).

ÜRÄN see **ÜREN**

ÜREGİR   Oghuz/Trkm. 13th c. **Üregir** [اورکیر / Урегир], Taγ-χan's son (Abulg./Kon. 520, 560, 610).

ÜREKEY   Tat. 1613 **Ürekey** [Урекей Чемекеевъ] (Zolotn. 159). ✧ 'Spool' cf. Crm., Turk. *öräkä* 'die Spule, Spindel' (Radl. I, 1218) + dim. suff. *-y*.

ÜREN   Hak. 19th c. **Ürän** [Ӳрäн], fem. (Katanov, Otč. 12); Alt. 19th-20th c. **Üren** [Ӳрен], fem. (OjrRS 213). ✧ 'Seed, kernel; descendant' cf. Alt., Hak. *ürän* 'id.' (Radl. I, 1827).

ÜRENČİ   Alt. 19th-20th c. **Ürenči** [Ӳренчи], fem. (OjrRS 213). ✧ 'Wagtail' (OjrRS) cf. Alt.(Kmd.) *üränčī* 'die Bachstelze' (Radl. I, 1829).

ÜRENEY   Chuv. 17th c. **Üreney** [Уренейко] (IOAIÊK XXIX, 348); Alt. 19th-20th c. **Üreney** [Ӳреней] (OjrRS 210). ⇨ **ÜREN** + dim. suff. *-ey*.

ÜREÑ   Kzk. 19th c. **Üreñ-bay** (<**Üreñk-bay?**) [Уренкъ-бай] (Grod., Pril. 52).

ÜREÑ-TAŠ   Khorezm.? **Üreñ-taš** [Уренгташ] (RaD II, 126). ⇨ **ÜREÑ** + **TAŠ.**

ÜRGEM-PAY see **ÜRGEN**

ÜRGEN   Kzk. 19th c. **Ürgem-pay** (<**Ürgen-pay**) [Ургемпай] (Pam. kn. Turg. 41).

ÜRGÜNİS   Kzk. 1823 **Ürgünis-bay** [Ургунисбай] (MIK IV, 443).

ÜRİKÄ   Hak. 19th-20th c. **Ürikä** [Ӳрика], fem. (HRS 355).

ÜRK see **ÜRÜK**

ÜRK-TOΓRÏL   Uyg. 12th c. - 14th c. **Ürk-toγrïl** [Ürk

Toγrïl] (Radl., USp. 214, 256). ⇨ ?+ **TOΓRÏL.**

ÜRKE   Tat.(Mish.) 1765 **Ürke** [Мухамметкул Уркин] (MIB IV/1, 108).

ÜRKEY   Tat. 1764 **Ürkey** [Рахманкул Уркеев] (MIB IV/1, 300); Bashk. 18th c. **Ürkey** [Абзан Уркеев] (MIB V, 71). ⇨ **ÜRKE** + dim. suff. -y.

ÜRKEL   Bashk. 1693 **Ürkel** [Уркел] (MIB I, 84).

ÜRKENČİ   Kzk. 19th c. **Ürkenči** [Уркенчи] (SOV 104). ⇨ **ÖRKEN?** + suff. -či.

ÜRKEŠ   Bashk. 1710 **Ürkeš** [Уркеш Кутлугуш] (MIB III, 56); Bashk. 1738 **Ürkeš** [Батал Уркешев] (MIB III, 337). ⇨ **ÜRKE?** + suff. -š.

ÜRKMES   Maml. 1464 **Ürkmes** [الجاموس الاشرفى اركماس] (Ibn Taghrīb. VIII, 482); Maml. 1497 **Ürkmes** [السيفى اركماس بن عبدالله] (Sauvaget: BEO III, 8). ✧ 'He won't be afraid' cf. Maml. ürk- 'erschrecken' (Qawānīn).

ÜRKÜČ   Turk. 1630 **Ürküč** [Urkucs], a „bölük-bašï" (Velics-Kamm. II, 739).

ÜRKÜM   Kzk. 19th c. **Ürküm-bay** [Уркумбай Акбергеновъ] (Grod., Pril. 62).

ÜRKÜTEY-MÜRKÜTEY   Alt. **Ürkütey-mürkütey** [Ӱркӱтей-Мӱркӱтей] (Nikiforov 148).

ÜRLÜK   Bashk. 1750 **Ürlük** [Тойчин Урлюков] (MIB III, 474).

ÜRMÄČ   Bashk. 1707 **Ürmäč** [Ирмяш Урмячев] (MIB III, 35).

ÜRMEKEY   Bashk. 1710 **Ürmekey** [Урмекей Кунгулдин] (MIB III, 60); Bashk. 1752 **Ürmekey** [Сатый Урмекеев] (MIB IV/1, 59). ✧ 'Creeper, trailer' cf. Tat. ürmä 'eine Schlingpflanze' (Radl. I, 1844) + suff. -key.

ÜRMEN   Bashk. 1714 **Ürmen / Urmen?** [Урмень Китяпов] (MIB I, 105).

ÜRMET see **QURMET**

ÜRPEK   Kzk. 19th c. **Ürpek** [Урпекъ] (AOAtb. 38). ✧ 'A pomp on a dress' cf. Kuman ürpäk 'ein Schmuck am Kleide' (Radl. I, 1844).

ÜRTEKE   Kzk. 1846 **Ürteke (<Yürteke?)** [Юртеке Баубеков] (MKOP 155).

ÜRTEMEY   Bashk. 1758 **Ürtemey** [Уртемей Бииндыков] (MIB IV/1, 168); Bashk. 1777 **Ürtemey** [Уртемей Сяпеев] (MIB V, 65). ✧ '(He) doesn't aggravate, (he) doesn't rag' cf. Tat. ürtä- 'necken' (Radl. I, 1842).

ÜRTÜKEY   Bashk. 1730 **Ürtükey / Yürtükey? / Yürtikey?** [Максим Юртюкеев / Юртыкеев] (MIB III, 273).

ÜRÜYA   Crm. **Ürüya** [Ӱрӱja] (Proben VII, 41).

ÜRÜK   Kzk. 19th c. **Örïk-pay / Örek-pay?** [Орекпай] (SODž. 148); Kzk. 19th c. **Ürk-bay / Ürik-bay** [Урькбай] (AOA 114); Bashk. 1740 **Ürük** [Мурзаш Урюков] (MIB I, 434); Kzk. 19th c. **Ürük** [Урюкъ], fem. (Grod. I, 98); Kzk. 19th c. **Ürük-pay** [Урюкпай]

(SODž. 152). ✧ 'Apricot; dried small apricot' cf. Kzk., East.T., Uzb. örük 'die wilde Aprikose' (Radl. I, 1223), Kzk. örïk 'урюк' (KzRS), Bashk. örök 'абрикос, урюк' (BRS).

ÜRÜÑ-ÄLKÄNÄY   Yak. **Ürüñ-älkänäy-toyon** [Ӱрӱҥ Äлкäнäи тоjон] (Pek.). ✧ 'White-kind/nice (master)' (Pek.).

ÜRÜÑ-ÜKÄYDÄN   Yak. **Ürüñ-ükäydän** [Ӱрӱҥ Ӱкäидäн-куо], fem. (Pek.).

ÜRÜÑ-ÜÖKÄYDÄN see **ÜRÜÑ-ÜKÄYDÄN**

ÜRÜÑ-ÜKÄYDÄN   Yak. **Ürüñ-ükäydän / Ürüñ-üökäydän** [Ӱрӱҥ Ӱкäидäн / Ӱрӱҥ Ӱökäидäн], fem. (Pek.). ✧ 'White-?'.

ÜRÜWEYDE   Oghuz/Trkm. 14th c. - 15th c. **Ürüweyde** [Ürüveyde] (DQorq./Rossi 100).

ÜS-TEMİR see **ÖZ-TEMİR**

ÜSÄDİK   Bashk. 1754 **Üsädik** [Усядык] (MIB IV/1, 81). ✧ 'Crowded' cf. Bashk. üsä- 'злорадствовать, проявлять' (BRS).

ÜSÄMBİ   Bulg. 927 **Üsämbi?** [Οὔσαμψις], a chief (Byz. Turc.).

ÜSÄN see **QUSAYİN**

ÜSÄNČİ   Bashk. 1731 **Üsänči** [Усянчи Олдашев] (MIB III, 287).

ÜSENKÄ   Bashk. 1664 **Üsenkä / Ösänkä** [Усенька Татлубаев] (MIB I, 187).

ÜSÄŠ   Bashk. 1749 **Üsäš** [Кады Усяшев] (MIB III, 465).

ÜSEY   Tat. 18th c. **Usey (<Üse?)** [Аитъ Усѣевъ] (Nepljuev 807, 825); Bashk. 1735 **Üsey** [Кутлубулатъ Усеевъ], a tarχan (Vel.-Zern., Bašk. 21, 22); Bashk. 1760 **Üsey** [Алиш Усеев] (MIB IV/1, 187); Bashk. 1760 **Üsey** [Казай Усеев] (MIB IV/1, 187); Bashk. 1769 **Üsey** [Кинзяфер (Канзяфер / Канзяфар / Канзафар) Усеев] (MIB IV/2, 389). ✧ 'He/she is growing (up)' cf. Tat. üs- 'wachsen' (Radl. I, 1877).

ÜSEK   Tat. 1624 **Üsek** [Усекъ Кулункѣевъ] (Pokrovskij 72). ⇨ **ÖSEK?**

ÜSEKEY   Bashk. 1706 **Üsekey** [Усекей Ембетев] (MIB III, 29); Bashk. 1740 **Üsekey** [Джiянгулъ Усѣкѣевъ] (Nepljuev 172). ⇨ **ÜSEK** + dim. suff. -ey.

ÜSEKTİN   Kzk. 19th c. **Üsektin-bay** [Усектынбай] (SODž. 150).

ÜSEM   Kzk. 19th c. **Üsem-bay** [Усембай] (SODž. 102). ✧ 'Growth, increase' cf. Kzk. ösim 'hayvan sayısının çoğalması, bir şeyin artması' (KzTS).

ÜSEN see **QUSAYİN**

ÜSEN-GİLDE   Tat.(Sib.) 1601 **Üsen-gilde(y)** [Кизылбай Усенгилдеев] (Miller, Ist. Sib. II, 169). ⇨ **ESÄN? + KELDİ.**

ÜSER see **ÖSER**

ÜSKEY   Chuv. 18th-19th c. **Üskey** [Ускей] (Magn. 89).

ÜSKEM-BAY see **ÖSKEN**

ÜSKÜ   Kzk. 19th c. **Üskü-bay** [Ускюбай] (SOV 12). ✧

'Awl' cf. Kzk. *üskö* 'eine grosse Ahle, ein Stechbohrer' (Radl. I, 1880).

ÜSLÜ Bashk. 1746 **Üslü-bay** [Услюбай] (MIB III, 435); Bashk. 1749, 1756, 1761 **Üslü-bay / Üslä-bay?** [Услюбай / Услябай Янабердин / Енабердин] (MIB III, 459, 464, IV/1, 112, 200). ✧ 'Avenger' cf. Bashk. *üs* 'месть, злоба' (BRS) + suff. *-lü*.

ÜSTÄÑ Uyg. 13th-14th c. **Üstäñ-täñrim / Üstäk-täñrim?** [Üstng Tngrim], fem. (Zieme, Mat. III, 275). ✧ 'Surpassing, prevailing' cf. Uyg. *üsdäñ / üstäñ* 'превосходящий, одерживающий верх' (DTS).

ÜSÜR Kzk. 19th c. **Üsür-bay** [Усюрбай] (SOK 32); *TN:* Kzk.? **Üsür-bay** [Usurbai], a burial mound south of Lake Balkhash at the confluence of the Qara-tal and Biše rivers (PM Ergh. 42); Uzb.? **Üsür-bay** [Усурбай], a tomb north-west of Tashkent (Karta JAR XIX). ⇨ **ÖSER?**

ÜŠ-AYAQ Kzk. 19th c. **Üš-ayaq** [Ушаякъ] (SODž. 150). ✧ 'Tripod' cf. Kzk. *üš ayaq* 'тренога, треножник' (RKzS). ⇨ **AYAQ.**

ÜŠ-ARAL Kzk. 19th c. **Üš-aral** [Ушаралъ] (SOV 146). ✧ 'Three-Aral' cf. Kzk. *üš* 'три' (KzRS). ⇨ **ARAL.**

ÜŠ-KEMPİR see **ÜČ-KEMPİR**

ÜŠ-QULAQ Maml. 14th c. **Üš-qulaq** [اوش قلق] (Sauvaget 39). ✧ 'Three ears; having three ears'. ⇨ **QULAQ.** See also **DÖRT-QULAQ.**

ÜŠÄ Uyg. 12th c. - 14th c. **Üšä** [Üšä / Üşä] (Radl., USp. 122, DTS, EUTS).

ÜŠKE Kzk. 19th c. **Üške** [Ушке] (SOV 54); Kzk. 19th c. **Üške?** [Ушко] (SODž. 12). ✧ 'Little Three' cf. Kzk. *üš* 'три' (KzRS) + suff. *-ke* <comp. *-ake.*

ÜŠLİK Kzk. 19th c. **Üšlik** [Ушликъ] (AOO 22). ✧ 'Of the value of three; threefold'? cf. Kzk. *üš* 'три' (KzRS) + suff. *-lik.*

ÜTÄ see **ÖTÄ**

ÜTÄ-BAŠ see **ÖTÄ-BAŠ**

ÜTÄGÄN see **ÖTÄGÄN**

ÜTÄY see **ÖTEY**

ÜTÄK see **ÖTEK**

ÜTÄL see **ÖTEL**

ÜTÄMİS see **ÖTÄMİŠ**

ÜTÄMİŠ see **ÖTÄMİŠ**

ÜTÄMİŠ-KERÄY Tat. 1549 **Ütämiš-keräy / Ütämiš-geräy?** [اوتامس كراى / Утямышъ-гирей (Мамшикирѣй, Александръ)], son of Safa-girey the Khan of Kazan (?) (PSRL XIX, 69, 318, 320, Vel.-Zern., Kasim. I, 335); Tat. 1549, 1552, 1564 **Ütemeš-kirey** [Утемешь-Кирѣй / Утѣмишь-Гирѣй / Утемишъ-гирей], Aleksandr Safa-Girejevič, prince of Kazan (PSRL XIII, 151, 161, AI I, 287, 330). ⇨ **ÜTÄMİŠ + KERÄY.**

ÜTÄN see **ÖTEN?**

ÜTÄP see **ÖTEP**

ÜTÄŠ see **ÖTEŠ**

ÜTÄW see **ÖTÄW**

ÜTÄW-BAQAWUL Uzb. 18th c. **Ütäw-baqawul** [Outaou-Bakaoul], from Ferghana (Nalivkin-Dozon 80). ⇨ **ÖTÄW.**

ÜTÄWLİ see **ÖTÄ**

ÜTEGEN see **ÖTÄGÄN**

ÜTEKEY Tat. 1764 **Ütäkey** [Утякей Кудашев] (MIB IV/1, 279); Tat. 1764 **Ütäkey** [Абдулрахим Утякеев] (MIB IV/1, 279); Bashk. 1735 **Ütekey** [Утекей Юлушевъ], a tarχan (Vel.-Zern., Bašk. 23); Bashk. 1745 **Ütekey** [Утекей Юлушев] (MIB III, 427); Bashk. 1746 **Ütekey** [Утекей Токаев] (MIB III, 435); Bashk. 1752 **Ütekey** [Кунзяп Утекеев] (MIB IV/1, 63); Bashk. 1767 **Ütekey** [Салават Утекеев] (MIB IV/1, 325). ⇨ **ÖTÄ** + dim. suff. *-käy / -key.*

ÜTEM-ALİ Nog. 20th c. **Ütem-alï-uwlï** [Йавдан Уьтемалы увлы / Явдан Утемалиев], father of one of Baskakov's informants from the aul of Nökis (Bask., Nog. 143). ⇨ **ALİ.**

ÜTEN-BERGEN Kzk. 19th c. **Üten-bergen** [Утенбергенъ] (SOK 20). ⇨ **ÖTEN + BERGEN.**

ÜTENEY Bashk. 1678 **Üteney** [Утенѣй Темешовъ] (DAI IX, 93). ⇨ **ÖTEN** + dim. suff. *-ey.*

ÜTMÄS Bashk. 1761 **Ütmäs** [Утмас Ямашев] (MIB IV/1, 216); Bashk. 1762 **Ütmes-qul** [Алимбеть Утмескулов] (MIB IV/1, 241). ✧ 'Won't pass away (won't die)' cf. Uyg., Kuman, Alt., Hak., Kzk., Kirg. etc. *öt-* 'hindurchgehen, vergehen, vorbeigehen' (Radl. I, 1260) + suff. *-mäs.*

ÜTMİŠ Chag. 16th c. **Ütmiš** [Утмиш], a mirza (Ivanov 299). ✧ 'Went (past) away' cf. cf. Uyg., Kuman, Alt., Hak., Kzk., Kirg. etc. *öt-* 'hindurchgehen, vergehen, vorbeigehen' (Radl. I, 1260) + suff. *-miš.*

ÜTRÄT Uyg. 13th-14th c. **Üträt / Öträt** [Üträt / Öträt], fem. (Müller, Uig. II, 76, DTS).

ÜTRİTMİŠ Uyg. 13th-14th c. **Ütritmiš**, fem. (Zieme, Mat. III, 280).

ÜTTEM Kzk. 19th c. **Üttem-bay?** [Утдембай] (AOAtb. 46).

ÜTÜGEN see **ÖTÄGÄN**

ÜTÜK Uyg. 1293 **Ütük** [Utuk] (Chwol., Syr.-nest. (NF) 12). ✧ 'Iron (tool)' cf. Karakh. *ütük* 'утюг' (DTS).

ÜTÜS Karg. **Ütüs** [Ӳтӳс] (Katanov, Otč. 8).

ÜZDÖN see **ÖZDEN**

ÜZEY Tat. 1702 **Üzey** [Телячко Узеевъ], a Tatar from Kungursk (Letop. ZAK II, 8). ⇨ **ÖZ?** + suff. *-ey.*

ÜZEM Kzk. 19th c. **Üzem-bay (<Üzen-bay)** [Узембай] (SODž. 114). ⇨ **ÜSEM?**

ÜZEM-BAY see **ÖZEN**

ÜZERİM Kzk. 19th c. **Üzerim** [Узеримъ] (SOK 158, 214).

ÜZİLDİK Kkalp. 20th c. **Üzildik** [Узилдик], fem. (KkRS 779). ✧ 'We separated; we detached ourselves' cf. Kkalp. *üzil-* 'обрываться, разрываться' (KkRS) +

suff. *-dik.

ÜZÖÑGÜ see **ZEÑİ**

ÜZÜ-GELDİ Bashk. 1675 **Üzü-geldi** [Карабаш Узюгелдин] (MIB I, 199). ✧ 'He himself has come'? ⇨ **ÖZ?** + **KELDİ** + poss. *-ü*.

ÜZÜBEK Bashk. 1752 **Üzübäk** [Усман Узюбяков] (MIB IV/2, 379); Bashk. 1735 **Üzübek** [Сеитъ Узюбековъ], a tarɣan (Vel.-Zern., Bašk. 24); Bashk. 1777 **Üzübek** [Узюбек Текумбетов] (MIB V, 53). ✧ 'Uzbeg / Özbek (ethnic name)'. ⇨ **ÖZÜ-BEK?**

ÜZÜK Uyg. 12th c. - 14th c. **Üzük** [üzük] (DTS); Kzk. 19th c. **Üzük** [Узукъ], fem. (Grod., Pril. 138). ✧ 'Cover of a yurta made of felt' cf. Kzk. *üzük* 'die Filzbekleidung der Jurte' (Radl. I, 1894); II. Uyg. *üzük* 'разорванный' (DTS), Alt.(Tel.), Kzk. *üzük* 'ein abgerissenes Stück, Zwischenraum' (Radl. I, 1895). See also **XUTLUΓ-ÜZÜK**.

ÜLMÄS see **ÖLMEZ**

V

VARİSAT Turk. 15th c. **Varisat-aɣa?** [Βαρισάταγας], an Ottoman governor (Byz. Turc. 87).

VATA Chuv. 18th-19th c. **Vata** [Вата] (Magn. 35).

VELET Yürük 1543 **Velet** [Veled] (Gökb., Rum. 180-240). ✧ 'Son, child' cf. Uzb. *väläd* (Ar.) 'das Kind' (Radl. IV, 1971), Turk. *velet* (Ar.) 'çocuk, evlât; oğul' (Özön), Turk. (slang) *velet* 'bastard; rascal' (TED).

VELİ Yürük 1543 **Veli** [Veli] (Gökb., Rum. 227); Tat. 1543 **Veli** [Veli] (Gökb., Rum. 237); Trkm. 20th c. **Velï** [Veli] (Zaj. 1971, 326); Trkm. 20th c. **Velï** [Вели] (TrkmRS 130); Kkalp. 20th c. **Wäliy** [Уэлий] (KkRS 776) ✧ 'Holy man; prophet; benefactor, guardian; owner, master, brother, relative' (Used also as a secondary component.); cf. Crm., Trkm., Uzb. *wäli* 'ein heiliger Mensch; der Wohlthäter' (Radl. IV, 1971), Turk. *veli* 'sahip; küçük çocuğun işlerine karışan, halinden sorumlu olan kimse; ermiş' (Özön), Kkalp. *wäliy* 'пророк; прорицатель, предсказатель' (KkRS) (<Ar.).

VENERA Tat. 20th c. **Venera** [Венера], fem. (Nikonov: OSA 158, Sattarov); Bashk. 20th c. **Venera** [Венера] (Nikonov: OSA 158); Kzk. 20th c. **Venera** [Венера], fem. (Nikonov: OSA 158); Kirg. 20th c. **Venera** [Венера], fem. (Nikonov: OSA 158). ✧ Venera (R.). See also **ČOLPAN, ZÖHRÄ**.

VENERKA Kirg. 20th c. **Venerka** [Венерка], fem. (Nikonov: OSA 158). ✧ Venerka (R.), derived from R. *Venera*.

VEÑAR Khorezm./Chag. 14th c. **Veñar-aɣa** [Vẽgaraga], one of Timur's wives (Clavijo 52).

VEPA Bashk. 1737-39 **Вара** [Бапа (Бепеня, Пепеня) мулла Турупкельди], a mulla (MIB I, 307, 317, 328 etc.); Kzk. 19th c. **Вара** [Бапа] (AOP 74); Trkm. 20th c. **Vepa** [Vepa] (Zaj. 1971, 329); Trkm. 20th c. **Vepā** [Вепа] (TrkmRS 130). ✧ 'Faith' cf. Trkm. *vepā* 'верность, преданность' (TrkmRS), East.T.(Tar.) *vapa* 'id.' (Radl. IV, 1965), cf. also Kzk. PNs *Bapa, Bafa* (Žanuzakov-Esbaeva) (<Ar.).

VEREK Chuv. 18th-19th c. **Verek** [Верекъ] (Magn. 36).

VERMİŠ see **BERMİŠ**

VÏRÏSKA Chuv. 18th-19th c. **Vïrïska** [Вырыска] (Magn. 36). ⇨ **VÏRUS** + suff. *-qa*.

VÏRUS see **URUS**

VOYVODA Turk. 19th c. **Voyvoda-oɣlu** [Vojvoda oɣlu], a Zeybek (Kúnos 1891, 119). ✧ 'Commander of town; governor' cf. Turk. *voyvoda* (<Slav) 'воевода' (TRS).

VURMANČU see **ORMANČÏ**

VURUSTAY see **URUSTAY**

VÜŠİ Trkm. 20th c. **Vüši** [Vüši] (Zaj. 1971, 333); Trkm. 20th c. **Vüši** [Вуши] (TrkmRS 133). ✧ 'Ill of trachoma' cf. Trkm. *vüši* 'трахомный' (TrkmRS).

W

WAYSİL-ATA Kirg. **Oysul-ata** [Ойсулата], protector-spirit of camels (Jud. 78, 563); Kirg. **Waysil-ata** [Вайсилата / Ойсулата], protector of camels (Jud. 175). ✧ 'Protector of camels; camel' (Jud.), cf. Kkalp. *oysil qara* 'покровитель верблюдов; (перен.) верблюд' (KkRS). ⇨ **ATA.** See also **OYSÏL-QARA.**

WALİ Trkm. 1881 **Wali** [Вали], a captain (Grod., Vojna IV, 18); Kzk. 19th c. **Wali-χan** [Čokan Čingisovič Valichanov] (Mende 27, AUK 158); Uzb. 1897 **Wali-χan-türä** [Chodja Walichan-Tjure], a χoja from Kokand (ArchKR XXII, 72); NUyg.(Tar.) **Wali-qan-törö** [Walikan Törö / Валикан Төпö] (Proben VI, 12 /15/). ✧ 'Governor' cf. Turk. *vali* (Ar.), Crm. *wali* 'der Generalgouverneur' (Radl. IV, 1962), Uzb. *wäli* 'правитель, наместник (UzbRS).

WÄLİY see **VELİ**

Z

ZABİT Turk. 20th c. **Zabit** (Önder, Hınıs). ✧ 'Ruler, officer, clerk' cf. Turk. *zabit* (Ar.) 'der Verwalter, der Offizier, der Beamte' (Radl. IV, 877).

ZADA see **ZĀDE**

ZAΓAN? Turk.? 1453 **Zaγan / Saγan?** [Заганъ], at the siege of Constantinople (PSRL XII, 92).

ZAHĬR Trkm. 20th c. **Zahïr** [Zahïr] (Zaj. 1971, 328); Trkm. 20th c. **Zāhïr** [Захыр] (TrkmRS 335). ✧ 'Evident, obvious, clear' cf. Trkm. *zāχïr* 'явный, очевидный' (TrkmRS) (<Ar.).

ZAHRAŠ Bulg. 1336 **Zahraš** [زهرش / Захраш] (Jusupov 24).

ZAXARYA Uyg. 12th c. - 14th c. **Zaχarya** [zaχarja] (DTS). ✧ Zakaria (Ar. <Gr. Zaharios), the biblical Zachariah (Ahmed).

ZAYĬS Bashk. 1773 **Zayis / Zays?** [Заис Ясасманов] (MIB IV/2, 413).

ZAYSA Bashk. 1792 **Zaysa** [Зайса Карабашев] (MIB V, 328).

ZAYSAN Bashk. 1742, 1759 **Zaysan** [Зайсан Юсупов] (MIB III, 513, IV/2, 22, 23); Bashk. 1745 **Zaysan** [Зайсан Акбаев] (MIB III, 428); Bashk. 1737-1739 **Zaysan / Zamsan / Yaysan / Yansan** [Зайсан / Яйсан / Замсан / Янсан Карабашев], a partaker of the revolt of 1737-39 (MIB I, 271, 318, 329 etc.). ⇨ **YAYSAN.**

ZAQ see **UZAQ**

ZALTĬY Bashk. 1779 **Zaltiy** [Залтий Таиров] (MIB V, 101).

ZAMAM-BEK see **ZAMAN**

ZAMAN Kzk. 19th c. **Zamam-bek (<Zaman-bek)** [Замамбекъ] (SODž. 76); Kzk. 19th c. **Zamam-bek (<Zaman-bek)** [Замамбекъ] (SOV 56); Turk. 16th c. **Zaman** [Zaman], fem. (Ongan, Ank. II); Trkm. 1628 **Zaman-bek** [Заман-бек], a „tüfängči-aγasï" from the Nazïr tribe (clan?) (MIT II, 103, 105, 106 etc.); Trkm. 1779 **Zaman-bek** [Заман-бек], from the Teke tribe (MIT II, 352); Trkm. 1826 **Zaman-bek** [Заман-бек], from the Salïr tribe (MIT II, 440); Kirg. **Zaman-bek** [Заманбек] (Jud. 37); Trkm. 1745 **Zaman-bek / Zaman-χan** [Мухаммед Заман-бек / Мухаммед Заман-хан], from the Qajar tribe (MIT II, 172, 173, 175, 176 etc.); Trkm. 1813 **Zaman-χan** [Заман-хан], „sadozay"(?) (MIT II, 209); Trkm. 1837/38 **Zaman-χan** [Заман-хан], from the Ǧemšid tribe (MIT II, 236); Trkm. 1838 **Zaman-χan** [Заман-хан], from the Čaraymaq tribe (clan?) (MIT II, 471, 472). ✧ 'Time' cf. Crm., Tat., Kar., Kzk. *zaman* 'id.' (Radl. IV, 880). See also **QUTLUΓ-ZAMAN.**

ZAMAS Kzk. 1823 **Zamas** [ضاماص / Замас] (MIK IV, 424, 429).

ZAMSAN see **ZAYSAN**

ZAN see **ĴAN**

ZAN-YUQLARĬ Balk. 20th c. **Zan-yuqlarï** [Zanjúqlari], family-name (Pröhle, Balk. 268). ✧ 'Heartless people'? ⇨ **ĴAN + YOQ** + plur. suff. *-lar* + poss. *-ï.*

ZAN-KĬŠĬLARĬ Balk. 20th c. **Zan-kišilarï** [Zankišilari], family-name (Pröhle, Balk. 268). ✧ 'Soul-Men' cf. Balk. *kiši [kišĭ]* 'Mann, Mannsbild, ein Mann wie er sein soll' (Pröhle, Balk. 229). ⇨ **ĴAN.**

ZANAY see **ĴANAY**

ZANT Tat. 1739 **Zant** [Зант] (Alatyr. 142).

ZAÑĬ Selj.? 1106 **Zañï** [Zângî Mawsîl], Yāγarmïš's son (Abulfar./Budge I, 240); Selj.? 1181 **Zañï** [Emâd ad-Dîn Zangî], lord of Sinjâr (Abulfar./Budge I, 311); Kzk. 19th c. **Zañï-bay** [Зангыбай] (SODž. 92). ⇨ **YAÑĬ?**

ZAR-MUXAMET Trkm. 19th c. **Zar-muχamet** [Зармухаметъ Талтаевъ] (Ščeglov IV, 164). ✧ 'Friend (of) Mukhammad' cf. Crm., Kzk., Tat., Turk. *zar* (P.) 'die Klage, der Jammer' (Radl. IV, 868), Trkm. *zār* 'рыдание, жалобный вопль' (TrkmRS). ⇨ **MUXAMMED.**

ZAR-NĬYAR Az. **Zar-niyar** [Зарнияр], fem. (Az. Skaz. 408). ✧ 'Sadness / sad / crying - Beauty' cf. Crm., Kzk., Tat., Turk. *zar* (P.) 'die Klage, der Jammer' (Radl. IV, 868), Trkm. *zār* 'рыдание, жалобный вопль' (TrkmRS). ⇨ **NĬGĀR.**

ZARĬL Kirg. **Zarïl** [Зарыл], fem. (Jud. 96). ✧ 'Needed, necessary, required' cf. Kirg. *zarïl* 'id.' (Jud.).

ZARLĬQ Kzk. 19th c. **Zarlïq** [Зарлыкъ] (AUK Dobavl. 12); Kkalp. 20th c. **Zarlïq** [Зарлык] (KkRS 774); Kkalp. 20th c. **Zarlïq-bay** [Зарлыкбай] (KkRS 774); Kzk. 1855 **Zarlïq-χan / Zarlïq-töre / Ĵarlïq-töre** / [Зарлык хан / Джарлык-тёре / Зарлык-тöре], a Kazak prince (töre) who became the khan of the Karakalpaks (MIKk. 86, 88, MIT II, 555, 558). ✧ 'Sadness, bitterness; crying' cf. Kkalp. *zar* 'печаль, скорбь; плач, рыдание; вопль, стон' (KkRS).

ZARSAN Kzk. 1884 **Zarsan-bay** [Зарсанбай Саксанбаевъ] (Grod., Pril. 94).

ZASATAY Bashk. 1693 **Zasatay** [Засатай], from Ufa (MIB I, 84). ✧ '?' (<R.).

ZAURA see **ZOHRA**

ZĀDE Bashk. 20th c. **Zada** [Зада] (Kusimova); Kkalp. 20th c. **Zada** [Зада], fem. (KkRS 777); Tat. 20th c. **Zadä** [Задə] (Sattarov). ✧ 'Child; son or daughter (male and female component); prince, princess (male and female title)' cf. Turk. *zadä* (P.) 'der Sohn' (Radl. IV, 876), Kzk. *zada* 'die Abkunft, die Herkunft' (Radl. IV, 876), (<P.) *zād* 'детеныш' (Miller).

ZĀY-QOWAQ Bashk. 1709 **Zäy-qowaq** [Зяйковаг Елмакаев] (MIB I, 264). ⇨ **YAY.**

ZĀYLĀ see **YAYLAQ**

ZĀYLĀW see **YAYLAQ**

ZĀLĬKEY Bashk. 1785 **Zälikey** [Зяликей Юртикеев] (MIB V, 559); Bashk. 1785 **Zälikey** [Зяликой / Зялятей Иманев] (MIB V, 559).

ZĀÑĬR Tat.(Mish.) 1755 **Zäñir** [Иман Зянгиров] (MIB IV/1, 93); Bashk. 1755 **Zäñir** [Зянгир Бердагулов] (MIB IV/1, 93); Kzk. 19th c. **Zeñir**

[Зенгеръ] (AOP 82). ✧ 'High / tall?' cf. Kzk. *zenger / zengir / zangar* 'yüksek, çok yüksek' (KzTS).

ZÄRİYPA   Kkalp. 20th c. **Zäriypa** [Зәрийпа], fem. (KkRS 777). ✧ Zarifa (Ar. fem.) 'elegant, witty, graceful' (Ahmed).

ZÄRİMBET   Kkalp. 20th c. **Zärimbet** [Зәримбет] (KkRS). ⇨ **ZERİ** + suff. *-imbet / -mbet*.

ZÄRİP   Kkalp. 20th c. **Zärip** [Зәрип] (KkRS 774); Kkalp. 20th c. **Zärip-bay** [Зәрипбай] (KkRS 774). ✧ 'Smart, elegant, fine' cf. Turk. *zarif* (Ar.) 'elegant, graciös, fein, geistreich' (Radl. IV, 871, HŞ).

ZÄRYÄR   Kzk. **Zäryär** [Särjär / Зәпјәп] (Proben III, 755 /846/).

ZEBİDAXAN   NUyg.(Tar.) 19th c. **Zebidaχan** [زبیده‌خان / Зебида-ханъ], fem. (Pantusov, Tar. 103). ⇨ **ZİBAYDA** + suff. *-χan(1)*.

ZEDENEY   Chuv.? 16th c. **Zedeney** [Зеденей], commander of the cavallery of Moscow in the war with Kazan (Zolotn. 157); Crm. 1506 **Zedenäy / Zeyn-ali** [Зеденай / Зеналей], a prince of the Crimea (PSRL VIII, 246).

ZEYLİ   Bashk. 1760 **Zeyli / Zeyle(y)?** [Куйбак Зеилеев] (MIB IV/2, 160).

ZEYN   Kzk. 19th c. **Zeyn-eke** [Зейнеке] (SOV 136). ✧ Zayn (Ar.) 'beautiful, pretty, beauty, grace' (Ahmed), cf. Tat. PN *Zäynä / Zäyne* (Sattarov).

ZEYNEL   Oghuz/Trkm. 13th c. **Zeynäl-γazi** [زینلغازی / Зейнал-Гази], Är-sarï-bay's son (Abulg./Kon. 1245, 1250); Turk. 1526 **Zeynel** [Ζεηνέλ], an Ottoman pasha (Byz. Turc. 130). ✧ Zeinel (Ar.).

ZEYNEP   Kzk. 19th c. **Zeyneb** [Зейнебъ], Čokan Čingisovič Valihanov's mother (Protok. Turk. IV, 52); Kkalp. 20th c. **Ziynep** [Зийнеп], fem. (KkRS 777). ✧ Zaynab (Ar. fem.) 'scented flower' (Ahmed).

ZEL   Kzk. 19th c. **Zel-bek** [Зельбекъ] (SOK 202).

ZENBİL   Khazar 623? **Zenbil** [Ζιεβήλ / Zenbīl], commander-in-chief of the Khazars, the first man after the χāqān (qaγan) (Justi 384-85).

ZEÑ-BABA see **ZEÑİ**

ZEÑİ   Kirg. 19th c. **Zeñ-baba** [Зенгъ-баба], protector-spirit of cows (Potanin II, 152); Selj. **Zeñi** [تاج الدین زنکی / Zengi], governor of Balkh (Ǯuwaynī II, 58); Selj. **Zeñi** [زنکی بن سعد / Zengi], an atabek (Ǯuwaynī II, 97); Selj. 11th c. - 12th c. **Zeñi** [زنکی بن اقسنر], an atabek, the lord of the emirs (Usāma 2, 74, 162); Selj. 1094 **Zeñi** [عماد الدین زنکی بن اقسنر قسیم الدولة], lord of Mosul (Ibn al-Athīr/Tornb. X, 157, 448-58, 474-78, XI, 2-9 etc.); Selj. 1095 **Zeñi** [زنکی بن اقسنر سلغری], the atabek of Syria (Qazw. 451, 472); Selj. 1099 **Zeñi** [بن برسق زنکی] (Ibn al-Athīr/Tornb. X, 196, 205, 340); Selj. 1106/07 **Zeñi** [زنکی بن جکرمیش / Zengi ibn Jagarmish], governor of Mosul (Ibn al-Athīr/Tornb. X,

293, Ibn al-Athīr: RHCHor I, 241, Abulfar. Or. (244-45) 372); Selj. 1115/16 **Zeñi** [زنکی / Zengui], Borsuq's (Borsoq's) brother, died in 1115/16 (Ibn al-Athīr: RHCHor I, 298); Selj. 1128 **Zeñi** [زنکی عماد الدین], he occupied Haleb (Abulfidā III, 430 etc.); Selj.? 1146/47 **Zeñi** [زنکی بن اقسنر / Zengui], an atabek died in 1146/47 (Ibn al-Athīr: RHCHor I, 266 etc., 456); Selj. 1147, 1152/53 **Zeñi** [زنکی الجاندار / زنگی جاندار / Zengui le Djendar] (Ibn al-Athīr/Tornb. XI, 76, 106, Ahbar 75, 76, 82, 89, Rāwandī 260, 261, Ibn al-Athīr, Atab.: RHCHor II/2, 187); Selj. 12th c. **Zeñi** [Zengi atabek] (Ahbar 108); Selj. 12th c. **Zeñi** [زنکی فخرالدین], an emir (Rāwandī 262); Selj. 12th c. **Zeñi** [زنکی / Zengui], Zengi I (Ibn al-Athīr, Atab.: RHCHor II/2, 30-37 etc.); Selj. 1153 **Zeñi** [زنکی بن علی / Зенги ибн Али ибн Халифа аш-Шейбани] (Ibn al-Athīr/Tornb. XI, 117, 202, MIT I, 389-403); Selj. 1161 **Zeñi** [بن دکلا السلغری] (Ibn al-Athīr/Tornb. XI, 177-78, 229); Selj. 1169/70, 1197/98 **Zeñi** [عمادالدین زنکی / Zengui], Zengi II, grand-son of Zengi I, lord of Haleb, died in 1197/98 (Ibn al-Athīr, Atab.: RHCHor II/2, 264, Ibn al-Athīr: RHCHor I, 573); Selj. 1175 **Zeñi** [زنگی بن مودود], an atabek in Fars, died in 1175 (Qazw. 505); Selj.? 1201 **Zeñi** [زنکی بن مسعود] (Ibn al-Athīr/Tornb. XII, 108, 114-15); Selj.? 1206 **Zeñi** [زنکی بن خرجوم] (Ibn al-Athīr/Tornb. XII, 147); Selj. 1260 **Zeñi** [عماد الدین زنکی بن اقسنر / Zengi / Имад-ад-дин Зенги ибн Аксонкур], lord of Mosul (RaD I/2, 82, Abulfar. Or. (250) 380, 381); Trkm.? 1851 **Zeñi-ata** [Зенги-ата], a sheykh (MIT II, 285); Kzk. 19th c. **Zeñi-ata** [Zengi-ata] (Ljutš 151); Kzk. **Zeñi-baba** [Зенги-баба], in a tale (TOOIK III, 159); Kzk. 19th c.? **Zeñi-baba** [Zengi-baba] (Atyns. 118); Kzk. 19th c. **Zeñi-baba** [Зенги-баба], protector-spirit of cattle (Potanin, Pred. 114); Kirg. **Zeñi-baba / Zeñgi-baba / Üzöñgü-baba** [Зенги баба / Узэнгу баба] (Jud. 90); Kzk. 19th c. **Zeñi-bay / Zeñī-bay** [Зенгебай] (AOK 118). ✧ 'Zeñi(-ata/-baba), the protector of cattle; cattle / cow' (Potanin, Jud.).

ZEÑİ-PARS   Selj. 12th c. **Zeñi-pars** [زنگی پارس / Zengi-pars] (Rāwandī 290). ⇨ **ZEÑİ?** + **BARS**.

ZEÑİJÄ see **ZEÑİJE**

ZEÑİJE   Kzk. 1920 **Zeñijä** [Zendkidja], fem. (Fox 172); Khorezm. 1220 **Zeñije** [زنکیجة / Zenkidja], fem. (Nasawī 41). ✧ 'Huge' cf. Kzk. *zengi* 'büyük, dev' (KzTS) + suff. *-je*.

ZERİXAN   Kkalp. 20th c. **Zeriχan** [Зерихан], fem. (KkRS 777). ⇨ **ZERİ** + suff. *-χan(1)*.

ZİBAYDA   Bulg. **Sübeyte / Söbäytä** [سُبَیتَ / Sübeyte / Cöбäйтä], fem. (Jusupov 43, Epigr. Bulg. 118, 119, Tekin 113); Kkalp. 20th c. **Zibayda** [Зибайда], fem.

(KkRS 777). ✧ 'Zubaida (elected, chosen; the noblest)'
cf. Ar. زبـيـده, also Tekin 206.

ZİFA Kkalp. 20th c. **Ziyba** [Зийба], fem. (KkRS 777);
Kkalp. 20th c. **Ziyba-gül** [Zyjba-gül / Зийбагул], fem.
(KkRS 777, Baskakov: OSA 140). ✧ 'Beautiful, pretty,
nice' cf. Tat. *zifa / zipa* (P.) 'stattlich, gut gewachsen'
(Radl. IV, 917), Turk. *ziba* 'beautiful, elegant' (TED).
See also **GÜZEL, HÄSEN, KÜRKLİ, KÖRKLÄ,
KÖRTLÄ, NİGĀR, SİLİГ, ZİFA.**

ZİYAQAY Bashk. 1776 **Ziyaqay / Žiyaqay** [Зиякай /
Жиякай Аптаков] (MIB V, 39, 41). ✧ 'Little gleam,
brightness' (Ar.) (Kusimova, Sattarov), cf. Turk. *ziya*
'das Licht, die Helle' (Radl. IV, 909).

ZİYAN Bashk. 18 th.c. **Seyan-ɣul (<Ziyan-ɣul)**
[Бепенъ Сеянгуловъ] (Nepljuev 141); Bashk. 1732
Ziyan [Сарба Зиянов] (MIB III, 302); Bashk. 1734
Ziyan [Зиян Мусин] (MIB III, 322); Bashk. 1738
Ziyan [Апак Зиянов] (MIB III, 383); Bashk. 1756
Ziyan [Якуп Зиянов] (MIB IV/1, 107); Bashk. 1756
Ziyan [Юсуп Зиянов] (MIB IV/1, 107); Bashk. 1758
Ziyan [Ангар Зиянов] (MIB IV/2, 20); Bashk. 1764
Ziyan [Науруз Зиянов] (MIB IV/1, 277); Bashk.
1738 **Ziyan-bay** [Зиян-бай] (MIB I, 361); Bashk.
1740 **Ziyan-čura** [Зианчюра Янтемиров] (MIB I,
401); Bashk. 1790 **Ziyan-čura / Zyan-čura** [Зиянчура
/ Зянчура Алдакаев] (MIB V, 279); Bashk. 1735
Ziyan-ɣul [Зьянгул Яушев] (MIB III, 331); Bashk.
1738 **Ziyan-ɣul** [Зиянгулов] (MIB I, 361); Bashk.
1738 **Ziyan-ɣul** [Зиянгул Кутлугулов] (MIB I, 361);
Bashk. 1756 **Ziyan-ɣul** [Зиянгул Ямчюрин] (MIB
IV/1, 123); Bashk. 1763 **Ziyan-ɣul** [Баикай
Зиянгулов] (MIB IV/1, 271); Bashk. 1788 **Ziyan-ɣul**
[Зиянгул Табулдин] (MIB V, 233); Bashk. 1789
Ziyan-ɣul [Таиш Зиянгулов] (MIB V, 255); Bashk.
1790 **Ziyan-ɣul** [Мурсалим Зиянгулов] (MIB V,
284). ✧ 'Loss, damage' cf. Tat., Turk. *zïyan / ziyan* (P.)
'Verlust, Schaden' (Radl. IV, 902, 909). See also **ALA-
ZİYAN, ALAŇ-ZİYAN.**

ZİYAN-ALÏ Bashk. 1697 **Ziyan-alï** [Кучанъ
Зьяналыевъ] (Vel.-Zern., Bašk. 31). ⇨ **ZİYAN +
ALİ.**

ZİYANBET Bashk. 1735 **Ziyambet (<Ziyanbet)**
[Исекей Зиямбетевъ], a prince (Vel.-Zern., Bašk.
17); Bashk. 1788 **Ziyanbet / Ziyambet** [Зиянбеть /
Зиямбеть Зиянгулов] (MIB V, 238). ⇨ **ZİYAN +
suff. -bet.**

ZİYARET Turk. 20th c. **Ziyaret** [Ziyaret], a village in
Turkey (TMİB 853); Turk. 20th c. **Ziyaret** [Ziyaret]
(TMİB 865). ✧ 'Visit, voluntary pilgrimage' (Erol II)
(<Ar.).

ZİYBA see **ZİFA**

ZİYÄŠ Bashk. 1732 **Ziyäš** [Зьяш Тоумбаев] (MIB III,
300). ✧ Zia (Ar.) 'light, glow, illumination' (Ahmed) +
dim. suff. -š.

ZİYNE Kkalp. 20th c. **Ziyne-gül** [Зийнегул], fem.
(KkRS 777, Baskakov: OSA 141). ✧ 'Pretty, elegant'
(Baskakov: Ziyne-gül 'narjadnaja roza', l. cit.), cf.
Turk. *zinät* (Ar.) 'der Schmuck, die Verschönerung'
(Radl. IV, 912).

ZİYNEP see **ZEYNEP**

ZİYNEŠ Kkalp. 20th c. **Ziyneš** [Зийнеш], fem. (KkRS
777). ⇨ **ZİYNE** + suff. -š.

ZİYTÏŠ Bashk. 1761 **Ziytïš** [Назар Зийтышев] (MIB
IV/1, 215).

ZİLİKEY Bashk. 1740, 1757 **Zilikey** [Полат
Зиликеев] (MIB I, 410, IV/1, 144).

ZİLİŠ Bashk. 1779 **Ziliš** [Байдагул Зилышев] (MIB
V, 88, 106).

ZİMAS Bashk. 1737 **Zimas** [Зимас Абдалов] (MIB I,
338).

ZİMİKEY Bashk. 1770 **Zimikey** [Кучукбай
Зимикеев] (MIB IV/1, 349).

ZİMUL Tat.(Sib.) 1609 **Zimul / Sim-ul?** [Зимуль]
(Miller, Ist. Sib. II, 212).

ZİNJİRLİ Crm.(Tat.) 19th c. **Zinjirli** [Zinğirli] (Mende
67). ✧ 'Chained' cf. Turk. *zincirli* 'chained; madman or
prisoner in chains; a gold coin' (TED).

ZİW-GİLDE Bashk. 1709 **Ziw-gilde / Ziw-gildey**
[Зивгилдей Исянев] (MIB I, 264). ⇨ **KELDİ.**

ZİTAN Kzk. **Zïtan?** [Sïtan / (?)], khan's son in the
legend (Proben III, 381(?) /454/).

ZİTUN Kzk. **Zïtun-batïr** [Sïtun Batyr / Зïтун батыр]
(Proben III, 400 /473/).

ZİLÏYXA see **ZULAYXA**

ZİLÏYQA see **ZULAYXA**

ZİMAQ-ULLARÏ Balk. 20th c. **Zïmaq-ullarï**
[Zimaqullari], earlier a slave family (Pröhle, Balk. 273).

ZYAN see **ZİYAN**

ZOHRA Kzk. 19th c. **Zaura** [Батпа, Заура], fem.
(Grod. I, 98); Kzk. 19th c. **Zohra** [Зохра], fem. (Grod.,
Pril. 123); NUyg.(Tar.) **Zora-χenim** [Sora Chenim /
Зора Хеním], fem. (Proben VI, 180 /237/); Kar.(Crm.)
Zöhrä [Даһыр iлäн Зöhpä], fem. (Proben VII, 327);
Trkm. 20th c. **Zöhre** [Zöhre], fem. (Zaj. 1971, 337);
Trkm. 20th c. **Zöhre / Zöhrä** [Зухра], fem. (TrkmRS
340); NUyg.(Tar.) 19th c. **Zuhra-χanïm / Zuhraχan**
[زهرا خان / Зугра-ханымъ], fem. (Pantusov, Tar. 47);
Kirg. 19th-20th c. **Zura-qan** [Zurákán] (Prinz 249);
Kirg. **Zūra** [Зуура], fem. (Jud. 943); Kkalp. 20th c.
Zühra [Зухра], fem. (KkRS 777). ✧ 'Venus' cf. Trkm.
zöhre 'id.' (TrkmRS) (<Ar.).

ZOR Kzk. 1817 **Zor-bay** [ظور باى / Зорбай] (MIK IV,
312, 319); Kzk. 19th c. **Zor-bay** [Зорбай] (SOK 22).
✧ 'Big, large' cf. Kar., Kirg., Kzk. *zor* (P.) 'gross,
erhaben' (Radl. IV, 898-899). See also **BOYŠAN,
DÄW, DUOLANTAY, KETTÄ, QOŽAQ, ULUГ.**

ZOR-MURUN Kzk. 19th c. **Zor-murun** [Зормурунъ]
(SOK 74). ✧ 'Big-nose(d)'. ⇨ **ZOR + BURUN.**

ZORA see **ZOHRA**

ZORBA Turk. 20th c. **Zorba** (Önder, Göle). ✧ 'Rebel' cf. Turk. *zorba* 'der Aufrührer, der Aufständige' (Radl. IV, 901).

ZORQ Kzk. 19th c. **Zorq-pay** [Зоркпай] (SOK 182).

ZORLUQ Kzk. 19th c. **Zorluq-pay** [Зорлукпай] (AOAtb. 46). ✧ 'Assault; violent' cf. Kzk., Turk. *zorluk* 'die Gewaltthätigkeit' (Radl. IV, 900).

ZORTMAQ Kzk. 18th c. - 19th c. **Zortmaq** [Зортмак], a clan? (Tynyšp. 75).

ZÖHRÄ see **ZOHRA**

ZUBAY-BERDİ Uzb. 20th c. **Zubay-berdi** [Зубайберди] (Begmatov 1984, 202). ⇨ **SUBAY?** + **BERDİ.**

ZUHRA see **ZOHRA**

ZUYUR Nog. 20th c. **Zuyur** [Абджуьр Зуйур увлы], father of one of Baskakov's informants from the aul of Nökis (Bask., Nog. 143).

ZULAY Bashk. 1740 **Zulay / Züläy?** [Минлигул Зюлаев] (MIB I, 424).

ZULAYXA Kkalp. 20th c. **Zïlïyχa** [Зылыйха], fem. (KkRS 777); Nog. **Zïlïyqa** [Зыпыйка], fem. (Sprav. Im.); Kirg. **Zulayqa** [Зулайка], fem. (Jud. 35, 752); Kmk. **Zuleyχa** [Зулейха] (Sprav. Im.); Bashk. 1712 **Züläyχa** [Зюлелехея], fem. (MIB III, 84); Bashk. 20th c. **Züläyχa** [Зөләйха], fem. (Kusimova); Crm.(Tat.) **Züläyχa / Zuleyχa** [Зюлейха / Зулейха] (Sprav. Im.); Kzk. 19th c. **Züleyχa** [Зюлейха], fem. (Grod., Pril. 151). ✧ Zulaikha / Zulaykha (P. < Ar. fem.) (Ahmed).

ZULAYQA see **ZULAYXA**

ZULEYXA see **ZULAYXA**

ZULΓUPUL Kzk. **Zulγupul** [Sulgupul / Зулгупул] (Proben III, 502 /427/).

ZUMA-GÜZÄ see **JUMA**

ZURA see **ZOHRA**

ZURAL Kzk. 19th c. **Zural** [Зуралъ] (SKSO VIII, 226).

ZURUM Crm. 1684 **Zurum** [Зурумъ], a messenger from the Crimea (DAI XI, 21). ✧ 'Army'? cf. Kar. *zurum* 'das Heer' (Radl. IV, 919). See also **ČERİ I.,** **ΓOŠUN, SÜ.**

ZUWAN see **JUBAN**

ZÜHRA see **ZOHRA**

ZÜLÄYXA see **ZULAYXA**

ZÜLQARNEY see **ZÜLQARNEYN**

ZÜLQARNEYN Bashk. 1785 **Zülqarney** [Зюлкарней Илкеев] (MIB V, 170); Karakh. **Zülqarneyn** [Zülkarneyn] (MK/Atalay 860). ✧ (Iskender) Zulkarnayin (<Ar.).

ZÜLPİQAR Kkalp. 20th c. **Zülpïqar** [Зулпыкар] (KkRS 774). ✧ Zulfikar (Ar.), the name of Prophet Ali's magic sword.

ZÜLÜY Karch. 20th c. **Zülüy** [Зülüj], fem. (Pröhle, Kar. 145).

ZÜS see **YÜZ**

ŽAY-TUWΓAN Kkalp. 20th c. **Žay-tuwγan** [Жайтуўған] (KkRS 773). ✧ 'Born easily, simply' cf. Kkalp. *žay* 'так себе, просто; медленно, спокойно' (KkRS). ⇨ **TUΓAN I.**

ŽAYÏLΓAN Kkalp. 20th c. **Žayïlγan** [Жайылган] (KkRS 773). ✧ 'Widespread' cf. Kkalp. *žayïlγan* разостланный; распространенный (KkRS).

ŽAYLAW see **YAYLAQ**

ŽAYLÏ Kkalp. 20th c. **Žaylï-bay** [Жайлыбай] (KkRS 773). ✧ 'Right, agreeable, good, pleasing' cf. Kkalp. *žaylï* 'удобный, подходящий, хороший; имеющий дом' (KkRS).

ŽAYLŌ see **YAYLAQ**

ŽAKEN Kzk. 20th c. **Žaken-ulï** [Мухъан Жакен-улы], a worker, Baskakov's informant (Bask., Kkalp. 138); Kkalp. 20th c. **Žäken** [Жәкен] (KkRS 773).

ŽAQÏP see **YAQUB**

ŽAQSÏ see **YAQŠÏ**

ŽAQSÏ-MURAT Kkalp. 20th c. **Žaqsï-mïrat** [Жақсымырат] (KkRS 773); Kkalp. 20th c. **Žaqsï-murat** [Жақсымурат] (KkRS 773). ⇨ **YAQŠÏ** + **MURAT.**

ŽAQSÏLÏQ see **YAQŠÏLÏQ**

ŽALDUZXAN Balk. 20th c. **Žalduzχan**, fem. (Pröhle, Balk. 276). ⇨ **ŽALDUZ** + suff. -*χan(1)*.

ŽALΓAS Kkalp. 20th c. **Žalγas** [Жалғас] (KkRS 773); Kkalp. 20th c. **Žalγas-bay** [Жалғасбай] (KkRS 773). ✧ 'Be helpful! Join us!' cf. Kkalp. *žalγas-* 'приходить на помощь вместе с кем либо' (KkRS).

ŽALΓÏZ Kkalp. 20th c. **Žalγïz** [Жалғыз] (KkRS 773). ✧ 'Single, lonesome' cf. Kkalp. *žalγïz* 'id.' (KkRS).

ŽALİMBET Kkalp. 20th c. **Žalimbet** [Жалимбет], Qalimbet' and Ker-boγa's brother (Bask., Kkalp. 15 /41/); Kkalp. 20th c. **Žalimbet / Jalimbet** [Жалимбет / Джалимбет] (Bask., Kkalp. 41); Kkalp. 20th c. **Žälimbet** [Жәлимбет] (KkRS 773). ⇨ **YAL** + suff. -*imbet / -imbet*.

ŽAMA see **JUMA**

ŽAMAL see **JAMAL**

ŽAMBÏL see **JAMBUL**

ŽAMΓÏRČİ see **YAMΓURČİ**

ŽAMÏYLA see **JÄMİYLÄ**

ŽAN see **JAN**

ŽAN-BOSÏN see **JAN-BOLSUN**

ŽAN-DÄWLET Kkalp. 20th c. **Žan-däwlet** [Жандәулет] (KkRS 773). ⇨ **JAN** + **DÄWLÄT.**

ŽAN-ÏZAQ see ĴAN-UZAQ

ŽAN-TUƔAN see ĴAN-TUƔAN

ŽAN-UZAQ see ĴAN-UZAQ

ŽANAQ   Kzk. 19th c.? **Žanaq** [Žanak] (Atyns. 124). ⇨ **ĴAN?** + suff. *-aq.*

ŽANÏ-BEK see ĴANÏ

ŽANÏM see ĴANÏM

ŽANÏŠ   Kirg. **Žanïš** [Жаныш] (Jud. 70). ⇨ **ĴAN?** + suff. *-ïš.*

ŽAÑÏL see ĴAÑÏL

ŽAPAQ see YAPAQ

ŽAR-BOL see YAR-BOL

ŽAR-BUL see YAR-BOL

ŽARÏLQAƔAN   Kkalp. 20th c. **Žarïlqaɣan** [Жарылқаған] (KkRS 773). ✧ 'Blessed; absolved' cf. Kkalp. *žarïlqa-* 'благословлять; прощать, отпускать грехи' (KkRS).

ŽARÏLQAP   Kkalp. 20th c. **Žarïlqap** [Жарылқап] (KkRS 773). ✧ 'Blessed, blessing; absolving' cf. Kkalp. *žarïlqa-* 'благословлять; прощать, отпускать грехи' (KkRS) + suff. *-p.*

ŽARÏLQASÏN   Kzk. 19th c. **Čarïqasïn / Čarïlqasïn?** [Чарикасинъ] (Grod., Pril. 107-108); Kzk. 19th c. **Yarïqasïm (<Yarïlqasïn)** [Ярыкасымъ Сатеновъ] (SKSO III, 190); Kkalp. 20th c. **Žarïlqasïn** [Жарылқасын] (KkRS 773). ✧ 'Thankfulness, gratefulness' cf. Kkalp. *žarïlqasïn* 'id.' (KkRS); 'Let him/her be thankful/grateful! Let him do god! Be him forgiven by God' cf. Kzk. *carïlka-* 'İyilik etmek, yetiştirmek; birisine duada bulunmak' (KzTS), Turk. *yarïlɣa-* 'vergeben (von Gott)' (Radl. III, 126), also Kzk. PN *Žarïlqasïn* (Žanuzakov-Esbaeva).

ŽARQÏN see YARQÏN

ŽASAƔAN-BERGEN   Kzk. 19th c. **Žasaɣan-bergen** [Жасаганберген Пирманов] (AUK 99). ✧ 'Lived-given / living-given'? cf. Kzk. *casa-* III 'yaşamak' (KzTS). ⇨ **BERGEN.**

ŽAW-BASAR see YAW-BASAR

ŽAWUZ   Bashk. 1740 **Žawuz-bay** [Жаузбай Кусюкбаев] (MIB I, 397). ✧ 'Wicked, fiend' cf. Kuman *yauz* 'niedrig' (Radl. III, 20), Bashk. *yawïz* 'злой; злодей' (BRS/Uraksin), Kzk. *žawïz* 'злой, злодей' (RKzS).

ŽAZÏQ   Kkalp. 20th c. **Žazïq-bay** [Жазықбай] (KkRS 773). ✧ 'Stretched; sin; crime'? cf. Kkalp. *žazïq* 'вина, проступок; равнина, плато; паспростертый, раскинувшийся' (KkRS).

ŽAŽDÏ   Kzk. **Žaždï-bay** [Žaždybaev] (Mende 145).

ŽÄDÏGER see YADÏƔAR

ŽÄKEN see ŽAKEN

ŽÄMÏYLE see ĴÄMÏYLÄ

ŽÄRÏMBET   Kkalp. 20th c. **Žärimbet** [Жәримбет] (KkRS 773). ⇨ **YAR** + suffixoid *-imbet.* See also **ĴAR-MAMBET, YARMÄT.**

ŽÄRMEN   Kkalp. 20th c. **Žärmen** [Жәрмен] (KkRS 773). ✧ 'Corrupt, venal; voracious, insatiable' cf. Kkalp. *žermen* 'взяточник, ненасытный' (KkRS).

ŽEKSEMBE see YEKŠENBE

ŽENEWÏT see ĴENEWÏT

ŽET-QATÏN see YETİ

ŽİBEK see ĴİBEK

ŽİDE see ĴİDÄ

ŽİYAQAY see ZİYAQAY

ŽİYÄN see ĴİYEN

ŽİYE-MÏRAT see ŽİYE-MURAT

ŽİYE-MURAT   Kkalp. 20th c. **Žiye-mïrat** [Жийемырат] (KkRS 773); Kkalp. 20th c. **Žiye-murat** [Жийемурат] (KkRS 773). ⇨ **?** + **MURAT.**

ŽİYEN see ĴİYEN

ŽİYRENČE-ČEŠÄN see YİRENŠE-ŠEŠEN

ŽİYRENŠE see ĴİYRENŠE

ŽÏƔA   Kkalp. 20th c. **Žïɣa-gül** [Жыгагул], fem. (KkRS 777, Baskakov: OSA 139). ✧ 'Feather-tuft (crest) of a shako' cf. Kkalp. *žïɣa* 'султан из птичьих перьев' (KkRS).

ŽÏLQÏ-AYDAR see ĴÏLQÏ-AYDAR

ŽÏÑÏL see ĴÏÑÏL

ŽOL see YOL

ŽOL-MAN see ĴOL-AMAN

ŽOLOY see YULAY

ŽOLUM see YOLUM

ŽOMART see ĴOMART

ŽUL-MAMBET see ĴOL-MAMBET

ŽUL-TAY see ĴUL-TAY

ŽUL-TANAY   Kzk. 18th c. **Žul-tanay** [Жултанай], a chief (Nepljuev 714). ⇨ **YOL** + **DANAY?**

ŽULDÏZAY see ĴULDUZAY

ŽUMA see ĴUMA

ŽUMA-MÏRAT see ŽUMA-MURAT

ŽUMA-MURAT   Kkalp. 20th c. **Žuma-mïrat** [Жумамырат] (KkRS 773); Kkalp. 20th c. **Žuma-murat** [Жумамурат] (KkRS 773). ⇨ **ĴUMA** + **MURAT.**

ŽUMA-NAZAR see ĴUMA-NAZAR

ŽUMA-NİYAZ see ĴUMA-NİYAZ

ŽUMA-TAY   Kzk. 19th c. **Žuma-tay** [Жуматай] (AUK 93). ⇨ **ĴUMA** + **TAY** or suff. *-tay(1,2)?*

ŽUMAN see YUMAN

ŽUMART see ĴOMART

ŽUMAŠ see ĴUMAŠ

ŽUN-BANÏŠ   Nog. **Žun-banïš** [Жунбаныш] (Žirm., Epos 395). ⇨ **?** + **BANÏ** + suff. *-š.*

ŽUPAR see YÏPAR

ŽURT see ĴURT

ŽÜNİS see ĴUNUŠ

ŽÜS see YÜZ

ŽÜZ see YÜZ

www.ingramcontent.com/pod-product-compliance
Lightning Source LLC
Chambersburg PA
CBHW052146020426
41879CB00036B/58